THE OFFICIAL ENCYCLOPEDIA OF MAJOR LEAGUE BASEBALL

TOTAL BASEBALL

FIFTH EDITION

EDITED BY

JOHN THORN, PETE PALMER,

MICHAEL GERSHMAN

AND DAVID PIETRUSZA

VIKING

VIKING

Published by the Penguin Group
Penguin Books USA Inc., 375 Hudson Street,
New York, New York 10014, U.S.A.
Penguin Books Ltd, 27 Wrights Lane,
London W8 5TZ, England
Penguin Books Australia Ltd, Ringwood,
Victoria, Australia
Penguin Books Canada Ltd, 10 Alcorn Avenue,
Toronto, Ontario, Canada M4V 3B2
Penguin Books (N.Z.) Ltd, 182–190 Wairau Road,
Auckland 10, New Zealand

Penguin Books Ltd, Registered Offices:
Harmondsworth, Middlesex, England

This edition published in 1997 by Viking Penguin,
a division of Penguin Books USA Inc.

10 9 8 7 6 5 4 3 2 1

Official Publication—Major League Baseball

ISBN 0-670-87511-2
CIP data available

This book is printed on acid-free paper.
∞

Printed in the United States of America
Set in Times Roman
Designed by Marc Cheshire

Contents

PART TWO

The Registers, Leaders, and Rosters

Appendixes

Acknowledgments

This fifth edition of *Total Baseball* could not have been published without the assistance of a legion of writers, researchers, and editorial/production staff. The principal contributors in these areas are credited on the table of contents; others may be acknowledged within the text or in the separate introductions to the various sections of Part 2. Still others provided vital inspiration, investigative tips, and production help, yet go unmentioned in the body of the book; this page is for them, especially those who took part in the launch of the book back in 1989 and our new colleagues at Major League Baseball and Viking.

This book would not exist in its current form without the clear vision and dedicated effort of Michael Bernstein, Director of Publishing at Major League Baseball Properties. Michael was an indispensable editorial adviser and his staff, Dana Nicole Williams, Cindy McManus, Jennifer Langness, and Gary Perkinson made the book better with their careful review of the manuscript. Rich Levin, Director of Public Relations in the Commissioner's Office of Major League Baseball, played a key role as well.

Seymour Siwoff and Steve Hirdt of the Elias Sports Bureau offered their aid toward creating a unified statistical database of Major League Baseball.

Al Silverman, our editor at Viking, was a key contributor in shaping the new features of this edition and in enlisting the support of the company's marketing group, led by Cathy Hemming and Laurie Rippon, ably abetted by Mary Ellen Curley and Paul Slovak. Similarly, Roni Axelrod, Larry Nevins, and Cynthia Achar were invaluable on the production end.

We were fortunate to extend our relationship with Starkey & Henricks, which has been the typographer for every edition of *Total Baseball*. To Peter and Doug Bird, and Peter Compton, George Galgoczi, and Ellen Curcio go our admiration and gratitude.

With this edition David Pietrusza joins us at the bottom of the page (and elsewhere, of course) as an unindicted co-editor, and passes his managerial torch to Matt Silverman, a promising rookie.

Marc Cheshire's splendid design for the first edition has stood the test of time. Gypsy da Silva earned the *croix de guerre* for her production work on the second edition; Jacquie Roland was important to the third edition, as Ray Shaw was to the fourth. In this fifth edition, James Charlton's mastery of the day-by-day history of baseball has informed our expanded Annual Record.

Thanks to Mark Nieker and all the people at Mindscape—notably Kevin Johnson, Dave Schenone, and Patrice Paul—who not only brought you *Total Baseball* on the enclosed CD-ROM, but also introduced us to the World Wide Web in 1996 in a blizzard of team sites as well as our central address:

http://www.totalbaseball.com

To our cyberpartners at Mindscape we added an indispensable production team closer to home in Kingston, New York: MediaFlow, Inc., headed by Joseph Flanigan.

We will not forget our friends at Sony, or Eric Pozzo and the pioneers at CMC (Creative Multimedia Corporation), who first published *Total Baseball* in electronic form back in 1991-92. Thanks as well to Microsoft, which incorporated much of this work in its *Complete Baseball*, and to Franklin Electronic Publishing, which also enlarged our audience.

We are indebted to David Reuther, our friend and associate in many other books. His contributions to the editorial, production, and business aspects of *Total Baseball*—both the original and second editions—were truly awesome.

For research help, particularly into the years before 1920, we extend heartfelt thanks (alphabetically) to SABR colleagues Bill Carle, Bob McConnell, David Neft, Bob Tiemann, and Frank Williams. Bill helped us with biographical data, especially debut dates. Bob McConnell lent his personal expertise and his knowledge of the John Tattersall research collection to clear up a variety of perplexing areas. David supplied us with heretofore unknown RBI data for the National League of 1880-1885 and inspired us by his example, as the man who headed the Information Concepts, Inc., team that produced *The Baseball Encyclopedia* of 1969. Bob Tiemann provided game scores and sites for a host of pre-1900 games that were most helpful in deriving, for the first time, home-road stats for the nineteenth century; he also headed the SABR research project that yielded new National Association data. And Frank Williams continued his remarkable efforts in correcting pitcher won-lost records before 1920.

Since our debut in 1989, a veritable army of readers has taken us up on our invitation to write with their corrections and suggestions, from the mathematical to the typographical; we thank them in the aggregate here and list them by name in the Notes on Contributors section near the end of the book. Deserving of special mention here, however, is Tim Cashion, whose amazingly thorough review of recent editions has made *Total Baseball* as close to error-free as human frailty will permit.

And last, we thank some giants of baseball research whose work informs these pages but who are no longer with us to receive the tribute: in no particular order, Ernie Lanigan, John Tattersall, S.C. Thompson, Alex Haas, Preston D. Orem, Len Gettelson, Lee Allen, and Harold Seymour.

J.T. *M.G.*
P.P. *D.P.*

This book is dedicated to the great pioneers of integrated baseball,
the men who made this a truly national pastime:

Bud Fowler

Fleet Walker

Rube Foster

Branch Rickey

Jackie Robinson

Larry Doby

Minnie Minoso

Introduction

When it first appeared, in 1989, *Total Baseball* was the most complete, most authoritative, and most informative—not to mention the biggest—baseball book ever published. It came into being because its creators saw that there was nothing else like it and because its publishers had faith that fans would want such a book—a virtual baseball library in one volume. In fact, it could be said that *Total Baseball* is the first true baseball encyclopedia because it offers not only the game's numbers but also the stories and statistical principles that underlie them.

In this fifth edition, *Total Baseball* builds upon that foundation to provide new stories, new stats, and a thorough review of all the data that went into the first four editions. We welcomed, in a dramatic new development, the endorsement of *Total Baseball* by Major League Baseball as the official encyclopedia of the game in 1995, and in that same year we also welcomed a new publishing partner in Viking.

This book is divided into two parts. The first consists of prose features on subjects of interest to all baseball fans, from the general reader who wishes to know more about the game's trivia and lore to the advanced fan who wants to know about its business and law. The origins of the farm system; black baseball before Jackie Robinson; complete balloting for the Hall of Fame and major awards; ballparks; women in baseball . . . but why tease you with the pleasures that await?

Simply be assured that *Total Baseball* will be totally absorbing. The writers gathered together here are experts in their fields, as befits an encyclopedic reference work, and even the most erudite reader will learn countless new things about our great game.

The same holds true for Part 2, which contains the playing and pitching registers, a variety of rosters, a year-by-year statistical summary of major league play since 1871, and more. The stats newly developed for this book—like the Total Player Ranking or Fielding Runs—will please the devotee of sabermetrics, who may know about Runs Created, Production, and the whole Linear Weights System but who has never before been offered these stats applied to all of baseball's 14,661 players. The traditional computations will appeal to baseball scholars, who know what a tangle of briars the historical record has become over the last two decades, as individual player records have been altered without corresponding changes to other players on the same team. (For more on this, see the essay, "The History of Major League Baseball Statistics.") And the cornucopia of stats old and new—for everyone from all-time leaders to cup-of-coffee nonentities—will provide days, months, and years of archaeological delight for baseball fans of all stripes.

Total Baseball joins the game's most knowledgeable writers, most of them members of the Society for American Baseball Research (SABR), with the game's great historical database, the one built up over two decades by Pete Palmer. Benefiting from the painstaking research of hundreds of friends and colleagues in SABR, we have corrected many errors and omissions in other reference works, relying not upon the numbers enshrined by tradition or official edict but upon the evidence. How many hours have been spent scanning the handwritten official records of the early years of the century, or reviewing box scores and scoresheets and game summaries! It would have been easier not to bother, to accept, for example, a game mistakenly entered twice in the record for 1910 so that Ty Cobb could keep his career total of 4,191 hits. But there can be no statute of limitations on historical error; the researcher and historian must go where the evidence leads them.

This book is as good as we know how to make it, but we do want to hear from you about our blunders (we know there will be some, as there were in the previous editions) or about your research (which may be as important to subsequent editions of *Total Baseball* as that of, say, Joe Wayman was for the fourth). We believe that history is process, not product, and our aim has been for *Total Baseball* to reflect the state of the art in baseball research and to convey its editors' love for the game.

## CHAPTER 1

Our Game

John Thorn

Baseball has been, most often for better but occasionally for worse, the American game. It has given our people rest and recreation, myths and memories, heroes and history and hope. It has mirrored our society, sometimes propelling it with models for democracy, community, commerce, and common humanity, sometimes lagging behind with equally instructive models of futility and resistance to change. And as our national game, baseball in no small measure defines us as Americans, connecting us with our countrymen across all barriers of generation, class, race, and creed.

Baseball in the Americas is more than a game, an observation to which the scope of this book is testimony and tribute. But it is first and foremost about *play*, a fact obscured amid today's ferment of free agency, salary caps, and threatened cataclysm. Some 150 years ago, an overly solemn America was first indebted to baseball for the freedom it gave to play. As overture to this volume's chronicle of baseball's history, let's look at how child's play came to be our national pastime.

America Learns to Play

Even when baseball was in its infancy in the 1850s—having just evolved from the boyhood game of rounders and its more formalized derivative, town ball—the sport was already shaping the life of the country. Americans of the previous generation had been blind to the virtue of play, much perplexing our European cousins. We permitted ourselves few amusements that could not be justified in terms of social or business utility, or "seriousness." Nonconformists like the Olympic Town Ball Club of Philadelphia in the 1830s had to put up with a lot of guff, as this contemporary account details:

The first day that the Philadelphia men took the field .... only four men were found to play, so they started in by playing a game called cat ball. All the players were over twenty-five years of age, and to see them playing a game like this caused much merriment among the friends of the players. It required "sand" in those days to go out on the field and play, as the prejudice against the game was very great. It took nearly a whole season to get men enough together to make a team, owing to the ridicule heaped upon the players for taking part in such childish sports.

What brought scorn upon the heads of these staunch devotees of town ball (also known as "Boston Ball" or the "Massachusetts Game") was that although the game had regularly positioned fielders and demanded a modicum of strategic play, it still bore the childish essence of rounders: the retirement of a baserunner by throwing the ball *at* him, which necessitated a softer, less resilient ball than that used in the manly sport of cricket. Who was the genius who came up with the idea of retiring a runner by touching him with the ball or securing it "in the hands of an adversary on the base"? Perhaps it was Alexander Cartwright, who is known to many as "the man who invented baseball," though baseball was not invented; it evolved. But it may have been Daniel Lucius Adams or William Wheaton or Lewis F. Wadsworth.

No matter—this was the first step toward making an American game that could challenge boys and men alike, and that could take its place in the life of our nation as cricket had done in England. Henry Chadwick, the English-born cricket reporter who coined the term "national pastime" and became known as the "Father of Baseball," wrote that early on he

... was struck with the idea that base ball was just the game for a national sport for Americans and ... that from this game of ball a powerful lever might be made by which our people could be lifted into a position of more devotion to physical exercise and healthful out-door recreation than they had, hitherto, been noted for.... In fact, as is well-known, we were the regular target for the shafts of raillery and even abuse from our outdoor-sport-loving cousins of England, in consequence of our national neglect of sports and pastimes, and our too great devotion to business and the "Almighty Dollar." But thanks to Base Ball ... we have been transformed into quite another people....

The transformation was from a hard-working but grim citizenry to a nation devoted to fresh air and exercise, not unlike the current rage for jogging, aerobics, and body building. Amateur baseball clubs sprang up like dandelions in the years immediately before the Civil War, but these were formed more for camaraderie and calisthenics than the pursuit of victory or the honing of skills. The demands of the new game on athleticism were few, as the one-bound rule remained in effect (an out was recorded if a ball was caught on a bounce), and a couple of weeks' practice were enough to make a novice of forty a creditable player. Men viewed baseball as a mild pastime, or relief from the mental strains of work; as a tonic, restorative of the physical energies needed for work; or as a release of the surplus nervous energy that impedes young men in their pursuit of purposeful work. America in the mid-1850s was learning how to play, but still viewed sport in terms of its salutary effects on commerce; not until the close of the War Between the States would the focus shift to learning how to play well—for its own sake.

The Charm of the Game

Today we think of baseball as an anachronism, a last vestige of America's agrarian paradise—an idyllic game that takes us back to a more innocent time. But baseball originated in New York City, not rural Cooperstown, and in truth it was an exercise in nostalgia from the beginning. Alexander Cartwright and his Knickerbockers began play in Madison Square in 1842, and the city's northward progress soon compelled them to move uptown to Murray Hill. When the grounds there were also threatened by the march of industry, the Knicks ferried across the Hudson River to the Elysian Fields of Hoboken, a landscaped retreat of picnic grounds and scenic vistas that was designed by its proprietors to relieve New Yorkers of city air and city care. In other words, the purpose of baseball's primal park was the same as that of New York's Central Park or, much later, Boston's Fenway Park—to give an increasingly urban populace a park within the city, a place reminiscent of the idealized farms that had sent all these lads to the metropolis.

Thus the attraction of the game in its earliest days was first the novelty and exhilaration of play; second the opportunity for deskbound city clerks to expend surplus energy in a sylvan setting, freed from the tyranny of the clock; and third, to harmonize with an American golden age that was almost entirely legendary.

Simple charms, simple pleasures. In the late 1860s, advancing skills led to heightened appetites for victory, which led to hot pursuit of the game's gifted players, which inevitably led to *sub rosa* payments and, by 1870, rampant professionalism. (Doesn't that chain reaction put one in mind of college football or basketball?) The gentlemanly players of baseball's first generation retreated from the field, shaking their heads in dismay at how greed had perverted the "grand old game"—now barely twenty years old—and probably ruined it forever.

Sound familiar? It should—the same dire and premature announcements of the demise of the game have been issued ever since, spurred by free-agent signings, long-term contracts, no-trade provisions, strikes and lockouts, integration, night ball, rival leagues, ad infinitum. The only conclusions a calm head might draw from this recurring cycle of disdain for the present and glorification of the past are that (a) things aren't what they used to be and never were; (b) accurate assessment of a present predicament is impossible, for it requires perspective; and (c) no matter what the owners or players or rulesmakers or fans do, they can't kill baseball. All three conclusions are correct. In baseball, the distinction between amateur and professional is not clear-cut: an amateur may play for devotion to the game (*amat* being the Latin for love), but a professional does not play for pursuit of gain alone; he plays for love, too.

Oh, don't you remember the game of base-ball we saw twenty years ago played,
When contests were true, and the sight free to all, and

home-runs in plenty were made?
When we lay on the grass, and with thrills of delight, watched the ball squarely pitched at the bat,
And easily hit, and then mount out of sight along with our cheers and our hat?
And then, while the fielders raced after the ball, the men on the bases flew round,
And came in together—four batters in all. Ah! That was the old game renowned.
Now salaried pitchers, who throw the ball curved at padded and masked catchers lame
And gate-money music and seats all reserved is all that is left of the game.
Oh, give us the glorious matches of old, when love of true sport made them great,
And not this new-fashioned affair always sold for the boodle they take at the gate.

                                                   H. C. Dodge

That doomsday ditty was published in 1886.

The National Pastime

America before the Civil War was still populated by a handful of veterans of the Revolutionary War and many who remembered vividly the War of 1812. The era of Anglo-American amity had not yet dawned; our country's spiritual separation from the Mother Country, though effected by treaty in 1783, was still in process. And having baseball to rival and replace cricket was an important step in that process. Moreover when England, seeking to maintain its supply of cotton from the American South, appeared over-cordial to the Confederate cause, anti-British feeling swept the North. An America long suffering from an inferiority complex toward England now turned against cricket and embraced baseball with increased fervor.

From 1856 on, Henry Chadwick had been eager for baseball to rise to the status in America that cricket held in his native England. He championed the game tirelessly, helping to refine its rules and practices to make it the equal of cricket as a "manly" and "scientific" game. And baseball soon became, in his words, like cricket "a game requiring the mental powers of judgment, calculation and quick perception to excel in it—while in its demands upon the vigor, endurance and courage of manhood, its requirements excel those requisite to become equally expert as a cricketer."

Chadwick invented a method of scorekeeping and statistical compilation patterned on those which were inaugurated in cricket. Baseball was an elemental game—pitch, hit, catch, throw—like other games of ball; but keeping records of the contests and later printing box scores and individual averages elevated it from rounders and placed it on an equal footing with its transatlantic counterpart. (As important, the records served to legitimize men's concern with what had been merely a boys' exercise by making it more systematic, like the numerically annotated world of business.) Today a baseball without records is inconceivable: They are what keep Babe Ruth and Ty Cobb and Walter Johnson alive in our minds in a way that President James K. Polk, Walter Reed, or

Admiral Dewey—arguably greater men—are not.

By the end of the Civil War cricket in this country remained a pastime for a shrinking band of Anglophiles, while the New York Game of Baseball (as it was then called to differentiate it from the nearly vanished Massachusetts Game) was spreading across the country, courtesy of returning veterans whose first exposure to baseball might have come in a prisoner-of-war camp. In the press, baseball was typically proclaimed The National Game— the same term Britons used for cricket.

Play for Pay

From its creation in 1871 to its crash five years later, the National Association had a rocky time as America's first professional league. Franchises came and went with dizzying speed, often folding in midseason. Schedules were not played out if a club slated to go on the road saw little prospect of gain. Drinking and gambling and game-fixing were rife. And the Boston Red Stockings of Al Spalding and the Wright brothers dominated play, going 71-8 in the last of their four straight championship seasons; their predictable and one-sided victories crushed the competition and at last, interest in the entire circuit.

But from the ashes of the National Association emerged the Red Stockings' model of success and the entrepreneurial genius of Chicago's William Hulbert. After raiding Boston to obtain four of the biggest stars in the game—Spalding, Ross Barnes, Deacon White, and Cal McVey—and lining up the services of the Philadelphia Athletics' Adrian Anson, the White Stockings were ready to roll in the National League of Professional Base Ball Clubs, founded on February 2, 1876 in New York's Grand Central Hotel.

The first five years of the NL were nearly as unsettled as the final years of the NA, with franchises appearing and then disappearing in such cities as Syracuse, Indianapolis, and Hartford while major cities like New York and Philadelphia were, after the league's inaugural year, unrepresented. In 1878 the fledgling circuit was forced to cut back to six teams: Milwaukee, Indianapolis, Chicago, Providence, Cincinnati, and Boston. *National* League? *National* Game? It seemed Americans had plenty of appetite for playing the game, but not much for watching it.

Yet as the National League suffered with growing pains, it was introducing some elements that were critical to the explosion of interest that came with the 1880s. It created a professional (paid) umpiring crew; insisted that the league schedule be honored; banned pool selling and hard-liquor consumption in the stands; and created a system of management-owned teams as opposed to the player-run cooperatives that had largely characterized the NA. As the public's renewed faith in the integrity of the game coincided with an upswing in the national economy, not only did the National League flourish; along came an interloper, the rival American Association, to offer patrons 25-cent baseball (NL admissions were 50 cents), Sunday games, and beer. With the public's new appetite for the game seeming insatiable, a group of investors led by St. Louis' Henry Lucas launched a *third* major league, the Union Association, for 1884.

As brash stars like Cap Anson, Tim Keefe, Dan Brouthers, and the larger-than-life King Kelly captured the newspaper headlines and the nation's imagination, the age of the baseball idol arrived. Before this decade, men like Jim Creighton, Joe Start, and George Wright had been admired in New York and New England, but now a baseball hero's image could be mass-produced for nationwide sale, or licensed for advertising, or inspire odes and songs. Kelly inspired "Slide, Kelly, Slide," its arcane references now largely forgotten but once the most popular song in the land:

> *Slide, Kelly, slide!*
> *Your running's a disgrace!*
> *Slide, Kelly, slide!*
> *Stay there, hold your base!*
> *If someone doesn't steal ya,*
> *And your batting doesn't fail ya,*
> *They'll take you to Australia!*
> *Slide, Kelly, slide!*

And although Ernest Lawrence Thayer always denied it, Kelly could well have been the model for "Casey at the Bat," the immortal lyric ballad Thayer penned in 1888. ("Casey" was sometimes reprinted in the newspapers of the 1880s as "Kelly at the Bat," changing the locale from Mudville to Beantown.)

Baseball was ascendant in the 1880s, and like the budding nation whose pastime it was, pretty cocksure of itself. In the same year that "Casey" made his debut, Albert Spalding led a contingent of baseball players on a round the world tour, spreading the gospel of bat and ball to such places as Egypt, Italy, England, Hawaii, and the above-mentioned Australia. Baseball, America thought, was too grand a game to be merely a national pastime; it ought to be the international pastime.

At a New York banquet for Spalding's returning "world tourists" in 1889, speaker Mark Twain declared, "Baseball is the very symbol, the outward and visible expression of the drive and push and rush and struggle of the raging, tearing, booming nineteenth century." Spalding himself later wrote:

I claim that Base Ball owes its prestige as our National Game to the fact that as no other form of sport it is the exponent of American Courage, Confidence, Combativeness; American Dash, Discipline, Determination; American Energy, Eagerness, Enthusiasm; American Pluck, Persistency, Performance; American Spirit, Sagacity, Success; American Vim, Vigor, Virility.

In fact baseball had become more than the mere reflection of our rising industrial and political power and its propensity for bluster and hokum: the national game was beginning to *supply* emblems for democracy, industry, and community that would change America and the world—not in the ways that Spalding's Tourists may have envisioned, but indisputably for the better.

A Model Institution

Father Chadwick had been typically prescient when he wrote in 1876, the inaugural year of the National League and the centenary of America's birth:

What Cricket is to an Englishman, Base-Ball has become to an American.... On the Cricket-field—and there only—the Peer and the Peasant meet on equal terms; the possession of courage, nerve, judgment, skill, endurance and activity alone giving the palm of superiority. In fact, a more democratic institution does not exist in Europe than this self-same Cricket; and as regards its popularity, the records of the thousands of Commoners, Divines and Lawyers, Legislators and Artisans, and Literateurs as well as Mechanics and Laborers, show how great a hold it has on the people. If this is the characteristic of Cricket in aristocratic and monarchical England, how much more will the same characteristics mark Base-Ball in democratic and republican America.

Chadwick's vision of baseball as a model democratic institution would have to wait for the turn of the century to be fully articulated, and for Jackie Robinson and Branch Rickey to be fully realized. But Chadwick's belief that baseball could be more than a game, could become a model of and for American life, presaged baseball's golden age of 1903-30.

The tumultuous 1890s witnessed a player revolt against high-handed and monopolistic management, epitomized by a cap on salaries, followed by a nearly ruinous contraction from three major leagues to one twelve-team circuit. The national economy suffered a panic in 1893 and a sluggish recovery thereafter; baseball attendance dwindled; and the lack of postseason interleague competition after 1890 (as there had been since 1884) was sorely felt. The game was in a period of consolidation, or hibernation, or stagnation; one's perspective depended upon whether he were an owner, fan, or player.

But then Ban Johnson came along, fired by the same vision of a rival league that had inflamed the Players League and the American and Union Associations before him, and that would beckon to the Federal and Continental Leagues later on. With the declaration by the American League that it would conduct business as a major league in 1901, and the signing of a peace treaty with the Nationals two years later, the World Series was resumed, prosperity returned, and the popularity and influence of the game exploded.

Baseball mania seized America as new heroes like Christy Mathewson, Honus Wagner, Ty Cobb, Walter Johnson, and Nap Lajoie found a public hungry for knowledge of their every action, their every thought. A fan's affiliation with his team could exceed in vigor his attachment to his church, his trade, his political party—all but family and country, and even these were wrapped up in baseball. The national pastime became the great repository of national ideals, the symbol of all that was good in American life: fair play (sportsmanship); the rule of law (objective arbitration of disputes); equal opportunity (each side has its innings); the brotherhood of man (bleacher harmony); and more.

The baseball boom of the early twentieth century built on the game's simple charms of exercise and communal celebration, adding the psychological and social complexities of vicarious play: civic pride, role models, and hero worship. It became routine for the President to throw out the first ball of the season. Supreme Court Justices had inning-by-inning scores from the World Series relayed to their chambers. Business leaders, perhaps disingenuously, praised baseball as a model of competition and fair play. "Baseball," opined a writer for *American Magazine* in 1913, "has given our public a fine lesson in commercial morals.... Some day all business will be reorganized and conducted by baseball standards."

Leaders of recent immigrant groups advised their peoples to learn the national game if they wanted to become Americans, and foreign-language newspapers devoted space to educating their readers about America's strange and wonderful game. (New York's *Staats-Zeitung,* for example, applauded *Kraftiges Schlagen*—hard hitting—and cautioned German fans not to kill the *Unparteiischer.*) As historian Harold Seymour wrote, "The argot of baseball supplied a common means of communication and strengthened the bond which the game helped to establish among those sorely in need of it—the mass of urban dwellers and immigrants living in the anonymity and impersonal vortex of large industrial cities.... With the loss of the traditional ties known in a rural society, baseball gave to many the feeling of belonging." And rooting for a baseball team permitted city folk, newcomers and native-born, the sense of pride in community that in former times—when they may have lived in small towns—was commonplace.

Thus baseball offered a model of how to be an American, to be part of the team: Baseball was "second only to death as a leveler," wrote essayist Allen Sangree. Even in those horrifically leveling years of 1941-45, when so many of our bravest and best gave their lives to defend American ideals, baseball's role as a vital enterprise was confirmed by President Franklin Delano Roosevelt's "green light" for continued play. Many of baseball's finest players—Ted Williams, Joe DiMaggio, Hank Greenberg, Bob Feller, to name a few—swapped their baseball gear for Uncle Sam's, and served with military distinction or helped to boost the nation's morale. Even oldtimers like Babe Ruth, Walter Johnson, and Ty Cobb donned uniforms in service of their country—baseball uniforms, as they staged exhibitions on behalf of war bonds. Servicemen overseas looked to letters from home and the box scores in *The Sporting News* to keep them in touch with what they had left behind, and what they were fighting for—an American way of life that was a beacon for a world in which the light of freedom had been nearly extinguished.

I was one of the countless immigrants who from the 1860s on saw baseball as the "open sesame" to the door of their adopted land. A Polish Jew born in occupied Germany to Holocaust survivors, I arrived on these shores at age two. After checking in at Ellis Island, I happened by chance to spend the first night in my new land in the no-longer-elegant hotel where in 1876 the National League had been founded. I learned to read by studying the backs of Topps baseball cards, and to be an American by attaching myself passionately to the Brooklyn Dodgers (who also taught me about the fickleness of love).

The Brooklyn Dodgers, in the persons particularly of Rickey and Robinson, also taught America a lesson: that baseball's integrative and democratic models, by the 1940s long held to be verities, were hollow at the core.

David Halberstam has written:

...it was part of our folklore, basic to our national democratic myth, that sports was the great American equalizer, that money and social status did not matter upon the playing fields. Elsewhere life was assumed to be unfair: those who had privilege passed it on to their children, who in turn had easier, softer lives. Those without privilege were doomed to accept the essential injustices of daily life. But according to the American myth, in sports the poor but honest kid from across the tracks could gain (often in competition with richer, snottier kids) recognition and acclaim for his talents.

Until October 23, 1945, when Robinson signed a contract to play for the Montreal Royals, Brooklyn's top farm club, the myth as far as African Americans were concerned was not a sustaining legend but a mere falsehood.

Rickey's rectitude and Robinson's courage have become central parables of baseball and America, exemplars of decency and strength that inspire all of us. Their "great experiment" came too late for such heroes of black ball as Josh Gibson and Oscar Charleston and Ray Dandridge, but its success has been complete. Once the integrative or leveling model of baseball—all America playing and working in harmony—was extended to African Americans, the effect on the nation was profound. Eighty years after the Civil War, America had proved itself unable to practice the values for which it was fought; baseball showed the way. This is what Commissioner Ford Frick said to the St. Louis Cardinals, rumored to be planning a strike in May 1947:

If you do this you will be suspended from the league. You will find that the friends you think you have in the press box will not support you, that you will be outcasts. I do not care if half the league strikes. Those who do it will encounter quick retribution. They will be suspended and I don't care if it wrecks the National League for five years. This is the United States of America, and one citizen has as much right to play as any other. The National League will go down the line with Robinson whatever the consequence.

As Monte Irvin said, "Baseball has done more to move America in the right direction than all the professional patriots with their billions of cheap words." The Supreme Court decision of *Brown v. Topeka Board of Education*; civil rights heroes like Martin Luther King, Jr., James Meredith, Thurgood Marshall, and others; the freedom marches and the voting rights act—all were vital to America's progress toward unity, but the title of one of Jackie Robinson's books may not overstate the case: *Baseball Has Done It.*

A final way in which baseball supplies models for America is one that has been present from the game's beginning: a model for children wishing to be grownups, wrestling with their insecurities and wondering, *What does it mean to be a man? What does a man do?* (Most of us old boys occasionally wonder this as well.) The answers in baseball, at least, are unequivocal; as Satchel Paige said in his later years, "I loved baseball. There wasn't no 'maybe so' about it."

Baseball gives children a sense of how wide the world is, in its possibilities but also in its geography. Reading the summations of minor-league ball in *The Sporting News* each week piqued the curiosity of baseball-mad boys like me: where were Kokomo and Mattoon and Thibodeaux and Nogales? How did people behave in Salinas or Rocky Mount? What did they eat in Artesia? How many exciting, exotic places this enormous country contained! But a note of comfort—they couldn't be all that strange if baseball was played there.

And to that other vast *terra incognita*—the world of adults—baseball also offered a road map. How many boys and girls learned to talk with adults, principally their fathers, by nodding wisely at an assessment of a shortstop's range or a pitcher's heart, and mock-confidently venturing an opinion about the hometown team's chances? Our dads are our first heroes (and, decades later, our last); but in between, baseball players are what we want to be. For heroes are larger than life, and when as adults we have taken the measure of ourselves and found we are no more than life-size, and on our bad days seemingly less than that, baseball can puff us up a bit.

Douglass Wallop put it nicely:

... only yesterday the fan was a kid of nine or ten bolting his breakfast on Saturday morning and hurtling from the house with a glove buttoned over his belt and a bat over his shoulder, rushing to the nearest vacant lot, perhaps the nearest alley, where the other guys were gathering, a place where it would always be spring. For him, baseball would always have the sound and look and smell of that morning and of other mornings just like it. Only by an accident of chance would he find himself, in the years to come, up in the grandstand, looking on. But for a quirk of fate, he himself would be down on that field; it would be his likeness on the television screen and his name in the newspaper high on the list of .300 hitters. He was a fan, but a fan only incidentally. He was, first and always, himself a baseball player.

The Fifties

If the America that was survives anywhere as more than a memory, it is in baseball, that strangely pastoral game in no matter what setting—domed stadium or Little League field. As hindsight improves upon foresight, memory improves upon reality, so that the endless monotony and grinding physical labor of small-town life before the Civil War are now thought quite romantic. For all our complaints today, it may likewise be argued that America is better than it ever was.

Given the calamitous labor-management war of 1994, there are few who would say the same about baseball. However, today's players *are* better than those in the game's golden age; the strategy of the game and even its execution are more adept (forget all that moaning about how nobody knows the "fundamentals" any more ... the average player of fifty years ago didn't know them either); and the opportunities to watch baseball, if not to play it, far exceed those of say, the 1950s, today broadly regarded as the game's halcyon era. (A golden age may be defined flexibly, it seems, so as to coincide with the period of one's youth.) For all its pull toward the good old days, for all its statistical illusions of an Olympian era when titans strode the basepaths, for all its seeming permanence in a world aswirl with change, baseball has in fact moved with America, and improved with it.

The period after World War II was a heady time for the nation and its pastime, both of them buoyed by returning veterans and removed restrictions. But in 1946 the major leagues still represented only the sixteen cities that had participated in the National Agreement of 1903, none west of St. Louis; a handful of African Americans were just entering the minor leagues after a half-century's exclusion; and because television was not yet a staple of the American home, most baseball fans had never seen *even a single big-league game.*

Women had been courted as patrons (even nonpaying patrons) ever since the game's dawn. Baseball management hoped that their presence would lend "tone" to the proceedings and keep a lid on the rowdies, in the stands and on the field. But women's participation in the game's labor force and management was even more limited than their role in the nation's business and industry—Rosie the Riveter and Eleanor Roosevelt as yet had no counterparts in Organized Baseball. The All-American Girls Baseball League made its debut in 1943, the brainchild of Chicago Cubs' owner Philip K. Wrigley. The women's "league of their own" won many admirers over the next decade, but the majors always regarded it as separate and unequal.

On the amateur level, while American Legion Junior Baseball had begun as early as 1928, and Little League in 1939, neither attained their heights until after the War ended. Naysayers will point out that baseball has lost ground as more kids today play football, basketball, soccer, and tennis than fifty years ago—but far more play baseball, too, and not only in America. The annual pursuit of the Little League championship in Williamsport, Pennsylvania (like the Pan-American Games), has become an international affair, an instrument of diplomacy that State Department officials envy. Indeed, baseball may yet hold the key to neighborly relations with all nations in the hemisphere.

Baseball in the colleges, now so vibrant and so fertile with major league talent, was on the path to extinction by the end of the War, only to be brought back from the brink by the G.I. Bill: the explosive growth in enrollment that the returning veterans produced also created a sudden need for expanded athletic programs, and baseball was the prime beneficiary. The NCAA's introduction of the College World Series in 1947 affirmed the game's recovery on campus, and since locating in Omaha three years later it has grown steadily.

In 1951 Major League Baseball, as dated from the inception of the National League in 1876, reached the august age of 75 and proclaimed its "diamond jubilee." Celebratory banquets were held, a plaque was erected at the old hotel where the league was founded, and all NL players wore a commemorative patch on their sleeves. (Coincidentally but less flashily the American League marked its fiftieth birthday as a major circuit.) Let's take a moment to look at where baseball stood at that point.

There was no question it was booming. On the professional level, a whopping 59 leagues contained 448 teams employing about 8,000 players—or 19 minor leaguers

competing for each of the then 400 spots in the big show. Little League would soon send its first alumnus to the majors, which had already accepted hundreds of graduates from Legion and other programs. Happy Chandler secured from television a then mind-boggling but now quaint $6 million for broadcast rights to the next six World Series. And with the game's most powerful teams bunched in New York City—the Yankees, the Dodgers, and the Giants—the publicity mills and the turnstiles were spinning as they had never spun before.

But the excitement of the first five postwar years was not confined to New York: even such perennial tailenders as the Boston Braves, the Philadelphia Phillies, and the Cleveland Indians fought their way into the World Series; and staid old Cleveland, under Bill Veeck's carnival-barker aegis, set staggering new attendance records. Many of the newly admitted African-American players had become stars and—satisfyingly, though few but Branch Rickey had predicted it—box-office attractions: Jackie Robinson, Roy Campanella, and Don Newcombe of the Dodgers; Monte Irvin and rookie Willie Mays of the Giants; Sam Jethroe of the Braves; Larry Doby and Satchel Paige of the Indians. Many prewar stars continued to shine, like Bob Feller, Stan Musial, and Ted Williams (though with the Korean War he answered Uncle Sam's call yet again), and new ones like Gotham's center field trio of Duke Snider, Mickey Mantle, and Mays replenished the stock as heroes like Joe DiMaggio hung up their spikes.

But most of these blessings had their downside. Opening the game to African Americans was indubitably right, but it killed the Negro Leagues, ruining owners and abruptly ending many playing careers. The increasing organization of youth baseball, particularly the rise of Little League, heightened the stress of the game at its formative levels and drained much of the fun, as driven parents began to see their Junior as tomorrow's big leaguer, not as just a boy having fun while learning a thing or two. The game on the field was dominated by the home run, making for a brand of ball that some might term dull. League champs registered such stolen-base totals as Dom DiMaggio's 15 or Jackie Jensen's 22; Early Wynn led the AL in ERA one year with a mark of 3.20; and the three-base hit, despite the big old parks still prevalent, went the way of the dodo. And the pennant domination by the three New York teams—principally the Yankees, of course—made the national pastime a rather parochial pleasure; it was hard for fans in Pittsburgh or Detroit to wax rhapsodic over a Subway Series. No, the blessings of the 1950s were not unmitigated, any more than on the national scene the tranquility of the Eisenhower years was without cost.

Take television, for instance: the revenues were great, and so was the publicity value of electronically extending major league play to people in southern and western areas. But the novelty of big-time heroes on the small screen kept those folks at home when formerly they had gone to the local ballpark. The minors began their long decline, one that didn't bottom out until 1964; by then the 59 leagues of 1951 had become 19, and the 8,000-odd professional players had dwindled to fewer than 2,500.

Moreover, television whetted the baseball appetites of Californians and Texans (and Georgians and Washingtonians and more). That demand plus the development of faster passenger planes gave ideas to owners of two of baseball's decaying franchises. Walter O'Malley, owner of the Brooklyn Dodgers, and Giants' owner Horace Stoneham had seen the solidarity of the original sixteen-city composition broken in 1953, when the venerable Boston Braves (a franchise established in the first year of the National Association, 1871) became the darlings of Milwaukee, and further weakened by the defections in 1954-55 of the St. Louis Browns to Baltimore and the Philadelphia Athletics to Kansas City. Amid weeping and gnashing of teeth that continue to this day, the Dodgers and Giants left for the Golden West in 1958.

In a strange twist, the architect of the move, Walter O'Malley, was (and in the East, still is) widely reviled as the man responsible for ending the grand old game's paradisical age. Yet the placement of franchises in California, as distressing as it was for Brooklyn and Manhattan and as roundly condemned as it was by traditionalists, may now be seen as the best thing to happen to baseball in the decade. And Walter O'Malley, if you will permit your mind a considerable stretch, may be viewed not as the snake offering baseball the mortal apple but as a latter-day Johnny Appleseed (in the footsteps of Alexander Cartwright, who in 1849 also headed for California in pursuit of gold, yet who is remembered not for his venality but for bringing the New York Game to the West).

It was imperative that baseball take the game to where the people were, precisely as it had in 1903. America's population had already begun the westward and southward shift that was to become so pronounced in the 1960s and '70s. The move to Los Angeles and San Francisco, rather than confirming those cities' stature as "big-league," as is so often written, brought baseball into step with America, which had long recognized them as such. Baseball could now call itself the national pastime without apology.

The Sixties

A chaotic decade for our country, the 1960s were worrisome, stormy years for baseball as well, with dramatic changes in league composition, playing styles, competitive balance and, most distressingly, the game's appeal to the American people. Baseball endured its ordeal by fire, and came through not unscathed but strengthened.

The departure of the Dodgers and Giants in 1958 created a vacuum in New York and an increased hunger for baseball in new boomtowns like Houston, Atlanta, and Minneapolis. Enter Branch Rickey, nearly eighty but still possessed of a keen nose for new opportunity. The great innovator who had already brought baseball the farm system and integration now created the Continental League, a paper league with paper franchises. Nonetheless, Rickey's mirage worried Organized Baseball into expansion.

Two of the Continental "franchises"—the future New York Mets and Houston Colt .45s—were admitted for 1962. The American League was authorized to commence its western foray one year earlier with the expansion-draft Los Angeles Angels and the relocated Minnesota Twins (the latter being the transplanted Wash-

ington Senators, who were replaced in the nation's capital by an ill-fated expansion team).

Other franchise shifts and startups in the decade saw baseball's original vagabonds, the Milwaukee Braves by way of Boston, move to Atlanta in 1966. Two years later the erstwhile Athletics of Philadelphia, having failed in Kansas City, directed their caravan toward Oakland.

The A's were quickly replaced in KC by the Royals, one of two new teams introduced in each league with the expansion of 1969. This in turn precipitated divisional play and the League Championship Series, both inventions much decried at the time but now generally applauded. And in one of baseball's more forgettable debacles, the expansion Pilots of 1969 lost their course in Seattle after only one year and ran aground in Milwaukee, where they were rechristened as the Brewers. The National League's expansion into San Diego and Montreal proceeded more smoothly, although Padres' attendance lagged expectations and the Expos' Olympic Stadium (replacing the stopgap Jarry Park) took longer to open its dome than Michelangelo took to paint St. Peter's.

On the field, the big-bang game of the 1950s was giving way to a pitching-and-defense formula, at least in the National League, which began to outstrip its long-time tormentor at the box office and in World Series and All Star confrontations. Speed returned to the equation, too, as personified by first Maury Wills and then Lou Brock (though both were preceded, in the AL, by Luis Aparicio). And a revolution in baseball strategy was brewing, as the 1959 success of such relievers as Larry Sherry, Lindy McDaniel, and Roy Face paved the way for the universal adoption of the bullpen stopper in the 1960s.

In the American League expansion year of 1961, the first played to a 162-game schedule, the Bronx Bombers hit a whopping 240 homers. Sluggers Harmon Killebrew, Norm Cash, and Rocky Colavito all hit more than 40 homers; Mickey Mantle hit more than 50. These totals were troubling to Commissioner Ford Frick, but nowhere near as consterning as the 61 homers struck by Roger Maris to top the game's most famous record, the 60 that Babe Ruth had walloped in 1927. After seeing the National League's scoring increase in 1962, its first year of expansion, Frick became concerned that pitchers were becoming an endangered species. He said:

I would even like the spitball to come back. Take a look at the batting, home run, and slugging record for recent seasons, and you become convinced that the pitchers need help urgently.

Disastrously, Frick convinced the owners to widen the strike zone for 1963 to its pre-1950 dimensions: top of the armpit to bottom of the knee. The result was to increase strikeouts, reduce walks, and shrink batting averages within five years to levels unseen since 1908, the nadir of the deadball era. The once-proud Yankees, who had continued their long domination of the American League to mid-decade, saw their team batting average sink to an incredible .214 in 1968. That year produced an overall AL mark of .230 and a batting champion, Carl Yastrzemski, with an average of .301.

As pitchers vanquished batters, seemingly for all eternity, the bottom line was that the fans stayed away in droves. Attendance in the National League, which in 1966 reached 15 million, fell by 1968 to only 11.7 million. In fact, despite the addition of four new clubs in 1961-62, attendance in 1968 was only 3 million more than it had been in 1960. Critics charged that baseball was a geriatric vestige of an America that had vanished, a game too slow for a nation that was rushing toward the moon; its decline would only steepen, they claimed, as that more with-it national pastime, pro football, extended its mastery of the airwaves.

But the sky was not falling, despite the alarms. The owners acted quickly to redress the game's balance between offense and defense, reducing the strike zone and lowering the pitcher's mound. But the most important change may have been one that was introduced in 1965 and was only beginning to take effect: the amateur free-agent draft. Typically successful teams like the Yankees, Dodgers, Braves, and Cardinals had stayed successful because of their attention to scouting. Consistently they were able to garner more top prospects for their farm systems than clubs with less deep pockets or more volatile management. Now, teams that had fallen on hard times need not look toward a generation of famine before returning to the feast. Now, dynasties—awe-inspiring but not healthy for the game—were suddenly rendered implausible. Now, baseball had a competitive balance that could produce a rotation of electrifying successes among the leagues' cities, like the ascension of the Boston Red Sox from ninth place in 1966 to the pennant the next, and the amazing rise of the New York Mets from the netherworld they had known to World Champions in 1969. The game would still have some hard rows to hoe in the 1970s, but there was no mistaking the reversal of its downturn: in the new age of "relevance," baseball was back.

The Seventies

The 1970s saw a continuation of the trend toward new stadium construction that had marked the 1960s and may well have triggered that decade's batting drought, as hitter's havens like Ebbets Field, the Polo Grounds, and Sportsman's Park fell to the wrecker's ball. The 1960s had brought new ballparks to eleven cities—San Francisco, Los Angeles, Washington, Bloomington (MN), New York (NL), Houston, Atlanta, Anaheim, St. Louis, Oakland, and San Diego. In 1970-71, baseball bade farewell to old friends Crosley Field, Forbes Field, and Shibe Park as new stadiums—artificial-turf clones of each other—sprang up in Cincinnati, Pittsburgh, and Philadelphia. Other new parks were built in Arlington, Kansas City, Montreal, Seattle, and Toronto (the latter two, expansion franchises added to the American League in 1977), and Yankee Stadium underwent a massive facelift.

All this construction activity seemed to bespeak the game's profitability. Indeed, attendance was climbing in almost all major league cities, as heroes like Henry Aaron, Johnny Bench, Reggie Jackson, and Pete Rose, to name but a few, gave the fans plenty to cheer about. And the controversial adoption of the designated hitter innovation by the American League in 1973 gave a further boost to hitting while giving fans much to argue about, which after all is one of the game's great pleasures.

But the game's financial health was imperiled by rising unrest over labor issues, centered on the reserve clause which bound a player to his team in perpetuity while denying him the opportunity to gauge his worth in the free market. The reformulation of the relationship between players and management became the hallmark of the decade and sorely tested fans' devotion to the game.

It began with the momentous case brought against Organized Baseball by veteran outfielder Curt Flood in 1970, challenging the legality of the reserve clause. The Supreme Court ruled against Flood the following year, but the tenor for the 1970s had been set. A thirteen-day player strike delayed the opening of the 1972 season, and arbitrator Peter Seitz ruled in 1975 (in what has come to be known as the Messersmith-McNally case) that a player could establish his right of free agency by playing out his option year without a signed contract. The writing on the wall was clear: free agency was the wave of the future.

Big-name players like Jim Hunter, Reggie Jackson, and Rich Gossage migrated to New York and lesser lights like Wayne Garland and Oscar Gamble signed elsewhere for figures that seemed incredible. In the race to sign available talent some owners spun out of control while others like Minnesota's Cal Griffith, without corporate coffers behind them, had no choice but to sit on the sidelines. Player movement among stars jeopardized fan allegiances, pundits alleged, as Gossage and Jackson played for three teams in three years and championship teams like the Oakland A's and Boston Red Sox were broken up through trades that were forced by the specter of impending—and uncompensated—free-agent departures.

(Comfortingly to the historian, all this hubbub had occurred in very much the same way in 1869-70, before the advent of the reserve clause, when Henry Chadwick was fulminating about the perniciousness of players "revolving" from one team to another simply to advance their fortunes. Also, baseball's first avowedly professional team, Harry Wright's Cincinnati Red Stockings of 1869-70, were roundly abused for constructing their powerhouse team with "mercenaries" from other states—thus scorning baseball's core appeal to civic pride.)

What actually compromised fan loyalties in the '70s was not player movement—it took Yankee fans, oh, maybe, ten minutes to regard Reggie as a born pinstriper—but player salaries. When the major-league minimum was under $5,000 or so and only a Mantle, Williams, Musial, and DiMaggio made $100,000 a year, fans saw with their heroes as, by and large, working colleagues who had the supreme good fortune to play ball for a living. If a star made a splendiferous salary, that was socially useful as a proof that any worker could make it big if only he had sufficient ability to emerge from the pack. But when stars began routinely to command seven-figure salaries, and more importantly the annual wage of the average major leaguer rose to six-figure levels, and eventually seven figures, many adult breadwinners struggled to remain fans.

That they succeeded is testament to their love of the game, for fans have had a difficult assignment in reshaping their views of baseball players along the lines of media stars. The princely compensations of actors and pop musicians have long been accepted by the public as the verdict of the marketplace. If the movie *The Termina-*

tor makes hundreds of millions of dollars for its studio and distributor, then Arnold Schwarzenegger's multimillion-dollar fee for the film seems not out of line. Analogously, if the Dodgers were fabulously lucrative for ownership, then a lofty salary for Steve Garvey ought not to have given rise in the 1970s to resentment among the fans. This sort of reeducation is by no means complete, but barroom banter about baseball in the 1990s is not as bitterly one-note about "greedy players" as it had been fifteen years previous.

And one didn't hear a peep about pro football replacing baseball as the national game.

The Eighties and Nineties

The game on the field in the 1970s had been marked by an unprecedented commingling of power and speed; the great teams of Cincinnati, Baltimore, and Oakland; the return to prominence of the Yankees; and the historic exploits of Henry Aaron and Pete Rose. The game in the '80s would begin with the Philadelphia Phillies, led by free-agent Rose and future Hall of Famers Mike Schmidt and Steve Carlton, ridding themselves of a historic stain. Until their victory over the Kansas City Royals, the Phils were the only one of the original sixteen major-league franchises never to have won a World Series (the St. Louis Browns had to accept the help of their modern incarnation, the Baltimore Orioles).

The next year brought baseball's darkest moment since the Brotherhood revolt and ensuing Players League of 1890, as major-league players walked off their jobs at the height of the season and didn't return for fifty days. By that time even diehard fans were thoroughly fed up with baseball's seeming inability to resolve its problems fairly and with dispatch. Talk of a fan boycott never amounted to much, but as players and management looked toward their Basic Agreement negotiation in 1989—the centenary of the Brotherhood's break with Organized Baseball—both reflected back on the damage wrought in 1981.

The 1980s brought unprecedented parity on the playing field and misery off it. The drug problem endemic in our society struck baseball, inevitably as well, and Pete Rose's itch for gambling disgraced him and the game. Baseball's victims are highly publicized and their fall from grace is judged more reprehensible for all the advantages that today's players enjoy—but the game is an American institution reflecting what is wrong with our people as well as what is right with them. Let's hope that in this most difficult area of addictive behavior baseball can again—as it did with integration—lead America rather than follow it.

The year of 1989 became a nightmare, with Commissioner Bart Giamatti's expulsion of Rose followed by his own sudden and shocking death days later, a second finding of collusion by owners to undermine the free-agent market, and a Bay Area World Series rudely interrupted by an earthquake. But baseball recovered even from these calamities, as well as a spring training lockout in 1990, to embark upon an era that gave promise of unprecedented prosperity. The attendance of the Toronto Blue Jays exceeded the 4 million mark while the team captured back-to-back World Series, the first such feat since the Cincinnati Reds of 1975-1976. And in 1993 the National League expanded to fourteen teams, welcoming franchises in Miami and Colorado that were instantly and wildly prosperous, with the Rockies setting an all-time attendance peak of nearly 4.5 million fans.

And then came 1994, a year of wonderment on the playing fields, as Ken Griffey, Jr., Matt Williams, Frank Thomas, Jeff Bagwell, Tony Gwynn, Greg Maddux and a host of others appeared to be initiating a new golden age of baseball ... until play stopped on August 12 and did not resume. The leagues, which had divided into three divisions for the first time, now had no opportunity to try out their new idea of an additional round of postseason play, with the introduction of a wild-card team that had not been a division winner.

As fans, we were presented with a dilemma: to side with the players, who went on strike hoping to extend their gains of the previous two decades? Or to side with the owners, who stood fast in insisting upon a balance between costs and revenues? As fans, we tried to side with the game of baseball, and wish that its most intense contests would soon reconvene to the field of play.

And they did, with splendid seasons in 1995 and 1996, though some fans continued to withhold their affections, hoping that baseball owners and players would give peace a chance—as at last they did.

Baseball is not a conventional industry. It belongs neither to the players nor management, but to all of us. It is our national pastime, our national symbol, and our national treasure.

Each of us has deplored the present state of things, and has thought back to his personal version of the good old days. But make no mistake about it—our game, the American game, will become stronger than before for having passed through its crucible of the mid-1990s.

The Weather of Our Lives

Ever changing in ways that are so small as to preserve the illusion that "nothing changes in baseball," the game has introduced, in the lifetime of many of us: night ball, plane travel, television, integration, bullpen stoppers, expansion, the amateur draft, competitive parity, indoor stadiums, artificial turf, free agency, the designated hitter, wild-card contestants, interleague contests and international play. Not far off, perhaps, are further expansion to thirty-two teams and intercontinental championships.

For fans accustomed to the game's languorous rhythms and conservative resistance to innovation, the changes of the past twenty years in particular seem positively frenetic. Yet for all its changes, baseball has not strayed far from its origins, and in fact has changed far less than other American institutions of equivalent antiquity. What sustains baseball in the hearts of Americans, finally, is not its responsiveness to changes in society nor its propensity for novelty, but its myths, its lore, its records, and its essential stability. As historian Bruce Catton noted in 1959:

A gaffer from the era of William McKinley, abruptly brought back to the second half of the twentieth century, would find very little in modern life that would not seem new, strange, and rather bewildering, but put in a good grandstand seat back of first base he would see nothing that was not completely familiar.

It's still a game of bat and ball, played without regard for the clock; a game of ninety-foot basepaths, nine innings, nine men in the field; three outs, all out; and three strikes still send you to the bench, no matter whom you know in city hall. It's the national anthem before every game; it's playing catch with your son or daughter; it's learning how to win and how to deal with loss, and how to connect with something larger than our selves.

"Baseball," wrote Thomas Wolfe, "has been not merely 'the great national game' but really a part of the whole weather of our lives, of the thing that is our own, of the whole fabric, the million memories of America." Spring comes in America not on the vernal equinox but on opening day; summer sets in with a Memorial Day doubleheader and does not truly end until the last out of the regular season. Winter begins the day after the World Series.

Where were you when Bobby Thomson hit the shot heard 'round the world? Or the night Carlton Fisk hit his homer in the twelfth? Or when the Mets, with batter after batter one strike away from their loss in the World Series, staged their famous rally? These are milestones in the lives of America and Americans.

We grow up with baseball; we mark—and, for a moment, stop—the passage of time with it; and we grow old with it. It is our game, for all our days.

## CHAPTER 2

Team Histories

Frederick Ivor-Campbell

When the National League awarded expansion franchises to Denver and Miami in June 1991, the number of major league clubs reached 14 in each league—the most since 1884. When the Colorado Rockies and Florida Marlins began play in 1993, they brought to 110 the number of clubs (plus those of the Negro major leagues) that have played major league ball at one time or another since baseball's first professional league—the National Association—was organized in 1871. Some of the early teams dropped out after only a few games, but several have played for more than a century, and one—the present Atlanta Braves—has played every season from 1871 to the present. The only existing franchise older than Atlanta's (which originated as the Boston Red Stockings, then became the Boston and Milwaukee Braves before moving to Atlanta) is the Chicago Cubs, which organized in 1870, a year before league play began. The White Stockings (as they were first known) missed two seasons (1872–1873) in the aftermath of the great Chicago fire, but have since then continuously represented the same city longer than any other club in baseball history.

Here are brief histories of the 28 current big-league clubs, arranged alphabetically by city or state. These are followed by summary histories of the 82 other clubs— now defunct—that at one time also represented their cities in the major leagues.

Atlanta Braves

The Atlanta Braves, who first played in 1871 as Boston's Red Stockings, are the only club to field a team every season of professional league baseball. When the game's first openly professional club, the Cincinnati Red Stockings, decided to revert to amateur status, manager/outfielder Harry Wright and three of his teammates took their talents (and club nickname) to Boston, where, with infielders Ross Barnes and Harry Schafer and pitcher Al Spalding, they formed the nucleus of a team that would dominate the five-year history of the first professional league, the National Association. After a close second-place finish in their first year, the Red Stockings won four pennants in convincing fashion, including a 71–8 record in 1875 with an .899 winning percentage that has never since been approached in major league ball.

When the National League replaced the NA in 1876, four of Boston's best players (including Spalding and Barnes) deserted the club for Chicago. But after a fourth-place finish in 1876, the Red Stockings lured pitcher

Tommy Bond from Hartford and finished at the top in 1877 and '78. Bond dominated NL pitching, winning 40 each year, 22 more than his nearest rival. Although he won another 43 in 1879, Boston slipped to second.

In 1880 the Red Stockings suffered their first losing season as they fell to sixth. After another sixth-place finish the next year, Wright left to manage Providence, but Boston rebounded to third in 1882 and surprised everyone in 1883 by outplaying favored Chicago and Providence to capture their seventh pennant.

Providence knocked them out of the race late in 1884, and Boston remained out of contention the next four seasons. In 1889, though, with several players signed from the defunct Detroit Wolverines (including batting champ Dan Brouthers), and 49 wins from pitcher John Clarkson, the Beaneaters (as they were now more commonly known) waged a two-team race for the championship with the New York Giants. Boston won as many games as the Giants, but lost two more and finished a game back.

Frank Selee, who had managed two straight minor league pennant winners, was hired from Omaha along with his star pitcher, Charles "Kid" Nichols. Their arrival in 1890 ushered in Boston's second golden era. Before they left the club twelve years later, the Beaneaters had won five more NL pennants. Nichols won 27 games in his rookie season, but Boston—decimated by defections to the outlaw Players League—finished only fifth. With the return of some of the defectors in 1891, Clarkson won 33 games, Nichols recorded the first of seven 30-win seasons, and the Beaneaters returned to the top.

When the NL expanded in 1892 from eight teams to twelve, the schedule too was expanded, and the season divided into two halves. Boston won the first half, and the Cleveland Spiders the second. In a World Series to determine the league champion, the Beaneaters (who at 102–48 had the best record) defeated the Spiders.

The split season was abandoned and the schedule reduced in 1893—and Boston captured its third straight pennant. Center fielder Hugh Duffy hit .363. The next year, when hitters exploded for a league BA of .309, Duffy led the way with a .440 that is still the major-league record. His Beaneaters didn't win the pennant, but they became the first club in a decade (and the last until 1920) to hit over 100 home runs. Five Beaneaters drove in 100 runs or more, and the team set a big league record for runs scored (1,220) that still stands.

Boston dropped out of contention for a couple of years, but bounced back in 1897 to edge Baltimore for the pennant by two games. In the Temple Cup series, though (played between the first- and second-place teams for the world title), the Orioles overwhelmed Boston four games to one. The next year the schedule was expanded again, and again (as in 1892) Boston won 102 games to lead the league, winning their twelfth pennant. But as the league had abandoned the four-year-old Temple Cup play, there was no World Series.

After coming in second in 1899, Boston dropped out of pennant contention for fourteen years, finishing as far back as 66½ games (in 1906) and losing as many as 108 (in 1909). Five times the club finished last, including the four years from 1909 to 1912. The Braves (as they were now known) rose to fifth in 1913 under new manager George Stallings, but seemed through the first half of 1914 to be securing for themselves another bed in the cellar.

In mid-July they stood a last-place eighth in a tight field. Six days and six wins later they were third. By mid-August they had climbed to second; on August 26 they replaced the New York Giants in first. For two weeks they alternated between first and second, then took off to win the pennant by 10½ games.

Boston's heroes were pitchers Dick Rudolph and Bill James, both in only their second full big league seasons. Rudolph won 26 games in 1914 and James won 26; then they added two more each in the Braves' World Series sweep of the heavily favored Philadelphia Athletics. But Rudolph crafted only one more 20-win season, and James won only 5 games in two final major-league campaigns.

Classy fielding kept the Braves competitive the next two years. In 1915 they spurted once again out of the cellar—but only to second place this time. They began their climb earlier the next year, but a seven-game losing streak in early September dropped them out of a tie for first. They rallied, but finished third. It was the Braves' last close race for thirty-two years.

In the twenty-nine years from 1917 through 1945 the Braves finished only three seasons as high as fourth, and only once as close as nine games from the top. With four years in the cellar and eleven in seventh place, the team finished near the bottom of the league more than half the time. In 1935 slugger Wally Berger led the league in home runs and RBI, but the Braves lost a club-record 115 games in their worst season ever.

In 1946, with dynamic new ownership headed by contractor Lou Perini, a new manager—Billy Southworth, who had led the Cardinals to three pennants and two world championships—and the return of war veterans like pitchers Warren Spahn and John Sain, the Braves neared the end of their long depression with their first winning season in eight years. At the end of the season Boston acquired third baseman Bob Elliott from Pittsburgh. He enjoyed a career year in 1947, powering the Braves to third place. Spahn and Sain won 21 games each.

Spahn dropped to 15 wins in 1948, but Sain won 24. Four veterans—plus rookie shortstop Alvin Dark—hit over .300. With the league's best pitching and hitting, the Braves moved out in front in June, and shook off their last challengers with a September spurt that made them champions by 6½ games.

But from there on, the Braves' path in Boston was downhill. Cleveland beat them in the World Series, and the club dropped to fourth for the next three years. South-

worth resigned part way into the 1951 season. In 1952 the team fell to seventh; home attendance was less than one-fifth what it had been four years earlier. The next spring Perini moved the franchise to Milwaukee in the league's first realignment since 1900.

The move was a spectacular success. Not only did the Braves rebound to second place, but attendance jumped 649 percent over their previous year in Boston to set an NL record of more than 1.8 million. The league's best pitching staff was led by the trio that would anchor Milwaukee's years of greatness: veteran Warren Spahn, sophomore Lew Burdette, and rookie Bob Buhl. Sophomore third baseman Eddie Mathews led the league in home runs; with outfielder Henry Aaron, who came up the next year, Mathews would give the Braves a consistent source of power through their Milwaukee years.

A July-August surge in 1954 pulled the Braves within a few games of the top before they slipped back, but they set another attendance record and became the first NL club to draw more than two million at home in a season. In 1955 the Braves finished a distant second to the Dodgers, but 1956 produced a great three-way race that found the Braves slightly ahead through much of the season until five straight losses in early September brought them even with the surging Dodgers. It was a dogfight the rest of the way, not settled until the final day, when a Dodger victory over Pittsburgh left Milwaukee a game back in second.

The acquisition of veteran second baseman Red Schoendienst from St. Louis in June 1957 steadied the infield and gave the team a frequent baserunner for Mathews and Aaron to drive in. In August the Braves drew away from the pack, and recovered from a September slump to win the pennant by a convincing 8 games over St. Louis. The Yankees took them to seven games in the World Series, but Burdette's shutout in the finale brought the Braves their first world championship in forty-three years.

Milwaukee repeated as league champions just as convincingly in 1958, but in the autumn classic, after taking the first two games from the Yankees, they lost the Series in seven. The race was much tighter in 1959 until the Giants moved away from the Dodgers and Braves in August. But in September the Giants faltered as the others surged past them, and the season ended with the Braves and Dodgers tied. In a best-of-three playoff, the Dodgers took the pennant in two games—but both by only one run and the second only after twelve innings.

A portent for the Braves' future could be seen in the crowd of under 20,000 that attended the first playoff game in Milwaukee. After setting a third NL record in 1957, Milwaukee attendance had gradually declined, dropping below two million in 1958, the club's second pennant year, and even farther in this year of the tight pennant race. As the Braves declined on the field to a more distant second in 1960, then successively to fourth, fifth, and sixth, so too did the decline continue in the stands to well under a million. Perini sold his majority interest in the club. A tighter race in 1964 stirred a little more fan interest, but when attendance dropped in 1965 to a new Milwaukee low of just over half a million, the club pulled up stakes again and moved to Atlanta.

The Braves' won-lost records in 1965 and '66 were nearly identical. But in Atlanta attendance improved by almost a million. Of the Braves who had brought glory to Milwaukee, most were gone from the club or in decline. But Aaron was still at the height of his powers, and younger players were beginning to make their mark. Reliever Phil Niekro, for example, was converted to a starter in 1967 and responded with the league's best ERA.

After finishing no higher than fifth in their first three seasons in Atlanta, the Braves celebrated 1969, the first year of divisional play, with a late-season drive that carried them out of a tight five-team race to the championship of the West. Veteran Orlando Cepeda, newly acquired from St. Louis, joined Aaron in supplying power, and Niekro won 23 games as the Braves won ten in a row to clinch the title in their next-to-last game. In the league's first Championship Series, though, the "Miracle" Mets of New York swept Atlanta in three games.

Aaron remained a presence in Atlanta for five more years, and Niekro, after a relatively dismal season in 1970, established himself over the years as one of the game's most durable and effective pitchers. But the team went nowhere. When they enjoyed an occasional good season (as in 1974, when they won 88 games), at least two other clubs did much better. Aaron returned to Milwaukee (to the AL Brewers) in 1975, and attendance sank to an Atlanta low. Yachtsman Ted Turner bought the club in 1976 and attendance rose, but the team sank to the bottom of the division for four years.

In 1982, though, with power from outfielder Dale Murphy and third baseman Bob Horner, and exceptional pitching from Niekro (17–4) and reliever Gene Garber (30 saves, a club record), Atlanta grabbed the division lead with a season-opening 13-game winning streak, and recovered from a midsummer collapse to edge Los Angeles by one game for their second divisional crown. But they were swept in the LCS, this time by St. Louis.

For the next two seasons Murphy's league-leading slugging carried the Braves to second place—a close 3 games behind Los Angeles in 1983 (in a race which pushed Atlanta attendance over two million for the first time), and a tie with Houston 12 games behind San Diego the next year. By 1986, though, they had sunk into the division cellar. Murphy boosted them up a notch in 1987 with the most productive season of his career, but as his power at the plate dropped the next year, the Braves sunk to their worst finish in fifty-three years. Fans fell away, and Atlanta became the first big-league club in three seasons to attract fewer than a million spectators to its home games.

Veteran outfielder Lonnie Smith broke out of a five-year slump in 1989, his second Atlanta season, to become one of baseball's most potent hitters, and in 1990 strong seasons by young sluggers Ron Gant and rookie Dave Justice gave Atlanta hope for the future. But Dale Murphy, in the third year of his decline, was traded to Philadelphia in August, and the Braves, mired in the cellar for their third straight season, remained the weakest draw in major league baseball.

With the first bottom-to-top comeback in NL history, the Braves captured the West in 1991. As Atlanta's home attendance zoomed back above 2 million, the Braves won a battle with Los Angeles that saw eleven ties or lead changes in the season's final weeks, then took the city's first pennant in a seven-game playoff against Pittsburgh.

Free agent Terry Pendleton joined Justice and Gant to power Atlanta's offense, while a trio of young pitchers— Tom Glavine, Steve Avery, and John Smoltz—anchored one of the league's best mound staffs.

In the World Series the Braves overcame a two-game deficit to take a Series lead before falling short by one extra-inning run in each of the final two games. Nineteen ninety-two was a near-repeat of 1991. Once again the Braves captured the NL East—although this time they built a more comfortable eight-game lead at the finish, after moving into first place in July with an eleven-game win streak. Once again they edged Pittsburgh for the pennant, although this time it took a come-from-behind win in the final at bat of Game Seven to do it. And once again they faltered in the World Series, this time succumbing to Toronto in six games.

For the third season in a row the Braves topped the NL West in 1993, this time charging from ten games back in July to a four-game lead in mid-September, then holding off resurgent San Francisco to clinch the crown on the season's final day. After building a 2-1 lead in the LCS, though, they fell to the Phillies in six games.

When the players' strike ended the 1994 season in August, pitcher Greg Maddux, en route to a record third consecutive Cy Young Award, was fashioning one of the greatest mound seasons in years. Atlanta's 68–46 record ranked second in the NL only to Montreal's 74–40. But a new divisional alignment had moved the Braves from the NL West to the East—Montreal's division—so they only finished second, six games behind the Expos.

Behind Maddux (19-2, 1.63 ERA), who won his fourth straight Cy Young, and rookie star Chipper Jones, the Braves bounced back in 1995, romping to the NL East title by a 21-game margin. Atlanta also charged past wild-card team Colorado in the first round of the new offseason format and swept the Reds in the NLCS. In the World Series the Braves met the Indians in a rematch of the 1948 Fall Classic. This time the results were far different as Atlanta triumphed 4-2.

The Braves won the NL East again in 1996, besting Montreal by 8 games. Atlanta's staff was paced this time by Cy Young Award winner John Smoltz (24-8, 276 strikeouts), Tom Glavine (15-10), and Mark Wohlers (39 saves); its offense was led by Chipper Jones (.309, 30 HR, 110 RBI), Ryan Klesko (34 HR, 93 RBI), and Fred McGriff (28 HR, 107 RBI). In the first round of the postseason Atlanta rolled over Los Angeles. In the NLCS, the club had its back to the wall. Down three games to one, it rallied with 12-1, 3-1, and 15-0 wins over Tony LaRussa's Cards. The Braves kept it up in the first two games of the World Series, stomping Joe Torre's Yankees 12-1 and 4-0—for an amazing five-game margin of victory of 46-3. The pundits were about to anoint the Braves as one of history's greatest teams. Then, suddenly, they ran out of gas, losing the next four straight to New York.

Arizona Diamondbacks

Along with the Tampa Bay Devil Rays, the Arizona Diamondbacks were granted a $130 million NL expansion franchise on March 9, 1995 and are scheduled to begin league play in 1998.

The Diamondbacks ownership group is headed by Phoenix Suns owner Jerry Colangelo. Minority investors included Nike chairman Phil Knight and comedian Billy Crystal. Joe Garagiola, Jr., a former player agent, was named the Diamondbacks' first General Manager; long-time baseball executive Roland Hemond was designated as Senior Executive Vice President of Baseball Operations. In November 1995 the Diamondbacks named former Yankees manager Buck Showalter as the franchise's first field manager. The Diamondbacks will play at 48,500-seat Bank One Ballpark, a $335 million retractable-roofed, natural grass facility just to the east of the NBA Suns' America West Arena in downtown Phoenix.

Baltimore Orioles

The history of major league baseball in Baltimore dates back to 1872, to the Lord Baltimores of the National Association, and includes the great National League Orioles of the 1890s. The city was also represented in the American League's first big league seasons, 1901–1902. But when those Orioles moved to New York in 1903 and became the Highlanders (later the Yankees), Baltimore was left without a big league club for more than half a century, until the transfer of the Browns from St. Louis in 1954.

The current Orioles didn't get their start in St. Louis, though. Their first home was Milwaukee, where they finished in the AL cellar in 1901. When they moved to St. Louis the next year, they lured several valuable players from the city's NL Cardinals—including 1901 batting champ Jesse Burkett, star shortstop Bobby Wallace, and the Cards' three best pitchers. They also took on the Cardinals' discarded nickname, becoming the new St. Louis Browns.

The Browns finished a strong second to the Philadelphia Athletics in their first St. Louis season, but fell to sixth the next year and, except for a fourth-place finish in 1908 (thanks to the pitching of newly acquired veteran Rube Waddell), remained mired in the second division until 1920. Late in the 1913 season a young Branch Rickey was hired to manage the Browns. In his two full seasons he was unable to lift the club out of the second division, but he did sign college star George Sisler (whom he had coached at the University of Michigan), who became, as the Browns' first baseman, one of the game's all-time greats.

In 1916, his first full season, Sisler led the Browns in hitting as they caught fire in August to record their first winning season in eight years. Pitcher Urban Shocker was obtained from the Yankees two years later and by 1920 had developed into a 20-game winner. Also in 1920, Sisler connected for what is still a major league record 257 hits and batted .407 to help move the Browns up to fourth, their first finish that high since 1908 (though their won-lost record of 76–77 remained on the losing side). The next year Shocker's 27 victories brought them a winning season and third place. And in 1922 the team recorded its finest record ever in St. Louis: 93 wins and a .604 winning percentage.

The 1922 Browns, led by Sisler's sizzling .420 BA, hit .313 as a team to lead the league. Left fielder Ken Williams ran away with the RBI title and beat out Babe Ruth and Tilly Walker for the home run crown. (Ruth, to be honest, did miss nearly a third of the season that year.) Sisler and Williams even finished one-two in AL stolen bases. And though Shocker slipped a bit to 24 wins, he led a pitching staff that recorded the league's lowest ERA. The team led the league in the standings throughout July and into August before the Yankees nudged ahead of them. The Browns hung close, but didn't regain the lead, remaining second, a heartbreaking single game back, at season's end.

Falling back to fifth the next year, as Sisler missed the whole season with a sinus infection, the Browns remained out of contention for the next twenty-one years, dropping to their lowest point in 1939, 64½ games out of first, with 111 losses. They recovered for three winning seasons in the war years 1942–1945, finishing a distant third in 1942, and capturing their only St. Louis pennant in 1944, edging the Detroit Tigers on the final day after trailing them through most of September. The World Series—an all-St. Louis affair—proved anticlimactic for the Browns as they lost to the Cardinals in six games.

The Browns finished third in 1945 before sinking back into the second division. Even the club's purchase by the dynamic Bill Veeck in July 1951 couldn't rouse them out of the depths. (A month after buying the Browns, Veeck made his best-remembered move, bringing in midget Eddie Gaedel for one plate appearance—he walked.)

Unable to earn either victories or money in St. Louis, Veeck in September 1953 sold the club to a Baltimore group, who moved the Browns and renamed them the Orioles. The new owners hired the brilliant Paul Richards to rebuild the team as manager, both in the front office and on the field. It took him (and Lee MacPhail, who became general manager and president in 1958) several years to move the Orioles above .500, but in 1960, young third baseman Brooks Robinson found he could hit as well as field, and rookie Jim Gentile drove in 98 runs; the team made its first run for the pennant since 1944. In first place in early September, they finished second when the Yanks won fifteen straight to pass them by.

The next year the O's did even better, winning six more games than they had in 1960 as Gentile hit 46 home runs and drove in 141. But it was an even better year for New York and Detroit, and Baltimore finished a distant third.

When Hank Bauer was brought in to manage the Orioles in 1964, the team entered its golden decades—twenty years which saw them win seven division titles, six pennants, and three world championships, with only two finishes below third. With Robinson driving in runs and left fielder Boog Powell slugging at a league-leading pace, the O's finished 1964 with wins in seven of their final eight games. But the White Sox won their last nine and the Yankees put together an eleven-game streak near the end to take the flag and leave Baltimore third, two games back.

After another third-place finish in 1965, the Orioles acquired slugging Frank Robinson from Cincinnati and moved second-year pitcher Jim Palmer into the starting rotation. Palmer won 15 to lead a balanced staff, and Frank Robinson captured the Triple Crown. With both Robinsons and Powell driving in 100 runs or more, the O's romped to their first Baltimore pennant. They continued the romp in the World Series, holding Los Angeles to just two runs as they swept to their first world title.

A drop in offensive production and the loss of Palmer to injuries for most of the season plunged Baltimore into a tie for sixth in 1967. Palmer was out the next year, too, but pitchers Dave McNally and Jim Hardin burst to the forefront with fine seasons to lift the club back to second.

Baltimore coach Earl Weaver, a pennant-winning manager in the O's farm system, replaced Hank Bauer at the Orioles' helm in mid-1968 to begin what became one of the longest and most successful managerial tenures of recent times. In fourteen full seasons Weaver led his club to six Eastern Division titles and six second-place finishes, with one season each in third and fourth. His teams featured fine hitters and fielders, but it is the pitching that stands out above the rest. In seven of the fourteen years the Oriole staff compiled the league's lowest ERA, including five consecutive seasons (1969-1973). Oriole pitchers put together in those fourteen years twenty-one 20-win seasons (eight of them by Jim Palmer), and garnered six Cy Young Awards.

In the first three years of divisional play (1969-71) Baltimore ran away with the East championship and swept to the pennant each time in the League Championship Series. The 1969 team (despite an embarrassingly easy loss to the New York Mets in the World Series) is often ranked among the greatest of all time. With overwhelming pitching and fielding, the Orioles took the division crown by 19 games, winning a club-record 109. In fielding, seven percentage points separated the AL's second-best team from the worst; the Orioles fielded three points better than the second-best team. And Oriole pitchers gave up nearly a run less per game than the league average.

Baltimore's performance in 1970 was nearly as impressive. Mike Cuellar and Dave McNally won 24 games each, and Jim Palmer contributed 20 more wins to the O's total of 108. This year they won the World Series as well as the pennant, rolling over Cincinnati in five games.

In the 1971 World Series, though, Pittsburgh came back from losses in the first two games to defeat the Orioles by a run in game seven. The O's captured divisional titles in 1973 and '74, but it was 1979 before they again triumphed in the LCS. Once again, however, they faced the Pittsburgh Pirates in the World Series, and once again took the Series lead, only to fall again in the seventh game.

The 1979 pennant was Weaver's last, as late-season Oriole surges in 1980 and '82 fell just short. But in 1983 the O's—paced by the pitching of veteran Scott McGregor and rookie Mike Boddicker, and the hitting and fielding of Cal Ripken, Jr., at short, and Eddie Murray at first—made new manager Joe Altobelli look good. After a comfortable divisional win, they trounced Chicago's White Sox in the LCS and the Philadelphia Phillies in the World Series.

Declining after 1983 despite the return of Earl Weaver in 1985–1986, the Orioles finished last in the East in 1986. Though they rose to sixth in 1987, their .414 winning percentage was their lowest in thirty-two years. Then in 1988 they hit rock bottom, not only finishing last but also beginning the season with an AL record-setting twenty-one consecutive defeats.

Baltimore's rebound was even more startling than its plummet. Under manager Frank Robinson (who had been handed the hapless O's early in the 1988 season) the 1989 Orioles took over first place in late April, held the lead through August, and stayed within the reach of the division title until Toronto defeated them in the season's penultimate game to clinch the crown. The newly potent bat of catcher Mickey Tettleton and splendid relief from rookie Gregg Olson highlighted the Baltimore resurgence. Olson remained effective in 1990, but the offense faltered, and an August-September slide dropped the Orioles out of the race.

The O's began slowly in 1991, and manager Robinson was replaced by coach Johnny Oates in May, with the club in last place. Although Cal Ripken put together an MVP season, the O's never caught fire, and finished sixth, 24 games out. In 1992, however, playing in the packed new Orioles Park at Camden Yards, Baltimore snapped back to challenge Toronto through much of the season before slipping to third, 7 games out.

At a bankruptcy auction in August 1993, a group led by Peter Angelos agreed to purchase the club for a record $173 million. On the field, 1993 was much like 1992. Only half a game out as late as September 9, the Orioles finished ten games back, tied for third with Detroit.

They challenged again in 1994; however, they slipped from just half a game behind the division-leading Yankees at midseason to 6½ games out by the time the players' strike brought the season to an early close in August. The second-place finish was not good enough to save manager Oates's job.

Nineteen ninety-five was the year of Cal Ripken, Jr., as he finally broke Lou Gehrig's consecutive game playing streak. But otherwise it was a disappointing season as Baltimore loaded up on such high-priced talent as Bobby Bonilla and Rafael Palmeiro but still finished only 71-73. Davey Johnson's 1996 Orioles (88-74) underperformed until midseason. Owner Angelos resisted temptations to break up the team and instead acquired veteran Eddie Murray, making possible a successful stretch run for a wildcard berth. Offense was the name of the game for this team as it slammed an ML record 257 homers. Oriole standouts included Brady Anderson (110 RBI and an ML-best 50 HR), Rafael Palmeiro (39 HR, 142 RBI), Roberto Alomar (22 HR, 94 RBI), Cal Ripken (26 HR, 102 RBI), and Mike Mussina (19-11).

Baltimore's postseason appearance (its first since 1983) was overshadowed, however, by Alomar's spitting on umpire John Hirschbeck. In the first round of the postseason, Baltimore upset the favored Indians, but in the ALCS (aided by a controversial Game One Yankee home run that should have been ruled fan interference) fell to Joe Torre's Yankees in five games.

Boston Red Sox

Since the end of World War Two, the Red Sox have won the American League pennant four times, only to lose the World Series each time in the seventh game. It was not always thus. In their first two decades they were the league's most successful club, winners of six pennants and five world championships. (No World Series was played the year of their second pennant.)

Organized in 1901 as one of four new eastern clubs in Ban Johnson's newly major league AL, Boston's Americans (or Pilgrims, Puritans, Plymouth Rocks, or Somersets, as they were variously called) quickly established themselves as one of the game's strongest teams. Star third baseman Jimmy Collins was lured from Boston's NL club to manage the new Americans, and he assembled a team that included such former NL standouts as slugger Buck Freeman and pitcher Cy Young. Finishing a strong second in the AL's inaugural major league season, the Pilgrims quickly supplanted their mediocre NL counterparts in the hearts and wallets of Boston fans.

After a third-place finish in 1902, the Pilgrims ran away from the rest of the league in 1903 to take their first pennant by 14½ games over Philadelphia. Young led the league in victories for the third straight season, Freeman took titles in home runs, total bases, and RBI, and second-year outfielder Patsy Dougherty finished first in hits and runs scored. In the first modern World Series, Boston overcame Pittsburgh's favored Pirates, thereby confirming the AL's claim to major league status.

Boston repeated as pennant winners in 1904, but by a much narrower margin, after a struggle with New York's Highlanders that wasn't settled until the next-to-last game of the season. The NL Giants refused to play Boston in a World Series that year.

Over the next few years, as the Pilgrims dropped into the league cellar, new owner John I. Taylor (whose father, *Boston Globe* publisher Charles Taylor, was said to have bought the club for his son to give him something useful to do) rid the team of many of the players who had brought it glory. Eventually Taylor was himself maneuvered out of the club presidency, but it turned out he had not been a wanton destroyer. In driving out the old guard he had been making room for new young players: pitcher Joe Wood, for example, and a sprightly outfield of Tris Speaker, Harry Hooper, and Duffy Lewis. The club—now known as the Red Sox—rose out of its depths in the final years of Taylor's presidency, even challenging the league leaders through much of 1909 before dropping away in late August. In 1911, in one of the last acts of his presidency, Taylor had, with his father, purchased land in Boston's Fenway section and built a new ballpark.

Sparked by the spectacular pitching of Joe Wood and Speaker's play at the bat and in center field, the Red Sox of 1912 took the league lead in early June and were never headed, finishing with a club-record 105 victories. In the World Series they edged John McGraw's Giants and Christy Mathewson in one of the most exciting Series ever, four games to three, with one tie. Three years later, with a staff that boasted the AL's four top pitchers in winning percentage (including rookie Babe Ruth), the Sox captured their fourth pennant, staving off a late-season surge by Detroit to finish 2½ games in front. After a first-game loss to the Phillies in the World Series, Boston recovered to sweep the next four by one run apiece.

Joe Wood's ailing arm finally gave out, and Tris Speaker was traded to Cleveland at the start of the 1916 season following a salary dispute. But with Ruth winning 23 games to lead the team, the Sox slid past the White Sox and Tigers in mid-September to take their fifth flag, and waltzed over Brooklyn in the Series.

Incipient disaster struck the Red Sox that December when New York theatrical entrepreneurs Hugh Ward and Harry Frazee bought the club. They put little cash into the deal, counting on future profits to pay the bulk of the purchase price. Ward sailed for Australia, leaving Frazee to run the club. For a while the future looked bright. After a second-place finish in 1917, Frazee hired minor league executive Ed Barrow as manager, and when many of the team's regulars left for military service in World War One, Frazee bought and traded for worthy replacements. In a season shortened a month because of the war, the Sox edged Cleveland for their sixth pennant and defeated the Chicago Cubs for their fifth and, as it turned out, last world championship.

Frazee's theater losses put him in a financial bind and gradually forced him to sell off the best of his players— mostly to the Yankees, who had plenty of money, and an office just a short hop from Frazee's New York theater. Though the Sox fell to sixth place in 1919, Babe Ruth kept attention fixed on the team as he went to the outfield and startled the baseball world with a record 29 home runs. But that winter Frazee sold Ruth to the Yankees for $100,000 and a $300,000 mortgage on Fenway Park.

The Red Sox were embarked on a fifteen-year sojourn in the second division that even a 1923 change in ownership was powerless to end. In the eleven years from 1922 through 1932 the Sox emerged from last place only twice. In 1932 they reached their nadir, losing 111 games and finishing 64 games out of first.

But in 1933, young, wealthy Tom Yawkey bought the club and promptly began what would be a lifetime effort to restore Boston to its former glory. His first efforts to buy success ready-made with such established stars as Lefty Grove, Jimmie Foxx, and Joe Cronin pulled the club out of the cellar but failed to lift it into pennant contention. But as general manager Eddie Collins began turning up young players to join the veterans, the Sox' fortunes rose. The emergence between 1938 and 1942 of players like Bobby Doerr, Ted Williams, and pitcher Tex Hughson brought Boston a level of success not seen since 1918. In four of the five years they finished second to the Yankees, achieving in 1942 their highest winning percentage since 1915.

The loss of most of these newcomers to military service in World War Two delayed further progress. But with the arrival of rookie pitching sensation Dave Ferriss in 1945, and the acquisition of slugging first baseman Rudy York that winter, the club was prepared for its returning war veterans to join in bringing Boston its greatest season since 1912. With 104 victories, the 1946 Sox won their long-delayed seventh pennant by 12 games over second-place Detroit. Only in the World Series was there disappointment as the heavily favored Sox bowed in Game Seven to the Cardinals by one run.

The Yankees ran away from the pack in 1947, but the three years that followed saw the Red Sox three times in the throes of pennant fever. In 1948, after falling back a bit in late September, the Sox won four at the very end to tie Cleveland for first—but lost the one-game playoff. The next year they were 12 games behind the Yankees on July 4, but pulled up gradually to take a one-game lead into the final two-game series in New York. One Sox win would give them the flag, but the Yankees took both games. In 1950 Boston played the league's best ball through July and August, to pull within a game of the Yankees on September 18, but then lost four in a row and all hope of the pennant.

In 1951 the Sox collapsed at season's end to finish third, 11 games back. They came no closer for the next fifteen years, finishing with eight consecutive losing seasons from 1959 through 1966, when they suffered their second successive ninth-place finish in a league now expanded to ten teams.

In 1967 the Sox awakened from their long slumber. A ten-game win streak in mid-July shot them out of mediocrity into the midst of a four-team race for the pennant that was not settled until Boston beat Minnesota and Detroit split a doubleheader on the final day, leaving the Sox on top. Carl Yastrzemski, who had replaced Ted Williams in left field seven years earlier, replaced him now in the fans' awe as he clinched the Triple Crown with a game-winning home run and six other hits in the final two must-win games. But Boston lost the World Series to St. Louis in seven games.

It was eight years before the Red Sox won another pennant, but they came close in 1972, losing the AL East crown by half a game to Detroit in the season's final series. They led the division two years later from mid-July through early September, then fell apart and finished third. But the next year, 1975, they maintained to the end the lead they first took in May, and swept Oakland in the League Championship Series for their ninth pennant. Television viewers will long remember Carlton Fisk's home run that won Game Six of the World Series from Cincinnati. But Red Sox fans also remember that the Sox lost Game Seven the next day, 4–3. Owner Tom Yawkey died the following July without the world championship he had sought for more than forty years.

Boston contended seriously in 1977 in a tight three-way race, pulling ahead for a time in June and again in August, but ultimately falling 2½ games short. The next year, though, the Sox pulled off another amazing finish. After blowing a 7½-game late-August lead to fall 3⅓ games behind New York in mid-September, they won their final eight scheduled games to tie the Yankees. But in the playoff, Yankee Bucky Dent's three-run pop-fly homer over Fenway's cozy left field wall proved Boston's ruin. The Sox rallied in the eighth to draw within a run, but with two out and a man on third in the ninth, Yastrzemski popped up and the season was history.

Yaz retired in 1983, full of years and honor, but outfielders Jim Rice and Dwight Evans remained from the 1975 champions. Joined by a new generation that included, in Wade Boggs, baseball's most consistent hitter since Ted Williams, and, in Roger Clemens, Boston's most exciting pitcher since Joe Wood, the Sox in 1986 won their tenth pennant, with an amazing comeback over California from a 3–1 deficit in the League Championship Series. In Game Six of the World Series they were within one pitch of capturing their first world title in 68 years. But they lost the game, and in Game Seven—once again—the Series.

When a pitching decline dropped the Sox to fifth place in 1987, and the All-Star break the next year found them barely above .500, manager John McNamara was replaced by coach Joe Morgan. The Sox responded with nineteen wins in their next twenty games and, despite a slump at season's end, took the title in the AL East by one game. In the LCS, though, Oakland swept to the pennant in four games.

In 1989 Boston moved to within half a game of the division lead in August before slipping back to third, but in 1990, with pitcher Clemens back in peak form after a season and a half below par, the Sox arrived at midseason in first place. After trading the lead back and forth with Toronto, they captured the crown of the East on the season's final day. But in the LCS Oakland again swept past them to the pennant.

Roger Clemens won his third Cy Young award in 1991 and the Sox came from 11½ games back in August to within half a game of first-place Toronto in September. But they dropped eleven of their remaining fourteen games to finish in a second-place tie with Detroit. Manager Joe Morgan was replaced by Butch Hobson for 1992, but the downhill slide continued. Dreadful hitting and fielding added insult to a season haunted by injury, and plunged the Sox into the AL East cellar for the first time since the advent of divisional play.

The team's best start in years, coupled with a mid-season surge after a long slump, saw the Sox in first place for three days in late July 1993. However, a late-season decline dropped them below .500, into fifth place.

Another strong start gave Boston the best record in the majors through the first month of the 1994 season. But, by the time the players' strike ended the season in August, they had sunk below .500 for the third year in a row. The Sox finished fourth, just one game ahead of last-place Detroit, and manager Hobson was fired.

His replacement, Kevin Kennedy, constantly juggled lineups to give the Sox the 1995 AL East by the surprisingly comfortable margin of seven games over New York. Key to the club's victory was AL RBI king Mo Vaughn, who captured MVP honors in a tight race over Cleveland's Albert Belle. Boston, however, was no match for the powerful Indians, falling to them 3-0 in the first round of the postseason, with Vaughn and Jose Canseco particularly ineffective at bat.

In 1996 the Sox got off to a sluggish start, but finished strong—not strong enough, however, to save manager Kennedy's job (he was replaced by longtime Braves coach Jimy Williams). Standouts for the third-place (85-77) Red Sox included Vaughn (44 HR, 143 RBI, 207 hits) and Clemens (an AL-best 257 strikeouts, including a record-tying 20 in one game against Detroit.)

California Angels

Of the ten teams added to the major leagues in the 1960s and '70s, the Angels were quickest to put together a winning season, finishing third in the American League in only their second year of play.

Former cowboy actor and singer Gene Autry brought the club into being as the Los Angeles Angels in December 1960. Playing their first season, 1961, in Los Angeles's Wrigley Field, a former minor league park with power alleys only five feet deeper than the foul poles, five Angels hit 20 or more home runs. Though the team finished seventh in the standings, they were second in homers only to the mighty Yankees.

What the Angels lost in home runs in 1962 (when they moved out of Wrigley Field into the L.A. Dodgers' new stadium), they more than made up in pitching. Paced by rookie Dean Chance, the Angels nearly doubled their wins on the road, and as late as mid-August stood in second place, within striking distance of New York. Though they tailed off in September, they finished a respectable third, 10 games back.

The team collapsed to ninth the next year, but in 1964 Chance's pitching and splendid relief by rookie Bob Lee overcame the Angels' continuing inertia at the bat to lift them back into the first division. Among Chance's league-leading 11 shutouts were six 1–0 victories.

Los Angeles became the California Angels in 1965 in anticipation of their move south to a new stadium in Anaheim the following year, but neither the name change nor the new location stirred them out of the second division. In 1967, though, with below-average run production but the league's third-best pitching, the Angels in mid-season shot up from ninth to third before leveling off to fifth. After dismal seasons in 1968–1969, career years in 1970 by pitcher Clyde Wright (22 wins, including a no-hitter) and newly acquired left fielder Alex Johnson (202 hits and a league-high .329 BA) helped the Angels snap back with an 86–76 record that matched their previous best (1962).

The seven losing seasons which followed 1970 were somewhat redeemed by the arrival in 1972 of pitcher Nolan Ryan, who burst into superstardom as an Angel, setting a modern record of 383 strikeouts in 1973 and hurling four no-hitters in three years (1973–1975). Ryan's effectiveness dipped in 1978, but the club as a whole came to life, contending closely for the Western Division title until Kansas City shot ahead in September.

In 1979 Don Baylor became the first (and, so far, only) DH to be named league MVP, as a renewed offense powered California to its first division title. Baltimore stopped the Angels in the LCS, though. The team's run production dropped off dramatically the next year and the club followed up its best season with its worst.

After another losing season in 1981 (during which Jim Fregosi was replaced as manager by twenty-year veteran Gene Mauch), California lured free-agent slugger Reggie Jackson from the Yankees. With Jackson leading a resurgent offense and Geoff Zahn headlining the league's second-best pitching staff, the Angels rebounded to a new team high of 93 wins in 1982, and their second division title. They defeated Milwaukee in the first two games of the LCS, but lost the next three. A disappointed Mauch retired.

Again, in 1983, the Angels followed a championship with a poor season—not quite as bad as 1980, but still their third worst to that point. In 1984 they rebounded to .500, good enough for second in a weak division. As a foretaste of continuing improvement, pitcher Mike Witt concluded his rise to staff ace with a perfect game on the season's last day.

Gene Mauch came out of retirement to manage the Angels again in 1985. With pitching that featured splendid relief from newly acquired Donnie Moore (31 saves; 1.92 ERA), the team led the division much of the season, but lost three games of four to Kansas City in the final week to fall a game behind the Royals into second.

With Witt's 18 wins and 2.84 ERA pacing the staff and rookie first baseman Wally Joyner leading a revitalized offense, California won the 1986 division crown with ease. In the LCS against Boston, the Angels took three of the first four games, and in Game Five were within one pitch of capturing their first pennant. But the Boston Red Sox rallied to win.

In 1987 California for the third time followed up their division championship with a losing season, this time dropping the season finale to tie for last place in the AL West. Manager Mauch retired again, this time for good. After another losing season brought them home a distant fourth in 1988, the Angels signed Doug Rader to manage the club. They also acquired a veteran pitcher—Bert Blyleven—who led a resurgence of Angel pitching that lifted the club to its third best won-lost record ever. But as the West was now the stronger AL division, the team's 91 wins carried them only into third place, eight games back. In 1990 they dropped just one place in the standings, but finished again below .500, 23 games out of first.

The Angels began strong in 1991, and moved into the division lead on July 3. But seven straight losses plunged them to fifth, and although they finished at .500 for the season, just 14 games out of first, they wound up in the division cellar. Their standing in the AL West improved in 1992 and 1993 with back-to-back ties for fifth place. But their won-lost records of 72-90 and 71-91, respectively, were their worst since 1983.

The Angels played even worse in strike-shortened 1994. Although they finished only 5½ games out of first in the weak AL West, their .409 winning percentage was the league's lowest, and the second lowest in club history.

Yet by 1995 manager Marcel Lachemann's Angels (paced by Jim Edmonds's 107 RBI and Mark Langston's 15-7 mark) led the AL West for most of the 1995 season, only to fade and finish in a tie in the division race with the upstart Seattle Mariners. The AL West title was decided by a special one-game playoff in which the Mariners' Randy Johnson made the difference. California's improvement made it one of only three ML clubs to register an increase in per-game attendance over 1994.

The Angels fell to last in 1996, resulting in Lachemann's firing and his replacement by interim pilot John McNamara and ultimately by former Astros pilot Terry Collins. Angels enjoying standout seasons included Troy Percival (36 saves) and Chuck Finley (215 strikeouts). In the offseason the club announced that it would be renamed the Anaheim Angels and sport a new winged logo.

Chicago Cubs

The Chicago Cubs have represented the same city in the major leagues longer than any other club. Organized in 1870 to provide a professional challenge to Cincinnati's Red Stockings, the next year the White Stockings (as they were originally known) were one of the founding members of the game's first professional league—the National Association.

Despite the great Chicago fire, which destroyed their ballpark, uniforms, and club business records late in the 1871 season, the White Stockings completed their schedule, finishing third to the Athletics of Philadelphia. But they dropped out of the NA for the next two years because of the fire's devastation. In 1875, in the midst of a second losing season following their return, the club arranged for four of champion Boston's best players to jump to Chicago for the 1876 season. That winter, White Stocking president William A. Hulbert and pitcher/manager Al Spalding (one of the jumpers) led in forming a new league to replace the NA.

Sparked by its Boston players and infielder Adrian "Cap" Anson (lured from the Athletics), the 1876 White Stockings outscored their opponents by more than five runs per game and handily won the first championship of the new National League. The next year, though, when Spalding (whose pitching had brought Chicago 47 of its 52 victories in 1876) switched over to first base, the club fell to fifth.

Spalding retired from the field in 1878 to attend to his young sporting goods firm (though he returned as club president from 1882 through 1891). In 1879 Anson was named to manage the team. Leading the league in batting, he restored the White Stockings to winning ways, and in 1880 back to the top.

For twelve years the White Stockings ranked among baseball's best, garnering five pennants (1880–1882, 1885–1886) and four second-place finishes. Anson's stern morality and strict discipline did not make him popular with his often rowdy teammates, but his consistency as a player set an example, and his innovative management made the most of his players' drive and aggressiveness. Anson's forcefulness, however, contributed to baseball's most grievous setback: his adamant refusal in the mid-1880s to take the field against black players prevented the racial integration of the major leagues that had up to then seemed imminent.

After a close finish behind Boston in 1891, the White Stockings' first era as an NL power ended. In each of the next eleven seasons they fell at least 15 games short of the top. The team's youthful ineptitude was reflected in the nicknames that succeeded "White Stockings": the "Colts," the "Orphans" (in 1898, after Anson—by then known as "Pop"—was fired after nineteen years at the helm), and finally, the "Cubs."

When Frank Selee (who had led Boston to greatness in the 1890s) was hired to manage the Cubs in 1902, he inherited a team that had ended the 1901 season 37 games out, its worst finish up to then. By 1903 he had turned catcher/outfielder Frank Chance into a first baseman, moved Joe Tinker from third to short, and brought up Johnny Evers from Troy to play second. The new double-play combination flourished not only in the field but at the bat. The Cubs finished third in 1903 with their best record since 1898.

That winter Selee traded for pitcher Mordecai "Three Finger" Brown, and in 1905 signed rookie hurler Ed Reulbach. After leading the Cubs to second place in 1904, Selee, ill with tuberculosis, took a leave of absence in the middle of the 1905 season. Chance took his place and brought the team to third.

Selee never returned, but he had gone a long way toward building a championship team. Trades for outfielder Jimmy Sheckard and third baseman Harry Steinfeldt, the signing of rookie pitcher Jack Pfiester, and

the acquisition during the 1906 season of pitchers Orval Overall and Jack Taylor completed one of the greatest teams of all time. The Cubs passed the Giants to take the lead early in May and kept on rising. New York and Pittsburgh made a race of it through July, but the Cubs won 55 of their final 65 games to finish with a record 116 victories, 20 games ahead of second-place New York. The hitting of Steinfeldt and Chance led the Cubs to the top of the league in batting and slugging, and the club topped all others in fielding. But it was Cub pitching that stood out most. Brown's 1.04 ERA was the league's best, with those of Pfiester and Reulbach second and third. The team ERA of 1.76 was the first below 2.00 since the pitching distance was increased to 60'6" in 1893. Over all, Chicago scored 80 more runs than its nearest rival, and yielded 89 fewer.

But in the World Series, the crosstown "hitless wonder" White Sox matched the Cubs' hitting and pitched twice as effectively to take the crown in six games. It was the third time the Cubs had failed to win the world title: in two of the earliest Series, they had tied the St. Louis Browns by 3–3–1 in 1885, and lost to them the next year, 2–4.

The Cubs' hitting and run production fell off in 1907, but their pitching did not (ERA: 1.73). With 107 wins, they captured their second straight pennant, by 17 games. This time their dominance carried over into the World Series as they swept Detroit after an opening-game tie.

The pennant race of 1908, in sharp contrast to those of the previous two years, was one of the tightest in baseball history. On September 22 the Cubs won two from the Giants to pull into a virtual tie for first (with Pittsburgh third, 1½ games back). The next day the Giants appeared to have beaten the Cubs with an RBI single in the last of the ninth. But young Fred Merkle, on first when the hit was made, seeing the runner on third cross the plate, failed to continue on to second himself and was forced out by alert Cub second baseman Johnny Evers for the third out, which negated the Giant run. Because of increasing darkness and the mood of excited fans on the field, the game was called and ruled a tie. After another week and a half in which all three teams took turns in front, Chicago defeated Pittsburgh to pull ahead by half a game, leaving the Pirates and Giants tied for second. But New York had one more game—and defeated the Boston Braves to pull into a tie with the Cubs. The "Merkle boner" game thus had to be replayed, and this time the Cubs won to take their third straight pennant. In the World Series they again beat Detroit in five games. Their second straight world title was also, to date, their last.

In 1909 the Cubs won 104 games as their pitching staff for the third time in four years recorded an ERA under 2.00, but the club trailed Pittsburgh throughout the season and finished second. In 1910, however, their 104 wins carried them to another pennant, by a comfortable 13 games. It was their last championship of the Chance era. After a World Series loss to the Philadelphia Athletics, and seasons in second and third place, Chance resigned, protesting the unwillingness of owner Charles Murphy to spend money for top players.

The Cubs got a new owner in 1916, and with him a new ballpark. Charles Weeghman, who had owned the Chicago Whales in the short-lived Federal League, purchased the Cubs when the FL went under, and moved them into the park he had built for the Whales. Although there was talk in the 1980s of moving the Cubs out of what is now known as Wrigley Field, the introduction of night baseball in 1988 assured continuing play in this crown jewel of ballparks.

The team that next carried Chicago to the pennant, in the war-shortened season of 1918, featured only one name familiar to Cubs fans from earlier championship seasons—Fred Merkle. The man whose rookie boner as a Giant had made possible their pennant in 1908 was now their leading run producer. As in earlier pennant-winning seasons, fine pitching predominated, with veteran James "Hippo" Vaughn the league's best pitcher on the league's top staff.

Several years of decline followed the Cubs' World Series loss to the Boston Red Sox. The club hit bottom in 1925 with its first cellar finish in fifty-three years of league play, but a new era of greatness was at hand. In 1921 wealthy chewing-gum manufacturer William Wrigley had purchased control of the Cubs, with a determination to spend whatever was needed to produce a pennant winner.

The seeds Wrigley planted eventually bore fruit. In 1926 he hired Joe McCarthy—a successful minor league manager—to lead the club, and drafted outfielder Lewis "Hack" Wilson from Toledo. Wilson immediately became one of the league's leading offensive threats, and the Cubs rebounded to the first division. In 1927 they even led the league through August before dropping back to fourth. A postseason trade brought them outfielder Hazen "Kiki" Cuyler, and a close third-place finish in 1928. Then the Cubs traded with the Braves for second baseman Rogers Hornsby, and in 1929 returned to the top. Led by Wilson's 159 RBI and Hornsby's 149, five Cubs drove in more than 90 runs each. After battling Pittsburgh for the lead through mid-July, the Cubs hurtled ahead to take the pennant by 10½ games, despite a late-season slump. The slump continued through the World Series, though, as Connie Mack's Philadelphia Athletics humbled the Cubs in five games.

Just four games from the end of the hot pennant race in 1930 (the year Wilson set the major league RBI record with 190), McCarthy—still smarting from criticism arising from the World Series loss—quit as manager. With Hornsby at the helm, the Cubs preserved a second-place finish. They dropped to third the next year, but returned to the top in 1932. Hornsby, near the end of his playing days, was dropped as manager in August, with the Cubs in second, and replaced by first baseman Charlie Grimm. Pitcher Lon Warneke, in his first full season as a starter, led the league in wins and ERA. The club enjoyed a hot streak in August to move out in front of slumping Pittsburgh and hung on to take the flag by four games. The Yankees provided the World Series humiliation this time, a four-game sweep that provided McCarthy (now the Yankee manager) with sweet revenge for the Chicago fans' criticism three years earlier.

It had become a pattern: three years, another pennant. In 1935 a balanced offense (led by catcher "Gabby" Hartnett and second baseman Billy Herman) and the league's best pitching brought the Cubs up from fourth in late June to first in September. They clinched the pennant with

three games to go, with their twentieth win of a 21-game streak. In the World Series, Detroit stopped the Cubs in six games.

After two seasons in second, it was time for another pennant. Bill Lee, the Cubs' top pitcher in 1935, was now the league's finest, as was the Cubs' staff. With the club languishing 6½ games back in midseason, Grimm quit as manager and was replaced by catcher Hartnett. In September the Cubs came to life, rising to second early in the month. They overtook Pittsburgh on September 28 with their ninth consecutive win—on Hartnett's homer against the Pirates in the growing darkness with two away in the bottom of the ninth—and clinched the pennant four games later, on the next-to-last day of the season. It was their fourth pennant at three-year intervals—and their sixth straight World Series loss, another New York Yankee sweep.

In 1940, after fourteen straight winning seasons, the Cubs began a five-year stretch below .500. Jimmie Wilson replaced Hartnett as manager in 1941; then Grimm returned near the start of the 1944 season. The club finished a distant fourth that year, but in 1945, after a middling start, they won twenty-six of thirty midseason games to take a lead they never relinquished. Balanced pitching (sparked by Hank Borowy, who went 11–2 after coming over from the Yankees in July) and the hitting of veteran first baseman Phil Cavarretta (.355) and center fielder Andy Pafko (110 RBI) held off the pressing St. Louis Cardinals to preserve a sixteenth Cub pennant. But although they battled Detroit through a full seven games in the World Series, they ended up losing again—their ninth defeat in twelve tries.

For the next twenty-three years the Cubs remained out of pennant contention. But in 1969, the first year of divisional play, under the lively management of Leo Durocher, they took an early lead in the NL East. With a potent offense led by veteran sluggers Ron Santo, Ernie Banks, and Billy Williams, the team continued rising through early August. But the New York Mets rose even faster and farther; they didn't pause when Chicago leveled off in late August, and while the Cubs were losing eight straight in September the Mets were winning ten in a row. The Cubs wound up eight games back.

The next year Chicago started well, slumped in late June, then fought back into the thick of the race in September before fading to another second-place finish. Three years later, in 1973, the Cubs entered July with a substantial lead. Although they fell to fifth by season's end, in the tightly packed division they were only five games back. It was to be their closest finish for eleven years.

In 1981 the Wrigley family, no longer able to bankroll a winner, sold the club to the Chicago Tribune Company. Three years later, with a new manager, Jim Frey, and an almost wholly different roster, the new management capped its rebuilding program with the acquisition from Cleveland, in mid-June 1984, of pitcher Rick Sutcliffe. As Sutcliffe fashioned a 16–1 record for his new club, the Cubs moved in front to stay on August 1, and kept on rising to capture their first division title by 6½ games.

Their fall was as rapid as their rise. After winning the first two games of the League Championship Series against San Diego, the pennant was swept out from under them as the Padres took the final three. Four losing seasons followed, in which the Cubs finished no closer than 18½ games behind the division winner.

But in 1989 the team, now managed by Don Zimmer, bounced back to duplicate its 1984 success. With a balanced offense and pitching vastly improved over the previous season, the Cubs took the NL East lead for good on August 7, and finished six games ahead of New York. Once again, though, they were unable to persevere to the pennant, losing the League Championship Series to San Francisco in five games.

As they had done in 1989, Andre Dawson, Mark Grace, and Ryne Sandberg continued to provide offensive clout over the next three years, and in 1992 Cy Young Award winner Greg Maddux and newly acquired Mike Morgan excelled on the mound. But the team could not carve out a winning season, finishing tied for fourth in 1990, and fourth by themselves in 1991 and '92. The Cub owners snarled when Commissioner Fay Vincent proposed transferring the club from the NL East to the West in 1993 (trading places with Atlanta), a logical move geographically. But the threat passed when Vincent, under pressure from owners dissatisfied with his leadership, resigned before the end of the 1992 season.

Free agents Dawson and Maddux left for greener pastures in 1993, but catcher Rick Wilkins and outfielder Sammy Sosa blossomed into power hitters, and newly acquired closer Randy Myers garnered a league record 53 saves. While the Cubs once again finished only fourth, they put together their first winning season in four years. The improvement wasn't enough to satisfy management, though, and second-year manager Jim Lefebvre was replaced by coach Tom Treblehorn at the end of the season.

Ryne Sandberg, claiming to have lost his competitive drive, retired during the 1994 season, and the Cubs followed suit, settling themselves firmly in the cellar of the newly formed Central division with eight losses in the ten games that preceded the season-ending strike.

Chicago, under manager Jim Riggleman, bounced back to third (73-71) in 1995 as Mark Grace led the NL with 51 doubles. And at season's end Sandberg, now 36, announced he was ending his retirement and returning to the Cubs. The 1996 Cubs sunk to fifth (76-86), just three games ahead of last-place Pittsburgh. Standouts included Mark Grace (.331) and Sammy Sosa (40 HR).

Chicago White Sox

When minor league owner Charlie Comiskey transferred his club from St. Paul to Chicago as part of the move to upgrade the American League to major league status, he called it the White Stockings, after the Chicago team that dominated the National League in its early years. The new Chicago team revived memories of the old White Stockings, winning the AL championship in 1900, and repeating the triumph in 1901, the league's first major league season. Manager Clark Griffith (who had jumped to the White Stockings from Chicago's NL Cubs) was the team's star pitcher in 1901, winning 24 of 31 decisions as his team took the lead in May and held off the threatening Boston Somersets the rest of the way.

Griffith's effectiveness fell off in 1902, as did the team,

(now called the White Sox) which took a sizable lead in July, only to slide back to fourth in August. Griffith left the next year and the White Sox sank to seventh. It would take eighteen years and baseball's greatest scandal for the Sox to finish that low again.

In 1904, after center fielder Fielder Jones replaced left fielder Nixey Callahan as manager, they rose into first place for a moment in August before settling back to third. The next year they made up a seven-game deficit in September to catch the Philadelphia Athletics, but the loss of two games to the A's stalled their drive and left them in second.

Nothing stalled the White Sox drive in 1906. Although they ranked at the very bottom of the league in hitting and entered June five games below .500, their pitching and hustle pulled them through. "Big Ed" Walsh, who had finally mastered the spitball after two years of trying, won 17 games, including a league-high 10 shutouts. Doc White contributed 18 wins with a league-best 1.52 ERA, and Frank Owen and Nick Altrock won 22 and 20, respectively. The Sox shot to the top in August with a 19-game win streak (including 8 shutouts). Early in September, New York's Highlanders passed them, but after the two teams had traded the lead back and forth for a couple of weeks the Sox spurted to take the pennant by 3 games. If the race was close, so were the individual games: the Sox achieved nearly one-third of their victories by the margin of a single run. The "hitless wonders" carried their momentum through the World Series, shocking the mighty crosstown Cubs (who had won a record 116 games that year) four games to two.

In 1907, after leading the league much of the first half, the Sox slipped to third. The next year Walsh pitched in the final seven games on his way to a career-high 40 wins. In a tight finish he pulled the Sox to within a half game of first-place Detroit before they dropped back to third with a loss to the Tigers on the final day.

It was 1915 before the Sox (piloted by rookie manager Clarence H. "Pants" Rowland) next finished that high, and 1916 before they again challenged seriously for the pennant. Comiskey, though accused of pinching pennies in his payment of players, was willing to spend what was needed to acquire them. After the 1914 season he purchased star second baseman Eddie Collins from the A's, and promising young Oscar "Happy" Felsch from minor league Milwaukee. The following August he acquired the great Joe Jackson from Cleveland. Together with the league's best pitching staff, they carried the Sox into the thick of a three-way race and a close second-place finish in 1916, and in 1917 to the pennant with the best winning percentage the club has ever compiled. Ten-year veteran pitcher Eddie Cicotte enjoyed his first 20-win season with a league-high 28 victories, and a league- and career-best 1.53 ERA. After dueling the Boston Red Sox most of the season, Chicago streaked out of reach in late August to finish with 100 wins and a 9-game lead. In the World Series against the New York Giants they captured their second (and, to date, their last) world title, in six games.

With several key players out much of 1918 for military or civilian war service, the White Sox finished out of the running, a dismal sixth. But in 1919, with the team back at full strength, the race once again went to Chicago. If their pitching didn't have quite the depth of the 1917 squad, its best hurlers were in peak form. Cicotte, after an off-year in 1918, attained a career high with 29 wins, as did Lefty Williams with 23 victories. Collins and Jackson enjoyed their best seasons in several years, and infielder Buck Weaver had never been better. Old-time pitcher/second baseman Kid Gleason was a rookie as a big league manager, but his Sox began strong and, after slipping briefly into second in midseason, pulled ahead in July to stay.

When the Sox lost the World Series to underdog Cincinnati, there were rumors of a fix, but nothing came to light for nearly a year. The White Sox looked better than ever in 1920. Though they fell back in May after a hot April, by mid-August they had risen to the thick of a tight three-team race. Felsch, Collins, and Weaver had never played better, Jackson was enjoying one of his very best seasons, and four pitchers were on their way to more than 20 wins. Chicago might not have caught Cleveland's rampaging Indians, but it didn't help that talk of a White Sox scandal revived late in the season, or that the grand jury convened only eight games from the end, or that eight Sox players were indicted and suspended with just three games to play. The team finished two games back, in second place.

The indicted players—among whom were Cicotte, Felsch, Jackson, Weaver, and Williams—were acquitted in court when three crucial confessions disappeared, but they were banned for life from organized baseball by Commissioner K. M. Landis. The White Sox did not soon recover from the loss. In 1921 they began fifteen years of wandering in the second division, including three seasons in the cellar and one seventh-place finish (in 1932) that, while not the league's most distant, remains the farthest out Chicago has ever finished, 56½ games behind champion New York.

Two of the club's greatest and most durable players arrived during these years: pitcher Ted Lyons (who won 260 games for the Sox over twenty-one years) in 1923, and in 1930 shortstop Luke Appling (who averaged .310 in his twenty years with the club). Owner Comiskey died in 1931, in the midst of his Sox's most dismal era, but Lyons and Appling were around long enough to enjoy a few fourth- and third-place seasons. But neither saw the Sox contend seriously for the pennant. After his playing career was over, Lyons managed the team for a few years—until 1948, when the Sox lost 101 games and finished last.

That year Frank Lane was lured from the presidency of the American Association to take charge as Chicago's general manager. He began reshaping the team, and after two more losing seasons the White Sox' fortunes began to rise. When Lane hired Paul Richards to manage the club in 1951, the Sox began what became a seventeen-year string of winning seasons.

In 1951, Richards's first season, the Sox spent a month in first place before drifting down to fourth, and the next year began a five-year stopover in third place. In 1954 they won 94 games but were out of the race by August— that was the year Cleveland won 111 and the second-place Yankees 103. Richards moved on to Baltimore, but Marty Marion, who replaced him, kept the Sox in third place. Their 91 wins in 1955 earned them a much tighter race than '54, one that found them in first place at the start of September, until four losses dropped them to third.

Frank Lane left at the end of the 1955 season, and young Chuck Comiskey (one of the grandchildren of Charlie Comiskey who now owned the club) took over the front office. A year later Comiskey replaced Marion with Al Lopez, who had piloted the great Cleveland club of 1954 and whose teams, in his six seasons of managing, had never finished below second. Lopez continued his success in Chicago: the Sox moved up to second (though well behind the Yankees) in 1957 and '58. In March 1959, Bill Veeck (who had in previous years owned the Cleveland Indians and the St. Louis Browns) bought a controlling interest in the White Sox from the Comiskey family and stepped into instant success.

With the Yankees suffering an off-year in 1959, Chicago and Cleveland battled for the lead throughout the summer, until the White Sox pulled away in late August. The same 94–60 record that had given them only a distant third in 1954 now carried them to their first pennant in forty years. The close and successful pennant race, and the club's dynamic new ownership, pushed Sox home attendance up more than 78 percent to a new club record.

As they had in 1906, pitching and hustle won the Sox their 1959 pennant. The league's best staff was led by veteran Early Wynn (enjoying his last big season with a league high of 22 wins) and young Bob Shaw (with a career high of 18), and featured the league's top relievers in Gerry Staley and Turk Lown. Shortstop Luis Aparicio, in the midst of a nine-year reign as stolen-base leader, set a personal high in runs scored as the club went 35–15 in one-run games. But in the World Series, Los Angeles stopped Chicago in six games.

The next year the Sox remained competitive until September, but finished third. After dropping to fourth and fifth the next two years (in a league now expanded to ten teams), they returned to second in 1963. The next year the Sox finished a season-long three-way race with nine straight wins, enough to pull them past Baltimore, but a game short of catching the Yankees, whose eleven-game streak a week earlier had put them out in front. After a third straight second-place finish in 1965, manager Lopez resigned for health reasons.

Under Eddie Stanky—and with the AL's stingiest pitching staff in forty-nine years—the Sox competed into the final week of a hot 1967 race, when five straight losses at the end dropped them to fourth. Only twice in the next thirteen years would they rise above .500; in 1970 they lost a club-record 106 games to finish at the bottom of the AL West. Two years later they took the division lead briefly in late August before dropping back to second, and in 1977 they held the lead through much of the summer before tailing off to third.

Bill Veeck had sold the club and repurchased it in 1976. But in January 1981, after three losing seasons and troubled by poor health and skyrocketing player salaries, he sold the Sox once again, to a group headed by Jerry Reinsdorf and Eddie Einhorn. With Reinsdorf heading the club's baseball operations and lawyer Tony LaRussa piloting the team on the field, the Sox became by 1983 one of the best teams in baseball. With their best record since 1920, the 1983 Sox carried the AL West by 20 games. Rookie slugger Ron Kittle led the attack, backed up by fourth-year outfielder Harold Baines and resurgent old-timers Greg Luzinski and Carlton Fisk. Pitchers La-

Marr Hoyt and Rich Dotson attained personal bests to lead the majors in wins (with 24 and 22), and White Sox home attendance for the first time topped two million. In the League Championship Series, though, after a close win over Baltimore in the opener, Chicago lost the next three games and the pennant. The Sox pitching and offense (except for Baines) collapsed the next season, and the team remained out of serious contention for six years.

Most forecasters predicted another dismal season for the Sox in 1990, but as fans watched a new Comiskey Park arise next door, they also saw their club celebrate its final year in the old yard with an astonishing resurgence. With their best start in decades, the Sox stayed close to mighty Oakland through the first half of the season, and even took over first place for brief periods in June and July before Oakland pulled away. Anchoring a strong bullpen, closer Bobby Thigpen shattered the major league record for saves, passing the old record of 46 with a month to go and finishing with 57.

First baseman Frank Thomas, confirming in his first full season the offensive powers he had demonstrated as a rookie in 1990, helped keep the Sox competitive through much of 1991, the inaugural season of their new park. Rookie Wilson Alvarez's August 11 no-hitter capped a seven-game win streak that pulled the team to just a game from the top, but fifteen losses in their next seventeen games stifled their pennant hopes. Thomas continued his awesome offense in 1992, and Jack McDowell showed himself one of the American League's best pitchers, but the team won one game fewer than the year before, and finished third.

McDowell, Alvarez, and Alex Fernandez led the league's stingiest pitching staff in 1993, and Thomas turned in an MVP season as the Sox carried a narrow lead into the All-Star break, held it into late September, then pulled away to an eight-game margin of victory at the finish. In the postseason, though, the Sox came up short, losing the AL pennant to Toronto in six games.

In 1994, Frank Thomas was rising to yet new heights and became the first American Leaguer since Roger Maris in 1960 and 1961 to be named MVP in back-to-back seasons. The Sox were hanging on to a slim first-place lead over Cleveland in the new Central division, when the players struck to end the season.

Despite another strong season by Thomas (.308, 40 HR, 111 RBI) the club slumped to third in 1995, 32 games back of Cleveland. In 1996, the Sox again finished second to the Tribe, but this time only by a 14.5 game margin. Once again Thomas (.349, 134 RBI) paced Chicago batters. Sox pitchers were led by Alex Fernandez (200 strikeouts), Wilson Alvarez (181 strikeouts), and Roberto Hernandez (38 saves). The offseason signing of free agent slugger Albert Belle gave Chisox fans hope for a pennant in 1997.

Cincinnati Reds

The Red Stockings was the nickname of two pioneering Cincinnati ballclubs—the first avowedly professional team, which was undefeated in 1869, and the charter member club in the National League of 1876–1880. After a year on the sidelines, the reformed Reds joined the new American Association and captured the 1882 pennant by 11½ games, with a .688 winning percentage that is still the club record. Seven Reds enjoyed career highs in batting, pitcher Will White led the association with 40 wins, and rookie second baseman John "Bid" McPhee proved himself already one of the game's classiest fielders. The Reds even won one of a pair of postseason exhibition games with Chicago's White Stockings, champions of the older and stronger National League.

McPhee remained eighteen years with the Reds and established himself as the finest second baseman of the nineteenth century. But the club would go thirty-seven years before it won another pennant. Twice in their seven remaining years in the AA the Reds finished second, and they enjoyed six winning seasons. Transferring from the AA to the NL in 1890, they finished fourth; at 10½ games out of first, it was their closest finish in the thirty-four years between 1884 and their next pennant-winning season, 1919.

The Reds wound up in the cellar for the first time in 1901. The next year club owner John T. Brush sold out to a group of Cincinnati's political bosses, who in mid-August named August "Garry" Herrmann (formerly head of the water works commission) to run it. Herrmann promptly acquired two outfielders from Baltimore—Cy Seymour and Joe Kelley, who was appointed team manager—who helped pull the Reds up to .500 and to fourth place by season's end. Three winning seasons followed, but then came eleven years in which the Reds finished above .500 only once (and then by only one game). Herrmann, meanwhile had found his calling in baseball administration. He not only remained president of the Reds for twenty-five years, but he also chaired the three-man National Commission that oversaw organized baseball, from its establishment in 1903 until 1920 (when his resignation brought about the commission's demise).

A midseason trade in 1916 brought the Reds Christy Mathewson (at the end of his pitching career) to manage the team, plus outfielder Edd Roush. The next year, with Roush leading the league in batting, the Reds edged above .500 and into fourth place. In 1918 an August spurt boosted the Reds into third place, in a season shortened by a month at the end because of the World War. Roush enjoyed another banner year, but Mathewson left for the Army just before the season ended.

First baseman Hal Chase—suspected of throwing games—was traded away after the season and replaced by veteran Jake Daubert. Southpaw Slim Sallee was purchased from the Giants and righthander Ray Fisher from the Yankees. Pat Moran (who had led the Phillies to a pennant in 1915) was hired to replace Mathewson at the Cincinnati helm. Thus fortified, the Reds in 1919 won their second pennant. Three pitchers—Sallee (21–7), Hod Eller (20–9), and Dutch Ruether (19–7, 1.82 ERA)—reached career peaks, Fisher (14–5) enjoyed one of his best years, Roush won another batting title and finished second in NL RBI, and three Reds finished in the league's top four in runs scored. The Reds broke quickly at the start, but faltered in May and didn't pass the Giants into first place for good until late July. But from then on, they increased their lead to the end, finishing 9 games in front. Rumors of a White Sox fix to throw the World Series clouded the Reds' Series triumph—and spoiled it entirely when, a year later, the scandal became public and the truth of the rumors was confirmed.

In 1920 Cincinnati led the league entering September, but Brooklyn spurted and the Reds slumped to a third-place finish, 10½ games out. They dropped to sixth in 1921, but recovered for five years in the first division, including three second-place finishes. But only in 1926 did the Reds contend closely for the flag. After leading the league much of the first half of the season, they found themselves in the second half tangled in a three-way battle with St. Louis and Pittsburgh. But after surging into a narrow lead with seven straight wins in mid-September, they lost their next five games and wound up 2 games back of the Cardinals in second place.

The Reds finished the eleven years after 1926 in the second division, hitting bottom with four straight cellar finishes in 1931–1934. President Herrmann retired after the 1927 season, and within two years a controlling interest in the Reds was sold to a wealthy Cincinnatian, Sidney Weil. But Weil lost his fortune in the stock market crash of 1929 and the Depression that followed. While he continued to run the Reds for four years, his stock in the club was held by the Central Trust Company. In his efforts to turn the club around, Weil acquired catcher Ernie Lombardi from Brooklyn in March 1932, and pitcher Paul Derringer from the St. Louis Cardinals the following May. Derringer lost 25 games in his first Red season and 21 the next, but both remained with the club long enough to star in its return to glory. Owner Weil, however, relinquished his control to the bank in 1933, at the depth of the Depression and of the team's fortunes.

The bank hired Larry MacPhail (who had rescued minor league Columbus by introducing night baseball there) to run the Reds. MacPhail in turn hired Frank Lane to develop a minor league farm system, and persuaded Cincinnati industrialist Powel Crosley, Jr., to invest in the club. On May 24, 1935, Crosley and MacPhail brought night ball to the major leagues (the Reds, with Derringer pitching, beat the Phillies 2–1), and with it a sharp upswing in attendance at Crosley Field. By June 1936, Crosley's increased investment in the Reds had made him the majority owner. The temperamental MacPhail quit suddenly in mid-September 1936, but the Reds replaced him with another successful minor league executive, Warren Giles, who ran the club until his selection in 1952 as president of the NL.

After rising to sixth place in 1935 and fifth the next year, the Reds dropped back into the cellar in 1937. But the following year, under new manager Bill McKechnie, they rose into the first division once again—even holding second place briefly in September before slipping to fourth. Derringer enjoyed the first of three peak seasons, young Johnny Vander Meer contributed 15 wins (including two consecutive no-hitters) and Bucky Walters, after his acquisition from the Phillies in June, compiled his first winning season since converting from third baseman to pitcher in 1935. Catcher Lombardi led the NL in batting, and first baseman Frank McCormick, in his first full season, led the team in RBI and the league in hits. The stage was set for the club's first back-to-back pennants.

Several Reds reached the apex of their careers in 1939, among them Walters (27–11) and Derringer (25–7), who between them topped most of the league's pitching stats, and Frank McCormick, who led the league in RBI and hits and finished second in batting. The club pulled out of the pack to the front before the end of May and held the lead to the end, although St. Louis closed the gap with a late-season surge before slipping 4½ games back.

Cincinnati's sweep by the Yankees in the World Series was something of a shock, but the club had recovered its poise by the next spring. Starting strong and—except for a small dip in August—pushing steadily upward throughout the season, the Reds shook off the persistent Dodgers in midseason and finished 12 games in front with their first 100-win season. McCormick and Lombardi powered the offense, and Walters for the second year in a row took NL crowns in wins and ERA. This time the team's triumph carried through the World Series as Walters and Derringer won two games apiece to edge the Detroit Tigers in seven games.

The Reds' pitching remained strong in 1941, but their hitting and run production fell off and the team struggled to finish third. They remained in the upper division through 1944, but then dropped into an eleven-year trough of losing seasons in which, while they never sank into the cellar, they never rose above fifth.

Ted Kluszewski was in his ninth season as the Reds' slugging first baseman when Cincinnati next offered a serious run for the pennant in 1956 under manager Birdie Tebbetts. Kluszewski led the club in hitting and RBI, but his 35 home runs were good enough only for third behind rookie Frank Robinson's 38 and Wally Post's 36 on a team that hammered 221 during the season to tie the then-major league record set nine years earlier by the Giants. The Reds' offense (they led the league in runs scored) kept them in the thick of a three-team race throughout the season, and they finished only 2 games out. That same year, for the first time ever they drew more than a million fans at home.

The Reds dropped out of a tight race in August 1957, and suffered losing seasons the next three years. After the 1960 season, Gabe Paul, who had succeeded Warren Giles as club president and general manager, left to help organize the new Houston club, and the following spring owner Crosley died. Bill DeWitt, who replaced Paul as president (and ultimately purchased control of the club), acquired pitcher Joey Jay from the Milwaukee Braves and third baseman Gene Freese from the White Sox. Jay in 1961 won twelve games more than his previous season high—tying for the league lead with 21, and Freese homered 26 times and drove in 87 runs—both career highs. Most of the team improved on their 1960 stats, and despite a poor start that saw them enter May in last place, the Reds had risen to the top by mid-June. The streaking Dodgers caught them briefly in August, but then fell away as the Reds pushed their pennant-winning margin to 4 games. In the World Series, though, it was the Yankees in five games.

The Reds next threatened in 1964 when, in a wild three-way finish, they won nine straight in late September to take first place for a day before slipping into a tie for second, one game behind St. Louis. In 1965 a young Pete Rose recorded the first of his ten 200-hit seasons as the Reds battled among the leaders through much of the summer before dropping off to fourth.

That December, after a decade of standout offense in

Cincinnati, Frank Robinson was traded to Baltimore. The next year, while Robinson won the Triple Crown in assisting his new team to the world championship, the Reds suffered their first losing season in six years and sank to seventh place. That winter, owner DeWitt completed the sale of the team to a group led by Cincinnati newspaper publisher Francis Dale, and including brothers James and William Williams who later acquired a controlling interest in the club.

In 1969, the first year of divisional play, the Reds rose, after a slow start, into the thick of a five-way race in the NL West before stumbling as Atlanta and San Francisco surged in the final three weeks. But the season provided a foretaste of the decade to come as the team captured league crowns in slugging and home runs.

At midseason in 1970 the Reds moved out of Crosley Field—their home for fifty-eight years—into the new Riverfront Stadium. Catcher Johnny Bench and third baseman Tony Perez, with the finest seasons of their long careers, paced an overwhelming Red offense as the team hammered out a new club-high 102 wins to reward rookie manager Sparky Anderson with victory in the NL West by 14½ games, and gain the appelation "Big Red Machine." In the League Championship Series the Reds continued their triumph with a three-game sweep of East winner Pittsburgh. But mighty Baltimore humbled the Reds in the World Series, 4–1.

Cincinnati's hitting and run production fell off sharply the next year, and the club dropped to fourth with their only losing season of the decade. But in 1972—spurred on after a slow start by Johnny Bench's recovery of power, Gary Nolan's finest season on the mound, and the all-around mastery of newly acquired second baseman Joe Morgan—the Reds rebounded after a slow start to take a lead in June and pull away from everyone in July for an easy division win. Victory in the LCS came harder, as powerful Pittsburgh carried the series to the full five games before handing the Reds the pennant with a wild pitch in the last of the ninth inning of the final game. Cincinnati's defeat in the World Series was also close: the Reds won three, and Oakland's four wins were each achieved by a margin of just one run.

The Reds repeated as division titlists in 1973 with a second-half surge from fourth place that carried them past front-runner Los Angeles in September. But the much weaker New York Mets ended Cincinnati's pennant hopes in the LCS, 3–2.

In 1974 the Reds trailed the Dodgers all season and finished 4 games back in second place. But over the next two years the Big Red Machine flattened all opposition. In 1975, after hovering around .500 through mid-May, the Reds began an ascent that carried them to what are still club records: 108 victories and a winning margin of 20 games. The team featured balanced pitching (six starters won ten or more games), a balanced offense in which every regular drove in more than 45 runs (averaging nearly 77 apiece), the best fielding in the majors, and a big NL lead in stolen bases. After a three-game sweep of Pittsburgh in the LCS, the Reds subdued the stubborn Boston Red Sox in seven games for their first world title in thirty-five years, and their third overall.

They won their fourth the next year. Joe Morgan, at the peak of his career, led the NL in slugging, finished second

to teammate George Foster in RBI, and stole 60 bases. Balanced pitching and offense again put the Reds in front to stay in June, carrying the team to 102 wins and a 10-game lead over Los Angeles at the finish. The LCS produced another sweep—of Philadelphia this time. The World Series was also a sweep as the Reds dispatched the Yankees, outscoring them nearly three to one.

Two years of second-place finishes followed, and the Reds replaced Sparky Anderson at the helm with John McNamara, who led the club back to the top of the NL West in 1979. Pete Rose, after sixteen years in Cincinnati, had signed with the Phillies as a free agent, but Ray Knight (who replaced Rose at third base) minimized the loss with a team-high .318 batting average. Houston led the division much of the summer, but a sustained Reds' surge in August brought them even, then pulled them ahead in early September, where they hung on to take the title by just 1½ games. But that was the end of the Reds' decade of splendor, for Pittsburgh swept past them to the pennant in the LCS.

Joe Morgan left the club after the season, returning as a free agent to Houston, whence he had come eight years earlier. In 1980 the Reds dipped in midseason, recovering to make a race of it in August, only to fade a bit and finish third. The next year, in a season shortened and split in two by a players' strike, the Reds compiled the best overall record in the majors. But they came away empty-handed by finishing half a game behind Los Angeles in the first half-season and 1½ games back of Houston in the second half, losing a chance at postseason play when the powers that be decided to pit the half-season winners against each other for the right to play in the LCS.

As a penurious front office continued to trade away its stars or lose them to free agency, the dispirited Reds dropped to the bottom of the NL West in 1982 with a club-worst 101 losses. Manager McNamara yielded in midseason to coach Russ Nixon, who was himself replaced by Vern Rapp after another last-place finish in 1983. Robert Howsam, Sr., whose shrewd trading as general manager had been instrumental in building the mighty Reds of the 1970s, was called out of semiretirement to restore the club to respectability. Howsam signed free-agent slugger Dave Parker from Pittsburgh, and late in the 1984 season brought Pete Rose back as player-manager. Early in 1985 the NL approved the sale of the Reds to Marge Schott, a Cincinnati automobile dealer. With Parker enjoying his most productive seasons in several years, and newcomers Eric Davis and John Franco developing respectively into one of the league's leading run producers and one of its best relief pitchers, owner Schott's public enthusiasm for her team was rewarded with four straight second-place finishes (and a return in 1987 to a home attendance over two million for the first time in seven years). In 1987 the team even spent two months at the top of the NL West, until an August slump dropped them into a hole from which a late-season rally could not extricate them.

Turmoil ruled the Reds in 1989. Disabling injuries to no fewer than twelve players, including such 1988 standouts as pitcher Danny Jackson (whose 23 wins tied for the league high) and infielders Barry Larkin and Chris Sabo, contributed most to the team's drop to fifth place. But baseball's investigation of manager Pete Rose on charges of gambling on baseball games and other offenses—an investigation which resulted in Rose's lifetime banishment from the game in August—did nothing to bolster Cincinnati's play on the field.

The distress of 1989 was all but forgotten in 1990 as the Reds, under new manager Lou Piniella, leaped to a 9–0 start and, surviving threats from San Francisco in August and Los Angeles in September, held on to first place through the entire season. Larkin and Sabo—whole again—anchored a balanced offense, while pitchers Randy Myers (acquired from the Mets in a trade for John Franco) and Rob Dibble provided All-Star relief to a solid core of starters. In the LCS, the Reds overcame an opening-game loss to capture the pennant from Pittsburgh in six games, then startled Oakland's heavily favored Athletics with a four-game sweep.

The Reds remained in the thick of the 1991 race through midseason, despite a 10-game losing streak in July. But as Atlanta rose to battle early leader Los Angeles, Cincinnati settled into a long decline that at the end left them 20 games back, in fifth place. Barry Larkin and Bip Roberts sparked the league's strongest offense in 1992, as the Reds rebounded to win 90 games. But they let a 6-game mid-season lead get away from them and finished 8 games behind repeat champion Atlanta.

Manager Piniella was replaced by Cincinnati hero—but managing novice—Tony Perez for 1993. Perez lasted only until May 24, when veteran manager Davey Johnson took his place. Meanwhile, Marge Schott's fellow NL owners banned her for the season from active participation in club affairs for making racial slurs. With their season further marred by injuries and backbiting, the Reds finished fifth, 31 games out.

With Kevin Mitchell pacing a strong, balanced offense, the Reds turned their fortunes around in 1994 and reached the All-Star break atop the new Central division by 2½ games. They were still clinging to a half-game lead over Houston when the season ended on August 12.

When play resumed in 1995 the Reds showed they had indeed been for real, winning the division by nine games. Standouts included MVP Barry Larkin (.319, 15 HR, 66 RBI), Mets discard Pete Schourek (18-7), Ron Gant (29 HR, 88 RBI), Reggie Sanders (28 HR, 99 RBI), and Jeff Brantley (28 saves). The Reds swept LA in the first round of playoffs but in turn were swept by the Braves in the NLCS. At season's end manager Davey Johnson left the team for the Baltimore Orioles and was replaced by former third base star Ray Knight. The 1996 season saw owner Schott again embroiled in controversy and the team fall to third place (81-81).

Cleveland Indians

Until their AL Championship 1995 season Cleveland remained without at least one divisional title. Since the advent of divisional play in 1969, the Indians have enjoyed only five winning seasons, finishing last in their old home, the AL East, eight times. Their record was not always this dismal. Though no other major league club with their longevity has won as few pennants, the Indians before 1969 ranked consistently among the league's better teams. They finished in the top half of the league

nearly 70 percent of the time through their first sixty-eight years, and only once (in 1914) wound up in the cellar.

The Indians (who were at first called the Blues because of the color of their uniforms) succeeded Cleveland's National League Spiders, who in 1899, their final season, lost a major league record 134 games. When the NL dropped the Spiders at the end of the season, Ban Johnson, president of the emerging American League, grasped the opportunity to move into this major market. In 1901, when Johnson proclaimed the AL a major league, Cleveland lured several players from NL clubs and played much better than the Spiders had, but still finished next-to-last in their first big league season. The next year the Bronchos (as they decided to call themselves) languished in last place through June. But during the season they acquired several players through trade and purchase—most notably star second baseman Napoleon "Nap" Lajoie and pitcher Bill Bernhard—who turned the Bronchos around in midseason and lifted them above .500 (and into fifth place) by season's end.

With Lajoie sparkling in the field and dominating the league at the plate, the fans soon settled on another nickname for the club—the Naps—that lasted as long as Lajoie remained in Cleveland. Late in the 1904 season, Lajoie was named manager. After enjoying moderate success in two of the next three seasons, the Naps in 1908 experienced their best year yet, and one of the team's most exciting finishes ever.

With a ten-game winning streak near the end of the season, they moved from fourth to first, only to be surpassed by Detroit's ten-game streak. Both teams won their season finale, but the Tigers, because they had not made up an earlier rainout, took the pennant by half a game. Cleveland protested that if Detroit had played the missed game and lost, Cleveland would have gained a tie, forcing a playoff that might have brought them the championship. The dispute eventually led to a rules change requiring ties or washouts to be replayed if their outcome could determine the pennant winner.

Poor seasons alternated with good the next few years. Lajoie quit as manager but remained as player. Pitching ace Addie Joss pitched a second no-hitter (he had hurled a perfect game at the height of the 1908 race), but before the start of the 1911 season, Joss was dead of tubercular meningitis. Outfielder Joe Jackson—acquired from the Athletics—hit .408 in his first full big league season. The club reached bottom in 1914 with a last-place finish that found them 18½ games out of *seventh* place, 48½ out of first. After the season Lajoie was waivered to Philadelphia (the fans then voted to rename the club the Indians), and the next August Jackson was sold to the Chicago White Sox as attendance dropped to its lowest level since 1901.

By the time the 1916 season began, though, new ownership had acquired the great Tris Speaker from Boston and brought up from the minors a pair of promising pitchers, Jim Bagby (Sr.) and Stan Coveleski. The club rose only one place that year, to sixth. But they stayed in the pennant fight through July and wound up winning 20 games more than they had the previous year. Attendance more than tripled over 1915.

Sparked by the three newcomers, the Indians rose to third in 1917, and to close second-place finishes the next two years. In 1920 everything came together. Speaker, who had taken over as manager the previous July, hit .388 and enjoyed one of his best years, as did Coveleski with 24 wins. Bagby, in the finest season of his career, led the league with 31 victories, and veteran pitcher Ray Caldwell (picked up from the Boston Red Sox the previous summer) added another 20. Six regulars hit over .300; the club as a whole hit .303.

Involved from mid-June in a close race with the Yankees, joined in August by the White Sox, Cleveland saw its home attendance climb above 900,000 for the first time, to set a club record that would last twenty-six years. The Yankees dropped back a bit in mid-September, but the White Sox hung close until the final week, when eight of their players were indicted and suspended as suspects in the Black Sox scandal of 1919. The Sox lost two of their final three games and all hope of tying Cleveland to force a playoff. The Indians defeated Brooklyn in a World Series that is best remembered for second baseman Bill Wambsganss's unassisted triple play in Game Five.

Cleveland led much of the way in 1921 before a late slump and a New York surge gave the Yankees their first pennant. Through the next quarter century the Indians came close to a pennant only twice. In 1926, with two veteran Georges—pitcher Uhle and first baseman Burns—enjoying their finest seasons, the Indians came to life in midseason and drew within three games of the Yankees by season's end. Fourteen years later, in 1940, behind the 27 wins of twenty-one-year-old Bob Feller and the inspired play (in the field and at the bat) of second-year shortstop Lou Boudreau, Cleveland made an even closer run for the flag. Throughout the summer the Indians were in or near first place, but six losses in nine games with a resurgent Detroit in late August and September left them a game back at the finish.

Two years later Boudreau, at age twenty-four, was named to manage the Tribe. His team stirred little interest through the war years. But in 1946, with Feller back from military service and pitching his best ever, Cleveland fans boosted home attendance above a million for the first time, even though the team's won-lost record was its worst in eighteen years. The next year, their first full season under new president Bill Veeck, the Indians climbed to fourth. More significantly, Veeck hired the league's first black player, Larry Doby, who became a mainstay of the Indians for the next eight years.

In 1948 the Indians began a nine-year era of excellence with a victory in one of the closest pennant races ever. Through June they ran a three-way race with the Yankees and the surprisingly lively Philadelphia Athletics; in July the Red Sox rose out of nowhere to make it a four-way struggle. In September the A's fell behind, but the three remaining clubs stayed close, and on September 24 found themselves in a three-way tie. Cleveland moved ahead with a four-game win streak, but Boston, after a pair of losses, won their final four (including two to eliminate New York). Cleveland's final-day loss to Detroit left them tied with Boston. In a one-game playoff in Boston the next day (the first playoff in AL history), manager-shortstop Boudreau capped his MVP season with two home runs to help give rookie Gene Bearden his twentieth win and the Tribe their second pennant. The exciting race drew more than 2.6 million Cleveland fans to Municipal Stadium, a new major league record. By contrast, the

World Series against the Boston Braves was anticlimactic—a Cleveland triumph in six games.

By 1951 both owner Veeck and manager Boudreau had moved on, but under new manager Al Lopez the Indians fashioned a six-year stretch in which they finished second to the Yankees five times, and in 1954 they won their third pennant with 111 victories—the most in AL history. The Lopez years, 1951–1956, were punctuated by the power of players like Doby, Luke Easter, Al Rosen, and Vic Wertz. But it was pitching that gave the team its consistency. Bob Lemon and Early Wynn won between 17 and 23 games in every one of the six years, as did Mike Garcia through 1954. As Garcia and Feller (who won 22 in 1951) faded, Art Houtteman was acquired from Detroit for a couple of good years, and Herb Score came along for his two explosive seasons.

The 1954 season—Cleveland's year to break the Yankee grip on the AL—was in fact New York's best season in the eighteen years from 1943 through 1960, a period in which they won twelve pennants. The Yankees kept the race close until early September, and finished with 103 wins. But the Indians won an AL-record 111 games to beat New York by 8. Wynn and Lemon tied for the league lead with 23 wins apiece, and Garcia copped the ERA crown. Doby led the league in homers and RBI, and second baseman Bobby Avila took the batting title. Heavily favored to defeat the Giants in the World Series, the Tribe and their fans were shocked when the NL champs swept them in four games.

After Lopez left to manage the White Sox in 1957, the Indians slipped below .500 for the first time in a decade. Rocky Colavito's power and Cal McLish's pitching brought them back in 1959, when they finished second to Lopez's Sox. Their next highest post-Lopez finish came nine years later, in 1968, when Luis Tiant and Sam McDowell pitched them into third.

From 1969 through 1989 the Indians completed every season in the bottom half of the AL East, rising above .500 in only four seasons while finishing seven years in the division cellar. In 1990, though, with three straight wins at season's end, they passed Baltimore by half a game to wind up a middle-of-the-divison fourth.

The effort proved too much. In July 1991 the Indians dropped into the cellar to stay, spiraling on down to a club-record 105 losses. With nowhere to go but up, the 1992 team, spurred by the offense of Carlos Baerga and Albert Belle, and the impressive pitching of Charles Nagy, played the best ball in the AL after the All Star break, lifting themselves out of the cellar into a fourth-place tie with the Yankees.

The tragic preseason deaths of relievers Tim Crews and Steve Olin—and severe injury to starter Bob Ojeda—in a boating accident cast a pall over the team's final season in Cleveland Stadium. With Nagy also out much of the season, the Indians' pitching was among the league's worst. Offensively, though, they ranked among the better clubs, paced by Baerga, Belle, and sophomore Kenny Lofton, whose league-leading 70 stolen bases set a new club record. The team finished sixth.

The Indians—playing in brand-new Jacobs Field— were up for 1994. Belle, who ranked among AL leaders in almost every offensive category, and Lofton, who added the league lead in hits to another stolen base title, paced a powerful offense that kept the team in the thick of a tight race with Chicago in the league's new Central division. With their best chance in decades to bring Cleveland a winner, the Indians trailed the White Sox by just one game when the season ended prematurely.

The Indians dominated the AL in 1995, rolling to a 100-44 record and capturing the AL Central division by a phenomenal 30 games. Paced by Albert Belle (who despite the shortened season led the AL with 50 homers, 121 runs, 377 total bases, 52 doubles, and a .690 slugging percentage), the Indians batted .291 and slugged 207 homers. Meanwhile Tribe pitchers posted a league-best 3.83 ERA (the only AL ERA under 4.00). Jose Mesa led league relievers with 46 saves.

The Indians swept the Red Sox in the first round of the postseason, then edged the upstart Mariners in the ALCS, before falling 4-2 to Atlanta in the World Series. Indian fans appreciated their team's superb effort, however, and in the offseason the club became the first to sell out every seat for the entire upcoming campaign.

Despite discarding Eddie Murray and Carlos Baerga in midseason, and integrating Jeff Kent and Jose Vizcaino, the 1996 Indians (99-62, with a league-leading .293 team batting average) repeated as East Division champions, with the best record in the AL. Team standouts included Albert Belle (48 HR and an AL-best 148 RBI), Kenny Lofton (.317 and a league-leading 75 SB), Jim Thome (38 HR), Jose Mesa (39 saves), and Charles Nagy (17-5, 3.41). The Tribe fell, however, to wild-card Baltimore in the first round of the postseason.

Colorado Rockies

Denver was one of two cities awarded a National League franchise in June 1991 (Miami was the other), in the league's first expansion since Montreal and San Diego were added in 1969. The new teams took the field for the first time in 1993, their rosters stocked primarily with players selected from the other major league clubs in a special expansion draft. Denver, which chose to call itself the Colorado Rockies, drew nearly 4.5 million fans to cavernous Mile High Stadium (its home until new Coors Field opened in 1995), the highest season attendance in the history of sport.

Though their 5.41 ERA was by far the worst in the majors, the Rockies, under rookie manager Don Baylor, not only avoided the NL West cellar, but set a new record for wins by a first-year expansion team, with 67. Andres Galarraga, Charlie Hayes, and Dante Bichette headed a solid offense, with Galarraga hitting more than one hundred points above his previous major league career average to lead the NL in batting at .370.

Galarraga was in the midst of another fine season in 1994 when a pitch broke his hand on July 28. Despite a 50–54 record, the Rockies stood in second place in the weak NL West, just half a game out of first. By the time the season ended two weeks later, though, they had slipped to third, 6½ games out.

In 1995 the Rockies moved into beautiful new Coors Field (drawing 3.3 million fans) and Baylor won NL Manager of the Year honors as Colorado finished just one game behind LA in the NL West and earned a wild card

playoff slot in the process. Key Rockies were Galarraga (31 HR, 106 RBI), Vinny Castilla (32 HR, 90 RBI, .309), Dante Bichette (.340 and a league-leading 40 HR, 128 RBI, 359 total bases, and a .620 slugging mark), Eric Young (.317 and an NL-leading 9 triples), and Larry Walker (36 HR, 101 RBI, .306). The dream ended in the first round of the playoffs, however, as Colorado fell to Atlanta, three games to one.

The 1996 Rockies finished third, 8 games behind surprising San Diego. Standouts included Galarraga (a league-leading 47 HR and 150 RBI), Bichette (141 RBI, 198 hits), Young (a league-leading 53 SB) and Ellis Burks (40 HR, .344, 211 hits, 128 RBI, and an NL-best 142 runs scored).

Detroit Tigers

One of the more successful clubs in the American League, the Tigers have enjoyed winning seasons nearly 70 percent of the time. In eighteen of their sixty-one winning seasons, they have remained in contention into the final days, eleven times emerging triumphant as league or division champions. They have finished last in the league or AL East only seven times, and have never had more than four losing seasons in a row.

Detroit was one of the clubs from Ban Johnson's Western League that (renamed the American League) raised itself to major league status in 1901 with a talent raid on the long-established National League. In their first six big league seasons, the Tigers displayed little bite, finishing four times in the second division and never threatening for the league lead.

In 1907 all that changed. Sparked by a young right fielder, Ty Cobb (who in his first full big league season led the league in batting, slugging, hits, RBI, and stolen bases) and led by a dynamic new manager, Hugh "Eeyah" Jennings (who knew enough not to try to tell Cobb how to play the game), the Tigers clawed their way to the pennant in a four-way race. The outcome might have been different if two late-season games with second-place Philadelphia had not been rained out and tied. Today's rules would require that the games be made up.

The 1908 race was even closer, with four teams contending into late September. The race wasn't settled until the final day, when Detroit beat Chicago to edge Cleveland by half a game. Once again the pennant hinged on a rainout that had not been made up. And once again Cobb dominated the league's hitters (though he slipped to fourth in stolen bases).

The Tigers had a slightly easier time of it the next year. It was a three-way race into September, but Detroit then pulled away to finish 3½ games ahead of Philadelphia. Cobb, in his best season yet, took the Triple Crown and returned to the top in stolen bases. But the Tigers were unable to win a World Series. In 1907, after an opening-game tie, the Chicago Cubs swept the next four. The Cubs lost Game Three the next year, but won the other four. And in 1909 Pittsburgh and Detroit alternated victories, with the Pirates emerging world champions in seven games.

Jennings managed Detroit for eleven more seasons; then Cobb took the reins for six years before leaving for

Philadelphia. But the Tigers won no more pennants in the Cobb era. Cobb himself continued to dominate the league offensively through 1919. In 1911 he achieved career highs in most offensive categories, including a batting average of .420, but the Tigers managed no better than a distant second to the Athletics. In 1915 they started strong and remained in the race throughout the season. Cobb stole what was for forty-seven years a modern-record 96 bases, and the team's 100 wins proved to be the highest total in their first thirty-three years. But after running neck and neck with the Red Sox through most of August, the Tigers slumped a bit in early September—just enough for the Sox to take the flag by 2½ games. A close third-place finish the next year marked the Tigers' last serious challenge for eighteen years.

In 1934, after six straight years in the second division, and only three years after their most distant finish ever (47 games out), the Tigers turned themselves around to win the pennant with a 101–53 record and a .656 winning percentage, the highest in Tiger history. Two newly acquired veterans—manager/catcher Mickey Cochrane and outfielder Goose Goslin—enjoyed fine seasons at the bat, as did first baseman Hank Greenberg (.339, 139 RBI) in his first full season, and long-time Tiger second baseman Charlie Gehringer (.356, 127 RBI). The two other infielders, third baseman Marv Owen and shortstop Billy Rogell enjoyed their finest seasons at the plate for a club whose batting average led the league at .300. It took the Tigers a month to get going, but by mid-July they had shot ahead of the Yankees, pulling farther away through August and September to win by 7 games. But once again, victory in the World Series eluded them as the St. Louis Cardinals blew them away 11–0 in Game Seven.

The Tigers' hitting fell off ten points in 1935, but their slugging jumped eleven points. Paced by Greenberg's 170 RBI, Detroit—after another slow start—shot up so sharply in July and August that even a September slump gave the Yankees no opportunity to catch them. And finally, in their fifth try, the Tigers won a world championship, overcoming Chicago in six games despite the loss of Greenberg, who broke his wrist in Game Two. Part-owner Frank Navin, who had run the club for three decades, had finally seen his Tigers reach the very top. A month later, after falling from a horse, he suffered a heart attack and died.

Del Baker had replaced Cochrane as manager when Detroit next made a run for the pennant in 1940. In a tight race the Tigers caught up with Cleveland in early September and traded the lead with them for two weeks before pulling ahead to stay with two wins in a three-game series. In the pennant clincher, Detroit's Floyd Giebell outdueled Cleveland great Bob Feller 2–0 for his third—and last—big league victory. In the World Series the Tigers lost once again, as Cincinnati came from behind in Game Seven for a 2–1 win.

Two losing seasons followed, and Steve O'Neill replaced Baker at the helm. In 1944, the wartime Tigers, behind the splendid pitching of workhorses Dizzy Trout and Hal Newhouser (one-two in ERA and innings pitched, and winners of 27 and 29 games), joined the race in late August and found themselves tied with the St. Louis Browns for first going into the last game of the season. But the Browns beat the Yankees and Detroit lost

to Washington as Trout failed in his try for a twenty-eighth win.

Hank Greenberg's release from military service in mid-1945 sparked another Tiger run for the pennant. They held the lead from mid-June through August, but in September a surging Washington Senators club caught up with them. The race once again went down to the final day, and the final inning, when Greenberg's grand slam home run overcame a St. Louis Browns' lead to give Detroit the flag over the idle Senators. Newhouser, with 25 wins and a 1.81 ERA, was named American League MVP for the second straight year. In the World Series his ERA shot up to 6.10, but he still managed to win two games (including the finale) as the Tigers took the Cubs in seven for their second world title.

In the twenty-three years that passed before their next pennant, the Tigers came close only twice. In 1950 they led the race through the middle of the season, but were caught by the Yankees late in August. After retaking the lead in early September, the two clubs ran neck-and-neck for a while before Detroit fell away to second.

Two years later the Tigers reached their nadir: their first cellar finish, their most losses ever (104), and their lowest winning percentage (.325). After a decade in which they finished no higher than fourth, they rebounded in 1961 as first baseman Norm Cash and left fielder Rocky Colavito both enjoyed the most explosive seasons of their careers. Compiling their best season record since 1934, Detroit led the league through parts of June and July. But this was the year of Maris and Mantle and 109 Yankee victories; when the season ended, the Tigers' 101 wins had earned them only second place.

They came much closer six years later in the great four-way race of 1967 that saw three clubs still contending on the final day, when the Tigers split a doubleheader to tie with Minnesota for second. If 1967 was a scramble, 1968 was all Detroit's. In what is now known as the year of the pitcher, Tiger Denny McLain won 31 games (the last major leaguer to win 30) to lead the team to a 103-win finish, 12 games ahead of Baltimore. Down 1–3 to the Cardinals in the World Series, the pitching of McLain in Game Six and Mickey Lolich in Games Five and Seven brought the Tigers back and gave them their third world championship.

A strike at the start of 1972 contributed to the Tigers' first divisional title, which culminated a four-way race in the AL East. Detroit defeated Boston two games out of three at season's end, to edge the Sox by half a game. But if the strike had not wiped out an unequal number of games, the end of the season could have seen the two clubs tied.

The Tigers lost the pennant to Oakland with a 1–2 loss in the finale of a close League Championship Series, and dropped out of contention for a decade. In 1974 they finished at the bottom of the division, and the next year lost 102 games to post the worst record in the majors.

Finally, after seven seasons in the second division, Detroit put together a strong second half in strike-divided 1981, fading only at the end to tie for second. Three years later the Tigers were back on top with one of their best years. Opening the season with 9 wins, they ended April at 18–2, stretched their mark to 35–5 by late May, and were never headed, finishing a team-record 15 games in front, with 104 wins, their most ever. Their balanced pitching staff led the league in ERA, even though none of their starters finished among the top ten. Tiger newcomer Willie Hernandez (who with Aurelio Lopez compiled a 19–4 record from the bullpen, with 46 saves) earned both Cy Young and MVP awards. After sweeping Kansas City in the LCS, the Tigers took the world championship—their fourth—from San Diego in five games.

In 1987 the Tigers caught Toronto's Blue Jays in the season's final series, tying them for the lead in the first game, moving to the front with a twelve-inning win in the second game, and clinching the division crown in the finale, 1–0. In the LCS, though, Minnesota stopped the favored Tigers, four games to one.

Injuries sidelined veteran keystoners Alan Trammell and Lou Whitaker more than a month each and derailed the season of starter Jeff Robinson in August just as he was emerging as ace of Detroit's pitchers. All the same, the Tigers led the AL East much of the 1988 season before falling back and rallied at season's end to finish second, one game behind Boston.

The next year, though, as new waves of injury broke over an aging lineup, the Tigers dropped into the division cellar in June and kept sinking, finishing with 103 losses and the worst record in the majors. But in 1990 Trammell rebounded from one of his worst seasons with one of his best and, with newly acquired first baseman Cecil Fielder, sparked a Tiger recovery to third place. Fielder, back in the AL after a season in Japan, topped the majors in home runs (with 51, the most in the AL since 1961), slugging percentage, and runs batted in.

The 1991 Tigers clawed their way back from an 8-game deficit in mid-July into a tie with first-place Toronto seven weeks later. But their grip wouldn't hold, and they finished tied for second with Boston. In 1992, for the third year in a row, Detroit led the AL in home runs, but this time their big bats couldn't lift the club above sixth place. Texas edged the Tigers for the home run crown in 1993, but Detroit challenged for their division lead through August and, after a dip in September, surged to tie Baltimore for third place. In strike-shortened 1994 they finished last in the AL East, 18 games out.

On the field in 1995 little of substance changed for the Tigers, as Fielder slammed 31 homers and the team finished a distant fourth (60-84), but momentous changes occurred off it. Sparky Anderson resigned as Tiger manager at season's end, and plans to replace Tiger Stadium with another downtown ballpark accelerated.

The Buddy Bell-led 1996 Tigers compiled baseball's worst record (53-109, 39 GB). The season saw Cecil Fielder leave for the Yankees in midseason and Alan Trammell retire at season's end.

Florida Marlins

One of two new clubs to join the National League in 1993, the Florida Marlins were formed after the selection, in June 1991, of Miami and Denver as cities for the league's first expansion teams since 1969. Headed by entertainment magnate H. Wayne Huizenga, the Marlins played in Joe Robbie Stadium (which Huizenga partially owns). In their first season the Marlins featured one of the game's

premier relievers in Bryan Harvey, whose 45 saves ranked third in the NL and contributed to seventy per cent of the club's 64 victories. Though the Marlins lost their final six games, they finished ahead of the New York Mets for sixth place in the NL East.

In the strike-shortened seasons of 1994 and 1995 they finished in the division cellar. In 1995, however, Pat Rapp showed signs of promise with a 14-7 mark and rookie second baseman Quilvio Veras led the NL with 56 stolen bases. Even though the Marlins fired manager Rene Lacheman in midseason 1996 (replacing him with interim manager John Boles) they moved up to third place (80-82) with help from Gary Sheffield (42 HR, 120 RBI, 118 runs scored), Al Leiter (200 strikeouts), and Robb Nen (35 saves). At season's end Florida scored a major coup by securing the services of veteran Pirates manager Jim Leyland.

Houston Astros

The Colt .45s (as the Astros were originally known) had hoped to begin their history in the Harris County Domed Stadium, but when the start of the vast project was delayed, a temporary outdoor park was built for them next door in time for their 1962 inaugural. Heat, humidity, and giant mosquitoes held Colt home attendance below a million in each of their three outdoor seasons, but when, in 1965, they brought big league baseball indoors for the first time, the fans arrived—more than two million the first year. The original grass under the dome was real, but when the skylight panels were coated over so fielders wouldn't lose sight of high flies, the grass died. In 1966 the club (now known as the Astros) and the stadium (now called the Astrodome) brought to baseball yet another innovation—AstroTurf.

The Houston franchise, conceived as an entry in the abortive Continental League, first took the field instead (along with New York's Mets) in the National League, as part of the league's first expansion since shrinking from twelve teams to eight in 1900. Shrewd player selection by general manager Paul Richards kept the new team from being as bad as the Mets. Although they suffered just as long playing below .500 (seven years), they finished only once below New York in the standings.

When the NL added two more teams in 1969 and split into two divisions, the Astros for the first time made a serious title run. Though they wound up fifth in the West (ahead of only the expansion San Diego Padres), they rose to within two games of the top in August, and again in September, before a six-game losing streak dropped them out of contention. With an 81–81 record, they finished out of the ranks of losers for the first time.

After dropping below .500 again in 1970 and '71, the Astros made their second run for the division title in 1972. At the end of June they were neck and neck with Cincinnati for the lead, but the Reds pulled away over the rest of the season while Houston leveled off for an eventual second-place finish 10½ games back. With a record of 84–69, the Astros had fashioned their first winning season.

In 1975 they endured their worst year ever, losing 97 games to finish at the bottom of the West, 43½ games behind the Reds. But the next year pitcher J. R. Richard, with the first of several fine seasons, brought the club up to third with his 20 wins. By 1979 Richard was the NL's most overwhelming pitcher, leading the league with 313 strikeouts and a 2.71 ERA. His 18 wins and teammate Joe Niekro's 21 sparked a team that spent much of the summer in first place before falling to 1½ games behind Cincinnati at the end.

Houston and Los Angeles battled back and forth for the division lead throughout 1980. Richard began strong and seemed headed for his finest year. With a 10–4 record, he was starting pitcher in the All-Star Game. But shortly after midseason he suffered a stroke that ended his big league career. Led by Joe Niekro and Vern Ruhle (who replaced Richard in the rotation and finished 12–4), the best pitching staff in baseball kept the Astros in the race to season's end, although three straight losses to the Dodgers had left the clubs tied for first. In a one-game playoff, Houston rebounded with a 7–1 win (Niekro's twentieth) to capture the division title. In the League Championship Series, the Astros took the Phillies to the tenth inning of the final game before bowing two games to three.

When a player strike cut the middle out of the 1981 season, intradivisional playoffs were scheduled between the winners of the two halves. Houston, the second-half champion, defeated first-half victor Los Angeles in the first two games, but lost the next three, and with them the division title.

After four years in the middle of the division, the Astros stormed back in 1986 with their best season ever, winning fifteen of their last nineteen games to conquer the West by ten games. Pitcher Mike Scott, who had developed a deceptive split-finger fastball, won 18 to pace a strong Astro staff, leading the league in strikeouts and ERA. On September 25 he clinched the division crown with a no-hitter. In the LCS the Astros lost to the Mets, two games to four—but they held the New Yorkers at bay for fifteen innings of the final game before falling by a run in the sixteenth.

In each of the next three seasons the Astros drew within ½ to 1½ games of first place in August, only to tumble out of the race in the season's final weeks. While the team never challenged for the division lead in 1990, they overcame—with a winning second half—the worst first half in the league to tie for fourth in the NL West.

Rookie first baseman Jeff Bagwell's strong performance at the plate gave Astros fans one of their few reasons to cheer in 1991 as their team plummeted to last place. In 1992 Bagwell's continuing offensive leadership, plus strong relief pitching (especially a career-best season from newly acquired Doug Jones) ignited a fiery final two months that lifted the Astros from sixteen games below .500 to an unexpected 81-81 fourth-place finish.

The offense set club records in batting average and home runs in 1993, and the pitching staff compiled the second lowest ERA in the majors, as ace Mark Portugal concluded his brilliant 18–4 season with 12 straight wins. But the Astros couldn't approach powerful Atlanta and San Francisco, and finished third in their division, 19 games out.

Free agent Portugal departed for San Francisco in 1994, but pitcher Doug Drabek rebounded after an off year and MVP Bagwell's slugging dominated the NL.

Playing in the Central division under new manager Terry Collins, the Astros struggled to catch division leader Cincinnati, and had drawn within half a game of the Reds when the season ended.

The following year was almost a replay of 1994, as the Astros again finished second to Cincinnati. In 1996 the Astros were bridesmaids again, this time finishing second (82-80), six games back of St. Louis, as the team collapsed in September. At season's end Astros broadcaster Larry Dierker replaced Collins as manager. Bagwell (.315, 31 HR, 120 RBI) paced the NL with 48 doubles. Derek Bell drove in a career-high 113 runs.

Kansas City Royals

Two years after the Athletics abandoned Kansas City for the West Coast, patent-medicine millionaire Ewing Kauffman bankrolled an expansion club for the city. Where the A's had been unable in thirteen years to fashion even one winning season, the Royals did it in 1971, their third year (when, ironically, they finished second in the AL West to the newly invincible Oakland A's). One of the most successful of all expansion clubs, the Royals in their first twenty years finished either first or second in their division fourteen times.

In their fifth season, 1973, the year they moved into new Royals Stadium, the Royals also made their first serious run for the division title. A midsummer spurt carried them into first place in August before they leveled off to another second-place finish behind Oakland.

After a third second-place race with Oakland in 1975 (during which manager Jack McKeon was replaced by Whitey Herzog), the Royals won the division crown in 1976, taking the lead two months into the season and holding it to the end. Third baseman George Brett won his first AL batting championship and carried his hot bat into the League Championship Series, but the Yankees snatched the pennant on Chris Chambliss's home run in the bottom of the ninth inning of the final game.

For two more years the Royals dominated the AL West but failed to stop the Yankees in the LCS. In 1977, with a pitching staff that led the league in ERA and a balanced offense that included four players with more than 20 home runs and 80 RBI, the Royals compiled a record of 102–60—their finest to date. Though they didn't move into the division lead until mid-August, they were nearly unstoppable the rest of the way. In the LCS they once again battled New York all the way, only to lose the Series and pennant for the second time in the final inning of game five.

The divisional race was a bit tighter in 1978, as California hung close to K.C. through much of August and into September, before the Royals finally pulled away. In the League Championship Series, the Royals tied the Series with a big win in Game Two, but the Yankees came back to take the next two by one run each for their third straight flag.

The Royals slipped to second place in 1979, but the next year (led now by rookie manager Jim Frey) they overwhelmed the rest of a weak division. Despite a month-long decline in September, K.C. finished the season 14 games ahead of Oakland for their fourth divisional title. This was the year Brett chased .400 (ending at .390, the highest major league average since Ted Williams hit .406 in 1941), reliever Dan Quisenberry enjoyed his first big season (12 wins, 33 saves), and starter Dennis Leonard came back from an off-year to record his third 20-win season in four years. It was also the year the Royals finally beat the Yankees to capture their first pennant—with a three-game sweep in the LCS. In the World Series, though, it was Philadelphia in six games.

The player strike of 1981 divided the season into two halves. In the first half the Royals finished fifth, but part way through the second half Dick Howser (who had managed the Yankees to the East title the previous year) replaced Frey as Royals manager and brought the club in first, a game ahead of Oakland. But in the special playoffs, the A's (who had won the first-half race) beat K.C. for the division title with a three-game sweep.

Two more second-place finishes in 1982 (a close race with California) and 1983 (20 games behind the Chicago White Sox) were followed in 1984 by a fifth division championship in a three-way race with California and Minnesota. But Detroit swept away the Royals' pennant hopes in the LCS, in the minimum three games.

For Kansas City, 1985 was a season of catching up. Few picked the Royals to win the West, but with starters Charlie Leibrandt (17–9) and Bret Saberhagen (20–6) finishing two-three in the league ERA race, reliever Quisenberry leading the league in saves for the fourth straight year, and veteran George Brett healthy and enjoying one of his best seasons ever, the Royals chased California throughout the summer and caught them in the final week to take their sixth division crown by a single game. In the LCS against Toronto, K.C. fell behind 1–3, which would have eliminated them in earlier years. But, saved by the expansion of the Series from five games to seven, they came back with three straight wins for their second pennant. Repeating the suspense in the World Series, the Royals again fell behind 1–3, to St. Louis, before rallying once again to win three straight for their first world championship.

During the 1986 season, manager Howser left the club after he was found to have a brain tumor. The Royals dropped below .500 and finished third, their lowest rank in a dozen years. Howser was unable to return to the helm in 1987 as he had hoped and died during the summer. The Royals rallied at season's end to pull themselves above .500 and finish (for the eighth time) runner-up in the West, 2 games behind Minnesota. Although they improved on their 1987 won-lost record in 1988, they finished in third place.

In 1989 Bret Saberhagen, with his most sparkling season yet (23–6, 2.16 ERA), hurled the Royals to their best record since 1980, but their 92 wins earned them only a ninth second-place finish. Confounding predictions of another strong season, following free agent acquisitions Mark Davis and Storm Davis, the Royals in 1990 floundered in the division cellar much of the summer. They wound up in sixth place, 27½ games out. Thirty-seven-year-old George Brett, though, rallied from the worst start of his career (.200 BA in early May) to hit .329 and capture his third AL batting title.

Slugging outfielder Danny Tartabull enjoyed a peak season in 1991 and helped lift K.C. back above .500. But

in the strong AL West no club suffered a losing season, so the Royals again had to settle for sixth. When Tartabull left for the Yankees in 1992, the Royals faltered again. But as the West was now the weaker division, the club's 72–90 record was good enough for a fifth-place tie.

In the twenty-first—and final—season of his playing career at Kansas City, George Brett led his team in RBI in 1993, and Kevin Appier led AL pitchers in ERA, as the Royals returned above .500 to finish third. Ewing Kauffman, the club's founder and owner, died in August, and Royals Stadium was renamed in his honor.

In 1994, after a sluggish first half, the Royals picked up the pace to challenge Chicago and Cleveland in the new AL Central division. At season's end, the Royals were still third but—thanks largely to Cy Young Award winner David Cone's 16–5 season—only four games behind first-place Chicago.

Manager Bob Boone's Royals finished second again in 1995—but this time 30 games back of Cleveland. Standouts included Gary Gaetti (35 HR), Wally Joyner (.310), Keith Lockhart (.321), and Kevin Appier (15-10). In 1996, playing on natural turf for the first time in Kaufman Stadium's history, the Royals finished last again (75-86, 24 games out).

Los Angeles Dodgers

When the Dodgers left Brooklyn for Los Angeles, an era ended. From baseball's earliest days Brooklyn had been prominent; the city's Atlantics were the nation's best in the mid-1860s, and since 1884 Brooklyn had been home to major league ball. But before the start of the 1958 season, its link to the big time was severed by an owner who saw greener fields to the west. He was right: the Dodgers in Los Angeles are one of the game's most profitable franchises, who have often attracted more than 3 million fans per year to Dodger Stadium.

The club's origins were modest. After winning the championship of the minor Inter-State Association in 1883, Brooklyn moved up to the major league American Association in 1884 and endured three losing seasons in its first four years. But in 1888, after signing three regulars from New York's newly defunct Mets and buying pitching/hitting stars Bob Caruthers and Dave Foutz from the AA champion St. Louis Browns, Brooklyn finished second to St. Louis, and the next year dethroned the Browns for their first big league pennant. In a projected ten-game World Series against the National League champion New York Giants, the Bridegrooms (as the Brooklyns had been nicknamed) won three of the first four games, but lost the next five.

Before the start of the 1890 season, Brooklyn transferred from the AA to the more prestigious NL. Many NL clubs performed below par that year, weakened by the loss of players to the outlaw Players League. But Brooklyn held on to most of its players and swept to its second straight pennant. In postseason play, poor weather and lack of fan support caused the World Series against AA winner Louisville to be called off after each team had won three games and tied one. The next year, with other NL teams renewed by players from the failed PL, Brooklyn finished sixth.

When the AA folded after the 1891 season, Brooklyn picked up slugger Dan Brouthers and pitcher George Haddock from pennant-winning Boston, and rebounded in 1892 to finish second and third in the two halves of a divided season. But for the next five years they finished no higher than fifth, and in 1898 sank to tenth in what was now a twelve-team league.

Help was on the way, however—help that today would be prohibited. Longtime Brooklyn president Charles Byrne had died, and the owners of the Baltimore Orioles—Harry Von der Horst and Ned Hanlon—seeing an opportunity to move into the more lucrative Brooklyn market, purchased a half interest in the Bridegrooms. Hanlon retained his Baltimore presidency, but took over as manager in Brooklyn, bringing along with him the core of his Oriole club—shortstop Hughie Jennings and outfielders Joe Kelley and Willie Keeler—plus its two best pitchers, Jim Hughes and Doc McJames.

The infusion of new talent worked wonders, as Brooklyn in 1899 (with a new nickname, the Superbas) took the NL lead in late May, during a twenty-two game winning streak, and held it the rest of the way. That winter, when Baltimore was dropped as the NL cut back from twelve teams to eight, Hanlon moved more Orioles to Brooklyn (including pitcher Joe "Iron Man" McGinnity), and once again led the Superbas to the pennant. That year they also won their first world championship in a series played with second-place Pittsburgh for the elegant Chronicle-Telegraph Cup.

Slow starts in 1901 and '02 kept the Superbas out of pennant contention, although they finished third and second. During this period Charley Ebbets, who had risen from ticket seller to president, took over majority ownership with the purchase of Von der Horst's stock, thereby quashing Hanlon's proposed move back to Baltimore. But Ebbets's clashes with Hanlon hastened the club's decline. In 1903 the team began a twelve-year sojourn in the second division, including a last-place finish in 1905 with their worst record ever (48–104, 56½ games out). Perhaps the most memorable events of these years were the change in nickname to Dodgers, and their move to brand-new Ebbets Field in 1913.

Hanlon was fired as manager after the disastrous 1905 season, but it was not until Wilbert Robinson took over in 1914 that the team began to pull out of its doldrums. Pitcher Jack Pfeffer, in his first full big-league season, won 23 games for the fifth-place Dodgers that year, and two years later led them to the pennant with 25 wins on a sparkling 1.92 ERA.

But the Dodgers lost the World Series to the Boston Red Sox, and in 1917 fell all the way to seventh. After three years in the second division, they bounced back in 1920, turning a three-way race into a rout with sixteen wins in their final eighteen games. After another World Series loss, to Cleveland, the Dodgers returned to the second division for another three years. In 1924 they began slowly, but leaped from twelve games back to an early-September lead, only to slip 1½ games behind the Giants at the finish.

Charley Ebbets died the following April, and Robinson was named to replace him. In his five years as president the club suffered on the field, finishing sixth each year. Fired as president but retained as manager, "Uncle Robbie" saw his Robins (as the Dodgers were now known) lead the league in 1930 most of the time from mid-May to a mid-August decline, then retake the lead for a day in mid-September before tailing off once more to finish fourth. That was Uncle Robbie's last hurrah. When the Robins provided no serious challenge in their fourth-place run the next year, he resigned after eighteen years at the wheel.

A succession of managers followed, but it was not until the Dodgers brought in the free-spending Larry MacPhail as general manager in 1938 that the club began to pull itself back into contention. The highlight of MacPhail's first year with the Dodgers was not the team's finish (seventh) but the introduction of night baseball to Ebbets Field (on June 15, when Cincinnati's Johnny Vander Meer defeated Brooklyn with his second consecutive no-hitter). MacPhail was also looking for new talent, and over the next couple of years he acquired a combination of youngsters and veterans that turned the Dodgers into one of the best teams in the league.

But MacPhail's most brilliant move may have been his conversion of shortstop Leo Durocher into manager Leo Durocher. The loud, driven Durocher alienated many (including MacPhail himself), but provided inspired leadership and a will to win that overcame complaints against him. After a third-place finish in 1939 and second place in 1940, the Dodgers battled the St. Louis Cardinals through all of 1941 before pulling ahead to clinch the pennant with just two games remaining. Veteran first baseman Dolf Camilli led the league in home runs and RBI, sophomore outfielder Pete Reiser led the league in batting, slugging, and runs scored, and pitchers Kirby Higbe and Whitlow Wyatt tied for the league lead with 22 wins apiece, as the Dodgers for the first time since 1899 won 100 games. Only their loss to the Yankees in the World Series marred their finest season in forty-two years.

In 1942 they played even better, winning 104 games. But a late-season five-game slump dropped them behind the surging Cardinals, and they finished 2 games short of the flag.

MacPhail and many of his players left for the war, and though the club finished third in 1943 and 1945, it was not until 1946 that the Dodgers again presented a serious challenge. Once again the Cards and Dodgers made a two-team race of it, but this time the race ended in a tie, forcing the first league playoff ever. St. Louis won the pennant with wins in the first two games.

When MacPhail left for the Army, Branch Rickey was hired to run the club. MacPhail had left the club financially sound and a big drawing card; Rickey set about to make it a consistent winner. Famed as the developer of the Cardinal farm system, he was determined at Brooklyn to tap the one source of talent that the major leagues had willfully neglected: black players. He signed Jackie Robinson to Montreal (Brooklyn's leading farm team), and after a year there promoted him to the Dodgers for the 1947 season. Thus began the club's golden Brooklyn decade: ten years in which they won six pennants and—in 1955—a World Series. Two other races went right to the wire—in 1950 and 1951—and only once did they finish as low as third.

With manager Durocher suspended from baseball for a year for consorting with gamblers, the Dodgers in 1947 were led by grandfatherly Burt Shotton, brought out of his Florida retirement. Robinson's hustle put him at the top of the league in stolen bases and second in runs scored. The team pulled up from fourth in June to first in July, and held the lead to the end. In the World Series they lost to the Yankees in an exciting seven games.

Durocher returned to the helm in 1948, but was replaced by Shotton in midsummer, with the Dodgers in fifth place. Shotton saw the team rise to third that season, then battle back and forth with the Cardinals throughout 1949 before edging them by a game on the final day. Robinson, in his finest season, led the NL in hitting and stolen bases, and finished among the leaders in most other offensive categories. Rookie pitcher Don Newcombe led the team in victories with 17, and Preacher Roe led the league in winning percentage. Again the World Series was a loss to the Yankees, this time in only five games.

In 1950 the Dodgers nearly caught the staggering Phillies, losing out only in the tenth inning of the final game. President Rickey left the club for Pittsburgh and was replaced by Walter O'Malley, who replaced manager Shotton with Charlie Dressen. The slugging of catcher Roy Campanella and first baseman Gil Hodges, and 20-win seasons by Roe (22–3) and Newcombe (20–9) kept the Dodgers in front through most of 1951, but New York's surging Giants closed from thirteen games back in August to tie for the lead at the finish. The teams split the first two playoff games. In Game Three the Dodgers were leading by three runs in the last of the ninth when Bobby Thomson's three-run homer gave New York the flag.

The next year, though, the Giants fell short and Brooklyn took the pennant with relative ease. But not the World Series. Although Brooklyn held a 3–2 lead after five games, the Yankees came back to take the final two.

The Dodgers repeated as NL champions in 1953 with their best season ever. Dodger bats overwhelmed the league, hitting 19 points and slugging 63 points above the league average, as the team outscored its nearest rival by more than a run per game. With a club-record 105 wins, the Dodgers cruised to the pennant by 13 games. But again the Yankees took the World Series, in six games.

Dressen wanted a three-year contract and was let go when he turned down another for only one year. Minor league manager Walter Alston wasn't so demanding, and signed for 1954 the first of a historic string of twenty-three one-year Dodger contracts that would see him into the Hall of Fame. After a second-place finish in Alston's rookie season, the Dodgers in 1955 took the lead from the start and—never challenged—walked away with their eleventh pennant. Outfielder Duke Snider, with one of his most productive seasons, led the league's most powerful squad; Newcombe (20–5) paced the league's best pitching staff.

Once more in the World Series, Brooklyn faced the Yankees, and once more the Series went seven games. But this time there was joy in Brooklyn—Johnny Podres shut out New York in the finale! In an exciting three-way fight in 1956, the Dodgers repeated as pennant-winners, taking their final three games to edge Milwaukee's Braves. Newcombe, in his greatest year, clinched the flag on the final day with his twenty-seventh win. In the World Series, though, it was *déjà vu* time—a sixth Yankee triumph, in seven games. The golden decade was over.

The Dodgers (despite the league's best pitching) vacated the 1957 race in August, finishing third. Before the start of the next season, they had vacated Brooklyn as well, for Los Angeles. Playing in Memorial Coliseum (a converted football stadium) the L.A. Dodgers sank to seventh place in 1958. But the next year the reawakened bats of aging Duke Snider and Gil Hodges, the fiery pitching of young Don Drysdale, and the late-season pitching heroics of Roger Craig (recalled from Spokane) kept the team in the thick of a tight race that found them tied with the Braves at season's end. The Dodgers won the first playoff game in Milwaukee, and captured big league baseball's first West Coast pennant at home the next day, in the twelfth inning. Then they defeated the Chicago White Sox to give the West its first World Series winner.

After finishes of fourth and second, the Dodgers produced record-breaking excitement in 1962 as they moved into brand-new Dodger Stadium in the hills above Los Angeles. Between the new ballpark and the excitement generated on the field, more than 2.75 million fans passed through the turnstiles—a new attendance record that would last until the Dodgers themselves broke it fifteen years later. As pitcher Don Drysdale and left fielder Tommy Davis ignited the league with career-high seasons, and shortstop Maury Wills became the first major leaguer of the century to steal 100 bases, the team locked into a season-long struggle for first place with archrival San Francisco. But after holding a narrow lead much of the season, the Dodgers dropped their last four games to finish in yet another tie—their fourth.

The playoff must have reminded fans of 1951. As they had then, the Giants and Dodgers split the first two games, and the Dodgers once again brought a 4–2 lead into the ninth inning of Game Three. This time, though, it was not a home run that undid them, but a bases-loaded walk.

Sandy Koufax—who had won 14 games in 1962 (and the first of five straight ERA crowns) despite losing half the year with circulation problems in his fingers—rose to dominate the world of pitching the next four years. For three of those years his Dodgers dominated the NL. In 1963 Koufax's 25–5 season carried Los Angeles into the World Series against the Yankees, where two more wins helped put the New Yorkers away in the minimum four games. The next year Koufax slipped to 19 wins, but the Dodgers fell all the way to a tie for sixth.

They rebounded to the top in 1965. Koufax won 26 and Drysdale 23 in a tight four-team race that saw them fall behind the Giants in early September, only to retake the lead for good later in the month with 13 straight wins. The World Series against Minnesota went to the seventh game before Koufax nailed down another world title with his second shutout in three days.

The race in 1966 was just as close as in '65, with three teams switching leads throughout the season. But the Dodgers, third at the end of August, put together streaks of five and seven wins in September to move to the top, where Koufax clinched the pennant on the final day with his twenty-seventh victory. And then it was all over. After a losing effort in Game Two of the World Series (a Baltimore sweep), Koufax, at age thirty, retired because of arthritis in his pitching elbow. The Dodgers sank to eighth the next year and rose only to seventh in 1968.

In 1969, the first season of divisional play, Los Angeles

found itself in the thick of a five-team race in the West until eight straight losses in late September dropped them to fourth. No one challenged Cincinnati in 1970, but the next year the Dodgers closed to within a game of the front-running Giants in September before their drive stalled.

A late-season Dodger slump let Cincinnati get to the top in 1973, but the Dodgers held their lead to the end in 1974. Newly acquired veteran outfielder Jimmy Wynn and first baseman Steve Garvey, in his first full season, led the club offensively; pitcher Mike Marshall set a modern major league record with 106 appearances in relief of a staff that was the league's best (which earned him the Cy Young award). The Dodgers beat Pittsburgh handily in the League Championship Series for their fifth Los Angeles pennant, but lost the World Series to Oakland in five games.

Cincinnati proved untouchable in 1975 and '76, but in 1977 the Dodgers—under new manager Tom Lasorda, who moved up from the coaching staff when Alston retired—jumped to an early lead and held it all the way. Garvey's 33 home runs led a balanced offense in which four players hit 30 or more homers and drove in over 85 runs. Again the Dodgers won the LCS (in four games, against Philadelphia), and again they lost the World Series (to the Yankees, in six games).

Although the divisional race was closer— and the Dodgers broke baseball's three million attendance barrier for the first time—1978 was in most respects a replay of 1977. Garvey again led the club offensively, the Dodgers again beat out Cincinnati in the West and Philadelphia in a four-game LCS, and the Yankees again defeated the Dodgers in a six-game World Series.

A season-long back-and-forth battle with Houston in 1980 ended in a tie for first—the fifth tie for the Dodgers, three more than any other club. In the playoff (reduced from three games to one to bring the NL into line with AL practice), Houston won easily.

When the players went out on strike part way through 1981, the Dodgers, paced by the spectacular pitching of rookie Fernando Valenzuela, found themselves half a game in front of Cincinnati. In a special playoff with poststrike leader Houston, the Dodgers defeated the Astros in five games for the division title, and also went the distance in beating Montreal for the pennant—their twenty-first. Facing the Yankees for the eleventh time in World Series play, they lost the first two games, but swept the next four games to capture their sixth world title.

In 1982, after a poor start, the Dodgers fought back to take the lead in August and again in September before dropping back to second, a game out. More successful drives in 1983 and '85 led to their fifth and sixth division titles, but culminated in defeat in the LCS—to Philadelphia in 1983 and St. Louis two years later. In 1986 and '87 they posted identical 73–89 won-lost records—the team's worst performance in two decades.

But then in 1988, with an infusion of talent from the American League—most notably slugger Kirk Gibson and relief ace Jay Howell—and a spectacular season from starter Orel Hershiser (who concluded his 23–8 year with a major-league record 59 consecutive scoreless innings), the Dodgers bounced back to the top of the NL West. It

took them the full seven games to down the favored Mets in the LCS for their twenty-second pennant, but in the World Series they humbled Oakland's powerful Athletics in just five games for their seventh world crown.

Hershiser (whose 15–15 record belied another strong season on the mound) led a 1989 Dodger pitching staff that yielded the fewest runs in the majors, but with an offense last among major league clubs in *scoring* runs, the Dodgers could finish no better than fourth in the West. Hershiser's 1990 season ended almost as soon as it began when he underwent shoulder surgery in late April, but young Ramon Martinez took up the slack, winning 20 games. With a revived offense that topped the NL West in runs scored, the Dodgers bounded back from a slow first half to draw within 3½ games of Cincinnati in late September and finish second, 5 games out.

From early May to late August 1991, the Dodgers occupied first place in their division, paced by the majors' stingiest pitching staff and the hot bats of free agent signees Brett Butler and Darryl Strawberry. But the team never enjoyed more than a 6-game lead, and with seven straight losses after the All-Star break, began their descent into a great struggle with ascendant Atlanta. From August 21 through season's end the two clubs stayed within two games of each other. With four games to go, Los Angeles held a one-game lead. But they lost their next three games and all hope of the division crown.

In 1992 everything fell apart. Unable to parry the twin blows of injury and inexperience, the Dodgers stumbled to the worst record in the majors, and finished last for only the second time in their 109 years of major league play. Rookie catcher Mike Piazza burst upon the scene in 1993 to rank among NL leaders in batting, slugging, home runs and RBI, as the Dodgers recovered to finish in fourth place. A final-game victory over San Francisco brought their season record to .500, and deprived the Giants of a tie for the division title.

In 1994, the Dodgers struggled to keep their record above .500. But their 58–56 record, while only the league's fifth best, was good enough for a 3½ game lead over runner-up San Francisco in the weak NL West.

Japanese rookie sensation Hideo Nomo paced the NL with 236 strikeouts in 1995 and led the Dodgers to the NL West division title—by just one game over the power-hitting Colorado Rockies. But in the first round of the postseason, Los Angeles fell to Cincinnati in three straight.

In mid-1996 a heart attacked felled Lasorda, and he handed over the club's reins to Bill Russell. Mike Piazza (.344, 36 HR, 105 RBI), Eric Karros (34 HR, 121 RBI), Raul Mondesi (.297, 24 HR) and Delino DeShields (48 SB) led the offense. Outfielder Todd Hollandsworth (.291) became the fifth consecutive Dodger to win NL Rookie of the Year honors. Ramon Martinez (15-6), Ismael Valdes (15-7), Hideo Nomo (16-11, 234 strikeouts), and Todd Worrell (44 saves) paced a staff that led the majors with a 3.46 ERA. Los Angeles (90-72) lost the West Division title to San Diego on the final day of the season but achieved a postseason berth via the wildcard route. The 1996 Dodgers faced Atlanta in the playoffs and met the same fate as the 1995 team had at the hands of the Reds: a humiliating three-game sweep.

Milwaukee Brewers

When in 1969 the new Seattle Pilots played their home opener in the refurbished minor league Sick's Stadium, 7,000 seats and the left field fence were still unfinished. The Pilots may not have needed the seats. Fewer than 700,000 fans came to see them play—the third worst attendance in the league—as they drifted into the cellar of the American League West with 98 losses. That winter the Pilots—renamed the Brewers—moved to Milwaukee, where a genuine big league stadium (vacated by the Braves five years earlier) awaited them.

Attendance improved nearly 38 percent in Milwaukee, although the Brewers of 1970 won only one game more than the Pilots had in Seattle. It would be eight more years before they experienced their first winning season. Meanwhile, in 1972, they switched divisions from West to East, trading places with the Washington Senators, who moved West to become the Texas Rangers.

At last—and with power—the Brewers broke their losing pattern in 1978. One key front-office move leading to the turnaround, the signing of free agent Larry Hisle (who the previous year with Minnesota had led the league in RBI), was also a giant step in the escalation of major league player compensation. With a signing bonus and deferred payments on top of salary, Hisle's six-year contract averaged out to eleven times what he was paid in Minnesota, an annual average figure that would have paid almost 40 percent of the Brewers' player payroll the previous year.

Hisle proved his worth in 1978, leading an offense that sprang to life under rookie manager George Bamberger to top the league in hitting, slugging, homers, and runs scored. On the mound Mike Caldwell won 22 games in the best season of his career. Although the Brewers never threatened the Boston Red Sox or the New York Yankees for the lead, they did rise from below .500 in early June to finish a solid third, 24 games above .500.

A shoulder injury the next April marked the beginning of the end of Hisle's career and perhaps cost Milwaukee the division title. Even without Hisle the team compiled what is still their best winning percentage (.590), as outfielder Gorman Thomas (45 home runs, 123 RBI) and several other Brewer hitters attained new career peaks of productivity. While they never seriously threatened front-running Baltimore, they rose past Boston in late August to finish second.

Most of the Milwaukee bats remained hot in 1980, but injuries, ragged pitching, and Bamberger's heart attack (which caused him to miss the first part of the season and retire in early September) contributed to a distant third-place finish. In strike-divided 1981, league-leading performances by two newly acquired pitchers—starter Pete Vuckovich (14–4) and reliever Rollie Fingers (28 saves)—helped give the Brewers the best overall record in the AL East, and the second-half championship. But in the special intradivisional playoffs with first-half winner New York, the Yankees captured the division crown three games to two.

The Brewers started slowly in 1982; at the end of May they were two games below .500, near the bottom of the division. A day later Buck Rodgers, the Milwaukee coach who had replaced Bamberger as manager two years ear-

lier, was himself replaced by coach Harvey Kuenn. By mid-July the team had risen to first place, and they led the West by more than six games as September neared. But Baltimore had cut the lead to three games by the time Milwaukee arrived for the season's final four games. One win would give the Brewers their first division championship, but they lost the first three games by five, six, and eight runs. Don Sutton, who had been acquired from Houston a month earlier, faced Oriole Jim Palmer in the season finale: the Brewers made Sutton's job easy, scoring ten runs to Baltimore's two.

Milwaukee's offense—"Harvey's Wallbangers"—had been awesome, scoring more than a run per game above the league average. Just about every offensive category featured one or two Brewers among the league's top three: in hits they took all three top spots. Shortstop Robin Yount, who finished first in slugging, hits, total bases, and doubles, was named major league player of the year.

In postseason play California took a 2–1 lead in the League Championship Series, but Milwaukee came back to take the final two games and the pennant. In the World Series against St. Louis, the Brewers twice took the lead in games, but a Cardinal come-from-behind win in Game Seven ended Brewer hopes.

Milwaukee dropped to fifth in 1983, then to a last-place seventh the next year, 36½ games back—their most distant finish ever. It was not until 1987 that they returned to the winning track, finishing third with 91 victories. Had they remained in the AL West where they started, they would have won the division championship by 6 games.

As veterans Robin Yount and Paul Molitor continued to spark the team's offense, and starter Ted Higuera and reliever Dan Plesac headlined the AL East's best pitching staff, the Brewers in 1988 rose above .500 to stay at the end of August, and finished in a tie for third, just two games behind champion Boston. With Yount and Molitor enjoying even more productive seasons in 1989, and reliever Plesac on a club-record pace for saves, the Brewers drew within half a game of first place in August. But injuries and league-worst fielding took their toll, and the club finished fourth, right at .500. In 1990, as poor fielding led to more than 100 unearned runs, the Brewers dropped to sixth.

Paul Molitor enjoyed a banner season in 1991, and from the first week in August to the finish the Brewers played at a torrid .750 clip. But they had begun their comeback 15 games behind, and too late to raise themselves past fourth, 8 games out. With another sterling season from Molitor in 1992, and another strong finish (after a better first half), Milwaukee drew within 2 games of ultimately victorious Toronto in the season's final week. Still, the Brewers' 92–70 record and second-place finish were their best since their pennant-winning season a decade earlier. In 1993, though, free agent Molitor departed for Toronto, sparking the Blue Jays' run for a second straight world championship as the Brewers fell into the AL East cellar, 26 games behind the Jays.

In 1994 the Brewers were one of five clubs inserted into the AL's new Central Division, thus becoming the only club to play in three different divisions. They finished last once again, dropping behind Minnesota just three days before the season concluded in August.

Only marginal improvement occurred in 1995 as manager Phil Garner's Brewers finished fourth (65-79) in the new AL Central Division. In 1996, despite slugger Greg Vaughn's midseason departure to San Diego, Milwaukee moved up to third (80-82). Other 1996 Brewer standouts included Dave Nilsson (.331) and Mike Fetters (32 saves).

Minnesota Twins

The Twins' beginnings as the Washington Senators were inauspicious. When American League president Ban Johnson established the Senators as part of his move in 1901 to raise the league to major league status, he staffed it with the manager and many of the players from his disbanded Kansas City franchise. Within a decade, four of the eight teams in the new major league had won two or more pennants, and three others had enjoyed at least one season in second place. But the Senators, after sixth-place finishes in their first two seasons, spent the next nine years in seventh or eighth. In 1904, their fourth season, they lost 113 games—still the team worst.

Even the arrival of promising young fireballer Walter Johnson didn't seem to help. By 1909 he was the league's second-best strikeout artist, but he lost 25 games and the Senators finished farther back than ever—56 games from the top. Johnson turned his record around the next two years, winning 25 games in 1910 and in 1911, but the team rose only to seventh.

When Clark Griffith—a forty-two-year-old former pitching great and one of the founders of the American League—was hired to manage the Senators after the 1911 season, the club's fortunes took an immediate turn for the better. Griffith revamped the lineup—most strikingly in the acquisition of first baseman Chick Gandil from minor league Montreal. The Senators in 1912 won seventeen straight games after Gandil was put into the lineup, and found themselves in the midst of a pennant race. Boston's Red Sox eventually ran away from the field, but the Senators held off Philadelphia for second place. Johnson won 33 games, and his 1.39 ERA led the league.

The next season was Johnson's finest. His league-leading 36 wins, 11 shutouts, and 1.14 ERA were also career bests and enabled Washington to overtake Cleveland late in the season for another second-place finish. But while Johnson continued to top 20 wins per season for several years before beginning to fade, his team was unable to stay competitive, only once in the next decade making a serious run at the pennant (in war-shortened 1918, when they finished 4 games back, in third).

Griffith wanted the Senators to spend more to attract good players; when his demands were rejected, he bought into a controlling interest in the club and named himself president. A year later, in 1921, he retired as field manager. Under a succession of veteran player-managers the team showed some improvement over the next three years, but Griffith's surprise appointment of twenty-seven-year-old second baseman Bucky Harris to manage the team in 1924 worked wonders. Left fielder Goose Goslin drove in more runs than Babe Ruth, and Walter Johnson put together his best season in years to head the league's best pitching staff. A hot streak in June shot the team from fifth to first, and a strong stretch drive in August and September brought them to the finish 2 games

ahead of the Yankees. In the World Series a ground ball's lucky bounce over the head of the Giants' third baseman brought the Senators victory in the last of the twelfth inning of the seventh game.

Though the Senators, aided by the acquisition of veteran pitcher Stan Coveleski from Cleveland, fought off the A's to repeat as pennant winners in 1925, they were less successful in postseason play. Once again the Series went the full seven games, but this time Pittsburgh won the world title.

The Senators enjoyed winning seasons in five of the next seven years, as Johnson retired from the mound and replaced Harris as manager. But it was not until 1933, when Johnson was replaced by twenty-six-year-old shortstop Joe Cronin, that the team again pursued the pennant beyond midseason. Two veteran pitchers at the top of their form—Alvin "General" Crowder and Earl Whitehill—and a balanced offense led by Cronin and first baseman Joe Kuhel kept the Senators close to New York through July, and then, as the Yankees leveled off in August, shot the team up out of reach. Although they tailed off a bit at the end, the Senators won the pennant handily, compiling a .651 winning percentage that is still the club record. The New York Giants, though, took Washington's measure in the World Series and overcame them in five games.

The following October, after a drop from third place in June to a distant seventh at season's end had plunged home attendance nearly 25 percent below the previous year, Griffith—always close to the edge financially—traded Joe Cronin, his manager, star shortstop, and (since September) son-in-law, to the Boston Red Sox for a lesser shortstop and $225,000.

Only twice in their remaining quarter century in Washington did the Senators rise higher than fourth or finish closer than 17 games from the top. In 1943 they placed second, 13½ games behind the runaway Yankees. And two years later, after a poor start, they caught up with frontrunner Detroit in September, only to stall and finish 1½ games out. In their final six Washington seasons, they wound up in the cellar four times.

Calvin Griffith, Clark's adopted son, assumed the club presidency when his father died in 1955. Within three years he was making plans to move the club to Minneapolis. There were threats from Congress and a plea from President Eisenhower not to move the Senators—and at first the league itself opposed the move. But Washington was not a good baseball town even when the Senators were playing well, and in October 1960 a solution was reached. The league would let Griffith move his club to Minnesota, and Washington would be granted a new expansion team.

Players like outfielders Bob Allison and Harmon Killebrew, and pitcher Camilo Pascual, who had enjoyed productive seasons before the move, were even more productive in Minnesota. Other standouts became regulars or joined the club after the move—Zoilo Versalles at shortstop, Rich Rollins at third, Jim Kaat on the mound, and (arriving in 1964) outfielder Tony Oliva and pitcher Jim "Mudcat" Grant. Infielder Rod Carew began his twelve-year stint with the Twins in 1967.

Former outfielder Sam Mele made his major league managerial debut during 1961, and in 1962 saw his Twins come close to catching the Yankees in mid-September, finishing second. The next year they didn't catch fire until August and wound up third. In 1964 they dropped below .500 into a tie for sixth. But after the end of June 1965 no one challenged them as they breezed to their first Minnesota pennant. Oliva led the league in batting for the second straight year, and Versalles (in what was far and away his finest season) led the league in total bases and runs scored. Mudcat Grant led the league with 21 victories (his only 20-win season) and 6 shutouts, and Kaat's 18 wins were the league's third best. In the World Series it took a three-hitter by Los Angeles's Sandy Koufax to stop the Twins in the seventh game.

After a poor start in 1966 that saw them enter July deep in fifth place, the Twins played better than anyone else the rest of the season to sneak ahead of Detroit into second. Killebrew, who had been injured much of the previous year, returned with his old power in '66, and Kaat enjoyed a career-high season with 25 wins.

The Twins began 1967 with another poor start. With the team in disarray and in sixth place, the easygoing Mele was replaced in June by hard-driving Cal Ermer, a longtime minor league manager. By mid-July the team had risen to second, and a month later (after dropping back to fourth) moved to the top in one of the greatest pennant races ever. Four clubs battled for the title, with three still in the running on the final day. But Boston defeated Minnesota to win the pennant, and Detroit split a doubleheader to tie the Twins for second. The next year Minnesota finished seventh.

Fiery rookie manager Billy Martin replaced Ermer in 1969 and, in this first season of divisional play, piloted the Twins to the championship of the West by a convincing 9 games. Killebrew exploded for the best season of his career (49 home runs, 140 runs driven in), and Carew won the first of his seven batting titles. The first League Championship Series, though, was a disaster for the Twins as Baltimore swept to the pennant in three games. Veteran manager Bill Rigney replaced the difficult Martin at the helm, and piloted Minnesota to an almost identical division crown in 1970, 9 games ahead of Oakland. Pitcher Jim Perry, with 24 victories, enjoyed his second straight 20-win season, and the best of his career. The LCS, though, was another repeat performance—a Baltimore sweep.

For the next thirteen years the Twins remained out of contention, although only in 1981 and '82 did they drop to the bottom of the division. Twice (in 1974 and '76) they recovered from poor starts to make a decent showing, and once (1979) they pushed into first in July before nosediving out of the race. But it was not until the flowering of a new generation of young players in 1984 that a Minnesota title threat could be taken seriously.

The Twins' decline on the field was matched by a decline in attendance, which even their move indoors in 1982 did not significantly redress. The Griffith family, unwilling to risk the high cost of luring proven talent, decided to give up the club after more than sixty years of family ownership. Early in 1984 a buyer was found in Carl Pohlad, a wealthy Minneapolis banker. By the time Pohlad's purchase was completed at the end of July, the Twins' young team had blossomed into the West's front-runner, paced by pitcher Frank Viola's sudden development into a winner, and by the arrival in May of rookie

centerfield sparkplug Kirby Puckett. Although the Twins leveled off in August and lost their final six games, to fall to .500 and a tie for second, they had brought the crowds back to the ballpark. The team in 1984 for the first time ever drew more than 1.5 million fans to their home games, and remained well above a million the next two years despite a pair of losing seasons.

In 1987 the Minnesota fans were rewarded for their faithfulness. Although the Twins lost their last five games to finish only eight above .500 (and two ahead of surging Kansas City), their winning record at home was the best in the league, and their title in the West was never in doubt. More surprising was their decisive triumph over favored Detroit in the LCS, four games to one. In the first World Series to feature indoor play, the Twins won the four games played in their Metrodome to capture Minnesota's first world baseball championship in seven games.

Although the Twins in 1988 improved on their 1987 won-lost record—and Frank Viola, Kirby Puckett, and relief ace Jeff Reardon enjoyed career peaks—they finished well back of Oakland in the race for the division crown. But their home attendance, which had jumped 66 percent in 1987 to top 2 million for the first time, bounded another 45 percent in 1988 to make the Twins the first AL club ever to attract more than 3 million fans in a season.

As the team suffered a general decline in pitching and hitting in 1989, Viola—in the middle of a disappointing season—was traded to the Mets; the Twins finished fifth. Reardon, a free agent, left for Boston after the season. The Twins continued their downhill slide in 1990, slipping from fifth place at midseason to their first cellar finish in eight years.

On May 27, 1991, the Twins stood sixth in the AL West. Three weeks later, after winning eighteen of nineteen games, they were first. There they finished, becoming (like Atlanta in the NL) the first AL team to rise from last place to first in successive seasons. Minnesota's attack featured a balanced offense in which seven players drove in 50 runs or more, and a pitching revival that starred veteran free agent Jack Morris and a pair of young hurlers in their first full seasons, Scott Erickson and Kevin Tapani. In the ALCS, the Twins overcame Toronto in five games, then came back from a 2–3 World Series deficit to defeat Atlanta with a pair of extra-inning victories.

After his single starring season in Minnesota, pitcher Morris moved on to Toronto to hurl the Blue Jays to the championship. The Twins, meanwhile, led the AL West into midseason, before drifting back into a second-place finish behind Oakland. Veteran superstar Dave Winfield left Toronto for Minnesota in 1993, where in September he passed the 3,000 hit mark. But the Twins slid out of contention early, and finished tied for fifth.

In early August 1994, now playing in the new Central Division, they finished fourth. No such heroics could save Minnesota in 1995. They tied Toronto for the majors' worst record (56-88) and saw attendance drop 38 percent from the previous season. The season was further marred at its end by Puckett's retirement due to glaucoma. Among the few bright spots were Chuck Knoblauch (.333) and AL Rookie of the Year Marty Cordova (24 HR, 84 RBI, .277).

Minnesota rebounded back to fourth (78-84) in 1996, helped largely by the efforts of Knoblauch and Paul Molitor (.341 and an AL-best 225 hits), who recorded his 3,000th hit during the season.

Montreal Expos

In the spring of 1969, in an unfinished "temporary" ballpark that would be the Expos' home for eight years, major league baseball came to Canada. One of two clubs added to the National League in this first year of divisional play—Montreal in the East and San Diego in the West—the Expos finished 48 games out of first. But although they matched San Diego's 52–110 record and last-place divisional finish, they outdrew the Padres by better than two to one, with a home attendance of more than 1.2 million fans.

After a second last-place (but much improved at 73–89) season in 1970, the Expos moved a notch out of the cellar to fifth in 1971 and '72, and into pennant contention in 1973. Outfielder Ken Singleton became the first Expo to drive in 100 or more runs, rookie pitcher Steve Rogers compiled a sparkling 1.54 ERA (and a 10–5 won-lost record), and reliever Mike Marshall set a new major-league record with 92 pitching appearances (winning 14 games and saving a league-high 31). In the tightest race of the century, all six clubs remained in contention into September, when Philadelphia dropped away. In mid-September Montreal won six straight to catch front-running Pittsburgh, only to lose nine of the next ten and drop back to fifth. Three wins in the final four games lifted them to fourth place, just 3½ games behind the champion New York Mets.

Center fielder Willie Davis (acquired from Los Angeles in a trade for Mike Marshall) led the Expos' offense in another fourth-place season in 1974, but the club sank back to a tie for last in 1975 and sole possession of the cellar a year later, with a 55–107 record nearly as bad as their first season (and a home attendance little more than half that of 1969).

But with the acquisition of heavy-hitting Tony Perez from Cincinnati, a new manager—the controversial Dick Williams—and strong seasons from catcher Gary Carter, sophomore outfielder Ellis Valentine, and rookie Andre Dawson, the club snapped back in 1977 to win 20 more games than the previous year and rise to fifth. And with their move into the new Olympic Stadium (built for the 1976 Olympics), Expo attendance rebounded from a club low to a new high.

After climbing another notch to fourth in 1978 (as the newly acquired Ross Grimsley became their first—and, to date, only—20-game winner), the Expos put on a run for the title that drove attendance in 1979 to over two million. Third baseman Larry Parrish, with a career-high season, led the club in batting and home runs in a balanced attack that saw five players drive in more than 70 runs. The pitching too was balanced, with six pitchers winning 10 games or more on a staff that compiled the league's lowest ERA. With a fast start in April, the Expos led the East through much of June and into July, when a surging Pittsburgh caught up with them. Both clubs climbed away from the pack to the end of the season. Montreal fell back a bit in August but caught up with the Pirates in September and carried the race to the final day before dropping off to second. The Expos' 95 victories remain the club record to date.

The 1980 race was just as exciting. A three-way struggle with Philadelphia and Pittsburgh through most of the summer narrowed to two teams in September as the Pirates fell away. In a crucial late-September series, the Expos beat the Phillies two games of three to take a half-game lead, but in the final series a week later Philadelphia won two games to clinch the crown.

In a 1981 season divided by a players' strike, Montreal finished the first part of the season in third place, but held off St. Louis to win the second part by half a game. The Expos then won the division championship in a special playoff with first-half winner Philadelphia—their first title—but lost the League Championship Series to Los Angeles.

As the Expos declined gradually over the next five years, most of the regulars left through trade, free agency, or retirement. But in 1987, two 1981 rookies who had remained in Montreal—outfielder Tim Raines and third baseman Tim Wallach—stood out in an Expo comeback that left them in third place, just four games back, with 91 wins and the second-best record up to that point.

Strong midsummer surges in 1988 and 1989 propelled the Expos into the thick of the race in the NL East, in 1989 lifting them into the lead for six straight weeks following the acquisition from Seattle of mound ace Mark Langston. But in both years, late-season slumps dropped the club to identical 81–81 finishes. In 1990 strong pitching (despite the loss of free-agents Langston, Bryan Smith, and Pascual Perez) kept the Expos competitive well into September before they fell out of the race.

The collapse of a huge cement beam at Olympic Stadium in September 1991—which forced the Expos to play all their remaining games on the road—was emblematic of the team's collapse into the cellar with their worst record in fifteen years. But the club revived in 1992 under new manager Felipe Alou (who was promoted from coach in late May), rising from fifth place to second behind the pitching of Ken Hill and veteran ace Dennis Martinez, and the offensive leadership of right fielder Larry Walker. The Expos finished an even closer second in 1993, just three games behind Philadelphia, with a record of 94–68, their second best ever.

On August 7, 1994, pitcher Hill moved into the NL lead with his sixteenth win of the season. Walker and Moises Alou—manager Felipe's son—dueled for the club's offensive leadership. Montreal stood atop the mountain with the best record in the majors. Five days later, the season was over.

Even though the club fell to last (66-78) in 1995, the club turned a $40,000 profit—a dramatic turnaround from 1994 when due to the strike the club lost an estimated $15.9 million. Helping the Expos balance sheet was the modesty of their payroll—just $10 million.

The Expos (88-74) challenged for a wildcard berth in 1996 but fell short in the final week despite the efforts of Henry Rodriguez (36 HR, 103 RBI), Mark Grudzielanek (.306, 201 hits), Jeff Fassero (15-11, 22 strikeouts), and Mel Rojas (36 saves).

New York Mets

Branch Rickey's projected Continental League never materialized, but its New York and Houston franchises were admitted to the National League, expanding the league to ten clubs in 1962. Few major league teams have been as inept as the New York Mets were in their first season. Despite the presence on the club of such New York favorites as manager Casey Stengel, pitcher Roger Craig, and first baseman Gil Hodges, and of players like outfielders Richie Ashburn and Frank Thomas who were still near peak form, the Mets finished at the bottom of the league in batting, fielding, and pitching. They won only one game in four and suffered a twentieth-century record 120 losses. But New York fans—deprived of National League baseball since the defection of the Dodgers and Giants to the West Coast four years earlier—found their ineptitude lovable. By their third season, having moved out of the old Polo Grounds into brand-new Shea Stadium, the last-place Mets were regularly outdrawing the pennant-bound Yankees.

Former New York Giants catcher Wes Westrum replaced the aging Stengel as manager part way through the 1965 season, and the next year saw the club rise out of the cellar for the first time. But they fell back to tenth in 1967 (despite rookie Tom Seaver's 16 wins—then a club record), and Westrum was replaced at the helm by Gil Hodges (who had retired from playing after a few games in 1963). With Jerry Koosman joining Seaver in the starting rotation and setting a new club record with 19 victories, Hodges led the Mets in 1968 back up to ninth place with their first season of more than 70 victories.

In 1969 the majors inaugurated divisional play, but the Mets got off to their usual indifferent start. At the end of May, however, they began to win consistently. By early June they were second in the NL East, though well back of the explosive Chicago Cubs. By September, though, the Cubs were faltering. The "Miracle Mets" caught and passed them with a ten-game winning streak and continued on to take the division title by eight games. Among the many Met heroes, Tom Seaver stands out. He won his last ten starts, sparking the team's final push to triumph and finishing with a league-high 25 wins that still stands as the club record. After a three-game sweep of West champion Atlanta in the league's first Championship Series, the Mets faced the mighty Baltimore Orioles—regarded by many as one of baseball's all-time greatest teams—for the world championship. The Met miracle continued as, after an opening game loss, the New Yorkers humbled the Orioles with four straight wins.

The Mets of 1970 remained competitive into mid-September as they sought to repeat their '69 triumph. But they fell back at the end while Pittsburgh spurted, and finished third. Two more third-place finishes followed in 1971 and '72. Just before the start of the 1972 season, Met coach Yogi Berra moved up to manage the club after Hodges suffered a fatal heart attack two days before his forty-eighth birthday.

In 1973 the NL East experienced the tightest major league race of the century. Chicago moved out in front of the pack early in the season, but folded in July and August. So did the Mets, who fell from third to a last-place sixth. But although they were last late in August, they

were less than seven games out of first. A series of bursts in September, culminating in a seven-game winning streak, shot the Mets through the division into first place by September 21. Although they finished the season only three games above .500, they topped the division by 1½ games. In the LCS they held off the favored Cincinnati Reds to take the pennant in the maximum five games, but lost the World Series when Oakland overcame a 2–3 deficit to win the final two contests.

The Mets then entered a decade-long decline. Though they won as often in 1975 and '76 as they had in 1973, they didn't come close to winning the East, and dropped into a seven-year trough in 1977 which included five seasons in last place. Seaver was traded to Cincinnati in 1977, and Koosman (after two disastrous seasons) was sent to Minnesota in the fall of 1978 (where he won 20 the next year). The heirs of original owner Joan Whitney Payson (who had died in 1975) sold the club to Nelson Doubleday (of the publishing company) and Fred Wilpon in January 1980. In February the new owners hired Frank Cashen as general manager, hoping he could rebuild the Mets as he had the Baltimore Orioles in the late 1960s.

It took a few years to achieve the right blend, but when outfielder Darryl Strawberry was brought up from the minors early in 1983 and first baseman Keith Hernandez was acquired from St. Louis in June, the mix had nearly all the needed ingredients. In 1984, under new manager Davey Johnson, and with rookie pitchers Dwight Gooden and Ron Darling combining for 29 wins, the Mets rebounded to second place with their second-best season record up till then.

The rise continued in 1985. With catcher Gary Carter (newly acquired from Montreal) leading the club in homers and RBI, and Gooden cementing his superstardom at age twenty with a phenomenal 24–4, 1.53 ERA season, the Mets won 98 games—eight more than the year before—and came within a game of tying St. Louis late in September before slipping 3 games back at the finish.

When the Mets acquired pitcher Bob Ojeda from the Boston Red Sox after the season, many predicted an easy division title for them in 1986. For once, the pundits were right. With Carter, Strawberry, and Hernandez powering the offense, and Ojeda, Darling, and Gooden all placing among the league's top five pitchers in ERA, the Mets won two of every three games (108 in all) to capture the division title by 21½ games.

The postseason battles were tougher. The Mets won the pennant from Houston with a 16-inning victory in Game Six of the LCS, but came within a strike of elimination by the Red Sox in Game Six of the World Series before rallying to take that game and the next for their second world crown.

Strawberry enjoyed his finest season yet in 1987, and pitchers Terry Leach and Rick Aguilera put together a combined won-lost record of 22–4. But Ojeda was lost to injury early in the season, and the Mets, though they hung close and posted 92 wins, lost out—as in 1985—to St. Louis by 3 games.

David Cone (20–3, 2.22 ERA) emerged in 1988 as the ace of the league's best pitching staff, which, with the power of Darryl Strawberry and Kevin McReynolds behind it, carried the Mets back to the top of the NL East, 15 games ahead of runner-up Pittsburgh. But after taking a

3-2 lead in the LCS, they lost the pennant to underdog Los Angeles in seven games.

With co-captains Carter and Hernandez injured and in decline, the Mets floundered through 1989, salvaging a narrow second-place finish over St. Louis with four wins in the season's final three days. The two captains were released after the season. Next May, with the Mets mired 9½ games out, manager Davey Johnson was replaced by coach Bud Harrelson. In June the team—ignited by Strawberry's suddenly hot bat—took off: with a flight that included a club-record eleven-game win streak, the Mets propelled themselves into first place before the end of the month. Through July and August the Mets and Pittsburgh lobbed the division lead back and forth, until the Pirates consigned the New Yorkers to second place for good with a three-game sweep in early September.

Free agent Strawberry signed with Los Angeles for 1991, but the Mets competed strongly into July before tumbling to fifth place with their first losing season in eight years. Manager Harrelson was replaced by Jeff Torborg for 1992, and ex-Pirate star Bobby Bonilla signed with the club as a free agent. But injuries plagued the team throughout the season, and the finish found them once again a distant fifth.

Things only got worse in 1993, and even a six-game win streak at the end of the season couldn't keep them from the worst record in the majors and, with 103 losses, the club's worst season in twenty-eight years.

In 1994, pitcher Bret Saberhagen's fifth comeback of his eleven-year career (14–4, 2.74 ERA) propelled the Mets to something of a comeback of their own. They finished just three games below .500, good enough for third place in the NL East.

The Mets stumbled out of the gate in 1995. When they rid themselves of such high-priced talent as Saberhagen, Bonilla, and center fielder Brett Butler, it appeared the club might hit a very deep bottom. Instead, new talent such as Bill Pulsipher and Jason Isringhausen lifted manager Dallas Green's young team to a surprising second place finish (69-75).

Adding another highly-rated pitching prospect, Paul Wilson, to the starting rotation gave Mets fans high hopes for 1996 but these were not realized. Despite standout seasons from Bernard Gilkey (.317, 117 RBI), Lance Johnson (.333, 227 hits, 21 triples), and Randy Hundley (a record 41 HRs for a catcher), the club faltered, and Bobby Valentine replaced Green as manager. New York's 71-91 record was good only for fourth place.

New York Yankees

In its first twenty seasons, the club that became the New York Yankees won no league championships, and finished second only twice. But for the next forty-four years the Yankees dominated the American League, winning nearly two of every three pennants and twenty World Series. After another pennant drought of twelve years, the club in six years won five division titles, four pennants, and their twenty-first and twenty-second World Series. Their next pennant drought, which ended in 1996, lasted fourteen years, and was the second longest in their history.

The Yankees began as the Baltimore Orioles in 1901.

But AL president Ban Johnson really wanted a club in New York and, after outmaneuvering the politically influential Giants (who didn't want a competing big league team in their city), Johnson moved the Orioles to the northern end of Manhattan in 1903.

In 1904 the Highlanders (as they were known during their first years in New York because of the high land on which their park was built) chased the Boston Pilgrims through midsummer, catching them in August and trading first place back and forth into October. But after Jack Chesbro defeated Boston 3–2 on October 7 to give New York a half-game lead (it was his forty-first win, a twentieth-century major league record), the Pilgrims came back to win the next two. In the fourth game of the series, with Chesbro again pitching and the score tied 2–2 in the top of the ninth, a wild pitch over the New York catcher's head let in Boston's pennant-clinching run.

The Highlanders again led the league in late September two years later, before tailing off to finish 3 games behind Chicago. But that was the last time they contended seriously for the title for fourteen years. Meanwhile they finished last twice, in 1908 losing a club-worst 103 games, and in 1912 suffering their most distant finish ever—55 games behind the pennant-winning Boston Red Sox.

In 1914 Colonel Jake Ruppert and Tillinghast Huston bought the Yankees, and the next year they purchased pitcher Bob Shawkey from the Philadelphia A's. Shawkey's 24 victories in 1916 led the Yankees to their first winning season in six years, and in 1919, on returning from military service, his 20 wins (plus the 9 of Carl Mays, who came to the club in a controversial midseason deal with the Red Sox) brought the Yankees to third—at 7½ games out, their closest finish in thirteen years.

That winter, on the recommendation of manager Miller Huggins, the Yankees paid a then-record $125,000 (plus a $300,000 loan) to the Red Sox for Babe Ruth. Ruth, with 54 home runs in 1920, obliterated the record of 29 he had set the year before, and Mays and Shawkey together won 46 games in a three-way pennant race that ended with New York a close third.

At season's end Ruppert hired Ed Barrow as Yankee general manager. While managing the Red Sox, Barrow had converted Ruth from a pitcher to outfielder. His December trade with Boston that gave the Yankees pitcher Waite Hoyt and catcher Wally Schang was just the improvement needed to bring the Yankees their first pennant in 1921. Ruth's 59 homers and his career-high 171 RBI didn't hurt, either.

The prickly Carl Mays, staff ace in 1921 with a 27–9 record, slipped to 13–14 the next year. But the Yankees continued to decimate the Red Sox roster with trades that brought them pitchers "Bullet Joe" Bush and "Sad Sam" Jones, and infielders Everett Scott and Joe Dugan. Bush's 26 wins in 1922 made up for Mays's decline, and the Yankees captured their second straight league championship.

Both races had been tight two-way struggles—with Cleveland in 1921 and the St. Louis Browns in 1922—and both pennants had been followed by a World Series loss to the Giants. But in 1923 the Yankees at last put everything together. After sharing the Giants' Polo

Grounds since 1913, they were at home in brand-new Yankee Stadium just across the Harlem River in the Bronx. With the addition of yet another pitcher from the Red Sox—Herb Pennock—and a .393 year from Ruth, they took the lead from the start and built it over the summer to a 16-game margin by the end. For the third time the Yankees faced the Giants in the World Series; this time they beat them, in six games, for their first world championship.

The Yankees lost a close race to Washington in 1924 and collapsed into seventh place in 1925—a year in which Ruth was lost much of the season to surgery and suspension. There were bright spots, though: center fielder Earle Combs, in his first full season, hit .342 to lead Yankee regulars, left fielder Bob Meusel filled Ruth's shoes as AL home run and RBI leader, and first baseman Lou Gehrig arrived to stay. With Ruth's return to full strength in 1926 and the establishment of a new middle infield of Tony Lazzeri and Mark Koenig, the Yankees took their fourth pennant in a race that was not as close as their 3-game winning margin would suggest. They lost a close World Series to the Cardinals.

Many observers rank the 1927 Yankees as baseball's greatest team ever. Certainly it was the Yankees' greatest team. They won more games (110) than any Yankee team before or since. Ruth hit his 60 home runs, and Gehrig drove in 175. Waite Hoyt led the league in ERA and rookie Wilcy Moore proved the league's premier reliever. As a team the Yankees led the league in hitting (.307) and slugging (.489, still a major league record); their pitchers compiled a 3.20 ERA that was ¾ of a run per game lower than the ERA of the next best team. In the World Series they swept the Pittsburgh Pirates.

The resurgent Athletics made the 1928 race much closer, but New York won three in a row from the A's in mid-September to pull ahead, and held on for their sixth pennant. Another Series sweep (this time against the Cardinals) gave them their third world title.

For three years the A's left the Yankees in the shade. An ill Huggins yielded the club's reins in September 1929 and died before the season had ended. By the time the Yankees returned to the top in 1932, their manager was Joe McCarthy. He had led Chicago's Cubs to the NL pennant in 1929; in fifteen seasons at New York he would lead his club to eight more pennants and seven world championships. Only once would his Yankees finish as low as fourth.

A Yankee pennant and World Series triumph over the Cubs in 1932 was followed by three second-place finishes to Washington (in 1933) and Detroit (in 1934 and 1935). Ruth had retired by the time the Bronx Bombers returned to the top in 1936, but Gehrig was still in top form, catcher Bill Dickey and outfielder George Selkirk developed into formidable sluggers, and Joe DiMaggio arrived to take over center field. New York finished a club-record 19½ games in front and buried the Giants in the World Series.

Three more pennants and three more world titles followed in 1937–1939. Lefty Gomez emerged as the league's premier pitcher in 1937, and DiMaggio picked up the home run and slugging crowns. Again the Giants were vanquished in the World Series. Rookie second baseman Joe Gordon and sophomore outfielder Tommy Henrich joined Dickey, DiMaggio, and a declining Gehrig in leading the slugging Yankees to the 1938 crown and a Series sweep of the Cubs. A balanced attack in 1939 saw seven of the eight starters (including Babe Dahlgren, who replaced the dying Gehrig at first) drive in 80 runs or more as the Yankees won 106 to run away with their eleventh pennant—and eighth World Series, another sweep, with Cincinnati the victim. For the fourth year in a row the offense topped the league in slugging, and overshadowed the steady—if unspectacular—Yankee pitchers, who for the *sixth* consecutive season compiled the league's stingiest ERA.

After catching the leaders with a 19–4 spurt in late summer, the 1940 Yankees fell away to finish a close third. But then came another three convincing pennant wins and a pair of Series triumphs as the nation moved into World War Two. Outfielders DiMaggio and Charlie Keller dominated the Yankee offense in 1941, and rookie shortstop Phil Rizzuto hit .307. Though no Yankee pitcher won more than 15 games, seven won 9 or more (and reliever Johnny Murphy won 8 while saving a league-high 15). With 101 victories the team was lost from view to the rest of a league in which six of the eight clubs failed to break .500. In the World Series Brooklyn was the loser in five games.

Keller, DiMaggio, and Gordon provided the power, and Tiny Bonham (with 21 wins), Spud Chandler, and rookie Hank Borowy headed the league-leading pitching staff that propelled the Yankees to 103 wins and another easy pennant in 1942. But after winning their previous eight World Series, the Yankees were finally stopped, in five games, by the St. Louis Cardinals.

By 1943 many Yankees were in military service. But pitchers Chandler, Bonham, Borowy, and Murphy were not, and they led the charge to the team's seventh pennant in eight years. In the Series the Yankees reversed the results of the previous year, turning back St. Louis in five.

When Jake Ruppert died in 1939, general manager Barrow succeeded him as president, a position he held until January 1945, when Dan Topping and Del Webb bought the club and installed Larry MacPhail as president, giving him a third of the club and a ten-year contract to run it. The volatile, innovative MacPhail had previously brought new life to Cincinnati and Brooklyn, and did bring night ball to Yankee Stadium. But manager McCarthy, who couldn't get along with MacPhail, quit early in the 1946 season, and the team finished a distant third.

DiMaggio and the others were back from the war by 1946, but it was not until 1947—under new manager Bucky Harris, and with sparkling pitching from Allie Reynolds (acquired from Cleveland), rookie Frank "Spec" Shea, and reliever Joe Page—that the Yankees returned to the top of the heap with an easy pennant win and a narrow World Series triumph over Brooklyn. On the day the Yankees won the Series, though, president MacPhail embarrassed the club and undid himself by brawling in public. Topping and Webb bought out his contract and share of the ownership. Topping took over the presidency, but promoted farm director George Weiss to run the club as general manager.

After the Yankees dropped a pair of season-ending games to the Red Sox to finish third in a tight 1948 race,

Weiss replaced manager Harris with Casey Stengel, who in nine years of managing the Braves and Dodgers had only twice seen his club finish as high as fifth. But with Weiss providing a steady stream of talented players via the farm system and canny trades, the Yankees under Stengel proved all but invincible into the '60s.

Stengel's Yankees began by putting together a record string of five world championships. No major league club had ever won five pennants in a row, let alone five World Series, and the Yankees didn't accomplish the feat easily. In 1949, for example, they saw the Red Sox come from 12 games back in midseason to pass them with a three-game series sweep in late September, only to rescue the flag with two close must-win victories over the Sox in the season's final games. In the World Series, Brooklyn was again the victim, in five games.

After losing much of 1949 to injury, DiMaggio returned with power in 1950, shortstop Rizzuto and catcher Yogi Berra enjoyed the finest seasons of their careers, and pitcher Whitey Ford broke into the majors, winning all nine of his decisions as a starter (he lost one game in relief). But the Yankees struggled even harder for the pennant than the year before, battling three other contenders before finally pulling in front to stay with five straight wins near to the end of the season. Though three of the games in the World Series were decided by just one run, New York took the Philadelphia Phillie "Whiz Kids" without a loss.

No Yankee drove in as many as 90 runs in 1951, and Whitey Ford was drafted for two years of military service. But the remaining pitchers doubled their shutout production and lowered the team ERA by more than half a run per game, enough to propel the club ahead of Cleveland in mid-September. In the World Series the Yankees shook the faith of the "miracle" Giants, four games to two. Cleveland challenged once again in 1952, and again fell just short, as did Brooklyn in carrying the World Series to seven games.

Finally, in 1953, Stengel's Yankees won with relative ease. Ford, back from the Army, won 18 to lead the club to a finish 8½ games up. Once again it was Brooklyn in the World Series, and once again the Yankees beat them.

In 1954 New York won 103 games—the most in Stengel's twelve-year tenure. But Cleveland won an AL-record 111 to take the flag by 8 games. In 1955, though, it was back to second place for Cleveland as New York, with Mickey Mantle now established as one of the game's most productive hitters, settled in for another four pennants. As August passed into September, three teams were within a game of each other at the top. But the Chicago White Sox faltered and fell away, leaving the Yankees and Indians to fight it out. With two weeks left, New York won eight straight to pass Cleveland for good. Facing the Dodgers in the World Series for the sixth time, the Yankees finally lost, as Johnny Podres shut them out in Game Seven to give Brooklyn its first world title since 1900.

From 1956 through 1958 the Yankees seldom found themselves out of first place. Only in 1957, when they leveled off in May before surging to the front in June, were they involved in anything resembling a close race. In postseason play, they went the full seven games all three years, winning twice—from the Dodgers for the sixth

time in 1956, and from the Milwaukee Braves in 1958, after losing to them the year before.

In 1959 the Yankees started poorly and never did rise much above .500, finishing a distant third with their worst won-lost record in thirty-four years. After the season, George Weiss sent an aging Hank Bauer to Kansas City in a trade that brought Roger Maris to New York. In 1960 Maris, with AL titles in slugging and RBI, won the MVP award. He and Mantle dominated the power stats and led the charge back to the top as the Yankees won their final fifteen games to bury the faltering Orioles.

New York's 1960 pennant was the first in another five-flag streak, but it was the last for Stengel. After Pittsburgh toppled the Yankees in the World Series on Bill Mazeroski's famous home run, president Topping retired both the seventy-year-old Stengel and general manager Weiss, sixty-five, who had been with the club for twenty-eight years.

With the season lengthened by eight games in 1961, Maris broke Ruth's home-run record and rookie manager Ralph Houk led the club to 109 wins, just one off the club record. Once again Maris and Mantle finished among the best in offensive power, and once again New York took the pennant by 8 games. Ford enjoyed a splendid 25–4 season and celebrated with two more wins in the World Series as the Yankees humbled Cincinnati in five games.

Pitcher Ralph Terry moved out of Ford's shadow in 1962 with 23 wins. Though the Yankees finished just five games ahead of Minnesota, there was little doubt about the outcome from midseason on. In a close World Series with San Francisco, Terry won two, including the clincher with a four-hit shutout.

Though New York won pennants the next two years, the 1962 world title was to be their last until the Steinbrenner era fifteen years later. Despite the loss to injuries of Mantle and Maris for much of 1963, New York dominated the AL, winning by 10½ games with 104 wins. But in postseason play the Yankees were themselves dominated by the Dodgers (now in Los Angeles), who held them to just four runs in a Series sweep.

Yogi Berra replaced Houk as manager for 1964. In a season-long three-way race with the White Sox and Orioles that found the clubs virtually tied in mid-September, only an eleven-game win streak gave the Yankees the space they needed for their final one-game margin of victory. Pitcher Jim Bouton won a pair in the World Series, but the Cardinals won in seven. Berra was fired.

During the 1964 season Topping had sold the Yankees to CBS. The next year the club, which had gone forty years without a losing season, dropped to sixth place, and in 1966 fell to a last-place tenth, their first cellar finish in more than half a century. Even Houk's return as manager in 1967—though it led to some winning seasons—failed to restore the once-proud club to pennant contention, except once, in 1972, when it was mid-September before they fell out of a tight race to finish fourth.

In January 1973 a syndicate headed by Cleveland shipping magnate George Steinbrenner purchased the Yankees from CBS. Although he had vowed not to take a prominent role in running the club, Steinbrenner soon emerged as one of baseball's most active owners. Through a series of shrewd trades, offers of big contracts to free agents, and what became a round robin of managerial changes, Steinbrenner's Yankees became competitive again in 1974 (finishing a close second to Baltimore after streaking from last in July to first in September) and returned to the top with three successive pennants and a pair of world championships.

Billy Martin (a former Yankee second baseman) in 1976, his first full season as manager, led the renewed club to a runaway division title. First baseman Chris Chambliss's homer in the last of the ninth of the final game of the League Championship Series gave the Yankees the pennant by the narrowest of margins over the Kansas City Royals. Cincinnati swept New York in the World Series, but the Yankees came back the next year to edge Baltimore and Boston in a three-way race that saw the teams shift back and forth in the standings throughout the season. Slugger Reggie Jackson, signed as a free agent the previous autumn, turned the club's power trio of Chambliss, Graig Nettles, and Thurman Munson into a quartet as the Yankees recorded their first hundred-victory season in fourteen years. After another ninth-inning win over Kansas City in the LCS finale, New York won the World Series in six games over Los Angeles, and Jackson became "Mr. October" with five home runs— three of them in successive at-bats in the final game.

The 1978 season provided as exciting a race as baseball is likely to see. In mid-July it looked like a Red Sox romp, but the fourth-place Yankees put on a great surge, catching the faltering Sox with a four-game series sweep in early September. Boston dropped 3½ games back, but won their final eight games to catch New York on the final day. In the one-game tiebreaker, Yankee shortstop Bucky Dent lofted a wind-blown three-run homer over Boston's close left field wall in the seventh, and Jackson homered an inning later for New York's final run in the 5–4 win. Again the Royals were the victims in the LCS, as were the Dodgers in the World Series.

After dropping to fourth in 1979, the Yankees held off Baltimore in 1980 to win their fourth division title—but this time Kansas City swept to the pennant in three games. In 1981 the Yankees found themselves in first place when the players struck in June and were thus admitted to an intradivisional playoff with the season's second-half winner, Milwaukee. Narrowly defeating the Brewers for the division title, New York swept Oakland for the pennant in the LCS. But after taking the first two games from Los Angeles in the World Series, they were stopped cold as the Dodgers won the next four.

The Yankees fell below .500 the next year, and although they revived to win 91 games in 1983, they failed to frighten the division leaders until 1985. First baseman Don Mattingly drove in more runs than any American leaguer since 1953 and newcomer (from Oakland) Rickey Henderson scored more often than any major leaguer since 1949—the team remained in the running until Toronto eliminated them with just one game to go.

But constant roster manipulation and managerial rotation (Billy Martin alone was hired and fired five times) at last set in motion a steady drop in Yankee effectiveness. While the team remained in the thick of a tight 1988 divisional race until three season-ending losses set them back into fifth place, their won-lost record showed a third straight season of decline. In 1989 the Yankees sank to their worst finish in twenty-two years and in 1990 they dropped to the floor of the AL East with the club's worst record since 1913.

Attempting to gain information damaging to longtime Yankee outfielder Dave Winfield, Steinbrenner dealt with a gambler named Howard Spira. As his penalty, Steinbrenner was forced to relinquish his controlling interest in the club in August 1990. The team improved a little over the next two years to finish fifth in 1991 and tie for fourth in 1992. But their string of consecutive losing seasons stretched to four, something that hadn't happened to the Yankees in seventy-six years. In 1993 the Yankees bounced back and—bolstered by the league's best hitting and a strong season from newly acquired pitcher Jimmy Key—contended seriously into September, finishing second to Toronto, seven games back.

They were even better in 1994. With Key in the midst of one of his best seasons ever, and a solid offense paced by right fielder Paul O'Neill (whose .603 slugging average stood 99 points above his previous career high), the Yankees were enjoying the league's best won-lost record and a 6½-game lead in the AL East when the players' strike cut the season short in August.

The 1995 Yankees earned the first-ever AL wild card slot. Standouts included Wade Boggs (.324), Paul O'Neill (24 HR), Bernie Williams (.307), David Cone (9-2 with New York after coming over from Toronto), and Black Jack McDowell (15-10). After taking a tough loss to Seattle in the division series, the Yankees saw the departure of McDowell, veteran Don Mattingly, and manager Buck Showalter (who became manager of the new Arizona Diamondbacks). Joe Torre replaced Showalter, continuing a tradition of managers—Casey Stengel, Yogi Berra, and Dallas Green—who have managed both the Mets and the Yankees.

In 1996, despite a late season swoon, Torre's Yankees (92-70) captured the AL East championship. Standout Yankees included Bernie Williams (.305, 29 HR, 102 RBI), Paul O'Neill (.302, 19 HR, 91 RBI), Tino Martinez (.292, 25 HR, 117 RBI), AL Rookie of the Year Derek Jeter (.314), Andy Pettite (21-8), and John Wetteland (43 saves). In the first round of the postseason, New York overcame Texas in four games.

In the ALCS, the Yanks rolled over Baltimore in five games, aided by Darryl Strawberry's three homers. Also assisting the Bronx Bombers was the "Angel in the Outfield," twelve-year old fan Jeffrey Maier, who in Game One caught Jeter's fly ball. Instead of fan interference being called, Jeter was credited with a pivotal homer.

In the first two games of the World Series against Atlanta the Yankees looked outclassed, losing 12-1 and 4-0. But New York rebounded to win the next four, including a ten-inning Game Four comeback from a 6-0 deficit and the clincher against Atlanta's Greg Maddux. The victory was particularly sweet for manager Torre, whose brother Frank, received a long-awaited heart transplant the day before.

Oakland Athletics

The history of the Athletics is a tale of three cities—a story of the best of teams and of the worst of teams. With a thirteen-year sojourn in Kansas City between residence in Philadelphia and Oakland, the A's are the only club to include a stop in Middle America in their trek from the East Coast to West. They have won fifteen American League pennants (plus four Western Division championships that didn't lead to a pennant), second in the AL only to the incomparable Yankees. But they have also finished last in the league or division twenty-seven times, and in sixteen seasons have lost 100 games or more—both AL worsts, by far. A club of extremes, they have been either at the top or at the bottom in nearly one season out of two.

When Ban Johnson in 1901 established four eastern clubs for his American League, he chose Connie Mack to manage the new Philadelphia Athletics and gave him a quarter ownership of the club. Mack, who had been managing the league's Milwaukee franchise, settled in at Philadelphia and set a record for managerial longevity—fifty years—that is unlikely ever to be surpassed.

In his first fourteen years the A's dominated the league, with six pennants and two close second-place finishes. After finishing fourth in 1901, the club won its first pennant the next year, pulling away from the field with spurts in August and September. Rube Waddell led the team with 24 wins, and six regulars hit over .300. The next two years saw the A's fade in August, but in 1905, after forging ahead in early August and hanging on to the lead with two crucial wins over Chicago's surging White Sox in late September, the A's opened October with a five-game winning streak to clinch their second flag. Waddell, with 26 wins, once again led the club (followed closely by Eddie Plank's 25) and compiled a league-leading 1.48 ERA. In the Athletics' first World Series appearance, though, New York's Christy Mathewson provided most of the pitching heroics, shutting out the A's three times in the Giants' 4–1 Series triumph.

Another August decline in 1906 was followed in 1907 by a comeback struggle from fifth place in late May to a 2½-game lead in mid-September. But the loss of a crucial game to Detroit several days later, and the failure to make up a rainout and a tie, left the A's 1½ games behind the Tigers at the finish.

In 1908 the A's suffered their first losing season, but they rebounded in 1909 to chase the Tigers throughout the summer before tailing off to second. In 1910, with a pitching staff that compiled a stunning 1.79 ERA (paced by Jack Coombs, whose 31 wins included 13 shutouts) and with league-leading fielding and hitting, the A's pulled ahead for good in June, increasing their lead through the rest of the season to finish 14½ games in front. In the World Series they continued to dominate, outscoring the Chicago Cubs 35–15 as they took their first world title, in five games. The A's repeated just as convincingly in 1911. With their "$100,000 infield" of Stuffy McInnis, Eddie Collins, Jack Barry, and Frank "Home Run" Baker averaging .323 at the bat, and Jack Coombs winning 28 games to again lead the club (and the league), the A's overtook Detroit in August to win by 13½ games. In the World Series, Baker hit two important home runs against the Giants, and the A's defeated Mathewson twice, avenging their 1905 humiliation with a victory in six games.

A third-place finish in 1912 broke the pennant streak, but the Athletics came back for two more in 1913 and '14, in both seasons pulling away in early June for easy wins.

In the 1913 World Series the A's again felled the Giants, this time in just five games, but the next year they were in turn humiliated by the upstart Boston Braves, who stunned Philadelphia with the first sweep since the renewal of World Series play in 1903.

That winter, Mack began to dismantle his championship club, selling second baseman Collins to the White Sox and releasing pitchers Coombs, Eddie Plank, and Chief Bender. (Third baseman Baker, homesick for the country life, sat out the 1915 season before moving on to the Yankees). Though Mack received $50,000 for Collins, his unconditional release of the three pitchers suggests that he had another reason than financial need for purging his club. (Suspicion of corrupt play in the 1914 World Series has been hinted.)

Whatever Mack's reasons, the changes did not help the club. The A's sank immediately to last place, where they remained for seven years. In 1915 they lost 109 games and finished 58½ games out. The next year they lost 117 games to set a league record for ineptitude that has never been equalled.

It was a decade before Mack was able to restore the club to respectability. In 1924 he brought up Al Simmons, and the next year Jimmie Foxx and pitcher Lefty Grove. Thus renewed, the A's in 1925 battled Washington to the end of August before backing off to second. In 1927 they won 91 games, though their second-place finish was 19 games back of the overwhelming Yankees. In 1928 the A's battled from well back of New York in midseason to overtake them for a day or two in September, only to lose three of four games in a critical Yankee series and slip back to second.

From 1929 through 1931, though, the A's interrupted New York's domination of the AL with three spectacular seasons. In 1929 sophomore pitcher George Earnshaw blossomed into the league's big winner with 24 victories and Grove led the league's stingiest staff with a league-low 2.81 ERA. Six players drove in 79 runs or more (led by Simmons' league-high 157) in powering the A's to 104 wins and an impressive finish 18 games ahead of the second-place Yankees.

After swamping the Cubs in the World Series, the A's repeated as pennant winners in 1930. Simmons led the league in batting (.381), and Grove led its pitchers in just about everything: wins (28), ERA, strikeouts—even saves (9). Again the World Series was no contest as the A's downed the Cardinals in six.

Earnshaw won more than 20 games for his third successive season in 1931, Simmons repeated as batting leader (.390), and Grove enjoyed what would be the finest season of his career (31–4, 2.06 ERA) in carrying the A's to 107 wins—their best record ever. But in Game Seven of the World Series their dominance of the baseball world ended in a Cardinal victory.

Following a second-place finish in 1932, Mack began selling off his stars again. This time the reason was primarily economic. Home attendance—never robust—fell off sharply after 1931, as the Great Depression and the A's decline made their impact felt. By 1935 the Athletics were back in the cellar, where they finished in ten of Mack's final sixteen years as manager.

In 1946 Mack, who since 1940 had been the A's majority stockholder, divided his shares among his three sons, provoking a family squabble over control of the club. In 1950 the two eldest, Roy and Earle, bought out Connie Jr. and pressured their eighty-seven-year-old father to retire. But with Connie Sr. gone, attendance (which had risen to new highs in the baseball boom that followed World War Two) dropped off again. When in 1954 the A's finished 60 games behind champion Cleveland and attendance dropped to an eighteen-year low, the Macks sold the club to Chicagoan Arnold Johnson, who moved it to Kansas City.

Attendance jumped more than a million the first season in Kansas City (putting the A's over one million for the first time ever), and the team rose a couple of places to sixth. But 1955 was the high point of their thirteen-year stay in the Midwest; the K.C. A's never again rose above seventh, and they finished last six times.

Owner Johnson died in March 1960, and that December his heirs sold the club to the enterprising but abrasive Charles O. Finley. Finley brought in a succession of new managers over the next few years, and in 1965 outfitted his players in new bright green-and-yellow uniforms. But with the league's expansion to ten teams in 1961, the A's had two places lower to sink—and did. After finishing tenth in 1967 for the third time in four years, Finley moved the club to Oakland, California.

Attendance was slow to improve in Oakland—unlike the team. In 1968, their first year on the coast, they put together their first winning season in sixteen years. The next year, with the start of divisional play, the A's took second in the AL West. Reggie Jackson, in only his second full big league season, enjoyed his finest year, with 47 home runs, 118 RBI, and AL highs in slugging (.608) and runs scored (123).

After another second-place finish in 1970, the A's were ready for a return to glory. In the next five years they won five division titles, winning both the AL pennant and the World Series in the three middle years, 1972–1974. In 1971, with a new manager, Dick Williams, and three pitchers (Vida Blue, Catfish Hunter, and reliever Rollie Fingers) who reached their prime all at once, the A's enjoyed their best season in forty years and won the West by 16 games. Baltimore swept them away in the League Championship Series, but they came back to take the West again the next year. Detroit took them to the limit in the LCS, as did Cincinnati in the World Series, but in both series the A's prevailed in the deciding game by the margin of a single run.

The next year, 1973, Jackson led the league in slugging, homers, and RBI, Ken Holtzman joined Blue and Hunter in the 20-win column, and home attendance crept over a million (by a few hundred souls) for the first time in Oakland as the A's ran their string of Western Division titles to three. Once again they were pushed to the limit in the postseason—by Baltimore in the LCS and the New York Mets in the World Series—and once again they emerged as world champions.

Manager Williams quit in a dispute with Finley and was replaced by Al Dark, but the outcome in 1974 (except for a drop in attendance to under a million) was the same. Hunter bore more of the pitching load and wound up tied for the AL lead with 25 wins. His 2.49 ERA also led the league, as the staff ended Baltimore's five-year hold on the ERA title. The A's toppled the Orioles in the LCS and

(in the first World Series held entirely on the West Coast) won their third consecutive world title in five closely fought games with Los Angeles.

Free-agent Catfish Hunter deserted to the Yankees, and Baltimore regained the ERA crown in 1975, but pitchers Paul Lindblad and newcomer Dick Bosman combined for a 20–5 record to supplement the efforts of Blue, Holtzman, and Fingers and carry Oakland to an unprecedented fifth straight division title. But there the magic stopped, as Boston swept to the pennant in the LCS.

In the off-season Finley, with moves reminiscent of Connie Mack, tried to sell off his star players: Blue, Jackson, Fingers, Holtzman, and outfielder/first baseman Joe Rudi, one of the team's steadiest hitters. The proposed sales made some sense: the players planned to leave the club at the end of their 1976 option year, and Finley by disposing of them before they played out their option could at least be compensated for his loss. The Jackson and Holtzman deals were approved, but baseball commissioner Bowie Kuhn blocked the sale of the others, citing the "best interests of baseball."

The weakened A's came back from a poor start to close within 2½ games of the Kansas City Royals in 1976, but they dropped to last place the next year. After another last-place finish in 1979, Finley hired fiery Billy Martin to manage the club. Martin brought the A's in second in 1980, and first in the first half of strike-divided 1981. They won the Western Division championship by sweeping Kansas City in the special intradivisional playoffs, but were in turn swept by the Yankees in the LCS.

Finley's sale of the club in 1981 to the folks who bring us Levi's jeans signaled a turn toward normalcy and popularity. Despite a losing season in 1982, the club set a home attendance record as over 1.7 million fans came to watch Rickey Henderson's successful assault on the stolen-base record. In 1987 the A's finished right at .500—for the first time in their history a perfectly average team.

The next season they inaugurated a new multiyear reign as the league's best. Starter Dave Stewart and closer Dennis Eckersley anchored the league's strongest pitching staff and "bash brothers" Jose Canseco and Mark McGwire headlined an awesome offense. In 1988–90 the A's took title to the AL West with the majors' best won-lost record, then sailed past the East champion to the pennant. In 1988 they built a 13-game margin of victory over runner-up Minnesota, winning 104 games and drawing more than 2 million fans to their home games for the first time. They swept Boston in the ALCS, but faltered in the World Series, losing to underdog L.A. in five games.

Injuries to several key players—especially Canseco, who missed the first half of the season with a broken wrist—kept the A's from dominating AL play through most of 1989. But the preseason signing of free agent starter Mike Moore had strengthened the pitching, and a June trade that brought Rickey Henderson back after more than four years with the Yankees gave the A's the push they needed to prevail. At full strength by season's end, the A's overwhelmed Toronto in five games for their fourteenth pennant, then swept San Francisco for their world title.

Only Chicago's surprising White Sox challenged Oakland in 1990, and they too fell away in the latter half of the season as the A's walked to the division title with 103 wins. The potent offense was made even more formidable by the late-season acquisition of Harold Baines from Texas and Willie McGee from St. Louis. But the key to Oakland's dominance was its pitchers, who for the third year in a row compiled the league's lowest earned run average. Bob Welch led the majors with 27 wins, Dave Stewart put together his fourth straight 20-win season, and Dennis Eckersley rebounded from an injury-hampered 1989 with his finest relief year yet. The A's swept over Boston to their third straight pennant, but—shades of 1988!—floundered in the World Series, succumbing in just four games to Cincinnati's aroused Reds.

In 1991 the A's stayed at or near the top into late June before slipping to fourth. Eckersley remained in top form, however, and in 1992 proved almost invincible, with 7 wins and 51 saves. Jose Canseco's trade to Texas late in the season severed the bash brothers' tandem offense, but Mark McGwire enjoyed a banner season at the bat. Despite a wave of injuries that would have sunk most teams, the A's stayed afloat near the front through the first half of the season and held steady in the second half to win their fourth division title in five years. In the LCS the A's fell to Toronto in six games.

With an injury to McGwire that sidelined him more than four months, plus a general decline on the mound and at the bat that saw the team finish with the league's worst batting and earned run averages, Oakland in 1993 did what only two major league clubs before them (the 1915 Athletics and 1885 St. Louis Maroons) had ever done: tumble into the cellar after a first-place finish the year before.

The A's weren't winning much more often in 1994 when the players' strike halted play in August, but in the weak AL West their 51–63 record was good enough to land them in second place, just a game out of first.

In 1995 their 67-77 mark earned them last place in the AL West. More significant, however, was the sale of the club by the Haas family to Bay Area businessmen Steve Schott and Ken Hofmann and the departures at season's end of Eckersley and manager Tony LaRussa. The power-hitting 1996 A's (78-84) edged up to third place, largely on the basis of McGwire's ML-best 52 homers.

Philadelphia Phillies

It took the Phillies thirty-two years to win their first pennant, and ninety-seven to win their first world championship. They have finished last in their league or division twenty-nine times—one season in four. In the nine years from 1975 through 1983, though, they were one of the most formidable teams in baseball.

Alfred J. Reach, a sporting goods entrepreneur and former player, and Colonel John Rogers, a Philadelphia lawyer and politician, organized the Phillies in 1883 to bring Philadelphia back into the National League after a six-year absence. In their first season, the Phillies won only 17 of 98 decisions to finish an eighth-place last, as far out of seventh as the seventh-place team was from first. Bad as the Phillies have sometimes been since, their 1883 winning percentage of .173 remains their very worst.

Reach hired the respected Harry Wright to manage the Phillies in 1884, and while Wright failed to lead them to a pennant in his ten years at the helm, he did make them respectable. His fourth-place 1886 team, in fact, compiled a winning percentage of .623 that remained the club's best for ninety years. In 1887 the Phillies, with three pitchers winning more than 20 games, finished second, just 3½ games behind Detroit—their closest finish until their first pennant twenty-eight years later.

The Phillies remained in the upper division twelve of the next fourteen years. For five years—1891–1895—they fielded an outfield of Ed Delahanty, Billy Hamilton, and Sam Thompson—Hall of Famers who rank among the top hitters of all time. In the three heavy-hitting seasons that followed the lengthening of the pitching distance to its present 60′6″ in 1893, Delahanty, Hamilton, and Thompson—with help from players like catcher Jack Clements (.394 in 1895) and utility outfielder Tuck Turner (.416 in 1894)—sparked the Phillies to three team batting titles with BAs of over .300. In 1894 the big three joined Turner in batting over .400 and the team hit .349—still the major league club record.

In 1899, with Delahanty's .410 leading the way, the Phillies once again topped .300 to lead the league. Though the team finished third, they won 94 games, a club high they would not surpass for seventy-seven years. President Reach sold his interest in the club after a dispute with co-owner Rogers, and Rogers lost star second baseman Larry Lajoie in a salary dispute to the Athletics (Philadelphia's new entry in the rival American League). But the Phillies chased front-runner Pittsburgh through much of 1901. Though they slumped in August, they recovered to finish second.

It was the end of an era. Delahanty deserted to the AL the next season, and the Phillies dropped to seventh. Rogers sold the club to a syndicate. By 1904 the team was in last place, losing 100 games for the first time.

They rose into the first division the next season, but didn't mount a serious pennant run until 1911, when the pitching of rookie Grover Cleveland Alexander kept them in the thick of the race into midseason. Two years later they enjoyed first place through most of June before fading to a distant second.

In 1915 Alexander brought his ERA down more than a run per game to a league- and career-best of 1.22, hurling 12 shutouts among his 31 wins. Right fielder Gavvy Cravath and first baseman Fred Luderus finished one-two among NL sluggers, and Cravath won home run and RBI crowns. For half a season all eight clubs were in the thick of a tight race, with the Cubs and Phillies at the top of the heap. But in July the Cubs folded, and in August and September the Phillies took off to outdistance the late-surging Boston Braves by 7 games for their first pennant.

The World Series was a Phillies' heartbreak. Four of the five games were decided by a single run—but the runs belonged to the Boston Red Sox, who swept four after the Phillies had taken the opener.

Alexander shut out a record-tying 16 opponents the following year, winning a career-high 33, and teammate Eppa Rixey had his first big year with 22 wins. Through most of the season, the club trailed the leading Dodgers, but caught them in September, only to fall away again in the final week.

After Alexander's 30 wins had brought the Phillies another second-place finish in 1917, the club dealt him to Chicago and embarked on thirty-one years of wandering in the desert. After fourteen losing seasons (eight of them in last place), they climbed to fourth, two games above .500, in 1932, but dropped back the next year into the second division (including nine last-place finishes) for sixteen more years.

Several outstanding players spent time in Philadelphia during these years: Dave Bancroft (a rookie in their pennant season), Cy Williams, Freddy Leach, Chuck Klein, Lefty O'Doul, and Dick Bartell. Of these, only Williams and Klein retired as Phillies. The financially strapped management traded away the others at the height of their careers in deals that included cash as well as players. Even Klein—perhaps the greatest of them all—was sold twice before returning a third time to Philly to end his career.

The Phillies in 1930 produced a season that ranks among the most extraordinary of all time. With Klein and O'Doul leading the way at .386 and .383, every regular hit at least .280, to give the Phillies a team BA of .315. But Phillie pitchers yielded a record 1199 runs while compiling the worst big league ERA ever—6.71. The club lost 102 games and finished last.

The Phillies' move in 1938 out of tiny, antiquated Baker Bowl into the Athletics' Shibe Park did nothing for attendance—or for performance, as the team strung together a club-record five consecutive last-place finishes from 1938 to 1942, in which they averaged 107 losses per season and finished between 43 and 62½ games out of first.

In February 1943 the league took control of the debt-ridden club and sold it to a group headed by New York sportsman William D. Cox. Cox didn't last long; before the year was out he was barred from baseball for betting on the Phillies. His controlling interest was sold to Robert M. Carpenter, who installed his son, Robert Jr., as president. The younger Carpenter hired former pitcher Herb Pennock as general manager with instructions to build a farm system, and a new era began in the club's history.

Outfielder Del Ennis had come up to hit .313 in 1946, but Pennock died (in January 1948) before he could see the full fruits of his labor. First baseman Dick Sisler would be purchased in March; rookie outfielder Richie Ashburn would lead Phillie batters in 1948 with a .333 BA. Willie Jones wouldn't nail down third base for another year, and rookie pitchers Robin Roberts and Curt Simmons wouldn't overawe the opposition for a couple of seasons yet. But the team that would be dubbed the "Whiz Kids" was gathering. Triple-A manager Eddie Sawyer was brought up in late July.

In 1949, the loss of first baseman Eddie Waitkus (shot in the chest by a crazed young woman) and midseason complacency threatened to strand the Phillies in the second division. But Sawyer fired up his players in a special team meeting, and the Phillies rallied to finish third with the club's best record in thirty-two years.

With new red-pinstripe uniforms and a recovered Eddie Waitkus, the 1950 Phillies pulled away from a tightly bunched first division in July and August, but late in September fell to within two games of onrushing Brooklyn. The Dodgers took the first game of a season-ending two-game series to narrow the gap to one. But in the finale

the Phillies' Sisler homered to break a tenth-inning tie. When Brooklyn failed to score in the bottom of the tenth, the Whiz Kids had their pennant.

Curt Simmons, who was called up for military service in September after winning 17 games, missed the World Series. As in 1915, the result for Philadelphia was frustration and heartbreak, as the Phillies were swept by the Yankees—in the first three games by a single run.

Roberts's pitching kept the Phillies in the first division for four of the next five years, but the team made no serious run at another pennant. And when Roberts began to lose his effectiveness the team sank farther, to fifth for two years, then to four years in the cellar, culminating in 1961 with the longest big league losing streak of the century: 23 games.

The club stuck with new manager Gene Mauch, and the 1962 Phillies edged above .500 for the first time in nine years (though finishing seventh in a league newly expanded to ten teams). In 1963 they moved up to fourth with a strong second half. In 1964, with the acquisition of pitcher Jim Bunning from Detroit and infielder Richie (later Dick) Allen's productive rookie season, Mauch's Phillies moved way out in front in August. But they blew their lead with ten straight losses in late September while Cincinnati was winning nine and St. Louis eight in a row. Only victories in their final two games salvaged a second-place tie.

The Phillies produced winning seasons the next three years but never challenged the leaders. With Mauch replaced as manager during the 1968 campaign, the team embarked on seven straight losing seasons, including three years at the bottom of the NL East.

Pitcher Steve Carlton, acquired from St. Louis in an off-season trade, accounted for nearly half the Phillies' 59 wins in 1972. His 27 victories for the league's worst team gave the club a ray of hope for the future and earned Carlton the Cy Young Award. Carlton lost a league-high 20 games the next year, but as he regained his form over the next three seasons, so too the Phillies gradually rose to the top of the division.

In 1974 sophomore third baseman Mike Schmidt burst to the forefront of the league's power hitters. The Phillies dropped out of contention in August, but wound up third, their best finish since the league split into divisions in 1969. The next year outfielder Greg Luzinski joined Schmidt among the league's top sluggers, and the club rose to second, with their first winning season since 1967.

The Phillies had entered their golden age—nine straight winning seasons (a club record), including five division titles, two pennants, and their first world championship. In 1976 they enjoyed their finest regular season ever. With Schmidt and Luzinski providing the power, Carlton returning to the ranks of 20-game winners and Jim Lonborg climaxing a long comeback with 18 wins, the Phillies took the division lead in May and pulled away, recovering from a late-season dive to finish well ahead of Pittsburgh. Their 101 wins, .624 winning percentage, and nine-game margin of victory remain club records.

The Phillies were swept by Cincinnati in the League Championship Series, but came back the next season to duplicate their record 101 wins for another comfortable first-place finish. Carlton won 23 (and his second Cy Young Award), and Luzinski enjoyed the best season of his career, driving in 130 runs. After defeating Los Angeles in the LCS opener, though, the Phillies lost the pennant with three straight losses.

In 1978, even though Schmidt and Carlton had off-years, the Phillies led much of the season and captured the division title a third straight time. But it was a tight race, and they barely survived a late-season Pittsburgh surge to finish 1½ games in front. For the third time, their triumph in the East was followed by defeat in the LCS—for the second time at the hands of Los Angeles in four games.

Danny Ozark, in his seventh year as Phillies manager, was replaced by Dallas Green late in a disappointing 1979 season that saw the club stumble after a strong start before rallying in September to finish fourth. But Schmidt was back in top form, and Pete Rose had arrived via free agency to add his bat and hustle.

In a three-way race in 1980 that remained close through August, the Phillies hung tight without being able to move into the lead. But as Pittsburgh folded in late August and early September, the Phillies edged in front briefly, then battled back and forth with Montreal. Tied with the Expos as the clubs met in Montreal for the season's final three games, Philadelphia took the first 2–1, then—in eleven innings—the second, to clinch their fourth division title in five years. Schmidt, with perhaps his finest season, drove in 121 runs and was named NL MVP; Carlton, with 24 wins, won his third Cy Young Award; and veteran reliever Tug McGraw enjoyed his best season in years.

In an LCS in which four of the five games went into extra innings, the Phillies prevailed over Houston, capturing their first pennant since the Whiz Kids era thirty years earlier. And in the World Series, fortune finally smiled on the team as they overcame Kansas City in six games.

The Phillies won the first half of the strike-divided 1981 season. In the special intradivisional playoff against Montreal, Philadelphia fought back to tie the series after losing the first two games—only to lose the finale.

The Carpenter family—citing the prohibitive cost of running a major league club—sold the team. Manager Dallas Green also left and was replaced by Pat Corrales, who kept the club in the thick of the 1982 race until the final month, when the Phillies slipped 3½ games back, to second. And Steve Carlton did it again: his 23 wins earned him a record fourth Cy Young trophy.

Mike Schmidt again dominated the Phillies' offense in 1983, but Carlton yielded to John Denny as the team's pitching ace. Newly acquired reliever Al Holland emerged as one of the league's best. After general manager Paul Owens took over for Corrales as manager in midseason, the Phillies came alive and took the division title by 6 games. Carlton dominated the LCS with an 0.66 ERA and two wins as the Phillies won their fourth pennant. But their golden age ended in the World Series, when Baltimore triumphed in five games.

The Phillies dropped to .500 and fourth place in 1984, and suffered a losing fifth-place season in 1985. They rebounded to second in 1986 (but 21½ games behind New York), then dropped back below .500 in 1987. Mike Schmidt continued to power the offense—the only member of the 1980 world champions still a Phillie. Despite an impressive lineup of everyday players in 1988, the Phils collapsed, finishing in the division cellar for the first time in fifteen years.

Unable to recover from a shoulder injury, Mike Schmidt retired in May 1989, and despite several mid-season trades the Phillies again finished last in the NL East. In 1990, though, the flaming start of one of the players acquired in mid-1989—outfielder Len Dykstra, who was batting above .400 as late as June—lit the Phillies' competitive fires. But as Dykstra cooled off to mere excellence, the Phillies fell out of contention and finished 18 games back, tied for fourth.

A thirteen-game win streak in July–August 1991 came too late to propel the Phillies into the thick of the race, and although they rose to third place in the season's final week, they finished 20 games out. In 1992 they played at the bottom of the NL East much of the season, and finished there for the third time in five years.

Strengthened by the signing of several free agents, and sustained by solid performances throughout the roster, the Phillies reversed course in 1993. Led by Dykstra's peak season at the plate, the team grabbed the division lead at the start of the year and never let go, fending off Montreal's late-season surge to take the NL East title by three games. In the LCS they won their fifth NL pennant, defeating Atlanta in six games, but in the World Series they blew a pair of late-inning leads and fell in six games to repeat champion Toronto. Plagued by illness and injury, the Phillies never caught fire in 1994, finishing a distant fourth in the NL East. In 1995 they finished tied for second (but 21 games back).

The following year saw the Phillies riddled by injuries and falling to last (67-95), with the worst record in the NL. The club's failure led to manager Jim Fregosi's firing at season's end. Standouts in the futile effort were outfielder Jim Eisenreich (.361), starter Curt Schilling (3.19 ERA), reliever Ricky Bottalico (34 saves), and catcher Benito Santiago (30 HR).

Pittsburgh Pirates

Pittsburgh became a big league city in 1882, when its Allegheny baseball club joined with five other teams to form the American Association. Allegheny president H. D. McKnight was named president of the new league, but Allegheny made little stir until the club hired Horace Phillips to manage it and replaced its team in 1885 with players from the defunct Columbus club, which had finished second in the AA the year before. The new Alleghenys finished a distant third in 1885, but after purchasing Pud Galvin from Buffalo they improved in 1886 to finish second behind the St. Louis Browns.

Flushed with success, Allegheny in 1887 became the first club to desert the AA for the older and more highly regarded National League. There they found the competition stiffer and sank back into the second division. In 1890, when most of the team jumped to the rival Pittsburgh Players' League club, Allegheny (known that year as the Innocents) suffered the worst season in Pittsburgh major league history, finishing last, 66½ games out of first place (and 23 out of seventh), with a won-lost record of 23–113.

When the PL folded after just one season, Allegheny merged with its PL counterpart to form the Pittsburgh Athletic Company, thereby retrieving many of its old regulars. The club also hired a second baseman—Lou Bierbauer—whose signing (or theft, as his old club saw it) gave the Innocents a new and more enduring nickname: the Pirates. The renewed club still finished last in 1891, but thirty-six games closer to the top than the year before, and only fractionally out of seventh place.

In 1893 a rules change moved the pitcher 10½ feet farther back from home plate. Of all the NL clubs, the Pirates benefited most from the change: their batting average jumped 63 points—28 more than that of the league as a whole—while their pitchers suffered less than most. The club finished second, with a .628 winning percentage that was their best of the century. Lefty Frank Killen, a twenty-two-year-old pitcher acquired from Washington, led the club's resurgence with a league-leading 34 wins.

Although catcher Connie Mack was called upon to manage the club toward the end of the 1894 season and led them to winning seasons the next two years, the Pirates did not make another serious run for the pennant until 1900. With a team transformed yet again by players from a defunct club—this time the Louisville Colonels—the Pirates battled Brooklyn's Superbas almost to the end of the season before dropping 4½ games back, a solid second. Although they lost the postseason *Chronicle-Telegraph* Cup games (that year's World Series) to the Superbas, the Pirates were embarked on an era of greatness.

In the merger that brought the Louisville players to Pittsburgh, the Colonels' owner Barney Dreyfuss acquired half ownership of the Pirates. A year later he bought the other half. His perennial hope for the club was a first-division finish; in twenty-six of his thirty-two years of Pirate ownership his hope was rewarded.

Four of the former Louisville players—outfielder-turned-shortstop Honus Wagner, outfielder/manager Fred Clarke, third baseman/outfielder Tommy Leach, and pitcher Deacon Phillippe—and one carryover from the old Pirates, pitcher Sam Leever, remained with Pittsburgh long enough to help lead them to four pennants and, in 1909, their first world championship. In the sixteen years Clarke managed the Pirates (a club record), they also finished second five times, and slipped out of the first division only in Clarke's final two seasons at the helm.

In contrast to the club's devastation by the Players' League raid of 1890, the Pirates were unaffected in 1901 by raiders from the American League (which that year turned itself into a major league largely by drawing off talent from National League clubs). Only third baseman Jimmy Williams defected to the Americans, and he was ably replaced by Tommy Leach, as the Pirates, with the league's best pitching (Jesse Tannehill and Deacon Phillippe finished one-two in ERA, and Jack Chesbro at 21–10 led in winning percentage), captured their first pennant by a comfortable 7½ games over the Philadelphia Phillies.

The Pirates repeated as pennant winners in 1902 and 1903. The 1902 team was one of the most overwhelming of all time. One Pirate or another led the league in nearly every offensive category: Ginger Beaumont in hits and batting; Tommy Leach in home runs (with 6); and Honus Wagner in slugging, RBI, runs scored, doubles, and stolen bases. Pitcher Jack Chesbro's 28 wins led the league, and the top five NL pitchers in winning percentage were all

Pirates. The club held the lead the whole season, finishing 27½ games ahead of second-place Brooklyn, still a national league record.

Pitchers Chesbro and Tannehill deserted to the AL's New York Highlanders the next season, but their loss merely made Pittsburgh's pennant-winning margin (6½ games) smaller than it might have been. Wagner beat out teammate Fred Clarke for the NL batting crown and finished second to Clarke in slugging. Beaumont took the titles in hits, runs, and total bases. Pitcher Sam Leever, with his finest season, led the club with 25 wins and the league in ERA and winning percentage. Owner Dreyfuss arranged with the AL champion Boston Pilgrims for a best-of-nine World Series—the first between NL and AL champions—but the Pirates lost it in eight games as their tired pitchers at last succumbed to overwork.

Although the Pirates twice finished second over the next four years, they didn't come close to capturing another pennant until 1908, when, in one of the tightest NL races ever, they were edged out by the Chicago Cubs and finished one game back, tied with New York's Giants for second. The following year, though, they moved in June into the new concrete-and-steel Forbes Field and celebrated by returning to the top of the league with a club record 110 wins—holding off the dogged Cubs throughout the season to take the flag by 6½ games. And this time they won the World Series, too, although they needed the full seven games to subdue Detroit's Tigers. Honus Wagner remained the league's dominant offensive force, but aging pitchers Leever and Phillippe were overshadowed by a new crop of standouts: Vic Willis, Howie Camnitz, Nick Maddox, and Lefty Leifield—and the astonishing rookie Babe Adams, who after going 12–3 (with a 1.11 ERA) during the season, won three more games in the World Series.

The Series triumph ended an era. Wagner was past his prime and wound down his long career over the next several seasons as the Pirates dropped out of contention for a dozen years, including four (1914–1917) in the hated second division. Only Babe Adams remained of the world championship team when Pittsburgh next made a contest of the pennant race in 1921, taking an early lead and holding it most of the summer until an August-September decline dropped them to second place, 4 games back.

Former Pirate infielder Bill McKechnie replaced George Gibson as manager during the following season with the club in fifth place, and saw the Pirates spurt to second before fading to third at the finish. Two more third-place seasons—with the Pirates finishing just 3 games out of first in 1924—paved the way for another pennant in 1925.

The 1925 Pirates fielded several stars: shortstop Glenn Wright, who led the club with 121 RBI; sophomore right fielder Kiki Cuyler, who led the team in hitting (.357) and the league in runs scored; third baseman Pie Traynor, who shone on the field and at the bat; and Max Carey, who beat out Cuyler for the league stolen base title and enjoyed his finest season (.343) at the plate. The team as a whole hit .307 to lead the league and ran away with the pennant, spurting to catch the front-running Giants in midseason and pushing ahead to an 8½-game lead by season's end. The World Series was tougher, but the Pirates prevailed over the Washington Senators, defeating veteran Walter Johnson in a seventh-game slugfest 9–7. Babe Adams, hero of the 1909 Series and now, at forty-three, nearing the end of his long career, pitched one shutout inning in Game Four.

Rookie outfielder Paul Waner arrived the next season and hit .336, but the team, which had led the race going into August, fell into decline late in the month and finished third, 4½ games out. Max Carey sparked an unsuccessful player uprising against the management and was sold to Brooklyn just before the Pirate collapse in August, and manager McKechnie was replaced after the season by former Washington manager Donie Bush.

In 1927, his first season at the helm, Bush sailed the Pirate ship to its sixth pennant, even though Kiki Cuyler was benched for half the season for refusing to bat second in the order. But Paul Waner's younger brother Lloyd arrived to join Paul in the outfield, and the pair tore up the league, finishing one-two in hits (237 and 223) as Paul also took crowns in batting (.380; Lloyd was third at .355), RBI and total bases, while Lloyd led in runs scored. In and out of first place throughout the season, the Pirates moved into the lead a final time at the start of September and held on to edge the St. Louis Cardinals by 1½ games. In the World Series, though (played with Cuyler on the bench), the Pirates were swept by a Yankee team widely acclaimed as the greatest of all time.

Barney Dreyfuss died in February 1932. Ownership of the Pirates passed to his widow, who named their son-in-law Bill Benswanger president. The team finished a competitive second in 1932 and 1933, but then fell back until 1938, when—with Pie Traynor now manager—they moved out in front in midseason and held their lead comfortably until late September, when ten straight Chicago victories (including three against Pittsburgh) dropped the Pirates to second place, where they finished, 2 games back.

The Pirates showcased some great players in their lean years, like shortstop Arky Vaughan in the 1930s and early '40s, and slugger Ralph Kiner, who won or shared the league home run title all seven of his seasons with Pittsburgh in the 1940s and '50s. But after 1938 the club finished no closer than eight games from the top for twenty-one years. They finished as high as second only twice (in 1944 and 1958), and in the eight years 1950–1957 wound up each season either last or next-to-last, reaching their nadir in 1952 with 112 losses and a last-place finish 54½ games out of first.

The Pirates had been purchased in 1946 by a four-man syndicate that included singer Bing Crosby and real estate tycoon John W. Galbreath. Galbreath later bought a majority interest in the club and, as president, hired Branch Rickey to rebuild the Pirates into contenders. Barney Dreyfuss had resisted the development of minor league farm systems (a Rickey innovation at St. Louis and Brooklyn), preferring to scour unaffiliated minor league teams himself for young talent. Rickey's ministrations helped build a foundation for the Pirate resurgence of 1958–1960.

No one threatened the 1958 Milwaukee Braves' preeminence in the NL after July, but Pittsburgh came closer than anyone, finishing second, eight games back. Six of the eight regulars who would lead the Pirates to their next

championship in 1960 were already in the lineup, including Dick Groat, Bill Mazeroski, and Roberto Clemente; and the leading pitchers of 1958—Bob Friend, Vern Law, and reliever Roy Face—topped the 1960 staff, too.

In 1959 the Pirates fell back to fourth place, barely above .500, but the next year they began strong and, shaking off their last challenger in late July, built up a 7-game margin of victory by season's end. League batting champion Groat paced a balanced offense that led the league in hitting, and pitcher Law, with 20 wins, enjoyed the finest season of his career. Facing the Yankees in the World Series, the Pirates were overwhelmed in the three games they lost, but they won the world title with four close wins, capped by Mazeroski's famous home run in the bottom of the ninth inning of the final game.

Pittsburgh again led the league in batting in 1961, with Clemente (whose .351 batting average led the league) and first baseman Dick Stuart (35 home runs, 117 RBI) enjoying especially fine seasons. But the Pirate pitching fell apart (Vern Law lost most of the season to arm trouble), and the club dropped to sixth place.

When the Pirates next made a serious run for the pennant, in 1966, Harry Walker managed the team and center fielder Matty Alou (newly acquired from San Francisco) won the batting crown. (His brother Felipe of Atlanta was runner-up—the only one-two brother finish ever.) In a season-long three-way race, the Pirates took a lead in August but lost it early in September and finished third, 3 games out. They dropped to sixth again the next season and remained out of the pennant race for three years.

In 1970 the majors experienced their second season of divisional play, John Galbreath's son Daniel was named Pirates' president, and Danny Murtaugh returned a third time to pilot the Pirates. (His second stint was for half a season in 1967.) The team began slowly and entered June with a record under .500. But they were already on their way up, and by mid-July, when they moved out of aging Forbes Field into the brand-new Three Rivers Stadium, they were at the top of the NL East. They slipped into a three-way tangle in mid-September, but shot ahead later in the month to take the division title by 5 games. Most of the team was new since 1960—the power was now supplied by first baseman Bob Robertson and outfielder Willie Stargell. But Roberto Clemente was still in top form, and Bill Mazeroski was still at second base, though nearing the end of his career.

In the 1970 League Championship Series, the Pirates were swept by Cincinnati. But they came back the next season to overwhelm the East in a race that was no race after June, then defeated San Francisco for their eighth pennant, three games to one. Their slugging—paced by Stargell's league-leading 48 home runs—led the league, and reliever Dave Giusti saved a league-leading 30 games in support of a balanced pitching staff. Clemente hit .414 in the World Series (with half his hits going for extra bases) as the Pirates overcame a 0–2 deficit to edge Baltimore in seven games for their fourth world title.

In 1972, after a slow start, Pittsburgh (now managed by their former center fielder Bill Virdon) rocketed to their third straight division championship—by 11 games over Chicago. The club lost, narrowly, to Cincinnati in the LCS, then suffered an even greater loss when Clemente was killed that winter in a plane crash. They played poorly the next season, yet even with a losing record finished third, only 2½ games behind the champion New York Mets in a five-way divisional race. Danny Murtaugh returned as manager a fourth (and final) time late in the season and piloted the club to two more NL East titles the next two years.

The 1974 championship drive featured a comeback from last place in early July to first by late August, followed by a nip-and-tuck race in September with St. Louis that was settled by a tenth-inning Pirate victory over Chicago in the season's final game. Stargell's bat was joined by those of Al Oliver and Richie Zisk as the Pirates outhit the rest of the league. In the LCS, though, the Los Angeles Dodgers overcame Pittsburgh handily, three games to one.

The Pirates won the 1975 race more easily, holding the lead from early June as right fielder Dave Parker, in his first full big league season, led the club in home runs and RBI, and the league in slugging. But once again, for the fourth time in five tries, Pittsburgh lost the pennant in the LCS—swept this time by the awesome Cincinnati Reds, winners of 108 regular season games.

A distant second-place finish in 1976 was followed that December by manager Murtaugh's untimely death. His successor, Chuck Tanner, kept the Pirates competitive in his first two seasons, steering them to within 5 games of the champion Phillies in 1977, then—with an amazing August-September spurt from way below .500—to within 1½ games of the Phillies in 1978.

In 1979 the Pirates again started slowly but began to move up in May and pushed to the front, ahead of Montreal, in late July. By mid-September, though, the Expos had caught up, and it was not until the final day that an Expo loss and Pirate win gave Pittsburgh its sixth NL East title. Parker and the aging Stargell (now called "Pops") were still the club's big bats, but submariner Kent Tekulve had emerged as the bullpen ace, and one of six Pirate pitchers to win 10 games or more.

In the National League Championship Series the Pirates repaid Cincinnati for their 1975 humiliation, sweeping to the pennant in three games. In the World Series they seemed to have met their match in the Baltimore Orioles of Earl Weaver, falling behind three games to one. But Pops rallied his "family" to victory in the final three must-win contests, and Pittsburgh for a fifth time reigned at the top of the baseball world.

For seven years the Pirates drifted downhill. The club's family spirit disintegrated, fans deserted the team, and it seemed for a time that the Pirates would leave Pittsburgh. But in 1985 a group of local corporations and individuals purchased the club from the Galbreaths, determined (with the assistance of a loan from the city of Pittsburgh) to keep the Pirates in town. Syd Thrift, a trader of consummate skill, was named general manager, and Chicago White Sox coach Jim Leyland was hired to his first job as a big league pilot. Under the new regime the club improved gradually, until in 1988 it once again proved itself a serious contender for the NL championship of the East. Thrift had built a team second only to New York's mighty Mets. But Thrift's unwillingness to share with his superiors the top-level decision making bulked larger, in the eyes of the Pirate directors, than his achievement and he was fired at the season's end.

Plagued all season by injuries, Pittsburgh plunged to fifth in 1989. But in 1990, as Doug Drabek put together a career season on the mound and the bats of Barry Bonds and Bobby Bonilla burst into full bloom, the Pirates arrived at the All-Star break in first place by half a game over New York. With Drabek and Zane Smith (newly acquired from Montreal) all but unbeatable down the stretch, the Pirates, after exchanging the lead with New York several times, swept a Met series in early September to extend a narrow lead and clinched the NL East title at the end of the month with eight straight wins.

The Pirates repeated as division champions in 1991 and 1992. Bonds and Bonilla again led the offense in 1991 and pitcher John Smiley won 20 games. In 1992, even the departure of Bonilla (who signed with the Mets as a free agent) and Smiley (dealt to Minnesota) didn't hamper the Pirates. Center fielder Andy Van Slyke took up the offensive slack with one of his best seasons, and pitcher Tim Wakefield rose from the minors at the end of July to compile an 8-1 record as the Pirate ship breezed to the title by 9 games. But the three-time division champions could not win a pennant. In the 1990 LCS they fell to Cincinnati in six games. The next year they built a 3–1 lead over Atlanta, but lost the final two games. And in 1992, down three games to two, they fought back to within one out of victory in Game Seven before an Atlanta pinch hit cut them down once again.

The departure of free agent Barry Bonds to San Francisco was the most crucial of many roster changes for 1993, which saw more than half the 1992 NL East championship squad replaced. The revamped Pirates fielded near the top of the league and batted near the middle, but their pitching fell apart and the team finished fifth.

When the strike ended the 1994 season, the Pirates' .465 winning percentage was only two points better than the year before, but in the NL's new Central Division, that was good enough for a third-place tie with St. Louis. However, financial problems continued to haunt the team, and the payroll was slashed to the bone in 1995, resulting in the Pirates posting the NL's worst record (58-78). In February 1996 thirty-two-year-old Sacramento newspaper heir Kevin McClatchy moved to purchase the club for $90 million.

Despite an 11-game winning streak in September, the Pirates (73-89) remained in the basement in 1996, prompting Jim Leyland to resign at season's end. Pacing the Buc offense were Jeff King (30 HR, 111 RBI) and Al Martin (.300, 38 SB).

St. Louis Cardinals

The club that is now the Cardinals first fielded a team in 1881, and the next season became a charter member of the American Association, a new major league formed in part to offer fans the beer and Sunday baseball forbidden by the older National League. Chris Von der Ahe, one of the club's founders and its first president, at first saw in baseball simply a source of customers for his St. Louis saloon and beer garden, but he developed a love for the game itself as his Brown Stockings—or Browns—developed into one of the era's greatest teams.

After a losing season in 1882, Von der Ahe hired Ted

Sullivan, a noted judge of baseball talent, to manage the Browns. Sullivan brought in third baseman Arlie Latham and pitcher Tony Mullane to strengthen a team that already boasted a fine pitcher in Jumbo McGinnis (25–18 in 1882) and one of the game's premier first baseman in Charlie Comiskey. Although Sullivan quit before the end of his first season because of the continued interference of the volatile Von der Ahe, the Browns finished second in the American Association, just a game behind champion Philadelphia.

When Mullane bolted the Browns in 1884, the club slipped to fourth. But help was on the way. In July Von der Ahe purchased the Bay City, Michigan, club to acquire its heavy-hitting pitcher Dave Foutz, and in September added another hitting pitcher, "Parisian Bob" Caruthers, to the roster. In 1885—with Comiskey now the manager, left fielder Tip O'Neill blossoming into one of baseball's best hitters, and Caruthers and Foutz winning 40 and 33 games—the Browns rose to the top, 16 games ahead of second-place Cincinnati. They finished on top four years in a row, tying Chicago's White Stockings (3–3–1) in the 1885 World Series and defeating them four games to two the next year for the AA's only Series triumph over their NL rivals.

Pitcher Silver King joined the club in 1887, and outfielder Tommy McCarthy arrived the following year. They helped keep the Browns at the top of the AA through 1888 (although the team lost the World Series both years). But Von der Ahe's sale of Foutz and Caruthers to Brooklyn following the 1887 season boosted Brooklyn to second place in 1888. The next year Brooklyn edged the Browns for the pennant, and the club's first era of greatness was over.

When the AA folded after the 1891 season, the Browns were taken into the NL, but fared poorly there, finishing ninth and eleventh of the twelve clubs in the divided season of 1892. They rose no higher than ninth in the remaining years of Von der Ahe's ownership, dropping into the cellar (63½ games out) in 1897 and returning to the bottom with a club-worst 111 losses the next season.

New owners Frank and Stanley Robison (who also controlled the Cleveland club) transferred the best Cleveland players and their manager to St. Louis in 1899. Dubbed the Perfectos, the revitalized St. Louis club fell short of perfection, but did rise to a first-division fifth place that year and (now known as the Cardinals) rose to fourth in 1901 before sinking back into the second division for a dozen years.

After Stanley Robison died in 1911 (his brother Frank had died in 1905), the club passed into the possession of Frank's daughter Helene Britton, who ran it behind the scenes until, in 1916, she sold it to a syndicate headed by her attorney James C. Jones. Jones hired Branch Rickey away from the AL Browns to run the club.

Rickey took over a team with two chief assets: manager Miller Huggins and a promising young infielder, Rogers Hornsby. Huggins had managed the Cards to third place in 1914, before Hornsby arrived, and after a pair of losing seasons brought them up to third again in 1917. Huggins was lost to the New York Yankees the next year, and Rickey left the club temporarily for military service in the Great War. When Rickey returned in 1919, he took over as manager himself, and in 1921 and 1922 saw the team

finish third, closer to the leaders than the club had finished since joining the NL in 1891. Led by Hornsby's .397 and .401 batting, the team hit over .300 both seasons.

Sam Breadon, one of the Jones group of owners, increased his investment in the Cardinals until by 1920 he was majority stockholder and club president, with Rickey as vice president and general manager. Breadon moved the Cards out of the inadequate wooden Cardinal Park during the 1920 season into the more modern Sportsman's Park, owned by the Browns (and built on the site of Von der Ahe's original grounds).

Early in the 1925 season, with the Cards in last place, Breadon replaced Rickey as field manager with second baseman Hornsby. The switch worked. In 1925 the Cards rebounded to fourth, and in 1926 they captured their first pennant since the glory days of the old Browns four decades earlier—edging Cincinnati in the final week of the season after an August spurt had shot them into pennant contention. The season was made perfect by victory in the World Series over Miller Huggins's Yankees.

But Breadon and his irascible player-manager had a falling out, and Hornsby found himself traded that winter to the New York Giants for second baseman Frank Frisch and pitcher Jimmy Ring. The trade enraged Cardinal fans, but the team finished a close second in 1927, and returned to the top (under new manager Bill McKechnie) in a tight race the following season.

McKechnie, fired after the Yankees swept the Cards in the 1928 World Series and rehired in the midst of a Cardinal slump the next season, left to manage the Boston Braves in 1930. Former catcher Gabby Street, who replaced him, led the Cards back to the top again for successive pennants in 1930 and 1931, and in 1931 to a World Series victory over the Philadelphia Athletics. The 1930 race saw the club shoot from below .500 in mid-June to 30 games above .500 by season's end, overtaking three other teams to clinch the flag just three games from the finish. The 1931 team ran away with the pennant, leading all the way and finishing 13 games in front. Outfielder Chick Hafey and first baseman Jim Bottomley finished first and third in NL batting, and pitcher Bill Hallahan led the league in strikeouts (for the second year in a row) and tied for the lead in wins, with 19. Four of the league's top five base stealers—led by Frank Frisch and including outfielder Pepper Martin in his first full season—were Cardinals.

When the Cards dropped to sixth place in 1932 and showed little improvement the following year, Breadon replaced manager Street with Frisch. As when he had named Hornsby to manage, Breadon's move paid immediate dividends. Though the club finished fifth that season, their record improved after Frisch took over, and the next year, in a season-long uphill struggle, the Cards won thirteen of their final fifteen games to pass the front-running New York Giants in the final week.

Writers labeled the 1934 Cardinals the "Gashouse Gang" for their rowdy and daring play. In addition to team veterans Frisch and Martin (who had been shifted from the outfield to third base), the gang included shortstop Leo Durocher, left fielder Joe "Ducky" Medwick, and the team's leading hitter and slugger, first baseman Rip Collins, who in a career-best season led the league in slugging average and tied for first in home runs.

Cardinal pitching was headed by the league-leading Jerome "Dizzy" Dean (30–7) and his rookie brother Paul (19–11). Of the team's final nine wins, Diz and Paul accounted for seven. Each won another pair in the Cards' World Series triumph over Detroit.

The next two seasons the Cardinals moved into the lead late in the season only to wind up second. After the team slipped into the second division in 1938, Breadon replaced Frisch as manager with Ray Blades, who led a late-season run for the flag in 1939 but finished second. When the Cards failed to contend in 1940, Breadon brought up Rochester manager Billy Southworth for a second time. Southworth had failed as McKechnie's replacement in 1929, but this time he stuck, becoming one of the club's greatest helmsmen.

Through all these years Branch Rickey was revolutionizing baseball as he built the game's first and most extensive "farm system" of minor league clubs. The Cardinals' farm teams would—until the other major league clubs caught on and caught up—provide St. Louis with a competitive advantage in the recruitment and development of young players.

In the closing days of the 1941 season, perhaps the Cardinal system's greatest product arrived at the big club: Stan Musial. Southworth brought the club in a close second that year after a season-long back-and-forth struggle with Brooklyn. The next year—Musial's first full season—the Cardinals enjoyed their winningest season ever: 106 victories. They needed them all, too, for Brooklyn won 104 games, leading the race until mid-September, when the Cardinals passed them and held on to a narrow lead by winning twelve of their final thirteen games. St. Louis pitchers Mort Cooper and Johnny Beazley finished one-two in National League wins and ERA, while Enos Slaughter and Musial paced the Cardinal offense. The club maintained its momentum in the World Series, taking the Yankees in five games.

St. Louis retained its preeminence for two more years as baseball gradually lost players to military service in World War Two. Slaughter and Beazley were gone by 1943. But Cooper remained to compile two more 20-plus winning seasons, and Musial was not called until after the 1944 season. With 105 wins in both 1943 and 1944, the Cards ran away with two more pennants, losing to the Yankees in the 1943 World Series, but taking their sixth world title the next year from their St. Louis landlords, the AL champion Browns.

Owner Breadon had fired Branch Rickey in 1942 (objecting to the personal profit Rickey made from selling the club's unneeded farm players), and Southworth left to manage the Boston Braves after the 1945 season (in which the Cards failed to catch the leading Chicago Cubs, finishing second). Rickey went to head the Brooklyn Dodgers, building for them a farm system and tapping the large reservoir of black players. In 1946, the last year of all-white major league ball, the Cards (managed now by Eddie Dyer) and the Dodgers waged a two-team pennant race, ending the season in the first major league tie for first place. St. Louis won the first two games in a best-of-three playoff and went on to surprise the favored Boston Red Sox in the World Series. With the war over, the team was back at full strength. Slaughter led the league in RBI, and Musial led it in most other offensive categories;

pitcher Howie Pollett led the league in ERA (as he had in 1943 before leaving for the war) and in wins, with 21.

But St. Louis was slow to integrate its club and lost ground to teams like Brooklyn, whose black players brought an immediate upswing in the club's success. The Cards began poorly in 1947, but recovered to finish second to Brooklyn, though never offering a serious challenge for the flag. After the season Breadon sold the club to Fred Saigh and Robert Hannegan (the U.S. Postmaster General). Musial enjoyed his finest season in 1948, but the club finished second again in a lackluster race. The next year, though, the Cards and Dodgers tangled in a season-long struggle for first place that was not resolved until the season's last day—with Brooklyn on top.

The Cardinals threatened to move to Milwaukee, but beer magnate August Busch, Jr., purchased the club early in 1953 and the same year bought Sportsman's Park from the Browns (who were moving to Baltimore). With Busch's infusion of money and enthusiasm, the club slowly revived. They made runs for the pennant in 1957, 1960, and 1963, but each time tailed off sharply in the final week of the season.

The Cards were playing below .500, in seventh place, in mid-June 1964 when the arrival (via a trade with the Cubs) of speedy young Lou Brock sparked a revival of both the team and player. Brock, who had been hitting .251 in Chicago, with 10 stolen bases, hit .348 the rest of the season and stole 33 more bases as the Cards hurtled into the midst of a four-way race for the pennant that was settled only when they took the flag with an 11–5 win on the final day. After surprising the Yankees in the World Series, the Cardinals were themselves surprised when manager Johnny Keane left to take the Yankee helm. The club slipped into the second division for a couple of years under the management of their great former second baseman Red Schoendienst.

But owner Busch built them a striking new stadium in 1966, and the next season the team rebounded to the top again, running away from the field in the last half of the season behind the heavy hitting of Orlando Cepeda, the bat and speed of Lou Brock, and a pitching staff of remarkable breadth and balance. Bob Gibson's three World Series wins over Boston edged the Cards to a ninth world title and set the stage for Gibson's astonishing season the following year.

With his 22 wins leading the Cards to another pennant in 1968, Gibson hurled 13 shutouts and compiled an ERA of just 1.12—both feats the best in more than half a century, both ranking among the top five big league performances ever. After winning two World Series games, Gibson lost Game Seven as Detroit took the crown.

Red Schoendienst continued as Cardinal manager through 1976—a club record twelve years—but led the team to no more championships. When divisional play was inaugurated in 1969, geography was ignored as the Cards were installed in the East to add strength to what seemed the weaker division. But it was fourteen years before they won their first divisional championship. Four times they finished second, losing twice by only 1½ games, in the back-to-back tight races of 1973 and 1974.

Dorrel "Whitey" Herzog was in his first full season as Cardinal manager before the club again finished that near the top. In the strike-shortened divided season of 1981, the Cards compiled the best overall record in the NL East, but because they had finished the two halves of the season second to Philadelphia and Montreal they were ineligible for postseason play.

With the defensive wizard shortstop Ozzie Smith (acquired from San Diego) and rookie speedster Willie McGee bolstering an already strong team, the Cardinals of 1982, after prevailing against the Phillies in the race for the East, swept West champion Atlanta for the pennant and captured their tenth World Series crown in a seven-game struggle with Milwaukee.

After two seasons out of the running, the Cards in 1985 gained the power of veteran Jack Clark (acquired from San Francisco) and the speed of rookie Vince Coleman. With career-best seasons from Willie McGee and newly acquired pitcher John Tudor, the team edged New York for the division title and defeated Los Angeles for the pennant—but lost the World Series to Kansas City.

Jack Clark missed two-thirds of the 1986 season to injury, and the Cards finished below .500, but they rebounded to edge the Mets again for the championship of the East in 1987 as Clark and Vince Coleman enjoyed their finest seasons at the bat. But the reinjured Clark made only a token appearance as the Cards edged San Francisco for the league championship, and he missed the World Series entirely as St. Louis bowed to Minnesota in seven games. That winter Clark signed as a free agent with the Yankees and in 1988 the Cardinals dropped to fifth place, 25 games out.

With solid pitching and hitting, and the league's best fielding, the 1989 Cardinals drew within half a game of the division lead on September 8, then fell out of the race with six straight losses, finishing third. As the season drew to its close, long-time owner August Busch, Jr., died at age ninety. The next July, with the club uncharacteristically mired at the bottom of the National League East, manager Whitey Herzog resigned. Under new manager Joe Torre the Cards revived briefly, but then dropped their final seven games to insure their first basement finish in seventy-two years.

Reliever Lee Smith provided the key to St. Louis's 1991 rebound to second place: his 47 saves—a new NL record—preserved more than half the wins of a team that won 37 of its games by a single run. Smith saved another 43 games in 1992, but this time the Cards finished third. The defense developed a leak in 1993, and the pitching faltered, but four regulars—Bernard Gilkey, Todd Zeile, and newcomers Gregg Jefferies and Mark Whiten—scaled new heights offensively to keep the Cardinals competitive through much of the season and give them another third place finish. In 1994 the team—now playing in the NL's new Central Division—performed below .500 for the first time since 1990.

The weak-hitting Cards slipped to fourth in 1995. Manager Joe Torre was fired as the season wound down and was replaced by interim manager Mike Jorgensen and ultimately by former A's pilot Tony LaRussa. The big news of the year, however, came in December when Anheuser-Busch sold the club for $150 million to an investment group headed by St. Louis banker Andrew Baur and William DeWitt Jr., whose father had once owned the Browns and the Reds.

In 1996, Ozzie Smith's last season, the LaRussa-led

Cards (88-74) outpaced Houston and Cincinnati for the NL Central championship. Aiding St. Louis's effort were Ron Gant (30 HR, 82 RBI), Brian Jordan (17 HR, 104 RBI), Andy Benes (18-10), and Dennis Eckersley (30 saves). In the first round of the postseason the Cards rolled over San Diego in three straight but in the NLCS ran into the Atlanta buzzsaw. Ahead three games to one, the Cards couldn't put away the pennant as the Braves rolled to 12-1, 3-1 and 15-0 victories in the last three games.

San Diego Padres

In their first fifteen years the Padres put together only one winning season. In their sixteenth, they won the National League pennant. Founded in the 1969 expansion that saw the two major leagues divide into East and West divisions, the Padres finished last in the six-team NL West their first six seasons, ending each year from 28½ to 42 games behind the division champion.

Their first season was their worst. With 110 losses, the Padres finished not only 41 games out of first but 29 games out of *fifth*. First baseman Nate Colbert, with 24 home runs, provided San Diego's brightest ray of hope. He proved to be one of the Padres' standout performers through their last-place years, and in 1972 became the first Padre to drive in more than 100 runs.

Big league baseball was not an instant hit in San Diego. Home attendance barely topped half a million in the Padres' first year, and though it rose a little over the next few seasons, the increase was not enough to make the club viable. Owner C. Arnholt Smith decided early in 1974 to sell the franchise to a buyer who planned to move the team to Washington, D.C. New uniforms had been manufactured and the club's files were packed for the move, when the builder of the McDonald's fast-food empire, longtime baseball fan Ray Kroc, stepped in with an offer to buy the Padres for cash and keep them in San Diego. His bid was accepted.

Though Kroc's 1974 Padres finished last with the same 60–102 record they had posted the year before, his sense of showmanship drew spectators. Home attendance shot up 76 percent, rising above a million for the first time. The Padres then began to draw fans on their own merits as they finally pulled themselves out of the cellar. Pitcher Randy Jones, who in 1974 had led the league with 22 losses, turned his record around and for two years shone as one of the game's finest pitchers. He halved his 1974 ERA to a league-leading 2.24, winning 20 games as the Padres rose to fourth place in 1975 and posted a winning percentage over .400 for the first time. The next year Jones won a league-high 22 games and earned the Cy Young Award—the first major award to come to a San Diego player.

Although 1976 proved to be Jones's last winning season, the Padres were by then attracting other top-quality players. Outfielder Dave Winfield came up as a rookie in 1973, and the following year became the team RBI leader, a position he held in six of his seven full seasons with the Padres. Reliever Rollie Fingers signed as a free agent. In each of his four seasons in San Diego (1977–1980) he led the team in saves, twice also leading the league. In 1978 the Padres acquired veteran pitcher Gaylord Perry from

Texas and installed rookie Ozzie Smith at shortstop. Perry's sparkling 21–6 season gave San Diego its second Cy Young winner, and together with Smith's play in the field, Winfield's bat (.308, 97 RBI) and Fingers's 37 saves, brought the Padres their first winning season.

All these stars had gone—and owner Kroc had recently died—by the time the Padres recorded a second winning season six years later, and won the division title and NL pennant with a new blend of experience and youth. Sparked by recently acquired veterans Steve Garvey at first, Graig Nettles at third, and Goose Gossage in the bullpen, and by a bevy of younger stars like batting champ Tony Gwynn and hard-hitting outfielder Kevin McReynolds, the Padres moved into first place to stay in early June. From August 3 to the end of the season, they played only .500 ball but still won the championship of the weak Western Division by 12 games. Underdogs in the League Championship Series, the Padres lost the first two games in Chicago, but pulled themselves together to take the pennant with three come-from-behind wins at home.

Their decline began with their World Series loss to Detroit. The end of 1985 saw them tied for third, and in 1986 they slipped below .500 and into fourth place. In 1987 Gwynn won his second batting title, and rookie catcher Benito Santiago capped the season with a 34-game hitting streak to cop Rookie of the Year honors. But with most of the 1984 standouts faded or traded, the Padres' decline was complete: the club for the ninth time in its nineteen years finished last.

In late May 1988, with the team at 16–30, Padre general manager Jack McKeon took over as field manager from Larry Bowa. Under McKeon the Padres went 67–48, with nine wins in their final ten games, shot from sixth place to third in the NL West.

In 1989 a trio of veteran pitchers—starters Bruce Hurst (lured from Boston as a free agent) and Ed Whitson, and closer Mark Davis—attained new peaks of performance. Slugger Jack Clark (newly acquired from the Yankees) turned on the power after a slow start to complement Tony Gwynn's fourth season as NL batting leader. The Padres stumbled through the first half, arriving at the All-Star break four games below .500, but climbed steadily through the final two months to a second-place finish with their second-best winning percentage ever.

With the loss of free agent Davis in 1990, plus injuries to Clark and catcher Santiago, even the new power of Joe Carter (traded from Cleveland) could not lift the club above a tie for fourth. New owners, headed by TV producer Tom Werner, took control of the Padres from Ray Kroc's widow Joan in mid-June. Jack McKeon resigned his managerial position, which went to coach Greg Riddoch a month later, and was fired as general manager in September.

Slugger Fred McGriff arrived for 1991 (in a trade that sent Carter to Toronto) and helped power the Padres into third place. In 1992 he was joined by Gary Sheffield, who revived after an injury-ridden season at Milwaukee to lead the NL in batting and rank with McGriff among the league leaders in home runs and RBI. The Padres again finished third. But Sheffield and McGriff were traded away during the 1993 season in cost-cutting moves that, combined with poor team pitching and fielding, dumped the Padres into the NL West cellar, a club record 43 games

out of first. Attendance also fell, to below 1.4 million, the club's lowest level in thirteen years.

Although the Padres had improved their winning percentage somewhat over 1993 by the time the 1994 season was cut short in August by the strike, their 47–70 record was the worst in the majors. One of San Diego's few reasons to cheer in 1994 was the hitting of Tony Gwynn, whose .394 batting average was the best in the NL since Bill Terry's .401 sixty-four years earlier.

In December 1994 a group led by Larry Lucchino and John Moores acquired the club. GM Randy Smith resigned in midseason 1995, but the club rebounded slightly to a third place finish (70-74) as Gwynn (.368) won his sixth batting title.

The 1996 Padres (91-71) surprised virtually everyone by catching the Dodgers and capturing the NL West title on the last day of the season. Standout Padres included Tony Gwynn (with a league-leading .353 average), MVP Ken Caminiti (40 HR, 130 RBI), Steve Finley (30 HR, 95 RBI), Rickey Henderson (37 SB), and Trevor Hoffman (42 saves). Their Cinderella season, however, came to an end in the first round of the postseason as they lost in three straight to St. Louis.

San Francisco Giants

The expulsion of Troy and Worcester from the National League after the 1882 season cleared the way for the league to reestablish clubs in the major markets of Philadelphia and New York. Manufacturer John B. Day was awarded the New York franchise. Purchasing the defunct Troy club, he divided their players between the new NL Gothams and his other club, the Metropolitans of the American Association, and set them up on adjoining grounds north of Central Park, on a field once used for polo.

The Mets fared better than the Gothams, finishing fourth in 1883 to the Gothams' sixth, and winning the AA pennant the next year while the Gothams rose only to fifth in the NL. Since the NL, with greater prestige and higher ticket prices, offered potentially greater profit, Day switched some of his Mets to the Gothams in 1885, including ace hurler Tim Keefe and manager Jim Mutrie. The results were immediate: the Mets sank to seventh place while the Gothams (dubbed "my Giants" by an enthusiastic Mutrie) rose to the thick of a pennant race with Chicago. At the finish Chicago was on top by two games, but the Giants had won more than three games out of four for a .759 winning percentage that is not only the club's best ever, but one of the highest in major-league history. Pitchers Keefe and Mickey Welch together won 76 of the team's 85 victories, and first-baseman Roger Connor led the league in batting.

The Giants won their first pennant in 1888 by nine games over Chicago, and their second the next year in a one-game squeaker over Boston. Keefe and Welch, still going strong, combined for 61 wins in '88 and 55 in '89. Continuing their winning ways in the World Series, the Giants triumphed easily over St. Louis in 1888, and overcame a 1-3 deficit to vanquish Brooklyn the next year.

In 1890, ravaged by the loss of players to the rival Players League, the Giants finished sixth, but they recovered several players when the PL folded at the end of the season. (They also moved into the PL ballpark, named it after their original Polo Grounds, and played there 67 years). They rose to third in 1891, but Day could no longer afford to maintain the team and sold out to financier Edward Talcott. Talcott brought back former Giant star J. M. Ward to manage the club, and in 1894 saw the team rise to a close second-place finish behind Baltimore. Pitchers Amos Rusie and Jouett Meekin tied for the league lead with 36 wins apiece. In postseason Temple Cup play, the Giants swept Baltimore in four games for their third world championship.

That winter Talcott sold control of the club to Tammany Hall politician Andrew Freedman. Giant fortunes sank under Freedman's abrasive and heavy-handed rule. As he ran through a succession of managers, the Giants fell to ninth (of twelve clubs) in 1895 and—apart from a third-place finish in 1897—rose no higher than seventh while he controlled the franchise. In 1902, his final year of ownership, the Giants suffered their lowest winning percentage—.353—and most distant finish ever—53½ games behind champion Pittsburgh.

In the midst of the 1902 season, though, a skirmish in the war between the NL and the upstart American League led to a Giant turnaround. John T. Brush, owner of the NL Cincinnati Reds, bought the AL Baltimore Orioles, then released Oriole manager John McGraw and several key players to sign with NL clubs. Five joined the Giants, including McGraw, catcher Roger Bresnahan, and pitcher Joe "Iron Man" McGinnity. That winter, Brush sold the Reds and Orioles and bought the Giants.

In 1903, with Bresnahan hitting .350 and McGinnity winning a league-high 31 games (closely followed by third-year Giant Christy Mathewson's 30 wins), manager McGraw saw his Giants win thirty-six more games than they had in 1902 and finish a solid second in the standings. In McGraw's twenty-nine full seasons at the helm, the team would win ten pennants and finish second eleven times.

Just two years after their worst season ever, McGraw in 1904 led the Giants to one of their best. Their 106 wins and 13-game winning margin remain Giant highs to this day. The club led the NL in pitching, hitting, fielding, and base stealing. McGinnity led league pitchers in several categories with a career-best 35–8, 1.61 ERA season. Mathewson, right behind with 33 wins, led the league in strikeouts.

The only Giant disappointment of 1904 was McGraw's refusal to face Boston in a World Series. His rejection of the AL champions as worthy opponents was the last shot fired in the war between the two leagues. By the time the Giants had repeated as NL pennant winners a year later, the World Series was an official and permanent feature of the baseball landscape. Mathewson led NL pitchers in 1905 with 31 wins and an ERA of 1.27, and outfielder "Turkey Mike" Donlin, acquired from Cincinnati the previous July, erupted with the best season of his career, batting a team-high .356 and scoring a league-high 124 runs. The Giants won only one game less than the year before and held a comfortable lead throughout the season. Matty's three shutouts against the Philadelphia Athletics in the World Series secured the club's fourth world crown.

It was 1911 before the Giants won their next pennant. Despite 96 wins in 1906 they finished a distant second to Chicago's mighty Cubs, who won a record 116 games. In 1908 the Giants came within a disputed play of the pennant. On September 23, playing Chicago (with whom they were tied at the top of a three-way race), Giant baserunner Fred Merkle failed to run to second on a single by Al Bridwell that would have driven in the winning run from third. Merkle was forced at second after the ball (or a second ball—the argument still rages) was recovered amid the horde of fans who overran the field. The force out at second negated the run, and the game was ruled a tie. At season's end, when the two clubs found themselves again tied at the top, the "Merkle boner" game was replayed. The Cubs won the game and flag, leaving the Giants in a second-place tie with Pittsburgh.

In 1911 the Giants pulled away from the Cubs in September for the first of three straight pennants. (Early in the season most of the Polo Grounds was rebuilt in concrete after fire destroyed the wooden stands.) The following year the Giants took the lead in May and held it comfortably the rest of the way. In 1913 they didn't move into first until late June, but then quickly put the flag out of reach and finished 12½ games ahead of the faltering Phillies. Mathewson led the team in victories over the three years, with 74, followed closely by Rube Marquard (who with 73 wins enjoyed the three best seasons of his career). Matty led the NL in ERA in 1911 and 1913; Giant rookie Jeff Tesreau took the honors in 1912 (winning 17 games that season and 22 the next). Giant pitching led the league all three seasons, as did their hitting, which featured a balanced offense paced by infielders Larry Doyle and Art Fletcher and catcher John "Chief" Meyers.

In the World Series, though, the Giants three times fell short of the title. Philadelphia's Athletics defeated them handily in 1911 and 1913, but the Giants carried the 1912 Series against the Boston Red Sox to the tenth inning of the final game before a pair of Giant fielding lapses enabled Boston to rally for the win.

Boston's "miracle" Braves, in their 1914 surge from last place to the pennant, passed the front-running Giants for good in early September. The next year, five of the eight NL clubs found themselves bunched within 3½ games of one another at the lower end of the standings as the season ended—with the Giants at the very bottom. And in a 1916 Giant season characterized by dips and surges, even a 26-game winning streak in September couldn't raise the team higher than fourth. But in 1917 a balanced pitching staff—paced by Ferdie Schupp's one big season (21–7, 1.95 ERA)—hurled the Giants to the front early in June and kept them there to the finish. Once more, though, the World Series proved a disappointment, with a loss to the Chicago White Sox in six games.

Three years of second-place finishes followed, in the midst of which the Giants changed owners. Brush had died in 1912 and was succeeded as president by his son-in-law Harry Hempstead. But in January 1919 Brush's heirs sold the club to financier and racehorse fancier Charles A. Stoneham, with manager McGraw a minority stockholder.

In 1921 McGraw brought home the first of four straight winners for Stoneham. Seven regulars hit over .300 (led by third baseman Frank Frisch's .341); first baseman

George Kelly's 23 home runs topped the NL. The club hung close to Pittsburgh through August, then broke into a lead which the fading Pirates could not challenge. In postseason play the Giants lost the first two games to the Yankees, but charged back to win their fifth world title. The next year outfielder Emil "Irish" Meusel celebrated his first full season in New York with a team-high 132 RBI, as the Giants fended off a midseason challenge from St. Louis to pull away to a comfortable margin at the end. The World Series was especially sweet: a four-game sweep of the Yankees.

Cincinnati and Pittsburgh hung just behind the Giants through much of 1923, but never quite caught up. The Giants' league-leading offense was led by individual NL highs in RBI (Meusel), runs scored (outfielder Ross Youngs), and hits and total bases (Frisch). But the Yankees finally caught the Giants in the World Series, 4–2.

George Kelly took the NL RBI title in 1924. The club's hitting remained the league's best, and by early August the Giants had taken a ten-game lead. But they then leveled off while Brooklyn and Pittsburgh surged. Brooklyn, in fact, took over the lead for a day in early September, but the Giants emerged triumphant at the end by 1½ games. The World Series, though, was as heartbreaking as the pennant race had been heartstopping: the Giants lost to Washington in the last of the twelfth inning of the seventh game when a Senator grounder bounced over the head of rookie third baseman Fred Lindstrom to drive in the Series-ending run.

Close finishes—2 games out—in 1927 and 1928 were the nearest McGraw's Giants came to another pennant. Player relations with the demanding manager had seldom been harmonious, and they had reached a low point when, ill and tired, he quit early in the 1932 season with the team in last place, naming first baseman Bill Terry to replace him. Under Terry the Giants rose only to sixth that season, but McGraw had built a squad fit for a new era of greatness. He had persuaded Terry to leave a career with Standard Oil for one with the Giants; he had saved Mel Ott's unique but effective batting stance from revision by well-meaning minor league managers by keeping Ott out of the minors; and he had rescued pitcher Carl Hubbell from mediocrity by encouraging the screwball pitch other managers had tried to suppress.

Hubbell and Ott formed the heart of the club that would win a trio of pennants under Terry's management. In 1933 the Giants moved to the front in June and, despite a late-September slump, finished well ahead of runner-up Pittsburgh. Ott, with what was for him an off-year, powered the Giant offense with 23 homers and 103 RBI, while Hubbell led the league in wins, shutouts, and ERA. Hubbell also hurled two wins against Washington in the World Series, and Ott won it all for New York with a tenth-inning home run in Game Five. McGraw, still the club's vice president, threw a party for "his" Giants after the Series. The following February he died, at age sixty.

As they had the previous season, the Giants of 1934 emerged from the crowd to take and hold first place into late September. They rose higher than they had in 1933 and didn't slump as far at the end. But their five end-of-season losses were enough to drop them 2 games behind the surging Cardinals at the finish. Again in 1935 they led the league much of the season. But they had begun to level off in mid-July and finished the season well back in third. Charles Stoneham died in January 1936, and his son Horace—who at age thirty-three had already run the club for a year—assumed the club presidency.

In 1936, and again in 1937, the Giants came from behind to take the flag. Hubbell sparked their second-half resurgence in 1936, winning his final 16 decisions of the season as the Giants rose from fourth to first. In the World Series, though, Hubbell, after one win, was stopped by the Yankees in his try for a second. The Yankees took the Series in six games.

Again the next year the Giants hid behind the leaders most of the season until a surge in late August coincided with a Chicago decline and shot the Giants to the front. The Cubs recovered, but New York continued its winning ways and finished ahead by 3 games. But again the Yankees dominated the World Series, winning in five games.

Hubbell's years of greatness were now over, and while the Giants led the NL through the first half of 1938, they finished third, 5 games out. It would be twelve years before they again finished that close to the top. Mel Ott replaced Terry as manager in 1942, but the Giants sank to the cellar in 1943 with their second-worst season ever, and finished last again three years later. One bright spot: in 1947 they rose to fourth with a barrage of 221 home runs (led by Johnny Mize's 51) that remained the major league record (though tied by Cincinnati in 1956) until the 1961 Yankees topped it with 240.

Halfway through the 1948 season the baseball world was startled to learn that Leo Durocher, the fiery manager of the Brooklyn Dodgers, had switched his allegiance to their arch foes, the Giants. Durocher discarded the three top Giant home run hitters of 1947 (but presciently retained the fourth, Bobby Thomson), and added agile infielders Alvin Dark and Eddie Stanky to the roster. By 1950, with the blossoming of Sal Maglie into a first-rank pitcher and the timely midseason purchase of hurler Jim Hearn, the Giants were once more a challenger, spurting in the second half from below .500 to within 5 games of the top.

After losing their first eleven games the next year, the Giants began a long climb. A sixteen-game August winning streak and a seven-game streak at season's end tied them with Brooklyn and forced a three-game playoff. After a win and a loss, the Giants entered the last of the ninth inning of Game Three trailing 1–4. Two singles and a double cut the deficit by a run and brought on Dodger Ralph Branca to face Bobby Thomson, whose two-run homer had provided the Giants' margin of victory in Game One. Thomson homered again, and the Giants won the pennant. Their defeat by the Yankees in the World Series dimmed the miracle a bit, but couldn't detract from the career bests of pitchers Maglie and Larry Jansen, who tied for the NL lead with 23 wins apiece, and of former Negro League great Monte Irvin, who hit .312 and led the league in RBI.

The next year Irvin was lost until August with a broken ankle, Jansen (with a back problem) fell off to 11–11, and Willie Mays—a promising rookie in 1951—left early in the season for a hitch in the Army. Still, the Giants hung close to Brooklyn for much of the summer and finished second. In 1953, though, they fell apart in midseason and wound up in fifth, 35 games out.

Mays returned in 1954 to enjoy one of his strongest seasons at the bat, and pitchers Johnny Antonelli (newly acquired from Milwaukee), sophomore Ruben Gomez, and reliever Marv Grissom all burst forth with the best seasons of their careers. The Giants pulled away from Brooklyn in July and held on with a late-season rush to finish 5 games up. Underdogs to powerful Cleveland in the World Series, they stunned the Indians (and the rest of the baseball world) with a four-game sweep. It was their eighth world title—and, so far, their last.

Manager Durocher retired after a distant third-place finish in 1955, and Bill Rigney, who replaced him (the first of seven straight rookie managers to be hired by the Giants over the next twenty years), presided over a pair of sixth-place seasons in the club's final years in New York. Persuaded by the Dodgers' Walter O'Malley that California was the land of baseball opportunity, Giant owner Horace Stoneham announced in August 1957 his decision to move the club to San Francisco before the next season.

The move succeeded. Home attendance doubled, even though the team had to play in a former minor league park that seated fewer than 23,000 fans. When new Candlestick Park opened in 1960 attendance climbed to nearly 1.8 million, a new club high. Better still, rookie sensations like Orlando Cepeda in 1958 and Willie McCovey in 1959, plus the continuing mastery of Willie Mays, made the Giants competitive once again. In their first fourteen San Francisco seasons, they compiled winning records— a longer string than they had known in all their years in New York.

Candlestick Park, though, proved a cold and windy place to watch baseball, and after its inaugural season fans began to drift away. Attendance picked up some in 1962, however, as the Giants battled for first all summer with the Los Angeles Dodgers. Mays, Cepeda, and Felipe Alou headlined the league's best offense, and a pair of veteran pitchers—Jack Sanford and Billy O'Dell—garnered the most wins of their careers (24 and 19) as part of a balanced staff that also got 16 wins from veteran Billy Pierce and 18 from the emerging great Juan Marichal. Still, the Giants trailed the Dodgers most of the season until a Dodger loss and Giant win on the final day threw the teams into a tie and another playoff. As in 1951, the Giants won the first game and lost the second, and overcame a ninth-inning deficit in the finale to win the pennant. Also as in 1951, they lost the World Series to the Yankees, although this time they held on until the final out of Game Seven—a screaming liner off the bat of Willie McCovey into the glove of Bobby Richardson—before losing their grip on the crown.

The 1963 Giants offered little challenge to the leaders after June, but the next three years found them locked to the end in tight struggles for the flag. Although they finished fourth in 1964, they were still in contention with just two games to play, in one of the closest four-way races ever. The next year they took the lead from the Dodgers early in September, only to lose it in the final week. And in 1966, in a season-long three-way race with the Dodgers and Pirates, the Giants weren't eliminated until the final day.

The turbulence of these races was reflected in the team itself. Cepeda (until traded to St. Louis in 1966) continually railed against his managers and his low pay. Alvin Dark, after four winning seasons as manager, was fired in 1964 when some of his racist comments ended up in print. And Marichal was fined and suspended for nine days in 1965 for hitting Dodger catcher John Roseboro over the head with his bat.

After a pair of distant second-place finishes, the Giants in 1969 (with the fine work of Marichal and McCovey augmented by the speed and power of young outfielder Bobby Bonds) found themselves in the thick of a five-way race for the championship of the newly created NL West. The race wasn't settled until the final week, when Atlanta's ten-game winning streak knocked the Giants out of first. Two years later, with Bonds the chief source of offensive power and fine pitching from starters Marichal and Gaylord Perry and reliever Jerry Johnson, the Giants moved out in front at the start of the season and held their lead all the way. A September slump coinciding with a Dodger surge narrowed the lead to one game in midmonth, but the Giants held on for the division crown. In their first experiences with a League Championship Series, though, they succumbed to Pittsburgh with three losses after an opening-game win.

The LCS loss signaled the end of an era. McCovey was past his prime and Marichal had enjoyed his last big year. Mays, after twenty Giant seasons, was sold to the Mets in 1972 so he could close out his career in New York, where it began. That year the Giants suffered their first losing season in San Francisco, and attendance for the first time dropped below what it had been in their final New York season.

Attendance had reached such a low point by the mid-1970s that Stoneham negotiated the club's sale to a Canadian brewery which planned to move it to Toronto. But San Francisco's mayor George Moscone delayed the sale until a buyer could be found who would keep the Giants in the city. San Francisco realtor Robert Lurie stepped forth with half the purchase price, and Arizona cattleman Arthur "Bud" Herseth provided the rest. (Toronto settled for an expansion club, the Blue Jays.)

After six years out of the running, the Giants in 1978 played at the top of the NL East through much of the summer before dropping to third (and home attendance jumped more than a million above the previous year). But they fell below .500 the next two years—making seven losing seasons in the nine that followed their division title of 1971.

In 1982 the Giants—paced by the slugging of Jack Clark and Greg Minton's sparkling relief pitching—made one of the most impressive comebacks since divisional play was instituted in 1969, driving from ten games below .500 in late June to just 2 games from champion Atlanta at season's end. But they dropped to fifth the following year, and to a last-place sixth in 1984 and 1985.

When Roger Craig was called on to manage the final weeks of the 1985 season, there was no stopping the Giants' slide to a club-record 100 losses. But the next year, inspiring a "can do" spirit among the players, Craig turned the club around. Veteran hurler Mike Krukow won a career-high 20 games, eight players contributed more than 40 RBI each, and the team captured 26 of their 83 wins in their final at-bat. In first place at midseason, the Giants slipped (in part because of injuries) to third by season's end, but the fans were back—over 700,000 more than a year earlier.

The club set a new home attendance record of more than 1.9 million in 1987 as it returned to the top of the NL West for the first time in sixteen years. Sophomore first baseman Will Clark led a balanced offense, and several shrewd in-season acquisitions by the front office spurred a second-half drive from five games back to a 6-game lead at the finish. But after taking a 3–2 advantage over St. Louis in the LCS, the Giants failed to score in the final two games and the Cardinals captured the flag.

Injuries contributed to the Giants' decline to fourth place the next year, but in 1989 Will Clark enjoyed his strongest season yet, and left fielder Kevin Mitchell erupted with league-high power (47 HRs, 125 RBI, .635 slugging) to lead another successful Giant assault on the division title. For the first time, the Giants passed the 2 million mark in home attendance. After holding first place from mid-June to the finish, they pushed past the stubborn Cubs in the LCS to their first pennant in twenty-seven years, their nineteenth over all. But the earthquake that delayed Game 3 of the World Series only postponed a sweep by mighty Oakland.

The Giants' downward slide over the next three years—to third place in 1990, fourth in 1991, and fifth in 1992—coincided with futile efforts to persuade Bay area voters to approve public funding for a new stadium to replace unpopular Candlestick Park. In August 1992, Giant owner Bob Lurie arranged to sell the club to a group of investors who planned to move it to St. Petersburg, Florida. In November, though, the sale and move were blocked by the other major league owners.

The signing of free agent Barry Bonds ignited a Giant turnaround in 1993. As Bonds put together another Ruthian season, and Matt Williams rebounded from his worst season to his best, starting pitchers John Burkett and Bill Swift developed into twenty-game winners and closer Rod Beck saved the second most games (48) in NL history. The Giants lost their once-big lead to surging Atlanta in September, but revived to tie the Braves with three games to go. Although a final-game loss to Los Angeles cost them the division title, their 103 wins tied for third best in club history.

On August 11, 1994, the Giants stood five games below .500, but only 3½ games out of first place in the weak NL West. Barry Bonds was enjoying another fine season at the bat, but Matt Williams stole the headlines: with 43 home runs he was challenging Roger Maris's major league single season record of 61. When the players went out on strike the next day, one of the most exciting offensive seasons ever went down the drain.

In 1995 manager Dusty Baker's Giants fell to last (67-77) despite Barry Bonds's 33 homers and 104 RBI. The Giants (68-94) remained in the NL basement in 1996 as Bonds again compiled superstar numbers.

Seattle Mariners

The Mariners began play in 1977, returning major league baseball to the Pacific Northwest eight years after the

Seattle Pilots had moved to Milwaukee after only one season. With a 64–98 inaugural season, the Mariners avoided last place in the American League West only because the Oakland A's had plummeted faster and farther. The hitting of first baseman Dan Meyer, outfielder Leroy Stanton, and rookie center fielder Ruppert Jones—who combined for 73 home runs—and the relief pitching of rookie Enrique (Romo) Romero, who contributed 16 saves and 8 wins, provided most of the high points of that first season.

There was less to cheer about the next year as the production of the first-season heroes fell off and the Mariners took possession of the cellar from mid-May on, losing a club-record 104 games. They finished 12 games out of sixth place, 35 out of first. Much of the offense that was generated came from outfielder Leon Roberts. Acquired from Houston over the winter, Roberts put together his best season and became the Mariners' first .300 hitter.

The club moved up a notch in 1979, to sixth place. Meyer and Jones regained much of their 1977 power, first baseman Bruce Bochte hit .316 and drove in 100 runs, and DH Willie Horton, near the end of a long career, enjoyed one of his finest seasons, driving in 106 runs and leading the club with 29 homers.

As the Mariners, with the league's weakest hitting, dropped back into the cellar the next season, attendance fell to a new low, and some of the original owners decided to sell out. In January 1981 California real-estate magnate George Argyros purchased control of the club, and later bought out the remaining partners to take sole ownership.

In strike-divided 1981 the Mariners finished sixth and fifth in the two halves of the season. Second baseman Julio Cruz continued among the league's top base stealers, and right fielder Tom Paciorek's second-place .326 BA put a Seattle hitter high among the league's best for the first time. Paciorek was traded away that winter, but his replacement, veteran Al Cowens, came through with one of his best seasons in 1982. And Mariner pitching improved dramatically—from the bottom of the league in ERA in 1981 to fourth best in '82. Newcomers Bill Caudill and rookie Ed Vande Berg, working in relief, combined for 21 wins and 31 saves. Starter Floyd Bannister led the league in strikeouts while winning 12 games (tying Caudill for the team lead), and veteran Gaylord Perry added 10 victories, including his 300th career win in May. The team finished above .450 for the first time, fourth in the AL West, a new high.

Caudill's 26 saves in 1983 couldn't prevent a slide back into last place. But the club's farm system was beginning to produce quality talent, and 1984 saw the arrival of two standouts: first baseman Alvin Davis, whose 27 homers and 116 RBI earned him AL Rookie of the Year honors, and pitcher Mark Langston, a 17-game winner in 1984 and AL strikeout leader in three of his first four seasons. Rookie third baseman Jim Presley hit 10 home runs in 70 games and proceeded to blossom into one of the Seattle club's leading power hitters the next year.

After sixth-place finishes in 1984 and '85, the Mariners fell off to last again in 1986. Langston's 19 wins led the team's 1987 rebound to fourth, with Lee Guetterman's 11–4 pitching and the power of Davis and Presley providing valuable assists. Infielder Harold Reynolds stole his sixtieth base in the final game to preserve his lead in that department and to give the Mariners their first league leader in an offensive category.

After dropping back into the cellar in 1988 and rising a notch to sixth in 1989, the Mariners revived under new ownership in 1990 to challenge the .500 barrier. Center fielder Ken Griffey, Jr., began to fulfill the promise he had shown as a nineteen-year-old rookie the previous summer. Sophomore hurler Erik Hanson—with 18 wins and an ERA among the league's best—replaced the traded Mark Langston as ace of a young pitching staff that compiled the league's third lowest ERA. The Mariners entered August third in the strong AL West, with a winning record which they maintained through mid-month before stumbling to fifth place with their fourteenth straight losing season.

At last, in 1991, Seattle produced its first winning season, rising from an even .500 with six wins in the final eight games. Griffey Jr. overcame a lackluster first half to reach new Mariner heights in batting (.327) and slugging (.527), but the club still finished fifth, and manager Jim Lefebvre was fired. It also continued to lose money, so in June 1992, as the Mariners sailed for the sixth time toward the bottom of the AL West, the club was sold. The new ownership group included (for the first time) substantial local representation, but as major financing came from Hiroshi Yamauchi, the Japanese president of computer game giant Nintendo, and his son-in-law, a Washington State resident but Japanese national, the sale was delayed until jingoistic opposition to it subsided. The deal was restructured to insure American control of the club. On the field Griffey enjoyed another strong season, and third baseman Edgar Martinez hit .343 to give Seattle its first league batting champion.

A torn hamstring sidelined Martinez much of 1993, but Griffey shone brighter than ever at the bat, and pitcher Randy Johnson finished with nine straight wins (for a 19–8 season record) and 308 strikeouts (a fifteen-year AL high). Their exploits lifted the Mariners into third place for a day in late September before they settled into fourth, with their second winning season ever.

In 1994 the Mariners again enjoyed stellar performances from Griffey and Johnson, but despite six straight wins before the season ended in August, they wound up fourteen games below .500. In the weak AL West, though, their ministreak brought them within two games of division leader Texas—and a third place finish, their highest ever.

After a long climb during the 1995 season, the Mariners (paced by Edgar Martinez's league-leading .356 average and Randy Johnson's league-leading 294 strikeouts and 2.48 ERA) caught the Angels in the AL West division race and forced a one-game playoff. Behind Johnson, Seattle took the game and went on to nip the wild-card New York Yankees in the first round of the postseason in one of the most exciting series in baseball history. But in the ALCS the powerhouse Indians proved too much for Seattle, defeating them 4-2.

Injuries to Johnson and Edgar Martinez hampered the 1996 Mariners and they slipped to second (85-76) despite shortstop Alex Rodriguez's ML-best .358 average and 54 doubles.

Tampa Bay Devil Rays

Along with the Arizona Diamondbacks, the Tampa Bay Devil Rays were granted a $130 million major league expansion franchise on March 9, 1995 and are scheduled to begin league play in 1998.

Several times the area had come close to winning a major league franchise. The White Sox had planned to move to St. Petersburg and only remained in the Windy City when funding was approved for a new Comiskey Park. The Mariners had considered moving to St. Petersburg in 1991. And in late 1992 a Tampa Bay group led by businessman Vince Naimoli thought it had purchased the San Francisco Giants from Bob Lurie for $115 million, but NL owners voted against moving the club from one Bay Area to another. Naimoli was eventually awarded the Devil Rays franchise and he named former Atlanta Braves Assistant GM Chuck LaMar as the club's first General Manager.

The team will play in St. Petersburg's ThunderDome (original cost: $150 million). It was estimated it would take another $50 million to prepare the facility for major league baseball.

Texas Rangers

As part of the first American League expansion, a new Washington club was added to the league in November 1960, to replace the old Senators, who were moving to Minnesota to become the Twins. The old Senators had languished in the second division their final 14 years in Washington, and the new Senators scarcely improved on that record. In each of their first four seasons they lost 100 games or more, tying for last place in 1961 and holding down the bottom all by themselves for two years before rising to ninth in 1964.

Although as an expansion team the new Senators had to make do at first with expendable players from the established clubs, they were not devoid of talent. In their first season, pitcher Dick Donovan led the league with a 2.40 earned run average, though injuries and the lack of offensive support held his won-lost record to 10–10. Perhaps their most promising player, he was traded with two teammates to Cleveland for outfielder Jimmy Piersall. Piersall proved a major disappointment in Washington, batting only .244 while Donovan was winning 20 games for his new club.

Not all the Senators' trades proved disastrous. In late 1964 they sent another promising pitcher—Claude Osteen—to the Dodgers in a deal that brought them five players, including third baseman Ken McMullen and outfielder Frank Howard. Osteen blossomed into a consistent winner in Los Angeles, but at the same time, McMullen brought strength to the Washington infield and Howard became one of the league's offensive stars.

The Senators' blend of youth and experience jelled in 1969 under rookie manager Ted Williams, as several key players—including McMullen and Howard—enjoyed career-best seasons. The club finished above .500 for the first time, driving with a late-season spurt to within a game of third-place Boston in the league's Eastern Division.

But 1969 was a one-year phenomenon. After losing seasons in 1970 and '71 (and the loss of much of their fan support), owner Bob Short pulled up stakes and moved the club to Arlington, Texas (midway between Fort Worth and Dallas), where, as the Texas Rangers, they have been ever since. Their first summer in Texas resembled their first in Washington: they lost 100 games (despite a strike-shortened season) and finished last. Williams was replaced by a new rookie manager—Whitey Herzog—but the club did no better in 1973.

Before the season's end Herzog gave way to Billy Martin. Martin came too late to save the Rangers from another lost season, but the next year he spurred the team to the kind of turnaround Williams had managed five years earlier. Behind the 25–12 pitching of Ferguson Jenkins (acquired in the offseason from the Cubs) and the hitting of league MVP Jeff Burroughs and rookie first baseman Mike Hargrove, the Rangers spurted in the second half of 1974 from a sub-.500 record to second place in the American League West, only 5 games behind Oakland.

Since 1974 the Rangers' fortunes have been up and down. After two losing seasons they rebounded in 1977 to their finest season yet (94–68, .580) and second place, behind strong pitching and the blooming of Jim Sundberg as a hitter to go along with his league-leading catching. Fergie Jenkins's return to the club (after two years in Boston), the sparkling 11–5 season of rookie Steve Comer, and a September surge kept the club competitive in 1978. Jim Kern's brilliant relief work the next season helped the club recover from a nosedive in July and August to edge the Minnesota Twins for a strong third-place finish.

After a losing season in 1980, the Rangers bounced back in 1981 to record their second-best winning percentage ever (.543)—and finishes of second and third in the two halves of the strike-divided season. Then they slipped below .500 again for four more years. Pitcher Charlie Hough's knuckleball, and strong seasons at the bat from Pete O'Brien, Larry Parrish, Scott Fletcher and rookie Pete Incaviglia helped new manager Bobby Valentine turn the Rangers around once again in 1986, lifting them to the club's fifth second-place finish after last-place seasons in 1984 and '85.

Once more, though, the turnaround was brief: in 1987 losses in their final games of the season dropped the Rangers into a tie at the bottom of the division, and in 1988 they finished only two games out of the cellar, in sixth place.

A group of investors headed by George W. Bush—the President's son—purchased control of the Rangers in March 1989, and strikeout king Nolan Ryan returned to the American League as a Ranger after nine years in Houston. The strong arms of starter Ryan (who recorded his 5,000th career strikeout during the season) and reliever Jeff Russell, the potent bats of outfielder Ruben Sierra and second baseman Julio Franco (newly acquired from the Cleveland Indians), and a 10–1 start that put the club in first place for a month highlighted a Ranger return to the winning side of the ledger. In 1990 Ryan hurled his 300th win and sixth no-hitter, first baseman Rafael Palmeiro peaked at the plate, and pitcher Bobby Witt enjoyed his finest season, with 17 wins. After a slow first

half, the Rangers rose from sixth place to third, compiling an 83–79 record identical to that of the year before.

A fourteen-game win streak in May 1991 boosted the Rangers into first place for several days, although they again finished third. Jose Guzman joined Ryan (who threw a sixth no-hitter) among the league's top pitchers, and young slugger Juan Gonzalez formed with Franco, Palmeiro, and Sierra a powerful quartet that made the Rangers the top scoring team in the majors. In 1992 pitcher Kevin Brown won 21 games, and Gonzalez topped the majors in home runs. But an overall decline in offense, coupled with disastrous fielding and relief pitching, dropped the team below .500 after a competitive first half. In the year's biggest in-season trade, the club acquired Jose Canseco from Oakland for Sierra, Witt, and Russell.

The Rangers surged to within a game of first place in mid-July 1993, and remained competitive into September, finishing second, eight games out. Canseco injured his elbow in a relief pitching stint in June and was lost for the season, but Gonzalez again led the league in home runs (with 46), while also leading his team in batting and RBI. Nolan Ryan retired after an injury-shortened season, and as the Rangers ended their tenure at Texas Stadium, their new home—"The Ballpark At Arlington"—arose on the other side of the parking lot.

In the weak American League West of 1994, it didn't matter that the Rangers played losing ball in their new park. Despite their worst record in six years—a .456 winning percentage that would have consigned them to the cellar of the East or Central divisions—season's end found the Rangers a game ahead of the Oakland Athletics, improbably in first place.

Texas's won-lost percentage improved to .538 in 1995 but that was only good enough for third. Ranger standouts included Mickey Tettleton (32 HR), Will Clark (92 RBI), and Kenny Rogers (17-7).

In 1996 the Rangers (90-72) won their first division title on the heavy hitting of MVP Juan Gonzalez (47 HR, 144 RBI), Dean Palmer (38 HR, 107 RBI), and Kevin Elster (24 HR, 99 RBI). The Rangers boasted an unusually well-balanced rotation—Ken Hill (16-10), Roger Pavlik (15-8), Bobby Witt (16-12), and Darren Oliver (14-6)—along with reliever Mike Henneman (31 saves) and late season addition John Burkett (5-2). The Yankees, however, rolled over Texas in the first round of the postseason.

Toronto Blue Jays

For a while, in February 1976, it looked as if the National League's San Francisco Giants would move to Toronto, where there were buyers eager for the club. But when the Giants were sold in March to new owners determined to keep them in San Francisco, the American League jumped in to establish Toronto as an American League city, setting up an expansion club, the Blue Jays, who began play the next year.

It took seven years for the Jays to lift themselves out of last place in the seven-team AL East. For five years they had the cellar all to themselves, never finishing closer than 11 games behind the *sixth*-place club.

In their first season, the Jays' 107 losses left them 45½ games out of first, as the team performed at the bottom of the division in hitting, fielding, and pitching. In 1978 their fielding improved dramatically, but the Jays still lost over 100 games, and there was little doubt after April who would finish last.

The next year was the team's worst ever. While every other Eastern Division club was compiling a winning record, Toronto plunged relentlessly downward and, despite a brief rally in September, finished 28½ games out of sixth place (50½ out of first), with 109 losses.

The club's turnaround began in 1980. It was late June before the Jays began their drop away from the rest of the division, and for the first time they finished with fewer than 100 losses. Pitchers Jim Clancy and Dave Stieb lowered their ERAs below 4.00 for the first time, and newly acquired second baseman Damaso Garcia combined with shortstop Alfredo Griffin to form the league's best double-play combination. There were still two more seasons in the cellar, but in strike-divided 1981 the Jays played a creditable second half for the first time, and in 1982 they spurted in September to tie the Indians for sixth at season's end. Garcia in 1982 became a .300 hitter and a leading base stealer, Clancy put together his first winning season and Stieb his second, and Stieb's five shutouts led the league.

In 1983, with seven of the Blue Jays' eight principal pitchers enjoying winning seasons, and the Jays' hitters leading the league in team batting and slugging, Toronto recorded its first winning season—in fourth place, only 9 games out of first. Their balanced pitching and offense carried them to a repeat 89–73 record in 1984—this time for second place (though they finished a distant 15 games behind Detroit).

In 1985 the Blue Jays topped their division with 99 victories, edging the Yankees by 2 games. Their pitching was better than ever. Doyle Alexander won 17 games, Jimmy Key and Dave Stieb contributed 14 each, and reliever Dennis Lamp compiled an impressive 11–0 record. Stieb led the league in ERA, with Key fourth. Tony Fernandez, in his first full big league season, sparkled as expected at short, but also proved unexpectedly solid at the bat. Eight Jays drove in more than 50 runs, with outfielders George Bell (95), Jesse Barfield (84), and Lloyd Moseby (71) pacing the club's balanced attack.

In the LCS the Jays won three of their first four games against Kansas City, but lost the next three—and the pennant. Equally discouraging was their drop to fourth place in 1986. Barfield, Bell, and Fernandez all improved at the plate, but the league-leading pitchers of 1985 dropped back to the middle of the pack in '86 (though rookie Mark Eichorn sparkled in long relief).

Toronto sprang back stronger than ever in 1987. Jim Clancy (15–11, 3.54 ERA) enjoyed his best season yet, as did Jimmy Key (17–8), whose 2.76 ERA led the league. Once again, as in 1985, the team ERA was the league's lowest. And the offense remained strong. (George Bell, league RBI leader with 134, was named the American League MVP at season's end.) The Jays led their division going into the season's final series against second-place Detroit, though four straight losses had reduced the lead to just one game. Needing to win two of the three games to take the AL East title, or one to tie the Tigers and force

a playoff, the Jays' slumping bats remained quiet, and Toronto lost the first two games. In the season finale, Jimmy Key hurled a three-hitter, striking out eight. But one of the hits was a home run—the only run of the game, as it turned out. Toronto's seven-game losing streak had cost them what would have been their second title in three years.

In 1988, a rocky season made worse by George Bell's feud with manager Jimy Williams (who wanted the unwilling outfielder to serve as designated hitter), the Jays surged at the end—with six straight wins—into a tie for third place, only two games out of first. The season was highlighted by the emergence of Fred McGriff as one of the game's most powerful batsmen, and by ace Dave Stieb's two successive one-hitters in late September—both of which were no-hitters through 8⅔ innings.

When Toronto's front office replaced manager Williams with batting coach Cito Gaston in mid-May 1989, the Jays were drowning near the bottom of the AL East with a record of 12–24. By mid-August they had bobbed above .500 to stay, and on September 1 replaced Baltimore in first place. With a pair of one-run victories over the Orioles at the end of September, the Jays preserved their narrow lead and clinched the division title. But Oakland outplayed them in the LCS, taking the pennant in five games.

From mid-June 1990 to the final day of the season, the Blue Jays battled Boston for the division lead before settling for second. Dave Stieb (after two more one-hitters in 1989) at last hurled a no-hitter, and third baseman Kelly Gruber confirmed a place with Bell and McGriff among Toronto's power elite. But the brightest Toronto star of 1989–90 was the new SkyDome, with its 11,000-ton retractable roof and its restaurants and hotel rooms above the outfield wall. After the Jays moved into the Dome on June 5, 1989, attendance zoomed, and by season's end the club set a new American League home attendance record of nearly 3.4 million. In 1990, with a full season in the Dome, the Jays attracted over a half million more fans than the year before, for a new major league record of 3,885,284.

SkyDome attendance continued to set new records in 1991 and 1992 as it rose above 4 million. McGriff and Bell had departed by 1991, but an improved Devon White, plus newly acquired slugger Joe Carter and second baseman Roberto Alomar, led an offense that—together with the league's stingiest pitching staff—brought the Jays to their third divisional title. For the third time, though, they crashed in the LCS, this time trampled by Minnesota in five games. With the addition of a pair of free-agent veterans—pitcher Jack Morris (who went 21–6) and DH–outfielder Dave Winfield (108 RBI)—Toronto in 1992 finally completed the puzzle. The Jays sported a balanced offense (six players drove in 60 runs or more) and outstanding pitching from starter Juan Guzman (16–5; 2.64 ERA) and relievers Tom Henke and Duane Ward. Thus armed, they fended off Baltimore's challenge for the lead through much of the summer and resisted Milwaukee's late-season surge to repeat as AL East titlists. They then felled Oakland in six games to bring Canada its first major league baseball pennant, and stopped stubborn Atlanta in six games to carry home the championship of the world.

Nearly half the team was new in 1993, but after a tight battle with several clubs through most of the season, the Blue Jays pulled away to capture their fourth divisional title in five years, by a comfortable seven-game margin. John Olerud, with his first full .300 season at the bat, hit over .400 through the first half of the season and finished with a league-high .363. Paul Molitor, signed from Milwaukee as a free agent, hit better than anyone else in the league from midseason on, and finished second over all. Together with Roberto Alomar, Olerud and Molitor became the first teammates since 1893 to take the top three spots in a major league batting race. In postseason play the Jays repeated their success of the previous year, with six-game victories over the Chicago White Sox for the AL pennant and over Philadelphia for the world title.

The glory faded fast in 1994. At the July All-Star break the Blue Jays lay at the bottom of the AL East. While they pulled themselves up to third before the players' strike ended the season in August, they remained sixteen games out of first, their most distant finish and first losing season in a dozen years. The losing continued in 1995 as the Jays stripped their roster of most of the veterans of its World Championship squad. Toronto tied Minnesota for the dubious honor of posting MLB's worst record (56-88).

Toronto edged up slightly in 1996, to fourth (74-88) in the AL East. Standouts included Cy Young winner Pat Hentgen (20-10, 181 strikeouts) and Mike Timlin (31 saves).

Defunct Clubs

In addition to the many Negro League teams, some 110 ballclubs have played in the major leagues since the first professional association was formed in 1871. The twenty-eight that still do are described above; here are the other eighty-two, listed according to the league and year in which they first played major league baseball. The official club names precede the name of the city; nicknames follow.

National Association, 1871–1875

Two of the twenty-three clubs that played at one time or another in baseball's first professional league still play in the majors: the Atlanta Braves (then the Boston Red Stockings) and the Chicago Cubs (then the White Stockings). The other twenty-one:

Athletic of Philadelphia: NA 1871–1875, NL 1876. Organized in 1860 as an amateur club, the Athletics became one of the dominant teams of the decade. As professionals they won the first NA pennant in 1871. After one year in the NL, they were expelled for failing to make the final western trip of the season.

Forest City of Cleveland, NA 1871–1872. In the midst of a second losing season, the club disbanded in August 1872.

Forest City of Rockford, Ill., NA 1871. As an amateur club, Forest City (with its sixteen-year-old pitcher Al Spalding) was the only team to defeat the famous Washington Nationals on their pioneering midwestern tour of 1867. As professionals, Forest City finished seventh of the nine NA teams in 1871.

Kekionga of Fort Wayne, NA 1871. The Kekiongas won the first NA game ever played, but dropped out of the association before the end of the season.

Mutual of New York, NA 1871–1875, NL 1876. Organized as an amateur club in 1857, the Mutuals were said to be backed financially by New York's notorious William M. "Boss" Tweed. Frequently accused of corrupt practices, the club was one of the leading eastern teams of the late 1860s. They were declared national champions of 1868, and proclaimed themselves national champions of 1870. On the demise of the NA the Mutuals entered the NL, but were expelled after one season (along with the Athletics) for failing to play their final games in the West.

Olympic of Washington, D.C., NA 1871–1872. Unsuccessful in 1872 after playing well the year before, the Olympics disbanded about midseason.

Union of Troy, N.Y., NA 1871–1872. The Haymakers, as they were popularly known, dropped out of the NA halfway through the 1872 season.

Atlantic of Brooklyn, NA 1872–1875. One of the greatest of the amateur clubs, the Atlantics (organized in 1855) went undefeated in 1864 and 1865, and won three successive national championships, 1864–1866. But in four NA seasons their combined won-lost record was only 49–139, including a dismal 2–42 in 1875.

Eckford of Brooklyn, NA 1872. Another great early amateur club—like the Atlantics, organized in 1855—they won the national championship in 1862, and again (with an undefeated season of ten games) the next year. The Eckfords actually joined the NA in August 1871, replacing Kekionga, but their 1871 games were later erased from the record because they had failed to enter the association at the start of the season.

Lord Baltimore of Baltimore, NA 1872–1874. After twice finishing third, the Lord Baltimores (or "Canaries," for their yellow silk jerseys) disbanded two games before the end of the 1874 season, while in last place.

Mansfield of Middletown, Ct., NA 1872. Disbanded in late August.

National of Washington, D.C., NA 1872–1873, 1875. Organized as amateurs in 1859, the Nationals were the first eastern club to tour as far west as Chicago and St. Louis. After skipping the 1874 race, the Nationals re-entered the NA in 1875, but dropped out in July.

Maryland of Baltimore, NA 1873. Dropped out after only six games.

Philadelphia, NA 1873–1875. Known successively as the "White Stockings," "Pearls," and "Phillies," the team finished a strong second to Boston in their first season, but slipped to fourth and fifth the next two years.

Resolute of Elizabeth, N.J., NA 1873. Disbanded in August with a 2–21 record.

Hartford Dark Blues, NA 1874–1875, NL 1876–1877. After a weak first year, Hartford finished third in its next three seasons, as standings are reckoned today. But by the 1876 guidelines (which used the number of games won rather than winning percentage), Hartford that year placed second. In 1877 the club played its home games in Brooklyn, N.Y.

Centennial of Philadelphia, NA 1875. Dropped out in late May.

New Haven Elm Citys, NA 1875. Failed to play out their schedule.

St. Louis Brown Stockings, NA 1875, NL 1876–1877. George Bradley pitched all but 5 of the Browns' 39 wins in 1875, when they finished fourth, and all 45 victories in 1876, when they finished a strong third (in number of victories; they were second in winning percentage). With Bradley lost to Chicago the next year, St. Louis dropped below .500—and out of the league.

St. Louis Red Stockings, NA 1875. A successful amateur club that decided to take a fling at pro ball, the Red Stockings played only a few games in the NA.

Western of Keokuk, Iowa, NA 1875. Disbanded in mid-June.

National League, 1876–

When the NL was founded to replace the ill-organized NA, it included six of the stronger NA clubs plus independent clubs in Cincinnati and Louisville. The league's composition was in continual flux to the end of the century as clubs were dropped and added, shrinking the league to as few as six teams and expanding it to as many as twelve. Two clubs that first played major league ball in the NL still do: the Philadelphia Phillies and the San Francisco (originally New York) Giants, both organized in 1883. (The Boston and Chicago franchises—that continue to this day as the Atlanta Braves and Chicago Cubs—had their starts in the National Association.) Those that have not survived:

Cincinnati Red Stockings, NL 1876–1880. From last place in 1876 (and 1877, when their games were not counted because of the club's reorganization and failure to pay its dues), the Reds—with seven new regulars—rose to second in 1878, only to fall back to fifth in 1879, and last again in 1880. That fall, when they refused to accept a new rule abolishing liquor sales and Sunday baseball, they were dropped from league membership.

Louisville Grays, NL 1876–1877. The strong Louisville team led the league in mid-August, 1877, but seven suspicious losses to chief rivals Boston and Hartford dropped the Grays out of first place. After Boston clinched the pennant, Louisville revived to secure second place, but four players—including pitching ace Jim Devlin—were expelled from baseball for throwing games. Their expulsion showed the NL's determination to wipe out corruption, but it also caused the St. Louis Browns, who had planned to sign three of the four Louisville players for 1878, to resign from the league. Louisville, too, dropped out of the league before the next season, unable to find adequate replacements for the four.

Indianapolis Browns, NL 1878. Finished fifth of six teams.

Milwaukee Grays (or Cream Citys), NL 1878. Finished a last-place sixth.

Providence Grays, NL 1878–1885. One of the great teams in the NL's early years, Providence won pennants in 1879 and 1884, finishing no lower than third in seven of their eight seasons. In 1884, pitcher Charlie "Old Hoss" Radbourn won a record 59 games, then pitched the Grays to victory in baseball's first World Series with a three-game sweep of the American Association champion New York Mets. But as they dropped to fourth place the next year, finishing for the first time below .500, their fans deserted them. Late that autumn the club was dissolved.

Buffalo Bisons, NL 1879–1885. Buffalo moved up to the majors after winning the International Association pennant in 1878. Jim "Pud" Galvin pitched nearly 70 percent of Buffalo's victories as he led them to four first-division finishes in seven big league seasons. First baseman Dan Brouthers, in his five years with Buffalo, twice won the batting title and led NL sluggers five times.

Cleveland Blues, NL 1879–1884. Cleveland's fortunes rested in large measure with pitcher Jim McCormick (who also managed the club their first two seasons). In 1880, their best season, McCormick won a career-high 45 games to bring the Blues in third. In 1883 Cleveland was in first place when McCormick's injured arm put him out for the season after he had won twenty-three games. The Blues dropped to fourth. The club folded after a seventh-place finish in 1884, a season that saw McCormick and two other Blues jump to the UA.

Star of Syracuse, NL 1879. After finishing a close second to Buffalo in the International League in 1878, the Stars moved up with the Bisons to the NL, but disbanded after a single unsuccessful season.

Troy, N.Y., Trojans, NL 1879–1882. After four losing seasons the franchise was expelled to make room for a club in New York City.

Worcester, Mass., Brown Stockings, NL 1880–1882. After a pair of losing minor league seasons, Worcester was admitted to the NL to replace the defunct Stars of Syracuse. After finishing a respectable fifth in 1880, Worcester dropped into the cellar for two seasons before being ousted in 1883 for a new Philadelphia club.

Detroit Wolverines, NL 1881–1888. Buffalo's sale of its "big four" (Dan Brouthers, Hardy Richardson, Jack Rowe, and Deacon White) to Detroit late in 1885 transformed a perennial also-ran into a contender. The club finished second in 1886 and won the pennant in 1887. In a World Series played in ten different cities, the Wolverines trounced St. Louis ten games to five. In 1888, after finishing fifth, they expired.

Kansas City Cowboys, NL 1886. They finished seventh, 58½ games out.

Washington Senators, NL 1886–1889. In their four seasons, the Senators finished out of the cellar only once: next to last in 1887.

Indianapolis Hoosiers, NL 1887–1889. After dropping below Washington into the cellar in 1887, the Hoosiers and Senators traded places for their final two years.

American Association, 1882–1891

Three of the six clubs that formed the AA in 1882 still represent their cities in the majors today: Allegheny (Pittsburgh), Cincinnati, and St. Louis. Brooklyn, which entered the AA two years later, today represents Los Angeles. The others:

Athletic of Philadelphia, AA 1882–1890. After finishing a distant second in the AA's first season, the Athletics in 1883 took the pennant from St. Louis by a single game. First baseman Harry Stovey, who led AA batters in most offensive categories that year, was even more productive in 1884. But the A's dropped to seventh and never again challenged for the crown. Expelled from the AA after the 1890 season for financial reasons, they were replaced by the Philadelphia club from the defunct Players League.

Baltimore Orioles, AA 1882–1889, 1890–1891, NL 1892–1899. After eight seasons out of pennant contention (including four in last place), the Orioles dropped out of the AA to play minor league ball in 1890. But toward the end of the season, when Brooklyn's new franchise went under, the Orioles returned to complete Brooklyn's season (finishing a combined last). After rising to third in 1891, the AA's final year, the Orioles were invited into the expanding NL, where they dropped to a twelfth-place last (54½ games out) in 1892.

Ned Hanlon, hired to manage Baltimore early in the 1892 season, set about building a championship club. By 1894, with a lineup that included six future Hall of Famers, Hanlon led his club to a narrow pennant victory over New York, though the Giants swept the Orioles in the first Temple Cup World Series, 4–0.

For five years Hanlon's brand of scrappy, hustling play made the Orioles the terror of the NL. Led by shortstop Hughie Jennings and outfielders Willie Keeler and Joe Kelley, the club repeated as NL champions in 1895 and 1896, and finished second to Boston the next two years. They lost the Temple Cup to Cleveland (1–4) in 1895, but swept the Spiders the next year 4–0, and took the cup again in 1897, defeating Boston 4–1 in what turned out to be the Series swan song.

Baltimore owners Hanlon and Harry Von der Horst purchased a half-interest in the Brooklyn club in 1899 (retaining a half-interest in Baltimore), and switched Jennings, Kelley, and Keeler to Brooklyn. Hanlon also went over as manager, leaving third baseman John McGraw in charge of the Orioles. McGraw hit .391 and rookie pitcher Joe McGinnity won 28 games to bring the team in fourth. But Hanlon's Superbas won the pennant, and when the NL cut back to eight teams after the season, Baltimore got the ax.

Eclipse of Louisville/Louisville Colonels (or Cyclones), AA 1882–1891, NL 1892–1899. The club, which changed its official name from Eclipse to Louisville after the 1883 season, was one of only two teams to play all ten seasons of the major league AA. (St. Louis—the present Cardinals—was the other.) Louisville finished above .500 in five of its first six years, but only once in that time closed within ten games of the top—in 1884, when Guy Hecker's 52 wins brought the team in third. Slugger Pete Browning paced the Colonel offense in their early years, winning batting titles in 1882 (his rookie season), 1885 and 1886, and hammering a second-best .402 in 1887. (A bat made for him by woodworker John Hillerich inspired the creation of the Louisville Slugger.)

By 1889, though, the club had sunk to last place, finishing 66½ games out of first, with 111 losses. The next year, although Hecker and Browning defected to the outlaw PL, the club was less affected by deserters than other AA teams. The Colonels (paced by the league's best hitter, William "Chicken" Wolf, and its best pitcher, Scott Stratton) made one of the greatest turnarounds in big league history, winning the pennant by 10 games over second-place Columbus. In the World Series against Brooklyn, poor weather and small crowds ended play after the teams had tied once and won three apiece.

Even though the Colonels finished next to last in 1891, they were one of four clubs taken into the NL after the AA folded. They never finished higher than ninth in the NL,

and for three straight years (1894–1896) they occupied the cellar. When the league cut back from twelve teams to eight after the 1899 season, Louisville merged with the Pittsburgh Pirates.

Columbus Colts (or Senators), AA 1883–1884. From sixth place in 1883, Columbus climbed to second in 1884 behind the 34–13 pitching of rookie Ed Morris. But when the AA dropped back from twelve clubs to eight in 1885, Columbus was out.

Metropolitan of New York, AA 1883–1887. After success in minor league and independent play since 1880, the Mets entered the AA in 1883 as the association expanded from six clubs to eight. With 41 victories from pitcher Tim Keefe (who was picked up from disbanded Troy), the Mets finished fourth. The next season, with first baseman Dave Orr hitting .354 in his first full major league season and pitcher Jack Lynch matching Keefe with 37 wins apiece, the Mets won the AA pennant handily. But they lost baseball's first World Series to the Providence Grays. When manager Jim Mutrie, third baseman Dude Esterbrook, and pitcher Keefe were transferred in 1885 to the New York Giants (the two clubs had the same owner), the Mets sank to seventh place, where they finished in their final three seasons.

Indianapolis Blues, AA 1884. Finished eleventh of twelve clubs, 46 games behind.

Toledo Blue Stockings, AA 1884. Catcher Fleet Walker (who played in 42 games) and his brother Welday (5 games) were the major leagues' first black players—and the only blacks until Jackie Robinson broke the color bar for good in 1947.

Washington, D.C., AA 1884. The popularity of the city's UA Nationals proved too much for this inept AA club, which went under in early August.

Virginia of Richmond, AA 1884. When Washington disbanded in August, the Wilmington club of the Eastern League was invited to join the AA as its replacement. Wilmington declined (and later jumped to the UA), but Virginia—also a member of the EL—accepted the invitation and took over Washington's remaining games. Washington-Virginia finished a combined 24–81, in last place.

Cleveland Spiders, AA 1887–1888, NL 1889–1899. After two losing seasons in the AA, the Spiders moved to the NL, where they continued below .500 for three more years. But in 1892 Cy Young's league-leading pitching brought them the second-half championship of the league's experimental split season. Cleveland lost the World Series to first-half winner Boston, losing five after tying the first game.

Second-place finishes in 1895 and 1896 qualified the Spiders for the Temple Cup series against champion Baltimore. In 1895 they beat the Orioles for the world title four games to one, but were swept the next year 0–4.

In 1899, when owner Frank Robison transferred all the team's best players to St. Louis (which he also owned), Cleveland suffered the worst season in major league history, winning only 20 games while losing a record 134. They finished 35 games behind eleventh-place Washington and 84 games out of first. After the season the Spiders died, as the National League cut back from twelve teams to eight.

Kansas City Blues, AA 1888–1889. Finished last in 1888, next to last in 1889.

Columbus Colts (or Solons), AA 1889–1891. In 1890, with the AA weakened by the replacement of half its franchises with new clubs and by defections to the outlaw PL, Columbus (which retained several of its regulars) rose from its 1889 sixth-place finish to second behind Louisville. When the PL folded and the defectors returned in 1891, Columbus dropped back to sixth.

Brooklyn Gladiators, AA 1890. Formed as a replacement for the Brooklyn club that forsook the AA for the NL in 1890, the Gladiators floundered and were replaced by Baltimore late in the season.

Rochesters, AA 1890. Played .500 ball, finishing fifth.

Syracuse Stars, AA 1890. Finished sixth.

Toledo Maumees, AA 1890. Finished fourth.

Cincinnati Porkers, AA 1891. Also known as "Kelly's Killers" for their manager Mike "King" Kelly, the club went bankrupt in August and was replaced by Milwaukee.

Milwaukee Brewers, AA 1891. This Western League club moved up to the AA in August. Taking five players and the 43–57 record from the defunct Cincinnati club, Milwaukee went 21–15 the rest of the way to lift the Cincinnati-Milwaukee combination from seventh to fifth by season's end.

Washington Senators, AA 1891, NL 1892–1899. Despite a cellar finish in the AA's final year, the Senators were taken into the expanding NL. Of its nine losing seasons, the best was a tie for sixth in the twelve-team NL of 1897.

Union Association, 1884

Formed in opposition to the reserve rule that governed players in the NL and AA, the UA struggled through one season. The first eight clubs listed here began the season. The other five are listed according to the month they entered the UA as replacement teams. All thirteen—like the UA itself—are long extinct:

Altoona, Pa., Unions, UA 1884. The first of several UA clubs to drop out of competition during the season, Altoona disbanded on May 31, but reorganized as an independent club two days later with many of the same players.

Baltimore Unions, UA 1884. Bill Sweeney's league-leading 40 wins accounted for 70 percent of third-place Baltimore's victories.

Boston Unions, UA 1884. Outfielder Tom McCarthy, the UA's only Hall of Famer, hit .215 in this, his rookie big league season. Boston finished fourth.

Chicago Browns/Pittsburgh Stogies, UA 1884. Financial woes caused the Chicago Browns to relocate in Pittsburgh in late August, but the club quit altogether less than a month later.

Cincinnati Outlaw Reds, UA 1884. With three 20-game winners—including Jim McCormick, who won 21 after defecting from the NL in midseason—Cincinnati compiled a strong 69–36 record, but still finished 21 games behind champion St. Louis.

Keystone of Philadelphia, UA 1884. In early August Keystone dropped out of the league and reorganized as an independent semipro club.

National of Washington, D.C., UA 1884. Finished sixth, 46½ games back.

St. Louis Maroons, UA 1884, NL 1885–1886. Batting 47 points above the league average, the Maroons scored 184 runs more than the next-best club to run away with the pennant. They were the only UA club to survive 1884 as a major league team, but in the NL, where they were dubbed "the black diamonds" because of their previously expelled players, they were unable to fashion a winning season or finish higher than sixth.

Kansas City Unions, UA 1884. Formed to replace Altoona, Kansas City went 16–63 in its partial season.

Wilmington, Del., UA 1884. After Wilmington had gone 51–12 to sew up the Eastern League championship, they jumped to the UA in August to replace Philadelphia's Keystones. But as several players failed to make the jump with them, the move was a disaster on the field (2–16) and financially. They failed in mid-September.

Milwaukee Grays, UA 1884. One of only two teams left in the deteriorating Northwestern League, Milwaukee moved up to the UA in September to complete the schedule of dropout Pittsburgh.

St. Paul White Caps, UA 1884. With the disbanding of the Northwestern League in September, St. Paul joined the UA to take over Wilmington's remaining games.

Players League, 1890

Formed in rebellion against the Brush classification plan, a scheme to limit players' pay, the PL drew many of the finest players from the NL and AA, and proved the most popular league with the fans. But when only one club turned a profit, the clubs' financial backers deserted and the league died. Two clubs were admitted to the AA, and many of the rest merged with their NL counterparts:

Boston Red Stockings, PL 1890, AA 1891. Boston won the PL pennant with such stars as Dan Brouthers, Old Hoss Radbourne, Hardy Richardson, and manager King Kelly. The only PL club to make money, Boston joined the AA the next year and won another pennant. But when the popular Kelly defected to Boston's NL Beaneaters (who also won a pennant for the city in 1891), the fans defected too, and the Red Stockings died along with the AA at the end of the season.

Brooklyn Wonders, PL 1890. At the end of a season in which they edged New York for second place, the Wonders merged with Brooklyn's NL pennant-winners.

Buffalo Bisons, PL 1890. After a last-place finish 20 games back of their nearest competitor, the Bisons simply went out of business.

Chicago Pirates, PL 1890. Mark Baldwin, with a league-high 34 wins, and Charles "Silver" King, with 30, pitched Chicago into fourth place. Both went to Pittsburgh the next year, although the franchise was absorbed by Chicago's NL Colts.

Cleveland Infants, PL 1890. Like Cleveland's NL Spiders of 1890, the Infants finished next to last. But one of their three managers, infielder Oliver Wendell "Patsy" Tebeau, would go on to lead the Spiders to their finest seasons.

Philadelphia Quakers, PL 1890, *Athletic* AA 1891. Although they finished sixth in their PL season, the Quakers compiled a winning record. When the Athletics of the AA were expelled following the 1890 season, the Quakers were admitted in their place and awarded the name "Athletic." The team finished fourth in 1891, but was not among the four clubs taken into the NL when the AA folded, because Philadelphia already had an NL team (the Phillies).

New York Giants, PL 1890. Paced by the hitting of first baseman Roger Connor and outfielder Jim O'Rourke, New York's PL Giants finished third. In November the club merged with the city's NL Giants.

Pittsburgh Burghers, PL 1890. After a sixth-place finish, the Pittsburgh PL club and the NL Allegheny Club combined to form the new Pittsburgh Athletic Club, which still represents Pittsburgh in the NL.

American League, 1901–

When Western League president Ban Johnson renamed the circuit in 1900 and proclaimed it a major league the next year, he little knew how stable it would be. For over half a century (1903–1953) the same eight clubs represented the same eight cities. Even today, although the league has expanded and several clubs have moved to new cities, not one franchise has perished.

Federal League, 1914–1915

After an inaugural season as a six-team minor league in 1913, the FL expanded to eight teams and declared war on the NL and AL for their players. After two big league seasons, and despite two of the game's most exciting pennant races ever, the league died for lack of patronage, and with it went its eight franchises:

Baltimore Terrapins, FL 1914–1915. Jack Quinn and George Suggs, with 26 and 25 wins, pitched Baltimore to third place in 1914. But when Quinn and Suggs lost their stuff the next year, the club sank out of sight, 24 games behind seventh-place Brooklyn.

Brooklyn Tip-Tops (or Brookfeds), FL 1914–1915. The Brookfeds finished fifth in 1915 and not even the acquisition of batting and base-stealing champ Benny Kauff could stop Brooklyn from slipping to seventh the next year.

Buffalo Buffeds, FL 1914–1915. Finished fourth in 1914, sixth the next year.

Chicago Chifeds (or Whales), FL 1914–1915. After leading the league through July and much of August in 1914, only to lose out after a late-season struggle with Indianapolis, the Whales came back in 1915 to triumph in an even tighter race that saw the three top teams separated at the finish by only half a game. Owner Charles Weeghman was permitted to buy the NL Cubs in 1916, and many Whales joined the Cubs in play at what was then Weeghman Park and now is known as Wrigley Field.

Indianapolis Federals (or Hoosiers), FL 1914; *Newark Peps,* FL 1915. Five regulars hit over .300 (paced by Benny Kauff's league-leading .370) in 1914, and the team as a whole hit twenty-two points above the league average. From fourth place in August the Hoosiers fought back to capture the flag from Chicago by 1½ games, with seven consecutive wins at the end. The only major league pennant-winner to move to a new city the next year, the Hoosiers became the Peps in 1915. Though they remained competitive into September, an eight-game losing streak dropped them out of the race and they finished fifth.

Kansas City Packers, FL 1914–1915. After a sixth-place finish in 1914, the Packers competed in a five-way race through much of 1915. But from first place on August 21 they dropped to fifth a week later and finished fourth.

Pittsburgh Rebels, FL 1914–1915. After avoiding last place in 1914 only by St. Louis's late-season nosedive, Pittsburgh turned itself around the next year, luring first baseman Ed Konetchy from their NL rival Pirates, and pitcher Frank Allen from the NL Brooklyn Robins. Both enjoyed the best season of their careers to lead the Rebels into first place in late August, where they remained until they were dropped to third by losing three out of four at the end to the champion Whales.

St. Louis Terriers, FL 1914–1915. After finishing last in 1914, St. Louis added veteran pitcher Eddie Plank to its roster. From a club with two 20-game losers, the Terriers became in 1915 a team with three 20-game winners (including Plank), pulling up from fifth late in August to catch the leaders with a nine-game winning streak. At the finish, though, they ranked second—by less than one percentage point, the narrowest big league pennant margin ever. For 1916, Terriers' owner Phil Ball took over the AL St. Louis Browns.

## CHAPTER 3

Ballparks

Philip J. Lowry

What follows are the vital statistics of each of the current twenty-eight major league baseball stadiums and a selection of the storied parks of the past. My book, *Green Cathedrals,* from which much of this section is taken, encompasses the whole of major league history, from 1871 to the present, including the extraordinary variety of early playing sites, from cricket grounds and polo fields to agricultural fairgrounds and cow pastures. That book also covers Negro League ballparks in a depth beyond the scope possible here, including the vast array of barnstorming sites, even for official league games, that was characteristic of impoverished ballclubs looking to maximize their gate receipts in any way possible. All the same, despite the space constraints imposed upon this entry, the primary Negro League parks will be covered, as well as classic shrines such as Ebbets Field, Griffith Stadium, Forbes Field, and others.

The focus here is on ballpark geometry and the oddities in play that resulted from the unique configuration of the park. Dimensional changes are catalogued and dated, particularly in outfield fence distances and heights. This subject is crucial to an understanding of the statistical history of baseball, whether or not one is a devotee of the park-adjusted figures on display in this volume.

The following leagues are covered by this study. The accompanying abbreviations may be employed for the twentieth century's principal leagues:

NL National League, 1876–
AL American League, 1901–
FL Federal League, 1914–1915
NNL Negro National League, 1920–1931, 1933–1948
ECL Eastern Colored League, 1923–1928
NAL Negro American League, 1929, 1937–1950
NSL Negro Southern League, 1932
NEWL Negro East-West League, 1932

Before 1900, most parks were small wooden grandstands hastily constructed around recreation fields that often were not even enclosed by outfield fences. Beginning with the erection of Shibe Park and Forbes Field in 1909, however, concrete-and-steel ballparks became the rule. These palaces signaled the growing prominence of baseball and constituted to my mind the best in ballpark design; the term I have applied to this type of park is "Major League Classic." Beginning in the 1950s, multipurpose stadiums were developed. "Multipurpose" means, for this essay, that a stadium was used for both football and baseball, a marriage not made in heaven.

"New Major League Classic" reflects the return to asymmetrical, baseball-only parks—in Baltimore, Cleveland, Texas, and Denver.

Using the Outlines

"Style" defines the structural design of the park.

"A.K.A." (Also Known As) lists alternate names and nicknames used for the ballpark.

"Occupant" lists teams using the park in chronological order. Inclusive dates of play within the league follow.

"Event" contains neutral site and All-Star Games.

"Location" lists the surrounding streets. When possible, fields and bases are associated with the streets. Geographical directions, (N) for North, (S) for South, (E) for East, and (W) for West, are provided when available.

Because all older stadiums had grass "surfaces," information concerning carpet or grass is included only for modern ballparks.

Under "Dimensions" the distance is given in feet from home plate to the fences, and to the backstop. Dates, in parentheses, denote the *first* month and/or year when the boundaries stood at the stated distance.

"Fences" lists the heights of the outfield fences in feet. Dates denote the *first* time the fences stood at the stated height.

"Former Use" describes how the site was utilized before stadium construction. Similarly, "Current Use" chronicles the development of the site after a ballpark was demolished or abandoned.

"Phenomena" is a more general category for historical data. Included here will be special features of the park's physical plant, important changes over the years, and events of note throughout the years of operation.

ANAHEIM, CALIFORNIA

ANAHEIM STADIUM

STYLE Multipurpose
A.K.A. Big A 1966, Bigger A 1980
OCCUPANT AL Angels April 19, 1966 to date
EVENT All-Star Game 1967, 1989
LOCATION *Left Field (N)* Katella Avenue; *3rd Base (W)* 2000 State College Boulevard, then Interstate 5; *1st Base (S)* Orangewood Avenue, then Santa Ana River; *Center Field (E)* Orange Freeway
SURFACE Bluegrass
DIMENSIONS *Foul Lines:* 333; *Bullpens:* 362; *Power*

Alleys: 375 (1966), 369 (1973), 374 (1974), 370 (1989); *Deep Alleys:* 386; *Center Field:* 406 (1966), 402 (1973), 404 (1974); *Backstop:* 55 (1966), 60.5 (1973)

FENCES *Majority of the Fence:* 10 (wire 1966), 7.86 (wire 1973), 7.86 (padded 1981); *Corners Between Foul Poles and Bullpens:* 4.75 (steel 1966); *Left-center Between 386 and 404 Marks:* 7.5 (padded 1981); *Padded Posts at the Left Sides of Both Left and Right Field; Bullpen Gates:* 9 (padded 1981); *Bullpen Gates:* 9.95 (wire 1966)

FORMER USE Four farms—Camille Allec's 39 acres of orange and eucalyptus trees, Roland Reynolds' 70 acres of alfalfa, John Knutgen's 20 acres of corn, Bill Ross and George Lenney's 19 acres of corn

CAPACITY 64,593

PHENOMENA

• Power hitter's park, the ball carries well.

• Huge 230-foot-high letter "A" stood behind the fence in left as a scoreboard support until 1980, then it was moved to the parking lot. The letter has a gold halo at its top.

• Sections 69 and 70 in center covered by green-canvas batters' background.

• Two thin black TV cables run in fair territory on the warning track from the left field corner bullpen gate to the foul pole, and then along the wall in foul territory about 50 feet toward third base, then into the stands.

• Outfield enclosed and tripledecked in 1980; new owner (Disney) plans to un-enclose it, and rip out the distant outfield structure.

• 6 doors on ivy-covered wall in deep left-center behind outfield fence labeled: "warning track," "skin material," "screen clay mounds," "raw clay," "sand," "equipment."

ATLANTA, GEORGIA

TURNER FIELD

STYLE Traditional Baseball Only

OCCUPANT NL Braves April 4, 1997

LOCATION (N) Ralph Abernathy Boulevard; (E) Capital Avenue; (S) Love Street; (W) Washington Street

SURFACE Grass

DIMENSIONS *Left Field:* 335; *Left Center:* 380; *Center Field:* 400; *Right Center:* 385; *Right Field:* 330; *Backstop:* 53.

FENCES 8

CAPACITY 50,528

PHENOMENA

• Stadium built to host 1996 Summer Olympics.

• A hand-operated scoreboard posts out-of-town scores above the left field stands.

• Upper level seats afford view of downtown Atlanta.

• Atlanta-Fulton County Stadium razed to create parking for Turner Field.

ATLANTA-FULTON COUNTY STADIUM

STYLE Multipurpose

A.K.A. Atlanta Stadium 1965-74, Launching Pad

OCCUPANT NL Braves April 12, 1966 to October 24, 1996

EVENT All-Star Game 1972

LOCATION *Left Field (NE)* Pullman Street and Interstate 20; *3rd Base (NW)* Washington Street and Interstate

75/85 and Georgia Avenue; *1st Base (SW)* 521 Capitol Avenue; *Right Field (SE)* Fulton Street

SURFACE Grass

DIMENSIONS *Foul Lines:* 325 (1966), 330 (1967); *Power Alleys:* 385 (1966), 375 (1969), 385 (1974); *Center Field:* 402 (1966), 400 (1969), 402 (1973); Back Stop: 59.92 (1973); *Foul Territory:* Large (1966), Medium (1977)

FENCES 6 (wire 1966), 10 (4 plexiglass above 6 wire 1983), 10 (plexiglass 1985)

CAPACITY 52,270

PHENOMENA

• Three statues outside the stadium honor Ty Cobb, Hank Aaron, and Phil Niekro.

• Being replaced in 1997 by Olympic Stadium.

• Big Victor, a large totem-pole-styled figure, stood in the stadium in 1966. The huge head tilted and the eyes rolled whenever a Brave hit a home run.

• Chief Noc-A-Homa's Wigwam replaced Big Victor in 1967.

• Only park to close with a World Series contest.

BALTIMORE, MARYLAND

ORIOLE PARK AT CAMDEN YARDS

STYLE New Major League Classic

A.K.A. Camden Yards

OCCUPANT AL Orioles April 6, 1992 to date

EVENT All-Star Game 1993

LOCATION (N) Camden Street; (W) Russell Street; (E) Howard Street; (S) Martin Luther King Boulevard

SURFACE Maryland Bluegrass ("Prescription Athletic Turf")

DIMENSIONS *Left Field:* 333; *Left Center:* 364; *Deepest Left Center:* 410; *Center Field:* 400; *Right Center:* 373; *Right Field:* 318; *Backstop:* 57.5

FENCES 25 in right, 7 elsewhere

FORMER USE Le Comte de Rochambeau, French general, camped his troops here on the way to Yorktown in 1781; former station of Baltimore & Ohio Railroad

CAPACITY 48,262

PHENOMENA

• Camden Yards complex includes the Baltimore & Ohio Warehouse, longest building on the East Coast (1,016 feet long but only 51 feet wide). Houses Orioles offices as well as a cafeteria, sports bar, and the exclusive Camden Club. Banks of lights are mounted on roof.

• Each aisle seat features an 1890s Orioles logo.

• Unique doubledecked bullpens in left-center field.

• Hearing-impaired persons may hook into "hearing assistance channels" at their seats.

• Playing field is 16 feet below street level.

• Located only two blocks from Babe Ruth's birthplace; Babe's father operated Ruth's Cafe at 406 Conway Street, the site of which is now located in center field.

• Designed by HOK Sports Facility Group.

• Site of unique three league triple header on June 6, 1992. Fans could take in a morning game at Hagerstown, Md., an afternoon contest at Frederick, Md., and end up under the lights at Camden Yards.

• Large Babe Ruth statue has the Bambino incorrectly wearing a right-handed fielder's glove.

- Faced with brick to present a traditional appearance.
- Football stadium to be built adjacent to Camden Yards.
- Warehouse is 432 feet from home plate.
- Sportswriter John Steadman's unofficial measurements revealed that LCF is 352 rather than 364, deepest LCF is 397 rather than 410, and RCF is 363 rather than 373.

BOSTON, MASSACHUSETTS

FENWAY PARK

STYLE   Major League Classic
OCCUPANT   AL Red Sox April 20, 1912 to date
EVENT   NL Braves vs. New York April 19, May 30, 1913; August 1 and 8, September 7 to 29, 1914; 1914 World Series; April 14 to July 26, 1915; All-Star Game 1946, 1961
LOCATION   *Left Field (N)* Lansdowne Street, Boston & Albany Railroad tracks, and Mass. Turnpike/Interstate 90; *3rd Base (W)* Brookline Avenue and 24 Jersey Street, renamed 24 Yawkey Way in 1976, also bowling alley building attached to park; *1st Base (S)* Van Ness Street (built after park was done); *Right Field (E)* Ipswich Street and Fenway Garage building
SURFACE   Bluegrass
DIMENSIONS   *Left Field:* 324 (1921), 320.5 (1926), 320 (1930), 318 (1931), 320 (1933), 312 (1934), 315 (1936), 310 (1995); *Left-Center:* 379 (1934); *Deep Left-Center at Flagpole:* 388 (1934); *Flagpole Removed from Field of Play in 1970; Centerfield:* 488 (1922), 468 (1930), 388.67 (1934), 389.67 (1954); *Deepest Corner, Just Right of Center:* 550 (1922), 593 (1931), 420 (1934) [Note: 593 is cited in 1931-33 Bluebooks; this could be a misprint.] *Right-Center, Just Right of Deepest Corner Where the Bullpen Begins:* 380 (1938), 383 (1955); *Right of Right Center:* 405 (1939), 382 (1940), 381 (1942), 380 (1943); *Right Field:* 313.5 (1921), 358.5 (1926), 358 (1930), 325 (1931) 358 (1933), 334 (1934), 332 (1936), 322 (1938), 332 (1939), 304 (1940), 302 (1942); *Back-stop:* 68 (1912), 60 (1934); *Foul Territory:* Very small, smallest in the majors
FENCES   *Left Field:* 25 (wood 1912), 37.17 (tin over wood over concrete lower section 1934), 37.17 (hard plastic 1976); *Left Field Wall to Center Bleacher Wall Behind Flagpole:* 18 sloping to 17 (concrete 1934), (padding 1976) crash pad added from 18 inches to 6 feet on left and center field walls (1976); *Center Field to Bullpen Fence:* 8.75 (wood 1940); *Right-Center Bullpen Fence:* 5.25 (wood 1940); *Right Field Wall and Railing:* Bullpen 3.42 sloping to 5.37 at foul pole (steel 1940); *Right Field Belly:* the low railing and wall curve out sharply from the 302 marker at the right field foul pole into deep right field—many a right fielder has run toward the foul line and watched helplessly as a 302-foot pop fly falls over the railing for a home run.
CAPACITY   33,871
PHENOMENA
- Seats made of oak.
- 1976 electronic scoreboard significantly altered the wind currents.
- 43 private 28-seat rooftop boxes added 1984.
- Duffy's Cliff was a 10-foot-high mound which formed an incline in front of the left field wall from 1912 to 1933,

extending from the left field foul pole to the flag pole in center—named after Red Sox left fielder Duffy Lewis, who was the acknowledged master of defensive play on the cliff. It was greatly reduced but not completely eliminated in 1934.
- The Green Monster Wall in left completely dominates the field of play—now all green, it used to be covered with advertisements.
- Ladder starts near upper-left corner of scoreboard, 13 feet above ground, and rises to top of the Green Monster to allow groundskeeper to remove batting practice home run balls from the netting above the Wall.
- Scoreboard numbers—runs and hits: 16 inches by 16 inches, 3 pounds; errors, innings, pitcher's numbers: 12 inches by 16 inches, 2 pounds.
- No ball has ever been hit over the right field roof.
- Balls that hit uprights above the Wall, and should have been homers, have been declared in play by the umpires.
- Wooden bleachers stood down the left field line in foul territory in the 1910s and 1920s, but burned down on May 8, 1926. The charred remains were removed, increasing the size of foul territory there. Wooden bleachers were completed in center and right-center by the 1912 World Series.
- Infield grass was transplanted from Huntington Avenue Baseball Grounds to Fenway in 1912.
- During the winter of 1933-34, all the wooden grandstands were replaced with concrete and steel. A big fire on January 5, 1934, destroyed much of what had already been built, but all was finished for the 1934 season opener on April 17.
- In 1936, a 23-foot seven-inch net was placed atop the wall in left to protect windows on Landsowne Street.
- Wind usually helps the batters. New pressbox built in late 1980s above home plate causes wind swirl which pushes foul balls back into fair territory. This is the park with the tiniest foul territory in the majors.
- When tin covered the two-by-fours on the Wall, balls hitting the tin over two-by-fours had a live bounce, but balls hitting between the two-by-fours were dead and just dropped straight down.
- In 1940, in an effort to help Ted Williams hit home runs, the Red Sox added the right field bullpens, called Williamsburg, which reduced the distance to the fence by 23 feet.
- In 1947 all advertisements were removed from the left field wall, which was painted green.
- Tom A. Yawkey's and his wife Jean R. Yawkey's initials, TAY and JRY, appear in Morse code in two vertical stripes on the scoreboard in left. The 1946 roof boxes were replaced in 1982.
- The screen behind home plate, designed to protect fans and allow foul balls to roll back down onto the field of play, was the first of its kind in the majors.
- Left field scoreboard installed on the Wall in 1934, moved 20 feet to the right in 1976.
- The low concrete base of the left and center field walls was padded after the 1975 World Series, during which Fred Lynn crashed into the concrete wall in center.
- The left field foul line was measured by Art Keefe and George Sullivan, authors of *The Picture History of the Boston Red Sox,* in October 1975 as 309 feet 5 inches. On October 19, 1975, the Boston *Globe* used aerial photogra-

phy and measured it at 304.779 feet. Osborn Engineering Co. blueprints document the distance at 308 feet. The sign was changed from 315 to 310 in 1995.

• Fenway—"where you can sit for hours and feel a security that does not exist anywhere else in the world."

CHICAGO, ILLINOIS

NEW COMISKEY PARK
STYLE   Superstructure with natural surface
A.K.A.   Comiskey II
OCCUPANT   AL White Sox April 18, 1991 to date
LOCATION   West 36th Street (South); 333 West 35th Street (North); Dan Ryan Expressway (East); Wentworth Ave. (West)
SURFACE   Natural Grass (Bluegrass)
DIMENSIONS   *Left field:* 347; *Power Alleys:* 383; (1991), 375 (1992); *Center Field:* 400; *Right Field:* 347; *Backstop:* 60
FENCES   8
FORMER USE   Approximately 80 privately owned residential buildings
CAPACITY   44,321
PHENOMENA

• Unlike the Picnic Area at old Comiskey Park, entry to the new Picnic Area's buffet costs $30 over the ticket price.

• Echoing the nickname of Charles Comiskey, food court contains a shop called Old Roman Pizza.

• Management boasts "Ratio of washroom fixtures to fan capacity, one of the best in baseball" but fans complain of long washroom lines.

• During construction was visible from former Comiskey Park, to which it was adjacent.

• Large scoreboard in center field replicates one designed by Bill Veeck at former Comiskey Park.

• Infield dirt transported here from old park.

• Built at a cost of $134.9 million; paid for in large part by a new hotel tax.

• Park's exterior is of precast colored concrete and features arched windows reminiscent of former park.

• Seats in front row of the upper deck are farther from home plate than those in last row at old Comiskey.

WRIGLEY FIELD
STYLE   Major League Classic
A.K.A.   North Side Ball Park, 1914; Weeghman Park, 1914-15; Cubs' Park, 1916-26; Whales Park, 1915; Eddie Dorr's House
OCCUPANT   FL Whales April 23, 1914 to October 3, 1915; NL Cubs April 20, 1916 to date
EVENT   All-Star Game 1947, 1962, 1990
LOCATION   *Left Field (N)* West Waveland Avenue; *3rd Base (W)* Seminary Avenue; *Home Plate (SW)* North Clark Street; *1st Base (S)* 1060 West Addison Street; *Right Field (E)* North Sheffield Avenue
SURFACE   Grass, mixture of Merion Bluegrass and clover
DIMENSIONS   *Left Field:* 310 (April 1914), 335 (May 1914), 327 (June 1914), 343 (1921), 325 (1923), 348 (1926), 364 (1928), 355 (1938); *Left-Center Deepest:* 357 (1938); *Power Alleys:* 364 (1914), 368 (1938); *Center*

Field: 440 (1914), 447 (1923), 436 (1928), 400 (1938); *Right-Center Deepest:* 363 (1938); *Right Field:* 356 (April 1914), 345 (June 1914), 321 (1915), 298 (1921), 399 (1922), 318 (1923), 321 (1928), 353 (1938); *Backstop:* 62.42 (1930), 60.5 (1957), 62.42 (1982), 60.5 (1993); *Foul Territory:* Very small
FENCES   *Left Field Corner:* 15.92 (11.33 brick with Boston and Bittersweet Ivy, below 4.59 plywood), 3 wire basket in front 1985 (does not change height of fence); *Transition Between Left Field Corner and Bleachers:* 12.5 (screen and yellow railing on top of brick wall); *Left-Center to Right-Center:* 8 (screen 1914), 11.33 (brick with ivy 1938); in front is wire basket (May 1970); *Left Field Scoreboard:* 40 (wood July 9 to September 3, 1937); *Center Field Screen:* 1933 (8 wire above 11.33 brick June 18, 1963 to October 1964); *Right Center Triangle:* 17.5 in front of catwalk steps sloping down to 15.5 (screen 1928, plywood 1979, removed 1985); *Right Field Corner:* 15.5 (11.33 brick with ivy, below 4.17 plywood), wire basket in front (1985)
CAPACITY   38,765
PHENOMENA

• IBM Home Run Distance calculation appears on center field scoreboard after a home run.

• The only remaining Federal League ballpark.

• Beautiful ivy vines on the outfield wall.

• After the game, a blue flag with a white W flying from the center field flag pole signifies a Cub win, a white flag with a blue L a Cub loss.

• Sea breeze off the lake favors pitchers.

• 452 seats added July 1985 to catwalks near foul pole, in fair territory.

• The center field 400 sign is slightly right of straight-away center.

• The only park where it's more difficult to hit a homer down the foul line than to hit one 50 or so feet out in fair territory because the bleachers protrude into the outfield.

• In 1923, the foul lines were shifted slightly amidst park renovations.

• From 1923 through 1930s Bobby Dorr, the ground superintendent, lived in a 6 room apartment at the ballpark, adjacent to the left field corner gate; the apartment is still there.

• Eight-foot-high batter's background wire fence, 64 feet wide, stood on top of the center field wall from June 18, 1963 through the end of the 1964 season. Called the Whitlow fence because Cub Athletic Director Robert Whitlow put it up. The screen prevented 10 homers, 4 by Cubs and 6 by visitors, 1 each by 500+ homer hitters Ernie Banks and Willie McCovey.

• Current green Astroturf cover on center field seats used for batters' background and debuted on May 18, 1967.

• In the winter of 1924-25, the left field bleachers were removed, the grandstand was doubledecked, and the playing area was lowered several feet.

• For World Series in 1929, 1932, and 1935, extra bleachers were built on the street on Waveland and Sheffield.

• The park was located so it would be easy for fans to get there on the Milwaukee Road train.

• The 27-foot-high, 75-foot-wide scoreboard was built in 1937 by Bill Veeck. Its top is 85 feet above the field. The 10 foot diameter clock was added in 1941.

• In 1937, the bleacher stairstep was created to allow

potted plants and eight huge Chinese elm trees to grow, complementing the ivy. The trees were eventually removed.

• Ivy planted on the outfield walls in 1937 by Bill Veeck. Originally 350 Japanese bittersweet plants and 200 Boston ivy plants.

• During the 1937 season, new outfield bleachers were built, and the six gates in the brick wall were emplaced. They were red, repainted blue in 1981, then green in the mid-1980s.

• The bleachers were expanded to their present state in the 1940s; famous Bleacher Bums formed here in 1966 by 10 bleacher fans.

• Lights were inside the park in the early 1940s ready to be installed, but Mr. Wrigley donated them to the war effort instead on December 8, 1941, thus allowing Wrigley Field to remain dark at night until 1988.

• The right field wall was remodeled in 1950-51.

• On April 14, 1976, Met Dave "King Kong" Kingman hit a homer 550 feet over Waveland and against a frame house 3 doors down on the east side of Kenmore Avenue. If the ball had carried 3 feet higher, it would have crashed through a window and smashed a TV screen on which Ms. Naomi Martinez was watching Mr. Kingman round the bases.

• Park is affected by wind conditions more than any other major league park, with the possible exception of Candlestick.

• More home runs than normal are caused by high altitude of over 600 feet above sea level, and by the heat involved in playing so many daylight games.

• William F. Wrigley, Jr. Water fountain moved to the Cub Hall of Fame under the first base stands, near the Friendly Confines cafe.

• Arched dormers on the roof.

• Outfield wall distances before 1981 were marked on plywood markers screwed into the brick. Since then they have been painted directly on the brick.

• Foul pole screens have distances marked on plywood vertically "355" and "353."

• The most distant current outfield measurement sign is at Wrigley Field. On the roof of a house across Sheffield Avenue in right-center, the sign says "495."

• Winds blowing toward the lake take homers with them.

CINCINNATI, OHIO

SYNERGY FIELD

STYLE Multipurpose
OCCUPANT NL Reds June 30, 1970 to date
A.K.A. Riverfront Stadium
EVENT All-Star Game 1970
LOCATION *Left Field (E)* Riverfront Coliseum, Central Bridge and Broadway; *3rd Base (N)* 201 East Second Street, renamed Pete Rose Way on September 10, 1985; *1st Base (W)* Interstate 71 Suspension Bridge Approach Ramp; *Right Field (S)* Mehring Way, railroad tracks, and Ohio River
SURFACE Astroturf—hard, balls bounce high off it
DIMENSIONS *Foul Lines:* 330; *Power Alleys:* 375; *Center Field:* 404; *Backstop:* 51; *Foul Territory:* Small
FENCES 12 (wood, 1970); 8 (wood, 1984)

CAPACITY 52,952
PHENOMENA

• First to paint metric distances on outfield walls: 100.58 down the lines, 114.30 to the alleys, 123.13 to center.

• Uses Crosley Field's home plate.

• Parking garage beneath stadium.

• 4,192 circle in left center commemorates Pete Rose's 4,192nd hit here on 9/10/85 vs. the Padres.

• Reds and Pirates played slowest game ever here 8/30/78—80.6 minutes per inning, called off after 3½ innings and 3½ hours of rain delays at 12:47 A.M.

• Winds help righthanded hitters.

CLEVELAND, OHIO

JACOBS FIELD

STYLE New Major League Classic
OCCUPANT Cleveland Indians, April 4, 1994 to present
A.K.A. Gateway, The Jake
LOCATION *Left Field (SW):* Ontario Avenue; *First Base (SE)* Carnegie Avenue; *Right Field (NE)* East 9th Street
SURFACE Natural Grass
DIMENSIONS *Left Field:* 325; *Left Center:* 368; *Deepest Center Field:* 410; *Center Field:* 405; *Right Center:* 375; *Right Field:* 325; *Backstop:* 59; *Foul Territory:* Small.
FENCES *Left Field:* 19; *Center and Right Field:* 8; *Right Field corner at the foul line:* 14.
CAPACITY 42,865
PHENOMENA

• Original plan was for a downtown domed stadium but local voters rejected an increase in property taxes to fund the proposal.

• Base of exterior facade consists of Atlantic green granite; remainder is Kasota stone, limestone, and buff-colored brick.

• Picnic Plaza located beyond center field fence.

• Executive Offices located in separate building in back of left field stands.

• Adjacent to home of NBA's Cleveland Cavaliers.

• Scoreboard located in left field.

• Indians bullpen in deep right center field; visitors in right field corner; each with 3 pitching mounds.

• Bullpens elevated 4'6" above playing field.

• Features "Kidsland" near the family seating area.

• Home plate from Cleveland Stadium transplanted at end of 1993 season.

• Indians have a batting cage under the stands, behind their dugout.

DALLAS, TEXAS

THE BALLPARK AT ARLINGTON

STYLE New Major League Classic
OCCUPANT Texas Rangers, April 11, 1994 to present
EVENT All-Star Game 1995
LOCATION Northwest corner of Stadium Drive and Randol Road

SURFACE Natural Grass
DIMENSIONS *Left Field:* 332; *Left Center:* 388; *Center Field:* 400; *Deepest Right Center:* 403; *Right Center:* 381; *Right Field:* 325; *Backstop:* 60; *Foul Territory:* Small.
FENCES *Left Field:* 14; *Center and Right Field:* 8
CAPACITY 49,178
PHENOMENA
• Granite and brick facade.
• Covered pavilion porch in right field features pillars reminiscent of Tiger Stadium.
• Playing field is 22 feet below street level.
• Wind helps carry balls hit to right center.
• Bullpens raised five feet above playing surface so fans can see who is warming up.
• Part of a complex that includes two manmade lakes and a Riverwalk area featuring shops and restaurants.
• Picnic area in front of four-story office building in center field.
• Outfield has many nooks and crannies reminiscent of Ebbets Field in Brooklyn.
• Rangers have a warning track under the stands behind their dugout for players to warm up on.

DENVER, COLORADO

COORS FIELD
STYLE New Major League Classic
OCCUPANT NL Rockies, April 26, 1995 to date
LOCATION 20th and Blake
SURFACE Bluegrass with strains of rye
DIMENSIONS *Left field:* 347; *Left Center:* 390; *Deepest Left Center:* 420; *Center Field:* 415; *Right Center:* 375; *Deepest Right Center:* 424; *Right Field Corner:* 358; *Right Field:* 350; *Backstop:* 56.33
FENCES *Left Field Corner to Right-Center:* 8; *Right Field (Manual Scoreboard):* 14
FORMER USE Rail Yard
CAPACITY 50,200
PHENOMENA
• Originally designed for 43,800 capacity but increased due to huge crowds at temporary Mile High Stadium, where the Rockies drew well over 4 million, and once had a single game crowd of 80,227.
• Club level features 22″-wide seats and waiter/waitress service.
• Bleachers known as the "Rockpile."
• 10 miles of handrails throughout the park.
• Over 500 wheelchair seats available daily.
• The 21st row of the upper deck is marked in purple to indicate it is 5,280 feet above sea level — mile high.
• Home and visitors bullpens are back-to-back in center field.
• Warning track is 90% crushed lava, 10% red clay.
• Features spectacular view of Rocky Mountains from first base and right field seats.
• First two games were exhibitions featuring "replacement" Yankees and Rockies.
• Exceptional hitting park because of altitude.

DETROIT, MICHIGAN

TIGER STADIUM
STYLE Major League Classic
A.K.A. Navin Field 1912 to 1937, Briggs Stadium 1938 to 1960
OCCUPANT AL Tigers April 20, 1912 to date, NNL Stars 1920-31, NEWL Wolves 1932, NNL Stars 1933, NAL Stars 1937
EVENT All-Star Game 1941, 1951, 1971
LOCATION *Left Field (NW)* Cherry Street, later Kaline Drive, and Interstate 75; *3rd Base (SW)* National Avenue, later Cochrane Avenue; *1st Base (SE)* Michigan Avenue; *Right Field (NE)* 2121 Trumbull Avenue, same site as Bennett park but turned around 90 degrees, in the Corktown neighborhood
SURFACE Bluegrass
DIMENSIONS *Left Field:* 345 (1921), 340.58 (1926), 339 (1930), 367 (1931), 339 (1934), 340 (1938), 342 (1939), 340 (1942); *Left Center:* 365 (1942); *Center Field:* 467 (1927), 455 (1930), 464 (1931), 459 (1936), 450 (1937), 440 (1938), 450 (1939), 420 (1942), 440 (1944); *Right Center:* 370 (1942), 375 (1982); *Right Field:* 370 (1921), 370.91 (1926), 372 (1930), 367 (1931), 325 (1936), 315 (1939), 325 (1942), 302 (1954), 325 (1955); *Backstop:* 54.35 (1954), 66 (1955); *Foul Territory:* Small
FENCES *All Fences:* 5 concrete topped by screen; *Left Field:* 20 (1935), 30 (1937), 10 (1938), 12 (1940), 15 (1946), 12 (1953), 14 (1954), 12 (1955), 11 (1958), 9 (1962); *Center Field:* 9 (1940), 15 (1946), 11 (1950), 9 (1953), 14 (1954), 9 (1955); *Right of Flag Pole:* 7 (1946); *Right Field:* 8 (1940), 30 (1944), 10 (1945), 20 (1950), 8 (1953), 9 (1958), 30 (1961), 9 (1962); *Flag Pole:* 125 in play (5 feet in front of fence in center field, just left of dead center)
CAPACITY 52,416
PHENOMENA
• First named for Frank Navin, a Tiger president.
• Right field second deck overhangs the lower deck by 10 feet. Screen in right in 1944 and in 1961 required balls to be hit into the second deck to be home runs.
• Only doubledecked bleachers in the majors—upper deck from left-center to center, lower deck from center to right-center.
• 125-foot-high flag pole in play in deep center, just to the left of the 440 mark—highest outfield obstacle ever in play in baseball history. The scoreboard now on the left field fence was originally placed at the 440 mark in dead center in 1961 but was moved when Norm Cash, Al Kaline, and Charlie Maxwell complained that it hindered the batters' view of the pitch.
• There is a string of spotlights mounted under the overhang to illuminate the right field warning track which is shadowed from the normal light standards.
• Cobb's Lake—area in front of plate which was always soaked with water by the groundskeepers to slow down Ty Cobb's bunts.
• When slugging teams came to visit, manager Ty Cobb had the groundskeepers put in temporary bleachers in the outfield, turning long drives into ground-rule doubles.
• Sign above entrance to visitors' clubhouse: "Visitors' Clubhouse—No Visitors Allowed."

• Doubledecked in 1923-24 from first to third base.
• Capacity increased in winter of 1935-36 by doubledecking the right field stands, and in the winter of 1937-38 by doubledecking both the left field stands and the center field bleachers.
• In the 1930s and 1940s, there was a 315 marker on the second deck in right field.
• In 1942 and 1943, the center field distance was only 420. The notches just left and right of dead center were closer than 420, at 405.
• Next-to-last classic old ballyard to put in lights, in 1948.
• Saved in 1974 when owner John Fetzer told the Pontiac Silverdome committee, "This franchise belongs to the inner city of Detroit; I'm just the caretaker." Now that mantle of caretaker has been passed on to the Tiger Stadium Fan Club and the Cochrane Plan, an architectural plan to preserve the ballpark.
• First homer at Navin Field, on May 5, 1912, came on a fluke bounce which hopped through the side door of the left-center scoreboard.
• Home plate and batters' boxes oriented towards right-center rather than straight out to the mound. This tends to give righthanded pitchers more outside corner strike calls and can disorient visiting batters.

HOUSTON, TEXAS

ASTRODOME

STYLE Dome
A.K.A. Harris County Domed Stadium 1965, Eighth Wonder of the World 1960s
OCCUPANT NL Astros April 12, 1965 to date
EVENT All-Star Game 1968, 1986
LOCATION *Center Field (E)* Fannin Street; *3rd Base (N)* Old Spanish Trail; *Home Plate (W)* Kirby Drive; *1st Base (S)* South Loop Freeway/Interstate 610; *Above:* Domed roof of 4796 Lucite panels and steel girders
SURFACE *Infield:* Grass (1965) Tifway 419 Bermuda grass specially selected for indoor play—died; Astroturf, fast on all but the part normally dirt 1966-70; on all the infield except for sliding pits 1971 to date); *Outfield:* Grass (April 12, 1965 to July 19, 1966)—died too; Astroturf, fast (July 19, 1966 to date)
DIMENSIONS *Foul Lines:* 340 (1965), 330 (1972), 340 (1977), 330 (1985), 325 (1992), 330 (1993), 325 (1994); *Power Alleys:* 375 (1965), 390 (1966), 378 (1972), 390 (1977), 378 (1985), 375 (1992), 380 (1993), 375 (1994); *Center Field:* 406 (1965), 400 (1972), 406 (1977), 400 (1985); *Apex of Dome:* 208; *Backstop:* 60.5 (1965), 67 (1990), 52 (1993)
FENCES *Left and Right Field:* 16 (9 concrete below 3 wire, 2 concrete, and 2 wire plus railing, 1965), 12 (concrete, 1969), 10 (concrete, 1977); 10 (canvas, 1990); 19.5 (concrete, 1991); 10 canvas (1992); Between foul poles and scoreboards: 8 (canvas, 1994), Scoreboards 16 (canvas, 1994); *Center Field* 12 (concrete, 1965), 10 (concrete, 1977), 10 (canvas 1990)
CAPACITY 54,350
PHENOMENA
• The second major league covered stadium, the first being the field under the Queensboro 59th Street Bridge in New York City used by the New York Cubans of the Negro National League in the 1930s.
• Maximum height of the dome is 208 feet, just beyond second base.
• The roof had 4,796 clear panes of glass originally, but they caused a glare which prevented fielders from seeing the ball, thus two of the eight roof sections were painted white. This killed the grass and unfortunately introduced the world to Astroturf.
• Excepting Yankee Stadium's Death Valley, the most distant power alleys in the majors at 390 feet, until changed in 1985.
• Too much yellow, orange, and red.
• Hard to see through the screen from behind the plate.
• Site of 1992 Republican convention.
• In its inaugural season of 1965, the Astrodome was the scene of a unique groundskeeping argument. The New York Mets claimed that the groundskeepers were roof-keeping as well by manipulating the air conditioning system so that the air currents helped Astro long balls and hindered visitors' long balls.
• The first game on a carpet was versus the Dodgers on April 8, 1966.
• Shoeshine stands behind home plate in lower deck.
• On April 28, 1965, Met announcer Lindsey Nelson broadcast a game from a gondola suspended from the apex of the dome.
• On June 10, 1974, Phillie Mike Schmidt hit the public address speaker 117 feet up and 329 feet from home—what would have been a 500-plus-foot homer ended up as a single as the ball dropped in center field.
• On June 15, 1976, a game was rained out because of flooding in the streets.
• The old location of Colt Stadium (now rebuilt in Torreon, Mexico) is just northwest of the Astrodome; Astrohall and Astroarena are just south of the Astrodome.

KANSAS CITY, MISSOURI

KAUFFMAN STADIUM

STYLE Superstructure with Natural Surface
A.K.A. Harry S. Truman Sports Complex, Royals Stadium 1973 to 1993
OCCUPANT AL Royals April 10, 1973 to date
EVENT All-Star Game 1973
LOCATION *Center Field (N)* Spectacular Drive, then Interstate 70; *3rd Base (W)* Lancer Lane, then Dutton Brookfield Drive; *Home Plate (S)* Royal Way, then Chiefs Way, Arrowhead Stadium, Raytown Road, and CRI&P Railroad tracks; *1st Base (E)* Red Coat Drive, then Blue Ridge Cut-Off; Stadium Drive encircles the park
SURFACE Astroturf—very fast (1973-1994); Grass 1995
DIMENSIONS *Foul Lines:* 330 (1973); 320 (1995); *Power Alleys:* 375 (1973); 385 (1990); 375 (1995); *Center Field:* 405 (1973); 410 (1980); 400 (1995); *Backstop:* 60; *Foul Territory:* Small
FENCES 12 (canvas, 1973), 9 (canvas, 1995)
CAPACITY 40,625
PHENOMENA
• Waterfalls and fountains run for 322 feet on the embankment overlooking right-center.

• Best visibility for hitters in the majors.

• Homers few here because alleys are deep and the fence cuts away sharply from the 330 foul poles.

• Kenny Pippin, in his frogman suit, cleans the pond periodically in right-center.

• Royals 1985 World Series cup and other trophies are on display through the sixth inning of each game at Section 107.

• Upper deck fans near foul poles are in relative darkness.

• Before 1996, when grass replaced the hated carpet, the best groundskeeper in baseball had the ironic job of maintaining an ugly plastic carpet. He kept busy maintaining the Runway and the Baja, the grassy running area and the 125-tree forest beyond the left-center fence.

LOS ANGELES, CALIFORNIA

DODGER STADIUM
STYLE Traditional Baseball Only
A.K.A. Chavez Ravine during AL use 1962 to 1965 by Los Angeles Angels, Taj O'Malley, O'Malley's Golden Gulch
OCCUPANT NL Dodgers April 10, 1962 to date; AL Angels April 17, 1962 to September 22, 1965
EVENT All-Star Game 1980
LOCATION *Left Field (NW)* Glendale Boulevard; *3rd Base (SW)* Sunset Boulevard; *Home Plate (S)* 1000 Elysian Park Avenue; *1st Base (SE)* Pasadena Freeway; *Right Field (NE)* Los Angeles Police Academy, Elysian Park, and Golden State Freeway/Interstate; Stadium Way encircles the park; in Chavez Ravine, on a hill overlooking downtown Los Angeles
SURFACE Santa Ana Bermuda grass
DIMENSIONS *Foul Lines:* 330; *Power Alleys:* 380 (1962), 370 (1969), 385 (1983); *Center Field:* 410 (1962), 400 (1969); *Back Stop:* 65 (1962), 68.19 (1963), 75 (1969); *Foul Territory:* Large
FENCES *Left-Center to Right-Center:* 10 (wood 1962), 8 (1973); *Foul Poles to Bullpens in Left and Right Field Corners:* 3.75 (steel 1962), 3.83 (1969); *The Dip:* (where low corner steel wall and screen bullpen fence meet) 3.42 (1962), 3.5 (1969)
FORMER USE Used by squatters and goats.
CAPACITY 56,000
PHENOMENA
• A classic pitcher's park.

• Dugout level box seats behind the plate patterned after Tokyo's Korakuen Stadium.

• Designed by architect Emil Praeger to be expandable to 85,000 seats.

• Painted every offseason, cleanest ballpark, bar none.

• Infield dirt and outfield warning track made of 70 percent crushed red building brick and 30 percent mountain clay and calcium chlorate. Palm trees beyond the fence down the foul lines.

• See-through windows in bullpen fence installed in 1974.

• Although the center field 400 sign came down in 1980, the distance is still 400 to center; the two 395 signs are left and right of dead center.

• No drinking-water fountains when first built. Original design had a huge fountain in center field, like that in right-center at Royals Stadium.

• When foul poles were installed in 1962, discovered that they were positioned completely foul. Special dispensation was received from National League so they were recognized as fair, but the next year plate was moved so that poles are now actually fair.

MIAMI, FLORIDA

PRO PLAYER STADIUM
STYLE Multipurpose
OCCUPANT Florida Marlins April 5, 1993 to present
A.K.A. Joe Robbie Stadium
LOCATION 2269 N.W. 199th Street
SURFACE Natural Grass ("Bermuda 419")
DIMENSIONS *Left Field:* 335; *Power Alleys:* 380; *Center Field:* 410; *Right Field:* 345; *Backstop:* 58
FENCES *Left Center scoreboard:* 33; *everywhere else:* 8
CAPACITY 41,855
PHENOMENA
• Opening Day for football: August 16, 1987 (Bears vs. Dolphins).

• First baseball game: Los Angeles Dodgers vs. Baltimore Orioles on March 11, 1988.

• A helipad site in the parking lot.

• All the second-deck outfield seats are covered by canvas and are not used.

• Many fans speak Spanish, with a Cuban-American accent.

MILWAUKEE, WISCONSIN

COUNTY STADIUM
STYLE Multipurpose
OCCUPANT NL Braves April 14, 1953 to September 22, 1965; AL White Sox for nine 1968 games and eleven in 1969; games from May 15, 1968 to September 26, 1969; AL Brewers April 7, 1970 to date
EVENT All-Star Game 1955, 1975
LOCATION *Left Field (E)* Menominee River and South 44th Street, later US-41 Stadium Freeway; *3rd Base (N)* Story Parkway and Interstate 94; *1st Base (W)* General Mitchell Boulevard; *Right Field (S)* West National Avenue and the National Soldiers Home
SURFACE Bluegrass
DIMENSIONS *Left Field:* 320 (1953), 315 (1975); *Power Alleys:* 355 (1953), 362 (1962); *Deep Alleys:* 397 (1953), 392 (1955); *Center Field:* 404 (1953), 410 (1954), 402 (1955); *Right Field:* 320 (1953), 315.37 (1954); *Backstop:* 60
FENCES *Left Field:* 4 (1953), 8 (1955), 8.33 (1959), 10 (1985); *Center Field:* 4 (1953), 8 (1955), 8.33 (1959), 10 (1985); *Right Field:* 4 (1953), 10 (1955)
FORMER USE Stone Quarry
CAPACITY 53,192
PHENOMENA
• Surveyor's mark on right field foul pole: "315.37."

• Before the park was expanded from 1953 to 1973, hospital patients at the National Soldiers Home V.A.

Hospital sat outside their rooms on Mockingbird Hill overlooking right field and watched the game for free.
• Perini's Woods, spruce and fir trees behind center field fence, planted in 1954, replaced by bleachers in 1961.
• Braves Reservation, a picnic area down the left field line, was inaugurated in 1961.
• Bernie Brewer slides into a huge beer stein in right-center whenever a Brewer hits a homer.
• Only homer ever hit over left field roof was hit by Cecil Fielder.
• Scene of Midwest League minor league game on August 27, 1966 between Fox Cities and Wisconsin Rapids.
• Braves hosted both the Reds and the Cards on September 24, 1954. The first game was the finish of a game two days earlier whose conclusion on a disputed double play was successfully protested by the Reds. The Reds tied the game after the protested game's resumption, but the Braves won 4-3 in the bottom of the ninth, and then beat the Cards 4-2.

MINNEAPOLIS, MINNESOTA

HUBERT H. HUMPHREY METRODOME

STYLE Dome
A.K.A. Minnedome, Bounce Dome, Hump Dome, Homer Dome, Hubie Dome, Sweat Box (before June 28, 1983, when air conditioning arrived), Thunderdome
OCCUPANT AL Twins April 6, 1982 to date
EVENT All-Star Game 1985
LOCATION *Left Field (SW)* Fourth Street South; *3rd Base (NW)* 501 Chicago Avenue South; *1st Base (NE)* Sixth Street South; *Right Field (SE)* Tenth Avenue South; *Above:* Domed roof
SURFACE SporTurf (1982 to 1986—liveliest bounce ever), Astroturf (1987 to date)
DIMENSIONS *Apex of Dome:* 186; *Left Field:* 344 (1982), 343 (1983); *Left-Center:* 385; *Center Field:* 407 (1982), 408 (1983); *Right Center:* 367; *Right Field:* 327; *Backstop:* 60; *Foul Territory:* Small
FENCES *Left Field:* 7 (canvas 1982), 13 (6 plexiglass above 7 canvas 1983), 7 (canvas 1994); *Center Field:* 7 (canvas 1982); *Right Field:* 7 (canvas 1982), 13 (canvas early in 1983), 23 (canvas later in 1983)
CAPACITY 44,457
PHENOMENA
• A power hitter's park.
• Right field wall called Hefty Bag.
• Almost an exact duplicate of the domed stadiums in Seattle, Pontiac, and Vancouver. All four were built by the same engineering firm.
• Game on April 26, 1986 delayed as violent rainstorm knocked out the lights and had the scoreboard and roof swaying.
• The white air-supported fabric Teflon roof makes it difficult to see the ball when hit high in the air.
• Playoffs and World Series of 1991 set new decibel records for sound in the Thunderdome.
• Sections 107 to 113 are football seats which in baseball season are tilted up and back to create a 40-foot wall behind the right field fence.
• The roof collapsed on April 14, 1983 from the weight of heavy snow.

• Twin batter Randy Bush hit a ball off the roof in 1983. The ball was caught foul for an out by Blue Jays catcher Buck Martinez. Rob Deer hit two such fly-ball outs to shortstop on consecutive at bats on May 30, 1992.
• On May 4, 1984, in the top of the fourth inning, A's batter Dave Kingman hit a ball through the roof. It should have been a homer, but Kingman got only a double.
• Balls bounced very high off the carpet used from 1982 to 1986.
• More home runs tend to be hit when the air conditioning is turned off.
• Curvature of wall behind plate causes wild pitches and passed balls to bounce directly toward first base.

MONTREAL, QUEBEC

STADE OLYMPIQUE

STYLE Summer Olympics Stadium/Dome
A.K.A. Olympic Stadium, Big O, Big Owe
OCCUPANT NL Expos April 15, 1977 to date
EVENT All-Star Game 1982
LOCATION *Left Field (NW)* rue Sherbrooke; *3rd Base (SW)* boulevard Pie-IX; *1st Base (SE)* 4549, avenue Pierre-de-Coubertin; *Right Field (NE)* boulevard Viau
SURFACE Astroturf
DIMENSIONS *Foul Lines:* 325 (1977), 330 (1981), 325 (1983); *Power Alleys:* 375; *Center Field:* 404 (1977), 405 (1979), 404 (1980), 400 (1981), 404 (1983); *Apex of Dome:* 180; *Backstop:* 62 (1977), 65 (1983), 53 (1989); *Foul Territory:* Large
FENCES 12 (wood 1977), 12 (foam 1989)
CAPACITY 46,500
PHENOMENA
• Labatt's Noise-Meter high above right field is baseball's answer to the old NBA Sacramento Kings' Arco Arena Noise-Meter.
• Roof improves offense by keeping out extreme cold.
• Built for 1976 Olympics.
• Plaque inside and statue of Jackie Robinson at main entrance. Robinson starred at the Delorimer Downs for the IL Montreal Royals in 1946. Huge 623-foot-high umbrella tower in center field from section 766 in left-center to section 767 in right-center stood half finished from 1976 to 1987. Became a fixed-dome stadium in 1989. The once retractable dome is silver on top, and orange on the bottom, with 26 white cones which link the roof to the tower. It consists of 60,696 square feet of Kevlar, weighing 50 tons. Retractable roof not actually retractable until 1988 due to generator problems, then became balky and decision was made to keep it closed.
• Parts of the concrete upper section of the stadium fell down in 1991, forcing the Expos to reschedule their September home games for the road.

NEW YORK, NEW YORK

YANKEE STADIUM

STYLE Major League Classic
A.K.A. House That Ruth Built
OCCUPANT AL Yankees April 18, 1923 to September 30, 1973; NNL Black Yankees 1946 to 1948; Negro

League World Series 3rd game, 1942; 1st game 1947; AL
Yankees April 15, 1976 to date
EVENT   All-Star Game 1939, 1960, 1977
LOCATION   *Left Field (NE)* East 161st Street; *3rd
Base (NW)* Doughty Street, later Ruppert Place; *Home
Plate (W)* Major Degan Expressway/Interstate 87 and
Harlem River; *1st Base (SW)* East 157th Street; *Right
Field (SE)* River Avenue and IRT elevated tracks; In the
southwest Bronx
SURFACE   Grass—Merion Bluegrass
DIMENSIONS   *Left Field:* 280.58 (1923), 301 (1928),
312 (1976), 318 (1988); *Left Side of Bullpen Gate in
Short Left-Center:* 395 (1923), 402 (1928), 387 (1976),
379 (1985); *Right Side of Bullpen Gate:* 415 (1937);
Deepest Left-Center: 500 (1923), 490 (1924), 457 (1937),
430 (1976), 411 (1985), 399 (1988); *Left Side of Center
Field Screen:* 466 (1937); *Center Field:* 487 (1923), 461
(1937), 463 (1967), 417 (1976), 410 (1985), 408 (1988);
Deepest Right Center: 429 (1923), 407 (1937), 385
(1976); *Left Side of Bullpen Gate in Short Right Center:*
350 (1923), 367 (1937), 353 (1976); *Right Side of Bullpen
Gate:* 344 (1937); *Right Field:* 294.75 (1923), 295
(1930), 296 (1939), 310 (1976), 314 (1988); *Backstop:* 82
(1942), 80 (1953), 84 (1976); *Foul Territory:* Large for
the catcher behind home plate, but small for fielders down
the foul lines
FENCES   *Left Field–Foul Line:* 3.92 (3 wire above .92
concrete 1923), 8 (canvas 1976); *Left Center–Left of Visitors' Bullpen:* 3.58 (3 wire above .58 concrete); *Right of
Visitors' Bullpen:* 7.83 (3 wire above 4.83 concrete), 7
(canvas 1976); *Center Field-Left Screen When Up for
Hitters' Background:* 20 (1953), 22.25 (1959), 22.42
(1954); *Screen When Down:* 13.83,7 (canvas 1976); *Right
Center-Right of Screen:* 14.5 (3 wire above 11.5 concrete
1923); *Left of Home Bullpen:* 7.83 (3 wire above 4.83
concrete 1923); *Right of Home Bullpen:* 3.58 (3 wire
above .58 concrete 1923), 8 (canvas 1976), 9 (canvas
1979); *Right Field-Foul Line:* 3.75 (3 wire above .75
concrete 1923), 10 (canvas 1976)
CAPACITY   57,545
FORMER USE   City plot 2106, lot 100, a farm granted
to John Lion Gardiner before the Revolutionary War.
PHENOMENA
• Left-center field monuments and plaques: Yankee Sta-
dium (I)
• Monuments in fair territory, Lou Gehrig on the left,
Miller Huggins in the middle, Babe Ruth on the right;
Yankee Stadium (II) Monuments beyond the fence; same
as Yankee Stadium I (plus Mickey Mantle in 1996). Pla-
ques beyond the fence, Ed Barrow, Jacob Ruppert, Joe
DiMaggio, Mickey Mantle, Casey Stengel, Joe McCar-
thy, Pope Paul VI, Thurman Munson, Pope John Paul II,
Billy Martin, Whitey Ford, Lefty Gomez, Roger Maris,
Allie Reynolds, Elston Howard, Phil Rizzuto, Bill
Dickey, Thurman Munson, and Yogi Berra.
• A ball hitting the foul pole in the 1930s was in play, not
a homer.
• "Death Valley" in left-center.
• Green curtain in center sometimes raised and lowered
like a window shade to force visiting batters to face a
background of white-shirted bleacher fans but allow Yan-
kee hitters to face a dark green background. Removed in
World Series to sell more seats.

• Bleachers in right-center often called Ruthville and
Gehrigville.
• Warning track red cinders; later on, red brick dust.
• Extra grass kept near monuments in center, in play.
• Underneath second base in Yankee Stadium (I), there
was a 15-foot-deep brick-lined vault with electrical, telephone, and telegraphic connections for boxing events.
• As originally constructed, from May 5, 1922, to April
18, 1923, three concrete decks extended from behind
home plate to each corner, with a single deck in left-
center, and wooden bleachers around the rest of the
outfield.
• In the winter of 1927-28, second and third decks were
added to left-center, and several rows of box seats were
removed in left, extending the foul pole from 281 to 301.
• During the 1936 season, the winter of 1936-37, and
continuing through the 1937 season, the wooden bleachers were replaced with concrete ones. During the 1937
season, second and third decks were added in right-
center. The bleacher changes shortened straightaway
center from 490 to 461 and reduced seating capacity from
the 80,000s to the 70,000s.
• As the outfield bench seats were gradually replaced
with chair seats, in the 1930s and 1940s, the seating
capacity gradually dropped from over 70,000 to about
67,000.
• Bloody Angle—between bleachers and RF foul line in
1923 season was very asymmetric and caused crazy
bounces. Eliminating this in 1924 caused the plate to be
moved 13 feet, and the deepest left center corner to
change from 500 to 490.
• Auxiliary scoreboards were built in the late 1940s,
which covered up the 367 right-center sign and the 415
left-center sign.
• Minor modifications were made in the winter of 1966-
67. During this work, a new 463 sign and a 433 sign
appeared in the power alleys, and the exterior was painted
blue and white.
• During 1974-75 renovation, iron third deck distinctive
facade was removed, and a portion was placed in the
bleachers.
• Home dugout switched from third base to first base on
April 19, 1946.

SHEA STADIUM
STYLE   Multipurpose
A.K.A.   William A. Shea Municipal Stadium
OCCUPANT   NL Mets April 17, 1964 to date; AL
Yankees, April 6, 1974 to September 28, 1975
EVENT   All-Star Game 1964
LOCATION   *Centerfield (E)* 126th Street; *3rd Base (N)*
Whitestone Expressway/Interstate 678, and Flushing Bay;
Home Plate (W) Grand Central Parkway; *1st Base (S)*
Roosevelt Avenue; In Queens, near Flushing Meadow
Park, site of 1939 and 1964 World's Fairs, just southeast
of La Guardia Airport
SURFACE   Bluegrass
DIMENSIONS   *Foul Line:* 330 (marked 1964), 341
(actual 1964), 341 (1965), 338 (1979); *Power Alleys:* 371;
Center Field: 410; *Backstop:* 80 (1964); *Foul Territory:*
Very large
FENCES   *Foul Lines:* 16.33 (4 wire and railing above
12.33 brick 1964), 12.33 (brick 1965), 8 (wood 1979);

Power Alleys: 8 (wood); *Center Field:* Small section 8.75 (wood), most 8 (wood)

CAPACITY 55,777

PHENOMENA

• Designed to be expandable to 90,000 seats.

• Noisiest outdoor ballpark; frequent La Guardia Airport air traffic noise overhead.

• Named for attorney William Shea, who obtained the Mets franchise for New York by organizing the Continental League.

• Right-center scoreboard is largest in majors, 86 feet high with Bulova clock on top, about 25 feet behind the outfield fence, and 175 feet long.

• Practice facilities under the right field stands.

• Behind fence in center, just to the right of the 410 mark, is a Mets Magic Top Hat. When a Met hits a homer, a red Big Apple rises out of the black top hat, which actually looks more like a big kettle.

• Foul lines from 1965 to 1978 had an orange home run line painted at the top of the 12-foot, 4-inch brick wall. Above this was a 4-foot wire screen and railing. A ball was a homer if it hit above the line. Like a similar ground rule at Crosley Field in center field, this caused many controversies, so in 1979 an inner 8-foot wooden fence was installed.

• Worst visibility for hitters in the majors.

• Churchlike spire beyond center field fence formerly graced "Serval Zippers" sign.

• Outfield fences also marked as 358 and 396. From 1973 to 1979, there were also distance markers, outside the field of play, on the rear bullpen walls at 428, base of left-center light tower at 442, bottom edge of right-center scoreboard at 405 on right field end and 420 on center field end.

• 1964 Mets Banner Day—"Mongolia Loves The Mets" (in Mongolian) banner carried by the author; other banners included "E=mc2" (or Errors = Mets times customers squared),"Eamus Metropoli" (Let's go Mets in Latin).

• Christened April 16, 1964 with Dodger Holy Water from the Gowanus Canal in Brooklyn and Giant Holy Water from the Harlem River at the exact location where it passed the old Polo Grounds.

OAKLAND, CALIFORNIA

OAKLAND-ALAMEDA COUNTY COLISEUM

STYLE Multipurpose

A.K.A. Oakland Coliseum Complex, Oakland Mausoleum

OCCUPANT AL Athletics April 17, 1968 to date

EVENT All-Star Game 1987

LOCATION *Center Field (NE)* San Leandro Street and Southern Pacific Railroad tracks; *3rd Base (NW)* 66th Avenue; *Home Plate (SW)* Oakland-Alameda County Coliseum Arena, Nimitz Freeway, and San Leandro Bay; *1st Base (SE)* Hegenberger Drive

SURFACE Bluegrass

DIMENSIONS *Foul Lines:* 330; *Power Alleys:* 378 (1968), 375 (1969), 372 (1981); *Center Field:* 410 (1968), 400 (1969), 396 (1981), 397 (1982), 400 (1990); *Backstop:* 90 (1968), 60 (1969); *Foul Territory:* Huge, largest in the majors

FENCES 8 (plywood 1968), 10 (canvas over plywood and plexiglass 1981), 8 (1986)

CAPACITY 39,875

PHENOMENA

• Surrounded by beautiful green ivy slope.

• Backstop is a notch cut in stands.

• Possible to watch game for free from concourse behind the field seats by peering between wooden slats on cyclone fence.

• Steel shell of pitcher's mound was exposed on Opening Day April 17, 1968 and had to keep being covered between innings.

• Right field scoreboard installed June 1968.

• Finley Fun Board put in for 1969 season—24 feet high and 126 feet long.

• Named the Mausoleum in the 1970s when the scoreboard didn't work, the entire stadium was gray concrete in color, and the A's were terrible.

• Huge foul territory area reduces batting average by roughly 5 to 7 points, making this the best pitcher's park in the AL.

• Fun picnic atmosphere is the very best in the majors of all new concrete circular ugly ashtray stadia.

• Best food in baseball.

• Winds favor lefthanded batters.

• Next door to Jewel Box, home of the NBA Golden State Warriors.

• Scoreboard shows upcoming home stands, with A's annihilating the opposition.

• Fans sitting at the foul poles can catch home run fair balls by reaching in front of the foul pole screens.

• Hand-operated scoreboard showing major league line scores installed in 1986.

• Renovated and expanded for Raiders football during 1996 season.

PHILADELPHIA, PENNSYLVANIA

VETERANS STADIUM

STYLE Multipurpose

A.K.A. Vet

OCCUPANT April 10, 1971 to date

EVENT All-Star Game 1976

LOCATION *Left Field (NE)* Packer Street and Interstate 76; *3rd Base (NW)* Broad Street and Philadelphia Naval Hospital; *1st Base (SW)* Pattison Avenue, Spectrum, and JFK Stadium; *Right Field (SE)* Tenth Street

SURFACE Astroturf—fast, but slower since 1977

DIMENSIONS *Foul Lines:* 330; *Power Alleys:* 371; *Center Field:* 408; *Backstop:* 60; *Foul Territory:* Large

FENCES 6 (wood April 1972); 8 (wood June 1971); 12 (6 plexiglass above 6 wood 1972)

CAPACITY 62,238

PHENOMENA

• The park's rounded rectangular shape is called an octorad by the architects.

• Connie Mack Stadium's home plate was transplanted here.

• Plastic tarp covered unfinished right field wall in April 1971.

• "Liberty Bell" used to hang from center field roof in fourth level—hit only by Greg Luzinski on May 16, 1972.

• First ball dropped from a helicopter on April 10, 1971.
• Smallest hot dogs and loudest boos in baseball.
• Statues of Connie Mack and a sliding runner outside the park.

PITTSBURGH, PENNSYLVANIA

THREE RIVERS STADIUM

STYLE Multipurpose
A.K.A. House That Clemente Built
OCCUPANT NL Pirates July 16, 1970 to date
EVENT All-Star Game 1974
LOCATION *Left Field (E)* Interstate 279 Fort Duquesne Bridge approach ramp; *3rd Base (N)* Reedsdale Street; *1st Base (W)* Allegheny Avenue, Ohio River, and the original point where the Monongahela River joins the Allegheny River to form the Ohio River; *Right Field (S)* North Shore Avenue, Roberto Clemente Memorial Park, Allegheny River; Stadium Circle encircles the park
SURFACE Carpet—Tartanturf 1970 to 1982; Astroturf 1983 to date
DIMENSIONS *Foul Lines:* 340 (1970), 335 (1975); *Power Alleys:* 385 (1970), 375 (1975); *Center Field:* 410 (1970), 400 (1975); *Backstop:* 60; *Foul Territory:* Large
FENCES 10 (wood)
CAPACITY 48,044
PHENOMENA
• Roberto Clemente statue dedicated here in 1994.
• On a site that was an island during the French and Indian Wars. It had been an Indian burial ground, a fact discovered when the Big Flood of 1763 uncovered many graves. Named Kilbuck Island after a friendly Delaware Indian chief. Back channels filled with silt, and it was no longer an island in 1852.
• Numbers painted on seats in right field upper deck where Willie Stargell's homers landed.
• Without the inner fence, the outfield would be 342 down the lines and 434 to center.
• The Honus Wagner statue, which used to stand outside of Forbes Field, now stands outside of Three Rivers Stadium.
• An 8- by 12-foot area of the 406 marker section of the Forbes Field brick wall, 12 Romanesque window frames, and the Babe Ruth plaque showing where his 714th home run landed are in the Allegheny Club at Three Rivers.
• Original design by Erik Sirko was for a "Stadium Over the Monongahela," with stadium above two parking lot levels, all sitting above the Monongahela River with plenty of room for boats to pass beneath on the river.

ST. LOUIS, MISSOURI

BUSCH STADIUM (II)

STYLE Multipurpose
A.K.A. Civic Center Stadium 1966, Busch Memorial Stadium 1966 to 1983
OCCUPANT NL Cardinals May 12, 1966 to date
EVENT All-Star Game 1966
LOCATION *Left Field (E)* Broadway, Interstate 70, Gateway Arch and Mississippi River; *3rd Base (N)* Walnut Street; *1st Base (W)* Seventh Street and 300 Stadium Plaza; *Right Field (S)* Spruce Street; Stadium Plaza surrounds the park
SURFACE Grass 1966 to 1969. Carpet—very fast—1970 to date. From 1970 to 1976, the entire field was carpeted except for the part of the infield that is normally dirt on a grass field. In 1977, this was carpeted except for the sliding pits. This is one of only two instances where there was a full dirt infield, with an otherwise fully carpeted field, the other being Candlestick in 1971.
DIMENSIONS *Foul Lines:* 330; *Power Alleys:* 386 (1966), 376 (1973), 386 (1977), 383 (July 1983), 375 (1992); *Center Field:* 414 (1966), 410 (1971), 414 (1972), 404 (1973), 414 (1977), 402 (1992); *Backstop:* 64 (Vin Scully's unofficial measurement during 1985 World Series showed this to be 50 rather than 64); *Foul Territory:* Large
FENCES *Left and Right Fields:* 10.5 (padded concrete), 8 (padded canvas 1992); *Center Field:* 10.5 (padded concrete 1966), 8 (wood 1973), 10.5 (padded concrete 1977), 8 (padded canvas 1992)
CAPACITY 57,078
PHENOMENA
• A line drive park because of the deep alleys and deep center field and the quick turf.
• Open arches surround the field just below the roof.
• From 1966 to 1982 right field scoreboard lights showed a cardinal in flight when a Cardinal hit a home run; same show was put on each time Lou Brock set a new base-stealing record.
• Home plate transplanted from old Busch Stadium at opener on May 12, 1966.
• Next to the Gateway Arch and the Mississippi River; you can see the Arch from the top deck in right field.
• Statue of "Stan the Man" Musial outside the stadium was unveiled in 1968.
• Small sections of bleachers in the outfield.
• Chicken wire basket (à la Wrigley Field in Chicago), installed in front of left-center and right-center bleacher sections in July 1983, is 2 feet high and reduces distance to fence by 3 feet (386 to 383 in power alleys). It does not raise the height of the 10½ foot wall. No basket in center field bleacher section since it was used only for professional football.
• At league direction, the site designated for any Cubs playoffs or World Series home games from 1986 until 1988, when Wrigley Field got lights.
• Most fans at the stadium seem to be wearing Cardinal red.
• Seventh inning brought the Clydesdale horses to the scoreboard.
• When Anheuser-Busch owned the Cards played "King of Beers" theme song on the organ during the seventh inning stretch instead of "Take Me Out to the Ballgame."

SAN DIEGO, CALIFORNIA

SAN DIEGO JACK MURPHY STADIUM

STYLE Multipurpose
A.K.A. San Diego Stadium 1969 to 1980, Jack Murphy Stadium thereafter
OCCUPANT NL Padres April 8, 1969 to date
EVENT All-Star Games 1978, 1992

LOCATION *Left Field (N)* 9449 Friars Road; *3rd Base (W)* Stadium Way and a quarry; *1st Base (S)* San Diego River, Camino del Rio North, and Interstate 8; *Right Field (E)* Interstate 15
SURFACE Santa Ana Bermuda grass
DIMENSIONS *Foul Lines:* 330 (1969), fence 327 (1982), foul poles 329 (1982); *Power Alleys:* 375 (1969), 370 (1982); *Center Field:* 420 (1969), 410 (1973), 420 (1978), 405 (1982); *Backstop:* 80 (1969), 75 (1982)
FENCES *Left and Right Fields:* 17.5 (concrete 1969), 9 (line painted on concrete 1973), 18 (concrete 1974), 8.5 (canvas 1982); *Center Field:* 17.5 (concrete 1969), 10 (wood 1973), 18 (concrete 1978), 8.5 (canvas 1982), one section in right center 9 (canvas 1982)
FORMER USE San Diego River ran through the area, which was then a marshy swampland.
CAPACITY 47,750
PHENOMENA
• Named for sports editor who campaigned to bring major league baseball to San Diego.
• Noticeable lack of Spanish-speaking fans and Spanish language advertisements in the only major league ballpark on the Mexican border.
• The stadium is circular but open in right.
• Foul poles sit two feet behind the fence, and one foot in front of the wall.
• The right-center scoreboard sits directly behind the right center seats, and is so hot that fans there feel the heat on their backs.
• Only park where bullpen dirt area touches the foul lines.
• Only park where a foul ball can be caught out of sight of all umpires and most players. Location is in either bullpen near the foul poles.
• After 1981 season, the plate was moved 5 feet back toward the backstop.
• Expanded during 1983 football season by adding seats in right and right-center.
• Ivy put on center field fence in 1980.
• 20-foot-wide black batter's eye section on both center field wall and fence July-October 1982.

SAN FRANCISCO, CALIFORNIA

3COM PARK

STYLE Multipurpose
OCCUPANT NL Giants April 12, 1960 to date
A.K.A. Candlestick Park
EVENT All-Star Game 1961, 1984
LOCATION *Left Field (NW)* Giants Drive; *3rd Base (SW)* Jamestown Avenue and Bay View Hill; *1st Base (SE)* Jamestown Avenue, Candlestick Point and San Francisco; *Right Field (NE)* Hunters Point Expressway and San Francisco Bay; Candlestick Point, with its rock outcroppings, was leveled to fill in the water for the parking lots.
SURFACE Grass (1960), Carpet (1971), Bluegrass (1979)
DIMENSIONS *Left Field:* 330 (1960), 335 (1968); *Left-Center:* 397 (1960), 365 (1961); *Center Field:* 420 (1960), 410 (1961); *Right-Center:* 397 (1960), 365 (1961); *Right Field:* 330 (1965), 335 (1968), 330 (1991), 328 (1993); *Backstop:* 73 (1960), 70 (1961), 55 (1975), 65 (1982), 66 (1985); *Foul Territory:* Very large
FENCES 10 (wire 1960); 8 (wire 1972); 12 (6 canvas below 6 plexiglass 1975); 9 (6 canvas below 3 plexiglass 1982); 9 (wire 1984), 9.5 (fence posts 1984); 8 (canvas 1993)
CAPACITY 63,000
PHENOMENA
• Named for jagged rocks and trees which rise from the tidelands like giant candlesticks.
• Bay View Hill overlooks the park from behind 3rd base.
• Many fans arrived by boat in 1960s.
• Only hot-water-heated open-air stadium in the majors.
• Before the bleachers were enclosed, so many fans would stream out of the bleachers in right-center when Mays and McCovey batted and crowd up against the flimsy cyclone fence, that a white line was painted on the asphalt 20 feet behind the fence. Fans had to stand behind this line.
• Fifty-nine posts every 20 feet or so on the outfield fence can cause strange bounces—their tips extend 6 inches above the 9 foot wire fence.
• Wind, wind, and more wind! Before the stadium was enclosed, wind blew in from left-center and out toward right-center. Now that it is enclosed, the wind is a swirling monster, just as strong as before.
• Six Giants retired numbers on white baseballs on the right field fence.
• Maury's Lake—the basepath between first and second was drenched before the game to make it more difficult for Dodger Maury Wills to steal second.
• Umps protested location of foul poles completely in fair territory in third inning of opening game on April 12, 1960.
• Stu Miller was blown off the mound by the wind in the 1961 All-Star Game.
• The stadium was enlarged and fully enclosed in the winter of 1971-72 to house the 49ers.
• Architect John Bolles' boomerang-shaped concrete shell baffle behind the upper tier's last row of seats was intended to protect the park from wind; it didn't work.
• In the winter of 1978-79, the Giants ripped up their carpet and replaced it with grass.
• Coldest park in the majors, resulting in fewer home runs.
• Croix de Candlestick pin awarded to fans at conclusion of night extra-inning games because of extreme wind chill conditions.

SEATTLE, WASHINGTON

KINGDOME

STYLE Dome
A.K.A. King County Stadium, The Tomb (1980s), Puget Puke (1980s)
OCCUPANT AL Mariners April 6, 1977 to date
EVENT All-Star Game 1979
LOCATION *Left Field (N)* 201 South King Street; *3rd Base (W)* 589 Occidental Avenue South; *1st Base (S)* South Royal Brougham Way; *Right Field (E)* Fourth Avenue South and Burlington Northern Railroad tracks;

Above: Domed roof

DIMENSIONS *Left Field:* 315 (1977), 316 (marked 1978), 314 (actual 1978), 324 (1990), 331 (1991); *Left Center:* 375 (1977), 365 (1978), 357 (1981), 362 (1990), 376 (1991); *Deep Left-Center:* 385 (1990), 389 (1991); *Center Field:* 405 (1977), 410 (1978), 405 (1981), 410 (1986), 405 (1991); *Deep Right Center:* 375 (1990), 380 (1991); *Right Center:* 375 (1977), 365 (1978), 357 (1981), 352 (1990); *Right Field:* 315 (1977), 316 (1978), 314 (1990), 312 (1991); *Speakers in Left (3), Left Center, and Center:* 110 (1977), 133.5 (1981); 11 other speakers 130; *Backstop:* 63; *Apex of Dome:* 250; *Foul Territory:* Large

FENCES *Left Field:* 11.5 (wood 1977), 17.5 (6 plexiglass over wood 1988), 11.5 (wood 1990); *Center Field:* 11.5 (wood 1977); *Right Field:* 11.5 (wood 1977), 23.25 (wood 1982), 11.5 (wood 1988)

CAPACITY 59,166

PHENOMENA

• Large American flag flies above the concrete dome.

• 23-foot Mini-Green Monster in right and right-center is called the Walla Walla.

• Carpet is rolled out by the Rhinoceros machine, and smoothed by the Grasshopper machine after it has been zipped together.

• Baby-changing areas in aisles 111, 113, 201, 203.

• Domed roof looks from below like it's made of thousands of bricks.

• Sick's Stadium home plate on display in Royal Brougham trophy case.

• In the winter of 1980-81, the three speakers above left, left-center, and center were raised from 102 to 133.5 feet to reduce the chance of their being hit again.

• Two foul balls have gone up but never come down: August 4, 1979—Ruppert Jones of Mariners hit a foul ball that stuck in the speaker above the first base dugout, thus disproving the old adage of physics that what goes up must come down. On May 20, 1983, Brewer Ricky Nelson did the same. By some arcane logic, both fly balls were ruled strikes.

• Four foul balls have bounced off speakers and been caught for outs: August 3, 1979, caught by A's pitcher Matt Keough; September 3, 1979, caught by Mariners' first baseman; May 19, 1980, caught by Mariners' first baseman; April 25, 1985, caught by Mariners' pitcher Mark Langston.

• Other foul balls have bounced off the Supersonics basketball speakers above first base and the basketball scoreboard above and behind home plate, without being caught.

• One fair ball bounced off a roof support wire and remained in play on April 11, 1985—a ball hit by Dave Kingman of A's was caught for an out in deep left: it would have been a home run. One fair ball has struck the right field speaker—Ken Phelps of the Mariners hit a tape-measure homer on August 13, 1987—the ball landed foul.

• Seven fair balls have bounced off speakers and remained in play.

• Called the Tomb by visiting sportswriters because it was sickeningly gray concrete and quiet in the 1980s.

• Roof's hanging red, white, and blue streamers can tangle up an infield fly and deflect it from the pitcher's mound to behind second base.

• U.S.S. *Mariner*—a huge yellow sailing ship behind the center-field fence which fires a cannon after every Mariner homer.

• 42 air-conditioning units, 16 in fair territory, 26 in foul territory, 8 ducts in each unit. These blow air in toward the field which means fewer home runs in what would normally be a "Homer Dome" because of the short 357 foot power alleys.

• Outfield distances marked on fences in both feet and fathoms 1977-80 (1 fathom = 6 feet).

• Third deck highest at third base and in right field. AL East and AL West standings posted on right field third deck facade.

• Plate moved 10 feet toward first base dugout in 1990 in a change that altered outfield distances.

• New classic "in-play" 123-feet by 11½-foot scoreboard placed on right field wall in 1990 in dramatic facelift.

• Scene of Funny Nose-Eye Glasses night.

• Mariners played home games on the road just before the players' strike in 1994 after tiles fell off roof.

TORONTO, ONTARIO

SKYDOME

STYLE Retractable Dome

OCCUPANT AL Blue Jays June 5, 1989 to date

EVENT All-Star Game 1991

LOCATION *Center Field (N)* Front Street West; *3rd Base (W)* Spadina Avenue; *Home Plate (S)* Gardiner Expressway; *1st Base (E)* John Street and CN Tower, the world's largest free-standing structure

SURFACE Astroturf

DIMENSIONS *Left Field:* 328; *Left Center:* 375; *Center Field:* 400; *Right Center:* 375; *Right Field:* 328; *Apex of Dome:* 282

FENCES 10 (canvas)

FORMER USE Water Supply pumping station where second base is now

CAPACITY 50,516

PHENOMENA

• 400-foot sign in center is actually right of dead center.

• 31 stories high (Astrodome is just 18).

• SkyDome's Jumbotron scoreboard is the world's biggest video display board (115 by 33 feet).

• Hotel inside SkyDome has 348 rooms, 70 with a view of (and by) the stadium.

• SkyDome Fitness Club boasts the world's largest indoor running track (2.2 lap per mile circuit) at the top of the stadium.

• First park to draw over 4 million fans in a season.

• SkyDome's retractable four-panel, 11,000-ton roof takes twenty minutes to open or close; uses $500 in electricity in doing so.

• When roof is opened 91 percent of all seats are exposed to sky.

• Facilities include a Hard Rock Cafe and the 650-seat Windows on SkyDome restaurant.

• Site of first World Series games played outside United States.

• Also home to the Toronto Argonauts of the Canadian Football League.

Storied Parks of the Past

BALTIMORE, MARYLAND

MEMORIAL STADIUM

STYLE Multipurpose
OCCUPANT AL Orioles April 15, 1954 to September 30, 1991
EVENT All-Star Game 1958
LOCATION *Center Field (N)* East 36th Street; *3rd Base (W)* Ellerslie Avenue; *Home Plate (S)* 1000 East 33rd Street, section of 33rd Street near ballpark is known as Babe Ruth Plaza; *1st Base (E)* Ednor Road
SURFACE Bluegrass
DIMENSIONS *Foul Lines:* 309; where the 7-foot fence meets the 14-foot wall, 360; *Power Alleys:* 446 (1954), 447 (1955), 405 (1956), 380 (1958), 370 (1962), 385 (1970), 375 (1976), 378 (1977), 376 (1980), 378 (1990); *Center Field:* 445 (1954), 450 (1955), 425 (1956), 410 (1958), 400 (1976), 405 (1977), 410 (1978), 405 (1980); *Backstop:* 78 (1954), 58 (1961), 54 (1980), 75 (1987); *Foul Territory:* Large
FENCES *Foul Line Corners:* 11.33 (concrete 1954), 14 (11 concrete below 3 plywood 1959); these walls bounce balls toward center, reducing triples; *Left-Center to Right-Center:* 10 (hedges April and May, 1954), 8 (wire June 1954), 7 (wire 1955), 6 (wire 1958), 14 (wire 1961), 6 (wire 1963), 7 (canvas 1977)
FORMER USE Venable Stadium
PHENOMENA
• Beautiful trees on an embankment beyond the fence in center.
• Oriole Landing was a picnic area in the upper deck in the 1960s.
• At the beginning of the 1954 season, hedges served as the center field fence. In June 1954 a wire fence was erected which stood right in front of a row of high hedges. The top 6 feet of the fence were covered with canvas padding in 1958 after Harvey Kuenn cut his face trying to catch a home run ball by climbing the fence. The walls in the left and right field corners were also padded after Curt Blefary injured his hip chasing a Max Alvis fly.
• Fans yelled "O" (for Orioles) in unison when "The Star-Spangled Banner" reaches "O say does that star-spangled banner yet wave . . ."
• Wind usually helps lefthanded hitters.
• Venable Stadium, a football stadium also used for baseball after the July 4, 1944 fire destroyed Oriole Park (V), was torn down to make way for Memorial Stadium. Home plate was moved from where it had been in the north to its current location in the south.
• Home of the best crabcakes in baseball; crab races in the bottom of the sixth on the scoreboard between Wee Willie in orange, Paco in blue, and Mugsy in yellow.
• Inscribed into the concrete facade: "Dedicated as a memorial to all who so valiantly fought in the world wars with eternal gratitude to those who made the supreme sacrifice to preserve equality and freedom throughout the world—time will not dim the glory of their deeds."
• Used for Eastern League Bowie Baysox games in 1993.

BLOOMINGTON, MINNESOTA

METROPOLITAN STADIUM

STYLE Expanded Minor League
A.K.A. Met
OCCUPANT AL Twins April 21, 1961 to September 30, 1981
LOCATION *Left Field (E)* 24th Avenue South, and a cornfield during the 1960s; *3rd Base (N)* Interstate 494; *1st Base (W)* 8001 Cedar Avenue; *Right Field (S)* West 78th Street, later named Killebrew Drive in 1973
SURFACE Grass
DIMENSIONS *Left Field:* 329 (1961), 330 (1962), 344 (1965), 346 (1967), 330 (1975), 343 (1977); *Short Left Center:* 365 (1961), 360 (1966), 373 (1972), 350 (1975), 346 (1976), 360 (1977); *Deep Left Center:* 402 (1961), 435 (1965), 430 (1968), 410 (1975), 406 (1976); *Deep Left Center Corner:* 430 (1965), 406 (1975); *Center Field:* 412 (1961), 430 (1965), 425 (1968), 410 (1975), 402 (1977); *Deep Right Center Corner:* 430 (1965); *Deep Right Center:* 402 (1961), 435 (1965), 430 (1968), 410 (1977); *Short Right Center:* 365 (1961), 373 (1968), 365 (1972), 370 (1977); *Right Field:* 329 (1961), 330 (1962); *Backstop:* 60
FENCES *Left Field:* 8 (wire 1961), 12 (1964), 7 (1974), 12 (1977); *Center Field:* 8 (wire 1961); *Right Field:* 8 (wire 1961), 12 (1964), 8 (1970)
FORMER USE Opened on April 24, 1956 by minor league Millers
CURRENT USE Razed 1984-1985. Future site of Convention Center and amusement park
PHENOMENA
• The 330 foot marker was curiously far away from the foul pole in right, raising the distinct possibility that the distance to right was actually less than 330.
• Most poorly maintained ballpark in the majors. In 1981, broken railings on the third deck overlooking the left field bleachers created a distinct safety hazard.
• First modern stadium to be abandoned.

BOSTON, MASSACHUSETTS

HUNTINGTON AVENUE BASEBALL GROUNDS

STYLE Wooden
OCCUPANT AL Red Sox May 8, 1901 to October 7, 1911
LOCATION *Left Field (N)* Huntington Avenue; *3rd Base (W)* Rogers Avenue, later Forsyth Street; *1st Base (S)* New York, New Haven and Hartford Railroad Tracks; *Right Field (E)* New Gravely Street and Gainsborough Street; just north of South End Grounds
DIMENSIONS *Left Field:* 440; *Center Field:* 635; *Right Field:* 280; *Backstop:* 60
FORMER USE Circuses and carnivals
CURRENT USE Northeastern University's indoor athletic building, known officially as Godfrey Lowell Cabot Physical Education Center and informally as Cabot Cage. A room there, devoted to mementos of the 1901 to 1911 era, is called the World Series Exhibit Room. A plaque commemorating the former location of the right field foul pole was unveiled in May 1956.

PHENOMENA
- Scene of the first NL-AL World Series in 1903.
- The 635 distance to center is an approximation by Bob Bluthardt, working from a scale drawing.

BRAVES FIELD

STYLE   Major League Classic
A.K.A.   National League Field, 1936 to 1940; National League Ball Park, 1936 to 1940; Bee Hive, 1936 to 1940; Wigwam, Nickerson Field
OCCUPANT   NL Braves August 18, 1915 to September 21, 1952 AL Red Sox 1915 and 1916 World Series, and Sunday games 1929 to June 1932
LOCATION   *Left Field (NW)* Boston and Albany R.R. tracks, Storrow Drive, and Charles River; *3rd Base (SW)* Babcock Street; *1st Base (SE)* Commonwealth Avenue; *Right Field (NE)* 34 Gaffney Street
DIMENSIONS   *Left Field:* 402.5 (early 1915), 396 (late 1915), 402.42 (1921), 404 (1922), 402.5 (1926), 320 (April 1928), 353.5 (July 1928), 340 (1930), 353.67 (1931), 359 (1933), 353.67 (1934), 368 (1936), 350 (1940), 337 (1941), 334 (1942), 340 (1943), 337 (1944); *Left Center:* 330 (April, 1928), 359 (July, 1928), 365 (1942); *Center Field:* 520 (1926), 387 (April 1928), 417 (July 1928), 387.17 (1929), 394.5 (1930), 387.25 (1931), 417 (1933), 426 (1936), 407 (1937), 408 (1939), 385 (1940), 401 (1941), 375 (1942), 370 (1943), 390 (1944), 380 (1945), 370 (1946); *Deepest Center Field corner,* just right of straightaway center: 550 (1915), 401 (1942), 390 (1943); *Right Center:* 362 (1942), 355 (1943); *Right Field:* 402 (early 1915), 375 (late 1915), 365 (1921), 364 (1928), 297.75 (1929), 297.92 (1931), 364 (1933), 297 (1936) 376 (1937), 378 (1938), 350 (1940), 340 (early 1943), 320 (late 1943), 340 (April 1944), 320 (May 1944), 340 (April 1946), 320 (May 1946), 318 (1947), 320 (1948), 319 (1948); *Backstop:* 75 (1915), 60 (1936)
FENCES   *Left Field to Right Center:* 10 (concrete 1915), 8 (wood 1928), 20 (wood 1946), 25 (wood 1948), 19 (wood 1953); *Left Field scoreboard sides:* 64 (1949); *middle arch:* 68 (1949); *Left Center:* 1 (gravestones July, 1928); *Right Center:* exit gate 8 (wire); *Right Field:* 10 (6 screen above 4 wood)
FORMER USE   Allston Golf Club
CURRENT USE   Nickerson Field, a football stadium serving as home for the B.U. Terriers and the 1983 USFL Boston Breakers. Also Myles Standish Dorms, three Boston University dorm towers near 3rd base.

PHENOMENA
- In 1915, there was a ground level scoreboard in left.
- In 1928, plate was turned towards right and inner fences were added.
- The infield grass was transported from the old South End Grounds in 1915, and was kept very long by the groundskeepers.
- Left field bleachers installed April 1928, removed slowly in a process that took from mid-June to the end of the season. Scoreboard moved from top of the left center wall to the rear of right field in 1928; later moved to Kansas City Municipal Stadium in 1955.
- Jury Box—small bleachers section behind the fence in right with very vocal fans.
- In 1936, home plate was moved 15 feet closer to the backstop.

- In the 1940s, fir trees were planted beyond the fence in center in an unsuccessful attempt to hide from the fans the huge clouds of railroad locomotive smoke belching from the Boston and Albany tracks in left and center.
- In 1946, the field was turned again slightly toward right. In 1937, a notch was cut in the right field bleachers, which can still be seen today in the former home of the United States Football League Breakers, Nickerson Field.
- In 1946, 5,000 fans left the home opener with green paint on their clothing because that morning's paint job on the seats had not yet dried—the Braves paid $6,000 in claims to irate fans, and played the rest of their April home games at Fenway.
- In June, 1947, the field was lowered by 18 inches.
- Boston University purchased the field in the 1950s, and laid out a football carpet from the first base dugout to right center.
- The right field foul line bleachers, extending from first base to the right field foul pole, still stand.
- The Gaffney Street first base entrance still stands.
- The concrete outer wall in right and center still stands.

BROOKLYN, NEW YORK

EBBETS FIELD

STYLE   Major League Classic
OCCUPANT   NL Dodgers April 9, 1913 to September 24, 1957, NNL Eagles 1935
EVENT   All-Star Game 1949
LOCATION   *Left Field (NE)* Montgomery Street; *3rd Base (NW)* Franklin Avenue, later Cedar Place, later McKeever Place; *1st Base (SW)* 55 Sullivan Place; *Right Field (SE)* Bedford Avenue; in the Pigtown/Crown Heights district of Flatbush, near the Gowanus Canal.
DIMENSIONS   *Left Field:* 419 (1913), 410 (1914), 418.75 (1921), 383.67 (1926), 382.83 (1930), 384 (1931), 353 (1932), 356.33 (1934), 365 (1938), 357 (1939), 365 (1940), 356 (1942), 357 (1947), 343 (1948), 348 (1953), 343 (1955), 348 (1957). There is some confusion about distances because the left field foul line and grandstand wall were the same near the corner between the 343 and 357 markers. *Left-Center:* 365 (1932), 351 (1948); *Deep Left-Center at Bend in Wall:* 407 (1932), 393 (1948), 395 (1954); *Center Field:* 450 (1914), 466 (1930), 460.79 (early 1931), 447 (late 1931), 399.42 (1932), 399 (1936), 402 (1938), 400 (1939), 399 (1947), 384 (1948), 393 (1955); *Right Side of Center Field Grandstand:* 390 (1932), 376 (1948); *Right-Center's Deepest Corner:* 500 (1913), 476.75 (1926), 415 (1932), 403 (1948), 405 (1950), 403 (1955); *Right Side of Right-Center Field Exit Gate:* 399 (1932); *Right-Center:* 352; *Scoreboard:* left side 344, right side 318; *Right Field:* 301 (1913), 300 (1914), 296.17 (1921), 292 (1922), 301 (1926), 296.08 (1930), 295.92 (1931), 296.5 (1934), 297 (1938); *Backstop:* 64 (1942), 70.5 (1954), 72 (1957)
FENCES   *Left Field to Left-Center:* 20 (1913), 3 (wood 1920), 9.87 (concrete 1931); *Center Field:* 20 (1913), 393 marker: 9.87 (concrete 1931) sloping upward; 376 marker: 15 (concrete 1931); *Right-Center:* 9 (concrete 1913), from 376 point to screen: 15 sloping upward to 19, then down to 13; *Right-Center to Right Field:* 38 (top 19

screen, bottom 19 concave concrete wall, bent at 9.5 midpoint, vertical top half, concave angled bottom half); *Screen in Center Field:* 20 (screen above sloping concrete 1920s); *Right Field Before the Screen:* 9 (concrete 1913)

FORMER USE   The Pigtown garbage dump

CURRENT USE   Scoreboard clock now sits on top of right field scoreboard at McCormick Field, Asheville, North Carolina. Ebbets Field Apartments housing development built in 1963 and the I.S. 320 Intermediate School is across the road. Apartments renamed Jackie Robinson Apartments at Ebbets Field in 1972; renamed Ebbets Field Apartments in mid-1970s. Jackie Robinson School, previously known as Crown Heights, houses the Brooklyn Dodger Hall of Fame.

PHENOMENA

• Rotunda was 80-foot circle enclosed in Italian marble with floor tiled with stitches of a baseball, a chandelier with 12 baseball-bat arms holding 12 globes shaped like baseballs. There were 12 turnstiles and 12 gilded ticket windows. The domed ceiling was 27 feet high at its center.

• Little kids watched the game through a gap under the metal gate in right-center.

• Cobblestoned Bedford Avenue was a hill, climbing from a low point in right field to higher ground in center field.

• Right field wall and scoreboard had approximately 289 different angles—the scoreboard jutted out 5 feet from the wall at a 45-degree angle. Overhang of the center field second deck hung out over the field. Scoreboard built after 1930.

• Schaefer Beer sign on the top of the right-center scoreboard notified fans of official scorer's decision—the "H" in Schaefer lit up for a hit, an "E" for an error—the sign was erected after World War II.

• Abe Stark sign offered a free suit at 1514 Pitkin Avenue to any batter hitting the 3-foot-by-30-foot sign.

• Opened on April 5, 1913 for an exhibition game vs. the Yankees; it was discovered that the flag, a press box, and the keys to the bleachers had been forgotten. A press box was finally added in 1929.

• In the winter of 1931-32, the double deck was extended from 3rd base to the left field corner and across to center field.

• According to Roger Kahn, the park was "a narrow cockpit of iron and concrete along a steep cobblestone slope."

• In the winter of 1937-38, box seats were added in center field.

• In the winter of 1947-48, more seats were added to left and center.

• Demolition began on February 23, 1960. Same wrecking ball used 4 years later to demolish Polo Grounds. Eight light towers were moved to Downing Stadium on Randall's Island.

• George Cutshaw of Dodgers hit groundball home run in 1916 which bounced crazily up the concave wall in right and over the fence, to the amazement of Phillies rightfielder Gavvy Cravath.

CHICAGO, ILLINOIS

COMISKEY PARK

STYLE   Major League Classic

A.K.A.   White Sox Park (II) 1910 to 1912, Charles A. Comiskey's Baseball Palace 1910, White Sox Park(III) May 1962 to 1975

OCCUPANT   AL White Sox July 1, 1910 through September 30, 1990; NL Cubs 1918 World Series; NAL American Giants 1941 to 1950

EVENT   First major league All-Star Game, 1933; all Negro League East-West All-Star games, 1933 to 1950; Negro League World Series, eighth through tenth games, 1926; third game, 1943; fifth game, 1946; fourth game, 1947

LOCATION   *Left Field (N)* West 34th; *3rd Base (W)* Portland Avenue, later called South Shield's Avenue; *1st Base (S)* 324 West 35th Street; *Right Field (E)* South Wentworth Avenue, later Dan Ryan Expressway/I-94

SURFACE   *Outfield:* Grass; *Infield:* Grass (1910), Carpet (1969), Grass (1976)

DIMENSIONS   *Foul Lines:* 363 (1910), 362 (1911), 365 (1927), 362 (1930), 342 (1934), 353 (1935), 340 (1936), 352 (1937), 332 (April 22, 1949), 352 (May 5, 1949), 335 (1969), 352 (marked 1971), 349 (actual 1971), 341 (1983), 347 (1986); *Power Alleys:* 382 (1910), 375 (1927), 370 (1934), 382 (1942), 362 (April 22, 1949), 375 (May 5, 1949), 382 (1954), 365 (1955), 375 (1956), 365 (1959), 375 (1968), 370 (1969), 375 (marked 1971), 382 (actual 1971), 374 (1983), 382 (1986); *Center Field:* 420 (1910), 450 (1926), 455 (1927), 450 (1930), 436 (1934), 422 (1936), 440 (1937), 420 (April 22, 1949), 415 (May 5, 1949), 410 (1951), 415 (1952), 400 (1969), 440 (1976), 445 (1977), 402 (marked 1981), 409 (actual 1981), 401 (1983), 409 (1986); *Backstop:* 98 (1910), 71 (1933), 85 (1934), 86 (1955); *Foul Territory:* Large

FENCES   *Foul Lines and Power Alleys:* 12 (concrete 1955), 9.83 (concrete 1959), 5 (wire 1969), 9.83 (concrete 1971); *Center Field:* 15 (1927), 30 (1948), 17 (1976), 18 (1980); *Left-Center to Right-Center Inner Fences:* 5 (canvas 1949), 6.5 (24-foot section in front of bullpens 1969), 9 (1974), 7 (canvas 1981), 7.5 (1982), 11 (1984), 7.5 (1986)

FORMER USE   A truck garden owned by Signor Scavado, and/or a city dump. South Side Park (II) was almost on the same site, across Wentworth Avenue.

PHENOMENA

• Foul lines were old water hoses, painted white and squished flat.

• In 1910, there were bleachers in left and right, but not in center.

• In the winter of 1926-27, wooden bleachers were replaced with concrete and steel, and the pavilions from left around home plate to right were doubledecked. The scoreboard was moved from right center to two locations on the left field and right field walls.

• Center field bleachers were eliminated in 1947 to improve batter's visibility.

• Section of grandstand collapsed May 17, 1913.

• Special elevator for Lou Comiskey, in use from 1931 to 1982, had an inlaid tile floor.

• In 1950 the bullpens were moved from foul territory

down the lines to behind the center field fence.

• In 1960 Bill Veeck installed the first exploding scoreboard in the majors, high above the bleachers in center. In 1982, when the Diamond Vision Board replaced the original, the pinwheels were retained.

• Green cornerstone laid on St. Patrick's Day in 1910 stayed green until 1960 when the exterior was painted all white by Bill Veeck.

• Scene of many masterful groundskeeping tricks by Roger, Gene, and Emil Bossard: (a) Camp Swampy in 1967 referred to the area in front of the plate, dug up and soaked with water when White Sox sinkerball pitchers were on the mound, but mixed with clay and gasoline and burned to provide hard soil if a sinkerballer was pitching for the visiting team. (b) Opposing team bullpen mounds were lowered or raised from the standard 10-inch height to upset visiting pitchers' rhythm. (c) Under Eddie Stanky's managerial tenure, the grass in front of shortstop was cut long because the Sox shortstop had limited range, but at second the grass was cut short because the Sox second sacker had very good range. (d) When the Sox had a lousy defensive outfield, the grass was cut long to turn triples into doubles. (e) When the Sox had speedy line drive hitters, the outfield grass was cut long to turn singles into doubles. (f) When the Sox had good bunters, more paint was added to the foul line in order to tilt the ball back fair.

• Nine speaker horns on the center field bleacher wall.

• Clock on wall in center to left of flag pole.

• Picnic areas, including Bullring in left and Bullpens I and II in right and right-center, Bavarian and Mexican restaurants and beer halls under the stands behind the plate.

• Showers in the bleachers in center.

• Foul poles bend back slightly to join the top of the roof.

• 540 center field listing in 1931-33 *Baseball Guides* is a misprint.

• Organist Nancy Faust played "Na-na-na-na, hey-hey, Good bye."

• Open arches between first and second decks.

CINCINNATI, OHIO

CROSLEY FIELD

STYLE   Major League Classic
A.K.A.   Redland Field 1912 to 1933
OCCUPANT   NL Cincinnati Reds April 11, 1912 to June 24, 1970; NAL Tigers 1937; NAL Clowns 1942 to 1945
EVENT   All-Star Games 1938, 1953
LOCATION   *Left Field* (N) York Street; *3rd Base* (W) McLean Avenue; *1st Base* (S) Findlay Street; *Center Field* (NE) Western Avenue
DIMENSIONS   *Left field:* 360 (1912), 320 (321), 352 (1926), 339 (1927), 328 (1938); *Scoreboard in Left Center* 380383 feet left to right; *Center Field:* 420 (1912), 417 (1926), 395 (1927), 393 (1930), 407 (1931), 393 (1933), 407 (1936), 387 (1938), 380 (1939), 387 (1940), 390 (1944), 387 (1955); *Right Center Field:* 383 (1955); *Deepest Corner:* 387 (1944); *Right Field:* 360 (1912), 384 (1921), 400 (1926), 383 (early 1927), 377 (late 1927), 366 (1938), 366 (1938), 342 (1942), 366 (June 30, 1950),

342 (1953), 366 (1958); *Backstop* 38 (1912), 58 (1927), 66 (1943), 78 (1953)
FENCES   *Center Field* Canvas shield above fence to protect against street light glare (1935 to June 7, 1940); *Left Field* 18 (1938), 12 (1957), 14 (1962), 18 (1963); *Clock on top of the Scoreboard* 58 (1957), 45 (1967); *Left Center to Right Center* 18 (1954), 14 (1962), 13.5 (1963), 23 (9.5 plywood over 13.5 concrete 1965); *Right Field 7.5 (4.5 wire above 3 concrete 1938), 7.5 (4.5 wire above 3 wood 1942), 10 (7 wire above 3 wood 1949), 12 (9 wire above 3 concrete (June 30, 1950), 10 (7 wire above 3 wood 1953), 10 (7 wire above 3 concrete 1958), 9 (6 wire above 3 concrete 1959); Flagpole in left center 82, in play*
FORMER USE   Brickyard, League Park (1884-1901), Palace of the Fans (1902-1911)
CURRENT USE   Reconstructed on farm near Union, Kentucky (a replica has also been constructed at Blue Ash, Ohio). Site used for an industrial park.
PHENOMENA

• Designed by Harry Hake; built at cost of $225,000.

• In the 1920s rented out for movies and dancing, leading to complaints of "immoral dancing" and "vulgar conduct between boys and girls in unlighted portions of the grandstand."

• Steep incline in front of the fence all around the outfield; a pratfall on it by Babe Ruth on May 28, 1935 helped speed his retirement.

• Renamed for Reds owner Powel Crosley, manufacturer of radios, refrigerators and autos.

• Scene of first major league night game (vs. Phillies) on May 24, 1935.

• In January 1937 the Mill Creek flooded, covering the playing field with twenty-one feet of water. Pitcher Lee Grissom and Reds traveling secretary John McDonald rowed a boat over the center field fence.

• Pressbox was not erected until 1938. Prior to that sportswriters sat in the front row of the second deck.

• Both home and visitor clubhouses were located behind left field stands.

• *"Hit this sign and win a Siebler suit"* prominently displayed on Superior Towel & Linen Service Building across street.

• Capacity rose from 20,000 in 1912 to 29,488 in 1970 (yet largest crowd was 36,691 for an April 27, 1947 doubleheader).

• A 65 ×50.2 foot scoreboard installed in left center field in 1957.

PALACE OF THE FANS

STYLE   Wooden
A.K.A.   League Park (III)
OCCUPANT   NL Reds April 17, 1902 to October 6, 1911
LOCATION   *Left Field* (N) York Street; *3rd Base* (W) McLean Avenue; *1st Base* (S) Findlay Street; *Right Field* (E) Western Avenue; *Center Field* (NE) Western Avenue
PHENOMENA

• Pillars and columns patterned after those of the 1893 Columbian Exposition in Chicago.

• Rooters Row—beer drinkers' area next to the field down both foul lines.

• Burned down in the fall of 1911.

CLEVELAND, OHIO

CLEVELAND STADIUM

STYLE Summer Olympics Stadium

A.K.A. Lakefront Stadium 1930s, Cleveland Public Municipal Stadium 1930s, Municipal Stadium 1940s and 1950s

OCCUPANT AL Indians July 31, 1932 to September 24, 1933; August 2, 1936 vs. New York; AL Indians May 30 to September 6, 1937 Sundays and holidays only between Memorial Day and Labor Day; April 1938 to June 1939 Sundays, holidays and selected important games only; AL Indians June 27, 1939 to September 1947 nights, Sundays, holidays, and selected important games (this was a majority of home games in 1940, 1942-46); AL Indians April 15, 1947 to September 26, 1993.

EVENT All-Star Game 1935, 1954, 1963, 1981

LOCATION *Center Field (NE)* East Ninth Street; *3rd Base (NW)* Erieside Avenue and Donald Gray Lakefront Gardens Port Authority Dock 28 and Lake Erie; *Home Plate (SW)* West Third Street; *1st Base (SE)* Cleveland Memorial Shoreway, Amtrak/Conrail railroad tracks; Boudreau Boulevard encircles the park

SURFACE Bluegrass

DIMENSIONS *Foul Lines:* 322 (1932), 320 (1933), 321 (1948), 320 (1953); *Corners Where Inner Fence Meets Stadium Walls:* 362 (1947), 370 (1980); *Power Alleys:* 435 (1932), 365 (1947), 362 (1948), 385 (1949), 380 (1954), 400 (1965), 390 (1967), 395 (1968), 385 (1970), 395 (1991); *Left Center:* 377 (1980); *Right-Center:* 385 (1980); *Deep Left-Center:* 387 (1980); *Deep Right Center:* 395 (1980); *Bleacher Corners:* 463 (1932); *Grandstand Corners:* 435 (1932); *Center Field:* 470 (1932), 467 (1938), 450 (1939), 410 (April 27, 1947), 408 (1966), 407 (1967), 410 (1968), 400 (1970), 415 (1990), 404 (1992); *Backstop:* 60; *Foul Territory:* Large

FENCES *Left and Right Field:* 5.25 (concrete 1932), 5.5 (wire April 27, 1947), 5.25 (concrete June 6, 1947), 6 (1955), 9 (1976), 8 (1977), 8 (canvas 1984)

PHENOMENA

- Architectural style has been called "stripped classicism," and has been compared to later Memorial and County Stadiums in Baltimore and Milwaukee.
- Groundskeepers' tools kept in foul territory in 1930s and 1940s.
- Before the inner fences were installed on April 27 after the first two weeks of the 1947 season, there was an incline in front of the center field bleacher wall; strange shape in power alleys caused by the end of the double-decked grandstand, where the fence jumped abruptly deeper to the bleacher wall in center. The April 27 inner fence curved all the way to the foul poles. On June 6, 1947, it was changed so the inner fence just stretched across center field, hitting the permanent wall at 362 mark.
- Teepees erected in 1946 in center.
- Foul poles were 32 feet 8 inches high, 27 inches wide, and the screen on them is 22 inches wide.
- No one ever hit a ball into the center field bleachers.
- Music bandstand in center field between fence and bleachers set up in 1953.
- Wind usually blew out toward the lake.
- Center field standing-room area was a garden in 1957.
- Field was lowered 2 feet in 1976.
- Cleveland Stadium/League Park ratio of home games from 1936 to 1946—1/77, 15/63, 18/58, 30/47, 49/33, 32/45, 46/34, 48/29, 44/34, 46/31, 41/36.
- Featured in two movies—*The Kid from Cleveland* in 1949, *Fortune Cookie* in mid-1960s.
- Opened formally on July 1, 1931—13 months before the Indians' first home game on July 31, 1932.
- Largest regular season crowd ever—86,563 (84,587 paid)—for doubleheader against Yankees, September 12, 1954.
- Torn down in 1996-97, after the NFL Browns left for Baltimore to become the Ravens.

LEAGUE PARK

STYLE Major League Classic

A.K.A. Dunn Field 1916 to 1927

OCCUPANT AL Indians April 21, 1910 to July 1932; AL Indians April 1934 to September 21, 1946; NAL Bears 1939 to 1940; NAL Buckeyes 1943 to 1948, 1950; Negro League World Series 1st game 1945; 2nd and 5th games 1947

LOCATION *Left Field (E)* East 70th Street; *3rd Base (N)* Linwood Avenue; *1st Base (W)* Dunham Street, later East 66th Street; *Right Field (S)* Lexington Avenue Northeast

DIMENSIONS *Left Field:* 385 (1910), 376 (1921), 374 (1930), 373 (1934) 374 (1938) 375 (1942); *Left Center:* 415 (1942); *Deepest corner, just left of Center Field:* 450 (1926), 467 (1930), 465 (1938), 460 (1939); *Center Field:* 420; *Right Center:* 400 (1942); *Right Field:* 290 (1921), 240 (when roped off for overflow crowds); *Backstop:* 76 (1910), 60 (1942)

FENCES *Left Field:* 5 (concrete); *Left Center:* 10 (7 screen above 3 concrete); *Center Field Scoreboard:* 35; *Right Center Clock:* 20 (left and right sides), 22 (center of clock); *Right Field:* 45 (20 concrete topped by 25 screen 1920), 40 (20 concrete topped by 20 screen 1934)

CURRENT USE Public park, stands were razed in 1950

PHENOMENA

- Named after owner James Dunn (1916 to 1927).
- Seats added in left and center in August 1920 which considerably reduced fence distances. Until that time, center field fence was as distant as center field at Polo Grounds.
- Steel beams protruded from the wall in right, causing balls to bounce at crazy angles. Only here did left fielders handle doubles to right field.
- Large green scoreboard in center field, and a clock just to the right of the scoreboard.
- Megaphone speakers on left center wall.
- Tepees erected in 1946.
- Ticket booths and part of left field stands remain as League Park Community Center.

DALLAS, TEXAS

ARLINGTON STADIUM

STYLE Expanded Minor League

A.K.A. Turnpike Stadium, 1965 to 1971

OCCUPANT AL Rangers April 21, 1972 to October 3, 1993.

LOCATION Arlington, Texas—between Dallas and Fort Worth; *Left Field (E)* Stadium Drive East and Six Flags Over Texas Amusement Park; *3rd Base (N)* 1500 South Copeland Road; *1st Base (W)* Stadium Drive West; *Right Field (S)* Randol Mill Road
SURFACE 419 Bermuda grass
DIMENSIONS *Foul Lines:* 330; *Power Alleys:* 380 (1972), 370 (1974), 383 (1981), 380 (1982); *Center Field:* 400; *Backstop:* 60; *Foul Territory:* Small
FENCES 11 (1972), 12 (1981), 11 (1986)
FORMER USE Minor league ballpark from 1965 to 1971 called Turnpike Stadium
PHENOMENA
• Built in 1965 as Turnpike Stadium.
• Like Dodger Stadium, the field was below the surrounding parking lots. Before 1978, when the upper deck was added, fans would walk in at the top of the stadium.
• Wind blew in directly from the outfield.
• Hottest park in the majors, which increased the number of home runs hit here since the warm humid air is not as dense as cooler drier air elsewhere and therefore does not offer as much resistance to the ball in flight.
• More advertising signs than any other major league park.
• The Lone Ranger on Diamond Vision scoreboard rooted for the Rangers.

DENVER, COLORADO

MILE HIGH STADIUM
STYLE Expanded Minor League
A.K.A. Bears Stadium 1948-1967
OCCUPANT Colorado Rockies, April 9, 1993 to August 11, 1994
LOCATION Interstate 25, Routes 88 and 287, and Routes 70, 287 and 40; Left Field Clay Street; 3rd Base West 20th Street; 1st Base Elliot Street
SURFACE Natural Grass ("Prescription Athletic Turf")
DIMENSIONS *Left field:* 335; *Left Center:* 375; *Center Field:* 423; *Right Center:* 400; *Right Field:* 370
FENCES 10 (padded)
CAPACITY 19,000 (1960), 43,103 (1975), 75,123 (1985), 76,037 (1993)
PHENOMENA
• Home of American Association and Pacific Coast League's Denver Bears/Zephyrs, 1948-1992.
• Also home of NFL's Denver Broncos; former home of United States Football League's Denver Gold.
• Near McNichols Sports Arena, home of NBA Nuggets.
• Rockies drew largest ever season attendance of 4,483,350 in 1993.
• Entire east stands (built in 1977; capacity 21,000) are movable to accommodate both football and baseball; conversion time to football is ten hours; back to baseball, twelve hours.
• Playing field is heated electrically to prevent surface freezing and to allow year-round growth.
• First "fully distributed sound system" in any major US stadium—delivers "near stereo quality sound."
• Largest NL regular season paid crowd ever—80,227—against Expos on April 9, 1993.

The only bigger AL regular season paid crowds have been:
84,587—September 12, 1954—Cleveland Stadium
82,871—June 20, 1948—Cleveland Stadium
81,841—May 30, 1938—Yankee Stadium
81,622—September 9, 1928—Yankee Stadium

HOUSTON, TEXAS

COLT STADIUM
STYLE For Temporary Use
A.K.A. Mosquito Heaven
OCCUPANT NL Colt .45s April 10, 1962 to September 27, 1964
LOCATION *(N)* East/West Utility Road; *(E)* North Stadium Drive; *1st Base (S)* Astrodome—future site; *3rd Base* Loop 610 South, also called South Main Street; Home Plate Kirby Drive
DIMENSIONS *Foul Lines:* 360; *Power Alleys:* 395; *Center Field:* 420; *Deepest corners in center just left and right of straightaway center:* 427; *Backstop:* 60
FENCES Left and Right 8; Center Field Screen 30
CURRENT USE Blacktop in northern Astrodome parking lot
PHENOMENA
• Scoreboard in center on both sides of 30-foot-high batters' background.
• Stiff wind blew in from right toward home.
• Power alley measurements not marked on the wall
• Home of largest and peskiest mosquitoes in major league history. Park was regularly sprayed by the ground crew between innings.
• Lay in decay until early 1970s when it was bought and moved to Torreon, Mexico by a Mexican League team.

KANSAS CITY, MISSOURI

MUNICIPAL STADIUM
STYLE Expanded Minor League
A.K.A. Muehlebach Field 1923 to 1937, Ruppert Stadium 1938 to 1942, Blues Stadium 1943 to 1954
OCCUPANT NAL Monarchs 1923 to 1950; AL Athletics April 12, 1955 to September 27, 1967; AL Royals April 8, 1969 to October 4, 1972; Negro World Series, Games 5-7, 1924; 1-4, 1925; 4, 1942; 3-4, 1946
LOCATION Left Field (N) 21st Street; 3rd Base (W) Euclid Avenue; 1st Base (S) 22nd Street; Right Field (E) 2128 Brooklyn Avenue
DIMENSIONS *Left Field:* 350 (1923), 312 (1955), 330 (1956), 370 (1961), 353 (1962), 331 (1963), 370 (1965), 369 (1967); *Left Center:* 408 (1923), 382 (1955), 375 (1957), 390 (1961), 364 (1963), 392 (1964), 409 (1965), 408 (1969); *Center Field:* 450 (1923), 432 (1950), 430 (1955), 421 (1956), 410 (1964), 421 (1965); *Right Center:* 382 (1955), 387 (1957), 364 (1962), 360 (1963), 392 (1964), 360 (1965), 382 (1969); *Right Field:* 350 (1923), 347 (1955), 352 (1956), 353 (1957), 338 (1963), 325 (1965), 338 (1966); *Backstop:* 60 (1955), 70 (1963)
FENCES *Left Field:* 24 (screen 1956), 18.5 (concrete 1958), 38.5 (20 screen over 18.5 concrete 1959), 10

(1961), 13.5 (1962), 10 (1963), 22 (1967), 13 (1969); *Center Field:* 12 (1958), 14 (1959), 12 (1961), 13.5 (1962), 10 (1963), 22 (screen 1966), 40 (screen 1969), 22 (screen 1970); *Right Field:* 12 (1956), 14 (1959), 12 (1961), 13.5 (1962), 10 (1963), 4.5 (plywood 1965), 40 (screen 1966), 13 (1969), 12 (screen 1970)

FORMER USE Swimming hole, frog pond, and ash heap

PHENOMENA
- Opened on July 23, 1923.
- Originally named for owner George Muehlebach
- When rebuilt for 1955, home plate was moved 25 feet toward the outfield.
- In the spring of 1955, the right center field scoreboard was put into position. It had previously stood in Boston's Braves Field.
- The bottom of the left center light tower was in play—the warning track detoured around it.
- Right field embankment zoo—the mule Charlie O., sheep, China golden pheasants, Capuchin monkeys, German checker rabbits, peafowl, and a German shorthaired pointer dog all lived out there.
- Little Blowhard was a subterranean device that blew compressed air through the middle of the plate so that the umpire didn't have to brush it off.
- Harvey the Mechanical Rabbit rose out of the ground to the right of the plate to offer the umpire new baseballs from a basket between his ears.
- Pennant Porch: Charles O. Finley believed that one reason the Yankees won so many pennants was their 296-foot right field porch. In April 1965, he created his own 296-foot pennant porch in Municipal Stadium's right field.

LAS VEGAS, NEVADA

CASHMAN FIELD

STYLE Minor League
A.K.A. Cashman Field Center
OCCUPANT AL A's April 1-7, 1996
LOCATION Las Vegas Boulevard
DIMENSIONS *Foul Lines:* 328; *Power Alleys:* 364; *Center Field:* 433; *Backstop:* 43
FENCES Left and Right 20; Center 22
CAPACITY 9,353
PHENOMENA
- A's played two series here because their Coliseum was torn up by construction to accommodate the returning NFL Raiders.
- Grassy embankment on the hill behind left field was filled with picnicking fans.
- Usherettes danced the polka in the aisles between innings.
- Home of Las Vegas PCL franchise.
- Most billboards ever at a major league park—47 in fair territory, 9 in foul territory, including Caesar's Palace Magical Empire, Anderson Dairy—Since 1907, Arizona Charlie's—Hit Charlie $ Win Dinner for 2, 92.3 KOMP Rocks Vegas.

LOS ANGELES, CALIFORNIA

LOS ANGELES MEMORIAL COLISEUM

STYLE Summer Olympics Stadium
A.K.A. O'Malley's Chinese Theatre, O'Malley's Alley
OCCUPANT NL Dodgers April 18, 1958 to September 20, 1961
EVENT All-Star Game 1959
LOCATION *Left Field (N)* Exposition Boulevard and museums; *3rd Base (W)* Merlo Avenue and Los Angeles Olympic Swimming Stadium; *1st Base (S)* Santa Barbara Avenue, now Martin Luther King, Jr. Drive; *Right Field (E)* 3911 South Figueroa Street and Los Angeles Memorial Sports Arena
DIMENSIONS *Left Field:* 250 (1958), 251.6 (1959); *Left-Center:* 320 at end of screen rectangle; *Left-Center Where Fence Met Wall:* 425 (1958), 417 (1959); *Center Field:* 425 (1958), 420 (1959); *Right-Center:* 440 (1958), 375 (1959), 394 (1960), 380 (1961); *Right Field Where Fence Met Wall:* 390 (1958), 333 (1959), 340 (1960); *Right Field:* 301 (1958), 300 (1959); *Back-stop:* 60 (1958), 66 (1959); *Foul Territory:* Large; tremendous area on 3rd base line, but almost none on 1st base line
FENCES *Left Field:* 40 (screen 1958), 42 (screen 1959); 60 (2 support towers for screen 1958); *Left Center:* 40 (fence (1958); from foul pole 140 feet into left center, 42 sloping to ground at 30 degree angle from 320 mark to 348 mark for a distance of 24 feet (1959 to 1960); 4 steps down from 42 to 8: 1st step left corner 42 sloping to 41, 2nd step 31, 3rd step 20, 4th step 12 (1961); *Right of Screen in Left-Center:* 8 (wire); *Center Field to Right Field Corner:* 6 (wire); *Right Field Corner:* 4 (concrete)
FORMER USE Agriculture Park in 1890s—fairs, livestock shows, amusement park booths, horse-racing track and barns, saloons. Exposition Park—armory, museum, gardens from 1908 to 1921 along with gravel pit
PHENOMENA
- Wall in left-center jutted out twice, going from chest to thigh level, jutting out to ankle level, jutting out to thigh level, then back again to chest level.
- Concrete wall in the right field corner was the wall surrounding the football field. It sloped sharply away, creating a Fenway-like belly, and allowing a situation where a long drive near the right field foul line would be an out but a short fly down the line would be a home run.
- Huge tunnel behind home plate.
- First used for baseball by USC Trojans, who worked out here before the Dodgers opened the 1958 season.
- O'Malley considered using the Rose Bowl in Pasadena for the first years after the move from Brooklyn and before the Dodgers' Stadium opened. It would have been laid out differently from the Coliseum. Ten rows would have been removed in right and left to deepen the foul lines to 300 feet, and center field would have been 460. The field would have been symmetrical, because home plate would have been in one endzone and center field in the other endzone. Box seats were to have been added behind the plate and between 1st and 3rd.
- The 42-foot screen in left placed to prevent 251 foot popups from becoming homers.
- Commissioner Ford Frick attempted to order the Dodgers to construct a second screen in left, in the seats at 333 feet. A ball clearing both screens would be a home run,

but a ball clearing just the shorter screen would be a double. The California Earthquake Law made construction of such a screen illegal.
- 79 rows of seats.
- 700 feet to furthest seats under peristylum.
- Two stones are on exhibit under the peristylum atop the bleachers in right-center at one end of the oval—the one on the left from Altis, Olympia, Greece, and the one on the right from the Colosseum, Rome, Italy.
- Rim of stadium 110 feet above ground level, field 33 feet below ground level.
- Cable and towers and wires above screen in play.
- Small green light pole in field of play in right field.
- 74,000 seats built from 1921 to 1923, expanded to 105,000 seats for the 1932 Olympic games.
- The right-center fence was shortened in 1959 after 182 homers were hit to left but only 3 to center and 8 to right. In 1959, there were 132 homers to left, 1 to center, 39 to right. In 1960, 155 to left, 3 to center, 28 to right. In 1961, 147 to left, 7 to center, 38 to right.
- Largest World Series crowd ever—92,706 against White Sox on October 6, 1959.

WRIGLEY FIELD

STYLE Minor League
OCCUPANT AL Angels April 27 to October 1, 1961
LOCATION *Left Field (E)* Avalon Boulevard; *3rd Base (S)* East 42nd Place; *1st Base (W)* San Pedro Street; *Right Field (N)* East 41st Place
DIMENSIONS *Left Field:* 340; *Power Alleys:* 345; *Center Field:* 412; *Right Field:* 338.5; *Backstop:* 56
FENCES *Left Field to Center Field:* 14.5 (concrete); *Center Field to Right Field:* 9 (6 wire above 3 concrete)
CURRENT USE Gilbert Lindsay Park, a public playground, and City Center Community Mental Health Facility
PHENOMENA
- Dedicated on September 27, 1925.
- Named for Cubs owner William Wrigley when Los Angeles was a Cub farm team.
- In its minor league days, there were two walls and a picnic area in right. A large office tower stood just to the first base side of home plate above the grandstand. The bottom of the light tower in left center was in play.
- Rear wall at foul pole was 346.58 in 1961.
- In 1961, Wrigley Field set the current record for most homers in one park in one season—248. The reason was that the power alleys were only 5 feet more distant than the foul pole in left.
- Demolished in 1966.

MONTERREY, NUEVO LEON, MEXICO

ESTADIO MONTERREY

STYLE Minor League
OCCUPANT NL Padres vs. Mets August 16-18, 1996
DIMENSIONS *Foul Lines:* 325
FENCES 8 (wire 1969), 5 (wire 1970), 8 (wire 1976)
CAPACITY 25,644
PHENOMENA
- Site of first ML game played outside US or Canada.
- Mexico's Fernando Valenzuela pitched and won first game of "La Primera Serie."

- Fireworks after every homer.
- Modeled after San Diego's Jack Murphy Stadium.
- Next to Monterrey's soccer stadium.
- Harp Music over P.A. after every strikeout.
- Home of Monterrey's Mexican League franchise.

MONTREAL, QUEBEC

PARC JARRY

STYLE For Temporary Use
A.K.A. Jarry Park
OCCUPANT NL Expos April 14, 1969 to September 26, 1976
LOCATION *Left Field (NW)* rue Jarry; *3rd Base (SW)* Canadian Pacific Railroad tracks; *1st Base (SE)* 285, ouest rue Faillon; *Right Field (NE)* rue St. Laurent and a public swimming pool
DIMENSIONS *Left Field:* 340; *Left Center:* 368; *Center Field:* 415 (1969), 417 (1971), 420 (1974); *Right Center:* 368; *Right Field:* 340; *Backstop:* 62
FENCES 8 (wire 1969), 5 (wire 1970), 8 (wire 1976)
CURRENT USE Municipal facility for athletic events
PHENOMENA
- Still under construction during the first two months of Expos home games in April and May 1969.
- Jet stream wind helped drives to left center. Homers to right landed in a swimming pool.
- On April 13, 1971, opening day, fans stood on snow plowed high in mounds behind the 8½-foot wall that stood behind the 5-foot wire screen fence in right field and viewed the game free.

NEW YORK, NEW YORK

HILLTOP PARK

STYLE Wooden
A.K.A. Highlanders Park, New York American League Ballpark, Rockpile, The Hilltop
OCCUPANT AL Highlanders-Yankees April 30, 1903 to October 5, 1912; NL Giants April 15 to May 30, 1911
LOCATION *(N)* West 168th Street; *(W)* Fort Washington Avenue; *(SW)* Deaf and Dumb Asylum; *(S)* West 165th Street; *(E)* Broadway
DIMENSIONS *Left Field:* 365; *Center Field:* 542; *Right Field:* 400
CURRENT USE Columbia Presbyterian Hospital
PHENOMENA
- Excellent view of the Hudson River and the New Jersey Palisades from the upper seats behind the plate.
- Scoreboard in left.
- Large exit gate in right from which fans left after the game.
- Bull Durham sign shaped like a bull in right center in 1909, twice the height of the rest of the fence.
- Memorial dedicated at site of home plate in 1993 through cooperation of the Society for American Baseball Research (SABR), the New York Yankees, and Columbia Presbyterian Hospital.

POLO GROUNDS (IV)

STYLE Major League Classic

A.K.A. Brush Stadium 1911 to 1919, Coogan's Bluff, Coogan's Hollow, Matty Schwab's House, Harlem Meadow

OCCUPANT NL Giants June 28, 1911 to September 29, 1957; AL Yankees May 30, 1912 (morning game); April 17, 1913 to October 8, 1922; NL Mets April 13, 1962 to September 18, 1963

EVENT Negro League World Series first game, 1946; All-Star Game 1934, 1942

LOCATION *Center Field (SE)* Eighth Avenue, then IRT elevated tracks, Harlem River and Harlem River Drive; *3rd Base (NE)* West 159th Street and IRT Rail Yards; *Home Plate (NW)* Bridge Park, then Harlem River Speedway, Coogan's Bluff, and Croton Aqueduct; *1st Base (SW)* West 157th Street trace; Same site as Polo Grounds (III); In Coogan's Hollow, 115 feet below Coogan's Bluff, the last remaining portion of a farm granted to Mr. John Lion Gardiner by the King of England in the seventeenth century

DIMENSIONS *Left Field:* 277 (1911), 286.67 (1921), 279.67 (1923), 279 (1930), 280 (1943), 279 (1955); *Left Field, Second Deck:* 250; *Left Center, Left of Bullpen:* 447; *Left-Center, Right of Bullpen:* 455; *Front Clubhouse Steps:* 460; *Center Field:* 433 (1911), 483 (1923), 484.75 (1927), 505 (1930), 430 (1931), 480 (1934), 430 (1938), 505 (1940), 490 (1943), 505 (1944), 480 (1945), 490 (1946), 484 (1947), 505 (1949), 483 (1952), 480 (1953), 483 (1954), 480 (1955), 475 (1962), 483 (1963); *Bleacher Corners:* 475; *Right-Center, Left of Bullpen:* 449; *Right-Center, Right of Bullpen:* 440; *Right Field:* 256.25 (1921), 257.67 (1923), 257.5 (1931), 257.67 (1942), 259 (1943), 257.67 (1944); *Right Field Photographers Perch:* 249; *Backstop:* 65 (1942), 70 (1943), 65 (1944), 70 (1946), 74 (1949), 65 (1954), 74 (1955), 65 (1962); *Foul Territory:* Very large. There's a lot of confusion here. During the Giants' stay it was 483 to the front of the clubhouse, and probably 505 to the rear clubhouse wall above the overhang. Why the 483 marker sometimes was changed to 480 or 475, is not known but it could have been due to remeasurements or a slight shift of home plate's location. Or it could have been a measurement to the base of the Eddie Grant Memorial. In the Giants' time, reading from left to right, the markers read 315, 360, 414, 447, 455, 483, 455, 449, 395, 338, 294. In the Mets' time, they read 306, 405, 475, 405, 281. The foul lines were never marked. One possibility is that it was 433 feet to the front of the bleachers, 475 to the beginning of the clubhouse overhang, 483 to the rear wall under the overhang, and 505 to the front of the high wall. The 21-foot overhang of the second deck in left reduced the distance to the second deck from 279 to 250, not 258, because of the angle involved.

FENCES—1911-22 *Left to Center:* 10 (concrete); *Center:* 20 (tarp); *Right-Center:* 10 (concrete); *Right Field:* 12 sloping to 11 at pole (concrete)

FENCES—1923-63 *Left Field:* 16.81 (concrete); *Left-Center:* 18 (concrete); *Where Left-Center Wall Ended at Bleachers:* 12 (concrete); *Center Field Bleachers Wall:* 8.5 (4.25 wire on top of 4.25 concrete) on both sides of clubhouse runway; *Center Field Hitters' Background:* 16.5 on both sides of clubhouse runway; *Center Field Clubhouse:* 60 high and 60 wide—50 high in 1963; *Center Field Top of Longines Clock:* 80; *Center Field Top of Right Side of Scoreboard:* 71; *Center Field Top of Left Side of Scoreboard:* 68; *Center Field Top of Middle of Scoreboard:* 64; *Center Field Top of 5 Right Scoreboard Windows:* 57; *Center Field Top of 4 Left Scoreboard Windows:* 55; *Center Field Bottom of 5 Right Scoreboard Windows:* 53; *Center Field Bottom of 4 Left Scoreboard Windows:* 48; *Center Field Bottom of Clubhouse Scoreboard:* 31; *Center Field Top of Rear Clubhouse Wall:* 28; *Center Field Top of Front Clubhouse Wall:* 19; *Center Field Top of 14 Lower Clubhouse Windows:* 16; *Center Field Bottom of 14 Lower Clubhouse Windows:* 11; *Center Field Clubhouse floor Overhang:* 8; *Center Field Top of Eddie Grant Memorial:* 5; *Center Field Width of Little Office on Top of Lower Clubhouse:* 10; *Right Center:* 12 (concrete); *Right Field:* 10.64 (concrete)

FORMER USE Underneath the Harlem River until filled in with dirt in the late 1870s.

CURRENT USE Polo Grounds Towers—four 30-story apartment buildings. Willie Mays Field—an asphalt playground with 6 basketball backboards where center field used to be, a brass historical marker in place.

PHENOMENA

- Originally named for owner John T. Brush.
- Second deck in right had 9-foot photographer's perch overhang 60 feet from foul pole out into right-center.
- Bullpens in fair territory in left-center and right-center.
- There was no line on the 60-foot-high center field clubhouse above which a ball would be a home run.
- The outfield was slightly sunken. A manager, standing in his dugout, could see only the top half of his outfielders. At the wall, the field was 8 feet below the infield.
- The left field second deck overhang meant that a homer to left was easier than a homer to right, even though the wall in left was 279 and the wall in right was 258. The overhang was 21 feet, but it effectively shortened the distance required for a pop-fly homer to the second deck in left to 250 feet because of the angle involved.
- The overhangs here and at Tiger Stadium and Shibe Park have more significance than one might suspect, according to research published by the professional society for physicists, the American Physical Society. The batted ball's trajectory consists of two component vectors, horizontal and vertical. The vertical deceleration is constant over time due to gravity, but the horizontal deceleration increases over time due to wind resistance and atmospheric drag. Near the end of its flight, the ball is coming down sharply, rather than arcing down as it arched up, as would occur in a vacuum. So many outfielders have watched helplessly as a ball they could catch dropped into the 2nd deck.
- Hitter's background extended beyond the end of the bleacher wall, several feet into the clubhouse gap.
- The field sloped in a "turtle back" just beyond the infield dirt. It sloped down 1.5 feet to drains about 20 feet into the outfield, then back up again.
- Right-center wall sloped gradually from 11 feet at pole to 12 feet at the bleachers.
- Left-center wall sloped from 16 feet 9.75 inches at the pole to 18 feet in left center, then abruptly fell to 16 feet and then to 14 feet and sloped gradually to 12 feet at the bleachers. When ad signs were removed in the 1940s, the

abrupt changes in height in left-center disappeared.
• After the all-wooden Polo Grounds (III) burned down April 14, 1911, Polo Grounds (IV) was built with temporary stands for 1911. The infield stands were rebuilt with concrete for 1912, and the outfield concrete double deck was finished in 1922. The bleachers in left-center and center were wood remaining from before the fire.
• In 1914, there were 2 bends in the wall in right-center.
• In 1917, the fans exited from the field through gates under the center field bleachers.
• Morris James Mansion sat up on Coogan's Bluff, overlooking the ballpark.
• Brush Stairway led down from Coogan's Bluff to the Speedway and the ticket booths behind home plate.
• Coats of arms of all the teams in the National League on the top of the grandstand. Removed in the 1920s.
• Dedicated on May 30, 1921, to a former Giant killed in World War I, the Eddie Grant Memorial stood in center at the base of the clubhouse wall. It was 5 feet high. The Memorial reads:

In Memory of
Capt. Edward Leslie Grant
307th Infantry - 77th Division
A.E.F.
Soldier - Scholar - Athlete
Killed in action
Argonne Forest
October 5, 1918
Philadelphia Nationals
1907-1908-1909-1910
Cincinnati Reds
1911-1912-1913
New York Giants
1913-1914-1915
Erected by friends in Baseball,
Journalism, and the Service.

• In the winter of 1922-23, the concrete double decks were extended all the way to either side of the new concrete bleachers in center, housing the clubhouse. Unfortunately, the Roman Colosseum facade frescoes were removed during that winter also.
• Bleachers in center remodeled in 1923.
• In 1929, the first attempt was made to wire the umpires for sound and reconnect them into the PA system. It didn't work too well.
• Speaker placed above Grant Memorial in 1931.
• Field raised 4½ feet in 1949 to help with drainage. In 1609 and 1874 maps, the location is shown to be underneath the Harlem River. The water table was only 2-6 feet below the playing surface, and drainage was complicated by rainwater cascading off the 115-foot-high Coogan's Bluff down onto the site.
• During the 1950s, groundskeeper Matty Schwab and his family lived in an apartment under Section 3 of the left field stands built for him by Horace Stoneham. The apartment was the main bait in Mr. Stoneham's successful offer to grab Mr. Schwab away from the hated Dodgers in 1950.
• A two-foot-square section of sod from center field was removed and taken to San Francisco in the fall of 1957.
• Home plate was moved out toward center several feet by the Mets in the winter of 1961-62.
• During the Mets' stay in 1962 and 1963, Johnny McCarthy and his crew of groundskeepers painted Schwab's

four rooms pink, installed a shower and plywood on the floor and lockers, and called it their Pink Room.
• In 1962 and 1963, the Howard Clothes sign on the outfield wall promised a boat to any player hitting it.
• Demolition started on April 10, 1964, with same wrecking ball that demolished Ebbets Field.

PHILADELPHIA, PENNSYLVANIA

BAKER BOWL

STYLE   Major League Classic
A.K.A.   Huntingdon Street Baseball Grounds 1895 to July 1913, National League Park (III) 1895 to 1938, Hump, Cigar Box, Band Box, Philadelphia Park
OCCUPANT   NL Phillies April 14, 1904 to May 14, 1927; NL Phillies June 24, 1927 to June 20, 1938; also neutral use by NL Cleveland versus Baltimore July 29, July 30, and August 11, 1898; and versus Washington August 5, 6, and 8, 1898
EVENT   Negro League World Series first and second games 1924, fifth and sixth games 1925, fourth and fifth games 1926
LOCATION   *Left Field (N)* West Lehigh Avenue; *3rd Base (W)* North 15th Street; *1st Base (S)* West Huntingdon Street; *Right Field (E)* North Broad Street; *Beneath* Philadelphia and Reading Railroad tracks in a tunnel
DIMENSIONS   *Left Field:* 335 (1921), 341.5 (1926), 341 (1930), 341.5 (1931); *Center Field:* 408; *Right-Center:* 300; *Right Field:* 272 (1921), 279.5 (1924), 280.5 (1925); *Backstop:* 60
FENCES   *Left Field:* 4 (1895), 12 July (1929); *Left-Center Field Clubhouse to Right-Center:* 35 (1895), 47 (with 12 screen on top 1915); *Right Field:* 40 (tin over brick 1895), 60 (40 tin over brick, topped by 20 screen 1915)
CURRENT USE   Parking lot and car wash in right-center, gas station in center, bus garage from home down right field foul line
PHENOMENA
• Named after Phillie owner William F. Baker.
• Named the Hump because it was on an elevated piece of ground that had a railroad tunnel underneath the outfield.
• Swimming pool in the basement of the center field clubhouse prior to World War I.
• Coke and "Health Soap Stops B.O." Lifebuoy signs on the high right field wall.
• Extra seats added in front of the fence in center for the 1915 World Series led directly to the Phillies losing the Series' last game.
• During Prohibition, the outfield wall liquor ads were boarded over with dirty grimy blank boards.
• Home plate moved back a foot in 1925, making the right field foul pole 280.5 rather than 279.5.
• Torn down in 1950.

SHIBE PARK

STYLE   Major League Classic
A.K.A.   Connie Mack Stadium 1953 to 1970
OCCUPANT   AL Athletics April 12, 1909 to September 19, 1954; NL Phillies May 16 to May 28, 1927; NL Phillies July 4, 1938 to October 1, 1970

EVENT Negro League World Series fifth game 1942; fourth game 1945; third game 1947; All-Star Game 1943, 1952

LOCATION *Left Field (N)* West Somerset Street; *3rd Base (W)* North 21st Street; *1st Base (S)* West Lehigh Avenue; *Right Field (E)* North 20th Street

DIMENSIONS *Left Field:* 360 (1909), 378 (late 1909), 380 (1921), 334 (1922), 312 (1926), 334 (1930); *Center:* 515 (1909), 502 (late 1909), 468 (1922), 448 (1950), 440 (1951), 460 (1953), 468 (1954), 447 (1956), 410 (1969); *Right Center:* 393 (1909), 390 (1969); *Right Center, Left of Scoreboard:* 400 (1942); *Right Field:* 360 (1909), 340 (late 1909), 380 (1921), 307 (1926), 331 (1931), 331 (to lower 1934), 329 (to upper iron fence 1934); *Backstop:* 90 (1942), 86 (1943), 78 (1956), 64 (1960)

FENCES *Left Field to Left Center:* 12 (4 screen above 8 concrete 1949); *Center Field, Small Section:* 20 (1955), 8 (wood 1956), 3 (canvas 1969); *Right-Center Scoreboard:* 50 (top of black scoreboard 1956), 60 (top of Ballantine Beer sign 1956); *Right Field:* 12 (concrete 1909), 34 (22 corrugated iron above 12 concrete 1935), 30 (1943), 50 (1949), 40 (1953), 30 (1954), 40 (1955), 32 (1956)

FORMER USE City dog pound, also a brickyard in the Swampoodle neighborhood nearby

CURRENT USE Vacant site. Several hundred of the seats are being used now in Duncan Park, former home of the Sally League Phillies in Spartanburg, South Carolina, and in War Memorial Stadium, Greensboro, North Carolina

PHENOMENA
• The first concrete and steel stadium in the majors.
• Named for Ben Shibe, an A's stockholder and baseball manufacturer.
• French Renaissance churchlike dome on exterior roof behind the plate which housed Connie Mack's office.
• Sod transplanted here from Columbia Park.
• Highest pitcher's mound—20 inches high.
• Batting cage sat behind short fence in center when the measurement was only 447.
• Corrugated iron fence in right—balls bounced at crazy angles off it—top 22 feet of 34-foot fence—2-foot-deep frame—was 329 to front of frame, 231 to rear of frame where iron sheets were.
• Conduit on right field wall was in play.
• Slopes in front of the outfield fences in early years.
• Ladder in front of left field scoreboard, 1909—went all the way to the top.
• Doubledecked in 1925; also in that year left field stands added.
• Mezzanine added in 1929.
• Right field wall reinforcement in 1934 reduced distance to front of the frame from 331 to 329, but sign wasn't changed until 1956.
• Before 1935, 20th Street residents could sit in their front bedroom or on their roof and see the game free over the 12-foot right-field fence. Fans could see the lines of laundry on the roof of 20th Street houses. Connie Mack lost a suit to prevent this, so he built the high right-field fence.
• 1948 plans to add 18,000 seats in right field and reduce foul line to 315 feet never materialized.

• In 1956, the old Yankee Stadium scoreboard may have been installed in front of the right-center wall; later a clock was added—balls hitting the clock were homers—top of clock was 75 feet high; top of Ballantine Beer sign, 60 feet high.
• In 1956 the normal screen was replaced by see-through plexiglass—protected the fans behind the plate from foul balls.
• Home plate moved to Veterans Stadium in 1971.
• Fire damaged it on August 20, 1971.
• Last game on October 1, 1970.
• Torn down in June 1976.

PITTSBURGH, PENNSYLVANIA

FORBES FIELD

STYLE Major League Classic

A.K.A. Oakland Orchard, Dreyfuss' Folly

OCCUPANT NL Pirates June 30, 1909 to June 28, 1970; NNL Grays 1939 to 1948

EVENT Negro League World Series second game 1942; fourth and fifth games 1944; second game in 1945; All-Star Game 1944, 1959

LOCATION *Left Field (NE)* Schenley Park, then Bigelow Boulevard; *3rd Base (NW)* Sennott (also spelled "Sonnett" at times) Street, then Cathedral of Learning; *1st Base (SW)* Boquet (also spelled "Bouquet" at times) Street; *Right Field (SE)* Joncaire Street, Pierre Ravine, Junction Hollow, Junction Railroad tracks

DIMENSIONS *Left Field:* 360 (1909), 356.5 (1921), 356 (1922), 360 (1926), 365 (1930), 335 (1947), 365 (1954); *Deepest Corner, Left of Straightaway Center, at the Flag Pole:* 462 (1909), 457 (1930); *Center Field:* 442 (1926), 435 (1930); *Right-Center, Right Side of Exit Gate:* 416 (1955); *Right-Center:* 375 (1942); *Bend at Left End of Screen:* 375; *Right Field:* 376 (1909), 376.5 (1921), 376 (1922), 300 (1925); *Backstop:* 110 (1909), 84 (1938), 80 (1947), 84 (1953), 75 (1959)

FENCES *Left Field Front Fence:* 8 (5 screen above 3 wood 1947), 12 (9 screen on top of 3 wood 1949), 14 (screen 1950); *Left Field Wall:* 12 (1909), 12 (brick and ivy 1946); *Left Field Scoreboard:* 25.42 (steel left and right sides), 27 (middle); *Wooden Marine Sergeant at Parade Rest to Right of Scoreboard:* 32 (June 26, 1943 to end of season); *Side Wall Angling Back to Meet Brick Wall in Left-Center:* 12 (wood, when front fence was up); *Cages Around Light Tower Just Right of Scoreboard and in Power Alleys:* 16.5; *Center Field:* 12 (wood 1909), 12 (brick and ivy 1946); *Right-Center:* 9.5 (concrete 1925); *Screen—Left Side at 375 Mark:* 24 (14.5 wire above 9.5 concrete 1932); *Screen—Right Side at Flag Pole:* 27.67 (18.17 wire above 9.5 concrete 1932)

FORMER USE Part of Schenley Farms, a hothouse and livery stable. Land for grazing cows. Ravine where right field would be. Football site for University of Pennsylvania vs. Carnegie Tech October 31, 1908, game. Penn won on the rocky field.

CURRENT USE Mervis Hall, out in right field, and the University of Pittsburgh's Forbes Quadrangle in the infield. The center field and right-center brick walls still stand, along with the base of the flag pole. Mazeroski Field, a Little League diamond beyond the left field brick wall, still remains. Roberto Clemente Drive now bisects the site, and runs about 10 feet under what used to be the playing surface of the infield.

PHENOMENA

• 1st base by a misspelled street: Boquet Street was named for General Henry Bouquet, a Swiss soldier who fought for the British in the French and Indian War's decisive battle at Fort Duquesne.

• Named for General John Forbes, a British general in the French and Indian War who captured Fort Duquesne and renamed it Fort Pitt in 1758.

• Ivy-covered brick wall in left and left-center.

• The 14-foot Longines clock with speaker horns on top of the left field scoreboard were out of play—a drive hitting it was a home run.

• Fans in the upper left corner of the left field bleachers could not see the plate because of the third base grandstand, which stood between them and the plate. Right field roof was 86 feet high.

• During World War II, the right field screen could not be replaced due to the priority given to the war effort. It deteriorated badly.

• No no-hitter was ever pitched here.

• Home plate remains in almost its exact original location, only now it is encased in glass on the first-floor walkway of the University of Pittsburgh's Forbes Quadrangle.

• The bottoms of the light-tower cages in left-center, center, and right-center were in play, as was the bottom of the center field flag pole.

• Just to the left of the flag pole stood the batting cage, also in play. Before being placed in left-center, it stood behind home plate.

• Very hard infield surface—ask Tony Kubek!

• Back in the 1910s, there was a small scoreboard on the center field wall.

• In 1920s, cars and trucks were repaired and sold beneath the left field bleachers.

• Right field stands built in 1925, reducing distance to right field foul pole by 76.5 feet. Right field screen added in 1932. It was taken down for a short period once, then put back up.

• Barney Dreyfuss Monument was just to the left of the exit gate in right-center where fans exited the ballpark into Schenley Park after a game. It was installed on June 30, 1934, on the park's 25th anniversary, and was made of granite with a bronze tablet.

• Greenberg Gardens, also called Kiner's Korner: the area between the scoreboard and a chicken coop wire short fence in left put there to increase home run production from 1947 to 1953—called Greenberg Gardens 1947, Kiner's Korner 1948 to 1953.

• When Greenberg Gardens were in place, a Western Union clock stood on top of the scoreboard, to the right of the familiar Gruen Clock. Torn down in 1972 and 1973.

• In 1938, with the Buccos apparently on their way to the World Series, they built a third deck of seats behind the plate called the Crow's Nest, which had the major leagues' first elevator. Bucs finally made the Series 22 years later.

• During World War II, from June 26 through the end of the 1943 season, a huge U.S. Marine made of wood stood against the left field wall, just to the right of the scoreboard. Standing at parade rest, the Marine sergeant was 32 feet high, 15 feet wide across his feet, and in play.

• Honus Wagner statue in Schenley Park erected 1955—18 feet high, 1,800 pounds—moved to Three Rivers with Bucs in 1970.

• A plaque today marks the spot where Bill Mazeroski's World Series-winning homer left the park in 1960 and flew into the trees above Yogi Berra's head.

• Green foam rubber crash pads placed on concrete wall in right and right-center, first in majors. Wooden walls installed in left and center in 1909, replaced with brick and ivy in 1946.

• Street deadending into Sennott Street by 3rd base was called at various times Pennant Place and Forbes Field Avenue.

• Fires damaged park December 24, 1970, and July 17, 1971. Destruction began July 28, 1971.

• Site also occupied today by Deliverance Evangelistic Church.

ST. LOUIS, MISSOURI

SPORTSMAN'S PARK (IV)

STYLE Major League Classic

A.K.A. Busch Stadium (I) 1953 to 1966, Bill Veeck's House

OCCUPANT AL Browns April 14, 1909 to September 27, 1953; NL Cardinals July 1, 1920 to May 8, 1966; NAL New Orleans–St. Louis Stars one game 1941

EVENT All-Star Game 1940, 1948, 1957

LOCATION *Left Field (NE)* Sullivan Avenue; *3rd Base (NW)* North Spring Avenue; *1st Base (SW)* 3623 Dodier Street; *Right Field (SE)* 2911 North Grand Avenue, later North Grand Boulevard. Same as earlier Sportsman's Parks, but turned around so that home plate was in the west-southwest corner

DIMENSIONS *Left Field:* 368 (1909), 340 (1921), 356 (1923), 355 (1926), 360 (1930), 351.1 (1931); *Left Center:* 379; *Center Field:* 430 (1926), 450 (1930), 445 (1931), 420 (1938), 422 (1939); *Deepest Corner Just Left of Dead Center:* 426 (1938); *Deepest Corner Just Right of Dead Center:* 422 (1938); *Right Center:* 354 (1942); *Right Field:* 335 (1909), 315 (1921), 320 (1926), 310 (1931), 332 (1938), 309.5 (1939); *Backstop:* 75 (1942), 67 (1953)

FENCES *Left to Center:* 11.5 (concrete); *354 Mark in Right-Center to Right:* 11.5 (1909), 33 (11.5 concrete below 21.5 wire July 5, 1929), 11.5 (1955), 36.67 (11.5 concrete below 25.17 wire 1956)

CURRENT USE Herbert Hoover Boys' Club, with a baseball diamond where the major league one used to be

PHENOMENA

• The local newspaper, the *Globe-Democrat*, had an ad on the right-center wall which showed the star of the previous game. Just to the right of this ad, the league standings for both leagues were listed.

• The Busch eagle would flap its wings after a Cardinal home run. It sat on top of the left-center scoreboard. During World War II, there was a War Chest sign there.

• Cards office was at 3623 Dodier, Browns office was at 2911 North Grand.

• Pavilion seats in the power alley in right center.

- Second deck from first to third added in 1909.
- Second deck expanded to foul poles in 1925.
- Bleachers were added to parts of outfield in 1926.
- Beginning in the 1940s, the outfield signs were 351, 358, 379, 400, 426, 425, 422, 422, 405, 354, 322, and 310. In the mid 1950s, the 426 and the right 422 signs that marked the corners just left and right of straightaway center were removed.
- Flag pole in fair territory until removed in the 1950s.
- Bill Veeck's family lived in an apartment under the stands in the 1950s.
- When he bought the stadium from the Browns in 1953, Card owner Gussie Busch almost named it Budweiser Stadium, but was prevented by league pressure.
- The wire screen in front of the right field pavilion was removed for the entire 1955 season. It had been installed on July 5, 1929.
- A helicopter carried home plate to Busch Memorial Stadium after the last game on May 8, 1966.
- The old 1902–8 grandstand behind home plate became the left field pavilion in this park from 1909 to 1925 when it was replaced.

SAN FRANCISCO, CALIFORNIA

SEALS STADIUM
STYLE Minor League
A.K.A. Home Plate Mine
OCCUPANT NL Giants April 15, 1958 to September 20, 1959
LOCATION *Left Field (E)* Potrero Avenue; *3rd Base (N)* Alameda Street; *1st Base (W)* Bryant Street; *Right Field (S)* 16th Street and Franklin Square Park
DIMENSIONS *Left Field:* 365 (1958), 361 (1959); *Left Center:* 375 (1958), 364 (1959); *Just Left of Straightaway Center in the Corner:* 404; *Center Field:* 410 (1958), 400 (1959); *Just Right of Straightaway Center in the Corner:* 415; *Just Right of the 415 Mark Where the Seats Jutted Out:* 397; *Right Field:* 355 (1958), 350 (1959); *Back Stop:* 55.42
FENCES *Left Field:* 15 (5 concrete below 10 wire); *Center Field Scoreboard:* 30.5; *Right Field:* 16 (5 concrete below 11 wire)
CURRENT USE San Francisco Auto Center
PHENOMENA
- Opened April 7, 1931.
- The original deed for the land under the park was listed as "Home Plate Mine."
- No warning track.
- Wind blew from right to left.
- Nearby Hamms Brewery still standing.

SEATTLE, WASHINGTON

SICK'S STADIUM
STYLE Expanded Minor League
A.K.A. Sick's Select Stadium 1940s, Seattle Stadium 1940s
OCCUPANT AL Pilots April 11 to October 2, 1969
LOCATION *Left Field (E)* Empire Way South; *3rd Base (N)* South Bayview Street; *1st Base (W)* 2700 Ranier Avenue South; *Right Field (S)* South McClellan Street
DIMENSIONS *Left Field:* 305; *Power Alleys:* 345;

Corners just right and left of center: 405; *Center Field:* 402; *Right Field:* 320; *Backstop:* 54
FENCES *Left Field:* 8 (3 concrete below 5 wire); *Center Field:* 12.55 (3 concrete below 9.55 wire); *Right Field:* 8 (3 concrete below 5 wire)
PHENOMENA
- Opened June 15, 1938 for PCL franchise.
- Bleachers down the left field line just as at Forbes Field. Fans could see Mt. Rainier in the distance.
- On April 11, 1969, fans could get a free view of the Pilots' opening day game by looking through numerous openings in the unfinished left field fence. Seven thousand seats were unfinished and 700 fans had to wait an hour before they could take their seats while the carpenters finished their work.
- Insufficient water pressure if crowd was large.
- Used by Class A teams in early 1970s.

WASHINGTON, D.C.

GRIFFITH STADIUM
STYLE Major League Classic
A.K.A. National Park (III) 1911 to 1921, Clark Griffith Park 1922
OCCUPANT AL Senators (I) April 12, 1911 to October 2, 1960; ECL Potomacs 1924; NEWL Pilots 1932; NNL Elite Giants 1936 to 1937; NNL Washington-Homestead Grays half of their home games 1937 to 1948; NNL Black Senators 1938; AL Senators (II) April 10 to September 21, 1961; Negro League World Series first game 1942, first and second games 1943; third game 1945
EVENT All-Star Game 1937, 1956
LOCATION *Left Field (E)* Larch Street, later Fifth Street NW; *3rd Base (N)* Howard University, then W Street NW; *1st Base (W)* J. Frank Kelley Lumber and Mill Works, then Georgia Avenue NW, also called Seventh Street NW; *Right Field (S)* Spruce Street, later U Street NW
DIMENSIONS *Left Field:* 407 (1911), 424 (1921), 358 (1926), 407 (1931), 402 (1936), 405 (1942), 375 (Opening Day 1947), 405 (remainder 1947), 402 (1948), 386 (1950), 408 (1951), 405 (1952), 388 (1954), 386 (1956), 350 (1957), 388 (1961); *Left of Left-Center at Corner:* 383 (1931), 366 (1954), 360 (1956); *Right of Left-Center at Bend in Bleachers: 409 (1942), 398 (1954), 383 (1955), 380 (1956); Left-Center:* 391 (1911), 380 (1950); *Center Field:* 421; *Center Field Corner to Left of Building Protection Wall:* 423 (1926), 441 (1930), 422 (1931), 426 (1936), 420 (1942), 426 (1948), 420 (1950), 394 (1951), 420 (1952) 421 (1953), 426 (1954), 421 (1955), 426 (1961); *Inner Tip of Building Protection Wall:* 409 (1943), 408 (1953); *Deepest Corner—Right End of Building Protection Wall*; *Right Center:* 378 (1954), 372 (1955), 373 (1956); *Right Field:* 328 (1909), 326 (1921), 328 (marked 1926), 320 (actual 1926), 320 (1956); *Backstop:* 61
FENCES *Left Field:* 11.25 (foul pole to 408 mark concrete 1953), 12 (from 410 corner near left field foul pole to 408 mark just right of dead center 1954), 8 to 10 (wood in the corner in front of the bullpen at the foul pole 1955), 6.5 (wire and plywood in front of bullpen 1956); *Center Field:* 30 (concrete 408 mark to 457 mark 1953), 31 (concrete 408 mark to 457 mark 1954), 6 (wire and ply-

wood 1956); *Right-Center*: to the left of the scoreboard in front of the bullpen: 4 (wood from 457 mark to 435 mark 1953), 10 (wood 1955), 4 (wood 1959); *Right Center Scoreboard:* 41 (1946); *National Bohemian Beer Bottle:* 56 (1946); *Right Field:* 30 (concrete 1953), 31 (concrete 1954)

CURRENT USE   Howard University Medical Center and Howard University College of Dentistry, 909 seats now in use at Tinker Field in Orlando, Florida

PHENOMENA

• Loudspeaker horn high on the wall in center.

• The center field wall detoured around 5 houses and a huge tree in center, jutting into the field of play.

• Right field foul line was the grandstand wall for the last 15 or so feet in front of the foul pole, so there was no way to catch a foul ball there.

• It was downhill from the plate to first base, supposedly to help save a step for slow Washington batters.

• Right field clock out of play.

• Ball rolling between top of scoreboard and bottom of the clock was in play: if it didn't come out, it was a homer; if it did, the outfielder could throw it back into play.

• U.S. presidents traditionally opened each season here by throwing out the first ball.

• Memorials honoring Walter Johnson and Clark Griffith stood outside the main entrance to the first base grandstand. The former now stands at Walter Johnson High School in Bethesda, Maryland; the latter at RFK Stadium.

• Height of National Bohemian Beer Bottle, above right-center scoreboard, approximately 50 feet.

• Park rebuilt after March 17, 1911 fire; completed on July 24, 1911.

• Doubledecked in 1920 from the bases down to the foul poles with a roof higher than the original second deck roof behind the plate.

• Temporary seats placed in front of left field bleachers for the 1924 World Series.

• In 1954, the visitor's bullpen was enclosed behind a screen fence in the left field corner in fair territory.

• Clark Calvin Griffith Memorial, dedicated by Vice President Nixon on August 8, 1956, was later moved to R.F.K. Stadium.

• In 1956, all the distances to the outfield fences were remeasured, and it was discovered that right field had lost 8 feet over the years!

• Also in 1956, 10 rows of temporary seats were added in front of the left field bleacher section.

• Park demolished from January 26 to August 14, 1965.

Negro League and Auxilliary Major League Baseball Sites

ATLANTA, GEORGIA

PONCE DE LEON PARK

STYLE   Minor League

A.K.A.   Spiller Park 1924 to 1932, Poncey

OCCUPANT   NSL Black Crackers 1932; NAL Black Crackers 1938

LOCATION   *Left Field (N)* Parking lot; *3rd Base (W)* North Boulevard; *1st Base (S)* 650 Ponce de Leon Boulevard; *Right Field (E)* Southern Railroad tracks

DIMENSIONS   *Left Field: 365 (1932), 330 (1949); Left-Center, Left Side of Scoreboard:* 525; *Center Field:* 462 (1932), 448 (1938), 410 (1949); *Right Field:* 321 (1932), 324 (1938)

FENCES   *Left Field:*2 (hedge, April 1949), 4 (cyclone fence, May 1949); *Left-Center:* 25 (scoreboard); *Center Field:* 6; *Right-Center:* Magnolia Tree halfway up very steep embankment, no fence; *Right Field:* 15

CURRENT USE   Parking lot opposite Sears department store since being torn down in 1967

PHENOMENA

• First Ponce de Leon Park, built in 1907, burned down September 9, 1923.

• A 2-foot-high hedge formed the outfield fence from the left field line to the right side of the left-center scoreboard in 1949. It reduced the foul line from 365 to 330 and caused numerous arguments because a left fielder had to stay within the hedge. If he fell over it, the hit was a homer.

BROOKLYN, NEW YORK

DEXTER PARK

STYLE   Negro League

A.K.A.   Sterling Oval

OCCUPANT   ECL Royal Giants 1923 to 1927

LOCATION   Woodhaven, Long Island *Left (N)* Simpson Street, now called Park Lane South; *3rd Base (NW)* Cypress Hills Cemetery; *1st Base (W)* Elderta Lane and 75th Street; *Center Field (E)* Lott Avenue, now called 76th Street

PHENOMENA

• Had probably the most creative outfield wall billboard ever. An optician's ad read: "Don't Kill the Umpire— Maybe It's Your Eyes."

• Owners Max and Milt Rosner operated the semipro Brooklyn Bushwicks.

• Huge incline in right field caused by horse buried under the grass.

• First lights installed on east coast, 1930.

CHICAGO, ILLINOIS

SOUTH SIDE PARK (III)

STYLE   Cricket Ground

A.K.A.   39th Street Grounds (II), White Stocking Park (III) 1901 to 1903, Chicago Cricket Club, White Sox Park (I) 1904 to 1910, American Giants Field 1911 to 1940, Schorling's Park 1920 to 1940

OCCUPANT   AL White Sox April 24, 1901 to June 27, 1910; NNL Giants 1920; NNL American Giants 1920 to 1931, 1933 to 1935; NSL American Giants 1932; NAL American Giants 1937 to 1940; Neutral site use by NNL Cleveland Tigers 1928, by NNL Kansas City Monarchs in 1920s, by NNL Cuban Stars West in 1920s

LOCATION   *Left Field (N)* West 38th Street; *3rd Base (W)* South Princeton Avenue; *1st Base (S)* West 39th Street, now West Pershing Road; *Right Field (E)* Wentworth Avenue

DIMENSIONS   *Left Field:* 355; *Left Center:* 400; *Center Field:* 450

FORMER USE   Home of Wanderers cricket team

CURRENT USE Housing project three blocks from Comiskey Park

PHENOMENA
- Opened in 1900.
- Overhanging roof added in 1902.
- Fence cut back sharply around J. F. Kidwell Greenhouse buildings in right center, making right-center relatively short compared to center and right.
- Used as a dog racing track during the summer of 1933, forcing the NNL American Giants to move all their home games from May 28 through the end of the 1933 season to Indianapolis.
- Burned down Christmas Day 1940.

EAST ORANGE, NEW JERSEY

GROVE STREET OVAL

STYLE Negro League

A.K.A. Grove Street Senior Ball Diamond, Monte Irvin Field, East Orange Oval

OCCUPANT NNL Cubans 1940 to 1948; NAL Cubans 1949 to 1950; also neutral site used by NNL Newark Eagles 1936 to 1948

LOCATION East Orange, New Jersey *Left Field (E)* Greenwood Avenue; *3rd Base (N)* Grove Place; *1st Base (W)* Grove Street North; *Right Field (S)* Eaton Place;

DIMENSIONS *Left Field:* 240; *Center Field:* 360 to the water fountain; *Right Field:* 280

FENCES *Left Field:* 25 (garage walls); *Center Field:* 4 (water fountain); *Right Field:* None

CURRENT USE Still used as a community ball diamond

PHENOMENA
- No fence in center field where there were some hedges.
- Water fountain in play in deepest center field.
- Trees in right, as well as tennis courts beyond.
- Scoreboard in left, as well as poplar trees.
- Clubhouse down right field line in foul territory.
- "Bujum" Jud Wilson hit longest ball ever hit over water fountain in center.
- Property purchased by city in October 1907 and park dedicated Labor Day 1908 in a game between the New Jersey State Senate and the New Jersey State General Assembly.
- Fire destroyed the first grandstand at 4 AM, May 3, 1925; new grandstand dedicated May 1, 1926.
- Renamed Monte Irvin Field at June 6, 1986 ceremony in culmination of 4 years effort initiated by this author and the SABR Negro Leagues Committee, who designed the plaque marking the site.

JERSEY CITY, NEW JERSEY

ROOSEVELT STADIUM

STYLE Minor League

OCCUPANT NL Dodgers for seven 1956 games and eight 1957 games from April 19, 1956 to September 3, 1957; some NNL New York Black Yankees games in 1940s

LOCATION *Left Field (NE)* Hackensack River; *3rd Base (NW)* Newark Bay; *1st Base (SW)* Danforth Avenue; *Right Field (SE)* State Highway 440; at Droyers Point

DIMENSIONS *Foul lines:* 330; *Power Alleys:* 397; *Center Field:* 411; *Backstop:* 60

FENCES *Foul Line Corners:* 11; *Left Field to Center Field:* 4; *Right-Center to Right Field:* 7

FORMER USE A landfill for dirt excavated from Holland Tunnel

PHENOMENA
- Built as a WPA project in 1937 and named for FDR.
- Newark Bay brought mosquitoes and mist into the outfield.
- Thanksgiving morning football games between St. Peter's and Dickinson were always sold out in the 1940s.
- Torn down in 1984.

NASHVILLE, TENNESSEE

SULPHUR DELL (II)

STYLE Minor League

A.K.A. Sulphur Springs Bottom, Sulphur Dell Park, Athletic Park, Dump, Suffer Hell

OCCUPANT NNL Elite Giants 1933 to 1934

LOCATION *Left Field (N)* Jackson Street; *3rd Base (W)* Summer Street, later 900 Fifth Avenue North; *1st Base (S)* Tennessee Central Railroad tracks; *Right Field (E)* Cherry Street, later Fourth Avenue North

DIMENSIONS *Left Field:* 334; *Center Field:* 421; *Right Field:* 262 (235 when fans sat behind ropes on the bank)

FENCES *All Around:* 16 (wood 1927); *Left and Center:* 16 (wood 1931); *Right Field:* 38.5 to 46 (16 wood below 22.5 to 30 screen to a point 186 feet from the right field foul line)

PHENOMENA
- Only one-quarter mile from the Cumberland River, the park was often flooded.
- Nicknamed "the Dump" in honor of the exceptional fragrance that drifted over from the nearby smoldering city dump and lent a unique character to Sulphur Dell hot dogs!
- Sulphur Dell had the craziest right field in history. Right fielders were called mountain goats because they had to go up and down the irregular hills in right-center and right. The incline in right rose 25 feet, beginning gradually behind first, then rising sharply at a 45-degree angle, then leveling off at a 10-foot-wide shelf one-third of the way up the incline, and then continuing at a 45-degree angle to the fence.
- Fielders used to play on the shelf, 235 feet from the plate. When overflow crowds were attracted to a game, a rope was extended in front of the shelf, and fans sat on the upper two thirds of the incline, reducing right field to 235 rather than 262.
- The stands were very close to the pancake-shaped diamond. First base was 42 feet from the seats; third base was 26 feet from the seats.
- Embankments began in left at 301 and in right at 224.
- Casey Stengel once joked that he hit a bunt home run down the 1st base line.

NEW YORK, NEW YORK

DYCKMAN OVAL

STYLE Negro League
OCCUPANT NNL Cuban Stars 1922; ECL Cuban Stars East 1923 to 1928; ECL Bachrach Giants many games 1923 to 1928; NAL Cuban Stars East 1929; NNL Cuban House of David 1931; NEWL Cuban Stars 1932
LOCATION *Left Field (NE)* West 204th Street; *3rd Base (NW)* Nagle Avenue; *1st Base (SW)* Academy Street; *Right Field (SE)* Tenth Avenue. In Upper Manhattan, 8 blocks east of the Henry Hudson Parkway, 5 blocks east of Inwood Hill Park, south of the Harlem Ship Canal, 4 blocks north of Dyckman Street, in Dyckman section
PHENOMENA
• The first major league park in New York to have lights for evening games. They were installed in 1930 by Cuban Stars owner Alex Pompez.

CAPITAL TEXTURE

STYLE Negro League
OCCUPANT ECL Lincoln Giants 1928; NAL Lincoln Giants 1929
LOCATION *(N)* East 138th Street; *(W)* Fifth Avenue; *(S)* East 135th Street; *(E)* Madison Avenue
CURRENT USE Riverton Apartments

CATHOLIC PROTECTORY OVAL

STYLE Amateur
OCCUPANT ECL Lincoln Giants 1923 to 1926; NNL Cubans 1935 to 1936
LOCATION *Left Field (E)* Hoguet Avenue; *3rd Base (N)* East Tremont Avenue; *1st Base (W)* White Plains Road; *Right Field (S)* McGraw Avenue. Bronx, 5 miles northeast of Yankee Stadium
CURRENT USE Parkchester Apartments, built by the Metropolitan Life Insurance Company—Unionport Road now crosses the site from home plate to center field; Metropolitan Avenue now runs from right field in to second base and then curves out to left field.
PHENOMENA
• The Protectory was a Catholic home and school for impoverished boys whose 50-piece marching band was much in demand. One of the students, Hank Greenberg, is now in the Hall of Fame.
• No grass in the infield.
• Leveled in 1939 so that Parkchester Apartments could be built.

TRIBOROUGH STADIUM

STYLE Football Stadium
A.K.A. Randall's Island Stadium, J. J. Downing Memorial Stadium
OCCUPANT NNL Black Yankees 1938
LOCATION *(N)* Bronx Kills and Harlem River, Eastern Parkway and Triborough Bridge; *(W)* House of Refuge, Vesta Avenue; *(S)* Little Hell Gate, East River, and Ward's Island, Sutter Avenue; *(E)* Sunken Meadow, Powell Street, Triborough Bridge
CURRENT USE Still standing, was used for WFL Stars football games in 1974 and NASL Cosmos soccer games in 1975

PHENOMENA
• A U-shaped stadium, open at the southwest end.
• Eight Ebbets Field light towers were moved here when Ebbets had new lights installed.

PATERSON, NEW JERSEY

HINCHCLIFFE STADIUM

STYLE Football Stadium
OCCUPANT NNL Black Yankees 1936 to 1937, 1939 to 1945
LOCATION Paterson, New Jersey *Center Field (SE)* Passaic River; *3rd Base (NE)* Redwood Avenue; *Home Plate (NW)* Liberty Street; *1st Base (SW)* Maple Street
CURRENT USE Community baseball, still standing, opened 1932

PHILADELPHIA, PENNSYLVANIA

HILLDALE PARK

STYLE High School
A.K.A. Darby Catholic School Stadium
OCCUPANT ECL Hilldales 1923 to 1927; NAL Hilldales 1929; NEWL Hilldales 1932
LOCATION Yeadon, Pennsylvania *Left Field (N)* Bunting Lane, later MacDade Boulevard; *3rd Base (W)* Greenhouses and Cedar Avenue; *1st Base (S)* Chester Avenue; *Right Field (E)* Yeadon School In the suburbs of Philadelphia at a Catholic school on the Darby-Yeadon borderline
DIMENSIONS *Left Field:* 315; *Right Center:* 400; *Right Field:* 370
CURRENT USE Acme Super Saver supermarket and drive-in bank
PHENOMENA
• A huge tree sat beyond the fence in right-center; branches hung over the fence and were in play.

PITTSBURGH, PENNSYLVANIA

GUS GREENLEE FIELD

STYLE Negro League
OCCUPANT NEWL Grays 1932; NEWL Crawfords 1932; NNL Grays 1933, 1935 to 1938; NNL Crawfords 1933 to 1938
LOCATION In the Hill District *Left Field (N)* Ridgeway Street; *3rd Base (W)* Junilla Street; *1st Base (S)* 2500 Bedford Avenue; *Right Field (E)* Municipal Hospital and Francis Street
FORMER USE Entress Brick Company factory
CURRENT USE Pittsburgh Housing Authority projects
PHENOMENA
• Opened on April 29, 1932.
• Tin fence in outfield.
• Left field foul line was longer than at Forbes Field, where it was 365.
• The structure was torn down on December 10, 1938.

## CHAPTER 4

Major League Attendance
Robert L. Tiemann and Pete Palmer

If you have the patience to sift through them, the figures on the following pages, dating from 1890 through 1996, tell a remarkable story. Season attendance has approached 4.5 million in Colorado in 1993, and it has been as little as 6,088 in Cleveland in 1899, when the awful Spiders went 20–134. The first club to pass the million mark was the New York Yankees of 1920, featuring a newcomer named Ruth and a ballpark borrowed from the Giants (who did not reach the mark themselves until 1945). In the depths of the Depression, the St. Louis Browns posted annual attendance figures (80,922 in 1935; 88,113 in 1933) below what a weekend set produces in many major-league venues.

Why did attendance stagnate in the 1890s? How much did the entry of the American League into National League strongholds New York, Chicago, Philadelphia, and St. Louis hurt the senior franchises? Were the Dodgers justified in leaving Brooklyn? How did baseball survive in Washington as long as it did, surpassing the million mark only once from 1892 to 1971? Did anyone notice that Atlanta's attendance of 1990 doubled, and then tripled, over the next two years? Or that while major league attendance increased by 25.8 percent from 1992 to 1993, almost all of that gain came from the senior circuit? (The American League rose a modest 5 percent while the National League posted a whopping gain of 53 percent; even if we subtract expansion clubs Florida and Colorado, the NL increase was an impressive 21.8 percent.)

You get the picture. There's stuff here that permits you to chart trends in baseball that you already know about, and if you are eagle-eyed you may pick up an anomalous figure that prompts you to rethink what you thought you knew.

A researcher's goldmine, the tables that follow tell an interesting story for the average fan as well. Does winning a pennant correlate with higher attendance? Are first-division teams more profitable than those in the second division? What is the impact on attendance of a new stadium?

By the time the next edition rolls around we may be able to gather figures going back to the dawn of professional baseball. Here are some scattered tidbits:

• In their first year of existence, 1871, the Boston Red Stockings counted 32,600 fans in 18 home games.
• In 1882, the last year of its existence as an NL franchise, the Troy Haymakers drew a whopping 26,000 attendees for its 42 home games, with one late season date posting a recorded crowd of 12 (that's not a typo).
• The 1891 American Association, in its final year of operation, counted 1,296,000 fans, or an average of 162,000 per team, a figure very comparable to the 169,060 of the National League. In 1892, with the AA gone and the NL a twelve-team circuit, the average team attendance was less than 152,000. Is there a lesson to be drawn from this?

Yes, and the lesson is plain for magnates no less than for fans and students of the game.

	1890	1891	1892	1893	1894	1895	1896	1897	1898	1899
NATIONAL LEAGUE										
BAL			93,589	143,000	328,000	293,000	249,448	273,046	123,416	121,935
BOS	147,539	184,472	146,421	193,300	152,800	242,000	240,000	334,800	229,275	200,384
BRO	121,412	181,477	183,727	235,000	214,000	230,000	201,000	220,831	122,514	269,641
CHI	102,536	201,188	109,067	223,500	239,000	382,300	317,500	327,160	424,352	352,130
CIN	131,980	97,500	196,473	194,250	158,000	281,000	373,000	336,800	336,378	259,536
CLE	47,478	132,000	139,928	130,000	82,000	143,000	152,000	115,250	70,496	6,088
LOU			131,159	53,683	75,000	92,000	133,000	145,210	128,980	109,319
NY	60,667	210,568	130,566	290,000	387,000	240,000	274,000	390,340	206,700	121,384
PHI	148,366	217,282	193,731	293,019	352,773	474,971	357,025	290,027	265,414	388,933
PIT	16,064	128,000	177,205	184,000	159,000	188,000	197,000	165,950	150,900	251,834
STL			192,442	195,000	155,000	170,000	184,000	136,400	151,700	373,909
WAS			128,279	90,000	125,000	153,000	223,000	151,028	103,250	86,392
TOT	776,042	1,352,487	1,822,587	2,224,752	2,427,573	2,889,271	2,900,973	2,886,842	2,313,375	2,541,485
ML	776,042	1,352,487	1,822,587	2,224,752	2,427,573	2,889,271	2,900,973	2,886,842	2,313,375	2,541,485

	1900	1901	1902	1903	1904	1905	1906	1907	1908	1909
AMERICAN LEAGUE										
BAL		141,952	174,606							
BOS		289,448	348,567	379,338	623,295	468,828	410,209	436,777	473,048	668,965
CHI		354,350	337,898	286,183	557,123	687,419	585,202	666,307	636,096	478,400
CLE		131,380	275,395	311,280	264,749	316,306	325,733	382,046	422,262	354,627
DET		259,430	189,469	224,523	177,796	193,384	174,043	297,079	436,199	490,490
MIL		139,034								
NY				211,808	438,919	309,100	434,700	350,020	305,500	501,700
PHI		206,329	420,078	422,473	512,294	554,576	489,129	625,581	455,062	674,915
STL			272,283	380,405	318,108	339,112	389,157	419,025	618,947	366,274
WAS		161,661	188,158	128,878	131,744	252,027	129,903	221,929	264,252	205,199
TOT		1,683,584	2,206,454	2,344,888	3,024,028	3,120,752	2,938,076	3,398,764	3,611,366	3,740,570
NATIONAL LEAGUE										
BOS	202,000	146,502	116,960	143,155	140,694	150,003	143,280	203,221	253,750	195,188
BRO	183,000	198,200	199,868	224,670	214,600	227,924	277,400	312,500	275,600	321,300
CHI	248,577	205,071	263,700	386,205	439,100	509,900	654,300	422,550	665,325	633,480
CIN	170,000	205,728	217,300	351,680	391,915	313,927	330,056	317,500	399,200	424,643
NY	190,000	297,650	302,875	579,530	609,826	552,700	402,850	538,350	910,000	783,700
PHI	301,913	234,937	112,066	151,729	140,771	317,932	294,680	341,216	420,660	303,177
PIT	264,000	251,955	243,826	326,855	340,615	369,124	394,877	319,506	382,444	534,950
STL	270,000	379,988	226,417	226,538	386,750	292,800	283,770	185,377	205,129	299,982
TOT	1,829,490	1,920,031	1,683,012	2,390,362	2,664,271	2,734,310	2,781,213	2,640,220	3,512,108	3,496,420
ML	1,829,490	3,603,615	3,889,466	4,735,250	5,688,299	5,855,062	5,719,289	6,038,984	7,123,474	7,236,990

	1910	1911	1912	1913	1914	1915	1916	1917	1918	1919
AMERICAN LEAGUE										
BOS	584,619	503,961	597,096	437,194	481,359	539,885	496,397	387,856	249,513	417,291
CHI	552,084	583,208	602,241	644,501	469,290	539,461	679,923	684,521	195,081	627,186
CLE	293,456	406,296	336,844	541,000	185,997	159,285	492,106	477,298	295,515	538,135
DET	391,288	484,988	402,870	398,502	416,225	476,105	616,772	457,289	203,719	643,805
NY	355,857	302,444	242,194	357,551	359,477	256,035	469,211	330,294	282,047	619,164
PHI	588,905	605,749	517,653	571,896	346,641	146,223	184,471	221,432	177,926	225,209
STL	249,889	207,984	214,070	250,330	244,714	150,358	335,740	210,486	122,076	349,350
WAS	254,591	244,884	350,663	325,831	243,888	167,332	177,265	89,682	182,122	234,096
TOT	3,270,689	3,339,514	3,263,631	3,526,805	2,747,591	2,434,684	3,451,885	2,858,858	1,707,999	3,654,236
NATIONAL LEAGUE										
BOS	149,027	116,000	121,000	208,000	382,913	376,283	313,495	174,253	84,938	167,401
BRO	279,321	269,000	243,000	347,000	122,671	297,766	447,747	221,619	83,831	360,721
CHI	526,152	576,000	514,000	419,000	202,516	217,058	453,685	360,218	337,256	424,430
CIN	380,622	300,000	344,000	258,000	100,791	218,878	255,846	269,056	163,009	532,501
NY	511,785	675,000	638,000	630,000	364,313	391,850	552,056	500,264	256,618	708,857
PHI	296,597	416,000	250,000	470,000	138,474	449,898	515,365	354,428	122,266	240,424
PIT	436,586	432,000	384,000	296,000	139,620	225,743	289,132	192,807	213,610	276,810
STL	355,668	447,768	241,759	203,531	256,099	252,666	224,308	288,491	110,599	167,059
TOT	2,935,758	3,231,768	2,735,759	2,831,531	1,707,397	2,430,142	3,051,634	2,361,136	1,372,127	2,878,203
ML	6,206,447	6,571,282	5,999,390	6,358,336	4,454,988	4,864,826	6,503,519	5,219,994	3,080,126	6,532,439

	1920	1921	1922	1923	1924	1925	1926	1927	1928	1929
AMERICAN LEAGUE										
BOS	402,445	279,273	259,184	229,688	448,556	267,782	285,155	305,275	396,920	394,620
CHI	833,492	543,650	602,860	573,778	606,658	832,231	710,339	614,423	494,152	426,795
CLE	912,832	748,705	528,145	558,856	481,905	419,005	627,426	373,138	375,907	536,210
DET	579,650	661,527	861,206	911,377	1,015,136	820,766	711,914	773,716	474,323	869,318
NY	1,289,422	1,230,696	1,026,134	1,007,066	1,053,533	697,267	1,027,675	1,164,015	1,072,132	960,148
PHI	287,888	344,430	425,356	534,122	531,992	869,703	714,508	605,529	689,756	839,176
STL	419,311	355,978	712,918	430,296	533,349	462,898	283,986	247,879	339,497	280,697
WAS	359,260	456,069	458,552	357,406	584,310	817,199	551,580	528,976	378,501	355,506
TOT	5,084,300	4,620,328	4,874,355	4,602,589	5,255,439	5,186,851	4,912,583	4,612,951	4,221,188	4,662,470

	1920	1921	1922	1923	1924	1925	1926	1927	1928	1929
NATIONAL LEAGUE										
BOS	162,483	318,627	167,965	227,802	177,478	313,528	303,598	288,685	227,001	372,351
BRO	808,722	613,245	498,865	564,666	818,883	659,435	650,819	637,230	664,863	731,886
CHI	480,783	410,107	542,283	703,705	716,922	622,610	885,063	1,159,168	1,143,740	1,485,166
CIN	568,107	311,227	493,754	575,063	473,707	464,920	672,987	442,164	490,490	295,040
NY	929,609	973,477	945,809	820,780	844,068	778,993	700,362	858,190	916,191	868,806
PHI	330,998	273,961	232,471	228,168	299,818	304,905	240,600	305,420	182,168	281,200
PIT	429,037	701,567	523,675	611,082	736,883	804,354	798,542	869,720	495,070	491,377
STL	326,836	384,773	536,998	338,551	272,885	404,959	668,428	749,340	761,574	399,887
TOT	4,036,575	3,986,984	3,941,820	4,069,817	4,340,644	4,353,704	4,920,399	5,309,917	4,881,097	4,925,713
ML	9,120,875	8,607,312	8,816,175	8,672,406	9,596,083	9,540,555	9,832,982	9,922,868	9,102,285	9,588,183

	1930	1931	1932	1933	1934	1935	1936	1937	1938	1939
AMERICAN LEAGUE										
BOS	444,045	350,975	182,150	268,715	610,640	558,568	626,895	559,659	646,459	573,070
CHI	406,123	403,550	233,198	397,789	236,559	470,281	440,810	589,245	338,278	594,104
CLE	528,657	483,027	468,953	387,936	391,338	397,615	500,391	564,849	652,006	563,926
DET	649,450	434,056	397,157	320,972	919,161	1,034,929	875,948	1,072,276	799,557	836,279
NY	1,169,230	912,437	962,320	728,014	854,682	657,508	976,913	998,148	970,916	859,785
PHI	721,663	627,464	405,500	297,138	305,847	233,173	285,173	430,738	385,357	395,022
STL	152,088	179,126	112,558	88,113	115,305	80,922	93,267	123,121	130,417	109,159
WAS	614,474	492,657	371,396	437,533	330,074	255,011	379,525	397,799	522,694	339,257
TOT	4,685,730	3,883,292	3,133,232	2,926,210	3,763,606	3,688,007	4,178,922	4,735,835	4,445,684	4,270,602
NATIONAL LEAGUE										
BOS	464,835	515,005	507,606	517,803	303,205	232,754	340,585	385,339	341,149	285,994
BRO	1,097,329	753,133	681,827	526,815	434,188	470,517	489,618	482,481	663,087	955,668
CHI	1,463,624	1,086,422	974,688	594,112	707,525	692,604	699,370	895,020	951,640	726,663
CIN	386,727	263,316	356,950	218,281	206,773	448,247	466,345	411,221	706,756	981,443
NY	868,714	812,163	484,868	604,471	730,851	748,748	837,952	926,887	799,633	702,457
PHI	299,007	284,849	268,914	156,421	169,885	205,470	249,219	212,790	166,111	277,973
PIT	357,795	260,392	287,262	288,747	322,622	352,885	372,524	459,679	641,033	376,734
STL	508,501	608,535	279,219	256,171	325,056	506,084	448,078	430,811	291,418	400,245
TOT	5,446,532	4,583,815	3,841,334	3,162,821	3,200,105	3,657,309	3,903,691	4,204,228	4,560,827	4,707,177
ML	10,132,262	8,467,107	6,974,566	6,089,031	6,963,711	7,345,316	8,082,613	8,940,063	9,006,511	8,977,779

	1940	1941	1942	1943	1944	1945	1946	1947	1948	1949
AMERICAN LEAGUE										
BOS	716,234	718,497	730,340	358,275	506,975	603,794	1,416,944	1,427,315	1,558,798	1,596,650
CHI	660,336	677,077	425,734	508,962	563,539	657,981	983,403	876,948	777,844	937,151
CLE	902,576	745,948	459,447	438,894	475,272	558,182	1,057,289	1,521,978	2,620,627	2,233,771
DET	1,112,693	684,915	580,087	606,287	923,176	1,280,341	1,722,590	1,398,093	1,743,035	1,821,204
NY	988,975	964,722	922,011	618,330	789,995	881,845	2,265,512	2,178,937	2,373,901	2,283,676
PHI	432,145	528,894	423,487	376,735	505,322	462,631	621,793	911,566	945,076	816,514
STL	239,591	176,240	255,617	214,392	508,644	482,986	526,435	320,474	335,564	270,936
WAS	381,241	415,663	403,493	574,694	525,235	652,660	1,027,216	850,758	795,254	770,745
TOT	5,433,791	4,911,956	4,200,216	3,696,569	4,798,158	5,580,420	9,621,182	9,486,069	11,150,099	10,730,647
NATIONAL LEAGUE										
BOS	241,616	263,680	285,332	271,289	208,691	374,178	969,673	1,277,361	1,455,439	1,081,795
BRO	975,978	1,214,910	1,037,765	661,739	605,905	1,059,220	1,796,824	1,807,526	1,398,967	1,633,747
CHI	534,878	545,159	590,972	508,247	640,110	1,036,386	1,342,970	1,364,039	1,237,792	1,143,139
CIN	850,180	643,513	427,031	379,122	409,567	290,070	715,751	899,975	823,386	707,782
NY	747,852	763,098	779,621	466,095	674,483	1,016,468	1,219,873	1,600,793	1,459,269	1,218,446
PHI	207,177	231,401	230,183	466,975	369,586	285,057	1,045,247	907,332	767,429	819,698
PIT	507,934	482,241	448,897	498,740	604,278	604,694	749,962	1,283,531	1,517,021	1,449,435
STL	324,078	633,645	553,552	517,135	461,968	594,630	1,061,807	1,247,913	1,111,440	1,430,676
TOT	4,389,693	4,777,647	4,353,353	3,769,342	3,974,588	5,260,703	8,902,107	10,388,470	9,770,743	9,484,718
ML	9,823,484	9,689,603	8,553,569	7,465,911	8,772,746	10,841,123	18,523,289	19,874,539	20,920,842	20,215,365

	1950	1951	1952	1953	1954	1955	1956	1957	1958	1959
AMERICAN LEAGUE										
BAL					1,060,910	852,039	901,201	1,029,581	829,991	891,926
BOS	1,344,080	1,312,282	1,115,750	1,026,133	931,127	1,203,200	1,137,158	1,181,087	1,077,047	984,102
CHI	781,330	1,328,234	1,231,675	1,191,353	1,231,629	1,175,684	1,000,090	1,135,668	797,451	1,423,144
CLE	1,727,464	1,704,984	1,444,607	1,069,176	1,335,472	1,221,780	865,467	722,256	663,805	1,497,976
DET	1,951,474	1,132,641	1,026,846	884,658	1,079,847	1,181,838	1,051,182	1,272,346	1,098,924	1,221,221
KC						1,393,054	1,015,154	901,067	925,090	963,683
NY	2,081,380	1,950,107	1,629,665	1,537,811	1,475,171	1,490,138	1,491,784	1,497,134	1,428,438	1,552,030
PHI	309,805	465,469	627,100	362,113	304,666					
STL	247,131	293,790	518,796	297,238						
WAS	699,697	695,167	699,457	595,594	503,542	425,238	431,647	457,079	475,288	615,372
TOT	9,142,361	8,882,674	8,293,896	6,964,076	7,922,364	8,942,971	7,893,683	8,196,218	7,296,034	9,149,454
NATIONAL LEAGUE										
BOS	944,391	487,475	281,278							
BRO	1,185,896	1,282,628	1,088,704	1,163,419	1,020,531	1,033,589	1,213,562	1,028,258		
CHI	1,165,944	894,415	1,024,826	763,658	748,183	875,800	720,118	670,629	979,904	858,255

	1950	1951	1952	1953	1954	1955	1956	1957	1958	1959
CIN	538,794	588,268	604,197	548,086	704,167	693,662	1,125,928	1,070,850	788,582	801,298
LA									1,845,556	2,071,045
MIL				1,826,397	2,131,388	2,005,836	2,046,331	2,215,404	1,971,101	1,749,112
NY	1,008,878	1,059,539	984,940	811,518	1,155,067	824,112	629,179	653,923		
PHI	1,217,035	937,658	755,417	853,644	738,991	922,886	934,798	1,146,230	931,110	802,815
PIT	1,166,267	980,590	686,673	572,757	475,494	469,397	949,878	850,732	1,311,988	1,359,917
STL	1,093,411	1,013,429	913,113	880,242	1,039,698	849,130	1,029,773	1,183,575	1,063,730	929,953
SF									1,272,625	1,422,130
TOT	8,320,616	7,244,002	6,339,148	7,419,721	8,013,519	7,674,412	8,649,567	8,819,601	10,164,596	9,994,525
ML	17,462,977	16,126,676	14,633,044	14,383,797	15,935,883	16,617,383	16,543,250	17,015,819	17,460,630	19,143,979

	1960	1961	1962	1963	1964	1965	1966	1967	1968	1969
AMERICAN LEAGUE										
BAL	1,187,849	951,089	790,254	774,343	1,116,215	781,649	1,203,366	955,053	943,977	1,062,069
BOS	1,129,866	850,589	733,080	942,642	883,276	652,201	811,172	1,727,832	1,940,788	1,833,246
CAL						566,727	1,400,321	1,317,713	1,025,956	758,388
CHI	1,644,460	1,146,019	1,131,562	1,158,848	1,250,053	1,130,519	990,016	985,634	803,775	589,546
CLE	950,985	725,547	716,076	562,507	653,293	934,786	903,359	662,980	857,994	619,970
DET	1,167,669	1,600,710	1,207,881	821,952	816,139	1,029,645	1,124,293	1,447,143	2,031,847	1,577,481
KC	774,944	683,817	635,675	762,364	642,478	528,344	773,929	726,639		902,414
LA		603,510	1,144,063	821,015	760,439					
MIN		1,256,723	1,433,116	1,406,652	1,207,514	1,463,258	1,259,374	1,483,547	1,143,257	1,349,328
NY	1,627,349	1,747,725	1,493,574	1,308,920	1,305,638	1,213,552	1,124,648	1,259,514	1,185,666	1,067,996
OAK									837,466	778,232
SEA										677,944
WAS	743,404	597,287	729,775	535,604	600,106	560,083	576,260	770,868	546,661	918,106
TOT	9,226,526	10,163,016	10,015,056	9,094,847	9,235,151	8,860,764	10,166,738	11,336,923	11,317,387	12,134,720
NATIONAL LEAGUE										
ATL							1,539,801	1,389,222	1,126,540	1,458,320
CHI	809,770	673,057	609,802	979,551	751,647	641,361	635,891	977,226	1,043,409	1,674,993
CIN	663,486	1,117,603	982,095	858,805	862,466	1,047,824	742,958	958,300	733,354	987,991
HOU			924,456	719,502	725,773	2,151,470	1,872,108	1,348,303	1,312,887	1,442,995
LA	2,253,887	1,804,250	2,755,184	2,538,602	2,228,751	2,553,577	2,617,029	1,664,362	1,581,093	1,784,527
MIL	1,497,799	1,101,441	766,921	773,018	910,911	555,584				
MON										1,212,608
NY			922,530	1,080,108	1,732,597	1,768,389	1,932,693	1,565,492	1,781,657	2,175,373
PHI	862,205	590,039	762,034	907,141	1,425,891	1,166,376	1,108,201	828,888	664,546	519,414
PIT	1,705,828	1,199,128	1,090,648	783,648	759,496	909,279	1,196,618	907,012	693,485	769,369
STL	1,096,632	855,305	953,895	1,170,546	1,143,294	1,241,201	1,712,980	2,090,145	2,011,167	1,682,783
SD										512,970
SF	1,795,356	1,390,679	1,592,594	1,571,306	1,504,364	1,546,075	1,657,192	1,242,480	837,220	873,603
TOT	10,684,963	8,731,502	11,360,159	11,382,227	12,045,190	13,581,136	15,015,471	12,971,430	11,785,358	15,094,946
ML	19,911,489	18,894,518	21,375,215	20,477,074	21,280,341	22,441,900	25,182,209	24,308,353	23,102,745	27,229,666

	1970	1971	1972	1973	1974	1975	1976	1977	1978	1979
AMERICAN LEAGUE										
BAL	1,057,069	1,023,037	899,950	958,667	962,572	1,002,157	1,058,609	1,195,769	1,051,724	1,681,009
BOS	1,595,278	1,678,732	1,441,718	1,481,002	1,556,411	1,748,587	1,895,846	2,074,549	2,320,643	2,353,114
CAL	1,077,741	926,373	744,190	1,058,206	917,269	1,058,163	1,006,774	1,432,633	1,755,386	2,523,575
CHI	495,355	833,891	1,177,318	1,302,527	1,149,596	750,802	914,945	1,657,135	1,491,100	1,280,702
CLE	729,752	591,361	626,354	615,107	1,114,262	977,039	948,776	900,365	800,584	1,011,644
DET	1,501,293	1,591,073	1,892,386	1,724,146	1,243,080	1,058,836	1,467,020	1,359,856	1,714,893	1,630,929
KC	693,047	910,784	707,656	1,345,341	1,173,292	1,151,836	1,680,265	1,852,603	2,255,493	2,261,845
MIL	933,690	731,531	600,440	1,092,158	955,741	1,213,357	1,012,164	1,114,938	1,601,406	1,918,343
MIN	1,261,887	940,858	797,901	907,499	662,401	737,156	715,394	1,162,727	787,878	1,070,521
NY	1,136,879	1,070,771	966,328	1,262,103	1,273,075	1,288,048	2,012,434	2,103,092	2,335,871	2,537,765
OAK	778,355	914,993	921,323	1,000,763	845,693	1,075,518	780,593	495,599	526,999	306,763
SEA								1,338,511	877,440	844,447
TEX			662,974	686,085	1,193,902	1,127,924	1,164,982	1,250,722	1,447,963	1,519,671
TOR								1,701,052	1,562,585	1,431,651
WAS	824,789	655,156								
TOT	12,085,135	11,868,560	11,438,538	13,433,604	13,047,294	13,189,423	14,657,802	19,639,551	20,529,965	22,371,979
NATIONAL LEAGUE										
ATL	1,078,848	1,006,320	752,973	800,655	981,085	534,672	818,179	872,464	904,494	769,465
CHI	1,642,705	1,653,007	1,299,163	1,351,705	1,015,378	1,034,819	1,026,217	1,439,834	1,525,311	1,648,587
CIN	1,803,568	1,501,122	1,611,459	2,017,601	2,164,307	2,315,603	2,629,708	2,519,670	2,532,497	2,356,933
HOU	1,253,444	1,261,589	1,469,247	1,394,004	1,090,728	858,002	886,146	1,109,560	1,126,145	1,900,312
LA	1,697,142	2,064,594	1,860,858	2,136,192	2,632,474	2,539,349	2,386,301	2,955,087	3,347,845	2,860,954
MON	1,424,683	1,290,963	1,142,145	1,246,863	1,019,134	908,292	646,704	1,433,757	1,427,007	2,102,173
NY	2,697,479	2,266,680	2,134,185	1,912,390	1,722,209	1,730,566	1,468,754	1,066,825	1,007,328	788,905
PHI	708,247	1,511,223	1,343,329	1,475,934	1,808,648	1,909,233	2,480,150	2,700,070	2,583,389	2,775,011
PIT	1,341,947	1,501,132	1,427,460	1,319,913	1,110,552	1,270,018	1,025,945	1,237,349	964,106	1,435,454
STL	1,629,736	1,604,671	1,196,894	1,574,046	1,838,413	1,695,270	1,207,079	1,659,287	1,278,215	1,627,256
SD	643,679	557,513	644,273	611,826	1,075,399	1,281,747	1,458,478	1,376,269	1,670,107	1,456,967
SF	740,720	1,106,043	647,744	834,193	519,987	522,919	626,868	700,056	1,740,477	1,456,402
TOT	16,662,198	17,324,857	15,529,730	16,675,322	16,978,314	16,600,490	16,660,529	19,070,228	20,106,921	21,178,419

	1970	1971	1972	1973	1974	1975	1976	1977	1978	1979
ML	28,747,333	29,193,417	26,968,268	30,108,926	30,025,608	29,789,913	31,318,331	38,709,779	40,636,886	43,550,398

	1980	1981	1982	1983	1984	1985	1986	1987	1988	1989
AMERICAN LEAGUE										
BAL	1,797,438	1,024,247	1,613,031	2,042,071	2,045,784	2,132,387	1,973,176	1,835,692	1,660,738	2,535,208
BOS	1,956,092	1,060,379	1,950,124	1,782,285	1,661,618	1,786,633	2,147,641	2,231,551	2,464,851	2,510,012
CAL	2,297,327	1,441,545	2,807,360	2,555,016	2,402,997	2,567,427	2,655,872	2,696,299	2,340,925	2,647,291
CHI	1,200,365	946,651	1,567,787	2,132,821	2,136,988	1,669,888	1,424,313	1,208,060	1,115,749	1,045,651
CLE	1,033,827	661,395	1,044,021	768,941	734,079	655,181	1,471,805	1,077,898	1,411,610	1,285,542
DET	1,785,293	1,149,144	1,636,058	1,829,636	2,704,794	2,286,609	1,899,437	2,061,830	2,081,162	1,543,656
KC	2,288,714	1,279,403	2,284,464	1,963,875	1,810,018	2,162,717	2,320,794	2,392,471	2,350,181	2,477,700
MIL	1,857,408	874,292	1,978,896	2,397,131	1,608,509	1,360,265	1,265,041	1,909,244	1,923,238	1,970,735
MIN	769,206	469,090	921,186	858,939	1,598,692	1,651,814	1,255,453	2,081,976	3,030,672	2,277,438
NY	2,627,417	1,614,353	2,041,219	2,257,976	1,821,815	2,214,587	2,268,030	2,427,672	2,633,701	2,170,485
OAK	842,259	1,304,052	1,735,489	1,294,941	1,353,281	1,334,599	1,314,646	1,678,921	2,287,335	2,667,225
SEA	836,204	636,276	1,070,404	813,537	870,372	1,128,696	1,029,045	1,134,255	1,022,398	1,298,443
TEX	1,198,175	850,076	1,154,432	1,363,469	1,102,471	1,112,497	1,692,002	1,763,053	1,581,901	2,043,993
TOR	1,400,327	755,083	1,275,978	1,930,415	2,110,009	2,468,925	2,455,477	2,778,429	2,595,175	3,375,883
TOT	21,890,052	14,065,986	23,080,449	23,991,053	23,961,427	24,532,225	25,172,732	27,277,351	28,499,636	29,849,262
NATIONAL LEAGUE										
ATL	1,048,411	535,418	1,801,985	2,119,935	1,724,892	1,350,137	1,387,181	1,217,402	848,089	984,930
CHI	1,206,776	565,637	1,249,278	1,479,717	2,107,655	2,161,534	1,859,102	2,035,130	2,089,034	2,491,942
CIN	2,022,450	1,093,730	1,326,528	1,190,419	1,275,887	1,834,619	1,692,432	2,185,205	2,072,528	1,979,320
HOU	2,278,217	1,321,282	1,558,555	1,351,962	1,229,862	1,184,314	1,734,276	1,909,902	1,933,505	1,834,908
LA	3,249,287	2,381,292	3,608,881	3,510,313	3,134,824	3,264,593	3,023,208	2,797,409	2,980,262	2,944,653
MON	2,208,175	1,534,564	2,318,292	2,320,651	1,606,531	1,502,494	1,128,981	1,850,324	1,478,659	1,783,533
NY	1,192,073	704,244	1,323,036	1,112,774	1,842,695	2,761,601	2,767,601	3,034,129	3,055,445	2,918,710
PHI	2,651,650	1,638,752	2,376,394	2,128,339	2,062,693	1,830,350	1,933,335	2,100,110	1,990,041	1,861,985
PIT	1,646,757	541,789	1,024,106	1,225,916	773,500	735,900	1,000,917	1,161,193	1,866,713	1,374,141
STL	1,385,147	1,010,247	2,111,906	2,317,914	2,037,448	2,637,563	2,471,974	3,072,122	2,892,799	3,080,980
SD	1,139,026	519,161	1,607,516	1,539,815	1,983,904	2,210,352	1,805,716	1,454,061	1,506,896	2,009,031
SF	1,096,115	632,274	1,200,948	1,251,530	1,001,545	818,697	1,528,748	1,917,168	1,785,297	2,059,701
TOT	21,124,084	12,478,390	21,507,425	21,549,285	20,781,436	22,292,154	22,333,471	24,734,155	24,499,268	25,323,834
ML	43,014,136	26,544,376	44,587,874	45,540,338	44,742,863	46,824,379	47,506,203	52,011,506	52,998,904	55,173,096

	1990	1991	1992	1993	1994	1995	1996			
AMERICAN LEAGUE										
BAL	2,415,189	2,552,753	3,567,819	3,644,965	2,535,359	3,098,475	3,646,950			
BOS	2,528,986	2,562,435	2,468,574	2,422,021	1,775,826	2,164,378	2,315,233			
CAL	2,555,688	2,416,236	2,065,444	2,057,460	1,512,622	1,748,680	1,820,532			
CHI	2,002,357	2,934,154	2,681,156	2,581,091	1,697,398	1,609,773	1,676,416			
CLE	1,225,240	1,051,863	1,224,094	2,177,908	1,995,174	2,842,725	3,318,174			
DET	1,495,783	1,641,661	1,423,963	1,971,421	1,184,783	1,180,979	1,168,610			
KC	2,244,956	2,161,537	1,867,689	1,934,578	1,400,494	1,232,969	1,436,007			
MIL	1,752,900	1,478,729	1,857,351	1,688,080	1,268,397	1,087,560	1,327,155			
MIN	1,751,584	2,293,842	2,482,428	2,048,673	1,398,565	1,057,667	1,437,352			
NY	2,006,436	1,863,733	1,748,737	2,416,942	1,675,557	1,705,257	2,250,839			
OAK	2,900,217	2,713,493	2,494,160	2,035,025	1,242,692	1,174,310	1,148,380			
SEA	1,509,727	2,147,905	1,651,367	2,052,638	1,103,798	1,640,992	2,722,392			
TEX	2,057,911	2,297,720	2,198,231	2,244,616	2,502,538	1,985,910	2,888,920			
TOR	3,885,284	4,001,527	4,028,318	4,057,947	2,907,933	2,826,483	2,559,563			
TOT	30,332,260	32,117,588	31,759,331	33,333,365	24,201,136	25,356,158	29,716,523			
NATIONAL LEAGUE										
ATL	980,129	2,140,217	3,077,400	3,884,720	2,539,240	2,561,831	2,901,242			
CHI	2,243,791	2,314,250	2,126,720	2,653,763	1,845,208	1,918,265	2,219,110			
CIN	2,400,892	2,372,377	2,315,946	2,453,232	1,897,681	1,843,649	1,861,428			
COL				4,483,350	3,281,511	3,390,037	3,891,014			
FLA				3,064,847	1,937,467	1,700,466	1,746,767			
HOU	1,310,927	1,196,152	1,211,412	2,084,618	1,561,136	1,363,801	1,975,888			
LA	3,002,396	3,348,170	2,473,266	3,170,393	2,279,355	2,766,251	3,188,454			
MON	1,373,087	934,742	1,669,127	1,641,437	1,276,250	1,309,618	1,618,573			
NY	2,732,745	2,284,484	1,779,534	1,873,183	1,151,471	1,273,183	1,588,323			
PHI	1,992,484	2,050,012	1,927,448	3,137,674	2,290,971	2,043,588	1,801,677			
PIT	2,049,908	2,065,302	1,829,395	1,650,593	1,222,520	905,517	1,326,640			
STL	2,573,225	2,448,699	2,418,483	2,844,977	1,866,544	1,748,709	2,659,239			
SD	1,856,396	1,804,289	1,721,406	1,375,432	953,857	1,041,805	2,187,886			
SF	1,975,528	1,737,478	1,560,998	2,606,354	1,704,608	1,241,497	1,413,687			
TOT	24,491,508	24,696,172	24,111,135	36,924,573	25,807,819	25,108,217	30,379,928			
ML	54,823,768	56,813,760	55,870,466	70,257,938	50,008,955	50,464,375	60,096,451			

CHAPTER 5

The True Father of Baseball

John Thorn

The history of baseball is a lie from beginning to end, from its creation myth to its rosy models of commerce, community, and fair play. The game's epic feats and revered figures, its pieties about racial harmony and bleacher democracy, its artful blurring of sport and business—all of it is bunk, tossed up with a wink and a nudge. Yet Abner Doubleday, for example, will not be consigned to the dustbin of baseball history no matter how convincingly one argues that he did not invent baseball.

But if the history of baseball is a lie, it is a glorious, vibrant and, in the grand scheme of life, harmless lie, gripping us in a way that good, gray fact seldom can. The bearer of fact cannot hope to annihilate the legends in baseball's Elysian Fields, but simply to play alongside them, occasionally getting a turn at bat.

I believe that the conventional tale of the game's birth is substantially incorrect. By this I refer not to the Doubleday fable, pointless to attack, but to the scarcely less legendary development of the Knickerbocker game, ostensibly sired by Alexander Cartwright.

Let's look at the delicate condition of baseball's paternity. There would have been no need to establish Alexander Cartwright as a baseball deity had the Mills Commission report of 1907—created by Albert Spalding not to explore the origins of the game but to confirm its American roots—not named Abner Doubleday the father of the game; however, the absurdity of the Doubleday claim agitated Cartwright's son Bruce so much that he protested to Spalding, and to *Collier's* writer Will Irwin, that baseball did not exist before the advent of Cartwright and the Knickerbocker Base Ball Club of New York City. This claim came at a time when men were still alive who had seen some rural variant of baseball in the 1820s or 1830s or who had even played baseball in an urban setting with one of the several ball clubs that had preceded the formation of the Knicks in 1845, such as the New York Base Ball Club, the Brooklyn Ball Club, the Eagles of New York, or the Olympics of Philadelphia.

Earlier histories of baseball—from those published annually by Henry Chadwick in the Beadle, DeWitt, and Spalding Guides to book-length histories such as Charles Peverelly's *Book of American Pastimes* (1866) and Jacob Morse's *Sphere and Ash* (1888)—gave credit to the Knickerbockers for the eventual ascendance of the New York Game of baseball over the competing Massachusetts Game, but did not single out Cartwright as the sole creator. In 1860, in the premier edition of the Beadle *Dime Base Ball Player,* Chadwick acknowledged the existence of the New York Base Ball Club prior to the organization of the Knicks, but stated "we shall not be far wrong if we award to the Knickerbocker the honor of being the pioneers of the present game of base ball." Still, he never swerved from his assertion in that same essay that it was rounders, the English childhood game, "from which base ball is derived." Only in the next century did Cartwright become—no less than Doubleday—a tool of those who wished to establish baseball as the product of an identifiable spark of American ingenuity, without foreign or Darwinian taint.

What *did* Cartwright do? He suggested that the Knickerbockers, who had been playing informally since at least 1842, be organized as a club, with a constitution and playing rules that he did much to formulate (although not alone—three other Knickerbockers were equally involved in drafting the original fourteen playing rules). Notable among these rules—which simply codified the game that the Knicks were already playing—were the laying out of baseball on a "diamond" rather than a square, the concept of foul territory, and the elimination of the rounders and town-ball practice of retiring a runner by throwing the ball *at* him. These are critical differences from earlier games, sufficient in and of themselves to term the Knickerbocker game a landmark in the evolution of baseball. But what Cartwright assuredly did *not* do was any of the three central things credited to him on his plaque in the Baseball Hall of Fame: "Set bases 90 feet apart. Established 9 innings as a game and 9 players as a team." (More on this in a moment.) He also did not create the forty-five-foot pitching distance, nor the requirement that a ball be caught on the fly to register an out, nor a system for calling balls and strikes.

The truth of the paternity question? Eighty-year-old Henry Chadwick had it right when he said in 1904, only one year before the formation of the Mills Commission, "Like Topsy, baseball never had no 'fadder'; it jest growed." In fact, until Papa Doubleday was pulled out of the hat, it was Chadwick himself who had most frequently been honored with the sobriquet "Father of Baseball," not for any powers of invention but for his role in popularizing and shaping the game. Others to have been accorded patriarchal honors were Harry Wright, who organized the first openly professional team; Albert Spalding, the tireless player, magnate, and tour promoter; William Hulbert, founder of the National League in 1876; and Daniel L. Adams, whose name today is scarcely known. Allow me to introduce him.

Daniel Lucius Adams was born on November 1, 1814, in Mt. Vernon, New Hampshire, the younger of two sons of Dr. Daniel Adams and Nancy Mulliken Adams. He spent his first two years of college at Amherst, then graduated from Yale in 1835. Afterwards came a medical degree from Harvard in 1838, then a general practice in New York City, coupled with an active involvement with treating the poor at the New York Dispensaries. He resided and practiced at 14 Bond Street.

"Doc" Adams, as he was known to all, began to play baseball in 1839. "I was always interested in athletics while in college and afterward," he told an interviewer at the age of eighty-one, "and soon after going to New York I began to play base ball just for exercise, with a number of other young medical men. Before that there had been a club called the New York Base Ball Club, but it had no very definite organization and did not last long. Some of the younger members of that club got together and formed the Knickerbocker Base Ball Club, September 24, 1845 [actually September 23]. The players included merchants, lawyers, Union Bank clerks [like Cartwright], insurance clerks and others who were at liberty after 3 o'clock in the afternoon. They went into it just for exercise and enjoyment, and I think they used to get a good deal more solid fun out of it than the players in the big games do nowadays.

"About a month after the organization of this club, several of us medical fellows joined it, myself among the number. The following year I was made President and served as long as I was willing to retain the office."

What's new here? Plenty. According to Adams, the New York Base Ball Club not only preceded the Knickerbocker, but formed it; for example, such early New York Base Ball Club members as James Lee, Abraham Tucker, and William Wheaton all became Knickerbockers in 1845–1846. As early as 1840, Adams played a game in New York that he understood to be baseball. It was the same game as that played by the men who would become the Knickerbockers, played on a square, at first with eleven men on a side, as in cricket and perhaps the Massachusetts Game. This game—called base ball and not rounders or town ball—was played in New York City as early as 1832 by two clubs, one composed of residents of the first ward (the lower part of the city), the other in the upper part of the city (ninth and fifteenth wards). By 1843, when the Knicks were still playing at their original site in Madison Square, the teams had been reduced to eight—which included a "pitch," a "behind," three basemen and three in the field—and the playing field had been changed from a square to a diamond, as in rounders. According to Alphonse Martin, a prominent pitcher in the 1860s who left an unpublished manuscript "History of Base Ball," it was Cartwright who prompted this move. In later years, when asked how the game of baseball originated, Doc Adams declined to identify a distinct starting point; he believed it grew from rounders.

Actually, baseball as played by the Knicks in the years 1845–1849 (Cartwright left for California in the gold-rush spring of 1849) was almost never a nine-man game— eight, ten, and eleven were all more frequently employed numbers to the side. Play was conducted in accord with Cartwright's model of only three basemen, and on the rare occasions when nine or more fielding positions were created by a surfeit of players, the "extras" were put into the outfield. In a game in late May 1847, for example, when eleven men were available to each side, the Knickerbockers' response was to play with nine, including four outfielders, and hold two men out as substitutes.

The advent of the short fielder, or shortstop, was a crucial break with rounders, and this position was created in 1849 or 1850 by Adams. "I used to play shortstop," he reminisced, "and I believe I was the first one to occupy that place, as it had formerly been left uncovered." But when Adams first went out to short, it was not to bolster the infield but to assist in relays from the outfield. The early Knickerbocker ball was so light that it could not be thrown even 200 feet; thus the need for a short fielder to send the ball in to the pitcher's point.

"We had a great deal of trouble in getting balls made," Adams recalled, "and for six or seven years I made all the balls myself, not only for our club but also for other clubs when they were organized. [He also supervised the turning of the bats during this period.] I went all over New York to find someone who would undertake this work, but no one could be induced to try it for love or money. Finally I found a Scotch saddler who was able to show me a good way to cover the balls with horsehide, such as was used for whip lashes. I used to make the stuffing out of three or four ounces of rubber cuttings, wound with yarn and then covered with the leather. Those balls were, of course, a great deal softer than the balls now in use."

When the ball was wound tighter, gaining more hardness and resilience, it could be hit farther and, crucially, thrown farther. This permitted the shortstop to come into the infield, which Adams did. Even more important, the introduction of the hard ball permitted a change in the dimensions of the playing field. The Knickerbocker rules of 1845 had specified no pitching distance, and no baseline length; all that was indicated was: "from 'home' to second base, forty-two paces; from first to third base, forty-two paces, equidistant." It has been presumed by scholars that when a three-foot pace is plugged in, the resulting baselines of eighty-nine feet are close enough to the present ninety so that we can proclaim Cartwright's genius. In fact, the pace in 1845 was either an imprecise and variable measure—to gauge distances by "stepping off"—or precisely two and a half feet, in which case the distance from home to second would have been 105 feet and the Cartwright basepaths would have been 74.25 feet. The pace of 1845 could not have been interpreted as the equivalent of three feet. The alternate definition of a pace as a three-foot measure did not come into practice until much later in the century. (Here is the definition of a pace from *An American Dictionary of the English Language,* by Noah Webster, 1828: Pace: "1. A step. 2. The space between the two feet in walking, estimated at two feet and a half. But the geometrical pace is five feet, or the whole space passed over by the same foot from one step to another." This definition was not changed for Webster's 1853 revised edition.)

My research indicates that 75-foot basepaths were the norm well into the mid-1850s—when the basepaths were first prescribed as "42 paces or yards"—and were the standard for youth play well into the next decade.

In 1848 Adams, as Knickerbocker president, headed the Committee to Revise the Constitution and By-Laws; Alexander Cartwright served under him. Adams' interest in refining the rules of the game, already evident, was further piqued by the formation of additional clubs, beginning with the Washington Base Ball Club in 1850, which was constructed around several former New York

Base Ball Club members. In 1852 the Washingtons were renamed the Gothams and took in additional players, and the Eagle Club, which had been organized to play town ball in 1840, reconstituted itself to become the Eagle Base Ball Club. "The playing rules remained very crude up to this time," Adams said, "but in 1853 the three clubs united in a revision of the rules and regulations. At the close of 1856 there were twelve clubs in existence, and it was decided to hold a convention of delegates from all of these for the purpose of establishing a permanent code of rules by which all should be governed. A call was therefore issued, signed by the officers of the Knickerbocker Club as the senior organization, and the result was the assembling of the first convention of base ball players in May, 1857. I was elected presiding officer." It was at this meeting, eight years after Cartwright's western expedition, that the winner of a game was defined as the team that was ahead at the conclusion of nine innings, rather than the first team to score twenty-one runs. "In March of the next year the second convention was held, and at this meeting the annual convention was declared a permanent organization, and with the requisite constitution and by-laws became the 'National Association of Ball Players.'

"I was chairman of the Committee on Rules and Regulations from the start and so long as I retained membership. I presented the first draft of rules, prepared after much careful study of the matter, and it was in the main adopted. The distance between bases I fixed at 30 yards— the only previous determination of distance being 'the bases shall be from home to second base 42 paces, from first to third base 42 paces equidistant'—which was rather vague. In every meeting of the National Association while a member, I advocated the fly-game—that is, not to allow first-bound catches—but I was always defeated on the vote. The change was made, however, soon after I left, as I predicted in my last speech on the subject before the convention.

"The distance from home to pitcher's base I made 45 feet. Many of the old rules, such as those defining a foul, remain substantially the same today," he concluded in 1896, "while others are changed and, of course, many new ones added. I resigned in 1862, but not before thousands were present to witness matches, and any number of outside players standing ready to take a hand on regular playing days." In the 1840s players could not be relied upon to show up for practice. Adams recalled that the Knickerbockers frequently went to Hoboken to find only two or three members present, and were often obliged to take their exercise "in the form of 'old cat,' 'one' or 'two' as the case might be." But, he summed up in 1896, "we pioneers never expected to see the game so universal as it has now become."

On May 7, 1861, Adams married Cornelia A. Cook. Less than a year later he resigned from the Knickerbocker Base Ball Club, and in 1865 he retired from his practice in New York and moved to Ridgefield, Connecticut. He played his last formal game of baseball on September 27, 1875, in an oldtimers' contest arranged by longtime Knickerbocker comrade James Whyte Davis. Adams played backyard ball with his sons even into his eighth decade, when he moved his family to New Haven, where the boys attended Sheffield Scientific School. On January 3, 1899, Daniel Lucius Adams died in his home at 146 Edwards Street.

Success has many fathers, failure none. For his role in making baseball the success it is, Doc Adams may be counted as first among the Fathers of Baseball.

## CHAPTER 6

The 100 Greatest Players
Michael Gershman

Picking baseball's hundred greatest players looks easy, which is why it's been tried more often than a Cub fan's patience. But in fact it requires the hand of a sculptor, the eye of an eagle, the nose of a sommelier, and the sensitivity of a redistricted Congressman up for reelection. Lacking these attributes, brass will suffice.

Part of the problem revolves around packing a hundred great players into just nine positions. It is easy to be blinded by power and pick just fireballing pitchers or slugging left fielders. Balance requires a different approach, with proper attention paid to fielding, baserunning, longevity, and other factors unrelated solely to batting or pitching statistics.

Accordingly, after poring over the contents of this volume, I have selected the players I considered the best:

• eight at each corner position (first and third base, left and right field);
• ten at each interior position (catcher, second base, shortstop, and center field);
• four who logged quality time in both infield and outfield (like Pete Rose);
• twenty-four pitchers (with representation for relievers).

One of the problems with this approach is that the eleventh best shortstop may very well be a better all-around ballplayer than the eighth best left fielder. Nevertheless, drawing the line—and thus obtaining focus—is what this exercise is all about. The great ones are easy to identify; the problem comes in separating the near great from the very good. Some of the players who didn't make the list were very good indeed—Johnny Mize, Pee Wee Reese, Early Wynn, and more.

It was tempting to pick a hundred Hall of Famers and let it go at that. But such a procedure would necessarily exclude players of today who are sure bets to make the Hall—such as Carlton Fisk, Nolan Ryan, and Ryne Sandberg. A second problem with an all-Hall top hundred is that I have the advantage of the records in this book, which are seemingly unfamiliar to those on the Hall of Fame Veterans Committee who place a Pop Haines in Cooperstown while keeping a Bid McPhee out, or those writers who persist in their snubs of Bill Mazeroski and Ron Santo.

Some members of the Baseball Hall of Fame are merely famous for being famous—like Candy Cummings, who may have invented the curveball—or famous for being pulled into the Hall by their more illustrious teammates, like the infield of the New York Giants of the 1920s. Such Hall of Famers are easy enough to exclude from any list of the top 100 baseball figures. But if fame alone is not enough to make the cut, how about great stats? While statistics are the lifeblood of *Total Baseball,* numbers can never adequately reflect the accomplishments of the game's pioneers, white or black. Dan Brouthers was the greatest offensive force in the game before 1900. His numbers would probably be very different if he were beamed down to play today, but then again he would not be playing the game of yesterday, and it could be said that he would not even be Dan Brouthers anymore. It is safe to assume, I believe, that while an average player of a century ago probably could not play in the 1990s, a star of an earlier period would be a star today. And as for Negro League baseball, statistics—even the scattered and fragmentary numbers unearthed by the Society for American Baseball Research—can only hint at the greatness of an Oscar Charleston or a Pop Lloyd. Such men were excluded during their active careers; they cannot be excluded here.

Having delivered the requisite caveats, it is now time to deliver the goods. I have tried to go beyond the stats and convey in each of these profiles a sense of the man, the era in which he performed, and why he deserves to be included in a list more elite than the roll call of the Baseball Hall of Fame.

Humorist Robert Benchley once said of baseball that "one of the chief duties of the fan is to engage in arguments with the man behind him. This department of the game has been allowed to run down fearfully." I hope this top hundred list stimulates a whole new bunch of arguments.

First Base (8)	*Second Base* (10)	Morgan, Joe	Maranville, Rabbit
Anson, Cap	Collins, Eddie	Sandberg, Ryne	Ripken, Cal
Brouthers, Dan	Evers, Johnny		Smith, Ozzie
Foxx, Jimmie	Frisch, Frankie	*Shortstop* (10)	Vaughan, Arky
Gehrig, Lou	Gehringer, Charlie	Aparicio, Luis	Wagner, Honus
Greenberg, Hank	Hornsby, Rogers	Appling, Luke	
Killebrew, Harmon	Lajoie, Nap	Banks, Ernie	*Third Base* (8)
McCovey, Willie	Mazeroski, Bill	Cronin, Joe	Baker, Home Run
Sisler, George	McPhee, Bid	Lloyd, John Henry	Boggs, Wade

Brett, George
Mathews, Eddie
Robinson, Brooks
Santo, Ron
Schmidt, Mike
Traynor, Pie

DiMaggio, Joe
Hamilton, Billy
Mantle, Mickey
Mays, Willie
Murphy, Dale
Snider, Duke
Speaker, Tris

Rose, Pete
Yount, Robin

Catchers (10)
Bench, Johnny
Berra, Yogi
Campanella, Roy
Carter, Gary
Cochrane, Mickey
Dickey, Bill
Ewing, Buck
Fisk, Carlton
Gibson, Josh
Hartnett, Gabby

Fingers, Rollie
Ford, Whitey
Gibson, Bob
Grove, Lefty
Hubbell, Carl
Keefe, Tim
Johnson, Walter
Koufax, Sandy
Mathewson, Christy
Nichols, Kid
Paige, Satchel
Palmer, Jim
Rusie, Amos
Ryan, Nolan
Seaver, Tom
Spahn, Warren
Walsh, Ed
Wilhelm, Hoyt
Young, Cy

Left Field (8)
Brock, Lou
Henderson, Rickey
Jackson, Joe
Kiner, Ralph
Musial, Stan
Simmons, Al
Stargell, Willie
Williams, Ted

Right Field (8)
Aaron, Hank
Clemente, Roberto
Jackson, Reggie
Kaline, Al
Robinson, Frank
Ruth, Babe
Thompson, Sam
Winfield, Dave

Pitchers (24)
Alexander, Grover
Brown, Mordecai
Carlton, Steve
Clemens, Roger
Feller, Bob

Center Field (10)
Ashburn, Richie
Charleston, Oscar
Cobb, Ty

Utility (4)
Bell, Cool Papa
Robinson, Jackie

HANK AARON

Right Field. Born Feb. 5, 1934 Mobile, Ala. Holds major league record for most lifetime home runs (755). NL MVP 1957.

Even though he led the NL in hits and batting average in 1956, Henry Louis Aaron, Jr., was pictured backward—batting lefthanded—on his 1957 baseball card.

That was fitting symbolism for the man who did everything quietly, except break Babe Ruth's record for career home runs. Hank Aaron integrated the Sally League, set records for career RBI (2,297) and total bases (6,856), won two batting titles and four RBI crowns, and hit .300 or better in fourteen seasons—all very quietly.

No one exclaimed over his fielding, either, although Aaron played errorless defense in fourteen World Series games, won three Gold Gloves, led the league's outfielders three times in double plays, and twice in fielding runs. According to the Total Baseball Ranking, he was baseball's leading player from 1961 to 1990 and fifth overall, behind only Babe Ruth, Napoleon Lajoie, Ty Cobb, and Ted Williams.

Aaron hit crosshanded in Mobile, Alabama, and with the Indianapolis Clowns of the Negro AL. After the Braves bought his contract, he hit .326 in the Northern League and .362 to lead the Sally League. When Bobby Thomson broke his ankle in spring training in 1954, Aaron became a major league regular at age twenty.

Three years later, with characteristically little fanfare, he was named the NL's MVP as the Braves won the pennant, and he hit .393 in the World Series, including 3 home runs to lead all batters. Always rising to the occasion, Aaron hit home runs in two of the twenty-four All-Star Games in which he played, homered in all three playoff games in 1969, and amassed a lifetime World Series average of .364.

Number 44 attracted attention only with his home runs, hitting 44 in four different seasons; he won three National League home run crowns and tied for a fourth. In 1973 he hit 40 home runs in just 392 at bats. He broke Ruth's record the following year with a rocket off Al

Downing in Atlanta, and finished his career with a record 755.

Although many fans discovered Aaron after most of his career was over, his colleagues knew how special he was. Stan Musial jumped onto the field to congratulate him when he joined the 3,000 hit club, and Mickey Mantle said of him, "Aaron was to my time what Joe DiMaggio was to the era when he played."

He was elected to the Hall of Fame in 1982.

GROVER CLEVELAND ALEXANDER

Pitcher. Born Feb. 26, 1887 St. Paul, Neb. Died Nov. 4, 1950 St. Paul,. Neb. Holds NL records for lifetime shutouts (90) and lifetime complete games (436).

Grover Cleveland Alexander got his big break when he was traded for a vote.

Charles Carr, owner of the American Association's Indianapolis team, had invested in a company that manufactured baseballs. Anxious to have his ball used in the New York State League, he told the owner of the Syracuse team, "If you'll vote for my ball, I'll give you a good pitcher for nothing."

The pitcher, Alexander, suffered from double vision at the time but recovered enough to win 29 games for Syracuse—13 of them shutouts. Drafted by the Phillies, he no-hit the Athletics in a five-inning exhibition game and won 28 games in 1911 to set the rookie record. He won 19, 22, and 27 his next three years to set the stage for the most successful three-year run enjoyed by any pitcher.

In 1915 he won 31 games (12 shutouts and a record 4 one-hitters) and outdid himself a year later by winning 33 games, 16 of them shutouts. In 1917 he won 30, two of them complete games in a Labor Day doubleheader against the Dodgers. If there were a "Triple Crown" for pitchers, as many have suggested, Alexander would have won it twice, leading the league in most wins, strikeouts, and lowest ERA for 1916 and 1920. The second time occurred after he returned from military duty deaf in one ear and suffering from epilepsy.

Occasional neurological fits and an eventually crippling fondness for liquor didn't ruin his pitching. He led the league in ERA twice after his trade to the Chicago Cubs, for whom he won 27 games in 1920. Waived to the Cardinals six years later, he pitched the 15–1 underdogs to complete game victories in the second and sixth games and recorded the most dramatic "save" in Series history, striking out Tony Lazzeri with the bases loaded in the seventh inning of the seventh game.

Alex averaged 19.6 wins for nineteen years, pitched 90 lifetime shutouts (second only to Walter Johnson's 110), and won 373 games to tie Christy Mathewson as the NL lifetime leader. Even more impressive, he recorded the bulk of them at hitter-friendly parks—Philadelphia's Baker Bowl with its 290-foot right field fence and Wrigley Field. He joined the other immortals in Cooperstown in 1938.

ADRIAN "CAP" ANSON

First Baseman. Born Apr. 11, 1852 Marshalltown, Ia. Died Apr. 14, 1922 Chicago. Holds NL record for most seasons batting .300 or more (18). Most seasons of big-league play, 27 (5 NA, 22, NL).

Adrian Constantine "Cap" Anson was the first man to reach 3,000 hits, the first manager to rotate pitchers, and the first player to draw the color line against blacks in baseball.

A hard-driving disciplinarian, Anson was perhaps the most influential player in the nineteenth century. He played in the first professional league, the National Association, from its inception in 1871 and hit .331 in the NL twenty-five years later. Using a split grip, he hit .300 or better in twenty-five seasons, won two batting titles and eight RBI crowns, averaging an RBI every five at-bats over the course of his career.

Anson spent a year at Notre Dame, turned pro with the NA Rockford Forest Citys, played third base for the Philadelphia Athletics for four years, and joined Chicago when White Stockings owner William Hulbert formed the NL. Anson became the White Sox captain in 1878 and switched to first base exclusively when he took over as manager in 1879.

He managed Chicago to pennants from 1880 to 1882, 1884, and 1885, rotating his pitchers and using signals to his hitters and fielders. He has a claim to originating platooning and initiated preseason training. He also was fined regularly by umpires and league officials, earning the nickname "Baby" (for crybaby) before cleaning up his act to earn the nickname "Cap" (for captain). He used bed checks to keep tabs on his charges but also got them first-class hotel rooms and personally marched them onto the field single file before every game.

In 1883, Anson refused to play in an exhibition game at Toledo because the home team had a black catcher, Moses Fleetwood Walker. Although Anson backed down when threatened with forfeiture of the gate, he used his position and popularity to ban black pitcher George Stovey in 1887 when John Montgomery Ward tried to sign him to the Giants; no one tried to upset this "gentleman's agreement" until 1947.

Despite this black mark on his character, Anson later mellowed and eventually became known as "Pop" Anson. When he was fired in 1897, Chicago briefly became known as the Orphans, because they'd lost their Pop.

Anson managed the Giants for just twenty-five days, turned down $50,000 donated by Chicago fans, opened a billiard saloon, tried to organize a rival major league—the abortive American Association of 1899, entered vaudeville (doing skits written by Ring Lardner), and served a term as city clerk in Chicago. He was voted into the Hall of Fame in 1939.

LUIS APARICIO

Shortstop. Born Apr. 29, 1934 Maracaibo, Venezuela. Holds major league records for most games at shortstop (2,581), assists (8,016), and double plays (1,553).

Hank Greenberg had a choice of Venezuelan shortstops in the 1950s and guessed wrong. The Indians' general manager didn't think Luis Aparicio was worth a $10,000 bonus and traded instead for his countryman, Alfonso "Chico" Carrasquel. Carrasquel's career ended in 1959, the same year Aparicio led the "Go-Go Sox" to a pennant, the first for Chicago since the scandal year of 1919.

While Maury Wills is generally given credit with reinventing the stolen base in 1962, Aparicio had made pilferage pay six years earlier. In his rookie year, Aparicio led the league in stolen bases with 21, handled more chances than any AL shortstop, and was named Rookie of the Year. Aparicio led the league in stolen bases his first nine years in the AL (1956–1964), once stole 26 consecutive bases, and was successful on 79 percent of his base stealing attempts.

In truth, Aparicio was not a prototypical leadoff man, sporting an on base average of only .313. Part of his success was due to the bat-handling ability of second baseman and second-place hitter Nelson Fox. Looie hollered like Fox, spat tobacco juice like Fox, and named his son for Fox. When Fox won the MVP award in 1959, the year the Sox won the pennant, Aparicio was right behind him in second place.

Fox and Aparicio won more fielding titles together than any other double play combination, and no shortstop ever led his league in the major defensive categories as often as Looie. He won nine Gold Gloves, was selected to the *Sporting News* All-Star team five times, and the All-Star fielding team ten times. Aparicio attributed his success to using a heavier glove in infield practice to make his own feel lighter during the game.

In January 1963, the White Sox broke up the double play combination, trading Looie to the Orioles. Aparicio provided some of the leadership that enabled the Orioles to win the 1966 pennant and sweep the World Series. He began a second hitch with the White Sox in 1968, hit better than .300 for the only time in his career in 1970 (.313), and finished up playing three years for the Red Sox, giving him eighteen consecutive seasons in which he played 100 or more games. Aparicio was voted into the Hall of Fame in 1984.

LUKE APPLING

Shortstop. Born Apr. 2, 1907 High Point, N.C. Died Jan. 3, 1991 Cumming, Ga. Won two batting titles, including a record for shortstops of .388 in 1936.

They called him Old Aches and Pains, Fumblefoot, and Old Tanglehoof. But by the time he had retired, Luke Appling had hit .300 or better nine straight years and sixteen times in all; had set a major league record by leading the AL in assists seven seasons in a row, and had played more games at shortstop than any ALer.

The hypochondriacal Appling would complain to White Sox manager Jimmy Dykes, saying "Honest, Jimmy, I'm dying." In actuality, over his long career Appling only broke a finger in 1930 and a leg in 1938. "Old Aches and Pains" was hung on him when he roomed with Chicago's trainer. The roomies would get to Comiskey Park early, and Appling would catch forty winks on the rubbing table; inquiring mates were told he was getting "special treatment for a muscle pull."

Lucius Benjamin Appling was healthy enough to consider pro football after playing fullback at Oglethorpe College, but joined the Atlanta Crackers instead. After hitting .326 in 104 games, he was told that the Cubs had bought his contract; however, Bill Veeck, Sr., had second thoughts, and Appling wound up with the Chicago White Sox instead.

Veeck must have felt relieved when the rookie started 1931 0-for-28 and averaged an error every other day; manager Lew Fonseca tried to trade him to no avail. He told Appling, "You're going to play 154 games if you hit .154 and field .154." By 1933, Luke was leading the AL in errors for the first of a record five times, but he also tied Billy Rogell for the lead in total chances and hit .322.

In 1936 he went 4-for-4 the final day of the season to become the first AL shortstop to win a batting title. He won his second in 1943 (.328) before going into the service. By 1949 he had become, at 42, the oldest regular shortstop in baseball history. He eclipsed Rabbit Maranville's record of 2,154 games at short, and retired with a career batting average of .310.

Appling won pennants managing Memphis (Southern Association) and Indianapolis (American Association) and managed the Kansas City A's in 1967. Elected to the Hall of Fame in 1964, he made an appearance in the Cracker Jack All-Star Game in 1984, homering at age 75 against Warren Spahn.

RICHIE ASHBURN
Center Field. Born Mar. 19, 1927 Tilden, Neb. Holds major league records for most years with 400 or more putouts (9) and 500 or more putouts (4).
When Richie Ashburn reported to spring training in 1948, all he had to do to win the center field job for the Phillies was beat out the man who had won the previous year's batting championship by 46 points—Harry "The Hat" Walker.

But Walker fouled a pitch off his foot one morning and was out of the lineup through May. By then, Ashburn was hitting .346 and had unseated him as the Phils' center fielder. The only rookie voted to the 1948 All-Star team, Ashburn had a pair of singles and a stolen base. Even though he broke a finger in August, no injury could spoil a year in which he had a 23-game hitting streak, led the league with 32 stolen bases, hit .333, and was named Rookie of the Year.

Some skeptics pointed out that, "He's not hitting .333; he's hitting .133 and running .200." But in a fifteen-year career, Ashburn hit .300 or better nine times, won two batting titles, got on base about 40 percent of the time, and posted a .308 career average, topping Pete Rose, Willie Mays, and Hank Aaron, among others. As an out-fielder he set records by recording 500 or more putouts in four different seasons and 400 or more putouts in nine different seasons. He tied Max Carey's major league records by leading the league in that department nine times; he accepted the most chances nine times; he ranks fifth behind Carey, Willie Mays, Tris Speaker, and Ty Cobb in both career putouts and total chances.

"Whitey" Ashburn won batting titles in 1955 (.338) and 1958 (.350), but his greatest moment as a Phillie came in the field. On the last day of the 1950 season, the Dodgers, trailing Philadelphia by a game, played them at Ebbets Field. With the score tied, 1–1, in the bottom of the ninth inning, Brooklyn's Cal Abrams tried to score from second on Duke Snider's single; Ashburn cut him down by twenty feet, setting the stage for Dick Sisler's tenth-inning homer and clinching the Phils' first flag in thirty-five years.

Traded to the Cubs in 1961, Ashburn became one of the original Mets in 1962 and the expansion team's first All-Star, the fifth time he'd been named to an All-Star squad. Since retiring as a player, allegedly because the Mets were so bad at the time, Ashburn has become the Phillies' longest-running broadcaster.

FRANK "HOME RUN" BAKER
Third Baseman. Born Mar. 13, 1886 Trappe, Md., Died Jun. 28, 1963 Trappe, Md.
By the end of the 1910 season, Frank Baker had hit just six home runs in 1,133 at bats. Up to that point, he was more noted as a base stealer than a power hitter, having stolen 20 or more bases every year and having led the league in triples in 1909 with 19.

Then Baker hit 11 homers in 1911 to lead the league for the first of four straight years and helped Connie Mack's Athletics to their second straight pennant. In the World Series, the Giants' Christy Mathewson won the opener, 2–1. Game Two was tied 1–1 in the sixth; New York's Rube Marquard had retired thirteen batters in a row; but, after Eddie Collins doubled, Baker pulled an inside pitch over the short right field wall at the Polo Grounds to give the A's a 3–1 win. The next day, Mathewson's ghost writer, John Wheeler, second-guessed Marquard and advised that "Baker should be pitched *outside*." Later that day, in Game Three, Mathewson retired Baker on two harmless grounders and a fly ball. When Baker came to bat for the fourth time, with the Giants ahead 1–0 with one out in the ninth, Mathewson got two strikes, but then Baker pulled an outside pitch into the right field seats; the A's won, 3–1 in 11 innings, and Frank Baker suddenly became "Home Run" Baker.

Baker batted cleanup, behind Eddie Collins, and sportswriters suggested that Collins's antics on the basepaths made Baker a better hitter. Collins laughed. "When it came to hitting," he said, "Baker needed help like Carnegie needed money." A .300 hitter in six different seasons, he led the league in RBI twice and might have done even more damage if he hadn't missed two whole seasons.

When the A's were swept in the 1914 Series, Mack decided to punish his players with stiff pay cuts; Baker sat out the season instead and was sold to the Yankees. He also didn't play in 1920, the year his wife died, but helped New York win pennants in 1921 and 1922 as a spot player.

In 1961 sportswriter Joe Williams asked Baker how many homers he would hit today. He replied, "I'd say 50 anyway. The year I hit 12, I also hit the right field fence at Shibe Park 38 times; all of those would have been home runs with the lively ball."

ERNIE "MR. CUB" BANKS

Shortstop/First Baseman. Born Jan. 31, 1931 Dallas, Tex. NL MVP 1958, 1959. Holds major league shortstop record for home runs in a season (47).

To the victors go the spoils—and most of the MVP Awards. Yet, once in baseball history, the shortstop of a club tied for fifth was named MVP two straight years. In 1958 Ernie Banks led the league in home runs (47), RBI (129), and slugging percentage (.614), and played in every game. A year later, Banks led the league again with 143 ribbies. He hit 20 or more homers in thirteen seasons, hit .300 or better three times, and drove in 100 or more runs eight times. He led the league's shortstops in fielding three times and, after moving to first base in 1962, led all first basemen in putouts five times.

Banks never played minor league ball, jumping directly from the Kansas City Monarchs of the Negro AL to the Chicago Cubs. He hit .314 in ten games in 1953, took over as the Cubs' starting shortstop the following year, and had his first great season in 1955, knocking in 117 runs and hitting 44 homers, a record for shortstops; five of them came with the bases loaded, then a record (since broken by Don Mattingly).

By 1957 he was one of the most feared power hitters in the league. The late umpire Tom Gorman once recalled that, "in 1957 Banks was knocked down four times by four different pitchers—Don Drysdale, Bob Purkey, Bob Friend, and Jack Sanford. And each time he was knocked down, Banks hit their next pitch out of the park."

He led the league in RBI in 1959 and homers again in 1960 (41). Only Eddie Mathews's 46th homer in a 1959 playoff game kept Banks, who had 45, from a share of three consecutive home run titles. He hit more home runs than any shortstop in the history of the game (293) and wound up with 512 for his career. Prior to his retirement in 1971, he was voted the Greatest Cub Player of All Time.

After becoming a minor league instructor for the Cubs, Banks belied his goody-two-shoes image by saying things like, "I like my players to be married and in debt. That's the way you motivate them." But Cub fans will always remember him as the ballplayer who said, "What a great day for baseball. Let's play two!"

JAMES "COOL PAPA" BELL

Infielder/Outfielder. Negro Leagues 1922–46; St. Louis Stars, Pittsburgh Crawfords, Detroit Wolves, Kansas City Monarchs, Chicago American Giants, Memphis Red Sox, Homestead Grays. Born May 17, 1903 Starkville, Miss. Died March 7, 1991 St. Louis, Mo.

Cool Papa Bell may have been the headiest and fastest baserunner of his time, and, maybe, all time.

He is credited with stealing 175 bases in 1933 and is said to have once rounded the bases in 12 seconds. (The official record is 13.3 seconds, set by Evar Swanson of the Reds in 1931.) Bell scored from first on a sacrifice in a 1940s exhibition against major leaguers. Satchel Paige bunted him over to second, then seeing third uncovered, Bell took off; catcher Roy Partee gave chase, but Bell slid home safely; he was forty-five at the time.

Originally a righthanded batter, Bell taught himself to switch hit and is credited with hitting .437 for Torreon of the Mexican League in 1940. Over an 89-game season, he led the league in runs (119), hits (167), triples (15), home runs (12) and RBI (79). According to incomplete records, he hit .407 in 1944 and .402 in 1946.

Bill Veeck said, "Defensively, he was the equal of Tris Speaker, Joe DiMaggio or Willie Mays." Pro basketball pioneer and baseball scout Eddie Gottlieb said, "If he had played in the major leagues, he would have reminded the fans of Willie Keeler as a hitter and Ty Cobb as a baserunner—and he might have exceeded both."

Born in Starkville, Mississippi, James Bell played semipro ball with four of his brothers on the Compton Hill Cubs in St. Louis, breaking in as a lefthanded pitcher. After a particularly strong game in 1922, the St. Louis Stars signed him for $90 a month and switched him to the outfield to take advantage of his speed every day.

Named Cool Papa for his unflappability, he performed up to par in his few appearances against major league opposition. In 1929 he and other black stars barnstormed against a team headed by Hall of Famers Charlie Gehringer, Al Simmons, and Heinie Manush and won six games out of eight.

When his playing days were over, Bell had a hand in the development of Ernie Banks and others. Banks credits Bell with taking him from the Texas sandlots to Kansas City, and both Lou Brock and Maury Wills give Bell credit for helping them steal bases. He was elected to the Hall of Fame in 1974.

JOHNNY BENCH

Catcher. Born Dec. 7, 1947 Oklahoma City, Okla. NL MVP 1970, 1972.

Ted Williams has signed many autographs but none as prescient as one penned in spring training in 1965: "To Johnny Bench, a sure Hall of Famer."

Bench was named to the NL All-Star team fourteen times, played in every game from 1968 to 1975, and hit .409 with 3 home runs. He set a major league record for home runs by a catcher (327 plus 62 playing elsewhere), later broken by Carlton Fisk; won two home run crowns; led the league in RBI three times; and was chosen MVP twice.

While Bench is remembered most for his offense, he may have had his greatest impact behind the bat. He was the first receiver to use a protective helmet in the field, popularized catching onehanded, kept his throwing hand behind his back to protect it from foul tips, and said his father "taught me to throw 254 feet—twice the distance to second base—from a crouch."

Not known for keeping his counsel, Bench once said flatly, "I can throw out any runner alive," and brashly predicted that he would be the first catcher to be named Rookie of the Year. He did just that in 1968, caught 154 games, a rookie record, and won the first of ten straight Gold Gloves. Bench hit 45 homers and was chosen MVP for the first time in 1970, the year Bob Hunter, a Los Angeles sportswriter, first called Cincinnati "the Big Red Machine."

That year, the Reds ran into Brooks Robinson and, the second time Bench was named MVP, in 1972, the Big Red Machine was derailed by the Oakland A's Mustache Gang. When the Reds squared off against the New York Yankees in 1976, the press played up the confrontation between Bench and the Yankees' catcher and captain, Thurman Munson.

Bench caught Mickey Rivers stealing in Game One, New York's only attempted theft in the Series, got two hits in each of the first three games, and hit two home runs in Game Four to lead the Reds to their first World Series sweep. Munson hit .529 with 2 RBI; Bench hit .533 and knocked in 6 runs. Munson gave Bench his due, "The man deserves all the credit in the world."

Bench made Williams's prediction come true in 1989, the first year he was eligible. He is currently a broadcaster with CBS radio nationally and local station WLWT in Cincinnati.

LAWRENCE "YOGI" BERRA
Catcher. Born May 12, 1925 St. Louis, Mo. AL MVP, 1951, 1954, 1955.
Branch Rickey didn't make many mistakes, but declining to sign Yogi Berra for all of $250 was a real beaut.

In 1942 Rickey was the Cardinals' general manager and offered Berra $250 to sign, refusing to pay him the same $500 offered to his friend, Joe Garagiola. Berra turned down the $250 and, a year later, the Yankees signed him for the very same $500; not very long thereafter, they turned down a $50,000 offer from Giant manager Mel Ott, who had seen Berra play for the International League Newark Bears.

Berra eventually became a fifteen-time All-Star, a three-time MVP, and a Hall of Famer. He also holds numerous World Series records including games by a catcher (63), hits (71), and times on the winning team (10). Though lightly regarded as a manager, he was the first big league skipper to win pennants in both leagues in nearly forty years.

Born in "the Hill" section of St. Louis, Berra got his nickname when childhood friends watching a movie noted Berra's resemblance to a Hindu practicing yoga. Following stints in the navy and the minors, Yogi became a Yankee and shared catching duties with Aaron Robinson and Sherman Lollar until the Dodgers ran him ragged in the 1947 World Series. After being tutored by Bill Dickey, however, he became a standout catcher and accepted 950 errorless chances from July 28, 1957 to May 10, 1959.

Berra led AL catchers in putouts eight times, assists and fielding three times each, and handled the Yankee pitching staff masterfully. Although he never led the league in home runs or RBI, Berra, a notorious bad-ball hitter, was a constant threat offensively, particularly with men on base; he was named Most Valuable Player in 1951, repeated in 1954 and 1955, and retired with a .285 lifetime average.

Named to manage the Yankees in 1964, he won the pennant but lost both a seven-game Series and his job to Johnny Keane. He joined the Mets as a coach and became the manager in 1973, taking them from fifth place to the pennant, ultimately losing the Series again in seven games, to the A's. He returned to the Yankees as coach and manager, was elected to the Hall of Fame in 1972 and ended his career as a coach with the Astros.

WADE BOGGS
Third Baseman. Born June 15, 1958 Omaha, Neb. Won four straight AL batting titles, 1985–1988, five straight on base percentage titles, 1985–1989.
After undergoing a horrendous slump at the end of 1996, Wade Boggs finally earned a ring and can add World Champion to a resume already highlighted by "five-time batting champion." His lifetime average is still a robust .333, which places him twenty-fourth.

Boggs scored 100 or more runs seven straight times, led the AL in batting five times, and notched 200 or more hits in seven straight seasons, a modern record. Named to the All-Star team in 1985, he has been a starter every year from 1986 to 1994.

The son of a retired Marine, Boggs grew up an all-state kicker in Tampa, Florida, signed with the Red Sox in 1976, and was playing for Elmira of the NY-Penn League shortly after graduating from high school. In 1980 he lost the International League batting title on the last day of the season but won it the next year on the last day of the season. Boggs became a regular in 1982 when Carney Lansford was injured. He booted the first two ground balls hit to him in the majors but hit .349, splitting his time between first base and third.

In 1983 he made 27 errors but led the majors in hitting (.361) and on-base percentage (.449). A year later, he topped all AL third basemen in errors but also had the most chances, double plays, assists, putouts, and fielding runs. In 1985 he hit .368 to win the first of four straight batting titles, reached base safely 340 times, and had 240 hits, the most since Babe Herman's 241 in 1930. He batted .357 to help the Red Sox win the pennant in 1986 and has hit .311 in three playoffs and World Series, with the Red Sox and the Yankees.

The "Chicken Man," so named by Jim Rice for his love of fowl, lives a disciplined life, getting up at the same time, going to the ballpark at the same time, eating chicken daily, and doing the same things the same way as often as possible. He fields exactly 150 grounders in practice, steps into the batting cage at 5:17 and, after private time in the clubhouse bouncing a baseball off a wall, hits the field at precisely 7:17 for wind sprints.

Boggs says his eyesight is his greatest asset. He told *Newsweek*, "I can observe the spin on a breaking ball. If it happens to be a fastball, I can still hit it to left. And if the pitch happens to be off-speed enough, believe it or not, I'll pull it."

GEORGE BRETT
Third Baseman. May 15, 1953 Glen Dale, W. Va. In 1980 had highest batting average since Ted Williams' .406 of 1941.
George Brett joined the exclusive 3,000-hit club on September 30, 1992. He was already the only player to win batting titles in three different decades, a thirteen-time All-Star, and the last modern player to make a serious run at hitting .400.

The younger brother of pitcher Ken Brett, he led the league in hits and triples in 1975, repeated in both categories in 1976, and added his first batting title that year, hitting .333 to edge Rod Carew and teammate Hal McRae, later his manager. From 1976 to 1978 the Royals lost three straight playoffs to the Yankees despite Brett's three-run homer in 1976 and his three consecutive homers off Catfish Hunter in 1978.

Just before the All-Star break in 1980 Brett was hitting .337 when he strained ankle ligaments trying to steal a base; however, he got hot in July and even hotter in August, going 4-for-4 on the 17th to reach the magic figure of .400. With two weeks left, he slumped but finished strong (10-for-19), ending the season at .390; he also led the league in slugging (.664) and, to absolutely no one's surprise, was named MVP.

That year, the Royals broke the playoff jinx against the Yankees as Brett homered in Game One and hit an upper deck home run off Goose Gossage to win Game Three. Although the Phils beat KC in a six-game Series, Brett homered and went 9-for-24 in the Series. The Royals finally won a championship in 1985 as Brett starred offensively and defensively; he went 4-for-5 in Game Seven, robbed the Cardinals of five potential hits and went 10-for-27, scoring five runs.

On July 24, 1983, Brett made history in a different way. With New York leading Kansas City 4-3 in the ninth inning at Yankee Stadium, he homered with two out and a man on to put the Royals in front, 5-4. Yankee manager Billy Martin contended that Brett should be declared out and the runs shouldn't count, because his bat had pine tar more than 18 inches from the knob to the barrel; the umpires agreed, awarding the win to the Yankees. The Royals protested, however, and AL president Lee Mac-Phail ended the Great Pine Tar Incident by overruling his own umpires and declaring a resumption of play at a later date.

Brett won his third batting title in 1990.

He retired after the 1993 season and became a member of the Royals' front office.

LOU BROCK

Left Field. Born Jun. 18, 1939 ElDorado, Ark. Holds major league record for most consecutive years 50 or more stolen bases (12).

In 1978 the NL announced that its annual stolen base leader would receive the Lou Brock Award, making Brock the first active player to have an award named after him. The greatest base stealer baseball had produced to that time, Lou went on to break Ty Cobb's "modern" career record of 891 with 938 (Billy Hamilton had 912 in 1888–1901) although the record was eventually eclipsed, in turn, by Rickey Henderson.

Brock ensured that he'd get numerous chances to run by joining the exclusive 3,000-hit club (3,023) and finishing a nineteen-year career with seven .300 seasons and a lifetime batting average of .293. In 1968 he led the league in doubles, triples, and steals, the first National League player to accomplish that feat since Honus Wagner did it in 1908.

Lou could run, hit, and even hit with power occasionally; in 1967 he led the Cardinals in extra-base hits and knocked in 76 runs as a leadoff man. As a youngster with the Chicago Cubs, Brock even blasted a home run into the center field stands at the Polo Grounds, a startling feat that had been accomplished only once before, by certified slugger Joe Adcock.

After being traded from the Cubs to the Cardinals for Ernie Broglio in June 1964, he hit .348 and scored 81 runs in 103 games; during the stretch run, when the Phillies folded, he hit .461 to help the Cardinals win their first pennant in eighteen years. Although he hit .300, 1964 would prove to be his poorest offensive Series. In 1967 he batted .414 with 12 hits, stole a record 7 bases, and went 4-for-4 in Game One. A year later, he stole 7 bases again and improved to .464 with 13 hits, tying Bobby Richardson's record; his 14 steals is a World Series career record, tying Eddie Collins.

In 1966 he broke Maury Wills's stranglehold on the stolen base championship with 74 thefts. That was the first of four straight base-stealing crowns, and, after Bobby Tolan interrupted his string in 1970, Lou won four more in a row. In 1974 he smashed Maury Wills's season mark of 104 stolen bases, ending with 118, and was named Man of the Year by *The Sporting News*. He was elected to the Hall of Fame in 1985.

DENNIS "BIG DAN" BROUTHERS

First Baseman. Born May 8, 1858 Sylvan Lake, N.Y. Died Aug. 3, 1932 East Orange, N.J. Highest slugging average of any player to perform before 1900; led NL in slugging six years in a row (1881–1886).

Big Dan Brouthers holds the highest lifetime average of any first baseman (.342), batting .300 or better for fourteen straight years. He played on champions in three leagues, won five batting titles, and topped the NL in slugging six straight times.

Although he hit just 106 homers, the lefthanded Brouthers (rhymes with "soothers") was "the Babe Ruth of his era." John McGraw, his Oriole teammate, said, "When I first went with Baltimore there were little flags stuck on the fences of the different parks to show where Brouthers had driven balls out."

Brouthers got his baseball baptism with the semipro Wappingers Falls Actives. The Troy Haymakers brought him to the big leagues but, after he made 34 errors in 39 games in 1879, returned him to the minors. In 1881 Big Dan shuffled off to Buffalo, where he led the NL in homers (8) and topped all batsmen in 1882 (.368) and 1883 (.374).

Brouthers, James "Deacon" White, Hardy "Old True Blue" Richardson, and Jack Rowe constituted Buffalo's "Big Four." Although they failed to bring Buffalo a pennant, the quartet—sold as a unit to the Wolverines after the 1885 season—brought Detroit its first flag in 1887. Brouthers led the league in runs, doubles, and on-base percentage.

When the Wolverines disbanded a year later, Brouthers was awarded to the Boston Beaneaters, with whom he won his third batting title (.373) in 1889. The next year, he jumped to the Boston Reds, a Players League team; when it, too, disbanded, he joined a team of the same name that captured the American Association pennant and won the batting title again in 1891 (.350). Big Dan "revolved" (changed teams) and became a Brooklyn Superba, copped his fifth batting crown in 1892 (.335), and was traded to the Orioles with Willie Keeler. Brouthers had his last great year in 1894, hitting .347 and providing 128 RBI to lead Baltimore to its first pennant.

After brief stops in Louisville and Philadelphia he continued his slugging exploits in the minors, winning the batting title of the Class D Hudson River League in 1904 at the age of 46, capping that incredible year with a two-game return to the big leagues for McGraw's Giants. He served as a press box attendant at the Polo Grounds until he died in 1932. He was elected to the Hall of Fame in 1945.

MORDECAI "THREE FINGER" BROWN

Pitcher. Born Oct. 19, 1876 Nyesville, Ind. Died Feb. 14, 1948 Terre Haute, Ind. ERA of 1.06 in 1906 stands as NL best since 1880.

Mordecai Brown's colorful nickname often obscures what a great pitcher he was.

He ranks third behind Ed Walsh and Addie Joss in lifetime ERA (2.06) and trails only Walsh, Joss, and Christy Mathewson in allowing the fewest runners per nine innings (9.80). Ty Cobb said of Brown's breaking ball, "It was the most devastating pitch I ever faced. Christy Mathewson's fadeaway was good, but it was nothing like that curve Three-Fingered Brown threw at you."

Brown was seven when he put the index finger of his right hand into his uncle's corn shredder; it was amputated just above the knuckle. A few weeks later he broke his third and fourth fingers while chasing a hog; they healed into a gnarled, unnatural shape. Despite his handicap, Brown became a semipro infielder. One day, the team's star pitcher broke his arm and Brown took over; in five innings, he struck out fourteen, using a curve ball that broke unusually because of the shape of his hand.

"Miner" Brown (so named because he was a coal miner before he became a ballplayer) joined the Cardinals, going 9–13 in his rookie season. The Cubs saw great potential and traded for the man Frank Chance called "the greatest fielding pitcher the game ever had." Brown won 15 games in 1904, 18 in 1905, and 26 in 1906, posting a 1.04 ERA.

In 1908 Brown won 29 games against 9 losses, threw four consecutive shutouts, and helped Chicago catch the slumping Giants by winning both ends of a September doubleheader. The next day, Fred Merkle's baserunning boner turned a Giant victory in a tie, ultimately necessitating a playoff game. When the first three Giants hit safely and the next two walked, Brown took over from Jack Pfiester without warming up. He shut the Giants out the rest of the way and the Cubs won the game, 4–2, and the pennant.

In 1909 he led the league in wins (27), complete games (32), and saves (7) but wrenched a ligament in his right leg. He remained effective in 1910, but the glory years were behind him. Traded to the Reds in 1913, he won only 5 games. Following a stretch managing the St. Louis Federals, he rejoined the Cubs, and he and Mathewson pitched their finales against each other, Mathewson winning the atypically inept contest 10–7.

The great pitchers thus concluded their personal rivalry with Mathewson winning thirteen times against Brown's eleven. Matty was an original inductee into the Hall of Fame in 1936; Brown had to wait thirteen more years.

ROY CAMPANELLA

Catcher. Born Nov. 19, 1921 Philadelphia, Pa. Died Jun. 23, 1993 Woodland Hills, Cal. NL MVP 1951, 1953, 1955.

Baseball's all-time record crowd wasn't attracted by a red-hot playoff or a World Series game. Instead, 93,103 fans filled the Los Angeles Coliseum on May 7, 1959, to honor Roy Campanella, whose baseball career had ended the previous year when the car he was driving skidded into a telephone pole, leaving him paralyzed.

A decade after that unique tribute, Campanella received baseball's ultimate honor and was inducted into the Hall of Fame despite a major league career that had lasted a mere ten years. Then again, Campy was named MVP in three of the nine full seasons in which he played; 1951, 1953, and 1955 to rank with Stan Musial and Mike Schmidt as the only three-time MVPs in the NL.

An outstanding handler of pitchers, Campanella caught three no-hitters, led the league in putouts six times, caught 100 or more games a year his last nine years in the majors, and nailed two of every three runners that tried to steal on him. Although his batting average oscillated wildly (.312 to .207 to .318 to .219 between 1953 and 1956), he was more consistent at the power game, averaging 27 homers between 1949 and 1956.

He joined the Negro NL's Baltimore Elite Giants right out of high school and eventually made $3,000 a month as a full-fledged star, being named to All-Star teams in 1941, 1944, and 1945. After that season he became Brooklyn's second black signee, taking $185 a month to play with Nashua in the New England League; by 1949 he was the Dodgers' regular catcher.

In 1951 he hit .325 with 33 homers and 108 RBI but pulled a leg muscle in the final regular season game, missing the last two games of the playoff. Monte Irvin says, "If Campanella hadn't injured himself in Philadelphia, he might have settled Ralph Branca down after one high strike to Bobby Thomson."

After a modest 1952 season, Campy hit 41 homers in 1953 (40 as a catcher to set the since-broken major league record), batted .312, and led the league with 142 RBI. In 1955 he hit .318 with 32 homers and 107 RBI and was named to *The Sporting News* All-Star Team for the fourth time. He hit two home runs as Brooklyn won its only World Series.

STEVE CARLTON

Pitcher. Born Dec. 22, 1944 Miami, Fla. NL Cy Young Award 1972, 1977, 1980, 1982.

Steve Carlton never won the hearts and minds of baseball writers, but he led the NL in innings pitched and strikeouts five times each, won 329 games, and captured four Cy Young Awards.

He trained by using isometrics, kung fu, and twisting his hands in three-foot deep buckets of rice. The powerful lefty made 30 or more starts in 16 seasons. "I've never paced myself," he said, "I've always thrown everything as hard as I can for as long as I can."

Offered $4,000 by the Pirates as a junior college freshman, Carlton was signed by Cards' scout Howie Pollet for $5,000. On a Cards trip to Japan in 1968, he began developing the slider that became his "out" pitch. He fanned 19 Mets in a September 1969 game to set an National League record, finished the season 17–11, and won 20 games in 1971.

Instead of the big raise he expected, Carlton got traded to the Phillies and responded with a historic season. Lefty won 27 games for the last place Phils, notching a modern record 45 percent of the team's wins. A Triple Crown pitcher, he also led in ERA (1.97) and strikeouts (310), won his first Cy Young Award, and negotiated a salary of $167,000, then a record for pitchers.

The bounces didn't go his way the next year and he became a 20-game loser. He bounced back to win 59 games as the Phils won division titles in 1976, 1977, and 1978. In 1980, Carlton was 24–9 in the regular season, captured his third Cy Young Award, and beat the Royals twice in the World Series to give the Phillies their only world championship.

Three years after his last Cy Young Award (1982), Carlton went on the DL for the first time and was released by the Phils a year later. He pitched briefly for the Giants, White Sox, Indians, and Twins before retiring in 1988 as the NL leader in career strikeouts (4,000) and the leading lefty in the majors (4,136).

GARY CARTER

Catcher. Born Apr. 8, 1954 Culver City, Cal. All-Star Game MVP 1981, 1984.

In an earlier edition of *Total Baseball*, Bob Carroll wrote of Gary Carter, "The guy is friendly, open, cooperative, thoughtful, enthusiastic and has never been involved in a scandal. What's he hiding?"

Carter's gee-whiz personality has led observers to discount his achievements; clearly, however, he was the National League's leading catcher since Johnny Bench. A three-time Gold Glover, Carter led the league five times in assists and six straight years in games and putouts. Offensively, he drove in more than a hundred runs four times and hit 20 or more homers nine times.

Carter passed on more than a hundred football scholarship offers to sign with the Montreal Expos and was shocked to discover that they saw him not as a shortstop but as a catcher. In the beginning, Carter says, "I was the worst catcher you ever saw—a real joke." (One of his minor league managers charged him a quarter for every ball he dropped and often collected three or four dollars a game.)

He caught and played first and the outfield until the Expos traded Barry Foote in 1977. In 1978 he set a major league record by allowing just a single passed ball in 157 games. By 1981, "Kid" was the All-Star starter and homered off Ken Forsch and Ron Davis to be named MVP, joining Al Rosen, Arky Vaughan, Willie McCovey, and Ted Williams as the only men to homer twice in an All-Star Game. That fall, Carter hit .421 against the Phils in the divisional playoff and .438 against the Dodgers in the NLCS.

In the 1984 All-Star Game Carter homered off Dave Stieb to break a 1–1 tie and win his second All-Star MVP award. That season, despite knee problems which required postseason surgery, he tied Mike Schmidt for the RBI crown (106) and hit 27 homers. Traded to the Mets, he hit 24 homers to help the Mets win the pennant in 1986, drove in 3 runs in both Games Three and Four of the World Series, and singled to ignite the come-from-behind rally that won Game Six. After being released by the Mets in 1989, he played a year each with the Giants, Dodgers, and Expos. In 1993 he became part of the original broadcasting crew for the expansion Florida Marlins, an alliance he continues to this day.

OSCAR CHARLESTON

Center Fielder. Born Oct. 14, 1896 Indianapolis, Ind. Died Oct. 5, 1954 Philadelphia, Pa. Batted .434 in the Negro National League of 1921.

Oscar Charleston is generally regarded as the greatest of all Negro League players.

It diminishes Negro Leaguers to equate them with white players as the "black" this or that; however, Charleston's preeminence is such that he is known equally as "the black Tris Speaker" for his fielding, "the black Ty Cobb" for his baserunning, and "the black Babe Ruth" for his hitting. John McGraw said that he was simply the best, adding, "If only I could calcimine him."

He started out as batboy for the Indianapolis ABCs in his home town, joined the army at age fifteen, and was stationed in the Philippines with the all-black 24th Infantry. Even at that age, he was skilled enough to play in the otherwise all-white Manila League. He also ran track and was timed at the 220-yard dash in 23 seconds flat, giving rise to his nickname, "the Hoosier Comet."

He started professional play with the Indianapolis ABC's in 1915 and later moved on to the Chicago American Giants and St. Louis Giants. In a five-game series between Charleston's St. Louis Giants and the white St. Louis Cardinals, he is reported to have hit four home runs in one game, two of them off Jesse "Pop" Haines.

Charleston became player-manager of the Eastern Colored League Harrisburg Giants from 1922 to 1925 and moved to Philadelphia, where he became friends with catcher Biz Mackey and third baseman Judy Johnson. After stints with the Hilldales and the Homestead Grays, Johnson and Charleston moved to Pittsburgh when Gus Greenlee persuaded Charleston to manage and play for the Crawfords. Charleston hit .363, second only to Josh Gibson, and led the team to a 99–36 record, with the help of Gibson, Johnson, and Satchel Paige.

When the Crawfords moved to Toledo and Indianapolis, Charleston stayed with them through 1940, moving on to the Philadelphia Stars in 1941. After the war, Charleston was signed to Branch Rickey's Brooklyn Brown Dodgers, where he had a hand in corralling both Jackie Robinson and Roy Campanella. He joined them in the Hall of Fame in 1976.

ROGER CLEMENS

Pitcher. Born Aug. 4, 1962 Dayton, Oh. AL Cy Young Award 1986, 1987, 1991.

On September 18, 1996, Rocket Man turned Time Traveler. Roger Clemens turned the clock back a decade and fanned 20 Tigers in a single game, equaling his 1986 feat of striking out 20 Mariners.

No stranger to the spotlight, in 1987 Roger Clemens became the third pitcher, along with Sandy Koufax and Jim Palmer, to win back-to-back Cy Young Awards outright (Denny McLain won the award in 1968 and tied for it in 1969). He picked up his third Cy Young in 1991. Nicknamed "Rocket," or "Rocket Man," after an Elton

John song, Clemens burst on the scene the night of April 29, 1986, when he struck out 20 Mariners, breaking the nine-inning record previously held by Tom Seaver, Steve Carlton, and Clemens's idol, Nolan Ryan.

Clemens was destined for stardom. Offered $1,500 by the Twins, Clemens instead entered San Jacinto Junior College, then turned down a $20,000 bonus offered by the Mets and transferred to the University of Texas. (There he joined Bruce Ruffin, Calvin Schiraldi, and Greg Swindell.) After beating Alabama, 4–3, in the finals in 1983, Rocket became the Red Sox first pick in the June draft, signing for $121,000.

Called up the following May, Clemens was 9–4 in August when he strained a tendon in his right forearm and missed the rest of the season. He suffered a second arm injury in 1985 and required arthroscopic surgery in the rotator cuff of his right shoulder; yet eight months later he was striking out 20 Mariners on his way to winning his first 14 decisions. Starting for the American League in the All-Star Game, he retired nine straight batters to be named MVP. Clemens finished the 1986 season 24–4 to lead Boston to a division title and was the unanimous winner of the Cy Young Award. Pitching with the flu on three days' rest, Clemens beat the Angels, 8–1, to clinch the pennant. He left two World Series games ahead, 6–3 (after 4⅓ innings in Game Two) and 3–2 after 7 innings of the ill-fated Game Six.

In 1990 Clemens put together a 21–6 season but missed most of September because of a shoulder injury. The Sox won their division and Clemens left Game One of the playoffs after six shutout innings and got no decision. He gave up three runs in Game Four and was ejected after arguing with plate umpire Terry Cooney.

ROBERTO CLEMENTE

Right Field. Born Aug. 18, 1934 Carolina, P.R. Died Dec. 31, 1972 San Juan, P.R. NL MVP, 1966.

When Roberto Clemente graduated from high school in Puerto Rico, he received not only the best wishes of his friends and family but also blessings in person from scouts for ten different big league teams.

He had played for Santurce in the Puerto Rican Winter League while still a student and had quickly attracted bird dogs with his hitting, fielding, and throwing ability. Although the Milwaukee Braves offered him a $30,000 signing bonus, he kept an earlier commitment to the Dodgers and signed for $10,000.

However, he never played for Brooklyn or Los Angeles. A rule then in effect required that any player signing for more than $4,000 be put on the big league roster after a year in the minors; otherwise, he could be signed by any other club for $4,000. Although the Dodgers tried to hide Clemente on their Montreal roster by not playing him, he was claimed by the Pirates on November 22, 1954, for $4,000.

It was the Bucs' best investment since Honus Wagner. Clemente batted over .300 in thirteen seasons, won four NL batting crowns, finished with an even 3,000 hits, and ended an eighteen-year career with a lifetime average of .317. The NL MVP in 1966, he was also selected for the All-Star game twelve times.

A textbook right fielder, Clemente won twelve straight Gold Gloves. In 1958 he threw out 22 runners to win the first of a NL record five assists titles. A World Series star, he led the Bucs to championships in 1960 and 1971 and hit safely in every World Series game in which he played. In 1971 he homered in the sixth and seventh games, hit .414 with 12 hits, fielded flawlessly, and was chosen the Series MVP.

Throughout his career Clemente was plagued by back injuries, the result of an arthritic spine caused by an automobile accident. He died in an airplane crash on New Year's Eve, 1972, carrying food and medical supplies to earthquake-stricken Nicaragua.

The customary five-year waiting period was waived, and in 1973 he became the first Hispanic member of the Hall of Fame. Later he became the second baseball player, after Jackie Robinson, to be pictured on a U.S. postage stamp.

TY COBB

Center Field. Born Dec. 18, 1886 Narrows, Ga. Died July 17, 1961 Atlanta. Holds major league record for lifetime batting average (.366), most years leading league in batting (12) and hits (8).

When Ty Cobb was eighteen, his mother shot his father fatally at her bedroom window; some say she mistook him for a burglar, others that he suspected her of infidelity.

Either way, the tragedy probably spurred Cobb to become the fiercest competitor in baseball as well as the game's greatest hitter. Since 1947, only Stan Musial, Ted Williams, Rod Carew, George Brett, Tony Gwynn, Wade Boggs, Andres Galarraga, and Jeff Bagwell have, in single seasons, outhit Cobb's career average of .366. Virtually overlooked is his feat of leading the league in RBI four out of five years and bettering 100 RBI seven times, mostly in the dead-ball era.

One of the original five players elected to the Hall of Fame (he got seven more votes than Babe Ruth), Cobb is the only ALer to hit .400 or better in three different seasons. The Georgia Peach hit .300 or better every year from 1906 to 1928 and won the AL batting championship every year from 1907 to 1915 and from 1917 to 1919. (He slumped to .371 in 1916, when Tris Speaker hit .386.) Revisionist historians have deprived him of the batting titles in 1910 and 1914, but Cobb went to his grave with twelve batting championships.

While serving as player-manager of the Tigers in the mid-1920s Cobb benched himself when he was hitting .392. At the time, the Tigers had an all-.400 hitting outfield—Heinie Manush (.402), Fats Fothergill (.406), and Harry Heilmann (.410)—and Cobb didn't want to tamper with such statistics.

Although Pete Rose eclipsed Cobb's record for career hits, and Maury Wills, Lou Brock, and Rickey Henderson have broken most of his baserunning records, Cobb remains the career leader in steals of home (35); he also stole second, third, and home in the same inning three different times. While it cannot be documented statistically, his aggressive style produced balks, throwing errors, and lapses of concentration that counted as runs.

Cobb was shrewd as well as belligerent. He started the practice of swinging several bats in the on-deck circle so that one would feel light when it came time to hit. Similarly, he hunted in lead-weighted boots in the winter, practiced in them all spring, and switched to paper-thin shoes once the season started. (That same shrewdness led him to buy Coca-Cola at $1.18 a share and build a considerable fortune.)

Although Detroit won three straight pennants from 1907 to 1909, Cobb was never part of a world championship team and, as a manager, he never brought the Bengals home higher than second.

GORDON "MICKEY" COCHRANE

Catcher. Born Apr. 6, 1903 Bridgewater, Mass. Died Jun. 28, 1962 Lake Forest, Ill. AL MVP 1928, 1934.

Mickey Cochrane was a franchise player—literally. In 1924, Cochrane had hit .333 for Portland in the Pacific Coast League and carried a stiff $50,000 price tag. When Connie Mack found the whole club could be had for $200,000, he bought the franchise, sold the other players at a profit, and got Cochrane at a bargain price.

"Black Mike" hit .331, .357 and .349 from 1929 to 1931 to lead the A's to three pennants. A lifetime .320 hitter, he hit .300 or better nine times in his career. After he was sold to the Tigers in 1934 as a player-manager, he led them to a pennant in 1934 and a world championship in 1935.

Cochrane hit .400 in the 1929 Series, but Commissioner Landis threatened to suspend him for his brutal bench jockeying. Chastened, Cochrane greeted the Cubs with , "Hello, sweethearts! We're gonna serve tea this afternoon." After the A's won Game Five to secure the championship, Landis congratulated every Athletic except Cochrane. Just before he left, the Judge said to Mickey, "Hello, sweetheart. I came in after my tea. Will you pour?"

Mack sold Cochrane to the Tigers after the 1933 season. Just as he had sparked the A's, Black Mike led a fifth place team to the pennant his first year. As the season wore on, the exhausted Cochrane played but spent the night in a nearby hospital. The Gashouse Gang won the 1934 classic in seven games. Next year it was Cochrane's turn. He scored the run that clinched the World Series and later said, "It was my greatest day in baseball."

There would not be too many others. In a game against the Yankees in May 1937, Cochrane homered off Bump Hadley. On his next trip to the plate he took a fastball to his right temple and collapsed in a heap. He was unconscious for ten days but finally pulled through; he never played again. Elected to the Hall of Fame in 1947, he went on to serve as general manager of the A's under Mack and became a Tiger VP in 1961.

EDDIE "COCKY" COLLINS

Second Baseman. Born May 2, 1887 Millerton, N.Y. Died Mar. 25, 1951 Boston, Mass. Holds major league record for most years leading league in fielding (9). AL MVP 1914.

Eddie Collins may have been "Cocky," but as a member of four world championship teams he'd earned the right to be confident about his abilities. He hit an even .333 lifetime and batted .300 or better every year from 1909 to 1916 and the period 1919–1928.

Had Ty Cobb not been so dominant while Collins was playing, he might have enjoyed even greater recognition. As it was, Cocky hit .369, .365, and .360 without ever winning a batting title. He did lead the league in stolen bases four times, winding up with 744 career steals, behind only Cobb and Billy Hamilton during his lifetime.

Defensively he played more games (2,650) and had more putouts (6,526), assists (7,630) and total chances (14,591) than any other second baseman. Collins won nine fielding titles and, with the exception of 1918 when he missed 57 games because of injuries, he led the league in one or another fielding category every year from 1909 to 1922.

In 1906, he made his debut under the name Sullivan until it was revealed that Sullivan was, in reality, Columbia University's junior quarterback and star infielder Eddie Collins. He was allowed to continue at Columbia as nonplaying captain and joined the A's after graduation.

Collins quickly became the keystone of the A's infield. When shortstop Jack Barry, third baseman Frank "Home Run" Baker and first baseman John "Stuffy" McInnis joined the A's, the quartet became known as the "$100,000 infield" because Mack "wouldn't take that sum for all of them." The A's proceeded to roll to pennants in 1910, 1911, 1913, and 1914.

Sold to the White Sox in 1915 after winning the Chalmers Award as MVP in 1914, he hit .409 in the 1917 Series and scored the deciding run by slipping out of a rundown between third and home to beat the Giants' third baseman to the unprotected plate. Dispirited by some of his teammates' play in the Black Sox World Series of 1919, Collins batted only .226 but still stole a base to give him 14 career World Series thefts.

Inevitably, he became a manager, piloting the White Sox in 1925 and 1926 before returning to the Athletics as a pinch hitter—and leading the league in that department with a .353 average. He served as a highly placed Red Sox executive from 1932 until his death in 1951. Collins was elected to the Hall of Fame in 1939.

JOE CRONIN

Shortstop. Born Oct. 12, 1906 San Francisco, Cal. Died Sept. 7, 1984. AL MVP 1930.

Joe Cronin had 11 .300-plus seasons, hit .301 lifetime, won the Washington Senators' last pennant as a player-manager and, as a nonplaying manager, led the Red Sox to their only pennant in the 1940s.

Cronin grew up in San Francisco and signed with the Pirates but cooled his heels in the minors because the Bucs already had the league's leading shortstop in Glenn Wright. After Cronin signed with the Kansas City Blues, Joe Engel bought his contract for the Senators.

He finished 1928 in the big leagues, bettered .300 and 100 RBI from 1930 to 1933, and also led the league in triples in 1932 (18) and in doubles in 1933 (45). Moreover, Cronin was the league's best shortstop in that time span, three times leading in putouts, assists, and double plays. Senators' owner Clark Griffith made him the manager at age twenty-six to replace Walter Johnson. Hailed as the Boy Manager, Cronin won the pennant in his first season, though the Senators lost the Series in five games to the Giants.

The Nats nosedived to seventh in 1934, and the high point of Cronin's season was marrying Griffith's adopted daughter, Mildred Robinson. While the two honeymooned, Red Sox boss Tom Yawkey angled to buy Cronin. When he offered a record $225,000 and shortstop

Lyn Lary, the Boy Manager gave the go-ahead; in one move, Griffith had gotten rid of his shortstop, his manager and his son-in-law.

In 1938 Cronin hit a career high .325 and also led the league in doubles; however, the Sox finished second in four out of the five years between 1938 and 1942. Cronin stepped aside as shortstop in favor of Johnny Pesky, and prospered as a part-time player and pinch hitter, leading the league in 1943 with 18 hits in 42 at-bats, a .426 average. On one occasion he pinch hit home runs in both halves of a doubleheader. Ironically, the year he removed himself from the roster, 1946, the Red Sox won their first pennant since 1918, only to lose a seven-game Series to the Cardinals.

Cronin moved to the front office in 1948 and served as Boston's general manager until 1959 when he became American League president. He was named to the Hall of Fame in 1956.

BILL DICKEY

Catcher. Born Jun. 6, 1907 Bastrop, Ga. Died Nov. 12, 1993 Little Rock, Ark. Hit .362 in 1936, highest average for a catcher in this century.

Bill Dickey was the only Yankee quiet enough to play in the shadow of his roommate, the painfully shy Lou Gehrig, who had himself played in Babe Ruth's shadow.

Yet, with the passage of the years, it becomes clear that while Ruth started the Yankee mystique with his power and personality, the pinstriped legacy was passed along by quiet men—Gehrig, Dickey, Joe DiMaggio. An admiring Dan Daniel once wrote of him, "Dickey isn't just a catcher. He's a ball club. He isn't just a player. He's an influence."

With the Yanks and Reds scoreless in the ninth inning of the 1939 World Series opener, Charlie Keller tripled and Reds pitcher Paul Derringer walked Joe DiMaggio intentionally. Tommy Henrich says, "When I saw that—and this is the absolute gospel truth—I turned around and picked up my glove, because I knew the game was going to be over right now. And it was." (Dickey singled.)

One of the few nonpitchers in the Hall of Fame who never led the league in a single offensive category, he hit .300 or better eleven times—in 1936 a lofty .362, the highest mark for a backstop in this century—and compiled a lifetime average of .313. In the course of 6,300 at bats, he struck out only 289 times. As a bonus, Dickey caught 100 games in thirteen straight seasons, a record later tied by Johnny Bench.

At his best in October, Dickey hit .438 in the 1932 Classic, went 4-for-4 to open the 1938 edition, knocked in at least one run in every game in 1939, and finished off the Cardinals in Game Five of the 1943 Series with a two-run homer in the ninth.

Signed by Yankee scout Lena Blackburne on the back of an Elks Club card, Dickey tried to impress manager Miller Huggins with his home run swing. Huggins told him, "Stop unbuttoning your shirt on every pitch." With Ruth, Gehrig, and Lazzeri, the Yankees didn't need power from Dickey. What they wanted was steadiness. Dickey provided it, leading AL catchers three times each in assists and fielding and five times in putouts.

Given the job of turning Yogi Berra into a catcher, he looked up one day to find Joe Garagiola and Roy Campanella listening. In Yogi's phrase, Dickey "learned them all his experiences," too.

JOE DiMAGGIO

Center Field. Born Nov. 25, 1914 Martinez, Cal. Holds major league record for hitting in 56 consecutive games.

Babe Ruth played on seven pennant winners and four championship teams in his fifteen years as a Yankee; Joe DiMaggio played on ten pennant winners and nine championship teams in thirteen years.

At nineteen, he hit in 61 straight games for the San Francisco Seals, a Pacific Coast League record that still stands. Bought by the Yankees in 1936, he hit .323 as a rookie, led the league in home runs and runs scored the following year, and in 1939 led the league in batting and was named MVP for the first time.

He won the batting crown again in 1940 and the RBI title in 1941, the year he hit in 56 straight games, winning the MVP award despite Ted Williams' mark of .406. A disc jockey wrote a hit song called "Joltin' Joe DiMaggio." A Cincinnati high school class was asked to name the greatest American of all time; George Washington finished second to DiMaggio.

After his return from military service, DiMaggio had a sub-par 1946, hitting only .290. The next spring, he was almost traded for Williams. DiMaggio responded by winning his third MVP award in 1947 and blasting two home runs in the World Series.

On February 7, 1949, DiMaggio became the first $100,000 ballplayer and, despite serious injuries, helped the Yanks win the pennant. In 1951 he retired with a .325 career batting average, having played on All-Star teams in every year of major league service. He was named to the Hall of Fame in 1955.

Despite serving on the boards of the A's and Orioles, a turbulent marriage to Marilyn Monroe, commercials for banks and coffeemakers, and an involvement in signing memorabilia for profit, DiMaggio retains his aura of heroism. In 1989 former All-Star outfielder Andy Pafko said, "Even today I look up to him. And he's never disappointed me."

JOHNNY EVERS

Second Baseman. Born July 21, 1881 Troy, N.Y. Died Mar. 28, 1947 Albany, N.Y. NL MVP 1914.

When Johnny Evers joined the Cubs in 1902 he played both ends of a Labor Day doubleheader; yet his mates thought so little of him that they refused to let him on the team bus; he had to ride on top instead.

As things turned out, Evers was a Hall of Fame second baseman and a winner in every sinew of his 125-pound body. An early incarnation of Eddie Stanky or Billy Martin, Evers single-mindedly drove himself and his mates to victory and his opponents to distraction. He was on five pennant winners, and three of the four times he played his team won the Series. (A broken leg kept him out of the 1910 Series, which the Cubs lost.)

Born in Troy, he was "the Trojan," but that nickname soon gave way to "the Crab." Like many other bantam-sized battlers, Evers had a chip on his shoulder and never ran from a fight. He and shortstop Joe Tinker had a falling out on September 14, 1905, when Evers took a cab to the park without waiting for Tinker; although they didn't speak for thirty-three years, they won three championships together.

The third championship came in 1908 when Evers batted 1.000 in the rules department. On September 4, with one out in the bottom of the tenth of a scoreless tie, the Pirates loaded the bases; Owen "Chief" Wilson singled, Fred Clarke scored the winning run, and Warren Gill, the runner on first, started for the clubhouse. Evers called for the ball, touched second, and told umpire Hank O'Day the side had been retired because Gill had been "forced." O'Day disallowed that protest but, when the same situation arose on September 23, Evers's alertness caused the controversial "Merkle boner" game to end in a tie and, after a one-game playoff to break a final-day tie, give Chicago its third straight pennant.

In February 1914, Evers was sold to the Braves. He and Rabbit Maranville led the Miracle Braves from last place to the pennant, and Evers was named MVP and shone in the World Series, hitting .438 to lead the Braves to a sweep. He ended his career in Philadelphia, although he played one game each for the Braves and White Sox while coaching with them. He, Tinker, and Frank Chance were reunited in the Hall of Fame in 1946.

WILLIAM "BUCK" EWING

Catcher. Born Oct. 17, 1859 Hoaglands, Oh. Died Oct. 20, 1906, Cincinnati, Oh.
In the 1919 *Reach Guide*, sportswriter Francis Richter picked the three greatest players of all time—Ty Cobb, Honus Wagner, and Buck Ewing—and said that, in his prime (1884–1890), Ewing was "the greatest player of the game." In the 1930 *Spalding Guide*, editor John Foster said Ewing "was the greatest all-around player ever connected with the game."

For one thing, Ewing did play all around literally, all nine positions. In addition to catching 636 games and leading all catchers in assists three times and double plays twice, he played 253 at first, 212 at the other infield slots, and 112 in the outfield. Finally, with the Giants involved in the pennant race in 1889 and short of pitchers, Ewing even pitched and won two games.

A lifetime .303 hitter, Ewing was fast enough to lead the league in triples in 1884 (20), and strong enough to outhomer it in 1883 (10). One of the few catchers to bat leadoff and be considered a real threat to run, Ewing stole 40 or more bases four times in his career. In one famous instance, he stole second, stole third, announced, "Now I'm stealing home," and made it. The moment was later immortalized in a famous lithograph.

But Ewing's greatest fame came as a defensive catcher and strategist. Mickey Welch, a Hall of Fame pitcher, said Ewing was "the thinking man's player" and credited him with inventing the pregame clubhouse meeting. It is said that Ewing also originated the practice of throwing from a crouch, saving precious fractions of a second to catch larcenous runners.

In 1888 John Montgomery Ward resigned as team captain, a position closer to today's manager, and Ewing took over and led the Giants to their first pennant. For the 1889 season, Ewing was paid $5,000, a princely sum, and hit .327 as the Giants repeated. When the Players League was founded, Ewing jumped to be player-manager of the New York team, rejoined the Giants when the league folded,

and later played at Cleveland and Cincinnati, where he succeeded Charles Comiskey as the Reds' manager.

Ewing died a wealthy man from real estate investments. In 1936 he tied Cap Anson for the most "old-timer" votes in the intial selection of men for the Hall of Fame, and three years later, when the new museum opened, he and his old rival were immortalized with plaques.

BOB FELLER

Pitcher. Born Nov. 3, 1918 Van Meter, Ia. Threw three no-hitters and twelve one-hitters.
Bob Feller struck out 17 Athletics in a major league game in 1936, tying Dizzy Dean's record; then he went back to Van Meter, Iowa, to finish high school.

Feller generated statewide publicity at sixteen, and the Indians signed him to a contract before he completed high school, a violation of baseball rules.

Without any minor league experience, he faced the Cardinals in an exhibition game on July 6, 1936, and fanned eight members of the Gashouse Gang in three innings. "Rapid Robert" won his first big league start, 4–1, striking out 15 St. Louis Browns. After the season concluded, Cleveland's rights to Feller were questioned—despite Feller's ardent desire to remain with the club. Commissioner Landis finally ruled Feller could remain with the Indians and fined Cleveland $7,500.

On the last day of the 1938 season, 30,000 people came to see Hank Greenberg try to break Babe Ruth's record of 60 home runs in a season. Instead, they saw Feller strike out 18 Tigers to set the major league record (since broken) and win the AL strikeout title, beating out Bobo Newsom. (He also led in bases on balls.)

By the time he was twenty-three Feller had won 107 games. He enlisted in the Navy the day after Pearl Harbor and was sworn in by former heavyweight champ Gene Tunney. Pitching anti-aircraft shells from the deck of the battleship *Alabama,* Feller missed nearly four full seasons but earned six battle citations as a gun crew chief.

Returning to baseball at the end of 1945, he had his best season ever in 1946, winning 26 games, striking out a record 348 batters in 371 innings, and recording 10 shutouts with an ERA of 2.18. In 1948, he two-hit the Braves in his only World Series game but lost. In 1951, he still had enough stuff to throw his third no-hitter and lead the league with a record of 22–8.

By the time he retired, Feller had pitched twelve one-hitters, won 20 or more games six times and rolled up 2,581 career strikeouts. Satchel Paige summed up his career this way: "If anybody threw that ball any harder than Rapid Robert, then the human eye couldn't follow it." He was elected to the Hall of Fame in 1962.

ROLLIE FINGERS

Pitcher. Born Aug. 25, 1946 Steubenville, Oh. AL Cy Young Award and MVP, 1981. Established major league record for saves, 341 (since surpassed).
If he hadn't been such a worrywart, Rollie Fingers might have been an average starter; instead, he fretted himself right into the bullpen and became a Hall of Fame fireman.

"I would plan my pitches days in advance of my start and get so wound up I couldn't sleep the night before my turn," he recalled. After finishing only four of thirty-five starts, he took immediately to the relief role in 1971 and finished with 17 saves. In 1972, he led the league with 11 relief wins and 21 saves to help Oakland win the division.

Fingers pitched in six of the seven games in the 1972 World Series, earning saves in Games Two and Seven and a win in Game Four. One year later, he pitched 3⅓ hitless innings in the Series opener against the Mets, saved Game Three for Paul Lindblad and Game Six for Catfish Hunter, and yielded only one unearned run in 3⅓ innings of relief in the finale.

In 1974, he led the A's to a third straight world championship. He got the win in Game One; for a change, Catfish Hunter got the save. The roles were reversed in Game Three when Fingers saved Hunter. Rollie got a second save the next day, and was named Series MVP.

When Fingers and the A's reached a contract impasse, owner Charlie Finley sold him to Boston, but Commissioner Bowie Kuhn voided the sale. With San Diego in 1977, Fingers appeared in 78 games and saved 35 (league-leading figures), and earned National League Fireman of the Year honors.

Four days after being traded to St. Louis in 1980, he moved again, to Milwaukee. During the strike-shortened 1981 season, he notched a league-leading 28 saves and posted a brilliant 1.04 ERA. Fingers won his fourth Fireman of the Year award, won the Cy Young Award, and was also named MVP.

After posting 29 saves in 1982, Fingers missed the World Series and the entire 1983 season because of tendinitis. He came back to notch 23 saves by July, 1984, when a herniated disk ended his season and career. He ranks first in wins plus saves (430) and was inducted into the Hall of Fame in 1992.

CARLTON FISK

Catcher. Born Dec. 26, 1947 Bellows Falls, Vt. Holds major league record for lifetime home runs by a catcher (351). Holds major league record for games caught (2,226).

During a Yankees–White Sox game in May 1990, Carlton Fisk blasted Deion Sanders for not running out a pop fly, starting a brawl but enhancing Fisk's role as Defender of the Game. Moreover, it came at a time when Fisk, a ten-time All-Star, was trying to push an unknown pitching staff to a division title.

That year Fisk, already the oldest regular catcher in baseball history, hit 18 homers to pass Johnny Bench as baseball's leading home run-hitting catcher, extended his AL record of games caught, and added to his total as modern baseball's best base-stealing catcher. Fisk, Bench, and Yogi Berra are the only three receivers to hit 300 homers and both score and drive in 1,000 runs.

Carlton Ernest Fisk grew up in Charlestown, New Hampshire on the heavy side (5'4", 155) and was dubbed "Pudge" by a female relative. A three-sport MVP in high school, he earned a basketball scholarship to the University of New Hampshire but signed instead with the Red Sox in 1967.

Brought up late in 1971 for a look-see, he was the All-Star catcher by the summer of '72. That fall he became the first AL Rookie of the Year to be chosen unanimously. In 1975 injuries limited him to only 79 games during the regular season, but he created one of baseball's enduring

moments in the World Series with a twelfth-inning, body English home run off the Reds' Pat Darcy to end the now fabled Game Six.

After the 1980 season, free agent Fisk signed with the White Sox. He had worn number 27 in Boston but sported number 72 in Chicago, because "it represents a turn-around in my career." Following a workmanlike 1982 season, Fisk slumped in early 1983 and was hitting only .136. Replaced in both halves of a June 12 doubleheader in Oakland, Fisk jawed with manager Tony LaRussa. LaRussa said, "He came out fighting, the way a winner reacts to a challenge." In the next 71 games, Fisk hit 16 homers, drove in 49 runs, raised his average more than 100 points, and helped Chicago clinch the division.

An Opening Day abdominal muscle pull hampered him in 1984. The next year, however, at age thirty-seven, Fisk had his greatest campaign, knocking in 107 runs and hitting 37 homers.

ED "WHITEY" FORD

Pitcher. Born Oct. 21, 1928 New York, N.Y. Holds record for World Series wins (10); AL Cy Young Award, 1961.

Whitey Ford won 236 games and lost only 106 to register a lifetime .690 won-lost percentage, the highest recorded by any pitcher since 1900. He also broke Babe Ruth's forty-five-year-old record of 29⅔ scoreless innings in World Series competition, ending up with 32. Ford also holds the records for most Series wins (10), strikeouts (94), and innings pitched (146).

Ford's Series stats are so impressive that his regular season numbers tend to get buried. He won 20 games only twice in sixteen seasons; however, from 1953 to 1960, he averaged nearly 16 wins against 7 losses. Casey Stengel, who manipulated the rotation so Ford faced the toughies (though he kept him out of Boston's Fenway Park), said, "If you had one game to win and your life depended on it, you'd want him to pitch it."

Even though he led the league in wins, innings pitched, and won-lost percentage and won the Cy Young Award in 1961, Ford's 25–4 record was almost overshadowed by Roger Maris's quest for home run number 61. He got more recognition by going 24–7 in 1963 and repeating in all three categories.

Ford was inducted into the Hall of Fame on August 12, 1974, along with Mickey Mantle, his partner in the long-running "Mick and Slick" Show. When writers recalled the spitter Ford used to strike out Willie Mays in the 1964 All-Star Game, Ford said, "Look, they didn't call me Slick for nothing."

JIMMIE FOXX

First Baseman. Born Oct. 22, 1907 Sudlersville, Md. Died July 21, 1967 Miami, Fla. Holds major league record for most consecutive years with 30 or more home runs (12). AL MVP 1932, 1933, 1938.

Jimmie Foxx hit some of baseball's most awesome home runs. He homered over the two-tiered left field stands in Shibe Park, drove a ball out of Comiskey Park some 600 feet from home plate, broke a seat in the upper deck of left field at Yankee Stadium, and hit what he considered his longest shot over the left-center field fence in Sportsman's Park to win Game Five of the 1930 Series. Ted Williams, not known for admiring other hitters, said of

Foxx, "I never saw anyone hit a baseball harder."

Nicknamed "The Beast" and "Double X," Foxx won three MVP awards (1932, 1933, 1938), knocked in 100 or more runs in thirteen straight seasons, won five slugging titles, hit .300 or better thirteen times, and ended his career with a lifetime batting average of .325, 534 homers, and 1,922 RBI. He also set a record by hitting 30 or more home runs in 12 consecutive seasons.

Appropriately enough this great home run hitter was discovered at age sixteen by none other than Home Run Baker. He entered Organized Baseball as a catcher. After several .300-plus seasons as a utility player, Foxx was installed at first base in 1929 and hit .354 with 33 homers. In 1932 he mounted the first serious challenge to Babe Ruth's season record of 60 home runs with 58. (According to writer Fred Lieb, Foxx hit five doubles against the right field screen in Sportsman's Park, which hadn't been there in 1927 when Ruth hit 60 homers.) Foxx failed to win the Triple Crown when Dale Alexander was named batting champ, even though he didn't have 400 at bats. Nevertheless, the Beast led the league in homers (58), runs scored (151), RBI (169), total bases (438) and slugging (.749) and finished second in batting average (.364) and hits (213) to win his first MVP award.

In 1933 he repeated as MVP, topped the league with a slugging percentage of .703, and captured the Triple Crown, hitting 48 homers, driving in 163 runs, and hitting .356. After tying Hank Greenberg for the home run crown in 1935, he was sold to the Red Sox. Foxx responded with another MVP year in 1938, leading the league with 175 RBI and hitting 50 homers, second to Greenberg's 58.

Foxx entered the pantheon at Cooperstown in 1951.

FRANKIE FRISCH

Second Baseman. Born Sept. 9, 1898 New York, N.Y. Died Mar. 12, 1973 Wilmington, Del. Holds major league records for most assists (641) and chances accepted (1,037) in a season, 1927; NL MVP 1931.

Frank Frisch, "The Fordham Flash," had something to prove in 1927.

Giants manager John McGraw, the man who had taken Frisch from Fordham to stardom, had traded him to the Cardinals after the 1926 season for Rogers Hornsby. McGraw had taught Frisch how to switch hit and play the hitters, and had been a father figure for Frisch, giving the trade a personal twist.

Frisch spent the winter toughening up and came out charging. He hit .337, led the league in steals, handled a record 1,037 chances (including a record 641 assists), made the most double plays, and just missed being named MVP, finishing second to Paul Waner. Cardinal catcher Bob O'Farrell, the MVP a year before, said, "The greatest player I ever saw in any one season was Frankie Frisch in 1927."

He'd served as captain of the baseball, football and basketball teams at Fordham and been a second-team All-America halfback when he joined the Giants in 1919. Frisch led the league in stolen bases in 1921 and hits in 1923, and the Giants won pennants every year from 1921–1924. He went 4-for-4 in the 1921 Series opener and averaged .363 in his first four Series.

The Flash also brought the Cardinals to three World Series as a player and one as a player-manager. The Yanks swept St. Louis in 1928 and the A's took them in six games in 1930, so 1931 was doubly sweet. Frisch sparked the Cardinals to a seventh-game win over the A's and was also named MVP. In the first All-Star Game, in 1933, Frisch singled and hit the first NL homer.

Shortly thereafter, he took over as player-manager of the Gashouse Gang, riding herd over Pepper Martin, Dizzy Dean, and company. In 1934 he hit .305 (one of thirteen times he hit .300 or better) and led the Redbirds to a pennant. In Game Seven of the Series, the Tigers intentionally walked Jack Rothrock to load the bases; Frisch unloaded them with a double and the Cardinals went on to a rout, 11–0.

After retiring as a player to devote himself to managing full time, Frisch never won another pennant with the Cardinals, Pirates, or Cubs; however, in 1947 he began a third successful career as a Giants broadcaster. In that same year he was reunited with McGraw in the Hall of Fame.

LOU GEHRIG

First Base. Born Jun. 19, 1903 New York, N.Y. Died June 2, 1941 Riverdale, N.Y. Holds major league record for grand slams (23); AL MVP 1927, 1936.

Playing in Babe Ruth's shadow may have robbed Lou Gehrig of the spotlight, but, as he himself said, "It's a pretty big shadow. It gives me lots of room to spread myself." The year Ruth retired (1935), Gehrig began a three-year streak of leading the league in walks, a good measure of the respect pitchers still had for him when he was in his mid-thirties.

Gehrig had 200 or more hits in eight seasons, never hit below .300 from 1926 to 1937, and had a career average of .340. He tied Ruth for the RBI lead in 1928 and led the league outright four times; his 184 ribbies in 1931 is still the league record. The "Iron Horse" led in homers in 1934 and 1936 and tied Ruth for the lead in 1931 with 46, when Lyn Lary's baserunning mistake—passing a runner on the bases—robbed him of his 47th. He also holds the record for career grand slams (23). On June 3, 1932, he was the first modern slugger to hit four home runs in a game, an achievement that was somewhat eclipsed because it happened on the same day as John McGraw's retirement.

Although Gehrig originally went to Columbia on a football scholarship, Giant manager John McGraw persuaded him to play pro baseball under an assumed name (Lewis) in 1921, making him ineligible for college ball; however, Gehrig's coach, Andy Coakley, persuaded the faculty to give Lou another chance. The contract was dissolved, and Gehrig resumed collegiate play.

In 1934, Ruth's last year as a Yankee, Gehrig won the Triple Crown, leading the AL in homers (49), RBI (165), and batting average (.363). He batted .361 in World Series play, averaging an RBI a game for 34 games with 43 hits, 10 of them homers.

Suffering from the effects of amyotrophic lateral sclerosis, Gehrig took himself out of the lineup on May 2, 1939, after playing in a then-record 2,130 consecutive games. He entered the Hall of Fame later that year when the Baseball Writers Association waived the existing rule which required a player to be retired one year before he could be elected.

On Lou Gehrig Day at Yankee Stadium, the stoical slugger told a packed house, "I may have been given a bad break, but with all this I have a lot to live for. I consider myself the luckiest man on the face of the earth."

CHARLIE GEHRINGER

Second Baseman. Born May 11, 1903 Fowlerville, Mich. Died Jan. 21, 1993 Bloomfield Hills, Mich. American League MVP 1937.

Describing Charlie Gehringer, Mickey Cochrane said of his teammate, "He says hello on opening day and goodbye on closing day, and in between he hits .350."

Gehringer was so quiet that when he was given a "Day," the lefthander was given a set of righthanded golf clubs and learned to play the game righthanded. He celebrated the Day by homering on the first pitch thrown to him, getting three other hits, and stealing home to win the game.

"The Mechanical Man" had 200 or more hits seven times, bettered .300 fourteen times, and knocked in 100 or more runs seven times. In the field, he led the AL in fielding six times, putouts three times, and assists a record seven times. A measure of Gehringer's all-around excellence is the 1929 season, when he led the league in stolen bases, doubles, triples, hits, runs, games, putouts, and fielding while hitting .339. As for consistency, he hit .320 lifetime and .320 in twenty World Series games.

Like Bob Feller, Gehringer played his first baseball on a field carved out of a family farm. A third baseman at the University of Michigan, Gehringer was discovered by Tiger great Bobby Veach and, despite his quiet nature, became a favorite of manager Ty Cobb. Cobb resisted all efforts to change Gehringer's swing and said that, aside from Eddie Collins, Gehringer was "the best second baseman I ever saw."

After brief callups in 1924 and 1925, Gehringer became the Tigers' regular second baseman in 1926. In 1933 he started a string of six straight starts for the AL in the All-Star Game. He is the midsummer classic's lifetime batting leader with an even .500 average (10 for 20).

This splendid ballplaying machine was equally sparkling in World Series play, hitting .379, leading all Tiger hitters in a losing effort in 1934. In 1935, however, Detroit's "G-Men"—Hank Greenberg, Gehringer, and Goose Goslin—became champions, beating the Cubs as Gehringer hit .375 and handled 39 chances flawlessly.

In 1937 Gehringer reached the high-water mark of his career, hitting .371 and being named MVP. After three more .300-plus seasons, he played out the string during World War II. Elected to the Hall of Fame in 1949, he served as the Tigers' general manager from 1951 to 1953 and a vice president until 1959.

BOB GIBSON

Pitcher. Born Nov. 9, 1935 Omaha, Neb. Holds major league season record for lowest ERA in 300 or more innings (1.12), 1968. NL MVP 1968, Cy Young Award 1968, 1970.

Bob Gibson was a winner whether he was using his arm, his bat, or his glove.

In a fifteen-year career, he won 251 games, posted 56 shutouts, became the first major leaguer to strike out 200 or more in nine seasons, and posted a lifetime ERA of 2.91. He also hit 24 regular season home runs and earned a Gold Glove every year from 1965 to 1973.

Gibson suffered from rickets and asthma while growing up in Omaha and because of a heart murmur needed a doctor's permission to play ball. Nevertheless, he starred as the switch-hitting catcher-shortstop of a YMCA team, won a basketball scholarship to Creighton University, played with the Harlem Globetrotters for a year, joined the Cards for good in 1961, and had his first big year in 1963, going 18–9.

In 1964 his 19–12 record helped the Cards win the pennant, and he began an unprecedented streak of seven straight World Series wins by taking Game Five and, on two days' rest, Game Seven. On his way to another big year in 1967 (13 wins), Gibson was out when Roberto Clemente's smash fractured his left leg. Incredibly, after being sidelined for eight weeks, he came back to win three World Series games against the Red Sox, allowing just three earned runs and pitching three complete games.

In 1968 he was even better, posting a record of 22–9 with an ERA of 1.12, breaking Walter Johnson's 1913 record for the lowest ERA with 300 or more innings pitched. That year Gibson pitched 13 shutouts, and surrendered just 2 runs during one 95-inning stretch during the regular season to win both the MVP and Cy Young Awards. Awesome in the 1968 Series, he struck out 17 Tigers, a World Series record, while winning the opener.

In 1970 he was 23–7 and took his second Cy Young Award. On July 17, 1974, he became only the second pitcher (Walter Johnson was the first) to notch 3,000 strikeouts. Shortly before Gibson retired, 55,000 people at Busch Stadium gave him a ten-minute standing ovation. He was named to the Hall of Fame in 1981.

JOSH GIBSON

Catcher. Born Dec. 21, 1911 Buena Vista, Ga. Died Jan. 20, 1947 Pittsburgh, Pa.

Josh Gibson may have been the greatest catcher of all time. Walter Johnson said of him, "He hits the ball a mile. Throws like a rifle. Bill Dickey isn't as good a catcher." Roy Campanella, who saw Gibson at his peak, said, "When I broke in with the Baltimore Elite Giants in 1937 there were already a thousand legends about him; once you saw him play you knew they were all true."

According to a 1967 article in *The Sporting News,* Gibson hit a ball two feet from the top of the stadium wall circling the bleachers at Yankee Stadium, some 580 feet from home plate. His Hall of Fame plaque credits him with "almost 800 home runs," and various authorities say he hit 69, 75, 84, and 89 home runs in a season, albeit sometimes against semipro pitching. Gibson could also hit for average, compiling a .412 mark in 34 at bats against big league pitching. And, while he wasn't a great handler of pitchers or catcher of popups, few baserunners tried to steal on him because of his great arm.

He was born in Buena Vista, Georgia, and moved to Pittsburgh when he was twelve. As a youngster he won numerous swimming medals. At maturity, he stood 6' 2" and weighed 210.

Unable to break into the lineup of Pittsburgh's Homestead Grays, Gibson organized the semipro Crawford Colored Giants; He was in the stands when the Grays' regular catcher, Buck Ewing, split a finger in June 1930;

he changed into a uniform and never left the lineup again.

In 1931 Gus Greenlee founded the Pittsburgh Crawfords, signed Gibson and Satchel Paige, and wrote ads that promised, "Josh Gibson will hit a home run and Satchel Paige will strike out the side on nine pitches." They nearly always delivered. Gibson also played winter ball extensively and said his greatest thrill was being chosen MVP of the Puerto Rican League in 1941.

Pirate owner Bill Benswanger reportedly signed him to a contract in 1943, but Commissioner Landis vetoed the signing. On January 20, 1947, three months before Jackie Robinson's major league debut, Gibson died of a stroke. He was elected to the Hall of Fame in 1972.

HANK GREENBERG

First Baseman. Born Jan. 1, 1911 New York, N.Y. Died Sept. 4, 1986 Beverly Hills, Cal. AL MVP 1935, 1940.

In 1934, the big question in Detroit was, "Should Hank Greenberg play on Rosh Hashanah and Yom Kippur?"

With the Tigers involved in a hot pennant race with the Yankees, the Jewish slugger sought spiritual guidance. After due deliberation, Rabbi Leo Franklin ruled that Greenberg should play on Rosh Hashanah, the Jewish New Year, a happy occasion; he did and hit a tenth-inning homer to win the game. However, Rabbi Franklin said the slugger should pray, not play, on Yom Kippur, the Day of Atonement. Greenberg acquiesced. Poet Edgar Guest commented:

We shall miss him in the infield and shall miss him at the bat
But he's true to his religion—and I honor him for that.

The Tigers won the pennant, and Greenberg homered in the World Series, as he would in all four Series in which he played. A year later, his 36 homers and 170 RBI earned him the MVP award, but he missed the last four games of the Series with a broken wrist. Greenberg had a null year in 1936—67 at bats; however, in 1937, he drove in a mind-boggling 183 runs and, in 1938 fell just short of Babe Ruth's season home run record, with 58.

After hitting 33 homers and knocking in 112 runs in 1939, he was forced to take a $10,000 pay cut—if he stayed at first base. Instead he moved to the outfield, making way for good-hit, no-field Rudy York, and got a $10,000 raise. He was named MVP again in 1940, when the Tigers lost the Series in seven games to Cincinnati.

In May 1941 Greenberg was drafted into the Army and returned in July 1945, winning the pennant for the Tigers on the last day of the season with a grand slam in the bottom of the ninth inning. In 1947 he had a last fling with the Pirates, hitting 25 homers and knocking in 74 runs in his only NL season. When he retired that fall, he had led the league in RBI four times, won home run honors outright four times and tied for the lead once, and hit 331 career home runs, even though he had lost four and a half seasons to the war and injury. He was elected to the Hall of Fame in 1956.

ROBERT "LEFTY" GROVE

Pitcher. Born Mar. 6, 1900 Lonaconing, Md. Died May 22, 1975 Norwalk, Oh. AL MVP 1931.

In 1931 Lefty Grove was en route to his seventeenth straight victory, which would have broken the AL record then shared by Walter Johnson and Smoky Joe Wood. Al Simmons had taken the day off, and the rookie outfielder subbing for him misjudged a fly ball, leading to an unearned run; Grove lost, 1–0. He said, "After that game I went in and tore the clubhouse up. Wrecked the place. Tore those stall lockers off the wall, giving Al Simmons hell all the while."

Grove recovered his composure, won another eight straight, was named MVP, and ended the season 31–4, possibly the single greatest season enjoyed by any hurler. The dominant pitcher of his era, he was the AL's strikeout leader his first seven years, led in ERA a record nine times, and went on to compile a won-lost record of 300–141, a winning percentage of .680. Normalized for league average and adjusted for home park, his 3.06 ERA is, quite simply, the best in baseball history.

He started in Organized Ball with Martinsburg, West Virginia, of the Blue Ridge League and joined the International League Orioles when Baltimore bartered for him, paying cash for Martinsburg's new center field fence. Owner Jack Dunn knew what he had in Grove and delayed his entry to the big leagues until the southpaw was twenty-five; he sold Grove to Connie Mack's A's for $100,600—$600 more than the Red Sox had paid for Babe Ruth in 1914.

Like Sandy Koufax after him, Grove had his troubles initially, winning 10 and losing 12 in 1925, his rookie year; however, the following year his ERA improved from 4.75 to 2.51, good enough to lead the league for the first time. By 1927, he was ready for his first 20-win season and tied George Pipgras for the league lead in wins (24) while losing only 8.

From 1929 to 1931 Grove was an awesome 79–15, and the A's won pennants every year as well as the Series the first two. By the time he was sold to the Red Sox for $125,000 in 1933, he had won 20, 24, 20, 28, 31, 25, and 24 games in seven consecutive seasons. Yet success didn't mellow him; in batting practice a teammate once hit a ball back through the box; on the next pitch the batter hit the dust. Grove was elected to the Hall of Fame in 1947.

"SLIDING BILLY" HAMILTON

Center Fielder. Born Feb. 16, 1866 Newark, N.J. Died Dec. 16, 1940 Worcester, Mass. Holds major league record for runs scored in a season (196), 1894; stole 912 bases, a mark that stood for nine decades.

Although he was nicknamed for his daring, head-first slides, looking at the records, it's clear that Billy Hamilton should have been nicknamed "Scoring Billy."

Hamilton notched a record 1,690 runs in 1,591 games, making him the most effective leadoff man of all time. (For comparison, Rickey Henderson had, at the end of the 1996 season, 1,829 in 2,340 games.) What's more, Billy could hit as well as run. He missed hitting .300 only in his first and last seasons, led the league in hitting twice, and retired with a lifetime average of .344.

He was also a part of history's only all-.400 outfield, the Phillies' 1894 edition; Hamilton's puny .404 was dwarfed by the lusty .407 achieved by both his oversized garden mates, "Big Sam" Thompson and "Big Ed" Delahanty. (Incredibly, spare outfielder Tuck Turner, in over 300 at bats, hit for .416.)

Equally oversized is Hamilton's stolen base total. The record credits him with 912 steals—100-plus each in the years from 1889 to 1891. At the time, however, if a runner tagged up on a fly ball, went from first to third on a single, or moved up on a ground ball to the right side, he was credited with a stolen base. Beginning in 1892, steals were awarded to a runner only if there were "a possible chance and a palpable attempt made to retire him." Sliding Billy slid to only 57 and 43 steals the next two years but rebounded with 98 and 97 in 1894 and 1895 to lead the league. He also topped all NLers in bases on balls, runs scored (a record 192 in 1894), and on-base percentage. In fact, his on-base percentage of .455 over nearly 1600 games is probably a greater achievement than all the stolen bases; he trails only Ted Williams, Babe Ruth, and John McGraw in this department.

Hamilton moved over to the Boston Beaneaters in 1896. He missed 59 games in 1899 because of injuries and played his last major league season in 1901. Far from ready to retire, he played ten more years in the Tri-State and New England Leagues. After becoming a Red Sox scout, he bought part of the Worcester team. Sliding Billy was named to the Hall of Fame in 1961.

CHARLES "GABBY" HARTNETT
Catcher. Born Dec. 20, 1900 Woonsocket, R.I. Died Dec. 20, 1972 Park Ridge, Ill. NL MVP 1935.
Gabby Hartnett had an active role in three of baseball's greatest moments. He caught Charlie Root when Babe Ruth "called his shot" in the 1932 World Series; flashed the signs when Carl Hubbell fanned Ruth and four other Hall of Fame sluggers in order in the 1934 All-Star Game; and, hit the "Homer in the Gloamin'" that put the Cubs ahead to stay in the 1938 pennant race.

The NL Bill Dickey, Hartnett was resilient, reliable, clever at picking pitches, and blessed with a shotgun for an arm. He caught 100 or more games twelve times, had a career average of .297, and set the standard for NL catchers defensively, leading four times in putouts, six times in assists, and six times in fielding percentage.

Hartnett was born in Woonsocket, Rhode Island to an unusual family; his mother had seven boys in a row and then seven girls in a row. Signed by the Cubs in high school, he was silent on his first train trip west to Catalina in 1922, and a reporter promptly dubbed him Gabby. His father had played semipro ball with Grover Cleveland Alexander, the Cubs' reigning star. Alexander insisted that Hartnett catch him on Opening Day, and Hartnett called the pitches for most of his starts thereafter.

By 1924 Gabby was doing the bulk of the catching, and Bob O'Farrell was traded to the Cardinals. Joe McCarthy became the Cubs' manager in 1926 and brought them a pennant winner in 1929 without Hartnett, who due to a dead arm caught in only one game. Hartnett's mother thought the pain in his arm was related to his wife's pregnancy; when the baby was born in December, the pain went away.

Hartnett came out charging in 1930. He led all the fielding categories, hit .339, and knocked in a career-high 122 runs; in 1935, he hit .344 and was named MVP. With the Cubs 5½ games behind Pittsburgh in July 1938, he became player-manager. On September 28, with darkness falling at Wrigley Field, Hartnett's homer to left in the

bottom of the ninth off Pittsburgh's Mace Brown gave them a half-game lead they never relinquished. The famous blow was the highlight of a stretch drive that saw the Cubs leapfrog over three teams to win the National League pennant.

The Cubs faltered the next two years, and Hartnett was released, eventually catching on as a player-coach with Bill Terry's Giants. He later managed in the minors and was elected to the Hall of Fame in 1955.

RICKEY HENDERSON
Left Field. Born Dec. 25, 1958 Chicago, Ill. Holds major league records for stolen bases season (130), 1982, and lifetime (1,186). AL MVP, 1990.
Rickey Henderson is baseball's version of the Energizer bunny. He just keeps stealing and stealing and stealing and had logged 1,186 stolen bases by the end of 1996, his first National League season.

The most powerful leadoff man in history, Henderson broke Bobby Bonds's career record for leadoff homers in 1989 and had 70 at the end of the 1996 season. He was named the American League MVP in 1990, broke Lou Brock's record for career steals on May 1, 1991, and, a year later to the day, became the first man to steal 1,000 bases.

None of this surprised long-time Henderson watchers, who became convinced of his gifts when he played for Modesto of the California League. In 1977 Henderson stole a record 95 bases, led league outfielders in total chances (313), hit .345 to be named MVP, and became only the fourth man in professional baseball to steal seven bases in a single game.

Brought up to Oakland in 1979, the "Man of Steal" absconded with 33 bases in 89 games and, a year later, became the first ALer to steal 100 bases in a season, was second in the AL in walks, third in on-base percentage, and fourth in runs scored. A year later, during the strike-shortened 1981 season, he led the league in hits (135), runs (89), and steals (56); he also led the league's outfielders in putouts and total chances and won a Gold Glove, the first of many.

In 1982 Henderson broke Lou Brock's record of 118 steals in a season, set in 1974, winding up with 130. After the 1984 season he became a Yankee in exchange for Tim Birtsas, Eric Plunk, Stan Javier, Jay Howell, and Jose Rijo. Although he missed the first 10 games of the 1985 season with a sprained left ankle, he hit 24 homers, knocked in 72 runs, batted .314, and led the league in runs scored (146) for the second time, the highest total since Ted Williams scored 150 in 1949.

Henderson led the league in steals every year from 1980 to 1990 except in 1987, when he missed 57 games due to injuries. Traded back to Oakland in June 1989, Henderson helped the A's win the division and starred in the playoffs, tying Jim Rice's record of 8 runs scored in a single series, stealing a record 8 bases, and being named MVP. He was chosen World Series MVP as well and was named regular season MVP in 1990 when he hit .325 and hit 28 homers. In 1993 he was traded to the Blue Jays and helped them to their second straight championship. He has the highest Total Player Rating among active players and, with some years of optimum performance ahead, is already the twelfth best player of all time.

ROGERS HORNSBY

Second Baseman. Born Apr. 27, 1896 Winters, Tex. Died Jan. 5, 1963 Chicago, Ill. Holds modern major league record for highest batting average in a season (.424), 1924, and NL record for batting average, lifetime (.358).
Rogers Hornsby was suspicious, short-tempered, and the greatest righthanded hitter that ever lived.

The Rajah hit .300 or better in fourteen full seasons, won the NL batting title six straight years (1920–1925), is the only righthanded hitter to bat .400 or better three times and ended his career with a lifetime average of .358, second only to Ty Cobb. Like Cobb, he was thorny and idiosyncratic, reserving the right to bet on horses and refusing to read books or see movies for fear it would hurt his eyesight.

His career didn't begin auspiciously; Hornsby made 58 errors at shortstop in the Texas League and was unimpressive in 18 games with the Cardinals in 1915. Manager Miller Huggins told him to put on weight and, 25 pounds heavier, the Rajah hit .313 to lead the Cardinals in 1916.

By the mid-1920s he was the dominant player in the NL, winning the Triple Crown in both 1922 and 1925, when he became the Cardinals player-manager and was also named MVP for the first time. For the five-year period 1921–1925 his batting average exceeded .400! In 1926 he slumped to .317 but he gave the Cardinals their first pennant and helped upset the Yanks in a seven-game Series.

Two months after his great triumph, on December 20, 1926, he was traded to the Giants for Frankie Frisch and Jimmy Ring. Before the trade could go through, Hornsby had to sell 1,000 shares of St. Louis stock lest a Giants player own stock in the Cardinals; he nearly tripled his money, finally settling for $120,000.

He was traded again to the Braves and then the Cubs. With Chicago in 1929, he hit .380 with 39 homers and 149 RBI, to win his second MVP award in his last full year as a player. Hornsby managed the Cubs from the end of 1930 until August 2, 1932, when he was replaced by Charlie Grimm; the Cubs went on to win the pennant and demonstrated their affection for Hornsby by cutting him out of the World Series pool.

The Rajah finished up with the Browns and managed in the minor leagues for fifteen years before coming back to lead the Browns in 1952 and the Reds in 1953. He ended his career as a Mets scout and coach. Hornsby was elected to the Hall of Fame in 1942.

CARL HUBBELL

Pitcher. Born Jun. 22, 1903 Carthage, Mo. Died Nov. 21, 1988 Scottsdale, Ariz. NL MVP 1933, 1936.
Ty Cobb was convinced that Carl Hubbell's screwball, which Cobb called the "butterfly pitch," would ruin his arm and forbade Hubbell to throw it—even though the Tigers had paid Oklahoma City $20,000 for his services. The man who would later be known as the Giants' "Meal Ticket" languished without his favorite pitch and was eventually given his outright release.

Hubbell picked up the scroogie again with Beaumont of the Texas League and was signed by Dick Kinsella, a part-time Giant scout and bored Illinois delegate to the 1928 Democratic Convention in Houston. Hubbell won 10 of his 16 decisions that first season, no-hit the Pirates,

11–0, in his sophomore year, and really hit his stride in 1933. That year King Carl six-hit the Cardinals, 1–0, over eighteen innings, led the league in innings pitched (309), wins (23), shutouts (10), and ERA (1.66), and was MVP.

In the World Series he beat Joe Cronin's Senators twice, 4–2 and 2–1, and pitched twenty innings without allowing an earned run as the Giants won in five games. On July 10, 1934, Hubbell started the second All-Star Game by giving up a single to Charlie Gehringer and walking Heinie Manush. He then struck out Babe Ruth, Lou Gehrig, and Jimmie Foxx consecutively to end the first inning and got Al Simmons and Joe Cronin to start the second, one of baseball's greatest feats.

Equally commanding during the regular season that year, Hubbell led the league with a 2.30 ERA and a 21–12 record, the second of five straight 20-game seasons. In 1936, he went 26–6 and was named MVP again. That July 17, he started a string of 24 straight victories over two seasons, eventually snapped by the Dodgers on May 27, 1937; he also won games in both the 1936 and 1937 World Series to post a 1.97 ERA in October.

In 1938, Hubbell experienced arm trouble and won only 13 games; in four more years he would never win more than 11, and he finally ended his pitching career at age 40 with 253 wins and 36 shutouts. Named to the Hall of Fame in 1947, he ran the Giants' farm system, directing player development from 1943 to 1977 and scouting from 1978 to 1985, eventually seeing fellow Hall of Famers like Willie Mays, Willie McCovey, and Juan Marichal take his place as the Giants' meal tickets.

"SHOELESS JOE" JACKSON

Outfielder. Born July 16, 1888 Brandon Mills, S.C. Died Dec. 5, 1951 Greenville, S.C. In ten years as a regular, 1911–1920, never hit below .300.
Babe Ruth once said, "I decided to pick out the greatest hitter to watch and study and Jackson was good enough for me."

Joseph Jefferson Jackson never learned to read or write, but he could hit, field, and run. He hit .356 lifetime (third highest behind Cobb and Rogers Hornsby), and his glove was named "the place triples go to die." Yet he remains under a cloud for his part in the Black Sox series of 1919.

Signed by the A's but assailed by homesickness, Shoeless Joe blossomed in Cleveland, making the biggest rookie splash in history by hitting .408 in 1911 and finishing second only to Ty Cobb in batting, slugging, hits, doubles, and total bases. Although his stats were nearly as good in 1912 (.395) and 1913 (.373), Cleveland was a last place club; sold to Chicago in the middle of 1915, Jackson helped the Sox win the pennant in 1917 and the World Series.

When Sox first baseman Chick Gandil approached Jackson about throwing the 1919 Series, Jackson called owner Charles Comiskey and asked to be benched, but Comiskey refused to hear him out. While Jackson was the leading hitter (.375), set a Series record for hits (12), and knocked in 6 runs, pitcher Lefty Williams gave Jackson $5,000 for his part in the fix, and, to his eternal discredit, Jackson took it.

In 1920 Jackson hit .382 but, that September, a Chicago grand jury investigated the fix; Jackson confessed, denied doing anything to throw the Series, but admitted taking the money. Although acquitted after their confessions "disappeared," Jackson and the other Black Sox were barred from baseball for life by Commissioner Landis. Shoeless Joe sued Comiskey for back pay and won a judgment for $16,711.04, but it was overturned; the sitting judge ordered him to jail for perjury and, after a brief stay, he accepted a small settlement from Comiskey,

Jackson ran several successful businesses in his home town of Brandon Mills, South Carolina. When the Cleveland Hall of Fame was started, in 1951, Jackson became the fourth highest vote-getter even though his name wasn't on the ballot. TV host Ed Sullivan heard the story and asked Jackson to be on the show; the day before he was scheduled to appear, Jackson died of a heart attack.

REGGIE JACKSON
Right Field. Born May 18, 1946 Wyncote, Pa. AL MVP 1973.
The only player to be named MVP in two World Series, Reggie Jackson earned the nickname "Mr. October" by setting a Series record for slugging percentage (.755).

He's also baseball's all-time strikeout king, fanning 2,597 times, once every four at-bats. In addition to being all-or-nothing on offense, Jackson was next-to-nothing on defense. He is tied with Burt Shotton for leading the AL in errors the most times (five). Yet, from 1971 to 1982, Jackson helped three different clubs win ten division titles, six pennants, and five championships.

In 1968 he hit 29 homers, led the league in assists (14) and errors (12), and struck out 171 times in 553 at bats. In July 1969 he was two weeks ahead of Roger Maris's pace with 40, then hit only 7 more for the rest of the season and finished second to Harmon Killebrew. In 1973 he won the first of four home run crowns.

Jackson made his 1973 World Series debut memorable with four hits in Game Two, doubled twice to knock in both runs of Game Six, and hit a home run and made two spectacular catches to help Oakland win Game Seven; Jackson was voted MVP of the Series to go along with the MVP award he had won in the regular season.

He also homered in the opener of the 1974 Series, doubled in Game Two, and threw out a key base runner in Game Five. In the fall of 1977, Jackson fulfilled his destiny and truly became Mr. October. He homered in Games Four and Five and homered on three consecutive pitches in Game Six. Since he'd hit a homer on his last swing of Game Five and walked his first time up in Game Six, Jackson had hit four straight homers in four official at bats off four different pitchers. He set other Series records for homers (5), runs scored (10), and total bases (25).

After getting his name on a candy bar, Jackson won a third home run crown in 1980 with the Yankees, a fourth in 1982 with the Angels, and ended his career with the A's in 1987, retiring with 563 career homers to place sixth on the all-time list. Jackson was elected to the Hall of Fame in 1993.

WALTER JOHNSON
Pitcher. Born Nov. 6, 1887 Humboldt, Kan. Died Dec. 10, 1946 Washington, D.C. Holds major league record for lifetime shutouts (110). AL MVP 1913, 1924.
Walter Johnson and the Senators were baseball's odd

couple. From 1907 to 1927, Johnson compiled a record of 417–279 while the Senators won just two pennants. He lost 27 games by the score of 1–0; in all, he lost 65 games in which his team failed to score.

Not that he needed much support. On thirty-eight occasions when the Senators managed only a single run, Johnson held the opposition scoreless. He pitched seven Opening Day shutouts and wound up with more career whitewashes (110) than most big league pitchers have career wins.

Twelve of those shutouts came in 1913, when he was at his peak, finishing 36–7 to win his first MVP award. His 1.14 ERA was a record for fifty-five years, and he struck out 243 batters in 346 innings. "Barney" (after race driver Barney Oldfield) led the league in wins, ERA, and strikeouts again in 1918 and 1924, won 20 games or more in ten straight seasons, and had the lowest lifetime ERA (2.17) among AL pitchers with more than 2,000 innings. Considering all pitchers in all eras, Johnson ranks first in Total Pitcher Index.

A high school sensation, Johnson was ready to sign with the Pirates but was refused a $9 signing bonus; instead, he agreed to sign with the Senators on the condition that they pay his way home to Fullerton, California, if he didn't make it in the big leagues. He made his debut on August 2, 1907, losing a five-hitter to Ty Cobb and the Tigers, 3–2. The following year, the "Big Train" arrived, shutting out the New York Highlanders (Yankees) three times in a four-day weekend series on four, three, and two hits.

Seventeen years later, when he should have been washed up, Johnson went 23–7 to win his second MVP award, and the hapless Senators finally reached the World Series. After losing twice to the Giants, Johnson won his first Series game by pitching four scoreless innings of relief in Game 7 as Washington beat the Giants, 4–3, in twelve innings. In the 1925 Series, Johnson won two games against the Pirates but lost the finale, 9–7, as his mates allowed four unearned runs.

When the first election was held for the Hall of Fame, Johnson joined Cobb, Babe Ruth, Honus Wagner, and Christy Mathewson as charter members, the "Five Immortals."

AL KALINE
Right Field. Born Dec. 19, 1934 Baltimore, Md. Won batting championship at age twenty.
He was never named MVP, never led the league in home runs or RBI, and managed to win only one batting title in twenty-two major league seasons. Yet, in 1980, Al Kaline became only the tenth player named to the Hall of Fame in his first year of eligibility.

Kaline had 100 or more hits eighteen times, hit 20 or more home runs nine times, hit .300 or better eight times. The first player to win Gold Gloves at two positions, he won ten in all. In 1971 at age thirty-six, Kaline played the entire season errorless as part of a 242-game streak without a miscue.

One week after signing with the Tigers on his high school graduation day, Kaline got into the lineup when Steve Souchock broke his wrist. Soon after, in a game against the White Sox, Kaline threw runners out at second, third, and home in successive innings. the next year he became the youngest player to win the batting title (.340) and was named AL Player of the Year by *The Sporting News.*

He started in the All-Star Game for the first of ten times in 1955 and played in sixteen summer classics without committing an error, hit .324, and homered in the 1959 Game and the second Game in 1960. He also won the slugging championship in 1959 (.530) and was named *The Sporting News* Player of the Year a second time in 1963.

A's pitcher Lew Krausse hit him with a pitch in 1968, breaking his arm; six weeks later, Kaline returned as a first baseman and played the outfield during the Series. Down three games to one, the Tigers came back in Game Five when Kaline singled in the tying and go-ahead runs. In Game Six he singled twice in the ten-run third inning as the Tigers romped, 13–1. He wound up leading the eventual Champs with a .379 average and 8 RBI.

In 1974 Kaline needed 139 hits to reach 3,000 and became a full-time DH. He got his 3,000th, doubling off Dave McNally, and retired with 3,007. While no Tiger uniform had been retired in deference to Ty Cobb, who didn't wear numerals, Kaline's number 6 was taken out of circulation in August 1980, after his election to the Hall of Fame.

TIM KEEFE
Pitcher. Born Jan. 1, 1857 Cambridge, Mass. Died Apr. 23, 1933 Cambridge, Mass. Posted all-time-low ERA of 0.80 in 1880.
The Mets' first great pitcher wasn't Tom Seaver. It was Tim Keefe, who won 41 games his first year and 37 in his second for the New York Metropolitans of the American Association.

Keefe notched 342 victories in just fourteen years, with a career ERA of 2.62, and established a major league record (since tied) by winning 19 straight games. In the 600 games Keefe pitched, he held the opposition to six or fewer hits on 235 occasions, more than a third of the time. In his streak season (1888), he managed this feat twenty-eight times in fifty-one starts, more than half the time.

His success depended partly on the changeup, of which he was the acknowledged pioneer, and partly on keeping meticulous records of opposing hitters in his own system of notation. (When fellow Giant John Montgomery Ward organized the Players League in 1890, Keefe was named secretary because he could take shorthand.)

Born in Cambridge, Massachusetts, he played with a string of semipro and minor-league New England teams before joining the Troy Haymakers in 1880. He first attracted national attention by going 41–27 with the Mets in 1883—including both ends of a doubleheader, a one-hitter and a two-hitter. He enjoyed even greater success with Jim Mutrie's New York Giants (42–20 in 1886) and became known as "Sir Timothy" for his pitching and manner.

Sir Tim's streak started on June 23, 1888, when he beat the Quakers (Phillies), 7–6, at the Baker Bowl. He went forty-five days before losing again, to the White Stockings (Cubs), 4–2, at the Polo Grounds. To cap off a dream season, Keefe was 4–0 in the World Series, yielding the American Association St. Louis Browns just 18 hits and 2 earned runs in 35 innings.

After jumping to the Players League, Keefe ended his playing days with the Phillies. He umpired in the NL before becoming a real estate mogul. He was elected to the Hall of Fame in 1964 and was proclaimed Cambridge's All-Time Greatest Athlete in a 1976 poll conducted by the Cambridge *Chronicle.*

HARMON KILLEBREW
First Baseman. Born Jun. 29, 1936 Payette, Ida. Holds AL record for most lifetime home runs, righthanded batter (573). AL MVP 1969.
Harmon Killebrew averaged a homer every 14.22 at-bats, more frequently than anyone but Babe Ruth and Ralph Kiner.

The fact is that Killebrew was better at hitting home runs than Ruth and Kiner—half the time—and worse than Rabbit Maranville and Nellie Fox the other half. Baseball has had many streak hitters for average, but Killebrew was a bonafide streak hitter for power.

In 1962 the Killer beat Norm Cash for the home run title, 48 to 39; after a horrendous summer slump, he hit 11 homers in the last eleven games to beat Cash. In 1963 he pulled the same stunt, missing twenty games with a twisted knee, then hit seven homers in the last six games to outhomer Dick Stuart, 45 to 42. In all, he hit 573 homers to place fifth on the all-time list. He led the league in homers five times.

Killebrew is also the only Washington Senator to be discovered by an Idaho senator. The Honorable Herman Welker tipped Clark Griffith about Killebrew in 1954, comparing him to Mickey Mantle. The last time Welker had boasted about an Idaho boy, it had been Vernon Law, and Griffith hadn't listened. This time he sent Ossie Bluege to investigate, and Bluege signed Killebrew the day he first saw him.

In 1959 the Senators gave Killebrew the third base job; he responded with five two-homer games from May 1 through May 17 and ended the year with 42 to tie Rocky Colavito for the league lead. The Senators moved him to first base for two years, then to the outfield the year after moving to Minnesota. From 1962 through 1964, he led the league with 48, 45, and 49 homers.

When the Twins won their first pennant in 1965, he missed 48 games with a dislocated elbow but still hit 25 homers and won a fifth home run crown in 1967 (44). After missing nearly half the 1968 season with injuries, he had a banner year in 1969, leading the league in homers (49) and RBI (140) and helped bring the Twins a Western Division title.

He hit 41 homers in 1970, his eighth 40-plus year, homered in his third All-Star Game in 1971 and ended his career in a Kansas City uniform; he was elected to the Hall of Fame in 1984.

RALPH KINER
Left Field. Born Oct. 27, 1922 Santa Rita, N.M. Hit home runs at a clip (home run percentage) faster than anyone except Babe Ruth.
Ralph Kiner set a home run record that even Babe Ruth and Hank Aaron couldn't top by leading or tying for the league lead in home runs the first seven years of his career. He is also the only player who hit home runs in three consecutive All-Star Games (1949–1951), averaged

35 homers a year in his ten-year major league career, and tied Rogers Hornsby for the then National League record in career grand slams with 12.

Never noted for his finesse with either arm or glove, Kiner ushered in the era of the pure slugger. Kiner had led the NL in 1946 with 23 home runs, the first rookie to do so since Harry Lumley in 1906; however, he really blossomed after slugger Hank Greenberg joined the Pirates in 1947. "Hank put me in a better position in the batter's box, which enabled me to pull outside pitches, and changed my stance and my whole approach to hitting, getting me not to swing at bad pitches," Kiner recalls. He hit 51 homers in 1947, 48 of them after June 1.

The good-looking Kiner also attracted a new kind of woman fan to baseball and became linked with movie stars like Elizabeth Taylor. He began doing personal appearances and became one of the first ballplayers to host his own local TV show.

Kiner reached his peak as a long ball hitter in 1949, hitting 54 homers, four of them grand slams. His mighty blasts attracted fans despite the Pirates' second-division finishes, and, by 1951, Kiner topped Stan Musial as the league's highest salaried player, at $90,000. Two years later the romance was over, and Kiner was traded to the Cubs. He ended his playing career with Cleveland, retiring at thirty-three when a back sprain held him to just 18 homers in 113 games.

Adept at putting people in the seats, he learned the business side of baseball as general manager of the San Diego Padres of the Pacific Coast League from 1955 to 1960. After a year as the radio voice of the White Sox, Kiner became part of the expansion Mets' announcing troika, with Lindsey Nelson and Bob Murphy. Named to the Hall of Fame in 1975, Kiner remained a Mets announcer through the close of the 1996 season.

SANFORD "SANDY" KOUFAX
Pitcher. Born Dec. 30, 1935 Brooklyn, N.Y. Holds major league record for most consecutive years leading league in ERA (five). NL MVP 1963 and Cy Young Award 1963, 1965, 1966.

Sandy Koufax was the best pitcher in baseball for five seasons. From 1962 to 1966, he was 111–34 with 100 complete games, 33 of them shutouts. He led the NL in ERA all five years, in wins and strikeouts in 1963, 1965, and 1966, and won the Cy Young Award all three years.

Born Sanford Braun, he took the name of his stepfather, attorney Irving Koufax. He went to the University of Cincinnati on a basketball scholarship, but chose baseball after striking out 51 batters in 32 innings. In 1955 the nineteen-year old lefty joined the Dodgers and mopped up for three seasons. The first sign that he might be special came on August 31, 1959, when Koufax struck out 18 Cubs to tie Bob Feller's record; yet, frustrated with his progress, he nearly quit in 1960 after going 8–13.

One day, scout Kenny Meyers and catcher Norm Sherry asked him to throw at a spot and noticed that Koufax's motion obstructed his vision. Meyers said, "How can you hit that spot when you can't even see it?" Sherry persuaded Koufax to throw more deliberately, and controlling the speed of his delivery made all the difference between getting behind the hitters and throwing strikes.

In 1961, Koufax was 18–13, leading the league with 269 strikeouts. He blossomed fully in 1963, winning 25 of 30 regular season decisions and taking the first and last games of the World Series sweep of the Yankees. He also won the Cy Young Award and was named MVP.

Adhesions in his pitching arm broke loose in 1964, leading to the traumatic arthritis which would end his career. After throwing his third no-hitter in late August, Koufax was forced to stop pitching with a record of 19–5 and an ERA of 1.74. On medical orders, he didn't throw between starts in 1965 and went 26–8, crowning the regular season by pitching a perfect game against the Cubs on September 9; he shut out Minnesota twice in the World Series as the Dodgers won in seven games.

Koufax's final season was 1966, when he won 27 and lost 9 and led the league in ERA for the fifth year in a row (1.73). In 1972 he became the youngest player ever elected to the Hall of Fame and was also named Player of the Decade in the 1960s.

NAPOLEON "LARRY" LAJOIE
Second Baseman. Born Sept. 5, 1875 Woonsocket, R.I. Died Feb. 7, 1959 Daytona Beach, Fla. Holds AL record for highest season batting average, (.426), 1901.

Napoleon Lajoie was the complete package. No other second baseman has ever shone so brilliantly in so many ways for so long (twenty-one years).

In addition to leading ALers in every fielding category in two different seasons, Lajoie won a Triple Crown and four batting titles, compiled 3,242 career hits and a lifetime batting average of .338. At one time or another, he led both leagues in RBI, slugging average, and fielding percentage, and was so well-loved that his team adopted his nickname as its own.

Originally signed by the Phillies, Lajoie hit .361 in 1897 and won the slugging championship (.569). By 1900 he had gathered five straight .300 plus seasons but was earning only $2,400, the NL maximum. When Connie Mack offered him $4,000, he jumped to the new AL and won the Triple Crown in 1901, hitting .426 (still an AL record) with 14 home runs and 125 RBI; it is a measure of his versatility that he also led in runs scored (145), hits (232), doubles (48) and slugging percentage (.643), putouts (395) and fielding percentage (.960).

The Phils sued Mack, and eventually the Pennsylvania Supreme Court enjoined Lajoie from playing with the Athletics. AL president Ban Johnson ordered that Lajoie be transferred to Cleveland where he could avoid Pennsylvania's jurisdiction but could still play in the AL; for the first few years, Lajoie always remained behind or went on to the next road stop when the Bronchos (Indians) traveled to Philadelphia.

He won batting titles in 1903 (.344) and 1904 (.376) and was named Cleveland's player-manager in 1905; the team was renamed the Naps in his honor. Although the Naps improved, they never won a pennant under Lajoie, who resigned during the 1909 season to concentrate on playing.

Nap might have won a fourth, albeit tainted batting championship when he got six bunt singles on the last day of the 1910 season, all because of the opposing manager's hatred for Cobb, who was four points ahead. In retaliation, sportswriter Hugh Fullerton changed his ruling on a

Cobb smash that he had ruled an error earlier in the season, helping to give Cobb a single extra hit and the championship. Seven decades later the controversy erupted anew as it was discovered that Cobb had been the beneficiary of a double entry of a game in which he had gone 2-for-3; Larry had the higher batting average in 1910, after all.

Lajoie was elected to the Hall of Fame in 1937.

JOHN HENRY "POP" LLOYD

Shortstop. Born Apr. 25, 1884 Palatka, Fla. Died Mar. 19, 1965 Atlantic City, N.J. At age forty-four, hit .564 and led the Negro NL in home runs.

Pop Lloyd was frequently called "the Black Honus Wagner." There is no record that Wagner was ever called "the white Pop Lloyd," but to have done so would have been high compliment indeed.

Wagner once commented about Lloyd, "After I saw him play, I felt honored that they should name such a great ballplayer after me." Connie Mack added, "You could put Wagner and Lloyd in a bag together and whichever one you pulled out, you couldn't go wrong."

Lloyd may have been the single greatest black player of all time. A lefthanded line drive hitter, he was a gifted base runner and base stealer in both the United States and Cuba, where he played for twelve years and was an idol to fans and youngsters. They called him "El Cuchara"—"the Shovel," and writers talk of him scooping ground balls with dirt, twigs, and anything else that populated the primitive infields.

Born in Florida, he played semipro ball in Georgia with the Macon Acmes and moved on to the Cuban-X Giants. In Cuba he played against Ty Cobb in an exhibition game, tagging him out three times on attempted steals with catcher Bruce Petway delivering the ball. Lloyd also outhit Cobb, .500 to .369, and Cobb was so embarrassed that he vowed never to play against blacks again.

Perhaps the highlight of Lloyd's playing career came from 1914 to 1917 when he played for Rube Foster's Chicago American Giants and batted cleanup on a team that included Oscar Charleston, Bingo DeMoss, Smokey Joe Williams, and Cannonball Dick Redding.

As Lloyd's legs began to go, he switched to first base and signed on with the Brooklyn Royal Giants as player-manager for three seasons. From 1921 to 1928, he played with the Columbus Buckeyes, Hilldale, the Bacharach Giants, and the New York Lincoln Giants. At age forty-four he hit .564 and led the league in home runs.

When announced Graham McNamee asked Babe Ruth to name the greatest player of all time, Ruth said, "You mean major leaguers?" "No," replied McNamee, "the greatest player anywhere." "In that case," said Ruth, "I'd pick John Henry Lloyd." Lloyd was elected to the Hall of Fame in 1977.

MICKEY MANTLE

Center Field. Born Oct. 20, 1931 Spavinaw, Okla. Died Aug. 13, 1995 Dallas Tex. AL MVP 1956, 1957, 1962.

Despite a chronic bone infection in his legs and operations on both knees, Mickey Mantle became baseball's most powerful switch hitter, hitting 536 home runs in the regular season and setting a World Series record with 18.

Named for Mickey Cochrane, his father's favorite player, Mantle learned to switch hit at age five and starred in high school baseball and football, developing osteomyelitis after bruising a leg in a football game. After a short (and error-filled) career as a minor league shortstop, he became the Yankees' regular right fielder before his twentieth birthday. He suffered his first serious injury during the 1951 Series against the Giants when he tripped on a drain at Yankee Stadium and required surgery for torn knee cartilage.

Joe DiMaggio retired that fall, and Mantle moved to center field, hitting .311 in 142 games. He led the league in home runs (37) in 1955 and, a year later, won the Triple Crown, hitting 52 homers, knocking in 130 runs, and batting .353. The only player besides Jimmie Foxx to hit 50 homers and win a batting title, Mantle won the MVP award and shone in the World Series, hitting three homers as the Yanks beat Brooklyn in seven games.

In 1957 he was chosen MVP again as he hit .365. He won home run crowns again in 1958 (42) and 1960 (40), finishing second to Roger Maris's 61 homers in 1961 with 54. Mantle was named MVP a third time in 1962 when he hit .321. On June 5, 1963, he broke his left foot in Baltimore, ending a season in which he had 15 home runs in 172 at-bats, although he returned in time to hit a home run in the World Series.

His personal choice for most memorable homer was his ninth-inning shot off Cardinal Barney Schultz in 1964, which broke Babe Ruth's record for lifetime Series home runs and won Game Three. Mickey went on to hit two more in that Series, his last, and wound up his tenth Series with 18 homers, 42 runs scored, 123 total bases, and 40 RBI—all records.

Despite his injuries, Mantle holds the Yankee record for games played—2,401. He retired during spring training in 1969, and, on June 8, received a ten-minute standing ovation at Yankee Stadium. He was named to the Hall of Fame in 1974.

WALTER "RABBIT" MARANVILLE

Shortstop. Born Nov. 11, 1891 Springfield, Mass. Died Jan. 5, 1954 New York, N.Y. Holds major league shortstop record for most years leading league in putouts (6) and lifetime putouts (5,133).

If you thought Jimmy Blake was, in the words of *Casey at the Bat,* "much-despised," consider Walter James Vincent "Rabbit" Maranville.

Every time suggestions are made to "prune" the Hall of Fame of its many undeserving members, Maranville's name is invariably suggested, mostly due to his limitations with the bat. The possessor of just 28 career home runs in more than 10,000 at bats, "Rabbit" bettered .300 just once in seventeen seasons as a regular, and never led the league in an offensive category.

Yet, in 1914 and again in 1919, Maranville led the league in both Fielding Runs and Total Player Rating. He saved 50 runs more than an average shortstop in 1914 and personally accounted for more wins than any player in the league. Casey Stengel, who later managed Maranville, said of him, "Shortstops who stay around more than twenty years are not clowns."

Maranville finished a close second to fellow Miracle Brave Johnny Evers in the voting for the Chalmers (MVP) Award. There was no MVP voting for the NL in 1919, but

Maranville was third in 1913 and finished in the top twenty in MVP voting no less than seven times.

The colorful Maranville invented the "basket catch," but many of his antics were inspired by alcohol. He jumped into a water fountain fully clothed; dangled a teammate out of a twelfth-story hotel window; and, named manager of the Cubs in 1925, celebrated by pouring ice water on all his sleeping teammates. Waived to the Brooklyn Robins, Maranville was demoted to Rochester of the International League.

That's when he resolved to quit drinking. Asked to comment on the effects of Prohibition, he said, "There is much less drinking now than there was before 1927, because I quit drinking on May 24, 1927."

He joined the Cardinals later that year, started for the pennant-winning 1928 team, and hit .308 in the World Series. Back with the Braves in 1929, he started playing more second base; in 1932, at the age of forty-one, he led the league at that position in putouts and fielding. He still holds the major league record for career putouts by a shortstop and was elected to the Hall of Fame shortly after his death in 1954.

EDDIE MATHEWS

Third Baseman. Born Oct. 13, 1931 Texarkana, Tex. Holds NL record, most consecutive years with 30 or more home runs (nine).

Eddie Mathews played a game-within-the-game. He said, "I'd take on the other third baseman ... I wanted to beat him in every department—fielding, hitting, running the bases. I played that game all my life, and it kept me on my toes."

It did indeed. Mathews was a seven-time All-Star. He hit 30 or more homers for nine straight seasons and 512 lifetime, led the NL's third basemen three times in assists, and teamed with Henry Aaron to form the greatest one-two home run punch in baseball history; as Braves teammates, they accounted for 863 homers.

The only Brave to play in Boston, Milwaukee and Atlanta, Mathews could have had his choice of teams. He was scouted by nine, but because Boston had the oldest third baseman (Bob Elliott), Mathews became a Brave at 12: 01 a.m. the day following his high school graduation in 1949 and was sent to Atlanta, where Dixie Walker was the manager. Walker helped Mathews deal with left-handed pitchers and Billy Jurges polished his fielding. By the fall of 1951, Ty Cobb said, "I've seen three or four perfect swings in my time. This lad has one of them."

In April 1952 Elliott was traded to the Giants, and Steady Eddie got his job. He became the first rookie to homer three times in a game, hit 25 homers, and proved there was no sophomore jinx by winning the home run title the following year with 47 round-trippers, finishing second only to Roy Campanella in the MVP voting.

Mathews starred in the 1957 World Series although the Yankees walked him eight times. He won Game Four with a tenth-inning homer, scored the only run in Game Five, and doubled in the first two runs of Game Seven; with the bases loaded and two out in the bottom of the ninth, he made a lunging stop on Bill Skowron's shot down the line and stepped on third to give the Milwaukee Braves their only championship.

In 1959 Mathews won his second home run crown. He was traded to the Astros on New Year's Eve, 1967, moved on to the Tigers, and played in his final World Series in 1968. He managed the Braves from 1972 to 1974 and entered the Hall of Fame in 1978.

CHRISTY MATHEWSON

Pitcher. Born Aug. 12, 1880 Factoryville, Pa. Died Oct. 7, 1925 Saranac Lake, N.Y. Holds NL record for most years winning 20 or more games (12).

If Mattel had made Barbie dolls in 1903, Christy Mathewson might have been the model for Ken.

Handsome, clean-cut, intelligent, clean-living, and heroic, Mathewson was one of the first players to attract women and children to the ballpark. An All-America college football player for Bucknell, he was nationally known as a checkers expert, too. Oh yes. He won 373 games in his major league career even though he didn't normally pitch on Sundays. (His mother had wanted him to become a minister.)

One of the "Five Immortals" elected when the Hall of Fame was established in 1936, Mathewson was called "Big Six" because his fastball reminded reporters of a famous New York fire engine. Nevertheless, it was his fadeaway (screwball) that drove National Leaguers crazy. He won 30 or more games four times, finished 434 of the 551 games he started, and completed 10 of 11 World Series games while posting an ERA of 1.15. A control whiz, he pitched 68 consecutive innings in 1913 without walking a batter.

Born to well-to-do parents in Factoryville, Pennsylvania, Mathewson studied forestry at Bucknell, headed two literary societies, was elected class president, and was the kicker on Walter Camp's 1900 All-America team. He became a Giant that fall, won 20 games in 1901, and became baseball's dominant pitcher starting in 1903, the first of three straight years in which he won 30 or more.

In the 1905 World Series, Mathewson became a household name; in a Series decided entirely by shutouts, Matty contributed three—in five days. He four-hit Connie Mack's A's in the opener and, two days after Chief Bender blanked the Giants, four-hit the Mackmen again. Two days later Matty wound up the Series, giving up six hits this time, but nevertheless pitching his third shutout in six days. In 27 innings, Mathewson walked one man and struck out 18.

Over the next ten years, Mathewson won at least 20 games a season. When the fadeaway began to fade, Mathewson's manager and best friend, John McGraw, arranged a trade to Cincinnati so he could take the helm of the Reds. Joining a chemical warfare unit in France during World War I, he was accidentally exposed to poison gas that weakened his lungs; he later contracted tuberculosis, which ultimately proved fatal. He had served as general manager of the Braves despite his poor health but died on the opening day of the 1925 World Series.

WILLIE MAYS

Center Field. Born May 6, 1931 Westfield, Ala. NL Rookie of the Year 1951, MVP 1954, 1965.

In 1951 Willie Mays chased a 457-foot shot to dead center in Forbes Field, hit the warning track, saw the ball hook right, and, with no time to reach across his body, made the catch bare-handed. Pirates general manager Branch

Rickey, in his forty-eighth year of baseball, sent Mays a note: "That was the finest catch I have ever seen and the finest catch I ever hope to see."

Mays started with the Birmingham Black Barons of the Negro AL and, after hitting .477 in the opening months of the 1951 season with the Minneapolis Millers, was promoted to the Giants. When Mays had trouble hitting big league pitching, manager Leo Durocher assured him that center field was his—whether he hit or not. Mays responded by leading the Giants to the pennant and was named Rookie of the Year.

He spent most of 1952 and all of 1953 in the service, returning in 1954 to win his only batting title (.345) and to belt 41 homers. The Giants won another pennant and Mays collected his first MVP award. In Game One of the World Series, Mays made one of baseball's most famous catches, snaring Vic Wertz's drive to deep center over his shoulder to keep the game tied, 3–3; the Giants swept the Indians, and Mays won the Hickok Belt as Pro Athlete of the Year.

The "Say Hey Kid" only got better, winning the first of four home run titles in 1955 and becoming the complete player in 1957—winning a Gold Glove, stealing a league-leading 38 bases, and hitting 26 doubles, 20 triples, and 35 homers. He hit four home runs in a game on April 30, 1961, and hit 49 homers in 1962 to lead the league and drive the Giants to another pennant.

Voted the All-Star MVP in 1963 and 1968, he holds the All-Star Game record for career hits (23) and stolen bases (6) and says the best catch he ever made was one that robbed Ted Williams of a home run in the 1955 game at Milwaukee's County Stadium.

Willie earned eleven Gold Gloves, set records for career putouts and total chances, was the first man to hit 300 home runs and steal 300 bases, had 660 lifetime homers, and a batting average of .302. He has considerable support as the best ever to play the game. He was elected to the Hall of Fame in 1979, his first year of eligibility.

BILL MAZEROSKI

Second Baseman. Born Sept. 5, 1936 Wheeling, West Va. Holds major league record for lifetime double plays by a second baseman (1,706).

Bill Mazeroski, remembered best for his Series-winning home run in 1960, may have been baseball's best fielder. In *Baseball Ratings*, Charles Faber awards points for percentage, assists, chances, and range factor to all players with ten years' experience; Mazeroski leads every player from every era, regardless of position.

He set records for second basemen by leading his league the most years in assists (9) and double plays (8) and holds the record for career double plays by a second baseman (1706). Only three *first basemen* took part in more double plays; Lou Gehrig, for instance, played in one game more and figured in 136 fewer double plays.

Mazeroski won the first of eight Gold Gloves in 1956 and became an All-Star for the first of seven times in 1958. After hitting 19 home runs that year, he tried to pull everything and wound up with just seven homers and thirty-four-point drop in his batting average. When the slump continued into 1960, George Sisler made him stand deeper in the box to hit curveballs after they broke. Hitting .237 on August 3, Mazeroski ended the regular sea-

son at .273 as the Pirates won their first pennant in thirty-three years.

He started a double play in the first inning of Game One, hit a two-run homer in the fourth inning (the margin of victory in a 6–4 Pirate win), and turned his third double play in the ninth inning to end the game. With the Yanks and Pirates even in the Series, in the seventh game the Pirates went ahead, 9–7, in the eighth inning. The Yankees tied it in the top of the ninth, but, leading off in the bottom, Mazeroski hit Ralph Terry's second pitch over the left field wall to win the Series.

Maz set an NL record for double plays by a second baseman (144) in 1961 and smashed Gerry Priddy's ML record of 150 double plays in 1966; that year, he (161) and Gene Alley (128) recorded the most double plays for a shortstop and a second baseman in a season. A utility man in 1971, he retired in 1972. He later became an unofficial infield instructor for the Expos, and the Pirates retired his number 9 in 1987.

WILLIE "STRETCH" McCOVEY

First Baseman. Born Jan. 10, 1938 Mobile, Ala. Holds National League record for most lifetime home runs by a lefthanded batter (521). NL Rookie of the Year 1959, MVP 1969.

The man who left his heart in San Francisco wasn't Tony Bennett but Willie McCovey. After three seasons in San Diego and 11 games in Oakland, McCovey returned on Opening Day in 1977 and received a standing ovation that moved him to tears. He responded to the fans by hitting 28 homers at age thirty-nine and was named Comeback Player of the Year.

The love affair began on July 30, 1959, when McCovey made a spectacular debut. Called up from Phoenix, where he'd been tutored by Ted Williams, McCovey went 4-for-4 against Robin Roberts with two singles and two triples. But there was a problem. The Giants already had a first baseman, Orlando Cepeda, who had been named Rookie of the Year the year before. McCovey won the same honor in 1959, hitting .354, and the two see-sawed back and forth between first and the outfield; Cepeda got the first base job until he was injured in 1965, then was traded to the Cardinals.

By then McCovey was a star, having led the league with 44 homers in 1963. When he returned to first base full time, Willie led the league in 1968 with 36 homers, 105 RBI, and a .545 slugging average. For an encore, he headed the same categories in 1969 with even better numbers—45 homers, 126 RBI and a .656 slugging average.

NL pitchers, rather than pitch to McCovey in 1970, decided to walk him instead—a league-leading 137 times, including a record 45 intentional walks. "Stretch" (for his ability to keep one foot on the bag and reach off-the-mark throws) still hit 39 homers and led the league in slugging for the third straight year.

A series of injuries plagued him in the 1970s, and when he did play, pitchers continued to pitch around him. The Giants traded him and he played for three teams without leaving California. When he hung up his spikes in 1980, McCovey had played in four decades and hit 521 homers to tie Ted Williams, his idol and former mentor, for ninth on the all-time list. He also set the NL career record for grand slams (18), second only to Lou Gehrig's 23. He was elected to the Hall of Fame in 1985.

JOHN "BID" McPHEE
Second Baseman. Born Nov. 1, 1859 Messina, N.Y. Died Jan. 3, 1943 San Diego, Cal. Holds major league record for putouts by a second baseman (6,545).

John Alexander "Bid" McPhee made more putouts than any other major league second baseman, ranks fifth in Fielding Wins, ahead of star glove men like Tris Speaker and Ozzie Smith, stole more bases than Davey Lopes or Luis Aparicio. and, in Total Player Rating, beats out Hall of Fame second basemen Frankie Frisch, Bobby Doerr, and Billy Herman.

So how come you never heard of this guy?

Sometimes greatness can be boring, and that's certainly the case with "King Bid," as he was known. As historian Bob Carroll has noted, "In all of his eighteen years he was never fined. He was never even thrown out of a game!... McPhee showed up every day in shape, stayed sober, did his job, and went home to a good night's sleep." About the only thing that made him colorful was the fact that he was the best defensive second baseman in the nineteenth century and for fourteen (of his eighteen) seasons he did it barehanded.

McPhee, who stood 5'8" and weighed 152 on a good day, was "biddy"—small. He joined the brand-new Cincinnati Reds of the brand-new American Association in 1882, leading the league in putouts, double plays, and fielding average, a habit he never quite broke. He was the double play champ eleven times and led in fielding nine times.

As you might expect, McPhee was a pesky hitter (.271 lifetime), speedy enough to steal 95 bases in 1887 and 568 lifetime. What might surprise is that Bid once "cranked out" 8 homers to lead the league in 1886. (Yes, they were all inside the park.) The other surprise is that McPhee's on-base percentage is .354, relatively low for a guy who walked 981 times.

When his contemporaries began using mitts, McPhee refused to go along. Although he toughened his hands every spring, he was no longer leading the league; however, he began 1896 with a sore finger and finally gave in. The results were instructive; at age 37, McPhee's fielding average was .978, a full 10 points above the recognized mark. The record stood until 1925 when Sparky Adams broke it.

He retired after the 1899 season, briefly managed the Reds, and scouted for them in Los Angeles, where he settled.

JOE MORGAN
Second Baseman. Born Sept. 19, 1943 Bonham, Tex. Holds major league record for seasons by a second baseman (22). NL MVP 1975, 1976.

When the Big Red Machine was operating in the 1970s, Joe Morgan was its generator. He got on base 41 percent of the time and, on a team with Johnny Bench and Pete Rose, was named MVP in both 1975 and 1976.

From 1972 through 1977, he averaged 60 stolen bases, scored more than 100 runs each year, and averaged 21 homers and 84 RBI with a .301 batting average. Moreover, Little Joe won Gold Gloves in 1973–1977. Over

twenty-two years, he helped his teammates win six divisional titles, four pennants and two world championships.

Born in Bonham, Texas, Morgan signed with the Astros and was named NL Rookie of the Year in 1965 by *The Sporting News*. Traded to Cincinnati before the 1972 season, he topped NL second basemen in putouts and fielding and led in walks (115) and runs scored (122).

In 1975 he hit .327, led all second basemen in fielding percentage, and stole 67 bases to be named MVP (he added six steals in the postseason). Morgan won Game Three of the World Series with a single in the bottom of the tenth and Game Seven with a single in the top of the ninth to give the Reds their first championship in thirty-five years.

The Reds repeated in 1976 and Morgan became the first back-to-back MVP since Ernie Banks. Little Joe won the slugging title (.576) and was runner-up in RBI (111), runs scored (113), and steals (60). Morgan set a record for second basemen in 1977, making just five errors, but tailed off offensively in 1978 and 1979. He helped the Astros win their division in 1980 and went on to two solid years with the San Francisco Giants. Reunited with Pete Rose and Tony Perez in Philadelphia for 1983, he hit 16 homers to help the Phillies win the pennant and homered twice in the World Series.

He made his 1984 farewell with Oakland memorable by replacing Rogers Hornsby as the most prolific home-run hitting second baseman of all time (268). A first-year selection to the Hall of Fame in 1990, Morgan has also been successful as a broadcaster for ESPN.

DALE MURPHY
Center Field. Born Mar. 12, 1956 Portland, Ore. NL MVP 1982, 1983.

Dale Murphy hit 20 or more homers in twelve seasons, played in at least 154 games from 1982 to 1990, and became in 1983 the youngest player to be chosen MVP in two consecutive seasons.

He was the Braves' first-round draft choice two months after Hank Aaron set the record for career home runs. A catcher at the time, Murphy had impressed Atlanta management with his home run swing and rifle arm and was touted as "the next Johnny Bench." For a while, he wasn't even the next Biff Pocoroba. Shortly after being brought up to Atlanta, he developed a mysterious mental block about throwing to second base, and even tossing back to the pitcher.

Rather than let him languish behind Pocoroba and Bruce Benedict, manager Bobby Cox moved Murphy to first base, and he hit 23 homers in 1978. Moved again, to center field in 1980, Murphy became a superstar, hitting 33 homers and, two years later, leading the Braves to the Western Division championship. Murph finished second that year in homers (36 to Dave Kingman's 37), tied Al Oliver for the RBI lead with 109, won his first of five Gold Gloves, and was named MVP. Nolan Ryan said, "I can't imagine Joe DiMaggio was a better all-around player than Dale Murphy."

Five weeks later, he was working on his hitting; new manager Joe Torre was convinced that Murphy could become an even better hitter with two strikes. In 1983 he hit 36 home runs again, added 21 points to his batting average, and struck out 24 fewer times. He also stole 30 bases to become only the sixth 30–30 man in major league history. He was named MVP again at age twenty-seven—joining Ernie Banks, Joe Morgan, and Mike Schmidt as the only NLers to be named MVP in back-to-back seasons.

In 1984 Murphy hit 36 home runs yet again to tie Mike Schmidt for the league lead; a year later, he led the league in walks (90), runs scored (118), and home runs (37). After perhaps his best all-around season in 1987, when he hit 44 homers and achieved personal bests in slugging (.580) and on base percentage (.420), Murphy had calamitous declines in 1988–1990. In August 1990 he was traded to Philadelphia.

Dealt to the expansion Rockies in 1993, Murphy concluded his career with 398 lifetime homers to rank him twenty-fourth on the all-time list.

STAN "THE MAN" MUSIAL

Left Field. Born Nov. 21, 1920 Donora, Pa. Holds modern NL record for most years (seventeen) and consecutive years (sixteen) hitting .300 or better. NL MVP 1943, 1946, 1948.

In the bottom of the twelfth inning of the 1955 All-Star Game, Yogi Berra complained, "My feet are killing me." Stan Musial said, "Relax, I'll have you home in a minute." He hit a home run on the next pitch to win the game.

Musial's magic lit up twenty-four All-Star Games, and he holds the record for most All-Star homers (6), extra-base hits (8), and total bases (40). During the regular season he hit .300 or better in 17 of his 21 full years, won seven batting titles, and had a lifetime average of .331, with 475 homers and 1,951 RBI.

His bat and glove helped the Cardinals reign over the NL in the 1940s as St. Louis won the pennant in 1943 and the World Series in 1942, 1944, and 1946. Musial was named MVP in 1942, 1946, and 1948 and won three straight batting titles from 1950 to 1952, around the time a Dodger fan nicknamed him by saying, "Uh, oh. Here comes that man again."

Musial's splendid hitting redeemed a promising pitching career that was ended by a shoulder injury. In 1940, Musial was 18–5 in the Florida State League when he fell on his arm and it went numb. Branch Rickey converted him to the outfield, and Musial's hitting got him to the big leagues in time to hit .426 in 12 games in 1941.

In twenty-two seasons as a Cardinal, he led the National League in runs scored five times, sharing the record with Rogers Hornsby and George Burns, and led the major leagues in total bases six times. At his retirement, he held major league records for most extra-base hits and total bases and the NL records for runs, hits, doubles, and RBI.

Musial said his secret was memory. "I consciously memorized the speed at which every pitcher in the league threw his fastball, curve, and slider; then, I'd pick up the speed of the ball in the first thirty feet of its flight and knew how it would move once it had crossed the plate."

When he retired, he became a Cardinal VP. The club honored him with a statue outside Busch Memorial Stadium in 1968, and he entered the Hall of Fame in 1969. Fully ten years later, when consumers were asked whose endorsement they would trust, Stan the Man still ranked first among athletes.

CHARLES "KID" NICHOLS

Pitcher. Born Sep. 14, 1869 Madison, Wis. Died Apr. 11, 1953 Kansas City, Mo. Won 30 games or more in seven of eight straight years (1891–1898).

Little recalled today, Kid Nichols won 361 games, completed 531 (as many as Walter Johnson), and finished behind only Johnson and Cy Young in Adjusted Pitching Runs, a measurement of how many runs a pitcher saved his team, beyond what an average pitcher would have done in his stead.

No pitcher has had more 30-win seasons than Nichols (seven), who pitched with no wind-up and, scorning the curveball, changed speeds with surpassing skill. The righthander led the Boston Beaneaters to five pre-1900 pennants and became the youngest pitcher to win 300 games, marking the anniversary before his thirty-first birthday.

He made his debut with Kansas City in 1887, when that city was in the Western League, and made his mark two years later with Omaha of the Western Association, winning 36 games. When his manager, Frank Selee, went to Boston to manage the Beaneaters, Nichols went along and was an immediate sensation, winning 27 games his rookie year.

Called "Kid" for his slight build and baby face, Nichols soon became the workhorse of his era. He pitched more than 400 innings in each of his first five years, 300 or more in his first ten, and holds the record for most seasons with 300 innings pitched (twelve). He was relieved in only 24 of the 501 starts he made for Boston. Late in 1892, a year in which he finished at 35–16 in 453 innings, he pitched complete game wins three days in a row.

Named "Nervy Nick" for beating the Orioles twice in three days to win the 1897 pennant, Nichols held out for more than $2,400, the maximum allowable at the time, and was given a $285 bonus for winning the 1898 pennant. Nevertheless, he left the majors to buy a piece of the Kansas City team and returned after a two-year hiatus as player-manager of the Cardinals. Fading from the big leagues after the 1906 campaign, he returned to Kansas City and coached amateur clubs, one of which had a player named Charles Dillon "Casey" Stengel.

A vigorous man, he won the Kansas City bowling championship at age sixty-four and bowled competitively into his seventies. Elected to the Hall of Fame in 1949, he died in Kansas City four years later at the age of eighty-three.

LEROY "SATCHEL" PAIGE

Pitcher. Born July 7, 1905 Mobile, Ala. Died June 8, 1982 Kansas City, Mo. Pitched professionally from 1924 to 1959.

When the Cleveland Indians signed Satchel Paige to a contract in 1948, J.G. Taylor Spink, publisher of *The Sporting News,* wrote, "To bring in a pitching rookie of Paige's age is to demean the standards of baseball." Two days later, Paige demeaned the White Sox, holding them scoreless in two innings of relief. He pitched a shutout in his second start and finished his first big league season 6–1; since the Indians wound up in a tie with the Red Sox, they literally could not have won the pennant without him.

Satchel Paige had made it to the majors, but not when he was the best pitcher in baseball. In 1930 he struck out

22 big leaguers, including Hack Wilson and Babe Herman, in an exhibition game. A year later he joined the Pittsburgh Crawfords, who advertised—truthfully—that "Josh Gibson will hit two home runs and Satchel Paige will strike out the first nine batters."

As a member of the Crawfords in 1933 he was 31–4, winning 21 games in a row and once racking up 62 straight scoreless innings. In 1938 a sore arm threatened to put him out of baseball, but he learned to throw curves, and gradually his arm came back. He pitched the Kansas City Monarchs to five pennants, and, when one of his teammates, Jackie Robinson, made it to the majors, Paige figured rightly that his time had come.

After his sensational start with the Indians, Paige had a subpar season in 1949 and, following owner Bill Veeck's departure, was released. He rejoined Veeck as a member of the lowly Browns and, incredibly, became the AL's leading reliever in 1952 at age 46, winning 12 games and saving 10.

When the team moved to Baltimore, Satch pitched in the minors for seven more years. He came back at 59 to pitch three scoreless innings for the Kansas City A's in 1965. He was signed as a pitching coach in 1968 by the Braves to qualify for his pension. Fittingly, he was the first man elected to the Hall of Fame by the Committee on Negro Leagues formed in 1971.

JIM PALMER
Pitcher. Born Oct. 15, 1945 New York, N.Y. AL Cy Young Award 1973, 1975, 1976.

The best pitchers win the big ones. Jim Palmer clinched the first four pennants in Baltimore's post-1900 history and had a record of 8–3 and an ERA of 2.61 in postseason play. In 1983 he became the only pitcher to win a World Series game in three different decades.

Over eighteen years, Palmer won the Cy Young Award three times (1973, 1975, and 1976) and set Oriole records for career wins (268), shutouts (53), and complete games (211). He is, along with Walter Johnson and Lefty Grove, the only AL pitcher to win 20 games in eight or more seasons, and his ERA (2.86) ranks fifth among pitchers with 3,000 innings or more.

Palmer averaged 288 innings for nine straight years and led the league in that department four times. Despite this durability, he was frequently injured and acquired a reputation as a hypochondriac. When Oriole pitcher Steve Stone saw Palmer reading *Doctor Zhivago,* he quipped, "It must be about an elbow specialist."

Palmer led the Orioles in wins with 15 in 1966 and, before his twenty-first birthday, beat the Dodgers and Sandy Koufax in the southpaw's last game, 6–0, to become the youngest pitcher to throw a World Series shutout. The game was an apt symbol to divide the old and new orders of pitchers, but Palmer suffered a sore arm and was out of the majors for nearly two years.

He won 20 games eight out of nine years, from 1970 to 1973 and from 1975 to 1978. Numerous arm injuries slowed him down, and, when he sported an ERA of 7.44 in May 1982, it looked as though that might be his last year; however, Palmer recovered and won 11 in a row, nearly leading the Orioles to another pennant. When the O's won in 1983, Palmer pitched only once, winning Game Three as a relief pitcher.

After starting the 1984 season 0–3, Palmer pitched his last game on May 12. Although his plan to make a comeback in 1991—one year after he was inducted into the Hall of Fame!—never materialized, he remains in the public eye as a TV talk show host and corporate spokesman.

CAL RIPKEN, JR.
Shortstop. Born Aug. 24, 1960 Havre De Grace, Md. AL Rookie of the Year 1982, American League MVP 1983, 1991. Major league record of 2,316 consecutive games played through 1996 season.

On September 6, 1995 at Camden Yards, Cal Ripken, Jr. played in his 2,131st consecutive game to break Lou Gehrig's record for consecutive games played. He had played in 2,316 straight by the end of the 1996 season. Cal Ripken, Jr., hasn't been out of the Orioles' starting lineup since May 29, 1982, when he started at short in the second game of a doubleheader. On July 15, 1996 after 2,216 consecutive games at shortstop, he moved to third base, the first time Ripken hadn't started at shortstop since 1982.

Ripken has taken criticism for keeping the streak alive, when he might not have been healthy enough to play effectively. Nevertheless, the streak has pushed Ripken beyond ordinary physical limits, sometimes with gratifying results. In 1983, he hurt his hand sliding on artificial turf in Seattle and was unable to grip the bat at first; he somehow gritted his teeth and got five hits that night, two of them home runs, and thirteen total bases to tie an Oriole club record.

At 6'4", he is the tallest regular shortstop in major league history and one of the most powerful. In 1986, Ripken became the only shortstop besides Ernie Banks to hit 20 or more homers in six straight seasons. (His streak of ten straight seasons was finally broken in 1992.) The first AL shortstop to start more than three straight All-Star Games (seven in all), he has also led the league four times in putouts and double plays, six times in assists, and set a new AL assist record (534) in 1983.

Although Ripken played 44 errorless games at third base and homered in his first at-bat in 1982, he suffered a deep batting slump (7-for-60). Reggie Jackson told him, "You look like you're fighting yourself ... stick with what got you here." Moved to shortstop on July 1 to fill Mark Belanger's shoes for good, he wound up with 28 homers and 93 RBI to be named Rookie of the Year.

In 1983, Ripken led the majors in hits and doubles and the league in runs, extra base hits, assists, total chances, and double plays. He was named MVP and led Baltimore to a division title. He played errorless ball as the O's beat the White Sox in the playoffs and Philadelphia in the World Series.

BROOKS "HOOVER" ROBINSON
Third Baseman. Born May 18, 1937 Little Rock, Ark. Holds major league third baseman records for highest fielding average (.971), putouts (2,697), assists (6,205), and double plays (618). AL MVP 1964.

Brooks Calbert Robinson, Jr. wasn't nicknamed "Hoover" for his resemblance to Herbert or J. Edgar but rather for his ability to suck up everything hit towards third base.

He won Gold Gloves every year from 1960 to 1975, led

AL third basemen eleven times in fielding and eight times each in putouts and assists, and made more putouts, assists, chances, and double plays than any third baseman in history. He also spent a record twenty-three years with one team, the Orioles. Sportswriter Gordon Beard said, "He never asked anyone to name a candy bar after him. In Baltimore people name their children after him."

Robinson made his debut as an Oriole in 1955 and collected 2,848 hits in the regular season; however, no amount of work could make up for his basic lack of speed; he grounded into more double plays than any other ALer (297) and stole only 28 bases in his entire career.

He won the MVP award in 1964, hitting .317 with 28 homers and shone in postseason play. In 39 playoff and World Series games, he hit 5 homers and went 44-for-145, a .303 average. He hit an even .500 in the 1969 playoffs and .583 in 1970 as the O's crushed the Twins.

The 1970 World Series was the Brooks Robinson Show. In the opener he backhanded Lee May's bullet to keep the go-ahead run off base in the sixth inning and, with the score tied 3–3 in the seventh, homered over the left field fence to give the Birds a 4–3 win; in Game Two he knocked in the game-winner in a 6–5 squeaker.

All that was prologue to Game Three when Robinson did for fielding what Esther Williams did for swimsuits. He made sparkling plays on Tony Perez's shot down the line in the first, Tommy Helms's slow roller in the second, Johnny Bench's line drive in the sixth. He went 4-for-4 in Game Four and was named MVP when the Orioles won Game Five and the Series. The ultimate accolade came from Johnny Bench: "I will become a lefthanded hitter to keep the ball away from that guy."

When he retired in 1977, the Orioles gave credit where it was due by holding Thanks Brooks Day on September 18. The occasion drew the largest regular season crowd in Memorial Stadium's history. He entered the Hall of Fame in 1983.

FRANK ROBINSON

Right Field. Born Aug. 31, 1935 Beaumont, Tex. NL Rookie of the Year 1956, MVP 1961. Won AL MVP and Triple Crown 1966.

Frank Robinson was in a class by himself as a two-league player. He's the only man to be chosen MVP in both leagues, to hit All-Star Game homers for both, to hit 200 or more home runs in both, and to become the first black manager in both, piloting Cleveland from 1975 to 1977 and San Francisco from 1981 to 1984. In 1989, while managing Baltimore, he matched the Manager of the Year award he'd won in 1982 with the Giants.

Robinson also holds the record for hitting home runs in the most ballparks and, while his 586 homers place him fourth on the all-time list, Robinson also ranks in the top ten in career runs, RBI, and total bases. The complete player, he stole 20 bases or more three times, and even led the majors in intentional walks in four straight years (1961–1964).

Like all professionals, he produced under pressure. Robby made a dramatic debut as a player-manager, homering in his first at bat for the Indians. Similarly, he won the hearts of Baltimore fans shortly after joining the Orioles by hitting the first home run—a 540-foot shot—out of Memorial Stadium.

Robinson broke in with Cincinnati in 1956, tied Wally Berger's rookie record by hitting 38 homers, and was named Rookie of the Year. The first MVP award came in 1961, when he hit .323 with 37 homers, and stole 22 bases. In 1966 he hit 49 homers, knocked in 122 runs, and hit .316 to win the Triple Crown; that year he led Baltimore to a pennant and earned his second MVP award. Robby's home run off Don Drysdale in the World Series provided the only run in Game Four of an Oriole sweep, and he was named MVP of the Series as well.

He played in six All-Star Games for the National League and five for the American League. Yet, he will probably always be remembered as an Oriole. When he was traded to the Dodgers, number 20 became the first Baltimore uniform to be retired, and it's the one he wears in his 1982 Hall of Fame portrait.

JACKIE ROBINSON

Infielder/Outfielder. Born Jan. 31, 1919 Cairo, Ga. Died Oct. 24, 1972 Stamford, Conn. First black player in twentieth-century major leagues. NL Rookie of the Year 1947, MVP 1949.

If all Jackie Robinson did was to integrate baseball, that alone would have ensured his place in the game's history. For the story of his valiant effort and his role not only in baseball's history but that of our nation as well, see the essay by Jules Tygiel in this volume.

But Jackie Robinson did so much more than make baseball truly the national pastime. It is easy to overlook what a fabulous baseball player he was. He led the Brooklyn Dodgers to six pennants in ten years (plus their only world championship) and was named Rookie of the Year in 1947 and MVP in 1949.

While the Dodgers also had Hall of Famers Duke Snider, Pee Wee Reese, and Roy Campanella, Robinson forced them, by his example, to elevate their game, as he did all his other teammates. Cardinal second baseman Red Schoendienst once said, "If it wasn't for him, the Dodgers would be in the second division."

Driven by history and temperament, Robinson rattled pitchers by dancing off first base and had enough speed to steal home 19 times, 5 times in one season. He bettered .300 for six straight seasons, and retired with a .311 average. He was a regular at first, second, and third base and left field and led the league's second basemen in double plays four straight years (1949–1952).

UCLA's first four-letter man (baseball, basketball, football, and track), he went on to join the Army's Officer Candidate School. There he was court martialed, then acquitted, for refusing to sit in the back of a bus. After stints with the Kansas City Monarchs and the Dodgers' Montreal Royals farm club, he made his major league debut with the Dodgers in 1947 at the advanced age of twenty-eight; Robby hit .297, scored 125 runs, and led them to a pennant. That fall he finished second in a poll only to crooner Bing Crosby as the most popular man in America.

Robinson, in just his second year, became the Dodgers' team leader. He started on the All-Star team for the first of five times (four as a second baseman) in 1949, led the league in hitting, was named MVP, and led the Dodgers to another pennant.

On the last day of the 1951 season, with Brooklyn

needing to win to force a playoff with the Giants, Robinson made a spectacular, game-saving grab of Eddie Waitkus's liner to send the game into extra innings, then won it with a homer in the fourteenth. The Dodgers fell short of the pennant that year thanks to Bobby Thomson, but recaptured the flag in four of Robinson's final five seasons.

Fifteen years after he'd integrated baseball, Robinson integrated the Baseball Hall of Fame.

PETE ROSE

Infielder/Outfielder. Born Apr. 14, 1941 Cincinnati, Oh. NL Rookie of the Year 1963, MVP 1973. Holds major league records for games played (3,562); most seasons, 200 or more hits (10); most lifetime hits (4,256).

In 1989 Commissioner A. Bartlett Giamatti suspended Pete Rose from baseball for life for gambling. In 1990 Rose served five months in prison for tax evasion. It all seemed a long way since spring training in 1963, when Rose ran out a walk and Whitey Ford dubbed him "Charlie Hustle."

Sadly, Rose is ineligible to be voted into the Hall of Fame, an honor he deserves for his accomplishments on the field. Rose was named Player of the Decade (1970–1979) by *The Sporting News,* played in sixteen All-Star Games, and holds the record for starting at most different positions (five)—first, second, and third bases, and left and right fields. He also played on three championship teams in six years—the 1975 and 1976 Reds and the 1980 Phillies. Rose holds playoff records for most hits (45) and batted .381 in 118 playoff at bats.

He grew up in Cincinnati and credited his father Harry, a former semipro football player, with influencing him to become an athlete. "He wanted me to share his love of sports and I did. One time Mom sent him to the store to buy a pair of shoes for my sister. Instead, he came back with a pair of boxing gloves for me."

In 1963 Rose hustled his way onto the Reds and turned out to be the sparkplug of the developing Big Red Machine. In 1970 Rose led the league in hits (205) for the third time. He repeated in 1972 and, in 1975 and 1976, he led the league in doubles and runs scored both times. In each of those years the Reds won the pennant.

In December 1978, the man who once said, "I'd go through hell in a gasoline suit to keep playing baseball," signed a four-year 3.2 million contract with the Phils to become the highest-paid player in team sports. Six years later, after playing briefly with the Expos, he returned to Cincinnati where he became a player-manager, breaking Ty Cobb's record for career hits. He retired as a player after the 1986 season and in six years as manager brought the Reds home second three times without winning a division title.

AMOS RUSIE

Pitcher. Born May 31, 1871 Indianapolis, Ind. Died Dec. 6, 1942 Seattle, Wash.

When Walter Johnson came along in 1907, writers seeking to compliment the young fireballer called him "another Rusie."

Baseball paid Rusie the ultimate compliment in 1893 when it changed the rules because of him. The mound was moved back from 50 feet to 60 feet, 6 inches, and several

authorities claim the change was intended to make Rusie's heat less intimidating. (Rusie's first catcher, Dick Buckley, padded his glove with a thin sheet of lead to help absorb the impact of Rusie's hummer.) The Hoosier led the league in strikeouts five years out of six and won 30 games or more four years in a row.

The stocky righthander (6'1", 200) beat Boston and Washington in exhibition games before joining Indianapolis of the NL in 1889; when the franchise folded, Rusie and seven other players became Giants for $60,000. He arrived as a star in 1890, striking out 341 batters to lead the league. The media hero of his day, "the Hoosier Thunderbolt" was mentioned in a Mr. Dooley story as well as a Weber and Fields vaudeville skit; Lillian Russell, the sex symbol of that era, begged for an introduction to Rusie and got it.

At the end of the 1892 season the Giants, hoping to save half a month's pay, released him under a "gentlemen's agreement" that no club would sign him . . . but the White Stockings did, for $6,250 plus a $2,000 bonus. The Giants eventually bought the contract back, then tried to count the bonus as part of Rusie's salary.

Rusie prevailed but in crossing swords with Giant boss Andrew Freedman he had bought a heap of trouble. Rusie later was fined for missing curfew and for thumbing his nose at Freedman in public, who withheld $200 from his last paycheck of 1895. Rusie pioneered the holdout, missing the entire 1896 season. He sued for damages and, just before the 1897 season, the NL owners pooled $5,000 to settle the suit.

Rusie picked up where he'd left off and went 28–10. He won 20 in 1898; however, he hurt his arm making a pickoff throw, and 1898 was his last full season. He stayed home in Washington State to tend to his ailing wife and was disciplined by the Giants yet again. After sitting out a two-year suspension, he was traded to the Reds for Christy Mathewson. Matty at this point had no major league wins behind him but 373 ahead; Rusie had 245 in his pocket but, alas, none ahead. He started just two games, was blasted as he had never been in his prime, and retired. He was elected to the Hall of Fame in 1977.

GEORGE HERMAN "BABE" RUTH

Right Field. Born Feb. 6, 1895 Baltimore, Md. Died Aug. 16, 1948 New York, N.Y. Holds major league records for highest slugging percentage, season (.847, 1920) and lifetime (.690), most home runs by lefthanded batter (714), most years leading league in home runs (twelve).

Babe Ruth was one of baseball's best pitchers, its greatest player, greatest public figure, and the greatest hero in American sports.

When he was seven, George Herman Ruth was committed to Baltimore's St. Mary's Industrial School for repeated theft. Father Gilbert of St. Mary's later released him to pitch for the International League Baltimore Orioles and persuaded Orioles' owner-manager, Jack Dunn, to become Ruth's guardian, making Ruth his "Babe."

In 1914 Ruth was bought by the Red Sox, farmed out to Providence, and brought back to Boston after winning 22 games. He won 18 games for the big club in 1915, followed up with 23 wins in 1916, and pitched the longest complete game victory in World Series history that fall, a fourteen-inning 2–1 win over the Dodgers. The Babe became primarily an outfielder in 1918 (though he still pitched enough to go 13–7 in 1918 and 9–5 the following year). He left the mound in 1919 (not counting five cameo appearances over the next fourteen years, each of which he won) as the only man to have pitched more than 1,000 innings and have a lifetime batting average over .300 (.304).

In 1918 Ruth led the league in home runs (with 11) for the first of a record twelve times. Harry Frazee, Red Sox owner and a theatrical producer deep in debt, was forced to sell him to the Yankees that December. Now playing his home games in the friendly Polo Grounds, which the Yanks shared with the Giants, Ruth changed the game by hitting 54 homers; the rest of the American League had only 315. His slugging average of .847 has never been approached, except by the Babe himself the following year, when he produced a mark of .846.

Fans rushed to see him in his first year in New York, producing the first million-plus attendance in baseball history and spurring the Yankees to erect a superstadium in 1923, "The House That Ruth Built." That year he hit .393 to lead the Yankees to their third straight pennant and first World Series their first of twenty-two World Series titles. He dominated the 1923 Series, hitting three home runs and batting .368.

From 1926 to 1930, he led the league in home runs every year and tied Lou Gehrig for the lead in 1931. Three years later, Ruth asked to manage the Yankees and was chagrined when owner Jacob Ruppert offered him New York's top farm club instead. He signed with the Braves and had a final moment of glory on May 25, 1935, hitting 3 home runs in a game, one of them a prodigious shot over the right-field roof at Pittsburgh's Forbes Field. The Babe retired a few weeks later with 714 home runs, a lifetime average of .342, and the highest slugging percentage in history (.690). In the inaugural ballot for the Hall of Fame the following year, he became one of the Founding Five members.

NOLAN RYAN
Pitcher. Born Jan. 31, 1947 Refugio, Tex. Holds major league record for no-hitters (7) and lifetime strikeouts (5,714). Add up the lifetime strikeouts of Vida Blue (2,175), Hal Newhouser (1,796), and Carl Hubbell (1,677), and you still have 66 fewer than Nolan Ryan had all by himself.
The career of baseball's strikeout king parallels that of Sandy Koufax—the great fastball and overpowering curve, the control problems, early failure, final success— with Ryan's longevity being the obvious difference. Koufax retired at thirty-two, an age at which Ryan was leading the league in strikeouts for the sixth of twelve times.

Lynn Nolan Ryan was selected by the Mets on the eighth round of the free-agent draft in June 1965, when Tom Seaver was graduating from USC. In 1969 Seaver was the toast of the baseball world after winning 25 games in the regular season; Ryan was, by contrast, 6–3 as a relief pitcher although he saved Game Three of the World Series.

Traded to the Angels for Jim Fregosi, Ryan blossomed all at once, just as Koufax had a decade earlier. From 1972 to 1974, Ryan had a record of 62–48, with 1,079 strike-

outs in 943 innings. In an eight-day period in 1972 he fanned 15 Rangers, 16 Red Sox, and 16 A's, on his way to winning 19 games, 9 of them shutouts. In 1973 he was even better, no-hitting the Royals and the Tigers. Despite a torn calf muscle, he fanned Rich Reese for his 383rd and final K of the season, breaking Koufax's record for strikeouts in a season.

On August 12, 1974, he struck out 19 Red Sox to tie the record held by former teammate Tom Seaver and Steve Carlton. One month later he notched his third no-hitter, against the Twins. He tied Koufax with number four on June 1, 1975, beating the Orioles, 1-0. In 1979 Ryan signed with the Houston Astros as a free agent.

Back in the NL, he eclipsed Koufax's record for no-hitters by beating the Dodgers, 5–0, at the Astrodome on September 26, 1981 and he led NL pitchers in that strike-shortened year with a 1.69 ERA. In 1983 he broke Walter Johnson's record for career strikeouts. Signing with the Texas Rangers after the 1988 season for what was antici-pated to be his fading farewell tour, Ryan instead turned up the heat. He added a sixth no-hitter in 1990 on the road against the A's and a seventh at home against Toronto.

RYNE SANDBERG
Second Baseman. Born Sept. 18, 1959 Spokane, Wash. NL MVP 1984.
The Cubs weren't looked upon as a contender in 1984, but Ryne Sandberg changed that in a nationally televised game against the Cardinals. In both the ninth and tenth innings, Sandberg homered against Bruce Sutter to tie the game and went 5-for-6 with seven RBI in a game the Cubs won, 12–11. Cards manager Whitey Herzog said, "One day I thought he was one of the best players in the NL. The next day I think he's one of the best players I've ever seen."

Sandberg attracted a lot of attention for his defense in 1990, by which time he'd gone nearly a year without making an error. The streak started on June 21, 1989, and ended on May 17, 1990; by that time, Sandberg had played in 123 consecutive games and accepted 582 chances without making an error, both records for all infielders except first basemen. Even more incredible, Sandberg put together streaks of 30 or more errorless games fifteen times.

He grew up in Spokane, where he was the quarterback on *Parade* magazine's high school All-America team. Drafted by the Phillies, he played at Wichita, Spartan-burg, and Reading and spent winter ball learning all the infield positions, because the Phillies saw him as a utility man. Dealt to Chicago as a throw-in in a swap of short-stops Larry Bowa and Ivan DeJesus, Sandberg made the team as a third baseman, moving to second in 1983 when the Cubs signed Ron Cey.

Second baseman Sandberg became the first player to change positions and win a Gold Glove; he has since won eight more. In 1984 Jim Frey signed on as the manager and convinced Sandberg that he could become a power hitter by turning on 2–0 or 3–1 pitches. "Coaches and managers had always told me to hit the ball on the ground. He told me to swing for power and gave me confidence." Not coincidentally, the Cubs caught fire as a team, took the Eastern Division, and narrowly missed winning the pennant; Sandberg was named MVP.

After the 1991 season, Sandberg signed a contract which paid him $7.1 million a year. In 1992, he hit .304, his fourth .300-plus season, and hit 26 homers for the second straight year.

He retired early in the 1994 season but returned to the Cubs in 1996.

RON SANTO

Third Baseman. Born Feb. 25, 1940 Seattle, Wash. Holds major league record for most times leading the league in total chances (nine), third baseman .

Ron Santo was the NL's best third baseman in the 1960s, the senior circuit's version of Brooks Robinson.

Although he won fewer Gold Gloves than Robinson, he set a major league record by leading third basemen in total chances the most times (nine) and shares NL records for leading the most times in putouts and assists (7) and double plays (6).

With 342 career homers, he was also a disciplined batter who led the league in walks four times and twice in on-base percentage.

The durable Santo missed just 23 games in a ten-year period and played from 1961 to 1971 without injury. Bill James has plumped for Santo as a Hall of Famer, as have the editors of *Total Baseball*; James ranks him as the seventy-first best player of all time, ahead of contemporaries Roberto Clemente and Billy Williams.

When Santo started out at San Antonio, he had such a wild arm, according to pitcher Jim Brosnan, that the GM "was going to sell first base box seats at a premium since fans who sat there were pretty sure to get a ball." Santo benefited from the coaching of Grady Hatton and was a polished third sacker by the time he reached Chicago. in his Cub debut he also knocked in five runs in a doubleheader.

If Billy Williams played in the shadow of Ernie Banks, Santo was even more invisible. Using the Total Player Rating, Santo was the best player in the NL in both 1966 and 1967 by a wide margin, yet finished thirteenth and fourth respectively in MVP voting. When the Cubbies came close to winning the division, in 1969, Santo led the league in runs produced (191) and drove in a career-high 123 runs.

Santo was also a success in business. He owned a printing company, started a baseball school, and got the rights to sell Pro's Pizza at Wrigley Field. (Every cover had a round baseball card of a Cub hero.) When the Cubs had a Day for him, he revealed that he had been diabetic since age eighteen; Santo buttons were sold, and all proceeds went to the Diabetes Association.

On December 11, 1973, he became the first ten-year veteran to veto a trade to another team, the Angels. (Given the timing, wits called this contract provision the "Santo clause.") Santo instead moved to the South Side and played second base with the White Sox, retiring after an unsatisfying 1974 season. He joined the Cub broadcast team in 1990.

MIKE SCHMIDT

Third Baseman. Born Sept. 27, 1949 Dayton, Oh. Holds major league record for most home runs by a third baseman (509 of his total 548).

Philadelphia's famous boobirds even booed baseball's greatest third baseman in 1978. They held Mike Schmidt's light hitting accountable for playoff losses to the Reds in 1976 and the Dodgers in 1977 and 1978.

When the Phillies beat Houston to face Kansas City in the 1980 World Series, Schmidt turned the boos to cheers. He:

• scored two runs in Game One;
• doubled in the winning run in Game Two;
• homered in a losing cause in Game Three;
• hit a two-run homer and singled to start a rally in the ninth inning of Game Five;
• singled in the first two runs in Game Six to win the championship.

Schmidt hit .381 and was named MVP of the Series to match the MVP award he'd won in the regular season, the first of three he earned. Over eighteen seasons, Schmidt homered more often than any other third baseman (509), hit 30 or more homers thirteen times, started seven All-Star Games, and won ten Gold Gloves, nine of them consecutively.

The shortstop on *The Sporting News* College All-America team for 1971 and the Pacific Coast League's All-Star second baseman the next year, he became the Phils' regular third baseman in 1973. He had a disastrous year, striking out 136 times in 367 at bats and hitting .196, the lowest average compiled that season by any major league regular.

One year later he led the NL in homers (36) for the first of three consecutive seasons and batted in 116 runs. He told *Sport* that winter ball in Puerto Rico had made the difference. "I found a swing that made things happen . . . I was standing at the plate nice and relaxed and that sucker went off my bat a mile."

On April 17, 1976, he became the tenth major leaguer to hit four home runs in a game, as the Phillies beat the Cubs, 18–16. That same year he set a record for assists in a 162-game season (404) and topped the NL six more times to tie Ron Santo's record, as well as tying him in leading the league in double plays with six.

In the strike-shortened 1981 season, he led the majors in homers (31), RBI (91), slugging (.644), and total bases (228) to earn his second consecutive MVP award. Fans named him the greatest Phillies player ever in 1983. Three years later, he led the league in homers (37) and RBI (119) and became the only three-time NL MVP besides Stan Musial and Roy Campanella. He retired in 1989 and was named to the Hall of Fame in 1995.

TOM SEAVER

Pitcher. Born Nov. 17, 1944 Fresno, Cal. Holds major league record for most consecutive years with 200 or more strikeouts (9). NL Cy Young Award 1969, 1973, 1975.

Tom Seaver almost single-handedly turned the Mets from laughingstock to champion.

In their first four years, the Mets had a winning percentage of .294; four years later, thanks to Seaver, they won 100 games, swept the Braves in the playoffs, and stunned the Orioles in five games to become world champions. Over a decade after he last pitched for them, Seaver remains the Mets' team leader in wins (198), shutouts (44), and strikeouts (2,541). He won 311 games in all and three Cy Young Awards, and struck out a record 200 batters in nine straight seasons (1968-76).

He almost began his career as a Brave, signing a contract with Atlanta that violated baseball's college rule, according to Commissioner William Eckert. Three clubs wanted to sign him—the Indians, Phillies, and Mets. On April 3, 1966, Eckert picked the Mets' name out of a hat, and the Mets signed Seaver to a $50,000 bonus and assigned him to Jacksonville.

Sixteen months later he made his first of eight All-Star Game appearances and capped the season by by being named National League Rookie of the Year. Seaver won 16 games each of his first two years and, in 1969, he was 25-7 to lead the Mets to the World Series. In the Mets' five-game defeat of the Baltimore Orioles, he won Game 4, 2-1 in ten innings.

On April 22, 1970, Seaver was presented with his first Cy Young Award at Shea Stadium and celebrated by setting the record for consecutive strikeouts in one game, fanning the last 10 Padres to reach a game total of 19. Seaver won 20 games or more in 1971, 1972, 1975, and 1977, when he was unexpectedly traded to the Reds.

He no-hit the Cardinals in 1978, and went 14-2 in 1981, his best won-lost percentage; however, injuries made 1982 his worst—a 5-13 record and a 5.50 ERA—and he improved only slightly upon his return to the Mets in 1983. After joining the White Sox, Tom turned Terrific again, and, at 39, wound up leading the Sox in wins (15) and shutouts (4), never missing a turn in the rotation. In 1985 he was even better, winning 16 games, among them his 300th.

He retired after the 1986 season with 61 career shutouts (seventh on the all-time list); was fourth in career strikeouts; and compiled a sterling 2.85 ERA. He entered the Hall of Fame in 1992.

AL SIMMONS
Left Field. Born May 22, 1902 Milwaukee, Wis. Died May 26, 1956 Milwaukee, Wis. AL MVP 1929.
Striding toward third base, leaving the impression that he hit with his "foot in the bucket" (a venerable baseball term for a frightened batter, going back to the days when a water bucket sat at the end of the players' bench) didn't bother Al Simmons. He bettered .300 for eleven straight years, won back-to-back batting titles, hit .329 in nineteen World Series games, and .334 lifetime. Though unheralded for his defense, Simmons led the league in fielding twice. Joe Cronin said, "There never was a better left fielder in hustling to the foul line to turn a double into a single."

Born Aloysius Szymanski in Milwaukee in 1902, he turned pro with the Milwaukee Brewers in 1922, taking the name Simmons from a newspaper ad. Sold to the A's, Simmons worried that Connie Mack would change his stance, but Mack told him, "You can hold the bat in your teeth, provided you hit safely and often." Simmons hit .387 as a sophomore and led the league in hits (253), still a record for righthanded batsmen.

In 1929, he helped the A's to a pennant with 34 homers and a league-leading 157 RBI and was named MVP. He drove in four runs in Game Two of the Series with a single and a homer, homered to start the famous ten-run rally in Game Four, and singled and doubled in Game Seven, scoring the Series-winning run on Bing Miller's double. If anything, Simmons improved in 1930, leading the league in runs (152) and hitting (.381), and homering in Games One and Six as the A's won their second straight championship.

Simmons held out in 1931, and, on Opening Day, Mack announced he would not play for the A's. Taking a cab to Shibe Park, Mack reached into his pocket to pay; the driver declined, saying, "If you can't afford Simmons, you can't afford me either." Hours later, Simmons signed a three-year contract and homered on the first pitch thrown to him.

In 1931, the Duke of Milwaukee hit .390 to lead the league for the second straight year and homered twice in the World Series, but he never again reached such heights. He said later, "When I finally decided I had it made, I was never again the ballplayer I was when I was hungry." Simmons went on to play with six other teams before finishing his career in a third tour of duty with the A's. He was named to the Hall of Fame in 1953.

GEORGE SISLER
First Baseman. Born Mar. 24, 1893 Manchester, Oh. Died Mar. 26, 1973 St. Louis, Mo. Holds major league record for hits in a season (257); AL MVP 1922.
George Sisler had the defensive ability, foot speed, and batting prowess to equal any first baseman. Originally a pitcher, Sisler was clearly more valuable as an everyday player. He led the league's first basemen in assists a record seven times, stole home nineteen times, and compiled a .340 career average.

In 1920 he played every inning of every game, had 140 assists, started 13 first-to-short-to-first double plays, stole 42 bases, batted .407, banged out 19 homers, and established what may be an unbeatable major league record with 257 hits. Two years later he led the league in hits, runs, doubles, and average, batting .420. Although Sisler earned the first League Award (MVP), the Yanks won the pennant by a single game, a sad end to a great season; Sisler never came close to another chance to play in a World Series.

Born in Manchester, Ohio, Sisler was an all-around athlete and signed with Akron of the Ohio-Penn League, although he received no money and never played for Akron. (He reported but was told the team didn't have a uniform small enough.) Instead, he starred for Branch Rickey at the University of Michigan. Rickey became a Browns scout in 1912, moved up to manager a year later, and signed Sisler when he graduated in 1915 with a degree in mechanical engineering.

The Pirates, who had purchased the Akron contract from Columbus, also claimed Sisler, and the case was brought before the three-man National Commission, a predecessor of the commissioner's office. The NL and AL presidents voted along party lines, but Reds president Garry Herrmann broke ranks; Sisler became a Brown.

As great as he was, Sisler might have been even better had he not contracted poisonous sinusitis and missed the entire 1923 season. Although he had three more 200-plus-hit seasons thereafter, he said, "I didn't consider that real good hitting." He once told *Baseball* magazine that his ambition was to "hang up a higher average than Ty Cobb's," and, indeed, Sisler's .41979 average in 1922 did edge the .41962 Cobb had in 1911. In fact, Cobb called him "the nearest thing to a perfect ballplayer."

Sisler was elected to the Hall of Fame in 1939, and in the 1940s and 1950s tutored two other Hall of Famers—Duke Snider and Roberto Clemente.

OZZIE SMITH

Shortstop. Born Dec. 26, 1954 Mobile, Ala. Holds NL record for most Gold Gloves (13).

At his retirement after the 1996 season, Ozzie Smith was in a class by himself at shortstop. Thomas Boswell of the *Washington Post* once wrote of him, "Instead of '1' his number should be '8,' but turned sideways because the possibilities he brings to his position are almost infinite."

The NL's career leader in Gold Gloves and arguably baseball's best-fielding shortstop of all time, Smith has also made himself into an above-average hitter and high-average base-stealer. But what makes him a lock for the Hall of Fame when he hangs up his glove is . . . his glove. In the course of his career, he saved his teams 242 runs beyond what an average shortstop would have done, a mark unequaled at the position in this century.

"The Wizard of Oz" attended Locke High School in Los Angeles with Eddie Murray, and the Padres picked him in the fourth round of the 1977 free agent draft. After winning two Gold Gloves for San Diego and setting a record for assists in 1980 (621), Smith was traded to the Cardinals. Two years later, the Cardinals won their first championship in fifteen years as Smith led the league's shortstops in fielding for the first of a record seven times. (He also whacked two home runs, doubling his four-year output in San Diego.)

Learning to fit his talents to Busch Stadium, the switch-hitting Smith improved his batting average to .276 by 1985, when the Cardinals won their division again. Smith blossomed in the playoffs against the Dodgers, batting .435. With the score tied, 2–2, in Game Five, he homered in the bottom of the ninth to give the Cardinals a 3–2 edge in games.

In 1987, for the fifth time in Smith's six years in St. Louis, the Cardinals led the league in team fielding. They won another pennant but lost a seven-game Series to the Royals. That year, the Wizard of Ahs finally reached the .300 mark (.303), won the accustomed Gold Glove, and finished second to Andre Dawson in voting for the Most Valuable Player.

In 1991 he set a record for NL shortstops, committing just 8 errors in 150 games, and won his thirteenth consecutive Gold Glove in 1992 to break a tie with Willie Mays and Roberto Clemente. At retirement, he had amassed 580 stolen bases and was major league baseball's career leader in assists for shortstops.

EDWIN "DUKE" SNIDER

Center Field. Born Sept. 19, 1926 Los Angeles, Cal. Hit 40 or more home runs in five consecutive seasons (1952-56).

When New York had Willie (Mays), Mickey (Mantle), and the Duke (Snider), Snider always got third billing. Yet he hit more home runs in the 1950s than Mays, Mantle, or any other major leaguer (326) and tied Ralph Kiner's NL record of hitting 40 or more homers in five straight seasons. Kiner said of his fielding, "I'd say Duke covers

more ground, wastes less motion, and is more consistent than anyone since DiMaggio."

Snider chose the Dodgers because of his admiration for Pete Reiser and Pee Wee Reese. General manager Branch Rickey put him in the batting cage three hours every day with Hall of Famer George Sisler—but not to hit. Snider recalls, "I was just supposed to call every pitch, ball or strike. It was amazing how wrong I was at the beginning. But I learned."

The Duke became a regular in 1949, hitting .292 with 23 homers, and clinched the pennant on the last day of the season by driving in the winning run. His World Series debut was a disaster (a .143 average and 8 strikeouts), but he redeemed himself in the 1952 World Series with ten hits, four of them home runs to tie the mark then shared by Babe Ruth and Lou Gehrig.

In 1955 Snider led the league in RBI (136), led for a third time in runs scored (126), hit .309, and had 42 homers. He hit four more homers in the 1955 Series as Brooklyn won its only World Series and became the only man to hit four dingers in a Series twice. After the season, he was named Player of the Year by *The Sporting News*.

He led the league in home runs (43) in 1956, the only time he did so. The Dodgers moved to Los Angeles for the 1958 season, depriving the Duke of the cozy dimensions of Ebbets Field. In 1959 he still had enough muscle to send out 23 homers and propel Los Angeles to the world championship, in which he homered again. That was Snider's last Series; he still holds the NL record for career World Series homers (11) and RBI (26).

After two seasons as a Met and, even more incongruously, as a Giant, he retired with a lifetime batting average of .295 and 407 homers. He managed several Dodger farm teams, scouted for the Dodgers and Padres, and broadcast games for those two teams as well as the Expos. He was elected to the Hall of Fame in 1980.

WARREN SPAHN

Pitcher. Born Apr. 23, 1921 Buffalo, N.Y. Holds major league record for most games won by lefthanded pitcher (363).

Stan Musial once said, "I don't think Spahn will ever get into the Hall of Fame. He'll never stop pitching."

Musial's point was well taken. Warren Spahn pitched long enough to be a Brave under Casey Stengel in 1942 and a Met under Stengel again in 1965. In between, he became the winningest lefthander in major league history, emerging victorious in 363 games. He put 15,741 batters out of their misery, won 20 games or more in thirteen seasons, and had a lifetime ERA of 3.09.

Not regarded as a strikeout artist, he nonetheless recorded 2,583 whiffs in his career and led the NL four straight years, from 1949 to 1952. He led the league in wins five times outright, had the most shutouts four times, and compiled the lowest ERA three times. He also started more double plays than any other major league pitcher (82) and also leads all NL pitchers in hitting home runs (35).

Brought up to the Boston Braves in 1942, he was sent back down when Stengel ordered him to throw at Pee Wee Reese and he refused. He enlisted in the Army, suffered shrapnel wounds in a battle along the Rhine, and was awarded the Purple Heart. He made his mark in 1947 by posting a 21–10 record, leading the league in ERA (2.33) and innings pitched (289⅔).

In 1948 the Braves won the pennant, fueled by the hopes for "Spahn and Sain and two days of rain." The franchise moved to Milwaukee in 1953. That year Spahn pitched in his third of seven All-Star Games and got the win. When the Braves won pennants in 1957 and 1958, he led the league in wins both years. He was given the Cy Young Award in 1957 (when there was only one award for both leagues) and won two games in the 1958 Series, shutting out the Yanks in Game 4.

When the 1960 season started, Spahn had won 267 major league games without pitching a no-hitter. He remedied this oversight on September 15, striking out 15 Phillies to win his 20th game of the season. Five days after his fortieth birthday, in 1961, Spahn pitched his second no-hitter.

After a losing season in 1964 (his first) and brief stays with the Mets and Giants in 1965, he coached in Mexico City and Japan. In line with Musial's prediction, Spahn interrupted his retirement to pitch in the Mexican League, thus delaying the onset of the mandatory five-year inactive period before induction into the Hall of Fame. Finally, however, Spahn left the mound for good and was elected to the Hall of Fame in 1973.

TRIS SPEAKER

Center Fielder. Born Apr. 4, 1888 Hubbard City, Tex. Died Dec. 8, 1958 Lake Whitney, Tex. Holds records for assists (450) and double plays (135) by an outfielder.

Like a wide receiver anticipating the throw of the quarterback, Tris Speaker revolutionized center fielding by moving before the pitch.

He acquired the knack as a Red Sox rookie, fielding fungos hit by Cy Young and trying to figure out which way the ball would go. He says, "In a few days I knew just by the way he swung whether the ball would go to my right or left. Then I began to study the batter during a game; when he started his swing, I knew if he would hit to my left or right and I was on my way."

Getting a head start allowed him to play shallow. The "Gray Eagle" participated in a record four unassisted double plays and set a record for outfielders with 448 career assists. He led AL outfielders seven times in putouts, five times in double plays (some of them 4–8–3 or 6–8–3), three times in assists, and twice in fielding. Just as much a threat offensively, Speaker hit .345 during a twenty-two-year career, had eighteen .300-plus seasons, and compiled 3,514 hits.

Two of baseball's shrewdest operators didn't sign him: Pirate boss Barney Dreyfuss because "he smoked cigarettes"; and Giant manager John McGraw because "I had all the outfielders I needed." Speaker paid his way to the Red Sox training camp in Little Rock, Arkansas. Boston optioned Speaker and bartered him to Little Rock in lieu of their $400 rental fee. Several months later, he was burning up the league and became the Red Sox starting center fielder in 1909.

A star by 1912, Speaker tied Home Run Baker for most home runs (10) that year, led the league in doubles (53), hit .383, and won the Chalmers Award (a forerunner of the MVP award), and hit .340 as the Red Sox beat the Giants in the World Series. In 1916 Speaker, newly arrived in Cleveland, won the batting title (.386) from Ty Cobb, interrupting what would have been an uninterrupted string of 13 titles, and also led the league in doubles (41), hits (211), and slugging percentage (.503).

He took over as manager of the Indians during the 1919 season; a year later he steered them to a pennant and a World Series win over the Dodgers. Speaker was elected to the Hall of Fame in 1937 and returned to the Tribe as a coach during the Bill Veeck era.

WILVER "WILLIE" STARGELL

Left Field. Born Mar. 6, 1941. Earlsboro, Okla. NL co-MVP 1979.

Wilver Stargell was the Pittsburgh Pirates' Gold Star Father in 1979.

When a teammate distinguished himself with a clutch hit, heads-up move on the basepaths, or fielding gem, "Pops" Stargell marked the occasion with a gold star ceremony. Soon ballplayers earning $300,000 a year were putting out a little bit extra to get a gold "Stargell Star" and by the end of the season, the Pirates had the whole country singing "We Are Family," earning enough gold stars to become World Champions.

At thirty-nine, two years after his career had apparently ended, Stargell set a record for most MVP awards in a season. He was named MVP of both the playoffs and the World Series, divided regular season MVP honors with Keith Hernandez, and shared *Sports Illustrated*'s Sportsman of the Year award with Steeler Terry Bradshaw.

Many of his 475 career home runs were titanic. Only eighteen balls were hit out of Forbes Field in sixty-one years (beginning with Babe Ruth's epic blast on May 25, 1935); Stargell hit seven of them. Only one player hit a ball completely out of Dodger Stadium—Stargell, who did it twice.

Stargell's 1977 season was plagued with injuries, but Pops hit 28 homers and drove in 97 runs in 1978 to earn Comeback Player of the Year. After the gold stars came out during spring training in 1979, Stargell hit 32 homers and the Pirates won the division, finishing two games ahead of Montreal.

In the playoffs against Cincinnati, he broke an 11-inning 2–2 tie with a three-run homer and homered again in Game Three as Pittsburgh swept the Big Red Machine. In the World Series against Baltimore, Stargell homered as the Orioles won the opener and went 3-for-5 with a homer in Game Four; however, Baltimore came up with six runs in the eighth inning to win, 9–6, and open up a 3–1 lead in games.

With the Pirates trailing, 1–0, in the bottom of the sixth inning of Game 5, Stargell hit a sacrifice fly to even the score and later singled to start a three-run inning. The Pirates won, 7–1. After John Candelaria and Kent Tekulve shut Baltimore out in Game Six to bring the Buccos even, Stargell put on a batting show in the finale, going 4-for-5 with a two-run homer. Overall, he set a Series record with seven extra-base hits. He became a Hall of Famer in 1988.

SAM THOMPSON

Right Field. Born Mar. 5, 1860 Danville, Ind. Died Nov. 7, 1922 Detroit, Mich.

Sam Thompson was the power hitter par excellence of the nineteenth century and set a record for lifetime home runs that wasn't broken until Babe Ruth came along. Also possessed of a legendary throwing arm, "Big Sam" Thompson was still so highly regarded that he played eight games alongside rookie Ty Cobb in the Tiger outfield in 1906—at age 46.

The fifth of eleven children, Thompson started his big league career late. He played on the Danville team and worked in his father's carpentry business. When a scout offered to pay him the magnificent sum of $2.50 per game, Thompson joined Evansville of the Northwest League and hit .391 before the league folded. He signed with Indianapolis and, at age twenty-five, joined the NL Detroit Wolverines. When Gene Moriarty crashed into an outfield wall, Thompson took over and got 11 hits in his first 26 at bats. Moriarty never played again for Detroit.

Thompson was an innovator in the outfield, too. Possessed of a rifle arm, he is said to have originated the one-hop throw to the plate, trying to catch a runner from third. He was so successful at this technique that in 1886 he led the league's outfielders in double plays (11) for the first of two times. In 1887, "Big Sam" (6'2", 207) had an awesome season at the bat, leading the league in hits (203), triples (23), batting (.372), and slugging (.571). He drove in an astounding 1.31 runs per game. This was a record that only he would ever surpass, with 1.42 in 1894 and 1.39 in 1895; for comparison, Hack Wilson, when he drove in 190 in 1930, had a mark of 1.23.

A sore arm sidelined him for most of 1888, and he was unceremoniously sold to the Philadelphia Quakers (Phillies). In 1889 Thompson rebounded with 20 home runs to lead the league, picked up another hit crown in 1890 (172), and in 1891 managed to accumulate 32 assists. In 1894 he led the league in fielding (.977) and hit .407 as part of an all-.400-hitting outfield, along with Ed Delahanty, Billy Hamilton, and Tuck Turner. His last great offensive year was 1895, when Big Sam led the league in homers (18), RBI (165), and slugging (.654).

He still holds the major league record for ratio of RBI to games played (.923, nipping Lou Gehrig) and was named to the Hall of Fame in 1974.

HAROLD "PIE" TRAYNOR

Third Baseman. Born Nov. 11, 1899 Framingham, Mass. Died Mar. 16, 1972 Pittsburgh, Pa. Holds NL record for lifetime putouts by third baseman (2,288).

Pie Traynor was the first third baseman whom the baseball writers voted into the Hall of Fame. (The Veterans' Committee previously selected Jimmy Collins.)

Traynor was also named the major leagues' outstanding third baseman by *The Sporting News* seven times and finished in the top ten in MVP voting six times between 1925 and 1933. While some analysts downplay his offensive accomplishments today, Hall of Famers of his era—Mickey Cochrane, Bill Dickey, Charlie Gehringer, Rogers Hornsby, and Carl Hubbell—named him to their All-Time All-Star teams.

Traynor hit .320 lifetime with ten seasons above .300, knocked in 100 or more runs seven times, and never struck out more than 28 times in seventeen seasons. In the field, he led in assists three times, double plays four straight years, led in putouts seven times (a record tied by Puddin' Head Jones and Ron Santo), and set the NL record for career putouts (2,289).

As a child Traynor yearned to play for the Somerville, Massachusetts, parish team coached by Father Nangle; instead, he chased balls. Taken to the grocery store as a reward, he would invariably say, "I'll take pie, Father," the source of his nickname. He was originally a shortstop, but after Traynor made 12 errors in his 17-game trial in 1920, the Pirates acquired Rabbit Maranville. Traynor's fielding improved when he moved to third base, and he began to hit with more power when Rogers Hornsby switched him to a forty-two-ounce bat.

The Pirates won the pennant in 1925. Traynor singled and homered against Walter Johnson in his first two World Series at bats and hit .346 as the Pirates won in seven. The Pie Man's bases-loaded single on the last day of the 1927 season gave the Pirates another pennant, but the Bucs were swept by the Yankees of Ruth and Gehrig.

Traynor hit .356 in 1929 and had his best batting average, .366, in 1930, but his career was essentially ended in 1934 when catcher Jimmy Wilson fell across his right arm and broke it. Pie took over as player-manager and just missed leading Pittsburgh to a pennant in 1938, when the Cubs' Gabby Hartnett hit his "Homer in the Gloamin'."

In retirement, Traynor ran a sporting goods store with Honus Wagner, coached at Duquesne, and was active as a sportscaster in Pittsburgh for thirty-three years. He was elected to the Hall of Fame in 1948.

ARKY VAUGHAN

Shortstop. Born Mar. 9, 1912 Clifty, Ark. Died Aug. 30, 1952 Eagleville, Cal. His .385 average of 1935 is the NL record for shortstops in this century.

Arky Vaughan was, according to his Total Player Rating, the NL's leading player four times from 1934–1940.

Using a unique flat-footed stance, Vaughan hit well over .300 ten straight years, twelve times in all, and set an all-time record for the league's shortstops by hitting .385 in 1935. Although it has become chic to deride Vaughan's fielding, he led the league three times each in putouts and assists (and, yes, errors) when such slick-fielding shortstops as Billy Jurges, Dick Bartell, and Eddie Miller were in their prime.

Born in Clifty, Arkansas (hence his nickname), Joseph Floyd Vaughan grew up in California and was a football star at Fullerton High School. (Fellow student Richard M. Nixon picked Vaughan for his All-Time All-Stars.) Signed by the Pirates, he led the league in errors his first two years but improved with help from his roommate, coach Honus Wagner, and from Pie Traynor.

Vaughan was named to the All-Star team for the first of seven times in 1934 and became the first man to homer twice in the midsummer classic, in 1941. His lifetime All-Star Game average was .364.

Traded to the Dodgers after the 1941 season, Vaughan became embroiled in a dispute between pitcher Bobo Newsom and catcher Bobby Bragan in 1943. Manager Leo Durocher suspended Newsom, and Vaughan led a successful "strike," after which Durocher backed down. Despite leading the league in runs scored for the third time, Vaughan was fed up and retired.

When Durocher was suspended in 1947, Vaughan came back and hit .325 to help the Dodgers win a pennant. Jackie Robinson said, "He went out of his way to be nice to me when I was a rookie. I needed it." After a subpar 1948, he played briefly for San Francisco and retired.

On August 30, 1952, while fishing in Lost Lake, his companion tipped the boat over; Vaughan tried to rescue him but both went under and drowned. He was elected to the Hall of Fame in 1985. Among Hall of Fame shortstops, only Honus Wagner (.329) has a higher lifetime batting average than Vaughan (.318).

JOHN PETER "HONUS" WAGNER

Shortstop. Born Feb. 24, 1874 Carnegie, Pa. Died Dec. 6, 1955 Carnegie, Pa. Holds NL records for most years leading league in batting (eight) and most consecutive years hitting .300 or better (seventeen).

Honus Wagner and Babe Ruth finished in a tie behind Ty Cobb when the first players were voted into the Hall of Fame in 1936. The fan of today may look at the stats of these men and wonder why Wagner stands alongside the other two. Yet Bill Deane, in his "Awards and Honors" piece in this volume, credits Wagner with six "hypothetical" MVP awards during his career—for the years 1900–1903, 1907, and 1909, years in which no award was given. Only Babe Ruth dominated a league for so long a time.

John Peter Wagner became "Johannes" and, later, "Honus" or "Hans," just as Wagner's nationality, German (a "Deutschman") became "Dutchman," hence Wagner's nickname, "the Flying Dutchman." Bowlegged, he "looked like a hoop rolling down the baselines" but reached the majors with Louisville. When the city was dropped from the league, owner Barney Dreyfuss bought Pittsburgh and took Wagner with him.

In 1900 Wagner won his first of eight batting titles, an NL record. He was stationed all over the diamond until Frederick "Bones" Ely, the regular shortstop, begged off. Wagner made three errors in an inning, then got lucky. With men on first and second, he gave the signal for a pickoff play and dashed toward second; the pitcher delivered to the plate instead, resulting in a one-hopper that Wagner turned into a double play. Wagner called it "the best play I ever made."

The Dutchman led the Pirates to pennants in 1901, 1902, 1903, and 1909, when he outplayed Cobb, and his batting average didn't fall below .300 until 1914. Wagner led the league five times in RBI and stolen bases, six times in slugging, and seven times in doubles. When he retired as a player in 1917, he led the NL in hits, runs, singles, doubles, and triples.

After coaching at Carnegie Tech and owning a sporting goods store with Pie Traynor, Wagner fell on hard times. Early in 1933, Fred Lieb wrote a column about Wagner's plight, and new Pirate owner Bill Benswanger made him a coach. Honus boosted attendance and was given "Days," even in opposing cities.

In Larry Ritter's *The Glory of Their Times*, Paul Waner remembered, "He must have been sixty.... [He'd] get out there every once in a while [and take infield practice] ... a hush would come over the whole ballpark, and every player on both teams would stand there, like a bunch of little kids ... I'll never forget it."

ED WALSH

Pitcher. Born May 14, 1881 Plains, Pa. Died May 26, 1959 Pompano Beach, Fla. Holds major league record for lowest lifetime ERA (1.82).

Ty Cobb said of Ed Walsh, "When this big moose had his stuff, he was just unbeatable, that's all."

The big spitballer (6'1", 193) won 40 games one year, led the league in saves five times, and is baseball's all-time leader in career ERA (1.82). He also set several fielding records for pitchers and was the first AL pitcher to steal home twice. Walsh, who also helped design Comiskey Park, pleased the crowds by fungoing balls into the stands and was not entirely unaware of his talents. Sportswriter Charlie Dryden said of him, "He's the only man I ever saw who could strut standing still." He is thought by many students of the game and literature to have been Ring Lardner's model for Jack Keefe, the cocksure narrator of *You Know Me, Al.*

Walsh joined the White Sox soon after Elmer Stricklett taught him how to throw the spitball in 1904. Exhibiting the endurance which marked his career, he pitched two complete game wins against the Red Sox on September 6, 1905, and led the league in 1906 with 10 shutouts in the regular season. He also won two World Series games, striking out 12 Cubs in Game Three, a record which stood until 1929, and taking Game Five even though the "Hitless Wonders" made five errors behind him.

In 1907 lack of offense hurt Walsh, who was shut out eight times but still posted a 24–18 record and set major league records for assists and total chances by a pitcher.

He had a nearly perfect year in 1908, leading the league in wins (40), shutouts (11), starts, complete games, strikeouts, and saves and set a post-1900 record for innings pitched (464) which still stands.

Chicago, Detroit, St. Louis, and Cleveland were neck-and-neck all season long, and Walsh pitched seven times in the last nine games. He won a doubleheader against Boston September 29 but lost his best-pitched game of the season on October 2; Walsh struck out 15 in eight innings only to lose 1–0 to Addie Joss's perfect game.

Bedeviled by a lack of offense again in 1910, Walsh became the only pitcher to lead the league in ERA (1.27) and lose 20 games. His team hit 7 homers all season long, batted .211, and made 314 errors.

After winning 27 games in both 1911 and 1912, he suffered arm trouble and retired in 1917. Walsh was named to the Hall of Fame in 1946.

HOYT WILHELM

Pitcher. Born July 26, 1923 Huntersville, N.C. Holds major league record for games pitched (1,070) and most games won as a relief pitcher (124).

Hoyt Wilhelm, the first relief pitcher elected to the Hall of Fame, threw 36,000 knuckleballs to get there.

Pitching in twenty-one seasons, Wilhelm delivered those dipsy-doodles as an NL reliever, AL starter, and AL reliever. All told, he pitched in more games than any player in history (1,070), won the most in relief, (123) and finished the most (651).

After languishing in the minors, Wilhelm stuck with the Giants as a twenty-nine-year-old rookie and made a sensational debut in 1952, going 15–3 with 11 saves. He led the league in won-lost percentage (.833) and ERA (2.43) to become the first rookie ever to top his league in those two categories and the only rookie ever to win an ERA crown.

In 1955, Wilhelm was 4–1 but hadn't posted a single

save in 59 appearances. He was traded to St. Louis, sold to Cleveland, and was picked up on waivers by Baltimore, mostly because Oriole manager Paul Richards had caught knuckleballer Dutch Leonard; after he lost three starts, Knuckles knew his days as an Oriole were numbered.

With his career hanging by a thread, Wilhelm got one last chance on September 20, 1958, against the Yankees. He pitched a no-hitter, winning 1–0 on Gus Triandos's homer. In 1959 he won his first nine starts and went on to lead the league in ERA (2.19), thus becoming the only pitcher to turn the trick in both circuits.

Traded to the White Sox, Wilhelm began his third career, posting a 2.64 ERA and a career-high 21 saves in 1963 and outdoing himself in 1964 with 27 saves, 12 wins and an ultra-stingy 1.99 ERA; his ERA didn't rise above 2.00 for four more seasons as he compiled 98 saves and 41 wins with the White Sox.

In the expansion draft of 1969 he was picked by the new Kansas City Royals, traded to the Angels, and passed along to the Braves, helping them take their division by winning 2 games and saving 4 in 8 appearances. After stints with the Cubs and Dodgers, he was released five days short of his 49th birthday. He was elected to the Hall of Fame in 1985.

TED WILLIAMS

Left Field. Born Aug. 30, 1918 San Diego, Cal. AL MVP 1946, 1949. Highest on base percentage of all time (.483), second only to Babe Ruth in slugging percentage and production.

He'll never be remembered for his fielding, throwing, running, or leadership, but by any measure Ted Williams is the greatest hitter of his era and perhaps of all time.

Despite missing five seasons to military service, the "Splendid Splinter" holds the records for most consecutive years leading the league in runs scored (five) and walks (six) and for career on-base percentage (.483) He also won four home run crowns, six batting titles, led the AL in slugging nine times, and finished with a career batting average of .344 and 521 home runs. At the close of the 1950s *The Sporting News* named him Player of the Decade.

Williams broke in with the San Diego Padres of the Pacific Coast League in 1936. In 1938 he won the Triple Crown at Minneapolis and became the Red Sox regular right fielder in 1939, moving to left later on. He set the rookie record for RBI (145) to lead the AL. In 1941 his two-out, three-run homer off Claude Passeau won the All-Star Game and he concluded the year with a .406 batting average. He could have safeguarded his .400 average on the final day by sitting out, but instead he chose to play both ends of a doubleheader, going 6-for-8. He became the last player to top the magic number of .400, and the only one since 1930.

After winning the Triple Crown in 1942, the "Thumper" played for Uncle Sam from 1943 to 1945. He returned to star in the 1946 All-Star Game, hitting 2 homers and 2 singles, led the league in runs scored and slugging percentage, helped the Red Sox win the pennant, and was named Most Valuable Player. He won his second Triple Crown in 1947. In 1949 he led the league in homers (43) and RBI (159), hit .343, and was named Most Valuable Player for a second time.

At thirty-four, he flew thirty-nine combat missions for the Marines in Korea and returned late in 1953 to hit .407 with 13 homers in 37 games. He had one of his greatest seasons at age thirty-nine in 1957, hitting .388 to become the oldest player ever to lead the league in hitting. To prove it was no fluke, he led the league again in hitting in 1958 at age 40, hitting .328, and ended his career at 42, hitting .316 with 29 home runs, including one in his last at-bat. He entered the Hall of Fame in 1966.

DAVE WINFIELD

Right Field. Born Oct. 3, 1951 St. Paul, Minn. Oldest player to drive in 100 or more runs, 1992.

Dave Winfield was given a second chance and made the most of it.

Bedeviled by the memory a 1-for-22 batting slump in the 1981 World Series with the Yankees (and George Steinbrenner's subsequent characterization of him as "Mr. May," for his inability to produce in October), Winfield came to bat in the eleventh inning of Game Six in the 1992 Fall Classic as a member of the Toronto Blue Jays. With the score tied, 2–2, and two out, Winfield doubled down the left field line to give the Jays a 4–2 lead, and they hung on to win their first world championship.

It was sweet vindication for a man who had won seven Gold Gloves (two with the Padres, five with the Yankees), was an All-Star every year from 1977 to 1988, started All-Star Games in 1979, 1981, and every year from 1983 to 1988, and batted .361 in the twelve games.

Known as "Daddy Longlegs," the six-foot six-inch Winfield was a pitcher at the University of Minnesota, finished his senior year 13–1 and hit .400, and was the MVP of the College World Series. Drafted by the NBA's Atlanta Hawks, the ABA's Utah Stars, and the NFL's Minnesota Vikings—even though he had not played college football—Winfield was also selected by the Padres on June 5, 1973. Like Sandy Koufax and Al Kaline, Winfield had no minor league experience, and made his major league debut two weeks later.

In 1980, after leading the NL in RBI (118), he signed a ten-year free agent contract with the Yankees; however, misinterpreting a cost-of-living clause led Steinbrenner to owe Winfield an extra $7 million and started a simmering feud which resulted in the Yankee owner paying a convicted felon, Howard Spira, for allegedly damaging information about Winfield. The damage instead was done to Steinbrenner, who was banished from baseball by Commissioner Fay Vincent.

Despite his problems with Steinbrenner, Winfield knocked in 100 runs or more from 1982 to 1986, the first Yankee to turn the trick in five consecutive seasons since Joe DiMaggio. In 1984, Winfield consciously shortened his stroke in an attempt to win a batting title and came close, hitting .340 to finish three points behind Don Mattingly. He underwent back surgery and missed the 1989 season; he joined the Angels for 1990. With the Angels, he drove in 72 runs in 112 games and won the Comeback Player of the Year Award. He closed his career in 1995 with Cleveland, finishing with 465 career home runs, nineteenth behind Stan Musial and Willie Stargell on the all-time list.

In 1996, Winfield moved up to the broadcast booth as an analyst for Fox TV.

DENTON TRUE "CY" YOUNG

Pitcher. Born Mar. 29, 1867 Gilmore, Oh. Died Nov. 4, 1955 Newcomerstown, Oh. Holds major league records for wins (511), starts (815), and complete games (749).

Had the honor been presented during his career, baseball's winningest pitcher might have had a shot at winning half a dozen Cy Young Awards.

He won at least 30 games in five seasons and, although he won a mere 26 in 1904, Young put together a string of 44 consecutive scoreless innings—23 of them hitless as well. He started with two hitless innings on April 25 against the A's, six on April 30 against Washington, and nine in the first post-1900 perfect game ever pitched, on May 5 against the A's. The streak ended on May 11 after he'd pitched six more hitless innings against the Tigers. (He did shut them out for fifteen innings.)

Pitching at a time when complete games were the rule, Young finished what he'd started 749 times. He'd take twelve warmup tosses and be ready to go. He pitched more than 400 innings in a season five times, more than 300 eleven other times, and said, "I never had a sore arm, and I pitched every third day. Once I pitched every other day for eighteen days."

Denton True Young was an instant sensation at Canton of the Tri-State League and got the name Cyclone (later shortened to Cy) after his pregame pitches splintered the fence that served as an outfield barrier.

Young threw a three-hitter in his big-league debut in 1890 and pitched both ends of a doubleheader that October, winning 5–1 and 7–3. In 1891, his first full season, he won 27 for the Cleveland Spiders, the first of nine straight seasons in which he won 20 games or more.

In 1897 Cy pitched the first of his three no-hitters. In 1903 he won two games for the Boston Pilgrims (Red Sox) in the first World Series between the American and National leagues. He rebounded from losing seasons in 1905 and 1906 to win 21 games in 1907 and, at age forty-one, pitched his third no-hitter in 1908.

He retired with the most career victories (511), losses (316), innings pitched (7,354), and complete games (749) in history. In 1937 he was voted into the Hall of Fame.

ROBIN YOUNT

Infielder/Outfielder. Born Sept. 16, 1955 Danville, Ill. AL MVP 1982, 1989; joined 3,000-hit club in 1992.

Unlike the slowing veteran who moves from the outfield to first base, Robin Yount made a different move with different results. Seven years after being chosen MVP at one demanding defensive position, shortstop, Yount was selected as MVP again at another demanding position—center field.

After 1974 Yount was consistency itself, hitting in the high .280s (and over .300 six times) and playing 150 or more games eight times. He won fielding titles at both positions, led the league in doubles, triples, and runs created twice each, and reached the 3,000 hit mark in 1992.

A high school All-America in Woodland Hills, California, Yount was the Brewers' number one pick in 1973 and the third player picked overall, behind David Clyde and John Stearns (and just ahead of Dave Winfield). He hit .285 at Newark, New York, in the New York–Penn League and went to spring training with the Brewers in 1974. When Brewers manager Del Crandall saw Yount play, he won the starting job; by the age of twenty-two, Yount had already qualified for his big league pension by playing for four years. During spring training in 1978, he left the Brewers briefly to become a pro golfer, returned a few months later, and has been with the Brewers ever since. In 1981, he led the league in fielding (.985) and fielding runs (28) and batted .316 in the divisional playoff series.

In 1982 Yount was the starting shortstop in the All-Star Game and had a career year; he became the first shortstop to lead the league in slugging and total bases and also topped his colleagues in hits, doubles, production, and Total Player Rating. He batted .414 with 6 RBI in the World Series, although the Brewers lost to the Cardinals, and was named MVP in the off-season.

An All-Star starter again in 1983, Yount suffered back problems so severe that he was briefly shifted to DH. He moved to the outfield in 1985 and led the league's outfielders in fielding (.997), making just one error. On September 9, 1992, he joined baseball's exclusive 3,000-hit club by singling against Cleveland's Jose Mesa in Milwaukee. He finished the 1993 season with 3,142 hits and retired.

## CHAPTER 7

Baseball Families

Larry Amman

Just as the Wright brothers were first in flight, so were Wright brothers first in baseball. In the National Association's inaugural season of 1871, the Boston team featured Harry Wright as manager and reserve outfielder, and George at shortstop. Brother Sam joined them on the bench for the 1876 season, after an apprenticeship in New Haven the year before.

Since then there have been 348 brother combinations in the majors. The only season in which there was not at least one such pair was 1899. There were three new ones in 1995 and two in 1996.

The first thing that strikes the eye as one reads the list is the large number who were teammates, however briefly— more than 25 percent.

Another observation one must make is how one-sided the big league performance was between so many of the combinations. For example, there are twenty-five members of the Hall of Fame who had brothers in the majors. Yet how many baseball fans have ever heard of the brothers of Bill Dickey, Christy Mathewson, or Honus Wagner? As another example, how many people remember the brothers of Steve Sax, Robin Yount, or Eddie Murray? These big names have brothers who played in the majors briefly.

Of course, being the brother of a major leaguer never guarantees success, nor even a shot at the big leagues. The five Delahantys, the three Boyers, and the two Ferrells all had other brothers who played minor league ball only.

Because the combinations in which more than one brother excelled are so rare, we can focus on the more outstanding ones.

In terms of balanced, outstanding achievement no group of three or more brothers can match the DiMaggios. The enduring folk hero status of Joe DiMaggio unfortunately has not done anything to keep alive the memory of his brothers, Vince and Dom. All three were gifted outfielders, good hitters, and fine all-around athletes. Vince, the oldest of these sons of a San Francisco fisherman, played for five different National League teams. In 1941 he had 21 homers and 100 RBI for Pittsburgh. Four years later he hit four grand slams for the Phillies.

Dom DiMaggio was the youngest and smallest of the three brothers. Although lacking any of the power of the other two, he was the fastest on the bases and yielded nothing to his two brothers in the grace and skill he exhibited in the outfield. His lifetime batting average was just under .300.

In the 1941 All-Star Game, Dom went to right field as a late-inning substitute to play alongside Joe in center. This was a first in the midsummer classic. In the eighth inning, Joe doubled and Dom singled him home. In the 1949 All-Star Game, Joe drove in Dom with what proved to be the margin of victory for the junior circuit.

Dominic, or the "Little Professor" as he was called, started four different All-Star games, including the 1946 contest. That year he was voted to start in center field ahead of his brother. On the season, Dom outhit Joe by 26 points (.316 to .290).

In the 1943 All-Star Game, Vince went 3 for 3, including a ninth-inning home run. While Joe and Dom were away in the military, Vince was ". . . maintaining the family tradition of excellence in All-Star Games."

The first time two brothers played against each other in an All-Star Game was in 1969. Carlos May of the White Sox came to bat as a pinch-hitter with brother Lee of the Reds playing first base. In the 1990 midsummer classic, television cameras showed Sandy Alomar, Jr., at bat while Roberto Alomar set himself at second base, ready to field anything his brother might have hit his way. Both men were teammates for the junior circuit in the 1991, 1992, and 1996 games.

For the title of the best brother pitching combination, the competition is very close between the Niekros of Ohio and the Perrys of Williamston, North Carolina. In 1987 the ancient knuckleballing duo of Phil and Joe Niekro passed Jim and Gaylord Perry in wins. The two families remain very close in most statistical categories.

The Perry brothers had one full season as teammates— 1974 with Cleveland, when the two combined for 39 victories, almost half of the team total. A year earlier, when Jim was with Detroit, the two made their only start against each other. Gaylord took the loss for Cleveland. Jim got a no-decision. In the 1970 All-Star Game, the National League pitcher in the sixth and seventh innings was Gaylord Perry of the Giants. On the mound for the American League in the seventh and eighth innings was Jim Perry of the Twins. This is the only time two brothers were rival pitchers in the midsummer classic. Both have also won the Cy Young Award.

For Joe and Phil Niekro, pitching against each other was not that uncommon. It happened nine different times. The most noteworthy occasion came on September 26, 1978, in Atlanta. Before this, his last start of the season, Phil was 19–17 for the Braves; Joe was 12–14 for the Astros. Houston won 2–0, much to the dismay of victor Joe. He loathed the idea of pitching against his brother in these circumstances.

Harry and Stan Coveleski of the coal-mining country

in Pennsylvania were brother hurlers who refused to start games against each other. Stan, the younger, was in his first full season in the majors in 1916 at Cleveland while Harry was winning 20 for the third consecutive year at Detroit. Harry developed arm trouble and did not pitch another full season, but Stan went on to five 20-win seasons and a niche in the Hall of Fame.

Virtually every baseball fan has heard of the game on September 15, 1963, in which Felipe, Matty, and Jesus Alou formed the San Francisco outfield for one inning. A better story about this Dominican family, however, is the race for the 1966 National League batting title.

Going into the season, Felipe, with the Atlanta Braves, had established himself as a hitter of high average and respectable power. Younger brother Matty's career so far had been disappointing. With no power, his lifetime batting average was .260. In the off-season the Giants had traded him to Pittsburgh.

With the Bucs, Matty came under the special tutelage of manager Harry Walker. "Harry the Hat" taught his pupil to chop down on the ball and to hit to left field instead of trying to pull. This, plus over 20 bunt and 30 infield singles, propelled Matty to the top of the league batting race. Second or third to him almost all year was Atlanta leadoff man and first baseman Felipe Alou. Matty won the crown with a .342 average, while Felipe finished second at .327. The elder brother, however, led the circuit in runs, hits, and total bases.

It was only fitting that Harry Walker was the cause of the enormous jump in Matty's batting average. In 1947 Harry Walker the outfielder was traded from the Cardinals to the Phillies early in the season. There he won the batting title with an average 100 points higher than the year before. This was the second batting title in the family. In 1944 older brother Dixie had led the senior circuit with a .357 mark at Brooklyn.

Brother rivalries and brother teammates come into very sharp focus under the media glare of the World Series. The fall classics from 1921 to 1932 featured Bob Meusel of the Yankees versus older brother Emil or "Irish" of the Giants. These two outfielders were very similar in physical appearance and in capabilities.

Before the 1921 Series one writer summed up the pair:

Bob hits harder than Emil though he is not as consistent in garnering his hits. Bob also excels Emil as a thrower, but Emil is the more finished fielder. Bob is a left field hitter, and Emil often hits to right, so the play of "Meusel flied to Meusel" may be repeated frequently during the Series.

Indeed, it was so in all three series. In Game Three of the 1923 fall classic, each brother robbed the other of an extra-base hit. Over all, Irish emerged superior to Bob in every category—even in extra-base hits. Bob, however, had the last laugh, driving in the go-ahead run in Game Six of 1923 to give the Yankees their first world title.

For their entire careers, the Meusels startle the observer with the closeness of all their statistics. Irish averaged .310 to Bob's .309, both for 11 seasons. Bob leads in all other categories, but not by much. If Irish's totals were increased by prorating them based on his 100 fewer games, the two would look like clones. Each man led his league in RBI one time.

Two brothers whose lifetime batting averages are identical are Bob and Roy Johnson. Both of these Oklahoma Indians hit .296 as American League outfielders in the 1930s. Bob amassed 2,000 hits and almost 300 home runs, playing mostly for Connie Mack. Elder brother Roy was a speedy singles and doubles hitter. He exceeded his brother only in stolen bases in his shorter career.

The 1927 World Series featured Lloyd Waner leading off and playing center field for Pittsburgh while older brother Paul hit third and patrolled right field. In just his second season, Paul had won the batting title. Rookie Lloyd finished second in hits and third in batting average. The two combined for 460 hits during the season and were 11 for 30 in the World Series as the Yankees swept the Pirates in four games.

The Waners played parts of 16 seasons together, much longer than any other pair. Paul hit 17 points higher in batting and almost 70 points higher in slugging. However, "Big Poison" was actually shorter than Lloyd. Paul's moniker came from all the doubles and triples he delivered.

In 1934 Dizzy and Paul Dean had the greatest year any pitching brothers have ever enjoyed. "Me 'n' Paul" together won 49 games during the regular season and all four of the games the Cardinals won from the Tigers in the World Series. In 1935 their combined victory total was only two less. These two 19-win seasons were Paul's only full years in the majors.

An even more memorable year in St. Louis Cardinal history was 1942. In the last week of August, the Red Birds were five games behind the defending champion Brooklyn Dodgers. Five weeks later the Cardinals clinched first place with a record September rush. Winning five games in the last month for a total of 22 on the season was Mort Cooper. Catching him was younger brother Walker, in his first season as a regular. Mort won his September games with great flair. He was called the "fashion plate" for wearing the number on his back which equaled the victory he was seeking that day. The Cardinals beat the Yankees in a five-game World Series to shock all of baseball. Walker Cooper contributed several timely hits to the Series upset.

Mort also won 20 for the 1943 and 1944 pennant winners and had a victory in each of the World Series. Both brothers were named to *The Sporting News* All-Star team in 1944. Walker hit an even .300 for three Fall Classics.

The Coopers may have been the best of the 15 brother battery combinations, but Wes and Rick Ferrell have to be a close second. Rick caught his younger brother for five straight seasons. Wes won 20 the first two years together.

The next great brother act in the World Series was in 1964, when Ken and Clete Boyer were the opposing third basemen. Elder brother Ken was the National League's Most Valuable Player with a league-leading 119 RBI for St. Louis. Clete had hit an anemic .219 for the Yankees. Still, this was his chance to show the baseball world he was Ken's equal in the field.

Although neither hit for a high average in the seven games, both did well with the glove. Ken gave his team all its runs in Game Four with a grand-slam homer. St. Louis won that contest 4–3. In the seventh game, Ken scored the first run and later homered. Brother Clete helped make the finish exciting as he hit one of the two solo home runs off Bob Gibson in the ninth inning. Like the Coopers, the

Boyers were born and raised in the "Show Me" state. Both parents were in the stands maintaining their strict neutrality and feeling great pride.

The integrity of play when brothers square off against each other has been taken for granted for many years. This wasn't always the case. In 1933 Joe Sewell, playing third base for the Yankees, and Luke Sewell, catching for Washington, found themselves on opposite sides of a hot pennant race. They had been teammates at Cleveland for a number of years.

Reporting on a crucial game in the 1933 AL race, Shirley Povich of the Washington *Post* wrote:

> It was brother versus brother in the seventh when Joe Sewell made a whale of a stop and throw to cut down Luke. It's things like that help prove the honesty of baseball.

The shadow of the Black Sox Scandal still hung over the game.

Now for a trivia windup: There have been five brother shortstop–second base combinations in big league history: Granny and Garvin Hamner of the 1945 Phillies, Lou and Dino Chiozza of the 1935 Phillies, Milt and Frank Bolling of the 1958 Tigers, Eddie and Johnny O'Brien of the Pirates in the mid-1950s, and Cal and Bill Ripken of the Orioles from 1987 to 1992 and again in 1996. The O'Briens were one of seven sets of twins in the majors.

Josh Clarke with Louisville in the National League in 1898 and George "White Wings" Tebeau of Cleveland in 1894–1895 must have felt some sense of constraint in criticizing their managers. In both cases it was a brother: Fred Clarke and Patsy Tebeau. Both pilots were regular players those seasons as well. Ed Hengle, who never played in the majors, managed his brother Moxie in the Union Association for the entry that began the season in Chicago. By the end of the campaign, both Mengels were gone, and the club had moved to Pittsburgh.

Wes and Rick Ferrell have something in common with Jesse and Lee Tannehill. In each case the pitching brother—Wes and Jesse—had a higher career batting average and more home runs than the brother who played every day.

No, Henry and Tommie Aaron were not the first "soul-brother" brother combination in major-league baseball. The game's first black siblings were Fleet and Welday Walker, who both played for Toledo of the American Association in 1884. That circuit was then considered a major league.

Fathers and Sons

Shortly after breaking into the majors, Dale Berra was asked about similarities between himself and his famous father, Yogi. The younger Berra replied, "Our similarities are different."

Like the many malapropisms of Yogi Berra, this one by his son may appear foolish on the surface, but it contains quite a bit of underlying wisdom. In fact, it can serve as a metaphor for father-son combinations in major league baseball.

Of the 139 combinations, only 44 feature both genera-

tions at the same position. There are twenty father-son pitcher combinations, five cases where both father and son caught, one where both played first, three where both played shortstop, and fourteen where both father and son were outfielders. Very few fathers and sons at any position have career totals that are at all close.

Another important generalization is the great increase in father-son combinations since World War Two, especially in the last twenty years. The first son of a former big leaguer to break into the majors was Jack Doscher in 1903 as a pitcher for the Chicago Cubs—one of the three teams with whom his father, Herm, had toiled as a utility player twenty years earlier. By 1945 the number of father-son combinations was 36. In 1965 the total was 66. That means almost 40 percent of today's number has been added in the last two decades.

Is the son of a big league ballplayer more apt to develop into a major leaguer than the average boy? Some people think not. In the 1950s, Hall of Famer George Sisler was asked this very question. The two-time .400 hitter shook his head over how two of his offspring had made the majors. He pointed out that baseball players are absentee fathers. They don't have much opportunity to teach their boys the fundamentals or to practice with them.

If not their fathers, perhaps other well-qualified professionals have instructed the second generation. A worthwhile study could be conducted to determine how many second-generation players who have broken in during the last two decades attended baseball camps as boys. If the number is significant, this could explain the big increase during this period.

Certainly, the Sisler family deserves special attention. Father George broke into the majors just before World War One as a pitcher for the St. Louis Browns. After being switched to first base, he spent fifteen years as one of the greatest performers ever at that position. Accordingly, it is only fitting that he should have one son, Dick, who was a good hitter and another son, Dave, who pitched in the majors briefly. Dick's home run on the last day of the 1950 season, which gave the Philadelphia Whiz Kids the pennant, has given him an identity independent of his father. Also, these two men both managed in the majors for a short time. The Sislers and the Macks are the only families in which both father and son managed in the majors.

Baseball families fall into one of three categories: famous fathers only, famous sons only, and equals.

Let us consider the famous son category first. Another way of describing these men would be to call them "fathers of . . ." Two families stand out in this category. They are the Muellers and the Walkers.

Walter Mueller was a reserve outfielder for the Pirates for four seasons in the 1920s. His son, Don, hit .296 in twelve seasons as a National League outfielder. In 1954 Mueller and teammate Willie Mays battled all season for the batting title on the pennant-winning Giants. Mays finished first in hitting by three points, but Mueller led the league in hits with 212.

Dixie Walker was a pitcher for the Washington team from 1909 through 1912. His lifetime record was 24–30. Both his sons, Fred (or "Dixie") and Harry, won batting titles. These two are the only clear cases of a son of All-Star quality who had a father whose career in the majors was forgettable. Other families with "fathers of . . ." are Coleman, Grimsley, and Smalley.

In contrast, the list of "sons of . . . " is a long one. There are eight baseball fathers in the Hall of Fame. Averill, Berra, Collins, Lindstrom, Mack, O'Rourke and Walsh had offspring who fit this category. Four more families—Bagby, Camilli, Trosky, and Wood—had fathers of All-Star quality and sons who are footnotes to their careers. Hegan, Wills, and Trout are families where the sons had respectable careers and characteristics similar to those of the fathers, but the older generation was clearly superior.

We must consider first whether some of the "sons of..." got to the majors, or second, stayed longer than they merited, because of the family name. I would cite Collins, Walsh, and Wood to prove the former proposition, and Dale Berra and Marc Sullivan as support for the latter.

The younger Berra and Sullivan not only had the temerity to go into their father's business, but, like Bill and Cal Ripken, Jr., of Baltimore, they had dad for their boss. The Ripkens (in 1988) and Dale Berra (in 1985) saw their fathers dismissed as managers early in the season. Cal Ripken, Sr., was not only the first father to manage two sons at once, but the first without major league playing experience to manage his sons.

Sullivan, whose father owned part of the Red Sox, traded his son to the Houston Astros organization before the 1988 season, where he could commiserate with the Berras on the difficulties of combining a baseball career with family obligations.

By far the most interesting category is that of the fathers and sons whose careers parallel each other.

The two Billy Sullivans caught for both the White Sox and the Tigers. Both played other positions as well as caught in one World Series. Sullivan Senior caught the older Ed Walsh; Junior caught the younger Ed Walsh—both at Chicago. Junior hit for what appears a much higher average, but we must remember that Senior played in the Dead-Ball Era, and Junior in the high-hitting 1930s.

Jim and Mike Hegan were a father-son combination well known for defensive ability. Father Jim was a great handler of pitchers for Cleveland. Mike played first base and the outfield for several American League teams. Both appeared in two World Series. Mike broke into the majors just four seasons after his father's finale.

The father-son pitching combinations have few parallels. Both Thornton and Don Lee gave up home runs to Ted Williams. Only three families have had both father and son pitch in a World Series. Jim Bagby, Sr. pitched for Cleveland in the 1920 Series and his son for the Red Sox in 1946. Mel Stottlemyre went 1–1 for the Yankees in the 1964 Series. Todd Stottlemyre pitched for Toronto in the 1992 and 1993 fall classics. In the 1995 Fall Classic Pedro Borbon, Jr. came in for Atlanta in relief. Pedro Senior pitched for the Reds in four Series.

Joe Schultz, Junior, received some unwanted publicity in Jim Bouton's book *Ball Four,* for being Bouton's manager. Schultz and his father, Joe Senior, each spent almost a decade in the majors as reserve players. Senior was 46 for 170 as a pinch-hitter. Junior went 43 for 160 in that same role.

It is only fitting that Buddy Bell spent a portion of his fine career with the Cincinnati Reds, the team on which his father Gus spent his best years. The two ended their careers with nearly identical batting averages and home run totals.

Ten father-son combinations have been named to play in All-Star Games. Prior to 1990 only the Bell, Boone, Tresh, and Hegan families could have made that boast. Then Barry Bonds, Ken Griffey, Jr., both Alomar sons, Todd Hundley, and Moises Alou made their debuts in the midsummer classic. The senior Tresh and the junior Hegan were named to the All-Star squads but did not play. The Bells and Boones have similar statistics. Gus was 2 for 6, hitting a home run his first time up; Buddy was 1 for 7, hitting a triple in his first plate appearance. Ray Boone went 1 for 5 in All-Star games with a homer; Bob was 2 for 5 in three games. Both Griffeys have been Most Valuable Player in an All Star Game: Senior in 1980 and Junior in 1992. Currently the Seattle center fielder is 8 for 14 in the midsummer classic. His father was 5 for 7 in three games. Each has a home run to his credit. Barry Bonds is now 4 for 16 in All-Star competition. His father, Bobby, went 2 for 6 in three contests and was MVP in 1972.

Felipe Alou may have had some feelings of regret mixed with the great pride he felt when his son Moises drove in the winning run in the 1994 All-Star Game. Felipe's one appearance was in 1968. He played one inning in left field and did not have an official time at bat. In the 1996 Game Mets catcher Todd Hundley went 0 for 1 to become the tenth combination. His father, Randy, went 0 for 1 in the 1969 game.

In Game One of the 1984 World Series, a two-run double by San Diego catcher Terry Kennedy was noted by the television announcers as something significant. This was the first time in the history of the fall classic that both a father and son had a World Series RBI. Terry's father, Bob, knocked in a run for Cleveland as an outfielder in the 1948 Series. There have been seven families in which the father and son both played in a World Series. Five have been mentioned already; there is also Ernie and Don Johnson. The father was a substitute infielder for the Yankees in the 1923 Series. Don was the regular second baseman for the Cubs in the 1945 fall classic. Stan Javier in 1988 and 1989 with Oakland makes seven; his father, Julian, played in four World Series.

An interesting father-son parallel to watch for in the future is that between Bobby and Barry Bonds. The son, an outfielder for San Francisco, has his father's penchant for home runs, stolen bases, and strikeouts.

The Bondses are not the first black father-son combination. That honor goes to the Hairstons. Father Sam caught two games for the White Sox in 1951. Son Jerry was a respected pinch-hitter for that team for over a decade.

Since the first edition of this book two significant events have taken place. In September 1990 Ken Griffey, Senior took a place in the Seattle Mariner outfield next to his son. Late in the 1992 season, Bret Boone made his major league debut as the Seattle second baseman. Baseball now has a three-generation family. Bret's father was Bob Boone and his grandfather was Ray Boone. In 1995 David Bell, son of Buddy and grandson of Gus, made his major league debut for the second three-generation family. It is hard to imagine what could top these two events in fan interest, but we are sure to see many more family combinations in the years to come.

Brothers' Combined Totals (*Still active)

Seasons		Games		Hits		Doubles		Triples	
Alou	47	Alou	5,129	Waner	5,611	DiMaggio	906	Waner	308
Niekro	46	Waner	4,541	Alou	5,094	Waner	884	Delahanty	280
Delahanty	41	DiMaggio	4,245	DiMaggio	4,853	Delahanty	769	Wagner	256
Perry	39	Boyer	3,872	Delahanty	4,211	Alou	765	Clarke	233
Waner	38	Aaron	3,735	Aaron	3,987	Sewell	709	Connor	225
Boyer	36	Delahanty	3,595	Sewell	3,619	Johnson	671	DiMaggio	212
Sewell	35	Sewell	3,532	Boyer	3,559	Wagner	658	Johnson	178
Brett	35	May	3,236	Wagner	3,489	Brett	643	Ewing	178
DiMaggio	34	*Ripken	3,195	Johnson	3,343	Meusel	618	Wheat	177
Ferrell	33	Cruz	3,077	*Murray	3,262				
Forsch	32	Johnson	3,016	Brett	3,245				
				Meusel	3,214				

Home Runs		Runs		RBI		Batting Average (10 seasons)		Steals	
Aaron	768	DiMaggio	2,927	DiMaggio	2,739	Manush	.329	Wagner	726
DiMaggio	573	Waner	2,827	Aaron	2,391	*Gwynn	.328	Delahanty	685
*Murray	505	Delahanty	2,309	Delahanty	2,153	Wagner	.326	Clarke	557
Boyer	444	Aaron	2,276	*Murray	1,924	Waner	.325	Milan	501
May	444	Alou	2,213	Waner	1,907	Connor	.314	Sax	444
Nettles	406	Johnson	1,956	Meusel	1,887	Delahanty	.311	Cruz	322
*Ripken	370	Sewell	1,794	Johnson	1,839	Meusel	.309	*Nixon	545
Allen	358	Wagner	1,762	Boyer	1,803	Wheat	.309	*Alomar	335
Johnson	346	Boyer	1,761	May	1,780	Clarke	.308	*Gwynn	298
Brett	327	Clarke	1,744	Wagner	1,750	O'Rourke	.308	Alou	294
				Sewell	1,747	Kell	.304	Yount	271
						Brett	.303	Meusel	253
								Moriarty	250
								Aaron	249

Brother Pitching Totals

Games		Innings		Wins		Losses		Strikeouts		Shutouts		Complete Games	
Niekro	1,566	Niekro	8,988	Niekro	539	Niekro	478	Perry	5,110	Perry	85	Clarkson	571
Perry	1,407	Perry	8,637	Perry	529	Perry	439	Niekro	5,089	Niekro	74	Weyhing	455
Forsch	1,019	Clarkson	5,616	Clarkson	383	Forsch	249	Mathewson	2,504	Coveleski	51	Mathewson	436
McDaniel	1,006	Forsch	4,921	Coveleski	296	Weyhing	239	Clarkson	2,326	Clarkson	43	Perry	412
Reuschel	755	Mathewson	4,793	Forsch	282	Clarkson	232	*Maddux	2,209	Forsch	37	Niekro	352
		Reuschel	3,865									Coveleski	308

Father-Son Hitters

	Years	Games	Runs	Hits	Homers	RBI	BA	Steals
ALOMAR								
Sandy, Sr.	15	1,481	588	1,168	13	282	.245	227
Robby	9	1,304	829	1,522	99	593	.301	313
Sandy, Jr.	9	617	246	561	52	259	.270	22
ALOU								
Felipe	17	2,082	985	2,101	206	852	.286	107
Moises	6	610	343	627	64	373	.291	53
AVERILL								
Earl, Sr.	13	1,669	1,224	2,020	238	1,165	.318	69
Earl, Jr.	9	449	137	249	44	159	.242	3
BELL								
Gus	15	1,741	865	1,823	206	942	.281	30
Buddy	18	2,405	1,150	2,514	201	1,106	.279	55
BERRA								
Yogi	19	2,120	1,175	2,150	358	1,430	.285	30
Dale	11	853	236	603	49	278	.236	32

	Years	Games	Runs	Hits	Homers	RBI	BA	Steals
BONDS								
Bobby	14	1,849	1,258	1,886	332	1,024	.268	461
Barry	11	1,583	1,121	1,595	334	993	.288	380
BOONE								
Ray	13	1,373	645	1,260	151	737	.275	21
Bob	19	2,264	679	1,838	105	826	.254	38
Bret	5	497	224	473	55	258	.260	14
CAMILLI								
Dolf	12	1,490	936	1,482	239	950	.277	60
Doug	9	313	56	153	18	80	.199	0
GRIFFEY								
Ken, Sr.	19	2,090	1,129	2,143	152	859	.296	200
Ken, Jr.	8	1,057	695	1,204	238	725	.302	108

	Years	Games	Runs	Hits	Homers	RBI	BA	Steals
HEGAN								
Jim	17	1,666	550	1,087	92	525	.228	15
Mike	12	965	281	504	53	229	.242	28
HUNDLEY								
Randy	14	1,061	311	813	82	381	.236	12
Todd	7	644	254	478	91	299	.238	8
KENNEDY								
Bob	16	1,483	514	1,176	63	514	.254	45
Terry	14	1,491	474	1,313	113	628	.264	6
McRAE								
Hal	19	2,084	940	2,091	191	1,097	.290	109
Brian	7	908	522	966	59	362	.268	362
SCHOFIELD								
Ducky	19	1,321	394	699	21	211	.227	12
Dick	13	1,355	502	985	56	353	.230	119

	Years	Games	Runs	Hits	Homers	RBI	BA	Steals
SISLER								
George	15	2,055	1,283	2,812	99	1,175	.340	375
Dick	8	799	302	720	55	360	.276	6
SMALLEY								
Roy, Jr.	11	872	277	601	61	305	.227	4
Roy, III	13	1,653	745	1,454	163	694	.257	27
SULLIVAN								
Billy, Sr.	16	1,146	363	777	20	378	.212	98
Billy, Jr.	12	962	347	820	29	388	.289	30
TRESH								
Mike	12	1,027	326	788	2	297	.249	19
Tom	9	1,192	595	1,041	153	530	.245	45
WILLS								
Maury	14	1,942	1,067	2,134	20	458	.281	586
Bump	6	831	472	807	36	302	.266	196

Father-Son Pitchers

	Years	Games	W–L	SO	CG	ERA		Years	Games	W–L	SO	CG	ERA
BAGBY							**QUEEN**						
Jim, Sr.	9	316	127–89	450	132	3.10	Mel, Sr.	8	146	27–40	328	15	5.09
Jim, Jr.	10	303	97–96	431	84	3.96	Mel, Jr.	9	140	20–17	302	6	3.14
COLEMAN							**SISLER**						
Joe, Sr.	10	223	52–76	444	60	4.38	George	7	24	5–6	63	9	2.35
Joe, Jr.	15	484	142–135	1728	94	3.69	Dave	7	247	38–44	355	12	4.33
KRAUSSE							**STOTTLEMYRE**						
Lew, Sr.	2	23	5–1	17	3	4.48	Mel, Sr.	11	360	164–139	1,257	152	2.97
Lew, Jr.	12	321	68–91	721	21	4.00	Todd	9	271	97-88	1,061	31	4.33
LEE							**TROUT**						
Thornton	16	374	117–124	937	155	3.56	Paul	15	521	170–161	1,256	158	3.23
Don	9	244	40–44	467	13	3.61	Steve	12	301	88–92	656	32	4.18
PILLETTE							**WALSH**						
Herman	4	107	34–32	148	33	3.45	Ed, Sr.	14	430	195–126	2,346	250	1.82
Duane	8	188	38–66	305	34	4.40	Ed, Jr.	4	79	11–24	107	15	5.57

Baseball Families

KEY

tm teammates
F-S father-son

BROTHERS

AARON   Henry & Tommie *tm*
ACOSTA   Jose & Merito
ADAMS   Bobby & Dick *F-S also*
ALLEN   Dick, Hank & Ron *tm*
ALLISON   Art & Doug *tm*
ALOMAR   Roberto & Sandy Jr. *tm*
ALOU   Felipe, *F-S also*
     Matty & Jesus *tm*
ANDERSON   Kent & Mike
ANDREWS   Rob & Mike
ARMAS   Tony & Marcos
ASPROMONTE   Bob & Ken

BAILEY   Ed & Jim *tm*
BAKER   Dave & Doug
BANDO   Chris & Sal
BANNON   Jimmy & Tom
BARNES   Jesse & Virgil
BARRETT   Marty & Tom
BAXES   Jim & Mike
BELL   Charlie & Frank
BELL   George & Juan
BENES   Alan & Andy *tm*
BENNETT   Dave & Dennis *tm*
BERGEN   Bill & Marty
BIGBEE   Carson & Lyle *tm*
BLANKENSHIP   Homer & Ted *tm*
BLUEGE   Ossie & Otto
BOLLING   Frank & Milt *tm*
BOONE   Danny & Ike
BOYER   Clete, Ken & Cloyd *tm*
BOYLE   Buzz & Jim
BOYLE   Eddie & Jack
BRASHEAR   Kitty & Roy
BREEDEN   Danny & Hal
BRETT   George & Ken *tm*
BREWER   Mike & Tony
BRINKMAN   Chuck & Ed
BROWN   Dick & Larry
BROWN   Jackie & Paul
BROWN   Oscar & Ollie
BROWN   Curtis & Leon

CAMNITZ   Harry & Howie *tm*
CAMP   Kid & Llewellan *tm*
CAMPBELL   Hugh & Mat *tm*
CANSECO   Jose & Ozzie (twins) *tm*
CANTWELL   Mike & Tom
CARLYLE   Cleo & Roy
CASEY   Dan & Dennis *tm*
CEDENO   Andujar & Domingo
CHIOZZA   Dino & Lou *tm*
CHRISTOPHER   Lloyd & Russ
CLAPP   Aaron & John
CLARK   Jerald & Phil
CLARKE   Fred & Josh *tm*
CLARKE   Sumpter & Rufe
CLARKSON   Dad, John &
    Walter *tm*
CLIBURN   Stan & Stew (twins)
COFFMAN   Dick & Slick
COHEN   Andy & Syd
CONIGLIARO   Billy & Tony
CONNELL   Gene & Joe
CONNOR   Joe & Roger

CONWAY   Jim & Pete
CONWAY   Bill & Dick *tm*
COONEY   Jimmy & Johnny *tm*
    F-S also
COOPER   Mort & Walker *tm*
CORCORAN   Larry & Mike *tm*
COSCARART   Joe & Pete
COVELESKI   Harry & Stan
COVINGTON   Sam & Tex
CROSS   Amos, Frank & Lave *tm*
CRUZ   Hector, Jose & Tommy *tm*
CUCCINELLO   Al & Tony

DAILY   Con & Ed
DALY   Joe & Tom
DANNING   Harry & Ike
DARINGER   Cliff & Rolla
DARWIN   Jeff & Danny
DAVALILLO   Vic & Yo-Yo
DAVENPORT   Claude & Dave
DAVIS   Mark & Mike
DEAN   Dizzy & Paul *tm*
DEASLEY   John & Pat
DELAHANTY   Ed, Frank, Jim,
    Joe & Tom *tm*
DEMONTREVILLE   Gene & Lee
DICKEY   Bill & George
DILLON   Packy & John *tm*
DIMAGGIO   Vince, Joe & Dom
DONAHUE   Jiggs & Pat
DONNELLY   Pete & John
DONOVAN   Jerry & Tom
DORGAN   Jerry & Mike
DOWNS   Kelly & Dave
DOYLE   Brian & Denny
DRAKE   Sammy & Solly
DUGAN   Bill & Ed *tm*

EDWARDS   Dave, Marshall & Mike
    (twins)
ENS   Jewel & Mutz
ERAUTT   Eddie & Joe
EVERS   Joe & Johnny
EWING   Buck & John *tm*

FALK   Bibb & Chet
FARMER   Michael & Howard
FERRELL   Rick & Wes *tm*
FERRY   Cy & Jack
FINNEY   Hal & Lou
FISHER   Bob & Newt
FISHER   Chauncey & Tom
FOGARTY   Jim & Joe
FORD   Gene & Russ
FOREMAN   Brownie & Frank *tm*
FORSCH   Bob & Ken
FOUTZ   Dave & Frank
FOWLER   Art & Jesse
FREESE   Gene & George
FRIEL   Bill & Pat
FULLER   Harry & Shorty
FULMER   Chick & Washington

GAGLIANO   Phil & Ralph
GANZEL   Charlie & John *F-S also*
GARBARK   Bob & Mike
GARDELLA   Al & Danny *tm*
GARRETT   Adrian & Wayne
GASTON   Alex & Milt *tm*
GEISS   Bill & Emil
GENTRY   Harvey & Rufe
GILBERT   Harry & John *tm*

GILBERT   Charlie & Tookie
    F-S also
GLEASON   Bill & Jack *tm*
GLEASON   Harry & Kid
GRABOWSKI   Al & Reggie
GRAVES   Joe & Sid
GREGG   Dave & Vean
GRIMES   Ray & Roy (twins)
    F-S also
GRISSOM   Lee & Marv
GROH   Heinie & Lew
GUMBERT   Ad & Billy
GWYNN   Chris & Tony

HACKETT   Mert & Walter *tm*
HAFEY   Bud & Tom
HAIRSTON   Jerry & John *F-S also*
HAMNER   Garvin & Granny *tm*
HAMMOND   Chris & Steve
HANDLEY   Gene & Lee
HARGRAVE   Bubbles & Pinky
HATFIELD   Gil & John
HAYWORTH   Ray & Red
HEMPHILL   Charlie & Frank
HEVING   Joe & Johnnie
HIGH   Andy, Charlie & Hugh
HILL   Hugh & Still Bill
HINCHMAN   Bill & Harry *tm*
HITCHCOCK   Billy & Jim
HOFFMAN   Glenn & Trevor
HOGAN   George & Happy
HOLBERT   Aaron & Ray
HOLMAN   Brian & Brad
HOVLIK   Hick & Joe
HOWARD   Del & Ivon
HUGHES   Jim & Mickey
HUGHES   Ed & Tom
HUNTER   Bill & George (twins)

IGNASIAK   Gary & Mike
IORG   Dane & Garth
IRWIN   Arthur & John

JEFFCOAT   George & Hal
JIMENEZ   Elvio & Manny
JOHNSON   Bob & Roy
JOHNSON   Chet & Earl
JOHNSTON   Doc & Jimmy
JONES   Darryl & Lynn
JONES   Gary & Steve
JONNARD   Bubber & Claude
    (twins)
JORGENS   Arndt & Orville

KAPPEL   Heinie & Joe
KELL   George & Skeeter
KELLER   Charlie & Hal
KELLNER   Alex & Walt *tm*
KELLY   George & Ren
KENNEDY   Jim & Junior
KEOUGH   Marty & Joe *F-S also*
KIEFER   Steve & Mark
KILLEFER   Bill & Red
KILROY   Matt & Mike *tm*
KLAUS   Billy & Bobby
KLING   Bill & Johnny
KNODE   Mike & Ray
KNOTHE   Fritz & George
KOPF   Larry & Wally
KRSNICH   Mike & Rocky

LACHEMANN   Marcel & Rene
LANNING   Johnny & Tom

LANSFORD   Carney & Joe
LARY   Al & Frank
LAWTON   Matt & Mareus
LEITER   Al & Mark
LELIVELT   Bill & Jack
LILLARD   Bill & Gene *tm*
LOBERT   Frank & Hans
LOOK   Bruce & Dean
LOWDERMILK   Grover & Lou *tm*
LUSH   Billy & Ernie

MACHA   Ken & Mike
MACK   Quinn & Shane
MADDUX   Greg & Mike
MAHLER   Mickey & Rick *tm*
MAISEL   Fritz & George
MANCUSO   Frank & Gus
MANGUAL   Angel & Pepe
MANSELL   John, Mike & Tom *tm*
MANUSH   Frank & Heine
MANZANILLO   Josias & Ravelo
MARION   Marty & Red
MARTINEZ   Pedro & Ramon *tm*
MASKREY   Harry & Leech *tm*
MATHEWSON   Christy & Henry *tm*
MATTOX   Cloy & Jim
MAY   Carlos & Lee
MAYER   Erskine & Sam
MCDANIEL   Lindy & Von *tm*
MCFARLAN   Alex & Dan
MCFARLAND   Lamont & Charles
MCGEEHAN   Connie & Dan
MCLAUGHLIN   Barney & Frank *tm*
MEUSEL   Bob & Irish
MILAN   Clyde & Horace *tm*
MILLER   Jake & Russ
MILLER   Bing & Ralph *tm*
MITCHELL   John & Charlie
MOFFETT   Joe & Sam
MORIARTY   Bill & George
MORRISON   Johnny & Phil *tm*
MORRISSEY   John & Tom
MOTA   Andy & Jose *F-S also*
MURRAY   Eddie & Rich
MYERS   Billy & Lynn

NETTLES   Graig & Jim
NEWKIRK   Floyd & Joel
NIEKRO   Joe & Phil *tm*
NIXON   Otis & Donnell
NYMAN   Chris & Nyls

O'BRIEN   Eddie & Johnny
    (twins) *tm*
OGDEN   Curley & Jack
OLIVO   Chi Chi & Diomedes *F-S*
    also
O'NEILL   Jack, Jim, Mike &
    Steve *tm*
ONSLOW   Eddie & Jack
O'ROURKE   Jim & John *F-S also*
ORTIZ   Baby & Roberto *tm*
O'TOOLE   Denny & Jim
OWEN   Dave & Spike

PACIOREK   John, Tom & Jim
PARKER   Jay & Doc
PARROTT   Jiggs & Tom *tm*
PASCUAL   Camilo & Carlos
PATTERSON   Ham & Pat
PEITZ   Heine & Joe *tm*
PENA   Ramon & Tony

PEPLOSKI　Henry & Pepper
PEREZ　Pascual, Melido & Melido
PERRY　Gaylord & Jim *tm*
PFEFFER　Big Jeff & Jeff
PIERSON　Dave & Dick
PIKE　Jay & Lip
PIPGRAS　Ed & George
POTTER　Dykes & Squire

RAJSICH　Dave & Gary
REACH　Al & Bob
RECCIUS　John & Phil *tm*
REUSCHEL　Paul & Rick *tm*
REYNOLDS　Harold & Don
RICKETTS　Dick & Dave
RIDDLE　Elmer & Johnny *tm*
RIPKEN　Cal & Billy *tm*
ROBINSON　Bruce & Dave
ROBINSON　Fred & Wilbert
ROENICKE　Gary & Ron
ROETTGER　Oscar & Wally
ROMO　Vicente & Romero Enrique
ROOF　Gene & Phil
ROSENBERG　Harry & Lou
ROTH　Braggo & Frank
ROWE　Dave & Jack
ROY　Charlie & Luther
RUSSELL　Allan & Lefty

SADOWSKI　Bob, Eddie & Ted
SAUER　Ed & Hank
SAX　Dave & Steve *tm*
SAY　Jimmie & Lou *tm*
SCANLAN　Doc & Frank
SCHANG　Bobby & Wally
SCHAREIN　Art & George
SCHMIDT　Boss & Walter
SCHULTE　Herman & Leonard
SEWELL　Luke, Joe & Tommie *tm*
SHAFFER　Orator & Taylor *tm*
SHANNON　Joe & Red (twins) *tm*
SHANTZ　Billy & Bobby *tm*
SHERLOCK　Monk & Vince
SHERRY　Larry & Norm *tm*
SISLER　Dave & Dick *F-S also*
SMITH　Charlie & Fred
SOWDERS　Bill, John & Len
STAFFORD　John & Jim
STANICEK　Steve & Pete
STANLEY　Buck & Joe
STOTTLEMYRE　Mel, Jr. & Todd
STOVALL　George & Jessie
SURHOFF　B.J. & Rick
SUTHERLAND　Darrell & Gary

TANNEHILL　Jesse & Lee
TEBEAU　Patsy & White Wings *tm*
THIELMAN　Henry & Jake
THOBE　John & Thomas
THOMAS　Bill & Roy *tm*
THOMPSON　Homer & Tommy *tm*
THRONEBERRY　Faye & Marv
TOBIN　Jim & Johnny
TORRE　Frank & Joe *tm*
TRAFFLEY　Bill & John
TREACEY　Fred & Pete *tm*
TREVINO　Alex & Bobby
TWOMBLY　Babe & George
TYLER　Fred & Lefty *tm*

TYRONE　Jim & Wayne

UNDERWOOD　Pat & Tom
UPTON　Bill & Tom

VAN CUYK　Chris & Johnny

WADE　Ben & Jake
WAGNER　Butts & Honus
WALKER　Dixie Sr. & Ernie *F-S also*
WALKER　Dixie Jr. & Harry
WALKER　Gee & Hub *tm*
WALKER　Fleet & Welday *tm*
WANER　Lloyd & Paul *tm*
WATT　Al & Frank
WEILAND　Bob & Ed
WESTLAKE　Jim & Wally
WEYHING　Gus & John
WHEAT　Mack & Zack
WHITE　Deacon & Will *tm*
WHITNEY　Art & Frank
WILLIAMS　Gus & Harry
WILTSE　Hooks & Snake
WINGO　Al & Ivy
WOOD　Fred & Pete *tm*
WORRELL　Todd & Tim
WRIGHT　George, Harry & Sam *tm*
YOCHIM　Len & Ray
YOUNT　Larry & Robin

FATHERS-SONS

ADAMS　Bobby-Mike
ALOMAR　Sandy-Roberto & Sandy Jr.
ALOU　Felipe-Moises
AMARO　Ruben Sr. & Jr.
ARAGON　Angel-Jack
AVERILL　Earl-Earl

BAGBY　Jim Sr. & Jr.
BARNHART　Clyde-Vic
BEAMON　Charlie-Charlie
BELL　Buddy-David
BELL　Gus-Buddy
BERRA　Yogi-Dale
BERRY　Charlie-Charlie
BERRY　Joe-Joe
BONDS　Bobby-Barry
BOONE　Ray-Bob
BOONE　Bob-Bret
BORBON　Pedro-Pedro
BRICKELL　Fred-Fritzie
BRUCKER　Earle Sr. & Jr.
BRUMLEY　Mike-Mike
BUFORD　Don-Damon

CAMILLI　Dolf-Doug
CAMPANIS　Alex-Jim
CARREON　Camilo-Mark
COLEMAN　Joe-Joe
COLLINS　Ed Sr. & Jr.
CONNOLLY　Ed Sr. & Jr.
COONEY　Jimmy-Jimmy & Johnny
CORRIDEN　Red-John
CROUCH　Bill-Wilmer

DOSCHER　Herm-Jack

ELLSWORTH　Dick-Steve
ESCHEN　Jim-Larry

FLETCHER　Tom-Darrin
FRANCONA　Tito-Terry

GABRIELSON　Len-Len
GANZEL　Charlie-Babe
GILBERT　Larry-Charlie & Tookie
GRAHAM　Peaches-Jack
GREEN　Fred-Gary
GRIFFEY　Ken Sr. & Jr. *tm*
GRIMES　Ray-Oscar
GRIMSLEY　Ross-Ross

HAIRSTON　Sam-Jerry & John
HANEY　Larry-Chris
HEGAN　Jim-Mike
HEINTZELMAN　Ken-Tom
HOOD　Wally Sr. & Jr.
HOWARD　Bruce-David
HUNDLEY　Randy-Todd

JAVIER　Julian-Stan
JETER　Johnny-Shawn
JOHNSON　Adam-Adam
JOHNSON　Ernie-Don

KENDALL　Jason-Fred
KENNEDY　Bob-Terry
KEOUGH　Marty-Matt
KESSINGER　Don-Keith
KRAUSE　Lew Sr. & Jr.
KUNKEL　Bill-Jeff

LANDRUM　Joe-Bill
LANIER　Max-Hal
LAW　Vern-Vance
LEE　Thornton-Don
LERCHEN　Dutch-George
LIEBHARDT　Glenn-Glenn
LINDSTROM　Fred-Charlie
LIVELY　Jack-Bud

MACK　Connie-Earle
MAGGERT　Harl-Harl
MALAY　Charlie-Joe
MARTIN　Barney-Jerry
MATHEWS　Nelson-T.J.
MATTICK　Wally-Bobby
MAY　Dave-Derrick
MAY　Pinky-Milt
McAndrew　Jim-Jamie
McKNIGHT　Jim-Jeff
McRAE　Hal-Brian
MEINKE　Frank-Bob
MILLS　Willie-Art
MONTEAGUDO　Rene-Aurelio
MOORE　Eugene Sr. & Jr.
MORTON　Guy Sr. & Jr.
MOTA　Manny-Andy & Jose
MUELLER　Walter-Don

NARLESKI　Bill-Ray
NAVARRO　Julio-Jaime
NEN　Dick-Robert
NICHOLS　Chet Sr. & Jr.
NORTHEY　Ron-Scott

O'DONOGHUE　John Sr. & Jr.
OKRIE　Frank-Len
OLIVARES　Ed-Omar
OLIVER　Bob-Darren
OLIVO　Diomedes-Gilbert Rondon

O'ROURKE　Patsy-Joe
O'ROURKE　Jim-Queenie
OSBORNE　Tiny-Bobo

PARTENHEIMER　Steve-Stan
PEREZ　Tony-Eduardo
PILLETTE　Herman-Duane

QUEEN　Mel-Mel

RIPLEY　Walt-Allen

SAVIDGE　Ralph-Don
SCHOFIELD　Ducky-Dick
SCHULTZ　Joe Sr. & Jr.
SEGUI　Diego-David
SHEELY　Earl-Bud
SHEELY　Earl-Bub
SIEBERT　Dick-Paul
SISLER　George-Dick & Dave
SKINNER　Bob-Joel
SMALLEY　Roy Jr.-Roy III
SPIEZIO　Ed-Scott
SPRAGUE　Ed Sr. & Jr.
ST. CLAIRE　Ebba-Randy
STENHOUSE　Dave-Mike
STEPHENSON　Joe-Jerry
STILLWELL　Ron-Kurt
STOTTLEMYRE　Mel-Todd & Mel Jr. *F-S also*
SULLIVAN　Billy Sr.-Jr.
SULLIVAN　Haywood-Marc
SUSCE　George-George

TANNER　Chuck-Bruce
TARTABULL　Jose-Danny
TORRES　Ricardo-Gil
TRESH　Mike-Tom
TROSKY　Hal Sr. & Jr.
TROUT　Paul-Steve

UNSER　Al-Del

VIRGIL　Ozzie Sr. & Jr.

WAKEFIELD　Howard-Dick
WALKER　Dixie-Dixie & Harry
WALSH　Ed-Ed
WHITE　JoJo-Mike
WILLS　Maury-Bump
WINE　Bobby-Robbie
WOOD　Joe-Joe

YOUNG　Del-Del

GREAT GRANDFATHER-GREAT GRANDSON

Jim Bluejacket & Bill Wilkinson

GRANDFATHER-GRANDSON

George Rooks-Lou Possehl
Shano Collins-Bob Gallagher
Bill Brubaker-Dennis Rasmussen
Marty & Ed Herrmann
Ben & Jim Spencer
Lennie & Matt Merullo
Ray & Bret Boone
Bill & Roger Salkeld
Bobby Estalella-Robert Estalella

## CHAPTER 8

Tragedies and Shortened Careers

Joseph M. Overfield

If, of all words of tongue and pen,
The saddest are, "It might have been,"
More sad are these we daily see:
"It is, but hadn't ought to be."
　　　　　　　　—Bret Harte

In the eleventh century in the reign of William the Conqueror, detailed information about the landowners of England and their assets was gathered and then recorded in what were called *Domesday Books.* Much of what is known of the demographics of early England is derived from these books.

Baseball also has its *Domesday Books,* but they are called *Encyclopedias.* They list the name, vital statistics, and records of every player who ever appeared in a major league game, beginning with the formation of the National Association in 1871. So assiduously have baseball's *Domesday Books* been corrected, refined, and updated, it is safe to say that detailed information is more readily available about ballplayers, even the most obscure, than it is for statesmen, authors, artists, poets, or captains of industry.

Informative as they are, the *Encyclopedias* still leave much unsaid. For example, why did Bert Shepard play but a single game, while Jim McGuire played for twenty-six seasons? Short careers, like Shepard's, usually mean a lack of ability or, perhaps, the failure to receive a fair opportunity; but often they are short for other reasons— death, illness, injury, accident, suicide, or even murder. It is with such tragically shortened careers that this chapter will deal. Although the subject was carefully researched, no assertion of 100 percent completeness is proffered.

Since baseball's *Domesday Books* are limited to major league players and managers, no listing will be found there for minor leaguers like Bill Thomas of the 1906 Buffalo Bisons or Ralph Worrell of the 1918 Baltimore Orioles or Jeff Hoffman of the 1992 Albany-Colonie Yankees.

James Creighton was the star pitcher of the Excelsior Club, a famous Brooklyn amateur nine of the 1850s and 1860s. Before Creighton's day, it was customary for pitchers to toss the ball gently to the plate. Creighton changed all this by developing a snap throw that gave speed and spin to the ball. In addition, he was one of the most powerful hitters of his day. It is said that he completed one entire season without being put out. On October 14, 1862, the Excelsiors were playing the Union Club of Morrisania in their final match of the season. Creighton, at bat for the Excelsiors, swung mightily and sent the ball beyond the reach of the outfielders. As he crossed first base, he collapsed, obviously in great pain. Legend has it that he staggered around the bases for a home run. He was immediately taken home by his teammates. Four days later, the twenty-one-year-old pitcher was dead. According to an account in the *Brooklyn Eagle,* headlined "Obsequies of a Celebrated Ballplayer," Creighton had ruptured his bladder with the force of his final swing and died from internal bleeding.

A. G. Spalding, in his book *Baseball, America's National Game,* devoted two pages to Creighton, with his picture and a view of the towering granite monument his teammates erected in his memory on Tulip Hill in Brooklyn's Greenwood Cemetery. The monument is embossed with crossed bats, a cap, a base, and a scorebook.

The circumstances of the death of Bill Thomas, a twenty-five-year-old Buffalo pitcher, in April 1906, are still a mystery. Thomas had been a big winner in the Pacific Coast League, and manager George Stallings of Buffalo had brought him east to test his mettle in the stronger Eastern League. He was successful in his first start at Baltimore. The Bisons then finished a series at Providence and took a train to New Bedford, Massachusetts, from which point they boarded the night boat *Richard Peck,* en route to New York City. Thomas had left word with the porter and with his roommate, pitcher Joe Galaski, that he wanted an early call so he could see the New York skyline at sunrise. In the morning, when the porter came into the stateroom, the Thomas bunk, which had been slept in, was empty. Thomas was never seen again.

In 1918 Ralph Worrell, only nineteen, won 25 games for Jack Dunn's Baltimore Orioles, but he never pitched again. Instead of becoming another Lefty Grove (also a Jack Dunn discovery), Worrell failed to survive the winter, dying in the terrible World War One flu epidemic.

Just as tragic was the death of twenty-nine-year-old Yankee farmhand Jeff Hoffman of the Albany-Colonie Yankees, August 29, 1992. The young righthanded pitcher collapsed in his Binghamton (N.Y.) hotel room and died later that day in a local hospital. There was no evidence of foul play or drug or alcohol use. After several days it was determined he had died from a heart deficiency, previously undetected. He left his wife Teresa, who was expecting their first child.

The deaths of young, vigorous, and supposedly healthy athletes like Creighton, Thomas, Worrell, and Hoffman are sad and decidedly against the odds, but in the muster rolls of major league players in baseball's *Domesday Books*, such cases are far from rare.

Fatal Illnesses of Players and Managers

Elmer White was long thought to be a brother of James "Deacon" White and Will White. The early encyclopedias listed him as playing 15 games for the Forest Cities of Cleveland in 1872, but nothing more. A trip by the writer to the village of Caton in New York's southern tier and to the cemetery behind the Methodist Church there resulted in the finding of Elmer White's grave. The inscription on the tombstone, which showed he was Jim's and Will's cousin, not a brother, told with great economy of words the story of a short life and a short baseball career: "Born December 7, 1850. Died March 17, 1873."

Of all the deaths of active major leaguers to be recounted here, significantly, only one—that of Ray Chapman, who was killed by a Carl Mays pitch—resulted directly from activity on the diamond. Many of the deaths, especially those in the first fifty years, were from illnesses routinely controlled today. Typhoid fever, for example, killed first baseman Alex McKinnon of Pittsburgh (NL) on July 24, 1887. He played in the July 4 game, complained of not feeling well, and was taken home. He died twenty days later at the age of thirty. Less than a year later, on April 29, 1888, Charlie Ferguson, an outstanding young pitcher who had won 21, 26, 30, and 22 games for Philadelphia (NL) from 1884 through 1887 and was a strong hitter as well (.288 in four seasons), died from the same disease, twelve days after his twenty-fifth birthday.

On May 14, 1892 in a game at Boston, twenty-eight-old Brooklyn outfielder Hub Collins, who had played in the major leagues since 1886 and had led the American Association in doubles in 1888 and the National League in 1890, was pinch hit for because he was not feeling well. Five days later he died in Brooklyn, a victim of typhoid fever.

Edward "Sy" Sutcliffe, a catcher for most of his career, had shifted to first base for Baltimore (NL) in 1892 and had done quite well, batting .279 in 66 games. In the off-season, the twenty-nine-year-old native of Wheaton, Illinois, developed Bright's disease. He died February 13, 1893.

Joe Cassidy, an infielder for the Washington Senators in 1904 and 1905, was a fourth victim of the deadly typhoid. He was only twenty-three when he died at his home in Chester, Pennsylvania, March 25, 1906. Just a year and four days later, March 29, 1907, Patrick Henry "Cozy" Dolan, a nine-year outfielder in the majors, most recently with Boston (NL), also died of typhoid. He took ill during Boston's spring training trip, and died in a Louisville hospital, at age thirty-four. News of his death was overshadowed in the Boston papers by the extensive coverage given to the sensational suicide of manager Chick Stahl of the other Boston club, the day before in West Baden, Indiana.

Mike Powers, who caught in the majors from 1898 to 1909, mainly with the Philadelphia Athletics, was an anomaly in those hard-bitten days of the game's history, in that he held a degree from Holy Cross College and had also attended Notre Dame Medical School. Powers, incidentally, recruited the legendary Louis "Chief" Sockalexis for both of his alma maters, as shall be seen later. Powers was not a strong hitter (.216 lifetime), but he was considered a fine defensive catcher. He was behind the plate in an early season game in 1909, when he complained of nausea and asked to be taken to a hospital. He underwent three stomach operations, and then gangrene set in. "Doc" Powers died April 26, 1909, at the age of thirty-eight.

Alan Storke was an infielder for Pittsburgh and St. Louis (NL) from 1906 through 1909. He never made it to spring training in 1910. He was a mere twenty-five when he died in Newton, Massachusetts, March 18, 1910, following a lung operation. Less than two years later, February 1, 1912, another National League infielder, thirty-year-old Jimmy Doyle, who had batted .282 for the Cubs in 1911, died in Syracuse, New York, after an appendicitis operation.

Addie Joss pitched in the majors only eight seasons and part of a ninth, but his record was so extraordinary that he was elected to the Hall of Fame (in 1978), despite his short tenure. With Cleveland from 1902 to 1910, he won 160 games, lost 97, and compiled an ERA of 1.88 (second on the all-time list). He pitched a perfect game on October 2, 1908, defeating Big Ed Walsh, 1–0, with first place on the line. Joss had another no-hitter on April 20, 1910, also against the White Sox, just before his health began to fail.

Joss made only 13 appearances in 1910, and still felt weak when he went south in 1911. He collapsed on the bench during an exhibition game at Chattanooga, Tennessee, then became ill again when the team reached Cincinnati. Doctors said it was pleurisy and sent him home to Toledo. On April 14, 1911, two days after his team had opened the season in St. Louis, he died at the age of thirty-one. The cause of his death was given as tubercular meningitis. Famed ballplayer-preacher Billy Sunday presided at his funeral, said to have been the biggest ever seen in Toledo.

Leonard "King" Cole, a righthanded pitcher who had won 20 games for the Cubs in 1910 and 18 the following season, was, like Charlie Ferguson, to have a brilliant career nipped in the bud by a fatal illness. During the 1915 season, when Cole was with the Yankees, it was discovered that he had been suffering from tuberculosis. He returned to his home in Bay City, Michigan, where he died on January 6, 1916, at twenty-nine. He left a splendid 56–27 (.675) won–lost record.

Joe Leonard, a twenty-five-year-old infielder who began with Pittsburgh in 1914 and played for Washington in 1916, 1917, and 1919, appeared in only one game for the Senators in 1920, became ill, and was taken to George Washington Hospital. He died there on May 1, following an appendicitis operation.

In 1922, the St. Louis Cardinals lost two young ballplayers within nine months. First to go was William "Pickles" Dillhoefer, who had caught in the majors since 1917, usually in a backup role. He was twenty-seven when he died in a St. Louis hospital, February 22, 1922, of that old bugaboo, typhoid fever. Outfielder Austin McHenry had started with the Cardinals in 1918, but had not really blossomed until 1921, when he batted .350 and hit 37 doubles, 8 triples, and 17 home runs. The following year he began to have difficulties in judging fly balls. Manager Branch Rickey sent him to a doctor, who diagnosed his problem as a brain tumor. An operation proved unsuccessful, and he died at Jefferson Township, Ohio,

November 27, 1922. He was twenty-seven, the same age as Dillhoefer.

The 1924 season saw the deaths of two veterans of the Cincinnati Reds within eight months. Pat Moran was a catcher in the majors from 1901 to 1914 and then a highly successful manager, first with the Phillies and then with the Reds. In nine managerial seasons, he compiled a record of 748–586 and won a pennant with each team. His 1915 Phillies lost the World Series to the Boston Red Sox, in five games, while his 1919 Reds won the tainted 1919 Series from the White Sox, 5–3. Moran was forty-eight when he died of Bright's disease at Orlando, Florida, March 7, 1924, while at spring training with the Reds. The second Red to die that year was Jake Daubert, a fancy-fielding first baseman who could hit (.303 in fifteen years with the Dodgers and the Reds). Although forty years old, he played 102 games for the Reds in 1924, batted .281 and fielded .990. He became ill in October and was taken to Good Samaritan Hospital in Cincinnati, where he died on October 9 following an appendicitis operation, just as Jimmy Doyle and Joe Leonard had before him.

Legendary New York Giants outfielder and future Hall of Famer Ross Youngs was at the height of his career when he was struck down by Bright's disease, diagnosed during spring training in 1926. Despite his illness, he played 95 games and batted .306. All through the season, he was accompanied by a male nurse hired by manager John McGraw. Youngs was bedridden for the entire 1927 season and died on October 22 at the age of thirty. Despite his relatively short career, nine seasons and part of another, his record was impressive enough to earn him election to the Hall of Fame in 1972. McGraw said he was the greatest outfielder he had ever seen.

Urban Shocker was an outstanding pitcher for the great Yankee teams of the 1925–1927 period. His record was 18–6 for the 1927 Yankees, but illness kept him out of the World Series. His thirteen-year record with the St. Louis Browns and the Yankees is in Hall of Fame country— 187–117 (.615)—and he never had a losing season. His health continued to fail in 1928, and he appeared in only one game before being released. On September 9, 1928, in Denver, he died of heart disease and pneumonia. He was thirty-eight.

Shocker's manager, Miller Huggins, was to survive him little more than a year. On September 20, 1929, Huggins, who had managed the Yankees since 1918 and had won six pennants and three world's championships, asked coach Art Fletcher to take over for him, so that he could check into a hospital. Five days later, he was dead of erysipelas, a streptococcal skin infection. Huggins, who was of Munchkin size at 5'6" and 140 pounds, had been in the majors since 1904, batting a career .265, and winning 1,413 games and losing 1,134 as a manager. His showdowns with his rambunctious slugger, Babe Ruth, are part of baseball lore. Huggins was elected to the Hall of Fame in 1964.

On May 28, 1930, Hal Carlson, thirty-eight-year-old righthanded pitcher of the Chicago Cubs, and a fourteen-year veteran of the National League, called several of his teammates to his apartment in a Chicago hotel, saying that he was in severe pain. Shortly after the team physician arrived, Carlson was dead from what was described

as "an internal hemorrhage." He left a three-year-old son and his wife, who was expecting another child.

Twenty-nine-year-old infielder Mickey Finn, who had played for the Dodgers from 1930 to 1932 and then for the Phillies, became ill midway through the 1933 season. Owner Gerry Nugent of the Phillies summoned his brother-in-law, Dr. H. P. Boyle, who diagnosed Finn's trouble as a duodenal ulcer. Surgery was performed in an Allentown, Pennsylvania, hospital. He seemed on the road to recovery, but unforeseen medical problems arose, leading to his death on July 7, 1933.

On August 28, 1949, Ernie Bonham, who had pitched seven seasons for the Yankees and appeared in three World Series, but who was now with the Pirates, pitched his team to an 8–2 win over the Phillies. He had complained of some discomfort during the game, and as a precaution was taken to a Pittsburgh hospital, where appendicitis was diagnosed. The normally routine operation extended for three hours when complications developed. He was very weak when manager Billy Meyer visited him a few days later. "Billy, they are hitting me all over the field, and I can't get anybody out," he mumbled. On September 15, minutes before Meyer and coach Goldie Holt arrived for another visit, he passed away. Bonham, who was thirty-six, left an impressive 103–72 record.

Perhaps the closest parallel to the death of James Creighton in the preprofessional era was the shocking and tragic passing of first baseman Harry Agganis of the Boston Red Sox, on June 27, 1955 at the age of twenty-five. Like Creighton, Agganis was young and talented, with a glorious career seemingly assured.

At 6'2", 200 pounds, and lefthanded, Agganis was a drawing-board first baseman. "The Golden Greek," as he was called, was the most publicized athlete to come out of Boston University since Mickey Cochrane in 1923. Such were Agganis's skills as a quarterback that he was a first-round draft pick of the Cleveland Browns, who offered him $25,000 to sign. When the Boston Red Sox upped this figure by $10,000, he chose baseball. After the 1953 season at Louisville (American Association), where he batted .281, had 23 home runs, 108 RBIs, and played in 155 games, he took over at first base for the parent club in 1954. He batted only .251 his first season. In the early going in 1955, he was over .300 when he developed pneumonia and was hospitalized for ten days. He returned to the lineup, but became ill again in Kansas City. He flew back to Boston and checked into Santa Maria Hospital in nearby Cambridge. He was thought to be recovering nicely, when suddenly on June 27, he died. The cause of his death was given as a massive pulmonary embolism.

Agganis's body lay in state at St. George's Greek Orthodox Church in his home town of Lynn, Massachusetts. On the day before the funeral, ten thousand mourners passed the bier.

Righthanded pitcher Jim Umbricht of Houston underwent a cancer operation on March 8, 1963. By May 9 he was back in uniform, and he finished the year with a 4–3 record and an ERA of 2.61 in 35 appearances. He did not make it into the next season. The malignancy spread, and he died on April 8, 1964, at age thirty-three.

On April 13, 1965, twenty-five-year-old righthander Dick Wantz made his major league debut with the California Angels, giving up three hits and two runs in one inning of relief. Exactly one month later, he was dead, following an operation for a brain tumor.

According to present information, two active major leaguers succumbed to leukemia. Both were twenty-nine when they died and both at one time played with Minnesota. The first was giant 6'7" Walter Bond, who started with Cleveland in 1960, moved to Houston in 1964 and then to Minnesota in 1967, when illness forced him to quit. He died in Houston, September 14, 1967.

The second, infielder Danny Thompson, who broke in with Minnesota in 1970, had played for three years in the majors when he learned he had leukemia. He continued to play, however, and on June 1, 1976, he was involved in one of the big trades of the year, when he was bundled with pitcher Bert Blyleven and shipped to Texas for Roy Smalley, Bill Singer, Mike Cubbage, Jim Gideon, and $250,000. Thompson finished the season with Texas, but it was to be his last. Baseball's Most Courageous Performer (he was so voted in 1974) was only twenty-nine when he died December 10, 1976, at Rochester, Minnesota.

In a single year, 1966, the Detroit Tigers lost two managers to illness and subsequent death, a tragic sequence not duplicated in major league history. On May 16 Charley Dressen, who had managed in the majors for sixteen seasons, suffered a heart attack and was succeeded by coach Bob Swift. Dressen died three months later at the age of sixty-seven. Swift himself became ill in July and was hospitalized, with another coach, Frank Skaff, taking over. It was found that Swift had an advanced case of lung cancer. He died October 16 at the age of fifty-one.

Quiet, efficient, and soft-spoken Dick Howser was an American League infielder from 1961 to 1968 with Kansas City, Cleveland, and New York. He became manager of the Yankees in 1980 and led them to 103 wins and a division title. After the Yankees lost the league championship series to Kansas City, 0–3, owner George Steinbrenner made things so uncomfortable for Howser that he resigned. He moved to Kansas City in 1981, winning a division title in 1984, then a pennant and a world's championship in 1985.

Early in the 1986 season, Howser began to suffer from headaches and to experience visual and memory problems. On July 18, he learned he had a malignant brain tumor. Operations followed, and he recovered sufficiently to return to uniform in 1987. But his health continued to deteriorate and he was forced to give up his managerial duties. He was fifty years old when he died, June 17, 1987.

Suicides and Other Violent Deaths

According to present information, five active major leaguers and one league president ended their lives by their own hands. Four others killed themselves in the year after they had been sent to the minors. Another Johnny Mostil, attempted suicide but recovered. There is also some intimation that the violent deaths of Len Koenecke and Ed Delahanty might have been "death wish" situations.

On February 28, 1894, Edgar McNabb, a pitcher who had won eight games for the Baltimore Orioles in 1893, checked in at the Eiffel Hotel on Smithfield Street in Pittsburgh. He told the clerk that his wife had gone to Braddock to visit her ailing parents and that he should give her the room key when she returned. Earlier that day, the McNabbs had run into a friend, one Louis Gillen, and the three had agreed to attend the theater that evening.

When the agreed time for the meeting passed, Gillen became concerned and went to the McNabbs' room. As he stood outside the door, he heard a woman's screams. He called for help, and when the room clerk opened the door, the two were shocked and sickened by the bloody and grisly scene before them. Mrs. McNabb lay on the floor, bleeding horribly from bullet holes in her neck and head, but still breathing. Lying beside her, dead, with bullet holes in the head, was Edgar McNabb. A pistol was still in his hand.

As the story unfolded, it became more than a tragic domestic confrontation. The dying woman was not Mrs. McNabb at all. She was Mrs. R. E. Rockwell, whose husband was a well-known West Coast baseball figure and had once been president of the Pacific Northwest Baseball League. She was an actress by profession and used the stage name of Louise Kellogg.

It appeared that Miss Kellogg, who had just finished a theatrical engagement in New York, had asked McNabb to meet her in Pittsburgh. According to a newspaper account, she was planning to break off her relationship with the ballplayer. Letters found in the room indicated that she had been sending him money to tide him over the winter, and further that there had been recent disagreements between them. In the judgment of the police who investigated, an argument had developed, culminating in McNabb's shooting of Miss Kellogg and then turning the gun on himself.

Among McNabb's possessions on the scene was a copy of a message which read: IN GREAT TROUBLE, TELEGRAPH $100 IMMEDIATELY. SEE YOU IN TWO WEEKS. It was probably this message that led Edgar McNabb and Louise Kellogg to their fateful rendezvous at the Eiffel Hotel. Miss Kellogg miraculously survived her wounds but was paralyzed.

Even more shocking than the McNabb affair was the sad denouement of Marty Bergen, first-string catcher for Frank Selee's Boston (NL) club from 1896 to 1899.

On the morning of January 19, 1900, Marty's father, Michael Bergen, who was staying at the house of a neighbor, walked to his son's property, which was called "Snowball Farm," to get some milk. Seeing no activity around the house, he left. He returned at noon and still saw no signs of life. He walked through the unlocked kitchen door, only to be confronted by a scene of unspeakable horror. On the kitchen floor, lay the body of his six-year-old granddaughter Florence. In the adjoining room, he found the body of his daughter-in-law Harriet Bergen and next to her that of her three-year-old son Joseph. Mrs. Bergen's hands were raised as though in supplication or as though trying to ward off a blow. A bloody ax, the apparent murder weapon, was found on the scene. Bergen himself had committed suicide with a straight razor, almost severing his head from his body.

Dr. W. E. Norwood, the medical examiner, made an almost on-the-spot judgment, ruling that the crime had been committed "in a fit of insanity," and that no autopsies would be necessary. According to the account in *The Sporting Life,* the funeral service at St. Joseph's Church in North Brookfield was somber and brief, and "only a few words suitable to the occasion were spoken." The only prominent baseball people present were Connie Mack of the Milwaukee club and Billy Hamilton, a Bergen teammate.

What triggered the carnage at Snowball Farm will never be known. Bergen's manager, Frank Selee, said that he seemed, at times, to act irrationally and to be pursued by hallucinations. It was also revealed that he had sought help from his pastor and his doctor, and that on one occasion he had accused the latter of trying to kill him. Bergen was not a drinker and apparently had no pressing money problems. He was buying the farm on the installment plan and had $2,000 in cash.

On January 12, 1903, not quite three years after the Bergen murder-suicide, the baseball world was stunned by the self-inflicted death of another prominent player. George Barclay "Win" Mercer was a versatile performer who had played every position but catcher in nine years in the majors, winning 131 games as a pitcher and batting .285. He was manager-designate for Detroit, where he had played in 1902.

Mercer was on the West Coast for a series of exhibition games between teams from the American and National leagues. A small man with striking good looks, he had a weakness for fast women and slow horses, a deadly combination that apparently was to do him in. On the fatal day, he did not appear when expected in the dining room of the San Francisco hotel where the players were staying. When the door of his room was opened, Mercer's body was found. A rubber hose was connected to a gas jet. He had died of self-inflicted asphyxiation.

Mercer left a suicide note in which he warned of the evils of women and gambling. He also left a note for his mother and one for his fiancée in East Liverpool, Ohio. Another letter was addressed to Tip O'Neill, manager of the ballplayer troupe, for which Mercer was in charge of finances. Even though Mercer had recently incurred heavy gambling losses, it was reported that his baseball accounts were in order.

Charles "Chick" Stahl had batted .307 in ten major league seasons and was considered one of the game's premier defensive outfielders. Stahl, a Marty Bergen teammate at Boston (NL) from 1897 to 1899, had been named manager of the Boston Puritans (AL) late in the 1906 season, succeeding his friend and roommate Jimmy Collins. Stahl was handsome, popular, well paid for his era, and recently married. Despite his oft-expressed distaste for managing and a recent attempt to resign, it seemed he had almost every reason to be on top of the world; but on March 28, 1907, in his room at the West Baden Hotel in West Baden, Indiana, he ingested a lethal dose of carbolic acid. As he staggered toward his bed, roommate Collins went to his assistance, just in time to hear him gasp: "Boys, I couldn't help it; it drove me to it."

For years, baseball historians pondered Stahl's cryptic words, then usually concluded it was the pressure of managing that forced him to swallow the poison. Dissenting was Harold Seymour, who, in his *Baseball, The Early Years,* strongly hints at the real reason: *cherchez la femme.* In the May 1986 issue of *Boston Magazine,* author Glenn

Stout dug out the rest of the Stahl story and wrote it.

Stahl, according to Stout, although in love with a young lady named Julia Harmon of Roxbury, Massachusetts, was also attracted to other young ladies, the groupies of his day. Furthermore, according to Stout, one of his admirers, a Lulu Ortman, demanded that Stahl marry her. When he spurned her, she twice tried to shoot him but missed. Meanwhile, on November 14, 1906, Stahl had married Miss Harmon at St. Francis de Sales Church in Roxbury. It seems that he had also been involved, late in the 1906 season, with another woman, who now claimed to be pregnant by him. She pressured Stahl to marry her on pain of exposure. He told her that marriage was impossible, since he was already married. She persisted that spring, and it was this pressure, concludes Stout, not the pressure of managing, that led to his suicide.

A sad postscript to the Stahl suicide was the fate of his wife, Julia. Shortly after his death, she attempted suicide herself, but survived. On November 15, 1908, she was found dead in the doorway of a house in South Boston, after a night on the town. An autopsy showed that she had died of edema of the brain.

Little more than two years after the Stahl tragedy, another suicide rocked the game, but it had none of the nasty characteristics of the McNabb, Bergen, or Stahl cases.

Richard Cory, in Edwin Arlington Robinson's poem of the same name, was young, elegant, and well thought of, but one summer night he "went home and put a bullet through his head." Harry Clay Pulliam, president of the National League, was baseball's Richard Cory. On June 28, 1909, Pulliam went to his room in the New York Athletic Club and fired a shot through his head. He died the next morning. The forty-year-old bachelor left no suicide note. Presumably it was a combination of poor health (he had been on leave of absence for health reasons) and the burdens of his job that caused him to do it.

On December 13, 1910, Dennis "Dan" McGann, former captain of the New York Giants and a premier first baseman for thirteen seasons, but most recently a member of the Milwaukee club of the American Association, was found dead in a Louisville hotel room, a bullet hole in his heart and a revolver in his hand. He had been seen around the hotel during the day and had appeared to be in good spirits. One explanation was that he was depressed over the suicide of a brother the past summer.

On March 28, 1927, at the Youree Hotel in Shreveport, Louisiana, spring training headquarters of the Chicago White Sox, Johnny Mostil, the team's star center fielder, slashed both wrists and wounded himself in the chest, throat, and legs with a razor blade and a knife. Early reports, giving him little chance to survive, were wrong. He did recover, played later that same season, and two more seasons thereafter, followed by a long career in the game as a scout. The only explanation for his act seems to have been his hypochondriacal nature. He constantly worried and brooded over his health, although a physical examination that spring had revealed no serious problems.

In eight major league seasons, Cincinnati righthander Benny Frey had struggled to a 57–82 record. At the end of the 1936 season, the best of his career (he was 10–8), he was sent to Nashville to work an ailing arm back into shape. Apparently despondent over the failure of his arm to recover, Frey, on November 1, 1937, at Jackson, Michigan, sat in his car with the motor running and a rubber hose attached to the exhaust pipe. When police found the thirty-one-year-old pitcher, he was dead from carbon monoxide poisoning.

It was August 3, 1940, and the Cincinnati Reds were in Boston. Pleading illness, catcher Willard Hershberger told his roommate, Bill Baker (some accounts say it was Lew Riggs), that he would not be able to come to the ballpark until later. When he did not appear and his telephone was not answered, manager Bill McKechnie sent Dan Cohen, Hershberger's close friend, to the hotel to get him. When the room was entered, Hershberger's body was found in the bathroom, his jugular vein severed by a razor.

Hershberger was young (just thirty), successful, and single, and there seemed no apparent reason for his act. As in the McGann case, there had been a previous suicide in the family. Hershberger's father had shot himself to death in 1928. It has been theorized that the catcher was depressed over his recent failures on the diamond. He had gone hitless in a crucial game, and on another occasion had supposedly called a wrong pitch to Harry Danning of the Giants, who then had hit a home run to beat the Reds in the ninth inning. On the other hand, it was no secret that he had been contemplating suicide. He had told manager McKechnie as much in recent weeks. Also, he had recently purchased a $500 bond, placed it in the hotel safe, and asked that it be given to his mother "if anything happens to me."

With all the obvious planning, it is curious that no suicide note was found. Suicidal tendencies notwithstanding, a hitless game and the call of a wrong pitch hardly seem sufficient to have provoked the deed. It took almost eighty years for the truth to be revealed about the Stahl suicide. Someday, perhaps, more light will be shed on the Hershberger story.

In seven seasons with the Chicago White Sox, Mexican-born righthander Francisco Barrios compiled a 38–38 record. After the 1981 season, during which he had entered a Chicago hospital for drug and alcohol treatment, he was released. On April 4, 1982, he died at his parents' home in Hermosillo, Mexico, of heart failure brought on by an overdose of heroin.

Donnie Ray Moore had a combined 52 saves in 1985 and 1986 for the California Angels, only to become the goat of the 1986 championship series loss to Boston when he gave up a two-out, two-run home run to Dave Henderson that helped cost the Angels the title. He spent most of the next season on the disabled list, was released by the Angels in 1988 and then signed with Omaha of the American Association. He was released by the Royals on June 12 after seven appearances and a 1–2 record. On July 18 he shot his estranged wife (she recovered) and then killed himself with a bullet to the brain as his ten-year-old son watched in horror. Moore's agent attributed all of Moore's troubles to his brooding over the Henderson home run.

Over the years, ballplayers have died violently, other than by suicide. The bizarre death of Hall of Famer Ed Delahanty is a case in point. In 1903 he was with Washington of the American League, but wanted to be with the Giants in New York, where he felt he could earn more money. He dealt with his unhappiness by consuming generous doses of alcohol, starting with a drinking spree in Cleveland. Later, in Detroit, where he took out an accident policy in favor of his daughter, he was heard to threaten to take his own life.

On July 2, 1903, Delahanty boarded a Michigan Central train at Detroit with a ticket to Buffalo, from where, it is believed, he planned to catch another train to Washington to meet his wife. The conductor said Delahanty was "under the weather" when he got on at Detroit and that he had downed at least five shots of whiskey along the way. Not only was he boisterous, but he also threatened some passengers with a razor. At Bridgeburg, Ontario, just across the Niagara River from Buffalo, the conductor ejected him from the train. Delahanty, in the darkness, began to walk across the International Bridge, a railroad bridge connecting Bridgeburg and Buffalo. Bridge watchman Sam Kingston had just escorted a freight across the bridge and, lantern in hand, was walking back to the Canadian side when he confronted Delahanty. Words were exchanged and a scuffle ensued. It is not clear (Kingston told conflicting stories) if Delahanty fell, jumped, or was pushed into the river. Eight days later, his body was found at Niagara Falls, below the Horseshoe Falls.

Subsequently, Delahanty's widow filed suit in the Ontario courts against the Michigan Central Railroad, seeking $20,000 damages for the wrongful death of her husband. She was awarded $3,000, and her daughter received $2,000.

When Walter "Big Ed" Morris won 19 games for the last-place Boston Red Sox in 1928 and then came back with 14 wins for another cellar Boston club in 1929, he became one of the most sought-after pitchers in the league. One story had the Red Sox turning down a $100,000 offer. A sore arm slowed Morris in 1930 and 1931, and his record retrogressed to 4–9 and 5–7. Confident that his arm had regained its strength, he prepared to go to spring training in 1932. As a going-away present, some of his buddies arranged a party for him at a tavern in Century, Florida, just across the state line from Morris's hometown of Flomaton, Alabama. Unfortunately, the party began to get out of hand, and soon the guest of honor was involved in a fight with Joe White, a gas station attendant from Brewton, Alabama. When Morris slipped to the floor, White pulled a knife and stabbed him twice, fatally. Morris was thirty-one and left a widow and two children.

Len Koenecke was an impressive-looking athlete—broad of shoulder, slim of waist, and ruggedly handsome. He was said to have been the last player personally scouted by John McGraw, who arranged for his purchase from Indianapolis (American Association) in 1931 for players valued at $75,000. The young outfielder failed to live up to his minor league billings and was farmed to Jersey City in 1932 and to Buffalo in 1933. An outstanding season for the Bisons in 1933 led to his sale to Brooklyn, where in 1934 he batted .320 and fielded a league-leading .994. But he slumped in 1935, and late that year manager Casey Stengel sent Koenecke and two other players home from St. Louis so that he could try out some young prospects.

On the flight from St. Louis to Detroit, Koenecke, who

had been drinking, created a disturbance, and when the airport was reached he was ordered off the plane. Although it was late in the evening, he decided to charter a private plane and fly to Buffalo, where he had friends. The plane he chartered had an interesting past. It had once been owned by Smith Reynolds of the tobacco family and his wife, torch singer Libby Holman, who were principals in one of the most sensational murder cases of the 1930s. When Reynolds was shot to death at the family estate in Winston-Salem, N.C., his wife was charged with the crime but was later cleared.

While the plane was still over Canada, Koenecke tried to take over the controls from pilot William Mulqueeny. Irwin Davis, the copilot, attempted to restrain the husky ballplayer but was pushed to the floor. Mulqueeny, while trying to guide the plane with one hand, picked up a fire extinguisher with the other and bludgeoned Koenecke until he was dead. Mulqueeny had no idea where he was until he spotted the lights of Toronto. Seeing a racetrack on the outskirts of the city, he decided to use the backstretch as an airport and brought the plane safely down. Then, to cap their night of terror, the two men were attacked by watch dogs as they left the plane. The dogs eventually backed off, and they were able to summon help.

After two hearings in Canadian courts, Mulqueeny and Davis were absolved of all blame in Koenecke's death. Blood tests had shown that the dead ballplayer was drunk. At one of the hearings, Edward J. Murphy, attorney for the pilots, alleged that Koenecke was trying to commit suicide and to do it "in a grand and glorious manner."

In the early hours of January 5, 1975, Don Wilson, star righthanded pitcher of the Houston Astros, who had won 104 games in nine major league seasons and pitched two no-hitters, drove his luxury car into the garage of his suburban Houston home and left the motor running. At one P.M. his lifeless body was found slumped in the passenger seat. The ignition was on, the battery was dead, the gas tank was empty, and there were exhaust-fume stains on the garage floor. In the room above the garage, his five-year-old son Alexander was dead from the fumes. His wife, Bernice, and his daughter, Denise, were taken to the hospital in serious condition. Bernice Wilson also had a badly bruised jaw, which was never explained, but which could have been caused by a fall.

Mrs. Wilson and her daughter both recovered. Tests on the twenty-nine-year-old Don Wilson revealed a blood-alcohol content of .167. On February 5, 1975, the medical examiner ruled the deaths of father and son were accidental.

Mickey Fuentes, a righthanded pitcher who was 1–3 for Seattle in 1969, never made it to spring training in 1970. He was shot to death in a tavern brawl in his native Loiza Aldea, Puerto Rico, January 29, 1970, He was only twenty years old.

With Lyman Bostock, who had starred for Minnesota (in 1975–1977) and then had signed a lucrative free-agent contract with California, it was a case of being in the wrong place at the wrong time. On September 23, 1978, in Gary, Indiana, he was in a car being driven by his uncle when he was shot by a man named Leonard Smith, whose apparent target was Smith's estranged wife, seated next to Bostock in the back seat. Three hours after the assault, the twenty-seven-year-old Bostock was dead. There was whispering that something was going on between Bostock and Mrs. Smith. Actually they had met only twenty minutes before and were heading for different destinations.

Leonard Smith was twice tried for murder. The first trial, in which insanity was pleaded, ended in a hung jury. In the second trial, he was found not guilty by reason of insanity, spent six months in a mental hospital, and then was a free man. Outrage over the outcome of the two trials resulted in a change in the Indiana law, whereby an accused can now be judged both insane and guilty of a crime.

Planes, Cars, Trucks, and a Dune Buggy

When superstars Roberto Clemente and Thurman Munson lost their lives in air crashes, it was front-page news all over the country. In Clemente's case, the coverage was international in scope because of the mercy mission in which he was involved.

Clemente and Munson were not the first active major leaguers to perish in airplane accidents. There were at least six prior air fatalities—seven if Koenecke is included. Marvin Goodwin, a righthanded spitball pitcher who saw action with the Senators, Cardinals, and Reds from 1916 through 1925, was the first. In 1925, nearing the end of his career, he was pitcher-manager of Houston of the Texas League, on assignment from the Cardinals. He did so well at Houston (21–9) that Cincinnati purchased him conditionally late in the season, with the understanding that final payment on the deal would be made only if he lasted thirty days into the 1926 season. He made four September appearances for the Reds with no wins and no losses.

Goodwin had been a flying instructor in World War One and was still a lieutenant in the reserve. On October 18, 1925, he took off on a practice flight from Ellington Field, near Houston, with a mechanic on board. The engine failed at 200 feet, and the plane crashed. The mechanic miraculously survived, but Goodwin, who suffered two broken legs and internal injuries, died four days later. The fatality had a ghoulish aftermath. The following year, the Cardinals demanded full payment for Goodwin's contract. The Reds refused on the grounds that he was not on their roster thirty days into the 1926 season. The case was referred to the commissioner's office. Judge Landis, citing the terms of the contract, ruled in favor of the Reds.

Elmer Joseph Gedeon played in the outfield for the Washington Senators in 1939. He had been a track star at the University of Michigan and had given up a chance to run in the Olympic Games to go into baseball. But then World War Two came along, and Gedeon gave up baseball to become an early volunteer in the Air Corps. He died April 15, 1944, when his plane was shot down over France. (Two others who played in the majors in 1939 also died in battle. Bob Neighbors, a shortstop for seven games with the St. Louis Browns, died in North Korea in 1952, and Harry O'Neill, who caught one game for the Philadelphia Athletics, perished in the assault on Iwo Jima in 1945.)

After his graduation from Boston University in 1955,

catcher Tom Gastall pocketed a $40,000 bonus from the Baltimore Orioles. He was used sparingly, playing 20 games in 1955 and 32 in 1956. On September 20, 1956, he took off in a light plane from Harbor Field, near Baltimore. He landed at Easton, from where he later took off for the return flight over the Chesapeake Bay. Five days later, his body and the wreckage of the plane were found in the water off Riviera Beach. Gastall was just twenty-four.

A little over two months later, on November 27, 1956, outfielder Charlie Peete, who had played 23 games for the St. Louis Cardinals that summer, died in a plane crash in the mountains of Venezuela, near Caracas, while en route to play winter ball. His wife and three children also perished in the crash.

Another victim of a Venezuelan air disaster was twenty-one-year-old Nestor Chavez, a San Francisco Giant farmhand who played in two games for the Giants in 1967. On March 16, 1969, the young pitcher was on his way to join the Giants' Phoenix farm club when his plane crashed, killing 155 passengers. It was one of the worst accidents in aviation history.

Ken Hubbs, playing 160 games for the Chicago Cubs in 1962, handled 148 consecutive chances without an error and was Rookie of the Year. He tailed off in 1963 but was still rated one of the game's rising young stars. At the end of the 1963 season, he began to take flying lessons. In early February 1964, shortly after he had received his license, Hubbs, who lived in Colton, California, flew to Provo, Utah, with a friend, Dennis Doyle, to visit Doyle's in-laws. On February 15, Hubbs and Doyle took off in a snowstorm for their return trip to California. Only five miles from Provo, the plane crashed into Utah Lake, killing Hubbs and Doyle.

After investigation, the Civil Aeronautics Board reported the probable cause as "Hubbs's attempt to continue visual flight into an area of adverse weather." The twenty-two-year-old Hubbs, who was not licensed for instrument flying, left a log book which showed he had flown just 71 hours, 16 minutes.

On September 30, 1972, Roberto Clemente, who had batted .317 in eighteen seasons with Pittsburgh, touched Jon Matlack of the Mets for a base hit. It was Clemente's 3,000th and last hit. On December 31, 1972, Clemente and four others were killed when a plane carrying food, clothing, and medical supplies to earthquake-stricken Nicaragua crashed moments after takeoff from San Juan, Puerto Rico.

Clemente's career had all the elements of a Horatio Alger tale. Born August 18, 1934, in Carolina, Puerto Rico, the son of a sugar plantation foreman, he was signed by Al Campanis of the Dodgers as a teenager. The Dodgers tried to cover him up on the Montreal (International League) roster, but Pittsburgh general manager Branch Rickey, who knew all about him from his days with the Dodgers, drafted him for a piddling $4,000. It was one of the greatest bargains in baseball history. Clemente immediately became a regular and won all manner of plaudits for his hitting, fielding, and magnificent throwing arm. He was Most Valuable Player in 1966, batted .310 and .414 in two World Series (1960, 1971), and was *The Sporting News*'s Gold Glove outfielder twelve times. Twice he hit three home runs in one game, and five times he led

National League outfielders in assists.

Clemente was voted into the Baseball Hall of Fame in 1973 in a special election, with the usual five-year waiting period waived by a change of the voting rules.

Thurman Munson was the only New York Yankee to win both Rookie of the Year (1970) and Most Valuable Player (1976) awards. He was the regular Yankee catcher from 1970, averaging more than 140 games a year, despite aching knees, a beaning, and a foul ball in the throat. He was one of the league's top clutch hitters, with 701 RBIs and a .292 average over eleven seasons. His clashes with new teammate Reggie Jackson over which of them was the straw that stirred the Yankee drink drew national attention.

On August 2, 1979, an off-day, Munson flew his new Cessna Citation jet from New York to Canton, Ohio, to visit his family. Late in the afternoon, he was practicing takeoffs and landings at the Akron-Canton Airport when the plane crashed a thousand feet short of the runway. Munson's flying companions, David Hall and Jerry Anderson, survived and at great danger to themselves, attempted to pull Munson from the flaming wreckage. But there was no chance. Munson, who was thirty-two, left his wife, Diane, and three children, not to mention millions of mourning baseball fans. On August 6 of that year, 51,000 fans at Yankee Stadium participated in an impressive nine-minute salute to the Yankee captain, who, with a few more years under his belt, could well have been a good bet for the Hall of Fame.

As far as is known, the first active major leaguer to die in a vehicular accident was Norman Boeckel, a .298 hitter for the 1923 Boston Braves. The thirty-one-year-old third baseman died February 16, 1924, in a San Diego hospital, from pelvic injuries sustained the day before, when he was standing alongside his car after it had been involved in a collision with a truck and he was struck by a passing motorist. Earlier, Boeckel had played a fringe role in another piece of baseball history. He had submitted an affidavit to National League President John Heydler, attesting that he had heard pitcher Rube Benton boast of winning $3,200 on the 1919 World Series on a tip from Hal Chase. Benton was thrown out of baseball, but was later reinstated by Judge Landis.

The year 1929 saw the deaths of two major leaguers in vehicular accidents. Denny Williams, a twenty-nine-year-old outfielder, who had played with the Reds in 1921 and the Red Sox in 1924, 1925 and 1928, was killed in Los Angeles, March 21. Seven months later, on October 22, Walter "Peck" Lerian, regular catcher for the Phillies in 1928 and 1929, died in a Baltimore hospital, after being hit by a truck that vaulted over a curb and pinned him against the wall of a building.

Catcher Al Montgomery was only twenty years old when he appeared in 42 games for the Boston Braves in 1941. While returning from spring training on April 26, 1942, having been assigned to Hartford of the Eastern League, he was involved in a car accident near Waverly, Virginia, and killed.

While Paul Edmondson, a twenty-seven-year-old pitcher who had been 1–6 with the 1969 White Sox, was en route to spring training, he was involved in a fatal auto accident February 13, 1970, near Santa Barbara, California. Another victim of a California crash was Chico Ruiz, who had been in the majors for eight years, first with Cincinnati and most recently with California. He was killed in San Diego February 9, 1972.

The pitching career of Bob Moose was a series of highs and lows. In ten years with the Pirates, he won 76 games and lost 71. One of his wins was a no-hitter against the New York Mets on September 20, 1969. On the other side of the coin is the wild pitch he uncorked in the final game of the 1972 league championship series that permitted Cincinnati to defeat Pittsburgh. He also made three appearances in the 1971 World Series, but had no decisions. On October 9, 1976, at Martin's Ferry, Ohio, he suffered fatal injuries in an automobile accident. It was his twenty-ninth birthday.

Righthanded pitcher Danny Frisella, who in ten years in the majors saw action with the Mets, Braves, Padres, Cardinals, and Brewers (34–40), took a dune buggy out in the desert near Phoenix on New Year's Day, 1977. When the buggy overturned, he was killed instantly.

Just six days later, on January 6, Mike Miley, a twenty-three-year-old shortstop with California in 1975 and 1976, was killed in a car crash at Baton Rouge.

On Friday night, December 19, 1986, Honolulu native Joe DeSa hit four doubles to help his Ponce Lions defeat the Mayaguez Indians, 11–8, in a Puerto Rico winter league game. At four A.M. on December 20, DeSa was killed in a head-on crash on the Las Americas Expressway. DeSa, who had played for Buffalo (American Association) in 1985 and 1986 and was the team's most valuable player in the latter year, had signed with Kansas City and was due to report in the spring for his third hitch in the majors.

The two known deaths of active players by drowning are separated by almost one hundred years. The first was England-born Al Thake, second baseman for the Brooklyn Atlantics. He drowned off Fort Hamilton, New York, while fishing, September 1, 1872. Almost a century later, on December 14, 1970, Herman Hill, twenty-five-year-old outfielder with Minnesota in 1969 and 1970, was in Venezuela to play winter ball when he drowned off Valencia.

On March 22, 1993, after a day of fishing on Little Lake Nellie, 27 miles north of Winter Haven, Florida, Cleveland Indians pitchers Tim Crews, Steve Olin, and Bob Ojeda were returning to shore in an open, eighteen-foot-base boat. In the darkness, Crews, who was returning the boat, did not see a dock that extended some 250 feet into the lake. He rammed it while traveling at an estimated 39 miles per hour. Olin was killed instantly and Crews died a few hours later. Ojeda came within an inch of having the top of his head sheared off, but though grievously injured did recover and returned to the mound late in the 1993 season, but is now out of baseball. Evidence in the boat and through blood tests indicated that alcohol was involved. Crews and Olin each left a wife and three small children. It was the only instance in major league history in which two players were killed in one accident.

Cleveland's cup of sorrow overflowed in the 1993 off-season as another member of its pitching staff lost his life in an accident. Reliever Cliff Young, a twenty-nine year-old veteran of three major league campaigns, was fatally injured in a November car crash.

Bean Balls

Every time a batter steps to the plate, it is an act of courage. With pitches hurtling toward him at 90 miles per hour, he has but a fraction of a second to decide if he should swing, take, or bail out. Modern helmets with ear flaps have removed much of the peril, but not all. Prior to the 1950s, batters had no head protection at all; and before 1893 the risk was even greater, since the pitching distance was only 50 feet.

Considering the danger involved, it is somewhat of a miracle that only one batter has been killed by a pitched ball in the long history of major league baseball. No definitive statistics are available, but it is known that many have been killed at the amateur level and at least seven in minor league play.

Major league baseball's only bean ball fatality, and its only diamond fatality for any reason, occurred on August 16, 1920, at the Polo Grounds, New York, in a game between the New York Yankees and the Cleveland Indians. It was the first half of the fifth inning, and shortstop Ray Chapman of the Indians was at bat, faced by Yankee submarine-baller Carl Mays. Chapman liked to crowd the plate and crouch over it. Mays, who had a mean streak, was not averse to throwing at any batter who encroached on his territory. Mays's first pitch was a strike, his second a ball, as Chapman seemed to edge even closer to the plate. Predictably the third pitch was high and inside. There was an ominous crack that was heard all over the Polo Grounds. Mays, thinking his pitch had hit Chapman's bat, fielded the ball and started to throw to Wally Pipp at first base, but then he saw Chapman slumped in the arms of catcher Muddy Ruel and he knew the batter had been hit. A doctor was summoned from the stands and Chapman was temporarily revived. Assisted by two of his teammates, he began the long walk to the clubhouse in center field, but he soon collapsed and was carried the rest of the way.

When a preliminary examination in the clubhouse showed the injury was extremely serious, he was taken to nearby St. Lawrence Hospital, where an operation was performed. He was still under ether when he died at five A.M. the following day, August 17.

The repercussions were immediate and furious. Mays, a surly sort and never popular among his peers, was strongly criticized. Detroit and Boston players demanded that he be barred for life, while those on the Washington and St. Louis clubs threatened to strike if Mays was allowed to pitch again. But Mays did have his defenders. Cleveland pitcher Ray Caldwell, a former Yankee, said it seemed to him that Chapman had turned his head right into the ball. Connie Mack, venerable skipper of the Philadelphia Athletics, while deploring the fatal accident, pleaded for sympathy for Mays. Catcher Muddy Ruel, who caught Chapman when he fell, said in later years that the pitch could have been a strike.

Mays appeared before the district attorney and, after a deposition, was cleared of any criminal charges. He said he was not trying to hit Chapman, only to pitch him tight. That spring, Mays pointed out, he had seen Yankee infielder Chick Fewster nearly killed by a pitch delivered by Jeff Pfeffer of the Dodgers, and from that time on he had been reluctant even to throw inside pitches, let alone throw at batters. He then suggested the fatality might have been averted had plate umpire Tom Connolly not refused to remove from play the scuffed ball that hit Chapman. This drew a sharp rejoinder from American League umpires Billy Evans and Bill Dinneen, who charged that Mays was one of the league's most notorious scuffers. They said further that club owners had complained to Ban Johnson, league president, that too many balls were being thrown out, and that Johnson had responded by sending out a directive, instructing umpires to keep balls in play, "except those which are dangerous."

In the *New York Times* of August 19, there was an impassioned plea for the development and use of batting helmets, but it was to be more than thirty years before this advice would be heeded.

Chapman was the only major leaguer to die directly from action on the diamond, but Opening Day fans at Cincinnati's Riverfront Stadium on April 1, 1996, watched in horror as 328-pound umpire John McSherry collapsed on the field with a massive heart attack. Less than an hour later, he was pronounced dead at University Hospital. He was fifty-one years old.

At least seven minor leaguers have been killed by pitched balls. On August 9, 1906, Joe Yaeger of Fall River of the New England League hit Tom Burke of Lynn in the head with a pitch. Two days later, Burke was dead. Two days after attending Burke's funeral, Yaeger took his turn on the mound, only to be arrested by Lynn police on a manslaughter charge. Shortly thereafter, the charges were dropped. Jaeger, who had pitched for six years in the majors with Brooklyn and Detroit, completed the season with a 15–19 record.

In the second game of a Central League doubleheader, played in gathering darkness at Dayton, September 14, 1909, Charles "Cupid" Pinkney, twenty-year-old Dayton second baseman, was beaned by Casey Hageman of Grand Rapids. At first, it was thought he would recover, but his condition deteriorated, and he died following an operation. Pinkney's father, who had traveled from Cleveland to watch his son play, was at his side when he died.

On June 18, 1916, Johnny Dodge, infielder for Mobile of the Southern Association, was hit on the head by Tom "Shotgun" Rogers of Nashville and died the next day of a fractured skull. It is believed that Dodge was thrown at in retaliation for the beaning of a Nashville player the previous day. By the strangest of coincidences, Rogers and Carl Mays were to be teammates briefly on the 1921 Yankees.

On July 4, 1933, at Omaha, Jesse Batterton, nineteen-year-old third baseman for Springfield of the Western League, suffered a fractured skull when hit by a pitch thrown by Omaha's Floyd "Swede" Carlson. He was able to get to his feet and walk to the clubhouse, but then collapsed and was taken to a hospital. He died there following an operation, with pitcher Carlson at his bedside.

On July 21, 1938, Linus "Skeeter" Ebnet, twenty-three-year-old shortstop for Winnipeg of the Northern League, died in a Winnipeg hospital, five days after being hit by a pitched ball in a game against Grand Forks.

Twenty-year-old James (Stormy) Davis was off to a great start for Ballinger (Texas) of the Longhorn League.

In 48 games he had hit 19 home runs and had 59 RBIs. On July 3, 1947 he was beaned by Stan (Midnight) Wilson of Sweetwater. The young outfielder died a week later.

A seventh fatality occurred in the Alabama-Florida League on June 2, 1951. Lefty Jack Clifton of Headland hit Ottis Johnson of the Dothan Browns on the head and killed him. In his next start, Clifton, who had already hit twelve batters that season, pitched a no-hit, no-run game against Panama City. According to Ken Brooks in his book *The Last Rebel Yell,* every Panama City batter had one foot in the dugout.

In major league history there have been countless beanings. In most cases, the batters came back, but often were not the same hitters as before. Lowell Reidenbaugh, in his *Cooperstown,* writes that Hughie Jennings survived three skull fractures. His most serious injury was from a pitch delivered by Amos Rusie of New York, said to have been the swiftest pitcher of his day. The blow left Jennings near death and unconscious for four days. Some historians say it was Rusie's speed and the fear that he might kill someone that brought about the lengthening of the pitching distance in 1893 to the present 60 feet, 6 inches.

At Ebbets Field on September 3, 1932, Giants shortstop Ed Marshall was beaned by a Van Lingle Mungo fastball. He survived despite lapsing into "unsafe condition." The incident ended his major league career although Marshall did play thereafter in the minors.

On May 25, 1937, future Hall of Famer Mickey Cochrane, player-manager of the Detroit Tigers, lost sight of a pitch by Bump Hadley of the Yankees. It hit him in the right temple and fractured his skull. He lay unconscious for ten days but eventually recovered, although he never played again. He did, however, resume his managerial duties and also served with distinction in the Navy in World War Two.

Tony Conigliaro of the Boston Red Sox, who hit 166 home runs in six full seasons and parts of two others (all with the Red Sox, except for 74 games and 4 home runs for California in 1971), surely would have racked up more impressive numbers had he not been hit in the face and nearly killed by a Jack Hamilton (of California) pitch on August 18, 1967. He was out of the game for a year and a half, but then came back to hit 20 home runs in 1969 and 36 in 1970. On October 11, 1970, in a most controversial deal, he was traded to California, where he was to see only limited duty. He returned to Boston for 21 games in 1975 and then was out of baseball. He died February 24, 1990.

Dickie Thon was the All-Star National League shortstop for Houston in 1983 and also led the league in game-winning hits. In the fifth game of the 1984 season, he was hit in the eye by a Mike Torrez (Mets) fastball. Despite permanent damage to his eye, he was able to return to action and played more or less regularly for the Texas Rangers in 1992 and then briefly for the Milwaukee Brewers in 1993.

Don Zimmer, a Yankees coach in 1996, suffered two serious beanings and still carries a metal plate in his head from the injuries. Paul Blair, center field magician of the Baltimore Orioles, Minnie Minoso of the White Sox, and Wayne Terwilliger, utility player for several clubs, were others whose careers were interrupted or affected by bean balls.

Sore Arms, Illnesses, Injuries, and Accidents

Up to this point, the subject has been (with a few exceptions) deaths off or on the diamond. But fatalities are only part of the story. Many a baseball career has aborted for reasons not resulting in death, at least, not at once.

In the old days, sore arms were usually rested. If there was any treatment at all, it was by the likes of John D. "Bonesetter" Reese, a self-trained muscle manipulator of Youngstown, Ohio. Nobody ever heard of the rotator cuff or even dreamed of such sophisticated operations as those which prolonged the careers of Tommy John, Ken Dayley, and others.

Charles "Lady" Baldwin was one old-timer who could have used a Tommy John bionic arm. In 1886 he won 42 games for Detroit (NL) and pitched 487 innings. He then developed arm trouble and dropped to 13 wins in 1887 and to 3 each in 1888 and 1890, after which he retired for good to his Michigan farm. Hall of Famer Christy Mathewson's arm went dead in 1916, but by then he was thirty-eight, had won 373 games, and had achieved immortality. Smoky Joe Wood was another sore arm victim, but he did beat the rap in a way. After winning 23 games for the Red Sox in 1911 and then 34 in 1912, including 16 in a row, he developed a sore arm the following spring. His days as an intimidating fireballer were over, although he did win 35 games for the Sox over the next three seasons. Realizing he could no longer pitch, he decided to become a sore-armed outfielder, and played that position with fair success for Cleveland through the 1922 season. Altogether he played in fourteen major league seasons and left a 116–57 pitching record and a career batting mark of .283.

Undocumented are the names of countless other pitchers of the game's early years who dropped out prematurely because of so-called dead arms. More is known of modern pitchers, like Dave Ferris and Karl Spooner. Ferris joined the Boston Red Sox in 1945, having been mustered out of the Army because of asthma. He raised plenty of eyebrows with a 21–10 record in the last year of wartime baseball, but then made believers out of everyone by winning 25 and losing just 6 in 1946. But in a night game in Cleveland in June of 1947, he suffered a shoulder injury, from which he never fully recovered although he did hang on until 1950. His career log shows 65–30 for a phenomenal .684 percentage.

No pitcher ever made a more dazzling entrance or faded as fast as Karl Spooner. The twenty-three-year-old lefthander was called up by Brooklyn from Fort Worth (Texas), late in the 1954 season. He pitched shutouts against New York and Pittsburgh in his first two starts, allowing just 7 hits and striking out 27. Hampered by a sore arm, he struggled to an 8–6 record in 1955, made two appearances in the World Series (0–1), then never pitched again.

In 1966 another Dodger lefthander, Hall of Famer Sandy Koufax was 27–9, with 5 shutouts and an ERA of 1.73 in 323 innings of work. Talk about going out on top! No pitcher in major league history ever matched that in a final season. He pitched against Baltimore in the 1966 World Series (0–1), but at the age of thirty his career was over. Traumatic arthritis in the left elbow, triggered by a fall on his left arm when attempting a pickoff during the 1964 season, made it impossible for him to continue. Had

Koufax been able to pitch as long as, say Warren Spahn, there is no telling what his record might have been. As it was, he left an imposing mark of 165–87 (.655) and an ERA of 2.76.

Mark Fidrych, the colorful Detroit pitcher known as "the Bird," was 19–9 in 1976 and was the starting pitcher in the All-Star game. But plagued by arm trouble, he faded to a combined 10–11 record over the next four seasons. He was only twenty-six when he pitched his final big league game in 1980. Twice he tried comebacks in the minors, but failed.

Lefty Don Gullett, the only man to pitch the opening game in successive World Series for two different teams (Cincinnati Reds, 1976; and New York Yankees, 1977), was just twenty-seven when his career ended with a bad arm after the 1978 season. He had been one of the first free agents signed by the Yankees, and was certainly one of their most expensive, costing them $2 million for his 18 wins in two seasons.

Righthander Wayne Garland of the Indians was operated on for a rotator cuff tear on May 5, 1978. He had won 33 games the two previous seasons. After the operation, he came back, hanging on until 1981, but he was never the same pitcher. And like Gullett, he was working on a lucrative long-term contract.

The previous pages have told of the surprising number of active major leaguers who succumbed to illness. Many others became ill and were forced to give up the game or see their baseball livelihoods interrupted. An early example was Jimmy Wood, who played for Chicago, Brooklyn, and Philadelphia in the National Association from 1871 to 1873. In 1873 he developed a leg abscess which he attempted to lance with a penknife. A severe infection developed, resulting in the loss of his leg. His playing days, of course, were over, but he did return as a manager in 1874 and 1875.

In 1890 first baseman Dave Orr of Brooklyn (in the Players' League) batted .373, hit 32 doubles, 13 triples, and 6 home runs, while striking out only 11 times. For a nonpitcher, this was the ultimate in final seasons. In the off-season, the thirty-one-year-old Orr suffered a stroke and never played again. He died in Brooklyn on June 3, 1915.

Hall of Famer Amos Rusie won 243 games in nine seasons and part of a tenth, but saw his career shrouded by misfortune, some of his own making. The so-called "Hoosier Thunderbolt," who almost killed Hughie Jennings with a bean ball, himself took a line drive to the head which permanently damaged his hearing. He threw out his arm in 1898 and was out of the game for two years. He compounded his other problems with heavy drinking. Although he tried to come back in 1901, he failed. At the age of thirty he was through.

The aforementioned Jennings, another Hall of Famer, had a baseball life replete with illness and adversity. In addition to the almost fatal beaning by Rusie, he suffered a nervous breakdown in 1925, after taking over as manager of the New York Giants when John McGraw became ill. Jennings died of spinal meningitis in 1928 at the age of fifty-eight.

Often documented is the tragic accident that terminated the career of catcher Charley Bennett, who played in the majors from 1878 to 1893 (except for 1879). In January of 1894, while on a hunting trip, he tried to catch and board a moving train at Wellsville, Kansas, but lost his grip and fell under the wheels, losing both legs.

Shortstop Charlie Hollocher, who played for the Cubs from 1918 to 1924, was constantly bedeviled by illness, real and imaginary, blunting what some observers feel could have been a Hall of Fame–level career. His tormented life came to an end on August 14, 1940, when he parked his car on a quiet Clayton, Missouri, street, then tore his throat apart with a blast from a sixteen-gauge shotgun.

One of the strangest cases in which illness terminated a career involved pitcher-turned-outfielder Erwin (Zeke) Harvey. After batting .333 for Chicago and Cleveland of the new American League in 1901 and starting the 1902 season at a .348 clip in 12 games, he quit baseball, claiming he had such serious stomach pains that he could no longer play ball. He never returned to the diamond. Instead he became an entomologist on the west coast. He died in Santa Monica, in 1954 at the age of seventy-five.

On September 25, 1905, Dave Fultz was playing center field for the New York Highlanders when he collided with shortstop Norman "Kid" Elberfeld. His nose and jaw were broken, injuries which would end his baseball career. He had been studying law and he opened his own office in 1906. In 1912 he formed the Players Fraternity and later secured many benefits for players. In 1919 and 1920 he served as president of the International League.

Jackie Hayes, outstanding second baseman and shortstop for the Senators and the White Sox (1927–1940), was 3 for 3 in a 1940 Sox spring game; then in the shower room he noticed a cloudiness in one eye. He played 18 games that year, but by August he had lost his sight in the clouded eye. In a matter of three years, he had lost his sight in the other. Similarly, George "Specs" Toporcer, a former major league infielder, had lost his sight while managing Buffalo (International League) in 1951. Both men learned to live with their blindness and went on to lead productive lives, Hayes as the tax collector of Chilton County, Alabama, and Toporcer as a writer and lecturer.

In 1996, fifty-six years after Hayes was forced to quit, an eye affliction ended the playing career of Minnesota outfielder Kirby Puckett, one of the game's superstars and one of its most charismatic and popular players. Even before spring training he began to notice cloudiness in his right eye. Medical examination revealed he was suffering from a form of glaucoma. Two surgical procedures failed to alleviate the problem and July 12 he announced his retirement. At the same time, it was announced that Puckett would remain with the Twins in an undetermined front office capacity.

Righthanded pitcher Monty Stratton (15–5 and 15–9 for the Chicago White Sox in 1937 and 1938) was hunting rabbits near his mother's home in Greenville, Texas, after the 1938 season, when he accidentally discharged a .22-caliber pistol. The slug lodged in his right knee, severing the main artery and necessitating amputation of the leg. Stratton did not pitch again in the majors, but he was a White Sox coach for three seasons. In 1946 he pitched for Sherman in the Class C East Texas League, where, remarkably, he won 18 games. Hollywood thought it saw a story in the courageous way he had faced his tragedy and made a much-acclaimed movie of his life, *The Stratton Story*, starring Jimmy Stewart and June Allyson.

A third victim of a leg injury was Joe Cronin, Hall of Fame shortstop who played twenty years for Washington and Boston, and probably would have played a few more had he not fractured his leg three games into the 1945 season. He never played again, but continued in the game for many years as a manager, front office executive, and as American League president.

He looked so indestructible that they called him "The Iron Horse." Henry Louis Gehrig, in seventeen years at first base for the New York Yankees, averaged .340, hit 535 doubles, 162 triples, and 493 home runs. He scored 1,888 runs, had 1,990 RBIs, and posted a slugging percentage of .632. His incredible record of playing in 2,130 consecutive games at one time seemed unassailable, but has since been broken by Cal Ripken, Jr., of the Baltimore Orioles. On May 2, 1939, Gehrig approached manager Joe McCarthy, told him he was not feeling well. Gehrig thought he was hurting the team, and he asked to be taken from the lineup. McCarthy, of course, complied, and so for the first time since pinch-hitting for Pee-Wee Wanninger on May 31, 1925, Gehrig missed a Yankee game.

A few months later the bad news came from the Mayo Clinic. The indestructible one, "The Iron Horse," had been stricken with amyotrophic lateral sclerosis, a disease of the central nervous system for which no cure was known. On July 4, 1939, 61,000 gathered at Yankee Stadium for a gigantic Gehrig tribute. There he spoke his memorable words: "I consider myself the luckiest man on the face of the earth."

In the short time left to him, Gehrig devoted himself to public service. On June 2, 1941, exactly sixteen years from the day he replaced Wally Pipp at first base, he died. He was thirty-seven years old. The malady that killed him is now generally referred to as Lou Gehrig's disease. Unfortunately it is almost as much a medical mystery today as it was fifty years ago when it struck him.

Catcher Bill DeLancey was a product of the St. Louis Cardinal farm system. After playing eight games for the parent club in 1932 and then spending a year at Columbus (American Association), he became a regular member of the "Gas House Gang" in 1934. In 1935 he found that he had tuberculosis and faced a long recovery period. It was not until 1940 that he made it back, and then it was just for 15 games. By then, he knew it was no use. His career was over. He died November 28, 1946, on his thirty-fifth birthday.

When Don Black went to the mound for the Cleveland Indians against the St. Louis Browns on September 13, 1948, he could have looked back on an undistinguished six-year record with the Athletics and Indians (34–55). But there were two victories—one off the diamond—that he could recall with pride. The first was against the bottle; the second was a no-hit, no-run game against the Philadelphia Athletics on July 10, 1947.

In the late-season game against the Browns, upon retiring the Browns in the first two innings, Black came to bat against Bill Kennedy. After swinging mightily at the first pitch and fouling it back, he began to stagger and finally sank to his knees. Umpire Bill Summers bent over to assist Black and heard him whisper, "That last pitch to [Ed] Pellagrini did it." (He had struck out the Browns' shortstop with a curve ball to end the top of the second.)

Apparently, that pitch plus the force of his swing had caused an aneurysm to rupture, sending blood to his brain and spinal cord. (Shades of James Creighton, who had injured himself fatally while batting on August 14, 1862.) An eminent neurosurgeon was summoned. He ruled out surgery as too risky, but said Black had just a 50-50 chance of surviving. But Black did survive and on September 22 he was recipient of a large purse from a benefit game against the Red Sox that attracted a crowd of 76,772.

The Indians went on to win the pennant and then defeated the Boston Braves in the World Series, but without Black, who never pitched again. He died April 21, 1959 at the age of 42.

Baseball's *Domesday Books* credit lefthanded pitcher Bert Shepard with one major league appearance. What the books do not say is that this game was pitched by a one-legged man. When Shepard's call to World War Two service came, he was a promising young pitcher. The fortunes of war took him to the European front, where he was downed over Germany on his thirty-fifth mission and taken prisoner. Doctors removed his shattered right leg, after which a fellow prisoner of war fashioned him a wooden leg. After his recapture and return to the States, he was signed by the Washington Senators as a batting practice pitcher. In his one appearance in a regular game, he allowed one run in 5⅓ innings for an ERA of 1.69.

Lou Brissie, like Bert Shepard, was a victim of World War Two combat. Brissie, who joined the Army in 1942 as a teenager, was badly wounded on the Italian front and forced to undergo twenty-three operations. Despite the handicap of a steel leg brace and a leather guard, he never gave up his dream of becoming a major league pitcher. In 1947, for Savannah of the Sally League, he won 23 games and earned a late-season call-up from the Philadelphia Athletics. From 1947 to 1953, he won 44 games for the A's and the Indians, to whom he was traded in 1951. His best year was 1949, when he won 16 games and pitched in the All-Star Game. He was only twenty-nine when his career came to a close. He then became national director of the American Legion baseball program.

Herb Score was a third American League lefty to see his career abbreviated by injury. In 1955, Score won 16 games for Cleveland and struck out 245; then in 1956 he improved to 20 wins and 263 strikeouts. Along the banks of Lake Erie, he was hailed as a lefthanded Bob Feller. But it was not to be. On May 7, 1957, at Municipal Stadium in Cleveland, he was hit in the eye by a torrid line drive off the bat of Gil McDougald of the New York Yankees and seriously injured.

His recovery was slow, and he did not return to the Indians until 1958 and then only for 12 games. On April 18, 1960, he was traded to the White Sox for Barry Latman. After three seasons of limited duty for the Sox, he called it a day. He remains in baseball as the play-by-play announcer for the Indians.

Brooklyn catcher Roy Campanella was thirty-six and in the twilight of a remarkable career that had seen him win three Most Valuable Player awards, when disaster struck on a January night in 1958. He was driving to his Long Island home in the early hours of the morning when his borrowed car skidded on a slippery spot in the road and slammed into a utility pole. The two broken vertebrae

he suffered doomed him to a long and excruciatingly painful period of recovery and rehabilitation, not to mention lifelong confinement to a wheelchair.

On May 7, 1959, before a crowd of 93,103 fans at the Los Angeles Coliseum, the Dodgers and the Yankees met in a mammoth benefit for the paralyzed Campanella. It was an emotional affair, rivaling similar tributes to Yankee greats Gehrig and Ruth at Yankee Stadium.

The courage Campanella displayed in his rehabilitation was an inspiration to many others who suffered severe spinal injuries. He received baseball's highest honor in 1969—election to the Hall of Fame.

Mike Pazik, a lefthander from Lynn, Mass., who appeared briefly for Minnesota in 1975, 1976, and 1977, saw his pitching career terminated when he suffered multiple fractures of both legs in a 1977 automobile accident. He returned to the game in 1980 as a coach for the White Sox. Later, he served four years as a roving pitching instructor for the Milwaukee Brewers, and then in late 1987 he was named pitching coach for Charlotte of the Double-A Southern League.

Houston righthander J. R. Richard, at 6′8″ and 222 pounds, was an intimidating figure on the mound. From 1976 through 1979, his strikeout log showed 214, 214, 303, and 313, respectively, while his victories totaled 74. In 1980, even though slowed by arm and shoulder injuries, he was chosen to start for the National League in the All-Star Game at Los Angeles. But, as fate would have it, he was to pitch just two more innings for the Astros before being laid low by a stroke. The rehabilitation was painfully slow, but there always seemed to be hope that his career could be salvaged, but such hopes proved to be futile. Twice (in 1982 and 1983) he tried to pitch in the lower minors, but the illness had taken too great a toll.

In 1988, while with the San Francisco Giants, lefty Dave Dravecky developed a cancerous growth on his pitching arm. An operation and a long recuperation followed. He tried to come back in 1989, but in a late-season game against Montreal his pitching arm broke as he was delivering a pitch. Subsequently his arm was amputated, bringing to an end a once promising career. His major league record was 64–57 with an ERA of 3.13.

First baseman Nick Esasky enjoyed a career year with the Boston Red Sox in 1989, with 30 home runs and 108 RBIs. He then signed a lucrative free agent contract with the Atlanta Braves. During spring training he began to suffer from vertigo. He played only nine regular season games in 1990 before being disabled. His failure to recover baffled a horde of medical experts. He did not play at all in 1991, tried to come back in '92, but was eventually released by the Braves.

Bo Jackson of the Kansas City Royals was one of the most exciting players to hit the majors in years. He could run, throw, field, and hit with power. He was also a superstar in football and that proved to be his downfall. An innocent-looking sideline tackle while he was playing for the Los Angeles Raiders in 1990 resulted in a serious hip injury. Released by the Royals, he was given another chance by the White Sox in 1991. He played in only 23 late-season games, batting .225 with three home runs. His hip continued to deteriorate and eventually had to be surgically replaced. He did not play at all in 1992, but, miraculously, returned to action in 1993, playing the entire season for the White Sox, mainly as a designated hitter, then in 1994 signed and played with the California Angels. He is now out of baseball.

Careers cut short for psychological reasons are not common, but there have been a few. Steve Blass, hero of the 1971 Pittsburgh World Series victory over Baltimore and winner of 19 games in 1972, suddenly could not throw strikes. So severe was the mental block that his baseball life ended in 1974 when he was only thirty-two. Kevin Saucier, a lefthanded relief pitcher for Detroit, had 13 saves and 4 wins in 1981; then, inexplicably, he developed the Steve Blass syndrome and could not throw strikes. In his case it was a fear of hitting and injuring a batter. He could not overcome the problem, and at twenty-six he was out of baseball. Joe Cowley, who pitched for the Braves, Yankees, White Sox, and Phillies, and who has a no-hit game to his credit, simply could not throw strikes and was sent to the minors by the Phillies in 1987. He could not throw strikes there either and finally was sent home.

Catcher Mike Ivie was the number one pick by the Padres in the 1970 draft. The record shows he played in 857 major league games over eleven seasons, but just nine as a catcher. He developed a phobia about throwing the ball back to the pitcher and never could overcome it. He walked away from the game on three occasions and spent two terms on the disabled list due to what was called "mental exhaustion." His career ended in 1983 when the Tigers released him. He was thirty years old. Buzzy Bavasi said of Ivie: "He could have been one of the greatest catchers of all time."

At least one career came to a premature end because of a fear of flying. Jackie Jensen, who hit 199 home runs in eleven seasons with the Yankees, Senators, and Red Sox, retired first in 1959, tried again in 1961, but then quit for good at the age of thirty-four.

It was on July 30, 1991, eleven years to the day on which J. R. Richard of the Houston Astros was hit by a massive stroke, that twenty-eight-year-old Jeff Gray, Boston Red Sox pitcher, met the same fate. Stricken while sitting in front of his locker at Fenway Park, suddenly he was unable to walk, talk, or grip a baseball. After two years of excruciating rehabilitation, in which he had to relearn almost every normal activity, he even reached the point of being able to pitch with some authority, although not at his former level. In 1994 he was named a minor league pitching coach by the Red Sox.

On May 3, 1996, Dodger center fielder Brett Butler entered the hospital for what was expected to be a routine tonsillectomy. Instead, cancer was found and major surgery and extensive follow-up treatment ensued. Miraculously, he was able to return to the Dodgers on September 3. Four days later, however, he suffered a broken wrist when hit by a pitch. His baseball future hangs in the balance, but he insists he will be back.

The summer of 1996 also saw the resignation of long-time Dodger manager Tommy LaSorda, following hospitalization and treatment for a heart ailment. He will continue to bleed Dodger blue in a front office capacity.

Alcohol and Drugs

It is impossible to put a number on the baseball careers shortened or adversely affected by the excessive use of alcohol. In at least four cases (Delahanty, Koenecke, Morris, and Wilson), dealt with elsewhere in this chapter, fatalities resulted. Countless players of the game's early years were lushes. Liquor was readily available to them, often on the house, and there was plenty of time for carousing, especially when on the road. Some of the worst offenders were quietly blacklisted and faded from the game. Others who were heavy drinkers continued in uniform, because they were star players and the owners winked at their alcoholic escapades. Future Hall of Famer Michael "King" Kelly, for example, drank as hard as he played; yet in 1887 Boston paid an unheard of $10,000 to Chicago for his contract. Toward the end of his career, he opened a saloon in New York, which was like putting the fox in charge of the chicken coop. His performance level deteriorated rapidly, and by 1894 he was in the minors. That fall he developed pneumonia, and on November 8 he died at the age of thirty-six.

Terry Larkin, who won 29 games for Hartford in 1877, and 29 and 31, respectively, for Chicago in 1878 and 1879, was another nineteenth-century player whose career self-destructed from the ravages of strong drink. In 1883, while drunk, he shot his wife (she recovered) and then tried to commit suicide in jail. In 1886, while employed as a bartender in Brooklyn, he showed up for work with two pistols and challenged his employer to a duel. Police were called and he was thrown into jail until he sobered up. He died in Brooklyn in 1894.

Equally melancholy is the story of James (The Troy Terrier) Egan, who pitched, caught and played the outfield for Troy (NL) in 1882 and then was blacklisted for drunkenness. Supposedly rehabilitated, he was given a chance with Brooklyn (AA) in 1884, but before he played a game he was arrested for theft and jailed. He died of what was described as "brain fever" in a New Haven, Connecticut, jail, September 26, 1884.

Few players have come to the majors with more raw talent than Louis Sockalexis, a Penobscot Indian from Old Towne, Maine. He played college baseball at both Holy Cross and Notre Dame. While at the latter school in 1897, he and a companion broke up an establishment run by a certain "Popcorn Jennie" and threw the furniture out the windows. When the good fathers who ran Notre Dame read about this caper in the *South Bend Tribune,* they promptly threw him out. Future major league catcher Mike Powers, who had been instrumental in getting Sockalexis into both Holy Cross and Notre Dame, wired the Cleveland Club, with whom the Indian had signed a contract to take effect at the end of the school year, and suggested it send someone to South Bend to bail him out. Manager Patsy Tebeau caught the next train west, and in a few days Sockalexis was in a Cleveland uniform. He impressed with his strength, speed, and magnificent arm. In later years, both John McGraw and Hughie Jennings said he was the greatest natural talent they had ever seen. Even allowing for the hyperbole that often accompanies such reminiscence, it is apparent that he was a player of exceptional ability. But just as exceptional was his appetite for strong drink. Frequently interrupted by binges and injuries (once he jumped from a second-floor window and severely injured an ankle), his major league career was limited to 94 games in three seasons.

Sockalexis died in Burlington, Maine, on December 24, 1913, at the age of forty-two. His baseball monument is not his .313 batting average but the Cleveland Indians baseball club, which was nicknamed after him.

Hall of Famer Rube Waddell gained almost as much notoriety for his drinking as he did recognition for his pitching. Lowell Reidenbaugh, in his *Cooperstown,* tells how Waddell would come into a bar, penniless, and whisper to the bartender, "Give me a drink, and I will give you the ball I used to defeat Cy Young in twenty innings." According to Reidenbaugh, hundreds of bartenders "displayed what they considered to be the historic souvenir."

Despite the abuse he gave his body, the Rube lasted for thirteen major league seasons and won 191 games. But his indiscretions led to tuberculosis and he died in San Antonio, Texas, on April Fool's Day, 1914, at the age of thirty-seven.

Waddell contemporary Arthur (Bugs) Raymond was not the pitcher the Rube was, but he was his equal in the drinking department. The efforts of Giant manager John McGraw to rein him in are a part of the lore and legend of baseball. Raymond finally became so uncontrollable that the Giants let him go in the spring of 1912. Later that year Raymond, while drunk, was watching a sandlot game in Chicago when a spectator picked up a broken piece of pottery and threw it, hitting Raymond in the face. A fight ensued in which Raymond was badly beaten up. He went back to his hotel room, where six days later he died of a cerebral hemorrhage, caused by a skull fracture. He was only thirty years old. One former teammate said of him, "Bugs paid too much too soon for too many drinks."

The problem of alcoholism continues in the modern game, but added to it is an affliction even more virulent— the use of illegal drugs. Careers are being shortened or interrupted by excessive drinking or the ingestion of drugs, or by a combination of both. In the old days, when a player drank too much, he was either shunted aside or his problem was swept under the rug. Now, the usual pattern is a confession of the problem, or exposure, followed by treatment, rehabilitation, sometimes suspension, but then a return to the game.

In 1983 the baseball world was rocked by the news that four players on the Kansas City Royals—Willie Wilson, Willie Aikens, Jerry Martin, and Vida Blue (no longer with the team)—had been involved with illegal drugs. All were suspended for one year by Commissioner Bowie Kuhn, although later an arbitrator reduced the suspensions, except for Blue's. Meanwhile, indictments were handed down and all were convicted and sentenced to one year in jail, with the last nine months suspended. Eventually Wilson returned to the Royals. Aikens was traded to Toronto but then went to the minors. Martin and Blue soon faded from baseball.

Pitcher Steve Howe of the Los Angeles Dodgers was suspended for the 1984 season for alleged drug use and did not challenge it. After at least two relapses, he was signed by the Texas Rangers and appeared for them late in the 1987 season. He was out of baseball in '88 and '89, but made a comeback in 1991 and eventually worked himself up to a prominent place in the New York Yankee bullpen. After his conviction in 1992 in Kalispell, Montana, for drug possession, he was barred from baseball "for life" by Commissioner Fay Vincent, but was given yet another chance to play in 1993, by virtue of a ruling by an arbitrator. He pitched the entire season for the Yankees, with spotty results, and presumably passed all his required blood tests. In 1994 he became the ace of the Yankee bullpen. He was released by the Yankees in the summer of 1996.

Atlanta pitcher Pascual Perez spent three months in a Dominican Republic jail on drug charges during the 1983–1984 off-season and was also suspended by Commissioner Kuhn. Arbitrator Richard I. Bloch, who had also ruled in the Willie Wilson et al. cases, subsequently threw out the Perez suspension because of lack of evidence.

Also in 1983, pitcher Dickie Noles of the Cubs spent time in jail after a drunken brawl in Cincinnati. Outfielder Ron LeFlore was arrested on drug and weapons charges in 1982 while with the Chicago White Sox. Although found not guilty, he was released by the Sox in April 1983.

Bob Welch, talented righthanded pitcher of the Dodgers, best remembered for his classic confrontation with Reggie Jackson of the Yankees in the 1978 World Series, revealed that he had been an alcoholic for many years. After rehabilitation and relegation to the minors, he returned to the Dodgers in 1986 and Oakland two years later. He has written a book about his experiences, *Five O'Clock Comes Early.*

A much-publicized drug trial that began in Pittsburgh on September 5, 1985, exposed the drug involvement of numerous players, including Keith Hernandez of the Mets (formerly with the Cardinals) and Dave Parker of the Reds (formerly with the Pirates). After the trial, Commissioner Peter Ueberroth meted out penalties to twenty-one players, ranging from heavy fines to be paid to drug prevention programs, orders to participate in random drug testing, and the performance of drug-related community service.

The shocking disclosures of widespread drug use that came out of the 1985 trial and the severe penalties that followed seemed to have a favorable impact on the drug problem, but did not eliminate it entirely. In 1986 San Diego pitcher LaMarr Hoyt, a Cy Young Award winner in 1983 when he was with the White Sox, was arrested three times on drug-related charges, and after the third was sentenced to forty-five days in federal prison. Hoyt's suspension from baseball was later overturned, and he was ordered reinstated with back pay, much to the dismay of the baseball hierarchy.

Hoyt then signed with his old club, the Chicago White Sox, but his troubles were far from over. He tested positive for cocaine three times in October 1987, and then on December 4 he was arrested in his Columbia, S.C., apartment and charged with intent to distribute cocaine and marijuana. He was convicted the following year and sentenced to one year in prison. How widespread has been the use of illegal drugs by major league players? In a recent book, *Baseball Babylon,* author Dan Gutman lists eighty-three players who have been so involved, including such superstars as Dwight Gooden and Darryl Strawberry, whose problems surfaced again in 1994. After several chances and subsequent failures, both Gooden and Strawberry, apparently with their problems under control, wound up as key players on the 1996 Yankees, with

Gooden pitching a no-hit, no-run game and Strawberry finding his home run stroke.

The list of tragedies and shortened careers has been a long one and sad. It has included paragons and playboys, teetotalers and tosspots, the great, the near-great, and the never-were; some who self-destructed and many more who were simply the victims of the cruelest of bad luck. However classified, for each player the hypothetical question remains: Had his tragedy not occurred, what might have been?

Careers Shortened by Blacklisting or Expulsion

Listed below, but not discussed in this chapter, are players blacklisted or expelled from baseball for gambling, dishonest play (or knowledge of same), criminal activity, or, in one case—that of Ray Fisher—violation of a contract. The players involved in the 1877 Louisville and 1919

Chicago White Sox scandals, all of whom were barred for life, are grouped; the others are listed alphabetically:

1877 Louisville players   Bill Craver, Jim Devlin, George Hall, Al Nichols.

1919 Chicago White Sox players   Eddie Cicotte, Oscar Felsch, Chick Gandil, Joe Jackson, Fred McMullin, Swede Risberg, Buck Weaver, Claude Williams.

Others   George Bechtel, Rube Benton (who was later reinstated and returned to the majors), Hal Chase, Cozy Dolan, Phil Douglas, Jean Dubuc (who returned as a coach with Detroit in 1931), Ray Fisher, Joe Gedeon, Claude Hendrix, Richard Higham (umpire), Benny Kauff, Hubert Leonard, Lee Magee, Jimmy O'Connell, Eugene Paulette, Pete Rose, Heinie Zimmerman. [Former major leaguers banned from baseball for their activities in the minor leagues include Babe Borton, Gene Dale, Jess Levan, Harl Maggert, Tom Seaton and Joe Tipton.]

## CHAPTER 9

From Greenberg to Green: Jewish Ballplayers

David Spaner

During the Depression, when Hank Greenberg chased home run records and ominous reports emanated from Germany, Shawn Green's grandfather changed the family name from Greenberg. In many ways, the changes Jewish ballplayers have experienced since the beginnings of major league baseball reflect the changes in North American Jewish communities, and during those years numerous Jews, like the game, have "gone from Greenberg to Green."

On April 25, 1933, in Washington, Ben Chapman, noted for his sharp spikes and sharp bigoted tongue, slid hard into second base, knocking down Washington Senator Buddy Myer. The Jewish Senator, long a target of this southern Yankee, came up brawling and the toe-to-toe combat almost became a riot, involving more players and hundreds of spectators.

That same baseball season, four months later, a slope alongside the first base line at Toronto's Christie Pits ballpark filled with supporters of Harbord, a Jewish nine playing St. Peter's for the city championship. Supporters of St. Peter's crowded together along the third base line at Toronto's Christie.

As the game ended, some supporters of the St. Peter's team shouted "Heil Hitler" and unfurled a huge swastika flag. Harbord supporters poured toward the flag, intent on capturing it. Ballplayers also joined in the brawl, which would spread throughout the park and into the streets. Jewish youths ripped up the flag, but the street war would go into the night, moving into the surrounding neighborhoods.

The riot at Christie Pits was not an isolated event in Toronto, following frequent harassment and the organizing that summer of a "Swastika Club." It was, however, the first time North American Jews had, en masse, fought back against the rising anti-Semitic movement of the 1930s. In the riot's aftermath, some in the older Jewish community, convinced they should rely on the goodwill of the non-Jewish authorities to defend them, were critical of the young Jews.

"It was unfortunate that the Jewish youths considered it necessary to take matters into their own hands, for the police, I am sure, would have handled the situation properly," announced Meyer Steinglass of the *Jewish Standard.*

But a rioter named Ben Steiner, in the *Toronto Star,* expressed the sentiments of much of a second Jewish generation, raised in Toronto: "Rather than submit to the outrages that have been perpetrated against our race, we would die on the streets. This is the feeling amongst the younger element of our people."

Sammy Luftspring, who was the No. 3 contender for the welterweight crown before an eye injury ended his boxing career, was at Christie Pits. "Damn right I was proud," the member of the Canadian Sports Hall of Fame told *Total Baseball,* recalling how the neighborhood stood together. "You have no idea how proud you would be if you saw what happened there. We were just fighting with our hands. They were hitting us with baseball bats, iron pipes, and whatever. We were up against it. It was pretty tough being Jewish at that time. They'd grab older Jews and throw them to the ground, you'd walk down the street and they'd call you dirty Jew. We had to finally do something or otherwise we were nothing."

Along with a new mood, these children of immigrants had a new sport: Baseball. Participants in the Christie Pits riot recall the significant role the game had in the lives of young Toronto Jews during the 1930s. "Baseball was a big thing," says Luftspring. "I played second base, and I was tickled pink when I got on the school team. Baseball was something we all did."

It had been the sport of entry. The bulk of Jewish immigration from Eastern Europe, from the 1880s to the 1920s, coincided with the development of baseball as "the national pastime." And the immigrants settled primarily in cities in the East and Midwest where the major leagues were based and baseball was by far the most popular sport.

"It makes sense to teach a child to play dominoes or chess. But what is the point of a crazy game like baseball?" an immigrant wrote the *Jewish Daily Forward.* "I want my boy to grow up to be a *mensch,* not a wild American runner. But he cries his head off."

The newspaper's editor responded: "Let your boys play baseball and play it well, as long as it does not interfere with their education or get them into bad company. Half the parents in the Jewish quarter have this problem. Chess is good, but the body needs to develop also."

At first, it had been called the New York game, and the city at the heart of Jewish immigration also happened to be the heart of baseball, where each morning, with the studiousness of Talmudic scholars, young Jews would study the box scores of three major league teams. The hold baseball had on these immigrants' children would result in Jews being active in every aspect of the game—broadcasters, executives, journalists, umpires, clowns, gamblers, novelists, coaches, union leaders. "Like most of my friends," wrote Brooklyn's Marvin Miller, the longtime executive director of the players association, "I could recite the vital statistics of every Dodger—and of most of their competition too."

There were players too. First up, in the story of Jewish ballplayers, is the question, who to include? Several ballplayers listed as Jewish in other publications have, through subsequent research and interviews with descendants, proven not to be, including Ed Reulbach, Johnny Kling, Levi Meyerle, George Stone, Jim Roseman, Sammy Strang, Mickey Harris, Benny Kauff, Rod Carew, and John Lowenstein. But research has also turned up many ballplayers who haven't been listed as Jewish before. In order to reflect the full range of Jewish experience in baseball, this article and the accompanying roster take a broad ethnic definition of who is a Jew, rather than the traditional religious definition that a Jew is the child of a Jewish mother. Thus, it includes any ballplayers with Jewish fathers and non-Jewish mothers. It also includes players who converted to Judaism.

The early years of major league baseball came before the waves of Eastern European immigration, and Jewish players were a rarity. But there were some, most notably Lipman Pike of Brooklyn. A noted baserunner and hitter, Pike was an original member of the National Association, the first league composed entirely of professionals. After hitting .321 during his NA years, Pike joined the National League's St. Louis club in 1876, the year the NL was founded, and he led the league in home runs the following season. Francis Richter, editor of the *Sporting Life,* selected Pike as an outfielder on his 1870-80 all-star team.

There were other early Jewish ballplayers beyond the reaches of the professional game. Out west, for example, there was the pioneering Mensor family of Jacksonville, Oregon. Morris and Matilda Mensor operated Mensor's New York Store, and had 17 children, including several adept at baseball. The December 26, 1879 edition of the *Jacksonville Democratic Times* announced: "CHALLENGE ACCEPTED: Some weeks since we published a challenge from Judge Fenton to match his family of boys against any other family in the State in the national game—baseball. The *Roseberg Star* accepts the challenge, naming the Mensor family, of Jacksonville, as the opposing nine and offers to bet two to one on them." Henry Mensor was the ace pitcher on the family team and Jacksonville's town team. His son, Eddie, would play for the Pittsburgh Pirates.

There was a handful of nineteenth century Jewish professional ballplayers, but it would be the second generation, the children of the Eastern European immigrants, who would have an impact on the game. Education came before athletics in most of the working-class homes in the Jewish immigrant neighborhoods, and there was often parental opposition when someone wanted to play ball for a living. But Jewish players did come from the urban *shtetls* as the twentieth century began.

The best of the first years of the century were Barney Pelty, who fashioned a 2.62 ERA during a ten-year career, and Erskine Mayer, a two-time 20-game winner. Abe Kiviat, a silver medalist in the 1,500-meter run at the 1912 Olympics, went 2-for-4 with a triple as a member of the first U.S. Olympic baseball team, which played an exhibition contest during the Stockholm Games that year. Al Schacht had a brief career as a pitcher with the Washington Senators, then spent four decades as baseball's "clown prince," taking his baggy uniforms and slapstick to the troops during the Second World War and to ballparks across North America.

As the children of the Jewish immigrants, the second generation, came of ballplaying age, there wasn't a massive influx into the pro game, but there was a steady sprinkling from the turn of the century. The actual number is impossible to determine because many names were changed. "There must have been at least half a hundred Jews in the game but we'll never know their real names," Ford Frick wrote in 1925. "During the early days of this century the Jewish boys had tough sledding in the majors and many of them changed their name."

At least five Cohens played in the major leagues under different names during the early years of baseball's second century. In 1980, Dorothy Corey Pinzger, the widow of Edward Corey, who pitched for the White Sox in 1918, explained her husband's decision. "The name was changed from Cohen to Corey due to the ethnic slurs. . . . We have a clipping in the scrapbook which noted that in his appearance in one of the Midwest League games, Ed was loudly and continuously derided about his ethnic background from a few of the unintelligent fans. The clipping further noted that the greatest majority of the fans were 'good sports,' but just those few harassed him. The name was changed by this method: The H in COHEN was dropped and the R inserted; likewise the N was dropped, and the Y inserted, and the name became COREY."

Michael Myron Silverman left Cleveland and his family's clothing business to be a ballplayer. As Jesse Baker, he got his shot in 1919, starting at short with the Washington Senators in a game against Detroit. But Ty Cobb spiked the infielder at second, and Silverman/Baker had to leave the game, returning to the minors without an at-bat. After his brief major league experience, Silverman/Baker bounced around the minors, then wound up in Los Angeles, becoming a fixture at the racetrack and boxing ring, a favorite of Damon Runyon and Walter Winchell. "If you knew my husband there was nothing but adventure," his widow, Elizabeth, told *Total Baseball,* recalling, for example, his attempt to turn heavyweight Sam Cohen into a champion. "He was such a good fighter. The Marx Brothers wanted part of that fighter. Each wanted 10 per cent. Mike said, 'My God, it's a good thing there isn't another brother, there'd be nothing left.' They were crazy anyway. They were going to call him the Canvass Duck. They had all these big plans."

Sometimes the name-changes surprised other Jews. When Jimmy Reese was playing in the Pacific Coast League, he appeared in a celebrity game in which the other team had a Jewish battery of pitcher-songwriter Harry Ruby and catcher Ike Danning, brother of Harry Danning. Instead of using signals, Danning called the game in Yiddish, figuring none of the opposing players would understand. Reese slammed four hits, and after the game Ruby said to him, "I didn't know you were that good a hitter, Jimmie."

"You also didn't know," Reese said, "that my name was Hymie Solomon."

A Solomon (Mose) did play for the Giants in 1923, and there were other players who refused to changed their names. In the majors in the early decades of the twentieth century there were, along with other Jewish names, some Cohens, including Andrew, from El Paso, Texas. Andy Cohen was the first player celebrated for his Jewishness. New York Giants manager John McGraw had been searching for a player who would attract the city's massive Jewish population to the ballpark. The second baseman, who had batted .353 the previous year in Triple A, was unveiled opening day, 1928, and he delivered three hits, two RBI and two runs in a 5-2 Giants' victory over the Boston Braves.

"For the moment at least he is the baseball hero of New York," *Times* sportswriter James R. Harrison declared. "He will pull them in at the gate like a Babe Ruth—partly because he is, for the present anyway, the long-sought Jewish star on a New York team." But Cohen's star would fade quickly, at least in the eyes of McGraw, who dispatched him to the minors although the infielder hit .274 and .294 in his seasons with the Giants.

In the wake of the publicity surrounding Cohen's arrival, the press joined in the search for Jewish players. "McGraw's Hunt for a *Yiddish Star* Might have Ended with Marine's Visit, Except for Rejection by Bresnahan," *The Sporting News* announced in 1932. The story detailed Jim Levey's experience in 1928 when, as a U.S. Marine, he arrived for a tryout with the Giants and was told by Roger Bresnahan, McGraw's assistant: "No equipment, no workout. You'd better beat it." *The Sporting News* said Levey, who hit .280 for the St. Louis Browns in 1932, was "destined to become one of the great infielders." And Levey, a two-sport athlete who also played three seasons in the National Football League, explained he was "the son of Mr. and Mrs. Solomon Levey. . . . We were a happy family and our religion played an important part in our home life."

There would be other attempts by New York clubs to find a Jewish gate attraction. The Yankees even reversed the discarding of Jewish names by having Ed Whitner use his stepfather's name of Levy in the early 1940s. "You may be Whitner to the rest of the world," said Yankee general manager Ed Barrow, "but if you are going to play with the Yankees you'll be Ed Levy, understand."

But by that time, Barrow needn't have bothered. In the 1930s there were several Jews emerging as fine players, such as Hank Greenberg, Harry Danning, Buddy Myer, Moe Berg, Goody Rosen, Lou Boudreau, Sid Gordon, Phil Weintraub, and Morrie Arnovich.

Myer hit .303 during a seventeen-year career, including nine .300 seasons, and he led AL second basemen in fielding and the league in stolen bases. Following the 1935 season when the second baseman hit .349 to lead the AL, a *Sporting News* headline read, "YANKS HOPE TO DRESS IN MYER A TAILOR-MADE JEWISH STAR."

Myer stayed in Washington, but Danning would be the Jewish Giant the New York NL club had looked for. He was a four-time all-star, and in 1939, Giants manager Bill Terry said: "Danning will be the best catcher in the National League this year, possibly in baseball, and I include Hartnett and Dickey." That year Danning hit .313 with 16 home runs.

Gordon, a slugging outfielder born and raised in Brooklyn, was revered in his home borough despite playing for the rival Giants. A "Sid Gordon Day" was held in Ebbets Field, a practically sacrilegious affair for a visiting player. Gordon received a Chrysler, then showed his gratitude by hitting two homers against Brooklyn, where, he said, "If 30,000 fans were in the stands, I knew 25,000 of them."

There was a close bond between second-generation Jewish players and fans, who would hold "days" at the ballpark in their honor. Morrie Arnovich, for instance, received his day in Philadelphia in 1939, the year he hit .324. Arnovich, from Superior, Wisconsin, had his parents, immigrants from Poland, on hand to see him receive fishing gear and be guest of honor at a banquet.

The intense connection between the era's Jewish fans and players was prompted by the first significant influx of Jewish players into the game, coming during a period in which fascist, anti-Semitic movements were growing. And many of the players came from the same kind of neighborhoods as the fans—they had the same concerns and they literally spoke the same language.

The connection between players and fans was particularly close in Brooklyn, and Toronto's Goody Rosen became a Jewish hero when he starred for the Dodgers, hitting .325 as the National League's all-star center fielder in 1945. When Rosen and a couple of his teammates appeared at a fundraiser for a Brooklyn orphanage, he was so moved by a judge's plea for funds to buy sports equipment, he said: "If someone will donate $100, I'll tell a story in Jewish." Rosen's offer was accepted, his Yiddish tale received thunderous applause, and he announced he would make a donation too.

Most of the Jewish players of the era weren't stars, making cameo appearances in the majors like Harry Shuman or Sam Nahem. Shuman grew up in Philadelphia during the Depression and had a couple cups of coffee in the early 1940s. About the time Rosen was becoming a hero in Brooklyn, Shuman became a hero in Rosen's home town, when he played for the Triple A Toronto Maple Leafs.

"My wife came up to visit me from Philadelphia, and we stayed at the Victoria Hotel on Yonge Street. At the next table were two men, one older and one younger, and at another table was a group of Jewish people celebrating something. The older man said to me, 'Don't you hate those Jews over there?' He walked out in the lobby and I followed him and said, 'You ought to be ashamed of yourself. There's people dying over in Europe.' The younger man threw a punch at me. I blocked it, and threw a punch and knocked him out. He slid 10-15 feet across the marble floor. The old man—I later found out he was a leading banker in Toronto—apologized. The next night the box seats were full of Jewish people and when I stepped on the field they all stood up and applauded. There was a big Jewish population in Toronto. They had heard what happened."

When Sam Nahem met Moe Berg at the wedding of a Boston Red Sox player in the late 1930s, it was meeting of two of the game's unique ballplayers. Berg's story is well-known—major league catcher, lawyer, linguist, spy behind enemy lines during the Second World War. But Nahem was also a lawyer playing pro ball. "One summer during law school, I said to my mother I was leaving to play baseball. She said, 'Isn't it time you stopped playing games?' I said, 'I'm going to make $200 a month.' She said, 'Go and play baseball.' "

When he was a star pitcher at Brooklyn College, Nahem developed a passion for another American pastime of the 1930s: political activism. He was a right-handed pitcher with a leftie pitch. "I felt baseball was a separate aspect of my life and my political life was different," says Nahem. "I was left. I marched, I contributed to the Republican side in the Spanish Civil War, gave fund-raising parties, was involved in the fight around the Rosenbergs, was chairman of the negotiating committee for the union at the Standard Oil plant in Richmond, California."

Blanche Schacter also grew up in Brooklyn and played ball in the 1940s, in the first women's professional league. "I was always good athletically. I was brought up Orthodox, played for the temple. I heard they were having tryouts in New Jersey, and I asked my mom, 'What do you think?' She said, 'Blanche, go.' She was all for it. It's still on the pictures of me in my uniform—'Dear Mom, Love Blanche.' It was thrilling for someone like me who eats it, sleeps it. I loved it." A torn knee cartilage shortened Schacter's tenure in the All-American Girls Professional Baseball League.

Tiby Eisen left a job in a war-time shipyard in Los Angeles to join the league in its inaugural 1944 season. She starred in the league for nine years, her best season coming in 1946 when she made the all-star team, led the league in triples, and stole 128 bases for the Peoria Redwings. "We played a big charity game in Chicago for a Jewish hospital," Eisen recalls. "My name and picture was in every Jewish paper. My uncle had said, 'You shouldn't be playing baseball, you'll get a bad reputation, a bad name.' He was in the stands and he was just bursting with pride that I was there."

In 1929, John McGraw just missed getting his Jewish star when Hank Greenberg was rebuffed in a tryout with his home-town Giants. He would go on to become the Detroit Tigers' Hammerin' Hank, leading the American League in home runs four times and challenging Babe Ruth's 60 in 1938 when he slammed 58. His .92 RBI per at-bat is third highest in major league history, and he had seasons of 170 and 183.

When Greenberg decided not to play on Yom Kippur in 1934, poet Edgar Guest wrote:

Come Yom Kippur—holy fast day world wide over to the Jew—
And Hank Greenberg to his teaching and the old tradition true,
Spent the day among his people and he didn't come to play.
Said Murphy to Mulrooney, 'We shall lose the game today!
We shall miss him in the infield and shall miss him at the bat.
But he's true to his religion—and I honor him for that!'

Greenberg was met by verbal abuse from fans and opposing players day-after-day. He answered his critics with his bat, and on occasion his fists, and was revered among Jews. With mythical characters, sometimes it's difficult to separate fact from fiction. Actor Walter Matthau, who grew up on New York's Lower East Side idolizing Greenberg, later became his friend and gave a eulogy at his funeral.

"For 30 years I told a story which I read in the newspapers, about Hank Greenberg at a port of embarkation during World War II," Matthau said. "The story had it that there was a soldier who had had a little too much to drink, and he was weaving around all the soldiers sitting there. He was quite a big fella. And he said in a very loud voice, 'Anybody here named Goldberg or Ginsberg? I'll kick the livin' daylights out of him.' Or words to that effect. Hank had been sitting on his helmet, and he stood up and said, 'My name is Greenberg, soldier.' The soldier looked at him from head to foot and said, 'Well, I said nothin' about Greenberg, I said Goldberg or Ginsberg.' I told this to Hank when I met him at the club. He said it never happened. I told him I didn't care to hear that. I was going to continue to tell that story because I liked it. He said, 'OK, whatever you say, Walter.' "

Greenberg entered the Army in 1941, and when he returned four years later the Tigers were in a pennant fight. "In October of 1944, I was in India, listening to the World Series between the Cards and the Browns," he said. "By July of the following year, I was back with the Tigers. Going into the last day of the season, our fate was in our own hands. If we beat the Browns, we clinch the pennant. If we lose, Washington ties us for first place."

With the Tigers down 3-2 in the ninth, they loaded the bases with one out, and the returning soldier promptly belted one over the left-field fence. The Tigers poured on to the field, the city of Detroit poured into the streets, cheering Greenberg.

Greenberg wasn't just a Jewish hero. He was a baseball hero, a towering figure in an era of great sluggers. And he arrived as Jews were under attack in Europe and North America, performing his heroics in the city from which the fascist sympathizer Father Charles Coughlin broadcast across the country his diatribes against Jews.

In a letter to the *New York Times* after Greenberg's death in 1986, a non-Jewish Detroiter named Rosemary LeBoeuf said: "He was becoming a hero to *goyim,* too. I . . . grew up in Catholic Detroit. To my classmates' recital of Jewish faults, I had always the last word: 'Yeah? What about Hank Greenberg?' "

Former Dodger pitcher Joe Black, who came across the color line shortly after Jackie Robinson broke it, recalled in the documentary *Boys of Summer* that as a high school phenom he asked a major league scout why he was signing other players but not him. "Colored guys don't play in the big leagues," Black was told, and he ran home, up to the attic, opened his scrapbook. "And he was right, there wasn't a face of color there. And I tore them all up, except Greenberg. And just laid in the bed and just cried."

When Robinson broke the line in 1947 he was abused by fans and players wherever he went. That year, Greenberg had moved to Pittsburgh for his last season, and when his team played the Dodgers for the first time, his teammates lit into Robinson. "He got a hit and stood beside me on first base with his chin up, like a prince," Greenberg said. "I had a feeling for him because of the way I had been treated. I remember saying to him, 'Don't let them get you down. You're doing fine. Keep it up.' "

The next day, the headline in the *New York Times* said: HANK GREENBERG A HERO TO DODGERS' NEGRO STAR. "Class tells," Robinson said. "It sticks out all over Mr. Greenberg."

Later, Greenberg would be a baseball owner and general manager. He was also considered for the job of executive director of the players association. Greenberg and Bill Veeck were the only former owners to testify for Curt Flood in his case against the reserve clause.

"It's a strange thing," Greenberg would reflect in retirement. "When I was playing I used to resent being singled out as a Jewish ballplayer. I wanted to be known as a great ballplayer, period. I'm not sure why or when I changed, because I'm still not a particularly religious person. Lately, though, I find myself wanting to be remembered not only as a great ballplayer, but even more as a great Jewish ballplayer. I realize now, more than I used to, how important a part I played in the lives of a generation of Jewish kids who grew up in the '30s."

The 1950s were a transitional time when the last of the second generation Jews appeared in the majors, and a new generation—the children of the children of immigrants—made their arrival. Al Rosen grew up in Miami, and recalls sitting in the back seat of a car with other students trying out for his high school football team, when the coach turned from the front seat. "He said, 'Rosen, what are you doing out for football?' I said, 'I love it.' 'Well, I didn't know you Jewboys liked contact.' I remember it as if it happened this morning. I remember the coach's name. I was not going to accept that premise, and I was bound and determined to dispel that image. I was proud, and when I was in the majors, uppermost in my mind was conducting myself in a way that would give Jewish people someone to be proud of, something to cheer about."

Rosen became a superb schoolboy athlete, starring in baseball, football and basketball, and was Florida's high school middleweight boxing champ. He grew up a battler, working his way to Cleveland where in 1950 he set a record for most home runs (37) by an American League rookie. Saul Rogovin, a Jewish pitcher who led the AL in ERA in 1951, recalled a night when he was with the White Sox and a teammate yelled at Rosen as he passed the Sox dugout: " 'Well, we got you that time, you Jew bastard.' . . . Al walked over to our dugout and said, 'That son of a bitch that called me a Jew bastard, would he care to say that again?' Everybody just sat there. I felt very funny, because there I was, an opposing player and also a Jew. I had mixed feelings over that. I felt good for Al, thinking, 'Thattaboy Al, give it to them,' and I also felt sort of disloyal, because Al was an opposing player."

In 1953, Rosen just missed the Triple Crown, leading the AL in home runs (43), RBI (143) and missing the batting title by .001 (.336 to Mickey Vernon's .337). Vernon conceded it would be "a dog-gone crime" if Rosen wasn't voted Most Valuable Player. And he was the first unanimous selection for the award, beating by 12 votes the record set in 1948 by another Cleveland Indian with a Jewish mom, Lou Boudreau, who hit .355 that year.

A seven-time all-star, Boudreau set shortstop fielding records and led the AL in hitting at .327 in 1944. In 1942, he was named player/manager of the Indians at the age of twenty-four, and was an innovator, devising the "Boudreau Shift" in which he positioned three infielders between first and second to face Ted Williams. In 1948, as player/manager he led the Indians to a World Series victory and was named AL MVP.

"Both of my mother's parents were Jewish, and they kept special plates for holidays," Boudreau says, adding that he also lived with his French-American father when his parents separated and had little Jewish influence from a young age living in small-town Illinois.

Rosen was the last of the outstanding second-generation ballplayers. Others such as Gordon and Rogovin and Cal Abrams would continue into the 1950s, but by the last half of that decade the next generation had arrived, featuring players such as Larry and Norm Sherry, Barry Latman, Bo Belinsky, and Sandy Koufax. And the heart of Jewish baseball had shifted from New York to Los Angeles. The Sherrys and Latman attended L.A.'s Fairfax High School, and Belinsky (L.A. Angels) and Koufax (L.A. Dodgers) were transplanted easterners.

There were still instances of anti-Semitism but in the post-Holocaust aftershock it was more muted inside baseball, in no small part due to battles fought by Greenberg, Rosen, and other earlier players. Prejudice against Jewish ballplayers doesn't exist in the major leagues, Larry Sherry said in a 1963 interview, adding that he had encountered some in the minors, "but if I let those people bother me, I'd be getting down to their level."

Sherry arrived with a bang, picking up two wins and two saves as a Los Angeles Dodger rookie in the 1959 World Series. His brother, Norm, became a big league manager and coach after his playing career. When he was managing the Angels, Sherry was hit above the eye by a wild throw. "My head was exploding and I thought I was going to die. I kept moaning, my temple, my temple," Sherry said. A concerned Angels pitching coach, Billy Muffett, leaned over Sherry, and whispered comfortingly, "Norm, today is Sunday. Temple is on Saturday."

Norm Sherry's most lasting legacy was his role in developing Sandy Koufax, a struggling flamethrower in 1961 when Sherry, a Dodger catcher, told him to "quit trying to always throw the ball through a wall," Koufax said. "He convinced me I could throw just as fast without trying so hard. That, I think, is when I became a pitcher."

In 1954, Koufax was signed by his home-town Brooklyn Dodgers. He didn't pitch regularly until the Dodgers moved to L.A. Although there had been flashes of greatness—such as an 18-strikeout game in 1959—he wouldn't emerge until 1961. When he did, he led the Dodgers to two World Series victories, and he won three Cy Young Awards and five straight ERA titles, tossed four no-hitters, and led the majors in strikeouts four times. He retired after a painful 1966 season (when he won 26 games with a 1.73 ERA and 323 strikeouts) because arthritis in his elbow threatened permanent disability.

"Koufax is the most overpowering pitcher I ever faced," Stan Musial said. "There were some hard-throwing pitchers . . . but none of them threw harder than Sandy and none of them had his curve. Sandy has one of the best curves I ever saw. . . . That's what makes Koufax great. He has the great fastball and the great curve. He just overpowers you with them."

In Game 1 of the 1963 World Series, Koufax struck out the first five Yankees he faced, and the rest of the afternoon fans were in awe as Yankees lunged helplessly at his pinpoint fastball and curve, watching him set a World Series strikeout record (15).

"How come he only won 25?" asked Yankee Bobby Richardson. "If Koufax is this consistent, I've never seen anyone like him."

"Everything," Mickey Mantle concluded, "they were writing about him is true."

People filled ballparks everywhere to watch him pitch, and he drew the respect of fans and players. Once when NBC wanted to pay him $10,000 to do an hour-long special, recalled Dodger reliever Phil Regan, "he wouldn't do it unless the network gave $1,000 to each Dodger player. He thought his teammates were very important to his success."

Like Greenberg and Rosen before him, Koufax sat out Yom Kippur, and after he decided not to pitch the first game of the 1965 series versus Minnesota, which the Twins won 8-2, a Minnesota fan at the ballpark before Game 2 was quoted, "What this country needs is more Jewish holidays."

"He would not pitch under the circumstances and I would not ask him to," said Dodger manager Walter Alston, who reportedly kept on his desk a calendar with Jewish holidays circled. "I don't know," Koufax said, "why people insist upon making something big out of that. I am not devout, but I have religious principles by which I've lived and by which I intend to keep living."

Koufax became an idol to the Jewish baby boom generation, which had followed their parents out of the urban neighborhoods, into the suburbs. And their parents adored him too. Tiby Eisen returned to L.A. after her ballplaying days, and was a Dodger fan during the Koufax years. "He was cool and collected and never seemed to get into trouble. The teammates and everyone loved him," says Eisen, adding that she was also drawn by his Jewishness. "I feel we've been picked on quite a bit. There's a lot of prejudice. When you find out someone is Jewish and they've succeeded, it's a good feeling, you have kind of a camaraderie with them."

Sam Nahem notes: "I've been mentioned in the same breath as Koufax. The breath usually is, 'Sam Nahem is no Sandy Koufax.' "

"My dad followed Koufax's career and was a fan of his," says Hank Greenberg's son, Steve, who served as baseball's deputy commissioner in the early 1990s. "He was proud of him as a Jew and, more than that, he thought he was a good human being and obviously a great, great pitcher."

Koufax and Greenberg teamed to support publicly the 1965 U.S. team for the Maccabiah Games, the "Jewish Olympics" held every four years in Israel. "We talked only briefly," Koufax would recall of the few times he met Greenberg. "What I remember about Hank was that he was a terribly nice man."

"If that young fellow," Casey Stengel said of Koufax's popularity, "was running for office in Israel, they'd have a whole new government over there." But a popular bumpersticker of the day expressed the sentiments of many fans of the 1960s: "You Don't Have To Be Jewish To Love Sandy."

Koufax retired in 1966, as another generation was emerging, players such as Art Shamsky, Ron Blomberg,

Mike Epstein, Ken Holtzman, Richie Scheinblum, and Steve Stone.

Shamsky arrived with a bang, hitting home runs in four consecutive plate appearances to tie a record in 1966, and was a favorite in New York when he hit .300 with the 1969 Miracle Mets. When Ron Blomberg joined the Yankees, Shamsky's teammate Tom Seaver noted, "That should take some of the pressure off Shamsky." Blomberg and Mike Epstein were the most heralded of the Jewish baby boomers. Epstein, born in the Bronx and raised in L.A.'s Fairfax district, was said to have unlimited potential when he came to the Baltimore Orioles after being named, in only his second professional season, the International League's MVP. Epstein penciled a Star of David on his glove, and after he blasted a homer for Stockton his manager, Rocky Bridges, dubbed him Superjew, a nickname reminiscent of earlier handles such as Barney (The Yiddish Curver) Pelty and Mose (The Rabbi of Swat) Solomon. He took pride in the nickname, but acknowledged: "I don't think there's a Super Jew or a Super Christian or a Super Negro. If there was anybody it had to be Sandy Koufax or Hank Greenberg."

The *Baltimore Jewish Times* headlined Epstein's arrival: "The Orioles' Hank Greenberg." The story quoted Epstein's manager at Triple A, Earl Weaver: "He's the best prospect I've ever had." Epstein did produce, but he couldn't live up to the expectations, and bounced from Baltimore to Washington to Oakland to Texas to California. When he was with Washington, manager Ted Williams had told the press: "That's my prodigy. That Epstein ought to hit 40 home runs a year."

"From then on, I always felt that nothing I did was enough. People compared me to Mickey Mantle and I knew I couldn't carry his jock. When I was playing, nothing was ever good enough for me. I probably tried too hard for my own good. Now I finally have perspective. I realize I was really a bear-down guy. How much better could I have been?" Epstein retired after nine seasons and 130 home runs. He hit 50 homers in 833 at-bats his last two complete seasons as a Senator, and there was talk the Yankees and Mets were interested in bringing the slugger to New York as a gate attraction, but he wound up in Oakland, where he hit 26 homers for the 1972 world champions.

Blomberg was the No. 1 pick overall in the 1967 baseball draft, signed out of an Atlanta high school, noted for his bat, his speed, and his distant family ties to Jerry Lewis. "I feel that Ronnie is the best pro prospect to come along in several years," said Yankee GM Lee MacPhail. "A JEWISH MANTLE?" *The Sporting News* asked.

His parents didn't take his baseball obsession seriously until scouts started hovering before the draft. "Two or three years ago I asked him what he wanted to become," said his father, Sol, after the draft. "He said a professional baseball player. I told him, come on, be serious. I didn't believe him until six weeks ago."

By the time Blomberg arrived, many in the close-knit urban Jewish neighborhoods had left for the suburbs, and Bob Fishel, the Yankees public relations director, said: "For many years, we made a conscious effort to find a Jewish player. After all, the Jewish community in New York is immense. Now, however, we've seen so many changes, here and nationally, that I'm not sure how important the ethnic element is. We certainly didn't draft Blomberg for the reason that he was Jewish. We had first pick that year and we felt he was the best player in the country." When told that much of the Bronx's Jewish population had moved to the suburbs, Blomberg said: "That's all right. I'll bring them back." And Jewish fans, suburban or not, did respond to the "Yiddish Yankee."

"Can Blomberg Lead Yanks Out of Desert?" the *New York Post* headline read, and Blomberg received invitations to speak to Jewish organizations, was sent mezuzahs in the mail, was asked to do commercials for Hebrew National salami. In 1971, Blomberg made sure he'd be home by the start of the Jewish New Year, with a ninth-inning hit that gave the Yanks a 3-2 win. "It's my day," he said after the game. "Why do you think I did it? I knew sundown was coming. I could only stay another hour. If the count had been 3-2 and the sun went down, I would have left."

The following spring, Yankee manager Ralph Houk said: "Can't you imagine what a drawing card he'll be in Yankee Stadium if he keeps developing? He has speed, size and strength. He's a naturally outgoing personality. He takes care of himself. And he's Jewish. Last year, when I sat him down against lefthanders, I was deluged by mail from Jewish people."

In 1973 he was hitting .400 halfway through the season, the first player to hit that high that late in 25 years, and wound up at .329. That year, his bat was sent to Cooperstown after opening day when he became the first designated hitter to appear in a major league game. He wound up hitting .293 over eight seasons, but there were injuries, and managers wouldn't let him hit lefties, so in the end, despite the hoopla and highlights, he had a checkered career.

"I was going to be the new Hank Greenberg," Blomberg recalled after he'd left baseball. "The day they put my name up on the scoreboard after the Yankees signed me, and I was there to watch the game with my parents, a big cheer went up. Must have been all those Jewish fans, from Paramus to Riverdale, they all stood up to cheer me."

Kenny Holtzman hit the headlines for the first time in 1966, when as a twenty-year-old rookie Chicago Cub, he outdueled his baseball hero, Sandy Koufax. Holtzman came within three outs of a no-hitter, going on to win 2-1, handing Koufax the last regular-season defeat of his career. "Imagine beating Koufax in a game like this," Holtzman said. "[Manager] Leo [Durocher] told me Sandy's the greatest who ever pitched and I beat him. That's the big thrill. Imagine beating Koufax."

Headlines and stories read "The New Koufax" so often that it seemed to be his nickname. "I know people say this and mean to be complimentary," Holtzman said. "And I know there is a similarity. We're both Jewish and we're both lefthanded pitchers. However, after that, we are miles apart. He was the greatest."

"He's not the 'new Sandy Koufax,'" Koufax said. "He's the first Kenny Holtzman."

Holtzman would have a fine career in his own right. In 1969 he won 17 and pitched a no-hitter, and he notched a second no-hitter in 1971. The next year, he became a mainstay in the starting rotation of the Oakland A's team that would win three World Series. From 1972 to 1975, he won 77 games for Oakland, including 21 in 1973, the year he was named *Sporting News* AL lefthanded pitcher of the year. He also won four World Series games.

In 1970, Holtzman said, "I think the reason my being Jewish has never been the subject of any harsh barbs is because of the great respect players had for Sandy Koufax." But in 1984, Reggie Jackson in his autobiography accused several former Yankees of making comments that were anti-black and anti-Semitic. They would watch Holtzman run laps, "making Jewish jokes . . . crude, juvenile stuff," wrote Jackson, who had worn a black armband, along with teammates Epstein and Holtzman, when Israeli athletes were murdered at the 1972 Olympics. When the issue of anti-Semitism was raised earlier, Billy Martin, who was among those named by Jackson, had denied he was prejudiced, adding, "I happen to be in love with a Jew by the name of Jesus Christ."

Jackson wasn't the first in the baseball world to show Jews they weren't alone when they faced anti-Semitism. Just as Greenberg had stood with Robinson, others had stood with Jewish ballplayers. For instance, pitcher Bob Gibson told a player who made an anti-Jewish comment not to speak with him again, "and if I ever pitch against you, I'm going to hit you on the coconut with my first pitch." And umpire George Moriarty was fined by commissioner Kenesaw Mountain Landis for stopping a World Series game to engage in a heated exchange with the Chicago Cubs bench, which had been hurling ethnic slurs at Greenberg. "I told [Cubs manager Charlie] Grimm at Detroit if I heard any more such profanity as they yelled at Greenberg that I'd chase five of them off the bench with Grimm leading the procession," Moriarty said.

"My grandfather was an extraordinary man," actor Michael Moriarty, who starred in the baseball movie *Bang the Drum Slowly,* told *Total Baseball.* "He set a family code for the Moriarty family. Baseball in the Moriarty family is a sacred thing, and my grandfather didn't allow anyone to drag it into the gutter with something as despicable as racism. Gilda Radner's father in Windsor, Canada, got together a bunch of Jewish people to pay my grandfather's fine. I met her when she was doing *Saturday Night Live.* She said, 'My father and your grandfather knew each other,' and she showed me newspaper clippings about it. They sent him a check for $250. He sent it back and told them to send it to his favorite charity. He was a highly principled man. There's a term for what he was: 'Righteous gentile.'"

Like Holtzman, Steve Stone of Ohio wore Koufax's No. 32. Stone credits Koufax with turning his fortunes around early in his minor league career. "I read his biography," Stone said. "I was struggling with a 3-10 record and a 6.00 ERA, even though I was averaging 12 strikeouts every nine innings. In his book, Sandy said the most important pitch was not the fastball, curve, or slider, but strike one." His ERA and strikeout totals came down, and Stone went up to the majors the next season.

Like many of the Jewish ballplayers, Stone is secular, observing his Jewishness as a cultural, ethnic tradition (such as his mother's "best matzoh ball soup this side of Tel Aviv") as much as a religion. "I'm proud of the fact that I'm a Jew, but I don't belong to a temple," Stone said. "I observe Judaism in my own way without the organized aspects." Until 1980, Stone had a solid, but unspectacular career as a starter, with a high of 15 wins. That year, with the Baltimore Orioles, he went 25-7, including 14 wins in a row, and won the Cy Young Award. He also started the All-Star Game, pitching three perfect innings. It would be Stone's last complete season, as he retired after the 1981 season because of tendinitis.

Baseball's baby-boom era, reflecting the rising numbers of intermarriages in the Jewish community, included several ballplayers who had converted to Judaism—Lloyd Allen, Skip Jutze, Elliot Maddox, Joel Horlen, Steve Yeager, and Jeff Newman. As well, some recent ballplayers with Jewish or partially Jewish backgrounds practice other religions, including Bob Melvin, Jon Perlman, Ryan Karp and Doug Johns.

Horlen won 116 games and led the AL with a 2.06 ERA in 1967, when he went 19-7 for the White Sox. He converted after marrying Lois Eisenstein in San Antonio, Texas. "I had always been interested in the history of the Jews and Judaism," he says, noting that when he told his old teammate Mike Epstein about his conversion at an oldtimers game, "He said, 'Welcome to the tribe.' "

Outfielder Elliot Maddox converted in 1974 when he hit .303 with the New York Yankees. The black ballplayer had close Jewish friends growing up in Union, New Jersey, and took Judaic studies courses while attending the University of Michigan. "In studying Judaism and tying it in to things I already knew, I started to see a very strong correlation between the black experience in America with that of the Jews. . . . I don't think there is nearly as much dislike and distrust of Jews among blacks as is written about in the media. Blacks generally view Jews with a much closer bond than they do any other white group," Maddox said.

Until the 1960s there had been just a handful of ballplayers with one Jewish parent—most notably Buddy Myer and Lou Boudreau—but more children of mixed marriages entered the game in the '60s and '70s, including Bo Belinsky, whose mother was Jewish, and Dave Roberts, Greg Goossen, and Mike LaCoss, who had Jewish fathers.

Belinsky tossed a no-hitter shortly after he joined the Angels in 1962, but he was better known for his flamboyant personality and unrelenting partying than for pitching in L.A. "It was quite a town, and it was mine for one year," he said.

Roberts won 103 games in a thirteen-year career, and Goossen hit 10 homers in 139 at-bats for the expansion 1969 Seattle Pilots. In 1995, Goossen could be seen acting in the movie *Get Shorty*. Born Michael Marks, LaCoss, who won 98 games, took his stepfather's name after his parents separated.

By the 1980s, Jewish ballplayers had long discarded the old name-change routine, and if a player's name had been Anglicized, the change likely went back to grandparents or earlier. Any stigma baseball had held as a profession had largely vanished. Although there is still an emphasis on education in Jewish families, in the '80s and '90s, with the emphasis on recruiting from colleges, Jewish ballplayers can answer the old concerns of their parents by getting an education and playing baseball. And current players are often the children of baseball players or fans, and the grandchildren of the urban Jews whose parents worried about them because of their devotion to the game.

When Mark Gilbert came up to the White Sox in 1985, not only did he please his father, Herbert, who had made it to Triple A, but he thrilled his grandfather, Joseph. "I've still got a letter from Connie Mack," the eighty-five-year-old said when his grandson got the call to the ChiSox. "He wrote it in 1919. I keep it in an envelope in my desk at the store. Connie wanted to give me a chance to pitch for the old Philadelphia A's. I showed the letter to my father and he said, 'Joe, ballplayers are bums. If you want to play ball, go ahead. But you'll have to move out of the house. You can't live here anymore.' "

From when Mark was a young boy, Joseph Gilbert shared his knowledge of the game with his grandson, who had made him proud. "My time is up," the grandfather said, "and now I'm very happy."

In the 1990s, Jewish players are almost as likely to have intermarried parents as not, and the decades of assimilation, conversion and name-changing has made it so a Jewish major leaguer is as liable to be named Jose Bautista, Andrew Lorraine, or Brad Ausmus, as he is to be named Alan Levine, Steve Rosenberg, or Wayne Rosenthal. Outfielder Ruben Amaro Jr., son of the black Cuban/Mexican ballplayer and a Jewish mother, said: "I didn't attend Hebrew school or have a bar mitzvah, but we did Chanukah and Passover. I knew how to recite the Chanukah blessings and did so for years before I went off to college."

There was a paucity of Jewish players in the 1980s, but the numbers increased in the 1990s, when the children of the baby boomers came of age. The early players had largely come from northeastern cities, primarily New York, and now baseball was drawing from another area with a large Jewish population, California—not L.A.'s urban sections that spawned the Dannings and the Sherrys, but the suburban sprawl.

Andrew Lorraine's grandmother left Poland for England before the Nazis marched in, but most of her family didn't survive. She had two sons—one became a rabbi outside London, the other moved to suburban southern California, where Lorraine was born in 1972. When Lorraine was fourteen, the two brothers took their families to Israel, where they visited Yad Vashem, the memorial to the Holocaust dead. "It was overwhelming," Lorraine says. "You could look up records that showed what happened to each Jewish community. It was sad to see the town where my grandmother lived. There were no survivors. They were all taken to Treblinka. I'm proud of my family, and being Jewish is what I share with my sister, my parents. Personally, it's deeper than anything else."

Lorraine graduated from Stanford with a BA in 1994, the year he was named the Pacific Coast League's No. 1 pitching prospect by *Baseball America*. Since then, he's had stints with the California Angels and Chicago White Sox. He grew up on anecdotes about Sandy Koufax and identifies with the Hall of Famer, an icon to many of the Jewish players of the '90s, much as Hispanic players identify with Roberto Clemente.

Mike Zimmerman likes Koufax too, and he's pitching proof that today's Jewish ballplayers aren't all from California. He is from Brooklyn, drafted by Pittsburgh in the first round in 1990 after a sensational pitching career at

South Alabama University, and had made it as far as Triple A as of the middle of the 1996 season. His father Jerry, a onetime member of the N.Y. State handball championship team, attended the same high school as Koufax, and watched him pitch for the Dodgers of both coasts.

"He's a diehard Brooklyn Dodger fan. One day I brought a Yankees hat into the house and he threw it out," Mike Zimmerman says, crediting much of his pitching ability to hours spent playing ball with his father every day after school. The Zimmermans are a close family who attended ball games ("Mets," he stresses) and often get together when Mike's in Brooklyn during the off-season. "We'd go out to dinner two-three times a week and every time my dad's telling stories about Sandy Koufax and the Brooklyn Dodgers. I'd like to meet him some day."

Shawn Green has received more hype than any Jewish ballplayer since Epstein and Blomberg. A first-round draft pick, he quickly rose to lead the International League in hitting in 1994 (.344). The next year, as a Toronto Blue Jay, he hit .288 with 15 homers and led the team in slugging percentage after being named the majors' No.1 rookie in *Baseball America's* preseason listing. "I like everything about him," an opposing IL manager, Richmond's Grady Little, told *Baseball America*. "He has

a chance to be a great player."

After being drafted, Green continued his education, taking classes at Stanford in the offseason. "My mother (Judy Schneider Green) was more 'go to school, get your education,' in the beginning. They both wanted me to do what was best for me." Green's father, Ira Green, who played NCAA basketball, notes that his father, Leo, changed the family name from Greenberg in the 1930s. The mainstream media is less interested in players' ethnicity than it once was, but the Jewish press has welcomed Green, articles appearing with headlines such as "The Natural" and "Shawn Green following in Greenberg's steps." As well, much of Toronto's large Jewish community has embraced the young outfielder, and he receives many letters from Jewish fans and has spoken before Jewish organizations.

"I see it building," Green says of the Jewish fan support. "I think it's fine. It's great to have people pulling for me. A lot of Jewish fans can relate to a Jewish ballplayer. It's almost like family.

"They come from the same heritage, go through the same experiences. Jewish people feel a closeness, a connection when they see another Jewish person doing well. I'm proud of who I am."

Jewish Baseball Roster

Major Leagues

Cal Abrams OF
1949-56 BKN, CIN, PIT, BAL, CHI-A
Lloyd Cecil Allen P
1969-75 CAL, TEX, CHI-A
Ruben Amaro Jr. OF
1991-1996 CAL, PHI, CLE
Morrie Arnovich OF
1936-41, 1946 PHI-N, CIN, NY-N
Brad Ausmus C
1993-96 SD, DET
Jesse Baker (Michael Myron Silverman) SS
1919 WAS
Brian Bark P
1995 BOS
Ross Baumgarten P
1978-82 CHI-A, PIT
Jose Bautista P
1988-91, 1993-96 BAL, CHI-N, SF
Bo Belinsky P
1962-67, 1969-70 LA-A, PHI, HOU, PIT, CIN
Joe Bennett (Joseph Rosenblum) 3B
1923 PHI-N
Moe Berg C
1923, 1926-39 BKN, CHI-A, CLE, WAS, BOS-A
Nathan Berkenstock OF
1871 PHI-NA
Bob Berman C
1918 WAS
Cy Block 3B/2B
1942, 1945-46 CHI-N
Ron Blomberg DH/1B/OF
1969, 1971-76, 1978 NY-A, CHI-A
Sammy Bohne (Sammy Arthur Cohen) 2B/SS/3B
1916, 1921-26 STL-N, CIN, BKN
Henry Bostick (Henry Lifsit) 3B
1915 PHI-A
Louis Boudreau SS
1938-52 CLE, BOS-A
Lou Brower SS
1931 DET
Conrad Cardinal P
1963 HOU
Harry Chozen C
1937 CIN
Alta Cohen OF
1931-33 BKN, PHI-N

Andy Cohen 2B
1926-28, 1929 NY-N
Hy Cohen P
1955 CHI-N
Sid Cohen P
1934, 1936-37 WAS
Richard Conger P
1940-43 DET, PIT, PHI-N
Phil Cooney (Phillip Clarence Cohen) 3B
1905 NY-A
Ed Corey (Edward Norman Cohen) P
1918 CHI-A
Bill Cristall P
1901 CLE
Harry Danning C
1933-42 NY-N
Ike Danning C
1928 STL-A
Harry Eisenstat P
1935-42 BKN, DET, CLE
Mike Epstein 1B
1966-74 BAL, WAS, OAK, CAL
Reuben Ewing (Reuben Cohen) SS
1921 STL-N
Al Federoff 2B
1951-52 DET
Eddie Feinberg SS/2B/OF
1938-39 PHI-
Harry Feldman P
1941-46 NY-N
Leo Fishel P
1899 NY-N
Happy Foreman P
1924, 1926 CHI-A, BOS-A
Murray Franklin SS/2B
1941-42 DET
Milt Galatzer OF
1933-36, 1939 CLE, CIN
Mark Gilbert OF
1985 CHI-A
Joe Ginsberg C
1948, 1950-54, 1956-62 DET, CLE, BALT, CHI-A, BOS-A, NY-N
Jonah Goldman SS/3B
1928, 1930-31 CLE
Izzy Goldstein P
1932 DET
Jake Goodman 1B
1878, 1882 MIL-N, PIT-AA

Greg Goossen 1B/C
1965-70 NY-N, SEA, MIL-A, WAS
Sid Gordon OF/3B
1941-43, 1946-55 NY-N, BOS-N, MIL-N, P
Herb Gorman OF
1952 STL-N
Shawn Green OF
1993-96 TOR
Hank Greenberg 1B/OF
1930, 1933-1941, 1945-47 DET, PIT
Eric Helfand C
1993-95 OAK
Steve Hertz 3B
1964 HOU
Ken Holtzman P
1965-79 CHI-N, OAK, BAL, NY-A
Joel Horlen P
1961-72 CHI-A, OAK
Doug Johns P
1995-96 OAK
Skip Jutze C
1972-77 STL, HOU, SEA
Harry Kane (Harry Cohen) P
1902-03, 1905-06 STL-A, DET, PHI-N
Ryan Karp P
1995 PHI
Herb Karpel P
1946 NY-A
Alan Koch P
1963-64 DET, WAS
Brian Kowitz OF
1995 ATL
Sandy Koufax P
1955-66 BKN, LA-N
Mike LaCoss (Michael Marks) P
1978-90 CIN, HOU, KC, SF
Barry Latman P
1957-67 CHI-A, CLE, LA-A, CAL, HOU
Jim Levey SS
1930-33 STL-A
Alan Levine P
1996 CHI-A
Jesse Levis C
1992-96 CLE, MIL
Lou Limmer 1B
1951, 1954 PHI-A
Andrew Lorraine P
1994-95 CAL, CHI-A
Elliott Maddox OF/2B

1970-80 DET, WAS, TEX, NY-A, BAL, NY-N
Cy Malis P
1934 PHI-N
Moxie Manuel P
1905, 1908 WAS, CHI-A
Duke Markell (Harry Duquesne Makowsky) P
1951 STL-A
Ed Mayer P
1957-58 CHI-N
Erskine Mayer P
1912-19 PHI-NL, CHI-AL
Sam Mayer OF/P
1915 WAS
Bob Melvin C
1985-94 DET, SF, BAL, KC, BOS, NY, CHI-A
Mike Milchin P
1996 MIN, BAL
Norm Miller OF
1965-74 HOU, ATL
Buddy Myer 2B/SS/3B
1925-41 WAS, BOS-A
Sam Nahem P
1938, 1941-42, 1948 BKN, STL-N, PHI-N
Jeff Newman C/1B
1976-84 OAK, BOS
Barney Pelty P
1903-12 STL-A, WAS
Jon Perlman P
1985, 1987 CHI-N, SF
Jacob Pike OF
1877 HAR-N
Lipman Pike OF/2B
1871-78, 1881, 1887 TROY-NA, BAL-NA, HAR-NA, STL-NA, STL-N, CIN-N, PRO-N, WOR-N, NY-AA
Jake Pitler 2B
1917-18 PIT
Scott Radinsky P
1990-93, 1995-96 CHI-A, LA
Steve Ratzer P
1980-81 MON
Jimmy Reese 2B
1930-32 NY-
Al Richter SS
1951, 1953 BOS-A
Dave Roberts P

1969-81 SD, HOU, DET, CHI-N, SF,
  PIT, SEA, NY-N
Saul Rogovin P
  1949-53, 1955-57 DET, CHI-A, BAL,
  PHI-N
Al Rosen 3B
  1947-56 CLE
Goody Rosen OF
  1937-39, 1944-46 BKN, NY-N
Harry Rosenberg OF
  1930 NY-N
Lou Rosenberg 2B
  1923 CHI-A
Steve Rosenberg P
  1988-91 CHI-A, SD
Max Rosenfeld OF
  1931-33 BKN
Wayne Rosenthal P
  1991-92 TEX
Si Rosenthal OF
  1925-26 BOS-A
Marv Rotblatt P
  1948, 1950-51 CHI-A

Larry Rothschild P
  1981-82 DET
Mickey Rutner 3B
  1947 PHI-A
Roger Samuels P
  1988-89 SF, PIT
Ike Samuls 3B/SS
  1895 STL-N
Moe Savransky P
  1954 CIN
Al Schacht P
  1919-21 WAS
Sid Schacht P
  1950-51 STL-A, BOS-N
Hal Schacker P
  1945 BOS-N
Heinie Scheer 2B/3B
  1922-23 PHI-A
Richie Scheinblum OF
  1965, 1967-74 CLE, WAS, KC, CIN,
  CAL, STL-N
Mike Schemer 1B

1945-46 NY-N
Bill Schwarz C
  1914 NY-A
Art Shamsky OF/1B
  1965-72 CIN, NY-N, CHI-N, OAK
Dick Sharon OF
  1973-75 DET, SD
Larry Sherry P
  1958-68 LA-N, DET, HOU, CAL
Norm Sherry C
  1959-63 LA-N, NY-N
Harry Shuman P
  1942-44 PIT, PHI-N
Al Silvera OF
  1955-56 CIN
Fred Sington OF
  1934-39 WAS, BKN
Mose Solomon OF
  1923 NY-N
Bill Starr C
  1935-36 WAS
Steve Stone P

1971-81 SF, CHI-A, CHI-N, BAL
Bud Swartz P
  1947 STL-A
Don Taussig OF
  1958, 1961-62 SF, STL-N, HOU
Eddie Turchin 3B/SS
  1943 CLE
Steve Wapnick P
  1990-91 DET, CHI-A
Phil Weintraub 1B/OF
  1933-35, 1937-38, 1944-45 NY-N,
  CIN, PHI-N
Ed Wineapple P
  1929 WAS
Steve Yeager C
  1972-86 LA-N, SEA
Larry Yellen P
  1963-64 HOU
Guy Zinn OF
  1911-15 NY-A, BOS-N, BAL-F
Eddie Zosky SS
  1991-92, 1995 TOR, FLA

All-American Girls Professional Baseball League

Tiby Eisen OF
  1944-52 Milwaukee, Grand Rapids,
  Peoria, Fort Wayne

Anita Foss 2B
  1948-49 Muskegon, Grand Rapids

Blanche Schacter OF
  1949 Kenosha

Margaret Wisinger OF
  1944-46 Minneapolis, Rockford

Olympics: U.S. Team

Abe Kiviat, 1912

Herman Goldberg,
  1936

Mike Schemer, 1940
  (Games cancelled)

Mike Epstein, 1964

Mike Milchin, 1988

Skip Bertman
  (head coach), 1996

## CHAPTER 10

Streaks and Feats

Jack Kavanagh

The past of baseball is accented by feats of accomplishment. The heroics of individual players or collective efforts of teams are listed in record books as bare statistics. It is the purpose of this section to clothe these with accounts of how such records were made.

These are the achievements of mortals whom we have made into heroes by giving great value to things they have done. Deeds of baseball players are valued more highly than scholarship, skills in creative crafts, or sustaining a precarious balance of world peace. We can name more Cy Young Award winners than we can list those given the Nobel Peace Prize; we can rattle off batting champions but not name holders of the Pulitzer Prize.

It is axiomatic that all records are made to be broken, yet it is wasteful to throw away old records which have been cherished by generations of fans and only replace them with a newly minted line of agate type. Those who have been on the top of the list, or came close to the peak, have been recognized by relying on lists which sustain enough depth to single out the most noteworthy performances in the many categories which are represented.

As the former mayor of New York City, the dapper, perceptive Jimmy Walker, once admonished Babe Ruth when he had fallen from grace in the eyes of fans, "The cheers of yesterday have a short echo."

The Streaks

Most records are, eventually, displaced by new ones. Some survive because the conditions under which they were made have been altered by changing circumstances in baseball. Some, such as the accumulation of sheer totals, are pushed higher. This is not so much a matter of accomplishment as it is of perseverance and lengthened seasons.

Consecutive Games Played

When the first edition of *Total Baseball* was written, the Streaks section led off with a review of Joe DiMaggio's consecutive game hitting streak. It dismissed the likelihood there would be a plausible challenge to Lou Gehrig's ironman feat of playing in 2,130 consecutive games. It seemed that among the prominent streaks, DiMaggio's was a record likely to be assaulted every season. His 56 consecutive game hitting streak loomed as an annual challenge. DiMaggio's feat had been accomplished in a season which produced largely normal cumulative stats for Jolting Joe. In no offensive category did he

have a career high, and largely due to Ted Williams's phenomonal season, hitting .406, DiMaggio led in only one 1941 category, RBI with 125. Surely, someone would be able to string together base hits in more than 56 games. No one has yet come close.

Compared to Gehrig's accomplishment of being in the lineup game after game, DiMaggio seemed much more likely to be challenged by someone on a long hot streak. Gehrig's challengers had already fallen short or were distant blips on the screen. Among those was a young shortstop, Cal Ripken, Jr., off to an impressive early career, but not yet a focus for speculation to outlast Lou Gehrig for daily durability. Subsequent editions of *Total Baseball* eventually showed Ripken's name on the list. Finally, he became the only active player on that list and moved relentlessly toward Gehrig's place at the top. He became baseball's antidote to the shaky health of the national pastime.

A good portion of Ripken's charm was his blue collar identity. It takes a talented player to achieve Hall of Fame statistics. It takes a durable and determined one to show up for work every day and play baseball with workmanlike technique. Ripken is a rare species in an era in which players limp onto the disabled list in droves.

Beyond Ripken's durability is a viewpoint formed by his baseball-wise father, Cal Ripken, Sr. He managed in the minors, coached, handled special assignments, and became the third base coach of the parent team. When his sons, Billy and Cal, Jr., reached the major league team, they knew most of the older system-developed Orioles. They had been bat boys for them in the lower leagues. They also knew how to play the game, correctly in every nuance. There are far flashier infielders than Cal Ripken, Jr. There are none whose positioning in anticipation of where a ball will be batted is so expert.

Statistics do not define Cal Ripken, Jr. as they do most players. Only the on-going consecutive game appearances streak is important. By the end of the 1996 season it had reached 2,316 regular season games. The event came a few weeks after the death of the era's most charismatic player, Mickey Mantle. No two men could have approached baseball and life more differently. Mantle's self-destructive life ended at age sixty-three. Ripken might still be playing every day at that age.

In 1995 the most serious threat to his record came when the major leagues prepared to open the season with replacement players. With other members of the players union, Ripken stood firm. He would surrender his opportunity to break Gehrig's record if the American League began the season with a replacement player at shortstop. Owner Peter Angelos added to the complication by refusing to sign replacement players and offering to forfeit games as a result.

When the strike was settled, a 144-game season was finally achieved and baseball's promoters began to set a probable date for Ripken to catch and then pass Gehrig. It happened, to the delight of owner Angelos and the team's stockholders and fans, at the Camden Yards.

The record was tied on September 5 and a new one began on the sixth. Ripken rose to the occasion. It was a national event, covered by world-wide television attention. He batted a combined 5-for-9 with a home run in each game. He accepted the plaudits modestly, shared the moment with the fans by circling the ball park to shake hands with those who crowded against the railings. He endlessly answered the same questions from reporters. When he had satisfied all demands, he dressed and went home to celebrate with his father, brother Bill, and wife and children. The next day he went to work as usual. By season's end the new record had reached 2,153 games. In 1996 he methodically added 163 games to extend the run of consecutive appearances to 2,316. The streak will end sometime and be proclaimed unbreakable.

This time, unlike Lou Gehrig's string, it might be true.

Gehrig's Streak

On May 31, 1925, no one thought the young substitute pinch-hitting for the New York Yankees was launching the most extraordinary streak of durability the game has yet seen. The next day Lou Gehrig took the place of the team's star first baseman, Wally Pipp, and continued his uncertain start toward a goal so distant it was unimaginable.

Gehrig had played for Hartford in the Eastern League after the Yankees signed him off the campus of Columbia University. It was thought he would make the major league grade, but he had not been handed a starting job. Only when Pipp complained of a headache and was given the day off by manager Miller Huggins did Gehrig get a chance to start a game. So uncertain of the rookie's skills was management that two days later Aaron Ward pinch-hit for Gehrig and Pipp finished the game in the field.

Before June ended, Gehrig had been taken out of games three times for pinch hitters, although he continued to start games. On July 5 he wasn't even the starting first baseman. Fred Merkle, who in 1908, as a rookie himself, had failed to run to second on what appeared to be a game-winning single, started the game. Merkle, whose gaffe eventually cost the New York Giants a pennant to the Chicago Cubs, had been forever more labeled Bone-head by unforgiving fans. Gehrig was destined for adulation. This day he made a ninth-inning appearance, an unsuspected extension of a fledgling feat.

Of course at the time there was no suspicion that young Lou Gehrig had launched a string of consecutive-game appearances which wouldn't end until fourteen years later. He began it as a young giant in the prime of his life and ended it a dying man, forced out of the lineup with a rare disease. From start to finish it became a matter of drama as the survival of the string became a compelling goal which Gehrig sustained despite injury, sickness, accident, and managed to avoid ending inadvertently.

Gehrig is remembered, or known to people who never saw him play, as the gentle giant who was portrayed by actor Gary Cooper in the movie *The Pride of the Yankees*. In reality, particularly in his early years, Gehrig was a hard-nosed, competitive player who would readily leap into argument with umpires and enemy players. He was ejected from a major league game a half dozen times without drawing a suspension which would have ended his string of games.

Durable, yes. Gehrig was well dubbed "the Iron Horse" for his rawboned toughness. However, he never spared himself. A statistic which astonishes fans is that he stole home 15 times, risking crashing into a plate-blocking catcher. He ran the bases with surprising speed and fearless abandon. Babe Ruth and Lou Gehrig are remembered for the home runs they hit; yet they were also daring baserunners.

Once Gehrig's penchant for never missing a game was established, just being in the boxscore was the goal. He could have simultaneously set records for consecutive games played at first base, while extending his string of boxscore appearances. However, while in the sixth year of his developing string, in a late-season game, the Yankees promoted a game in which Babe Ruth would pitch while Lou Gehrig took his place in the outfield. Harry Rice, an outfielder who sometimes spelled Gehrig late in one-sided games, played first base.

Gehrig's 2,130-game skein, stretched over fourteen seasons, was not simply a matter of having him go out to first base day after day. For one thing, there were times when he could hardly play. When the Iron Horse was no longer a frisky colt, he developed lumbago, and it hobbled him from time to time. In midseason of 1934, Lou was seized by an attack and, immobilized, had to be helped off the field.

There was an acute awareness on the part of the Yankees of the consecutive games Gehrig played, and this was kept alive by the sportswriters who covered the team. Everett Scott had astonished baseball with his consecutive-game appearances at shortstop, ending a string of 1,307 in 1925, the season Gehrig, his rookie roommate, began his string. Scott had started his run of games with the Boston Red Sox, and when he was bought by the Yankees in 1923, he carried on the string without interruption. He slowed down drastically early in 1925 and was first benched, then sold to the Senators. Unlike Scott, Lou Gehrig, the Iron Horse, would never be put out to pasture. However, Scott had left a legend behind, and it served to lead Gehrig toward new standards of durability.

The day after Gehrig had been helped off the field, with his string at 1,426, and Scott's record broken, he made a contrived appearance in the lineup. Hardly able to stand, he was in the lineup of the visiting Yankees in Detroit as the leadoff batter, penciled in to play shortstop. Despite his pain, he lined out a single and, with his appearance established in the boxscore, gave way to pinch runner Red Rolfe, who finished the game at short while Gehrig took his aching back to the hotel. Jack Saltzgaver, a utility infielder who, over the years, replaced Gehrig at first base more often than any other player, filled in at first that day.

Gehrig was back in the regular lineup the next day, collecting four hits, three of them doubles. He was on his way to the only batting title he ever won and the Triple Crown for 1934. But it wasn't a pain-free future ahead for

Lou. Lumbago continued to be a problem. He left games early because he was feeling ill, and he had a thumb injury in 1938 which he ignored to keep his string going.

It was during 1938 that the perpetual machine began to show signs of wearing out. For the first time he batted below .300; his stats—a .295 average, 29 home runs, and 107 runs batted in—would have pleased most players. But they were substandard for Lou, and so was his general play. Just age catching up, it was thought, just the way it had slowed Everett Scott in 1925 when Gehrig was starting out.

In spring training the next season, it was evident that something was amiss, but manager Joe McCarthy left it to Gehrig to decide when to call it quits. It was on May 2, 1939, after eight feebly played games had brought his string to 2,130, that Gehrig advised McCarthy to replace him.

The longest streak of its kind, seemingly impossible to ever exceed despite the longer seasons, ended. For fourteen years Gehrig had played despite a broken thumb, a broken toe, back spasms, frequent colds, and recurring attacks of lumbago. He had been forced from the lineup by something no one could foresee and almost no one had ever heard about. When the tests at Mayo Clinic proved that he had amyotrophic lateral sclerosis, it was so singular an affliction that it was renamed Lou Gehrig's Disease. It was incurable then and still is. Gehrig was a doomed man. He knew it, as did his wife, Eleanor. They bravely pretended to each other that Lou would regain his strength.

He continued to carry the lineup card to home plate during the 1939 pennant-winning season, as the team captain, but soon he had to surrender even that role. On July 4, 1939, a Lou Gehrig Day was arranged at Yankee Stadium. The scene was repeated in the Gary Cooper movie and is seen often in filmed highlights of baseball history.

Babe Ruth, who had broken relations with Gehrig during a 1934 postseason tour to the Pacific and Japan, embraced his former teammate, and the occasion came to a climax as Gehrig, a man who knew his life was nearly over, stood at a microphone, surrounded by the Yankees who had been his fellow players. He told a choked-up audience, "Today, I consider myself the luckiest man on the face of the earth." He died on June 2, 1941.

Far in the Distance

Everett Scott, whose record Gehrig had eclipsed, now is third on the list, just ahead of Steve Garvey's 1,207 games. For many years, Joe Sewell ranked third behind Scott. Sewell is best remembered for his avoidance of strikeouts. Twice he fanned only 4 times in a whole season. Once he went 115 games without striking out in 437 times at bat. He set his consecutive-game string with Cleveland, later moving to the Yankees where he played for three years as Lou Gehrig's teammate. He was elected to the Hall of Fame in 1977.

During the 1930s, Gus Suhr, a fine-fielding first baseman for the Pittsburgh Pirates, reached 822 consecutive games played. It was dwarfed, even as he made it, by Gehrig's string in progress, but he far exceeded earlier National League marks.

Gus Suhr's National League record was broken by Stan Musial, who played in 895 straight games, ending in 1957 at age thirty-six. This provided a target for Billy Williams when his career with the Cubs got under way in 1963 and daily appearances were part of his routine. He sailed past Musial to claim the National League record at 1,117. He stopped in 1970, and the occasional rest did him good. He led the National League in batting in 1972 and his career ended with Oakland in 1975. He has been elected to the Hall of Fame.

Williams' new National League record provided an attainable goal for Steve Garvey, who had the stamina and will power required to catch Gehrig. He just didn't get started soon enough. Gehrig was twenty-two when his streak began; Garvey was twenty-six.

Also, Garvey did not become an everyday regular with the Los Angeles Dodgers until 1975, his sixth season with the team. He had been regarded as erratic at third base but, once moved across the diamond in 1974, he delivered with consistency in the field, at the bat, with power, and refused to budge from the lineup.

He left the Dodgers with his string intact after the 1982 season and took his Iron Man act to San Diego. A hand injury took him out of the lineup on July 29, 1983. He had broken Billy Williams' record the previous season, and all told he played in 1,207 consecutive games.

A special recognition is due to Pete Rose. Had he not paused to catch his breath during the 1978 season, when he was thirty-seven years old, he would hold the National League record. In 1978 Rose had more realistic aims than Gehrig's too distant goal. During that season he reached the 3,000-hit mark and set aim on Ty Cobb's all-time total. He also captured the headlines with his assault on Joe DiMaggio's 56-game hitting streak.

The year 1978 was also Rose's last season with the Cincinnati Reds and, in a celebrated case of free agency, he moved to Philadelphia. There he not only resumed his climb toward Cobb's hit totals, but played again on a daily basis. When he sat down for two games in 1978 with the Reds, he snapped a somewhat modest run of 678 games. When he finally left the daily lineup in Philadelphia, in 1983, he had run off an even longer string of 745 games. Add them together and Rose's total is 1,423 games, longer than anyone's stretch except Gehrig's and now Ripken's.

The following table shows the men who have played in the most consecutive games:

2,316	Cal Ripken, Jr. (through 1996)
2,130	Lou Gehrig
1,307	Everett Scott
1,207	Steve Garvey
1,117	Billy Williams
1,103	Joe Sewell
895	Stan Musial
829	Eddie Yost
822	Gus Suhr
798	Nellie Fox

Longest Hitting Streaks

Joe DiMaggio's streak of hitting safely in 56 games in a row is mind-boggling in its length, yet temptingly attainable by batters capable of hitting for high averages. And any player might get on a hot streak and sustain it long enough to challenge DiMaggio's total. However, those who have set extended streaks did it while accomplishing a high season's average. The trick is to string those games with base hits together. The more games in which a batter has hit safely, the greater the possibility these will come in succession for long stretches.

Until the New York press, wire services, and broadcast industry made Joe DiMaggio's consecutive-game hitting streak a matter of national awareness and interest, this kind of feat was not noted with a daily fanaticism. Streaks drew comment, but this was mostly reserved to be relished during the winter's Hot Stove League sessions among sport-starved fans.

Although Willie Keeler's consecutive-game string became the target for future attempts to exceed it, it might have been only one of the records made under special circumstances. Keeler's 44 consecutive games might only be unusual in retrospect because the string began on Opening Day, 1897. Had Bad Bill Dahlen not had a most peculiar bad day on August 7, 1894, even Joe DiMaggio's 56-game streak would only be a "modern record" set after 1900. As it is, Bill Dahlen appears high on the list with the 42 games in which he hit safely.

DiMaggio was stopped by stellar infield play. Bill Dahlen was stopped by his own inability to fatten his record in a game in which almost everyone else did. Dahlen's team, the Chicago Colts, had 17 hits, winning a ten-inning game from Cincinnati 13–11. Dahlen's blanking was more evident because it was sandwiched between the feats that day of his teammates, Jimmy Ryan and Walter Wilmot. Ryan, the leadoff batter, had five hits, three of them doubles, and Walter Wilmot, who followed Dahlen in the batting order, also had five hits, two of them triples.

Dahlen was at bat a half dozen times, but the Reds' pitchers, Chauncey Fisher and Tom Parrott, found him, uniquely that day, an easy out. Dahlen's feat was obscured when Willie Keeler, a star of greater national awareness, hit safely in 44 games three years later. The eclipsed record was simply noted but not recounted in the detail which was later paid to the strings which exceeded it. Although appearing in 121 games and batting .362, Dahlen was not a regular shortstop at that time, dividing his games between short and third.

It was Keeler's feat which caught the public fancy, particularly as it began on Opening Day, April 22, 1897, and continued for 44 games into the season. He was eventually stopped on June 18. Until then, it seemed he had found an unending series of opportunities to "hit 'em where they ain't"—his simplistic explanation for his base-hit totals. Keeler's record not only stood the test of time until Joe DiMaggio broke it in 1941, it still stands as the National League record, tied only by Pete Rose in 1978.

It wasn't until 1922 that the feat of hitting successfully in successive games became a real target for seekers of new records. Keeler's streak had been regarded more as evidence of his great ability to rap out base hits than as a model of daily consistency. He was a widely admired player, the leadoff batter for the Baltimore Orioles, three times pennant winners prior to the 1897 season.

When Ty Cobb came along, the fact that he nearly equaled Keeler's mark in 1911, when he set an American League record with 40 successive games in which he got at least one hit, was also taken as a sign of his superiority, not necessarily observed as a model event.

But in 1922 the public and press were ready for new records, and they had popular heroes to set them. In 1922 both George Sisler and Rogers Hornsby created new marks in hitting safely in consecutive games. Sisler broke Cobb's American League record and Hornsby notched 33 games in a row in which he had a base hit.

This was hailed as a new record for righthanded batters, at least since 1900. Dahlen's 42 had been made before the turn of the century. While such a demarcation might be a dubious distinction, it serves to create new records. (Eventually those who are insatiable for "new records" will draw a line across some point in the twentieth century and begin proclaiming new records by ignoring those which, like DiMaggio's 56-game streak, seem unbreakable.)

Consider, too, that Ty Cobb, the American League record holder, whose 1911 mark was Sisler's target, was still quite capable of breaking his own record in 1922. Although the hit which raised his final average that year to .401 was argued about, he was still a high-average batter and needed only to string enough games together to set a new mark. Hitting safely in consecutive games was a trademark for Cobb. He hit in 20 or more games in a row seven times during his career.

George Sisler was a very popular player. A college product when the campus was not a direct line to the major leagues, with superlative skills and a gentlemanly manner, he was widely admired. In addition, his team, the St. Louis Browns, was engaged in a hot pennant battle with the New York Yankees.

Sisler began his string on July 27 and continued through August and past Labor Day, getting his base hit in game after game. Then, with his targets in sight—Cobb's American League record and Keeler's major league record, set in the National League—Sisler injured his right shoulder. It was thought at first that not only might he not be able to keep his consecutive string going, but he might not be able to finish the season.

Ironically Sisler found himself at the threshold of Cobb's record while playing against the Detroit Tigers, managed by Cobb, who patrolled center field. Sisler notched games 37 and 38 when the Tigers came to Sportsman's Park in St. Louis. On September 11, struggling to keep his streak alive, Sisler tried for game 39, one short of Cobb's record.

Sisler had been granted a streak-extending single by a generous scorer on a fly ball which Bobby Veach had reached but couldn't hold, but in 1922 there were no message boards or public address systems to inform fans of scorer's decisions. So Cobb, playing center field, was too far away from the press box to see the scorer hold up one finger, the traditional sign of a safe hit. He didn't know Veach's muff had been ruled a hit. As far as he knew, Sisler, coming to bat in the bottom of the ninth, with two out, a runner on first, and the score 4–3 in favor of Detroit, was hitless.

Manager Cobb had a choice. He could order Sisler, the Browns' most dangerous hitter, walked. This would move the tying run into scoring position and put the winning run on base. It would have been bad baseball and worse sportsmanship to order an intentional walk. Cobb might have been tempted to deny his rival what he thought was a last chance, but he didn't. He did take the precaution of removing Bob "Fatty" Fothergill, a slow-footed fielder, and replacing him in right with a better defensive player, Ira Flagstead. Then he signaled Howard Ehmke to pitch. He did, and Sisler lined a triple between Cobb and Flagstead. He scored the game-winning run a moment later on a Marty McManus single. Cobb had lost a game he might have won by passing Sisler, and George had moved to within one game of tying Ty's record.

At this point Sisler's shoulder ached so much he couldn't play the next four games, a series against the last-place Boston Red Sox. It was one of those "might have been" situations. He might have set a new American League record then against the Red Sox. However, it was much more dramatically attained when the Yankees, a half game ahead of the Browns in a torrid pennant race's final stages, came to St. Louis for a crucial three-game series.

Sisler played. His shoulder and right arm were bandaged, and he could only swing his bat with one hand. But, he played and, in a 2–1 loss, he managed a lone hit off Bob Shawkey to tie Cobb's record. The next day, September 17, the Browns evened the series as Babe Ruth's nemesis, Hub Pruett, stopped the Yankees. Ruth did get a home run, but more importantly Sisler managed another one-handed base hit to break Cobb's record.

The final game of the series was won by the Yankees as Joe Bush gained his twenty-fifth victory and Sisler went hitless in four plate appearances, never making solid contact. The Yankees left town with an increased lead they nursed to a pennant by a one-game margin. With his team still in contention, Sisler was unable to play. He pinch-hit unsuccessfully the next day, as Walter Johnson defeated the Browns, then sat out games until he returned to action with a hit against the Athletics on September 23. He hit safely the next day, and then, in a peculiarity of the 1922 season, the whole league was idle for four days.

When the league resumed for the final Friday, Saturday, and Sunday, the Browns were unable to catch the Yankees, although George Sisler hit safely in the three final games. Leave out the pinch-hit effort against Walter Johnson, a desperate attempt by a player who, if he had been swinging with two hands, would have played the full game. Without an injured shoulder, Sisler arguably might have kept his string alive against Joe Bush. He might not have missed those four games against the pitching-poor Red Sox or the two final games against the Senators. He might have hit safely in all of those games as well as the three he added at the season's end. If he had, he would have finished the season, with no more games to play to extend his streak, with 52 games in which he hit consecutively. Think what a target that would have been for Joe DiMaggio in 1941.

The DiMaggio Streak

Joe DiMaggio was playing poorly when his epochal feat began. He wasn't thinking about hitting in 56 straight games; he was worrying about getting a hit in the game of May 15. In spring training DiMaggio hit safely in every exhibition game, a forecast of the record-setting year ahead. His momentum carried through the first eight games of the 1941 season. Then he was thrown into a slump by a junk-ball pitcher, Lester McCrabbe of the Philadelphia Athletics.

By mid-May DiMaggio was still floundering, hitting below .300 and without his usual authority. On May 15 he managed a scratch single. It was an unimpressive handle hit off Cotton Ed Smith of the Chicago White Sox. However, it began a streak that wouldn't end until another pitcher named Smith, Al Smith, paired with Jim Bagby, Jr., held Joe hitless in a game against the Cleveland Indians.

The well-known DiMaggio batting eye that had produced batting championships the two preceding seasons, grew sharper, although in most games he made only a single hit. There were to be 34 games in which the string was kept alive with a lone hit. Not only was this a precarious way to sustain a batting streak, it did not, in its opening stages, draw attention to the feat that was under way. Fans followed Joe's rising batting average but not his successive daily contributions to it. He was thought to be in a contest with Ted Williams, not with the ghosts of record holders whose feats had been both unchallenged and unnoticed since the 1920s. He never caught Williams, who was enjoying the last season a champion would bat over .400.

As DiMaggio's string lengthened, the days of another Yankee immortal, Lou Gehrig, grew fewer. The Iron Horse, who had set another sort of consecutive streak by appearing in 2,130 games, died on June 2, as DiMaggio's skein reached 19.

As the string stretched into the twenties, reporters began digging into record books. The last time this arcane event excited interest had been in 1922, when George Sisler broke Ty Cobb's American League record but was stopped short of Willie Keeler's total. In 1938 another St. Louis Browns first baseman, George McQuinn, had run off a string of 34 games in which he had hit safely. Since McQuinn was playing in the anonymity of the second division, little attention was paid to his challenge.

Because there are two major leagues, record setters have two targets. DiMaggio was required first to set a league mark at 42 and then proceed to reach 45 and set an all-time mark by breaking Keeler's total set in the past century.

By regarding DiMaggio first as a righthanded batter, he could challenge the closer record of Rogers Hornsby, who had hit in 33 straight games in 1922. No mention was made of Bill Dahlen's record of 1894. Perhaps the reporters assumed it had been made under different playing conditions and shouldn't count. They were wrong; the pitching distance had been established at sixty feet, six inches in 1893, and bunts fouled off counted as strikes from 1894. In any case, Dahlen's 42 games was less than Keeler's total, which became the ultimate target.

When DiMaggio passed Rogers Hornsby's total, the public's attention was heightened. Sisler's American League record was only a week's play away. The hype went into full swing. Les Brown's orchestra hurried a phonograph record onto the market, "Jolting Joe DiMaggio." As banal a tune as ever came from Tin Pan Alley, the song became a pep rally number as the band chanted,

"Joe, Joe, DiMaggio, we want you on our side."

Bill "Bojangles" Robinson, who had tap-danced in movies with little Shirley Temple, did routines atop the Yankees dugout while he sprinkled what he called "goofer dust" to enhance DiMaggio's luck.

Despite the distractions of people pressing their attention on the reserved, unemotional DiMaggio, he continued his consistent, game-after-game pursuit of the next milestone, Sisler's league record. At the same time, he was carrying the Yankees toward a pennant. They had lost the title in 1940 after four successive world championships under manager Joe McCarthy. They were out to recapture their league's title.

Interest in Joe DiMaggio's quest went beyond the readers of the sports pages. The wire services carried stories assuring newspaper readers that Joe had extended his string before they gave the account of the game in which he did it. Radio newscasts began with bulletins about Joe's progress.

Cynics and debunkers, who concentrated their suspicions on anything coming out of New York, particularly if it gave credit to the Yankees, watched closely for scoring decisions which would give DiMaggio a favored ruling.

Rival managers juggled pitching rotations to bring their best to the mound when DiMaggio and the Yankees came to town.

Dan Daniel, a prolific and conscientious sportswriter and editor, was the official scorer for games at Yankee Stadium in 1941, and he covered the team on the road for his paper. He has written extensively about DiMaggio's 56-game hitting streak. He saw every game.

The scorer's circumstances at Yankee Stadium, as described by Daniel, placed him in view of rabid Yankee supporters who gathered behind him to demand a base hit no matter how glaring the error which allowed DiMaggio to reach base.

Daniel wrote afterward that he had to have his home phone number changed. He also insisted both he and the other scorers around the league became hyperattentive every time DiMaggio came to bat once his string had become established as a potential record breaker.

Daniel also explained that players on the opposing teams were keyed up when DiMaggio batted, none wanting to contribute to extending the string by loafing on a ball and turning it into a hit. DiMaggio's streak lifted the quality of play, umpiring, and press coverage. Everyone, including DiMaggio, wanted him to earn a new record.

Years afterward, DiMaggio looked back on the 56 games and could only find one where he wished the play had not been as judgmental as it was. It came in the thirtieth game, when he was still short of Hornsby's record. The White Sox came to the Stadium, and Johnny Rigney was the pitcher. He had twice been DiMaggio's victim in earlier games in the streak but on this day had stopped the Yankee Clipper until the seventh inning.

Then DiMaggio hit a routine grounder to Luke Appling. The future Hall of Fame shortstop moved for the ball, but it took a bad bounce, hitting him in the shoulder. In his rush to recover, Appling grabbed at the ball, dropped it, then threw too late. A bad-hop single? Butterfingered retrieval? The official scorer, Dan Daniel, ruled it a hit. Lucky for Joe and fortunate for legend, too, because on his last time up, in the ninth, Taft Wright made a

leaping catch to snatch a home run out of the right field stands. Joe would have been blanked.

The next day DiMaggio got another streak-extending break, almost the same way. This time the ball was hard hit and Appling could only knock it down. He couldn't make a throw. Too hard to handle? Scorer Daniel ruled so and the fans relaxed. A few days later Hornsby's record for righthanded batters would be broken and DiMaggio would be headed for Sisler's mark. However, it took another break for DiMaggio to get there.

Eldon Auker, a St. Louis submarine-ball pitcher, held Joe hitless until the eighth inning at Yankee Stadium. Unless one of the first three batters kept the inning alive, Joe, due up fourth, would not bat again. The Yankees were ahead by two runs, and it did not appear as though there would be a bottom of the ninth.

Johnny Sturm popped up, but Red Rolfe drew a walk. Tommy Henrich, the next batter, had a dilemma. He could still deprive Joe of a chance to bat if he hit into a double play. With manager McCarthy's consent, Henrich bunted and moved Rolfe to second base. Now, with first base open, it was Auker who had a dilemma. He could walk DiMaggio, hit him with a pitch (a strategy as underhanded as his delivery), or pitch to him.

DiMaggio stood at the plate, unruffled. Coolly he smashed the first pitch into left field for a double. It was a close call, but now Sisler's record was in reach.

In a Sunday doubleheader with Washington at Griffith Stadium, on June 29, DiMaggio tied Sisler's record in the first game and broke it in the nightcap. The record-tying hit came off knuckleballer Dutch Leonard and was broken with a last-chance single off the unknown Arnold Anderson. DiMaggio was two games short of tying Willie Keeler's 1897 record.

The only mark left for DiMaggio to eclipse was tied in the second game of a July 1 doubleheader with the Boston Red Sox and broken the next day.

The day DiMaggio claimed the American League record was marked by two extremes of luck. It was fortunate his record-tying hit came early in the game because a downpour deluged Yankee Stadium and the game was called after five innings. It was unfortunate that during the rain delay no one kept an eye on the bat rack. A souvenir hunter reached over the dugout and pulled out a bat. He grabbed DiMaggio's favorite club.

Although he was upset, the man who rarely showed emotion quietly borrowed a bat from teammate Tommy Henrich the next day. It was an identical thirty-six-inch, thirty-six-ounce bat, and Joe used it to break Keeler's record. His record-smashing hit was a prodigeous home run off Dick Newsome, a 19-game winner for the Red Sox. It carried high over the head of his rival, Ted Williams, into the left field stands.

Joe DiMaggio did not rest on his laurels. Actually, with the pressure to produce at least one base hit each game lifted, he began pounding out hits in clusters. He passed the 50-game mark and his luck still held. In the fifty-fourth game, he again came up against Johnny Rigney of the White Sox. This time he would have been stopped except for a topped roller. A typical lusty swing sent a dribbler slowly toward third base where Bob Kennedy was playing fearfully deep, a precaution normally taken by rival third baseman against DiMaggio. It worked to

Joe's advantage that day as he beat out the slowly hit ball for his only hit. However, it would work to his disadvantage a few days later in Cleveland.

Although Joe DiMaggio said after his streak had ended, "I wish it could have gone on forever," like all good things it had to come to an end. Joe had reached 56 games when the kind of luck which occasionally had sustained him, such as the topped roller against Chicago, turned around. The Yankees came into Cleveland and crowds came, divided between fans' wishes to witness the streak extended and hometeam rooters' hopes that their team could bring the mighty DiMaggio to a halt.

What could only be a matter of time happened. As a minor league star in his native San Francisco, a nineteen-year-old Joe DiMaggio had been stopped after hitting in 61 consecutive games. After the 1941 streak ended, the *San Francisco Chronicle,* which had made daily reports of DiMaggio's record-breaking games, observed that the Pacific Coast League string had been ended by the son of a former major league pitching star, Bob Walsh, whose father, Big Ed Walsh, would be elected to the Hall of Fame. It was pointed out that DiMaggio's major league string was ended, in part, by Jim Bagby, Jr., another son of a successful major leaguer, a 31-game winner for the 1920 world champion Cleveland Indians.

It wasn't so much the pitching of starter Al Smith or reliever Bagby that halted DiMaggio as the glove work on the left side of the Indians' infield. Twice Ken Keltner, playing a very deep third base, took drives down the baseline and turned them into outs. And Joe's last chance found him deserted by luck on a bad bounce. A ball headed up the middle took an erratic hop, and shortstop Lou Boudreau grabbed it and flipped to second to start a double play that closed off DiMaggio's chance to keep safely intact the stretch of games in which he had hit.

Although the DiMaggio streak had been stopped, he was still a hot hitter, and even his favorite bat was back. An embarrassed fan from Newark admitted the theft and returned the bat, and Joe used it to continue his torrid hitting. He kept pounding out hits on a daily basis until he had hit safely in 16 more consecutive games. This meant he would have reached an incredible 73 games had not Keltner and Boudreau pulled off outstanding defensive plays after game 56.

As it is, hitting safely in 72 of 73 games is almost unimaginable. Historians had to go back to the over-looked Bad Bill Dahlen to find a comparable feat for DiMaggio to eclipse almost half a century later. Back in 1894, after he had run up a string of 42 games, Dahlen ran off another stretch of 28 games in which he hit safely. He had left a neglected legacy of hitting in 70 of 71 games for DiMaggio to top with 72 in 73.

During his 56-game streak, Joe DiMaggio batted .408. Although he finished the 1941 season with a .357 average, he was second to Ted Williams's league-leading .406. However, DiMaggio had led his team to a championship and this, with the incredible feat of hitting in 56 straight games, earned him the Most Valuable Player Award by a close margin.

Those whose interest in statistics match, if not exceed, a curiosity about the drama of making them, will want to know that, in hitting .408 during the 56 games, DiMaggio scored 56 runs and batted in 55. He hit 15 home runs, half

his season's total, and had 35 extra-base hits among the 91 hits he collected in 223 at-bats. He walked 21 times, was hit by a pitch twice, and struck out only 7 times.

The Yankees went on to defeat the Brooklyn Dodgers in the World Series and, as the Japanese went on to bomb Pearl Harbor and involve the United States in World War Two, Joe was asked to take a $2,500 cut in salary for 1942. He managed to get a $5,000 raise and play the 1942 season before entering military service in possession of a unique feat which still attracts its new challengers.

Joe DiMaggio's 1941 Hitting Streak

Game No.	Date	Club and Pitcher	AB	R	H
1	5-15	White Sox, Smith	4	0	1
2	5-16	White Sox, Lee	4	2	2
3	5-17	White Sox, Rigney	3	1	1
4	5-18	Browns, Harris, Niggeling	3	3	3
5	5-19	Browns, Galehouse	3	0	1
6	5-20	Browns, Auker	5	1	1
7	5-21	Tigers, Rowe, Benton	5	0	2
8	5-22	Tigers, McKain	4	0	1
9	5-23	Red Sox, Newsome	5	0	1
10	5-24	Red Sox, Johnson	4	2	1
11	5-25	Red Sox, Grove	4	0	1
12	5-27	Senators, Chase, Anderson, Carrasquel	5	3	4
13	5-28	Senators, Hudson	4	1	1
14	5-29	Senators, Sundra	3	1	1
15	5-30	Red Sox, Johnson	2	1	1
16	5-30	Red Sox, Harris	3	0	1
17	6-1	Indians, Milnar	4	1	1
18	6-1	Indians, Harder	4	0	1
19	6-2	Indians, Feller	4	2	2
20	6-3	Tigers, Trout	4	1	1
21	6-5	Tigers, Newhouser	5	1	1
22	6-7	Browns, Muncrief, Allen, Caster	5	2	3
23	6-8	Browns, Auker	4	3	2
24	6-8	Browns, Caster, Kramer	4	1	2
25	6-10	White Sox, Rigney	5	1	1
26	6-12	White Sox, Lee	4	1	2
27	6-14	Indians, Feller	2	0	1
28	6-15	Indians, Bagby	3	1	1
29	6-16	Indians, Milnar	5	0	1
30	6-17	White Sox, Rigney	4	1	1
31	6-18	White Sox, Lee	3	0	1
32	6-19	White Sox, Smith, Ross	3	2	3
33	6-20	Tigers, Newsom, McKain	5	3	4
34	6-21	Tigers, Trout	4	0	1
35	6-22	Tigers, Newhouser, Newsom	5	1	2
36	6-24	Browns, Muncrief	4	1	1
37	6-25	Browns, Galehouse	4	1	1
38	6-26	Browns, Auker	4	0	1
39	6-27	Athletics, Dean	3	1	2
40	6-28	Athletics, Babich, Harris	5	1	2
41	6-29	Senators, Leonard	4	1	1
42	6-29	Senators, Anderson	5	1	1
43	7-1	Red Sox, Harris, Ryba	4	0	2
44	7-1	Red Sox, Wilson	3	1	1
45	7-2	Red Sox, Newsome	5	1	1
46	7-5	Athletics, Marchildon	4	2	1
47	7-6	Athletics, Babich, Hadley	5	2	4
48	7-6	Athletics, Knott	4	0	2
49	7-10	Browns, Niggling	2	0	1
50	7-11	Browns, Harris, Kramer	5	1	4
51	7-12	Browns, Auker, Muncrief	5	1	2
52	7-13	White Sox, Lyons, Hallett	4	2	3
53	7-13	White Sox, Lee	4	0	1
54	7-14	White Sox, Rigney	3	0	1
55	7-15	White Sox, Smith	4	1	2
56	7-16	Indians, Milnar, Krakauskas	4	3	3
Totals			223	56	91

The Pete Rose Challenge

The year 1978 was a tremendous one for Pete Rose, whose career with the Cincinnati Reds qualified him as a potential challenger for Joe DiMaggio's record of hitting safely in 56 consecutive games. Although he did not hit for the high averages of the other streakers who had held records—Keeler, Sisler, Hornsby, and DiMaggio—Rose batted leadoff and had amassed 10 seasons with 200 or more hits. Even more, he was the kind of player who would rise to any occasion. He loved a challenge.

Longest Hitting Streaks, NL

Player	Team	Year	G
Willie Keeler	BAL	1897	44
Pete Rose	CIN	1978	44
Bill Dahlen	CHI	1894	42
Tommy Holmes	BOS	1945	37
Billy Hamilton	PHI	1894	36
Fred Clarke	LOU	1895	35
Benito Santiago	SD	1987	34
George Davis	NY	1893	33
Rogers Hornsby	STL	1922	32
Ed Delahanty	PHI	1899	31
Willie Davis	LA	1969	31
Rico Carty	ATL	1970	31
Elmer Smith	CIN	1898	30
Stan Musial	STL	1950	30
Jerome Walton	CHI	1989	30

Longest Hitting Streaks, AL

Player r	Team	Year	G
Joe DiMaggio	NY	1941	56
George Sisler	STL	1922	41
Ty Cobb	DET	1911	40
Paul Molitor	MIL	1987	39
Ty Cobb	DET	1917	35
George Sisler	STL	1925	34
George McQuinn	STL	1938	34
Dom DiMaggio	BOS	1949	34
Hal Chase	NY	1907	33
Heinie Manush	WAS	1933	33
Nap Lajoie	CLE	1906	31
Sam Rice	WAS	1924	31
Ken Landreaux	MIN	1980	31
Tris Speaker	BOS	1912	30
Bing Miller	PHI	1929	30
Goose Goslin	DET	1934	30
Ron LeFlore	DET	1976	30
George Brett	KC	1980	30

Before he got around to taking a swing at DiMaggio's record, Rose had, as his first order of business, the matter of making his 3,000th career base hit. He opened the 1978 season needing 34 hits to reach a plateau only twelve others had gained. On May 5 Rose reached 3,000 with a single off Montreal pitcher Steve Rogers, before a hometown crowd at Riverfront Stadium.

"Charlie Hustle" was having an epoch-making season and, with one landmark reached, he soon found himself en route to another. Consecutive-game hitting streaks begin without signaling their advent. It is only as they grow that they attract attention.

Pete Rose was only batting .267 when he got a pair of hits against the Cubs on June 14. He kept adding hits in the games he played and, eventually, it was decided he had enough in a row to start looking for a record to be broken.

DiMaggio's 56-game streak in 1941 loomed far beyond expectation. However, the record keepers had gerrymandered Willie Keeler, holder of the National League record at 44, out of the books. There was a modern mark of 37, set during the wartime year of 1945, by Tommy Holmes of the Boston Braves.

Pete Rose hustled onward and, as luck would have it, came into Shea Stadium for a series with the Mets on the verge of knocking Holmes out of the record book. The patron saint of hype was on the ball, and a now sixty-one-year-old Tommy Holmes was on hand to root for Rose. He was there in a dual capacity. Tommy Holmes was also the Mets' community relations director.

There was another reward in having Pete Rose break Holmes's record in front of the Mets' fans. In 1973 Pete had been *persona non grata* when he had wrestled on the ground with skinny shortstop Bud Harrelson in a League Championship game after a takeout slide by Rose at second base. The Mets fans remembered Rose calling them "animals" as they threatened to avenge the honor of the team by challenging the wives and children of the Reds' players in field boxes behind the Cincinnati dugout. However, hype places a statute of limitations on vengeance in New York. Whipped to a frenzy of impartiality by the Mets' announcers and a record-hungry press, people filled Shea Stadium ready to cheer Rose on while trusting he'd not be so unappreciative as to make his record-extending safety a game-winning hit.

On July 24 Pete Rose equaled the record of Tommy Holmes and to chants of "Go, Pete, Go!" broke it the next night against Craig Swan. An appreciative Holmes, pleased to have been a short-term celebrity, came onto the field to shake the hand of the man who had erased him from the record books. Pete now held the "modern" National League record for hitting safely in consecutive games. In fairness, he would now try to reach Willie Keeler's mark of 44, a feat turned before the century began.

Pete continued his quest. He had the skill, the competitive instincts, and the attitude to do it. He was unruffled by press attention, accustomed to it as the consequence of being the game's most colorful player of his time. Would he break DiMaggio's seemingly unreachable mark? If anyone could, Pete Rose could do it. But first he had to lay the ghost of Willie Keeler and his 81-year-old record.

Willie Keeler's 1897 Hitting Streak

Game No.	Date	AB	R	H
1	April 22	5	2	2
2	April 23	4	1	2
3	April 24	4	1	2
4	April 26	4	0	1
5	April 27	5	2	2
6	April 28	5	1	3
7	April 29	4	1	2
8	April 20	4	3	3
9	May 3	4	0	1
10	May 4	4	0	2
11	May 5	4	0	1
12	May 6	5	0	3
13	May 7	6	2	1
14	May 8	3	1	1
15	May 10	4	0	1
16	May 11	5	1	2
17	May 12	5	0	3
18	May 14	6	2	2
19	May 15	6	2	2
20	May 16	6	3	3
21	May 17	4	1	2
22	May 18	6	1	1
23	May 19	4	1	1
24	May 20	4	1	3
25	May 21	3	1	2
26	May 22	4	2	2
27	May 25	5	0	1
28	May 26	5	1	2
29	May 27	5	1	3
30	May 29	6	2	2
31	May 30	4	0	1
32	May 31	4	1	1
33	May 31	5	2	1

34	June 2	5	1	4
35	June 5	5	1	1
36	June 7	4	1	1
37	June 9	5	2	2
38	June 10	4	0	2
39	June 11	4	0	2
40	June 12	5	2	2
41	June 14	5	1	2
42	June 15	3	0	1
43	June 16	5	2	1
44	June 18	4	3	3
Totals		201	49	82

It was a struggle, as the whole streak had been, but Rose reached Keeler's mark on July 31 in Atlanta. His record-equaling hit came off the knuckleball pitching of Phil Niekro, a man whose own feats as a middle-aged ballplayer also merited recognition.

Keeler had been caught. Would he be passed? No. The next night a rookie lefthander, Larry McWilliams, held Pete Rose hitless through most of the game, and reliever Gene Garber provided the final denial. He struck Rose out.

Pete Rose is joined with Willie Keeler, linked now, regardless of the era when the feat was accomplished, as coholders of the National League record for hitting safely in consecutive games.

Pete Rose's 1978 Hitting Streak

Game No.	Date	Club and Pitcher	AB	R	H
1	6-14	Cubs, Roberts	4	1	2
2	6-16	Cardinals, Denny	4	1	2
3	6-17	Cardinals, Vuckovich, Schultz	4	2	2
4	6-18	Cardinals, Martinez	4	1	1
5	6-20	Giants, Montefusco	5	2	2
6	6-21	Giants, Halicki	4	0	1
7	6-22	Giants, Knepper	4	0	1
8	6-23	Dodgers, Hooton	4	0	1
9	6-24	Dodgers, Welch	5	1	4
10	6-25	Dodgers, John	3	1	2
11	6-26	Astros, Lemongello	5	1	2
12	6-27	Astros, Niekro	4	1	1
13	6-28	Astros, Dixon	4	0	1
14	6-29	Astros, Bannister	3	0	1
15	6-30	Dodgers, Rautzhan	4	1	1
16	6-30	Dodgers, Welch, Forster, Hough	5	1	3
17	7-1	Dodgers, Rhoden	5	0	1
18	7-2	Dodgers, Rau	4	1	1
19	7-3	Astros, Bannister, McLaughlin	5	1	3
20	7-4	Astros, Richard	4	1	1
21	7-5	Astros, Niekro	4	0	1
22	7-6	Giants, Blue, Curtis	5	1	3
23	7-7	Giants, Barr	4	0	1
24	7-8	Giants, Montefusco	4	1	1
25	7-9	Giants, Halicki, Knepper	4	1	3
26	7-13	Mets, Koosman, Lockwood	5	0	2
27	7-14	Mets, Zachry	5	0	2
28	7-15	Mets, Swan	2	2	1
29	7-16	Mets, Siebert	5	1	1
30	7-17	Expos, Bahnsen	4	0	1
31	7-18	Expos, Dues	4	0	2
32	7-19	Phillies, Reed	4	1	1
33	7-20	Phillies, Kaat	5	1	1
34	7-21	Expos, Grimsley	3	1	1
35	7-22	Expos, Schatzeder	3	0	1
36	7-23	Expos, Rogers, Knowles	6	0	2
37	7-24	Mets, Zachry, Lockwood	5	2	2
38	7-25	Mets, Swan	4	1	3
39	7-26	Mets, Espinosa	3	0	1
40	7-28	Phillies, Lerch	2	1	1
41	7-28	Phillies, Carlton	4	0	1
42	7-29	Phillies, Lonborg, Kaat	4	1	3
43	7-30	Phillies, Christenson	5	0	2
44	7-31	Braves, Niekro	4	0	1
Totals			182	30	70

Successive Pitching Victories

The 1912 baseball season produced a bumper crop of pitchers winning successive victories. Rube Marquard of the New York Giants topped everyone by running up a total of 19. This tied the record set by Tim Keefe, also of New York. Keefe had won his games in 1888, when the pitching distance was only fifty feet between pitcher and batter, but he had won them in a row and that is the measurement of this feat. The present distance of sixty feet, six inches (actually, this is only about 55 feet from the pitcher's point of release) was set in 1893, Keefe's last season.

Marquard's mark remains unmatched within the confines of a single season. The record for consecutive wins beginning in the midst of one season and extending into the next season is held by Carl Hubbell, whose 24 consecutive victories, starting in 1936 and continuing into 1937, tops the list.

However, 1912 produced more than just Marquard's record. It also produced a new American League record and an immediate challenger to it. Even while Rube Marquard was engaged in his run in the National League, Walter Johnson, almost concurrently, was setting the American League record at 16. And by the time he was stopped, another streak was under way, this one by Smokey Joe Wood of the Boston Red Sox.

No one could ask for a better matchup in 1912 than the one which brought Walter Johnson, the record holder, to the mound at Fenway Park to face Joe Wood the challenger. Johnson was the premier pitcher in the American League and its strikeout king. Wood had dazzled the baseball world while en route to a 34–5 season, with 10 shutouts. He won three more games in the 1912 World Series. Then he injured his arm and never returned to his single-season pinnacle.

Walter Johnson, himself a 33-game winner in 1912, had broken the former American League record of 14 straight, set by Jack Chesbro in 1904. By winning his sixteenth straight game on August 23, he had set a new league mark and had his sights on the brand-new record of Rube Marquard. The New York lefthander had won his 19 by July 3. Johnson never caught Marquard.

Johnson was a victim of both bad luck and a scoring rule which today would not have cost him a loss. He lost a game in relief, taking over in the seventh inning of a tie game. There were two runners on base, and before Johnson could get the side out, one of them scored the winning run. Today the loss would be charged to the starting pitcher, Tom Hughes, who had allowed the runner to get on base. At that time the loss went against whoever was pitching when the winning run scored.

Even so, in 1912 the scorer's decision was denounced by the press and sympathetic fans. However, Ban Johnson, not only president of the American League but its iron-fisted founder, decreed the loss be placed against Walter Johnson's record, and there it remains forever. He had been stopped at 16.

When the 1912 penchant for pitchers winning consecutive victories identified the next challenger as Smokey Joe Wood of the pennant-bound Boston Red Sox, Johnson was called upon to stop him personally. The schedule brought the Washington Senators to Fenway Park to play the Red Sox, and the management was well aware they had a great gate attraction. Both Johnson and Wood had pitched four days earlier.

Whatever the capacity of Fenway Park in 1912, it was far exceeded when, on a weekday, over 30,000 baseball fans crowded the park. The crowd overflowed the stands. In fact, the players could not sit in their dugouts. Instead, they sat on chairs arranged in front of the throngs that stood just outside the baselines. Thousands more people stood in the outfield, behind ropes, reducing the area for the great Red Sox outfield to cover. Tris Speaker, Duffy Lewis, and Harry Hooper would not be able to roam back to catch deep fly balls. These would be automatic doubles if they reached the crowd herded behind the ropes.

Walter Johnson held the American League record, a string of 16 straight victories. Joe Wood had drawn nearer to Johnson's mark in his last start, beating New York on September 2 for his thirteenth win without a loss during the streak. Today he was after his fourteenth straight, Chesbro's old mark, and Walter Johnson didn't want him to get it. Unless Johnson himself stopped Wood, his own record, and possibly Marquard's, were in danger.

The game lived up to expectations. It was a pitcher's battle. Great defensive plays snuffed out rallies, and both pitchers stopped scoring threats with clutch strikeouts. A scoreless tie was broken in the sixth inning, when Tris Speaker hit a fly ball that reached the roped-back crowd for a ground-rule double and Duffy Lewis hit an opposite-field double down the right field foul line. It just eluded the grab of Danny Moeller and Speaker scored. And that was it. The game ended 1–0 as Walter Johnson lost another game in which his team failed to get him any runs. He lost 65 games during his career when his team was shut out.

When Wood pitched next, in Chicago, he was not in top form but held a 5–3 lead going into the bottom of the ninth. When the first two White Sox batters reached base with hits, manager Jake Stahl replaced Wood with reliever Charles "Sea Lion" Hall. A sacrifice fly made the final score 5–4, but Hall retired the White Sox without further damage and Joe Wood was within one game of tying Walter Johnson.

The Red Sox rode on to St. Louis in Pullman cars for a game on September 15, and Joe Wood pitched another strong game, a 2–1 victory in eight innings to tie Johnson's record. Darkness caused the game to be called after Wood himself had scored the go-ahead run in the top of the eighth inning.

It all came to an end on September 20 in Detroit. Wood failed to break Walter Johnson's mark. He went the distance but mostly on the sufferance of manager Jake Stahl. Although two of the Tigers' runs were unearned, the 6–4 final score indicated Joe Wood's fastball lacked its usual smoke that day.

The Marquard Inheritance

When Rube Marquard wrote his way into the record books in 1912, with 19 consecutive victories, he established a benchmark which has been approached but never equaled, or excelled, since that time. Although Walter Johnson's American League mark, itself never beaten, took on extra importance because of the affection and awe

he inspired in baseball fans, Marquard set the standard for all others to challenge.

The Johnson-Wood confrontation excited the imagination, and other challenges have created their own temporary focus, but always there stands the record of Marquard. It is the pinnacle toward which others climb and never reach, on a single-season, starting pitcher basis. It has only been exceeded by joining the end of one season to the start of the next.

Perhaps even more than the way Walter Johnson was revered in the American League, Rube Marquard's teammate, Christy Mathewson, overshadowed everyone. Marquard's record was the sort of achievement Matty should have had. Until 1912 all the heroics on the Giants' staff had been his. Rube's emergence took everyone by surprise; he was still living down the onerous nickname "the $11,000 Lemon."

Just a kid pitcher, only eighteen, when the Giants bought him from Indianapolis where he had won 28 games in 1908, Marquard had been a disappointment. He benefited in 1911 when manager John McGraw brought Wilbert Robinson to spring training as a coach to tame the wild throwing Rube. Robbie produced a 24-game winner. Then in 1912 Marquard began his streak with his first start of the season and, as he added to it, he began to attract favorable attention for the first time. When he won his sixth game, he exceeded any previous high; when he won the tenth game, he had won more than he had in his first two seasons combined.

Marquard had shed the label, "The $11,000 Lemon," the year before his record-breaking string, by winning 24 games and leading the league with a .774 winning percentage. Until then he had disappointed Giant fans, who had expected another Mathewson when John McGraw paid the largest amount shelled out for a player to date. The Giant manager had purposely topped the $10,000 price tag paid for Mike "King" Kelly, the leading nineteenth century gate attraction. In 1912, Marquard displaced Matty as the leading winner on the staff. While Mathewson won 23 games, Marquard led the league with 26, the first 19 of them in a row. He won his first start on April 11 and did not lose a game until July 8.

Actually, under the present scoring rules, Marquard's record would total 20 consecutive victories. McGraw inserted Rube in the eighth inning of a game at the Polo Grounds, against the Brooklyn Dodgers, which was tied at 3–3. Marquard inherited a bases-loaded situation but stopped Zack Wheat and Jake Daubert, both to become batting champions, and retired George Cutshaw, without a run being scored. The Giants won the game in the bottom of the ninth, but the rules then gave the victory to the starting pitcher.

The Giants, in 1912, were winning the middle of three successive pennants, and Marquard joined with Christy Mathewson to lead the Giants' staff. He was called "Rube," a nickname often given to lefthanders with a superior fastball. This was a tribute to Rube Waddell and had no bucolic significance: Marquard was no innocent country boy turned loose on Broadway.

Marquard married a vaudeville headliner, Blossom Seeley, who was even more popular than he was. Her life story was later made into a motion picture which ignored Marquard in favor of Blossom's subsequent husband, song-and-dance man Benny Fields.

However, Rube had held up his end of the vaudeville act, serving as a straight man for the comedienne and added female impersonations, in which he sang and danced as well. This too is a performance unlikely to be duplicated by a modern player.

Streakers Blurred by Time

Although it is convenient to separate the "modern era" of baseball from its ancient past at 1900, the better dividing line would be 1893. That year the pitcher was moved back from fifty feet to the still-prevailing sixty feet, six inches. He had been allowed to throw overhand since 1884.

Until the 1890s, teams rarely used more than two principal pitchers. More open dates existed in the schedules, and two strong-armed men could carry the bulk of the work. A third pitcher, or a general substitute, could help out in doubleheaders. However, the regular duo met most occasions and had many more opportunities to reel off long strings of victories.

When Tim Keefe set the mark at 19 straight, he required only seven weeks to do it. Between June 23 and August 10, 1888, he won all his starts, 17 of them complete games. He alternated on the mound with Mickey Welch, himself the owner of an impressive winning streak. In 1885 Smiling Mickey had run off 17 in a row. That had been one less than the record Hoss Radbourn set in 1884. Pitchers in those years were capable of putting together long winning streaks.

Another contemporary, Jim McCormick of Chicago, won 14 in a row in 1885 and 16 straight the next year. When Keefe set his mark in 1888, the public was impressed but not stunned by its magnitude. After all, it only topped the recent mark of Radbourn's by one.

The New York Giants of 1888 were the toast of the town. They were led by Jim Mutrie, who had dubbed them "my Giants," marveling at the magnitude of the star players. Such stalwarts as Roger Connor, Montgomery Ward, and Buck Ewing—all future Hall of Fame members— were in the lineup. Keefe and Welch, pitching in tandem, were also destined for Cooperstown and immortality. The Giants were easy pennant winners over Cap Anson's Chicago team.

Tim Keefe began his 19-game winning streak on June 23. He had lost his previous start to yet another star pitcher, John Clarkson. Also elected to the Hall of Fame, even before Keefe and Welch, Clarkson had won 13 straight in 1885.

Keefe's first win was a squeaker, 7–6, over Philadelphia. Then he marched along, and when he won his twelfth in a row, his opponent was Clarkson. During the streak Tim Keefe pitched 17 complete games. The two he failed to finish included one in which he was hit on the arm by a line drive while leading 8–3 in the sixth inning. A replacement with a name more domineering than the record he left behind, Cannonball Eddie Crane, held on for a 9–6 victory credited to Keefe.

The other incomplete game would not have been added to his string by today's scoring rules. On July 16, while leading Chicago 9–0, Keefe was excused for the day after two innings. The practices of the time gave him the win.

Tim Keefe's string came to an end on August 14, when

his defense betrayed him and two unearned runs were the difference in a 4–2 loss. Gus Krock, of the Chicago White Stockings, was a lefthanded rookie who soon disappeared from the major leagues, but he had the satisfaction of stopping Keefe at 19.

Considering the winning streaks his contemporaries had run off, it was probably thought that Keefe's record was temporary. Had it not been for the victory gained in that two-inning start, it would have been. He would have been tied with Hoss Radbourn at 18 and eclipsed when Rube Marquard reached 19 in 1912. As it is, more than a century after his feat, Tim Keefe stands beside Marquard with a total no one has surpassed.

American League Record Tied

It wasn't until 1931 that the lesser American League record of 16 consecutive pitching victories was challenged. Lefty Grove came very close to setting a new record in the American League and narrowly missed being the pitcher to break Marquard's mark of 19. Grove had a 31–4 season, figures which could have accommodated both record-breaking streaks.

However, the luck even the best must have to sustain a long streak deserted Grove at the critical point. He was luckless in the game which would have moved him past Walter Johnson and Smokey Joe Wood, coholders of the American League mark.

The 1931 Philadelphia Athletics were awesome. Connie Mack's last championship team won its third pennant in a row. Responding to Depression-related financial pressures, Mack would break up the team, selling off its stars, including Grove, who went to the Red Sox. Future Hall of Famers Jimmie Foxx, Mickey Cochrane, Al Simmons, and Grove himself were at the peak of their careers. The members of the supporting cast—Max Bishop, Jimmie Dykes, Mule Haas, Bing Miller, and others—were all excellent role players. This was a team which did not beat itself.

As the season advanced into August, the Athletics were virtually coasting to a pennant. They would win 107 games and distance the runner-up New York Yankees by 13 games. Grove, pitching every fourth game and appearing in relief when needed, was on his personal roll. For the first time in many years, it appeared the American League record for consecutive victories could be broken by a pitcher. It was possible to project that Grove might go on and also catch Marquard's record. There was enough time left.

Lefty Grove tied the American League record on August 19 and was expected to break it four days later with his seventeenth straight win. The day the record coheld by Walter Johnson and Joe Wood since 1912 was to fall was Sunday, August 23.

The St. Louis Browns, a second-division team and perennial victim, would provide only token opposition, and the unheralded Dick Coffman would be the sacrificial pitching opponent. Grove pitched with close to his usual brilliance, limiting the Browns to six hits, allowing only one run, and striking out six.

However, Dick Coffman, on that particular day, out-pitched Grove and shut out the Athletics with only three hits. Grove's streak came to an end at 16 straight victories. He had only joined Johnson and Wood at the top of the American League's list.

Lefty Grove had never been a gracious, philosophical loser. He refused to accept defeat gracefully. He blamed the loss on the absence of Al Simmons from the lineup. True, Simmons was at home, in Milwaukee, seeing a doctor, and his replacement, Jim Moore, was far from being a sure-handed defensive player. When Moore misjudged a fly ball, which became the game-winning hit, Grove fumed that Simmons would have caught the ball. Further, he complained, Simmons, the league-leading batter, would surely have knocked in a few runs as well as preventing the Browns from scoring a tainted one.

Grove complained every time he was asked about the end of his streak, and the image of Simmons idling away the afternoon, thumbing through *National Geographic*s in a doctor's waiting room, persisted. Actually, Simmons had an infected ankle and had already been out of the lineup for a week.

What made the defeat more bitter in retrospect was that Grove went on to win his next five starts. These victories would have put the record at 21, eclipsing not only the American League record but topping Marquard's all-time total of 19. (Grove won his next two starts, incidentally, with Simmons still missing from the lineup.) He did not lose until the final game of the season, on September 27.

Schoolboy Rowe's Row

It was only a few years later, in 1934, when the next assault was made on the American League record, now held by Lefty Grove as well as by Walter Johnson and Joe Wood. This time it was the colorful Schoolboy Rowe, blessed with a rural candor that the press found refreshing and the public fascinating, who made the run.

Mickey Cochrane, Grove's former battery mate, was a first-term manager, having been sold by the Athletics to Detroit. Still a great player and catcher, Cochrane had his team headed for the pennant and Schoolboy Rowe led the way. Rowe had been a pitcher of promise and Cochrane had brought about its fulfillment. Rowe had made a slow start, splitting his first eight decisions. His inauspicious beginning offered no portent that when, on June 15, he won his fifth victory, it was the start of a record-equaling skein. During the summer months Rowe shared the spotlight with Dizzy Dean of the National League. However, while Dean was garnering the victories which would eventually reach 30 for the season, he did not string them together the way Rowe did.

Rowe won his sixteenth straight game on August 26 but then ran into the barrier which had blocked other American League pitchers at that point. He joined Grove, Johnson, and Wood at the top of the list but also joined them among the frustrated who could not go past that point.

Rowe stumbled from the path toward a new record on August 29, when the Tigers met the now lowly Philadelphia Athletics in a doubleheader. Gone from Connie Mack's A's were Lefty Grove, Mickey Cochrane, Al Simmons, George Earnshaw, and Rube Walberg. Only Jimmie Foxx remained from the recent championship teams.

It was the second game of an August 29 doubleheader, and Rowe was far off form. He was knocked out in the sixth inning. Unlike the contentious Lefty Grove, Rowe blamed no one but himself, saying without rancor that he'd just had an off-day. He refused the alibi offered by his manager, Mickey Cochrane, who contended that the demands of the press and public on the young pitcher had produced more turmoil than Schoolboy could handle. Rowe scoffed at the idea and went on to finish the season with 24 wins. He didn't face Dizzy Dean in the 1934 World Series, but he split two decisions, as the Cardinals won a seven-game series from Detroit. Another pennant year followed for Detroit, with Rowe winning 19 games. After that a chronic arm problem hindered his career, although he lasted a long while in the major leagues, winning 158 games, with a .610 winning average, over fifteen years.

Carl Hubbell's Fabulous Streak

When one adds the start of one season to the end of the preceding one, one finds a 17-game streak for Cleveland's Johnny Allen in 1936–1937 and another for Baltimore's Dave McNally in 1969–1970. But in this area Carl Hubbell claims all the records.

In the quirky way that records for consecutive victories by pitchers seem to come almost simultaneously, the same two seasons which provided Johnny Allen's 17 straight wins, also produced one of the most fabulous feats of all time. As had been the case with 1912, there was a magic about 1936–1937.

Carl Hubbell, between July 17, 1936, and May 27, 1937, won 24 games in a row. He won his last 16 decisions in 1936 and added 8 more victories before losing a game in 1937.

Carl Hubbell, and the team which would support him in his quest for a record, the New York Giants, were at their best in 1936 and 1937. They were the best in the National League at a time when their crosstown rivals, the Yankees, were dominant in the American League and also in the World Series. They beat the Giants both years despite Hubbell's presence. The Giants won only three World Series games in the two years and Hubbell won two of them.

Carl Hubbell was the ace of the Giants staff and the National League's most valuable player in 1936. He led the league in 1936 with 26 victories, an .813 winning percentage, and a 2.31 ERA. In 1937 he again topped the league in wins with 22 and percentage with .733 and added the strikeout crown with 159, his career high.

It was this kind of consistency that earned Carl Hubbell the nickname "the Meal Ticket." His manager, Bill Terry, knew Hubbell would pitch in rotation and stop any losing streak before it gained momentum.

The Giants were off to a bad start in 1936, although Hubbell was winning two of every three decisions. The day Hubbell's winning streak began, July 17, the Giants were in fifth place, barely over .500 at 42–41 and 10 games behind the defending champion Chicago Cubs. Hubbell had lost his last start, a tough two-hit 1–0 game, to the Cubs' Big Bill Lee. Chicago's run was unearned.

Appropriately Hubbell got the Giants back on a winning track by shutting out Pittsburgh, 6–0. The game contained a streak of another kind. In the first inning Joe Moore, Mel Ott, and Hank Leiber hit successive triples.

Before the inning ended, Eddie Mayo, a utility infielder, added another triple. Not only was Hubbell off on a personal winning streak that wouldn't end until the next year, the Giants had found their own victory pace.

Oddly, considering the magnitude of Hubbell's record, the streak-starting shutout was the last one he pitched in 1936. He had a season-opening shutout the next year.

Pitchers with 12 or More Straight Victories in Season

National League		
Year	Pitcher	Won
1888	Timothy Keefe, N.Y.	19
1912	Richard Marquard, N.Y.	19
1884	Charles Radbourn, Provi.	18
1885	Michael Welch, N.Y.	17
1890	John Luby, Chi.	17
1959	El Roy Face, Pitts.	17
1886	James McCormick, Chi.	16
1936	Carl Hubbell, N.Y.	16
1947	Ewell Blackwell, Cinn.	16
1962	John Sanford, S.F.	16
1924	Arthur Vance, Brook.	15
1968	Robert Gibson, St. L.	15
1972	Steven Carlton, Phila.	15
1885	James McCormick, Chi.	14
1886	John Flynn, Chi.	14
1904	Joseph McGinnity, N.Y.	14
1909	Edward Reulbach, Chi.	14
1984	Richard Sutcliffe, Chi.	14
1985	Dwight Gooden, N.Y.	14
1996	John Smoltz, Atl.	14
1880	Lawrence Corcoran, Chi.	13
1884	Charles Buffinton, Bos.	13
1885	John Clarkson, Chi.	13
1892	Denton Young, Cleve.	13
1893	Frank Killen, Pitts.	13
1896	Frank Dwyer, Cin.	13
1897	Fred Klobedanz, Bos.	13
1898	Ted Lewis, Bos.	13
1909	Chris. Mathewson, N.Y.	13
1910	Charles Phillippe, Pitts.	13
1927	Burleigh Grimes, N.Y.	13
1956	Brooks Lawrence, Cin.	13
1966	Philip Regan, L.A.	13
1971	Dock Ellis, Pitts.	13
1992	Tom Glavine, Atl.	13
1886	Charles Ferguson, Phila.	12
1902	John Chesbro, Pitts.	12
1904	George Wiltse, N.Y.	12
1906	Edward Reulbach, Chi.	12
1975	Burt Hooton, L.A.	12
1992	Tom Glavine, Atl.	12
1992	Mark Portugal, Hou.	12

American League		
Year	Pitcher	Won
1912	Walter Johnson, Wash.	16
1912	Joseph Wood, Bos.	16
1931	Robert Grove, Phila.	16
1934	Lynwood Rowe, Det.	16
1932	Alvin Crowder, Wash.	15
1937	John Allen, Cleve.	15
1969	David McNally, Balt.	15
1974	Gaylord Perry, Cleve.	15
1904	John Chesbro, N.Y.	14
1913	Walter Johnson, Wash.	14
1914	Charles Bender, Phila.	14
1928	Robert Grove, Phila.	14
1961	Edward Ford, N.Y.	14
1980	Steven Stone, Balt.	14
1986	W. Roger Clemens, Bos.	14
1924	Walter Johnson, Wash.	13
1925	Stanley Coveleski, Wash.	13
1930	Wesley Ferrell, Cleve.	13
1940	Louis Newsom, Det.	13
1949	Ellis Kinder, Bos.	13
1971	David McNally, Balt.	13
1973	James Hunter, Oak.	13
1978	Ronald Guidry, N.Y.	13
1983	D. LaMarr Hoyt, Chi.	13
1990	Bobby Witt, Tex.	13
1991	Scott Erickson, Minn.	13
1901	Denton Young, Bos.	12
1910	Russell Ford, N.Y.	12
1914	Hubert Leonard, Bos.	12
1929	Jonathan Zachary, N.Y.	12
1931	George Earnshaw, Phila.	12
1938	John Allen, Cleve.	12
1939	Atley Donald, N.Y.	12
1946	David Ferriss, Bos.	12
1961	Luis Arroyo, N.Y.	12
1963	Edward Ford, N.Y.	12
1968	David McNally, Balt.	12
1971	Patrick Dobson, Balt.	12
1985	Ronald Guidry, N.Y.	12
1991	Scott Erickson, Min.	12
1992	Bobby Witt, Texas	12

However, low-run games predominated, and he produced an ERA of 1.95 for the run of 24 games.

Carl Hubbell's great rival was Dizzy Dean, and duels between the two were matchups between two titans. Hubbell's lefthanded screwball was matched against the fastball of the colorful screwball of the Cardinals. These confrontations were arranged as often as possible for their gate appeal, and Dean tried to head off Hubbell's march toward glory three times during the string.

Twice he failed gloriously and once ingloriously. During the 1936 portion of the skein, Dean lost 2–1 in an extra-inning game and lost another 2–1 game in the regulation nine innings. These were typical Hubbell-Dean matchups, with both pitchers rising to the occasion. Hubbell, over the years, rose higher more often.

Probably in frustration, when the streak reached 22 on May 19, 1937, Dean lost both the game and his temper when umpire George Barr called a balk against Dizzy for the third time. It gave a reprieve to the batter, Giant shortstop Dick Bartell, who had flied out. He then hit a line drive which Pepper Martin dropped, and a flurry of runs followed.

Dean's retaliation was to throw beanballs at every Giant batter who dared step to the plate. In this pre-helmet time such tactics were not viewed kindly, and outfielder Jimmy

Ripple offered to take Dean on in a one-to-one fistfight. Dean, who spent a career vainly trying to find someone he could lick, accepted the challenge. He was engulfed by Giant bodies, topped by players in Cardinal uniforms, in what turned into one of the best displays of belligerence ever seen on a ballfield. Individual fights ranged all around the diamond. There were no peacemakers among the players. Among the few who chose to be spectators was Carl Hubbell. He had better use for his arm than swinging it at someone. When order was restored, Hubbell finished pitching a one-run, seven-hit game.

Dean protested his subsequent fine and threatened to boycott the upcoming All Star Game. As usual his threat was unfulfilled. It would have been far better for him if he had stayed away. It was in the 1937 All Star Game that Dean was hit on the foot by an Earl Averill line drive. He tried to pitch while favoring a broken toe and ruined a great right arm.

The end of Hubbell's streak came on May 31 at the hands of the team which considered any victory over the Giants as compensation for an otherwise dismal season. The Brooklyn Dodgers invaded the Polo Grounds for a doubleheader which drew the second-largest crowd that had ever crammed into the Giants home field.

The Dodgers had always been a tough team for Hubbell. He had beaten them five times during his 24-game streak, twice in relief, but in the opening game of the doubleheader Brooklyn closed the door on Hubbell's feat.

Carl Hubbell took the long walk from the mound to the clubhouse in center field during the third inning. Five runs had scored. There had been seven hits and three walks. In came Dick Coffman, who had been Lefty Grove's nemesis. It would have been fitting if he had stopped the Dodgers in their tracks and the Giants had rallied to save Hubbell's streak so he could extend it the next time. Neither happened; Brooklyn scored five more runs, the Giants only tallied three runs for the whole game.

Lost in the Crowd

By winning 24 games in a row over two seasons, Carl Hubbell obscured the feat of Roy Face in 1958 and 1959 when the forkballer won 22 consecutive games, all in relief. That stands as the best achievement for a reliever. Also in 1959, Face equaled Johnny Allen's mark of 17 consecutive wins, doing it all in one season.

Roy Face, only five-eight and weighing just 160 pounds, didn't lose his first decision in 1959 until September 11. He had entered the game in relief and gave up the winning run in the ninth inning of a game at Los Angeles when Charlie Neal hit a single. Until then, it appeared that Roy Face was destined to never lose a game. Even when his forkball wasn't working its usual magic, he won.

A modest man, Face would point to six or seven games when the Pirates' hitters bailed him out. The most extreme of these times came in a June 11 game, when the San Francisco Giants played Pittsburgh. Face came in to protect a 7–5 lead in the eighth inning. The Giants had two men on base and Willie Mays came up as a pinch hitter. He homered and the Giants led, 8–7. In the bottom of the inning, the Pirates erupted with five runs and Face had a win instead of a loss.

During his string, Face won eleven of his games in extra innings.

Consecutive Base Hits

The feat of making a dozen consecutive base hits has been accomplished only twice in all the years major league baseball has been played. The record has rested there for over forty years and might never see the time when a batter delivers a baker's dozen to provide a new record. The hitter who reaches 13 will cap a slow, gradual climb toward a peak shared by Pinky Higgins and Walt Dropo, both American Leaguers. The National League's record is 10.

The history of consecutive base hits goes back to 1897, when Ed Delahanty, whom you would expect to set such standards, and Jake Gettman, whom you wouldn't, each got ten hits in a row during the season. Delahanty, one of five major-league-playing brothers, batted .377 for Philadelphia in 129 games. Gettman, who only played one season as a regular, got his ten straight while appearing in only 36 games for Washington. He hit .315 overall. The National League record is still 10 consecutive hits, and seven others have joined the original pair.

Tris Speaker was the first to top 10, getting 11 straight hits in 1920. Speaker had eclipsed Doc Johnson's American League total of 9, hit in 1919, the same season Brooklyn's Ed Konetchy had joined Delahanty and Gettman with 10.

The next year, when Speaker moved the major league record up a notch, his feat came amid the epoch record-setting of Babe Ruth's 54 home runs. This had broken Ruth's own mark of 29 set the season before. It dwarfed Speaker's rattling off 11 straight hits. In fact, Speaker's own accomplishment, leading the Cleveland Indians to a World Series victory despite the loss of shortstop Ray Chapman to a fatal beaning during the pennant chase, overshadowed his own batting feats. This included a runner-up .388 to George Sisler's league-leading batting average of .407.

However, Speaker's 11 straight stood the test of time. During the 1920s others made a run at the record but couldn't get beyond 10 straight hits. They included Sisler in 1921 and Harry Heilmann in 1922. Kiki Cuyler in 1925 and Chick Hafey in 1929, all future Hall of Famers, got up to 10 straight in the National League. In 1936 another Hall of Famer to be, Joe Medwick, hit in 10 straight times at bat.

One outsider who edged onto the list with those headed for baseball's Hall of Fame was a reserve catcher, Harry McCurdy. A rookie with the White Sox in 1926, he only played in 33 games, but cracked out 10 straight hits while batting .326. He might have played in more games, but he had a month's vacation in August. He was claimed by the Yankees on waivers, but when New York discovered this included an obligation for the rookie's bonus of $30,000, they refused to complete the deal. The White Sox insisted they were honor-bound. As is usual in baseball, honor lost and McCurdy remained a substitute catcher with Chicago.

Speaker's record finally tumbled in 1938, when Mike "Pinky" Higgins, the Boston Red Sox third baseman, began by going 4 for 4 against the White Sox in Chicago. The next day the team was in Detroit to play a doubleheader with the Tigers. When Higgins went 4 for 4, with a walk, against Roxie Lawson in the first game, and singled his first time up in the second game, Cal Hubbard, umpiring on the bases, observed, "That makes you 5 for 5 for the day."

Higgins told Hubbard he was 9 for 9, counting the previous day in Chicago. It wasn't enough that Higgins put pressure on himself, but after he got his tenth straight hit, the field announcer at Briggs Field, Ty Tyson, made a public-address announcement that Higgins could tie Speaker's record if he got another hit the next time up.

Higgins shook off the hex and got the hit and, with everyone knowing a new record was on the line, ripped a single off Tommy Bridges, the best curveballer in the league, the next time up. It was an unlucky 13, however, as Higgins fanned his last time at bat. The catcher in both games of the doubleheader was Rudy York. It was the year the Tigers tried to find a place for him to play.

Even though he was to be described by Tom Meany as "part Indian, part first baseman," when Hank Greenberg moved to the outfield so York could play where he'd do the least damage, the one season as a catcher had been a disaster. Higgins later confided he had little trouble guessing a fastball was coming as York had become known to avoid complications by refusing to call for curveballs.

In 1952 the slugging first baseman of the Red Sox, Walt Dropo, tied Higgins's record. He had debuted in 1950 with a sensational season, hitting .322, but he never hit above .300 again. Dropo had begun the season with Boston, but in a multiplayer deal in June, he had been traded to Detroit. Going along with Dropo was Johnny Pesky, longtime shortstop for the Red Sox and, in the way of coincidences in record setting, had reached 11 straight hits, one behind Higgins's record, in 1946. Pesky was at shortstop in the games when Dropo tied him first for runner-up, a spot he now shared with Speaker. He watched as Dropo got his twelfth straight.

Like Higgins, Walt Dropo made his run in a doubleheader. He had gone 5 for 5 against the Yankees in a single game on July 14, and the next day, in Griffith Stadium, he had four straight in the first game. All the hits had been singles, but starting off in the first inning of the nightcap, the powerful Dropo hit a triple with the bases loaded.

In the third inning he had his eleventh straight hit, another single, and Mickey Vernon, the Washington first baseman, told him he could tie the record with a hit the next time at bat. He did with a double. And he had another time at bat coming, in the seventh inning. Despite Dropo's hitting, the Tigers trailed, 7–6. He swung from the heels but only lifted a foul fly which catcher Mickey Grasso caught at the edge of the field boxes. The streak was over. Dropo added a single in the ninth inning but had to settle for a shared record which has stood against more recent assaults.

Ken Singleton of Baltimore got 10 in 1981, and Bip Roberts of Cincinnati managed the feat in 1992.

Most Consecutive Hits

American League

Player	Team	Year	H
Pinky Higgins	Bos.	1938	12
Walt Dropo	Det.	1952	12
Tris Speaker	Cleve.	1920	11
Johnny Pesky	Bos.	1946	11
George Sisler	St.L.	1921	10
Harry Heilmann	Det.	1922	10
Harry McCurdy	Chi.	1926	10
Rip Radcliff	Chi.	1938	10
Ken Singleton	Balt.	1981	10
Doc Johnston	Cleve.	1919	9
Ty Cobb	Det.	1925	9
Sam Rice	Wash.	1925	9
Hal Trosky	Cleve.	1936	9
Ted Williams	Bos.	1939	9
Tony Oliva	Minn.	1967	9
Jorge Orta	Cleve.	1980	9
Mickey Hatcher	Minn.	1985	9
Lance Johnson	Chi.	1995	9

National League

Player	Team	Year	H
Ed Delahanty	Phila.	1897	10
Jake Gettman	Wash.	1897	10
Ed Konetchy	Brook.	1919	10
Kiki Cuyler	Pitts.	1925	10
Chick Hafey	St.L.	1929	10
Joe Medwick	St.L.	1936	10
Buddy Hassett	Bos.	1940	10
Woody Williams	Cin.	1943	10
Bip Roberts	Cin.	1992	10
Joe Kelley	Balt.	1894	9
Rogers Hornsby	St.L.	1924	9
Taylor Douthit	St.L.	1926	9

Babe Herman	Brook.	1926	9
Bill Jurges	N.Y.	1941	9
Terry Moore	St.L.	1947	9
Dick Sisler	Phila.	1950	9
Eddie Waitkus	Phila.	1950	9
Dave Philley	Phila.	1958-59	9
Felipe Alou	S.F.	1962	9
Willie Stargell	Pitts.	1966	9
Rennie Stennett	Pitts.	1975	9
Ron Cey	L.A.	1977	9
Andres Galarraga	Col.	1993	9
Sammy Sosa	Chi.	1991	9
Jose Vizcaino	N.Y.	1996	9

Team Winning Streaks

The two longest winning streaks by teams had different outcomes. Twice National League clubs won 21 in a row and the pennant. When the Chicago White Stockings did it, under Cap Anson, in 1880, they were simply running away from the pack. They won the pennant by 15 games.

However, when their descendants, the Chicago Cubs, won 21 in a row in 1935, the drive capped a sensational stretch battle that caught and passed their rivals, the St. Louis Cardinals, within a few days of the season's end.

These two 21-game streaks are not the longest on record. The record of 26 games won in a row by the 1916 New York Giants stands as the most perverse record of achievement in baseball. No other team has won so many games so convincingly to such little purpose. The Giants came in fourth, despite having had another win streak the same season of 17 straight. Even more peculiarly, the 26 games in a row were all played at home. Maybe the Giants could only win at the Polo Grounds? No. The 17 straight were all won on the road.

John McGraw did a remarkable thing in 1916. He rebuilt the team well into the season, after they had won 17 in a row. The season had started dismally, and before they hit their stride, they had lost thirteen of the first fifteen games played. When they ran off a streak of wins, it only made up for previously lost ground. Then they flattened out again. McGraw acted.

He had a flawed infield. Shortstop Art Fletcher was a gem, but the other positions were played by former stars, Fred Merkle at first and Larry Doyle at second. Bill McKechnie, the third baseman, would someday be a Hall of Famer, but as a manager.

John McGraw had a love-hate relationship with Buck Herzog. He loved him as a player, but hated him as an individual. Herzog had been a rookie with the Giants and was traded away to the Braves, then swapped back again to star on three successive pennant winners, in 1911 through 1913. Then he was exiled again.

McGraw coveted Herzog, an unrepentant infielder who could hit and play any place with superb skill. They met privately, agreed that the money and opportunity involved was more important than any blood feud, and McGraw swapped the immortal Christy Mathewson, whose fade-away pitch had failed, to Cincinnati, where he would become manager. He sent McKechnie along and a young outfielder of promise but little playing time, Edd Roush. The next year and two years later Roush won the batting championships. McGraw never regretted his move. He had laid the groundwork for the 1917 pennant.

Even though the season was well along, McGraw shipped his former captain, Larry Doyle, to Chicago for Heinie Zimmerman. Doyle, who had shouted in boyish enthusiasm, "It's great to be young and a Giant," was no longer young and no longer a Giant.

Fred Merkle, forgiven the blunder of 1908, when he failed to touch second as an apparent winning run scored and cost the Giants a pennant, had also grown old in McGraw's service and was shipped out. When Zimmerman arrived, Herzog was shifted to second, and double plays began to be turned, base hits became infield outs, and the pitchers relished their new-found support. The Giants' drive began as late as September 7, when they were in fourth place, twelve-and-a-half games out of third. Ferdie Schupp came out of nowhere to emerge as a star pitcher and won six games in the string. Pol Perritt won the first game of a doubleheader on September 9 and enjoyed it so much he came back and pitched a shutout in the second game. Regulars won, and rookies debuted and won. The Giants won, but moved up only as far as third.

The Giants ripped off 12 in a row and then paused for a rain-stopped tie game, 1–1, as Burleigh Grimes, who lost 13 in a row that season, managed a tie game for Pittsburgh. The streak resumed the next day and went on and on, although the Giants could never catch first-place Brooklyn. It was the Phillies who were breathing on the necks of the Dodgers, catching them on September 30 but then falling back.

The Giants' streak was stopped in their last home game of the season, when they lost to the Boston Braves. They crossed the bridge to Brooklyn to close out the season on October 2, and McGraw set off wide speculation in the press by leaving the bench during the game and intimating afterward that the Giants had deliberately lost the game to ensure a Dodger pennant. Brooklyn was managed by Wilbert Robinson, once McGraw's closest crony, his coach and developer of pitchers. Some argument, some twist to the volatile McGraw temper had made them enemies. McGraw, who hated to lose, loathed losing to Brooklyn and Uncle Robbie. Maybe that's all there was to it, just another symptom of McGraw being a sore loser. Yet just ahead was the Black Sox scandal, and playing for the Giants were two non-Chicago players who were to be swept out of baseball when Judge Landis purged its suspect characters—Heinie Zimmerman and Bennie Kauff. McGraw's 1916 Giants finished in fourth place—right where they were when they began their 26-game streak!—and 7 games out of first place.

The 1935 Chicago Cubs' 21 straight wins carried them to a pennant, although they faced a task made tougher by the schedule. The St. Louis Cardinals, the Gas House Gang world champions from 1934, not only led by 2 games, but the indomitable Deans, Dizzy and Paul, headed the staff. Even more comforting for the Cards, the schedule called for the Cubs to play the last five games of the season at Sportsman's Park in St. Louis.

In 1935 the Cubs picked up momentum, and it took them past the Cards in the middle of the streak. They took the lead on September 14 as they won their eleventh game and were three games ahead of the crumbling Cards when they reached St. Louis for the final five games. Lon Warneke beat Paul Dean 1–0 in the opener, and Bill Lee won his twentieth game of the season, beating Dizzy Dean 6–3 to clinch the pennant. It was the first game of a doubleheader, and the Cubs reached 21 straight by taking the nightcap.

They lost the next game, a meaningless one in the pennant race, in extra innings on Joe Medwick's second home run of the game. The Cards won the season's finale, 2–1, but it was the Cubs who went on to the World Series.

The next year was also a season of streaks. Again the Cubs got in gear with an impressive run of victories, taking 15 straight before midseason was reached. It did not lead to a pennant. Another 15-game winning streak, by the New York Giants, brought the championship to the Polo Grounds.

It was a streak that started late in the season and ran, in part, concurrently with Carl Hubbell's own string of 16 wins. While the Giants were racking up 15 straight, Hubbell appeared in ten consecutive games. He never ran out of steam. The season ended with Hubbell experiencing a 16-game streak. He extended it by winning his first 8 decisions the next year to reach 24 straight wins over two seasons.

Other very long winning streaks in the National League that added late-season zest to pennant races were those of the 1924 Dodgers and, of course, the 1951 Giants. The Dodgers came up short, unable to catch the leading Giants, who added a fourth straight pennant in 1924, when Brooklyn's 15 straight and Dazzy Vance's MVP season were not enough.

In 1951 the same traditional rivals reversed roles, but not results. It was the Dodgers who were far in front when the Giants, managed by former Dodger skipper Leo Durocher, began a late-season drive. The Giants had started with the wrong kind of a streak. They lost their first 11 games and spent the season trying to catch the fast-flying Dodgers. They were 13 games behind when they won the first of 16 straight decisions on August 12 and began to close the gap the Dodgers had opened.

The Giants slowly edged closer and into a tie with a game to play. When both teams won their final games, the Dodgers on Jackie Robinson's extra-inning heroics in Philadelphia, the stage was set for a playoff series. It was won by Bobby Thomson's dramatic home run in the last of the ninth of the third, and decisive, game.

The 1906 American League season produced long strings of wins by two teams locked in a hotly contested pennant race. The Chicago White Sox set a record, since tied by the 1947 Yankees, of 19 straight wins.

Dubbed "the Hitless Wonders" because of a .230 team batting average, the White Sox engaged in a dramatic scenario with the New York team, then called the Highlanders.

In early August the White Sox were in fourth place. Ahead of them were Philadelphia, New York, and Cleveland. Day after day the White Sox chipped away at the lead held by the teams ahead of them. They eventually passed Philadelphia and Cleveland.

The Highlanders benefited from two winning streaks of their own, 11 and 15 in a row. However, in the final surge of the pennant race, it was the White Sox who came home in first place. New York became the first of only two teams (the 1912 Senators being the second) to win 15 in a row and not win a pennant in the American League. In the National League since 1900, four teams have won at least 15 in a row and not won the pennant. The most glaring example, of course, was the 1916 Giants, winners of 26 and 17 straight. The 1936 Cubs won 15 in a row and finished second to the Giants, also winners of 15 straight. The 1907 Giants had the poorest finish. Despite 17 straight wins, they finished fourth, 25 games out.

One might think that if a team wants to ensure winning a pennant, a good way to do it is rack up 15 or more consecutive victories along the way, preferably in the stretch run. But actually there is no correlation between a streak start date and chances of winning a flag. Streaks of 15 or more wins that start before Memorial Day have led to 7 out of 10 pennants (70%); such streaks that start between Memorial Day and August 1 have won 9 of 13 pennants; and streaks occurring in the stretch run, after August 1, have won 10 of 14 pennants.

Fifteen Game Team Winning Streaks

	Tie	Team		Year	Start End	Manager	Spoiler
21	*2	CHI	NL	1880	6/02 - 7/10	Anson	@CLE(McCormick)
20		STL	UA	1884	4/20 - 5/24	Sullivan	BOS(Bond)
20		PRO	NL	1884	8/07 - 9/09	Bancroft	BUF(Galvin)
18		CHI	NL	1885	6/01 - 6/25	Anson	PHI(Daily)
15		DET	NL	1886	5/10 - 5/31	Watkins	@NY(Keefe)
15		STL	AA	1887	4/24 - 5/17	Comiskey	PHI(Seward)
16	*16	PHI	NL	1887	9/15 - 10/8	Wright	BOS(Clarkson) '88
16		PHI	NL	1890	7/08 - 7/28	Allen	@CHI(Hutchison)
18	*2	BOS	NL	1891	9/16 - 10/3	Selee	@PHI(Keefe)
16		PHI	NL	1892	6/10 - 6/29	Wright	BOS(Nichols)
18		BAL	NL	1894	8/24 - 9/16	Hanlon	@CIN(Parrott)
17		BOS	NL	1897	5/31 - 6/22	Selee	@BKN(Kennedy)
15		PIT	NL	1903	6/02 - 6/25	Clarke	@PHI(Mitchell)
18		NY	AL	1904	6/16 - 7/05	McGraw	@PHI(Fraser)
19	*12	CHI	AL	1906	8/02 - 8/25	Jones	@WAS(C. Smith)
15		NY	AL	1906	8/29 - 9/10	Griffith	BOS(Winter)
17		NY	NL	1907	4/25 - 5/20	McGraw	STL(C. Brown)
16		PIT	NL	1909	9/09 - 9/27	Clarke	NY(Wiltse)
17		WS	AL	1912	5/30 - 6/19	Griffith	@PHI(Coombs)
16		NY	NL	1912	6/19 - 7/04	McGraw	BKN(Ragan)
15		PHI	AL	1913	5/27 - 6/11	Mack	STL(Stone)
15		IND	FL	1914	6/11 - 6/25	Phillips	KC(Harris)
17		NY	NL	1916	5/09 - 5/30	McGraw	@PHI(Demaree)
26	*13	NY	NL	1916	9/07 - 9/30	McGraw	BOS(Tyler)
15		BKN	NL	1924	8/25 - 9/06	Robinson	@BOS(Genewich)
16		NY	AL	1926	5/10 - 5/28	Huggins	PHI(Grove)
17		PHI	AL	1931	5/05 - 5/26	Mack	NY(Gomez)
21		CHI	NL	1935	9/04 - 9/28	Grimm	@STL(Walker)
15		CHI	NL	1936	6/04 - 6/21	Grimm	@BKN(Mungo)
15		NY	NL	1936	8/11 - 8/29	Terry	@PIT(Lucas)
15		BOS	AL	1946	4/25 - 5/11	Cronin	@NY(Bonham)
19		NY	AL	1947	6/29 - 7/18	Harris	@DET(Hutchinson)
16		NY	AL	1951	8/12 - 8/28	Durocher	PIT(Pollet)
18		NY	AL	1953	5/27 - 6/16	Stengel	STL(Pillette)
16		KC	AL	1977	8/31 - 9/16	Herzog	SEA(Medich)
15		MIN	AL	1991	6/01 - 6/17	Kelly	@BAL(Williamson)

(Chart Courtesy of Frank Vaccaro)
*Indicates tie in game number noted.

The Feats

What follows is a celebration of three of baseball's most rare and heroic feats: the triple crowns of batting and pitching, and the triple putout by one player, better known as the unassisted triple play. These feats do not rank with the central records of the game: Henry Aaron's 755 homers, Cy Young's 511 wins, Pete Rose's 4,256 hits, Ty Cobb's lifetime batting average of .366. They are not as distant in memory as a .400 hitter or a 40-game winner. But they are remarkable achievements and—unlike those mentioned above—are not evident from a perusal of the leaders tables found later in this book.

Triple Crown Winners—Batting

Baseball's first Triple Crown winner, Paul Hines, waited ninety years to be enthroned. The crown consists of three jewels: the batting, home run, and runs-batted-in titles must be won in a single season. The RBI count was a late starter among baseball stats and had to be reconstructed for earlier seasons. However, it was not for lack of the RBI distinction that Hines, of the Providence Grays, waited for belated recognition. His feat went unacknowledged until researchers turned up information which made him the true 1878 batting champion.

A special Baseball Records Committee met in 1968 and put a stamp of approval on statistics which had been in dispute or unverified from baseball's past. The new information appeared the next year when Macmillan published the first edition of *The Baseball Encyclopedia.*

Abner Dalrymple had gone to his grave in 1939, the year the Baseball Hall of Fame Museum opened in Cooperstown, New York, with one baseball honor to his name. He had won the National League batting championship in 1878. Paul Hines, who died in 1935, was remembered only as the winner of the 1879 title. But new data—coming from the two tie games he played and the one for Dalrymple—have revealed that Hines ought to have been a repeat batting champion, too, for under modern scoring rules, his batting average of .358 was higher than Dalrymple's .356.

Paul Hines enjoyed that distinction from 1969 through 1994, then lost it as Major League Baseball and *Total Baseball* adopted a new stance, acknowledging that the individual marks amassed in tie games were not counted in the NL of 1878, *by the practices of the day*—and thus the championship should return to Dalrymple, despite his lower average under modern reconstruction. Thus with hindsight, we can award Hines 1879 batting-average supremacy (though not the championship), the RBI leadership which resulted from reconstructed states, and the small but clearly superior total of 4 home runs. Thus Paul Hines can be said to have attained the first Triple Crown. In addition, when he won the batting title again in 1879, again through later research efforts, he became the first to repeat as hitting leader.

Another nineteenth-century player, Hugh Duffy, had—since 1969, when his RBI data first were published—been considered the first to wear the Triple Crown. In 1894 he had won the three necessary titles but had almost obscured his own feat by batting .438, later corrected upward to .440. This remains the highest batting average of all time and in Duffy's later years had always interested interviewers more than the Triple Crown. Duffy's 18 home runs and 145 runs batted in led the league in these departments in 1894, but the idea of linking them as a diadem had not yet been formed. No one knew Paul Hines had done it and few cared that Hugh Duffy had. Although the RBI was known as a baseball stat as early as 1879, it was not commonly used until the 1910s, and not an official measure until 1920.

Hugh Duffy, a twinkle-eyed New Englander, told about his batting record for the fifty subsequent years that he spent in major league baseball, the last several decades as a coach for the Boston Red Sox. When a rookie named Ted Williams arrived in the big leagues in 1939, Hugh

Duffy became his first mentor. Duffy proclaimed Williams as the greatest hitter he ever saw and watched while Williams won two Triple Crowns and missed a third by the closest margin possible.

Another recently discovered Triple Crown was Tip O'Neill's of 1887. The American Association's RBI totals for that season were not calculated until 1996. Then it was discovered his 123 RBI led the circuit and (along with his 14 HR and .435 BA) gave him a Triple Crown. O'Neill also paced the American Association in runs, hits, doubles, triples, on base average, production, and slugging percentage.

The player who placed the stamp of the superstar most firmly on the concept of the Triple Crown was Nap Lajoie, who was the dominant player in the game when the American League was formed and ushered in twentieth-century baseball. The great Napoleon Lajoie had become the star of the Philadelphia Phillies as the nineteenth century closed. He was the prize recruit for the new league, remaining in Philadelphia where Connie Mack was establishing a new franchise. Lajoie put the team and the American League on the baseball map in 1901, when he provided the league-leading totals in the three prize categories. He batted .426, hit 14 home runs in the dead-ball era of the time, as later research showed, and, batted in 145 runs. It was the greatest season the immortal would ever have. He would win two more batting titles and again lead the league in RBI. However, home runs were not his specialty.

Still, his Triple Crown brought instant respect to the new league and, together with other stars who had switched leagues, forced acceptance that the American League was a full-fledged major league and would be part of the basis of baseball's structure from then on.

Lajoie was succeeded as the American League's superstar by Ty Cobb, who also laid claim to the Triple Crown in 1909. As with Lajoie, hitting home runs was not Cobb's dominant ability, and despite ten batting championships and four RBI titles, he wore the Triple Crown but once. He came close two other times, in 1907 and 1911, finishing second in home runs each of those years.

Cobb's great rival was the National League's Honus Wagner, who never wore the Triple Crown, although he too missed it by a close margin. In 1908 he was second in home runs, the most difficult final jewel for the superstars of the dead-ball era to achieve. Wagner's eight batting titles and four RBI championships were never accompanied by a home run leadership.

While the list of those who have won the Triple Crown is short, it is a quality list. All but one Triple Crown holder in this century—the suspect Heinie Zimmerman—are in the Hall of Fame.

In 1912 Heinie Zimmerman, one of the best major league third basemen, put together the greatest season he would ever have. Honus Wagner failed to repeat as batting champion, and his 102 RBI total was one less than Zimmerman's, according to the tabulations of Ernie Lanigan. The 14 home runs Zimmerman hit edged teammate Wildfire Schulte, who had led the league in four-baggers the two previous seasons, by one. Only in batting average, where Zimmerman's .372 far distanced the field, did he have a clear superiority, but a Triple Crown by any measure is a rare treasure and it was Heinie's without dispute,

that is until the researchers of Information Concepts, Inc., the group that compiled *The Baseball Encyclopedia,* downgraded his RBI total to 99. Later, an editor of *The Baseball Encyclopedia* fudged Zim's RBI count back up to 103 to restore his Triple Crown, but we cannot subscribe to such an arbitrary change.

It was 1922 before the Triple Crown would again rest on a player's head, but when it did, it landed on the brow of the royally nicknamed "Rajah" Hornsby and just eluded Babe Ruth, "the Sultan of Swat."

Hornsby strung together six successive batting titles, from 1920 through 1925, and added another in 1928. Although he had home run power to go with his high averages, the title escaped him in 1921, when George Kelly outhomered him by two. It would have been the first Triple Crown for the Rajah and would have given him an eventual three, a total no one has ever achieved.

Babe Ruth, who got two legs up on the Triple Crown seven times without ever winning one, had many home run titles and frequently topped the league in RBI. However, the competition for batting championships in the 1920s, when Cobb, Sisler, and Heilmann topped .400 and Heilmann alone accounted for four batting titles, was tough. Ruth managed one hitting title but lost the RBI leg that year, 1924, to Goose Goslin. The Babe won many honors, but the Triple Crown was not among them.

In the 1930s a quartet of superstars and future Hall of Fame members competed for the Triple Crown during most of the decade, and each took a single turn wearing it.

The American League had two great first baseman, Jimmie Foxx and Lou Gehrig. Each was a threat to claim the Crown every year, but when Foxx narrowly failed on two occasions, it was not Gehrig who stymied him. In 1932 Jimmie came frustratingly close. He was edged out of the batting title by the clumsy-fielding Dale Alexander in 1932. Called "Moose," Alexander split the season between Detroit and Boston, the first player to win a batting title while appearing with two teams. Alexander barely qualified for the championship, but his .367 topped the .364 by Foxx. The following year, 1933, Foxx won his lone Triple Crown.

Alexander was long gone back to the minor leagues before Jimmie Foxx had his second near-miss of the Triple Crown in 1938. This time it was the home run lead that eluded him. Although Foxx hit 50 home runs in 1938, while winning the batting and RBI honors, Hank Greenberg hit 58 homers to almost equal Babe Ruth's record of 60.

While Gehrig and Foxx were trying on the Triple Crown for size in the American League, two sluggers in the National League were sharing domination of their league. Chuck Klein was the league's outstanding batter during the early 1930s and Joe Medwick took over for the final half of the decade. Both wore the Triple Crown, Klein getting his in 1933 when Jimmie Foxx was doing likewise. It was the only year that each league produced a Triple Crown winner. Medwick won his in 1937.

The next to claim the Triple Crown was Ted Williams. A brash rookie when he reported to the Boston Red Sox in 1939, he had little to learn from the old guy hitting fungos in practice. Hugh Duffy took one look at Williams's swing and knew the only part he could serve was as a role model. Williams had his eye on hitting .400. When he did it, in 1941, his .406 was far short of Duffy's .440, the all-time record.

Williams was also one leg short of the Triple Crown in 1941. He added the home run title to his batting championship, but his main rival, Joe DiMaggio, had topped the RBI column. DiMaggio had piled up his runs-batted-in totals largely during his 56-game hitting streak that season.

Ted Williams won all three titles for the Triple Crown the next season, 1942, and then went off to serve in World War Two. Several wartime players won two legs of the Triple Crown: Rudy York, with the Detroit Tigers in 1943, and Bill Nicholson, a Chicago Cubs outfielder in 1943 and 1944. Both hit home runs and batted in runs at league-leading levels, but they were far outdistanced for the batting-average honors.

Ted Williams returned from the war in 1946 and finished second in each of the Triple Crown categories. Mickey Vernon beat him out for the batting title, and Hank Greenberg, who had blocked Jimmie Foxx in 1938, had his last hurrah with the Tigers, topping Williams in both home runs and runs batted in.

The next year, with Greenberg gone to the National League, Ted Williams claimed his second Triple Crown. No one was close to him in any of the three prize categories, and despite three prime seasons lost to wartime service, the Red Sox star seemed most likely to be the first to wear the Triple Crown three times. He had won in 1942 and 1947.

In 1948 his old nemesis, Joe DiMaggio, who was never to win a Triple Crown, picked off two of the crown jewels, leading the American League in home runs with 39 and in runs batted in with 155. Ted Williams was far ahead of the pack as batting champion with a .369 average.

It was 1949 that proved the greatest disappointment to Williams. DiMaggio was injured much of the season and did not compete for individual honors. However, the pennant race was tightly contested between the Yankees and Red Sox, and more interest was focused on that than on the seemingly assured third Triple Crown to be worn by Ted Williams.

As the season reached the final weekend, Boston came to New York for two games between the Red Sox and Yankees. Boston was a game ahead and needed to win only one to gain the pennant. They lost on Saturday, and the teams were tied when Sunday's game began.

The biggest threat to Ted Williams' third Triple Crown came from teammate Vern Stephens, a slugging shortstop who was tied with Ted for RBI. Williams held a small but probably secure batting lead over George Kell of the Detroit Tigers.

However, Williams and the Red Sox were in a slump, and it cost both the team and the individual their honors. The final game of the season between the Yankees and Red Sox was one of the most exciting of all time, if you were a Yankee fan. If you were among the generations of faithful Red Sox followers who have seen their team fail in the final situation, one frustrating season after another, it was a bitter end. The Yankees staved off a three-run Red Sox rally to win 5–3.

Williams had gone hitless and ended up not only missing a World Series appearance but his third Triple Crown. While Williams had sputtered in the final games, George

Kell, who had missed two stretches of games with injuries, got back in the lineup for Detroit's final three games. With only a batting title at stake, Kell had two hits in his final game. When the final statistics were known, George Kell had batted .3429 and Ted Williams .3427. It was the closest any player ever came to a Triple Crown without actually winning it and the closest anyone has come to earning the honor three times.

The year before, in the National League, Stan Musial had narrowly missed his bid for a Triple Crown, when he was one behind Johnny Mize and Ralph Kiner, who tied for the home run title with 40.

In 1953 Al Rosen had a near-miss almost as tight as Ted Williams had had in 1949. Rosen won the home run and RBI titles but was edged out, .337 to .336, for the batting championship by Mickey Vernon, of the Washington Senators, who had blocked Williams's bid in that category in 1946.

Mickey Mantle hit his peak in 1956 when he put the necessary ingredients together to win a Triple Crown. He hit .353 for the only batting title he would win, had top totals in home runs with 52, and piled up 130 runs batted in.

Ten years later, in 1966, Frank Robinson reacted to being traded out of the National League by winning the Triple Crown in the American League. His .316 batting average was one of only two above .300 that year in the American League. He had switched leagues just in time. A .316 average wouldn't have made the top five in the National League in 1966. He won the home run and RBI titles comfortably.

In 1967, the year of the Red Sox "Impossible Dream," the team was driven to a surprise championship by the captain, Carl Yastrzemski, who had an astounding year. Yaz won the only home run title of his career and also the lone RBI championship he would record. He joined these with one of his three batting crowns and ended the season with what was to become an elusive honor, the Triple Crown.

He is the last player to wear the title, although a number of players have gained two legs, including Yaz's teammate, Jim Rice, who did this twice. In the American League the inability of power hitters to achieve a high batting average has resulted in a parade of sluggers leading in home runs and runs batted in but falling short in base-hit percentage.

Harmon Killebrew, who tied with Yaz for home runs in Yastrzemski's crown-winning season, Frank Howard, Dick Allen, Reggie Jackson, George Scott, Eddie Murray, Tony Armas, and Jose Canseco have won two legs but failed the batting title.

Since Yaz won the last Triple Crown, two National Leaguers have won batting titles and the RBI championship, but failed in home runs. Joe Torre in 1971 and Al Oliver in 1982 earned two legs one way, and Johnny Bench, Willie Stargell, George Foster, Andre Dawson, and Mike Schmidt have done it with the home run and RBI crowns. Foster did it twice and Schmidt four times.

Combining a high batting average with power is a rare characteristic in contemporary baseball. Players such as Rod Carew and Wade Boggs, who won frequent batting championships without expectation of adding the other elements of the Triple Crown, served to reduce the likelihood that a pure power hitter would also annex a batting title, especially in the course of the same season.

Carl Yastrzemski might not have been just part of a vanishing breed. He might have been the last example of a breed that has already vanished.

Triple Crown Hitters

American League

Player	Team	Year	HR	RBI	BA
Nap Lajoie	Phila.	1901	14	125	.422
Ty Cobb	Det.	1909	9	115	.377
Jimmie Foxx	Phila.	1933	48	163	.356
Lou Gehrig	N.Y.	1934	49	165	.363
Ted Williams	Bos.	1942	36	137	.356
	Bos.	1947	32	114	.343
Mickey Mantle	N.Y.	1956	52	130	.353
Frank Robinson	Bal.	1966	49	122	.316
Carl Yastrzemski	Bos.	1967	44	121	.326

National League

Player	Team	Year	HR	RBI	BA
Paul Hines*	Prov.	1878	4	50	.358
Hugh Duffy	Bos.	1894	18	145	.438
Heinie Zimmerman**	Chi.	1912	14	103	.372
Rogers Hornsby	St.L.	1922	42	152	.401
	St. L.	1925	39	143	.403
Chuck Klein	Phila.	1933	28	120	.368
Joe Medwick	St.L.	1937	31	154	.374

American Association

Player	Team	Year	HR	RBI	BA
Tip O'Neill	St.L.	1887	14	123	.435

*Hines's batting average was the highest in the NL, but Abner Dalrymple retains his title.

**Zimmerman ranked first in RBI as calculated by Ernie Lanigan, but only third as calculated by ICI research in 1969.

Triple Crown Winners—Pitching

Tommy Bond, the only nineteenth-century pitcher on the list of Triple Crown Winners who is not in the Hall of Fame, has, at least, the honor of turning the feat first. When the National League was formed in 1876, Bond was an established star in the National Association. The others who eventually won the pitchers' Triple Crown, for the most wins and strikeouts and the lowest ERA in a single season, began their careers in the National League.

Although he was only twenty-one when he won the Triple Crown in 1877, Bond had been pitching for prominent teams since he had been sixteen and joined the Athletics of Brooklyn. He entered the National League with Hartford but moved to Boston for his best seasons. He was Boston's only pitcher during 1877 and 1878 and pitched the great majority of games in 1879. He won 123 of the 204 games Boston played in those early years of short schedules.

Bond, who later coached baseball at Harvard, was celebrated for his victories and strikeouts. The measurement of earned runs was done retroactively.

As Bond's career lapsed, the next to claim the Triple Crown of pitching emerged. Old Hoss Radbourn reached the peak year that gave him his nickname for durability in 1884. He pitched the Providence Grays to the National League pennant, almost singlehandedly, after Charlie Sweeney's departure had left only Radbourn as the team's pitcher.

His 59 victories is the most ever won by a pitcher in a season. It shines brightest among all such jewels in the Triple Crowns worn by those who came after him. Radbourn won 309 games in his big league career, but the 59 he totaled in his 1884 season—including a streak of 26 wins in 27 decisions—gave him a celebrity which was recognized when he was named to the Hall of Fame in its opening year, 1939.

A Triple Crown is an exacting measurement of a pitcher's superiority at any time. However, because of the circumstance that he started so many games for the league's best team, Radbourn's win totals and strikeout numbers can largely be attributed to opportunity. However, it is his 1.38 ERA at a time when the league mark was 2.98 that stamps Old Hoss as truly remarkable.

Tim Keefe, the next pitcher to annex a Triple Crown, wore his for a season that has kept his name in the active files of modern baseball writers. Whenever a pitcher runs off a string of victories, this prompts a review of the record book, and Keefe's 19 in a row is remembered as the highest total, shared with Rube Marquard's 1912 season total of 19 straight. In all, Tim Keefe won 35 games for the New York Giants in 1888, just edging out the man who would take the Triple Crown the next year.

John Clarkson pitched Boston to a pennant in 1889, winning the Triple Crown as the workhorse of a staff which included the worn Old Hoss Radbourn. Clarkson won 49 games and Radbourn 20.

Clarkson's career was overlapped by that of Amos Rusie, the most awesome pitcher of the 1890s. A burly farm boy, "the Hoosier Thunderbolt" was the principal reason the distance of the pitcher's box was pushed back in 1893. Rusie responded the following year by continuing to dominate the league in strikeouts, while topping all pitchers with 36 wins and an ERA of 2.78.

Probably because of the increased pitching distance, the league ERA ballooned to 5.32 and batters averaged .309 in 1894. This was the year Hugh Duffy won the batter's Triple Crown and set a still-unexcelled .440 batting record.

Rusie's career peaked in 1894. The next season one of the most oppressive men to own a big league team, Andrew Freedman, bought the Giants and began a blood feud with Rusie. Rusie sat out the 1896 season, but returned as a reluctant star for two more 20-game-winning seasons. Then he tore his arm muscles and retired. A token appearance in 1901 was the tenth season which qualified him for election to the Hall of Fame.

Just as Nap Lajoie marked the American League's inaugural in 1901 by winning a Triple Crown for batters, another established star, Cy Young, did the same for the pitchers' version. Young, in midcareer as a big league pitcher, won 33 games, a total almost dwarfed among the 511 he won in his career. This latter is a mark certain to stand permanently.

With two major leagues now offering the potential of a Triple Crown winner each year, it took only until 1905 to have both the American and National Leagues produce such winners. Christy Mathewson won the first of the two Triple Crowns he would win for the New York Giants, and the eccentric Rube Waddell had his last great year with the Philadelphia Athletics.

Matty won 31 games, struck out 206, and had an ERA of 1.43. The Rube produced 26 wins, 287 strikeouts, and an ERA of 1.48. The World Series, inaugurated in 1903 but boycotted by the Giants in 1904, was resumed in 1905. It would have provided marvelous theater for the two Triple Crown winners. The confrontation would have been the only one of its kind. Never since have two pennant winners also had pitching's Triple Crown winners. Alas, the colorful Rube Waddell injured his arm while wrestling a teammate just before the Series began.

Without Waddell to oppose him, Christy Mathewson won three games, all shutouts, and the Giants took the Series in five. Matty won the Triple Crown again in 1908 but lost his last start when the Chicago Cubs won the playoff game of a season which had ended in a tie. It was the failure of Fred Merkle to reach second as the winning run scored, resulting in his becoming an inning-ending force out, that deprived Matty of a second opportunity to wear his Triple Crown into a World Series.

Walter Johnson, the next to sport a Triple Crown, won three at widely spaced intervals in his long career. The first came in 1913, the next in 1918, and the last in 1924 when, in his eighteenth season, Johnson once more topped the American League in the three prize categories. This time it also brought a pennant to the Senators, the first in their history. The World Series came close to being a disappointing anticlimax for Johnson. He lost the opener to the Giants in extra innings, then lost again, but salvaged glory by winning the seventh game in relief.

Earlier, during Walter Johnson's widely spaced crown jewels, Grover Alexander produced the most impressive reign ever enjoyed by a Triple Crown winner. Pitching for the Philadelphia Phillies, he had three successive seasons with 30 or more victories, starting with the pennant-winning 1915 season; each time he led the NL in ERA and K's as well. What stopped Alexander's run of mastery was World War One. Old Pete swapped his baseball uniform for the khaki of the Army and his Triple Crown honors for a sergeant's stripes.

While Pete was in the Army, another pitcher claimed the Triple Crown. Hippo Vaughn in 1917 had achieved immortality by engaging in a double no-hit game, losing in the tenth inning. In 1918, with Alexander away, Vaughn won the Triple Crown pitching for the Cubs.

Ironically Grover Alexander had served his Army hitch as a new member of the Cubs. With his battery mate, Reindeer Bill Killefer, he had been sold to Chicago after winning his third Triple Crown, in 1917. He pitched only three games in 1918 while Vaughn was in the star's role, and in 1919 the two teammates competed for the Triple Crown. Alexander led the league in ERA and Vaughn in strikeouts. Between them they won 37 games, but neither came close to topping the league.

However, in 1920 Grover Alexander again emerged as the Triple Crown winner. It was his fourth, the most ever won by a pitcher. He continued to star, despite personal and physical problems, during the 1920s without again leading in any of the categories which make up the diadem of the Triple Crown.

Next to wear the Triple Crown of pitchers was Dazzy Vance. Like Rusie, Waddell, and Johnson, Vance began with expectation of finishing each season with a league-leading total in strikeouts. In 1924 he won the Most Valuable Player Award, even though the Brooklyn Dodgers as a team could not win the pennant. To his strikeout superiority, the Dazzler added leadership in wins with 24

and an ERA of 2.16. His domination of the league can best be measured by comparing his ERA to a league total of 3.87 as the lively ball bounded off hitters' bats.

Lefty Grove of the Philadelphia Athletics won back to back Triple Crowns in 1930 and 1931, having missed one of the three legs in 1929. The A's won pennants all three of those years, and Grove was their leading pitcher. In 1929 teammate George Earnshaw topped him in wins, 24 to 20, as Grove missed getting decisions in an unusual number of games.

Another southpaw ace, Lefty Gomez, succeeded Lefty Grove as a Triple Crown winner. Like Grove, he wore the title twice, but not consecutively. He won his first Triple Crown, oddly, in a season when his team, the New York Yankees, didn't win a pennant, 1934. His next came in 1937 as the Yankees were in the midst of a run of four straight pennants.

Gomez was only a spot starter in 1939, when the Yankees met the Reds in the World Series, but Cincinnati had a converted third baseman, Bucky Walters heading their staff, the first National Leaguer to win the Triple Crown in fifteen years.

During World War Two, Hal Newhouser emerged as a superlative pitcher who might have been equally impressive against peacetime competition. He missed the Triple Crown in 1944, winning two legs but coming in second to Detroit Tiger teammate Dizzy Trout for ERA honors. In 1945, the final wartime year, Newhouser topped the American League in the three prize categories, and winning the Triple Crown went into a long hiatus when the 1946 season resumed with the star pitchers back from service.

Despite leading the league in victories six times and in strikeouts seven, Bob Feller never won an official ERA title to match up with the other components of the Triple Crown. Although Feller's ERA in 1940 is today regarded as the lowest for that year, at that time Ernie Bonham won the title despite pitching only 99 innings.

Warren Spahn topped the National League in victories eight times, led in strikeouts four times, and even took ERA honors three times, but he could never link them up in a single season.

Robin Roberts, like Feller, never won an ERA title, so despite leading in victories four times and strikeouts twice, the singular honor of the Triple Crown eluded him, as it did all other pitchers once baseball had returned to the normalcy of peacetime play.

It wasn't until Sandy Koufax reached stardom when the Dodgers were transplanted to Los Angeles and notched three Triple Crown titles that the distinction was again achieved. Koufax topped the three needed categories in 1963, 1965, and 1966. Unlike any other winner of the Triple Crown, Koufax retired with the honor. An aching arthritic arm caused his early retirement, leaving a final season of 27 victories, 317 strikeouts, and an ERA of 1.73.

A Triple Crown-winning pitcher has not always meant a pennant for his team, although the two have gone together more often than not. However, in 1972 Steve Carlton took the honor despite pitching for a last-place team. There has never been such a contrast in the success of a team's best pitcher and the rest of its staff. The Phillies won 59 games, and Carlton was responsible for 27 of them. He also led, for the only time, in ERA, with 1.97, and struck out 310.

Again a drought followed, despite the presence of such star pitchers as Tom Seaver, Fergie Jenkins, Juan Marichal, Jim Palmer, Gaylord Perry, and others who led in some of the prize-earning stats. Then in 1985 the New York Mets' Dwight Gooden took up the challenge and claimed the Triple Crown with a remarkable record: 24-4, 1.53, and 268 strikeouts. Gooden faltered the next year, but Roger Clemens came forward to just miss the honor by finishing second in strikeouts while winning the other two legs.

Triple Crown Pitchers

American League

Player	Team	Year	W	L	SO	ERA
Cy Young	Bos.	1901	33	10	158	1.62
Rube Waddell	Phila.	1905	26	11	287	1.48
Walter Johnson	Wash.	1913	36	7	303	1.09
	Wash.	1918	23	13	162	1.27
	Wash.	1924	23	7	158	2.72
Lefty Grove	Phila.	1930	28	5	209	2.54
	Phila.	1931	31	4	175	2.06
Lefty Gomez	N.Y.	1934	26	5	158	2.33
	N.Y.	1937	21	11	194	2.33
Hal Newhouser	Det.	1945	25	9	212	1.81

National League

Player	Team	Year	W	L	SO	ERA
Tommy Bond	Bos.	1877	40	17	170	2.11
Old Hoss Radbourn	Prov.	1884	59	12	441	1.38
Tim Keefe	N.Y.	1888	35	12	333	1.74
John Clarkson	Bos.	1889	49	19	284	2.73
Amos Rusie	N.Y.	1894	36	13	195	2.78
Christy Mathewson	N.Y.	1905	31	8	206	1.27
	N.Y.	1908	37	11	259	1.43
Grover Alexander	Phila.	1915	31	10	241	1.22
	Phila.	1916	33	12	167	1.55
	Phila.	1917	30	13	201	1.86
Hippo Vaughn	Chi.	1918	22	10	148	1.74
Grover Alexander	Chi.	1920	27	14	173	1.91
Dazzy Vance	Brook	1924	28	6	262	2.16
Bucky Walters	Cin.	1939	27	11	137	2.29
Sandy Koufax	L.A.	1963	25	5	306	1.88
	L.A.	1965	26	8	382	2.04
	L.A.	1966	27	9	317	1.73
Steve Carlton	Phila.	1972	27	10	310	1.97
Dwight Gooden	N.Y.	1985	24	4	268	1.53

The Unassisted Triple Play

The unassisted triple play has been turned in regular season major league play only ten times in this century and just one questionable time in the nineteenth. (It also happened once in World Series play.)

On May 30, 1987, family and friends of ninety-three-year-old Jimmy Cooney gathered at his home to celebrate the sixtieth anniversary of his unassisted triple play. Rare? It was the last one made in the NL at that time.

Fate waited until Jimmy Cooney died two years later before ending the drought of TP-6UA scorebook entries. However, as wellwishers celebrated his sixty-year-old feat it seemed as though it might stand forever. Letters of congratulation had come for the the occasion from NL president A. Bartlett Giamatti and Dallas Green, the general manager of the Chicago Cubs. Cooney had worn a Chicago Cubs uniform the day destiny had decreed he be in the right place at the right time. A much-traveled infielder, he had worn six major league uniforms in seven seasons. It was a happy coincidence that he was Chicago's shortstop when he made his unassisted triple play.

His father, the first Jimmy Cooney, had been Chicago's shortstop in 1890, '91, and part of '92.

Jimmy's younger brother John had logged twenty years in the big leagues as a pitcher, and after his arm went lame, he had become an outfielder and first baseman.

Jimmy Cooney was no stranger to unassisted triple plays. Two seasons earlier, when he was shortstop for the St. Louis Cardinals, he was doubled off second by the Pirate shortstop Glenn Wright, who next tagged out Rogers Hornsby coming from first base. Wright had snared a line drive off the bat of Jim Bottomley to start his triple play. He watched from the Pirates' bench the day Cooney emulated his feat in much the same manner.

Paul Waner provided the line drive to make the first out, with Cooney snaring it as he ran toward second base. Clyde Barnhart had broken for second on the pitch, and Lloyd Waner, the runner on second, had dashed for third as his brother, Paul, swung. Lloyd was doubled off second, and Cooney simply tagged the startled Barnhart, who thought the ball had gone into center field for a base hit.

There are certain similarities among ten of the eleven unassisted triple plays which have been recorded. These have occurred with runners on first and second, have been made by infielders, and have required the complicity of baserunners either attempting a double steal or were running on a hit-and-run play. The eleventh—which is soon to be revealed—was by an outfielder, with runners on second and third.

Even the most celebrated unassisted-triple-play feat had an explanation that almost absolved the victims, the Brooklyn Dodgers, of bonehead base running. This was the only such event to happen in a World Series, and it was turned in by Bill Wambsganss, the Cleveland Indian second baseman in 1920. Those who have examined the boxscore have questioned the tactics of Uncle Wilbert Robinson, the Brooklyn manager whose strategies often were charitably called "unusual." It was the fifth inning, and Brooklyn, behind 7–0, had the first two runners on base. Play it safe? Not Uncle Robbie.

Despite being scoreless, the Dodgers had been hitting the Cleveland pitcher, Jim Bagby, hard. It was a game in which they made thirteen hits and scored a lone run. Bill Wambsganss, who told the story hundreds of times, explained that he chose to play very deep when Clarence Mitchell, a very good-hitting pitcher came to bat in the fifth inning. He didn't think a seven-run lead was too secure the way the Dodgers had been hitting.

When Mitchell cracked the ball on a line, the batters took off, not thinking that Wamby was where the ball was going. He was and ran over and doubled Kilduff off second and turned and found a dumbfounded Otto Miller standing in the baseline. He tagged him out and, as has been the case after every unassisted triple play, trotted off the field in silence. It always takes the crowd a minute or more to realize what has happened.

In the early years of baseball, outfielder Paul Hines of the Providence Grays, had been credited with making an unassisted triple play. Later-day research indicated Hines had made an unassisted double play but had thrown to a base for the third out. But according to the rules of 1878, Hines did indeed register an unassisted triple play.

In 1928, Providence sportswriter W. D. "Bill" Perrin—

who at that time had covered the Providence Grays for nearly half a century—described Hines' actions in the game played on May 8, 1878, in Providence. "The circumstances of this play have afforded more arguments than any other known play. That the play was made is not disputed, but whether Hines made the play unassisted or whether [second baseman Charles] Sweasy completed it by retiring the third man. . . . Here is what happened: [Jim] O'Rourke drew a base on balls and scored when Sweasy threw [Jack] Manning's drive over [Providence first baseman Tim] Murnane's head, Manning going to third on the error. Murnane muffed [Ezra] Sutton's fly, Manning holding third [as Sutton took second]. [Jack] Burdock was next up and dropped the ball just over [shortstop Tom] Carey's head for what looked like a safe hit. . . .

"The story in the *Providence Journal* of the next day thus describes the play: 'Manning and Sutton proceeded to the home plate,' meaning that both rounded third. 'Hines ran in and caught the ball, and kept going to tag third.' The rule then as now requires that when a base runner is forced to retrace his steps he must retouch the bases passed in reverse order. As Hines touched third with the ball in his hand, after making the catch, before either Manning or Sutton could get back, both were out automatically. It is true that Hines then on a signal from Sweasy threw the ball to second, but this was unnecessary as both runners were out at third."

To confirm Perrin's view, let's look at the playing rules for 1878, the year in which Hines made his celebrated play. Rule V, Section 1 reads: "Players running the bases must touch each base in regular order, viz., first, second, third, and home bases; and when obliged to return to bases they have occupied they must retouch them in reverse order. . . ." And Rule V, Section 15 reads: "Any base-runner failing to touch the base he runs for shall be declared out if the ball be held by a fielder, while touching said base, before the base-runner returns and touches it." Chadwick's gloss on the rule stated: ". . . it is only necessary for a fielder to hold the ball on the base, which should have been touched, in order to put the runner out."

Eureka! The controversy of over a century is thus resolved, and in favor of Paul Hines and his unassisted triple play. Rewrite the record books!

Johnny Neun had read in the morning paper of May 31, 1927, about Jimmy Cooney's unassisted triple play in the National League. As first baseman for the Detroit Tigers, known for his fielding and base stealing, Neun was alert to all possibilities when Homer Summa's line drive landed in his glove. Charlie Jamieson was a dead duck, caught off first and easily tagged for the second out. Shortstop Jackie Tavener was jumping up and down at second base calling for the ball. Slow-footed Glen Myatt was lumbering back from third base.

Neun waved his shortstop out of the way and raced toward second base, implausibly shouting, "I'm running into the Hall of Fame."

In a nice touch of journalistic enterprise, *Sports Illustrated,* in 1987, noted that both Jimmy Cooney and Johnny Neun were still alive and arranged for them to talk on the telephone about their unique plays made sixty years earlier. They had been contemporaries but had played in different leagues and had never met. When each had gone back to the minor leagues, they

played against each other in the International League but simply passed each other without fraternal comment, despite having shared such an extremely rare experience. They had a very nice talk, and months later, when Jimmy reached his anniversary a day ahead of Johnny, it was Neun who called to extend congratulations.

On July 30, 1968, Ron Hansen, playing shortstop for the Washington Senators, made an unassisted triple play, following the process all other shortstops have used. He grabbed a line drive off the bat of Joe Azcue, stepped on second to retire Dave Nelson, and tagged Russ Snyder coming from first. It was the first time the feat had been pulled since 1927, forty-one years earlier.

It was the most memorable event of Hansen's week, which was an unusual one in other ways as well. Following his play, he struck out six consecutive times, perhaps still stunned by the event. Then he regained his batting eye to hit a grand-slam home run. His unassisted triple play had been made on a road trip. He could expect applause when he came to bat the first time before hometown Washington fans when the team returned home. But he didn't get this. Instead, he was traded to the White Sox.

The first unassisted triple play of the twentieth century was made on July 19, 1909, by a Cleveland shortstop, Neal Ball. Overall Cleveland has been involved in five of the eleven unassisted triple plays in the major leagues. Three times the event has taken place there, twice executed by Cleveland players, and in all a Cleveland player has been involved somewhere five times. It all began with Neal Ball, who snagged a liner hit by Boston's Amby McConnell and retired Charley Wagner and Jake Stahl on the basepaths.

George Burns, playing for the Boston Red Sox between stints as a member of the Indians, turned the tables for Boston and made Cleveland the victim in 1923. He caught Frank Brower's liner, tagged Rube Lutzke off first, and ran to second to get Riggs Stephenson before he could return.

Burns made his play on September 14, and on October 6 another unassisted triple play occurred, making the feat which had been so rare appear almost commonplace, for a while. This time Ernie Padgett, a redheaded shortstop for the Boston Braves, turned the trick. Again the play was made in typical fashion—a line drive, a runner doubled off second base, and a surprised baserunner from first being tagged out.

Jimmy Cooney's claim on the last NL unassisted triple play ended late in the 1992 season. Rookie second baseman Mickey Morandini of the Philadelphia Phillies made a diving catch of a line drive off the bat of Pittsburgh's Jeff King. Morandini scrambled to second base to double off Andy Van Slyke. Then Barry Bonds, running from first base, bumbled into the surprised second baseman, who pushed him away with a climaxing third-out tag. Unaware of the rarity of his sudden feat, the rookie infielder rolled the ball toward the mound. The ball that was used to make the first play of its kind in the big leagues in twenty-four seasons was put into play the next inning.

In 1994 Boston's John Valentin replaced Ron Hansen as the last American Leaguer to perform the three-ply putout singlehandedly. On July 15 the Red Sox shortstop had an extraordinary day in an exceptionally well-played game. In the top of the sixth inning, after the Minnesota

Twins had put the first two runners on base, Valentin speared Marc Newfield's line drive with the runners moving. He stepped on second to erase Mike Blowers, then noticed Keith Mitchell was about to run past him. It appeared as if the shortstop felt he had done enough to make an unassisted double play and only tagged the runner just in case the inning wasn't really over. As Morandini had done, Valentin nonchalantly dropped the ball on the mound and trotted off the field. Unlike Morandini, whose ball had negligently been put back into play, Valentin retrieved the ball and took it home as a souvenir.

In 1968 Ron Hansen had struck out six straight times after his one-man triple play, but Valentin homered to lead off the bottom of the sixth. The game ended with three game-saving defensive plays. Scott Cooper made a diving stop at third, and Tim Naehring sprawled to dig his throw out of the dirt. Lee Tinsley then made a Game of the Week super catch, grabbing a low line drive in right center, and, finally Wes Chamberlain went to the bullpen fence, leaped high in the air, and came down with a home run ball in the webbing of his glove. Sox fans left Fenway wondering if they would ever see the home team make so many defensive gems in one game again. Not likely.

Unassisted Triple Plays

Player/Team	Date	Pos.	Opp.	Opp. Batter
Paul Hines, Prov.	May 8, 1878	OF	Bos.	Jack Burdock
Neal Ball, Cleve.	July 19, 1909	SS	Bos.	Amby McConnell
Bill Wambsganss, Cleve.	October 10, 1920	2B	Brook.	Clarence Mitchell
George Burns, Bos.	September 14, 1923	1B	Cleve.	Frank Brower
Ernie Padgett, Bos.	October 6, 1923	SS	Phila.	Walter Holke
Glenn Wright, Pitts.	May 7, 1925	SS	St.L.	Jim Bottomley
Jimmy Cooney, Chi.	May 30, 1927	SS	Pitts.	Paul Waner
Johnny Neun, Det.	May 31, 1927	1B	Cleve.	Homer Summa
Ron Hansen, Wash.	July 29, 1968	SS	Cleve.	Joe Azcue
Mickey Morandini, Phi.	September 23, 1992	2B	Pitt.	Jeff King
John Valentin, Bos.	July 15, 1994	SS	Minn.	Marc Newfield

The No-Hitters

What follows is the traditional honor roll of the 200-plus pitchers who have attained the no-hit heights. Also provided is a list of those handful of ugly-duckling no-hitters that didn't go nine innings, and those 36 games in which a pitcher retired 27 or more batters in succession. Concerning the last-named group, only 14 are officially recognized as perfect games—the rest were deprived of perfection by their fielding support, their stars, or like Dick Bosman, simply themselves. Pitchers whose no-hitters are no longer officially credited appear with an asterisk.

No-hit games, nine or more innings.

(Number to left is career total if greater than one)
(Home team is that of pitcher, unless team is in italics)

Joe Borden, Phi vs. Chi NA, 4-0; July 28, 1875.
George Bradley, StL vs. Har NL, 2-0; July 15, 1876.
Lee Richmond, Wor vs. Cle NL, 1-0; June 12, 1880 (perfect game).
John Ward, Pro vs. Buf NL, 5-0; June 17, 1880.
Larry Corcoran, Chi vs. Bos NL, 6-0; August 19, 1880.
Jim Galvin, Buf vs. *Wor* NL, 1-0; August 20, 1880.
Tony Mullane, Lou vs. *Cin* AA, 2-0; September 11, 1882.
Guy Hecker, Lou vs. *Pit* AA, 3-1; September 19, 1882

2   Larry Corcoran, Chi vs. Wor NL, 5-0; September 20, 1882
    Hoss Radbourn, Pro vs. Cle NL, 8-0; July 25, 1883
    Hugh (One Arm). Daily, Cle vs. *Phi* NL, 1-0; September 13, 1883.
    Al Atkisson, Phi vs. Pit AA, 10-1; May 24, 1884.
    Ed Morris, Col vs. *Pit* AA, 5-0; May 29, 1884.
    Frank Mountain, Col vs. *Was* AA, 12-0; June 5, 1884.
3   Larry Corcoran, Chi vs. Pro NL, 6-0; June 27, 1884.
2   Jim Galvin, Buf vs. *Det* NL, 18-0; August 4, 1884.
    Dick Burns, Cin vs. *KC* UA, 3-1; August 26, 1884.
    Ed Cushman, Mil vs. Was UA, 5-0; September 28, 1884.
    Sam Kimber, Bro vs. Tol AA, 0-0; October 4, 1884 (10 innings, tie).
    John Clarkson, Chi vs. *Pro* NL, 4-0; July 27, 1885.
    Charlie Ferguson, Phi vs. Pro NL, 1-0; August 29, 1885.
2   Al Atkisson, Phi vs. NY AA, 3-2; May 1, 1886.
    Adonis Terry, Bro vs. StL AA, 1-0; July 24, 1886.
    Matt Kilroy, Bal vs. *Pit* AA, 6-0; October 6, 1886.
2   Adonis Terry, Bro vs. Lou AA, 4-0; May 27, 1888.
    Henry Porter, KC vs. *Bal* AA, 4-0; June 6, 1888.
    Ed Seward, Phi vs. Cin AA, 12-2; July 26, 1888.
    Gus Weyhing, Phi vs. KC AA, 4-0; July 31, 1888.
*   Silver King, eight innings, Chi vs. Bro PL, 0-1; June 21, 1890.
    Cannonball Titcomb, Roch vs. Syr AA, 7-0; September 15, 1890.
    Tom Lovett, Bro vs. NY NL, 4-0; June 22, 1891.
    Amos Rusie, NY vs. Bro NL, 6-0; July 31, 1891.
    Ted Breitenstein, StL vs. Lou AA, 8-0; October 4, 1891 (1st game). (first start in the major leagues).
    Jack Stivetts, Bos vs. Bro NL, 11-0; August 6, 1892.
    Ben Sanders, Lou vs. Bal NL, 6-2; August 22, 1892.
    Bumpus Jones, Cin vs. Pit NL, 7-1; October 15, 1892. (first game in the major leagues).
    Bill Hawke, Bal vs. Was NL, 5-0; August 16, 1893.
    Cy Young, Cle vs. Cin NL, 6-0; September 18, 1897 (1st game).
2   Ted Breitenstein, Cin vs. Pit NL, 11-0; April 22, 1898.
    Jim Hughes, Bal vs. Bos NL, 8-0; April 22, 1898.
    Red Donahue, Phi vs. Bos NL, 5-0; July 8, 1898.
    Walter Thornton, Chi vs. Bro NL, 2-0; August 21, 1898 (2nd game).
    Deacon Phillippe, Lou vs. NY NL, 7-0; May 25, 1899.
    Noodles Hahn, Cin vs. Phi NL, 4-0; July 12, 1900.
*   Earl Moore, Cle vs. Chi AL, 2-4; May 9, 1901 (lost on two hits in 10th).
    Christy Mathewson, NY vs. *StL* NL, 5-0; July 15, 1901.
    Jim Callahan, Chi vs. Det AL, 3-0; September 20, 1902 (1st game).
    Chick Fraser, Phi vs. *Chi* NL, 10-0; September 18, 1903 (2nd game).
2   Cy Young, Bos vs. Phi AL, 3-0; May 5, 1904 (perfect game).
*   Bob Wicker, Chi vs. *NY* NL, 1-0; June 11, 1904. (won in 12 innings after allowing one hit in the 10th).
    Jesse Tannehill, Bos vs. *Chi* AL, 6-0; August 17, 1904.
2   Christy Mathewson, NY vs. *Chi* NL, 1-0; June 13, 1905.
    Weldon Henley, Phi vs. *StL* AL, 6-0; July 22, 1905 (1st game).
    Frank Smith, Chi vs. *Det* AL, 15-0; September 6, 1905 (2nd game).
    Bill Dinneen, Bos vs. Chi AL, 2-0; September 27, 1905 (1st game).
    Johnny Lush, Phi vs. *Bro* NL, 6-0; May 1, 1906.
    Mal Eason, Bro vs. *StL* NL, 2-0; July 20, 1906.
*   Harry McIntyre, Bro vs. Pit NL, 0-1; August 1, 1906. (lost on four hits in 13 innings after allowing first hit in 11th).
    Frank (Jeff). Pfeffer, Bos vs. Cin NL, 6-0; May 8, 1907.
    Nick Maddox, Pit vs. Bro NL, 2-1; September 20, 1907.
3   Cy Young, Bos vs. *NY* AL, 8-0; June 30, 1908.
    Hooks Wiltse, NY vs. Phi NL, 1-0; July 4, 1908 (first game, ten innings).
    Nap Rucker, Bro vs. Bos NL, 6-0; September 5, 1908 (2nd game).
    Dusty Rhoades, Cle vs. Bos AL, 2-1; September 18, 1908.
2   Frank Smith, Chi vs. Phi AL, 1-0; September 20, 1908.
    Addie Joss, Cle vs. *Chi AL*, 1-0; October 2, 1908 (perfect game).
*   Red Ames, NY vs. Bro NL, 0-3; April 15, 1909. (lost on seven hits in 13 innings after allowing first hit in 10th).
2   Addie Joss, Cle vs. Chi AL, 1-0; April 20, 1910.
    Chief Bender, Phi vs. Cle AL, 4-0; May 12, 1910.
*   Tom L. Hughes, NY vs. Cle AL, 0-5; August 30, 1910 (2nd game). (lost on seven hits in 11 innings after allowing first hit in 10th).
    Joe Wood, Bos vs StL AL, 5-0; July 29, 1911 (1st game).
    Ed Walsh, Chi vs. Bos AL, 5-0; August 27, 1911.
    George Mullin, Det vs. StL AL, 7-0; July 4, 1912 (2nd game).
    Earl Hamilton, StL vs. *Det* AL, 5-1; August 30, 1912.
    Jeff Tesreau, NY vs. *Phi* NL, 3-0; September 6, 1912 (1st game).
*   Jim Scott, Chi vs. *Was* AL, 0-1; May 14, 1914 (lost on 2 two hits in 10th).
    Joe Benz, Chi vs. Cle Al, 6-1; May 31, 1914.
    George Davis, Bos vs. Phi NL, 7-0; September 9, 1914 (2nd game).
    Ed Lafitte, Bro vs. KC FL, 6-2; September 19, 1914.
    Rube Marquard, NY vs. Bro NL, 2-0; April 15, 1915.
    Frank Allen, Pit vs. *StL* FL, 2-0; April 24, 1915
    Claude Hendrix, Chi vs. *Pit* FL, 10-0; May 15, 1915.
    Alex Main, KC vs *Buf* FL, 5-0; August 16, 1915.
    Jimmy Lavender, Chi vs. *NY* NL, 2-0; August 31, 1915 (1st game).
    Dave Davenport, StL vs. Chi FL, 3-0; September 7, 1915.
2   Tom L. Hughes, Bos vs. Pit NL, 2-0; June 16, 1916.
    Rube Foster, Bos vs. NY AL, 2-0; June 16, 1916.
    Joe Bush, Phi vs. Cle AL, 5-0; August 26, 1916.
    Hubert (Dutch) Leonard, Bos vs. StL AL, 4-0; August 30, 1916
    Eddie Cicotte, Chi vs. *StL* AL, 11-0; April 14, 1917.
    George Mogridge, NY vs. *Bos* AL, 2-1; April 24, 1917.
    Fred Toney, Cin vs. *Chi* NL, 1-0; May 2, 1917 (10 innings).
*   Hippo Vaughn, Chi vs. Cin NL, 0-1; May 2, 1917. (lost on two hits in 10th; Toney pitched a no-hitter in this game).
    Ernie Koob, StL vs. Chi AL, 1-0; May 5, 1917.

Bob Groom, StL vs. Chi AL, 3-0; May 6, 1917 (2nd game).
* Ernie Shore, Bos vs. Was AL, 4-0; June 23, 1917 (1st game). (perfect game). (Shore relieved Babe Ruth in the first inning after Ruth had been thrown out of the game for protesting a walk to the first batter. The runner was caught stealing and Shore retired the remaining 26 batters in order).
2 Hubert (Dutch). Leonard, Bos vs. Det AL, 5-0; June 3, 1918.
Hod Eller, Cin vs. StL NL, 6-0; May 11, 1919.
Ray Caldwell, Cle vs. NY AL, 3-0; September 10, 1919 (1st game).
Walter Johnson, Was vs. Bos AL, 1-0; July 1, 1920.
Charlie Robertson, Chi vs. Det AL, 2-0; April 30, 1922 (perfect game).
Jesse Barnes, NY vs. Phi NL, 6-0; May 7, 1922.
Sam Jones, NY vs. Phi AL, 2-0; September 4, 1923.
Howard Ehmke, Bos vs. Phi AL, 4-0; September 7, 1923.
Jesse Haines, StL vs Bos NL, 5-0; July 17, 1924.
Dazzy Vance, Bro vs. Phi NL, 10-1; September 13, 1925 (1st game).
Ted Lyons, Chi vs. Bos AL, 6-0; August 21, 1926.
Carl Hubbell, NY vs. Pit NL, 11-0; May 8, 1929.
Wes Ferrell, Cle vs. StL AL, 9-0; April 29, 1931.
Bobby Burke, Was vs. Bos AL, 5-0; August 8, 1931.
* Bobo Newsom, StL vs Bos AL, 1-2; September 18, 1934 (lost on one hit in 10th).
Paul Dean, StL vs. Bro NL, 3-0; September 21, 1934 (2nd game).
Vern Kennedy, Chi vs. Cle AL, 5-0; August 31, 1935.
Bill Dietrich, Chi vs. StL AL, 8-0; June 1, 1937.
Johnny Vander Meer, Cin vs. Bos NL, 3-0; June 11, 1938.
2 Johnny Vander Meer, Cin vs. Bro NL, 6-0; June 15, 1938 (next start after June 11).
Monte Pearson, NY vs. Cle AL, 13-0; August 27, 1938 (2nd game).
Bob Feller, Cle vs. Chi AL, 1-0; April 16, 1940 (opening day).
Tex Carleton, Bro vs. Cin NL, 3-0; April 30, 1940.
Lon Warneke, StL vs. Cin NL, 2-0; August 30, 1941.
Jim Tobin, Bos vs. Bro NL, 2-0; April 27, 1944.
Clyde Shoun, Cin vs. Bos NL, 1-0; May 15, 1944.
Dick Fowler, Phi vs. StL AL, 1-0; September 9, 1945 (2nd game).
Ed Head, Bro vs. Bos NL, 5-0; April 23, 1946.
2 Bob Feller, Cle vs. NY AL, 1-0; April 30, 1946.
Ewell Blackwell, Cin vs. Bos NL, 6-0; June 18, 1947.
Don Black, Cle vs. Phi AL, 3-0; July 10, 1947 (1st game).
Bill McCahan, Phi vs. Was AL, 3-0; September 3, 1947.
Bob Lemon, Cle vs. Det AL, 2-0; June 30, 1948.
Rex Barney, Bro vs. NY NL, 2-0; September 9, 1948.
Vern Bickford, Bos vs. Bro NL, 7-0; August 11, 1950.
Cliff Chambers, Pit vs. Bos NL, 3-0; May 6, 1951 (2nd game).
3 Bob Feller, Cle vs. Det AL, 2-1; July 1, 1951 (1st game).
Allie Reynolds, NY vs. Cle AL, 1-0; July 12, 1951.
2 Allie Reynolds, NY vs. Bos AL, 8-0; September 28, 1951 (1st game).
Virgil Trucks, Det vs. Was AL, 1-0; May 15, 1952.
Carl Erskine, Bro vs. Chi NL, 5-0; June 19, 1952.
2 Virgil Trucks, Det vs. NY AL, 1-0; August 25, 1952.
Bobo Holloman, StL vs. Phi AL, 6-0; May 6, 1953 (first start in the major leagues).
Jim Wilson, Mil vs. Phi NL, 2-0; June 12, 1954.
Sam Jones, Chi vs Pit NL, 4-0; May 12, 1955.
2 Carl Erskine, Bro vs. NY NL, 3-0; May 12, 1956.
* Johnny Klippstein (7 innings), Hershell Freeman (1 inning) and Joe Black (3 innings)., Cin vs. Mil NL, 1-2; May 26, 1956. (lost on three hits in 11 innings after allowing first hit in 10th).
Mel Parnell, Bos vs. Chi AL, 4-0; July 14, 1956.
Sal Maglie, Bro vs. Phi NL, 5-0; September 25, 1956.
Don Larsen, NY AL vs. Bro NL, 2-0; October 8, 1956. (World Series). (perfect game).
Bob Keegan, Chi vs. Was AL, 6-0; August 20, 1957 (2nd game).
Jim Bunning, Det vs. Bos AL, 3-0; July 20, 1958 (1st game).
Hoyt Wilhelm, Bal vs. NY AL, 1-0; September 20, 1958.
* Harvey Haddix, Pit vs. Mil NL, 0-1; May 26, 1959 (lost on one hit in 13 innings after pitching 12 perfect innings).
Don Cardwell, Chi vs. StL NL, 4-0; May 15, 1960 (2nd game).
Lew Burdette, Mil vs. Phi NL, 1-0; August 18, 1960.
Warren Spahn, Mil vs. Phi NL, 4-0; September 16, 1960.
2 Warren Spahn, Mil vs. SF NL, 1-0; April 28, 1961.
Bo Belinsky, LA vs. Bal AL, 2-0; May 5, 1962.
Earl Wilson, Bos vs. LA AL, 2-0; June 26, 1962.
Sandy Koufax, LA vs. NY NL, 5-0; June 30, 1962.
Bill Monbouquette, Bos vs. Chi AL, 1-0; August 1, 1962.
Jack Kralick, Min vs. KC AL, 1-0; August 26, 1962.
2 Sandy Koufax, LA vs. SF NL, 8-0; May 11, 1963.
Don Nottebart, Hou vs. Phi NL, 4-1; May 17, 1963.
Juan Marichal, SF vs. Hou NL, 1-0; June 15, 1963.
Ken T. Johnson, Hou vs. Cin NL, 0-1; April 23, 1964 (lost game).
3 Sandy Koufax, LA vs. Phi NL, 3-0; June 4, 1964.
2 Jim Bunning, Phi vs. NY NL, 6-0; June 21, 1964 (1st game; perfect game).
* Jim Maloney, Cin vs. NY NL, 0-1; June 14, 1965 (lost on two hits in 11 innings after pitching 10 hitless innings).
Jim Maloney, Cin vs. Chi NL, 1-0; August 19, 1965 (1st game; 10 innings).
4 Sandy Koufax, LA vs. Chi NL, 1-0; September 9, 1965 (perfect game).
Dave Morehead, Bos vs. Cle AL, 2-0; September 16, 1965.
Sonny Siebert, Cle vs. Was AL, 2-0; June 10, 1966.
Steve D. Barber (8⅔ innings). and Stu Miller (⅓ inning) Bal vs. Det AL, 1-2; April 30, 1967 (1st game; lost game).
Don Wilson, Hou vs. Atl NL, 2-0; June 18, 1967.
Dean Chance, Min vs. Cle AL, 2-1; August 25, 1967 (2nd game).
Joe Horlen, Chi vs. Det AL, 6-0; September 10, 1967 (1st game).

Tom Phoebus, Bal vs. Bos AL, 6-0; April 27, 1968.
Catfish Hunter, Oak vs. Min AL, 4-0; May 8, 1968 (perfect game).
George Culver, Cin vs. Phi NL, 6-1; July 29, 1968 (2nd game).
Gaylord Perry, SF vs. StL NL, 1-0; Sept. 17, 1968.
Ray Washburn, StL vs. SF NL, 2-0; September 18, 1968.
Bill Stoneman, Mon vs. Phi NL, 7-0; April 17, 1969.
3 Jim Maloney, Cin vs. Hou NL, 10-0; April 30, 1969.
2 Don Wilson, Hou vs. Cin NL, 4-0; May 1, 1969.
Jim Palmer, Bal vs. Oak AL, 8-0; August 13, 1969.
Ken Holtzman, Chi vs. Atl NL, 3-0; August 19, 1969.
Bob Moose, Pit vs. NY NL, 4-0; September 20, 1969.
Dock Ellis, Pit vs. SD NL, 2-0; June 12, 1970 (1st game).
Clyde Wright, Cal vs. Oak AL, 4-0; July 3, 1970.
Bill Singer, LA vs. Phi NL, 5-0; July 20, 1970.
Vida Blue, Oak vs. Min AL, 6-0; September 21, 1970.
2 Ken Holtzman, Chi vs. Cin NL, 1-0; June 3, 1971.
Rick Wise, Phi vs. Cin NL, 4-0; June 23, 1971.
Bob Gibson, StL vs. Pit NL, 11-0; August 14, 1971.
Burt Hooton, Chi vs. Phi NL, 4-0; April 16, 1972.
Milt Pappas, Chi vs. SD NL, 8-0; September 2, 1972.
2 Bill Stoneman, Mon vs. NY NL, 7-0; October 2, 1972 (1st game).
Steve Busby, KC vs. Det AL, 3-0; April 27, 1973.
Nolan Ryan, Cal vs. KC AL, 3-0; May 15, 1973.
2 Nolan Ryan, Cal vs. Det AL, 6-0; July 15, 1973.
Jim Bibby, Tex vs. Oak AL, 6-0; July 20, 1973.
Phil Niekro, Atl vs. SD NL, 9-0; August 5, 1973.
2 Steve Busby, KC vs. Mil AL, 2-0; June 19, 1974.
Dick Bosman, Cle vs. Oak AL, 4-0; July 19, 1974.
3 Nolan Ryan, Cal vs. Min AL, 4-0; September 28, 1974
4 Nolan Ryan, Cal vs. Bal AL, 1-0; June 1, 1975.
Ed Halicki, SF vs. NY NL, 6-0; August 24, 1975 (2nd game).
Vida Blue (5 innings), Glenn Abbott (1 inning), Paul Lindblad (1 inning), and Rollie Fingers (2 innings), Oak vs. Cal AL, 5-0; September 28, 1975.
Larry Dierker, Hou vs. Mon NL, 5-0; July 9, 1976.
Blue Moon Odom (5 innings) and Francisco Barrios (4 innings), Chi vs. Oak AL, 6-0; July 28, 1976.
John Candelaria, Pit vs. LA NL, 2-0; August 9, 1976.
John Montefusco, SF vs. Atl NL, 9-0; September 29, 1976.
Jim Colborn, KC vs. Tex AL, 6-0; May 14, 1977.
Dennis Eckersley, Cle vs. Cal AL, 1-0; May 30, 1977.
Bert Blyleven, Tex vs. Cal AL, 6-0; September 22, 1977.
Bob Forsch, StL vs. Phi NL, 5-0; April 16, 1978.
Tom Seaver, Cin vs. StL NL, 4-0; June 16, 1978.
Ken Forsch, Hou vs. Atl NL, 6-0; April 7, 1979.
Jerry Reuss, LA vs. SF NL, 8-0; June 27, 1980.
Charlie Lea, Mon vs. SF NL, 4-0; May 10, 1981 (2nd game).
Len Barker, Cle vs. Tor AL, 3-0; May 15, 1981 (perfect game).
5 Nolan Ryan, Hou vs. LA NL, 5-0; September 26, 1981.
Dave Righetti, NY vs. Bos AL, 4-0; July 4, 1983.
2 Bob Forsch, StL vs. Mon NL, 3-0; September 26, 1983.
Mike Warren, Oak vs. Chi AL, 3-0; September 29, 1983.
Jack Morris, Det vs. Chi AL, 4-0; April 7, 1984.
Mike Witt, Cal vs. Tex AL, 1-0; September 30, 1984 (perfect game).
Joe Cowley, Chi vs. Cal AL, 7-1; September 19, 1986.
Mike Scott, Hou vs. SF NL, 2-0; September 25, 1986.
Juan Nieves, Mil vs. Bal AL, 7-0; April 15, 1987.
Tom Browning, Cin vs. LA NL, 1-0; September 16, 1988 (perfect game).
Mark Langston (7 innings) and Mike Witt (2 innings), Cal vs Sea AL, 1-0; April 11, 1990.
Randy Johnson, Sea vs. Det AL, 2-0; June 2, 1990.
6 Nolan Ryan, Tex vs. Oak AL, 5-0; June 11, 1990.
Dave Stewart, Oak vs. Tor AL, 5-0; June 29, 1990.
Fernando Valenzuela, LA vs. StL NL, 6-0; June 29, 1990.
* Andy Hawkins, NY vs. Chi AL, 0-4; July 1, 1990 (8 innings, lost the game).
Terry Mulholland, Phi vs. SF NL, 6-0; August 15, 1990.
Dave Stieb, Tor vs. Det AL, 3-0; September 2, 1990.
7 Nolan Ryan, Tex vs. Tor AL, 3-0; May 1, 1991.
Tommy Greene, Phi vs. Mon NL, 2-0; May 23, 1991.
Bob Milacki, Bal (6 innings), Mike Flanagan (1 inning), Mark Williamson (1 inning), Gregg Olson (1 inning) vs. Oak AL, 2-0; July 13, 1991.
* Mark Gardner, Mon vs. LA NL, 0-1; July 26, 1991 (9 innings, lost game in 10th).
Dennis Martinez, Mon vs. LA NL, 2-0; July 28, 1991 (perfect game).
Wilson Alvarez, Chi vs. Bal AL, 7-0; August 11, 1991.
Bret Saberhagen, KC vs. Chi AL, 7-0; August 26, 1991.
Kent Mercker (6 innings), Mark Wohlers (2 innings), Alejandro Pena (1 inning), Atl vs. SD NL, 1-0; September 11, 1991.
* Matt Young, Bos vs. Cle AL, 1-2; April 12, 1992 (8 innings, lost game).
Kevin Gross, LA vs. SF NL, 2-0; August 17, 1992.
Chris Bosio, Sea vs. Bos AL, 7-0; April 22, 1993.
Jim Abbott, NY vs. Cle AL, 4-0; September 4, 1993.
Darryl Kile, Hou vs. NY NL, 7-1; September 8, 1993.
Kent Mercker, Atl vs. LA, NL, 6-0; April 8, 1994.
Scott Erickson, Minn vs. Mil AL, 6-0; April 27, 1994.
Kenny Rogers, Tex vs. Cal AL, 4-0; July 29, 1994 (perfect game).
* Pedro Martinez (9 innings) and Mel Rojas (1 inning), Mon. vs. S.D. NL; 1-0; June 3, 1995 (Martinez pitched 9 perfect innings, but allowed a hit in the tenth, Rojas relieved and finished the game).
Ramon Martinez, L.A. vs. Fla. NL, 7-0, July 14, 1995
Al Leiter, Fla. vs. Col. NL, 11-0; May 11, 1996
Dwight Gooden, NY vs. Sea. AL, 2-0; May 14, 1996
Hideo Nomo, L.A. vs. Col. NL, 9-0, September 17, 1996

No-hit games, fewer than nine innings

(Home team is that of pitcher, unless team is in italics)

* Larry McKeon, six innings, Ind vs. *Cin* AA, 0-0; May 6, 1884.
* Charlie Gagus, eight innings, Was vs. *Wil* UA, 12-1; August 21, 1884.
* Charlie Getzien, six innings, Det vs. Phi NL, 1-0; October 1, 1884.
* Charlie Sweeney (3 innings) and Henry Boyle (2 innings), five innings, StL vs. StP U.A., 0-1; October 5, 1884.
* Dupee Shaw, five innings, Pro vs. *Buf* NL, 4-0; October 7, 1885 (1st game).
* George Van Haltren, six innings, Chi vs. Pit NL, 1-0; June 21, 1888.
* Cannonball Crane, seven innings, NY vs. Was NL, 3-0; September 27, 1888.
* Matt Kilroy, seven innings, Bal vs. StL AA, 0-0; July 29, 1889 (2nd game).
* George Nicol, seven innings, StL vs. Phi AA, 21-2; September 23, 1890.
* Hank Gastright, eight innings, Col vs. Tol AA, 6-0; October 12, 1890.
* Jack Stivetts, five innings, Bos vs. *Was* NL, 6-0; October 15, 1892 (2nd game).
* Elton Chamberlain, seven innings, Cin vs. Bos NL, 6-0; September 23, 1893 (2nd game).
* Ed Stein, six innings, Bro vs. Chi NL, 6-0; June 2, 1894.
* Red Ames, five innings, NY vs. *StL* NL, 5-0; September 14, 1903 (2nd game).
* Rube Waddell, five innings, Phi vs. StL AL, 2-0; August 15, 1905.
* Jake Weimer, seven innings, Cin vs. Bro NL, 1-0; August 24, 1906 (2nd game).
* Jimmy Dygert (3 innings) and Rube Waddell (2 innings), five innings, Phi vs. Chi, AL, 4-3; August 29, 1906.

* Stoney McGlynn, seven innings, StL vs. *Bro* NL, 1-1; September 24, 1906 (2nd game).
* Lefty Leifield, six innings, Pit vs. *Phi* NL, 8-0; September 26, 1906, (2nd game).
* Ed Walsh, five innings, Chi vs. NY AL, 8-1; May 26, 1907.
* Ed Karger, seven perfect innings, StL vs. Bos NL, 4-0; August 11, 1907 (2nd game).
* Howie Camnitz, five innings, Pit vs. *NY* NL, 1-0; August 23, 1907 (2nd game).
* Rube Vickers, five perfect innings, Phi vs. *Was* AL, 4-0; October 5, 1907 (2nd game).
* Johnny Lush, six innings, StL vs. *Bro* NL, 2-0; August 6, 1908.
* King Cole, seven innings, Chi vs. *StL* NL, 4-0; July 31, 1910 (2nd game).
* Jay Cashion, six innings, Was vs. Cle AL, 2-0; August 20, 1910 (2nd game).
* Walter Johnson, seven innings, Was vs. StL Al, 2-0; August 25, 1910.
* Fred Frankhouse, seven and two-thirds innings, Bro vs. Cin NL, 5-0; August 27, 1937.
* John Whitehead, six innings, StL vs. Det AL, 4-0; August 5, 1940 (2nd game).
* Jim Tobin, five innings, Bos vs. Phi NL, 7-0; June 22, 1944 (2nd game).
* Mike McCormick, five innings, SF vs. *Phi* NL, 3-0; June 12, 1959.
* Sam Jones, seven innings, SF vs. *StL* NL, 4-0; September 26, 1959.
* Dean Chance, five perfect innings, Min vs. Bos AL, 2-0; August 6, 1967.
* Dave Palmer, five perfect innings, Mon vs. *StL* NL, 4-0; April 21, 1984 (2nd game).
* Pascual Perez, five innings, Mon vs. *Phi* NL, 1-0; September 24, 1988.
* Melido Perez, five innings, rain, Chi vs. NY AL, 8-0; July 12, 1990.

Perfection Plus

Year	Pitcher	Batters	Opponent	Notes
1959	Harvey Haddix	36	Milwaukee	(12 innings)
1919	Waite Hoyt	34	Yanks	(2nd-13th inning)
1880	Pud Galvin	33	Worcester	(6 errors)
1884	Charlie Buffinton	32	Providence	(5 errors)
1971	Rick Wise	32	Chicago	(2nd-12th inning)
1908	Nap Rucker	30	Braves	(3 errors)
1885	John Clarkson	29	Providence	(3 errors, 1 DP)
1883	Hoss Radbourn	28	Cleveland	(1 error)
1884	Pud Galvin	28	Detroit	(1 error)
1905	Christy Mathewson	28	Cubs	(2 errors, one DP)
1910	Tom Hughes	28	Cleveland	(1 error)
1919	Walter Johnson	28**	New York	
1920	Walter Johnson	28	Red Sox	(1 error)
1947	Bill McCahan	28	Washington	(1 error)
1974	Dick Bosman	28	Oakland	(1 error, his own)
1980	Jerry Reuss	28	San Francisco	(1 error)
1880	J. L. Richmond	27	Cleveland	
1880	J. M. Ward	27	Buffalo	
1904	Cy Young	27	Philadelphia	
1906	Lefty Leifield	27	Cubs	(8 innings, 3 errors)
1908	Addie Joss	27	White Sox	

Year	Pitcher	Batters	Opponent	Notes
1919	Walter Johnson	28**	New York	
1922	Charlie Robertson	27	Detroit	
1953	Curt Simmons	27*	Milwaukee	
1956	Don Larsen	27	Brooklyn	
1964	Jim Bunning	27	Mets	
1965	Sandy Koufax	27	Cubs	
1968	Catfish Hunter	27	Minnesota	
1981	Len Barker	27	Toronto	
1984	Mike Witt	27	Texas	
1988	Tom Browning	27	Los Angeles	
1991	Dennis Martinez	27	Los Angeles	
1994	Kenny Rogers	27	California	
1954	Robin Roberts	27*	Cincinnati	
1981	Jim Bibby	27*	Atlanta	
1990	Terry Mulholland	27	San Francisco	(1 error, 1 DP)
1995	Pedro J. Martinez	27	San Diego	
1917	Ernie Shore	26†	Washington	

*Retired last twenty-seven batters in a row after giving up a hit to leadoff man.
**Retired twenty-eight batters in a row after allowing a one-out single in the first inning, then allowed a two-out single in the tenth.
†Starter Babe Ruth walked the first man and promptly slugged the umpire in the jaw and was banished. Ernie Shore rushed in from the bull pen, got the runner on a steal attempt, and retired the next twenty-six.
Note: Hooks Wiltse in 1908 and Lew Burdette in 1960 missed perfection because each hit a batter, with Wiltse hitting the *last* batter—the opposing pitcher—with an 0-2 count.

## CHAPTER 11

Awards and Honors

Bill Deane

This chapter presents the history and voting results of baseball's most prestigious awards and honors, including the complete balloting and current constituency of the Baseball Hall of Fame. This material will be of interest to the fan who wonders how a player of the past was viewed by his contemporaries. I have ventured an additional section of "what if" awards: what if the Cy Young Award had been instituted long before its actual inception in 1956, or the Rookie of the Year before its real debut in 1947, and so on. What follows is divided into seven sections:

MVP Award: history and balloting.
Rookie of the Year Award: history and balloting.
Cy Young Award: history and balloting.
Hypothetical Awards: explanation and selections.
Gold Glove Award: history, discussion, and list of winners.
Special MVP Awards: All-Star Game, League Championship Series, World Series.
Hall of Fame: history of elections and balloting.

Balloting tables and lists of winners include each player's first initial, last name, and club city abbreviation (and point total, if applicable).

Most Valuable Player Award: History

The concept of most valuable player awards dates back more than a century. The first documented MVP-type honor in pro ball was bestowed upon James "Deacon" White of the 1875 Boston Red Stockings in the National Association. Catcher White sparked Boston to a remarkable 71–8 record that year, scoring 77 runs in 80 games and batting .355. An ardent Red Stockings' admirer presented Deacon with a silver tray, water pitcher, and loving cup inscribed with the words: WON BY JIM WHITE AS MOST VALUABLE PLAYER TO BOSTON TEAM, 1875.

The first official MVP honor was initiated some thirty-five years later. Prior to the 1910 season, baseball fan Hugh Chalmers, president and general manager of the Chalmers Motor Company, announced that he would present one of his company's automobiles—a Chalmers "30"—to the major league player who compiled the highest batting average. What appeared to be a harmless promotional gimmick was to soon turn into a public relations disaster.

The rules specified that players must accumulate a specific minimum number of times at bat, depending on position, to qualify for the award. For infielders and outfielders, it was a minimum of 350 at-bats; for catchers,

250 at-bats; and for pitchers, 100 at-bats. Interest in the award was tremendous from the outset. Ty Cobb, who already owned a Chalmers "30" roadster, wrote: "I am glad that something besides medals and trophies is offered for the championship in batting. I think the offer of a Chalmers "30" is simply great and I hope to be lucky enough to own a new Chalmers next fall."

It developed into a two-man race, with Detroit's Cobb and Cleveland's Napoleon Lajoie, both American Leaguers, the only serious challengers for the coveted prize. Throughout the season there were charges and counter-charges of favoritism by scorers in various cities. Furthermore, the general consensus of the press was that Cobb's selfish pursuit of this individual honor had cost his team the pennant. The controversy was capped by scandalous circumstances on the final day of the season.

Through games of September 16, Cobb held a solid lead over Lajoie, .368 to .357 (although, because of the era's sloppy record keeping, few actually knew the official figures at the time). From then through October 8, Cobb batted a torrid .532 (25 for 47) to seemingly lock up the crown with a .383 average. But Lajoie refused to surrender, going 30 for 54 (.556) in that same span to enter the final day, October 9, with a .376 mark. Cobb chose to sit out his final game, while Lajoie played the infamous doubleheader with the St. Louis Browns in which he went 8 for 8, including *seven bunt hits*—remarkable for a slow-footed slugger—to apparently edge out Cobb in the batting race. Browns' manager Jack O'Connor had instructed his rookie third baseman, Red Corriden, to play deep on Lajoie, advice with which Corriden complied. Lajoie took advantage of the strange defensive arrangement with the repeated safe bunts. Although neither Lajoie nor Corriden were implicated, there were charges of a Browns' frame-up to give the coveted batting title (and car) to the respected Lajoie over the disliked Cobb.

O'Connor lost his job due to his role in the alleged fix. Subsequently, AL President Ban Johnson announced that a "discrepancy" had been found in the official records, and that Cobb had actually won the batting crown after all (although this point is challenged by many current researchers, who have evidence that Cobb was credited wrongly for a 2 for 3 game). Meanwhile, Hugh Chalmers, attempting to divorce himself from the controversy, presented autos to both Cobb and Lajoie. It was generally acknowledged that this fiasco doomed the future of individual awards of any kind.

Hoping to salvage some goodwill out of the whole idea, Chalmers came up with a new proposal for the 1911 season. This time he would award an auto to one player in each league who "should prove himself as the most important and useful player to his club and to the league at large in point of deportment and value of services rendered." The decision for this honor was to be made by a committee of baseball writers, one writer from each club city in each league. Each writer was to make eight selections, with a first-place ballot scoring eight points, on down to an eighth-place vote counting one point. Thus was born the short-lived Chalmers Award, with Ty Cobb and Frank Schulte earning recognition in 1911. Both Cobb and Schulte voluntarily withdrew from the competition in 1912, although the former received seventeen points anyway.

Interest in the award diminished within a few years. By 1914 the public was distracted by baseball's battles with the new Federal League and the escalation of the World War in Europe. The timing was right for the Chalmers Award to quietly disappear; it was noted that Mr. Chalmers had agreed to present vehicles for five years and that the 1914 awards marked the fifth presentations.

On July 15, 1922, the newly formed American League Trophy Committee adopted a set of rules governing the selection of an annual award-winner. The rules specified that "the purpose of the American League Trophy is to honor the baseball player who is of greatest all-round service to his club and credit to the sport during each season; to recognize and reward uncommon skill and ability when exercised by a player for the best interests of his team, and to perpetuate his memory." The rules further instructed voters to seek out the "winning ball player," reminding them that "combined offensive and defensive ability is not always indicated by any system of records."

Eight baseball writers, one from each AL city, were enfranchised, with each required to select exactly one player from each team, for a total of eight selections. Player-managers and previous winners were to be excluded from consideration. Points were distributed the same as in the Chalmers Award: eight for first place, down to one for eighth.

The intention of AL President Ban Johnson was to have a monument to baseball erected in East Potomac Park, Washington, D.C., engraved with the names of winners of the AL Award. This proposal was introduced as a congressional resolution in 1924, and passed in the House of Representatives before dying on the Senate Floor.

The AL voting rules led to growing criticism for several reasons, one of which was the limitation on the number of vote-getters from each team. For example, when the Browns' George Sisler won the first AL Award in 1922, he was named on all eight ballots—thus disqualifying his teammates from receiving any votes. As a result, fellow Brownie Ken Williams, who led the league in home runs (39), RBI (155), and total bases (367) and became the first player ever to have 30 homers and 30 stolen bases in the same season, was shut out in the League Award voting.

Secondly, the rule prohibiting player-managers from eligibility drew fire. In 1925, when this rule eliminated five solid candidates from consideration, *The New York Times* wrote, "to say that it is impossible or impractical to divorce a man's managerial skill from his talents purely as a player is to reflect on the intelligence of the committee that awards the prize."

The *Times* further editorialized on the fallacy of assuming that no player can be the "most valuable" more than one year: "the purpose, of course, is to pass the honor around, but the effect is to pass an empty honor around." This rule became increasingly ridiculous when it eliminated Babe Ruth (and his 60 home runs) from consideration in 1927; by the following year, both Ruth and teammate Lou Gehrig, who were in the process of finishing one-two in the AL home run derby in five consecutive seasons, were ineligible for the League Award.

In 1924 the National League instituted its own award, with radical differences in the selection method: each writer voted for ten players rather than eight (ten points for first place, and so on); he was not bound to vote for a certain number of players from each team; he was free to select a player-manager; and, later, he was allowed to consider previous winners of the award. Additionally, the NL offered a cash "present" of $1,000 to the award-winner.

At various times between 1925–51, writers were permitted to name "honorable mention" candidates, whose vote totals were listed but not counted in the balloting. Another feature of early voting reports was the listing of "cumulative vote leaders"—a forerunner to Bill James's "award shares"—over a period of years.

A number of factors led to the demise of the AL Award, including the award's loss of credibility due to the previously mentioned shortsighted voting rules. Secondly, Ban Johnson, having failed to secure the erection of his proposed monument, felt the award had fallen short of its aim. Finally, management was concerned with the efforts of award-winners to parlay their honors into substantial pay raises. The AL Award was officially voted out at a special league meeting on May 6, 1929.

The National League followed suit with the AL's decision, but agreed to continue its award through the 1929 season.

In October 1929, the Baseball Writers' Association of America (BBWAA) announced the results of an "unofficial" AL most valuable player poll, whose winner was Lew Fonseca of Cleveland. Two months later, *The Sporting News* (TSN) conducted a poll of the eight writers who had previously voted on the League Award, thereby reporting Al Simmons as the "unofficial" AL Award-winner. Combining the results of these two unofficial polls gives Fonseca 77 points, followed by Heinie Manush (57), Simmons (56), Tony Lazzeri (55) and Charlie Gehringer (44).

The Sporting News announced that, thereafter, they would take it upon themselves to conduct an annual poll to substitute for the defunct league awards. However, they retained the stipulation that each voter must select just one player on each team. In 1930, TSN chose Joe Cronin in the AL and Bill Terry in the NL. Earlier, the Associated Press also had a special committee of writers make an unofficial AL selection for 1930, while the BBWAA did the same for the NL (adding a check for $1,000 for the winner). The respective selections here were Cronin in the AL and Hack Wilson in the NL. Again combining the two sets of polls, the AL leaders were Cronin (100), Al Simmons (85), Lou Gehrig (68), Charlie Gehringer (67), and Ted Lyons (56). The NL pace-setters were Hack Wilson (111), Frankie Frisch (107), Bill Terry (105), Chuck Klein (57), and Floyd "Babe" Herman (52).

In an effort to standardize MVP voting, the BBWAA, in its annual winter meeting in New York on December 11, 1930, decided to appoint two committees (one in each league) to elect most valuable players, with the association to "award suitable emblems to the players selected." Thus was born what is considered the modern MVP Award, with most of the flaws of its forerunners eliminated.

TSN, however, continued to make its own selections in bitter competition with the BBWAA. Finally, beginning in 1938, TSN agreed to unify the award by abiding with BBWAA balloting, and presenting *The Sporting News* Trophy to the winner. Among the various prizes awarded to the winners were wristwatches and shotguns.

At a meeting during the 1944 World Series, the BBWAA decided to begin issuing its own trophy, the Kenesaw Mountain Landis Award, in honor of the ailing commissioner. Landis died a month later and the official MVP Award has born his name ever since. A plaque engraved with the names of the winners hangs in the National Baseball Library in Cooperstown, New York.

The Sporting News went back to naming its own MVPs in 1944 and '45. Then, at the request of the new commissioner, Happy Chandler, TSN "withdrew from the field to cooperate in making the Landis Awards, provided by the major leagues, the official designations of the year." In 1948, however, TSN went back to its own awards, selecting a Player of the Year and Pitcher of the Year in each league, as they have done ever since. For some reason, TSN awards have never received the public recognition that the BBWAA honors have.

Two major changes in the MVP voting began in 1938. The BBWAA began polling three writers in each major league city, rather than just one, which remained in effect until it was reduced to two writers per city, starting in 1961. Also in 1938, the process was initiated to award fourteen points for each first-place vote, rather than ten.

"Split votes," which have since infiltrated all the major awards, first appeared in MVP Awards in 1959. The American League MVP race that year, by consensus, was between second baseman Nellie Fox and shortstop Luis Aparicio of the champion Chicago White Sox. Late in the season, the suggestion often arose that the two ought to share the award. When the votes were in, Fox had received fourteen first-place votes, Aparicio had gotten six, and four writers had split their votes between the two. Tickled with the idea of a split vote, one NL writer also resorted to this option, dividing his first-place nomination between Ernie Banks and Ed Mathews. The cop-out vote, having been allowed in '59, has since surfaced in sixteen more MVP Awards, ten Rookie of the Year, and six Cy Young Award elections. The ultimate folly of this practice was best exemplified in 1979. One NL writer split his fourth-place vote between pitching brothers Phil and Joe Niekro, evidently convinced that the two were identical twins. But the writer was still permitted to make six more selections.

That meant that his fifth-, sixth-, and seventh-place selections received more points (six, five and four, respectively) than his fourth-place co-selections, who were credited with just three and a half points apiece!

There has long been debate about the consideration of pitchers for the MVP Award, the theory (by some) that a man who plays every fourth or fifth game cannot be as valuable as a man who plays every day. The debate escalated after the inception of the Cy Young Award in 1956, giving pitchers their own exclusive honor, and the increasing practice of five-man rotations in the 1970s, giving starting pitchers even less of a chance to contribute. As far as Jack Lang, executive secretary of the BBWAA, is concerned, there is no room for controversy. "The rules that are sent out to the voters on the [MVP] committee state: 'Keep in mind that all players are eligible. That includes pitchers, starters and relievers,' " says Lang. "Anybody on the committee that feels they cannot vote for a pitcher, we replace them. In my twenty-four years running the elections, only two writers have said that to me." Since 1931, pitchers have won the award ten times in the AL and nine times in the NL.

There have been fifteen occasions in which one player received all of the available first-place MVP votes in his league. The AL players so honored are Ty Cobb (1911), Babe Ruth (1923), Hank Greenberg (1935), Al Rosen (1953), Mickey Mantle (1956), Frank Robinson (1966), Denny McLain (1968), Reggie Jackson (1973), Jose Canseco (1988), and Frank Thomas (1993). The five unanimous NL selections are Carl Hubbell (1936), Orlando Cepeda (1967), Mike Schmidt (1980), Jeff Bagwell (1994) and Ken Caminiti (1996). Hubbell's distinction is disputable, as two of the eight writers did not submit ballots that year and were not replaced on the selection committee.

Following are the maximum possible point totals that could have been earned by an individual receiving the first-place nomination of every writer polled:

National League		American League	
1911–14	64	1911–14	64
1924–29	80	1922–28	64
1931–37	80	1931–37	80
1938–60	336	1938–60	336
1961	224	1961–68	280
1962–68	280	1969–76	336
1969–1992	336	1977–present	392
1993–present	392		

There have been numerous cases in which the MVP vote point totals did not add up to the correct figure. Reasons for this include inaccuracies in tabulation, inaccuracies in reporting, and writers who failed to vote or to complete their ballots. However, the total impact of all these errors is a small fraction of 1 percent of the total voting over the years.

Following is a complete tabulation of all the recognized MVP elections since 1911:

MVP Award
Chalmers Award, 1911–14

1911 NATIONAL

F. Schulte, CHI	29
C. Mathewson, NY	25
L. Doyle, NY	23
H. Wagner, PIT	23
G. Alexander, PHI	23
M. Huggins, SL	21
F. Merkle, NY	19
R. Marquard, NY	19
J. Daubert, BRO	16
J. Tinker, CHI	11
C. Meyers, NY	11
J. Sheckard, CHI	9
M. Mitchell, CIN	9
M. Doolan, PHI	6
B. Harmon, SL	6
J. Archer, CHI	5
H. Lobert, PHI	4
G. Gibson, PIT	4
M. Brown, CHI	4
B. Bescher, CIN	4
B. Sweeney, BOS	3
O. Knabe, PHI	2
E. Konetchy, SL	2
D. Hoblitzell, CIN	2
J. Walsh, PHI	2
J. Devore, NY	2
F. Luderus, PHI	1
J. Kling, BOS	1
B. Adams, PIT	1
N. Rucker, BRO	1

1911 AMERICAN

T. Cobb, DET	64
E. Walsh, CHI	35
E. Collins, PHI	32

J. Jackson, CLE 28
W. Johnson, WAS ... 19
B. Cree, NY 16
T. Speaker, BOS ... 16
I. Thomas, PHI 12
C. Milan, WAS 10
V. Gregg, CLE 9
F. Baker, PHI 8
J. Coombs, PHI 6
N. Lajoie, CLE 5
J. Knight, NY 4
S. Crawford, DET ... 4
B. Lord, PHI 4
D. Bush, DET 4
R. Ford, NY 3
J. Barry, PHI 3
J. Austin, SL 2
F. LaPorte, SL 2
S. McInnis, PHI 1
G. McBride, WAS 1

1912 NATIONAL
L. Doyle, NY 48
H. Wagner, PIT 43
C. Meyers, NY 25
J. Tinker, CHI 22
B. Bescher, CIN 17
B. Sweeney, BOS ... 16
H. Zimmerman, CHI . 16
R. Marquard, NY 13
O. Wilson, PIT 13

J. Daubert, BRO 13
O. Knabe, PHI 10
E. Konetchy, SL 8
C. Mathewson, NY .. 8
D. Paskert, PHI 6
J. Tesreau, NY 6
R. Murray, NY 5
M. Huggins, SL 5
A. Marsans, CIN 4
F. Merkle, NY 4
J. Evers, CHI 2
C. Hendrix, PIT 2
J. Archer, CHI 1
G. Alexander, PHI ... 1

1912 AMERICAN
T. Speaker, BOS 59
E. Walsh, CHI 30
W. Johnson, WAS ... 28
C. Milan, WAS 23
J. Wood, BOS 22
E. Collins, PHI 18
F. Baker, PHI 17
T. Cobb, DET 17
J. Jackson, CLE 16
H. Wagner, BOS 12
C. Gandil, WAS 7
B. Shotton, SL 6
D. Pratt, SL 5
E. Foster, WAS 4
L. Gardner, BOS 4

S. Crawford, DET 4
J. Barry, PHI 4
B. Carrigan, BOS 4
G. Moriarty, DET 3
J. Birmingham, CLE .. 2
D. Moeller, WAS 1
G. McBride, WAS 1
S. McInnis, PHI 1
B. Daniels, NY 1

1913 NATIONAL
J. Daubert, BRO 50
C. Cravath, PHI 40
R. Maranville, BOS... 23
C. Mathewson, NY... 21
C. Meyers, NY 20
V. Saier, CHI 15
L. Cheney, CHI 12
D. Miller, PIT 11
H. Wagner, PIT 11
J. Evers, CHI 10
T. Seaton, PHI 9
A. Fletcher, NY 7
J. Archer, CHI 6
M. Doolan, PHI 6
B. Sweeney, BOS ... 6
J. Viox, PIT 6
L. Doyle, NY 5
T. Shafer, NY 5
R. Murray, NY 4

H. Zimmerman, CHI .. 4
O. Knabe, PHI 4
B. Adams, PIT 3
C. Cutshaw, BRO.... 3
G. Burns, NY 2
A. Marsans, CIN 2
B. Humphries, CHI... 2
M. Brown, CIN 1

1913 AMERICAN
W. Johnson, WAS ... 54
J. Jackson, CLE 43
E. Collins, PHI 30
T. Speaker, BOS 26
F. Baker, PHI 21
C. Gandil, WAS 14
S. McInnis, PHI 12
W. Schang, PHI..... 11
C. Milan, WAS 8
J. Barry, PHI 8
N. Lajoie, CLE 7
D. Bush, DET 6
H. Wagner, BOS 6
R. Russell, CHI 5
B. Shotton, SL 5
G. McBride, WAS ... 5
J. Scott, CHI 5
G. Stovall, SL 5
S. Crawford, DET ... 5
T. Cobb, DET 3

R. Schalk, CHI 3
C. Bender, PHI 2
T. Turner, CLE 2
S. O'Neill, CLE 1
H. Hooper, BOS 1

1914 NATIONAL
J. Evers, BOS 50
R. Maranville, BOS... 44
B. James, BOS 33
G. Burns, NY 31
J. Miller, SL 18
J. Tesreau, NY 15
D. Rudolph, BOS ... 14
S. Magee, PHI 14
Z. Wheat, BRO 10
G. Alexander, PHI ... 9
R. Bresnahan, CHI .. 6
L. Magee, SL 5
B. Doak, SL 5
J. Viox, PIT 5
A. Fletcher, NY 4
C. Mathewson, NY .. 4
V. Saier, CHI 4
B. Schmidt, BOS ... 4
J. Daubert, BRO 4
L. McCarty, BRO ... 3
H. Groh, CIN 2
T. Clarke, CIN 1
G. Cravath, PHI 1

1914 AMERICAN
E. Collins, PHI 63
S. Crawford, DET ... 35
D. Bush, DET 17
F. Baker, PHI 17
J. Jackson, CLE 15
R. Schalk, CHI 13
E. Foster, WAS 11
B. Weaver, CHI 11
S. McInnis, PHI 11
D. Pratt, SL 10
W. Schang, PHI 10
T. Speaker, BOS.... 9
T. Walker, SL 9
T. Cobb, DET 7
E. Scott, BOS 7
J. Barry, PHI 6
D. Leonard, BOS ... 6
E. Plank, PHI 5
G. McBride, WAS ... 5
D. Lewis, BOS 4
H. Hooper, BOS ... 4
F. Maisel, NY 3
R. Peckinpaugh, NY . 2
C. Milan, WAS 2
S. Agnew, SL 2
R. Hartzell, NY 2
E. Cicotte, CHI 1
G. Moriarty, DET 1

(No official awards, 1915–21)

MVP Award
League Awards, 1922–29

1922 AMERICAN
G. Sisler, SL 59
E. Rommel, PHI..... 31
R. Schalk, CHI 26
L. Bush, NY 19
E. Collins, CHI 18
J. Bassler, DET 13
S. O'Neill, CLE 13
J. Judge, WAS...... 12

W. Pipp, NY 12
L. Blue, DET 11
G. Galloway, PHI 10
H. Heilmann, DET... 8
D. Pratt, BOS 7
W. Schang, NY 7
B. Meusel, NY 6
E. Scott, NY 6
W. Johnson, WAS ... 5

U. Shocker, SL 5
C. Jamieson, CLE ... 4
J. Sewell, CLE 4
G. Burns, BOS..... 2
J. Dykes, PHI 2
B. Harris, WAS 2
R. Peckinpaugh, WAS 2
B. Wambsganss, CLE 2
G. Cutshaw, DET ... 1

C. Perkins, PHI 1

1923 AMERICAN
B. Ruth, NY 64
E. Collins, CHI 37
H. Heilmann, DET... 31
W. Gerber, SL 20
J. Sewell, CLE 20
C. Jamieson, CLE ... 19

J. Bassler, DET 17
C. Galloway, PHI 13
G. Uhle, CLE 13
G. Burns, BOS..... 8
H. Ehmke, BOS.... 7
M. Ruel, WAS 7
R. Peckinpaugh, WAS 6
U. Shocker, SL 5

J. Judge, WAS........ 4
M. McManus, SL 4
K. Williams, SL 4
J. Harris, BOS 3
B. Harris, WAS 3
J. Hauser, PHI 1
W. Johnson, WAS ... 1
C. Perkins, PHI 1

(No National League awards, 1922–23)

1924 NATIONAL
D. Vance, BRO 74
R. Hornsby, SL 62
F. Frisch, NY 40
Z. Wheat, BRO 40
R. Youngs, NY 35
G. Kelly, NY 34
R. Maranville, PIT .. 33
K. Cuyler, PIT 25
J. Fournier, BRO..... 21
E. Roush, CIN 12
G. Wright, PIT 10
A. High, BRO 9
B. Pinelli, CIN 7
R. Bressler, CIN ... 5
G. Hartnett, CHI ... 5
B. Grimes, BRO ... 5
J. Bottomley, SL.... 4
J. Johnston, BRO ... 3
M. Carey, PIT 3
T. Jackson, NY 3
E. Yde, PIT 2
C. Williams, PHI ... 1
E. Rixey, CIN 1
G. Alexander, CHI .. 1
H. DeBerry, BRO ... 1

1924 AMERICAN
W. Johnson, WAS ... 55
E. Collins, CHI 49
C. Jamieson, CLE ... 25
H. Pennock, NY ... 24
J. Bassler, DET 22
H. Severeid, SL 13
J. Hauser, PHI 13
W. Jacobson, SL ... 11
H. Heilmann, DET... 9
J. Sewell, CLE 9
M. Ruel, WAS 7
W. Schang, NY 7
A. Simmons, PHI ... 7
W. Pipp, NY 6
H. Ehmke, BOS.... 5
I. Flagstead, BOS ... 5

W. Gerber, SL 4
E. Whitehill, DET 4
L. Blue, DET 3
I. Boone, BOS 2
J. Harris, BOS 2
C. Galloway, PHI ... 1
K. Williams, SL 1

1925 NATIONAL
R. Hornsby, SL 73
K. Cuyler, PIT...... 61
G. Kelly, NY 52
G. Wright, PIT 43
D. Vance, BRO 42
D. Bancroft, BOS .. 41
J. Bottomley, SL ... 28
P. Traynor, PIT 27
F. Frisch, NY 13
E. Roush, CIN 12
M. Carey, PIT 11
I. Meusel, NY 6
D. Luque, CIN 5
C. Grimm, CHI 5
Z. Wheat, BRO ... 4
P. Donohue, CIN ... 4
B. Hargrave, CIN .. 4
G. Harper, PHI 3
J. Sand, PHI 3
W. Gautreau, BOS .. 2
V. Aldridge, PIT 1

1925 AMERICAN
R. Peckinpaugh,
WAS 45
A. Simmons, PHI ... 41
J. Sewell, CLE 21
H. Heilmann, DET... 20
H. Rice, SL 18
E. Sheely, CHI 17
I. Flagstead, BOS ... 10
W. Jacobson, SL ... 10
J. Mostil, CHI 10
O. Bluege, WAS ... 8
M. Cochrane, PHI .. 8

L. Blue, DET 7
S. Coveleski, WAS... 7
W. Kamm, CHI 7
E. Rommel, PHI..... 7
R. Schalk, CHI 7
A. Wingo, DET 7
E. Combs, NY 6
B. Meusel, NY 6
T. Lyons, CHI 5
G. Burns, CLE 4
M. McManus, SL ... 4
H. Pennock, NY ... 4
B. Bengough, NY ... 2
H. Ehmke, BOS.... 2
L. Gehrig, NY 2
I. Boone, BOS 1
J. Dugan, NY 1
P. Todt, BOS 1

1926 NATIONAL
B. O'Farrell, SL 79
H. Critz, CIN 60
R. Kremer, PIT 32
T. Thevenow, SL ... 30
H. Wilson, CHI 25
L. Bell, SL 24
B. Hargrave, CIN .. 23
P. Rhem, SL 20
F. Lindstrom, NY ... 17
D. Bancroft, BOS .. 17
H. Carlson, PHI ... 16
P. Waner, PIT 15
P. Traynor, PIT 14
W. Pipp, CIN 10
E. Brown, BOS ... 10
F. Herman, BRO ... 8
R. Root, CHI 8
R. Hornsby, SL ... 7
J. Butler, BRO 5
B. Southworth, NY-SL 5
G. Alexander, CHI-SL 5
C. Mays, CIN 4
G. Kelly, NY 2
C. Walker, CIN 1

1926 AMERICAN
G. Burns, CLE 63
J. Mostil, CHI 33
H. Pennock, NY ... 32
S. Rice, WAS 18
H. Heilmann, DET... 16
H. Manush, DET ... 16
A. Simmons, PHI ... 16
L. Grove, PHI 12
G. Goslin, WAS ... 9
L. Gehrig, NY 7
T. Lazzeri, NY 7
B. Falk, CHI 6
F. Fothergill, DET ... 6
O. Melillo, SL 6
H. Rice, SL 6
O. Bluege, WAS ... 5
P. Todt, BOS 5
M. Cochrane, PHI .. 4
J. Judge, WAS 4
M. McManus, SL ... 4
B. Meusel, NY 3
E. Rigney, BOS ... 3
I. Flagstead, BOS ... 2
W. Gerber, SL 2
T. Zachary, SL 2
W. Jacobson, SL-BOS 1

1927 NATIONAL
P. Waner, PIT 72
F. Frisch, NY 66
R. Hornsby, NY ... 54
C. Root, CHI 46
T. Jackson, NY ... 42
L. Waner, PIT 25
P. Traynor, PIT 18
J. Haines, SL 16
R. Kremer, PIT 14
G. Hartnett, CHI ... 12
R. Lucas, CIN 10
H. Wilson, CHI 9
B. Terry, NY 6
J. Bottomley, SL ... 6
B. Hargrave, CIN .. 6

F. May, CIN 6
C. Williams, PHI 6
E. Farrell, NY-BOS... 4
B. Grimes, NY 4
M. Carey, BRO ... 3
R. Stephenson, CHI . 3
G. Alexander, SL ... 3
C. Hill, PIT 2
J. Petty, BRO 2
F. Ulrich, PHI 2
C. Hafey, SL 1

1927 AMERICAN
L. Gehrig, NY 56
H. Heilmann, DET... 35
T. Lyons, CHI 34
M. Cochrane, PHI .. 18
A. Simmons, PHI ... 18
G. Goslin, WAS ... 15
M. Ruel, WAS 15
J. Dykes, PHI 14
L. Sewell, CLE 13
J. Sewell, CLE 9
T. Lazzeri, NY 8
R. Reeves, WAS .. 7
F. O'Rourke, SL ... 6
J. Tavener, DET ... 6
H. Lisenbee, WAS .. 5
E. Miller, SL 5
A. Metzler, CHI ... 4
I. Flagstead, BOS .. 3
C. Jamieson, CLE .. 3
W. Schang, SL 3
F. Schulte, SL 3
W. Hudlin, CLE ... 2
W. Regan, BOS ... 2
J. Rothrock, BOS .. 2
B. Harriss, BOS ... 1
P. Todt, BOS 1

1928 NATIONAL
J. Bottomley, SL 76
F. Lindstrom, NY ... 70
B. Grimes, PIT 53

L. Benton, NY 37
H. Critz, CIN 37
P. Traynor, PIT 28
H. Wilson, CHI 21
S. Hogan, NY 17
T. Jackson, NY ... 16
R. Maranville, SL .. 14
D. Vance, BRO ... 13
C. Hafey, SL 11
R. Hornsby, BOS .. 10
G. Hartnett, CHI ... 6
P. Waner, PIT 5
L. Richbourg, BOS... 5
T. Douthit, SL 5
D. Bissonette, BRO . 3
D. Flowers, BRO ... 3
J. Wilson, PHI-SL .. 3
A. Whitney, PHI ... 3
H. Ford, CIN 2
L. Thompson, PHI .. 1

1928 AMERICAN
M. Cochrane, PHI ... 53
H. Manush, SL 51
J. Judge, WAS..... 27
T. Lazzeri, NY...... 27
W. Kamm, CHI 15
G. Goslin, WAS ... 13
E. Combs, NY 13
C. Gehringer, DET .. 12
C. Myer, BOS..... 11
W. Hoyt, NY 8
J. Foxx, PHI 7
J. Sewell, CLE 6
L. Sewell, CLE 6
I. Flagstead, BOS .. 5
E. Morris, BOS ... 4
H. Heilmann, DET .. 4
C. Lind, CLE 4
W. Cissell, CHI ... 4
A. Thomas, CHI.... 4
O. Carroll, DET ... 3
H. Rice, DET 3
L. Fonseca, CLE.... 2

T. Lyons, CHI 2
J. Hodapp, CLE 2
A. Metzler, CHI 1
W. Regan, BOS 1

1929 NATIONAL
R. Hornsby, CHI 60
L. O'Doul, PHI 54
B. Terry, NY 48
B. Grimes, PIT 35

L. Waner, PIT 30
R. Lucas, CIN 29
P. Traynor, PIT 27
H. Wilson, CHI 24
F. Herman, BRO 24

G. Bush, CHI 16
M. Ott, NY 15
C. Klein, PHI 15
T. Douthit, SL 14
C. Grimm, CHI 13

T. Jackson, NY 8
R. Maranville, BOS ... 8
H. Critz, CIN 5
B. Friberg, PHI 4
P. Malone, CHI 3

F. Frisch, SL 2
P. Whitney, PHI 2
J. Frederick, BRO 2
R. Stephenson, CHI ... 1
Z. Taylor, BOS-CHI ... 1

(There were no official selections for the American League in 1929 or for either league in 1930.)

MVP Award
Baseball Writers' Association of America Awards, 1931–Present

1931 NATIONAL
F. Frisch, SL 65
C. Klein, PHI 55
B. Terry, NY 53
W. English, CHI 30
C. Hafey, SL 29
J. Wilson, SL 28
T. Jackson, NY 24
C. Grimm, CHI 21
E. Adams, SL 18
E. Brandt, BOS 15
R. Maranville, BOS .. 15
K. Cuyler, CHI 14
P. Traynor, PIT 12
R. Lucas, CIN 10
L. Waner, PIT 8
J. Bottomley, SL 8
J. Elliott, PHI 6
J. Quinn, BRO 6
N. Finn, BRO 6
W. Clark, BRO 3
P. Derringer, SL 3
C. Root, CHI 3
D. Bartell, PHI 2
J. Vergez, NY 2
F. Fitzsimmons, NY ... 1
L. O'Doul, BRO 1
G. Wright, BRO 1
T. Cuccinello, CIN 1
C. Gelbert, SL 1

1931 AMERICAN
L. Grove, PHI 78
L. Gehrig, NY 59
A. Simmons, PHI ... 51
E. Averill, CLE 43
B. Ruth, NY 40
E. Webb, BOS 22
J. Cronin, WAS 18
O. Melillo, SL 17
S. West, WAS 16
M. Cochrane, PHI ... 16
G. Earnshaw, PHI ... 12
W. Ferrell, CLE 12
F. Marberry, WAS ... 11
H. Rhyne, BOS 10
B. Chapman, NY 7
J. Stone, DET 6
C. Gehringer, DET ... 4
L. Blue, CHI 4
R. Kress, SL 3
C. Reynolds, CHI 2
W. Stewart, SL 2
G. Goslin, SL 2
D. MacFayden, BOS .. 2
T. Oliver, BOS 2
J. Foxx, PHI 1

1932 NATIONAL
C. Klein, PHI 78
L. Warneke, CHI 68
L. O'Doul, BRO 58
P. Waner, PIT 37
R. Stephenson, CHI 32
B. Terry, NY 25
D. Hurst, PHI 24
P. Traynor, PIT 17
B. Herman, CHI 16
M. Ott, NY 15
R. Brown, BOS 10
F. Herman, CIN 8
L. Waner, PIT 6
W. Berger, BOS 6
H. Wilson, BRO 6
E. Orsatti, SL 6
R. Maranville, BOS ... 5
J. Wilson, SL 5
T. Cuccinello, BRO ... 4
J. Dean, SL 3
F. Frisch, SL 3
R. Collins, SL 3
A. Vaughan, PIT 1

G. Bush, CHI 1

1932 AMERICAN
J. Foxx, PHI 75
L. Gehrig, NY 55
H. Manush, WAS 41
E. Averill, CLE 37
L. Gomez, NY 27
J. Cronin, WAS 26
B. Ruth, NY 26
T. Lazzeri, NY 21
A. Simmons, PHI ... 13
C. Gehringer, DET ... 13
D. Alexander,
  DET-BOS 10
W. Cissell, CHI-CLE . 10
R. Ferrell, SL 9
L. Grove, PHI 8
J. Allen, NY 8
B. Dickey, NY 8
G. Goslin, SL 7
M. Weaver, WAS 6
H. Davis, DET 5
D. Harris, WAS 5
W. Ferrell, CLE 5
J. Levey, SL 5
T. Lyons, CHI 5
B. Sullivan, CHI 3
E. McNair, PHI 3
S. Jolley, CHI-BOS .. 3
G. Crowder, WAS 2
M. McManus, BOS ... 2
G. Walker, DET 1
J. Sewell, NY 1

1933 NATIONAL
C. Hubbell, NY 77
C. Klein, PHI 48
W. Berger, BOS 44
B. Terry, NY 35
P. Martin, SL 31
G. Mancuso, NY 24
J. Dean, SL 23
P. Traynor, PIT 20
B. Ryan, NY 19
A. Lopez, BRO 18
B. Cantwell, BOS ... 18
H. Schumacher, NY . 11
R. Maranville, BOS .. 11
G. Bush, CHI 11
L. French, PIT 10
F. Frisch, SL 7
J. Bottomley, CIN 6
J. Medwick, SL 5
G. Hartnett, CHI 5
L. Warneke, CHI 4
R. Lucas, CIN 3
D. Bartell, PHI 3
A. Vaughan, PIT 2
R. Moore, BOS 2
V. Davis, PHI 1
C. Hafey, CIN 1
D. Luque, NY 1

1933 AMERICAN
J. Foxx, PHI 74
J. Cronin, WAS 62
H. Manush, WAS 54
L. Gehrig, NY 39
L. Grove, PHI 35
C. Gehringer, DET ... 32
G. Crowder, WAS ... 28
A. Simmons, CHI ... 19
E. Whitehill, WAS ... 18
O. Melillo, SL 12
S. West, SL 11
R. Ferrell, SL-BOS ... 9
B. Dickey, NY 9
T. Lazzeri, NY 6
J. Kuhel, WAS 5
C. Averill, CLE 5
C. Myer, WAS 5

M. Cochrane, PHI 5
B. Johnson, PHI 5
B. Chapman, NY 4
M. Bishop, PHI 1
L. Appling, CHI 1
W. Kamm, CLE 1

1934 NATIONAL
J. Dean, SL 78
P. Waner, PIT 50
J. Moore, NY 42
T. Jackson, NY 39
M. Ott, NY 37
R. Collins, SL 32
B. Terry, NY 30
C. Davis, PHI 18
P. Dean, SL 16
H. Schumacher, NY . 16
L. Hubbell, NY 16
W. Berger, BOS 13
L. Warneke, CHI 10
G. Hartnett, CHI 9
G. Slade, CIN 5
K. Cuyler, CHI 4
B. Frey, CIN 4
F. Frankhouse, BOS .. 4
R. Boyle, BRO 4
B. Herman, CHI 4
F. Frisch, SL 4
W. Hoyt, PIT 2
A. Lopez, BRO 1
V. Mungo, BRO 1
A. Vaughan, PIT 1

1934 AMERICAN
M. Cochrane, DET ... 67
C. Gehringer, DET ... 65
L. Gomez, NY 60
S. Rowe, DET 59
L. Gehrig, NY 54
H. Greenberg, DET .. 29
H. Trosky, CLE 18
W. Ferrell, BOS 16
M. Owen, DET 13
J. Foxx, PHI 11
A. Simmons, CHI ... 9
B. Werber, BOS 8
R. Johnson, BOS 8
G. Goslin, DET 6
S. West, SL 6
M. Harder, CLE 4
F. Higgins, PHI 4
E. Averill, CLE 3
B. Knickerbocker,
  CLE 2

1935 NATIONAL
G. Hartnett, CHI 75
J. Dean, SL 66
A. Vaughan, PIT 45
B. Herman, CHI 38
J. Medwick, SL 37
C. Hubbell, NY 30
W. Berger, BOS 20
B. Terry, NY 20
J. Galan, CHI 18
P. Martin, SL 16
H. Leiber, NY 11
L. Warneke, CHI 9
E. Lombardi, CIN ... 8
F. Frisch, SL 7
C. Blanton, PIT 5
J. Moore, PHI 5
J. Allen, PHI 4
G. Mancuso, NY 4
P. Derringer, CIN ... 4
M. Ott, NY 3
P. Dean, SL 3
R. Collins, SL 2
C. Davis, PHI 2
P. Waner, PIT 1
B. Lee, CHI 1

T. Jackson, NY 1
D. Camilli, PHI 1

1935 AMERICAN
H. Greenberg, DET .. 80
W. Ferrell, BOS 62
J. Vosmik, CLE 39
C. Myer, WAS 36
L. Gehrig, NY 29
C. Gehringer, DET ... 26
M. Cochrane, DET ... 24
R. Cramer, PHI 18
M. Solters, BOS-SL .. 16
R. Hemsley, SL 16
J. Foxx, PHI 11
T. Bridges, DET 11
T. Lyons, CHI 10
L. Grove, BOS 8
Z. Bonura, CHI 7
L. Appling, CHI 7
L. Sewell, CHI 7
J. Allen, NY 5
J. Whitehead, CHI ... 4
F. Higgins, PHI 3
J. Marcum, PHI 3
E. Auker, DET 2
M. Harder, CLE 2
L. Lary, WAS-SL 1

1936 NATIONAL
C. Hubbell, NY 60
J. Dean, SL 53
B. Herman, CHI 37
J. Medwick, SL 30
P. Waner, PIT 29
M. Ott, NY 28
F. Demaree, CHI ... 17
G. Mancuso, NY 13
D. MacFayden, BOS . 12
L. Durocher, SL 8
P. Derringer, CIN ... 6
G. Hartnett, CHI 6
B. Whitehead, NY ... 6
A. Lopez, BOS 5
V. Mungo, BRO 5
W. Berger, BOS 4
D. Camilli, PHI 4
G. Phelps, BRO 3
D. Bartell, NY 2
E. Lombardi, CIN 1
T. Moore, SL 1

1936 AMERICAN
L. Gehrig, NY 73
L. Appling, CHI 65
E. Averill, CLE 48
C. Gehringer, DET ... 39
B. Dickey, NY 29
V. Kennedy, CHI 27
J. Kuhel, WAS 27
J. DiMaggio, NY 26
T. Bridges, DET 25
H. Trosky, CLE 19
J. Foxx, BOS 16
G. Walker, DET 14
B. Bell, SL 10
W. Moses, PHI 7
L. Grove, BOS 5
J. Dykes, CHI 3
R. Radcliff, CHI 3
W. West, SL 2
Z. Bonura, CHI 1
E. McNair, BOS 1

1937 NATIONAL
J. Medwick, SL 70
G. Hartnett, CHI 68
C. Hubbell, NY 52
J. Turner, BOS 30
L. Fette, BOS 29
D. Bartell, NY 26
M. Ott, NY 24

P. Waner, PIT 21
B. Herman, CHI 19
J. Mize, SL 18
C. Melton, NY 17
C. Root, CHI 15
P. Whitney, PHI 13
H. Danning, NY 10
F. Demaree, CHI ... 9
L. Warneke, SL 6
B. Jurges, CHI 4
J. Cooney, BRO 4
B. Myers, CIN 2
L. Grissom, CIN 2
H. Manush, BRO ... 1

1937 AMERICAN
C. Gehringer, DET ... 78
J. DiMaggio, NY 74
H. Greenberg, DET .. 48
L. Gehrig, NY 42
L. Sewell, CHI 22
B. Dickey, NY 22
J. Cronin, BOS 19
R. Ruffing, NY 18
L. Gomez, NY 14
M. Kreevich, CHI ... 13
C. Travis, WAS 12
W. Moses, PHI 12
J. Allen, CLE 11
H. Clift, SL 11
R. Radcliff, CHI 10
B. Lewis, WAS 7
L. Appling, CHI 5
B. Bell, SL 5
E. Averill, CLE 4
L. Lary, CLE 4
R. Lawson, DET 4
G. Walker, DET 3
R. York, DET 1
P. Fox, DET 1

1938 NATIONAL
E. Lombardi, CIN ... 229
B. Lee, CHI 166
A. Vaughan, PIT ... 163
M. Ott, NY 132
F. McCormick, CIN 130
J. Rizzo, PIT 96
S. Hack, CHI 87
P. Derringer, CIN ... 70
M. Brown, PIT 62
G. Hartnett, CHI 61
J. Medwick, SL 55
J. Mize, SL 28
T. Cuccinello, BOS .. 19
P. Young, PIT 19
C. Bryant, CHI 16
H. Danning, NY 11
I. Goodman, CIN 11
J. VanderMeer, CIN . 6
L. Durocher, BRO ... 6
D. Coffman, NY 6
A. Lopez, BOS 5
L. Waner, PIT 5
D. Garms, BOS 5
D. Camilli, BRO 5
C. Root, CHI 3
J. Moore, NY 3
J. Hudson, BRO 3
H. Mulcahy, PHI ... 3
L. Handley, PIT 1
L. Warneke, SL 1
F. Fitzsimmons, BRO 1
H. Martin, PHI 1

1938 AMERICAN
J. Foxx, BOS 305
B. Dickey, NY 196
H. Greenberg, DET . 162
R. Ruffing, NY 146
B. Newsom, SL 111
J. DiMaggio, NY ... 106

J. Cronin, BOS 92
E. Averill, CLE 34
C. Travis, WAS 33
C. Gehringer, DET .. 27
J. Heath, CLE 24
J. Gordon, NY 23
H. Trosky, CLE 22
K. Keltner, CLE 16
M. Stratton, CHI ... 15
M. Harder, CLE 14
B. Johnson, PHI 13
H. Clift, SL 11
L. Gehrig, NY 10
P. Fox, DET 9
J. Vosmik, BOS 7
G. McQuinn, SL ... 7
L. Grove, BOS 7
B. Lewis, WAS 5
R. Rolfe, NY 5
C. Myer, WAS 5
E. Brucker, PHI 5
J. Allen, CLE 3
F. Crosetti, NY 2
L. Gomez, NY 1
D. Cramer, BOS 1

1939 NATIONAL
B. Walters, CIN 303
J. Mize, SL 178
P. Derringer, CIN .. 174
F. McCormick, CIN 159
C. Davis, SL 106
J. Brown, SL 99
J. Medwick, SL 81
L. Durocher, BRO ... 52
H. Danning, NY 33
L. Hamlin, BRO 32
M. Ott, NY 21
B. Jurges, NY 20
D. Camilli, BRO 20
W. Myers, CIN 18
S. Hack, CHI 17
A. Galan, CHI 15
T. Moore, SL 15
M. Arnovich, PHI .. 10
L. Frey, CIN 8
B. Lee, CHI 8
E. Slaughter, SL 8
W. Werber, CIN 6
M. West, BOS 5
G. Hartnett, CHI ... 5
I. Goodman, CIN 4
B. Hassett, BOS 4
P. Coscarart, BRO ... 4
E. Fletcher, BOS-PIT . 4
C. Lavagetto, BRO .. 3
R. Bowman, SL 2
E. Miller, BOS 1
B. Herman, CHI 1

1939 AMERICAN
J. DiMaggio, NY ... 280
J. Foxx, BOS 170
B. Feller, CLE 155
T. Williams, BOS ... 126
R. Ruffing, NY 116
B. Dickey, NY 110
E. Leonard, WAS ... 71
B. Johnson, PHI 52
J. Gordon, NY 43
M. Kreevich, CHI .. 38
C. Brown, CHI 34
K. Keltner, CLE 26
G. McQuinn, SL ... 24
C. Gehringer, DET .. 21
L. Grove, BOS 17
J. Cronin, BOS 15
T. Lyons, CHI 13
H. Greenberg, DET . 12
B. Newsom, SL-DET. 11
J. Rigney, CHI 9
J. Kuhel, CHI 8

C. Keller, NY.......... 7
J. Heath, CLE......... 7
G. Walker, CHI......... 7
F. Hayes, PHI......... 7
T. Bridges, DET....... 7
R. Rolfe, NY......... 6
B. McCosky, DET..... 6
E. McNair, CHI 5
H. Trosky, CLE....... 4
G. Case, WAS 3
M. Hoag, SL 3
R. York, DET 1
L. Appling, CHI 1

1940 NATIONAL
F. McCormick, CIN ... 274
J. Mize, SL 209
B. Walters, CIN 146
P. Derringer, CIN ... 121
F. Fitzsimmons, BRO 84
D. Walker, BRO 71
H. Danning, NY 64
S. Hack, CHI 61
E. Lombardi, CIN 38
W. Werber, CIN 36
J. Cooney, BOS 31
D. Camilli, BRO 30
E. Miller, BOS 28
D. Garms, PIT 28
A. Vaughan, PIT 27
C. Passeau, CHI 26
J. Beggs, CIN 19
T. Moore, SL......... 18
E. Fletcher, PIT 16
B. Nicholson, CHI 12
K. Higbe, PHI 10
C. Rowell, BOS 10
A. Lopez, BOS-PIT ... 9
M. Van Robays, PIT... 8
R. Sewell, PIT........ 7
P. Reese, BRO 6
M. West, BOS 6
B. Young, NY 6
W. Wyatt, BRO 3
J. Rizzo, PHI 3
P. May, PHI 3
H. Mulcahy, PHI 3
J. Martin, SL......... 2
F. Gustine, PIT....... 1

1940 AMERICAN
H. Greenberg, DET .292
B. Feller, CLE.......222
J. DiMaggio, NY 151
B. Newsom, DET ...120
L. Boudreau, CLE....119
J. Foxx, BOS.......110
S. Rowe, DET 62
R. York, DET 61
R. Radcliff, SL 55
L. Appling, CHI 54
R. Weatherly, CLE ... 34
D. Bartell, DET 26
J. Kuhel, CHI 18
S. Hudson, WAS..... 16
T. Williams, BOS..... 16
B. McCosky, DET.... 11
E. Bonham, NY 8
W. Judnich, SL 6
J. Babich, PHI 5
M. Tresh, CHI 4
F. Hayes, PHI 4
R. Mack, CLE....... 4
J. Gordon, NY 3
C. Travis, WAS...... 3
B. Kennedy, CHI 3
C. Gehringer, DET ... 3
R. Hemsley, CLE 2
T. Lyons, CHI 2
L. Finney, BOS 1
E. Auker, SL 1

1941 NATIONAL
D. Camilli, BRO 300
P. Reiser, BRO 183
W. Wyatt, BRO 151
J. Brown, SL.......107
E. Riddle, CIN 98
E. White, SL 77
K. Higbe, BRO...... 64
J. Hopp, SL......... 61
J. Mize, SL 48
D. Walker, BRO 34
B. Herman, CHI-BRO 27
T. Moore, SL....... 26

S. Hack, CHI 26
E. Fletcher, PIT 22
J. Cooney, BOS 20
B. Nicholson, CHI ... 16
G. Mancuso, SL 14
F. Crespi, SL 13
M. Ott, NY 12
E. Slaughter, SL ... 12
B. Young, NY 10
V. DiMaggio, PIT.... 10
J. Tobin, BOS 10
A. Lopez, PIT 8
M. Marion, SL 8
M. Cooper, SL 8
L. Warneke, SL 7
N. Etten, PHI 6
B. Walters, CIN 6
B. Dahlgren, BOS-CHI 6
W. Werber, CIN 6
E. Crabtree, SL 5
J. Rucker, NY 4
B. Litwhiler, PHI ... 3
H. Danning, NY 2
C. Hubbell, NY 2
C. Lavagetto, BRO ... 2
A. Vaughan, PIT ... 2

1941 AMERICAN
J. DiMaggio, NY 291
T. Williams, BOS....254
B. Feller, CLE.......174
T. Lee, CHI 144
C. Keller, NY 126
C. Travis, WAS......101
J. Gordon, NY 60
J. Heath, CLE....... 37
H. Newsome, BOS .. 32
R. Cullenbine, SL ... 29
J. Cronin, BOS 26
S. Chapman, PHI ... 25
B. Dickey, NY....... 18
T. Henrich, NY 16
B. McCosky, DET ... 12
T. Lyons, CHI 12
D. Siebert, PHI...... 10
L. Boudreau, CLE... 10
A. Benton, DET 8
R. Pizzuto, NY 7
E. Leonard, WAS ... 7
B. Campbell, DET ... 4
R. York, DET 3
F. Hayes, PHI 3
T. Wright, CHI 2
R. Ruffing, NY 2
E. Auker, SL 1
F. Higgins, DET ... 1
D. DiMaggio, BOS ... 1

1942 NATIONAL
M. Cooper, SL......263
E. Slaughter, SL ...200
M. Ott, NY 190
A. Owen, BRO 103
J. Mize, NY 97
P. Reiser, BRO 91
M. Marion, SL 81
D. Camilli, BRO 42
E. Elliott, PIT 39
C. Passeau, CHI 33
W. Cooper, SL..... 28
S. Musial, SL 26
E. Lombardi, BOS .. 24
J. Beazley, SL 24
J. Brown, SL....... 24
W. Wyatt, BRO 22
J. Medwick, BRO ... 20
T. Moore, SL....... 15
B. Nicholson, CHI .. 14
S. Hack, CHI 11
J. VanderMeer, CIN.. 11
T. Hughes, PHI 10
R. Starr, CIN 9
L. French, BRO 7
P. Reese, BRO 6
W. Kurowski, SL ... 4
R. Lamanno, CIN ... 4
M. West, BOS 4
L. Frey, CIN....... 4
F. McCormick, CIN .. 4
A. Javery, BOS 3
E. Miller, BOS 1

1942 AMERICAN
J. Gordon, NY 270
T. Williams, BOS....249

J. Pesky, BOS 143
V. Stephens, SL 140
E. Bonham, NY 102
T. Hughson, BOS ... 92
J. DiMaggio, NY ... 86
S. Spence, WAS ... 65
P. Marchildon, PHI .. 39
L. Boudreau, CLE... 34
B. Doerr, BOS 24
T. Lyons, CHI 23
G. Case, WAS 17
K. Keltner, CLE 15
C. Keller, NY 15
W. Judnich, SL 14
B. Dickey, NY...... 12
D. Gutteridge, SL .. 12
P. Rizzuto, NY 9
C. Laabs, SL....... 9
R. Ferrell, SL 8
H. Borowy, NY 8
J. Bagby, CLE 6
T. Wright, CHI 6
L. Lupien BOS 4
L. Fleming, CLE 4
S. Chandler, NY ... 3
R. York, DET 3
B. McCosky, DET ... 1

1943 NATIONAL
S. Musial, SL 267
W. Cooper, SL......192
B. Nicholson, CHI ...181
B. Herman, BRO ...140
M. Cooper, SL......130
R. Sewell, PIT......127
E. Riddle, CIN 68
R. Elliott, PIT...... 52
F. McCormick, CIN .. 26
C. Shoun, CIN 24
E. Miller, CIN 24
M. Witek, NY 21
M. Marion, SL 20
S. Rowe, PHI 18
W. Wyatt, BRO 15
A. Vaughan, BRO ... 15
R. Mueller, CIN 12
A. Javery, BOS 12
S. Hack, CHI 10
M. Ott, NY 9
E. Fletcher, PIT 7
A. Adams, NY 7
L. Klein, SL 6
A. Galan, BRO 5
D. Walker, BRO 5
J. Tobin, BOS...... 5
D. Bartell, NY 5
P. Cavaretta, CHI ... 4
T. Holmes, BOS 2
R. Northey, PHI 2
B. Dahlgren, PHI.... 2
H. Bithorn, CHI 1
B. Walters, CIN 1
L. Frey, CIN........ 1

1943 AMERICAN
S. Chandler, NY 246
L. Appling, CHI 215
R. York, DET 152
W. Johnson, NY ...135
B. Johnson, WAS ...116
D. Wakefield, DET .. 72
N. Etten, NY 61
B. Dickey, NY 58
V. Stephens, SL 49
L. Boudreau, CLE... 40
D. Trout, DET 38
G. Case, WAS 37
C. Keller, NY 31
B. Doerr, BOS 21
A. Smith, CLE 19
G. Priddy, WAS 17
O. Hockett, CLE ... 14
D. Gutteridge, SL .. 13
E. Wynn, WAS 13
J. Bagby, CLE 11
R. Cramer, DET 8
F. Higgins, DET 8
C. Laabs, SL....... 6
J. Early, WAS 6
J. Gordon, NY 4
J. Wolff, PHI 4
L. Newsome, BOS .. 3
J. Cronin, BOS 3
J. Flores, PHI 3
G. Maltzberger, CHI .. 3

F. Crosetti, NY 2
K. Keltner, CLE 2
P. Fox, BOS 1
R. Hodgin, CHI 1
J. Murphy, NY 1
D. Siebert, PHI...... 1
J. Tabor, BOS 1
H. Wagner, PHI 1

1944 NATIONAL
M. Marion, SL 190
B. Nicholson, CHI ...189
D. Walker, BRO 145
S. Musial, SL 136
B. Walters, CIN 107
B. Voiselle, NY 107
R. Mueller, CIN 85
W. Cooper, SL..... 72
M. Cooper, SL..... 63
R. Elliott, PIT....... 57
R. Sewell, PIT...... 49
B. Dahlgren, PIT ... 33
F. McCormick, CIN .. 32
P. Cavaretta, CHI ... 27
R. Sanders, SL 25
M. Ott, NY 20
J. Tobin, BOS 13
J. Hopp, SL........ 10
R. Northey, PHI 10
J. Medwick, NY 9
J. Barrett, PIT 8
E. Miller, CIN 7
T. Holmes, BOS ... 6
T. Wilks, SL........ 4
T. Lupien, PHI 3
S. Hack, CHI 2
M. Lanier, SL 2
C. Ryan, BOS 2
A. Galan, BRO 1
W. Kurowski, SL ... 1
J. Heath, CLE...... 1
J. Russell, PIT 1

1944 AMERICAN
H. Newhouser, DET .236
D. Trout, DET 232
V. Stephens, SL 193
S. Stirnweiss, NY ...129
D. Wakefield, DET ..128
L. Boudreau, CLE... 84
B. Doerr, BOS 75
S. Spence, WAS ... 56
N. Potter, SL....... 52
B. Johnson, BOS ... 51
M. Christman, SL ... 27
T. Hughson, BOS ... 22
D. Cramer, DET 14
F. Hayes, PHI 13
P. Fox, BOS 12
J. Kramer, SL...... 9
J. Lindell, NY 8
J. Richards, DET ... 8
D. Gutteridge, SL .. 7
F. Higgins, DET 7
G. McQuinn, SL ... 7
G. Kell, PHI 6
R. Cullenbine, CLE .. 5
N. Etten, NY 5
R. York, DET 5
R. Hemsley, NY 4
M. Kreevich, SL 4
W. Moses, CHI 4
E. Mayo, DET 3
D. Siebert, PHI..... 3
H. Borowy, NY 2
F. Crosetti, NY 2
R. Hodgin, CHI 2
B. Muncrief, SL 1

1945 NATIONAL
P. Cavaretta, CHI ...279
T. Holmes, BOS ...175
C. Barrett, BOS-SL .151
A. Pafko, CHI 131
W. Kurowski, SL ... 90
H. Borowy, CHI ... 84
H. Wyse, CHI 72
M. Marion, SL 69
D. Walker, BRO 66
G. Rosen, BRO 56
S. Hack, CHI 42
H. Brecheen, SL ... 31
M. Ott, NY 22
A. Galan, BRO 18
J. Hopp, SL........ 17
R. Elliott, PIT 15

L. Olmo, BRO 13
B. Adams, PHI-SL .. 12
C. Passeau, CHI ... 9
J. Barrett, PIT 8
E. Heusser, CIN 7
D. Johnson, CHI ... 7
B. Kerr, NY 7
F. McCormick, CIN .. 6
B. Salkeld, PIT 6
P. Lowrey, CHI 5
A. Adams, NY 4
A. Karl, PHI 4
A. Lopez, PIT 2
P. Masi, BOS 2
E. Miller, CIN 2
V. DiMaggio, PHI ... 1
E. Stanky, BRO 1

1945 AMERICAN
H. Newhouser, DET .236
E. Mayo, DET 164
S. Stirnweiss, NY ...161
B. Ferriss, BOS 148
G. Myatt, WAS 98
V. Stephens, SL 94
R. Wolff, WAS 78
L. Boudreau, CLE... 70
G. Case, WAS 60
P. Richards, DET ... 35
M. Tresh, CHI 33
J. Kuhel, WAS 29
R. Cullenbine, DET .. 26
H. Greenberg, DET .. 25
E. Leonard, WAS ... 16
N. Etten, NY 21
T. Cuccinello, CHI .. 18
D. Trout, DET 17
R. Schalk, CHI 13
J. Heath, CLE...... 10
G. Binks, WAS 9
B. Muncrief, SL 8
A. Benton, DET 6
R. Ferrell, WAS 6
B. Johnson, BOS ... 6
M. Christman, SL ... 5
B. Estalella, PHI ... 5
F. Hayes, PHI-CLE .. 5
D. Cramer, DET 4
W. Moses, CHI 4
E. Lake, BOS 2
R. Christopher, PHI .. 1
L. Newsome, BOS .. 1
R. York, DET 1

1946 NATIONAL
S. Musial, SL 319
D. Walker, BRO 159
E. Slaughter, SL ...144
H. Pollet, SL......116
J. Sain, BOS 95
P. Reese, BRO 79
E. Stanky, BRO 67
D. Ennis, PHI 61
P. Reiser, BRO 58
P. Cavaretta, CHI ... 49
B. Kerr, NY 37
J. Hopp, BOS 34
E. Waitkus, CHI 21
B. Edwards, BRO ... 20
K. Higbe, BRO 18
H. Brecheen, SL ... 14
J. Mize, NY 14
G. Hatton, CIN 12
T. Holmes, BOS ... 11
J. Tabor, PHI...... 10
E. Verban, SL-PHI .. 10
H. Walker, SL 9
L. Rowe, PHI 8
P. Masi, BOS 7
J. VanderMeer, CIN .. 7
R. Schoendienst, SL.. 6
B. Cox, PIT 5
F. Gustine, PIT 4
M. Marion, SL 4
R. Kiner, PIT 3
W. Kurowski, SL ... 3
R. Mueller, CIN 3
J. Schmitz, CHI 3
P. Lowrey, CHI 3
F. McCormick, PHI .. 2
C. Furillo, BRO 1
O. Judd, PHI......... 1

1946 AMERICAN
T. Williams, BOS....224
H. Newhouser, DET .197
B. Doerr, BOS 158
J. Pesky, BOS 141
M. Vernon, WAS ...134
B. Feller, CLE......105
B. Ferriss, BOS 94
H. Greenberg, DET .. 91
D. DiMaggio, BOS .. 56
L. Boudreau, CLE... 37
R. York, BOS 28
L. Appling, CHI 26
T. Hughson, BOS ... 19
E. Caldwell, CHI 18
C. Keller, NY 17
G. Kell, PHI-DET ... 12
S. Chandler, NY ... 12
A. Robinson, NY ... 12
J. DiMaggio, NY ... 6
B. Newsom, PHI-WAS 6
V. Stephens, SL 6
P. Marchildon, PHI .. 5
B. Rosar, PHI 4
S. Spence, WAS ... 4
J. Berardino, SL ... 2
T. Henrich, NY 1
H. Wagner, BOS 1

1947 NATIONAL
R. Elliott, BOS 205
E. Blackwell, CIN ...175
J. Mize, NY 144
B. Edwards, BRO ...140
J. Robinson, BRO ..106
R. Kiner, PIT 101
L. Jansen, NY 91
P. Reese, BRO 80
W. Kurowski, SL ... 45
H. Walker, SL-PHI .. 45
R. Branca, BRO 40
H. Casey, BRO 37
E. Leonard, PHI 32
E. Stanky, BRO 32
W. Spahn, BOS 26
W. Marshall, NY 20
J. Sain, BOS....... 20
W. Cooper, NY 19
D. Walker, BRO 14
E. Slaughter, SL ... 12
S. Musial, SL 12
E. Verban, PHI 9
P. Cavaretta, CHI ... 6
P. Lowrey, CHI 2
E. Miller, CIN 2
A. Pafko, CHI 1

1947 AMERICAN
J. DiMaggio, NY 202
T. Williams, BOS....201
L. Boudreau, CLE...168
J. Page, NY 167
G. Kell, DET 132
G. McQuinn, NY ... 77
J. Gordon, CLE 59
B. Feller, CLE...... 58
P. Marchildon, PHI .. 47
L. Appling, CHI 43
E. Joost, PHI 35
B. McCosky, PHI ... 35
T. Henrich, NY 33
F. Shea, NY 23
Y. Berra, NY 18
A. Reynolds, NY ... 18
J. Dillinger, SL 13
J. Pesky, BOS 11
F. Fain, PHI....... 9
W. Johnson, NY ... 9
S. Spence, WAS ... 9
F. Hutchison, DET ... 8
E. Wynn, WAS 7
B. Doerr, BOS ... 6
B. Rosar, PHI 6
M. Christman, WAS .. 4
B. McCahan, PHI ... 4
D. Mitchell, CLE ... 4
R. Cullenbine, DET .. 3
J. Dobson, BOS ... 3
J. Heath, SL 1
E. Lopat, CHI 1
V. Stephens, SL 1
J. Wright, CHI 1

1948 NATIONAL
S. Musial, SL 303

J. Sain, BOS........223
A. Dark, BOS......174
S. Gordon, NY.....72
H. Brecheen, SL...61
P. Reese, BRO.....60
R. Kiner, PIT......55
E. Slaughter, SL...55
D. Murtaugh, PIT..52
S. Rojek, PIT......51
R. Ashburn, PHI...48
J. Schmitz, CHI....37
R. Elliott, BOS.....33
W. Spahn, BOS.....31
J. Robinson, BRO...30
A. Pafko, CHI.......25
J. Mize, NY.........22
R. Barney, BRO.....15
J. VanderMeer, CIN...13
J. Wyrostek, CIN.....9
R. Branca, BRO......8
R. Campanella, BRO..8
B. Chesnes, PIT......6
P. Cavaretta, CHI....6
E. Miller, PHI........4
D. Ennis, PHI........3
G. Hatton, CIN.......3
L. Jansen, NY........2
D. Walker, PIT.......2
G. Hodges, BRO......1
W. Lockman, NY.....1
H. Sauer, CIN........1

1948 AMERICAN
L. Boudreau, CLE...324
J. DiMaggio, NY....213
T. Williams, BOS...171
V. Stephens, BOS..121
B. Lemon, CLE.....101
J. Gordon, CLE......63
T. Henrich, NY.......63
G. Bearden, CLE.....52
H. Newhouser, DET..48
E. Joost, PHI........39
H. Majeski, PHI......23
B. Tebbetts, BOS.....23
V. Raschi, NY.......23
K. Keltner, CLE......18
J. Priddy, SL........16
G. Kell, DET.........14
W. Evers, DET.......13
A. Zarilla, SL........11
B. Doerr, BOS.......10
B. Dillinger, SL......10
J. Hegan, CLE.......10
L. Appling, CHI.......8
B. Feller, CLE........6
L. Brissie, PHI.......5
F. Fain, PHI..........5
J. Dobson, BOS......5
B. Goodman, BOS....4
B. McCosky, PHI.....3
Y. Berra, NY.........3
D. DiMaggio, BOS....3
L. Doby, CLE.........3
C. Fannin, SL.........2
P. Mullin, DET........1
P. Rizzuto, NY........1

1949 NATIONAL
J. Robinson, BRO..264
S. Musial, SL.......226
E. Slaughter, SL....181
R. Kiner, PIT.......133
P. Reese, BRO......118
C. Furillo, BRO......68
W. Spahn, BOS......60
D. Newcombe, BRO..55
K. Heintzelman, PHI..47
R. Schoendienst, SL..30
G. Hodges, BRO......29
H. Pollet, SL.........29
D. Ennis, PHI........28
B. Thomson, NY.....25
R. Campanella, BRO..24
P. Roe, BRO.........21
G. Hamner, PHI......9
W. Lockman, NY.....9
R. Meyer, PHI........8
K. Raffensberger, CIN..8
H. Sauer, CIN-CHI....8
T. Wilks, SL..........8
R. Ashburn, PHI......6
J. Schmitz, CHI.......6
A. Dark, BOS.........3
M. Marion, SL........3

W. Jones, PHI........2
W. Marshall, NY......2
E. Torgeson, BOS.....2
S. Gordon, NY........1
D. Sisler, PHI.........1

1949 AMERICAN
T. Williams, BOS....272
P. Rizzuto, NY.....175
J. Page, NY........166
M. Parnell, BOS...151
E. Kinder, BOS....122
T. Henrich, NY....121
V. Stephens, BOS..100
G. Kell, DET.........80
B. Lemon, CLE......57
V. Wertz, DET.......51
V. Raschi, NY.......19
J. DiMaggio, NY.....18
E. Joost, PHI........11
L. Boudreau, CLE....10
Y. Berra, NY.........9
D. DiMaggio, BOS....7
B. Doerr, BOS........7
A. Kellner, PHI.......6
E. Robinson, WAS....6
R. Sievers, SL........6
B. Tebbetts, BOS.....6
L. Appling, CHI.......3
A. Houtteman, DET...3
J. Priddy, SL.........3
J. Trucks, DET.......3
D. Mitchell, CLE......2
A. Reynolds, NY......2

1950 NATIONAL
J. Konstanty, PHI...286
S. Musial, SL.......158
E. Stanky, NY......144
D. Ennis, PHI.......104
R. Kiner, PIT........91
G. Hamner, PHI......79
R. Roberts, PHI......68
G. Hodges, BRO.....55
D. Snider, BRO......53
S. Maglie, NY........51
E. Blackwell, CIN.....41
A. Pafko, CHI.........38
R. Campanella, BRO..29
A. Seminick, PHI.....25
J. Robinson, BRO....23
C. Simmons, PHI.....22
P. Roe, BRO.........15
T. Kluszewski, CIN...14
W. Spahn, BOS......14
D. Newcombe, BRO..14
J. Sain, BOS.........12
S. Gordon, BOS......11
J. Hearn, SL-NY......10
P. Reese, BRO........8
E. Waitkus, PHI.......8
R. Elliott, BOS........8
E. Torgeson, BOS.....6
S. Jethroe, BOS.......5
H. Sauer, CHI.........5
V. Bickford, BOS......4
C. Furillo, BRO........4
W. Westrum, NY......3
D. Sisler, PHI.........2
H. Thompson, NY....2
L. Jansen, NY.........2
W. Jones, PHI.........1

1950 AMERICAN
P. Rizzuto, NY......284
B. Goodman, BOS..180
Y. Berra, NY.......146
G. Kell, DET........127
B. Lemon, CLE.....102
W. Dropo, BOS......75
V. Raschi, NY........63
L. Doby, CLE.........57
J. DiMaggio, NY......54
V. Wertz, DET........50
W. Evers, DET........38
C. Carrasquel, CHI...21
D. Trout, DET........21
D. DiMaggio, BOS....17
I. Noren, WAS........16
B. Doerr, BOS........15
J. Mize, NY..........11
J. Priddy, DET........11
A. Rosen, CLE........11

E. Yost, WAS.........8
M. Parnell, BOS.......7
W. Ford, NY..........7
T. Williams, BOS......7
N. Garver, SL.........6
V. Stephens, BOS.....6
A. Houtteman, DET...6
S. Lollar, SL..........4
E. Lopat, NY..........3
K. Wood, SL..........1
S. Dente, WAS........1
D. Philley, CHI........1

1951 NATIONAL
R. Campanella, BRO..243
S. Musial, SL.......191
M. Irvin, NY........166
S. Maglie, NY.......153
P. Roe, BRO........138
J. Robinson, BRO.....92
R. Ashburn, PHI......69
B. Thomson, NY......62
M. Dickson, PIT......59
R. Kiner, PIT.........49
W. Spahn, BOS.......45
A. Dark, NY..........30
R. Roberts, PHI......27
L. Jansen, NY........26
P. Reese, BRO........15
G. Hodges, BRO......10
S. Gordon, BOS.......10
K. Raffensberger, CIN..8
J. Wyrostek, CIN......6
E. Blackwell, CIN......6
C. Furillo, BRO........6
D. Newcombe, BRO...3
P. Cavaretta, CHI......1
H. Sauer, CHI.........1

1951 AMERICAN
Y. Berra, NY.......184
N. Garver, SL......157
A. Reynolds, NY....125
M. Minoso, CLE-CHI..120
B. Feller, CLE.......118
F. Fain, PHI.........103
E. Kinder, BOS.......66
V. Raschi, NY........64
M. McDougald, NY...63
B. Avila, CLE.........49
P. Rizzuto, NY........47
E. Lopat, NY.........44
T. Williams, BOS......35
E. Joost, PHI.........32
G. Kell, DET..........30
E. Wynn, CLE.........29
N. Fox, CHI..........25
B. Goodman, BOS....21
D. DiMaggio, BOS.....16
G. Zernial, CHI-PHI...15
B. Shantz, PHI........14
M. Garcia, CLE........11
G. Coan, WAS.........7
M. Parnell, BOS.......7
E. Robinson, CHI......7
G. Woodling, NY......5
J. Pesky, BOS.........5
I. Noren, WAS.........4
D. Mitchell, CLE.......4
V. Trucks, DET........2
E. Yost, WAS.........2
J. Busby, CHI.........2
J. Mize, NY...........2

1952 NATIONAL
H. Sauer, CHI.......226
R. Roberts, PHI.....211
J. Black, BRO.......208
H. Wilhelm, NY.....133
S. Musial, SL.......127
E. Slaughter, SL......92
J. Robinson, BRO.....31
P. Reese, BRO........29
D. Snider, BRO.......29
R. Campanella, BRO..25
R. Schoendienst, SL...25
A. Dark, NY..........24
M. Dickson, PIT......18
D. Ennis, PHI.........18
W. Lockman, NY......18
B. Thomson, NY......17
F. Baumholtz, CHI....16
T. Kluszewski, CIN....16

G. Hodges, BRO......15
R. McMillan, CIN......15
E. Mathews, BOS.....13
B. Adams, CIN.........9
B. Cox, BRO..........8
W. Hacker, CHI........8
R. Kiner, PIT..........8
S. Maglie, NY.........8
K. Raffensberger, CIN..8
W. Spahn, BOS........8
P. Roe, BRO..........7
S. Gordon, BOS.......6
G. Hamner, PHI........6
S. Hemus, SL.........5
M. Irvin, NY..........5
R. Shuba, BRO........5
E. Yuhas, SL..........5
A. Brazle, SL..........3
J. Logan, BOS.........3
T. Atwell, CHI.........2
C. Metkovich, PIT.....2
W. Cooper, BOS.......1

1952 AMERICAN
B. Shantz, PHI......280
A. Reynolds, NY....183
M. Mantle, NY......143
Y. Berra, NY........104
E. Wynn, CLE.........99
F. Fain, PHI..........66
N. Fox, CHI...........59
B. Lemon, CLE........58
M. Garcia, CLE........52
A. Rosen, CLE.........51
L. Doby, CLE..........46
L. Easter, CLE.........40
P. Rizzuto, NY........33
E. Joost, PHI..........20
B. Goodman, BOS....18
J. Jensen, NY-WAS...12
S. Paige, SL..........12
V. Raschi, NY.........12
H. Bauer, NY..........10
G. Woodling, NY......10
P. Runnels, WAS.......8
C. Courtney, NY.......7
D. Gernert, BOS.......6
W. Dropo, BOS-DET...5
S. Rogovin, CHI.......4
S. White, SL..........4
B. Avila, CLE..........3
B. Pierce, CHI.........3
J. Sain, NY...........3
B. Young, SL..........3
J. Collins, NY.........2
C. Marrero, WAS......1
B. Porterfield, WAS...1

1953 NATIONAL
R. Campanella, BRO..297
E. Mathews, MIL....216
D. Snider, BRO......157
R. Schoendienst, SL..155
W. Spahn, MIL.......120
R. Roberts, PHI......106
T. Kluszewski, CIN....69
S. Musial, SL.........62
C. Erskine, BRO.......54
C. Furillo, BRO........54
P. Reese, BRO........27
J. Robinson, BRO.....19
D. Ennis, PHI.........14
G. Hodges, BRO......13
M. Irvin, NY..........11
D. O'Connell, PIT.....10
H. Haddix, SL.........9
F. Thomas, PIT........6
R. Ashburn, PHI.......5
G. Bell, CIN...........3
J. Logan, MIL.........3
R. Gomez, NY.........2
G. Hamner, PHI.......2
D. Crandall, MIL.......1
H. Thompson, NY.....1

1953 AMERICAN
A. Rosen, CLE.......336
Y. Berra, NY........167
M. Vernon, WAS....162
M. Minoso, CHI......100
V. Trucks, SL-CHI.....81
P. Rizzuto, NY........76

B. Porterfield, WAS..64
R. Boone, CLE-DET..59
J. Piersall, BOS.......56
B. Pierce, CHI.........55
E. Kinder, BOS........41
H. Bauer, NY.........37
A. Reynolds, NY......37
M. Parnell, BOS.......27
H. Kuenn, DET........23
B. Lemon, CLE........22
E. Lopat, NY.........18
G. Zernial, PHI........16
D. Philley, PHI........11
W. Ford, NY..........8
B. Goodman, BOS.....5
M. Mantle, NY........5
G. Woodling, NY......3
E. Yost, WAS.........3
B. Martin, NY.........2
C. Carrasquel, CHI....1
G. Kell, BOS..........1
T. Williams, BOS......1

1954 NATIONAL
W. Mays, NY.......283
T. Kluszewski, CIN..217
J. Antonelli, NY....154
D. Snider, BRO.....135
A. Dark, NY........110
S. Musial, SL........97
R. Roberts, PHI......70
J. Adcock, MIL.......60
P. Reese, BRO.......53
G. Hodges, BRO.....40
W. Spahn, MIL.......38
D. Mueller, NY.......30
R. Schoendienst, SL..24
F. Thomas, PIT.......24
H. Wilhelm, NY......17
E. Banks, CHI........14
D. Crandall, MIL......13
J. Logan, MIL........13
E. Mathews, MIL......5
G. Hamner, PHI.......5
R. Ashburn, PHI......5
S. Maglie, NY.........4
G. Conley, MIL........3
M. Grissom, NY.......2
R. McMillan, CIN......2
D. Rhodes, NY........1
H. Sauer, CHI.........1

1954 AMERICAN
Y. Berra, NY.......230
L. Doby, CLE.......210
B. Avila, CLE.......203
M. Minoso, CHI.....186
B. Lemon, CLE.....179
E. Wynn, CLE........72
T. Williams, BOS.....65
H. Kuenn, DET........37
M. Vernon, WAS.....30
N. Fox, CHI..........30
B. Grim, NY..........25
J. Finigan, PHI.......19
V. Trucks, CHI.......19
J. Jensen, BOS.......17
M. Mantle, NY........16
I. Noren, NY.........16
A. Rosen, CLE........16
J. Busby, WAS.........7
J. Coleman, NY........6
B. Goodman, BOS.....6
M. Garcia, CLE........6
J. Hegan, CLE.........5
H. Bauer, NY.........4
A. Kaline, DET........4
B. Turley, BAL........4
S. Gromek, DET.......1
C. Abrams, BAL.......1
R. Boone, DET.........1
R. Sievers, WAS.......1

1955 NATIONAL
R. Campanella, BRO..226
D. Snider, BRO......221
E. Banks, CHI.......195
W. Mays, NY.......165
R. Roberts, PHI.....159
T. Kluszewski, CIN...111
D. Newcombe, BRO..89
S. Musial, SL........46
H. Aaron, MIL........36
P. Reese, BRO........36

J. Logan, MIL........24
W. Post, CIN.........23
D. Ennis, PHI.........21
R. Ashburn, PHI......17
C. Labine, BRO.......11
B. Friend, PIT........10
D. Crandall, MIL.......8
E. Mathews, MIL......6
D. Long, PIT..........3
J. Meyer, PHI.........3
G. Baker, CHI.........2
C. Furillo, BRO........2
V. Law, PIT..........1
F. Thomas, PIT.......1

1955 AMERICAN
Y. Berra, NY.......218
A. Kaline, DET......201
A. Smith, CLE.......200
T. Williams, BOS....143
M. Mantle, NY......113
R. Narleski, CLE......90
N. Fox, CHI..........84
H. Bauer, NY.........64
R. Power, KC.........53
J. Jensen, BOS.......39
S. Lollar, CHI.........37
M. McDougald, NY...34
B. Klaus, BOS.........27
T. Byrne, NY.........24
W. Ford, NY..........21
R. Boone, DET........16
R. Sievers, WAS.......9
H. Kuenn, DET........8
B. Pierce, CHI.........8
D. Philley, CLE-BAL....6
E. Wynn, CLE.........6
E. Valo, KC...........5
M. Vernon, WAS.......4
B. Hoeft, DET.........1
D. Mossi, CLE.........1
F. Sullivan, BOS.......1
G. Triandos, BAL......1
J. Valdivielso, WAS....1
S. White, BOS.........1

1956 NATIONAL
D. Newcombe, BRO...223
S. Maglie, BRO.....183
H. Aaron, MIL.......146
W. Spahn, MIL......126
J. Gilliam, BRO.....103
R. McMillan, CIN.....96
F. Robinson, CIN.....79
P. Reese, BRO.......71
S. Musial, SL........62
D. Snider, BRO.......55
J. Adcock, MIL.......54
B. Friend, PIT........38
H. Freeman, CIN......25
J. Antonelli, NY......18
T. Kluszewski, CIN...18
J. Robinson, BRO.....17
W. Mays, NY.........14
E. Bailey, CIN.........13
B. Virdon, SL-PIT.....13
S. Lopata, PHI........11
C. Furillo, BRO........9
L. Burdette, MIL.......8
B. Buhl, MIL..........7
R. Roberts, PHI.......7
B. Lawrence, CIN......6
D. Long, PIT..........4
W. Moon, SL.........3
E. Banks, CHI.........2
K. Boyer, SL..........2
C. Labine, BRO........1
J. Logan, MIL.........1
R. Ashburn, PHI.......1

1956 AMERICAN
M. Mantle, NY......336
Y. Berra, NY.......186
A. Kaline, DET......142
H. Kuenn, DET........80
B. Pierce, CHI.........75
T. Williams, BOS......70
B. Nieman, CHI-BAL..55
G. McDougald, NY....55
V. Wertz, CLE........45
B. Lemon, CLE........40
H. Simpson, KC.......37
W. Ford, NY..........33
E. Wynn, CLE.........32

J. Piersall, BOS 28
N. Fox, CHI 28
S. Lollar, CHI 27
F. Lary, DET 24
P. Runnels, WAS 24
H. Score, CLE 18
J. Jensen, BOS 15
M. Vernon, BOS 14
T. Brewer, BOS 11
H. Bauer, NY 8
C. Maxwell, DET 8
L. Aparicio, CHI 7
G. Triandos, BAL 6
F. Bolling, DET........ 3
M. Minoso, CHI 3
V. Power, KC 3
J. Kucks, NY 2
R. Sievers, WAS 1

1957 NATIONAL
H. Aaron, MIL.......239
S. Musial, SL 230
R. Schoendienst,
  NY-MIL 221
W. Mays, NY 174
W. Spahn, MIL 131
E. Banks, CHI 60
G. Hodges, BRO 54
E. Mathews, MIL 45
F. Robinson, CIN 42
J. Sanford, PHI 39
D. Hoak, CIN 37
D. Blasingame, SL 26
E. Bouchee, PHI 26
D. Buhl, MIL 15
D. Ennis, SL 13
D. Groat, PIT 13
A. Dark, SL 12
D. Snider, BRO 10
F. Thomas, PIT 8
D. Drysdale, BRO 6
R. McMillan, CIN 6
D. Drott, CHI 6
G. Hamner, PHI 3
L. Burdette, MIL 2
J. Logan, MIL 1
H. Anderson, PHI 1

1957 AMERICAN
M. Mantle, NY 233
T. Williams, BOS 209
R. Sievers, WAS 205
N. Fox, CHI 193
G. McDougald, NY ..165
V. Wertz, CLE 61
F. Malzone, BOS 58
M. Minoso, CHI 55
J. Bunning, DET 46
A. Kaline, DET 40
B. Pierce, CHI 35
B. Gardner, BAL 22
D. Donovan, CHI 19
Y. Berra, NY 18
G. Woodling, CLE 13
B. Grim, NY 9
B. Boyd, BAL 9
C. Maxwell, DET 5
W. Held, NY-KC 4
W. Ford, NY 4
V. Power, KC 3
J. Piersall, BOS 2
B. Skowron, NY 2
H. Kuenn, DET........ 2
S. Lollar, CHI 2
T. Kubek, NY 1
B. Shantz, NY 1

1958 NATIONAL
E. Banks, CHI 283
W. Mays, SF 185
H. Aaron, MIL 166
F. Thomas, PIT 143
W. Spahn, MIL 108
B. Friend, PIT 98
R. Ashburn, PHI 62
B. Mazeroski, PIT 61
O. Cepeda, SF 57
D. Crandall, MIL 48
L. Burdette, MIL 47
S. Musial, SL 39
K. Boyer, SL 31
J. Temple, CIN 26
B. Skinner, PIT 18
W. Covington, MIL ... 16
E. Face, PIT 8

H. Anderson, PHI 5
J. Gilliam, LA 4
B. Purkey, CIN 4
F. Robinson, CIN 4
J. Adcock, MIL 2
C. Furillo, LA......... 1

1958 AMERICAN
J. Jensen, BOS 233
B. Turley, NY 191
R. Colavito, CLE 181
B. Cerv, KC 164
M. Mantle, NY 127
R. Sievers, WAS 95
T. Williams, BOS 89
N. Fox, CHI 88
S. Lollar, CHI 57
P. Runnels, BOS 29
G. Triandos, BAL 27
D. Hyde, WAS 26
H. Kuenn, DET....... 24
C. McLish, CLE 18
V. Power, KC-CLE ... 15
F. Bolling, DET....... 10
E. Howard, NY 9
Y. Berra, NY 6
M. Minoso, CLE 6
A. Kaline, DET 5
G. McDougald, NY ... 5
R. Duren, NY 4
F. Lary, DET 3
J. Harshman, BAL ... 2
D. Donovan, CHI 1
F. Malzone, BOS 1

1959 NATIONAL
E. Banks, CHI 232½
E. Mathews, MIL ... 189½
H. Aaron, MIL 174
W. Moon, LA 161
S. Jones, SF 130
W. Mays, SF 85
E. Face, PIT 67
C. Neal, LA 64
F. Robinson, CIN ... 52
K. Boyer, SL 37
D. Crandall, MIL 27
L. Burdette, MIL 14
R. Craig, LA 12
J. Cunningham, SL .. 12
V. Pinson, CIN 11
J. Temple, CIN 8
D. Hoak, PIT 6
G. Hodges, LA 4
O. Cepeda, SF 3
V. Law, PIT 3
W. Spahn, MIL....... 3
G. Conley, PHI 1
W. McCovey, SF 1
D. Snider, LA 1

1959 AMERICAN
N. Fox, CHI 295
L. Aparicio, CHI 255
E. Wynn, CHI 123
R. Colavito, CLE 117
T. Francona, CLE 102
A. Kaline, DET 84
J. Landis, CHI 66
H. Kuenn, DET 64
S. Lollar, CHI 44
J. Jensen, BOS 40
C. McLish, CLE 35
Y. Berra, NY 26
M. Minoso, CLE 26
F. Malzone, BOS 24
H. Killebrew, WAS ... 21
G. Woodling, BAL ... 18
M. Mantle, NY 13
B. Richardson, NY ... 11
C. Pascual, WAS 9
B. Shaw, CHI 8
G. Triandos, BAL 8
B. Daley, KC 7
V. Power, CLE 5
B. Tuttle, KC 5
J. Lemon, WAS 4
P. Runnels, BOS 2
T. Williams, BOS 2
B. Allison, WAS 1
G. Staley, CHI 1

1960 NATIONAL
D. Groat, PIT 276
D. Hoak, PIT 162

W. Mays, SF 155
E. Banks, CHI 100
L. McDaniel, SL 95
K. Boyer, SL 80
V. Law, PIT 80
R. Clemente, PIT 62
E. Broglio, SL 58
E. Mathews, MIL 52
H. Aaron, MIL 49
E. Face, PIT 47
D. Crandall, MIL 31
W. Spahn, MIL....... 27
N. Larker, LA 21
S. Musial, SL 18
W. Mills, LA 7
V. Pinson, CIN 6
J. Adcock, MIL 5
S. Burgess, PIT 2
F. Robinson, CIN 2
L. Sherry, LA 2
P. Herrera, PHI 1

1960 AMERICAN
R. Maris, NY 225
M. Mantle, NY 222
B. Robinson, BAL 211
M. Minoso, CHI 141
R. Hansen, BAL 110
A. Smith, CHI 73
R. Sievers, CHI 58
E. Battey, WAS 57
B. Skowron, NY 56
J. Lemon, WAS 36
T. Kubek, NY 29
C. Estrada, BAL 28
T. Williams, BOS 25
V. Wertz, BOS 22
Y. Berra, NY 21
J. Gentile, BAL 21
P. Runnels, BOS..... 18
N. Fox, CHI 11
V. Power, CLE 11
S. Barber, BAL 7
L. Aparicio, CHI 6
J. Perry, CLE 6
G. Staley, CHI 4
J. Bunning, DET 3
G. Woodling, BAL ... 3
H. Kuenn, CLE 3
B. Daley, KC......... 3
M. Fornieles, BOS ... 2
C. Maxwell, DET 2
J. Piersall, CLE 2

1961 NATIONAL
F. Robinson, CIN ...219
O. Cepeda, SF 117
V. Pinson, CIN 104
R. Clemente, PIT 81
J. Jay, CIN 74
W. Mays, SF 70
K. Boyer, SL 43
H. Aaron, MIL........ 39
W. Mills, LA 36
J. O'Toole, CIN 31
W. Spahn, MIL....... 31
S. Miller, SF 26
W. Moon, LA 22
G. Altman, CHI 9
J. Podres, LA 9
R. McMillan, MIL 8
E. Mathews, MIL 7
S. Koufax, LA 5
J. Roseboro, LA 4
J. Brosnan, CIN 3
J. Torre, MIL 2
J. Jackson, SL 1
J. Lynch, CIN 1
B. Malkmus, PHI 1
D. Stuart, PIT 1

1961 AMERICAN
R. Maris, NY 202
M. Mantle, NY 198
J. Gentile, BAL 157
N. Cash, DET 151
W. Ford, NY 102
L. Arroyo, NY 95
F. Lary, DET 53
R. Colavito, DET ... 51
A. Kaline, DET 35
E. Howard, NY 30
H. Killebrew, MIN ... 29
L. Aparicio, CHI..... 16
J. Piersall, CLE 10

S. Barber, BAL 7
D. Schwall, BOS 7
N. Siebern, KC 7
D. Donovan, WAS 5
B. Phillips, CLE 5
B. Robinson, BAL 4
C. Schilling, BOS 4
T. Morgan, LA 3
A. Smith, CHI 3
Y. Berra, NY 2
B. Richardson, NY ... 1
J. Romano, CLE 1
L. Thomas, NY-LA ... 1
H. Wilhelm, BAL 1

1962 NATIONAL
M. Wills, LA.........209
W. Mays, SF 202
T. Davis, LA 175
F. Robinson, CIN ...164
D. Drysdale, LA 85
H. Aaron, MIL 72
J. Sanford, SF 62
B. Purkey, CIN 33
F. Alou, SF 10
B. White, SL 10
O. Cepeda, SF 9
D. Groat, PIT 9
R. Clemente, PIT 6
E. Banks, CHI 5
K. Boyer, SL 5
J. Callison, PHI 5
H. Kuenn, SF 5
J. Marichal, SF 4
B. Skinner, PIT 4
J. Davenport, SF 3
S. Koufax, LA 3
D. Crandall, MIL 2
A. Mahaffey, PHI ... 2
E. Roebuck, LA 2
E. Kasko, CIN 1
E. Mathews, MIL 1

1962 AMERICAN
M. Mantle, NY 234
B. Richardson, NY .. 152
H. Killebrew, MIN 99
L. Wagner, LA 85
D. Donovan, CLE 64
A. Kaline, DET 58
N. Siebern, KC 53
R. Rollins, MIN 47
B. Robinson, BAL.... 41
F. Robinson, CHI ... 33
L. Thomas, LA 32
T. Tresh, NY 30
B. Moran, LA 28
R. Terry, NY 19
C. Pascual, MIN 14
R. Colavito, DET 10
H. Aguirre, DET 10
J. Cunningham, CHI .. 9
P. Runnels, BOS 9
C. Yastrzemski, BOS .. 9
V. Power, MIN 8
D. Radatz, BOS 8
J. Bunning, DET 8
Z. Versalles, MIN..... 8
J. Lumpe, KC 7
E. Bressoud, BOS ... 6
B. Rodgers, LA 6
W. Ford, NY 6
R. Herbert, CHI 5
C. Hinton, WAS 5
F. Malzone, BOS 3
N. Cash, DET 3
A. Smith, CHI 1

1963 NATIONAL
S. Koufax, LA.......237
D. Groat, SL 190
H. Aaron, MIL 135
R. Perranoski, LA .. 130
W. Mays, SF 102
J. Gilliam, LA 62
B. White, SL 54
T. Davis, LA 41
R. Santo, CHI 41
V. Pinson, CIN 31
J. Marichal, SF 31
W. Spahn, MIL 30

K. Boyer, SL 19
R. Clemente, PIT 12
J. Callison, PHI 11
T. Taylor, PHI 10
W. McCovey, SF 9
M. Wills, LA 9
D. Ellsworth, CHI 7
J. Maloney, CIN 7
D. Demeter, PHI 3
D. Drysdale, LA 3
T. Gonzalez, PHI 2
C. Flood, SL 1

1963 AMERICAN
E. Howard, NY.......248
A. Kaline, DET 148
W. Ford, NY 125
H. Killebrew, MIN 85
D. Radatz, BOS 84
C. Yastrzemski, BOS 81
E. Battey, MIN 57
G. Peters, CHI 55
P. Ward, CHI 52
B. Richardson, NY ... 43
T. Tresh, NY 38
C. Pascual, MIN 29
D. Stuart, BOS 25
A. Pearson, LA 22
B. Allison, MIN 15
J. Bouton, NY 11
M. Alvis, CLE 10
J. Pepitone, NY 10
L. Wagner, LA 9
S. Miller, BAL 9
W. Causey, KC 5
R. Rollins, MIN 5
L. Aparicio, BAL 3
B. Dailey, MIN 3
J. Fregosi, LA 3
N. Fox, CHI 2
T. Kubek, NY 1
F. Robinson, CHI ... 1
N. Siebern, KC 1

1964 NATIONAL
K. Boyer, SL.........243
J. Callison, PHI 187
B. White, SL 106½
F. Robinson, CIN ... 98
J. Torre, MIL 85
W. Mays, SF 66
R. Allen, PHI 63
R. Santo, CHI 59
R. Clemente, PIT 56
L. Brock, CHI-SL 40
C. Flood, SL 38
L. Jackson, CHI 26
J. Bunning, PHI 23
H. Aaron, MIL 22
J. Marichal, SF 14
S. Ellis, CIN 13
S. Koufax, LA 7½
V. Pinson, CIN 6
J. Hart, SF 6
B. Williams, CHI 6
R. Amaro, PHI 5
T. Davis, LA 4
B. Gibson, SL 2
C. Short, PHI 2
B. Hunt, NY 1
B. Schultz, LA 1

1964 AMERICAN
B. Robinson, BAL...269
M. Mantle, NY 171
E. Howard, NY.....124
T. Oliva, MIN 99
D. Chance, LA 97
P. Ward, CHI 67½
B. Freehan, DET 44
G. Peters, CHI 44
D. Radatz, BOS...... 37
H. Killebrew, MIN ... 31
B. Powell, BAL 28
W. Bunker, BAL 23
J. Fregosi, LA 21
A. Kaline, DET 17
F. Robinson, CHI ... 14
R. Hansen, CHI 10
B. Richardson, NY ... 9
L. Wagner, CLE 9
J. Pizarro, CHI 8
J. Horlen, CHI 7
W. Ford, NY 7

B. Allison, MIN 5
R. Colavito, KC 5
M. Stottlemyre, NY ... 4
R. Maris, NY 4
W. Causey, KC 4
L. Aparicio, BAL 3½
D. Stuart, BOS 3
E. Bressoud, BOS ... 2
C. Osteen, WAS 2
D. Wickersham, DET.. 2
D. Lock, WAS........ 1

1965 NATIONAL
W. Mays, SF 224
S. Koufax, LA 177
M. Wills, LA 164
D. Johnson, CIN 108
D. Drysdale, LA 77
P. Rose, CIN 67
H. Aaron, MIL 58
R. Clemente, PIT 56
J. Marichal, SF 26
W. McCovey, SF 25
J. Torre, MIL 23
B. Williams, CHI 21
F. Linzy, SF 16
W. Stargell, PIT 15
C. Flood, SL 13
J. Hart, SF 13
V. Law, PIT 12
F. Robinson, CIN ... 11
R. Santo, CHI 11
E. Mathews, MIL 8
L. Cardenas, CIN ... 7
J. Maloney, CIN 7
L. Lefebvre, LA 7
J. Callison, PHI 6
L. Johnson, LA 5
C. Rojas, PHI 5
J. Roseboro, LA 5
R. Allen, PHI 4
T. Cloninger, MIL ... 4
J. Gilliam, LA 3
J. Morgan, HOU 1

1965 AMERICAN
Z. Versalles, MIN ...275
T. Oliva, MIN 174
B. Robinson, BAL...150
E. Fisher, CHI 122
R. Colavito, CLE 89
J. Grant, MIN 74
S. Miller, BAL 45
W. Horton, DET 24
T. Tresh, NY 23
E. Battey, MIN 22
D. Wert, DET 22
C. Yastrzemski, BOS 22
J. Hall, MIN 19
M. Stottlemyre, NY ... 17
H. Killebrew, MIN ... 15
A. Kaline, DET 9
J. Adair, BAL 7
R. Hansen, CHI 7
S. McDowell, CLE ... 7
B. Richardson, NY ... 6
V. Davalillo, CLE ... 5
J. Fregosi, CAL 5
F. Whitfield, CLE ... 5
B. Knoop, CAL 4
D. Buford, CHI 3
M. Mantle, NY 3
P. Richert, WAS 3
F. Robinson, CHI ... 3
B. Campaneris, KC ... 2
F. Howard, WAS 2
R. Kline, WAS....... 2
F. Mantilla, BOS 2
N. Cash, DET 1
T. Conigliaro, BOS ... 1

1966 NATIONAL
R. Clemente, PIT ...218
S. Koufax, LA 208
W. Mays, SF 111
R. Allen, PHI 107
F. Alou, ATL 83
J. Marichal, SF 74
P. Regan, LA 66
H. Aaron, ATL 57
M. Alou, PIT 36
P. Rose, CIN 31
G. Alley, PIT 24
R. Santo, CHI 23
J. Roseboro, LA 22

O. Cepeda, SF-SL ... 22
W. Stargell, PIT 19
J. Torre, ATL 18
W. McCovey, SF ... 12
J. Lefebvre, LA 8
G. Perry, SF 8
C. Flood, SL 7
M. Wills, LA 5
R. Staub, HOU 4
B. Mazeroski, PIT 3
G. Beckert, CHI 3
J. Maloney, CIN 3
B. White, PHI 3
L. Brock, SL 2
B. Shaw, SF-NY 1
C. Short, PHI 1
W. Davis, LA 1

1966 AMERICAN
F. Robinson, BAL ... 280
B. Robinson, BAL ... 153
B. Powell, BAL 122
H. Killebrew, MIN ... 96
J. Kaat, MIN 84
T. Oliva, MIN 71
A. Kaline, DET 66
T. Agee, CHI 63
L. Aparicio, BAL ... 51
B. Campaneris, KC .. 36
S. Miller, BAL 27
N. Cash, DET 23
J. Aker, KC 22
E. Wilson, BOS-DET . 13
D. McLain, DET 12
B. Freehan, DET 9
A. Etchebarren, BAL . 7
B. Knoop, CAL 6
M. Mantle, NY 5
T. Tresh, NY 5
J. Sanford, CAL 4
R. Reichardt, CAL ... 4
F. Valentine, WAS ... 4
W. Horton, DET 4
L. Wagner, CLE 4
P. Richert, WAS 3
J. Pepitone, NY 2
T. Conigliaro, BOS ... 1
S. Siebert, CLE 1
C. Yastrzemski, BOS   1
J. Fregosi, CAL 1

1967 NATIONAL
O. Cepeda, SL 280
T. McCarver, SL 136
R. Clemente, PIT ... 129
R. Santo, CHI 103
H. Aaron, ATL 79
M. McCormick, SF .. 73
L. Brock, SL 49
T. Perez, CIN 43
J. Javier, SL 41
P. Rose, CIN 40
J. Wynn, HOU 29
F. Jenkins, CHI 26
C. Flood, SL 24
E. Banks, CHI 22
N. Briles, SL 20
R. Staub, HOU 12
D. Hughes, SL 10
J. Hart, SF 10
R. Allen, PHI 9
T. Abernathy, CIN ... 8
C. Boyer, ATL 6
B. Gibson, SL 5
R. Hundley, CHI 5
J. Bunning, PHI 5
T. Seaver, NY 5
T. Davis, NY 3
G. Alley, PIT 3
T. Gonzalez, PHI ... 3
W. McCovey, SF 2

1967 AMERICAN
C. Yastrzemski,
  BOS 275
H. Killebrew, MIN ... 161
B. Freehan, DET ... 137
J. Horlen, CHI 91
A. Kaline, DET 88
J. Lonborg, BOS 82
C. Tovar, MIN 70
J. Fregosi, CAL 70
G. Peters, CHI 37
G. Scott, BOS 33
F. Robinson, BAL 31

E. Wilson, DET 20
D. Chance, MIN 19
R. Hansen, CHI 13
J. Adair, CHI-BOS ... 11
P. Blair, BAL 9
R. Petrocelli, BOS 7
E. Howard, NY-BOS .. 7
T. Oliva, MIN 6
J. Kaat, MIN 4
P. Casanova, WAS 3
D. Mincher, CAL 3
M. Lolich, DET 2
M. Rojas, CAL 1

1968 NATIONAL
B. Gibson, SL 242
P. Rose, CIN 205
W. McCovey, SF ... 135
C. Flood, SL 116
J. Marichal, SF 93
L. Brock, SL 73
M. Shannon, SL 55
B. Williams, CHI 48
G. Beckert, CHI 40
F. Alou, ATL 33
M. Alou, PIT 32
H. Aaron, ATL 19
W. Mays, SF 14
E. Banks, CHI 14
J. Koosman, NY 14
J. Bench, CIN 11
J. Regan, LA-CHI 7
F. Jenkins, CHI 6
T. Perez, CIN 5
N. Briles, SL 4
D. Maxvill, SL 4
S. Blass, PIT 3
T. Haller, LA 3
R. Santo, CHI 2
C. Carroll, ATL-CIN .. 1
T. Helms, CIN 1

1968 AMERICAN
D. McLain, DET 280
B. Freehan, DET ... 161
K. Harrelson, BOS .. 103
W. Horton, DET 102
D. McNally, BAL 78
L. Tiant, CLE 78
D. McAuliffe, DET ... 71
F. Howard, WAS 63
C. Yastrzemski, BOS . 50
M. Stottlemyre, NY .. 43
B. Campaneris, OAK . 39
R. White, NY 17
J. Northrup, DET 15
L. Aparicio, CHI 13
J. Fregosi, CAL 11
D. Buford, BAL 11
B. Robinson, BAL 8
R. Jackson, OAK 8
T. Oliva, MIN 5
D. Cater, OAK 5
M. Andrews, BOS 4
B. Powell, BAL 4
N. Cash, DET 3
C. Tovar, MIN 3
M. Stanley, DET 2
W. Wood, CHI 2
T. Uhlaender, MIN ... 1

1969 NATIONAL
W. McCovey, SF ... 265
T. Seaver, NY 243
H. Aaron, ATL 188
P. Rose, CIN 127
R. Santo, CHI 124
T. Agee, NY 89
C. Jones, NY 82
R. Clemente, PIT ... 51
P. Niekro, ATL 47
T. Perez, CIN 28
M. Wills, MON-LA ... 17
E. Banks, CHI 15
R. Carty, ATL 12
J. Bench, CIN 12
D. Kessinger, CHI ... 8
T. Gonzalez, SD-ATL . 8
R. Hunt, SF 8
D. Menke, HOU 8
W. Granger, CIN 8
J. Wynn, HOU 8
W. Davis, LA 7
W. Stargell, PIT 7
J. Marichal, SF 6

B. Williams, CHI 6
J. Koosman, NY 6
J. Torre, SL 6
M. Alou, PIT 6
L. Dierker, HOU 6
T. Haller, LA 3
B. Gibson, SL 2
R. Hundley, CHI 2
L. May, CIN 2
T. Sizemore, LA 2
W. Parker, LA 2
J. Edwards, HOU 1
R. Staub, MON 1
O. Cepeda, ATL 1

1969 AMERICAN
H. Killebrew, MIN ... 294
B. Powell, BAL 227
F. Robinson, BAL ... 162
F. Howard, WAS ... 115
R. Jackson, OAK ... 110
D. McLain, DET 85
R. Petrocelli, BOS ... 71
M. Cuellar, BAL 55
J. Perry, MIN 40
R. Carew, MIN 30
P. Blair, BAL 28
L. Cardenas, MIN ... 27
R. Perranoski, MIN .. 25
D. McNally, BAL 25
T. Oliva, MIN 21
B. Sando, OAK 18
C. Tovar, MIN 9
M. Stottlemyre, NY .. 8
C. Yastrzemski, BOS . 8
E. Brinkman, WAS ... 7
J. Fregosi, CAL 7
R. Smith, BOS 6
D. Unser, WAS 5
B. Robinson, BAL 5
M. Epstein, WAS 4
M. Andrews, BOS 3
D. Bosman, WAS 3
B. Freehan, DET 3
T. Harper, SEA 2
A. Messersmith, CAL . 2
R. Reese, MIN 2
K. Tatum, CAL 2
R. White, NY 2
M. Belanger, BAL 2
D. Green, OAK 1
J. Northrup, DET 1
L. Piniella, KC 1

1970 NATIONAL
J. Bench, CIN 326
B. Williams, CHI ... 218
T. Perez, CIN 149
B. Gibson, SL 110
W. Parker, LA 91
D. Giusti, PIT 72
P. Rose, CIN 54
J. Hickman, CHI 52
W. McCovey, SF 47
R. Carty, ATL 43
M. Sanguillen, PIT .. 36
B. Powell, BAL 33
D. Clendenon, NY ... 26
G. Perry, SF 24
W. Stargell, PIT 20
B. Tolan, CIN 17
H. Aaron, ATL 16
J. Torre, SL 15
T. Agee, NY 13
B. Harrelson, NY ... 10
F. Jenkins, CHI 8
J. Merritt, CIN 8
D. Kessinger, CHI ... 6
C. Gaston, SD 5
D. Johnson, PHI 4
L. Walker, PIT 4
C. Morton, MON 3
B. Robertson, PIT ... 3
T. Seaver, NY 2
W. Granger, CIN 1

1970 AMERICAN
B. Powell, BAL 234
T. Oliva, MIN 157
H. Killebrew, MIN .. 152
C. Yastrzemski,
  BOS 136
F. Howard, WAS 91
T. Harper, MIL 78

B. Robinson, BAL ... 75
A. Johnson, CAL ... 70
J. Perry, MIN 63
F. Robinson, BAL .. 60
M. Cuellar, BAL 45
R. Perranoski, MIN .. 35
J. Fregosi, CAL 35
R. White, NY 25
D. McNally, BAL ... 22
S. McDowell, CLE ... 22
C. Tovar, MIN 16
T. Munson, NY 15
D. Buford, BAL 12
C. Wright, CAL 8
L. McDaniel, NY 8
R. Fosse, CLE 7
B. Campaneris, OAK.. 5
J. Palmer, BAL 4
R. Smith, BOS 3
S. Bando, OAK 1
T. Horton, CLE 1
B. Oliver, KC 1

1971 NATIONAL
J. Torre, SL 318
W. Stargell, PIT ... 222
H. Aaron, ATL 180
B. Bonds, SF 139
R. Clemente, PIT .. 87
M. Wills, LA 74
F. Jenkins, CHI ... 71
M. Sanguillen, PIT . 49
T. Seaver, NY 46
A. Downing, LA 36
G. Beckert, CHI ... 35
L. May, CIN 28
L. Brock, SL 20
D. Giusti, PIT 16
W. McCovey, SF ... 15
T. Simmons, SL ... 13
W. Davis, LA 13
J. Johnson, SF 12
W. Mays, SF 11
R. Staub, MON 11
B. Williams, CHI .. 10
B. Harrelson, NY ... 4
B. Gibson, SL 3
R. Garr, ATL 3
D. Roberts, SD 1
P. Rose, CIN 1

1971 AMERICAN
V. Blue, OAK 268
S. Bando, OAK ... 182
F. Robinson, BAL .. 170
B. Robinson, BAL .. 163
M. Lolich, DET ... 155
F. Patek, KC 77
B. Murcer, NY 72
A. Otis, KC 67
W. Wood, CHI 54
T. Oliva, MIN 36
D. McNally, BAL ... 26
N. Cash, DET 21
B. Melton, CHI ... 18
R. Jackson, OAK .. 15
C. Rojas, KC 15
K. Sanders, MIL .. 13
P. Dobson, BAL ... 9
R. Smith, BOS 9
D. Johnson, BAL ... 8
M. Rettenmund, BAL . 8
H. Killebrew, MIN .. 5
J. Palmer, BAL ... 5
L. Cardenas, MIN .. 5
M. Cuellar, BAL ... 4
C. Tovar, MIN 4
G. Scott, BOS 3
D. Buford, BAL ... 2
J. Hunter, OAK ... 1
G. Nettles, CLE ... 1

1972 NATIONAL
J. Bench, CIN 263
B. Williams, CHI .. 211
W. Stargell, PIT .. 201
J. Morgan, CIN ... 197
S. Carlton, PHI .. 124
C. Cedeno, HOU .. 112
A. Oliver, PIT 52
N. Colbert, SD ... 45
L. May, HOU 30
T. Simmons, SL ... 22
M. Marshall, MON .. 22

P. Rose, CIN 19
R. Clemente, PIT ... 16
C. Carroll, CIN 16
L. Brock, SL 13
H. Aaron, ATL 12
M. Sanguillen, PIT .. 12
S. Blass, PIT 9
R. Garr, ATL 7
G. Clines, PIT 6
B. Tolan, CIN 6
D. Baker, ATL 5
M. Mota, LA 4
D. Kingman, SF ... 3
T. McGraw, NY 2
R. Staub, NY 2
T. Seaver, NY 2
J. Cardenal, CHI ... 1
F. Jenkins, CHI 1
C. Speier, SF 1

1972 AMERICAN
R. Allen, CHI 321
J. Rudi, OAK 164
S. Lyle, NY 158
C. Fisk, BOS 96
B. Murcer, NY 89
G. Perry, CLE 88
W. Wood, CHI 78
L. Tiant, BOS 70½
E. Brinkman, DET .. 62
M. Lolich, DET ... 60
J. Hunter, OAK ... 57
J. Mayberry, KC ... 27
J. Palmer, BAL ... 21
B. Grich, BAL 16
R. Carew, MIN ... 16
B. Campaneris, OAK. 11
M. Epstein, OAK .. 11
L. Aparicio, BOS .. 9½
R. Petrocelli, BOS . 9
R. Jackson, OAK .. 9
C. May, CHI 6
G. Scott, MIL 6
D. Thompson, MIN . 5
A. Kaline, DET ... 4
B. Freehan, DET .. 3
K. McMullen, CAL . 3
R. Robinson, BAL . 3
R. Smith, BOS 3
S. Bando, OAK ... 2
N. Ryan, CAL 2
A. Otis, KC 1
L. Piniella, KC ... 1

1973 NATIONAL
P. Rose, CIN 274
W. Stargell, PIT .. 250
B. Bonds, SF 174
J. Morgan, CIN .. 102
M. Marshall, MON . 93
L. Brock, SL 65
T. Perez, CIN 59
T. Seaver, NY 57
K. Singleton, MON . 52
J. Bench, CIN 41
C. Cedeno, HOU .. 39
H. Aaron, ATL ... 35
D. Johnson, ATL .. 34
T. Simmons, SL .. 20
T. McGraw, NY ... 17
F. Millan, NY 12
W. Davis, LA 12
D. Evans, ATL ... 11
L. May, HOU 9
T. Fuentes, SF ... 8
B. Watson, HOU .. 7
J. Ferguson LA ... 7
J. Cardenal, CHI .. 6
J. Billingham, CIN . 6
A. Oliver, PIT 6
R. Hunt, MON 5
R. Bryant, SF 5
G. Maddox, SF ... 3
B. Harrelson, NY .. 2
B. Williams, CHI .. 2
G. Luzinski, PHI .. 2
R. Russell, LA ... 1

1973 AMERICAN
R. Jackson, OAK .. 336
J. Palmer, BAL ... 172
A. Otis, KC 112
R. Carew, MIN ... 83
J. Hiller, DET 83

S. Bando, OAK 83
J. Mayberry, KC ... 76
D. May, MIL 65
B. Murcer, NY 53
T. Davis, BAL 47
J. Hunter, OAK ... 47
T. Munson, NY 43
T. Harper, BOS ... 33
G. Scott, MIL 25
O. Cepeda, BOS ... 21
F. Robinson, CAL .. 21
N. Ryan, CAL 20
C. Fisk, BOS 16
B. Grich, BAL 9
C. Yastrzemski, BOS . 9
M. Belanger, BAL .. 8
D. Johnson, OAK .. 8
J. Briggs, MIL 6
J. Coleman, DET .. 6
C. Rojas, KC 5
B. Blyleven, MIN ... 4
G. Perry, CLE 4
B. Campaneris, OAK.. 4
V. Blue, OAK 3
C. May, CHI 3
W. Horton, DET ... 3
B. North, OAK ... 3
P. Blair, BAL 2
D. Nelson, TEX ... 2
R. Allen, CHI 1

1974 NATIONAL
S. Garvey, LA 270
L. Brock, SL 233
M. Marshall, LA .. 146
J. Bench, CIN 141
J. Wynn, LA 137
M. Schmidt, PHI .. 136
A. Oliver, PIT 87
J. Morgan, CIN ... 72
R. Zisk, PIT 54
W. Stargell, PIT .. 43
R. Smith, SL 39
R. Garr, ATL 11
T. Simmons, SL .. 7
D. Cash, PHI 6
D. Concepcion, CIN . 5
J. Billingham, CIN . 4
C. Cedeno, HOU .. 4
A. Hrabosky, SL .. 4
A. Messersmith, LA . 4
B. Capra, ATL ... 3
L. McGlothen, SL .. 2
B. McBride, SL ... 2
R. Hebner, PIT ... 2
R. Stennett, PIT .. 2
B. Buckner, LA ... 1
R. Cey, LA 1

1974 AMERICAN
J. Burroughs, TEX . 248
J. Rudi, OAK 161½
S. Bando, OAK ... 143½
R. Jackson, OAK .. 119
F. Jenkins, TEX ... 118
J. Hunter, OAK ... 107
R. Carew, MIN ... 70
E. Maddox, NY ... 59
B. Grich, BAL 49
M. Cuellar, BAL .. 42
L. Tiant, BOS 41
R. Robinson, BAL . 30
P. Blair, BAL 27
N. Ryan, CAL 24
B. Campaneris, OAK. 23
R. Fingers, OAK .. 21
G. Perry, CLE 18
C. Yastrzemski, BOS 14
K. Henderson, CHI .. 12
J. Hiller, DET 11
L. Randle, TEX ... 10
B. Murcer, NY ... 10
L. Piniella, NY ... 8
R. Allen, CHI 8
S. Lyle, NY 7
T. Munson, NY ... 6
T. Davis, BAL 6
M. Belanger, BAL .. 6
D. Money, MIL ... 5
T. Murphy, MIL ... 3
H. McRae, KC ... 3
S. Busby, KC ... 3
G. Scott, MIL ... 2
P. Dobson, NY ... 1

1975 NATIONAL
J. Morgan, CIN ... 321½
G. Luzinski, PHI ... 154
D. Parker, PIT ... 120
J. Bench, CIN ... 117
P. Rose, CIN ... 114
T. Simmons, SL ... 103
W. Stargell, PIT ... 69
A. Hrabosky, SL ... 66
T. Seaver, NY ... 65
R. Jones, SD ... 54
S. Garvey, LA ... 50
B. Madlock, CHI ... 45
D. Cash, PHI ... 26
R. Staub, NY ... 20
T. Perez, CIN ... 18
M. Schmidt, PHI ... 16
M. Sanguillen, PIT ... 16
R. Cey, LA ... 11½
D. Kingman, NY ... 9
B. Watson, HOU ... 8
L. Brock, SL ... 6
L. Bowa, PHI ... 3
J. Reuss, PIT ... 2
A. Messersmith, LA ... 1
W. Montanez, PHI-SF. 1

1975 AMERICAN
F. Lynn, BOS ... 326
J. Mayberry, KC ... 157
J. Rice, BOS ... 154
R. Fingers, OAK ... 129
R. Jackson, OAK ... 118
J. Palmer, BAL ... 82
T. Munson, NY ... 69
G. Scott, MIL ... 64½
R. Carew, MIN ... 54½
K. Singleton, BAL ... 44
G. Brett, KC ... 37½
J. Hunter, NY ... 31
R. Burleson, BOS ... 28
C. Washington, OAK. 22
T. Harrah, TEX ... 16
M. Torrez, BAL ... 12
R. Gossage, CHI ... 11
P. Lindblad, OAK ... 9
G. Tenace, OAK ... 7
B. Powell, CLE ... 6½
D. Baylor, BAL ... 6
B. Campaneris, OAK.. 6
B. Lee, BOS ... 5
J. Todd, OAK ... 5
D. Doyle, CAL-BOS.. 5
R. Wise, BOS ... 4
J. Rudi, OAK ... 3
J. Kaat, CHI ... 2
L. May, BAL ... 2
B. Bonds, NY ... 1
C. Yastrzemski, BOS . 1

1976 NATIONAL
J. Morgan, CIN ... 311
G. Foster, CIN ... 221
M. Schmidt, PHI ... 179
P. Rose, CIN ... 131
G. Maddox, PHI ... 98
B. Madlock, CHI ... 51
S. Garvey, LA ... 51
G. Luzinski, PHI ... 49
K. Griffey, CIN ... 49
R. Jones, SD ... 48
B. Watson, HOU ... 38
A. Oliver, PIT ... 30
R. Eastwick, CIN ... 26
J. Koosman, NY ... 20
S. Carlton, PHI ... 16
D. Cash, PHI ... 15
J. Richard, HOU ... 12
R. Monday, CHI ... 11
D. Kingman, NY ... 11
D. Parker, PIT ... 10
B. Robinson, PIT ... 9
D. Sutton, LA ... 7
R. Cey, LA ... 6
W. Montanez, SF-ATL 4
L. Brock, SL ... 3
C. Cedeno, HOU ... 3
C. Geronimo, CIN ... 3
R. Zisk, PIT ... 3
L. Bowa, PHI ... 1

1976 AMERICAN
T. Munson, NY ... 304
G. Brett, KC ... 217
M. Rivers, NY ... 179½

H. McRae, KC ... 99
C. Chambliss, NY ... 71½
R. Carew, MIN ... 71
A. Otis, KC ... 58
B. Campbell, MIN ... 56
L. May, BAL ... 51
J. Palmer, BAL ... 47
M. Fidrych, DET ... 41
J. Rudi, OAK ... 35
S. Bando, OAK ... 31
C. Yastrzemski, BOS 26
F. Tanana, CAL ... 19
R. Jackson, BAL ... 17
G. Nettles, NY ... 17
G. Tenace, OAK ... 13
R. Fingers, OAK ... 12
V. Blue, OAK ... 10
E. Figueroa, NY ... 9
S. Lyle, NY ... 8
R. LeFlore, DET ... 6
M. Littell, KC ... 5
R. Carty, CLE ... 5
R. White, NY ... 3
L. Tiant, BOS ... 3
J. Mayberry, KC ... 1
B. Wynegar, MIN ... 1

1977 NATIONAL
G. Foster, CIN ... 291
G. Luzinski, PHI ... 255
D. Parker, PIT ... 156
R. Smith, LA ... 112
S. Carlton, PHI ... 100
S. Garvey, LA ... 98
B. Sutter, CHI ... 68
R. Cey, LA ... 60
T. Simmons, SL ... 58
M. Schmidt, PHI ... 48
B. Robinson, PIT ... 34
T. John, LA ... 33
G. Templeton, SL ... 20
R. Fingers, SD ... 17
P. Rose, CIN ... 15
J. Burroughs, ATL ... 9
A. Oliver, PIT ... 9
J. Candelaria, PIT ... 8
R. Stennett, PIT ... 7
W. McCovey, SF ... 5
J. Bench, CIN ... 3
R. Reuschel, CHI ... 3
E. Valentine, MON ... 3
T. McGraw, PHI ... 2
L. Bowa, PHI ... 1
T. Seaver, NY-CIN ... 1

1977 AMERICAN
R. Carew, MIN ... 273
A. Cowens, KC ... 217
K. Singleton, BAL ... 200
J. Rice, BOS ... 163
G. Nettles, NY ... 112
S. Lyle, NY ... 79
T. Munson, NY ... 70
R. Jackson, NY ... 67
C. Fisk, BOS ... 67
B. Campbell, BOS ... 65
M. Rivers, NY ... 59
H. Hisle, MIN ... 54
G. Brett, KC ... 51
R. Zisk, CHI ... 34
J. Sundberg, TEX ... 30
B. Bonds, CAL ... 28
C. Yastrzemski, BOS 25
R. Guidry, NY ... 11
J. Palmer, BAL ... 9
R. LeFlore, DET ... 7
J. Thompson, DET ... 6
R. Burleson, BOS ... 5
B. Hobson, BOS ... 4
N. Ryan, CAL ... 3
G. Scott, BOS ... 3
H. McRae, KC ... 3
L. Bostock, MIN ... 2
T. Johnson, MIN ... 2
C. Chambliss, NY ... 1
O. Gamble, CHI ... 1
D. Leonard, KC ... 1

1978 NATIONAL
D. Parker, PIT ... 320
S. Garvey, LA ... 194
L. Bowa, PHI ... 189
R. Smith, LA ... 164
J. Clark, SF ... 107
G. Foster, CIN ... 104

G. Luzinski, PHI ... 48
G. Perry, SD ... 45
W. Stargell, PIT ... 39
D. Winfield, SD ... 37
P. Rose, CIN ... 35
V. Blue, SF ... 33
K. Tekulve, PIT ... 23
R. Fingers, SD ... 16
B. Hooton, LA ... 15
D. Lopes, LA ... 12
P. Niekro, ATL ... 8
B. Buckner, CHI ... 7
J. Burroughs, ATL ... 7
B. Sutter, CHI ... 5
G. Maddox, PHI ... 4
E. Cabell, HOU ... 2
B. Boone, PHI ... 1

1978 AMERICAN
J. Rice, BOS ... 352
R. Guidry, NY ... 291
L. Hisle, MIL ... 201
A. Otis, KC ... 90
R. Staub, DET ... 88
G. Nettles, NY ... 86
D. Baylor, CAL ... 51
E. Murray, BAL ... 50
C. Fisk, BOS ... 49
D. Porter, KC ... 48
R. Carew, MIN ... 46
M. Caldwell, MIL ... 41
R. Gossage, NY ... 39
A. Oliver, TEX ... 26½
J. Sundberg, TEX ... 24
R. LeFlore, DET ... 21
R. Jackson, NY ... 18
C. Yastrzemski, BOS . .
... 17
G. Brett, KC ... 14
A. Thornton, CLE .. 12½
L. Piniella, NY ... 11
T. Munson, NY ... 9
L. Bostock, CAL ... 8
L. Gura, KC ... 8
F. Lynn, BOS ... 6
M. Rivers, NY ... 6
B. Stanley, BOS ... 6
D. LaRoche, CAL ... 6
D. Money, MIL ... 5
W. Randolph, NY ... 5
D. Eckersley, BOS ... 4
H. McRae, KC ... 4
L. Roberts, SEA ... 3
R. Gale, KC ... 2
K. Singleton, BAL ... 2
R. Burleson, BOS ... 1
F. Tanana, CAL ... 1

1979 NATIONAL
W. Stargell, PIT ... 216
K. Hernandez, SL ... 216
D. Winfield, SD ... 155
L. Parrish, MON ... 128
R. Knight, CIN ... 82
J. Niekro, HOU ... 75½
B. Sutter, CHI ... 69
K. Tekulve, PIT ... 64
D. Concepcion, CIN .. 63
D. Parker, PIT ... 56
D. Kingman, CHI ... 53
G. Foster, CIN ... 34
M. Schmidt, PHI ... 32
S. Garvey, LA ... 30
O. Moreno, PIT ... 23
P. Rose, PHI ... 23
G. Carter, MON ... 15
B. Madlock, SF-PIT ... 14
J. Richard, HOU ... 12
P. Niekro, ATL ... 11½
J. Sambito, HOU ... 9
T. Seaver, CIN ... 9
J. Bench, CIN ... 7
A. Dawson, MON ... 6
G. Templeton, SL ... 4
D. Matthews, ATL ... 4
D. Collins, CIN ... 3
B. Horner, ATL ... 1

1979 AMERICAN
D. Baylor, CAL ... 347
K. Singleton, BAL ... 241
G. Brett, KC ... 226
F. Lynn, BOS ... 160½
J. Rice, BOS ... 124
M. Flanagan, BAL .. 100

G. Thomas, MIL ... 87
G. Grich, CAL ... 58
D. Porter, KC ... 52
B. Bell, TEX ... 48
E. Murray, BAL ... 25½
J. Kern, TEX ... 25
M. Marshall, MIN ... 25
B. Downing, CAL ... 24
S. Lezcano, MIL ... 18
R. Smalley, MIN ... 16
W. Wilson, KC ... 15
S. Kemp, DET ... 15
M. Clear, CAL ... 12
P. Molitor, MIL ... 8
B. Burroughs, ATL ... 7
T. John, NY ... 5
C. Cooper, MIL ... 4
R. Jackson, NY ... 3
W. Horton, SEA ... 3
D. Ford, CAL ... 1
R. Guidry, NY ... 1
M. Hargrove, CLE ... 1

1980 NATIONAL
M. Schmidt, PHI ... 336
G. Carter, MON ... 193
J. Cruz, HOU ... 166
D. Baker, LA ... 138
S. Carlton, PHI ... 134
S. Garvey, LA ... 131
A. Dawson, MON ... 72
G. Hendrick, SL ... 50
B. Horner, ATL ... 42
B. McBride, PHI ... 32
K. Hernandez, SL ... 29
D. Murphy, ATL ... 23
C. Cedeno, HOU ... 14
J. Bibby, PIT ... 11
B. Buckner, CHI ... 11
T. McGraw, PHI ... 10
J. Bench, CIN ... 7
J. Clark, SF ... 6
J. Niekro, HOU ... 3
M. Easler, PIT ... 2
J. Reuss, LA ... 2
K. Griffey, CIN ... 1
R. LeFlore, MON ... 1
G. Richards, SD ... 1
R. Scott, MON ... 1

1980 AMERICAN
G. Brett, KC ... 335
R. Jackson, NY ... 234
R. Gossage, NY ... 218
W. Wilson, KC ... 169
C. Cooper, MIL ... 160
E. Murray, BAL ... 106
R. Cerone, NY ... 77
D. Quisenberry, KC 76½
S. Stone, BAL ... 53
R. Henderson, OAK.. 51
A. Oliver, TEX ... 31½
T. Armas, OAK ... 29
A. Bumbry, BAL ... 27
B. Oglivie, MIL ... 27
W. Randolph, NY ... 10
M. Norris, OAK ... 10
R. Yount, MIL ... 8
M. Rivers, TEX ... 7
B. Bell, TEX ... 7
A. Trammell, DET ... 6
K. Singleton, BAL ... 4
T. Perez, BOS ... 2
M. Dilone, CLE ... 2
F. Lynn, BOS ... 1
J. Wathan, KC ... 1

1981 NATIONAL
M. Schmidt, PHI ... 321
A. Dawson, MON ... 215
G. Foster, CIN ... 146
D. Concepcion, CIN 108
F. Valenzuela, LA ... 90
G. Carter, MON ... 77
D. Baker, LA ... 65
B. Sutter, SL ... 59
S. Carlton, PHI ... 41
T. Seaver, CIN ... 35
P. Rose, PHI ... 35
B. Buckner, CHI ... 35
G. Matthews, PHI ... 31
J. Cruz, HOU ... 25
G. Hendrick, SL ... 25
N. Ryan, HOU ... 23
B. Madlock, PIT ... 20

A. Howe, HOU ... 16
T. Raines, MON ... 15
R. Camp, ATL ... 9
K. Hernandez, SL ... 9
T. Herr, SL ... 7
G. Minton, SF ... 7
W. Cromartie, MON... 3
S. Garvey, LA ... 1
M. May, SF ... 1

1981 AMERICAN
R. Fingers, MIL ... 319
R. Henderson, OAK.308
D. Evans, BOS ... 140
T. Armas, OAK ... 139
E. Murray, BAL ... 137
C. Lansford, BOS ... 109
D. Winfield, NY ... 98
C. Cooper, MIL ... 96
R. Gossage, NY ... 62
T. Paciorek, SEA ... 46
D. Murphy, OAK ... 45
K. Gibson, DET ... 40
S. McCatty, OAK ... 22
B. Grich, CAL ... 19
J. Morris, DET ... 17
A. Oliver, TEX ... 8
R. Yount, MIL ... 7
B. Bell, TEX ... 7
B. Almon, CHI ... 6
J. Mumphrey, NY ... 5
M. Hargrove, CLE ... 4
A. Trammell, DET ... 4
K. Singleton, BAL ... 3
S. Kemp, DET ... 3
D. Martinez, BAL ... 3
G. Luzinski, CHI ... 3
D. Stieb, TOR ... 1
G. Brett, KC ... 1

1982 NATIONAL
D. Murphy, ATL ... 283
L. Smith, SL ... 218
P. Guerrero, LA ... 175
A. Oliver, MON ... 175
B. Sutter, SL ... 134
M. Schmidt, PHI ... 54
J. Clark, SF ... 53
G. Minton, SF ... 44
S. Carlton, PHI ... 41
B. Buckner, CHI ... 38
B. Madlock, PIT ... 37
G. Carter, MON ... 35
O. Smith, SL ... 25
G. Hendrick, SL ... 20
T. Kennedy, SD ... 20
J. Morgan, SF ... 17
K. Hernandez, SL ... 12
J. Thompson, PIT ... 12
G. Garber, ATL ... 6
J. Andujar, SL ... 6
F. Valenzuela, LA ... 3
A. Dawson, MON ... 3
C. Chambliss, ATL ... 2
G. Matthews, PHI ... 2
R. Knight, HOU ... 1

1982 AMERICAN
R. Yount, MIL ... 385
E. Murray, BAL ... 228
D. DeCinces, CAL ... 178
H. McRae, KC ... 175
C. Cooper, MIL ... 152
R. Jackson, CAL ... 107
D. Evans, BOS ... 57
G. Thomas, MIL ... 44½
D. Quisenberry, KC .. 39
R. Henderson, OAK.. 38
D. Winfield, NY ... 33
P. Molitor, MIL ... 29½
L. Parrish, DET ... 26
B. Downing, CAL ... 22
W. Wilson, KC ... 16
R. Fingers, MIL ... 12
B. Boone, CAL ... 12
P. Vuckovich, MIL ... 11
J. Rice, BOS ... 10
T. Harrah, CLE ... 9
H. Baines, CHI ... 9
G. Brett, KC ... 9
D. Baylor, CAL ... 8
A. Thornton, CLE ... 8
B. Stanley, BOS ... 6
J. Palmer, BAL ... 5
D. Garcia, TOR ... 5

R. Carew, CAL ... 5
B. Caudill, SEA ... 4
B. Bell, TEX ... 3
C. Ripken, BAL ... 3
C. Lansford, BOS ... 1
R. Sutcliffe, CLE ... 1
G. Ward, MIN ... 1

1983 NATIONAL
D. Murphy, ATL ... 318
A. Dawson, MON ... 213
M. Schmidt, PHI ... 191
P. Guerrero, LA ... 182
T. Raines, MON ... 83
J. Cruz, HOU ... 76
D. Thon, HOU ... 67
B. Madlock, PIT ... 45
A. Holland, PHI ... 42
T. Kennedy, SD ... 37
G. Hendrick, SL ... 33
T. Pena, PIT ... 25
J. Denny, PHI ... 24
M. Soto, CIN ... 16
D. Evans, SF ... 16
R. Ramirez, ATL ... 15
J. Orosco, NY ... 14
L. Smith, CHI ... 8½
A. Oliver, MON ... 3
J. Leonard, SF ... 2
L. Smith, SL ... 1½
J. Davis, CHI ... 1
K. Hernandez, SL-NY. 1
B. Horner, ATL ... 1
O. Smith, SL ... 1

1983 AMERICAN
C. Ripken, BAL ... 322
E. Murray, BAL ... 290
C. Fisk, CHI ... 209
J. Rice, BOS ... 150
C. Cooper, MIL ... 123
D. Quisenberry,
KC ... 107½
D. Winfield, NY ... 85
L. Whitaker, DET ... 84
L. Parrish, DET ... 66
H. Baines, CHI ... 49
W. Upshaw, TOR ... 41½
W. Boggs, BOS ... 25
L. Hoyt, CHI ... 24½
L. Moseby, TOR ... 21
B. Stanley, BOS ... 11½
A. Trammell, DET ... 11
G. Luzinski, CHI ... 9
R. Yount, MIL ... 6
T. Simmons, MIL ... 4
R. Dotson, CHI ... 3½
R. Law, CHI ... 2
R. Guidry, NY ... 2
J. Morris, DET ... 2
J. Cruz, SEA-CHI ... 1
R. Henderson, OAK... 1
G. Wright, TEX ... 1
T. Martinez, BAL ... ½

1984 NATIONAL
R. Sandberg, CHI ... 326
K. Hernandez, NY ... 195
T. Gwynn, SD ... 184
R. Sutcliffe, CHI ... 151
G. Matthews, CHI ... 70
B. Sutter, SL ... 67
M. Schmidt, PHI ... 55½
J. Cruz, HOU ... 53
D. Murphy, ATL ... 52½
J. Davis, CHI ... 49
T. Raines, MON ... 41
L. Durham, CHI ... 38
R. Gossage, SD ... 34
G. Carter, MON ... 32
D. Gooden, NY ... 28
A. Wiggins, SD ... 14
R. Cey, CHI ... 6
K. McReynolds, SD... 6
B. Dernier, CHI ... 6
S. Garvey, SD ... 5
B. Brenly, SF ... 1
J. Samuel, PHI ... 1
J. Leonard, SF ... 1

1984 AMERICAN
W. Hernandez, DET. 306
K. Hrbek, MIN ... 247
D. Quisenberry, KC . 235
E. Murray, BAL ... 197

D. Mattingly, NY 113
K. Gibson, DET 96
T. Armas, BOS 87½
D. Winfield, NY 83
A. Trammell, DET ..76½
W. Wilson, KC 61
D. Evans, BOS 39
A. Davis, SEA 26
H. Baines, CHI 10
D. Kingman, OAK ...10
L. Parrish, DET 8
W. Upshaw, TOR 8
B. Downing, CAL 6
S. Balboni, KC 5
A. Thornton, CLE 5
J. Bell, TOR...........5
B. Bell, TEX..........4
D. Stieb, TOR.........4
L. Moseby, TOR 4
J. Beniquez, CAL 2
M. Boddicker, BAL ...2
C. Ripken, BAL 1

1985 NATIONAL
W. McGee, SL 280
D. Parker, CIN 220
P. Guerrero, LA 208
D. Gooden, NY 162
T. Herr, SL.......119
G. Carter, NY 116
D. Murphy, ATL 63
K. Hernandez, NY ...61
J. Tudor, SL 61
J. Clark, SL 20
V. Coleman, SL 16
T. Raines, MON 16
R. Sandberg, CHI ...14
M. Marshall, LA 11
H. Brooks, MON 11
O. Hershiser, LA 9
K. Moreland, CHI 8
O. Smith, SL........5
M. Scioscia, LA 5
J. Reardon, MON 4
J. Cruz, HOU 2
B. Doran, HOU 2
M. Duncan, LA.......1
T. Gwynn, SD.......1
F. Valenzuela, LA 1
G. Wilson, PHI.......1

1985 AMERICAN
D. Mattingly, NY ...367
G. Brett, KC 274
R. Henderson, NY ...174
W. Boggs, BOS 159
E. Murray, BAL 130
D. Moore, CAL 96
J. Barfield, TOR......88
J. Bell, TOR........84
H. Baines, CHI.......49
B. Saberhagen, KC ...45
D. Quisenberry, KC ..39
D. Winfield, NY 35
C. Fisk, CHI 29
Da. Evans, DET 17
R. Guidry, NY.......15
P. Bradley, SEA 12
C. Ripken, BAL 9
K. Gibson, DET 7
S. Balboni, KC 6
T. Henke, TOR........5
D. Lamp, TOR 5
K. Puckett, MIN......3
D. Alexander, TOR....3
D. Garcia, TOR 2
R. Gedman, BOS 1

1986 NATIONAL
M. Schmidt, PHI ...287
G. Davis, HOU 231
G. Carter, NY 181
K. Hernandez, NY ..179
D. Parker, CIN 144
T. Raines, MON 99
K. Bass, HOU 73
V. Hayes, PHI.......41
T. Gwynn, SD.......36
M. Scott, HOU 33
B. Doran, HOU 32
E. Davis, CIN 21
S. Sax, LA 13
R. Knight, NY 9

M. Krukow, SF........8
T. Worrell, SL 7
R. McDowell, NY 5
D. Smith, HOU 5
F. Valenzuela, LA 4
L. Dykstra, NY 4
B. Ojeda, NY 2
D. Murphy, ATL 2
C. Maldonado, SF 2

1986 AMERICAN
R. Clemens, BOS ...339
D. Mattingly, NY ...258
J. Rice, BOS........241
J. Bell, TOR........125
J. Barfield, TOR.....107
K. Puckett, MIN.....105
W. Boggs, BOS 87
W. Joyner, CAL 74
J. Carter, CLE 72
D. Righetti, NY 71
D. DeCinces, CAL 56
M. Witt, CAL........34
D. Baylor, BOS 32
T. Fernandez, TOR ...17
T. Higuera, MIL 7
G. Gaetti, MIN 6
P. O'Brien, TEX 5
S. Fletcher, TEX 5
M. Barrett, BOS 5
J. Canseco, OAK 3
J. Presley, SEA 2
D. Schofield, CAL......1

1987 NATIONAL
A. Dawson, CHI 269
O. Smith, SL........193
J. Clark, SL 186
T. Wallach, MON ...165
W. Clark, SF 128
S. Strawberry, NY 95
T. Raines, MON 80
T. Gwynn, SD.......75
E. Davis, CIN 73
H. Johnson, NY 42
D. Murphy, ATL 34
V. Coleman, SL 20
J. Samuel, PHI.......19
M. Schmidt, PHI 13
P. Guerrero, LA 12
S. Bedrosian, PHI......6
M. Thompson, PHI.....4
B. Doran, HOU 1
T. Pendleton, SL......1

1987 AMERICAN
J. Bell, TOR........332
A. Trammell, DET ...311
K. Puckett, MIN.....201
Dw. Evans, BOS 127
P. Molitor, MIL......125
M. McGwire, OAK ..109
D. Mattingly, NY 92
T. Fernandez, TOR ...79
W. Boggs, BOS 64
G. Gaetti, MIN 47
J. Reardon, MIN 37
Da. Evans, DET 21
D. Alexander, DET ...17
T. Henke, TOR.......17
W. Joyner, CAL 17
K. Hrbek, MIN 11
D. Tartabull, KC 10
R. Yount, MIL 8
R. Clemens, BOS 7
J. Morris, DET 5
K. Seitzer, KC 5
R. Sierra, TEX........5
J. Canseco, OAK 4
M. Nokes, DET 1

1988 NATIONAL
K. Gibson, LA.......272
D. Strawberry, NY ..236
K. McReynolds,NY ..162
A. Van Slyke, PIT ...160
W. Clark, SF 135
O. Hershiser, LA 111
A. Galarraga, MON .105
G. Davis, HOU 72
D. Jackson, CIN 41
D. Cone, NY 37
T. Gwynn, SD.......29
J. Franco, CIN 23
E. Davis, CIN 14

B. Bonilla, PIT 7
A. Dawson, CHI 6
N. Myers, NY 5
B. Butler, SF 2
S. Sax, LA 1

1988 AMERICAN
J. Canseco, OAK ...392
M. Greenwell, BOS .242
K. Puckett, MIN.....219
D. Winfield, NY 164
D. Eckersley, OAK ..156
W. Boggs, BOS 107
A. Trammell, DET 62
P. Molitor, MIL.......50
Dw. Evans, BOS 49
F. Viola, MIN........39
R. Yount, MIL 34
G. Brett, KC 29
R. Henderson, OAK ..28
B. Hurst, BOS 15
D. Jones, CLE 11
J. Reardon, MIN 11
F. McGriff, TOR.......9
R. Henderson, NY 8
M. McGwire, OAK 6
J. Carter, CLE 5
L. Smith, BOS 4
G. Gaetti, MIN 3
D. Plesac, MIL 3
D. Stewart, OAK 3
J. Franco, CLE........2
T. Fernandez, TOR ...1

1989 NATIONAL
K. Mitchell, SF 314
W. Clark, SF 225
P. Guerrero. SL 190
R. Sandberg, CHI ...157
H. Johnson, NY.....153
M. Davis, SD 76
G. Davis, HOU 64
T. Gwynn, SD.......57
E. Davis, CIN 44
M. Williams, CHI 41
L. Smith, ATL 34
J. Clark, SD.........16
J. Walton, CHI 14
M. Grace, CHI 9
M. Scott, HOU 6
B. Bonilla, PIT 5
B. Butler, SF 3
T. Raines, MON 3
M. Thompson, SL 3
S. Garrelts, SF 2

1989 AMERICAN
R. Yount, MIL 256
R. Sierra, TEX......228
C. Ripken, BAL 216
J. Bell, TOR........205
D. Eckersley, OAK ..116
F. McGriff, TOR......96
K. Puckett, MIN......84
B. Saberhagen, KC ...82
R. Henderson,
   NY-OAK 67
B. Jackson, KC 46
D. Parker, OAK 44
G. Olson, BAL 35
B. Blyleven, CAL.....32
D. Stewart, OAK 30
D. Mattingly, NY 25
J. Carter, CLE 23
C. Lansford, OAK 20
N. Esasky, BOS 19
T. Fernandez, TOR ...17
M. Moore, OAK 6
W. Boggs, BOS 3
S. Sax, NY 3
A. Davis, SEA 3
N. Ryan, TEX........2
C. Davis, CAL 1
M. McGwire, OAK 1
M. Wilson, TOR 1

1990 NATIONAL
B. Bonds, PIT.......331
B. Bonilla, PIT 212
D. Strawberry, NY ..167
R. Sandberg, CHI ...151
E. Murray, LA.......123
M. Williams, SF 95
B. Larkin, CIN 82
D. Drabek, PIT 59

L. Dykstra, PHI 41
T. Wallach, MON 36
K. Mitchell, SF 20
E. Davis, CIN 12
C. Sabo, CIN 11
R. Gant, ATL 10
D. Gooden, NY 10
R. Martinez, LA 9
J. Carter, SD.........7
R. Myers, CIN 7
P. O'Neill, CIN 6
J. Rijo, CIN 6
A. Dawson, CHI 6
D. Magadan, NY 4
B. Santiago, SD 3
B. Butler, SF 2
D. Justice, ATL 2
P. Guerrero, SL 2
K. Daniels, LA 1
A. Van Slyke, PIT 1

1990 AMERICAN
R. Henderson, OAK 317
C. Fielder, DET 286
R. Clemens, BOS ...212
K. Gruber, TOR 175
B. Thigpen, CHI 170
D. Eckersley, OAK ..112
G. Brett, KC 60
D. Stewart, OAK 56
B. Welch, OAK 54
F. McGriff, TOR......30
M. McGwire, OAK ...29
J. Canseco, OAK 26
E. Burks, BOS 25
R. Palmeiro, TEX.....22
C. Fisk, CHI 16
D. Parker, MIL 11
O. Guillen, CHI 10
J. Reed, BOS 9
K. Griffey, Jr., SEA ...7
A. Trammell, DET 7
T. Pena, BOS 6
W. Boggs, BOS 5
J. Jones, CLE 3
C. Ripken, BAL 2
N. Ryan, TEX.........1
D. Stieb, TOR........1

1991 NATIONAL
T. Pendleton, ATL...274
B. Bonds, PIT.......259
B. Bonilla, PIT 191
W. Clark, SF 118
H. Johnson, NY.....112
R. Gant, ATL 110
B. Butler, LA 103
L. Smith, SL 89
D. Strawberry, LA ...76
F. McGriff, SD 23
G. Glavine, ATL 16
D. Justice, ATL 11
J. Bell, PIT 11
A. Dawson, CHI 5
J. Smiley, PIT 5
T. Gwynn, SD.........4
J. Kruk, PHI 2
R. Sandberg, CHI 2
B. Larkin, CIN 2
D. Martinez, MON 1
C. Sabo, CIN 1
O. Smith, SL.........1

1991 AMERICAN
C. Ripken, BAL 318
C. Fielder, DET 286
F. Thomas, CHI.....181
J. Canseco, OAK ...145
J. Carter, TOR 136
J. Alomar, TOR 128
K. Puckett, MIN......78
R. Sierra, TEX.......63
K. Griffey, Jr., SEA ..62
R. Clemens, BOS 57
P. Molitor, MIL.......51
D. Tartabull, KC 32
J. Morris, MIN 29
C. Davis, MIN 21
J. Franco, TEX.......17
D. White, TOR 15
S. Erickson, MIN 12
R. Aguilera, MIN 11
R. Palmeiro, TEX......6
R. Ventura, CHI 3
D. Henderson, OAK...1

1992 NATIONAL
B. Bonds, PIT.......304
T. Pendleton, ATL...232
G. Sheffield, SD 204
A. Van Slyke, PIT ...145
L. Walker, MON 111
D. Daulton, PHI.....100
F. McGriff, SD 100
B. Roberts, CIN 54
M. Grissom, MON 54
T. Glavine, ATL 18
G. Maddux, CHI 14
R. Sandberg, CHI 12
B. Larkin, CIN 12
J. Jones, HOU 8
M. Grace, PHI 6
D. DeShields, MON ...6
R. Lankford, SL 5
J. Bagwell, HOU 4
D. Hollins, PHI 3
B. Butler, LA 2
O. Smith, SL.........2
O. Nixon, ATL........1
J. Wetteland, MON ...1

1992 AMERICAN
D. Eckersley, OAK ..306
K. Puckett, MIN.....209
J. Carter, TOR 201
M. McGwire, OAK ..155
D. Winfield, TOR ...141
R. Alomar, TOR 118
M. Devereaux, BAL 109
F. Thomas, CHI.....108
C. Fielder, DET 83
P. Molitor, MIL.......63
C. Baerga, CLE 31
E. Martinez, SEA 29
J. Morris, TOR 18
R. Clemens, BOS 16
B. Anderson, BAL 16
J. Gonzalez, TEX 15
K. Griffey, Jr., SEA ..13
P. Listach, MIL 8
J. McDowell, CHI 5
J. Bell, CHI 3
M. Bordick, OAK......2
M. Mussina, BAL 2
A. Belle, CLE 1

1993 NATIONAL
B. Bonds, SF 372
L. Dykstra, PHI 267
D. Justice, ATL 183
F. McGriff, SD-ATL .177
R. Gant, ATL 176
M. Williams, SF 103
D. Daulton, PHI......79
M. Grissom, MON ...66
M. Piazza, LA 49
A. Galarraga, COL ...45
G. Jefferies, STL 28
R. Beck, SF 23
G. Maddux, ATL 17
J. Bagwell, HOU 3
T. Gwynn, SD.........2
R. Myers, CHI 2
J. Rijo, CIN 2
J. Burkett, SF 1
T. Glavine, ATL 1
J. Wetteland, MON ...1

1993 AMERICAN
F. Thomas, CHI.....392
P. Molitor, TOR 209
J. Olerud, TOR 198
J. Gonzalez, TEX ...185
K. Griffey, Jr., SEA .182
R. Alomar, TOR 102
A. Belle, CLE 81
R. Palmeiro, TEX.....52
J. McDowell, CHI 51
C. Baerga, CLE 50
J. Key, NY 29
J. Carter, TOR 25
M. Stanley, NY 15
J. Montgomery, KC ...15
K. Lofton, CLE 11

T. Phillips, DET 10
C. Hoiles, BAL 10
M. Vaughn, BOS 8
D. Mattingly, NY 7
C. Ripken, BAL 7
A. Fernandez, CHI 4
D. Ward, TOR 3
G. Gagne, KC 3
K. Appier, KC 1
C. Fielder, DET 1
R. Johnson, SEA 1

1994 NATIONAL
J. Bagwell, Hou 392
M. Williams, SF 201
M. Alou, Mtl 183
B. Bonds, SF 144
G. Maddux, Atl 133
M. Piazza, LA 121
T. Gwynn, SD.......112
F. McGriff, Atl 96
K. Mitchell, Cin 86
A. Galarraga, Col 42
L. Walker, Mtl 23
K. Hill, Mtl 22
M. Grissom, Mtl 22
D. Bichette, Col 19
H. Morris, Cin 18
C. Biggio, Hou 17
G. Jefferies, StL 5
J. Conine, Fla 4
T. Wallach, LA 4
J. Franco, NY 3
B. Boone, Cin 2
A. Benes, SD 1
B. Butler, LA 1
B. Saberhagen, NY ...1

1994 AMERICAN
F. Thomas, Chi 372
K. Griffey, Jr., Sea .233
A. Belle, Cle 225
K. Lofton, Cle 181
P. O'Neill, NY 150
J. Key, NY 102
K. Puckett, Min 100
J. Franco, Chi 49
D. Cone, KC 40
J. Carter, Tor 35
J. Canseco, Tex 27
C. Ripken, Bal 24
W. Boggs, NY 19
L. Smith, Bal.........18
W. Clark, Tex 17
R. Palmeiro, Bal 11
M. Vaughn, Bos......10
D. Mattingly, NY 9
P. Molitor, Tor 9
C. Knoblauch, Min ...8
M. Mussina, Bal 8
C. Davis, Cal 3
J. Bere, Chi 1
R. Sierra, Oak 1

1995 NATIONAL
B. Larkin, Cin 281
D. Bichette, Col 251
G. Maddux, Atl 249
M. Piazza, LA 214
E. Karros, LA 135
R. Sanders, Cin 120
L. Walker, Col 88
S. Sosa, Chi 81
T. Gwynn, SD.......72
C. Biggio, Hou 58
R. Gant, Cin 31
B. Bonds, SF 21
M. Grace, Chi.........14
D. Bell, Hou 12
J. Bagwell, Hou 5
C. Hayes, Phi 4
A. Galarraga, Col 4
C. Jones, Atl 3
V. Castilla, Col 2
F. McGriff, Atl 2
P. Schourek, Cin 2
J. Conine, Fla 1
T. Henke, StL 1

1995 AMERICAN
M. Vaughn, Bos 308
A. Belle, Cle 300
E. Martinez, Sea 244
J. Mesa, Cle 130
J. Buhner, Sea......120

R. Johnson, Sea 111
T. Salmon, Cal......110
F. Thomas, Chi 86
J. Valentin, Bos 57
G. Gaetti, KC 45
R. Palmeiro, Bal 34
M. Ramirez, Cle 30
T. Wakefield, Bos 20
J. Edmonds, Cal 18
P. O'Neill, NY 14
M. McGwire, Oak 7
C. Knoblauch, Min 5

W. Boggs, NY 5
G. DiSarcina, Cal 3
C. Ripken, Bal 3
K. Puckett, Min 2

1996 NATIONAL
K. Caminiti, SD 392
M. Piazza, LA 237
E. Burks, Col 186
C. Jones, Atl.........158
B. Bonds, SF 132

A. Galarraga, Col ...112
G. Sheffield, Fla 112
B. Jordan, StL 69
J. Bagwell, Hou......59
S. Finley, SD........38
J. Smoltz, Atl 33
B. Larkin, Cin 29
M. Grissom, Atl 23
B. Gilkey, NY 13
S. Sosa, Chi 12
E. Karros, LA 10

H. Rodriguez, Mon.... 9
T. Hundley, NY 7
L. Johnson, NY 7
D. Bichette, Col....... 6
T. Worrell, LA 3
K. Brown, Fla 2
T. Hoffman, SD 2
M. Alou, Mon 1

1996 AMERICAN
J. Gonzalez, Tex 290

A. Rodriguez, Sea ..228
A. Belle, Cle 228
K. Griffey, Sea ...188
M. Vaughn, Bos.....124
R. Palmeiro, Bal ...104
M. McGwire, Oak ...100
F. Thomas, Chi 88
B. Anderson, Bal ...53
I. Rodriguez, Tex ...52
K. Lofton, Cle........34

M. Duncan, NY 27
P. Molitor, Min 19
A. Pettitte, NY 11
J. Thome, Cle 9
C. Knoblauch, Min ... 8
J. Buhner, Sea 6
B. Williams, NY 4
J. Wetteland, NY...... 4
R. Alomar............. 3
T. Steinbach, Oak 1

Rookie of the Year Award: History

The Chicago chapter of the Baseball Writers' Association of America (BBWAA) established an award recognizing the major leagues' top rookie following the 1940 season, selecting Lou Boudreau for the honor. This procedure continued for six more years before going national. The subsequent winners of the Chicago chapter's award were Pete Reiser (1941), Johnny Beazley (1942), Bill Johnson (1943), Bill Voiselle (1944), Boo Ferriss (1945), and Eddie Waitkus (1946).

The Sporting News began naming its own Rookie of the Year in 1946, with the selection of Del Ennis of the Philadelphia Phillies. Their award has competed with that of the BBWAA ever since. In 1949 they began recognizing a winner from each league and in 1957 they started selecting both a rookie player and a rookie pitcher of the year for each league.

In 1947 thirty-three baseball writers were asked to name five rookies in order of preference, with votes distributed on a 5–4–3–2–1 basis. Thus, Jackie Robinson became the first nationally recognized winner of the BBWAA Rookie of the Year Award, or the J. Louis Comiskey Memorial Award, as it was called. During the 1987 Hall of Fame induction ceremony, Commissioner Peter Ueberroth announced that, hereafter, the Rookie of the Year Award would be officially known as the Jackie Robinson Award.

In 1948 forty-eight writers took part in the award, this time naming only a single candidate on each ballot. In 1949 the BBWAA began the process of choosing a top rookie in each league. Three writers from each league city, the same men who decided on the MVP Awards, participated in the voting. Voters were free to use their individual judgments as to the eligibility of rookie candidates, which created some problems, especially in 1950 when Al Rosen, and his league-leading 37 homers, was ignored by Rookie of the Year voters. Apparently they felt that Rosen's 58 previous major league at-bats were tantamount to veteran status, while winner Walt Dropo's 41 previous at-bats were not.

In 1957 formal guidelines were finally established for determining rookie status. A player could not have accumulated more than 75 at-bats, 45 innings pitched, or have been on a major league roster between May 15 and September 1 of any previous season. Shortly after, the guidelines were changed to 90 at-bats, 45 innings pitched or 45 days on a major league roster before September 1. Finally, in 1971, the guidelines were set at 130 at-bats, 50 innings, or 45 days on a roster.

There were several instances, especially in the early days of the award, in which some Rookie of the Year voters didn't bother to exercise their franchise. In 1961, as with the MVP Award, the number of voters was reduced from three to two writers from each league city.

Following two tie votes in four years (1976 NL, 1979 AL), the writers adopted the system used in Cy Young Award balloting: naming three rookies on each ballot, in order of preference, with votes distributed on a 5–3–1 basis. This system began in 1980, although it had been scheduled to start ten years earlier.

The maximum possible point total available to Rookie of the Year candidates was 165 in 1947, 48 in 1948, and 24 in each league in 1949–60. In the National League, it was 16 in 1961, 20 in 1962–68, 24 in 1969–79, 120 in 1980-92, and 140 from 1993 to the present. In the American League, it was 20 in 1961–68, 24 in 1969–76, 28 in 1977–79, and 140 from 1980 to the present.

There have been twelve unanimous Rookie of the Year selections since 1947: Frank Robinson (NL, 1956), Orlando Cepeda (NL, 1958), Willie McCovey (NL, 1959), Carlton Fisk (AL, 1972), Vince Coleman (NL, 1985), Benito Santiago (NL, 1987), Mark McGwire (AL, 1987), Sandy Alomar (AL, 1990), Mike Piazza (NL, 1993), Tim Salmon (AL, 1993), Raul Mondesi (NL, 1994) and Derek Jeter (1996). Technically, Tony Kubek's 1957 AL selection was also unanimous, as the lone dissenting vote went to an ineligible player.

Rookie of the Year Award

1947
J. Robinson, BRO
  (NL) 129
L. Jansen, NY (NL) ..105
F. Shea, NY (AL) 67
F. Fain, PHI (AL) 43
F. Baumholtz, CIN
  (NL) 42
(Rest of voting
  unknown)

1948
A. Dark, BOS (NL) ...27
G. Bearden, CLE (AL) . 8
R. Ashburn, PHI (NL).. 7
L. Brissie, PHI (AL) .. 3
B. Goodman, BOS
  (AL) 3

1949 NATIONAL
D. Newcombe, BRO . 21
D. Crandall, BOS 3

1949 AMERICAN
R. Sievers, SL 10
A. Kellner, PHI 5
G. Coleman, NY 4
B. Kuzava, CHI 1
J. Groth, DET 1
M. Garcia, CLE 1

1950 NATIONAL
S. Jethroe, BOS 11
B. Miller, PHI 5
D. O'Connell, PIT 4
E. Church, PHI 2
B. Serena, CHI........ 1

1950 AMERICAN
W. Dropo, BOS 15
W. Ford, NY 6
C. Carrasquel, CHI ... 2

1951 NATIONAL
W. Mays, NY 18
C. Nichols, BOS 4
C. Labine, BRO....... 2

1951 AMERICAN
G. McDougald, NY ..13
M. Minoso, CLE-CHI. 11

1952 NATIONAL
J. Black, BRO 19
H. Wilhelm, NY 9
D. Groat, PIT 1

E. Mathews, BOS..... 1

1952 AMERICAN
H. Byrd, PHI 9
C. Courtney, SL 8
S. White, BOS 7

1953 NATIONAL
J. Gilliam, BRO 11
H. Haddix, SL 4
R. Jablonski, SL 2
R. Repulski, SL 2
B. Bruton, MIL 2
F. Baczewski, CIN 1
J. Greengrass, CIN ... 1

1953 AMERICAN
H. Kuenn, DET.......23

T. Umphlett, BOS..... 1

1952 AMERICAN — *(see column)*

1954 NATIONAL
W. Moon, SL 17
E. Banks, CHI 4
G. Conley, MIL 2
H. Aaron, MIL 1

1954 AMERICAN
B. Grim, NY 15
J. Finigan, PHI 8
A. Kaline, DET 1

1955 NATIONAL
B. Virdon, SL 15
J. Meyer, PHI 7
D. Bessent, BRO 2

1955 AMERICAN
H. Score, CLE 18
B. Klaus, BOS 5
N. Zauchin, BOS...... 1

1956 NATIONAL
F. Robinson, CIN 24

1956 AMERICAN
L. Aparicio, CHI......22
T. Francona, BAL 1
R. Colavito, CLE 1

1957 NATIONAL
J. Sanford, PHI 16
E. Bouchee, PHI 4
D. Drott, CHI......... 3
B. Hazle, MIL......... 1

1957 AMERICAN
T. Kubek, NY 23
F. Malzone, BOS 1

1958 NATIONAL
O. Cepeda, SF ... 21

1958 AMERICAN
A. Pearson, WAS 14
R. Duren, NY 7
G. Bell, CLE 3

1959 NATIONAL
W. McCovey, SF ... 24

1959 AMERICAN
B. Allison, WAS 18
J. Perry, CLE 5
R. Snyder, KC 1

1960 NATIONAL
F. Howard, LA 12
P. Herrera, PHI 4
A. Mahaffey, PHI 3
R. Santo, CHI 2
T. Davis, LA 1

1960 AMERICAN
R. Hansen, BAL ... 22
C. Estrada, BAL 1
J. Gentile, BAL 1

1961 NATIONAL
B. Williams, CHI 10
J. Torre, MIL 5
J. Curtis, CHI 1

1961 AMERICAN
D. Schwall, BOS 7
D. Howser, KC 6
Fl. Robinson, CHI 2
C. Schilling, BOS 2
L. Thomas, LA 2
J. Wood, DET 1

1962 NATIONAL
K. Hubbs, CHI 19
D. Clendenon, PIT 1

1962 AMERICAN
T. Tresh, NY 13
B. Rodgers, LA 4
B. Allen, MIN 1
D. Chance, LA 1
D. Radatz, BOS 1

1963 NATIONAL
P. Rose, CIN......... 17
R. Hunt, NY 2
R. Culp, PHI 1

1963 AMERICAN
G. Peters, CHI 10
P. Ward, CHI 6
J. Hall, MIN 4

1964 NATIONAL
R. Allen, PHI 18
R. Carty, MIL 1
J. Hart, SF 1

1964 AMERICAN
T. Oliva, MIN 19
W. Bunker, BAL 1

1965 NATIONAL
J. Lefebvre, LA 13
J. Morgan, HOU 4
F. Linzy, SF 3

1965 AMERICAN
C. Blefary, BAL 12
M. Lopez, CAL 8

1966 NATIONAL
T. Helms, CIN 12
S. Jackson, HOU 3
T. Fuentes, SF 2
R. Hundley, CHI 1
C. Jones, NY 1
L. Jaster, SL 1

1966 AMERICAN
T. Agee, CHI 16
J. Nash, KC 2
D. Johnson, BAL 1
G. Scott, BOS 1

1967 NATIONAL
T. Seaver, NY 11
D. Hughes, SL 6
G. Nolan, CIN........ 3

1967 AMERICAN
R. Carew, MIN 19
R. Smith, BOS 1

1968 NATIONAL
J. Bench, CIN 10½
J. Koosman, NY ... 9½

1968 AMERICAN
S. Bahnsen, NY 17
D. Unser, WAS 3

1969 NATIONAL
T. Sizemore, LA 14
C. Laboy, MON 3
A. Oliver, PIT 3
B. Didier, ATL 2
L. Hisle, PHI 2

1969 AMERICAN
L. Piniella, KC 9
M. Nagy, BOS 6
C. May, CHI 5
K. Tatum, CAL 4

1970 NATIONAL
C. Morton, MON 11
B. Carbo, CIN 8
L. Bowa, PHI 3
W. Simpson, CIN 1
C. Cedeno, HOU 1

1970 AMERICAN
T. Munson, NY 23
R. Foster, CLE........ 1

1971 NATIONAL
E. Williams, ATL 18
W. Montanez, PHI 6

1971 AMERICAN
C. Chambliss, CLE .. 11
B. Parsons, MIL 5
A. Mangual, OAK 4
D. Griffin, BOS........ 3
P. Splittorff, KC 1

1972 NATIONAL
J. Matlack, NY 19
Dv. Rader, SF 4
J. Milner, NY.......... 1

1972 AMERICAN
C. Fisk, BOS......... 24

1973 NATIONAL
G. Matthews, SF..... 11
S. Rogers, MON 3½
B. Boone, PHI 2
E. Sosa, SF 2
D. Driessen, CIN 2
C. Cey, LA 1
D. Lopes, LA 1
J. Grubb, SD 1
R. Zisk, PIT .... ½

1973 AMERICAN
A. Bumbry, BAL ... 13½
P. Garcia, MIL 3
D. Porter, MIL 2
S. Busby, KC 2
D. Medich, NY 2
R. Coggins, BAL 1½

1974 NATIONAL
B. McBride, SL 16
G. Gross, HOU 7
B. Madlock CHI 1

1974 AMERICAN
M. Hargrove, TEX .. 16½
B. Dent, CHI 3
G. Brett, KC 2
R. Burleson, BOS ... 1½

J. Sundberg, TEX 1

1975 NATIONAL
J. Montefusco, SF ... 12
G. Carter, MON 9
Lr. Parrish, MON 1
R. Eastwick, CIN...... 1
M. Trillo, CHI.......... 1

1975 AMERICAN
F. Lynn, BOS 23½
J. Rice, BOS.......... ½

1976 NATIONAL
B. Metzger, SD 11
P. Zachry, CIN 11
H. Cruz, SL 2

1976 AMERICAN
M. Fidrych, DET 22
B. Wynegar, MIN 2

1977 NATIONAL
A. Dawson, MON 10
S. Henderson, NY 9
G. Richards, SD 4
F. Bannister, HOU ... 1

1977 AMERICAN
E. Murray, BAL 12½
M. Page, OAK 9½
B. Wills, TEX 4
D. Rozema, DET 2

1978 NATIONAL
B. Horner, ATL..... 12½
O. Smith, SD 8½
D. Robinson, PIT 3

1978 AMERICAN
L. Whitaker, DET.... 21
P. Molitor, MIL....... 3
C. Lansford, CAL 2
R. Gale, KC 1
A. Trammell, DET 1

1979 NATIONAL
R. Sutcliffe, LA...... 20
J. Leonard, HOU...... 3
S. Thompson, CHI 1

1979 AMERICAN
J. Castino, MIN 7
A. Griffin, TOR 7
M. Clear, CAL 5
R. Davis, NY 3
R. Baumgarten, CHI .. 3
P. Putnam, TEX 3

1980 NATIONAL
S. Howe, LA 80
B. Gullickson, MON .. 53
L. Smith, PHI 49
R. Oester, CIN 16
D. Smith, HOU 13
J. Reardon, NY 2
A. Holland, SF 1
L. Durham, SL 1
B. Walk, PHI 1

1980 AMERICAN
J. Charboneau, CLE 102
D. Stapleton, BOS ... 40
D. Corbett, MIN...... 38
D. Garcia, TOR 35
B. Burns, CHI........ 33
R. Peters, DET 3
J. Dotson, CHI 1

1981 NATIONAL
F. Valenzuela, LA .. 107
T. Raines, MON..... 85
H. Brooks, NY 8½
B. Berenyi, CIN 5
J. Bonilla, SD 5
T. Pena, PIT 4
M. Wilson, NY 1½

1981 AMERICAN
D. Righetti, NY...... 127
R. Gedman, BOS 64
B. Ojeda, BOS 36
M. Jones, KC 8
D. Engle, MIN 4½
M. Witt, CAL........ 4

S. Babitt, OAK 4
J. Bell, TOR.......... 2
G. Ward, MIN 1½
B. Havens, MIN...... 1

1982 NATIONAL
S. Sax, LA 63
J. Ray, PIT.......... 57
W. McGee, SL 39
C. Davis, SF 32
L. DeLeon, SD 10
R. Sandberg, CHI 9
S. Bedrosian, ATL 4
D. LaPoint, SL 1
E. Show, SD 1

1982 AMERICAN
C. Ripken, BAL 132
K. Hrbek, MIN 90
W. Boggs, BOS.... 10½
G. Vande Berg, SEA .. 9
M. Gaetti, MIN 5
D. Hostetler, TEX 3
V. Hayes, CLE 2
J. Barfield, TOR..... 1½

1983 NATIONAL
D. Strawberry, NY ..106
C. McMurtry, ATL ... 49
M. Hall, CHI 32
G. Redus, CIN 8
B. Doran, HOU 7
F. DiPino, HOU 6
G. Brock, LA......... 3
J. DeLeon, PIT 3
M. Thurmond, SD.... 1
L. Tunnell, PIT 1

1983 AMERICAN
R. Kittle, CHI 104
J. Franco, CLE....... 78
M. Boddicker, BAL .. 70

1984 NATIONAL
D. Gooden, NY 118
J. Samuel, PHI....... 67
O. Hershiser, LA 15
D. Gladden, SF 9
R. Darling, NY 3
C. Martinez, SD...... 2
J. Stone, PHI 1
T. Pendleton, SL..... 1

1984 AMERICAN
A. Davis, SEA.......134
M. Langston, SEA ... 82
K. Puckett, MIN 23
T. Teufel, MIN....... 5
M. Young, BAL 3
R. Clemens, BOS 2
M. Gubicza, KC 1
A. Nipper, BOS 1
R. Romanick, CAL.... 1

1985 NATIONAL
V. Coleman, SL.....120
T. Browning, CIN ... 72
M. Duncan, LA...... 9
C. Brown, SF 7
G. Davis, HOU 3
R. McDowell, NY 2
J. Orsulak, PIT 2
J. Hesketh, MON 1

1985 AMERICAN
O. Guillen, CHI 101
T. Higuera, MIL 67
E. Riles, MIL 29
O. McDowell, TEX ... 25
S. Cliburn, CAL 16
B. Fisher, NY 7
T. Henke, TOR....... 5
M. Salas, MIN 2

1986 NATIONAL
T. Worrell, SL 118
R. Thompson, SF 46
K. Mitchell, NY...... 22
C. Kerfeld, HOU 17
W. Clark, SF 5
B. Bonds, PIT........ 4
J. Deshaies, HOU 1
B. Larkin, CIN 1
B. Ruffin, PHI 1
J. Kruk, SD 1

1986 AMERICAN
J. Canseco, OAK ...110
W. Joyner, CAL 98
M. Eichhorn, TOR ... 23
C. Snyder, CLE 16
D. Tartabull, SEA 4
R. Sierra, TEX........ 1

1987 NATIONAL
B. Santiago, SD 120
M. Dunne, PIT 66
J. Magrane, SL 10
C. Candaele, MON ... 9
G. Young, HOU 7
J. James, PHI 1
L. Lancaster, CHI 1
G. Mathews, SL 1
R. Myers, NY 1

1987 AMERICAN
M. McGwire, OAK ..140
K. Seitzer, KC 64
M. Nokes, DET 32
M. Greenwell, BOS ... 9
D. White, CAL 5
M. Henneman, DET .. 1
N. Liriano, TOR 1

1988 NATIONAL
C. Sabo, CIN 79
M. Grace, CHI 61
T. Belcher, LA 35
R. Gant, ATL 22
R. Alomar, SD 11
D. Berryhill, CHI 3
G. Jefferies, NY 3
R. Jordan, PHI 2

1988 AMERICAN
W. Weiss, OAK 103
B. Harvey, CAL 49
J. Reed, BOS 48
D. August, MIL 22
D. Gallagher, CHI ... 18
M. Perez, CHI....... 9
M. Schooler, SEA ... 2
C. Espy, TEX 1

1989 NATIONAL
J. Walton, CHI 116
D. Smith, CHI 68
G. Jefferies, NY 18
D. Lilliquist, ATL 6
A. Benes, SD 3
C. Hayes, PHI 3
G. Harris, SD 2

1989 AMERICAN
G. Olson, BAL 136
T. Gordon, KC 67
K. Griffey, SEA...... 21
C. Worthington, BAL . 16
J. Abbott, CAL....... 10
K. Brown, TEX 2

1990 NATIONAL
D. Justice, ATL 118
D. DeShields, MON .. 60
H. Morris, CIN 13
J. Burkett, SF 12
M. Harkey, CHI 12
T. Zeile, SL 4
M. Grissom, MON ... 1
L. Walker, MON...... 1

1990 AMERICAN
S. Alomar, CLE 140
K. Maas, NY 47
K. Appier, KC........ 31
J. Olerud, TOR 13
K. Tapani, MIN 9
T. Fryman, DET 5
R. Ventura, CHI 3
B. McDonald, BAL ... 2
A. Cole, CLE......... 1
S. Radinsky, CHI 1

1991 NATIONAL
J. Bagwell, HOU 118
O. Merced, PIT...... 53
R. Lankford, SL...... 28
B. Hunter, ATL 7
B. Barberie, MON.... 3
W. Chamberlain, PHI . 3
C. McElroy, CHI 3

M. Stanton, ATL 1

1991 AMERICAN
C. Knoblauch, MIN . 136
J. Guzman, TOR 68
M. Cuyler, DET 22
I. Rodriguez, TEX 10
B. DeLucia, SEA 7
M. Timlin, TOR 2
M. Whiten, TOR-CLE . 2
L. Gomez, BAL 1
D. Henry, MIL 1
B. Mayne, KC 1
C. Nagy, CLE 1
P. Plantier, BOS 1

1992 NATIONAL
E. Karros, LA 116
M. Alou, MON 30
T. Wakefield, PIT..... 29
R. Sanders, CIN 23
D. Osborne, SL 12
M. Perez, SL 2
B. Rivera, PHI 1
F. Seminara, SD 1
B. Williams, HOU 1
M. Wohlers, ATL 1

1992 AMERICAN
P. Listach, MIL 122
K. Lofton, CLE 85
D. Fleming, SEA 23
C. Eldred, MIL 22

1993 NATIONAL
M. Piazza, LA 140
G. McMicheal, ATL .. 40
J. Conine, FLA....... 31
C. Carr, FLA 18
A. Martin, PIT......... 6
K. Stocker, PHI 4
W. Cordero, MON ... 3
K. Rueter, MON 3
C. Garcia, PIT 2
P. Martinez, LA 2
S. Cooke, PIT 1
R. Guttierrez, SD 1
A. Reynoso, COL..... 1

1993 AMERICAN
T. Salmon, CAL......140
J. Bere, CHI 59
A. Sele, BOS 19
W. Kirby, CLE 12
R. Amaral, SEA 8
B. Gates, OAK 7
T. Neel, OAK 5
J. DiPoto, CLE 1
D. Hulse, TEX 1

1994 NATIONAL
R. Mondesi, LA 140
J. Hudek, HOU 27
R. Klesko, ATL 25
S. Trachsel, CHI 22
C. Floyd, MON 10
J. Hamilton, SD 10
W. Van Landingham,
    SF 9
H. Carrasco, CIN 3
B. Jones, NY 3
J. Lopez, ATL 2
S. Reynolds, HOU ... 1

1994 AMERICAN
B. Hamelin, KC 134
M. Ramirez, CLE..... 44
R. Greer, TEX 42
D. Hall, TOR 9
C. Gomez, DET 6
B. Risley, SEA 6
J. Anderson, CAL ... 4
J. Edmonds, CAL ... 1
J. Valentin, MIL 1

1995 NATIONAL
H. Nomo, LA........118
C. Jones, ATL 104
Q. Veras, FLA........ 14
J. Isringhausen, NY .. 4
J. Mabry, STL 4
C. Perez, MON 4
C. Fonville, SF 1
B. Hunter, HOU 1

C. Johnson, FLA...... 1
I. Valdes, LA 1

1995 AMERICAN
M. Cordova, MIN ... 105
G. Anderson, CAL ... 99

A. Pettite, NY 16
T. Percival, CAL 13
S. Green, TOR 8
R. Durham, CHI 3
J. Tavarez, CLE 3
J. Nunnally, KC 2

T. Goodwin, KC 1
B. Radke, MIN 1
S. Sparks, MIL 1

1996 NATIONAL
Hollandsworth, LA .. 105

E. Renteria, FLA 84
J. Kendall, PIT 30
F. P. Santangelo,
  MON 15
R. Ordonez, NY 7

J. Dye, ATL 6
A. Benes, STL 5

1996 AMERICAN
D. Jeter, NY 140

J. Baldwin, CHI 64
T. Clark, DET 30
R. Cloppinger, BAL ... 6
J. Rosado, KC 6
D. Erstad, CAL....... 3

Cy Young Award: History

Commissioner Ford Frick, troubled by pitchers' lack of representation in MVP voting, spearheaded the 1956 effort to initiate a "most valuable pitcher" award. Cy Young, baseball's winningest pitcher, who had died the previous November, was the logical choice to name the honor after. At a special meeting on July 9, 1956, the Baseball Writers' Association of America approved, by the slim margin of 14-12, the establishment of the Cy Young Memorial Award, designed to honor the major leagues' outstanding pitcher each year beginning in '56. Ironically, the first winner, Brooklyn's Don Newcombe, also won his league's MVP Award.

One writer from each major league city participated in the balloting. In case of a tie vote, a second balloting was to be taken between the deadlocked pitchers. Hurlers were not to be eligible to win the award more than once, a rule which was evidently scrapped within two years.

Frick was adamantly opposed to the commonly voiced idea to recognize a Cy Young winner in each league but, not long after his December 1965 retirement, the idea became a reality. On March 1, 1967, Frick's successor William Eckert approved the plan for dual awards, with two writers from each league city to select.

The system of having each writer make only one selection prevailed until 1969, when Detroit's Denny McLain and Baltimore's Mike Cuellar tied for the AL Cy Young Award. Thereafter, writers were instructed to name three pitchers in each league, with 5 points allotted for each first-place vote, 3 for second, and 1 for third.

The maximum number of points available for one pitcher was 16 from 1956–60, 18 in 1961, 20 in 1962–68, 24 in 1969, 120 in 1970–76 (AL) and 1970–92 (NL), and 140 in 1977–present (AL) and 1993–present (NL). As with every other major award, there have been a few instances in Cy Young voting where at least one writer failed to return a ballot.

Unanimous winners of the Cy Young Award are Sandy Koufax (NL, 1963, '65, and '66), Bob Gibson (NL, 1968), Denny McLain (AL, 1968), Steve Carlton (NL, 1972), Ron Guidry (AL, 1978), Rick Sutcliffe (NL, 1984), Dwight Gooden (NL, 1985), Roger Clemens (AL, 1986), Orel Hershiser (NL, 1988), and Greg Maddux (NL, 1994-1995).

Relief pitchers, once overlooked in Cy Young balloting, have become strong candidates in recent years. Until 1970 only one reliever — Lindy McDaniel in 1960 — had received even a single vote. The new voting system helped open opportunities for bullpen aces and in 1974 the Dodgers' Mike Marshall became the first reliever to win the Cy Young Award. He has been followed in that distinction by Sparky Lyle (AL, 1977), Bruce Sutter (NL, 1979), Rollie Fingers (AL, 1981), Willie Hernández (AL, 1984), Steve Bedrosian (NL, 1987), Mark Davis (NL, 1989), and Dennis Eckersley (AL, 1992).

Cy Young Award

1956
D. Newcombe, BRO
  (NL) 10
S. Maglie, BRO (NL) .. 4
W. Spahn, MIL (NL) ... 1
W. Ford, NY (AL) 1

1957
W. Spahn, MIL (NL) .. 15
D. Donovan, CHI (AL) . 1

1958
B. Turley, NY (AL) 5
W. Spahn, MIL (NL) ... 4
B. Friend, PIT (NL) ... 3
L. Burdette, MIL (NL).. 3

1959
E. Wynn, CHI (AL).... 13
S. Jones, SF (NL) 2
B. Shaw, CHI (AL) 1

1960
V. Law, PIT (NL) 8
W. Spahn, MIL (NL) ... 4
E. Broglio, SL (NL) 1
L. McDaniel, SL (NL).. 1

1961
W. Ford, NY (AL) 9
W. Spahn, MIL (NL) ... 6
F. Lary, DET (AL)...... 2

1962
D. Drysdale, LA (NL) . 14
J. Sanford, SF (NL) ... 4
B. Purkey, CIN (NL) ... 1
B. Pierce, SF (NL)..... 1

1963
S. Koufax, LA (NL) ... 20

1964
D. Chance, LA (AL) .. 17
L. Jackson, CHI (NL).. 2
S. Koufax, LA (NL) 1

1965
S. Koufax, LA (NL) ... 20

1966
S. Koufax, LA (NL) ... 20

1967 NATIONAL
M. Mc Cormick, SF .. 18
F. Jenkins, CHI 1
J. Bunning, PHI 1

1967 AMERICAN
J. Lonborg, BOS..... 18
J. Horlen, CHI 2

1968 NATIONAL
B. Gibson, SL 20

1968 AMERICAN
D. McLain, DET 20

1969 NATIONAL
T. Seaver, NY 23
P. Niekro, ATL 1

1969 AMERICAN
M. Cuellar, BAL...... 10
D. McLain, DET 10
J. Perry, MIN 3
D. McNally, BAL 1

1970 NATIONAL
B. Gibson, SL 118
G. Perry, SF 51
F. Jenkins CHI 16
D. Giusti, PIT 8

J. Merritt, CIN 8
G. Nolan, CIN......... 5
T. Seaver, NY 4
W. Granger, CIN 3
C. Morton, MON 2
L. Walker, PIT 1

1970 AMERICAN
J. Perry, MIN 55
D. McNally, BAL 47
S. McDowell, CLE ... 45
M. Cuellar, BAL...... 44
J. Palmer, BAL 11
C. Wright, CAL 9
R. Perranoski, MIN .. 5

1971 NATIONAL
F. Jenkins, CHI 97
T. Seaver, NY 61
A. Downing, LA 40
D. Ellis, PIT 9
B. Gibson, SL 3
J. Johnson, SF 2
D. Roberts, SD 2
J. Marichal, SF 1
B. Stoneman, MON ... 1

1971 AMERICAN
V. Blue, OAK 98
M. Lolich, DET 85
W. Wood, CHI 23
D. McNally, BAL 8
D. Drago, KC 1
A. Messersmith, CAL . 1

1972 NATIONAL
S. Carlton, PHI 120
S. Blass, PIT......... 35
F. Jenkins, CHI 23
M. Marshall, MON ... 8
G. Nolan, CIN........ 6

T. Seaver, NY........ 6
C. Carroll, CIN 6
D. Sutton, LA 6
B. Gibson, SL 3
M. Pappas, CHI 3

1972 AMERICAN
G. Perry, CLE........ 64
W. Wood, CHI 58
M. Lolich, DET 27
J. Hunter, OAK 26
J. Palmer, BAL 20
L. Tiant, BOS 16
S. Lyle, NY 3
N. Ryan, CAL 2

1973 NATIONAL
T. Seaver, NY........ 71
M. Marshall, MON ... 54
R. Bryant, SF 50
J. Billingham, CIN ... 30
D. Sutton, LA 7
F. Norman, SD-CIN .. 3
D. Giusti, PIT 1

1973 AMERICAN
J. Palmer, BAL 88
N. Ryan, CAL 62
J. Hunter, OAK 52
J. Hiller, DET 6
W. Wood, CHI 3
J. Colborn, MIL 2
V. Blue, OAK 1
B. Blyleven, MIN 1
G. Perry, CLE........ 1

1974 NATIONAL
M. Marshall, LA 96
A. Messersmith, LA.. 66
P. Niekro, ATL 15
D. Sutton, LA 12

A. Hrabosky, SL 9
J. Billingham, CIN 8
D. Gullett, CIN 5
C. Carroll, CIN 2
D. Giusti, PIT 1
B. Capra, ATL 1
L. McGlothen, SL 1

1974 AMERICAN
J. Hunter, OAK 90
F. Jenkins, TEX 75
N. Ryan, CAL 28
G. Perry, CLE........ 8
L. Tiant, BOS 8
M. Cuellar, BAL...... 6
J. Hiller, DET 1

1975 NATIONAL
T. Seaver, NY 98
R. Jones, SD 80
A. Hrabosky, SL 33
J. Montefusco, SF ... 2
D. Gullett, CIN 1
A. Messersmith, LA . 1
D. Sutton, LA 1

1975 AMERICAN
J. Palmer, BAL 98
J. Hunter, NY 74
R. Fingers, OAK 25
F. Tanana, CAL 7
J. Kaat, CHI 7
V. Blue, OAK 2
R. Gossage, CHI..... 2
R. Wise, BOS 1

1976 NATIONAL
R. Jones, SD 96
J. Koosman, NY ... 69½
D. Sutton, LA 25½
S. Carlton, PHI 11

R. Eastwick, CIN...... 6
J. Matlack, NY 5
J. Richard, HOU 2
T. Seaver, NY 1

1976 AMERICAN
J. Palmer, BAL 108
M. Fidrych, DET 51
F. Tanana, CAL 18
E. Figueroa, NY 12
L. Tiant, BOS 10
V. Blue, OAK 8
B. Campbell, MIN.... 7
R. Fingers, OAK 1
W. Garland, BAL..... 1

1977 NATIONAL
S. Carlton, PHI 104
T. John, LA 54
T. Seaver, NY-CIN .. 18
R. Reuschel, CHI 18
J. Candelaria, PIT.... 17
B. Sutter, CHI........ 5

1977 AMERICAN
S. Lyle, NY 56½
J. Palmer, BAL 48
N. Ryan, CAL 46
D. Leonard, KC 45
B. Campbell, BOS . 25½
D. Goltz, MIN . 19
R. Guidry, NY........ 5
D. Rozema, DET 4
F. Tanana, CAL 3

1978 NATIONAL
G. Perry, SD 116
B. Hooton, LA 38
V. Blue, SF 17
J. Richard, HOU 13
K. Tekulve, PIT....... 12

P. Niekro, ATL 10
R. Grimsley, MON 7
R. Fingers, SD 1
T. John, LA 1
D. Robinson, PIT 1

1978 AMERICAN
R. Guidry, NY 140
M. Caldwell, MIL ... 76
J. Palmer, BAL 14
D. Eckersley, BOS ... 10
R. Gossage, NY 4
F. Jenkins, TEX 2
E. Figueroa, NY 1
L. Gura, KC 1
D. Leonard, KC 1
M. Marshall, MIN 1
P. Splittorff, KC 1
B. Stanley, BOS 1

1979 NATIONAL
B. Sutter, CHI 72
J. Niekro, HOU 66
J. Richard, HOU 41
T. Seaver, CIN 20
K. Tekulve, PIT 14
P. Niekro, ATL 3

1979 AMERICAN
M. Flanagan, BAL .. 136
T. John, NY 51
R. Guidry, NY 26
J. Kern, TEX 25
M. Marshall, MIN 7
J. Koosman, MIN 5
D. Eckersley, BOS ... 1
A. Lopez, DET 1

1980 NATIONAL
S. Carlton, PHI 118
J. Reuss, LA 55
J. Bibby, PIT 28
J. Niekro, HOU 11
T. McGraw, PHI 1
S. Rogers, MON 1
J. Sambito, HOU 1
M. Soto, CIN 1

1980 AMERICAN
S. Stone, BAL 100
M. Norris, OAK 91
R. Gossage, NY ... 37½
T. John, NY.......... 14
D. Quisenberry, KC 7½
L. Gura, KC........... 1
S. McGregor, BAL 1

1981 NATIONAL
F. Valenzuela, LA ... 70
T. Seaver, CIN 67

S. Carlton, PHI 50
N. Ryan, HOU 28
B. Sutter, SL....... 1

1981 AMERICAN
R. Fingers, MIL 126
S. McCatty, OAK .. 84½
J. Morris, DET 21
P. Vuckovich, MIL .. 8½
D. Martinez, BAL .. 3½
R. Gossage, NY 3
R. Guidry, NY 2½
B. Burns, CHI 2
L. Gura, KC.......... 1

1982 NATIONAL
S. Carlton, PHI 112
S. Rogers, MON 29
F. Valenzuela, LA .. 25½
B. Sutter, SL......... 25
P. Niekro, ATL 18
G. Minton, SF 4
J. Andujar, SL 1
G. Garber, ATL 1
M. Soto, CIN .... ½

1982 AMERICAN
P. Vuckovich, MIL ... 87
J. Palmer, BAL 59
D. Quisenberry, KC .. 40
D. Stieb, TOR 36
R. Sutcliffe, CLE ... 14
G. Zahn, CAL 7
B. Stanley, BOS 4
B. Caudill, SEA 4
D. Petry, DET 1

1983 NATIONAL
J. Denny, PHI 103
M. Soto, CIN 61
J. Orosco, NY 19
S. Rogers, MON 15
L. McWilliams, PIT ... 7
A. Holland, PHI 4
C. McMurtry, ATL 3
B. Welch, LA.......... 2
N. Ryan, HOU 1
L. Smith, CHI 1

1983 AMERICAN
L. Hoyt, CHI 116
D. Quisenberry, KC .. 81
J. Morris, DET 38
R. Dotson, CHI 9
R. Guidry, NY 5
S. McGregor, BAL 3

1984 NATIONAL
R. Sutcliffe, CHI 120
D. Gooden, NY 45

B. Sutter, SL........ 33½
J. Andujar, SL .. 12½
R. Gossage, SD 3
M. Soto, CIN 2

1984 AMERICAN
W. Hernandez, DET.. 88
D. Quisenberry, KC .. 71
B. Blyleven, CLE 45
M. Boddicker, BAL .. 41
D. Petry, DET 3
F. Viola, MIN 2
J. Morris, DET 1
D. Stieb, TOR......... 1

1985 NATIONAL
D. Gooden, NY 120
J. Tudor, SL 65
O. Hershiser, LA 17
J. Andujar, SL 6
F. Valenzuela, LA ... 4
T. Browning, CIN 3
J. Reardon, MON ... 1

1985 AMERICAN
B. Saberhagen, KC . 127
R. Guidry, NY 88
B. Blyleven, MIN 9
D. Quisenberry, KC .. 9
C. Leibrandt, KC 7
D. Alexander, TOR ... 5
B. Burns, CHI 2
D. Moore, CAL 2
D. Stieb, TOR 2
M. Moore, SEA 1

1986 NATIONAL
M. Scott, HOU 98
F. Valenzuela, LA ... 88
M. Krukow, SF 15
B. Ojeda, NY 9
R. Darling, NY 2
R. Rhoden, PIT 2
D. Gooden, NY 1
S. Fernandez, NY 1

1986 AMERICAN
R. Clemens, BOS ... 140
T. Higuera, MIL 42
M. Witt, CAL......... 35
D. Righetti, NY 20
J. Morris, DET 13
M. Eichhorn, TOR ... 2

1987 NATIONAL
S. Bedrosian, PHI ... 57
R. Sutcliffe, CHI 55
R. Reuschel, SF ... 54
O. Hershiser, LA 14
D. Gooden, NY 12

N. Ryan, HOU 12
M. Scott, HOU 9
B. Welch, LA........ 3

1987 AMERICAN
R. Clemens, BOS ...124
J. Key, TOR 64
D. Stewart, OAK 32
D. Alexander, DET ... 8
M. Langston, SEA ... 7
T. Higuera, MIL 5
F. Viola, MIN 5
J. Reardon, MIN 4
J. Morris, DET 3

1988 NATIONAL
O. Hershisher, LA ...120
D. Jackson, CIN 54
D. Cone, NY 42

1988 AMERICAN
F. Viola, MIN 138
D. Eckersley, OAK .. 52
M. Gubicza, KC...... 26
M. Langston, CAL 7
D. Stewart, OAK 16
B. Hurst, BOS 12
R. Clemens, BOS 8

1989 NATIONAL
M. Davis, SD 107
M. Scott, HOU 65
G. Maddux, CHI 17
O. Hershiser, LA 7
J. Magrane, SL 7
T. Belcher, LA 4
S. Garrelts, SF 4
R. Reuschel, SF 3
M. Bielecki, CHI 1
M. Williams, CHI 1

1989 AMERICAN
B. Saberhagen, KC . 138
D. Stewart, OAK 80
M. Moore, OAK 10
B. Blyleven, CAL.... 9
N. Ryan, TEX 5
J. Ballard, BAL...... 3
D. Eckersley, OAK ... 3
G. Olson, BAL 3
J. Russell, TEX 1

1990 NATIONAL
D. Drabek, PIT 118
R. Martinez, LA 70
F. Viola, NY 19
D. Gooden, NY 8
R. Myers, CIN 1

1990 AMERICAN
B. Welch, OAK......107

R. Clemens, BOS 77
D. Stewart, OAK 43
B. Thigpen, CHI 20
D. Eckersley, OAK ... 2
D. Stieb, TOR......... 2
C. Finley, CAL 1

1991 NATIONAL
T. Glavine, ATL 110
L. Smith, SL 60
J. Smiley, PIT 26
J. Rijo, CIN 13
D. Martinez, MON ... 4
S. Avery, ATL 1
A. Benes, SD 1
M. Williams, PHI 1

1991 AMERICAN
R. Clemens, BOS ...119
S. Erickson, MIN 56
J. Abbott, CAL...... 26
J. Morris, MIN 17
B. Harvey, CAL 10
M. Langston, CAL 7
K. Tapani, MIN 6
B. Gullickson, DET ... 5
J. McDowell, CHI 3
D. Ward, TOR........ 3

1992 NATIONAL
G. Maddux, CHI 112
T. Glavine, ATL 78
B. Tewksbury, SL .. 22
L. Smith, SL 3
D. Drabek, PIT 1

1992 AMERICAN
D. Eckersley, OAK . 107
J. McDowell, CHI ... 51
R. Clemens, BOS 48
M. Mussina, BAL 26
J. Morris, TOR 10
K. Brown, TEX 9
C. Nagy, CLE 1

1993 NATIONAL
G. Maddux, ATL 119
B. Swift, SF 61
T. Glavine, ATL 49
J. Burkett, SF 9
J. Rijo, CIN 8
T. Greene, PHI 3
M. Portugal, HOU ... 2
B. Harvey, FLA 1
R. Myers, CHI 1

1993 AMERICAN
J. McDowell, CHI ...124

R. Johnson SEA 75
K. Appier, KC 30
J. Key, NY 14
D. Ward, TOR........ 5
P. Hentgen, TOR 3
J. Guzman, TOR...... 1

1994 NATIONAL
G. Maddux, ATL 140
K. Hill, MON 56
B. Saberhagen, NY .. 42
M. Freeman, COL.... 4
D. Drabek, HOU 4
D. Jackson, PHI 3
J. Franco, NY........ 2
R. Beck, SF.......... 1

1994 AMERICAN
D. Cone, KC 108
J. Key, NY 96
R. Johnson, SEA 24
M. Mussina, BAL ... 23
L. Smith, BAL 1

1995 NATIONAL
G. Maddux, ATL 140
P. Schourek, CIN ... 55
T. Glavine, ATL 30
H. Nomo, LA........ 18
R. Martinez, LA 8

1995 AMERICAN
R. Johnson, SEA ...136
J. Mesa, CLE 54
D. Cone, TOR-NY .. 18
M. Mussina, BAL ... 14
C. Nagy, CLE......... 1

1996 NATIONAL
J. Smoltz, ATL 136
K. Brown, FLA 88
A. Benes, STL 9
H. Nomo, LA.......... 5
T. Hoffman, SD 3
G. Maddux, ATL 3
T. Worrell, LA 3

1996 AMERICAN
P. Hentgen, TOR ...110
A. Pettite, NY 104
M. Rivera, NY 18
C. Nagy, CLE........ 12
M. Mussina, BAL 5
A. Fernandez, CHI ... 1
R. Fernandez, CHI ... 1
K. Hill, TEX 1

Hypothetical Awards

As the "expert" in baseball award-voting, I have been asked to make a set of hypothetical award selections for the years no official honors were given; i.e., pre-1956 Cy Young, pre-1947 Rookie of the Year, and pre-1911 MVP Awards, along with awards for any other "missing" years.

While this assignment gave me unusual freedom, I felt a certain responsibility to make my selections consistent with the perceptions and voting trends of a particular era. For example, although there were better NL players than Cincinnati's Edd Roush in 1919, he did two things which, combined, would have virtually guaranteed him the MVP Award: he won the batting crown, which was *the* individual title in the dead-ball era; and he played on a pennant-winner, which has always been a key factor in MVP voting. Thus, I felt obliged to make Roush my hypothetical selection.

Besides my own opinions and intuitions, several sources were instrumental in my selection process, including:

1. SABR retroactive award surveys, which have been done for pre-1949 Rookie of the Year and pre-1967 Cy Young Awards. SABR (the Society for American Baseball Research) is comprised of more than six thousand hard-core fans, hundreds of whom chose to participate in these surveys. The ballots were tremendously helpful in screening candidates and the voting results were carefully compared to my own choices.

2. Linear Weights, an overall player rating system devised by Pete Palmer, first used in *The Hidden Game of Baseball* (Doubleday, 1984, 1985), and continued in *Total Baseball*.

3. MVP voting results, for comparing Cy Young and Rookie candidates. If rookie "A" receives 75 points in the MVP election, while comparable rookie "B" receives just 10, I am forced to conclude that the on-the-spot observers discerned some important difference that we can't see in the statistics and that "A" is probably the better choice. (Incidentally, the criteria used to determine rookies was a maximum of 90 at-bats or 45 innings pitched in any previous seasons.)

4. Unofficial awards, including 1940–46 Rookie and 1929–30 MVP selections.

5. Cy Young (1956–66) and Rookie of the Year (1947–48) balloting, for years in which one league had no official winner.

The resulting selections are not necessarily ones the average reader will agree with, nor even that the *writer* agrees with; rather, they are the ones which can be *best justified with the available evidence*. I am prepared to defend any of my choices.

In comparison with the Palmer system, my selections concurred 54 percent with top player selections and 59 percent with top pitcher nominations. In comparison with the SABR surveys, my selections agreed 84 percent in the Rookie of the Year Award and 79 percent in the Cy Young Award.

The big winner in the hypothetical awards is Christy Mathewson, who picks up a Rookie of the Year, two MVPs, and eight Cy Young Awards. Other pitchers cap-

turing at least three Cy Youngs are Walter Johnson (7); Lefty Grove (6, consecutively); Warren Spahn (4, to add to the one he actually did win); Grover Cleveland Alexander (4); Burleigh Grimes, Carl Hubbell, Bob Feller, Bucky Walters, Bob Lemon, and appropriately, Cy Young himself (3 each).

Notable Rookies of the Year include Grover Cleveland Alexander, Babe Ruth, Rogers Hornsby, Dizzy Dean, Joe DiMaggio, and Ted Williams.

Honus Wagner cops six MVP Awards, including four in succession. Three-time MVPs are Nap Lajoie, Alexander, Ruth, and Hornsby. Ruth (once) and Hornsby (twice) also won official MVP Awards.

The following pages contain my hypothetical Cy Young (124), Rookie of the Year (97), and MVP (42) selections for this century.

Hypothetical Cy Young Award

American League Pitcher/Club	Year	American League Pitcher/Club	Year	American League Pitcher/Club	Year	National League Pitcher/Club	Year	National League Pitcher/Club	Year	National League Pitcher/Club	Year
C. Young, BOS	1901	E. Rommel, PHI	1922	S. Chandler, NY	1943	J. Kaat, MIN	1966	G. Alexander, CHI	1920	B. Walters, CIN	1940
C. Young, BOS	1902	G. Uhle, CLE	1923	D. Trout, DET	1944	J. McGinnity, BRO	1900	B. Grimes, BRO	1921	W. Wyatt, BRO	1941
C. Young, BOS	1903	W. Johnson, WAS	1924	H. Newhouser, DET	1945	N. Hahn, CIN	1901	W. Cooper, PIT	1922	M. Cooper, SL	1942
J. Chesbro, NY	1904	S. Coveleski, WAS	1925	H. Newhouser, DET	1946	J. Taylor, CHI	1902	D. Luque, CIN	1923	M. Cooper, SL	1943
R. Waddell, PHI	1905	G. Uhle, CLE	1926	J. Page, NY	1947	C. Mathewson, NY	1903	D. Vance, BRO	1924	B. Walters, CIN	1944
A. Orth, NY	1906	W. Moore, NY	1927	B. Lemon, CLE	1948	J. McGinnity, NY	1904	D. Vance, BRO	1925	C. Barrett, BOS-SL	1945
E. Walsh, CHI	1907	L. Grove, PHI	1928	M. Parnell, BOS	1949	Mathewson, NY	1905	R. Kremer, PIT	1926	H. Pollet, SL	1946
E. Walsh, CHI	1908	L. Grove, PHI	1929	B. Lemon, CLE	1950	M. Brown, CHI	1906	C. Root, CHI	1927	E. Blackwell, CIN	1947
F. Smith, CHI	1909	L. Grove, PHI	1930	N. Garver, SL	1951	Mathewson, NY	1907	B. Grimes, PIT	1928	J. Sain, BOS	1948
J. Coombs, PHI	1910	L. Grove, PHI	1931	B. Shantz, PHI	1952	Mathewson, NY	1908	B. Grimes, PIT	1929	W. Spahn, BOS	1949
W. Johnson, WAS	1911	L. Grove, PHI	1932	B. Pierce, CHI	1953	Mathewson, NY	1909	P. Malone, CHI	1930	J. Konstanty, PHI	1950
J. Wood, BOS	1912	L. Grove, PHI	1933	B. Lemon, CLE	1954	Mathewson, NY	1910	E. Brandt, BOS	1931	S. Maglie, NY	1951
W. Johnson, WAS	1913	L. Gomez, NY	1934	R. Narleski, CLE	1955	Mathewson, NY	1911	L. Warneke, CHI	1932	R. Roberts, PHI	1952
W. Johnson, WAS	1914	W. Ferrell, BOS	1935	B. Pierce, CHI	1956	R. Marquard, NY	1912	C. Hubbell, NY	1933	W. Spahn, MIL	1953
W. Johnson, WAS	1915	T. Bridges, DET	1936	J. Bunning, DET	1957	Mathewson, NY	1913	D. Dean, SL	1934	J. Antonelli, NY	1954
B. Ruth, BOS	1916	L. Gomez, NY	1937	C. Estrada, BAL	1960	B. James, BOS	1914	D. Dean, SL	1935	R. Roberts, PHI	1955
E. Cicotte, CHI	1917	R. Ruffing, NY	1938	D. Donovan, CLE	1962	G. Alexander, PHI	1915	C. Hubbell, NY	1936	W. Spahn, MIL	1958
W. Johnson, WAS	1918	B. Feller, CLE	1939	W. Ford, NY	1963	G. Alexander, PHI	1916	C. Hubbell, NY	1937	S. Jones, SF	1959
W. Johnson, WAS	1919	B. Feller, CLE	1940	E. Fisher, CHI	1965	G. Alexander, PHI	1917	B. Lee, CHI	1938	W. Spahn, MIL	1961
J. Bagby, CLE	1920	B. Feller, CLE	1941			J. Vaughn, CHI	1918	B. Walters, CIN	1939	L. Jackson, CHI	1964
R. Faber, CHI	1921	T. Hughson, BOS	1942			J. Vaughn, CHI	1919				

Hypothetical Federal League Awards

	1914	1915
Most Valuable Player	B. Kauff, IND	D. Zwilling, CHI
Cy Young	C. Hendrix, CHI	G. McConnell, CHI
Rookie of the Year	B. Kauff, IND	E. Johnson, SL

Hypothetical Rookie of the Year Award

American League Player/Club	Year	American League Player/Club	Year	American League Player/Club	Year	National League Player/Club	Year	National League Player/Club	Year	National League Player/Club	Year
S. Seybold, PHI	1901	A. Sothoron, SL	1917	B. Johnson, PHI	1933	E. Scott, CIN	1900	R. Hornsby, SL	1916	P. Derringer, SL	1931
A. Joss, CLE	1902	S. Perry, PHI	1918	H. Trosky, CLE	1934	C. Mathewson, NY	1901	L. Cadore, BRO	1917	D. Dean, SL	1932
C. Bender, PHI	1903	D. Kerr, CHI	1919	J. Powell, WAS	1935	H. Smoot, SL	1902	C. Hollocher, CHI	1918	F. Demaree, CHI	1933
F. Glade, SL	1904	B. Meusel, NY	1920	J. DiMaggio, NY	1936	J. Weimer, CHI	1903	O. Tuero, SL	1919	C. Davis, PHI	1934
G. Stone, SL	1905	J. Sewell, CLE	1921	R. York, DET	1937	H. Lumley, BRO	1904	J. Haines, SL	1920	C. Blanton, PIT	1935
C. Rossman, CLE	1906	H. Pillette, DET	1922	K. Keltner, DET	1938	E. Reulbach, CHI	1905	R. Grimes, CHI	1921	J. Mize, SL	1936
S. Nicholls, PHI	1907	H. Summa, CLE	1923	T. Williams, BOS	1939	J. Pfiester, CHI	1906	H. Miller, CHI	1922	J. Turner, BOS	1937
E. Summers, DET	1908	A. Simmons, PHI	1924	W. Judnich, SL	1940	N. Rucker, BRO	1907	G. Grantham, CHI	1923	J. Rizzo, PIT	1938
F. Baker, PHI	1909	E. Combs, NY	1925	P. Rizzuto, NY	1941	G. McQuillan, PHI	1908	K. Cuyler, PIT	1924	H. Casey, BRO	1939
R. Ford, NY	1910	T. Lazzeri, NY	1926	J. Pesky, BOS	1942	D. Miller, PIT	1909	J. Welsh, BOS	1925	B. Young, NY	1940
V. Gregg, CLE	1911	W. Moore, NY	1927	B. Johnson, NY	1943	K. Cole, CHI	1910	P. Waner, PIT	1926	E. Riddle, CIN	1941
D. Pratt, SL	1912	E. Morris, BOS	1928	J. Berry, PHI	1944	G. Alexander, PHI	1911	L. Waner, PIT	1927	J. Beazley, SL	1942
R. Russell, CHI	1913	D. Alexander, DET	1929	B. Ferriss, BOS	1945	L. Cheney, CHI	1912	D. Bissonette, BRO	1928	L. Klein, CHI	1943
R. Bressler, PHI	1914	S. Jolley, CHI	1930	B. Lemon, CLE	1946	J. Viox, PIT	1913			B. Voiselle, NY	1944
B. Ruth, BOS	1915	J. Vosmik, CLE	1931	F. Shea, NY	1947	J. Pfeffer, BRO	1914	J. Frederick, BRO	1929	K. Burkhart, SL	1945
J. Bagby, CLE	1916	J. Allen, NY	1932	G. Bearden, CLE	1948	T. Long, SL	1915	W. Berger, BOS	1930	D. Ennis, PHI	1946

Hypothetical Most Valuable Player Award

American League Player/Club	Year	American League Player/Club	Year	American League Player/Club	Year	National League Player/Club	Year	National League Player/Club	Year	National League Player/Club	Year
N. Lajoie, PHI	1901	E. Walsh, CHI	1908	J. Jackson, CHI	1919	H. Wagner, PIT	1902	H. Wagner, PIT	1909	E. Roush, CIN	1919
C. Young, BOS	1902	T. Cobb, DET	1909	B. Ruth, NY	1920	H. Wagner, PIT	1903	S. Magee, PHI	1910	R. Hornsby, SL	1920
N. Lajoie, PHI	1903	J. Coombs, PHI	1910	B. Ruth, NY	1921	J. McGinnity, NY	1904	G. Alexander, PHI	1915	R. Hornsby, SL	1921
J. Chesbro, NY	1904	E. Collins, CHI	1915	L. Fonseca, CLE	1929	C. Mathewson, NY	1905	G. Alexander, PHI	1916	R. Hornsby, SL	1922
R. Waddell, PHI	1905	T. Speaker, CLE	1916	J. Cronin, WAS	1930	F. Chance, CHI	1906	G. Alexander, PHI	1917	D. Luque, CIN	1923
N. Lajoie, CLE	1906	E. Cicotte, CHI	1917	H. Wagner, PIT	1900	H. Wagner, PIT	1907	J. Vaughn, CHI	1918	H. Wilson, CHI	1930
T. Cobb, DET	1907	B. Ruth, BOS	1918	H. Wagner, PIT	1901	C. Mathewson, NY	1908				

Gold Glove Award: History

In a 1956 spring training survey, Elmer A. Blasco—employed by Rawlings Sporting Goods as advertising, public relations and sales manager—found that 83 percent of the active regular major league players wore Rawlings gloves or mitts. Noting that Hillerich & Bradsby (the major leagues' leading baseball bat supplier) awarded Silver Bats to the leagues' top hitters, Blasco reasoned that Rawlings ought to sponsor some sort of fielding award. After his idea was accepted by Rawlings' management, Blasco contacted the Brown Shoe Company of St. Louis and obtained from them a hide of gold lamé-tanned leather used to make ladies' formal slippers. A glove was crafted from this hide, laced and stamped as a regular fielders glove, and attached to a metal fixture on a walnut base with an appropriate engraved plate.

Thus was born the Gold Glove Award.

The October 2, 1957, edition of *The Sporting News* featured a full-page advertisement/announcement: "Recognizing the importance of superior individual fielding performance to the advancement of baseball as America's national game, Rawlings (Sporting Goods Company) has established Annual Gold Glove Awards beginning with the 1957 season.

"Each of the nine Major League players chosen for *The Sporting News* All-Star Fielding Team will be honored with a Rawlings Gold Glove Award. Selections will be made by a Committee named by *The Sporting News*.

"Awards will be Rawlings custom-built gloves or mitts hand-crafted of special metallic gold-finished leather, each mounted on a suitable hardwood stand bearing an engraved plate."

TSN publisher J. G. Taylor Spink appointed nineteen noted sportswriters for the selection task. They included Shirley Povich, Edgar Munzel, Hy Hurwitz, Earl Lawson, Bob Broeg, Allen Lewis, and Hal Lebowitz. A contest to predict the winners, open to baseball-playing boys, was sponsored by Rawlings.

The first Gold Glove winners were announced with great pomp and circumstance in the December 18, 1957, issue of TSN. "Too long neglected, the magicians of the defense have had no real recognition," the article explained, adding that the selections were made "solely on the basis of their defensive ability."

Rawlings and TSN also joined forces that year in the establishment of the Silver Glove Award, given to the top minor league fielder at each position—based entirely on fielding averages.

In 1958 the Gold Glove selection privilege was turned over to the major league players and an All-Star Fielding Team was selected for each league (as it still is).

In 1961 the method for selecting outfielders was changed. Rather than choosing a left-, center-, and right fielder for each league, each voter was instructed to name three outfielders regardless of position (still the practice today).

In 1965 the managers and coaches of each team took over the voting responsibility, which they have retained ever since. Voters are not permitted to select players on their own teams. In 1987, 139 different managers and coaches took part in the balloting.

Perhaps because of its originality, the Gold Glove is the one *Sporting News* award that has gained universal acceptance and prestige in the baseball world. However, as with any award, the selections often draw criticism.

One complaint is that too much importance is given to fielding average. Most of us realize that FA is not always a reliable indicator of defensive ability, but how much does it influence the Gold Glove voters?

Of the 366 FA leaders at the various positions between 1957–87 (discounting pitchers and counting only one outfielder per league each year), 118 (32 percent) also won their respective Gold Glove Awards (see Table 1). We can say, then, that if a player leads his league in FA, he has about a one-in-three chance of winning the Gold Glove—not an overwhelming correlation, but about four times better than random chance.

This raises some interesting questions. Since official fielding statistics are not published until months *after* Gold Gloves (although unofficial stats are readily available) are voted on, any voter relying on fielding stats would probably have to consult (or remember) the *previous* year's data. Therefore, if FA itself really does impress voters, we should expect to see many players winning a Gold Glove the year *after* they lead in FA. Do they? Well, no (see Table 2). The percentage here is 25 percent or one-in-four—again, considerably better than chance, but less of a factor than leading in FA in the current year.

And what about the influence of Gold Gloves on fielding averages? Is an official scorer less likely to charge an error against a player simply because he won a Gold Glove the previous year? Apparently not (see Table 3). The percentage of Gold Glove recipients leading in FA the following year is 23 percent.

"It is my belief that a lot more is considered than fielding percentage," said *TSN* editor Tom Barnidge, citing "range, throwing arm, the headiness of the ballplayer." Pete Rose, a two-time Gold Glove winner and later a voter, concurred: "There are a lot of intangibles involved in voting for the Gold Glove. Take an outfielder. The coaches and managers watch these guys all the time. How they play the hitters, how strong their arms are, how often they hit the cutoff man, and all that is taken into consideration—things that do not show up in the statistics."

Another criticism of the Gold Glove is that batting performance plays a role in the selections, contrary to the award's philosophy. As *USA Today* baseball editor Hal Bodley put it, "A player who is outstanding on defense and respectable on offense has a much better chance of getting a Gold Glove than a counterpart whose forte is fielding alone."

Other factors can be distractions to the voters: flashiness, reputations, and the selection process itself. For insight on some of these and their effects, I consulted an expert on the Gold Glove: Wes Parker, a six-time winner of the award at first base.

Parker, it should be noted, would seem to have no reason to gripe about the award. He grasped the honor from a seven-time winner; he won it even when he batted as low as .239; and he became one of only two nonpitchers (Roberto Clemente is the other) to win the award in his final major league season.

"I would say many, if not most, coaches and managers fail to take their voting responsibility seriously," said

Parker. "They don't treat it as a vital act. They are usually much more concerned with their team and the pennant race and, as a result, tend to zip through the ballots (distributed in September). So they wind up voting for the most recognizable names."

Parker brought out another rarely discussed procedural problem: "Since players [when they were voting] and coaches are forbidden to vote for anyone on their own team, they often won't vote for the guy who is contending with their team's leading candidate for the same award. That increases their teammate's chances."

On the subject of reputation, Parker asserted that it "has a lot to do with it, absolutely. In 1966, Bill White won the award (for the seventh consecutive time), although even White admitted that I probably deserved it. It takes a couple of years for your reputation to catch up with you, but that can work to your advantage at the end of your career.

"Flashiness is a factor too," continued Parker. "It puts the player's name in the forefront of the voter's minds." Wes also concurred with the theory that a player's bat can be the difference in winning this 'fielding' award.

"[Four-time Gold Glove winner Steve] Garvey is a good example of someone who won it with his bat and notoriety, a perfect example, in fact," opines Parker. "Garvey was vastly overrated defensively . . . he had no range, no arm, and no aggressiveness. He would hold the ball and allow opposing runners to take extra bases to avoid throwing errors. That's how he compiled his high [fielding] averages at first base. Remember, he was a terrible third baseman, worst I ever saw." (In 1972, Garvey's last season as a third-sacker, he led the NL with 28 errors in just 85 games, posting a woeful .902 percentage.)

"Amazingly, despite these prejudices," Parker concluded, "I think the Gold Glove choices have been excellent. At first base I think they have been perfect, with the exception of Garvey."

TABLE 1   Fielding Average Leaders Winning Gold Glove, 1957-87 (Maximum 61 Each Position).

POS.	NL	AL	TOT.	PCT.
C	7	7	14	23
1B	13	13	26	43
2B	14	5	19	31
3B	4	15	19	31
SS	14	12	26	43
OF	6	8	14	23
TOT.	58	60	118	32

TABLE 2   Fielding Average Leaders Winning Gold Glove in Following Season, 1956-86 (Maximum 61 Each Position).

POS.	NL	AL	TOT.	PCT.
C	7	7	14	23
1B	8	11	19	31
2B	9	6	15	25
3B	3	13	16	26
SS	11	9	20	33
OF	2	5	7	11
TOT.	40	51	91	25

TABLE 3   Fielding Average Leaders Who Won Gold Glove in Previous Season, 1958-87 (Maximum 59 Each Position).

POS.	NL	AL	TOT.	PCT.
C	3	7	10	17
1B	11	8	19	32
2B	8	2	10	17
3B	2	12	14	24
SS	10	9	19	32
OF	6	5	11	19
TOT.	40	43	83	23

While the Gold Glove Award has adequately filled the need for a subjective fielding award, there is still something to be said about fielding statistics. It is fashionable to say that fielding stats are meaningless, but, as analyst Bill James said, "If a baseball statistic is meaningless to you, that is simply because you don't know what it means."

With the understanding of which fielding statistics *are* meaningful for each position, it is possible to make a pretty reliable judgment of a player's defensive skills based on stats alone. In recent years, several analysts have attempted to measure individual fielding performance on the basis of numbers.

One newer method is Linear Weights, Pete Palmer's translation of individual batting, pitching, and fielding statistics into runs gained and thus games won. The fielding portion of the system, Fielding or Defensive Wins, incorporates data (variously weighted according to position) on putouts, assists, errors, and double plays, comparing a player's totals against the league averages.

The formula first determines how many runs a player saves (or costs) his team as compared to an "average" player at the same position. Runs are then translated into wins, based on the league average of runs per win. For example, second baseman Glenn Hubbard was computed to have won about three and a half games for the Braves with his glove in 1986, the top Defensive Wins total in the majors.

Of the sixty players identified by the Palmer system as the best fielders in their leagues between 1957–86, twenty-eight also won their respective Gold Glove Awards.

Palmer has drawn criticism for comparing players with average, rather than replacement-level, players; for over-emphasizing the double play; and for the use of arbitrary weighting schemes. It is particularly—and admittedly—inadequate in evaluating catchers.

Bill James has also presented a fielding measurement system, Defensive Won/Lost Percentage (DW/L%), although he hasn't used it since 1984. The formula varies from position to position, using four arbitrarily weighted components at each. These components range from readily available statistics (fielding average, assists per game, and so on) to abstruse estimations and calculations, using some data unavailable to the average researcher. The formula, however, is not designed for cross-era comparisons.

The results of these calculations produce the DW/L%, which in turn is translated into defensive wins and losses, based on still more arbitrary assignments of defensive games at each position (ranging from 3 at first base to 11 at shortstop).

Of the thirty-two players identified by DW/L% as the best at their positions and leagues for the 1983–84 seasons, twelve (38 percent) also won their respective Gold Gloves.

The use of a series of arbitrary values is the glaring flaw of DW/L%. Criticism is also due for the complexity and lack of adaptability of the system(s).

The Elias Sports Bureau has demonstrated a simple and generally effective system for evaluating fielders: comparing the number of runs scored per nine innings while a player is on the field to the number scored when he isn't. For example, Elias calculated that the 1982–86 Cardinals averaged allowing 3.85 runs per nine innings with Ozzie Smith at shortstop, as compared to 4.04 per game with other shortstops.

There is nothing new or brilliant about this concept; the

difference is that Elias has the data available to make this type of measurement, right down to thirds of an inning, at least since 1975. Since they generally choose not to share this data with the public, however, it is of no value at present. So, when all is said and done about modern statistical fielding measurements, a subjective measure-ment—the Gold Glove—is probably still the best tool we have available to rate fielders.

The following pages list the winners of the Gold Glove at each position since 1957. Complete balloting for Gold Glove elections is, unfortunately, neither available nor researchable.

Gold Glove Award

Pitchers

Year	National League	American League
1957	(No selection)	B. Shantz, NY
1958	H. Haddix, CIN	B. Shantz, NY
1959	H. Haddix, PIT	B. Shantz, NY
1960	H. Haddix, PIT	B. Shantz, NY
1961	B. Shantz, PIT	F. Lary, DET
1962	B. Shantz, SL	J. Kaat, MIN
1963	B. Shantz, SL	J. Kaat, MIN
1964	B. Shantz, PHI	J. Kaat, MIN
1965	B. Gibson, SL	J. Kaat, MIN
1966	B. Gibson, SL	J. Kaat, MIN
1967	B. Gibson, SL	J. Kaat, MIN
1968	B. Gibson, SL	J. Kaat, MIN
1969	B. Gibson, SL	J. Kaat, MIN
1970	B. Gibson, SL	J. Kaat, MIN
1971	B. Gibson, SL	J. Kaat, MIN
1972	B. Gibson, SL	J. Kaat, MIN
1973	B. Gibson, SL	J. Kaat, MIN
1974	A. Messersmith, LA	J. Kaat, CHI
1975	A. Messersmith, LA	J. Kaat, CHI
1976	J. Kaat, PHI	J. Palmer, BAL
1977	J. Kaat, PHI	J. Palmer, BAL
1978	P. Niekro, ATL	J. Palmer, BAL
1979	P. Niekro, ATL	J. Palmer, BAL
1980	P. Niekro, ATL	M. Norris, OAK
1981	S. Carlton, PHI	M. Norris, OAK
1982	P. Niekro, ATL	R. Guidry, NY
1983	P. Niekro, ATL	R. Guidry, NY
1984	J. Andujar, SL	R. Guidry, NY
1985	R. Reuschel, PIT	R. Guidry, NY
1986	F. Valenzuela, LA	R. Guidry, NY
1987	R. Reuschel, SF	M. Langston, SEA
1988	O. Hershiser, LA	M. Langston, SEA
1989	R. Darling, NY	B. Saberhagen, KC
1990	G. Maddux, CHI	M. Boddicker, BOS
1991	G. Maddux, CHI	M. Langston, CAL
1992	G. Maddux, CHI	M. Langston, CAL
1993	G. Maddux, ATL	M. Langston, CAL
1994	G. Maddux, ATL	M. Langston, CAL
1995	G. Maddux, ATL	M. Langston, CAL
1996	G. Maddux, ATL	M. Mussina, BAL

Catchers

Year	National League	American League
1957	(No selection)	S. Lollar, CHI
1958	D. Crandall, MIL	S. Lollar, CHI
1959	D. Crandall, MIL	S. Lollar, CHI
1960	D. Crandall, MIL	E. Battey, WAS
1961	J. Roseboro, LA	E. Battey, MIN
1962	D. Crandall, MIL	E. Battey, MIN
1963	J. Edwards, CIN	E. Howard, NY
1964	J. Edwards, CIN	E. Howard, NY
1965	J. Torre, MIL	B. Freehan, DET
1966	J. Roseboro, LA	B. Freehan, DET
1967	R. Hundley, CHI	B. Freehan, DET
1968	J. Bench, CIN	B. Freehan, DET
1969	J. Bench, CIN	B. Freehan, DET
1970	J. Bench, CIN	R. Fosse, CLE
1971	J. Bench, CIN	R. Fosse, CLE
1972	J. Bench, CIN	C. Fisk, BOS
1973	J. Bench, CIN	T. Munson, NY
1974	J. Bench, CIN	T. Munson, NY
1975	J. Bench, CIN	T. Munson, NY
1976	J. Bench, CIN	J. Sundberg, TEX
1977	J. Bench, CIN	J. Sundberg, TEX
1978	B. Boone, PHI	J. Sundberg, TEX
1979	B. Boone, PHI	J. Sundberg, TEX
1980	G. Carter, MON	J. Sundberg, TEX
1981	G. Carter, MON	J. Sundberg, TEX
1982	G. Carter, MON	B. Boone, CAL
1983	T. Pena, PIT	Lc. Parrish, DET
1984	T. Pena, PIT	Lc. Parrish, DET
1985	T. Pena, PIT	Lc. Parrish, DET
1986	J. Davis, CHI	B. Boone, CAL
1987	M. LaValliere, PIT	B. Boone, CAL
1988	B. Santiago, SD	B. Boone, CAL
1989	B. Santiago, SD	B. Boone, KC
1990	B. Santiago, SD	S. Alomar, CLE
1991	T. Pagnozzi, SL	T. Pena, BOS
1992	T. Pagnozzi, SL	I. Rodriguez, TEX
1993	K. Manwaring, SF	I. Rodriguez, TEX
1994	T. Pagnozzi, SL	I. Rodriguez, TEX
1995	C. Johnson, FLA	I. Rodriguez, TEX
1996	C. Johnson, FLA	I. Rodriguez, TEX

First Basemen

Year	National League	American League
1957	G. Hodges, BRO	(No selection)
1958	G. Hodges, LA	V. Power, CLE
1959	G. Hodges, LA	V. Power, CLE
1960	B. White, SL	V. Power, CLE
1961	B. White, SL	V. Power, CLE
1962	B. White, SL	V. Power, MIN
1963	B. White, SL	V. Power, MIN
1964	B. White, SL	V. Power, LA
1965	B. White, SL	J. Pepitone, NY
1966	B. White, PHI	J. Pepitone, NY
1967	W. Parker, LA	G. Scott, BOS
1968	W. Parker, LA	G. Scott, BOS
1969	W. Parker, LA	J. Pepitone, NY
1970	W. Parker, LA	J. Spencer, CAL
1971	W. Parker, LA	G. Scott, BOS
1972	W. Parker, LA	G. Scott, MIL
1973	M. Jorgensen, MON	G. Scott, MIL
1974	S. Garvey, LA	G. Scott, MIL
1975	S. Garvey, LA	G. Scott, MIL
1976	S. Garvey, LA	G. Scott, MIL
1977	S. Garvey, LA	J. Spencer, CHI
1978	K. Hernandez, SL	C. Chambliss, NY
1979	K. Hernandez, SL	C. Cooper, MIL
1980	K. Hernandez, SL	C. Cooper, MIL
1981	K. Hernandez, SL	M. Squires, CHI
1982	K. Hernandez, SL	E. Murray, BAL
1983	K. Hernandez, SL-NY	E. Murray, BAL
1984	K. Hernandez, NY	E. Murray, BAL
1985	K. Hernandez, NY	D. Mattingly, NY
1986	K. Hernandez, NY	D. Mattingly, NY
1987	K. Hernandez, NY	D. Mattingly, NY
1988	K. Hernandez, NY	D. Mattingly, NY
1989	A. Galarraga, MON	D. Mattingly, NY
1990	A. Galarraga, MON	M. McGwire, OAK
1991	W. Clark, SF	D. Mattingly, NY
1992	M. Grace, CHI	D. Mattingly, NY
1993	M. Grace, CHI	D. Mattingly, NY
1994	J. Bagwell, HOU	D. Mattingly, NY
1995	M. Grace, CHI	J. Snow, CAL
1996	M. Grace, CHI	J. Snow, CAL

Second Basemen

Year	National League	American League
1957	(No selection)	N. Fox, CHI
1958	B. Mazeroski, PIT	F. Bolling, DET
1959	C. Neal, LA	N. Fox, CHI
1960	B. Mazeroski, PIT	N. Fox, CHI
1961	B. Mazeroski, PIT	B. Richardson, NY
1962	K. Hubbs, CHI	B. Richardson, NY
1963	B. Mazeroski, PIT	B. Richardson, NY
1964	B. Mazeroski, PIT	B. Richardson, NY
1965	B. Mazeroski, PIT	B. Richardson, NY
1966	B. Mazeroski, PIT	B. Knoop, CAL
1967	B. Mazeroski, PIT	B. Knoop, CAL
1968	G. Beckert, CHI	B. Knoop, CAL
1969	F. Millan, ATL	D. Johnson, BAL
1970	T. Helms, CIN	D. Johnson, BAL
1971	T. Helms, CIN	D. Johnson, BAL
1972	F. Millan, ATL	D. Griffin, BOS
1973	J. Morgan, CIN	B. Grich, BAL
1974	J. Morgan, CIN	B. Grich, BAL
1975	J. Morgan, CIN	B. Grich, BAL
1976	J. Morgan, CIN	B. Grich, BAL
1977	J. Morgan, CIN	F. White, KC
1978	D. Lopes, LA	F. White, KC
1979	M. Trillo, PHI	F. White, KC
1980	D. Flynn, NY	F. White, KC
1981	M. Trillo, PHI	F. White, KC
1982	M. Trillo, PHI	F. White, KC
1983	R. Sandberg, CHI	L. Whitaker, DET
1984	R. Sandberg, CHI	L. Whitaker, DET
1985	R. Sandberg, CHI	L. Whitaker, DET
1986	R. Sandberg, CHI	F. White, KC
1987	R. Sandberg, CHI	F. White, KC
1988	R. Sandberg, CHI	H. Reynolds, SEA
1989	R. Sandberg, CHI	H. Reynolds, SEA
1990	R. Sandberg, CHI	H. Reynolds, SEA
1991	R. Sandberg, CHI	R. Alomar, TOR
1992	J. Lind, PIT	R. Alomar, TOR
1993	R. Thompson, SF	R. Alomar, TOR
1994	C. Biggio, HOU	R. Alomar, TOR
1995	C. Biggio, HOU	R. Alomar, TOR
1996	C. Biggio, HOU	R. Alomar, TOR

Third Basemen

Year	National League	American League
1957	(No selection)	F. Malzone, BOS
1958	K. Boyer, SL	F. Malzone, BOS
1959	K. Boyer, SL	F. Malzone, BOS
1960	K. Boyer, SL	B. Robinson, BAL
1961	K. Boyer, SL	B. Robinson, BAL
1962	J. Davenport, SF	B. Robinson, BAL
1963	K. Boyer, SL	B. Robinson, BAL
1964	R. Santo, CHI	B. Robinson, BAL
1965	R. Santo, CHI	B. Robinson, BAL
1966	R. Santo, CHI	B. Robinson, BAL
1967	R. Santo, CHI	B. Robinson, BAL
1968	R. Santo, CHI	B. Robinson, BAL
1969	C. Boyer, ATL	B. Robinson, BAL
1970	D. Rader, HOU	B. Robinson, BAL
1971	D. Rader, HOU	B. Robinson, BAL
1972	D. Rader, HOU	B. Robinson, BAL
1973	D. Rader, HOU	B. Robinson, BAL
1974	D. Rader, HOU	B. Robinson, BAL
1975	K. Reitz, SL	B. Robinson, BAL
1976	M. Schmidt, PHI	A. Rodriguez, DET
1977	M. Schmidt, PHI	G. Nettles, NY
1978	M. Schmidt, PHI	G. Nettles, NY
1979	M. Schmidt, PHI	B. Bell, TEX
1980	M. Schmidt, PHI	B. Bell, TEX
1981	M. Schmidt, PHI	B. Bell, TEX
1982	M. Schmidt, PHI	B. Bell, TEX
1983	M. Schmidt, PHI	B. Bell, TEX
1984	M. Schmidt, PHI	B. Bell, TEX
1985	T. Wallach, MON	G. Brett, KC
1986	M. Schmidt, PHI	G. Gaetti, MIN
1987	T. Pendleton, SL	G. Gaetti, MIN
1988	T. Wallach, MON	G. Gaetti, MIN
1989	T. Pendleton, SL	G. Gaetti, MIN
1990	T. Wallach, MON	K. Gruber, TOR
1991	M. Williams, SF	R. Ventura, CHI
1992	T. Pendleton, ATL	R. Ventura, CHI
1993	M. Williams, SF	R. Ventura, CHI
1994	M. Williams, SF	W. Boggs, NY
1995	K. Caminiti, SD	W. Boggs, NY
1996	K. Caminiti, SD	R. Ventura, CHI

Shortstops

Year	National League	American League
1957	R. McMillan, CIN	(No selection)
1958	R. McMillan, CIN	L. Aparicio, CHI
1959	R. McMillan, CIN	L. Aparicio, CHI
1960	E. Banks, CHI	L. Aparicio, CHI
1961	M. Wills, LA	L. Aparicio, CHI
1962	M. Wills, LA	L. Aparicio, CHI
1963	B. Wine, PHI	Z. Versalles, MIN
1964	R. Amaro, PHI	L. Aparicio, BAL
1965	L. Cardenas, CIN	Z. Versalles, MIN
1966	G. Alley, PIT	L. Aparicio, BAL
1967	G. Alley, PIT	J. Fregosi, CAL
1968	D. Maxvill, SL	L. Aparicio, CHI
1969	D. Kessinger, CHI	M. Belanger, BAL
1970	D. Kessinger, CHI	L. Aparicio, CHI
1971	B. Harrelson, NY	M. Belanger, BAL
1972	L. Bowa, PHI	E. Brinkman, DET
1973	R. Metzger, HOU	M. Belanger, BAL
1974	D. Concepcion, CIN	M. Belanger, BAL
1975	D. Concepcion, CIN	M. Belanger, BAL
1976	D. Concepcion, CIN	M. Belanger, BAL
1977	D. Concepcion, CIN	M. Belanger, BAL
1978	L. Bowa, PHI	M. Belanger, BAL
1979	D. Concepcion, CIN	R. Burleson, BOS
1980	O. Smith, SD	A. Trammell, DET
1981	O. Smith, SD	A. Trammell, DET
1982	O. Smith, SL	R. Yount, MIL
1983	O. Smith, SL	A. Trammell, DET
1984	O. Smith, SL	A. Trammell, DET
1985	O. Smith, SL	A. Griffin, OAK
1986	O. Smith, SL	T. Fernandez, TOR
1987	O. Smith, SL	T. Fernandez, TOR
1988	O. Smith, SL	T. Fernandez, TOR
1989	O. Smith, SL	T. Fernandez, TOR
1990	O. Smith, SL	O. Guillen, CHI
1991	O. Smith, SL	C. Ripken, BAL
1992	O. Smith, SL	C. Ripken, BAL
1993	J. Bell, PIT	O. Vizquel, SEA
1994	B. Larkin, CIN	O. Vizquel, SEA
1995	B. Larkin, CIN	O. Vizquel, CLE
1996	B. Larkin, CIN	O. Vizquel, CLE

National League Outfielders

YEAR	PLAYERS		
1957	W. Mays, NY (CF)	(No other selections)	
1958	F. Robinson, CIN (LF)	W. Mays, SF (CF)	H. Aaron, MIL (RF)
1959	J. Brandt, SF (LF)	W. Mays, SF (CF)	H. Aaron, MIL (RF)
1960	W. Moon, LA (LF)	W. Mays, SF (CF)	H. Aaron, MIL (RF)
1961	W. Mays, SF	R. Clemente, PIT	V. Pinson, CIN
1962	W. Mays, SF	R. Clemente, PIT	B. Virdon, PIT
1963	W. Mays, SF	R. Clemente, PIT	C. Flood, SL
1964	W. Mays, SF	R. Clemente, PIT	C. Flood, SL
1965	W. Mays, SF	R. Clemente, PIT	C. Flood, SL
1966	W. Mays, SF	C. Flood, SL	R. Clemente, PIT
1967	R. Clemente, PIT	C. Flood, SL	W. Mays, SF
1968	W. Mays, SF	R. Clemente, PIT	C. Flood, SL
1969	R. Clemente, PIT	C. Flood, SL	P. Rose, CIN
1970	R. Clemente, PIT	T. Agee, NY	P. Rose, CIN
1971	R. Clemente, PIT	B. Bonds, SF	W. Davis, LA
1972	R. Clemente, PIT	C. Cedeno, HOU	W. Davis, LA
1973	B. Bonds, SF	C. Cedeno, HOU	W. Davis, LA
1974	C. Cedeno, HOU	C. Geronimo, CIN	B. Bonds, SF
1975	C. Cedeno, HOU	C. Geronimo, CIN	G. Maddox, PHI
1976	C. Cedeno, HOU	C. Geronimo, CIN	G. Maddox, PHI
1977	C. Geronimo, CIN	G. Maddox, PHI	D. Parker, PIT
1978	G. Maddox, PHI	D. Parker, PIT	E. Valentine, MON
1979	G. Maddox, PHI	D. Parker, PIT	D. Winfield, SD
1980	A. Dawson, MON	G. Maddox, PHI	D. Winfield, SD
1981	A. Dawson, MON	G. Maddox, PHI	D. Baker, LA
1982	A. Dawson, MON	D. Murphy, ATL	G. Maddox, PHI
1983	A. Dawson, MON	D. Murphy, ATL	W. McGee, SL
1984	D. Murphy, ATL	B. Dernier, CHI	A. Dawson, MON
1985	W. McGee, SL	D. Murphy, ATL	A. Dawson, MON
1986	T. Gwynn, SD	D. Murphy, ATL	W. McGee, SL
1987	E. Davis, CIN	T. Gwynn, SD	A. Dawson, CHI
1988	A. Van Slyke, PIT	E. Davis, CIN	A. Dawson, CHI
1989	A. Van Slyke, PIT	E. Davis, CIN	T. Gwynn, SD
1990	A. Van Slyke, PIT	T. Gwynn, SD	B. Bonds, PIT
1991	A. Van Slyke, PIT	T. Gwynn, SD	B. Bonds, PIT
1992	A. Van Slyke, PIT	L. Walker, MON	B. Bonds, PIT
1993	B. Bonds, SF	L. Walker, MON	M. Grissom, MON
1994	B. Bonds, SF	D. Lewis, SF	M. Grissom, MON
1995	R. Mondesi, LA	M. Grissom, ATL	S. Finley, SD
1996	B. Bonds, SF	M. Grissom, ATL	S. Finley, SD

American League Outfielders

YEAR	PLAYERS		
1957	M. Minoso, CHI (LF)	A. Kaline, DET (RF)	(No other selection)
1958	N. Siebern, NY (LF)	J. Piersall, BOS (CF)	A. Kaline, DET (RF)
1959	M. Minoso, CLE (LF)	A. Kaline, DET (CF)	J. Jensen, BOS (RF)
1960	M. Minoso, CHI (LF)	J. Landis, CHI (CF)	R. Maris, NY (RF)
1961	A. Kaline, DET	J. Piersall, CLE	J. Landis, CHI
1962	J. Landis, CHI	M. Mantle, NY	A. Kaline, DET
1963	A. Kaline, DET	C. Yastrzemski, BOS	J. Landis, CHI
1964	A. Kaline, DET	J. Landis, CHI	V. Davalillo, CLE
1965	A. Kaline, DET	T. Tresh, NY	C. Yastrzemski, BOS
1966	A. Kaline, DET	T. Agee, CHI	T. Oliva, MIN
1967	C. Yastrzemski, BOS	P. Blair, BAL	A. Kaline, DET
1968	M. Stanley, DET	C. Yastrzemski, BOS	R. Smith, BOS
1969	P. Blair, BAL	M. Stanley, DET	C. Yastrzemski, BOS
1970	M. Stanley, DET	P. Blair, BAL	K. Berry, CHI
1971	P. Blair, BAL	A. Otis, KC	C. Yastrzemski, BOS
1972	P. Blair, BAL	B. Murcer, NY	K. Berry, CAL
1973	P. Blair, BAL	A. Otis, KC	M. Stanley, DET
1974	P. Blair, BAL	A. Otis, KC	J. Rudi, OAK
1975	P. Blair, BAL	J. Rudi, OAK	F. Lynn, BOS
1976	J. Rudi, OAK	Dw. Evans, BOS	R. Manning, CLE
1977	J. Beniquez, TEX	C. Yastrzemski, BOS	A. Cowens, KC
1978	F. Lynn, BOS	Dw. Evans, BOS	R. Miller, CAL
1979	Dw. Evans, BOS	S. Lezcano, MIL	F. Lynn, BOS
1980	F. Lynn, BOS	D. Murphy, OAK	W. Wilson, KC
1981	D. Murphy, OAK	Dw. Evans, BOS	R. Henderson, OAK
1982	Dw. Evans, BOS	D. Winfield, NY	D. Murphy, OAK
1983	Dw. Evans, BOS	D. Winfield, NY	D. Murphy, OAK
1984	Dw. Evans, BOS	D. Winfield, NY	D. Murphy, OAK
1985	G. Pettis, CAL	D. Winfield, NY	Dw. Evans, BOS & D. Murphy, OAK
1986	G. Pettis, CAL	J. Barfield, TOR	K. Puckett, MIN
1987	J. Barfield, TOR	K. Puckett, MIN	D. Winfield, NY
1988	K. Puckett, MIN	D. White, CAL	G. Pettis, DET
1989	D. White, CAL	G. Pettis, DET	K. Puckett, MIN
1990	G. Pettis, TEX	K. Griffey, Jr., SEA	E. Burks, BOS
1991	K. Puckett, MIN	K. Griffey, Jr., SEA	D. White, TOR
1992	K. Puckett, MIN	K. Griffey, Jr., SEA	D. White, TOR
1993	K. Griffey, Jr., SEA	D. White, TOR	K. Lofton, CLE
1994	K. Griffey, Jr., SEA	D. White, TOR	K. Lofton, CLE
1995	K. Griffey, Jr., SEA	K. Lofton, CLE	D. White, TOR
1996	K. Griffey, Jr., SEA	K. Lofton, CLE	J. Buhner, SEA

Special MVP Awards
The All-Star Game

The All-Star Game MVP Award began in 1962, the last year in which two All-Star Games were played. It was called the Arch Ward Memorial Award, in honor of the late Chicago newspaper writer credited with conceiving the Mid-Summer Classic. In Bowie Kuhn's tenure, 1970-84, the award was called the Commissioner's Trophy.

A committee of writers and executives in attendance votes on the recipient of the game's award. Only twice—Brooks Robinson in 1966 and Carl Yastrzemski in 1970—has a member of the losing team been honored. Two-time winners are Willie Mays, Steve Garvey, and Gary Carter.

Following are the winners of the All-Star Game MVP Awards. Complete voting breakdowns are not available.

1962	Maury Wills, LA (NL) [Game 1]	1971	Frank Robinson, BAL (AL)
	Leon Wagner, LA (AL) [Game 2]	1972	Joe Morgan, CIN (NL)
1963	Willie Mays, SF (NL)	1973	Bobby Bonds, SF (NL)
1964	Johnny Callison, PHI (NL)	1974	Steve Garvey, LA (NL)
1965	Juan Marichal, SF (NL)	1975	Bill Madlock, CHI (NL)
1966	Brooks Robinson, BAL (AL)		Jon Matlack, NY (NL)
1967	Tony Perez, CIN (NL)	1976	George Foster, CIN (NL)
1968	Willie Mays, SF (NL)	1977	Don Sutton, LA (NL)
1969	Willie McCovey, SF (NL)	1978	Steve Garvey, LA (NL)
1970	Carl Yastrzemski, BOS (AL)		

1979	Dave Parker, PIT (NL)	1988	Terry Steinbach, OAK (AL)
1980	Ken Griffey, CIN (NL)	1989	Bo Jackson, KC (AL)
1981	Gary Carter, MON (NL)	1990	Julio Franco, TEX (AL)
1982	Dave Concepcion, CIN (NL)	1991	Cal Ripken, BAL (AL)
1983	Fred Lynn, CAL (AL)	1992	Ken Griffey, Jr., SEA (AL)
1984	Gary Carter, MON (NL)	1993	Kirby Puckett, MIN (AL)
1985	LaMarr Hoyt, SD (NL)	1994	Fred McGriff, ATL (NL)
1986	Roger Clemens, BOS (AL)	1995	Jeff Conine, FLA (NL)
1987	Tim Raines, MON (NL)	1996	Mike Piazza, LA (NL)

League Championship Series

MVP Awards for the League Championship Series were instituted by the National League in 1977, and in the American three years later. A committee of writers and executives in attendance does the voting.

Steve Garvey and Dave Stewart are the only two-time winners thus far. Winners from losing teams are Fred Lynn (1982), Mike Scott (1986), and Jeffrey Leonard (1987).

Following are the winners of LCS MVP Awards. Complete voting breakdowns are not available.

Year	National League	American League
1977	Dusty Baker, LA	
1978	Steve Garvey, Dave Stewart & Orel Hershiser, LA	
1979	Willie Stargell, PIT	
1980	Manny Trillo, PHI	Frank White, KC
1981	Burt Hooton, LA	Graig Nettles, NY
1982	Darrell Porter, SL	Fred Lynn, CAL
1983	Gary Matthews, PHI	Mike Boddicker, BAL
1984	Steve Garvey, SD	Kirk Gibson, DET
1985	Ozzie Smith, SL	George Brett, KC
1986	Mike Scott, HOU	Marty Barrett, BOS

Year	National League	American League
1987	Jeffrey Leonard, SF	Gary Gaetti, MIN
1988	Orel Hershiser, LA	Dennis Eckersley, OAK
1989	Will Clark, SF	Rickey Henderson, OAK
1990	Rob Dibble, CIN Randy Myers, CIN	Dave Stewart, OAK
1991	Steve Avery, ATL	Kirby Puckett, MIN
1992	John Smoltz, ATL	Roberto Alomar, TOR
1993	Curt Schilling, PHI	Dave Stewart, TOR
1994	(No Series)	(No Series)
1995	Mike Devereaux, ATL	Orel Hershiser, CLE
1996	Javier Lopez, ATL	Bernie Williams, NY

World Series

There are two major World Series MVP Awards. The New York chapter of the Baseball Writers' Association of America established one in memory of Babe Ruth in 1949, the year after the Bambino's death. Six years later, *Sport* magazine introduced its version, presented in cooperation with the Chevrolet Motor Company (which typically presented a Corvette to the winner).

The winner of the *Sport* award was originally chosen by the magazine's editors, but the voting process eventually went to a committee of sports reporters and officials. The award is now sanctioned by Major League Baseball, and

has eclipsed the Babe Ruth Award in prestige and public recognition. The *Sport* award is voted on during the final game of the Series and presented immediately following its conclusion, whereas the Ruth Award is voted on during a local chapter meeting some time after the Series.

Following are the winners of the two World Series MVP Awards. Two-time winners of the *Sport* award are Sandy Koufax, Bob Gibson, and Reggie Jackson; double-winners of the Ruth award are Koufax and Jack Morris. Winners from losing teams are Bobby Richardson (*Sport*, 1960), and Luis Tiant (Ruth, 1975). Complete voting breakdowns on either award are not available.

Year	Babe Ruth Award	Sport Magazine Award
1949	Joe Page, NY (AL)	
1950	Jerry Coleman, NY (AL)	
1951	Phil Rizzuto, NY (AL)	
1952	Johnny Mize, NY (AL)	
1953	Billy Martin, NY (AL)	
1954	Dusty Rhodes, NY (NL)	
1955	Johnny Podres, BRO (NL)	Johnny Podres, BRO (NL)
1956	Don Larsen, NY (AL)	Don Larsen, NY (AL)
1957	Lew Burdette, MIL (NL)	Lew Burdette, MIL (NL)
1958	Elston Howard, NY (AL)	Bob Turley, NY (AL)
1959	Larry Sherry, LA (NL)	Larry Sherry, LA (NL)
1960	Bill Mazeroski, PIT (NL)	Bobby Richardson, NY (AL)
1961	Whitey Ford, NY (AL)	Whitey Ford, NY (AL)
1962	Ralph Terry, NY (AL)	Ralph Terry, NY (AL)
1963	Sandy Koufax, LA (NL)	Sandy Koufax, LA (NL)
1964	Bob Gibson, SL (NL)	Bob Gibson, SL (NL)
1965	Sandy Koufax, LA (NL)	Sandy Koufax, LA (NL)
1966	Frank Robinson, BAL (AL)	Frank Robinson, BAL (AL)
1967	Lou Brock, SL (NL)	Bob Gibson, SL (NL)
1968	Mickey Lolich, DET (AL)	Mickey Lolich, DET (AL)
1969	Al Weis, NY (NL)	Donn Clendenon, NY (NL)
1970	Brooks Robinson, BAL (AL)	Brooks Robinson, BAL (AL)
1971	Roberto Clemente, PIT (NL)	Roberto Clemente, PIT (NL)
1972	Gene Tenace, OAK (AL)	Gene Tenace, OAK (AL)
1973	Bert Campaneris, OAK (AL)	Reggie Jackson, OAK (AL)

Year	Babe Ruth Award	Sport Magazine Award
1974	Dick Green, OAK (AL)	Rollie Fingers, OAK (AL)
1975	Luis Tiant, BOS (AL)	Pete Rose, CIN (NL)
1976	Johnny Bench, CIN (NL)	Johnny Bench, CIN (NL)
1977	Reggie Jackson, NY (AL)	Reggie Jackson, NY (AL)
1978	Bucky Dent, NY (AL)	Bucky Dent, NY (AL)
1979	Willie Stargell, PIT (NL)	Willie Stargell, PIT (NL)
1980	Tug McGraw, PHI (NL)	Mike Schmidt, PHI (NL)
1981	Ron Cey, LA (NL)	Ron Cey, LA (NL)
		Pedro Guerrero, LA (NL)
		Steve Yeager, LA (NL)
1982	Bruce Sutter, SL (NL)	Darrell Porter, SL (NL)
1983	Rick Dempsey, BAL (AL)	Rick Dempsey, BAL (AL)
1984	Jack Morris, DET (AL)	Alan Trammell, DET (AL)
1985	Bret Saberhagen, KC (AL)	Bret Saberhagen, KC (AL)
1986	Ray Knight, NY (NL)	Ray Knight, NY (NL)
1987	Frank Viola, MIN (AL)	Frank Viola, MIN (AL)
1988	Orel Hershiser, LA (NL)	Orel Hershiser, LA (NL)
1989	Dave Stewart, OAK (AL)	Dave Stewart, OAK (AL)
1990	Billy Hatcher, CIN (NL)	Jose Rijo, CIN (NL)
1991	Jack Morris, MIN (AL)	Jack Morris, MIN (AL)
1992	Dave Winfield, TOR (AL)	Pat Borders, TOR (AL)
1993	Paul Molitor, TOR (AL)	Paul Molitor, TOR (AL)
1994	(No Series)	(No Series)
1995	Tom Glavine, ATL (NL)	Tom Glavine, ATL (NL)
1996	Cecil Fielder, NY (AL)	John Wetteland, NY (AL)

Hall of Fame Elections: History

In the 1930s plans were being made to celebrate baseball's 100th anniversary, based on the ill-advised findings of the Mills Commission three decades earlier: "The first scheme for playing baseball, according to the best evidence obtainable to date, was devised by Abner Doubleday at Cooperstown, New York, in 1839." A small-scale baseball museum was established in Cooperstown, and a Centennial Committee composed of six baseball bigwigs ordered the first Hall of Fame election. On January 29, 1936, the results of this election were announced, with five immortals qualifying for enshrinement (although actual induction was delayed until formal opening of the Hall on June 12, 1939).

Actually, there were two elections in 1936: one a poll of 226 members of the Baseball Writers' Association of America (BBWAA), and the other held by a special veterans' committee of 78 designed to choose from among "old-timers." No specific guidelines were set as to who was eligible for consideration (several active players received strong support), nor to which committee would consider whom (resulting in Cy Young's split vote: 49 percent in the writers' election, 41 percent in the veterans'). A 75 percent majority was necessary for election by either committee, a voting feature which survives.

Elections were held by both the BBWAA and an old-timers' committee for each of the next three years, resulting in a total of 26 inductees in 1939. After that, BBWAA elections were scheduled at three-year intervals, with only

one player elected in 1942 and none in 1945. A decision was made to hold annual elections beginning in 1946. This continued through 1956, when it was decided to hold elections only every other year. Annual elections were resumed a decade later and continue to this day.

A nominating system was installed after the 1945 election, providing for the top twenty vote-getters in a preliminary balloting to be listed alphabetically on a second and final ballot. The preliminary election's vote totals were not to be divulged until after the final balloting (so as not to influence voters), nor would they assure anyone of automatic election. However, this system proved an utter failure in 1946 and was amended in December of that year. Thereafter, anyone receiving 75 percent of the votes on the nominating ballot would be automatically elected, eliminating the runoff election.

No runoff was required until 1949, when Charlie Gehringer was elected on the second ballot. The nominating system was discontinued after that year but revived from 1960-68 (providing for reconsideration of the top thirty vote-getters), being put into practice in 1964-67.

Currently, an eligible candidate must have played at least ten seasons in the majors and been active at some point during a period beginning twenty years and ending five years before a given election (the former rule has been ignored in some recent cases). The five-year wait rule was first implemented in 1954 (excepting candidates who had already received 100 or more votes in a previous election); a one-year wait had been in effect from 1946–53, and no wait was specified before then (due to World War II, it was sometimes unclear who was still "active"). At the other end of the span, the twenty-year rule has been in effect since 1962; the cutoff was thirty years in 1956-62, and twenty-five years in 1946-56.

Following Roberto Clemente's tragic death, a rule was passed in 1973 providing for the immediate consideration of an eligible candidate who dies while still active, or before the five-year waiting period has elapsed. Clemente was inducted overwhelmingly (393 of 424 votes) in a special election held that March. A few months later, the new rule was amended to allow consideration at least six months after a player's death (or five years after his retirement, whichever is less).

The "Pete Rose Rule" was added to the books in February 1991: "Any player on Baseball's ineligible list shall not be an eligible candidate."

Ten-year active and honorary members of the BBWAA are eligible to vote in the annual election (the ten-year restriction was installed in 1947). About 450 writers submit ballots each year, voting for up to ten eligible candidates apiece. At various times over the past three decades, it has been suggested that the enfranchisement be limited to a few dozen of the top baseball writers.

A candidate Screening Committee was first employed in 1968, limiting the ballot to forty candidates. Standards were relaxed somewhat after former pitcher Milt Pappas vociferously objected to his elimination by this committee (Pappas was allowed on the ballot in 1979, receiving 5 of 432 votes). Nomination by two of the six members of the Screening Committee now ensures a candidate at least one try on the BBWAA ballot; however, if he receives less than 5 percent of the vote, he is eliminated from future consideration. (Fortunately for many, this rule has not always been existent; more than seventy current Hall of Famers received less than 5 percent of the vote in their first tries!)

The Baseball Hall of Fame Committee on Baseball Veterans was established in July 1953. Previously, special old-timers' committees had elected new members in 1936–39, 1944–46, and 1949.

The new committee was composed of eleven members. This number was increased to twelve in 1960, eighteen in 1979, and twenty in 1987; then it was reduced to 18 in 1988 and 15 in 1996. Elections were held every other year at first, but have been held annually since 1961.

In most years the committee has been limited to naming no more than two new inductees per election. Exceptions occurred in the elections of 1953 (six), 1963 (four), 1964 (six), 1970 (three), 1971 (seven), and 1972–77 (three each). Two additional slots opened for 1995-99, one for pre-1920 players, the other for Negro Leaguers. Voting details are not released to the public.

Individuals considered by the Veterans Committee include managers, umpires, executives, and certain players no longer eligible through the BBWAA (except members of the committee). For eligibility under the former three groups, a person must have been retired five years, or six months if he has reached the age of sixty-five (a rule tailor-made for Casey Stengel's election in 1966). For players, the minimum wait is twenty-three years; previously, it was twenty-five years (1953–56, 1974–84), thirty years (1957–62), or twenty years (1963–73).

On June 10, 1971, a nine-member Baseball Hall of Fame Committee on Negro Baseball Leagues was established. Candidates were to have totaled at least ten years of service in the pre-1946 Negro Leagues and/or the major leagues, without being eligible for BBWAA election. A rule specified that the "Committee shall serve until it shall dissolve itself of its own motion or until further notice from the Board of Directors" of the Hall.

At least one new member was inducted by this committee in each year between 1971 and 1977, after which the committee dissolved and was absorbed into the Veterans Committee. Only two Negro League representatives were enshrined between 1978-94.

As far back as 1944, it was suggested that a special "Roll of Honor," distinct from actual Hall of Fame induction, be established for distinguished baseball writers and similar contributors to the baseball world. In 1962 the J. G. Taylor Spink Award was initiated to honor individuals "for meritorious contributions to baseball writing." In 1978 the Ford C. Frick Award was established to dignify broadcasters "for major contributions to the game of Baseball." The awards are presented annually during the Hall of Fame induction ceremonies and the winners' names are engraved on a plaque hanging in the National Baseball Library (explaining references to a writers' or broadcasters' "wing" at the Hall of Fame). Through 1996 there had been forty-seven winners of the Spink Award, and twenty recipients of the Frick trophy. But, contrary to what you hear and read elsewhere, these men are not members of the Hall of Fame.

There have been a total of 228 men inducted into the National Baseball Hall of Fame and Museum through 1996, including 173 major league players, twenty-two classified as pioneers or executives, thirteen Negro Leaguers, thirteen managers and seven umpires (many of the latter four groups also played in the majors or minors); eighty-six individuals have been elected by the BBWAA, 133 by the various veterans committees, and nine by the Negro Leagues Committee.

What follows is, first, a roster of the 228 members of the Hall of Fame named between 1936 and early 1996; second, an index of every man who ever received so much as a single vote for the Hall of Fame, detailing each man's total for each year he received support; and third, the top ten finishers in the voting for each year of balloting since 1936. Men named to the Hall of Fame by special committee action, such as Alexander Cartwright or Josh Gibson, may not have received votes in an election, but they are included in this index as well. (There have been four such committee groupings: the Centennial Commission of 1937–1938, the Old Timers' Committee of 1939–1949, the Veterans Committee of 1953–present, and the Negro Leagues Committee of 1971–1977.)

Of special interest are some prominent players who were not elected or named to the Hall: Gil Hodges, who received the most votes for the Hall of Fame but remains outside it; Herman Long, who finished among the top ten vote-getters in the Veterans Ballot of 1936, which during later years produced twenty-nine future Hall of Famers; Hank Gowdy, who in the 1950s experienced a fate similar to Long's; and Marty Marion and Allie Reynolds, other long-term vote-getters who were not able to bunch their support in a given year. And don't get White Sox fans talking about Nellie Fox and the election of 1985, when, in his final year of eligibility for the Baseball Writers Election, Fox fell only two votes short of the 297 that would have granted him enshrinement—the closest any man has ever come without making it.

The Hall of Fame balloting results were researched and compiled by Pete Palmer.

Hall of Fame Roster

FIRST BASEMEN
Anson, Cap
Beckley, Jake
Bottomley, Jim
Brouthers, Dan
Chance, Frank
Connor, Roger
Foxx, Jimmie
Gehrig, Lou
Greenberg, Hank
Kelly, George
Killebrew, Harmon
McCovey, Willie
Mize, Johnny
Sisler, George
Terry, Bill

SECOND BASEMEN
Carew, Rod
Collins, Eddie
Doerr, Bobby
Evers, Johnny
Frisch, Frankie
Gehringer, Charlie
Herman, Billy
Hornsby, Rogers
Lajoie, Nap
Lazzeri, Tony
Morgan, Joe
Robinson, Jackie
Schoendienst, Red

SHORTSTOPS
Aparicio, Luis
Appling, Luke
Bancroft, Dave
Banks, Ernie
Boudreau, Lou
Cronin, Joe
Jackson, Travis
Jennings, Hugh
Maranville, Rabbit
Reese, Pee Wee
Rizzuto, Phil

Sewell, Joe
Tinker, Joe
Vaughan, Arky
Wagner, Honus
Wallace, Bobby
Ward, Monte

THIRD BASEMEN
Baker, Frank
Collins, Jimmy
Kell, George
Lindstrom, Fred
Mathews, Eddie
Robinson, Brooks
Schmidt, Mike
Traynor, Pie

LEFT FIELDERS
Brock, Lou
Burkett, Jesse
Clarke, Fred
Delahanty, Ed
Goslin, Goose
Hafey, Chick
Kelley, Joe
Kiner, Ralph
Manush, Heinie
Medwick, Joe
Musial, Stan
O'Rourke, Jim
Simmons, Al
Stargell, Willie
Wheat, Zack
Williams, Billy
Williams, Ted
Yastrzemski, Carl

CENTER FIELDERS
Ashburn, Richie
Averill, Earl
Carey, Max
Cobb, Ty
Combs, Earle
DiMaggio, Joe

Duffy, Hugh
Hamilton, Billy
Mantle, Mickey
Mays, Willie
Roush, Edd
Snider, Duke
Speaker, Tris
Waner, Lloyd
Wilson, Hack

RIGHT FIELDERS
Aaron, Hank
Clemente, Roberto
Crawford, Sam
Cuyler, Kiki
Flick, Elmer
Heilmann, Harry
Hooper, Harry
Kaline, Al
Keeler, Willie
Kelly, King
Klein, Chuck
McCarthy, Tommy
Ott, Mel
Rice, Sam
Robinson, Frank
Ruth, Babe
Slaughter, Enos
Thompson, Sam
Waner, Paul
Youngs, Ross

CATCHERS
Bench, Johnny
Berra, Yogi
Bresnahan, Roger
Campanella, Roy
Cochrane, Mickey
Dickey, Bill
Ewing, Buck
Ferrell, Rick
Hartnett, Gabby
Lombardi, Ernie

Schalk, Ray

PITCHERS
Alexander, Grover
Bender, Chief
Brown, Mordecai
Bunning, Jim
Carlton, Steve
Chesbro, Jack
Clarkson, John
Coveleski, Stan
Dean, Dizzy
Drysdale, Don
Faber, Red
Feller, Bob
Fingers, Rollie
Ford, Whitey
Galvin, Pud
Gibson, Bob
Gomez, Lefty
Grimes, Burleigh
Grove, Lefty
Haines, Jess
Hoyt, Waite
Hubbell, Carl
Hunter, Catfish
Jenkins, Fergie
Johnson, Walter
Joss, Addie
Keefe, Tim
Koufax, Sandy
Lemon, Bob
Lyons, Ted
Marichal, Juan
Marquard, Rube
Mathewson, Christy
McGinnity, Joe
Newhouser, Hal
Nichols, Kid
Palmer, Jim
Pennock, Herb

Perry, Gaylord
Plank, Eddie
Radbourn, Charles
Rixey, Eppa
Roberts, Robin
Ruffing, Red
Rusie, Amos
Seaver, Tom
Spahn, Warren
Vance, Dazzy
Waddell, Rube
Walsh, Ed
Welch, Mickey
Wilhelm, Hoyt
Willis, Vic
Wynn, Early
Young, Cy

FROM NEGRO LEAGUES
Bell, Cool Papa
Charleston, Oscar
Dandridge, Ray
Day, Leon
Dihigo, Martin
Foster, Bill
Foster, Rube
Gibson, Josh
Irvin, Monte
Johnson, Judy
Leonard, Buck
Lloyd, John
Paige, Satchel

MANAGERS
Alston, Walter
Durocher, Leo
Hanlon, Ned
Harris, Bucky
Huggins, Miller
Lopez, Al

Mack, Connie
McCarthy, Joe
McGraw, John
McKechnie, Bill
Robinson, Wilbert
Stengel, Casey
Weaver, Earl

UMPIRES
Barlick, Al
Conlan, Jocko
Connolly, Tom
Evans, Billy
Hubbard, Cal
Klem, Bill
McGowan, Bill

PIONEERS AND EXECUTIVES
Barrow, Ed
Bulkeley, Morgan
Cartwright, Alexander
Chadwick, Henry
Chandler, Albert
Comiskey, Charles
Cummings, Candy
Frick, Ford
Giles, Warren
Griffith, Clark
Harridge, Will
Hulbert, William
Johnson, Ban
Landis, Kenesaw
MacPhail, Larry
Rickey, Branch
Spalding, Al
Veeck, Bill
Weiss, George
Wright, George
Wright, Harry
Yawkey, Tom

Hall of Fame Balloting: Vote Totals of All Candidates

Hank Aaron
Inducted in 1982

1982	406

Babe Adams

1937	8
1938	11
1939	11
1942	11
1945	7
1946 NOM	6
1947	22
1948	4
1949	5
1950	6
1951	12
1952	9
1953	17
1954	13
1955	24

Sparky Adams

1958	1
1960	1

Bobby Adams

1966	1

Pete Alexander
Inducted in 1938

1936	55
1937	125
1938	212

Dick Allen

1983	14
1985	28
1986	41
1987	55
1988	52
1989	35
1990	58
1991	59
1992	69
1993	70
1994	66
1995	72
1996	89

Johnny Allen

1955	1

Doug Allison

1936 V	1

Felipe Alou

1980	3

Jesus Alou

1985	1

Matty Alou

1980	5

Walt Alston
Inducted in 1983
Manager

1983	Vet. Com.

Nick Altrock

1937	3
1938	7
1939	6
1953	1
1954	2
1958	20
1960	18

Cap Anson
Inducted in 1939

1936 V	40
1939	O/T Com.

Luis Aparicio
Inducted in 1984

1979	120
1980	124
1981	48
1982	174
1983	252
1984	341

Luke Appling
Inducted in 1964

1953	2
1955	3
1956	14
1958	77

1960	72
1962	48
1964	142
1964 RO	189

Jimmy Archer

1937	6
1938	7
1939	3

Richie Ashburn
Inducted in 1996

1968	6
1969	10
1970	11
1971	10
1972	11
1973	25
1974	56
1975	76
1976	85
1977	139
1978	158
1979	130
1980	134
1981	142
1982	126
1995	Vet. Comm.

Jimmy Austin

1958	1

Earl Averill
Inducted in 1975

1949	1
1952	2
1955	2
1956	3
1958	14
1960	11
1962	3
1975	Vet. Com.

Bob Bailey

1984	1

Dusty Baker

1992	4

Frank Baker
Inducted in 1955

1936	1
1937	13
1938	32
1939	30
1942	39
1945	26
1946 NOM	39
1946	36
1947	49
1948	4
1950	4
1951	8
1955	Vet. Com.

Dave Bancroft
Inducted in 1971

1937	3
1938	2
1939	1
1946 NOM	1
1948	4
1949	5
1950	9
1951	9
1952	11
1953	10
1954	10
1955	19
1956	15
1958	43
1960	30
1971	Vet. Com.

Sal Bando

1987	3

Ernie Banks
Inducted in 1977

1977	321

Al Barlick
Inducted in 1989
Umpire

1989	Vet. Com.

Ross Barnes

1936 V	3

Ed Barrow
Inducted in 1953
Executive
1953 .... Vet. Com.

Jack Barry
1938 3
1939 1

Dick Bartell
1948 1
1951 1
1958 1
1960 1

Joe Battin
1936 V 1

Hank Bauer
1967 23
1967 RO.............9

Don Baylor
1994 12
1995 12

Ginger Beaumont
1938 1
1942 1
1945 1
1946 NOM............1

Glenn Beckert
1981 1

Jake Beckley
Inducted in 1971
1936 V 1
1942 1
1971 .... Vet. Com.

Mark Belanger
1988 16

Buddy Bell
1995 8

Cool Papa Bell
Inducted in 1974
1974 .... Neg. Com.

Johnny Bench
Inducted in 1989
1989 431

Chief Bender
Inducted in 1953
1936 2
1937 17
1938 33
1939 40
1942 55
1945 40
1946 NOM...........39
1946 35
1947 72
1948 5
1949 2
1950 6
1951 35
1952 70
1953 104
1953 .... Vet. Com.

Charlie Bennett
1936 V 3

Larry Benton
1958 1

Moe Berg
1958 3
1960 5

Marty Bergen
1937 2
1938 1

Wally Berger
1956 1
1958 2

Yogi Berra
Inducted in 1972
1971 242
1972 339

Charlie Berry
1955 1
1958 3

Jim Bibby
1990 1

Carson Bigbee
1948 1

Jack Billingham
1986 1

Max Bishop
1955 1
1956 1
1958 4
1960 5

Ewell Blackwell
1968 5
1969 11
1970 14

Ray Blades
1958 1
1960 1

Paul Blair
1986 8

Steve Blass
1980 2

Lu Blue
1954 1

Vida Blue
1992 23
1993 37
1994 14
1995 26

Ossie Bluege
1948 2
1949 1
1954 1
1956 2
1958 2
1960 3

Ping Bodie
1937 2
1949 1

Joe Boley
1942 1

Tommy Bond
1936 V 1

Bobby Bonds
1987 24
1988 27
1989 29
1990 30
1991 39
1992 40
1993 45
1994 37
1995 35
1996 24

Bob Boone
1996 36

Jim Bottomley
Inducted in 1974
1948 4
1949 8
1950 8
1951 6
1952 7
1953 10
1954 16
1955 26
1956 42
1958 57
1960 89
1962 20
1974 .... Vet. Com.

Lou Boudreau
Inducted in 1970
1956 2
1958 64
1960 35
1962 12
1964 68
1964 RO.............43
1966 115
1967 143
1967 RO.............68
1968 146
1969 218
1970 232

Jim Bouton
1984 3

Larry Bowa
1991 11

Clete Boyer
1978 1
1979 3

Ken Boyer
1975 9
1976 15
1977 14
1978 18
1979 20
1985 68
1986 95
1987 96
1988 109
1989 62
1990 78
1991 58
1992 71
1993 69
1994 56

Bill Bradley
1936 1
1937 5
1938 1
1939 1
1942 1
1946 NOM...........1

Harry Brecheen
1960 7
1968 3
1969 2
1970 3
1971 7
1972 5
1973 3

Ted Breitenstein
1937 1

Roger Bresnahan
Inducted in 1945
1936 47
1937 43
1938 67
1939 67
1942 57
1945 133
1945 .... O/T Com.

Jim Brewer
1982 2

Tommy Bridges
1956 3
1958 11
1960 4
1962 1
1964 15
1964 RO.............1
1966 16

Lou Brock
Inducted in 1985
1985 315

Dan Brouthers
Inducted in 1945
1936 V 2
1945 .... O/T Com.

Gates Brown
1981 1

Mordecai Brown
Inducted in 1949
1936 6
1937 31
1938 54
1939 54
1942 63
1945 46
1946 NOM...........56
1946 48
1949 .... O/T Com.

Bill Bruton
1971 1

Bill Buckner
1996 10

Morgan Bulkeley
Inducted in 1937
Executive
1937 .... Cen. Com.

Jim Bunning
Inducted in 1996
1977 146
1978 181
1979 147
1980 177
1981 164
1982 138
1983 138
1984 201
1985 214
1986 279
1987 289
1988 317
1989 283
1990 257
1991 282
1996 .... Vet. Comm.

Lew Burdette
1973 12
1974 7
1975 11
1976 21
1977 85
1978 76
1979 53
1980 66
1981 48
1982 43
1983 43
1984 97
1985 82
1986 96
1987 96

Smoky Burgess
1973 1
1974 2

Jesse Burkett
Inducted in 1946
1936 V 1
1937 1
1938 2
1942 4

1945 2
1946 NOM............2
1946 .... O/T Com.

George J. Burns
1937 3
1938 3
1939 1
1949 1
1950 2

Jeff Burroughs
1991 1

Guy Bush
1956 2

Joe Bush
1958 5

Donie Bush
1937 1
1939 2
1942 2
1945 1
1946 NOM...........2
1953 1

Leon Cadore
1948 1

Johnny Callison
1979 1

Dolf Camilli
1948 1
1956 1
1958 4
1960 3

Howie Camnitz
1945 1

Roy Campanella
Inducted in 1969
1964 115
1964 RO.............138
1966 197
1967 204
1967 RO.............170
1968 205
1969 270

Bert Campaneris
1989 14

Bill Campbell
1993 1

Jose Cardenal
1986 1

Leo Cardenas
1981 1
1982 1

Rod Carew
Inducted in 1991
1991 401

Max Carey
Inducted in 1961
1937 6
1938 6
1939 7
1945 1
1948 9
1949 12
1950 14
1951 27
1952 36
1953 55
1954 55
1955 119
1956 65
1958 136
1961 .... Vet. Com.

Steve Carlton
Inducted in 1994
1994 436

Chico Carrasquel
1966 1

Bill Carrigan
1937 5
1938 4
1939 2
1945 3

Clay Carroll
1984 1

Rico Carty
1985 1

Alex Cartwright
Inducted in 1938
Pioneer
1938 .... Cen. Com.

George Case
1958 1
1960 1
1962 1
1964 2

Dave Cash
1986 2

Norm Cash
1980 6

Phil Cavaretta
1962 2
1964 22
1964 RO.............1
1966 9
1967 15
1967 RO.............4
1968 23
1969 37
1970 51
1971 83
1972 61
1973 73
1974 61
1975 129

Cesar Cedeno
1992 2

Orlando Cepeda
1980 48
1981 77
1982 42
1983 59
1984 124
1985 114
1986 152
1987 179
1988 199
1989 176
1990 211
1991 192
1992 246
1993 252
1994 335

Ron Cey
1993 8

Henry Chadwick
Inducted in 1938
Pioneer
1938 .... Cen. Com.

Frank Chance
Inducted in 1946
1936 5
1937 49
1938 133
1939 158
1942 136
1945 179

1946 NOM.......... 144
1946 150
1946 .... O/T Com.

Happy Chandler
Inducted in 1982
Executive

1982 .... Vet. Com.

Spud Chandler

1950 2
1951 1
1956 1
1962 2
1964 6

Ben Chapman

1949 1
1952 1

Ray Chapman

1938 1

Sam Chapman

1958 1

Oscar Charleston
Inducted in 1976

1976 .... Neg. Com.

Hal Chase

1936 11
1937 18

Jack Chesbro
Inducted in 1946

1937 1
1938 2
1939 6
1946 NOM............. 1
1946 .... O/T Com.

Bill Cissell

1937 1

Watty Clark

1958 1

Fred Clarke
Inducted in 1945

1936 V 9
1936 1
1937 22
1938 63
1939 59
1942 58
1945 53
1945 .... O/T Com.

John Clarkson
Inducted in 1963

1936 V 5
1946 NOM............. 1
1963 .... Vet. Com.

Roberto Clemente
Inducted in 1973

1973 .... Spec. El.

Andy Coakley

1938 1

Ty Cobb
Inducted in 1936

1936 222

Mickey Cochrane
Inducted in 1947

1936 80
1939 28
1942 88
1945 125
1946 NOM........... 80
1946 65
1947 128

Rocky Colavito

1974 2
1975 1

Eddie Collins
Inducted in 1939

1936 60
1937 115
1938 175
1939 213

Jimmy Collins
Inducted in 1945

1936 V 8
1936 58
1937 66
1938 79
1939 72
1942 68
1945 121
1945 .... O/T Com.

Shano Collins

1937 1

Earle Combs
Inducted in 1970

1937 4
1938 7
1939 3
1945 1
1948 6
1949 6
1950 3
1952 1
1953 3
1955 1
1956 14
1958 34
1960 43
1962 6
1970 .... Vet. Com.

Charlie Comiskey
Inducted in 1939
Executive

1936 V 6
1939 .... O/T Com.

Dave Concepcion

1994 31
1995 43
1996 63

Jocko Conlan
Inducted in 1974
Umpire

1974 .... Vet. Com.

Tommy Connolly
Inducted in 1953
Umpire

1953 .... Vet. Com.

Roger Connor
Inducted in 1976

1976 .... Vet. Com.

Wid Conroy

1945 1

Jack Coombs

1937 2
1938 2
1946 NOM............. 2
1948 2
1951 1

Mort Cooper

1956 2
1958 3
1960 1
1969 3

Walker Cooper

1968 8
1969 5
1970 9
1971 7

Wilbur Cooper

1938 1
1939 1
1948 2
1949 4
1951 1
1952 2
1953 9
1954 7
1955 11

Clint Courtney

1967 1

Stan Coveleski
Inducted in 1969

1938 1
1948 2
1949 3
1950 1
1958 34
1969 .... Vet. Com.

Billy Cox

1962 1

Doc Cramer

1956 4
1958 2
1960 1
1962 1
1964 12

Del Crandall

1976 15
1977 8
1978 6
1979 9

Doc Crandall

1938 1

Gavvy Cravath

1937 2
1938 2
1939 2
1946 NOM............. 1
1947 2

Sam Crawford
Inducted in 1957

1936 1
1937 5
1938 11
1939 6
1942 2
1945 4
1946 NOM............. 9
1957 .... Vet. Com.

Lou Criger

1936 V 1
1936 7
1937 16
1938 11
1939 2
1946 NOM............. 6

Hughie Critz

1956 2

Joe Cronin
Inducted in 1956

1947 6
1948 25
1949 33
1949 RO 16
1950 33
1951 44
1952 48
1953 69
1954 85
1955 135

Frank Crosetti

1950 1
1952 1
1956 1
1958 5
1960 8
1968 15

Lave Cross

1939 1
1942 1

Al Crowder

1958 1
1960 1

Walt Cruise

1938 1

Jose Cruz

1994 2

Tony Cuccinello

1956 1
1958 3

Candy Cummings
Inducted in 1939
Pioneer

1939 .... O/T Com.

Kiki Cuyler
Inducted in 1968

1948 3
1949 4
1950 11
1951 8
1952 10
1953 18
1954 20
1955 35
1956 55
1958 90
1960 72
1962 31
1968 .... Vet. Com.

Bill Dahlen

1936 V 1
1938 1

Ray Dandridge
Inducted in 1987

1987 .... Vet. Com.

Harry Danning

1958 1
1960 1

Alvin Dark

1966 17
1967 38
1967 RO 7
1968 36
1969 48
1970 55
1971 54
1972 55
1973 53
1974 54
1975 48
1976 62
1977 66
1978 60
1979 80
1980 43

Jake Daubert

1936 V 1
1937 2
1938 1
1939 1
1951 1
1955 1

Curt Davis

1958 1

Harry Davis

1945 1
1946 NOM............. 2

Tommy Davis

1982 5

Spud Davis

1948 1
1949 1

Leon Day
Inducted in 1995

1995 .... Vet. Comm.

Dizzy Dean
Inducted in 1953

1945 17
1946 NOM........... 40
1946 45
1947 88
1948 40
1949 88
1949 RO 81
1950 85
1951 145
1952 152
1953 209

Doug DeCinces

1993 2

Ed Delahanty
Inducted in 1945

1936 V 22
1936 17
1937 70
1938 132
1939 145
1942 104
1945 111
1945 .... O/T Com.

Jerry Denny

1936 V 6

Bucky Dent

1990 3

Paul Derringer

1948 1
1950 1
1951 1
1955 1
1956 12
1958 15
1960 8

Bill Dickey
Inducted in 1954

1945 17
1946 NOM........... 40
1946 32
1948 39
1949 65
1949 RO 39
1950 78
1951 118
1952 139
1953 179
1954 202

Martin Dihigo
Inducted in 1977

1977 .... Neg. Com.

Dom DiMaggio

1960 4
1962 2
1964 12
1968 8
1969 13
1970 15
1971 15
1972 36
1973 43

Joe DiMaggio
Inducted in 1955

1945 1
1953 117
1954 175
1955 223

Bill Dinneen

1938 4
1939 7
1942 1
1945 1
1946 NOM............. 1

Bill Doak

1958 3

Larry Doby

1966 7
1967 10
1967 RO 1

Bobby Doerr
Inducted in 1986

1953 2
1956 5
1958 25
1960 15
1962 10
1964 24
1964 RO 5
1966 30
1967 35
1967 RO 15
1968 48
1969 62
1970 75
1971 78
1986 .... Vet. Com.

Mike Donlin

1937 6
1938 5
1939 5
1945 1

Bill Donovan

1937 3
1938 1
1939 2
1945 3
1946 NOM............. 4

Red Dooin

1937 1
1938 1

Jack Doyle

1936 V 1

Larry Doyle

1937 2
1938 4
1939 1

Walt Dropo

1967 1

Don Drysdale
Inducted in 1984

1975 76
1976 114
1977 197
1978 219
1979 233
1980 238
1981 243
1982 233
1983 242
1984 316

Hugh Duffy
Inducted in 1945

1936 V 4
1937 7
1938 24
1939 34
1942 77
1945 64

1945 .... O/T Com.

Joe Dugan
1937 1
1938 1
1948 3
1949 2
1956 1
1958 5
1960 8

Fred Dunlap
1936 V 2

Jack Dunn
1942 1
1945 1
1946 NOM............1

Leo Durocher
Inducted in 1994
Manager
1948 1
1949 1
1952 1
1956 1
1958 28
1960 10
1962 1
1964 15
1964 RO.........2
1994 .... Vet. Com.

Eddie Dyer
1947 1

Jimmy Dykes
1948 5
1949 7
1950 2
1951 3
1952 5
1953 5
1955 1
1956 1
1958 26
1960 27
1962 6

George Earnshaw
1948 3
1949 2
1950 2
1955 2
1956 3

Hank Edwards
1960 2

Howard Ehmke
1938 1
1949 1
1951 1
1952 1
1953 4
1954 4
1955 8
1956 8
1958 7
1960 12

Kid Elberfeld
1936 1
1937 1
1938 2
1942 1
1945 2

Jumbo Elliott
1958 1

Bob Elliott
1960 2
1962 1
1964 4

Dock Ellis
1985 1

Del Ennis
1966 3
1967 2

Jewel Ens
1950 1

Carl Erskine
1966 6
1968 9
1969 4
1970 2
1971 3
1972 4
1973 4
1974 11

Billy Evans
Inducted in 1973
Umpire
1973 .... Vet. Com.

Darrell Evans
1995 8

Johnny Evers
Inducted in 1946
1936 6
1937 44
1938 91
1939 107
1942 91
1945 134
1946 NOM.........130
1946 110
1946 .... O/T Com.

Buck Ewing
Inducted in 1939
1936 V 40
1939 2
1939 .... O/T Com.

Red Faber
Inducted in 1964
1937 3
1938 1
1939 3
1942 1
1948 3
1949 6
1950 9
1951 8
1952 9
1953 9
1954 12
1955 27
1956 34
1958 68
1960 83
1962 30
1964 .... Vet. Com.

Elroy Face
1976 23
1977 33
1978 27
1979 35
1980 21
1981 23
1982 22
1983 32
1984 65
1985 62
1986 74
1987 78
1988 79
1989 47
1990 50

Ron Fairly
1985 3

Cy Falkenberg
1937 1

Bob Feller
Inducted in 1962
1962 150

Rick Ferrell
Inducted in 1984
1956 1
1958 1
1960 1
1984 .... Vet. Com.

Wes Ferrell
1948 1
1949 1
1956 7
1960 8
1962 1

Rollie Fingers
Inducted in 1992
1991 291
1992 349

Fred Fitzsimmons
1948 2
1949 2
1950 1
1956 3
1958 16
1960 13
1962 1

Art Fletcher
1937 2
1938 3
1939 1
1947 3
1948 3
1949 1
1950 1
1951 4

Elmer Flick
Inducted in 1963
1938 1
1963 .... Vet. Com.

Curt Flood
1977 16
1978 8
1979 14
1985 28
1986 45
1987 50
1988 48
1989 27
1990 35
1991 23
1992 42
1993 36
1994 40
1995 59
1996 71

Lew Fonseca
1948 1
1950 2
1956 3
1958 3
1960 3

Whitey Ford
Inducted in 1974
1973 255
1974 284

Bob Forsch
1995 2

Bill Foster
1996 .... Vet. Com.

Eddie Foster
1938 2

George Foster
1992 24
1993 29
1994 16
1995 19

Rube Foster
Inducted in 1981
Manager
1981 .... Vet. Com.

Nellie Fox
1971 39
1972 64
1973 73
1974 79
1975 76
1976 174
1977 152
1978 149
1979 174
1980 161
1981 168
1982 127
1983 173
1984 246
1985 295

Jimmie Foxx
Inducted in 1951
1936 21
1946 NOM..........26
1947 10
1948 50
1949 85
1949 RO.........89
1950 103
1951 179

Chick Fraser
1939 1

Bill Freehan
1982 2

Jim Fregosi
1984 4

Ford Frick
Inducted in 1970
Executive
1970 .... Vet. Com.

Frankie Frisch
Inducted in 1947
1936 14
1939 26
1942 84
1945 101
1946 NOM.........104
1946 67
1947 136

Carl Furillo
1966 2
1967 2
1970 2
1971 5
1972 2

Augie Galan
1968 2
1970 3

Jim Galvin
Inducted in 1965
1965 .... Vet. Com.

Phil Garner
1994 2

Ned Garver
1967 1

Steve Garvey
1993 176
1994 166
1995 196
1996 175

Lou Gehrig
Inducted in 1939
1936 51
1939 .... Spec. El.

Charlie Gehringer
Inducted in 1949
1945 10
1946 NOM.......... 43
1946 23
1947 105
1948 52
1949 102
1949 RO 159

Charlie Gelbert
1947 1
1949 2
1950 1
1951 1

Josh Gibson
Inducted in 1972
1972 .... Neg. Com.

Bob Gibson
Inducted in 1981
1981 337

Warren Giles
Inducted in 1979
Executive
1979 .... Vet. Com.

Dave Giusti
1983 1

Jack Glasscock
1936 V 2

Kid Gleason
1937 1
1938 1
1939 1
1945 1

Lefty Gomez
Inducted in 1972
1945 7
1946 NOM...........4
1947 1
1948 16
1949 17
1950 18
1951 23
1952 29
1953 35
1954 38
1955 71
1956 89
1958 76
1960 51
1962 20
1972 .... Vet. Com.

Mike Gonzales
1950 1
1952 1
1953 1
1958 3
1960 2

Joe Gordon
1945 1
1955 1
1956 4
1958 11
1960 11
1962 4
1964 30
1964 RO..........1
1966 31
1967 66
1967 RO.........13
1968 77
1969 97
1970 79

Goose Goslin
Inducted in 1968
1948 1
1949 4
1950 2
1954 1
1955 7

1956 26
1958 26
1960 30
1962 14
1968 .... Vet. Com.

Hank Gowdy
1937 2
1938 8
1939 4
1942 8
1945 3
1947 1
1948 3
1949 10
1950 6
1951 26
1952 34
1953 58
1954 51
1955 90
1956 49
1958 45
1960 38

Eddie Grant
1938 1
1939 2
1942 3
1945 2
1946 NOM...........1

George Grantham
1958 1

Hank Greenberg
Inducted in 1956
1945 3
1949 67
1949 RO..........44
1950 64
1951 67
1952 75
1953 80
1954 97
1955 157
1956 164

Bobby Grich
1992 11

Clark Griffith
Inducted in 1946
Executive
1937 4
1938 10
1939 20
1942 71
1945 108
1946 NOM..........73
1946 82
1946 .... O/T Com.

Burleigh Grimes
Inducted in 1964
1937 1
1938 1
1939 1
1948 7
1949 8
1950 6
1951 5
1952 9
1953 9
1955 3
1956 25
1958 71
1960 92
1962 43
1964 .... Vet. Com.

Charlie Grimm
1939 1
1945 1
1946 NOM...........1
1948 6
1949 10
1950 13
1951 9
1952 6
1953 9
1958 26

1960 13
1962 2

Marv Grissom
1966 2

Dick Groat
1973 7
1974 4
1975 4
1976 7
1977 4
1978 3

Heinie Groh
1937 1
1938 3
1945 1
1948 1
1950 2
1954 1
1955 5
1960 1

Steve Gromek
1964 1

Orval Grove
1958 5
1960 7

Lefty Grove
Inducted in 1947
1936 12
1945 28
1946 NOM 71
1946 61
1947 123

Ron Guidry
1994 24
1995 25
1996 37

Frank Gustine
1958 3

Mule Haas
1955 1
1956 1
1958 1
1960 1

Stan Hack
1948 2
1949 4
1950 8
1951 3
1956 1
1958 6
1960 6

Harvey Haddix
1971 10
1972 9
1973 1
1974 8
1975 8
1976 8
1977 7
1978 7
1979 8
1985 15

Chick Hafey
Inducted in 1971
1948 1
1949 2
1950 4
1951 1
1952 1
1953 2
1954 2
1955 4
1956 16
1958 12
1960 29
1962 7
1971 .... Vet. Com.

Noodles Hahn
1939 1

Jesse Haines
Inducted in 1970
1939 1
1947 1
1948 2
1949 2
1950 11
1953 4
1954 6
1955 10
1956 14
1958 22
1960 20
1962 3
1970 .... Vet. Com.

Bill Hallahan
1948 1
1956 1
1958 1
1960 2

Billy Hamilton
Inducted in 1961
1936 V 2
1942 1
1961 .... Vet. Com.

Ned Hanlon
Inducted in 1996
1996 .... Vet. Com.

Mel Harder
1949 4
1950 2
1951 1
1952 10
1953 8
1958 6
1960 12
1962 7
1964 51
1964 RO 14
1966 34
1967 52
1967 RO 14

Bubbles Hargrave
1947 1
1958 1
1960 1

Mike Hargrove
1991 1

Toby Harrah
1992 1

Bud Harrelson
1986 1

Will Harridge
Inducted in 1972
Executive
1972 .... Vet. Com.

Bucky Harris
Inducted in 1975
Manager
1938 1
1939 1
1948 3
1949 11
1950 4
1951 9
1952 12
1953 21
1958 45
1960 31
1975 .... Vet. Com.

Gabby Hartnett
Inducted in 1955
1945 2
1946 NOM 2
1947 2

1948 33
1949 35
1949 RO 7
1950 54
1951 57
1952 77
1953 104
1954 151
1955 195

Grady Hatton
1966 4
1967 1

Jim Hearn
1966 1
1967 1

Richie Hebner
1991 1

Jim Hegan
1966 5
1967 2

Harry Heilmann
Inducted in 1952
1937 10
1938 14
1939 8
1942 4
1945 5
1946 NOM 23
1947 65
1948 40
1949 59
1949 RO 52
1950 87
1951 153
1952 203

Tommy Helms
1983 1

Solly Hemus
1966 1

Tommy Henrich
1952 4
1953 10
1956 2
1958 11
1960 10
1962 3
1964 13
1968 22
1969 50
1970 62

Babe Herman
1942 1
1948 2
1949 5
1950 2
1951 1
1952 3
1953 2
1954 1
1955 5
1956 11
1958 13
1960 7

Billy Herman
Inducted in 1975
1948 1
1956 2
1958 7
1962 4
1964 26
1964 RO 9
1966 28
1967 59
1967 RO 14
1975 .... Vet. Com.

Keith Hernandez
1996 24

Willie Hernandez
1995 2

Buck Herzog
1938 1

Jim Hickman
1980 1

Mike Higgins
1950 2
1951 1
1958 6
1960 3

John Hiller
1986 11

Bill Hinchman
1937 1

Gil Hodges
1969 82
1970 145
1971 180
1972 161
1973 218
1974 198
1975 188
1976 233
1977 224
1978 226
1979 242
1980 230
1981 241
1982 205
1983 237

Tommy Holmes
1958 2
1960 2

Ken Holtzman
1985 4
1986 5

Harry Hooper
Inducted in 1971
1937 6
1938 4
1939 5
1948 2
1950 2
1951 3
1971 .... Vet. Com.

Burt Hooton
1991 1

Rogers Hornsby
Inducted in 1942
1936 105
1937 53
1938 46
1939 176
1942 182

Willie Horton
1986 4

Art Houtteman
1964 2

Elston Howard
1974 19
1975 23
1976 55
1977 43
1978 41
1979 30
1980 29
1981 83
1982 40
1983 32
1984 45
1985 54
1986 51
1987 44

1988 53

Frank Howard
1979 6

Waite Hoyt
Inducted in 1969
1939 1
1942 1
1946 NOM 1
1948 7
1949 7
1950 11
1951 13
1952 12
1953 14
1954 14
1955 33
1956 37
1958 37
1960 29
1962 18
1969 .... Vet. Com.

Al Hrabosky
1988 1

Cal Hubbard
Inducted in 1976
Umpire
1976 .... Vet. Com.

Carl Hubbell
Inducted in 1947
1945 24
1946 NOM 101
1946 75
1947 140

Miller Huggins
Inducted in 1964
Manager
1937 5
1938 48
1939 97
1942 111
1945 133
1946 NOM 129
1946 106
1948 4
1950 2
1964 .... Vet. Com.

William Hulbert
Inducted in 1995
1995 .... Vet. Com.

Catfish Hunter
Inducted in 1987
1985 212
1986 289
1987 315

Fred Hutchinson
1962 1
1964 10

Monte Irvin
Inducted in 1973
1973 .... Neg. Com.

Charlie Irwin
1938 1
1939 1

Joe Jackson
1936 2
1946 NOM 2

Reggie Jackson
Inducted in 1993
1993 396

Sonny Jackson
1980 1

Travis Jackson
Inducted in 1982
1948 5
1949 6
1950 6
1951 4
1952 1
1953 2
1954 1
1955 5
1956 14
1958 11
1960 11
1962 1
1982 .... Vet. Com.

Fergie Jenkins
Inducted in 1991
1989 234
1990 296
1991 334

Hughie Jennings
Inducted in 1945
1936 V 11
1937 4
1938 23
1939 33
1942 64
1945 92
1945 .... O/T Com.

Jackie Jensen
1967 3
1968 3
1969 1
1970 1
1971 2
1972 1

Tommy John
1995 98
1996 102

Ban Johnson
Inducted in 1937
Executive
1937 .... Cen. Com.

Dave Johnson
1984 3

Judy Johnson
Inducted in 1975
1975 .... Neg. Com.

Bob Johnson
1948 1
1956 1

Walter Johnson
Inducted in 1936
1936 189

Fielder Jones
1946 NOM 1

Sam P. Jones
1939 1
1955 1
1956 1

Tim Jordan
1951 1

Mike Jorgensen
1991 1

Addie Joss
Inducted in 1978
1937 11
1938 18
1939 28
1942 33
1945 23
1946 NOM 14
1960 1
1978 .... Vet. Com.

Joe Judge
1937 1
1938 2
1949 1
1955 2
1956 2
1958 9
1960 15

Billy Jurges
1949 2
1958 1

Jim Kaat
1989 87
1990 79
1991 62
1992 114
1993 125
1994 98
1995 100
1996 91

Al Kaline
Inducted in 1980
1980 340

Willie Kamm
1958 3
1960 1

Tim Keefe
Inducted in 1964
1936 V 1
1964 .... Vet. Com.

Willie Keeler
Inducted in 1939
1936 V 33
1936 40
1937 115
1938 177
1939 207

George Kell
Inducted in 1983
1964 33
1964 RO 8
1966 29
1967 40
1967 RO 11
1968 47
1969 60
1970 90
1971 105
1972 115
1973 114
1974 94
1975 114
1976 129
1977 141
1983 .... Vet. Com.

Charlie Keller
1953 1
1956 2
1958 9
1960 7
1962 1
1964 12
1968 11
1969 14
1970 7
1971 14
1972 24

Joe Kelley
Inducted in 1971
1939 1
1942 1
1971 .... Vet. Com.

George Kelly
Inducted in 1973
1947 1
1948 2
1949 1
1956 2
1958 2
1960 5

1962 1
1973 .... Vet. Com.

Mike Kelly
Inducted in 1945
1936 V 15
1945 .... O/T Com.

Ken Keltner
1958 1
1960 1

Dickie Kerr
1937 1
1938 3
1939 5
1942 1
1945 1
1949 1
1951 3
1952 9
1953 13
1954 13
1955 25

Don Kessinger
1985 2

Harmon Killebrew
Inducted in 1984
1981 239
1982 246
1983 269
1984 335

Bill Killefer
1946 NOM 1

Matt Kilroy
1936 V 1

Ellis Kinder
1964 3

Ralph Kiner
Inducted in 1975
1962 5
1964 31
1964 RO 3
1966 74
1967 124
1967 RO 41
1968 118
1969 137
1970 167
1971 212
1972 235
1973 235
1974 215
1975 273

Dave Kingman
1992 3

Chuck Klein
Inducted in 1980
1948 3
1949 9
1950 14
1951 15
1952 19
1954 11
1955 25
1956 44
1958 36
1960 37
1962 18
1964 56
1964 RO 18
1980 .... Vet. Com.

Bill Klem
Inducted in 1953
Umpire
1953 .... Vet. Com.

Johnny Kling
1936 8
1937 20

1938 26
1939 14
1942 15
1945 12
1946 NOM 20
1948 2
1953 1

Ted Kluszewski
1967 9
1968 14
1969 11
1970 8
1971 9
1972 10
1973 14
1974 28
1975 33
1976 50
1977 55
1978 51
1979 58
1980 50
1981 56

Otto Knabe
1939 1
1946 NOM 1

Ray Knight
1994 1

Jerry Koosman
1991 4

Sandy Koufax
Inducted in 1972
1972 344

Ray Kremer
1948 1
1958 2

Red Kress
1958 1
1960 3

Mike Krukow
1995 1

Harvey Kuenn
1977 57
1978 58
1979 63
1980 83
1981 93
1982 62
1983 77
1984 106
1985 125
1986 144
1987 144
1988 168
1989 115
1990 107
1991 100

Joe Kuhel
1956 1

Bob Kuzava
1964 1

Nap Lajoie
Inducted in 1937
1936 V 2
1936 146
1937 168

Judge Landis
Inducted in 1944
Executive
1944 .... O/T Com.

Bill Lange
1936 V 6
1953 1

Hal Lanier
1979 1

Don Larsen
1974 29
1975 23
1976 47
1977 39
1978 32
1979 53
1980 31
1981 33
1982 32
1983 22
1984 25
1985 32
1986 33
1987 30
1988 31

Arlie Latham
1936 V 1
1938 1
1942 1

Cookie Lavagetto
1958 4
1960 2

Vern Law
1973 9
1974 5
1975 6
1976 5
1977 5
1978 6
1979 9

Tony Lazzeri
Inducted in 1991
1945 1
1947 1
1948 21
1949 20
1949 RO 6
1950 21
1951 27
1952 29
1953 28
1954 30
1955 66
1956 64
1958 80
1960 59
1962 8
1991 .... Vet. Com.

Fred Leach
1958 2
1960 1

Tommy Leach
1937 1
1939 1

Bill Lee
1988 3

Sam Leever
1937 1

Bob Lemon
Inducted in 1976
1964 24
1964 RO 3
1966 21
1967 35
1967 RO 7
1968 47
1969 56
1970 70
1971 90
1972 117
1973 177
1974 190
1975 233
1976 305

Chet Lemon
1996 1

Buck Leonard
Inducted in 1972
1972 .... Neg. Com.

Dennis Leonard
1992 1

Emil Leonard
1960 2
1968 5
1969 4
1970 5
1971 3
1972 5
1973 6

Duffy Lewis
1937 3
1938 5
1939 6
1945 1
1951 2
1952 11
1953 20
1954 20
1955 34

Fred Lindstrom
Inducted in 1976
1949 1
1956 3
1958 5
1960 6
1962 7
1976 .... Vet. Com.

John Henry Lloyd
Inducted in 1977
1977 .... Neg. Com.

Hans Lobert
1937 2
1938 1
1939 2
1960 1

Whitey Lockman
1966 4

Mickey Lolich
1985 78
1986 86
1987 84
1988 109
1989 47
1990 27
1991 33
1992 45
1993 43
1994 23
1995 26
1996 33

Ernie Lombardi
Inducted in 1986
1950 3
1951 3
1956 8
1958 4
1960 6
1962 5
1964 33
1964 RO 9
1966 34
1967 43
1967 RO 25
1986 .... Vet. Com.

Jim Lonborg
1985 3
1986 3

Herman Long
1936 V 16
1937 1
1938 1
1939 1
1945 1
1946 NOM 1

Ed Lopat
1968 2
1969 2
1970 1
1971 4
1972 2

Davey Lopes
1993 2

Al Lopez
Inducted in 1977
Manager
1949 1
1952 2
1953 2
1956 1
1958 34
1960 26
1962 11
1964 57
1964 RO 34
1966 109
1967 114
1967 RO 50
1977 .... Vet. Com.

Bobby Lowe
1936 V 2
1942 1
1945 2

John Lowenstein
1991 1

Red Lucas
1949 2
1950 1
1958 1

Dolph Luque
1937 1
1938 1
1939 1
1950 1
1952 1
1953 1
1956 1
1958 15
1960 4

Greg Luzinski
1990 1

Sparky Lyle
1988 56
1989 25
1990 25
1991 15

Fred Lynn
1996 26

Ted Lyons
Inducted in 1955
1945 4
1946 NOM 3
1948 15
1949 29
1949 RO 14
1950 42
1951 71
1952 101
1953 139
1954 170
1955 217

Connie Mack
Inducted in 1937
Manager
1936 1
1937 .... Cen. Com.

Larry MacPhail
Inducted in 1978
Executive
1978 .... Vet. Com.

Bill Madlock
1993 ... 19

Sherry Magee
1937 ... 2
1938 ... 2
1939 ... 1
1942 ... 1
1945 ... 1
1946 NOM ... 1
1950 ... 1
1951 ... 2

Sal Maglie
1964 ... 13
1968 ... 11

Jim Maloney
1978 ... 2
1979 ... 2

Gus Mancuso
1958 ... 1

Mickey Mantle
Inducted in 1974
1974 ... 322

Heinie Manush
Inducted in 1964
1948 ... 1
1949 ... 1
1956 ... 13
1958 ... 22
1960 ... 20
1962 ... 15
1964 ... Vet. Com.

Rabbit Maranville
Inducted in 1954
1937 ... 25
1938 ... 73
1939 ... 82
1942 ... 66
1945 ... 51
1946 NOM ... 50
1946 ... 29
1947 ... 91
1948 ... 38
1949 ... 58
1949 RO ... 39
1950 ... 66
1951 ... 110
1952 ... 133
1953 ... 164
1954 ... 209

Firpo Marberry
1938 ... 1
1950 ... 1
1958 ... 5
1960 ... 2
1962 ... 2

Juan Marichal
Inducted in 1983
1981 ... 233
1982 ... 305
1983 ... 313

Marty Marion
1956 ... 1
1960 ... 37
1962 ... 16
1964 ... 50
1964 RO ... 17
1966 ... 86
1967 ... 90
1967 RO ... 22
1968 ... 89
1969 ... 112
1970 ... 120
1971 ... 123
1972 ... 120
1973 ... 127

Roger Maris
1974 ... 78
1975 ... 70
1976 ... 87

1977 ... 72
1978 ... 83
1979 ... 127
1980 ... 111
1981 ... 94
1982 ... 69
1983 ... 69
1984 ... 107
1985 ... 128
1986 ... 177
1987 ... 176
1988 ... 184

Rube Marquard
Inducted in 1971
1936 ... 1
1937 ... 13
1938 ... 10
1939 ... 4
1946 NOM ... 6
1947 ... 18
1948 ... 6
1949 ... 4
1951 ... 3
1952 ... 9
1953 ... 19
1954 ... 15
1955 ... 35
1971 ... Vet. Com.

Mike Marshall
1987 ... 6

Billy Martin
1967 ... 1

Pepper Martin
1942 ... 2
1945 ... 1
1946 NOM ... 1
1948 ... 7
1949 ... 16
1950 ... 7
1951 ... 19
1952 ... 31
1953 ... 43
1956 ... 7
1958 ... 46
1960 ... 29
1962 ... 6
1964 ... 19
1964 RO ... 5

Morrie Martin
1966 ... 2

Eddie Mathews
Inducted in 1978
1974 ... 118
1975 ... 148
1976 ... 189
1977 ... 239
1978 ... 301

Christy Mathewson
Inducted in 1936
1936 ... 205

Lee May
1988 ... 2

Carl Mays
1958 ... 6

Willie Mays
Inducted in 1979
1979 ... 409

Bill Mazeroski
1978 ... 23
1979 ... 36
1980 ... 33
1981 ... 38
1982 ... 28
1983 ... 48
1984 ... 74
1985 ... 87
1986 ... 100
1987 ... 125
1988 ... 143

1989 ... 134
1990 ... 131
1991 ... 142
1992 ... 182

Jim McAleer
1936 V ... 1

Joe McCarthy
Inducted in 1957
Manager
1939 ... 3
1947 ... 2
1951 ... 1
1953 ... 1
1958 ... 2
1957 ... Vet. Com.

Tommy McCarthy
Inducted in 1946
1936 V ... 1
1946 ... O/T Com.

Tim McCarver
1986 ... 16

Frank McCormick
1956 ... 3
1962 ... 1
1964 ... 6
1968 ... 3

Willie McCovey
Inducted in 1986
1986 ... 346

Lindy McDaniel
1981 ... 1
1982 ... 3

Gil McDougald
1966 ... 5
1967 ... 4
1968 ... 4
1969 ... 3
1970 ... 1
1971 ... 4
1972 ... 4
1973 ... 2
1974 ... 3

Joe McGinnity
Inducted in 1946
1937 ... 12
1938 ... 36
1939 ... 32
1942 ... 59
1945 ... 44
1946 NOM ... 53
1946 ... 47
1946 ... O/T Com.

Bill McGowan
Inducted in 1992
Umpire
1992 ... Vet. Com.

John McGraw
Inducted in 1937
Manager
1936 V ... 17
1936 ... 4
1937 ... 35
1937 ... Cen. Com.

Tug McGraw
1990 ... 6

Stuffy McInnis
1937 ... 1
1938 ... 4
1939 ... 4
1948 ... 5
1949 ... 8
1950 ... 1
1951 ... 3

Bill McKechnie
Inducted in 1962
Manager
1945 ... 2
1946 NOM ... 2
1950 ... 1
1951 ... 8
1962 ... Vet. Com.

Denny McLain
1978 ... 1
1979 ... 3
1985 ... 2

Larry McLean
1937 ... 1

Don McMahon
1980 ... 1

Marty McManus
1958 ... 2
1960 ... 2

Roy McMillan
1972 ... 9
1973 ... 5
1974 ... 4

Dave McNally
1981 ... 5
1982 ... 5
1985 ... 7
1986 ... 12

Cal McVey
1936 V ... 1

Lee Meadows
1958 ... 2

Ducky Medwick
Inducted in 1968
1948 ... 1
1956 ... 31
1958 ... 50
1960 ... 38
1962 ... 34
1964 ... 108
1964 RO ... 130
1966 ... 187
1967 ... 212
1967 RO ... 248
1968 ... 240

Andy Messersmith
1985 ... 3
1986 ... 3

Bob Meusel
1937 ... 1
1938 ... 1
1945 ... 1
1948 ... 6
1949 ... 3
1950 ... 2
1952 ... 1
1955 ... 2
1956 ... 1
1958 ... 5
1960 ... 10

Eddie Miksis
1964 ... 1

Clyde Milan
1938 ... 1
1950 ... 1
1951 ... 1
1952 ... 1
1953 ... 1
1954 ... 3
1955 ... 6

Felix Millan
1983 ... 1

Bing Miller
1958 ... 1
1960 ... 6

Dots Miller
1948 ... 1

Hack Miller
1937 ... 1

Minnie Minoso
1969 ... 6
1986 ... 89
1987 ... 82
1988 ... 90
1989 ... 59
1990 ... 51
1991 ... 38
1992 ... 69
1993 ... 67
1994 ... 45
1995 ... 66
1996 ... 62

Johnny Mize
Inducted in 1981
1960 ... 45
1962 ... 14
1964 ... 54
1964 RO ... 12
1966 ... 81
1967 ... 89
1967 RO ... 14
1968 ... 103
1969 ... 116
1970 ... 126
1971 ... 157
1972 ... 157
1973 ... 157
1981 ... Vet. Com.

Rick Monday
1990 ... 2

Don Money
1989 ... 1

Wally Moon
1971 ... 2

Jo-Jo Moore
1950 ... 1

Terry Moore
1950 ... 1
1953 ... 1
1958 ... 12
1960 ... 7
1962 ... 1
1964 ... 14
1967 ... 3
1968 ... 33

Pat Moran
1937 ... 1
1938 ... 1
1939 ... 1
1945 ... 1

Joe Morgan
Inducted in 1990
1990 ... 363

Wally Moses
1958 ... 1
1960 ... 1
1968 ... 4
1969 ... 4
1970 ... 5
1971 ... 7

Johnny Mostil
1956 ... 1
1958 ... 1

Manny Mota
1988 ... 18
1989 ... 9

Hugh Mulcahy
1948 ... 1

Van Mungo
1945 ... 1
1948 ... 1
1958 ... 2
1960 ... 2

Thurman Munson
1981 ... 62
1982 ... 26
1983 ... 18
1984 ... 29
1985 ... 32
1986 ... 35
1987 ... 28
1988 ... 32
1989 ... 31
1990 ... 33
1991 ... 28
1992 ... 32
1993 ... 40
1994 ... 31
1995 ... 30

Bobby Murcer
1989 ... 3

Danny Murphy
1937 ... 1
1945 ... 1

Red Murray
1937 ... 1
1938 ... 1

Stan Musial
Inducted in 1969
1969 ... 317

Buddy Myer
1949 ... 1

Art Nehf
1937 ... 3
1938 ... 5
1939 ... 1
1949 ... 1
1950 ... 2
1951 ... 4
1952 ... 3
1953 ... 4
1954 ... 7
1955 ... 7
1958 ... 13

Graig Nettles
1994 ... 38
1995 ... 28
1996 ... 37

Don Newcombe
1966 ... 7
1967 ... 18
1967 RO ... 2
1968 ... 9
1969 ... 3
1970 ... 5
1971 ... 8
1972 ... 7
1973 ... 11
1974 ... 7
1975 ... 11
1976 ... 21
1977 ... 43
1978 ... 48
1979 ... 52
1980 ... 59

Hal Newhouser
Inducted in 1992
1962 ... 4
1964 ... 26
1964 RO ... 3
1966 ... 32
1967 ... 62
1967 RO ... 13
1968 ... 67
1969 ... 82

1970 80
1971 94
1972 92
1973 79
1974 73
1975 155
1992 ....Vet. Com.

Bobo Newsom
1960 6
1962 3
1964 17
1964 RO....1
1966 25
1967 19
1967 RO....6
1968 22
1969 32
1970 12
1971 17
1972 31
1973 33

Kid Nichols
Inducted in 1949
1936 V 3
1938 3
1939 7
1942 5
1945 5
1946 NOM....1
1949 ....O/T Com.

Bill Nicholson
1960 1

Joe Niekro
1994 6

Phil Niekro
1993 278
1994 273
1995 286
1996 321

Ron Northey
1964 1

Jim Northrup
1981 1

Lefty O'Doul
1948 4
1949 4
1950 9
1951 13
1952 19
1953 11
1956 5
1958 27
1960 45
1962 13

Joe Oeschger
1948 1

Bob O'Farrell
1950 4
1958 3
1960 3

Charlie O'Leary
1953 1
1958 1
1960 1

Tony Oliva
1982 63
1983 75
1984 124
1985 114
1986 154
1987 160
1988 202
1989 135
1990 142
1991 160
1992 175
1993 157
1994 158

1995 149
1996 170

Al Oliver
1991 19

Steve O'Neill
1948 2
1949 6
1950 1
1951 3
1952 10
1953 13
1958 10

Jim O'Rourke
Inducted in 1945
1945 ....O/T Com.

Claude Osteen
1981 2

Mel Ott
Inducted in 1951
1949 94
1949 RO....128
1950 115
1951 197

Charlie Pabor
1936 V 1

Andy Pafko
1966 2
1967 1

Satchel Paige
Inducted in 1971
1951 1
1971 ....Neg. Com.

Jim Palmer
Inducted in 1990
1990 411

Milt Pappas
1979 5

Larry Parrish
1994 2

Camilo Pascual
1977 3
1978 1

Dode Paskert
1937 1

Monte Pearson
1958 1

Roger Peckinpaugh
1937 3
1938 2
1939 1
1942 2
1949 1
1952 2
1953 2
1954 1
1955 1

Heinie Peitz
1939 1

Herb Pennock
Inducted in 1948
1937 15
1938 37
1939 40
1942 72
1945 45
1946 NOM....41
1946 16
1947 86
1948 94

Hub Perdue
1938 1
1939 1

Tony Perez
1992 215
1993 233
1994 263
1995 259
1996 309

Cy Perkins
1958 2

Ron Perranoski
1979 6

Gaylord Perry
Inducted in 1991
1989 304
1990 320
1991 342

Jim Perry
1981 6
1983 7

Johnny Pesky
1960 1

Rico Petrocelli
1982 3

Deacon Phillippe
1939 1
1942 1
1945 2
1946 NOM....1

Billy Pierce
1970 5
1971 7
1972 4
1973 4
1974 4

Lip Pike
1936 V 1

Lou Piniella
1990 2

Vada Pinson
1981 18
1982 6
1983 12
1985 19
1986 43
1987 48
1988 67
1989 33
1990 36
1991 30
1992 36
1993 38
1994 46
1995 32
1996 51

Wally Pipp
1958 1

Eddie Plank
Inducted in 1946
1937 23
1938 38
1939 28
1942 63
1945 33
1946 NOM....34
1946 ....O/T Com.

Johnny Podres
1975 3
1976 2
1977 3

Bob Porterfield
1966 1

Boog Powell
1983 5

Vic Power
1971 2
1972 3

Herb Pruett
1949 1
1950 1
1951 1
1952 1
1953 1

Jack Quinn
1948 2
1958 9
1960 2

Dan Quisenberry
1996 18

Charlie Radbourn
Inducted in 1939
1936 V 16
1939 ....O/T Com.

Vic Raschi
1962 1
1964 8
1968 1
1969 3
1971 2
1972 7
1973 7
1974 3
1975 37

Bugs Raymond
1937 1

Pee Wee Reese
Inducted in 1984
1964 73
1964 RO....47
1966 95
1967 89
1967 RO....16
1968 81
1969 89
1970 97
1971 127
1972 129
1973 126
1974 141
1975 154
1976 186
1977 163
1978 169
1984 ....Vet. Com.

Pete Reiser
1958 6
1960 8

Jack Remsen
1936 V 1

Jerry Remy
1990 1

Jerry Reuss
1996 2

Allie Reynolds
1956 1
1960 24
1962 15
1964 35
1964 RO....6
1966 60
1967 77
1967 RO....19
1968 95
1969 98

1970 89
1971 110
1972 105
1973 93
1974 101

Del Rice
1966 2

Jim Rice
1995 137
1996 166

Sam Rice
Inducted in 1963
1938 1
1948 1
1949 3
1950 1
1951 1
1952 1
1953 3
1954 9
1955 28
1956 45
1958 90
1960 143
1962 81
1963 ....Vet. Com.

J. R. Richard
1986 7

Hardy Richardson
1936 V 1

Bobby Richardson
1972 8
1973 2
1974 5

Branch Rickey
Inducted in 1967
Executive
1942 3
1945 2
1967 ....Vet. Com.

Jimmy Ring
1949 1

Claude Ritchey
1945 1

Mickey Rivers
1990 2

Eppa Rixey
Inducted in 1963
1937 1
1938 2
1945 1
1947 1
1948 5
1949 4
1950 6
1951 5
1952 3
1953 3
1954 5
1955 8
1956 27
1958 32
1960 142
1962 49
1963 ....Vet. Com.

Phil Rizzuto
Inducted in 1994
1956 1
1962 44
1964 45
1964 RO....11
1966 54
1967 71
1967 RO....14
1968 74
1969 78
1970 79
1971 92

1972 103
1973 111
1974 111
1975 117
1976 149
1994 ....Vet. Com.

Robin Roberts
Inducted in 1976
1973 213
1974 224
1975 263
1976 337

Dave Robertson
1953 1

Brooks Robinson
Inducted in 1983
1983 344

Frank Robinson
Inducted in 1982
1982 370

Jackie Robinson
Inducted in 1962
1962 124

Wilbert Robinson
Inducted in 1945
Manager
1936 V 6
1937 5
1938 17
1939 46
1942 89
1945 81
1945 ....O/T Com.

Preacher Roe
1960 1
1962 1
1968 2
1970 1
1971 3
1972 2

Red Rolfe
1950 7
1951 6
1952 4
1953 5
1956 3
1958 13
1960 10
1962 1

Eddie Rommel
1948 3
1949 2
1950 1
1951 1
1952 2
1953 1
1958 7
1960 12

Charlie Root
1945 1
1948 3
1949 1
1950 1
1958 6
1960 2

Pete Rose
1992 41
1993 14
1994 19

Edd Roush
Inducted in 1962
1936 2
1937 10
1938 9
1939 8
1942 1
1945 5
1946 NOM....11

1947	25
1948	17
1949	14
1950	16
1951	21
1952	24
1953	32
1954	52
1955	97
1956	91
1958	112
1960	146
1962	Vet. Com.

Schoolboy Rowe

1958	12
1960	3
1968	6
1969	17

Nap Rucker

1936	1
1937	11
1938	12
1939	13
1942	15
1945	10
1946 NOM	13

Dick Rudolph

1937	1
1951	1

Muddy Ruel

1946 NOM	1
1950	4
1951	1
1952	1
1953	8
1954	5
1955	11
1956	16
1958	10
1960	9

Red Ruffing
Inducted in 1967

1948	4
1949	22
1949 RO	4
1950	12
1951	9
1952	10
1953	24
1954	29
1955	60
1956	97
1958	99
1960	86
1962	72
1964	141
1964 RO	184
1966	208
1967	212
1967 RO	266

Amos Rusie
Inducted in 1977

1936 V	12
1937	1
1938	8
1939	6
1942	1
1945	1
1977	Vet. Com.

Bill Russell

1992	3

Babe Ruth
Inducted in 1936

1936	215

Ray Sadecki

1983	2

Johnny Sain

1962	1
1964	3
1968	7
1969	8

1970	9
1971	11
1972	21
1973	47
1974	51
1975	123

Manny Sanguillen

1986	2

Ron Santo

1980	15
1985	53
1986	64
1987	78
1988	108
1989	75
1990	96
1991	116
1992	136
1993	155
1994	150
1995	139
1996	174

Hank Sauer

1966	4

Al Schacht

1939	1
1948	2
1951	4
1956	1

Germany Schaefer

1942	1
1953	1

Ray Schalk
Inducted in 1955

1936	4
1937	24
1938	45
1939	35
1942	53
1945	33
1946 NOM	36
1947	50
1948	22
1949	24
1949 RO	17
1950	16
1951	37
1952	44
1953	52
1954	54
1955	113
1955	Vet. Com.

Wally Schang

1948	1
1950	1
1956	1
1958	8
1960	11

Mike Schmidt
Inducted in 1995

1995	444

Red Schoendienst
Inducted in 1989

1969	65
1970	97
1971	123
1972	104
1973	96
1974	110
1975	94
1976	129
1977	105
1978	130
1979	159
1980	164
1981	166
1982	135
1983	146
1989	Vet. Com.

Ossie Schreckengost

1937	2

1938	2
1939	2

Frank Schulte

1937	1

Hal Schumacher

1948	1
1955	1
1956	2
1958	1
1960	11
1962	1
1964	10

Everett Scott

1937	2
1938	2
1939	1
1942	1
1947	1
1948	3
1949	3
1950	3
1951	2
1952	4
1953	5
1954	4
1955	8
1956	1

George Scott

1986	1

Jack Scott

1958	1

Tom Seaver
Inducted in 1992

1992	425

George Selkirk

1948	1
1949	1
1950	1
1951	2
1952	1
1953	1

Hank Severeid

1948	1

Joe Sewell
Inducted in 1977

1937	1
1948	1
1954	1
1955	1
1956	3
1958	1
1960	23
1977	Vet. Com.

Luke Sewell

1948	1
1958	3
1960	3
1962	1

Rip Sewell

1958	1
1962	1
1964	1

Cy Seymour

1945	1

Bobby Shantz

1970	7
1971	5
1972	9
1973	5
1974	3

Jim Sheckard

1938	1
1945	1
1946 NOM	1

Bill Sherdel

1948	1
1949	1
1950	1
1951	1
1953	1
1955	1
1956	1
1958	2
1960	2

Urban Shocker

1938	1
1939	1
1948	1
1949	2
1958	4

Chris Short

1979	1

Sonny Siebert

1981	1

Roy Sievers

1971	4
1972	3

Al Simmons
Inducted in 1953

1936	4
1946 NOM	1
1947	6
1948	60
1949	89
1949 RO	76
1950	90
1951	116
1952	141
1953	199

Curt Simmons

1973	5
1974	3

Ted Simmons

1994	17

George Sisler
Inducted in 1939

1936	77
1937	106
1938	179
1939	235

Sibby Sisti

1960	1

Enos Slaughter
Inducted in 1985

1966	100
1967	123
1967 RO	48
1968	129
1969	128
1970	133
1971	165
1972	149
1973	145
1974	145
1975	177
1976	197
1977	222
1978	261
1979	297
1985	Vet. Com.

Roy Smalley

1964	1

Earl Smith

1948	1
1956	1

Reggie Smith

1988	3

Sherry Smith

1948	1

Duke Snider
Inducted in 1980

1970	51
1971	89
1972	84
1973	101
1974	111
1975	129
1976	159
1977	212
1978	254
1979	308
1980	333

Billy Southworth

1945	1
1946 NOM	1
1949	7
1950	1
1951	4
1952	1
1953	1
1958	18

Warren Spahn
Inducted in 1973

1973	316

Al Spalding
Inducted in 1939
Pioneer

1936 V	4
1939	O/T Com.

Tully Sparks

1946 NOM	1

Tris Speaker
Inducted in 1937

1936	133
1937	165

Chris Speier

1995	1

Jake Stahl

1938	1
1939	1

Eddie Stanky

1960	3

Mickey Stanley

1984	2

Willie Stargell
Inducted in 1988

1988	352

Rusty Staub

1991	28
1992	26
1993	32
1994	36
1995	23
1996	24

Harry Steinfeldt

1937	1
1939	1
1942	1

Casey Stengel
Inducted in 1966
Manager

1938	2
1939	6
1945	2
1948	1
1949	3
1950	3
1951	8
1952	27
1953	61
1966	Vet. Com.

Riggs Stephenson

1956	2
1958	1
1960	4
1962	1

Mel Stottlemyre

1980	3

Harry Stovey

1936 V	6

Gabby Street

1937	1
1938	1
1953	1

Gus Suhr

1956	1
1958	1
1960	1

Clyde Sukeforth

1958	1

Billy Sullivan

1937	1
1946 NOM	1

Jim Sundberg

1995	1

Bruce Sutter

1994	109
1995	137
1996	137

Don Sutton

1994	259
1995	264
1996	300

Bill Sweeney

1945	1

Jess Tannehill

1946 NOM	1

Birdie Tebbetts

1958	8
1960	1

Kent Tekulve

1995	6

Gene Tenace

1989	1

Fred Tenney

1936 V	1
1937	5
1938	8
1939	3
1942	1
1946 NOM	1

Bill Terry
Inducted in 1954

1936	9
1938	7
1939	16
1942	36
1945	32
1946 NOM	31
1947	46
1948	52
1949	81
1949 RO	48
1950	105
1951	148
1952	155
1953	191
1954	195

Tommy Thevenow

1950	2

Ira Thomas
1938 1

Sam Thompson
Inducted in 1974
1974 .... Vet. Com.

Bobby Thomson
1966 12
1967 10
1967 RO 1
1968 13
1969 6
1970 4
1971 4
1972 10
1973 3
1974 6
1975 10
1976 9
1977 10
1978 5
1979 11

Andre Thornton
1993 2

Luis Tiant
1988 132
1989 47
1990 42
1991 32
1992 50
1993 62
1994 42
1995 45
1996 64

Joe Tinker
Inducted in 1946
1937 15
1938 16
1939 12
1942 36
1945 49
1946 NOM 55
1946 45
1946 .... O/T Com.

Jim Tobin
1956 2

Fred Toney
1949 1

Earl Torgeson
1967 2

Joe Torre
1983 20
1984 45
1985 44
1986 60
1987 47
1988 60
1989 40
1990 55
1991 41
1992 62
1993 63
1994 53
1995 50
1996 50

Mike Torrez
1990 1

Pie Traynor
Inducted in 1948
1936 16
1938 3
1939 10
1942 45
1945 81
1946 NOM 65
1946 53
1947 119
1948 93

Dizzy Trout
1964 1

Virgil Trucks
1964 4

John Tudor
1996 2

Jim Turner
1956 1

Terry Turner
1947 2

George Uhle
1956 1
1958 4
1960 4

Ellis Valentine
1991 1

Elmer Valo
1967 2

Dazzy Vance
Inducted in 1955
1936 1
1937 10
1938 10
1939 15
1942 37
1945 18
1946 NOM 31
1947 50
1948 23
1949 33
1949 RO 15
1950 52
1951 70
1952 105
1953 150
1954 158
1955 205

Johnny Vander Meer
1945 1
1956 3
1958 35
1960 31
1962 5
1964 51
1964 RO 20
1966 72
1967 87
1967 RO 35
1968 79
1969 95
1970 88
1971 98

George Van Haltren
1936 V 1

Arky Vaughan
Inducted in 1985
1953 1
1954 2
1955 4
1956 9
1958 6
1960 10
1962 6
1964 17
1964 RO 6
1966 36
1967 46
1967 RO 19
1968 82
1985 .... Vet. Com.

Bobby Veach
1937 1

Bill Veeck
Inducted in 1991
Executive
1991 .... Vet. Com.

Mickey Vernon
1966 20
1967 14
1967 RO 2
1968 22
1969 21
1970 10
1971 12
1972 12
1973 23
1974 27
1975 22
1976 52
1977 52
1978 66
1979 88
1980 96

Bill Virdon
1974 3
1975 1

Rube Waddell
Inducted in 1946
1936 33
1937 67
1938 148
1939 179
1942 126
1945 154
1946 NOM 122
1946 87
1946 .... O/T Com.

Honus Wagner
Inducted in 1936
1936 V 5
1936 215

Rube Walberg
1958 1
1960 1

Dixie Walker
1962 1
1964 6
1968 6
1969 9

Harry Walker
1958 1

Bobby Wallace
Inducted in 1953
1936 V 1
1937 1
1938 7
1939 5
1942 2
1945 3
1953 .... Vet. Com.

Ed Walsh
Inducted in 1946
1936 20
1937 56
1938 110
1939 132
1942 113
1945 137
1946 NOM 115
1946 106
1946 .... O/T Com.

Bucky Walters
1950 4
1952 3
1953 10
1956 36
1958 33
1960 19
1962 5
1964 35
1964 RO 8
1966 56
1967 65
1967 RO 24
1968 82
1969 20
1970 29

Bill Wambsganss
1942 1
1950 1
1953 1
1954 4
1955 5
1956 1

Lloyd Waner
Inducted in 1967
1949 3
1950 1
1951 1
1952 2
1956 18
1958 39
1960 22
1962 5
1964 47
1964 RO 12
1967 .... Vet. Com.

Paul Waner
Inducted in 1952
1946 NOM 4
1948 51
1949 73
1949 RO 63
1950 95
1951 162
1952 195

Monte Ward
Inducted in 1964
1936 V 3
1964 .... Vet. Com.

Lon Warneke
1949 2
1958 2
1960 4
1962 2
1964 13

Bob Watson
1990 3

Earl Weaver
Inducted in 1996
1996 .... Vet. Com.

George Weiss
Inducted in 1971
Executive
1971 .... Vet. Com.

Mickey Welch
Inducted in 1973
1973 .... Vet. Com.

Billy Werber
1949 1
1950 1
1952 1
1958 3

Vic Wertz
1970 2
1971 2
1972 4
1973 2
1974 5
1975 5
1976 5
1977 4
1978 4

Sam West
1948 1

Wes Westrum
1964 2

Zach Wheat
Inducted in 1959
1937 5
1938 7
1939 4
1942 3

1945 2
1946 NOM 6
1947 37
1948 15
1949 15
1950 17
1951 19
1952 30
1953 32
1954 33
1955 51
1956 26
1959 .... Vet. Com.

Deacon White
1936 V 1

Frank White
1996 18

Will White
1975 7
1976 7
1977 4

Burgess Whitehead
1956 1

Earl Whitehill
1956 1
1958 2
1960 3

Hoyt Wilhelm
Inducted in 1985
1978 158
1979 168
1980 209
1981 238
1982 236
1983 243
1984 290
1985 331

Billy Williams
Inducted in 1987
1982 97
1983 153
1984 202
1985 252
1986 315
1987 354

Fred Williams
1938 1
1945 1
1948 1
1949 2
1950 9
1951 7
1952 4
1953 4
1954 4
1955 3
1956 11
1958 6
1960 11

Ken Williams
1956 1
1958 1

Ted Williams
Inducted in 1966
1966 282

Ned Williamson
1936 V 2

Vic Willis
Inducted in 1995
1995 .... Vet. Com.

Maury Wills
1978 115
1979 166
1980 146
1981 163
1982 91

1983 77
1984 104
1985 93
1986 124
1987 113
1988 127
1989 95
1990 95
1991 61
1992 110

Jimmie Wilson
1948 8
1949 6
1950 4
1951 2
1952 7
1953 10
1954 8
1955 13
1956 17
1958 3
1960 6
1962 4

Jim Wilson
1964 2

Hack Wilson
Inducted in 1979
1937 1
1939 1
1942 1
1948 2
1949 24
1949 RO 12
1950 16
1951 21
1952 21
1953 43
1954 48
1955 81
1956 74
1958 94
1960 72
1962 39
1979 .... Vet. Com.

Whitey Witt
1949 1

Joe Wood
1937 13
1938 6
1939 2
1942 1
1946 NOM 5
1947 29
1948 5
1950 1
1951 5

Wilbur Wood
1984 14
1985 16
1986 23
1987 26
1988 30
1989 14

Glenn Wright
1948 2
1949 1
1950 2
1951 1
1952 1
1953 3
1954 1
1955 4
1956 3
1958 8
1960 18
1962 1

George Wright
Inducted in 1937
Pioneer
1936 V 6
1937 .... Cen. Com.

Harry Wright
Inducted in 1953
Pioneer
1953 .... Vet. Com.

Whit Wyatt
1958 1

Early Wynn
Inducted in 1972
1969 95
1970 140
1971 240
1972 301

Tom Yawkey
Inducted in 1980
Executive
1980 .... Vet. Com.

Carl Yastrzemski
Inducted in 1989
1989 423

Steve Yeager
1992 2

Steve Yerkes
1945 1

Rudy York
1962 1
1964 10

Cy Young
Inducted in 1937
1936 V 32
1936 111
1937 153

Pep Young
1958 1

Ross Youngs
Inducted in 1972
1936 10
1937 16
1938 40
1939 34
1942 44
1945 22
1946 NOM........ 25
1947 36
1948 19
1949 20
1949 RO........ 11
1950 17
1951 34
1952 34
1953 31
1954 34
1955 48
1956 19
1972 .... Vet. Com.

Tom Zachary
1958 1
1960 1

Chief Zimmer
1938 1

1936 Veterans
Needed to Elect: 59
Cap Anson 40
Buck Ewing.......... 40
Willie Keeler 33
Cy Young 32
Ed Delahanty 22
John McGraw 17
Herman Long 16
Charlie Radbourn.... 16
Mike Kelly 15
Amos Rusie 12

1936
Needed to Elect: 170
Ty Cobb 222

Babe Ruth.......... 215
Honus Wagner...... 215
Christy Mathewson . 205
Walter Johnson 189
Nap Lajoie 146
Tris Speaker 133
Cy Young 111
Rogers Hornsby 105
Mickey Cochrane 80

1937
Needed to Elect: 151
Nap Lajoie 168
Tris Speaker 165
Cy Young 153
Pete Alexander 125
Eddie Collins 115
Willie Keeler 115
George Sisler 106
Ed Delahanty 70
Rube Waddell 67
Jimmy Collins 66

1938
Needed to Elect: 197
Pete Alexander 212
George Sisler 179
Willie Keeler 177
Eddie Collins 175
Rube Waddell 148
Frank Chance 133
Ed Delahanty 132
Ed Walsh 110
Johnny Evers 91
Jimmy Collins 79

1939
Needed to Elect: 206
George Sisler 235
Eddie Collins 213
Willie Keeler 207
Rube Waddell 179
Rogers Hornsby 176
Frank Chance 158
Ed Delahanty 145
Ed Walsh 132
Johnny Evers 107
Miller Huggins 97

1942
Needed to Elect: 175
Rogers Hornsby 182
Frank Chance 136
Rube Waddell 126
Ed Walsh 113
Miller Huggins 111
Ed Delahanty 104
Johnny Evers 91
Wilbert Robinson ... 89
Mickey Cochrane ... 88
Frankie Frisch 84

1945
Needed to Elect: 186
Frank Chance 179
Rube Waddell 154
Ed Walsh 137
Johnny Evers 134
Roger Bresnahan ... 133
Miller Huggins 133
Mickey Cochrane ... 125
Jimmy Collins 121
Ed Delahanty 111
Clark Griffith 108

1946 Nominating Total Voting: 202
Frank Chance 144
Johnny Evers 130
Miller Huggins 129
Rube Waddell 122
Ed Walsh 115
Frankie Frisch 104
Carl Hubbell 101
Mickey Cochrane ... 80
Clark Griffith 73
Lefty Grove 71

1946
Needed to Elect: 198
Frank Chance 150
Johnny Evers 110

Miller Huggins 106
Ed Walsh 106
Rube Waddell 87
Clark Griffith 82
Carl Hubbell 75
Frankie Frisch 67
Mickey Cochrane ... 65
Lefty Grove 61

1947
Needed to Elect: 121
Carl Hubbell 140
Frankie Frisch 136
Mickey Cochrane ... 128
Lefty Grove 123
Pie Traynor 119
Charlie Gehringer ... 105
Rabbit Maranville ... 91
Dizzy Dean 88
Herb Pennock 86
Chief Bender 72

1948
Needed to Elect: 91
Herb Pennock 94
Pie Traynor 93
Al Simmons 60
Charlie Gehringer ... 52
Bill Terry 52
Paul Waner 51
Jimmie Foxx 50
Dizzy Dean 40
Harry Heilmann 40
Bill Dickey 39

1949
Needed to Elect: 115
Charlie Gehringer ... 102
Mel Ott 94
Al Simmons 89
Dizzy Dean 88
Jimmie Foxx 85
Bill Terry 81
Paul Waner 73
Hank Greenberg 67
Bill Dickey 65
Harry Heilmann 59

1949 Run Off
Needed to Elect: 141
One Player Maximum
Charlie Gehringer ... 159
Mel Ott 128
Jimmie Foxx 89
Dizzy Dean 81
Al Simmons 76
Paul Waner 63
Harry Heilmann 52
Bill Terry 48
Hank Greenberg 44
Bill Dickey 39
Rabbit Maranville ... 39

1950
Needed to Elect: 126
Mel Ott 115
Bill Terry 105
Jimmie Foxx 103
Paul Waner 95
Al Simmons 90
Harry Heilmann 87
Dizzy Dean 85
Bill Dickey 78
Rabbit Maranville ... 66
Hank Greenberg 64

1951
Needed to Elect: 170
Mel Ott 197
Jimmie Foxx 179
Paul Waner 162
Harry Heilmann 153
Bill Terry 148
Dizzy Dean 145
Bill Dickey 118
Al Simmons 116
Rabbit Maranville ... 110
Ted Lyons 71

1952
Needed to Elect: 176
Harry Heilmann 203

Paul Waner 195
Bill Terry 155
Dizzy Dean 152
Al Simmons 141
Bill Dickey 139
Rabbit Maranville ... 133
Dazzy Vance 105
Ted Lyons 101
Gabby Hartnett ... 77

1953
Needed to Elect: 198
Dizzy Dean 209
Al Simmons 199
Bill Terry 191
Bill Dickey 179
Rabbit Maranville ... 164
Dazzy Vance 150
Ted Lyons 139
Joe DiMaggio 117
Chief Bender 104
Gabby Hartnett 104

1954
Needed to Elect: 189
Rabbit Maranville ... 209
Bill Dickey 202
Bill Terry 195
Joe DiMaggio 175
Ted Lyons 170
Dazzy Vance 158
Gabby Hartnett ... 151
Hank Greenberg 97
Joe Cronin 85
Max Carey.......... 55

1955
Needed to Elect: 189
Joe DiMaggio 223
Ted Lyons 217
Dazzy Vance 205
Gabby Hartnett ... 195
Hank Greenberg ... 157
Joe Cronin 135
Max Carey 119
Ray Schalk 113
Edd Roush 97
Hank Gowdy 90

1956
Needed to Elect: 145
Hank Greenberg ... 164
Joe Cronin 152
Red Ruffing......... 97
Edd Roush 91
Lefty Gomez 89
Hack Wilson 74
Max Carey 65
Tony Lazzeri 64
Kiki Cuyler 55
Hank Gowdy 49

1958
Needed to Elect: 200
Max Carey.......... 136
Edd Roush 112
Red Ruffing......... 99
Hack Wilson 94
Kiki Cuyler 90
Sam Rice 90
Tony Lazzeri 80
Luke Appling 77
Lefty Gomez 76
Burleigh Grimes ... 71

1960
Needed to Elect: 202
Edd Roush 146
Sam Rice 143
Eppa Rixey 142
Burleigh Grimes 92
Jim Bottomley 89
Red Ruffing......... 86
Red Faber 83
Luke Appling 72
Kiki Cuyler 72
Hack Wilson 72

1962
Needed to Elect: 120
Bob Feller 150
Jackie Robinson.... 124

Sam Rice............. 81
Red Ruffing.......... 72
Eppa Rixey 49
Luke Appling 48
Phil Rizzuto 44
Burleigh Grimes ... 43
Hack Wilson 39
Ducky Medwick 34

1964
Needed to Elect: 151
Luke Appling 142
Red Ruffing......... 141
Roy Campanella ... 115
Ducky Medwick 108
Pee Wee Reese 73
Lou Boudreau 68
Al Lopez............. 57
Chuck Klein 56
Johnny Mize 54
Mel Harder 51
Johnny Vander Meer . 51

1964 Run Off
Needed to Elect: 170
One Player Maximum
Luke Appling 189
Red Ruffing......... 184
Roy Campanella ... 138
Ducky Medwick 130
Pee Wee Reese 47
Lou Boudreau 43
Al Lopez............. 34
Johnny Vander Meer . 20
Chuck Klein 18
Marty Marion 17

1966
Needed to Elect: 227
Ted Williams 282
Red Ruffing......... 208
Roy Campanella ... 197
Ducky Medwick 187
Lou Boudreau 115
Al Lopez............. 109
Enos Slaughter 100
Pee Wee Reese 95
Marty Marion 86
Johnny Mize......... 81

1967
Needed to Elect: 219
Ducky Medwick 212
Red Ruffing......... 212
Roy Campanella ... 204
Lou Boudreau 143
Ralph Kiner 124
Enos Slaughter 123
Al Lopez............. 114
Marty Marion 90
Johnny Mize 89
Pee Wee Reese...... 89

1967 Run Off
Needed to Elect: 230
One Player Maximum
Red Ruffing......... 266
Ducky Medwick 248
Roy Campanella ... 170
Lou Boudreau 68
Al Lopez............. 50
Enos Slaughter 48
Ralph Kiner 41
Johnny Vander Meer . 35
Ernie Lombardi 25
Bucky Walters 24

1968
Needed to Elect: 213
Ducky Medwick 240
Roy Campanella ... 205
Lou Boudreau 146
Enos Slaughter 129
Ralph Kiner 118
Johnny Mize 103
Allie Reynolds 95
Marty Marion 89
Arky Vaughan 82
Pee Wee Reese 81

1969
Needed to Elect: 255
Stan Musial 317
Roy Campanella ... 270
Lou Boudreau 218
Ralph Kiner 137
Enos Slaughter 128
Johnny Mize 116
Marty Marion 112
Allie Reynolds 98
Joe Gordon 97
Johnny Vander Meer . 95
Early Wynn 95

1970
Needed to Elect: 225
Lou Boudreau 232
Ralph Kiner 167
Gil Hodges 145
Early Wynn 140
Enos Slaughter 133
Johnny Mize 126
Marty Marion 120
Pee Wee Reese 97
Red Schoendienst ... 97
George Kell.......... 90

1971
Needed to Elect: 270
Yogi Berra 242
Early Wynn 240
Ralph Kiner 212
Gil Hodges 180
Enos Slaughter 165
Johnny Mize 157
Pee Wee Reese 127
Marty Marion 123
Red Schoendienst .. 123
Allie Reynolds 110

1972
Needed to Elect: 297
Sandy Koufax 344
Yogi Berra 339
Early Wynn 301
Ralph Kiner 235
Gil Hodges 161
Johnny Mize......... 157
Enos Slaughter 149
Pee Wee Reese 129
Marty Marion 120
Bob Lemon.......... 117

1973
Needed to Elect: 285
Warren Spahn 316
Whitey Ford 255
Ralph Kiner 235
Gil Hodges 218
Robin Roberts 213
Bob Lemon.......... 177
Johnny Mize 157
Enos Slaughter 145
Marty Marion 127
Pee Wee Reese..... 126

1974
Needed to Elect: 274
Mickey Mantle 322
Whitey Ford 284
Robin Roberts 224
Ralph Kiner 215
Gil Hodges 198
Bob Lemon.......... 190
Enos Slaughter 145
Pee Wee Reese..... 141
Eddie Mathews 118
Phil Rizzuto 111
Duke Snider 111

1975
Needed to Elect: 272
Ralph Kiner.......... 273
Robin Roberts 263
Bob Lemon.......... 233
Gil Hodges 188
Enos Slaughter 177
Hal Newhouser 155
Pee Wee Reese 154
Eddie Mathews 148
Phil Cavaretta 129
Duke Snider 129

1976
Needed to Elect: 291

Robin Roberts 337
Bob Lemon 305
Gil Hodges 233
Enos Slaughter 197
Eddie Mathews 189
Pee Wee Reese 186
Nellie Fox 174
Duke Snider 159
Phil Rizzuto 149
George Kell 129
Red Schoendienst .. 129

1977
Needed to Elect: 288

Ernie Banks 321
Eddie Mathews 239
Gil Hodges 224
Enos Slaughter 222
Duke Snider 212
Don Drysdale 197
Pee Wee Reese 163
Nellie Fox 152
Jim Bunning 146
George Kell 141

1978
Needed to Elect: 285

Eddie Mathews 301
Enos Slaughter 261
Duke Snider 254
Gil Hodges 226
Don Drysdale 219
Jim Bunning 181
Pee Wee Reese 169
Richie Ashburn 158
Hoyt Wilhelm 158
Nellie Fox 149

1979
Needed to Elect: 324

Willie Mays 409
Duke Snider 308
Enos Slaughter 297
Gil Hodges 242
Don Drysdale 233
Nellie Fox 174

Hoyt Wilhelm 168
Maury Wills 166
Red Schoendienst .. 159
Jim Bunning 147

1980
Needed to Elect: 289

Al Kaline 340
Duke Snider 333
Don Drysdale 238
Gil Hodges 230
Hoyt Wilhelm 209
Jim Bunning 177
Red Schoendienst .. 164
Nellie Fox 161
Maury Wills 146
Richie Ashburn 134

1981
Needed to Elect: 301

Bob Gibson 337
Don Drysdale 243
Gil Hodges 241
Harmon Killebrew ... 239
Hoyt Wilhelm 238
Juan Marichal 233
Nellie Fox 168
Red Schoendienst .. 166
Jim Bunning 164
Maury Wills 163

1982
Needed to Elect: 312

Hank Aaron 406
Frank Robinson 370
Juan Marichal 305
Harmon Killebrew .. 246
Hoyt Wilhelm 236
Don Drysdale 233
Gil Hodges 205
Luis Aparicio 174
Jim Bunning 138
Red Schoendienst .. 135

1983
Needed to Elect: 281

Brooks Robinson ... 344

Juan Marichal 313
Harmon Killebrew ... 269
Luis Aparicio 252
Hoyt Wilhelm 243
Don Drysdale 242
Gil Hodges 237
Nellie Fox 173
Billy Williams 153
Red Schoendienst .. 146

1984
Needed to Elect: 303

Luis Aparicio 341
Harmon Killebrew ... 335
Don Drysdale 316
Hoyt Wilhelm 290
Nellie Fox 246
Billy Williams 202
Jim Bunning 201
Orlando Cepeda 124
Tony Oliva 124
Roger Maris 107

1985
Needed to Elect: 297

Hoyt Wilhelm 331
Lou Brock 315
Nellie Fox 295
Billy Williams 252
Jim Bunning 214
Catfish Hunter 212
Roger Maris 128
Harvey Kuenn 125
Orlando Cepeda 114
Tony Oliva 114

1986
Needed to Elect: 319

Willie McCovey 346
Billy Williams 315
Catfish Hunter 289
Jim Bunning 279
Roger Maris 177
Tony Oliva 154
Orlando Cepeda 152
Harvey Kuenn 144
Maury Wills 124

Bill Mazeroski 100

1987
Needed to Elect: 310

Billy Williams 354
Catfish Hunter 315
Jim Bunning 289
Orlando Cepeda 179
Roger Maris 176
Tony Oliva 160
Harvey Kuenn 144
Bill Mazeroski 125
Maury Wills 113
Ken Boyer 96
Lew Burdette 96

1988
Needed to Elect: 321

Willie Stargell 352
Jim Bunning 317
Tony Oliva 202
Orlando Cepeda 199
Roger Maris 184
Harvey Kuenn 168
Bill Mazeroski 143
Luis Tiant 132
Maury Wills 127
Ken Boyer 109
Mickey Lolich 109

1989
Needed to Elect: 336

Johnny Bench 431
Carl Yastrzemski ... 423
Gaylord Perry 304
Jim Bunning 283
Fergie Jenkins 234
Orlando Cepeda 176
Tony Oliva 135
Bill Mazeroski 134
Harvey Kuenn 115
Maury Wills 95

1990
Needed to Elect: 333

Jim Palmer 411

Joe Morgan 363
Gaylord Perry 320
Fergie Jenkins 296
Jim Bunning 257
Orlando Cepeda 211
Tony Oliva 142
Bill Mazeroski 131
Harvey Kuenn 107
Ron Santo 96

1991
Needed to Elect: 333

Rod Carew 401
Gaylord Perry 342
Fergie Jenkins 334
Rollie Fingers 291
Jim Bunning 282
Orlando Cepeda 192
Tony Oliva 160
Bill Mazeroski 142
Ron Santo 116
Harvey Kuenn 100

1992
Needed to Elect: 323

Tom Seaver 425
Rollie Fingers 349
Orlando Cepeda 246
Tony Perez 215
Bill Mazeroski 182
Tony Oliva 175
Ron Santo 136
Jim Kaat 114
Maury Wills 110
Ken Boyer 71

1993
Needed to Elect: 318

Reggie Jackson 396
Phil Niekro 278
Orlando Cepeda 252
Tony Perez 233
Steve Garvey 176
Tony Oliva 157

Ron Santo 155
Jim Kaat 125
Dick Allen 70
Ken Boyer 69

1994
Needed to Elect: 342

Steve Carlton 436
Orlando Cepeda 335
Phil Niekro 273
Tony Perez 263
Don Sutton 259
Steve Garvey 166
Tony Oliva 158
Ron Santo 150
Bruce Sutter 109
Jim Kaat 98

1995
Needed to Elect: 345

Mike Schmidt 444
Phil Niekro 286
Don Sutton 264
Tony Perez 259
Steve Garvey 196
Tony Oliva 149
Ron Santo 139
Jim Rice 137
Bruce Sutter 137
Jim Kaat 100

1996
Needed to Elect: 353

Phil Niekro 321
Tony Perez 309
Don Sutton 300
Steve Garvey 175
Ron Santo 174
Tony Oliva 170
Jim Rice 166
Bruce Sutter 137
Tommy John 102
Jim Kaat 91

## CHAPTER 12

The All-Star Game

Frederick Ivor-Campbell

Although the tradition of All-Star Games in baseball dates back to an 1858 series between teams of stars from Brooklyn and New York (they were called "picked nines" in those days), the current All-Star series began when Arch Ward, sports editor of the *Chicago Tribune*, persuaded hesitant league owners to go along with his proposal for a game between stars from the American and National leagues, to be played in Chicago during that city's Century of Progress Exposition in 1933.

All-Star managers (who, except for the first game, have been the pilots of the previous year's pennant winners) shared with fans the selection of players for the first two games. From 1935 through 1946 the manager selected his whole squad. Since 1947, he has chosen his pitchers and all other players except the eight members of the starting lineup. The fans chose the starters in 1947–1957; after an incident of ballot-box stuffing by Cincinnati partisans in 1957, the major

league players, coaches, and managers made the choice in 1958–1969; in 1970 the selection of starting lineups was returned to the fans.

The American League dominated the early years of the series, winning the first three games, and extending their winning margin to eight games (12–4) by 1949. The National League cut the lead in half with four straight wins, and by 1964 had drawn even in the series (17–17–1). From 1965 through 1985 the National Leaguers continued their drive, winning 19 All-Star Games while losing only two, to build a commanding 36–19 lead in the series. In recent years, though, the American Leaguers began to come back, winning in 1993 their seventh game in eight years, and their sixth in a row. The National League won in 1994, though it took extra innings to break the American League streak, and they won in 1995 and 1996 as well.

GAME 1
Comiskey Park, Chicago
July 6, 1933
AL, 4–2

NL	000 002 000	2	8	0
AL	012 001 00X	4	9	1

Pitchers: HALLAHAN, Warneke (3), Hubbell (7) vs GOMEZ, Crowder (4), Grove (7)
Home Runs: Ruth-A, Frisch-N
Attendance: 49,200

Baseball's two grand old managers—Connie Mack and John Mc-Graw—were chosen to lead the American and National League squads in the first All-Star Game, and American starting pitcher Lefty Gomez of the Yankees took home honors both as the first All-Star winning pitcher and as the first player to drive in an All-Star run (singling in Jimmie Dykes in the second inning). But it was another "grand old man"—Babe Ruth—who made the game's headlines. At thirty-eight, in his next-to-last season as a Yankee, he lined a two-run homer in the third to make the score 3–0, and as right fielder in the eighth he robbed Chick Hafey of a hit with a remarkable running catch of Hafey's line drive.

Frank Frisch homered for the Nationals, following up Pepper Martin's RBI with a solo shot in the National League's two-run sixth. But the American stars countered with an insurance run in the bottom of the sixth, as Earl Averill singled in Joe Cronin to end the scoring. Carl Hubbell for the Nationals and Lefty Grove for the Americans blanked the opposition through the final innings.

GAME 2
Polo Grounds, New York
July 10, 1934
AL, 9–7

AL	000 261 000	9	14	1
NL	103 030 000	7	8	1

Pitchers: Gomez, Ruffing (4), HARDER (5) vs Hubbell, Warneke (4), MUNGO (5), J.Dean (6), Frankhouse (9)
Home Runs: Frisch-N, Medwick-N
Attendance: 48,363

This was the game in which Carl Hubbell struck out Babe Ruth, Lou Gehrig, Jimmie Foxx, Al Simmons, and Joe Cronin in order in the first two innings. Hubbell also walked two and gave up two hits in his three innings of work, but allowed no run to score as his Nationals took a 4–0 lead on homers by Frank Frisch in the first and Joe Medwick (for three runs) in the third off American starter (and first-game winner) Lefty Gomez.

But with Hubbell gone, the Americans pounced on Lon Warneke and Van Lingle Mungo for four runs each in the fourth and fifth innings. The Nationals battled back for three off Red Ruffing in their half of the fifth, to come within a run of tying the game. But Mel Harder relieved Ruffing with none out and put out the fire, one-hitting the National stars over the final five innings. The Americans picked up an insurance run in the sixth off Dizzy Dean before Dean and Fred Frankhouse shut them down, too, through the final three frames.

GAME 3
Municipal Stadium, Cleveland
July 8, 1935
AL, 4–1

NL	000 100 000	1	4	1
AL	210 010 00X	4	8	0

Pitchers: WALKER, Schumacher (3), Derringer (7), J.Dean (8) vs GOMEZ, Harder (7)
Home Runs: Foxx-A
Attendance: 69,812

Lefty Gomez started his third All-Star Game, and pitched a record six innings to pick up his second All-Star win. For three innings he shut out the Nationals as the Americans built a lead behind him on Jimmie Foxx's two-run homer in the first, and Rollie Hemsley's triple and Joe Cronin's run-scoring fly in the second.

The National Leaguers tried to catch up in the fourth, when they put together two of their three hits off Gomez—a double by Arky Vaughan and a single by Bill Terry—and scored a run. But an inning later Foxx nullified the National run, singling Joe Vosmik home for his third RBI.

Gomez blanked the National stars through two more innings before yielding to Mel Harder, who came in to close his second All-Star Game. Harder had created an All-Star record the previous year with his five consecutive scoreless innings pitched, and extended the record to eight, with three more shutout innings to end the game.

GAME 4
Braves Field, Boston
July 7, 1936
NL, 4–3

AL	000 000 300	3	7	1
NL	020 020 00X	4	9	0

Pitchers: GROVE, Rowe (4), Harder (7) vs J.DEAN, Hubbell (4), C.Davis (7), Warneke (7)
Home Runs: Galan-N, Gehrig-A
Attendance: 25,534

The National League, which had not yet won an All-Star Game, scored first in the second when Gabby Hartnett tripled in a run off Lefty Grove—rookie Joe DiMaggio missing his try for a shoe-top catch of Hartnett's drive to right field. Pinky Whitney then singled in Hartnett. Augie Galan homered off Schoolboy Rowe (and the right field foul pole) in the fifth, and DiMaggio's bobble of Billy Herman's single a batter later put Herman in position to score an unearned fourth run, on Joe Medwick's single, that proved to be the margin of victory.

The Americans, shut out through six by Dizzy Dean and Carl Hubbell, nearly tied the game in the seventh off Curt Davis as Lou Gehrig homered and Luke Appling singled in two more. But Lon Warneke took over and, after loading the bases with a walk, escaped disaster as shortstop Leo Durocher snared DiMaggio's vicious line drive to his right for the third out. Warneke shut the Americans out over the final two innings to preserve the one-run lead and the National League's first All-Star win.

GAME 5
Griffith Stadium, Washington
July 7, 1937
AL, 8–3

```
NL   000 111 000    3 13 0
AL   002 312 00X    8 13 2
```

Pitchers: J.DEAN, Hubbell (4),
   Blanton (4), Grissom (5), Mungo (6),
   Walters (8) vs GOMEZ, Bridges (4),
   Harder (7)
Home Runs: Gehrig-A
Attendance: 31,391

President Franklin Roosevelt attended the game. Lou Gehrig
homered and doubled to drive in
half the American League's eight
runs in an easy American win.
Lefty Gomez started his fourth
All-Star Game in five years, winning his third. And AL reliever Mel
Harder pitched the final innings for
the fourth All-Star Game in a row,
pushing his record for consecutive
All-Star shutout innings to 13. But
the game is remembered not for
any of these things, but for Earl
Averill's line drive in the third inning which fractured Dizzy Dean's
toe and led to the premature end of
his spectacular career. (Dean recovered from the broken toe, but
tried to resume his pitching too
soon. In favoring the toe, he
changed his delivery and irrepara-
bly injured his pitching arm.)

   The Americans began their scoring when Gehrig, who preceded
Averill in the batting order,
homered off Dean in the third, with
one aboard. They added to their
score in each of the next three innings, so that although the Nationals countered with single runs in
the three middle innings, they only
fell farther behind.

GAME 6
Crosley Field, Cincinnati
July 6, 1938
NL, 4–1

```
AL   000 000 001    1 7 4
NL   100 100 20X    4 8 0
```

Pitchers: GOMEZ, Allen (4), Grove (7)
   vs VANDER MEER, Lee (4),
   Brown (7)
Attendance: 27,607

For the fifth (and final) time, Lefty
Gomez started for the American
League, and although he gave up
only two hits and no earned runs in
his three innings, he was saddled
with the loss when an error by
shortstop Joe Cronin paved the way
for a National League run in the
first.

   The Nationals scored their only
earned run in the fourth when Mel
Ott tripled and Ernie Lombardi singled him home. But in the seventh
they recorded two more unearned
runs when Leo Durocher bunted to
move Frank McCormick to second.
Both McCormick and Durocher
scored as third baseman Jimmie
Foxx threw wildly to first and right
fielder Joe DiMaggio (who chased
the ball down) missed home plate
with his throw.

   In the ninth DiMaggio singled
and Cronin doubled him home in
partial atonement for their errors.
But as Johnny Vander Meer and
Big Bill Lee had each blanked the
American stars on one hit in their
three-inning stints, and some fine
outfield catches had kept them
from scoring more than this one
run off Mace Brown, the Americans' errors cost them the game.

GAME 7
Yankee Stadium, New York
July 11, 1939
AL, 3–1

```
NL   001 000 000    1 7 1
AL   000 210 00X    3 6 1
```

Pitchers: Derringer, LEE (4), Fette (7) vs
   Ruffing, BRIDGES (4), Feller (6)
Home Runs: J.DiMaggio-A
Attendance: 62,892

Six Yankees started for the American League, and one of them—Joe
DiMaggio—hit the game's only
home run. But it was a young
Cleveland pitcher—twenty
-year-old Bob Feller, playing in his
first All-Star Game—who turned in
the most memorable performance.

   The Nationals scored first, with a
run in the third on three hits off the
American League starter, Red Ruffing. But the Americans came back
with two runs in the fourth on a
walk, two singles, and a bobbled
grounder by shortstop Arky
Vaughan. DiMaggio hit his insurance homer an inning later.

   In the top of the sixth, after two
singles and an error had loaded the
bases with National stars, with only
one out, Feller replaced Tommy
Bridges to face Vaughan (who had
earlier singled and scored his
team's only run). One pitch got
Feller out of the inning as Vaughan
grounded into a 4–6–3 double play.
Feller shut out the National stars
over the final three innings, striking
out Johnny Mize and Stan Hack in
the ninth to end the game and give
the Americans their fifth All-Star
victory.

GAME 8
Sportsman's Park, St. Louis
July 9, 1940
NL, 4–0

```
AL   000 000 000    0 3 1
NL   300 000 01X    4 7 0
```

Pitchers: RUFFING, Newsom (4),
   Feller (7) vs DERRINGER,
   Walters (3), Wyatt (5), French (7),
   Hubbell (9)
Home Runs: West-N
Attendance: 32,373

The National Leaguers made short
work of the Americans, scoring
three times in the first inning and
holding the opposing stars to three
hits for the All-Star Game's first
shutout. Before American League
starter Red Ruffing retired a single
National batter in the bottom of the
first inning, three of the game's
four runs had been scored, on singles by Arky Vaughan and Billy
Herman and Max West's home run
to right center.

   Ruffing then settled down, and
he and Buck Newsom held the Nationals to just three additional hits
through the seventh. Bob Feller
gave up the Nationals' fourth run in
the eighth, on a walk, a sacrifice,
and Harry Danning's single.

   Five National League pitchers
combined for the shutout, permitting only five batters to reach base
while striking out seven. Starter
Paul Derringer, who struck out
three men in his two innings, was
awarded the win.

GAME 9
Briggs Stadium, Detroit
July 8, 1941
AL, 7–5

```
NL   000 001 220    5 10 2
AL   000 101 014    7 11 3
```

Pitchers: Wyatt, Derringer (3), Walters (5), PASSEAU (7) vs Feller, Lee (4), Hudson (7), SMITH (8)
Home Runs: Vaughn-N (2), Williams-A
Attendance: 54,674

The National Leaguers entered the last of the ninth with a 5–3 lead and hopes of nailing down their first back-to-back All-Star victories. The American stars had scored their first run in the fourth. The Nationals tied the score in the top of the sixth, but the Americans countered with a run later in the inning. The Nationals' Arky Vaughan then made a bid to be the game's hero, homering in the seventh off Sid Hudson with a man aboard to restore the National lead, and homering again an inning later off Edgar Smith for two more runs.

A double and single by the DiMaggio brothers Joe and Dom brought the Americans a run closer in the eighth, but they still needed two to tie as they faced Claude Passeau in the bottom of the ninth. Two one-out singles and a walk loaded the bases, and a force play at second (that just missed being a game-ending double play) scored Ken Keltner from third. With two men now out and the Americans still down a run, Ted Williams homered on a letter-high fastball against the upper parapet in right for three more runs and another American League victory.

GAME 10
Polo Grounds, New York
July 6, 1942
AL, 3–1

```
AL   300 000 000    3 7 0
NL   000 000 010    1 6 1
```

Pitchers: CHANDLER, Benton (5) vs M.COOPER, Vander Meer (4), Passeau (7), Walters (9)
Home Runs: Boudreau-A, York-A, Owen-N
Attendance: 33,694

Home runs accounted for all the scoring as the American League, in something of a reverse of the 1940 game, scored three times in the top of the first to defeat the Nationals. Lou Boudreau, leading off, hit the game winner off Mort Cooper's second pitch, into the upper deck in left field. A double and two outs later, Rudy York put one over the fence near the short right field foul line for two more runs.

The Americans hit safely only four more times, and scored no more runs, but they already had more than enough, as Spud Chandler and Al Benton combined to shut out the National League stars for seven innings, until Mickey Owen, pinch-hitting for pitcher Claude Passeau in the eighth, hit his only home run of the summer.

This was the second All-Star Game played in the Polo Grounds. It had been Brooklyn's turn to host the game at Ebbets Field, but because the proceeds were destined for the war effort, the site was shifted to the larger stadium. The game might as well have been held in Brooklyn, though, as a pregame rain held attendance to well below the Polo Grounds' capacity.

GAME 11
Shibe Park, Philadelphia
July 13, 1943
AL, 5–3

```
NL   100 000 101    3 10 3
AL   031 010 00X    5 8 1
```

Pitchers: M.COOPER, Vander Meer (3), Sewell (6), Javery (7) vs LEONARD, Newhouser (4), Hughson (7)
Home Runs: Doerr-A, V.DiMaggio-N
Attendance: 31,938

For the first time, the All-Star Game was played at night. And for the only time in All-Star history, no Yankee played—although six had been named to the American League squad. But Yankee Joe McCarthy (serving for the sixth time as American manager) was piqued by criticism that he favored his own players, and retaliated by keeping them all on the bench.

The only DiMaggio in this wartime game was Pittsburgh's Vince, and he provided most of the National League power—batting 3 for 3, with eight total bases and two of his team's three runs. But after the Nationals had jumped to a one-run lead in the first, Bobby Doerr of the Americans homered off Mort Cooper with two aboard in the second to put the American stars ahead. They added to their lead with a run in the third and another in the fifth. DiMaggio scored in the seventh after tripling off Tex Hughson and added a homer against Hughson in the ninth, but his heroics were not enough to overcome the American League's march to its third win in a row, and its eighth in eleven tries.

GAME 12
Forbes Field, Pittsburgh
July 11, 1944
NL, 7–1

```
AL   010 000 000    1 6 3
NL   000 040 21X    7 12 1
```

Pitchers: Borowy, HUGHSON (4), Muncrief (5), Newhouser (7), Newsom (8) vs Walters, RAFFENSBERGER (4), Sewell (6), Tobin (9)
Attendance: 29,589

For the second time the game was played at night, and for the seventh time Joe McCarthy managed the American League team. But this time—unlike Game 11—he let his Yankees play. He started Yankee pitcher Hank Borowy, who not only shut out the Nationals in his three innings but drove in a run in the second to give his team the lead.

But that was all the American stars got. For the first four innings it was enough, but in the fifth a double, four singles, a walk, an error, and a stolen base brought in four National League runs. In the seventh, Whitey Kurowski doubled in two more National runs, and in the eighth a missed third strike, two walks, and a fly ball produced a seventh and final tally.

No home runs were hit in the game, only the second time that had happened in All-Star play. But Phil Cavarretta of the Nationals tripled—and reached base four additional times on a single and three walks for a new All-Star on-base record.

GAME 13
Fenway Park, Boston
July 9, 1946
AL, 12–0

```
NL   000 000 000    0  3  0
AL   200 130 24X   12 14  1
```

Pitchers: PASSEAU, Higbe (4), Blackwell (5), Sewell (8) vs FELLER, Newhouser (4), Kramer (7)
Home Runs: Keller-A, Williams-A (2)
Attendance: 34,906

No All-Star Game was played in 1945 because of restrictions on wartime travel, but when the classic resumed in 1946 the American stars avenged their 1944 loss with the most decisive All-Star victory to date: 12–0. American pitchers Bob Feller, Hal Newhouser, and Jack Kramer combined to hold the National stars to three singles and a walk, as their teammates pounded National pitching for 14 hits, including two doubles and three home runs.

But the game belonged to Ted Williams. Back after three years at war, and playing before his hometown fans, he equaled Phil Cavarretta's 1944 on-base record in spectacular fashion, with one walk, two singles, and two home runs: one a drive into the center field bleachers and the other his first homer ever hit off Rip Sewell's looping "eephus" pitch. He scored the game's first run in the first inning as Charlie Keller followed his walk with a homer, and went on to break an All-Star record by scoring three more times, while driving in a record five runs.

GAME 14
Wrigley Field, Chicago
July 8, 1947
AL, 2–1

```
AL   000 001 100    2  8  0
NL   000 100 000    1  5  1
```

Pitchers: Newhouser, SHEA (4), Masterson (7), Page (8) vs Blackwell, Brecheen (4), SAIN (7), Spahn (8)
Home Runs: Mize-N
Attendance: 41,123

Johnny Mize homered for the National League off rookie Spec Shea in the fourth inning for the game's first run, after three one-hit innings by the two lanky starters, Ewell Blackwell of the Nationals and Hal Newhouser of the Americans. Mize's run remained the only score until the sixth inning, when the American Leaguers tied the game on two singles and a double-play grounder.

Sharp baserunning by Bobby Doerr—plus a little luck—led to the Americans' second run an inning later. Doerr singled, then stole second. He took third when pitcher Johnny Sain's pickoff throw bounced off Doerr's back into the outfield. Pinch hitter Stan Spence then singled Doerr home with what proved to be the game's final—and winning—run. The Nationals put men on first and third in the eighth, but shortstop Lou Boudreau's spectacular stop of a hot grounder and sharp throw to first retired the side and ended the threat.

GAME 15
Sportsman's Park, St. Louis
July 13, 1948
AL, 5–2

```
NL   200 000 000    2  8  0
AL   011 300 00X    5  6  0
```

Pitchers: Branca, SCHMITZ (4), Sain (4), Blackwell (6) vs Masterson, RASCHI (4), Coleman (7)
Home Runs: Musial-N, Evers-A
Attendance: 34,009

Vic Raschi pitched three shutout innings for the American stars and drove in two go-ahead runs with a fourth-inning single as the American League—for the third time since the All-Star Game originated in 1933—won its third classic in a row. The Nationals scored first on Stan Musial's two-run homer in the top of the first. But that was all they got, as starter Walt Masterson settled down and shut out the Nationals through the second and third innings. Raschi then came on for his shutout stint, and Joe Coleman stopped the Nationals without even a hit over the final three innings.

Meanwhile, the Americans scored a run in the second on Hoot Evers's homer, and tied the game with another run in the third on two walks, a double steal, and an outfield fly. Then in the fourth, when two walks and a single had loaded the bases, pitcher Raschi singled in the third and fourth American runs. Joe DiMaggio's pinch-hit fly scored a fifth run. Johnny Sain and Ewell Blackwell shut out the Americans the rest of the way, but the damage had been done.

GAME 16
Ebbets Field, Brooklyn
July 12, 1949
AL, 11–7

```
AL   400 202 300   11 13  1
NL   212 002 000    7 12  5
```

Pitchers: Parnell, TRUCKS (2), Brissie (4), Raschi (7) vs Spahn, NEWCOMBE (2), Munger (5), Bickford (6), Pollet (7), Blackwell (8), Roe (9)
Home Runs: Musial-N, Kiner-N
Attendance: 32,577

Each team scored seven earned runs in this game which saw a total of 25 hits, including seven doubles and two home runs. But two first-inning National League errors let in four unearned American runs to provide the margin for the American League's fourth consecutive All-Star win. Stan Musial and Ralph Kiner each drove in two National runs with homers, but Eddie Joost singled in two runs for the Americans and Joe DiMaggio singled and doubled in three more to lead the American attack. For the second year in a row, Vic Raschi shut out the National stars for three innings, this time holding the American lead over the final third of the game.

The game was notable as the first to include black players: three Dodgers (Jackie Robinson, Roy Campanella, and Don Newcombe) for the National League, and Larry Doby for the American. With the Americans now ahead 12–4, it also marked the farthest extent of American League domination of the midsummer classic.

GAME 17
Comiskey Park, Chicago
July 11, 1950
NL, 4–3

NL	020 000 001 000 01	4 10 0
AL	001 020 000 000 00	3 8 1

Pitchers: Roberts, Newcombe (4), Konstanty (6), Jansen (7), BLACKWELL (12) vs Raschi, Lemon (4), Houtteman (7), Reynolds (10), GRAY (13), Feller (14)
Home Runs: Kiner-N, Schoendienst-N
Attendance: 46,127

For the first time, the All-Star Game went into extra innings, and for the first time the National League won a game as the visiting team. Three pitchers each hurled three innings of shutout ball: Bob Lemon and Allie Reynolds for the American League and Ewell Blackwell (who finished the game and got the win) for the Nationals. But top pitching honors were earned by National Leaguer Larry Jansen, who struck out six and gave up only one hit over *five* shutout innings (7–11).

The National stars scored first with two runs in the second. The Americans came back with one in the third, and tied and took the lead in the fifth on George Kell's run-scoring fly and an RBI single by Ted Williams (who, it was later learned, had broken his left elbow making an off-the-wall catch in the first inning). But in the top of the ninth, Ralph Kiner of the Nationals hit a game-tying homer, and 4½ scoreless innings later Red Schoendienst—on the first pitch of the fourteenth inning—homered off American Ted Gray with what proved to be the game winner.

GAME 18
Briggs Stadium, Detroit
July 10, 1951
NL, 8–3

NL	100 302 110	8 12 1
AL	010 110 000	3 10 2

Pitchers: Roberts, MAGLIE (3), Newcombe (6), Blackwell (9) vs Garver, LOPAT (4), Hutchinson (5), Parnell (8), Lemon (9)
Home Runs: Musial-N, Elliott-N, Wertz-A, Kell-A, Hodges-N, Kiner-N
Attendance: 52,075

In a game moved from Philadelphia to help Detroit celebrate its 250th birthday, hometowners Vic Wertz and George Kell of the Tigers hit solo homers in the fourth and fifth innings to bring the American stars within a run of the Nationals. But they came no closer, as the National Leaguers pulled away for a convincing 8-3 victory.

The Nationals, aided by six innings of shutout pitching (including three by Don Newcombe), produced four home runs of their own to drive in six of their eight runs. With the score tied 1–1 going into the fourth inning, Stan Musial greeted Ed Lopat's first pitch with a shot to the right field upper deck, and Bob Elliott added two more runs later in the inning with a homer to left. Gil Hodges increased the National League lead to 6–3 with a two-run homer in the sixth, and Ralph Kiner concluded the Nationals' scoring with a solo upper-deck shot to left center in the eighth. For the first time in All-Star play, the National League had won two games in a row.

GAME 19
Shibe Park, Philadelphia
July 8, 1952
NL, 3–2

AL	000 20	2 5 0
NL	100 20	3 3 0

Pitchers: Raschi, LEMON (3), Shantz (5) vs Simmons, RUSH (4)
Home Runs: J.Robinson-N, Sauer-N
Attendance: 32,785

No sun shone for this rain-shortened game, but two hometown pitchers did. Curt Simmons of the Phillies held the American stars to one hit as he shut them out over the first three innings. And the Athletics' Bobby Shantz—in the midst of an MVP season—struck out the side in the fifth for the Americans.

But home runs and rain determined the final outcome. Jackie Robinson opened the scoring with a homer off Vic Raschi in the bottom of the first to give the Nationals a 1–0 lead. In the fourth the Americans came back to take the lead briefly with two runs on a double, a walk, and two singles off eventual winner Bob Rush. But in the bottom of the inning, Hank Sauer's home run off Bob Lemon with one aboard returned the lead to the National League. And there it stayed through a scoreless fifth, when the rain, which had fallen throughout the game, at last brought the soggy festivities to the All-Star series' first premature conclusion.

GAME 20
Crosley Field, Cincinnati
July 14, 1953
NL, 5–1

AL	000 000 001	1 5 0
NL	000 020 12X	5 10 0

Pitchers: Pierce, REYNOLDS (4), Garcia (6) Paige (8) vs Roberts, SPAHN (4), Simmons (6), Dickson (8)
Attendance: 30,846

For the first 4½ innings, pitchers for both sides held the opposition scoreless, with one hit each. Then the National Leaguers got to Allie Reynolds for two runs in the bottom of the fifth on a hit batsman, a walk, and two singles.

This proved margin enough for the National League's fourth consecutive victory, as four National pitchers held the Americans to just two hits through eight innings before three singles in the ninth gave the American Leaguers their only run. For good measure, though, the National stars added a run in the seventh, and two more in the eighth (with three singles and a walk off Satchel Paige in his only All-Star appearance).

Enos Slaughter of the Nationals provided much of the game's excitement. With two singles, a walk, and a stolen base, he drove in one run and scored two others, and defensively made a spectacular diving catch in right field. Pee Wee Reese's double in the seventh (scoring Slaughter) was the game's only extra-base hit.

GAME 21
Municipal Stadium, Cleveland
July 13, 1954
AL, 11–9

```
NL   000 520 020    9 14 0
AL   004 121 03X   11 17 1
```

Pitchers: Roberts, Antonelli (4), Spahn (6), Grissom (6), CONLEY (8), Erskine (8) vs Ford, Consuegra (4), Lemon (4), Porterfield (5), Keegan (8), STONE (8), Trucks (9)
Home Runs: Rosen-A (2), Boone-A, Kluszewski-N, Bell-N, Doby-A
Attendance: 68,751

American starter Whitey Ford gave up only one hit in three shutout innings, and National starter Robin Roberts shut out the American stars through two. But in the bottom of the third Al Rosen tagged Roberts for a three-run homer, and Ray Boone followed with a solo shot. By the end of the game new All-Star records had been set for hits (31), runs (20), and pitchers used (13), and the record of 6 home runs had been equaled.

The Nationals topped the American four-run third with five straight hits off Sandy Consuegra in the fourth, for five runs. The Americans tied the game with a run in their half of the fourth, but Ted Kluszewski homered in the fifth for two more National League runs. In the bottom of the fifth, Rosen homered again, for two, to bring the Americans even again.

A run in the sixth put the Americans ahead, but Gus Bell's two-run blast in the eighth returned the Nationals to the top by one. They were threatening to lengthen that lead when Dean Stone entered the contest in relief of Bob Keegan with two out and Red Schoendienst on third. Before Stone's first delivery, Schoendienst broke for home and was tagged out, setting the stage for Stone to become the winning pitcher without making a pitch. American Larry Doby tied it up again later in the eighth with a home run, and Nellie Fox drove in the game's final two runs a few batters later with a bases-loaded single.

In the ninth, the Nationals' Stan Musial blasted two over the fence—both foul—with a man aboard. But Virgil Trucks retired him and Gil Hodges, who followed, to preserve the American League's first victory in five games.

GAME 22
County Stadium, Milwaukee
July 12, 1955
NL, 6–5

```
AL   400 001 000 000    5 10 2
NL   000 000 230 001    6 13 1
```

Pitchers: Pierce, Wynn (4), Ford (7), SULLIVAN (8) vs Roberts, Haddix (4), Newcombe (7), Jones (8), Nuxhall (8), CONLEY (12)
Home Runs: Mantle-A, Musial-N
Attendance: 45,314

Down 5–0 in the seventh inning, the National Leaguers came back to tie the game and send it into extra innings. The Americans attacked early, scoring four runs off Robin Roberts (three of them on Mickey Mantle's home run to center) before the game's first out had been recorded. They added a fifth run in the sixth inning. Meanwhile, pitchers Billy Pierce and Early Wynn were shutting the Nationals down on four hits.

In the seventh, though, two singles, a walk, and an American error gave the Nationals two runs, and in the eighth, four two-out singles and another error tied the game. Joe Nuxhall for the Nationals and the Americans' Frank Sullivan prevented further scoring through the eleventh. In the top of the twelfth, Gene Conley replaced Nuxhall and struck out the side: Al Kaline, Mickey Vernon, and Al Rosen. Sullivan returned for the Americans to face Stan Musial in the bottom of the twelfth. Musial hit the first pitch—a fastball—over the screen in right and the game was over.

GAME 23
Griffith Stadium, Washington
July 10, 1956
NL, 7–3

```
NL   001 211 200    7 11 0
AL   000 003 000    3 11 0
```

Pitchers: FRIEND, Spahn (4), Antonelli (6) vs PIERCE, Ford (4), Wilson (5), Brewer (6), Score (8), Wynn (9)
Home Runs: Mays-N, Williams-A, Mantle-A, Musial-N
Attendance: 28,843

Four of the game's greatest sluggers—Willie Mays, Stan Musial, Ted Williams, and Mickey Mantle—hit home runs, three of them off two of the game's greatest pitchers—Whitey Ford and Warren Spahn. But the star of the game was National League third baseman Ken Boyer, who went 3 for 5, scoring one run and driving in another, while making three spectacular diving and leaping plays in the field.

The National stars scored five times—including twice in the fourth on Mays's homer off Ford—before the Americans put a run on the board. But in the bottom of the sixth, Williams homered for two runs off Spahn, and Mantle followed him with another homer to bring the Americans within two. But that was the end of their scoring, as Johnny Antonelli relieved Spahn to stop the American stars the rest of the way. The Nationals scored twice more in the seventh—one of the runs coming on Musial's homer—ensuring them a comfortable 7–3 victory.

GAME 24
Sportsman's Park, St. Louis
July 9, 1957
AL, 6–5

```
AL   020 001 003    6 10 0
NL   000 000 203    5  9 1
```

Pitchers: BUNNING, Loes (4), Wynn (7), Pierce (7), Mossi (9), Grim (9) vs SIMMONS, Burdette (2), Sanford (6), Jackson (7), Labine (9)
Attendance: 30,693

Cincinnati fans stuffed the ballot boxes and elected Reds to start everywhere but first base. Commissioner Ford Frick removed two elected starters, but left five Reds in the lineup. They could not bring the National League the victory, though.

The Americans scored twice in the second on singles and walks to take a lead they held to the finish. Although reliever Lew Burdette—after walking in the second run—stopped the American stars through the fifth, Jim Bunning and Billy Loes were combining to keep the Nationals from scoring through the first six innings. The Americans, meanwhile, added a third run in the top of the sixth on a double, a wild pitch, and a single.

The Nationals scored their first two in the seventh, on two singles and a double, to draw within a run of a tie. But in the top of the ninth the Americans combined two singles, an error, a sacrifice bunt, and Minnie Minoso's pinch double for three more runs. They needed them all, for the Nationals responded in their half of the ninth with three runs of their own on a blend of walks, hits (including Willie Mays's triple), and a wild pitch. With two out and a runner at second, Gil Hodges lined one deep to left center. But Minoso, now in left field, snared the drive on the run to end the game.

GAME 25
Memorial Stadium, Baltimore
July 8, 1958
AL, 4–3

```
NL   210 000 000   3 4 2
AL   110 011 00X   4 9 2
```
Pitchers: Spahn, FRIEND (4), Jackson (6), Farrell (7) vs Turley, Narleski (2), WYNN (6), O'Dell (7)
Attendance: 48,829

Although American League pitchers held the National Leaguers to only four hits (all singles), the Nationals took a quick lead, and held it for half the game before they were overtaken. Willie Mays and Stan Musial singled in the top of the first, both scoring as American starter Bob Turley proceeded to give up a sacrifice fly, hit a batter, walk a man, and unload a wild pitch.

The Americans came back with one run in their half of the first, but the Nationals drove Turley out with their third run as Mays (who had reached on a fielder's choice) worked his way around the bases on a steal, an error, and Bob Skinner's single. Once again the Americans answered with a run, but they didn't tie the game until Mickey Vernon scored on a bases-loaded ground out in the fifth. An inning later they took the lead when pinch hitter Gil McDougald singled home Frank Malzone.

Billy O'Dell set down the Nationals in order over the final three innings to preserve the lead and give the American Leaguers their second consecutive victory.

GAME 26
Forbes Field, Pittsburgh
July 7, 1959
NL, 5–4

```
AL   000 100 030   4 8 0
NL   100 000 22X   5 9 1
```
Pitchers: Wynn, Duren (4), Bunning (7), FORD (8), Daley (8) vs Drysdale, Burdette (4), Face (7), ANTONELLI (8), Elston (9)
Home Runs: Mathews-N, Kaline-A
Attendance: 35,277

For the third year in a row, the game was decided by one run, with the National League celebrating the city of Pittsburgh's bicentennial by breaking the American League's win streak at two.

Eddie Mathews homered for the Nationals in the bottom of the first for the only run in the first three innings, as Don Drysdale stopped the Americans without a hit or walk, fanning four. Al Kaline tied the game in the top of the fourth with an American home run for the only score of the middle three innings, as Ryne Duren one-hit the Nationals, like Drysdale striking out four.

In the last of the seventh, though, a double and two singles off Jim Bunning put the Nationals ahead by two runs. The NL lead lasted only briefly, however, as the Americans moved back into the lead with three runs in the eighth off Roy Face, with two singles, a walk, and a double after Face had retired the first two men. But in their half of the eighth the Nationals hit on Whitey Ford, tying the game with a single-sacrifice-single, and scoring the game winner on Willie Mays's triple to center.

GAME 27
Memorial Coliseum, Los Angeles
August 3, 1959
AL, 5–3

```
AL   012 000 110   5 6 0
NL   100 010 100   3 6 3
```
Pitchers: WALKER, Wynn (4), Wilhelm, (6), O'Dell (7), McLish (8) vs DRYSDALE, Conley (4), Jones (6), Face (8)
Home Runs: Malzone-A, Berra-A, F. Robinson-N, Gilliam-N, Colavito-A
Attendance: 55,105

To raise extra money for the players' pension fund and other causes, a second All-Star Game was scheduled for 1959, the first ever to be played in August, and the first on the West Coast. The American stars avenged their earlier defeat with a 5–3 win, out-homering the Nationals three to two.

The National Leaguers scored first on a first-inning double and sacrifice fly, but Frank Malzone tied the score with the game's first home run. Yogi Berra homered an inning later with one on for a 3–1 American lead, but Frank Robinson brought the Nationals back to within one with his homer in the fifth. The Americans replaced that run in the top of the seventh on a walk, two errors, and a single, but Junior Gilliam countered with a home run in the last of the inning. Rocky Colavito scored the game's final run for the Americans in the eighth with the game's final homer.

Don Drysdale, the pitching standout of the July game, struck out five this time, but also walked three and gave up three runs on homers to take the loss.

GAME 28
Municipal Stadium, Kansas City
July 11, 1960
NL, 5–3

```
NL   311 000 000   5 12 4
AL   000 001 020   3  6 1
```
Pitchers: FRIEND, McCormick (4), Face (6), Buhl (8), Law (9) vs MONBOUQUETTE, Estrada (3), Coates (4), Bell (6), Lary (8), Daley (9)
Home Runs: Banks-N, Crandall-N, Kaline-A
Attendance: 30,619

The day was hot—the temperature broke 100—and so were the National League bats. Willie Mays went 3 for 4, including a leadoff triple and a double; Ernie Banks homered and doubled; Del Crandall homered and singled; and Joe Adcock doubled and singled for three-fourths of the Nationals' 12 hits as the National League scored five unanswered runs in the first three innings to take an unbeatable lead. Starter Bob Friend, meanwhile, blanked the Americans on one hit through three innings and Mike McCormick held them scoreless for two more before yielding the first American run in the sixth on Nellie Fox's bases-loaded single. Roy Face then came on to douse the fire, getting Luis Aparicio to ground into a double play.

Four American League pitchers stopped the National stars after the third inning, and Al Kaline homered for two more American runs in the eighth. In the ninth the Americans put men on first and second with one away. But their comeback fell short, as Vern Law came on to retire Brooks Robinson and Harvey Kuenn and preserve the National victory.

GAME 29
Yankee Stadium, New York
July 13, 1960
NL, 6–0

NL	021	000	102	6	10	0
AL	000	000	000	0	8	0

Pitchers: LAW, Podres (3), S.Williams (5), Jackson (7), Henry (8), McDaniel (9) vs FORD, Wynn (4), Staley (6), Lary (8), Bell (9)
Home Runs: Mathews-N, Mays-N, Musial-N, Boyer-N
Attendance: 38,362

Only two days after the first All-Star Game, the squads met a second time before fewer than 39,000 fans in capacious Yankee Stadium. It was no contest. Vern Law, who had completed and saved the first game, started and won this one. His two shutout innings set the pace for the five National pitchers who followed him to fashion the first National League shutout in twenty years. The American stars got only two fewer hits than the Nationals (8 to 10), but only one was for extra bases, whereas four of the National League hits were home runs.

Eddie Mathews began the scoring with a two-run homer in the second, and Willie Mays (on his way to a second straight 3-for-4 game) homered for the third National run an inning later. No one scored through the three middle innings, but in the seventh Stan Musial broke his own record with his sixth All-Star homer—a mighty shot three tiers up in right—and in the ninth Ken Boyer completed the rout with a two-run shot to left.

GAME 30
Candlestick Park, San Francisco
July 11, 1961
NL, 5–4

AL	000	001	002	1	4	4	2
NL	010	100	010	2	5	11	5

Pitchers: Ford, Lary (4), Donovan (4), Bunning (6), Fornieles (8), WILHELM (8) vs Spahn, Purkey (4), McCormick (6), Face (9), Koufax (9), MILLER (9)
Home Runs: Killebrew-A, Altman-N
Attendance: 44,115

National League pitchers began the game where they had left off the year before. For five innings Warren Spahn and Bob Purkey shut out the American stars without a hit or base on balls. In the sixth, Harmon Killebrew homered off Mike Mc-Cormick to end the American drought, but it was the only hit Mc-Cormick yielded through the eighth.

Meanwhile, the Nationals had taken a 3–1 lead with runs in the second and fourth innings and George Altman's homer in the eighth. But in the top of the ninth, Candlestick's notorious winds helped put the Americans back in the game. Their second and third hits of the game brought in one run, and their fourth (and last) hit put another man on base. The tying run came in when the wind first of all blew pitcher Stu Miller off the mound for a balk to advance the runners, and then twisted a grounder out of third baseman Ken Boyer's grasp for a run-scoring error. In the tenth, the wind may have contributed to the Americans' go-ahead run as Boyer's throw to first sailed into the outfield, allowing Nellie Fox (who had walked) to score from first.

But in the last of the tenth the wind finally came to the aid of the Nationals, rendering useless the famous knuckleball of American reliever Hoyt Wilhelm, who gave up the tying run on hits by Hank Aaron and Willie Mays and lost the game when Roberto Clemente singled in Mays from second.

GAME 31
Fenway Park, Boston
July 31, 1961
Tie, 1–1

NL	000	001	000	1	5	1
AL	100	000	000	1	4	0

Pitchers: Purkey, Mahaffey (3), Koufax (5), Miller (7) vs Bunning, Schwall (4), Pascual (7)
Home Runs: Colavito-A
Attendance: 31,851

In the second All-Star Game of 1961, the weather again played a crucial role, as heavy rain at the end of the ninth inning forced the first (and, so far, only) All-Star tie.

Rocky Colavito's home run for the Americans in the first inning turned out to be his squad's only run, as four National League pitchers combined to shut out the American stars on only three singles the rest of the way. The American League pitching was just as effective, with starter Jim Bunning and finisher Camilo Pascual each pitching three no-hit innings. Don Schwall, who pitched the middle three innings, gave up all five National League hits and the Nationals' one run. But even that might have been prevented.

In the sixth, with two on and two out, American shortstop Luis Aparicio waited for a slow grounder, failing to get the ball in time to throw the batter out and end the inning. The Nationals scored on the next play, Bill White's hot ground single up the middle, which Aparicio stopped brilliantly to prevent more than one run from scoring, but which did drive in the game's tying—and final—run.

GAME 32
D.C. Stadium, Washington
July 10, 1962
NL, 3–1

NL	000	002	010	3	8	0
AL	000	001	000	1	4	0

Pitchers: Drysdale, MARICHAL (4), Purkey (6), Shaw (8) vs Bunning, PASCUAL (4), Donovan (7), Pappas (9)
Attendance: 45,480

The stadium was new, President Kennedy threw out the first ball, and starters Don Drysdale of the Nationals and Jim Bunning of the Americans both pitched three innings of one-hit shutout ball. But Maury Wills stole the show. Entering the game in the sixth inning to run for forty-one-year-old Stan Musial, who had singled, Wills stole second, then scored on Dick Groat's single up the middle for the game's first run. Another single, a long fly out, and a ground out scored Groat with the second (and, as it turned out, winning) run.

Two singles and a fly out by Roger Maris brought in an American run in the bottom of the sixth off Bob Purkey. But that was all they got, as Purkey and Bob Shaw one-hit the American stars through the final three innings.

In the eighth inning Wills manufactured an insurance run for the Nationals. On first with a leadoff single, he somehow reached third on Jim Davenport's single to short left, racing from second to third as left fielder Rocky Colavito threw in to second. He scored after tagging on a foul out to right.

GAME 33
Wrigley Field, Chicago
July 30, 1962
AL, 9–4

AL	001 201 302	9 10 0
NL	010 000 111	4 10 4

Pitchers: Stenhouse, HERBERT (3), Aguirre (6), Pappas (9) vs Podres, MAHAFFEY (3), Gibson (5), Farrell (7), Marichal (8)
Home Runs: Runnels-A, Wagner-A. Colavito-A, Roseboro-N
Attendance: 38,359

With this second game of 1962, the leagues ended their four-year experiment of playing two All-Star games a year. The Americans out-homered the Nationals to spoil the National League's attempt to even the series at 16 wins apiece. But no matter—the American stars would win only once again in the next twenty years.

The National stars scored first on a double and single in the second, but Pete Runnels evened the score in the third with a solo homer, and Leon Wagner put the Americans ahead with a two-run shot an inning later. After Tom Tresh doubled home a fourth American run in the sixth, Rocky Colavito put the game out of reach with a three-run blast in the seventh.

The Nationals tried to come back with runs in the seventh and eighth, but the Americans neutralized them with two more of their own in the ninth (on two errors, two Juan Marichal wild pitches, a double, and a long fly out). With the score now 9–3, John Roseboro's solo homer in the last of the ninth put the Nationals in the home-run column, but that was all.

GAME 34
Municipal Stadium, Cleveland
July 9, 1963
NL, 5–3

NL	012 010 010	5 6 0
AL	012 000 000	3 11 1

Pitchers: O'Toole, JACKSON (3), Culp (5), Woodeshick (6), Drysdale (8) vs McBride, BUNNING (4), Bouton (6), Pizarro (7), Radatz (8)
Attendance: 44,160

Willie Mays sparked the National League to victory with his baserunning and timely hitting. Although he had only one hit—a single—he scored two runs and drove in two others in the Nationals' 5–3 win.

The National stars scored first when Mays walked in the second inning, stole second, and came in on a single by Dick Groat. The Americans tied the game in the last of the second, but in the top of the third Mays singled in one run, stole second again, and scored his second run on Ed Bailey's single.

Once again the Americans came back in the bottom of the third to tie the game on Albie Pearson's double, followed by two singles sandwiched around an infield out. But these were their last runs, as four National pitchers shut them out on four singles the rest of the way. Meanwhile, Mays drove in what proved to be the winning run with a ground out in the fifth. In the eighth the Nationals scored a final run when Ron Santo singled home Bill White, who had singled and stolen second.

GAME 35
Shea Stadium, New York
July 7, 1964
NL, 7–4

AL	100 002 100	4 9 1
NL	000 210 004	7 8 0

Pitchers: Chance, Wyatt (4), Pascual (5), RADATZ (7) vs Drysdale, Bunning (4), Short (6), Farrell (7), MARICHAL (9)
Home Runs: B.Williams-N, Boyer-N, Callison-N
Attendance: 50,850

A new stadium in the midst of a World's Fair was the venue for this game in which the National League at last drew even with the American at 17 wins apiece.

The American stars jumped into the lead with an unearned run in the first, but the Nationals (after Dean Chance had shut them out through three innings) overtook the Americans in the fourth, on home runs by Billy Williams and Ken Boyer, and Dick Groat doubled in a third run in the fifth. In the top of the sixth the Americans tied the score when Brooks Robinson tripled in a pair, and took the lead again an inning later on a sacrifice fly that barely scored Elston Howard ahead of Willie Mays's throw from center.

The Americans held their slim lead into the bottom of the ninth. But Mays walked (after fouling off five third strikes), stole second, and scored the tying run on a single to short right and an errant throw home. One intentional walk and two outs later, Johnny Callison hit Dick Radatz's fastball over the fence in right to win the game.

GAME 36
Metropolitan Stadium, Bloomington, Minnesota
July 13, 1965
NL, 6–5

NL	320 000 100	6 11 0
AL	000 140 000	5 8 0

Pitchers: Marichal, Maloney (4), Drysdale (5), KOUFAX (6), Farrell (7), Gibson (8) vs Pappas, Grant (2), Richert (4), McDOWELL (6), Fisher (8)
Home Runs: Mays-N, Torre-N, Stargell-N, McAuliffe-A, Killebrew-A
Attendance: 46,706

For a while it looked as though the Nationals would run away with the game. Willie Mays led off with a home run in the first, and Joe Torre added two runs with a homer later in the inning. In the second Willie Stargell homered for two more runs to make the score 5–0. National starter Juan Marichal stopped the Americans on one hit through three innings.

But the American stars battled back. A single, a walk, and another single off Marichal's replacement, Jim Maloney, brought in one run in the fourth. Maloney retired the first two men in the fifth, but then he gave up a walk followed by a home run to Dick McAuliffe, and a scratch single followed by a Harmon Killebrew homer—and the score was tied at 5–5.

Only one more run was scored. In the seventh, Willie Mays, who had walked and gone to third on Hank Aaron's single, scored on Ron Santo's infield hit to short. The Nationals held off American threats in the eighth and ninth to take the All-Star series lead for the first time.

GAME 37
Busch Memorial Stadium, St. Louis
July 12, 1966
NL, 2–1

```
AL   010 000 000 0   1 6 0
NL   000 100 000 1   2 6 0
```

Pitchers: McLain, Kaat (4), Stottlemyre (6), Siebert (8), RICHERT (10) vs Koufax, Bunning (4), Marichal (6), G.PERRY (9)
Attendance: 49,936

The celebration of another new stadium and the city's bicentennial—and a temperature of 106 Fahrenheit—greeted participants in the 1966 classic. Pitching dominated: seven pitchers hurled two innings or more each of shutout ball. American starter Denny McLain threw three perfect innings, but the National League's Sandy Koufax gave the Americans a run in the second when he let loose a wild pitch after Brooks Robinson had tripled.

The Nationals tied the score in the fourth with three singles off Jim Kaat, but that ended the scoring for both sides through the regulation nine innings. In the top of the tenth, Gaylord Perry stopped the American stars. But in the last half of the inning, National Leaguer Tim McCarver singled off Pete Richert, was sacrified to second, and came across with the winning run on Maury Wills's single to right.

GAME 38
Anaheim Stadium, Anaheim, California
July 11, 1967
NL, 2–1

```
NL   010 000 000 000 001   2 9 0
AL   000 001 000 000 000   1 8 0
```

Pitchers: Marichal, Jenkins (4), Gibson (7), Short (9), Cuellar (11), DRYSDALE (13), Seaver (15) vs Chance, McGlothlin (4), Peters (6), Downing (9), HUNTER (11)
Home Runs: Allen-N, B.Robinson-A, Perez-N
Attendance: 46,309

This was a game of strikeouts, home runs, and extra innings. Every one of the twelve pitchers used in the game struck out at least one batter. American Leaguers Gary Peters (who pitched three perfect middle innings) and Catfish Hunter struck out four apiece, while Ferguson Jenkins of the Nationals tied the All-Star record with six. The game total of 30 strikeouts shattered the previous record of 20 set in 1955.

Apart from the splendid pitching, three home runs provided the only excitement—and the only scoring—in this longest All-Star Game. Richie Allen of the Nationals scored first, homering to center off Dean Chance in the second inning. The Americans' Brooks Robinson tied the score in the sixth with a shot off Jenkins. And 8½ innings later, in the top of the fifteenth, National Leaguer Tony Perez homered off Hunter for the game's third and final run. Tom Seaver set down the Americans in the bottom of the fifteenth, and the game—after a record 3 hours and 41 minutes—was history.

GAME 39
Astrodome, Houston
July 9, 1968
NL, 1–0

```
AL   000 000 000   0 3 1
NL   100 000 00X   1 5 0
```

Pitchers: TIANT, Odom (3), McLain (5), McDowell (7), Stottlemyre (8), John (8) vs DRYSDALE, Marichal (4), Carlton (6), Seaver (7), Reed (9), Koosman (9)
Attendance: 48,321

This game could be described by what was missing: fresh air and real grass (it was the first All-Star Game held indoors), hitting (the eight hits were a new low for a nine-inning All-Star Game), and earned runs (the game's only run came with the help of an error). In fact, if it weren't for thirty-seven-year-old Willie Mays, the game might not have had any runs at all. Starting only because of an injury to Pete Rose, National Leaguer Mays led off the bottom of the first with a single, and took second when first baseman Harmon Killebrew mishandled pitcher Luis Tiant's pickoff throw for an error. Mays took third as the rattled Tiant threw a wild pitch to walk Curt Flood, and scored when Willie McCovey grounded into a double play.

The pitching on both sides was superb, but the National Leaguers shone especially bright. Tom Seaver gave up two of the Americans' three hits (all of which were doubles), but struck out five in his two innings. Juan Marichal hurled two perfect innings, fanning three. And none of the six National pitchers walked a man. One American, Killebrew, couldn't walk. Stretching for a throw at first, the slugger tore a hamstring and missed the next two months, the most serious All-Star Game casualty since Ted Williams's broken elbow 18 years earlier.

GAME 40
R.F.K. Memorial Stadium, Washington, D.C.
July 23, 1969
NL, 9–3

```
NL   125 100 000   9 11 0
AL   011 100 000   3 6 2
```

Pitchers: CARLTON, Gibson (4), Singer (5), Koosman (7), Dierker (8), P.Niekro (9) vs STOTTLEMYRE, Odom (3), Knowles (3), McLain (4), McNally (5), McDowell (7), Culp (9)
Home Runs: Bench-N, Howard-A, McCovey-N (2), Freehan-A
Attendance: 45,259

After four one-run victories in a row, the National Leaguers finally broke loose, massing 10 of their 11 hits in the first four innings for nine runs and a crushing win. Scoring an unearned run in the first on a dropped outfield fly, and two in the second on Johnny Bench's home run, the Nationals erupted in the third for five runs off Blue Moon Odom before two outs had been recorded. Willie McCovey's two-run homer began the third-inning scoring, and an error, single, and two doubles added three more runs before Odom was mercifully relieved. McCovey homered again in the fourth for the Nationals' final tally.

The American bats were not wholly silent, but the solo homers by Frank Howard and Bill Freehan in the second and third, and a third run in the fourth, couldn't counter the Nationals' attack.

The final five innings of the game were as quiet as the opening four had been noisy. No runs scored, and the two teams together managed only three hits.

GAME 41
Riverfront Stadium, Cincinnati
July 14, 1970
NL, 5–4

AL	000 001 120 000	4	12 0
NL	000 000 103 001	5	10 0

Pitchers: Palmer, McDowell (4), J.Perry (7), Hunter (9), Peterson (9), Stottlemyre (9), WRIGHT (11) vs Seaver, Merritt (4), G.Perry (6), Gibson (8), OSTEEN (10)
Home Runs: Dietz-N
Attendance: 51,838

In a new stadium, opened only two weeks earlier, no one scored for the first five innings, as Jim Palmer and Sam McDowell of the Americans and Tom Seaver and Jim Merritt of the Nationals held the opposition to two hits per team. The Americans finally scored a run in the sixth, and another in the seventh. The Nationals got one back in the last of the seventh, but the Americans increased their lead to 4–1 in the eighth when Brooks Robinson tripled home two baserunners.

Fans had already begun to leave the park when the Nationals' Dick Dietz homered off Catfish Hunter to lead off the last of the ninth. Two pitchers, three singles, and a sacrifice fly later, the game was tied and headed for extra innings. Claude Osteen held the Americans scoreless from the tenth through the twelfth, and the Nationals also failed to score in the tenth and eleventh. But in the last of the twelfth, with two out, Pete Rose, Billy Grabarkewitz, and Jim Hickman singled. Hometowner Rose, racing home from second on Hickman's hit, crashed into catcher Ray Fosse with a force that injured both players and still provokes controversy—but which also gave the National League its eighth straight victory.

GAME 42
Tiger Stadium, Detroit
July 13, 1971
AL, 6–4

NL	021 000 010	4	5 0
AL	004 002 00X	6	7 0

Pitchers: ELLIS, Marichal (4), Jenkins (6), Wilson (7) vs BLUE, Palmer (4), Cuellar (6), Lolich (8)
Home Runs: Bench-N, Aaron-N, Jackson-A, F.Robinson-A, Killebrew-A, Clemente-N
Attendance: 53,559

With an assist from a favorable wind, six all-time greats homered to account for all the scoring as the American League broke its eight-game All-Star drought with a 6–4 victory. Johnny Bench put the Nationals in front with a two-run homer in the second inning off Vida Blue, and Hank Aaron—with his first All-Star home run—added a third run off Blue an inning later. But the Americans, shut out by Dock Ellis through the first two innings, rocked him in the bottom of the third as Reggie Jackson and Frank Robinson wrested the lead from the Nationals with a pair of two-run homers. (Robinson's made him the first player to hit an All-Star home run for both leagues.)

Ferguson Jenkins yielded the game's fifth homer, Harmon Killebrew's two-run shot for the Americans in the sixth. Roberto Clemente brought the Nationals a run closer with his solo homer off Mickey Lolich in the eighth, but that ended the team's scoring, and (for a year, anyway) the National League's All-Star stranglehold.

GAME 43
Atlanta-Fulton County Stadium, Atlanta
July 25, 1972
NL, 4–3

AL	001 000 020 0	3	6 0
NL	000 002 001 1	4	8 0

Pitchers: Palmer, Lolich (4), G.Perry (6), Wood (8), McNALLY (10) vs Gibson, Blass (3), Sutton (4), Carlton (6), Stoneman (7), McGRAW (9)
Home Runs: Aaron-N, Rojas-A
Attendance: 53,107

The American Leaguers tried to extend their All-Star win streak to two games, and for a time it looked as though they might do it. In the third, they scored the only run of the first half of the game as Jim Palmer and Mickey Lolich held the Nationals to two hits through the first five innings. In the sixth Hank Aaron thrilled the hometown crowd with a two-run homer deep to left to shift the lead to the National League. But Cookie Rojas restored the American lead with his own two-run shot in the eighth.

The Americans held their lead into the bottom of the ninth, but after two singles and a force out, the score was tied. Tug McGraw set down the American stars in order in the tenth, but American reliever Dave McNally was not so fortunate. He walked leadoff batter Nate Colbert, who was sacrificed to second. Joe Morgan then sent the American Leaguers back into the ranks of losers with a sharp RBI single to right center. His single also gave the Nationals their seventh win in seven extra-inning games.

GAME 44
Royals Stadium, Kansas City
July 24, 1973
NL, 7–1

NL	002 122 000	7	10 0
AL	010 000 000	1	5 0

Pitchers: WISE, Osteen (3), Sutton (5), Twitchell (6), Giusti (7), Seaver (8), Brewer (9) vs Hunter, Holtzman (2), BLYLEVEN (3), Singer (4), Ryan (6), Lyle (8), Fingers (9)
Home Runs: Bench-N, Bonds-N, W.Davis-N
Attendance: 40,849

Once again a new stadium was chosen to host the All-Star Game, and once again the National League emerged victorious. The Americans scored first, with a run in the second when Reggie Jackson scored from second on a single after doubling off the center field wall. But that was the beginning and end of their offense, as six National pitchers shut them out on three hits the rest of the way.

Meanwhile the National League hitters came to life, producing seven runs in four innings. Two walks and two singles in the third brought in two runs, and Johnny Bench's homer in the fourth made the score 3–1. In the fifth, Bobby Bonds—in the midst of his finest season—homered for two more National runs. And in the sixth, Willie Davis's home run completed the game's scoring, bringing in the Nationals' sixth and seventh runs.

The final third of the game was anticlimactic, as only two hits were made after the sixth inning. But Bonds brought the crowd to life briefly in the seventh, stretching one of those hits into a double with some audacious baserunning (ensuring his selection as the game's MVP).

GAME 45
Three Rivers Stadium, Pittsburgh
July 23, 1974
NL, 7–2

AL	002 000 000	2 4 1
NL	010 210 12X	7 10 1

Pitchers: G.Perry, TIANT (4), Hunter (6), Fingers (8) vs Messersmith, BRETT (4), Matlack (6), McGlothen (7), Marshall (8)
Home Runs: R.Smith-N
Attendance: 50,706

Steve Garvey, who was elected to the National League starting lineup on write-in votes (his name was omitted from the fans' All-Star ballot), sparked the Nationals to yet another convincing win over the hapless American stars. After singling in the second inning, he scored the game's first run on Ron Cey's double.

The Americans took the lead with two runs in the top of the third, capitalizing on two walks and an error sandwiched between Thurman Munson's leadoff double and Dick Allen's single. They might have scored more had not Garvey snared Bobby Murcer's hot grounder for an assist on the third out.

Garvey doubled in the tying run in the fourth, and Cey's RBI ground out restored the Nationals' lead. Lou Brock added a run in the fifth with a single and some inspired baserunning, and Reggie Smith homered for another in the seventh. Don Kessinger's triple and a wild pitch by Rollie Fingers in the eighth contributed to two final National League runs.

GAME 46
County Stadium, Milwaukee
July 15, 1975
NL, 6–3

NL	021 000 003	6 13 1
AL	000 003 000	3 10 1

Pitchers: Reuss, Sutton (4), Seaver (6), MATLACK (7), R.Jones (9) vs Blue, Busby (3), Kaat (5), HUNTER (7), Gossage (9)
Home Runs: Garvey-N, Wynn-N, Yastrzemski-A
Attendance: 51,480

When National stars Steve Garvey and Jim Wynn led off the second with back-to-back homers and their teammates added another run in the third, it looked as if the National League might be on its way to another easy win. But the American pitchers shut down the National League offense for the next five innings, and Carl Yastrzemski made a contest of it with a three-run homer in the sixth off Tom Seaver to tie the score.

In the top of the ninth, though, the Americans all but gave the game away. Left fielder Claudell Washington dropped a fly on the run (it was scored a hit) and misplayed a line drive that went for a double. Goose Gossage came in to relieve Catfish Hunter on the mound and hit the next batter to load the bases. Bill Madlock then drove in two of the baserunners with a single through the drawn-in infield, and Pete Rose knocked in the third run of the inning with a sacrifice fly.

Randy Jones set the Americans down in order in the bottom of the ninth, and—voilà!—the National League had won again.

GAME 47
Veterans Stadium, Philadelphia
July 13, 1976
NL, 7–1

AL	000 100 000	1 5 0
NL	202 000 03X	7 10 0

Pitchers: FIDRYCH, Hunter (3), Tiant (5), Tanana (7) vs R.JONES, Seaver (4), Montefusco (6), Rhoden (8), K.Forsch (9)
Home Runs: Foster-N, Lynn-A, Cedeno-N
Attendance: 63,974

Tom Seaver gave up a home run to Fred Lynn in the fourth inning, but that was the Americans' only score as the Nationals held the American stars to five hits while celebrating the nation's bicentennial with ten hits and seven runs.

Rookie standout Mark Fidrych was chosen to start for the Americans and was promptly rapped for two runs. Pete Rose led off with a single and was tripled home by Steve Garvey, who scored himself on a ground out. The Nationals doubled their score in the third inning as George Foster tagged Catfish Hunter for two runs with a mighty home run to left center, and capped their assault with three more in the eighth off Frank Tanana, including a two-run homer by Cesar Cedeno.

The fans had elected five members of Cincinnati's "big red machine" to the National League starting lineup, and Sparky Anderson, the Reds' and National squad's manager, added two more. They provided the bulk of the Nationals' offense, with seven hits, four RBI, and four runs scored.

GAME 48
Yankee Stadium, New York
July 19, 1977
NL, 7–5

NL	401 000 020	7 9 1
AL	000 002 102	5 8 0

Pitchers: SUTTON, Lavelle (4), Seaver (6), R.Reuschel (8), Gossage (9) vs PALMER, Kern (3), Eckersley (4), LaRoche (6), Campbell (7), Lyle (8)
Home Runs: Morgan-N, Luzinski-N, Garvey-N, Scott-A
Attendance: 56,683

The Nationals' Joe Morgan homered off Jim Palmer to open the game, and before Palmer escaped the first inning three more National Leaguers had crossed the plate on a single, double, and Greg Luzinski's homer. Palmer got through the second inning without further damage, but before he was relieved in the third Steve Garvey had homered to give the Nationals a 5–0 lead.

The Americans fought back against Tom Seaver in the sixth and seventh. Seaver retired two in the sixth, but then gave up two singles, and two runs as Richie Zisk doubled the runners home. Two more singles in the seventh produced a third American run.

But the Nationals—assisted by pitcher Sparky Lyle's wild pitch and hit batsman—put a sixth and seventh run on the board in the eighth with a double and single. The Americans added two final runs of their own in the bottom of the ninth on George Scott's homer off Goose Gossage, but fell short of victory once again.

GAME 49
San Diego Stadium,
July 11, 1978
NL, 7–3

AL	201 000 000	3 8 1
NL	003 000 04X	7 10 0

Pitchers: Palmer, Keough (3), Sorensen (4), Kern (7), Guidry (7), GOSSAGE (8) vs Blue, Rogers (4), Fingers (6), SUTTER (8), P. Niekro (9)
Attendance: 51,549

Rod Carew led off both the first and third innings with triples—an All-Star record— scoring both times as the Americans took a 3–0 lead into the bottom of the third. But then Jim Palmer, who had shut the Nationals out on one hit through the first two innings, lost his touch. After yielding a leadoff single, he retired two batters, but then issued three walks to force in a run, and when Steve Garvey singled past the shortstop two more runs scored to tie the game.

No one scored through the next 4½ innings, with Larry Sorensen turning in the game's top pitching performance as he shut the Nationals out on one hit through the three middle innings. But in the last of the eighth, Goose Gossage (the National League closer the previous year) took the mound this year for the Americans. Garvey greeted him with a leadoff triple and scored what proved to be the winning run on a wild pitch. A walk and three singles added three insurance runs before the inning ended. Bruce Sutter and Phil Niekro blanked the Americans in the ninth, and the Nationals had extended their current win streak to seven.

GAME 50
Kingdome, Seattle
July 17, 1979
NL, 7–6

NL	211 001 011	7 10 0
AL	302 001 000	6 10 0

Pitchers: Carlton, Andujar (2), Rogers (4), G. Perry (6), Sambito (6), LaCoss (6), SUTTER (8) vs Ryan, Stanley (3), Clear (5), KERN (7), Guidry (9)
Home Runs: Lynn-A, Mazzilli-N
Attendance: 58,905

Mike Schmidt tripled and George Foster doubled to drive in the game's first runs as the Nationals began their scoring in the top of the first. The Americans fought back to take the lead later in the inning as Don Baylor doubled home one run and Fred Lynn homered for two more. The Nationals tied the score with a run in the second and went ahead again in the third when Schmidt scored after doubling. But the Americans recaptured the lead in the bottom of the third, scoring twice on a single, wild pitch, ground out, hit batsman, single, and error.

Three innings later the Nationals again tied the game, but the Americans went ahead for the third time with a run in their half of the sixth. Outstanding throws by right fielder Dave Parker, who notched two assists, helped keep the Americans from pulling away. In the eighth the Nationals' Lee Mazzilli homered for yet another tie, and an inning later Ron Guidry walked Mazzilli with the bases loaded to force in the Nationals' go-ahead seventh run. When Bruce Sutter kept the Americans from scoring in the bottom of the ninth, the National Leaguers had for the second time defeated the Americans eight years in a row.

GAME 51
Dodger Stadium,
Los Angeles
July 8, 1980
NL, 4–2

AL	000 020 000	2 7 1
NL	000 012 10X	4 7 0

Pitchers: Stone, JOHN (4), Farmer (6), Stieb (7), Gossage (8) vs Richard, Welch (3), REUSS (6), Bibby (7), Sutter (8)
Home Runs: Lynn-A, Griffey-N
Attendance: 56,088

For 4⅔ innings J.R. Richard and Bob Welch held the American stars scoreless. But then Rod Carew singled and Fred Lynn drove in the game's first runs with his third All-Star homer.

The Americans' Steve Stone and Tommy John pitched even better, setting the Nationals down in order through four innings. John continued the perfect streak through the first two outs of the fifth, but then Ken Griffey homered, and the Americans' spell on the National Leaguers was broken.

While three National pitchers limited the Americans to a single and a walk over the final four innings, three singles and an error sent the Nationals into the lead in the sixth. A passed ball surrounded by two wild pitches moved Dave Concepcion around the bases in the seventh (he had reached on a fielder's choice) for the Nationals' fourth run. They didn't really need it, though, as Bruce Sutter—the winning pitcher in the two previous All-Star games—saved this one with two final innings of no-hit ball for the Nationals' ninth successive win.

GAME 52
Municipal Stadium,
Cleveland
August 9, 1981
NL, 5–4

NL	000 011 120	5 9 1
AL	010 003 000	4 11 1

Pitchers: Valenzuela, Seaver (2), Knepper (3), Hooton (5), Ruthven (6), BLUE (7), Ryan (8), Sutter (9) vs Morris, Barker (3), K.Forsch (5), Norris (6), Davis (7), FINGERS (8), Stieb (8)
Home Runs: Singleton-A, Carter-N (2), Parker-N, Schmidt-N
Attendance: 72,086

The game, delayed until August by the midseason players' strike, drew an All-Star record crowd of more than 72,000 fans, and the managers set a new record by using 56 players. But the game itself followed a familiar pattern.

The Americans scored first in the second inning on Ken Singleton's home run off Tom Seaver, and held their slim lead into the fifth on Len Barker's two innings of perfect pitching. But Ken Forsch replaced Barker in the fifth and Gary Carter homered off his first pitch to tie the score. Dave Parker's homer off Mike Norris an inning later put the Nationals ahead for the first time, but the Americans came right back in the bottom of the inning, putting together four singles and a sacrifice fly for three runs and a two-run advantage.

Gary Carter's second home run of the game—this time off Ron Davis's first pitch—brought the Nationals within one in the seventh, and Mike Schmidt's two-run blast off Rollie Fingers in the eighth restored their lead. Three National pitchers shut out the Americans without a hit over the final three innings as closer Bruce Sutter picked up his second consecutive All-Star save and the National Leaguers their tenth consecutive victory.

GAME 53
Olympic Stadium, Montreal
July 13, 1982
NL, 4–1

```
AL   100 000 000    1 8 2
NL   021 001 00X    4 8 1
```
Pitchers: ECKERSLEY, Clancy (4), Bannister (5), Quisenberry (6), Fingers (8) vs ROGERS, Carlton (4), Soto (6), Valenzuela (8), Minton (8), Howe (9), Hume (9)
Home Runs: Concepcion-N
Attendance: 59,057

In the first All-Star Game held outside the United States, the American League for the third year in a row put the first run on the board, but for the eleventh year in a row the final score showed the National League the winner. Two singles, a wild pitch, and a sacrifice fly gave the Americans a run in the top of the first. But starter Steve Rogers of the host Expos held the Americans scoreless for the remainder of his three innings while the Nationals struck back for two runs in the second on Dave Concepcion's home run, and added another in the third when Ruppert Jones—who had tripled to open the inning—scored on a sacrifice fly.

Six National League pitchers (and shortstop Ozzie Smith's spectacular stop and throw to first with two on in the eighth) joined Rogers in holding the American stars scoreless after the first inning. Two hometowners put together the Nationals' final run in the sixth. Al Oliver, leading off, doubled down the line in left and took third as the ball got by left fielder Rickey Henderson. Two outs later Gary Carter lined a pitch to center, scoring Oliver as Willie Wilson's dive for the ball came up short.

GAME 54
Comiskey Park, Chicago
July 6, 1983
AL, 13–3

```
NL   100 110 000    3 8 3
AL   117 000 22X   13 15 2
```
Pitchers: SOTO, Hammaker (3), Dawley (3), Dravecky (5), Perez (7), Orosco (7), L.Smith (8) vs STIEB, Honeycutt (4), Stanley (6), Young (8), Quisenberry (9)
Home Runs: Rice-A, Lynn-A
Attendance: 43,801

The game returned to the park where it had originated fifty years earlier, and the American League, after eleven years of All-Star losses, unleashed its pent-up fury to produce the greatest margin of victory in thirty-seven years. The game began, though, as an embarrassment of errors. American starter Dave Stieb struck out the side in the first, but along the way two errors (one of them Stieb's) let in a run. An unearned run in the bottom of the first tied the score and another in the second put the American League ahead for good (making a loser out of the unfortunate National starter Mario Soto).

The hitting began in earnest in the last of the third as the Americans scored seven times for a new one-inning record. Among their six hits (also a record for an All-Star inning) were a homer by Jim Rice, a triple by George Brett, and a bases-loaded blast by Fred Lynn—his fourth All-Star home run and the first grand slam in All-Star history. With the score now 9–1, the National League's single runs in the fourth and fifth were exercises in futility, and the Americans' two each in the seventh and eighth served chiefly to boost the winning total to 13—another All-Star high.

GAME 55
Candlestick Park,
San Francisco
July 10, 1984
NL, 3–1

```
AL   010 000 000    1 7 2
NL   110 000 01X    3 8 0
```
Pitchers: STIEB, Morris (3), Dotson (5), Caudill (7), Hernandez (8) vs LEA, Valenzuela (3), Gooden (5), Soto (7), Gossage (9)
Home Runs: Brett-A, Carter-N, Murphy-N
Attendance: 57,756

Only four times in the previous fifty-four All-Star Games had a pitcher struck out the side in order. In this game, three more pitchers did it. And, on this fiftieth anniversary of Carl Hubbell's five consecutive strikeouts, two of those pitchers combined to break Hubbell's record with six back-to-back whiffs. Hubbell, who threw out the first ball, also saw an All-Star nine-inning record set with 21 total Ks (11 by National League pitchers, 10 by American).

In the fourth inning, National star Fernando Valenzuela mowed down three of the game's premier sluggers: Dave Winfield, Reggie Jackson, and George Brett. If the three men Dwight Gooden retired on strikes an inning later (Lance Parrish, Chet Lemon, and rookie Alvin Davis) were slightly less formidable, still, it was an impressive performance for a nineteen-year-old rookie (the youngest player in All-Star history). The three that American Leaguer Bill Caudill struck out in the seventh were no slouches either: Tim Raines, Ryne Sandberg (in the midst of an MVP season), and Keith Hernandez.

Three of the four runs scored in the game were homers. The National League's run in the first was unearned, but the Americans' George Brett homered to center to tie the game in the second, and the Nationals' go-ahead run later in the inning came on Gary Carter's blast to left. In the eighth, National Leaguer Dale Murphy also put one over the left field fence to end the scoring.

GAME 56
H. Humphrey Metrodome,
Minneapolis
July 16, 1985
NL, 6–1

```
NL   011 020 002    6 9 1
AL   100 000 000    1 5 0
```
Pitchers: HOYT, Ryan (4), Valenzuela (7), Reardon (8), Gossage (9) vs MORRIS, Key (3), Blyleven (4), Stieb (6), Moore (7), Petry (9), Hernandez (9)
Attendance: 54,960

The American Leaguers scored first, as Rickey Henderson led off the bottom of the first with a single and circled the bases on a steal, error, and sacrifice fly. But the five National pitchers blanked the Americans the rest of the way on only four more singles.

Meanwhile, the National stars methodically dismantled the Americans for their thirty-sixth All-Star victory. In the top of the second, after Darryl Strawberry singled and stole second, Terry Kennedy, whose error had led to the American League run, redeemed himself by singling Strawberry home. An inning later, with two out, Tom Herr doubled and scored the go-ahead (and winning) run on Steve Garvey's single.

In the fifth the Nationals scored two more runs on a hit batsman, Tim Wallach's ground-rule double, and Ozzie Virgil's single, and finished their scoring in the ninth with another pair on three walks and Willie McGee's double—another ground-rule bounce out of play off the lively Metrodome surface. Goose Gossage struck out the final two American batters in the bottom of the ninth, and the Nationals had increased their winning margin in the series to a new high of seventeen games.

GAME 57
Astrodome, Houston
July 15, 1986
AL, 3–2

```
AL  020 000 100   3 5 0
NL  000 000 020   2 5 1
```

Pitchers: CLEMENS, Higuera (4), Hough (7), Righetti (8), Aase (9) vs GOODEN, Valenzuela (4), Scott (7), Fernandez (8), Krukow (9)
Home Runs: Whitaker-A, White-A
Attendance: 45,774

National League pitchers struck out 12 Americans, led by Fernando Valenzuela's five in a row, which matched the mark set by Carl Hubbell in 1934. (Two years earlier Valenzuela had helped set a multipitcher All-Star record of six consecutive strikeouts.) In the eighth inning Sid Fernandez, after walking two, struck out the next three.

Though the American Leaguers struck out fewer men, their pitching was more effective over all. Starter Roger Clemens hurled three perfect innings (3 balls and 21 strikes), and Teddy Higuera one-hit the Nationals over the next three. Charlie Hough struck out three in the eighth after yielding the Nationals' only extra-base hit (a double) to Chris Brown. But catcher Rich Gedman couldn't handle Hough's knuckleball, and Brown advanced to third on the first strikeout (ruled a wild pitch) and scored on the second, a passed ball which also enabled batter Hubie Brooks to reach first safely. Brooks moved up on a balk and scored the Nationals' second run on Steve Sax's single.

But home runs had already undone the Nationals. With two gone in the second, Dave Winfield doubled off starter Dwight Gooden, and Lou Whitaker clubbed an 0–2 pitch over the fence in right. And in the seventh, Frank White (hitting for Whitaker) knocked Mike Scott's 0–2 pitch over the fence in left center for what proved the margin of American League victory.

GAME 58
Oakland-Alameda County
Stadium, Oakland
July 14, 1987
NL, 2–0

```
NL  000 000 000 000 2   2 8 2
AL  000 000 000 000 0   0 6 1
```

Pitchers: Scott, Sutcliffe (3), Hershiser (5), R.Reuschel (7), Franco (8), Bedrosian (9), L.SMITH (10), S. Fernandez (13) vs Saberhagen, Morris (4), Langston (6), Plesac (8), Righetti (9), Henke (9), J.HOWELL (12)
Attendance: 49,671

None of the previous fifty-seven All-Star Games had gone more than five innings without at least one run crossing the plate. But this game went more than twice that before National Leaguer Tim Raines tripled in two runs in the top of the thirteenth for the game's only scoring. It was the National League's eighth win in eight extra-inning All-Star games.

Both teams missed scoring opportunities in the ninth inning. Raines singled for the Nationals with only one out, and became the game's first runner to reach third when a throw from first on his attempted steal went into center field. But a fly to short right and a foul out left him stranded. In the bottom of the ninth, the Americans came close to winning the game as Dave Winfield headed for home from second on a missed 4–6–1 double play. But National pitcher Steve Bedrosian, covering first, snared the off-center throw from short and fired it home to catch Winfield for the third out.

The Americans again reached third in the eleventh as Larry Parrish singled and moved around on a sacrifice and ground out. But pitcher Lee Smith (whose three shutout innings earned him the win) struck out Tony Fernandez to end the threat.

GAME 59
Riverfront Stadium,
Cincinnati
July 12, 1988
AL, 2–1

```
AL  001 100 000   2 6 2
NL  000 100 000   1 5 0
```

Pitchers: VIOLA, Clemens (3), Gubicza (4), Stieb (6), Russell (7), Jones (8), Plesac (8), Eckersley (9) vs GOODEN, Knepper (4), Cone (5), Gross (6), Davis (7), Walk (7), Hershiser (8), Worrell (9)
Home Run: Steinbach-A
Attendance: 55,837

Oakland's Terry Steinbach was not among the ten top American League catchers in batting; because of time lost to injuries, he was not even his club's leading catcher in games played. But the fans voted him to start in the All-Star Game, and he won it for the American Leaguers with a home run in his first trip to the plate and a sacrifice fly his next time up. Steinbach's homer—a drive off Dwight Gooden that led off the third inning—caromed off the glove of a leaping Darryl Strawberry over the wall in right for the game's first score. His sacrifice fly—high and deep to left in the fourth inning—scored Dave Winfield (aboard with his record seventh All-Star double) to put the Americans ahead 2–0.

Steinbach also contributed negatively to the National League run later in the fourth. His throwing error on Vince Coleman's steal of second enabled Coleman to advance to third, whence he scored on a wild pitch by Mark Gubicza.

American starter Frank Viola, the midseason league leader in wins, was awarded the victory for his two perfect innings pitched. Dennis Eckersley, the majors' top reliever, preserved the win for the Americans with a perfect ninth inning.

GAME 60
Anaheim Stadium,
Anaheim
July 11, 1989
AL, 5–3

```
NL  200 000 010   3 9 1
AL  212 000 00X   5 12 0
```

Pitchers: Reuschel, SMOLTZ (2), Sutcliffe (3), Burke (4), M. Davis (6), Howell (7), Williams (8) vs Stewart, RYAN (2), Gubicza (4), Moore (5), Swindell (6), Russell (7), Plesac (8), Jones (8)
Home Runs: Jackson-A, Boggs-A
Attendance: 64,036

The National stars struck early with a pair of two-out runs in the top of the first inning, and a double steal put two more runners in scoring position. But left fielder Bo Jackson stifled the assault with a fine running catch, then opened the American half of the first with a massive home run to center field off Rick Reuschel. Wade Boggs, the next man up, added insult to the forty-year-old Reuschel's first All-Star start, tying the game with another homer. In the second inning Jackson drove in the American League's go-ahead run with a slow grounder off young John Smoltz, and an inning later four American singles produced two more runs. A quartet of National League pitchers held the Americans scoreless on just three hits over the final six innings, and their teammates rallied for a third National run in the eighth. But Doug Jones (the majors' top reliever in 1989) came on to get the final out of the eighth, and in the ninth preserved the American lead to give the American Leaguers their first repeat All-Star victory in thirty-one years.

National League hurler Smoltz, at age twenty-two the youngest player in the lineup, took the loss. Nolan Ryan, back in the American League after nine National League seasons, earned the win with two shutout innings. Not only was he the oldest player on either side, at forty-two he was the oldest All-Star winning pitcher ever.

GAME 61
Wrigley Field, Chicago
July 10, 1990
AL, 2–0

```
AL   000 000 200   2 7 0
NL   000 000 000   0 2 1
```

Pitchers: Welch, Stieb (3), SABERHAGEN (5), Thigpen (7), Finley (8), Eckersley (9) vs Armstrong, R. Martinez (3), D. Martinez (4), Viola (5), D. Smith (6), BRANTLEY (6), Dibble (7), Myers (8), Franco (9)
Attendance: 39,071

Back-to-back American League singles off Jeff Brantley had put men on third and first and brought Julio Franco to the plate in the seventh inning, when heavy rain halted the game for more than an hour. During the delay Brantley's side stiffened, so when Franco finally got his turn at bat he faced a new National pitcher, Rob Dibble. Franco lined Dibble's third pitch into the gap in right center for a double—the only extra-base hit of the game—driving in what proved to be the game's only runs.

Damp air and a stiff breeze in from left field helped tame the offense. American League batters managed to accumulate seven hits, but the Nationals were held to two—an All-Star all-time low. No runner advanced as far as third base until the sixth inning, when American stars Kelly Gruber and Jose Canseco pulled off a double steal. No National Leaguer reached that far, and if it weren't for Barry Larkin's third-inning steal, no National runner would even have stood on second base.

American hurler Bret Saberhagen's two perfect middle innings earned him the win, and Dennis Eckersley, after yielding a leadoff hit in the ninth, retired the final three batters to record his second All-Star save in three years. The victory was the third in a row for the American Leaguers, the first time they had put together such a string of triumphs in forty-one years.

GAME 62
SkyDome, Toronto
July 9, 1991
AL, 4–2

```
NL   100 100 000   2 10 1
AL   003 000 10X   4 8 0
```

Pitchers: Glavine, MARTINEZ (3), Viola (5), Harnisch (6), Smiley (7), Dibble (7), Morgan (8) vs Morris, KEY (3), Clemens (4), McDowell (5), Reardon (7), Aguilera (7), Eckersley (9)
Home Runs: Ripken-A, Dawson-N
Attendance: 52,383

The National League took an early 1–0 lead on singles by Tony Gwynn, Will Clark, and Bobby Bonilla in the top of the first, and held it for two innings on Tom Glavine's strong pitching, which included three strikeouts. But Dennis Martinez yielded successive singles to Rickey Henderson and Wade Boggs in the third inning, and the next batter, Cal Ripken, Jr., homered to center to give the Americans all the runs they would need for victory.

National Leaguer Andre Dawson led off the fourth inning with a massive home run to center off Roger Clemens. This brought the Nationals within a run of tying the game, but they scored no more, as a succession of American pitchers shut them down on a walk and four singles the rest of the way. In the seventh inning the Americans added an insurance run when Joe Carter singled and moved around the bases on a call of catcher interference (the first in All-Star history), a sacrifice bunt, and Harold Baines's sacrifice liner to right.

Jimmy Key, the pitcher of record when Ripken's three-run homer put the American League ahead, was awarded the win. Dennis Eckersley, who pitched a perfect ninth, earned a record third All-Star save.

It was only the second time in All-Star history that the American League had won four games in a row.

GAME 63
Jack Murphy Stadium, San Diego
July 14, 1992
AL, 13–6

```
AL   411 004 030   13 19 1
NL   000 001 032    6 12 1
```

Pitchers: BROWN, McDowell (2), Guzman (3), Clemens (4), Mussina (5), Langston (6), Nagy (7), Montgomery (8), Aguilera (8), Eckersley (9) vs GLAVINE, Maddux (2), Cone (4), Tewksbury (5), Smoltz (6), Martinez (7), Jones (8), Charlton (9)
Home Runs: Sierra-A, Griffey-A, Clark-N
Attendance: 59,372

By the time the National Leaguers pushed across their first run in the sixth inning, the Americans had already scored ten times, and although National bats caught fire for five more runs in the eighth and ninth, they were powerless to prevent the American League from stretching its All-Star win streak to five games. National starting pitcher Tom Glavine could not repeat his strong 1991 start: before his relief after 1⅔ innings he was tagged for nine singles and five runs. In the third inning, Ken Griffey, Jr., who had driven in one of the first-inning runs, added the sixth American score with a homer off Greg Maddux. When he came up again to lead off the sixth inning, Griffey doubled to initiate a new American scoring spree, which included two-out doubles by Carlos Baerga and Robin Ventura, capped by Ruben Sierra's home run—all off Bob Tewksbury, who had set down the Americans 1–2–3 an inning earlier. Travis Fryman's RBI single and Roberto Kelly's two-run double in the eighth closed out the American League scoring.

Will Clark's two-out blast off Rick Aguilera in the last of the eighth was the National League's first three-run homer since 1964, but it was too little to make more than a dent in the American lead. With two men out in the ninth, a pair of singles off Dennis Eckersley loaded the bases, and Bip Roberts' single drove in two of the baserunners to bring the NL run total to six (enough to have defeated the AL in the seven previous All-Star Games).

Starter Kevin Brown was awarded the win; Glavine took the loss.

GAME 64
Oriole Park at Camden Yards, Baltimore
July 13, 1993
AL, 9–3

```
AL   011 033 10X   910
NL   200 001 000   372
```

Pitchers: Mulholland, Benes (3), BURKETT (5), Avery (5), Smoltz (6), Beck (7), Harvey (8) vs Langston, Johnson (3), McDOWELL (5), Key (6), Montgomery (7), Aguilera (8), Ward (9)
Home Runs: Sheffield-N, Alomar-A, Puckett-A
Attendance: 48,147

Barry Bonds doubled off Mark Langston with one out in the first inning and Gary Sheffield followed with a home run to left that gave the National League two runs before the American Leaguers came to bat. In the bottom of the second inning, though, Kirby Puckett's solo shot over the center field wall off Terry Mulholland narrowed the gap, and an inning later Roberto Alomar led off with a homer to right off Andy Benes that evened the score.

The Americans pushed ahead in the last of the fifth when, with John Burkett pitching, Ivan Rodriguez lined a ground rule double to left and Albert Belle singled him home. Belle took second on an error, and scored on Ken Griffey Jr.'s single; Griffey scored on Puckett's double into the gap at left center. A half inning later, Barry Larkin drove Bonds home with a sacrifice fly to narrow the score to 5–3, but the Americans blew the game open in the sixth with a trio of unearned runs. After shortstop Jeff Blauser failed to field a grounder by Carlos Baerga—depriving pitcher Steve Avery of a 1–2–3 inning—Avery walked Belle and Devon White doubled, sending Baerga home and Bell to third. John Smoltz, who relieved Avery, unloaded a pair of wild pitches that enabled Belle and White to score.

In the bottom of the seventh inning, Terry Steinbach tagged Rod Beck for a double high off the wall in right to drive in the ninth—and final—AL run. The Nationals got runners to second and third in the eighth with just one out, but failed to score, and when they fell to closer Duane Ward in order in the ninth, the American League had its sixth straight All-Star victory.

GAME 65
Three Rivers Stadium, Pittsburgh
July 12, 1994
NL, 8–7

AL	100 003 300 0	7	15	0
NL	103 001 002 1	8	12	1

Pitchers: Key, Cone (3), Mussina (5), Johnson (6) Hentgen (7), Alvarez (8), Smith (9), BERE (10) vs Maddux, Hill (4), Drabek (6), Hudek (6), Jackson (7), Beck (7), Myers (9), JONES (10)
Home Runs: Grissom-N, McGriff-N
Attendance: 59,568

A blend of youth and experience enabled the National League to snap the American Leaguers' six-game winning streak with one of the tightest finishes in All-Star history. In the bottom of the tenth inning, with the score tied, 7–7, Tony Gwynn, a veteran of ten All-Star games, led off by chopping a single to center off Jason Bere. He took off when novice All-Star Moises Alou drove Bere's second pitch to the base of the wall in left center. AL catcher Ivan Rodriguez received the ball—relayed sharply from the outfield—just as Gwynn slipped between the catcher's legs with the winning run.

It was a close game all the way. The teams traded single runs in the first inning. In the third, the National Leaguers grabbed the biggest lead of the evening when they sandwiched a hit batsman and Gwynn's double between a pair of singles to knock David Cone for three runs. In the top of the sixth the Americans evened the score again with a trio of runs off Doug Drabek. Then Marquis Grissom hit a home run off Randy Johnson a half inning later.

Once again the Americans knotted the game when Scott Cooper doubled home Ivan Rodriguez in the seventh and took their first (and, as it turned out, only) lead when Ken Lofton singled to score Chuck Knoblauch and Cooper. A fourth run would have scored in the seventh, however, if shortstop Ozzie Smith—thirty-nine years old and playing in his thirteenth All-Star contest—had not made a spectacular diving stop of Knoblauch's drive and recovered to force Mickey Tettleton at second. The run prevented by Smith's play would have given the American Leaguers their seventh straight victory.

The Americans maintained their 7–5 advantage into the last of the ninth. Pinch hitter Fred McGriff, after fouling off a third strike, brought National League fans to their feet with a game-tying home run. NL closer Doug Jones held the Americans scoreless in the top of the tenth, and the stage was set for the Gwynn–Alou finish.

GAME 66
The Ballpark at Arlington, Texas
July 11, 1995
NL, 3–2

NL	000 001 110	3	3	0
AL	000 200 000	2	8	0

MVP: Jeff Conine, FLA (NL)
Pitchers: Neagle (6), Perez (7), SLOCUMB (7), Henke (8), Myers (9) vs Johnson, Appier (3), Martinez (5), Rogers (7), ONTIVEROS (8), Wells (8), Mesa (9)
Home Runs: Thomas-A, Biggio-N, Piazza-N, Conine-N
Attendance: 50,920

On a ninety-six degree evening at The Ballpark in Arlington, Texas, the National League made the most of just three hits (the lowest for a winning squad since 1952) in defeating the AL 3-2. The key: all three were home runs.

After 5⅔ innings it certainly didn't appear the NL would triumph. AL pitchers Randy Johnson, Kevin Appier, and Dennis Martinez combined to no-hit Senior Circuit batters. Not until Houston's Craig Biggio homered off Martinez did the National Leaguers collect their first hit.

That cut the AL's margin to 2-1, since Frank Thomas had delivered a monster two-run homer off John Smiley in the fourth. The ball landed in a left field luxury box and was eventually retrieved by Donald Fehr's nine-year-old nephew.

Mike Piazza tied the game an inning later by homering off Kenny Rogers. In the eighth inning Jeff Conine pinch hit for DH Ron Gant. Facing Steve Ontiveros, who had also just entered the game, the 29-year-old Conine delivered a 410-foot homer to the lower deck in left. That was all the National League needed to win—and it earned Conine All-Star MVP honors.

Pregame excitement centered about the figure of Dodgers rookie Hideo Nomo. Nomo, the first Japanese national to appear in an All-Star Game, was also the first rookie to start since Fernando Valenzuela in 1981. Much of his native land stopped work (it was 9 AM in Japan) to watch—and cheer—Nomo's performance as he allowed just one hit in two innings and struck out Kenny Lofton, Edgar Martinez, and Albert Belle.

GAME 67
Veterans Stadium, Philadelphia
July 9, 1996
NL, 6–0

AL	000 000 000	0	7	0
NL	121 002 00X	6	12	1

MVP: Mike Piazza, LA (NL)
Pitchers: NAGY, Finley (3), Pavlik (5), Percival (7), Hernandez (8) vs. SMOLTZ, Brown (3), Glavine (4), Bottalico (5), Martinez (6), Trachsel (7), Worrell (8), Wohlers (9), Leiter (9)
Home Runs: Piazza-N, Caminiti-N
Attendance: 62,670

Mike Piazza, a native of nearby Norristown, Pa., homered his first time up, doubled in his next at bat, and called the signals behind the plate as nine pitchers combined to shut down the potent AL lineup, 6-0.

Indian manager Mike Hargrove's power-packed AL lineup, which had Baltimore's Brady Anderson batting eighth, managed only seven singles against the NL's parade of pitchers.

Atlanta's John Smoltz, like his counterpart Charles Nagy of Cleveland, was making his first All-Star start. Smoltz allowed only two hits and a walk in two innings to get the win. Nagy, on the other hand, was touched for four hits and three runs, including a 445-foot home run by Piazza leading off the second.

Met center fielder Lance Johnson, who started and played the entire game in place of injured Tony Gwynn, had three hits and a stolen base. He set the tone for the game by legging out a double on the first pitch from Nagy, taking third on a groundout by Barry Larkin and scoring on a groundout by Barry Bonds. Following Piazza's homer, Chipper Jones singled and went to second on a groundout by Craig Biggio. Jones scored on a single by Henry Rodriguez. Piazza brought home the NL's fourth run with a double off Chuck Finley to score Larkin. Ken Caminiti homered to right off Roger Pavlik in the sixth and Craig Biggio delivered the final run later in the inning. Ozzie Smith, playing his 15th and final All-Star Game, stole the show in the latter innings. Smith, who announced earlier this year that 1996 was his final season, received a long standing ovation when he came to bat in the seventh. He also started a double play at shortstop in the ninth.

## CHAPTER 13

Postseason Play: Introduction

Frederick Ivor-Campbell

When Major League Baseball and the striking players were unable to work out a settlement of their dispute in 1994, they interrupted a tradition of major league postseason play that traced back to 1871, the first year there was a professional league. National Association teams in the 1870s typically followed the conclusion of their championship (regularly scheduled) season with exhibition games against amateur clubs. In the 1880s nearly every major league club played a couple of weeks of postseason games, generally against major- and minor-league teams they hadn't faced during the regular season. In the twentieth century there had been a World Series every year for ninety years, prefaced since 1969 by League Championship Series to determine the American and National League pennant winners.

Before there was a World Series there were city and regional series. In 1882 Cleveland defeated Cincinnati for the championship of Ohio, and the next year teams in Philadelphia and New York played for the championships of those cities. These were informal series, arranged by the clubs themselves without official league sanction, and varied in the number of games scheduled according to the desires of the clubs involved.

The same held true for the early World Series, which had their beginnings in 1884. Two years earlier, the champions of the National League and the brand-new American Association played a pair of postseason contests (in which each team recorded a shutout against the other). Some would like to call these games the first World Series, but no one in 1882 saw them as more than exhibition games. In fact, because the NL didn't yet recognize the legitimacy of the AA and forbade its clubs to play those of the new league, the NL champion Chicago White Stockings had to release their players from their season contracts so they could face AA champion Cincinnati as technically independent players.

That winter the two major leagues made their peace, and although a proposed series between the 1883 NL and AA titlists was called off, the 1884 champion Providence Grays (NL) and the Metropolitan Club of New York (AA) played three games "for the championship of the United States." The winning Grays were acclaimed in the press as "champions of the world," and the World Series was born.

The brief 1884 Series set the stage for more elaborate World Series to follow. From 1885 through 1890 the NL and AA pennant-winners met in Series that ranged in length from six games to fifteen.

The demise of the AA after the 1891 season caused a one-year gap in World Series play. When the National League expanded from eight clubs to twelve the next year (by absorbing four teams from the defunct AA), it divided the regular season into two halves, with the first-half winner playing the winner of the second half for the world title. Boston defeated Cleveland in the first official World Series, but the unpopular divided season was not repeated (that is, until the strike year of 1981).

Two years later a new World Series scheme was devised when one William C. Temple offered a prize cup to the winner of a postseason series between the first- and second-place finishers in the NL. For four years these best-of-seven Temple Cup games served as the officially recognized world championship. But by the end of four lopsided Series (only one of which was won by the pennant-winning club), fan interest—never robust—had declined so much that the trophy was returned to its donor and the series abandoned.

In 1900, partisans of second-place Pittsburgh felt that their Pirates were the equal of pennant-winning Brooklyn, and a Pittsburgh newspaper, the *Chronicle-Telegraph*, offered a silver trophy cup to the winner of a best-of-five series between the clubs, to be played entirely in Pittsburgh. Described in the press as the "world's championship series," the games confirmed the superiority of Brooklyn's Superbas, who needed only four games to subdue the hometown Pirates.

The upgrading of the American League from minor- to major-league status in 1901 made a return to interleague World Series play theoretically possible, but it was not until after the NL and AL had made peace in 1903 that the first modern Series was contested. The owners of NL champion Pittsburgh and AL champion Boston arranged a best-of-nine postseason Series in 1903, which proved both popular and financially successful—a firm foundation for future Series. When the NL pennant-winning Giants refused to meet repeating AL titlist Boston in 1904, press and fan disappointment led baseball's National Commission to establish the World Series officially in 1905.

The end of the 1903 season saw not only the first modern World Series, but also a revival of city and regional series (which had lapsed when the AA folded) in Chicago, Philadelphia, St. Louis, and Ohio. In 1905 the National Commission offered to oversee these series, too, and give them the stability of official sanction. Until the manpower needs of the World War halted the 1918 season a month early (discouraging postseason play apart from the World Series), most of the city and regional series—and occasional series between other clubs, like Cleveland

and Pittsburgh, and the Boston Red Sox and New York Giants—were played under National Commission auspices.

After the war's end, only Chicago's Cubs and White Sox resumed a city series; they played sixteen series between 1921 and 1942, when World War II intervened. For twenty-six years thereafter the World Series alone remained of the once multifaceted major-league postseason—until the AL and NL split into two divisions each in 1969 and ushered in a new layer of playoffs: the League Championship Series. (In 1981, to recoup some of the money and fan interest lost during a midseason players' strike that split the season in half, a one-time third layer of postseason playoffs was added, pitting the first-half and second-half winners in each division against each other for the division titles—an aberration that made the divisional races even more surreal than the strike itself had done.) From 1969 through 1984 the LCS were played as best-of-five series, but in 1985 they were expanded to match the best-of-seven World Series.

In 1993, the club owners voted to realign each league into three divisions—East, Central, and West—and to install a preliminary layer of playoffs for each league. The three divisional champions and the second-place team with the best record would determine, through a pair of best-of-five series, which two teams would compete for the pennant in the League Championship Series. When the 1994 postseason was cancelled, however, the introduction of the new playoffs was among the casualties.

Key to the Statistics

The statistics in this section of *Total Baseball* are standard—there is little point in applying newer analytical measures to performances that run to seven games or fewer. We do offer, however, stats that were not standard at the time, such as earned run averages for years before 1912 and runs batted in before 1920 (which were deter-mined from box scores and play-by-plays) and saves before 1969. Beyond our powers of reconstruction were the following: runs batted in, stolen bases, and batter strike-outs for the World Series of 1885.

Ignoring the odd 1887 custom of counting walks as base hits, we present the cumulative box score for that year's World Series in accordance with modern practice. Other curiosities of early postseason play include the use of neutral sites for some games in 1885 and 1888 and for the majority of games in 1887, and the use of players who did not appear in so much as an inning for that team during the regular season (Tom Forster, New York Mets, 1884; Bug Holliday, Chicago, 1885; Sy Sutcliffe, Detroit, 1887; Jumbo Davis, Brooklyn 1889).

The length of the World Series varied from three games in 1884 all the way up to fifteen in 1887 and ten the following year. The best-of-seven format came in with the Temple Cup Series of 1894 and has been the norm for World Series ever since (excepting 1900, 1903, and 1919–1921). In recent years this format has become the norm for League Championship Series as well.

If a player appeared at more than one position during the Series, the number of games he played at each is noted (for example, a man who divided seven games at short-stop and third base would carry the notation *ss-4, 3b-3*). Other abbreviations are as follows:

POS	Position	SB	Stolen Bases
AVG	Batting average	W	Wins
G	Games	L	Losses
AB	At bats	ERA	Earned run average
R	Runs	GS	Games started
H	Hits	CG	Complete games
2B	Doubles	SHO	Shutouts
3B	Triples	SV	Saves
HR	Home runs	IP	Innings pitched
RB	Runs batted in	ER	Earned runs
BB	Bases on Balls	SO	Strikeouts

After a flurry of boasts and challenges, Met manager Jim Mutrie and the Grays' Frank Bancroft arranged a three-game series in New York to determine which team was the nation's best. These were not the first games between NL and AA pennant winners. In 1882, the AA's first season, champion Cincinnati met NL titlist Chicago twice as part of its postseason schedule, in games viewed simply as exhibition contests. (Each team won one). The next year a postseason series was proposed between champions Boston (NL) and the Athletics of Philadelphia (AA), but the Athletics fared so poorly in exhibitions against lesser NL teams that they refused to face Boston.

The 1884 Series was touted as "for the championship of the United States," but the influential weekly *Sporting Life* established precedent for future Series hype by naming victorious Providence "Champions of the World." The weather turned cold and windy as the Series got under way. A hardy opening game crowd of 2,500 saw the Grays' great Charlie "Old Hoss" Radbourn blank the Mets on two singles. Met pitcher Tim Keefe, wild at the start, paved the way for two first-inning Providence runs by hitting the first two men to face him and assisted them around the bases with a pair of wild pitches. Paul Hines singled in the third for the Grays' first hit and scored as a passed ball and two more wild pitches brought him home. Keefe yielded only four other hits, but they came back to back in the seventh to produce the Grays' final three runs.

The 1,000 spectators at Game Two witnessed the Series' closest contest. Keefe and Radbourn overwhelmed their opposition for four innings, but in the top of the fifth the Grays bunched three of their five hits for three two-out runs as Jerry Denny homered over the center field fence. The Mets responded with a run in the last of the fifth, but scored no more before darkness ended the game after seven innings.

The Grays had clinched the championship with their second win, and when they saw only a few hundred diehards in the stands for Game Three, they wanted to go home. The Mets must have regretted their insistence on playing the game. Although darkness halted it after only six innings, rookie Met pitcher Buck Becannon (replacing Keefe, who umpired) and awful Mets fielding gave Providence eleven or twelve runs (scorers disagreed), while Radbourn held the New Yorkers to a pair of unearned tallies.

Providence Grays (NL), 3; New York Mets (AA), 0

PRO (N)

PLAYER/POS	AVG	G	AB	R	H	2B	3B	HR	RB	BB	SO	SB
Cliff Carroll, of	.100	3	10	2	1	0	0	0	1	1	1	0
Jerry Denny, 3b	.444	3	9	3	4	0	1	1	2	0	3	0
Jack Farrell, 2b	.444	3	9	3	4	2	0	0	0	0	0	1
Barney Gilligan, c	.444	3	9	3	4	2	0	0	2	0	1	0
Paul Hines, of	.250	3	8	5	2	0	0	0	1	3	0	2
Arthur Irwin, ss	.222	3	9	2	2	0	1	0	2	0	2	0
Charlie Radbourn, p	.100	3	10	1	1	0	0	0	2	1	3	0
Paul Radford, of	.000	3	7	1	0	0	0	0	1	0	1	0
Joe Start, 1b	.100	3	10	0	1	0	0	0	1	0	2	0
TOTAL	.235		81	20	19	4	2	1	12	5	13	3

PITCHER	W	L	ERA	G	GS	CG	SV	SHO	IP	H	ER	BB	SO
Charlie Radbourn	3	0	0.00	3	3	3	0	1	22.0	11	0	0	16
TOTAL	3	0	0.00	3	3	3	0	1	22.0	11	0	0	16

NY (A)

PLAYER/POS	AVG	G	AB	R	H	2B	3B	HR	RB	BB	SO	SB
Buck Becannon, p	.500	1	2	0	1	0	0	0	0	0	0	0
Steve Brady, of	.000	3	10	1	0	0	0	0	0	0	1	0
Dude Esterbrook, 3b	.300	3	10	0	3	1	0	0	0	0	3	1
Tom Forster, 2b	.000	1	3	0	0	0	0	0	0	0	1	0
Bill Holbert, c	.000	1	2	0	0	0	0	0	0	0	1	0
Tim Keefe, p	.200	2	5	0	1	0	0	0	0	0	4	0
Ed Kennedy, of	.000	3	7	0	0	0	0	0	0	0	2	0
Candy Nelson, ss	.100	3	10	0	1	0	0	0	0	0	1	0
Dave Orr, 1b	.111	3	9	0	1	0	0	0	0	0	0	0
Charlie Reipschlager, c	.000	2	5	1	0	0	0	0	0	0	1	0
Chief Roseman, of	.333	3	9	1	3	0	0	0	1	0	1	0
Dasher Troy, 2b	.200	2	5	0	1	0	0	0	1	0	1	0
TOTAL	.143		77	3	11	1	0	0	2	0	16	1

PITCHER	W	L	ERA	G	GS	CG	SV	SHO	IP	H	ER	BB	SO
Buck Becannon	0	1	10.50	1	1	1	0	0	6.0	9	7	2	1
Tim Keefe	0	2	3.60	2	2	2	0	0	15.0	10	6	3	12
TOTAL	0	3	5.57	3	3	3	0	0	21.0	19	13	5	13

GAME 1 AT NY OCT 23

NY	000 000 000	0 2 0
PRO	201 000 30X	6 5 2

Pitchers: KEEFE vs RADBOURN
Attendance: 2,500

GAME 2 AT NY OCT 24

PRO	000 030 0	3 5 4
NY	000 010 0	1 3 1

Pitchers: RADBOURN vs KEEFE
Home Runs: Denny-PRO
Attendance: 1,000
(Game called at end of seventh, darkness)

GAME 3 AT NY OCT 25

PRO	120 144	12 9 3
NY	000 011	2 6 9

Pitchers: RADBOURN vs BECANNON
Attendance: 300
(Game called at end of sixth, darkness)

Before the start of the final game, the two clubs agreed to throw out Game Two, which had been forfeited to Chicago, leaving the Series tied at two wins apiece, plus the one tie. But after the Browns won the seventh game for their third victory, Chicago manager Cap Anson decided his club should retain its forfeit win after all, and a select committee agreed, leaving the Series in a tie instead of a White Stocking defeat.

Game One, in Chicago, was called for darkness after eight innings, with the score tied 5–5. The Browns scored first with a run in the second and added four more in the top of the fourth. But Chicago came back with a run in the last of the fourth, and in the bottom of the eighth scored four more on a walk, two singles, and Fred Pfeffer's game-tying three-run homer.

The Series moved to St. Louis for the next three games. Chicago was leading 5–4 in the sixth inning of Game Two when Browns manager Charlie Comiskey pulled his team off the field, objecting to the umpiring of David Sullivan. Umpire Sullivan later forfeited the game to the White Stockings; he worked no more in the Series. The Browns won Game Three, scoring five unearned runs with two out in the top of the first, and holding on for a 7–4 win. Chicago lost again the next day in a much closer game. The Browns scored first with a run in the third inning, but Abner Dalrymple's two-run homer in the fifth gave the White Stockings a 2–1 lead. In the bottom of the eighth, however, St. Louis scored twice and held on for the 3–2 win.

The Series took to the road for its final three games. In Pittsburgh for Game Five, Chicago overwhelmed the Browns 9–2, scoring four runs in the first inning, and their final three just before darkness ended the game after seven innings.

Game Six and Seven were played in Cincinnati. The White Stockings won the sixth game by the same 9–2 score as Game Five. The Browns' two runs were unearned, as Chicago's Jim Mc-Cormick stopped St. Louis on just two hits, both singles. The Browns' victory in the finale was a runaway 13–4, called in the eighth for darkness. St. Louis' six-run fourth inning typified the game's sloppy play, the runs scoring on five hits, four errors, and two passed balls.

Chicago White Stockings (NL), 3; St. Louis Browns (AA), 3; tie, 1

CHI (N)

PLAYER/POS	AVG	G	AB	R	H	2B	3B	HR	RB	BB	SO	SB
Cap Anson, 1b	.423	7	26	8	11	1	1	0		2		
Tom Burns, ss-4,3b-3	.080	7	25	3	2	0	1	0		0		
John Clarkson, p-2,of-2	.154	4	13	1	2	1	0	0		0		
Abner Dalrymple, of	.269	7	26	4	7	2	0	1		2		
Silver Flint, c	.143	4	14	0	2	0	0	0		0		
George Gore, of	.000	1	3	1	0	0	0	0		1		
Bug Holliday, of	.000	1	4	0	0	0	0	0		0		
King Kelly, of-4,c-3	.346	7	26	9	9	3	1	0		2		
Jim McCormick, p	.176	5	17	1	3	0	0	0		0		
Fred Pfeffer, 2b	.407	7	27	5	11	2	0	1		0		
Billy Sunday, of	.273	6	22	5	6	2	0	0		2		
N. Williamson, 3b-4,ss-3	.087	7	23	1	2	0	0	0		4		
TOTAL	.243		226	38	55	11	3	2		13		

PITCHER	W	L	ERA	G	GS	CG	SV	SHO	IP	H	ER	BB	SO
John Clarkson	0	1	1.13	2	2	2	0	0	16.0	15	2	1	15
Jim McCormick	3	2	2.00	5	5	5	0	0	36.0	27	8	6	19
TOTAL	3	3	1.73	7	7	7	0	0	52.0	42	10	7	34

STL (A)

PLAYER/POS	AVG	G	AB	R	H	2B	3B	HR	RB	BB	SO	SB
Sam Barkley, 2b	.087	7	23	3	2	0	0	0		2		
Doc Bushong, c	.154	4	13	1	2	0	0	0		0		
Bob Caruthers, p-3,of-2	.200	5	15	1	3	0	1	0		1		
Charlie Comiskey, 1b	.292	7	24	6	7	0	0	0		0		
Dave Foutz, p	.167	4	12	1	2	0	0	0		0		
Bill Gleason, ss	.231	7	26	5	6	2	0	0		1		
Arlie Latham, 3b	.318	7	22	5	7	3	0	0		2		
Hugh Nicol, of	.000	1	2	0	0	0	0	0		0		
Tip O'Neill, of	.208	7	24	4	5	0	0	0		0		
Yank Robinson, of-4,c-3	.174	7	23	5	4	0	1	0		1		
Curt Welch, of	.148	7	27	5	4	1	1	0		0		
TOTAL	.199		211	36	42	6	3	0		7		

PITCHER	W	L	ERA	G	GS	CG	SV	SHO	IP	H	ER	BB	SO
Bob Caruthers	1	1	2.42	3	3	3	0	0	26.0	25	7	4	16
Dave Foutz	2	2	0.61	4	4	4	0	0	29.1	30	2	9	14
TOTAL	3	3	1.46	7	7	7	0	0	55.1	55	9	13	30

GAME 1 AT CHI OCT 14

STL	010 400 00	5	7	2
CHI	000 100 04	5	5	10

Pitchers: CARUTHERS vs CLARKSON
Home Runs: Pfeffer-CHI
Attendance: 2,000
(Game called at end of eighth, darkness)

GAME 2 AT STL OCT 15

CHI	110 003	5	6	5
STL	300 10X	4	2	4

Pitchers: McCORMICK vs FOUTZ
Attendance: 2,000
(Game forfeited to Chicago in bottom of sixth)

GAME 3 AT STL OCT 16

CHI	111 000 001	4	8	7
STL	500 002 00X	7	8	4

Pitchers: CLARKSON vs CARUTHERS
Attendance: 3,000

GAME 4 AT STL OCT 17

CHI	000 020 000	2	8	3
STL	001 000 02X	3	6	7

Pitchers: McCORMICK vs FOUTZ
Home Runs: Dalrymple-CHI
Attendance: 3,000

GAME 5 AT PIT A OCT 22

CHI	400 110 3	9	7	1
STL	010 000 1	2	4	7

Pitchers: CLARKSON vs FOUTZ
Attendance: 500
(Game called at end of seventh, darkness)

GAME 6 AT CIN A OCT 23

CHI	200 111 040	9	11	7
STL	002 000 000	2	2	7

Pitchers: McCORMICK vs CARUTHERS
Attendance: 1,500

GAME 7 AT CIN A OCT 24

CHI	200 020 00	4	9	9
STL	004 621 0X	13	13	5

Pitchers: McCORMICK vs FOUTZ
Attendance: 1,200
(Game called in eighth, darkness)

It was a winner-take-all Series, with the club that won four games pocketing the entire proceeds. Attendance, very good for those days, averaged over 7,000 per game and brought the victorious Browns about $14,000.

The first three games were played in Chicago. The White Stockings won the opener on a sparkling five-hit shutout by their ace John Clarkson. But St. Louis's Bob Caruthers improved on Clarkson's performance the next day, blanking Chicago on just two singles as his Browns turned thirteen hits and thirteen Chicago errors into twelve runs (in a game shortened by darkness to eight innings). The White Stockings improved their fielding in the next game (which was also called after eight innings), and this time their bats came alive. With eleven hits (including home runs by Mike "King" Kelly and George Gore) combining with seven St. Louis errors, they regained the Series advantage with an easy 11–4 win.

When the venue shifted to St. Louis, though, the Browns battled back. In a back-and-forth battle in Game Four, Chicago tied the game at 5–5 with a pair of runs in the sixth, but St. Louis scored three final runs a half inning later, winning when darkness ended play in the middle of the seventh.

Game Five repeated Game Two's innovation: two umpires (instead of the usual one), plus a "referee" who stood between the pitcher and second base. The umpiring satisfied everyone, but Chicago, handicapped by their scheduled pitcher's sore arm, lost when they sent shortstop Ned Williamson and right fielder Jimmy Ryan into the box. In the 6½ innings before dark, St. Louis got to Williamson and Ryan for eleven hits and ten runs as their Nat Hudson held Chicago batters to three hits and three unearned runs.

The finale proved to be the Series' best-played and closest game. Chicago's Clarkson shut out the Browns through seven innings as his mates built a three-run lead—one of them scored on Fred's Pfeffer's homer in the fourth. Rain (and a rowdy crowd which poured onto the field) halted play for a while in the fifth. But the game resumed and the rain subsided. In the last of the eighth, Charlie Comiskey scored the Browns' first run on a single, errant throw and run-scoring fly out, and Arlie Latham tripled home two more runners later in the inning to tie the game. The score remained 3–3 into the last of the tenth, when the Browns' Curt Welch singled (for

St. Louis Browns (AA), 4; Chicago White Stockings (NL), 2

STL (A)

PLAYER/POS	AVG	G	AB	R	H	2B	3B	HR	RB	BB	SO	SB
Doc Bushong, c	.188	6	16	4	3	1	0	0	2	4	5	0
Bob Caruthers, p-3,of-3	.250	6	24	6	6	1	2	0	5	1	4	1
Charlie Comiskey, 1b	.292	6	24	2	7	1	0	0	2	0	4	0
Dave Foutz, p-2,of-2	.200	4	15	2	3	1	1	0	3	0	3	0
Bill Gleason, ss	.208	6	24	3	5	0	0	0	5	1	3	0
Nat Hudson, p-1,of-1	.167	2	6	1	1	0	1	0	0	1	3	0
Arlie Latham, 3b-6,c-1	.174	6	23	4	4	0	1	0	3	3	4	2
Tip O'Neill, of	.400	6	20	4	8	0	2	2	5	4	5	2
Yank Robinson, 2b	.316	6	19	5	6	1	1	0	3	3	2	2
Curt Welch, of	.350	6	20	7	7	2	0	0	1	3	4	2
TOTAL	.262		191	38	50	7	8	2	29	19	38	9

PITCHER	W	L	ERA	G	GS	CG	SV	SHO	IP	H	ER	BB	SO
Bob Caruthers	2	1	2.42	3	3	3	0	1	26.0	18	7	6	12
Dave Foutz	1	1	3.60	2	2	2	0	0	15.0	16	6	6	7
Nat Hudson	1	0	2.57	1	1	1	0	0	7.0	3	2	3	3
TOTAL	4	2	2.81	6	6	6	0	1	48.0	37	15	15	22

CHI (N)

PLAYER/POS	AVG	G	AB	R	H	2B	3B	HR	RB	BB	SO	SB
Cap Anson, 1b-6,c-2	.238	6	21	3	5	1	0	0	1	4	0	1
Tom Burns, 3b-6,of-1	.286	6	21	2	6	2	1	0	1	0	2	0
John Clarkson, p-4,of-1	.067	4	15	0	1	0	0	0	1	0	2	1
Abner Dalrymple, of	.190	6	21	2	4	1	1	0	2	0	5	1
Silver Flint, c	.000	1	3	0	0	0	0	0	0	1	0	1
George Gore, of	.174	6	23	4	4	0	0	1	2	3	3	0
King Kelly, c-5,ss-2,1b-1,3b-1	.208	6	24	4	5	0	0	1	1	2	2	1
Jim McCormick, p	.000	1	3	0	0	0	0	0	0	0	0	0
Fred Pfeffer, 2b	.286	6	21	7	6	0	0	1	4	2	1	2
Jimmy Ryan, of-6,p-1,ss-1	.250	6	20	4	5	1	0	0	2	0	1	1
Ned Williamson, ss-6,p-2,c-1,of-1	.056	6	18	2	1	0	1	0	3	4	5	1
TOTAL	.195		190	28	37	5	3	3	18	15	22	8

PITCHER	W	L	ERA	G	GS	CG	SV	SHO	IP	H	ER	BB	SO
John Clarkson	2	2	2.01	4	4	3	0	1	31.1	25	7	12	28
Jim McCormick	0	1	6.75	1	1	1	0	0	8.0	13	6	2	4
Jimmy Ryan	0	0	9.00	1	0	0	0	0	5.0	8	5	4	4
Ned Williamson	0	1	4.50	2	1	0	0	0	2.0	4	1	1	2
TOTAL	2	4	3.69	8	6	4	0	1	46.1	50	19	19	38

only the fourth St. Louis hit), went to second on an infield hit, and took third on a sacrifice. Welch then attempted to steal home but catcher Kelly had smelled out the play and called for a pitch out. Clarkson's delivery was poor and bobbled by Kelly, allowing Welch to steal home with a "$15,000 slide" for the Browns' triumph.

GAME 1 AT CHI OCT 18

STL	000 000 000	0	5	3
CHI	200 001 03X	6	10	4

Pitchers: FOUTZ vs CLARKSON
Attendance: 6,000

GAME 2 AT CHI OCT 19

STL	200 230 50	12	13	2
CHI	000 000 00	0	2	10

Pitchers: CARUTHERS vs McCORMICK
Home Runs: O'Neill-STL (2)
Attendance: 8,000
(Game called at end of eighth, darkness)

GAME 3 AT CHI OCT 20

CHI	200 112 32	11	11	2
STL	010 002 01	4	9	7

Pitchers: CLARKSON, Williamson (8) vs CARUTHERS
Home Runs: Kelly-CHI, Gore-CHI
Attendance: 6,000
(Game called at end of eighth, darkness)

GAME 4 AT STL OCT 21

CHI	300 002 0	5	6	4
STL	011 033 X	8	7	4

Pitchers: CLARKSON vs FOUTZ
Attendance: 8,000
(Game called in seventh, darkness)

GAME 5 AT STL OCT 22

CHI	011 100 00	3	3	3
STL	214 003 0X	10	11	3

Pitchers: WILLIAMSON, Ryan (2) vs HUDSON
Attendance: 10,000
(Game called in eighth, darkness)

GAME 6 AT STL OCT 23

CHI	010 101 000 0	3	6	2
STL	000 000 030 1	4	5	3

Pitchers: CLARKSON vs CARUTHERS
Home Runs: Pfeffer-CHI
Attendance: 8,000

Even though their star slugger Dan Brouthers was sidelined for all but one game by a sprained ankle, the Wolverines—in baseball's longest World Series, played in ten different cities—followed up their only pennant with an easy triumph over repeating AA champion St. Louis. The Browns won the opener at home, though, 6–1. They played errorless ball (rare in that era) as pitcher Bob Caruthers held Detroit scoreless until the ninth inning, and drove in the Browns' second run himself with a first-inning single.

The Wolverines came back to win the next three games. They took an early lead in Game Two and held on for a 5–3 win in St. Louis to even the Series. Then, in the Series' tightest game (played in Detroit) the Wolverines defeated Caruthers 2–1 in the last of the thirteenth when their pitcher Charlie Getzien led off with a single, advanced to second and third on ground outs, and scored on an infield error. In Game Four (in Pittsburgh) Detroit's Charles "Lady" Baldwin stopped the Browns on two hits for an easy 8–0 win.

Caruthers hurled a seven-hitter in Brooklyn for St. Louis's second win, but Detroit took the next four. Getzien contributed a two-hit shutout in New York, and Baldwin overcame Caruthers 3–1 in Philadelphia the next day. Getzien yielded eight hits the day after that in Boston, but Caruthers gave up thirteen, including two home runs to Sam Thompson, and Detroit took the game 9–2. Back in Philadelphia for Game Nine, St. Louis broke a 1–1 tie with a run in the top of the sixth. But the Wolverines scored two in the seventh and a final run in the eighth. The win gave Detroit a 7–2 Series advantage.

Game Ten, scheduled for the next day in Washington, was postponed because of rain until the following morning. Detroit's Hardy Richardson opened the game with a home run, but the Wolverines lost an opportunity to clinch the Series as the Browns overwhelmed Getzien with sixteen hits for an 11–4 victory featuring a triple play. But that afternoon, in Baltimore, Detroit took the deciding game as decisively as they had lost in the morning, knocking the Browns' Dave Foutz for fourteen hits (including four by Richardson and three—including a home run—by Larry Twitchell) as Baldwin held St. Louis to two hits in a 13–3 win.

The Browns and Wolverines split the final four meaningless games, played in Brooklyn,

Detroit Wolverines (NL), 10; St. Louis Browns (AA), 5

DET (N)

PLAYER/POS	AVG	G	AB	R	H	2B	3B	HR	RB	BB	SO	SB
Lady Baldwin, p	.235	5	17	1	4	1	0	0	1	2	2	1
Charlie Bennett, c-10,1b-3	.262	11	42	6	11	2	1	0	9	3	5	5
Dan Brouthers, 1b	.667	1	3	0	2	0	0	0	0	0	0	0
Pete Conway, p	.000	4	12	0	0	0	0	0	0	0	2	0
Fred Dunlap, 2b	.150	11	40	5	6	0	1	0	1	0	4	4
Charlie Ganzel, 1b-10,c-7	.224	14	58	5	13	1	0	0	2	1	2	3
Charlie Getzien, p	.300	6	20	5	6	2	0	0	2	3	6	1
Ned Hanlon, of	.220	15	50	5	11	1	1	0	4	5	1	7
Hardy Richardson, of-10,2b-5,3b-1	.197	15	66	12	13	5	2	1	4	1	9	7
Jack Rowe, ss	.333	15	63	12	21	1	1	0	7	2	1	5
Cy Sutcliffe, 1b-3,c-1	.091	4	11	1	1	0	0	0	0	1	1	1
Sam Thompson, of	.362	15	58	8	21	2	0	2	7	3	3	5
Larry Twitchell, of	.250	6	20	5	5	1	0	1	3	0	1	1
Deacon White, 3b-14,1b-1	.207	15	58	8	12	1	1	0	3	2	0	2
TOTAL	.243		518	73	126	17	7	4	43	23	37	42

PITCHER	W	L	ERA	G	GS	CG	SV	SHO	IP	H	ER	BB	SO
Lady Baldwin	4	1	1.50	5	5	5	0	1	42.0	28	7	10	4
Pete Conway	2	2	3.00	4	4	4	0	0	33.0	31	11	6	10
Charlie Getzien	4	2	2.48	6	6	6	0	1	58.0	61	16	15	17
TOTAL	10	5	2.30	15	15	15	0	2	133.0	120	34	31	31

STL (A)

PLAYER/POS	AVG	G	AB	R	H	2B	3B	HR	RB	BB	SO	SB
Jack Boyle, c	.208	6	24	1	5	0	0	0	1	0	4	0
Doc Bushong, c	.241	9	29	3	7	0	0	0	1	4	1	0
Bob Caruthers, p-8,of-3	.239	10	46	2	11	0	0	0	3	1	1	3
Charlie Comiskey, 1b-14,of-1	.306	15	62	8	19	2	0	0	2	1	1	4
Dave Foutz, of-11,p-3,1b-1	.169	15	59	4	10	2	1	0	1	2	3	0
Bill Gleason, ss	.163	13	49	3	8	0	0	0	1	3	2	1
Silver King, p	.071	4	14	0	1	0	0	0	0	0	3	0
Arlie Latham, 3b	.293	15	58	12	17	1	0	1	9	2	15	
Harry Lyons, ss	.286	2	7	3	2	0	0	0	0	1	0	0
Tip O'Neill, of	.200	15	65	7	13	2	1	1	5	0	2	0
Yank Robinson, 2b	.326	15	46	5	15	5	1	0	4	10	6	4
Curt Welch, of	.207	15	58	6	12	3	1	1	6	0	2	1
TOTAL	.232		517	54	120	15	4	2	25	31	27	28

PITCHER	W	L	ERA	G	GS	CG	SV	SHO	IP	H	ER	BB	SO
Bob Caruthers	4	4	2.13	8	8	8	0	0	71.2	64	17	12	19
Dave Foutz	0	3	3.46	3	3	3	0	0	26.0	36	10	9	6
Silver King	1	3	2.03	4	4	4	0	0	31.0	26	7	2	21
TOTAL	5	10	2.38	15	15	15	0	0	128.2	126	34	23	46

Detroit, Chicago, and St. Louis. For the first time in a World Series, two umpires officiated at all the games.

GAME 1 AT STL OCT 10

STL	200 040 000	6	12	0
DET	000 000 001	1	4	5

Pitchers: CARUTHERS vs GETZIEN
Attendance: 4,208

GAME 2 AT STL OCT 11

DET	022 000 100	5	10	2
STL	000 000 120	3	8	7

Pitchers: CONWAY vs FOUTZ
Attendance: 6,408

GAME 3 AT DET OCT 12

STL	010 000 000 000 0	1	13	7
DET	000 000 010 000 1	2	6	1

Pitchers: CARUTHERS vs GETZIEN
Attendance: 4,509

GAME 4 AT PIT OCT 13

DET	410 012 000	8	11	1
STL	000 000 000	0	2	6

Pitchers: BALDWIN vs KING
Attendance: 2,447

GAME 5 AT BRO OCT 14

STL	200 002 100	5	5	4
DET	000 020 000	2	7	5

Pitchers: CARUTHERS vs CONWAY
Attendance: 6,796

GAME 6 AT NY OCT 15

DET	330 000 003	9	12	1
STL	000 000 000	0	2	8

Pitchers: GETZIEN vs FOUTZ
Attendance: 5,797

GAME 7 AT PHI OCT 17

STL	000 000 001	1	8	1
DET	030 000 00X	3	6	1

Pitchers: CARUTHERS vs BALDWIN
Home Runs: O'Neill-STL
Attendance: 6,478

GAME 8 AT BOS OCT 18

DET	031 003 200	9	13	2
STL	100 001 000	2	8	5

Pitchers: GETZIEN vs CARUTHERS
Home Runs: Thompson-DET (2)
Attendance: 2,891

GAME 9 AT PHI OCT 19

STL	000 101 000	2	9	2
DET	000 100 21X	4	6	3

Pitchers: KING vs CONWAY
Attendance: 2,389

GAME 10 AT WAS OCT 21 (AM)

DET	200 010 001	4	8	3
STL	200 031 41X	11	16	5

Pitchers: GETZIEN vs CARUTHERS
Home Runs: Latham-STL, Welch-STL, Richardson-DET
Attendance: 1,261

GAME 11 AT BAL OCT 21 (PM)

STL	110 010 000	3	2	7
DET	100 344 10X	13	14	7

Pitchers: FOUTZ vs BALDWIN
Home Runs: Twitchell-DET
Attendance: 2,707
(Detroit wins best of 15 series 8 to 3)

GAME 12 AT BRO OCT 22

DET	000 100 0	1	5	3
STL	410 000 X	5	10	2

Pitchers: CONWAY vs KING
Attendance: 1,138
(Game called in seventh, darkness)

GAME 13 AT DET OCT 24

DET	020 100 120	6	12	3
STL	100 010 001	3	4	5

Pitchers: BALDWIN vs CARUTHERS
Attendance: 3,389

GAME 14 AT CHI OCT 25

STL	000 002 100	3	10	5
DET	300 010 00X	4	4	4

Pitchers: KING vs GETZIEN
Attendance: 378

GAME 15 AT STL OCT 26

STL	340 110	9	11	5
DET	011 000	2	8	7

Pitchers: CARUTHERS vs BALDWIN
Attendance: 659
(Game called after sixth, cold)

St. Louis, AA champions for the fourth straight year, battled the Giants closely through several games, but blowout losses in Games Six and Eight undid them. The first three games were played in New York. In a splendidly pitched opener, Brown ace Charles "Silver" King held New York to two hits and a walk while Giant ace Tim Keefe limited the Browns to three hits and a walk, striking out nine on his way to a narrow 2–1 win. St. Louis evened the Series in Game Two behind the shutout pitching of Elton "Icebox" Chamberlain. Tommy McCarthy scored the Browns' first run in the second inning when, after singling, he moved around to third on two passed balls by Giant catcher Buck Ewing and came home on Ewing's failed attempt to throw out a runner stealing second. Two more runs in the ninth gave St. Louis more than enough insurance for the win.

The Giants scored twice in the first inning of Game Three, and increased their lead to 4–0 before allowing St. Louis a pair of harmless runs in the final innings. They also scored first and led all the way in Game Four (played in Brooklyn) as another St. Louis rally fell short. The Browns took a 4–1 lead into the bottom of the eighth in Game Five (in New York), but a five-run Giant rally reversed the lead—and the outcome—as the game was called for darkness with St. Louis at bat in the ninth.

Giant Mickey Welch hurled a three-hitter (in Philadelphia) two days later, but St. Louis, capitalizing on walks and a questionable "safe" call at home, carried a 4–1 lead into the sixth inning. New York exploded in the late innings for 11 runs, however, and when darkness ended the game after eight the Giants were just one win away from the title.

The final four games were played in St. Louis. The Browns spoiled New York's hope of quick victory in Game Seven, coming from behind to tie the score with three runs in the fourth, and—after New York had scored twice in the sixth—recovering again with a four-run eighth for a 7–5 lead before darkness again halted play after eight innings. But the Browns' win only delayed the inevitable. The Giants hammered Icebox Chamberlain for twelve hits in Game Eight (including home runs by Buck Ewing and Mike Tiernan) to clinch their first world championship with an 11–3 win.

The final two games meant nothing to the outcome, and both clubs used reserve pitchers in Game Nine. But St. Louis rewarded the small crowd with a two-run rally in the ninth to tie the game at 11-all and scored three more runs in the tenth to win it. The finale the next day again featured heavy hitting on both sides, including a trio of home runs (one of them Tip O'Neill's second in two days) and an 18–7 St. Louis romp.

New York Giants (NL), 6; St. Louis Browns (AA), 4

NY (N)

PLAYER/POS	AVG	G	AB	R	H	2B	3B	HR	RB	BB	SO	SB
Willard Brown, c	.375	2	8	1	3	1	0	0	0	0	0	0
Roger Connor, 1b	.304	7	23	7	7	1	2	0	3	4	0	4
Ed Crane, p	.143	2	7	1	1	0	0	0	2	0	1	0
Buck Ewing, c-6,1b-1	.346	7	26	5	9	0	2	1	6	1	3	5
Bill George, p-1,1b-1	.333	2	9	2	3	1	0	1	4	0	2	0
George Gore, of-2,3b-1	.455	3	11	5	5	1	0	0	0	2	2	2
Gil Hatfield, p-1,2b-1,ss-1	.250	2	8	2	2	0	0	0	1	1	2	1
Tim Keefe, p	.091	4	11	2	1	0	0	0	0	2	2	1
Pat Murphy, c	.100	3	10	1	1	0	0	0	1	0	0	0
Jim O'Rourke, of-7,1b-2,ss-1	.222	10	36	4	8	0	0	0	1	4	2	3
Danny Richardson, 2b	.167	9	36	6	6	2	0	0	6	3	5	3
Mike Slattery, of-10,2b-1	.205	10	39	6	8	2	0	0	5	0	5	6
Mike Tiernan, of	.342	10	38	8	13	0	0	1	6	8	2	5
Ledell Titcomb, p-1,of-1	.500	1	4	1	2	1	0	0	1	0	0	0
Monte Ward, ss	.379	8	29	4	11	1	0	0	6	1	0	6
Mickey Welch, p	.286	2	7	2	2	0	0	0	1	0	0	0
Art Whitney, 3b-9,of-1	.324	10	37	7	12	0	1	0	12	1	4	2
TOTAL	.277		339	64	94	10	5	3	55	27	30	38

PITCHER	W	L	ERA	G	GS	CG	SV	SHO	IP	H	ER	BB	SO
Ed Crane	1	1	2.12	2	2	2	0	0	17.0	15	4	6	12
Bill George	0	1	7.20	1	1	1	0	0	10.0	15	8	3	4
Gil Hatfield	0	0	12.60	1	0	0	0	0	5.0	12	7	3	2
Tim Keefe	4	0	0.51	4	4	4	0	0	35.0	18	2	9	30
Ledell Titcomb	0	1	6.75	1	1	0	0	0	4.0	5	3	2	2
Mickey Welch	1	1	2.65	2	2	2	0	0	17.0	10	5	9	2
TOTAL	6	4	2.97	11	10	9	0	0	88.0	75	29	32	52

STL (A)

PLAYER/POS	AVG	G	AB	R	H	2B	3B	HR	RB	BB	SO	SB
Jack Boyle, c-4,of-1	.438	4	16	4	7	0	1	0	4	2	2	3
Icebox Chamberlain, p	.000	5	13	3	0	0	0	0	0	4	3	1
Charlie Comiskey, 1b-10,of-1	.268	10	41	6	11	1	1	0	3	1	1	4
Jim Devlin, p	.000	1	3	0	0	0	0	0	0	0	0	0
Ed Herr, of	.091	3	11	2	1	0	0	0	0	0	5	1
Silver King, p	.067	5	15	1	1	0	0	0	0	1	6	0
Arlie Latham, 3b	.250	10	40	10	10	0	0	0	3	5	6	11
Harry Lyons, of	.118	5	17	0	2	0	0	0	1	1	5	0
Tommy McCarthy, of	.244	10	41	10	10	1	0	1	9	0	0	6
Jocko Milligan, c-8,1b-1	.400	8	25	5	10	2	1	0	4	3	3	0
Tip O'Neill, of	.243	10	37	8	9	1	0	2	11	6	3	0
Yank Robinson, 2b	.250	10	36	7	9	2	1	0	7	6	12	2
Bill White, ss	.143	10	35	4	5	1	0	0	4	3	6	1
TOTAL	.227		330	60	75	8	4	3	46	32	52	29

PITCHER	W	L	ERA	G	GS	CG	SV	SHO	IP	H	ER	BB	SO
Icebox Chamberlain	2	3	5.32	5	5	5	0	1	44.0	52	26	16	13
Jim Devlin	1	0	2.57	1	0	0	0	0	7.0	5	2	2	5
Silver King	1	3	2.31	5	5	4	0	0	35.0	37	9	9	12
TOTAL	4	6	3.87	11	10	9	0	1	86.0	94	37	27	30

Six wins was the magic number this year, and it was agreed that—unlike most previous Series—play would not continue beyond the deciding game. At first it seemed Brooklyn might prevail, with an assist from the dark of night. The Giants wanted the opening game called for darkness after the seventh inning, when they led 10–8. But the umpires held off until Brooklyn, in the deepening gloom, had scored four runs in the last of the eighth to go ahead 12–10.

The next day, in Brooklyn before more than 16,000 spectators (by far the largest World Series crowd to that time), Giant Ed "Cannonball" Crane held the Grooms to four hits as New York evened the Series. But Brooklyn won the next two for a 3–1 Series advantage. In Game Three, ahead 8–7 in the sixth inning, the Grooms began stalling, waiting for darkness to fall. The score was still 8–7 when the game was finally halted in the top of the ninth with one out and three Giants on base.

Darkness for a third time gave Brooklyn the victory in Game Four. New York overcame a 7–2 Bridegroom lead to tie the score with five runs in the top of the sixth, but in the bottom of the inning Brooklyn's Tom "Oyster" Burns homered in the dark for three runs. The umpires then halted the game.

The five remaining contests went the distance, and the Giants won them all. Cannonball Crane in Game Five gave up eight hits, but homered in his own behalf, driving in two runs in his Giants' 11–3 rout. Game Six was a pitching duel between New York's Hank O'Day and Brooklyn's William "Adonis" Terry. The Grooms scored a run in the second inning, but New York tied the game with two outs in the last of the ninth (when Monte Ward singled, stole second and third, and scored on Roger Connor's single), and won it with two away in the eleventh as Ward drove in a speedy Mike Slattery from second with an infield hit.

Back-to-back homers by Giants Dan Richardson and Jim O'Rourke highlighted an eight-run second inning in Game Seven. The Giants' eventual 11–7 win gave them their first Series advantage. In Game Eight, two of Brooklyn's five hits were home runs. But the Giants outscored the Grooms 12–2 over the first four innings and beat them 16–7.

With their backs to the wall, the Bridegrooms scored first in

New York Giants (NL), 6; Brooklyn Bridegrooms (AA), 3

NY (N)

PLAYER/POS	AVG	G	AB	R	H	2B	3B	HR	RB	BB	SO	SB
Willard Brown, c	.600	1	5	3	3	0	0	1	2	0	0	0
Roger Connor, 1b	.343	9	35	9	12	2	2	0	12	3	2	8
Ed Crane, p	.278	5	18	3	5	1	1	1	5	1	2	0
Buck Ewing, c	.250	8	36	5	9	4	0	0	7	2	5	1
George Gore, of	.333	5	21	5	7	1	1	0	1	3	0	2
Tim Keefe, p	.500	2	4	1	2	1	0	0	0	1	1	0
Hank O'Day, p	.167	3	6	0	1	0	0	0	0	2	2	0
Jim O'Rourke, of	.389	9	36	7	14	2	2	2	7	2	2	3
Danny Richardson, 2b	.314	9	35	8	11	1	1	3	8	3	5	3
Mike Slattery, of	.188	4	16	6	3	0	0	0	1	3	1	1
Mike Tiernan, of	.289	9	38	12	11	1	1	1	5	5	3	3
Monte Ward, ss	.417	9	36	10	15	0	1	0	7	5	2	10
Mickey Welch, p	.333	3	0	1	1	0	0	0	0	0	1	0
Art Whitney, 3b	.229	9	35	4	8	2	1	0	3	1	0	0
TOTAL	.315		324	73	102	16	10	8	58	31	26	31

PITCHER	W	L	ERA	G	GS	CG	SV	SHO	IP	H	ER	BB	SO
Ed Crane	4	1	3.72	5	5	4	0	0	38.2	29	16	32	19
Tim Keefe	0	1	8.18	2	1	1	1	0	11.0	17	10	2	4
Hank O'Day	2	0	1.17	3	2	2	0	0	23.0	10	3	14	12
Mickey Welch	0	1	9.00	1	1	0	0	0	5.0	11	5	3	1
TOTAL	6	3	3.94	11	9	7	1	0	77.2	67	34	51	36

BRO (A)

PLAYER/POS	AVG	G	AB	R	H	2B	3B	HR	RB	BB	SO	SB
Oyster Burns, of	.229	9	35	8	8	3	0	2	11	5	6	0
Doc Bushong, c	.000	3	8	0	0	0	0	0	0	1	0	0
Bob Caruthers, p	.250	4	8	1	2	0	0	0	1	3	3	0
Bob Clark, c	.417	4	12	3	5	2	0	0	3	2	2	0
Hub Collins, 2b	.371	9	35	13	13	3	0	1	2	7	5	6
Pop Corkhill, of	.208	9	24	4	5	1	0	1	5	6	2	1
Jumbo Davis, ss	.000	1	4	0	0	0	0	0	0	0	0	0
Dave Foutz, 1b-9,p-1	.286	9	35	7	10	2	0	1	9	4	2	3
Mickey Hughes, p	.333	1	3	1	1	1	0	0	0	1	2	0
Tom Lovett, p	.000	1	1	0	0	0	0	0	0	0	0	0
Darby O'Brien, of	.161	9	31	8	5	0	1	0	4	12	6	6
George Pinckney, 3b	.258	9	31	2	8	2	0	0	3	4	2	2
Germany Smith, ss	.172	8	29	2	5	2	1	0	2	3	2	2
Adonis Terry, p-5,1b-1	.167	5	18	1	3	0	0	0	1	1	1	1
Joe Visner, c-3,of-2	.125	5	16	2	2	1	0	0	0	2	3	0
TOTAL	.231		290	52	67	17	2	5	41	51	36	21

PITCHER	W	L	ERA	G	GS	CG	SV	SHO	IP	H	ER	BB	SO
Bob Caruthers	0	2	3.75	4	2	2	1	0	24.0	28	10	6	6
Dave Foutz	0	0	7.20	1	0	0	0	0	5.0	5	4	2	2
Mickey Hughes	1	0	7.71	1	1	0	0	0	7.0	14	6	3	3
Tom Lovett	0	1	24.00	1	1	0	0	0	3.0	8	8	2	1
Adonis Terry	2	3	5.97	5	5	4	0	0	37.2	47	25	18	14
TOTAL	3	6	6.22	12	9	6	1	0	76.2	102	53	31	26

Game Nine and held a 2–1 lead after five innings. But New York tied the score in the sixth and went ahead 3–2 on a passed ball in the seventh. Meanwhile Giant pitcher Hank O'Day (although he walked five batters) blanked the Grooms on just two hits after the first inning to bring New York its second straight world championship.

GAME 1 AT NY OCT 18

| NY | 020 210 50 | 10 12 2 |
| **BRO** | 510 000 24 | 12 16 3 |

Pitchers: KEEFE vs TERRY
Home Runs: Collins-BRO, Richardson-NY
Attendance: 8,848
(Game called at end of eighth, darkness)

GAME 2 AT BRO OCT 19

| **NY** | 111 120 000 | 6 10 4 |
| BRO | 110 000 000 | 2 4 8 |

Pitchers: CRANE vs CARUTHERS
Attendance: 16,172

GAME 3 AT NY OCT 22

| NY | 200 032 00 | 7 15 2 |
| BRO | 023 120 00 | 8 12 3 |

Pitchers: WELCH, O'Day (6) vs HUGHES, Caruthers (8)
Home Runs: Corkhill-BRO, O'Rourke-NY
Attendance: 5,181
(Game called at end of eighth, darkness)

GAME 4 AT BRO OCT 23

| NY | 001 105 | 7 9 8 |
| **BRO** | 202 033 | 10 7 1 |

Pitchers: CRANE vs TERRY
Home Runs: Burns-BRO
Attendance: 3,045
(Game called at end of sixth, darkness)

GAME 5 AT BRO OCT 24

| **NY** | 004 040 021 | 11 12 2 |
| BRO | 000 111 000 | 3 8 2 |

Pitchers: CRANE vs CARUTHERS
Home Runs: Brown-NY, Richardson-NY, Crane-NY
Attendance: 2,901

GAME 6 AT NY OCT 25

| BRO | 010 000 000 00 | 1 6 4 |
| **NY** | 000 000 001 01 | 2 7 1 |

Pitchers: TERRY vs O'DAY
Attendance: 2,556

GAME 7 AT NY OCT 26

| BRO | 004 030 000 | 7 5 3 |
| **NY** | 180 001 10X | 11 14 4 |

Pitchers: LOVETT, Caruthers (4) vs CRANE, Keefe (5)
Home Runs: Richardson-NY, O'Rourke-NY
Attendance: 3,312

GAME 8 AT BRO OCT 28

| NY | 541 203 001 | 16 15 4 |
| BRO | 200 000 023 | 7 5 4 |

Pitchers: CRANE vs TERRY, Foutz (5)
Home Runs: Foutz-BRO, Tiernan-NY, Burns-BRO
Attendance: 2,584

GAME 9 AT NY OCT 29

| BRO | 200 000 000 | 2 4 2 |
| **NY** | 100 001 10X | 3 8 5 |

Pitchers: TERRY vs O'DAY
Attendance: 3,067

The Bridegrooms, AA pennant winners in 1889, switched to the NL and returned to World Series play as champions of their new league. Louisville, meanwhile, rose from a last-place finish in 1889 to replace Brooklyn at the top of the AA. The Series, though, seemed meaningless to many who believed that pennant-winning Boston of the outlaw Players League (which had drawn off many of the best NL and AA players) could beat both Louisville and Brooklyn if given the opportunity.

The first four games of the Series were played in Louisville before an ever decreasing number of spectators. The largest crowd—5,600—saw the Cyclones humiliated in the opener 9–0 as Brooklyn's Adonis Terry stopped them on two singles. The Grooms won the second game, too, breaking a 2–2 tie with a pair of runs in the fourth and holding on for a 5–3 win.

Louisville played catch-up throughout Game Three and entered the last of the eighth still behind 7–4. But a walk, three hits, a sacrifice fly, and a passed ball brought to score to 7-all—where it remained when darkness ended the game. Only 1,050 spectators attended the final contest in Louisville, but they saw the first Louisville win. The Cyclones scored three runs in the first inning, but Brooklyn countered with three an inning later, and both teams scored single runs in the third. Louisville's Red Ehret blanked the Grooms the rest of the way, but Brooklyn's Tom Lovett yielded the Cyclones a winning run in the seventh when Tim Shinnick tripled and was sacrificed home.

Rain postponed the first game in Brooklyn for two days, but when it was played—on a cold, muddy day before a small crowd of 1,000—the Grooms took the lead on Oyster Burns's two-run homer in the first inning and held it all the way for their third win. As the weather grew colder, the crowds declined for the final two games. Louisville captured its second win by a 9–8 margin when a three-run Brooklyn rally in the eighth inning of Game Six stalled one run short of a tie. Only abut 300 diehards saw the Cyclones even the Series in the finale, 6–2 behind Red Ehret's four-hitter. A tie-breaking eighth game seemed called for, but there was not enough interest in playing any further in the bitter cold.

Brooklyn Bridegrooms (NL), 3; Louisville Cyclones (AA), 3; tie, 1

BRO (N)

PLAYER/POS	AVG	G	AB	R	H	2B	3B	HR	RB	BB	SO	SB
Oyster Burns, of-4,3b-3	.222	7	27	6	6	2	0	1	5	3	4	0
Doc Bushong, c	.000	2	6	0	0	0	0	0	0	0	1	0
Bob Caruthers, of	.000	2	6	0	0	0	0	0	0	2	0	0
Bob Clark, c	.667	1	3	2	2	0	1	0	1	0	0	0
Hub Collins, 2b	.310	7	29	7	9	0	1	0	1	3	0	2
Tom Daly, c-6,1b-1	.182	6	22	1	4	2	0	0	3	0	4	2
Patsy Donovan, of	.471	5	17	5	8	1	0	0	3	2	1	3
Dave Foutz, 1b-7,of-1	.300	7	30	6	9	2	1	0	4	0	1	1
Tom Lovett, p-4,of-1	.067	5	15	0	1	0	0	0	0	0	4	0
Darby O'Brien, of	.125	6	24	3	3	0	1	0	3	1	5	3
George Pinckney, 3b	.357	4	14	4	5	0	2	0	3	2	1	1
Germany Smith, ss	.276	7	29	3	8	0	2	0	7	0	3	1
Adonis Terry, p-3,of-3	.050	6	20	5	1	1	0	0	0	6	3	1
TOTAL	.231		242	42	56	8	8	1	30	19	27	14

PITCHER	W	L	ERA	G	GS	CG	SV	SHO	IP	H	ER	BB	SO
Tom Lovett	2	2	2.83	4	4	4	0	0	35.0	29	11	6	14
Adonis Terry	1	1	3.60	3	3	3	0	1	25.0	25	10	10	8
TOTAL	3	3	3.15	7	7	7	0	1	60.0	54	21	16	22

LOU (A)

PLAYER/POS	AVG	G	AB	R	H	2B	3B	HR	RB	BB	SO	SB
Ned Bligh, c	.000	2	3	0	0	0	0	0	0	0	1	0
Ed Daily, of-4,p-2	.136	6	22	1	3	1	1	0	3	1	2	2
Red Ehret, p	.429	3	7	1	3	0	1	0	0	0	0	0
Charlie Hamburg, of	.269	7	26	3	7	1	0	0	2	0	3	0
George Meakim, p	.500	1	2	0	1	0	0	0	0	0	0	0
Harry Raymond, ss-5,ss-3	.148	7	27	5	4	1	1	0	1	2	5	1
John Ryan, c	.053	6	19	0	1	0	0	0	2	0	1	1
Tim Shinnick, 2b	.292	7	24	3	7	1	1	0	3	2	2	2
Scott Stratton, p-3,of-1	.222	4	9	4	2	1	0	0	0	2	1	3
Harry Taylor, 1b	.300	7	30	6	9	1	0	0	2	3	3	3
Phil Tomney, ss	.200	3	5	1	1	0	0	0	0	3	1	0
Farmer Weaver, of	.259	7	27	4	7	1	0	0	4	1	2	5
Pete Weckbecker, c	.000	1	4	0	0	0	0	0	0	0	2	0
Chicken Wolf, 3b-5,of-3	.360	7	25	4	9	3	1	0	8	3	0	2
TOTAL	.235		230	32	54	10	5	0	25	16	22	19

PITCHER	W	L	ERA	G	GS	CG	SV	SHO	IP	H	ER	BB	SO
Ed Daily	0	2	2.65	2	2	2	0	0	17.0	12	5	8	5
Red Ehret	2	0	1.35	3	2	2	1	0	20.0	12	3	6	13
George Meakim	0	0	0.00	1	0	0	0	0	4.0	6	0	1	1
Scott Stratton	1	1	2.37	3	3	1	0	0	19.0	26	5	4	8
TOTAL	3	3	1.95	9	7	5	1	0	60.0	56	13	19	27

GAME 1 AT LOU OCT 17

BRO	300 030 30	9	11	1
LOU	000 000 00	0	2	6

Pitchers: TERRY vs STRATTON
Attendance: 5,600

GAME 2 AT LOU OCT 18

BRO	020 201 000	5	5	3
LOU	101 000 001	3	6	5

Pitchers: LOVETT vs DAILY
Attendance: 2,860

GAME 3 AT LOU OCT 20

BRO	020 130 10	7	10	2
LOU	001 012 03	7	11	3

Pitchers: Terry vs Stratton, Meakim (4)
Attendance: 2,500
(Game called at end of eighth, darkness)

GAME 4 AT LOU OCT 21

BRO	031 000 000	4	7	2
LOU	301 000 10X	5	9	2

Pitchers: LOVETT vs EHRET
Attendance: 1,050

GAME 5 AT BRO OCT 25

LOU	010 010 000	2	5	6
BRO	210 200 20X	7	7	0

Pitchers: DAILY vs LOVETT
Home Runs: Burns-BRO
Attendance: 1,000

GAME 6 AT BRO OCT 27

LOU	012 101 220	9	13	3
BRO	100 004 030	8	12	3

Pitchers: STRATTON, Ehret (7) vs TERRY
Attendance: 600

GAME 7 AT BRO OCT 28

LOU	103 000 020	6	8	3
BRO	200 000 000	2	4	1

Pitchers: EHRET vs LOVETT
Attendance: 300

Interleague squabbling prevented a World Series in 1891, and the AA folded before the next season. Four AA clubs were taken into the NL, expanding the NL to twelve teams. To create a postseason championship series, the regular season was divided in half, with first-half winner Boston meeting second-half victor Cleveland for both the league and world titles.

The first game, in Cleveland, was a pitching and fielding classic. Boston's Jack Stivetts and Cleveland's Cy Young blanked the opposition for eleven innings before darkness halted the game. Young yielded just six hits and Stivetts four—all singles. Just as remarkable in an era when errors were commonplace, Cleveland committed only one and Boston none; several outstanding plays were made in the field.

Boston center fielder Hugh Duffy was the offensive and defensive star of Game Two. He drove in three of the Beaneaters' four runs (with a fly out, a triple, and a double), and scored the fourth himself after tripling a second time. And in the bottom of the ninth he snared a leadoff liner with a great running catch. As it was, Cleveland scored once in the inning to pull within a run of a tie; Duffy's catch prevented a certain tie and a possible Cleveland win. Game Three was just as close. Pitchers Stivetts and Young each gave up two early runs, but then blanked their foes until the seventh inning, when Boston's Tommy McCarthy singled in Stivetts (who had doubled) with what proved the winning run.

The Series moved to Boston for the next three games. In Game Four, Boston ace Kid Nichols shut out the Spiders, scattering seven hits and fanning eight. Cleveland's Nig Cuppy yielded only six hits, but one was a home run ball to Hugh Duffy for two runs in the third inning, and another was a two-run single to Joe Quinn in the sixth. Cleveland pitcher John Clarkson helped his own cause the next day with a three-run homer in the Spider's six-run second inning. But Boston pitcher Jack Stivetts—with the score now 7–5 Cleveland in the sixth—tripled in a run and scored the tying run. In the seventh, Stivetts scored Boston's twelfth (and final) run after singling, while holding Cleveland scoreless through the final four innings.

Two days later the Beaneaters brought the Series to an end with their fifth straight win. The Spiders scored first, with a three-run third, but pitcher Kid Nichols held them

scoreless after that and singled home Boston's tying and go-ahead runs himself as the Beaneaters tagged Cy Young for eight runs over the final six innings.

Boston Beaneaters, 5; Cleveland Spiders, 0; tie, 1

BOS (N)

PLAYER/POS	AVG	G	AB	R	H	2B	3B	HR	RB	BB	SO	SB
Charlie Bennett, c	.286	2	7	2	2	0	0	1	1	0	2	1
Hugh Duffy, of	.462	6	26	3	12	3	2	1	9	1	0	3
Charlie Ganzel, c	.500	2	8	1	4	0	0	0	2	1	0	0
King Kelly, c	.000	2	8	0	0	0	0	0	0	0	2	1
Herman Long, ss	.222	6	27	4	6	0	0	0	1	0	0	2
Bobby Lowe, of	.130	6	23	8	3	0	0	0	0	1	2	1
Tommy McCarthy, of	.381	6	21	2	8	2	0	0	2	6	1	3
Billy Nash, 3b	.167	6	24	3	4	0	0	0	4	2	3	2
Kid Nichols, p	.286	2	7	1	2	0	0	0	2	0	1	1
Joe Quinn, 2b	.286	6	21	2	6	1	1	0	4	1	2	0
Harry Staley, p	.000	1	4	0	0	0	0	0	0	0	3	0
Jack Stivetts, p	.250	3	12	3	3	1	1	0	1	0	2	0
Tommy Tucker, 1b	.261	6	23	2	6	0	0	1	2	0	1	0
TOTAL	.265		211	31	56	7	4	3	28	12	19	14

PITCHER	W	L	ERA	G	GS	CG	SV	SHO	IP	H	ER	BB	SO
Kid Nichols	2	0	1.00	2	2	2	0	1	18.0	17	2	4	13
Harry Staley	1	0	3.00	1	1	1	0	0	9.0	10	3	1	0
Jack Stivetts	2	0	0.93	3	3	3	0	1	29.0	21	3	7	17
TOTAL	5	0	1.29	6	6	6	0	2	56.0	48	8	12	30

CLE (N)

PLAYER/POS	AVG	G	AB	R	H	2B	3B	HR	RB	BB	SO	SB
Jesse Burkett, of	.320	6	25	3	8	1	0	0	1	0	2	4
Cupid Childs, 2b	.409	6	22	3	9	0	2	0	0	5	1	0
John Clarkson, p	.250	2	8	1	2	0	0	1	3	0	1	0
Nig Cuppy, p	.000	1	3	0	0	0	0	0	0	0	2	0
George Davis, 3b-2	.167	3	6	0	1	0	0	0	0	0	1	0
Jimmy McAleer, of	.182	6	22	0	4	0	0	0	1	2	2	1
Ed McKean, ss	.440	6	25	2	11	0	0	0	6	1	3	0
Jack O'Connor, of	.136	6	22	1	3	0	0	0	0	2	3	0
Patsy Tebeau, 3b	.000	5	18	1	0	0	0	0	0	0	2	1
Jake Virtue, 1b	.125	6	24	1	3	0	0	0	0	2	5	1
Cy Young, p	.091	3	11	1	1	0	0	0	0	0	5	0
Chief Zimmer, c	.261	6	23	2	6	1	1	0	2	0	3	0
TOTAL	.230		209	15	48	2	3	1	13	12	30	7

PITCHER	W	L	ERA	G	GS	CG	SV	SHO	IP	H	ER	BB	SO
John Clarkson	0	2	5.29	2	2	2	0	0	17.0	24	10	5	9
Nig Cuppy	0	1	1.13	1	1	1	0	0	8.0	6	1	4	1
Cy Young	0	2	3.00	3	3	3	0	1	27.0	26	9	3	9
TOTAL	0	5	3.46	6	6	6	0	1	52.0	56	20	12	19

GAME 1 AT CLE OCT 17

CLE	000	000	000	00	0	4	1
BOS	000	000	000	00	0	6	0

Pitchers: YOUNG vs STIVETTS
Attendance: 6,000
(Game called at end of eleventh, darkness)

GAME 2 AT CLE OCT 18

BOS	101	010	010	4	10	2
CLE	001	100	001	3	10	2

Pitchers: STALEY vs CLARKSON
Attendance: 6,700

GAME 3 AT CLE OCT 19

CLE	200	000	000	2	8	0
BOS	110	000	10X	3	9	2

Pitchers: YOUNG vs STIVETTS
Attendance: 5,000

GAME 4 AT BOS OCT 21

CLE	000	000	000	0	7	3
BOS	002	002	00X	4	6	0

Pitchers: CUPPY vs NICHOLS
Home Runs: Duffy-BOS
Attendance: 6,547

GAME 5 AT BOS OCT 22

CLE	060	010	000	7	9	4
BOS	000	324	30X	12	14	3

Pitchers: CLARKSON vs STIVETTS
Home Runs: Clarkson-CLE, Tucker-BOS
Attendance: 3,466

GAME 6 AT BOS OCT 24

CLE	003	000	000	3	10	5
BOS	002	211	11X	8	11	5

Pitchers: YOUNG vs NICHOLS
Home Runs: Bennett-BOS
Attendance: 2,300

As the divided season of 1892 was not repeated, no "world series" was held in 1893. But in 1894 Pittsburgh sportsman William C. Temple offered an elegant trophy to the winner of a series between the NL's first- and second-place finishers. For four years the Temple Cup games determined the world championship. In this first matchup, second-place New York swept the feisty pennant-winning Orioles.

Game One, in Baltimore, was a shutout through four innings as New York's Amos Rusie and Baltimore's Duke Esper held their opponents at bay. But Giant George Van Haltren tripled in the fifth inning and scored the game's first run on a fly to left. The Giants also scored single runs in the sixth, seventh, and eighth innings, while Rusie continued his shutout pitching through the eighth. In the ninth Oriole John McGraw singled, and he came around on a sacrifice, stolen base, and single to spoil the shutout. But the Oriole effort was too little to deprive Rusie of his win.

Some two hundred policemen patrolled the second game the next day to protect the umpires and New York's players and fans from the abusive Orioles and the crowd in the stands whom the Oriole players egged on. Baltimore scored first with two runs in the second and, after losing and regaining the lead, completed the eighth inning tied 5–5. But in the top of the ninth, the Giants put together their second four-run inning of the game. Once again the Orioles came up with a run in the last of the ninth, but once again came up short.

More than 22,000 spectators showed up for Game Three as the Series shifted to New York—a huge crowd for that era, even for a Saturday. As in Game One, the Giants' Amos Rusie hurled a 4–1 victory. New York broke a 1–1 tie with a run in the fifth on a throwing error and a ground out, and scored the game's final runs an inning later. Threatening weather held down attendance at Game Four to about 12,000. Baltimore jumped to a quick lead with two runs in the top of the first, but New York pitcher Jouett Meekin held the Orioles to just one run after that as the Giants piled up runs for a 16–3 advantage by the time darkness forced an end to play after eight innings. Meekin, in winning his second game of the Series, connected for three hits himself—half as many as he permitted the whole Oriole team.

New York Giants, 4;
Baltimore Orioles, 0

NY (N)

PLAYER/POS	AVG	G	AB	R	H	2B	3B	HR	RB	BB	SO	SB
Eddie Burke, of	.389	4	18	3	7	1	0	0	2	1	0	1
George Davis, 3b	.313	4	16	5	5	2	2	0	5	2	0	2
Jack Doyle, 1b	.588	4	17	4	10	1	1	0	6	1	1	6
Duke Farrell, c	.400	4	15	5	6	0	0	0	2	1	1	1
Shorty Fuller, ss	.286	4	14	4	4	0	0	0	2	2	0	1
Jouett Meekin, p	.556	2	9	2	5	0	0	0	3	0	1	0
Yale Murphy, of	.000	1	1	0	0	0	0	0	0	0	0	0
Amos Rusie, p	.429	2	7	1	3	1	0	0	1	0	1	0
Mike Tiernan, of	.294	4	17	5	5	0	1	0	3	2	2	0
George Van Haltren, of	.500	4	14	3	7	1	1	0	0	2	2	2
Monte Ward, 2b	.294	4	17	1	5	0	0	0	6	0	0	0
TOTAL	.393		145	33	57	6	5	0	30	11	8	13

PITCHER	W	L	ERA	G	GS	CG	SV	SHO	IP	H	ER	BB	SO
Jouett Meekin	2	0	1.59	2	2	2	0	0	17.0	13	3	8	6
Amos Rusie	2	0	0.50	2	2	2	0	0	18.0	14	1	3	9
TOTAL	4	0	1.03	4	4	4	0	0	35.0	27	4	11	15

BAL (N)

PLAYER/POS	AVG	G	AB	R	H	2B	3B	HR	RB	BB	SO	SB
Frank Bonner, ss-1,of-1	.000	2	5	0	0	0	0	0	0	0	2	0
Steve Brodie, of	.000	4	15	2	0	0	0	0	0	2	1	1
Dan Brouthers, 1b	.188	4	16	2	3	0	0	0	0	1	0	3
Duke Esper, p	.000	1	2	0	0	0	0	0	0	1	1	0
Kid Gleason, p	.200	2	5	0	1	0	1	0	1	0	1	0
Bill Hawke, p	.000	1	2	0	0	0	0	0	0	0	1	0
George Hemming, p	.000	1	3	0	0	0	0	0	0	1	1	0
Hughie Jennings, ss	.143	4	14	0	2	0	0	0	1	0	2	0
Willie Keeler, of	.250	3	12	1	3	0	0	0	1	1	0	0
Joe Kelley, of	.333	4	15	2	5	1	1	0	3	2	1	1
John McGraw, 3b	.250	4	16	2	4	0	0	0	2	0	0	1
Heinie Reitz, 2b	.333	4	15	1	5	0	0	0	4	1	3	1
Wilbert Robinson, c	.267	4	15	1	4	0	0	0	1	1	1	1
TOTAL	.200		135	11	27	1	2	0	10	11	15	8

PITCHER	W	L	ERA	G	GS	CG	SV	SHO	IP	H	ER	BB	SO
Duke Esper	0	1	4.00	1	1	1	0	0	9.0	13	4	1	3
Kid Gleason	0	1	9.69	2	1	1	0	0	13.0	25	14	6	3
Bill Hawke	0	1	9.00	1	1	0	0	0	4.0	9	4	1	0
George Hemming	0	1	1.13	1	1	1	0	0	8.0	10	1	3	2
TOTAL	0	4	6.09	5	4	3	0	0	34.0	57	23	11	8

GAME 1 AT BAL OCT 4

| NY | 000 011 110 | 4 13 2 |
| BAL | 000 000 001 | 1 7 1 |

Pitchers: RUSIE vs ESPER
Attendance: 9,000

GAME 2 AT BAL OCT 5

| NY | 004 000 014 | 9 14 3 |
| BAL | 022 000 101 | 6 7 2 |

Pitchers: MEEKIN vs GLEASON
Attendance: 11,000

GAME 3 AT NY OCT 6

| BAL | 000 100 000 | 1 7 4 |
| NY | 100 012 00X | 4 10 4 |

Pitchers: HEMMING vs RUSIE
Attendance: 22,000

GAME 4 AT NY OCT 8

| BAL | 201 000 00 | 3 6 3 |
| NY | 101 351 50 | 16 20 4 |

Pitchers: HAWKE, Gleason (5) vs
    MEEKIN
Attendance: 12,000
(Game called at end of eighth, darkness)

Baltimore, repeating as NL pennant winner, returned to Temple Cup play against new runner-up Cleveland. The first 4½ innings of the opener—played in Cleveland—featured a scoreless duel between Baltimore veteran John "Sadie" McMahon and the Spiders' great Cy Young. After Cleveland scored the game's first run in the last of the fifth, the teams traded runs and the lead, completing the eighth inning tied 3–3. In the top of the ninth, doubles by Wilbert Robinson and John McGraw restored the edge to Baltimore. But in the bottom of the inning, four straight Spider hits pushed across the tying run and filled the bases. One runner was forced at home for the first out, but a grounder that just missed being a double-play ball drove in the winning Cleveland run.

The next three games were not so closely contested. A large and enthusiastic Cleveland crowd watched its Spiders jump on Baltimore for three runs in the bottom of the first inning of Game Two and coast to a 7–2 win behind the strong pitching of Nig Cuppy, who held the Orioles to five singles. Cleveland repeated itself in Game Three, again exploding for three runs in the bottom of the first on the way to a seven-run total. Cy Young was just as effective in the box as Cuppy had been, scattering four hits over seven shutout innings before Baltimore put together three singles in the eighth for their only run.

When the teams shifted to Baltimore for Game Four, the Orioles sprang to life. While their pitcher Duke Esper strangled the Spiders on just five singles—only two Cleveland runners advanced as far as second base—Oriole batters tagged Nig Cuppy for five runs and their first Temple Cup win in two years of trying.

It proved to be their only win of the Series. The next day, in the first close struggle since the opener, Cy Young and Baltimore's rookie ace Bill Hoffer dueled scorelessly through six innings. But in the top of the seventh, Young doubled to start what became a three-run rally, and an inning later the Spiders scored twice more. Baltimore scored a single run in the last of the seventh, and, with two out in the ninth, loaded the bases on two walks and a hit batsman. A Cleveland error brought in the Orioles' second run as the bases remained full for Steve Brodie. But despite the pleas of Baltimore partisans to hit a homer or triple, Brodie "failed miserably" and Cleveland copped the cup.

Cleveland Spiders, 4; Baltimore Orioles, 1

CLE (N)

PLAYER/POS	AVG	G	AB	R	H	2B	3B	HR	RB	BB	SO	SB
Harry Blake, of	.250	5	20	1	5	3	0	0	2	0	2	0
Jesse Burkett, of	.450	5	20	3	9	2	0	0	2	0	0	1
Cupid Childs, 2b	.190	5	21	4	4	1	0	0	2	1	0	1
Nig Cuppy, p	.167	2	6	1	1	1	0	0	1	0	0	0
Jimmy McAleer, of	.286	5	21	2	6	0	0	0	2	0	0	1
Chippy McGarr, 3b	.368	5	19	3	7	2	0	0	1	1	0	2
Ed McKean, ss	.300	5	20	2	6	1	1	0	4	3	0	1
Patsy Tebeau, 1b	.286	5	21	3	6	1	0	0	3	1	1	0
Cy Young, p	.250	3	12	3	3	1	0	0	1	0	1	0
Chief Zimmer, c	.333	4	18	2	6	2	0	0	3	3	4	0
TOTAL	.298		178	24	53	14	1	0	21	9	9*	6

PITCHER	W	L	ERA	G	GS	CG	SV	SHO	IP	H	ER	BB	SO
Nig Cuppy	1	1	3.18	2	2	2	0	0	17.0	14	6	4	6
Cy Young	3	0	2.33	3	3	3	0	0	27.0	28	7	4	2
TOTAL	4	1	2.66	5	5	5	0	0	44.0	42	13	8	8

BAL (N)

PLAYER/POS	AVG	G	AB	R	H	2B	3B	HR	RB	BB	SO	SB
Steve Brodie, of	.200	5	20	1	4	0	0	0	2	0	0	0
Scoops Carey, 1b	.263	5	19	0	5	1	0	0	1	0	0	0
Boileryard Clarke, c	.286	2	7	1	2	0	0	0	0	0	0	2
Duke Esper, p	.000	1	3	0	0	0	0	0	0	1	2	0
Kid Gleason, 2b	.105	5	19	0	2	0	0	0	0	0	1	0
Bill Hoffer, p	.000	2	7	0	0	0	0	0	0	0	2	0
Hughie Jennings, ss	.368	5	19	3	7	2	0	0	2	1	0	1
Willie Keeler, of	.235	5	17	3	4	0	0	0	1	3	1	0
Joe Kelley, of	.368	5	19	1	7	0	0	0	5	1	1	1
John McGraw, 3b	.400	5	20	4	8	2	0	0	1	2	0	2
Sadie McMahon, p	.000	2	7	0	0	0	0	0	0	0	0	0
Wilbert Robinson, c	.250	3	12	1	3	1	0	0	0	0	1	0
TOTAL	.249		169	14	42	6	0	0	12	8	8	6

PITCHER	W	L	ERA	G	GS	CG	SV	SHO	IP	H	ER	BB	SO
Duke Esper	1	0	0.00	1	1	1	0	1	9.0	5	0	0	3
Bill Hoffer	0	2	4.24	2	2	2	0	0	17.0	21	8	6	4
Sadie McMahon	0	2	5.94	2	2	2	0	0	16.2	27	11	3	2
TOTAL	1	4	4.01	5	5	5	0	1	42.2	53	19	9	9

* While the total strikeouts for the team have been confirmed as 9, research has failed, to this point, to identify the missing batter strikeout.

Baltimore captured its third consecutive pennant and for the second year in a row faced runner-up Cleveland in the Temple Cup games. But this time the Orioles emerged triumphant—with a sweep in which their margin of victory was never less than four runs.

Aces Bill Hoffer of Baltimore and the Spiders' Cy Young faced each other in the opener, in Baltimore. Hoffer walked four men, but gave up only five hits while the Orioles bombarded Young for thirteen. When the game ended, Hoffer and Baltimore had a 7–1 win.

Bobby Wallace (who had not yet discovered his role at shortstop that would propel him into the Hall of Fame) pitched for Cleveland in Game Two. He lost the game in the first inning when two Spider errors, a hit batsman, three hits, and a steal of home put four Baltimore runs on the board. The Orioles added two runs in the third and another in the fifth, while their promising twenty-year-old pitcher Joe Corbett held the Spiders to two runs on seven hits.

The Orioles' Hoffer gave up ten hits to Cleveland in Game Three—two more than the Birds made off Spider Nig Cuppy. But all the hits off Hoffer were singles, and he walked only one. Half of Cleveland's hits went toward producing just two runs. Their second run tied the score in the fifth inning, but in the sixth Baltimore regained the lead as John McGraw singled, stole second, took third on an error, and came home on an outfield fly. In the eighth the Orioles bunched four of their eight hits for three insurance runs.

The Series moved to Cleveland for the fourth game. Young Joe Corbett was again sent into the box for Baltimore, this time to face Nig Cuppy. For six innings the game was a scoreless duel. Baltimore hit safely in every inning but the second, but failed to score until the seventh, when Joe Kelley's double and Jack Doyle's single scored the only run they would need. But the Orioles added a second run in that inning and three more in the eighth. Two of the four Cleveland hits against Corbett put men on base in the eighth inning, and Corbett walked two in the ninth to raise Cleveland's hopes. But no Spider scored, and with the 5–0 win the Orioles were world champions at last.

Baltimore Orioles, 4; Cleveland Spiders, 0

BAL (N)

PLAYER/POS	AVG	G	AB	R	H	2B	3B	HR	RB	BB	SO	SB
Steve Brodie, of	.067	4	15	1	1	0	0	0	3	0	0	1
Joe Corbett, p	.500	2	6	1	3	1	0	0	0	1	1	0
Jack Doyle, 1b	.294	4	17	3	5	1	0	0	4	0	0	2
Bill Hoffer, p	.286	2	7	1	2	0	2	0	0	0	1	0
Hughie Jennings, ss	.333	4	15	5	5	2	0	0	3	1	2	1
Willie Keeler, of	.471	4	17	4	8	1	2	0	4	0	0	1
Joe Kelley, of	.471	4	17	3	8	1	0	0	4	0	1	2
John McGraw, 3b	.267	4	15	4	4	0	0	0	1	0	0	4
Joe Quinn, 2b	.000	1	3	1	0	0	0	0	0	0	0	0
Heinie Reitz, 2b	.133	4	15	1	2	0	0	0	2	1	0	0
Wilbert Robinson, c	.267	4	15	1	4	1	0	0	2	0	3	0
TOTAL	.296		142	25	42	7	4	0	23	3	8	11

PITCHER	W	L	ERA	G	GS	CG	SV	SHO	IP	H	ER	BB	SO
Joe Corbett	2	0	0.50	2	2	2	0	1	18.0	11	1	7	10
Bill Hoffer	2	0	1.50	2	2	2	0	0	18.0	15	3	5	10
TOTAL	4	0	1.00	4	4	4	0	1	36.0	26	4	12	20

CLE (N)

PLAYER/POS	AVG	G	AB	R	H	2B	3B	HR	RB	BB	SO	SB
Harry Blake, of	.071	4	14	1	1	0	0	0	0	1	1	1
Jesse Burkett, of	.333	4	15	1	5	0	0	0	0	2	3	0
Cupid Childs, 2b	.231	4	13	2	3	0	0	0	0	4	0	1
Nig Cuppy, p	.143	2	7	0	1	0	0	0	0	0	1	0
Jimmy McAleer, of	.133	4	15	0	2	0	0	0	1	1	2	1
Chippy McGarr, 3b	.063	4	16	0	1	0	0	0	0	0	3	2
Ed McKean, ss	.313	4	16	0	5	1	1	0	1	1	2	1
Jack O'Connor, 1b	.286	4	14	1	4	0	0	0	1	1	2	0
Patsy Tebeau, 1b	.000	1	1	0	0	0	0	0	0	0	0	0
Bobby Wallace, p-1	.200	3	5	0	1	0	0	0	0	0	0	0
Cy Young, p	.000	1	3	0	0	0	0	0	0	0	0	0
Chief Zimmer, c	.214	4	14	0	3	1	0	0	1	2	6	0
TOTAL	.195		133	5	26	2	1	0	4	12	20	6

PITCHER	W	L	ERA	G	GS	CG	SV	SHO	IP	H	ER	BB	SO
Nig Cuppy	0	2	4.76	2	2	2	0	0	17.0	19	9	0	4
Bobby Wallace	0	1	4.50	1	1	1	0	0	8.0	10	4	2	4
Cy Young	0	1	6.00	1	1	1	0	0	9.0	13	6	1	0
TOTAL	0	4	5.03	4	4	4	0	0	34.0	42	19	3	8

GAME 1 AT BAL OCT 2

BAL	002 001 310	7 13 1
CLE	000 001 000	1 5 4

Pitchers: HOFFER vs YOUNG
Attendance: 4,000

GAME 2 AT BAL OCT 3

BAL	402 010 00	7 10 3
CLE	001 001 00	2 7 3

Pitchers: CORBETT vs WALLACE
Attendance: 3,100
(Game called at end of eighth, darkness)

GAME 3 AT BAL OCT 5

BAL	011 001 030	6 8 2
CLE	001 010 000	2 10 2

Pitchers: HOFFER vs CUPPY
Attendance: 2,000

GAME 4 AT CLE OCT 8

CLE	000 000 000	0 4 2
BAL	000 000 23X	5 11 1

Pitchers: CUPPY vs CORBETT
Attendance: 1,500

Boston had edged Baltimore in a close race for the NL pennant, but the Orioles turned the tables on the Beaneaters in Temple Cup play. The Series was a high-scoring affair, the winner of each game averaging eleven runs, the loser eight.

The opener, in Boston, set the tone for the games. Baltimore sent four runners across the plate in the top of the first inning, and Boston followed in its half with three. The Beaneaters recorded only twelve hits in the game to the Orioles' twenty, but they also received seven walks from Baltimore hurler Jerry Nops, and five of those runners scored. The lead switched back and forth in the middle innings, but Boston scored two final runs in the eighth and hung on for a 13–12 win.

Baltimore's Joe Corbett gave up sixteen hits (one a home run) and four walks in Game Two as Boston scored eleven times. But Boston's two pitchers, Fred Klobedanz and Jack Stivetts, were even more generous, handing out seventeen hits (including three homers—one of them to opposing pitcher Corbett, who also hit a double and two singles) and five walks as the Orioles evened the Series with their thirteen-run attack.

Game Three was the Series' lowest in run production, with Baltimore scoring four in the second inning and another four in the third for an 8–3 win. But rain ended the game before Boston could complete its time at bat in the last of the eighth, which erased from the record four more Oriole runs scored earlier in the inning. Rather than waste the two free days before the Series resumed in Baltimore, the two clubs played a pair of exhibition games in Worcester and Springfield, Massachusetts. Baltimore won them both, 11–10 and 8–6.

The Orioles continued their roll in Series Game Four, with another close but high-scoring victory, 12–11. It looked at first like a blowout as Baltimore scored six runs in the first inning and five more in the second. But Ted Lewis relieved Boston starter Jack Stivetts and held Baltimore to just one further run as the Beaneaters fought back to within one run of a tie before faltering in the ninth.

Boston batters hit Oriole Bill Hoffer safely fifteen times in Game Five, but only three Beaneaters scored. Baltimore, with two fewer hits, garnered six more runs than Boston and, with their fourth win, the right to hold the cup for another year. But attendance at the final game was so small the embarrassed Baltimore management refused to release the figures, and the league gave the cup back to Mr. Temple rather than sponsor another unprofitable Series. There was no postseason championship contest in 1898 or 1899.

Baltimore Orioles, 4; Boston Beaneaters, 1

BAL (N)

PLAYER/POS	AVG	G	AB	R	H	2B	3B	HR	RB	BB	SO	SB
Frank Bowerman, c-1,1b-1	.500	2	8	2	4	0	1	0	4	0	0	0
Boileryard Clarke, c	.563	4	16	5	9	1	1	1	4	1	0	0
Joe Corbett, p	.667	2	6	2	4	1	0	1	2	0	1	0
Jack Doyle, 1b	.526	5	19	7	10	2	0	0	9	0	1	2
Bill Hoffer, p	.250	2	8	2	2	1	0	0	0	0	0	0
Hughie Jennings, ss	.318	5	22	5	7	2	0	0	3	4	0	0
Willie Keeler, of	.391	5	23	5	9	2	0	0	2	4	0	0
Joe Kelley, of	.313	4	16	7	5	3	0	0	5	5	0	0
John McGraw, 3b	.300	5	20	6	6	1	1	0	6	7	0	0
Jerry Nops, p	.286	2	7	0	2	0	0	0	1	1	5	0
Tom O'Brien, of	.400	1	5	2	2	1	0	0	0	0	0	0
Heinie Reitz, 2b	.250	5	20	4	5	1	0	1	4	2	0	0
Jake Stenzel, of	.381	5	21	7	8	1	1	0	3	2	0	2
TOTAL	.382		191	54	73	16	4	3	43	26	7	4

PITCHER	W	L	ERA	G	GS	CG	SV	SHO	IP	H	ER	BB	SO
Joe Corbett	1	0	9.00	2	1	1	0	0	12.0	21	12	8	5
Bill Hoffer	2	0	3.38	2	2	2	0	0	16.0	25	6	4	2
Jerry Nops	1	1	12.86	2	2	1	0	0	14.0	23	20	9	3
TOTAL	4	1	8.14	6	5	4	0	0	42.0	69	38	21	10

BOS (N)

PLAYER/POS	AVG	G	AB	R	H	2B	3B	HR	RB	BB	SO	SB
Marty Bergen, c	.500	1	4	0	2	0	0	0	1	0	1	1
Jimmy Collins, 3b	.182	5	22	4	4	0	0	0	4	1	0	0
Hugh Duffy, of	.524	5	21	6	11	2	0	0	7	1	0	0
Billy Hamilton, of	.500	4	16	6	8	1	0	0	2	5	3	2
Charlie Hickman, p-1,of-1	.250	1	4	0	1	1	0	0	1	0	0	0
Fred Klobedanz, p	1.000	2	5	3	5	0	0	0	1	0	0	0
Fred Lake, c	.000	1	3	0	0	0	0	0	0	0	1	0
Ted Lewis, p	.500	3	6	1	3	1	0	0	1	1	0	0
Herman Long, ss	.286	5	21	4	6	1	1	1	5	2	2	1
Bobby Lowe, 2b	.391	5	23	6	9	2	0	0	6	1	0	1
Kid Nichols, p	.000	1	3	0	0	0	0	0	1	0	0	0
Chick Stahl, of	.381	5	21	6	8	1	0	0	6	3	2	2
Jack Stivetts, p-2,of-1	.000	3	7	1	0	0	0	0	0	1	0	1
Jim Sullivan, p	.000	1	1	0	0	0	0	0	0	0	0	0
Fred Tenney, 1b	.286	5	21	4	6	0	0	0	2	4	1	2
George Yeager, c	.500	3	12	2	6	1	1	0	2	2	0	0
TOTAL	.365		189	41	69	10	2	1	38	21	10	10

PITCHER	W	L	ERA	G	GS	CG	SV	SHO	IP	H	ER	BB	SO
Charlie Hickman	0	1	3.60	1	1	0	0	0	5.0	7	2	2	0
Fred Klobedanz	0	1	9.35	2	1	0	0	0	8.2	12	9	8	0
Ted Lewis	1	1	6.00	3	1	0	0	0	12	18	8	9	4
Kid Nichols	0	0	12.00	1	1	0	0	0	6.0	14	8	0	3
Jack Stivetts	0	1	18.47	2	1	0	0	0	6.1	16	13	7	0
Jim Sullivan	0	0	3.00	1	0	0	0	0	3.0	6	1	0	0
TOTAL	1	4	9.00	10	5	0	0	0	41.0	73	41	26	7

GAME 1 AT BOS OCT 4

BAL	401	023	200	12	20	4
BOS	300	125	02X	13	12	4

Pitchers: NOPS vs Nichols, LEWIS (7)
Attendance: 9,600

GAME 2 AT BOS OCT 5

BAL	130	160	110	13	17	2
BOS	002	620	100	11	16	3

Pitchers: CORBETT vs KLOBEDANZ, Stivetts (5)
Home Runs: Reitz-BAL, Clarke-BAL, Corbett-BAL, Long-BOS
Attendance: 6,500

GAME 3 AT BOS OCT 6

BAL	044	000	0	8	9	2
BOS	003	000	0	3	10	2

Pitchers: HOFFER vs LEWIS, Klobedanz (3)
Attendance: 5,000
(Game called in eighth, rain)

GAME 4 AT BAL OCT 9

BOS	000	024	320	11	16	3
BAL	650	001	00X	12	14	3

Pitchers: STIVETTS, Lewis (2) vs NOPS, Corbett (7)
Attendance: 2,500

GAME 5 AT BAL OCT 11

BOS	020	000	001	3	15	3
BAL	023	000	22X	9	13	2

Pitchers: HICKMAN, Sullivan (7) vs HOFFER
Attendance: 700

Pennant-winning Brooklyn led the NL in hitting, but runner-up Pittsburgh claimed the best pitching. Honus Wagner was the only Pirate regular to hit over .300, but he enjoyed what turned out to be his finest season offensively, leading the league with a .381 batting average. Pittsburghers believed their club superior to Brooklyn and a best-of-five "world championship" series was arranged, with all the games to be played in Pittsburgh for a silver cup donated by the *Pittsburgh Chronicle-Telegraph*. Brooklyn, however, proved that its pennant was no fluke.

Two of the game's best pitchers faced off in the opener: Pittsburgh's Rube Waddell, who had led the league in ERA, and Joe "Iron Man" McGinnity, whose 28 regular-season wins totaled eight more than those of the league's runners-up. McGinnity prevailed, shutting out the Pirates until two unearned runs came across in the top of the ninth. Pirate errors also gave Brooklyn a pair of unearned runs, but Waddell lost the game on hits—thirteen in all, including six in the Superbas' three-run third inning.

In Game Two, Brooklyn's Frank Kitson held Pittsburgh to four hits, and although his Superbas scored only one earned run, six Pirate errors gave them their second win, 4–2.

The Pirates staved off a Series sweep with sharp pitching and heavy hitting in Game Three. Deacon Phillippe shut out Brooklyn on six hits as the Pirates jumped on Harry Howell for thirteen. All the Pirate hits were singles, but combined with Brooklyn errors they were good for ten runs, seven of them unearned.

Three Brooklyn singles and a fumble by Pirate pitcher Sam Leever in the fourth inning of Game Four gave the Superbas three runs and a 4–0 lead the Pirates could not overcome. Brooklyn hurler McGinnity scattered nine Pirate hits and, supported by flawless fielding, held Pittsburgh to a single run to bring Brooklyn its first World Series triumph in three tries—and its last until 1955. The Brooklyn players voted to award their trophy to McGinnity for his fine pitching. The cup may be seen today—along with the Temple Cup and the current World Series trophy—at the Baseball Hall of Fame in Cooperstown.

Brooklyn Superbas, 3; Pittsburgh Pirates, 1

BRO (N)

PLAYER/POS	AVG	G	AB	R	H	2B	3B	HR	RB	BB	SO	SB
Lave Cross, 3b	.278	4	18	2	5	0	1	0	1	0	0	1
Bill Dahlen, ss	.176	4	17	3	3	0	1	0	2	0	3	1
Tom Daly, 2b	.154	4	13	2	2	1	0	0	1	3	1	0
Duke Farrell, c	.375	2	8	0	3	0	0	0	1	0	0	1
Harry Howell, p	.000	1	3	0	0	0	0	0	0	0	2	0
Hughie Jennings, 1b	.167	4	18	1	3	1	0	0	2	1	1	0
Fielder Jones, of	.278	4	18	3	5	0	0	0	4	1	1	1
Willie Keeler, of	.353	4	17	0	6	0	0	0	0	1	0	0
Joe Kelley, of	.176	4	17	2	3	0	0	0	1	2	3	0
Frank Kitson, p	.000	1	3	0	0	0	0	0	0	1	2	0
Joe McGinnity, p	.143	2	7	1	1	0	0	0	0	1	0	2	0
Deacon McGuire, c	.375	2	8	1	3	1	0	0	0	0	1	0
TOTAL	.231		147	15	34	3	2	0	13	9	16	4

PITCHER	W	L	ERA	G	GS	CG	SV	SHO	IP	H	ER	BB	SO
Harry Howell	0	1	3.38	1	1	1	0	0	8.0	13	3	2	3
Frank Kitson	1	0	1.00	1	1	1	0	0	9.0	4	1	1	2
Joe McGinnity	2	0	0.00	2	2	2	0	0	18.0	14	0	3	5
TOTAL	3	1	1.03	4	4	4	0	0	35.0	31	4	6	10

PIT (N)

PLAYER/POS	AVG	G	AB	R	H	2B	3B	HR	RB	BB	SO	SB
Ginger Beaumont, of	.267	4	15	2	4	0	0	0	1	1	0	1
Fred Ely, ss	.286	4	14	1	4	1	0	0	0	1	1	2
Tommy Leach, of	.176	4	17	4	3	0	0	0	1	1	2	0
Sam Leever, p	.250	2	4	0	1	0	0	0	0	0	1	1
Tom O'Brien, 1b	.125	4	16	1	2	1	0	0	2	0	1	0
Jack O'Connor, c	.250	2	4	0	1	0	0	0	1	1	0	0
Deacon Phillippe, p	.000	1	4	1	0	0	0	0	0	0	1	0
Claude Ritchey, 2b	.333	4	15	3	5	1	0	0	1	1	0	0
Pop Schriver, ph	.000	1	1	0	0	0	0	0	0	0	0	0
Rube Waddell, p	.200	2	5	0	1	0	0	0	0	0	1	0
Honus Wagner, of	.400	4	15	2	6	1	0	0	3	0	1	2
Jimmy Williams, 3b	.214	4	14	0	3	0	0	0	0	1	0	0
Chief Zimmer, c	.111	3	9	1	1	0	0	0	1	0	2	1
TOTAL	.233		133	15	31	4	0	0	10	6	10	7

PITCHER	W	L	ERA	G	GS	CG	SV	SHO	IP	H	ER	BB	SO
Sam Leever	0	2	1.38	2	2	1	0	0	13.0	13	2	4	4
Deacon Phillippe	1	0	0.00	1	1	1	0	1	9.0	6	0	2	5
Rube Waddell	0	1	1.93	2	1	1	0	0	14.0	15	3	3	7
TOTAL	1	3	1.25	5	4	3	0	1	36.0	34	5	9	16

GAME 1 AT PIT OCT 15

BRO	003 101 000	5 13 1
PIT	000 000 002	2 5 4

Pitchers: McGINNITY vs WADDELL
Attendance: 4,000

GAME 2 AT PIT OCT 16

BRO	010 003 000	4 7 0
PIT	000 100 100	2 4 6

Pitchers: KITSON vs LEEVER
Attendance: 1,800

GAME 3 AT PIT OCT 17

BRO	000 000 000	0 6 3
PIT	310 020 13X	10 13 1

Pitchers: HOWELL vs PHILLIPPE
Attendance: 2,500

GAME 4 AT PIT OCT 18

BRO	100 311 000	6 8 0
PIT	000 001 000	1 9 3

Pitchers: McGINNITY vs LEEVER, Waddell (5)
Attendance: 2,335

When the Boston Pilgrims of the young American League accepted a challenge from owner Barney Dreyfuss of the National League Pirates, the modern World Series was born. (In 1901–02, the National and American Leagues were warring, and did not stage a postseason series.) Pittsburgh was favored to win but entered the Series weakened by injuries to pitching ace Sam Leever and shortstop Honus Wagner, and by the loss of pitcher Ed Doheny to mental illness.

Deacon Phillippe, the Pirates' one healthy starter, faced Cy Young in the opener, winning handily as Pirate batters, with two out in the top of the first, jumped on Young (and a porous defense) for four runs. Right fielder Jimmy Sebring starred offensively for the Pirates, with four RBIs and the Series's first home run. Boston came back in Game Two as Bill Dinneen shut out the Pirates on three hits. His teammates scored three runs off the sore-armed Leever and reliever Bucky Veil, two coming on homers by Patsy Dougherty. (They were the last World Series home runs for five years.)

Phillippe, with only a day's rest, started Game Three and again pitched Pittsburgh into the Series lead, holding Boston to four hits. After a Sunday travel day to Pittsburgh and a day of rain, Phillippe defeated Boston a third time, though he yielded three ninth-inning runs before emerging with a 5–4 win.

The tide began to turn against the Pirates the next day, as Boston knocked five ground-rule triples into the overflow crowd, scoring ten runs in the sixth and seventh innings to give Young an 11–2 victory. Dinneen bested Leever for a second time in Game Six, holding the Pirates scoreless in eight of their nine innings for a 6–3 win. And in Game Seven, Phillippe finally lost, Young winning his second game as Boston numbered 5 more triples among its 11 hits.

After another travel Sunday and another rainout, Phillippe for the fifth time faced the Pilgrims. He pitched well, giving up three runs (only two of them earned). But Bill Dinneen pitched better, holding the Pirates to four hits as he shut them out for the second time to give Boston the Series.

Boston Pilgrims (AL), 5; Pittsburgh Pirates (NL), 3

BOS (A)

PLAYER/POS	AVG	G	AB	R	H	2B	3B	HR	RB	BB	SO	SB
Jimmy Collins, 3b	.250	8	36	5	9	1	2	0	1	1	1	3
Lou Criger, c	.231	8	26	1	6	0	0	0	4	2	3	0
Bill Dinneen, p	.250	4	12	1	3	0	0	0	0	2	2	0
Patsy Dougherty, of	.235	8	34	3	8	0	2	2	5	2	6	0
Duke Farrell, ph	.000	2	2	0	0	0	0	0	1	0	0	0
Hobe Ferris, 2b	.290	8	31	3	9	0	1	0	5	0	6	0
Buck Freeman, of	.281	8	32	6	9	0	3	0	4	2	2	0
Tom Hughes, p	.000	1	0	0	0	0	0	0	0	0	0	0
Candy La Chance, 1b	.222	8	27	5	6	2	1	0	4	3	2	0
Jack O'Ben, ph	.000	2	2	0	0	0	0	0	0	0	1	0
Freddy Parent, ss	.281	8	32	8	9	0	3	0	4	1	1	0
Chick Stahl, of	.303	8	33	6	10	1	3	0	3	1	2	2
Cy Young, p	.133	4	15	1	2	0	1	0	3	0	3	0
TOTAL	.252		282	39	71	4	16	2	34	14	29	5

PITCHER	W	L	ERA	G	GS	CG	SV	SHO	IP	H	ER	BB	SO
Bill Dinneen	3	1	2.06	4	4	4	0	2	35.0	29	8	8	28
Tom Hughes	0	1	9.00	1	1	0	0	0	2.0	4	2	2	0
Cy Young	2	1	1.85	4	3	3	0	0	34.0	31	7	4	17
TOTAL	5	3	2.15	9	8	7	0	2	71.0	64	17	14	45

PIT (N)

PLAYER/POS	AVG	G	AB	R	H	2B	3B	HR	RB	BB	SO	SB
Ginger Beaumont, of	.265	8	34	6	9	0	1	0	1	2	4	2
Kitty Bransfield, 1b	.207	8	29	3	6	0	2	0	1	1	6	1
Fred Clarke, of	.265	8	34	3	9	2	1	0	2	1	5	1
Brickyard Kennedy, p	.500	1	2	0	1	1	0	0	0	0	0	0
Tommy Leach, 3b	.273	8	33	3	9	0	4	0	7	1	4	1
Sam Leever, p	.000	2	4	0	0	0	0	0	0	0	0	0
Ed Phelps, c-7	.231	8	26	1	6	2	0	0	1	1	6	0
Deacon Phillippe, p	.222	5	18	1	4	0	0	0	1	0	3	0
Claude Ritchey, 2b	.111	8	27	2	3	1	0	0	2	4	7	1
Jimmy Sebring, of	.367	8	30	3	11	0	1	1	3	1	4	0
Harry Smith, c	.000	1	3	0	0	0	0	0	0	0	0	0
Gus Thompson, p	.000	1	1	0	0	0	0	0	0	0	2	0
Bucky Veil, p	.000	1	2	0	0	0	0	0	0	0	2	0
Honus Wagner, ss	.222	8	27	2	6	1	0	0	3	3	4	3
TOTAL	.237		270	24	64	7	9	1	21	14	45	9

PITCHER	W	L	ERA	G	GS	CG	SV	SHO	IP	H	ER	BB	SO
Brickyard Kennedy	0	1	5.14	1	1	0	0	0	7.0	11	4	3	3
Sam Leever	0	2	5.40	2	2	1	0	0	10.0	13	6	3	2
Deacon Phillippe	3	2	2.86	5	5	5	0	0	44.0	38	14	3	22
Gus Thompson	0	0	4.50	1	0	0	0	0	2.0	3	1	0	1
Bucky Veil	0	0	1.29	1	0	0	0	0	7.0	6	1	5	1
TOTAL	3	5	3.34	10	8	6	0	0	70.0	71	26	14	29

GAME 1 AT BOS OCT 1

PIT	401	100	100	7	12	2
BOS	000	000	201	3	6	4

Pitchers: PHILLIPPE vs YOUNG
Home Runs: Sebring-PIT
Attendance: 16,242

GAME 2 AT BOS OCT 2

PIT	000	000	000	0	3	2
BOS	200	001	00X	3	9	0

Pitchers: LEEVER, Vail (2) vs DINNEEN
Home Runs: Dougherty-BOS(2)
Attendance: 9,415

GAME 3 AT BOS OCT 3

PIT	012	000	010	4	7	0
BOS	000	100	010	2	4	2

Pitchers: PHILLIPPE vs HUGHES, Young (3)
Attendance: 18,801

GAME 4 AT PIT OCT 6

BOS	000	010	003	4	9	1
PIT	100	010	30X	5	12	1

Pitchers: DINNEEN vs PHILLIPPE
Attendance: 7,600

GAME 5 AT PIT OCT 7

BOS	000	006	410	11	14	2
PIT	000	000	020	2	6	4

Pitchers: YOUNG vs KENNEDY, Thompson (8)
Attendance: 12,322

GAME 6 AT PIT OCT 8

BOS	003	020	100	6	10	1
PIT	000	000	300	3	10	3

Pitchers: DINNEEN vs LEEVER
Attendance: 11,556

GAME 7 AT PIT OCT 10

BOS	200	202	010	7	11	4
PIT	000	101	001	3	10	3

Pitchers: YOUNG vs PHILLIPPE
Attendance: 17,038

GAME 8 AT BOS OCT 13

PIT	000	000	000	0	4	3
BOS	000	201	00X	3	8	0

Pitchers: PHILLIPPE vs DINNEEN
Attendance: 7,455

After a year's gap caused by the Giants' refusal to play the American League champion Boston Pilgrims, the World Series—now established on an official and permanent basis—resumed with a pitching classic. Even though the A's ERA league leader Rube Waddell had ostensibly injured his shoulder and could not pitch in the Series—rumor had it that gamblers had reached him—the Philadelphia staff recorded a Series ERA of only 1.47. But the Giants' staff—led by Christy Mathewson's three shutouts—registered a matchless ERA of 0.00, permitting only three unearned runs to score in their only Series loss. Every victory in the Series was a shutout.

Mathewson, a 31-game winner in the regular season, continued his winning ways in the Series opener. Though three of the four hits he yielded were doubles, he permitted no more than one hit in any inning, and stopped the only scoring threat, fielding a squeeze bunt to throw out the runner at the plate in the sixth inning.

The A's came back to tie the Series the next day. This time it was Chief Bender's turn to hurl a four-hit shutout. Joe McGinnity also pitched well for the Giants, but New York errors in the third and eighth innings let in three unearned runs—the only runs, as it turned out, to be scored against the Giants in the Series.

Mathewson, pitching with only two days' rest in Game Three, once again permitted only four hits (all singles this time), and Philadelphia's flawed fielding let in seven unearned runs to help give Matty an easy 9–0 win. In Game Four, McGinnity, the hard-luck loser of Game Two, tried again. This time the Giants supported him almost flawlessly, while he gave up only five singles on his way to victory in the Series' tightest game. An A's error led to a single Giant run, and a loss for Eddie Plank, who had pitched even better than McGinnity, giving up only four hits while fanning six.

Chief Bender, the A's winner in Game Two, pitched a five-hitter in Game Six, but he also yielded three walks, all of which contributed to the two Giant runs. Mathewson, though he gave up six hits, walked none, retiring the final ten batters to conclude his record third shutout—and the Series.

New York Giants (NL), 4; Philadelphia Athletics (AL), 1

NY (N)

PLAYER/POS	AVG	G	AB	R	H	2B	3B	HR	RB	BB	SO	SB
Red Ames, p	.000	1	0	0	0	0	0	0	0	0	0	0
Roger Bresnahan, c	.313	5	16	3	5	2	0	0	1	4	0	1
George Browne, of	.182	5	22	2	4	0	0	0	1	0	2	2
Bill Dahlen, ss	.000	5	15	1	0	0	0	0	1	3	2	3
Art Devlin, 3b	.250	5	16	0	4	1	0	0	1	1	3	3
Mike Donlin, of	.263	5	19	4	5	1	0	0	1	2	1	2
Billy Gilbert, 2b	.235	5	17	1	4	0	0	0	2	0	2	1
Christy Mathewson, p	.250	3	8	1	2	0	0	0	0	1	1	0
Dan McGann, 1b	.235	5	17	1	4	2	0	0	4	2	7	0
Joe McGinnity, p	.000	2	5	0	0	0	0	0	0	0	2	0
Sam Mertes, of	.176	5	17	2	3	1	0	0	2	2	5	0
Sammy Strang, ph	.000	1	1	0	0	0	0	0	0	0	1	0
TOTAL	.203		153	15	31	7	0	0	13	15	26	12

PITCHER	W	L	ERA	G	GS	CG	SV	SHO	IP	H	ER	BB	SO
Red Ames	0	0	0.00	1	0	0	0	0	1.0	1	0	1	1
Christy Mathewson	3	0	0.00	3	3	3	0	3	27.0	14	0	1	18
Joe McGinnity	1	1	0.00	2	2	1	0	1	17.0	10	0	3	6
TOTAL	4	1	0.00	6	5	4	0	4	45.0	25	0	5	25

PHI (A)

PLAYER/POS	AVG	G	AB	R	H	2B	3B	HR	RB	BB	SO	SB
Chief Bender, p	.000	2	5	0	0	0	0	0	0	0	1	0
Andy Coakley, p	.000	1	2	0	0	0	0	0	0	0	1	0
Lave Cross, 3b	.105	5	19	0	2	0	0	0	0	1	1	0
Monte Cross, ss	.176	5	17	0	3	0	0	0	0	0	7	0
Harry Davis, 1b	.200	5	20	0	4	1	0	0	0	0	1	0
Topsy Hartsel, of	.294	5	17	1	5	1	0	0	0	2	1	2
Danny Hoffman, ph	.000	1	1	0	0	0	0	0	0	0	1	0
Bris Lord, of	.100	5	20	0	2	0	0	0	2	0	5	0
Danny Murphy, 2b	.188	5	16	0	3	1	0	0	0	0	2	0
Eddie Plank, p	.167	2	6	0	1	0	0	0	0	0	2	0
Mike Powers, c	.143	3	7	0	1	1	0	0	0	0	0	0
Ossee Schreckengost, c	.222	3	9	2	2	1	0	0	0	0	0	0
Socks Seybold, of	.125	5	16	0	2	0	0	0	0	2	3	0
TOTAL	.161		155	3	25	5	0	0	2	5	25	2

PITCHER	W	L	ERA	G	GS	CG	SV	SHO	IP	H	ER	BB	SO
Chief Bender	1	1	1.06	2	2	2	0	1	17.0	9	2	6	13
Andy Coakley	0	1	2.00	1	1	1	0	0	9.0	8	2	5	2
Eddie Plank	0	2	1.59	2	2	2	0	0	17.0	14	3	4	11
TOTAL	1	4	1.47	5	5	5	0	1	43.0	31	7	15	26

The Cubs and White Sox have played more postseason City Series than any other clubs, but this was their only all-Chicago World Series. The Cubs were the clear favorites: league leaders in batting, fielding, and pitching (with a team ERA of only 1.76). They were one of baseball's greatest teams ever, with a still-record 116 wins, finishing 20 games ahead of the second-place Giants. The White Sox, by contrast, although their pitching and fielding were good enough to rank second in the American League, were the junior circuit's weakest hitters, batting as a team only .230, 32 points below the Cubs. But in the Series the "hitless wonders" prevailed. Though they hit only .198 and yielded eight unearned runs to the Cubs' two, the Sox bunched their hits for 20 earned runs—double the Cubs' total. Meanwhile, Sox pitchers held the Cubs to a .196 BA, and produced a team ERA less than half that of Cub pitchers.

Game One was a pitcher's duel as the Cubs' Mordecai (Three Finger) Brown and the Sox' Nick Altrock traded four-hitters and one earned run apiece. But Brown lost the game when his error in the seventh led to the Sox' second run. The Cubs snapped back to take Game Two on Ed Reulbach's one-hit 7–1 win. Although Reulbach issued six walks, he didn't really need the five unearned runs handed his club by Sox errors.

In Game Three the Sox regained the Series lead as Ed Walsh two-hit the Cubs, fanning 12 for the Series' first shutout. The Cubs' Jack Pfiester also pitched shutout ball in eight of his nine innings, but George Rohe's bases-loaded triple in the sixth gave the Sox more than enough to defeat him. Brown brought the Cubs back the next day, evening the Series with a two-hit shutout of his own, winning when Altrock yielded his only run on pairs of singles and sacrifice bunts in the seventh.

The rest of the Series belonged to the hitless wonders, who rocked three Cub pitchers for 12 hits and eight runs to take Game Five, and buried Brown and Orval Overall under 14 hits and another eight runs in Game Six to capture their first world championship.

Chicago White Sox (AL), 4; Chicago Cubs (NL), 2

CHI (A)

PLAYER/POS	AVG	G	AB	R	H	2B	3B	HR	RB	BB	SO	SB
Nick Altrock, p	.250	2	4	0	1	0	0	0	0	0	1	0
George Davis, ss	.308	3	13	4	4	3	0	0	6	0	1	1
Jiggs Donahue, 1b	.333	6	18	0	6	2	1	0	4	3	3	0
Patsy Dougherty, of	.100	6	20	1	2	0	0	0	1	3	4	2
Eddie Hahn, of	.273	6	22	4	6	0	0	0	0	1	1	0
Frank Isbell, 2b	.308	6	26	4	8	4	0	0	4	0	6	1
Fielder Jones, of	.095	6	21	4	2	0	0	0	0	3	3	0
Ed McFarland, ph	.000	1	0	0	0	0	0	0	0	0	0	0
Bill O'Neill, of	.000	1	1	1	0	0	0	0	0	0	0	0
Frank Owen, p	.000	1	2	0	0	0	0	0	0	0	1	0
George Rohe, 3b	.333	6	21	2	7	1	2	0	4	3	1	2
Billy Sullivan, c	.000	6	21	0	0	0	0	0	0	0	9	0
Lee Tannehill, ss	.111	3	9	1	1	0	0	0	0	0	2	0
Babe Towne, ph	.000	1	1	0	0	0	0	0	0	0	0	0
Ed Walsh, p	.000	2	4	1	0	0	0	0	0	0	3	0
Doc White, p	.000	3	3	0	0	0	0	0	0	1	0	0
TOTAL	.198		187	22	37	10	3	0	19	18	35	6

PITCHER	W	L	ERA	G	GS	CG	SV	SHO	IP	H	ER	BB	SO
Nick Altrock	1	1	1.00	2	2	2	0	0	18.0	11	2	2	5
Frank Owen	0	0	3.00	1	0	0	0	0	6.0	6	2	3	2
Ed Walsh	2	0	1.20	2	2	1	0	1	15.0	7	2	6	17
Doc White	1	1	1.80	3	2	1	1	0	15.0	12	3	7	4
TOTAL	4	2	1.50	8	6	4	1	1	54.0	36	9	18	28

CHI (N)

PLAYER/POS	AVG	G	AB	R	H	2B	3B	HR	RB	BB	SO	SB
Mordecai Brown, p	.333	3	6	0	2	0	0	0	0	0	4	0
Frank Chance, 1b	.238	6	21	3	5	1	0	0	0	2	1	2
Johnny Evers, 2b	.150	6	20	2	3	1	0	0	1	1	3	2
Doc Gessler, ph	.000	2	1	0	0	0	0	0	0	1	0	0
Solly Hofman, of	.304	6	23	3	7	1	0	0	2	3	5	1
Johnny Kling, c	.176	6	17	2	3	1	0	0	0	4	3	0
Pat Moran, ph	.000	2	2	0	0	0	0	0	0	0	0	0
Orval Overall, p	.250	2	4	1	1	1	0	0	0	1	1	0
Jack Pfiester, p	.000	2	2	0	0	0	0	0	0	0	0	0
Ed Reulbach, p	.000	2	3	0	0	0	0	0	0	1	0	0
Frank Schulte, of	.269	6	26	1	7	3	0	0	3	1	3	0
Jimmy Sheckard, of	.000	6	21	0	0	0	0	0	1	2	4	1
Harry Steinfeldt, 3b	.250	6	20	2	5	1	0	0	2	1	0	0
Joe Tinker, ss	.167	6	18	4	3	0	0	0	1	2	2	3
TOTAL	.196		184	18	36	9	0	0	11	18	28	9

PITCHER	W	L	ERA	G	GS	CG	SV	SHO	IP	H	ER	BB	SO
Mordecai Brown	1	2	3.20	3	3	2	0	1	19.2	14	7	4	12
Orval Overall	0	0	2.25	2	0	0	0	0	12.0	10	3	3	8
Jack Pfiester	0	2	6.10	2	1	1	0	0	10.1	7	7	3	11
Ed Reulbach	1	0	2.45	2	2	1	0	0	11.0	6	3	8	4
TOTAL	2	4	3.40	9	6	4	0	1	53.0	37	20	18	35

GAME 1 AT CHI-N OCT 9

CHI-A	000 011 000	2	4	1
CHI-N	000 001 000	1	4	2

Pitchers: ALTROCK vs BROWN
Attendance: 12,693

GAME 2 AT CHI-A OCT 10

CHI-N	031 001 020	7	10	2
CHI-A	000 010 000	1	1	2

Pitchers: REULBACH vs WHITE, Owen (4)
Attendance: 12,595

GAME 3 AT CHI-N OCT 11

CHI-A	000 003 000	3	4	1
CHI-N	000 000 000	0	2	2

Pitchers: WALSH vs PFIESTER
Attendance: 13,667

GAME 4 AT CHI-A OCT 12

CHI-N	000 000 100	1	7	1
CHI-A	000 000 000	0	2	1

Pitchers: BROWN vs ALTROCK
Attendance: 18,385

GAME 5 AT CHI-N OCT 13

CHI-A	102 401 000	8	12	6
CHI-N	300 102 000	6	6	0

Pitchers: WALSH, White (7) vs Reulbach, PFIESTER (3), Overall (4)
Attendance: 23,257

GAME 6 AT CHI-A OCT 14

CHI-N	100 010 001	3	7	0
CHI-A	340 000 01X	8	14	3

Pitchers: BROWN, Overall (2) vs WHITE
Attendance: 19,249

The two-run lead that Detroit took into the bottom of the ninth inning of Game One proved to be its biggest of the Series. And it was short-lived, as Chicago—after Frank Chance's leadoff single—took advantage of a hit batsman, a fumble at third base, and a dropped third strike to even the score. Three scoreless extra innings later, darkness ended the game in a 3–3 tie.

The Tigers pitched well enough in the Series. Wild Bill Donovan and George Mullin, who provided more than 80 percent of Detroit's pitching, allowed only four earned runs each for a combined 1.89 ERA. But Cub pitchers gave up only four earned runs *as a team,* suffocating the Tigers with a team ERA of 0.75. And while Tiger fielders made one less error than the Cubs, their misplays proved more costly, permitting eight unearned runs to the Cubs' two.

Detroit's three-run eighth in the opener provided half of their Series scoring. Nine Tiger hits in Game Two produced only one run, while the Cubs bunched six of their nine hits into two innings for three runs and the Series' first win. In Games Three and Four, while the Tigers were twice again limited to a single run, the Cubs increased their run production to five and six, clustering 40 percent of their hits into two three-run innings, one in each game. Mordecai (Three Finger) Brown wrapped up the Series for Chicago with a shutout, as his Cubs blended a hit in each of the first two innings with three stolen bases and a Tiger error for the game's only two runs.

Detroit's twenty-year-old Ty Cobb, the American League batting, RBI, and stolen base leader in his first full big league season, hit an anemic .200 in the World Series, stealing no bases and driving in no Tiger runs. If there was an offensive hero, it was Cub centerfielder Jimmy Slagle. At age thirty-four, nearing the end of a ten-year major league career, he led both clubs with four RBIs (nearly quadruple his season's per-game output) and six stolen bases.

Chicago Cubs (NL), 4;
Detroit Tigers (AL), 0; tie, 1

CHI (N)

PLAYER/POS	AVG	G	AB	R	H	2B	3B	HR	RB	BB	SO	SB
Mordecai Brown, p	.000	1	3	0	0	0	0	0	0	1	0	0
Frank Chance, 1b	.214	4	14	3	3	1	0	0	0	3	2	3
Johnny Evers, 2b-5,ss-1	.350	5	20	2	7	2	0	0	1	0	1	3
Del Howard, 1b-1	.200	2	5	0	1	0	0	0	0	0	2	1
Johnny Kling, c	.211	5	19	2	4	0	0	0	1	1	4	0
Pat Moran, ph	.000	1	0	0	0	0	0	0	0	0	0	0
Orval Overall, p	.200	2	5	0	1	0	0	0	2	0	1	0
Jack Pfiester, p	.000	2	2	0	0	0	0	0	0	0	1	0
Ed Reulbach, p	.200	2	5	0	1	0	0	0	1	0	0	0
Frank Schulte, of	.250	5	20	3	5	0	0	0	2	1	2	0
Jimmy Sheckard, of	.238	5	21	0	5	2	0	0	2	0	4	1
Jimmy Slagle, of	.273	5	22	3	6	0	0	0	4	2	3	6
Harry Steinfeldt, 3b	.471	5	17	2	8	1	1	0	2	1	2	1
Joe Tinker, ss	.154	5	13	4	2	0	0	0	1	3	3	1
Heinie Zimmerman, 2b	.000	1	1	0	0	0	0	0	0	0	1	0
TOTAL	.257		167	19	43	6	1	0	16	12	26	16

PITCHER	W	L	ERA	G	GS	CG	SV	SHO	IP	H	ER	BB	SO
Mordecai Brown	1	0	0.00	1	1	1	0	1	9.0	7	0	1	4
Orval Overall	1	0	1.00	2	2	1	0	0	18.0	14	2	4	11
Jack Pfiester	1	0	1.00	1	1	1	0	0	9.0	9	1	1	3
Ed Reulbach	1	0	0.75	2	1	1	0	0	12.0	6	1	3	4
TOTAL	4	0	0.75	6	5	4	0	1	48.0	36	4	9	22

DET (A)

PLAYER/POS	AVG	G	AB	R	H	2B	3B	HR	RB	BB	SO	SB
Jimmy Archer, c	.000	1	3	0	0	0	0	0	0	0	1	0
Ty Cobb, of	.200	5	20	1	4	0	1	0	0	0	3	0
Bill Coughlin, 3b	.250	5	20	0	5	0	0	0	0	1	4	1
Sam Crawford, of	.238	5	21	1	5	1	0	0	3	0	3	0
Bill Donovan, p	.000	2	8	0	0	0	0	0	0	0	3	0
Davy Jones, of	.353	5	17	1	6	0	0	0	0	4	0	3
Ed Killian, p	.500	1	2	1	1	0	0	0	0	0	0	0
George Mullin, p	.000	2	6	0	0	0	0	0	0	0	1	0
Charley O'Leary, ss	.059	5	17	0	1	0	0	0	0	1	3	0
Fred Payne, c-1	.250	2	4	0	1	0	0	0	1	0	0	1
Claude Rossman, 1b	.400	5	20	1	8	0	1	0	2	1	0	1
Germany Schaefer, 2b	.143	5	21	1	3	0	0	0	0	0	3	0
Boss Schmidt, c-3	.167	4	12	0	2	0	0	0	0	2	1	0
Ed Siever, p	.000	1	1	0	0	0	0	0	0	0	0	0
TOTAL	.209		172	6	36	1	2	0	6	9	22	6

PITCHER	W	L	ERA	G	GS	CG	SV	SHO	IP	H	ER	BB	SO
Bill Donovan	0	1	1.71	2	2	2	0	0	21.0	17	4	5	16
Ed Killian	0	0	2.25	1	0	0	0	0	4.0	3	1	1	1
George Mullin	0	2	2.12	2	2	2	0	0	17.0	16	4	6	8
Ed Siever	0	1	4.50	1	1	0	0	0	4.0	7	2	0	1
TOTAL	0	4	2.15	6	5	4	0	0	46.0	43	11	12	26

GAME 1 AT CHI OCT 8

```
DET   000 000 030 000   3  9  3
CHI   000 100 002 000   3 10  5
```
Pitchers: Donovan vs Overall, Reulbach (10)
Attendance: 24,377
(Game called at end of twelfth, darkness)

GAME 2 AT CHI OCT 9

```
DET   010 000 000   1  9  1
CHI   010 200 00X   3  9  1
```
Pitchers: MULLIN vs PFIESTER
Attendance: 21,901

GAME 3 AT CHI OCT 10

```
DET   000 001 000   1  6  1
CHI   010 310 00X   5 10  1
```
Pitchers: SIEVER, Killian (5) vs REULBACH
Attendance: 13,114

GAME 4 AT DET OCT 11

```
CHI   000 020 301   6  7  2
DET   000 100 000   1  5  2
```
Pitchers: OVERALL vs DONOVAN
Attendance: 11,306

GAME 5 AT DET OCT 12

```
CHI   110 000 000   2  7  1
DET   000 000 000   0  7  2
```
Pitchers: BROWN vs MULLIN
Attendance: 7,370

The Tigers won their final game of the season to take their second straight pennant, and the Cubs won their third pennant in a row by defeating the Giants in a replay of an earlier tie. Ty Cobb and Detroit improved on their 1907 Series performance, as Cobb led his club in batting, hits, and RBIs, and the Tigers won a game. But the Cubs as a team hit 90 percentage points higher than Detroit, and outscored them 24–15, to take the Series with relative ease.

In Game One, the Tigers took advantage of the Cubs' ragged fielding to score two runs in the eighth for a 6–5 lead. But in the top of the ninth, the Cubs erupted for five runs on six consecutive singles and a double steal, to win the game. The next day Chicago's Orval Overall held Detroit to four hits and one ninth-inning run. The Tigers' Wild Bill Donovan pitched even better for seven innings, holding Pittsburgh to a single in the sixth. But in the eighth, Joe Tinker's two-run homer—the first in a World Series since 1903—began an assault that ended only after six Cubs had crossed the plate.

Detroit finally manufactured a Series win, pummeling Jack Pfiester in Game Three for ten hits (six of them in the sixth inning) and an 8–3 victory. But that was their last burst. As the Series moved to Detroit for Games Four and Five, the Tiger offense collapsed. Three Finger Brown, the winner as a reliever in Game One, won Game Four as a starter, shutting out the Tigers on four hits. The Cubs needed only three of their ten hits, combining them with a couple of walks and stolen bases, and a muffed fly ball, to score twice in the third inning and once in the ninth.

Only 6,210 spectators—the smallest World Series crowd of the century—saw Overall strike out four Tigers in the first inning of Game Five (one reached first on a wild pitch) in what became a three-hit shutout. Meanwhile, his Cubs unloaded for ten hits, defeating Donovan a second time, scoring runs in the first and fifth innings. Overall—after yielding a leadoff walk to Cobb in the fifth—retired Cobb on a force play and set down the final 11 men to face him.

Chicago Cubs (NL), 4; Detroit Tigers (AL), 1

CHI (N)

PLAYER/POS	AVG	G	AB	R	H	2B	3B	HR	RB	BB	SO	SB
Mordecai Brown, p	.000	2	4	0	0	0	0	0	0	0	2	0
Frank Chance, 1b	.421	5	19	4	8	0	0	0	2	3	1	5
Johnny Evers, 2b	.350	5	20	5	7	1	0	0	2	1	2	2
Solly Hofman, of	.316	5	19	2	6	0	1	0	4	1	4	2
Del Howard, of	.000	1	1	0	0	0	0	0	0	0	0	0
Johnny Kling, c	.250	5	16	2	4	1	0	0	2	2	2	0
Orval Overall, p	.333	3	6	0	2	0	0	0	0	0	1	0
Jack Pfiester, p	.000	1	2	0	0	0	0	0	0	0	2	0
Ed Reulbach, p	.000	2	3	0	0	0	0	0	0	0	1	0
Frank Schulte, of	.389	5	18	4	7	0	1	0	2	2	1	2
Jimmy Sheckard, of	.238	5	21	2	5	2	0	0	1	2	3	1
Harry Steinfeldt, 3b	.250	5	16	3	4	0	0	0	3	2	5	1
Joe Tinker, ss	.263	5	19	2	5	0	0	1	4	0	2	2
TOTAL	.293		164	24	48	4	2	1	20	13	26	15

PITCHER	W	L	ERA	G	GS	CG	SV	SHO	IP	H	ER	BB	SO
Mordecai Brown	2	0	0.00	2	1	1	0	1	11.0	6	0	1	5
Orval Overall	2	0	0.98	3	2	2	0	1	18.1	7	2	7	15
Jack Pfiester	0	1	7.87	1	1	0	0	0	8.0	10	7	3	1
Ed Reulbach	0	0	4.70	2	1	0	0	0	7.2	9	4	1	5
TOTAL	4	1	2.60	8	5	3	0	2	45.0	32	13	12	26

DET (A)

PLAYER/POS	AVG	G	AB	R	H	2B	3B	HR	RB	BB	SO	SB
Ty Cobb, of	.368	5	19	3	7	1	0	0	4	1	2	2
Bill Coughlin, 3b	.125	3	8	0	1	0	0	0	1	0	1	0
Sam Crawford, of	.238	5	21	2	5	1	0	0	1	1	2	0
Bill Donovan, p	.000	2	4	0	0	0	0	0	0	1	1	1
Red Downs, 2b	.167	2	6	1	1	1	0	0	1	1	2	0
Davy Jones, ph	.000	3	2	1	0	0	0	0	0	1	1	0
Ed Killian, p	.000	1	0	0	0	0	0	0	0	0	0	0
Matty McIntyre, of	.222	5	18	2	4	1	0	0	0	3	2	1
George Mullin, p	.333	1	3	1	1	0	0	0	1	1	0	0
Charley O'Leary, ss	.158	5	19	2	3	0	0	0	0	0	3	0
Claude Rossman, 1b	.211	5	19	3	4	0	0	0	3	1	4	1
Germany Schaefer, 2b-3,3b-2	.125	5	16	0	2	0	0	0	0	1	4	1
Boss Schmidt, c	.071	4	14	0	1	0	0	0	1	0	2	0
Ed Summers, p	.200	2	5	0	1	0	0	0	1	0	2	0
Ira Thomas, c-1	.500	2	4	0	2	1	0	0	1	1	0	0
George Winter, p-1	.000	2	0	0	0	0	0	0	0	0	0	0
TOTAL	.203		158	15	32	5	0	0	14	12	26	6

PITCHER	W	L	ERA	G	GS	CG	SV	SHO	IP	H	ER	BB	SO
Bill Donovan	0	2	4.24	2	2	2	0	0	17.0	17	8	4	10
Ed Killian	0	0	11.57	1	1	0	0	0	2.1	5	3	3	1
George Mullin	1	0	0.00	1	1	1	0	0	9.0	7	0	1	8
Ed Summers	0	2	4.30	2	1	0	0	0	14.2	18	7	4	7
George Winter	0	0	0.00	1	0	0	0	0	1.0	1	0	1	0
TOTAL	1	4	3.68	7	5	3	0	0	44.0	48	18	13	26

GAME 1 AT DET OCT 10

CHI	004	000	105	10	14	2
DET	100	000	320	6	10	4

Pitchers: Reulbach, Overall (7), BROWN (8) vs Killian, SUMMERS (3)
Attendance: 10,812

GAME 2 AT CHI OCT 11

DET	000	000	001	1	4	1
CHI	000	000	06X	6	7	1

Pitchers: DONOVAN vs OVERALL
Home Runs: Tinker-CHI
Attendance: 17,760

GAME 3 AT CHI OCT 12

DET	100	005	020	8	11	4
CHI	000	300	000	3	7	2

Pitchers: MULLIN vs PFIESTER, Reulbach (9)
Attendance: 14,543

GAME 4 AT DET OCT 13

CHI	002	000	001	3	10	0
DET	000	000	000	0	4	1

Pitchers: BROWN vs SUMMERS, Winter (9)
Attendance: 12,907

GAME 5 AT DET OCT 14

CHI	100	010	000	2	10	0
DET	000	000	000	0	3	0

Pitchers: OVERALL vs DONOVAN
Attendance: 6,210

Babe Adams, a twenty-seven-year-old rookie pitcher, was only the fifth biggest winner on the Pittsburgh staff. But his fine 12–3 record was supported by a team-best 1.11 ERA, and manager Fred Clarke started him in the Series opener against Detroit's ace George Mullin (who had led the American League with a career-high 29 wins). Mullin pitched well, giving up only one earned run—manager/outfielder Clarke's homer in the fourth inning. But four Tiger errors led to three Pirate runs in the fifth and sixth. Meanwhile, Adams, after yielding a run in the first, pitched shutout ball the rest of the way for the win.

Detroit came back in Game Two with seven runs (including Ty Cobb's theft of home) as Wild Bill Donovan held the Pirates to two runs on five hits. In Game Three the Pirates took an early lead, which Detroit, despite rallies in the seventh and ninth innings, was unable to overcome. Errors determined most of the scoring, as only one of Detroit's six runs and two of Pittsburgh's eight were earned.

Mullin shut out the Pirates on five hits in Game Four, striking out ten men as Detroit scored five runs (all earned, despite Pittsburgh's six errors) to drive out starter Lefty Leifield after four innings. The seesaw Series continued in Game Five, with Babe Adams winning his second game behind his Pirates' ten-hit, eight-run attack. Adams gave up leadoff homers to Davy Jones in the first and Sam Crawford in the eighth. But Pittsburgh's Clarke more than countered these with his three-run shot in the seventh. (All three homers were hit into temporary seats in center field.)

Back in Detroit for Game Six, the Tigers evened the Series for the third time, Mullin winning his second game in a close contest that saw Pittsburgh pull within a run of tying the game in the ninth before a runner thrown out at home and a game-ending double play cut their rally dead.

In the finale it was Babe Adams once again, scattering six Tiger hits for an easy 8–0 win, his third of the Series. Detroit had done better than ever, but still lost their third World Series in three consecutive attempts. A quarter century would pass before they would have a chance to try again.

Pittsburgh Pirates (NL), 4;
Detroit Tigers (AL), 3

PIT (N)

PLAYER/POS	AVG	G	AB	R	H	2B	3B	HR	RB	BB	SO	SB
Ed Abbaticchio, ph	.000	1	1	0	0	0	0	0	0	0	0	0
Bill Abstein, 1b	.231	7	26	3	6	2	0	0	2	3	10	1
Babe Adams, p	.000	3	9	0	0	0	0	0	0	0	1	0
Bobby Byrne, 3b	.250	7	24	5	6	1	0	0	0	1	4	1
Howie Camnitz, p	.000	2	1	0	0	0	0	0	0	0	0	0
Fred Clarke, of	.211	7	19	7	4	0	0	2	7	5	3	3
George Gibson, c	.240	7	25	2	6	2	0	0	2	1	1	2
Ham Hyatt, of-1	.000	2	1	0	0	0	0	0	1	1	0	0
Tommy Leach, of-7,3b-1	.360	7	25	8	9	4	0	0	2	2	1	1
Lefty Leifield, p	.000	1	1	0	0	0	0	0	0	0	1	0
Nick Maddox, p	.000	1	4	0	0	0	0	0	0	0	1	0
Dots Miller, 2b	.250	7	28	2	7	1	0	0	4	2	5	3
Paddy O'Connor, ph	.000	1	1	0	0	0	0	0	0	0	0	0
Deacon Phillippe, p	.000	2	1	0	0	0	0	0	0	0	1	0
Honus Wagner, ss	.333	7	24	4	8	2	1	0	6	4	2	6
Vic Willis, p	.000	2	4	0	0	0	0	0	0	0	1	0
Chief Wilson, of	.154	7	26	2	4	1	0	0	1	0	2	1
TOTAL	.224		223	34	50	13	1	2	25	20	34	18

PITCHER	W	L	ERA	G	GS	CG	SV	SHO	IP	H	ER	BB	SO
Babe Adams	3	0	1.33	3	3	3	0	1	27.0	18	4	6	11
Howie Camnitz	0	1	9.82	2	1	0	0	0	3.2	8	4	2	2
Lefty Leifield	0	1	11.25	1	1	0	0	0	4.0	7	5	1	0
Nick Maddox	1	0	1.00	1	1	1	0	0	9.0	10	1	2	4
Deacon Phillippe	0	0	0.00	2	0	0	0	0	6.0	2	0	1	2
Vic Willis	0	1	3.97	2	1	0	0	0	11.1	10	5	8	3
TOTAL	4	3	2.80	11	7	4	0	1	61.0	55	19	20	22

DET (A)

PLAYER/POS	AVG	G	AB	R	H	2B	3B	HR	RB	BB	SO	SB
Donie Bush, ss	.261	7	23	5	6	1	0	0	3	5	3	1
Ty Cobb, of	.231	7	26	3	6	3	0	0	5	2	2	2
Sam Crawford, of-7,1b-1	.250	7	28	4	7	3	0	1	4	1	1	1
Jim Delahanty, 2b	.346	7	26	2	9	4	0	0	4	2	5	0
Bill Donovan, p	.000	2	4	0	0	0	0	0	0	0	1	0
Davy Jones, of	.233	7	30	6	7	0	0	1	1	2	1	1
Tom Jones, 1b	.250	7	24	3	6	1	0	0	2	2	0	1
Matty McIntyre, of-1	.000	4	4	0	0	0	0	0	0	0	1	0
George Moriarty, 3b	.273	7	22	4	6	1	0	0	1	3	1	0
George Mullin, p-4	.188	6	16	1	3	0	0	0	0	1	3	0
Charley O'Leary, 3b	.000	1	3	0	0	0	0	0	0	0	0	0
Boss Schmidt, c	.222	6	18	0	4	2	0	0	4	2	0	0
Oscar Stanage, c	.200	2	5	0	1	0	0	0	2	0	2	0
Ed Summers, p	.000	2	3	0	0	0	0	0	0	0	2	0
Ed Willett, p	.000	2	2	0	0	0	0	0	0	0	0	0
Ralph Works, p	.000	1	0	0	0	0	0	0	0	0	0	0
TOTAL	.236		233	28	55	16	0	2	26	20	22	6

PITCHER	W	L	ERA	G	GS	CG	SV	SHO	IP	H	ER	BB	SO
Bill Donovan	1	1	3.00	2	2	1	0	0	12.0	7	4	8	7
George Mullin	2	1	2.25	4	3	3	0	1	32.0	23	8	8	20
Ed Summers	0	2	8.59	2	2	0	0	0	7.1	13	7	4	4
Ed Willett	0	0	0.00	2	0	0	0	0	7.2	3	0	0	1
Ralph Works	0	0	9.00	1	0	0	0	0	2.0	4	2	0	2
TOTAL	3	4	3.10	11	7	4	0	1	61.0	50	21	20	34

GAME 1 AT PIT OCT 8

DET	100 000 000	1	6	4
PIT	000 121 00X	4	5	0

Pitchers: MULLIN vs ADAMS
Home Runs: Clarke-PIT
Attendance: 29,264

GAME 2 AT PIT OCT 9

DET	023 020 000	7	9	3
PIT	200 000 000	2	5	1

Pitchers: DONOVAN vs CAMNITZ, Willis (3)
Attendance: 30,915

GAME 3 AT DET OCT 11

PIT	510 000 002	8	10	3
DET	000 000 402	6	10	5

Pitchers: MADDOX vs SUMMERS, Willett (1), Works (8)
Attendance: 18,277

GAME 4 AT DET OCT 12

PIT	000 000 000	0	5	6
DET	020 300 00X	5	8	0

Pitchers: LEIFIELD, Phillippe (5) vs MULLIN
Attendance: 17,036

GAME 5 AT PIT OCT 13

DET	100 002 010	4	6	1
PIT	111 000 41X	8	10	2

Pitchers: SUMMERS, Willett (8) vs ADAMS
Home Runs: D.Jones-DET, Crawford-DET, Clarke-PIT
Attendance: 21,706

GAME 6 AT DET OCT 14

PIT	300 000 001	4	7	3
DET	100 211 00X	5	10	3

Pitchers: WILLIS, Camnitz (6), Phillippe (7) vs MULLIN
Attendance: 10,535

GAME 7 AT DET OCT 16

PIT	020 203 010	8	7	0
DET	000 000 000	0	6	3

Pitchers: ADAMS vs DONOVAN, Mullin (4)
Attendance: 17,562

Pitcher Jack Coombs burst into stardom in 1910, emerging as the ace of a Philadelphia pitching staff which dominated the American League with an ERA of only 1.79. Coombs himself led league pitchers with 31 wins and 13 shutouts, and finished second to Chicago's Ed Walsh with an ERA of 1.30—all career bests. He continued his domination into the World Series, pitching three complete-game victories in the Athletics' surprisingly easy triumph over the Cubs.

The Series' finest pitching performance, though, was turned in by the A's Chief Bender in the opener. Only two batters reached base over the first eight innings—on a single and walk—and both of them were cut down trying to steal second. In the ninth, two Cub singles and two Athletic errors produced an unearned run, but as the A's had scored four runs (Bender himself providing the margin of victory with the game's second RBI in the second inning), the Cubs' run did no damage.

Coombs started Game Two and gave up a Cub run in the top of the first inning. But Athletic bats were hot in the Series (their team .316 batting average stood as a Series record for fifty years), and their 14 hits in this game (including four doubles and six runs in the seventh) sank Three Finger Brown and gave Coombs an easy win. Connie Mack also started Coombs in Game Three, two days later, and again the result was a lopsided win. Coombs himself drove in three of his team's 12 runs, and right fielder Danny Murphy added three more with the Series' only home run.

Bender pitched Game Four and suffered the A's only loss, as the Cubs tied the game at 3–3 with a run in the bottom of the ninth, and won it for reliever Three Finger Brown with a two-out RBI single an inning later.

Coombs faced Brown a second time in Game Five. Both clubs made nine hits, but the A's put four of them together with a walk, a wild pitch, and two stolen bases for five runs in the eighth to sink Brown as they had in Game Two, breaking a tight game wide open for Coombs's third win and the Athletics' first world championship.

Philadelphia Athletics (AL), 4; Chicago Cubs (NL), 1

PHI (A)

PLAYER/POS	AVG	G	AB	R	H	2B	3B	HR	RB	BB	SO	SB
Frank Baker, 3b	.409	5	22	6	9	3	0	0	4	2	1	0
Jack Barry, ss	.235	5	17	3	4	2	0	0	3	1	3	0
Chief Bender, p	.333	2	6	1	2	0	0	0	1	1	1	0
Eddie Collins, 2b	.429	5	21	5	9	4	0	0	3	2	0	4
Jack Coombs, p	.385	3	13	0	5	1	0	0	3	0	3	0
Harry Davis, 1b	.353	5	17	5	6	3	0	0	2	3	4	0
Topsy Hartsel, of	.200	1	5	2	1	0	0	0	0	0	1	2
Jack Lapp, c	.250	1	4	0	1	0	0	0	1	0	2	0
Bris Lord, of	.182	5	22	3	4	2	0	0	1	1	3	0
Danny Murphy, of	.350	5	20	6	7	3	0	1	9	1	0	1
Amos Strunk, of	.278	4	18	2	5	1	1	0	2	2	5	0
Ira Thomas, c	.250	4	12	2	3	0	0	0	1	4	1	0
TOTAL	.316		177	35	56	19	1	1	30	17	24	7

PITCHER	W	L	ERA	G	GS	CG	SV	SHO	IP	H	ER	BB	SO
Chief Bender	1	1	1.93	2	2	2	0	0	18.2	12	4	4	14
Jack Coombs	3	0	3.33	3	3	3	0	0	27.0	23	10	14	17
TOTAL	4	1	2.76	5	5	5	0	0	45.2	35	14	18	31

CHI (N)

PLAYER/POS	AVG	G	AB	R	H	2B	3B	HR	RB	BB	SO	SB
Jimmy Archer, c-2,1b-1	.182	3	11	1	2	1	0	0	0	0	3	0
Ginger Beaumont, ph	.000	3	2	1	0	0	0	0	0	1	1	0
Mordecai Brown, p	.000	3	7	0	0	0	0	0	0	0	1	0
Frank Chance, 1b	.353	5	17	1	6	1	1	0	4	0	3	0
King Cole, p	.000	1	2	0	0	0	0	0	0	0	2	0
Solly Hofman, of	.267	5	15	2	4	0	0	0	2	4	3	0
Johnny Kane, pr	.000	1	0	0	0	0	0	0	0	0	0	0
Johnny Kling, c-3	.077	5	13	0	1	0	0	0	1	1	2	0
Harry McIntire, p	.000	2	1	0	0	0	0	0	0	0	1	0
Tom Needham, ph	.000	1	1	0	0	0	0	0	0	0	0	0
Orval Ovall, p	.000	1	1	0	0	0	0	0	0	0	0	0
Jack Pfiester, p	.000	1	2	0	0	0	0	0	0	0	1	0
Ed Reulbach, p	.000	1	0	0	0	0	0	0	0	0	0	0
Lew Richie, p	.000	1	0	0	0	0	0	0	0	0	0	0
Frank Schulte, of	.353	5	17	3	6	3	0	0	2	2	3	0
Jimmy Sheckard, of	.286	5	14	5	4	2	0	0	1	7	2	1
Harry Steinfeldt, 3b	.100	5	20	0	2	1	0	0	1	0	4	0
Joe Tinker, ss	.333	5	18	2	6	2	0	0	0	0	2	1
Heinie Zimmerman, 2b	.235	5	17	0	4	1	0	0	2	1	3	1
TOTAL	.222		158	15	35	11	1	0	13	18	31	3

PITCHER	W	L	ERA	G	GS	CG	SV	SHO	IP	H	ER	BB	SO
Mordecai Brown	1	2	5.50	3	2	1	0	0	18.0	23	11	7	14
King Cole	0	0	3.38	1	1	0	0	0	8.0	10	3	3	5
Harry Mc Intire	0	1	6.75	2	0	0	0	0	5.1	4	4	3	3
Orval Overall	0	1	9.00	1	1	0	0	0	3.0	6	3	1	1
Jack Pfiester	0	0	0.00	1	0	0	0	0	6.2	9	0	1	1
Ed Reulbach	0	0	9.00	1	1	0	0	0	2.0	3	2	2	0
Lew Richie	0	0	0.00	1	0	0	0	0	1.0	1	0	0	0
TOTAL	1	4	4.70	10	5	1	0	0	44.0	56	23	17	24

GAME 1 AT PHI OCT 17

CHI	000	000	001	1	3	1
PHI	021	000	01X	4	7	2

Pitchers: OVERALL, McIntire (4) vs BENDER
Attendance: 26,891

GAME 2 AT PHI OCT 18

CHI	100	000	101	3	8	3
PHI	002	010	60X	9	14	4

Pitchers: BROWN, Richie (8) vs COOMBS
Attendance: 24,597

GAME 3 AT CHI OCT 20

PHI	125	000	400	12	15	1
CHI	120	000	020	5	6	5

Pitchers: COOMBS vs Reulbach, McINTIRE (3), Pfiester (3)
Home Runs: Murphy-PHI
Attendance: 26,210

GAME 4 AT CHI OCT 22

PHI	001	200	000 0	3	11	3
CHI	100	100	001 1	4	9	1

Pitchers: BENDER vs Cole, BROWN (9)
Attendance: 19,150

GAME 5 AT CHI OCT 23

PHI	100	010	050	7	9	1
CHI	010	000	010	2	9	2

Pitchers: COOMBS vs BROWN
Attendance: 27,374

Connie Mack's pitching aces out-dueled Christy Mathewson, and Frank Baker hit two crucial home runs to become "Home Run" Baker forever more, as the A's avenged their 1905 Series loss to the Giants. Game One, though, belonged to Matty and New York. Philadelphia scored first, but the Giants tied the game with an unearned run in the fourth inning, and won it with two doubles in the seventh, setting at naught Chief Bender's otherwise splendid 11-strikeout performance.

The A's came back to take three in a row. In Game Two Eddie Plank held the Giants to one run and Baker hit the first of his homers, breaking a tie in the sixth with a two-run blast off Rube Marquard. The next day, the A's and Jack Coombs handed Mathewson his first World Series loss. Both pitchers went the distance in an 11-inning duel that saw Matty hold the A's scoreless through eight, only to give up a game-tying home run to Baker in the ninth, and two unearned runs in the eleventh. Coombs, meanwhile, pitched two-hit, one-run ball through ten innings. In the last of the eleventh, a third Giant hit and an A's error let in a second Giant run, but the rally died when Beals Becker was cut down for the final out trying to steal second.

After a week of rain, Mathewson and Bender squared off in Game Four. The Giants jumped on Bender for two runs in the first, and held the lead until the fourth. But in the last of the fourth, three successive A's doubles and a run-scoring fly put the A's in front to stay as Bender held New York scoreless over the final 8 innings.

In Game Five, a three-run homer by the A's Rube Oldring off Rube Marquard in the third provided the only scoring through 6½ innings. But the Giants crept back with one run in the seventh, and two more in the last of the ninth tied the score. Plank replaced Coombs for the A's in the tenth and took the loss as Larry Doyle led off with a double, took third on a missed force play, and scored on Fred Merkle's fly to deep right.

After five closely contested games, Game Six was a laugher. It, too, was close at first—tied 1–1 after 3½ innings. But the A's scored four runs in the fourth on singles and errors, once in the sixth, and seven times in the seventh on a barrage of hits, an error, and a two-run wild pitch. Chief Bender, who gave up only four hits and two unearned runs, was the beneficiary of this largesse, taking his second win of the Series and giving the A's their second consecutive world title.

Philadelphia Athletics (AL), 4;
New York Giants (NL), 2

PHI (A)

PLAYER/POS	AVG	G	AB	R	H	2B	3B	HR	RB	BB	SO	SB
Frank Baker, 3b	.375	6	24	7	9	2	0	2	5	1	5	0
Jack Barry, ss	.368	6	19	2	7	4	0	0	2	0	2	2
Chief Bender, p	.091	3	11	0	1	0	0	0	0	0	1	0
Eddie Collins, 2b	.286	6	21	4	6	1	0	0	1	2	2	2
Jack Coombs, p	.250	2	8	1	2	0	0	0	0	0	0	0
Harry Davis, 1b	.208	6	24	3	5	1	0	0	5	0	3	0
Jack Lapp, c	.250	2	8	1	2	0	0	0	0	0	1	0
Bris Lord, of	.185	6	27	2	5	2	0	0	1	0	5	0
Stuffy McInnis, 1b	.000	1	0	0	0	0	0	0	0	0	0	0
Danny Murphy, of	.304	6	23	4	7	3	0	0	3	0	3	0
Rube Oldring, of	.200	6	25	2	5	2	0	1	3	0	5	0
Eddie Plank, p	.000	2	3	0	0	0	0	0	0	0	2	0
Amos Strunk, pr	.000	1	0	0	0	0	0	0	0	0	0	0
Ira Thomas, c	.083	4	12	1	1	0	0	0	1	1	2	0
TOTAL	.244		205	27	50	15	0	3	21	4	31	4

PITCHER	W	L	ERA	G	GS	CG	SV	SHO	IP	H	ER	BB	SO
Chief Bender	2	1	1.04	3	3	3	0	0	26.0	16	3	8	20
Jack Coombs	1	0	1.35	2	2	1	0	0	20.0	11	3	6	16
Eddie Plank	1	1	1.86	2	1	1	0	0	9.2	6	2	0	8
TOTAL	4	2	1.29	7	6	5	0	0	55.2	33	8	14	44

NY (N)

PLAYER/POS	AVG	G	AB	R	H	2B	3B	HR	RB	BB	SO	SB
Red Ames, p	.500	2	2	0	1	0	0	0	0	0	1	0
Beals Becker, ph	.000	3	3	0	0	0	0	0	0	0	0	0
Doc Crandall, p-2	.500	3	2	1	1	1	0	0	1	2	0	0
Josh Devore, of	.167	6	24	1	4	1	0	0	3	1	8	0
Larry Doyle, 2b	.304	6	23	3	7	3	1	0	1	2	1	2
Art Fletcher, ss	.130	6	23	1	3	1	0	0	1	0	4	0
Buck Herzog, 3b	.190	6	21	3	4	2	0	0	0	2	3	2
Rube Marquard, p	.000	3	2	0	0	0	0	0	0	0	2	0
Christy Mathewson, p	.286	3	7	0	2	0	0	0	0	1	3	0
Fred Merkle, 1b	.150	6	20	1	3	1	0	0	1	2	6	0
Chief Meyers, c	.300	6	20	2	6	2	0	0	2	0	3	0
Red Murray, of	.000	6	21	0	0	0	0	0	0	2	5	0
Fred Snodgrass, of	.105	6	19	1	2	0	0	0	1	2	7	0
Art Wilson, c	.000	1	1	0	0	0	0	0	0	0	0	0
Hooks Wiltse, p	.000	2	1	0	0	0	0	0	0	0	1	0
TOTAL	.175		189	13	33	11	1	0	10	14	44	4

PITCHER	W	L	ERA	G	GS	CG	SV	SHO	IP	H	ER	BB	SO
Red Ames	0	1	2.25	2	1	0	0	0	8.0	6	2	1	6
Doc Crandall	1	0	0.00	2	0	0	0	0	4.0	2	0	0	2
Rube Marquard	0	1	1.54	3	2	0	0	0	11.2	9	2	1	8
Christy Mathewson	1	2	2.00	3	3	2	0	0	27.0	25	6	2	13
Hooks Wiltse	0	0	18.90	2	0	0	0	0	3.1	8	7	0	2
TOTAL	2	4	2.83	12	6	2	0	0	54.0	50	17	4	31

GAME 1 AT NY OCT 14

PHI	010	000	000	1	6	2
NY	000	100	10X	2	5	0

Pitchers: BENDER vs MATHEWSON
Attendance: 38,281

GAME 2 AT PHI OCT 16

NY	010	000	000	1	5	3
PHI	100	002	00X	3	4	0

Pitchers: MARQUARD, Crandall (8) vs PLANK
Home Runs: Baker-PHI
Attendance: 26,286

GAME 3 AT NY OCT 17

PHI	000	000	001	02	3	9	2
NY	001	000	000	01	2	3	5

Pitchers: COOMBS vs MATHEWSON
Home Runs: Baker-PHI
Attendance: 37,216

GAME 4 AT PHI OCT 24

NY	200	000	000	2	7	3
PHI	000	310	00X	4	11	1

Pitchers: MATHEWSON, Wiltse (8) vs BENDER
Attendance: 24,355

GAME 5 AT NY OCT 25

PHI	003	000	000	0	3	7	1
NY	000	000	102	1	4	9	2

Pitchers: Coombs, PLANK (10) vs Marquard, Ames (4), CRANDALL (8)
Home Runs: Oldring-PHI
Attendance: 33,228

GAME 6 AT PHI OCT 26

NY	100	000	001	2	4	3
PHI	001	401	70X	13	13	5

Pitchers: AMES, Wiltse (5), Marquard (7) vs BENDER
Attendance: 20,485

The Giants outhit the Red Sox by 50 percentage points, and their pitchers let in one less earned run per game. But this was the Series in which Fred Snodgrass's famous muff of a routine fly to center in the tenth inning of the final game helped turn a slim Giant lead into a Red Sox world championship. In all fairness, it must be admitted that Snodgrass followed his muff with a brilliant catch off the next batter, and indecision by the catcher and first baseman permitted a pop foul to drop, keeping the Sox alive to score the tying and winning runs. For that matter, this final game might not have been needed at all if Snodgrass and Beals Becker hadn't both been cut down trying to steal second in the eleventh inning of Game Two, which ended in a tie because of darkness. If either had gone on to score, the Giants would have won the Series in seven games.

Boston's Smokey Joe Wood followed up his spectacular 34–5 regular season with Series wins in Games One and Four, before being rocked for six runs in the first inning of Game Seven for a loss. Relieving in the eighth inning of the finale, he stopped the Giants for two innings, but gave up what would have been the losing run in the tenth had not the Giants' fielding in the last of the inning turned the game around, giving Wood the win and the Sox the Series.

Although Wood won three games, the best pitching of the Series was turned in by the Giants' Rube Marquard and Boston's Hugh Bedient. Marquard (who in the regular season had tied a major league record with 19 consecutive wins) won two of his club's three victories (Games Three and Six), allowing three runs—only one of them earned. Bedient, in two starts and two relief appearances, matched Marquard's 0.50 earned run average, winning a duel with Christy Mathewson in Game Five, and hurling seven effective innings against Matty in the finale.

Mathewson was the Series' hard-luck pitcher: his one tie and two losses were all decided by unearned runs.

Boston Red Sox (AL), 4;
New York Giants (NL), 3; tie, 1

BOS (A)

PLAYER/POS	AVG	G	AB	R	H	2B	3B	HR	RB	BB	SO	SB
Neal Ball, ph	.000	1	1	0	0	0	0	0	0	0	1	0
Hugh Bedient, p	.000	4	6	0	0	0	0	0	0	0	0	0
Hick Cady, c	.136	7	22	1	3	0	0	0	1	0	3	0
Bill Carrigan, c	.000	2	7	0	0	0	0	0	0	0	0	0
Ray Collins, p	.000	2	5	0	0	0	0	0	0	0	2	0
Clyde Engle, ph	.333	3	3	1	1	1	0	0	2	0	0	0
Larry Gardner, 3b	.179	8	28	4	5	2	1	1	4	2	5	0
Charley Hall, p	.750	2	4	0	3	1	0	0	0	1	0	0
Olaf Henricksen, ph	1.000	2	1	0	1	1	0	0	1	0	0	0
Harry Hooper, of	.290	8	31	3	9	2	1	0	2	4	4	2
Duffy Lewis, of	.156	8	32	4	5	3	0	0	2	2	2	0
Buck O'Brien, p	.000	2	2	0	0	0	0	0	0	0	2	0
Tris Speaker, of	.300	8	30	4	9	1	2	0	2	4	2	1
Jake Stahl, 1b	.281	8	32	3	9	2	0	0	2	0	6	2
Heinie Wagner, ss	.167	8	30	1	5	1	0	0	0	3	6	1
Joe Wood, p	.286	4	7	1	2	0	0	0	1	1	0	0
Steve Yerkes, 2b	.250	8	32	3	8	0	2	0	4	2	3	0
TOTAL	.220		273	25	60	14	6	1	21	19	36	6

PITCHER	W	L	ERA	G	GS	CG	SV	SHO	IP	H	ER	BB	SO
Hugh Bedient	1	0	0.50	4	2	1	0	0	18.0	10	1	7	7
Ray Collins	0	0	1.88	2	1	0	0	0	14.1	14	3	0	6
Charley Hall	0	0	3.38	2	0	0	0	0	10.2	11	4	9	1
Buck O'Brien	0	2	5.00	2	2	0	0	0	9.0	12	5	3	4
Joe Wood	3	1	3.68	4	3	2	0	0	22.0	27	9	3	21
TOTAL	4	3	2.68	14	8	3	0	0	74.0	74	22	22	39

NY (N)

PLAYER/POS	AVG	G	AB	R	H	2B	3B	HR	RB	BB	SO	SB
Red Ames, p	.000	1	0	0	0	0	0	0	0	0	0	0
Beals Becker, of-1	.000	2	4	1	0	0	0	0	0	2	0	0
Doc Crandall, p	.000	1	0	0	0	0	0	0	0	0	1	0
Josh Devore, of	.250	7	24	4	6	0	0	0	0	7	5	4
Larry Doyle, 2b	.242	8	33	5	8	1	0	1	2	3	2	2
Art Fletcher, ss	.179	8	28	1	5	1	0	0	3	1	4	1
Buck Herzog, 3b	.400	8	30	6	12	4	1	0	4	1	3	2
Rube Marquard, p	.000	2	4	0	0	0	0	0	0	1	0	0
Christy Mathewson, p	.167	3	12	0	2	0	0	0	0	0	4	0
Moose McCormick, ph	.250	5	4	0	1	0	0	0	1	0	0	0
Fred Merkle, 1b	.273	8	33	5	9	2	1	0	3	0	7	1
Chief Meyers, c	.357	8	28	2	10	0	1	0	3	2	3	1
Red Murray, of	.323	8	31	5	10	4	1	0	5	2	2	0
Tillie Shafer, ss	.000	3	0	0	0	0	0	0	0	0	0	0
Fred Snodgrass, of	.212	8	33	2	7	2	0	0	2	2	5	1
Jeff Tesreau, p	.375	3	8	0	3	0	0	0	0	2	1	0
Art Wilson, c	1.000	2	1	0	1	0	0	0	0	0	0	0
TOTAL	.270		274	31	74	14	4	1	25	22	39	12

PITCHER	W	L	ERA	G	GS	CG	SV	SHO	IP	H	ER	BB	SO
Red Ames	0	0	4.50	1	0	0	0	0	2.0	3	1	1	0
Doc Crandall	0	0	0.00	1	0	0	0	0	2.0	1	0	0	2
Rube Marquard	2	0	0.50	2	2	2	0	0	18.0	14	1	2	9
Christy Mathewson	0	2	1.26	3	3	3	0	0	28.2	23	4	5	10
Jeff Tesreau	1	2	3.13	3	3	1	0	0	23.0	19	8	11	15
TOTAL	3	4	1.71	10	8	6	0	0	73.2	60	14	19	36

GAME 1 AT NY OCT 8

BOS	000 001 300	4	6	1
NY	002 000 001	3	8	1

Pitchers: WOOD vs TESREAU, Crandall (8)
Attendance: 35,730

GAME 2 AT BOS OCT 9

NY	010 100 030 10	6	11	5
BOS	300 010 010 10	6	10	1

Pitchers: Mathewson vs Collins, Hall (8), Bedient (11)
Attendance: 30,148
(Game called at end of eleventh, darkness)

GAME 3 AT BOS OCT 10

NY	010 010 000	2	7	1
BOS	000 000 001	1	7	0

Pitchers: MARQUARD vs O'BRIEN, Bedient (9)
Attendance: 34,624

GAME 4 AT NY OCT 11

BOS	010 100 001	3	8	1
NY	000 000 100	1	9	1

Pitchers: WOOD vs TESREAU, Ames (8)
Attendance: 36,502

GAME 5 AT BOS OCT 12

NY	000 000 100	1	3	1
BOS	002 000 00X	2	5	1

Pitchers: MATHEWSON vs BEDIENT
Attendance: 34,683

GAME 6 AT NY OCT 14

BOS	020 000 000	2	7	2
NY	500 000 00X	5	11	2

Pitchers: O'BRIEN, Collins (2) vs MARQUARD
Attendance: 30,622

GAME 7 AT BOS OCT 15

NY	610 002 101	11	16	4
BOS	010 000 210	4	9	3

Pitchers: TESREAU vs WOOD, Hall (2)
Home Runs: Doyle-NY, Gardner-BOS
Attendance: 32,694

GAME 8 AT BOS OCT 16

NY	001 000 000 1	2	9	2
BOS	000 000 100 2	3	8	5

Pitchers: MATHEWSON vs Bedient, WOOD (8)
Attendance: 17,034

Third baseman Frank Baker and catcher Wally Schang drove in more than 60 percent of the Athletics' runs, as Philadelphia dispatched the Giants in five games. Chief Bender led A's pitchers with two wins, and rookie Bullet Joe Bush hurled a nifty five-hitter in Game Three, but the Series highlights were two duels between the A's Eddie Plank and the Giant's Christy Mathewson. The A's heavy hitting made Bender's wins possible and Bush's win easy, but pitching dominated the Plank-Matty games.

Bender yielded 11 hits in the opener, as did the Giants' pitchers. But five of the game's six extra-base hits belonged to the A's—including Baker's two-run homer and triples by Schang and Eddie Collins—and Bender emerged victorious. In Game Two, Plank and Mathewson pitched shutout ball through nine innings, but in the top of the tenth Matty himself singled in the game's first run and scored the second. Taking a 3–0 lead into the bottom of the inning, he set the A's down in order for New York's only Series win.

In Game Three, Schang's solo homer and Collins's three hits (including his second Series triple) and three RBIs led a 12-hit A's attack which, with Bush's fine pitching, put Philadelphia back into the Series lead. Bender won again in Game Four, shutting out the Giants through six innings as his A's scored six runs. But in the seventh, New York's Fred Merkle homered for three runs, and a single, double, and triple in the eighth brought in two more Giant runs. With his lead cut to a single run, Bender bore down in the ninth and retired the side in order.

Plank avenged his earlier loss with a brilliant two-hitter in Game Five, facing the minimum three batters in eight of the nine innings. (His own error in the fifth—a dropped pop-up—led to the Giants' only run.) Mathewson pitched well, too, yielding only six singles. But four of them came in the first and third innings, combining with two sacrifice flies and an error for three runs. Only one Athletic batter reached base in the final six innings, but with Plank pitching as he was, the game and the title were in Philadelphia's pocket.

Philadelphia Athletics (AL), 4;
New York Giants (NL), 1

PHI (A)

PLAYER/POS	AVG	G	AB	R	H	2B	3B	HR	RB	BB	SO	SB
Frank Baker, 3b	.450	5	20	2	9	0	0	1	7	0	2	1
Jack Barry, ss	.300	5	20	3	6	3	0	0	2	0	0	0
Chief Bender, p	.000	2	8	0	0	0	0	0	1	0	1	0
Joe Bush, p	.250	1	4	0	1	0	0	0	0	0	1	0
Eddie Collins, 2b	.421	5	19	5	8	0	2	0	3	1	2	3
Jack Lapp, c	.250	1	4	0	1	0	0	0	0	0	1	0
Stuffy McInnis, 1b	.118	5	17	1	2	1	0	0	2	0	2	0
Eddie Murphy, of	.227	5	22	2	5	0	0	0	0	2	0	0
Rube Oldring, of	.273	5	22	5	6	0	1	0	0	0	1	1
Eddie Plank, p	.143	2	7	0	1	0	0	0	0	0	0	0
Wally Schang, c	.357	4	14	2	5	0	1	1	6	2	4	0
Amos Strunk, of	.118	5	17	3	2	0	0	0	0	2	2	0
TOTAL	.264		174	23	46	4	4	2	21	7	16	5

PITCHER	W	L	ERA	G	GS	CG	SV	SHO	IP	H	ER	BB	SO
Chief Bender	2	0	4.00	2	2	2	0	0	18.0	19	8	1	9
Joe Bush	1	0	1.00	1	1	1	0	0	9.0	5	1	4	3
Eddie Plank	1	1	0.95	2	2	2	0	0	19.0	9	2	3	7
TOTAL	4	1	2.15	5	5	5	0	0	46.0	33	11	8	19

NY (N)

PLAYER/POS	AVG	G	AB	R	H	2B	3B	HR	RB	BB	SO	SB
George Burns, of	.158	5	19	2	3	2	0	0	1	1	5	1
Claude Cooper, pr	.000	2	0	0	0	0	0	0	0	0	0	1
Doc Crandall, p-2	.000	4	4	0	0	0	0	0	0	0	0	0
Al Demaree, p	.000	1	1	0	0	0	0	0	0	0	0	0
Larry Doyle, 2b	.150	5	20	1	3	0	0	0	2	0	1	0
Art Fletcher, ss	.278	5	18	1	5	0	0	0	4	1	1	1
Eddie Grant, ph	.000	2	1	0	0	0	0	0	0	0	0	0
Buck Herzog, 3b	.053	5	19	1	1	0	0	0	0	0	1	0
Rube Marquard, p	.000	2	1	0	0	0	0	0	0	0	0	0
Christy Mathewson, p	.600	2	5	1	3	0	0	0	1	1	0	0
Moose McCormick, ph	.500	2	2	1	1	0	0	0	0	0	0	0
Larry McLean, c-4	.500	5	12	0	6	0	0	0	2	0	0	0
Fred Merkle, 1b	.231	4	13	3	3	0	0	1	3	1	2	0
Chief Meyers, c	.000	1	4	0	0	0	0	0	0	0	0	0
Red Murray, of	.250	5	16	2	4	0	0	0	1	2	2	0
Tillie Shafer, of-5,3b-1	.158	5	19	2	3	1	1	0	1	2	3	0
Fred Snodgrass, 1b-1,of-1	.333	2	3	0	1	0	0	0	0	0	0	0
Jeff Tesreau, p	.000	2	2	0	0	0	0	0	0	0	1	0
Art Wilson, c	.000	3	3	0	0	0	0	0	0	0	2	0
Hooks Wiltse, 1b	.000	2	2	0	0	0	0	0	0	0	1	0
TOTAL	.201		164	15	33	3	1	1	15	8	19	5

PITCHER	W	L	ERA	G	GS	CG	SV	SHO	IP	H	ER	BB	SO
Doc Crandall	0	0	3.86	2	0	0	0	0	4.2	4	2	0	2
Al Demaree	0	1	4.50	1	1	0	0	0	4.0	7	2	1	0
Rube Marquard	0	1	7.00	2	1	0	0	0	9.0	10	7	3	3
Christy Mathewson	1	1	0.95	2	2	2	0	1	19.0	14	2	2	7
Jeff Tesreau	0	1	6.48	2	1	0	0	0	8.1	11	6	1	4
TOTAL	1	4	3.80	9	5	2	0	1	45.0	46	19	7	16

GAME 1 AT NY OCT 7

PHI	000 320 010	6 11 1
NY	001 030 000	4 11 0

Pitchers: BENDER vs MARQUARD, Crandall (6), Tesreau (8)
Home Runs: Baker-PHI
Attendance: 36,291

GAME 2 AT PHI OCT 8

NY	000 000 000 3	3 7 2
PHI	000 000 000 0	0 8 2

Pitchers: MATHEWSON vs PLANK
Attendance: 20,563

GAME 3 AT NY OCT 9

PHI	320 000 210	8 12 1
NY	000 010 100	2 5 1

Pitchers: BUSH vs TESREAU, Crandall (7)
Home Runs: Schang-PHI
Attendance: 36,896

GAME 4 AT PHI OCT 10

NY	000 000 320	5 8 2
PHI	010 320 00X	6 9 0

Pitchers: DEMAREE, Marquard (5) vs BENDER
Home Runs: Merkle-NY
Attendance: 20,568

GAME 5 AT NY OCT 11

PHI	102 000 000	3 6 1
NY	000 010 000	1 2 2

Pitchers: PLANK vs MATHEWSON
Attendance: 36,682

The Athletics, easy winners of their fourth pennant in five years, were clear favorites over Boston. But the "Miracle Braves"—who moved from last place to first between July 18 and August 25 and kept going to take the pennant by 10½ games—had the momentum and swept the Series.

Boston pitcher Dick Rudolph (who won 27 games during the season) limited the A's to five hits and an unearned run, to take the opener behind the Braves' heavy hitting, 7–1. But the rest of the games were not won so easily.

Philadelphia's Eddie Plank held the Braves scoreless through eight innings of Game Two, and gave up only one run in the ninth. But the Braves' Bill James (26–7 during the season) allowed only two hits and no runs at all.

Game Three was a seesaw affair not settled until the twelfth inning. Through ten innings, starters Lefty Tyler of Boston and Joe Bush of the A's traded runs. Philadelphia scored one in the top of the first, but Braves' catcher Hank Gowdy doubled in the tying run in the second. The teams traded runs again in the fourth, but no one else crossed the plate until the tenth, when Frank Baker's bases-loaded single drove in two. For the third time, the Braves came back to tie it up. Gowdy opened the last of the tenth with the Series' only home run, and after a walk and single, a sacrifice fly knotted the score. Bill James came on to pitch no-hit ball through the eleventh and twelfth. Bush remained in for the A's, retiring the side in the eleventh. But an inning later Gowdy opened with his third crucial hit of the game, a double. Les Mann replaced him as runner, and after a walk, bunt, and wild throw to third, Mann scampered home with the winning run.

Two of Connie Mack's most promising young pitchers, Bob Shawkey and Herb Pennock (who would later find stardom as New York Yankees), shared the A's pitching in Game Four, and gave up only six hits between them. But a walk and an error led to a Boston run in the fourth, and although Shawkey himself doubled in the tying run a half inning later, two more Braves scored in the last of the fifth on Johnny Evers's single. Pennock came on to pitch three innings of shutout relief, but Rudolph held the A's hitless over the final four innings to preserve his second win and the Braves' crown.

Boston Braves (NL), 4; Philadelphia Athletics (AL), 0

BOS (N)

PLAYER/POS	AVG	G	AB	R	H	2B	3B	HR	RB	BB	SO	SB
Ted Cather, of	.000	1	5	0	0	0	0	0	0	0	1	0
Joe Connolly, of	.111	3	9	1	1	0	0	0	1	1	1	0
Charlie Deal, 3b	.125	4	16	1	2	2	0	0	0	0	0	2
Josh Devore, ph	.000	1	1	0	0	0	0	0	0	0	1	0
Johnny Evers, 2b	.438	4	16	2	7	0	0	0	2	2	2	1
Larry Gilbert, ph	.000	1	0	0	0	0	0	0	0	1	0	0
Hank Gowdy, c	.545	4	11	3	6	3	1	1	3	5	1	1
Bill James, p	.000	2	4	0	0	0	0	0	0	0	4	0
Les Mann, of-2	.286	3	7	1	2	0	0	0	1	0	1	0
Rabbit Maranville, ss	.308	4	13	1	4	0	0	0	3	1	1	2
Herbie Moran, of	.077	3	13	2	1	1	0	0	0	1	1	1
Dick Rudolph, p	.333	2	6	1	2	0	0	0	0	1	1	0
Butch Schmidt, 1b	.294	4	17	2	5	0	0	0	2	0	2	1
Lefty Tyler, p	.000	1	3	0	0	0	0	0	0	0	1	0
Possum Whitted, of	.214	4	14	2	3	0	1	0	2	3	1	1
TOTAL	.244		135	16	33	6	2	1	14	15	18	9

PITCHER	W	L	ERA	G	GS	CG	SV	SHO	IP	H	ER	BB	SO
Bill James	2	0	0.00	2	1	1	0	1	11.0	2	0	6	9
Dick Rudolph	2	0	0.50	2	2	2	0	0	18.0	12	1	4	15
Lefty Tyler	0	0	3.60	1	1	0	0	0	10.0	8	4	3	4
TOTAL	4	0	1.15	5	4	3	0	1	39.0	22	5	13	28

PHI (A)

PLAYER/POS	AVG	G	AB	R	H	2B	3B	HR	RB	BB	SO	SB
Frank Baker, 3b	.250	4	16	0	4	2	0	0	2	1	3	0
Jack Barry, ss	.071	4	14	1	1	0	0	0	0	1	3	1
Chief Bender, p	.000	1	2	0	0	0	0	0	0	0	0	0
Joe Bush, p	.000	1	5	0	0	0	0	0	0	0	2	0
Eddie Collins, 2b	.214	4	14	0	3	0	0	0	1	2	1	1
Jack Lapp, c	.000	1	1	0	0	0	0	0	0	0	0	0
Stuffy McInnis, 1b	.143	4	14	2	2	1	0	0	3	3	0	0
Eddie Murphy, of	.188	4	16	2	3	2	0	0	0	2	2	0
Rube Oldring, of	.067	4	15	0	1	0	0	0	0	0	5	0
Herb Pennock, p	.000	1	1	0	0	0	0	0	0	0	0	0
Eddie Plank, p	.000	1	1	0	0	0	0	0	0	0	1	0
Wally Schang, c	.167	4	12	1	2	1	0	0	0	1	4	0
Bob Shawkey, p	.500	1	2	0	1	1	0	0	1	0	1	0
Amos Strunk, of	.286	2	7	0	2	0	0	0	0	0	2	0
Jimmy Walsh, of-2	.333	3	6	0	2	1	0	0	1	3	1	0
Weldon Wyckoff, p	1.000	1	1	0	1	1	0	0	0	0	0	0
TOTAL	.172		128	6	22	9	0	0	5	13	28	2

PITCHER	W	L	ERA	G	GS	CG	SV	SHO	IP	H	ER	BB	SO
Chief Bender	0	1	10.13	1	1	0	0	0	5.1	8	6	2	3
Joe Bush	0	1	3.27	1	1	1	0	0	11.0	9	4	4	4
Herb Pennock	0	0	0.00	1	0	0	0	0	3.0	2	0	2	3
Eddie Plank	0	1	1.00	1	1	1	0	0	9.0	7	1	4	6
Bob Shawkey	0	1	3.60	1	1	0	0	0	5.0	4	2	2	0
Weldon Wyckoff	0	0	2.45	1	0	0	0	0	3.2	3	1	1	2
TOTAL	0	4	3.41	6	4	2	0	0	37.0	33	14	15	18

GAME 1 AT PHI OCT 9

BOS	020 013 010	7	11	2
PHI	010 000 000	1	5	0

Pitchers: RUDOLPH vs BENDER, Wyckoff (6)
Attendance: 20,562

GAME 2 AT PHI OCT 10

BOS	000 000 001	1	7	1
PHI	000 000 000	0	2	1

Pitchers: JAMES vs PLANK
Attendance: 20,562

GAME 3 AT BOS OCT 12

PHI	100 100 000 200	4	8	2
BOS	010 100 000 201	5	9	1

Pitchers: BUSH vs Tyler, JAMES (11)
Home Runs: Gowdy-BOS
Attendance: 35,520

GAME 4 AT BOS OCT 13

PHI	000 010 000	1	7	0
BOS	000 120 00X	3	6	0

Pitchers: SHAWKEY, Pennock (6) vs RUDOLPH
Attendance: 34,365

In a Series characterized by outstanding pitching, Boston's five runs in Game Five were the most scored by either team. It was also one of the most closely contested Series: the deciding run was not scored until the ninth inning in three of the games, and only in Game One was the margin of victory as much as two runs.

Grover Cleveland Alexander pitched the opener for the Phillies, and while the Red Sox tagged him for eight hits, they were all singles, and not until the eighth inning did one manage to drive a runner home. Boston's Ernie Shore pitched just as well, giving up only five singles and four walks. But two Phillie hits produced a run in the fourth, and an alternating pair of walks and infield hits in the eighth broke the tie with two runs for the Phillies' only win.

The next three games were 2–1 Boston victories. Rube Foster held the Phillies to three hits in Game Two, and led his team at the bat, going 3 for 4, including a double in the fifth. But it was his single in the ninth with a man on second that produced what proved to be the winning run as he retired the side in the bottom of the ninth to preserve his win. Dutch Leonard duplicated Foster's three-hit pitching two days later as the Series moved to Boston's spacious new Braves Field for Game Three. Before a new Series record crowd of 42,300, Leonard defeated the great Alexander, as the Sox' Duffy Lewis—with his third hit of the game—singled over second base to score Harry Hooper from third with two out in the bottom of the ninth.

Ernie Shore returned to the mound for Boston in Game Four, and although he gave up more hits (seven) than he had in Game One, his Sox had scored their two runs before the Phillies put across their one in the eighth.

Rube Foster was not as effective in Game Five as he had been in Game Two, twice giving the Phillies a two-run lead as Phillie first baseman Fred Luderus drove in three runs with a double and a home run. But from the fifth inning on, Foster held Philadelphia scoreless on two hits, while Duffy Lewis evened the score with a two-run homer in the eighth, and Harry Hooper (who had tied the score earlier with a home run in the third) won the game and the Series with a second homer in the top of the ninth.

Boston Red Sox (AL), 4;
Philadelphia Phillies (NL), 1

BOS (A)

PLAYER/POS	AVG	G	AB	R	H	2B	3B	HR	RB	BB	SO	SB
Jack Barry, 2b	.176	5	17	1	3	0	0	0	1	1	2	0
Hick Cady, c	.333	4	6	0	2	0	0	0	0	1	2	0
Bill Carrigan, c	.000	1	2	0	0	0	0	0	0	1	1	0
Rube Foster, p	.500	2	8	0	4	1	0	0	1	0	2	0
Del Gainer, 1b	.333	1	3	1	1	0	0	0	0	0	0	0
Larry Gardner, 3b	.235	5	17	2	4	0	1	0	0	1	0	0
Olaf Henricksen, ph	.000	2	2	0	0	0	0	0	0	0	0	0
Dick Hoblitzel, 1b	.313	5	16	1	5	0	0	0	1	0	1	1
Harry Hooper, of	.350	5	20	4	7	0	0	2	3	2	4	0
Hal Janvrin, ss	.000	1	1	0	0	0	0	0	0	0	0	0
Dutch Leonard, p	.000	1	3	0	0	0	0	0	0	0	2	0
Duffy Lewis, of	.444	5	18	1	8	1	0	1	5	1	4	0
Babe Ruth, ph	.000	1	1	0	0	0	0	0	0	0	0	0
Everett Scott, ss	.056	5	18	0	1	0	0	0	0	0	3	0
Ernie Shore, p	.200	2	5	0	1	0	0	0	0	0	3	0
Tris Speaker, of	.294	5	17	2	5	0	1	0	0	4	1	0
Pinch Thomas, c	.200	2	5	0	1	0	0	0	0	0	0	0
TOTAL	.264		159	12	42	2	2	3	11	11	25	1

PITCHER	W	L	ERA	G	GS	CG	SV	SHO	IP	H	ER	BB	SO
Rube Foster	2	0	2.00	2	2	2	0	0	18.0	12	4	2	13
Dutch Leonard	1	0	1.00	1	1	1	0	0	9.0	3	1	0	6
Ernie Shore	1	1	2.12	2	2	2	0	0	17.0	12	4	8	6
TOTAL	4	1	1.84	5	5	5	0	0	44.0	27	9	10	25

PHI (N)

PLAYER/POS	AVG	G	AB	R	H	2B	3B	HR	RB	BB	SO	SB
Pete Alexander, p	.200	2	5	0	1	0	0	0	0	0	1	0
Dave Bancroft, ss	.294	5	17	2	5	0	0	0	1	2	2	0
Beals Becker, of	.000	2	0	0	0	0	0	0	0	0	0	0
Ed Burns, c	.188	5	16	1	3	0	0	0	0	1	2	0
Bobby Byrne, ph	.000	1	1	0	0	0	0	0	0	0	0	0
George Chalmers, p	.333	1	3	0	1	0	0	0	0	0	1	0
Gavvy Cravath, of	.125	5	16	2	2	1	1	0	1	2	6	0
Oscar Dugey, pr	.000	2	0	0	0	0	0	0	0	0	0	1
Bill Killefer, ph	.000	1	1	0	0	0	0	0	0	0	0	0
Fred Luderus, 1b	.438	5	16	1	7	2	0	1	6	1	4	0
Erskine Mayer, p	.000	2	4	0	0	0	0	0	0	0	2	0
Bert Niehoff, 2b	.063	5	16	1	1	0	0	0	0	1	5	0
Dode Paskert, of	.158	5	19	2	3	0	0	0	0	1	2	0
Eppa Rixey, p	.500	1	2	0	1	0	0	0	0	0	0	0
Milt Stock, 3b	.118	5	17	1	2	0	0	0	0	1	0	0
Possum Whitted, of-5,1b-1	.067	5	15	0	1	0	0	0	1	1	0	1
TOTAL	.182		148	10	27	4	1	1	9	10	25	2

PITCHER	W	L	ERA	G	GS	CG	SV	SHO	IP	H	ER	BB	SO
Pete Alexander	1	1	1.53	2	2	2	0	0	17.2	14	3	4	10
George Chalmers	0	1	2.25	1	1	1	0	0	8.0	8	2	3	6
Erskine Mayer	0	1	2.38	2	2	1	0	0	11.1	16	3	2	7
Eppa Rixey	0	1	4.05	1	0	0	0	0	6.2	4	3	2	2
TOTAL	1	4	2.27	6	5	4	0	0	43.2	42	11	11	25

GAME 1 AT PHI OCT 8

BOS	000	000	010	1	8 1
PHI	000	100	02X	3	5 1

Pitchers: SHORE vs ALEXANDER
Attendance: 19,343

GAME 2 AT PHI OCT 9

BOS	100	000	001	2	10 0
PHI	000	010	000	1	3 1

Pitchers: FOSTER vs MAYER
Attendance: 20,306

GAME 3 AT BOS OCT 11

PHI	001	000	000	1	3 0
BOS	000	100	001	2	6 1

Pitchers: ALEXANDER vs LEONARD
Attendance: 42,300

GAME 4 AT BOS OCT 12

PHI	000	000	010	1	7 0
BOS	001	001	00X	2	8 1

Pitchers: CHALMERS vs SHORE
Attendance: 41,096

GAME 5 AT PHI OCT 13

BOS	011	000	021	5	10 1
PHI	200	200	000	4	9 1

Pitchers: FOSTER vs Mayer, RIXEY (3)
Home Runs: Hooper-BOS (2),
  Lewis-BOS, Luderus-PHI
Attendance: 20,306

In close pennant races, the Red Sox repeated as league champions and Brooklyn won its first pennant since 1900. The first three games of the Series were tightly contested, and the outcomes were determined by only one run apiece. For 6½ innings in the opener, Brooklyn's Rube Marquard dueled Boston's Ernie Shore about equally. But in the last of the seventh the Sox capitalized on a double, some sloppy Brooklyn fielding, and a couple of sacrifice hits for three runs, adding another off reliever Jeff Pfeffer in the eighth for a 6–1 lead. The Robins fought back in the ninth, driving out Shore and drawing within one run of a tie before reliever Carl Mays retired the final man with the bases loaded.

Game Two was even tighter. Boston starter Babe Ruth gave up a first-inning inside-the-park homer to Hy Myers, but in the third he drove in Everett Scott (who had tripled) to tie the game at 1–1. Then for the next ten innings he and Robin pitcher Sherry Smith shut off all scoring. Ruth continued to blank Brooklyn in the fourteenth, and in the last of the inning a walk, sacrifice, and single over the head of the third baseman gave Boston and Ruth the victory.

Brooklyn veteran Jack Coombs took a 4–0 lead into the sixth inning of Game Three before weakening. But after giving up a third Boston run on Larry Gardner's one-out homer in the seventh, he was relieved by Jeff Pfeffer, who set the Sox down in order the rest of the way. In saving what proved to be Coombs's last World Series appearance (as well as the Robins' only Series win), Pfeffer preserved Coombs's perfect Series won-lost record at 5–0.

Games Four and Five proved anticlimactic. In Game Four, Gardner's second homer of the Series—inside the park for three runs in the second inning—overcame the Robins' two runs in the first. The Sox added a run here and there to increase their lead, while Sox starter Dutch Leonard shut Brooklyn out through the final eight innings for a comfortable 6–2 win. And in what became the Series finale, Ernie Shore held the Robins to three singles and one unearned run as his Sox took advantage of a bad-hop triple in the second and two third-inning errors by Robin shortstop Ivy Olson to take the lead—and their fourth world championship.

Boston Red Sox (AL), 4; Brooklyn Robins (NL), 1

BOS (A)

PLAYER/POS	AVG	G	AB	R	H	2B	3B	HR	RB	BB	SO	SB
Hick Cady, c	.250	2	4	1	1	0	0	0	0	3	0	0
Bill Carrigan, c	.667	1	3	0	2	0	0	0	1	0	1	0
Rube Foster, p	.000	1	1	0	0	0	0	0	0	0	1	0
Del Gainer, ph	1.000	1	1	0	1	0	0	0	1	0	0	0
Larry Gardner, 3b	.176	5	17	2	3	0	0	2	6	0	2	0
Olaf Henricksen, ph	.000	1	0	1	0	0	0	0	0	1	0	0
Dick Hoblitzel, 1b	.235	5	17	3	4	1	1	0	2	6	0	0
Harry Hooper, of	.333	5	21	6	7	1	1	0	1	3	1	1
Hal Janvrin, 2b	.217	5	23	2	5	3	0	0	1	0	6	0
Dutch Leonard, p	.000	1	3	0	0	0	0	0	0	0	3	0
Duffy Lewis, of	.353	5	17	3	6	2	1	0	1	2	1	0
Carl Mays, p	.000	2	1	0	0	0	0	0	0	0	0	0
Mike McNally, pr	.000	1	0	1	0	0	0	0	0	0	0	0
Babe Ruth, p	.000	1	5	0	0	0	0	0	1	0	2	0
Everett Scott, ss	.125	5	16	1	2	0	1	0	1	1	1	0
Ernie Shore, p	.000	2	7	0	0	0	0	0	0	0	2	0
Chick Shorten, of	.571	2	7	0	4	0	0	0	2	0	1	0
Pinch Thomas, c	.143	3	7	0	1	0	1	0	0	0	1	0
Tilly Walker, of	.273	3	11	1	3	0	1	0	1	1	2	0
Jimmy Walsh, of	.000	1	3	0	0	0	0	0	0	0	0	0
TOTAL	.238		164	21	39	7	6	2	18	18	25	1

PITCHER	W	L	ERA	G	GS	CG	SV	SHO	IP	H	ER	BB	SO
Rube Foster	0	0	0.00	1	0	0	0	0	3.0	3	0	0	1
Dutch Leonard	1	0	1.00	1	1	1	0	0	9.0	5	1	4	3
Carl Mays	0	1	5.06	2	1	0	1	0	5.1	8	3	3	2
Babe Ruth	1	0	0.64	1	1	1	0	0	14.0	6	1	3	4
Ernie Shore	2	0	1.53	2	2	1	0	0	17.2	12	3	4	9
TOTAL	4	1	1.47	7	5	3	1	0	49.0	34	8	14	19

BRO (N)

PLAYER/POS	AVG	G	AB	R	H	2B	3B	HR	RB	BB	SO	SB
Larry Cheney, p	.000	1	0	0	0	0	0	0	0	0	0	0
Jack Coombs, p	.333	1	3	0	1	0	0	0	1	0	0	0
George Cutshaw, 2b	.105	5	19	2	2	1	0	0	2	1	1	0
Jake Daubert, 1b	.176	4	17	1	3	0	1	0	0	2	3	0
Wheezer Dell, p	.000	1	0	0	0	0	0	0	0	0	0	0
Gus Getz, ph	.000	1	1	0	0	0	0	0	0	0	0	0
Jimmy Johnston, of-2	.300	3	10	1	3	0	1	0	0	1	0	0
Rube Marquard, p	.000	2	3	0	0	0	0	0	0	0	1	0
Fred Merkle, 1b-1	.250	3	4	0	1	0	0	0	1	2	0	0
Chief Meyers, c	.200	3	10	0	2	0	1	0	0	1	0	0
Otto Miller, c	.125	2	8	0	1	0	0	0	0	0	1	0
Harry Mowery, 3b	.176	5	17	2	3	0	0	0	1	3	2	0
Hy Myers, of	.182	5	22	2	4	0	1	1	3	0	3	0
Ivy Olson, ss	.250	5	16	1	4	0	1	0	2	2	2	0
Ollie O'Mara, ph	.000	1	1	0	0	0	0	0	0	0	1	0
Jeff Pfeffer, p-3	.250	4	4	0	1	0	0	0	0	0	2	0
Nap Rucker, p	.000	1	0	0	0	0	0	0	0	0	0	0
Sherry Smith, p	.200	1	5	0	1	1	0	0	0	0	0	0
Casey Stengel, of-3	.364	4	11	2	4	0	0	0	0	0	1	0
Zack Wheat, of	.211	5	19	2	4	0	1	0	1	2	2	1
TOTAL	.200		170	13	34	2	5	1	11	14	19	1

PITCHER	W	L	ERA	G	GS	CG	SV	SHO	IP	H	ER	BB	SO
Larry Cheney	0	0	3.00	1	0	0	0	0	3.0	4	1	1	5
Jack Coombs	1	0	4.26	1	1	0	0	0	6.1	7	3	1	1
Wheezer Dell	0	0	0.00	1	0	0	0	0	1.0	1	0	0	0
Rube Marquard	0	2	6.55	2	2	0	0	0	11.0	12	8	6	9
Jeff Pfeffer	0	1	1.69	3	1	0	1	0	10.2	7	2	4	5
Nap Rucker	0	0	0.00	1	0	0	0	0	2.0	1	0	0	3
Sherry Smith	0	1	1.35	1	1	1	0	0	13.1	7	2	6	2
TOTAL	1	4	3.04	10	5	1	1	0	47.1	39	16	18	25

GAME 1 AT BOS OCT 7

BRO	000	100	004	5	10	4
BOS	001	010	31X	6	8	1

Pitchers: MARQUARD, Pfeffer (8) vs SHORE, Mays (9)
Attendance: 36,117

GAME 2 AT BOS OCT 9

BRO	100 000 000 000 00	1	6	2
BOS	001 000 000 000 01	2	7	1

Pitchers: SMITH vs RUTH
Home Runs: H.Myers-BRO
Attendance: 41,373

GAME 3 AT BRO OCT 10

BOS	000	002	100	3	7	1
BRO	001	120	00X	4	10	0

Pitchers: MAYS, Foster (6) vs COOMBS, Pfeffer (7)
Home Runs: Gardner-BOS
Attendance: 21,087

GAME 4 AT BRO OCT 11

BOS	030	110	100	6	10	1
BRO	200	000	000	2	5	4

Pitchers: LEONARD vs MARQUARD, Cheney (5), Rucker (8)
Home Runs: Gardner-BOS
Attendance: 21,662

GAME 5 AT BOS OCT 12

BRO	010	000	000	1	3	3
BOS	012	010	00X	4	7	2

Pitchers: PFEFFER, Dell (8) vs SHORE
Attendance: 42,620

Easy winners in their pennant races, the White Sox and Giants traded pairs of victories in the Series before the Sox came up with a second pair to take the title in six games. In the opener, Happy Felsch's solo homer in the fourth inning gave Sox starter Eddie Cicotte the margin he needed to defeat Giant Slim Sallee 2–1, and in Game Two Red Faber went all the way, as his Sox broke a 2–2 tie in the fourth inning with five runs on six singles for Chicago's second win.

The clubs traveled to New York for Games Three and Four, and Giant pitchers rewarded their fans with a pair of shutouts to even the Series. In Game Three, a triple, double, and single against the Sox' Cicotte in the fourth inning produced the only scoring, as Giant Rube Benton blanked the Sox on five hits, walking none. Giant ace Ferdie Schupp (a 21-game winner during the season) did the honors in Game Four, scattering seven hits, as teammate Benny Kauff, with his first Series hit in the fourth inning, homered inside the park to deep center against Red Faber for the deciding run. Two later runs against Faber and two more in the eighth (on Kauff's second homer) against reliever Dave Danforth made Schupp's win easy.

But Faber, the loser in Game Four, came in to pitch two innings of perfect relief two days later in Chicago for his second win, as the Sox rebounded from a 2–5 deficit with three runs in the bottom of the seventh to tie the game and three more an inning later to win it.

After a day of rest and a return to New York, Faber was given his third start. He pitched well enough, but his third win and the Series clincher was really the gift of some infamous Giant fielding. In the fourth inning, the first two Sox batters—Eddie Collins and Joe Jackson—reached on a high throw to first and a dropped fly. Happy Felsch, the third man up, reached on a fielder's choice as Giant third baseman Heinie Zimmerman chased Collins across the plate in a botched rundown. Jackson and Felsch scored the second and third unearned runs as Chick Gandil singled off the hapless Rube Benton. The Giants recovered to score two runs an inning later, but Faber shut them out the rest of the way to give his Sox the Series.

Chicago White Sox (AL), 4; New York Giants (NL), 2

CHI (A)

PLAYER/POS	AVG	G	AB	R	H	2B	3B	HR	RB	BB	SO	SB
Eddie Cicotte, p	.143	3	7	0	1	0	0	0	0	0	1	2	0
Eddie Collins, 2b	.409	6	22	4	9	1	0	0	2	2	3	3
Shano Collins, of	.286	6	21	2	6	1	0	0	0	0	2	0
Dave Danforth, p	.000	1	0	0	0	0	0	0	0	0	0	0
Red Faber, p	.143	4	7	0	1	0	0	0	0	2	3	0
Happy Felsch, of	.273	6	22	4	6	1	0	1	3	1	5	0
Chick Gandil, 1b	.261	6	23	1	6	1	0	0	5	0	2	1
Joe Jackson, of	.304	6	23	4	7	0	0	0	2	1	0	1
Nemo Leibold, of	.400	2	5	1	2	0	0	0	2	1	1	0
Byrd Lynn, ph	.000	1	1	0	0	0	0	0	0	0	1	0
Fred McMullin, 3b	.125	6	24	1	3	1	0	0	2	1	6	0
Swede Risberg, ph	.500	2	2	0	1	0	0	0	1	0	0	0
Reb Russell, p	.000	1	0	0	0	0	0	0	0	0	0	0
Ray Schalk, c	.263	6	19	1	5	0	0	0	0	2	1	1
Buck Weaver, ss	.333	6	21	3	7	1	0	0	1	0	2	0
Lefty Williams, p	.000	1	0	0	0	0	0	0	0	0	0	0
TOTAL	.274		197	21	54	6	0	1	18	11	28	6

PITCHER	W	L	ERA	G	GS	CG	SV	SHO	IP	H	ER	BB	SO
Eddie Cicotte	1	1	1.96	3	2	2	0	0	23.0	23	5	2	13
Dave Danforth	0	0	18.00	1	0	0	0	0	1.0	3	2	0	2
Red Faber	3	1	2.33	4	3	2	0	0	27.0	21	7	3	9
Reb Russell	0	0	∞	1	1	0	0	0	0.0	2	1	1	0
Lefty Williams	0	0	9.00	1	0	0	0	0	1.0	2	1	0	3
TOTAL	4	2	2.77	10	6	4	0	0	52.0	51	16	6	27

NY (N)

PLAYER/POS	AVG	G	AB	R	H	2B	3B	HR	RB	BB	SO	SB
Fred Anderson, p	.000	1	0	0	0	0	0	0	0	0	0	0
Rube Benton, p	.000	2	4	0	0	0	0	0	0	0	3	0
George Burns, of	.227	6	22	3	5	0	0	0	2	2	6	1
Art Fletcher, ss	.200	6	25	2	5	1	0	0	0	0	2	0
Buck Herzog, 2b	.250	6	24	1	6	0	1	0	2	1	4	0
Walter Holke, 1b	.286	6	21	2	6	2	0	0	1	0	6	0
Benny Kauff, of	.160	6	25	2	4	1	0	2	5	0	2	1
Lew McCarty, c-2	.400	3	5	1	2	0	1	0	1	0	0	0
Pol Perritt, p	1.000	3	2	0	2	0	0	0	0	0	0	0
Bill Rariden, c	.385	5	13	2	5	0	0	0	2	2	1	0
Dave Robertson, of	.500	6	22	3	11	1	1	0	1	0	0	2
Slim Sallee, p	.167	2	6	0	1	0	0	0	0	0	2	0
Ferdie Schupp, p	.250	2	4	0	1	0	0	0	1	0	1	0
Jeff Tesreau, p	.000	1	0	0	0	0	0	0	0	0	0	0
Jim Thorpe, of	.000	1	0	0	0	0	0	0	0	0	0	0
Joe Wilhoit, ph	.000	2	1	0	0	0	0	0	0	1	0	0
Heinie Zimmerman, 3b	.120	6	25	1	3	0	1	0	0	0	0	0
TOTAL	.256		199	17	51	5	4	2	16	6	27	4

PITCHER	W	L	ERA	G	GS	CG	SV	SHO	IP	H	ER	BB	SO
Fred Anderson	0	1	18.00	1	0	0	0	0	2.0	5	4	0	3
Rube Benton	1	1	0.00	2	2	1	0	1	14.0	9	0	1	8
Pol Perritt	0	0	2.16	3	0	0	0	0	8.1	9	2	3	3
Slim Sallee	0	2	5.28	2	2	1	0	0	15.1	20	9	4	4
Ferdie Schupp	1	0	1.74	2	2	1	0	1	10.1	11	2	2	9
Jeff Tesreau	0	0	0.00	1	0	0	0	0	1.0	0	0	1	1
TOTAL	2	4	3.00	11	6	3	0	2	51.0	54	17	11	28

Although both clubs had lost key players to military service, so had other major league teams, and after a season shortened by a month because of the war, the Red Sox and Cubs found themselves opponents in an early-September World Series.

In the opener, Babe Ruth pushed his string of consecutive scoreless World Series innings to 22, holding the Cubs to six singles as he went the distance. The Cubs' Hippo Vaughn pitched just as well, but two of the five singles he yielded followed a leadoff walk in the fourth and produced the game's only run. Chicago evened the Series in Game Two, bunching four of their seven hits after a walk in the second inning to take a 3–0 lead. Successive triples in Boston's ninth spoiled Lefty Tyler's shutout but not his victory.

Hippo Vaughn lost another close one in Game Three when he gave up two runs in the fourth inning on a hit batsman and a succession of singles. The Cubs got him one run back in the fifth, but the Sox' Carl Mays held Chicago to that one run as he hurled Boston back into the Series lead. Ruth pushed the Sox farther ahead the next day in another squeaker. As he continued his mastery over Cub hitters, he drove Boston into the lead with a two-run triple in the fourth inning (his only Series hit). But in the eighth a run-scoring ground out ended his record setting string of scoreless innings at 29⅔, and a single drove in another run to tie the game. The Sox, though, scored a third run on a Chicago error in the last of the eighth, and reliever Bullet Joe Bush shut down a threat in the ninth to save Ruth's win.

Vaughn, in his third start, finally found what was needed for victory—a shutout, on five hits, as the Cubs added hits to walks from Boston's Sad Sam Jones in the third and eighth to push across their three runs. But in Game Six the Sox scored two unearned runs on a dropped line drive to right in the third inning. It was their only scoring off Lefty Tyler, but Boston's Carl Mays was on his way to a one-run three-hitter that brought the Red Sox their fifth world championship in five tries. To date, although they have tried four more times, they have not won a sixth.

Boston Red Sox (AL), 4; Chicago Cubs (NL), 2

BOS (A)

PLAYER/POS	AVG	G	AB	R	H	2B	3B	HR	RB	BB	SO	SB
Sam Agnew, c	.000	4	9	0	0	0	0	0	0	0	0	0
Joe Bush, p	.000	2	2	0	0	0	0	0	0	1	0	0
Jean Dubuc, ph	.000	1	1	0	0	0	0	0	0	0	1	0
Harry Hooper, of	.200	6	20	0	4	0	0	0	0	2	2	0
Sam Jones, p	.000	1	1	0	0	0	0	0	0	1	0	0
Carl Mays, p	.200	2	5	1	1	0	0	0	0	1	0	0
Stuffy McInnis, 1b	.250	6	20	2	5	0	0	0	1	1	1	0
Hack Miller, ph	.000	1	1	0	0	0	0	0	0	0	0	0
Babe Ruth, p-2,of-2	.200	3	5	0	1	0	1	0	2	0	2	0
Wally Schang, c	.444	5	9	1	4	0	0	0	1	2	3	1
Everett Scott, ss	.095	6	21	0	2	0	0	0	0	1	1	0
Dave Shean, 2b	.211	6	19	2	4	1	0	0	0	4	3	1
Amos Strunk, of	.174	6	23	1	4	1	1	0	0	0	5	0
Fred Thomas, 3b	.125	6	16	0	2	0	0	0	0	1	2	0
George Whiteman, of	.250	6	20	2	5	0	1	0	1	2	1	1
TOTAL	.186		172	9	32	2	3	0	6	16	21	3

PITCHER	W	L	ERA	G	GS	CG	SV	SHO	IP	H	ER	BB	SO
Joe Bush	0	1	3.00	2	1	1	1	0	9.0	7	3	3	0
Sam Jones	0	1	3.00	1	1	1	0	0	9.0	7	3	5	5
Carl Mays	2	0	1.00	2	2	2	0	0	18.0	10	2	3	5
Babe Ruth	2	0	1.06	2	2	1	0	1	17.0	13	2	7	4
TOTAL	4	2	1.70	7	6	5	1	1	53.0	37	10	18	14

CHI (N)

PLAYER/POS	AVG	G	AB	R	H	2B	3B	HR	RB	BB	SO	SB
Turner Barber, ph	.000	3	2	0	0	0	0	0	0	0	0	0
Charlie Deal, 3b	.176	6	17	0	3	0	0	0	0	0	1	0
Phil Douglas, p	.000	1	0	0	0	0	0	0	0	0	0	0
Max Flack, of	.263	6	19	2	5	0	0	0	0	4	1	1
Claude Hendrix, p-1	1.000	2	1	0	1	0	0	0	0	0	0	0
Charlie Hollocher, ss	.190	6	21	2	4	0	1	0	1	1	1	1
Bill Killefer, c	.118	6	17	2	2	1	0	0	2	2	0	0
Les Mann, of	.227	6	22	0	5	2	0	0	2	0	0	0
Bill McCabe, ph	.000	3	1	1	0	0	0	0	0	0	0	0
Fred Merkle, 1b	.278	6	18	1	5	0	0	0	1	4	3	0
Bob O'Farrell, c-1	.000	3	3	0	0	0	0	0	0	0	0	0
Dode Paskert, of	.190	6	21	0	4	1	0	0	2	2	2	0
Charlie Pick, 2b	.389	6	18	2	7	1	0	0	0	1	1	1
Lefty Tyler, p	.200	3	5	0	1	0	0	0	2	2	0	0
Hippo Vaughn, p	.000	3	10	0	0	0	0	0	0	0	5	0
Chuck Wortman, 2b	.000	1	1	0	0	0	0	0	0	0	0	0
Rollie Zeider, 3b	.000	2	0	0	0	0	0	0	0	2	0	0
TOTAL	.210		176	10	37	5	1	0	10	18	14	3

PITCHER	W	L	ERA	G	GS	CG	SV	SHO	IP	H	ER	BB	SO
Phil Douglas	0	1	0.00	1	0	0	0	0	1.0	1	0	0	0
Claude Hendrix	0	0	0.00	1	0	0	0	0	1.0	0	0	0	0
Lefty Tyler	1	1	1.17	3	3	1	0	0	23.0	14	3	11	4
Hippo Vaughn	1	2	1.00	3	3	3	0	1	27.0	17	3	5	17
TOTAL	2	4	1.04	8	6	4	0	1	52.0	32	6	16	21

GAME 1 AT CHI SEPT 5

BOS	000	100	000	1	5	0
CHI	000	000	000	0	6	0

Pitchers: RUTH vs VAUGHN
Attendance: 19,274

GAME 2 AT CHI SEPT 6

BOS	000	000	001	1	6	1
CHI	030	000	000	3	7	1

Pitchers: BUSH vs TYLER
Attendance: 20,040

GAME 3 AT CHI SEPT 7

BOS	000	200	000	2	7	0
CHI	000	010	000	1	7	1

Pitchers: MAYS vs VAUGHN
Attendance: 27,054

GAME 4 AT BOS SEPT 9

CHI	000	000	020	2	7	1
BOS	000	200	01X	3	4	0

Pitchers: Tyler, DOUGLAS (8) vs RUTH, Bush (9)
Attendance: 22,183

GAME 5 AT BOS SEPT 10

CHI	001	000	002	3	7	0
BOS	000	000	000	0	5	0

Pitchers: VAUGHN vs JONES
Attendance: 24,694

GAME 6 AT BOS SEPT 11

CHI	000	100	000	1	3	2
BOS	002	000	00X	2	5	0

Pitchers: TYLER, Hendrix (8) vs MAYS
Attendance: 15,238

In the bottom of the first inning of Game One, White Sox pitcher Eddie Cicotte hit the first batter to face him, a prearranged signal to gamblers that "the fix was on"—that the Sox would throw the Series. The eight Chicago conspirators—pitching aces Cicotte and Lefty Williams, outfielders Joe Jackson and Happy Felsch, and infielders Chick Gandil, Buck Weaver, Fred McMullin and Swede Risberg—received no more than a fraction of the $100,000 promised them but "honored" their end of the deal. Cicotte (winner of 29 regular-season games, with a 1.82 ERA) gave up seven hits and six runs in the opening innings of Game One en route to a 1–9 loss, and Williams, though he held the Reds to four hits in Game Two, uncharacteristically walked six and fanned only one, a performance bad enough for a 2–4 loss.

Dickie Kerr, Chicago's third-best pitcher and not in on the fix, won Game Three with a three-hit shutout. But although Cicotte pitched well in Game Four, Chicago lost a third time as the Reds' Jimmy Ring hurled a three-hit shutout of his own (all three hits coming, ironically, off the bats of conspirators Jackson, Felsch, and Gandil).

Cincinnati's Hod Eller beat Chicago in Game Five with the Series' third successive three-hit shutout. Loser Lefty Williams once again yielded only four hits, but three came in a four-run sixth inning which also saw a walk and a throwing error by Felsch. (The win, the Reds' fourth, did not decide the Series, which had been expanded to the best five of nine in the exuberance which followed the end of the Great War.)

Chicago exerted itself to win the next two games. In Game Six, Kerr's second win depended on crucial hits by Jackson and Gandil in the tenth inning; and in Game Seven Cicotte held the Reds to one run as Jackson and Felsch drove in all the Sox' four.

But in Game Eight, Williams gave up two singles and two doubles before being pulled with only one away in the first. Jackson homered in the third. And he doubled and Gandil tripled to drive in three Chicago runs in the eighth. But by then the Reds had scored ten runs on their way to an easy win and their tainted world title.

Cincinnati Reds (NL), 5; Chicago White Sox (AL), 3

CIN (N)

PLAYER/POS	AVG	G	AB	R	H	2B	3B	HR	RB	BB	SO	SB
Jake Daubert, 1b	.241	8	29	4	7	0	1	0	1	1	2	1
Pat Duncan, of	.269	8	26	3	7	2	0	0	8	2	2	0
Hod Eller, p	.286	2	7	2	2	1	0	0	0	0	2	0
Ray Fisher, p	.500	2	2	0	1	0	0	0	0	0	0	0
Heinie Groh, 3b	.172	8	29	6	5	2	0	0	2	6	4	0
Larry Kopf, ss	.222	8	27	3	6	0	2	0	2	3	2	0
Dolf Luque, p	.000	2	1	0	0	0	0	0	0	0	1	0
Sherry Magee, ph	.500	2	2	0	1	0	0	0	0	0	0	0
Greasy Neale, of	.357	8	28	3	10	1	1	0	4	2	5	1
Bill Rariden, c	.211	5	19	0	4	0	0	0	2	0	0	1
Morrie Rath, 2b	.226	8	31	5	7	1	0	0	2	4	1	2
Jimmy Ring, p	.000	2	5	0	0	0	0	0	0	0	2	0
Edd Roush, of	.214	8	28	6	6	2	1	0	7	3	0	2
Dutch Ruether, p-2	.667	3	6	2	4	1	2	0	4	1	0	0
Slim Sallee, p	.000	2	4	0	0	0	0	0	0	0	0	0
Jimmy Smith, pr	.000	1	0	0	0	0	0	0	0	0	0	0
Ivey Wingo, c	.571	3	7	1	4	0	0	0	1	3	1	0
TOTAL	.255		251	35	64	10	7	0	33	25	22	7

PITCHER	W	L	ERA	G	GS	CG	SV	SHO	IP	H	ER	BB	SO
Hod Eller	2	0	2.00	2	2	2	0	1	18.0	13	4	2	15
Ray Fisher	0	1	2.35	2	1	0	0	0	7.2	7	2	2	2
Dolf Luque	0	0	0.00	2	0	0	0	0	5.0	1	0	0	6
Jimmy Ring	1	1	0.64	2	1	1	0	1	14.0	7	1	6	4
Dutch Ruether	1	0	2.57	2	2	1	0	0	14.0	12	4	4	1
Slim Sallee	1	1	1.35	2	2	1	0	0	13.1	19	2	1	2
TOTAL	5	3	1.63	12	8	5	0	2	72.0	59	13	15	30

CHI (A)

PLAYER/POS	AVG	G	AB	R	H	2B	3B	HR	RB	BB	SO	SB
Eddie Cicotte, p	.000	3	8	0	0	0	0	0	0	0	3	0
Eddie Collins, 2b	.226	8	31	2	7	1	0	0	1	1	2	1
Shano Collins, of	.250	4	16	2	4	1	0	0	0	0	0	0
Happy Felsch, of	.192	8	26	2	5	1	0	0	3	1	4	0
Chick Gandil, 1b	.233	8	30	1	7	0	1	0	5	1	3	1
Joe Jackson, of	.375	8	32	5	12	3	0	1	6	1	2	0
Bill James, p	.000	1	2	0	0	0	0	0	0	0	1	0
Dickie Kerr, p	.167	2	6	0	1	0	0	0	0	0	0	0
Nemo Leibold, of	.056	5	18	0	1	0	0	0	0	2	3	1
Grover Lowdermilk, p	.000	1	0	0	0	0	0	0	0	0	0	0
Byrd Lynn, c	.000	1	1	0	0	0	0	0	0	0	0	0
Erskine Mayer, p	.000	1	0	0	0	0	0	0	0	0	0	0
Fred McMullin, ph	.500	2	2	0	1	0	0	0	0	0	0	0
Eddie Murphy, ph	.000	3	2	0	0	0	0	0	0	0	1	0
Swede Risberg, ss	.080	8	25	3	2	0	1	0	0	5	3	1
Ray Schalk, c	.304	8	23	1	7	0	0	0	2	4	2	1
Buck Weaver, 3b	.324	8	34	4	11	4	1	0	0	0	2	0
Roy Wilkinson, p	.000	2	2	0	0	0	0	0	0	0	1	0
Lefty Williams, p	.200	3	5	0	1	0	0	0	0	0	3	0
TOTAL	.224		263	20	59	10	3	1	17	15	30	5

PITCHER	W	L	ERA	G	GS	CG	SV	SHO	IP	H	ER	BB	SO
Eddie Cicotte	1	2	2.91	3	3	2	0	0	21.2	19	7	5	7
Bill James	0	0	5.79	1	0	0	0	0	4.2	8	3	3	2
Dickie Kerr	2	0	1.42	2	2	2	0	1	19.0	14	3	3	6
Grover Lowdermilk	0	0	9.00	1	0	0	0	0	1.0	2	1	1	0
Erskine Mayer	0	0	0.00	1	0	0	0	0	1.0	0	0	1	0
Roy Wilkinson	0	0	1.23	2	0	0	0	0	7.1	9	1	4	3
Lefty Williams	0	3	6.61	3	3	1	0	0	16.1	12	12	8	4
TOTAL	3	5	3.42	13	8	5	0	1	71.0	64	27	25	22

GAME 1 AT CIN OCT 1

CHI	010 000 000	1 6 1
CIN	100 500 21X	9 14 1

Pitchers: CICOTTE, Wilkinson (4), Lowdermilk (8) vs RUETHER
Attendance: 30,511

GAME 2 AT CIN OCT 2

CHI	000 000 200	2 10 1
CIN	000 301 00X	4 4 2

Pitchers: WILLIAMS vs SALLEE
Attendance: 29,690

GAME 3 AT CHI OCT 3

CIN	000 000 000	0 3 1
CHI	020 100 00X	3 7 0

Pitchers: FISHER, Luque (8) vs KERR
Attendance: 29,126

GAME 4 AT CHI OCT 4

CIN	000 020 000	2 5 2
CHI	000 000 000	0 3 2

Pitchers: RING vs CICOTTE
Attendance: 34,363

GAME 5 AT CHI OCT 6

CIN	000 004 001	5 4 0
CHI	000 000 000	0 3 3

Pitchers: ELLER vs WILLIAMS, Mayer (9)
Attendance: 34,379

GAME 6 AT CIN OCT 7

CHI	000 013 000 1	5 10 3
CIN	002 200 000 0	4 11 0

Pitchers: KERR vs Ruether, RING (6)
Attendance: 32,006

GAME 7 AT CIN OCT 8

CHI	101 020 000	4 10 1
CIN	000 001 000	1 7 4

Pitchers: CICOTTE vs SALLEE, Fisher (5), Luque (6)
Attendance: 13,923

GAME 8 AT CHI OCT 9

CIN	410 013 010	10 16 2
CHI	001 000 040	5 10 1

Pitchers: ELLER vs WILLIAMS, James (1), Wilkinson (6)
Home Runs: Jackson-CHI
Attendance: 32,930

The Indians outscored the Robins in the Series, 21 runs to 8. Yet after losing the opener in Brooklyn, the Robins fought back to take the next two, and held the Series lead as the teams traveled to Cleveland for the next four games.

Both clubs garnered five hits in Game One, but an error, walk, single, and double gave the Indians two runs in the second and a lead they never yielded, as Stan Coveleski outlasted Rube Marquard for the win. In Game Two, both clubs increased their hit totals to seven, but the Robins bunched six of theirs into three innings for three runs, while Burleigh Grimes, only once yielding two hits in an inning, shut the Indians out. The two runs Brooklyn scored in the first inning of Game Three were all Sherry Smith needed to give the Robins their second win behind his three-hit pitching. But Brooklyn scored only twice more in the Series as the Indians swept to the championship with four wins in Cleveland.

With the Indians scoring four runs in Game Four before Brooklyn put its one run on the board, Coveleski breezed to his second five-hit Series run. Jim Bagby had it even easier the next day. The Robins tagged him for 13 hits, but not until the ninth inning were they able to put them together for a run. Meanwhile Bagby and his teammates were registering a couple of Series firsts as they moved to an eight-run lead. Right fielder Elmer Smith opened the scoring in the first inning with the first World Series grand slam, and Bagby himself homered for three more in the fourth—the first pitcher to hit a Series home run.

But the 1920 Series is best remembered for second baseman Bill Wambsganss's unassisted triple play in the fifth inning. With runners on first and second going on pitcher Clarence Mitchell's liner, Wambsganss snared the ball for the first out, stepped on second to force one runner, and tagged the runner coming in from first to retire the side.

In Game Six Duster Mails, a late-season addition to the team, shut out Brooklyn on three hits in a 1–0 squeaker over Sherry Smith. Coveleski won the clincher the next day, also via the shutout, with his third five-hitter of the Series and his third Series win.

Cleveland Indians (AL), 5;
Brooklyn Robins (NL), 2

CLE (A)

PLAYER/POS	AVG	G	AB	R	H	2B	3B	HR	RB	BB	SO	SB
Jim Bagby, p	.333	2	6	1	2	0	0	1	3	0	0	0
George Burns, 1b-4	.300	5	10	1	3	1	0	0	2	3	3	0
Ray Caldwell, p	.000	1	0	0	0	0	0	0	0	0	0	0
Stan Coveleski, p	.100	3	10	2	1	0	0	0	0	0	4	0
Joe Evans, of	.308	4	13	0	4	0	0	0	0	1	0	0
Larry Gardner, 3b	.208	7	24	1	5	1	0	0	2	1	1	0
Jack Graney, of-2	.000	3	3	0	0	0	0	0	0	0	2	0
Charlie Jamieson, of-5	.333	6	15	2	5	1	0	0	1	1	0	1
Doc Johnston, 1b	.273	5	11	1	3	0	0	0	0	2	1	1
Harry Lunte, 2b	.000	1	0	0	0	0	0	0	0	0	0	0
Duster Mails, p	.000	2	5	0	0	0	0	0	0	0	1	0
Les Nunamaker, c-1	.500	2	2	0	1	0	0	0	0	0	0	0
Steve O'Neill, c	.333	7	21	1	7	3	0	0	2	4	3	0
Joe Sewell, ss	.174	7	23	0	4	0	0	0	0	2	1	0
Elmer Smith, of	.308	5	13	1	4	0	1	1	5	1	1	0
Tris Speaker, of	.320	7	25	6	8	2	1	0	1	3	1	0
Pinch Thomas, c	.000	1	0	0	0	0	0	0	0	0	0	0
George Uhle, p	.000	2	0	0	0	0	0	0	0	0	0	0
Bill Wambsganss, 2b	.154	7	26	3	4	0	0	0	1	2	1	0
Joe Wood, of	.200	4	10	2	2	1	0	0	0	1	2	0
TOTAL	.244		217	21	53	9	2	2	17	21	21	2

PITCHER	W	L	ERA	G	GS	CG	SV	SHO	IP	H	ER	BB	SO
Jim Bagby	1	1	1.80	2	2	1	0	0	15.0	20	3	1	3
Ray Caldwell	0	1	27.00	1	1	0	0	0	0.1	2	1	1	0
Stan Coveleski	3	0	0.67	3	3	3	0	1	27.0	15	2	2	8
Duster Mails	1	0	0.00	2	1	1	0	1	15.2	6	0	6	6
George Uhle	0	0	0.00	2	0	0	0	0	3.0	1	0	0	3
TOTAL	5	2	0.89	10	7	5	0	2	61.0	44	6	10	20

BRO (N)

PLAYER/POS	AVG	G	AB	R	H	2B	3B	HR	RB	BB	SO	SB
Leon Cadore, p	.000	2	0	0	0	0	0	0	0	0	0	0
Tommy Griffith, of	.190	7	21	1	4	2	0	0	3	0	2	0
Burleigh Grimes, p	.333	3	6	1	2	0	0	0	0	0	0	0
Jimmy Johnston, 3b	.214	4	14	2	3	0	0	0	0	0	2	1
Pete Kilduff, 2b	.095	7	21	0	2	0	0	0	0	1	4	0
Ed Konetchy, 1b	.174	7	23	0	4	0	1	0	2	3	2	0
Ernie Krueger, c-3	.167	4	6	0	1	0	0	0	0	0	0	0
Bill Lamar, ph	.000	3	3	0	0	0	0	0	0	0	0	0
Al Mamaux, p	.000	3	1	0	0	0	0	0	0	0	1	0
Rube Marquard, p	.000	2	1	0	0	0	0	0	0	0	0	0
Bill McCabe, pr	.000	1	0	0	0	0	0	0	0	0	0	0
Otto Miller, c	.143	6	14	0	2	0	0	0	0	1	2	0
Clarence Mitchell, p-1	.333	2	3	0	1	0	0	0	0	0	0	0
Hy Myers, of	.231	7	26	0	6	0	0	0	1	0	1	0
Bernie Neis, of-2	.000	4	5	0	0	0	0	0	0	1	0	0
Ivy Olson, ss	.320	7	25	2	8	1	0	0	0	3	1	0
Jeff Pfeffer, p	.000	1	1	0	0	0	0	0	0	0	0	0
Ray Schmandt, ph	.000	1	1	0	0	0	0	0	0	0	0	0
Jack Sheehan, 3b	.182	3	11	0	2	0	0	0	0	0	1	0
Sherry Smith, p	.000	2	6	0	0	0	0	0	0	0	2	0
Zack Wheat, of	.333	7	27	2	9	2	0	0	2	1	2	0
TOTAL	.205		215	8	44	5	1	0	8	10	20	1

PITCHER	W	L	ERA	G	GS	CG	SV	SHO	IP	H	ER	BB	SO
Leon Cadore	0	1	9.00	2	1	0	0	0	2.0	4	2	1	1
Burleigh Grimes	1	2	4.19	3	3	1	0	1	19.1	23	9	9	4
Al Mamaux	0	0	4.50	3	0	0	0	0	4.0	2	2	0	5
Rube Marquard	0	1	1.00	2	1	0	0	0	9.0	7	1	3	6
Clarence Mitchell	0	0	0.00	1	0	0	0	0	4.2	3	0	2	1
Jeff Pfeffer	0	0	3.00	1	0	0	0	0	3.0	4	1	2	1
Sherry Smith	1	1	0.53	2	2	2	0	0	17.0	10	1	3	3
TOTAL	2	5	2.44	14	7	3	0	1	59.0	53	16	21	21

GAME 1 AT BRO OCT 5

CLE	020	100	000	3	5	0
BRO	000	000	100	1	5	1

Pitchers: COVELESKI vs MARQUARD, Mamaux (7), Cadore (9)
Attendance: 23,753

GAME 2 AT BRO OCT 6

CLE	000	000	000	0	7	1
BRO	101	010	00X	3	7	0

Pitchers: BAGBY, Uhle (7) vs GRIMES
Attendance: 22,559

GAME 3 AT BRO OCT 7

CLE	000	100	000	1	3	1
BRO	200	000	00X	2	6	1

Pitchers: CALDWELL, Mails (1), Uhle (8) vs SMITH
Attendance: 25,088

GAME 4 AT CLE OCT 9

BRO	000	100	000	1	5	1
CLE	202	001	00X	5	12	2

Pitchers: CADORE, Mamaux (2), Marquard (3), Pfeffer (6) vs COVELESKI
Attendance: 25,734

GAME 5 AT CLE OCT 10

BRO	000	000	001	1	13	1
CLE	400	310	00X	8	12	2

Pitchers: GRIMES, Mitchell (4) vs BAGBY
Home Runs: E.Smith-CLE, Bagby-CLE
Attendance: 26,884

GAME 6 AT CLE OCT 11

BRO	000	000	000	0	3	0
CLE	000	001	00X	1	7	3

Pitchers: SMITH vs MAILS
Attendance: 27,194

GAME 7 AT CLE OCT 12

BRO	000	000	000	0	5	2
CLE	000	110	10X	3	7	3

Pitchers: GRIMES, Mamaux (8) vs COVELESKI
Attendance: 27,525

Since both the Giants and Yankees called the Polo Grounds home, all eight games were played there, with the two clubs alternating from game to game as the hometeam. Pitching dominated the first two games—especially Yankee pitching. In Game One, Giant third baseman Frank Frisch went 4 for 4 against Carl Mays. But Mays gave up only one other hit and walked no one, to fashion a shutout. The next day Art Nehf of the Giants allowed the Yankees only three singles. But the Yankees capitalized on two of them, together with one of Nehf's seven walks, a couple of Giant errors, and Bob Meusel's steal of home to score three times, as pitcher Waite Hoyt shut out the Giants on two singles to put the Yanks two up in the Series.

In Game Three the hitters finally came alive. With the score tied 4–4 in the last of the seventh, the Giants unloaded for eight hits which, with two walks and a sacrifice fly, produced eight runs and the first Giant win. They evened the Series the next day, scoring three runs in the eighth to take a 3–1 lead, adding another in the ninth. Babe Ruth's first World Series home run, a solo shot in the bottom of the ninth, thrilled the fans but had no effect on the game's outcome.

The Yankees regained the Series lead in Game Five. Waite Hoyt was not as sharp as he had been in the opener, yielding ten hits. But the only run scored against him came as the result of a first-inning error, a deficit his Yankee teammates overcame for a 3–1 win. In Game Six the Yankees took a quick 3–0 lead in the first. The Giants tied it in the top of the second on home runs by Irish Meusel and Frank Snyder, but Chick Fewster hit a two-run shot a half inning later to restore the Yankee lead. In the fourth inning, though, the Giants parlayed four singles and an error into four runs and a lead that held up for a Series-tying win.

The Yankees scored only one run the rest of the way as the Giants took the final two games on unearned runs. In Game Seven, Mays and the Giants' Phil Douglas dueled into the seventh tied 1–1. But in the last of the seventh, Giant Frank Snyder's double drove in Johnny Rawlings, who had reached on an error, for the game's deciding run. In Game Eight, Hoyt held the Giants to four hits and completed his third game without giving up an earned run. But a Giant runner had scored in the first inning when a grounder shot through the legs of shortstop Roger Peckinpaugh. It turned out to be the game's only run, as Art Nehf and his Giants' flawless fielding blanked the Yankees to give manager John McGraw his first world championship since 1905.

New York Giants (NL), 5; New York Yankees (AL), 3

NY (N)

PLAYER/POS	AVG	G	AB	R	H	2B	3B	HR	RB	BB	SO	SB
Dave Bancroft, ss	.152	8	33	3	5	1	0	0	3	1	5	0
Jesse Barnes, p	.444	3	9	3	4	0	0	0	0	0	0	0
George Burns, of	.333	8	33	2	11	4	1	0	2	3	5	1
Phil Douglas, p	.000	3	7	0	0	0	0	0	0	0	2	0
Frankie Frisch, 3b	.300	8	30	5	9	0	1	0	1	4	3	3
George Kelly, 1b	.233	8	30	3	7	1	0	0	4	3	10	0
Irish Meusel, of	.345	8	29	4	10	2	1	1	7	2	3	1
Art Nehf, p	.000	3	9	0	0	0	0	0	0	1	3	0
Johnny Rawlings, 2b	.333	8	30	2	10	3	0	0	4	0	3	0
Earl Smith, c-2	.000	3	7	0	0	0	0	0	0	1	0	0
Frank Snyder, c-6	.364	7	22	4	8	1	0	1	3	0	2	0
Fred Toney, p	.000	2	0	0	0	0	0	0	0	0	0	0
Ross Youngs, of	.280	8	25	3	7	1	1	0	4	7	2	2
TOTAL	.269		264	29	71	13	4	2	28	22	38	7

PITCHER	W	L	ERA	G	GS	CG	SV	SHO	IP	H	ER	BB	SO
Jesse Barnes	2	0	1.65	3	0	0	0	0	16.1	10	3	6	18
Phil Douglas	2	1	2.08	3	3	2	0	0	26.0	20	6	5	17
Art Nehf	1	2	1.38	3	3	3	0	1	26.0	13	4	13	8
Fred Toney	0	0	23.63	2	2	0	0	0	2.2	7	7	3	1
TOTAL	5	3	2.54	11	8	5	0	1	71.0	50	20	27	44

NY (A)

PLAYER/POS	AVG	G	AB	R	H	2B	3B	HR	RB	BB	SO	SB
Frank Baker, 3b-2	.250	4	8	0	2	0	0	0	0	1	0	0
Rip Collins, p	.000	1	0	0	0	0	0	0	0	0	0	0
Al DeVormer, c-1	.000	2	1	0	0	0	0	0	0	0	0	0
Chick Fewster, of	.200	4	10	3	2	0	0	1	2	3	3	0
Harry Harper, p	.000	1	0	0	0	0	0	0	0	0	0	0
Waite Hoyt, p	.222	3	9	0	2	0	0	0	1	0	1	0
Carl Mays, p	.111	3	9	0	1	0	0	0	0	0	1	0
Mike McNally, 3b	.200	7	20	3	4	1	0	0	1	1	3	2
Bob Meusel, of	.200	8	30	3	6	2	0	0	3	2	5	1
Elmer Miller, of	.161	8	31	3	5	1	0	0	2	5	5	0
Roger Peckinpaugh, ss	.179	8	28	2	5	1	0	0	0	4	3	0
Bill Piercy, p	.000	1	0	0	0	0	0	0	0	0	0	0
Wally Pipp, 1b	.154	8	26	1	4	1	0	0	2	2	3	1
Jack Quinn, p	.000	1	2	0	0	0	0	0	0	0	1	0
Tom Rogers, p	.000	1	0	0	0	0	0	0	0	0	0	0
Babe Ruth, of	.313	6	16	3	5	0	0	1	4	5	8	2
Wally Schang, c	.286	8	21	1	6	1	1	0	1	5	4	0
Bob Shawkey, p	.500	2	4	2	2	0	0	0	0	0	1	0
Aaron Ward, 2b	.231	8	26	1	6	0	0	0	4	2	6	0
TOTAL	.207		241	22	50	7	1	2	20	27	44	6

PITCHER	W	L	ERA	G	GS	CG	SV	SHO	IP	H	ER	BB	SO
Rip Collins	0	0	54.00	1	0	0	0	0	0.2	4	4	1	0
Harry Harper	0	0	20.25	1	1	0	0	0	1.1	3	3	2	1
Waite Hoyt	2	1	0.00	3	3	3	0	1	27.0	18	0	11	18
Carl Mays	1	2	1.73	3	3	3	0	1	26.0	20	5	0	9
Bill Piercy	0	0	0.00	1	0	0	0	0	1.0	2	0	0	2
Jack Quinn	0	1	9.82	1	0	0	0	0	3.2	8	4	2	2
Tom Rogers	0	0	6.75	1	0	0	0	0	1.1	3	1	0	1
Bob Shawkey	0	1	7.00	2	1	0	0	0	9.0	13	7	6	5
TOTAL	3	5	3.09	13	8	6	0	2	70.0	71	24	22	38

GAME 1 AT NY -N OCT 5

NY-A	100 011 000	3	7	0
NY-N	000 000 000	0	5	0

Pitchers: MAYS vs DOUGLAS, Barnes (9)
Attendance: 30,202

GAME 2 AT NY -A OCT 6

NY-N	000 000 000	0	2	3
NY-A	000 100 02X	3	3	0

Pitchers: NEHF vs HOYT
Attendance: 34,939

GAME 3 AT NY -N OCT 7

NY-A	004 000 010	5	8	0
NY-N	004 000 81X	13	20	0

Pitchers: Shawkey, QUINN (3), Collins (7), Rogers (8) vs Toney, BARNES (3)
Attendance: 36,509

GAME 4 AT NY -A OCT 9

NY-N	000 000 031	4	9	1
NY-A	000 010 001	2	7	1

Pitchers: DOUGLAS vs MAYS
Home Runs: Ruth-NY(A)
Attendance: 36,372

GAME 5 AT NY -N OCT 10

NY-A	001 200 000	3	6	1
NY-N	100 000 000	1	10	1

Pitchers: HOYT vs NEHF
Attendance: 35,758

GAME 6 AT NY -A OCT 11

NY-N	030 401 000	8	13	0
NY-A	320 000 000	5	7	2

Pitchers: Toney, BARNES (1) vs Harper, SHAWKEY (2), Piercy (9)
Home Runs: E.Meusel-NY(N), Snyder-NY(N), Fewster-NY(A)
Attendance: 34,283

GAME 7 AT NY -N OCT 12

NY-A	010 000 000	1	8	1
NY-N	000 100 10X	2	6	0

Pitchers: MAYS vs DOUGLAS
Attendance: 36,503

GAME 8 AT NY -A OCT 13

NY-N	100 000 000	1	6	0
NY-A	000 000 000	0	4	1

Pitchers: NEHF vs HOYT
Attendance: 25,410

The Giants didn't quite sweep the Series—a tie in Game Two interrupted their string of victories—but they shut down the Yankee offense, holding Yankee scoring to three runs or less per game, and Babe Ruth to two hits and a .118 BA. This Series restored the best-of-seven-games format after three years of best-of-nine.

The Giants had to come from behind to take Game One. Yankee Bullet Joe Bush and Giant Art Nehf hurled shutout ball through five innings before the Yankees scored single runs in the sixth and seventh innings (Ruth driving in the Series' first run for the second year in a row with his single in the sixth). But in the eighth, Bush gave up four straight singles and two runs before Waite Hoyt relieved him with the score tied and men on first and third. Hoyt set down all three men he faced, but the first out—Ross Youngs's fly to center —drove in what proved to be the Giants' winning run.

The Giants led off Game Two with three first-inning runs on Irish Meusel's home run, but scored no more as Bob Shawkey stopped them for nine innings while his Yankees picked up runs in the first, fourth (on Aaron Ward's homer), and eighth to tie it all up. At the end of the tenth, with forty-five minutes left before sundown, the umpires called the game for darkness and provoked a storm of seat cushions and bottles from the stands.

The Giants resumed their winning ways in Game Three behind Jack Scott's shutout. Scott— picked up by the Giants in midseason—gave up only four Yankee hits, walking one, in the Series' top pitching performance. In Game Four the Yankees scored twice in the first inning, but in the fifth the Giants pounced on Carl Mays for four hits and two runs before the first out was recorded. Before the inning ended, a ground out and another hit had brought two more Giants across the plate, enough to survive Aaron Ward's second Series home run for a 4–3 win.

Game Five, the clincher, showed Nehf the winner by two runs at game's end, but the game went back and forth before the outcome was decided. Nehf gave up only five hits—all singles—but all of them contributed toward scoring Yankee runs in the first, fifth, and seventh innings. The Giants took the lead in the second with a pair of runs, but again fell behind until four hits and a walk in the eighth undid Yankee pitcher Joe Bush's fine effort, giving the Giants three additional runs and John McGraw his third world title.

New York Giants (NL), 4;
New York Yankees (AL), 0; tie, 1

NY (N)

PLAYER/POS	AVG	G	AB	R	H	2B	3B	HR	RBI	BB	SO	SB
Dave Bancroft, ss	.211	5	19	4	4	0	0	0	2	2	1	0
Jesse Barnes, p	.000	1	4	0	0	0	0	0	0	0	1	0
Bill Cunningham, of	.200	4	10	0	2	0	0	0	2	2	1	0
Frankie Frisch, 2b	.471	5	17	3	8	1	0	0	2	1	0	1
Heinie Groh, 3b	.474	5	19	4	9	0	1	0	0	2	1	0
George Kelly, 1b	.278	5	18	0	5	0	0	0	2	0	3	0
Lee King, of	1.000	2	1	0	1	0	0	0	1	0	0	0
Hugh McQuillan, p	.250	1	4	1	1	1	0	0	0	0	1	0
Irish Meusel, of	.250	5	20	3	5	0	0	1	7	0	1	0
Art Nehf, p	.000	2	3	0	0	0	0	0	0	2	0	0
Rosy Ryan, p	.000	1	0	0	0	0	0	0	0	0	0	0
Jack Scott, p	.250	1	4	0	1	0	0	0	0	0	1	0
Earl Smith, c-1	.143	4	7	0	1	0	0	0	0	0	2	0
Frank Snyder, c	.333	4	15	1	5	0	0	0	0	0	1	0
Casey Stengel, of	.400	2	5	0	2	0	0	0	0	0	1	0
Ross Youngs, of	.375	5	16	2	6	0	0	0	2	3	1	0
TOTAL	.309		162	18	50	2	1	1	18	12	15	1

PITCHER	W	L	ERA	G	GS	CG	SV	SHO	IP	H	ER	BB	SO
Jesse Barnes	0	0	1.80	1	1	1	0	0	10.0	8	2	2	6
Hugh McQuillan	1	0	3.00	1	1	1	0	0	9.0	8	3	2	4
Art Nehf	1	0	2.25	2	2	1	0	0	16.0	11	4	3	6
Rosy Ryan	1	0	0.00	1	0	0	0	0	2.0	1	0	2	2
Jack Scott	1	0	0.00	1	1	1	0	1	9.0	4	0	1	2
TOTAL	4	0	1.76	6	5	4	0	1	46.0	32	9	8	20

NY (A)

PLAYER/POS	AVG	G	AB	R	H	2B	3B	HR	RBI	BB	SO	SB
Frank Baker, ph	.000	1	1	0	0	0	0	0	0	0	0	0
Joe Bush, p	.167	2	6	0	1	0	0	0	1	0	0	0
Joe Dugan, 3b	.250	5	20	4	5	1	0	0	0	0	1	0
Waite Hoyt, p	.500	2	2	0	1	0	0	0	0	0	0	0
Sam Jones, p	.000	2	0	0	0	0	0	0	0	0	0	0
Carl Mays, p	.000	1	2	0	0	0	0	0	0	0	0	0
Norm McMillan, of	.000	1	2	0	0	0	0	0	0	0	0	0
Mike McNally, 2b	.000	1	0	0	0	0	0	0	0	0	0	0
Bob Meusel, of	.300	5	20	2	6	1	0	0	2	1	3	1
Wally Pipp, 1b	.286	5	21	0	6	1	0	0	3	0	2	1
Babe Ruth, of	.118	5	17	1	2	1	0	0	1	2	3	0
Wally Schang, c	.188	5	16	0	3	1	0	0	0	0	3	0
Everett Scott, ss	.143	5	14	0	2	0	0	0	1	1	0	0
Bob Shawkey, p	.000	1	4	0	0	0	0	0	0	0	1	0
Elmer Smith, ph	.000	2	2	0	0	0	0	0	0	0	2	0
Aaron Ward, 2b	.154	5	13	3	2	0	0	2	3	3	3	0
Whitey Witt, of	.222	5	18	1	4	1	0	0	0	1	2	0
TOTAL	.203		158	11	32	6	1	2	11	8	20	2

PITCHER	W	L	ERA	G	GS	CG	SV	SHO	IP	H	ER	BB	SO
Joe Bush	0	2	4.80	2	2	1	0	0	15.0	21	8	5	6
Waite Hoyt	0	1	1.13	2	1	0	0	0	8.0	11	1	2	4
Sam Jones	0	0	0.00	2	0	0	0	0	2.0	1	0	1	0
Carl Mays	0	1	4.50	1	1	0	0	0	8.0	9	4	2	1
Bob Shawkey	0	0	2.70	1	1	1	0	0	10.0	8	3	2	4
TOTAL	0	4	3.35	8	5	2	0	0	43.0	50	16	12	15

GAME 1 AT NY -N OCT 4

```
NY-A   000 001 100   2 7 0
NY-N   000 000 03X   3 11 3
```
Pitchers: BUSH, Hoyt (8) vs Nehf, RYAN (8)
Attendance: 36,514

GAME 2 AT NY -A OCT 5

```
NY-N   300 000 000 0   3 8 1
NY-A   100 100 010 0   3 8 0
```
Pitchers: Barnes vs Shawkey
Home Runs: E.Meusel-NY(N), Ward-NY(A)
Attendance: 37,020

GAME 3 AT NY -N OCT 6

```
NY-A   000 000 000   0 4 1
NY-N   002 000 10X   3 12 1
```
Pitchers: HOYT, Jones (8) vs J.SCOTT
Attendance: 37,620

GAME 4 AT NY -A OCT 7

```
NY-N   000 040 000   4 9 1
NY-A   200 000 100   3 8 0
```
Pitchers: McQUILLAN vs MAYS, Jones (9)
Home Runs: Ward-NY(A)
Attendance: 36,242

GAME 5 AT NY -N OCT 8

```
NY-A   100 010 100   3 5 0
NY-N   020 000 03X   5 10 0
```
Pitchers: BUSH vs NEHF
Attendance: 38,551

After two Series played entirely in the Polo Grounds, the Giants and Yankees in 1923 had Yankee Stadium across the river to play alternate games in. Celebrating the opener in the new "house that Ruth built," the Yankees took an early three-run lead. In the third inning, though, the Giants drove out starter Waite Hoyt, emerging with four runs. Yankee reliever Joe Bush prevented further Giant scoring for several innings as the Yankees picked up a tying run in the seventh. But with the game still knotted in the top of the ninth, Giant Casey Stengel legged out an inside-the-park homer to win it.

Babe Ruth gave Herb Pennock his first World Series win with a pair of homers in Game Two. The first, a solo blast over the roof in right, broke a 1–1 tie in the fourth, and the second, an inning later, concluded Yankee scoring in their 4–2 win that evened the Series. Stengel sent the Giants ahead in the seventh inning of Game Three, lifting a home run over the fence this time for the game's only score. The run gave Art Nehf the win in his duel with Sad Sam Jones, and again gave the Giants the Series lead.

Giant Ross Youngs's fourth hit of Game Four, an inside-the-park homer into the Polo Grounds' deep outfield, gave the Giants a fourth run to lead off the bottom of the ninth, but as a rally it fell short; the Yankees, who had already scored eight, took the game to even the Series. In Game Five Joe Bush gave up only three Giant hits—a single, double, and triple to Irish Meusel. Irish scored the only Giant run, but his Yankee brother Bob drove in three runs with his three hits—sharing RBI honors with Joe Dugan, whose four hits included the Series' third inside-the-park home run, a three-run shot in the second inning. Final score: 8–1.

In Game Six, Herb Pennock yielded four Giant runs in his seven innings on the mound and seemed on the edge of defeat. But in the top of the eighth, Art Nehf (who had pitched one-hit ball since Ruth homered for a Yankee run in the first) lost his stuff. With one out, two singles followed by two walks (on eight pitches) forced in a run. Rosy Ryan replaced Nehf and walked in another run. Ruth struck out, but Bob Meusel's single and a wild throw from center cleared the bases to put the Yankees ahead 6–4, where they remained to game's end for the first of their twenty-two world championships.

New York Yankees (AL), 4;
New York Giants (NL), 2

NY (A)

PLAYER/POS	AVG	G	AB	R	H	2B	3B	HR	RB	BB	SO	SB
Joe Bush, p-3	.429	4	7	2	3	1	0	0	1	1	1	0
Joe Dugan, 3b	.280	6	25	5	7	2	1	1	5	3	0	0
Hinky Haines, of	.000	2	1	1	0	0	0	0	0	0	0	0
Harvey Hendrick, ph	.000	1	1	0	0	0	0	0	0	0	0	0
Fred Hofmann, ph	.000	2	1	0	0	0	0	0	0	1	0	0
Waite Hoyt, p	.000	1	1	0	0	0	0	0	0	0	1	0
Ernie Johnson, ss-1	.000	2	0	1	0	0	0	0	0	0	0	0
Sam Jones, p	.000	2	2	0	0	0	0	0	0	0	1	0
Bob Meusel, of	.269	6	26	1	7	1	2	0	8	0	3	0
Herb Pennock, p	.000	3	6	0	0	0	0	0	0	0	2	0
Wally Pipp, 1b	.250	6	20	2	5	0	0	0	2	4	1	0
Babe Ruth, of-6,1b-1	.368	6	19	8	7	1	1	3	3	8	6	0
Wally Schang, c	.318	6	22	3	7	1	0	0	1	0	2	0
Everett Scott, ss	.318	6	22	2	7	0	0	0	3	0	1	0
Bob Shawkey, p	.333	1	3	0	1	0	0	0	1	0	0	0
Aaron Ward, 2b	.417	6	24	4	10	0	0	1	2	1	3	1
Whitey Witt, of	.240	6	25	1	6	2	0	0	4	1	1	0
TOTAL	.293		205	30	60	8	4	5	29	20	22	1

PITCHER	W	L	ERA	G	GS	CG	SV	SHO	IP	H	ER	BB	SO
Joe Bush	1	1	1.08	3	1	1	0	0	16.2	7	2	4	5
Waite Hoyt	0	0	15.43	1	1	0	0	0	2.1	4	4	1	0
Sam Jones	0	1	0.90	2	1	0	1	0	10.0	5	1	2	3
Herb Pennock	2	0	3.63	3	2	1	1	0	17.1	19	7	1	8
Bob Shawkey	1	0	3.52	1	1	0	0	0	7.2	12	3	4	2
TOTAL	4	2	2.83	10	6	2	2	0	54.0	47	17	12	18

NY (N)

PLAYER/POS	AVG	G	AB	R	H	2B	3B	HR	RB	BB	SO	SB
Dave Bancroft, ss	.083	6	24	1	2	0	0	0	1	1	2	1
Virgil Barnes, p	.000	2	1	0	0	0	0	0	0	0	1	0
Jack Bentley, p-2	.600	5	5	0	3	1	0	0	3	0	0	0
Bill Cunningham, of-3	.143	4	7	0	1	0	0	0	1	0	1	0
Frankie Frisch, 2b	.400	6	25	2	10	0	1	0	1	0	0	0
Dinty Gearin, pr	.000	1	0	0	0	0	0	0	0	0	0	0
Hank Gowdy, c-2	.000	3	4	0	0	0	0	0	0	1	0	0
Heinie Groh, 3b	.182	6	22	3	4	0	1	0	2	3	1	0
Travis Jackson, ph	.000	1	1	0	0	0	0	0	0	0	0	0
Claude Jonnard, p	.000	2	0	0	0	0	0	0	0	0	0	0
George Kelly, 1b	.182	6	22	1	4	0	0	0	1	1	2	0
Freddie Maguire, pr	.000	2	0	1	0	0	0	0	0	0	0	0
Hugh McQuillan, p	.000	2	3	0	0	0	0	0	0	0	1	0
Irish Meusel, of	.280	6	25	3	7	1	1	1	2	0	2	0
Art Nehf, p	.167	2	6	0	1	0	0	0	0	0	4	0
Jimmy O'Connell, ph	.000	2	1	0	0	0	0	0	0	0	1	0
Rosy Ryan, p	.000	3	2	0	0	0	0	0	0	0	1	0
Jack Scott, p	.000	2	1	0	0	0	0	0	0	0	0	0
Frank Snyder, c	.118	5	17	1	2	0	0	1	2	0	2	0
Casey Stengel, of	.417	6	12	3	5	0	0	2	4	4	0	0
Mule Watson, p	.000	1	0	0	0	0	0	0	0	0	0	0
Ross Youngs, of	.348	6	23	2	8	0	0	1	3	2	0	1
TOTAL	.234		201	17	47	2	3	5	17	12	18	1

PITCHER	W	L	ERA	G	GS	CG	SV	SHO	IP	H	ER	BB	SO
Virgil Barnes	0	0	0.00	2	0	0	0	0	4.2	4	0	0	4
Jack Bentley	0	1	9.45	2	1	0	0	0	6.2	10	7	4	1
Claude Jonnard	0	0	0.00	2	0	0	0	0	2.0	1	0	1	1
Hugh McQuillan	0	1	5.00	2	1	0	0	0	9.0	11	5	4	3
Art Nehf	1	1	2.76	2	2	1	0	1	16.1	10	5	6	7
Rosy Ryan	1	0	0.96	3	0	0	0	0	9.1	11	1	3	3
Jack Scott	0	1	12.00	2	1	0	0	0	3.0	9	4	1	2
Mule Watson	0	0	13.50	1	1	0	0	0	2.0	4	3	1	1
TOTAL	2	4	4.25	16	6	1	0	1	53.0	60	25	20	

GAME 1 AT NY -A OCT 10

NY-N	004	000	001	5	8	0
NY-A	120	000	100	4	12	1

Pitchers: Watson, RYAN (3) vs Hoyt, BUSH (3)
Home Runs: Stengel-NY(N)
Attendance: 55,307

GAME 2 AT NY -N OCT 11

NY-A	010	210	000	4	10	0
NY-N	010	001	000	2	9	2

Pitchers: PENNOCK vs McQUILLAN, Bentley (4)
Home Runs: Ward-NY(A), E.Meusel-NY(N), Ruth-NY(A) (2)
Attendance: 40,402

GAME 3 AT NY -A OCT 12

NY-N	000	000	100	1	4	0
NY-A	000	000	000	0	6	1

Pitchers: NEHF vs JONES, Bush (9)
Home Runs: Stengel-NY(N)
Attendance: 62,430

GAME 4 AT NY -N OCT 13

NY-A	061	100	000	8	13	1
NY-N	000	000	031	4	13	1

Pitchers: SHAWKEY, Pennock (8) vs J.SCOTT, Ryan (2), McQuillan (2), Jonnard (8), Barnes (9)
Home Runs: Youngs-NY(N)
Attendance: 46,302

GAME 5 AT NY -A OCT 14

NY-N	010	000	000	1	3	2
NY-A	340	100	00X	8	14	0

Pitchers: BENTLEY, J.Scott (2), Barnes (4), Jonnard (8) vs BUSH
Home Runs: Dugan-NY(A)
Attendance: 62,817

GAME 6 AT NY -N OCT 15

NY-A	100	000	050	6	5	0
NY-N	100	111	000	4	10	1

Pitchers: PENNOCK, Jones (8) vs NEHF, Ryan (8)
Home Runs: Ruth-NY(A), Snyder-NY(N)
Attendance: 34,172

Four of the seven games in this exciting Series were decided by one run—two of them after twelve innings. Pitcher Walter Johnson, in his first World Series after eighteen big-league seasons and 376 victories, opened for Washington against the Giants' Art Nehf. Although fourteen Giants reached base on hits or walks in the first nine innings, only two scored—George Kelly and Bill Terry, both of whom homered. In the bottom of the ninth, the Senators scored their second run to send the game into extra innings. Johnson shut out the Giants for two more frames, but in the top of the twelfth, two walks and three singles put New York ahead by two. Washington came back with a run and had a man on third. But Kelly at second base stopped Goose Goslin's grounder with his bare hand, and Nehf had the Giants' first win.

Goslin and manager/second baseman Bucky Harris homered in Game Two to give the Senators a 3–0 lead through six innings. The Giants scored once in the seventh and drove out starter Tom Zachary with two more in the ninth to tie the game, but in the last of the ninth Senator Roger Peckinpaugh doubled in the tie breaker to even the Series.

The Giants took an early lead in Game Three and held it to retake the Series lead, but Washington (led by Goslin's three-run homer in the third) unleashed a 13-hit, seven-run attack the next day to even the Series once more. In Game Five, though, New York pulled ahead again, defeating Johnson a second time as winning pitcher Jack Bentley put the Giants into the lead for good with a two-run homer in the fifth. In Game Six, Washington's two runs in the fifth inning overcame a first-inning Giant run and gave Tom Zachary all he needed for the Senators' third win, which set the stage for one of the most memorable games in Series history.

Washington scored first in Game Seven on manager Harris's homer in the fourth inning, but the Giants scored three runs in the sixth (two of them on Senator errors) to go ahead 3–1. In the last of the eighth, though, Harris's grounder to third bounced over the head of rookie Freddie Lindstrom for two more Senator runs and a 3–3 tie. Walter Johnson came in to face the Giants in the ninth, and shut them out through the twelfth, fanning five. Then in the bottom of the twelfth, with one out, Muddy Ruel (given a second chance after Giant catcher Hank Gowdy caught his foot in his mask and missed Ruel's pop foul) doubled to left. Pitcher Johnson then reached first when shortstop Travis Jackson bobbled what ought to have been a third-out grounder.

Washington Senators (AL), 4; New York Giants (NL), 3

WAS (A)

PLAYER/POS	AVG	G	AB	R	H	2B	3B	HR	RB	BB	SO	SB
Ossie Bluege, ss-5,3b-4	.192	7	26	2	5	0	0	0	2	3	4	1
Goose Goslin, of	.344	7	32	4	11	1	0	3	7	0	7	0
Bucky Harris, 2b	.333	7	33	5	11	0	0	2	7	1	4	0
Walter Johnson, p	.111	3	9	0	1	0	0	0	0	0	0	0
Joe Judge, 1b	.385	7	26	4	10	1	0	0	0	5	2	0
Nemo Leibold, of-1	.167	3	6	1	1	1	0	0	0	1	0	0
Firpo Marberry, p	.000	4	2	0	0	0	0	0	0	0	0	0
Joe Martina, p	.000	1	0	0	0	0	0	0	0	0	0	0
Earl McNeely, of	.222	7	27	4	6	3	0	0	1	4	4	1
Ralph Miller, 3b	.182	4	11	0	2	0	0	0	2	1	0	0
George Mogridge, p	.000	2	5	0	0	0	0	0	0	0	5	0
Curly Ogden, p	.000	1	0	0	0	0	0	0	0	0	0	0
Roger Peckinpaugh, ss	.417	4	12	1	5	2	0	0	2	1	0	1
Sam Rice, of	.207	7	29	2	6	0	0	0	1	3	2	2
Muddy Ruel, c	.095	7	21	2	2	1	0	0	0	6	1	0
Allan Russell, p	.000	1	0	0	0	0	0	0	0	0	0	0
Mule Shirley, ph	.500	3	2	1	1	0	0	0	0	0	0	0
By Speece, p	.000	1	0	0	0	0	0	0	0	0	0	0
Bennie Tate, ph	.000	3	0	0	0	0	0	0	1	3	0	0
Tommy Taylor, 3b	.000	3	0	0	0	0	0	0	0	0	2	0
Tom Zachary, p	.000	2	5	0	0	0	0	0	0	1	3	0
TOTAL	.246		248	26	61	9	0	5	24	29	34	5

PITCHER	W	L	ERA	G	GS	CG	SV	SHO	IP	H	ER	BB	SO
Walter Johnson	1	2	2.25	3	2	2	0	0	24.0	30	6	11	20
Firpo Marberry	0	1	1.13	4	1	0	2	0	8.0	9	1	4	10
Joe Martina	0	0	0.00	1	0	0	0	0	1.0	0	0	0	1
George Mogridge	1	0	2.25	2	1	0	0	0	12.0	7	3	6	5
Curly Ogden	0	0	0.00	1	1	0	0	0	0.1	0	0	1	1
Allan Russell	0	0	3.00	1	0	0	0	0	3.0	4	1	0	0
By Speece	0	0	9.00	1	0	0	0	0	1.0	3	1	0	0
Tom Zachary	2	0	2.04	2	2	1	0	0	17.2	13	4	3	3
TOTAL	4	3	2.15	15	7	3	2	0	67.0	66	16	25	40

NY (N)

PLAYER/POS	AVG	G	AB	R	H	2B	3B	HR	RB	BB	SO	SB
Harry Baldwin, p	.000	1	0	0	0	0	0	0	0	0	0	0
Virgil Barnes, p	.000	2	4	0	0	0	0	0	0	1	2	0
Jack Bentley, p-3	.286	5	7	1	2	0	0	1	2	1	1	0
Wayland Dean, p	.000	1	0	0	0	0	0	0	0	0	0	0
Frankie Frisch, 2b-7,3b-1	.333	7	30	1	10	4	1	0	0	4	1	1
Hank Gowdy, c	.259	7	27	4	7	0	0	0	1	2	2	0
Heinie Groh, ph	1.000	1	1	0	1	0	0	0	0	0	0	0
Travis Jackson, ss	.074	7	27	3	2	0	0	0	1	1	4	1
Claude Jonnard, p	.000	1	0	0	0	0	0	0	0	0	0	0
George Kelly, 1b-4,2b-1	.290	7	31	7	9	1	0	1	4	1	8	0
Fred Lindstrom, 3b	.333	7	30	1	10	2	0	0	4	3	6	0
Hugh McQuillan, p	1.000	3	1	0	1	0	0	0	1	1	0	0
Irish Meusel, of	.154	4	13	0	2	0	0	0	1	2	0	0
Art Nehf, p	.429	3	7	1	3	0	0	0	0	0	0	0
Rosy Ryan, p	.500	2	2	1	1	0	0	1	2	0	0	0
Frank Snyder, ph	.000	1	1	0	0	0	0	0	0	0	0	0
Billy Southworth, of-2	.000	5	1	0	0	0	0	0	0	0	0	0
Bill Terry, 1b-4	.429	5	14	3	6	0	1	1	3	1	0	0
Mule Watson, p	.000	1	0	0	0	0	0	0	0	0	0	0
Hack Wilson, of	.233	7	30	1	7	1	0	0	3	1	9	0
Ross Youngs, of	.185	7	27	3	5	1	0	0	2	5	6	1
TOTAL	.261		253	27	66	9	2	4	22	25	40	3

PITCHER	W	L	ERA	G	GS	CG	SV	SHO	IP	H	ER	BB	SO
Harry Baldwin	0	0	0.00	1	0	0	0	0	2.0	1	0	0	1
Virgil Barnes	0	1	5.68	2	2	0	0	0	12.2	15	8	1	9
Jack Bentley	1	2	3.71	3	2	1	0	0	17.0	18	7	8	10
Wayland Dean	0	0	4.50	1	0	0	0	0	2.0	3	1	0	2
Claude Jonnard	0	0	–	1	0	0	0	0	0.0	0	0	0	0
Hugh McQuillan	0	1	2.57	3	1	0	1	0	7.0	2	2	6	2
Art Nehf	1	1	1.83	3	2	1	0	0	19.2	15	4	9	7
Rosy Ryan	0	0	3.18	2	0	0	0	0	5.2	7	2	4	3
Mule Watson	0	0	0.00	1	0	0	1	0	0.2	0	0	1	0
TOTAL	3	4	3.24	17	7	2	2	0	66.2	61	24	29	34

With men on second and first, Earl McNeely bounced to Lindstrom at third. But again the ball bounded over Lindstrom's head, and Ruel raced home with Johnson's first Series win and Washington's only world championship.

GAME 1 AT WAS OCT 4

NY	010 100 000 002	4 14 1
WAS	000 001 001 001	3 10 1

Pitchers: NEHF vs JOHNSON
Home Runs: Kelly-NY, Terry-NY
Attendance: 35,760

GAME 2 AT WAS OCT 5

NY	000 000 102	3 6 0
WAS	200 010 001	4 6 1

Pitchers: BENTLEY vs ZACHARY, Marberry (9)
Home Runs: Goslin-WAS, Harris-WAS
Attendance: 35,922

GAME 3 AT NY OCT 6

WAS	000 200 011	4 9 2
NY	021 101 01X	6 12 0

Pitchers: MARBERRY, Russell (4), Martina (7), Speece (8) vs McQUILLAN, Ryan (4), Jonnard (9), Watson (9)
Home Runs: Ryan-NY
Attendance: 47,608

GAME 4 AT NY OCT 7

WAS	003 020 020	7 13 3
NY	100 001 011	4 6 1

Pitchers: MOGRIDGE, Marberry (8) vs BARNES, Baldwin (6), Dean (8)
Home Runs: Goslin-WAS
Attendance: 49,243

GAME 5 AT NY OCT 8

WAS	000 100 010	2 9 1
NY	001 020 03X	6 13 0

Pitchers: JOHNSON vs BENTLEY, McQuillan (8)
Home Runs: Bentley-NY, Goslin-WAS
Attendance: 49,211

GAME 6 AT WAS OCT 9

NY	100 000 000	1 7 1
WAS	000 020 00X	2 4 0

Pitchers: NEHF, Ryan (8) vs ZACHARY
Attendance: 34,254

GAME 7 AT WAS OCT 10

NY	000 003 000 000	3 8 3
WAS	000 100 020 001	4 10 4

Pitchers: Barnes, McQuillan (8), Nehf (10), BENTLEY (11) vs Ogden, Mogridge (1), Marberry (6), JOHNSON (9)
Home Runs: Harris-WAS
Attendance: 31,667

Repeating as pennant winners, the Senators found themselves again locked in a tight Series, this time with the Pirates, who hadn't won a pennant since 1909. Again Walter Johnson pitched the Series opener, winning this time with a strong five-hit, ten-strikeout performance, giving up only one run on Pie Traynor's homer in the fifth. Home runs by Pirates Kiki Cuyler and Glenn Wright and Senator Joe Judge accounted for four of the five runs scored in Game Two, in which Pirate Vic Aldridge dueled Senator Stan Coveleski to a narrow 3–2 win, evening the Series.

Washington took Games Three and Four, though, for a 3–1 Series advantage, Goose Goslin's solo homer in the sixth inning providing the margin of victory in Game Three, and homers by Goslin (for three runs) and Joe Harris the next day providing all the scoring as Johnson shut the Pirates out.

Harris hit his third Series homer in Game Five, but Pirate bats overwhelmed Coveleski as he lost to Aldridge for a second time. And although Goslin's third homer gave the Senators an early lead in Game Six, Pittsburgh's Ray Kremer shut Washington out from the third inning on as his teammates pulled even with two runs in the bottom of the third, and Eddie Moore's homer in the fifth gave him the run he needed for a win that sent the Series into a seventh game.

Both clubs went with their best in the finale as Johnson, winner of Games One and Four, faced Aldridge, victor in Games Two and Five. But Aldridge was wild, issuing three walks and two wild pitches in addition to two hits before being yanked with only one out in the top of the first. Johnson was hardly more effective: although he lasted the whole game, he gave up 15 hits and five earned runs. But if there was a Series goat, it would have to be Senator shortstop Roger Peckinpaugh, the American League MVP. Though he drove in a run in the first and homered for another in the eighth, his dropped pop fly in the seventh and wild throw in the eighth (his seventh and eighth errors of the Series) opened the way to four unearned runs and Pittsburgh's 9–7 triumph.

Pittsburgh Pirates (NL), 4;
Washington Senators (AL), 3

PIT (N)

PLAYER/POS	AVG	G	AB	R	H	2B	3B	HR	RB	BB	SO	SB
Babe Adams, p	.000	1	0	0	0	0	0	0	0	0	0	0
Vic Aldridge, p	.000	3	7	0	0	0	0	0	0	0	0	0
Clyde Barnhart, of	.250	7	28	1	7	1	0	0	5	3	5	1
Carson Bigbee, of-1	.333	4	3	1	1	1	0	0	1	0	0	1
Max Carey, of	.458	7	24	6	11	4	0	0	2	2	3	3
Kiki Cuyler, of	.269	7	26	3	7	3	0	1	6	1	4	0
Johnny Gooch, c	.000	3	3	0	0	0	0	0	0	0	0	0
George Grantham, 1b-4	.133	5	15	0	2	0	0	0	0	0	3	1
Ray Kremer, p	.143	3	7	0	1	0	0	0	1	0	5	0
Stuffy McInnis, 1b-3	.286	4	14	0	4	0	0	0	1	0	2	0
Lee Meadows, p	.000	1	1	0	0	0	0	0	0	0	1	0
Eddie Moore, 2b	.231	7	26	7	6	1	0	1	2	5	2	0
Johnny Morrison, p	.500	3	2	1	1	0	0	0	0	0	0	0
Red Oldham, p	.000	1	0	0	0	0	0	0	0	0	0	0
Earl Smith, c	.350	6	20	0	7	1	0	0	0	1	2	0
Pie Traynor, 3b	.346	7	26	2	9	0	2	1	4	3	1	1
Glenn Wright, ss	.185	7	27	3	5	1	0	1	3	1	4	0
Emil Yde, p-1	.000	2	1	1	0	0	0	0	0	0	0	0
TOTAL	.265		230	25	61	12	2	4	25	17	32	7

PITCHER	W	L	ERA	G	GS	CG	SV	SHO	IP	H	ER	BB	SO
Babe Adams	0	0	0.00	1	0	0	0	0	1.0	2	0	0	0
Vic Aldridge	2	0	4.42	3	3	2	0	0	18.1	18	9	9	9
Ray Kremer	2	1	3.00	3	2	2	0	0	21.0	17	7	4	9
Lee Meadows	0	1	3.38	1	1	0	0	0	8.0	6	3	0	4
Johnny Morrison	0	0	2.89	3	0	0	0	0	9.1	11	3	1	7
Red Oldham	0	0	0.00	1	0	0	1	0	1.0	0	0	0	2
Emil Yde	0	1	11.57	1	1	0	0	0	2.1	5	3	3	1
TOTAL	4	1	3.69	13	7	4	1	0	61.0	59	25	17	32

WAS (A)

PLAYER/POS	AVG	G	AB	R	H	2B	3B	HR	RB	BB	SO	SB
Spencer Adams, 2b-1	.000	2	1	0	0	0	0	0	0	0	0	0
Win Ballou, p	.000	2	0	0	0	0	0	0	0	0	0	0
Ossie Bluege, 3b	.278	5	18	2	5	1	0	0	2	0	4	0
Stan Coveleski, p	.000	2	3	0	0	0	0	0	0	1	2	0
Alex Ferguson, p	.000	2	4	0	0	0	0	0	0	0	3	0
Goose Goslin, of	.308	7	26	6	8	1	0	3	6	3	3	0
Joe Harris, of	.440	7	25	5	11	2	0	3	6	3	4	0
Bucky Harris, 2b	.087	7	23	2	2	0	0	0	0	1	3	0
Walter Johnson, p	.091	3	11	0	1	0	0	0	0	0	0	0
Joe Judge, 1b	.174	7	23	2	4	1	0	1	3	3	2	0
Nemo Leibold, ph	.500	3	2	1	1	1	0	0	0	1	0	0
Firpo Marberry, p	.000	2	0	0	0	0	0	0	0	0	0	0
Earl McNeely, of-2	.000	2	0	2	0	0	0	0	0	0	0	1
Buddy Myer, 3b	.250	3	8	0	2	0	0	0	0	1	2	0
Roger Peckinpaugh, ss	.250	7	24	1	6	1	0	1	3	1	2	0
Sam Rice, of	.364	7	33	5	12	0	0	0	3	0	1	0
Muddy Ruel, c	.316	7	19	0	6	1	0	0	1	3	2	0
Dutch Ruether, ph	.000	1	1	0	0	0	0	0	0	0	1	0
Hank Severeid, c	.333	1	3	0	1	0	0	0	0	0	0	0
Bobby Veach, ph	.000	2	1	0	0	0	0	0	0	1	0	0
Tom Zachary, p	.000	1	0	0	0	0	0	0	0	0	0	0
TOTAL	.262		225	26	59	8	0	8	25	17	32	2

PITCHER	W	L	ERA	G	GS	CG	SV	SHO	IP	H	ER	BB	SO
Win Ballou	0	0	0.00	2	0	0	0	0	1.2	0	0	1	1
Stan Coveleski	0	2	3.77	2	2	1	0	0	14.1	16	6	5	3
Alex Ferguson	1	1	3.21	2	2	0	0	0	14.0	13	5	6	11
Walter Johnson	2	1	2.08	3	3	3	0	1	26.0	26	6	4	15
Firpo Marberry	0	0	0.00	2	0	0	1	0	2.1	3	0	0	2
Tom Zachary	0	0	10.80	1	0	0	0	0	1.2	3	2	1	0
TOTAL	3	4	2.85	12	7	4	1	1	60.0	61	19	17	32

GAME 1 AT PIT OCT 7

WAS	010	020	001	4	8 1
PIT	000	010	000	1	5 0

Pitchers: JOHNSON vs MEADOWS, Morrison (9)
Home Runs: J.Harris-WAS, Traynor-PIT
Attendance: 41,723

GAME 2 AT PIT OCT 8

WAS	010	000	001	2	8 2
PIT	000	100	02X	3	7 0

Pitchers: COVELESKI vs ALDRIDGE
Home Runs: Judge-WAS, Wright-PIT, Cuyler-PIT
Attendance: 43,364

GAME 3 AT WAS OCT 10

PIT	010	101	000	3	8 3
WAS	001	001	20X	4	10 1

Pitchers: KREMER vs FERGUSON, Marberry (8)
Home Runs: Goslin-WAS
Attendance: 36,495

GAME 4 AT WAS OCT 11

PIT	000	000	000	0	6 1
WAS	004	000	00X	4	12 0

Pitchers: YDE, Morrison (3), Adams (8) vs JOHNSON
Home Runs: Goslin-WAS, J.Harris-WAS
Attendance: 38,701

GAME 5 AT WAS OCT 12

PIT	002	000	211	6	13 0
WAS	100	100	100	3	8 1

Pitchers: ALDRIDGE vs COVELESKI, Ballou (7), Zachary (8), Marberry (9)
Home Runs: J.Harris-WAS
Attendance: 35,899

GAME 6 AT PIT OCT 13

WAS	110	000	000	2	6 2
PIT	002	010	00X	3	7 1

Pitchers: FERGUSON, Ballou (8) vs KREMER
Home Runs: Goslin-WAS, Moore-PIT
Attendance: 43,810

GAME 7 AT PIT OCT 15

WAS	400	200	010	7	7 2
PIT	003	010	23X	9	15 2

Pitchers: JOHNSON vs Aldridge, Morrison (1), KREMER (5), Oldham (9)
Home Runs: Peckinpaugh-WAS
Attendance: 42,856

The Yankees, returning to the World Series after a two-year absence, faced the Cardinals, who had won their first pennant since joining the National League in 1892. Both clubs led their league in slugging and runs scored; this power erupted occasionally in the Series, but over all, pitching dominated as each staff bettered its regular-season earned run average by nearly a run per game.

Herb Pennock of the Yankees pitched a splendid three-hitter in the opener. After yielding two hits and a run in the first inning, he shut out the Cards the rest of the way, holding them hitless until the ninth. Cardinal starter Bill Sherdel also pitched effectively, but three walks in the first and a hit-sacrifice-hit sandwich in the sixth brought in enough runs to beat him.

In Game Two, the veteran Grover Cleveland Alexander evened the Series, striking out ten and holding the Yankees to four singles (three of them in the two-run second) as Billy Southworth and Tommy Thevenow homered for four of St. Louis's six runs. Two days later Jesse Haines put the Cards into the lead, winning the game both ways with a five-hit shutout and a two-run homer.

New York's big bats finally awoke in Game Four. Five Yankees doubled, and Babe Ruth hit three home runs (a World Series record) in a 14-hit, 10-run assault on half the Cardinal pitching staff. Yankee pitcher Waite Hoyt also gave up 14 hits, but 12 were singles and only five runs scored. In contrast, Game Five was a pitchers' duel. Pennock and Sherdel again faced each other and held the opposition to two runs apiece through nine innings. But in the tenth, rookie Tony Lazzeri's sacrifice fly gave New York a 3–2 lead, which Pennock held in the last of the tenth for his second win.

With St. Louis down three games to two, the Series moved to hostile New York for the final games. This didn't seem to trouble the Cardinals, who erupted in Game Six for their own ten-run game, four of them driven in by Les Bell's first-inning single and seventh-inning home run. Alexander pitched a complete game for his second Series win, and came back the next day to relieve Haines in the seventh with a 3–2 lead and the bases full. He struck out Lazzeri to end the inning and kept the Yankees off the bases until he issued Babe Ruth his eleventh Series walk with two away in the ninth. But Ruth, trying to steal second, was caught, and the Cards were world champions.

St. Louis Cardinals (NL), 4;
New York Yankees (AL), 3

STL (N)

PLAYER/POS	AVG	G	AB	R	H	2B	3B	HR	RB	BB	SO	SB
Pete Alexander, p	.000	3	7	1	0	0	0	0	0	0	2	0
Hi Bell, p	.000	1	0	0	0	0	0	0	0	0	0	0
Les Bell, 3b	.259	7	27	4	7	1	0	1	6	2	5	0
Jim Bottomley, 1b	.345	7	29	4	10	3	0	0	5	1	2	0
Taylor Douthit, of	.267	4	15	3	4	2	0	0	1	3	2	0
Jake Flowers, ph	.000	3	3	0	0	0	0	0	0	0	1	0
Chick Hafey, of	.185	7	27	2	5	2	0	0	0	0	7	0
Jesse Haines, p	.600	3	5	1	3	0	0	1	2	0	1	0
Bill Hallahan, p	.000	1	0	0	0	0	0	0	0	0	0	0
Wattie Holm, of-4	.125	5	16	1	2	0	0	0	1	1	2	0
Rogers Hornsby, 2b	.250	7	28	2	7	1	0	0	4	2	2	1
Vic Keen, p	.000	1	0	0	0	0	0	0	0	0	0	0
Bob O'Farrell, c	.304	7	23	2	7	1	0	0	2	2	2	0
Art Reinhart, p	.000	1	0	0	0	0	0	0	0	0	0	0
Flint Rhem, p	.000	1	1	0	0	0	0	0	0	0	1	0
Bill Sherdel, p	.000	2	5	0	0	0	0	0	0	0	2	0
Billy Southworth, of	.345	7	29	6	10	1	1	1	4	0	0	1
Tommy Thevenow, ss	.417	7	24	5	10	1	0	1	4	0	1	0
Specs Toporcer, ph	.000	1	0	0	0	0	0	0	0	1	0	0
TOTAL	.272		239	31	65	12	1	4	30	11	30	2

PITCHER	W	L	ERA	G	GS	CG	SV	SHO	IP	H	ER	BB	SO
Pete Alexander	2	0	1.33	3	2	2	1	0	20.1	12	3	4	17
Hi Bell	0	0	9.00	1	0	0	0	0	2.0	4	2	1	1
Jesse Haines	2	0	1.08	3	2	1	0	1	16.2	13	2	9	5
Bill Hallahan	0	0	4.50	1	0	0	0	0	2.0	2	1	3	1
Vic Keen	0	0	0.00	1	0	0	0	0	1.0	0	0	4	0
Art Reinhart	0	1	∞	1	0	0	0	0	0.0	1	4	4	0
Flint Rhem	0	0	6.75	1	1	0	0	0	4.0	7	3	2	4
Bill Sherdel	0	2	2.12	2	2	1	0	0	17.0	15	4	8	3
TOTAL	4	3	2.71	13	7	4	1	1	63.0	54	19	31	31

NY (A)

PLAYER/POS	AVG	G	AB	R	H	2B	3B	HR	RB	BB	SO	SB
Spencer Adams, ph	.000	2	0	0	0	0	0	0	0	0	0	0
Pat Collins, c	.000	3	2	0	0	0	0	0	0	0	1	0
Earle Combs, of	.357	7	28	3	10	2	0	0	2	5	2	0
Joe Dugan, 3b	.333	7	24	2	8	1	0	0	2	1	1	0
Mike Gazella, 3b	.000	1	0	0	0	0	0	0	0	0	0	0
Lou Gehrig, 1b	.348	7	23	1	8	2	0	0	4	5	4	0
Waite Hoyt, p	.000	2	6	0	0	0	0	0	0	0	1	0
Sam Jones, p	.000	1	0	0	0	0	0	0	0	0	0	0
Mark Koenig, ss	.125	7	32	2	4	1	0	0	2	0	6	0
Tony Lazzeri, 2b	.192	7	26	2	5	1	0	0	3	1	6	0
Bob Meusel, of	.238	7	21	3	5	1	1	0	0	6	1	0
Ben Paschal, ph	.250	5	4	0	1	0	0	0	1	1	2	0
Herb Pennock, p	.143	3	7	1	1	1	0	0	0	0	0	0
Dutch Ruether, p-1	.000	3	4	0	0	0	0	0	0	0	0	0
Babe Ruth, of	.300	7	20	6	6	0	0	4	5	11	2	1
Hank Severeid, c	.273	7	22	1	6	1	0	0	1	1	2	0
Bob Shawkey, p	.000	3	2	0	0	0	0	0	0	0	1	0
Urban Shocker, p	.000	2	2	0	0	0	0	0	0	0	0	0
Myles Thomas, p	.000	2	0	0	0	0	0	0	0	0	0	0
TOTAL	.242		223	21	54	10	1	4	20	31	31	1

PITCHER	W	L	ERA	G	GS	CG	SV	SHO	IP	H	ER	BB	SO
Waite Hoyt	1	1	1.20	2	2	1	0	0	15.0	19	2	1	10
Sam Jones	0	0	9.00	1	0	0	0	0	1.0	2	1	2	1
Herb Pennock	2	0	1.23	3	2	2	0	0	22.0	13	3	4	8
Dutch Ruether	0	1	4.15	1	1	0	0	0	4.1	7	2	2	1
Bob Shawkey	0	1	5.40	3	1	0	0	0	10.0	8	6	2	7
Urban Shocker	0	1	5.87	2	1	0	0	0	7.2	13	5	0	3
Myles Thomas	0	0	3.00	2	0	0	0	0	3.0	3	1	0	0
TOTAL	3	4	2.86	14	7	3	0	0	63.0	65	20	11	30

GAME 1 AT NY OCT 2

STL	100 000 000	1	3	1
NY	100 001 00X	2	6	0

Pitchers: SHERDEL, Haines (8) vs PENNOCK
Attendance: 61,658

GAME 2 AT NY OCT 3

STL	002 000 301	6	12	1
NY	020 000 000	2	4	0

Pitchers: ALEXANDER vs SHOCKER, Shawkey (8), Jones (9)
Home Runs: Southworth-STL, Thevenow-STL
Attendance: 63,600

GAME 3 AT STL OCT 5

NY	000 000 000	0	5	1
STL	000 310 00X	4	8	0

Pitchers: RUETHER, Shawkey (5), Thomas (8) vs HAINES
Home Runs: Haines-STL
Attendance: 37,708

GAME 4 AT STL OCT 6

NY	101 142 100	10	14	1
STL	100 300 001	5	14	0

Pitchers: HOYT vs Rhem, REINHART (5), H.Bell (5), Hallahan (7), Keen (9)
Home Runs: Ruth-NY (3)
Attendance: 38,825

GAME 5 AT STL OCT 7

NY	000 001 001 1	3	9	1
STL	000 100 100 0	2	7	1

Pitchers: PENNOCK vs SHERDEL
Attendance: 39,552

GAME 6 AT NY OCT 9

STL	300 010 501	10	13	2
NY	000 100 100	2	8	1

Pitchers: ALEXANDER vs SHAWKEY, Shocker (7), Thomas (8)
Home Runs: L.Bell-STL
Attendance: 48,615

GAME 7 AT NY OCT 10

STL	000 300 000	3	8	0
NY	001 001 000	2	8	3

Pitchers: HAINES, Alexander (7) vs HOYT, Pennock (7)
Home Runs: Ruth-NY
Attendance: 38,093

The Pirates, who struggled to a narrow pennant win in a four-team race, were no slouches at the bat. Their team BA of .305 led the National League, and in the Waner brothers—Paul and Lloyd—and Pie Traynor they had three of the league's five top hitters. But in the World Series they came up against a Yankee team that is still widely regarded as the game's greatest ever. With 110 season victories and a 19-game margin over second-place Philadelphia, the Yankees led the American League in nearly every offensive category. Three Yankees—Earle Combs, Lou Gehrig, and Babe Ruth—hit over .350, and divided among them league crowns in runs, hits, doubles, triples, home runs (Ruth's 60), RBIs, and slugging average. The Yankees not only hit: their pitching staff boasted the league's lowest earned run average.

In the Series, though, it was Pittsburgh's erratic play that brought about the first American League sweep. The Pirates scored four times off Yankee starter Waite Hoyt in Game One, and might have won the game. But Paul Waner misplayed a Gehrig fly for a run-scoring triple in the first, and in the third, two Pirate errors led to three more Yankee runs. A final run in the fifth was all New York needed to win, 5–4.

The Yankees won the next two games more convincingly, with strong pitching and timely hitting. George Pipgras held Pittsburgh to two runs in Game Two as his Yankees bunched seven of their 11 hits into the third and eighth innings (also taking advantage of two walks and a hit batsman in the eighth) for their six runs. And in Game Three—as Herb Pennock pitched perfectly into the eighth inning before yielding two hits and a run—Yankee batters again bunched most of their hits into two innings, scoring two runs on Gehrig's first-inning triple and six more in the seventh, climaxed by Ruth's three-run homer.

Pittsburgh took advantage of two Yankee errors in the seventh inning of Game Four to score two runs and tie the game at three-all. But in the last of the ninth, after the Pirates' Johnny Miljus had struck out Gehrig and Bob Meusel with the bases loaded, his second wild pitch of the inning undid him— Combs scored from third with the Series' winning run.

New York Yankees (AL), 4;
Pittsburgh Pirates (NL), 0

NY (A)

PLAYER/POS	AVG	G	AB	R	H	2B	3B	HR	RB	BB	SO	SB
Benny Bengough, c	.000	2	4	1	0	0	0	0	0	1	0	0
Pat Collins, c	.600	2	5	0	3	1	0	0	0	3	0	0
Earle Combs, of	.313	4	16	6	5	0	0	0	2	1	2	0
Joe Dugan, 3b	.200	4	15	2	3	0	0	0	0	0	0	0
Cedric Durst, ph	.000	1	1	0	0	0	0	0	0	0	0	0
Lou Gehrig, 1b	.308	4	13	2	4	2	2	0	4	3	3	0
Johnny Grabowski, c	.000	1	2	0	0	0	0	0	0	0	0	0
Waite Hoyt, p	.000	1	3	0	0	0	0	0	0	0	0	0
Mark Koenig, ss	.500	4	18	5	9	2	0	0	2	0	2	0
Tony Lazzeri, 2b	.267	4	15	1	4	1	0	0	2	1	4	0
Bob Meusel, of	.118	4	17	1	2	0	0	0	1	1	7	1
Wilcy Moore, p	.200	2	5	0	1	0	0	0	0	0	3	0
Herb Pennock, p	.000	1	4	1	0	0	0	0	0	1	0	0
George Pipgras, p	.333	1	3	0	1	0	0	0	0	0	1	0
Babe Ruth, of	.400	4	15	4	6	0	0	2	7	2	2	1
TOTAL	.279		136	23	38	6	2	2	19	13	25	2

PITCHER	W	L	ERA	G	GS	CG	SV	SHO	IP	H	ER	BB	SO
Waite Hoyt	1	0	4.91	1	1	0	0	0	7.1	8	4	1	2
Wilcy Moore	1	0	0.84	2	1	1	1	0	10.2	11	1	2	2
Herb Pennock	1	0	1.00	1	1	1	0	0	9.0	3	1	0	1
George Pipgras	1	0	2.00	1	1	1	0	0	9.0	7	2	1	2
TOTAL	4	0	2.00	5	4	3	1	0	36.0	29	8	4	7

PIT (N)

PLAYER/POS	AVG	G	AB	R	H	2B	3B	HR	RB	BB	SO	SB
Vic Aldridge, p	.000	1	2	0	0	0	0	0	0	0	0	0
Clyde Barnhart, of	.313	4	16	0	5	1	0	0	4	0	0	0
Fred Brickell, ph	.000	2	2	1	0	0	0	0	0	0	0	0
Mike Cvengros, p	.000	2	0	0	0	0	0	0	0	0	0	0
Joe Dawson, p	.000	1	0	0	0	0	0	0	0	0	0	0
Johnny Gooch, c	.000	3	5	0	0	0	0	0	0	1	1	0
George Grantham, 2b	.364	3	11	0	4	1	0	0	0	1	1	0
Heinie Groh, ph	.000	1	1	0	0	0	0	0	0	0	0	0
Joe Harris, 1b	.200	4	15	0	3	0	0	0	1	0	0	0
Carmen Hill, p	.000	1	1	0	0	0	0	0	0	1	0	0
Ray Kremer, p	.500	1	2	1	1	1	0	0	0	0	1	0
Lee Meadows, p	.000	1	2	0	0	0	0	0	0	0	0	0
Johnny Miljus, p	.000	2	2	0	0	0	0	0	0	0	2	0
Hal Rhyne, 2b	.000	1	4	0	0	0	0	0	0	0	0	0
Earl Smith, c-2	.000	3	8	0	0	0	0	0	0	0	0	0
Roy Spencer, c	.000	1	1	0	0	0	0	0	0	0	0	0
Pie Traynor, 3b	.200	4	15	1	3	1	0	0	0	0	1	0
Lloyd Waner, of	.400	4	15	5	6	1	1	0	0	1	0	0
Paul Waner, of	.333	4	15	0	5	0	0	0	3	0	1	0
Glenn Wright, ss	.154	4	13	1	2	0	0	0	2	0	0	0
Emil Yde, pr	.000	1	0	0	0	0	0	0	0	0	0	0
TOTAL	.223		130	10	29	6	1	0	10	4	7	0

PITCHER	W	L	ERA	G	GS	CG	SV	SHO	IP	H	ER	BB	SO
Vic Aldridge	0	1	7.36	1	1	0	0	0	7.1	10	6	4	4
Mike Cvengros	0	0	3.86	2	0	0	0	0	2.1	3	1	0	2
Joe Dawson	0	0	0.00	1	0	0	0	0	1.0	0	0	0	0
Carmen Hill	0	0	4.50	1	1	0	0	0	6.0	9	3	1	6
Ray Kremer	0	1	3.60	1	1	0	0	0	5.0	5	2	3	1
Lee Meadows	0	1	9.95	1	1	0	0	0	6.1	7	7	1	6
Johnny Miljus	0	1	1.35	2	0	0	0	0	6.2	4	1	4	6
TOTAL	0	4	5.19	9	4	0	0	0	34.2	38	20	13	25

GAME 1 AT PIT OCT 5

NY	103	010	000	5	6	1
PIT	101	010	010	4	9	2

Pitchers: HOYT, Moore (8) vs KREMER, Miljus (6)
Attendance: 41,467

GAME 2 AT PIT OCT 6

NY	003	000	030	6	11	0
PIT	100	000	010	2	7	2

Pitchers: PIPGRAS vs ALDRIDGE, Cvengros (8), Dawson (9)
Attendance: 41,634

GAME 3 AT NY OCT 7

PIT	000	000	010	1	3	1
NY	200	000	60X	8	9	0

Pitchers: MEADOWS, Cvengros (7) vs PENNOCK
Home Runs: Ruth-NY
Attendance: 60,695

GAME 4 AT NY OCT 8

PIT	100	000	200	3	10	1
NY	100	020	001	4	12	2

Pitchers: Hill, MILJUS (7) vs MOORE
Home Runs: Ruth-NY
Attendance: 57,909

After squandering a 13½-game lead and falling briefly behind the Athletics in early September, the Yankees recovered to meet the Cardinals—winners of another tight National League race—in the Series. With Herb Pennock lost to arm trouble, the Yankees made do with just three pitchers in extending their Series win streak to eight games.

The four games offered little suspense, but for Yankee fans there were thrills aplenty. The Bronx Bombers' nine home runs (including four by Lou Gehrig and three by Babe Ruth) nearly equalled St. Louis's total scoring (ten runs), and Gehrig himself drove in as many runs (nine) as the entire Cardinal offense. Ruth and Gehrig started things off with successive doubles and a run in the first inning of the opener, and when Bob Meusel followed Ruth's second double with a home run in the fourth, the Yanks had more than they would need to support Waite Hoyt's three-hitter. The Cardinals' Jim Bottomley homered off Hoyt in the seventh, but successive singles by Mark Koenig, Ruth, and Gehrig produced a fourth Yankee run and concluded the scoring.

Gehrig homered in the first inning of Game Two to get New York off to a 3–0 lead against forty-one-year-old Grover Cleveland Alexander. The Cards snapped back to tie the game, but the Yankees retook the lead with a run in the last of the second and put together four hits, two walks, and a hit batsman for four more in the third. A final Yankee run in the seventh capped a 9–3 four-hit win for pitcher George Pipgras.

Jim Bottomley gave St. Louis its first lead of the Series with a two-run triple in the first inning of Game Three. But Yankee Tom Zachary gave up only one more run, taking the third Yankee win as Gehrig drove in three runs with homers in the second and fourth, and his teammates scored three more in the sixth (thanks in large part to two Cardinal errors and Meusel's steal of home) and a final (unearned) run an inning later.

New York completed its second straight Series sweep with another 7–3 win two days later. Waite Hoyt gained his second victory, mostly on the strength of five solo Yankee homers, including three by Babe Ruth.

New York Yankees (AL), 4;
St. Louis Cardinals (NL), 0

NY (A)

PLAYER/POS	AVG	G	AB	R	H	2B	3B	HR	RBI	BB	SO	SB
Benny Bengough, c	.231	4	13	1	3	0	0	0	0	1	1	1
Pat Collins, c	1.000	1	1	0	1	1	0	0	0	0	0	0
Earle Combs, ph	.000	1	0	0	0	0	0	0	0	1	0	0
Joe Dugan, 3b	.167	3	6	0	1	0	0	0	1	0	0	0
Leo Durocher, 2b	.000	4	2	0	0	0	0	0	0	0	1	0
Cedric Durst, of	.375	4	8	3	3	0	0	1	2	0	1	0
Lou Gehrig, 1b	.545	4	11	5	6	1	0	4	9	6	0	0
Waite Hoyt, p	.143	2	7	0	1	0	0	0	0	0	0	0
Mark Koenig, ss	.158	4	19	1	3	0	0	0	0	0	1	0
Tony Lazzeri, 2b	.250	4	12	2	3	1	0	0	0	1	0	2
Bob Meusel, of	.200	4	15	5	3	1	0	1	3	2	5	2
Ben Paschal, ph	.200	3	10	0	2	0	0	0	1	1	0	0
George Pipgras, p	.000	1	2	0	0	0	0	0	0	1	0	0
Gene Robertson, 3b	.125	3	8	1	1	0	0	0	2	1	0	0
Babe Ruth, of	.625	4	16	9	10	3	0	3	4	1	2	0
Tom Zachary, p	.000	1	4	0	0	0	0	0	0	0	1	0
TOTAL	.276		134	27	37	7	0	9	25	13	12	4

PITCHER	W	L	ERA	G	GS	CG	SV	SHO	IP	H	ER	BB	SO
Waite Hoyt	2	0	1.50	2	2	2	0	0	18.0	14	3	6	14
George Pipgras	1	0	2.00	1	1	1	0	0	9.0	4	2	4	8
Tom Zachary	1	0	3.00	1	1	1	0	0	9.0	9	3	1	7
TOTAL	4	0	2.00	4	4	4	0	0	36.0	27	8	11	29

STL (N)

PLAYER/POS	AVG	G	AB	R	H	2B	3B	HR	RBI	BB	SO	SB
Pete Alexander, p	.000	2	1	0	0	0	0	0	0	1	0	0
Ray Blades, ph	.000	1	1	0	0	0	0	0	0	0	1	0
Jim Bottomley, 1b	.214	4	14	1	3	0	1	1	3	2	6	0
Taylor Douthit, of	.091	3	11	1	1	0	0	0	1	1	1	0
Frankie Frisch, 2b	.231	4	13	1	3	0	0	0	1	2	2	0
Chick Hafey, of	.200	4	15	0	3	0	0	0	0	1	4	0
Jesse Haines, p	.000	1	2	0	0	0	0	0	0	0	0	0
George Harper, of	.111	3	9	1	1	0	0	0	0	2	2	0
Andy High, 3b	.294	4	17	1	5	2	0	0	1	1	3	0
Wattie Holm, of-1	.167	3	6	0	1	0	0	0	1	0	1	0
Syl Johnson, p	.000	2	0	0	0	0	0	0	0	0	0	0
Rabbit Maranville, ss	.308	4	13	2	4	1	0	0	0	1	1	1
Pepper Martin, pr	.000	1	0	1	0	0	0	0	0	0	0	0
Clarence Mitchell, p	.000	1	2	0	0	0	0	0	0	0	2	0
Ernie Orsatti, of-1	.286	4	7	1	2	1	0	0	0	1	3	0
Flint Rhem, p	.000	1	0	0	0	0	0	0	0	0	0	0
Bill Sherdel, p	.000	2	5	0	0	0	0	0	0	0	2	0
Earl Smith, c	.750	4	4	0	3	0	0	0	0	0	0	0
Tommy Thevenow, ss	.000	1	0	0	0	0	0	0	0	0	0	0
Jimmie Wilson, c	.091	3	11	1	1	1	0	0	1	0	3	0
TOTAL	.206		131	10	27	5	1	1	9	11	29	3

PITCHER	W	L	ERA	G	GS	CG	SV	SHO	IP	H	ER	BB	SO
Pete Alexander	0	1	19.80	2	1	0	0	0	5.0	10	11	4	2
Jesse Haines	0	1	4.50	1	1	0	0	0	6.0	6	3	3	3
Syl Johnson	0	0	4.50	2	0	0	0	0	2.0	4	1	1	1
Clarence Mitchell	0	0	1.59	1	0	0	0	0	5.2	2	1	2	2
Flint Rhem	0	0	0.00	1	0	0	0	0	2.0	0	0	0	1
Bill Sherdel	0	2	4.72	2	2	0	0	0	13.1	15	7	3	3
TOTAL	0	4	6.09	9	4	0	0	0	34.0	37	23	13	12

GAME 1 AT NY OCT 4

STL	000 000 100	1 3 1
NY	100 200 01X	4 7 0

Pitchers: SHERDEL, Johnson (8) vs HOYT
Home Runs: Meusel-NY, Bottomley-STL
Attendance: 61,425

GAME 2 AT NY OCT 5

STL	030 000 000	3 4 1
NY	314 000 10X	9 8 2

Pitchers: ALEXANDER, Mitchell (3) vs PIPGRAS
Home Runs: Gehrig-NY
Attendance: 60,714

GAME 3 AT STL OCT 7

NY	010 203 100	7 7 2
STL	200 010 000	3 9 3

Pitchers: ZACHARY vs HAINES, Johnson (7), Rhem (8)
Home Runs: Gehrig-NY (2)
Attendance: 39,602

GAME 4 AT STL OCT 9

NY	000 100 420	7 15 2
STL	001 100 001	3 11 0

Pitchers: HOYT vs SHERDEL, Alexander (7)
Home Runs: Ruth-NY (3), Durst-NY, Gehrig-NY
Attendance: 37,331

The surprising success of a surprise starter and the ultimate in big innings highlighted the return of the Athletics to World Series play after a gap of fifteen years. In the opener, A's manager Connie Mack passed over the aces of his pitching staff in favor of Howard Ehmke, an aging journeyman who that season had started only eight times and pitched under 55 innings. But Ehmke, who (per Mack's instructions) had studied the Cubs' hitters in a series of late-season games, held the Cubs scoreless through the first eight innings of Game One (yielding an unearned run in the last of the ninth) while fanning 13 batters for a new Series record. Chicago's Charlie Root also pitched effectively until Jimmie Foxx's solo homer in the seventh gave the A's the game's first score. A pair of errors by Cub shortstop Woody English in the ninth set up two unearned runs against reliever Guy Bush and gave Ehmke and the A's all the lead they needed.

Home runs by Foxx and Al Simmons drove in five of the A's nine runs in Game Two as Philadelphia took a 2–0 Series lead. But Guy Bush held Mack's sluggers to nine singles and one run in Game Three as his Cubs scored three runs in the sixth to take their first win.

The Cubs seemed well on their way to tying the Series in Game Four as they entered the last of the seventh with an 8–0 lead. But Simmons led off with a homer to erase Charlie Root's shutout, and five of the next six batters singled. Art Nehf relieved Root, but the first batter to face him—Mule Haas—lofted a fly to center which Hack Wilson lost in the sun for a three-run inside-the-park homer, and the score was 8–7. After walking Mickey Cochrane, Nehf was replaced by Sheriff Blake, who gave up two singles and saw the tying run come home before Pat Malone took the mound with two men still on base and only one away. Malone struck out two in a row to end the inning—but not until he first hit a batter and gave up a double by Jimmy Dykes for the two runs that gave the A's a 10–8 win and a 3–1 Series advantage.

Game Five, although inevitably anticlimactic, was not decided until the final at-bat. Chicago scored twice off Ehmke in the fourth as Malone shut out the A's with only two hits through eight. But in the last of the ninth a single and Haas's home run tied the score, and—with two men out—Simmons doubled, Foxx was walked intentionally, Bing Miller doubled, and the Series was history.

Philadelphia Athletics (AL), 4; Chicago Cubs (NL), 1

PHI (A)

PLAYER/POS	AVG	G	AB	R	H	2B	3B	HR	RB	BB	SO	SB
Max Bishop, 2b	.190	5	21	2	4	0	0	0	1	2	3	0
Joe Boley, ss	.235	5	17	1	4	0	0	0	1	0	3	0
George Burns, ph	.000	1	2	0	0	0	0	0	0	0	1	0
Mickey Cochrane, c	.400	5	15	5	6	1	0	0	0	7	0	0
Jimmy Dykes, 3b	.421	5	19	2	8	1	0	0	4	1	1	0
George Earnshaw, p	.000	2	5	1	0	0	0	0	0	0	4	0
Howard Ehmke, p	.200	2	5	0	1	0	0	0	0	0	0	0
Jimmie Foxx, 1b	.350	5	20	5	7	1	0	2	5	1	1	0
Walter French, ph	.000	1	1	0	0	0	0	0	0	0	1	0
Lefty Grove, p	.000	2	2	0	0	0	0	0	0	0	1	0
Mule Haas, of	.238	5	21	3	5	0	0	2	6	1	3	0
Bing Miller, of	.368	5	19	1	7	1	0	0	4	0	2	0
Jack Quinn, p	.000	1	2	0	0	0	0	0	0	0	2	0
Eddie Rommel, p	.000	1	0	0	0	0	0	0	0	0	0	0
Al Simmons, of	.300	5	20	6	6	1	0	2	5	1	4	0
Homer Summa, ph	.000	1	1	0	0	0	0	0	0	0	1	0
Rube Walberg, p	.000	2	1	0	0	0	0	0	0	0	0	0
TOTAL	.281		171	26	48	5	0	6	26	13	27	0

PITCHER	W	L	ERA	G	GS	CG	SV	SHO	IP	H	ER	BB	SO
George Earnshaw	1	1	2.63	2	2	1	0	0	13.2	14	4	6	17
Howard Ehmke	1	0	1.42	2	2	1	0	0	12.2	14	2	3	13
Lefty Grove	0	0	0.00	2	0	0	2	0	6.1	3	0	1	10
Jack Quinn	0	0	9.00	1	1	0	0	0	5.0	7	5	2	2
Eddie Rommel	1	0	9.00	1	0	0	0	0	1.0	2	1	1	0
Rube Walberg	1	0	0.00	2	0	0	0	0	6.1	3	0	0	8
TOTAL	4	1	2.40	10	5	2	2		45.0	43	12	13	50

CHI (N)

PLAYER/POS	AVG	G	AB	R	H	2B	3B	HR	RB	BB	SO	SB
Footsie Blair, ph	.000	1	1	0	0	0	0	0	0	0	0	0
Sheriff Blake, p	1.000	2	1	0	1	0	0	0	0	0	0	0
Guy Bush, p	.000	2	3	1	0	0	0	0	0	1	3	0
Hal Carlson, p	.000	2	0	0	0	0	0	0	0	0	0	0
Kiki Cuyler, of	.300	5	20	4	6	1	0	0	4	1	7	0
Woody English, ss	.190	5	21	1	4	2	0	0	0	1	6	0
Mike Gonzalez, c-1	.000	2	1	0	0	0	0	0	0	0	1	0
Charlie Grimm, 1b	.389	5	18	2	7	0	0	1	4	1	2	0
Gabby Hartnett, ph	.000	3	3	0	0	0	0	0	0	0	3	0
Cliff Heathcote, ph	.000	2	1	0	0	0	0	0	0	0	0	0
Rogers Hornsby, 2b	.238	5	21	4	5	1	1	0	1	1	8	0
Pat Malone, p	.250	3	4	0	1	1	0	0	0	0	2	0
Norm McMillan, 3b	.100	5	20	0	2	0	0	0	0	2	6	1
Art Nehf, p	.000	2	0	0	0	0	0	0	0	0	0	0
Charlie Root, p	.000	2	5	0	0	0	0	0	0	0	3	0
Riggs Stephenson, of	.316	5	19	3	6	1	0	0	3	2	2	0
Zack Taylor, c	.176	5	17	0	3	0	0	0	0	3	0	0
Chick Tolson, ph	.000	1	1	0	0	0	0	0	0	0	0	0
Hack Wilson, of	.471	5	17	2	8	0	1	0	4	3	0	0
TOTAL	.249		173	17	43	6	2	1	15	13	50	1

PITCHER	W	L	ERA	G	GS	CG	SV	SHO	IP	H	ER	BB	SO
Sheriff Blake	0	1	13.50	2	0	0	0	0	1.1	4	2	0	1
Guy Bush	1	0	0.82	2	1	1	0	0	11.0	12	1	2	4
Hal Carlson	0	0	6.75	2	0	0	0	0	4.0	7	3	1	3
Pat Malone	0	2	4.15	3	2	1	0	0	13.0	12	6	7	11
Art Nehf	0	0	18.00	2	0	0	0	0	1.0	1	2	1	0
Charlie Root	0	1	4.72	2	2	0	0	0	13.1	12	7	2	8
TOTAL	1	4	4.33	13	5	2	0	0	43.2	48	21	13	27

GAME 1 AT CHI OCT 8

PHI	000 000 102	3	6	1
CHI	000 000 001	1	8	2

Pitchers: EHMKE vs ROOT, Bush (8)
Home Runs: Foxx-PHI
Attendance: 50,740

GAME 2 AT CHI OCT 9

PHI	003 300 120	9	12	0
CHI	000 030 000	3	11	1

Pitchers: EARNSHAW, Grove (5) vs MALONE, Blake (4), Carlson (6), Nehf (9)
Home Runs: Simmons-PHI, Foxx-PHI
Attendance: 49,987

GAME 3 AT PHI OCT 11

CHI	000 003 000	3	6	1
PHI	000 010 000	1	9	1

Pitchers: BUSH vs EARNSHAW
Attendance: 29,921

GAME 4 AT PHI OCT 12

CHI	000 205 100	8	10	2
PHI	000 000 10X	10	15	2

Pitchers: Root, Nehf (7), BLAKE (7), Malone (7), Carlson (8) vs Quinn, Walberg (6), ROMMEL (7), Grove (8)
Home Runs: Grimm-CHI, Haas-PHI, Simmons-PHI
Attendance: 29,921

GAME 5 AT PHI OCT 14

CHI	002 000 000	2	8	1
PHI	000 000 003	3	6	0

Pitchers: MALONE vs Ehmke, WALBERG (4)
Home Runs: Haas-PHI
Attendance: 29,921

Pitching 85 percent of the Series with a combined ERA of 1.02, Philadelphia aces George Earnshaw and Lefty Grove chilled the hot Cardinals, who had hit .314 and averaged 6½ runs per game during the season. The A's hit only .197 themselves in the Series, but more than half their hits went for extra bases as they outscored St. Louis 21–12 and took their second consecutive world championship in six games.

Grove faced Cardinal spitballer Burleigh Grimes in the opener, giving up nine hits, including four singles in the Cards' two-run third. The Athletics, for their part, touched Grimes for only five hits, all in separate innings. But every hit—a double, two triples, and home runs by Al Simmons and Mike Cochrane—resulted in a run, and Grove and the A's emerged 5–2 victors. In the first inning of Game Two, Cochrane again homered, sending Earnshaw on his way to Philadelphia's second win, 6–1.

When the Series moved to St. Louis, though, the Cards came alive. Wild Bill Hallahan (their leading winner during the season, with 15) spaced seven hits for a shutout. Taylor Douthit's fourth-inning home run off Rube Walberg was the first Cardinal hit, but the Cards knocked out nine more for four more runs before they were finished. A pair of unearned runs evened the Series the next day when A's third baseman Jimmy Dykes's wild throw to first in the fourth inning let in a tie-breaking second Cardinal run and led to a third against the ultimate loser Lefty Grove. Meanwhile, Cardinal veteran Jesse Haines, after yielding three Philadelphia hits and a run in the first inning, shut out the A's on one hit the rest of the way.

Earnshaw and Grove combined to restore the Series lead to the Athletics in Game Five with a three-hit shutout. Grove, who took over when Earnshaw left for a pinch hitter in the eighth, garnered his second Series win as Jimmie Foxx homered off Grimes in the top of the ninth for the game's only runs. After a travel day to Philadelphia, Earnshaw pitched again for the A's in Game Six, and pushed the Cardinals' scoreless streak to 21 innings before allowing them a token run in the ninth. But by then seven A's had crossed the plate and the Series was theirs.

Philadelphia Athletics (AL), 4; St. Louis Cardinals (NL), 2

PHI (A)

PLAYER/POS	AVG	G	AB	R	H	2B	3B	HR	RB	BB	SO	SB
Max Bishop, 2b	.222	6	18	5	4	0	0	0	0	7	3	0
Joe Boley, ss	.095	6	21	1	2	0	0	0	1	0	1	0
Mickey Cochrane, c	.222	6	18	5	4	1	0	2	4	5	2	0
Jimmy Dykes, 3b	.222	6	18	2	4	3	0	1	5	5	3	0
George Earnshaw, p	.000	3	9	0	0	0	0	0	0	0	5	0
Jimmie Foxx, 1b	.333	6	21	3	7	2	1	1	3	2	4	0
Lefty Grove, p	.000	3	6	0	0	0	0	0	0	0	3	0
Mule Haas, of	.111	6	18	1	2	0	1	0	1	1	3	0
Eric McNair, ph	.000	1	1	0	0	0	0	0	0	0	0	0
Bing Miller, of	.143	6	21	0	3	0	0	0	3	0	4	0
Jim Moore, of-1	.333	3	3	0	1	0	0	0	0	1	1	0
Jack Quinn, p	.000	1	0	0	0	0	0	0	0	0	0	0
Bill Shores, p	.000	1	0	0	0	0	0	0	0	0	1	0
Al Simmons, of	.364	6	22	4	8	2	0	2	4	2	2	0
Rube Walberg, p	.000	1	2	0	0	0	0	0	0	0	1	0
TOTAL	.197		178	21	35	10	2	6	21	24	32	0

PITCHER	W	L	ERA	G	GS	CG	SV	SHO	IP	H	ER	BB	SO
George Earnshaw	2	0	0.72	3	3	2	0	0	25.0	13	2	7	19
Lefty Grove	2	1	1.42	3	2	2	0	0	19.0	15	3	3	10
Jack Quinn	0	0	4.50	1	0	0	0	0	2.0	3	1	0	1
Bill Shores	0	0	13.50	1	0	0	0	0	1.1	3	2	0	0
Rube Walberg	0	1	3.86	1	1	0	0	0	4.2	4	2	1	3
TOTAL	4	2	1.73	9	6	4	0	0	52.0	38	10	11	33

STL (N)

PLAYER/POS	AVG	G	AB	R	H	2B	3B	HR	RB	BB	SO	SB
Sparky Adams, 3b	.143	6	21	0	3	0	0	0	1	0	4	0
Hi Bell, p	.000	1	0	0	0	0	0	0	0	0	0	0
Ray Blades, of-3	.111	5	9	2	1	0	0	0	0	2	2	0
Jim Bottomley, 1b	.045	6	22	1	1	1	0	0	0	2	9	0
Taylor Douthit, of	.083	6	24	1	2	0	0	1	2	0	2	0
George Fisher, ph	.500	2	2	0	1	1	0	0	0	0	1	0
Frankie Frisch, 2b	.208	6	24	0	5	2	0	0	0	0	0	1
Charlie Gelbert, ss	.353	6	17	2	6	0	1	0	2	3	3	0
Burleigh Grimes, p	.400	2	5	0	2	0	0	0	0	0	1	0
Chick Hafey, of	.273	6	22	2	6	5	0	0	2	1	3	0
Jesse Haines, p	.500	1	2	0	1	0	0	0	1	0	0	0
Bill Hallahan, p	.000	2	2	0	0	0	0	0	0	1	1	0
Andy High, 3b	.500	1	2	1	1	0	0	0	0	0	0	0
Syl Johnson, p	.000	2	0	0	0	0	0	0	0	0	0	0
Jim Lindsey, p	1.000	2	1	0	1	0	0	0	0	0	0	0
Gus Mancuso, c	.286	2	7	1	2	0	0	0	0	1	2	0
Ernie Orsatti, ph	.000	1	1	0	0	0	0	0	0	0	0	0
George Puccinelli, ph	.000	1	1	0	0	0	0	0	0	0	0	0
Flint Rhem, p	.000	1	1	0	0	0	0	0	0	0	0	0
George Watkins, of	.167	4	12	2	2	0	0	1	1	1	3	0
Jimmie Wilson, c	.267	4	15	0	4	1	0	0	2	0	1	0
TOTAL	.200		190	12	38	10	1	2	11	11	33	1

PITCHER	W	L	ERA	G	GS	CG	SV	SHO	IP	H	ER	BB	SO
Hi Bell	0	0	0.00	1	0	0	0	0	1.0	0	0	0	0
Burleigh Grimes	0	2	3.71	2	2	2	0	0	17.0	10	7	6	13
Jesse Haines	1	0	1.00	1	1	1	0	0	9.0	4	1	4	2
Bill Hallahan	1	1	1.64	2	2	1	0	1	11.0	9	2	8	8
Syl Johnson	0	0	7.20	2	0	0	0	0	5.0	4	4	3	4
Jim Lindsey	0	0	1.93	2	0	0	0	0	4.2	1	1	1	2
Flint Rhem	0	1	10.80	1	1	0	0	0	3.1	7	4	2	3
TOTAL	2	4	3.35	11	6	4	0	1	51.0	35	19	24	32

GAME 1 AT PHI OCT 1

STL	002	000	000	2	9 0
PHI	010	101	11X	5	5 0

Pitchers: GRIMES vs GROVE
Home Runs: Cochrane-PHI, Simmons-PHI
Attendance: 32,295

GAME 2 AT PHI OCT 2

STL	010	000	000	1	6 2
PHI	202	200	00X	6	7 2

Pitchers: RHEM, Lindsey (4), Johnson (7) vs EARNSHAW
Home Runs: Cochrane-PHI, Watkins-STL
Attendance: 32,295

GAME 3 AT STL OCT 4

PHI	000	000	000	0	7 0
STL	000	110	21X	5	10 0

Pitchers: WALBERG, Shores (5), Quinn (7) vs HALLAHAN
Home Runs: Douthit-STL
Attendance: 36,944

GAME 4 AT STL OCT 5

PHI	100	000	000	1	4 1
STL	001	200	00X	3	5 1

Pitchers: GROVE vs HAINES
Attendance: 39,946

GAME 5 AT STL OCT 6

PHI	000	000	002	2	5 0
STL	000	000	000	0	3 1

Pitchers: Earnshaw, GROVE (8) vs GRIMES
Home Runs: Foxx-PHI
Attendance: 38,844

GAME 6 AT PHI OCT 8

STL	000	000	001	1	5 1
PHI	201	211	00X	7	7 0

Pitchers: HALLAHAN, Johnson (3), Lindsey (6), Bell (8) vs EARNSHAW
Home Runs: Dykes-PHI, Simmons-PHI
Attendance: 32,295

For the second year in a row, the A's met the Cardinals in the Series, and once again pitchers Lefty Grove and George Earnshaw provided more than 80 percent of the Athletics' pitching, performing splendidly and winning three games between them. But this time Cardinal pitchers Wild Bill Hallahan and Burleigh Grimes outshone them, winning two games apiece to bring St. Louis the world championship.

Grove gave up four hits and two runs in the first inning of the opener, but shut out the Cards the rest of the way as the A's scored six off Paul Derringer to take the Series lead. Earnshaw also held St. Louis to two runs the next day—both manufactured by Pepper Martin's daring baserunning. But they were more than enough for Hallahan, who shut out the A's on three singles.

The Cardinals took their first Series lead in Game Three, scoring five times off Grove and reliever Roy Mahaffey while Grimes held the A's hitless through seven innings and scoreless through eight before giving up a harmless two-run homer to Al Simmons in the bottom of the ninth. But the A's came back to even the Series the next day on Earnshaw's two-hit shutout.

Pepper Martin, the Cardinal hero of Game Two, homered for two runs in Game Five, and drove in two more of St. Louis's five runs with a sacrifice fly and a single. Meanwhile pitcher Hallahan held Philadelphia to a lone run, returning the Series lead to the Cardinals with his second win.

Game Six pitted Grove and Derringer against each other again as in the opener, and again Grove emerged the victor, holding the Cardinals to one run and five hits. The Athletics scored four unearned runs in the fifth off the unfortunate Derringer who, after an error put a runner on base to open the inning, gave up two singles and walked four, including two with the bases full, before leaving the game. Four more Philadelphia runs in the seventh (two of them scoring on a dropped fly ball) gave the A's the Series' only lopsided win.

In the finale, Grimes once again held the A's scoreless through eight before giving up two runs in the ninth. And once again the runs proved harmless against an early Cardinal lead, as Hallahan came on to retire Max Bishop for the final out.

St. Louis Cardinals (NL), 4; Philadelphia Athletics (AL), 3

STL (N)

PLAYER/POS	AVG	G	AB	R	H	2B	3B	HR	RB	BB	SO	SB
Sparky Adams, 3b	.250	2	4	0	1	0	0	0	0	0	1	0
Ray Blades, ph	.000	2	2	0	0	0	0	0	0	0	2	0
Jim Bottomley, 1b	.160	7	25	2	4	1	0	0	2	2	5	0
Ripper Collins, ph	.000	2	2	0	0	0	0	0	0	0	1	0
Paul Derringer, p	.000	3	2	0	0	0	0	0	0	0	1	0
Jake Flowers, 3b-4	.091	5	11	1	1	1	0	0	0	1	0	0
Frankie Frisch, 2b	.259	7	27	2	7	2	0	0	1	1	2	1
Charlie Gelbert, ss	.261	7	23	0	6	1	0	0	3	0	4	0
Burleigh Grimes, p	.286	2	7	0	2	0	0	0	2	0	2	0
Chick Hafey, of	.167	6	24	1	4	0	0	0	0	0	5	1
Bill Hallahan, p	.000	3	6	0	0	0	0	0	0	0	3	0
Andy High, 3b	.267	4	15	3	4	0	0	0	0	0	2	0
Syl Johnson, p	.000	3	2	0	0	0	0	0	0	0	2	0
Jim Lindsey, p	.000	2	0	0	0	0	0	0	0	0	0	0
Gus Mancuso, c-1	.000	2	1	0	0	0	0	0	0	0	0	0
Pepper Martin, of	.500	7	24	5	12	4	0	1	5	2	3	5
Ernie Orsatti, of	.000	1	3	0	0	0	0	0	0	0	3	0
Flint Rhem, p	.000	1	0	0	0	0	0	0	0	0	0	0
Wally Roettger, of	.286	3	14	1	4	1	0	0	0	0	3	0
George Watkins, of	.286	5	14	4	4	1	0	1	2	2	1	1
Jimmie Wilson, c	.217	7	23	0	5	0	0	0	2	1	1	0
TOTAL	.236	7	229	19	54	11	0	2	17	9	41	8

PITCHER	W	L	ERA	G	GS	CG	SV	SHO	IP	H	ER	BB	SO
Paul Derringer	0	2	4.26	3	2	0	0	0	12.2	14	6	7	14
Burleigh Grimes	2	0	2.04	2	2	1	0	0	17.2	9	4	9	11
Bill Hallahan	2	0	0.49	3	2	2	1	1	18.1	12	1	8	12
Syl Johnson	0	1	3.00	3	1	0	0	0	9.0	10	3	1	6
Jim Lindsey	0	0	5.40	2	0	0	0	0	3.1	4	2	3	2
Flint Rhem	0	0	0.00	1	0	0	0	0	1.0	1	0	0	1
TOTAL	4	3	2.32	14	7	3	1	1	62.0	50	16	28	46

PHI (A)

PLAYER/POS	AVG	G	AB	R	H	2B	3B	HR	RB	BB	SO	SB
Max Bishop, 2b	.148	7	27	4	4	0	0	0	0	3	5	0
Joe Boley, ph	.000	1	1	0	0	0	0	0	0	0	1	0
Mickey Cochrane, c	.160	7	25	2	4	0	0	0	1	5	2	0
Doc Cramer, ph	.500	2	2	0	1	0	0	0	2	0	0	0
Jimmy Dykes, 3b	.227	7	22	2	5	0	0	0	2	5	1	0
George Earnshaw, p	.000	3	8	0	0	0	0	0	0	0	2	0
Jimmie Foxx, 1b	.348	7	23	3	8	0	0	1	3	6	5	0
Lefty Grove, p	.000	3	10	0	0	0	0	0	0	0	7	0
Mule Haas, of	.130	7	23	1	3	1	0	0	2	3	5	0
Johnnie Heving, ph	.000	1	1	0	0	0	0	0	0	0	0	0
Waite Hoyt, p	.000	1	0	0	0	0	0	0	0	0	0	0
Roy Mahaffey, p	.000	1	0	0	0	0	0	0	0	0	0	0
Eric McNair, 2b-1	.000	2	2	1	0	0	0	0	0	0	1	0
Bing Miller, of	.269	7	26	3	7	1	0	0	1	0	4	0
Jim Moore, of-1	.333	2	3	0	1	0	0	0	0	0	1	0
Eddie Rommel, p	.000	1	0	0	0	0	0	0	0	0	0	0
Al Simmons, of	.333	7	27	4	9	2	0	2	8	3	3	0
Phil Todt, ph	.000	1	1	0	0	0	0	0	0	1	0	0
Rube Walberg, p	.000	2	0	0	0	0	0	0	0	0	0	0
Dib Williams, ss	.320	7	25	2	8	1	0	0	1	2	9	0
TOTAL	.220	7	227	22	50	5	0	3	20	28	46	0

PITCHER	W	L	ERA	G	GS	CG	SV	SHO	IP	H	ER	BB	SO
George Earnshaw	1	2	1.88	3	3	2	0	1	24.0	12	5	4	20
Lefty Grove	2	1	2.42	3	3	2	0	0	26.0	28	7	2	16
Waite Hoyt	0	1	4.50	1	1	0	0	0	6.0	7	3	0	1
Roy Mahaffey	0	0	9.00	1	0	0	0	0	1.0	1	1	1	0
Eddie Rommel	0	0	9.00	1	0	0	0	0	1.0	3	1	0	0
Rube Walberg	0	0	3.00	2	0	0	0	0	3.0	3	1	2	4
TOTAL	3	4	2.66	11	7	4	0	1	61.0	54	18	9	41

GAME 1 AT STL OCT 1

PHI	004 000 200	6	11	0
STL	200 000 000	2	12	0

Pitchers: GROVE vs DERRINGER, Johnson (8)
Home Runs: Simmons-PHI
Attendance: 38,529

GAME 2 AT STL OCT 2

PHI	000 000 000	0	3	0
STL	010 000 10X	2	6	1

Pitchers: EARNSHAW vs HALLAHAN
Attendance: 35,947

GAME 3 AT PHI OCT 5

STL	020 200 001	5	12	0
PHI	000 000 002	2	2	0

Pitchers: GRIMES vs GROVE, Mahaffey (9)
Home Runs: Simmons-PHI
Attendance: 32,295

GAME 4 AT PHI OCT 6

STL	000 000 000	0	2	1
PHI	100 002 00X	3	10	0

Pitchers: JOHNSON, Lindsey (6), Derringer (8) vs EARNSHAW
Home Runs: Foxx-PHI
Attendance: 32,295

GAME 5 AT PHI OCT 7

STL	100 002 011	5	12	0
PHI	000 000 100	1	9	0

Pitchers: HALLAHAN vs HOYT, Walberg (7), Rommel (9)
Home Runs: Martin-STL, Watkins-STL
Attendance: 32,295

GAME 6 AT STL OCT 9

PHI	000 040 400	8	8	1
STL	000 001 000	1	5	2

Pitchers: GROVE vs DERRINGER, Johnson (5), Lindsey (7), Rhem (9)
Attendance: 39,401

GAME 7 AT STL OCT 10

PHI	000 000 002	2	7	1
STL	202 000 00X	4	5	0

Pitchers: EARNSHAW, Walberg (8) vs GRIMES, Hallahan (9)
Attendance: 20,805

Lou Gehrig, who hit .529 and scored nearly a quarter of New York's runs, led both clubs in batting, slugging, hits, runs, and RBI as the Yankees crushed the Cubs in four games. But the Series is best remembered for Babe Ruth's "called" shot in Game Three, when he pointed his bat at pitcher Charlie Root in the fifth inning and broke the game's 4–4 tie a moment later with a massive home run into the center field bleachers. Debate has raged ever since about whether Ruth intended his gesture as a home run prediction. Whether intended or not, it erased from public memory Gehrig's home run that followed Ruth's (and the homers both men had hit earlier in the game), and made memorable an otherwise undistinguished Series.

Chicago scored in the first inning of each game, taking early leads in three of the four, but held no lead beyond the sixth inning. In Game One, the Cubs connected for ten hits to the Yankees' eight, but managed to score only half as many runs as the New Yorkers, who put what had been a close game out of reach with five runs in the sixth (on four walks, two singles, and a ground out) and three more in the seventh (a walk, two singles, a hit batsman, a sacrifice fly, and a wild pitch).

Chicago's Lon Warneke walked four batters in Game Two, and three of them went on to score as the Yankees countered single Cub runs in the first and third with pairs of their own on two walks and two singles in each frame. (A fifth Yankee run—on two singles without bases on balls—concluded the scoring for the game.)

Game Three featured not only the two homers each by Ruth and Gehrig, but home runs by the Cubs' Kiki Cuyler and Gabby Hartnett. Hartnett's solo shot in the last of the ninth brought Chicago to within two runs of New York for the Series' closest finish.

Four first-inning singles, Frank Demaree's three-run homer, and a Yankee error gave the Cubs a 4–1 advantage early in Game Four—their biggest lead of the Series. But by game's end, 19 Yankee hits (including two home runs by Tony Lazzeri and one by Earle Combs) had created 13 Yankee runs, and the world title was theirs.

New York Yankees (AL), 4; Chicago Cubs (NL), 0

NY (A)

PLAYER/POS	AVG	G	AB	R	H	2B	3B	HR	RB	BB	SO	SB
Johnny Allen, p	.000	1	0	0	0	0	0	0	0	0	0	0
Sammy Byrd, of	.000	1	0	0	0	0	0	0	0	0	0	0
Ben Chapman, of	.294	4	17	1	5	2	0	0	6	2	4	0
Earle Combs, of	.375	4	16	8	6	1	0	1	4	4	3	0
Frankie Crosetti, ss	.133	4	15	2	2	1	0	0	0	2	3	0
Bill Dickey, c	.438	4	16	2	7	0	0	0	4	2	1	0
Lou Gehrig, 1b	.529	4	17	9	9	1	0	3	8	2	1	0
Lefty Gomez, p	.000	1	3	0	0	0	0	0	0	0	2	0
Myril Hoag, pr	.000	1	0	1	0	0	0	0	0	0	0	0
Tony Lazzeri, 2b	.294	4	17	4	5	0	0	2	5	2	1	0
Wilcy Moore, p	.333	1	3	0	1	0	0	0	0	0	2	0
Herb Pennock, p	.000	2	1	0	0	0	0	0	0	0	0	0
George Pipgras, p	.000	1	5	0	0	0	0	0	0	0	5	0
Red Ruffing, p-1	.000	2	4	0	0	0	0	0	0	1	1	0
Babe Ruth, of	.333	4	15	6	5	0	0	2	6	4	3	0
Joe Sewell, 3b	.333	4	15	4	5	1	0	0	3	4	0	0
TOTAL	.313		144	37	45	6	0	8	36	23	26	0

PITCHER	W	L	ERA	G	GS	CG	SV	SHO	IP	H	ER	BB	SO
Johnny Allen	0	0	40.50	1	1	0	0	0	0.2	5	3	0	0
Lefty Gomez	1	0	1.00	1	1	1	0	0	9.0	9	1	1	8
Wilcy Moore	1	0	0.00	1	0	0	0	0	5.1	2	0	0	1
Herb Pennock	0	0	2.25	2	0	0	2	0	4.0	2	1	1	4
George Pipgras	1	0	4.50	1	1	0	0	0	8.0	9	4	3	1
Red Ruffing	1	0	4.00	1	1	1	0	0	9.0	10	4	6	10
TOTAL	4	0	3.25	7	4	2	2	0	36.0	37	13	11	24

CHI (N)

PLAYER/POS	AVG	G	AB	R	H	2B	3B	HR	RB	BB	SO	SB
Guy Bush, p	.000	2	1	0	0	0	0	0	0	1	0	0
Kiki Cuyler, of	.278	4	18	2	5	1	1	1	2	0	3	1
Frank Demaree, of	.286	2	7	1	2	0	0	1	4	1	0	0
Woody English, 3b	.176	4	17	2	3	0	0	0	1	2	2	0
Burleigh Grimes, p	.000	2	1	0	0	0	0	0	0	0	1	0
Charlie Grimm, 1b	.333	4	15	2	5	2	0	0	1	2	2	0
Marv Gudat, ph	.000	2	2	0	0	0	0	0	0	0	1	0
Stan Hack, ph	.000	1	0	0	0	0	0	0	0	0	0	0
Gabby Hartnett, c	.313	4	16	2	5	2	0	1	1	1	3	0
Rollie Hemsley, c-1	.000	3	3	0	0	0	0	0	0	0	3	0
Billy Herman, 2b	.222	4	18	5	4	1	0	0	1	1	3	0
Billy Jurges, ss	.364	3	11	1	4	1	0	0	1	0	1	2
Mark Koenig, ss-1	.250	2	4	1	1	0	1	0	1	1	0	0
Pat Malone, p	.000	1	0	0	0	0	0	0	0	0	0	0
Jakie May, p	.000	2	2	0	0	0	0	0	0	0	0	0
Johnny Moore, of	.000	2	7	1	0	0	0	0	0	2	1	0
Charlie Root, p	.000	1	2	0	0	0	0	0	0	0	1	0
Bob Smith, p	.000	1	0	0	0	0	0	0	0	0	0	0
Riggs Stephenson, of	.444	4	18	2	8	1	0	0	4	0	0	0
Bud Tinning, p	.000	2	0	0	0	0	0	0	0	0	0	0
Lon Warneke, p	.000	2	4	0	0	0	0	0	0	0	3	0
TOTAL	.253		146	19	37	8	2	3	16	11	24	3

PITCHER	W	L	ERA	G	GS	CG	SV	SHO	IP	H	ER	BB	SO
Guy Bush	0	1	14.29	2	2	0	0	0	5.2	5	9	6	2
Burleigh Grimes	0	0	23.63	2	0	0	0	0	2.2	7	7	2	0
Pat Malone	0	0	0.00	1	0	0	0	0	2.2	1	0	4	4
Jakie May	0	1	11.57	2	0	0	0	0	4.2	9	6	3	4
Charlie Root	0	1	10.38	1	1	0	0	0	4.1	6	5	3	4
Bob Smith	0	0	9.00	1	0	0	0	0	1.0	2	1	0	1
Bud Tinning	0	0	0.00	2	0	0	0	0	2.1	0	0	3	3
Lon Warneke	0	1	5.91	2	1	1	0	0	10.2	15	7	5	8
TOTAL	0	4	9.26	13	4	1	0	0	34.0	45	35	23	26

GAME 1 AT NY SEPT 28

CHI	200	000	220	6	10	1
NY	000	305	31X	12	8	2

Pitchers: BUSH, Grimes (6), Smith (8) vs RUFFING
Home Runs: Gehrig-NY
Attendance: 41,459

GAME 2 AT NY SEPT 29

CHI	101	000	000	2	9	0
NY	202	010	00X	5	10	1

Pitchers: WARNEKE vs GOMEZ
Attendance: 50,709

GAME 3 AT CHI OCT 1

NY	301	020	001	7	8	1
CHI	102	100	001	5	9	4

Pitchers: PIPGRAS, Pennock (9) vs ROOT, Malone (5), May (7), Tinning (9)
Home Runs: Ruth-NY (2), Gehrig-NY (2), Cuyler-CHI, Hartnett-CHI
Attendance: 49,986

GAME 4 AT CHI OCT 2

NY	102	002	404	13	19	4
CHI	400	001	001	6	9	1

Pitchers: Allen, MOORE (1), Pennock (7) vs Bush, Warneke (1), MAY (4), Tinning (7), Grimes (9)
Home Runs: Demaree-CHI, Lazzeri-NY (2), Combs-NY
Attendance: 49,844

Although John McGraw had retired from managing the Giants in 1932, he continued to regard them as "his" team. Led now by first baseman Bill Terry, the Giants faced a club also led by an active player, shortstop Joe Cronin in his rookie managerial season.

Giant ace Carl Hubbell dominated the first game, striking out ten while limiting the Senators to five singles and a pair of unearned runs. Mel Ott set the tone for New York with a two-out two-run homer in the first inning, and singled home a third Giant run in the third to build a lead Washington would not overcome. The next day the Senators scored first, on Goose Goslin's solo homer in the third. But that was the only run scored off Giant pitcher Hal Schumacher, and when the Giants drove out Senator starter Alvin Crowder with six runs in the sixth they had their second win well in hand.

The Senators revived when the Series moved to Washington for Game Three. Each of second baseman Buddy Myer's three hits scored or drove in a run, providing a growing cushion for pitcher Earl Whitehill, who recorded the Series' only shutout.

Games Four and Five went to New York, but not without a struggle. In the fourth game, manager Terry's home run broke the ice in the fourth inning, but Giant pitcher Hubbell muffed a bunt in the seventh which led to the tying run. Hubbell and Senator starter Monty Weaver dueled without further scoring until shortstop Blondy Ryan's single in the top of the eleventh put New York up by one. Hubbell let men reach second and third with one out in the last of the eleventh, but an intentional walk set up the hoped-for double play to end the game.

New York had built a three-run lead in Game Five when Senator Fred Schulte evened the score in the last of the sixth with a three-run homer. Relievers Jack Russell and Dolf Luque then dueled scorelessly into the tenth, when Giant Mel Ott (whose homer had begun the Series' scoring in the first inning of Game One) homered once again for what proved the Series' final run. Luque shut down the Senators in their half of the tenth, and "McGraw's Giants" were for the fourth time the world's finest. But before the advent of another spring, McGraw was dead.

New York Giants (NL), 4; Washington Senators (AL), 1

NY (N)

PLAYER/POS	AVG	G	AB	R	H	2B	3B	HR	RB	BB	SO	SB
Hi Bell, p	.000	1	0	0	0	0	0	0	0	0	0	0
Hughie Critz, 2b	.136	5	22	2	3	0	0	0	0	1	0	0
Kiddo Davis, of	.368	5	19	1	7	1	0	0	0	0	3	0
Freddie Fitzsimmons, p	.500	1	2	0	1	0	0	0	0	0	0	0
Carl Hubbell, p	.286	2	7	0	2	0	0	0	0	0	0	0
Travis Jackson, 3b	.222	5	18	3	4	1	0	0	2	1	3	0
Dolf Luque, p	1.000	1	1	0	1	0	0	0	0	0	0	0
Gus Mancuso, c	.118	5	17	2	2	1	0	0	2	3	0	0
Jo-Jo Moore, of	.227	5	22	1	5	1	0	0	1	1	1	0
Lefty O'Doul, ph	1.000	1	1	1	1	0	0	0	2	0	0	0
Mel Ott, of	.389	5	18	3	7	0	0	2	4	4	4	0
Homer Peel, of-1	.500	2	2	0	1	0	0	0	0	0	0	0
Blondy Ryan, ss	.278	5	18	0	5	0	0	0	1	1	5	0
Hal Schumacher, p	.286	2	7	0	2	0	0	0	3	0	3	0
Bill Terry, 1b	.273	5	22	3	6	1	0	1	1	0	0	0
TOTAL	.267		176	16	47	5	0	3	16	11	21	0

PITCHER	W	L	ERA	G	GS	CG	SV	SHO	IP	H	ER	BB	SO
Hi Bell	0	0	0.00	1	0	0	0	0	1.0	0	0	0	0
Freddie Fitzsimmons	0	1	5.14	1	1	0	0	0	7.0	9	4	0	2
Carl Hubbell	2	0	0.00	2	2	2	0	0	20.0	13	0	6	15
Dolf Luque	1	0	0.00	1	0	0	0	0	4.1	2	0	2	5
Hal Schumacher	1	0	2.45	2	2	1	0	0	14.2	13	4	5	3
TOTAL	4	1	1.53	7	5	3	0	0	47.0	37	8	13	25

WAS (A)

PLAYER/POS	AVG	G	AB	R	H	2B	3B	HR	RB	BB	SO	SB
Ossie Bluege, 3b	.125	5	16	1	2	1	0	0	0	1	6	0
Cliff Bolton, ph	.000	2	2	0	0	0	0	0	0	0	0	0
Joe Cronin, ss	.318	5	22	1	7	0	0	0	2	0	2	0
General Crowder, p	.250	2	4	0	1	0	0	0	0	0	0	0
Goose Goslin, of	.250	5	20	2	5	1	0	1	1	1	3	0
Dave Harris, of-1	.000	3	5	0	0	0	0	0	0	2	0	0
John Kerr, pr	.000	1	0	1	0	0	0	0	0	0	0	0
Joe Kuhel, 1b	.150	5	20	1	3	0	0	0	1	1	4	0
Heinie Manush, of	.111	5	18	2	2	0	0	0	0	2	1	0
Alex McColl, p	.000	2	0	0	0	0	0	0	0	0	0	0
Buddy Myer, 2b	.300	5	20	2	6	1	0	0	2	2	3	0
Sam Rice, ph	1.000	1	1	0	1	0	0	0	0	0	0	0
Jack Russell, p	.000	3	2	0	0	0	0	0	0	1	2	0
Fred Schulte, of	.333	5	21	1	7	1	0	1	4	1	1	0
Luke Sewell, c	.176	5	17	1	3	0	0	0	1	2	0	1
Lefty Stewart, p	.000	1	1	0	0	0	0	0	0	0	1	0
Tommy Thomas, p	.000	2	0	0	0	0	0	0	0	0	0	0
Monte Weaver, p	.000	1	4	0	0	0	0	0	0	0	2	0
Earl Whitehill, p	.000	1	3	0	0	0	0	0	0	0	0	0
TOTAL	.214		173	11	37	4	0	2	11	13	25	1

PITCHER	W	L	ERA	G	GS	CG	SV	SHO	IP	H	ER	BB	SO
General Crowder	0	1	7.36	2	2	0	0	0	11.0	16	9	5	7
Alex McColl	0	0	0.00	2	0	0	0	0	2.0	0	0	0	0
Jack Russell	0	1	0.87	3	0	0	0	0	10.1	8	1	0	7
Lefty Stewart	0	1	9.00	1	1	0	0	0	2.0	6	2	0	0
Tommy Thomas	0	0	0.00	2	0	0	0	0	1.1	1	0	0	2
Monte Weaver	0	1	1.74	1	1	0	0	0	10.1	11	2	4	3
Earl Whitehill	1	0	0.00	1	1	1	0	1	9.0	5	0	2	2
TOTAL	1	4	2.74	11	5	1	0	1	46.0	47	14	11	21

GAME 1 AT NY OCT 3

WAS	000	100	001	2	5	3
NY	202	000	00X	4	10	2

Pitchers: STEWART, Russell (3), Thomas (8) vs HUBBELL
Home Runs: Ott-NY
Attendance: 46,672

GAME 2 AT NY OCT 4

WAS	001	000	000	1	5	0
NY	000	006	00X	6	10	0

Pitchers: CROWDER, Thomas (6), McColl (7) vs SCHUMACHER
Home Runs: Goslin-WAS
Attendance: 35,461

GAME 3 AT WAS OCT 5

NY	000	000	000	0	5	0
WAS	210	000	10X	4	9	1

Pitchers: FITZSIMMONS, Bell (8) vs WHITEHILL
Attendance: 25,727

GAME 4 AT WAS OCT 6

NY	000	100	000	01	2	11	1
WAS	000	000	100	00	1	8	0

Pitchers: HUBBELL vs WEAVER, Russell (11)
Home Runs: Terry-NY
Attendance: 26,762

GAME 5 AT WAS OCT 7

NY	020	001	000	1	4	11	1
WAS	000	003	000	0	3	10	0

Pitchers: Schumacher, LUQUE (6) vs Crowder, RUSSELL (6)
Home Runs: Schulte-WAS, Ott-NY
Attendance: 28,454

Pitching brothers Dizzy and Paul Dean won seven games in ten days to give the Cardinals the pennant on the final day of the season. In the Series they continued their winning ways, chalking up all four Cardinal victories. Dizzy pitched the opener in Detroit. Given a 3–0 lead, thanks to five Tiger errors in the first three innings, he breezed to an 8–3 win.

Detroit's Schoolboy Rowe brought the Tigers back with a pitching masterpiece in Game Two. After giving up single runs in the second and third innings, he allowed only one runner to reach base over the next nine as his Tigers tied the score in the ninth, and won it on two walks and a single in the twelfth.

Paul Dean nearly pitched a shutout in Game Three, yielding a harmless run with two out in the ninth after the Cards had built him a 4–0 lead. Brother Diz figured in a curious and painful play in Game Four. Pinch-running in the fourth inning, he was beaned by a would-be double-play throw as he ran to second. The tying run scored from third on the play, but Detroit's pitcher Eldon Auker shut out the Cards through the final five innings, and his teammates scored six more runs to bury St. Louis 10–4, evening the Series at two apiece. Diz was rushed to the hospital, but as no damage was found he started Game Five the next day. He pitched well enough, but Detroit's Tommy Bridges pitched better, giving the Cardinals only one run to the Tigers' three.

Paul Dean evened the Series again with a win against Rowe in a closely contested sixth game. A grounder through Dean's legs allowed the Tigers to tie the game in the sixth inning, but Paul redeemed his error in the seventh when he singled in the tie-breaking—and as it turned out, winning—run. Dizzy came back after only a day's rest to hurl a six-hit shutout in the finale. He also scored the game's first run and drove in the sixth with a double and single in his team's seven-run third. Three innings later, frustrated Tiger fans, angered by Cardinal Joe Medwick's rough slide into their third baseman, pelted Medwick with food and bottles, halting the game for twenty minutes until Commissioner Landis ordered Medwick from the game. The delay only forestalled Detroit's defeat, as the Cards took the title game 11–0.

St. Louis Cardinals (NL), 4; Detroit Tigers (AL), 3

STL (N)

PLAYER/POS	AVG	G	AB	R	H	2B	3B	HR	RB	BB	SO	SB
Tex Carleton, p	.000	2	1	0	0	0	0	0	0	0	0	0
Ripper Collins, 1b	.367	7	30	4	11	1	0	0	3	1	2	0
Pat Crawford, ph	.000	2	2	0	0	0	0	0	0	0	0	0
Spud Davis, ph	1.000	2	2	0	2	0	0	0	1	0	0	0
Dizzy Dean, p-3	.250	4	12	3	3	2	0	0	1	0	3	0
Paul Dean, p	.167	2	6	0	1	0	0	0	2	0	1	0
Bill DeLancey, c	.172	7	29	3	5	3	0	1	4	2	8	0
Leo Durocher, ss	.259	7	27	4	7	1	1	0	0	0	0	0
Frankie Frisch, 2b	.194	7	31	2	6	1	0	0	4	0	1	0
Chick Fullis, of	.400	3	5	0	2	0	0	0	0	0	0	0
Jesse Haines, p	.000	1	0	0	0	0	0	0	0	0	0	0
Bill Hallahan, p	.000	1	3	0	0	0	0	0	0	0	1	0
Pepper Martin, 3b	.355	7	31	8	11	3	1	0	4	3	3	2
Joe Medwick, of	.379	7	29	4	11	0	1	1	5	1	7	0
Jim Mooney, p	.000	1	0	0	0	0	0	0	0	0	0	0
Ernie Orsatti, of	.318	7	22	3	7	0	1	0	2	3	1	0
Jack Rothrock, of	.233	7	30	3	7	3	1	0	6	1	2	0
Dazzy Vance, p	.000	1	0	0	0	0	0	0	0	0	0	0
Bill Walker, p	.000	2	2	0	0	0	0	0	0	0	2	0
Burgess Whitehead, ss	.000	1	0	0	0	0	0	0	0	0	0	0
TOTAL	.279		262	34	73	14	5	2	32	11	31	2

PITCHER	W	L	ERA	G	GS	CG	SV	SHO	IP	H	ER	BB	SO
Tex Carleton	0	0	7.36	2	1	0	0	0	3.2	5	3	2	2
Dizzy Dean	2	1	1.73	3	3	2	0	1	26.0	20	5	5	17
Paul Dean	2	0	1.00	2	2	2	0	0	18.0	15	2	7	11
Jesse Haines	0	0	0.00	1	0	0	0	0	0.2	1	0	0	2
Bill Hallahan	0	0	2.16	1	1	0	0	0	8.1	6	2	4	6
Jim Mooney	0	0	0.00	1	0	0	0	0	1.0	1	0	0	0
Dazzy Vance	0	0	0.00	1	0	0	0	0	1.1	1	0	1	3
Bill Walker	0	2	7.11	2	0	0	0	0	6.1	6	5	6	2
TOTAL	4	3	2.34	13	7	4	0	1	65.1	56	17	25	43

DET (A)

PLAYER/POS	AVG	G	AB	R	H	2B	3B	HR	RB	BB	SO	SB
Eldon Auker, p	.000	2	4	0	0	0	0	0	0	0	2	0
Tommy Bridges, p	.143	3	7	0	1	0	0	0	0	1	4	0
Mickey Cochrane, c	.214	7	28	2	6	1	0	0	1	4	3	0
General Crowder, p	.000	2	1	0	0	0	0	0	0	0	0	0
Frank Doljack, of-1	.000	2	2	0	0	0	0	0	0	0	0	0
Pete Fox, of	.286	7	28	1	8	6	0	0	2	1	4	0
Charlie Gehringer, 2b	.379	7	29	5	11	1	0	1	2	3	0	1
Goose Goslin, of	.241	7	29	2	7	1	0	0	2	3	1	0
Hank Greenberg, 1b	.321	7	28	4	9	2	1	1	7	4	9	1
Ray Hayworth, c	.000	1	0	0	0	0	0	0	0	0	0	0
Chief Hogsett, p	.000	3	0	0	0	0	0	0	0	0	1	0
Firpo Marberry, p	.000	2	0	0	0	0	0	0	0	0	0	0
Marv Owen, 3b	.069	7	29	0	2	0	0	0	1	0	5	1
Billy Rogell, ss	.276	7	29	3	8	1	0	0	4	1	4	1
Schoolboy Rowe, p	.000	3	7	0	0	0	0	0	0	0	5	0
Gee Walker, ph	.333	3	3	0	1	0	0	0	1	0	1	0
Jo-Jo White, of	.130	7	23	6	3	0	0	0	0	8	4	1
TOTAL	.224		250	23	56	12	1	2	20	25	43	5

PITCHER	W	L	ERA	G	GS	CG	SV	SHO	IP	H	ER	BB	SO
Eldon Auker	1	1	5.56	2	2	1	0	0	11.1	16	7	5	2
Tommy Bridges	1	1	3.63	3	2	1	0	0	17.1	21	7	1	12
General Crowder	0	1	1.50	2	1	0	0	0	6.0	6	1	1	2
Chief Hogsett	0	0	1.23	3	0	0	0	0	7.1	6	1	3	3
Firpo Marberry	0	0	21.60	2	0	0	0	0	1.2	5	4	1	0
Schoolboy Rowe	1	1	2.95	3	2	2	0	0	21.1	19	7	0	12
TOTAL	3	4	3.74	15	7	4	0	0	65.0	73	27	11	31

GAME 1 AT DET OCT 3

STL 021 014 000   8 13 2
DET 001 001 010   3 8 5

Pitchers: J.DEAN vs CROWDER, Marberry (6), Hogsett (6)
Home Runs: Medwick-STL, Greenberg-DET
Attendance: 42,505

GAME 2 AT DET OCT 4

STL 011 000 000 000   2 7 3
DET 001 100 001 001   3 7 0

Pitchers: Hallahan, W.WALKER (9) vs ROWE
Attendance: 43,451

GAME 3 AT STL OCT 5

DET 000 000 001   1 8 2
STL 110 020 00X   4 9 1

Pitchers: BRIDGES, Hogsett (5) vs P.DEAN
Attendance: 34,073

GAME 4 AT STL OCT 6

DET 003 100 150   10 13 1
STL 011 200 000   4 10 5

Pitchers: AUKER vs Carleton, Vance (3), W.WALKER (5), Haines (8), Mooney (9)
Attendance: 37,492

GAME 5 AT STL OCT 7

DET 010 002 000   3 7 0
STL 000 000 100   1 7 1

Pitchers: BRIDGES vs J.DEAN, Carleton (9)
Home Runs: Gehringer-DET, Delancey-STL
Attendance: 38,536

GAME 6 AT DET OCT 8

STL 100 020 100   4 10 2
DET 001 002 000   3 7 1

Pitchers: P.DEAN vs ROWE
Attendance: 44,551

GAME 7 AT DET OCT 9

STL 007 002 200   11 17 1
DET 000 000 000   0 6 3

Pitchers: J.DEAN vs AUKER, Rowe (3), Hogsett (3), Bridges (4), Marberry (8), Crowder (9)
Attendance: 40,902

With a 21-game September winning streak, the Cubs vaulted over the Giants and Cardinals to face Detroit in the Series, and for a moment it seemed as if their momentum might carry them past the Tigers as well. Chicago scored two runs off Schoolboy Rowe in the top of the first in the opener, and right fielder Frank Demaree homered to open the ninth as Lon Warneke blanked the Tigers on four hits. But Detroit retaliated quickly in Game Two, driving out starter Charlie Root in the first inning with four runs (including Hank Greenberg's two-run homer) before Root had had a chance to record even one out. Tiger pitcher Rocky Bridges gained an easy 8–3 win, but Greenberg broke a wrist and was finished for the Series.

In Game Three the Cubs scored three times before Detroit countered with their first run in the sixth. But a walk and four Tiger hits in the eighth put the Bengals ahead 4–3, and Billy Rogell's baserunning as he turned a foiled steal into a rundown permitted a fifth Tiger to cross the plate. Two Cub runs in the last of the ninth tied the score, but Detroit pulled out the victory in the eleventh as a pair of singles sandwiched Fred Lindstrom's error at third to give them an unearned run.

Detroit's Alvin "General" Crowder followed up the Tigers' advantage the next day with a neat five-hit 2–1 win. Once again the Cubs bobbled away the game, this time with two sixth-inning errors that enabled Detroit to score the winning run without a hit. Chuck Klein's two-run homer saved Chicago from elimination in Game Five as Lon Warneke and Bill Lee shut out the Tigers through eight before letting in a harmless run in the ninth.

Chicago's Larry French and Tiger Rocky Bridges yielded 12 hits apiece in Game Six. Cub second baseman Billy Herman singled in a run in the third to tie the score, and homered for two more runs in the fifth to put the Cubs ahead. But the Tigers tied it up an inning later, and took their first world title ever when Goose Goslin singled in Mickey Cochrane with two out in the bottom of the ninth.

Detroit Tigers (AL), 4; Chicago Cubs (NL), 2

DET (A)

PLAYER/POS	AVG	G	AB	R	H	2B	3B	HR	RB	BB	SO	SB
Eldon Auker, p	.000	1	2	0	0	0	0	0	0	0	1	0
Tommy Bridges, p	.125	2	8	1	1	0	0	0	1	0	3	0
Flea Clifton, 3b	.000	4	16	1	0	0	0	0	0	2	4	0
Mickey Cochrane, c	.292	6	24	3	7	1	0	0	1	4	1	0
General Crowder, p	.333	1	3	1	1	0	0	0	0	0	0	0
Pete Fox, of	.385	6	26	1	10	3	1	0	4	0	1	0
Charlie Gehringer, 2b	.375	6	24	4	9	3	0	0	4	2	1	1
Goose Goslin, of	.273	6	22	2	6	1	0	0	3	5	0	0
Hank Greenberg, 1b	.167	2	6	1	1	0	0	1	2	1	0	0
Chief Hogsett, p	.000	1	0	0	0	0	0	0	0	0	0	0
Marv Owen, 1b-4,3b-2	.050	6	20	2	1	0	0	0	1	2	3	0
Billy Rogell, ss	.292	6	24	1	7	2	0	0	1	2	5	0
Schoolboy Rowe, p	.250	3	8	0	2	1	0	0	0	0	1	0
Gee Walker, of-1	.250	3	4	1	1	0	0	0	0	1	0	0
Jo-Jo White, of	.263	5	19	3	5	0	0	0	1	5	7	0
TOTAL	.248		206	21	51	11	1	1	18	25	27	1

PITCHER	W	L	ERA	G	GS	CG	SV	SHO	IP	H	ER	BB	SO
Eldon Auker	0	0	3.00	1	1	0	0	0	6.0	6	2	2	1
Tommy Bridges	2	0	2.50	2	2	2	0	0	18.0	18	5	4	9
General Crowder	1	0	1.00	1	1	1	0	0	9.0	5	1	3	5
Chief Hogsett	0	0	0.00	1	0	0	0	0	1.0	0	0	1	0
Schoolboy Rowe	1	2	2.57	3	2	2	0	0	21.0	19	6	1	14
TOTAL	4	2	2.29	8	6	5	0	0	55.0	48	14	11	29

CHI (N)

PLAYER/POS	AVG	G	AB	R	H	2B	3B	HR	RB	BB	SO	SB
Tex Carleton, p	.000	1	1	0	0	0	0	0	0	1	1	0
Phil Cavaretta, 1b	.125	6	24	1	3	0	0	0	0	0	5	0
Frank Demaree, of	.250	6	24	2	6	1	0	2	2	1	4	0
Larry French, p	.250	2	4	1	1	0	0	0	0	0	2	0
Augie Galan, of	.160	6	25	2	4	1	0	0	2	2	2	0
Stan Hack, 3b-6,ss-1	.227	6	22	2	5	1	1	0	0	2	2	1
Gabby Hartnett, c	.292	6	24	1	7	0	0	1	2	0	3	0
Roy Henshaw, p	.000	1	1	0	0	0	0	0	0	0	0	0
Billy Herman, 2b	.333	6	24	3	8	2	1	1	6	0	2	0
Billy Jurges, ss	.250	6	16	3	4	0	0	0	1	4	4	0
Chuck Klein, of-3	.333	5	12	2	4	0	0	1	2	0	2	0
Fabian Kowalik, p	.500	1	2	1	0	0	0	0	0	0	0	0
Bill Lee, p	.000	2	1	0	0	0	0	0	1	0	0	0
Fred Lindstrom, of-4,3b-1	.200	4	15	0	3	1	0	0	0	1	1	0
Ken O'Dea, ph	1.000	1	1	0	1	0	0	0	1	0	0	0
Charlie Root, p	.000	2	0	0	0	0	0	0	0	0	0	0
Walter Stephenson, ph	.000	1	1	0	0	0	0	0	0	0	1	0
Lon Warneke, p	.200	3	5	0	1	0	0	0	0	0	0	0
TOTAL	.238		202	18	48	6	2	5	17	11	29	1

PITCHER	W	L	ERA	G	GS	CG	SV	SHO	IP	H	ER	BB	SO
Tex Carleton	0	1	1.29	1	1	0	0	0	7.0	6	1	7	4
Larry French	0	2	3.38	2	1	1	0	0	10.2	15	4	2	8
Roy Henshaw	0	0	7.36	1	0	0	0	0	3.2	2	3	5	2
Fabian Kowalik	0	0	2.08	1	0	0	0	0	4.1	3	1	1	1
Bill Lee	0	0	3.48	2	1	0	1	0	10.1	11	4	5	5
Charlie Root	0	1	18.00	2	1	0	0	0	2.0	5	4	1	2
Lon Warneke	2	0	0.54	3	2	1	0	1	16.2	9	1	4	5
TOTAL	2	4	2.96	12	6	2	1	1	54.2	51	18	25	27

GAME 1 AT DET OCT 2

CHI	200	000	001	3	7	0
DET	000	000	000	0	4	3

Pitchers: WARNEKE vs ROWE
Home Runs: Demaree-CHI
Attendance: 47,391

GAME 2 AT DET OCT 3

CHI	000	010	200	3	6	1
DET	400	300	10X	8	9	2

Pitchers: ROOT, Henshaw (1), Kowalik (4) vs BRIDGES
Home Runs: Greenberg-DET
Attendance: 46,742

GAME 3 AT CHI OCT 4

DET	000	001	040 01	6	12	2
CHI	020	010	002 00	5	10	3

Pitchers: Auker, Hogsett (7), ROWE (8) vs Lee, Warneke (8), FRENCH (10)
Home Runs: Demaree-CHI
Attendance: 45,532

GAME 4 AT CHI OCT 5

DET	001	001	000	2	7	0
CHI	010	000	000	1	5	2

Pitchers: CROWDER vs CARLETON, Root (8)
Home Runs: Hartnett-CHI
Attendance: 49,350

GAME 5 AT CHI OCT 6

DET	000	000	001	1	7	1
CHI	002	000	10X	3	8	0

Pitchers: ROWE vs WARNEKE, Lee (7)
Home Runs: Klein-CHI
Attendance: 49,237

GAME 6 AT DET OCT 7

CHI	001	020	000	3	12	0
DET	100	101	001	4	12	1

Pitchers: FRENCH vs BRIDGES
Home Runs: Herman-CHI
Attendance: 48,420

The Giants managed to win two games, but this first Series between the cross-river rivals in thirteen years was really no contest. Babe Ruth was gone, but Lou Gehrig was still there, and Joe DiMaggio had arrived. The Yankees outhit the Giants by 56 percentage points and outscored them by 20 runs.

Giant ace Carl Hubbell, who had won his final 16 decisions of the regular season, continued his streak in the Series opener. The Yankees scored first on George Selkirk's third-inning homer, but Giant shortstop Dick Bartell homered to even things in the fifth. Hubbell held the Yankees to that one run, but the Giants roughed up Red Ruffing for five more runs, to give the Polo Grounders a brief Series advantage.

Game Two was a Yankee blowout, as the Yankees hammered five Giant pitchers for 18 runs—four of them on Tony Lazzeri's grand slam in the third—to give Lefty Gomez an easy win. By contrast, Game Three was a pitchers' duel. Although the Giants touched Bump Hadley and Pat Malone for 11 hits, only Jimmy Ripple's fifth-inning homer produced a run. Giant Freddie Fitzsimmons was much more stingy with hits, yielding only four. But one was Gehrig's home run in the second inning, and another was Frank Crosetti's game-winning RBI single in the eighth.

Gehrig homered again in the third inning of Game Four to give the Yankees an insurmountable lead—and Hubbell his first loss in months. Down three games to one, the Giants struggled back in Game Five. They took a first-inning 3–0 lead, but the Yankees clawed their way back, and by the end of six the score was 4–4. There it stayed until the tenth, when a double, sacrifice, and fly to center put the Giants ahead by a run. Hal Schumacher, who had pitched the whole game, held the Yankees scoreless one more time for the win.

Fitzsimmons, who had pitched so well in his third-game loss, didn't last four innings in Game Six. Though the Giants scored first, Yankee Jake Powell (who led all Series hitters at .455) tied the game with a two-run homer in the top of the second. Two more runs in the fourth drove out Fitzsimmons, but the game stayed close until the top of the ninth, when five Yankees singles and three walks produced seven runs and a Series-ending 13–5 rout.

New York Yankees (AL), 4;
New York Giants (NL), 2

NY (A)

PLAYER/POS	AVG	G	AB	R	H	2B	3B	HR	RB	BB	SO	SB
Frankie Crosetti, ss	.269	6	26	5	7	2	0	0	3	3	5	0
Bill Dickey, c	.120	6	25	5	3	0	0	1	5	3	4	0
Joe DiMaggio, of	.346	6	26	3	9	3	0	0	3	1	3	0
Lou Gehrig, 1b	.292	6	24	5	7	1	0	2	7	3	2	0
Lefty Gomez, p	.250	2	8	1	2	0	0	0	3	0	3	0
Bump Hadley, p	.000	1	2	0	0	0	0	0	0	0	1	0
Roy Johnson, ph	.000	2	1	0	0	0	0	0	0	0	1	0
Tony Lazzeri, 2b	.250	6	20	4	5	0	0	1	7	4	4	0
Pat Malone, p	1.000	2	1	0	1	0	0	0	0	0	0	0
Johnny Murphy, p	.500	1	2	1	1	0	0	0	0	1	0	0
Monte Pearson, p	.500	1	4	0	2	1	0	0	0	0	0	0
Jake Powell, of	.455	6	22	8	10	1	0	1	5	4	4	1
Red Rolfe, 3b	.400	6	25	5	10	0	0	0	4	3	1	0
Red Ruffing, p-2	.000	3	5	0	0	0	0	0	0	1	2	0
Bob Seeds, pr	.000	1	0	0	0	0	0	0	0	0	0	0
George Selkirk, of	.333	6	24	6	8	0	1	2	3	4	4	0
TOTAL	.302		215	43	65	8	1	7	41	26	35	1

PITCHER	W	L	ERA	G	GS	CG	SV	SHO	IP	H	ER	BB	SO
Lefty Gomez	2	0	4.70	2	2	1	0	0	15.1	14	8	11	9
Bump Hadley	1	0	1.13	1	1	0	0	0	8.0	10	1	1	2
Pat Malone	0	1	1.80	2	0	0	1	0	5.0	2	1	1	2
Johnny Murphy	0	0	3.38	1	0	0	0	0	2.2	1	1	1	1
Monte Pearson	1	0	2.00	1	1	1	0	0	9.0	7	2	2	7
Red Ruffing	0	1	4.50	2	2	1	0	0	14.0	16	7	5	12
TOTAL	4	2	3.33	9	6	3	2	0	54.0	50	20	21	33

NY (N)

PLAYER/POS	AVG	G	AB	R	H	2B	3B	HR	RB	BB	SO	SB
Dick Bartell, ss	.381	6	21	5	8	3	0	1	3	4	4	0
Slick Castleman, p	.500	1	2	0	1	0	0	0	0	0	0	0
Dick Coffman, p	.000	2	0	0	0	0	0	0	0	0	0	0
Harry Danning, c-1	.000	2	2	0	0	0	0	0	0	0	1	0
Kiddo Davis, ph	.500	4	2	2	1	0	0	0	0	0	0	0
Freddie Fitzsimmons, p	.500	2	4	0	2	0	0	0	0	0	1	0
Frank Gabler, p	.000	2	0	0	0	0	0	0	0	1	0	0
Harry Gumbert, p	.000	2	0	0	0	0	0	0	0	0	0	0
Carl Hubbell, p	.333	2	6	0	2	0	0	0	1	0	0	0
Travis Jackson, 3b	.190	6	21	1	4	0	0	0	1	1	3	0
Mark Koenig, 2b-1	.333	3	3	0	1	0	0	0	0	0	1	0
Hank Leiber, of	.000	2	6	0	0	0	0	0	0	2	2	0
Sam Leslie, ph	.667	3	3	0	2	0	0	0	0	0	0	0
Gus Mancuso, c	.263	6	19	3	5	2	0	0	1	3	3	0
Eddie Mayo, 3b	.000	1	1	0	0	0	0	0	0	0	0	0
Jo-Jo Moore, of	.214	6	28	4	6	2	0	1	1	1	4	0
Mel Ott, of	.304	6	23	4	7	2	0	1	3	3	1	0
Jimmy Ripple, of	.333	5	12	2	4	0	0	1	3	3	3	0
Hal Schumacher, p	.000	2	4	0	0	0	0	0	0	1	3	0
Al Smith, p	.000	1	0	0	0	0	0	0	0	0	0	0
Bill Terry, 1b	.240	6	25	1	6	0	0	0	5	1	4	0
Burgess Whitehead, 2b	.048	6	21	1	1	0	0	0	2	1	3	0
TOTAL	.246		203	23	50	9	0	4	20	21	33	0

PITCHER	W	L	ERA	G	GS	CG	SV	SHO	IP	H	ER	BB	SO
Slick Castleman	0	0	2.08	1	0	0	0	0	4.1	3	1	2	5
Dick Coffman	0	0	32.40	2	0	0	0	0	1.2	5	6	1	1
Freddie Fitzsimmons	0	2	5.40	2	2	1	0	0	11.2	13	7	2	6
Frank Gabler	0	0	7.20	2	0	0	0	0	5.0	7	4	4	0
Harry Gumbert	0	0	36.00	2	0	0	0	0	2.0	7	8	4	2
Carl Hubbell	1	1	2.25	2	2	1	0	0	16.0	15	4	2	10
Hal Schumacher	1	1	5.25	2	2	1	0	0	12.0	13	7	10	11
Al Smith	0	0	81.00	1	0	0	0	0	0.1	3	3	1	0
TOTAL	2	4	6.79	14	6	3	0	0	53.0	65	40	26	35

GAME 1 AT NY -N SEPT 30

```
NY-A   001 000 000    1  7  2
NY-N   000 011 04X    6  9  1
```
Pitchers: RUFFING vs HUBBELL
Home Runs: Bartell-NY(N), Selkirk-NY(A)
Attendance: 39,419

GAME 2 AT NY -N OCT 2

```
NY-A   207 001 206   18 17  0
NY-N   010 300 000    4  6  1
```
Pitchers: GOMEZ vs SCHUMACHER, Smith (3), Coffman (3), Gabler (5), Gumbert (9)
Home Runs: Dickey-NY(A), Lazzeri-NY(A)
Attendance: 43,543

GAME 3 AT NY -A OCT 3

```
NY-N   000 010 000    1 11  0
NY-A   010 000 01X    2  4  0
```
Pitchers: FITZSIMMONS vs HADLEY, Malone (9)
Home Runs: Gerhig-NY(A), Ripple-NY(N)
Attendance: 64,842

GAME 4 AT NY -A OCT 4

```
NY-N   000 100 010    2  7  1
NY-A   013 000 01X    5 10  1
```
Pitchers: HUBBELL, Gabler (8) vs PEARSON
Home Runs: Gehrig-NY(A)
Attendance: 66,669

GAME 5 AT NY -A OCT 5

```
NY-N   300 001 000 1    5  8  3
NY-A   011 002 000 0    4 10  1
```
Pitchers: SCHUMACHER vs Ruffing, MALONE (7)
Home Runs: Selkirk-NY(A)
Attendance: 50,024

GAME 6 AT NY -N OCT 6

```
NY-A   021 200 017   13 17  2
NY-N   200 010 110    5  9  1
```
Pitchers: GOMEZ, Murphy (7) vs FITZSIMMONS, Castleman (4), Coffman (9), Gumbert (9)
Home Runs: Moore-NY(N), Ott-NY(N), Powell-NY(A)
Attendance: 38,427

For the second year in a row, the Yankees overwhelmed the Giants, this time in just five games. Giant ace Carl Hubbell, who took the opener in 1936, was unable to repeat this year. For five innings he held the Yankees to one hit. But in the sixth everything fell apart. Before Hubbell was taken out, two walks, five singles, and a Giant error had let in five runs. And the two runners Hubbell left on base scored later on a second Giant error and two walks by reliever Dick Coffman. The Yankees' Lefty Gomez also yielded six hits, but wider spacing and better field support held the Giants to one run in the fifth. Tony Lazzeri's homer in the eighth made the final score 8–1.

The Yankees spread their runs a bit more evenly in Game Two. For the second time the Giants gained a 1–0 lead. Rookie phenom Cliff Melton held the Yankees scoreless through four, but four straight hits for two runs at the start of the fifth drove him out. Reliever Ad Gumbert stopped the Yankees in the rest of the inning but gave up four more hits—and four more runs—in the sixth before Coffman stepped in to stop the assault. But Coffman gave up two final Yankee runs in the seventh, to complete a second straight 8–1 Yankee win, as Red Ruffing held the Giants scoreless through the final eight innings.

The Yankees had scored five times off Hal Schumacher in Game Three before the Giants got their one run in the seventh. But Yankee starter Monte Pearson made the game tighter as he yielded a single and two walks to load the bases in the ninth before Johnny Murphy came on to record the final out.

Giant bats finally came alive in the second inning of Game Four. Seven singles, plus a walk and a missed play at the plate gave the club a 6–1 lead, which starter Hubbell protected for the only Giant win of the Series.

Solo homers by Myril Hoag in the second and Joe DiMaggio in the third gave the Yankees a 2–0 lead early in Game Five, but Giant Mel Ott tied it up with a two-run shot off Lefty Gomez in the last of the third. But Gomez shut the Giants down the rest of the way, and singled in Lazzeri in the fifth with what proved the game winner (scoring himself on Lou Gehrig's double for the final run of the Series).

New York Yankees (AL), 4;
New York Giants (NL), 1

NY (A)

PLAYER/POS	AVG	G	AB	R	H	2B	3B	HR	RB	BB	SO	SB
Ivy Andrews, p	.000	1	2	0	0	0	0	0	0	0	1	0
Frankie Crosetti, ss	.048	5	21	2	1	0	0	0	0	3	2	0
Bill Dickey, c	.211	5	19	3	4	0	1	0	3	2	2	0
Joe DiMaggio, of	.273	5	22	2	6	0	0	1	4	0	3	0
Lou Gehrig, 1b	.294	5	17	4	5	1	1	1	3	5	4	0
Lefty Gomez, p	.167	2	6	2	1	0	0	0	1	2	1	0
Bump Hadley, p	.000	1	0	0	0	0	0	0	0	0	0	0
Myril Hoag, of	.300	5	20	4	6	1	0	1	2	0	1	0
Tony Lazzeri, 2b	.400	5	15	3	6	0	1	1	2	3	3	0
Johnny Murphy, p	.000	1	0	0	0	0	0	0	0	0	0	0
Monte Pearson, p	.000	1	3	0	0	0	0	0	0	1	1	0
Jake Powell, ph	.000	1	1	0	0	0	0	0	0	0	0	0
Red Rolfe, 3b	.300	5	20	3	6	2	1	0	1	3	2	0
Red Ruffing, p	.500	1	4	0	2	1	0	0	3	0	0	0
George Selkirk, of	.263	5	19	5	5	1	0	0	6	2	0	0
Kemp Wicker, p	.000	1	0	0	0	0	0	0	0	0	0	0
TOTAL	.249		169	28	42	6	4	4	25	21	21	0

PITCHER	W	L	ERA	G	GS	CG	SV	SHO	IP	H	ER	BB	SO
Ivy Andrews	0	0	3.18	1	0	0	0	0	5.2	6	2	4	1
Lefty Gomez	2	0	1.50	2	2	2	0	0	18.0	16	3	2	8
Bump Hadley	0	1	33.75	1	1	0	0	0	1.1	6	5	0	0
Johnny Murphy	0	0	0.00	1	0	0	1	0	0.1	0	0	0	0
Monte Pearson	1	0	1.04	1	1	0	0	0	8.2	5	1	2	4
Red Ruffing	1	0	1.00	1	1	1	0	0	9.0	7	1	3	8
Kemp Wicker	0	0	0.00	1	0	0	0	0	1.0	0	0	0	0
TOTAL	4	1	2.45	8	5	3	1	0	44.0	40	12	11	21

NY (N)

PLAYER/POS	AVG	G	AB	R	H	2B	3B	HR	RB	BB	SO	SB
Dick Bartell, ss	.238	5	21	3	5	1	0	0	1	0	3	0
Wally Berger, ph	.000	3	3	0	0	0	0	0	0	0	1	0
Don Brennan, p	.000	2	0	0	0	0	0	0	0	0	0	0
Lou Chiozza, of	.286	2	7	0	2	0	0	0	0	1	1	0
Dick Coffman, p	.000	2	1	0	0	0	0	0	0	0	1	0
Harry Danning, c	.250	3	12	0	3	1	0	0	2	0	2	0
Harry Gumbert, p	.000	2	0	0	0	0	0	0	0	0	0	0
Carl Hubbell, p	.000	2	6	1	0	0	0	0	1	0	0	0
Hank Leiber, of	.364	3	11	2	4	0	0	0	2	1	1	0
Sam Leslie, ph	.000	2	1	0	0	0	0	0	0	1	0	0
Gus Mancuso, c-2	.000	3	8	0	0	0	0	0	0	1	0	1
Johnny McCarthy, 1b	.211	5	19	1	4	1	0	0	1	1	2	0
Cliff Melton, p	.000	3	2	0	0	0	0	0	0	0	1	0
Jo-Jo Moore, of	.391	5	23	1	9	1	0	0	1	0	1	0
Mel Ott, 3b	.200	5	20	1	4	0	0	1	3	1	4	0
Jimmy Ripple, of	.294	5	17	2	5	0	0	0	0	3	1	0
Blondy Ryan, ph	.000	1	1	0	0	0	0	0	0	0	1	0
Hal Schumacher, p	.000	1	1	0	0	0	0	0	0	0	1	0
Al Smith, p	.000	2	0	0	0	0	0	0	0	0	0	0
Burgess Whitehead, 2b	.250	5	16	1	4	2	0	0	0	2	0	1
TOTAL	.237		169	12	40	6	0	1	12	11	21	1

PITCHER	W	L	ERA	G	GS	CG	SV	SHO	IP	H	ER	BB	SO
Don Brennan	0	0	0.00	2	0	0	0	0	3.0	1	0	1	1
Dick Coffman	0	0	4.15	2	0	0	0	0	4.1	2	2	5	1
Harry Gumbert	0	0	27.00	2	0	0	0	0	1.1	4	4	1	1
Carl Hubbell	1	1	3.77	2	2	1	0	0	14.1	12	6	4	7
Cliff Melton	0	2	4.91	3	2	0	0	0	11.0	12	6	6	7
Hal Schumacher	0	1	6.00	1	1	0	0	0	6.0	9	4	4	3
Al Smith	0	0	3.00	2	0	0	0	0	3.0	2	1	0	1
TOTAL	1	4	4.81	14	5	1	0	0	43.0	42	23	21	21

GAME 1 AT NY -A OCT 6

NY-N	000	010	000	1	6	2
NY-A	000	007	01X	8	7	0

Pitchers: HUBBELL, Gumbert (6), Coffman (6), Smith (8) vs GOMEZ
Home Runs: Lazzeri-NY(A)
Attendance: 60,573

GAME 2 AT NY -A OCT 7

NY-N	100	000	000	1	7	0
NY-A	000	024	20X	8	12	0

Pitchers: MELTON, Gumbert (5), Coffman (6) vs RUFFING
Attendance: 57,675

GAME 3 AT NY -N OCT 8

NY-A	012	110	000	5	9	0
NY-N	000	000	100	1	5	4

Pitchers: PEARSON, Murphy (9) vs SCHUMACHER, Melton (7), Brennan (9)
Attendance: 37,385

GAME 4 AT NY -N OCT 9

NY-A	101	000	001	3	6	0
NY-N	060	000	10X	7	12	3

Pitchers: HADLEY, Andrews (2), Wicker (8) vs HUBBELL
Home Runs: Gehrig-NY(A)
Attendance: 44,293

GAME 5 AT NY -N OCT 10

NY-A	011	020	000	4	8	0
NY-N	002	000	000	2	10	0

Pitchers: GOMEZ vs MELTON, Smith (6), Brennan (8)
Home Runs: DiMaggio-NY(A), Hoag-NY(A), Ott-NY(N)
Attendance: 38,216

As they had six years earlier, the Cubs faced the Yankees in the World Series, and as they had six years earlier, New York swept the Series in four games. Although Cub batters made nearly as many hits as the Yankees, they did much less damage, driving in 13 fewer runs. In Game One, Yankee ace Red Ruffing scattered nine Cub hits, holding Chicago to a single run. The Cubs' Bill Lee was nearly as effective in scattering hits, but a base on balls in the second (the game's only walk) followed by a pair of singles sandwiched around an error accounted for two runs— all the Yankees would need for the win (though they scored once more in the sixth).

In Game Two the Cubs outhit the Yankees 11 to 7, but scored only half as many runs as the New Yorkers. Chicago's Dizzy Dean, pitching on craft and guile with his fastball gone, managed to keep the game close until the final innings. With a 3–2 lead going into the eighth, though, he gave up a two-run homer to Frank Crosetti, and the same to Joe DiMaggio in the ninth before being relieved. Yankee fireman Johnny Murphy, meanwhile, held Chicago scoreless over the final two innings to preserve Lefty Gomez's win.

Utility outfielder Joe Marty drove in both Chicago runs in Game Three with a grounder to third in the fifth and a homer in the eighth. (His .500 BA was tops for both teams, and he drove in five of the Cubs' nine Series runs.) But again the Cubs fell short, as Yankee rookie second baseman Joe Gordon homered to tie the score in the bottom of the fifth with the first of what would be five Yankee runs by the time Bill Dickey's homer in the eighth ended the scoring for the day.

Cub second baseman Billy Herman's wild throw with two out in the second inning of Game Four led to three unearned runs, and a Yankee lead they would not relinquish. Though their lead was cut to one run (4–3) when Chicago scored twice in the top of the eighth, the Yankees took advantage of two wild pitches and two walks to turn their four hits into four runs that crushed Cub hopes and gave the New Yorkers a record third consecutive world championship.

New York Yankees (AL), 4; Chicago Cubs (NL), 0

NY (A)

PLAYER/POS	AVG	G	AB	R	H	2B	3B	HR	RB	BB	SO	SB
Frankie Crosetti, ss	.250	4	16	1	4	2	1	1	6	2	4	0
Bill Dickey, c	.400	4	15	2	6	0	0	1	2	1	0	1
Joe DiMaggio, of	.267	4	15	4	4	0	0	1	2	1	1	0
Lou Gehrig, 1b	.286	4	14	4	4	0	0	0	0	2	3	0
Lefty Gomez, p	.000	1	2	0	0	0	0	0	0	0	0	0
Joe Gordon, 2b	.400	4	15	3	6	2	0	1	6	1	3	1
Tommy Henrich, of	.250	4	16	3	4	1	0	1	1	0	1	0
Myril Hoag, of-1	.400	2	5	3	2	1	0	0	1	0	0	0
Johnny Murphy, p	.000	1	0	0	0	0	0	0	0	0	0	0
Monte Pearson, p	.333	1	3	1	1	0	0	0	0	1	0	0
Jake Powell, of	.000	1	0	0	0	0	0	0	0	0	0	0
Red Rolfe, 3b	.167	4	18	0	3	0	0	0	1	0	3	1
Red Ruffing, p	.167	2	6	1	1	0	0	0	1	1	0	0
George Selkirk, of	.200	3	10	0	2	0	0	0	1	2	1	0
TOTAL	.274		135	22	37	6	1	5	21	11	16	3

PITCHER	W	L	ERA	G	GS	CG	SV	SHO	IP	H	ER	BB	SO
Lefty Gomez	1	0	3.86	1	1	0	0	0	7.0	9	3	1	5
Johnny Murphy	0	0	0.00	1	0	0	1	0	2.0	2	0	1	1
Monte Pearson	1	0	1.00	1	1	1	0	0	9.0	5	1	2	9
Red Ruffing	2	0	1.50	2	2	2	0	0	18.0	17	3	2	11
TOTAL	4	0	1.75	5	4	3	1	0	36.0	33	7	6	26

CHI (N)

PLAYER/POS	AVG	G	AB	R	H	2B	3B	HR	RB	BB	SO	SB
Clay Bryant, p	.000	1	2	0	0	0	0	0	0	0	1	0
Tex Carleton, p	.000	1	0	0	0	0	0	0	0	0	0	0
Phil Cavaretta, of-3	.462	4	13	1	6	1	0	0	0	0	1	0
Ripper Collins, 1b	.133	4	15	1	2	0	0	0	0	0	3	0
Dizzy Dean, p	.667	2	3	0	2	0	0	0	0	0	0	0
Frank Demaree, of	.100	3	10	1	1	0	0	0	0	1	2	0
Larry French, p	.000	3	0	0	0	0	0	0	0	0	0	0
Augie Galan, ph	.000	2	2	0	0	0	0	0	0	0	1	0
Stan Hack, 3b	.471	4	17	3	8	1	0	0	1	1	2	0
Gabby Hartnett, c	.091	3	11	0	1	0	1	0	0	0	2	0
Billy Herman, 2b	.188	4	16	1	3	0	0	0	0	1	4	0
Billy Jurges, ss	.231	4	13	0	3	1	0	0	0	1	3	0
Tony Lazzeri, ph	.000	2	2	0	0	0	0	0	0	0	1	0
Bill Lee, p	.000	2	3	0	0	0	0	0	0	0	0	0
Joe Marty, of	.500	3	12	1	6	1	0	1	5	0	2	0
Ken O'Dea, c-1	.200	3	5	1	1	0	0	1	2	1	0	0
Vance Page, p	.000	1	0	0	0	0	0	0	0	0	0	0
Carl Reynolds, of-3	.000	4	12	0	0	0	0	0	0	0	3	0
Charlie Root, p	.000	1	0	0	0	0	0	0	0	0	0	0
Jack Russell, p	.000	2	0	0	0	0	0	0	0	0	0	0
TOTAL	.243		136	9	33	4	1	2	8	6	26	0

PITCHER	W	L	ERA	G	GS	CG	SV	SHO	IP	H	ER	BB	SO
Clay Bryant	0	1	6.75	1	1	0	0	0	5.1	6	4	5	3
Tex Carleton	0	0	∞	1	0	0	0	0	0.0	1	2	2	0
Dizzy Dean	0	1	6.48	2	1	0	0	0	8.1	8	6	1	2
Larry French	0	0	2.70	3	0	0	0	0	3.1	1	1	1	2
Bill Lee	0	2	2.45	2	2	0	0	0	11.0	15	3	1	8
Vance Page	0	0	13.50	1	0	0	0	0	1.1	2	2	0	0
Charlie Root	0	0	3.00	1	0	0	0	0	3.0	3	1	0	0
Jack Russell	0	0	0.00	2	0	0	0	0	1.2	1	0	1	0
TOTAL	0	4	5.03	13	4	0	0	0	34.0	37	19	11	16

GAME 1 AT CHI OCT 5

NY	020	000	100	3	12 1
CHI	001	000	000	1	9 1

Pitchers: RUFFING vs LEE, Russell (9)
Attendance: 43,642

GAME 2 AT CHI OCT 6

NY	020	000	022	6	7 2
CHI	102	000	000	3	11 0

Pitchers: GOMEZ, Murphy (8) vs
  J.DEAN, French (9)
Home Runs: Crosetti-NY,
  DiMaggio-NY
Attendance: 42,108

GAME 3 AT NY OCT 8

CHI	000	010	010	2	5 1
NY	000	022	01X	5	7 2

Pitchers: BRYANT, Russell (6),
  French (7) vs PEARSON
Home Runs: Dickey-NY, Gordon-NY,
  Marty-CHI
Attendance: 55,236

GAME 4 AT NY OCT 9

CHI	000	100	020	3	8 1
NY	030	001	04X	8	11 1

Pitchers: LEE, Root (4), Page (7),
  French (8), Carleton (8), J.Dean (8) vs
  RUFFING
Home Runs: Henrich-NY, O'Dea-CHI
Attendance: 59,847

The Yankees won their fourth consecutive World Series with their second sweep in a row. This time the victim was Cincinnati, in the Series for the first time since their tainted triumph over the Black Sox two decades earlier. New York had lost the power of Lou Gehrig (whose illness forced his retirement early in the season), but in the Series rookie outfielder Charlie Keller took up the slack. He led both clubs in batting, slugging, home runs, RBI, hits, and runs, and hit one of the Series' two triples. His eight runs scored equalled those of the whole Cincinnati team.

The Yankees' Red Ruffing and Cincinnati's Paul Derringer hurled matching four-hitters through eight innings of Game One. With the score tied 1–1, Ruffing set the Reds down in order in the ninth. But in the bottom of the ninth Keller tripled off Derringer with one away, and scored the deciding run on catcher Bill Dickey's single.

Babe Dahlgren, Gehrig's replacement at first base, doubled in the third and later scored the Yankees' first run in Game Two, and homered in the next inning for New York's fourth and final run of the game. Red starter Bucky Walters stopped the Yankees after that, but they had more than enough runs for the win, as Monte Pearson held the Reds hitless through seven and wound up with a two-hit shutout.

Keller provided the margin of victory with a pair of two-run homers in the first and fifth innings of Game Three. Joe DiMaggio's two-run homer in the third and Bill Dickey's solo shot that followed Keller's homer in the fifth accounted for the rest of New York's runs in their 7–3 win.

No one scored through six innings of Game Four. Keller and Dickey then homered in the top of the seventh, but Red Rolfe's error at third in the last of the inning opened the way for the Reds to go ahead with three unearned runs. They earned a fourth run an inning later, but the Yankees tied it up with two in the ninth (one unearned) and took the lead in the tenth with three more runs (two unearned) on a walk, a single, and three more Red errors. Reliever Johnny Murphy held off a Red threat in the last of the tenth and the Series was over.

New York Yankees (AL), 4; Cincinnati Reds (NL), 0

NY (A)

PLAYER/POS	AVG	G	AB	R	H	2B	3B	HR	RB	BB	SO	SB
Frankie Crosetti, ss	.063	4	16	2	1	0	0	0	1	2	2	0
Babe Dahlgren, 1b	.214	4	14	2	3	2	0	1	2	0	4	0
Bill Dickey, c	.267	4	15	2	4	0	0	2	5	1	2	0
Joe DiMaggio, of	.313	4	16	3	5	0	0	1	3	1	1	0
Lefty Gomez, p	.000	1	0	0	0	0	0	0	0	0	1	0
Joe Gordon, 2b	.143	4	14	1	2	0	0	0	1	0	2	0
Bump Hadley, p	.000	1	3	0	0	0	0	0	0	0	0	0
Oral Hildebrand, p	.000	1	0	0	0	0	0	0	0	0	1	0
Charlie Keller, of	.438	4	16	8	7	1	1	3	6	1	2	0
Johnny Murphy, p	.000	1	2	0	0	0	0	0	0	0	0	0
Monte Pearson, p	.000	1	2	0	0	0	0	0	0	0	1	0
Red Rolfe, 3b	.125	4	16	2	2	0	0	0	0	0	0	0
Red Ruffing, p	.333	1	3	0	1	0	0	0	0	0	1	0
George Selkirk, of	.167	4	12	0	2	1	0	0	0	3	2	0
TOTAL	.206		131	20	27	4	1	7	18	9	20	0

PITCHER	W	L	ERA	G	GS	CG	SV	SHO	IP	H	ER	BB	SO
Lefty Gomez	0	0	9.00	1	1	0	0	0	1.0	3	1	0	1
Bump Hadley	1	0	2.25	1	0	0	0	0	8.0	7	2	3	2
Oral Hildebrand	0	0	0.00	1	1	0	0	0	4.0	2	0	0	3
Johnny Murphy	1	0	2.70	1	0	0	0	0	3.1	5	1	0	2
Monte Pearson	1	0	0.00	1	1	1	0	1	9.0	2	0	1	8
Red Ruffing	1	0	1.00	1	1	1	0	0	9.0	4	1	1	4
Steve Sundra	0	0	0.00	1	0	0	0	0	2.2	4	0	1	2
TOTAL	4	0	1.22	7	4	2	0	1	37.0	27	5	6	22

CIN (N)

PLAYER/POS	AVG	G	AB	R	H	2B	3B	HR	RB	BB	SO	SB
Wally Berger, of	.000	4	15	0	0	0	0	0	1	0	4	0
Nino Bongiovanni, ph	.000	1	1	0	0	0	0	0	0	0	0	0
Frenchy Bordagaray, pr	.000	2	0	0	0	0	0	0	0	0	0	0
Harry Craft, of	.091	4	11	0	1	0	0	0	0	0	6	0
Paul Derringer, p	.200	2	5	0	1	0	0	0	0	0	0	0
Lonny Frey, 2b	.000	4	17	0	0	0	0	0	0	1	4	0
Lee Gamble, ph	.000	1	1	0	0	0	0	0	0	0	1	0
Ival Goodman, of	.333	4	15	3	5	1	0	0	1	1	2	1
Lee Grissom, p	.000	1	0	0	0	0	0	0	0	0	0	0
Willard Hershberger, c-2	.500	3	2	0	1	0	0	0	0	0	0	0
Ernie Lombardi, c	.214	4	14	0	3	0	0	0	2	0	1	0
Frank McCormick, 1b	.400	4	15	1	6	1	0	0	1	0	1	0
Whitey Moore, p	.000	1	1	0	0	0	0	0	0	0	0	0
Billy Myers, ss	.333	4	12	2	4	0	1	0	0	2	3	0
Al Simmons, of	.250	1	4	1	1	1	0	0	0	0	0	0
Junior Thompson, p	1.000	1	1	0	1	0	0	0	0	0	0	0
Bucky Walters, p	.000	2	3	0	0	0	0	0	0	0	0	0
Billy Werber, 3b	.250	4	16	1	4	0	0	0	2	2	0	0
TOTAL	.203		133	8	27	3	1	0	8	6	22	1

PITCHER	W	L	ERA	G	GS	CG	SV	SHO	IP	H	ER	BB	SO
Paul Derringer	0	1	2.35	2	2	1	0	0	15.1	9	4	3	9
Lee Grissom	0	0	0.00	1	0	0	0	0	1.1	0	0	1	0
Whitey Moore	0	0	0.00	1	0	0	0	0	3.0	0	0	0	2
Junior Thompson	0	1	13.50	1	1	0	0	0	4.2	5	7	4	3
Bucky Walters	0	2	4.91	2	1	1	0	0	11.0	13	6	1	6
TOTAL	0	4	4.33	7	4	2	0	0	35.1	27	17	9	20

GAME 1 AT NY OCT 4

CIN	000 100 000	1	4	0
NY	000 010 001	2	6	0

Pitchers: DERRINGER vs RUFFING
Attendance: 58,541

GAME 2 AT NY OCT 5

CIN	000 000 000	0	2	0
NY	003 100 00X	4	9	0

Pitchers: WALTERS vs PEARSON
Home Runs: Dalhgren-NY
Attendance: 59,791

GAME 3 AT CIN OCT 7

NY	202 030 000	7	5	1
CIN	120 000 000	3	10	0

Pitchers: Gomez, HADLEY (2) vs
  THOMPSON, Grissom (5), Moore (7)
Home Runs: Keller-NY (2),
  DiMaggio-NY, Dickey-NY
Attendance: 32,723

GAME 4 AT CIN OCT 8

NY	000 000 202 3	7	7	1
CIN	000 000 310 0	4	11	4

Pitchers: Hildebrand, Sundra (5),
  MURPHY (7) vs Derringer,
  WALTERS (8)
Home Runs: Keller-NY, Dickey-NY
Attendance: 32,794

The Tigers outpitched and out-slugged the Reds, and scored six more runs than the Reds did. What they failed to do was win the Series.

Tiger ace Bobo Newsom, who had enjoyed what would be his finest season in a long career, carried his mastery into the Series opener. Detroit gave him an early lead, driving out Red starter Paul Derringer with five runs in the second inning, and added a pair of runs in the fifth on Bruce Campbell's home run. Newsom, meanwhile, held the Reds to single runs in the fourth and eighth.

Cincinnati's Bucky Walters walked the first two Tigers he faced in Game Two, and both scored. But two Red runs in the second tied the game, Jimmy Ripple's two-run homer an inning later gave them the lead, and pitcher Walters scored an insurance run in the fourth after doubling. Another Tiger walk in the sixth led to their third run, but Walters retired the remaining Tigers in order.

The Series moved to Detroit and the lead to the Tigers in Game Three. Detroit's Rocky Bridges yielded ten hits and four runs, but his teammates responded with 13 hits and seven runs, including a pair of two-run homers by Rudy York and Pinky Higgins in the seventh. Cincinnati again evened the Series the next day, though, with five runs to support Derringer's five-hit, two-run pitching. Although Newsom's father had suffered a fatal heart attack the day after seeing his son win the opener, the son pitched Game Five, and improved on his previous performance with a three-hit shutout. Hank Greenberg's homer in the third inning accounted for the first three of the Tigers' eight runs in their lopsided win.

The Reds returned home needing to win the final two games. Like Newsom, Bucky Walters bettered his earlier win with a shutout in Game Six, and drove in two of the Reds' four runs, one with a solo homer in the eighth. In the Series finale, Newsom and Derringer found themselves evenly matched. The Tigers scored a run in the third, while Newsom held Cincinnati scoreless through six. But in the seventh, leadoff doubles by Frank McCormick and Jimmy Ripple, plus a successful bunt and a fly to deep center, gave the Reds two runs—all they needed as Derringer stopped the Tigers through the final six innings for the victory.

Cincinnati Reds (NL), 4; Detroit Tigers (AL), 3

CIN (N)

PLAYER/POS	AVG	G	AB	R	H	2B	3B	HR	RB	BB	SO	SB
Morrie Arnovich, of	.000	1	1	0	0	0	0	0	0	0	0	0
Bill Baker, c	.250	3	4	1	1	0	0	0	0	0	1	0
Joe Beggs, p	.000	1	0	0	0	0	0	0	0	0	0	0
Harry Craft, ph	.000	1	1	0	0	0	0	0	0	0	0	0
Paul Derringer, p	.000	3	7	0	0	0	0	0	0	0	1	0
Lonny Frey, ph	.000	3	2	0	0	0	0	0	0	0	0	0
Ival Goodman, of	.276	7	29	5	8	2	0	0	5	0	3	0
Johnny Hutchings, p	.000	1	0	0	0	0	0	0	0	0	0	0
Eddie Joost, 2b	.200	7	25	0	5	0	0	0	2	1	2	0
Ernie Lombardi, c-1	.333	2	3	0	1	1	0	0	0	1	0	0
Frank McCormick, 1b	.214	7	28	2	6	1	0	0	0	1	1	0
Mike McCormick, of	.310	7	29	1	9	3	0	0	2	1	6	0
Whitey Moore, p	.000	3	2	0	0	0	0	0	0	0	1	0
Billy Myers, ss	.130	7	23	0	3	0	0	0	2	2	5	0
Elmer Riddle, p	.000	1	0	0	0	0	0	0	0	0	0	0
Lew Riggs, ph	.000	3	3	1	0	0	0	0	0	0	2	0
Jimmy Ripple, of	.333	7	21	3	7	2	0	1	6	4	2	0
Junior Thompson, p	.000	1	1	0	0	0	0	0	0	0	1	0
Jim Turner, p	.000	1	2	0	0	0	0	0	0	0	0	0
Johnny Vander Meer, p	.000	1	0	0	0	0	0	0	0	0	0	0
Bucky Walters, p	.286	2	7	2	2	1	0	1	2	0	1	0
Billy Werber, 3b	.370	7	27	5	10	4	0	0	2	4	2	0
Jimmie Wilson, c	.353	6	17	2	6	0	0	0	0	1	2	1
TOTAL	.250		232	22	58	14	0	2	21	15	30	1

PITCHER	W	L	ERA	G	GS	CG	SV	SHO	IP	H	ER	BB	SO
Joe Beggs	0	0	9.00	1	0	0	0	0	1.0	3	1	0	1
Paul Derringer	2	1	2.79	3	3	2	0	0	19.1	17	6	10	6
Johnny Hutchings	0	0	9.00	1	0	0	0	0	1.0	2	1	1	0
Whitey Moore	0	0	3.24	3	0	0	0	0	8.1	8	3	6	7
Elmer Riddle	0	0	0.00	1	0	0	0	0	1.0	0	0	2	0
Junior Thompson	0	1	16.20	1	1	0	0	0	3.1	8	6	4	2
Jim Turner	0	1	7.50	1	1	0	0	0	6.0	8	5	0	4
Johnny Vander Meer	0	0	0.00	1	0	0	0	0	3.0	2	0	3	2
Bucky Walters	2	0	1.50	2	2	2	0	1	18.0	8	3	6	6
TOTAL	4	3	3.69	14	7	4	0	1	61.0	56	25	30	30

DET (A)

PLAYER/POS	AVG	G	AB	R	H	2B	3B	HR	RB	BB	SO	SB
Earl Averill, ph	.000	3	3	0	0	0	0	0	0	0	0	0
Dick Bartell, ss	.269	7	26	2	7	2	0	0	3	3	3	0
Tommy Bridges, p	.000	1	3	0	0	0	0	0	0	0	1	0
Bruce Campbell, of	.360	7	25	4	9	1	0	1	5	4	4	0
Frank Croucher, ss	.000	1	0	0	0	0	0	0	0	0	0	0
Pete Fox, ph	.000	1	1	0	0	0	0	0	0	0	0	0
Charlie Gehringer, 2b	.214	7	28	3	6	0	0	0	1	2	0	0
Johnny Gorsica, p	.000	2	4	0	0	0	0	0	0	0	2	0
Hank Greenberg, of	.357	7	28	5	10	2	1	1	6	2	5	0
Pinky Higgins, 3b	.333	7	24	2	8	3	1	1	6	3	3	0
Fred Hutchinson, p	.000	1	0	0	0	0	0	0	0	0	0	0
Barney McCosky, of	.304	7	23	5	7	1	0	0	1	7	0	0
Archie McKain, p	.000	1	0	0	0	0	0	0	0	0	0	0
Bobo Newsom, p	.100	3	10	1	1	0	0	0	0	0	1	0
Schoolboy Rowe, p	.000	2	1	0	0	0	0	0	0	0	1	0
Clay Smith, p	.000	1	1	0	0	0	0	0	0	0	1	0
Billy Sullivan, c-4	.154	5	13	3	2	0	0	0	0	5	2	0
Birdie Tebbetts, c-3	.000	4	11	0	0	0	0	0	0	0	0	0
Dizzy Trout, p	.000	1	1	0	0	0	0	0	0	0	0	0
Rudy York, 1b	.231	7	26	3	6	0	1	1	2	4	7	0
TOTAL	.246		228	28	56	9	3	4	24	30	30	0

PITCHER	W	L	ERA	G	GS	CG	SV	SHO	IP	H	ER	BB	SO
Tommy Bridges	1	0	3.00	1	1	1	0	0	9.0	10	3	1	5
Johnny Gorsica	0	0	0.79	2	0	0	0	0	11.1	6	1	4	4
Fred Hutchinson	0	0	9.00	1	0	0	0	0	1.0	1	1	1	1
Archie McKain	0	0	3.00	1	0	0	0	0	3.0	4	1	0	0
Bobo Newsom	2	1	1.38	3	3	3	0	1	26.0	18	4	4	17
Schoolboy Rowe	0	2	17.18	2	2	0	0	0	3.2	12	7	1	1
Clay Smith	0	0	2.25	1	0	0	0	0	4.0	1	1	3	1
Dizzy Trout	0	1	9.00	1	1	0	0	0	2.0	6	2	1	1
TOTAL	3	4	3.00	12	7	4	0	1	60.0	58	20	15	30

GAME 1 AT CIN OCT 2

DET	050 020 000	7 10 1
CIN	000 100 010	2 8 3

Pitchers: NEWSOM vs DERRINGER, Moore (2), Riddle (9)
Home Runs: Campbell-DET
Attendance: 31,793

GAME 2 AT CIN OCT 3

DET	200 001 000	3 3 1
CIN	022 100 00X	5 9 0

Pitchers: ROWE, Gorsica (4) vs WALTERS
Home Runs: Ripple-CIN
Attendance: 30,640

GAME 3 AT DET OCT 4

CIN	100 000 012	4 10 1
DET	000 100 42X	7 13 1

Pitchers: TURNER, Moore (7), Beggs (8) vs BRIDGES
Home Runs: York-DET, Higgins-DET
Attendance: 52,877

GAME 4 AT DET OCT 5

CIN	201 100 010	5 11 1
DET	001 001 000	2 5 1

Pitchers: DERRINGER vs TROUT, Smith (3), McKain (7)
Attendance: 54,093

GAME 5 AT DET OCT 6

CIN	000 000 000	0 3 0
DET	003 400 01X	8 13 0

Pitchers: THOMPSON, Moore (4), Vander Meer (5), Hutchings (8) vs NEWSOM
Home Runs: Greenberg-DET
Attendance: 55,189

GAME 6 AT CIN OCT 7

DET	000 000 000	0 5 0
CIN	200 001 01X	4 10 2

Pitchers: ROWE, Gorsica (1), Hutchinson (8) vs WALTERS
Home Runs: Walters-CIN
Attendance: 30,481

GAME 7 AT CIN OCT 8

DET	001 000 000	1 7 0
CIN	000 000 20X	2 7 1

Pitchers: NEWSOM vs DERRINGER
Attendance: 26,854

Dodger catcher Mickey Owen's dropped third strike in Game Four was the Series' memorable boner, but it was not the chief cause of Brooklyn's downfall. Yankee pitching was. Three Yankee starters hurled complete-game wins, with each giving the Dodgers only one earned run. And relief ace Johnny Murphy hurled two-hit shutout ball in six innings over two games, winning one.

Yankee Joe Gordon opened the Series scoring with a solo homer in the second inning of Game One, and the Yankees added runs in the fourth and sixth. Owen tripled in the Dodgers' first run in the fifth, and pinch hitter Lew Riggs singled in an unearned run in the seventh. But Yankee starter Red Ruffing held on to his slim lead through the final two innings for the win.

Dodger ace Whitlow Wyatt gave the Yankees single runs in the second and third innings of Game Two, but held them scoreless the rest of the way. Meanwhile, the Dodgers tied the game in the fifth, and scored an unearned run in the sixth to finish the scoring and give Brooklyn its only win of the Series.

Freddie Fitzsimmons, with the Dodgers' best pitching of the Series, dueled Yankee Marius Russo through seven scoreless innings in Game Three. But Fitzsimmons's final out of the seventh—a line drive by Russo that bounced off Fitzsimmons's leg into the glove of shortstop Pee Wee Reese—broke his kneecap. Hugh Casey, who replaced Fitzsimmons in the eighth, retired the first batter, but then gave up four straight singles for two runs before being removed. The Yankees scored no more, and Brooklyn came up with a run in the last of the eighth. But Russo stopped the Dodgers in order in the ninth to preserve his lead for the Yankees' second win.

In Game Four, for the first time in the Series, the margin of victory was more than one run, thanks to catcher Owen's famous boner. Brooklyn held the lead 4–3 with two out in the top of the ninth. Dodger reliever Casey, who had shut out the Yankees since coming on in the fifth inning, then struck out Tommy Henrich for what should have been the game-ending out. But Owen let the ball get by him, and before the third out was recorded Casey had given up a single, two doubles, and two walks—and four runs, for Brooklyn's third loss.

The Yankees scored twice off Wyatt in the second inning of Game Five, and once more in the fifth (on Henrich's home run), as Tiny Bonham held Brooklyn to four hits and a single run to clinch the ninth Yankee world title.

New York Yankees (AL), 4;
Brooklyn Dodgers (NL), 1

NY (A)

PLAYER/POS	AVG	G	AB	R	H	2B	3B	HR	RB	BB	SO	SB
Tiny Bonham, p	.000	1	4	0	0	0	0	0	0	0	4	0
Frenchy Bordagaray, pr	.000	1	0	0	0	0	0	0	0	0	0	0
Marv Breuer, p	.000	1	1	0	0	0	0	0	0	0	0	0
Spud Chandler, p	.500	1	2	0	1	0	0	0	1	0	0	0
Bill Dickey, c	.167	5	18	3	3	1	0	0	1	3	1	0
Joe DiMaggio, of	.263	5	19	1	5	0	0	0	1	2	2	0
Atley Donald, p	.000	1	2	0	0	0	0	0	0	0	1	0
Joe Gordon, 2b	.500	5	14	2	7	1	1	1	5	7	0	0
Tommy Henrich, of	.167	5	18	4	3	1	0	1	1	3	3	0
Charlie Keller, of	.389	5	18	5	7	2	0	0	5	3	1	0
Johnny Murphy, p	.000	2	2	0	0	0	0	0	0	0	1	0
Phil Rizzuto, ss	.111	5	18	0	2	0	0	0	0	3	1	1
Red Rolfe, 3b	.300	5	20	2	6	0	0	0	0	2	1	0
Buddy Rosar, c	.000	1	0	0	0	0	0	0	0	0	0	0
Red Ruffing, p	.000	1	3	0	0	0	0	0	0	0	0	0
Marius Russo, p	.000	1	4	0	0	0	0	0	0	0	1	0
George Selkirk, ph	.500	2	2	0	1	0	0	0	0	0	0	0
Johnny Sturm, 1b	.286	5	21	0	6	0	0	0	0	2	2	1
TOTAL	.247		166	17	41	5	1	2	16	23	18	2

PITCHER	W	L	ERA	G	GS	CG	SV	SHO	IP	H	ER	BB	SO
Tiny Bonham	1	0	1.00	1	1	1	0	0	9.0	4	1	2	2
Marv Breuer	0	0	0.00	1	0	0	0	0	3.0	3	0	1	2
Spud Chandler	0	1	3.60	1	1	0	0	0	5.0	4	2	2	2
Atley Donald	0	0	9.00	1	1	0	0	0	4.0	6	4	3	2
Johnny Murphy	1	0	0.00	2	0	0	0	0	6.0	2	0	1	3
Red Ruffing	1	0	1.00	1	1	1	0	0	9.0	6	1	3	5
Marius Russo	1	0	1.00	1	1	1	0	0	9.0	4	1	2	5
TOTAL	4	1	1.80	8	5	3	0	0	45.0	29	9	14	21

BRO (N)

PLAYER/POS	AVG	G	AB	R	H	2B	3B	HR	RB	BB	SO	SB
Johnny Allen, p	.000	3	0	0	0	0	0	0	0	0	0	0
Dolph Camilli, 1b	.167	5	18	1	3	1	0	0	1	1	6	0
Hugh Casey, p	.500	3	2	0	1	0	0	0	0	0	1	0
Pete Coscarart, 2b	.000	3	7	1	0	0	0	0	0	1	2	0
Curt Davis, p	.000	1	2	0	0	0	0	0	0	0	0	0
Freddie Fitzsimmons, p	.000	1	2	0	0	0	0	0	0	0	0	0
Herman Franks, c	.000	1	0	0	0	0	0	0	0	0	0	0
Larry French, p	.000	2	0	0	0	0	0	0	0	0	0	0
Augie Galan, ph	.000	2	2	0	0	0	0	0	0	1	0	0
Billy Herman, 2b	.125	4	8	0	1	0	0	0	0	2	0	0
Kirby Higbe, p	1.000	1	1	0	1	0	0	0	0	0	0	0
Cookie Lavagetto, 3b	.100	3	10	1	1	0	0	0	0	2	0	0
Joe Medwick, of	.235	5	17	1	4	1	0	0	0	1	2	0
Mickey Owen, c	.167	5	12	1	2	0	1	0	2	3	0	0
Pee Wee Reese, ss	.200	5	20	1	4	0	0	0	2	0	0	0
Pete Reiser, of	.200	5	20	1	4	1	1	1	3	1	6	0
Lew Riggs, 3b-2	.250	3	8	0	2	0	0	0	1	1	1	0
Dixie Walker, of	.222	5	18	3	4	2	0	0	0	2	1	0
Jimmy Wasdell, of-1	.200	3	5	0	1	1	0	0	2	0	1	0
Whit Wyatt, p	.167	2	6	1	1	1	0	0	0	0	1	0
TOTAL	.182		159	11	29	7	2	1	11	14	21	0

PITCHER	W	L	ERA	G	GS	CG	SV	SHO	IP	H	ER	BB	SO
Johnny Allen	0	0	0.00	3	0	0	0	0	3.2	1	0	3	0
Hugh Casey	0	2	3.38	3	0	0	0	0	5.1	9	2	1	1
Curt Davis	0	1	5.06	1	1	0	0	0	5.1	6	3	3	1
Freddie Fitzsimmons	0	0	0.00	1	1	0	0	0	7.0	4	0	3	1
Larry French	0	0	0.00	2	0	0	0	0	1.0	0	0	0	0
Kirby Higbe	0	0	7.36	1	1	0	0	0	3.2	6	3	2	1
Whit Wyatt	1	1	2.50	2	2	2	0	0	18.0	15	5	10	14
TOTAL	1	4	2.66	13	5	2	0	0	44.0	41	13	23	18

Cardinal rookies Stan Musial and Whitey Kurowski drove in game-winning runs for rookie-pitcher Johnny Beazley in Games Two and Five as the major leagues' youngest team upset the Yankees. New York won only the opener, building a seven-run lead for starter Red Ruffing, who shut out St. Louis on one hit through 8⅓ innings before giving up four hits and four harmless runs in the last of the ninth.

The Cardinals scored first in Game Two on catcher Walker Cooper's two-run double in the first inning. Kurowski tripled in a third Cardinal run in the seventh, but pitcher Beazley, after holding the Yankees scoreless through seven innings, gave up three runs in the eighth on two singles and Charlie Keller's two-run homer. St. Louis regained the lead a half inning later when Musial singled home Enos Slaughter (who had doubled), and stifled a threat in the ninth as Slaughter's great throw from right field nailed a Yankee runner at third.

Second-year Cardinal pitcher Ernie White turned in the Series' top mound performance with a six-single, no-walk shutout in Game Three (aided by outfielders Musial and Slaughter, who hauled in a pair of potential home run blasts in the seventh inning). The Cards managed only five singles themselves, but they combined one with a walk, sacrifice, and ground out for a run in the third, and sandwiched a Yankee error with two hits in the nineth for an unearned insurance run.

Game Four saw the Series' heaviest hitting. New York scored once in the first, but the Cards exploded in the fourth for six runs on six hits and two walks. The Yankees tied it up two innings later, with Keller's three-run homer the feature of the five-run inning. St. Louis took the lead for good with two runs in the seventh, and added a ninth run in the ninth.

Beazley and Ruffing tangled in Game Five. Phil Rizzuto's solo homer put New York ahead in the first inning. Slaughter's fourth-inning home run tied the score, but the Yankees regained the lead with a run later in the inning. The Cards retied the game in the sixth, and took the final lead when Kurowski homered for two runs in the top of the ninth. The Yankees threatened in the last of the ninth, putting their first two men on with a single and error. But catcher Cooper picked a runner off second, second baseman Jimmy Brown redeemed his earlier error with a sparkling catch, then fielded a routine grounder for the final out and the Cardinal triumph.

St. Louis Cardinals (NL), 4; New York Yankees (AL), 1

STL (N)

PLAYER/POS	AVG	G	AB	R	H	2B	3B	HR	RB	BB	SO	SB
Johnny Beazley, p	.143	2	7	0	1	0	0	0	0	0	5	0
Jimmy Brown, 2b	.300	5	20	2	6	0	0	0	1	3	0	0
Mort Cooper, p	.200	2	5	1	1	0	0	0	2	0	1	0
Walker Cooper, c	.286	5	21	3	6	1	0	0	4	0	1	0
Creepy Crespi, pr	.000	1	0	1	0	0	0	0	0	0	0	0
Harry Gumbert, p	.000	2	0	0	0	0	0	0	0	0	0	0
Johnny Hopp, 1b	.176	5	17	3	3	0	0	0	0	1	1	0
Whitey Kurowski, 3b	.267	5	15	3	4	0	1	1	5	2	3	0
Max Lanier, p	1.000	2	1	0	1	0	0	0	1	0	0	0
Marty Marion, ss	.111	5	18	2	2	0	1	0	3	1	2	0
Terry Moore, of	.294	5	17	2	5	1	0	0	2	2	3	0
Stan Musial, of	.222	5	18	2	4	1	0	0	2	4	0	0
Ken O'Dea, ph	1.000	1	1	0	1	0	0	0	1	0	0	0
Howie Pollet, p	.000	1	0	0	0	0	0	0	0	0	0	0
Ray Sanders, ph	.000	2	1	1	0	0	0	0	0	1	0	0
Enos Slaughter, of	.263	5	19	3	5	1	0	1	2	3	2	0
Harry Walker, ph	.000	1	1	0	0	0	0	0	0	0	1	0
Ernie White, p	.000	1	2	0	0	0	0	0	0	0	0	0
TOTAL	.239		163	23	39	4	2	2	23	17	19	0

PITCHER	W	L	ERA	G	GS	CG	SV	SHO	IP	H	ER	BB	SO
Johnny Beazley	2	0	2.50	2	2	2	0	0	18.0	17	5	3	6
Mort Cooper	0	1	5.54	2	2	0	0	0	13.0	17	8	4	9
Harry Gumbert	0	0	0.00	2	0	0	0	0	0.2	1	0	0	0
Max Lanier	1	0	0.00	2	0	0	0	0	4.0	3	0	1	1
Howie Pollet	0	0	0.00	1	0	0	0	0	0.1	0	0	0	0
Ernie White	1	0	0.00	1	1	1	0	1	9.0	6	0	0	6
TOTAL	4	1	2.60	10	5	3	0	1	45.0	44	13	8	22

NY (A)

PLAYER/POS	AVG	G	AB	R	H	2B	3B	HR	RB	BB	SO	SB
Tiny Bonham, p	.000	2	2	0	0	0	0	0	0	0	1	0
Hank Borowy, p	.000	1	1	0	0	0	0	0	0	0	1	0
Marv Breuer, p	.000	1	0	0	0	0	0	0	0	0	0	0
Spud Chandler, p	.000	2	2	0	0	0	0	0	0	0	1	0
Frankie Crosetti, 3b	.000	1	3	0	0	0	0	0	0	0	1	0
Roy Cullenbine, of	.263	5	19	3	5	1	0	0	2	1	2	1
Bill Dickey, c	.263	5	19	1	5	0	0	0	0	1	0	0
Joe DiMaggio, of	.333	5	21	3	7	0	0	0	3	0	1	0
Atley Donald, p	.000	1	2	0	0	0	0	0	0	0	0	0
Joe Gordon, 2b	.095	5	21	1	2	1	0	0	0	0	7	0
Buddy Hassett, 1b	.333	3	9	1	3	1	0	0	2	0	1	0
Charlie Keller, of	.200	5	20	2	4	0	0	2	5	1	3	0
Jerry Priddy, 1b-3,3b-1	.100	3	10	0	1	1	0	0	1	1	0	0
Phil Rizzuto, ss	.381	5	21	2	8	0	0	1	1	2	1	2
Red Rolfe, 3b	.353	4	17	5	6	2	0	0	0	1	2	0
Buddy Rosar, ph	1.000	1	1	0	1	0	0	0	0	0	0	0
Red Ruffing, p-2	.222	4	9	0	2	0	0	0	0	0	2	0
George Selkirk, ph	.000	1	1	0	0	0	0	0	0	0	1	0
Tuck Stainback, pr	.000	2	0	0	0	0	0	0	0	0	0	0
Jim Turner, p	.000	1	0	0	0	0	0	0	0	0	0	0
TOTAL	.247		178	18	44	6	0	3	14	8	22	3

PITCHER	W	L	ERA	G	GS	CG	SV	SHO	IP	H	ER	BB	SO
Tiny Bonham	0	1	4.09	2	1	1	0	0	11.0	9	5	3	3
Hank Borowy	0	0	18.00	1	1	0	0	0	3.0	6	6	3	1
Marv Breuer	0	0	–	1	0	0	0	0	0.0	2	0	0	0
Spud Chandler	0	1	1.08	2	1	0	1	0	8.1	5	1	1	3
Atley Donald	0	1	6.00	1	0	0	0	0	3.0	3	2	2	1
Red Ruffing	1	1	4.08	2	2	1	0	0	17.2	14	8	7	11
Jim Turner	0	0	0.00	1	0	0	0	0	1.0	0	0	1	0
TOTAL	1	4	4.50	10	5	2	1	0	44.0	39	22	17	19

GAME 1 AT STL SEPT 30

NY	000	110	032	7	11	0
STL	000	000	004	4	7	4

Pitchers: RUFFING, Chandler (9) vs M.COOPER, Gumbert (8), Lanier (9)
Attendance: 34,769

GAME 2 AT STL OCT 1

NY	000	000	030	3	10	2
STL	200	000	11X	4	6	0

Pitchers: BONHAM vs BEAZLEY
Home Runs: Keller-NY
Attendance: 34,255

GAME 3 AT NY OCT 2

STL	001	000	001	2	5	1
NY	000	000	000	0	6	1

Pitchers: WHITE vs CHANDLER, Breuer (9), Turner (9)
Attendance: 69,123

GAME 4 AT NY OCT 4

STL	000	600	201	9	12	1
NY	100	005	000	6	10	1

Pitchers: M.Cooper, Gumbert (6), Pollet (6), LANIER (7) vs Borowy, DONALD (4), Bonham (7)
Home Runs: Keller-NY
Attendance: 69,902

GAME 5 AT NY OCT 5

STL	000	101	002	4	9	4
NY	100	100	000	2	7	1

Pitchers: BEAZLEY vs RUFFING
Home Runs: Rizzuto-NY, Slaughter-STL, Kurowski-STL
Attendance: 69,052

Although both clubs had lost players to military service since the previous World Series, history seemed to be repeating itself. The Cardinals lost to the Yankees in the opener and won the second game, as they had the previous year. But this year it was the Yankees who took the next three games and the Series, as fine Cardinal pitching gave way to even finer Yankee mound work.

Yankee pitcher Spurgeon (Spud) Chandler, coming off his finest season (20–4, 1.64 ERA), continued to overwhelm the opposition in the Series. He held the Cards to two runs (only one earned) in Game One, and the Yankees took advantage of a wild pitch to score two runs of their own in the sixth inning, breaking a 2–2 tie for a 4–2 win. Cardinal shortstop Marty Marion homered in the third inning for the first Cardinal run the next day, and first baseman Ray Sanders homered for two more runs in a three-run fourth. Cardinal ace Mort Cooper held New York to one run on four hits through eight innings, but he weakened in the last of the ninth, giving up a double and triple to the first two batters. But only two runs scored as he retired the next three men for St. Louis's only victory.

The Cardinals carried a 2–1 lead into the last of the eighth inning of Game Three, when a pair of errors, two walks, and five Yankee hits (including Billy Johnson's three-run triple) undid them. Yankee fireman Johnny Murphy retired the Cards in order in the ninth to save Hank Borowy's win. Max Lanier and Harry Brecheen held New York to just two runs (and six hits) in Game Four, but Yankee pitcher Marius Russo gave up only one run—and that was scored only because of two Yankee errors in the seventh inning.

In the fifth and (as it turned out) final game, St. Louis couldn't score even an unearned run, although they knocked Spud Chandler for ten hits. But they were all singles and were spaced harmlessly over eight of the nine innings. Three St. Louis pitchers held the Yankees to just seven hits, six of them singles. But in the sixth inning Bill Dickey followed one of the Yankee singles with the game's only extra-base hit—a home run—to produce the game's only scoring, and bring the Yankees yet another world championship, their tenth.

New York Yankees (AL), 4;
St. Louis Cardinals (NL), 1

NY (A)

PLAYER/POS	AVG	G	AB	R	H	2B	3B	HR	RB	BB	SO	SB
Tiny Bonham, p	.000	1	2	0	0	0	0	0	0	0	0	0
Hank Borowy, p	.500	1	2	1	1	1	0	0	0	0	1	0
Spud Chandler, p	.167	2	6	0	1	0	0	0	0	0	2	0
Frankie Crosetti, ss	.278	5	18	4	5	0	0	0	1	2	3	1
Bill Dickey, c	.278	5	18	1	5	0	0	1	4	2	2	0
Nick Etten, 1b	.105	5	19	0	2	0	0	0	2	1	2	0
Joe Gordon, 2b	.235	5	17	2	4	1	0	1	2	3	3	0
Billy Johnson, 3b	.300	5	20	3	6	1	1	0	3	0	3	0
Charlie Keller, of	.222	5	18	3	4	0	1	0	2	2	5	1
Johnny Lindell, of	.111	4	9	1	1	0	0	0	0	1	4	0
Bud Metheny, of	.125	2	8	0	1	0	0	0	0	0	2	0
Johnny Murphy, p	.000	2	0	0	0	0	0	0	0	0	0	0
Marius Russo, p	.667	1	3	1	2	2	0	0	0	0	1	0
Tuck Stainback, of	.176	5	17	0	3	0	0	0	0	0	2	0
Snuffy Stirnweiss, ph	.000	1	1	1	0	0	0	0	0	0	0	0
Roy Weatherly, ph	.000	1	1	0	0	0	0	0	0	0	0	0
TOTAL	.220		159	17	35	5	2	2	14	12	30	2

PITCHER	W	L	ERA	G	GS	CG	SV	SHO	IP	H	ER	BB	SO
Tiny Bonham	0	1	4.50	1	1	0	0	0	8.0	6	4	3	9
Hank Borowy	1	0	2.25	1	1	0	0	0	8.0	6	2	3	4
Spud Chandler	2	0	0.50	2	2	2	0	1	18.0	17	1	3	10
Johnny Murphy	0	0	0.00	2	0	0	1	0	2.0	1	0	1	1
Marius Russo	1	0	0.00	1	1	1	0	0	9.0	7	0	1	2
TOTAL	4	1	1.40	7	5	3	1	1	45.0	37	7	11	26

STL (N)

PLAYER/POS	AVG	G	AB	R	H	2B	3B	HR	RB	BB	SO	SB
Al Brazle, p	.000	1	3	0	0	0	0	0	0	0	1	0
Harry Brecheen, p	.000	3	0	0	0	0	0	0	0	0	0	0
Mort Cooper, p	.000	2	5	0	0	0	0	0	0	0	3	0
Walker Cooper, c	.294	5	17	1	5	0	0	0	0	0	1	0
Frank Demaree, ph	.000	1	1	0	0	0	0	0	0	0	0	0
Murry Dickson, p	.000	1	0	0	0	0	0	0	0	0	0	0
Debs Garms, of-1	.000	2	5	0	0	0	0	0	0	0	2	0
Johnny Hopp, of	.000	1	4	0	0	0	0	0	0	0	1	0
Lou Klein, 2b	.136	5	22	0	3	0	0	0	0	1	2	0
Howie Krist, p	.000	1	0	0	0	0	0	0	0	0	0	0
Whitey Kurowski, 3b	.222	5	18	2	4	1	0	0	1	0	3	0
Max Lanier, p	.250	3	4	0	1	0	0	0	1	0	0	0
Danny Litwhiler, of-4	.267	5	15	0	4	1	0	0	2	2	4	0
Marty Marion, ss	.357	5	14	1	5	2	0	1	2	3	1	1
Stan Musial, of	.278	5	18	2	5	0	0	0	0	2	2	0
Sam Narron, ph	.000	1	1	0	0	0	0	0	0	0	0	0
Ken O'Dea, c-1	.667	2	3	0	2	0	0	0	0	0	0	0
Ray Sanders, 1b	.294	5	17	3	5	0	0	1	2	3	4	0
Harry Walker, of	.167	5	18	0	3	0	0	0	0	0	2	0
Ernie White, pr	.000	1	0	0	0	0	0	0	0	0	0	0
TOTAL	.224		165	9	37	5	0	2	8	11	26	1

PITCHER	W	L	ERA	G	GS	CG	SV	SHO	IP	H	ER	BB	SO
Al Brazle	0	1	3.68	1	1	0	0	0	7.1	5	3	2	4
Harry Brecheen	0	1	2.45	3	0	0	0	0	3.2	5	1	3	3
Mort Cooper	1	1	2.81	2	2	1	0	0	16.0	11	5	3	10
Murry Dickson	0	0	0.00	1	0	0	0	0	0.2	0	0	1	0
Howie Krist	0	0	—	1	0	0	0	0	0.0	1	0	0	0
Max Lanier	0	1	1.76	3	2	0	0	0	15.1	13	3	3	13
TOTAL	1	4	2.51	11	5	1	0	0	43.0	35	12	12	30

GAME 1 AT NY OCT 5

STL	010 010 000	2 7 2
NY	000 202 00X	4 8 2

Pitchers: LANIER, Brecheen (8) vs CHANDLER
Home Runs: Gordon-NY
Attendance: 68,676

GAME 2 AT NY OCT 6

STL	001 300 000	4 7 2
NY	000 100 002	3 6 0

Pitchers: M.COOPER vs BONHAM, Murphy (9)
Home Runs: Marion-STL, Sanders-STL
Attendance: 68,578

GAME 3 AT NY OCT 7

STL	000 200 000	2 6 4
NY	000 001 05X	6 8 0

Pitchers: BRAZLE, Krist (8), Brecheen (8) vs BOROWY, Murphy (9)
Attendance: 69,990

GAME 4 AT STL OCT 10

NY	000 100 010	2 6 2
STL	000 000 100	1 7 1

Pitchers: RUSSO vs Lanier, BRECHEEN (8)
Attendance: 36,196

GAME 5 AT STL OCT 11

NY	000 002 000	2 7 1
STL	000 000 000	0 10 1

Pitchers: CHANDLER vs M.COOPER, Lanier (8), Dickson (9)
Home Runs: Dickey-NY
Attendance: 33,872

The Cardinals—a much stronger team in the regular season—entered the World Series against their landlord Browns (who owned Sportsman's Park, where both teams played) as clear favorites. They won the Series in six games, but if the Browns' fielding had been as good as their pitching the outcome might have been different.

The Browns won the opener on Denny Galehouse's strong pitching. Galehouse gave up seven hits and four walks, but held the Cards scoreless for 8⅔ innings before yielding a run in the ninth. Cardinal ace Mort Cooper also pitched well in six of his seven innings. He allowed the Browns only two hits, but they came back to back in the fourth inning—a single followed by George McQuinn's home run—to give the Browns all the scoring they needed.

Brown pitcher Nelson Potter's two errors (a fumble and a wild throw) on a bunt in the third inning of Game Two led to an unearned run, and third baseman Mark Christman's fumble an inning later set up a second unearned run. The Browns tied the score with a pair of runs on three two-out hits in the seventh—enough to have won an error-free game—but lost when the Cardinals singled a run across in the last of the eleventh.

Two Brown errors led to a pair of unearned runs in Game Three, but Jack Kramer held the Cards scoreless apart from that, striking out ten. Meanwhile, Brown hitters tied together five singles with two out in the third inning for three runs, adding a fourth run on a wild pitch before the inning ended. In the seventh the Browns tacked on two more runs for a comfortable win and a 2–1 Series advantage.

The Cardinals came back to earn victory in Games Four and Five, knocking three Brown pitchers for 12 hits in Game Four (including Stan Musial's two-run homer in the first) and a 5–1 win for pitcher Harry Brecheen, then rapping Denny Galehouse for two solo homers in Game Five (by Danny Litwhiler and Ray Sanders) for the game's only scoring as Mort Cooper fanned 12 Browns while shutting them out.

Two of the Cardinals' three runs in the fourth inning of Game Six were made possible by Brown shortstop Vern Stephens's throwing error. They provided the margin of victory, as Cardinal pitchers Max Lanier and Ted Wilks held the Browns to three hits and a single run, and brought the Cards their second world title in three years.

St. Louis Cardinals (NL), 4; St. Louis Browns (AL), 2

STL (N)

PLAYER/POS	AVG	G	AB	R	H	2B	3B	HR	RBI	BB	SO	SB
Augie Bergamo, of-2	.000	3	6	0	0	0	0	0	0	1	2	3	0
Harry Brecheen, p	.000	1	4	0	0	0	0	0	0	0	1	0
Bud Byerly, p	.000	1	0	0	0	0	0	0	0	0	0	0
Mort Cooper, p	.000	2	4	0	0	0	0	0	0	0	2	0
Walker Cooper, c	.318	6	22	1	7	2	1	0	2	3	2	0
Blix Donnelly, p	.000	2	1	0	0	0	0	0	0	0	1	0
George Fallon, 2b	.000	2	2	0	0	0	0	0	0	0	0	0
Debs Garms, ph	.000	2	2	0	0	0	0	0	0	0	0	0
Johnny Hopp, of	.185	6	27	2	5	0	0	0	0	0	8	0
Al Jurisich, p	.000	1	0	0	0	0	0	0	0	0	0	0
Whitey Kurowski, 3b	.217	6	23	2	5	1	0	0	1	1	4	0
Max Lanier, p	.500	2	4	0	2	0	0	0	1	0	0	0
Danny Litwhiler, of	.200	5	20	2	4	1	0	1	1	1	7	0
Marty Marion, ss	.227	6	22	1	5	3	0	0	2	2	3	0
Stan Musial, of	.304	6	23	2	7	2	0	1	2	2	2	0
Ken O'Dea, ph	.333	3	3	0	1	0	0	0	2	0	0	0
Ray Sanders, 1b	.286	6	21	5	6	0	0	1	1	5	8	0
Freddy Schmidt, p	.000	1	1	0	0	0	0	0	0	0	1	0
Emil Verban, 2b	.412	6	17	1	7	0	0	0	2	2	0	0
Ted Wilks, p	.000	2	2	0	0	0	0	0	0	0	2	0
TOTAL	.240		204	16	49	9	1	3	15	19	43	0

PITCHER	W	L	ERA	G	GS	CG	SV	SHO	IP	H	ER	BB	SO
Harry Brecheen	1	0	1.00	1	1	1	0	0	9.0	9	1	4	4
Bud Byerly	0	0	0.00	1	0	0	0	0	1.1	0	0	0	1
Mort Cooper	1	1	1.13	2	2	1	0	1	16.0	9	2	5	16
Blix Donnelly	1	0	0.00	2	0	0	0	0	6.0	2	0	1	9
Al Jurisich	0	0	27.00	1	0	0	0	0	0.2	2	2	1	0
Max Lanier	1	0	2.19	2	2	0	0	0	12.1	8	3	8	11
Freddy Schmidt	0	0	0.00	1	0	0	0	0	3.1	1	0	1	1
Ted Wilks	0	1	5.68	2	1	0	1	0	6.1	5	4	3	7
TOTAL	4	2	1.96	12	6	2	1	1	55.0	36	12	23	49

STL (A)

PLAYER/POS	AVG	G	AB	R	H	2B	3B	HR	RBI	BB	SO	SB
Floyd Baker, 2b	.000	2	2	0	0	0	0	0	0	0	2	0
Milt Byrnes, ph	.000	3	2	0	0	0	0	0	0	1	2	0
Mike Chartak, ph	.000	2	2	0	0	0	0	0	0	0	2	0
Mark Christman, 3b	.091	6	22	0	2	0	0	0	1	0	6	0
Ellis Clary, ph	.000	1	1	0	0	0	0	0	0	0	0	0
Denny Galehouse, p	.200	2	5	0	1	0	0	0	0	1	1	0
Don Gutteridge, 2b	.143	6	21	1	3	1	0	0	0	3	5	0
Red Hayworth, c	.118	6	17	1	2	1	0	0	1	3	1	0
Al Hollingsworth, p	.000	1	1	0	0	0	0	0	0	0	0	0
Sig Jakucki, p	.000	1	1	0	0	0	0	0	0	0	0	0
Jack Kramer, p	.000	2	4	0	0	0	0	0	0	0	2	0
Mike Kreevich, of	.231	6	26	0	6	3	0	0	0	0	5	0
Chet Laabs, of-4	.200	5	15	1	3	1	1	0	0	2	6	0
Frank Mancuso, c-1	.667	2	3	0	2	0	0	0	1	0	0	0
George McQuinn, 1b	.438	6	16	2	7	2	0	1	5	7	2	0
Gene Moore, of	.182	6	22	4	4	0	0	0	0	3	6	0
Bob Muncrief, p	.000	2	1	0	0	0	0	0	0	0	1	0
Nelson Potter, p	.000	2	4	0	0	0	0	0	0	0	1	0
Tex Shirley, p	.000	2	0	0	0	0	0	0	0	0	0	0
Vern Stephens, ss	.227	6	22	2	5	1	0	0	3	3	3	0
Tom Turner, ph	.000	1	1	0	0	0	0	0	0	0	0	0
Al Zarilla, of-3	.100	4	10	1	1	0	0	0	1	0	4	0
TOTAL	.183		197	12	36	9	1	1	9	23	49	0

PITCHER	W	L	ERA	G	GS	CG	SV	SHO	IP	H	ER	BB	SO
Denny Galehouse	1	1	1.50	2	2	2	0	0	18.0	13	3	5	15
Al Hollingsworth	0	0	2.25	1	0	0	0	0	4.0	5	1	2	1
Sig Jakucki	0	1	9.00	1	1	0	0	0	3.0	5	3	0	4
Jack Kramer	1	0	0.00	2	1	1	0	0	11.0	9	0	4	12
Bob Muncrief	0	1	1.35	2	0	0	0	0	6.2	5	1	4	4
Nelson Potter	0	1	0.93	2	2	0	0	0	9.2	10	1	3	6
Tex Shirley	0	0	0.00	1	0	0	0	0	2.0	2	0	1	1
TOTAL	2	4	1.49	11	6	3	0	0	54.1	49	9	19	43

GAME 1 AT STL-N OCT 4

STL-A	000	200	000	2	2	0
STL-N	000	000	001	1	7	0

Pitchers: GALEHOUSE vs M.COOPER, Donnelly (8)
Home Runs: McQuinn-STL(A)
Attendance: 33,242

GAME 2 AT STL-N OCT 5

STL-A	000	000	200	00	2	7	4
STL-N	001	100	000	01	3	7	0

Pitchers: Potter, MUNCRIEF (7) vs Lanier, DONNELLY (8)
Attendance: 35,076

GAME 3 AT STL-A OCT 6

STL-N	100	000	100	2	7	0
STL-A	004	000	20X	6	8	2

Pitchers: WILKS, Schmidt (3), Jurisich (7), Byerly (7) vs KRAMER
Attendance: 34,737

GAME 4 AT STL-A OCT 7

STL-N	202	001	000	5	12	0
STL-A	000	000	010	1	9	1

Pitchers: BRECHEEN vs JAKUCKI, Hollingsworth (4), Shirley (8)
Home Runs: Musial-STL(N)
Attendance: 35,455

GAME 5 AT STL-A OCT 8

STL-N	000	001	010	2	6	1
STL-A	000	000	000	0	7	1

Pitchers: M.COOPER vs GALEHOUSE
Home Runs: Sanders-STL(N), Litwhiler-STL(N)
Attendance: 36,568

GAME 6 AT STL-N OCT 9

STL-A	010	000	000	1	3	2
STL-N	000	300	00X	3	10	0

Pitchers: POTTER, Muncrief (4), Kramer (7) vs LANIER, Wilks (6)
Attendance: 31,630

As World War Two ended during the summer, military major leaguers began returning to their clubs. Hank Greenberg's return in July provided the spark needed for Detroit's narrow pennant victory, and his three-run homer in Game Two of the World Series proved to be the decisive blow in the Tigers' successful struggle for the world title.

Chicago started strong as Cub ace Hank Borowy shut out the Tigers on six singles while his teammates drove out Tiger ace Hal Newhouser with seven runs in the first three innings, to win 9–0. Chicago continued its assault the next day with a run in the top of the fourth, but in the fifth inning Tiger Doc Cramer—with two out and two on—singled in the tying run, and Greenberg followed with his tie-breaking homer for three additional runs. Detroit pitcher Virgil Trucks (who had returned from the Navy in time to pitch in the regular-season finale) held the Cubs scoreless after the fourth inning for the Tiger win.

Chicago's Claude Passeau moved the Cubs back into the Series lead with a one-hit shutout in Game Three, but Tiger Dizzy Trout's five-hitter in Game Four again evened the Series. The Tigers bunched four of their seven hits in the fourth inning for all four of their runs.

Detroit took the Series lead for the first time with an 8–4 win in Game Five. Borowy and Newhouser faced each other as they had in the opener, but this time Borowy was hit hard. Driven out when four Tigers opened the sixth inning with safe hits, he took the loss as Newhouser went the distance for the win.

In Game Six, Chicago concluded the seventh inning of a heavy-hitting game leading 7–3. Detroit tied the score with four runs in the top of the eighth (capped by Greenberg's home run), but in the last of the twelfth the Cubs' Stan Hack doubled home the winning run to keep Chicago's hopes alive.

Two days later in the finale, Cub manager Charlie Grimm started Borowy, who had relieved for four shutout innings to win Game Six. But this third appearance in four days proved too much. Removed after the first three batters to face him singled, he took the loss, as the Tigers went on to score nine runs to the Cubs' three.

Detroit Tigers (AL), 4;
Chicago Cubs (NL), 3

DET (A)

PLAYER/POS	AVG	G	AB	R	H	2B	3B	HR	RB	BB	SO	SB
Al Benton, p	.000	3	0	0	0	0	0	0	0	0	0	0
Red Borom, ph	.000	2	1	0	0	0	0	0	0	0	0	0
Tommy Bridges, p	.000	1	0	0	0	0	0	0	0	0	0	0
George Caster, p	.000	1	0	0	0	0	0	0	0	0	0	0
Doc Cramer, of	.379	7	29	7	11	0	0	0	4	1	0	1
Roy Cullenbine, of	.227	7	22	5	5	2	0	0	4	8	2	1
Zeb Eaton, ph	.000	1	1	0	0	0	0	0	0	0	1	0
Hank Greenberg, of	.304	7	23	7	7	3	0	2	7	6	5	0
Joe Hoover, ss	.333	1	3	1	1	0	0	0	1	0	0	0
Chuck Hostetler, ph	.000	3	3	0	0	0	0	0	0	0	0	0
Bob Maier, ph	1.000	1	1	0	1	0	0	0	0	0	0	0
Eddie Mayo, 2b	.250	7	28	4	7	1	0	0	2	2	2	0
John McHale, ph	.000	3	3	0	0	0	0	0	0	0	1	0
Ed Mierkowicz, of	.000	1	0	0	0	0	0	0	0	0	0	0
Les Mueller, p	.000	1	0	0	0	0	0	0	0	0	0	0
Hal Newhouser, p	.000	3	8	0	0	0	0	0	0	1	1	0
Jimmy Outlaw, 3b	.179	7	28	1	5	0	0	0	3	2	1	1
Stubby Overmire, p	.000	1	1	0	0	0	0	0	0	0	0	0
Paul Richards, c	.211	7	19	0	4	2	0	0	6	4	3	0
Bob Swift, c	.250	3	4	1	1	0	0	0	0	2	0	0
Jim Tobin, p	.000	1	1	0	0	0	0	0	0	0	0	0
Dizzy Trout, p	.167	2	6	0	1	0	0	0	0	0	0	0
Virgil Trucks, p	.000	2	4	0	0	0	0	0	0	0	1	0
Hub Walker, ph	.500	2	2	1	1	0	0	0	0	0	0	0
Skeeter Webb, ss	.185	7	27	4	5	0	0	0	1	3	1	0
Rudy York, 1b	.179	7	28	1	5	1	0	1	3	3	4	0
TOTAL	.223		242	32	54	10	0	2	32	33	22	3

PITCHER	W	L	ERA	G	GS	CG	SV	SHO	IP	H	ER	BB	SO
Al Benton	0	0	1.93	3	0	0	0	0	4.2	6	1	0	5
Tommy Bridges	0	0	16.20	1	0	0	0	0	1.2	3	3	3	1
George Caster	0	0	0.00	1	0	0	0	0	0.2	0	0	0	1
Les Mueller	0	0	0.00	1	0	0	0	0	2.0	0	0	1	1
Hal Newhouser	2	1	6.10	3	3	2	0	0	20.2	25	14	4	22
Stubby Overmire	0	1	3.00	1	1	0	0	0	6.0	4	2	2	2
Jim Tobin	0	0	6.00	1	0	0	0	0	3.0	4	2	1	0
Dizzy Trout	1	1	0.66	2	1	1	0	0	13.2	9	1	3	9
Virgil Trucks	1	0	3.38	2	2	1	0	0	13.1	14	5	5	7
TOTAL	4	3	3.84	15	7	4	0	0	65.2	65	28	19	48

CHI (N)

PLAYER/POS	AVG	G	AB	R	H	2B	3B	HR	RB	BB	SO	SB
Heinz Becker, ph	.500	3	2	0	1	0	0	0	0	1	1	0
Cy Block, pr	.000	1	0	0	0	0	0	0	0	0	0	0
Hank Borowy, p	.167	4	6	1	1	1	0	0	0	0	3	0
Phil Cavaretta, 1b	.423	7	26	7	11	2	0	1	5	4	3	0
Bob Chipman, p	.000	1	0	0	0	0	0	0	0	0	0	0
Paul Derringer, p	.000	3	0	0	0	0	0	0	0	0	0	0
Paul Erickson, p	.000	4	0	0	0	0	0	0	0	0	0	0
Paul Gillespie, c-1	.000	3	5	0	0	0	0	0	0	0	0	0
Stan Hack, 3b	.367	7	30	1	11	3	0	0	4	4	2	0
Roy Hughes, ss	.294	6	17	1	5	1	0	0	3	4	5	0
Don Johnson, 2b	.172	7	29	4	5	2	1	0	0	0	8	1
Mickey Livingston, c	.364	6	22	3	8	3	0	0	4	1	1	0
Peanuts Lowrey, of	.310	7	29	4	9	1	0	0	2	1	2	0
Clyde McCullough, ph	.000	1	1	0	0	0	0	0	0	0	1	0
Lennie Merullo, ss	.000	3	2	0	0	0	0	0	0	0	1	0
Bill Nicholson, of	.214	7	28	1	6	1	0	0	8	2	5	0
Andy Pafko, of	.214	7	28	5	6	2	1	0	2	2	5	1
Claude Passeau, p	.000	3	7	1	0	0	0	0	1	0	4	0
Ray Prim, p	.000	2	0	0	0	0	0	0	0	0	0	0
Ed Sauer, ph	.000	2	2	0	0	0	0	0	0	0	0	0
Bill Schuster, ss-1	.000	2	1	1	0	0	0	0	0	0	0	0
Frank Secory, ph	.200	5	5	0	1	0	0	0	0	0	2	0
Hy Vandenberg, p	.000	3	1	0	0	0	0	0	0	0	0	0
Dewey Williams, c-1	.000	2	2	0	0	0	0	0	0	0	1	0
Hank Wyse, p	.000	3	3	0	0	0	0	0	0	0	2	0
TOTAL	.259		247	29	64	16	3	1	27	19	48	2

PITCHER	W	L	ERA	G	GS	CG	SV	SHO	IP	H	ER	BB	SO
Hank Borowy	2	2	4.00	4	3	1	0	1	18.0	21	8	6	8
Bob Chipman	0	0	0.00	1	0	0	0	0	0.1	0	0	1	0
Paul Derringer	0	0	6.75	3	0	0	0	0	5.1	5	4	7	1
Paul Erickson	0	0	3.86	4	0	0	0	0	7.0	8	3	3	5
Claude Passeau	1	0	2.70	3	2	1	0	1	16.2	7	5	8	3
Ray Prim	0	1	9.00	2	1	0	0	0	4.0	4	4	1	1
Hy Vandenberg	0	0	0.00	3	0	0	0	0	6.0	1	0	3	3
Hank Wyse	0	1	7.04	3	1	0	0	0	7.2	8	6	4	1
TOTAL	3	4	4.15	23	7	2	0	2	65.0	54	30	33	22

GAME 1 AT DET OCT 3

CHI	403	000	200	9 13 0
DET	000	000	000	0 6 0

Pitchers: BOROWY vs NEWHOUSER, Benton (3), Tobin (5), Mueller (8)
Home Runs: Cavaretta-CHI
Attendance: 54,637

GAME 2 AT DET OCT 4

CHI	000	100	000	1 7 0
DET	000	040	00X	4 7 0

Pitchers: WYSE, Erickson (7) vs TRUCKS
Home Runs: Greenberg-DET
Attendance: 53,636

GAME 3 AT DET OCT 5

CHI	000	200	100	3 8 0
DET	000	000	000	0 1 2

Pitchers: PASSEAU vs OVERMIRE, Benton (7)
Attendance: 55,500

GAME 4 AT CHI OCT 6

DET	000	400	000	4 7 1
CHI	000	001	000	1 5 1

Pitchers: TROUT vs PRIM, Derringer (4), Vandenberg (6), Erickson (8)
Attendance: 42,923

GAME 5 AT CHI OCT 7

DET	001	004	102	8 11 0
CHI	001	000	201	4 7 2

Pitchers: NEWHOUSER vs BOROWY, Vandenberg (6), Chipman (6), Derringer (7), Erickson (9)
Attendance: 43,463

GAME 6 AT CHI OCT 8

DET	010	000	240	000	7 13 1
CHI	000	041	200	001	8 15 3

Pitchers: Trucks, Caster (5), Bridges (6), Benton (7), TROUT (8) vs Passeau, Wyse (7), Prim (8), BOROWY (9)
Home Runs: Greenberg-DET
Attendance: 41,708

GAME 7 AT CHI OCT 10

DET	510	000	120	9 9 1
CHI	100	100	010	3 10 0

Pitchers: NEWHOUSER vs BOROWY, Derringer (1), Vandenberg (2), Erickson (6), Passeau (8), Wyse (9)
Attendance: 41,590

With World War Two over, the majors were at full strength for the first time in five years. Boston's big bats were back, and the Sox ran away with the American League pennant. St. Louis had Stan Musial back, but they struggled to their pennant, finishing the regular schedule tied with Brooklyn, and defeating them in the first major league tie-breaker playoff, two games to none.

Favored Boston edged St. Louis in the opener, but it took a home run by Rudy York in the top of the tenth to spoil Cardinal ace Howie Pollet's strong showing. Harry Brecheen brought the Cards back the next day with the first of his three Series wins—a four-hit shutout.

Boston regained the lead in Game Three. Sox ace Dave Ferriss spaced six hits and a walk, one per inning, in shutting out the Cardinals, and Rudy York hit his second game-winning homer, this time a three-run shot in the first inning. The next day, though, St. Louis exploded for a record-tying 20 hits—four apiece by Enos Slaughter, Joe Garagiola and Whitey Kurowski—to give Cardinal pitcher George Munger (who had completed only two of his seven regular-season starts) an easy complete-game 12–3 victory.

For the third time the Red Sox took the Series lead, winning Game Five 6–3 behind Joe Dobson's four-hit pitching (the Cards' three runs were unearned), but St. Louis tied the Series for the third time with a win in Game Six. Brecheen, in his second start, again pitched splendidly, holding Boston to a single run in the seventh inning, long after the Cards had driven out Sox starter Mickey Harris with three runs in the third.

The final game, like the Series itself, was a seesaw battle. Boston scored the first run in the top of the first, but St. Louis tied the score an inning later. The Cards took a two-run lead on three hits in the fifth, but the Sox came back in the eighth to tie it up as Dom DiMaggio doubled off reliever Brecheen to drive in a pair of pinch hitters who had singled and doubled off starter Murry Dickson. The Series' final run came a half inning later. Slaughter opened with a single, but moved no farther as the next two batters were retired. Then Harry Walker hit a liner over short. Slaughter, off with the crack of the bat, never paused and beat the relay to the plate with what proved the winning run, as Brecheen held the Sox in the ninth for his third win of the Series and the Cardinals' seventh world title.

St. Louis Cardinals (NL), 4;
Boston Red Sox (AL), 3

STL (N)

PLAYER/POS	AVG	G	AB	R	H	2B	3B	HR	RB	BB	SO	SB
Johnny Beazley, p	.000	1	0	0	0	0	0	0	0	0	0	0
Al Brazle, p	.000	1	2	0	0	0	0	0	0	0	0	0
Harry Brecheen, p	.125	3	8	2	1	0	0	0	1	0	1	0
Murry Dickson, p	.400	2	5	1	2	2	0	0	1	0	1	0
Erv Dusak, of	.250	4	4	0	1	0	0	0	0	2	2	0
Joe Garagiola, c	.316	5	19	2	6	2	0	0	4	0	3	0
Nippy Jones, ph	.000	1	1	0	0	0	0	0	0	0	1	0
Whitey Kurowski, 3b	.296	7	27	5	8	3	0	0	2	0	3	0
Marty Marion, ss	.250	7	24	1	6	2	0	0	4	1	1	0
Terry Moore, of	.148	7	27	1	4	0	0	0	2	2	6	0
Red Munger, p	.250	1	4	0	1	0	0	0	0	0	2	0
Stan Musial, 1b	.222	7	27	3	6	4	1	0	4	4	2	1
Howie Pollet, p	.000	2	4	0	0	0	0	0	0	0	1	0
Del Rice, c	.500	3	6	2	3	1	0	0	2	0	0	0
Red Schoendienst, 2b	.233	7	30	3	7	1	0	0	1	0	2	1
Dick Sisler, ph	.000	2	2	0	0	0	0	0	0	0	0	0
Enos Slaughter, of	.320	7	25	5	8	1	1	1	2	4	3	1
Harry Walker, of	.412	7	17	3	7	2	0	0	6	4	2	0
Ted Wilks, p	.000	1	0	0	0	0	0	0	0	0	0	0
TOTAL	.259		232	28	60	19	2	1	27	19	30	3

PITCHER	W	L	ERA	G	GS	CG	SV	SHO	IP	H	ER	BB	SO
Johnny Beazley	0	0	0.00	1	0	0	0	0	1.0	1	0	0	1
Al Brazle	0	1	5.40	1	0	0	0	0	6.2	7	4	6	4
Harry Brecheen	3	0	0.45	3	2	2	0	1	20.0	14	1	5	11
Murry Dickson	0	1	3.86	2	2	0	0	0	14.0	11	6	4	7
Red Munger	1	0	1.00	1	1	1	0	0	9.0	9	1	3	2
Howie Pollet	0	1	3.48	2	2	1	0	0	10.1	12	4	4	3
Ted Wilks	0	0	0.00	1	0	0	0	0	1.0	2	0	0	0
TOTAL	4	3	2.32	11	7	4	0	1	62.0	56	16	22	28

BOS (A)

PLAYER/POS	AVG	G	AB	R	H	2B	3B	HR	RB	BB	SO	SB
Jim Bagby, p	.000	1	1	0	0	0	0	0	0	0	0	0
Mace Brown, p	.000	1	0	0	0	0	0	0	0	0	0	0
Paul Campbell, pr	.000	1	0	0	0	0	0	0	0	0	0	0
Leon Culberson, of-3	.222	5	9	1	2	0	0	1	1	1	2	1
Dom DiMaggio, of	.259	7	27	2	7	3	0	0	3	2	2	0
Joe Dobson, p	.000	3	3	0	0	0	0	0	0	0	2	0
Bobby Doerr, 2b	.409	6	22	1	9	1	0	1	3	2	2	0
Clem Dreisewerd, p	.000	1	0	0	0	0	0	0	0	0	0	0
Dave Ferriss, p	.000	2	6	0	0	0	0	0	0	0	1	0
Don Gutteridge, 2b-2	.400	3	5	1	2	0	0	0	1	0	0	0
Mickey Harris, p	.333	2	3	0	1	0	0	0	0	0	1	0
Pinky Higgins, 3b	.208	7	24	1	5	1	0	0	2	2	0	0
Tex Hughson, p	.333	3	3	0	1	0	0	0	0	0	1	0
Earl Johnson, p	.000	3	1	0	0	0	0	0	0	0	0	0
Bob Klinger, p	.000	1	0	0	0	0	0	0	0	0	0	0
Tom McBride, of-2	.167	5	12	0	2	0	0	0	1	0	1	0
Catfish Metkovich, ph	.500	2	2	1	1	1	0	0	0	0	0	0
Wally Moses, of	.417	4	12	1	5	0	0	0	0	1	2	0
Roy Partee, c	.100	5	10	1	1	0	0	0	1	1	2	0
Johnny Pesky, ss	.233	7	30	2	7	0	0	0	0	1	3	1
Rip Russell, 3b-1	1.000	2	2	1	2	0	0	0	1	0	0	0
Mike Ryba, p	.000	1	0	0	0	0	0	0	0	0	0	0
Hal Wagner, c	.000	5	13	0	0	0	0	0	0	0	1	0
Ted Williams, of	.200	7	25	2	5	0	0	0	1	5	5	0
Rudy York, 1b	.261	7	23	6	6	1	0	2	5	6	4	0
Bill Zuber, p	.000	1	0	0	0	0	0	0	0	0	0	0
TOTAL	.240		233	20	56	7	1	4	18	22	28	2

PITCHER	W	L	ERA	G	GS	CG	SV	SHO	IP	H	ER	BB	SO
Jim Bagby	0	0	3.00	1	0	0	0	0	3.0	6	1	1	1
Mace Brown	0	0	27.00	1	0	0	0	0	1.0	4	3	1	0
Joe Dobson	1	0	0.00	3	1	1	0	0	12.2	4	0	3	10
Clem Dreisewerd	0	0	0.00	1	0	0	0	0	0.1	0	0	0	0
Dave Ferriss	1	0	2.03	2	2	1	0	1	13.1	13	3	2	4
Mickey Harris	0	2	3.72	2	2	0	0	0	9.2	11	4	4	5
Tex Hughson	0	1	3.14	3	2	0	0	0	14.1	14	5	3	8
Earl Johnson	1	0	2.70	3	0	0	0	0	3.1	1	1	2	1
Bob Klinger	0	1	13.50	1	0	0	0	0	0.2	2	1	1	0
Mike Ryba	0	0	13.50	1	0	0	0	0	0.2	2	1	1	0
Bill Zuber	0	0	4.50	1	0	0	0	0	2.0	3	1	1	1
TOTAL	3	4	2.95	19	7	2	0	1	61.0	60	20	19	30

GAME 1 AT STL OCT 6

BOS	010 000 001 1	3	9	2
STL	000 001 010 0	2	7	0

Pitchers: Hughson, JOHNSON (9) vs POLLET
Home Runs: York-BOS
Attendance: 36,218

GAME 2 AT STL OCT 7

BOS	000 000 000	0	4	1
STL	001 020 00X	3	6	0

Pitchers: HARRIS, Dobson (8) vs BRECHEEN
Attendance: 35,815

GAME 3 AT BOS OCT 9

STL	000 000 000	0	6	1
BOS	300 000 01X	4	8	0

Pitchers: DICKSON, Wilks (8) vs FERRISS
Home Runs: York-BOS
Attendance: 34,500

GAME 4 AT BOS OCT 10

STL	033 010 104	12	20	1
BOS	000 100 020	3	9	4

Pitchers: MUNGER vs HUGHSON, Bagby (3), Zuber (6), Brown (8), Ryba (9), Dreisewerd (9)
Home Runs: Slaughter-STL, Doerr-BOS
Attendance: 35,645

GAME 5 AT BOS OCT 11

STL	010 000 002	3	4	1
BOS	110 001 30X	6	11	3

Pitchers: Pollet, BRAZLE (1), Beazley (8) vs DOBSON
Home Runs: Culberson-BOS
Attendance: 35,982

GAME 6 AT STL OCT 13

BOS	000 000 100	1	7	0
STL	003 000 01X	4	8	0

Pitchers: HARRIS, Hughson (3), Johnson (8) vs BRECHEEN
Attendance: 35,768

GAME 7 AT STL OCT 15

BOS	100 000 020	3	8	0
STL	010 020 01X	4	9	1

Pitchers: Ferriss, Dobson (5), KLINGER (8), Johnson (8) vs Dickson, BRECHEEN (8)
Attendance: 36,143

Two of the most memorable plays in World Series history brought Brooklyn victory in Games Four and Six, but when the Series had ended the Yankees were world champions for the eleventh time. Dodger ace Ralph Branca set New York down in order through the first four innings of Game One. But the first five batters to face him in the fifth inning reached base. Branca was lifted, but before the inning was over five Yankees had crossed the plate—more than enough for their first win.

The Yankees went two-up the next day, rocking four Brooklyn pitchers for 15 hits and an easy 10–3 win. Brooklyn finally made its presence felt in Game Three, another heavy-hitting affair, scoring six times in the second inning to establish a lead the Yankees could not overcome. Both teams recorded 13 hits, but Dodger fireman Hugh Casey extinguished the last Yankee flame in the seventh inning, and preserved a narrow 9–8 Dodger lead the rest of the way.

Shortstop Pee Wee Reese's error and a bases-loaded walk gave the Yankees an unearned run in the first inning of Game Four, and they earned a second run in the fourth. Meanwhile, Yankee pitcher Bill Bevens, although he averaged a walk an inning, had allowed no Dodger hits and only one run as the game entered the last of the ninth. Bevens retired two in the ninth, but walked his ninth and tenth batters (one intentionally), then lost both his no-hitter and the game as Dodger pinch hitter Cookie Lavagetto doubled home the two baserunners to even the Series at two-all.

Yankee Spec Shea (the winning pitcher in Game One) held Brooklyn to four hits and one run in Game Five. Joe DiMaggio homered in the fifth inning for New York's second run, enough to put the Yankees back in the Series lead. The Dodgers rebounded in Game Six to build an early 4–0 lead. But the Yankees tied the score in the last of the third and took a lead in the fourth. Brooklyn regained the lead in the sixth with four runs, but when DiMaggio hit a long fly to left with two on in the Yankee half of the inning, it looked as if the score would be tied. But substitute left fielder Al Gionfriddo (in what turned out to be his last big league game) raced to the bullpen fence 415 feet out to rob DiMag of the home run. New York scored a run in the ninth, but thanks to Gionfriddo's catch it was not enough to win the game.

Brooklyn scored first in the finale with a pair of second-inning runs, but Yankee relievers Bill Bevens and Joe Page shut them out

New York Yankees (AL), 4; Brooklyn Dodgers (NL), 3

NY (A)

PLAYER/POS	AVG	G	AB	R	H	2B	3B	HR	RB	BB	SO	SB
Yogi Berra, c-4,of-2	.158	6	19	2	3	0	0	1	2	1	2	0
Bill Bevens, p	.000	2	4	0	0	0	0	0	0	0	2	0
Bobby Brown, ph	1.000	4	3	2	3	2	0	0	3	1	0	0
Spud Chandler, p	.000	1	0	0	0	0	0	0	0	0	0	0
Allie Clark, of-1	.500	3	2	1	1	0	0	0	1	1	0	0
Joe DiMaggio, of	.231	7	26	4	6	0	0	2	5	6	2	0
Karl Drews, p	.000	2	2	0	0	0	0	0	0	0	2	0
Lonny Frey, ph	.000	1	1	0	0	0	0	0	1	0	0	0
Tommy Henrich, of	.323	7	31	2	10	2	0	1	5	2	3	0
Ralph Houk, ph	1.000	1	1	0	1	0	0	0	0	0	0	0
Billy Johnson, 3b	.269	7	26	8	7	0	3	0	2	3	4	0
Johnny Lindell, of	.500	6	18	3	9	3	1	0	7	5	2	0
Sherm Lollar, c	.750	2	4	3	3	2	0	0	1	0	0	0
George McQuinn, 1b	.130	7	23	3	3	0	0	0	1	5	8	0
Bobo Newsom, p	.000	2	0	0	0	0	0	0	0	0	0	0
Joe Page, p	.000	4	4	0	0	0	0	0	0	0	1	0
Jack Phillips, 1b-1	.000	2	2	0	0	0	0	0	0	0	0	0
Vic Raschi, p	.000	2	0	0	0	0	0	0	0	0	0	0
Allie Reynolds, p	.500	2	4	2	2	0	0	0	1	0	0	0
Phil Rizzuto, ss	.308	7	26	3	8	1	0	0	2	4	0	2
Aaron Robinson, c	.200	3	10	2	2	0	0	0	1	2	1	0
Spec Shea, p	.400	3	5	0	2	1	0	0	1	0	2	0
Snuffy Stirnweiss, 2b	.259	7	27	3	7	0	1	0	3	8	8	0
Butch Wensloff, p	.000	1	0	0	0	0	0	0	0	0	0	0
TOTAL	.282		238	38	67	11	5	4	36	38	37	2

PITCHER	W	L	ERA	G	GS	CG	SV	SHO	IP	H	ER	BB	SO
Bill Bevens	0	1	2.38	2	1	1	0	0	11.1	3	3	11	7
Spud Chandler	0	0	9.00	1	0	0	0	0	2.0	2	2	3	1
Karl Drews	0	0	3.00	2	0	0	0	0	3.0	2	1	1	0
Bobo Newsom	0	1	19.29	2	1	0	0	0	2.1	6	5	2	0
Joe Page	1	1	4.15	4	0	0	1	0	13.0	12	6	2	7
Vic Raschi	0	0	6.75	2	0	0	0	0	1.1	2	1	0	1
Allie Reynolds	1	0	4.76	2	2	1	0	0	11.1	15	6	3	6
Spec Shea	2	0	2.35	3	3	1	0	0	15.1	10	4	8	10
Butch Wensloff	0	0	0.00	1	0	0	0	0	2.0	0	0	0	0
TOTAL	4	3	4.09	19	7	3	1	0	61.2	52	28	30	32

BRO (N)

PLAYER/POS	AVG	G	AB	R	H	2B	3B	HR	RB	BB	SO	SB
Dan Bankhead, pr	.000	1	0	1	0	0	0	0	0	0	0	0
Rex Barney, p	.000	3	1	0	0	0	0	0	0	0	0	0
Hank Behrman, p	.000	5	0	0	0	0	0	0	0	0	0	0
Bobby Bragan, ph	1.000	1	1	0	1	1	0	0	1	0	0	0
Ralph Branca, p	.000	3	4	0	0	0	0	0	0	0	1	0
Hugh Casey, p	.000	6	1	0	0	0	0	0	0	0	1	0
Bruce Edwards, c	.222	7	27	3	6	1	0	0	2	2	7	0
Carl Furillo, of	.353	6	17	2	6	2	0	0	3	3	0	0
Al Gionfriddo, of-1	.000	4	3	2	0	0	0	0	0	1	0	1
Hal Gregg, p	.000	3	3	0	0	0	0	0	0	1	1	0
Joe Hatten, p	.333	4	3	1	1	0	0	0	0	0	0	0
Gene Hermanski, of	.158	7	19	4	3	0	1	0	1	3	3	0
Gil Hodges, ph	.000	1	1	0	0	0	0	0	0	1	0	0
Spider Jorgensen, 3b	.200	7	20	1	4	2	0	0	3	2	4	0
Cookie Lavagetto, 3b-3	.143	5	7	0	1	1	0	0	3	2	0	0
Vic Lombardi, p-2	.000	3	3	0	0	0	0	0	0	0	1	0
Eddie Miksis, 2b-1,of-1	.250	5	4	1	1	0	0	0	0	0	1	0
Pee Wee Reese, ss	.304	7	23	5	7	1	0	0	4	6	3	3
Pete Reiser, of-3	.250	5	8	1	2	0	0	0	0	3	1	0
Jackie Robinson, 1b	.259	7	27	3	7	2	0	0	3	2	4	2
Eddie Stanky, 2b	.240	7	25	4	6	1	0	0	2	3	2	0
Harry Taylor, p	.000	1	0	0	0	0	0	0	0	0	0	0
Arky Vaughan, ph	.500	3	2	0	1	0	0	0	0	1	0	0
Dixie Walker, of	.222	7	27	1	6	1	0	1	4	3	1	1
TOTAL	.230		226	29	52	13	1	1	26	30	32	7

PITCHER	W	L	ERA	G	GS	CG	SV	SHO	IP	H	ER	BB	SO
Rex Barney	0	1	2.70	3	1	0	0	0	6.2	4	2	10	3
Hank Behrman	0	0	7.11	5	0	0	0	0	6.1	9	5	5	3
Ralph Branca	1	1	8.64	3	1	0	0	0	8.1	12	8	5	8
Hugh Casey	2	0	0.87	6	0	0	1	0	10.1	5	1	1	3
Hal Gregg	0	1	3.55	3	1	0	0	0	12.2	9	5	8	10
Joe Hatten	0	0	7.00	4	1	0	0	0	9.0	12	7	7	5
Vic Lombardi	0	1	12.15	2	2	0	0	0	6.2	14	9	1	5
Harry Taylor	0	0	—	1	1	0	0	0	0.0	2	0	1	0
TOTAL	3	4	5.55	27	7	0	1	0	60.0	67	37	38	37

through the final seven innings as their teammates gradually built a Series-clinching 5–2 victory.

GAME 1 AT NY SEPT 30

BRO	100	001	100	3	6	0
NY	000	050	00X	5	4	0

Pitchers: BRANCA, Behrman (5), Casey (7) vs SHEA, Page (6)
Attendance: 73,365

GAME 2 AT NY OCT 1

BRO	001	100	001	3	9	2
NY	101	121	40X	10	15	1

Pitchers: LOMBARDI, Gregg (5), Behrman (7), Barney (7) vs REYNOLDS
Home Runs: Walker-BRO, Henrich-NY
Attendance: 69,865

GAME 3 AT BRO OCT 2

NY	002	221	100	8	13	0
BRO	061	200	00X	9	13	1

Pitchers: NEWSOM, Raschi (2), Drews (3), Chandler (4), Page (6) vs Hatten, Branca (5), CASEY (7)
Home Runs: DiMaggio-NY, Berra-NY
Attendance: 33,098

GAME 4 AT BRO OCT 3

NY	100	100	000	2	8	1
BRO	000	010	002	3	1	3

Pitchers: BEVENS vs Taylor, Gregg (1), Behrman (8), CASEY (9)
Attendance: 33,443

GAME 5 AT BRO OCT 4

NY	000	110	000	2	5	0
BRO	000	001	000	1	4	1

Pitchers: SHEA vs BARNEY, Hatten (5), Behrman (7), Casey (8)
Home Runs: DiMaggio-NY
Attendance: 34,379

GAME 6 AT NY OCT 5

BRO	202	004	000	8	12	1
NY	004	100	001	6	15	2

Pitchers: Lombardi, BRANCA (3), Hatten (6), Casey (9) vs Reynolds, Drews (3), PAGE (5), Newsom (6), Raschi (7), Wensloff (8)
Attendance: 74,065

GAME 7 AT NY OCT 6

BRO	020	000	000	2	7	0
NY	010	201	10X	5	7	0

Pitchers: GREGG, Behrman (4), Hatten (6), Barney (6), Casey (7) vs Shea, Bevens (2), PAGE (5)
Attendance: 71,548

Boston outpitched and outhit Cleveland, and the clubs tied in runs scored. But the Braves scored most of their runs in one game, and the Indians, spreading theirs more evenly, took the Series. Boston ace Johnny Sain dueled Bob Feller in the opener. Feller gave up only two singles, but one of them followed a walk and a sacrifice (and a controversial pickoff play at second, in which the Boston runner was ruled safe although photos later showed him clearly out) and drove in the game's only run. Both teams registered eight hits in Game Two, but Cleveland's led to four runs, while Indian hurler Bob Lemon held Boston to just one—and that was unearned.

Cleveland's rookie sensation Gene Bearden shut out the Braves on five hits in Game Three as the Series moved to Cleveland's huge Municipal Stadium. Bearden himself, after doubling in the third, scored on a Boston error what proved to be the winning run. A record 81,897 fans saw Sain face Steve Gromek in Game Four. Only five Indians hit Sain safely, but a first-inning single and double put Cleveland on the board, and Larry Doby's home run two innings later made the score 2–0. Boston's Marv Rickert homered in the seventh to narrow Cleveland's lead, but that ended the scoring.

Another attendance record was set at Game Five as 86,288 fans gathered to watch Bob Feller sew up the title for Cleveland. They went home disappointed. In a game that featured five of the Series' eight home runs, Boston jumped ahead on Bob Elliott's three-run blast in the first. Dale Mitchell opened Cleveland's half of the inning with a home run, but Elliott neutralized it in the third with his second homer. The Indians drove out Boston starter Nelson Potter with four runs in the fourth inning (three coming on Jim Hegan's homer). But Warren Spahn (who had lost Game Two) hurled one-hit shutout relief over the final five frames as his Braves tied the game on Bill Salkeld's homer in the sixth, and blew out Feller and two relievers with six runs in the seventh. The fourth Indian pitcher, Satchel Paige (in his only World Series appearance), retired two batters to end the inning, but the damage had been done.

A day later though, back in Boston, Cleveland edged the Braves 4–3 for the title. Gene Bearden's relief pitching allowed two inherited baserunners to score in the eighth, but halted Boston's rally one run short of a tie.

Cleveland Indians (AL), 4;
Boston Braves (NL), 2

CLE (A)

PLAYER/POS	AVG	G	AB	R	H	2B	3B	HR	RB	BB	SO	SB
Gene Bearden, p	.500	2	4	1	2	1	0	0	0	0	1	0
Ray Boone, ph	.000	1	1	0	0	0	0	0	0	0	1	0
Lou Boudreau, ss	.273	6	22	1	6	4	0	0	3	1	1	0
Russ Christopher, p	.000	1	0	0	0	0	0	0	0	0	0	0
Allie Clark, of	.000	1	3	0	0	0	0	0	0	0	1	0
Larry Doby, of	.318	6	22	1	7	1	0	1	2	2	4	0
Bob Feller, p	.000	2	4	0	0	0	0	0	0	0	2	0
Joe Gordon, 2b	.182	6	22	3	4	0	0	1	2	1	2	1
Steve Gromek, p	.000	1	3	0	0	0	0	0	0	0	1	0
Jim Hegan, c	.211	6	19	2	4	0	0	1	5	1	4	1
Wally Judnich, of	.077	4	13	1	1	0	0	0	1	1	4	0
Ken Keltner, 3b	.095	6	21	3	2	0	0	0	0	2	3	0
Bob Kennedy, of	.500	3	2	0	1	0	0	0	1	0	0	0
Ed Klieman, p	.000	1	0	0	0	0	0	0	0	0	0	0
Bob Lemon, p	.000	2	7	0	0	0	0	0	0	0	0	0
Dale Mitchell, of	.174	6	23	4	4	1	0	1	1	2	0	0
Bob Muncrief, p	.000	1	0	0	0	0	0	0	0	0	0	0
Satchel Paige, p	.000	1	0	0	0	0	0	0	0	0	0	0
Hal Peck, of	.000	1	0	0	0	0	0	0	0	0	0	0
Eddie Robinson, 1b	.300	6	20	0	6	0	0	0	1	1	0	0
Al Rosen, ph	.000	1	1	0	0	0	0	0	0	0	0	0
Joe Tipton, ph	.000	1	1	0	0	0	0	0	0	0	1	0
Thurman Tucker, of	.333	1	3	1	1	0	0	0	0	1	0	0
TOTAL	.199		191	17	38	7	0	4	16	12	26	2

PITCHER	W	L	ERA	G	GS	CG	SV	SHO	IP	H	ER	BB	SO
Gene Bearden	1	0	0.00	2	1	1	1	1	10.2	6	0	1	4
Russ Christopher	0	0	∞	1	0	0	0	0	0.0	2	1	0	0
Bob Feller	0	2	5.02	2	2	1	0	0	14.1	10	8	5	7
Steve Gromek	1	0	1.00	1	1	1	0	0	9.0	7	1	1	2
Ed Klieman	0	0	∞	1	0	0	0	0	0.0	1	3	2	0
Bob Lemon	2	0	1.65	2	2	1	0	0	16.1	16	3	7	6
Bob Muncrief	0	0	0.00	1	0	0	0	0	2.0	1	0	0	0
Satchel Paige	0	0	0.00	1	0	0	0	0	0.2	0	0	0	0
TOTAL	4	2	2.72	11	6	4	1	1	53.0	43	16	16	19

BOS (N)

PLAYER/POS	AVG	G	AB	R	H	2B	3B	HR	RB	BB	SO	SB
Red Barrett, p	.000	2	0	0	0	0	0	0	0	0	0	0
Vern Bickford, p	.000	1	0	0	0	0	0	0	0	0	0	0
Clint Conatser, of	.000	2	4	0	0	0	0	0	1	0	0	0
Alvin Dark, ss	.167	6	24	2	4	1	0	0	0	0	2	0
Bob Elliott, 3b	.333	6	21	4	7	0	0	2	5	2	2	0
Tommy Holmes, of	.192	6	26	3	5	0	0	0	1	0	0	0
Phil Masi, c	.125	5	8	1	1	1	0	0	1	0	0	0
Frank McCormick, 1b-1	.200	3	5	0	1	0	0	0	0	0	2	0
Mike McCormick, of	.261	6	23	1	6	0	0	0	2	0	4	0
Nelson Potter, p	.500	2	2	0	1	0	0	0	0	0	1	0
Marv Rickert, of	.211	5	19	2	4	0	0	1	2	0	4	0
Connie Ryan, ph	.000	2	1	0	0	0	0	0	0	1	0	0
Johnny Sain, p	.200	2	5	0	1	0	0	0	0	0	0	0
Bill Salkeld, c	.222	5	9	2	2	0	0	1	1	1	5	0
Ray Sanders, ph	.000	1	1	0	0	0	0	0	0	0	0	0
Sibby Sisti, 2b	.000	2	1	0	0	0	0	0	0	0	0	0
Warren Spahn, p	.000	3	4	0	0	0	0	0	1	0	0	0
Eddie Stanky, 2b	.286	6	14	0	4	1	0	0	1	7	1	0
Earl Torgeson, 1b	.389	5	18	2	7	3	0	0	1	2	1	1
Bill Voiselle, p	.000	2	2	0	0	0	0	0	0	0	0	0
TOTAL	.230		187	17	43	6	0	4	16	16	19	1

PITCHER	W	L	ERA	G	GS	CG	SV	SHO	IP	H	ER	BB	SO
Red Barrett	0	0	0.00	2	0	0	0	0	3.2	1	0	0	1
Vern Bickford	0	1	2.70	1	1	0	0	0	3.1	4	1	5	1
Nelson Potter	0	0	8.44	2	1	0	0	0	5.1	6	5	2	1
Johnny Sain	1	1	1.06	2	2	2	0	1	17.0	9	2	0	9
Warren Spahn	1	1	3.00	3	1	0	0	0	12.0	10	4	3	12
Bill Voiselle	0	1	2.53	2	1	0	0	0	10.2	8	3	2	2
TOTAL	2	4	2.60	12	6	2	0	1	52.0	38	15	12	26

GAME 1 AT BOS OCT 6

CLE	000 000 000	0	4	0
BOS	000 000 01X	1	2	2

Pitchers: FELLER vs SAIN
Attendance: 40,135

GAME 2 AT BOS OCT 7

CLE	000 210 001	4	8	1
BOS	100 000 000	1	8	3

Pitchers: LEMON vs SPAHN, Barrett (5), Potter (8)
Attendance: 39,633

GAME 3 AT CLE OCT 8

BOS	000 000 000	0	5	1
CLE	001 100 00X	2	5	0

Pitchers: BICKFORD, Voiselle (4), Barrett (8) vs BEARDEN
Attendance: 70,306

GAME 4 AT CLE OCT 9

BOS	000 000 100	1	7	0
CLE	101 000 00X	2	5	0

Pitchers: SAIN vs GROMEK
Home Runs: Doby-CLE, Rickert-BOS
Attendance: 81,897

GAME 5 AT CLE OCT 10

BOS	301 001 600	11	12	0
CLE	100 400 000	5	6	2

Pitchers: Potter, SPAHN (4) vs FELLER, Klieman (7), Christopher (7), Paige (7), Muncrief (8)
Home Runs: Elliott-BOS (2), Mitchell-CLE, Hegan-CLE, Salkeld-BOS
Attendance: 86,288

GAME 6 AT BOS OCT 11

CLE	001 002 010	4	10	0
BOS	000 100 020	3	9	0

Pitchers: LEMON, Bearden (8) vs VOISELLE, Spahn (8)
Home Runs: Gordon-CLE
Attendance: 40,103

Casey Stengel, in the first of his twelve years as Yankee manager, edged his team past the Boston Red Sox for his first of ten American League pennants, then past the Dodgers for his first of seven world championships. New York and Brooklyn traded 1–0 wins to begin the Series. In Game One Yankee Allie Reynolds dueled Dodger rookie Don Newcombe scorelessly through 8½ innings—until Tommy Henrich led off the last of the ninth with a Yankee home run. Dodger Jackie Robinson scored after doubling off Vic Raschi in the second inning of Game Two for that game's only score, while Dodger ace Preacher Roe permitted the Yankees just six scattered hits—never more than one per inning.

The teams entered the ninth inning of Game Three tied 1–1. But in the top of the ninth, Dodger starter Ralph Branca, after loading the bases on two walks and a single, gave up another single to pinch hitter Johnny Mize for two runs. Jerry Coleman's single off reliever Jack Banta drove in another run before the third out was made. In the last of the ninth, Yankee fireman Joe Page (who had held Brooklyn scoreless since coming on with the bases loaded in the fourth) finally weakened. But after yielding solo homers to Luis Olmo and Roy Campanella, he struck out pinch hitter Bruce Edwards for New York's second win.

The Yankees' victory in Game Four came a little easier. They scored first, driving out starter Don Newcombe with three runs in the fourth, and rapping reliever Joe Hatten for three more runs an inning later. Brooklyn retaliated in the sixth, sending Yankee starter Ed Lopat to the showers with seven singles for four runs. But Allie Reynolds came on for 3⅓ innings of no-hit relief to preserve the Yankees lead—and his Series 0.00 earned run average.

After four closely contested games, the Yankees erupted in Game Five for ten runs in the first six innings as Brooklyn was held to just two. In the last of the seventh, the Dodgers came back, driving out starter Vic Raschi with a four-run rally, capped by Gil Hodges's three-run homer. But Joe Page came on to get the final out of the seventh, and held the Dodgers scoreless over the final two innings to bring the Yankees' world titles to an even dozen.

New York Yankees (AL), 4;
Brooklyn Dodgers (NL), 1

NY (A)

PLAYER/POS	AVG	G	AB	R	H	2B	3B	HR	RB	BB	SO	SB
Hank Bauer, of	.167	3	6	0	1	0	0	0	0	0	0	0
Yogi Berra, c	.063	4	16	2	1	0	0	0	1	1	3	0
Bobby Brown, 3b-3	.500	4	12	4	6	1	2	0	5	2	2	0
Tommy Byrne, p	1.000	1	1	0	1	0	0	0	0	0	0	0
Gerry Coleman, 2b	.250	5	20	0	5	3	0	0	4	0	4	0
Joe DiMaggio, of	.111	5	18	2	2	0	0	1	2	3	5	0
Tommy Henrich, 1b	.263	5	19	4	5	0	0	1	1	3	0	0
Billy Johnson, 3b	.143	2	7	0	1	0	0	0	0	0	2	1
Johnny Lindell, of	.143	2	7	0	1	0	0	0	0	0	2	0
Ed Lopat, p	.333	1	3	0	1	1	0	0	1	0	0	0
Cliff Mapes, of	.100	4	10	3	1	1	0	0	2	2	4	0
Johnny Mize, ph	1.000	2	2	0	2	0	0	0	2	0	0	0
Gus Niarhos, c	.000	1	0	0	0	0	0	0	0	0	0	0
Joe Page, p	.000	3	4	0	0	0	0	0	0	0	2	0
Vic Raschi, p	.200	2	5	0	1	0	0	0	1	1	1	0
Allie Reynolds, p	.500	2	4	2	2	1	0	0	0	0	1	0
Phil Rizzuto, ss	.167	5	18	2	3	0	0	0	1	3	1	1
Charlie Silvera, c	.000	1	2	0	0	0	0	0	0	0	0	0
Snuffy Stirnweiss, ph	.000	1	0	0	0	0	0	0	0	0	0	0
Gene Woodling, of	.400	3	10	4	4	3	0	0	0	3	0	0
TOTAL	.226		164	21	37	10	2	2	20	18	27	2

PITCHER	W	L	ERA	G	GS	CG	SV	SHO	IP	H	ER	BB	SO
Tommy Byrne	0	0	2.70	1	1	0	0	0	3.1	2	1	2	1
Ed Lopat	1	0	6.35	1	1	0	0	0	5.2	9	4	1	4
Joe Page	1	0	2.00	3	0	0	1	0	9.0	6	2	8	8
Vic Raschi	1	1	4.30	2	2	0	0	0	14.2	15	7	5	11
Allie Reynolds	1	0	0.00	2	1	1	1	1	12.1	2	0	4	14
TOTAL	4	1	2.80	9	5	1	2	1	45.0	34	14	15	38

BRO (N)

PLAYER/POS	AVG	G	AB	R	H	2B	3B	HR	RB	BB	SO	SB
Jack Banta, p	.000	3	1	0	0	0	0	0	0	0	0	0
Rex Barney, p	.000	1	0	0	0	0	0	0	0	0	0	0
Ralph Branca, p	.000	1	3	0	0	0	0	0	0	0	3	0
Tommy Brown, ph	.000	2	2	0	0	0	0	0	0	0	1	0
Roy Campanella, c	.267	5	15	2	4	1	0	1	2	3	1	0
Billy Cox, 3b-1	.333	2	3	0	1	0	0	0	0	0	1	0
Bruce Edwards, ph	.500	2	2	0	1	0	0	0	0	0	1	0
Carl Erskine, p	.000	2	0	0	0	0	0	0	0	0	0	0
Carl Furillo, of-2	.125	2	8	0	1	0	0	0	0	1	0	0
Joe Hatten, p	.000	2	0	0	0	0	0	0	0	0	0	0
Gene Hermanski, of	.308	4	13	1	4	0	1	0	2	3	3	0
Gil Hodges, 1b	.235	5	17	2	4	0	0	1	4	1	4	0
Spider Jorgensen, 3b-3	.182	4	11	1	2	2	0	0	0	2	2	0
Mike McCormick, of	.000	1	0	0	0	0	0	0	0	0	0	0
Eddie Miksis, 3b-2	.286	3	7	0	2	0	0	0	0	0	1	0
Paul Minner, p	.000	1	0	0	0	0	0	0	0	0	0	0
Don Newcombe, p	.000	2	4	0	0	0	0	0	0	0	3	0
Luis Olmo, of	.273	4	11	2	3	0	0	1	2	0	2	0
Erv Palica, p	.000	1	0	0	0	0	0	0	0	0	0	0
Marv Rackley, of	.000	2	5	0	0	0	0	0	0	0	2	0
Pee Wee Reese, ss	.316	5	19	2	6	1	0	1	2	1	0	1
Jackie Robinson, 2b	.188	5	16	2	3	1	0	0	2	4	2	0
Preacher Roe, p	.000	1	3	0	0	0	0	0	0	0	3	0
Duke Snider, of	.143	5	21	2	3	1	0	0	0	0	8	0
Dick Whitman, ph	.000	1	1	0	0	0	0	0	0	0	1	0
TOTAL	.210		162	14	34	7	1	4	14	15	38	1

PITCHER	W	L	ERA	G	GS	CG	SV	SHO	IP	H	ER	BB	SO
Jack Banta	0	0	3.18	3	0	0	0	0	5.2	5	2	1	4
Rex Barney	0	1	16.88	1	1	0	0	0	2.2	3	5	6	2
Ralph Branca	0	1	4.15	1	1	0	0	0	8.2	4	4	4	6
Carl Erskine	0	0	16.20	2	0	0	0	0	1.2	3	3	1	0
Joe Hatten	0	0	16.20	2	0	0	0	0	1.2	4	3	2	0
Paul Minner	0	0	0.00	1	0	0	0	0	1.0	1	0	0	0
Don Newcombe	0	2	3.09	2	2	1	0	0	11.2	10	4	3	11
Erv Palica	0	0	0.00	1	0	0	0	0	2.0	1	0	1	1
Preacher Roe	1	0	0.00	1	1	1	0	1	9.0	6	0	0	3
TOTAL	1	4	4.30	14	5	2	0	1	44.0	37	21	18	27

GAME 1 AT NY OCT 5

BRO	000	000	000	0	2	0
NY	000	000	001	1	5	1

Pitchers: NEWCOMBE vs REYNOLDS
Home Runs: Henrich-NY
Attendance: 66,224

GAME 2 AT NY OCT 6

BRO	010	000	000	1	7	2
NY	000	000	000	0	6	1

Pitchers: ROE vs RASCHI, Page (9)
Attendance: 70,053

GAME 3 AT BRO OCT 7

NY	001	000	003	4	5	0
BRO	000	100	002	3	5	0

Pitchers: Byrne, PAGE (4) vs BRANCA, Banta (9)
Home Runs: Reese-BRO, Olmo-BRO, Campanella-BRO
Attendance: 32,788

GAME 4 AT BRO OCT 8

NY	000	330	000	6	10	0
BRO	000	004	000	4	9	1

Pitchers: LOPAT, Reynolds (6) vs NEWCOMBE, Hatten (4), Erskine (6), Banta (7)
Attendance: 33,934

GAME 5 AT BRO OCT 9

NY	203	113	000	10	11	1
BRO	001	001	400	6	11	2

Pitchers: RASCHI, Page (7) vs BARNEY, Banta (3), Erskine (6), Hatten (6), Palica (7), Minner (9)
Home Runs: DiMaggio-NY, Hodges-BRO
Attendance: 33,711

Philadelphia's Whiz Kids, who had capped an exciting pennant race with the Phillies' first flag in thirty-five years, carried the excitement into the World Series but couldn't quite catch up with the Yankees. New York scored only one run in the opener; Philadelphia didn't score any. The Phillies did score a run in the second game, but the Yankees scored two. In Game Three the Phillies scored two runs, the Yankees three.

Jim Konstanty, the National League's ace reliever (and MVP), started his first major league game in four years to lead off the Series, and held the Yankees to just four hits in eight innings of work. But Bobby Brown's double in the fourth was followed by two long flies which moved Brown around to the plate—all the scoring New York needed as Vic Raschi held the Phillies to two singles and a walk.

Robin Roberts and Allie Reynolds dueled in Game Two. New York scored first with a run on a walk and two singles in the second inning, but two Phillie singles and a fly to left tied the game in the last of the fifth. There matters stood until the top of the tenth, when Joe DiMaggio led off with a home run to the upper deck in left. Reynolds held the Phillies in the bottom of the tenth for the second Yankee win.

The Phillies took a lead for the only time in the Series when they broke a 1–1 tie with a run in the seventh inning of Game Three. But New York scored on a Phillie error to tie the game again in the eighth, and in the last of the ninth—with two outs—Yankees Gene Woodling, Phil Rizzuto, and Jerry Coleman singled to produce the winning run.

Rookie sensation Whitey Ford started Game Four and held Philadelphia scoreless into the ninth inning as his Yankees scored twice in the first and three more times in the sixth. He was taken out with two away in the ninth after two singles, a hit batsman, and a Yankee error had permitted two Phillies to score. But reliever Allie Reynolds struck out the final batter to secure for the Yankees a Series sweep.

New York Yankees (AL), 4;
Philadelphia Phillies (NL), 0

NY (A)

PLAYER/POS	AVG	G	AB	R	H	2B	3B	HR	RB	BB	SO	SB
Hank Bauer, of	.133	4	15	0	2	0	0	0	1	0	0	0
Yogi Berra, c	.200	4	15	2	3	0	0	1	2	2	1	0
Bobby Brown, 3b	.333	4	12	2	4	1	1	0	1	0	0	0
Gerry Coleman, 2b	.286	4	14	2	4	1	0	0	3	2	0	0
Joe Collins, 1b	.000	1	0	0	0	0	0	0	0	0	0	0
Joe DiMaggio, of	.308	4	13	2	4	1	0	1	2	3	1	0
Tom Ferrick, p	.000	1	0	0	0	0	0	0	0	0	0	0
Whitey Ford, p	.000	1	3	0	0	0	0	0	0	0	2	0
Johnny Hopp, 1b	.000	3	2	0	0	0	0	0	0	0	0	0
Jackie Jensen, pr	.000	1	0	0	0	0	0	0	0	0	0	0
Billy Johnson, 3b	.000	4	6	0	0	0	0	0	0	0	3	0
Ed Lopat, p	.500	1	2	0	1	0	0	0	0	0	1	0
Cliff Mapes, of	.000	1	4	0	0	0	0	0	0	0	0	0
Johnny Mize, 1b	.133	4	15	0	2	0	0	0	0	0	1	0
Vic Raschi, p	.333	1	3	0	1	0	0	0	0	0	0	0
Allie Reynolds, p	.333	2	3	0	1	0	0	0	0	1	2	0
Phil Rizzuto, ss	.143	4	14	1	2	0	0	0	0	3	0	1
Gene Woodling, of	.429	4	14	2	6	0	0	0	1	2	0	0
TOTAL	.222		135	11	30	3	1	2	10	13	12	1

PITCHER	W	L	ERA	G	GS	CG	SV	SHO	IP	H	ER	BB	SO
Tom Ferrick	1	0	0.00	1	0	0	0	0	1.0	1	0	1	0
Whitey Ford	1	0	0.00	1	1	0	0	0	8.2	7	0	1	7
Ed Lopat	0	0	2.25	1	1	0	0	0	8.0	9	2	0	5
Vic Raschi	1	0	0.00	1	1	1	0	1	9.0	2	0	1	5
Allie Reynolds	1	0	0.87	2	1	1	1	0	10.1	7	1	4	7
TOTAL	4	0	0.73	6	4	2	1	1	37.0	26	3	7	24

PHI (N)

PLAYER/POS	AVG	G	AB	R	H	2B	3B	HR	RB	BB	SO	SB
Richie Ashburn, of	.176	4	17	0	3	1	0	0	1	0	4	0
Jimmy Bloodworth, 2b	.000	1	0	0	0	0	0	0	0	0	0	0
Putsy Caballero, ph	.000	3	1	0	0	0	0	0	0	0	1	0
Del Ennis, of	.143	4	14	1	2	1	0	0	0	0	1	0
Mike Goliat, 2b	.214	4	14	1	3	0	0	0	1	1	2	0
Granny Hamner, ss	.429	4	14	1	6	2	1	0	1	1	2	1
Ken Heintzelman, p	.000	1	2	0	0	0	0	0	0	0	0	0
Ken Johnson, pr	.000	1	0	1	0	0	0	0	0	0	0	0
Willie Jones, 3b	.286	4	14	1	4	1	0	0	0	0	3	0
Jim Konstanty, p	.250	3	4	0	1	0	0	0	0	0	0	0
Stan Lopata, c-1	.000	2	1	0	0	0	0	0	0	0	1	0
Jackie Mayo, of-1	.000	3	0	0	0	0	0	0	0	1	0	0
Russ Meyer, p	.000	2	0	0	0	0	0	0	0	0	0	0
Bob Miller, p	.000	1	0	0	0	0	0	0	0	0	0	0
Robin Roberts, p	.000	2	2	0	0	0	0	0	0	0	1	0
Andy Seminick, c	.182	4	11	0	2	0	0	0	0	1	3	0
Ken Silvestri, c	.000	1	0	0	0	0	0	0	0	0	0	0
Dick Sisler, of	.059	4	17	0	1	0	0	0	1	0	5	0
Eddie Waitkus, 1b	.267	4	15	0	4	1	0	0	0	2	0	0
Dick Whitman, ph	.000	3	2	0	0	0	0	0	0	0	1	0
TOTAL	.203		128	5	26	6	1	0	3	7	24	1

PITCHER	W	L	ERA	G	GS	CG	SV	SHO	IP	H	ER	BB	SO
Ken Heintzelman	0	0	1.17	1	1	0	0	0	7.2	4	1	6	3
Jim Konstanty	0	1	2.40	3	1	0	0	0	15.0	9	4	4	3
Russ Meyer	0	1	5.40	2	0	0	0	0	1.2	4	1	0	1
Bob Miller	0	1	27.00	1	1	0	0	0	0.1	2	1	0	0
Robin Roberts	0	1	1.64	2	1	1	0	0	11.0	11	2	3	5
TOTAL	0	4	2.27	9	4	1	0	0	35.2	30	9	13	12

GAME 1 AT PHI OCT 4

NY	000 100 000	1 5 0
PHI	000 000 000	0 2 1

Pitchers: RASCHI vs KONSTANTY, Meyer (9)
Attendance: 30,746

GAME 2 AT PHI OCT 5

NY	010 000 000 1	2 10 0
PHI	000 010 000 0	1 7 0

Pitchers: REYNOLDS vs ROBERTS
Home Runs: DiMaggio-NY
Attendance: 32,660

GAME 3 AT NY OCT 6

PHI	000 001 100	2 10 2
NY	001 000 011	3 7 0

Pitchers: Heintzelman, Konstanty (8), MEYER (9) vs Lopat, FERRICK (9)
Attendance: 64,505

GAME 4 AT NY OCT 7

PHI	000 000 002	2 7 1
NY	200 003 00X	5 8 2

Pitchers: MILLER, Konstanty (1), Roberts (8) vs FORD, Reynolds (9)
Home Runs: Berra-NY
Attendance: 68,098

The Giants—who caught Brooklyn with a tremendous late-season drive, then defeated them for the pennant on Bobby Thomson's ninth-inning home run in Game Three of the tie-breaker playoff series—carried their momentum through Game Three of the World Series before bowing to the Yankees. Dave Koslo (the only Giant starter not to see action in the playoff) pitched the Series opener and held the Yankees to one run. Monte Irvin's steal of home for the Giants' second run in the top of the first was enough for the win, but Al Dark made Koslo's lead more secure with a three-run homer in the sixth.

The Yankees evened the Series in Game Two, scoring two early runs (one of them Joe Collins's home run) off Larry Jansen, and holding on for the win behind Ed Lopat's five-hit pitching. But the Giants regained the lead in Game Three with five unearned runs (three of them on Whitey Lockman's homer) in a fifth inning prolonged by two Yankee errors, as pitchers Jim Hearn and Sheldon Jones combined to hold the Bronx Bombers to five hits and a pair of runs (though Hearn issued eight walks).

But that was the end of the Giants' drive. Although they scored first in games Four and Five with first-inning runs, they couldn't hold the lead either time. In Game Four Allie Reynolds held the Giants to two runs as his Yankees scored six—including a two-run homer by Joe DiMaggio in the fifth inning that proved to be the last home run of his career. DiMag drove in three more Yankee runs in Game Five, as did Phil Rizzuto, and rookie infielder Gil McDougald contributed a grand slam as the Bombers earned their nickname in obliterating Giant pitching with 13 runs. Ed Lopat, meanwhile, hurled his second five-hitter of the Series for his second win.

Yankee Hank Bauer tripled with the bases full in the sixth inning of Game Six to break a tie and give the Yankees a 4–1 lead. The Giants loaded the bases with three straight singles to open the top of the ninth, and scored two runners on successive flies to left, to come within one run of a tie. But pinch hitter Sal Yvars (in his only Series at-bat) lined out to right and the Yankees had their fourteenth world title.

New York Yankees (AL), 4;
New York Giants (NL), 2

NY (A)

PLAYER/POS	AVG	G	AB	R	H	2B	3B	HR	RB	BB	SO	SB
Hank Bauer, of	.167	6	18	0	3	0	1	0	3	1	1	0
Yogi Berra, c	.261	6	23	4	6	1	0	0	0	2	1	0
Bobby Brown, 3b-4	.357	5	14	1	5	1	0	0	0	2	1	0
Gerry Coleman, 2b	.250	5	8	2	2	0	0	0	0	1	2	0
Joe Collins, 1b-6,of-1	.222	6	18	2	4	0	0	1	3	2	1	0
Joe DiMaggio, of	.261	6	23	3	6	2	0	1	5	2	4	0
Bobby Hogue, p	.000	2	0	0	0	0	0	0	0	0	0	0
Johnny Hopp, ph	.000	1	0	0	0	0	0	0	0	1	0	0
Bob Kuzava, p	.000	1	0	0	0	0	0	0	0	0	0	0
Ed Lopat, p	.125	2	8	0	1	0	0	0	0	1	0	0
Mickey Mantle, of	.200	2	5	1	1	0	0	0	0	2	1	0
Billy Martin, pr	.000	1	0	1	0	0	0	0	0	0	0	0
Gil McDougald, 3b-5,2b-4	.261	6	23	2	6	1	0	1	7	2	2	0
Johnny Mize, 1b-2	.286	4	7	2	2	1	0	0	1	2	0	0
Tom Morgan, p	.000	1	0	0	0	0	0	0	0	0	0	0
Joe Ostrowski, p	.000	1	0	0	0	0	0	0	0	0	0	0
Vic Raschi, p	.000	2	2	0	0	0	0	0	0	2	1	0
Allie Reynolds, p	.333	2	6	0	2	0	0	0	1	0	1	0
Phil Rizzuto, ss	.320	6	25	5	8	0	0	1	3	2	3	0
Johnny Sain, p	.000	1	1	0	0	0	0	0	0	0	0	0
Gene Woodling, of-5	.167	6	18	6	3	1	1	1	1	5	3	0
TOTAL	.246		199	29	49	7	2	5	25	26	23	0

PITCHER	W	L	ERA	G	GS	CG	SV	SHO	IP	H	ER	BB	SO
Bobby Hogue	0	0	0.00	2	0	0	0	0	2.2	1	0	0	0
Bob Kuzava	0	0	0.00	1	0	0	1	0	1.0	1	0	0	0
Ed Lopat	2	0	0.50	2	2	2	0	0	18.0	10	1	3	4
Tom Morgan	0	0	0.00	1	0	0	0	0	2.0	2	0	1	3
Joe Ostrowski	0	0	0.00	1	0	0	0	0	2.0	1	0	0	1
Vic Raschi	1	1	0.87	2	2	0	0	0	10.1	12	1	8	4
Allie Reynolds	1	1	4.20	2	2	1	0	0	15.0	16	7	11	8
Johnny Sain	0	0	9.00	1	0	0	0	0	2.0	4	2	2	2
TOTAL	4	2	1.87	12	6	3	1	0	53.0	46	11	25	22

NY (N)

PLAYER/POS	AVG	G	AB	R	H	2B	3B	HR	RB	BB	SO	SB
Al Corwin, p	.000	1	0	0	0	0	0	0	0	0	0	0
Alvin Dark, ss	.417	6	24	5	10	3	0	1	4	2	3	0
Clint Hartung, of	.000	2	4	0	0	0	0	0	0	0	0	0
Jim Hearn, p	.000	2	3	0	0	0	0	0	0	0	1	0
Monte Irvin, of	.458	6	24	3	11	0	1	0	2	2	1	2
Larry Jansen, p	.000	3	2	0	0	0	0	0	0	0	0	0
Sheldon Jones, p	.000	2	0	0	0	0	0	0	0	0	0	0
Monte Kennedy, p	.000	2	0	0	0	0	0	0	0	0	0	0
Alex Konikowski, p	.000	1	0	0	0	0	0	0	0	0	0	0
Dave Koslo, p	.000	2	5	0	0	0	0	0	0	0	2	0
Whitey Lockman, 1b	.240	6	25	1	6	2	0	1	4	1	2	0
Jack Lohrke, ph	.000	2	2	0	0	0	0	0	0	0	1	0
Sal Maglie, p	.000	1	1	0	0	0	0	0	0	0	1	0
Willie Mays, of	.182	6	22	1	4	0	0	0	1	2	2	0
Ray Noble, c	.000	2	2	0	0	0	0	0	0	0	1	0
Bill Rigney, ph	.250	4	4	0	1	0	0	0	0	1	0	0
Hank Schenz, pr	.000	1	0	0	0	0	0	0	0	0	0	0
George Spencer, p	.000	2	0	0	0	0	0	0	0	0	0	0
Eddie Stanky, 2b	.136	6	22	3	3	0	0	0	1	3	2	0
Hank Thompson, 3b	.143	5	14	3	2	0	0	0	0	5	2	0
Bobby Thomson, 3b	.238	6	21	3	5	1	0	0	2	5	0	0
Wes Westrum, c	.235	6	17	1	4	1	0	0	0	5	3	0
Davey Williams, ph	.000	2	1	0	0	0	0	0	0	0	0	0
Sal Yvars, ph	.000	1	1	0	0	0	0	0	0	0	0	0
TOTAL	.237		194	18	46	7	1	2	15	25	22	2

PITCHER	W	L	ERA	G	GS	CG	SV	SHO	IP	H	ER	BB	SO
Al Corwin	0	0	0.00	1	0	0	0	0	1.2	1	0	0	1
Jim Hearn	1	0	1.04	2	1	0	0	0	8.2	5	1	8	1
Larry Jansen	0	2	6.30	3	2	0	0	0	10.0	8	7	4	6
Sheldon Jones	0	0	2.08	2	0	0	1	0	4.1	5	1	1	2
Monte Kennedy	0	0	6.00	2	0	0	0	0	3.0	3	2	1	4
Alex Konikowski	0	0	0.00	1	0	0	0	0	1.0	1	0	0	0
Dave Koslo	1	1	3.00	2	2	1	0	0	15.0	12	5	7	6
Sal Maglie	0	1	7.20	1	1	0	0	0	5.0	8	4	2	3
George Spencer	0	0	18.90	2	0	0	0	0	3.1	6	7	3	0
TOTAL	2	4	4.67	16	6	1	1	0	52.0	49	27	26	23

GAME 1 AT NY-A OCT 4

NY-N	200 003 000	5	10	1
NY-A	010 000 000	1	7	1

Pitchers: KOSLO vs REYNOLDS, Hogue (7), Morgan (8)
Home Runs: Dark-NY(N)
Attendance: 65,673

GAME 2 AT NY-A OCT 5

NY-N	000 000 100	1	5	1
NY-A	110 000 01X	3	6	0

Pitchers: JANSEN, Spencer (7) vs LOPAT
Home Runs: Collins-NY(A)
Attendance: 66,018

GAME 3 AT NY-N OCT 6

NY-A	000 000 011	2	5	2
NY-N	010 050 00X	6	7	2

Pitchers: RASCHI, Hogue (5), Ostrowski (7) vs HEARN, Jones (8)
Home Runs: Lockman-NY(N), Woodling-NY(A)
Attendance: 52,035

GAME 4 AT NY-N OCT 8

NY-A	010 120 200	6	12	0
NY-N	100 000 001	2	8	2

Pitchers: REYNOLDS vs MAGLIE, Jones (6), Kennedy (9)
Home Runs: DiMaggio-NY(A)
Attendance: 49,010

GAME 5 AT NY-N OCT 9

NY-A	005 202 400	13	12	1
NY-N	100 000 000	1	5	3

Pitchers: LOPAT vs JANSEN, Kennedy (4), Spencer (6), Corwin (7), Konikowski (9)
Home Runs: McDougald-NY(A), Rizzuto-NY(A)
Attendance: 47,530

GAME 6 AT NY-A OCT 10

NY-N	000 010 002	3	11	1
NY-A	100 003 00X	4	7	0

Pitchers: KOSLO, Hearn (7), Jansen (8) vs RASCHI, Sain (7), Kuzava (9)
Attendance: 61,711

In four of the seven games, home runs provided the margin of victory. Homers accounted for five of the six runs scored in the opener, with Duke Snider's two-run blast in the sixth putting Brooklyn ahead to stay. Star Dodger reliever Joe Black, in only his third start of the year, held New York to six hits and two runs in defeating Yankee ace Allie Reynolds.

Four home runs enlivened the next three games but did not govern the outcomes. Billy Martin's three-run shot was the centerpiece of the Yankee assault in Game Two, but New York would have won without it behind Vic Raschi's one-run three-hitter. Brooklyn needed no homers to regain the Series advantage in Game Three. In the top of the ninth, with the Dodgers leading by a run, Pee Wee Reese and Jackie Robinson singled (driving out starter Ed Lopat) and pulled a double steal. Both then scored on a passed ball. Yankee pinch hitter Johnny Mize homered in the last of the ninth, but Preacher Roe escaped without further scoring for a complete-game 5–3 win.

Black opposed Reynolds again in Game Four and bettered his earlier performance, holding New York to three hits and one run (a Mize homer) in seven innings. But Reynolds improved even more, fanning ten as he shut the Dodgers out.

Snider hit his second homer of the Series and Mize his third in the fifth inning of Game Five. Mize's shot put New York ahead, but Brooklyn tied the game in the seventh and took a 6–5 lead when Snider doubled home a run in the eleventh. Dodger right fielder Carl Furillo's leaping catch in the last of the eleventh robbed Mize of another home run, and starter Carl Erskine held on for the win, giving Brooklyn a 3–2 Series lead.

Snider's home run in the last of the sixth ended Vic Raschi's shutout in Game Six, but Yogi Berra, the first Yankee up in the seventh, tied the game and spoiled Billy Loes's shutout with his home run, and pitcher Raschi singled home the go-ahead run two outs later. Yankee sophomore Mickey Mantle's blast in the eighth (the first of his record 18 World Series home runs) made the score 3–1. Snider's fourth homer of the Series gave the Dodgers a second run in the eighth, but Allie Reynolds relieved Raschi and prevented further scoring, sending the Series to a seventh game.

Joe Black traded three shutout innings with Yankee Ed Lopat in the finale before both clubs scored single runs in the fourth and fifth innings. Mantle homered off Black in the sixth for a third Yankee run that proved the Series winner, as three Yankee relievers held Brooklyn scoreless through the final four frames.

New York Yankees (AL), 4; Brooklyn Dodgers (NL), 3

NY (A)

PLAYER/POS	AVG	G	AB	R	H	2B	3B	HR	RB	BB	SO	SB
Hank Bauer, of	.056	7	18	2	1	0	0	0	1	4	3	0
Yogi Berra, c	.214	7	28	2	6	1	0	2	3	2	4	0
Ewell Blackwell, p	.000	1	1	0	0	0	0	0	0	0	0	0
Joe Collins, 1b	.000	6	12	1	0	0	0	0	0	1	3	0
Tom Gorman, p	.000	1	0	0	0	0	0	0	0	0	0	0
Ralph Houk, ph	.000	1	1	0	0	0	0	0	0	0	0	0
Bob Kuzava, p	.000	1	1	0	0	0	0	0	0	0	0	0
Ed Lopat, p	.333	2	3	0	1	0	0	0	0	1	1	0
Mickey Mantle, of	.345	7	29	5	10	1	1	2	3	3	4	0
Billy Martin, 2b	.217	7	23	2	5	0	0	1	4	2	2	0
Gil McDougald, 3b	.200	7	25	5	5	0	0	1	3	5	2	1
Johnny Mize, 1b-4	.400	5	15	3	6	1	0	3	6	3	1	0
Irv Noren, of-3	.300	4	10	0	3	0	0	0	1	1	3	0
Vic Raschi, p	.167	3	6	0	1	0	0	0	0	1	2	0
Allie Reynolds, p	.000	4	7	0	0	0	0	0	0	0	2	0
Phil Rizzuto, ss	.148	7	27	2	4	1	0	0	0	5	2	0
Johnny Sain, p-1	.000	2	3	0	0	0	0	0	0	0	0	0
Ray Scarborough, p	.000	1	0	0	0	0	0	0	0	0	0	0
Gene Woodling, of-6	.348	7	23	4	8	1	1	1	1	3	3	0
TOTAL	.216		232	26	50	5	2	10	24	31	32	1

PITCHER	W	L	ERA	G	GS	CG	SV	SHO	IP	H	ER	BB	SO
Ewell Blackwell	0	0	7.20	1	1	0	0	0	5.0	4	4	3	4
Tom Gorman	0	0	0.00	1	0	0	0	0	0.2	1	0	0	0
Bob Kuzava	0	0	0.00	1	0	0	1	0	2.2	0	0	0	2
Ed Lopat	0	1	4.76	2	2	0	0	0	11.1	14	6	4	3
Vic Raschi	2	0	1.59	3	2	1	0	0	17.0	12	3	8	18
Allie Reynolds	2	1	1.77	4	2	1	1	1	20.1	12	4	6	18
Johnny Sain	0	1	3.00	1	1	0	0	0	6.0	6	2	3	3
Ray Scarborough	0	0	9.00	1	0	0	0	0	1.0	1	1	0	1
TOTAL	4	3	2.81	14	7	2	2	1	64.0	50	20	24	49

BRO (N)

PLAYER/POS	AVG	G	AB	R	H	2B	3B	HR	RB	BB	SO	SB
Sandy Amoros, ph	.000	1	0	0	0	0	0	0	0	0	0	0
Joe Black, p	.000	3	6	0	0	0	0	0	0	1	6	0
Roy Campanella, c	.214	7	28	0	6	0	0	0	1	1	6	0
Billy Cox, 3b	.296	7	27	4	8	2	0	0	0	3	4	0
Carl Erskine, p	.000	3	6	1	0	0	0	0	0	0	1	0
Carl Furillo, of	.174	7	23	1	4	2	0	0	0	3	3	0
Gil Hodges, 1b	.000	7	21	1	0	0	0	0	1	5	6	0
Tommy Holmes, of	.000	3	1	0	0	0	0	0	0	0	0	0
Ken Lehman, p	.000	1	0	0	0	0	0	0	0	0	0	0
Billy Loes, p	.333	2	3	0	1	0	0	0	0	0	1	1
Bobby Morgan, 3b	.000	2	1	0	0	0	0	0	0	0	1	0
Rocky Nelson, ph	.000	4	3	0	0	0	0	0	0	1	2	0
Andy Pafko, of-5	.190	7	21	0	4	0	0	0	2	0	4	0
Pee Wee Reese, ss	.345	7	29	4	10	0	0	1	4	2	2	1
Jackie Robinson, 2b	.174	7	23	4	4	0	0	1	2	7	5	2
Preacher Roe, p	.000	3	2	0	0	0	0	0	0	0	0	0
Johnny Rutherford, p	.000	1	0	0	0	0	0	0	0	0	0	0
George Shuba, of-3	.300	4	10	0	3	1	0	0	0	0	4	0
Duke Snider, of	.345	7	29	5	10	2	0	4	8	1	5	0
TOTAL	.215		233	20	50	7	0	6	18	24	49	5

PITCHER	W	L	ERA	G	GS	CG	SV	SHO	IP	H	ER	BB	SO
Joe Black	1	2	2.53	3	3	1	0	0	21.1	15	6	8	9
Carl Erskine	1	1	4.50	3	2	1	0	0	18.0	12	9	10	10
Ken Lehman	0	0	0.00	1	0	0	0	0	2.0	2	0	1	0
Billy Loes	0	1	4.35	2	1	0	0	0	10.1	11	5	5	5
Preacher Roe	1	0	3.18	3	1	1	0	0	11.1	9	4	6	7
Johnny Rutherford	0	0	9.00	1	0	0	0	0	1.0	1	1	1	1
TOTAL	3	4	3.52	13	7	3	0	0	64.0	50	25	31	32

GAME 1 AT BRO OCT 1

NY	010 000 010	2	6	2
BRO	010 002 01X	4	6	0

Pitchers: REYNOLDS, Scarborough (8) vs BLACK
Home Runs: Robinson-BRO, Snider-BRO, Reese-BRO, McDougald-NY
Attendance: 34,861

GAME 2 AT BRO OCT 2

NY	000 115 000	7	10	4
BRO	001 000 000	1	3	1

Pitchers: RASCHI vs ERSKINE, Loes (6), Lehman (8)
Home Runs: Martin-NY
Attendance: 33,792

GAME 3 AT NY OCT 3

BRO	001 010 012	5	11	0
NY	010 000 011	3	6	2

Pitchers: ROE vs LOPAT, Gorman (9)
Home Runs: Berra-NY, Mize-NY
Attendance: 66,698

GAME 4 AT NY OCT 4

BRO	000 000 000	0	4	1
NY	000 100 01X	2	4	1

Pitchers: BLACK, Rutherford (8) vs REYNOLDS
Home Runs: Mize-NY
Attendance: 71,787

GAME 5 AT NY OCT 5

BRO	010 030 100 01	6	10	0
NY	000 050 000 00	5	5	1

Pitchers: ERSKINE vs Blackwell, SAIN (6)
Home Runs: Snider-BRO, Mize-NY
Attendance: 70,536

GAME 6 AT BRO OCT 6

NY	000 000 210	3	9	0
BRO	000 001 010	2	8	1

Pitchers: RASCHI, Reynolds (8) vs LOES, Roe (9)
Home Runs: Snider-BRO (2), Berra-NY, Mantle-NY
Attendance: 30,037

GAME 7 AT BRO OCT 7

NY	000 111 100	4	10	4
BRO	000 110 000	2	8	1

Pitchers: Lopat, REYNOLDS (4), Raschi (7), Kuzava (7) vs BLACK, Roe (6), Erskine (8)
Home Runs: Woodling-NY, Mantle-NY
Attendance: 33,195

Although the Yankees easily won the American League pennant, the Dodgers seemed even more overwhelming, with a team batting average of .285 and a club-record 105 season wins. But when the Series was over, the Yankees had added a record fifth straight world championship to their record fifth straight pennant.

Dodger ace Carl Erskine lasted only one inning of the Series opener, giving up three walks and two triples for four Yankee runs. By the middle of the seventh inning, the Dodgers had tied the score at 5–5. But Yankee Joe Collins homered to break the tie in the last of the seventh, and reliever Johnny Sain ensured his own win with a two-run double an inning later. The Dodgers outhit New York in Game Two, and held a 2–1 lead entering the bottom of the seventh. But Billy Martin (who hit .500 and slugged .958 in the Series) tied the game with a leadoff homer in the seventh, and Mickey Mantle won it with a two-run blast in the eighth.

Down 0–2, Brooklyn evened the Series at home with victories in Games Three and Four. Erskine redeemed his poor start in Game One with a record-setting 14-strikeout performance in Game Three. But it was a narrow win, settled only when Roy Campanella homered in the last of the eighth to break a 2–2 tie. In Game Four, Duke Snider made Billy Loes's three-run pitching a winning performance, driving in four of the Dodgers' seven runs with two doubles and a homer.

But Brooklyn never even took the lead in the final two games. Four Yankee home runs (including a Mantle grand slam) rocked Dodger pitching in Game Five as the Bombers built a lead which Dodger home runs in the eighth and ninth were unable to overcome. In Game Six the Yankees built a 3–0 lead over Erskine in the first two innings. Brooklyn fought back with a run in the sixth, and tied the game on Carl Furillo's two-run homer in the top of the ninth. But with men on first and second in the last of the ninth, Yankee Billy Martin singled in the game-ending, Series-winning run. It was Martin's twelfth hit, a new record for a six-game Series.

New York Yankees (AL), 4; Brooklyn Dodgers (NL), 2

NY (A)

PLAYER/POS	AVG	G	AB	R	H	2B	3B	HR	RB	BB	SO	SB
Hank Bauer, of	.261	6	23	6	6	0	1	0	1	2	4	0
Yogi Berra, c	.429	6	21	3	9	1	0	1	4	3	3	0
Don Bollweg, 1b-1	.000	3	2	0	0	0	0	0	0	0	2	0
Joe Collins, 1b	.167	6	24	4	4	1	0	1	2	3	8	0
Whitey Ford, p	.333	2	3	0	1	0	0	0	0	0	0	0
Tom Gorman, p	.000	1	1	0	0	0	0	0	0	0	1	0
Bob Kuzava, p	.000	1	1	0	0	0	0	0	0	0	1	0
Ed Lopat, p	.000	1	3	0	0	0	0	0	0	0	2	0
Mickey Mantle, of	.208	6	24	3	5	0	0	2	7	3	8	0
Billy Martin, 2b	.500	6	24	5	12	1	2	2	8	1	2	1
Jim McDonald, p	.500	1	2	0	1	1	0	0	1	1	1	0
Gil McDougald, 3b	.167	6	24	2	4	0	1	2	4	1	3	0
Johnny Mize, ph	.000	3	3	0	0	0	0	0	0	0	1	0
Irv Noren, ph	.000	2	1	0	0	0	0	0	0	1	0	0
Vic Raschi, p	.000	1	2	0	0	0	0	0	0	0	1	0
Allie Reynolds, p	.500	3	2	1	1	0	0	0	0	1	1	0
Phil Rizzuto, ss	.316	6	19	4	6	1	0	0	3	2	1	0
Johnny Sain, p	.500	2	2	1	1	1	0	0	2	0	1	0
Art Schallock, p	.000	1	0	0	0	0	0	0	0	0	0	0
Gene Woodling, of	.300	6	20	5	6	0	0	1	3	6	2	0
TOTAL	.279		201	33	56	6	4	9	32	25	43	2

PITCHER	W	L	ERA	G	GS	CG	SV	SHO	IP	H	ER	BB	SO
Whitey Ford	0	1	4.50	2	2	0	0	0	8.0	9	4	2	7
Tom Gorman	0	0	3.00	1	0	0	0	0	3.0	4	1	0	1
Bob Kuzava	0	0	13.50	1	0	0	0	0	0.2	2	1	0	1
Ed Lopat	1	0	2.00	1	1	1	0	0	9.0	9	2	4	3
Jim McDonald	1	0	5.87	1	1	0	0	0	7.2	12	5	0	3
Vic Raschi	0	1	3.38	1	1	1	0	0	8.0	9	3	3	4
Allie Reynolds	1	0	6.75	3	1	0	1	0	8.0	9	6	4	9
Johnny Sain	1	0	4.76	2	0	0	0	0	5.2	8	3	1	1
Art Schallock	0	0	4.50	1	0	0	0	0	2.0	2	1	1	1
TOTAL	4	2	4.50	13	6	2	1	0	52.0	64	26	15	30

BRO (N)

PLAYER/POS	AVG	G	AB	R	H	2B	3B	HR	RB	BB	SO	SB
Wayne Belardi, ph	.000	2	2	0	0	0	0	0	0	0	1	0
Joe Black, p	.000	1	0	0	0	0	0	0	0	0	0	0
Roy Campanella, c	.273	6	22	6	6	0	0	1	2	2	3	0
Billy Cox, 3b	.304	6	23	3	7	3	0	1	6	1	4	0
Carl Erskine, p	.250	3	4	0	1	0	0	0	0	0	1	0
Carl Furillo, of	.333	6	24	4	8	2	0	1	4	1	3	0
Jim Gilliam, 2b	.296	6	27	4	8	3	0	2	4	0	2	0
Gil Hodges, 1b	.364	6	22	3	8	0	0	1	1	3	3	1
Jim Hughes, p	.000	1	1	0	0	0	0	0	0	0	0	0
Clem Labine, p	.000	3	2	0	0	0	0	0	0	0	1	0
Billy Loes, p	.667	1	3	0	2	0	0	0	0	0	1	0
Russ Meyer, p	.000	1	1	0	0	0	0	0	0	0	1	0
Bob Milliken, p	.000	1	0	0	0	0	0	0	0	0	0	0
Bobby Morgan, ph	.000	1	1	0	0	0	0	0	0	0	0	0
Johnny Podres, p	1.000	1	1	0	1	0	0	0	0	0	0	0
Pee Wee Reese, ss	.208	6	24	0	5	0	1	0	0	4	1	0
Jackie Robinson, of	.320	6	25	3	8	2	0	0	2	1	0	1
Preacher Roe, p	.000	1	3	0	0	0	0	0	0	0	0	0
George Shuba, ph	1.000	2	1	1	1	0	0	1	2	0	0	0
Duke Snider, of	.320	6	25	3	8	3	0	1	5	2	6	0
Don Thompson, of	.000	2	0	0	0	0	0	0	0	0	0	0
Ben Wade, p	.000	2	2	0	0	0	0	0	0	0	0	0
Dick Williams, ph	.500	3	2	0	1	0	0	0	0	1	1	0
TOTAL	.300		213	27	64	13	1	8	26	15	30	2

PITCHER	W	L	ERA	G	GS	CG	SV	SHO	IP	H	ER	BB	SO
Joe Black	0	0	9.00	1	0	0	0	0	1.0	1	1	0	2
Carl Erskine	1	0	5.79	3	3	1	0	0	14.0	14	9	9	16
Jim Hughes	0	0	2.25	1	0	0	0	0	4.0	3	1	1	3
Clem Labine	0	2	3.60	3	0	0	1	0	5.0	10	2	1	3
Billy Loes	1	0	3.38	1	1	0	0	0	8.0	8	3	2	8
Russ Meyer	0	0	6.23	1	0	0	0	0	4.1	8	3	4	5
Bob Milliken	0	0	0.00	1	0	0	0	0	2.0	2	0	1	0
Johnny Podres	0	1	3.38	1	1	0	0	0	2.2	1	1	2	0
Preacher Roe	0	1	4.50	1	1	1	0	0	8.0	5	4	4	4
Ben Wade	0	0	15.43	2	0	0	0	0	2.1	4	4	1	2
TOTAL	2	4	4.91	15	6	2	1	0	51.1	56	28	25	43

GAME 1 AT NY SEPT 30

BRO	000	013	100	5 12 2
NY	400	010	13X	9 12 0

Pitchers: Erskine, Hughes (2), LABINE (6), Wade (8) vs Reynolds, SAIN (6)
Home Runs: Gilliam-BRO, Hodges-BRO, Shuba-BRO, Berra-NY, Collins-NY
Attendance: 69,374

GAME 2 AT NY OCT 1

BRO	000	200	000	2 9 1
NY	100	000	12X	4 5 0

Pitchers: ROE vs LOPAT
Home Runs: Martin-NY, Mantle-NY
Attendance: 66,786

GAME 3 AT BRO OCT 2

NY	000	010	010	2 6 0
BRO	000	011	01X	3 9 0

Pitchers: RASCHI vs ERSKINE
Home Runs: Campanella-BRO
Attendance: 35,270

GAME 4 AT BRO OCT 3

NY	000	020	001	3 9 0
BRO	300	102	10X	7 12 0

Pitchers: FORD, Gorman (2), Sain (5), Schallock (7) vs LOES, Labine (9)
Home Runs: McDougald-NY, Snider-BRO
Attendance: 36,775

GAME 5 AT BRO OCT 4

NY	105	000	311	11 11 1
BRO	010	010	041	7 14 1

Pitchers: McDONALD, Kuzava (8), Reynolds (9) vs PODRES, Meyer (3), Wade (8), Black (9)
Home Runs: Woodling-NY, Mantle-NY, Martin-NY, McDougald-NY, Cox-BRO, Gilliam-BRO
Attendance: 36,775

GAME 6 AT NY OCT 5

BRO	000	001	002	3 8 3
NY	210	000	001	4 13 0

Pitchers: Erskine, Milliken (5), LABINE (7) vs Ford, REYNOLDS (8)
Home Runs: Furillo-BRO
Attendance: 62,370

The Indians, who had won a league-record 111 games to break the American League domination of the New York Yankees, entered the World Series as strong favorites to humble the Giants. It was not to be.

Cleveland would have won the opener had it not been played in New York's Polo Grounds, with their short foul lines and deep center field. Most of the game was a pitchers' duel. Vic Wertz (the only Indian to hit safely in all four games) tripled off Sal Maglie to give Cleveland a two-run lead in the top of the first, but three Giant singles and a walk in the third off Bob Lemon tied the score. Lemon then settled down to hold New York scoreless through the ninth. Cleveland threatened in the eighth when the first two batters reached base, bringing Wertz to the plate. As he had already hit Maglie safely three times, Don Liddle was brought in to pitch to him. Wertz responded with a fly to deep center that would have been a home run in Cleveland, but in New York turned into the most famous catch in World Series history as Willie Mays raced out and tracked down the ball about 425 feet from the plate. Marv Grissom replaced Liddle on the mound and issued a walk to load the bases, but he retired the next two batters and (despite Wertz's double in the top of the tenth) held Cleveland scoreless the rest of the way. In the last of the tenth, Lemon retired the first batter, but Mays walked and stole second, and Hank Thompson was walked intentionally to set up the double play. Pinch hitter Dusty Rhodes then entered the hall of heroes with a short fly to right that—though it would have been an out in Cleveland—fell into the Polo Grounds stands for three runs and a Giant victory.

The rest of the Series was anti-climax. In the second game Rhodes, with half the Giants' four hits, drove in two runs on a single and another homer, providing the margin of victory for Giant ace Johnny Antonelli, who allowed only one of Cleveland's 14 baserunners to score. Game Three was no contest. New York had scored all six of its runs before the Indians managed to come up with single runs in both the seventh and eighth. Pinch hitter Hank Majeski's three-run homer put Cleveland on the board in the fifth inning of Game Four. But as New York had already scored seven times, even a fourth Cleveland run in the seventh proved too little to prevent a Giant sweep.

New York Giants (NL), 4; Cleveland Indians (AL), 0

NY (N)

PLAYER/POS	AVG	G	AB	R	H	2B	3B	HR	RB	BB	SO	SB
Johnny Antonelli, p	.000	2	3	0	0	0	0	0	0	1	0	0
Alvin Dark, ss	.412	4	17	2	7	0	0	0	0	1	1	0
Ruben Gomez, p	.000	1	4	0	0	0	0	0	0	0	2	0
Marv Grissom, p	.000	1	1	0	0	0	0	0	0	0	1	0
Monte Irvin, of	.222	4	9	1	2	1	0	0	2	0	3	0
Don Liddle, p	.000	2	3	0	0	0	0	0	0	0	2	0
Whitey Lockman, 1b	.111	4	18	2	2	0	0	0	0	1	2	0
Sal Maglie, p	.000	1	3	0	0	0	0	0	0	0	0	0
Willie Mays, of	.286	4	14	4	4	1	0	0	3	4	1	1
Don Mueller, of	.389	4	18	4	7	0	0	0	1	0	1	0
Dusty Rhodes, of-2	.667	3	6	2	4	0	0	2	7	1	2	0
Hank Thompson, 3b	.364	4	11	6	4	1	0	0	2	7	1	0
Wes Westrum, c	.273	4	11	0	3	0	0	0	3	1	3	0
Hoyt Wilhelm, p	.000	2	1	0	0	0	0	0	0	0	1	0
Davey Williams, 2b	.000	4	11	0	0	0	0	0	1	2	2	0
TOTAL	.254		130	21	33	3	0	2	20	17	24	1

PITCHER	W	L	ERA	G	GS	CG	SV	SHO	IP	H	ER	BB	SO
Johnny Antonelli	1	0	0.84	2	1	1	1	0	10.2	8	1	7	12
Ruben Gomez	1	0	2.45	1	1	0	0	0	7.1	4	2	3	2
Marv Grissom	1	0	0.00	1	0	0	0	0	2.2	1	0	3	2
Don Liddle	1	0	1.29	2	1	0	0	0	7.0	5	1	1	2
Sal Maglie	0	0	2.57	1	1	0	0	0	7.0	7	2	2	2
Hoyt Wilhelm	0	0	0.00	2	0	0	1	0	2.1	1	0	0	3
TOTAL	4	0	1.46	9	4	1	2	0	37.0	26	6	16	23

CLE (A)

PLAYER/POS	AVG	G	AB	R	H	2B	3B	HR	RB	BB	SO	SB
Bobby Avila, 2b	.133	4	15	1	2	0	0	0	0	2	1	0
Sam Dente, ss	.000	3	3	1	0	0	0	0	0	1	0	0
Larry Doby, of	.125	4	16	0	2	0	0	0	0	2	4	0
Mike Garcia, p	.000	2	0	0	0	0	0	0	0	0	0	0
Bill Glynn, 1b-1	.500	2	2	1	1	1	0	0	0	0	1	0
Mickey Grasso, c	.000	1	0	0	0	0	0	0	0	0	0	0
Jim Hegan, c	.154	4	13	1	2	1	0	0	0	1	1	0
Art Houtteman, p	.000	1	0	0	0	0	0	0	0	0	0	0
Bob Lemon, p-2	.000	3	6	0	0	0	0	0	0	1	1	0
Hank Majeski, 3b-1	.167	4	6	1	1	0	0	1	3	0	1	0
Dale Mitchell, ph	.000	3	2	0	0	0	0	0	0	1	0	0
Don Mossi, p	.000	3	0	0	0	0	0	0	0	0	0	0
Hal Naragon, c	.000	1	0	0	0	0	0	0	0	0	0	0
Ray Narleski, p	.000	2	0	0	0	0	0	0	0	0	0	0
Hal Newhouser, p	.000	1	0	0	0	0	0	0	0	0	0	0
Dave Philley, of-2	.125	4	8	0	1	0	0	0	0	1	3	0
Dave Pope, of-2	.000	3	3	0	0	0	0	0	0	1	1	0
Rudy Regalado, 3b-1	.333	4	3	0	1	0	0	0	0	1	0	0
Al Rosen, 3b	.250	3	12	0	3	0	0	0	0	1	0	0
Al Smith, of	.214	4	14	2	3	0	0	1	2	2	2	0
George Strickland, ss	.000	3	9	0	0	0	0	0	0	0	2	0
Vic Wertz, 1b	.500	4	16	2	8	2	1	1	3	2	2	0
Wally Westlake, of	.143	2	7	0	1	0	0	0	0	1	1	0
Early Wynn, p	.500	2	2	0	1	1	0	0	0	0	1	0
TOTAL	.190		137	9	26	5	1	3	9	16	23	0

PITCHER	W	L	ERA	G	GS	CG	SV	SHO	IP	H	ER	BB	SO
Mike Garcia	0	1	5.40	2	1	0	0	0	5.0	6	3	4	4
Art Houtteman	0	0	4.50	1	0	0	0	0	2.0	2	1	1	1
Bob Lemon	0	2	6.75	2	2	1	0	0	13.1	16	10	8	11
Don Mossi	0	0	0.00	3	0	0	0	0	4.0	3	0	0	1
Ray Narleski	0	0	2.25	2	0	0	0	0	4.0	1	1	1	2
Hal Newhouser	0	0	∞	1	0	0	0	0	0.0	1	1	1	0
Early Wynn	0	1	3.86	1	1	0	0	0	7.0	4	3	2	5
TOTAL	0	4	4.84	12	4	1	0	0	35.1	33	19	17	24

GAME 1 AT NY SEPT 29

CLE	200 000 000 0	2	8	0
NY	002 000 000 3	5	9	3

Pitchers: LEMON vs Maglie, Liddle (8), GRISSOM (8)
Home Runs: Rhodes-NY
Attendance: 52,751

GAME 2 AT NY SEPT 30

CLE	100 000 000	1	8	0
NY	000 020 10X	3	4	0

Pitchers: WYNN, Mossi (8) vs ANTONELLI
Home Runs: Smith-CLE, Rhodes-NY
Attendance: 49,099

GAME 3 AT CLE OCT 1

NY	103 011 000	6	10	1
CLE	000 000 110	2	4	2

Pitchers: GOMEZ, Wilhelm (7) vs GARCIA, Houtteman (4), Narleski (6), Mossi (9)
Home Runs: Wertz-CLE
Attendance: 71,555

GAME 4 AT CLE OCT 2

NY	021 040 000	7	10	3
CLE	000 030 100	4	6	2

Pitchers: LIDDLE, Wilhelm (7), Antonelli (8) vs LEMON, Newhouser (5), Narleski (5), Mossi (6), Garcia (8)
Home Runs: Majeski-CLE
Attendance: 78,102

The Dodgers and Yankees, after a year's absence, faced each other again in the World Series—their sixth Series confrontation in fifteen years. And after Brooklyn had lost the first two games it began to look as though 1955 might also mark the Yankees' sixth Series triumph over the Dodgers. But this was Brooklyn's year.

The opener was a hitters' game, but closely contested. Both teams scored twice in the second inning and once in the third, but Yankee first baseman Joe Collins's leadoff homer in the last of the fourth gave New York its first lead of the game, and his two-run blast in the sixth made the score 6–3. Brooklyn clawed back in the eighth for two runs—including Jackie Robinson's steal of home—to pull within one run of a tie, but they came no closer. In Game Two, Yankee pitcher Tommy Byrne held the Dodgers to five hits and two runs, and won his own game at the bat with a two-run single that capped the Yankees' four-run fourth.

The Series turned around as the Dodgers captured the next three games in Brooklyn. Roy Campanella's two-run homer in the first inning of Game Three gave Brooklyn a quick lead. New York tied the game with a pair of runs in the second (one of them a homer by Mickey Mantle, who appeared in only three Series games because of a leg injury). But two more Dodger runs in the last of the second drove out Yankee starter Bob Turley and put them ahead to stay as Dodger hurler Johnny Podres held the Yankees to three runs. Home runs by Campanella, Gil Hodges, and Duke Snider accounted for six of Brooklyn's eight runs in Game Four as the Dodgers evened the Series at two-all. Sandy Amoros's second-inning homer initiated the scoring in Game Five, and Snider's blasts in the third and fifth (which made him the first player to hit four home runs in two different Series) gave Brooklyn a 4–1 lead, which even late-inning Yankee homers by Bob Cerv and Yogi Berra could not overcome.

New York bounced back in Game Six, scoring all five of their runs in the first inning (including three on Bill Skowron's homer) to give Whitey Ford a comfortable lead, which he held with a one-run four-hitter. But in the finale, Gil Hodges drove in two Brooklyn runs with a single in the fourth and a sacrifice fly in the sixth. They were all Brooklyn got, but they proved more than enough to carry the Dodgers to their first world title in fifty-five years, as left fielder Sandy Amoros stifled New York's only real scoring threat with a spectacular running catch in the sixth that started a double play and preserved Johnny Podres's second Series win.

Brooklyn Dodgers (NL), 4; New York Yankees (AL), 3

BRO (N)

PLAYER/POS	AVG	G	AB	R	H	2B	3B	HR	RB	BB	SO	SB
Sandy Amoros, of	.333	5	12	3	4	0	0	1	3	4	4	0
Don Bessent, p	.000	3	1	0	0	0	0	0	0	0	1	0
Roy Campanella, c	.259	7	27	4	7	3	0	2	4	3	3	0
Roger Craig, p	.000	1	0	0	0	0	0	0	0	1	0	0
Carl Erskine, p	.000	1	1	0	0	0	0	0	0	0	0	0
Carl Furillo, of	.296	7	27	4	8	1	0	1	3	3	5	0
Jim Gilliam, 2b-5,of-4	.292	7	24	2	7	1	0	0	3	8	1	1
Don Hoak, 3b-1	.333	3	3	0	1	0	0	0	0	2	0	0
Gil Hodges, 1b	.292	7	24	2	7	0	0	1	5	3	2	0
Frank Kellert, ph	.333	3	3	0	1	0	0	0	0	0	0	0
Clem Labine, p	.000	4	4	0	0	0	0	0	0	0	3	0
Billy Loes, p	.000	1	1	0	0	0	0	0	0	0	0	0
Russ Meyer, p	.000	1	2	0	0	0	0	0	0	0	1	0
Don Newcombe, p	.000	1	3	0	0	0	0	0	0	0	0	0
Johnny Podres, p	.143	2	7	1	1	0	0	0	0	0	1	0
Pee Wee Reese, ss	.296	7	27	5	8	1	0	0	2	3	5	0
Jackie Robinson, 3b	.182	6	22	5	4	1	1	0	1	2	1	1
Ed Roebuck, p	.000	1	0	0	0	0	0	0	0	0	0	0
George Shuba, ph	.000	1	1	0	0	0	0	0	0	0	0	0
Duke Snider, of	.320	7	25	5	8	1	0	4	7	2	6	0
Karl Spooner, p	.000	2	0	0	0	0	0	0	0	0	0	0
Don Zimmer, 2b	.222	4	9	0	2	0	0	0	2	2	5	0
TOTAL	.260		223	31	58	8	1	9	30	33	38	2

PITCHER	W	L	ERA	G	GS	CG	SV	SHO	IP	H	ER	BB	SO
Don Bessent	0	0	0.00	3	0	0	0	0	3.1	3	0	1	1
Roger Craig	1	0	3.00	1	1	0	0	0	6.0	4	2	5	4
Carl Erskine	0	0	9.00	1	1	0	0	0	3.0	3	3	2	3
Clem Labine	1	0	2.89	4	0	0	1	0	9.1	6	3	2	2
Billy Loes	0	1	9.82	1	1	0	0	0	3.2	7	4	1	5
Russ Meyer	0	0	0.00	1	0	0	0	0	5.2	4	0	2	4
Don Newcombe	0	1	9.53	1	1	0	0	0	5.2	8	6	2	4
Johnny Podres	2	0	1.00	2	2	2	0	1	18.0	15	2	4	10
Ed Roebuck	0	0	0.00	1	0	0	0	0	2.0	1	0	0	0
Karl Spooner	0	1	13.50	2	1	0	0	0	3.1	4	5	3	6
TOTAL	4	3	3.75	17	7	2	1	1	60.0	55	25	22	39

NY (A)

PLAYER/POS	AVG	G	AB	R	H	2B	3B	HR	RB	BB	SO	SB
Hank Bauer, of-5	.429	6	14	1	6	0	0	0	1	0	1	0
Yogi Berra, c	.417	7	24	5	10	1	0	1	2	3	1	0
Tommy Byrne, p-2	.167	3	6	0	1	0	0	0	2	0	2	0
Andy Carey, ph	.500	2	2	0	1	0	1	0	1	0	0	0
Tom Carroll, pr	.000	2	0	0	0	0	0	0	0	0	0	0
Bob Cerv, of-4	.125	5	16	1	2	0	0	1	1	0	4	0
Gerry Coleman, ss	.000	3	3	0	0	0	0	0	0	0	1	0
Rip Coleman, p	.000	2	0	0	0	0	0	0	0	0	0	0
Joe Collins, 1b-5,of-1	.167	5	12	6	2	0	0	2	3	6	4	1
Whitey Ford, p	.000	2	6	1	0	0	0	0	0	1	1	0
Bob Grim, p	.000	3	2	0	0	0	0	0	0	0	0	0
Elston Howard, of	.192	7	26	3	5	0	0	1	3	1	8	0
Johnny Kucks, p	.000	2	0	0	0	0	0	0	0	0	0	0
Don Larsen, p	.000	1	2	0	0	0	0	0	0	0	0	0
Mickey Mantle, of-2	.200	3	10	1	2	0	0	1	1	0	2	0
Billy Martin, 2b	.320	7	25	2	8	1	1	0	4	1	5	0
Gil McDougald, 3b	.259	7	27	2	7	0	0	1	1	2	6	0
Tom Morgan, p	.000	2	0	0	0	0	0	0	0	0	0	0
Irv Noren, of	.063	5	16	0	1	0	0	0	0	1	1	0
Phil Rizzuto, ss	.267	7	15	2	4	0	0	0	1	5	1	2
Eddie Robinson, 1b-1	.667	4	3	0	2	0	0	0	1	2	1	0
Bill Skowron, 1b-3	.333	5	12	2	4	2	0	1	3	0	1	0
Tom Sturdivant, p	.000	2	0	0	0	0	0	0	0	0	0	0
Bob Turley, p	.000	3	1	0	0	0	0	0	0	0	0	0
TOTAL	.248		222	26	55	4	2	8	25	22	39	3

PITCHER	W	L	ERA	G	GS	CG	SV	SHO	IP	H	ER	BB	SO
Tommy Byrne	1	1	1.88	2	2	1	0	0	14.1	8	3	8	8
Rip Coleman	0	0	9.00	1	0	0	0	0	1.0	5	1	0	1
Whitey Ford	2	0	2.12	2	2	1	0	0	17.0	13	4	8	10
Bob Grim	0	1	4.15	3	1	0	0	1	8.2	8	4	5	8
Johnny Kucks	0	0	6.00	2	0	0	0	0	3.0	4	2	1	1
Don Larsen	0	1	11.25	1	1	0	0	0	4.0	5	5	2	2
Tom Morgan	0	0	4.91	2	0	0	0	0	3.2	3	2	3	1
Tom Sturdivant	0	0	6.00	2	0	0	0	0	3.0	5	2	2	0
Bob Turley	0	1	8.44	3	1	0	0	0	5.1	7	5	4	7
TOTAL	3	4	4.20	18	7	2	1	0	60.0	58	28	33	38

GAME 1 AT NY SEPT 28

BRO	021	000	020	5	10	0
NY	021	102	00X	6	9	1

Pitchers: NEWCOMBE, Bessent (6), Labine (8) vs FORD, Grim (9)
Home Runs: Furillo-BRO, Snider-BRO, Howard-NY, Collins-NY (2)
Attendance: 63,869

GAME 2 AT NY SEPT 29

BRO	000	110	000	2	5	2
NY	000	400	00X	4	8	0

Pitchers: LOES, Bessent (4), Spooner (5), Labine (8) vs BYRNE
Attendance: 64,707

GAME 3 AT BRO SEPT 30

NY	020	000	100	3	7	0
BRO	220	200	20X	8	11	1

Pitchers: TURLEY, Morgan (2), Kucks (5), Sturdivant (7) vs PODRES
Home Runs: Campanella-BRO, Mantle-NY
Attendance: 34,209

GAME 4 AT BRO OCT 1

NY	110	102	000	5	9	0
BRO	001	330	10X	8	14	0

Pitchers: LARSEN, Kucks (5), R.Coleman (6), Morgan (7), Sturdivant (8) vs Erskine, Bessent (4), LABINE (5)
Home Runs: McDougald-NY, Campanella-BRO, Hodges-BRO, Snider-BRO
Attendance: 36,242

GAME 5 AT BRO OCT 2

NY	000	100	110	3	6	0
BRO	021	010	01X	5	9	2

Pitchers: GRIM, Turley (7) vs CRAIG, Labine (7)
Home Runs: Cerv-NY, Berra-NY, Amoros-BRO, Snider-BRO (2)
Attendance: 36,796

GAME 6 AT NY OCT 3

BRO	000	100	000	1	4	1
NY	500	000	00X	5	8	0

Pitchers: SPOONER, Meyer (1), Roebuck (7) vs FORD
Home Runs: Skowron-NY
Attendance: 64,022

GAME 7 AT NY OCT 4

BRO	000	101	000	2	5	0
NY	000	000	000	0	8	1

Pitchers: PODRES vs BYRNE, Grim (6), Turley (8)
Attendance: 62,465

The 1956 Series was a mirror image of 1955. With both teams repeaters as league champions, the Yankees this year followed Brooklyn's winning pattern of the previous Series: losing the first two games, winning the next three, then splitting the final pair.

Sal Maglie outlasted Yankee ace Whitey Ford in the opener. Maglie gave up nine hits and three runs (on homers by Mickey Mantle and Billy Martin), but struck out ten and took the win as Jackie Robinson and Gil Hodges contributed homers for four of Brooklyn's six runs. Dodger ace Don Newcombe was blown out by six Yankee runs (capped by Yogi Berra's grand slam) in the first two innings of Game Two. But Brooklyn came back with six unearned runs in their half of the second (three of them on Duke Snider's homer) and proceeded to run through seven Yankee pitchers for a 13–8 win and a two-game Series edge.

Whitey Ford tried again in Game Three, and this time held on for a complete-game 5–3 win, supported by Billy Martin's game-tying solo homer in the second and forty-year-old Enos Slaughter's go-ahead three-run shot in the sixth. Tom Sturdivant duplicated Ford's effectiveness and success the next day with a six-hit 6–2 win to even the Series.

Sal Maglie pitched Game Five for Brooklyn and improved on his winning performance of Game One, yielding only two runs and holding New York hitless until Mantle's two-out homer in the fourth inning. But no one was a match for Yankee pitcher Don Larsen that day. There was a close out on a deflected Dodger liner in the second inning, and center fielder Mantle made a fine running catch to prevent a hit in the fifth. But Larsen retired the rest routinely, and when Dale Mitchell fanned in the ninth Larsen had his perfect game—a feat still unique in World Series history.

Brooklyn reliever Clem Labine was started in Game Six against Yankee fastballer Bob Turley. No runner scored for either side until the last of the tenth inning when, with two out, Jackie Robinson lined a Turley pitch over the head of the left fielder, scoring Jim Gilliam from second and forcing New York into a seventh game.

The finale proved an anticlimactic disaster for Brooklyn. Once again Dodger starter Newcombe was driven out—this time by Yogi Berra's two two-run homers and Elston Howard's solo shot. By the time it was over, Bill Skowron had increased the Yankee run total to nine with a grand slam, and Yankee starter Johnny Kucks had shut Brooklyn out on three singles. For

New York it was world title number seventeen.

New York Yankees (AL), 4; Brooklyn Dodgers (NL), 3

NY (A)

PLAYER/POS	AVG	G	AB	R	H	2B	3B	HR	RB	BB	SO	SB
Hank Bauer, of	.281	7	32	3	9	0	0	1	3	0	5	1
Yogi Berra, c	.360	7	25	5	9	2	0	3	10	4	1	0
Tommy Byrne, p-1	.000	2	1	0	0	0	0	0	0	0	0	0
Andy Carey, 3b	.158	7	19	2	3	0	0	0	0	1	6	0
Bob Cerv, ph	1.000	1	1	0	1	0	0	0	0	0	0	0
Gerry Coleman, 2b	.000	2	2	0	0	0	0	0	0	0	0	0
Joe Collins, 1b-5	.238	6	21	2	5	2	0	2	2	2	3	0
Whitey Ford, p	.000	2	4	0	0	0	0	0	0	0	3	0
Elston Howard, of	.400	1	5	1	2	1	0	1	1	0	0	0
Johnny Kucks, p	.000	3	3	0	0	0	0	0	0	0	1	0
Don Larsen, p	.333	2	3	1	1	0	0	0	0	1	0	0
Mickey Mantle, of	.250	7	24	6	6	1	0	3	4	6	5	1
Billy Martin, 2b-7,3b-1	.296	7	27	5	8	0	0	2	3	1	6	0
Maury McDermott, p	1.000	1	1	0	1	0	0	0	0	0	0	0
Gil McDougald, ss	.143	7	21	0	3	0	0	0	1	3	6	0
Tom Morgan, p	1.000	2	1	1	1	0	0	0	0	0	0	0
Norm Siebern, ph	.000	1	1	0	0	0	0	0	0	0	1	0
Bill Skowron, 1b-2	.100	3	10	1	1	0	0	1	4	0	3	0
Enos Slaughter, of	.350	6	20	6	7	0	0	1	4	4	0	0
Tom Sturdivant, p	.333	2	3	0	1	0	0	0	0	0	1	0
Bob Turley, p	.000	3	4	0	0	0	0	0	0	0	1	0
George Wilson, ph	.000	1	1	0	0	0	0	0	0	0	1	0
TOTAL	.253		229	33	58	6	0	12	33	21	43	2

PITCHER	W	L	ERA	G	GS	CG	SV	SHO	IP	H	ER	BB	SO
Tommy Byrne	0	0	0.00	1	0	0	0	0	0.1	1	0	0	1
Whitey Ford	1	1	5.25	2	2	1	0	0	12.0	14	7	2	8
Johnny Kucks	1	0	0.82	3	1	1	0	1	11.0	6	1	3	2
Don Larsen	1	0	0.00	2	2	1	0	1	10.2	1	0	4	7
Maury McDermott	0	0	3.00	1	0	0	0	0	3.0	2	1	3	3
Tom Morgan	0	1	9.00	2	0	0	0	0	4.0	6	4	4	3
Tom Sturdivant	1	0	2.79	2	1	1	0	0	9.2	8	3	8	9
Bob Turley	0	1	0.82	3	1	1	0	0	11.0	4	1	8	14
TOTAL	4	3	2.48	16	7	5	0	2	61.2	42	17	32	47

BRO (N)

PLAYER/POS	AVG	G	AB	R	H	2B	3B	HR	RB	BB	SO	SB
Sandy Amoros, of	.053	6	19	1	1	0	0	0	0	1	2	4	0
Don Bessent, p	.500	2	2	0	1	0	0	0	1	1	1	0
Roy Campanella, c	.182	7	22	2	4	1	0	0	3	3	7	0
Gino Cimoli, of	.000	1	0	0	0	0	0	0	0	0	0	0
Roger Craig, p	.500	2	2	0	1	0	0	0	0	0	0	0
Don Drysdale, p	.000	1	0	0	0	0	0	0	0	0	0	0
Carl Erskine, p	.000	2	1	0	0	0	0	0	0	0	1	0
Carl Furillo, of	.240	7	25	2	6	2	0	0	1	2	3	0
Jim Gilliam, 2b-6,of-1	.083	7	24	2	2	0	0	0	2	7	3	1
Gil Hodges, 1b	.304	7	23	5	7	2	0	1	8	4	4	0
Ransom Jackson, ph	.000	3	3	0	0	0	0	0	0	0	2	0
Clem Labine, p	.250	2	4	0	1	1	0	0	0	0	2	0
Sal Maglie, p	.000	2	5	0	0	0	0	0	0	0	2	0
Dale Mitchell, ph	.000	4	4	0	0	0	0	0	0	1	0	0
Charlie Neal, 2b	.000	1	4	0	0	0	0	0	0	0	1	0
Don Newcombe, p	.000	2	1	0	0	0	0	0	0	0	0	0
Pee Wee Reese, ss	.222	7	27	3	6	0	1	0	2	2	6	0
Jackie Robinson, 3b	.250	7	24	5	6	1	0	1	2	5	2	0
Ed Roebuck, p	.000	3	0	0	0	0	0	0	0	0	0	0
Duke Snider, of	.304	7	23	5	7	1	0	1	4	6	8	0
Rube Walker, ph	.000	2	2	0	0	0	0	0	0	0	0	0
TOTAL	.195		215	25	42	8	1	3	24	32	47	1

PITCHER	W	L	ERA	G	GS	CG	SV	SHO	IP	H	ER	BB	SO
Don Bessent	1	0	1.80	2	0	0	0	0	10.0	8	2	3	5
Roger Craig	0	1	12.00	2	1	0	0	0	6.0	10	8	3	4
Don Drysdale	0	0	9.00	1	0	0	0	0	2.0	2	2	1	1
Carl Erskine	0	1	5.40	2	1	0	0	0	5.0	4	3	2	2
Clem Labine	1	0	0.00	2	1	1	0	1	12.0	8	0	3	7
Sal Maglie	1	1	2.65	2	2	2	0	0	17.0	14	5	6	15
Don Newcombe	0	1	21.21	2	2	0	0	0	4.2	11	11	3	4
Ed Roebuck	0	0	2.08	3	0	0	0	0	4.1	1	1	0	5
TOTAL	3	4	4.72	16	7	3	0	1	61.0	58	32	21	43

New York it was world title number seventeen.

GAME 1 AT BRO OCT 3

NY	200 100 000	3	9	1
BRO	023 100 00X	6	9	0

Pitchers: FORD, Kucks (4), Morgan (6), Turley (8) vs MAGLIE
Home Runs: Mantle-NY, Robinson-BRO, Hodges-BRO, Martin-NY
Attendance: 34,479

GAME 2 AT BRO OCT 5

NY	150 100 001	8	12	2
BRO	061 220 02X	13	12	0

Pitchers: Larsen, Kucks (2), Byrne (2), Sturdivant (3), MORGAN (3), Turley (5), McDermott (6) vs Newcombe, Roebuck (2), BESSENT (3)
Home Runs: Berra-NY, Snider-BRO
Attendance: 36,217

GAME 3 AT NY OCT 6

BRO	010 001 100	3	8	1
NY	010 003 01X	5	8	1

Pitchers: CRAIG, Labine (7) vs FORD
Home Runs: Martin-NY, Slaughter-NY
Attendance: 73,977

GAME 4 AT NY OCT 7

BRO	000 100 001	2	6	0
NY	100 201 20X	6	7	2

Pitchers: ERSKINE, Roebuck (5), Drysdale (7) vs STURDIVANT
Home Runs: Mantle-NY, Bauer-NY
Attendance: 69,705

GAME 5 AT NY OCT 8

BRO	000 000 000	0	0	0
NY	000 101 00X	2	5	0

Pitchers: MAGLIE vs LARSEN
Home Runs: Mantle-NY
Attendance: 64,519

GAME 6 AT BRO OCT 9

NY	000 000 000 0	0	7	0
BRO	000 000 000 1	1	4	0

Pitchers: TURLEY vs LABINE
Attendance: 33,224

GAME 7 AT BRO OCT 10

NY	202 100 400	9	10	0
BRO	000 000 000	0	3	1

Pitchers: KUCKS vs NEWCOMBE, Bessent (4), Craig (7), Roebuck (7), Erskine (9)
Home Runs: Berra-NY (2), Howard-NY, Skowron-NY
Attendance: 33,782

Overall, the Yankees pitched better, hit oftener, and scored more runs than the Braves. But the Braves had Lew Burdette, and with him they won the Series.

The opener pitted the Braves' established great Warren Spahn against New York's Whitey Ford. Ford prevailed, with a five-hit 3–1 win as Spahn was chased in the sixth. Burdette, winner of 17 regular-season games, started Game Two against veteran Bobby Shantz, the American League ERA leader. After a scoreless first inning, both pitchers gave up a run in the second and another in the third. Two go-ahead runs in the top of the fourth ended the Braves' scoring, but they were enough, as Burdette blanked New York through the final six innings to even the Series. Before he was finished, Burdette would stretch his consecutive scoreless innings streak to 24.

The Yankees exploded in Game Three, in Milwaukee, running through six Brave pitchers for a 12–3 rout. Braves fans even ended up cheering Yankee second baseman Tony Kubek—a Milwaukee native—who opened the scoring with a solo homer in the first, scored again after singling in the fourth (on Mickey Mantle's home run), and concluded the Yankee scoring in the seventh with his second homer, with two aboard.

Warren Spahn carried a 4–1 Braves lead into the ninth inning of Game Four, but after retiring the first two batters in the ninth, he gave up singles to Yogi Berra and Gil McDougald, and a game-tying home run to Elston Howard. In the top of the tenth, Hank Bauer tripled in a go-ahead Yankee run, but Milwaukee's Johnny Logan doubled to tie it up in the last of the tenth, and Eddie Mathews homered to give Spahn a shaky victory.

Burdette faced Ford in Game Five. In the sixth inning the Braves put half their hits—three singles—back to back for a run. It was all they needed as Burdette spaced seven singles for the shutout. Back in New York two days later, all the scoring came on home runs. Each club hit a pair, but Berra's in the third was the only one with a man aboard. Brave blasts in the fifth (Frank Torre) and seventh (Hank Aaron) tied the score, but Bauer answered Aaron's homer in the last of the seventh with what proved the winning shot. Bob Turley, who yielded just four hits while fanning eight (the Series high) claimed the Yankee victory.

In the finale, Burdette, with only two days' rest, scattered four hits over the first eight innings as the Braves gave him a 5–0 lead. In the bottom of the ninth, though, three Yankee singles loaded the bases with two out. But third baseman Eddie Mathews snared Bil Skow-

Milwaukee Braves (NL), 4; New York Yankees (AL), 3

MIL (N)

PLAYER/POS	AVG	G	AB	R	H	2B	3B	HR	RB	BB	SO	SB
Hank Aaron, of	.393	7	28	5	11	0	1	3	7	1	6	0
Joe Adcock, 1b	.200	5	15	1	3	0	0	0	2	0	2	0
Bob Buhl, p	.000	2	1	0	0	0	0	0	0	0	1	0
Lew Burdette, p	.000	3	8	0	0	0	0	0	0	1	2	0
Gene Conley, p	.000	1	0	0	0	0	0	0	0	0	0	0
Wes Covington, of	.208	7	24	1	5	1	0	0	1	2	6	1
Del Crandall, c	.211	6	19	1	4	0	0	1	1	1	1	0
John De Merit, pr	.000	1	0	0	0	0	0	0	0	0	0	0
Bob Hazle, of	.154	4	13	2	2	0	0	0	0	1	2	0
Ernie Johnson, p	.000	3	1	0	0	0	0	0	0	0	1	0
Nippy Jones, ph	.000	3	2	0	0	0	0	0	0	0	0	0
Johnny Logan, ss	.185	7	27	5	5	1	0	1	2	3	6	0
Felix Mantilla, 2b-3	.000	4	10	1	0	0	0	0	0	1	0	0
Eddie Mathews, 3b	.227	7	22	4	5	3	0	1	4	8	5	0
Don McMahon, p	.000	3	0	0	0	0	0	0	0	0	0	0
Andy Pafko, of-5	.214	6	14	1	3	0	0	0	0	0	1	0
Juan Pizarro, p	.000	1	1	0	0	0	0	0	0	0	0	0
Del Rice, c	.167	2	6	0	1	0	0	0	0	1	2	0
Carl Sawatski, ph	.000	2	2	0	0	0	0	0	0	0	2	0
Red Schoendienst, 2b	.278	5	18	0	5	1	0	0	2	1	0	0
Warren Spahn, p	.000	2	4	0	0	0	0	0	0	1	2	0
Frank Torre, 1b	.300	7	10	2	3	0	0	2	3	2	0	0
Bob Trowbridge, p	.000	1	0	0	0	0	0	0	0	0	0	0
TOTAL	.209		225	23	47	6	1	8	22	22	40	1

PITCHER	W	L	ERA	G	GS	CG	SV	SHO	IP	H	ER	BB	SO
Bob Buhl	0	1	10.80	2	2	0	0	0	3.1	6	4	6	4
Lew Burdette	3	0	0.67	3	3	3	0	2	27.0	21	2	4	13
Gene Conley	0	0	10.80	1	0	0	0	0	1.2	2	2	1	0
Ernie Johnson	0	1	1.29	3	0	0	0	0	7.0	2	1	1	8
Don McMahon	0	0	0.00	3	0	0	0	0	5.0	3	0	3	5
Juan Pizarro	0	0	10.80	1	0	0	0	0	1.2	3	2	2	1
Warren Spahn	1	1	4.70	2	2	1	0	0	15.1	18	8	2	2
Bob Trowbridge	0	0	45.00	1	0	0	0	0	1.0	2	5	3	1
TOTAL	4	3	3.48	16	7	4	0	2	62.0	57	24	22	34

NY (A)

PLAYER/POS	AVG	G	AB	R	H	2B	3B	HR	RB	BB	SO	SB
Hank Bauer, of	.258	7	31	3	8	2	1	2	6	1	6	0
Yogi Berra, c	.320	7	25	5	8	1	0	1	2	4	0	0
Tommy Byrne, p	.500	2	2	0	1	0	0	0	0	0	1	0
Andy Carey, 3b	.286	2	7	0	2	1	0	0	1	1	0	0
Gerry Coleman, 2b	.364	7	22	2	8	2	0	0	2	3	1	0
Joe Collins, 1b-5	.000	6	5	0	0	0	0	0	0	0	3	0
Art Ditmar, p	.000	2	1	0	0	0	0	0	0	0	1	0
Whitey Ford, p	.000	2	5	0	0	0	0	0	0	0	1	0
Bob Grim, p	.000	2	0	0	0	0	0	0	0	0	0	0
Elston Howard, 1b-3	.273	6	11	2	3	0	0	1	3	1	3	0
Tony Kubek, of-5,3b-2	.286	7	28	4	8	0	0	2	4	0	4	0
Johnny Kucks, p	.000	1	0	0	0	0	0	0	0	0	0	0
Don Larsen, p	.000	2	2	1	0	0	0	0	0	2	1	0
Jerry Lumpe, 3b-3	.286	6	14	0	4	0	0	0	2	1	1	0
Mickey Mantle, of-5	.263	6	19	3	5	0	0	1	2	3	1	0
Gil McDougald, ss	.250	7	24	3	6	0	0	0	2	3	3	1
Bobby Richardson, 2b-1	.000	2	0	0	0	0	0	0	0	0	0	0
Bobby Shantz, p	.000	3	1	0	0	0	0	0	0	0	0	0
Harry Simpson, 1b-4	.083	5	12	0	1	0	0	0	1	0	4	0
Bill Skowron, 1b	.000	2	4	0	0	0	0	0	0	0	0	0
Enos Slaughter, of	.250	5	12	2	3	1	0	0	3	2	0	0
Tom Sturdivant, p	.000	2	1	0	0	0	0	0	0	0	0	0
Bob Turley, p	.000	3	4	0	0	0	0	0	0	0	2	0
TOTAL	.248		230	25	57	7	1	7	25	22	34	1

PITCHER	W	L	ERA	G	GS	CG	SV	SHO	IP	H	ER	BB	SO
Tommy Byrne	0	0	5.40	2	0	0	0	0	3.1	1	2	2	1
Art Ditmar	0	0	0.00	2	0	0	0	0	6.0	2	0	0	2
Whitey Ford	1	1	1.13	2	2	1	0	0	16.0	11	2	5	7
Bob Grim	0	1	7.71	2	0	0	0	0	2.1	3	2	0	2
Johnny Kucks	0	0	0.00	1	0	0	0	0	0.2	1	0	1	1
Don Larsen	1	1	3.72	2	1	0	0	0	9.2	8	4	5	6
Bobby Shantz	0	1	4.05	3	1	0	0	0	6.2	8	3	2	7
Tom Sturdivant	0	0	6.00	2	1	0	0	0	6.0	6	4	1	2
Bob Turley	1	0	2.31	3	2	1	0	0	11.2	7	3	6	12
TOTAL	3	4	2.89	19	7	2	0	0	62.1	47	20	22	40

ron's sharp grounder and stepped on the bag for a force out that preserved Burdette's second shutout and gave Milwaukee its first world championship.

GAME 1 AT NY OCT 2

MIL	000 000 100	1	5	0
NY	000 012 00X	3	9	1

Pitchers: SPAHN, Johnson (6), McMahon (7) vs FORD
Attendance: 69,476

GAME 2 AT NY OCT 3

MIL	011 200 000	4	8	0
NY	011 000 000	2	7	2

Pitchers: BURDETTE vs SHANTZ, Ditmar (4), Grim (8)
Home Runs: Logan-MIL, Bauer-NY
Attendance: 65,202

GAME 3 AT MIL OCT 5

NY	302 200 500	12	9	0
MIL	010 020 000	3	8	1

Pitchers: Turley, LARSEN (2) vs BUHL, Pizarro (1), Conley (3), Johnson (5), Trowbridge (7), McMahon (8)
Home Runs: Kubek-NY (2), Mantle-NY, Aaron-MIL
Attendance: 45,804

GAME 4 AT MIL OCT 6

NY	100 000 003 1	5	11	0
MIL	000 400 000 3	7	7	0

Pitchers: Sturdivant, Shantz (5), Kucks (8), Byrne (8), GRIM (10) vs SPAHN
Home Runs: Aaron-MIL, Torre-MIL, Howard-NY, Mathews-MIL
Attendance: 45,804

GAME 5 AT MIL OCT 7

NY	000 000 000	0	7	0
MIL	000 001 00X	1	6	1

Pitchers: FORD, Turley (8) vs BURDETTE
Attendance: 45,811

GAME 6 AT NY OCT 9

MIL	000 010 100	2	4	0
NY	002 000 10X	3	7	0

Pitchers: Buhl, JOHNSON (3), McMahon (8) vs TURLEY
Home Runs: Berra-NY, Torre-MIL, Aaron-MIL, Bauer-NY
Attendance: 61,408

GAME 7 AT NY OCT 10

MIL	004 000 010	5	9	1
NY	000 000 000	0	7	3

Pitchers: BURDETTE vs LARSEN, Shantz (3), Ditmar (4), Sturdivant (6), Byrne (8)
Home Runs: Crandall-MIL
Attendance: 61,207

After four games, Milwaukee held a 3–1 Series advantage, but New York rebounded to take the final three games and avenge their loss to the Braves the year before. As in the previous series, Warren Spahn faced Whitey Ford in the opener. The durable Spahn emerged the victor when Bill Bruton singled home the Braves' winning run off reliever Ryne Duren in the last of the tenth. In Game Two, home runs by Bruton and pitcher Lew Burdette (for three runs) helped put the Braves ahead 7–1 in the first inning. Milwaukee scored off five Yankee hurlers in their eventual 13–5 win.

Don Larsen and Ryne Duren combined for a shutout in Game Three to give New York its first victory. Hank Bauer drove in all four Yankee runs with a two-run single in the fifth and his third home run in three games in the seventh. Warren Spahn held Bauer hitless in Game Four, blanking New York on two hits to defeat Whitey Ford and bring Milwaukee within a win of the championship.

Yankee Bob Turley came up with a shutout of his own the next day, though, fanning ten men along the way. Gil McDougald's solo homer in the third inning was all the offense Turley needed, but as insurance the Yankees bunched six of their ten hits into the sixth inning for six more runs.

Spahn and Ford, with only two days' rest, confronted each other a third time in Game Six. Ford lasted less than two innings, but Spahn (despite Hank Bauer's fourth Series home run in the first inning) endured into extra innings, when McDougald put New York ahead with a leadoff homer in the tenth. Two outs and two hits later, Spahn was removed, and Bill Skowron's single off reliever Don McMahon drove home another Yankee run. Milwaukee scored once in the last of the tenth and threatened further damage with men on first and third. But Bob Turley came on to retire the final batter and send the Series to a seventh game.

In the sixth inning of the finale, the Braves' Del Crandall homered against Turley (who had relieved Don Larsen in the third) to tie the game 2–2. But four Yankee runs off starter Lew Burdette in the top of the eighth (including Skowron's three-run homer) made the score 6–2, where it remained, as Turley held on to bring Casey Stengel his seventh (and last) Series triumph—and the Yankees their eighteenth.

New York Yankees (AL), 4; Milwaukee Braves (NL), 3

NY (A)

PLAYER/POS	AVG	G	AB	R	H	2B	3B	HR	RB	BB	SO	SB
Hank Bauer, of	.323	7	31	6	10	0	0	4	8	0	5	0
Yogi Berra, c	.222	7	27	3	6	3	0	0	2	1	0	0
Andy Carey, 3b	.083	5	12	1	1	0	0	0	0	0	3	0
Murry Dickson, p	.000	2	0	0	0	0	0	0	0	0	0	0
Art Ditmar, p	.000	1	1	0	0	0	0	0	0	0	0	0
Ryne Duren, p	.000	3	3	0	0	0	0	0	0	0	2	0
Whitey Ford, p	.000	3	4	1	0	0	0	0	0	0	2	0
Elston Howard, of	.222	6	18	4	4	0	0	0	2	1	4	1
Tony Kubek, ss	.048	7	21	0	1	0	0	0	1	1	7	0
Johnny Kucks, p	1.000	2	1	0	1	0	0	0	0	0	0	0
Don Larsen, p	.000	2	2	0	0	0	0	0	0	0	1	0
Jerry Lumpe, 3b-3,ss-2	.167	6	12	0	2	0	0	0	0	0	2	0
Duke Maas, p	.000	1	0	0	0	0	0	0	0	0	0	0
Mickey Mantle, of	.250	7	24	4	6	0	1	2	3	7	4	0
Gil McDougald, 2b	.321	7	28	5	9	2	0	2	4	2	4	0
Zach Monroe, p	.000	1	0	0	0	0	0	0	0	0	0	0
Bobby Richardson, 3b	.000	4	5	0	0	0	0	0	0	0	0	0
Norm Siebern, of	.125	3	8	1	1	0	0	0	0	0	3	0
Bill Skowron, 1b	.259	7	27	3	7	0	0	2	7	1	4	0
Enos Slaughter, ph	.000	4	3	0	0	0	0	0	0	1	1	0
Marv Throneberry, ph	.000	1	1	0	0	0	0	0	0	0	1	0
Bob Turley, p	.200	4	5	0	1	0	0	0	2	0	1	0
TOTAL	.210		233	29	49	5	1	10	29	21	42	1

PITCHER	W	L	ERA	G	GS	CG	SV	SHO	IP	H	ER	BB	SO
Murry Dickson	0	0	4.50	2	0	0	0	0	4.0	4	2	0	1
Art Ditmar	0	0	0.00	1	0	0	0	0	3.2	2	0	0	2
Ryne Duren	1	1	1.93	3	0	0	1	0	9.1	7	2	6	14
Whitey Ford	0	1	4.11	3	3	0	0	0	15.1	19	7	5	16
Johnny Kucks	0	0	2.08	2	0	0	0	0	4.1	4	1	0	0
Don Larsen	1	0	0.96	2	2	0	0	0	9.1	9	1	6	9
Duke Maas	0	0	81.00	1	0	0	0	0	0.1	2	3	1	0
Zach Monroe	0	0	27.00	1	0	0	0	0	1.0	3	3	1	1
Bob Turley	2	1	2.76	4	2	1	1	1	16.1	10	5	7	13
TOTAL	4	3	3.39	19	7	1	2	1	63.2	60	24	27	56

MIL (N)

PLAYER/POS	AVG	G	AB	R	H	2B	3B	HR	RB	BB	SO	SB
Hank Aaron, of	.333	7	27	3	9	2	0	0	2	4	6	0
Joe Adcock, 1b	.308	4	13	1	4	0	0	0	0	1	3	0
Billy Bruton, of	.412	7	17	2	7	0	0	1	2	5	5	0
Lew Burdette, p	.111	3	9	1	1	0	0	1	3	0	3	0
Wes Covington, of	.269	7	26	2	7	0	0	0	4	2	4	0
Del Crandall, c	.240	7	25	4	6	0	0	1	3	3	10	0
Harry Hanebrink, ph	.000	2	2	0	0	0	0	0	0	0	0	0
Johnny Logan, ss	.120	7	25	3	3	2	0	0	2	2	4	0
Felix Mantilla, ss-1	.000	4	0	1	0	0	0	0	0	0	0	0
Eddie Mathews, 3b	.160	7	25	3	4	2	0	0	3	6	11	1
Don McMahon, p	.000	3	0	0	0	0	0	0	0	0	0	0
Andy Pafko, of	.333	4	9	0	3	1	0	0	1	0	0	0
Juan Pizarro, p	.000	1	0	0	0	0	0	0	0	0	0	0
Bob Rush, p	.000	1	2	0	0	0	0	0	0	0	2	0
Red Schoendienst, 2b	.300	7	30	5	9	3	0	0	0	2	1	0
Warren Spahn, p	.333	3	12	0	4	0	0	0	3	0	6	0
Frank Torre, 1b	.176	7	17	0	3	0	0	0	1	2	0	0
Carl Willey, p	.000	1	0	0	0	0	0	0	0	0	0	0
Casey Wise, ph	.000	2	1	0	0	0	0	0	0	0	1	0
TOTAL	.250		240	25	60	10	1	3	24	27	56	1

PITCHER	W	L	ERA	G	GS	CG	SV	SHO	IP	H	ER	BB	SO
Lew Burdette	1	2	5.64	3	3	1	0	0	22.1	22	14	4	12
Don McMahon	0	0	5.40	3	0	0	0	0	3.1	3	2	3	5
Juan Pizarro	0	0	5.40	2	0	0	0	0	1.2	2	1	1	3
Bob Rush	0	1	3.00	1	1	0	0	0	6.0	3	2	5	2
Warren Spahn	2	1	2.20	3	3	2	0	1	28.2	19	7	8	18
Carl Willey	0	0	0.00	1	0	0	0	0	1.0	0	0	0	2
TOTAL	3	4	3.71	12	7	3	0	1	63.0	49	26	21	42

GAME 1 AT MIL OCT 1

NY	000 120 000 0	3	8	1
MIL	000 200 010 1	4	10	0

Pitchers: Ford, DUREN (8) vs SPAHN
Home Runs: Skowron-NY, Bauer-NY
Attendance: 46,367

GAME 2 AT MIL OCT 2

NY	100 100 003	5	7	0
MIL	710 000 23X	13	15	1

Pitchers: TURLEY, Maas (1), Kucks (1), Dickson (5), Monroe (8) vs BURDETTE
Home Runs: Bruton-MIL, Burdette-MIL, Mantle-NY (2), Bauer-NY
Attendance: 46,367

GAME 3 AT NY OCT 4

MIL	000 000 000	0	6	0
NY	000 020 20X	4	4	0

Pitchers: RUSH, McMahon (7) vs LARSEN, Duren (8)
Home Runs: Bauer-NY
Attendance: 71,599

GAME 4 AT NY OCT 5

MIL	000 001 110	3	9	0
NY	000 000 000	0	2	1

Pitchers: SPAHN vs FORD, Kucks (8), Dickson (9)
Attendance: 71,563

GAME 5 AT NY OCT 6

MIL	000 000 000	0	5	0
NY	001 006 00X	7	10	0

Pitchers: BURDETTE, Pizarro (6), Willey (8) vs TURLEY
Home Runs: McDougald-NY
Attendance: 65,279

GAME 6 AT MIL OCT 8

NY	100 001 000 2	4	10	1
MIL	110 000 000 1	3	10	4

Pitchers: Ford, Ditmar (2), DUREN (6), Turley (10) vs SPAHN, McMahon (10)
Home Runs: Bauer-NY, McDougald-NY
Attendance: 46,367

GAME 7 AT MIL OCT 9

NY	020 000 040	6	8	0
MIL	100 001 000	2	5	2

Pitchers: Larsen, TURLEY (3) vs BURDETTE, McMahon (8)
Home Runs: Crandall-MIL, Skowron-NY
Attendance: 46,367

It took a nosedive from first to third by San Francisco and a Dodger playoff victory over Milwaukee (who had finished the season tied with the Dodgers), to bring Los Angeles the city's first major league pennant. But once they had made it to the Series, the Dodgers dispatched the White Sox in six games.

The opener, though, belonged to Chicago. In their first World Series in forty years, the White Sox overwhelmed Los Angeles with 11 runs in the first four innings as pitchers Early Wynn and Gerry Staley combined to blank the Dodgers. Chicago's big gun was veteran slugger Ted Kluszewski (acquired from Pittsburgh in late August), whose single and two homers drove in five runs. Chicago scored twice in the first inning the next day, but Dodger starter Johnny Podres settled down to blank the Sox over the next five innings as home runs by Charlie Neal in the fifth and pinch hitter Chuck Essegian and Neal (again) in the seventh put the Dodgers ahead by two. Rookie reliever Larry Sherry gave up a third Chicago run in the eighth on Al Smith's double, but a second runner was nailed at the plate, and Sherry set down the side in the ninth to save Podres's win.

When the Series moved to Los Angeles' cavernous Coliseum for the West Coast's first World Series games ever, fans turned out in record numbers, setting a new Series mark in each of the next three games. Dodger starter Don Drysdale yielded 11 hits and four walks in Game Three, but the only run scored against him came on a double-play after Larry Sherry had relieved him with two men on in the eighth. As Los Angeles had already scored twice, and added a third run in their half of the eighth, Drysdale emerged with the win and Sherry with his second save. In Game Four, the Sox's Sherm Lollar's three-run homer had tied the score by the time Sherry relieved Dodger starter Roger Craig in the eighth, so Gil Hodges's solo homer in the last of the eighth gave Sherry the win this time—and Los Angeles a 3–1 Series advantage.

Chicago's Bob Shaw dueled Dodger Sandy Koufax through seven innings of Game Five before 92,706 spectators (still a Series high). The Sox scored only once off Koufax, but one run was enough for their second win as a pair of Sox relievers continued Shaw's shutout through the final two innings.

Back in Chicago for Game Six, the Dodgers unloaded on Early Wynn and Dick Donovan for eight runs in the third and fourth innings. Ted Kluszewski's three-run homer in the last of the fourth led to Larry Sherry's fourth relief appear-

ance—and his second Series win, as he held the Sox scoreless the rest of the game to bring the world championship to the West Coast for the first time.

Los Angeles Dodgers (NL), 4; Chicago White Sox (AL), 2

LA (N)

PLAYER/POS	AVG	G	AB	R	H	2B	3B	HR	RB	BB	SO	SB
Chuck Churn, p	.000	1	0	0	0	0	0	0	0	0	0	0
Roger Craig, p	.000	2	3	0	0	0	0	0	0	0	2	0
Don Demeter, of	.250	6	12	2	3	0	0	0	0	1	3	0
Don Drysdale, p	.000	1	2	0	0	0	0	0	0	0	2	0
Chuck Essegian, ph	.667	4	3	2	2	0	0	2	2	1	1	0
Ron Fairly, of-4	.000	6	3	0	0	0	0	0	0	0	1	0
Carl Furillo, of-1	.250	4	4	0	1	0	0	0	2	0	1	0
Jim Gilliam, 3b	.240	6	25	2	6	0	0	0	0	2	2	2
Gil Hodges, 1b	.391	6	23	2	9	0	1	1	2	1	2	0
Johnny Klippstein, p	.000	1	0	0	0	0	0	0	0	0	0	0
Sandy Koufax, p	.000	2	2	0	0	0	0	0	0	0	1	0
Clem Labine, p	.000	1	0	0	0	0	0	0	0	0	0	0
Norm Larker, of	.188	6	16	2	3	0	0	0	0	0	2	0
Wally Moon, of	.261	6	23	3	6	0	0	1	2	2	2	1
Charlie Neal, 2b	.370	6	27	4	10	2	0	2	6	0	1	1
Joe Pignatano, c	.000	1	0	0	0	0	0	0	0	0	0	0
Johnny Podres, p-2	.500	3	4	1	2	1	0	0	1	0	0	0
Rip Repulski, of	.000	1	0	0	0	0	0	0	0	1	0	0
Johnny Roseboro, c	.095	6	21	0	2	0	0	0	1	0	0	0
Larry Sherry, p-4	.500	5	4	0	2	0	0	0	0	0	1	0
Duke Snider, of-3	.200	4	10	1	2	0	0	1	2	2	0	0
Stan Williams, p	.000	1	0	0	0	0	0	0	0	0	0	0
Maury Wills, ss	.250	6	20	2	5	0	0	0	1	0	3	1
Don Zimmer, ss	.000	1	1	0	0	0	0	0	0	0	0	0
TOTAL	.261		203	21	53	3	1	7	19	12	27	5

PITCHER	W	L	ERA	G	GS	CG	SV	SHO	IP	H	ER	BB	SO
Chuck Churn	0	0	27.00	1	0	0	0	0	0.2	5	2	0	0
Roger Craig	0	1	8.68	2	2	0	0	0	9.1	15	9	5	8
Don Drysdale	1	0	1.29	1	1	0	0	0	7.0	11	1	4	5
Johnny Klippstein	0	0	0.00	1	0	0	0	0	2.0	1	0	0	2
Sandy Koufax	0	1	1.00	2	1	0	0	0	9.0	5	1	1	7
Clem Labine	0	0	0.00	1	0	0	0	0	1.0	0	0	0	1
Johnny Podres	1	0	4.82	2	2	0	0	0	9.1	7	5	6	4
Larry Sherry	2	0	0.71	4	0	0	2	0	12.2	8	1	2	5
Stan Williams	0	0	0.00	1	0	0	0	0	2.0	0	0	2	1
TOTAL	4	2	3.23	15	6	0	2	0	53.0	52	19	20	33

CHI (A)

PLAYER/POS	AVG	G	AB	R	H	2B	3B	HR	RB	BB	SO	SB
Luis Aparicio, ss	.308	6	26	1	8	1	0	0	0	2	3	1
Norm Cash, ph	.000	4	4	0	0	0	0	0	0	0	2	0
Dick Donovan, p	.333	3	3	0	1	0	0	0	0	0	1	0
Sammy Esposito, 3b	.000	2	2	0	0	0	0	0	0	0	1	0
Nellie Fox, 2b	.375	6	24	4	9	3	0	0	0	4	1	0
Billy Goodman, 3b	.231	5	13	1	3	0	0	0	1	0	5	0
Ted Kluszewski, 1b	.391	6	23	5	9	1	0	3	10	2	0	0
Jim Landis, of	.292	6	24	6	7	0	0	0	1	1	7	1
Sherm Lollar, c	.227	6	22	3	5	0	0	1	5	1	3	0
Turk Lown, p	.000	3	0	0	0	0	0	0	0	0	0	0
Jim McAnany, of	.000	3	5	0	0	0	0	0	0	1	0	0
Ray Moore, p	.000	1	0	0	0	0	0	0	0	0	0	0
Bubba Phillips, 3b-3,of-1	.300	3	10	0	3	1	0	0	0	0	0	0
Billy Pierce, p	.000	3	0	0	0	0	0	0	0	0	0	0
Jim Rivera, of	.000	5	11	1	0	0	0	0	0	3	1	0
Johnny Romano, ph	.000	1	1	0	0	0	0	0	0	0	0	0
Bob Shaw, p	.250	2	4	0	1	0	0	0	0	0	2	0
Al Smith, of	.250	6	20	1	5	3	0	0	1	4	4	0
Gerry Staley, p	.000	4	1	0	0	0	0	0	0	1	1	0
Earl Torgeson, 1b-1	.000	3	1	1	0	0	0	0	0	1	0	0
Early Wynn, p	.200	3	5	0	1	1	0	0	1	0	2	0
TOTAL	.261		199	23	52	10	0	4	19	20	33	2

PITCHER	W	L	ERA	G	GS	CG	SV	SHO	IP	H	ER	BB	SO
Dick Donovan	0	1	5.40	3	1	0	1	0	8.1	4	5	3	5
Turk Lown	0	0	0.00	3	0	0	0	0	3.1	2	0	1	3
Ray Moore	0	0	9.00	1	0	0	0	0	1.0	1	1	0	1
Billy Pierce	0	0	0.00	3	0	0	0	0	4.0	2	0	2	3
Bob Shaw	1	1	2.57	2	2	0	0	0	14.0	17	4	2	2
Gerry Staley	0	1	2.16	4	0	0	1	0	8.1	8	2	0	3
Early Wynn	1	1	5.54	3	3	0	0	0	13.0	19	8	4	10
TOTAL	2	4	3.46	19	6	0	2	0	52.0	53	20	12	27

GAME 1 AT CHI OCT 1

LA	000 000 000	0	8 3
CHI	207 200 00X	11	11 0

Pitchers: CRAIG, Churn (3), Labine (4), Koufax (5), Klippstein (7) vs WYNN, Staley (8)
Home Runs: Kluszewski-CHI (2)
Attendance: 48,013

GAME 2 AT CHI OCT 2

LA	000 010 300	4	9 1
CHI	200 000 010	3	8 0

Pitchers: PODRES, Sherry (7) vs SHAW, Lown (7)
Home Runs: Neal-LA (2), Essegian-LA
Attendance: 47,368

GAME 3 AT LA OCT 4

CHI	000 000 010	1	12 0
LA	000 000 21X	3	5 0

Pitchers: DONOVAN, Staley (7) vs DRYSDALE, Sherry (8)
Attendance: 92,394

GAME 4 AT LA OCT 5

CHI	000 000 400	4	10 3
LA	004 000 01X	5	9 0

Pitchers: Wynn, Lown (3), Pierce (4), STALEY (7) vs Craig, SHERRY (8)
Home Runs: Lollar-CHI, Hodges-LA
Attendance: 92,650

GAME 5 AT LA OCT 6

CHI	000 100 000	1	5 0
LA	000 000 000	0	9 0

Pitchers: SHAW, Pierce (7), Donovan (8) vs KOUFAX, Williams (8)
Attendance: 92,706

GAME 6 AT CHI OCT 8

LA	002 600 001	9	13 0
CHI	000 300 000	3	6 1

Pitchers: Podres, SHERRY (4) vs WYNN, Donovan (4), Staley (5), Pierce (8), Moore (9)
Home Runs: Snider-LA, Moon-LA, Kluszewski-CHI, Essegian-LA
Attendance: 47,653

Through six games and 8½ innings of the seventh, the Yankees had outscored the Pirates by 29 runs. But as Pirate second baseman Bill Mazeroski stepped to the plate to open the last of the ninth, the Series was even at three games apiece, and Game Seven was tied 9–9. The stage was set for Mazeroski to fulfill that ultimate baseball fantasy, and he did, on pitcher Ralph Terry's second pitch.

Yankee Roger Maris opened the Series scoring with a solo homer in the first inning of Game One, and Elston Howard added two more Yankee runs with a homer in the ninth. But between the home runs New York scored only one run to the Pirates' six (including a two-run homer by Mazeroski in the fourth).

The Yankees avenged their first-game loss with a blowout in Game Two—their first of three. Pittsburgh hit safely 13 times, but scored only three runs. New York, though, turned 19 hits (and a Pirate error) into 16 runs—five of them driven in by Mickey Mantle's two home runs. Continuing their assault in New York the next day, the Bronx Bombers scored six runs in the first inning and four in the fourth as Whitey Ford blanked the Pirates on four hits. Mantle homered again, and second baseman Bobby Richardson drove in a Series single-game record six runs with a grand slam and a single.

Pirate ace Vernon Law—the winner of Game One—started Game Four and, with relief help once again from Roy Face, held the Yankees to two runs to even the Series. Law's bat proved crucial, too, as he doubled in Pittsburgh's first run and scored the third in a three-run fifth that provided all the Pirate scoring. In Game Five, the Pirates' Mazeroski doubled in what proved the two decisive runs in a three-run second as Harvey Haddix and Roy Face (who recorded his third save of the Series) duplicated the previous day's achievement of limiting New York to two runs.

But once again the Yankees came back. Bobby Richardson drove in three of New York's 12 runs with two triples to establish a new Series record of 12 RBI as the Yankees, behind Whitey Ford's second shutout, sent the Series into a seventh game.

Home runs dominated the finale. Rocky Nelson's two-run shot in the first opened the scoring, and Yankee homers by Bill Skowron in the fifth and Yogi Berra in the sixth contributed four of the five runs that put New York ahead 5–4. Pirate Hal Smith's three-run homer in the bottom of the eighth restored the lead to Pittsburgh, 9–7, and after the Yankees had tied the game

Pittsburgh Pirates (NL), 4;
New York Yankees (AL), 3

PIT (N)

PLAYER/POS	AVG	G	AB	R	H	2B	3B	HR	RB	BB	SO	SB
Gene Baker, ph	.000	3	3	0	0	0	0	0	0	0	1	0
Smoky Burgess, c	.333	5	18	2	6	1	0	0	0	2	1	0
Tom Cheney, p	.000	3	0	0	0	0	0	0	0	0	0	0
Joe Christopher, ph	.000	3	0	2	0	0	0	0	0	0	0	0
Gino Cimoli, of-6	.250	7	20	4	5	0	0	0	1	2	4	0
Roberto Clemente, of	.310	7	29	1	9	0	0	0	3	0	4	0
Roy Face, p	.000	4	3	0	0	0	0	0	0	0	2	0
Bob Friend, p	.000	3	1	0	0	0	0	0	0	0	0	0
Joe Gibbon, p	.000	2	0	0	0	0	0	0	0	0	0	0
Fred Green, p	.000	3	1	0	0	0	0	0	0	0	0	0
Dick Groat, ss	.214	7	28	3	6	2	0	0	2	0	1	0
Harvey Haddix, p	.333	2	3	0	1	0	0	0	0	0	0	0
Don Hoak, 3b	.217	7	23	3	5	2	0	0	3	4	1	0
Clem Labine, p	.000	3	0	0	0	0	0	0	0	0	0	0
Vern Law, p	.333	3	6	1	2	1	0	0	1	0	1	0
Bill Mazeroski, 2b	.320	7	25	4	8	2	0	2	5	0	3	0
Vinegar Bend Mizell, p	.000	2	0	0	0	0	0	0	0	0	0	0
Rocky Nelson, 1b-3	.333	4	9	2	3	0	0	1	2	1	1	0
Bob Oldis, c	.000	3	0	0	0	0	0	0	0	0	0	0
Dick Schofield, ss-2	.333	3	3	0	1	0	0	0	0	0	0	0
Bob Skinner, of	.200	5	2	5	1	0	0	0	1	1	0	1
Hal Smith, c	.375	3	8	1	3	0	0	1	3	0	1	0
Dick Stuart, 1b	.150	5	20	0	3	0	0	0	0	0	3	0
Bill Virdon, of	.241	7	29	2	7	3	0	0	5	1	3	1
George Witt, p	.000	3	0	0	0	0	0	0	0	0	0	0
TOTAL	.256		234	27	60	11	0	4	26	12	26	2

PITCHER	W	L	ERA	G	GS	CG	SV	SHO	IP	H	ER	BB	SO
Tom Cheney	0	0	4.50	3	0	0	0	0	4.0	4	2	1	6
Roy Face	0	0	5.23	4	0	0	3	0	10.1	9	6	2	4
Bob Friend	0	2	13.50	3	2	0	0	0	6.0	13	9	3	7
Joe Gibbon	0	0	9.00	2	0	0	0	0	3.0	4	3	1	2
Fred Green	0	0	22.50	3	0	0	0	0	4.0	11	10	1	3
Harvey Haddix	2	0	2.45	2	1	0	0	0	7.1	6	2	2	6
Clem Labine	0	0	13.50	3	0	0	0	0	4.0	13	6	1	2
Vern Law	2	0	3.44	3	3	0	0	0	18.1	22	7	3	8
Vinegar Bend Mizell	0	1	15.43	2	1	0	0	0	2.1	4	4	2	1
George Witt	0	0	0.00	3	0	0	0	0	2.2	5	0	2	1
TOTAL	4	3	7.11	28	7	0	3	0	62.0	91	49	18	40

NY (A)

PLAYER/POS	AVG	G	AB	R	H	2B	3B	HR	RB	BB	SO	SB
Luis Arroyo, p	.000	1	1	0	0	0	0	0	0	0	0	0
Yogi Berra, of-4,c-3	.318	7	22	6	7	0	0	1	8	2	0	0
Johnny Blanchard, c-2	.455	5	11	2	5	2	0	0	2	0	0	0
Clete Boyer, 3b-4,ss-1	.250	4	12	1	3	2	1	0	1	0	1	0
Bob Cerv, of-3	.357	4	14	1	5	0	0	0	0	0	3	0
Jim Coates, p	.000	3	1	0	0	0	0	0	0	0	0	0
Joe De Maestri, ss-3	.500	4	2	1	1	0	0	0	0	0	0	0
Art Ditmar, p	.000	2	0	0	0	0	0	0	0	0	0	0
Ryne Duren, p	.000	2	0	0	0	0	0	0	0	0	0	0
Whitey Ford, p	.250	2	8	1	2	0	0	0	0	2	2	0
Eli Grba, pr	.000	1	0	0	0	0	0	0	0	0	0	0
Elston Howard, c-4	.462	7	13	6	6	1	1	1	4	1	4	0
Tony Kubek, ss-7,of-2	.333	7	30	6	10	1	0	0	3	2	2	0
Dale Long, ph	.333	3	3	0	1	0	0	0	0	0	0	0
Hector Lopez, of-1	.429	3	7	0	3	0	0	0	0	0	0	0
Duke Maas, p	.000	1	0	0	0	0	0	0	0	0	0	0
Mickey Mantle, of	.400	7	25	8	10	1	0	3	11	8	9	0
Roger Maris, of	.267	7	30	6	8	1	0	2	2	2	4	0
Gil McDougald, 3b	.278	6	18	4	5	0	0	0	2	2	3	0
Bobby Richardson, 2b	.367	7	30	8	11	2	2	1	12	1	1	0
Bobby Shantz, p	.333	3	3	0	1	0	0	0	0	0	0	0
Bill Skowron, 1b	.375	7	32	7	12	0	0	2	6	0	6	0
Bill Stafford, p	.000	2	1	0	0	0	0	0	0	0	1	0
Ralph Terry, p	.000	2	2	0	0	0	0	0	0	0	1	0
Bob Turley, p	.250	2	4	0	1	0	0	0	0	1	1	0
TOTAL	.338		269	55	91	13	4	10	54	18	40	0

PITCHER	W	L	ERA	G	GS	CG	SV	SHO	IP	H	ER	BB	SO
Luis Arroyo	0	0	13.50	1	0	0	0	0	0.2	2	1	0	0
Jim Coates	0	0	5.68	3	0	0	0	0	6.1	6	4	1	3
Art Ditmar	0	2	21.60	2	2	0	0	0	1.2	6	4	1	0
Ryne Duren	0	0	2.25	2	0	0	0	0	4.0	2	1	5	4
Whitey Ford	2	0	0.00	2	2	2	0	2	18.0	11	0	2	8
Duke Maas	0	0	4.50	2	0	0	0	0	2.0	2	1	0	1
Bobby Shantz	0	0	4.26	2	0	0	1	0	6.1	4	3	1	1
Bill Stafford	0	0	1.50	2	0	0	0	0	6.0	5	1	1	2
Ralph Terry	0	2	5.40	3	0	0	0	0	6.2	7	4	1	5
Bob Turley	1	0	4.82	2	2	0	0	0	9.1	15	5	4	2
TOTAL	3	4	3.54	20	7	2	1	2	61.0	60	24	12	26

in the top of the ninth (on three singles and a ground out), Mazeroski's immortal shot over the wall in left gave Pittsburgh its first world championship in thirty-five years.

GAME 1 AT PIT OCT 5

NY	100	100	002	4	13 2
PIT	300	201	00X	6	8 0

Pitchers: DITMAR, Coates (1), Maas (5), Duren (7) vs LAW, Face (8)
Home Runs: Maris-NY, Mazeroski-PIT, Howard-NY
Attendance: 36,676

GAME 2 AT PIT OCT 6

NY	002	127	301	16	19 1
PIT	000	100	002	3	13 1

Pitchers: TURLEY, Shantz (9) vs FRIEND, Green (5), Labine (6), Witt (6), Gibbon (7), Cheney (9)
Home Runs: Mantle-NY (2)
Attendance: 37,308

GAME 3 AT NY OCT 8

PIT	000	000	000	0	4 0
NY	600	400	00X	10	16 1

Pitchers: MIZELL, Labine (1), Green (1), Witt (4), Cheney (6), Gibbon (8) vs FORD
Home Runs: Richardson-NY, Mantle-NY
Attendance: 70,001

GAME 4 AT NY OCT 9

PIT	000	030	000	3	7 0
NY	000	100	100	2	8 0

Pitchers: LAW, Face (7) vs TERRY, Shantz (7), Coates (8)
Home Runs: Skowron-NY
Attendance: 67,812

GAME 5 AT NY OCT 10

PIT	031	000	001	5	10 2
NY	011	000	000	2	5 2

Pitchers: HADDIX, Face (7) vs DITMAR, Arroyo (2), Stafford (3), Duren (8)
Home Runs: Maris-NY
Attendance: 62,753

GAME 6 AT PIT OCT 12

NY	015	002	220	12	17 1
PIT	000	000	000	0	7 1

Pitchers: FORD vs FRIEND, Cheney (3), Mizell (4), Green (6), Labine (6), Witt (9)
Attendance: 38,580

GAME 7 AT PIT OCT 13

NY	000	014	022	9	13 1
PIT	220	000	051	10	11 0

Pitchers: Turley, Stafford (2), Shantz (3), Coates (8), TERRY (8) vs Law, Face (6), Friend (9), HADDIX (9)
Home Runs: Nelson-PIT, Skowron-NY, Berra-NY, Smith-PIT, Mazeroski-PIT
Attendance: 36,683

Slugger Mickey Mantle sat out most of the Series with a thigh infection, but rookie manager Ralph Houk enjoyed an otherwise splendid finish to a splendid season as his Yankees mauled the Reds, 27 runs to 13. Yankee ace Whitey Ford, coming off one of his finest seasons (25–4), carried his mound mastery into the Series opener, holding Cincinnati to two singles and a walk as he hurled his third straight World Series shutout. New York recorded only six hits, but two of them were home runs by Elston Howard and Bill Skowron.

Gordy Coleman's two-run homer the next day in the top of the fourth inning broke Cincinnati's scoring drought and gave the Reds a 2–0 lead. Yogi Berra tied the score half an inning later with a two-run blast for New York, but that was all they would get. Red starter Joey Jay blanked the Yankees the rest of the way as his teammates put across four more runs to even the Series. Bob Purkey pitched for the Reds in Game Three and blanked New York on one hit through the first six innings, taking a 1–0 lead into the top of the seventh. A pair of Yankee singles sandwiched around a passed ball evened the score, but the Reds regained the lead with a run in the last of the seventh. But Yankee pinch hitter Johnny Blanchard homered to re-tie the game in the eighth and—while Yankee relief ace Luis Arroyo stopped the Reds through the final two innings—Roger Maris hit his sixty-second home run of the year to win the game and regain the Series lead for New York.

Cincinnati never again threatened. In Game Four, Whitey Ford held the Reds to four harmless singles until he was removed in the sixth because of an ankle injury. (In the third inning he passed Babe Ruth's World Series record of 29⅔ consecutive scoreless innings.) Reliever Jim Coates continued Ford's shutout as the Yankees scored seven runs for the decisive win. The fifth and final game also was no contest. Cincinnati did score five runs—three on Frank Robinson's third-inning home run and two on Wally Post's shot in the fifth. But the Yankees ran through eight Red pitchers, scoring 13 times. Seven of their 15 hits went for extra bases, including Johnny Blanchard's second home run of the Series, and a triple and homer by utility outfielder Hector Lopez.

New York Yankees (AL), 4;
Cincinnati Reds (NL), 1

NY (A)

PLAYER/POS	AVG	G	AB	R	H	2B	3B	HR	RB	BB	SO	SB
Luis Arroyo, p	.000	2	0	0	0	0	0	0	0	0	0	0
Yogi Berra, of	.273	4	11	2	3	0	0	1	3	5	1	0
Johnny Blanchard, of-2	.400	4	10	4	4	1	0	2	3	2	0	0
Clete Boyer, 3b	.267	5	15	0	4	2	0	0	3	4	0	0
Jim Coates, p	.000	1	1	0	0	0	0	0	0	0	0	0
Buddy Daley, p	.000	2	1	0	0	0	0	0	1	0	0	0
Whitey Ford, p	.000	2	5	1	0	0	0	0	0	1	0	0
Billy Gardner, ph	.000	1	1	0	0	0	0	0	0	0	0	0
Elston Howard, c	.250	5	20	5	5	3	0	1	1	2	3	0
Tony Kubek, ss	.227	5	22	3	5	0	0	0	1	1	4	0
Hector Lopez, of-3	.333	4	9	3	3	0	1	1	7	2	3	0
Mickey Mantle, of	.167	2	6	0	1	0	0	0	0	0	2	0
Roger Maris, of	.105	5	19	4	2	1	0	1	2	4	6	0
Jack Reed, of	.000	3	0	0	0	0	0	0	0	0	0	0
Bobby Richardson, 2b	.391	5	23	2	9	1	0	0	0	0	0	1
Bill Skowron, 1b	.353	5	17	3	6	0	0	1	5	3	4	0
Bill Stafford, p	.000	1	2	0	0	0	0	0	0	0	0	0
Ralph Terry, p	.000	2	3	0	0	0	0	0	0	0	1	0
TOTAL	.255		165	27	42	8	1	7	26	24	25	1

PITCHER	W	L	ERA	G	GS	CG	SV	SHO	IP	H	ER	BB	SO
Luis Arroyo	1	0	2.25	2	0	0	0	0	4.0	4	1	2	3
Jim Coates	0	0	0.00	1	0	0	1	0	4.0	1	0	1	2
Buddy Daley	1	0	0.00	2	0	0	0	0	7.0	5	0	0	3
Whitey Ford	2	0	0.00	2	2	1	0	1	14.0	6	0	1	7
Bill Stafford	0	0	2.70	1	1	0	0	0	6.2	7	2	2	5
Ralph Terry	0	1	4.82	2	2	0	0	0	9.1	12	5	2	7
TOTAL	4	1	1.60	10	5	1	1	1	45.0	35	8	8	27

CIN (N)

PLAYER/POS	AVG	G	AB	R	H	2B	3B	HR	RB	BB	SO	SB
Gus Bell, ph	.000	3	3	0	0	0	0	0	0	0	0	0
Don Blasingame, 2b	.143	3	7	1	1	0	0	0	0	0	3	0
Jim Brosnan, p	.000	3	0	0	0	0	0	0	0	0	0	0
Leo Cardenas, ph	.333	3	3	0	1	1	0	0	0	0	1	0
Elio Chacon, 2b-3	.250	4	12	3	0	0	0	0	0	1	2	0
Gordie Coleman, 1b	.250	5	20	2	5	0	0	1	2	0	1	0
Johnny Edwards, c	.364	3	11	1	4	2	0	0	2	0	0	0
Gene Freese, 3b	.063	5	16	0	1	1	0	0	0	3	4	0
Dick Gernert, ph	.000	4	4	0	0	0	0	0	0	0	1	0
Bill Henry, p	.000	2	0	0	0	0	0	0	0	0	0	0
Ken Hunt, p	.000	1	0	0	0	0	0	0	0	0	0	0
Joey Jay, p	.000	2	4	0	0	0	0	0	0	0	2	0
Darrell Johnson, c	.500	2	4	0	2	0	0	0	0	0	0	0
Ken Johnson, p	.000	1	0	0	0	0	0	0	0	0	0	0
Sherman Jones, p	.000	1	0	0	0	0	0	0	0	0	0	0
Eddie Kasko, ss	.318	5	22	1	7	0	0	0	1	0	2	0
Jerry Lynch, ph	.000	4	3	0	0	0	0	0	0	1	1	0
Jim Maloney, p	.000	1	0	0	0	0	0	0	0	0	0	0
Jim O'Toole, p	.000	2	3	0	0	0	0	0	0	0	1	0
Vada Pinson, of	.091	5	22	0	2	1	0	0	0	0	1	0
Wally Post, of	.333	5	18	3	6	1	0	1	2	0	1	0
Bob Purkey, p	.000	2	3	0	0	0	0	0	0	0	3	0
Frank Robinson, of	.200	5	15	3	3	2	0	1	4	3	4	0
Jerry Zimmerman, c	.000	2	0	0	0	0	0	0	0	0	0	0
TOTAL	.206		170	13	35	8	0	3	11	8	27	0

PITCHER	W	L	ERA	G	GS	CG	SV	SHO	IP	H	ER	BB	SO
Jim Brosnan	0	0	7.50	3	0	0	0	0	6.0	9	5	4	5
Bill Henry	0	0	19.29	2	0	0	0	0	2.1	4	5	2	3
Ken Hunt	0	0	0.00	1	0	0	0	0	1.0	0	0	1	1
Joey Jay	1	1	5.59	2	2	1	0	0	9.2	8	6	6	6
Ken Johnson	0	0	0.00	1	0	0	0	0	0.2	0	0	0	0
Sherman Jones	0	0	0.00	1	0	0	0	0	0.2	0	0	0	0
Jim Maloney	0	0	27.00	1	0	0	0	0	0.2	4	2	1	1
Jim O'Toole	0	2	3.00	2	2	0	0	0	12.0	11	4	7	4
Bob Purkey	0	1	1.64	2	1	1	0	0	11.0	6	2	3	5
TOTAL	1	4	4.91	15	5	2	0	0	44.0	42	24	24	25

GAME 1 AT NY OCT 4

CIN	000	000	000	0	2 0
NY	000	101	00X	2	6 0

Pitchers: O'TOOLE, Brosnan (8) vs FORD
Home Runs: Howard-NY, Skowron-NY
Attendance: 62,397

GAME 2 AT NY OCT 5

CIN	000	211	020	6	9 0
NY	000	200	000	2	4 3

Pitchers: JAY vs TERRY, Arroyo (8)
Home Runs: Coleman-CIN, Berra-NY
Attendance: 63,083

GAME 3 AT CIN OCT 7

NY	000	000	111	3	6 1
CIN	001	000	100	2	8 0

Pitchers: Stafford, Daley (7), ARROYO (8) vs PURKEY
Home Runs: Blanchard-NY, Maris-NY
Attendance: 32,589

GAME 4 AT CIN OCT 8

NY	000	112	300	7	11 0
CIN	000	000	000	0	5 1

Pitchers: FORD, Coates (6) vs O'TOOLE, Brosnan (6), Henry (9)
Attendance: 32,589

GAME 5 AT CIN OCT 9

NY	510	502	000	13	15 1
CIN	003	020	000	5	11 3

Pitchers: Terry, DALEY (3) vs JAY, Maloney (1), K.Johnson (2), Henry (3), Jones (4), Purkey (5), Brosnan (7), Hunt (9)
Home Runs: Blanchard-NY, Robinson-CIN, Lopez-NY, Post-CIN
Attendance: 32,589

After edging Los Angeles for the pennant in a three-game playoff to break a regular-season tie, San Francisco battled to the final out of Game Seven before falling to New York in the World Series. The teams alternated wins throughout the Series. In the opener Roger Maris doubled two runs home for a quick Yankee lead. Whitey Ford gave up a run in the second (ending his record streak for consecutive scoreless World Series innings pitched at 33⅔) and a tying run an inning later. But he blanked the Giants after that, and won the game on Clete Boyer's homer in the seventh.

Giant Jack Sanford blanked the Yankees on three hits in Game Two, but in Game Three Yankee Bill Stafford restored the Series edge to New York with a four-hit 3–2 win (a shutout until Giant Ed Bailey's ninth-inning home run). Both clubs hit safely nine times in Game Four. But one of the Giants' hits was Chuck Hiller's tie-breaking grand slam in the seventh—more than enough for a Giant win and another Series tie. In Game Five Sanford brought a three-hit 2–2 tie into the last of the eighth. But after he had notched his tenth strikeout, two singles and Tom Tresh's home run drove him out and gave Yankee pitcher Ralph Terry all the margin he needed to avenge his second-game loss to Sanford, and put the Yankees ahead in the Series for the third time.

When play resumed in San Francisco after several days of rain, Billy Pierce held New York to just three hits. One was Roger Maris's solo homer in the fifth, but Pierce's Giants unloaded on Whitey Ford for five runs, driving Ford out and keeping Giant hopes alive.

The finale pitted Terry against Sanford for the third time. Both pitched effectively, but Terry carried a 1–0 lead into the last of the ninth. Pinch hitter Matty Alou led off with a bunt single, but Terry fanned the next two batters. Then Willie Mays doubled to right, but Roger Maris's slick fielding stopped Alou at third. As Terry faced Willie McCovey (who had homered off him in Game Two), he pondered the home run he had given up to Bill Mazeroski two years earlier to lose the 1960 World Series to Pittsburgh. McCovey lined Terry's third pitch toward right—but right at second baseman Bobby Richardson, who grabbed it for the Yankees' twentieth world title. It would be fifteen years before they saw another.

New York Yankees (AL), 4;
San Francisco Giants (NL) 3

NY (A)

PLAYER/POS	AVG	G	AB	R	H	2B	3B	HR	RB	BB	SO	SB
Yogi Berra, c-1	.000	2	2	0	0	0	0	0	0	0	2	0
Johnny Blanchard, ph	.000	1	1	0	0	0	0	0	0	0	1	0
Clete Boyer, 3b	.318	7	22	2	7	1	0	1	4	1	3	0
Marshall Bridges, p	.000	2	0	0	0	0	0	0	0	0	0	0
Jim Coates, p	.000	2	0	0	0	0	0	0	0	0	0	0
Buddy Daley, p	.000	1	0	0	0	0	0	0	0	0	0	0
Whitey Ford, p	.000	3	7	0	0	0	0	0	0	0	1	0
Elston Howard, c	.143	6	21	1	3	1	0	0	1	1	4	0
Tony Kubek, ss	.276	7	29	2	8	1	0	0	1	1	3	0
Dale Long, 1b	.200	2	5	0	1	0	0	0	0	1	1	0
Hector Lopez, ph	.000	2	2	0	0	0	0	0	0	0	0	0
Mickey Mantle, of	.120	7	25	2	3	1	0	0	0	4	5	2
Roger Maris, of	.174	7	23	4	4	1	0	1	5	5	2	0
Bobby Richardson, 2b	.148	7	27	3	4	0	0	0	0	3	1	0
Bill Skowron, 1b	.222	6	18	1	4	0	1	0	1	1	5	0
Bill Stafford, p	.000	1	3	0	0	0	0	0	0	0	1	0
Ralph Terry, p	.125	3	8	0	1	0	0	0	0	0	6	0
Tom Tresh, of	.321	7	28	5	9	1	0	1	4	1	4	2
TOTAL	.199		221	20	44	6	1	3	17	21	39	4

PITCHER	W	L	ERA	G	GS	CG	SV	SHO	IP	H	ER	BB	SO
Marshall Bridges	0	0	4.91	2	0	0	0	0	3.2	4	2	2	3
Jim Coates	0	1	6.75	2	0	0	0	0	2.2	1	2	1	3
Buddy Daley	0	0	0.00	1	0	0	0	0	1.0	1	0	1	0
Whitey Ford	1	1	4.12	3	3	1	0	0	19.2	24	9	4	12
Bill Stafford	1	0	2.00	1	1	1	0	0	9.0	4	2	2	5
Ralph Terry	2	1	1.80	3	3	2	0	1	25.0	17	5	2	16
TOTAL	4	3	2.95	12	7	4	0	1	61.0	51	20	12	39

SF (N)

PLAYER/POS	AVG	G	AB	R	H	2B	3B	HR	RB	BB	SO	SB
Felipe Alou, of	.269	7	26	2	7	1	1	0	1	1	4	0
Matty Alou, of-4	.333	6	12	2	4	1	0	0	1	0	1	0
Ed Bailey, c-3	.071	6	14	1	1	0	0	1	2	0	3	0
Bobby Bolin, p	.000	2	0	0	0	0	0	0	0	0	0	0
Ernie Bowman, ss-1	.000	2	1	1	0	0	0	0	0	0	0	0
Orlando Cepeda, 1b	.158	5	19	1	3	1	0	0	2	0	4	0
Jim Davenport, 3b	.136	7	22	1	3	1	0	0	1	4	7	0
Tom Haller, c	.286	4	14	1	4	1	0	1	3	0	2	0
Chuck Hiller, 2b	.269	7	26	4	7	3	0	1	5	3	4	0
Harvey Kuenn, of	.083	3	12	1	1	0	0	0	0	1	1	0
Don Larsen, p	.000	3	0	0	0	0	0	0	0	0	0	0
Juan Marichal, p	.000	1	2	0	0	0	0	0	0	0	1	0
Willie Mays, of	.250	7	28	3	7	2	0	0	1	1	5	1
Willie McCovey, 1b-2,of-2	.200	4	15	2	3	0	1	1	1	1	3	0
Stu Miller, p	.000	2	0	0	0	0	0	0	0	0	0	0
Bob Nieman, ph	.000	1	0	0	0	0	0	0	0	1	0	0
Billy O'Dell, p	.333	3	3	0	1	0	0	0	0	0	0	0
John Orsino, c	.000	1	1	0	0	0	0	0	0	0	0	0
Jose Pagan, ss	.368	7	19	2	7	0	0	1	2	0	1	0
Billy Pierce, p	.000	2	5	0	0	0	0	0	0	0	1	0
Jack Sanford, p	.429	3	7	0	3	0	0	0	0	0	2	0
TOTAL	.226		226	21	51	10	2	5	19	12	39	1

PITCHER	W	L	ERA	G	GS	CG	SV	SHO	IP	H	ER	BB	SO
Bobby Bolin	0	0	6.75	2	0	0	0	0	2.2	4	2	2	2
Don Larsen	1	0	3.86	3	0	0	0	0	2.1	1	1	2	0
Juan Marichal	0	0	0.00	1	1	0	0	0	4.0	2	0	2	4
Stu Miller	0	0	0.00	2	0	0	0	0	1.1	1	0	2	0
Billy O'Dell	0	1	4.38	3	1	0	1	0	12.1	12	6	3	9
Billy Pierce	1	1	2.40	2	2	1	0	0	15.0	8	4	2	5
Jack Sanford	1	2	1.93	3	3	1	0	1	23.1	16	5	8	19
TOTAL	3	4	2.66	16	7	2	1	1	61.0	44	18	21	39

GAME 1 AT SF OCT 4

NY	200 000 121	6	11	0
SF	011 000 000	2	10	0

Pitchers: FORD vs O'DELL, Larsen (7), Miller (9)
Home Runs: Boyer-NY
Attendance: 43,852

GAME 2 AT SF OCT 5

NY	000 000 000	0	3	1
SF	100 000 10X	2	6	0

Pitchers: TERRY, Daley (8) vs SANFORD
Home Runs: McCovey-SF
Attendance: 43,910

GAME 3 AT NY OCT 7

SF	000 000 002	2	4	3
NY	000 000 30X	3	5	1

Pitchers: PIERCE, Larsen (7), Bolin (8) vs STAFFORD
Home Runs: Bailey-SF
Attendance: 71,434

GAME 4 AT NY OCT 8

SF	020 000 401	7	9	1
NY	000 002 001	3	9	1

Pitchers: Marichal, Bolin (5), LARSEN (6), O'Dell (7) vs Ford, COATES (7), Bridges (7)
Home Runs: Haller-SF, Hiller-SF
Attendance: 66,607

GAME 5 AT NY OCT 10

SF	001 010 001	3	8	2
NY	000 101 03X	5	6	0

Pitchers: SANFORD, Miller (8) vs TERRY
Home Runs: Pagan-SF, Tresh-NY
Attendance: 63,165

GAME 6 AT SF OCT 15

NY	000 010 010	2	3	2
SF	000 320 00X	5	10	1

Pitchers: FORD, Coates (5), Bridges (8) vs PIERCE
Home Runs: Maris-NY
Attendance: 43,948

GAME 7 AT SF OCT 16

NY	000 100 000	1	7	0
SF	000 000 000	0	4	1

Pitchers: TERRY vs SANFORD, O'Dell (8)
Attendance: 43,948

The Yankees won the American League pennant by 10½ games, but in the Series they were overwhelmed by Dodger pitching. The opener pitted two all-time greats against each other: Yankee Whitey Ford (24–7 that season) and Sandy Koufax (25–5). For an inning it was close. Ford fanned two of the first three batters to face him, and Koufax struck out the side. But in the top of the second the Dodgers' Frank Howard doubled with one out, and before Ford could record the second out, two singles and John Roseboro's home run had put four Dodger runs across. Koufax ran his consecutive Ks to five and had tied the Series single-game record of 14 by the time Tom Tresh tagged him for a two-run homer in the eighth. That was New York's only scoring, and Koufax ended the game with a new-record fifteenth strikeout an inning later.

Veteran Johnny Podres pitched shutout ball through 8⅓ innings of Game Two as his Dodgers built him a four-run lead (one of the runs a homer by ex-Yankee Bill Skowron). New York scored a run in the last of the ninth, but it was not enough to keep the Dodgers from returning to Los Angeles with a 2–0 Series advantage.

A first-inning walk, a wild pitch, and a single moved Dodger Jim Gilliam around the bases for the only scoring in Game Three as Yankee Jim Bouton hooked up in a duel with Don Drysdale. Bouton left after seven innings for Yankee relief ace Hal Reniff, who held Los Angeles hitless through the final frames. When Drysdale completed his shutout, only three singles had been hit against him, and he had struck out nine.

Ford and Koufax tangled again in the fourth game. Ford pitched much more impressively than he had in the opener, walking just one and yielding only two hits in seven innings. One of the Dodger hits was Frank Howard's solo homer in the fifth inning, but Mickey Mantle evened the score with a home run off Koufax in the seventh. But in the last of the seventh, Yankee first baseman Joe Pepitone lost sight of a throw from the third baseman for an error that sent batter Jim Gilliam all the way to third, and Willie Davis followed with a fly to center that scored Gilliam with the go-ahead run. No one else scored against Ford (or Reniff, who relieved him in the eighth), but no other Yankee scored against Koufax either, and the Dodgers, with just two hits, captured the game and the Series.

Los Angeles Dodgers (NL), 4; New York Yankees (AL), 0

LA (N)

PLAYER/POS	AVG	G	AB	R	H	2B	3B	HR	RB	BB	SO	SB
Tommy Davis, of	.400	4	15	0	6	0	2	0	2	0	2	1
Willie Davis, of	.167	4	12	2	2	2	0	0	3	0	6	0
Don Drysdale, p	.000	1	1	0	0	0	0	0	0	0	2	0
Ron Fairly, of	.000	4	1	0	0	0	0	0	0	3	0	0
Jim Gilliam, 3b	.154	4	13	3	2	0	0	0	0	3	1	0
Frank Howard, of	.300	3	10	2	3	1	0	1	1	0	2	0
Sandy Koufax, p	.000	2	6	0	0	0	0	0	0	0	2	0
Ron Perranoski, p	.000	1	0	0	0	0	0	0	0	0	0	0
Johnny Podres, p	.250	1	4	0	1	0	0	0	0	0	0	0
Johnny Roseboro, c	.143	4	14	1	2	0	0	1	3	0	4	0
Bill Skowron, 1b	.385	4	13	2	5	0	0	1	3	1	3	0
Dick Tracewski, 2b	.154	4	13	1	2	0	0	0	0	1	2	0
Maury Wills, ss	.133	4	15	1	2	0	0	0	0	1	3	1
TOTAL	.214		117	12	25	3	2	3	12	11	25	2

PITCHER	W	L	ERA	G	GS	CG	SV	SHO	IP	H	ER	BB	SO
Don Drysdale	1	0	0.00	1	1	1	0	1	9.0	3	0	1	9
Sandy Koufax	2	0	1.50	2	2	2	0	0	18.0	12	3	3	23
Ron Perranoski	0	0	0.00	1	0	0	1	0	0.2	1	0	0	1
Johnny Podres	1	0	1.08	1	1	0	0	0	8.1	6	1	1	4
TOTAL	4	0	1.00	5	4	3	1	1	36.0	22	4	5	37

NY (A)

PLAYER/POS	AVG	G	AB	R	H	2B	3B	HR	RB	BB	SO	SB
Yogi Berra, ph	.000	1	1	0	0	0	0	0	0	0	0	0
Johnny Blanchard, of-1	.000	1	3	0	0	0	0	0	0	0	0	0
Jim Bouton, p	.000	1	2	0	0	0	0	0	0	0	2	0
Clete Boyer, 3b	.077	4	13	0	1	0	0	0	0	1	6	0
Harry Bright, ph	.000	2	2	0	0	0	0	0	0	0	2	0
Al Downing, p	.000	1	1	0	0	0	0	0	0	0	1	0
Whitey Ford, p	.000	2	3	0	0	0	0	0	0	0	0	0
Steve Hamilton, p	.000	1	0	0	0	0	0	0	0	0	0	0
Elston Howard, c	.333	4	15	0	5	0	0	0	1	0	3	0
Tony Kubek, ss	.188	4	16	1	3	0	0	0	0	0	3	0
Phil Linz, ph	.333	3	3	0	1	0	0	0	0	0	1	0
Hector Lopez, of-2	.250	3	8	1	2	2	0	0	0	0	1	0
Mickey Mantle, of	.133	4	15	1	2	0	0	1	1	1	5	0
Roger Maris, of	.000	2	5	0	0	0	0	0	0	0	1	0
Joe Pepitone, 1b	.154	4	13	0	2	0	0	0	0	1	3	0
Hal Reniff, p	.000	3	0	0	0	0	0	0	0	0	0	0
Bobby Richardson, 2b	.214	4	14	0	3	1	0	0	0	1	3	0
Ralph Terry, p	.000	1	0	0	0	0	0	0	0	0	0	0
Tom Tresh, of	.200	4	15	1	3	0	0	1	2	1	6	0
Stan Williams, p	.000	1	0	0	0	0	0	0	0	0	0	0
TOTAL	.171		129	4	22	3	0	2	4	5	37	0

PITCHER	W	L	ERA	G	GS	CG	SV	SHO	IP	H	ER	BB	SO
Jim Bouton	0	1	1.29	1	1	0	0	0	7.0	4	1	5	4
Al Downing	0	1	5.40	1	1	0	0	0	5.0	7	3	1	6
Whitey Ford	0	2	4.50	2	2	0	0	0	12.0	10	6	3	8
Steve Hamilton	0	0	0.00	1	0	0	0	0	1.0	0	0	0	1
Hal Reniff	0	0	0.00	3	0	0	0	0	3.0	0	0	1	1
Ralph Terry	0	0	3.00	1	0	0	0	0	3.0	3	1	1	0
Stan Williams	0	0	0.00	1	0	0	0	0	3.0	1	0	0	5
TOTAL	0	4	2.91	10	4	0	0	0	34.0	25	11	11	25

GAME 1 AT NY OCT 2

LA	041 000 000	5 9 0
NY	000 000 020	2 6 0

Pitchers: KOUFAX vs FORD, Williams (6), Hamilton (9)
Home Runs: Roseboro-LA, Tresh-NY
Attendance: 69,000

GAME 2 AT NY OCT 3

LA	200 100 010	4 10 1
NY	000 000 001	1 7 0

Pitchers: PODRES, Perranoski (9) vs DOWNING, Terry (6), Reniff (9)
Home Runs: Skowron-LA
Attendance: 66,455

GAME 3 AT LA OCT 5

NY	000 000 000	0 3 0
LA	100 000 00X	1 4 1

Pitchers: BOUTON, Reniff (8) vs DRYSDALE
Attendance: 55,912

GAME 4 AT LA OCT 6

NY	000 000 100	1 6 1
LA	000 010 10X	2 2 1

Pitchers: FORD, Reniff (8) vs KOUFAX
Home Runs: F.Howard-LA, Mantle-NY
Attendance: 55,912

With late-season spurts the Cardinals edged the Reds and Phillies for their first pennant in eighteen years and the Yankees overtook the White Sox and Orioles for their fifteenth in eighteen years and their twenty-ninth over all. But when the Series was over, the long era of Yankee dominance had come to an end.

St. Louis won the opener, a 24-hit slugfest in which Curt Flood's RBI triple in the sixth proved the decisive blow. But New York came back to take the next two games. Rookie Mel Stottlemyre won Game Two, holding the Cards to three runs as his Yankees scored eight. (Loser Bob Gibson struck out nine Yankees, though, on his way to a new Series record of 31.) Game Three, by contrast, featured a pitchers' duel between Jim Bouton and Cardinal veteran Curt Simmons. Cardinal reliever Barney Schultz, who replaced Simmons for the last of the ninth with the score 1–1, lost the game on his first pitch when Mickey Mantle homered to deep right (his sixteenth World Series home run, which moved him ahead of Babe Ruth into the all-time Series lead).

Cardinal Ray Sadecki (the winner in Game One) left with one out in the first inning of Game Four after four Yankee batters hit safely, but relievers Roger Craig and Ron Taylor stopped New York on just two singles the rest of the way. The Cards were also held to six hits, but one was Ken Boyer's grand slam in the sixth, which erased a 3–0 Yankee lead and gave St. Louis runs enough to even the Series at two games apiece.

Gibson and Stottlemyre faced off a second time in Game Five. Gibson carried a 2–0 lead into the last of the ninth, when with two out Tom Tresh tagged him for a game-tying home run. In the top of the tenth, though, the Cards regained the lead on Tim McCarver's three-run homer and held on for the win as Gibson notched his thirteenth K of the game.

Bouton and Simmons tangled again in Game Six. Another 1–1 duel was shattered this time in the top of the sixth when Roger Maris and Mantle tagged Simmons for back-to-back home runs. New York put the game away in the eighth with five runs off Cardinal relievers—four of them on Joe Pepitone's grand slam.

With the series tied 3–3, Gibson and Stottlemyre were called upon to settle the title. Gibson pitched the whole game, striking out nine. Mantle touched him for a three-run homer in the sixth inning, and Clete Boyer and Phil Linz hit solo shots in the ninth. But as St. Louis had scored six times off Stottlemyre and his replacement Al Downing before the Yankees

scored their first runs, the game ended with the Cards victors and world champions. Yogi Berra, New York's rookie manager, was fired the next day. The following season the Yankees finished sixth.

St. Louis Cardinals (NL), 4;
New York Yankees (AL), 3

STL (N)

PLAYER/POS	AVG	G	AB	R	H	2B	3B	HR	RB	BB	SO	SB
Ken Boyer, 3b	.222	7	27	5	6	1	0	2	6	1	5	0
Lou Brock, of	.300	7	30	2	9	2	0	1	5	0	3	0
Gerry Buchek, 2b	1.000	4	1	1	1	0	0	0	0	0	0	0
Roger Craig, p	.000	2	1	0	0	0	0	0	0	0	0	0
Curt Flood, of	.200	7	30	5	6	0	1	0	3	3	1	0
Bob Gibson, p	.222	3	9	1	2	0	0	0	0	0	3	0
Dick Groat, ss	.192	7	26	3	5	1	1	0	1	4	3	0
Bob Humphreys, p	.000	1	0	0	0	0	0	0	0	0	0	0
Charlie James, ph	.000	3	3	0	0	0	0	0	0	0	1	0
Julian Javier, 2b	.000	1	0	1	0	0	0	0	0	0	0	0
Dal Maxvill, 2b	.200	7	20	0	4	1	0	0	1	1	4	0
Tim McCarver, c	.478	7	23	4	11	1	1	1	5	5	1	1
Gordie Richardson, p	.000	2	0	0	0	0	0	0	0	0	0	0
Ray Sadecki, p	.500	2	2	0	1	0	0	0	0	1	0	1
Barney Schultz, p	.000	4	1	0	0	0	0	0	0	0	0	0
Mike Shannon, of	.214	7	28	6	6	0	0	1	2	0	9	1
Curt Simmons, p	.500	2	4	0	2	0	0	0	0	1	0	0
Bob Skinner, ph	.667	4	3	0	2	1	0	0	1	1	0	0
Ron Taylor, p	.000	2	1	0	0	0	0	0	0	0	1	0
Carl Warwick, ph	.750	5	4	2	3	0	0	0	1	1	0	0
Bill White, 1b	.111	7	27	2	3	1	0	0	2	2	6	1
TOTAL	.254		240	32	61	8	3	5	29	18	39	3

PITCHER	W	L	ERA	G	GS	CG	SV	SHO	IP	H	ER	BB	SO
Roger Craig	1	0	0.00	2	0	0	0	0	5.0	2	0	3	9
Bob Gibson	2	1	3.00	3	3	2	0	0	27.0	23	9	8	31
Bob Humphreys	0	0	0.00	1	0	0	0	0	1.0	0	0	0	1
Gordie Richardson	0	0	40.50	2	0	0	0	0	0.2	3	3	2	0
Ray Sadecki	1	0	8.53	2	2	0	0	0	6.1	12	6	5	2
Barney Schultz	0	1	18.00	4	0	0	1	0	4.0	9	8	3	1
Curt Simmons	0	1	2.51	2	2	0	0	0	14.1	11	4	3	8
Ron Taylor	0	0	0.00	2	0	0	1	0	4.2	0	0	1	2
TOTAL	4	3	4.29	18	7	2	2		63.0	60	30	25	54

NY (A)

PLAYER/POS	AVG	G	AB	R	H	2B	3B	HR	RB	BB	SO	SB
Johnny Blanchard, ph	.250	4	4	0	1	1	0	0	0	0	1	0
Jim Bouton, p	.143	2	7	0	1	0	0	0	1	0	2	0
Clete Boyer, 3b	.208	7	24	2	5	1	0	1	3	1	5	1
Al Downing, p	.000	3	2	0	0	0	0	0	0	0	2	0
Whitey Ford, p	1.000	1	1	0	1	0	0	0	1	2	0	0
Pedro Gonzalez, 3b	.000	1	1	0	0	0	0	0	0	0	0	0
Steve Hamilton, p	.000	2	0	0	0	0	0	0	0	0	0	0
Mike Hegan, ph	.000	3	1	0	0	0	0	0	0	1	0	0
Elston Howard, c	.292	7	24	5	7	1	0	0	2	4	6	0
Phil Linz, ss	.226	7	31	5	7	1	0	2	2	2	5	0
Hector Lopez, of-1	.000	3	2	0	0	0	0	0	0	0	2	0
Mickey Mantle, of	.333	7	24	8	8	2	0	3	8	6	8	0
Roger Maris, of	.200	7	30	4	6	0	0	1	1	1	4	0
Pete Mikkelsen, p	.000	4	0	0	0	0	0	0	0	0	0	0
Joe Pepitone, 1b	.154	7	26	1	4	1	0	1	5	2	3	0
Hal Reniff, p	.000	1	0	0	0	0	0	0	0	0	0	0
Bobby Richardson, 2b	.406	7	32	3	13	2	0	0	3	0	2	1
Rollie Sheldon, p	.000	2	0	0	0	0	0	0	0	0	0	0
Mel Stottlemyre, p	.125	3	8	0	1	0	0	0	0	0	6	0
Ralph Terry, p	.000	1	0	0	0	0	0	0	0	0	0	0
Tom Tresh, of	.273	7	22	4	6	2	0	2	7	6	7	0
TOTAL	.251		239	33	60	11	0	10	33	25	54	2

PITCHER	W	L	ERA	G	GS	CG	SV	SHO	IP	H	ER	BB	SO
Jim Bouton	2	0	1.56	2	2	1	0	0	17.1	15	3	5	7
Al Downing	0	1	8.22	3	1	0	0	0	7.2	9	7	2	5
Whitey Ford	0	1	8.44	1	1	0	0	0	5.1	8	5	1	4
Steve Hamilton	0	0	4.50	2	0	0	1	0	4.0	3	2	1	2
Pete Mikkelsen	0	1	5.79	4	0	0	0	0	4.2	4	3	2	4
Hal Reniff	0	0	0.00	1	0	0	0	0	0.1	2	0	0	0
Rollie Sheldon	0	0	0.00	2	0	0	0	0	2.2	0	0	2	3
Mel Stottlemyre	1	1	3.15	3	3	1	0	0	20.0	18	7	6	12
Ralph Terry	0	0	0.00	1	0	0	0	0	2.0	2	0	0	3
TOTAL	3	4	3.77	19	7	2	1	0	62.0	61	26	18	39

GAME 1 AT STL OCT 7

NY	030 010 010	5 12 2
STL	110 004 03X	9 12 0

Pitchers: FORD, Downing (6), Sheldon (8), Mikkelsen (9) vs SADECKI, Schultz (7)
Home Runs: Tresh-NY, Shannon-STL
Attendance: 30,805

GAME 2 AT STL OCT 8

NY	000 101 204	8 12 0
STL	001 000 011	3 7 0

Pitchers: STOTTLEMYRE vs GIBSON, Schultz (9), Craig (9), Richardson (9)
Home Runs: Linz-NY
Attendance: 30,805

GAME 3 AT NY OCT 10

STL	000 010 000	1 6 0
NY	010 000 001	2 5 2

Pitchers: Simmons, SCHULTZ (9) vs BOUTON
Home Runs: Mantle-NY
Attendance: 67,101

GAME 4 AT NY OCT 11

STL	000 004 000	4 6 1
NY	300 000 000	3 6 1

Pitchers: Sadecki, CRAIG (1), Taylor (6) vs DOWNING, Mikkelsen (7), Terry (8)
Home Runs: K.Boyer-STL
Attendance: 66,312

GAME 5 AT NY OCT 12

STL	000 020 000 3	5 10 1
NY	000 000 002 0	2 6 2

Pitchers: GIBSON vs Stottlemyre, Reniff (8), MIKKELSEN (8)
Home Runs: Tresh-NY, McCarver-STL
Attendance: 65,633

GAME 6 AT STL OCT 14

NY	000 012 050	8 10 0
STL	100 000 011	3 10 1

Pitchers: BOUTON, Hamilton (9) vs SIMMONS, Taylor (7), Schultz (8), Richardson (8), Humphreys (9)
Home Runs: Maris-NY, Mantle-NY, Pepitone-NY
Attendance: 30,805

GAME 7 AT STL OCT 15

NY	000 003 002	5 9 2
STL	000 330 10X	7 10 1

Pitchers: STOTTLEMYRE, Downing (5), Sheldon (5), Hamilton (7), Mikkelsen (8) vs GIBSON
Home Runs: Brock-STL, Mantle-NY, K.Boyer-STL, C.Boyer-NY, Linz-NY
Attendance: 30,346

The Twins (bringing the World Series to Minnesota for the first time ever) featured heavy hitting, while Dodger hopes rested on great pitching and speed on the bases. For a while it looked as if batting power would triumph as the Twins took the first two games at home. They drove out Dodger starter Don Drysdale with seven runs in the first three innings of the opener—including home runs by Don Mincher and Zoilo Versalles—on the way to a convincing 8–2 win, and followed up with a 5–1 triumph the next day over Dodger ace Sandy Koufax (who had declined to pitch Game One on Yom Kippur, the holiest day of the Jewish year) and star reliever Ron Perranoski, who was tagged for three of the Twins' runs.

But when the Series moved to Los Angeles, Dodger pitching began to assert itself. Claude Osteen held Minnesota to five hits and no runs, while Los Angeles bunched seven of their ten hits in the middle three innings for four runs. Drysdale evened the Series in Game Four, avenging his first-game pounding with a second Dodger five-hitter. Twins Harmon Killebrew and Tony Oliva tagged him for a pair of solo homers, but that was Minnesota's only scoring—more than balanced by seven Dodger runs, including homers by Wes Parker and Lou Johnson. In Game Five the next day, Koufax avenged his earlier loss, carrying Los Angeles to its first Series lead with a shutout in which he allowed only four singles and a walk, while fanning ten Twins. Speedster Willie Davis stole three bases and Maury Wills stole another as the Dodgers parlayed fourteen hits into a 7–0 victory.

Back in Minnesota for Game Six, the Twins rallied, using the long ball to even the Series again with a 5–1 win. Bob Allison opened the scoring with a two-run shot off Dodger starter Claude Osteen in the fourth, and Minnesota pitcher Mudcat Grant insured his own win with a three-run blast two innings later.

In the finale, though, the visiting team won for the only time in the Series. Koufax again struck out ten men, stopping the Twins on three hits for his second shutout. Lou Johnson's second Series homer (a fourth-inning solo shot to left off Twin starter Jim Kaat that was barely fair) was all the Dodgers needed for their fifth world championship, but Ron Fairly followed Johnson with a double and Wes Parker singled home an insurance run that drove Kaat out and concluded the Series scoring.

Los Angeles Dodgers (NL), 4;
Minnesota Twins (AL), 3

LA (N)

PLAYER/POS	AVG	G	AB	R	H	2B	3B	HR	RB	BB	SO	SB
Jim Brewer, p	.000	1	0	0	0	0	0	0	0	0	0	0
Willie Crawford, ph	.500	2	2	0	1	0	0	0	0	0	1	0
Willie Davis, of	.231	7	26	3	6	0	0	0	0	0	2	3
Don Drysdale, p-2	.000	3	5	0	0	0	0	0	0	0	4	0
Ron Fairly, of	.379	7	29	7	11	3	0	2	6	0	1	0
Jim Gilliam, 3b	.214	7	28	2	6	1	0	0	2	1	0	0
Lou Johnson, of	.296	7	27	3	8	2	0	2	4	1	3	0
John Kennedy, 3b	.000	4	1	0	0	0	0	0	0	0	0	0
Sandy Koufax, p	.111	3	9	0	1	0	0	0	1	1	5	0
Jim Lefebvre, 2b	.400	3	10	2	4	0	0	0	0	0	0	0
Don LeJohn, ph	.000	1	1	0	0	0	0	0	0	0	1	0
Bob Miller, p	.000	2	0	0	0	0	0	0	0	0	0	0
Wally Moon, ph	.000	2	2	0	0	0	0	0	0	0	0	0
Claude Osteen, p	.333	2	3	0	1	0	0	0	0	0	0	0
Wes Parker, 1b	.304	7	23	3	7	0	1	1	2	3	3	2
Ron Perranoski, p	.000	2	0	0	0	0	0	0	0	0	0	0
Howie Reed, p	.000	2	0	0	0	0	0	0	0	0	0	0
Johnny Roseboro, c	.286	7	21	1	6	1	0	0	3	5	3	1
Dick Tracewski, 2b	.118	6	17	0	2	0	0	0	0	1	5	0
Maury Wills, ss	.367	7	30	3	11	3	0	0	3	1	3	3
TOTAL	.274		234	24	64	10	1	5	21	13	31	9

PITCHER	W	L	ERA	G	GS	CG	SV	SHO	IP	H	ER	BB	SO
Jim Brewer	0	0	4.50	1	0	0	0	0	2.0	3	1	0	1
Don Drysdale	1	1	3.86	2	2	1	0	0	11.2	12	5	3	15
Sandy Koufax	2	1	0.38	3	3	2	0	2	24.0	13	1	5	29
Bob Miller	0	0	0.00	2	0	0	0	0	1.1	0	0	0	0
Claude Osteen	1	1	0.64	2	2	1	0	1	14.0	9	1	5	4
Ron Perranoski	0	0	7.36	2	0	0	0	0	3.2	3	3	4	1
Howie Reed	0	0	8.10	2	0	0	0	0	3.1	2	3	2	4
TOTAL	4	3	2.10	14	7	4	0	3	60.0	42	14	19	54

MIN (A)

PLAYER/POS	AVG	G	AB	R	H	2B	3B	HR	RB	BB	SO	SB
Bob Allison, of	.125	5	16	3	2	1	0	1	2	2	9	1
Earl Battey, c	.120	7	25	1	3	0	1	0	2	0	5	0
Dave Boswell, p	.000	1	0	0	0	0	0	0	0	0	0	0
Mudcat Grant, p	.250	3	8	3	2	1	0	1	3	0	1	0
Jimmie Hall, of	.143	2	7	0	1	0	0	0	0	1	5	0
Jim Kaat, p	.167	3	6	0	1	0	0	0	2	0	5	0
Harmon Killebrew, 3b	.286	7	21	2	6	0	0	1	2	6	4	0
Johnny Klippstein, p	.000	2	0	0	0	0	0	0	0	0	0	0
Jim Merritt, p	.000	2	0	0	0	0	0	0	0	0	0	0
Don Mincher, 1b	.130	7	23	3	3	0	0	1	1	2	7	0
Joe Nossek, of-5	.200	6	20	0	4	0	0	0	0	0	1	0
Tony Oliva, of	.192	7	26	2	5	1	0	1	2	1	6	0
Camilo Pascual, p	.000	1	1	0	0	0	0	0	0	0	0	0
Jim Perry, p	.000	2	0	0	0	0	0	0	0	0	0	0
Bill Pleis, p	.000	1	0	0	0	0	0	0	0	0	0	0
Frank Quilici, 2b	.200	7	20	2	4	2	0	0	1	4	3	0
Rich Rollins, ph	.000	3	2	0	0	0	0	0	0	1	0	0
Sandy Valdespino, of-2	.273	5	11	1	3	1	0	0	0	0	1	0
Zoilo Versalles, ss	.286	7	28	3	8	1	1	1	4	2	7	1
Al Worthington, p	.000	2	0	0	0	0	0	0	0	0	0	0
Jerry Zimmerman, c	.000	2	1	0	0	0	0	0	0	0	0	0
TOTAL	.195		215	20	42	7	2	6	19	19	54	2

PITCHER	W	L	ERA	G	GS	CG	SV	SHO	IP	H	ER	BB	SO
Dave Boswell	0	0	3.38	1	0	0	0	0	2.2	3	1	2	3
Mudcat Grant	2	1	2.74	3	3	2	0	0	23.0	22	7	2	12
Jim Kaat	1	2	3.77	3	3	1	0	0	14.1	18	6	2	6
Johnny Klippstein	0	0	0.00	2	0	0	0	0	2.2	2	0	2	3
Jim Merritt	0	0	2.70	2	0	0	0	0	3.1	2	1	0	1
Camilo Pascual	0	1	5.40	1	1	0	0	0	5.0	8	3	1	0
Jim Perry	0	0	4.50	2	0	0	0	0	4.0	5	2	2	4
Bill Pleis	0	0	9.00	1	0	0	0	0	1.0	2	1	0	0
Al Worthington	0	0	0.00	2	0	0	0	0	4.0	2	0	2	2
TOTAL	3	4	3.15	17	7	3	0	0	60.0	64	21	13	31

GAME 1 AT MIN OCT 6

LA	010 000 001	2	10	1
MIN	016 001 00X	8	10	0

Pitchers: DRYSDALE, Reed (3), Brewer (5), Perranoski (7) vs GRANT
Home Runs: Fairly-LA, Mincher-MIN, Versalles-MIN
Attendance: 47,797

GAME 2 AT MIN OCT 7

LA	000 000 100	1	7	3
MIN	000 002 12X	5	9	0

Pitchers: KOUFAX, Perranoski (7), Miller (8) vs KAAT
Attendance: 48,700

GAME 3 AT LA OCT 9

MIN	000 000 000	0	5	0
LA	000 211 00X	4	10	1

Pitchers: PASCUAL, Merritt (6), Klippstein (8) vs OSTEEN
Attendance: 55,934

GAME 4 AT LA OCT 10

MIN	000 101 000	2	5	2
LA	110 103 01X	7	10	0

Pitchers: GRANT, Worthington (6), Pleis (8) vs DRYSDALE
Home Runs: Killebrew-MIN, Parker-LA, Oliva-MIN, Johnson-LA
Attendance: 55,920

GAME 5 AT LA OCT 11

MIN	000 000 000	0	4	1
LA	202 100 20X	7	14	0

Pitchers: KAAT, Boswell (3), Perry (6) vs KOUFAX
Attendance: 55,801

GAME 6 AT MIN OCT 13

LA	000 000 100	1	6	1
MIN	000 203 00X	5	6	1

Pitchers: OSTEEN, Reed (6), Miller (8) vs GRANT
Home Runs: Allison-MIN, Grant-MIN, Fairly-LA
Attendance: 49,578

GAME 7 AT MIN OCT 14

LA	000 200 000	2	7	0
MIN	000 000 000	0	3	1

Pitchers: KOUFAX vs KAAT, Worthington (4), Klippstein (6), Merritt (7), Perry (9)
Home Runs: Johnson-LA
Attendance: 50,596

The Orioles, with their first pennant since moving from St. Louis in 1954, won the franchise's first World Series ever, crushing NL repeater Los Angeles in four games. Back-to-back home runs by Frank and Brooks Robinson in the top of the first inning of the opener gave Baltimore a quick three-run lead, and the O's added a fourth run an inning later before the Dodgers attempted to come back with single runs in the second and third innings. But by then Oriole reliever Moe Drabowsky had come on to pitch, and he stopped the Dodgers on one hit the rest of the way, striking out eleven (including six in a row in the fourth and fifth innings). The Dodgers would not score again in the Series.

Sophomore Jim Palmer (a week shy of his twenty-first birthday) hurled a four-hit shutout at Los Angeles in Game Two, defeating the great—but critically sore-armed—Sandy Koufax, who, though only thirty years old himself, was pitching the final game of his career. Three errors by center fielder Willie Davis in the fifth (including a pair of flies lost in the sun) led to three unearned runs—the first scoring against Koufax. Frank Robinson's leadoff triple in the sixth and Boog Powell's single gave the Orioles an earned run before a double play ended the inning. Koufax was replaced after the inning by a succession of Dodger relievers as Baltimore went on to win 6–0.

Wally Bunker did the honors for the Orioles in Game Three, emerging the victor of a pitching duel with Dodger Claude Osteen on the strength of a fifth-inning home run by Paul Blair, a tremendous 430-foot shot to left. Osteen yielded only two other Orioles hits—both singles—in his seven innings, and Dodger reliever Phil Regan retired the side in the eighth. But one run was all Bunker needed for his shutout win.

Dave McNally, who had given up the Dodgers' only Series runs in Game One, mended his ways with a four-hit shutout in Game Four. He needed the shutout for the Oriole sweep, for Dodger Don Drysdale was also in top form. Drysdale, too, gave up only four hits. But one of them was Frank Robinson's second home run of the Series, a fourth-inning solo shot to left for the game's only scoring.

Baltimore Orioles (AL), 4;
Los Angeles Dodgers (NL) 0

BAL (A)

PLAYER/POS	AVG	G	AB	R	H	2B	3B	HR	RB	BB	SO	SB
Luis Aparicio, ss	.250	4	16	0	4	1	0	0	0	2	0	0
Paul Blair, of	.167	4	6	2	1	0	0	1	1	1	0	0
Curt Blefary, of	.077	4	13	0	1	0	0	0	0	2	3	0
Wally Bunker, p	.000	1	2	0	0	0	0	0	0	0	1	0
Moe Drabowsky, p	.000	1	2	0	0	0	0	0	0	1	1	0
Andy Etchebarren, c	.083	4	12	2	1	0	0	0	0	2	4	0
Davey Johnson, 2b	.286	4	14	1	4	1	0	0	1	0	1	0
Dave McNally, p	.000	2	3	0	0	0	0	0	0	0	1	0
Jim Palmer, p	.000	1	2	0	0	0	0	0	0	0	2	0
Boog Powell, 1b	.357	4	14	1	5	1	0	0	1	0	1	0
Brooks Robinson, 3b	.214	4	14	2	3	0	0	1	1	1	0	0
Frank Robinson, of	.286	4	14	4	4	0	1	2	3	2	3	0
Russ Snyder, of	.167	3	6	1	1	0	0	0	1	0	2	0
TOTAL	.200		120	13	24	3	1	4	10	11	17	0

PITCHER	W	L	ERA	G	GS	CG	SV	SHO	IP	H	ER	BB	SO
Wally Bunker	1	0	0.00	1	1	1	0	1	9.0	6	0	1	6
Moe Drabowsky	1	0	0.00	1	0	0	0	0	6.2	1	0	2	11
Dave McNally	1	0	1.59	2	2	1	0	1	11.1	6	2	7	5
Jim Palmer	1	0	0.00	1	1	1	0	1	9.0	4	0	3	6
TOTAL	4	0	0.50	5	4	3	0	3	36.0	17	2	13	28

LA (N)

PLAYER/POS	AVG	G	AB	R	H	2B	3B	HR	RB	BB	SO	SB
Jim Barbieri, ph	.000	1	1	0	0	0	0	0	0	0	1	0
Jim Brewer, p	.000	1	0	0	0	0	0	0	0	0	0	0
Wes Covington, ph	.000	1	1	0	0	0	0	0	0	0	1	0
Tommy Davis, of-3	.250	4	8	0	2	0	0	0	0	1	1	0
Willie Davis, of	.063	4	16	0	1	0	0	0	0	0	4	0
Don Drysdale, p	.000	2	2	0	0	0	0	0	0	0	1	0
Ron Fairly, of-2,1b-1	.143	3	7	0	1	0	0	0	0	2	4	0
Al Ferrara, ph	1.000	1	1	0	1	0	0	0	0	0	0	0
Jim Gilliam, 3b	.000	2	6	0	0	0	0	0	0	1	2	0
Lou Johnson, of	.267	4	15	1	4	1	0	0	0	1	1	0
John Kennedy, 3b	.200	2	5	0	1	0	0	0	0	0	0	0
Sandy Koufax, p	.000	1	2	0	0	0	0	0	0	0	0	0
Jim Lefebvre, 2b	.167	4	12	1	2	0	0	1	1	3	4	0
Bob Miller, p	.000	1	0	0	0	0	0	0	0	0	0	0
Joe Moeller, p	.000	1	0	0	0	0	0	0	0	0	0	0
Nate Oliver, pr	.000	1	0	0	0	0	0	0	0	0	0	0
Claude Osteen, p	.000	1	2	0	0	0	0	0	0	0	1	0
Wes Parker, 1b	.231	4	13	0	3	2	0	0	0	1	3	0
Ron Perranoski, p	.000	2	0	0	0	0	0	0	0	0	0	0
Phil Regan, p	.000	2	0	0	0	0	0	0	0	0	0	0
Johnny Roseboro, c	.071	4	14	0	1	0	0	0	0	0	0	0
Dick Stuart, ph	.000	2	2	0	0	0	0	0	0	0	1	0
Maury Wills, ss	.077	4	13	0	1	0	0	0	0	3	3	1
TOTAL	.142		120	2	17	3	0	1	2	13	28	1

PITCHER	W	L	ERA	G	GS	CG	SV	SHO	IP	H	ER	BB	SO
Jim Brewer	0	0	0.00	1	0	0	0	0	1.0	0	0	0	1
Don Drysdale	0	2	4.50	2	2	1	0	0	10.0	8	5	3	6
Sandy Koufax	0	1	1.50	1	1	0	0	0	6.0	6	1	2	2
Bob Miller	0	0	0.00	1	0	0	0	0	3.0	2	0	2	1
Joe Moeller	0	0	4.50	1	0	0	0	0	2.0	1	1	1	0
Claude Osteen	0	1	1.29	1	1	0	0	0	7.0	3	1	1	3
Ron Perranoski	0	0	5.40	2	0	0	0	0	3.1	4	2	1	2
Phil Regan	0	0	0.00	2	0	0	0	0	1.2	0	0	1	2
TOTAL	0	4	2.65	11	4	1	0	0	34.0	24	10	11	17

GAME 1 AT LA OCT 5

BAL	310 100 000	5	9	0
LA	011 000 000	2	3	0

Pitchers: McNally, DRABOWSKY (3) vs DRYSDALE, Moeller (3), Miller (5), Perranoski (8)
Home Runs: F.Robinson-BAL, B.Robinson-BAL, Lefebvre-LA
Attendance: 55,941

GAME 2 AT LA OCT 6

BAL	000 031 020	6	8	0
LA	000 000 000	0	4	6

Pitchers: PALMER vs KOUFAX, Perranoski (7), Regan (8), Brewer (9)
Attendance: 55,947

GAME 3 AT BAL OCT 8

LA	000 000 000	0	6	0
BAL	000 010 00X	1	3	0

Pitchers: OSTEEN, Regan (8) vs BUNKER
Home Runs: Blair-BAL
Attendance: 54,445

GAME 4 AT BAL OCT 9

LA	000 000 000	0	4	0
BAL	000 100 00X	1	4	0

Pitchers: DRYSDALE vs McNALLY
Home Runs: F.Robinson-BAL
Attendance: 54,458

The Cardinals cruised into the Series leading by 10½ games, whereas the Red Sox eked out their pennant over Minnesota and Detroit only by a dramatic win at season's end. The Sox continued to claw their way through six games of the Series before finally falling to superior pitching and hitting in the seventh game. Cardinal hurler Bob Gibson (who had missed a third of the season with a broken leg) edged Boston in the opener 2–1 with a six-hitter that included ten strikeouts. The only run against him came on a solo homer by opposing pitcher Jose Santiago in the third that tied the game. But Santiago was undone when Cardinal Lou Brock singled off him to open the seventh, then stole second, and moved around to score on a pair of ground outs.

Boston ace Jim Lonborg evened the Series the next day with a brilliant one-hit shutout. Sox Triple Crown winner Carl Yastrzemski accounted for four of Boston's five runs with homers in the fourth and seventh innings. Cardinal Nelson Briles outlasted a succession of Boston pitchers for a go-ahead 5–2 win in Game Three, and Gibson, with a five-hit shutout in Game Four, put St. Louis up three games to one.

But Boston's Lonborg kept Red Sox hopes alive with another pitching gem—a three-hitter in which the only extra-base hit was Roger Maris's harmless home run in the last of the ninth, after the Sox had already scored three runs (two of them unearned). Boston's bats came alive as the Series moved to Boston for Game Six, and the Sox evened the Series with an 8–4 win. The Cards used eight pitchers in a futile effort to hold off the Boston assault. Boston's score would have been greater had not all four Boston homers (including three in the fourth inning by Yastrzemski, Reggie Smith, and Rico Petrocelli—his second of the game) been solo shots.

With the Series tied at three-all, the Series' two-game winners, Gibson and Lonborg, faced off in the finale. It turned out to be no contest. Lonborg gave up ten hits and seven runs (including a homer by pitcher Gibson in the fifth and a three-run blast by Julian Javier an inning later) in six innings. Four Boston relievers held the Cards scoreless the rest of the game, but it was too late. Gibson's three-hitter included ten strikeouts and yielded only two Boston runs.

St. Louis Cardinals (NL), 4;
Boston Red Sox (AL) 3

STL (N)

PLAYER/POS	AVG	G	AB	R	H	2B	3B	HR	RB	BB	SO	SB
Eddie Bressoud, ss	.000	2	0	0	0	0	0	0	0	0	0	0
Nelson Briles, p	.000	2	3	0	0	0	0	0	0	0	0	0
Lou Brock, of	.414	7	29	8	12	2	1	1	3	2	3	7
Steve Carlton, p	.000	1	1	0	0	0	0	0	0	0	0	0
Orlando Cepeda, 1b	.103	7	29	1	3	2	0	0	1	0	4	0
Curt Flood, of	.179	7	28	2	5	1	0	0	3	3	3	0
Phil Gagliano, ph	.000	1	1	0	0	0	0	0	0	0	0	0
Bob Gibson, p	.091	3	11	1	1	0	0	1	1	1	2	0
Joe Hoerner, p	.000	2	0	0	0	0	0	0	0	0	0	0
Dick Hughes, p	.000	2	3	0	0	0	0	0	0	0	3	0
Larry Jaster, p	.000	1	0	0	0	0	0	0	0	0	0	0
Julian Javier, 2b	.360	7	25	2	9	3	0	1	4	0	6	0
Jack Lamabe, p	.000	3	0	0	0	0	0	0	0	0	0	0
Roger Maris, of	.385	7	26	3	10	1	0	1	7	3	1	0
Dal Maxvill, ss	.158	7	19	1	3	0	1	0	1	4	1	0
Tim McCarver, c	.125	7	24	3	3	1	0	0	2	2	2	0
Dave Ricketts, ph	.000	3	3	0	0	0	0	0	0	0	0	0
Mike Shannon, 3b	.208	7	24	3	5	1	0	1	2	1	4	0
Ed Spiezio, ph	.000	1	1	0	0	0	0	0	0	0	0	0
Bobby Tolan, ph	.000	3	2	1	0	0	0	0	0	1	1	0
Ray Washburn, p	.000	2	0	0	0	0	0	0	0	0	0	0
Ron Willis, p	.000	3	0	0	0	0	0	0	0	0	0	0
Hal Woodeshick, p	.000	1	0	0	0	0	0	0	0	0	0	0
TOTAL	.223		229	25	51	11	2	5	24	17	30	7

PITCHER	W	L	ERA	G	GS	CG	SV	SHO	IP	H	ER	BB	SO
Nelson Briles	1	0	1.64	2	1	1	0	0	11.0	7	2	1	4
Steve Carlton	0	1	0.00	1	1	0	0	0	6.0	3	0	2	5
Bob Gibson	3	0	1.00	3	3	3	0	1	27.0	14	3	5	26
Joe Hoerner	0	0	40.50	2	0	0	0	0	0.2	4	3	1	0
Dick Hughes	0	1	5.00	2	2	0	0	0	9.0	9	5	3	7
Larry Jaster	0	0	0.00	1	0	0	0	0	0.1	2	0	0	0
Jack Lamabe	0	1	6.75	3	0	0	0	0	2.2	5	2	0	4
Ray Washburn	0	0	0.00	2	0	0	0	0	2.1	1	0	1	2
Ron Willis	0	0	27.00	3	0	0	0	0	1.0	2	3	4	1
Hal Woodeshick	0	0	0.00	1	0	0	0	0	1.0	1	0	0	0
TOTAL	4	3	2.66	20	7	4	0	1	61.0	48	18	17	49

BOS (A)

PLAYER/POS	AVG	G	AB	R	H	2B	3B	HR	RB	BB	SO	SB
Jerry Adair, 2b-4	.125	5	16	0	2	0	0	0	1	0	3	1
Mike Andrews, 2b-3	.308	5	13	2	4	0	0	0	1	0	1	0
Gary Bell, p	.000	3	0	0	0	0	0	0	0	0	0	0
Ken Brett, p	.000	2	0	0	0	0	0	0	0	0	0	0
Joe Foy, 3b-3	.133	6	15	2	2	1	0	0	1	1	5	0
Russ Gibson, c	.000	2	2	0	0	0	0	0	0	0	0	0
Ken Harrelson, of	.077	4	13	0	1	0	0	0	0	1	3	0
Elston Howard, c	.111	7	18	0	2	0	0	0	1	1	2	0
Dalton Jones, 3b-4	.389	6	18	2	7	0	0	0	1	1	3	0
Jim Lonborg, p	.000	3	9	0	0	0	0	0	0	0	7	0
Dave Morehead, p	.000	2	0	0	0	0	0	0	0	0	0	0
Dan Osinski, p	.000	2	0	0	0	0	0	0	0	0	0	0
Rico Petrocelli, ss	.200	7	20	3	4	1	0	2	3	3	8	0
Mike Ryan, c	.000	1	2	0	0	0	0	0	0	0	1	0
Jose Santiago, p	.500	3	2	1	1	0	0	1	1	0	1	0
George Scott, 1b	.231	7	26	3	6	1	1	0	0	3	6	0
Norm Siebern, of-1	.333	3	3	0	1	0	0	0	0	1	0	0
Reggie Smith, of	.250	7	24	3	6	1	0	2	3	2	2	0
Lee Stange, p	.000	1	0	0	0	0	0	0	0	0	0	0
Jerry Stephenson, p	.000	1	0	0	0	0	0	0	0	0	0	0
Jose Tartabull, of-6	.154	7	13	1	2	0	0	0	0	1	2	0
George Thomas, of-1	.000	2	2	0	0	0	0	0	0	0	1	0
Gary Waslewski, p	.000	2	1	0	0	0	0	0	0	0	1	0
John Wyatt, p	.000	2	0	0	0	0	0	0	0	0	0	0
Carl Yastrzemski, of	.400	7	25	4	10	2	0	3	5	4	1	0
TOTAL	.216		222	21	48	6	1	8	19	17	49	1

PITCHER	W	L	ERA	G	GS	CG	SV	SHO	IP	H	ER	BB	SO
Gary Bell	0	1	5.06	3	1	0	1	0	5.1	8	3	1	1
Ken Brett	0	0	0.00	2	0	0	0	0	1.1	0	0	1	1
Jim Lonborg	2	1	2.63	3	3	2	0	1	24.0	14	7	2	11
Dave Morehead	0	0	0.00	2	0	0	0	0	3.1	0	0	4	3
Dan Osinski	0	0	6.75	2	0	0	0	0	1.1	2	1	0	0
Jose Santiago	0	2	5.59	3	2	0	0	0	9.2	16	6	3	6
Lee Stange	0	0	0.00	1	0	0	0	0	2.0	3	0	0	0
Jerry Stephenson	0	0	9.00	1	0	0	0	0	2.0	3	2	1	0
Gary Waslewski	0	0	2.16	2	1	0	0	0	8.1	4	2	2	7
John Wyatt	1	0	4.91	2	0	0	0	0	3.2	1	2	3	1
TOTAL	3	4	3.39	21	7	2	1	1	61.0	51	23	17	30

GAME 1 AT BOS OCT 4

STL	001	000	100	2	10 0
BOS	001	000	000	1	6 0

Pitchers: GIBSON vs SANTIAGO, Wyatt (8)
Home Runs: Santiago-BOS
Attendance: 34,796

GAME 2 AT BOS OCT 5

STL	000	000	000	0	1 1
BOS	000	101	30X	5	9 0

Pitchers: HUGHES, Willis (6), Hoerner (7), Lamabe (7) vs LONBORG
Home Runs: Yastrzemski (2)
Attendance: 35,188

GAME 3 AT STL OCT 7

BOS	000	001	100	2	7 1
STL	120	001	01X	5	10 0

Pitchers: BELL, Waslewski (3), Stange (6), Osinski (8) vs BRILES
Home Runs: Shannon-STL, Smith-BOS
Attendance: 54,575

GAME 4 AT STL OCT 8

BOS	000	000	000	0	5 0
STL	402	000	00X	6	9 0

Pitchers: SANTIAGO, Bell (1), Stephenson (3), Morehead (5), Brett (8) vs GIBSON
Attendance: 54,575

GAME 5 AT STL OCT 9

BOS	001	000	002	3	6 1
STL	000	000	001	1	3 2

Pitchers: LONBORG vs CARLTON, Washburn (7), Willis (9), Lamabe (9)
Home Runs: Maris-STL
Attendance: 54,575

GAME 6 AT BOS OCT 11

STL	002	000	200	4	8 0
BOS	010	300	40X	8	12 1

Pitchers: Hughes, Willis (4), Briles (5), LAMABE (7), Hoerner (7), Jaster (7), Washburn (7), Woodeshick (8) vs Waslewski, WYATT (6), Bell (8)
Home Runs: Petrocelli-BOS (2), Yastrzemski-BOS, Smith-BOS, Brock-STL
Attendance: 35,188

GAME 7 AT BOS OCT 12

STL	002	023	000	7	10 1
BOS	000	010	010	2	3 1

Pitchers: GIBSON vs LONBORG, Santiago (7), Morehead (9), Osinski (9), Brett (9)
Home Runs: Gibson-STL, Javier-STL
Attendance: 35,188

In this "year of the pitcher," Tiger Denny McLain's 31 wins were the most for a major leaguer in thirty-seven years. Cardinal Bob Gibson's 1.12 ERA was the majors' best since Dutch Leonard's 1.01 in 1914, and his 13 season shutouts tied for third best of all time. In the Series, though, it was Detroit's second-best pitcher—Mickey Lolich—who emerged as the hero.

McLain came off second-best against Gibson in the opener. He yielded only three hits in his five innings, but two Cardinal singles in the fourth combined with a pair of walks and a Tiger error for three runs. Gibson, meanwhile, was in the process of striking out a Series-record 17 batters on the way to a five-hit shutout. But Lolich brought Detroit back in Game Two. He struck out nine, and his third-inning home run (the only one of his major league career) for the second Tiger run provided all the scoring needed for a Detroit victory, although the Tigers kept putting runs across for an eventual 8–1 win.

Home runs accounted for most of the scoring in Game Three. Veteran Al Kaline's two-run shot in the third opened the scoring, but Cardinal Tim McCarver's three-run blast in the fifth put St. Louis ahead. Tiger Dick McAuliffe's solo shot later in the inning brought Detroit within one run of a tie, but the Cardinals put the game away on Orlando Cepeda's three-run homer in the seventh.

McLain faced Gibson again in Game Four, and again came off second-best. Cardinal Lou Brock led off the game with a home run, and before the end of the third inning McLain was gone. Gibson gave up a solo homer to Tiger Jim Northrup in the fourth, but that was the only Detroit run he allowed. Gibson homered himself and struck out ten in an easy 10–1 win.

Down three games to one, the Tigers were saved from elimination by Lolich's arm. Although three Cardinal hits in the top of the first (including Orlando Cepeda's second homer of the Series) gave St. Louis a quick three runs, Lolich held the Cards scoreless the rest of the game as his Tigers fought back with two runs in the fourth and three more in the seventh (with a rally started by Lolich's single). McLain finally came through in Game Six, evening the Series with an easy 13–1 victory, in which Jim Northrup's grand slam provided the big blow of a ten-run third inning.

Lolich and Gibson—both 2–0 in the Series—faced off in the finale. Gibson broke his own World Series strikeout record in the third inning (finishing with 8 for the game and 35 for the Series), and both pitchers hurled shutout ball through six

innings. But four two-out Tiger hits in the top of the seventh—including a misplayed fly ball in center field—put three runs on the board, and another run in the ninth made the score 4–0. In the last of the ninth, Mike Shannon's solo homer spoiled Lolich's shutout, but not his third Series win—or the Tigers' comeback world title.

Detroit Tigers (AL), 4;
St. Louis Cardinals (NL) 3

DET (A)

PLAYER/POS	AVG	G	AB	R	H	2B	3B	HR	RB	BB	SO	SB
Gates Brown, ph	.000	1	1	0	0	0	0	0	0	0	0	0
Norm Cash, 1b	.385	7	26	5	10	0	0	1	5	3	5	0
Wayne Comer, ph	1.000	1	1	0	1	0	0	0	0	0	0	0
Pat Dobson, p	.000	3	0	0	0	0	0	0	0	0	0	0
Bill Freehan, c	.083	7	24	0	2	1	0	0	2	4	8	0
John Hiller, p	.000	2	0	0	0	0	0	0	0	0	0	0
Willie Horton, of	.304	7	23	6	7	1	1	1	3	5	6	0
Al Kaline, of	.379	7	29	6	11	2	0	2	8	0	7	0
Fred Lasher, p	.000	1	0	0	0	0	0	0	0	0	0	0
Mickey Lolich, p	.250	3	12	2	3	0	0	1	2	1	5	0
Tom Matchick, ph	.000	3	3	0	0	0	0	0	0	0	1	0
Eddie Mathews, 3b-1	.333	2	3	0	1	0	0	0	0	1	1	0
Dick McAuliffe, 2b	.222	7	27	5	6	0	0	1	3	4	6	0
Denny McLain, p	.000	3	6	0	0	0	0	0	0	0	4	0
Don McMahon, p	.000	2	0	0	0	0	0	0	0	0	0	0
Jim Northrup, of	.250	7	28	4	7	0	1	2	8	1	5	0
Ray Oyler, ss	.000	4	0	0	0	0	0	0	0	0	0	0
Daryl Patterson, p	.000	2	0	0	0	0	0	0	0	0	0	0
Jim Price, ph	.000	2	2	0	0	0	0	0	0	0	1	0
Joe Sparma, p	.000	1	0	0	0	0	0	0	0	0	0	0
Mickey Stanley, ss-7,of-4	.214	7	28	4	6	0	1	0	0	2	4	0
Dick Tracewski, 3b-1	.000	2	0	1	0	0	0	0	0	0	0	0
Don Wert, 3b	.118	6	17	1	2	0	0	0	2	6	5	0
Earl Wilson, p	.000	1	1	0	0	0	0	0	0	0	1	0
TOTAL	.242		231	34	56	4	3	8	33	27	59	0

PITCHER	W	L	ERA	G	GS	CG	SV	SHO	IP	H	ER	BB	SO
Pat Dobson	0	0	3.86	3	0	0	0	0	4.2	5	2	1	0
John Hiller	0	0	13.50	2	0	0	0	0	2.0	6	3	3	1
Fred Lasher	0	0	0	1	0	0	0	0	2.0	1	0	0	1
Mickey Lolich	3	0	1.67	3	3	3	0	0	27.0	20	5	6	21
Denny McLain	1	2	3.24	3	3	1	0	0	16.2	18	6	4	13
Don McMahon	0	0	13.50	2	0	0	0	0	2.0	4	3	0	1
Daryl Patterson	0	0	0.00	2	0	0	0	0	3.0	1	0	4	0
Joe Sparma	0	0	54.00	1	0	0	0	0	0.1	2	2	0	0
Earl Wilson	0	1	6.23	1	1	0	0	0	4.1	4	3	6	3
TOTAL	4	3	3.48	18	7	4	0		62.0	61	24	21	40

STL (N)

PLAYER/POS	AVG	G	AB	R	H	2B	3B	HR	RB	BB	SO	SB
Nelson Briles, p	.000	2	4	0	0	0	0	0	0	0	4	0
Lou Brock, of	.464	7	28	6	13	3	1	2	5	3	4	7
Steve Carlton, p	.000	2	0	0	0	0	0	0	0	0	0	0
Orlando Cepeda, 1b	.250	7	28	2	7	0	0	2	6	2	3	0
Ron Davis, of	.000	2	7	0	0	0	0	0	0	0	2	0
Johnny Edwards, ph	.000	1	1	0	0	0	0	0	0	0	1	0
Curt Flood, of	.286	7	28	4	8	1	0	0	2	2	2	3
Phil Gagliano, ph	.000	3	3	0	0	0	0	0	0	0	0	0
Bob Gibson, p	.125	3	8	2	1	0	0	1	2	1	2	0
Wayne Granger, p	.000	1	0	0	0	0	0	0	0	0	0	0
Joe Hoerner, p	.500	3	2	0	1	0	0	0	0	0	1	0
Dick Hughes, p	.000	1	0	0	0	0	0	0	0	0	0	0
Larry Jaster, p	.000	1	0	0	0	0	0	0	0	0	0	0
Julian Javier, 2b	.333	7	27	1	9	1	0	0	3	3	4	1
Roger Maris, of-5	.158	6	19	5	3	1	0	0	1	3	3	0
Dal Maxvill, ss	.000	7	22	1	0	0	0	0	0	3	5	0
Tim McCarver, c	.333	7	27	3	9	0	2	1	4	3	2	0
Mel Nelson, p	.000	1	0	0	0	0	0	0	0	0	0	0
Dave Ricketts, ph	1.000	1	1	0	1	0	0	0	0	0	0	0
Dick Schofield, ss-1	.000	2	0	0	0	0	0	0	0	0	0	0
Mike Shannon, 3b	.276	7	29	3	8	1	0	1	4	1	5	0
Ed Spiezio, ph	1.000	1	1	0	1	0	0	0	0	0	0	0
Bobby Tolan, ph	.000	1	1	0	0	0	0	0	0	0	0	0
Ray Washburn, p	.000	2	3	0	0	0	0	0	0	0	0	0
Ron Willis, p	.000	3	0	0	0	0	0	0	0	0	0	0
TOTAL	.255		239	27	61	7	3	7	27	21	40	11

PITCHER	W	L	ERA	G	GS	CG	SV	SHO	IP	H	ER	BB	SO
Nelson Briles	0	1	5.56	2	2	0	0	0	11.1	13	7	4	7
Steve Carlton	0	0	6.75	2	0	0	0	0	4.0	7	3	1	3
Bob Gibson	2	1	1.67	3	3	3	0	1	27.0	18	5	4	35
Wayne Granger	0	0	0.00	1	0	0	0	0	2.0	0	0	1	1
Joe Hoerner	0	1	3.86	3	0	0	1	0	4.2	5	2	5	3
Dick Hughes	0	0	0.00	1	0	0	0	0	0.1	0	0	0	0
Larry Jaster	0	0	∞	1	0	0	0	0	0.0	2	3	1	0
Mel Nelson	0	0	0.00	1	0	0	0	0	1.0	0	0	1	0
Ray Washburn	1	1	9.82	2	2	0	0	0	7.1	7	8	7	6
Ron Willis	0	0	8.31	3	0	0	0	0	4.1	4	4	4	3
TOTAL	3	4	4.65	19	7	3	1	1	62.0	56	32	27	59

GAME 1 AT STL OCT 2

DET	000 000 000	0 5 3
STL	000 300 10X	4 6 0

Pitchers: McLAIN, Dobson (6), McMahon (8) vs GIBSON
Home Runs: Brock-STL
Attendance: 54,692

GAME 2 AT STL OCT 3

DET	011 003 102	8 13 1
STL	000 001 000	1 6 1

Pitchers: LOLICH vs BRILES, Carlton (6), Willis (7), Hoerner (9)
Home Runs: Horton-DET, Lolich-DET, Cash-DET
Attendance: 54,692

GAME 3 AT DET OCT 5

STL	000 040 300	7 13 0
DET	002 010 000	3 4 0

Pitchers: WASHBURN, Hoerner (6) vs WILSON, Dobson (5), McMahon (6), Patterson (7), Hiller (8)
Home Runs: Kaline-DET, McCarver-STL, McAuliffe-DET, Cepeda-STL
Attendance: 53,634

GAME 4 AT DET OCT 6

STL	202 200 040	10 13 0
DET	000 100 000	1 5 4

Pitchers: GIBSON vs McLAIN, Sparma (3), Patterson (4), Lasher (6), Hiller (8), Dobson (8)
Home Runs: Brock-STL, Gibson-STL, Northrup-DET
Attendance: 53,634

GAME 5 AT DET OCT 7

STL	300 000 000	3 9 0
DET	000 200 30X	5 9 1

Pitchers: Briles, HOERNER (7), Willis (7) vs LOLICH
Home Runs: Cepeda-STL
Attendance: 53,634

GAME 6 AT STL OCT 9

DET	0 2 10 010 000	13 12 1
STL	0 0 0 000 001	1 9 1

Pitchers: McLAIN vs WASHBURN, Jaster (3), Willis (3), Hughes (3), Carlton (4), Granger (7), Nelson (9)
Home Runs: Northrup-DET, Kaline-DET
Attendance: 54,692

GAME 7 AT STL OCT 10

DET	000 000 301	4 8 1
STL	000 000 001	1 5 0

Pitchers: LOLICH vs GIBSON
Home Runs: Shannon-STL
Attendance: 54,692

Atlanta's Hank Aaron homered in each game and drove in a series-high seven runs. But the "Miracle Mets" as a team outhomered the Braves six to five, outhit them by seventy-two percentage points, and scored nearly twice as many runs.

Twice in the first game the Braves came from behind to lead by a run, but in the top of the eighth, five New York hits and poor Atlanta fielding buried starter Phil Niekro under five runs. In Game Two, home runs by Tommie Agee and Ken Boswell helped New York take an early 8–0 lead that even Aaron's three-run homer in the fifth couldn't damage.

In the third game the lead changed hands three times on home runs. Aaron began the barrage with a two-run shot in the first inning. Agee's homer in the third followed by Boswell's for two runs in the fourth put the Mets ahead—until Orlando Cepeda's two-run homer in the fifth gave Atlanta another lead. But in the bottom of the fifth, Met rookie Wayne Garrett's two-run blast reversed the lead one last time and, after four final shutout innings by twenty-two-year-old reliever Nolan Ryan, the Mets had swept to their first pennant.

New York Mets (East), 3; Atlanta Braves (West) 0

NY (E)

PLAYER/POS	AVG	G	AB	R	H	2B	3B	HR	RB	BB	SO	SB
Tommie Agee, of	.357	3	14	4	5	1	0	2	4	2	5	2
Ken Boswell, 2b	.333	3	12	4	4	0	0	2	5	1	2	0
Wayne Garrett, 3b	.385	3	13	3	5	2	0	1	3	2	2	1
Rod Gaspar, of	.000	3	0	0	0	0	0	0	0	0	0	0
Gary Gentry, p	.000	1	0	0	0	0	0	0	0	0	0	0
Jerry Grote, c	.167	3	12	3	2	1	0	0	1	1	4	0
Bud Harrelson, ss	.182	3	11	2	2	1	1	0	3	1	2	0
Cleon Jones, of	.429	3	14	4	6	2	0	1	4	1	2	2
Jerry Koosman, p	.000	1	2	1	0	0	0	0	0	1	2	0
Ed Kranepool, 1b	.250	3	12	2	3	1	0	0	1	1	2	0
J. C. Martin, ph	.500	2	2	0	1	0	0	0	2	0	0	0
Tug McGraw, p	.000	1	0	0	0	0	0	0	0	0	0	0
Nolan Ryan, p	.500	1	4	1	2	0	0	0	0	0	1	0
Tom Seaver, p	.000	1	3	0	0	0	0	0	0	0	2	0
Art Shamsky, of	.538	3	13	3	7	0	0	0	1	0	3	0
Ron Taylor, p	.000	2	0	0	0	0	0	0	0	0	0	0
Al Weis, 2b	.000	3	1	0	0	0	0	0	0	0	0	0
TOTAL	.327		113	27	37	8	1	6	24	10	25	5

PITCHER	W	L	ERA	G	GS	CG	SV	SHO	IP	H	ER	BB	SO
Gary Gentry	0	0	9.00	1	1	0	0	0	2.0	5	2	1	1
Jerry Koosman	0	0	11.57	1	1	0	0	0	4.2	7	6	4	5
Tug McGraw	0	0	0.00	1	0	0	1	0	3.0	1	0	1	1
Nolan Ryan	1	0	2.57	1	0	0	0	0	7.0	3	2	2	7
Tom Seaver	1	0	6.43	1	1	0	0	0	7.0	8	5	3	2
Ron Taylor	1	0	0.00	2	0	0	1	0	3.1	3	0	0	4
TOTAL	3	0	5.00	7	3	0	2	0	27.0	27	15	11	20

ATL (W)

PLAYER/POS	AVG	G	AB	R	H	2B	3B	HR	RB	BB	SO	SB
Hank Aaron, of	.357	3	14	3	5	2	0	3	7	0	1	0
Tommie Aaron, ph	.000	1	1	0	0	0	0	0	0	0	0	0
Felipe Alou, ph	.000	1	1	0	0	0	0	0	0	0	0	0
Bob Aspromonte, ph	.000	3	3	0	0	0	0	0	0	0	0	0
Clete Boyer, 3b	.111	3	9	0	1	0	0	0	3	2	3	0
Jim Britton, p	.000	1	0	0	0	0	0	0	0	0	0	0
Rico Carty, of	.300	3	10	4	3	2	0	0	0	3	1	0
Orlando Cepeda, 1b	.455	3	11	2	5	2	0	1	3	1	2	1
Bob Didier, c	.000	3	11	0	0	0	0	0	0	0	2	0
Paul Doyle, p	.000	1	0	0	0	0	0	0	0	0	0	0
Gil Garrido, ss	.200	3	10	0	2	0	0	0	0	1	1	0
Tony Gonzalez, of	.357	3	14	4	5	1	0	1	2	1	4	0
Sonny Jackson, ss	.000	1	0	0	0	0	0	0	0	0	0	0
Pat Jarvis, p	.000	1	2	0	0	0	0	0	0	0	2	0
Mike Lum, of-1	1.000	2	2	0	2	1	0	0	0	0	0	0
Felix Millan, 2b	.333	3	12	2	4	1	0	0	0	3	0	0
Gary Neibauer, p	.000	1	0	0	0	0	0	0	0	0	0	0
Phil Niekro, p	.000	1	3	0	0	0	0	0	0	0	1	0
Milt Pappas, p	.000	1	1	0	0	0	0	0	0	0	1	0
Ron Reed, p	.000	1	0	0	0	0	0	0	0	0	0	0
George Stone, p	.000	1	1	0	0	0	0	0	0	0	1	0
Bob Tillman, c	.000	1	0	0	0	0	0	0	0	0	0	0
Cecil Upshaw, p	.000	3	1	0	0	0	0	0	0	0	1	0
TOTAL	.255		106	15	27	9	0	5	15	11	20	1

PITCHER	W	L	ERA	G	GS	CG	SV	SHO	IP	H	ER	BB	SO
Jim Britton	0	0	0.00	1	0	0	0	0	0.1	0	0	1	0
Paul Doyle	0	0	0.00	1	0	0	0	0	1.0	2	0	1	3
Pat Jarvis	0	1	12.46	1	1	0	0	0	4.1	10	6	0	6
Gary Neibauer	0	0	0.00	1	0	0	0	0	1.0	0	0	0	1
Phil Niekro	0	1	4.50	1	1	0	0	0	8.0	9	4	4	4
Milt Pappas	0	0	11.57	1	0	0	0	0	2.1	4	3	0	4
Ron Reed	0	1	21.60	1	1	0	0	0	1.2	5	4	3	3
George Stone	0	0	9.00	1	0	0	0	0	1.0	2	1	0	0
Cecil Upshaw	0	0	2.84	3	0	0	0	0	6.1	5	2	1	4
TOTAL	0	3	6.92	11	3	0	0	0	26.0	37	20	10	25

GAME 1 AT ATL OCT 4

NY	020 200 050	9 10 1
ATL	012 010 100	5 10 2

Pitchers: SEAVER, Taylor (8) vs NIEKRO, Upshaw (9)
Home Runs: Gonzalez-ATL, H.Aaron-ATL
Attendance: 50,122

GAME 2 AT ATL OCT 5

NY	132 210 200	11 13 1
ATL	000 150 000	6 9 3

Pitchers: Koosman, TAYLOR (5), McGraw (7) vs REED, Doyle (2), Pappas (3), Britton (6), Upshaw (6), Neibauer (9)
Home Runs: Agee-NY, Boswell-NY, H.Aaron-ATL, Jones-NY
Attendance: 50,270

GAME 3 AT NY OCT 6

ATL	200 020 000	4 8 1
NY	001 231 00X	7 14 0

Pitchers: JARVIS, Stone (5), Upshaw (6) vs Gentry, RYAN (3)
Home Runs: H.Aaron-ATL, Agee-NY, Boswell-NY, Cepeda-ATL, Garrett-NY
Attendance: 53,195

Minnesota led the league in batting, Baltimore in pitching. In the LCS, pitching prevailed as the Twins were held to a series batting average 113 points below their season mark.

Still, Minnesota nearly won the first game with three runs on only four hits. But the Orioles tied the score on Boog Powell's homer in the bottom of the ninth and won the game three innings later on Paul Blair's suicide squeeze bunt with two away. In Game Two, Minnesota's Dave Boswell scattered seven Baltimore hits over 10⅔ scoreless innings before giving way to Ron Perranoski in the eleventh. But Oriole pitcher Dave McNally was more than a match for Boswell. He gave up only three Twin hits—none in the final 7⅔ innings of the 11 he pitched—and took the win when Baltimore pinch hitter Curt Motton lined a single off Perranoski to score Powell from second with the game's only run.

In the third game, the Twins fell apart as the Orioles battered seven Minnesota pitchers for eighteen hits. Baltimore's Jim Palmer gave up more than a hit an inning himself, but coasted to the pennant 11–2.

Baltimore Orioles (East), 3;
Minnesota Twins (West) 0

BAL (E)

PLAYER/POS	AVG	G	AB	R	H	2B	3B	HR	RB	BB	SO	SB
Mark Belanger, ss	.267	3	15	4	4	0	1	1	1	0	0	0
Paul Blair, of	.400	3	15	1	6	2	0	1	6	2	2	0
Don Buford, of	.286	3	14	3	4	1	0	0	1	3	0	0
Mike Cuellar, p	.000	1	2	0	0	0	0	0	0	0	1	0
Andy Etchebarren, c	.000	2	4	0	0	0	0	0	0	0	0	0
Dick Hall, p	.000	1	0	0	0	0	0	0	0	0	0	0
Elrod Hendricks, c	.250	3	8	2	2	2	0	0	3	1	2	0
Davey Johnson, 2b	.231	3	13	2	3	0	0	0	0	2	1	0
Marcelino Lopez, p	.000	1	0	0	0	0	0	0	0	0	0	0
Dave May, ph	.000	1	1	0	0	0	0	0	0	0	0	0
Dave McNally, p	.000	1	4	0	0	0	0	0	0	0	2	0
Curt Motton, ph	.500	2	2	0	1	0	0	0	1	0	0	0
Jim Palmer, p	.000	1	5	0	0	0	0	0	0	0	3	0
Boog Powell, 1b	.385	3	13	2	5	0	0	1	2	2	0	0
Merv Rettenmund, ph	.000	1	0	0	0	0	0	0	0	0	0	0
Pete Richert, p	.000	1	0	0	0	0	0	0	0	0	0	0
Brooks Robinson, 3b	.500	3	14	1	7	1	0	0	0	0	0	0
Frank Robinson, of	.333	3	12	1	4	2	0	1	2	3	3	0
Chico Salmon, ph	.000	1	1	0	0	0	0	0	0	0	0	0
Eddie Watt, p	.000	1	0	0	0	0	0	0	0	0	0	0
TOTAL	.293		123	16	36	8	1	4	15	13	14	0

PITCHER	W	L	ERA	G	GS	CG	SV	SHO	IP	H	ER	BB	SO
Mike Cuellar	0	0	2.25	1	1	0	0	0	8.0	3	2	1	7
Dick Hall	1	0	0.00	1	0	0	0	0	0.2	0	0	0	1
Marcelino Lopez	0	0	0.00	1	0	0	0	0	0.1	1	0	2	0
Dave McNally	1	0	0.00	1	1	0	0	1	11.0	3	0	5	11
Jim Palmer	1	0	2.00	1	1	1	0	0	9.0	10	2	2	4
Pete Richert	0	0	0.00	1	0	0	0	0	1.0	0	0	2	2
Eddie Watt	0	0	0.00	1	0	0	0	0	2.0	0	0	0	2
TOTAL	3	0	1.13	7	3	2	0	1	32.0	17	4	12	27

MIN (W)

PLAYER/POS	AVG	G	AB	R	H	2B	3B	HR	RB	BB	SO	SB
Bob Allison, of	.000	2	8	0	0	0	0	0	0	1	0	0
Dave Boswell, p	.000	1	4	0	0	0	0	0	0	0	4	0
Leo Cardenas, ss	.154	3	13	0	2	0	1	0	0	0	7	0
Rod Carew, 2b	.071	3	14	0	1	0	0	0	0	1	4	0
Dean Chance, p	.000	1	0	0	0	0	0	0	0	0	0	0
Joe Grzenda, p	.000	1	0	0	0	0	0	0	0	0	0	0
Tom Hall, p	.000	1	0	0	0	0	0	0	0	0	0	0
Harmon Killebrew, 3b	.125	3	8	2	1	1	0	0	0	6	2	0
Chuck Manuel, ph	.000	1	0	0	0	0	0	0	0	1	0	0
Bob Miller, p	.000	1	0	0	0	0	0	0	0	0	0	0
George Mitterwald, c	.143	2	7	0	1	0	0	0	0	0	3	0
Graig Nettles, ph	1.000	1	1	0	1	0	0	0	0	0	0	0
Tony Oliva, of	.385	3	13	3	5	2	0	1	2	1	3	1
Ron Perranoski, p	.000	3	1	0	0	0	0	0	0	0	1	0
Jim Perry, p	.000	1	3	0	0	0	0	0	0	0	0	0
Rich Reese, 1b	.167	3	12	0	2	0	0	0	2	1	1	0
Rich Renick, ph	.000	1	1	0	0	0	0	0	0	0	0	0
John Roseboro, c	.200	2	5	0	1	0	0	0	0	0	0	0
Cesar Tovar, of	.077	3	13	0	1	0	0	0	0	1	2	1
Ted Uhlaender, of	.167	2	6	0	1	0	0	0	0	0	0	0
Dick Woodson, p	1.000	1	1	0	1	0	0	0	0	0	0	0
Al Worthington, p	.000	1	0	0	0	0	0	0	0	0	0	0
TOTAL	.155		110	5	17	3	1	1	5	12	27	2

PITCHER	W	L	ERA	G	GS	CG	SV	SHO	IP	H	ER	BB	SO
Dave Boswell	0	1	0.84	1	1	0	0	0	10.2	7	1	7	4
Dean Chance	0	0	13.50	1	0	0	0	0	2.0	4	3	0	2
Joe Grzenda	0	0	0.00	1	0	0	0	0	0.2	0	0	0	0
Tom Hall	0	0	0.00	1	0	0	0	0	0.2	0	0	0	0
Bob Miller	0	1	5.40	1	1	0	0	0	1.2	5	1	0	0
Ron Perranoski	0	1	5.79	3	0	0	0	0	4.2	8	3	0	2
Jim Perry	0	0	3.38	1	1	0	0	0	8.0	6	3	3	3
Dick Woodson	0	0	10.80	1	0	0	0	0	1.2	3	2	3	2
Al Worthington	0	0	6.75	1	0	0	0	0	1.1	3	1	0	1
TOTAL	0	3	4.02	11	3	0	0	0	31.1	36	14	13	14

GAME 1 AT BAL OCT 4

MIN   000 010 200 000   3 4 2
BAL   000 110 001 001   4 10 1

Pitchers: Perry, PERRANOSKI (9) vs
   Cuellar, Richert (9), Watt (10),
   Lopez (12), HALL (12)
Home Runs: F.Robinson-BAL,
   Belanger-BAL, Oliva-MIN,
   Powell-BAL
Attendance: 39,324

GAME 2 AT BAL OCT 5

MIN   000 000 000 00   0 3 1
BAL   000 000 000 01   1 8 0

Pitchers: BOSWELL, Perranoski (11) vs
   McNALLY
Attendance: 41,704

GAME 3 AT MIN OCT 6

BAL   030 201 023   11 18 0
MIN   100 010 000   2 10 2

Pitchers: PALMER vs MILLER,
   Woodson (2), Hall (4), Worthington (5),
   Grzenda (6), Chance (7),
   Perranoski (9)
Home Runs: Blair-BAL
Attendance: 32,735

The heavy-hitting, slick-fielding Orioles, who also boasted the majors' top pitching staff, entered the Series clear favorites against the upstart Mets. But the "Miracle Mets," after losing the opener, polished off Baltimore with four straight wins.

The clubs' big winners, Met Tom Seaver (25–7) and Mike Cuellar (23–11) faced each other in the opener. Baltimore's leadoff batter, Don Buford, greeted Seaver with a home run, and a three-run Oriole rally with two out in the fourth made the score 4–0 before the Mets scored their first Series run in the seventh. Cuellar held New York to that one run for the victory.

No one scored for three innings of Game Two off Oriole Dave McNally or even hit Met Jerry Koosman safely. But Met Donn Clendenon led off the fourth with a home run as Koosman continued to no-hit Baltimore for three more innings. In the seventh, though, Baltimore's Paul Blair spoiled Koosman's no-hitter with a leadoff single, and after stealing second, scored the tying run on Brooks Robinson's single. But those were the only hits the O's would get, and in the top of the ninth three successive two-out Met singles produced what proved to be the winning run.

Met pitchers Gary Gentry and Nolan Ryan (with the assist of two spectacular catches by center fielder Tommie Agee that saved a total of five runs) combined for a shutout in Game Three. Agee's leadoff homer against Jim Palmer in the first was all the scoring the Mets would need, but they added four more runs before the game ended. Game Four was the Series' tightest. Seaver went the distance for the win, holding a 1–0 lead until a sacrifice fly scored the tying Baltimore run in the top of the ninth. In the bottom of the tenth, the Mets finally won it as a bunt thrown to first hit the runner and bounded away, allowing pinch runner Rod Gaspar to score all the way from second.

Dave McNally and Jerry Koosman tangled a second time in Game Five, and again Koosman and the Mets emerged victorious. McNally's two-run homer in the third gave him a lead which Frank Robinson expanded with a solo shot. But in an eerie sixth inning reprise of Game Four of the 1957 World Series featuring Nippy Jones, the Mets' Cleon Jones was struck by a pitch on the foot and awarded first base after inspection by the home plate umpire revealed tell-tale shoe polish on the ball. Each Jones produced a key run, Cleon coming home on Donn Clendenon's home run which followed immediately. Al Weis homered in the seventh for a 3–3 tie. With McNally now gone, two

New York Mets (NL), 4; Baltimore Orioles (AL) 1

NY (N)

PLAYER/POS	AVG	G	AB	R	H	2B	3B	HR	RB	BB	SO	SB
Tommie Agee, of	.167	5	18	1	3	0	0	1	1	1	2	5	1
Ken Boswell, 2b	.333	1	3	1	1	0	0	0	0	0	0	0
Don Cardwell, p	.000	1	0	0	0	0	0	0	0	0	0	0
Ed Charles, 3b	.133	4	15	1	2	1	0	0	0	0	2	0
Donn Clendenon, 1b	.357	4	14	4	5	1	0	3	4	2	6	0
Duffy Dyer, ph	.000	1	1	0	0	0	0	0	0	0	0	0
Wayne Garrett, 3b	.000	2	1	0	0	0	0	0	0	2	1	0
Rod Gaspar, of-1	.000	3	2	1	0	0	0	0	0	0	0	0
Gary Gentry, p	.333	1	3	0	1	1	0	0	2	0	2	0
Jerry Grote, c	.211	5	19	1	4	2	0	0	1	1	3	0
Bud Harrelson, ss	.176	5	17	1	3	0	0	0	0	3	4	0
Cleon Jones, of	.158	5	19	2	3	1	0	0	0	0	1	0
Jerry Koosman, p	.143	2	7	0	1	1	0	0	0	0	4	0
Ed Kranepool, 1b	.250	1	4	1	1	0	0	1	1	0	0	0
J.C. Martin, ph	.000	1	0	0	0	0	0	0	0	0	0	0
Nolan Ryan, p	.000	1	0	0	0	0	0	0	0	0	0	0
Tom Seaver, p	.000	2	4	0	0	0	0	0	0	0	2	0
Art Shamsky, of-1	.000	3	6	0	0	0	0	0	0	0	0	0
Ron Swoboda, of	.400	4	15	1	6	1	0	0	1	1	3	0
Ron Taylor, p	.000	2	0	0	0	0	0	0	0	0	0	0
Al Weis, 2b	.455	5	11	1	5	0	0	1	3	4	2	0
TOTAL	.220		159	15	35	8	0	6	13	15	35	1

PITCHER	W	L	ERA	G	GS	CG	SV	SHO	IP	H	ER	BB	SO
Don Cardwell	0	0	0.00	1	0	0	0	0	1.0	0	0	0	0
Gary Gentry	1	0	0.00	1	1	0	0	0	6.2	3	0	5	4
Jerry Koosman	2	0	2.04	2	2	1	0	0	17.2	7	4	4	9
Nolan Ryan	0	0	0.00	1	0	0	1	0	2.1	1	0	2	3
Tom Seaver	1	1	3.00	2	2	1	0	0	15.0	12	5	3	9
Ron Taylor	0	0	0.00	2	0	0	1	0	2.1	0	0	1	3
TOTAL	4	1	1.80	9	5	2	2	0	45.0	23	9	15	28

BAL (A)

PLAYER/POS	AVG	G	AB	R	H	2B	3B	HR	RB	BB	SO	SB
Mark Belanger, ss	.200	5	15	2	3	0	0	0	1	2	1	0
Paul Blair, of	.100	5	20	1	2	0	0	0	0	2	5	1
Don Buford, of	.100	5	20	1	2	1	0	1	2	2	4	0
Mike Cuellar, p	.400	2	5	0	2	0	0	0	1	0	3	0
Clay Dalrymple, ph	1.000	2	2	0	2	0	0	0	0	0	0	0
Andy Etchebarren, c	.000	2	6	0	0	0	0	0	0	0	1	0
Dick Hall, p	.000	1	0	0	0	0	0	0	0	0	0	0
Elrod Hendricks, c	.100	3	10	1	1	0	0	0	0	1	0	0
Davey Johnson, 2b	.063	5	16	1	1	0	0	0	0	2	1	0
Dave Leonhard, p	.000	1	0	0	0	0	0	0	0	0	0	0
Dave May, ph	.000	2	1	0	0	0	0	0	0	1	1	0
Dave McNally, p	.200	2	5	1	1	0	0	1	2	0	2	0
Curt Motton, ph	.000	1	1	0	0	0	0	0	0	0	0	0
Jim Palmer, p	.000	1	2	0	0	0	0	0	0	0	0	0
Boog Powell, 1b	.263	5	19	0	5	0	0	0	1	4	0
Merv Rettenmund, pr	.000	1	0	0	0	0	0	0	0	0	0	0
Pete Richert, p	.000	1	0	0	0	0	0	0	0	0	0	0
Brooks Robinson, 3b	.053	5	19	1	1	0	0	0	2	0	3	0
Frank Robinson, of	.188	5	16	2	3	0	0	1	1	4	3	0
Chico Salmon, pr	.000	2	0	0	0	0	0	0	0	0	0	0
Eddie Watt, p	.000	2	0	0	0	0	0	0	0	0	0	0
TOTAL	.146		157	9	23	1	0	3	9	15	28	1

PITCHER	W	L	ERA	G	GS	CG	SV	SHO	IP	H	ER	BB	SO
Mike Cuellar	1	0	1.13	2	2	1	0	0	16.0	13	2	4	13
Dick Hall	0	1	–	1	0	0	0	0	0.0	1	0	1	0
Dave Leonhard	0	0	4.50	1	0	0	0	0	2.0	1	1	1	1
Dave McNally	0	1	2.81	2	2	1	0	0	16.0	11	5	5	13
Jim Palmer	0	1	6.00	1	1	0	0	0	6.0	5	4	4	5
Pete Richert	0	0	–	1	0	0	0	0	0.0	0	0	0	0
Eddie Watt	0	1	3.00	2	0	0	0	0	3.0	4	1	0	3
TOTAL	1	4	2.72	10	5	2	0	0	43.0	35	13	15	35

doubles off Eddie Watt in the eighth brought in the go-ahead Met run, and a pair of errors let in a run for insurance. Koosman held Baltimore scoreless in the ninth and the Met miracle was complete.

GAME 1 AT BAL OCT 11

NY	000 000 100	1 6 1
BAL	100 300 00X	4 6 0

Pitchers: SEAVER, Cardwell (6), Taylor (7) vs CUELLAR
Home Runs: Buford-BAL
Attendance: 50,429

GAME 2 AT BAL OCT 12

NY	000 100 001	2 6 0
BAL	000 000 100	1 2 0

Pitchers: KOOSMAN, Taylor (9) vs McNALLY
Home Runs: Clendenon-NY
Attendance: 50,850

GAME 3 AT NY OCT 14

BAL	000 000 000	0 4 1
NY	120 001 01X	5 6 0

Pitchers: PALMER, Leonhard (7) vs GENTRY, Ryan (7)
Home Runs: Agee-NY, Kranepool-NY
Attendance: 56,335

GAME 4 AT NY OCT 15

BAL	000 000 001 0	1 6 1
NY	010 000 000 1	2 10 1

Pitchers: Cuellar, Watt (8), HALL (10), Richert (10) vs SEAVER
Home Runs: Clendenon-NY
Attendance: 57,367

GAME 5 AT NY OCT 16

BAL	003 000 000	3 5 2
NY	000 002 12X	5 7 0

Pitchers: McNally, WATT (8) vs KOOSMAN
Home Runs: McNally-BAL, F.Robinson-BAL, Clendenon-NY, Weis-NY
Attendance: 57,397

Pitching was the game and three the magic number, as Cincinnati swept Pittsburgh, scoring three runs in each game while holding the Pirates to just three runs for the whole series.

Pirate pitcher Dock Ellis matched the Reds' Gary Nolan for nine scoreless innings in Game One before a pinch-hit triple, a single, and a double undid him for three runs in the top of the tenth. In Game Two Pittsburgh scored its first series run, but Red center fielder Bobby Tolan scored three for Baltimore—including a home run—to give Cincinnati its second win.

The Pirates took a lead for the only time in the series with a run in the top of the first inning of Game Three. But Tony Perez and Johnny Bench homered in the bottom of the inning to put the Reds up 2–1. The Pirates tied the score in the fifth, but three Red relievers combined to shut them out over the final four innings, while Tolan sank the Pirate ship with his second game-winner in two days: a single in the eighth that drove in Cincinnati's third—and final—run.

Cincinnati Reds (West), 3;
Pittsburgh Pirates (East) 0

CIN (W)

PLAYER/POS	AVG	G	AB	R	H	2B	3B	HR	RB	BB	SO	SB
Johnny Bench, c	.222	3	9	2	2	0	0	1	1	3	1	0
Angel Bravo, ph	.000	1	1	0	0	0	0	0	0	0	0	0
Bernie Carbo, of	.000	2	6	0	0	0	0	0	0	0	3	0
Clay Carroll, p	.000	2	0	0	0	0	0	0	0	0	0	0
Ty Cline, of-1	1.000	2	1	2	1	0	1	0	0	1	0	0
Tony Cloninger, p	.000	1	1	0	0	0	0	0	0	1	0	0
Dave Concepcion, ss	.000	3	0	0	0	0	0	0	0	0	0	0
Wayne Granger, p	.000	1	0	0	0	0	0	0	0	0	0	0
Don Gullett, p	.000	2	1	0	0	0	0	0	0	0	0	0
Tommy Helms, 2b	.273	3	11	0	3	0	0	0	0	0	1	0
Lee May, 1b	.167	3	12	0	2	1	0	0	2	0	2	0
Hal McRae, of-1	.000	2	4	0	0	0	0	0	0	0	1	0
Jim Merritt, p	.000	1	2	0	0	0	0	0	0	0	2	0
Gary Nolan, p	.333	1	3	0	1	0	0	0	0	0	0	0
Tony Perez, 3b-3,1b-1	.333	3	12	1	4	2	0	1	2	1	1	0
Pete Rose, of	.231	3	13	1	3	0	0	0	1	0	0	0
Jimmy Stewart, of	.000	1	2	0	0	0	0	0	0	0	0	0
Bobby Tolan, of	.417	3	12	3	5	0	0	1	2	1	1	1
Milt Wilcox, p	.000	1	0	0	0	0	0	0	0	0	0	0
Woody Woodward, ss-3,3b-3	.100	3	10	0	1	0	0	0	0	1	0	0
TOTAL	.220		100	9	22	3	1	3	8	8	12	1

PITCHER	W	L	ERA	G	GS	CG	SV	SHO	IP	H	ER	BB	SO
Clay Carroll	0	0	0.00	2	0	0	1	0	1.1	2	0	0	2
Tony Cloninger	0	0	3.60	1	1	0	0	0	5.0	7	2	4	1
Wayne Granger	0	0	0.00	1	0	0	0	0	0.2	1	0	0	0
Don Gullett	0	0	0.00	2	0	0	2	0	3.2	1	0	2	3
Jim Merritt	1	0	1.69	1	1	0	0	0	5.1	3	1	0	2
Gary Nolan	1	0	0.00	1	1	0	0	0	9.0	8	0	4	6
Milt Wilcox	1	0	0.00	1	0	0	0	0	3.0	1	0	2	5
TOTAL	3	0	0.96	9	3	0	3	0	28.0	23	3	12	19

PIT (E)

PLAYER/POS	AVG	G	AB	R	H	2B	3B	HR	RB	BB	SO	SB
Gene Alley, ss	.000	2	7	0	0	0	0	0	0	1	2	0
Matty Alou, of	.250	3	12	1	3	1	0	0	0	2	1	0
Dave Cash, 2b	.125	2	8	1	1	1	0	0	0	1	1	0
Roberto Clemente, of	.214	3	14	1	3	0	0	0	1	0	4	0
Dock Ellis, p	.000	1	2	0	0	0	0	0	0	0	1	0
Joe Gibbon, p	.000	2	0	0	0	0	0	0	0	0	0	0
Dave Giusti, p	.000	2	0	0	0	0	0	0	0	0	0	0
Richie Hebner, 3b	.667	2	6	0	4	2	0	0	0	2	1	0
Johnny Jeter, of-1	.000	3	2	0	0	0	0	0	0	0	2	0
Bill Mazeroski, 2b	.000	1	2	0	0	0	0	0	0	2	0	0
Bob Moose, p	.000	1	0	0	0	0	0	0	0	0	1	0
Al Oliver, 1b	.250	2	8	0	2	0	0	0	1	1	0	0
Jose Pagan, 3b	.333	1	3	0	1	0	0	0	0	1	1	0
Freddie Patek, ss	.000	1	3	0	0	0	0	0	0	1	2	0
Bob Robertson, 1b-1	.200	2	5	0	1	1	0	0	0	0	0	0
Manny Sanguillen, c	.167	3	12	0	2	0	0	0	0	0	1	0
Willie Stargell, of	.500	3	12	0	6	1	0	0	1	1	1	0
Luke Walker, p	.000	1	2	0	0	0	0	0	0	0	1	0
TOTAL	.225		102	3	23	6	0	0	3	12	19	0

PITCHER	W	L	ERA	G	GS	CG	SV	SHO	IP	H	ER	BB	SO
Dock Ellis	0	1	2.79	1	1	0	0	0	9.2	9	3	4	1
Joe Gibbon	0	0	0.00	2	0	0	0	0	0.1	1	0	0	1
Dave Giusti	0	0	3.86	2	0	0	0	0	2.1	3	1	1	1
Bob Moose	0	1	3.52	1	1	0	0	0	7.2	4	3	2	4
Luke Walker	0	1	1.29	1	1	0	0	0	7.0	5	1	1	5
TOTAL	0	3	2.67	7	3	0	0	0	27.0	22	8	8	12

For the second year in a row, Baltimore swept Minnesota in the LCS. In the first two games the Orioles' attack featured the big inning. The score was tied 2–2 in the first game as the Orioles came to bat in the top of the fourth. But by the time the Twins came to bat in the inning, they were seven runs behind—thanks in part to a grand slam by Baltimore pitcher Mike Cuellar. Harmon Killebrew's two-run homer in the fifth helped bring the Twins within three, but they came no closer.

Except for home runs to Killebrew and Tony Oliva in the fourth inning, Oriole pitcher Dave McNally stopped the Twins in Game Two, and Baltimore held a close 4–3 lead after eight. If they had been playing at home, they wouldn't have needed to bat at all in the ninth. But they did come to bat in the top of the ninth, and once again buried Minnesota under a seven-run inning.

In the third game, for the second year in a row, Oriole pitcher Jim Palmer breezed through the series clincher. Baltimore scored five runs for him in the first three innings, and another in the eighth—four more than he needed to carry his club to another pennant.

Baltimore Orioles (East), 3; Minnesota Twins (West) 0

BAL (E)

PLAYER/POS	AVG	G	AB	R	H	2B	3B	HR	RB	BB	SO	SB
Mark Belanger, ss	.333	3	12	5	4	0	0	0	1	1	0	0
Paul Blair, of	.077	3	13	0	1	0	0	0	0	1	4	0
Don Buford, of	.429	2	7	2	3	1	0	1	3	2	0	0
Mike Cuellar, p	.500	1	2	1	1	0	0	1	4	0	1	0
Andy Etchebarren, c	.111	2	9	1	1	0	0	0	0	0	3	0
Dick Hall, p	.500	1	2	1	1	0	0	0	0	0	1	0
Elrod Hendricks, c	.400	1	5	2	2	0	0	0	0	0	1	0
Davey Johnson, 2b	.364	3	11	4	4	0	0	2	4	1	1	0
Dave McNally, p	.400	1	5	1	2	1	0	0	1	0	1	0
Jim Palmer, p	.250	1	4	1	1	1	0	0	1	0	0	0
Boog Powell, 1b	.429	3	14	2	6	2	0	1	6	0	3	0
Merv Rettenmund, of	.333	1	3	1	1	0	0	0	1	2	1	1
Brooks Robinson, 3b	.583	3	12	3	7	2	0	0	1	0	1	0
Frank Robinson, of	.200	3	10	3	2	0	0	1	2	5	2	0
TOTAL	.330		109	27	36	7	0	6	24	12	19	1

PITCHER	W	L	ERA	G	GS	CG	SV	SHO	IP	H	ER	BB	SO
Mike Cuellar	0	0	12.46	1	1	0	0	0	4.1	10	6	1	2
Dick Hall	1	0	0.00	1	0	0	0	0	4.2	1	0	0	3
Dave McNally	1	0	3.00	1	1	1	0	0	9.0	6	3	5	5
Jim Palmer	1	0	1.00	1	1	1	0	0	9.0	7	1	3	12
TOTAL	3	0	3.33	4	3	2	0	0	27.0	24	10	9	22

MIN (W)

PLAYER/POS	AVG	G	AB	R	H	2B	3B	HR	RB	BB	SO	SB
Bob Allison, ph	.000	3	2	0	0	0	0	0	0	1	1	0
Brant Alyea, of-2	.000	3	7	1	0	0	0	0	0	2	3	0
Bert Blyleven, p	.000	1	0	0	0	0	0	0	0	0	0	0
Leo Cardenas, ss	.182	3	11	1	2	0	0	0	1	1	1	0
Rod Carew, ph	.000	2	2	0	0	0	0	0	0	0	1	0
Tom Hall, p	.000	2	1	0	0	0	0	0	0	0	1	0
Jim Holt, of	.000	3	5	0	0	0	0	0	0	0	2	0
Jim Kaat, p	.000	1	1	0	0	0	0	0	0	0	0	0
Harmon Killebrew, 3b-2,1b-1	.273	3	11	2	3	0	0	2	4	2	4	0
Chuck Manuel, ph	.000	1	1	0	0	0	0	0	0	0	1	0
George Mitterwald, c	.500	2	8	2	4	1	0	0	2	0	2	0
Tony Oliva, of	.500	3	12	2	6	2	0	1	1	0	1	0
Ron Perranoski, p	.000	2	0	0	0	0	0	0	0	0	0	0
Jim Perry, p	.000	2	1	0	0	0	0	0	1	0	1	0
Frank Quilici, 2b-2	.000	3	2	0	0	0	0	0	0	0	1	0
Paul Ratliff, c	.250	1	4	0	1	0	0	0	0	0	1	0
Rich Reese, 1b	.143	2	7	0	1	0	0	0	0	1	1	0
Rich Renick, 3b-1	.200	2	5	0	1	0	0	0	0	0	1	0
Danny Thompson, 2b	.125	3	8	0	1	0	0	0	0	1	0	0
Luis Tiant, p-1	.000	2	0	0	0	0	0	0	0	0	0	0
Cesar Tovar, of-3,2b-1	.385	3	13	2	5	0	1	0	1	0	0	0
Stan Williams, p	.000	2	0	0	0	0	0	0	0	0	1	0
Dick Woodson, p	.000	1	0	0	0	0	0	0	0	0	0	0
Bill Zepp, p	.000	2	0	0	0	0	0	0	0	0	0	0
TOTAL	.238		101	10	24	4	1	3	10	9	22	0

PITCHER	W	L	ERA	G	GS	CG	SV	SHO	IP	H	ER	BB	SO
Bert Blyleven	0	0	0.00	1	0	0	0	0	2.0	2	0	0	2
Tom Hall	0	1	6.75	2	1	0	0	0	5.1	6	4	4	6
Jim Kaat	0	1	9.00	1	1	0	0	0	2.0	6	2	2	1
Ron Perranoski	0	0	19.29	2	0	0	0	0	2.1	5	5	1	3
Jim Perry	0	1	13.50	2	1	0	0	0	5.1	10	8	1	3
Luis Tiant	0	0	13.50	1	0	0	0	0	0.2	1	1	0	0
Stan Williams	0	0	0.00	2	0	0	0	0	6.0	2	0	1	2
Dick Woodson	0	0	9.00	1	0	0	0	0	1.0	2	1	1	0
Bill Zepp	0	0	6.75	2	0	0	0	0	1.1	2	1	2	2
TOTAL	0	3	7.62	14	3	0	0	0	26.0	36	22	12	19

GAME 1 AT MIN OCT 3

BAL	020	701	000	10	13	0
MIN	110	130	000	6	11	2

Pitchers: Cuellar, HALL (5) vs PERRY, Zepp (4), Woodson (5), Williams (6), Perranoski (9)
Home Runs: Cuellar-BAL, Buford-BAL, Powell-BAL, Killebrew-MIN
Attendance: 26,847

GAME 2 AT MIN OCT 4

BAL	102	100	007	11	13	0
MIN	000	300	000	3	6	2

Pitchers: McNALLY vs HALL, Zepp (4), Williams (5), Perranoski (8), Tiant (9)
Home Runs: F.Robinson-BAL, Killebrew-MIN, Oliva-MIN, Johnson-BAL
Attendance: 27,490

GAME 3 AT BAL OCT 5

MIN	000	010	000	1	7	2
BAL	113	000	10X	6	10	0

Pitchers: KAAT, Blyleven (3), Hall (5), Perry (7) vs PALMER
Home Runs: Johnson-BAL
Attendance: 27,608

With a near-sweep of Cincinnati, the Orioles helped Baltimore fans forget their 1969 Series humiliation by the New York Mets. Baltimore's first two wins, though, were closely contested. In the opener in Cincinnati (the first World Series game played on artificial grass), a Red run in the first inning and Lee May's third-inning two-run homer off Oriole starter Jim Palmer gave Cincinnati a 3–0 lead. But Orioles Boog Powell and Elrod Hendricks tagged Red starter Gary Nolan for home runs in the fourth and fifth that evened the score, and Brooks Robinson—whose other-worldly defense at third gave Reds right-handed hitters nightmares throughout the Series—homered in the seventh for a one-run Baltimore lead that held up as Palmer settled down to pitch one-hit ball from the fourth inning until he was relieved for the final out of the ninth.

Game Two was just as close. The Reds scored four runs in the first three innings, but Baltimore came back with six in the fourth and fifth. Johnny Bench's leadoff homer in the last of the sixth brought the Reds within one, but that was the end of the scoring for either side. In Game Three Oriole Dave McNally gave up nine hits and three runs. But he himself hit a grand slam in the sixth inning to cement what became a 9–3 victory.

On the verge of a Series sweep, the Orioles scored three runs in the last of the third inning of Game Four to take a 4–2 lead. But the Reds' Pete Rose homered in the fifth, and although Baltimore got the run back in the sixth, Lee May's three-run blast in the eighth overcame the Oriole lead and gave the Reds a narrow 6–5 win as Red reliever Clay Carroll permitted only one Oriole to hit safely over the final 3⅔ innings.

Mike Cuellar, driven out of Game Two in the third inning, hurled the complete game for Baltimore in Game Five, even though Cincinnati hammered him for four hits (three of them doubles) and three runs in the top of the first inning. But as Oriole home runs by Frank Robinson and Merv Rettenmund highlighted a Baltimore onslaught that produced fifteen hits and nine runs, Cuellar settled down, holding Cincinnati to a walk and a pair of harmless singles over the final eight innings to bring Baltimore its second world title in five years.

Baltimore Orioles (AL), 4; Cincinnati Reds (NL) 1

BAL (A)

PLAYER/POS	AVG	G	AB	R	H	2B	3B	HR	RB	BB	SO	SB
Mark Belanger, ss	.105	5	19	0	2	0	0	0	0	1	1	2	0
Paul Blair, of	.474	5	19	5	9	1	0	0	3	2	4	0
Don Buford, of	.267	4	15	3	4	0	0	1	1	3	2	0
Terry Crowley, ph	.000	1	1	0	0	0	0	0	0	0	0	0
Mike Cuellar, p	.000	2	4	0	0	0	0	0	0	0	2	0
Moe Drabowsky, p	.000	2	1	0	0	0	0	0	0	0	1	0
Andy Etchebarren, c	.143	2	7	1	1	0	0	0	0	2	3	0
Dick Hall, p	.000	1	1	0	0	0	0	0	0	0	1	0
Elrod Hendricks, c	.364	3	11	1	4	1	0	1	4	1	2	0
Davy Johnson, 2b	.313	5	16	2	5	2	0	0	2	5	2	0
Marcelino Lopez, p	.000	1	0	0	0	0	0	0	0	0	0	0
Dave McNally, p	.250	1	4	1	1	0	0	1	4	0	2	0
Jim Palmer, p	.143	2	7	1	1	0	0	0	0	0	3	0
Tom Phoebus, p	.000	1	0	0	0	0	0	0	0	0	0	0
Boog Powell, 1b	.294	5	17	6	5	1	0	2	5	5	2	0
Merv Rettenmund, of-1	.400	2	5	2	2	0	0	1	2	1	0	0
Pete Richert, p	.000	1	0	0	0	0	0	0	0	0	0	0
Brooks Robinson, 3b	.429	5	21	5	9	2	0	2	6	0	2	0
Frank Robinson, of	.273	5	22	5	6	0	0	2	4	0	5	0
Chico Salmon, ph	1.000	1	1	1	1	0	0	0	0	0	0	0
Eddie Watt, p	.000	1	0	0	0	0	0	0	0	0	0	0
TOTAL	.292		171	33	50	7	0	10	32	20	33	0

PITCHER	W	L	ERA	G	GS	CG	SV	SHO	IP	H	ER	BB	SO
Mike Cuellar	1	0	3.18	2	2	1	0	0	11.1	10	4	2	5
Moe Drabowsky	0	0	2.70	2	0	0	0	0	3.1	2	1	1	1
Dick Hall	0	0	0.00	1	0	0	1	0	2.1	0	0	0	0
Marcelino Lopez	0	0	0.00	1	0	0	0	0	0.1	0	0	0	0
Dave McNally	1	0	3.00	1	1	1	0	0	9.0	9	3	2	5
Jim Palmer	1	0	4.60	2	2	0	0	0	15.2	11	8	9	9
Tom Phoebus	1	0	0.00	1	0	0	0	0	1.2	1	0	0	0
Pete Richert	0	0	0.00	1	0	0	1	0	0.1	0	0	0	0
Eddie Watt	0	1	9.00	1	0	0	0	0	1.0	2	1	1	3
TOTAL	4	1	3.40	12	5	2	2	0	45.0	35	17	15	23

CIN (N)

PLAYER/POS	AVG	G	AB	R	H	2B	3B	HR	RB	BB	SO	SB
Johnny Bench, c	.211	5	19	3	4	0	0	1	3	1	2	0
Angel Bravo, ph	.000	4	2	0	0	0	0	0	0	1	1	0
Bernie Carbo, of-2	.000	4	8	0	0	0	0	0	0	2	3	0
Clay Carroll, p	.000	4	1	0	0	0	0	0	0	0	1	0
Darrel Chaney, ss	.000	3	1	0	0	0	0	0	0	0	1	0
Ty Cline, ph	.333	3	3	0	1	0	0	0	0	0	0	0
Tony Cloninger, p	.000	2	2	0	0	0	0	0	0	0	0	0
Dave Concepcion, ss	.333	3	9	0	3	0	1	0	3	0	0	0
Pat Corrales, ph	.000	1	1	0	0	0	0	0	0	0	0	0
Wayne Granger, p	.000	2	0	0	0	0	0	0	0	0	0	0
Don Gullett, p	.000	3	1	0	0	0	0	0	0	0	1	0
Tommy Helms, 2b	.222	5	18	1	4	0	0	0	0	1	1	0
Lee May, 1b	.389	5	18	6	7	2	0	2	8	2	2	0
Jim McGlothlin, p	.000	1	2	0	0	0	0	0	0	0	1	0
Hal McRae, of	.455	3	11	1	5	2	0	0	3	0	1	0
Jim Merritt, p	.000	1	1	0	0	0	0	0	0	0	1	0
Gary Nolan, p	.000	2	3	0	0	0	0	0	0	0	1	0
Tony Perez, 3b	.056	5	18	2	1	0	0	0	0	3	4	0
Pete Rose, of	.250	5	20	2	5	1	0	1	2	2	0	0
Jimmy Stewart, ph	.000	2	2	0	0	0	0	0	0	0	1	0
Bobby Tolan, of	.211	5	19	5	4	1	0	1	1	3	2	1
Ray Washburn, p	.000	1	0	0	0	0	0	0	0	0	0	0
Milt Wilcox, p	.000	2	0	0	0	0	0	0	0	0	0	0
Woody Woodward, ss-3	.200	4	5	0	1	0	0	0	0	0	0	0
TOTAL	.213		164	20	35	6	1	5	20	15	23	1

PITCHER	W	L	ERA	G	GS	CG	SV	SHO	IP	H	ER	BB	SO
Clay Carroll	1	0	0.00	4	0	0	0	0	9.0	5	0	2	11
Tony Cloninger	0	1	7.36	2	1	0	0	0	7.1	10	6	5	4
Wayne Granger	0	0	33.75	2	0	0	0	0	1.1	7	5	1	1
Don Gullett	0	0	1.35	3	0	0	0	0	6.2	5	1	4	4
Jim McGlothlin	0	0	8.31	1	1	0	0	0	4.1	6	4	2	2
Jim Merritt	0	1	21.60	1	1	0	0	0	1.2	3	4	1	0
Gary Nolan	0	1	7.71	2	2	0	0	0	9.1	9	8	3	9
Ray Washburn	0	0	13.50	1	0	0	0	0	1.1	2	2	2	0
Milt Wilcox	0	1	9.00	2	0	0	0	0	2.0	3	2	0	2
TOTAL	1	4	6.70	18	5	0	0	0	43.0	50	32	20	33

GAME 1 AT CIN OCT 10

BAL	000 210 100	4	7	2
CIN	102 000 000	3	5	0

Pitchers: PALMER, Richert (9) vs NOLAN, Carroll (7)
Home Runs: May-CIN, Powell-BAL, Hendricks-BAL, B.Robinson-BAL
Attendance: 51,531

GAME 2 AT CIN OCT 11

BAL	000 150 000	6	10	2
CIN	301 001 000	5	7	0

Pitchers: Cuellar, PHOEBUS (3), Drabowsky (5), Lopez (7), Hall (7) vs McGlothlin, WILCOX (5), Carroll (5), Gullett (8)
Home Runs: Tolan-CIN, Powell-BAL, Bench-CIN
Attendance: 51,531

GAME 3 AT BAL OCT 13

CIN	010 000 200	3	9	0
BAL	201 014 10X	9	10	1

Pitchers: CLONINGER, Granger (6), Gullett (7) vs McNALLY
Home Runs: F.Robinson-BAL, Buford-BAL, McNally-BAL
Attendance: 51,773

GAME 4 AT BAL OCT 14

CIN	011 010 030	6	8	3
BAL	013 001 000	5	8	0

Pitchers: Nolan, Gullett (3), CARROLL (6) vs Palmer, WATT (8), Drabowsky (9)
Home Runs: B.Robinson-BAL, Rose-CIN, May-CIN
Attendance: 53,007

GAME 5 AT BAL OCT 15

CIN	300 000 000	3	6	0
BAL	222 010 02X	9	15	0

Pitchers: MERRITT, Granger (2), Wilcox (3), Cloninger (5), Washburn (7), Carroll (8) vs CUELLAR
Home Runs: F.Robinson-BAL, Rettenmund-BAL
Attendance: 45,341

For the first time, an LCS went more than the minimum three games, as Pittsburgh rebounded from a loss in the opener to take the next three from San Francisco.

The Pirates scored first, with two runs in the third inning of Game One, but the Giants came back with a run in the bottom of the inning and put the game away in the fifth as Tito Fuentes and Willie McCovey both hit two-out two-run homers. Pirate first baseman Bob Robertson avenged his club's opening-game defeat the next day, battering four of the Giants' six pitchers for three home runs and a double—and five RBIs—in the Pirates' 9–5 win. Robertson continued his assault in Game Three, homering off Juan Marichal in the second. The Giants came back with a run in the sixth, but third baseman Richie Hebner put the game away with a second Pirate home run off Marichal in the eighth.

Both clubs scored five times in the first two innings of Game Four. But Pirate relievers Bruce Kison and Dave Giusti then pinned the Giants down for the final seven innings, while Roberto Clemente and Al Oliver combined for four RBIs in the sixth to capture the flag.

Pittsburgh Pirates (East), 3; San Francisco Giants (West), 1

PIT (E)

PLAYER/POS	AVG	G	AB	R	H	2B	3B	HR	RB	BB	SO	SB
Gene Alley, ss	.500	1	2	1	1	0	0	0	0	0	0	0
Steve Blass, p	.000	2	1	0	0	0	0	0	0	0	1	0
Dave Cash, 2b	.421	4	19	5	8	2	0	0	1	0	1	1
Roberto Clemente, of	.333	4	18	2	6	0	0	0	4	1	6	0
Gene Clines, of	.333	1	3	1	1	0	0	1	1	0	1	0
Vic Davalillo, ph	.000	2	2	0	0	0	0	0	0	0	1	0
Dock Ellis, p	.000	1	3	0	0	0	0	0	0	0	2	0
Dave Giusti, p	.000	4	1	0	0	0	0	0	0	0	0	0
Richie Hebner, 3b	.294	4	17	3	5	1	0	2	4	0	4	0
Jackie Hernandez, ss	.231	4	13	2	3	0	0	0	1	0	4	0
Bob Johnson, p	.000	1	2	0	0	0	0	0	0	0	0	0
Bruce Kison, p	.000	1	2	0	0	0	0	0	0	0	0	0
Milt May, ph	.000	1	1	0	0	0	0	0	0	0	0	0
Bill Mazeroski, ph	1.000	1	1	1	1	0	0	0	0	0	0	0
Bob Miller, p	.000	1	1	0	0	0	0	0	0	0	0	0
Bob Moose, p	.000	1	0	0	0	0	0	0	0	0	0	0
Al Oliver, of	.250	4	12	2	3	0	0	1	5	1	3	0
Jose Pagan, 3b	.000	1	1	0	0	0	0	0	0	0	0	0
Bob Robertson, 1b	.438	4	16	5	7	1	0	4	6	0	2	0
Manny Sanguillen, c	.267	4	15	1	4	0	0	0	1	1	1	1
Willie Stargell, of	.000	4	14	1	0	0	0	0	0	2	6	0
TOTAL	.271		144	24	39	4	0	8	23	5	33	2

PITCHER	W	L	ERA	G	GS	CG	SV	SHO	IP	H	ER	BB	SO
Steve Blass	0	1	11.57	2	2	0	0	0	7.0	14	9	2	11
Dock Ellis	1	0	3.60	1	1	0	0	0	5.0	6	2	4	1
Dave Giusti	0	0	0.00	4	0	0	3	0	5.1	1	0	2	3
Bob Johnson	1	0	0.00	1	1	0	0	0	8.0	5	0	3	7
Bruce Kison	1	0	0.00	1	0	0	0	0	4.2	2	0	2	3
Bob Miller	0	0	6.00	1	0	0	0	0	3.0	3	2	3	3
Bob Moose	0	0	0.00	1	0	0	0	0	2.0	0	0	0	0
TOTAL	3	1	3.34	11	4	0	3	0	35.0	31	13	16	28

SF (W)

PLAYER/POS	AVG	G	AB	R	H	2B	3B	HR	RB	BB	SO	SB
Jim Barr, p	.000	1	1	0	0	0	0	0	0	0	0	0
Bobby Bonds, of	.250	3	8	0	2	0	0	0	0	2	4	0
Ron Bryant, p	.000	1	0	0	0	0	0	0	0	0	0	0
Don Carrithers, p	.000	1	0	0	0	0	0	0	0	0	0	0
John Cumberland, p	.000	1	0	0	0	0	0	0	0	0	0	0
Dick Dietz, c	.067	4	15	0	1	0	0	0	0	2	5	0
Frank Duffy, ph	.000	1	1	0	0	0	0	0	0	0	1	0
Tito Fuentes, 2b	.313	4	16	4	5	1	0	1	2	1	3	0
Alan Gallagher, 3b	.100	4	10	0	1	0	0	0	0	0	0	0
Steve Hamilton, p	.000	1	0	0	0	0	0	0	0	0	0	0
Jim Ray Hart, 3b-1	.000	3	5	0	0	0	0	0	0	0	2	0
Ken Henderson, of	.313	4	16	3	5	1	0	0	2	2	1	1
Jerry Johnson, p	.000	1	0	0	0	0	0	0	0	0	0	0
Dave Kingman, of-2	.111	4	9	0	1	0	0	0	0	1	3	0
Hal Lanier, 3b	.000	1	1	0	0	0	0	0	0	0	0	0
Juan Marichal, p	.000	1	3	0	0	0	0	0	0	0	1	0
Willie Mays, of	.267	4	15	2	4	2	0	1	3	3	3	1
Willie McCovey, 1b	.429	4	14	2	6	0	0	2	6	4	2	0
Don McMahon, p	.000	2	0	0	0	0	0	0	0	0	0	0
Gaylord Perry, p	.250	2	4	0	1	0	0	0	0	0	0	0
Jimmy Rosario, pr	.000	1	0	0	0	0	0	0	0	0	0	0
Chris Speier, ss	.357	4	14	4	5	1	0	1	1	1	1	0
TOTAL	.235		132	15	31	5	0	5	14	16	28	2

PITCHER	W	L	ERA	G	GS	CG	SV	SHO	IP	H	ER	BB	SO
Jim Barr	0	0	9.00	1	0	0	0	0	1.0	3	1	0	2
Ron Bryant	0	0	4.50	1	0	0	0	0	2.0	1	1	1	2
Don Carrithers	0	0	∞	1	0	0	0	0	0.0	3	3	0	0
John Cumberland	0	1	9.00	1	1	0	0	0	3.0	7	3	0	4
Steve Hamilton	0	0	9.00	1	0	0	0	0	1.0	1	1	0	3
Jerry Johnson	0	0	13.50	1	0	0	0	0	1.1	1	2	1	2
Juan Marichal	0	1	2.25	1	1	1	0	0	8.0	4	2	0	6
Don McMahon	0	0	0.00	2	0	0	0	0	3.0	0	0	0	3
Gaylord Perry	1	1	6.14	2	2	1	0	0	14.2	19	10	3	11
TOTAL	1	3	6.09	11	4	2	0	0	34.0	39	23	5	33

Baltimore, dividing its fifteen runs evenly among the three games, swept the ALCS for the third year in a row.

Oakland's Vida Blue took a 3–1 lead into the seventh inning of Game One, but with two away and men on first and third, an Oriole single and two doubles pushed across four runs to beat him 5–3, as Oriole starter Dave McNally and reliever Eddie Watt held the A's scoreless from the fifth inning on. In the second game Oakland managed only one run off Mike Cuellar, while the Orioles hammered Catfish Hunter for five runs on four homers—two of them by Boog Powell, including one in the eighth with a man aboard.

Reggie Jackson retaliated for the A's in Game Three with two home runs off Jim Palmer, and Sal Bando added a third. But Palmer permitted no other A's to score, and—supported by a Baltimore run in the first and two each in the fifth and seventh—preserved an Oriole lead throughout the game, for the third year in a row clinching the pennant for Baltimore with a complete-game victory.

Baltimore Orioles (East), 3;
Oakland A's (West) 0

BAL (E)

PLAYER/POS	AVG	G	AB	R	H	2B	3B	HR	RB	BB	SO	SB
Mark Belanger, ss	.250	3	8	1	2	0	0	0	1	3	2	0
Paul Blair, of	.333	3	9	1	3	1	0	0	2	0	3	0
Don Buford, of	.429	2	7	1	3	0	1	0	0	2	1	0
Mike Cuellar, p	.333	1	3	0	1	0	0	0	0	0	0	0
Andy Etchebarren, c	.000	2	5	0	0	0	0	0	0	0	0	0
Elrod Hendricks, c	.500	2	4	1	2	0	0	1	2	1	1	0
Davey Johnson, 2b	.300	3	10	2	3	2	0	0	0	3	1	0
Dave McNally, p	.000	1	2	0	0	0	0	0	0	0	0	0
Curt Motton, ph	1.000	1	1	0	1	1	0	0	1	0	0	0
Jim Palmer, p-1	.200	2	5	1	1	0	0	0	0	0	1	0
Boog Powell, 1b	.300	3	10	4	3	0	0	2	3	3	3	0
Merv Rettenmund, of	.250	3	8	0	2	1	0	0	1	0	3	0
Brooks Robinson, 3b	.364	3	11	2	4	1	0	1	3	0	1	0
Frank Robinson, of	.083	3	12	2	1	1	0	0	1	1	4	0
Eddie Watt, p	.000	1	0	0	0	0	0	0	0	0	0	0
TOTAL	.274		95	15	26	7	1	4	14	13	22	0

PITCHER	W	L	ERA	G	GS	CG	SV	SHO	IP	H	ER	BB	SO
Mike Cuellar	1	0	1.00	1	1	1	0	0	9.0	6	1	1	2
Dave McNally	1	0	3.86	1	1	0	0	0	7.0	7	3	1	5
Jim Palmer	1	0	3.00	1	1	1	0	0	9.0	7	3	3	8
Eddie Watt	0	0	0.00	1	0	0	1	0	2.0	2	0	0	1
TOTAL	3	0	2.33	4	3	2	1	0	27.0	22	7	5	16

OAK (W)

PLAYER/POS	AVG	G	AB	R	H	2B	3B	HR	RB	BB	SO	SB
Sal Bando, 3b	.364	3	11	3	4	2	0	1	1	1	0	0
Curt Blefary, ph	.000	1	1	0	0	0	0	0	0	0	1	0
Vida Blue, p	.000	1	3	0	0	0	0	0	0	0	3	0
Bert Campaneris, ss	.167	3	12	0	2	1	0	0	0	0	1	0
Tommy Davis, 1b-2	.375	3	8	1	3	1	0	0	0	0	0	0
Dave Duncan, c	.500	2	6	0	3	1	0	0	2	0	0	0
Mike Epstein, 1b-1	.200	2	5	0	1	0	0	0	0	0	3	0
Rollie Fingers, p	.000	2	0	0	0	0	0	0	0	0	0	0
Mudcat Grant, p	.000	1	0	0	0	0	0	0	0	0	0	0
Dick Green, 2b	.286	3	7	0	2	0	0	0	0	1	1	0
Mike Hegan, ph	.000	1	1	0	0	0	0	0	0	0	1	0
Catfish Hunter, p	.000	1	3	0	0	0	0	0	0	0	1	0
Reggie Jackson, of	.333	3	12	2	4	1	0	2	2	0	1	0
Darold Knowles, p	.000	1	0	0	0	0	0	0	0	0	0	0
Bob Locker, p	.000	1	0	0	0	0	0	0	0	0	0	0
Angel Mangual, of	.167	3	12	1	2	1	1	0	2	0	1	0
Rick Monday, of	.000	3	3	0	0	0	0	0	0	1	2	0
Joe Rudi, of	.143	2	7	0	1	1	0	0	0	1	0	0
Diego Segui, p	.000	1	2	0	0	0	0	0	0	0	0	0
Gene Tenace, c	.000	1	3	0	0	0	0	0	0	1	1	0
TOTAL	.229		96	7	22	8	1	3	7	5	16	0

PITCHER	W	L	ERA	G	GS	CG	SV	SHO	IP	H	ER	BB	SO
Vida Blue	0	1	6.43	1	1	0	0	0	7.0	7	5	2	8
Rollie Fingers	0	0	7.71	2	0	0	0	0	2.1	2	2	1	2
Mudcat Grant	0	0	0.00	1	0	0	0	0	2.0	3	0	0	2
Catfish Hunter	0	1	5.63	1	1	1	0	0	8.0	7	5	2	6
Darold Knowles	0	0	0.00	1	0	0	0	0	0.1	1	0	0	0
Bob Locker	0	0	0.00	1	0	0	0	0	0.2	0	0	2	0
Diego Segui	0	1	5.79	1	1	0	0	0	4.2	6	3	6	4
TOTAL	0	3	5.40	8	3	1	0	0	25.0	26	15	13	22

GAME 1 AT BAL OCT 3

OAK	020	100	000	3	9	0
BAL	000	100	40X	5	7	1

Pitchers: BLUE, Fingers (8) vs
 McNALLY, Watt (8)
Attendance: 42,621

GAME 2 AT BAL OCT 4

OAK	000	100	000	1	6	0
BAL	011	000	12X	5	7	0

Pitchers: HUNTER vs CUELLAR
Home Runs: B.Robinson-BAL,
 Powell-BAL (2), Hendricks-BAL
Attendance: 35,003

GAME 3 AT OAK OCT 5

BAL	100	020	200	5	12	0
OAK	001	001	010	3	7	0

Pitchers: PALMER vs SEGUI,
 Fingers (5), Knowles (7), Locker (7),
 Grant (8)
Home Runs: Jackson-OAK (2),
 Bando-OAK
Attendance: 33,176

In its third successive Series, Baltimore faced its third different opponent and beat the Pirates in the first two games. A walk, a wild pitch, two Baltimore errors, and a single in the second inning of the opener gave Pittsburgh an early 3–0 lead. But Oriole pitcher Dave McNally shut out the Pirates on two hits the rest of the game as Frank Robinson, Merv Rettenmund and Don Buford homered to give Baltimore a 5–3 victory. Jim Palmer took the win in Game Two as Baltimore hammered Pirate pitching for fourteen hits and eleven runs before Palmer issued Richie Hebner a three-run homer—Pittsburgh's only scoring—in the eighth.

The Pirates overtook the Orioles when the Series moved to Pittsburgh. Steve Blass pitched a three-hitter in Game Three, and while Frank Robinson's solo homer in the seventh ended Blass's shutout, a three-run shot by Pirate Bob Robertson in the last of the inning cemented a 5–1 Pittsburgh win. The next evening (in the first World Series night game ever), Baltimore scored three times in the top of the first inning, but two Pirate runs later in the inning and another run in the third tied the game. It remained tied until Pirate pinch hitter Milt May singled home the game winner with two away in the seventh.

With the Series now even at two wins apiece, Pittsburgh's Nelson Briles stopped the Orioles in Game Five on a pair of singles. Bob Robertson's leadoff homer in the second proved all the Pirates needed for the win, but Briles himself drove in an insurance run later in the inning and Pittsburgh went on to win 4–0.

The Pirates tried to win it all in Game Six, scoring single runs against the O's Jim Palmer in the second inning and the third (Roberto Clemente's home run). But Pirate starter Bob Moose was replaced after giving up a solo homer to Don Buford in the sixth, and a tying Baltimore run came home an inning later. A ninth-inning pinch hitter for Palmer produced nothing, but Baltimore won in the last of the tenth, when Frank Robinson scored on Brooks Robinson's sacrifice fly to shallow center.

Steve Blass, who had defeated Oriole Mike Cuellar in Game Three, faced him again in the finale and again emerged the victor of a pitching duel. Clemente's two-out homer in the fourth inning provided the game's only run until the eighth, when both teams scored single runs. Blass retired Baltimore in order in the ninth and the Pirates were world champions.

Pittsburgh Pirates (NL), 4; Baltimore Orioles (AL) 3

PIT (N)

PLAYER/POS	AVG	G	AB	R	H	2B	3B	HR	RB	BB	SO	SB
Gene Alley, ss	.000	2	2	0	0	0	0	0	0	1	0	0
Steve Blass, p	.000	2	7	0	0	0	0	0	0	0	1	0
Nelson Briles, p	.500	1	2	0	1	0	0	0	1	0	1	0
Dave Cash, 2b	.133	7	30	2	4	1	0	0	1	3	1	1
Roberto Clemente, of	.414	7	29	3	12	2	1	2	4	2	2	0
Gene Clines, of	.091	3	11	2	1	0	1	0	0	1	1	1
Vic Davalillo, of-2	.333	3	3	1	1	0	0	0	0	0	0	0
Dock Ellis, p	.000	1	1	0	0	0	0	0	0	0	1	0
Dave Giusti, p	.000	3	0	0	0	0	0	0	0	0	0	0
Richie Hebner, 3b	.167	3	12	2	2	0	0	1	3	3	3	0
Jackie Hernandez, ss	.222	7	18	2	4	0	0	0	1	2	5	1
Bob Johnson, p	.000	2	3	0	0	0	0	0	0	0	2	0
Bruce Kison, p	.000	2	2	0	0	0	0	0	0	0	2	0
Milt May, ph	.500	2	2	0	1	0	0	0	1	0	0	0
Bill Mazeroski, ph	.000	1	1	0	0	0	0	0	0	0	0	0
Bob Miller, p	.000	3	0	0	0	0	0	0	0	0	0	0
Bob Moose, p	.000	3	2	0	0	0	0	0	0	0	1	0
Al Oliver, of-4	.211	5	19	1	4	2	0	0	2	2	5	0
Jose Pagan, 3b	.267	4	15	0	4	2	0	0	2	0	1	0
Bob Robertson, 1b	.240	7	25	4	6	0	0	2	5	4	8	0
Charlie Sands, ph	.000	1	1	0	0	0	0	0	0	0	1	0
Manny Sanguillen, c	.379	7	29	3	11	1	0	0	0	0	3	2
Willie Stargell, of	.208	7	24	3	5	1	0	0	1	7	9	0
Bob Veale, p	.000	1	0	0	0	0	0	0	0	0	0	0
Luke Walker, p	.000	1	0	0	0	0	0	0	0	0	0	0
TOTAL	.235		238	23	56	9	2	5	21	26	47	5

PITCHER	W	L	ERA	G	GS	CG	SV	SHO	IP	H	ER	BB	SO
Steve Blass	2	0	1.00	2	2	2	0	0	18.0	7	2	4	13
Nelson Briles	1	0	0.00	1	1	1	0	1	9.0	2	0	2	2
Dock Ellis	0	1	15.43	1	1	0	0	0	2.1	4	4	1	1
Dave Giusti	0	0	0.00	3	0	0	1	0	5.1	3	0	2	4
Bob Johnson	0	1	9.00	2	1	0	0	0	5.0	5	5	3	3
Bruce Kison	1	0	0.00	2	0	0	0	0	6.1	1	0	2	3
Bob Miller	0	1	3.86	3	0	0	0	0	4.2	7	2	1	2
Bob Moose	0	0	6.52	3	1	0	0	0	9.2	12	7	2	7
Bob Veale	0	0	13.50	1	0	0	0	0	0.2	1	1	2	0
Luke Walker	0	0	40.50	1	1	0	0	0	0.2	3	3	1	0
TOTAL	4	3	3.50	19	7	3	1	1	61.2	45	24	20	35

BAL (A)

PLAYER/POS	AVG	G	AB	R	H	2B	3B	HR	RB	BB	SO	SB
Mark Belanger, ss	.238	7	21	4	5	0	1	0	0	5	2	1
Paul Blair, of-3	.333	4	9	2	3	1	0	0	0	0	1	0
Don Buford, of	.261	6	23	3	6	1	0	2	4	3	3	0
Mike Cuellar, p	.000	2	3	0	0	0	0	0	0	1	2	0
Pat Dobson, p	.000	3	2	0	0	0	0	0	0	0	2	0
Tom Dukes, p	.000	2	0	0	0	0	0	0	0	0	0	0
Andy Etchebarren, c	.000	1	2	0	0	0	0	0	0	0	0	0
Dick Hall, p	.000	1	0	0	0	0	0	0	0	0	0	0
Elrod Hendricks, c	.263	6	19	3	5	1	0	0	1	3	3	0
Grant Jackson, p	.000	1	0	0	0	0	0	0	0	0	0	0
Davy Johnson, 2b	.148	7	27	1	4	0	0	0	3	0	1	0
Dave Leonhard, p	.000	1	0	0	0	0	0	0	0	0	0	0
Dave McNally, p	.000	4	4	0	0	0	0	0	0	0	3	0
Jim Palmer, p	.000	2	4	0	0	0	0	0	0	2	2	0
Boog Powell, 1b	.111	7	27	1	3	0	0	0	1	1	3	0
Merv Rettenmund, of-6	.185	7	27	3	5	0	0	1	4	0	4	0
Pete Richert, p	.000	1	0	0	0	0	0	0	0	0	0	0
Brooks Robinson, 3b	.318	7	22	2	7	0	0	0	5	3	1	0
Frank Robinson, of	.280	7	25	5	7	0	0	2	2	2	8	0
Tom Shopay, ph	.000	5	4	0	0	0	0	0	0	0	0	0
Eddie Watt, p	.000	2	0	0	0	0	0	0	0	0	0	0
TOTAL	.205		219	24	45	3	1	5	22	20	35	1

PITCHER	W	L	ERA	G	GS	CG	SV	SHO	IP	H	ER	BB	SO
Mike Cuellar	0	2	3.86	2	2	0	0	0	14.0	11	6	6	10
Pat Dobson	0	0	4.05	3	1	0	0	0	6.2	13	3	4	6
Tom Dukes	0	0	0.00	2	0	0	0	0	4.0	2	0	0	1
Dick Hall	0	0	0.00	1	0	0	0	1	1.0	1	0	0	0
Grant Jackson	0	0	0.00	1	0	0	0	0	0.2	0	0	1	0
Dave Leonhard	0	0	0.00	1	0	0	0	0	1.0	0	0	1	0
Dave McNally	2	1	1.98	4	2	1	0	0	13.2	10	3	5	12
Jim Palmer	1	0	2.65	2	2	0	0	0	17.0	15	5	9	15
Pete Richert	0	0	0.00	1	0	0	0	0	0.2	0	0	0	1
Eddie Watt	0	1	3.86	2	0	0	0	0	2.1	4	1	0	2
TOTAL	3	4	2.66	19	7	1	1	0	61.0	56	18	26	47

GAME 1 AT BAL OCT 9

PIT	030	000	000	3	3	0
BAL	013	010	00X	5	10	3

Pitchers: ELLIS, Moose (3), Miller (7) vs McNALLY
Home Runs: F.Robinson-BAL, Rettenmund-BAL, Buford-BAL
Attendance: 53,229

GAME 2 AT BAL OCT 11

PIT	000	000	030	3	8	1
BAL	010	361	00X	11	14	1

Pitchers: R.JOHNSON, Kison (4), Moose (4), Veale (5), Miller (6), Giusti (8) vs PALMER, Hall (9)
Home Runs: Hebner-PIT
Attendance: 53,239

GAME 3 AT PIT OCT 12

BAL	000	000	100	1	3	3
PIT	100	001	30X	5	7	0

Pitchers: CUELLAR, Dukes (7), Watt (8) vs BLASS
Home Runs: F.Robinson-BAL, Robertson-PIT
Attendance: 50,403

GAME 4 AT PIT OCT 13

BAL	300	000	000	3	4	1
PIT	201	000	10X	4	14	0

Pitchers: Dobson, Jackson (6), WATT (7), Richert (8) vs Walker, KISON (1), Giusti (8)
Attendance: 51,378

GAME 5 AT PIT OCT 14

BAL	000	000	000	0	2	1
PIT	021	010	00X	4	9	0

Pitchers: McNALLY, Leonhard (5), Dukes (6) vs BRILES
Home Runs: Robertson-PIT
Attendance: 51,377

GAME 6 AT BAL OCT 16

PIT	011	000	000	0	2	9	1
BAL	000	001	100	1	3	8	0

Pitchers: Moose, R.Johnson (6), Giusti (7), MILLER (10) vs Palmer, Dobson (10), McNALLY (10)
Home Runs: Clemente-PIT, Buford-BAL
Attendance: 44,174

GAME 7 AT BAL OCT 17

PIT	000	100	010	2	6	1
BAL	000	000	010	1	4	0

Pitchers: BLASS vs CUELLAR, Dobson (9), McNally (9)
Home Runs: Clemente-PIT
Attendance: 47,291

Pittsburgh traded wins with Cincinnati through the first four games—winning the first and third—and took a lead into the ninth inning of the fifth game before a home run and a wild pitch undid them.

Cincinnati got eight hits in each of the first two games. In the first game, though, only Joe Morgan's first-inning homer produced a run, and the Reds lost 5–1. But the next day, five first-inning hits gave the Reds four runs and a lead the Pirates could not overcome.

Pirate catcher Manny Sanguillen brought Pittsburgh back in Game Three with a home run in the fifth and the game-winning RBI in the eighth. But Reds pitcher Ross Grimsley evened the series for Cincinnati the next day with a two-hitter, in the series' only complete-game performance.

Game Five was Pittsburgh's for 8½ innings. The Pirates scored first, and held the lead into the bottom of the ninth. But Johnny Bench opened the Reds' half of the ninth with a game-tying home run, and Tony Perez and Denis Menke followed him with singles. Bob Moose came in and retired the next two men, though George Foster (running for Perez) took third on a fly to right. Moose then threw away the pennant with a run-scoring, series-ending wild pitch.

Cincinnati Reds (West), 3; Pittsburgh Pirates (East) 2

CIN (W)

PLAYER/POS	AVG	G	AB	R	H	2B	3B	HR	RB	BB	SO	SB
Johnny Bench, c	.333	5	18	3	6	1	1	1	2	1	3	2
Jack Billingham, p	.000	1	2	0	0	0	0	0	0	0	1	0
Pedro Borbon, p	.000	3	0	0	0	0	0	0	0	0	0	0
Clay Carroll, p	.000	2	0	0	0	0	0	0	0	0	0	0
Darrel Chaney, ss	.188	5	16	3	3	0	0	0	1	1	1	1
Dave Concepcion, ss-1	.000	3	2	0	0	0	0	0	0	0	0	0
George Foster, pr	.000	1	0	1	0	0	0	0	0	0	0	0
Cesar Geronimo, of	.100	5	20	2	2	0	0	1	1	0	2	0
Ross Grimsley, p	.500	1	4	0	2	1	0	0	1	0	1	0
Don Gullett, p	.500	2	2	0	1	0	0	0	0	0	0	0
Joe Hague, ph	.000	3	1	0	0	0	0	0	0	2	1	0
Tom Hall, p	.000	2	1	0	0	0	0	0	0	0	0	0
Jim McGlothlin, p	.000	1	0	0	0	0	0	0	0	0	0	0
Hal McRae, ph	.000	1	0	0	0	0	0	0	0	0	0	0
Denis Menke, 3b	.250	5	16	1	4	1	0	0	0	4	3	0
Joe Morgan, 2b	.263	5	19	5	5	0	0	2	3	1	2	1
Gary Nolan, p	.000	1	2	0	0	0	0	0	0	0	1	0
Tony Perez, 1b	.200	5	20	0	4	1	0	0	2	0	7	0
Pete Rose, of	.450	5	20	1	9	4	0	0	2	1	2	0
Bobby Tolan, of	.238	5	21	3	5	1	1	0	4	0	4	0
Ted Uhlaender, ph	.500	2	2	0	1	0	0	0	0	0	0	0
TOTAL	.253		166	19	42	9	2	4	16	10	28	4

PITCHER	W	L	ERA	G	GS	CG	SV	SHO	IP	H	ER	BB	SO
Jack Billingham	0	0	3.86	1	1	0	0	0	4.2	5	2	2	4
Pedro Borbon	0	0	2.08	3	0	0	0	0	4.1	2	1	0	1
Clay Carroll	1	1	3.38	2	0	0	0	0	2.2	1	1	3	0
Ross Grimsley	1	0	1.00	1	1	1	0	0	9.0	2	1	0	5
Don Gullett	0	1	8.00	2	2	0	0	0	9.0	12	8	0	5
Tom Hall	1	0	1.23	2	0	0	0	0	7.1	3	1	3	8
Jim McGlothlin	0	0	0.00	1	0	0	0	0	1.0	0	0	0	0
Gary Nolan	0	0	1.50	1	1	0	0	0	6.0	4	1	1	4
TOTAL	3	2	3.07	13	5	1	0	0	44.0	30	15	9	27

PIT (E)

PLAYER/POS	AVG	G	AB	R	H	2B	3B	HR	RB	BB	SO	SB
Gene Alley, ss	.000	5	16	1	0	0	0	0	0	0	3	0
Steve Blass, p	.000	2	6	0	0	0	0	0	0	0	3	0
Nelson Briles, p	.000	1	2	0	0	0	0	0	0	0	1	0
Dave Cash, 2b	.211	5	19	4	4	0	0	0	3	0	0	0
Roberto Clemente, of	.235	5	17	1	4	1	0	1	2	3	5	0
Gene Clines, ph	.000	3	2	1	0	0	0	0	0	0	1	0
Vic Davalillo, ph	.000	1	1	0	0	0	0	0	0	1	0	0
Dock Ellis, p-1	.000	3	1	0	0	0	0	0	0	0	0	0
Dave Giusti, p	.000	3	1	0	0	0	0	0	0	0	0	0
Richie Hebner, 3b	.188	5	16	2	3	1	0	0	1	1	3	0
Ramon Hernandez, p	.000	5	0	0	0	0	0	0	0	0	0	0
Bob Johnson, p	.000	2	1	0	0	0	0	0	0	1	0	0
Bruce Kison, p	.000	2	0	0	0	0	0	0	0	0	0	0
Milt May, c	.500	1	2	0	1	0	0	0	1	0	0	0
Bill Mazeroski, ph	.500	2	2	0	1	0	0	0	0	0	1	0
Bob Miller, p	.000	1	0	0	0	0	0	0	0	0	0	0
Bob Moose, p	.000	2	2	0	0	0	0	0	0	0	0	0
Al Oliver, of	.250	5	20	3	5	2	1	1	3	0	4	0
Bob Robertson, 1b	.000	4	0	0	0	0	0	0	0	0	1	0
Manny Sanguillen, c	.313	5	16	4	5	1	0	1	2	0	0	0
Willie Stargell, 1b-5,of-1	.063	5	16	1	1	1	0	0	1	2	5	0
Rennie Stennett, of-5,2b-1	.286	5	21	2	6	0	0	0	1	1	0	0
Luke Walker, p	.000	1	0	0	0	0	0	0	0	0	0	0
TOTAL	.190		158	15	30	6	1	3	14	9	27	0

PITCHER	W	L	ERA	G	GS	CG	SV	SHO	IP	H	ER	BB	SO
Steve Blass	1	0	1.72	2	2	0	0	0	15.2	12	3	6	5
Nelson Briles	0	0	3.00	1	1	0	0	0	6.0	6	2	1	3
Dock Ellis	0	1	0.00	1	1	0	0	0	5.0	5	0	1	3
Dave Giusti	0	1	6.75	3	0	0	1	0	2.2	5	2	0	3
Ramon Hernandez	0	0	2.70	3	0	0	1	0	3.1	1	1	0	3
Bob Johnson	0	0	3.00	2	0	0	0	0	6.0	4	2	2	7
Bruce Kison	1	0	0.00	2	0	0	0	0	2.1	1	0	0	3
Bob Miller	0	0	0.00	1	0	0	0	0	1.0	0	0	0	1
Bob Moose	0	1	54.00	2	1	0	0	0	0.2	5	4	0	0
Luke Walker	0	0	18.00	1	0	0	0	0	1.0	3	2	0	0
TOTAL	2	3	3.30	18	5	0	2	0	43.2	42	16	10	28

GAME 1 AT PIT OCT 7

CIN	100 000 000	1 8 0
PIT	**300 020 00X**	**5 6 0**

Pitchers: GULLETT, Borbon (7) vs BLASS, R.Hernandez (9)
Home Runs: Morgan-CIN, Oliver-PIT
Attendance: 50,476

GAME 2 AT PIT OCT 8

CIN	400 000 010	5 8 1
PIT	000 111 000	3 7 1

Pitchers: Billingham, HALL (5) vs MOOSE, Johnson (6), R.Hernandez (7), Giusti (9)
Home Runs: Morgan-CIN
Attendance: 50,584

GAME 3 AT CIN OCT 9

PIT	000 010 110	3 7 0
CIN	002 000 000	2 8 1

Pitchers: Briles, KISON (7), Giusti (8) vs Nolan, Borbon (7), CARROLL (7), McGlothlin (9)
Home Runs: Sanguillen-PIT
Attendance: 52,420

GAME 4 AT CIN OCT 10

PIT	000 000 100	1 2 3
CIN	100 000 00X	7 11 1

Pitchers: ELLIS, Johnson (6), Walker (7), Miller (8) vs GRIMSLEY
Home Runs: Clemente-PIT
Attendance: 39,447

GAME 5 AT CIN OCT 11

PIT	020 100 000	3 8 0
CIN	001 010 002	4 7 1

Pitchers: Blass, R.Hernandez (8), GIUSTI (9), Moose (9) vs Gullett, Borbon (4), Hall (6), CARROLL (9)
Home Runs: Geronimo-CIN, Bench-CIN
Attendance: 41,887

Oakland turned back the Tigers in the first two games, but Detroit evened the series before succumbing in the fifth game.

In Game One, Tiger Al Kaline homered off Rollie Fingers in the eleventh to give starter Mickey Lolich a 2–1 lead. But in the last of the inning, pinch hitter Gonzalo Marquez singled off Tiger reliever Chuck Seelbach with two on to drive in the tying run, and Gene Tenace scored to win it on the same play as right fielder Kaline threw the ball away. Blue Moon Odom increased the A's series lead with a three-hit shutout in Game Two, but Detroit's Joe Coleman retaliated with 14 strikeouts and a shutout of his own to save the Tigers from elimination in Game Three.

In Game Four the A's pulled out of a 1–1 tie with two runs in the top of the tenth. But Detroit in its half of the inning went through three Oakland relievers for three runs and the win. In the finale, after Odom, the A's starter, had given Detroit a run and a brief lead in the first, he and Vida Blue divided eight shutout innings between them as the A's scored twice to capture their first pennant since Connie Mack won his last in Philadelphia forty-one years earlier.

Oakland A's (West), 3; Detroit Tigers (East) 2

OAK (W)

PLAYER/POS	AVG	G	AB	R	H	2B	3B	HR	RB	BB	SO	SB
Matty Alou, of	.381	5	21	2	8	4	0	0	2	0	2	1
Sal Bando, 3b	.200	5	20	0	4	0	0	0	0	0	3	0
Vida Blue, p	.000	4	1	0	0	0	0	0	0	0	0	0
Bert Campaneris, ss	.429	2	7	3	3	0	0	0	0	1	0	2
Tim Cullen, ss	.000	2	1	0	0	0	0	0	0	0	0	0
Dave Duncan, c	.000	2	2	0	0	0	0	0	0	1	1	0
Mike Epstein, 1b	.188	5	16	1	3	0	0	1	1	4	5	1
Rollie Fingers, p	.000	3	1	0	0	0	0	0	0	0	0	0
Dick Green, 2b	.125	5	8	0	1	1	0	0	0	0	0	0
Dave Hamilton, p	.000	1	0	0	0	0	0	0	0	0	0	0
Mike Hegan, 1b-1	.000	3	1	1	0	0	0	0	0	0	0	0
George Hendrick, of-1	.143	5	7	2	1	0	0	0	0	0	1	0
Ken Holtzman, p	.000	1	1	0	0	0	0	0	0	0	1	0
Joe Horlen, p	.000	1	0	0	0	0	0	0	0	0	0	0
Catfish Hunter, p	.167	2	6	0	1	0	0	0	0	0	2	0
Reggie Jackson, of	.278	5	18	1	5	1	0	0	2	1	6	2
Ted Kubiak, 2b-3,ss-1	.500	4	4	0	2	0	0	0	1	0	0	0
Bob Locker, p	.000	2	0	0	0	0	0	0	0	0	0	0
Angel Mangual, ph	.000	3	3	0	0	0	0	0	0	0	1	0
Gonzalo Marquez, ph	.667	3	3	1	2	0	0	0	1	0	0	0
Dal Maxvill, ss-4,2b-1	.125	5	8	0	1	0	0	0	0	1	2	1
Don Mincher, ph	.000	1	1	0	0	0	0	0	0	0	1	0
Blue Moon Odom, p-2	.250	3	4	0	1	1	0	0	0	0	1	0
Joe Rudi, of	.250	5	20	1	5	1	0	0	2	1	4	0
Gene Tenace, c-5,2b-2	.059	5	17	1	1	0	0	0	1	3	5	0
TOTAL	.224		170	13	38	8	0	1	10	12	35	7

PITCHER	W	L	ERA	G	GS	CG	SV	SHO	IP	H	ER	BB	SO
Vida Blue	0	0	0.00	4	0	0	1	0	5.1	4	0	1	5
Rollie Fingers	1	0	1.69	3	0	0	0	0	5.1	4	1	1	3
Dave Hamilton	0	0	∞	1	0	0	0	0	0.0	1	0	1	0
Ken Holtzman	0	1	4.50	1	1	0	0	0	4.0	4	2	2	2
Joe Horlen	0	1	∞	1	0	0	0	0	0.0	0	1	1	0
Catfish Hunter	0	0	1.17	2	2	0	0	0	15.1	10	2	5	9
Bob Locker	0	0	13.50	2	0	0	0	0	2.0	4	3	0	1
Blue Moon Odom	2	0	0.00	2	2	1	0	1	14.0	5	0	2	5
TOTAL	3	2	1.76	16	5	1	1	1	46.0	32	9	13	25

DET (E)

PLAYER/POS	AVG	G	AB	R	H	2B	3B	HR	RB	BB	SO	SB
Ed Brinkman, ss	.250	1	4	0	1	1	0	0	0	0	0	0
Ike Brown, 1b	.500	1	2	0	1	0	0	0	2	0	1	0
Gates Brown, ph	.000	3	2	1	0	0	0	0	0	1	0	0
Norm Cash, 1b	.267	5	15	1	4	0	0	1	2	2	3	0
Joe Coleman, p	.500	1	2	0	1	0	0	0	0	1	0	0
Bill Freehan, c	.250	3	12	2	3	1	0	1	3	0	1	0
Woody Fryman, p	.000	2	3	0	0	0	0	0	0	0	0	0
Tom Haller, ph	.000	1	1	0	0	0	0	0	0	0	0	0
John Hiller, p	.000	3	0	0	0	0	0	0	0	0	0	0
Willie Horton, of-3	.100	5	10	0	1	0	0	0	0	1	3	0
Al Kaline, of	.263	5	19	3	5	0	0	1	1	2	2	0
John Knox, pr	.000	1	0	0	0	0	0	0	0	0	0	0
Lerrin La Grow, p	.000	1	0	0	0	0	0	0	0	0	0	0
Mickey Lolich, p	.000	2	7	0	0	0	0	0	0	0	2	0
Dick McAuliffe, ss-4,2b-1	.200	5	20	3	4	0	0	1	1	1	4	0
Joe Niekro, pr	.000	0	0	0	0	0	0	0	0	0	0	0
Jim Northrup, of	.357	5	14	0	5	0	0	0	1	2	3	0
Aurelio Rodriguez, 3b	.000	5	16	0	0	0	0	0	0	2	2	0
Fred Scherman, p	.000	1	0	0	0	0	0	0	0	0	0	0
Chuck Seelbach, p	.000	2	0	0	0	0	0	0	0	0	0	0
Duke Sims, c-2,of-2	.214	4	14	0	3	2	1	0	0	1	2	0
Mickey Stanley, of-3	.333	4	6	0	2	0	0	0	0	0	0	0
Tony Taylor, 2b	.133	4	15	0	2	2	0	0	0	0	2	0
Chris Zachary, p	.000	1	0	0	0	0	0	0	0	0	0	0
TOTAL	.198		162	10	32	6	1	4	10	13	25	0

PITCHER	W	L	ERA	G	GS	CG	SV	SHO	IP	H	ER	BB	SO
Joe Coleman	1	0	0.00	1	1	1	0	1	9.0	7	0	3	14
Woody Fryman	0	2	3.65	2	2	0	0	0	12.1	11	5	2	8
John Hiller	1	0	0.00	3	0	0	0	0	3.1	1	0	1	1
Lerrin La Grow	0	0	0.00	1	0	0	0	0	1.0	0	0	0	1
Mickey Lolich	0	1	1.42	2	2	0	0	0	19.0	14	3	5	10
Fred Scherman	0	0	0.00	1	0	0	0	0	0.2	1	0	0	1
Chuck Seelbach	0	0	18.00	2	0	0	0	0	1.0	4	2	0	0
Chris Zachary	0	0	∞	1	0	0	0	0	0.0	0	1	1	0
TOTAL	2	3	2.14	13	5	1	0	1	46.1	38	11	12	35

GAME 1 AT OAK OCT 7

DET	010 000 000 01	2	6	2
OAK	001 000 000 02	3	10	1

Pitchers: LOLICH, Seelbach (11) vs Hunter, Blue (9), FINGERS (9)
Home Runs: Cash-DET, Kaline-DET
Attendance: 29,536

GAME 2 AT OAK OCT 8

DET	000 000 000	0	3	1
OAK	100 040 00X	5	8	0

Pitchers: FRYMAN, Zachary (5), Scherman (5), LaGrow (6), Hiller (7) vs ODOM
Attendance: 31,088

GAME 3 AT DET OCT 10

OAK	000 000 000	0	7	0
DET	000 200 01X	3	8	1

Pitchers: HOLTZMAN, Fingers (5), Blue (6), Locker (7) vs COLEMAN
Home Runs: Freehan-DET
Attendance: 41,156

GAME 4 AT DET OCT 11

OAK	000 000 100 2	3	9	2
DET	001 000 000 3	4	10	1

Pitchers: Hunter, Fingers (8), Blue (9), Locker (10), HORLEN (10), Hamilton (10) vs Lolich, Seelbach (10), HILLER (10)
Home Runs: McAuliffe-DET, Epstein-OAK
Attendance: 37,615

GAME 5 AT DET OCT 12

OAK	010 100 000	2	4	0
DET	100 000 000	1	5	2

Pitchers: ODOM, Blue (6) vs FRYMAN, Hiller (9)
Attendance: 50,276

Oakland slugger Reggie Jackson missed the Series with a pulled hamstring, but Gene Tenace (the A's backup catcher during the season) took up the slack, hitting four of the club's five homers and driving in nine of their sixteen runs.

Six of the seven games were decided by a single run. Oakland won the first two in Cincinnati, 3–2 and 2–1. Tenace made the difference in the opener, driving in all the A's runs with a two-run homer in the second inning and a solo shot in the fifth. In the second game, A's starting pitcher Catfish Hunter singled in a run in the second inning which proved the margin of his victory. His 8⅔-inning performance was the longest mound outing in a Series which saw the two clubs together use nearly seven pitchers per game.

Cincinnati took the first game in Oakland, 1–0. The A's' Blue Moon Odom dueled the Reds' Jack Billingham scorelessly on one hit through six innings before giving up the game's only run on a single-sacrifice-single in the seventh. Billingham, too, yielded only three hits in eight-plus innings before yielding to ace reliever Clay Carroll, who retired the side in the ninth.

Oakland won Game Four, 3–2. Tenace opened the scoring with a solo homer in the fifth. The Reds' Bobby Tolan doubled in a pair in the eighth to put Cincinnati ahead, but in the last of the ninth four successive A's singles scored two runs, with Tenace scoring the game winner on pinch hitter Angel Mangual's hit. Tenace homered again in Game Five for three runs, but it wasn't enough as the Reds tied the score in the eighth and won on Pete Rose's RBI single in the ninth.

The Reds produced the Series' only blowout with five runs in the seventh inning of Game Six to make the score 8–1, where it remained. The finale saw Tenace drive in a run in the top of the first for a narrow Oakland lead which held until the Reds tied the game in the fifth. In the sixth the A's scored twice—Tenace doubling in the go-ahead run. Cincinnati scored once more in the eighth as a runner inherited by A's reliever Rollie Fingers came home on a sacrifice fly. But Fingers permitted no other runs to score, and the A's took the crown with their fourth one-run victory.

Oakland Athletics (AL), 4; Cincinnati Reds (NL) 3

OAK (A)

PLAYER/POS	AVG	G	AB	R	H	2B	3B	HR	RB	BB	SO	SB
Matty Alou, of	.042	7	24	0	1	0	0	0	0	0	3	0	1
Sal Bando, 3b	.269	7	26	2	7	1	0	0	1	2	5	0
Vida Blue, p	.000	4	1	0	0	0	0	0	0	2	1	0
Bert Campaneris, ss	.179	7	28	1	5	0	0	0	0	1	4	0
Dave Duncan, c-1	.200	3	5	0	1	0	0	0	0	0	3	0
Mike Epstein, 1b	.000	6	16	1	0	0	0	0	0	5	3	0
Rollie Fingers, p	.000	6	1	0	0	0	0	0	0	0	0	0
Dick Green, 2b	.333	7	18	0	6	2	0	0	1	0	4	0
Dave Hamilton, p	.000	2	0	0	0	0	0	0	0	0	0	0
Mike Hegan, 1b-5	.200	6	5	0	1	0	0	0	0	0	2	0
George Hendrick, of	.133	5	15	3	2	0	0	0	0	1	2	0
Ken Holtzman, p	.000	3	5	0	0	0	0	0	0	0	0	0
Joe Horlen, p	.000	1	0	0	0	0	0	0	0	0	0	0
Catfish Hunter, p	.200	3	5	0	1	0	0	0	1	2	1	0
Ted Kubiak, 2b	.333	4	3	0	1	0	0	0	0	0	0	0
Allan Lewis, pr	.000	6	0	0	0	0	0	0	0	0	0	0
Bob Locker, p	.000	1	0	0	0	0	0	0	0	0	0	0
Angel Mangual, of-2	.300	4	10	1	3	0	0	0	0	1	0	0
Gonzalo Marquez, ph	.600	5	5	0	3	0	0	0	0	1	0	0
Don Mincher, ph	1.000	3	1	0	1	0	0	0	1	0	0	0
Blue Moon Odom, p-2	.000	4	4	0	0	0	0	0	0	0	3	0
Joe Rudi, of	.240	7	25	1	6	0	0	1	1	2	5	0
Gene Tenace, c-6,1b-1	.348	7	23	5	8	1	0	4	9	2	4	0
TOTAL	.209		220	16	46	4	0	5	16	21	37	1

PITCHER	W	L	ERA	G	GS	CG	SV	SHO	IP	H	ER	BB	SO
Vida Blue	0	1	4.15	4	1	0	1	0	8.2	8	4	5	5
Rollie Fingers	1	1	1.74	6	0	0	2	0	10.1	4	2	4	11
Dave Hamilton	0	0	27.00	2	0	0	0	0	1.1	3	4	1	1
Ken Holtzman	1	0	2.13	3	2	0	0	0	12.2	11	3	3	4
Joe Horlen	0	0	6.75	1	0	0	0	0	1.1	2	1	2	1
Catfish Hunter	2	0	2.81	3	2	0	0	0	16.0	12	5	6	11
Bob Locker	0	0	0.00	1	0	0	0	0	0.1	1	0	0	0
Blue Moon Odom	0	1	1.59	2	2	0	0	0	11.1	5	2	6	13
TOTAL	4	3	3.05	22	7	0	3	0	62.0	46	21	27	46

CIN (N)

PLAYER/POS	AVG	G	AB	R	H	2B	3B	HR	RB	BB	SO	SB
Johnny Bench, c	.261	7	23	4	6	1	0	1	1	5	5	2
Jack Billingham, p	.000	3	5	0	0	0	0	0	0	0	4	0
Pedro Borbon, p	.000	6	0	0	0	0	0	0	0	0	0	0
Clay Carroll, p	.000	5	0	0	0	0	0	0	0	0	0	0
Darrel Chaney, ss-3	.000	4	7	0	0	0	0	0	0	2	2	0
Dave Concepcion, ss-5	.308	6	13	2	4	0	1	0	2	2	2	1
George Foster, of-1	.000	2	0	0	0	0	0	0	0	0	0	0
Cesar Geronimo, of	.158	7	19	1	3	0	0	0	3	1	4	1
Ross Grimsley, p	.000	4	0	0	0	0	0	0	0	0	2	0
Don Gullett, p	.000	1	2	0	0	0	0	0	0	0	0	0
Joe Hague, of-1	.000	3	3	0	0	0	0	0	0	0	1	0
Tom Hall, p	.000	4	2	0	0	0	0	0	0	0	0	0
Julian Javier, ph	.000	2	2	0	0	0	0	0	0	0	0	0
Jim McGlothlin, p	.000	1	1	0	0	0	0	0	0	0	1	0
Hal McRae, of-2	.444	5	9	1	4	1	0	0	2	0	1	0
Denis Menke, 3b	.083	7	24	1	2	0	0	1	2	2	6	0
Joe Morgan, 2b	.125	7	24	4	3	2	0	0	1	6	3	2
Gary Nolan, p	.000	2	3	0	0	0	0	0	0	0	3	0
Tony Perez, 1b	.435	7	23	3	10	2	0	0	2	4	4	0
Pete Rose, of	.214	7	28	3	6	0	0	1	2	4	4	1
Bobby Tolan, of	.269	7	26	2	7	1	0	0	6	1	4	5
Ted Uhlaender, ph	.250	4	4	0	1	0	0	0	0	0	1	0
TOTAL	.209		220	21	46	8	1	3	21	27	46	12

PITCHER	W	L	ERA	G	GS	CG	SV	SHO	IP	H	ER	BB	SO
Jack Billingham	1	0	0.00	3	2	0	1	0	13.2	6	0	4	11
Pedro Borbon	0	1	3.86	6	0	0	0	0	7.0	7	3	2	4
Clay Carroll	0	1	1.59	5	0	0	1	0	5.2	6	1	4	3
Ross Grimsley	2	1	2.57	4	1	0	0	0	7.0	7	2	3	2
Don Gullett	0	0	1.29	1	1	0	0	0	7.0	5	1	2	4
Tom Hall	0	0	0.00	4	0	0	1	0	8.1	6	0	2	7
Jim McGlothlin	0	0	12.00	1	1	0	0	0	3.0	2	4	2	3
Gary Nolan	0	1	3.38	2	2	0	0	0	10.2	7	4	2	3
TOTAL	3	2	2.17	26	7	0	3	0	62.1	46	15	21	37

GAME 1 AT CIN OCT 14

OAK	020 010 000	3 4 0
CIN	010 100 000	2 7 0

Pitchers: HOLTZMAN, Fingers (6), Blue (7) vs NOLAN, Borbon (7), Carroll (8)
Home Runs: Tenace-OAK (2)
Attendance: 52,918

GAME 2 AT CIN OCT 15

OAK	011 000 000	2 9 2
CIN	000 000 001	1 6 0

Pitchers: HUNTER, Fingers (9) vs GRIMSLEY, Borbon (6), Hall (8)
Home Runs: Rudi-OAK
Attendance: 53,224

GAME 3 AT OAK OCT 18

CIN	000 000 100	1 4 2
OAK	000 000 000	0 3 2

Pitchers: BILLINGHAM, Carroll (9) vs ODOM, Blue (8), Fingers (8)
Attendance: 49,410

GAME 4 AT OAK OCT 19

CIN	000 000 020	2 7 1
OAK	000 010 002	3 10 1

Pitchers: Gullett, Borbon (8), CARROLL (9) vs Holtzman, Blue (8), FINGERS (9)
Home Runs: Tenace-OAK
Attendance: 49,410

GAME 5 AT OAK OCT 20

CIN	100 110 011	5 8 0
OAK	030 100 000	4 7 2

Pitchers: McGlothlin, Borbon (4), Hall (5), Carroll (7), GRIMSLEY (8), Billingham (9) vs Hunter, FINGERS (5), Hamilton (9)
Home Runs: Rose-CIN, Tenace-OAK, Menke-CIN
Attendance: 49,410

GAME 6 AT CIN OCT 21

OAK	000 010 000	1 7 1
CIN	000 111 50X	8 10 0

Pitchers: BLUE, Locker (6), Hamilton (7), Horlen (7) vs Nolan, GRIMSLEY (5), Borbon (6), Hall (7)
Home Runs: Bench-CIN
Attendance: 52,737

GAME 7 AT CIN OCT 22

OAK	100 002 000	3 6 1
CIN	000 010 010	2 4 2

Pitchers: Odom, HUNTER (5), Holtzman (8), Fingers (8) vs Billingham, BORBON (6), Carroll (6), Grimsley (7), Hall (8)
Attendance: 56,040

The Mets received strong pitching throughout the series, and their offense came through just often enough to defeat Cincinnati in five games.

Though three Reds pitchers held New York to three hits in Game One, the single Met run in the second seemed for a time enough for a win. But Tom Seaver gave up a home run to Pete Rose in the eighth and lost the game in the ninth when Johnny Bench homered. Not wanting another last-inning loss in Game Two, the Mets unloaded for four runs in the top of the ninth to add to their one in the fourth. But this time one would have been enough as Jon Matlack blanked the Reds on two hits.

The Mets made it easy for Jerry Koosman in Game Three in New York, scoring nine times in the first four innings. Things were more difficult for shortstop Bud Harrelson, who exchanged blows with Pete Rose following Rose's hard slide in the fifth inning. A bench-clearing melee ensued, and fans in the left field stands showered Rose with debris until a delegation of Tom Seaver, Willie Mays and Rusty Staub visited the area to calm nerves and eliminate the threat of a forfeit. In Game Four, though, Met bats were stifled once again as four Reds pitchers combined for a 12-inning three-hitter. The Reds won the game and tied the series on Rose's sweetly vengeful twelfth-inning homer.

In the finale the Mets took a quick two-run lead. Cincinnati tied the game in the top of the fifth, but New York retaliated with four more in the bottom of the inning. Seaver—and Tug McGraw in the ninth—held the Reds scoreless the rest of the way.

New York Mets (East), 3; Cincinnati Reds (West) 2

NY (E)

PLAYER/POS	AVG	G	AB	R	H	2B	3B	HR	RB	BB	SO	SB
Ken Boswell, ph	.000	1	1	0	0	0	0	0	0	0	0	0
Wayne Garrett, 3b	.087	5	23	1	2	1	0	0	1	0	5	0
Jerry Grote, c	.211	5	19	2	4	0	0	0	2	1	3	0
Don Hahn, of	.235	5	17	2	4	0	0	0	1	2	4	0
Bud Harrelson, ss	.167	5	18	1	3	0	0	0	2	1	1	0
Cleon Jones, of	.300	5	20	3	6	2	0	0	3	2	4	0
Jerry Koosman, p	.500	1	4	1	2	0	0	0	1	0	0	0
Ed Kranepool, of	.500	1	2	0	1	0	0	0	2	0	0	0
Jon Matlack, p	.000	2	2	0	0	0	0	0	0	1	2	0
Willie Mays, of	.333	1	3	1	1	0	0	0	1	0	0	0
Tug McGraw, p	.000	2	1	0	0	0	0	0	0	0	1	0
Felix Millan, 2b	.316	5	19	5	6	0	0	0	0	2	1	0
John Milner, 1b	.176	5	17	2	3	0	0	0	1	5	3	0
Harry Parker, p	.000	1	0	0	0	0	0	0	0	0	0	0
Tom Seaver, p	.333	2	6	1	2	2	0	0	1	1	1	0
Rusty Staub, of	.200	4	15	4	3	0	0	3	5	3	2	0
George Stone, p	.000	1	0	0	0	0	0	0	0	1	1	0
TOTAL	.220		168	23	37	5	0	3	22	19	28	0

PITCHER	W	L	ERA	G	GS	CG	SV	SHO	IP	H	ER	BB	SO
Jerry Koosman	1	0	2.00	1	1	1	0	0	9.0	8	2	0	9
Jon Matlack	1	0	0.00	1	1	1	0	1	9.0	2	0	3	9
Tug McGraw	0	0	0.00	2	0	0	1	0	5.0	4	0	3	3
Harry Parker	0	1	9.00	1	0	0	0	0	1.0	1	1	0	0
Tom Seaver	1	1	1.62	2	2	1	0	0	16.2	13	3	5	17
George Stone	0	0	1.35	1	1	0	0	0	6.2	3	1	2	4
TOTAL	3	2	1.33	8	5	3	1	1	47.1	31	7	13	42

CIN (W)

PLAYER/POS	AVG	G	AB	R	H	2B	3B	HR	RB	BB	SO	SB
Ed Armbrister, of-1	.167	3	6	0	1	0	0	0	0	0	5	0
Johnny Bench, c	.263	5	19	1	5	2	0	1	1	2	2	0
Jack Billingham, p	.000	2	3	0	0	0	0	0	0	0	1	0
Pedro Borbon, p	.000	4	0	0	0	0	0	0	0	0	0	0
Clay Carroll, p	.000	3	0	0	0	0	0	0	0	0	0	0
Darrel Chaney, ph	.000	5	9	0	0	0	0	0	0	3	4	0
Ed Crosby, ss-2	.500	3	2	0	1	0	0	0	0	0	1	0
Dan Driessen, 3b	.167	4	12	0	2	1	0	0	1	0	2	0
Phil Gagliano, ph	.000	3	3	0	0	0	0	0	0	0	2	0
Cesar Geronimo, of	.067	4	15	0	1	0	0	0	0	0	7	0
Ken Griffey, of-2	.143	3	7	0	1	1	0	0	0	0	1	0
Ross Grimsley, p	.000	2	0	0	0	0	0	0	0	0	0	0
Don Gullett, p	.000	3	1	0	0	0	0	0	0	0	0	0
Tom Hall, p	.000	3	0	0	0	0	0	0	0	0	0	0
Hal King, ph	.500	3	2	0	1	0	0	0	0	1	0	0
Andy Kosco, of	.300	3	10	0	3	0	0	0	0	2	3	0
Denis Menke, ss-2,3b-2	.222	3	9	1	2	0	0	1	1	1	2	0
Joe Morgan, 2b	.100	5	20	1	2	1	0	0	1	2	2	0
Roger Nelson, p	.000	1	0	0	0	0	0	0	0	0	0	0
Fred Norman, p	.000	1	1	0	0	0	0	0	0	0	1	0
Tony Perez, 1b	.091	5	22	1	2	0	0	1	2	0	4	0
Pete Rose, of	.381	5	21	3	8	1	0	2	2	2	2	0
Larry Stahl, ph	.500	4	4	1	2	0	0	0	0	0	1	0
Dave Tomlin, p	.000	1	0	0	0	0	0	0	0	0	0	0
TOTAL	.186		167	8	31	6	0	5	8	13	42	0

PITCHER	W	L	ERA	G	GS	CG	SV	SHO	IP	H	ER	BB	SO
Jack Billingham	0	1	4.50	2	2	0	0	0	12.0	9	6	4	9
Pedro Borbon	1	0	0.00	4	0	0	1	0	4.2	3	0	3	3
Clay Carroll	1	0	1.29	3	0	0	0	0	7.0	5	1	1	2
Ross Grimsley	0	1	12.27	2	1	0	0	0	3.2	7	5	2	3
Don Gullett	0	1	2.00	3	1	0	0	0	9.0	4	2	3	6
Tom Hall	0	0	67.50	3	0	0	0	0	0.2	3	5	4	1
Roger Nelson	0	0	0.00	1	0	0	0	0	2.1	0	0	1	0
Fred Norman	0	0	1.80	1	0	0	0	0	5.0	1	1	3	3
Dave Tomlin	0	0	16.20	1	0	0	0	0	1.2	5	3	1	1
TOTAL	2	3	4.50	20	5	0	1	0	46.0	37	23	19	28

GAME 1 AT CIN OCT 6

NY	010 000 000	1 3 0
CIN	000 000 011	2 6 0

Pitchers: SEAVER vs Billingham, Hall (9), BORBON (9)
Home Runs: Rose-CIN, Bench-CIN
Attendance: 53,431

GAME 2 AT CIN OCT 7

NY	000 100 004	5 7 0
CIN	000 000 000	0 2 0

Pitchers: MATLACK vs GULLETT, Carroll (9), Hall (9), Borbon (9)
Home Runs: Staub-NY
Attendance: 54,041

GAME 3 AT NY OCT 8

CIN	002 000 000	2 8 1
NY	151 200 00X	9 11 1

Pitchers: GRIMSLEY, Hall (2), Tomlin (3), Nelson (4), Borbon (7) vs KOOSMAN
Home Runs: Staub-NY (2), Menke-CIN
Attendance: 53,967

GAME 4 AT NY OCT 9

CIN	000 000 100 001	2 8 0
NY	001 000 000 000	1 3 2

Pitchers: Norman, Gullett (6), CARROLL (10), Borbon (12) vs Stone, McGraw (7), PARKER (12)
Home Runs: Perez-CIN, Rose-CIN
Attendance: 50,786

GAME 5 AT NY OCT 10

CIN	001 010 000	2 7 1
NY	200 041 00X	7 13 1

Pitchers: BILLINGHAM, Gullett (5), Carroll (5), Grimsley (7) vs SEAVER, McGraw (9)
Attendance: 50,323

The Orioles finally met their match in an LCS as Oakland took its second consecutive pennant. Baltimore started strong, chasing A's starter Vida Blue with four runs in the first inning as Jim Palmer—pitching the series opener for a change—blanked the A's on five hits. But Oakland snapped back in Game Two, with five of their six runs coming on homers by Sal Bando (two, for three runs), Joe Rudi, and Bert Campaneris.

Oriole Mike Cuellar and the A's Ken Holtzman cut down opposing batters for 10½ innings in Game Three before Oakland's Campaneris broke the 1–1 tie in the bottom of the eleventh with a leadoff home run. The next day Jim Palmer was driven out in the second inning by three Oakland runs, and the A's added to their lead with another run in the sixth. But Andy Etchebarren led a four-run Oriole comeback in the seventh with a three-run homer, and Bobby Grich's solo shot in the next inning gave the Orioles the margin they needed to win the game and tie the series.

The A's took it all in the finale, though, needing only one of their three runs as Catfish Hunter stopped Baltimore cold on five scattered hits.

Oakland A's (West), 3;
Baltimore Orioles (East) 2

OAK (W)

PLAYER/POS	AVG	G	AB	R	H	2B	3B	HR	RB	BB	SO	SB
Jesus Alou, dh-1	.333	4	6	0	2	0	0	0	1	0	1	0
Mike Andrews, 1b-1,dh-1	.000	2	1	0	0	0	0	0	0	0	0	0
Sal Bando, 3b	.167	5	18	2	3	0	0	2	3	3	6	0
Vida Blue, p	.000	2	0	0	0	0	0	0	0	0	0	0
Pat Bourque, dh	.000	2	1	0	0	0	0	0	0	1	1	0
Bert Campaneris, ss	.333	5	21	3	7	1	0	2	3	2	2	3
Billy Conigliaro, of	.000	1	4	0	0	0	0	0	0	0	2	0
Vic Davalillo, 1b-2,of-2	.625	4	8	2	5	1	1	0	1	1	0	0
Rollie Fingers, p	.000	3	0	0	0	0	0	0	0	0	0	0
Ray Fosse, c	.091	5	11	2	1	1	0	0	3	2	2	0
Dick Green, 2b	.077	5	13	0	1	1	0	0	1	1	4	0
Ken Holtzman, p	.000	1	0	0	0	0	0	0	0	0	0	0
Catfish Hunter, p	.000	2	0	0	0	0	0	0	0	0	0	0
Reggie Jackson, of	.143	5	21	0	3	0	0	0	0	0	6	0
Deron Johnson, dh	.100	4	10	0	1	0	0	0	0	2	6	0
Ted Kubiak, 2b	.000	3	2	0	0	0	0	0	0	0	1	0
Allan Lewis, pr	.000	2	0	1	0	0	0	0	0	0	0	0
Angel Mangual, of	.111	3	9	1	1	0	0	0	0	0	3	0
Blue Moon Odom, p	.000	1	0	0	0	0	0	0	0	0	0	0
Horacio Pina, p	.000	1	0	0	0	0	0	0	0	0	0	0
Joe Rudi, of	.222	5	18	1	4	0	0	1	3	3	1	0
Gene Tenace, 1b-5,c-3	.235	5	17	3	4	1	0	0	0	2	4	0
TOTAL	.200		160	15	32	5	1	5	15	17	39	3

PITCHER	W	L	ERA	G	GS	CG	SV	SHO	IP	H	ER	BB	SO
Vida Blue	0	1	10.29	2	2	0	0	0	7.0	8	8	5	3
Rollie Fingers	0	1	1.93	3	0	0	1	0	4.2	4	1	2	4
Ken Holtzman	1	0	0.82	1	1	1	0	0	11.0	3	1	1	7
Catfish Hunter	2	0	1.65	2	2	1	0	0	16.1	12	3	6	6
Blue Moon Odom	0	0	1.80	1	0	0	0	0	5.0	6	1	2	4
Horacio Pina	0	0	0.00	1	0	0	0	0	2.0	3	0	1	1
TOTAL	3	2	2.74	10	5	2	1	0	46.0	36	14	16	25

BAL (E)

PLAYER/POS	AVG	G	AB	R	H	2B	3B	HR	RB	BB	SO	SB
Doyle Alexander, p	.000	1	0	0	0	0	0	0	0	0	0	0
Frank Baker, ss	.000	2	0	0	0	0	0	0	0	0	0	0
Don Baylor, of-3	.273	4	11	3	3	0	0	0	1	3	5	0
Mark Belanger, ss	.125	5	16	0	2	0	0	0	1	1	1	0
Paul Blair, of	.167	5	18	2	3	0	0	0	0	1	5	0
Larry Brown, 3b	.000	1	0	0	0	0	0	0	0	0	0	0
Al Bumbry, of	.000	2	7	1	0	0	0	0	0	2	2	1
Rich Coggins, of	.444	2	9	1	4	0	0	0	0	0	0	0
Terry Crowley, of-1	.000	2	2	0	0	0	0	0	0	0	0	0
Mike Cuellar, p	.000	1	0	0	0	0	0	0	0	0	0	0
Tommy Davis, dh	.286	5	21	1	6	0	0	0	2	1	0	0
Andy Etchebarren, c	.357	4	14	1	5	1	0	1	4	0	1	0
Bobby Grich, 2b	.100	5	20	1	2	0	0	1	1	2	5	0
Don Hood, pr	.000	0	0	0	0	0	0	0	0	0	0	0
Grant Jackson, p	.000	2	0	0	0	0	0	0	0	0	0	0
Dave McNally, p	.000	1	0	0	0	0	0	0	0	0	0	0
Jim Palmer, p	.000	3	0	0	0	0	0	0	0	0	0	0
Boog Powell, 1b	.000	1	4	1	0	0	0	0	0	0	1	0
Merv Rettenmund, of	.091	3	11	1	1	0	0	0	0	3	2	0
Bob Reynolds, p	.000	2	0	0	0	0	0	0	0	0	0	0
Brooks Robinson, 3b	.250	5	20	1	5	2	0	0	2	1	1	0
Eddie Watt, p	.000	1	0	0	0	0	0	0	0	0	0	0
Earl Williams, 1b-4,c-1	.278	5	18	2	5	2	0	1	4	2	2	0
TOTAL	.211		171	15	36	7	0	3	15	16	25	1

PITCHER	W	L	ERA	G	GS	CG	SV	SHO	IP	H	ER	BB	SO
Doyle Alexander	0	1	4.91	1	1	0	0	0	3.2	5	2	0	1
Mike Cuellar	0	1	1.80	1	1	1	0	0	10.0	4	2	3	11
Grant Jackson	1	0	0.00	2	0	0	0	0	3.0	0	0	1	0
Dave McNally	0	1	5.87	1	1	0	0	0	7.2	7	5	2	7
Jim Palmer	1	0	1.84	3	2	1	0	1	14.2	11	3	8	15
Bob Reynolds	0	0	3.18	2	0	0	0	0	5.2	5	2	3	5
Eddie Watt	0	0	0.00	1	0	0	0	0	0.1	0	0	0	0
TOTAL	2	3	2.80	11	5	2	0	1	45.0	32	14	17	39

GAME 1 AT BAL OCT 6

OAK	000	000	000	0	5	1
BAL	400	000	11X	6	12	0

Pitchers: BLUE, Pina (1), Odom (3), Fingers (8) vs PALMER
Attendance: 41,279

GAME 2 AT BAL OCT 7

OAK	100	002	021	6	9	0
BAL	100	001	010	3	8	0

Pitchers: HUNTER, Fingers (8) vs McNALLY, Reynolds (8), G.Jackson (9)
Home Runs: Campaneris-OAK, Rudi-OAK, Bando-OAK (2)
Attendance: 48,425

GAME 3 AT OAK OCT 9

BAL	010	000	000	00	1	3	0
OAK	000	000	010	01	2	4	3

Pitchers: CUELLAR vs HOLTZMAN
Home Runs: Williams-BAL, Campaneris-OAK
Attendance: 34,367

GAME 4 AT OAK OCT 10

BAL	000	000	410	5	8	0
OAK	030	001	000	4	7	0

Pitchers: Palmer, Reynolds (2), Watt (7), G.JACKSON (7) vs Blue, FINGERS (7)
Home Runs: Etchebarren-BAL, Grich-BAL
Attendance: 27,497

GAME 5 AT OAK OCT 11

BAL	000	000	000	0	5	2
OAK	001	200	00X	3	7	0

Pitchers: ALEXANDER, Palmer (4) vs HUNTER
Attendance: 24,265

For the second year in a row, the A's were outpitched and outscored by their Series opposition, and this time they were outhit as well. But again, when the dust of Game Seven had settled, they still wore the crown. A's starter Ken Holtzman, who because of the American League's new designated hitter rule had not batted all season, doubled for the A's first hit in the third inning of Game One and scored the first Oakland run on a Met error. The A's scored again in the inning, enough for the win as Holtzman and two relievers held New York to a single run.

The Mets evened things in a Game Two that lasted a then-record 4 hours 13 minutes, scoring four runs with two out in the top of the twelfth inning for a lead the A's were not able to overcome. (Three of the runs scored on a pair of errors by second-baseman Mike Andrews, prompting a flap that rocked the baseball world as A's owner Charlie Finley tried—unsuccessfully—to "fire" Andrews by declaring him injured.) Final score of the slugfest: 10–7.

In a somewhat more normal third game, the Mets grabbed an early lead on Wayne Garrett's lead-off homer in the bottom of the first and scored a second run on two singles and wild pitch for a 2–0 lead that held up until Oakland tied the game in the eighth. In the eleventh, the A's Ted Kubiak worked his way around the bases on a walk, passed ball, and single for a lead that reliever Rollie Fingers held in the bottom of the inning.

New York evened the Series on Rusty Staub's three-run homer in the first inning of Game Four (scoring three more times later for a 6–1 win). The Mets moved in front on a sparkling 2–0 three-hitter by Jerry Koosman and Tug McGraw in Game Five, but lost their edge as the Series returned to Oakland for Game Six, losing when Reggie Jackson's doubles in the first and third drove in two runs to give the A's a lead New York was unable to overtake.

Oakland made the finale look easy. Bert Campaneris and Jackson both hit two-run homers in the third inning, and Campaneris scored a fifth run two innings later before New York finally got on the board in the sixth. In the ninth inning the Mets scored a second run with two outs, but reliever Darold Knowles came on for a record seventh pitching appearance and retired the final batter for his second Series save.

Oakland Athletics (AL), 4; New York Mets (NL) 3

OAK (A)

PLAYER/POS	AVG	G	AB	R	H	2B	3B	HR	RB	BB	SO	SB
Jesus Alou, of-6	.158	7	19	0	3	1	0	0	3	0	0	0
Mike Andrews, 2b-1	.000	2	3	0	0	0	0	0	0	1	1	0
Sal Bando, 3b	.231	7	26	5	6	1	1	0	1	4	7	0
Vida Blue, p	.000	2	4	0	0	0	0	0	0	0	4	0
Pat Bourque, 1b	.500	2	2	0	1	0	0	0	0	0	0	0
Bert Campaneris, ss	.290	7	31	6	9	0	1	1	3	1	7	3
Billy Conigliaro, ph	.000	3	3	0	0	0	0	0	0	0	1	0
Vic Davalillo, of-4,1b-1	.091	6	11	0	1	0	0	0	0	2	1	0
Rollie Fingers, p	.333	6	3	0	1	0	0	0	0	0	1	0
Ray Fosse, c	.158	7	19	0	3	1	0	0	0	1	4	0
Dick Green, 2b	.063	7	16	0	1	0	0	0	0	0	6	0
Ken Holtzman, p	.667	3	3	2	2	2	0	0	0	0	0	0
Catfish Hunter, p	.000	2	5	0	0	0	0	0	0	0	3	0
Reggie Jackson, of	.310	7	29	3	9	3	1	1	6	2	7	0
Deron Johnson, 1b-2	.300	6	10	0	3	1	0	0	0	1	4	0
Darold Knowles, p	.000	7	0	0	0	0	0	0	0	0	0	0
Ted Kubiak, 2b	.000	4	3	1	0	0	0	0	0	1	1	0
Allan Lewis, pr	.000	3	0	1	0	0	0	0	0	0	0	0
Paul Lindblad, p	.000	3	1	0	0	0	0	0	0	0	0	0
Angel Mangual, of-1	.000	5	6	0	0	0	0	0	0	0	3	0
Blue Moon Odom, p-2	.000	3	1	0	0	0	0	0	0	0	1	0
Horacio Pina, p	.000	2	0	0	0	0	0	0	0	0	0	0
Joe Rudi, of	.333	7	27	3	9	2	0	0	4	3	4	0
Gene Tenace, 1b-7,c-3	.158	7	19	0	3	1	0	0	3	11	7	0
TOTAL	.212		241	21	51	12	3	2	20	28	62	3

PITCHER	W	L	ERA	G	GS	CG	SV	SHO	IP	H	ER	BB	SO
Vida Blue	0	1	4.91	2	2	0	0	0	11.0	10	6	3	8
Rollie Fingers	0	1	0.66	6	0	0	2	0	13.2	13	1	4	8
Ken Holtzman	2	1	4.22	3	3	0	0	0	10.2	13	5	5	6
Catfish Hunter	1	0	2.03	2	2	0	0	0	13.1	11	3	4	6
Darold Knowles	0	0	0.00	7	0	0	2	0	6.1	4	0	5	5
Paul Lindblad	1	0	0.00	3	0	0	0	0	3.1	4	0	1	1
Blue Moon Odom	0	0	3.86	2	0	0	0	0	4.2	5	2	2	2
Horacio Pina	0	0	0.00	2	0	0	0	0	3.0	6	0	2	0
TOTAL	4	3	2.32	27	7	0	4	0	66.0	66	17	26	36

NY (N)

PLAYER/POS	AVG	G	AB	R	H	2B	3B	HR	RB	BB	SO	SB
Jim Beauchamp, ph	.000	4	4	0	0	0	0	0	0	0	1	0
Ken Boswell, ph	1.000	3	3	1	3	0	0	0	0	0	0	0
Wayne Garrett, 3b	.167	7	30	4	5	0	0	2	2	5	11	0
Jerry Grote, c	.267	7	30	2	8	0	0	0	0	0	1	0
Don Hahn, of	.241	7	29	2	7	1	1	0	2	1	6	0
Bud Harrelson, ss	.250	7	24	2	6	1	0	0	1	5	3	0
Ron Hodges, ph	.000	1	0	0	0	0	0	0	0	1	0	0
Cleon Jones, of	.286	7	28	5	8	2	0	1	1	4	2	0
Jerry Koosman, p	.000	2	4	0	0	0	0	0	0	0	3	0
Ed Kranepool, ph	.000	4	3	0	0	0	0	0	0	0	0	0
Ted Martinez, pr	.000	2	0	0	0	0	0	0	0	0	0	0
Jon Matlack, p	.250	3	4	0	1	0	0	0	0	2	1	0
Willie Mays, of-2	.286	3	7	1	2	0	0	0	1	0	1	0
Tug McGraw, p	.333	5	3	1	1	0	0	0	0	0	0	0
Felix Millan, 2b	.188	7	32	3	6	1	1	0	1	1	1	0
John Milner, 1b	.296	7	27	2	8	0	0	0	2	5	1	0
Harry Parker, p	.000	3	0	0	0	0	0	0	0	0	0	0
Ray Sadecki, p	.000	4	0	0	0	0	0	0	0	0	0	0
Tom Seaver, p	.000	2	5	0	0	0	0	0	0	0	2	0
Rusty Staub, of	.423	7	26	1	11	2	0	1	6	2	2	0
George Stone, p	.000	2	0	0	0	0	0	0	0	0	0	0
George Theodore, of-1	.000	2	2	0	0	0	0	0	0	0	0	0
TOTAL	.253		261	24	66	7	2	4	16	26	36	0

PITCHER	W	L	ERA	G	GS	CG	SV	SHO	IP	H	ER	BB	SO
Jerry Koosman	1	0	3.12	2	2	0	0	0	8.2	9	3	7	8
Jon Matlack	1	2	2.16	3	3	0	0	0	16.2	10	4	5	11
Tug McGraw	1	0	2.63	5	0	0	1	0	13.2	13	4	9	14
Harry Parker	0	1	0.00	3	0	0	0	0	3.1	2	0	2	2
Ray Sadecki	0	0	1.93	4	0	0	1	0	4.2	5	1	1	6
Tom Seaver	0	1	2.40	2	2	0	0	0	15.0	13	4	3	18
George Stone	0	0	0.00	2	0	0	1	0	3.0	0	0	1	3
TOTAL	3	4	2.22	21	7	0	3	0	65.0	51	16	28	62

GAME 1 AT OAK OCT 13

NY	000	100	000	1	7	2
OAK	002	000	00X	2	4	0

Pitchers: MATLACK, McGraw (7) vs HOLTZMAN, Fingers (6), Knowles (9)
Attendance: 46,021

GAME 2 AT OAK OCT 14

NY	011	004	000	004	10	15	1
OAK	210	000	102	001	7	13	5

Pitchers: Koosman, Sadecki (3), Parker (5), McGRAW (6), Stone (12) vs Blue, Pina (6), Knowles (6), Odom (8), FINGERS (10), Lindblad (12)
Home Runs: Jones-NY, Garrett-NY
Attendance: 49,151

GAME 3 AT NY OCT 16

OAK	000	001	010	01	3	10	1
NY	200	000	000	00	2	10	2

Pitchers: Hunter, Knowles (7), LINDBLAD (9), Fingers (11) vs Seaver, Sadecki (9), McGraw (9), PARKER (11)
Home Runs: Garrett-NY
Attendance: 54,817

GAME 4 AT NY OCT 17

OAK	000	100	000	1	5	1
NY	300	300	00X	6	13	1

Pitchers: HOLTZMAN, Odom (1), Knowles (4), Pina (5), Lindblad (8) vs MATLACK, Sadecki (9)
Home Runs: Staub-NY
Attendance: 54,817

GAME 5 AT NY OCT 18

OAK	000	000	000	0	3	1
NY	010	001	00X	2	7	1

Pitchers: BLUE, Knowles (6), Fingers (7) vs KOOSMAN, McGraw (7)
Attendance: 54,817

GAME 6 AT OAK OCT 20

NY	000	000	010	1	6	2
OAK	101	000	01X	3	7	0

Pitchers: SEAVER, McGraw (8) vs HUNTER, Knowles (8), Fingers (8)
Attendance: 49,333

GAME 7 AT OAK OCT 21

NY	000	001	001	2	8	1
OAK	004	010	00X	5	9	1

Pitchers: MATLACK, Parker (3), Sadecki (5), Stone (7) vs HOLTZMAN, Fingers (6), Knowles (9)
Home Runs: Campaneris-OAK, Jackson-OAK
Attendance: 49,333

Dodger pitcher Don Sutton—who had brought his won-lost record from 10–9 to 19–9 with a nine-game winning streak in the regular season—continued his winning ways in the LCS, surrendering only seven hits and one run in seventeen innings and taking both the opener and clincher of the four-game series. Los Angeles's Andy Messersmith followed up Sutton's opening-game shutout with six shutout innings of his own in Game Two before Pittsburgh scored its first two runs of the series in the seventh. They tied the score, but the Dodgers countered with three more in the top of the eighth to assure their second win.

The Pirates captured their only victory in Game Three, as Richie Hebner and Willie Stargell homered for five of the Bucs' seven runs, while Bruce Kison and Ramon Hernandez shut out the Dodgers on four hits.

Pittsburgh finally got to Sutton for a run when Stargell homered in the seventh inning of Game Four. But it was too little, and too late to stem a twelve-run Dodger attack led by Steve Garvey's four hits (two of them home runs) and four RBI.

Los Angeles Dodgers (West), 3; Pittsburgh Pirates (East) 1

LA (W)

PLAYER/POS	AVG	G	AB	R	H	2B	3B	HR	RB	BB	SO	SB
Rick Auerbach, ph	1.000	1	1	0	1	1	0	0	0	0	0	0
Bill Buckner, of	.167	4	18	0	3	1	0	0	0	0	2	0
Ron Cey, 3b	.313	4	16	2	5	3	0	1	1	3	2	0
Willie Crawford, of	.250	2	4	1	1	0	0	0	1	1	1	0
Al Downing, p	.000	1	1	0	0	0	0	0	0	0	0	0
Joe Ferguson, of-3,c-2	.231	4	13	3	3	0	0	0	2	5	1	0
Steve Garvey, 1b	.389	4	18	4	7	1	0	2	5	1	1	0
Charlie Hough, p	.000	1	0	0	0	0	0	0	0	0	0	0
Von Joshua, ph	.000	1	0	0	0	0	0	0	0	1	0	0
Lee Lacy, pr	.000	1	0	0	0	0	0	0	0	0	0	0
Davey Lopes, 2b	.267	4	15	4	4	0	1	0	3	5	1	3
Mike Marshall, p	.000	2	0	0	0	0	0	0	0	0	0	0
Ken McMullen, ph	.000	1	1	0	0	0	0	0	0	0	1	0
Andy Messersmith, p	.000	1	3	0	0	0	0	0	0	0	1	0
Manny Mota, of-1	.333	3	3	0	1	0	0	0	1	0	0	0
Tom Paciorek, of	1.000	1	1	0	1	0	0	0	0	0	0	0
Doug Rau, p	.000	1	0	0	0	0	0	0	0	0	0	0
Bill Russell, ss	.389	4	18	1	7	0	0	0	3	1	0	0
Eddie Solomon, p	.000	1	0	0	0	0	0	0	0	0	0	0
Don Sutton, p	.286	2	7	0	2	0	0	0	1	1	2	0
Jimmy Wynn, of	.200	4	10	4	2	2	0	0	2	9	1	1
Steve Yeager, c	.000	3	9	1	0	0	0	0	0	3	3	1
TOTAL	.268		138	20	37	8	1	3	19	30	16	5

PITCHER	W	L	ERA	G	GS	CG	SV	SHO	IP	H	ER	BB	SO
Al Downing	0	0	0.00	1	0	0	0	0	4.0	1	0	1	0
Charlie Hough	0	0	7.71	1	0	0	0	0	2.1	4	2	0	2
Mike Marshall	0	0	0.00	2	0	0	0	0	3.0	0	0	0	1
Andy Messersmith	1	0	2.57	1	1	0	0	0	7.0	8	2	3	0
Doug Rau	0	1	40.50	1	1	0	0	0	0.2	3	3	1	0
Eddie Solomon	0	0	0.00	1	0	0	0	0	2.0	2	0	1	1
Don Sutton	2	0	0.53	2	2	1	0	1	17.0	7	1	2	13
TOTAL	3	1	2.00	9	4	1	0	1	36.0	25	8	8	17

PIT (E)

PLAYER/POS	AVG	G	AB	R	H	2B	3B	HR	RB	BB	SO	SB
Ken Brett, p	.000	1	1	0	0	0	0	0	0	0	1	0
Gene Clines, of	.000	2	1	1	0	0	0	0	0	0	0	0
Larry Demery, p	.000	2	0	0	0	0	0	0	0	0	0	0
Dave Giusti, p	.000	3	0	0	0	0	0	0	0	0	0	0
Richie Hebner, 3b	.231	4	13	1	3	0	0	1	4	1	4	0
Ramon Hernandez, p	.000	2	1	0	0	0	0	0	0	0	1	0
Art Howe, ph	.000	1	1	0	0	0	0	0	0	0	0	0
Ed Kirkpatrick, 1b	.000	3	9	0	0	0	0	0	0	2	0	0
Bruce Kison, p	.000	1	3	0	0	0	0	0	0	0	2	0
Mario Mendoza, ss	.200	3	5	0	1	0	0	0	1	1	0	0
Al Oliver, of	.143	4	14	1	2	0	0	0	1	2	2	0
Dave Parker, of-2	.125	3	8	0	1	0	0	0	0	0	1	0
Juan Pizarro, p	.000	1	0	0	0	0	0	0	0	0	0	0
Paul Popovich, ss	.600	3	5	1	3	0	0	0	0	0	0	0
Jerry Reuss, p	.000	2	2	0	0	0	0	0	0	0	0	0
Bob Robertson, 1b	.000	1	5	1	0	0	0	0	0	0	1	0
Jim Rooker, p	.500	1	2	0	1	0	0	0	0	0	0	0
Manny Sanguillen, c	.250	4	16	0	4	1	0	0	0	0	0	0
Willie Stargell, of	.400	4	15	3	6	0	0	2	4	1	2	0
Rennie Stennett, 2b	.063	4	16	1	1	0	0	0	0	1	1	0
Frank Taveras, ss	.000	2	2	0	0	0	0	0	0	0	0	1
Richie Zisk, of-2	.300	3	10	1	3	0	0	0	0	0	3	0
TOTAL	.194		129	10	25	1	0	3	10	8	17	1

PITCHER	W	L	ERA	G	GS	CG	SV	SHO	IP	H	ER	BB	SO
Ken Brett	0	0	7.71	1	0	0	0	0	2.1	3	2	2	1
Larry Demery	0	0	36.00	2	0	0	0	0	1.0	3	4	2	0
Dave Giusti	0	1	21.60	3	0	0	0	0	3.1	13	8	5	1
Ramon Hernandez	0	0	0.00	2	0	0	0	0	4.1	3	0	1	2
Bruce Kison	1	0	0.00	1	1	0	0	0	6.2	2	0	6	5
Juan Pizarro	0	0	0.00	1	0	0	0	0	0.2	0	0	1	0
Jerry Reuss	0	2	3.72	2	2	0	0	0	9.2	7	4	8	3
Jim Rooker	0	0	2.57	1	1	0	0	0	7.0	6	2	5	4
TOTAL	1	3	5.14	13	4	0	0	0	35.0	37	20	30	16

GAME 1 AT PIT OCT 5

LA	010	000	002	3	9	2
PIT	000	000	000	0	4	0

Pitchers: SUTTON vs REUSS, Giusti (8)
Attendance: 40,638

GAME 2 AT PIT OCT 6

LA	100	100	030	5	12	0
PIT	000	000	200	2	8	3

Pitchers: MESSERSMITH, Marshall (8) vs Rooker, GIUSTI (8), Demery (8), Hernandez (8)
Home Runs: Cey-LA
Attendance: 49,247

GAME 3 AT LA OCT 8

PIT	502	000	000	7	10	0
LA	000	000	000	0	4	5

Pitchers: KISON, Hernandez (7) vs RAU, Hough (1), Downing (4), Solomon (8)
Home Runs: Stargell-PIT, Hebner-PIT
Attendance: 55,953

GAME 4 AT LA OCT 9

PIT	000	000	100	1	3	1
LA	102	022	23X	12	12	0

Pitchers: REUSS, Brett (3), Demery (6), Giusti (7), Pizarro (8) vs SUTTON, Marshall (9)
Home Runs: Garvey-LA (2), Stargell-PIT
Attendance: 54,424

After spotting Baltimore a win in the opener, Oakland took the next three games and their third consecutive pennant. Although the A's got nine hits in Game One—their series high—the Orioles hit harder, burying Oakland under home runs by Paul Blair, Brooks Robinson, and Bobby Grich. In Game Two, though, Ken Holtzman shut out Baltimore on five hits as Sal Bando and Ray Fosse homered. Bando homered again in the third game for the only Oakland run as Jim Palmer limited the A's to four hits. But one run was enough to defeat Baltimore, for Vida Blue shut them out on a masterly two-hitter.

Oriole starter Mike Cuellar walked nine men in 4⅔ innings of Game Four, including four in the fifth to force in Oakland's first run. Two innings later Reggie Jackson's double (the only Oakland hit of the game) off reliever Ross Grimsley drove in Oakland's second run, while starter Catfish Hunter was blanking the O's through seven-plus innings. After failing to score for thirty consecutive innings, the Orioles got to reliever Rollie Fingers for a run with two out in the bottom of the ninth. But Fingers then struck out Don Baylor, and the A's had their pennant.

Oakland A's (West), 3;
Baltimore Orioles (East) 1

OAK (W)

PLAYER/POS	AVG	G	AB	R	H	2B	3B	HR	RB	BB	SO	SB
Jesus Alou, ph	1.000	1	1	0	1	0	0	0	0	0	0	0
Sal Bando, 3b	.231	4	13	4	3	0	0	2	2	4	0	0
Vida Blue, p	.000	1	0	0	0	0	0	0	0	0	0	0
Bert Campaneris, ss	.176	4	17	0	3	0	0	0	3	0	3	1
Rollie Fingers, p	.000	2	0	0	0	0	0	0	0	0	0	0
Ray Fosse, c	.333	4	12	1	4	1	0	1	3	1	2	0
Dick Green, 2b	.222	4	9	0	2	0	0	0	0	2	1	0
Jim Holt, 1b-1	.000	1	0	0	0	0	0	0	0	1	0	0
Ken Holtzman, p	.000	1	0	0	0	0	0	0	0	0	0	0
Catfish Hunter, p	.000	2	0	0	0	0	0	0	0	0	0	0
Reggie Jackson, dh-3,of-1	.167	4	12	0	2	1	0	0	1	5	2	0
Angel Mangual, dh	.250	1	4	0	1	0	0	0	0	0	0	0
Dal Maxvill, 2b	.000	1	1	0	0	0	0	0	0	0	1	0
Billy North, of	.063	4	16	3	1	1	0	0	0	2	1	0
Blue Moon Odom, p-1	.000	3	0	0	0	0	0	0	0	0	0	0
Joe Rudi, of	.154	4	13	0	2	0	1	0	1	3	2	0
Gene Tenace, 1b	.000	4	11	1	0	0	0	0	1	4	4	1
Manny Trillo, pr	.000	1	0	1	0	0	0	0	0	0	0	0
Claudell Washington, of-3	.273	4	11	1	3	1	0	0	0	0	0	0
Herb Washington, pr	.000	2	0	0	0	0	0	0	0	0	0	0
TOTAL	.183		120	11	22	4	1	3	11	22	16	3

PITCHER	W	L	ERA	G	GS	CG	SV	SHO	IP	H	ER	BB	SO
Vida Blue	1	0	0.00	1	1	1	0	1	9.0	2	0	0	7
Rollie Fingers	0	0	3.00	2	0	0	1	0	3.0	3	1	1	3
Ken Holtzman	1	0	0.00	1	1	1	0	1	9.0	5	0	2	3
Catfish Hunter	1	1	4.63	2	2	0	0	0	11.2	11	6	2	6
Blue Moon Odom	0	0	0.00	1	0	0	0	0	3.1	1	0	0	1
TOTAL	3	1	1.75	7	4	2	1	2	36.0	22	7	5	20

BAL (E)

PLAYER/POS	AVG	G	AB	R	H	2B	3B	HR	RB	BB	SO	SB
Frank Baker, ss	.000	2	0	0	0	0	0	0	0	0	0	0
Don Baylor, of	.267	4	15	0	4	0	0	0	0	0	2	0
Mark Belanger, ss	.000	4	9	0	0	0	0	0	0	1	3	0
Paul Blair, of	.286	4	14	3	4	0	0	1	2	2	2	0
Al Bumbry, ph	.000	2	1	0	0	0	0	0	0	0	1	0
Enos Cabell, of-1	.250	3	4	0	1	0	0	0	0	0	2	0
Rich Coggins, of	.000	3	11	0	0	0	0	0	0	0	3	0
Mike Cuellar, p	.000	2	0	0	0	0	0	0	0	0	0	0
Tommy Davis, dh	.267	4	15	0	4	0	0	0	1	0	1	0
Andy Etchebarren, c	.333	2	6	0	2	0	0	0	0	0	0	0
Wayne Garland, p	.000	1	0	0	0	0	0	0	0	0	0	0
Bobby Grich, 2b	.250	4	16	2	4	1	0	1	2	0	1	0
Ross Grimsley, p	.000	2	0	0	0	0	0	0	0	0	0	0
Elrod Hendricks, c	.167	3	6	1	1	0	0	0	0	1	3	0
Grant Jackson, p	.000	1	0	0	0	0	0	0	0	0	0	0
Dave McNally, p	.000	1	0	0	0	0	0	0	0	0	0	0
Curt Motton, ph	.000	1	1	0	0	0	0	0	0	0	0	0
Jim Palmer, p-1	.000	2	0	0	0	0	0	0	0	0	0	0
Boog Powell, 1b	.125	2	8	0	1	0	0	0	1	0	0	0
Bob Reynolds, p	.000	1	0	0	0	0	0	0	0	0	0	0
Brooks Robinson, 3b	.083	4	12	1	1	0	0	1	1	1	0	0
Earl Williams, 1b	.000	2	6	0	0	0	0	0	0	0	2	0
TOTAL	.177		124	7	22	1	0	3	7	5	20	0

PITCHER	W	L	ERA	G	GS	CG	SV	SHO	IP	H	ER	BB	SO
Mike Cuellar	1	1	2.84	2	2	0	0	0	12.2	9	4	13	6
Wayne Garland	0	0	0.00	1	0	0	0	0	0.2	0	0	1	0
Ross Grimsley	0	0	1.69	2	0	0	0	0	5.1	1	1	2	2
Grant Jackson	0	0	0.00	1	0	0	0	0	0.1	1	0	0	1
Dave McNally	0	1	1.59	1	1	0	0	0	5.2	6	1	2	2
Jim Palmer	0	1	1.00	1	1	1	0	0	9.0	4	1	1	4
Bob Reynolds	0	0	0.00	1	0	0	0	0	1.1	1	0	3	1
TOTAL	1	3	1.80	9	4	1	0	0	35.0	22	7	22	16

GAME 1 AT OAK OCT 5

BAL	100 140 000	6	10 0
OAK	001 010 001	3	9 0

Pitchers: CUELLAR, Grimsley (9) vs HUNTER, Odom (5), Fingers (9)
Home Runs: Blair-BAL, Robinson-BAL, Grich-BAL
Attendance: 41,609

GAME 2 AT OAK OCT 6

BAL	000 000 000	0	5 2
OAK	000 101 03X	5	8 0

Pitchers: McNALLY, Garland (6), Reynolds (7), G.Jackson (8) vs HOLTZMAN
Home Runs: Bando-OAK, Fosse-OAK
Attendance: 42,810

GAME 3 AT BAL OCT 8

OAK	000 100 000	1	4 2
BAL	000 000 000	0	2 1

Pitchers: BLUE vs PALMER
Home Runs: Bando-OAK
Attendance: 32,060

GAME 4 AT BAL OCT 9

OAK	000 010 100	2	1 0
BAL	000 000 001	1	5 1

Pitchers: HUNTER, Fingers (8) vs CUELLAR, Grimsley (5)
Attendance: 28,136

Although the A's were in a turmoil of dislike for owner Charlie Finley—and for each other—they played well enough together to take their third consecutive world championship in just five games. Still, victory didn't come easily, as three of Oakland's wins came by identical 3–2 scores (as did the Dodgers' one victory), and their biggest winning margin was three runs in Game Four. It was the first World Series held entirely on the West Coast.

The A's and Dodgers split the first two games in Los Angeles. Oakland won the opener on the strength of Reggie Jackson's home run in the second inning, pitcher Ken Holtzman's double in the fifth (he moved around on a wild pitch and squeeze bunt), and a Dodger throwing error in the eighth. The Dodgers evened the Series on Joe Ferguson's two-run homer in the sixth inning of the second game, which gave Los Angeles a 3–0 lead that an Oakland rally in the ninth failed to catch.

Los Angeles outhit Oakland in Game Three, but two of the A's runs were unearned, coming after Dodger catcher Ferguson bobbled what should have been a third-out play in the third inning.

Pitcher Ken Holtzman, who had now gone two regular seasons without a time at bat, produced in Game Four his second hit of the Series, this one a homer in the third inning for the game's first run. The Dodgers' Bill Russell tripled off him for two runs a half inning later, but in the last of the sixth inning Oakland regained the lead on three walks interspersed with a pair of singles and an RBI grounder to short. Four runs scored—more in this one inning than either team scored in any of the other four games.

Oakland took an early 2–0 lead in Game Five, with single runs in the first and second innings (the latter a Ray Fosse home run). The Dodgers put together a pinch-hit double, a walk, a pair of sacrifices (bunt and fly), and a single to tie the score in the sixth. But Joe Rudi hit the first pitch of Oakland's half of the seventh into the stands in left for the run that decided the game and the Series.

Oakland Athletics (AL), 4; Los Angeles Dodgers (NL) 1

OAK (A)

PLAYER/POS	AVG	G	AB	R	H	2B	3B	HR	RB	BB	SO	SB
Jesus Alou, ph	.000	1	1	0	0	0	0	0	0	0	1	0
Sal Bando, 3b	.063	5	16	3	1	0	0	0	2	2	5	0
Vida Blue, p	.000	2	4	0	0	0	0	0	0	0	4	0
Bert Campaneris, ss	.353	5	17	1	6	2	0	0	2	0	2	1
Rollie Fingers, p	.000	4	2	0	0	0	0	0	0	0	1	0
Ray Fosse, c	.143	5	14	1	2	0	0	1	1	1	5	0
Dick Green, 2b	.000	5	13	1	0	0	0	0	1	1	4	0
Larry Haney, c	.000	2	0	0	0	0	0	0	0	0	0	0
Jim Holt, 1b-1	.667	4	3	0	2	0	0	0	2	0	0	0
Ken Holtzman, p	.500	2	4	2	2	1	0	1	1	1	1	0
Catfish Hunter, p	.000	2	2	0	0	0	0	0	0	0	0	0
Reggie Jackson, of	.286	5	14	3	4	1	0	1	1	5	3	1
Angel Mangual, ph	.000	1	1	0	0	0	0	0	0	0	1	0
Dal Maxvill, 2b	.000	2	0	0	0	0	0	0	0	0	0	0
Billy North, of	.059	5	17	3	1	0	0	0	0	2	5	1
Blue Moon Odom, p	.000	2	0	0	0	0	0	0	0	0	0	0
Joe Rudi, of-5,1b-2	.333	5	18	1	6	0	0	1	4	0	3	0
Gene Tenace, 1b	.222	5	9	0	2	0	0	0	0	3	4	0
Claudell Washington, of	.571	5	7	1	4	0	0	0	0	0	1	0
Herb Washington, pr	.000	3	0	0	0	0	0	0	0	0	0	0
TOTAL	.211		142	16	30	4	0	4	14	16	42	3

PITCHER	W	L	ERA	G	GS	CG	SV	SHO	IP	H	ER	BB	SO
Vida Blue	0	1	3.29	2	2	0	0	0	13.2	10	5	7	9
Rollie Fingers	1	0	1.93	4	0	0	2	0	9.1	8	2	2	6
Ken Holtzman	1	0	1.50	2	2	0	0	0	12.0	13	2	4	10
Catfish Hunter	1	0	1.17	2	1	0	1	0	7.2	5	1	2	5
Blue Moon Odom	1	0	0.00	2	0	0	0	0	1.1	0	0	1	2
TOTAL	4	1	2.05	12	5	0	3	0	44.0	36	10	16	32

LA (N)

PLAYER/POS	AVG	G	AB	R	H	2B	3B	HR	RB	BB	SO	SB
Rick Auerbach, pr	.000	1	0	0	0	0	0	0	0	0	0	0
Jim Brewer, p	.000	1	0	0	0	0	0	0	0	0	0	0
Bill Buckner, of	.250	5	20	1	5	1	0	1	1	0	1	0
Ron Cey, 3b	.176	5	17	1	3	0	0	0	0	3	3	0
Willie Crawford, of-2	.333	3	6	1	2	0	0	1	1	0	0	0
Al Downing, p	.000	1	0	0	0	0	0	0	0	0	0	0
Joe Ferguson, of-4,c-2	.125	5	16	2	2	0	0	1	2	4	6	1
Steve Garvey, 1b	.381	5	21	2	8	0	0	0	1	0	3	0
Charlie Hough, p	.000	1	0	0	0	0	0	0	0	0	0	0
Von Joshua, ph	.000	4	4	0	0	0	0	0	0	0	0	0
Lee Lacy, ph	.000	1	1	0	0	0	0	0	0	0	0	0
Davey Lopes, 2b	.111	5	18	2	2	0	0	0	0	3	4	2
Mike Marshall, p	.000	5	0	0	0	0	0	0	0	1	0	0
Andy Messersmith, p	.500	2	4	0	2	0	0	0	0	0	0	0
Tom Paciorek, ph	.500	3	2	1	1	1	0	0	0	0	0	0
Bill Russell, ss	.222	5	18	0	4	0	1	0	2	0	2	0
Don Sutton, p	.000	2	3	0	0	0	0	0	0	0	2	0
Jimmy Wynn, of	.188	5	16	1	3	1	0	1	2	4	4	0
Steve Yeager, c	.364	4	11	0	4	1	0	0	1	1	4	0
TOTAL	.228		158	11	36	4	1	4	10	16	32	3

PITCHER	W	L	ERA	G	GS	CG	SV	SHO	IP	H	ER	BB	SO
Jim Brewer	0	0	0.00	1	0	0	0	0	0.1	0	0	0	1
Al Downing	0	1	2.45	1	1	0	0	0	3.2	4	1	4	3
Charlie Hough	0	0	0.00	1	0	0	0	0	2.0	0	0	1	4
Mike Marshall	0	1	1.00	5	0	0	1	0	9.0	6	1	1	10
Andy Messersmith	0	2	4.50	2	2	0	0	0	14.0	11	7	7	12
Don Sutton	1	0	2.77	2	2	0	0	0	13.0	9	4	3	12
TOTAL	1	4	2.79	12	5	0	1	0	42.0	30	13	16	42

GAME 1 AT LA OCT 12

OAK	010 010 010	3	6	2
LA	000 010 001	2	11	1

Pitchers: Holtzman, FINGERS (5), Hunter (9) vs MESSERSMITH, Marshall (9)
Home Runs: Jackson-OAK, Wynn-LA
Attendance: 55,974

GAME 2 AT LA OCT 13

OAK	000 000 002	2	6	0
LA	010 002 00X	3	6	1

Pitchers: BLUE, Odom (8) vs SUTTON, Marshall (9)
Home Runs: Ferguson-LA
Attendance: 55,989

GAME 3 AT OAK OCT 15

LA	000 000 011	2	7	2
OAK	002 100 00X	3	5	2

Pitchers: DOWNING, Brewer (4), Hough (5), Marshall (7) vs HUNTER, Fingers (8)
Home Runs: Buckner-LA, Crawford-LA
Attendance: 49,347

GAME 4 AT OAK OCT 16

LA	000 200 000	2	7	1
OAK	001 004 00X	5	7	0

Pitchers: MESSERSMITH, Marshall (7) vs HOLTZMAN, Fingers (8)
Home Runs: Holtzman-OAK
Attendance: 49,347

GAME 5 AT OAK OCT 17

LA	000 002 000	2	5	1
OAK	110 000 10X	3	6	1

Pitchers: Sutton, MARSHALL (6) vs Blue, ODOM (7), Fingers (8)
Home Runs: Fosse-OAK, Rudi-OAK
Attendance: 49,347

The Reds, who had steamrolled the National League during the season, continued their roll in the LCS. Red pitcher Don Gullett gave up three Pirate runs in the first game, but he drove in three himself with a home run and a single. Pitching the series' only complete game, he won easily behind his club's twelve-hit, eight-run attack. The Reds won just as handily in Game Two, with Fred Norman and reliever Rawley Eastwick holding the Pirates to one run as Tony Perez drove in half the Reds' six runs—two of them with a first-inning homer.

In Game Three the Pirates struggled gamely against elimination. Cincinnati scored first in the second, but in the sixth Al Oliver put Pittsburgh ahead with a two-run homer. In the eighth, though, Pete Rose restored the Reds' lead (and nullified rookie John Candelaria's fourteen-strikeout effort over 7⅔ innings) with his two-run shot. The Pirates were granted a brief reprieve when Red reliever Eastwick walked in the tying run in the bottom of the ninth. But in the tenth the Reds scored twice on three hits, and when Eastwick's replacement Pedro Borbon shut the Pirates down in the bottom of the tenth, Cincinnati had its series sweep.

Cincinnati Reds (West), 3; Pittsburgh Pirates (East) 0

CIN (W)

PLAYER/POS	AVG	G	AB	R	H	2B	3B	HR	RB	BB	SO	SB
Ed Armbrister, ph	.000	2	0	0	0	0	0	0	0	1	0	0
Johnny Bench, c	.077	3	13	1	1	0	0	0	0	1	6	1
Pedro Borbon, p	.000	1	0	0	0	0	0	0	0	0	0	0
Clay Carroll, p	.000	1	0	0	0	0	0	0	0	0	0	0
Dave Concepcion, ss	.455	3	11	2	5	0	0	1	1	1	2	2
Terry Crowley, ph	.000	1	0	0	0	0	0	0	0	0	0	0
Rawly Eastwick, p	.000	2	0	0	0	0	0	0	0	0	0	0
George Foster, of	.364	3	11	3	4	0	0	0	0	1	2	1
Cesar Geronimo, of	.000	3	10	0	0	0	0	0	1	1	7	0
Ken Griffey, of	.333	3	12	3	4	1	0	0	4	0	3	3
Don Gullett, p	.500	1	4	1	2	0	0	1	3	0	0	0
Will McEnaney, p	.000	1	0	0	0	0	0	0	0	0	0	0
Joe Morgan, 2b	.273	3	11	2	3	3	0	0	1	3	2	4
Gary Nolan, p	.000	1	2	0	0	0	0	0	0	0	0	0
Fred Norman, p	.000	1	0	0	0	0	0	0	0	1	0	0
Tony Perez, 1b	.417	3	12	3	5	0	0	1	4	1	2	0
Merv Rettenmund, ph	.000	2	1	1	0	0	0	0	0	1	0	0
Pete Rose, 3b	.357	3	14	3	5	0	0	1	2	2	0	0
TOTAL	.284		102	19	29	4	0	4	18	9	28	11

PITCHER	W	L	ERA	G	GS	CG	SV	SHO	IP	H	ER	BB	SO
Pedro Borbon	0	0	0.00	1	0	0	1	0	1.0	0	0	0	1
Clay Carroll	0	0	0.00	1	0	0	0	0	1.0	0	0	1	1
Rawly Eastwick	1	0	0.00	2	0	0	1	0	3.2	2	0	2	1
Don Gullett	1	0	3.00	1	1	1	0	0	9.0	8	3	2	5
Will McEnaney	0	0	6.75	1	0	0	0	0	1.1	1	1	0	1
Gary Nolan	0	0	3.00	1	1	0	0	0	6.0	5	2	0	5
Fred Norman	1	0	1.50	1	1	0	0	0	6.0	4	1	5	4
TOTAL	3	0	2.25	8	3	1	2	0	28.0	20	7	10	18

PIT (E)

PLAYER/POS	AVG	G	AB	R	H	2B	3B	HR	RB	BB	SO	SB
Ken Brett, p	.000	2	0	0	0	0	0	0	0	0	0	0
John Candelaria, p	.000	1	3	0	0	0	0	0	0	0	3	0
Larry Demery, p	.000	1	0	0	0	0	0	0	0	0	0	0
Duffy Dyer, ph	.000	1	0	0	0	0	0	0	0	1	1	0
Dock Ellis, p	.000	1	0	0	0	0	0	0	0	0	0	0
Dave Giusti, p	.000	1	0	0	0	0	0	0	0	0	0	0
Richie Hebner, 3b	.333	3	12	2	4	1	0	0	2	1	1	0
Ramon Hernandez, p	.000	1	0	0	0	0	0	0	0	0	0	0
Ed Kirkpatrick, ph	.000	2	2	0	0	0	0	0	0	0	0	0
Bruce Kison, p	.000	1	0	0	0	0	0	0	0	0	0	0
Al Oliver, of	.182	3	11	1	2	0	0	1	2	2	0	0
Dave Parker, of	.000	3	10	2	0	0	0	0	0	1	3	0
Willie Randolph, 2b-1	.000	2	2	1	0	0	0	0	0	0	1	0
Jerry Reuss, p	.000	1	1	0	0	0	0	0	0	0	0	0
Craig Reynolds, ss-1	.000	2	1	0	0	0	0	0	0	0	0	0
Bob Robertson, 1b-1	.500	3	2	0	1	0	0	0	1	1	0	0
Bill Robinson, ph	.000	2	2	0	0	0	0	0	0	0	1	0
Jim Rooker, p	.000	1	1	0	0	0	0	0	0	0	1	0
Manny Sanguillen, c	.167	3	12	0	2	0	0	0	0	0	0	0
Willie Stargell, 1b	.182	3	11	1	2	1	0	0	0	1	3	0
Rennie Stennett, 2b-3,ss-1	.214	3	14	0	3	0	0	0	0	0	1	0
Frank Taveras, ss	.143	3	7	0	1	0	0	0	1	1	2	0
Kent Tekulve, p	.000	2	0	0	0	0	0	0	0	0	0	0
Richie Zisk, of	.500	3	10	0	5	1	0	0	0	2	2	0
TOTAL	.198		101	7	20	3	0	1	7	10	18	0

PITCHER	W	L	ERA	G	GS	CG	SV	SHO	IP	H	ER	BB	SO
Ken Brett	0	0	0.00	2	0	0	0	0	2.1	1	0	0	1
John Candelaria	0	0	3.52	1	1	0	0	0	7.2	3	3	2	14
Larry Demery	0	0	18.00	1	0	0	0	0	2.0	4	4	1	1
Dock Ellis	0	0	0.00	1	0	0	0	0	2.0	2	0	0	2
Dave Giusti	0	0	0.00	1	0	0	0	0	1.1	0	0	0	1
Ramon Hernandez	0	1	27.00	1	0	0	0	0	0.2	3	2	0	0
Bruce Kison	0	0	4.50	1	0	0	0	0	2.0	2	1	1	1
Jerry Reuss	0	1	13.50	1	1	0	0	0	2.2	4	4	4	1
Jim Rooker	0	1	9.00	1	1	0	0	0	4.0	7	4	0	5
Kent Tekulve	0	0	6.75	2	0	0	0	0	1.1	3	1	1	2
TOTAL	0	3	6.58	12	3	0	0	0	26.0	29	19	9	28

GAME 1 AT CIN OCT 4

PIT	020	000	001	3	8	0
CIN	013	040	00X	8	11	0

Pitchers: REUSS, Brett (3), Demery (5), Ellis (7) vs GULLETT
Home Runs: Gullett-CIN
Attendance: 54,633

GAME 2 AT CIN OCT 5

PIT	000	100	000	1	5	0
CIN	200	201	10X	6	12	1

Pitchers: ROOKER, Tekulve (5), Brett (6), Kison (7) vs NORMAN, Eastwick (7)
Home Runs: Perez-CIN
Attendance: 54,752

GAME 3 AT PIT OCT 7

CIN	010	000	020	2	5	6	0
PIT	000	002	001	0	3	7	2

Pitchers: NOLAN, C.Carroll (7), McEnaney (8), EASTWICK (9), Borbon (10) vs Candelaria, Giusti (8), HERNANDEZ (10), Tekulve (10)
Home Runs: Concepcion-CIN, Oliver-PIT, Rose-CIN
Attendance: 46,355

The Oakland A's ran their domination of the American League West to five years, but an aroused Boston team stifled their try for a fourth straight pennant.

In the first game Luis Tiant held Oakland to three hits as his teammates—aided by four Oakland errors—scored seven times before giving the A's an unearned run in the eighth. Oakland scored first in Game Two on Reggie Jackson's two-run homer in the first inning and added a run in the fourth. But Carl Yastrzemski's two-run shot in the last of the fourth, followed by a Carlton Fisk double and a Fred Lynn single, drove out A's starter Vida Blue, and the tying run scored on a double play. Single Boston runs in the sixth, seventh, and eighth put the game away.

The A's started Ken Holtzman for the second time in Game Three, after only two days of rest. He held the Sox scoreless for three innings, but was driven from the game in the fifth. Boston scored four times before Oakland put a run on the board, and retained the lead to the game's conclusion.

Boston Red Sox (East), 3;
Oakland A's (West) 0

BOS (E)

PLAYER/POS	AVG	G	AB	R	H	2B	3B	HR	RB	BB	SO	SB
Juan Beniquez, dh	.250	3	12	2	3	0	0	0	1	0	1	2
Rick Burleson, ss	.444	3	9	2	4	2	0	0	1	1	0	0
Reggie Cleveland, p	.000	1	0	0	0	0	0	0	0	0	0	0
Cecil Cooper, 1b	.400	3	10	0	4	2	0	0	1	0	2	0
Denny Doyle, 2b	.273	3	11	3	3	0	0	0	1	0	1	0
Dick Drago, p	.000	2	0	0	0	0	0	0	0	0	0	0
Dwight Evans, of	.100	3	10	1	1	1	0	0	1	1	2	0
Carlton Fisk, c	.417	3	12	4	5	1	0	0	2	0	2	1
Fred Lynn, of	.364	3	11	1	4	1	0	0	3	0	0	0
Roger Moret, p	.000	1	0	0	0	0	0	0	0	0	0	0
Rico Petrocelli, 3b	.167	3	12	1	2	0	0	1	2	0	3	0
Luis Tiant, p	.000	1	0	0	0	0	0	0	0	0	0	0
Rick Wise, p	.000	1	0	0	0	0	0	0	0	0	0	0
Carl Yastrzemski, of	.455	3	11	4	5	1	0	1	2	1	1	0
TOTAL	.316		98	18	31	8	0	2	14	3	12	3

PITCHER	W	L	ERA	G	GS	CG	SV	SHO	IP	H	ER	BB	SO
Reggie Cleveland	0	0	5.40	1	1	0	0	0	5.0	7	3	1	2
Dick Drago	0	0	0.00	2	0	0	2	0	4.2	2	0	1	2
Roger Moret	1	0	0.00	1	0	0	0	0	1.0	1	0	1	0
Luis Tiant	1	0	0.00	1	1	1	0	0	9.0	3	0	3	8
Rick Wise	1	0	2.45	1	1	0	0	0	7.1	6	2	3	2
TOTAL	3	0	1.67	6	3	1	2	0	27.0	19	5	9	14

OAK (W)

PLAYER/POS	AVG	G	AB	R	H	2B	3B	HR	RB	BB	SO	SB
Glenn Abbott, p	.000	1	0	0	0	0	0	0	0	0	0	0
Sal Bando, 3b	.500	3	12	1	6	2	0	0	2	0	3	0
Vida Blue, p	.000	1	0	0	0	0	0	0	0	0	0	0
Dick Bosman, p	.000	1	0	0	0	0	0	0	0	0	0	0
Bert Campaneris, ss	.000	3	11	1	0	0	0	0	0	1	1	0
Rollie Fingers, p	.000	1	0	0	0	0	0	0	0	0	0	0
Ray Fosse, c	.000	1	2	0	0	0	0	0	0	0	1	0
Phil Garner, 2b	.000	3	5	0	0	0	0	0	0	0	1	0
Tommy Harper, ph	.000	1	0	0	0	0	0	0	0	1	0	0
Jim Holt, 1b-1	.333	3	3	0	1	1	0	0	0	0	0	0
Ken Holtzman, p	.000	2	0	0	0	0	0	0	0	0	0	0
Don Hopkins, dh	.000	1	0	0	0	0	0	0	0	0	0	0
Reggie Jackson, of	.417	3	12	1	5	0	0	1	3	0	2	0
Paul Lindblad, p	.000	2	0	0	0	0	0	0	0	0	0	0
Ted Martinez, 2b	.000	3	0	0	0	0	0	0	0	0	0	0
Billy North, of	.000	3	10	0	0	0	0	0	0	1	2	0
Joe Rudi, 1b-2,of-1	.250	3	12	1	3	2	0	0	0	0	1	0
Gene Tenace, c-3,1b-1	.000	3	9	0	0	0	0	0	0	3	2	0
Jim Todd, p	.000	3	0	0	0	0	0	0	0	0	0	0
Cesar Tovar, 2b-1	.500	2	2	1	1	0	0	0	0	1	0	0
Claudell Washington, of-2,dh-1	.250	3	12	1	3	1	0	0	1	0	2	0
Billy Williams, dh-2	.000	3	8	0	0	0	0	0	0	1	1	0
TOTAL	.194		98	7	19	6	0	1	7	9	14	0

PITCHER	W	L	ERA	G	GS	CG	SV	SHO	IP	H	ER	BB	SO
Glenn Abbott	0	0	0.00	1	0	0	0	0	1.0	0	0	0	0
Vida Blue	0	0	9.00	1	1	0	0	0	3.0	6	3	0	2
Dick Bosman	0	0	0.00	1	0	0	0	0	0.1	0	0	0	0
Rollie Fingers	0	1	6.75	1	0	0	0	0	4.0	5	3	1	3
Ken Holtzman	0	2	4.09	2	2	0	0	0	11.0	12	5	1	7
Paul Lindblad	0	0	0.00	2	0	0	0	0	4.2	5	0	1	0
Jim Todd	0	0	9.00	3	0	0	0	0	1.0	3	1	0	0
TOTAL	0	3	4.32	11	3	0	0	0	25.0	31	12	3	12

The Red Sox entered the Series as underdogs to the mighty Reds, who had won 108 regular-season games. In the opening game, though, the Reds were surprised by veteran Sox starter Luis Tiant, who shut them out on five hits with the Series' first complete-game pitching effort in four years. Tiant also opened the Boston seventh with a single, starting a rally that ended only when he fouled out to end the inning after six runs had scored.

Boston took a 2–1 lead into the ninth inning of Game Two before Johnny Bench doubled to drive out starter Bill Lee, and Dave Concepcion and Ken Griffey drove in runs off reliever Dick Drago to turn the tide for Cincinnati. The Reds moved ahead in the Series with a tenth-inning victory in Game Three, a slugfest in which each club hit three home runs and used five pitchers. Boston tied the score on Dwight Evans's two-run homer in the ninth, but in the last of the tenth, the Reds' Joe Morgan drove one over the center fielder's head with the bases full to end the game.

Tiant pitched Game Four for Boston. Four of the nine hits against him went for extra bases, and each drove in a run. But the Sox bunched six of their eleven hits in the fourth inning for five runs—their only scoring, but enough for the win. Tiant himself scored the fifth run after singling. The Reds moved nearer the title in Game Five, though, as Tony Perez homered twice for four runs in a 6–2 win for a 3–2 Series advantage.

A day of travel to Boston and three days of rain between Games Five and Six brought Tiant back to the mound for a third time. Rookie standout Fred Lynn gave Tiant a three-run lead with a first-inning homer, but Ken Griffey's triple and Johnny Bench's long single drove in the tying Red runs in the fifth. Two more Red runs in the seventh and Cesar Geronimo's leadoff homer in the eighth drove out Tiant, but Boston pinch hitter Bernie Carbo homered to center in the last of the eighth for three runs that tied the score again. After a trio of Boston relievers had held Cincinnati in check through the top of the twelfth inning, the Sox leadoff hitter in the last of the twelfth, Carlton Fisk, ended the game dramatically with a home run to left on the first pitch that came within inches of being foul.

After the pyrotechnics of Game Six (ranked by some as the greatest World Series game ever), the seventh game, close as it was, came as an anticlimax. Boston scored three runs in the third inning, but the Reds began their comeback with

Cincinnati Reds (NL), 4;
Boston Red Sox (AL) 3

CIN (N)

PLAYER/POS	AVG	G	AB	R	H	2B	3B	HR	RB	BB	SO	SB
Ed Armbrister, ph	.000	4	1	1	0	0	0	0	0	2	0	0
Johnny Bench, c	.207	7	29	5	6	2	0	1	4	2	4	0
Jack Billingham, p	.000	3	2	0	0	0	0	0	0	0	0	0
Pedro Borbon, p	.000	3	1	0	0	0	0	0	0	0	0	0
Clay Carroll, p	.000	5	0	0	0	0	0	0	0	0	0	0
Darrel Chaney, ph	.000	2	2	0	0	0	0	0	0	0	1	0
Dave Concepcion, ss	.179	7	28	3	5	1	0	1	4	0	1	3
Terry Crowley, ph	.500	2	2	0	1	0	0	0	0	0	1	0
Pat Darcy, p	.000	2	1	0	0	0	0	0	0	0	1	0
Dan Driessen, ph	.000	2	2	0	0	0	0	0	0	0	0	0
Rawly Eastwick, p	.000	5	1	0	0	0	0	0	0	0	0	0
George Foster, of	.276	7	29	1	8	1	0	0	2	1	1	1
Cesar Geronimo, of	.280	7	25	3	7	0	1	2	3	3	5	0
Ken Griffey, of	.269	7	26	4	7	3	1	0	4	4	2	2
Don Gullett, p	.286	3	7	1	2	0	0	0	0	0	2	0
Will McEnaney, p	1.000	5	1	0	1	0	0	0	0	0	0	0
Joe Morgan, 2b	.259	7	27	4	7	1	0	0	3	5	1	2
Gary Nolan, p	.000	2	1	0	0	0	0	0	0	0	0	0
Fred Norman, p	.000	2	1	0	0	0	0	0	0	0	0	0
Tony Perez, 1b	.179	7	28	4	5	0	0	3	7	3	9	1
Merv Rettenmund, ph	.000	3	3	0	0	0	0	0	0	0	1	0
Pete Rose, 3b	.370	7	27	3	10	1	1	0	2	5	1	0
TOTAL	.242		244	29	59	9	3	7	29	25	30	9

PITCHER	W	L	ERA	G	GS	CG	SV	SHO	IP	H	ER	BB	SO
Jack Billingham	0	0	1.00	3	1	0	0	0	9.0	8	1	5	7
Pedro Borbon	0	0	6.00	3	0	0	0	0	3.0	3	2	2	1
Clay Carroll	1	0	3.18	5	0	0	0	0	5.2	4	2	2	3
Pat Darcy	0	1	4.50	2	0	0	0	0	4.0	3	2	2	1
Rawly Eastwick	2	0	2.25	5	0	0	1	0	8.0	6	2	3	4
Don Gullett	1	1	4.34	3	3	0	0	0	18.2	19	9	10	15
Will McEnaney	0	0	2.70	5	0	0	1	0	6.2	3	2	2	5
Gary Nolan	0	0	6.00	2	2	0	0	0	6.0	6	4	1	2
Fred Norman	0	1	9.00	2	1	0	0	0	4.0	8	4	3	2
TOTAL	4	3	3.88	30	7	0	2	0	65.0	60	28	30	40

BOS (A)

PLAYER/POS	AVG	G	AB	R	H	2B	3B	HR	RB	BB	SO	SB
Juan Beniquez, of-2	.125	3	8	0	1	0	0	0	0	1	1	0
Rick Burleson, ss	.292	7	24	1	7	1	0	0	2	4	2	0
Jim Burton, p	.000	2	0	0	0	0	0	0	0	0	0	0
Bernie Carbo, of-2	.429	4	7	3	3	1	0	2	4	1	1	0
Reggie Cleveland, p	.000	3	2	0	0	0	0	0	0	0	2	0
Cecil Cooper, 1b	.053	5	19	0	1	1	0	0	1	0	3	0
Denny Doyle, 2b	.267	7	30	3	8	1	1	0	0	2	1	0
Dick Drago, p	.000	2	0	0	0	0	0	0	0	0	0	0
Dwight Evans, of	.292	7	24	3	7	1	1	1	5	3	4	0
Carlton Fisk, c	.240	7	25	5	6	0	0	2	4	7	7	0
Doug Griffin, ph	.000	1	1	0	0	0	0	0	0	0	0	0
Bill Lee, p	.167	2	6	0	1	0	0	0	0	0	3	0
Fred Lynn, of	.280	7	25	3	7	1	0	1	5	3	5	0
Rick Miller, of-2	.000	3	2	0	0	0	0	0	0	0	0	0
Bob Montgomery, ph	.000	1	1	0	0	0	0	0	0	0	0	0
Roger Moret, p	.000	3	0	0	0	0	0	0	0	0	0	0
Rico Petrocelli, 3b	.308	7	26	3	8	1	0	0	4	3	6	0
Dick Pole, p	.000	1	0	0	0	0	0	0	0	0	0	0
Diego Segui, p	.000	1	0	0	0	0	0	0	0	0	0	0
Luis Tiant, p	.250	3	8	2	2	0	0	0	0	0	4	0
Jim Willoughby, p	.000	3	0	0	0	0	0	0	0	0	0	0
Rick Wise, p	.000	2	2	0	0	0	0	0	0	0	0	0
Carl Yastrzemski, 1b-4,of-4	.310	7	29	7	9	0	0	0	4	4	1	0
TOTAL	.251		239	30	60	7	2	6	30	30	40	0

PITCHER	W	L	ERA	G	GS	CG	SV	SHO	IP	H	ER	BB	SO
Jim Burton	0	1	9.00	2	0	0	0	0	1.0	1	1	3	0
Reggie Cleveland	0	1	6.75	3	1	0	0	0	6.2	7	5	3	5
Dick Drago	0	1	2.25	2	0	0	0	0	4.0	3	1	1	1
Bill Lee	0	0	3.14	2	2	0	0	0	14.1	12	5	3	7
Roger Moret	0	0	0.00	3	0	0	0	0	1.2	2	0	3	1
Dick Pole	0	0	INF	1	0	0	0	0	0.0	0	1	2	0
Diego Segui	0	0	0.00	1	0	0	0	0	1.0	0	0	0	0
Luis Tiant	2	0	3.60	3	3	2	0	1	25.0	25	10	8	12
Jim Willoughby	0	1	0.00	3	0	0	0	0	6.1	3	0	0	2
Rick Wise	1	0	8.44	2	1	0	0	0	5.1	6	5	2	2
TOTAL	3	4	3.86	22	7	2	0	1	65.1	59	28	25	30

Tony Perez's two-run homer in the sixth, tied the game an inning later, and took a 4–3 lead on Joe Morgan's bloop RBI single in the ninth. Red reliever Will McEnaney came on to set the Sox down in order in the last of the ninth, and the Reds went home with their first world title in thirty-five years.

GAME 1 AT BOS OCT 11

CIN	000 000 000	0	5	0
BOS	000 000 60X	6	12	0

Pitchers: GULLETT, Carroll (7), McEnaney (7) vs TIANT
Attendance: 35,205

GAME 2 AT BOS OCT 12

CIN	000 100 002	3	7	1
BOS	100 001 000	2	7	0

Pitchers: Billingham, Borbon (6), McEnaney (7), EASTWICK (8) vs Lee, Drago (9)
Attendance: 35,205

GAME 3 AT CIN OCT 14

BOS	010 001 102 0	5	10	2
CIN	000 230 000 1	6	7	0

Pitchers: Wise, Burton (5), Cleveland (5), WILLOUGHBY (7), Moret (10) vs Nolan, Darcy (5), Carroll (7), McEnaney (7), EASTWICK (9)
Home Runs: Fisk-BOS, Bench-CIN, Concepcion-CIN, Geronimo-CIN, Carbo-BOS, Evans-BOS
Attendance: 55,392

GAME 4 AT CIN OCT 15

BOS	000 500 000	5	11	1
CIN	200 200 000	4	9	1

Pitchers: TIANT vs NORMAN, Borbon (4), Carroll (5), Eastwick (7)
Attendance: 55,667

GAME 5 AT CIN OCT 16

BOS	100 000 001	2	5	0
CIN	000 113 01X	6	8	0

Pitchers: CLEVELAND, Willoughby (6), Pole (8), Segui (8) vs GULLETT, Eastwick (9)
Home Runs: Perez-CIN (2)
Attendance: 56,393

GAME 6 AT BOS OCT 21

CIN	000 030 210 000	6	14	0
BOS	300 000 030 001	7	10	1

Pitchers: Nolan, Norman (3), Billingham (3), Carroll (5), Borbon (6), Eastwick (8), McEnaney (9), DARCY (10) vs Tiant, Moret (8), Drago (9), WISE (12)
Home Runs: Lynn-BOS, Geronimo-CIN, Carbo-BOS, Fisk-BOS
Attendance: 35,205

GAME 7 AT BOS OCT 22

CIN	000 002 101	4	9	0
BOS	003 000 000	3	5	2

Pitchers: Gullett, Billingham (5), CARROLL (7), McEnaney (9) vs Lee, Moret (7), Willoughby (7), BURTON (9), Cleveland (9)
Home Runs: Perez-CIN
Attendance: 35,205

Philadelphia outhit Cincinnati in two of the three games, but couldn't turn enough hits into runs, as the Reds for the second year in a row swept the LCS. The Phillies scored first in Game One with a run in the first inning. But pitcher Don Gullett held them scoreless for the next seven innings as his Reds caught up in the third, moved ahead in the sixth, and took a five-run lead into the last of the ninth. The Phillies scored twice in their half of the inning, but the rally fell short.

In the second game the Phillies outhit the Reds ten to six, scoring the game's first two runs while their starter Jim Lonborg threw a no-hitter for five innings. But in the sixth a walk and two singles drove Lonborg out and set the Reds off on a two-inning six-run spree for their second win.

Again in Game Three the Phillies outhit the Reds, this time going into the last of the ninth ahead by two runs. But George Foster and Johnny Bench hit back-to-back homers off Ron Reed to tie the score, and two relievers (and a single and two walks) later, the Reds brought home another pennant as Ken Griffey's high-bouncing chop glanced off first baseman Bobby Tolan's outstretched glove.

Cincinnati Reds (West), 3; Philadelphia Phillies (East) 0

CIN (W)

PLAYER/POS	AVG	G	AB	R	H	2B	3B	HR	RB	BB	SO	SB
Ed Armbrister, ph	.000	1	0	0	0	0	0	0	0	0	0	0
Johnny Bench, c	.333	3	12	3	4	1	0	1	1	1	2	1
Pedro Borbon, p	.000	2	2	1	0	0	0	0	0	0	2	0
Dave Concepcion, ss	.200	3	10	4	2	1	0	0	0	2	1	0
Dan Driessen, ph	.000	1	1	0	0	0	0	0	0	0	0	0
Rawly Eastwick, p	.000	2	0	0	0	0	0	0	0	0	0	0
Doug Flynn, 2b	.000	1	0	0	0	0	0	0	0	0	0	0
George Foster, of	.167	3	12	2	2	0	0	2	4	0	4	0
Cesar Geronimo, of	.182	3	11	0	2	0	1	0	2	1	3	0
Ken Griffey, of	.385	3	13	2	5	0	1	0	2	2	1	2
Don Gullett, p	.500	1	4	1	2	1	0	0	3	0	0	0
Mike Lum, ph	.000	1	1	0	0	0	0	0	0	0	0	0
Joe Morgan, 2b	.000	3	7	2	0	0	0	0	0	6	1	2
Gary Nolan, p	.000	1	0	0	0	0	0	0	0	1	0	0
Tony Perez, 1b	.200	3	10	1	2	0	0	0	3	1	2	0
Pete Rose, 3b	.429	3	14	3	6	2	1	0	2	1	0	0
Manny Sarmiento, p	.000	1	1	0	0	0	0	0	0	0	0	0
Pat Zachry, p	.000	1	1	0	0	0	0	0	0	0	0	0
TOTAL	.253		99	19	25	5	3	3	17	15	16	5

PITCHER	W	L	ERA	G	GS	CG	SV	SHO	IP	H	ER	BB	SO
Pedro Borbon	0	0	0.00	2	0	0	1	0	4.1	4	0	1	0
Rawly Eastwick	1	0	12.00	2	0	0	0	0	3.0	7	4	2	1
Don Gullett	1	0	1.13	1	1	0	0	0	8.0	2	1	3	4
Gary Nolan	0	0	1.59	1	1	0	0	0	5.2	6	1	2	1
Manny Sarmiento	0	0	18.00	1	0	0	0	0	1.0	2	2	1	0
Pat Zachry	1	0	3.60	1	1	0	0	0	5.0	6	2	3	3
TOTAL	3	0	3.33	8	3	0	1	0	27.0	27	10	12	9

PHI (E)

PLAYER/POS	AVG	G	AB	R	H	2B	3B	HR	RB	BB	SO	SB
Richie Allen, 1b	.222	3	9	1	2	0	0	0	0	3	2	0
Bob Boone, c	.286	3	7	0	2	0	0	0	1	1	0	0
Larry Bowa, ss	.125	3	8	1	1	1	0	0	1	3	0	0
Ollie Brown, of	.000	1	2	0	0	0	0	0	0	1	1	0
Steve Carlton, p	.000	1	2	0	0	0	0	0	0	0	0	0
Dave Cash, 2b	.308	3	13	1	4	1	0	0	1	0	0	0
Gene Garber, p	.000	2	0	0	0	0	0	0	0	0	0	0
Terry Harmon, pr	.000	1	0	1	0	0	0	0	0	0	0	0
Tom Hutton, ph	.000	1	1	0	0	0	0	0	0	0	0	0
Jay Johnstone, of-2	.778	3	9	1	7	1	1	0	2	1	0	0
Jim Kaat, p	.500	1	2	0	1	0	0	0	0	0	0	0
Jim Lonborg, p	.000	1	1	0	0	0	0	0	0	0	0	0
Greg Luzinski, of	.273	3	11	2	3	2	0	1	2	1	4	0
Garry Maddox, of	.231	3	13	2	3	1	0	0	2	2	0	0
Jerry Martin, of	.000	1	1	1	0	0	0	0	0	0	0	0
Tim McCarver, c-1	.000	2	4	0	0	0	0	0	0	0	1	0
Tug McGraw, p	.000	2	0	0	0	0	0	0	0	0	0	0
Johnny Oates, c	.000	1	1	0	0	0	0	0	0	0	0	0
Ron Reed, p	.000	2	1	0	0	0	0	0	0	0	0	0
Mike Schmidt, 3b	.308	3	13	1	4	2	0	0	2	0	1	0
Bobby Tolan, 1b-1,of-1	.000	3	2	0	0	0	0	0	0	0	0	0
Tom Underwood, p	.000	1	0	0	0	0	0	0	0	0	0	0
TOTAL	.270		100	11	27	8	1	1	11	12	9	0

PITCHER	W	L	ERA	G	GS	CG	SV	SHO	IP	H	ER	BB	SO
Steve Carlton	0	1	5.14	1	1	0	0	0	7.0	8	4	5	6
Gene Garber	0	1	13.50	2	0	0	0	0	0.2	2	1	1	0
Jim Kaat	0	0	3.00	1	1	0	0	0	6.0	2	2	2	1
Jim Lonborg	0	1	1.69	1	1	0	0	0	5.1	2	1	2	2
Tug McGraw	0	0	11.57	2	0	0	0	0	2.1	4	3	1	5
Ron Reed	0	0	7.71	2	0	0	0	0	4.2	6	4	2	2
Tom Underwood	0	0	0.00	1	0	0	0	0	0.1	1	0	2	0
TOTAL	0	3	5.13	10	3	0	0	0	26.1	25	15	15	16

GAME 1 AT PHI OCT 9

CIN	001 002 030	6 10 0
PHI	100 000 002	3 6 1

Pitchers: GULLETT, Eastwick (9) vs CARLTON, McGraw (8)
Home Runs: Foster-CIN
Attendance: 62,640

GAME 2 AT PHI OCT 10

CIN	000 004 200	6 6 0
PHI	010 010 000	2 10 1

Pitchers: ZACHRY, Borbon (6) vs LONBORG, Garber (6), McGraw (7), Reed (7)
Home Runs: Luzinski-PHI
Attendance: 62,651

GAME 3 AT CIN OCT 12

PHI	000 100 221	6 11 0
CIN	000 000 403	7 9 2

Pitchers: Kaat, Reed (7), GARBER (9), Underwood (9) vs Nolan, Sarmiento (6), Borbon (7), EASTWICK (8)
Home Runs: Foster-CIN, Bench-CIN
Attendance: 55,047

Returning to postseason play after a dozen years' absence, the Yankees found themselves evenly matched with the first-time-champion Royals. They didn't really need their two ninth-inning runs in the first game: the two they scored in the first inning proved cushion enough for Catfish Hunter's one-run five-hitter. But Kansas City came back the next day, scoring first, losing the lead in the third, then regaining it for good in the sixth.

The Royals again took a first-inning lead in Game Three, but this time the Yankees, once they went ahead in the sixth, didn't let go. Kansas City held on to its early lead in Game Four, building on it throughout the game for a second win, despite Yankee Graig Nettles' two home runs.

But Game Five—like the series itself—was a seesaw affair. For the fourth time the Royals scored first, with a pair in the first on John Mayberry's home run. But the Yankees tied the game when they came to bat, and K.C. retook the lead in the second. New York went ahead again in the third and increased its lead to 6–3 in the sixth. But in the top of the eighth, George Brett's three-run homer tied the score once again, setting the stage for Chris Chambliss to win for the Yankees their thirtieth American League pennant with his first-pitch home run in the bottom of the ninth.

New York Yankees (East), 3; Kansas City Royals (West) 2

NY (E)

PLAYER/POS	AVG	G	AB	R	H	2B	3B	HR	RB	BB	SO	SB
Sandy Alomar, dh-1	.000	2	1	0	0	0	0	0	0	0	0	0
Chris Chambliss, 1b	.524	5	21	5	11	1	1	2	8	0	1	2
Dock Ellis, p	.000	1	0	0	0	0	0	0	0	0	0	0
Ed Figueroa, p	.000	2	0	0	0	0	0	0	0	0	0	0
Oscar Gamble, of	.250	3	8	1	2	1	0	0	1	1	1	0
Ron Guidry, pr	.000	1	0	0	0	0	0	0	0	0	0	0
Elrod Hendricks, ph	1.000	1	1	0	1	0	0	0	0	0	0	0
Catfish Hunter, p	.000	2	0	0	0	0	0	0	0	0	0	0
Grant Jackson, p	.000	2	0	0	0	0	0	0	0	0	0	0
Sparky Lyle, p	.000	1	0	0	0	0	0	0	0	0	0	0
Elliott Maddox, of	.222	3	9	0	2	1	0	0	1	0	1	0
Jim Mason, ss	.000	2	0	0	0	0	0	0	0	0	0	0
Carlos May, dh	.200	3	10	1	2	1	0	0	0	1	4	0
Thurman Munson, c	.435	5	23	3	10	2	0	0	3	0	1	0
Graig Nettles, 3b	.235	5	17	2	4	1	0	2	4	3	3	0
Lou Piniella, dh-3	.273	4	11	1	3	1	0	0	0	0	1	0
Willie Randolph, 2b	.118	5	17	0	2	0	0	0	1	3	1	1
Mickey Rivers, of	.348	5	23	5	8	0	1	0	0	1	1	0
Fred Stanley, ss	.333	5	15	1	5	2	0	0	0	2	0	0
Dick Tidrow, p	.000	3	0	0	0	0	0	0	0	0	0	0
Otto Velez, ph	.000	1	1	0	0	0	0	0	0	0	0	0
Roy White, of	.294	5	17	4	5	3	0	0	3	5	1	1
TOTAL	.316		174	23	55	13	2	4	21	16	15	4

PITCHER	W	L	ERA	G	GS	CG	SV	SHO	IP	H	ER	BB	SO
Dock Ellis	1	0	3.38	1	1	0	0	0	8.0	6	3	2	5
Ed Figueroa	0	1	5.84	2	2	0	0	0	12.1	14	8	2	5
Catfish Hunter	1	1	4.50	2	2	1	0	0	12.0	10	6	1	5
Grant Jackson	0	0	8.10	2	0	0	0	0	3.1	4	3	1	3
Sparky Lyle	0	0	0.00	1	0	0	1	0	1.0	0	0	1	0
Dick Tidrow	1	0	3.68	3	0	0	0	0	7.1	6	3	4	0
TOTAL	3	2	4.70	11	5	1	1	0	44.0	40	23	11	18

KC (W)

PLAYER/POS	AVG	G	AB	R	H	2B	3B	HR	RB	BB	SO	SB
Doug Bird, p	.000	1	0	0	0	0	0	0	0	0	0	0
George Brett, 3b	.444	5	18	4	8	1	1	1	5	2	1	0
Al Cowens, of	.190	5	21	3	4	0	1	0	0	1	1	2
Larry Gura, p	.000	2	0	0	0	0	0	0	0	0	0	0
Tom Hall, p	.000	1	0	0	0	0	0	0	0	0	0	0
Andy Hassler, p	.000	2	0	0	0	0	0	0	0	0	0	0
Dennis Leonard, p	.000	2	0	0	0	0	0	0	0	0	0	0
Mark Littell, p	.000	3	0	0	0	0	0	0	0	0	0	0
Buck Martinez, c	.333	5	15	0	5	0	0	0	4	1	3	0
John Mayberry, 1b	.222	5	18	4	4	0	0	1	3	1	0	0
Hal McRae, dh-3,of-2	.118	5	17	2	2	1	1	0	1	1	4	0
Steve Mingori, p	.000	3	0	0	0	0	0	0	0	0	0	0
Dave Nelson, dh-1	.000	2	0	0	0	0	0	0	0	0	1	0
Amos Otis, of	.000	1	1	0	0	0	0	0	0	0	0	0
Freddie Patek, ss	.389	5	18	2	7	2	0	0	4	0	1	0
Marty Pattin, p	.000	2	0	0	0	0	0	0	0	0	0	0
Tom Poquette, of	.188	5	16	1	3	2	0	0	4	2	3	0
Jamie Quirk, dh-2	.143	4	7	1	1	0	1	0	2	0	2	0
Cookie Rojas, 2b	.333	4	9	2	3	0	0	0	1	0	0	1
Paul Splittorff, p	.000	2	0	0	0	0	0	0	0	0	0	0
Bob Stinson, c-1	.000	2	1	0	0	0	0	0	0	0	0	0
John Wathan, c	.000	1	0	0	0	0	0	0	0	0	0	0
Frank White, 2b	.125	4	8	2	1	0	0	0	0	0	1	0
Jim Wohlford, of	.182	5	11	3	2	0	0	0	0	3	1	2
TOTAL	.247		162	24	40	6	4	2	24	11	18	5

PITCHER	W	L	ERA	G	GS	CG	SV	SHO	IP	H	ER	BB	SO
Doug Bird	1	0	1.93	1	0	0	0	0	4.2	4	1	0	1
Larry Gura	0	1	4.22	2	2	0	0	0	10.2	18	5	1	4
Tom Hall	0	0	0.00	1	0	0	0	0	0.1	0	0	0	0
Andy Hassler	0	1	6.14	2	1	0	0	0	7.1	8	5	6	4
Dennis Leonard	0	0	19.29	2	2	0	0	0	2.1	9	5	2	0
Mark Littell	0	1	1.93	3	0	0	0	0	4.2	4	1	1	3
Steve Mingori	0	0	2.70	3	0	0	0	0	3.1	4	1	0	1
Marty Pattin	0	0	27.00	2	0	0	0	0	0.1	0	1	0	0
Paul Splittorff	1	0	1.93	2	0	0	0	0	9.1	7	2	5	2
TOTAL	2	3	4.40	18	5	0	1	0	43.0	55	21	16	15

GAME 1 AT KC OCT 9

NY	200	000	002	4	12	0
KC	000	000	010	1	5	2

Pitchers: HUNTER vs GURA, Littell (9)
Attendance: 41,077

GAME 2 AT KC OCT 10

NY	012	000	000	3	12	5
KC	200	002	03X	7	9	0

Pitchers: FIGUEROA, Tidrow (6) vs Leonard, SPLITTORFF (3), Mingori (9)
Attendance: 41,091

GAME 3 AT NY OCT 12

KC	300	000	000	3	6	0
NY	000	203	00X	5	9	0

Pitchers: HASSLER, Pattin (6), Hall (6), Mingori (6), Littell (6) vs ELLIS, Lyle (9)
Home Runs: Chambliss-NY
Attendance: 56,808

GAME 4 AT NY OCT 13

KC	030	201	010	7	9	1
NY	020	000	101	4	11	0

Pitchers: Gura, BIRD (3), Mingori (7) vs HUNTER, Tidrow (4), Jackson (7)
Home Runs: Nettles-NY (2)
Attendance: 56,355

GAME 5 AT NY OCT 14

KC	210	000	030	6	11	1
NY	202	002	001	7	11	1

Pitchers: Leonard, Splittorff (1), Pattin (4), Hassler (5), LITTELL (7) vs Figueroa, Jackson (8), TIDROW (9)
Home Runs: Mayberry-KC, Brett-KC, Chambliss-NY
Attendance: 56,821

The Reds led the National League in virtually every offensive category and in fielding as well. In the Series (which, incidentally, was the first to employ the designated hitter), the Big Red Machine continued its roll over the Yankees to become the first National League club in fifty-four years to repeat as world champions, as well as the first team to sweep both a League Championship and World Series. Red catcher Johnny Bench led the attack with eight hits, half of them for extra bases, for a batting average of .533 and a 1.133 average in slugging.

Joe Morgan's home run for Cincinnati in the first inning of Game One was the first hit of the Series, but New York pushed across a tying run half an inning later on a sacrifice fly. Red pitchers Don Gullett and Pedro Borbon held the Yankees scoreless after that as the Reds regained the lead with a run in the third and extended it in the sixth and seventh for a 5–1 win.

Game Two turned out to be the Reds' only narrow victory. They scored first, with three runs in the second inning. In the fourth the Yankees scored their first run, and they tied the score with two more runs in the seventh. But with two men out in the last of the ninth, a throwing error by Yankee shortstop Fred Stanley allowed the Reds' batter Ken Griffey to reach second, from where he scored the winning run on Tony Perez's line single to left.

In Game Three, four hits and a pair of stolen bases put Cincinnati ahead 3–0 in the second inning, and Dan Driessen homered in the fourth to make it 4–0 before the Yankees scored their first run. Another quartet of hits in the eighth gave the Reds two more runs and a 6–2 win.

New York took the lead for the only time in the Series when Chris Chambliss doubled in Thurman Munson in the first inning of Game Four. (Munson had singled with the third of what became six straight hits.) But the Reds' George Foster drove in a tying run in the fourth, and Johnny Bench followed him with a two-run homer. New York scored again an inning later to come close, but Bench's second home run, a three-run blast in the ninth, put the game out of reach, and a pair of ground-rule doubles touched by New York fans nailed the final run in the Yankee coffin.

Cincinnati Reds (NL), 4;
New York Yankees (AL) 0

CIN (N)

PLAYER/POS	AVG	G	AB	R	H	2B	3B	HR	RB	BB	SO	SB
Johnny Bench, c	.533	4	15	4	8	1	1	2	6	0	1	0
Jack Billingham, p	.000	1	0	0	0	0	0	0	0	0	0	0
Pedro Borbon, p	.000	1	0	0	0	0	0	0	0	0	0	0
Dave Concepcion, ss	.357	4	14	1	5	1	1	0	3	1	3	1
Dan Driessen, dh	.357	4	14	4	5	2	0	1	1	2	0	1
George Foster, of	.429	4	14	3	6	1	0	0	4	2	3	0
Cesar Geronimo, of	.308	4	13	3	4	2	0	0	1	2	2	2
Ken Griffey, of	.059	4	17	2	1	0	0	0	1	0	1	1
Don Gullett, p	.000	1	0	0	0	0	0	0	0	0	0	0
Will McEnaney, p	.000	2	0	0	0	0	0	0	0	0	0	0
Joe Morgan, 2b	.333	4	15	3	5	1	1	1	2	2	2	2
Gary Nolan, p	.000	1	0	0	0	0	0	0	0	0	0	0
Fred Norman, p	.000	1	0	0	0	0	0	0	0	0	0	0
Tony Perez, 1b	.313	4	16	1	5	1	0	0	2	1	2	0
Pete Rose, 3b	.188	4	16	1	3	1	0	0	1	2	2	0
Pat Zachry, p	.000	1	0	0	0	0	0	0	0	0	0	0
TOTAL	.313		134	22	42	10	3	4	21	12	16	7

PITCHER	W	L	ERA	G	GS	CG	SV	SHO	IP	H	ER	BB	SO
Jack Billingham	1	0	0.00	1	0	0	0	0	2.2	0	0	0	1
Pedro Borbon	0	0	0.00	1	0	0	0	0	1.2	0	0	0	0
Don Gullett	1	0	1.23	1	1	0	0	0	7.1	5	1	3	4
Will McEnaney	0	0	0.00	2	0	0	2	0	4.2	2	0	1	2
Gary Nolan	1	0	2.70	1	1	0	0	0	6.2	8	2	1	1
Fred Norman	0	0	4.26	1	1	0	0	0	6.1	9	3	2	2
Pat Zachry	1	0	2.70	1	1	0	0	0	6.2	6	2	5	6
TOTAL	4	0	2.00	8	4	0	2	0	36.0	30	8	12	16

NY (A)

PLAYER/POS	AVG	G	AB	R	H	2B	3B	HR	RB	BB	SO	SB
Doyle Alexander, p	.000	1	0	0	0	0	0	0	0	0	0	0
Chris Chambliss, 1b	.313	4	16	1	5	1	0	0	1	0	2	0
Dock Ellis, p	.000	1	0	0	0	0	0	0	0	0	0	0
Ed Figueroa, p	.000	1	0	0	0	0	0	0	0	0	0	0
Oscar Gamble, of-2	.125	3	8	0	1	0	0	0	1	0	0	0
Elrod Hendricks, ph	.000	2	2	0	0	0	0	0	0	0	0	0
Catfish Hunter, p	.000	1	0	0	0	0	0	0	0	0	0	0
Grant Jackson, p	.000	1	0	0	0	0	0	0	0	0	0	0
Sparky Lyle, p	.000	2	0	0	0	0	0	0	0	0	0	0
Elliott Maddox, of-1,dh-1	.200	2	5	0	1	0	1	0	0	1	2	0
Jim Mason, ss	1.000	3	1	1	1	0	0	1	1	0	0	0
Carlos May, dh	.000	4	9	0	0	0	0	0	0	0	1	0
Thurman Munson, c	.529	4	17	2	9	0	0	0	2	0	1	0
Graig Nettles, 3b	.250	4	12	0	3	0	0	0	2	3	1	0
Lou Piniella, of-2,dh-2	.333	4	9	1	3	1	0	0	0	0	0	0
Willie Randolph, 2b	.071	4	14	1	1	0	0	0	0	1	3	0
Mickey Rivers, of	.167	4	18	1	3	0	0	0	0	1	2	1
Fred Stanley, ss	.167	4	6	1	1	0	0	0	1	3	1	0
Dick Tidrow, p	.000	2	0	0	0	0	0	0	0	0	0	0
Otto Velez, ph	.000	3	3	0	0	0	0	0	0	0	3	0
Roy White, of	.133	4	15	0	2	0	0	0	0	3	0	0
TOTAL	.222		135	8	30	3	1	1	8	12	16	1

PITCHER	W	L	ERA	G	GS	CG	SV	SHO	IP	H	ER	BB	SO
Doyle Alexander	0	1	7.50	1	1	0	0	0	6.0	9	5	2	1
Dock Ellis	0	1	10.80	1	1	0	0	0	3.1	7	4	0	1
Ed Figueroa	0	1	5.63	1	1	0	0	0	8.0	6	5	5	2
Catfish Hunter	0	1	3.12	1	1	1	0	0	8.2	10	3	4	5
Grant Jackson	0	0	4.91	1	0	0	0	0	3.2	4	2	0	3
Sparky Lyle	0	0	0.00	2	0	0	0	0	2.2	1	0	0	3
Dick Tidrow	0	0	7.71	2	0	0	0	0	2.1	5	2	1	1
TOTAL	0	4	5.45	9	4	1	0	0	34.2	42	21	12	16

GAME 1 AT CIN OCT 16

NY	010	000	000	1	5	1
CIN	101	001	20X	5	10	1

Pitchers: ALEXANDER, Lyle (7) vs GULLETT, Borbon (8)
Home Runs: Morgan-CIN
Attendance: 54,826

GAME 2 AT CIN OCT 17

NY	000	100	200	3	9	1
CIN	030	000	001	4	10	0

Pitchers: HUNTER vs Norman, BILLINGHAM (7)
Attendance: 54,816

GAME 3 AT NY OCT 19

CIN	030	100	020	6	13	2
NY	000	100	100	2	8	0

Pitchers: ZACHRY, McEnaney (7) vs ELLIS, Jackson (4), Tidrow (8)
Home Runs: Driessen-CIN, Mason-NY
Attendance: 56,667

GAME 4 AT NY OCT 21

CIN	000	300	004	7	9	2
NY	100	010	000	2	8	0

Pitchers: NOLAN, McEnaney (7) vs FIGUEROA, Tidrow (9), Lyle (9)
Home Runs: Bench-CIN (2)
Attendance: 56,700

The Phillies took the first game, but the Dodgers proved better over all at turning hits into runs and swept the next three. Philadelphia jumped ahead in the first inning of Game One, and had built a 5–1 lead by the seventh, when Ron Cey tied the score with a Dodger grand slam. But the Phillies came back with two runs on three singles in the top of the ninth and held on for the win. As in Game One, both clubs again got nine hits apiece in Game Two, but this time Dodger pitcher Don Sutton scattered the Phillies' hits for a single run over nine innings, while Phillie starter Jim Lonborg—in the four innings he pitched—yielded five runs, including a grand slam to Dusty Baker.

In Game Three Los Angeles outhit the Phillies, but the Dodgers were nearly undone when starter Burt Hooton walked in three Philadelphia runs in the second inning. The Phillies took a two-run lead into the ninth, but after two men were out the Dodgers rebounded, thanks largely to a couple of old pros. Pinch hitter Vic Davalillo, age 38, beat out a drag bunt on a disputed call, and 39-year-old Manny Mota doubled to deep left. Two more Dodger singles scored three runs that proved enough for the win.

The Dodgers didn't even need all of their five hits to take the final game behind Tommy John's one-run seven-hitter, for one of those hits was another Dusty Baker home run with a man aboard.

Los Angeles Dodgers (West), 3;
Philadelphia Phillies (East) 1

LA (W)

PLAYER/POS	AVG	G	AB	R	H	2B	3B	HR	RB	BB	SO	SB
Dusty Baker, of	.357	4	14	4	5	1	0	2	8	2	3	0
Glenn Burke, of	.000	4	7	0	0	0	0	0	0	0	3	0
Ron Cey, 3b	.308	4	13	4	4	1	0	1	4	2	4	1
Vic Davalillo, ph	1.000	1	1	1	1	0	0	0	0	0	0	0
Mike Garman, p	.000	2	0	0	0	0	0	0	0	0	0	0
Steve Garvey, 1b	.308	4	13	2	4	0	0	0	0	2	1	0
Ed Goodson, ph	.000	1	1	0	0	0	0	0	0	0	0	0
Jerry Grote, c-1	.000	2	0	0	0	0	0	0	0	1	0	0
Burt Hooton, p	1.000	1	1	0	1	0	1	0	0	0	0	0
Charlie Hough, p	.000	1	0	0	0	0	0	0	0	0	0	0
Tommy John, p	.200	2	5	0	1	0	0	0	0	0	2	0
Lee Lacy, ph	1.000	1	1	1	1	0	0	0	0	0	0	0
Davey Lopes, 2b	.235	4	17	2	4	0	0	0	3	2	0	0
Rick Monday, of	.286	3	7	1	2	1	0	0	0	2	1	0
Manny Mota, ph	1.000	1	1	1	1	1	0	0	0	0	0	0
Doug Rau, p	.000	1	0	0	0	0	0	0	0	0	0	0
Lance Rautzhan, p	.000	1	0	0	0	0	0	0	0	0	0	0
Rick Rhoden, p	.000	1	1	0	0	0	0	0	0	0	0	0
Bill Russell, ss	.278	4	18	3	5	1	0	0	2	0	0	0
Reggie Smith, of	.188	4	16	2	3	0	1	0	1	2	5	1
Elias Sosa, p	.000	2	1	0	0	0	0	0	0	0	0	0
Don Sutton, p	.000	1	3	0	0	0	0	0	0	0	0	0
Steve Yeager, c	.231	4	13	1	3	0	0	0	2	1	3	0
TOTAL	.263		133	22	35	6	1	3	20	14	22	3

PITCHER	W	L	ERA	G	GS	CG	SV	SHO	IP	H	ER	BB	SO
Mike Garman	0	0	0.00	2	0	0	1	0	1.1	0	0	0	1
Burt Hooton	0	0	16.20	1	1	0	0	0	1.2	2	3	4	1
Charlie Hough	0	0	4.50	1	0	0	0	0	2.0	2	1	0	3
Tommy John	1	0	0.66	2	2	1	0	0	13.2	11	1	5	11
Doug Rau	0	0	0.00	1	0	0	0	0	1.0	0	0	0	1
Lance Rautzhan	1	0	0.00	1	0	0	0	0	0.1	0	0	0	0
Rick Rhoden	0	0	0.00	1	0	0	0	0	4.1	2	0	2	0
Elias Sosa	0	1	10.13	2	0	0	0	0	2.2	5	3	0	0
Don Sutton	1	0	1.00	1	1	1	0	0	9.0	9	1	0	4
TOTAL	3	1	2.25	12	4	2	1	0	36.0	31	9	11	21

PHI (E)

PLAYER/POS	AVG	G	AB	R	H	2B	3B	HR	RB	BB	SO	SB
Bob Boone, c	.400	4	10	1	4	0	0	0	0	0	0	0
Larry Bowa, ss	.118	4	17	2	2	0	0	0	1	1	0	0
Ollie Brown, ph	.000	2	2	0	0	0	0	0	0	0	1	0
Warren Brusstar, p	.000	2	0	0	0	0	0	0	0	0	0	0
Steve Carlton, p	.500	2	4	0	2	0	0	0	1	0	2	0
Larry Christenson, p	.000	1	0	0	0	0	0	0	0	1	0	0
Gene Garber, p	.000	3	0	0	0	0	0	0	0	0	0	0
Richie Hebner, 1b-3	.357	4	14	2	5	0	0	0	0	0	1	0
Tom Hutton, 1b-1	.000	3	3	0	0	0	0	0	0	0	0	0
Davey Johnson, 1b	.250	1	4	0	1	0	0	0	2	0	1	0
Jay Johnstone, of	.200	2	5	0	1	0	0	0	0	0	1	0
Jim Lonborg, p	.000	1	1	0	0	0	0	0	0	0	1	0
Greg Luzinski, of	.286	4	14	2	4	1	0	1	2	3	3	1
Garry Maddox, of	.429	2	7	1	3	0	0	0	2	0	1	0
Jerry Martin, of-1	.000	3	4	0	0	0	0	0	0	0	2	0
Bake McBride, of	.222	4	18	2	4	0	0	1	2	1	2	0
Tim McCarver, c-2	.167	3	6	1	1	0	0	0	0	1	3	0
Tug McGraw, p	.000	2	0	0	0	0	0	0	0	0	0	0
Ron Reed, p	.000	3	0	0	0	0	0	0	0	0	0	0
Mike Schmidt, 3b	.063	4	16	1	1	0	0	0	1	2	3	0
Ted Sizemore, 2b	.231	4	13	1	3	0	0	0	0	2	0	0
TOTAL	.225		138	14	31	3	0	2	12	11	21	1

PITCHER	W	L	ERA	G	GS	CG	SV	SHO	IP	H	ER	BB	SO
Warren Brusstar	0	0	3.38	2	0	0	0	0	2.2	2	1	1	2
Steve Carlton	0	1	6.94	2	2	0	0	0	11.2	13	9	8	6
Larry Christenson	0	0	8.10	1	1	0	0	0	3.1	7	3	0	2
Gene Garber	1	1	3.38	3	0	0	0	0	5.1	4	2	0	3
Jim Lonborg	0	1	11.25	1	1	0	0	0	4.0	5	5	1	1
Tug McGraw	0	0	0.00	2	0	0	1	0	3.0	1	0	2	3
Ron Reed	0	0	1.80	3	0	0	0	0	5.0	3	1	2	5
TOTAL	1	3	5.40	14	4	0	1	0	35.0	35	21	14	22

GAME 1 AT LA OCT 4

PHI	200 021 002	7 9 0
LA	000 010 400	5 9 2

Pitchers: Carlton, GARBER (7), McGraw (9) vs John, Garman (5), Hough (6), SOSA (8)
Home Runs: Luzinski-PHI, Cey-LA
Attendance: 55,968

GAME 2 AT LA OCT 5

PHI	001 000 000	1 9 1
LA	001 401 10X	7 9 1

Pitchers: LONBORG, Reed (5), Brusstar (7) vs SUTTON
Home Runs: McBride-PHI, Baker-LA
Attendance: 55,973

GAME 3 AT PHI OCT 7

LA	020 100 003	6 12 2
PHI	030 000 020	5 6 2

Pitchers: Hooton, Rhoden (2), Rau (7), Sosa (8), RAUTZHAN (8), Garman (9) vs Christenson, Brusstar (4), Reed (5), GARBER (7)
Attendance: 63,719

GAME 4 AT PHI OCT 8

LA	020 020 000	4 5 0
PHI	000 100 000	1 7 0

Pitchers: JOHN vs CARLTON, Reed (6), McGraw (7), Garber (9)
Home Runs: Baker-LA
Attendance: 64,924

As in 1976, the Royals met the Yankees in the LCS, and as in 1976 the series went five games, with the Royals outscoring New York by a single run. But this time Kansas City won the first game, and as the teams traded victories through the first four games and K.C. took a lead into the ninth inning of Game Five, it began to look as though this year the Royals might take the pennant.

Royal hitters began things with a bang, scoring six of their seven runs in Game One in the first three innings for an insurmountable lead. New York came back to take the second game 6–2 behind Ron Guidry's three-hitter, but the Royals reversed the score the next day as Dennis Leonard limited the Yankees to four hits. Yankee reliever Sparky Lyle shut K.C. down over the final five innings of Game Four after the Royals had drawn within a run of New York in the fourth inning, and the series was tied.

In the finale, Kansas City drew first blood with two runs in the bottom of the first and led by one run after eight. But with the pennant in sight, the Royals gave up three Yankee runs in the top of the ninth, scoring nothing themselves as reliever Lyle held them off to give the Yankees their thirty-first flag.

New York Yankees (East), 3; Kansas City Royals (West) 2

NY (E)

PLAYER/POS	AVG	G	AB	R	H	2B	3B	HR	RB	BB	SO	SB
Paul Blair, of	.400	3	5	1	2	0	0	0	0	0	0	0
Chris Chambliss, 1b	.059	5	17	0	1	0	0	0	0	3	4	0
Bucky Dent, ss	.214	5	14	1	3	1	0	0	2	1	0	0
Ed Figueroa, p	.000	1	0	0	0	0	0	0	0	0	0	0
Ron Guidry, p	.000	2	0	0	0	0	0	0	0	0	0	0
Don Gullett, p	.000	1	0	0	0	0	0	0	0	0	0	0
Reggie Jackson, of-4,dh-1	.125	5	16	1	2	0	0	0	1	2	2	1
Cliff Johnson, dh-4	.400	5	15	2	6	2	0	1	2	1	2	0
Sparky Lyle, p	.000	4	0	0	0	0	0	0	0	0	0	0
Thurman Munson, c	.286	5	21	3	6	1	0	1	5	0	2	0
Graig Nettles, 3b	.150	5	20	1	3	0	0	0	1	0	3	0
Lou Piniella, of-4,dh-1	.333	5	21	1	7	3	0	0	2	0	1	0
Willie Randolph, 2b	.278	5	18	4	5	1	0	0	2	1	0	0
Mickey Rivers, of	.391	5	23	5	9	2	0	0	2	0	2	1
Fred Stanley, ss	.000	2	0	0	0	0	0	0	0	0	0	0
Dick Tidrow, p	.000	2	0	0	0	0	0	0	0	0	0	0
Mike Torrez, p	.000	2	0	0	0	0	0	0	0	0	0	0
Roy White, of-1,dh-1	.400	4	5	2	2	2	0	0	0	1	0	0
TOTAL	.263		175	21	46	12	0	2	17	9	16	2

PITCHER	W	L	ERA	G	GS	CG	SV	SHO	IP	H	ER	BB	SO
Ed Figueroa	0	0	10.80	1	1	0	0	0	3.1	5	4	2	3
Ron Guidry	1	0	3.97	2	2	1	0	0	11.1	9	5	3	8
Don Gullett	0	1	18.00	1	1	0	0	0	2.0	4	4	2	0
Sparky Lyle	2	0	0.96	4	0	0	0	0	9.1	7	1	0	3
Dick Tidrow	0	0	3.86	2	0	0	0	0	7.0	6	3	3	3
Mike Torrez	0	1	4.09	2	2	0	0	0	11.0	11	5	5	5
TOTAL	3	2	4.50	12	5	1	0	0	44.0	42	22	15	22

KC (W)

PLAYER/POS	AVG	G	AB	R	H	2B	3B	HR	RB	BB	SO	SB
Doug Bird, p	.000	3	0	0	0	0	0	0	0	0	0	0
George Brett, 3b	.300	5	20	2	6	0	2	0	2	1	0	0
Al Cowens, of	.263	5	19	2	5	0	0	1	5	1	3	0
Larry Gura, p	.000	2	0	0	0	0	0	0	0	0	0	0
Andy Hassler, p	.000	1	0	0	0	0	0	0	0	0	0	0
Pete LaCock, 1b	.000	1	1	0	0	0	0	0	0	1	1	0
Joe Lahoud, dh	.000	1	2	0	0	0	0	0	0	2	0	0
Dennis Leonard, p	.000	2	0	0	0	0	0	0	0	0	0	0
Mark Littell, p	.000	2	0	0	0	0	0	0	0	0	0	0
John Mayberry, 1b	.167	4	12	1	2	1	0	1	3	1	2	0
Hal McRae, dh-3,of-2	.444	5	18	6	8	3	0	1	2	3	1	0
Steve Mingori, p	.000	3	0	0	0	0	0	0	0	0	0	0
Amos Otis, of	.125	5	16	1	2	1	0	0	2	2	3	2
Freddie Patek, ss	.389	5	18	4	7	3	1	0	5	1	2	0
Marty Pattin, p	.000	1	0	0	0	0	0	0	0	0	0	0
Tom Poquette, of	.167	2	6	0	1	0	0	0	0	0	0	0
Darrell Porter, c	.333	5	15	3	5	0	0	0	0	3	0	0
Cookie Rojas, dh	.250	1	4	0	1	0	0	0	0	0	1	1
Paul Splittorff, p	.000	2	0	0	0	0	0	0	0	0	0	0
John Wathan, 1b-2,c-1,dh-1	.000	4	6	0	0	0	0	0	0	0	3	0
Frank White, 2b	.278	5	18	1	5	1	0	0	2	0	4	1
Joe Zdeb, of	.000	4	9	0	0	0	0	0	0	0	2	1
TOTAL	.258		163	22	42	9	3	3	21	15	22	5

PITCHER	W	L	ERA	G	GS	CG	SV	SHO	IP	H	ER	BB	SO
Doug Bird	0	0	0.00	3	0	0	0	0	2.0	4	0	0	1
Larry Gura	0	1	18.00	2	1	0	0	0	2.0	7	4	1	2
Andy Hassler	0	1	4.76	1	1	0	0	0	5.2	5	3	0	3
Dennis Leonard	1	1	3.00	2	1	1	0	0	9.0	5	3	2	4
Mark Littell	0	0	3.00	2	0	0	0	0	3.0	5	1	3	1
Steve Mingori	0	0	0.00	3	0	0	0	0	1.1	0	0	0	1
Marty Pattin	0	0	1.50	1	0	0	0	0	6.0	6	1	0	0
Paul Splittorff	1	0	2.40	2	2	0	0	0	15.0	14	4	3	4
TOTAL	2	3	3.27	16	5	1	0	0	44.0	46	16	9	16

GAME 1 AT NY OCT 5

KC	222	000	010	7	9	0
NY	002	000	000	2	9	0

Pitchers: SPLITTORFF, Bird (9) vs GULLETT. Tidrow (3), Lyle (9)
Home Runs: McRae-KC, Mayberry-KC, Munson-NY, Cowens-KC
Attendance: 54,930

GAME 2 AT NY OCT 6

KC	001	001	000	2	3	1
NY	000	023	01X	6	10	1

Pitchers: HASSLER, Littell (6), Mingori (8) vs GUIDRY
Home Runs: Johnson-NY
Attendance: 56,230

GAME 3 AT KC OCT 7

NY	000	010	001	2	4	1
KC	011	012	10X	6	12	1

Pitchers: TORREZ, Lyle (6) vs LEONARD
Attendance: 41,285

GAME 4 AT KC OCT 8

NY	121	100	001	6	13	0
KC	002	200	000	4	8	2

Pitchers: Figueroa, Tidrow (4), LYLE (4) vs GURA, Pattin (3), Mingori (9), Bird (9)
Attendance: 41,135

GAME 5 AT KC OCT 9

NY	001	000	013	5	10	0
KC	201	000	000	3	10	1

Pitchers: Guidry, Torrez (3), LYLE (8) vs Splittorff, Bird (8), Mingori (8), LEONARD (9), Gura (9), Littell (9)
Attendance: 41,133

This was the Series in which Yankee Reggie Jackson established his reputation as "Mr. October" with a record five home runs, including three in successive at-bats in the final game, and the Yankees showed that after a decade or so of decline they were once again the world's best. Los Angeles scored first in the opening game with a pair of first-inning runs. But New York gained back half the ground in the bottom of the first and tied the game on Willie Randolph's leadoff homer in the sixth. The clubs traded runs in the eighth and ninth to take the game into extra innings. The impasse was not breached until the last of the twelfth, when Randolph doubled and Paul Blair singled him home.

Game Two, by contrast, was a runaway Dodger victory. Home runs in the first three innings by Ron Cey, Steve Yeager, and Reggie Smith made the score 5–0 before New York scored its lone run in the fourth. Burt Hooton hurled the Dodger win, a five-hitter. And for good measure, Dodger Steve Garvey homered in the ninth inning. The Yankees returned to form two days later in Los Angeles, though, scoring three runs in the top of the first on pairs of doubles and singles (and a Dodger error). Dodger Dusty Baker's three-run homer tied the game in the third, but single Yankee runs in the next two innings provided pitcher Mike Torrez with runs enough for the win.

Two of the four hits yielded by emerging Yankee ace Ron Guidry in Game Four were pitcher Rick Rhoden's double followed by Davey Lopes's home run in the third inning. But the Yankees had already scored three times in the second, and Reggie Jackson homered in the sixth as Guidry held Los Angeles scoreless after the third for a 4–2 win. A Yankee assault against Dodger pitcher Don Sutton in Game Five included back-to-back home runs by Thurman Munson and Jackson in the eighth inning. But Los Angeles rocked Yankee pitching even harder, with homers by Steve Yeager and Reggie Smith producing five of the Dodgers' ten runs as the club evaded elimination with its second win.

The Dodgers scored first in the sixth game when Steve Garvey's first-inning triple drove in two runners. Yankee Chris Chambliss matched that an inning later with a two-run homer. Smith restored the lead to Los Angeles with a solo shot in the third inning, but Jackson put the Yankees back in front with the first of his three home runs, a two-run blast in the fourth. By the time he had homered again for two in the fifth and for the third time in the eighth, the Yankees' twenty-first world title was well in hand.

New York Yankees (AL), 4;
Los Angeles Dodgers (NL) 2

NY (A)

PLAYER/POS	AVG	G	AB	R	H	2B	3B	HR	RB	BB	SO	SB
Paul Blair, of-3	.250	4	4	0	1	0	0	0	1	1	0	0
Chris Chambliss, 1b	.292	6	24	4	7	2	0	1	4	0	2	0
Ken Clay, p	.000	2	0	0	0	0	0	0	0	0	0	0
Bucky Dent, ss	.263	6	19	0	5	0	0	0	2	2	1	0
Ron Guidry, p	.000	1	2	0	0	0	0	0	0	0	1	0
Don Gullett, p	.000	2	2	0	0	0	0	0	0	0	2	0
Catfish Hunter, p	.000	2	0	0	0	0	0	0	0	0	0	0
Reggie Jackson, of	.450	6	20	10	9	1	0	5	8	3	4	0
Cliff Johnson, c-1	.000	2	1	0	0	0	0	0	0	0	0	0
Sparky Lyle, p	.000	2	2	0	0	0	0	0	0	0	2	0
Thurman Munson, c	.320	6	25	4	8	2	0	1	3	2	8	0
Graig Nettles, 3b	.190	6	21	1	4	1	0	0	2	2	3	0
Lou Piniella, of	.273	6	22	1	6	0	0	0	3	0	3	0
Willie Randolph, 2b	.160	6	25	5	4	2	0	1	1	2	2	0
Mickey Rivers, of	.222	6	27	1	6	2	0	0	1	0	2	1
Fred Stanley, ss	.000	1	0	0	0	0	0	0	0	0	0	0
Dick Tidrow, p	.000	2	1	0	0	0	0	0	0	0	1	0
Mike Torrez, p	.000	2	6	0	0	0	0	0	0	0	4	0
Roy White, ph	.000	2	2	0	0	0	0	0	0	0	0	0
George Zeber, ph	.000	2	2	0	0	0	0	0	0	0	2	0
TOTAL	.244		205	26	50	10	0	8	25	11	37	1

PITCHER	W	L	ERA	G	GS	CG	SV	SHO	IP	H	ER	BB	SO
Ken Clay	0	0	2.45	2	0	0	0	0	3.2	2	1	1	0
Ron Guidry	1	0	2.00	1	1	1	0	0	9.0	4	2	3	7
Don Gullett	0	1	6.39	2	2	0	0	0	12.2	13	9	7	10
Catfish Hunter	0	1	10.38	2	1	0	0	0	4.1	6	5	0	1
Sparky Lyle	1	0	1.93	2	0	0	0	0	4.2	2	1	0	2
Dick Tidrow	0	0	4.91	2	0	0	0	0	3.2	5	2	0	1
Mike Torrez	2	0	2.50	2	2	2	0	0	18.0	16	5	5	15
TOTAL	4	2	4.02	13	6	3	0	0	56.0	48	25	16	36

LA (N)

PLAYER/POS	AVG	G	AB	R	H	2B	3B	HR	RB	BB	SO	SB
Dusty Baker, of	.292	6	24	4	7	0	0	1	5	0	2	0
Glenn Burke, of	.200	3	5	0	1	0	0	0	0	0	1	0
Ron Cey, 3b	.190	6	21	2	4	1	0	1	3	3	5	0
Vic Davalillo, ph	.333	3	3	0	1	0	0	0	1	0	0	0
Mike Garman, p	.000	2	0	0	0	0	0	0	0	0	0	0
Steve Garvey, 1b	.375	6	24	5	9	1	1	1	3	1	4	0
Ed Goodson, ph	.000	1	1	0	0	0	0	0	0	1	0	0
Jerry Grote, c	.000	1	1	0	0	0	0	0	0	0	0	0
Burt Hooton, p	.000	2	5	0	0	0	0	0	0	0	2	0
Charlie Hough, p	.000	2	0	0	0	0	0	0	0	0	0	0
Tommy John, p	.000	1	2	0	0	0	0	0	0	0	2	0
Lee Lacy, of-2	.429	4	7	1	3	0	0	0	2	1	1	0
Rafael Landestoy, pr	.000	1	0	0	0	0	0	0	0	0	0	0
Davey Lopes, 2b	.167	6	24	3	4	0	1	1	2	4	3	2
Rick Monday, of	.167	4	12	0	2	0	0	0	0	0	3	0
Manny Mota, ph	.000	3	3	0	0	0	0	0	0	0	0	0
Johnny Oates, c	.000	1	1	0	0	0	0	0	0	0	0	0
Doug Rau, p	.000	2	0	0	0	0	0	0	0	0	0	0
Lance Rautzhan, p	.000	1	0	0	0	0	0	0	0	0	0	0
Rick Rhoden, p	.500	2	2	1	1	1	0	0	0	0	0	0
Bill Russell, ss	.154	6	26	3	4	0	1	0	2	1	3	0
Reggie Smith, of	.273	6	22	7	6	1	0	3	5	4	3	0
Elias Sosa, p	.000	2	0	0	0	0	0	0	0	0	0	0
Don Sutton, p	.000	2	6	0	0	0	0	0	0	1	4	0
Steve Yeager, c	.316	6	19	2	6	1	0	2	5	5	1	0
TOTAL	.231		208	28	48	5	3	9	28	16	36	2

PITCHER	W	L	ERA	G	GS	CG	SV	SHO	IP	H	ER	BB	SO
Mike Garman	0	0	0.00	2	0	0	0	0	4.0	2	0	1	3
Burt Hooton	1	1	3.75	2	2	1	0	0	12.0	8	5	2	9
Charlie Hough	0	0	1.80	2	0	0	0	0	5.0	3	1	0	5
Tommy John	0	1	6.00	1	1	0	0	0	6.0	9	4	3	7
Doug Rau	0	1	11.57	2	1	0	0	0	2.1	4	3	0	1
Lance Rautzhan	0	0	0.00	1	0	0	0	0	0.1	0	0	2	0
Rick Rhoden	0	1	2.57	2	0	0	0	0	7.0	4	2	1	5
Elias Sosa	0	0	11.57	2	0	0	0	0	2.1	3	3	1	1
Don Sutton	1	0	3.94	2	2	1	0	0	16.0	17	7	1	6
TOTAL	2	4	4.09	16	6	2	0	0	55.0	50	25	11	37

GAME 1 AT NY OCT 11

LA	200 000 001 000	3	6	0
NY	100 001 010 001	4	11	0

Pitchers: Sutton, Rautzhan (8), Sosa (8), Garman (9), RHODEN (12) vs Gullett, LYLE (9)
Home Runs: Randolph-NY
Attendance: 56,668

GAME 2 AT NY OCT 12

LA	212 000 001	6	9	0
NY	000 100 000	1	5	0

Pitchers: HOOTON vs HUNTER, Tidrow (3), Clay (6), Lyle (9)
Home Runs: Cey-LA, Yeager-LA, Smith-LA, Garvey-LA
Attendance: 56,691

GAME 3 AT LA OCT 14

NY	300 110 000	5	10	0
LA	003 000 000	3	7	1

Pitchers: TORREZ vs JOHN, Hough (7)
Home Runs: Baker-LA
Attendance: 55,992

GAME 4 AT LA OCT 15

NY	030 001 000	4	7	0
LA	002 000 000	2	4	0

Pitchers: GUIDRY vs RAU, Rhoden (2), Garman (9)
Home Runs: Lopes-LA, Jackson-NY
Attendance: 55,995

GAME 5 AT LA OCT 16

NY	000 000 220	4	9	2
LA	100 432 00X	10	13	0

Pitchers: GULLETT, Clay (5), Tidrow (6), Hunter (7) vs SUTTON
Home Runs: Yeager-LA, Smith-LA, Munson-NY, Jackson-NY
Attendance: 55,955

GAME 6 AT NY OCT 18

LA	201 000 001	4	9	0
NY	020 320 01X	8	8	1

Pitchers: HOOTON, Sosa (4), Rau (5), Hough (7) vs TORREZ
Home Runs: Chambliss-NY, Smith-LA, Jackson-NY (3)
Attendance: 56,407

Steve Garvey hit half the Dodgers' eight home runs and Tommy John hurled the first LCS shutout in four years as Los Angeles, for the second year in a row, defeated the Phillies for the pennant in four games. Philadelphia's five runs in Game One would have been enough to win any of the other games, but not this one as the Dodgers outhomered the Phillies four to one (including two by Garvey) and scored nine times. Dodger Davey Lopes hit the game's only home run the next day (with a man aboard), but it was more than enough support for John's four-hit shutout.

The series' most decisive win went to the Phillies in Game Three. Steve Carlton allowed four Dodger runs to score, but he made up for it by driving in his own four runs on a homer and sacrifice fly. His teammates added five more, rendering futile Garvey's third series home run.

But Garvey's fourth homer, in Game Four, helped carry the Dodgers into the tenth inning, when Bill Russell—capitalizing on Gary Maddox's muff of Ron Cey's fly to center—singled home Cey with the Dodgers' unearned pennant winner.

Los Angeles Dodgers (West), 3; Philadelphia Phillies (East), 1

LA (W)

PLAYER/POS	AVG	G	AB	R	H	2B	3B	HR	RB	BB	SO	SB
Dusty Baker, of	.467	4	15	1	7	2	0	0	1	3	0	0
Ron Cey, 3b	.313	4	16	4	5	1	0	1	3	2	4	0
Joe Ferguson, ph	.000	2	2	0	0	0	0	0	0	0	1	0
Terry Forster, p	.000	1	0	0	0	0	0	0	0	0	0	0
Steve Garvey, 1b	.389	4	18	6	7	1	1	4	7	0	1	0
Jerry Grote, c	.000	1	0	0	0	0	0	0	0	0	0	0
Burt Hooton, p	.000	1	2	0	0	0	0	0	0	0	1	0
Charlie Hough, p	.000	1	0	0	0	0	0	0	0	0	0	0
Tommy John, p	.000	1	3	0	0	0	0	0	0	0	0	0
Lee Lacy, ph	.000	2	2	0	0	0	0	0	0	0	0	0
Davey Lopes, 2b	.389	4	18	3	7	1	1	2	5	0	1	1
Rick Monday, of	.200	3	10	2	2	0	1	0	0	1	5	0
Manny Mota, ph	1.000	2	1	0	1	1	0	0	0	0	0	0
Billy North, of	.000	4	8	0	0	0	0	0	0	0	1	0
Doug Rau, p	.000	1	1	0	0	0	0	0	0	0	0	0
Lance Rautzhan, p	.000	1	0	0	0	0	0	0	0	0	0	0
Rick Rhoden, p	.000	1	1	0	0	0	0	0	0	0	0	0
Bill Russell, ss	.412	4	17	1	7	1	0	0	2	1	1	0
Reggie Smith, of	.188	4	16	2	3	1	0	0	1	0	2	0
Don Sutton, p	.000	1	2	0	0	0	0	0	0	0	2	0
Bob Welch, p	.000	1	2	0	0	0	0	0	0	0	1	0
Steve Yeager, c	.231	4	13	2	3	0	0	1	2	2	2	1
TOTAL	.286		147	21	42	8	3	8	21	9	22	2

PITCHER	W	L	ERA	G	GS	CG	SV	SHO	IP	H	ER	BB	SO
Terry Forster	1	0	0.00	1	0	0	0	0	1.0	1	0	0	2
Burt Hooton	0	0	7.71	1	1	0	0	0	4.2	10	4	0	5
Charlie Hough	0	0	4.50	1	0	0	0	0	2.0	1	1	0	1
Tommy John	1	0	0.00	1	1	1	0	1	9.0	4	0	2	4
Doug Rau	0	0	3.60	1	1	0	0	0	5.0	5	2	2	1
Lance Rautzhan	0	0	6.75	1	0	0	0	0	1.1	3	1	2	0
Rick Rhoden	0	0	2.25	1	0	0	0	0	4.0	2	1	1	3
Don Sutton	0	1	6.35	1	1	0	0	0	5.2	7	4	2	0
Bob Welch	1	0	2.08	1	0	0	0	0	4.1	2	1	0	5
TOTAL	3	1	3.41	9	4	1	0	1	37.0	35	14	9	21

PHI (E)

PLAYER/POS	AVG	G	AB	R	H	2B	3B	HR	RB	BB	SO	SB
Bob Boone, c	.182	3	11	0	2	0	0	0	0	0	1	0
Larry Bowa, ss	.333	4	18	2	6	0	0	0	0	1	2	0
Warren Brusstar, p	.000	3	0	0	0	0	0	0	0	0	0	0
Jose Cardenal, 1b	.167	2	6	0	1	0	0	0	0	1	1	0
Steve Carlton, p	.500	1	4	2	2	0	0	1	4	0	0	0
Larry Christenson, p	.000	1	0	0	0	0	0	0	0	0	1	0
Rawly Eastwick, p	.000	1	0	0	0	0	0	0	0	0	0	0
Barry Foote, ph	.000	1	1	0	0	0	0	0	0	0	1	0
Orlando Gonzalez, ph	.000	1	1	0	0	0	0	0	0	0	0	0
Richie Hebner, 1b-2	.111	3	9	0	1	0	0	0	1	0	0	0
Randy Lerch, p	.000	1	2	0	0	0	0	0	0	0	0	0
Greg Luzinski, of	.375	4	16	3	6	0	1	2	3	1	2	0
Garry Maddox, of	.263	4	19	1	5	0	0	0	2	0	3	0
Jerry Martin, of-3	.222	4	9	1	2	1	0	1	2	1	3	0
Bake McBride, of-2	.222	3	9	2	2	0	0	1	1	0	2	0
Tim McCarver, c-1	.000	2	4	2	0	0	0	0	1	2	0	0
Tug McGraw, p	.000	3	0	0	0	0	0	0	0	0	0	0
Jim Morrison, ph	.000	1	1	0	0	0	0	0	0	0	1	0
Ron Reed, p	.000	2	0	0	0	0	0	0	0	0	0	0
Dick Ruthven, p	.000	1	1	0	0	0	0	0	0	0	1	0
Mike Schmidt, 3b	.200	4	15	1	3	2	0	0	1	2	2	0
Ted Sizemore, 2b	.385	4	13	3	5	0	1	0	1	1	0	0
TOTAL	.250		140	17	35	3	2	5	16	9	21	0

PITCHER	W	L	ERA	G	GS	CG	SV	SHO	IP	H	ER	BB	SO
Warren Brusstar	0	0	0.00	3	0	0	0	0	2.2	2	0	1	0
Steve Carlton	1	0	4.00	1	1	1	0	0	9.0	8	4	2	8
Larry Christenson	0	1	12.46	1	1	0	0	0	4.1	7	6	1	3
Rawly Eastwick	0	0	9.00	1	0	0	0	0	1.0	3	1	0	1
Randy Lerch	0	0	5.06	1	1	0	0	0	5.1	7	3	0	0
Tug McGraw	0	1	1.59	3	0	0	0	0	5.2	3	1	5	5
Ron Reed	0	0	2.25	2	0	0	0	0	4.0	6	1	0	2
Dick Ruthven	0	1	5.79	1	1	0	0	0	4.2	6	3	0	3
TOTAL	1	3	4.66	13	4	1	0	0	36.2	42	19	9	22

GAME 1 AT PHI OCT 4

LA	004	211	001	9	13 1
PHI	010	030	001	5	12 1

Pitchers: Hooton, WELCH (5) vs CHRISTENSEN, Brusstar (5), Eastwick (6), McGraw (7)
Home Runs: Garvey-LA (2), Lopes-LA, Yeager-LA, Martin-PHI
Attendance: 63,460

GAME 2 AT PHI OCT 5

LA	000	120	100	4	8 0
PHI	000	000	000	0	4 0

Pitchers: JOHN vs RUTHVEN, Brusstar (5), Reed (7), McGraw (9)
Home Runs: Lopes-LA
Attendance: 60,642

GAME 3 AT LA OCT 6

PHI	040	003	101	9	11 1
LA	012	000	010	4	8 2

Pitchers: CARLTON vs SUTTON, Rautzhan (6), Hough (8)
Home Runs: Carlton-PHI, Luzinski-PHI, Garvey-LA
Attendance: 55,043

GAME 4 AT LA OCT 7

PHI	002	000	100	0	3 8 2
LA	010	101	000	1	4 13 0

Pitchers: Lerch, Brusstar (6), Reed (7), McGRAW (9) vs Rau, Rhoden (6), FORSTER (10)
Home Runs: Luzinski-PHI, Cey-LA, Garvey-LA, McBride-PHI
Attendance: 55,124

It took Bucky Dent's pop-fly home run against Boston in an Eastern Division tiebreaker to carry the Yankees into the LCS. But once there they took the pennant, downing the Royals for the third year in a row. Reggie Jackson's three-run homer in the eighth inning of Game One capped a sixteen-hit, seven-run Yankee attack, as pitchers Jim Beattie and Ken Clay combined to limit Kansas City to two hits and a single run. The Royals, though, made it look just as easy the next day as their own sixteen hits and ten runs evened the series.

Twice in Game Three George Brett gave the Royals a lead with a home run, and he tied the game with a third homer in the fifth. But Jackson's two-run homer in the fourth brought the Yankees back, and Thurman Munson's two-run shot in the eighth gave New York a close win. Game Four was just as close, but more of a pitcher's duel. Dennis Leonard, who went the distance, gave up only four hits, but two of them were home runs to Graig Nettles and Roy White. Yankee starter Ron Guidry allowed a run in the first, but shut out the Royals for the next seven innings. Goose Gossage preserved Guidry's good work—and the pennant—in the ninth.

New York Yankees (East), 3; Kansas City Royals (West), 1

NY (E)

PLAYER/POS	AVG	G	AB	R	H	2B	3B	HR	RB	BB	SO	SB
Jim Beattie, p	.000	1	0	0	0	0	0	0	0	0	0	0
Paul Blair, of-3,2b-1	.000	4	6	1	0	0	0	0	0	0	1	0
Chris Chambliss, 1b	.400	4	15	1	6	0	0	0	2	0	4	0
Ken Clay, p	.000	1	0	0	0	0	0	0	0	0	0	0
Bucky Dent, ss	.200	4	15	0	3	0	0	0	4	0	0	0
Brian Doyle, 2b	.286	3	7	0	2	0	0	0	1	1	1	0
Ed Figueroa, p	.000	1	0	0	0	0	0	0	0	0	0	0
Rich Gossage, p	.000	2	0	0	0	0	0	0	0	0	0	0
Ron Guidry, p	.000	1	0	0	0	0	0	0	0	0	0	0
Catfish Hunter, p	.000	1	0	0	0	0	0	0	0	0	0	0
Reggie Jackson, dh-3,of-1	.462	4	13	5	6	1	0	2	6	3	4	0
Cliff Johnson, ph	.000	1	1	0	0	0	0	0	0	0	0	0
Sparky Lyle, p	.000	1	0	0	0	0	0	0	0	0	0	0
Thurman Munson, c	.278	4	18	2	5	1	0	1	2	0	0	0
Graig Nettles, 3b	.333	4	15	3	5	0	1	1	2	0	1	0
Lou Piniella, of	.235	4	17	2	4	0	0	0	0	0	3	0
Mickey Rivers, of	.455	4	11	0	5	0	0	0	0	2	0	0
Fred Stanley, 2b	.200	2	5	0	1	0	0	0	0	0	2	0
Gary Thomasson, of	.000	3	1	0	0	0	0	0	0	0	0	0
Dick Tidrow, p	.000	1	0	0	0	0	0	0	0	0	0	0
Roy White, of-3,dh-1	.313	4	16	5	5	1	0	1	1	1	2	0
TOTAL	.300		140	19	42	3	1	5	18	7	18	0

PITCHER	W	L	ERA	G	GS	CG	SV	SHO	IP	H	ER	BB	SO
Jim Beattie	1	0	1.69	1	1	0	0	0	5.1	2	1	5	3
Ken Clay	0	0	0.00	1	0	0	1	0	3.2	0	0	3	2
Ed Figueroa	0	1	27.00	1	1	0	0	0	1.0	5	3	0	0
Rich Gossage	1	0	4.50	2	0	0	1	0	4.0	3	2	0	3
Ron Guidry	1	0	1.13	1	1	0	0	0	8.0	7	1	1	7
Catfish Hunter	0	0	4.50	1	1	0	0	0	6.0	7	3	3	5
Sparky Lyle	0	0	13.50	1	0	0	0	0	1.1	3	2	0	0
Dick Tidrow	0	0	4.76	1	0	0	0	0	5.2	8	3	2	1
TOTAL	3	1	3.86	9	4	0	2	0	35.0	35	15	14	21

KC (W)

PLAYER/POS	AVG	G	AB	R	H	2B	3B	HR	RB	BB	SO	SB
Doug Bird, p	.000	2	0	0	0	0	0	0	0	0	0	0
Steve Braun, of-1	.000	2	5	0	0	0	0	0	0	0	1	0
George Brett, 3b	.389	4	18	7	7	1	1	3	3	0	1	0
Al Cowens, of	.133	4	15	2	2	0	0	0	1	0	2	0
Larry Gura, p	.000	1	0	0	0	0	0	0	0	0	0	0
Al Hrabosky, p	.000	3	0	0	0	0	0	0	0	0	0	0
Clint Hurdle, of-2	.375	4	8	1	3	0	1	0	1	2	3	0
Pete LaCock, 1b-3	.364	4	11	1	4	2	1	0	1	3	1	1
Dennis Leonard, p	.000	2	0	0	0	0	0	0	0	0	0	0
Hal McRae, dh	.214	4	14	0	3	0	0	0	2	2	1	1
Steve Mingori, p	.000	1	0	0	0	0	0	0	0	0	0	0
Amos Otis, of	.429	4	14	2	6	2	0	0	1	3	5	4
Freddie Patek, ss	.077	4	13	2	1	0	0	1	2	1	4	0
Marty Pattin, p	.000	1	0	0	0	0	0	0	0	0	0	0
Tom Poquette, ph	.000	1	1	0	0	0	0	0	0	0	0	0
Darrell Porter, c	.357	4	14	1	5	1	0	0	3	2	0	0
Paul Splittorff, p	.000	1	0	0	0	0	0	0	0	0	0	0
John Wathan, 1b	.000	1	3	0	0	0	0	0	0	0	0	0
Frank White, 2b	.231	4	13	1	3	0	0	0	2	0	0	0
Willie Wilson, of	.250	3	4	0	1	0	0	0	0	0	2	0
TOTAL	.263		133	17	35	6	3	4	16	14	21	6

PITCHER	W	L	ERA	G	GS	CG	SV	SHO	IP	H	ER	BB	SO
Doug Bird	0	1	9.00	2	0	0	0	0	1.0	2	1	0	1
Larry Gura	1	0	2.84	1	1	0	0	0	6.1	8	2	2	2
Al Hrabosky	0	0	3.00	3	0	0	0	0	3.0	3	1	0	2
Dennis Leonard	0	2	3.75	2	2	1	0	0	12.0	13	5	2	11
Steve Mingori	0	0	7.36	1	0	0	0	0	3.2	5	3	3	0
Marty Pattin	0	0	27.00	1	0	0	0	0	0.2	2	2	0	0
Paul Splittorff	0	0	4.91	1	1	0	0	0	7.1	9	4	0	2
TOTAL	1	3	4.76	11	4	1	0	0	34.0	42	18	7	18

GAME 1 AT KC OCT 3

NY	011	020	030	7	16 0
KC	000	001	000	1	2 2

Pitchers: BEATTIE, Clay (6) vs LEONARD, Mingori (5), Hrabosky (8), Bird (9)
Home Runs: Jackson-NY
Attendance: 41,143

GAME 2 AT KC OCT 4

NY	000	000	220	4	12 1
KC	140	000	32X	10	16 1

Pitchers: FIGUEROA, Tidrow (2), Lyle (7) vs GURA, Pattin (7), Hrabosky (8)
Home Runs: Patek-KC
Attendance: 41,158

GAME 3 AT NY OCT 6

KC	101	010	020	5	10 1
NY	010	201	02X	6	10 0

Pitchers: Splittorff, BIRD (8), Hrabosky (8) vs Hunter, GOSSAGE (7)
Home Runs: Brett-KC (3), Jackson-NY, Munson-NY
Attendance: 55,535

GAME 4 AT NY OCT 7

KC	100	000	000	1	7 0
NY	010	001	00X	2	4 0

Pitchers: LEONARD vs GUIDRY, Gossage (9)
Home Runs: Nettles-NY, R.White-NY
Attendance: 56,356

The outcome was the same as in 1977: the Yankees over the Dodgers in six games. But this year New York overcame a two-game deficit by sweeping the next four, a feat never before achieved in a World Series.

Los Angeles overwhelmed New York in the opener. Home runs in the second and fourth innings by Dusty Baker and Davey Lopes (two, for five RBI), and another run in the fifth, gave the Dodgers a 7–0 lead before Reggie Jackson's lead-off homer in the seventh gave New York its first score. The Yankees scored four more times, but so did the Dodgers for an 11–5 win. Game Two was closer. The Yankees scored first and held a lead through the top of the sixth, but Ron Cey's three-run homer in the bottom of the inning gave Los Angeles the runs they needed to win 4–3.

Yankee Ron Guidry, coming off a spectacular 25–3 regular season, pitched Game Three as the Series moved to New York. He gave up eight hits and issued seven walks. But only one baserunner scored, thanks in large part to several memorable stops and throws by third baseman Graig Nettles. Meanwhile, Roy White's home run in the first inning began Yankee scoring in what would become a 5–1 win.

It took ten innings for New York to win Game Four. Starters Tommy John and Ed Figueroa hurled shutout ball until Dodger Reggie Smith tagged Figueroa for a three-run homer in the top of the fifth. The Yankees clawed back in the sixth. Reggie Jackson singled in one run, then—in a play that stirred great controversy—got in the way (the Dodgers claimed intentionally) of a throw from second on an attempted double play, deflecting the ball to the outfield and permitting a second run to score. In the eighth, Thurman Munson doubled home the tying Yankee run, and in the last of the tenth Lou Piniella's two-out drive to center scored baserunner Roy White with the game winner.

Game Five was a Yankee blowout. No one hit home runs, but the Yankees hit sixteen singles (a Series record) and two doubles for twelve runs (five of them driven in by Munson's three hits) to give Yankee pitcher Jim Beattie (nine hits, two runs) an easy win. Back in Los Angeles for the sixth game, the Yankees won the crown on the hitting of two men at the bottom of the batting order: Denny Doyle and Bucky Dent. With three hits each, they combined for five RBI in the 7–2 win. For good measure, Reggie Jackson concluded the Series scoring with a mighty two-run homer in the seventh.

New York Yankees (AL), 4;
Los Angeles Dodgers (NL), 2

NY (A)

PLAYER/POS	AVG	G	AB	R	H	2B	3B	HR	RB	BB	SO	SB
Jim Beattie, p	.000	1	0	0	0	0	0	0	0	0	0	0
Paul Blair, cf	.375	6	8	2	3	1	0	0	0	1	4	0
Chris Chambliss, 1b	.182	3	11	1	2	0	0	0	0	1	1	0
Ken Clay, p	.000	1	0	0	0	0	0	0	0	0	0	0
Bucky Dent, ss	.417	6	24	3	10	1	0	0	7	1	2	0
Brian Doyle, 2b	.438	6	16	4	7	1	0	0	2	0	0	0
Ed Figueroa, p	.000	2	0	0	0	0	0	0	0	0	0	0
Rich Gossage, p	.000	3	0	0	0	0	0	0	0	0	0	0
Ron Guidry, p	.000	1	0	0	0	0	0	0	0	0	0	0
Mike Heath, c	.000	1	0	0	0	0	0	0	0	0	0	0
Catfish Hunter, p	.000	2	0	0	0	0	0	0	0	0	0	0
Reggie Jackson, dh	.391	6	23	2	9	1	0	2	8	3	7	0
Cliff Johnson, ph	.000	2	2	0	0	0	0	0	0	0	1	0
Jay Johnstone, of	.000	2	0	0	0	0	0	0	0	0	0	0
Paul Lindblad, p	.000	1	0	0	0	0	0	0	0	0	0	0
Thurman Munson, c	.320	6	25	5	8	3	0	0	7	3	7	1
Graig Nettles, 3b	.160	6	25	2	4	0	0	0	1	0	6	0
Lou Piniella, of	.280	6	25	3	7	0	0	0	4	0	0	1
Mickey Rivers, of-4	.333	5	18	2	6	0	0	0	1	0	2	1
Jim Spencer, 1b-3	.167	4	12	3	2	0	0	0	0	2	4	0
Fred Stanley, 2b	.200	3	5	0	1	1	0	0	0	1	0	0
Gary Thomasson, of	.250	3	4	0	1	0	0	0	0	0	1	0
Dick Tidrow, p	.000	2	0	0	0	0	0	0	0	0	0	0
Roy White, of	.333	6	24	9	8	0	0	1	4	4	5	2
TOTAL	.306		222	36	68	8	0	3	34	16	40	5

PITCHER	W	L	ERA	G	GS	CG	SV	SHO	IP	H	ER	BB	SO
Jim Beattie	1	0	2.00	1	1	1	0	0	9.0	9	2	4	8
Ken Clay	0	0	11.57	1	0	0	0	0	2.1	4	3	2	2
Ed Figueroa	0	1	8.10	2	2	0	0	0	6.2	9	6	5	2
Rich Gossage	1	0	0.00	3	0	0	0	0	6.0	1	0	1	4
Ron Guidry	1	0	1.00	1	1	1	0	0	9.0	8	1	7	4
Catfish Hunter	1	1	4.15	2	2	0	0	0	13.0	13	6	1	5
Paul Lindblad	0	0	11.57	1	0	0	0	0	2.1	4	3	0	1
Dick Tidrow	0	0	1.93	2	0	0	0	0	4.2	4	1	0	5
TOTAL	4	2	3.74	13	6	2	0	0	53.0	52	22	20	31

LA (N)

PLAYER/POS	AVG	G	AB	R	H	2B	3B	HR	RB	BB	SO	SB
Dusty Baker, of	.238	6	21	2	5	0	0	1	1	1	3	0
Ron Cey, 3b	.286	6	21	2	6	0	0	1	4	3	3	0
Vic Davalillo, dh-1	.333	2	3	0	1	0	0	0	0	0	0	0
Joe Ferguson, c	.500	2	4	1	2	2	0	0	0	0	1	0
Terry Forster, p	.000	3	0	0	0	0	0	0	0	0	0	0
Steve Garvey, 1b	.208	6	24	1	5	1	0	0	1	1	7	1
Jerry Grote, c	.000	2	0	0	0	0	0	0	0	0	0	0
Burt Hooton, p	.000	2	0	0	0	0	0	0	0	0	0	0
Charlie Hough, p	.000	2	0	0	0	0	0	0	0	0	0	0
Tommy John, p	.000	2	0	0	0	0	0	0	0	0	0	0
Lee Lacy, dh	.143	4	14	0	2	0	0	0	1	1	3	0
Davey Lopes, 2b	.308	6	26	7	8	0	0	3	7	2	1	2
Rick Monday, of-4,dh-1	.154	5	13	2	2	1	0	0	4	3	0	0
Manny Mota, ph	.000	1	0	0	0	0	0	0	0	1	0	0
Billy North, of	.125	4	8	2	1	1	0	0	2	1	0	1
Johnny Oates, c	1.000	1	1	0	1	0	0	0	0	1	0	0
Doug Rau, p	.000	1	0	0	0	0	0	0	0	0	0	0
Lance Rautzhan, p	.000	2	0	0	0	0	0	0	0	0	0	0
Bill Russell, ss	.423	6	26	1	11	2	0	0	2	2	2	1
Reggie Smith, of	.200	6	25	3	5	0	0	1	5	2	6	0
Don Sutton, p	.000	2	0	0	0	0	0	0	0	0	0	0
Bob Welch, p	.000	3	0	0	0	0	0	0	0	0	0	0
Steve Yeager, c	.231	5	13	2	3	1	0	0	1	1	2	0
TOTAL	.261		199	23	52	8	0	6	22	20	31	5

PITCHER	W	L	ERA	G	GS	CG	SV	SHO	IP	H	ER	BB	SO
Terry Forster	0	0	0.00	3	0	0	0	0	4.0	5	0	1	6
Burt Hooton	1	1	6.48	2	2	0	0	0	8.1	13	6	3	6
Charlie Hough	0	0	8.44	2	0	0	0	0	5.1	10	5	2	5
Tommy John	1	0	3.07	2	2	0	0	0	14.2	14	5	4	6
Doug Rau	0	0	0.00	1	0	0	0	0	2.0	1	0	0	3
Lance Rautzhan	0	0	13.50	2	0	0	0	0	2.0	4	3	0	0
Don Sutton	0	2	7.50	2	2	0	0	0	12.0	17	10	4	8
Bob Welch	0	1	6.23	3	0	0	0	1	4.1	4	3	2	6
TOTAL	2	4	5.47	17	6	0	1	0	52.2	68	32	16	40

GAME 1 AT LA OCT 10

NY	000	000	320		5	9	1
LA	030	310	31X		11	15	2

Pitchers: FIGUEROA, Clay (2), Lindblad (5), Tidrow (7) vs JOHN, Forster (8)
Home Runs: Baker-LA, Lopes-LA (2), Jackson-NY
Attendance: 55,997

GAME 2 AT LA OCT 11

NY	002	000	100		3	11	0
LA	000	103	00X		4	7	0

Pitchers: HUNTER, Gossage (7) vs HOOTON, Forster (7), Welch (9)
Home Runs: Cey-LA
Attendance: 55,982

GAME 3 AT NY OCT 13

LA	001	000	000		1	8	0
NY	110	000	30X		5	10	1

Pitchers: SUTTON, Rautzhan (7), Hough (8) vs GUIDRY
Home Runs: White-NY
Attendance: 56,447

GAME 4 AT NY OCT 14

LA	000	030	000 0		3	6	1
NY	000	002	010 1		4	9	0

Pitchers: John, Forster (8), WELCH (8) vs Figueroa, Tidrow (6), GOSSAGE (9)
Home Runs: Smith-LA
Attendance: 56,445

GAME 5 AT NY OCT 15

LA	101	000	000		2	9	3
NY	004	300	41X		12	18	0

Pitchers: HOOTON, Rautzhan (3), Hough (4) vs BEATTIE
Attendance: 56,448

GAME 6 AT LA OCT 17

NY	030	002	200		7	11	0
LA	101	000	000		2	7	1

Pitchers: HUNTER, Gossage (8) vs SUTTON, Welch (7), Rau (8)
Home Runs: Lopes-LA, Jackson-NY
Attendance: 55,985

The Pirates—with a better season's record than Cincinnati and stronger hitting and pitching—proved their superiority in the LCS as well, dominating the statistics and sweeping the series. Yet the games were closer than the stats alone would suggest. Pittsburgh won the first game by three runs—but they didn't come until Willie Stargell's homer in the eleventh inning broke a 2–2 tie.

In Game Two, Cincinnati scored first. The Pirates tied the game with a run in the fourth and took a narrow lead with another in the fifth. But the Reds came back on a game-tying pair of doubles in the ninth, and it wasn't until the tenth that Pittsburgh eked out its victory with a run on two singles and Don Robinson's shutout relief.

Only in the third game did the Pirates take a commanding lead, with six runs in the first four innings (two of them on home runs by Stargell and Bill Madlock). The Reds outhit Pittsburgh eight to seven, but only Johnny Bench's homer brought them a run, as Bert Blyleven overcame them in the series' only complete-game pitching performance.

Pittsburgh Pirates (East), 3; Cincinnati Reds (West), 0

PIT (E)

PLAYER/POS	AVG	G	AB	R	H	2B	3B	HR	RB	BB	SO	SB
Matt Alexander, pr	.000	1	0	1	0	0	0	0	0	0	0	0
Jim Bibby, p	.000	1	0	0	0	0	0	0	0	1	0	0
Bert Blyleven, p	.333	1	3	1	1	0	0	0	0	0	1	0
John Candelaria, p	.000	1	3	0	0	0	0	0	0	0	2	0
Mike Easler, ph	.000	1	1	0	0	0	0	0	0	0	0	0
Tim Foli, ss	.333	3	12	1	4	1	0	0	3	0	0	0
Phil Garner, 2b-3,ss-1	.417	3	12	4	5	0	1	1	1	1	0	0
Grant Jackson, p	.000	2	1	0	0	0	0	0	0	0	0	0
Bill Madlock, 3b	.250	3	12	1	3	0	0	1	2	2	0	2
John Milner, of	.000	3	9	0	0	0	0	0	0	2	0	0
Omar Moreno, of	.250	3	12	3	3	0	1	0	0	2	2	1
Ed Ott, c	.231	3	13	0	3	0	0	0	0	0	2	0
Dave Parker, of	.333	3	12	2	4	0	0	0	2	2	3	1
Dave Roberts, p	.000	1	0	0	0	0	0	0	0	0	0	0
Don Robinson, p	.000	2	0	0	0	0	0	0	0	0	0	0
Bill Robinson, of	.000	3	3	0	0	0	0	0	0	0	0	0
Enrique Romo, p	.000	2	0	0	0	0	0	0	0	0	0	0
Willie Stargell, 1b	.455	3	11	2	5	2	0	2	6	3	2	0
Rennie Stennett, 2b	.000	1	0	0	0	0	0	0	0	0	0	0
Kent Tekulve, p	.000	2	1	0	0	0	0	0	0	0	1	0
TOTAL	.267		105	15	28	3	2	4	14	13	13	4

PITCHER	W	L	ERA	G	GS	CG	SV	SHO	IP	H	ER	BB	SO
Jim Bibby	0	0	1.29	1	1	0	0	0	7.0	4	1	4	5
Bert Blyleven	1	0	1.00	1	1	1	0	0	9.0	8	1	0	9
John Candelaria	0	0	2.57	1	1	0	0	0	7.0	5	2	1	4
Grant Jackson	1	0	0.00	2	0	0	0	0	2.0	1	0	1	2
Dave Roberts	0	0	∞	1	0	0	0	0	0.0	0	0	1	0
Don Robinson	1	0	0.00	2	0	0	1	0	2.0	0	0	1	3
Enrique Romo	0	0	0.00	2	0	0	0	0	0.1	3	0	1	1
Kent Tekulve	0	0	3.38	2	0	0	0	0	2.2	2	1	2	2
TOTAL	3	0	1.50	12	3	1	1	0	30	23	5	11	26

CIN (W)

PLAYER/POS	AVG	G	AB	R	H	2B	3B	HR	RB	BB	SO	SB
Rick Auerbach, ph	.000	2	2	0	0	0	0	0	0	0	1	0
Doug Bair, p	.000	1	0	0	0	0	0	0	0	0	0	0
Johnny Bench, c	.250	3	12	1	3	0	1	1	1	2	2	0
Dave Collins, of	.357	3	14	0	5	1	0	0	1	0	2	2
Dave Concepcion, ss	.429	3	14	1	6	1	0	0	0	0	3	0
Hector Cruz, of-1	.200	2	5	1	1	1	0	0	0	0	1	0
Dan Driessen, 1b	.083	3	12	1	1	0	0	0	0	1	3	0
George Foster, of	.200	3	10	1	2	0	0	1	2	4	3	0
Cesar Geronimo, of	.143	2	7	0	1	0	0	0	0	0	5	0
Tom Hume, p	.000	3	1	0	0	0	0	0	0	0	1	0
Ray Knight, 3b	.286	3	14	0	4	1	0	0	0	0	2	1
Mike LaCoss, p	.000	1	0	0	0	0	0	0	0	0	0	0
Charlie Leibrandt, p	.000	1	0	0	0	0	0	0	0	0	0	0
Joe Morgan, 2b	.000	3	11	0	0	0	0	0	0	3	1	1
Fred Norman, p	.000	1	1	0	0	0	0	0	0	0	1	0
Frank Pastore, p	.000	1	0	0	0	0	0	0	1	1	0	0
Tom Seaver, p	.000	1	2	0	0	0	0	0	0	0	1	0
Mario Soto, p	.000	1	0	0	0	0	0	0	0	0	0	0
Harry Spilman, ph	.000	2	2	0	0	0	0	0	0	0	0	0
Dave Tomlin, p	.000	3	0	0	0	0	0	0	0	0	0	0
TOTAL	.215		107	5	23	4	1	2	5	11	26	4

PITCHER	W	L	ERA	G	GS	CG	SV	SHO	IP	H	ER	BB	SO
Doug Bair	0	1	9.00	1	0	0	0	0	1.0	2	1	1	0
Tom Hume	0	1	6.75	3	0	0	0	0	4.0	6	3	0	2
Mike LaCoss	0	1	10.80	1	1	0	0	0	1.2	1	2	4	0
Charlie Leibrandt	0	0	0.00	1	0	0	0	0	0.1	0	0	0	0
Fred Norman	0	0	18.00	1	0	0	0	0	2.0	4	4	1	1
Frank Pastore	0	0	2.57	1	1	0	0	0	7.0	7	2	3	1
Tom Seaver	0	0	2.25	1	1	0	0	0	8.0	5	2	2	5
Mario Soto	0	0	0.00	1	0	0	0	0	2.0	0	0	0	1
Dave Tomlin	0	0	0.00	3	0	0	0	0	3.0	3	0	2	3
TOTAL	0	3	4.34	13	3	0	0	0	29.0	28	14	13	13

GAME 1 AT CIN OCT 2

PIT	002 000 000 03	5	10	0
CIN	000 000 000 00	2	7	0

Pitchers: Candelaria, Romo (8), Tekulve (8), JACKSON (10), D.Robinson (11) vs Seaver, HUME (9), Tomlin (11)
Home Runs: Garner-PIT, Foster-CIN, Stargell-PIT
Attendance: 55,006

GAME 2 AT CIN OCT 3

PIT	000 110 000 1	3	11	0
CIN	010 000 001 0	2	8	0

Pitchers: Bibby, Jackson (8), Romo (8), Tekulve (8), Roberts (9), D.ROBINSON (9) vs Pastore, Tomlin (8), Hume (8), BAIR (10)
Attendance: 55,000

GAME 3 AT PIT OCT 5

CIN	000 001 000	1	8	1
PIT	112 200 01X	7	7	0

Pitchers: LaCOSS, Norman (2), Leibrandt (4), Soto (5), Tomlin (7), Hume (8) vs BLYLEVEN
Home Runs: Stargell-PIT, Madlock-PIT, Bench-CIN
Attendance: 42,240

Baltimore, returning to postseason play after a four-year absence, struggled with first-timer California through three games before blowing them away in the fourth. Game One went into the last of the tenth, tied 3–3, when Oriole pinch hitter John Lowenstein, up with two men on, ended it with a two-out, two-strike shot that just cleared the left field wall.

Game Two looked like a blowout for Baltimore. Eddie Murray drove in four runs, and the rest of the team added five more to give the O's a 9–1 lead by the end of three. But California chipped away at the lead in the latter half of the game and drew within one in the ninth, before Brian Downing hit into a forceout with the bases full to end their scoring.

The Angels' late rally in Game Three was more successful. Down by a run in the bottom of the ninth, they scored twice, on a walk, a dropped outfield fly, and Larry Harlow's game-winning double. The final game, though, was all Baltimore's, as Scott McGregor—pitching the series' only complete game—blanked the Angels on six hits. The Orioles scored two in the third and another in the fourth, before Pat Kelly put Angel pennant hopes out of reach with a three-run homer in the O's five-run seventh.

Baltimore Orioles (East), 3; California Angels (West), 1

BAL (E)

PLAYER/POS	AVG	G	AB	R	H	2B	3B	HR	RB	BB	SO	SB
Mark Belanger, ss	.200	3	5	0	1	0	0	0	0	1	0	2	0
Al Bumbry, of	.250	4	16	5	4	0	1	0	0	4	3	2
Terry Crowley, ph	.500	2	2	0	1	0	0	0	1	0	0	0
Rich Dauer, 2b	.182	4	11	0	2	0	0	0	0	0	1	0
Doug DeCinces, 3b	.308	4	13	4	4	1	0	0	3	1	1	0
Rick Dempsey, c	.400	3	10	3	4	2	0	0	2	1	0	1
Mike Flanagan, p	.000	1	0	0	0	0	0	0	0	0	0	0
Kiko Garcia, ss	.273	3	11	1	3	0	0	0	0	2	4	0
Pat Kelly, dh-2,of-1	.364	3	11	3	4	0	0	1	4	1	3	2
John Lowenstein, of-3	.167	4	6	2	1	0	0	1	3	2	2	0
Dennis Martinez, p	.000	1	0	0	0	0	0	0	0	0	0	0
Lee May, dh	.143	2	7	0	1	0	0	0	1	1	3	0
Scott McGregor, p	.000	1	0	0	0	0	0	0	0	0	0	0
Eddie Murray, 1b	.417	4	12	3	5	0	0	1	5	5	2	0
Jim Palmer, p	.000	1	0	0	0	0	0	0	0	0	0	0
Gary Roenicke, of	.200	2	5	1	1	0	0	0	0	1	0	0
Ken Singleton, of	.375	4	16	4	6	2	0	0	2	1	2	0
Dave Skaggs, c	.000	1	4	0	0	0	0	0	0	0	0	0
Billy Smith, 2b	.000	1	4	0	0	0	0	0	0	0	1	0
Don Stanhouse, p	.000	3	0	0	0	0	0	0	0	0	0	0
TOTAL	.278		133	26	37	5	1	3	25	18	24	5

PITCHER	W	L	ERA	G	GS	CG	SV	SHO	IP	H	ER	BB	SO
Mike Flanagan	1	0	5.14	1	1	0	0	0	7.0	6	4	1	2
Dennis Martinez	0	0	3.24	1	1	0	0	0	8.1	8	3	0	4
Scott McGregor	1	0	0.00	1	1	1	0	1	9.0	6	0	1	4
Jim Palmer	0	0	3.00	1	1	0	0	0	9.0	7	3	2	3
Don Stanhouse	1	1	6.00	3	0	0	0	0	3.0	5	2	3	0
TOTAL	3	1	2.97	7	4	1	0	1	36.1	32	12	7	13

CAL (W)

PLAYER/POS	AVG	G	AB	R	H	2B	3B	HR	RB	BB	SO	SB
Don Aase, p	.000	2	0	0	0	0	0	0	0	0	0	0
Jim Anderson, ss	.091	4	11	0	1	0	0	0	0	0	1	0
Mike Barlow, p	.000	1	0	0	0	0	0	0	0	0	0	0
Don Baylor, dh-3,of-1	.188	4	16	2	3	0	0	1	2	1	2	0
Bert Campaneris, ss	.000	1	0	0	0	0	0	0	0	0	0	0
Rod Carew, 1b	.412	4	17	4	7	3	0	0	1	0	0	1
Bobby Clark, of	.000	1	3	0	0	0	0	0	0	0	2	0
Mark Clear, p	.000	1	0	0	0	0	0	0	0	0	0	0
Willie Davis, ph	.500	2	2	1	1	1	0	0	0	0	0	0
Brian Downing, c	.200	4	15	1	3	0	0	0	1	1	1	0
Dan Ford, of	.294	4	17	2	5	1	0	2	4	0	0	0
Dave Frost, p	.000	2	0	0	0	0	0	0	0	0	0	0
Bobby Grich, 2b	.154	4	13	0	2	0	0	0	2	1	1	0
Larry Harlow, of-2	.125	3	8	0	1	1	0	0	1	1	2	0
Chris Knapp, p	.000	1	0	0	0	0	0	0	0	0	0	0
Carney Lansford, 3b	.294	4	17	2	5	0	0	0	3	1	2	1
Dave LaRoche, p	.000	1	0	0	0	0	0	0	0	0	0	0
Rick Miller, of	.250	4	16	2	4	0	0	0	0	0	1	0
John Montague, p	.000	2	0	0	0	0	0	0	0	0	0	0
Merv Rettenmund, dh	.000	2	2	0	0	0	0	0	0	2	1	0
Nolan Ryan, p	.000	1	0	0	0	0	0	0	0	0	0	0
Frank Tanana, p	.000	1	0	0	0	0	0	0	0	0	0	0
Dickie Thon, ss	.000	1	0	1	0	0	0	0	0	0	0	0
TOTAL	.234		137	15	32	7	0	3	14	7	13	2

PITCHER	W	L	ERA	G	GS	CG	SV	SHO	IP	H	ER	BB	SO
Don Aase	1	0	1.80	2	0	0	0	0	5.0	4	1	2	6
Mike Barlow	0	0	0.00	1	0	0	0	0	1.0	0	0	0	0
Mark Clear	0	0	4.76	1	0	0	0	0	5.2	4	3	2	3
Dave Frost	0	1	18.69	2	1	0	0	0	4.1	8	9	5	1
Chris Knapp	0	1	7.71	1	1	0	0	0	2.1	5	2	1	0
Dave LaRoche	0	0	6.75	1	0	0	0	0	1.1	2	1	1	1
John Montague	0	1	9.00	2	0	0	0	0	4.0	4	4	2	2
Nolan Ryan	0	0	1.29	1	1	0	0	0	7.0	4	1	3	8
Frank Tanana	0	0	3.60	1	1	0	0	0	5.0	6	2	2	3
TOTAL	1	3	5.80	12	4	0	0	0	35.2	37	23	18	24

GAME 1 AT BAL OCT 3

CAL	101 001 000 0	3 7 1
BAL	002 100 000 3	6 6 0

Pitchers: Ryan, MONTAGUE (8) vs Palmer, STANHOUSE (10)
Home Runs: Ford-CAL, Lowenstein-BAL
Attendance: 52,787

GAME 2 AT BAL OCT 4

CAL	100 001 132	8 10 1
BAL	441 000 00X	9 11 1

Pitchers: FROST, Clear (2), Aase (8) vs FLANAGAN, Stanhouse (8)
Home Runs: Ford-CAL, Murray-BAL
Attendance: 52,108

GAME 3 AT CAL OCT 5

BAL	000 101 100	3 8 3
CAL	100 100 002	4 9 0

Pitchers: D.Martinez, STANHOUSE (9) vs Tanana, AASE (6)
Home Runs: Baylor-CAL
Attendance: 43,199

GAME 4 AT CAL OCT 6

BAL	002 100 500	8 12 1
CAL	000 000 000	0 6 0

Pitchers: McGREGOR vs KNAPP, LaRoche (3), Frost (4), Montague (7), Barlow (9)
Home Runs: Kelly-BAL
Attendance: 43,199

Veteran Willie Stargell was "Pops," and in the Series he showed his Pirate "family" the way. Seven of his twelve hits went for extra bases, and he drove in a Series-high seven runs. What Stargell began, submarine reliever Kent Tekulve finished, appearing in five of the seven games and recording a record-tying three saves.

Stargell drove in a pair of runs in the opener—one of them with an eighth-inning homer—but Pittsburgh's four runs fell short of the five Baltimore had scored in the first inning. The only extra-base hits in Game Two came from the bat of Eddie Murray, who homered and doubled to drive in both Baltimore runs. But three singles and a sacrifice fly had already given Pittsburgh two runs in the second inning, and two more Pirate singles and a walk in the top of the ninth made the score 3–2. Tekulve came on in the last of the ninth to preserve the lead, fanning two as he retired the side in order.

Baltimore bounced back, though, to take the next two games in convincing fashion. The score favored the Orioles 8–4 when Tekulve came on to set the birds down in order over the final two innings. But Baltimore starter Scott McGregor had by then settled into his groove, retiring the final eleven Pirates with relative ease to preserve his lead and the Oriole win. It took four Orioles pitchers to hold the Pirates in Game Four. Stargell led the Bucs' seventeen-hit attack with a homer, double, and single, and the Pirates led 6–3 entering the eighth inning. But Baltimore loaded the bases in the top of the eighth, prompting Pirate manager Chuck Tanner to bring Tekulve in again. This one time the strategy failed, as Tekulve saw six runs score before he retired his first batter.

Down three games to one, the Pirates rebounded in Game Five, scoring seven times in the final three innings for a 7–1 victory. Baltimore starter Jim Palmer matched John Candelaria's shutout pitching through six innings of Game Six before the Pirates tagged him for pairs of runs in the seventh and eighth. Tekulve, meanwhile, continued Candelaria's shutout through the final three innings, retiring the last seven men in order, four by strikeout. Baltimore scored first in the finale on Rich Dauer's leadoff home run in the third inning, but Stargell put the Pirates ahead with a two-run homer in the sixth. Tekulve came in with two Orioles on base in the eighth to stifle the threat, and (after the Pirates had scored a pair of insurance runs in the top of the ninth) set Baltimore down in order to complete the Pirate comeback.

Pittsburgh Pirates (NL), 4; Baltimore Orioles (AL), 3

PIT (N)

PLAYER/POS	AVG	G	AB	R	H	2B	3B	HR	RB	BB	SO	SB
Matt Alexander, of	.000	1	0	0	0	0	0	0	0	0	0	0
Jim Bibby, p	.000	2	4	0	0	0	0	0	0	0	1	0
Bert Blyleven, p	.000	2	3	0	0	0	0	0	0	0	0	0
John Candelaria, p	.333	2	3	0	1	0	0	0	0	0	2	0
Mike Easler, ph	.000	2	1	0	0	0	0	0	0	1	0	0
Tim Foli, ss	.333	7	30	6	10	1	1	0	3	2	0	0
Phil Garner, 2b	.500	7	24	4	12	4	0	0	5	3	1	0
Grant Jackson, p	.000	4	1	0	0	0	0	0	0	0	0	0
Bruce Kison, p	.000	1	0	0	0	0	0	0	0	0	0	0
Lee Lacy, ph	.250	4	4	0	1	0	0	0	0	0	1	0
Bill Madlock, 3b	.375	7	24	2	9	1	0	0	3	5	1	0
John Milner, of	.333	3	9	2	3	1	0	0	1	2	0	0
Omar Moreno, of	.333	7	33	4	11	2	0	0	3	1	7	0
Steve Nicosia, c	.063	4	16	1	1	0	0	0	0	0	2	0
Ed Ott, c	.333	3	12	2	4	1	0	0	3	0	2	0
Dave Parker, of	.345	7	29	2	10	3	0	0	4	2	7	0
Don Robinson, p	.000	4	0	0	0	0	0	0	0	0	0	0
Bill Robinson, of-6	.263	7	19	2	5	1	0	0	2	0	4	0
Enrique Romo, p	.000	2	1	0	0	0	0	0	0	0	0	0
Jim Rooker, p	.000	2	2	0	0	0	0	0	0	0	1	0
Manny Sanguillen, ph	.333	3	3	0	1	0	0	0	1	0	0	0
Willie Stargell, 1b	.400	7	30	7	12	4	0	3	7	0	6	0
Rennie Stennett, ph	1.000	1	1	0	1	0	0	0	0	0	0	0
Kent Tekulve, p	.000	5	2	0	0	0	0	0	0	0	0	0
TOTAL	.323		251	32	81	18	1	3	32	16	35	0

PITCHER	W	L	ERA	G	GS	CG	SV	SHO	IP	H	ER	BB	SO
Jim Bibby	0	0	2.61	2	2	0	0	0	10.1	10	3	2	10
Bert Blyleven	1	0	1.80	2	1	0	0	0	10.0	8	2	3	4
John Candelaria	1	1	5.00	2	2	0	0	0	9.0	14	5	2	4
Grant Jackson	1	0	0.00	4	0	0	0	0	4.2	1	0	2	2
Bruce Kison	0	1	108.00	1	1	0	0	0	0.1	3	4	2	0
Don Robinson	1	0	5.40	4	0	0	0	0	5.0	4	3	6	3
Enrique Romo	0	0	3.86	2	0	0	0	0	4.2	5	2	3	4
Jim Rooker	0	0	1.04	2	1	0	0	0	8.2	5	1	3	4
Kent Tekulve	0	1	2.89	5	0	0	3	0	9.1	4	3	3	10
TOTAL	4	3	3.34	24	7	0	3	0	62.0	54	23	26	41

BAL (A)

PLAYER/POS	AVG	G	AB	R	H	2B	3B	HR	RB	BB	SO	SB
Benny Ayala, of-3	.333	4	6	1	2	0	0	1	2	1	0	0
Mark Belanger, ss-4	.000	5	6	1	0	0	0	0	0	1	1	0
Al Bumbry, of	.143	7	21	3	3	0	0	0	1	2	1	0
Terry Crowley, ph	.250	5	4	0	1	1	0	0	2	1	0	0
Rich Dauer, 2b-5	.294	6	17	2	5	1	0	1	1	0	1	0
Doug DeCinces, 3b	.200	7	25	2	5	0	0	1	3	5	5	1
Rick Dempsey, c-6	.286	7	21	3	6	2	0	0	0	1	3	0
Mike Flanagan, p	.000	3	5	0	0	0	0	0	0	1	2	0
Kiko Garcia, ss	.400	6	20	4	8	2	1	0	6	1	3	0
Pat Kelly, ph	.250	5	4	0	1	0	0	0	0	1	1	0
John Lowenstein, of-3	.231	6	13	2	3	1	0	0	3	1	3	0
Tippy Martinez, p	.000	3	0	0	0	0	0	0	0	0	0	0
Dennis Martinez, p	.000	2	0	0	0	0	0	0	0	0	0	0
Lee May, ph	.000	2	1	0	0	0	0	0	0	1	1	0
Scott McGregor, p	.000	2	4	1	0	0	0	0	0	2	1	0
Eddie Murray, 1b	.154	7	26	3	4	1	0	1	2	4	4	1
Jim Palmer, p	.000	2	4	0	0	0	0	0	0	0	3	0
Gary Roenicke, of-5	.125	6	16	1	2	1	0	0	0	0	6	0
Ken Singleton, of	.357	7	28	1	10	1	0	0	2	5	5	0
Dave Skaggs, c	.333	1	3	1	1	0	0	0	0	0	0	0
Billy Smith, 2b-2	.286	4	7	1	2	0	0	0	0	2	0	0
Don Stanhouse, p	.000	3	0	0	0	0	0	0	0	0	0	0
Sammy Stewart, p	.000	1	1	0	0	0	0	0	0	0	1	0
Tim Stoddard, p	1.000	4	1	0	1	0	0	0	1	0	0	0
Steve Stone, p	.000	1	0	0	0	0	0	0	0	0	0	0
TOTAL	.232		233	26	54	10	1	4	23	26	41	2

PITCHER	W	L	ERA	G	GS	CG	SV	SHO	IP	H	ER	BB	SO
Mike Flanagan	1	1	3.00	3	2	1	0	0	15.0	18	5	2	13
Tippy Martinez	0	0	6.75	3	0	0	0	0	1.1	3	1	0	1
Dennis Martinez	0	0	18.00	2	1	0	0	0	2.0	6	4	0	0
Scott McGregor	1	1	3.18	2	2	1	0	0	17.0	16	6	2	8
Jim Palmer	0	1	3.60	2	2	0	0	0	15.0	18	6	5	8
Don Stanhouse	0	1	13.50	3	0	0	0	0	2.0	6	3	3	0
Sammy Stewart	0	0	0.00	1	0	0	0	0	2.2	4	0	1	0
Tim Stoddard	1	0	5.40	4	0	0	0	0	5.0	6	3	1	3
Steve Stone	0	0	9.00	1	0	0	0	0	2.0	4	2	2	2
TOTAL	3	4	4.35	21	7	2	0	0	62.0	81	30	16	35

GAME 1 AT BAL OCT 10

PIT	000 102 010	4	11	3
BAL	500 000 000	5	6	3

Pitchers: KISON, Rooker (1), Romo (5), D.Robinson (6), Jackson (8) vs FLANAGAN
Home Runs: Stargell-PIT, DeCinces-BAL
Attendance: 53,735

GAME 2 AT BAL OCT 11

PIT	020 000 001	3	11	2
BAL	010 001 000	2	6	1

Pitchers: Blyleven, D.ROBINSON (7), Tekulve (9) vs PALMER, T.Martinez (8), Stanhouse (8), T.Martinez (9)
Home Runs: Muuray-BAL
Attendance: 53,739

GAME 3 AT PIT OCT 12

BAL	002 500 100	8	13	0
PIT	120 010 000	4	9	2

Pitchers: McGREGOR vs CANDELARIA, Romo (4), Jackson (7), Tekulve (8)
Home Runs: Ayala-BAL
Attendance: 50,848

GAME 4 AT PIT OCT 13

BAL	003 000 060	9	12	0
PIT	040 011 000	6	17	1

Pitchers: D.Martinez, Stewart (2), Stone (5), STODDARD (7) vs Bibby, Jackson (6), D.Robinson (8), TEKULVE (8)
Home Runs: Stargell-PIT
Attendance: 50,883

GAME 5 AT PIT OCT 14

BAL	000 010 000	1	6	2
PIT	000 002 23X	7	13	1

Pitchers: FLANAGAN, Stoddard (7), T.Martinez (7), Stanhouse (8) vs Rooker, BLYLEVEN (6)
Attendance: 50,920

GAME 6 AT BAL OCT 16

PIT	000 000 220	4	10	0
BAL	000 000 000	0	7	1

Pitchers: CANDELARIA, Tekulve (7) vs PALMER, Stoddard (9)
Attendance: 53,739

GAME 7 AT BAL OCT 17

PIT	000 002 002	4	10	0
BAL	001 000 000	1	4	2

Pitchers: Bibby, D.Robinson (5), JACKSON (5), Tekulve (8) vs McGREGOR, Stoddard (9), Flanagan (9), Stanhouse (9), T.Martinez (9), D.Martinez (9)
Home Runs: Stargell-PIT, Dauer-BAL
Attendance: 53,733

In the tightest LCS yet, the Phillies took the opener 3–1 on the series' only home run—Greg Luzinski's two-run blast in the sixth inning. It was the only game not to go into extra innings.

The Astros evened the series in Game Two—demolishing a 3–3 tie with four runs in the tenth—and took the series lead in a Game Three pitchers' duel that saw Astro Joe Niekro hurl ten scoreless innings. Reliever Dave Smith continued the shutout and took the win as Joe Morgan's triple and Denny Walling's sacrifice fly off ace Phillie reliever Tug McGraw scored the game's only run in the bottom of the eleventh.

The Phillies rebounded, though, with their own set of extra-inning victories. In Game Four, a single and two doubles pushed across two go-ahead runs in the top of the tenth, and McGraw preserved the edge for his second series save. And in the finale—which saw the lead change hands three times—after Del Unser scored on Gary Maddox's tenth-inning double, Dick Ruthven held off Houston to bring the Phillies their first pennant in thirty years.

Philadelphia Phillies (East), 3; Houston Astros (West), 2

PHI (E)

PLAYER/POS	AVG	G	AB	R	H	2B	3B	HR	RB	BB	SO	SB
Ramon Aviles, pr	.000	1	0	1	0	0	0	0	0	0	0	0
Bob Boone, c	.222	5	18	1	4	0	0	0	2	1	2	0
Larry Bowa, ss	.316	5	19	2	6	0	0	0	0	3	3	1
Warren Brusstar, p	.000	2	1	0	0	0	0	0	0	0	1	0
Marty Bystrom, p	.000	1	2	0	0	0	0	0	0	0	1	0
Steve Carlton, p	.000	2	4	0	0	0	0	0	0	0	1	0
Larry Christenson, p	.000	1	2	0	0	0	0	0	0	0	1	0
Greg Gross, of-1	.750	4	4	2	3	0	0	0	1	0	0	0
Greg Luzinski, of	.294	5	17	3	5	2	0	1	4	0	6	0
Garry Maddox, of	.300	5	20	2	6	2	0	0	3	2	2	0
Bake McBride, of	.238	5	21	0	5	0	0	0	0	1	5	2
Tug McGraw, p	.000	5	1	0	0	0	0	0	0	0	0	0
Keith Moreland, c-1	.000	2	1	0	0	0	0	0	1	0	0	0
Dickie Noles, p	.000	2	1	0	0	0	0	0	0	0	0	0
Ron Reed, p	.000	3	0	0	0	0	0	0	0	0	0	0
Pete Rose, 1b	.400	5	20	3	8	0	0	0	2	5	3	0
Dick Ruthven, p	.000	2	2	0	0	0	0	0	0	0	2	0
Kevin Saucier, p	.000	2	0	0	0	0	0	0	0	0	0	0
Mike Schmidt, 3b	.208	5	24	1	5	1	0	0	1	1	6	1
Lonnie Smith, of-2	.600	3	5	2	3	0	0	0	0	0	0	1
Manny Trillo, 2b	.381	5	21	1	8	2	1	0	4	0	2	0
Del Unser, of-2	.400	5	5	2	2	1	0	0	1	0	2	0
George Vukovich, of-1	.000	4	3	0	0	0	0	0	0	0	0	0
TOTAL	.289		190	20	55	8	1	1	19	13	37	7

PITCHER	W	L	ERA	G	GS	CG	SV	SHO	IP	H	ER	BB	SO
Warren Brusstar	1	0	3.38	2	0	0	0	0	2.2	1	1	1	0
Marty Bystrom	0	0	1.69	1	1	0	0	0	5.1	7	1	2	1
Steve Carlton	1	0	2.19	2	2	0	0	0	12.1	11	3	8	6
Larry Christenson	0	0	4.05	1	1	0	0	0	6.2	5	3	5	2
Tug McGraw	0	1	4.50	5	0	0	2	0	8.0	8	4	4	5
Dickie Noles	0	0	0.00	2	0	0	0	0	2.2	1	0	0	0
Ron Reed	0	1	18.00	3	0	0	0	0	2.0	3	4	1	1
Dick Ruthven	1	0	2.00	2	1	0	0	0	9.0	3	2	5	4
Kevin Saucier	0	0	0.00	2	0	0	0	0	0.2	1	0	2	0
TOTAL	3	2	3.28	20	5	0	2	0	49.1	40	18	31	19

HOU (W)

PLAYER/POS	AVG	G	AB	R	H	2B	3B	HR	RB	BB	SO	SB
Joaquin Andujar, p	.000	1	0	0	0	0	0	0	0	0	0	0
Alan Ashby, c	.125	2	8	0	1	0	0	0	1	0	0	0
Dave Bergman, 1b	.333	4	3	0	1	0	1	0	2	0	0	0
Bruce Bochy, c	.000	1	1	0	0	0	0	0	0	0	0	0
Enos Cabell, 3b	.238	5	21	1	5	1	0	0	1	1	3	0
Cesar Cedeno, of	.182	3	11	1	2	0	0	0	1	1	0	0
Jose Cruz, of	.400	5	15	3	6	1	1	0	4	8	1	0
Ken Forsch, p	1.000	2	2	0	2	0	0	0	0	0	0	0
Danny Heep, ph	.000	1	1	0	0	0	0	0	0	0	0	0
Art Howe, 1b-4	.200	5	15	0	3	1	1	0	2	2	2	0
Frank LaCorte, p	.000	2	1	0	0	0	0	0	0	0	0	0
Rafael Landestoy, 2b-3,ss-1	.222	5	9	3	2	0	0	0	2	1	0	1
Jeffrey Leonard, of-1	.000	3	3	0	0	0	0	0	0	0	2	0
Joe Morgan, 2b	.154	4	13	1	2	1	1	0	0	6	1	0
Joe Niekro, p	.000	1	3	0	0	0	0	0	0	0	1	0
Terry Puhl, of-4	.526	5	19	4	10	2	0	0	3	3	2	2
Luis Pujols, c	.100	4	10	1	1	0	1	0	0	3	0	0
Craig Reynolds, ss	.154	4	13	2	2	1	0	0	0	3	1	0
Vern Ruhle, p	.000	1	3	0	0	0	0	0	0	0	1	0
Nolan Ryan, p	.000	2	4	1	0	0	0	0	0	1	2	0
Joe Sambito, p	.000	3	0	0	0	0	0	0	0	0	0	0
Dave Smith, p	.000	3	0	0	0	0	0	0	0	0	0	0
Denny Walling, of-2,1b-1	.111	3	9	2	1	0	0	0	2	1	0	0
Gary Woods, of-3	.250	4	8	0	2	0	0	0	1	1	3	1
TOTAL	.233		172	19	40	7	5	0	18	31	19	4

PITCHER	W	L	ERA	G	GS	CG	SV	SHO	IP	H	ER	BB	SO
Joaquin Andujar	0	0	0.00	1	0	0	1	0	1.0	0	0	1	0
Ken Forsch	0	1	4.15	2	1	1	0	0	8.2	10	4	1	6
Frank LaCorte	1	1	3.00	2	0	0	0	0	3.0	7	1	2	2
Joe Niekro	0	0	0.00	1	1	0	0	0	10.0	6	0	1	2
Vern Ruhle	0	0	3.86	1	1	0	0	0	7.0	8	3	1	3
Nolan Ryan	0	0	5.40	2	2	0	0	0	13.1	16	8	3	14
Joe Sambito	0	1	4.91	3	0	0	0	0	3.2	4	2	2	6
Dave Smith	1	0	3.86	3	0	0	0	0	2.1	4	1	2	4
TOTAL	2	3	3.49	15	5	1	1	0	49.0	55	19	13	37

GAME 1 AT PHI OCT 7

HOU	001 000 000	1	7	0
PHI	000 002 10X	3	8	1

Pitchers: FORSCH vs CARLTON, McGraw (8)
Home Runs: Luzinski-PHI
Attendance: 65,277

GAME 2 AT PHI OCT 8

HOU	001 000 110 4	7	8	1
PHI	000 200 010 1	4	14	2

Pitchers: Ryan, Sambito (7), D.Smith (7), LaCORTE (9), Andujar (10) vs Ruthven, McGraw (8), REED (9), Saucier (10)
Attendance: 65,476

GAME 3 AT HOU OCT 10

PHI	000 000 000 00	0	7	1
HOU	000 000 000 01	1	6	1

Pitchers: Christensen, Noles (7), McGRAW (8) vs Niekro, D.SMITH (11)
Attendance: 44,443

GAME 4 AT HOU OCT 11

PHI	000 000 030 2	5	13	0
HOU	000 110 001 0	3	5	1

Pitchers: Carlton, Noles (6), Saucier (7), Reed (7), BRUSSTAR (8), McGraw (10) vs Ruhle, D.Smith (8), SAMBITO (8)
Attendance: 44,952

GAME 5 AT HOU OCT 12

PHI	020 000 050 1	8	13	2
HOU	100 001 320 0	7	14	0

Pitchers: Bystrom, Brusstar (6), Christenson (7), Reed (7), McGraw (8), RUTHVEN (9) vs Ryan, Sambito (8), Forsch (8), LaCORTE (9)
Attendance: 44,802

Kansas City and New York met for the fourth time in the LCS, and this time the Royals swept to their first pennant. In the first game the Yankees scored first, with second-inning home runs by Rick Cerone and Lou Piniella, but the Royals' Frank White doubled in a pair later in the inning to tie it, and Willie Aikens's hit in the third gave K.C. the lead. They held it to the end as Larry Gura shut out New York the rest of the way.

The Royals scored three runs in the third inning of Game Two, on Willie Wilson's two-run triple and an RBI double by U. L. Washington. Yankee starter Rudy May stopped K.C. after that, but the Royals already had enough for the win as Dennis Leonard in eight innings held New York to two runs, and Dan Quisenberry kept the lid on in the ninth.

Game Three was decided by home runs. White scored first for the Royals with a solo shot in the fifth. New York took the lead briefly with a two-run sixth, but lost it—and the pennant—in the top of the seventh when Goose Gossage, relieving starter Tommy John with two out and a man on, gave up an infield single to Washington and a home run to George Brett.

Kansas City Royals (West), 3; New York Yankees (East), 0

KC (W)

PLAYER/POS	AVG	G	AB	R	H	2B	3B	HR	RB	BB	SO	SB
Willie Aikens, 1b	.364	3	11	0	4	0	0	0	2	0	1	0
George Brett, 3b	.273	3	11	3	3	1	0	2	4	1	0	0
Larry Gura, p	.000	1	0	0	0	0	0	0	0	0	0	0
Clint Hurdle, of	.000	3	2	0	0	0	0	0	0	0	1	0
Pete LaCock, 1b	.000	1	0	0	0	0	0	0	0	0	0	0
Dennis Leonard, p	.000	1	0	0	0	0	0	0	0	0	0	0
Hal McRae, dh	.200	3	10	0	2	0	0	0	0	1	3	0
Amos Otis, of	.333	3	12	2	4	1	0	0	0	0	3	2
Darrell Porter, c	.100	3	10	2	1	0	0	0	0	1	0	0
Dan Quisenberry, p	.000	2	0	0	0	0	0	0	0	0	0	0
Paul Splittorff, p	.000	1	0	0	0	0	0	0	0	0	0	0
U. L. Washington, ss	.364	3	11	1	4	1	0	0	1	2	3	0
John Wathan, of	.000	3	6	1	0	0	0	0	0	3	1	0
Frank White, 2b	.545	3	11	3	6	1	0	1	3	0	1	1
Willie Wilson, of	.308	3	13	2	4	2	1	0	4	1	2	0
TOTAL	.289		97	14	28	6	1	3	14	9	15	3

PITCHER	W	L	ERA	G	GS	CG	SV	SHO	IP	H	ER	BB	SO
Larry Gura	1	0	2.00	1	1	1	0	0	9.0	10	2	1	4
Dennis Leonard	1	0	2.25	1	1	0	0	0	8.0	7	2	1	8
Dan Quisenberry	1	0	0.00	2	0	0	1	0	4.2	4	0	2	1
Paul Splittorff	0	0	1.69	1	1	0	0	0	5.1	5	1	2	3
TOTAL	3	0	1.67	5	3	1	1	0	27.0	26	5	6	16

NY (E)

PLAYER/POS	AVG	G	AB	R	H	2B	3B	HR	RB	BB	SO	SB
Bobby Brown, of	.000	3	10	1	0	0	0	0	0	1	2	0
Rick Cerone, c	.333	3	12	1	4	0	0	1	2	0	1	0
Ron Davis, p	.000	1	0	0	0	0	0	0	0	0	0	0
Bucky Dent, ss	.182	3	11	0	2	0	0	0	0	0	1	0
Oscar Gamble, of-1,dh-1	.200	2	5	1	1	0	0	0	0	1	1	0
Rich Gossage, p	.000	1	0	0	0	0	0	0	0	0	0	0
Ron Guidry, p	.000	1	0	0	0	0	0	0	0	0	0	0
Reggie Jackson, of	.273	3	11	1	3	1	0	0	0	1	4	0
Tommy John, p	.000	1	0	0	0	0	0	0	0	0	0	0
Joe Lefebvre, of	.000	1	0	0	0	0	0	0	0	0	0	0
Rudy May, p	.000	1	0	0	0	0	0	0	0	0	0	0
Bobby Murcer, dh	.000	1	4	0	0	0	0	0	0	0	2	0
Graig Nettles, 3b	.167	2	6	1	1	0	0	1	1	0	1	0
Lou Piniella, of	.200	2	5	1	1	0	0	1	1	2	1	0
Willie Randolph, 2b	.385	3	13	0	5	2	0	0	1	1	3	0
Aurelio Rodriguez, 3b	.333	2	6	0	2	1	0	0	0	0	0	0
Eric Soderholm, dh	.167	2	6	0	1	0	0	0	0	0	0	0
Jim Spencer, ph	.000	1	1	0	0	0	0	0	0	0	0	0
Tom Underwood, p	.000	2	0	0	0	0	0	0	0	0	0	0
Bob Watson, 1b	.500	3	12	0	6	3	1	0	0	0	0	0
TOTAL	.255		102	6	26	7	1	3	5	6	16	0

PITCHER	W	L	ERA	G	GS	CG	SV	SHO	IP	H	ER	BB	SO
Ron Davis	0	0	2.25	1	0	0	0	0	4.0	3	1	1	3
Rich Gossage	0	1	54.00	1	0	0	0	0	0.1	3	2	0	0
Ron Guidry	0	1	12.00	1	1	0	0	0	3.0	5	4	4	2
Tommy John	0	0	2.70	1	1	0	0	0	6.2	8	2	1	3
Rudy May	0	1	3.38	1	1	1	0	0	8.0	6	3	3	4
Tom Underwood	0	0	0.00	2	0	0	0	0	3.0	3	0	0	3
TOTAL	0	3	4.32	7	3	1	0	0	25.0	28	12	9	15

GAME 1 AT KC OCT 8

NY	020	000	000	2	10	1
KC	022	000	12X	7	10	0

Pitchers: GUIDRY, Davis (4), Underwood (8) vs GURA
Home Runs: Cerone-NY, Piniella-NY, G.Brett-KC
Attendance: 42,598

GAME 2 AT KC OCT 9

NY	000	020	000	2	8	0
KC	003	000	00X	3	6	0

Pitchers: MAY vs LEONARD, Quisenberry (9)
Home Runs: Nettles-NY
Attendance: 42,633

GAME 3 AT NY OCT 10

KC	000	010	300	4	12	1
NY	000	002	000	2	8	0

Pitchers: Splittorff, QUISENBERRY (6) vs John, GOSSAGE (7), Underwood (8)
Home Runs: White-KC, G.Brett-KC
Attendance: 56,588

Both clubs had won divisional titles three years in a row—1976–1978—only to lose the League Championship Series. But both overcame the jinx in 1980 to face off in the World Series—the Phillies for the first time in thirty years, the Royals for the first time ever. Kansas City began with a rush in the opener, scoring two runs on Amos Otis's homer in the second inning and two more on Willie Aikens's blast an inning later. But the Phillies came back to take the lead in their half of the third with a five-run rally capped by Bake McBride's three-run homer. Single Phillie runs in each of the next two innings kept them out of reach of Aikens's second two-run shot in the eighth for a narrow 7–6 win. The Phillies extended their Series advantage with a 6–4 win in the second game, rebounding from a two-run deficit with four runs in the eighth inning.

The two clubs traded single runs throughout Game Three. Royal George Brett's first-inning homer began the scoring. The Phillies got the run back in the second inning, the Royals took the lead in the fourth, Phillie Mike Schmidt homered to tie it again in the fifth, Amos Otis countered with a homer in the seventh, and Pete Rose singled in another tying Phillie run in the eighth. Phillie reliever Tug McGraw (who had a save in the opening game) came on to pitch the last of the tenth inning, but couldn't hold the tie, though two men were out before Willie Aikens singled in the Royals' winning run. The Royals evened the Series with their second victory the next day, scoring four times in the first inning and once in the second (with Willie Aikens for the second time in the Series hitting two home runs in a game), then holding on for a 5–3 win.

But the Phillies recovered to win the next two, and their first world crown. Mike Schmidt's fourth-inning two-run homer began the Phillies' scoring in Game Five. The Royals replied with one run in the fifth, and Amos Otis's home run an inning later tied the game. A second K.C. run in the inning put the Royals ahead until the top of the ninth, when pinch hitter Del Unser doubled home Schmidt to tie the game, and Manny Trillo drove home Unser with the go-ahead run. Tug McGraw, who had held K.C. scoreless through two innings of relief, loaded the bases in the last of the ninth with three walks, but at last fanned Jose Cardenal for the final out. In Game Six, with the Phillies ahead 4–0 in the eighth inning, McGraw relieved starter Steve Carlton with two men on, and loaded the bases with a walk. One Royal scored on a sacrifice fly before McGraw got his third out. In

the ninth, another McGraw walk and two singles again loaded the bases with only one away, but Frank White popped out foul, the ball bouncing off Bob Boone's catcher's mitt into Pete Rose's hand, and Willie Wilson struck out for the twelfth time to end the Series.

Philadelphia Phillies (NL), 4; Kansas City Royals (AL), 2

PHI (N)

PLAYER/POS	AVG	G	AB	R	H	2B	3B	HR	RB	BB	SO	SB
Bob Boone, c	.412	6	17	3	7	2	0	0	4	4	0	0
Larry Bowa, ss	.375	6	24	3	9	1	0	0	2	0	0	3
Warren Brusstar, p	.000	1	0	0	0	0	0	0	0	0	0	0
Marty Bystrom, p	.000	1	0	0	0	0	0	0	0	0	0	0
Steve Carlton, p	.000	2	0	0	0	0	0	0	0	0	0	0
Larry Christenson, p	.000	1	0	0	0	0	0	0	0	0	0	0
Greg Gross, of-3	.000	4	2	0	0	0	0	0	0	0	0	0
Greg Luzinski, dh-2,of-1	.000	3	9	0	0	0	0	0	0	1	5	0
Garry Maddox, of	.227	6	22	1	5	2	0	0	1	1	3	0
Bake McBride, of	.304	6	23	3	7	1	0	1	5	2	1	0
Tug McGraw, p	.000	4	0	0	0	0	0	0	0	0	0	0
Keith Moreland, dh	.333	3	12	1	4	0	0	0	1	0	1	0
Dickie Noles, p	.000	1	0	0	0	0	0	0	0	0	0	0
Ron Reed, p	.000	2	0	0	0	0	0	0	0	0	0	0
Pete Rose, 1b	.261	6	23	2	6	1	0	0	1	2	2	0
Dick Ruthven, p	.000	1	0	0	0	0	0	0	0	0	0	0
Kevin Saucier, p	.000	1	0	0	0	0	0	0	0	0	0	0
Mike Schmidt, 3b	.381	6	21	6	8	1	0	2	7	4	3	0
Lonnie Smith, of-5,dh-1	.263	6	19	2	5	1	0	0	1	1	1	0
Manny Trillo, 2b	.217	6	23	4	5	2	0	0	2	0	0	0
Del Unser, of	.500	3	6	2	3	2	0	0	2	0	1	0
Bob Walk, p	.000	1	0	0	0	0	0	0	0	0	0	0
TOTAL	.294		201	27	59	13	0	3	26	15	17	3

PITCHER	W	L	ERA	G	GS	CG	SV	SHO	IP	H	ER	BB	SO
Warren Brusstar	0	0	0.00	1	0	0	0	0	2.1	0	0	1	0
Marty Bystrom	0	0	5.40	1	1	0	0	0	5.0	10	3	1	4
Steve Carlton	2	0	2.40	2	2	0	0	0	15.0	14	4	9	17
Larry Christenson	0	1	108.00	1	1	0	0	0	0.1	5	4	1	0
Tug McGraw	1	1	1.17	4	0	0	2	0	7.2	7	1	8	10
Dickie Noles	0	0	1.93	1	0	0	0	0	4.2	5	1	2	6
Ron Reed	0	0	0.00	2	0	0	1	0	2.0	2	0	0	2
Dick Ruthven	0	0	3.00	1	1	0	0	0	9.0	9	3	0	7
Kevin Saucier	0	0	0.00	1	0	0	0	0	0.2	0	0	2	0
Bob Walk	1	0	7.71	1	1	0	0	0	7.0	8	6	3	3
TOTAL	4	2	3.69	15	6	0	3	0	53.2	60	22	27	49

KC (A)

PLAYER/POS	AVG	G	AB	R	H	2B	3B	HR	RB	BB	SO	SB
Willie Aikens, 1b	.400	6	20	5	8	0	1	4	8	6	8	0
George Brett, 3b	.375	6	24	3	9	2	1	1	3	2	4	1
Jose Cardenal, of	.200	4	10	0	2	0	0	0	0	0	3	0
Dave Chalk, 3b	.000	1	0	1	0	0	0	0	0	1	0	1
Onix Concepcion, pr	.000	3	0	0	0	0	0	0	0	0	0	0
Rich Gale, p	.000	2	0	0	0	0	0	0	0	0	0	0
Larry Gura, p	.000	2	0	0	0	0	0	0	0	0	0	0
Clint Hurdle, of	.417	4	12	1	5	1	0	0	0	2	1	1
Pete LaCock, 1b	.000	1	0	0	0	0	0	0	0	0	0	0
Dennis Leonard, p	.000	2	0	0	0	0	0	0	0	0	0	0
Renie Martin, p	.000	3	0	0	0	0	0	0	0	0	0	0
Hal McRae, dh	.375	6	24	3	9	3	0	0	1	2	2	0
Amos Otis, of	.478	6	23	4	11	2	0	3	7	3	3	0
Marty Pattin, p	.000	1	0	0	0	0	0	0	0	0	0	0
Darrell Porter, c-4	.143	5	14	1	2	0	0	0	0	3	4	0
Dan Quisenberry, p	.000	6	0	0	0	0	0	0	0	0	0	0
Paul Splittorff, p	.000	1	0	0	0	0	0	0	0	0	0	0
U L Washington, ss	.273	6	22	1	6	0	0	0	0	2	6	0
John Wathan, c-2,of-1	.286	3	7	1	2	0	0	0	1	2	1	0
Frank White, 2b	.080	6	25	0	2	0	0	0	0	1	5	1
Willie Wilson, of	.154	6	26	3	4	1	0	0	0	4	12	2
TOTAL	.290		207	23	60	9	2	8	22	26	49	6

PITCHER	W	L	ERA	G	GS	CG	SV	SHO	IP	H	ER	BB	SO
Rich Gale	0	1	4.26	2	2	0	0	0	6.1	11	3	4	4
Larry Gura	0	0	2.19	2	2	0	0	0	12.1	8	3	3	4
Dennis Leonard	1	1	6.75	2	2	0	0	0	10.2	15	8	2	5
Renie Martin	0	0	2.79	3	0	0	0	0	9.2	11	3	3	2
Marty Pattin	0	0	0.00	1	0	0	0	0	1.0	0	0	0	2
Dan Quisenberry	1	2	5.23	6	0	0	1	0	10.1	10	6	3	0
Paul Splittorff	0	0	5.40	1	0	0	0	0	1.2	4	1	0	0
TOTAL	2	4	4.15	17	6	0	1	0	52.0	59	24	15	17

GAME 1 AT PHI OCT 14

```
KC    022 000 020   6 9 1
PHI   005 110 00X   7 11 0
```

Pitchers: LEONARD, Martin (4), Quisenberry (8) vs WALK, McGraw (8)
Home Runs: Otis-KC, Aikens-KC (2), McBride-PHI
Attendance: 65,791

GAME 2 AT PHI OCT 15

```
KC    000 001 300   4 11 0
PHI   000 020 04X   6 8 1
```

Pitchers: Gura, QUISENBERRY (7) vs CARLTON, Reed (9)
Attendance: 65,775

GAME 3 AT KC OCT 17

```
PHI   010 010 010 0   3 14 0
KC    100 100 100 1   4 11 0
```

Pitchers: Ruthven, McGRAW (10) vs Gale, Martin (5), QUISENBERRY (8)
Home Runs: Schmidt-PHI, G.Brett-KC, Otis-KC
Attendance: 42,380

GAME 4 AT KC OCT 18

```
PHI   010 000 110   3 10 1
KC    410 000 00X   5 10 2
```

Pitchers: CHRISTENSEN, Noles (1), Saucier (6), Brusstar (6) vs LEONARD, Quisenberry (8)
Home Runs: Aikens-KC (2)
Attendance: 42,363

GAME 5 AT KC OCT 19

```
PHI   000 200 002   4 7 0
KC    000 012 000   3 12 2
```

Pitchers: Bystrom, Reed (6), McGRAW (7) vs Gura, QUISENBERRY (7)
Home Runs: Schmidt-PHI, Otis-KC
Attendance: 42,369

GAME 6 AT PHI OCT 21

```
KC    000 000 010   1 7 2
PHI   002 011 00X   4 9 0
```

Pitchers: GALE, Martin (3), Splittorff (5), Pattin (7), Quisenberry (8) vs CARLTON, McGraw (8)
Attendance: 65,838

The Expos, who triumphed over the NL East in the second half of the season, won the first two playoff games at home by identical 3–1 scores over the first-half champion Phillies. The Phillies rapped Expo ace Steve Rogers for ten hits in Game One, but Keith Moreland's solo home run in the second was the only hit to produce a run. The homer tied the score briefly, but the Expos regained the lead in the last of the second inning on Chris Speier's double and increased it to 3–1, two innings later. The Expos scored their three runs early in Game Two on Speier's second-inning single and Gary Carter's two-run homer an inning later. Expo starter Bill Gullickson blanked the Phillies on three hits through 7⅔ innings, but three two-out hits in the eighth scored a Phillie run and brought on reliever Jeff Reardon, who ended the threat for his second save in as many days.

When the Series moved to Philadelphia, the Phillies recovered to even things with a pair of wins. After an easy 13-hit 6–2 victory in Game Three, they took a 4–0 lead into the fourth inning of Game Four. Montreal fought back to tie the game, fell behind again, then re-tied the score at 5–5 in the top of the seventh. The final innings featured a duel between relievers Tug McGraw and Jeff Reardon. McGraw stopped the Expos on one hit through three innings, and took the win when Reardon, after retiring eight Phillies in a row, gave up a leadoff homer to pinch hitter George Vukovich in the bottom of the tenth.

Steve Rogers won the division title for Montreal in the finale, hurling a six-hit shutout against the Phillies and driving in the first two of the Expos' three runs with a bases-loaded single through the box in the fifth inning.

Montreal Expos, 3; Philadelphia Phillies, 2

MON (E)

PLAYER/POS	AVG	G	AB	R	H	2B	3B	HR	RB	BB	SO	SB
Stan Bahnsen, p	.000	1	0	0	0	0	0	0	0	0	0	0
Ray Burris, p	.000	1	2	0	0	0	0	0	0	0	2	0
Gary Carter, c	.421	5	19	3	8	3	0	2	6	1	1	0
Warren Cromartie, 1b	.227	5	22	1	5	2	0	0	1	0	9	0
Andre Dawson, of	.300	5	20	1	6	0	1	0	0	1	6	2
Terry Francona, of	.333	5	12	0	4	0	0	0	0	2	2	2
Woody Fryman, p	.000	1	0	0	0	0	0	0	0	0	0	0
Bill Gullickson, p	.000	1	3	0	0	0	0	0	0	0	1	0
Wallace Johnson, ph	.500	2	2	0	1	0	0	0	1	0	0	0
Bill Lee, p	.000	1	0	0	0	0	0	0	0	0	0	0
Jerry Manuel, 2b	.071	5	14	0	1	0	0	0	0	0	2	5	0
Brad Mills, ph	.000	1	0	0	0	0	0	0	0	0	1	0
John Milner, ph	.500	2	2	0	1	0	0	0	1	0	0	0
Larry Parrish, 3b	.150	5	20	3	3	1	0	0	1	1	3	0
Mike Phillips, 2b	.000	1	1	0	0	0	0	0	0	0	0	0
Jeff Reardon, p	.000	3	1	0	0	0	0	0	0	0	1	0
Steve Rogers, p	.400	2	5	0	2	0	0	0	2	0	1	0
Scott Sanderson, p	.000	1	1	0	0	0	0	0	0	0	1	0
Elias Sosa, p	.000	2	0	0	0	0	0	0	0	0	0	0
Chris Speier, ss	.400	5	15	4	6	2	0	0	3	4	2	0
Tim Wallach, of-3	.250	4	4	1	1	0	0	0	0	4	0	0
Jerry White, of	.167	5	18	3	3	1	0	0	1	2	2	3
TOTAL	.255		161	16	41	10	1	2	16	18	36	7

PITCHER	W	L	ERA	G	GS	CG	SV	SHO	IP	H	ER	BB	SO
Stan Bahnsen	0	0	0.00	1	0	0	0	0	1.1	1	0	1	1
Ray Burris	0	1	5.06	1	1	0	0	0	5.1	7	3	4	4
Woody Fryman	0	0	6.75	1	0	0	0	0	1.1	3	1	1	0
Bill Gullickson	1	0	1.17	1	1	0	0	0	7.2	6	1	1	3
Bill Lee	0	0	0.00	1	0	0	0	0	0.2	1	0	0	1
Jeff Reardon	0	1	2.08	3	0	0	2	0	4.1	1	1	1	2
Steve Rogers	2	0	0.51	2	2	1	0	1	17.2	16	1	3	5
Scott Sanderson	0	0	6.75	1	1	0	0	0	2.2	4	2	2	2
Elias Sosa	0	0	3.00	2	0	0	0	0	3.0	4	1	0	1
TOTAL	3	2	2.05	13	5	1	2	1	44.0	44	10	13	19

PHI (E)

PLAYER/POS	AVG	G	AB	R	H	2B	3B	HR	RB	BB	SO	SB
Luis Aguayo, pr	.000	2	0	1	0	0	0	0	0	0	0	0
Ramon Aviles, ph	.000	1	0	0	0	0	0	0	0	1	0	0
Bob Boone, c	.000	3	5	0	0	0	0	0	0	0	0	0
Larry Bowa, ss	.176	5	17	0	3	1	0	0	1	0	0	0
Warren Brusstar, p	.000	2	0	0	0	0	0	0	0	0	0	0
Steve Carlton, p	.250	2	4	0	1	0	0	0	0	0	0	0
Larry Christenson, p	.000	1	2	0	0	0	0	0	0	0	1	0
Dick Davis, of	.000	1	2	0	0	0	0	0	0	0	1	0
Greg Gross, of-2	.000	4	4	0	0	0	0	0	0	0	0	0
Sparky Lyle, p	.000	3	0	0	0	0	0	0	0	0	0	0
Garry Maddox, of	.333	2	3	0	1	1	0	0	0	0	0	0
Gary Matthews, of	.400	5	20	3	8	0	1	1	1	0	2	0
Bake McBride, of	.200	4	15	1	3	1	0	0	0	0	5	0
Tug McGraw, p	.000	2	0	0	0	0	0	0	0	0	0	0
Keith Moreland, c	.462	4	13	2	6	0	0	1	3	1	1	0
Dickie Noles, p	.000	1	0	0	0	0	0	0	0	1	0	0
Ron Reed, p	.000	4	0	0	0	0	0	0	0	0	0	0
Pete Rose, 1b	.300	5	20	1	6	1	0	0	2	2	0	0
Dick Ruthven, p	.000	1	1	0	0	0	0	0	0	0	0	0
Mike Schmidt, 3b	.250	5	16	3	4	1	0	1	2	4	2	0
Lonnie Smith, of	.263	5	19	1	5	1	0	0	0	0	4	0
Manny Trillo, 2b	.188	5	16	1	3	0	0	0	1	4	0	0
George Vukovich, of-3	.444	5	9	1	4	0	0	1	2	0	3	0
TOTAL	.265		166	14	44	6	1	4	12	13	19	0

PITCHER	W	L	ERA	G	GS	CG	SV	SHO	IP	H	ER	BB	SO
Warren Brusstar	0	0	4.91	2	0	0	0	0	3.2	5	2	1	3
Steve Carlton	0	2	3.86	2	2	0	0	0	14.0	14	6	8	13
Larry Christenson	1	0	1.50	1	1	0	0	0	6.0	4	1	1	8
Sparky Lyle	0	0	0.00	3	0	0	0	0	2.1	4	0	2	1
Tug McGraw	1	0	0.00	2	0	0	0	0	4.0	2	0	0	2
Dickie Noles	0	0	4.50	1	1	0	0	0	4.0	4	2	2	5
Ron Reed	0	0	3.00	4	0	0	0	0	6.0	5	2	3	4
Dick Ruthven	0	1	4.50	1	1	0	0	0	4.0	3	2	1	0
TOTAL	2	3	3.07	16	5	0	0	0	44.0	41	15	18	36

GAME 1 AT MON OCT 7

PHI	010	000	000	1	10 1
MON	110	100	00X	3	8 0

Pitchers: CARLTON, R.Reed (7) vs ROGERS, Reardon (9)
Home Runs: Moreland-PHI
Attendance: 34,327

GAME 2 AT MON OCT 8

PHI	000	000	010	1	6 2
MON	012	000	00X	3	7 0

Pitchers: RUTHVEN, Brusstar (5), Lyle (7), McGraw (8) vs GULLICKSON, Reardon (8)
Home Runs: Carter-MON
Attendance: 45,896

GAME 3 AT PHI OCT 9

MON	010	000	010	2	8 4
PHI	020	002	20X	6	13 0

Pitchers: BURRIS, Lee (6), Sosa (7) vs CHRISTENSON, Lyle (7), R.Reed (8)
Attendance: 36,835

GAME 4 AT PHI OCT 10

MON	000	112	100	0	5	10 1
PHI	202	001	000	1	6	9 0

Pitchers: Sanderson, Bahnsen (3), Sosa (5), Fryman (6), REARDON (7) vs Noles, Brusstar (5), Lyle (6), R.Reed (7), McGRAW (8)
Home Runs: Carter-MON, Schmidt-PHI, Matthews-PHI, G.Vukovich-PHI
Attendance: 38,818

GAME 5 AT PHI OCT 11

MON	000	021	000	3	8 1
PHI	000	000	000	0	6 0

Pitchers: ROGERS vs CARLTON, R.Reed (9)
Attendance: 47,384

Cincinnati, with the league's best overall season record, failed to win either half season in the NL West, and watched from the sidelines as first-half winner Los Angeles, down 0–2, recovered to win the final three games—and the division title—from second-half victor Houston. In the opener, Astro Alan Ashby's two-run homer in the last of the ninth broke a 1–1 tie and gave Nolan Ryan a two-hit victory. The next day, Astro Denny Walling's two-out bases-loaded single in the last of the eleventh scored Phil Garner with the game's only run.

When the clubs shifted to Los Angeles for the remainder of the series, the Dodgers came alive. In Game Three, a first-inning double by Dusty Baker and home run by Steve Garvey drove in three Dodger runs. Pitcher Burt Hooton and two relievers held Houston to three hits in what became a 6–1 Dodger victory. The next day, Dodger Fernando Valenzuela and Astro Vern Ruhle hurled matching four-hitters. But Pedro Guerrero's home run in the fifth inning and a pair of Dodger singles sandwiched around a sacrifice and intentional walk in the seventh gave Los Angeles two runs, while Valenzuela held Houston to a single run in the ninth. In the finale, Jerry Reuss blanked the Astros on five hits while his Dodgers blended three of their seven hits with a walk and Astro error for three runs in the sixth. Two more hits produced a final run an inning later.

Los Angeles Dodgers, 3; Houston Astros, 2

LA (W)

PLAYER/POS	AVG	G	AB	R	H	2B	3B	HR	RB	BB	SO	SB
Dusty Baker, of	.167	5	18	2	3	1	0	0	1	2	0	0
Terry Forster, p	.000	1	0	0	0	0	0	0	0	0	0	0
Steve Garvey, 1b	.368	5	19	4	7	0	1	2	4	0	2	0
Pedro Guerrero, 3b	.176	5	17	1	3	1	0	1	1	2	4	1
Burt Hooton, p	.000	1	3	0	0	0	0	0	0	0	0	0
Steve Howe, p	.000	2	0	0	0	0	0	0	0	0	0	0
Jay Johnstone, ph	.000	1	1	0	0	0	0	0	0	0	0	0
Ken Landreaux, of	.200	5	20	1	4	1	0	0	1	0	1	0
Davey Lopes, 2b	.200	5	20	1	4	1	0	0	0	3	7	1
Mike Marshall, ph	.000	1	1	0	0	0	0	0	0	0	1	0
Rick Monday, of	.214	5	14	1	3	0	0	0	1	2	4	0
Tom Niedenfuer, p	.000	1	0	0	0	0	0	0	0	0	0	0
Jerry Reuss, p	.000	2	8	0	0	0	0	0	0	0	8	0
Bill Russell, ss	.250	5	16	1	4	1	0	0	2	3	1	0
Steve Sax, 2b	.000	1	0	0	0	0	0	0	0	0	0	0
Mike Scioscia, c	.154	4	13	0	2	0	0	0	1	1	2	0
Reggie Smith, ph	.000	2	1	0	0	0	0	0	0	1	0	0
Dave Stewart, p	.000	2	0	0	0	0	0	0	0	0	0	0
Derrel Thomas, of	.000	4	2	1	0	0	0	0	0	0	1	0
Fernando Valenzuela, p	.000	2	4	0	0	0	0	0	0	0	1	0
Bob Welch, p	.000	1	0	0	0	0	0	0	0	0	0	0
Steve Yeager, c	.400	2	5	1	2	1	0	0	0	0	1	0
TOTAL	.198		162	13	32	6	1	3	12	13	34	2

PITCHER	W	L	ERA	G	GS	CG	SV	SHO	IP	H	ER	BB	SO
Terry Forster	0	0	0.00	1	0	0	0	0	0.1	0	0	0	0
Burt Hooton	1	0	1.29	1	1	0	0	0	7.0	3	1	3	2
Steve Howe	0	0	0.00	2	0	0	0	0	2.0	1	0	0	2
Tom Niedenfuer	0	0	0.00	1	0	0	0	0	0.1	1	0	1	1
Jerry Reuss	1	0	0.00	2	2	1	0	1	18.0	10	0	5	7
Dave Stewart	0	2	40.50	2	0	0	0	0	0.2	4	3	0	1
Fernando Valenzuela	1	0	1.06	2	2	1	0	0	17.0	10	2	3	10
Bob Welch	0	0	0.00	1	0	0	0	0	1.0	0	0	1	1
TOTAL	3	2	1.17	12	5	2	0	1	46.1	29	6	13	24

HOU (W)

PLAYER/POS	AVG	G	AB	R	H	2B	3B	HR	RB	BB	SO	SB
Alan Ashby, c	.111	3	9	1	1	0	0	1	2	2	0	0
Cesar Cedeno, 1b	.231	4	13	0	3	1	0	0	0	2	2	2
Jose Cruz, of	.300	5	20	0	6	1	0	0	0	1	3	1
Kiko Garcia, ss-1	.000	2	4	0	0	0	0	0	0	0	1	0
Phil Garner, 2b	.111	5	18	1	2	0	0	0	0	3	3	0
Art Howe, 3b	.235	5	17	1	4	0	0	1	1	2	1	0
Bob Knepper, p	.000	1	1	0	0	0	0	0	0	0	0	0
Frank LaCorte, p	.000	2	0	0	0	0	0	0	0	0	0	0
Joe Niekro, p	.000	1	2	0	0	0	0	0	0	0	0	0
Joe Pittman, ph	.000	2	2	0	0	0	0	0	0	0	0	0
Terry Puhl, of	.190	5	21	2	4	1	0	0	0	0	1	1
Luis Pujols, c	.000	2	6	0	0	0	0	0	0	0	1	0
Craig Reynolds, ss-1	.333	2	3	1	1	0	0	0	0	0	1	0
Dave Roberts, ph	.000	1	1	0	0	0	0	0	0	0	1	0
Vern Ruhle, p	.000	1	1	0	0	0	0	0	0	0	0	0
Nolan Ryan, p	.250	2	4	0	1	0	0	0	0	1	1	0
Joe Sambito, p	.000	2	0	0	0	0	0	0	0	0	0	0
Tony Scott, of	.150	5	20	0	3	0	0	0	2	1	6	0
Billy Smith, p	.000	1	0	0	0	0	0	0	0	0	0	0
Dave Smith, p	.000	2	0	0	0	0	0	0	0	0	0	0
Harry Spilman, ph	.000	1	1	0	0	0	0	0	0	0	0	0
Dickie Thon, ss	.182	4	11	0	2	0	0	0	0	1	0	0
Denny Walling, 1b-2	.333	3	6	0	2	0	0	0	1	0	1	0
Gary Woods, ph	.000	2	2	0	0	0	0	0	0	0	0	0
TOTAL	.179		162	6	29	3	0	2	6	13	24	4

PITCHER	W	L	ERA	G	GS	CG	SV	SHO	IP	H	ER	BB	SO
Bob Knepper	0	1	5.40	1	1	0	0	0	5.0	6	3	2	4
Frank LaCorte	0	0	0.00	2	0	0	0	0	3.2	2	0	1	5
Joe Niekro	0	0	0.00	1	1	0	0	0	8.0	7	0	3	4
Vern Ruhle	0	1	2.25	1	1	1	0	0	8.0	4	2	2	1
Nolan Ryan	1	1	1.80	2	2	1	0	0	15.0	6	3	3	14
Joe Sambito	1	0	16.20	2	0	0	0	0	1.2	5	3	2	2
Billy Smith	0	0	0.00	1	0	0	0	0	0.1	0	0	0	0
Dave Smith	0	0	3.86	2	0	0	0	0	2.1	2	1	0	4
TOTAL	2	3	2.45	12	5	2	0	0	44.0	32	12	13	34

GAME 1 AT HOU OCT 6

LA	000 000 100	1	2	0
HOU	000 001 002	3	8	0

Pitchers: Valenzuela, STEWART (9) vs RYAN
Home Runs: Garvey-LA, Ashby-HOU
Attendance: 44,836

GAME 2 AT HOU OCT 7

LA	000 000 000 00	0	9	1
HOU	000 000 000 01	1	9	0

Pitchers: Reuss, S.Howe (10), STEWART (11), Forster (11), Niedenfuer (11) vs Niekro, D.Smith (9), SAMBITO (11)
Attendance: 42,398

GAME 3 AT LA OCT 9

HOU	001 000 000	1	3	2
LA	300 000 03X	6	10	0

Pitchers: KNEPPER, LaCorte (6), Sambito (8), B.Smith (8) vs HOOTON, S.Howe (8), Welch (9)
Home Runs: Garvey-LA, A.Howe-HOU
Attendance: 46,820

GAME 4 AT LA OCT 10

HOU	000 000 001	1	4	0
LA	000 010 10X	2	4	0

Pitchers: RUHLE vs VALENZUELA
Home Runs: Guerrero-LA
Attendance: 55,983

GAME 5 AT LA OCT 11

HOU	000 000 000	0	5	3
LA	100 003 10X	4	7	2

Pitchers: RYAN, D.Smith (7), LaCorte (7) vs REUSS
Attendance: 55,979

The home field didn't seem to offer any advantage. First-half winner New York captured both games played in Milwaukee, but when the Series moved to Yankee Stadium for the final three games, the second-half champion Brewers evened the series.

Milwaukee took a 2–0 lead early in the opener, but New York erupted for four runs in the fourth on Oscar Gamble's two-run homer and Rick Cerone's double, and held on to win 5–3. In Game Two, rookie starter Dave Righetti fanned ten Brewers in his six innings and Goose Gossage's brilliant relief earned him his second save in two days as the Yankees took a 3–0 win on homers by Lou Piniella and Reggie Jackson.

Milwaukee, struggling against elimination, took the lead in the seventh inning of Game Three on Ted Simmons' two-run homer. New York tied the score at 3–3 in their half of the inning, but Paul Molitor broke the tie in the eighth with a solo homer. Simmons doubled home an insurance run later in the inning for a 5–3 Brewer win. The Brewers tagged Yankee pitching for only four hits in Game Four, but three of them came in the fourth inning and combined with a sacrifice fly to produce the Brewers' two runs. New York scored once in the sixth, but baserunning errors an inning later ended their only other scoring threat.

In the finale Milwaukee scored two early runs, but the Yankees (as they had done in the opener) took the lead with a four-run fourth—this time on home runs by Reggie Jackson and Oscar Gamble, and Rick Cerone's single. Cerone later hit an insurance homer, as the home team finally won a game—and captured the division crown.

New York Yankees, 3;
Milwaukee Brewers, 2

NY (E)

PLAYER/POS	AVG	G	AB	R	H	2B	3B	HR	RB	BB	SO	SB
Bobby Brown, pr	.000	1	0	0	0	0	0	0	0	0	0	0
Rick Cerone, c	.333	5	18	1	6	2	0	1	5	0	2	0
Ron Davis, p	.000	3	0	0	0	0	0	0	0	0	0	0
Barry Foote, ph	.000	1	0	0	0	0	0	0	0	0	0	0
Oscar Gamble, dh	.556	4	9	2	5	1	0	2	3	1	2	0
Rich Gossage, p	.000	3	0	0	0	0	0	0	0	0	0	0
Ron Guidry, p	.000	2	0	0	0	0	0	0	0	0	0	0
Reggie Jackson, of	.300	5	20	4	6	0	0	2	4	1	5	0
Tommy John, p	.000	1	0	0	0	0	0	0	0	0	0	0
Rudy May, p	.000	1	0	0	0	0	0	0	0	0	0	0
Larry Milbourne, ss	.316	5	19	4	6	1	0	0	0	0	1	0
Jerry Mumphrey, of	.095	5	21	2	2	0	0	0	0	0	1	1
Bobby Murcer, ph	.000	2	1	0	0	0	0	0	0	1	0	0
Graig Nettles, 3b	.059	5	17	1	1	0	0	0	1	3	1	0
Lou Piniella, dh	.200	4	10	1	2	1	0	1	3	0	0	0
Willie Randolph, 2b	.200	5	20	0	4	0	0	0	1	1	4	0
Rick Reuschel, p	.000	1	0	0	0	0	0	0	0	0	0	0
Dave Revering, 1b	.000	2	0	0	0	0	0	0	0	0	0	0
Dave Righetti, p	.000	2	0	0	0	0	0	0	0	0	0	0
Bob Watson, 1b	.438	5	16	2	7	0	0	0	1	1	1	0
Dave Winfield, of	.350	5	20	2	7	3	0	0	0	1	5	0
TOTAL	.269		171	19	46	8	0	6	18	9	22	1

PITCHER	W	L	ERA	G	GS	CG	SV	SHO	IP	H	ER	BB	SO
Ron Davis	1	0	0.00	3	0	0	0	0	6.0	1	0	2	6
Rich Gossage	0	0	0.00	3	0	0	3	0	6.2	3	0	2	8
Ron Guidry	0	0	5.40	2	2	0	0	0	8.1	11	5	3	8
Tommy John	0	1	6.43	1	1	0	0	0	7.0	8	5	2	0
Rudy May	0	0	0.00	1	0	0	0	0	2.0	1	0	1	1
Rick Reuschel	0	1	3.00	1	1	0	0	0	6.0	4	2	1	3
Dave Righetti	2	0	1.00	2	1	0	0	0	9.0	8	1	3	13
TOTAL	3	2	2.60	13	5	0	3	0	45.0	36	13	13	39

MIL (E)

PLAYER/POS	AVG	G	AB	R	H	2B	3B	HR	RB	BB	SO	SB
Sal Bando, 3b	.294	5	17	1	5	3	0	0	1	2	3	0
Dwight Bernard, p	.000	2	0	0	0	0	0	0	0	0	0	0
Thad Bosley, dh	.000	1	0	0	0	0	0	0	0	0	0	0
Mike Caldwell, p	.000	2	0	0	0	0	0	0	0	0	0	0
Cecil Cooper, 1b	.222	5	18	1	4	0	0	0	3	1	3	0
Jamie Easterly, p	.000	2	0	0	0	0	0	0	0	0	0	0
Marshall Edwards, of	.000	2	1	0	0	0	0	0	0	0	1	0
Rollie Fingers, p	.000	3	0	0	0	0	0	0	0	0	0	0
Jim Gantner, 2b	.143	4	14	1	2	1	0	0	0	0	2	0
Moose Haas, p	.000	2	0	0	0	0	0	0	0	0	0	0
Roy Howell, dh-3	.400	4	5	0	2	0	0	0	0	2	0	0
Randy Lerch, p	.000	1	0	0	0	0	0	0	0	0	0	0
Bob McClure, p	.000	3	0	0	0	0	0	0	0	0	0	0
Paul Molitor, of	.250	5	20	2	5	0	0	1	1	2	5	0
Don Money, 2b-1,dh-1	.000	2	3	0	0	0	0	0	0	0	0	0
Charlie Moore, of-2,dh-2	.222	4	9	0	2	0	0	0	1	1	2	0
Ben Oglivie, of	.167	5	18	0	3	1	0	0	1	0	7	0
Ed Romero, 2b	.500	1	2	1	1	0	0	0	0	0	1	0
Ted Simmons, c	.211	5	19	1	4	1	0	1	4	2	2	0
Jim Slaton, p	.000	4	0	0	0	0	0	0	0	0	0	0
Gorman Thomas, of-3,dh-2	.118	5	17	2	2	0	0	1	1	1	9	0
Pete Vuckovich, p	.000	2	0	0	0	0	0	0	0	0	0	0
Robin Yount, ss	.316	5	19	4	6	0	1	0	1	2	2	1
TOTAL	.222		162	13	36	6	1	3	13	13	39	1

PITCHER	W	L	ERA	G	GS	CG	SV	SHO	IP	H	ER	BB	SO
Dwight Bernard	0	0	0.00	2	0	0	0	0	2.1	0	0	0	0
Mike Caldwell	0	1	4.32	2	1	0	0	0	8.1	9	4	0	4
Jamie Easterly	0	0	6.75	2	0	0	0	0	1.1	2	1	0	1
Rollie Fingers	1	0	3.86	3	0	0	1	0	4.2	7	2	1	5
Moose Haas	0	2	9.45	2	2	0	0	0	6.2	13	7	1	4
Randy Lerch	0	0	1.50	1	1	0	0	0	6.0	3	1	4	3
Bob McClure	0	0	0.00	3	0	0	0	0	3.1	4	0	0	2
Jim Slaton	0	0	3.00	4	0	0	0	0	6.0	6	2	0	2
Pete Vuckovich	1	0	5.27	2	1	0	0	0	5.1	2	0	3	4
TOTAL	2	3	3.48	21	5	0	1	0	44.0	46	17	9	22

GAME 1 AT MIL OCT 7

NY	000 400 001	5	13	1
MIL	011 010 000	3	8	3

Pitchers: Guidry, DAVIS (5), Gossage (8) vs HAAS, Bernard (4), McClure (5), Slaton (6), Fingers (8)
Home Runs: Gamble-NY
Attendance: 35,064

GAME 2 AT MIL OCT 8

NY	000 100 002	3	7	0
MIL	000 000 000	0	7	0

Pitchers: RIGHETTI, Davis (7), Gossage (7) vs CALDWELL, Slaton (9)
Home Runs: Piniella-NY, Jackson-NY
Attendance: 26,395

GAME 3 AT NY OCT 9

MIL	000 000 320	5	9	0
NY	000 100 200	3	8	2

Pitchers: Lerch, FINGERS (7) vs JOHN, May (8)
Home Runs: Simmons-MIL, Molitor-MIL
Attendance: 56,411

GAME 4 AT NY OCT 10

MIL	000 200 000	2	4	2
NY	000 001 000	1	5	0

Pitchers: VUCKOVICH, Easterly (6), Slaton (7), McClure (8), Fingers (9) vs REUSCHEL, Davis (7)
Attendance: 52,077

GAME 5 AT NY OCT 11

MIL	011 000 100	3	8	0
NY	000 400 12X	7	13	0

Pitchers: HAAS, Caldwell (4), Bernard (4), McClure (6), Slaton (7), Easterly (8), Vuckovich (8) vs Guidry, RIGHETTI (5), Gossage (8)
Home Runs: Thomas-MIL, Jackson-NY, Gamble-NY, Cerone-NY
Attendance: 47,505

First-half winner Oakland, with the league's best win-loss record over the full season, swept the division title from second-half champ Kansas City (who, with a full-season record of 50–53, had become the only club in major-league history to qualify for postseason play with a losing record). Twice in the opener the Royals loaded the bases against Mike Norris with fewer than two outs, but both times failed to score. Meanwhile, after a Royal error had prolonged the A's fourth inning, Wayne Gross homered for three unearned Oakland runs. Dwayne Murphy's eighth-inning solo shot gave the A's a fourth run. The game ended with Norris possessor of a four-hit shutout.

Game Two was closer. Oakland's Tony Armas doubled in a run in the top of the first, and doubled home another in the eighth (his fourth hit of the game) to break a 1–1 tie and provide the margin needed for pitcher Steve McCatty's six-hit win. The A's Rick Langford yielded ten hits in Game Three (including Kansas City's only extra-base hit of the series, a double), but only one Royal scored, meanwhile the A's were sending four runs across the plate—three of them by Rickey Henderson, who reached base four times on pairs of hits and walks.

Oakland Athletics, 3;
Kansas City Royals, 0

KC (W)

PLAYER/POS	AVG	G	AB	R	H	2B	3B	HR	RB	BB	SO	SB
Willie Aikens, 1b	.333	3	9	0	3	0	0	0	0	3	2	0
George Brett, 3b	.167	3	12	0	2	0	0	0	0	0	0	0
Cesar Geronimo, pr	.000	1	0	0	0	0	0	0	0	0	0	0
Larry Gura, p	.000	1	0	0	0	0	0	0	0	0	0	0
Clint Hurdle, of	.273	3	11	0	3	0	0	0	0	1	1	0
Mike Jones, p	.000	1	0	0	0	0	0	0	0	0	0	0
Dennis Leonard, p	.000	1	0	0	0	0	0	0	0	0	0	0
Renie Martin, p	.000	2	0	0	0	0	0	0	0	0	0	0
Lee May, 1b	.000	1	0	0	0	0	0	0	0	0	0	0
Hal McRae, dh	.091	3	11	0	1	1	0	0	0	1	1	0
Amos Otis, of	.000	3	12	0	0	0	0	0	1	0	4	0
Dan Quisenberry, p	.000	1	0	0	0	0	0	0	0	0	0	0
U. L. Washington, ss	.222	3	9	0	2	0	0	0	0	0	0	0
John Wathan, c	.300	3	10	1	3	0	0	0	0	1	1	0
Frank White, 2b	.182	3	11	1	2	0	0	0	0	1	1	0
Willie Wilson, of	.308	3	13	0	4	0	0	0	0	1	0	0
TOTAL	.204		98	2	20	1	0	0	2	7	11	0

PITCHER	W	L	ERA	G	GS	CG	SV	SHO	IP	H	ER	BB	SO
Larry Gura	0	1	7.36	1	1	0	0	0	3.2	7	3	3	3
Mike Jones	0	1	2.25	1	1	0	0	0	8.0	9	2	0	2
Dennis Leonard	0	1	1.13	1	1	0	0	0	8.0	7	1	1	3
Renie Martin	0	0	0.00	2	0	0	0	0	5.1	1	0	2	2
Dan Quisenberry	0	0	0.00	1	0	0	0	0	1.0	1	0	0	0
TOTAL	0	3	2.08	6	3	0	0	0	26.0	25	6	6	10

OAK (W)

PLAYER/POS	AVG	G	AB	R	H	2B	3B	HR	RB	BB	SO	SB
Tony Armas, of	.545	3	11	1	6	2	0	0	3	1	1	0
Dave Beard, p	.000	1	0	0	0	0	0	0	0	0	0	0
Rick Bosetti, of	.000	1	0	0	0	0	0	0	0	0	0	0
Keith Drumright, dh	.250	1	4	0	1	0	0	0	0	0	0	0
Wayne Gross, 3b-1	.400	2	5	1	2	0	0	1	3	0	0	0
Mike Heath, c	.000	2	8	0	0	0	0	0	0	0	1	0
Rickey Henderson, of	.182	3	11	3	2	0	0	0	0	2	0	2
Cliff Johnson, dh	.286	2	7	0	2	1	0	0	0	0	1	0
Mickey Klutts, 3b	.143	2	7	0	1	0	0	0	0	0	1	0
Rick Langford, p	.000	1	0	0	0	0	0	0	0	0	0	0
Steve McCatty, p	.000	1	0	0	0	0	0	0	0	0	0	0
Dave McKay, 2b	.273	3	11	1	3	0	0	1	1	1	1	0
Kelvin Moore, 1b	.000	2	8	0	0	0	0	0	0	0	2	0
Dwayne Murphy, of	.545	3	11	4	6	1	0	1	2	1	1	0
Jeff Newman, c	.000	1	3	0	0	0	0	0	0	0	1	0
Mike Norris, p	.000	1	0	0	0	0	0	0	0	0	0	0
Rob Picciolo, ss	.333	1	3	0	1	0	0	0	0	0	0	0
Jim Spencer, 1b	.250	1	4	0	1	1	0	0	0	0	0	0
Fred Stanley, ss	.000	3	6	0	0	0	0	0	0	1	1	0
Tom Underwood, p	.000	1	0	0	0	0	0	0	0	0	0	0
TOTAL	.253		99	10	25	5	0	3	9	6	10	2

PITCHER	W	L	ERA	G	GS	CG	SV	SHO	IP	H	ER	BB	SO
Dave Beard	0	0	0.00	1	0	0	1	0	1.1	0	0	0	2
Rick Langford	1	0	1.23	1	1	0	0	0	7.1	10	1	0	3
Steve McCatty	1	0	1.00	1	1	1	0	0	9.0	6	1	4	3
Mike Norris	1	0	0.00	1	1	1	0	1	9.0	4	0	3	2
Tom Underwood	0	0	0.00	1	0	0	0	0	0.1	0	0	0	1
TOTAL	3	0	0.67	5	3	2	1	1	27.0	20	2	7	11

GAME 1 AT KC OCT 6

OAK	000	300	010	4	8	2
KC	000	000	000	0	4	1

Pitchers: NORRIS vs LEONARD, Martin (9)
Home Runs: Gross-OAK, Murphy-OAK
Attendance: 40,592

GAME 2 AT KC OCT 7

OAK	100	000	010	2	10	1
KC	000	010	000	1	6	0

Pitchers: McCATTY vs JONES, Quisenberry (9)
Attendance: 40,274

GAME 3 AT OAK OCT 9

KC	000	100	000	1	10	3
OAK	101	200	00X	4	7	0

Pitchers: GURA, Martin (4) vs LANGFORD, Underwood (8), Beard (8)
Home Runs: McKay-OAK
Attendance: 40,002

Fine pitching characterized the series, with the losing team held to one run in four of the five games. In the exception Expo Ray Burris hurled a shutout.

Montreal put men on base in each inning of the opener. But the pitching of Burt Hooton and Bob Welch—plus some fine Dodger fielding—kept the Expos from scoring until the ninth, when their one run was too little to overcome the Dodger lead. Burris's shutout evened the series in Game Two as the Expos scored three times against rookie sensation Fernando Valenzuela. The Expos took the series lead in Game Three, overcoming a 0–1 deficit with a two-out four-run burst in the sixth (capped by Jerry White's three-run homer).

In the end, though, the Dodgers prevailed. Through seven innings of Game Four, Hooton and the Expos' Bill Gullickson dueled at 1–1. But in the top of the eighth, Steve Garvey homered with a man aboard, and four more Dodger runs in the ninth put the game away. The finale—Burris vs. Valenzuela again—featured another 1–1 duel, this one reaching into the top of the ninth when, with two out, Dodger Rick Monday homered off reliever Steve Rogers. In the bottom of the ninth, Valenzuela walked two batters after retiring two, but Welch came on to save the game and the pennant.

Los Angeles Dodgers (West), 3; Montreal Expos (East), 2

LA (W)

PLAYER/POS	AVG	G	AB	R	H	2B	3B	HR	RB	BB	SO	SB
Dusty Baker, of	.316	5	19	3	6	1	0	0	3	1	0	0
Bobby Castillo, p	.000	1	0	0	0	0	0	0	0	0	0	0
Ron Cey, 3b	.278	5	18	1	5	1	0	0	3	3	2	0
Terry Forster, p	.000	1	0	0	0	0	0	0	0	0	0	0
Steve Garvey, 1b	.286	5	21	2	6	0	0	1	2	0	4	0
Pedro Guerrero, of	.105	5	19	1	2	0	0	1	2	1	4	0
Burt Hooton, p	.000	2	5	0	0	0	0	0	0	0	2	0
Steve Howe, p	.000	2	0	0	0	0	0	0	0	0	0	0
Jay Johnstone, ph	.000	2	2	0	0	0	0	0	0	0	0	0
Ken Landreaux, of-3	.100	5	10	0	1	1	0	0	0	3	2	0
Davey Lopes, 2b	.278	5	18	0	5	0	0	0	0	1	3	5
Rick Monday, of-2	.333	3	9	2	3	0	0	1	1	0	4	0
Tom Niedenfuer, p	.000	1	0	0	0	0	0	0	0	0	0	0
Alejandro Pena, p	.000	2	0	0	0	0	0	0	0	0	0	0
Jerry Reuss, p	.000	1	2	0	0	0	0	0	0	0	0	0
Bill Russell, ss	.313	5	16	2	5	0	1	0	1	1	1	0
Steve Sax, 2b	.000	1	0	0	0	0	0	0	0	0	0	0
Mike Scioscia, c	.133	5	15	1	2	0	0	1	1	2	1	0
Reggie Smith, ph	1.000	1	1	0	1	0	0	0	1	0	0	0
Derrel Thomas, 3b-1,of-1	1.000	2	1	2	1	0	0	0	0	0	0	0
Fernando Valenzuela, p	.000	2	5	0	0	0	0	0	0	1	0	0
Bob Welch, p	.000	3	0	0	0	0	0	0	0	0	0	0
Steve Yeager, c	.500	1	2	1	1	0	0	0	0	0	0	0
TOTAL	.233		163	15	38	3	1	4	15	12	23	5

PITCHER	W	L	ERA	G	GS	CG	SV	SHO	IP	H	ER	BB	SO
Bobby Castillo	0	0	0.00	1	0	0	0	0	1.0	0	0	0	1
Terry Forster	0	0	0.00	1	0	0	0	0	0.1	0	0	0	1
Burt Hooton	2	0	0.00	2	2	0	0	0	14.2	11	0	6	7
Steve Howe	0	0	0.00	2	0	0	0	0	2.0	1	0	0	2
Tom Niedenfuer	0	0	0.00	1	0	0	0	0	0.1	2	0	0	0
Alejandro Pena	0	0	0.00	2	0	0	0	0	2.1	1	0	0	0
Jerry Reuss	0	1	5.14	1	1	0	0	0	7.0	7	4	1	2
Fernando Valenzuela	1	1	2.45	2	2	0	0	0	14.2	10	4	5	10
Bob Welch	0	0	5.40	3	0	0	1	0	1.2	2	1	0	2
TOTAL	3	2	1.84	15	5	0	1	0	44.0	34	9	12	25

MON (E)

PLAYER/POS	AVG	G	AB	R	H	2B	3B	HR	RB	BB	SO	SB
Ray Burris, p	.000	2	6	0	0	0	0	0	0	0	4	0
Gary Carter, c	.438	5	16	3	7	1	0	0	0	4	2	0
Warren Cromartie, 1b	.167	5	18	3	3	1	0	0	2	0	2	0
Andre Dawson, of	.150	5	20	2	3	0	0	0	0	0	4	0
Terry Francona, of-1	.000	2	1	0	0	0	0	0	0	0	1	0
Woody Fryman, p	.000	1	0	0	0	0	0	0	0	0	0	0
Bill Gullickson, p	.000	2	3	0	0	0	0	0	0	1	2	0
Bill Lee, p	.000	1	0	0	0	0	0	0	0	0	0	0
Jerry Manuel, pr	.000	1	0	0	0	0	0	0	0	0	0	0
John Milner, ph	.000	1	1	0	0	0	0	0	0	0	0	0
Larry Parrish, 3b	.263	5	19	2	5	2	0	0	2	1	1	0
Tim Raines, of	.238	5	21	1	5	2	0	0	1	0	3	0
Jeff Reardon, p	.000	1	0	0	0	0	0	0	0	0	0	0
Steve Rogers, p	.000	2	2	0	0	0	0	0	0	0	1	0
Rodney Scott, 2b	.167	5	18	0	3	0	0	0	0	1	3	1
Elias Sosa, p	.000	2	0	0	0	0	0	0	0	0	0	0
Chris Speier, ss	.188	5	16	0	3	0	0	0	0	2	0	0
Tim Wallach, ph	.000	1	1	0	0	0	0	0	0	0	0	0
Jerry White, of	.313	5	16	2	5	1	0	1	3	3	1	1
TOTAL	.215		158	10	34	7	0	1	8	12	25	2

PITCHER	W	L	ERA	G	GS	CG	SV	SHO	IP	H	ER	BB	SO
Ray Burris	1	0	0.53	2	2	1	0	1	17.0	10	1	3	4
Woody Fryman	0	0	36.00	1	0	0	0	0	1.0	3	4	1	1
Bill Gullickson	0	2	2.51	2	2	0	0	0	14.1	12	4	6	12
Bill Lee	0	0	0.00	1	0	0	0	0	0.1	0	0	0	0
Jeff Reardon	0	0	27.00	1	0	0	0	0	1.0	3	3	0	0
Steve Rogers	1	1	1.80	2	1	1	0	0	10.0	8	2	1	6
Elias Sosa	0	0	0.00	2	0	0	0	0	0.1	1	0	1	0
TOTAL	2	3	2.86	10	5	2	0	1	44.0	38	14	12	23

GAME 1 AT LA OCT 13

MON	000	000	001	1	9	0
LA	020	000	03X	5	8	0

Pitchers: GULLICKSON, Reardon (8) vs HOOTON, Welch (8), Howe (9)
Home Runs: Guerrero-LA, Scioscia-LA
Attendance: 51,273

GAME 2 AT LA OCT 14

MON	020	001	000	3	10	1
LA	000	000	000	0	5	1

Pitchers: BURRIS vs VALENZUELA, Niedenfuer (7), Forster (7), Pena (7), Castillo (9)
Attendance: 53,463

GAME 3 AT MON OCT 16

LA	000	100	000	1	7	0
MON	000	004	00X	4	7	1

Pitchers: REUSS, Pena (8) vs ROGERS
Home Runs: White-MON
Attendance: 54,372

GAME 4 AT MON OCT 17

LA	001	000	024	7	12	1
MON	000	100	000	1	5	1

Pitchers: HOOTON, Welch (8), Howe (9) vs GULLICKSON, Fryman (8), Sosa (9), Lee (9)
Home Runs: Garvey-LA
Attendance: 54,499

GAME 5 AT MON OCT 19

LA	000	010	001	2	6	0
MON	100	000	000	1	3	1

Pitchers: VALENZUELA, Welch (9) vs Burris, ROGERS (9)
Home Runs: Monday-LA
Attendance: 36,491

The A's scored only four runs to their opponents' twenty as the Yankees swept the series. And only two of the six Yankee pitchers permitted an Oakland runner to score, while not one of Oakland's eight pitchers held New York scoreless. Even so, two of the three games were closely contested.

Oakland's Mike Norris gave up a bases-loaded double to Graig Nettles in the first inning of Game One before settling down to pitch shutout ball. But the three runs Nettles drove in were more than enough, as Tommy John and two relievers held the A's to a single run.

Game Two was the series' only blowout, and even it remained close for three innings. But, led by a pair of three-run homers from Nettles and Lou Piniella, the Yankees parlayed nineteen hits into thirteen runs as Yankee reliever George Frazier held the A's scoreless over the final five frames.

Game Three remained tight until the ninth. Through eight innings the only run came on Yankee Willie Randolph's homer off Oakland starter Matt Keough. But in the top of the ninth, Graig Nettles tagged reliever Tom Underwood for his second bases-clearing double of the series. The three runs weren't really needed, as Dave Righetti, Ron Davis, and Goose Gossage combined to shut out the A's for the full nine.

New York Yankees (East), 3; Oakland A's (West), 0

NY (E)

PLAYER/POS	AVG	G	AB	R	H	2B	3B	HR	RB	BB	SO	SB
Bobby Brown, of-2	1.000	3	1	2	1	0	0	0	0	0	0	0
Rick Cerone, c	.100	3	10	1	1	0	0	0	0	0	0	0
Ron Davis, p	.000	2	0	0	0	0	0	0	0	0	0	0
Barry Foote, c-1	1.000	2	1	0	1	0	0	0	0	0	0	0
George Frazier, p	.000	1	0	0	0	0	0	0	0	0	0	0
Oscar Gamble, dh-2,of-1	.167	3	6	2	1	0	0	0	1	5	3	0
Rich Gossage, p	.000	2	0	0	0	0	0	0	0	0	0	0
Reggie Jackson, of	.000	2	4	1	0	0	0	0	1	1	0	1
Tommy John, p	.000	1	0	0	0	0	0	0	0	0	0	0
Rudy May, p	.000	1	0	0	0	0	0	0	0	0	0	0
Larry Milbourne, ss	.462	3	13	4	6	0	0	0	1	0	0	0
Jerry Mumphrey, of	.500	3	12	2	6	1	0	0	0	3	2	0
Bobby Murcer, dh	.333	1	3	0	1	0	0	0	0	1	1	0
Graig Nettles, 3b	.500	3	12	2	6	2	0	1	9	1	0	0
Lou Piniella, dh-2,of-1	.600	3	5	2	3	0	0	1	3	0	0	0
Willie Randolph, 2b	.333	3	12	2	4	0	0	1	2	0	1	0
Dave Revering, 1b	.500	2	2	0	1	0	0	0	0	0	0	0
Dave Righetti, p	.000	1	0	0	0	0	0	0	0	0	0	0
Andre Robertson, ss	.000	1	1	0	0	0	0	0	0	0	0	0
Aurelio Rodriguez, 3b	.000	1	0	0	0	0	0	0	0	0	0	0
Bob Watson, 1b	.250	3	12	0	3	0	0	0	1	0	1	0
Dave Winfield, of	.154	3	13	2	2	1	0	0	2	2	2	1
TOTAL	.336		107	20	36	4	0	3	20	13	10	2

PITCHER	W	L	ERA	G	GS	CG	SV	SHO	IP	H	ER	BB	SO
Ron Davis	0	0	0.00	2	0	0	0	0	3.1	0	0	2	4
George Frazier	1	0	0.00	1	0	0	0	0	5.2	5	0	1	5
Rich Gossage	0	0	0.00	2	0	0	1	0	2.2	1	0	0	2
Tommy John	1	0	1.50	1	1	0	0	0	6.0	6	1	1	3
Rudy May	0	0	8.10	1	0	0	0	0	3.1	6	3	0	5
Dave Righetti	1	0	0.00	1	1	0	0	0	6.0	4	0	2	4
TOTAL	3	0	1.33	8	2	0	1	0	27.0	22	4	6	23

OAK (W)

PLAYER/POS	AVG	G	AB	R	H	2B	3B	HR	RB	BB	SO	SB
Tony Armas, of	.167	3	12	0	2	0	0	0	0	0	5	0
Dave Beard, p	.000	1	0	0	0	0	0	0	0	0	0	0
Rick Bosetti, of-1,dh-1	.250	2	4	1	1	1	0	0	0	0	1	0
Mike Davis, ph	1.000	1	1	0	1	0	0	0	0	0	0	0
Keith Drumright, dh-1	.000	3	4	0	0	0	0	0	0	0	1	0
Wayne Gross, 3b	.000	3	5	0	0	0	0	0	0	0	0	0
Mike Heath, c-2,of-1	.333	3	6	1	2	0	0	0	0	0	1	0
Rickey Henderson, of	.364	3	11	0	4	2	1	0	1	1	2	2
Cliff Johnson, dh	.000	2	6	0	0	0	0	0	0	2	2	0
Jeff Jones, p	.000	1	0	0	0	0	0	0	0	0	0	0
Matt Keough, p	.000	1	0	0	0	0	0	0	0	0	0	0
Brian Kingman, p	.000	1	0	0	0	0	0	0	0	0	0	0
Mickey Klutts, 3b	.429	3	7	1	3	0	0	0	0	0	1	0
Steve McCatty, p	.000	1	0	0	0	0	0	0	0	0	0	0
Dave McKay, 2b	.273	3	11	0	3	0	0	0	1	0	2	0
Kelvin Moore, 1b	.250	3	8	0	2	0	0	0	0	0	1	0
Dwayne Murphy, of	.250	3	8	0	2	1	0	0	1	2	3	0
Jeff Newman, c	.000	2	5	0	0	0	0	0	0	0	2	0
Mike Norris, p	.000	1	0	0	0	0	0	0	0	0	0	0
Bob Owchinko, p	.000	1	0	0	0	0	0	0	0	0	0	0
Rob Picciolo, ss	.200	2	5	1	1	0	0	0	0	0	2	0
Jim Spencer, 1b	.000	2	3	0	0	0	0	0	0	0	0	0
Fred Stanley, ss	.333	2	3	0	1	0	0	0	0	1	0	0
Tom Underwood, p	.000	2	0	0	0	0	0	0	0	0	0	0
TOTAL	.222		99	4	22	4	1	0	4	6	23	2

PITCHER	W	L	ERA	G	GS	CG	SV	SHO	IP	H	ER	BB	SO
Dave Beard	0	0	40.50	1	0	0	0	0	0.2	5	3	0	0
Jeff Jones	0	0	4.50	1	0	0	0	0	2.0	2	1	1	0
Matt Keough	0	1	1.08	1	1	0	0	0	8.1	7	1	6	4
Brian Kingman	0	0	81.00	1	0	0	0	0	0.1	3	3	0	0
Steve McCatty	0	1	13.50	1	1	0	0	0	3.1	6	5	2	2
Mike Norris	0	1	3.68	1	1	0	0	0	7.1	8	3	2	4
Bob Owchinko	0	0	5.40	1	0	0	0	0	1.2	3	1	0	0
Tom Underwood	0	0	13.50	2	0	0	0	0	1.1	4	2	2	0
TOTAL	0	3	6.84	9	3	0	0	0	25.0	36	19	13	10

What the Yankees had done to the Dodgers three years earlier, the Dodgers now did to the Yankees in this, their eleventh meeting in the Series: they took the crown with four straight wins after losing the first two games. In the opener Bob Watson's first-inning three-run homer gave New York an insurmountable lead. Yankee starter Ron Guidry pitched seven strong innings, yielding just one run on a Steve Yeager homer, but two eighth-inning Dodger runs charged to reliever Ron Davis made things exciting until Yankee third baseman Graig Nettles dampened the rally with a splendid diving catch of Steve Garvey's line drive. In Game Two, Tommy John (now a Yankee) shut out his old teammates on three hits for seven innings. Reliever Goose Gossage completed the shutout, earning his second save in two days in the 3–0 Yankee victory.

But as the Series moved to Los Angeles, the Dodgers took the upper hand. Rookie ace Fernando Valenzuela experienced rocky going in the early innings of Game Three, yielding six hits (including home runs to Bob Watson and Rick Cerone) and four runs in the second and third innings. But Ron Cey's first-inning home run had given Los Angeles three early runs, and Dodger hitters added two more in the fifth as Valenzuela settled down to blank New York on three hits over the final six innings. The next day the Dodgers evened the Series with another close win. New York scored four times before the Dodgers got their first runs, but L.A. tied the game at 6–6 in the sixth and took an 8–6 lead an inning later. Reggie Jackson homered in the eighth to bring New York within one run of a tie, but they came no closer.

In Game Five, for the third day in a row, the Dodgers ovecame a Yankee lead to claim a one-run victory. Dodger pitcher Jerry Reuss gave the Yankees a run on two hits in the second inning, but shut them out on just three additional hits the rest of the way. Yankee starter Ron Guidry, meanwhile, stopped the Dodgers on two hits through the first six innings, but then gave up back-to-back homers to Pedro Guerrero and Steve Yeager in the seventh—runs enough for a 2–1 Dodger win. The final game was close for four innings, but in the fifth and sixth the Dodgers broke it open with seven runs and coasted in on Steve Howe's 3⅔ innings of shutout relief to a 9–2 win and, including 1900, their sixth world championship.

Los Angeles Dodgers (NL), 4; New York Yankees (AL), 2

LA (N)

PLAYER/POS	AVG	G	AB	R	H	2B	3B	HR	RB	BB	SO	SB
Dusty Baker, of	.167	6	24	3	4	0	0	0	1	1	6	0
Bobby Castillo, p	.000	1	0	0	0	0	0	0	0	0	0	0
Ron Cey, 3b	.350	6	20	3	7	0	0	1	6	3	3	0
Terry Forster, p	.000	2	0	0	0	0	0	0	0	0	0	0
Steve Garvey, 1b	.417	6	24	3	10	1	0	0	0	2	5	0
Dave Goltz, p	.000	2	0	0	0	0	0	0	0	0	0	0
Pedro Guerrero, of	.333	6	21	2	7	1	1	2	7	2	6	0
Burt Hooton, p	.000	2	4	1	0	0	0	0	0	1	3	0
Steve Howe, p	.000	3	2	0	0	0	0	0	0	0	2	0
Jay Johnstone, ph	.667	3	3	1	2	0	0	1	3	0	0	0
Ken Landreaux, of-3	.167	5	6	1	1	1	0	0	0	0	2	1
Davey Lopes, 2b	.227	6	22	6	5	1	0	0	2	4	3	4
Rick Monday, of-4	.231	5	13	1	3	1	0	0	0	3	6	0
Tom Niedenfuer, p	.000	2	0	0	0	0	0	0	0	0	0	0
Jerry Reuss, p	.000	2	3	0	0	0	0	0	0	1	2	0
Bill Russell, ss	.240	6	25	1	6	0	0	0	2	0	1	1
Steve Sax, 2b-1	.000	2	1	0	0	0	0	0	0	0	0	0
Mike Scioscia, c	.250	3	4	1	1	0	0	0	0	1	0	0
Reggie Smith, ph	.500	2	2	0	1	0	0	0	0	0	1	0
Dave Stewart, p	.000	2	0	0	0	0	0	0	0	0	0	0
Derrel Thomas, of-3,3b-2,ss-1	.000	5	7	2	0	0	0	0	1	1	2	0
Fernando Valenzuela, p	.000	1	3	0	0	0	0	0	0	1	0	0
Bob Welch, p	.000	1	0	0	0	0	0	0	0	0	0	0
Steve Yeager, c	.286	6	14	2	4	1	0	2	4	0	2	0
TOTAL	.258		198	27	51	6	1	6	26	20	44	6

PITCHER	W	L	ERA	G	GS	CG	SV	SHO	IP	H	ER	BB	SO
Bobby Castillo	0	0	9.00	1	0	0	0	0	1.0	0	1	5	0
Terry Forster	0	0	0.00	2	0	0	0	0	2.0	1	0	3	0
Dave Goltz	0	0	5.40	2	0	0	0	0	3.1	4	2	1	2
Burt Hooton	1	1	1.59	2	2	0	0	0	11.1	8	2	9	3
Steve Howe	1	0	3.86	3	0	0	1	0	7.0	7	3	1	4
Tom Niedenfuer	0	0	0.00	2	0	0	0	0	5.0	3	0	1	0
Jerry Reuss	1	1	3.86	2	2	1	0	0	11.2	10	5	3	8
Dave Stewart	0	0	0.00	2	0	0	0	0	1.2	1	0	2	1
Fernando Valenzuela	1	0	4.00	1	1	1	0	0	9.0	9	4	7	6
Bob Welch	0	0	∞	1	1	0	0	0	0.0	3	2	1	0
TOTAL	4	2	3.29	18	6	2	1	0	52.0	46	19	33	24

NY (A)

PLAYER/POS	AVG	G	AB	R	H	2B	3B	HR	RB	BB	SO	SB
Bobby Brown, of-2	.000	4	1	1	0	0	0	0	0	0	1	0
Rick Cerone, c	.190	6	21	2	4	1	0	1	3	4	2	0
Ron Davis, p	.000	4	0	0	0	0	0	0	0	0	0	0
Barry Foote, ph	.000	1	1	0	0	0	0	0	0	0	1	0
George Frazier, p	.000	3	0	0	0	0	0	0	0	0	1	0
Oscar Gamble, of-2	.333	3	6	1	2	0	0	0	1	1	0	0
Rich Gossage, p	.000	3	1	0	0	0	0	0	0	0	1	0
Ron Guidry, p	.000	2	5	0	0	0	0	0	0	0	3	0
Reggie Jackson, of	.333	3	12	3	4	1	0	1	1	2	3	0
Tommy John, p	.000	3	2	0	0	0	0	0	0	0	0	0
Dave LaRoche, p	.000	1	0	0	0	0	0	0	0	0	0	0
Rudy May, p	.000	3	1	0	0	0	0	0	0	0	0	0
Larry Milbourne, ss	.250	6	20	2	5	2	0	0	3	4	0	0
Jerry Mumphrey, of	.200	5	15	2	3	0	0	0	0	3	2	1
Bobby Murcer, of	.000	4	3	0	0	0	0	0	0	0	0	0
Graig Nettles, 3b	.400	3	10	1	4	1	0	0	0	1	1	0
Lou Piniella, of-3	.438	6	16	2	7	1	0	0	3	0	1	1
Willie Randolph, 2b	.222	6	18	5	4	1	1	2	3	9	0	1
Rick Reuschel, p	.000	2	2	0	0	0	0	0	0	0	1	0
Dave Righetti, p	.000	1	1	0	0	0	0	0	0	0	1	0
Andre Robertson, pr	.000	1	0	0	0	0	0	0	0	0	0	0
Aurelio Rodriguez, 3b-3	.417	4	12	1	5	0	0	0	0	1	2	0
Bob Watson, 1b	.318	6	22	2	7	1	0	2	7	3	0	0
Dave Winfield, of	.045	6	22	0	1	0	0	0	1	5	4	1
TOTAL	.238		193	22	46	8	1	6	22	33	24	4

PITCHER	W	L	ERA	G	GS	CG	SV	SHO	IP	H	ER	BB	SO
Ron Davis	0	0	23.14	4	0	0	0	0	2.1	4	6	5	4
George Frazier	0	3	17.18	3	0	0	0	0	3.2	9	7	3	2
Rich Gossage	0	0	0.00	3	0	0	2	0	5.0	2	0	2	5
Ron Guidry	1	1	1.93	2	2	0	0	0	14.0	8	3	4	15
Tommy John	1	0	0.69	3	2	0	0	0	13.0	11	1	0	8
Dave LaRoche	0	0	0.00	1	0	0	0	0	1.0	0	0	0	2
Rudy May	0	0	2.84	3	0	0	0	0	6.1	5	2	1	5
Rick Reuschel	0	0	4.91	2	1	0	0	0	3.2	7	2	3	2
Dave Righetti	0	0	13.50	1	1	0	0	0	2.0	5	3	2	1
TOTAL	2	4	4.24	22	6	0	2	0	51.0	51	24	20	44

GAME 1 AT NY OCT 20

LA	000	010	020	3	5	0
NY	301	100	00X	5	6	0

Pitchers: REUSS, Castillo (3), Goltz (4), Niedenfuer (5), Stewart (8) vs GUIDRY, Davis (8), Gossage (8)
Home Runs: Watson-NY, Yeager-LA
Attendance: 56,470

GAME 2 AT NY OCT 21

LA	000	000	000	0	4	2
NY	000	010	02X	3	6	1

Pitchers: HOOTON, Forster (7), Howe (8), Stewart (8) vs JOHN, Gossage (8)
Attendance: 56,505

GAME 3 AT LA OCT 23

NY	022	000	000	4	9	0
LA	300	020	00X	5	11	1

Pitchers: Righetti, FRAZIER (3), May (5), Davis (8) vs VALENZUELA
Home Runs: Cey-LA, Watson-NY, Cerone-NY
Attendance: 56,236

GAME 4 AT LA OCT 24

NY	211	002	010	7	13	1
LA	002	013	20X	8	14	2

Pitchers: Reuschel, May (4), Davis (5), FRAZIER (5), John (7) vs Welch, Goltz (1), Forster (4), Niedenfuer (5), HOWE (7)
Home Runs: Johnstone-LA, Randolph-NY, Jackson-NY
Attendance: 56,242

GAME 5 AT LA OCT 25

NY	010	000	000	1	5	0
LA	000	000	20X	2	4	3

Pitchers: GUIDRY, Gossage (8) vs REUSS
Home Runs: Guerrero-LA, Yeager-LA
Attendance: 56,115

GAME 6 AT NY OCT 28

LA	000	134	010	9	13	1
NY	001	001	000	2	7	2

Pitchers: HOOTON, Howe (6) vs John, FRAZIER (5), Davis (6), Reuschel (6), May (7), LaRoche (9)
Home Runs: Guerrero-LA, Randolph-NY
Attendance: 56,513

The official records show Atlanta ahead and threatening only once in a three-game series swept by the Cardinals. But in the original Game One, Phil Niekro held a slim 1–0 Atlanta lead in the fifth inning when rain wiped out the game just before it could become official.

In the first official game, the Braves scored nothing at all as Bob Forsch held them to three hits. Atlanta's Pascual Perez gave up only one run through the first five innings, but the Cardinals exploded for five runs in the sixth to put the game away. Following another rainout, Niekro tried again in Game Two. He gave up a run in the first, but Atlanta came back with three before he yielded a second run in the sixth. Gene Garber, who relieved Niekro, gave up the tying run in the eighth and lost the game in the bottom of the ninth on Ken Oberkfell's RBI liner over the center fielder's head.

Joaquin Andujar shut out the Braves through six innings of Game Three before giving up two runs in the seventh. But by then St. Louis had scored five times. Bruce Sutter retired the last seven Braves in relief of Andujar, and the Cardinals had their pennant.

St. Louis Cardinals (East), 3; Atlanta Braves (West), 0

STL (E)

PLAYER/POS	AVG	G	AB	R	H	2B	3B	HR	RB	BB	SO	SB
Joaquin Andujar, p	.000	1	1	0	0	0	0	0	0	0	1	0
Doug Bair, p	.000	1	0	0	0	0	0	0	0	0	0	0
Steve Braun, ph	.000	1	1	0	0	0	0	0	0	0	0	0
Bob Forsch, p	.667	1	3	1	2	0	0	0	1	0	0	0
David Green, of	1.000	2	1	1	1	0	0	0	0	0	0	0
George Hendrick, of	.308	3	13	2	4	0	0	0	2	1	2	0
Keith Hernandez, 1b	.333	3	12	3	4	0	0	0	1	2	3	0
Tommy Herr, 2b	.231	3	13	1	3	1	0	0	0	1	2	0
Willie McGee, of	.308	3	13	4	4	0	2	1	5	0	5	0
Ken Oberkfell, 3b	.200	3	15	1	3	0	0	0	2	0	0	0
Darrell Porter, c	.556	3	9	3	5	3	0	0	1	5	2	0
Lonnie Smith, of	.273	3	11	1	3	0	0	0	1	0	1	0
Ozzie Smith, ss	.556	3	9	0	5	0	0	0	3	3	0	1
John Stuper, p	.000	1	1	0	0	0	0	0	0	0	0	0
Bruce Sutter, p	.000	2	1	0	0	0	0	0	0	0	0	0
TOTAL	.330		103	17	34	4	2	1	16	12	16	1

PITCHER	W	L	ERA	G	GS	CG	SV	SHO	IP	H	ER	BB	SO
Joaquin Andujar	1	0	2.70	1	1	0	0	0	6.2	6	2	2	4
Doug Bair	0	0	0.00	1	0	0	0	0	1.0	2	0	3	0
Bob Forsch	1	0	0.00	1	1	1	0	1	9.0	3	0	0	6
John Stuper	0	0	3.00	1	1	0	0	0	6.0	4	2	1	4
Bruce Sutter	1	0	0.00	2	0	0	1	0	4.1	0	0	0	1
TOTAL	3	0	1.33	6	3	1	1	1	27.0	15	4	6	15

ATL (W)

PLAYER/POS	AVG	G	AB	R	H	2B	3B	HR	RB	BB	SO	SB
Steve Bedrosian, p	.000	2	0	0	0	0	0	0	0	0	0	0
Bruce Benedict, c	.250	3	8	1	2	1	0	0	0	2	1	0
Brett Butler, of-1	.000	2	1	0	0	0	0	0	0	0	0	0
Rick Camp, p	.000	1	0	0	0	0	0	0	0	0	0	0
Chris Chambliss, 1b	.000	3	10	0	0	0	0	0	0	1	0	0
Gene Garber, p	.000	2	1	0	0	0	0	0	0	0	0	0
Terry Harper, of	.000	1	1	1	0	0	0	0	0	0	0	0
Bob Horner, 3b	.091	3	11	0	1	0	0	0	0	0	2	0
Glenn Hubbard, 2b	.222	3	9	1	2	0	0	0	1	0	3	0
Rick Mahler, p	.000	1	0	0	0	0	0	0	0	0	0	0
Donnie Moore, p	.000	2	0	0	0	0	0	0	0	0	0	0
Dale Murphy, of	.273	3	11	1	3	0	0	0	0	0	2	1
Phil Niekro, p	.000	1	0	0	0	0	0	0	1	0	0	0
Pascual Perez, p	.000	2	3	0	0	0	0	0	0	0	1	0
Biff Pocoroba, ph	.000	1	1	0	0	0	0	0	0	0	0	0
Rafael Ramirez, ss	.182	3	11	2	2	0	0	0	1	1	1	0
Jerry Royster, of-3,3b-1	.182	3	11	0	2	0	0	0	0	0	2	0
Bob Walk, p	.000	1	0	0	0	0	0	0	0	0	0	0
Claudell Washington, of	.333	3	9	0	3	0	0	0	0	2	2	0
Larry Whisenton, ph	.000	2	2	0	0	0	0	0	0	0	1	0
TOTAL	.169		89	5	15	1	0	0	3	6	15	1

PITCHER	W	L	ERA	G	GS	CG	SV	SHO	IP	H	ER	BB	SO
Steve Bedrosian	0	0	18.00	2	0	0	0	0	1.0	3	2	1	2
Rick Camp	0	1	36.00	1	1	0	0	0	1.0	4	4	1	0
Gene Garber	0	1	8.10	2	0	0	0	0	3.1	4	3	1	3
Rick Mahler	0	0	0.00	1	0	0	0	0	1.2	3	0	2	0
Donnie Moore	0	0	0.00	2	0	0	0	0	2.2	2	0	0	1
Phil Niekro	0	0	3.00	1	1	0	0	0	6.0	6	2	4	5
Pascual Perez	0	1	5.19	2	1	0	0	0	8.2	10	5	2	4
Bob Walk	0	0	9.00	1	1	0	0	0	1.0	2	1	1	1
TOTAL	0	3	6.04	12	3	0	0	0	25.1	34	17	12	16

GAME 1 AT STL OCT 7

ATL	000	000	000	0	3	0
STL	001	005	01X	7	13	1

Pitchers: PEREZ, Bedrosian (6), Moore (6), Walk (8) vs FORSCH
Attendance: 53,008

GAME 2 AT STL OCT 9

ATL	002	010	000	3	6	0
STL	100	001	011	4	9	1

Pitchers: Niekro, GARBER (7) vs Stuper, Bair (7), SUTTER (8)
Attendance: 53,408

GAME 3 AT ATL OCT 10

STL	040	010	001	6	12	0
ATL	000	000	200	2	6	1

Pitchers: ANDUJAR, Sutter (7) vs CAMP, Perez (2), Moore (5), Mahler (7), Bedrosian (8), Garber (9)
Home Runs: McGee-STL
Attendance: 52,173

For the first time in LCS play, a club won the first two games but lost the series. The Angels overcame a 1–3 deficit to take Game One, with four runs in the third and three more later, while starter Tommy John settled down to stop the Brewers through the final six innings. In Game Two Bruce Kison prevailed, as the Angels built a 4–0 lead over Milwaukee and Pete Vuckovich before Kison gave up what proved to be a harmless two-run homer to Paul Molitor in the fifth.

With three chances to clinch the pennant, California three times fell short. In the third game, their three eighth-inning runs couldn't catch the Brewers, who already had five. In Game Four, Don Baylor's eighth-inning grand slam completed Angel scoring at five runs, but Milwaukee had already scored seven, and they added two more. In the finale, Kison held a 3–2 lead when he was relieved after five innings. But Cecil Cooper singled off Luis Sanchez in the seventh (with two out and the bases loaded) for two runs and a Brewer lead. Bob McClure and Pete Ladd held off the Angels through the final two innings, and the Brewers were on their way to their first World Series.

Milwaukee Brewers (East), 3; California Angels (West), 2

MIL (E)

PLAYER/POS	AVG	G	AB	R	H	2B	3B	HR	RBI	BB	SO	SB
Dwight Bernard, p	.000	1	0	0	0	0	0	0	0	0	0	0
Mark Brouhard, of	.750	1	4	4	3	1	0	1	3	0	0	0
Mike Caldwell, p	.000	1	0	0	0	0	0	0	0	0	0	0
Cecil Cooper, 1b	.150	5	20	1	3	2	0	0	4	0	6	0
Marshall Edwards, dh-2,of-1	.000	3	1	2	0	0	0	0	0	0	0	1
Jim Gantner, 2b	.188	5	16	1	3	0	0	0	2	1	1	0
Moose Haas, p	.000	1	0	0	0	0	0	0	0	0	0	0
Roy Howell, dh	.000	1	3	0	0	0	0	0	0	0	1	0
Pete Ladd, p	.000	3	0	0	0	0	0	0	0	0	0	0
Bob McClure, p	.000	1	0	0	0	0	0	0	0	0	0	0
Paul Molitor, 3b	.316	5	19	4	6	1	0	2	5	2	3	1
Don Money, dh	.182	4	11	2	2	0	0	0	1	3	1	0
Charlie Moore, of	.462	5	13	3	6	0	0	0	0	1	2	0
Ben Oglivie, of	.133	4	15	1	2	0	0	1	1	0	3	0
Ted Simmons, c	.167	5	18	3	3	0	0	0	1	1	4	0
Jim Slaton, p	.000	2	0	0	0	0	0	0	0	0	0	0
Don Sutton, p	.000	1	0	0	0	0	0	0	0	0	0	0
Gorman Thomas, of	.067	5	15	1	1	0	0	1	3	2	7	0
Pete Vuckovich, p	.000	2	0	0	0	0	0	0	0	0	0	0
Robin Yount, ss	.250	5	16	1	4	0	0	0	0	5	0	0
TOTAL	.219		151	23	33	4	0	5	20	15	28	2

PITCHER	W	L	ERA	G	GS	CG	SV	SHO	IP	H	ER	BB	SO
Dwight Bernard	0	0	0.00	1	0	0	0	0	1.0	0	0	0	0
Mike Caldwell	0	1	15.00	1	1	0	0	0	3.0	7	5	1	2
Moose Haas	1	0	4.91	1	1	0	0	0	7.1	5	4	5	7
Pete Ladd	0	0	0.00	3	0	0	2	0	3.1	0	0	0	5
Bob McClure	1	0	0.00	1	0	0	0	0	1.2	2	0	0	0
Jim Slaton	0	0	1.93	2	0	0	1	0	4.2	3	1	1	3
Don Sutton	1	0	3.52	1	1	0	0	0	7.2	8	3	2	9
Pete Vuckovich	0	1	4.40	2	2	1	0	0	14.1	15	7	7	8
TOTAL	3	2	4.19	12	5	1	3	0	43.0	40	20	16	34

CAL (W)

PLAYER/POS	AVG	G	AB	R	H	2B	3B	HR	RBI	BB	SO	SB
Don Baylor, dh	.294	5	17	2	5	1	1	1	10	2	0	0
Juan Beniquez, of	.000	2	0	0	0	0	0	0	0	0	0	0
Bob Boone, c	.250	5	16	3	4	0	0	1	4	0	2	0
Rod Carew, 1b	.176	5	17	2	3	1	0	0	0	4	4	1
Bobby Clark, of	.000	2	0	0	0	0	0	0	0	0	0	0
Doug De Cinces, 3b	.316	5	19	5	6	2	0	0	0	1	5	0
Brian Downing, of	.158	5	19	4	3	1	0	0	0	3	2	0
Tim Foli, ss	.125	5	16	2	2	0	0	0	1	0	3	0
Dave Goltz, p	.000	1	0	0	0	0	0	0	0	0	0	0
Bobby Grich, 2b	.200	5	15	1	3	1	0	0	1	2	7	0
Andy Hassler, p	.000	2	0	0	0	0	0	0	0	0	0	0
Reggie Jackson, of	.111	5	18	2	2	0	0	1	2	2	7	0
Ron Jackson, ph	1.000	1	1	0	1	0	0	0	0	0	0	0
Tommy John, p	.000	2	0	0	0	0	0	0	0	0	0	0
Bruce Kison, p	.000	2	0	0	0	0	0	0	0	0	0	0
Fred Lynn, of	.611	5	18	4	11	2	0	1	5	2	3	0
Luis Sanchez, p	.000	2	0	0	0	0	0	0	0	0	0	0
Rob Wilfong, ph	.000	2	1	0	0	0	0	0	0	0	1	0
Mike Witt, p	.000	1	0	0	0	0	0	0	0	0	0	0
Geoff Zahn, p	.000	1	0	0	0	0	0	0	0	0	0	0
TOTAL	.255		157	23	40	8	1	4	23	16	34	1

PITCHER	W	L	ERA	G	GS	CG	SV	SHO	IP	H	ER	BB	SO
Dave Goltz	0	0	7.36	1	0	0	0	0	3.2	4	3	2	2
Andy Hassler	0	0	0.00	2	0	0	0	0	2.2	0	0	0	2
Tommy John	1	1	5.11	2	2	1	0	0	12.1	11	7	6	6
Bruce Kison	1	0	1.93	2	2	1	0	0	14.0	8	3	3	12
Luis Sanchez	0	1	6.75	2	0	0	0	0	2.2	4	2	1	1
Mike Witt	0	0	6.00	1	0	0	0	0	3.0	2	2	2	3
Geoff Zahn	0	1	7.36	1	1	0	0	0	3.2	4	3	1	2
TOTAL	2	3	4.29	11	5	2	0	0	42.0	33	20	15	28

GAME 1 AT CAL OCT 5

MIL	021	000	000	3	7 2
CAL	104	210	00X	8	10 0

Pitchers: CALDWELL, Slaton (4), Ladd (7), Bernard (8) vs JOHN
Home Runs: Thomas-MIL, Lynn-CAL
Attendance: 64,406

GAME 2 AT CAL OCT 6

MIL	000	020	000	2	5 0
CAL	021	100	00X	4	6 0

Pitchers: VUCKOVICH vs KISON
Home Runs: Re.Jackson-CAL, Molitor-MIL
Attendance: 64,179

GAME 3 AT MIL OCT 8

CAL	000	000	030	3	8 0
MIL	000	300	20X	5	6 0

Pitchers: ZAHN, Witt (4), Hassler (7) vs SUTTON, Ladd (8)
Home Runs: Molitor-MIL, Boone-CAL
Attendance: 50,135

GAME 4 AT MIL OCT 9

CAL	000	001	040	5	5 3
MIL	030	301	02X	9	9 2

Pitchers: JOHN, Goltz (4), Sanchez (8) vs HAAS, Slaton (8)
Home Runs: Baylor-CAL, Brouhard-MIL
Attendance: 51,003

GAME 5 AT MIL OCT 10

CAL	101	100	000	3	11 1
MIL	100	100	20X	4	6 4

Pitchers: Kison, SANCHEZ (6), Hassler (7) vs Vuckovich, McCLURE (7), Ladd (9)
Home Runs: Oglivie-MIL
Attendance: 54,968

The Series was anticipated as a matchup of Cardinal speed and Brewer power. In the event, though, St. Louis outslugged the Brewers and wound up with their tenth world championship.

The Brewers, in their first World Series, looked unstoppable in the opening game. Hammering four Cardinal pitchers for seventeen hits (including a record five for Paul Molitor), they scored ten runs while pitcher Mike Caldwell was shutting out the Cards on three hits. In the second game Milwaukee continued the onslaught, building an early 3–0 lead. But St. Louis finally got on the scoreboard with two runs in the last of the third, and tied the game at 4–4 in the sixth on Darrell Porter's two-RBI double. And the Cards won the game on a bases-loaded walk in the eighth as relievers Doug Bair and Bruce Sutter held the Brewers scoreless over the final four innings.

St. Louis pushed into the Series lead in Game Three, thanks mostly to the 6⅓ shutout innings of starter Joaquin Andujar and the fielding and batting of center fielder Willie McGee. McGee drove in four of the six Cardinal runs with a pair of homers and prevented an extra-base hit and a two-run Brewer homer with leaping catches in the first and final innings. The Cards pressed their advantage in Game Four with four early runs. But in the last of the seventh (with the score now 5–1), an error by Cardinal pitcher Dave LaPoint opened the way for Milwaukee to win the game with six two-out runs on a barrage of hits (and the added assistance of a pair of walks and a wild pitch).

Brewer pitcher Mike Caldwell wasn't as effective in Game Five as he had been in the opener, yielding fourteen hits and four runs in 8⅓ innings of work. But he was never behind in the game as his teammates, with eleven hits of their own (four of them by Robin Yount, including a home run) and several fielding gems put Milwaukee ahead again in the Series with a 6–4 win.

The Cards had their backs to the wall as the Series moved to St. Louis for the final games. But in Game Six the Cards responded to their opening-game humiliation with a laugher of their own, 13–1, on John Stuper's four-hitter. And in the finale they rocked Brewer ace Pete Vuckovich and three relievers for fifteen hits and a 6–3 victory that gave starter Joaquin Andujar his second Series win and reliever Bruce Sutter his second save.

St. Louis Cardinals (NL), 4; Milwaukee Brewers (AL), 3

STL (N)

PLAYER/POS	AVG	G	AB	R	H	2B	3B	HR	RB	BB	SO	SB
Joaquin Andujar, p	.000	2	0	0	0	0	0	0	0	0	0	0
Doug Bair, p	.000	3	0	0	0	0	0	0	0	0	0	0
Steve Braun, dh	.500	2	2	0	1	0	0	0	2	1	0	0
Glenn Brummer, c	.000	1	0	0	0	0	0	0	0	0	0	0
Bob Forsch, p	.000	2	0	0	0	0	0	0	0	0	0	0
David Green, of-4,dh-3	.200	7	10	3	2	1	1	0	0	1	3	0
George Hendrick, of	.321	7	28	5	9	0	0	0	5	2	2	0
Keith Hernandez, 1b	.259	7	27	4	7	2	0	1	8	4	2	0
Tommy Herr, 2b	.160	7	25	2	4	2	0	0	5	3	3	0
Dane Iorg, dh	.529	5	17	4	9	4	1	0	1	0	0	0
Jim Kaat, p	.000	4	0	0	0	0	0	0	0	0	0	0
Jeff Lahti, p	.000	2	0	0	0	0	0	0	0	0	0	0
Dave LaPoint, p	.000	2	0	0	0	0	0	0	0	0	0	0
Willie McGee, of	.240	6	25	6	6	0	0	2	5	1	3	2
Ken Oberkfell, 3b	.292	7	24	4	7	1	0	0	1	2	1	2
Darrell Porter, c	.286	7	28	1	8	2	0	1	5	1	4	0
Mike Ramsey, 3b-2	.000	3	1	1	0	0	0	0	0	0	1	0
Lonnie Smith, of-6,dh-1	.321	7	28	6	9	4	1	0	1	1	5	2
Ozzie Smith, ss	.208	7	24	3	5	0	0	0	1	3	0	1
John Stuper, p	.000	2	0	0	0	0	0	0	0	0	0	0
Bruce Sutter, p	.000	4	0	0	0	0	0	0	0	0	0	0
Gene Tenace, dh-1	.000	5	6	0	0	0	0	0	0	1	2	0
TOTAL	.273		245	39	67	16	3	4	34	20	26	7

PITCHER	W	L	ERA	G	GS	CG	SV	SHO	IP	H	ER	BB	SO
Joaquin Andujar	2	0	1.35	2	2	0	0	0	13.1	10	2	1	4
Doug Bair	0	1	9.00	3	0	0	0	0	2.0	2	2	2	3
Bob Forsch	0	2	4.97	2	2	0	0	0	12.2	18	7	3	4
Jim Kaat	0	0	3.86	4	0	0	0	0	2.1	4	1	2	2
Jeff Lahti	0	0	10.80	2	0	0	0	0	1.2	4	2	1	1
Dave LaPoint	0	0	3.24	2	1	0	0	0	8.1	10	3	2	3
John Stuper	1	0	3.46	2	2	1	0	0	13.0	10	5	5	5
Bruce Sutter	1	0	4.70	4	0	0	2	0	7.2	6	4	3	6
TOTAL	4	3	3.84	21	7	1	2	0	61.0	64	26	19	28

MIL (A)

PLAYER/POS	AVG	G	AB	R	H	2B	3B	HR	RB	BB	SO	SB
Dwight Bernard, p	.000	1	0	0	0	0	0	0	0	0	0	0
Mike Caldwell, p	.000	3	0	0	0	0	0	0	0	0	0	0
Cecil Cooper, 1b	.286	7	28	3	8	1	0	1	6	1	1	0
Marshall Edwards, of	.000	1	0	0	0	0	0	0	0	0	0	0
Jim Gantner, 2b	.333	7	24	5	8	4	1	0	4	1	1	0
Moose Haas, p	.000	2	0	0	0	0	0	0	0	0	0	0
Roy Howell, dh	.000	4	11	1	0	0	0	0	0	0	3	0
Pete Ladd, p	.000	1	0	0	0	0	0	0	0	0	0	0
Bob McClure, p	.000	5	0	0	0	0	0	0	0	0	0	0
Doc Medich, p	.000	1	0	0	0	0	0	0	0	0	0	0
Paul Molitor, 3b	.355	7	31	5	11	0	0	0	3	2	4	1
Don Money, dh-4	.231	5	13	4	3	1	0	0	1	2	0	0
Charlie Moore, of	.346	7	26	3	9	3	0	0	2	1	0	0
Ben Oglivie, of	.222	7	27	4	6	0	1	1	1	2	4	0
Ted Simmons, c	.174	7	23	2	4	0	0	2	3	5	3	0
Jim Slaton, p	.000	2	0	0	0	0	0	0	0	0	0	0
Don Sutton, p	.000	2	0	0	0	0	0	0	0	0	0	0
Gorman Thomas, of	.115	7	26	0	3	0	0	0	3	2	7	0
Pete Vuckovich, p	.000	2	0	0	0	0	0	0	0	0	0	0
Ned Yost, c	.000	1	0	0	0	0	0	0	0	1	0	0
Robin Yount, ss	.414	7	29	6	12	3	0	1	6	2	2	0
TOTAL	.269		238	33	64	12	2	5	29	19	28	1

PITCHER	W	L	ERA	G	GS	CG	SV	SHO	IP	H	ER	BB	SO
Dwight Bernard	0	0	0.00	1	0	0	0	0	1.0	0	0	0	1
Mike Caldwell	2	0	2.04	3	2	1	0	1	17.2	19	4	3	6
Moose Haas	0	0	7.36	2	1	0	0	0	7.1	8	6	3	4
Pete Ladd	0	0	0.00	1	0	0	0	0	0.2	1	0	2	0
Bob McClure	0	2	4.15	5	0	0	2	0	4.1	5	2	3	5
Doc Medich	0	0	18.00	1	0	0	0	0	2.0	5	4	1	0
Jim Slaton	1	0	0.00	2	0	0	0	0	2.2	1	0	2	1
Don Sutton	0	1	7.84	2	2	0	0	0	10.1	12	9	1	5
Pete Vuckovich	0	1	4.50	2	2	0	0	0	14.0	16	7	5	4
TOTAL	3	4	4.80	19	7	1	2	0	60.0	67	32	20	26

GAME 1 AT STL OCT 12

MIL	200	112	004	10	17 0
STL	000	000	000	0	3 1

Pitchers: CALDWELL vs FORSCH, Kaat (6), LaPoint (8), Lahti (9)
Home Runs: Simmons-MIL
Attendance: 53,723

GAME 2 AT STL OCT 13

MIL	012	010	000	4	10 1
STL	002	002	01X	5	8 0

Pitchers: Sutton, McCLURE (7), Ladd (8) vs Stuper, Kaat (5), Bair (5), SUTTER (7)
Home Runs: Simmons-MIL
Attendance: 53,723

GAME 3 AT MIL OCT 15

STL	000	030	201	6	6 1
MIL	000	000	020	2	5 3

Pitchers: ANDUJAR, Kaat (7), Bair (7), Sutter (7) vs VUCKOVICH, McClure (9)
Home Runs: McGee-STL (2), Cooper-MIL
Attendance: 56,556

GAME 4 AT MIL OCT 16

STL	130	001	000	5	8 1
MIL	000	010	60X	7	10 2

Pitchers: LaPoint, BAIR (7), Kaat (7), Lahti (7) vs Haas, SLATON (6), McClure (8)
Attendance: 56,560

GAME 5 AT MIL OCT 17

STL	001	000	102	4	15 2
MIL	101	010	12X	6	11 1

Pitchers: FORSCH, Sutter (8) vs CALDWELL, McClure (9)
Home Runs: Yount-MIL
Attendance: 56,562

GAME 6 AT STL OCT 19

MIL	000	000	001	1	4 4
STL	020	326	00X	13	12 1

Pitchers: SUTTON, Slaton (5), Medich (6), Bernard (8) vs STUPER
Home Runs: Porter-STL, Hernandez-STL
Attendance: 53,723

GAME 7 AT STL OCT 20

MIL	000	012	000	3	7 0
STL	000	103	02X	6	15 1

Pitchers: Vuckovich, McCLURE (6), Haas (6), Caldwell (8) vs ANDUJAR, Sutter (8)
Home Runs: Oglivie-MIL
Attendance: 53,723

The Dodgers earned only four runs off Philadelphia pitching, and even though they doubled their run total to eight on unearned runs, the Phillies scored twice that number to take the pennant in four games.

Mike Schmidt homered off Jerry Reuss in the first inning of the opener for the game's only run. Phillie starter Steve Carlton loaded the bases in the eighth, but Al Holland came on to get the third out and preserve the shutout. The Phillies also scored only one run in the second game, on Gary Matthews's homer off Fernando Valenzuela in the second. But this time the run only tied the score, and in the fifth Pedro Guerrero tripled in two unearned runs to give Valenzuela the Dodgers' only win.

The Phillies' Charlie Hudson hurled the series' only complete game—a four-hitter—to win Game Three. Gary Matthews's four hits in Game Three and Four included his second and third series homers, and drove in half the Phillies' fourteen runs as they took the two games by identical 7–2 scores.

Philadelphia Phillies (East), 3; Los Angeles Dodgers (West), 1

PHI (E)

PLAYER/POS	AVG	G	AB	R	H	2B	3B	HR	RB	BB	SO	SB
Steve Carlton, p	.200	2	5	0	1	0	0	0	0	0	3	0
Ivan DeJesus, ss	.250	4	12	0	3	0	0	0	1	3	3	0
John Denny, p	.000	1	1	0	0	0	0	0	0	0	0	0
Bob Dernier, of	.000	1	0	0	0	0	0	0	0	0	0	0
Bo Diaz, c	.154	4	13	0	2	1	0	0	0	2	1	0
Greg Gross, of-3	.000	4	5	1	0	0	0	0	0	2	2	0
Von Hayes, of-1	.000	2	0	0	0	0	0	0	0	0	0	0
Al Holland, p	.000	2	0	0	0	0	0	0	0	0	0	0
Charles Hudson, p	.000	1	4	0	0	0	0	0	0	0	3	0
Joe Lefebvre, of-1	.000	2	2	0	0	0	0	0	1	0	1	0
Sixto Lezcano, of	.308	4	13	2	4	0	0	1	2	1	1	0
Garry Maddox, of	.273	3	11	0	3	1	0	0	1	0	1	0
Gary Matthews, of	.429	4	14	4	6	0	0	3	8	2	1	1
Joe Morgan, 2b	.067	4	15	1	1	0	0	0	0	2	1	0
Tony Perez, ph	1.000	1	1	0	1	0	0	0	0	0	0	0
Ron Reed, p	.000	2	0	0	0	0	0	0	0	0	0	0
Pete Rose, 1b	.375	4	16	3	6	0	0	0	0	1	1	1
Juan Samuel, pr	.000	1	0	0	0	0	0	0	0	0	0	0
Mike Schmidt, 3b	.467	4	15	5	7	2	0	1	2	2	3	0
Ossie Virgil, ph	.000	1	1	0	0	0	0	0	0	0	1	0
TOTAL	.262		130	16	34	4	0	5	15	15	22	2

PITCHER	W	L	ERA	G	GS	CG	SV	SHO	IP	H	ER	BB	SO
Steve Carlton	2	0	0.66	2	2	0	0	0	13.2	13	1	5	13
John Denny	0	1	0.00	1	1	0	0	0	6.0	5	0	3	3
Al Holland	0	0	0.00	2	0	0	1	0	3.0	1	0	0	3
Charles Hudson	1	0	2.00	1	1	1	0	0	9.0	4	2	2	9
Ron Reed	0	0	2.70	2	0	0	0	0	3.1	4	1	1	3
TOTAL	3	1	1.03	8	4	1	1	0	35.0	27	4	11	31

LA (W)

PLAYER/POS	AVG	G	AB	R	H	2B	3B	HR	RB	BB	SO	SB
Dusty Baker, of	.357	4	14	4	5	1	0	1	1	2	0	0
Joe Beckwith, p	.000	2	0	0	0	0	0	0	0	0	0	0
Greg Brock, 1b	.000	3	9	1	0	0	0	0	0	0	3	0
Jack Fimple, c	.143	3	7	0	1	0	0	0	1	0	3	0
Pedro Guerrero, 3b	.250	4	12	1	3	1	1	0	2	3	3	0
Rick Honeycutt, p	.000	2	0	0	0	0	0	0	0	0	0	0
Rafael Landestoy, ph	.000	2	2	0	0	0	0	0	0	0	1	0
Ken Landreaux, of	.143	4	14	0	2	0	0	0	1	1	3	0
Candy Maldonado, ph	.000	2	2	0	0	0	0	0	0	0	1	0
Mike Marshall, 1b-3,of-2	.133	4	15	1	2	1	0	1	2	1	6	0
Rick Monday, ph	.000	1	0	0	0	0	0	0	0	0	0	0
Jose Morales, ph	.000	2	2	0	0	0	0	0	0	0	1	0
Tom Niedenfuer, p	.000	2	0	0	0	0	0	0	0	0	0	0
Alejandro Pena, p	1.000	1	1	0	1	0	0	0	0	0	0	0
Jerry Reuss, p	.000	2	3	0	0	0	0	0	0	0	3	0
Bill Russell, ss	.286	4	14	1	4	0	0	0	0	2	4	1
Steve Sax, 2b	.250	4	16	0	4	0	0	0	0	1	0	1
Derrel Thomas, of	.444	4	9	0	4	1	0	0	0	0	3	1
Fernando Valenzuela, p	.000	1	3	0	0	0	0	0	0	1	0	0
Bob Welch, p	.000	1	0	0	0	0	0	0	0	0	0	0
Steve Yeager, c	.167	2	6	0	1	1	0	0	0	0	0	0
Pat Zachry, p	.000	2	0	0	0	0	0	0	0	0	0	0
TOTAL	.209		129	8	27	5	1	2	7	11	31	3

PITCHER	W	L	ERA	G	GS	CG	SV	SHO	IP	H	ER	BB	SO
Joe Beckwith	0	0	0.00	2	0	0	0	0	2.1	1	0	2	3
Rick Honeycutt	0	0	21.60	2	0	0	0	0	1.2	4	4	0	2
Tom Niedenfuer	0	0	0.00	2	0	0	1	0	2.0	0	0	1	3
Alejandro Pena	0	0	6.75	1	0	0	0	0	2.2	4	2	1	3
Jerry Reuss	0	2	4.50	2	2	0	0	0	12.0	14	6	3	4
Fernando Valenzuela	1	0	1.13	1	1	0	0	0	8.0	7	1	4	5
Bob Welch	0	1	6.75	1	1	0	0	0	1.1	0	1	2	0
Pat Zachry	0	0	2.25	2	0	0	0	0	4.0	4	1	2	2
TOTAL	1	3	3.97	13	4	0	1	0	34.0	34	15	15	22

GAME 1 AT LA OCT 4

PHI	100	000	000	1	5	1
LA	000	000	000	0	7	0

Pitchers: CARLTON, Holland (8) vs REUSS, Niedenfuer (9)
Home Runs: Schmidt-PHI
Attendance: 49,963

GAME 2 AT LA OCT 5

PHI	010	000	000	1	7	2
LA	100	000	01X	4	6	1

Pitchers: DENNY, Reed (7) vs VALENZUELA, Niedenfuer (9)
Home Runs: Matthews-PHI
Attendance: 55,967

GAME 3 AT PHI OCT 7

LA	000	200	000	2	4	0
PHI	021	120	10X	7	9	1

Pitchers: WELCH, Pena (2), Honeycutt (5), Beckwith (5), Zachry (7) vs HUDSON
Home Runs: Marshall-LA, Matthews-PHI
Attendance: 53,490

GAME 4 AT PHI OCT 8

LA	000	100	010	2	10	1
PHI	300	022	00X	7	13	1

Pitchers: REUSS, Beckwith (5), Honeycutt (5), Zachry (7) vs CARLTON, Reed (7), Holland (8)
Home Runs: Matthews-PHI, Baker-LA, Lezcano-PHI
Attendance: 64,494

The White Sox and Orioles entered the LCS evenly matched, with similar season's records and stats. But in the LCS, Baltimore all but shut down Chicago's run production. Both teams had 28 hits, but the Sox, held to four for extra bases, found themselves outslugged by 116 percentage points and outscored by 16 runs.

Chicago won the first game, scoring two of their three series runs as LaMarr Hoyt shut Baltimore out for eight innings before letting in a run in the ninth. But the White Sox had concluded their effective scoring. In Game Two, Oriole rookie Mike Boddicker shut them out on five hits, striking out fourteen. In Game Three the Sox scored their final run. The Orioles got only two more hits than Chicago, but blended them with nine walks, a hit batsman, and a Sox error to score eleven runs. In the fourth game, Oriole pitchers Storm Davis and Tippy Martinez saw that ten Chicago hits scored no runs. Britt Burns held Baltimore scoreless, too, through nine innings. But Tito Landrum's solo homer in the top of the tenth drove Burns out, and two more Oriole runs provided more than enough scoring to win Baltimore the flag.

Baltimore Orioles (East), 3; Chicago White Sox (West), 1

BAL (E)

PLAYER/POS	AVG	G	AB	R	H	2B	3B	HR	RB	BB	SO	SB
Benny Ayala, dh	.000	1	0	0	0	0	0	0	0	1	0	0
Mike Boddicker, p	.000	1	0	0	0	0	0	0	0	0	0	0
Al Bumbry, of	.125	3	8	0	1	1	0	0	1	0	2	0
Todd Cruz, 3b	.133	4	15	0	2	0	0	0	1	0	5	0
Rich Dauer, 2b	.000	4	14	0	0	0	0	0	0	1	0	0
Storm Davis, p	.000	1	0	0	0	0	0	0	0	0	0	0
Rick Dempsey, c	.167	4	12	1	2	0	0	0	0	1	1	0
Jim Dwyer, of-1	.250	2	4	1	1	1	0	0	0	1	0	0
Mike Flanagan, p	.000	1	0	0	0	0	0	0	0	0	0	0
Dan Ford, of-1	.200	2	5	0	1	1	0	0	0	0	1	0
Tito Landrum, of-3	.200	4	10	2	2	0	0	1	1	0	2	0
John Lowenstein, of-2	.167	3	6	0	1	1	0	0	0	1	2	0
Tippy Martinez, p	.000	2	0	0	0	0	0	0	0	0	0	0
Scott McGregor, p	.000	1	0	0	0	0	0	0	0	0	0	0
Eddie Murray, 1b	.267	4	15	5	4	0	0	1	3	3	3	1
Joe Nolan, ph	.000	1	0	0	0	0	0	0	1	0	0	0
Jim Palmer, pr	.000	1	0	0	0	0	0	0	0	0	0	0
Cal Ripken, ss	.400	4	15	5	6	2	0	0	1	2	3	0
Gary Roenicke, of	.750	3	4	4	3	1	0	1	4	5	0	0
John Shelby, of-2	.222	3	9	1	2	0	0	0	0	1	3	1
Ken Singleton, dh	.250	4	12	0	3	2	0	0	1	2	2	0
Sammy Stewart, p	.000	2	0	0	0	0	0	0	0	0	0	0
TOTAL	.217		129	19	28	9	0	3	17	16	24	2

PITCHER	W	L	ERA	G	GS	CG	SV	SHO	IP	H	ER	BB	SO
Mike Boddicker	1	0	0.00	1	1	1	0	1	9.0	5	0	3	14
Storm Davis	0	0	0.00	1	1	0	0	0	6.0	5	0	2	2
Mike Flanagan	1	0	1.80	1	1	0	0	0	5.0	5	1	0	1
Tippy Martinez	1	0	0.00	2	0	0	0	0	6.0	5	0	3	5
Scott McGregor	0	1	1.35	1	1	0	0	0	6.2	6	1	3	2
Sammy Stewart	0	0	0.00	2	0	0	1	0	4.1	2	0	1	2
TOTAL	3	1	0.49	8	4	1	1	1	37.0	28	2	12	26

CHI (W)

PLAYER/POS	AVG	G	AB	R	H	2B	3B	HR	RB	BB	SO	SB
Juan Agosto, p	.000	1	0	0	0	0	0	0	0	0	0	0
Harold Baines, of	.125	4	16	0	2	0	0	0	0	1	3	0
Floyd Bannister, p	.000	1	0	0	0	0	0	0	0	0	0	0
Salome Barojas, p	.000	2	0	0	0	0	0	0	0	0	0	0
Britt Burns, p	.000	1	0	0	0	0	0	0	0	0	0	0
Julio Cruz, 2b	.333	4	12	0	4	0	0	0	0	3	4	2
Richard Dotson, p	.000	1	0	0	0	0	0	0	0	0	0	0
Jerry Dybzinski, ss	.250	2	4	0	1	0	0	0	0	0	0	0
Carlton Fisk, c	.176	4	17	0	3	1	0	0	0	1	3	0
Scott Fletcher, ss	.000	3	7	0	0	0	0	0	0	1	0	0
Jerry Hairston, of	.000	2	3	0	0	0	0	0	0	1	1	0
LaMarr Hoyt, p	.000	1	0	0	0	0	0	0	0	0	0	0
Ron Kittle, of	.286	3	7	1	2	1	0	0	0	1	2	0
Jerry Koosman, p	.000	1	0	0	0	0	0	0	0	0	0	0
Dennis Lamp, p	.000	3	0	0	0	0	0	0	0	0	0	0
Rudy Law, of	.389	4	18	1	7	1	0	0	0	0	1	2
Vance Law, 3b	.182	4	11	0	2	0	0	0	0	1	3	0
Greg Luzinski, dh	.133	4	15	0	2	1	0	0	0	1	5	0
Tom Paciorek, 1b-3,of-2	.250	4	16	1	4	0	0	0	1	1	2	0
Aurelio Rodriguez, 3b	.000	2	0	0	0	0	0	0	0	0	0	0
Mike Squires, 1b-3	.000	4	4	0	0	0	0	0	0	0	0	0
Dick Tidrow, p	.000	1	0	0	0	0	0	0	0	0	0	0
Greg Walker, 1b-1	.333	2	3	0	1	0	0	0	0	1	2	0
TOTAL	.211		133	3	28	4	0	0	2	12	26	4

PITCHER	W	L	ERA	G	GS	CG	SV	SHO	IP	H	ER	BB	SO
Juan Agosto	0	0	0.00	1	0	0	0	0	0.1	0	0	0	0
Floyd Bannister	0	1	4.50	1	1	0	0	0	6.0	5	3	1	5
Salome Barojas	0	0	18.00	2	0	0	0	0	1.0	4	2	0	0
Britt Burns	0	1	0.96	1	1	0	0	0	9.1	6	1	5	8
Richard Dotson	0	1	10.80	1	1	0	0	0	5.0	6	6	3	3
LaMarr Hoyt	1	0	1.00	1	1	0	0	0	9.0	5	1	0	4
Jerry Koosman	0	0	54.00	1	0	0	0	0	0.1	1	2	0	0
Dennis Lamp	0	0	0.00	3	0	0	0	0	2.0	0	0	2	1
Dick Tidrow	0	0	3.00	1	0	0	0	0	3.0	1	1	3	3
TOTAL	1	3	4.00	12	4	1	0	0	36.0	28	16	16	24

GAME 1 AT BAL OCT 5

CHI	001	001	000	2	7	0
BAL	000	000	001	1	5	1

Pitchers: HOYT vs McGREGOR, Stewart (7), T.Martinez (8)
Attendance: 51,289

GAME 2 AT BAL OCT 6

CHI	000	000	000	0	5	2
BAL	010	102	00X	4	6	0

Pitchers: BANNISTER, Barojas (7), Lamp (8) vs BODDICKER
Home Runs: Roenicke-BAL
Attendance: 52,347

GAME 3 AT CHI OCT 7

BAL	310	020	014	11	8	1
CHI	010	000	000	1	6	1

Pitchers: FLANAGAN, Stewart (6) vs DOTSON, Tidrow (6), Koosman (9), Lamp (9)
Home Runs: Murray-BAL
Attendance: 46,635

GAME 4 AT CHI OCT 8

BAL	000	000	000	3	3	9	0
CHI	000	000	000	0	0	10	0

Pitchers: Davis, T.MARTINEZ (7) vs BURNS, Barojas (10), Agosto (10), Lamp (10)
Home Runs: Landrum-BAL
Attendance: 45,477

Near neighbors Baltimore and Philadelphia met in a World Series for the first time. Both clubs were led by new managers: Baltimore by Joe Altobelli, who inherited a team built under longtime Oriole manager Earl Weaver; and the Phillies by general manager Paul Owens, who replaced Pat Corrales with himself in midseason. Both started their top game winners in the opener, and the result was a pitchers' duel, with all three runs scored on solo homers. Phillie John Denny gave up the first home run to Jim Dwyer in the first inning, but after that (with late-inning help from Al Holland) he blanked the Orioles, while Baltimore's Scott McGregor, after 5⅔ scoreless innings gave up home runs to Joe Morgan and (the game-loser two innings later) to Garry Maddox.

The Orioles swept the next four games. In Game Two, Mike Boddicker yielded just three singles (and no walks) to Phillie batters. Though one of the singles led to a run in the fourth inning, giving the Phillies a 1–0 lead, Oriole John Lowenstein tied the score with a home run in the fifth. Three more Oriole hits in the inning and a sacrifice fly made the score 3–1, and three two-out singles in the seventh inning brought in a fourth Baltimore run.

Philadelphia again scored first in Game Three, on leadoff home runs in the second and third innings by Gary Matthews and Joe Morgan. But the Orioles finally got to veteran starter Steve Carlton in the sixth for one run and drove him out after a second run scored an inning later. Carlton suffered the loss when the baserunner he left scored the tie-breaking run from second on an error by shortstop Ivan DeJesus.

The Phillies also lost Game Four by a single run. Baltimore scored first with two runs in the top of the fourth, but Philadelphia recovered with one run in the fourth and two an inning later. They would not lead again in the Series. Baltimore scored twice in the sixth to go ahead again, and once more in the seventh. The Phillies scored once more with two down in the last of the ninth to draw within one run of a tie, but Joe Morgan lined out to second to end the game.

Home runs by Rick Dempsey and Eddie Murray (who hit two) accounted for four of Baltimore's five runs in the final game—more than enough to support Scott McGregor's five-hit shutout pitching.

Baltimore Orioles (AL), 4; Philadelphia Phillies (NL), 1

BAL (A)

PLAYER/POS	AVG	G	AB	R	H	2B	3B	HR	RB	BB	SO	SB
Benny Ayala, ph	1.000	1	1	1	1	0	0	0	1	0	0	0
Mike Boddicker, p	.000	1	3	0	0	0	0	0	1	0	1	0
Al Bumbry, of	.091	4	11	0	1	1	0	0	1	0	1	0
Todd Cruz, 3b	.125	5	16	1	2	0	0	0	0	1	3	0
Rich Dauer, 2b	.211	5	19	2	4	1	0	0	3	0	3	0
Storm Davis, p	.000	1	2	0	0	0	0	0	0	0	2	0
Rick Dempsey, c	.385	5	13	3	5	4	0	1	2	2	2	0
Jim Dwyer, of	.375	2	8	3	3	1	0	1	1	0	0	0
Mike Flanagan, p	.000	1	1	0	0	0	0	0	0	0	1	0
Dan Ford, of-4	.167	5	12	1	2	0	0	1	1	1	5	0
Tito Landrum, of	.000	3	0	0	0	0	0	0	0	0	0	1
John Lowenstein, of	.385	4	13	2	5	1	0	1	1	0	3	0
Tippy Martinez, p	.000	3	0	0	0	0	0	0	0	0	0	0
Scott McGregor, p	.000	2	5	0	0	0	0	0	0	0	0	0
Eddie Murray, 1b	.250	5	20	2	5	0	0	2	3	1	4	0
Joe Nolan, c	.000	2	2	0	0	0	0	0	0	1	0	0
Jim Palmer, p	.000	1	0	0	0	0	0	0	0	0	0	0
Cal Ripken, ss	.167	5	18	2	3	0	0	0	1	3	4	0
Gary Roenicke, of-2	.000	3	7	0	0	0	0	0	0	0	0	0
Len Sakata, 2b	.000	1	1	0	0	0	0	0	0	0	0	0
John Shelby, of	.444	5	9	1	4	0	0	0	1	0	4	0
Ken Singleton, ph	.000	2	1	0	0	0	0	0	0	1	1	0
Sammy Stewart, p	.000	3	2	0	0	0	0	0	0	0	0	0
TOTAL	.213		164	18	35	8	0	6	17	10	37	1

PITCHER	W	L	ERA	G	GS	CG	SV	SHO	IP	H	ER	BB	SO
Mike Boddicker	1	0	0.00	1	1	1	0	0	9.0	3	0	0	6
Storm Davis	1	0	5.40	1	1	0	0	0	5.0	6	3	1	3
Mike Flanagan	0	0	4.50	1	1	0	0	0	4.0	6	2	1	1
Tippy Martinez	0	0	0.00	3	0	0	2	0	3.0	3	1	0	0
Scott McGregor	1	1	1.06	2	2	1	0	1	17.0	9	2	2	12
Jim Palmer	1	0	0.00	1	0	0	0	0	2.0	2	0	1	1
Sammy Stewart	0	0	0.00	3	0	0	0	0	5.0	2	0	2	6
TOTAL	4	1	1.60	12	5	2	2	1	45.0	31	8	7	29

PHI (N)

PLAYER/POS	AVG	G	AB	R	H	2B	3B	HR	RB	BB	SO	SB
Larry Andersen, p	.000	2	0	0	0	0	0	0	0	0	0	0
Marty Bystrom, p	.000	1	0	0	0	0	0	0	0	0	1	0
Steve Carlton, p	.000	1	3	0	0	0	0	0	0	0	1	0
Ivan DeJesus, ss	.125	5	16	0	2	0	0	0	0	1	2	0
John Denny, p	.200	2	5	1	1	0	0	0	1	0	1	0
Bob Dernier, pr	.000	1	0	1	0	0	0	0	0	0	0	0
Bo Diaz, c	.333	5	15	1	5	1	0	0	0	1	2	0
Greg Gross, of	.000	2	6	0	0	0	0	0	0	0	0	0
Von Hayes, of-1	.000	4	3	0	0	0	0	0	0	1	0	0
Willie Hernandez, p	.000	3	0	0	0	0	0	0	0	0	0	0
Al Holland, p	.000	2	0	0	0	0	0	0	0	0	0	0
Charles Hudson, p	.000	2	2	0	0	0	0	0	0	0	1	0
Joe Lefebvre, of-2	.200	3	5	0	1	1	0	0	2	0	1	0
Sixto Lezcano, of-3	.125	4	8	0	1	0	0	0	0	0	2	0
Garry Maddox, of-3	.250	4	12	1	3	1	0	1	1	0	2	0
Gary Matthews, of	.250	5	16	1	4	0	0	1	1	2	2	0
Joe Morgan, 2b	.263	5	19	3	5	0	1	2	2	2	3	1
Tony Perez, 1b-2	.200	4	10	0	2	0	0	0	0	0	2	0
Ron Reed, p	.000	3	0	0	0	0	0	0	0	0	0	0
Pete Rose, 1b-3,of-1	.313	5	16	1	5	1	0	0	1	1	3	0
Juan Samuel, ph	.000	3	1	0	0	0	0	0	0	0	0	0
Mike Schmidt, 3b	.050	5	20	0	1	0	0	0	0	0	6	0
Ossie Virgil, c-1	.500	3	2	0	1	0	0	0	1	0	1	0
TOTAL	.195		159	9	31	4	1	4	9	7	29	1

PITCHER	W	L	ERA	G	GS	CG	SV	SHO	IP	H	ER	BB	SO
Larry Andersen	0	0	2.25	2	0	0	0	0	4.0	4	1	0	1
Marty Bystrom	0	0	0.00	1	0	0	0	0	1.0	0	0	0	1
Steve Carlton	0	1	2.70	1	1	0	0	0	6.2	5	2	3	7
John Denny	1	1	3.46	2	2	0	0	0	13.0	12	5	3	9
Willie Hernandez	0	0	0.00	3	0	0	0	0	4.0	0	0	1	4
Al Holland	0	0	0.00	2	0	0	1	0	3.2	1	0	0	5
Charles Hudson	0	2	8.64	2	2	0	0	0	8.1	9	8	1	6
Ron Reed	0	0	2.70	3	0	0	0	0	3.1	4	1	2	4
TOTAL	1	4	3.48	16	5	0	1	0	44.0	35	17	10	37

GAME 1 AT BAL OCT 11

PHI	000 001 010	2 5 0
BAL	100 000 000	1 5 1

Pitchers: DENNY, Holland (8) vs McGREGOR, Stewart (9), T.Martinez (9)
Home Runs: Morgan-PHI, Maddox-PHI, Dwyer-BAL
Attendance: 52,204

GAME 2 AT BAL OCT 12

PHI	000 100 000	1 3 0
BAL	000 030 10X	4 9 1

Pitchers: HUDSON, Hernandez (5), Andersen (6), Reed (8) vs BODDICKER
Home Runs: Lowenstein-BAL
Attendance: 52,132

GAME 3 AT PHI OCT 14

BAL	000 001 200	3 6 1
PHI	011 000 000	2 8 2

Pitchers: Flanagan, PALMER (5), Stewart (7), T.Martinez (9) vs CARLTON, Holland (7)
Home Runs: Matthews-PHI, Morgan-PHI, Ford-BAL
Attendance: 65,792

GAME 4 AT PHI OCT 15

BAL	000 202 100	5 10 1
PHI	000 120 001	4 10 0

Pitchers: DAVIS, Stewart (6), T.Martinez (8) vs DENNY, Hernandez (6), Reed (6), Andersen (8)
Attendance: 66,947

GAME 5 AT PHI OCT 16

BAL	011 210 000	5 5 0
PHI	000 000 000	0 5 1

Pitchers: McGREGOR vs HUDSON, Bystrom (5), Hernandez (6), Reed (9)
Home Runs: Murray-BAL (2), Dempsey-BAL
Attendance: 67,064

After two games in Chicago, the Cubs appeared headed for their first pennant in thirty-nine years. Rick Sutcliffe and Warren Brusstar shut out the Padres 13–0 in an opener enlivened by five Cub home runs. In a quieter second game, the Cubs built a 4–1 lead over the first four innings and held on for the win.

When the series moved to San Diego, though, the Padres came to life. In the fifth and sixth innings of Game Three, they obliterated a 1–0 Cub lead with seven runs, as Ed Whitson and Goose Gossage held the Cubs scoreless after the second inning for what turned into an easy Padres win.

Game Four was not so easy. San Diego scored first in the third inning, lost their lead in the fourth, tied in the fifth, went ahead in the seventh, and fell back into a 5–5 tie in the eighth. But in the bottom of the ninth, Padre Steve Garvey's two-run homer sent the series into a fifth game.

Leon Durham put the Cubs ahead with a two-run homer in the first inning of the finale, and Jody Davis added to the lead with a solo shot in the second. Rick Sutcliffe, meanwhile, was setting down Padres as he added five shutout innings to his seven from Game One. But he gave up two runs in the sixth, and after first baseman Durham saw a grounder go through his legs to let in the tying run in the seventh, the Cubs watched the pennant slip away as Tony Gwynn's double and Garvey's single drove in the game's three final runs.

San Diego Padres (West), 3; Chicago Cubs (East), 2

SD (W)

PLAYER/POS	AVG	G	AB	R	H	2B	3B	HR	RB	BB	SO	SB
Kurt Bevacqua, ph	.000	2	2	0	0	0	0	0	0	0	0	0
Greg Booker, p	.000	1	0	0	0	0	0	0	0	0	0	0
Bobby Brown, of	.000	3	4	1	0	0	0	0	0	1	2	1
Dave Dravecky, p	.000	3	0	0	0	0	0	0	0	0	0	0
Tim Flannery, ph	.500	3	2	2	1	0	0	0	0	0	0	0
Steve Garvey, 1b	.400	5	20	1	8	1	0	1	7	1	2	0
Rich Gossage, p	.000	3	0	0	0	0	0	0	0	0	0	0
Tony Gwynn, of	.368	5	19	6	7	3	0	0	3	1	2	0
Greg Harris, p	.000	1	0	0	0	0	0	0	0	0	0	0
Andy Hawkins, p	.000	3	0	0	0	0	0	0	0	0	0	0
Terry Kennedy, c	.222	5	18	2	4	0	0	0	1	1	3	0
Craig Lefferts, p	.000	3	0	0	0	0	0	0	0	0	0	0
Tim Lollar, p	.000	1	0	0	0	0	0	0	0	0	1	0
Carmelo Martinez, of	.176	5	17	1	3	0	0	0	0	2	4	0
Kevin McReynolds, of	.300	4	10	2	3	0	0	1	4	3	1	0
Graig Nettles, 3b	.143	4	14	1	2	0	0	0	2	1	1	0
Mario Ramirez, ph	.000	2	2	0	0	0	0	0	0	0	0	0
Luis Salazar, of-2,3b-1	.200	3	5	0	1	0	1	0	0	0	1	0
Eric Show, p	.000	2	1	0	0	0	0	0	0	0	1	0
Champ Summers, ph	.000	2	2	0	0	0	0	0	0	0	1	0
Garry Templeton, ss	.333	5	15	2	5	1	0	0	2	2	0	1
Mark Thurmond, p	1.000	1	1	0	1	0	0	0	0	0	0	0
Ed Whitson, p	.000	3	3	0	0	0	0	0	0	0	1	0
Alan Wiggins, 2b	.316	5	19	4	6	0	0	0	1	2	2	0
TOTAL	.265		155	22	41	5	1	2	20	14	22	2

PITCHER	W	L	ERA	G	GS	CG	SV	SHO	IP	H	ER	BB	SO
Greg Booker	0	0	0.00	1	0	0	0	0	2.0	2	0	1	2
Dave Dravecky	0	0	0.00	3	0	0	0	0	6.0	2	0	0	5
Rich Gossage	0	0	4.50	3	0	0	1	0	4.0	5	2	1	5
Greg Harris	0	0	31.50	1	0	0	0	0	2.0	9	7	3	2
Andy Hawkins	0	0	0.00	3	0	0	0	0	3.2	0	0	2	1
Craig Lefferts	2	0	0.00	3	0	0	0	0	4.0	1	0	1	1
Tim Lollar	0	0	6.23	1	1	0	0	0	4.1	3	3	4	3
Eric Show	0	1	13.50	2	2	0	0	0	5.1	8	8	4	2
Mark Thurmond	0	1	9.82	1	1	0	0	0	3.2	7	4	2	1
Ed Whitson	1	0	1.13	1	1	0	0	0	8.0	5	1	2	6
TOTAL	3	2	5.23	19	5	0	1	0	43.0	42	25	20	28

CHI (E)

PLAYER/POS	AVG	G	AB	R	H	2B	3B	HR	RB	BB	SO	SB
Thad Bosley, ph	.000	2	2	0	0	0	0	0	0	0	2	0
Larry Bowa, ss	.200	5	15	1	3	1	0	0	1	1	0	0
Warren Brusstar, p	.000	3	1	0	0	0	0	0	0	0	0	0
Ron Cey, 3b	.158	5	19	3	3	1	0	1	3	3	3	0
Henry Cotto, of	1.000	3	1	1	1	0	0	0	0	0	0	0
Jody Davis, c	.389	5	18	3	7	2	0	2	6	0	3	0
Bob Dernier, of	.235	5	17	5	4	2	0	1	1	5	4	2
Leon Durham, 1b	.150	5	20	2	3	0	0	2	4	1	4	0
Dennis Eckersley, p	.000	1	2	0	0	0	0	0	0	0	1	0
George Frazier, p	.000	1	0	0	0	0	0	0	0	0	0	0
Richie Hebner, ph	.000	2	1	0	0	0	0	0	0	0	0	0
Steve Lake, c	1.000	1	1	0	1	1	0	0	0	0	0	0
Davey Lopes, of-1	.000	2	1	0	0	0	0	0	0	0	0	0
Gary Matthews, of	.200	5	15	4	3	0	0	2	5	6	4	1
Keith Moreland, of	.333	5	18	3	6	2	0	0	2	1	1	0
Ryne Sandberg, 2b	.368	5	19	3	7	2	0	0	2	3	2	3
Scott Sanderson, p	.000	1	2	0	0	0	0	0	0	0	1	0
Lee Smith, p	.000	2	0	0	0	0	0	0	0	0	0	0
Tim Stoddard, p	.000	2	0	0	0	0	0	0	0	0	0	0
Rick Sutcliffe, p	.500	2	6	1	3	0	0	1	1	0	2	0
Steve Trout, p	.500	2	2	0	1	0	0	0	0	0	0	0
Tom Veryzer, ss-2,3b-1	.000	3	1	0	0	0	0	0	0	0	0	0
Gary Woods, of	.000	1	1	0	0	0	0	0	0	0	1	0
TOTAL	.259		162	26	42	11	0	9	25	20	28	6

PITCHER	W	L	ERA	G	GS	CG	SV	SHO	IP	H	ER	BB	SO
Warren Brusstar	0	0	0.00	3	0	0	0	0	4.1	6	0	0	1
Dennis Eckersley	0	1	8.44	1	1	0	0	0	5.1	9	5	0	0
George Frazier	0	0	10.80	1	0	0	0	0	1.2	2	2	0	1
Scott Sanderson	0	0	5.79	1	1	0	0	0	4.2	6	3	1	2
Lee Smith	0	1	9.00	2	0	0	1	0	2.0	3	2	0	3
Tim Stoddard	0	0	4.50	2	0	0	0	0	2.0	1	1	2	2
Rick Sutcliffe	1	1	3.38	2	2	0	0	0	13.1	9	5	8	10
Steve Trout	1	0	2.00	2	1	0	0	0	9.0	5	2	3	3
TOTAL	2	3	4.25	14	5	0	1	0	42.1	41	20	14	22

GAME 1 AT CHI OCT 2

```
SD    000 000 000   0  6  1
CHI   203 062 00X  13 16  0
```
Pitchers: SHOW, Harris (5), Booker (7) vs SUTCLIFFE, Brusstar (8)
Home Runs: Dernier-CHI, Matthews-CHI (2), Sutcliffe-CHI, Cey-CHI
Attendance: 36,282

GAME 2 AT CHI OCT 3

```
SD    000 101 000   2  5  0
CHI   102 100 00X   4  8  1
```
Pitchers: THURMOND, Hawkins (4), Dravecky (6), Lefferts (8) vs TROUT, Smith (9)
Attendance: 36,282

GAME 3 AT SD OCT 4

```
CHI   010 000 000   1  5  0
SD    000 034 00X   7 11  0
```
Pitchers: ECKERSLEY, Frazier (6), Stoddard (8) vs WHITSON, Gossage (9)
Home Runs: McReynolds-SD
Attendance: 58,346

GAME 4 AT SD OCT 6

```
CHI   000 300 020   5  8  1
SD    002 010 202   7 11  0
```
Pitchers: Sanderson, Brusstar (5), Stoddard (7), SMITH (8) vs Lollar, Hawkins (5), Dravecky (6), Gossage (8), LEFFERTS (9)
Home Runs: Davis-CHI, Durham-CHI, Garvey-SD
Attendance: 58,354

GAME 5 AT SD OCT 7

```
CHI   210 000 000   3  5  1
SD    000 002 40X   6  8  0
```
Pitchers: SUTCLIFFE, Trout (7), Brusstar (8) vs Show, Hawkins (2), Dravecky (4), LEFFERTS (6), Gossage (8)
Home Runs: Durham-CHI, Davis-CHI
Attendance: 58,359

The heavily favored Tigers swept the series, but not without difficulty, despite a fourteen-hit, three-homer, 8–1 romp in the opener.

Games Two and Three were much tighter. In the second game, after Detroit had built a 3–0 lead over the first three innings, Royal rookie starter Bret Saberhagen settled down and blanked the Tigers for the next five innings as K.C. inched its way to a tie with runs in the fourth, seventh, and eighth. Through the ninth and tenth innings, Tiger reliever Aurelio Lopez and Royal Dan Quisenberry dueled scorelessly, but in the top of the eleventh Johnny Grubb doubled home two Tiger runs. Lopez struggled but held the Royals scoreless in the last of the eleventh for the win.

In Game Three, the Royals' Charlie Leibrandt and Tigers' Milt Wilcox hurled matching three-hitters. But the Tigers secured the game—and the pennant—when Chet Lemon scored on a broken double play in the second inning for the game's only run.

Detroit Tigers (East), 3;
Kansas City Royals (West), 0

DET (E)

PLAYER/POS	AVG	G	AB	R	H	2B	3B	HR	RB	BB	SO	SB
Doug Baker, ss	.000	1	0	0	0	0	0	0	0	0	0	0
Dave Bergman, 1b-1	1.000	2	1	1	1	0	0	0	0	0	0	1
Tom Brookens, 2b-1,3b-1	.000	2	2	0	0	0	0	0	0	0	1	0
Marty Castillo, 3b	.250	3	8	0	2	0	0	0	2	0	3	1
Darrell Evans, 1b-3,b-1	.300	3	10	1	3	1	0	0	1	1	0	1
Barbaro Garbey, dh-2	.333	3	9	1	3	0	0	0	0	0	1	0
Kirk Gibson, of	.417	3	12	2	5	1	0	1	2	2	1	1
Johnny Grubb, dh	.250	1	4	0	1	1	0	0	2	0	0	0
Willie Hernandez, p	.000	3	0	0	0	0	0	0	0	0	0	0
Larry Herndon, of	.200	2	5	1	1	0	0	1	1	1	2	0
Ruppert Jones, of	.000	2	5	1	0	0	0	0	0	1	1	0
Rusty Kuntz, of	.000	1	1	0	0	0	0	0	0	0	0	0
Chet Lemon, of	.000	3	13	1	0	0	0	0	0	0	1	0
Aurelio Lopez, p	.000	1	0	0	0	0	0	0	0	0	0	0
Jack Morris, p	.000	1	0	0	0	0	0	0	0	0	0	0
Lance Parrish, c	.250	3	12	1	3	0	0	1	3	0	3	0
Dan Petry, p	.000	1	0	0	0	0	0	0	0	0	0	0
Alan Trammell, ss	.364	3	11	2	4	0	1	1	3	3	1	0
Lou Whitaker, 2b	.143	3	14	3	2	0	0	0	0	0	3	0
Milt Wilcox, p	.000	1	0	0	0	0	0	0	0	0	0	0
TOTAL	.234		107	14	25	4	1	4	14	8	17	4

PITCHER	W	L	ERA	G	GS	CG	SV	SHO	IP	H	ER	BB	SO
Willie Hernandez	0	0	2.25	3	0	0	1	0	4.0	3	1	1	3
Aurelio Lopez	1	0	0.00	1	0	0	0	0	3.0	4	0	1	2
Jack Morris	1	0	1.29	1	1	0	0	0	7.0	5	1	1	4
Dan Petry	0	0	2.57	1	1	0	0	0	7.0	4	2	1	4
Milt Wilcox	1	0	0.00	1	1	0	0	0	8.0	2	0	2	8
TOTAL	3	0	1.24	7	3	0	1	0	29.0	18	4	6	21

KC (W)

PLAYER/POS	AVG	G	AB	R	H	2B	3B	HR	RB	BB	SO	SB
Steve Balboni, 1b	.091	3	11	0	1	0	0	0	0	1	4	0
Buddy Biancalana, ss	.000	2	1	0	0	0	0	0	0	0	1	0
Bud Black, p	.000	1	0	0	0	0	0	0	0	0	0	0
George Brett, 3b	.231	3	13	0	3	0	0	0	0	0	2	0
Onix Concepcion, ss	.000	3	7	0	0	0	0	0	0	0	0	0
Mark Huismann, p	.000	1	0	0	0	0	0	0	0	0	0	0
Dane Iorg, ph	.500	2	2	0	1	0	0	0	1	0	0	0
Lynn Jones, of-2	.200	3	5	1	1	0	0	0	0	0	0	0
Mike Jones, p	.000	1	0	0	0	0	0	0	0	0	0	0
Charlie Leibrandt, p	.000	1	0	0	0	0	0	0	0	0	0	0
Hal McRae, ph	1.000	2	2	0	2	1	0	0	1	0	0	0
Darryl Motley, of	.167	3	12	0	2	0	0	0	1	1	3	0
Jorge Orta, dh	.100	3	10	1	1	0	1	0	1	0	2	0
Greg Pryor, 3b	.000	1	0	0	0	0	0	0	0	0	0	0
Dan Quisenberry, p	.000	2	0	0	0	0	0	0	0	0	0	0
Bret Saberhagen, p	.000	1	0	0	0	0	0	0	0	0	0	0
Pat Sheridan, of	.000	3	6	1	0	0	0	0	0	3	3	0
Don Slaught, c	.364	3	11	0	4	0	0	0	0	0	0	0
U. L. Washington, ph	.000	2	1	0	0	0	0	0	0	0	1	0
John Wathan, dh	.000	1	1	0	0	0	0	0	0	0	0	0
Frank White, 2b	.091	3	11	1	1	0	0	0	0	0	3	0
Willie Wilson, of	.154	3	13	0	2	0	0	0	0	0	1	2	0
TOTAL	.170		106	4	18	1	1	0	4	6	21	0

PITCHER	W	L	ERA	G	GS	CG	SV	SHO	IP	H	ER	BB	SO
Bud Black	0	1	7.20	1	1	0	0	0	5.0	7	4	1	3
Mark Huismann	0	0	6.75	1	0	0	0	0	2.2	6	2	1	2
Mike Jones	0	0	6.75	1	0	0	0	0	1.1	1	1	0	0
Charlie Leibrandt	0	1	1.13	1	1	1	0	0	8.0	3	1	4	6
Dan Quisenberry	0	1	3.00	2	0	0	0	0	3.0	2	1	1	1
Bret Saberhagen	0	0	2.25	1	1	0	0	0	8.0	6	2	1	5
TOTAL	0	3	3.54	6	3	1	0	0	28.0	25	11	8	17

Few objective observers expected the Padres (playing in their first World Series) to best the mighty Tigers—and they didn't. Detroit's first two batters in Game One hit safely to produce the Series' first scoring before an out had been recorded. San Diego countered with three two-out hits in their half of the first to go ahead 2–1. But Detroit starter Jack Morris settled down to shut out the Padres over the final eight innings, and his Tigers scored the tying and winning runs in the fifth on Larry Herndon's two-run homer. The Tigers scored again in Game Two before the first out was recorded and drove out Padre starter Ed Whitson with three first-inning runs on five singles. But this time Detroit was shut out (by relievers Andy Hawkins and Craig Lefferts) over the final eight, while San Diego scored single runs in the first and fourth and the winning runs in the fifth on a three-run homer by the normally light-hitting Kurt Bevacqua.

The Tigers won Game Three on walks—a Series-record eleven—as the Series moved to Detroit. After scoring their first two runs in the second on a single and Marty Castillo's home run, they continued on to put across two more in the inning on a pair of hits alternated with three walks (the last with the bases full). Three more walks an inning later, followed by a hit batsman, gave Detroit its final run in what became a 5–2 win.

Alan Trammell's two-run homer in the first inning of Game Four put the Tigers ahead to stay. Tiger pitcher Jack Morris gave up a solo home run to Terry Kennedy in the second, but Trammell swatted a second two-run shot an inning later for a 4–1 lead. Morris let a second Padre runner score on a wild pitch in the ninth, but then retired Kennedy for the third out and his second Series win. Kirk Gibson's two home runs framed Tiger scoring in the final game. His two-run shot in the first inning opened the game's scoring. San Diego tied it up with runs in the third and fourth, but Detroit took a 5–3 lead with runs in the fifth and seventh (the latter on Lance Parrish's homer). The unlikely Kurt Bevacqua brought the Padres within a run of tying the game with his second Series homer in the eighth (doubling his regular-season total), but Gibson ended the scoring—and Padre hopes—with a three-run blast half an inning later.

Detroit Tigers (AL), 4;
San Diego Padres (NL), 1

DET (A)

PLAYER/POS	AVG	G	AB	R	H	2B	3B	HR	RB	BB	SO	SB
Doug Bair, p	.000	1	0	0	0	0	0	0	0	0	0	0
Dave Bergman, 1b	.000	5	5	0	0	0	0	0	0	0	1	0
Tom Brookens, 3b	.000	3	3	0	0	0	0	0	0	0	1	0
Marty Castillo, 3b	.333	3	9	2	3	0	0	1	2	2	1	0
Darrell Evans, 1b-4,3b-2	.067	5	15	1	1	0	0	0	1	4	4	0
Barbaro Garbey, dh-3	.000	4	12	0	0	0	0	0	0	0	2	0
Kirk Gibson, of	.333	5	18	4	6	0	0	2	7	4	4	3
Johnny Grubb, dh-2	.333	4	3	0	1	0	0	0	0	0	0	0
Willie Hernandez, p	.000	3	0	0	0	0	0	0	0	0	0	0
Larry Herndon, of	.333	5	15	1	5	0	0	1	3	3	2	0
Howard Johnson, ph	.000	1	1	0	0	0	0	0	0	0	0	0
Ruppert Jones, of	.000	2	3	0	0	0	0	0	0	0	1	0
Rusty Kuntz, ph	.000	2	1	0	0	0	0	0	0	1	1	0
Chet Lemon, of	.294	5	17	1	5	0	0	0	1	2	2	2
Aurelio Lopez, p	.000	2	0	0	0	0	0	0	0	0	0	0
Jack Morris, p	.000	2	0	0	0	0	0	0	0	0	0	0
Lance Parrish, c	.278	5	18	3	5	1	0	1	2	3	2	1
Dan Petry, p	.000	2	0	0	0	0	0	0	0	0	0	0
Bill Scherrer, p	.000	3	0	0	0	0	0	0	0	0	0	0
Alan Trammell, ss	.450	5	20	5	9	1	0	2	6	2	2	1
Lou Whitaker, 2b	.278	5	18	6	5	2	0	0	4	4	4	0
Milt Wilcox, p	.000	1	0	0	0	0	0	0	0	0	0	0
TOTAL	.253		158	23	40	4	0	7	23	24	27	7

PITCHER	W	L	ERA	G	GS	CG	SV	SHO	IP	H	ER	BB	SO
Doug Bair	0	0	0.00	1	0	0	0	0	0.2	0	0	0	1
Willie Hernandez	0	0	1.69	3	0	0	2	0	5.1	4	1	0	0
Aurelio Lopez	1	0	0.00	2	0	0	0	0	3.0	1	0	1	4
Jack Morris	2	0	2.00	2	2	2	0	0	18.0	13	4	3	13
Dan Petry	0	1	9.00	2	2	0	0	0	8.0	14	8	5	4
Bill Scherrer	0	0	3.00	3	0	0	0	0	3.0	5	1	0	0
Milt Wilcox	1	0	1.50	1	1	0	0	0	6.0	7	1	2	4
TOTAL	4	1	3.07	14	5	2	2	0	44.0	44	15	11	26

SD (N)

PLAYER/POS	AVG	G	AB	R	H	2B	3B	HR	RB	BB	SO	SB
Kurt Bevacqua, dh	.412	5	17	4	7	2	0	2	4	1	2	0
Bruce Bochy, ph	1.000	1	1	0	1	0	0	0	0	0	0	0
Greg Booker, p	.000	1	0	0	0	0	0	0	0	0	0	0
Bobby Brown, of	.067	5	15	1	1	0	0	0	2	0	4	0
Dave Dravecky, p	.000	2	0	0	0	0	0	0	0	0	0	0
Tim Flannery, 2b	1.000	1	1	0	1	0	0	0	0	0	0	0
Steve Garvey, 1b	.200	5	20	2	4	2	0	0	2	0	2	0
Rich Gossage, p	.000	2	0	0	0	0	0	0	0	0	0	0
Tony Gwynn, of	.263	5	19	1	5	0	0	0	0	3	2	1
Greg Harris, p	.000	1	0	0	0	0	0	0	0	0	0	0
Andy Hawkins, p	.000	3	0	0	0	0	0	0	0	0	0	0
Terry Kennedy, c	.211	5	19	2	4	1	0	1	3	1	1	0
Craig Lefferts, p	.000	3	0	0	0	0	0	0	0	0	0	0
Tim Lollar, p	.000	1	0	0	0	0	0	0	0	0	0	0
Carmelo Martinez, of	.176	5	17	0	3	0	0	0	0	1	9	0
Graig Nettles, 3b	.250	5	12	2	3	0	0	0	2	5	0	0
Ron Roenicke, of-1	.000	2	0	0	0	0	0	0	0	0	0	0
Luis Salazar, of-2,3b-1	.333	4	3	0	1	0	0	0	0	0	0	0
Eric Show, p	.000	1	0	0	0	0	0	0	0	0	0	0
Champ Summers, ph	.000	1	1	0	0	0	0	0	0	0	1	0
Garry Templeton, ss	.316	5	19	1	6	1	0	0	0	0	3	0
Mark Thurmond, p	.000	2	0	0	0	0	0	0	0	0	0	0
Ed Whitson, p	.000	1	0	0	0	0	0	0	0	0	0	0
Alan Wiggins, 2b	.364	5	22	2	8	1	0	0	1	0	2	1
TOTAL	.265		166	15	44	7	0	3	14	11	26	2

PITCHER	W	L	ERA	G	GS	CG	SV	SHO	IP	H	ER	BB	SO
Greg Booker	0	0	9.00	1	0	0	0	0	1.0	0	1	4	0
Dave Dravecky	0	0	0.00	2	0	0	0	0	4.2	3	0	1	5
Rich Gossage	0	0	13.50	2	0	0	0	0	2.2	3	4	1	2
Greg Harris	0	0	0.00	1	0	0	0	0	5.1	3	0	3	5
Andy Hawkins	1	1	0.75	3	0	0	0	0	12.0	4	1	6	4
Craig Lefferts	0	0	0.00	3	0	0	0	1	6.0	2	0	1	7
Tim Lollar	0	1	21.60	1	1	0	0	0	1.2	4	4	4	0
Eric Show	0	1	10.13	1	1	0	0	0	2.2	4	3	1	2
Mark Thurmond	0	1	10.13	2	2	0	0	0	5.1	12	6	3	2
Ed Whitson	0	0	40.50	1	1	0	0	0	0.2	5	3	0	0
TOTAL	1	4	4.71	17	5	0	1	0	42.0	40	22	24	27

GAME 1 AT SD OCT 9

DET	100 020 000	3 8 0
SD	200 000 000	2 8 1

Pitchers: MORRIS vs THURMOND, Hawkins (6), Dravecky (8)
Home Runs: Herndon-DET
Attendance: 57,908

GAME 2 AT SD OCT 10

DET	300 000 000	3 7 3
SD	100 130 00X	5 11 4

Pitchers: PETRY, Lopez (5), Scherrer (6), Bair (7), Hernandez (8) vs Whitson, HAWKINS (1), Lefferts (7)
Home Runs: Bevacqua-SD
Attendance: 57,911

GAME 3 AT DET OCT 12

SD	001 000 100	2 5 0
DET	041 000 00X	5 7 0

Pitchers: LOLLAR, Booker (2), Harris (3) vs WILCOX, Scherrer (7), Hernandez (7)
Home Runs: Castillo-DET
Attendance: 51,970

GAME 4 AT DET OCT 13

SD	010 000 001	2 10 2
DET	202 000 00X	4 7 0

Pitchers: SHOW, Dravecky (3), Lefferts (7), Gossage (8) vs MORRIS
Home Runs: Trammell-DET (2), Kennedy-SD
Attendance: 52,130

GAME 5 AT DET OCT 14

SD	001 200 010	4 10 1
DET	300 010 13X	8 11 1

Pitchers: Thurmond, HAWKINS (1), Lefferts (5), Gossage (7) vs Petry, Scherrer (4), LOPEZ (5), Hernandez (8)
Home Runs: Gibson-DET (2), Parrish-DET, Bevacqua-SD
Attendance: 51,901

The Dodgers' league-leading pitchers held St. Louis to three runs over the first two games, even though the Cardinals recorded eight hits per game. But the Cards' league-leading hitters put their blows to better advantage in the next four games of the expanded LCS, scoring twenty-six times for four wins and the pennant.

Fernando Valenzuela captured Game One for the Dodgers, thanks in part to some ragged fielding by the usually sharp Cardinal infield. And as Orel Hershiser was holding St. Louis to two runs in Game Two, an errant Cardinal pickoff throw and heavy Dodger hitting gave him an increasingly comfortable lead.

When the series shifted to St. Louis for Game Three, the Cardinals revived, scoring twice in each of the first two innings for a quick lead, which they held for their first win. In Game Four they unloaded for nine runs in the second inning, and in Game Five—with the game and series tied in the bottom of the ninth—Ozzie Smith hit his first lefthanded home run ever to give St. Louis the series lead.

Back in Los Angeles, the Dodgers scored first in Game Six, and held a 4–1 lead after six innings. But three Cardinals scored on four hits in the seventh, and though Dodger Mike Marshall's eighth-inning home run restored the lead to Los Angeles, Cardinal Jack Clark settled things with a three-run homer in the ninth.

St. Louis Cardinals (East), 4; Los Angeles Dodgers (West), 2

STL (E)

PLAYER/POS	AVG	G	AB	R	H	2B	3B	HR	RB	BB	SO	SB
Joaquin Andujar, p	.250	2	4	1	1	1	0	0	0	0	1	0
Steve Braun, ph	.000	2	2	0	0	0	0	0	0	0	0	0
Bill Campbell, p	.000	3	0	0	0	0	0	0	0	0	0	0
Cesar Cedeno, of-4	.167	5	12	2	2	1	0	0	0	0	2	3	0
Jack Clark, 1b	.381	6	21	4	8	0	0	1	4	5	5	0
Vince Coleman, of	.286	3	14	2	4	0	0	0	0	1	0	2	1
Danny Cox, p	.000	1	2	0	0	0	0	0	0	1	1	0
Ken Dayley, p	.500	5	2	0	1	0	0	0	0	0	0	0
Bob Forsch, p	.000	1	0	0	0	0	0	0	0	0	0	0
Brian Harper, ph	.000	1	1	0	0	0	0	0	0	0	0	0
Tommy Herr, 2b	.333	6	21	2	7	4	0	1	6	5	2	1
Rick Horton, p	.000	3	0	0	0	0	0	0	0	0	0	0
Mike Jorgensen, ph	.000	2	2	0	0	0	0	0	0	0	1	0
Jeff Lahti, p	.000	2	0	0	0	0	0	0	0	0	0	0
Tito Landrum, of-4	.429	5	14	2	6	0	0	0	4	1	1	1
Willie McGee, of	.269	6	26	6	7	1	0	0	3	3	6	2
Tom Nieto, c	.000	3	3	1	0	0	0	0	0	1	2	0
Terry Pendleton, 3b	.208	6	24	2	5	1	0	0	4	1	3	0
Darrell Porter, c	.267	5	15	1	4	1	0	0	0	5	4	0
Ozzie Smith, ss	.435	6	23	4	10	1	1	1	3	3	1	1
John Tudor, p	.000	2	4	1	0	0	0	0	0	0	1	0
Andy Van Slyke, of	.091	5	11	1	1	0	0	0	1	2	1	0
Todd Worrell, p	.000	4	0	0	0	0	0	0	0	0	0	0
TOTAL	.279		201	29	56	10	1	3	26	30	34	6

PITCHER	W	L	ERA	G	GS	CG	SV	SHO	IP	H	ER	BB	SO
Joaquin Andujar	0	1	6.97	2	2	0	0	0	10.1	14	8	4	9
Bill Campbell	0	0	0.00	3	0	0	0	0	2.1	3	0	0	2
Danny Cox	1	0	3.00	1	1	0	0	0	6.0	4	2	5	4
Ken Dayley	0	0	0.00	5	0	0	2	0	6.0	2	0	1	3
Bob Forsch	0	0	5.40	1	1	0	0	0	3.1	3	2	2	0
Rick Horton	0	0	9.00	3	0	0	0	0	3.0	4	3	2	1
Jeff Lahti	1	0	0.00	2	0	0	0	0	2.0	2	0	0	1
John Tudor	1	1	2.84	2	2	0	0	0	12.2	10	4	3	8
Todd Worrell	1	0	1.42	4	0	0	0	0	6.1	4	1	2	3
TOTAL	4	2	3.46	23	6	0	2	0	52.0	46	20	19	31

LA (W)

PLAYER/POS	AVG	G	AB	R	H	2B	3B	HR	RB	BB	SO	SB
Dave Anderson, ss-3,3b-1	.000	4	5	1	0	0	0	0	0	3	1	0
Bob Bailor, 3b	.000	2	1	0	0	0	0	0	0	0	0	0
Greg Brock, 1b-4	.083	5	12	2	1	0	0	1	2	2	2	0
Enos Cabell, 1b-3	.077	5	13	1	1	0	0	0	0	0	3	0
Bobby Castillo, p	.000	1	2	0	0	0	0	0	0	0	1	0
Carlos Diaz, p	.000	2	0	0	0	0	0	0	0	0	0	0
Mariano Duncan, ss	.222	5	18	2	4	2	1	0	1	1	3	1
Pedro Guerrero, of	.250	6	20	2	5	1	0	0	4	5	2	2
Orel Hershiser, p	.286	2	7	1	2	0	0	0	1	0	2	0
Rick Honeycutt, p	.000	2	0	0	0	0	0	0	0	0	0	0
Ken Howell, p	.000	1	0	0	0	0	0	0	0	0	0	0
Jay Johnstone, ph	.000	1	1	0	0	0	0	0	0	0	0	0
Ken Landreaux, of	.389	5	18	4	7	3	0	0	2	1	1	0
Bill Madlock, 3b	.333	6	24	5	8	1	0	3	7	0	2	1
Candy Maldonado, of-3	.143	4	7	0	1	0	0	0	1	0	3	0
Mike Marshall, of	.217	6	23	1	5	2	0	1	3	1	3	0
Len Matuszek, 1b-1,of-1	1.000	3	1	1	1	0	0	0	0	0	0	0
Tom Niedenfuer, p	.000	3	1	0	0	0	0	0	0	0	1	0
Jerry Reuss, p	.000	1	0	0	0	0	0	0	0	0	0	0
Steve Sax, 2b	.300	6	20	1	6	3	0	0	1	1	5	0
Mike Scioscia, c	.250	6	16	2	4	0	0	0	1	4	0	0
Fernando Valenzuela, p	.200	2	5	0	1	0	0	0	0	0	1	0
Bob Welch, p	.000	1	1	0	0	0	0	0	0	0	1	0
Terry Whitfield, ph	.000	1	0	0	0	0	0	0	0	0	0	0
Steve Yeager, c	.000	2	2	0	0	0	0	0	0	0	1	1	0
TOTAL	.234		197	23	46	12	1	5	23	19	31	4

PITCHER	W	L	ERA	G	GS	CG	SV	SHO	IP	H	ER	BB	SO
Bobby Castillo	0	0	3.38	1	0	0	0	0	5.1	4	2	2	4
Carlos Diaz	0	0	3.00	2	0	0	0	0	3.0	5	1	1	2
Orel Hershiser	1	0	3.52	2	2	1	0	0	15.1	17	6	6	5
Rick Honeycutt	0	0	13.50	2	0	0	0	0	1.1	4	2	2	1
Ken Howell	0	0	0.00	1	0	0	0	0	2.0	0	0	0	2
Tom Niedenfuer	0	2	6.35	3	0	0	1	0	5.2	5	4	2	5
Jerry Reuss	0	1	10.80	1	1	0	0	0	1.2	5	2	1	0
F. Valenzuela	1	0	1.88	2	2	0	0	0	14.1	11	3	10	13
Bob Welch	0	1	6.75	1	1	0	0	0	2.2	5	2	6	2
TOTAL	2	4	3.86	15	6	1	1	0	51.1	56	22	30	34

GAME 1 AT LA OCT 9

```
STL   000 000 100    1  8  1
LA    000 103 00X    4  8  0
```
Pitchers: TUDOR, Dayley (6), Campbell (7), Worrell (8) vs VALENZUELA, Niedenfuer (7)
Attendance: 55,270

GAME 2 AT LA OCT 10

```
STL   001 000 001    2  8  1
LA    003 212 00X    8 13  1
```
Pitchers: ANDUJAR, Horton (5), Campbell (6), Dayley (7), Lahti (8) vs HERSHISER
Home Runs: Brock-LA
Attendance: 55,222

GAME 3 AT STL OCT 12

```
LA    000 100 100    2  7  2
STL   220 000 00X    4  8  0
```
Pitchers: WELCH, Honeycutt (3), Diaz (5), Howell (7) vs COX, Horton (7), Worrell (7), Dayley (9)
Home Runs: Herr-STL
Attendance: 53,708

GAME 4 AT STL OCT 13

```
LA    000 000 110    2  5  2
STL   090 110 01X   12 15  0
```
Pitchers: REUSS, Honeycutt (2), Castillo (2), Diaz (8) vs TUDOR, Horton (8), Campbell (9)
Home Runs: Madlock-LA
Attendance: 53,708

GAME 5 AT STL OCT 14

```
LA    000 200 000    2  5  1
STL   200 000 001    3  5  1
```
Pitchers: Valenzuela, NIEDENFUER (9) vs Forsch, Dayley (4), Worrell (7), LAHTI (9)
Home Runs: Madlock-LA, Smith-STL
Attendance: 53,708

GAME 6 AT LA OCT 16

```
STL   001 000 303    7 12  1
LA    110 020 010    5  8  0
```
Pitchers: Andujar, WORRELL (7), Dayley (9) vs Hershiser, NIEDENFUER (7)
Home Runs: Madlock-LA, Marshall-LA, Clark-STL
Attendance: 55,208

Were it not for the expansion of the LCS to a best-of-seven series, the Blue Jays would have won the pennant. But after winning three of the first four games, the Jays lost their steam and K.C. swept to their second pennant.

The pitching of Toronto ace Dave Stieb proved a key to the club's fortunes. Three times he started for the Jays. In the opener he threw eight shutout innings as the Jays won easily. In Game Four he continued to dominate batters, though three walks in the sixth helped the Royals score a go-ahead run before Toronto pulled it out (for reliever Tom Henke) with a three-run ninth. Had the series ended there, Stieb would have been a hero. But it didn't, and he was called upon again for Game Seven—perhaps with inadequate rest. This time he faltered. After giving up single runs in the second and fourth innings, he loaded the bases in the sixth with two walks and a hit batsman. Jim Sundberg unloaded them with a wind-blown triple, later scoring himself, and the Royals were on the road to victory.

George Brett keyed Kansas City's triumph. His four hits in Game Three (including two home runs) gave the club its first victory, and his RBI ground out in Game Five and go-ahead homer in Game Six proved game-winners in contests the Royals had to win.

Kansas City Royals (West), 4; Toronto Blue Jays (East), 3

KC (W)

PLAYER/POS	AVG	G	AB	R	H	2B	3B	HR	RB	BB	SO	SB
Steve Balboni, 1b	.120	7	25	1	3	0	0	0	1	2	8	0
Buddy Biancalana, ss	.222	7	18	2	4	1	0	0	1	1	6	0
Bud Black, p	.000	3	0	0	0	0	0	0	0	0	0	0
George Brett, 3b	.348	7	23	6	8	2	0	3	5	7	5	0
Onix Concepcion, ss	.000	4	1	0	0	0	0	0	0	0	0	0
Steve Farr, p	.000	2	0	0	0	0	0	0	0	0	0	0
Mark Gubicza, p	.000	2	0	0	0	0	0	0	0	0	0	0
Dane Iorg, ph	.500	4	2	0	1	1	0	0	0	2	0	0
Danny Jackson, p	.000	2	0	0	0	0	0	0	0	0	0	0
Lynn Jones, of	.000	5	0	0	0	0	0	0	0	0	0	0
Charlie Leibrandt, p	.000	3	0	0	0	0	0	0	0	0	0	0
Hal McRae, dh	.261	6	23	1	6	2	0	0	3	1	6	0
Darryl Motley, of	.333	2	3	1	1	0	0	0	1	1	2	0
Jorge Orta, dh-1	.000	2	5	0	0	0	0	0	0	0	1	0
Jamie Quirk, ph	.000	1	1	0	0	0	0	0	0	0	0	0
Dan Quisenberry, p	.000	4	0	0	0	0	0	0	0	0	0	0
Bret Saberhagen, p	.000	2	0	0	0	0	0	0	0	0	0	0
Pat Sheridan, of	.150	7	20	4	3	0	0	2	3	2	3	0
Lonnie Smith, of	.250	7	28	2	7	2	0	0	1	3	6	1
Jim Sundberg, c	.167	7	24	3	4	1	1	1	6	1	7	0
Frank White, 2b	.200	7	25	1	5	0	0	0	3	1	2	0
Willie Wilson, of	.310	7	29	5	9	0	0	1	2	1	5	1
TOTAL	.225		227	26	51	9	1	7	26	22	51	2

PITCHER	W	L	ERA	G	GS	CG	SV	SHO	IP	H	ER	BB	SO
Bud Black	0	0	1.69	3	1	0	0	0	10.2	11	2	4	8
Steve Farr	1	0	1.42	2	0	0	0	0	6.1	4	1	1	3
Mark Gubicza	1	0	3.24	2	1	0	0	0	8.1	4	3	4	4
Danny Jackson	1	0	0.00	2	1	1	0	1	10.0	10	0	1	7
Charlie Leibrandt	1	2	5.28	3	2	0	0	0	15.1	17	9	4	6
Dan Quisenberry	0	1	3.86	4	0	0	1	0	4.2	7	2	0	3
Bret Saberhagen	0	0	6.14	2	2	0	0	0	7.1	12	5	2	6
TOTAL	4	3	3.16	18	7	1	1	1	62.2	65	22	16	37

TOR (E)

PLAYER/POS	AVG	G	AB	R	H	2B	3B	HR	RB	BB	SO	SB
Jim Acker, p	.000	2	0	0	0	0	0	0	0	0	0	0
Doyle Alexander, p	.000	2	0	0	0	0	0	0	0	0	0	0
Jesse Barfield, of	.280	7	25	3	7	1	0	1	4	3	7	1
George Bell, of	.321	7	28	4	9	3	0	0	1	0	4	0
Jeff Burroughs, ph	.000	1	1	0	0	0	0	0	0	0	0	0
Jim Clancy, p	.000	1	0	0	0	0	0	0	0	0	0	0
Tony Fernandez, ss	.333	7	24	2	8	2	0	0	2	1	2	0
Cecil Fielder, ph	.333	3	3	0	1	1	0	0	0	0	1	0
Damaso Garcia, 2b	.233	7	30	4	7	4	0	0	1	3	3	0
Jeff Hearron, c	.000	2	0	0	0	0	0	0	0	0	0	0
Tom Henke, p	.000	3	0	0	0	0	0	0	0	0	0	0
Garth Iorg, 3b	.133	6	15	1	2	0	0	0	0	1	3	0
Cliff Johnson, dh	.368	7	19	1	7	2	0	0	2	1	4	0
Jimmy Key, p	.000	2	0	0	0	0	0	0	0	0	0	0
Dennis Lamp, p	.000	3	0	0	0	0	0	0	0	0	0	0
Gary Lavelle, p	.000	1	0	0	0	0	0	0	0	0	0	0
Manny Lee, 2b	.000	1	1	0	0	0	0	0	0	0	0	0
Lloyd Moseby, of	.226	7	31	5	7	1	0	0	4	2	3	1
Rance Mulliniks, 3b	.364	5	11	1	4	1	0	1	3	2	2	0
Al Oliver, dh	.375	5	8	0	3	1	0	0	3	0	0	0
Dave Stieb, p	.000	3	0	0	0	0	0	0	0	0	0	0
Lou Thornton, pr	.000	2	0	1	0	0	0	0	0	0	0	0
Willie Upshaw, 1b	.231	7	26	2	6	2	0	0	1	1	4	0
Ernie Whitt, c	.190	7	21	1	4	1	0	0	2	2	4	0
TOTAL	.269		242	25	65	19	0	2	23	16	37	2

PITCHER	W	L	ERA	G	GS	CG	SV	SHO	IP	H	ER	BB	SO
Jim Acker	0	0	0.00	2	0	0	0	0	6.0	2	0	0	5
Doyle Alexander	0	1	8.71	2	2	0	0	0	10.1	14	10	3	9
Jim Clancy	0	1	9.00	1	0	0	0	0	1.0	2	1	1	0
Tom Henke	2	0	4.26	3	0	0	0	0	6.1	5	3	4	4
Jimmy Key	0	1	5.19	2	2	0	0	0	8.2	15	5	2	5
Dennis Lamp	0	0	0.00	3	0	0	0	0	9.1	2	0	1	10
Gary Lavelle	0	0	—	1	0	0	0	0	0.0	0	0	1	0
Dave Stieb	1	1	3.10	3	3	0	0	0	20.1	11	7	10	18
TOTAL	3	4	3.77	17	7	0	0	0	62.0	51	26	22	51

GAME 1 AT TOR OCT 8

```
KC    000 000 001    1   5  1
TOR   023 100 00X    6  11  0
```
Pitchers: LEIBRANDT, Farr (3), Gubicza (5), Jackson (8) vs STIEB, Henke (9)
Attendance: 39,115

GAME 2 AT TOR OCT 9

```
KC    002 100 001 1    5  10  3
TOR   000 102 010 2    6  10  0
```
Pitchers: Black, QUISENBERRY (8) vs Key, Lamp (4), Lavelle (8), HENKE (8)
Home Runs: Wilson-KC, Sheridan-KC
Attendance: 34,029

GAME 3 AT KC OCT 11

```
TOR   000 050 000    5  13  1
KC    100 112 01X    6  10  1
```
Pitchers: Alexander, Lamp (6), CLANCY (8) vs Saberhagen, Black (5), FARR (5)
Home Runs: Brett-KC (2), Barfield-TOR, Mulliniks-TOR, Sundberg-KC
Attendance: 40,224

GAME 4 AT KC OCT 12

```
TOR   000 000 003    3   7  0
KC    000 001 000    1   2  0
```
Pitchers: Stieb, HENKE (7) vs LEIBRANDT, Quisenberry (9)
Attendance: 41,112

GAME 5 AT KC OCT 13

```
TOR   000 000 000    0   8  0
KC    110 000 00X    2   8  0
```
Pitchers: KEY, Acker (6) vs JACKSON
Attendance: 40,046

GAME 6 AT TOR OCT 15

```
KC    101 012 000    5   8  1
TOR   101 001 000    3   8  2
```
Pitchers: GUBICZA, Black (6), Quisenberry (9) vs ALEXANDER, Lamp (6)
Home Runs: Brett-KC
Attendance: 37,557

GAME 7 AT TOR OCT 16

```
KC    010 104 000    6   8  0
TOR   000 010 001    2   8  1
```
Pitchers: Saberhagen, LEIBRANDT (4), Quisenberry (9) vs STIEB, Acker (6)
Home Runs: Sheridan-KC
Attendance: 32,084

The underdog Royals surprised St. Louis with superior hitting and pitching, and even outstole the speedy Cards six bases to two. Still, had an umpire not muffed a call at first base in Game Six, St. Louis might have emerged from the fray wearing the world crown.

The Cardinals broke a 1–1 tie in the fourth inning of the opener with back-to-back doubles off Royal starter Danny Jackson, and held on behind the strong pitching of John Tudor and reliever Todd Worrell for a 3–1 win. In Game Two, except for the fourth inning, when he yielded a single and two doubles (for two runs) before retiring his first batter, Cardinal starter Danny Cox held the Royals in check. Royal starter Charlie Leibrandt hurled even more effectively, holding St. Louis to two hits—until the ninth inning, when four Cardinal hits (three of them doubles) produced four runs and a second Card victory.

Kansas City finally demonstrated its punch in Game Three. Frank White hit a two-run homer in the fifth, and the Royals scored four more times to win behind the six-hit hurling of sophomore sensation Bret Saberhagen. The next day, though, Royal bats died again against John Tudor, who shut them out on five hits. Three Royal pitchers yielded only six hits to Cardinal batters, but two were home runs to Tito Landrum and Willie McGee, and one was a triple to Terry Pendleton, who scored on a sacrifice squeeze.

Down three games to one, the Royals hammered eleven hits in Game Five for six runs to win behind Danny Jackson's five-hitter. Seven Royal hits in the first eight innings of Game Six, though, scored no runs against Cardinal starter Danny Cox and reliever Ken Dayley. But in the last of the ninth, with the Cards ahead 1–0 and Todd Worrell now pitching, Royal pinch hitter Jorge Orta was ruled safe at first on what the cameras showed clearly as an out. This miscall, followed by a pop foul that first baseman Jack Clark should have caught but didn't, opened the door to Cardinal disintegration. A single and passed ball put Royals at second and third, and after an intentional walk to set up the double play, pinch hitter Dane Iorg singled home the tying and winning Royal runs.

The Cardinals threw seven pitchers at Kansas City in the finale in a vain attempt to halt the Royals' fourteen-hit, eleven-run attack, while Bret Saberhagen stopped the Cards cold on five hits to bring the Royals their first world title.

Kansas City Royals (AL), 4;
St. Louis Cardinals (NL), 3

KC (A)

PLAYER/POS	AVG	G	AB	R	H	2B	3B	HR	RBI	BB	SO	SB
Steve Balboni, 1b	.320	7	25	2	8	0	0	0	3	5	4	0
Joe Beckwith, p	.000	1	0	0	0	0	0	0	0	0	0	0
Buddy Biancalana, ss	.278	7	18	2	5	0	0	0	2	5	4	0
Bud Black, p	.000	2	1	0	0	0	0	0	0	0	1	0
George Brett, 3b	.370	7	27	5	10	1	0	0	1	4	7	1
Onix Concepcion, ss-2	.000	3	0	1	0	0	0	0	0	0	0	0
Dane Iorg, ph	.500	2	2	0	1	0	0	0	2	0	0	0
Danny Jackson, p	.000	2	6	0	0	0	0	0	0	0	5	0
Lynn Jones, of-4	.667	6	3	0	2	1	1	0	0	0	0	0
Charlie Leibrandt, p	.000	2	4	0	0	0	0	0	0	0	2	0
Hal McRae, ph	.000	3	1	0	0	0	0	0	0	1	0	0
Darryl Motley, of-4	.364	5	11	1	4	0	0	1	3	0	1	0
Jorge Orta, ph	.333	3	3	0	1	0	0	0	0	0	0	0
Greg Pryor, 3b	.000	1	0	0	0	0	0	0	0	0	0	0
Dan Quisenberry, p	.000	4	0	0	0	0	0	0	0	0	0	0
Bret Saberhagen, p	.000	2	7	1	0	0	0	0	0	0	4	0
Pat Sheridan, of-4	.222	5	18	0	4	2	0	0	1	0	7	0
Lonnie Smith, of	.333	7	27	4	9	3	0	0	4	3	8	2
Jim Sundberg, c	.250	7	24	6	6	2	0	0	1	6	4	0
John Wathan, ph	.000	2	1	0	0	0	0	0	0	0	1	0
Frank White, 2b	.250	7	28	4	7	3	0	1	6	3	4	1
Willie Wilson, of	.367	7	30	2	11	0	1	0	3	1	4	3
TOTAL	.288		236	28	68	12	2	2	26	28	56	7

PITCHER	W	L	ERA	G	GS	CG	SV	SHO	IP	H	ER	BB	SO
Joe Beckwith	0	0	0.00	1	0	0	0	0	2.0	1	0	0	3
Bud Black	0	1	5.06	2	1	0	0	0	5.1	4	3	5	4
Danny Jackson	1	1	1.69	2	2	1	0	0	16.0	9	3	5	12
Charlie Leibrandt	0	1	2.76	2	2	0	0	0	16.1	10	5	4	10
Dan Quisenberry	1	0	2.08	4	0	0	0	0	4.1	5	1	3	3
Bret Saberhagen	2	0	0.50	2	2	2	0	1	18.0	11	1	1	10
TOTAL	4	3	1.89	13	7	3	0	1	62.0	40	13	18	42

STL (N)

PLAYER/POS	AVG	G	AB	R	H	2B	3B	HR	RBI	BB	SO	SB
Joaquin Andujar, p	.000	2	1	0	0	0	0	0	0	0	1	0
Steve Braun, ph	.000	1	1	0	0	0	0	0	0	0	0	0
Bill Campbell, p	.000	3	0	0	0	0	0	0	0	0	0	0
Cesar Cedeno, of	.133	5	15	1	2	1	0	0	1	2	2	0
Jack Clark, 1b	.240	7	25	1	6	2	0	0	4	3	9	0
Danny Cox, p	.000	2	4	0	0	0	0	0	0	0	2	0
Ken Dayley, p	.000	4	0	0	0	0	0	0	0	0	0	0
Ivan DeJesus, ph	.000	1	1	0	0	0	0	0	0	0	0	0
Bob Forsch, p	.000	2	4	0	0	0	0	0	0	0	0	0
Brian Harper, ph	.250	4	4	0	1	0	0	0	1	0	1	0
Tommy Herr, 2b	.154	7	26	2	4	2	0	0	2	2	2	0
Rick Horton, p	.000	3	1	0	0	0	0	0	0	0	1	0
Mike Jorgensen, of-1	.000	2	3	0	0	0	0	0	0	0	0	0
Jeff Lahti, p	.000	3	0	0	0	0	0	0	0	0	0	0
Tito Landrum, of	.360	7	25	4	9	3	0	1	1	1	2	0
Tom Lawless, pr	.000	1	0	0	0	0	0	0	0	0	0	0
Willie McGee, of	.259	7	27	2	7	2	0	1	2	1	3	1
Tom Nieto, c	.000	2	5	0	0	0	0	0	0	1	2	0
Terry Pendleton, 3b	.261	7	23	3	6	1	1	0	3	3	2	0
Darrell Porter, c	.133	5	15	0	2	0	0	0	0	2	5	0
Ozzie Smith, ss	.087	7	23	1	2	0	0	0	0	4	0	1
John Tudor, p	.000	3	5	0	0	0	0	0	0	0	4	0
Andy Van Slyke, of	.091	6	11	0	1	0	0	0	0	0	5	0
Todd Worrell, p	.000	3	1	0	0	0	0	0	0	0	1	0
TOTAL	.185		216	13	40	10	1	2	13	18	42	2

PITCHER	W	L	ERA	G	GS	CG	SV	SHO	IP	H	ER	BB	SO
Joaquin Andujar	0	1	9.00	2	1	0	0	0	4.0	10	4	4	3
Bill Campbell	0	0	2.25	3	0	0	0	0	4.0	4	1	2	5
Danny Cox	0	0	1.29	2	2	0	0	0	14.0	14	2	4	13
Ken Dayley	1	0	0.00	4	0	0	0	0	6.0	1	0	3	5
Bob Forsch	0	1	12.00	2	1	0	0	0	3.0	6	4	1	3
Rick Horton	0	0	6.75	3	0	0	0	0	4.0	4	3	5	5
Jeff Lahti	0	0	12.27	3	0	0	1	0	3.2	10	5	0	2
John Tudor	2	1	3.00	3	3	1	0	1	18.0	15	6	7	14
Todd Worrell	0	1	3.86	3	0	0	1	0	4.2	4	2	2	6
TOTAL	3	4	3.96	25	7	1	2	1	61.1	68	27	28	56

Houston pitcher Mike Scott overwhelmed the Mets in Games One and Four, and would have faced them a third time in Game Seven if the Astros had won Game Six. They tried, scoring three runs in the first as Bob Knepper shut out the Mets on two hits through eight innings. But in the top of the ninth New York tied the game and held on into extra innings. No one scored again until the Mets put a run across in the fourteenth. Astro Billy Hatcher tied it up again later in the fourteenth with a home run just inside the left field foul pole. Two innings later the Mets (aided by a pair of wild pitches) scored three runs. Again the Astros came back, scoring twice, but fell just short as Jesse Orosco struck out Kevin Bass with two men on base to win his third game of the series and give New York the pennant.

In the series opener Houston scored just one run off Dwight Gooden, but it was enough, as Mike Scott, fanning fourteen, shut out the Mets on five hits. New York came back with five runs in Game Two to win behind Bob Ojeda, who gave up ten hits but only one run. In Game Three the Astros held the lead into the last of the sixth, when New York tied the score with four runs. Houston retook the lead in the seventh with a run, but Met Len Dykstra won it for New York with a two-run homer in the bottom of the ninth.

The Astros' win in Game Four evened the series. Houston had scored three runs by the time Scott (on his way to a three-hitter) gave the Mets their only run in the eighth. Houston's Nolan Ryan gave up only two hits in the first nine innings of Game Five (one of them Darryl Strawberry's game-tying solo homer in the fifth), striking out twelve. But New York's Gooden also yielded only one run in ten innings of work. Astro Charlie Kerfeld shut out the Mets in the tenth and eleventh, and the Mets' Orosco stopped Houston in the eleventh and twelfth. But in the last of the twelfth, Met catcher Gary Carter singled home a run off Kerfeld to end the game (and his series-long batting slump)—setting the stage for the sixteen-inning marathon the next day.

New York Mets (East), 4; Houston Astros (West), 2

NY (E)

PLAYER/POS	AVG	G	AB	R	H	2B	3B	HR	RB	BB	SO	SB
Rick Aguilera, p	.000	2	0	0	0	0	0	0	0	0	0	0
Wally Backman, 2b	.238	6	21	5	5	0	0	0	2	2	4	1
Gary Carter, c	.148	6	27	1	4	1	0	0	2	2	5	0
Ron Darling, p	.000	1	1	0	0	0	0	0	0	0	0	0
Lenny Dykstra, of	.304	6	23	3	7	1	1	1	3	2	4	1
Kevin Elster, ss	.000	4	3	0	0	0	0	0	0	0	1	0
Sid Fernandez, p	.000	1	1	0	0	0	0	0	0	0	0	0
Dwight Gooden, p	.000	2	5	0	0	0	0	0	0	0	2	0
Danny Heep, of-1	.250	5	4	0	1	0	0	0	1	0	2	0
Keith Hernandez, 1b	.269	6	26	3	7	1	1	0	3	3	6	0
Howard Johnson, ph	.000	2	2	0	0	0	0	0	0	0	0	0
Ray Knight, 3b	.167	6	24	1	4	0	0	0	2	1	5	0
Lee Mazzilli, ph	.200	5	5	0	1	0	0	0	0	0	3	0
Roger McDowell, p	.000	2	1	0	0	0	0	0	0	0	0	0
Kevin Mitchell, of	.250	2	8	1	2	0	0	0	0	0	1	0
Bob Ojeda, p	.000	2	5	1	0	0	0	0	0	0	0	0
Jesse Orosco, p	.000	4	0	0	0	0	0	0	0	0	0	0
Rafael Santana, ss	.176	6	17	0	3	0	0	0	0	0	3	0
Doug Sisk, p	.000	1	0	0	0	0	0	0	0	0	0	0
Darryl Strawberry, of	.227	6	22	4	5	1	0	2	5	3	12	1
Tim Teufel, 2b	.167	2	6	0	1	0	0	0	0	0	0	0
Mookie Wilson, of	.115	6	26	2	3	0	0	0	1	1	7	1
TOTAL	.189		227	21	43	4	2	3	19	14	57	4

PITCHER	W	L	ERA	G	GS	CG	SV	SHO	IP	H	ER	BB	SO
Rick Aguilera	0	0	0.00	2	0	0	0	0	5.0	2	0	2	2
Ron Darling	0	0	7.20	1	1	0	0	0	5.0	6	4	2	5
Sid Fernandez	0	1	4.50	1	1	0	0	0	6.0	3	3	1	5
Dwight Gooden	0	1	1.06	2	2	0	0	0	17.0	16	2	5	9
Roger McDowell	0	0	0.00	2	0	0	0	0	7.0	1	0	0	3
Bob Ojeda	1	0	2.57	2	2	1	0	0	14.0	15	4	4	6
Jesse Orosco	3	0	3.38	4	0	0	0	0	8.0	5	3	2	10
Doug Sisk	0	0	0.00	1	0	0	0	0	1.0	1	0	1	0
TOTAL	4	2	2.29	15	6	1	0	0	63.0	49	16	17	40

HOU (W)

PLAYER/POS	AVG	G	AB	R	H	2B	3B	HR	RB	BB	SO	SB
Larry Andersen, p	.000	2	0	0	0	0	0	0	0	0	0	0
Alan Ashby, c	.130	6	23	2	3	1	0	1	2	2	1	0
Kevin Bass, of	.292	6	24	0	7	2	0	0	4	4	2	2
Jeff Calhoun, p	.000	2	0	0	0	0	0	0	0	0	0	0
Jose Cruz, of	.192	6	26	0	5	0	0	0	2	1	8	0
Glenn Davis, 1b	.269	6	26	3	7	1	0	1	3	1	3	0
Bill Doran, 2b	.222	6	27	3	6	0	0	1	3	2	2	2
Phil Garner, 3b	.222	3	9	1	2	1	0	0	2	1	2	0
Billy Hatcher, of	.280	6	25	4	7	0	0	1	2	3	2	3
Charlie Kerfeld, p	.000	3	0	0	0	0	0	0	0	0	0	0
Bob Knepper, p	.000	2	5	0	0	0	0	0	0	1	2	0
Davey Lopes, ph	.000	3	2	1	0	0	0	0	0	1	0	0
Aurelio Lopez, p	.000	2	0	0	0	0	0	0	0	0	0	0
Jim Pankovits, ph	.000	2	2	0	0	0	0	0	0	0	1	0
Terry Puhl, ph	.667	3	3	0	2	0	0	0	0	0	0	1
Craig Reynolds, ss	.333	4	12	1	4	0	0	0	0	1	3	0
Nolan Ryan, p	.000	2	4	0	0	0	0	0	0	0	2	0
Mike Scott, p	.000	2	6	0	0	0	0	0	0	0	5	0
Dave Smith, p	.000	2	0	0	0	0	0	0	0	0	0	0
Dickie Thon, ss	.250	6	12	1	3	0	0	0	1	1	0	1
Denny Walling, 3b	.158	5	19	1	3	1	0	0	2	2	4	0
TOTAL	.218		225	17	49	6	0	5	17	17	40	8

PITCHER	W	L	ERA	G	GS	CG	SV	SHO	IP	H	ER	BB	SO
Larry Andersen	0	0	0.00	2	0	0	0	0	5.0	1	0	2	3
Jeff Calhoun	0	0	9.00	1	0	0	0	0	1.0	1	1	1	0
Charlie Kerfeld	0	1	2.25	3	0	0	0	0	4.0	2	1	1	4
Bob Knepper	0	0	3.52	2	2	0	0	0	15.1	13	6	1	9
Aurelio Lopez	0	1	8.10	2	0	0	0	0	3.1	7	3	4	3
Nolan Ryan	0	1	3.86	2	2	0	0	0	14.0	9	6	1	17
Mike Scott	2	0	0.50	2	2	2	0	1	18.0	8	1	1	19
Dave Smith	0	1	9.00	2	0	0	0	0	2.0	2	2	3	2
TOTAL	2	4	2.87	16	6	2	0	1	62.2	43	20	14	57

GAME 1 AT HOU OCT 8

NY	000	000	000	0	5	0
HOU	010	000	00X	1	7	1

Pitchers: GOODEN, Orosco (8) vs SCOTT
Home Runs: Davis-HOU
Attendance: 44,131

GAME 2 AT HOU OCT 9

NY	000	230	000	5	10	0
HOU	000	000	100	1	10	2

Pitchers: OJEDA vs RYAN, Andersen (6), Lopez (8), Kerfeld (9)
Attendance: 44,391

GAME 3 AT NY OCT 11

HOU	220	000	100	5	8	1
NY	000	004	002	6	10	1

Pitchers: Knepper, Kerfeld (8), SMITH (9) vs Darling, Aguilera (6), OROSCO (8)
Home Runs: Doran-HOU, Strawberry-NY, Dykstra-NY
Attendance: 55,052

GAME 4 AT NY OCT 12

HOU	020	010	000	3	4	1
NY	000	000	010	1	3	0

Pitchers: SCOTT vs FERNANDEZ, McDowell (7), Sisk (9)
Home Runs: Ashby-HOU, Thon-HOU
Attendance: 55,038

GAME 5 AT NY OCT 14

HOU	000	010	000	000	1	9	1
NY	000	010	000	001	2	4	0

Pitchers: Ryan, KERFELD (10) vs Gooden, OROSCO (11)
Home Runs: Strawberry-NY
Attendance: 54,986

GAME 6 AT HOU OCT 15

NY	000	000	003	000	010	3	7	11	0
HOU	300	000	000	000	010	2	6	11	1

Pitchers: Ojeda, Aguilera (6), McDowell (9), OROSCO (14) vs Knepper, Smith (9), Andersen (11), LOPEZ (14), Calhoun (16)
Home Runs: Hatcher-HOU
Attendance: 45,718

For the second time in the two years of the expanded LCS, a club that would have been eliminated in a five-game series came back to take the pennant in seven games. The first two games were one-sided. California scored five early runs off Roger Clemens and breezed to an easy 8–1 win in the opener. Boston retaliated in Game Two with nine runs, breaking the game open with six unanswered runs in the seventh and eighth innings.

Game Three was close until the Angels homered twice for three runs with two out in the seventh to break a 1–1 tie. In Game Four, the Angels were handed a tie in the last of the ninth when Boston reliever Calvin Schiraldi hit a batter with the bases loaded and won in the eleventh on Bobby Grich's RBI single.

The Red Sox, down three games to one, were on the brink of elimination in Game Five, with two out in the ninth, when Dave Henderson, after fouling off one third-strike pitch, hit the next for a two-run homer that gave Boston a one-run lead. The Angels tied the game in the last of the ninth, but Henderson's sacrifice fly in the eleventh put the Sox ahead for good.

Boston needed two more wins and got them with surprising ease, 10–4 and 8–1, as Oil Can Boyd and Clemens redeemed their earlier losses.

Boston Red Sox (East), 4; California Angels (West), 3

BOS (E)

PLAYER/POS	AVG	G	AB	R	H	2B	3B	HR	RB	BB	SO	SB
Tony Armas, of	.125	5	16	1	2	1	0	0	0	0	2	0
Marty Barrett, 2b	.367	7	30	4	11	2	0	0	5	2	2	0
Don Baylor, dh	.346	7	26	6	9	3	0	1	2	4	5	0
Wade Boggs, 3b	.233	7	30	3	7	1	1	0	2	4	1	0
Oil Can Boyd, p	.000	2	0	0	0	0	0	0	0	0	0	0
Bill Buckner, 1b	.214	7	28	3	6	1	0	0	3	0	2	0
Roger Clemens, p	.000	3	0	0	0	0	0	0	0	0	0	0
Steve Crawford, p	.000	1	0	0	0	0	0	0	0	0	0	0
Dwight Evans, of	.214	7	28	2	6	1	0	1	4	3	3	0
Rich Gedman, c	.357	7	28	4	10	1	0	1	6	0	4	0
Mike Greenwell, ph	.500	2	2	0	1	0	0	0	0	0	0	0
Dave Henderson, of	.111	5	9	3	1	0	0	1	4	2	2	0
Bruce Hurst, p	.000	2	0	0	0	0	0	0	0	0	0	0
Spike Owen, ss	.429	7	21	5	9	0	1	0	3	2	2	1
Jim Rice, of	.161	7	31	8	5	1	0	2	6	1	8	0
Ed Romero, ss	.000	1	2	0	0	0	0	0	0	0	1	0
Joe Sambito, p	.000	3	0	0	0	0	0	0	0	0	0	0
Calvin Schiraldi, p	.000	4	0	0	0	0	0	0	0	0	0	0
Bob Stanley, p	.000	3	0	0	0	0	0	0	0	0	0	0
Dave Stapleton, 1b	.667	4	3	2	2	0	0	0	0	0	1	0
TOTAL	.272		254	41	69	11	2	6	35	19	31	1

PITCHER	W	L	ERA	G	GS	CG	SV	SHO	IP	H	ER	BB	SO
Oil Can Boyd	1	1	4.61	2	2	0	0	0	13.2	17	7	3	8
Roger Clemens	1	1	4.37	3	3	0	0	0	22.2	22	11	7	17
Steve Crawford	1	0	0.00	1	0	0	0	0	1.2	1	0	2	1
Bruce Hurst	1	0	2.40	2	2	1	0	0	15.0	18	4	1	8
Joe Sambito	0	0	0.00	3	0	0	0	0	0.2	1	0	1	0
Calvin Schiraldi	0	1	1.50	4	0	0	1	0	6.0	5	1	3	9
Bob Stanley	0	0	4.76	3	0	0	0	0	5.2	7	3	3	1
TOTAL	4	3	3.58	18	7	1	1	0	65.1	71	26	20	44

CAL (W)

PLAYER/POS	AVG	G	AB	R	H	2B	3B	HR	RB	BB	SO	SB
Bob Boone, c	.455	7	22	4	10	0	0	1	2	1	3	0
Rick Burleson, 2b-2,dh-1	.273	4	11	0	3	0	0	0	0	0	0	0
John Candelaria, p	.000	2	0	0	0	0	0	0	0	0	0	0
Doug Corbett, p	.000	3	0	0	0	0	0	0	0	0	0	0
Doug DeCinces, 3b	.281	7	32	2	9	3	0	1	3	0	2	0
Brian Downing, of	.222	7	27	2	6	0	0	1	7	4	5	0
Chuck Finley, p	.000	3	0	0	0	0	0	0	0	0	0	0
Bobby Grich, 2b-3,1b-3	.208	6	24	1	5	0	0	1	3	0	8	0
George Hendrick, of-2,1b-1	.083	3	12	0	1	0	0	0	0	0	2	0
Jack Howell, ph	.000	2	1	0	0	0	0	0	0	1	1	0
Reggie Jackson, dh	.192	6	26	2	5	2	0	0	2	2	7	0
Ruppert Jones, of-5	.176	6	17	4	3	1	0	0	2	5	2	0
Wally Joyner, 1b	.455	3	11	3	5	2	0	1	2	2	0	0
Gary Lucas, p	.000	4	0	0	0	0	0	0	0	0	0	0
Kirk McCaskill, p	.000	2	0	0	0	0	0	0	0	0	0	0
Donnie Moore, p	.000	3	0	0	0	0	0	0	0	0	0	0
Jerry Narron, c-3	.500	4	2	1	1	0	0	0	0	1	1	0
Gary Pettis, of	.346	7	26	4	9	1	0	1	4	3	5	0
Vern Ruhle, p	.000	2	0	0	0	0	0	0	0	0	0	0
Dick Schofield, ss	.300	7	30	4	9	1	0	1	2	1	5	1
Don Sutton, p	.000	2	0	0	0	0	0	0	0	0	0	0
Devon White, of-3	.500	4	2	1	1	0	0	0	0	0	1	0
Rob Wilfong, 2b	.308	4	13	1	4	1	0	0	2	0	2	0
Mike Witt, p	.000	2	0	0	0	0	0	0	0	0	0	0
TOTAL	.277		256	30	71	11	0	7	29	20	44	1

PITCHER	W	L	ERA	G	GS	CG	SV	SHO	IP	H	ER	BB	SO
John Candelaria	1	1	0.84	2	2	0	0	0	10.2	11	1	6	7
Doug Corbett	1	0	5.40	3	0	0	0	0	6.2	9	4	2	2
Chuck Finley	0	0	0.00	3	0	0	0	0	2.0	1	0	0	1
Gary Lucas	0	0	11.57	4	0	0	0	0	2.1	3	3	1	2
Kirk McCaskill	0	2	7.71	2	2	0	0	0	9.1	16	8	5	7
Donnie Moore	0	1	7.20	3	0	0	1	0	5.0	8	4	2	0
Vern Ruhle	0	0	13.50	1	0	0	0	0	0.2	2	1	0	0
Don Sutton	0	0	1.86	2	1	0	0	0	9.2	6	2	1	4
Mike Witt	1	0	2.55	2	2	1	0	0	17.2	13	5	2	8
TOTAL	3	4	3.94	22	7	1	1	0	64.0	69	28	19	31

GAME 1 AT BOS OCT 7

CAL	041	000	030	8	11	0
BOS	000	001	000	1	5	1

Pitchers: WITT vs CLEMENS, Sambito (8), Stanley (8)
Attendance: 32,993

GAME 2 AT BOS OCT 8

CAL	000	110	000	2	11	3
BOS	110	010	33X	9	13	2

Pitchers: McCASKILL, Lucas (8), Corbett (8) vs HURST
Home Runs: Joyner-CAL, Rice-BOS
Attendance: 32,786

GAME 3 AT CAL OCT 10

BOS	010	000	020	3	9	1
CAL	000	001	31X	5	8	0

Pitchers: BOYD, Sambito (7), Schiraldi (8) vs CANDELARIA, Moore (8)
Home Runs: Schofield-CAL, Pettis-CAL
Attendance: 64,206

GAME 4 AT CAL OCT 11

BOS	000	001	020	00	3	6	1
CAL	000	000	003	01	4	11	2

Pitchers: Clemens, SCHIRALDI (9) vs Sutton, Lucas (7), Ruhle (7), Finley (8), CORBETT (8)
Home Runs: DeCinces-CAL
Attendance: 64,223

GAME 5 AT CAL OCT 12

BOS	020	000	004	01	7	12	0
CAL	001	002	201	00	6	13	0

Pitchers: Hurst, Stanley (7), Sambito (9), CRAWFORD (9), Schiraldi (11) vs Witt, Lucas (9), MOORE (9), Finley (11)
Home Runs: Gedman-BOS, Boone-CAL, Grich-CAL, Baylor-BOS, Henderson-BOS
Attendance: 64,223

GAME 6 AT BOS OCT 14

CAL	200	000	110	4	11	1
BOS	205	010	20X	10	16	1

Pitchers: McCASKILL, Lucas (3), Corbett (4), Finley (7) vs BOYD, Stanley (8)
Home Runs: Downing-CAL
Attendance: 32,998

GAME 7 AT BOS OCT 15

CAL	000	000	010	1	6	2
BOS	030	400	10X	8	8	1

Pitchers: CANDELARIA, Sutton (4), Moore (8) vs CLEMENS, Schiraldi (8)
Home Runs: Rice-BOS, Evans-BOS
Attendance: 33,001

In their three most recent Series appearances—1946, 1967, and 1975—the Red Sox had battled to a seventh game, only to lose. This time they came within one strike of winning the crown in the sixth game—but wound up losing again in Game Seven.

Boston surprised the favored Mets by taking the first two games in New York. Bruce Hurst (with relief from Calvin Schiraldi in the ninth) pitched a four-hitter. New York's Ron Darling hurled just as well but lost when a seventh-inning walk, a wild pitch, and an error by second baseman Tim Teufel moved Jim Rice around the bases with the game's only run. Game Two, close for three innings, turned into a 9–3 Boston blowout as the Sox racked four of the five Met pitchers for eighteen hits, including home runs by Dave Henderson and Dwight Evans.

When the Series moved to Boston, though, the Mets revived to rap Sox starter Oil Can Boyd and two relievers for thirteen hits and seven runs (starting with Len Dykstra's leadoff home run in the first inning) as former Sox pitcher Bob Ojeda subdued his old teammates, giving up just one run on five hits in his seven innings of work. The next day Ron Darling redeemed his first-game loss with seven shutout innings as his teammates built him a 6–0 lead (five of the runs scoring on homers by Dykstra and a pair by Gary Carter). The game ended at 6–2, with the Series even at two wins apiece.

Boston recovered in its final home appearance, taking a 4–0 lead and holding it until Teufel spoiled Bruce Hurst's try for a second shutout by homering in the eighth inning. Hurst yielded a second run with two out in the ninth, but struck out Len Dykstra on three pitches to seal his second win.

The ninth inning of Game Six ended with the score tied 3–3. Boston's Dave Henderson led off the tenth with a home run and two more Sox hits made the score 5–3. Boston reliever Calvin Schiraldi retired the first two Mets in the last of the tenth on long flies, but then three Mets singled, driving in one run and driving out Schiraldi. Bob Stanley, his replacement, had two strikes on Mookie Wilson when a wild pitch let in the tying run, and then Wilson's grounder went through first baseman Bill Buckner's legs as the winning Met bounded across the plate.

The Red Sox nearly recovered in Game Seven. Second-inning home runs by Dwight Evans and Rich Gedman, a walk, sacrifice, and single gave Boston a 3–0 lead which they held into the sixth inning. But then starter Bruce Hurst lost his touch: four hits and a walk later the

score was tied. A succession of five Sox relievers tried to hold the line, but the Mets scored five runs to Boston's two in the final innings for an 8–5 triumph.

New York Mets (NL), 4; Boston Red Sox (AL), 3

NY (N)

PLAYER/POS	AVG	G	AB	R	H	2B	3B	HR	RB	BB	SO	SB
Rick Aguilera, p	.000	1	0	0	0	0	0	0	0	0	0	0
Wally Backman, 2b	.333	6	18	4	6	0	0	0	1	3	2	1
Gary Carter, c	.276	7	29	4	8	2	0	2	9	0	4	0
Ron Darling, p	.000	3	3	0	0	0	0	0	0	0	1	0
Lenny Dykstra, of	.296	7	27	4	8	0	0	2	3	3	2	7	0
Kevin Elster, ss	.000	1	1	0	0	0	0	0	0	0	0	0
Sid Fernandez, p	.000	3	0	0	0	0	0	0	0	0	0	0
Dwight Gooden, p	.500	2	2	1	1	0	0	0	0	0	0	0
Danny Heep, dh-2,of-1	.091	5	11	0	1	0	0	0	2	1	1	0
Keith Hernandez, 1b	.231	7	26	1	6	0	0	0	4	5	1	0
Howard Johnson, 3b-1,ss-1	.000	2	5	0	0	0	0	0	0	0	2	0
Ray Knight, 3b	.391	6	23	4	9	1	0	1	5	2	2	0
Lee Mazzilli, of-1	.400	4	5	2	2	0	0	0	0	0	0	0
Roger McDowell, p	.000	5	0	0	0	0	0	0	0	0	0	0
Kevin Mitchell, of-2,dh-1	.250	5	8	1	2	0	0	0	0	0	3	0
Bob Ojeda, p	.000	2	2	0	0	0	0	0	0	0	1	0
Jesse Orosco, p	1.000	4	1	0	1	0	0	0	1	0	0	0
Rafael Santana, ss	.250	7	20	3	5	0	0	0	2	2	5	0
Doug Sisk, p	.000	1	0	0	0	0	0	0	0	0	0	0
Darryl Strawberry, of	.208	7	24	4	5	1	0	1	1	4	6	3
Tim Teufel, 2b	.444	3	9	1	4	1	0	1	1	1	2	0
Mookie Wilson, of	.269	7	26	3	7	1	0	0	0	1	6	3
TOTAL	.271		240	32	65	6	0	7	29	21	43	7

PITCHER	W	L	ERA	G	GS	CG	SV	SHO	IP	H	ER	BB	SO
Rick Aguilera	1	0	12.00	1	0	0	0	0	3.0	8	4	1	4
Ron Darling	1	1	1.53	3	3	0	0	0	17.2	13	3	10	12
Sid Fernandez	0	0	1.35	3	0	0	0	0	6.2	6	1	1	10
Dwight Gooden	0	2	8.00	2	2	0	0	0	9.0	17	8	4	9
Roger McDowell	1	0	4.91	5	0	0	0	0	7.1	10	4	6	2
Bob Ojeda	1	0	2.08	2	2	0	0	0	13.0	13	3	5	9
Jesse Orosco	0	0	0.00	4	0	0	2	0	5.2	2	0	0	6
Doug Sisk	0	0	0.00	1	0	0	0	0	0.2	0	0	1	1
TOTAL	4	3	3.29	21	7	0	2	0	63.0	69	23	28	53

BOS (A)

PLAYER/POS	AVG	G	AB	R	H	2B	3B	HR	RB	BB	SO	SB
Tony Armas, ph	.000	1	1	0	0	0	0	0	0	0	1	0
Marty Barrett, 2b	.433	7	30	1	13	2	0	0	4	5	2	0
Don Baylor, dh-3	.182	4	11	1	2	1	0	1	1	1	3	0
Wade Boggs, 3b	.290	7	31	3	9	3	0	0	3	4	2	0
Oil Can Boyd, p	.000	1	0	0	0	0	0	0	0	0	0	0
Bill Buckner, 1b	.188	7	32	2	6	0	0	0	1	0	3	0
Roger Clemens, p	.000	2	4	1	0	0	0	0	0	0	1	0
Steve Crawford, p	.000	3	1	0	0	0	0	0	0	0	0	0
Dwight Evans, of	.308	7	26	4	8	2	0	2	9	4	3	0
Rich Gedman, c	.200	7	30	1	6	1	0	1	1	0	10	0
Mike Greenwell, ph	.000	4	3	0	0	0	0	0	0	1	2	0
Dave Henderson, of	.400	7	25	6	10	1	1	2	5	2	6	0
Bruce Hurst, p	.000	3	3	0	0	0	0	0	0	0	3	0
Al Nipper, p	.000	2	0	0	0	0	0	0	0	0	0	0
Spike Owen, ss	.300	7	20	2	6	0	0	0	2	5	6	0
Jim Rice, of	.333	7	27	6	9	1	1	0	6	9	9	0
Ed Romero, ss	.000	3	1	0	0	0	0	0	0	0	0	0
Joe Sambito, p	.000	2	0	0	0	0	0	0	0	0	0	0
Calvin Schiraldi, p	.000	3	1	0	0	0	0	0	0	0	1	0
Bob Stanley, p	.000	5	1	0	0	0	0	0	0	0	1	0
Dave Stapleton, 1b	.000	3	1	0	0	0	0	0	0	0	0	0
TOTAL	.278		248	27	69	11	2	5	26	28	53	0

PITCHER	W	L	ERA	G	GS	CG	SV	SHO	IP	H	ER	BB	SO
Oil Can Boyd	0	1	7.71	1	1	0	0	0	7.0	9	6	1	3
Roger Clemens	0	0	3.18	2	2	0	0	0	11.1	9	4	6	11
Steve Crawford	1	0	6.23	3	0	0	0	0	4.1	5	3	0	4
Bruce Hurst	2	0	1.96	3	3	1	0	0	23.0	18	5	6	17
Al Nipper	0	1	7.11	2	1	0	0	0	6.1	10	5	2	2
Joe Sambito	0	0	27.00	2	0	0	0	0	0.1	2	1	2	0
Calvin Schiraldi	0	2	13.50	3	0	0	1	0	4.0	7	6	3	2
Bob Stanley	0	0	0.00	5	0	0	1	0	6.1	5	0	1	4
TOTAL	3	4	4.31	21	7	1	2	0	62.2	65	30	21	43

GAME 1 AT NY OCT 18

BOS 000 000 100   1 5 0
NY   000 000 000   0 4 1

Pitchers: HURST, Schiraldi (9) vs DARLING, McDowell (8)
Attendance: 55,076

GAME 2 AT NY OCT 19

BOS 003 120 201   9 18 0
NY   002 010 000   3 8 1

Pitchers: Clemens, CRAWFORD (5), Stanley (7) vs GOODEN, Aguilera (6), Orosco (7), Fernandez (9), Home Runs: Henderson-BOS, Evans-BOS
Attendance: 55,063

GAME 3 AT BOS OCT 21

NY   400 000 210   7 13 0
BOS   001 000 000   1 5 0

Pitchers: OJEDA, McDowell (8) vs BOYD, Sambito (8), Stanley (8)
Home Runs: Dykstra-NY
Attendance: 33,595

GAME 4 AT BOS OCT 22

NY   000 300 210   6 12 0
BOS   000 000 020   2 7 1

Pitchers: DARLING, McDowell (7), Orosco (7) vs NIPPER, Crawford (7), Stanley (9)
Home Runs: Dykstra-NY, Carter-NY (2)
Attendance: 33,920

GAME 5 AT BOS OCT 23

NY   000 000 011   2 10 1
BOS 011 020 00X   4 12 0

Pitchers: GOODEN, Fernandez (5) vs HURST
Home Runs: Teufel-NY
Attendance: 34,010

GAME 6 AT NY OCT 25

BOS   110 000 100 2   5 13 3
NY   000 020 010 3   6 8 2

Pitchers: Clemens, SCHIRALDI (8), Stanley (10) vs Ojeda, McDowell (7), Orosco (8), AGUILERA (9)
Home Runs: Henderson-BOS
Attendance: 55,078

GAME 7 AT NY OCT 27

BOS   030 000 020   5 9 0
NY   000 003 32X   8 10 0

Pitchers: Hurst, SCHIRALDI (7), Sambito (7), Stanley (7), Nipper (8), Crawford (8) vs Darling, Fernandez (4), McDOWELL (8), Orosco (9)
Home Runs: Evans-BOS, Gedman-BOS, Knight-NY, Strawberry-NY
Attendance: 55,032

The Giants scored four times in the fourth inning of Game Five, winning the game and taking a 3–2 series advantage. But Cardinal pitchers shut them out the rest of the series (an NLCS record 22 innings) to capture the flag.

St. Louis won the opener 5–3, with pitcher Greg Mathews's two-run single in the sixth providing his margin of victory. The Giants came back in Game Two, supporting Dave Dravecky's two-hit shutout with home runs by Will Clark and Jeffrey Leonard. But the Cards retook the series lead in Game Three, overcoming a 4–0 deficit with two runs on Jim Lindeman's homer in the sixth and four more in the seventh (capped by Lindeman's sacrifice fly) for an eventual 6–5 win.

The Giants snapped back with a pair of wins, scoring four runs on three homers in Game Four (including Leonard's fourth in successive games—an LCS record), and six runs in Game Five. But Dravecky and the Giants lost a heartbreaker in Game Six when right fielder Candy Maldonado lost Tony Pena's fly in the lights for a triple. Pena scored on a sacrifice fly for the game's only run, as John Tudor and two late-inning relievers blanked the Giants. Danny Cox pitched an easier shutout in the finale as his Cardinals hammered seven Giant pitchers for twelve hits and six runs.

St. Louis Cardinals (East), 4; San Francisco Giants (West) 3

STL (E)

PLAYER/POS	AVG	G	AB	R	H	2B	3B	HR	RB	BB	SO	SB
Jack Clark, ph	.000	1	1	0	0	0	0	0	0	0	1	0
Vince Coleman, of	.269	7	26	3	7	1	0	0	4	4	6	1
Danny Cox, p	.333	2	6	0	2	0	0	0	1	0	2	0
Ken Dayley, p	.000	3	0	0	0	0	0	0	0	0	0	0
Dan Driessen, 1b-4	.250	5	12	1	3	2	0	0	1	1	1	0
Curt Ford, of	.333	4	9	2	3	0	0	0	0	1	1	0
Bob Forsch, p	.000	3	0	0	0	0	0	0	0	0	0	0
Tommy Herr, 2b	.222	7	27	0	6	0	0	0	3	0	1	1
Rick Horton, p	.000	1	0	0	0	0	0	0	0	0	0	0
Lance Johnson, pr	.000	1	0	1	0	0	0	0	0	0	0	1
Tom Lawless, 3b-2,of-1	.333	3	6	0	2	0	0	0	0	1	1	0
Jim Lindeman, 1b	.308	5	13	1	4	0	0	1	3	0	3	0
Joe Magrane, p	.000	1	1	0	0	0	0	0	0	0	0	0
Greg Mathews, p	1.000	2	2	0	2	0	0	0	2	0	0	0
Willie McGee, of	.308	7	26	2	8	1	1	0	2	0	5	0
John Morris, of	.000	2	3	0	0	0	0	0	0	0	0	0
Jose Oquendo, of-5,3b-1	.167	5	12	3	2	0	0	1	4	3	2	0
Tom Pagnozzi, ph	.000	1	1	0	0	0	0	0	0	0	0	0
Tony Pena, c	.381	7	21	5	8	0	1	0	3	4	1	0
Terry Pendleton, 3b	.211	6	19	3	4	0	1	0	1	0	6	0
Ozzie Smith, ss	.200	7	25	2	5	0	1	0	1	3	4	0
John Tudor, p	.000	2	4	0	0	0	0	0	0	0	4	0
Todd Worrell, p-3,of-1	.000	3	1	0	0	0	0	0	0	0	1	0
TOTAL	.260		215	23	56	4	4	2	22	16	42	4

PITCHER	W	L	ERA	G	GS	CG	SV	SHO	IP	H	ER	BB	SO
Danny Cox	1	1	2.12	2	2	2	0	1	17.0	17	4	3	11
Ken Dayley	0	0	0.00	3	0	0	2	0	4.0	1	0	2	4
Bob Forsch	1	1	12.00	3	0	0	0	0	3.0	4	4	1	3
Rick Horton	0	0	0.00	1	0	0	0	0	3.0	2	0	0	2
Joe Magrane	0	0	9.00	1	1	0	0	0	4.0	4	4	2	3
Greg Mathews	1	0	3.48	2	2	0	0	0	10.1	6	4	3	10
John Tudor	1	1	1.76	2	2	0	0	0	15.1	16	3	5	12
Todd Worrell	0	0	2.08	3	0	0	1	0	4.1	4	1	1	6
TOTAL	4	3	2.95	17	7	2	3	1	61.0	54	20	17	51

SF (W)

PLAYER/POS	AVG	G	AB	R	H	2B	3B	HR	RB	BB	SO	SB
Mike Aldrete, of-3	.100	5	10	1	1	0	0	0	1	0	2	0
Bob Brenly, c	.235	6	17	3	4	1	0	1	2	3	7	0
Will Clark, 1b	.360	7	25	3	9	2	0	1	3	3	6	1
Chili Davis, of	.150	6	20	2	3	1	0	0	0	1	4	0
Kelly Downs, p	.000	1	0	0	0	0	0	0	0	0	0	0
Dave Dravecky, p	.167	2	6	0	1	0	0	0	0	0	1	0
Scott Garrelts, p	.000	2	0	0	0	0	0	0	0	0	0	0
Atlee Hammaker, p	.000	2	3	0	0	0	0	0	0	0	2	0
Mike Krukow, p	.000	1	0	0	0	0	0	0	0	1	0	0
Mike LaCoss, p	.000	2	0	0	0	0	0	0	0	0	0	0
Craig Lefferts, p	.000	3	0	0	0	0	0	0	0	0	0	0
Jeffrey Leonard, of	.417	7	24	5	10	0	0	4	5	3	4	0
Candy Maldonado, of	.211	5	19	2	4	1	0	0	2	0	3	0
Bob Melvin, c-2	.429	3	7	0	3	0	0	0	0	1	1	0
Eddie Milner, of-4	.143	6	7	0	1	0	0	0	0	0	3	0
Kevin Mitchell, 3b	.267	7	30	2	8	1	0	1	2	0	3	1
Joe Price, p	.000	2	1	0	0	0	0	0	0	0	1	0
Rick Reuschel, p	.000	2	2	0	0	0	0	0	0	0	1	0
Don Robinson, p	.000	3	0	0	0	0	0	0	0	0	0	0
Chris Speier, 2b-1	.000	3	5	0	0	0	0	0	0	0	2	0
Harry Spilman, ph	.500	3	2	1	1	0	0	1	1	0	0	0
Rob Thompson, 2b-6	.100	7	20	4	2	0	1	1	2	5	7	2
Jose Uribe, ss	.269	7	26	1	7	1	0	0	2	0	4	1
TOTAL	.239		226	23	54	7	1	9	20	17	51	5

PITCHER	W	L	ERA	G	GS	CG	SV	SHO	IP	H	ER	BB	SO
Kelly Downs	0	0	0.00	1	0	0	0	0	1.1	1	0	0	0
Dave Dravecky	1	1	0.60	2	2	1	0	1	15.0	7	1	4	14
Scott Garrelts	0	0	6.75	2	0	0	0	0	2.2	2	2	4	4
Atlee Hammaker	0	1	7.87	2	2	0	0	0	8.0	12	7	0	7
Mike Krukow	1	0	2.00	1	1	1	0	0	9.0	9	2	1	3
Mike LaCoss	0	0	0.00	2	0	0	0	0	3.1	1	0	3	2
Craig Lefferts	0	0	0.00	3	0	0	0	0	2.0	3	0	1	0
Joe Price	1	0	0.00	2	0	0	0	0	5.2	3	0	1	7
Rick Reuschel	0	1	6.30	2	2	0	0	0	10.0	15	7	2	2
Don Robinson	0	1	9.00	3	0	0	0	0	3.0	3	3	0	3
TOTAL	3	4	3.30	20	7	2	0	1	60.0	56	22	16	42

GAME 1 AT STL OCT 6

SF	100	100	010	3	7	1
STL	001	103	00X	5	10	1

Pitchers: REUSCHEL, Lefferts (7), Garrelts (8) vs MATHEWS, Worrell (8), Dayley (8)
Home Runs: Leonard-SF
Attendance: 55,331

GAME 2 AT STL OCT 7

SF	020	100	020	5	10	0
STL	000	000	000	0	2	1

Pitchers: DRAVECKY vs TUDOR, Forsch (9)
Home Runs: Clark-SF, Leonard-SF
Attendance: 55,331

GAME 3 AT SF OCT 9

STL	000	002	400	6	11	1
SF	031	000	001	5	7	1

Pitchers: Magrane, FORSCH (5), Worrell (7) vs Hammaker, D.ROBINSON (7), Lefferts (7), LaCoss (8)
Home Runs: Lindeman-STL, Leonard-SF, Spilman-SF
Attendance: 57,913

GAME 4 AT SF OCT 10

STL	020	000	000	2	9	0
SF	000	120	01X	4	9	2

Pitchers: COX vs KRUKOW
Home Runs: Thompson-SF, Leonard-SF, Brenly-SF
Attendance: 57,997

GAME 5 AT SF OCT 11

STL	101	100	000	3	7	0
SF	101	400	00X	6	7	1

Pitchers: Mathews, FORSCH (4), Horton (4), Dayley (7) vs Reuschel, PRICE (5)
Home Runs: Mitchell-SF
Attendance: 59,363

GAME 6 AT STL OCT 13

SF	000	000	000	0	6	0
STL	010	000	00X	1	5	0

Pitchers: DRAVECKY, D.Robinson (7) vs TUDOR, Worrell (8), Dayley (9)
Attendance: 55,331

GAME 7 AT STL OCT 14

SF	000	000	000	0	8	1
STL	040	002	00X	6	12	0

Pitchers: HAMMAKER, Price (3), Downs (3), Garrelts (5), Lefferts (6), LaCoss (6), D.Robinson (8) vs COX
Home Runs: Oquendo-STL
Attendance: 55,331

The Tigers, with the best over-all won-lost record in the majors, were favored to defeat the ninth-ranked Twins, although Minnesota held the home field advantage and the major leagues' best record at home. Tiger pitcher Doyle Alexander—he had been 9–0 since joining Detroit in mid-August—took a 5–4 lead into the last of the eighth in Game One. But a single and double drove him out, and before the inning was over three more Twins had scored to sew up their first win. Detroit scored twice in the second inning the next day, but the Twins responded later in the inning with three runs, two on Tim Laudner's double off Tiger ace Jack Morris, and increased their lead in the fourth and fifth to seal Morris's first loss in Minnesota after eleven wins.

The Tigers won a game after the series moved to Detroit, when Pat Sheridan's two-run homer in the eighth inning of Game Three restored a lead they had squandered in the middle innings. But that was it for Detroit, as the Twins surprised everyone by subduing the Tigers in their den. In Game Four they took the lead for good on Greg Gagne's fourth-inning home run. And in Game Five, after initiating the scoring with four runs in the second, Minnesota pushed on to a 9–5 win and their first pennant in twenty-two years.

Minnesota Twins (West) 4; Detroit Tigers (East), 1

MIN (W)

PLAYER/POS	AVG	G	AB	R	H	2B	3B	HR	RB	BB	SO	SB
Keith Atherton, p	.000	1	0	0	0	0	0	0	0	0	0	0
Don Baylor, dh	.400	2	5	0	2	0	0	0	1	0	0	0
Juan Berenguer, p	.000	4	0	0	0	0	0	0	0	0	0	0
Bert Blyleven, p	.000	2	0	0	0	0	0	0	0	0	0	0
Tom Brunansky, of	.412	5	17	5	7	4	0	2	9	4	3	0
Randy Bush, dh	.250	4	12	4	3	0	1	0	2	3	2	3
Sal Butera, c	.667	1	3	0	2	0	0	0	0	0	0	0
Mark Davidson, pr	.000	1	0	0	0	0	0	0	0	0	0	0
Gary Gaetti, 3b	.300	5	20	5	6	1	0	2	5	5	1	3	0
Greg Gagne, ss	.278	5	18	5	5	3	0	2	3	3	4	0
Dan Gladden, of	.350	5	20	5	7	2	0	0	5	2	1	0
Kent Hrbek, 1b	.150	5	20	4	3	0	0	1	1	3	0	0
Gene Larkin, ph	1.000	1	1	0	1	1	0	0	1	0	0	0
Tim Laudner, c	.071	5	14	1	1	1	0	0	2	2	5	0
Steve Lombardozzi, 2b	.267	5	15	2	4	0	0	0	1	2	2	0
Al Newman, 2b	.000	1	2	0	0	0	0	0	0	0	0	0
Kirby Puckett, of	.208	5	24	3	5	1	0	1	3	0	5	1
Jeff Reardon, p	.000	4	0	0	0	0	0	0	0	0	0	0
Dan Schatzeder, p	.000	2	0	0	0	0	0	0	0	0	0	0
Les Straker, p	.000	1	0	0	0	0	0	0	0	0	0	0
Frank Viola, p	.000	2	0	0	0	0	0	0	0	0	0	0
TOTAL	.269		171	34	46	13	1	8	33	20	25	4

PITCHER	W	L	ERA	G	GS	CG	SV	SHO	IP	H	ER	BB	SO
Keith Atherton	0	0	0.00	1	0	0	0	0	0.1	1	0	0	0
Juan Berenguer	0	0	1.50	4	0	0	1	0	6.0	1	1	3	6
Bert Blyleven	2	0	4.05	2	2	0	0	0	13.1	12	6	3	9
Jeff Reardon	1	1	5.06	4	0	0	2	0	5.1	7	3	3	5
Dan Schatzeder	0	0	0.00	2	0	0	0	0	4.1	2	0	0	5
Les Straker	0	0	16.88	1	1	0	0	0	2.2	3	5	4	1
Frank Viola	1	0	5.25	2	2	0	0	0	12.0	14	7	5	9
TOTAL	4	1	4.50	16	5	0	3	0	44.0	40	22	18	35

DET (E)

PLAYER/POS	AVG	G	AB	R	H	2B	3B	HR	RB	BB	SO	SB
Doyle Alexander, p	.000	2	0	0	0	0	0	0	0	0	0	0
Dave Bergman, 1b-1,dh-1	.250	4	4	0	1	0	0	0	2	0	1	0
Tom Brookens, 3b	.000	5	13	0	0	0	0	0	0	0	3	0
Darrell Evans, 1b-5,3b-1	.294	5	17	0	5	0	0	0	0	4	2	0
Kirk Gibson, of	.286	5	21	4	6	1	0	1	4	3	8	3
Johnny Grubb, dh-1	.571	4	7	0	4	0	0	0	0	0	1	0
Mike Heath, c	.286	3	7	1	2	0	0	1	2	0	0	0
Mike Henneman, p	.000	3	0	0	0	0	0	0	0	0	0	0
Willie Hernandez, p	.000	1	0	0	0	0	0	0	0	0	0	0
Larry Herndon, of-2,dh-1	.333	3	9	1	3	0	0	0	2	1	1	0
Eric King, p	.000	2	0	0	0	0	0	0	0	0	0	0
Chet Lemon, of	.278	5	18	4	5	0	0	2	4	1	4	0
Bill Madlock, dh	.000	1	5	0	0	0	0	0	0	0	3	0
Jack Morris, p-1,dh-1	.000	2	0	1	0	0	0	0	0	0	0	0
Jim Morrison, 3b-1,dh-1	.400	2	5	1	2	0	0	0	0	0	1	0
Matt Nokes, c-3,dh-2	.143	5	14	2	2	0	0	1	2	1	4	0
Dan Petry, p	.000	1	0	0	0	0	0	0	0	0	0	0
Jeff Robinson, p	.000	1	0	0	0	0	0	0	0	0	0	0
Pat Sheridan, of-4	.300	5	10	2	3	1	0	1	2	0	2	1
Frank Tanana, p	.000	1	0	0	0	0	0	0	0	0	0	0
Walt Terrell, p	.000	1	0	0	0	0	0	0	0	0	0	0
Mark Thurmond, p	.000	1	0	0	0	0	0	0	0	0	0	0
Alan Trammell, ss	.200	5	20	3	4	1	0	0	2	1	2	0
Lou Whitaker, 2b	.176	5	17	4	3	0	0	0	1	1	3	1
TOTAL	.240		167	23	40	4	0	7	21	18	35	5

PITCHER	W	L	ERA	G	GS	CG	SV	SHO	IP	H	ER	BB	SO
Doyle Alexander	0	2	10.00	2	2	0	0	0	9.0	14	10	1	5
Mike Henneman	1	0	10.80	3	0	0	0	0	5.0	6	6	6	3
Willie Hernandez	0	0	0.00	1	0	0	0	0	0.1	2	0	0	0
Eric King	0	0	1.69	2	0	0	0	0	5.1	3	1	2	4
Jack Morris	0	1	6.75	1	1	1	0	0	8.0	6	6	3	7
Dan Petry	0	0	0.00	1	0	0	0	0	3.1	1	0	0	1
Jeff Robinson	0	0	0.00	1	0	0	0	0	0.1	1	0	0	0
Frank Tanana	0	1	5.06	1	1	0	0	0	5.1	6	3	4	1
Walt Terrell	0	1	9.00	1	1	0	0	0	6.0	7	6	4	4
Mark Thurmond	0	0	0.00	1	0	0	0	0	0.1	1	0	0	0
TOTAL	1	4	6.70	14	5	1	0	0	43.0	46	32	20	25

GAME 1 AT MIN OCT 7

DET   001 001 120   5 10 0
MIN   010 030 04X   8 10 0

Pitchers: ALEXANDER, Henneman (8), Hernandez (8), King (8) vs Viola, REARDON (8)
Home Runs: Heath-DET, Gibson-DET, Gaetti-MIN (2)
Attendance: 53,269

GAME 2 AT MIN OCT 8

DET   020 000 010   3 7 1
MIN   030 210 00X   6 6 0

Pitchers: MORRIS vs BLYLEVEN, Berenguer (8)
Home Runs: Lemon-DET, Whitaker-DET, Hrbek-MIN
Attendance: 55,245

GAME 3 AT DET OCT 10

MIN   000 202 200   6 8 1
DET   005 000 02X   7 7 0

Pitchers: Straker, Schatzeder (3), Berenguer (7), REARDON (8) vs Terrell, HENNEMAN (7)
Home Runs: Gagne-MIN, Brunansky-MIN, Sheridan-DET
Attendance: 49,730

GAME 4 AT DET OCT 11

MIN   001 111 010   5 7 1
DET   100 011 000   3 7 3

Pitchers: VIOLA, Atherton (6), Berenguer (6), Reardon (9) vs TANANA, Petry (6), Thurmond (9)
Home Runs: Puckett-MIN, Gagne-MIN
Attendance: 51,939

GAME 5 AT DET OCT 12

MIN   040 000 113   9 15 1
DET   000 300 011   5 9 1

Pitchers: BLYLEVEN, Schatzeder (7), Berenguer (8), Reardon (8) vs ALEXANDER, King (2), Henneman (7), Robinson (9)
Home Runs: Brunansky-MIN, Nokes-DET, Lemon-DET
Attendance: 47,448

Although the Twins compiled a dismal record on the road during the season (29–52), their play at home (56–25) topped the majors. In postseason play they won all six games played in their Metrodome, including the four that won them the world championship. They overwhelmed St. Louis in the Series opener, the first World Series game ever played indoors. The Cardinals scored first, in the second inning, but Twin ace Frank Viola (with relief from Keith Atherton in the ninth) stopped them after that as his teammates unloaded for seven runs in the fourth inning (capped by Dan Gladden's grand slam) on their way to a 10–1 win. The Cardinals scored four runs in Game Two, but again the Twins enjoyed a big fourth inning—bunching six of their ten hits together for six runs—and scored two other runs on homers by Gary Gaetti and Tim Laudner.

When the Series moved to St. Louis, the Cardinals grabbed the home advantage to post their three wins. In Game Three, Cardinal pitchers John Tudor and Todd Worrell combined for a five-hitter as the Cards came from behind with a three-run seventh to win 3–1. The next day St. Louis broke a 1–1 tie with their own fourth-inning explosion, for six runs. The big blow was a three-run homer by utility infielder Tom Lawless—only the second home run of his big league career. Final score: 7–2. After five scoreless innings in Game Five, St. Louis moved out to a 4–0 lead in the sixth and seventh innings. Gaetti's eighth-inning triple put two Minnesota runs across, but the Cards held on for a 4–2 win.

Back in Minneapolis, St. Louis built up a 5–2 lead in Game Six before the Twins retaliated with four runs in the fifth inning (with Don Baylor's three-run homer providing the tying runs) and four more an inning later on Kent Hrbek's grand slam. A final Twins run in the eighth ended the scoring at 11–5.

The Cardinals scored first in Game Seven, with a pair of runs in the second inning, but the Twins edged their way to a tie with single runs in the second and fifth, and an inning later took the lead on three walks and an infield single. As Twin starter Frank Viola held St. Louis scoreless on two hits after the second inning, Minnesota made the score 4–2 with a final run in the eighth, and ace reliever Jeff Reardon retired the Cards in order in the ninth to bring Minnesota its first world championship.

Minnesota Twins (AL) 4; St. Louis Cardinals (NL), 3

MIN (A)

PLAYER/POS	AVG	G	AB	R	H	2B	3B	HR	RB	BB	SO	SB
Keith Atherton, p	.000	2	0	0	0	0	0	0	0	0	0	0
Don Baylor, dh-3	.385	5	13	3	5	0	0	1	3	1	1	0
Juan Berenguer, p	.000	3	0	0	0	0	0	0	0	0	0	0
Bert Blyleven, p	.000	2	1	0	0	0	0	0	0	0	1	0
Tom Brunansky, of	.200	7	25	5	5	0	0	0	2	4	4	1
Randy Bush, dh-2	.167	4	6	1	1	1	0	0	2	0	1	0
Sal Butera, c	.000	1	0	0	0	0	0	0	0	0	0	0
Mark Davidson, of-1	.000	2	0	0	0	0	0	0	0	0	0	0
George Frazier, p	.000	1	0	0	0	0	0	0	0	0	0	0
Gary Gaetti, 3b	.259	7	27	4	7	2	1	1	4	2	5	2
Greg Gagne, ss	.200	7	30	5	6	1	0	1	3	1	6	0
Dan Gladden, of	.290	7	31	3	9	2	1	1	7	3	4	2
Kent Hrbek, 1b-1,dh-1	.208	7	24	4	5	0	0	1	6	5	3	0
Gene Larkin, 1b-1,dh-1	.000	5	3	1	0	0	0	0	0	1	0	0
Tim Laudner, c	.318	7	22	4	7	1	0	1	4	5	3	0
Steve Lombardozzi, 2b	.412	6	17	3	7	1	0	1	4	2	3	0
Al Newman, 2b-3	.200	4	5	0	1	0	0	0	0	1	1	0
Joe Niekro, p	.000	1	0	0	0	0	0	0	0	0	0	0
Kirby Puckett, of	.357	7	28	5	10	1	1	0	3	2	1	1
Jeff Reardon, p	.000	4	0	0	0	0	0	0	0	0	0	0
Dan Schatzeder, p	.000	3	0	0	0	0	0	0	0	0	0	0
Roy Smalley, ph	.500	4	2	0	1	1	0	0	0	0	2	0
Les Straker, p	.000	2	2	0	0	0	0	0	0	0	0	0
Frank Viola, p	.000	3	1	0	0	0	0	0	0	0	1	0
TOTAL	.269		238	38	64	10	3	7	38	29	36	6

PITCHER	W	L	ERA	G	GS	CG	SV	SHO	IP	H	ER	BB	SO
Keith Atherton	0	0	6.75	2	0	0	0	0	1.1	0	1	1	0
Juan Berenguer	0	1	10.38	3	0	0	0	0	4.1	10	5	0	1
Bert Blyleven	1	1	2.77	2	2	0	0	0	13.0	13	4	2	12
George Frazier	0	0	0.00	2	0	0	0	0	2.0	1	0	0	2
Joe Niekro	0	0	0.00	1	0	0	0	0	2.0	1	0	1	1
Jeff Reardon	0	0	0.00	4	0	0	1	0	4.2	5	0	3	3
Dan Schatzeder	1	0	6.23	3	0	0	0	0	4.1	4	3	3	3
Les Straker	0	0	4.00	2	2	0	0	0	9.0	9	4	3	6
Frank Viola	2	1	3.72	3	3	0	0	0	19.1	17	8	3	16
TOTAL	4	3	3.75	21	7	0	1	0	60.0	60	25	13	44

STL (N)

PLAYER/POS	AVG	G	AB	R	H	2B	3B	HR	RB	BB	SO	SB
Vince Coleman, of	.143	7	28	5	4	2	0	0	2	2	10	6
Danny Cox, p	.000	3	2	0	0	0	0	0	0	0	1	0
Ken Dayley, p	.000	4	1	0	0	0	0	0	0	0	1	0
Dan Driessen, 1b	.231	4	13	3	3	2	0	0	1	1	1	0
Curt Ford, of-4	.308	5	13	1	4	0	0	0	2	1	1	0
Bob Forsch, p	.000	3	2	0	0	0	0	0	0	0	0	0
Tommy Herr, 2b	.250	7	28	2	7	0	0	1	1	2	2	0
Rick Horton, p	.000	2	0	0	0	0	0	0	0	0	0	0
Lance Johnson, pr	.000	1	0	0	0	0	0	0	0	0	0	1
Steve Lake, c	.333	3	3	0	1	0	0	0	1	0	0	0
Tom Lawless, 3b	.100	3	10	1	1	0	0	1	3	0	4	0
Jim Lindeman, 1b-6,of-1	.333	6	15	3	5	1	0	0	2	0	3	0
Joe Magrane, p	.000	2	0	0	0	0	0	0	0	0	0	0
Greg Mathews, p	.000	1	1	0	0	0	0	0	0	0	0	0
Willie McGee, of	.370	7	27	2	10	2	0	0	4	0	9	0
John Morris, of	.000	2	0	0	0	0	0	0	0	0	0	0
Jose Oquendo, 3b-4,of-3	.250	7	24	2	6	0	0	0	2	1	4	0
Tom Pagnozzi, dh-1	.250	2	4	0	1	0	0	0	0	0	0	0
Tony Pena, c-6,dh-1	.409	7	22	2	9	1	0	0	4	3	2	1
Terry Pendleton, dh-2	.429	3	7	2	3	0	0	0	1	1	1	2
Ozzie Smith, ss	.214	7	28	3	6	0	0	0	2	2	3	2
John Tudor, p	.000	2	3	0	0	0	0	0	0	0	2	0
Lee Tunnell, p	.000	2	0	0	0	0	0	0	0	0	0	0
Todd Worrell, p	.000	4	0	0	0	0	0	0	0	0	0	0
TOTAL	.259		232	26	60	8	0	2	25	13	44	12

PITCHER	W	L	ERA	G	GS	CG	SV	SHO	IP	H	ER	BB	SO
Danny Cox	1	2	7.71	3	2	0	0	0	11.2	13	10	8	9
Ken Dayley	0	0	1.93	4	0	0	1	0	4.2	2	1	0	3
Bob Forsch	1	0	9.95	3	0	0	0	0	6.1	8	7	5	3
Rick Horton	0	0	6.00	2	0	0	0	0	3.0	5	2	0	1
Joe Magrane	0	1	8.59	2	2	0	0	0	7.1	9	7	5	5
Greg Mathews	0	0	2.45	1	1	0	0	0	3.2	2	1	2	3
John Tudor	1	1	5.73	2	2	0	0	0	11.0	15	7	3	8
Lee Tunnell	0	0	2.08	2	0	0	0	0	4.1	4	1	2	1
Todd Worrell	0	0	1.29	4	0	0	2	0	7.0	6	1	4	3
TOTAL	3	4	5.64	23	7	0	3	0	59.0	64	37	29	36

GAME 1 AT MIN OCT 17

STL	010	000	000	1	5	1
MIN	000	720	10X	10	11	0

Pitchers: MAGRANE, Forsch (4), Horton (7) vs VIOLA, Atherton (9)
Home Runs: Gladden-MIN, Lombardozzi-MIN
Attendance: 55,171

GAME 2 AT MIN OCT 18

STL	000	010	120	4	9	0
MIN	010	601	00X	8	10	0

Pitchers: COX, Tunnell (4), Dayley (7), Worrell (8) vs BLYLEVEN, Berenguer (8), Reardon (9)
Home Runs: Gaetti-MIN, Laudner-MIN
Attendance: 55,257

GAME 3 AT STL OCT 20

MIN	000	001	000	1	5	1
STL	000	000	30X	3	9	1

Pitchers: Straker, BERENGUER (7), Schatzeder (7) vs TUDOR, Worrell (8)
Attendance: 55,347

GAME 4 AT STL OCT 21

MIN	001	010	000	2	7	1
STL	001	600	00X	7	10	1

Pitchers: VIOLA, Schatzeder (4), Niekro (5), Frazier (7) vs Mathews, FORSCH (4), Dayley (7)
Home Runs: Gagne-MIN, Lawless-STL
Attendance: 55,347

GAME 5 AT STL OCT 22

MIN	000	000	020	2	6	1
STL	000	003	10X	4	10	0

Pitchers: BLYLEVEN, Atherton (7), Reardon (7) vs COX, Dayley (8), Worrell (8)
Attendance: 55,347

GAME 6 AT MIN OCT 24

STL	110	210	000	5	11	2
MIN	200	044	01X	11	15	0

Pitchers: TUDOR, Horton (5), Forsch (6), Dayley (6), Tunnell (7) vs Straker, SCHATZEDER (4), Berenguer (6), Reardon (9)
Home Runs: Herr-STL, Baylor-MIN, Hrbek-MIN
Attendance: 55,293

GAME 7 AT MIN OCT 25

STL	020	000	000	2	6	1
MIN	010	011	01X	4	10	0

Pitchers: Magrane, COX (5), Worrell (6) vs VIOLA, Reardon (9)
Attendance: 55,376

The Mets had defeated the Dodgers in 10 of 11 regular season games, but in the LCS the pitching of Dodger ace Orel Hershiser and rookie Tim Belcher, and the timely hitting of Mike Scioscia and Kirk Gibson, propelled L.A. to the pennant. The Dodgers scored a first-inning run in the opener and carried a 2–0 lead into the ninth. But three Met runs in the top of the ninth (the final two scoring with two outs on a fly to short center that bounced off the glove of a diving John Shelby) gave New York the victory.

Dodger pitcher Tim Belcher singled with two away in the second inning of Game Two to start a four-run rally—the margin of victory in Belcher's 6–3 win. In Game Three (played in a steady downpour after a rainout the night before), the Mets overcame a 4–3 deficit, rapping four Dodger pitchers for five runs in the last of the eighth to take the series lead.

Kirk Gibson's twelfth-inning solo homer the next night put the Dodgers ahead 5–4, after Mike Scioscia's ninth-inning home run had pulled them into a tie. In the last of the twelfth, Orel Hershiser (who had pitched seven innings to no decision in the previous game) took the mound with two out and the bases full, and saved the game as center fielder Shelby, on the run, snared Kevin McReynolds' looping fly.

Gibson homered again in Game Four—for three runs that provided the winning margin in a 7–4 Dodger victory. One game from the pennant, as the series moved back to Los Angeles, the Dodgers for the first time failed to score first and saw the series evened a third time as David Cone held them to five hits and one run while the Mets scored five. But in the finale, the Dodgers unloaded on Ron Darling for six runs in the first two innings and Hershiser blanked the Mets on five hits.

Los Angeles Dodgers (West), 4; New York Mets (East), 3

LA (W)

PLAYER/POS	AVG	G	AB	R	H	2B	3B	HR	RB	BB	SO	SB
Tim Belcher, p	.125	2	8	1	1	0	0	0	0	0	3	0
Mike Davis, ph	.000	4	2	0	0	0	0	0	0	1	0	0
Rick Dempsey, c-3	.400	4	5	1	2	2	0	0	2	1	0	0
Kirk Gibson, of	.154	7	26	2	4	0	0	2	6	3	6	2
Jose Gonzalez, of-4	.000	5	0	2	0	0	0	0	0	0	0	0
Alfredo Griffin, ss	.160	7	25	1	4	1	0	0	3	0	5	0
Jeff Hamilton, 3b	.217	7	23	2	5	0	0	0	1	3	4	0
Mickey Hatcher, 1b-6,of-1	.238	6	21	4	5	2	0	0	3	3	0	0
Danny Heep, ph	.000	3	1	0	0	0	0	0	0	1	1	0
Orel Hershiser, p	.000	4	9	1	0	0	0	0	0	1	2	0
Brian Holton, p	1.000	3	1	1	1	0	0	0	0	0	0	0
Rick Horton, p	.000	4	0	0	0	0	0	0	0	0	0	0
Jay Howell, p	.000	2	0	0	0	0	0	0	0	0	0	0
Tim Leary, p	.000	2	1	0	0	0	0	0	0	0	0	0
Mike Marshall, of	.233	7	30	3	7	1	1	0	5	2	9	0
Jesse Orosco, p	.000	4	0	0	0	0	0	0	0	0	0	0
Alejandro Pena, p	.000	3	0	0	0	0	0	0	0	0	0	0
Steve Sax, 2b	.267	7	30	7	8	0	0	0	3	3	3	0
Mike Scioscia, c	.364	7	22	3	8	1	0	1	2	1	2	0
Mike Sharperson, ss-1,3b-1	.000	2	1	0	0	0	0	0	0	1	1	0
John Shelby, of	.167	7	24	3	4	0	0	0	3	5	12	2
Franklin Stubbs, 1b-3	.250	4	8	0	2	0	0	0	0	0	4	0
John Tudor, p	.000	1	2	0	0	0	0	0	0	0	2	0
Tracy Woodson, 1b	.250	3	4	0	1	0	0	0	0	0	1	0
TOTAL	.214		243	31	52	7	1	3	30	25	54	9

PITCHER	W	L	ERA	G	GS	CG	SV	SHO	IP	H	ER	BB	SO
Tim Belcher	2	0	4.11	2	2	0	0	0	15.1	12	7	4	16
Orel Hershiser	1	0	1.09	4	3	1	1	1	24.2	18	3	7	15
Brian Holton	0	0	2.25	3	0	0	1	0	4.0	2	1	1	2
Rick Horton	0	0	0.00	4	0	0	0	0	4.1	4	0	2	3
Jay Howell	0	1	27.00	2	0	0	0	0	0.2	1	2	2	1
Tim Leary	0	1	6.23	2	1	0	0	0	4.1	8	3	3	3
Jesse Orosco	0	0	7.71	4	0	0	0	0	2.1	4	2	3	0
Alejandro Pena	1	1	4.15	3	0	0	1	0	4.1	1	2	5	1
John Tudor	0	0	7.20	1	1	0	0	0	5.0	8	4	1	1
TOTAL	4	3	3.32	25	7	1	3	1	65.0	58	24	28	42

NY (E)

PLAYER/POS	AVG	G	AB	R	H	2B	3B	HR	RB	BB	SO	SB
Rick Aguilera, p	.000	3	1	0	0	0	0	0	0	0	1	0
Wally Backman, 2b	.273	7	22	2	6	1	0	0	2	2	5	1
Gary Carter, c	.222	7	27	0	6	1	1	0	4	1	3	0
David Cone, p	.000	3	4	0	0	0	0	0	0	0	0	0
Ron Darling, p-2	.000	2	3	0	0	0	0	0	0	0	2	0
Lennie Dykstra, of	.429	7	14	6	6	3	0	1	3	4	0	0
Kevin Elster, ss	.250	5	8	1	2	1	0	0	1	3	0	0
Sid Fernandez, p	.000	1	1	0	0	0	0	0	0	0	0	0
Dwight Gooden, p	.200	3	5	0	1	0	0	0	0	0	2	0
Keith Hernandez, 1b	.269	7	26	2	7	0	0	1	5	6	7	1
Gregg Jefferies, 3b	.333	7	27	2	9	2	0	0	1	4	0	0
Howard Johnson, ss-5,3b-1	.056	6	18	3	1	0	0	0	0	1	6	1
Terry Leach, p	.000	3	0	0	0	0	0	0	0	0	0	0
Dave Magadan, ph	.000	3	3	0	0	0	0	0	0	0	2	0
Lee Mazzilli, ph	.500	3	2	0	1	0	0	0	0	0	0	1
Roger McDowell, p	.000	4	0	0	0	0	0	0	0	0	0	0
Kevin McReynolds, of	.250	7	28	4	7	2	0	2	4	3	5	2
Randy Myers, p	.000	5	0	0	0	0	0	0	0	0	0	0
Mackey Sasser, c-1	.200	4	5	0	1	0	0	0	0	0	1	0
Darryl Strawberry, of	.300	7	30	5	9	2	0	1	6	2	5	0
Tim Teufel, 2b	.000	2	1	0	0	0	0	0	0	0	1	0
Mookie Wilson, of-3	.154	4	13	2	2	0	0	0	1	2	2	0
TOTAL	.242		240	27	58	12	1	5	27	28	42	6

PITCHER	W	L	ERA	G	GS	CG	SV	SHO	IP	H	ER	BB	SO
Rick Aguilera	0	0	1.29	3	0	0	0	0	7.0	3	1	2	4
David Cone	1	1	4.50	3	2	1	0	0	12.0	10	6	5	9
Ron Darling	0	1	7.71	2	2	0	0	0	7.0	11	6	4	7
Sid Fernandez	0	1	13.50	1	1	0	0	0	4.0	7	6	1	5
Dwight Gooden	0	0	2.95	3	2	0	0	0	18.1	10	6	8	20
Terry Leach	0	0	0.00	3	0	0	0	0	5.0	4	0	1	4
Roger McDowell	0	1	4.50	4	0	0	0	0	6.0	6	3	2	5
Randy Myers	2	0	0.00	5	0	0	0	0	4.2	1	0	2	0
TOTAL	3	4	3.94	22	7	1	0	0	64.0	52	28	25	54

Jose Canseco's three home runs and Dennis Eckersley's sparkling relief pitching highlighted Oakland's sweep to the pennant. In his six shutout innings, Eckersley gave up just one hit and a pair of walks while fanning five, to record an LCS record four saves.

Canseco's fourth-inning solo shot off the Sox' Bruce Hurst put the A's out in front in Game One. Boston tied it up in the seventh, but two former Boston players—Carney Lansford, who doubled, and Dave Henderson, who singled him home—put Oakland back in front in the eighth, and Eckersley (also an ex-Bostonian) held the Sox through the final two innings.

Oakland's Storm Davis and Boston's Roger Clemens dueled scorelessly through five innings of Game Two. The Sox took advantage of an Oakland error to score twice in the sixth, but four Oakland hits in the seventh (including a two-run homer by Canseco), a balk, and a wild pitch put the A's up 3–2. Rich Gedman's home run for Boston in the last of the seventh tied the score, but in the ninth Oakland's rookie shortstop Walt Weiss singled home what proved the game winner off Sox ace reliever Lee Smith.

Boston unloaded for five runs in the first two innings of Game Three. But Weiss's double and home runs by Mark McGwire and Carney Lansford in the last of the second brought the A's within one run of a tie, and Ron Hassey's two-run homer an inning later gave the A's a lead that they held to the end. Dave Henderson's two-run blast in the eighth capped the A's 10–6 victory.

Canseco's first-inning homer in Game Four put the A's ahead to stay, as starter Dave Stewart and relievers Rick Honeycutt and Eckersley combined for a four-hit, 4–1 pennant clincher.

Oakland Athletics (West), 4;
Boston Red Sox (East), 0

OAK (W)

PLAYER/POS	AVG	G	AB	R	H	2B	3B	HR	RB	BB	SO	SB
Don Baylor, dh	.000	2	6	0	0	0	0	0	0	1	2	0
Greg Cadaret, p	.000	1	0	0	0	0	0	0	0	0	0	0
Jose Canseco, of	.313	4	16	4	5	1	0	3	4	1	2	1
Storm Davis, p	.000	1	0	0	0	0	0	0	0	0	0	0
Dennis Eckersley, p	.000	4	0	0	0	0	0	0	0	0	0	0
Mike Gallego, 2b	.083	4	12	1	1	0	0	0	0	0	3	0
Ron Hassey, c	.500	4	8	2	4	1	0	1	3	1	1	0
Dave Henderson, of	.375	4	16	2	6	1	0	1	4	1	7	0
Rick Honeycutt, p	.000	3	0	0	0	0	0	0	0	0	0	0
Stan Javier, of	.500	2	4	0	2	0	0	0	1	1	0	0
Carney Lansford, 3b	.294	4	17	4	5	1	0	1	2	0	2	0
Mark McGwire, 1b	.333	4	15	4	5	0	0	1	3	1	5	0
Gene Nelson, p	.000	2	0	0	0	0	0	0	0	0	0	0
Dave Parker, dh-2,of-1	.250	3	12	1	3	1	0	0	0	0	4	0
Tony Phillips, of-2,2b-1	.286	2	7	0	2	1	0	0	0	1	4	0
Eric Plunk, p	.000	1	0	0	0	0	0	0	0	0	0	0
Luis Polonia, of-1	.400	3	5	0	2	0	0	0	0	1	1	0
Terry Steinbach, c	.250	2	4	0	1	0	0	0	0	2	0	0
Dave Stewart, p	.000	2	0	0	0	0	0	0	0	0	0	0
Walt Weiss, ss	.333	4	15	2	5	2	0	0	2	0	4	0
Bob Welch, p	.000	1	0	0	0	0	0	0	0	0	0	0
Curt Young, p	.000	1	0	0	0	0	0	0	0	0	0	0
TOTAL	.299		137	20	41	8	0	7	20	10	35	1

PITCHER	W	L	ERA	G	GS	CG	SV	SHO	IP	H	ER	BB	SO
Greg Cadaret	0	0	27.00	1	0	0	0	0	0.1	1	1	0	0
Storm Davis	0	0	0.00	1	1	0	0	0	6.1	2	0	5	4
Dennis Eckersley	0	0	0.00	4	0	0	4	0	6.0	1	0	2	5
Rick Honeycutt	1	0	0.00	3	0	0	0	0	2.0	0	0	2	0
Gene Nelson	2	0	0.00	2	0	0	0	0	4.2	5	0	1	0
Eric Plunk	0	0	0.00	1	0	0	0	0	0.1	1	0	0	1
Dave Stewart	1	0	1.35	2	2	0	0	0	13.1	9	2	6	11
Bob Welch	0	0	27.00	1	1	0	0	0	1.2	6	5	2	0
Curt Young	0	0	0.00	1	0	0	0	0	1.1	1	0	0	2
TOTAL	4	0	2.00	16	4	0	4	0	36.0	26	8	18	23

BOS (E)

PLAYER/POS	AVG	G	AB	R	H	2B	3B	HR	RB	BB	SO	SB
Marty Barrett, 2b	.067	4	15	2	1	0	0	0	0	1	0	0
Todd Benzinger, 1b-3	.091	4	11	0	1	0	0	0	0	1	3	0
Mike Boddicker, p	.000	1	0	0	0	0	0	0	0	0	0	0
Wade Boggs, 3b	.385	4	13	2	5	0	0	0	3	3	4	0
Ellis Burks, of	.235	4	17	2	4	1	0	0	1	0	3	0
Roger Clemens, p	.000	1	0	0	0	0	0	0	0	0	0	0
Dwight Evans, of	.167	4	12	1	2	1	0	0	1	3	5	0
Wes Gardner, p	.000	1	0	0	0	0	0	0	0	0	0	0
Rich Gedman, c	.357	4	14	1	5	0	0	1	1	2	1	0
Mike Greenwell, of	.214	4	14	2	3	1	0	1	3	3	0	0
Bruce Hurst, p	.000	2	0	0	0	0	0	0	0	0	0	0
Spike Owen, dh	.000	1	0	0	0	0	0	0	0	1	0	0
Larry Parrish, 1b-2	.000	4	6	0	0	0	0	0	0	0	2	0
Jody Reed, ss	.273	4	11	0	3	1	0	0	0	2	1	0
Jim Rice, dh	.154	4	13	0	2	0	0	0	1	2	4	0
Ed Romero, pr	.000	1	0	0	0	0	0	0	0	0	0	0
Kevin Romine, pr	.000	2	0	1	0	0	0	0	0	0	0	0
Lee Smith, p	.000	2	0	0	0	0	0	0	0	0	0	0
Mike Smithson, p	.000	1	0	0	0	0	0	0	0	0	0	0
Bob Stanley, p	.000	2	0	0	0	0	0	0	0	0	0	0
TOTAL	.206		126	11	26	4	0	2	10	18	23	0

PITCHER	W	L	ERA	G	GS	CG	SV	SHO	IP	H	ER	BB	SO
Mike Boddicker	0	1	20.25	1	1	0	0	0	2.2	8	6	1	2
Roger Clemens	0	0	3.86	1	1	0	0	0	7.0	6	3	0	8
Wes Gardner	0	0	5.79	1	0	0	0	0	4.2	6	3	2	8
Bruce Hurst	0	2	2.77	2	2	1	0	0	13.0	10	4	5	12
Lee Smith	0	1	8.10	2	0	0	0	0	3.1	6	3	1	4
Mike Smithson	0	0	0.00	1	0	0	0	0	2.1	3	0	0	1
Bob Stanley	0	0	9.00	2	0	0	0	0	1.0	2	1	1	0
TOTAL	0	4	5.29	10	4	1	0	0	34.0	41	20	10	35

GAME 1 AT BOS OCT 5

OAK	000	100	010	2	6	0
BOS	000	000	100	1	6	0

Pitchers: Stewart, HONEYCUTT (7), Eckersley (8) vs HURST
Home Runs: Canseco-OAK
Attendance: 34,104

GAME 2 AT BOS OCT 6

OAK	000	000	301	4	10	1
BOS	000	002	100	3	4	1

Pitchers: Davis, Cadaret (7), NELSON (7), vs Clemens, Stanley (8), SMITH (8)
Home Runs: Canseco-OAK, Gedman-BOS
Attendance: 34,605

GAME 3 AT OAK OCT 8

BOS	320	000	100	6	12	0
OAK	042	010	12X	10	15	1

Pitchers: BODDICKER, Gardner (3), Stanley (8) vs Welch, NELSON (2), Young (6), Plunk (7), Honeycutt (7), Eckersley (8)
Home Runs: Greenwell-BOS, McGwire-OAK, Lansford-OAK, Hassey-OAK, Henderson-OAK
Attendance: 49,261

GAME 4 AT OAK OCT 9

BOS	000	001	000	1	4	0
OAK	101	000	02X	4	10	1

Pitchers: HURST, Smithson (5), Smith (7) vs STEWART, Honeycutt (8), Eckersley (9)
Home Runs: Canseco-OAK
Attendance: 49,406

Mickey Hatcher's home run in the first inning of Game One set the tone for the Dodgers' surprising triumph over Oakland's mighty A's. Hatcher, who homered only once during the season, initiated the Series scoring with a two-run blast to left center. Half an inning later the A's Jose Canseco—baseball's leading slugger, with 42 season homers—erased the Dodger lead with his first career grand slam. But while Hatcher went on to hit safely six more times in the Series—including another home run—Canseco's first hit was also his last, as he went 0 for 19 the rest of the way. The Dodgers scored once in the sixth inning to draw within one run of a tie, but remained behind until the last of the ninth when, with two out and one on, Kirk Gibson pinch hit for pitcher Alejandro Peña. Gibson, the Dodgers' top source of power during the season, was so hobbled by leg injuries that he had, till that moment, sat out the game in the training room. But with two strikes on him he belted a home run off baseball's premier reliever, Dennis Eckersley, to win the game. It was Gibson's only Series appearance.

Dodger ace Orel Hershiser blanked the A's on three hits in Game Two and led the offense with three hits of his own. His single in the third inning began a five-run Dodger rally (capped by Mike Marshall's three-run homer), and his fourth-inning double drove in the Dodgers' sixth and final run.

When the Series moved to Oakland, the A's recovered for a dramatic win in Game Three, as Mark McGwire (who had homered 32 times during the season) broke a 1–1 tie with his only Series hit, a solo homer in the last of the ninth. In Game Four, Dodger reliever Jay Howell, who had yielded the losing home run the day before, got McGwire to pop up with the bases full to end the seventh inning, and blanked the A's the rest of the way to preserve a narrow 4–3 Dodger victory.

Hershiser returned to pitch Game Five. He allowed two runs in his four-hitter, but Mickey Hatcher had given the Dodgers the lead with a two-run homer in the first inning, and Mike Davis (who had homered just twice during the season) drove a 3–0 pitch into the stands for two more runs in the fourth. Veteran catcher Rick Dempsey (substituting for injured first-stringer Mike Scioscia) doubled home a fifth Los Angeles run in the sixth, and the Dodgers were on their way to a seventh world title.

Los Angeles Dodgers (NL), 4; Oakland Athletics (AL), 1

LA (N)

PLAYER/POS	AVG	G	AB	R	H	2B	3B	HR	RB	BB	SO	SB
Dave Anderson, dh	.000	1	1	0	0	0	0	0	0	0	1	0
Tim Belcher, p	.000	2	0	0	0	0	0	0	0	0	0	0
Mike Davis, dh-2,of-1	.143	4	7	3	1	0	0	2	2	4	0	2
Rick Dempsey, c	.200	2	5	0	1	1	0	0	1	1	2	0
Kirk Gibson, ph	1.000	1	1	1	1	0	0	1	2	0	0	0
Jose Gonzalez, of-3	.000	4	2	0	0	0	0	0	0	0	2	0
Alfredo Griffin, ss	.188	5	16	2	3	0	0	0	0	2	4	0
Jeff Hamilton, 3b	.105	5	19	1	2	0	0	0	0	1	4	0
Mickey Hatcher, of	.368	5	19	5	7	1	0	2	5	1	3	0
Danny Heep, of-1,dh-1	.250	3	8	0	2	1	0	0	0	0	2	0
Orel Hershiser, p	1.000	2	3	1	3	2	0	0	1	0	0	0
Brian Holton, p	.000	1	0	0	0	0	0	0	0	0	0	0
Jay Howell, p	.000	2	0	0	0	0	0	0	0	0	0	0
Tim Leary, p	.000	2	0	0	0	0	0	0	0	0	0	0
Mike Marshall, of	.231	5	13	2	3	0	1	1	3	0	5	0
Alejandro Pena, p	.000	2	0	0	0	0	0	0	0	0	0	0
Steve Sax, 2b	.300	5	20	3	6	0	0	0	0	1	1	1
Mike Scioscia, c	.214	4	14	0	3	0	0	0	1	0	2	0
John Shelby, of	.222	5	18	0	4	1	0	0	1	2	7	1
Franklin Stubbs, 1b	.294	5	17	3	5	2	0	0	2	1	3	0
John Tudor, p	.000	1	0	0	0	0	0	0	0	0	0	0
Tracy Woodson, 1b-3	.000	4	4	0	0	0	0	0	0	1	0	0
TOTAL	.246		167	21	41	8	1	6	19	13	36	4

PITCHER	W	L	ERA	G	GS	CG	SV	SHO	IP	H	ER	BB	SO
Tim Belcher	1	0	6.23	2	2	0	0	0	8.2	10	6	6	10
Orel Hershiser	2	0	1.00	2	2	2	0	1	18.0	7	2	6	17
Brian Holton	0	0	0.00	1	0	0	0	0	2.0	0	0	1	0
Jay Howell	0	1	3.38	2	0	0	1	0	2.2	3	1	1	2
Tim Leary	0	0	1.35	2	0	0	0	0	6.2	6	1	2	4
Alejandro Pena	1	0	0.00	2	0	0	0	0	5.0	2	0	1	7
John Tudor	0	0	0.00	1	1	0	0	0	1.1	0	0	1	1
TOTAL	4	1	2.03	12	5	2	1	1	44.1	28	10	17	41

OAK (A)

PLAYER/POS	AVG	G	AB	R	H	2B	3B	HR	RB	BB	SO	SB
Don Baylor, ph	.000	1	1	0	0	0	0	0	0	0	1	0
Todd Burns, p	.000	1	0	0	0	0	0	0	0	0	0	0
Greg Cadaret, p	.000	3	0	0	0	0	0	0	0	0	0	0
Jose Canseco, of	.053	5	19	1	1	0	0	1	5	2	5	1
Storm Davis, p	.000	2	1	0	0	0	0	0	0	0	1	0
Dennis Eckersley, p	.000	2	0	0	0	0	0	0	0	0	0	0
Mike Gallego, 2b	.000	1	0	0	0	0	0	0	0	0	0	0
Ron Hassey, c-4	.250	5	8	0	2	0	0	0	1	3	3	0
Dave Henderson, of	.300	5	20	1	6	2	0	0	1	2	7	0
Rick Honeycutt, p	.000	3	0	0	0	0	0	0	0	0	0	0
Glenn Hubbard, 2b	.250	4	12	2	3	0	0	0	0	1	2	1
Stan Javier, of-2	.500	3	4	0	2	0	0	0	2	0	1	0
Carney Lansford, 3b	.167	5	18	2	3	0	0	0	1	2	2	0
Mark McGwire, 1b	.059	5	17	1	1	0	0	1	1	3	4	0
Gene Nelson, p	.000	3	0	0	0	0	0	0	0	0	0	0
Dave Parker, of-2,dh-2	.200	4	15	0	3	0	0	0	0	2	4	0
Tony Phillips, 2b-1,of-1	.250	2	4	1	1	0	0	0	0	1	2	0
Eric Plunk, p	.000	2	0	0	0	0	0	0	0	0	0	0
Luis Polonia, of-2	.111	3	9	1	1	0	0	0	0	0	2	0
Terry Steinbach, c-2,dh-1	.364	3	11	0	4	1	0	0	0	0	2	0
Dave Stewart, p	.000	2	3	1	0	0	0	0	0	1	3	0
Walt Weiss, ss	.063	5	16	1	1	0	0	0	0	0	2	1
Bob Welch, p	.000	1	0	0	0	0	0	0	0	0	0	0
Curt Young, p	.000	1	0	0	0	0	0	0	0	0	0	0
TOTAL	.177		158	11	28	3	0	2	11	17	41	3

PITCHER	W	L	ERA	G	GS	CG	SV	SHO	IP	H	ER	BB	SO
Todd Burns	0	0	0.00	1	0	0	0	0	0.1	0	0	0	0
Greg Cadaret	0	0	0.00	3	0	0	0	0	2.0	2	0	0	3
Storm Davis	0	2	11.25	2	2	0	0	0	8.0	14	10	1	7
Dennis Eckersley	0	1	10.80	2	0	0	0	0	1.2	2	2	1	2
Rick Honeycutt	1	0	0.00	3	0	0	0	0	3.1	0	0	0	5
Gene Nelson	0	0	1.42	3	0	0	0	0	6.1	4	1	3	3
Eric Plunk	0	0	0.00	2	0	0	0	0	1.2	0	0	3	3
Dave Stewart	0	1	3.14	2	2	0	0	0	14.1	12	5	5	5
Bob Welch	0	0	1.80	1	1	0	0	0	5.0	6	1	3	8
Curt Young	0	0	0.00	1	0	0	0	0	1.0	1	0	0	0
TOTAL	1	4	3.92	20	5	0	0	0	43.2	41	19	13	36

GAME 1 AT LA OCT 15

OAK	040 000 000	4	7	0
LA	200 001 002	5	7	0

Pitchers: Stewart, ECKERSLEY (9) vs Belcher, Leary (3), Holton (6), PENA (8) Home Runs: Hatcher-LA, Canseco-OAK, Gibson-LA
Attendance: 55,983

GAME 2 AT LA OCT 16

OAK	000 000 000	0	3	0
LA	005 100 00X	6	10	1

Pitchers: DAVIS, Nelson (4), Young (6), Plunk (7), Honeycutt (8) vs HERSHISER
Home Runs: Marshall-LA
Attendance: 56,051

GAME 3 AT OAK OCT 18

LA	000 010 000	1	8	1
OAK	001 000 001	2	5	0

Pitchers: Tudor, Leary (2), Pena (6), J.HOWELL (9) vs Welch, Cadaret (6), Nelson (6), HONEYCUTT (8)
Home Runs: McGwire-OAK
Attendance: 49,316

GAME 4 AT OAK OCT 19

LA	201 000 100	4	8	1
OAK	100 001 100	3	9	2

Pitchers: BELCHER, J.Howell (7) vs STEWART, Cadaret (7), Eckersley (9)
Attendance: 49,317

GAME 5 AT OAK OCT 20

LA	200 201 000	5	8	0
OAK	001 000 010	2	4	0

Pitchers: HERSHISER vs DAVIS, Cadaret (5), Nelson (5), Honeycutt (8), Plunk (9), Burns (9)
Home Runs: Hatcher-LA, Davis-LA
Attendance: 49,317

From the first inning of Game 1 when they drove in their teams' first runs, first basemen Will Clark of the Giants and Mark Grace of the Cubs dominated the offense, finishing with eight RBIs apiece and LCS record-shattering BAs of .650 and .647. Although Grace homered for two Chicago runs in the opener, the game belonged to Clark, whose four hits—two of them home runs, one a grand slam—drove in six of the eleven Giant runs.

Grace led the Cubs' retaliation the next day with his second three-hit game, driving in four of Chicago's nine runs with doubles in the first and sixth innings. Kevin Mitchell, Matt Williams, and Robby Thompson—runners-up to Clark for Giant offensive honors in the series—all homered in the losing cause.

Chicago scored first in the next three games but narrowly lost them all. Thompson's two-run homer in the last of the seventh put the Giants ahead for good in Game 3. The next day, Williams's two-run single in the third inning overcame Chicago's lead, and his two-run homer in the fifth broke a 4–4 tie to conclude the scoring.

Cub starter Mike Bielecki stopped San Francisco on a pair of singles through six innings of Game 5, and carried a 1–0 lead into the seventh, when Clark's triple and Mitchell's sacrifice fly tied the score. An inning later, after Bielecki loaded the bases with three two-out walks, relief ace Mitch Williams was called on to face Clark and got two strikes on him. But after fouling off a slider and fastball, Clark lined a single up the middle for two go-ahead Giant runs. San Francisco closer Steve Bedrosian yielded Chicago a second run in the ninth on a trio of two-out singles, but Ryne Sandberg (until then batting .421 in the series) grounded out, and the Giants owned their first pennant in twenty-seven years.

San Francisco Giants (West), 4; Chicago Cubs (East), 1

SF (W)

PLAYER/POS	AVG	G	AB	R	H	2B	3B	HR	RB	BB	SO	SB
Bill Bathe, ph	.000	2	1	0	0	0	0	0	0	0	1	0
Steve Bedrosian, p	.000	4	0	0	0	0	0	0	0	0	0	0
Jeff Brantley, p	.000	3	0	0	0	0	0	0	0	1	0	0
Brett Butler, of	.211	5	19	6	4	0	0	0	0	3	3	0
Will Clark, 1b	.650	5	20	8	13	3	1	2	8	2	2	0
Kelly Downs, p	.000	2	3	0	0	0	0	0	0	0	1	0
Scott Garrelts, p	.000	2	4	0	0	0	0	0	0	1	1	0
Atlee Hammaker, p	.000	1	0	0	0	0	0	0	0	0	0	0
Terry Kennedy, c	.188	5	16	0	3	1	0	0	0	1	4	0
Mike LaCoss, p	.000	1	1	0	0	0	0	0	0	0	0	0
Craig Lefferts, p	.000	2	0	0	0	0	0	0	0	0	0	0
Greg Litton, 3b	1.000	1	1	0	1	0	0	0	0	0	0	0
Candy Maldonado, of	.000	3	3	1	0	0	0	0	1	2	0	0
Kirt Manwaring, c	.000	3	2	0	0	0	0	0	0	0	0	0
Kevin Mitchell, of	.353	5	17	5	6	0	0	2	7	3	3	0
Donell Nixon, of-2	.000	3	3	0	0	0	0	0	0	0	1	1
Ken Oberkfell, 3b-1	.000	3	4	0	0	0	0	0	0	0	0	0
Rick Reuschel, p	.000	2	5	0	0	0	0	0	0	0	0	0
Ernest Riles, ph	.000	1	1	0	0	0	0	0	0	0	0	0
Don Robinson, p	.000	1	0	0	0	0	0	0	0	0	0	0
Pat Sheridan, of	.154	5	13	1	2	0	1	0	0	0	4	0
Robby Thompson, 2b	.278	5	18	5	5	0	0	2	3	3	2	0
Jose Uribe, ss	.235	5	17	2	4	1	0	0	1	1	5	1
Matt Williams, 3b-5,ss-1	.300	5	20	2	6	1	0	2	9	0	2	0
TOTAL	.267		165	30	44	6	2	8	29	17	29	2

PITCHER	W	L	ERA	G	GS	CG	SV	SHO	IP	H	ER	BB	SO
Steve Bedrosian	0	0	2.70	4	0	0	3	0	3.1	4	1	2	2
Jeff Brantley	0	0	0.00	3	0	0	0	0	5.0	1	0	2	3
Kelly Downs	1	0	3.12	2	0	0	0	0	8.2	8	3	6	6
Scott Garrelts	1	0	5.40	2	2	0	0	0	11.2	16	7	2	8
Atlee Hammaker	0	0	0.00	1	0	0	0	0	1.0	1	0	0	0
Mike LaCoss	0	0	9.00	1	1	0	0	0	3.0	7	3	0	2
Craig Lefferts	0	0	9.00	2	0	0	0	0	1.0	1	1	2	1
Rick Reuschel	1	1	5.19	2	2	0	0	0	8.2	12	5	2	5
Don Robinson	1	0	0.00	1	0	0	0	0	1.2	3	0	0	0
TOTAL	4	1	4.09	18	5	0	3	0	44.0	53	20	16	27

CHI (E)

PLAYER/POS	AVG	G	AB	R	H	2B	3B	HR	RB	BB	SO	SB
Paul Assenmacher, p	.000	2	0	0	0	0	0	0	0	0	0	0
Mike Bielecki, p	.200	2	5	0	1	0	0	0	2	0	2	0
Andre Dawson, of	.105	5	19	0	2	1	0	0	3	2	6	0
Shawon Dunston, ss	.316	5	19	2	6	0	0	0	0	1	1	1
Joe Girardi, c	.100	4	10	1	1	0	0	0	0	1	2	0
Mark Grace, 1b	.647	5	17	3	11	3	1	1	8	4	1	1
Paul Kilgus, p	.000	1	0	0	0	0	0	0	0	0	0	0
Lester Lancaster, p	.000	3	1	0	0	0	0	0	0	0	1	0
Vance Law, 3b-1	.000	2	3	0	0	0	0	0	0	0	3	0
Greg Maddux, p-2	.000	3	3	1	0	0	0	0	0	0	0	0
L. McClendon, c-2,of-1	.667	3	3	0	2	0	0	0	1	0	0	0
Domingo Ramos, ph	.000	1	1	0	0	0	0	0	0	0	0	0
Luis Salazar, 3b	.368	5	19	2	7	0	1	1	2	0	0	0
Ryne Sandberg, 2b	.400	5	20	6	8	3	1	1	4	3	4	0
Scott Sanderson, p	.000	1	0	0	0	0	0	0	0	0	0	0
Dwight Smith, of	.200	4	15	2	3	1	0	0	0	2	2	1
Rick Sutcliffe, p	.500	1	2	0	1	1	0	0	0	0	0	0
Jerome Walton, of	.364	5	22	4	8	0	0	0	2	2	2	0
Mitch Webster, of-2	.333	3	3	0	1	0	0	0	0	0	0	0
Curtis Wilkerson, 3b-1	.500	3	2	1	1	0	0	0	0	0	0	0
Mitch Williams, p	.000	2	0	0	0	0	0	0	0	0	0	0
Steve Wilson, p	.000	2	0	0	0	0	0	0	0	0	3	0
Rick Wrona, c	.000	2	5	0	0	0	0	0	0	0	3	0
Marvell Wynne, of-2	.167	4	6	0	1	0	0	0	0	0	0	0
TOTAL	.303		175	22	53	9	3	3	21	16	27	3

PITCHER	W	L	ERA	G	GS	CG	SV	SHO	IP	H	ER	BB	SO
P. Assenmacher	0	0	13.50	2	0	0	0	0	0.2	3	1	0	0
Mike Bielecki	0	1	3.65	2	2	0	0	0	12.1	7	5	6	11
Paul Kilgus	0	0	0.00	1	0	0	0	0	3.0	4	0	1	1
Lester Lancaster	0	0	6.00	3	0	0	0	0	6.0	6	4	1	3
Greg Maddux	0	1	13.50	2	2	0	0	0	7.1	13	11	4	5
Scott Sanderson	0	0	0.00	1	0	0	0	0	2.0	2	0	0	1
Rick Sutcliffe	0	0	4.50	1	1	0	0	0	6.0	5	3	4	2
Mitch Williams	0	0	0.00	2	0	0	0	0	1.0	1	0	0	0
Steve Wilson	0	1	4.91	2	0	0	0	0	3.2	3	2	1	4
TOTAL	1	4	5.57	16	5	0	0	0	42.0	44	26	17	29

GAME 1 AT CHI OCT 4

SF	301	400	030	11	13 0
CHI	201	000	000	3	10 1

Pitchers: GARRELTS, Brantley (8), Hammaker (9) vs MADDUX, Kilgus (5), Wilson (8)
Home Runs: Grace-CHI, Clark-SF (2), Sandberg-CHI, Mitchell-SF
Attendance: 39,195

GAME 2 AT CHI OCT 5

SF	000	200	021	5	10 0
CHI	600	003	00X	9	11 0

Pitchers: REUSCHEL, Downs (1), Lefferts (6), Brantley (7), Bedrosian (8) vs Bielecki, Assenmacher (5), LANCASTER (6)
Home Runs: Mitchell-SF, Williams-SF, Thompson-SF
Attendance: 39,195

GAME 3 AT SF OCT 7

CHI	200	100	100	4	10 0
SF	300	000	20X	5	8 3

Pitchers: Sutcliffe, Assenmacher (7), LANCASTER (7) vs LaCoss, Brantley (4), ROBINSON (7), Lefferts (8), Bedrosian (9)
Home Runs: Thompson-SF
Attendance: 62,065

GAME 4 AT SF OCT 8

CHI	110	020	000	4	12 1
SF	102	120	00X	6	9 1

Pitchers: Maddux, WILSON (4), Sanderson (6), Williams (8) vs Garrelts, DOWNS (5), Bedrosian (9)
Home Runs: Salazar-CHI, Williams-SF
Attendance: 62,078

GAME 5 AT SF OCT 9

CHI	001	000	001	2	10 1
SF	000	000	12X	3	4 1

Pitchers: BIELECKI, Williams (8), Lancaster (8) vs REUSCHEL, Bedrosian (9)
Attendance: 62,084

The awesome A's produced their share of heroes. Jose Canseco powered a truly heroic home run into the top deck of Toronto's SkyDome in Game 4; Dave Parker, in his seventh postseason series, at last hit his first postseason homer (and later his second); closer Dennis Eckersley added three saves to his four from 1988 to establish a new LCS record; and Carney Lansford was batting .455, with four RBIs, when a hamstring pull in Game 3 ended his series play. But the hero of heroes was leadoff batter Rickey Henderson.

Oakland might have won the opener without Henderson, even though his hard slide into second in the sixth inning broke up a double play and forced a wide throw that gave the A's two runs and their first lead of the game. And the A's might also have won the next day even if Henderson had not rattled Toronto with four stolen bases. The A's suffered their loss in Game 3 despite an early 2–0 lead with Henderson scoring both runs—the first after walking, the second after a double and stolen base.

But in the final two games, Rickey Henderson's contribution made the difference between defeat and victory. A pair of two-run Henderson homers (together with Canseco's memorable blast and later RBI single) gave the A's their 6–5 win in Game 4. And in the first inning of Game 5, Henderson, after walking, stole his eighth base—a postseason series record—before Canseco singled him home with the A's first run. Two innings later Henderson tripled home the second Oakland run. The A's scored twice more in the seventh, but Toronto had narrowed Oakland's lead to one run when Eckersley fanned a final Blue Jay to secure the second straight Oakland pennant. Rickey Henderson was the unanimous choice for series MVP.

Oakland Athletics (West), 4; Toronto Blue Jays (East), 1

OAK (W)

PLAYER/POS	AVG	G	AB	R	H	2B	3B	HR	RB	BB	SO	SB
Lance Blankenship, 2b	.000	1	0	0	0	0	0	0	0	0	0	0
Jose Canseco, of	.294	5	17	1	5	0	0	1	3	3	7	0
Storm Davis, p	.000	1	0	0	0	0	0	0	0	0	0	0
Dennis Eckersley, p	.000	4	0	0	0	0	0	0	0	0	0	0
Mike Gallego, 2b-2,ss-2	.273	4	11	3	3	1	0	0	1	0	2	0
Ron Hassey, c	.167	2	6	0	1	0	0	0	1	1	2	0
Dave Henderson, of	.263	5	19	4	5	3	0	1	1	2	5	0
Rickey Henderson, of	.400	5	15	8	6	1	1	2	5	7	0	8
Rick Honeycutt, p	.000	3	0	0	0	0	0	0	0	0	0	0
Stan Javier, of	.000	1	2	0	0	0	0	0	0	0	1	0
Carney Lansford, 3b	.455	3	11	2	5	0	0	0	4	2	1	2
Mark McGwire, 1b	.389	5	18	3	7	1	0	1	3	1	4	0
Mike Moore, p	.000	1	0	0	0	0	0	0	0	0	0	0
Gene Nelson, p	.000	2	0	0	0	0	0	0	0	0	0	0
Dave Parker, dh	.188	4	16	2	3	0	0	2	3	0	6	0
Ken Phelps, ph	1.000	1	1	0	1	1	0	0	0	0	0	0
Tony Phillips, 2b-3,3b-3	.167	5	18	1	3	0	0	0	1	2	4	0
Terry Steinbach, c-3,dh-1	.200	4	15	0	3	0	0	0	1	1	5	0
Dave Stewart, p	.000	2	0	0	0	0	0	0	0	0	0	0
Walt Weiss, ss	.111	4	9	2	1	1	0	0	0	1	1	0
Bob Welch, p	.000	1	0	0	0	0	0	0	0	0	0	0
Matt Young, p	.000	1	0	0	0	0	0	0	0	0	0	0
TOTAL	.272		158	26	43	9	1	7	23	20	32	13

PITCHER	W	L	ERA	G	GS	CG	SV	SHO	IP	H	ER	BB	SO
Storm Davis	0	1	7.11	1	1	0	0	0	6.1	5	5	2	3
Dennis Eckersley	0	0	1.59	4	0	0	3	0	5.2	4	1	0	2
Rick Honeycutt	0	0	32.40	3	0	0	0	0	1.2	6	6	5	1
Mike Moore	1	0	0.00	1	1	0	0	0	7.0	3	0	2	3
Gene Nelson	0	0	0.00	2	0	0	0	0	1.1	1	0	0	2
Dave Stewart	2	0	2.81	2	2	0	0	0	16.0	13	5	3	9
Bob Welch	1	0	3.18	1	1	0	0	0	5.2	8	2	1	4
Matt Young	0	0	0.00	1	0	0	0	0	0.1	0	0	2	0
TOTAL	4	1	3.89	14	5	0	3	0	44.0	40	19	15	24

TOR (E)

PLAYER/POS	AVG	G	AB	R	H	2B	3B	HR	RB	BB	SO	SB
Jim Acker, p	.000	5	0	0	0	0	0	0	0	0	0	0
George Bell, dh-3,of-2	.200	5	20	2	4	0	0	1	2	0	3	0
Pat Borders, c	1.000	1	1	0	1	0	0	0	0	0	0	0
John Cerutti, p	.000	2	0	0	0	0	0	0	0	0	0	0
Junior Felix, of	.273	3	11	3	3	1	0	0	3	0	2	0
Tony Fernandez, ss	.350	5	20	6	7	3	0	0	1	1	2	5
Mike Flanagan, p	.000	1	0	0	0	0	0	0	0	0	0	0
Kelly Gruber, 3b	.294	5	17	2	5	1	0	0	1	3	2	1
Tom Henke, p	.000	3	0	0	0	0	0	0	0	0	0	0
Jimmy Key, p	.000	1	0	0	0	0	0	0	0	0	0	0
Manny Lee, 2b	.250	2	8	2	2	0	0	0	0	0	1	0
Nelson Liriano, 2b	.429	3	7	1	3	0	0	0	1	2	0	3
Lee Mazzilli, dh-2	.000	3	8	0	0	0	0	0	0	0	2	0
Fred McGriff, 1b	.143	5	21	1	3	0	0	0	0	3	4	0
Lloyd Moseby, of	.313	5	16	4	5	0	0	1	2	5	2	1
Rance Mulliniks, ph	.000	1	1	0	0	0	0	0	0	0	1	0
Dave Stieb, p	.000	2	0	0	0	0	0	0	0	0	0	0
Todd Stottlemyre, p	.000	1	0	0	0	0	0	0	0	0	0	0
Duane Ward, p	.000	2	0	0	0	0	0	0	0	0	0	0
David Wells, p	.000	1	0	0	0	0	0	0	0	0	0	0
Ernie Whitt, c	.125	5	16	1	2	0	0	1	3	2	3	0
Mookie Wilson, of	.263	5	19	2	5	0	0	0	2	2	2	1
TOTAL	.242		165	21	40	5	0	3	19	15	24	11

PITCHER	W	L	ERA	G	GS	CG	SV	SHO	IP	H	ER	BB	SO
Jim Acker	0	0	1.42	5	0	0	0	0	6.1	4	1	1	4
John Cerutti	0	0	0.00	2	0	0	0	0	2.2	0	0	3	1
Mike Flanagan	0	1	10.38	1	1	0	0	0	4.1	7	5	1	3
Tom Henke	0	0	0.00	3	0	0	0	0	2.2	0	0	0	3
Jimmy Key	1	0	4.50	1	1	0	0	0	6.0	7	3	2	2
Dave Stieb	0	2	6.35	2	2	0	0	0	11.1	12	8	6	10
Todd Stottlemyre	0	1	7.20	1	1	0	0	0	5.0	7	4	2	3
Duane Ward	0	0	7.36	2	0	0	0	0	3.2	6	3	3	5
David Wells	0	0	0.00	1	0	0	0	0	1.0	0	0	2	1
TOTAL	1	4	5.02	18	5	0	0	0	43.0	43	24	20	32

GAME 1 AT OAK OCT 3

TOR 020 100 000   3 5 1
OAK 010 013 02X   7 11 0

Pitchers: STIEB, Acker (6), Ward (8) vs STEWART, Eckersley (9)
Home Runs: D.Henderson-OAK, Whitt-TOR, McGwire-OAK
Attendance: 49,435

GAME 2 AT OAK OCT 4

TOR 001 000 020   3 5 1
OAK 000 203 10X   6 9 1

Pitchers: STOTTLEMYRE, Acker (6), Wells (6), Henke (7), Cerutti (8) vs MOORE, Honeycutt (8), Eckersley (8)
Home Runs: Parker-OAK
Attendance: 49,444

GAME 3 AT TOR OCT 6

OAK 101 100 000   3 8 1
TOR 000 400 30X   7 8 0

Pitchers: DAVIS, Honeycutt (7), Nelson (7), M.Young (8) vs KEY, Acker (7), Henke (9)
Home Runs: Parker-OAK
Attendance: 50,268

GAME 4 AT TOR OCT 7

OAK 003 020 100   6 11 1
TOR 000 101 120   5 13 0

Pitchers: WELCH, Honeycutt (6), Eckersley (8) vs FLANAGAN, Ward (5), Cerutti (8), Acker (9)
Home Runs: R.Henderson-OAK (2), Canseco-OAK
Attendance: 50,076

GAME 5 AT TOR OCT 8

OAK 101 000 200   4 4 0
TOR 000 000 012   3 9 0

Pitchers: STEWART, Eckersley (9) vs STIEB, Acker (7), Henke (9)
Home Runs: Moseby-TOR, Bell-TOR
Attendance: 50,024

Not even the devastating earthquake that blindsided baseball's first San Francisco Bay World Series could halt the Oakland juggernaut. The A's scored first in every game and, except for 1½ innings of Game 2 in which the score stood at 1–1, held their lead to the finish.

Athletic ace Dave Stewart shut out the Giants on five hits in the opener. Three second-inning Oakland runs initiated the Series scoring, and Dave Parker and Walt Weiss expanded Stewart's margin of comfort with solo homers in the third and fourth. In Game 2, doubles by Carney Lansford in the first inning and Parker in the fourth drove home the two runs the A's would need for victory; Terry Steinbach's three-run blast later in the fourth added frosting to Oakland's cake. A's starter Mike Moore yielded a pair of singles and the first Giant run of the Series in the third inning but held the Giants to just two more singles in his seven-plus innings of work. Relievers Rick Honeycutt and Dennis Eckersley hurled perfect ball in the eighth and ninth.

After a day off, the Series shifted eleven miles across the Bay to San Francisco for Game 3. But just as fans were settling into their seats, the earthquake struck, knocking out power to Candlestick Park and (as gradually became known) killing 67 people in scattered pockets of destruction throughout the Bay Area. The fans were sent home, but despite the pleas of a few Eastern reporters that the rest of the Series be cancelled, the overwhelming desire of Bay Area residents prevailed, and Game 3 came off at last, ten days late. Starter Dave Stewart gave up three Giant runs in seven innings, but by the time he was relieved, his A's had sent nine men across the plate. Four more runs in the eighth completed the Oakland scoring. The Giants put together their first big inning of the Series, scoring four runs in the last of the ninth. Although the Giants' effort fell far short of what was needed, pinch hitter Bill Bathe's home run—the game's seventh, including five by the A's—set a new World Series record.

Game 4 began as yet another Giant humiliation. Oakland's Rickey Henderson led off the game with a home run, and by the time Giant Kevin Mitchell homered in his team's first pair of runs in the sixth inning, the A's had scored eight times. The Giants struggled back, though, scoring four times in the seventh on a walk and a cycle of hits—home run, triple, double, and single—to draw within two runs of a tie. But they came no closer. Oakland scored a ninth run an inning later, and Todd Burns and Dennis Eckersley hurled the Series to its conclusion with 2⅓ innings of perfect relief.

Oakland Athletics (AL), 4; San Francisco Giants (NL), 0

OAK (A)

PLAYER/POS	AVG	G	AB	R	H	2B	3B	HR	RB	BB	SO	SB
Lance Blankenship, 2b	.500	1	2	1	1	0	0	0	0	0	0	0
Todd Burns, p	.000	2	0	0	0	0	0	0	0	0	0	0
Jose Canseco, of	.357	4	14	5	5	0	0	1	3	4	3	1
Dennis Eckersley, p	.000	2	0	0	0	0	0	0	0	0	0	0
Mike Gallego, 2b-1,3b-1	.000	2	1	0	0	0	0	0	0	0	0	0
Dave Henderson, of	.308	4	13	6	4	2	0	2	4	4	3	0
Rickey Henderson, of	.474	4	19	4	9	1	2	1	3	2	2	3
Rick Honeycutt, p	.000	3	0	0	0	0	0	0	0	0	0	0
Stan Javier, of	.000	1	0	0	0	0	0	0	0	0	0	0
Carney Lansford, 3b	.438	4	16	5	7	1	0	1	4	3	1	0
Mark McGwire, 1b	.294	4	17	0	5	1	0	0	1	1	3	0
Mike Moore, p	.333	2	3	1	1	1	0	0	2	0	1	0
Gene Nelson, p	.000	2	0	0	0	0	0	0	0	0	0	0
Dave Parker, dh-2	.222	3	9	2	2	1	0	1	2	0	2	0
Ken Phelps, ph	.000	1	1	0	0	0	0	0	0	0	0	0
Tony Phillips, 2b-3,3b-2,of-1	.235	4	17	2	4	1	0	1	3	0	3	0
Terry Steinbach, c	.250	4	16	3	4	0	1	1	7	2	1	0
Dave Stewart, p	.000	2	3	0	0	0	0	0	0	0	1	0
Walt Weiss, ss	.133	4	15	3	2	0	0	1	1	2	2	0
TOTAL	.301		146	32	44	8	3	9	30	18	22	4

PITCHER	W	L	ERA	G	GS	CG	SV	SHO	IP	H	ER	BB	SO
Todd Burns	0	0	0.00	2	0	0	0	0	1.2	1	0	1	0
Dennis Eckersley	0	0	0.00	2	0	0	1	0	1.2	0	0	0	0
Rick Honeycutt	0	0	6.75	3	0	0	0	0	2.2	4	2	0	2
Mike Moore	2	0	2.08	2	2	0	0	0	13.0	9	3	3	10
Gene Nelson	0	0	54.00	2	0	0	0	0	1.0	4	6	2	1
Dave Stewart	2	0	1.69	2	2	1	0	1	16.0	10	3	2	14
TOTAL	4	0	3.50	13	4	1	1	1	36.0	28	14	8	27

SF (N)

PLAYER/POS	AVG	G	AB	R	H	2B	3B	HR	RB	BB	SO	SB
Bill Bathe, ph	.500	2	2	1	1	0	0	1	3	0	0	0
Steve Bedrosian, p	.000	2	0	0	0	0	0	0	0	0	0	0
Jeff Brantley, p	.000	3	0	0	0	0	0	0	0	0	0	0
Brett Butler, of	.286	4	14	1	4	0	0	0	1	2	1	2
Will Clark, 1b	.250	4	16	2	4	1	0	0	0	1	3	0
Kelly Downs, p	.000	3	0	0	0	0	0	0	0	0	1	0
Scott Garrelts, p	.000	2	1	0	0	0	0	0	0	0	1	0
Atlee Hammaker, p	.000	2	0	0	0	0	0	0	0	0	0	0
Terry Kennedy, c	.167	4	12	1	2	0	0	0	2	1	3	0
Mike LaCoss, p	.000	2	1	0	0	0	0	0	0	0	0	0
Craig Lefferts, p	.000	3	0	0	0	0	0	0	0	0	0	0
Greg Litton, 2b-2,3b-1	.500	2	6	1	3	1	0	1	3	0	0	0
Candy Maldonado, of-3	.091	4	11	1	1	0	1	0	0	0	4	0
Kirt Manwaring, c	1.000	1	1	1	1	1	0	0	0	0	0	0
Kevin Mitchell, of	.294	4	17	2	5	0	0	1	2	0	3	0
Donell Nixon, of	.200	2	5	1	1	0	0	0	0	1	1	0
Ken Oberkfell, 3b	.333	4	6	1	2	0	0	0	0	3	0	0
Rick Reuschel, p	.000	1	0	0	0	0	0	0	0	0	0	0
Ernie Riles, dh-2	.000	4	8	0	0	0	0	0	0	0	1	0
Don Robinson, p	.000	1	0	0	0	0	0	0	0	0	0	0
Pat Sheridan, of	.000	1	2	0	0	0	0	0	0	0	0	0
Robby Thompson, 2b	.091	4	11	0	1	0	0	0	0	2	4	0
Jose Uribe, ss	.200	3	5	1	1	0	0	0	1	0	6	0
Matt Williams, ss-4,ss-3	.125	4	16	1	2	0	0	1	1	0	6	0
TOTAL	.209		134	14	28	4	1	4	14	8	27	2

PITCHER	W	L	ERA	G	GS	CG	SV	SHO	IP	H	ER	BB	SO
Steve Bedrosian	0	0	0.00	2	0	0	0	0	2.2	0	0	2	2
Jeff Brantley	0	0	4.15	3	0	0	0	0	4.1	5	2	3	1
Kelly Downs	0	0	7.71	3	0	0	0	0	4.2	3	4	2	4
Scott Garrelts	0	2	9.82	2	2	0	0	0	7.1	13	8	1	8
Atlee Hammaker	0	0	15.43	2	0	0	0	0	2.1	8	4	0	2
Mike LaCoss	0	0	6.23	2	0	0	0	0	4.1	4	3	3	2
Craig Lefferts	0	0	3.38	3	0	0	0	0	2.2	2	1	2	1
Rick Reuschel	0	1	11.25	1	1	0	0	0	4.0	5	5	4	2
Don Robinson	0	1	21.60	1	1	0	0	0	1.2	4	4	1	0
TOTAL	0	4	8.21	19	4	0	0	0	34.0	44	31	18	22

GAME 1 AT OAK OCT 14

SF	000 000 000	0	5	1
OAK	031 100 00X	5	5	1

Pitchers: GARRELTS, Hammaker (5), Brantley (6), LaCoss (8) vs STEWART
Home Runs: Parker-OAK, Weiss-OAK
Attendance: 49,385

GAME 2 AT OAK OCT 15

SF	001 000 000	1	4	0
OAK	100 400 00X	5	7	0

Pitchers: REUSCHEL, Downs (5), Lefferts (7), Bedrosian (8) vs MOORE, Honeycutt (8), Eckersley (9)
Home Runs: Steinbach-OAK
Attendance: 49,388

GAME 3 AT SF OCT 27

OAK	200 241 040	13	14	0
SF	010 200 004	7	10	3

Pitchers: STEWART, Honeycutt (8), Nelson (9), Burns (9) vs GARRELTS, Downs (4), Brantley (5), Hammaker (8), Lefferts (9)
Home Runs: Williams-SF, D.Henderson-OAK (2), Phillips-OAK, Canseco-OAK, Lansford-OAK, Bathe-SF
Attendance: 62,038

GAME 4 AT SF OCT 28

OAK	130 031 010	9	12	0
SF	000 002 400	6	9	0

Pitchers: MOORE, Nelson (7), Honeycutt (7), Eckersley (9) vs ROBINSON, LaCoss (2), Brantley (6), Downs (6), Lefferts (8), Bedrosian (8)
Home Runs: R.Henderson-OAK, Mitchell-SF, Litton-SF
Attendance: 62,032

Fielding plays and misplays provided some of the most crucial moments of the series. After the Pirates had overcome a three-run deficit to tie the score in Game 1, for example, they won the game when Eric Davis misplayed Andy Van Slyke's fly to left field for a run-scoring double. Cincinnati right fielder Paul O'Neill evened the series in Game 2 by singling home the game's first run in the first inning, then (with the game tied 1–1 in the fifth) doubling in the go-ahead—and final—run on a fly Pirate left fielder Barry Bonds lost in the late afternoon sun. Finally, O'Neill gunned down Pittsburgh's potential tying run at third base when Van Slyke attempted to move up after Bonds's fly-out to right.

Two- and three-run homers by Reds Billy Hatcher and Mariano Duncan gave Cincinnati the series advantage in Game 3, and Chris Sabo's sacrifice fly and two-run blast proved the decisive blows a day later as the Reds pushed their series lead to 3–1. In that game left fielder Eric Davis, backing up Bobby Bonilla's double off the center field wall, prevented what would have become a game-tying run when, with a perfect throw to third, he nailed Bonilla trying for a triple.

The Pirates staved off elimination with a narrow 3–2 win in Game 5, a win preserved by a spectacular bases-loaded game-ending double play. But in Game 6, Pittsburgh's uncertain fielding in the first inning gave the Reds their first and, as it turned out, decisive run. In the ninth inning, with the Reds ahead 2–1, Reds right fielder Glen Braggs snared a deep fly with a leaping catch that prevented at least one, and perhaps two, Pirate runs from scoring. One strikeout later the Reds had snared the National League pennant.

Cincinnati Reds (West), 4;
Pittsburgh Pirates (East), 2

CIN (W)

PLAYER/POS	AVG	G	AB	R	H	2B	3B	HR	RB	BB	SO	SB
Billy Bates, pr	.000	2	0	1	0	0	0	0	0	0	0	0
Todd Benzinger, 1b-2	.333	5	9	0	3	0	0	0	0	2	0	0
Glenn Braggs, of	.200	2	5	0	1	0	0	0	0	0	1	0
Tom Browning, p	.000	2	3	0	0	0	0	0	0	0	1	0
Norm Charlton, p	.000	4	0	0	0	0	0	0	0	0	0	0
Eric Davis, of	.174	6	23	2	4	1	0	0	2	1	9	0
Rob Dibble, p	.000	4	2	0	0	0	0	0	0	0	1	0
Mariano Duncan, 2b	.300	6	20	1	6	0	0	1	4	0	8	0
Billy Hatcher, of	.333	4	15	2	5	1	0	1	2	0	2	0
Danny Jackson, p	.000	2	3	0	0	0	0	0	0	0	2	0
Barry Larkin, ss	.261	6	23	5	6	2	0	0	1	3	1	3
Rick Mahler, p	.000	1	0	0	0	0	0	0	0	0	0	0
Hal Morris, 1b-4	.417	5	12	3	5	1	0	0	1	1	0	0
Randy Myers, p	.000	4	0	0	0	0	0	0	0	0	0	0
Ron Oester, 2b-2	.333	4	3	1	1	0	0	0	0	0	1	0
Joe Oliver, c	.143	5	14	1	2	0	0	0	0	0	0	0
Paul O'Neill, of	.471	5	17	1	8	3	0	1	4	1	1	1
Luis Quinones, ph	.500	3	2	1	1	0	0	0	0	2	0	1
Jeff Reed, c	.000	4	7	0	0	0	0	0	0	0	2	0
Jose Rijo, p	.000	2	5	0	0	0	0	0	0	0	1	0
Chris Sabo, 3b	.227	6	22	1	5	0	0	1	3	1	4	0
Scott Scudder, p	.000	1	0	0	0	0	0	0	0	0	0	0
Herm Winningham, of-2	.286	3	7	1	2	1	0	0	1	1	1	1
TOTAL	.255		192	20	49	9	0	4	20	10	37	6

PITCHER	W	L	ERA	G	GS	CG	SV	SHO	IP	H	ER	BB	SO
Tom Browning	1	1	3.27	2	2	0	0	0	11.0	9	4	6	5
Norm Charlton	1	1	1.80	4	0	0	0	0	5.0	4	1	3	3
Rob Dibble	0	0	0.00	4	0	0	1	0	5.0	0	0	1	10
Danny Jackson	1	0	2.38	2	2	0	0	0	11.1	8	3	7	8
Rick Mahler	0	0	0.00	1	0	0	0	0	1.2	2	0	0	0
Randy Myers	0	0	0.00	4	0	0	3	0	5.2	2	0	3	7
Jose Rijo	1	0	4.38	2	2	0	0	0	12.1	10	6	7	15
Scott Scudder	0	0	0.00	1	0	0	0	0	1.0	1	0	0	1
TOTAL	4	2	2.38	20	6	0	4	0	53.0	36	14	27	49

PIT (E)

PLAYER/POS	AVG	G	AB	R	H	2B	3B	HR	RB	BB	SO	SB
Wally Backman, 3b-2	.143	3	7	1	1	1	0	0	0	1	3	1
Stan Belinda, p	.000	3	0	0	0	0	0	0	0	0	0	0
Jay Bell, ss	.250	6	20	3	5	1	0	1	1	4	3	0
Barry Bonds, of	.167	6	18	4	3	0	0	0	1	6	6	2
Bobby Bonilla, of-5,3b-3	.190	6	21	0	4	1	0	0	1	3	1	0
Sid Bream, 1b	.500	4	8	1	4	1	0	1	3	2	3	0
Doug Drabek, p	.167	2	6	0	1	0	0	0	0	0	2	0
Jeff King, 3b-4	.100	5	10	0	1	0	0	0	0	1	5	0
Bill Landrum, p	.000	2	0	0	0	0	0	0	0	0	0	0
Mike LaValliere, c	.000	3	6	1	0	0	0	0	0	3	1	0
Jose Lind, 2b	.238	6	21	1	5	1	1	1	2	1	4	0
Carmelo Martinez, 1b	.250	2	8	0	2	2	0	0	2	0	1	0
Bob Patterson, p	.000	2	0	0	0	0	0	0	0	0	0	0
Ted Power, p	.000	2	1	0	0	0	0	0	0	0	1	0
Gary Redus, 1b-2	.250	5	8	0	2	0	0	0	0	1	3	1
R. J. Reynolds, of-3	.200	6	10	0	2	0	0	0	0	2	1	1
Don Slaught, c	.091	4	11	0	1	1	0	0	1	2	3	0
John Smiley, p	.000	1	0	0	0	0	0	0	0	0	0	0
Zane Smith, p	.000	2	3	0	0	0	0	0	0	0	1	0
Andy Van Slyke, of	.208	6	24	3	5	1	1	0	3	1	6	1
Bob Walk, p	.000	2	4	0	0	0	0	0	0	0	0	0
TOTAL	.194		186	15	36	9	2	3	14	27	49	6

PITCHER	W	L	ERA	G	GS	CG	SV	SHO	IP	H	ER	BB	SO
Stan Belinda	0	0	2.45	3	0	0	0	0	3.2	3	1	0	4
Doug Drabek	1	1	1.65	2	2	1	0	0	16.1	12	3	3	13
Bill Landrum	0	0	0.00	2	0	0	0	0	2.0	0	0	0	1
Bob Patterson	0	0	0.00	2	0	0	1	0	1.0	1	0	2	0
Ted Power	0	0	3.60	2	1	0	1	0	5.0	6	2	2	3
John Smiley	0	0	0.00	1	0	0	0	0	2.0	2	0	0	0
Zane Smith	0	2	6.00	2	1	0	0	0	9.0	14	6	1	8
Bob Walk	1	1	4.85	2	2	0	0	0	13.0	11	7	2	8
TOTAL	2	4	3.29	16	6	1	2	0	52.0	49	19	10	37

GAME 1 AT CIN OCT 4

PIT	001	200	100		4	7	1
CIN	300	000	000		3	5	0

Pitchers: WALK, Belinda (7), Patterson (9), Power (9) vs Rijo, CHARLTON (6), Dibble (9)
Home Runs: Bream-PIT
Attendance: 55,700

GAME 2 AT CIN OCT 5

PIT	000	010	000		1	6	0
CIN	100	010	00X		2	5	0

Pitchers: DRABEK vs BROWNING, Dibble (7), Myers (8)
Home Runs: Lind-PIT
Attendance: 54,456

GAME 3 AT PIT OCT 8

CIN	020	030	001		6	13	1
PIT	000	200	010		3	8	0

Pitchers: JACKSON, Dibble (6), Charlton (8), Myers (9) vs SMITH, Landrum (6), Smiley (7), Belinda (9)
Home Runs: Duncan-CIN, Hatcher-CIN
Attendance: 45,611

GAME 4 AT PIT OCT 9

CIN	000	200	201		5	10	1
PIT	100	100	010		3	8	0

Pitchers: RIJO, Myers (8), Dibble (9) vs WALK, Power (8)
Home Runs: O'Neill-CIN, Sabo-CIN, Bell-PIT
Attendance: 50,461

GAME 5 AT PIT OCT 10

CIN	100	000	010		2	7	0
PIT	200	100	00X		3	6	1

Pitchers: BROWNING, Mahler (6), Charlton (7), Scudder (8) vs DRABEK, Patterson (9)
Attendance: 48,221

GAME 6 AT CIN OCT 12

PIT	000	010	000		1	1	3
CIN	100	000	10X		2	9	0

Pitchers: Power, SMITH (3), Belinda (7), Landrum (8) vs Jackson, CHARLTON (7), Myers (8)
Attendance: 56,079

The ejection of Boston ace Roger Clemens from Game 4 for mouthing off to an umpire provided a moment of raucous counterpoint to the surgical precision with which Oakland dismembered the Red Sox. While the A's pitchers anesthetized Boston's hitters, parceling out just one run per game, their batters sliced up the Sox with singles, steals, and sacrifices.

In the fourth inning of Game 1, Boston's Wade Boggs interrupted a pitchers' duel between Clemens and Oakland's Dave Stewart with the series' only home run. But in the top of the seventh—after a tiring Clemens had been relieved—the A's evened the score with a walk, single, and sacrifice fly, took the lead an inning later with a pair of singles sandwiched around a bunt and stolen base, then buried the Sox with seven runs in the ninth. DH Harold Baines provided Oakland's most productive offense in the second game, singling home the tying run in the fourth inning, driving in the tiebreaker with a groundout in the seventh, and doubling home a third run in the ninth. In Game 3, a double steal by Baines and Jose Canseco set up the A's tying and tiebreaking runs, which scored on a sacrifice fly and a single.

The A's scored first for the only time in the series in Game 4, on a pair of singles and a grounder to short in the second inning. Following the shouting match between the Sox and umpires that erupted when pitcher Clemens was thrown out for disputing a walk to the next batter, Mike Gallego doubled home two more Oakland runs. A trio of Boston relievers stopped the Athletics the rest of the way, and a pair of Red Sox hits in the ninth ended Dave Stewart's shutout bid. But Rick Honeycutt came on to preserve Stewart's second win of the series and sew up Oakland's third successive American League championship.

Oakland Athletics (West), 4;
Boston Red Sox (East), 0

OAK (W)

PLAYER/POS	AVG	G	AB	R	H	2B	3B	HR	RB	BB	SO	SB
Harold Baines, dh	.357	4	14	2	5	1	0	0	3	2	1	1
Lance Blankenship, dh	.000	3	0	1	0	0	0	0	0	0	0	1
Jose Canseco, of	.182	4	11	3	2	0	0	0	1	5	5	2
Dennis Eckersley, p	.000	3	0	0	0	0	0	0	0	0	0	0
Mike Gallego, ss-3,2b-2	.400	4	10	1	4	1	0	0	2	1	1	0
Ron Hassey, c-1,dh-1	.333	2	3	0	1	0	0	0	0	2	0	0
Dave Henderson, of	.167	2	6	0	1	0	0	0	1	0	2	1
Rickey Henderson, of	.294	4	17	1	5	0	0	0	3	1	2	2
Rick Honeycutt, p	.000	3	0	0	0	0	0	0	0	0	0	0
Doug Jennings, of	.000	1	1	0	0	0	0	0	0	0	0	0
Carney Lansford, 3b	.438	4	16	2	7	1	0	0	2	0	1	0
Willie McGee, of-2,dh-1	.222	3	9	3	2	1	0	0	0	1	2	2
Mark McGwire, 1b	.154	4	13	2	2	0	0	0	2	3	3	0
Mike Moore, p	.000	1	0	0	0	0	0	0	0	0	0	0
Gene Nelson, p	.000	1	0	0	0	0	0	0	0	0	0	0
Jamie Quirk, ph	1.000	1	1	0	1	0	0	0	0	0	0	0
Willie Randolph, 2b	.375	4	8	1	3	0	0	0	3	1	0	0
Terry Steinbach, c	.455	3	11	2	5	0	0	0	1	1	2	0
Dave Stewart, p	.000	2	0	0	0	0	0	0	0	0	0	0
Walt Weiss, ss	.000	2	7	2	0	0	0	0	0	2	2	0
Bob Welch, p	.000	1	0	0	0	0	0	0	0	0	0	0
TOTAL	.299		127	20	38	4	0	0	18	19	21	9

PITCHER	W	L	ERA	G	GS	CG	SV	SHO	IP	H	ER	BB	SO
Dennis Eckersley	0	0	0.00	3	0	0	2	0	3.1	2	0	0	3
Rick Honeycutt	0	0	0.00	3	0	0	1	0	1.2	0	0	0	0
Mike Moore	1	0	1.50	1	1	0	0	0	6.0	4	1	1	5
Gene Nelson	0	0	0.00	1	0	0	0	0	1.2	3	0	0	0
Dave Stewart	2	0	1.13	2	2	0	0	0	16.0	8	2	2	4
Bob Welch	1	0	1.23	1	1	0	0	0	7.1	6	1	3	4
TOTAL	4	0	1.00	11	4	0	3	0	36.0	23	4	6	16

BOS (E)

PLAYER/POS	AVG	G	AB	R	H	2B	3B	HR	RB	BB	SO	SB
Larry Andersen, p	.000	3	0	0	0	0	0	0	0	0	0	0
Marty Barrett, 2b	.000	3	0	0	0	0	0	0	0	0	0	0
Mike Boddicker, p	.000	1	0	0	0	0	0	0	0	0	0	0
Wade Boggs, 3b	.438	4	16	1	7	1	0	1	1	1	3	0
Tom Bolton, p	.000	2	0	0	0	0	0	0	0	0	0	0
Tom Brunansky, of	.083	4	12	0	1	0	0	0	1	1	3	0
Ellis Burks, of	.267	4	15	1	4	2	0	0	0	1	1	1
Roger Clemens, p	.000	2	0	0	0	0	0	0	0	0	0	0
Dwight Evans, dh	.231	4	13	0	3	1	0	0	0	1	3	0
Jeff Gray, p	.000	2	0	0	0	0	0	0	0	0	0	0
Mike Greenwell, of	.000	4	14	1	0	0	0	0	0	2	2	0
Greg Harris, p	.000	1	0	0	0	0	0	0	0	0	0	0
Danny Heep, ph	.000	2	2	0	0	0	0	0	0	0	0	0
Dana Kiecker, p	.000	1	0	0	0	0	0	0	0	0	0	0
Randy Kutcher, pr	.000	2	0	0	0	0	0	0	0	0	0	0
Dennis Lamp, p	.000	1	0	0	0	0	0	0	0	0	0	0
Mike Marshall, ph	.333	3	3	0	1	0	0	0	0	0	1	0
Rob Murphy, p	.000	3	0	0	0	0	0	0	0	0	0	0
Tony Pena, c	.214	4	14	0	3	0	0	0	0	0	0	0
Carlos Quintana, 1b	.000	4	13	0	0	0	0	0	1	1	0	0
Jeff Reardon, p	.000	1	0	0	0	0	0	0	0	0	0	0
Jody Reed, 2b-4,ss-3	.133	4	15	0	2	0	0	0	1	0	2	0
Luis Rivera, ss	.222	4	9	1	2	1	0	0	0	0	2	0
TOTAL	.183		126	4	23	5	0	1	4	6	16	1

PITCHER	W	L	ERA	G	GS	CG	SV	SHO	IP	H	ER	BB	SO
Larry Andersen	0	1	6.00	3	0	0	0	0	3.0	3	2	3	3
Mike Boddicker	0	1	2.25	1	1	1	0	0	8.0	6	2	3	7
Tom Bolton	0	0	0.00	2	0	0	0	0	3.0	2	0	2	3
Roger Clemens	0	1	3.52	2	2	0	0	0	7.2	7	3	5	4
Jeff Gray	0	0	2.70	2	0	0	0	0	3.1	4	1	1	2
Greg Harris	0	1	27.00	1	0	0	0	0	0.1	3	1	0	0
Dana Kiecker	0	0	1.59	1	1	0	0	0	5.2	6	1	1	2
Dennis Lamp	0	0	108.00	1	0	0	0	0	0.1	2	4	2	0
Rob Murphy	0	0	13.50	1	0	0	0	0	0.2	2	1	1	0
Jeff Reardon	0	0	9.00	1	0	0	0	0	2.0	3	2	1	0
TOTAL	0	4	4.50	15	4	1	0	0	34.0	38	17	19	21

GAME 1 AT BOS OCT 6

OAK	000	000	117	9	13	0
BOS	000	100	000	1	5	1

Pitchers: STEWART, Eckersley (9) vs Clemens, ANDERSEN (7), Bolton (8), Gray (8), Lamp (9), Murphy (9)
Home Runs: Boggs-BOS
Attendance: 35,192

GAME 2 AT BOS OCT 7

OAK	000	100	102	4	13	1
BOS	001	000	000	1	6	0

Pitchers: WELCH, Honeycutt (8), Eckersley (9) vs Kiecker, HARRIS (6), Andersen (7), Reardon (8)
Attendance: 35,070

GAME 3 AT OAK OCT 9

BOS	010	000	000	1	8	3
OAK	000	202	00X	4	6	0

Pitchers: BODDICKER vs MOORE, Nelson (7), Honeycutt (8), Eckersley (9)
Attendance: 49,026

GAME 4 AT OAK OCT 10

BOS	000	000	001	1	4	1
OAK	030	000	00X	3	6	0

Pitchers: CLEMENS, Bolton (2), Gray (5), Andersen (8) vs STEWART, Honeycutt (9)
Attendance: 49,052

In the most stunning World Series sweep since 1954, Cincinnati's fired-up Reds roasted the team many were proclaiming baseball's newest dynasty. Reds left fielder Eric Davis, playing despite shoulder and knee injuries, provided the A's their first hint of what was to come when—on the first pitch thrown to him in the first inning—he homered over the center field wall for two runs. Billy Hatcher, on base with a walk, scored ahead of Davis, the first of his Series-high six runs. Hatcher would not be retired at the plate until Game 3. Final score: 7–0. For Oakland starter Dave Stewart, the loss ended a personal postseason six-game win streak. For the club, the loss ended a streak of ten postseason wins.

The A's put up their best fight of the Series in Game 2, scoring first, then overcoming a 2–1 deficit in the third inning with three more runs for a 4–2 lead. Cincinnati narrowed the gap with a run in the fourth and tied the score in the eighth when Hatcher tripled—setting a World Series record with his seventh straight hit—and came home on a grounder to short. The A's held on until the tenth inning, when ace reliever Dennis Eckersley gave up three straight hits to lose the game.

Game 3 was another Cincinnati blowout, an 8–3 contest in which all eleven runs were scored in the second and third innings. Chris Sabo led the Reds assault with two home runs, and handled a Series-record ten chances at third base.

For seven innings of Game 4 the tide of battle seemed to be turning in Oakland's favor. Billy Hatcher —who was batting .750—left the game after a pitch hit his hand in the first inning. Later in the inning Eric Davis tore a kidney diving for a Willie McGee shot that went for a double. McGee went on to score, and Davis departed for the hospital. A renewed Dave Stewart, supported by sharp fielding, seemed capable of sustaining his 1–0 lead to the finish. But in the eighth the Reds, with just one solid hit, eked out the two runs they would need for victory. After loading the bases with a leadoff single, a third-strike bunt that went for a hit, and a sacrifice bunt that Stewart misplayed for an error, the Reds drove home the tying run with a grounder to short and took the lead on a sacrifice fly. Meanwhile Reds starter Jose Rijo held the A's hitless after the first inning, leveling twenty men in order from the second into the ninth, when ace closer Randy Myers relieved him for the final two outs of the splendid sweep.

Cincinnati Reds (NL), 4;
Oakland Athletics (AL), 0

CIN (N)

PLAYER/POS	AVG	G	AB	R	H	2B	3B	HR	RB	BB	SO	SB
Jack Armstrong, p	.000	1	0	0	0	0	0	0	0	0	0	0
Billy Bates, ph	1.000	1	1	1	1	0	0	0	0	0	0	0
Todd Benzinger, 1b-3	.182	4	11	1	2	0	0	0	0	0	0	0
Glenn Braggs, of-1	.000	2	4	0	0	0	0	0	2	1	0	0
Tom Browning, p	.000	1	0	0	0	0	0	0	0	0	0	0
Norm Charlton, p	.000	1	0	0	0	0	0	0	0	0	0	0
Eric Davis, of	.286	4	14	3	4	0	0	1	5	0	0	0
Rob Dibble, p	.000	3	0	0	0	0	0	0	0	0	0	0
Mariano Duncan, 2b	.143	4	14	1	2	0	0	0	1	2	2	1
Billy Hatcher, of	.750	4	12	6	9	4	1	0	2	2	0	0
Danny Jackson, p	.000	1	1	0	0	0	0	0	0	0	1	0
Barry Larkin, ss	.353	4	17	3	6	1	1	0	1	2	0	0
Hal Morris, 1b-2,dh-2	.071	4	14	0	1	0	0	0	2	1	1	0
Randy Myers, p	.000	3	0	0	0	0	0	0	0	0	0	0
Ron Oester, ph	1.000	1	1	0	1	0	0	0	0	1	0	0
Joe Oliver, c	.333	4	18	2	6	3	0	0	2	0	1	0
Paul O'Neill, of	.083	4	12	2	1	0	0	0	1	5	2	1
Jose Rijo, p	.333	2	3	0	1	0	0	0	0	0	0	0
Chris Sabo, 3b	.563	4	16	2	9	1	0	2	5	2	2	0
Scott Scudder, p	.000	1	0	0	0	0	0	0	0	0	0	0
Herm Winningham, of-1	.500	2	4	1	2	0	0	0	0	0	0	0
TOTAL	.317		142	22	45	9	2	3	22	15	9	2

PITCHER	W	L	ERA	G	GS	CG	SV	SHO	IP	H	ER	BB	SO
Jack Armstrong	0	0	0.00	1	0	0	0	0	3.0	1	0	0	3
Tom Browning	1	0	4.50	1	1	0	0	0	6.0	6	3	2	2
Norm Charlton	0	0	0.00	1	0	0	0	0	1.0	1	0	0	0
Rob Dibble	1	0	0.00	3	0	0	0	0	4.2	3	0	1	4
Danny Jackson	0	0	10.13	1	1	0	0	0	2.2	6	3	2	0
Randy Myers	0	0	0.00	3	0	0	1	0	3.0	2	0	0	3
Jose Rijo	2	0	0.59	2	2	0	0	0	15.1	9	1	5	14
Scott Scudder	0	0	0.00	1	0	0	0	0	1.1	0	0	2	2
TOTAL	4	0	1.70	13	4	0	1	0	37.0	28	7	12	28

OAK (A)

PLAYER/POS	AVG	G	AB	R	H	2B	3B	HR	RB	BB	SO	SB
Harold Baines, dh-2	.143	3	7	1	1	0	0	0	1	2	1	2	0
Lance Blankenship, ph	.000	1	1	0	0	0	0	0	0	0	1	0
Mike Bordick, ss	.000	3	0	0	0	0	0	0	0	0	0	0
Todd Burns, p	.000	2	0	0	0	0	0	0	0	0	0	0
Jose Canseco, of-3,dh-1	.083	4	12	1	1	0	0	1	2	2	3	0
Dennis Eckersley, p	.000	2	0	0	0	0	0	0	0	0	0	0
Mike Gallego, ss	.091	4	11	0	1	0	0	0	1	1	3	1
Ron Hassey, c-1	.333	3	6	0	2	0	0	0	1	0	0	0
Dave Henderson, of-3	.231	4	13	2	3	1	0	0	0	1	3	0
Rickey Henderson, of	.333	4	15	2	5	2	0	1	1	3	4	3
Rick Honeycutt, p	.000	1	0	0	0	0	0	0	0	0	0	0
Doug Jennings, ph	1.000	1	1	0	1	0	0	0	0	0	0	0
Joe Klink, p	.000	1	0	0	0	0	0	0	0	0	0	0
Carney Lansford, 3b	.267	4	15	0	4	0	0	0	1	1	0	1
Willie McGee, of-3	.200	4	10	1	2	1	0	0	0	2	1	0
Mark McGwire, 1b	.214	4	14	1	3	0	0	0	0	2	4	0
Mike Moore, p	.000	1	0	0	0	0	0	0	0	0	0	0
Gene Nelson, p	.000	2	0	0	0	0	0	0	0	0	0	0
Jamie Quirk, c	.000	1	3	0	0	0	0	0	0	0	2	0
Willie Randolph, 2b	.267	4	15	0	4	0	0	0	0	1	0	1
Scott Sanderson, p	.000	2	0	0	0	0	0	0	0	0	0	0
Terry Steinbach, c	.125	3	8	0	1	0	0	0	0	0	1	0
Dave Stewart, p	.000	2	1	0	0	0	0	0	0	0	0	0
Bob Welch, p	.000	1	3	0	0	0	0	0	0	0	2	0
Curt Young, p	.000	1	0	0	0	0	0	0	0	0	0	0
TOTAL	.207		135	8	28	4	0	3	8	12	28	7

PITCHER	W	L	ERA	G	GS	CG	SV	SHO	IP	H	ER	BB	SO
Todd Burns	0	0	16.20	2	0	0	0	0	1.2	5	3	2	0
Dennis Eckersley	0	1	6.75	2	0	0	0	0	1.1	3	1	0	1
Rick Honeycutt	0	0	0.00	1	0	0	0	0	1.2	2	0	1	0
Joe Klink	0	0	—	1	0	0	0	0	0.0	0	0	1	0
Mike Moore	0	1	6.75	1	1	0	0	0	2.2	8	2	0	1
Gene Nelson	0	0	0.00	2	0	0	0	0	5.0	3	0	2	0
Scott Sanderson	0	0	10.80	2	0	0	0	0	1.2	4	2	1	0
Dave Stewart	0	2	3.46	2	2	1	0	0	13.0	10	5	6	5
Bob Welch	0	0	4.91	1	1	0	0	0	7.1	9	4	2	2
Curt Young	0	0	0.00	1	0	0	0	0	1.0	1	0	0	0
TOTAL	0	4	4.33	15	4	1	0	0	35.1	45	17	15	9

GAME 1 AT CIN OCT 16

OAK	000	000	000	0	9 1
CIN	202	030	00X	7	10 0

Pitchers: STEWART, Burns (5), Nelson (5), Sanderson (7), Eckersley (8) vs RIJO, Dibble (8), Myers (9)
Home Runs: Davis-CIN
Attendance: 55,830

GAME 2 AT CIN OCT 17

OAK	103	000	000	0	4 10
CIN	200	100	010	1	5 14

Pitchers: Welch, Honeycutt (8), ECKERSLEY (10) vs Jackson, Scudder (3), Armstrong (5), Charlton (8), DIBBLE (9)
Home Runs: Canseco-OAK
Attendance: 55,832

GAME 3 AT OAK OCT 19

CIN	017	000	000	8 14 1
OAK	021	000	000	3 7 1

Pitchers: BROWNING, Dibble (7), Myers (8) vs MOORE, Sanderson (3), Klink (4), Nelson (4), Burns (8), Young (9)
Home Runs: Sabo-CIN (2), Baines-OAK, R.Henderson-OAK
Attendance: 48,269

GAME 4 AT OAK OCT 20

CIN	000	000	020	2 7 1
OAK	100	000	000	1 2 1

Pitchers: RIJO, Myers (9) vs STEWART
Attendance: 48,613

Pitching dominated this back-and-forth series which featured four shutouts, including three 1–0 games. Three times Atlanta hurlers blanked Pittsburgh on the Pirates' home grounds, including a pair of must-win victories that brought the Braves back from the brink of defeat. Andy Van Slyke opened the series scoring with a first-inning Pirate home run. Pirate starter Doug Drabek held the Braves scoreless through six innings of the opener, before injuring himself on the basepath. By the time David Justice homered in the ninth for Atlanta's only score, the Pirates had the game well in hand.

Atlanta evened the series with its first of three shutouts in Game Two behind the pitching of young Steve Avery and (for the final 2⁄3 inning) Alejandro Pena, and the bat and glove of Mark Lemke. The Braves' second baseman doubled home that game's only run in the sixth inning and prevented a Pittsburgh run from scoring in the eighth with a diving stop of a grounder up the middle. In Atlanta for Game Three, the Braves took the series lead with a 10–3 route that featured home runs by Ron Gant, Greg Olson, and Sid Bream. (Orlando Merced and Jay Bell homered for Pittsburgh.)

Game Four was much closer; this time three Pirate runs brought them victory. The Braves took a quick lead with two first-inning runs, but Pittsburgh scored once in the second and tied the game in the fifth on a throwing error as Pirate pitching shut down Atlanta's offense. In the top of the tenth, Andy Van Slyke led off with a walk. With two away he stole second, and then scored what proved the winning run on Don Slaught's double. With the series even again, Atlanta lost a run in Game Five when David Justice was ruled out for missing third base as he dashed home from second. An inning later the Pirates parlayed a walk and a pair of singles into the only run they would need to carry the series advantage back to Pittsburgh.

In Game Six, though, the Braves returned the favor, tying the series once more with a gem of their own. Avery and Pena combined for their second 1–0 victory, holding Atlanta to just four singles. Drabek held the Braves scoreless into the ninth, when Olson doubled home the game's only run.

In the finale, Braves starter John Smoltz enjoyed a three-run lead when he took the mound in the bottom of the first inning. Rookie first baseman Brian Hunter (who had homered for two of the first-inning runs) doubled in an additional Atlanta run in the fifth. Meanwhile Smoltz stopped the Pirates on six hits to bring the Braves their first pennant since their move to Atlanta in 1966.

Atlanta Braves (West), 4; Pittsburgh Pirates (East), 3

ATL (W)

PLAYER/POS	AVG	G	AB	R	H	2B	3B	HR	RB	BB	SO	SB
Steve Avery, p	.143	2	7	0	1	0	0	0	0	0	4	0
Rafael Belliard, ss	.211	7	19	0	4	0	0	0	1	3	3	0
Jeff Blauser, ss	.000	2	2	0	0	0	0	0	0	0	0	0
Sid Bream, 1b	.300	4	10	1	3	0	0	1	3	0	1	0
Jim Clancy, p	.000	1	0	0	0	0	0	0	0	0	0	0
Ron Gant, of	.259	7	27	4	7	1	0	1	3	2	4	7
Tom Glavine, p	.250	2	4	0	1	0	0	0	0	0	2	0
Tommy Gregg, ph	.250	4	4	0	1	0	0	0	0	0	2	0
Brian Hunter, 1b	.333	5	18	2	6	2	0	1	4	0	2	0
David Justice, of	.200	7	25	4	5	1	0	1	2	3	7	0
Charlie Leibrandt, p	.000	1	1	0	0	0	0	0	0	0	0	0
Mark Lemke, 2b	.200	7	20	1	4	1	0	0	1	4	0	0
Kent Mercker, p	.000	1	0	0	0	0	0	0	0	0	0	0
Keith Mitchell, of	.000	5	4	0	0	0	0	0	0	0	1	0
Greg Olson, c	.333	7	24	3	8	1	0	1	4	4	3	1
Alejandro Pena, p	.000	4	0	0	0	0	0	0	0	0	0	0
Terry Pendleton, 3b	.167	7	30	1	5	1	0	0	1	1	3	0
Lonnie Smith, of	.250	7	24	3	6	3	0	0	0	4	5	1
John Smoltz, p	.200	2	5	0	1	0	0	0	0	1	4	1
Mike Stanton, p	.000	3	0	0	0	0	0	0	0	0	0	0
Jeff Treadway, 2b	.333	1	3	0	1	0	0	0	0	0	0	0
Jerry Willard, ph	.000	2	2	0	0	0	0	0	0	0	1	0
Mark Wohlers, p	.000	3	0	0	0	0	0	0	0	0	0	0
TOTAL	.231		229	19	53	10	1	5	19	22	42	10

PITCHER	W	L	ERA	G	GS	CG	SV	SHO	IP	H	ER	BB	SO
Steve Avery	2	0	0.00	2	2	0	0	0	16.1	9	0	4	17
Jim Clancy	0	0	0.00	1	0	0	0	0	0.1	0	0	0	0
Tom Glavine	0	2	3.21	2	2	0	0	0	14.0	12	5	6	11
Charlie Leibrandt	0	0	1.35	1	1	0	0	0	6.2	8	1	3	6
Kent Mercker	0	1	13.50	1	0	0	0	0	0.2	0	1	2	0
Alejandro Pena	0	0	0.00	4	0	0	3	0	4.1	1	0	0	4
John Smoltz	2	0	1.76	2	2	1	0	1	15.1	14	3	3	15
Mike Stanton	0	0	2.45	3	0	0	0	0	3.2	4	1	3	3
Mark Wohlers	0	0	0.00	3	0	0	0	0	1.2	3	0	1	1
TOTAL	4	3	1.57	19	7	1	3	1	63.0	51	11	22	57

PIT (E)

PLAYER/POS	AVG	G	AB	R	H	2B	3B	HR	RB	BB	SO	SB
Stan Belinda, p	.000	3	0	0	0	0	0	0	0	0	0	0
Jay Bell, ss	.414	7	29	2	12	2	0	1	1	0	10	0
Barry Bonds, of	.148	7	27	1	4	1	0	0	0	2	4	3
Bobby Bonilla, of	.304	7	23	2	7	2	0	0	1	6	2	0
Steve Buechele, 3b	.304	7	23	2	7	2	0	0	0	4	6	0
Doug Drabek, p	.200	2	5	0	1	1	0	0	1	0	2	0
Cecil Espy, ph	.000	2	2	0	0	0	0	0	0	0	2	0
Bob Kipper, p	.000	1	0	0	0	0	0	0	0	0	0	0
Bill Landrum, p	.000	1	0	0	0	0	0	0	0	0	0	0
Mike LaValliere, c	.333	3	6	0	2	0	0	0	1	2	0	0
Jose Lind, 2b	.160	7	25	0	4	0	0	0	3	0	6	0
Roger Mason, p	.000	3	1	0	0	0	0	0	0	0	1	0
Lloyd McClendon, 1b-1	.000	3	2	0	0	0	0	0	0	1	0	0
Orlando Merced, 1b-2	.222	3	9	1	2	0	0	1	1	0	1	0
Bob Patterson, p	.000	1	0	0	0	0	0	0	0	0	0	0
Gary Redus, 1b	.158	5	19	1	3	0	0	0	0	1	4	2
Rosario Rodriguez, p	.000	1	0	0	0	0	0	0	0	0	0	0
Don Slaught, c	.235	6	17	0	4	0	0	0	1	1	4	0
John Smiley, p	.000	2	0	0	0	0	0	0	0	0	0	0
Zane Smith, p	.000	2	5	0	0	0	0	0	0	0	4	0
Randy Tomlin, p	.000	1	2	0	0	0	0	0	0	0	0	0
Andy Van Slyke, of	.160	7	25	3	4	2	0	1	2	5	5	1
Gary Varsho, ph	.500	2	2	0	1	0	0	0	0	0	1	0
Bob Walk, p	.000	3	2	0	0	0	0	0	0	0	2	0
Curtis Wilkerson, ph	.000	4	4	0	0	0	0	0	0	0	3	0
TOTAL	.224		228	12	51	10	0	3	11	22	57	6

PITCHER	W	L	ERA	G	GS	CG	SV	SHO	IP	H	ER	BB	SO
Stan Belinda	1	0	0.00	3	0	0	0	0	5.0	0	0	3	4
Doug Drabek	1	1	0.60	2	2	1	0	0	15.0	10	1	5	10
Bob Kipper	0	0	4.50	1	0	0	0	0	2.0	2	1	0	1
Bill Landrum	0	0	9.00	1	0	0	0	0	1.0	2	1	2	2
Roger Mason	0	0	0.00	3	0	0	1	0	4.1	3	0	1	2
Bob Patterson	0	0	0.00	1	0	0	0	0	2.0	1	0	0	3
Rosario Rodriguez	0	0	27.00	1	0	0	0	0	1.0	1	3	2	1
John Smiley	0	2	23.63	2	2	0	0	0	2.2	8	7	1	3
Zane Smith	1	1	0.61	2	2	0	0	0	14.2	15	1	3	10
Randy Tomlin	0	0	3.00	1	1	0	0	0	6.0	6	2	1	1
Bob Walk	0	0	1.93	3	0	0	1	0	9.1	5	2	3	5
TOTAL	3	4	2.57	20	7	1	2	0	63.0	53	18	22	42

GAME 1 AT PIT OCT 9

ATL	000	000	001	1	5	1
PIT	102	001	01X	5	8	1

Pitchers: GLAVINE, Wohlers (7), Stanton (8) vs DRABEK, Walk (7)
Home Runs: Van Slyke-PIT, Justice-ATL
Attendance: 57,347

GAME 2 AT PIT OCT 10

ATL	000	001	000	1	8	0
PIT	000	000	000	0	6	0

Pitchers: AVERY, Pena (9) vs SMITH, Mason (8), Belinda (9)
Attendance: 57,533

GAME 3 AT ATL OCT 12

PIT	100	100	100	3	10	2
ATL	411	000	13X	10	11	0

Pitchers: SMILEY, Landrum (3), Patterson (4), Kipper (6), Rodriguez (8) vs SMOLTZ, Stanton (7), Wohlers (8), Pena (8)
Home Runs: Merced-PIT, Bell-PIT, Gant-ATL, Olson-ATL, Bream-ATL
Attendance: 50,905

GAME 4 AT ATL OCT 13

PIT	010	010	000	1	3	11	1
ATL	200	000	000	0	2	7	1

Pitchers: Tomlin, Walk (7), BELINDA (9) vs Leibrandt, Clancy, Stanton (8), MERCKER (10), Wohlers (10)
Attendance: 51,109

GAME 5 AT ATL OCT 14

PIT	000	010	000	1	6	2
ATL	000	000	000	0	9	1

Pitchers: SMITH, Mason (8) vs GLAVINE, Pena (9)
Attendance: 51,109

GAME 6 AT PIT OCT 16

ATL	000	000	001	1	7	0
PIT	000	000	000	0	4	0

Pitchers: AVERY, Pena (9) vs DRABEK
Attendance: 54,508

GAME 7 AT PIT OCT 17

ATL	300	010	000	4	6	1
PIT	000	000	000	0	6	0

Pitchers: SMOLTZ vs SMILEY, Walk (1), Mason (6), Belinda (8)
Home Runs: Hunter-ATL
Attendance: 46,932

Minnesota struggled to achieve a 2–1 advantage in the first three games, then blew the Jays out of their SkyDome in the next two. Game One looked as though it would be an easy win for the Twins, who drove out starter Tom Candiotti with five runs on eight hits in the first 2⅔ innings. But Toronto scored once in the fourth and chased Twin starter Jack Morris in the sixth with five straight singles and three more runs. Relievers Carl Willis and Rick Aguilera, though, held Toronto to just one more single to preserve the victory for Minnesota.

The Jays scored three times in Game Two before Minnesota put its first run across in the last of the third, and scored twice more in the seventh, taking their first—and, as it turned out, only—win behind the strong pitching of rookie Juan Guzman and relievers Tom Henke and Duane Ward. Toronto again scored early in Game Three, with a pair of two-out runs (one of them Joe Carter's homer) in the first inning. Jays starter Jimmy Key held the Twins scoreless until they got to him for a run in the fifth, and another in the sixth which evened the score. Meanwhile a string of Minnesota pitchers stifled the Blue Jay bats from the second inning on. In the tenth, pinch hitter Mike Pagliarulo won it for the Twins with a home run to right.

For the third game in a row, Toronto scored first, with a run in the second inning of Game Four. But Minnesota's Kirby Puckett homered in the fourth to tie the score, and by the time Toronto scored again two innings later, the Twins had upped its run total to six. Puckett's home run in the first inning of Game Five gave the Twins the first of two early runs, but the Jays came back with three runs in the third and two more in the fourth to drive out starter Kevin Tapani. They scored no more, however, as three Twin relievers held them to one single in the final five frames. In the sixth inning, meanwhile, Minnesota reawakened to tie the game with a trio of runs, and salted it—and the pennant—away in the eighth: with two out, Puckett doubled home the go-ahead run, and Kent Hrbek singled in two more for insurance.

Minnesota Twins (West), 4;
Toronto Blue Jays (East), 1

MIN (W)

PLAYER/POS	AVG	G	AB	R	H	2B	3B	HR	RBI	BB	SO	SB
Rick Aguilera, p	.000	3	0	0	0	0	0	0	0	0	0	0
Steve Bedrosian, p	.000	2	0	0	0	0	0	0	0	0	0	0
Jarvis Brown, dh	.000	1	0	1	0	0	0	0	0	0	0	0
Chili Davis, dh	.294	5	17	3	5	2	0	0	2	5	8	1
Scott Erickson, p	.000	1	0	0	0	0	0	0	0	0	0	0
Greg Gagne, ss	.235	5	17	1	4	0	0	0	1	1	5	0
Dan Gladden, of	.261	5	23	4	6	0	0	0	3	1	3	3
Mark Guthrie, p	.000	2	0	0	0	0	0	0	0	0	0	0
Brian Harper, c	.278	5	18	1	5	2	0	0	1	0	2	0
Kent Hrbek, 1b	.143	5	21	0	3	0	0	0	3	1	3	0
Chuck Knoblauch, 2b	.350	5	20	5	7	2	0	0	3	3	3	2
Gene Larkin, ph	.000	3	3	0	0	0	0	0	0	0	1	0
Scott Leius, 3b	.000	3	4	0	0	0	0	0	0	1	1	0
Shane Mack, of	.333	5	18	4	6	1	1	0	3	2	4	2
Jack Morris, p	.000	2	0	0	0	0	0	0	0	0	0	0
Al Newman, 2b-1,3b-1	.000	2	0	0	0	0	0	0	0	0	0	0
Junior Ortiz, c	.000	3	3	0	0	0	0	0	0	0	0	0
Mike Pagliarulo, 3b	.333	5	15	4	5	1	0	1	3	0	2	0
Kirby Puckett, of	.429	5	21	4	9	1	0	2	6	1	4	0
Paul Sorrento, ph	.000	1	1	0	0	0	0	0	0	0	1	0
Kevin Tapani, p	.000	2	0	0	0	0	0	0	0	0	0	0
David West, p	.000	2	0	0	0	0	0	0	0	0	0	0
Carl Willis, p	.000	3	0	0	0	0	0	0	0	0	0	0
TOTAL	.276		181	27	50	9	1	3	25	15	37	8

PITCHER	W	L	ERA	G	GS	CG	SV	SHO	IP	H	ER	BB	SO
Rick Aguilera	0	0	0.00	3	0	0	3	0	3.1	1	0	0	3
Steve Bedrosian	0	0	0.00	2	0	0	0	0	1.1	3	0	2	2
Scott Erickson	0	0	4.50	1	1	0	0	0	4.0	3	2	5	2
Mark Guthrie	1	0	0.00	2	0	0	0	0	2.2	0	0	0	0
Jack Morris	2	0	4.05	2	2	0	0	0	13.1	17	6	1	7
Kevin Tapani	0	1	7.84	2	2	0	0	0	10.1	16	9	3	9
David West	1	0	0.00	2	0	0	0	0	5.2	1	0	4	4
Carl Willis	0	0	0.00	3	0	0	0	0	5.1	2	0	0	3
TOTAL	4	1	3.33	17	5	0	3	0	46.0	43	17	15	30

TOR (E)

PLAYER/POS	AVG	G	AB	R	H	2B	3B	HR	RBI	BB	SO	SB
Jim Acker, p	.000	1	0	0	0	0	0	0	0	0	0	0
Roberto Alomar, 2b	.474	5	19	3	9	0	0	0	4	2	3	2
Pat Borders, c	.263	5	19	0	5	1	0	0	2	0	0	0
Tom Candiotti, p	.000	2	0	0	0	0	0	0	0	0	0	0
Joe Carter, of-3,dh-2	.263	5	19	3	5	2	0	1	4	1	5	0
Rob Ducey, of	.000	1	1	0	0	0	0	0	0	0	0	0
Rene Gonzales, 1b-1,ss-1	.000	2	0	0	0	0	0	0	0	0	0	0
Kelly Gruber, 3b	.286	5	21	1	6	1	0	0	4	0	4	1
Juan Guzman, p	.000	1	0	0	0	0	0	0	0	0	0	0
Tom Henke, p	.000	2	0	0	0	0	0	0	0	0	0	0
Jimmy Key, p	.000	1	0	0	0	0	0	0	0	0	0	0
Manuel Lee, ss	.125	5	16	3	2	0	0	0	0	1	5	0
Rob MacDonald, p	.000	1	0	0	0	0	0	0	0	0	0	0
Candy Maldonado, of	.100	5	20	1	2	1	0	0	1	1	6	0
Rance Mulliniks, dh-3	.125	5	8	1	1	0	0	0	0	3	0	0
John Olerud, 1b	.153	5	19	1	3	0	0	0	3	3	1	0
Todd Stottlemyre, p	.000	1	0	0	0	0	0	0	0	0	0	0
Pat Tabler, dh	.000	2	1	0	0	0	0	0	0	1	0	0
Mike Timlin, p	.000	4	0	0	0	0	0	0	0	0	0	0
Duane Ward, p	.000	2	0	0	0	0	0	0	0	0	0	0
David Wells, p	.000	4	0	0	0	0	0	0	0	0	0	0
Devon White, of	.364	5	22	5	8	1	0	0	0	2	3	3
Mookie Wilson, of-2	.250	3	8	1	2	0	0	0	0	1	3	1
TOTAL	.249		173	19	43	6	0	1	18	15	30	7

PITCHER	W	L	ERA	G	GS	CG	SV	SHO	IP	H	ER	BB	SO
Jim Acker	0	0	0.00	1	0	0	0	0	0.2	1	0	0	1
Tom Candiotti	0	1	8.22	2	2	0	0	0	7.2	17	7	2	5
Juan Guzman	1	0	3.18	1	1	0	0	0	5.2	4	2	4	2
Tom Henke	0	0	0.00	2	0	0	0	0	2.2	0	0	1	5
Jimmy Key	0	0	3.00	1	1	0	0	0	6.0	5	2	1	1
Rob MacDonald	0	0	9.00	1	0	0	0	0	1.0	1	1	1	0
Todd Stottlemyre	0	1	9.82	1	1	0	0	0	3.2	7	4	1	3
Mike Timlin	0	1	3.18	4	0	0	0	0	5.2	5	2	2	5
Duane Ward	0	1	6.23	2	0	0	1	0	4.1	4	3	1	6
David Wells	0	0	2.35	4	0	0	0	0	7.2	6	2	2	9
TOTAL	1	4	4.60	19	5	0	1	0	45.0	50	23	15	37

By any measure, this World Series was one of the great ones. Five of the seven games were decided by a single run, three of them—including Games Six and Seven—in extra innings.

The opener in Minnesota gave no indication of the suspense to come, as the Twins opened up a 4–0 lead in the fifth inning en route to a 5–2 win. Game Two proved more difficult. Chili Davis put the Twins in front with a two-run homer in the first inning, but in the fifth Atlanta tied the score. Braves hurler Tom Glavine lost the game when the Twins' Scott Leius lofted a homer to lead off the eighth.

Minnesota took a quick lead in Game Three, but Atlanta tied the game an inning later, and went ahead on solo homers by David Justice in the fourth inning and Lonnie Smith in the fifth. Home runs by Kirby Puckett and Chili Davis in the fifth and sixth re-tied the score, which remained at 4–4 into the last of the eleventh inning, when Justice scored from second on Mark Lemke's two-out single. Lemke's heroics also made the difference in Game Four. Mike Pagliarulo drove in a pair of runs for Minnesota with a single in the second and a home run in the seventh, but Braves Terry Pendleton and Lonnie Smith neutralized the runs with solo homers in the third and seventh. Lemke came to bat in the bottom of the ninth with one out and the score still 2–2. He tripled, and scored in a tight play to even the Series.

In Game Five the Braves assaulted five Minnesota pitchers for fourteen runs and the Series lead, but when play returned to Minnesota for Game Six the Twins revived with two first-inning runs. In the third inning Puckett prevented two Atlanta runs with a leaping catch above the wall, but in the fifth, Atlanta's Terry Pendleton evened the score with a two-run homer. Later in the inning the Twins regained the lead on Puckett's sacrifice fly. Atlanta knotted the score again in the seventh, at 2–2. In the last of the eleventh, leadoff batter Puckett lined the ball over the wall near where he had earlier made his game-saving catch.

No one scored through 9½ innings of Game Seven as Minnesota's Jack Morris dueled John Smoltz, Mike Stanton, and Alejandro Pena. If the Braves had scored in the eighth as they could have, they would have won the game and the crown. Lonnie Smith singled to lead off the inning and could have come around on Terry Pendleton's double to the wall in left center. But, decoyed by the Twins' middle infielders into thinking there was a play at second, he paused just long enough after passing second to en-

able him to advance only to third. No one was out, but a grounder to first, an intentional walk to load the bases, and a smart 3–2–3 double play ended the Braves' threat.

Thus the game was still scoreless in the last of the tenth when Dan Gladden hustled his way into a broken-bat double and moved to third on Chuck Knoblauch's sacrifice bunt. Then, after the bases were loaded intentionally, pinch hitter Gene Larkin lobbed a hit over the head of the drawn-in left fielder. Gladden came home with the title for Minnesota.

Minnesota Twins (AL), 4; Atlanta Braves (NL), 3

MIN (A)

PLAYER/POS	AVG	G	AB	R	H	2B	3B	HR	RB	BB	SO	SB
Rick Aguilera, p	.000	4	1	0	0	0	0	0	0	0	0	0
Steve Bedrosian, p	.000	3	0	0	0	0	0	0	0	0	0	0
Jarvis Brown, of-2,dh-1	.000	3	2	0	0	0	0	0	0	0	0	0
Randy Bush, of-2	.250	3	4	0	1	0	0	0	0	0	1	0
Chili Davis, dh-4,of-1	.222	6	18	4	4	0	0	2	4	2	3	0
Scott Erickson, p	.000	2	1	0	0	0	0	0	0	0	1	0
Greg Gagne, ss	.167	7	24	1	4	1	0	1	3	0	7	0
Dan Gladden, of	.233	7	30	5	7	2	2	0	0	3	4	2
Mark Guthrie, p	.000	4	0	0	0	0	0	0	0	0	0	0
Brian Harper, c	.381	7	21	2	8	2	0	0	1	2	2	0
Kent Hrbek, 1b	.115	7	26	2	3	1	0	1	2	2	6	0
Chuck Knoblauch, 2b	.308	7	26	3	8	1	0	0	2	4	2	4
Gene Larkin, dh-1	.500	4	4	0	2	0	0	0	1	0	0	0
Terry Leach, p	.000	2	0	0	0	0	0	0	0	0	0	0
Scott Leius, 3b	.357	7	14	2	5	0	0	1	2	1	2	0
Shane Mack, of	.130	6	23	0	3	1	0	0	1	0	7	0
Jack Morris, p	.000	3	2	0	0	0	0	0	0	0	1	0
Al Newman, 3b-2,2b-1,ss-1	.500	4	2	0	1	0	1	0	1	0	0	0
Junior Ortiz, c	.200	3	5	0	1	0	0	0	0	1	0	0
Mike Pagliarulo, 3b	.273	6	11	1	3	0	0	1	2	1	2	0
Kirby Puckett, of	.250	7	24	4	6	0	1	2	4	5	7	1
Paul Sorrento, 1b-1	.000	3	2	0	0	0	0	0	0	1	2	0
Kevin Tapani, p	.000	2	1	0	0	0	0	0	0	0	0	0
David West, p	.000	2	0	0	0	0	0	0	0	0	0	0
Carl Willis, p	.000	4	0	0	0	0	0	0	0	0	0	0
TOTAL	.232		241	24	56	8	4	8	24	21	48	7

PITCHER	W	L	ERA	G	GS	CG	SV	SHO	IP	H	ER	BB	SO
Rick Aguilera	1	1	1.80	4	0	0	2	0	5.0	6	1	1	3
Steve Bedrosian	0	0	5.40	3	0	0	0	0	3.1	3	2	0	2
Scott Erickson	0	0	5.06	2	2	0	0	0	10.2	10	6	4	5
Mark Guthrie	0	1	2.25	4	0	0	0	0	4.0	3	1	4	3
Terry Leach	0	0	3.86	2	0	0	0	0	2.1	2	1	0	2
Jack Morris	2	0	1.17	3	3	1	0	1	23.0	18	3	9	15
Kevin Tapani	1	1	4.50	2	2	0	0	0	12.0	13	6	2	7
David West	0	0	∞	2	0	0	0	0	0.0	2	4	4	0
Carl Willis	0	0	5.14	4	0	0	0	0	7.0	6	4	2	2
TOTAL	4	3	3.74	26	7	1	2	1	67.1	63	28	26	39

ATL (N)

PLAYER/POS	AVG	G	AB	R	H	2B	3B	HR	RB	BB	SO	SB
Steve Avery, p	.000	2	3	0	0	0	0	0	0	0	2	0
Rafael Belliard, ss	.375	7	16	0	6	1	0	0	4	1	2	0
Jeff Blauser, ss	.167	5	6	0	1	0	0	0	0	1	1	0
Sid Bream, 1b	.125	7	24	0	3	2	0	0	0	3	4	0
Francisco Cabrera, c-1	.000	3	1	0	0	0	0	0	0	0	0	0
Jim Clancy, p	.000	3	1	0	0	0	0	0	0	0	0	0
Ron Gant, of	.267	7	30	3	8	0	1	0	4	2	3	1
Tom Glavine, p	.000	2	2	0	0	0	0	0	0	0	0	0
Tommy Gregg, ph	.000	4	3	0	0	0	0	0	0	0	0	0
Brian Hunter, 1b-4,of-4	.190	7	21	2	4	1	0	1	3	0	2	0
David Justice, of	.259	7	27	5	7	0	0	2	6	5	5	2
Charlie Leibrandt, p	.000	2	0	0	0	0	0	0	0	0	0	0
Mark Lemke, 2b	.417	6	24	4	10	1	3	0	4	2	4	0
Kent Mercker, p	.000	2	0	0	0	0	0	0	0	0	0	0
Keith Mitchell, of	.000	3	2	0	0	0	0	0	0	0	1	0
Greg Olson, c	.222	7	27	3	6	2	0	0	1	5	4	1
Alejandro Pena, p	.000	3	0	0	0	0	0	0	0	0	0	0
Terry Pendleton, 3b	.367	7	30	6	11	3	0	2	3	3	1	0
Randy St. Claire, p	.000	1	0	0	0	0	0	0	0	0	0	0
Lonnie Smith, dh-4,of-3	.231	7	26	5	6	0	0	3	3	3	4	1
John Smoltz, p	.000	2	2	0	0	0	0	0	0	0	0	0
Mike Stanton, p	.000	5	0	0	0	0	0	0	0	0	0	0
Jeff Treadway, 2b-1	.250	3	4	1	1	0	0	0	0	1	2	0
Jerry Willard, ph	.000	1	0	0	0	0	0	0	0	0	0	0
Mark Wohlers, p	.000	3	0	0	0	0	0	0	0	0	0	0
TOTAL	.253		249	29	63	10	4	8	29	26	39	5

PITCHER	W	L	ERA	G	GS	CG	SV	SHO	IP	H	ER	BB	SO
Steve Avery	0	0	3.46	2	2	0	0	0	13.0	10	5	1	8
Jim Clancy	1	0	4.15	3	0	0	0	0	4.1	3	2	4	2
Tom Glavine	1	1	2.70	2	2	1	0	0	13.1	8	4	7	8
Charlie Leibrandt	0	2	11.25	2	1	0	0	0	4.0	8	5	1	3
Kent Mercker	0	0	0.00	2	0	0	0	0	1.0	0	0	0	1
Alejandro Pena	0	1	3.38	3	0	0	0	0	5.1	6	2	3	7
Randy St. Claire	0	0	9.00	1	0	0	0	0	1.0	1	1	0	0
John Smoltz	0	0	1.26	2	2	0	0	0	14.1	13	2	1	11
Mike Stanton	1	0	0.00	5	0	0	0	0	7.1	5	0	2	1
Mark Wohlers	0	0	0.00	3	0	0	0	0	1.2	2	0	2	1
TOTAL	3	4	2.89	25	7	1	0	0	65.1	56	21	21	48

GAME 1 AT MIN OCT 19

```
ATL   000 001 010    2 6 1
MIN   001 031 00X    5 9 1
```
Pitchers: LEIBRANDT, Clancy (5), Wohlers (7), Stanton (8) vs MORRIS, Guthrie (8), Aguilera (8)
Home Runs: Gagne-MIN, Hrbek-MIN
Attendance: 55,108

GAME 2 AT MIN OCT 20

```
ATL   010 010 000    2 8 1
MIN   200 000 01X    3 4 1
```
Pitchers: GLAVINE vs TAPANI, Aguilera (9)
Home Runs: Davis-MIN, Leius-MIN
Attendance: 55,145

GAME 3 AT ATL OCT 22

```
MIN   100 000 120 000    4 10 1
ATL   010 120 000 001    5 8 2
```
Pitchers: Erickson, West (5), Leach (5), Bedrosian (6), Willis (8), Guthrie (8), AGUILERA (12) vs Avery, Pena (8), Stanton (10), Wohlers (12), Mercker (12), CLANCY (12)
Home Runs: Justice-ATL, Smith-ATL, Puckett-MIN, Davis-MIN
Attendance: 50,878

GAME 4 AT ATL OCT 23

```
MIN   010 000 100    2 7 0
ATL   001 000 101    3 8 0
```
Pitchers: Morris, Willis (7), GUTHRIE (8), Bedrosian (9) vs Smoltz, Wohlers (8), STANTON (8)
Home Runs: Pendleton-ATL, Pagliarulo-MIN, Smith-ATL
Attendance: 50,878

GAME 5 AT ATL OCT 24

```
MIN   000 003 011    5 7 1
ATL   000 410 63X    14 17 1
```
Pitchers: TAPANI, Leach (5), West (7), Bedrosian (7), Willis (8) vs GLAVINE, Mercker (6), Clancy (7), St. Claire (9)
Home Runs: Justice-ATL, Smith-ATL, Hunter-ATL
Attendance: 50,878

GAME 6 AT MIN OCT 26

```
ATL   000 020 100 00    3 9 1
MIN   200 010 000 01    4 9 0
```
Pitchers: Avery, Stanton (7), Pena (9), LEIBRANDT (11) vs Erickson, Guthrie (7), Willis (7), AGUILERA (10)
Home Runs: Pendleton-ATL, Puckett-MIN
Attendance: 55,155

GAME 7 AT MIN OCT 27

```
ATL   000 000 000 0    0 7 0
MIN   000 000 000 1    1 10 0
```
Pitchers: Smoltz, Stanton (8), PENA (9) vs MORRIS
Attendance: 55,118

Atlanta opened the series with a pair of one-sided wins but Pittsburgh pulled out a close victory in Game Three. After a third loss, the Pirates pummelled the Braves for two wins even more lopsided than their losses in the first two games. With the series now even, the stage was set for what turned out to be one of the most dramatic finishes in postseason history.

In Game One Pirate Jose Lind spoiled John Smoltz's shutout with his first home run of the season in the eighth inning. But by then the Braves had scored five times and held victory firmly in hand. Game Two was even easier. By the time the Pirates came up with four runs in the seventh inning (ending Steve Avery's LCS-record streak of scoreless innings at 22⅓), Atlanta had already compiled two four-run innings of their own (one of them on Ron Gant's grand slam). The Braves added five more runs in the last of the seventh to put the game out of reach.

At home for Game Three, the Pirates pulled themselves together behind the five-hit pitching of rookie knuckleballer Tim Wakefield. Sid Bream's solo homer in the fourth inning gave Atlanta a 1–0 lead, but Pirate Don Slaught homered to even the score an inning later and a pair of sixth-inning doubles put the Pirates ahead. Ron Gant's homer for Atlanta in the top of the seventh tied the score again, but a single, double, and sacrifice fly in the bottom of the inning put Pittsburgh on top to stay.

A 6–4 loss in Game Four brought the Pirates to the brink of elimination, but in Game Five they counterattacked, driving out Atlanta starter Steve Avery in the first inning with five hits (four of them doubles) and four runs, on their way to a 7–1 victory. With their feet still at the chasm's edge, the Pirates unloaded on Atlanta's Tom Glavine for eight runs in the second inning of Game Six before the first out was recorded, and pushed the assault to a 13–4 conclusion and a tied series.

While the Pirates scored single runs in the first and sixth innings of the final game, Pirate starter Doug Drabek (who had taken losses in Games One and Four) held Atlanta scoreless through eight innings. Then, in the last of the ninth, lead-off Brave Terry Pendleton doubled. He moved to third as David Justice reached on a grounder bobbled by the usually sure-handed second baseman Jose Lind. A walk to Sid Bream filled the bases. Stan Belinda replaced Drabek on the mound and retired Ron Gant on a fly to left, but Pendleton scored Atlanta's first run after the catch. Damon Berryhill walked to reload the bases, and pinch hitter Brian Hunter popped out. Had there been

no error, the game would have been over, with Pittsburgh waving the pennant. Instead, little-used pinch hitter Francisco Cabrera lined the ball safely to left, scoring Justice with the tying run and Bream with a repeat pennant for Atlanta.

Atlanta Braves (West), 4; Pittsburgh Pirates (East), 3

ATL (W)

PLAYER/POS	AVG	G	AB	R	H	2B	3B	HR	RB	BB	SO	SB
Steve Avery, p	.000	3	2	0	0	0	0	0	0	1	0	1	0
R. Belliard, ss-3,2b-1	.000	4	2	1	0	0	0	0	0	0	1	0
Damon Berryhill, c	.167	7	24	1	4	1	0	0	1	3	2	0
Jeff Blauser, ss	.208	7	24	3	5	0	1	1	4	3	2	0
Sid Bream, 1b	.273	7	22	5	6	3	0	1	2	3	0	0
Francisco Cabrera, ph	.500	2	2	0	1	0	0	0	2	0	0	0
Marvin Freeman, p	.000	3	0	0	0	0	0	0	0	0	0	0
Ron Gant, of	.182	7	22	5	4	0	0	2	6	4	4	1
Tom Glavine, p	.000	2	0	0	0	0	0	0	0	0	0	0
Brian Hunter, 1b-2	.200	3	5	1	1	0	0	0	0	0	1	0
David Justice, of	.280	7	25	5	7	1	0	2	6	6	4	0
Charlie Leibrandt, p	.000	2	1	0	0	0	0	0	0	0	1	0
Mark Lemke, 2b-7,3b-1	.333	7	21	2	7	1	0	0	2	5	3	0
Javier Lopez, c	.000	1	1	0	0	0	0	0	0	0	0	0
Kent Mercker, p	.000	2	0	0	0	0	0	0	0	0	0	0
Otis Nixon, of	.286	7	28	5	8	2	0	0	2	4	4	3
Terry Pendleton, 3b	.233	7	30	2	7	2	0	0	3	0	2	0
Jeff Reardon, p	.000	3	0	0	0	0	0	0	0	0	0	0
Deion Sanders, of-3	.000	4	5	0	0	0	0	0	0	0	3	0
Lonnie Smith, ph	.333	6	6	1	2	0	1	0	1	0	0	0
Pete Smith, p	.000	2	1	0	0	0	0	0	0	0	0	0
John Smoltz, p	.286	3	7	1	2	0	0	0	1	0	2	1
Mike Stanton, p	1.000	5	1	1	1	1	0	0	1	0	0	0
Jeff Treadway, 2b-1	.667	3	3	1	2	0	0	0	0	0	1	0
Mark Wohlers, p	.000	3	0	0	0	0	0	0	0	0	0	0
TOTAL	.244		234	34	57	11	2	6	32	29	28	5

PITCHER	W	L	ERA	G	GS	CG	SV	SHO	IP	H	ER	BB	SO
Steve Avery	1	1	9.00	3	2	0	0	0	8.0	13	8	2	3
Marvin Freeman	0	0	14.73	3	0	0	0	0	3.2	8	6	2	1
Tom Glavine	0	2	12.27	2	2	0	0	0	7.1	13	10	3	2
Charlie Leibrandt	0	0	1.93	4	0	0	0	0	4.2	4	1	3	3
Kent Mercker	0	0	0.00	2	0	0	0	0	3.0	1	0	1	1
Jeff Reardon	1	0	0.00	3	0	0	1	0	3.0	0	0	2	3
Pete Smith	0	0	2.45	2	0	0	0	0	3.2	2	1	3	3
John Smoltz	2	0	2.66	3	3	0	0	0	20.1	14	6	10	19
Mike Stanton	0	0	0.00	5	0	0	0	0	4.1	2	0	2	5
Mark Wohlers	0	0	0.00	3	0	0	0	0	3.0	2	0	1	2
TOTAL	4	3	4.72	28	7	0	1	0	61.0	59	32	29	42

PIT (E)

PLAYER/POS	AVG	G	AB	R	H	2B	3B	HR	RB	BB	SO	SB
Stan Belinda, p	.000	2	0	0	0	0	0	0	0	0	0	0
Jay Bell, ss	.172	7	29	3	5	2	0	1	4	3	4	0
Barry Bonds, of	.261	7	23	5	6	1	0	1	2	6	4	1
Alex Cole, of	.200	4	10	2	2	0	0	0	1	3	2	0
Danny Cox, p	.000	2	0	0	0	0	0	0	0	0	0	0
Doug Drabek, p	.000	3	6	0	0	0	0	0	0	1	4	0
Cecil Espy, of-2	.667	4	3	0	2	0	0	0	0	0	1	0
Carlos Garcia, 2b	.000	1	1	0	0	0	0	0	0	0	0	0
Danny Jackson, p	.000	1	0	0	0	0	0	0	0	0	0	0
Jeff King, 3b	.241	7	29	4	7	4	0	0	2	0	1	0
Mike LaValliere, c	.200	3	10	1	2	0	0	0	0	0	3	0
Jose Lind, 2b	.222	7	27	5	6	2	1	1	5	1	4	0
Roger Mason, p	.000	2	0	0	0	0	0	0	0	0	0	0
Lloyd McClendon, of	.727	5	11	4	8	2	0	1	4	4	1	0
Orlando Merced, 1b	.100	4	10	0	1	1	0	0	2	2	4	0
Denny Neagle, p	.000	2	0	0	0	0	0	0	0	0	0	0
Bob Patterson, p	.000	2	0	0	0	0	0	0	0	0	0	0
Gary Redus, 1b	.438	5	16	4	7	4	1	0	3	2	3	0
Don Slaught, c	.333	5	12	5	4	1	0	1	5	6	3	0
Randy Tomlin, p	.000	2	0	0	0	0	0	0	0	0	0	0
Andy Van Slyke, of	.276	7	29	1	8	3	1	0	4	1	5	0
Gary Varsho, of-1	.500	2	2	0	1	0	0	0	0	0	0	0
Tim Wakefield, p	.000	2	6	1	0	0	0	0	0	0	0	0
Bob Walk, p	.000	2	5	0	0	0	0	0	0	0	1	0
John Wehner, ph	.000	2	2	0	0	0	0	0	0	0	2	0
TOTAL	.255		231	35	59	20	3	5	32	29	42	1

PITCHER	W	L	ERA	G	GS	CG	SV	SHO	IP	H	ER	BB	SO
Stan Belinda	0	0	0.00	2	0	0	0	0	1.2	2	0	1	2
Danny Cox	0	0	0.00	2	0	0	0	0	1.1	1	0	1	1
Doug Drabek	0	3	3.71	3	3	0	0	0	17.0	18	7	6	10
Danny Jackson	0	1	21.60	1	1	0	0	0	1.2	4	4	2	0
Roger Mason	0	0	0.00	2	0	0	0	0	3.1	0	0	2	1
Denny Neagle	0	0	27.00	2	0	0	0	0	1.2	4	5	3	0
Bob Patterson	0	0	5.40	2	0	0	0	0	1.2	3	1	1	1
Randy Tomlin	0	0	6.75	2	0	0	0	0	2.2	5	2	1	0
Tim Wakefield	2	0	3.00	2	2	0	0	0	18.0	14	6	5	7
Bob Walk	1	0	3.86	2	1	1	0	0	11.2	6	5	7	6
TOTAL	3	4	4.45	20	7	3	0	0	60.2	57	30	29	28

GAME 1 AT ATL OCT 6

PIT	000	000	010	1	5	1
ATL	010	210	10X	5	8	0

Pitchers: DRABEK, Patterson (5), Neagle (7), Cox (8) vs SMOLTZ, Stanton (9)
Home Runs: Lind-PIT, Blauser-ATL
Attendance: 51,971

GAME 2 AT ATL OCT 7

PIT	000	000	410	5	7	0
ATL	040	040	50X	13	14	0

Pitchers: JACKSON, Mason (2), Walk (3), Tomlin (5), Neagle (7), Patterson (7), Belinda (8) vs AVERY, Freeman (7), Stanton (7), Wohlers (8), Reardon (9)
Home Runs: Gant-ATL
Attendance: 51,975

GAME 3 AT PIT OCT 9

ATL	000	100	100	2	5	0
PIT	000	011	10X	3	8	1

Pitchers: GLAVINE, Stanton (7), Wohlers (8) vs WAKEFIELD
Home Runs: Bream-ATL, Gant-ATL, Slaught-PIT
Attendance: 56,610

GAME 4 AT PIT OCT 10

ATL	020	022	000	6	11	1
PIT	021	000	100	4	6	1

Pitchers: SMOLTZ, Stanton (7), Reardon (9) vs DRABEK, Tomlin (5), Cox (6), Mason (7)
Attendance: 57,164

GAME 5 AT PIT OCT 11

ATL	000	000	010	1	3	0
PIT	401	001	10X	7	13	0

Pitchers: AVERY, Smith (1), Leibrandt (5), Freeman (6), Mercker (8) vs WALK
Attendance: 52,929

GAME 6 AT ATL OCT 13

PIT	080	041	000	13	13	1
ATL	000	100	102	4	9	1

Pitchers: WAKEFIELD vs GLAVINE, Leibrandt (2), Freeman (5), Mercker (7), Wohlers (9)
Home Runs: Bell-PIT, Bonds-PIT, McClendon-PIT, Justice-ATL (2)
Attendance: 51,975

GAME 7 AT ATL OCT 14

PIT	100	001	000	2	7	1
ATL	000	000	003	3	7	0

Pitchers: DRABEK, Belinda (9) vs Smoltz, Stanton (7), Smith (7), Avery (7), REARDON (9)
Attendance: 51,975

Oakland had competed in three League Championship Series in the previous four years and won them all. Toronto in its first fifteen seasons of existence had competed three times in the LCS and never won. In the first game of the 1992 matchup, the Athletics scored first on Mark McGwire's two-run homer and the next batter, Terry Steinbach, pushed the score to 3–0 with another home run. Toronto's Pat Borders and Dave Winfield retaliated with solo homers in the fifth and sixth innings to narrow the gap, and the Blue Jays tied the score in the eighth when Winfield, who had doubled with two outs, came home on John Olerud's single. But in the top of the ninth, Harold Baines led off with the game's fifth home run to put Oakland back into the lead, and A's reliever Dennis Eckersley preserved it for his tenth LCS save.

After this encouraging beginning, though, the A's went into a three-game decline. In Game Two, fireballer David Cone held Oakland scoreless through eight innings while the Jays built a 3–0 lead on Kelly Gruber's two-run homer in the fifth inning and a third score two innings later. Oakland finally touched Cone for a run in the ninth, but reliever Tom Henke smothered the threat. The A's recovered from an early deficit in Game Three to tie the score in the fourth inning, but fell behind on Candy Maldonado's leadoff homer in the sixth and never regained the lead. In Game Four the A's rocked Toronto starter Jack Morris for five runs in the fifth, and added another in the sixth to take a 6–1 lead. But in the eighth, reliever Eckersley, who came on with one run in and two on, yielded singles on his first two pitches to let in two more runs, and in the ninth gave up a leadoff single and a game-tying home run to Roberto Alomar. Toronto finally took the lead in the eleventh as Derek Bell fouled off several pitches before drawing a walk, took third on Maldonado's single, and scored on Pat Borders' fly to left. Reliever Tom Henke held the lead.

Down three games to one, Oakland came out slugging in Game Five. Ruben Sierra homered for a pair of runs in the first inning and the A's added a third run two innings later. Dave Winfield homered in the Toronto fourth, but the A's took advantage of two Toronto errors to score three more runs an inning later, putting the game out of the Blue Jays' reach. But they couldn't sustain their comeback. Joe Carter's two-run homer in the first inning of Game Six, and Candy Maldonado's three-run blast two innings later, highlighted a 9–2 Toronto romp that ended the team's string of

failed opportunities and carried the American League pennant to Canada for the first time.

Toronto Blue Jays (East), 4
Oakland Athletics (West), 2

TOR (E)

PLAYER/POS	AVG	G	AB	R	H	2B	3B	HR	RB	BB	SO	SB
Roberto Alomar, 2b	.423	6	26	4	11	1	0	2	4	2	1	5
Derek Bell, of	.000	2	0	1	0	0	0	0	0	1	0	0
Pat Borders, c	.318	6	22	3	7	0	0	1	3	1	1	0
Joe Carter, of-6,1b-2	.192	6	26	2	5	0	0	1	3	2	4	2
David Cone, p	.000	2	0	0	0	0	0	0	0	0	0	0
Mark Eichhorn, p	.000	1	0	0	0	0	0	0	0	0	0	0
Alfredo Griffin, ss-1	.000	2	2	0	0	0	0	0	0	0	0	0
Kelly Gruber, 3b	.091	6	22	3	2	1	0	1	2	2	3	0
Juan Guzman, p	.000	2	0	0	0	0	0	0	0	0	0	0
Tom Henke, p	.000	4	0	0	0	0	0	0	0	0	0	0
Jimmy Key, p	.000	1	0	0	0	0	0	0	0	0	0	0
Manuel Lee, ss	.278	6	18	2	5	1	1	0	3	1	2	0
Candy Maldonado, of	.273	6	22	3	6	0	0	2	6	2	4	0
Jack Morris, p	.000	2	0	0	0	0	0	0	0	0	0	0
John Olerud, 1b	.348	6	23	4	8	2	0	1	4	2	5	0
Ed Sprague, ph	.500	2	2	0	1	0	0	0	0	0	1	0
Todd Stottlemyre, p	.000	1	0	0	0	0	0	0	0	0	0	0
Mike Timlin, p	.000	2	0	0	0	0	0	0	0	0	0	0
Duane Ward, p	.000	3	0	0	0	0	0	0	0	0	0	0
Devon White, of	.348	6	23	2	8	2	0	0	2	5	6	0
Dave Winfield, dh	.250	6	24	7	6	1	0	2	3	5	2	0
TOTAL	.281		210	31	59	8	1	10	30	23	29	7

PITCHER	W	L	ERA	G	GS	CG	SV	SHO	IP	H	ER	BB	SO
David Cone	1	1	3.00	2	2	0	0	0	12.0	11	4	5	9
Mark Eichhorn	0	0	0.00	1	0	0	0	0	1.0	0	0	0	0
Juan Guzman	2	0	2.08	2	2	0	0	0	13.0	12	3	5	11
Tom Henke	0	0	0.00	4	0	0	3	0	4.2	4	0	2	2
Jimmy Key	0	0	0.00	1	0	0	0	0	3.0	2	0	2	1
Jack Morris	0	1	6.57	2	2	1	0	0	12.1	11	9	9	6
Todd Stottlemyre	0	0	2.45	1	0	0	0	0	3.2	3	1	0	1
Mike Timlin	0	0	6.75	2	0	0	0	0	1.1	4	1	0	1
Duane Ward	1	0	6.75	3	0	0	0	0	4.0	5	3	1	2
TOTAL	4	2	3.44	18	6	1	3	0	55.0	52	21	24	33

OAK (W)

PLAYER/POS	AVG	G	AB	R	H	2B	3B	HR	RB	BB	SO	SB
Harold Baines, dh	.440	6	25	6	11	2	0	1	4	0	3	0
Lance Blankenship, 2b	.231	5	13	2	3	0	0	0	0	3	4	1
Mike Bordick, ss-4,2b-2	.053	6	19	1	1	0	0	0	0	1	2	1
Jerry Browne, 3b-2,of-1	.400	4	10	3	4	0	0	0	2	2	0	0
Jim Corsi, p	.000	3	0	0	0	0	0	0	0	0	0	0
Ron Darling, p	.000	1	0	0	0	0	0	0	0	0	0	0
Kelly Downs, p	.000	2	0	0	0	0	0	0	0	0	0	0
Dennis Eckersley, p	.000	3	0	0	0	0	0	0	0	0	0	0
Eric Fox, of-1,dh-1	.000	4	1	0	0	0	0	0	0	0	0	0
Rickey Henderson, of	.261	6	23	5	6	0	0	0	1	4	4	2
Rick Honeycutt, p	.000	2	0	0	0	0	0	0	0	0	0	0
Carney Lansford, 3b	.167	5	23	2	8	3	0	0	1	1	1	0
Mark McGwire, 1b	.150	6	20	1	3	0	0	1	3	5	4	0
Mike Moore, p	.000	2	0	0	0	0	0	0	0	0	0	0
Jeff Parrett, p	.000	3	0	0	0	0	0	0	0	0	0	0
Jamie Quirk, ph	.000	1	1	0	0	0	0	0	0	0	0	0
Randy Ready, ph	.000	1	1	0	0	0	0	0	0	0	1	0
Jeff Russell, p	.000	3	0	0	0	0	0	0	0	0	0	0
Ruben Sierra, of	.333	6	24	4	8	2	1	1	7	2	1	1
Terry Steinbach, c	.292	6	24	1	7	0	0	1	5	2	7	0
Dave Stewart, p	.000	2	0	0	0	0	0	0	0	0	0	0
Walt Weiss, ss	.167	3	6	1	1	0	0	0	0	2	1	2
Bob Welch, p	.000	1	0	0	0	0	0	0	0	0	0	0
Willie Wilson, of	.227	6	22	0	5	1	0	0	0	0	5	7
Bobby Witt, p	.000	1	0	0	0	0	0	0	0	0	0	0
TOTAL	.251		207	24	52	5	1	4	23	24	33	16

PITCHER	W	L	ERA	G	GS	CG	SV	SHO	IP	H	ER	BB	SO
Jim Corsi	0	0	0.00	3	0	0	0	0	2.0	2	0	3	0
Ron Darling	0	1	3.00	1	1	0	0	0	6.0	4	2	2	3
Kelly Downs	0	1	3.86	2	0	0	0	0	2.1	3	1	1	0
Dennis Eckersley	0	0	6.00	3	0	0	1	0	3.0	8	2	0	2
Rick Honeycutt	0	0	0.00	2	0	0	0	0	2.0	0	0	0	1
Mike Moore	0	2	7.45	2	2	0	0	0	9.2	11	8	5	7
Jeff Parrett	0	0	11.57	3	0	0	0	0	2.1	6	3	0	1
Jeff Russell	1	0	9.00	3	0	0	0	0	2.0	2	2	4	0
Dave Stewart	1	0	2.70	2	2	1	0	0	16.2	14	5	6	7
Bob Welch	0	0	2.57	1	1	0	0	0	7.0	7	2	1	7
Bobby Witt	0	0	18.00	1	0	0	0	0	1.0	2	2	1	1
TOTAL	2	4	4.50	23	6	1	1	0	54.0	59	27	23	29

GAME 1 AT TOR OCT 7

OAK	030	000	001	4 6 1
TOR	000	011	010	3 9 0

Pitchers: Stewart, RUSSELL (8), Eckersley (9) vs MORRIS
Home Runs: Baines-OAK, McGwire-OAK, Steinbach-OAK, Winfield-TOR, Borders-TOR
Attendance: 51,039

GAME 2 AT TOR OCT 8

OAK	000	000	001	1 6 0
TOR	000	020	10X	3 4 0

Pitchers: MOORE, Corsi (8), Parrett (8) vs CONE, Henke (9)
Home Runs: Gruber-TOR
Attendance: 51,114

GAME 3 AT OAK OCT 10

TOR	010	110	211	7 9 1
OAK	000	200	210	5 13 3

Pitchers: GUZMAN, Ward (7), Timlin (8), Henke (8) vs DARLING, Downs (7), Corsi (8), Russell (8), Honeycutt (9), Eckersley (9)
Home Runs: Alomar-TOR, Maldonado-TOR
Attendance: 46,911

GAME 4 AT OAK OCT 11

TOR	010	000	032	01	7 17 4
OAK	005	001	000	00	6 12 2

Pitchers: Morris, Stottlemyre (4), Timlin (8), WARD (9), Henke (11) vs Welch, Parrett (8), Eckersley (8), Corsi (9), DOWNS (10)
Home Runs: Alomar-TOR, Olerud-TOR
Attendance: 47,732

GAME 5 AT OAK OCT 12

TOR	000	100	100	2 7 3
OAK	201	030	00X	6 8 0

Pitchers: CONE, Key (5), Eichhorn (8) vs STEWART
Home Runs: Winfield-TOR, Sierra-OAK
Attendance: 44,955

GAME 6 AT TOR OCT 14

OAK	000	001	010	2 7 1
TOR	204	010	02X	9 13 0

Pitchers: MOORE, Parrett (3), Honeycutt (5), Russell (7), Witt (8) vs GUZMAN, Ward (8), Henke (9)
Home Runs: Carter-TOR, Maldonado-TOR
Attendance: 51,335

Atlanta outscored Toronto in the Series 20 runs to 16, but the Blue Jays eked out four one-run victories to bring Canada its first world baseball championship. In the fourth inning of Game One, Atlanta's Tom Glavine gave up a leadoff homer to Joe Carter for the game's first run, but held the Jays to just one single the rest of the way. For five innings, meanwhile, Toronto starter Jack Morris shut out the Braves. But in the top of the sixth he gave up a deciding three-run homer to catcher Damon Berryhill. The next night, though, down 4–5 in the ninth inning, Toronto pinch hitter Derek Bell drew a walk from Braves closer Jeff Reardon, and pinch hitter Ed Sprague lined Reardon's first pitch over the left field wall.

Toronto moved ahead with another close victory in Game Three, the first World Series game ever played outside the United States. Atlanta threatened in the fourth inning when, with two on and none out, David Justice drove the ball to deep center. But in the defensive play of the Series, center fielder Devon White leaped high to snare the ball. Baserunner Terry Pendleton was ruled out for passing Deion Sanders on the basepath, and third baseman Kelly Gruber tagged Sanders, who was diving back into second base, to complete what seemed to be a triple play. The umpire didn't see the tag, however, and called Sanders safe. Still, no Brave scored, and Blue Jay Joe Carter homered for the game's first run in the last of the fourth. Atlanta tied the game in the sixth and took the lead in the top of the eighth. Gruber homered to retie it in the bottom of the inning, and after the Jays had filled the bases in the last of the ninth, Candy Maldonado tagged Reardon for a hit over the drawn-in outfield to bring home the winning run.

The Jays pushed their Series advantage to 3–1 in Game Four. Catcher Pat Borders opened the Toronto third with a home run, and Gruber scored from second on Devon White's seventh-inning single to push the Blue Jay lead to 2–0. The Braves got to Toronto starter Jimmy Key for a run in the eighth, but relievers Duane Ward and Tom Henke combined to stop them from scoring again.

In the fifth game the Blue Jays twice came from one run down to even the score. But in the fifth inning, after the Braves had once again built a one-run lead, Lonnie Smith extended it with a grand slam home run that sent the Series back to Atlanta.

Toronto Blue Jays (AL), 4; Atlanta Braves (NL), 2

TOR (A)

PLAYER/POS	AVG	G	AB	R	H	2B	3B	HR	RB	BB	SO	SB
Roberto Alomar, 2b	.208	6	24	3	5	1	0	0	0	3	3	3
Derek Bell, ph	.000	2	1	1	0	0	0	0	0	1	0	0
Pat Borders, c	.450	6	20	2	9	3	0	1	3	2	1	0
Joe Carter, of-4	.273	6	22	2	6	2	0	2	3	3	2	1
David Cone, p	.500	2	4	0	2	0	0	0	0	1	1	0
Mark Eichhorn, p	.000	1	0	0	0	0	0	0	0	0	0	0
Alfredo Griffin, ss	.000	2	0	0	0	0	0	0	0	0	0	0
Kelly Gruber, 3b	.105	6	19	2	2	0	0	1	1	2	5	1
Juan Guzman, p	.000	1	0	0	0	0	0	0	0	0	0	0
Tom Henke, p	.000	3	0	0	0	0	0	0	0	0	0	0
Jimmy Key, p	.000	2	1	0	0	0	0	0	0	0	0	0
Manuel Lee, ss	.105	6	19	1	2	0	0	0	0	1	2	0
Candy Maldonado, of-5	.158	6	19	1	3	0	0	1	2	2	5	0
Jack Morris, p	.000	2	2	0	0	0	0	0	0	0	2	0
John Olerud, 1b	.308	4	13	2	4	0	0	0	0	0	4	0
Ed Sprague, 1b-1	.500	3	2	1	1	0	0	1	2	1	0	0
Todd Stottlemyre, p	.000	4	0	0	0	0	0	0	0	0	0	0
Pat Tabler, ph	.000	2	0	0	0	0	0	0	0	0	0	0
Mike Timlin, p	.000	2	0	0	0	0	0	0	0	0	0	0
Duane Ward, p	.000	4	0	0	0	0	0	0	0	0	0	0
David Wells, p	.000	4	0	0	0	0	0	0	0	0	0	0
Devon White, of	.231	6	26	2	6	1	0	0	2	0	6	1
Dave Winfield, of-3,dh-3	.227	6	22	0	5	1	0	0	3	2	3	0
TOTAL	.230		196	17	45	8	0	6	17	18	33	6

PITCHER	W	L	ERA	G	GS	CG	SV	SHO	IP	H	ER	BB	SO
David Cone	0	0	3.48	2	2	0	0	0	10.1	9	4	8	8
Mark Eichhorn	0	0	0.00	1	0	0	0	0	1.0	0	0	0	1
Juan Guzman	0	0	1.13	1	1	0	0	0	8.0	8	1	1	7
Tom Henke	0	0	2.70	3	0	0	2	0	3.1	2	1	2	1
Jimmy Key	2	0	1.00	2	1	0	0	0	9.0	6	1	0	6
Jack Morris	0	2	8.44	2	2	0	0	0	10.2	13	10	6	12
Todd Stottlemyre	0	0	0.00	4	0	0	0	0	3.2	4	0	2	0
Mike Timlin	0	0	0.00	2	0	0	1	0	1.1	0	0	0	0
Duane Ward	2	0	0.00	4	0	0	0	0	3.1	1	0	1	6
David Wells	0	0	0.00	4	0	0	0	0	4.1	1	0	2	3
TOTAL	4	2	2.78	25	6	0	3	0	55	44	17	20	48

ATL (N)

PLAYER/POS	AVG	G	AB	R	H	2B	3B	HR	RB	BB	SO	SB
Steve Avery, p	.000	2	1	0	0	0	0	0	0	0	1	0
Rafael Belliard, ss-3,2b-1	.000	4	0	0	0	0	0	0	0	0	0	0
Damon Berryhill, c	.091	6	22	1	2	0	0	1	3	1	11	0
Jeff Blauser, ss	.250	6	24	2	6	0	0	0	0	1	9	2
Sid Bream, 1b	.200	5	15	1	3	0	0	0	0	4	0	0
Francisco Cabrera, ph	.000	1	1	0	0	0	0	0	1	0	0	0
Ron Gant, of-3	.125	4	8	2	1	1	0	0	0	1	2	2
Tom Glavine, p	.000	2	2	0	0	0	0	0	0	0	0	0
Brian Hunter, 1b-3	.200	4	5	0	1	0	0	0	2	0	1	0
David Justice, of	.158	6	19	4	3	0	0	1	3	6	5	1
Charlie Leibrandt, p	.000	1	0	0	0	0	0	0	0	0	0	0
Mark Lemke, 2b	.211	6	19	0	4	0	0	0	2	1	3	0
Otis Nixon, of	.296	6	27	3	8	1	0	0	1	1	3	5
Terry Pendleton, 3b	.240	6	25	2	6	2	0	0	2	1	5	0
Jeff Reardon, p	.000	2	0	0	0	0	0	0	0	0	0	0
Deion Sanders, of	.533	4	15	4	8	2	0	0	1	2	1	5
Lonnie Smith, dh-3	.167	5	12	1	2	0	0	1	5	1	4	0
Pete Smith, p	.000	1	1	0	0	0	0	0	0	0	1	0
John Smoltz, p-2	.000	3	3	0	0	0	0	0	0	0	0	0
Mike Stanton, p	.000	4	0	0	0	0	0	0	0	0	0	0
Jeff Treadway, ph	.000	1	1	0	0	0	0	0	0	0	0	0
Mark Wohlers, p	.000	2	0	0	0	0	0	0	0	0	0	0
TOTAL	.220		200	20	44	6	0	3	19	20	48	15

PITCHER	W	L	ERA	G	GS	CG	SV	SHO	IP	H	ER	BB	SO
Steve Avery	0	1	3.75	2	2	0	0	0	12.0	11	5	3	11
Tom Glavine	1	1	1.59	2	2	2	0	0	17.0	10	3	4	8
Charlie Leibrandt	0	1	9.00	1	0	0	0	0	2.0	3	2	0	0
Jeff Reardon	0	1	13.50	2	0	0	0	0	1.1	2	2	1	1
Pete Smith	0	0	0.00	1	1	0	0	0	3.0	3	0	0	0
John Smoltz	1	0	2.70	2	2	0	0	0	13.1	13	4	7	12
Mike Stanton	0	0	0.00	4	0	0	1	0	5.0	3	0	2	1
Mark Wohlers	0	0	0.00	2	0	0	0	0	0.2	0	0	1	0
TOTAL	2	4	2.65	16	6	2	1	0	54.1	45	16	18	33

Toronto scored a run in the first inning of Game Six. Atlanta tied the game in the third, but Candy Maldonado's leadoff homer in the fourth restored the advantage to Toronto. In the bottom of the ninth, the Braves scrabbled back to tie it up again. The score remained knotted at 2–2 until the top of the eleventh, when Toronto's Dave Winfield delivered runners from second and first with a two-out double into the left field corner. As it turned out, the Jays needed both runs, for Atlanta scored in the bottom of the eleventh. But with two out and the potential tying run on third, Otis Nixon, attempting a bunt single, just failed to reach safely, and the Series was over.

GAME 1 AT ATL OCT 17

TOR	000 100 000	1	4	0
ATL	000 003 00X	3	4	0

Pitchers: MORRIS, Stottlemyre (7), Wells (8) vs GLAVINE
Home Runs: Carter-TOR, Berryhill-ATL
Attendance: 51,763

GAME 2 AT ATL OCT 18

TOR	000 020 012	5	9	2
ATL	010 120 000	4	5	1

Pitchers: Cone, Wells (5), Stottlemyre (7), WARD (8), Henke (9) vs Smoltz, Stanton (8), REARDON (8)
Home Runs: Sprague-TOR
Attendance: 51,763

GAME 3 AT TOR OCT 20

ATL	000 001 010	2	9	0
TOR	000 100 011	3	6	1

Pitchers: AVERY, Wohlers (9), Stanton (9), Reardon (9) vs Guzman, WARD (9)
Home Runs: Carter-TOR, Gruber-TOR
Attendance: 51,813

GAME 4 AT TOR OCT 21

ATL	000 000 010	1	5	0
TOR	001 000 10X	2	6	0

Pitchers: GLAVINE vs KEY, Ward (8), Henke (9)
Home Runs: Borders-TOR
Attendance: 52,090

GAME 5 AT TOR OCT 22

ATL	100 150 000	7	13	0
TOR	010 100 000	2	6	0

Pitchers: SMOLTZ, Stanton (7) vs MORRIS, Wells (5), Timlin (7), Eichhorn (8), Stottlemyre (9)
Home Runs: Justice-ATL, L.Smith-ATL
Attendance: 52,268

GAME 6 AT ATL OCT 24

TOR	100 100 000 02	4	14	1
ATL	001 000 001 01	3	8	1

Pitchers: Cone, Stottlemyre (7), Wells (7), Ward (8), Henke (9), KEY (10), Timlin (11) vs Avery, P.Smith (5), Stanton (8), Wohlers (9), LEIBRANDT (10)
Home Runs: Maldonado-TOR
Attendance: 51,763

Atlanta outhit the Phillies by 47 percentage points, outscored them by ten runs, and yielded 1.6 fewer earned runs per game. But the Phillies won the pennant. In the opener, Philadelphia starter Curt Schilling fanned ten batters—including the first five he faced—and left the game after eight innings with a 3–2 lead. An errant throw by Phillie third baseman Kim Batiste (who had just entered the game to strengthen the defense) set up an unearned tying run in the ninth inning. But in the last of the tenth, after John Kruk had doubled, Batiste redeemed himself with a game-winning hit down the left field line, and was carried off the field on his teammates' shoulders.

While the Philadelphia offense remained steady over the next two games, the Braves erupted for 28 runs, quadrupling the Phillies' seven. By the time Philadelphia scored its first runs in the fourth inning of Game Two, Atlanta had already sent eight men across the plate. In Game Three the Phillies scored first, and held a 2–0 lead before the Braves destroyed them with five runs in the sixth inning and four more in the seventh.

Game Four featured only four fewer hits than Game Three, but ten fewer runs, as Philadelphia evened the series with its second close win. Phillie starter Danny Jackson yielded nine hits and a pair of walks in 7⅔ innings, but only one second-inning run. In the top of the fourth, Darren Daulton, who had reached on an infield error, took third on Milt Thompson's double and scored on Kevin Stocker's two-out single. Pitcher Jackson then singled home Thompson with what proved the winning run.

In the fifth game, Curt Schilling held Atlanta to four hits through eight innings, and carried a 3–0 lead into the bottom of the ninth. But when a walk and infield error put the first two men on, Mitch Williams relieved Schilling and gave up a trio of singles which tied the game. In the top of the tenth inning, though, Lenny Dykstra's solo homer restored the Phillies' lead, and veteran reliever Larry Andersen blanked the Braves in the bottom of the tenth—striking out the final two batters—to preserve the win.

After their two narrow wins on the road, the Phillies clinched the pennant with relative ease when the series returned to Philadelphia for Game Six. Darren Daulton's two-out double in the third inning put the Phillies up 2–0. Atlanta scored once in the fifth, but Dave Hollins' two-run homer in the last of the fifth increased the Phillies' lead to three runs, and Mickey Morandini's two-out two-run triple

an inning later pushed the score to 6–1, driving out Atlanta starter Greg Maddux. Atlanta's Jeff Blauser brought the score to 6–3 with a home run in the seventh inning, but Phillie relievers David West and Mitch Williams set the Braves down in order in the final two innings.

Philadelphia Phillies (East), 4; Atlanta Braves (West), 2

PHI (E)

PLAYER/POS	AVG	G	AB	R	H	2B	3B	HR	RB	BB	SO	SB
Larry Andersen, p	.000	3	0	0	0	0	0	0	0	0	0	0
Kim Batiste, 3b	1.000	4	1	0	1	0	0	0	1	0	0	0
Wes Chamberlain, of-2	.364	4	11	1	4	3	0	0	1	1	3	0
Darren Daulton, c	.263	6	19	2	5	1	0	1	3	6	3	0
Mariano Duncan, 2b	.267	3	15	3	4	0	2	0	0	0	5	0
Lenny Dykstra, of	.280	6	25	5	7	1	0	2	2	5	8	0
Jim Eisenreich, of-5	.133	6	15	2	2	1	0	0	1	0	2	0
Tommy Greene, p	.000	2	1	0	0	0	0	0	0	1	0	0
Dave Hollins, 3b	.200	4	20	2	4	1	0	2	4	5	4	1
Pete Incaviglia, of	.167	3	12	2	2	0	0	1	1	0	3	0
Danny Jackson, p	.250	1	4	0	1	0	0	0	1	0	3	0
Ricky Jordan, ph	.000	2	1	0	0	0	0	0	0	0	1	0
John Kruk, 1b	.250	6	24	4	6	2	1	1	5	4	5	0
Tony Longmire, ph	.000	1	1	0	0	0	0	0	0	0	1	0
Roger Mason, p	.000	2	0	0	0	0	0	0	0	0	0	0
Mickey Morandini, 2b	.250	4	16	1	4	0	1	0	2	0	3	1
Terry Mulholland, p	.000	1	2	0	0	0	0	0	0	0	1	0
Todd Pratt, c	.000	1	1	0	0	0	0	0	0	0	0	0
Ben Rivera, p	.000	1	0	0	0	0	0	0	0	0	0	0
Curt Schilling, p	.000	2	5	0	0	0	0	0	0	0	2	0
Kevin Stocker, ss	.182	6	22	0	4	1	0	0	1	2	5	0
Bobby Thigpen, p	.000	2	0	0	0	0	0	0	0	0	0	0
Milt Thompson, of-5	.231	6	13	2	3	1	0	0	0	1	2	0
David West, p	.000	3	0	0	0	0	0	0	0	0	0	0
Mitch Williams, p	.000	4	0	0	0	0	0	0	0	0	0	0
TOTAL	.227		207	23	47	11	4	7	22	26	51	2

PITCHER	W	L	ERA	G	GS	CG	SV	SHO	IP	H	ER	BB	SO
Larry Andersen	0	0	15.43	3	0	0	1	0	2.1	4	4	1	3
Tommy Greene	1	1	9.64	2	2	0	0	0	9.1	12	10	7	7
Danny Jackson	1	0	1.17	1	1	0	0	0	7.2	9	1	2	6
Roger Mason	0	0	0.00	2	0	0	0	0	3.0	1	0	0	2
Terry Mulholland	0	1	7.20	1	1	0	0	0	5.0	9	4	1	2
Ben Rivera	0	0	4.50	1	0	0	0	0	2.0	1	1	1	2
Curt Schilling	0	0	1.69	2	2	0	0	0	16.0	11	3	5	19
Bobby Thigpen	0	0	5.40	2	0	0	0	0	1.2	1	1	1	3
David West	0	0	13.50	3	0	0	0	0	2.2	5	4	2	5
Mitch Williams	2	0	1.69	4	0	0	2	0	5.1	6	1	2	5
TOTAL	4	2	4.75	21	6	0	3		55.0	59	29	22	54

ATL (W)

PLAYER/POS	AVG	G	AB	R	H	2B	3B	HR	RB	BB	SO	SB
Steve Avery, p	.500	2	4	1	2	1	0	0	0	0	1	0
Rafael Belliard, 2b-1,ss-1	.000	2	1	1	0	0	0	0	0	0	1	0
Damon Berryhill, c	.211	6	19	2	4	0	0	1	3	1	5	0
Jeff Blauser, ss	.280	6	25	5	7	1	0	2	4	4	7	0
Sid Bream, 1b	1.000	1	1	1	1	0	0	0	0	0	0	0
Francisco Cabrera, c-1	.667	3	3	0	2	0	0	0	1	0	1	0
Ron Gant, of	.185	6	27	4	5	3	0	0	3	2	9	0
Tom Glavine, p	.000	1	3	0	0	0	0	0	0	0	0	0
David Justice, of	.143	6	21	2	3	1	0	0	4	3	3	0
Mark Lemke, 2b	.208	6	24	2	5	2	0	0	4	1	6	0
Greg Maddux, p	.250	2	4	1	1	0	0	0	0	0	1	0
Fred McGriff, 1b	.435	6	23	6	10	2	0	1	4	4	7	0
Greg McMichael, p	.000	4	0	0	0	0	0	0	0	0	0	0
Kent Mercker, p	.000	5	0	0	0	0	0	0	0	0	0	0
Otis Nixon, of	.348	6	23	3	8	2	0	0	4	5	6	0
Greg Olson, c	.333	2	3	0	1	1	0	0	0	0	1	0
Bill Pecota, ph	.333	4	3	1	1	0	0	0	0	0	1	0
Terry Pendleton, 3b	.346	6	26	4	9	1	0	1	5	0	2	0
Deion Sanders, of-1	.000	5	3	0	0	0	0	0	0	0	1	0
John Smoltz, p	.000	1	1	0	0	0	0	0	0	0	1	0
Mike Stanton, p	.000	1	0	0	0	0	0	0	0	0	0	0
Tony Tarasco, of	.000	1	1	0	0	0	0	0	0	0	1	0
Mark Wohlers, p	.000	4	0	0	0	0	0	0	0	0	0	0
TOTAL	.274		215	33	59	14	0	5	32	22	54	0

PITCHER	W	L	ERA	G	GS	CG	SV	SHO	IP	H	ER	BB	SO
Steve Avery	0	0	2.77	2	2	0	0	0	13.0	9	4	6	10
Tom Glavine	1	0	2.57	1	1	0	0	0	7.0	6	2	0	5
Greg Maddux	1	1	4.97	2	2	0	0	0	12.2	11	7	7	11
Greg McMichael	0	1	6.75	4	0	0	0	0	4.0	7	3	2	1
Kent Mercker	0	0	1.80	5	0	0	0	0	5.0	3	1	2	4
John Smoltz	0	1	6.14	1	1	0	0	0	6.1	8	0	5	10
Mike Stanton	0	0	0.00	1	0	0	0	0	1.0	1	0	1	0
Mark Wohlers	0	1	3.38	5	0	0	0	0	5.1	2	2	3	10
TOTAL	2	4	3.15	20	6	0	0	0	54.1	47	19	26	51

GAME 1 AT PHI OCT 6

ATL	001	100	001	0			3	9	0
PHI	100	101	000	1			4	9	1

Pitchers: Avery, Mercker (7), McMICHAEL (9) vs Schilling, WILLIAMS (9)
Home Runs: Incaviglia-PHI
Attendance: 62,012

GAME 2 AT PHI OCT 7

ATL	206	010	041	14	16	0
PHI	000	200	001	3	7	2

Pitchers: MADDUX, Stanton (8), Wohlers (9) vs GREENE, Thigpen (3), Rivera (4), Mason (6), West (8), Andersen (9)
Home Runs: Blauser-ATL, McGriff-ATL, Pendleton-ATL, Berryhill-ATL, Dykstra-PHI, Hollins-PHI
Attendance: 62,436

GAME 3 AT ATL OCT 9

PHI	000	101	011	4	10	1
ATL	000	005	40X	9	12	0

Pitchers: MULHOLLAND, Mason (6), Andersen (7), West (7), Thigpen (8) vs GLAVINE, Mercker (8), McMichael (9)
Home Runs: Kruk-PHI
Attendance: 52,032

GAME 4 AT ATL OCT 10

PHI	000	200	000	2	8	1
ATL	010	000	000	1	10	1

Pitchers: JACKSON, Williams (8) vs SMOLTZ, Mercker (7), Wohlers (8)
Attendance: 52,032

GAME 5 AT ATL OCT 11

PHI	100	100	001	1	4	6	1
ATL	000	000	003	0	3	7	1

Pitchers: Schilling, WILLIAMS (9), Andersen (10) vs Avery, Mercker (8), McMichael (9), WOHLERS (10)
Home Runs: Dykstra-PHI, Daulton-PHI
Attendance: 52,032

GAME 6 AT PHI OCT 13

ATL	000	010	200	3	5	3
PHI	002	022	00X	6	7	1

Pitchers: MADDUX, Mercker (6), McMichael (7) vs GREENE, West (8), Williams (9)
Home Runs: Blauser-ATL, Hollins-PHI
Attendance: 62,502

The visiting team won the first four games of the series, but in Game Five, home team Toronto held off a ninth-inning White Sox rally to take a 3–2 series lead. Then, in Chicago two days later, the Jays put the Sox away with the series' fifth road victory in its six games.

In Chicago for the series opener, Toronto scored first when Ed Sprague tripled home a pair of runs in the fourth inning. The White Sox bounced ahead with three runs in the last of the fourth, but the Blue Jays regained the lead a half inning later on John Olerud's two-run double, then pulled away to a 17-hit 7–3 win. Toronto also scored first in Game Two, with an unearned run in the first inning. But in the last of the inning, Blue Jay pitcher Dave Stewart walked the bases full, then handed Chicago a tying run with a wild pitch. With two out in the fourth inning, though, back-to-back doubles by Paul Molitor and Tony Fernandez restored the lead to Toronto, and a walk, an infield hit and an error increased the Jays' lead to 3–1. This ended the scoring, although the White Sox loaded the bases in the sixth before Stewart retired the next three batters to stifle the threat.

The White Sox leaped to life when the series moved to Toronto for Game Three. After the first two men had been retired in the third inning, Sox batters combined five singles with a pair of walks for a 5–0 lead, which Chicago starter Wilson Alvarez held for a 6–1 complete game victory. Lance Johnson's two-run homer in the second inning of Game Four put Chicago ahead. The Jays overtook them with three runs an inning later, but in the sixth inning Frank Thomas homered to even the score at 3–3, and after two batters had been walked aboard, Johnson's two-out triple put the Sox ahead to stay.

In Game Five, the Blue Jays finally broke the visiting team's lock on victory, scoring single runs in each of the first four innings, and another in the seventh, while starter Juan Guzman held Chicago to three hits and a single run in his seven innings. Robin Ventura's two-run homer off Jays' reliever Duane Ward in the Chicago ninth narrowed Toronto's lead to 5–3, but Ward then retired Bo Jackson with his third swinging K of the inning to send the Jays back to Chicago with a 3–2 series advantage.

Errors ended the White Sox season in Game Six. With the score tied 2–2 in the fourth inning, a bobble by Chicago third baseman Robin Ventura put Paul Molitor on base. Molitor subsequently scored the go-ahead run when second baseman Joey Cora threw a ball

low to first into the dugout. Devon White homered in the ninth inning to stretch Toronto's lead to 4–2, and an error by Sox reliever Scott Radinsky on what should have been the third out set the stage for Molitor to triple home a pair of baserunners with the Jays' final runs. Warren Newson's leadoff homer against Toronto reliever Duane Ward in the bottom of the ninth narrowed the score to 6–3, but the White Sox came no closer. The win, starter Dave Stewart's second of the series, was his eighth triumph without a loss in LCS play.

Toronto Blue Jays (East), 4; Chicago White Sox (West), 2

TOR (E)

PLAYER/POS	AVG	G	AB	R	H	2B	3B	HR	RB	BB	SO	SB
Roberto Alomar, 2b	.292	6	24	3	7	1	0	0	4	4	3	4
Pat Borders, c	.250	6	24	1	6	1	0	0	3	0	6	1
Joe Carter, of	.259	6	27	2	7	0	0	0	2	1	5	0
Tony Castillo, p	.000	2	0	0	0	0	0	0	0	0	0	0
Danny Cox, p	.000	2	0	0	0	0	0	0	0	0	0	0
Mark Eichhorn, p	.000	1	0	0	0	0	0	0	0	0	0	0
Tony Fernandez, ss	.318	6	22	1	7	0	0	0	1	2	4	0
Juan Guzman, p	.000	2	0	0	0	0	0	0	0	0	0	0
Rickey Henderson, of	.120	6	25	4	3	2	0	0	0	4	5	2
Pat Hentgen, p	.000	1	0	0	0	0	0	0	0	0	0	0
Al Leiter, p	.000	2	0	0	0	0	0	0	0	0	0	0
Paul Molitor, dh	.391	6	23	7	9	2	1	1	5	3	3	0
John Olerud, 1b	.348	6	23	5	8	1	0	0	3	4	1	0
Ed Sprague, 3b	.286	6	21	0	6	0	1	0	4	2	4	0
Dave Stewart, p	.000	2	0	0	0	0	0	0	0	0	0	0
Todd Stottlemyre, p	.000	1	0	0	0	0	0	0	0	0	0	0
Mike Timlin, p	.000	1	0	0	0	0	0	0	0	0	0	0
Duane Ward, p	.000	4	0	0	0	0	0	0	0	0	0	0
Devon White, of	.444	6	27	3	12	1	1	1	2	1	5	0
TOTAL	.301		216	26	65	8	3	2	24	21	36	7

PITCHER	W	L	ERA	G	GS	CG	SV	SHO	IP	H	ER	BB	SO
Tony Castillo	0	0	0.00	2	0	0	0	0	2.0	0	0	1	1
Danny Cox	0	0	0.00	2	0	0	0	0	5.0	3	0	2	5
Mark Eichhorn	0	0	0.00	1	0	0	0	0	2.0	1	0	1	1
Juan Guzman	2	0	2.08	2	2	0	0	0	13.0	8	3	9	9
Pat Hentgen	0	1	18.00	1	1	0	0	0	3.0	9	6	2	3
Al Leiter	0	0	3.38	2	0	0	0	0	2.2	4	1	2	2
Dave Stewart	2	0	2.03	2	2	0	0	0	13.1	8	3	8	8
Todd Stottlemyre	0	1	7.50	1	1	0	0	0	6.0	6	5	4	4
Mike Timlin	0	0	3.86	1	0	0	0	0	2.1	3	1	0	2
Duane Ward	0	0	5.79	4	0	0	2	0	4.2	4	3	3	8
TOTAL	4	2	3.67	18	6	0	2	0	54.0	46	22	32	43

CHI (W)

PLAYER/POS	AVG	G	AB	R	H	2B	3B	HR	RB	BB	SO	SB
Wilson Alvarez, p	.000	1	0	0	0	0	0	0	0	0	0	0
Tim Belcher, p	.000	1	0	0	0	0	0	0	0	0	0	0
Jason Bere, p	.000	1	0	0	0	0	0	0	0	0	0	0
Ellis Burks, of	.304	6	23	4	7	1	0	1	3	3	5	0
Joey Cora, 2b	.136	6	22	1	3	0	0	0	1	3	6	0
Jose DeLeon, p	.000	2	0	0	0	0	0	0	0	0	0	0
Alex Fernandez, p	.000	2	0	0	0	0	0	0	0	0	0	0
Craig Grebeck, 3b	1.000	1	1	0	1	0	0	0	0	0	0	0
Ozzie Guillen, ss	.273	6	22	4	6	1	0	0	2	0	2	1
Roberto Hernandez, p	.000	4	0	0	0	0	0	0	0	0	0	0
Bo Jackson, dh	.000	3	10	1	0	0	0	0	0	3	6	0
Lance Johnson, of	.217	6	23	2	5	1	1	1	6	2	1	1
Ron Karkovice, c	.000	6	15	0	0	0	0	0	0	1	7	0
Mike LaValliere, c	.333	2	3	0	1	0	0	0	0	1	0	0
Kirk McCaskill, p	.000	3	0	0	0	0	0	0	0	0	0	0
Jack McDowell, p	.000	2	0	0	0	0	0	0	0	0	0	0
Warren Newson, dh-1	.200	2	5	1	1	0	0	1	1	0	1	0
Dan Pasqua, 1b	.000	2	6	1	0	0	0	0	0	1	2	0
Scott Radinsky, p	.000	4	0	0	0	0	0	0	0	0	0	0
Tim Raines, of	.444	6	27	5	12	3	0	0	1	2	2	1
Frank Thomas, 1b-4,dh-2	.353	6	17	2	6	0	0	1	3	10	5	0
Robin Ventura, 3b-6,1b-1	.200	6	20	2	4	0	0	1	5	6	6	0
TOTAL	.237		194	23	46	6	1	5	22	32	43	3

PITCHER	W	L	ERA	G	GS	CG	SV	SHO	IP	H	ER	BB	SO
Wilson Alvarez	1	0	1.00	1	1	0	0	0	9.0	7	1	2	6
Tim Belcher	1	0	2.45	1	0	0	0	0	3.2	3	1	3	1
Jason Bere	0	0	11.57	1	1	0	0	0	2.1	5	3	2	3
Jose DeLeon	0	0	1.93	2	0	0	0	0	4.2	7	1	1	6
Alex Fernandez	0	2	1.80	2	2	0	0	0	15.0	15	3	6	10
Roberto Hernandez	0	0	0.00	4	0	0	1	0	4.0	4	0	0	1
Kirk McCaskill	0	0	0.00	3	0	0	0	0	3.2	3	0	1	3
Jack McDowell	0	2	10.00	2	2	0	0	0	9.0	18	10	5	5
Scott Radinsky	0	0	10.80	4	0	0	0	0	1.2	3	2	1	1
TOTAL	1	4	3.57	20	6	0	1	0	53.0	65	21	21	36

GAME 1 AT CHI OCT 5

TOR	000 230 200	7 17 1
CHI	000 300 000	3 6 1

Pitchers: GUZMAN, Cox (7), Ward (9) vs McDOWELL, DeLeon (7), Radinsky (8), McCaskill (9)
Home Runs: Molitor-TOR
Attendance: 46,246

GAME 2 AT CHI OCT 6

TOR	100 200 000	3 8 0
CHI	100 000 000	1 7 2

Pitchers: STEWART, Leiter (7), Ward (9) vs FERNANDEZ, Hernandez (9)
Attendance: 46,101

GAME 3 AT TOR OCT 8

CHI	005 100 000	6 12 0
TOR	001 000 000	1 7 1

Pitchers: ALVAREZ vs HENTGEN, Cox (4), Eichhorn (7), Castillo (9)
Attendance: 51,783

GAME 4 AT TOR OCT 9

CHI	020 003 101	7 11 0
TOR	003 001 000	4 9 0

Pitchers: Bere, BELCHER (3), McCaskill (7), Radinsky (8), Hernandez (9) vs STOTTLEMYRE, Leiter (7), Timlin (7)
Home Runs: Thomas-CHI, Johnson-CHI
Attendance: 51,889

GAME 5 AT TOR OCT 10

CHI	000 010 002	3 5 1
TOR	111 100 10X	5 14 0

Pitchers: McDOWELL, DeLeon (3), Radinsky (7), Hernandez (7) vs GUZMAN, Castillo (8), Ward (9)
Home Runs: Ventura-CHI, Burks-CHI
Attendance: 51,375

GAME 6 AT CHI OCT 12

TOR	020 100 003	6 10 0
CHI	002 000 001	3 5 3

Pitchers: STEWART, Ward (8) vs FERNANDEZ, McCaskill (8), Radinsky (9), Hernandez (9)
Home Runs: White-TOR, Newson-CHI
Attendance: 45,527

The Phillies and Blue Jays split the first two games, played in Toronto. But the defending champions captured the lead when play moved to Philadelphia for Game Three. In a contest delayed more than an hour by rain, Paul Molitor tripled home two Blue Jay runs before the first out had been recorded, and the Jays pushed on from there to an easy 10–3 win.

By just about any measure except pitching effectiveness, Game Four—played in a steady drizzle that for a time increased to a downpour—was one of the great ones. At 4 hours 14 minutes, it was the longest in World Series history, and its 29 total runs scored established a new record for major league postseason championship play, as did Philadelphia's 14 runs for a losing team. Toronto scored three times after two men had been retired in the top of the first inning, but Philadelphia retaliated immediately with four two-out runs in the bottom of the inning, as Jays' starter Todd Stottlemyre walked four batters, and Milt Thompson tripled over the center fielder's head. Lenny Dykstra's two-run homer an inning later pushed the Phillies' lead to 6–3, but Toronto scrambled back to regain a 7–6 advantage in the third inning on two walks and four singles. Philadelphia scored a tying run in the fourth inning, then scored five times an inning later with a barrage of hits highlighted by Darren Daulton's two-run homer and Dykstra's second two-run blast of the game. Toronto scored twice in the sixth inning, but single Phillie runs in the sixth and seventh restored their five-run lead. Then, in the top of the eighth, the Blue Jays parlayed two walks, two singles and a two-base error (later changed by the official scorer to a double) into a pair of runs and a diamond full of baserunners. Phillie reliever Mitch Williams fanned Ed Sprague for the second out of the inning, but Rickey Henderson lined a two-run single to center to bring the Jays within one run of a tie, and Devon White looped a triple to right center for the tying and go-ahead runs. Relievers Mike Timlin and Duane Ward retired the final seven Phillie batters on five strikeouts and a pair of pop flies.

The Phillies salvaged their final home game, scoring single runs in the first two innings as Curt Schilling shut out the Blue Jays and forced the Series back to Toronto for a sixth game. Paul Molitor's RBI triple gave the Jays a first-inning lead, and his solo homer in the fifth stretched it to 5–1. Lenny Dykstra's three-run shot in the seventh (his fourth home run of the Series) brought Philadelphia to within a run of Toronto, however, and Mariano Duncan scored the ty-

ing run on Dave Hollins' single. Pinch hitter Pete Incaviglia's sacrifice fly gave the Phillies their first lead of the game, 6–5. In the bottom of the ninth, Phillie reliever Mitch Williams walked Rickey Henderson and, with one away, gave up a single to Molitor (which raised his Series batting average to .500). Molitor scored the Series-winning run when Joe Carter, the next man up, lined Williams' would-be third strike over the left field fence for an 8–6 victory.

Toronto Blue Jays, 4; Philadelphia Phillies, 2

TOR (A)

PLAYER/POS	AVG	G	AB	R	H	2B	3B	HR	RB	BB	SO	SB
Roberto Alomar, 2b	.480	6	25	5	12	2	1	0	6	2	3	4
Pat Borders, c	.304	6	23	2	7	0	0	0	1	2	1	0
Rob Butler, ph	.500	2	2	1	1	0	0	0	0	0	0	0
Willie Canate, pr	.000	1	0	0	0	0	0	0	0	0	0	0
Joe Carter, of	.280	6	25	6	7	1	0	2	8	0	4	0
Tony Castillo, p	.000	2	1	0	0	0	0	0	0	0	1	0
Danny Cox, p	.000	3	0	0	0	0	0	0	0	0	0	0
Mark Eichhorn, p	.000	1	0	0	0	0	0	0	0	0	0	0
Tony Fernandez, ss	.333	6	21	2	7	1	0	0	9	3	3	0
Alfredo Griffin, 3b-2	.000	3	0	0	0	0	0	0	0	0	0	0
Juan Guzman, p	.000	2	2	0	0	0	0	0	0	0	1	0
Rickey Henderson, of	.227	6	22	6	5	2	0	0	2	5	2	1
Pat Hentgen, p	.000	1	3	0	0	0	0	0	0	0	1	0
Randy Knorr, c	.000	1	0	0	0	0	0	0	0	0	0	0
Al Leiter, p	1.000	3	1	0	1	1	0	0	0	0	0	0
Paul Molitor, dh-3	.500	6	24	10	12	2	2	2	8	3	0	1
John Olerud, 1b	.235	5	17	5	4	1	0	1	2	4	1	0
Ed Sprague, 3b-4,1b-1	.067	5	15	0	1	0	0	0	2	1	6	0
Dave Stewart, p	.000	2	0	0	0	0	0	0	0	0	0	0
Todd Stottlemyre, p	.000	1	0	0	0	0	0	0	0	0	1	0
Mike Timlin, p	.000	2	0	0	0	0	0	0	0	0	0	0
Duane Ward, p	.000	4	0	0	0	0	0	0	0	0	0	0
Devon White, of	.292	6	24	8	7	3	2	1	7	4	7	1
TOTAL	.311		206	45	64	13	5	6	45	25	30	7

PITCHER	W	L	ERA	G	GS	CG	SV	SHO	IP	H	ER	BB	SO
Tony Castillo	1	0	8.10	2	0	0	0	0	3.1	6	3	3	1
Danny Cox	0	0	8.10	3	0	0	0	0	3.1	6	3	5	6
Mark Eichhorn	0	0	0.00	1	0	0	0	0	0.1	1	0	1	0
Juan Guzman	0	1	3.75	2	2	0	0	0	12.0	10	5	8	12
Pat Hentgen	1	0	1.50	1	1	0	0	0	6.0	5	1	3	6
Al Leiter	1	0	7.71	3	0	0	0	0	7.0	12	6	2	5
Dave Stewart	0	1	6.75	2	2	0	0	0	12.0	10	9	8	8
Todd Stottlemyre	0	0	27.00	1	1	0	0	0	2.0	3	6	4	1
Mike Timlin	0	0	0.00	2	0	0	0	0	2.1	2	0	0	4
Duane Ward	1	0	1.93	4	0	0	2	0	4.2	3	1	0	7
TOTAL	4	2	5.77	21	6	0	2	0	53.0	58	34	34	50

PHI (N)

PLAYER/POS	AVG	G	AB	R	H	2B	3B	HR	RB	BB	SO	SB
Larry Andersen, p	.000	4	0	0	0	0	0	0	0	0	0	0
Kim Batiste, 3b	.000	2	0	0	0	0	0	0	0	0	0	0
Wes Chamberlain, ph	.000	2	2	0	0	0	0	0	0	0	1	0
Darren Daulton, c	.217	6	23	4	5	2	0	1	4	4	5	0
Mariano Duncan, 2b-5,dh-1	.345	6	29	5	10	0	1	0	2	1	7	3
Lenny Dykstra, of	.348	6	23	9	8	1	0	4	8	7	4	4
Jim Eisenreich, of	.231	6	26	3	6	0	0	1	7	2	4	0
Tommy Greene, p	1.000	1	1	1	1	0	0	0	0	0	0	0
Dave Hollins, 3b	.261	6	23	5	6	1	0	0	2	6	5	0
Pete Incaviglia, of	.125	4	8	0	1	0	0	0	1	0	4	0
Danny Jackson, p	.000	1	1	0	0	0	0	0	0	0	0	0
Ricky Jordan, dh-2	.200	3	10	0	2	0	0	0	0	0	2	0
John Kruk, 1b	.348	6	23	4	8	1	0	0	4	7	7	0
Roger Mason, p	.000	4	0	0	0	0	0	0	0	0	0	0
Mickey Morandini, 2b-1	.200	3	5	1	1	0	0	0	0	1	2	0
Terry Mulholland, p	.000	2	2	0	0	0	0	0	0	0	0	0
Ben Rivera, p	.000	1	0	0	0	0	0	0	0	0	0	0
Curt Schilling, p	.500	2	2	0	1	0	0	0	0	0	1	0
Kevin Stocker, ss	.211	6	19	1	4	1	0	0	1	5	5	0
Bobby Thigpen, p	.000	2	0	0	0	0	0	0	0	0	0	0
Milt Thompson, of	.313	5	16	3	5	1	1	1	6	1	2	0
David West, p	.000	3	0	0	0	0	0	0	0	0	0	0
Mitch Williams, p	.000	3	0	0	0	0	0	0	0	0	0	0
TOTAL	.274		212	36	58	7	2	7	35	34	50	7

PITCHER	W	L	ERA	G	GS	CG	SV	SHO	IP	H	ER	BB	SO
Larry Andersen	0	0	12.27	4	0	0	0	0	3.2	5	5	3	3
Tommy Greene	0	0	27.00	1	1	0	0	0	2.1	7	7	4	1
Danny Jackson	0	1	7.20	1	1	0	0	0	5.0	6	4	1	1
Roger Mason	0	0	1.17	4	0	0	0	0	7.2	4	1	1	7
Terry Mulholland	1	0	6.75	2	2	0	0	0	10.2	14	8	3	5
Ben Rivera	0	0	27.00	1	0	0	0	0	1.1	4	4	2	3
Curt Schilling	1	1	3.52	2	2	1	0	1	15.1	13	6	5	9
Bobby Thigpen	0	0	0.00	2	0	0	0	0	2.2	1	0	1	0
David West	0	0	27.00	3	0	0	0	0	1.0	5	3	1	0
Mitch Williams	0	2	20.25	3	0	0	0	0	2.2	5	6	4	1
TOTAL	2	4	7.57	23	6	1	1	1	52.1	64	44	25	30

GAME 1 AT TOR OCT 16

PHI	201 010 001	5 11 1
TOR	021 011 30X	8 10 3

Pitchers: SCHILLING, West (7), Andersen (7), Mason (8) vs Guzman, LEITER (6), Ward (8)
Home Runs: White-TOR, Olerud-TOR
Attendance: 52,011

GAME 2 AT TOR OCT 17

PHI	005 000 100	6 12 0
TOR	000 201 010	4 8 0

Pitchers: MULHOLLAND, Mason (6), Williams (7) vs STEWART, Castillo (7), Eichhorn (8), Timlin (8)
Home Runs: Dykstra-PHI, Eisenreich-PHI, Carter-TOR
Attendance: 52,062

GAME 3 AT PHI OCT 19

TOR	301 001 302	10 13 1
PHI	000 010 101	3 9 0

Pitchers: HENTGEN, Cox (7), Ward (9) vs JACKSON, Rivera (6), Thigpen (7), Andersen (9)
Home Runs: Molitor-TOR, Thompson-PHI
Attendance: 62,689

GAME 4 AT PHI OCT 20

TOR	304 002 060	15 18 0
PHI	420 151 100	14 14 0

Pitchers: Stottlemyre, Leiter (3), CASTILLO (5), Timlin (8), Ward (8) vs Greene, Mason (3), West (4), Andersen (7), WILLIAMS (8), Thigpen (9)
Home Runs: Dykstra-PHI (2), Daulton-PHI
Attendance: 62,731

GAME 5 AT PHI OCT 21

TOR	000 000 000	0 5 1
PHI	110 000 00X	2 5 1

Pitchers: GUZMAN, Cox (8) vs SCHILLING
Attendance: 62,706

GAME 6 AT TOR OCT 23

PHI	000 100 500	6 7 0
TOR	300 100 003	8 10 2

Pitchers: Mulholland, Mason (6), West (8), Andersen (8), WILLIAMS (9) vs Stewart, Cox (7), Leiter (7), WARD (9)
Home Runs: Molitor-TOR, Dykstra-PHI, Carter-TOR
Attendance: 52,195

Pitching-rich Atlanta's appearance in the division playoffs surprised few, but the hard-hitting expansion Rockies made history by reaching the postseason in just their third year of existence.

Two individuals shared the spotlight in Game One: Braves rookie third baseman Chipper Jones and Rockies manager Don Baylor, but for wildly different reasons. Jones collected two homers and made a spectacular stop to rob Andres Galarraga of a double. Baylor was less fortunate. He ran out of hitters in the bottom of the ninth—having to use pitcher Lance Painter as his last batter—after Jones homered with two outs in the top of the inning. Atlanta won 5-4.

Atlanta trailed 4-3 going into the top of the ninth in Game Two, but came thundering back with four runs as Mike Mordecai pinch-homered and Rockies second baseman Eric Young botched a routine ground ball. The Braves triumphed 7-4, taking a 2-0 lead in the series.

In Game Three Atlanta came through in the ninth once more on pinch-hitter Luis Polonia's two-strike run-scoring single, and the game went into extra innings. But Colorado bounced back to score twice in the tenth on Dante Bichette's double down the left field line and run-scoring singles by Andres Galarraga and Vinny Castilla (who had homered in the sixth).

Cy Young Award winners battled in Game Four as Greg Maddux and Bret Saberhagen started, but Saberhagen was ineffective and Atlanta eliminated the Rockies with a 10-4 win. Maddux struck out seven and walked none before leaving for a pinch hitter in the seventh inning. Not helping Saberhagen was a controversial "safe" call on a play in which he attempted to cover first. Fred McGriff followed the play with the first of his two homers in the contest.

Atlanta had reached the NLCS for the fourth straight time—a National League record—and would now face Cincinnati in the NLCS.

Atlanta Braves (E), 3;
Colorado Rockies (WC), 1

ATL (E)

PLAYER/POS	AVG	G	AB	R	H	2B	3B	HR	RB	BB	SO	SB
Steve Avery, p	.000	1	0	0	0	0	0	0	0	0	0	0
Rafael Belliard, ss	.000	4	5	1	0	0	0	0	0	0	1	0
Jeff Blauser, ss	.000	3	6	0	0	0	0	0	0	1	3	0
Pedro Borbon, p	.000	1	0	0	0	0	0	0	0	0	0	0
Brad Clontz, p	.000	1	0	0	0	0	0	0	0	0	0	0
Mike Devereaux, of-3	.200	4	5	1	1	0	0	0	0	0	0	0
Tom Glavine, p	.333	1	3	0	1	0	0	0	0	0	1	0
Marquis Grissom, of	.524	4	21	5	11	2	0	3	4	0	3	2
Chipper Jones, 3b	.389	4	18	4	7	2	0	2	4	2	2	0
David Justice, of	.231	4	13	2	3	0	0	0	0	5	2	0
Ryan Klesko, of	.467	4	15	5	7	1	0	1	0	1	3	0
Mark Lemke, 2b	.211	4	19	3	4	1	0	0	1	1	3	0
Javy Lopez, c	.444	3	9	0	4	0	0	0	3	0	3	0
Greg Maddux, p	.167	2	6	1	1	0	0	0	0	0	1	0
Fred McGriff, 1b	.333	4	18	4	6	0	0	2	6	2	3	0
Greg McMichael, p	.000	2	0	0	0	0	0	0	0	0	0	0
Kent Mercker, p	.000	1	0	0	0	0	0	0	0	0	0	0
Mike Mordecai, ss-1	.667	2	3	1	2	1	0	0	2	0	0	0
Charlie O'Brien, c	.200	2	5	0	1	0	0	0	0	1	1	0
Alejandro Pena, p	.000	3	0	0	0	0	0	0	0	0	0	0
Luis Polonia, ph	.333	3	3	0	1	0	0	0	2	0	1	1
Dwight Smith, ph	.667	4	3	0	2	1	0	0	1	0	0	0
John Smoltz, p	.000	1	2	0	0	0	0	0	0	0	1	0
Mark Wohlers, p	.000	3	0	0	0	0	0	0	0	0	0	0
TOTAL	.331		154	27	51	8	0	7	24	12	27	3

PITCHER	W	L	ERA	G	GS	CG	SV	SHO	IP	H	ER	BB	SO
Steve Avery	0	0	13.50	1	0	0	0	0	0.2	1	1	0	1
Pedro Borbon	0	0	0.00	1	0	0	0	0	1.0	1	0	0	3
Brad Clontz	0	0	0.00	1	0	0	0	0	1.1	0	0	0	2
Tom Glavine	0	0	2.57	1	1	0	0	0	7.0	5	2	1	3
Greg Maddux	1	0	4.50	2	2	0	0	0	14.0	19	7	2	7
Greg McMichael	0	0	6.75	2	0	0	0	0	1.1	1	1	2	1
Kent Mercker	0	0	0.00	1	0	0	0	0	0.1	0	0	0	0
Alejandro Pena	2	0	0.00	3	0	0	0	0	3.0	3	0	1	2
John Smoltz	0	0	7.94	1	1	0	0	0	5.2	5	5	1	6
Mark Wohlers	0	1	6.75	3	0	0	2	0	2.2	6	2	2	4
TOTAL	3	1	4.38	16	4	0	2	0	37.0	41	18	9	29

COL (W)

PLAYER/POS	AVG	G	AB	R	H	2B	3B	HR	RB	BB	SO	SB
Jason Bates, 2b-1,3b-1	.250	4	4	0	1	0	0	0	0	0	0	0
Dante Bichette, of	.588	4	17	6	10	3	0	1	3	1	3	0
Ellis Burks, of	.333	2	6	1	2	1	0	0	2	0	1	0
Vinny Castilla, 3b	.467	4	15	3	7	1	0	3	6	0	1	0
Andres Galarraga, 1b	.278	4	18	1	5	1	0	0	6	0	6	0
Joe Girardi, c	.125	4	16	0	2	0	0	0	0	0	2	0
Darren Holmes, p	.000	3	0	0	0	0	0	0	0	0	0	0
Trenidad Hubbard, ph	.000	1	0	0	0	0	0	0	0	0	0	0
Mike Kingery, of	.200	4	10	1	2	0	0	0	0	0	1	0
Curt Leskanic, p	.000	3	0	0	0	0	0	0	0	0	0	0
Mike Munoz, p	.000	4	0	0	0	0	0	0	0	0	0	0
J Owens, c	.000	1	1	0	0	0	0	0	0	0	1	0
Lance Painter, p-1	.000	2	2	0	0	0	0	0	0	0	1	0
Steve Reed, p	.000	3	0	0	0	0	0	0	0	0	0	0
Armando Reynoso, p	.000	1	0	0	0	0	0	0	0	0	0	0
Kevin Ritz, p	.000	2	0	0	0	0	0	0	0	0	0	0
Bruce Ruffin, p	.000	4	0	0	0	0	0	0	0	0	0	0
Bret Saberhagen, p	.000	1	1	0	0	0	0	0	0	0	0	0
Bill Swift, p	.000	1	3	0	0	0	0	0	0	0	2	0
Mark Thompson, p	.000	1	0	0	0	0	0	0	0	0	0	0
John Vander Wal, ph	.000	4	4	0	0	0	0	0	0	0	2	0
Larry Walker, of	.214	4	14	3	3	0	0	1	3	3	4	1
Walt Weiss, ss	.167	4	12	1	2	0	0	0	0	3	3	1
Eric Young, 2b	.438	4	16	3	7	1	0	1	2	2	2	1
TOTAL	.287		143	19	41	7	0	6	18	9	29	3

PITCHER	W	L	ERA	G	GS	CG	SV	SHO	IP	H	ER	BB	SO
Darren Holmes	1	0	0.00	3	0	0	0	0	1.2	6	0	0	2
Curt Leskanic	0	1	6.00	3	0	0	0	0	3.0	3	2	0	4
Mike Munoz	0	1	13.50	4	0	0	0	0	1.1	4	2	1	1
Lance Painter	0	0	5.40	1	1	0	0	0	5.0	5	3	2	4
Steve Reed	0	0	0.00	3	0	0	0	0	2.2	2	0	1	3
Armando Reynoso	0	0	0.00	1	0	0	0	0	1.0	2	0	0	3
Kevin Ritz	0	0	7.71	2	1	0	0	0	7.0	12	6	3	5
Bruce Ruffin	0	0	2.70	4	0	0	0	0	3.1	3	1	2	2
Bret Saberhagen	0	1	11.25	1	1	0	0	0	4.0	7	5	1	3
Bill Swift	0	0	6.00	1	1	0	0	0	6.0	7	4	2	3
Mark Thompson	0	0	0.00	1	0	0	1	0	1.0	0	0	0	0
TOTAL	1	3	5.75	24	4	0	1	0	36.0	51	23	12	27

GAME 1 AT COL OCT 3

ATL	001	002	011	5	12	1
COL	000	300	010	4	13	4

Pitchers: Maddux, McMichael (8), PENA (8), Wohlers (9) vs Ritz, Reed (6), Ruffin (7), Munoz (8), Holmes (8), LESKANIC (9)
Home Runs: Grissom-ATL, Jones-ATL (2), Castilla-COL
Attendance: 50,040

GAME 2 AT COL OCT 4

ATL	101	100	004	7	13	1
COL	000	003	010	4	8	2

Pitchers: Glavine, Avery (8), PENA (8), Wohlers (9) vs Painter, Reed (6), Ruffin (7), Leskanic (8), MUNOZ (9), Holmes (9)
Home Runs: Grissom-ATL (2), Walker-COL
Attendance: 50,040

GAME 3 AT ATL OCT 6

COL	102	002	000	2	7	9	0
ATL	000	300	010	0	5	11	0

Pitchers: Swift, Reed (7), Munoz (7), Leskanic (7), Ruffin (8), HOLMES (9), Thompson (10) vs Smoltz, Clontz (6), Borbon (8), McMichael (9), WOHLERS (10), Mercker (10)
Home Runs: Young-COL, Castilla-COL
Attendance: 51,300

GAME 4 AT ATL OCT 7

COL	003	001	000	4	11	1
ATL	004	213	00X	10	15	0

Pitchers: SABERHAGEN, Ritz (5), Munoz (6), Reynoso (7), Ruffin (8) vs MADDUX, Pena (8)
Home Runs: Bichette-COL, Castilla-COL, McGriff-ATL (2)
Attendance: 50,027

Davey Johnson's Cincinnati Reds made short work of Tommy Lasorda's Los Angeles Dodgers in the 1995 NL division series, sweeping them 3-0 and outscoring them 22-7.

Game One saw the Reds score four times in the first inning as they walloped the Dodgers 7-2. Los Angeles starter Ramon Martinez was ineffective, being cuffed for 10 hits and 2 walks in just 4⅓ innings.

Game Two was a more even affair until the Los Angeles bullpen went to work. Barry Larkin's eighth-inning single to right broke open a 2-2 tie, and in the top of the ninth the Reds added two insurance runs. Mike Piazza delivered a two-run homer to left off Jeff Brantley in the bottom of the inning, but it wasn't enough to stave off defeat.

The Reds wrapped up the series by humiliating the Dodgers 10-1 in Game Three. The Dodgers had their chances in the contest, but squandered their opportunities, leaving 11 runners on base. The Reds broke the game open in the sixth as pinch-hitter Mark Lewis delivered a grand slam to left-center off Mark Guthrie.

Cincinnati Reds (C), 3; Los Angeles (W), 0

CIN (C)

PLAYER/POS	AVG	G	AB	R	H	2B	3B	HR	RB	BB	SO	SB
Bret Boone, 2b	.300	3	10	4	3	1	0	1	1	1	3	1
Jeff Branson, 3b	.286	3	7	0	2	1	0	0	2	2	0	0
Jeff Brantley, p	.000	3	0	0	0	0	0	0	0	0	0	0
Dave Burba, p	.000	1	0	0	0	0	0	0	0	0	0	0
Mariano Duncan, 2b-1	.667	2	3	1	2	0	0	0	1	0	0	1
Ron Gant, of	.231	3	13	3	3	0	0	1	2	0	3	0
Thomas Howard, of	.100	3	10	0	1	1	0	0	0	0	2	0
Mike Jackson, p	1.000	3	1	0	1	1	0	0	0	3	0	0
Barry Larkin, ss	.385	3	13	2	5	0	0	0	1	1	2	4
Darren Lewis, of	.000	3	3	0	0	0	0	0	0	0	1	0
Mark Lewis, 3b	.500	2	2	2	1	0	0	1	5	1	0	0
Hal Morris, 1b	.500	3	10	5	5	1	0	0	2	3	1	1
Reggie Sanders, of	.154	3	13	3	2	1	0	1	2	1	9	2
Benito Santiago, c	.333	3	9	2	3	0	0	1	3	3	3	0
Pete Schourek, p	.000	1	2	0	0	0	0	0	0	0	1	0
John Smiley, p	.000	1	2	0	0	0	0	0	0	0	1	0
Jerome Walton, of	.000	3	3	0	0	0	0	0	0	0	1	0
David Wells, p	.333	1	3	0	1	0	0	0	0	0	1	0
TOTAL	.279		104	22	29	6	0	5	22	13	28	9

PITCHER	W	L	ERA	G	GS	CG	SV	SHO	IP	H	ER	BB	SO
Jeff Brantley	0	0	6.00	3	0	0	1	0	3.0	5	2	0	2
Dave Burba	1	0	0.00	1	0	0	0	0	1.0	2	0	1	0
Mike Jackson	0	0	0.00	3	0	0	0	0	3.2	4	0	0	1
Pete Schourek	1	0	2.57	1	1	0	0	0	7.0	5	2	3	5
John Smiley	0	0	3.00	1	1	0	0	0	6.0	9	2	0	1
David Wells	1	0	0.00	1	1	0	0	0	6.1	6	0	1	8
TOTAL	3	0	2.00	10	3	0	1	0	27.0	31	6	5	17

LA (W)

PLAYER/POS	AVG	G	AB	R	H	2B	3B	HR	RB	BB	SO	SB
Billy Ashley, ph	.000	1	0	0	0	0	0	0	0	0	1	0
Pedro Astacio, p	.000	3	0	0	0	0	0	0	0	0	0	0
Brett Butler, of	.267	3	15	1	4	0	0	0	1	0	3	0
John Cummings, p	.000	2	0	0	0	0	0	0	0	0	0	0
Delino DeShields, 2b	.250	3	12	1	3	0	0	0	0	1	3	0
Chad Fonville, ss	.500	3	12	1	6	0	0	0	0	0	1	0
Mark Guthrie, p	.000	3	0	0	0	0	0	0	0	0	0	0
Chris Gwynn, ph	.000	1	1	0	0	0	0	0	0	0	1	0
Dave Hansen, ph	.667	3	3	0	2	0	0	0	0	0	0	0
Todd Hollandsworth, of	.000	2	2	0	0	0	0	0	0	0	0	0
Eric Karros, 1b	.500	3	12	3	6	1	0	2	4	1	0	0
Roberto Kelly, of	.364	3	11	0	4	0	0	0	0	0	1	0
Ramon Martinez, p	.000	1	1	0	0	0	0	0	0	0	0	0
Raul Mondesi, of	.222	3	9	0	2	0	0	0	1	0	2	0
Hideo Nomo, p	.000	1	2	0	0	0	0	0	0	0	2	0
Jose Offerman, pr	.000	1	0	0	0	0	0	0	0	0	0	0
Antonio Osuna, p	.000	3	0	0	0	0	0	0	0	0	0	0
Mike Piazza, c	.214	3	14	1	3	1	0	1	1	0	2	0
Kevin Tapani, p	.000	2	0	0	0	0	0	0	0	0	0	0
Ismael Valdes, p	.000	1	3	0	0	0	0	0	0	0	1	0
Tim Wallach, 3b	.083	3	12	0	1	0	0	0	0	0	3	0
Mitch Webster, ph	.000	2	2	0	0	0	0	0	0	0	0	0
TOTAL	.279		111	7	31	2	0	3	7	5	17	0

PITCHER	W	L	ERA	G	GS	CG	SV	SHO	IP	H	ER	BB	SO
Pedro Astacio	0	0	0.00	3	0	0	0	0	3.1	1	0	0	5
John Cummings	0	0	20.25	2	0	0	0	0	1.1	3	3	2	3
Mark Guthrie	0	0	6.75	3	0	0	0	0	1.1	2	1	1	1
Ramon Martinez	0	1	14.54	1	1	0	0	0	4.1	10	7	2	3
Hideo Nomo	0	1	9.00	1	1	0	0	0	5.0	7	5	2	6
Antonio Osuna	0	1	2.70	3	0	0	0	0	3.1	3	1	1	3
Kevin Tapani	0	0	81.00	2	0	0	0	0	0.1	0	3	4	1
Ismael Valdes	0	0	0.00	1	1	0	0	0	7.0	3	0	1	6
TOTAL	0	3	6.92	16	3	0	0	0	26.0	29	20	13	28

The Cleveland Indians had enjoyed a 100-44 record in the strike-shortened 1995 season and captured the AL's new Central Division by a record 30 games. Not surprisingly, they were heavily favored against the AL East champion Red Sox. And not surprisingly, the Curse of Rocky Colavito fell in three straight to the Curse of the Bambino—in other words, the Tribe won.

Yet there were moments of high drama in the series. Game One was a titanic struggle that had nearly everything: two rain delays (39 minutes at the start and 23 minutes in the eighth), three extra inning homers, and a controversial piece of lumber. The five hour and one minute game ended at 2:08 AM the next day. But no one in Cleveland was complaining.

Boston jumped off to a 2-0 lead on John Valentin's two-run homer, but Red Sox starter Roger Clemens surrendered three runs in the sixth. Boston's Luis Alicea evened the score up with a leadoff homer in the eighth.

In the top of the eleventh, Tim Naehring homered to give the Sox the lead, but Albert Belle retaliated in the bottom of the frame with a homer of his own. The next move was Boston's, which contended Belle's bat was corked. AL authorities confiscated it and sawed it in half but found no cork.

In the twelfth the Indians loaded the bases with one out but did not score. In the thirteenth former Red Sox catcher Tony Pena ended it all with an improbable homer off a 3-0 pitch from Zane Smith.

Game Two was a much easier Indian win as veteran Orel Hershiser faced Boston's Erik Hanson. Flashy Indian shortstop Omar Vizquel doubled in two runs in the fifth. Eddie Murray added a two-run homer off Hanson in the eighth. That was more than Hershiser needed as he struck out seven in 7⅓ innings while walking just two and allowing a mere three hits. In the eighth, Hershiser even managed himself, having Tribe pilot Mike Hargrove remove him after his thirty-seven-year-old back stiffened up. Key to the Indians' success was holding Boston sluggers Mo Vaughn and Jose Canseco in check. In Game Two they were hitless in eight at-bats, making them a combined 0-for-20 in the series' first two games.

Game Three moved from Jacobs Field to Fenway Park, but the home field proved to be no advantage. Red Sox knuckleballer Tim Wakefield surrendered seven runs in 5⅓ innings as the Indians, behind Charles Nagy, eliminated Boston

with an 8-2 win. Vaughn and Canseco went hitless again in seven at-bats, running their record to 0-for-27, with nine strikeouts. But Boston's defeat was not the duo's fault entirely. Overall, Sox batters were 2-for-28 with runners in scoring position during the series. Neither of those hits both singles scored a run.

The Red Sox not only went home for the winter but were saddled with a 13-game postseason losing streak, the major league record. Cleveland would now face the surprising but virtually exhausted Seattle Mariners.

Cleveland Indians (C), 3; Boston Red Sox (E), 0

CLE (C)

PLAYER/POS	AVG	G	AB	R	H	2B	3B	HR	RB	BB	SO	SB
Sandy Alomar, c	.182	3	11	1	2	1	0	0	1	0	1	0
Paul Assenmacher, p	.000	3	0	0	0	0	0	0	0	0	0	0
Carlos Baerga, 2b	.286	3	14	2	4	1	0	0	1	0	1	0
Albert Belle, of	.273	3	11	3	3	1	0	1	3	4	3	0
Alvaro Espinoza, 3b	.000	1	1	0	0	0	0	0	0	0	0	0
Orel Hershiser, p	.000	1	0	0	0	0	0	0	0	0	0	0
Ken Hill, p	.000	1	0	0	0	0	0	0	0	0	0	0
Wayne Kirby, of-2	1.000	3	1	0	1	0	0	0	0	0	0	0
Kenny Lofton, of	.154	3	13	1	2	0	0	0	0	1	3	0
Dennis Martinez, p	.000	1	0	0	0	0	0	0	0	0	0	0
Jose Mesa, p	.000	2	0	0	0	0	0	0	0	0	0	0
Eddie Murray, dh	.385	3	13	3	5	0	1	1	3	2	1	0
Charles Nagy, p	.000	1	0	0	0	0	0	0	0	0	0	0
Tony Pena, c	.500	2	2	1	1	0	0	1	1	0	0	0
Herb Perry, ph	.000	1	1	0	0	0	0	0	0	0	0	0
Eric Plunk, p	.000	1	0	0	0	0	0	0	0	0	0	0
Jim Poole, p	.000	1	0	0	0	0	0	0	0	0	0	0
Manny Ramirez, of	.000	3	12	1	0	0	0	0	0	1	2	0
Paul Sorrento, 1b	.300	3	10	2	3	0	0	0	1	2	3	0
Julian Tavarez, p	.000	3	0	0	0	0	0	0	0	0	0	0
Jim Thome, 3b	.154	3	13	1	2	0	0	1	3	1	6	0
Omar Vizquel, ss	.167	3	12	2	2	1	0	0	4	2	2	1
TOTAL	.219		114	17	25	4	1	4	17	13	22	1

PITCHER	W	L	ERA	G	GS	CG	SV	SHO	IP	H	ER	BB	SO
Paul Assenmacher	0	0	0.00	3	0	0	0	0	1.2	0	0	0	3
Orel Hershiser	1	0	0.00	1	1	0	0	0	7.1	3	0	2	7
Ken Hill	1	0	0.00	1	1	0	0	0	1.1	1	0	0	2
Dennis Martinez	0	0	3.00	1	1	0	0	0	6.0	5	2	0	2
Jose Mesa	0	0	0.00	2	0	0	0	0	2.0	0	0	2	0
Charles Nagy	1	0	1.29	1	1	0	0	0	7.0	4	1	5	6
Eric Plunk	0	0	0.00	1	0	0	0	0	1.1	1	0	1	1
Jim Poole	0	0	5.40	1	0	0	0	0	1.2	2	1	1	2
Julian Tavarez	0	0	6.75	3	0	0	0	0	2.2	5	2	0	3
TOTAL	3	0	1.74	14	3	0	0	0	31.0	21	6	11	26

BOS (E)

PLAYER/POS	AVG	G	AB	R	H	2B	3B	HR	RB	BB	SO	SB
Rick Aguilera, p	.000	1	0	0	0	0	0	0	0	0	0	0
Luis Alicea, 2b	.600	3	10	1	6	1	0	1	1	2	2	1
Stan Belinda, p	.000	1	0	0	0	0	0	0	0	0	0	0
Jose Canseco, dh-2,of-1	.000	3	13	0	0	0	0	0	0	2	5	0
Roger Clemens, p	.000	1	0	0	0	0	0	0	0	0	0	0
Rheal Cormier, p	.000	2	0	0	0	0	0	0	0	0	0	0
Mike Greenwell, of	.200	3	15	0	3	0	0	0	0	0	1	0
Erik Hanson, p	.000	1	0	0	0	0	0	0	0	0	0	0
Bill Haselman, c	.000	1	2	0	0	0	0	0	0	0	0	0
Dwayne Hosey, of	.000	3	12	1	0	0	0	0	0	2	3	1
Joe Hudson, p	.000	1	0	0	0	0	0	0	0	0	0	0
Reggie Jefferson, dh	.250	1	4	1	1	0	0	0	0	0	1	0
Mike Macfarlane, c	.333	3	9	0	3	0	0	0	1	0	3	0
Mike Maddux, p	.000	3	0	0	0	0	0	0	0	0	0	0
Willie McGee, of	.250	2	4	0	1	0	0	0	1	0	2	0
Tim Naehring, 3b	.308	3	13	2	4	0	0	1	1	1	1	0
Zane Smith, p	.000	1	0	0	0	0	0	0	0	0	0	0
Matt Stairs, ph	.000	1	1	0	0	0	0	0	0	0	1	0
Mike Stanton, p	.000	1	0	0	0	0	0	0	0	0	0	0
Lee Tinsley, of	.000	1	5	0	0	0	0	0	0	1	2	0
John Valentin, ss	.250	3	12	1	3	1	0	1	2	3	1	0
Mo Vaughn, 1b	.000	3	14	0	0	0	0	0	0	1	7	0
Tim Wakefield, p	.000	1	0	0	0	0	0	0	0	0	0	0
TOTAL	.184		114	6	21	2	0	3	6	11	26	2

PITCHER	W	L	ERA	G	GS	CG	SV	SHO	IP	H	ER	BB	SO
Rick Aguilera	0	0	13.50	1	0	0	0	0	0.2	3	1	0	1
Stan Belinda	0	0	0.00	1	0	0	0	0	0.1	0	0	0	0
Roger Clemens	0	0	3.86	1	1	0	0	0	7.0	5	3	1	5
Rheal Cormier	0	0	13.50	2	0	0	0	0	0.2	2	1	1	2
Erik Hanson	0	1	4.50	1	1	0	0	0	8.0	4	4	4	5
Joe Hudson	0	0	0.00	1	0	0	0	0	1.0	2	0	1	0
Mike Maddux	0	0	0.00	2	0	0	0	0	3.0	2	0	1	1
Zane Smith	0	1	6.75	1	0	0	0	0	1.1	1	1	0	0
Mike Stanton	0	0	0.00	1	0	0	0	0	2.1	1	0	0	4
Tim Wakefield	0	1	11.81	1	1	0	0	0	5.1	5	7	5	4
TOTAL	0	3	5.16	12	3	1	0	0	29.2	25	17	13	22

GAME 1 AT CLE OCT 3

BOS	002	000	010	010	0 4 11 2
CLE	000	003	000	010	1 5 10 2

Pitchers: Clemens, Cormier (8), Belinda (8), Stanton (8), Aguilera (11), Maddux (11), SMITH (12) vs Martinez, Tavarez (7), Assenmacher (8), Plunk (8), Mesa (10), Poole (11), HILL (12)
Home Runs: Valentin-BOS, Alicea-BOS, Naehring-BOS, Belle-CLE, Pena-CLE
Attendance: 44,218

GAME 2 AT CLE OCT 4

BOS	000	000	000	0 3 1
CLE	000	020	02X	4 4 2

Pitchers: HANSON vs HERSHISER, Tavarez (8), Assenmacher (8), Mesa (9)
Home Runs: Murray-CLE
Attendance: 44,264

GAME 3 AT BOS OCT 6

CLE	021	005	000	8 11 2
BOS	000	100	010	2 7 1

Pitchers: NAGY, Tavarez (8), Assenmacher (9) vs WAKEFIELD, Cormier (6), Maddux (6), Hudson (9)
Home Runs: Thome-CLE
Attendance: 34,211

The hitherto laughable Seattle Mariners shocked the New York Yankees in a gritty, exciting five-game division series that could only be likened to two prize fighters standing toe-to-toe and slugging it out for fifteen full rounds.

Seattle found its rotation askew after being forced into a one game playoff against California to determine the AL West championship. In Game One the Yankees' David Cone started against Seattle's Chris Bosio and triumphed 9-6 despite Ken Griffey, Jr.'s two homers. Ultimately, Griffey would hit five in the series.

The Yankees won Game Two by breaking open a 5-5 marathon on a two-run Jim Leyritz homer in the bottom of the fifteenth. In the twelfth Griffey had homered to right-center on a 3-1 pitch to give Seattle the lead, but New York evened it in the bottom of the inning on Ruben Sierra's run-scoring double to left.

Seattle's ace, Cy Young Award winner Randy Johnson, finally appeared in Game Three, striking out 10 in 7 innings, as Seattle won 7-6 before a delirious Kingdome crowd.

New York jumped off to a 5-0 lead in Game Four but Seattle battled back to even the series at 2-2. The big blow was Edgar Martinez's grand-slam to center in the Mariners' five-run eighth inning. The game went down to the last out as New York left runners on second and third in the ninth.

After Seattle scored twice in the eighth to deadlock deciding Game Five at 4-4, Mariners manager Lou Piniella brought in Randy Johnson (who had pitched seven innings just two days before) to shut the door on New York. Not to be outdone, Yankees manager Buck Showalter countered with starter Jack McDowell. Once again, Edgar Martinez (series average of .571) came through in the clutch, hitting a two-run double down the left field line to end the game—and the series.

Seattle Mariners (W), 3;
New York Yankees (WC), 0

SEA (W)

PLAYER/POS	AVG	G	AB	R	H	2B	3B	HR	RB	BB	SO	SB
Bobby Ayala, p	.000	2	0	0	0	0	0	0	0	0	0	0
Tim Belcher, p	.000	2	0	0	0	0	0	0	0	0	0	0
Andy Benes, p	.000	2	0	0	0	0	0	0	0	0	0	0
Mike Blowers, 3b-5,1b-1	.167	5	18	0	3	0	0	0	0	1	7	0
Chris Bosio, p	.000	2	0	0	0	0	0	0	0	0	0	0
Jay Buhner, of	.458	5	24	2	11	1	0	1	3	2	4	0
Norm Charlton, p	.000	4	0	0	0	0	0	0	0	0	0	0
Vince Coleman, of	.217	5	23	6	5	0	1	1	1	2	4	1
Joey Cora, 2b	.316	5	19	7	6	1	0	1	1	3	0	1
Alex Diaz, of-1	.333	2	3	0	1	0	0	0	0	1	1	0
Felix Fermin, ss-2,2b-1	.000	3	1	0	0	0	0	0	0	0	1	0
Ken Griffey, of	.391	5	23	9	9	0	0	5	7	2	4	1
Randy Johnson, p	.000	2	0	0	0	0	0	0	0	0	0	0
Tino Martinez, 1b	.409	5	22	4	9	1	0	1	5	3	4	0
Edgar Martinez, dh	.571	5	21	6	12	3	0	2	10	6	2	0
Jeff Nelson, p	.000	3	0	0	0	0	0	0	0	0	0	0
Warren Newson, ph	.000	1	1	0	0	0	0	0	0	0	1	0
Bill Risley, p	.000	4	0	0	0	0	0	0	0	0	0	0
Alex Rodriguez, ss	.000	1	1	1	0	0	0	0	0	0	0	0
Luis Sojo, ss	.250	5	20	0	5	0	0	0	0	3	0	3
Doug Strange, 3b	.000	2	4	0	0	0	0	0	0	1	1	0
Bob Wells, p	.000	1	0	0	0	0	0	0	0	0	0	0
Chris Widger, c	.000	2	3	0	0	0	0	0	0	0	3	0
Dan Wilson, c	.118	5	17	0	2	0	0	0	1	2	6	0
TOTAL	.315		200	35	63	6	1	11	33	25	41	3

PITCHER	W	L	ERA	G	GS	CG	SV	SHO	IP	H	ER	BB	SO
Bobby Ayala	0	0	54.00	2	0	0	0	0	0.2	6	4	1	0
Tim Belcher	0	1	6.23	2	0	0	0	0	4.1	4	3	5	0
Andy Benes	0	0	5.40	2	2	0	0	0	11.2	10	7	9	8
Chris Bosio	0	0	10.57	2	2	0	0	0	7.2	10	9	4	2
Norm Charlton	1	0	2.45	4	0	0	1	0	7.1	4	2	3	9
Randy Johnson	2	0	2.70	2	1	0	0	0	10.0	5	3	6	16
Jeff Nelson	0	1	3.18	3	0	0	0	0	5.2	7	2	3	7
Bill Risley	0	0	6.00	4	0	0	1	0	3.0	2	2	0	1
Bob Wells	0	0	9.00	1	0	0	0	0	1.0	2	1	0	0
TOTAL	3	2	5.79	22	5	0	2	0	51.1	50	33	32	43

NY (E)

PLAYER/POS	AVG	G	AB	R	H	2B	3B	HR	RB	BB	SO	SB
Wade Boggs, 3b	.263	4	19	4	5	2	0	1	3	3	5	0
David Cone, p	.000	2	0	0	0	0	0	0	0	0	0	0
Russ Davis, 3b	.200	2	5	0	1	0	0	0	0	0	2	0
Tony Fernandez, ss	.238	5	21	0	5	2	0	0	0	2	2	0
Sterling Hitchcock, p	.000	2	0	0	0	0	0	0	0	0	0	0
Steve Howe, p	.000	2	0	0	0	0	0	0	0	0	0	0
Dion James, of	.083	4	12	0	1	0	0	0	0	1	1	0
Scott Kamieniecki, p	.000	1	0	0	0	0	0	0	0	0	0	0
Pat Kelly, 2b-4	.000	5	3	3	0	0	0	0	0	1	3	0
Jim Leyritz, c	.143	2	7	1	1	0	0	1	2	0	1	0
Don Mattingly, 1b	.417	5	24	3	10	4	0	1	6	1	5	0
Jack McDowell, p	.000	2	0	0	0	0	0	0	0	0	0	0
Paul O'Neill, of	.333	5	18	5	6	0	0	3	6	5	5	0
Andy Pettitte, p	.000	1	0	0	0	0	0	0	0	0	0	0
Jorge Posada, pr	.000	1	0	1	0	0	0	0	0	0	0	0
Mariano Rivera, p	.000	3	0	0	0	0	0	0	0	0	0	0
Ruben Sierra, dh	.174	5	23	2	4	2	0	2	5	2	7	0
Mike Stanley, c	.313	5	16	2	5	0	0	1	3	2	1	0
Darryl Strawberry, ph	.000	2	2	0	0	0	0	0	0	0	1	0
Randy Velarde, 2b-4, 3b-2,of-2	.176	5	17	3	3	0	0	0	1	6	4	0
John Wetteland, p	.000	3	0	0	0	0	0	0	0	0	0	0
Bob Wickman, p	.000	3	0	0	0	0	0	0	0	0	0	0
Bernie Williams, of	.429	5	21	8	9	2	0	2	5	7	3	1
Gerald Williams, of	.000	5	5	1	0	0	0	0	0	0	3	0
TOTAL	.259		193	33	50	12	0	11	32	32	43	1

PITCHER	W	L	ERA	G	GS	CG	SV	SHO	IP	H	ER	BB	SO
David Cone	1	0	4.60	2	2	0	0	0	15.2	15	8	9	14
Sterling Hitchcock	0	0	5.40	2	0	0	0	0	1.2	2	1	2	1
Steve Howe	0	0	18.00	2	0	0	0	0	1.0	4	2	0	1
Scott Kamieniecki	0	0	7.20	1	1	0	0	0	5.0	9	4	4	4
Jack McDowell	0	2	9.00	2	1	0	0	0	7.0	8	7	4	6
Andy Pettitte	0	0	5.14	1	1	0	0	0	7.0	9	4	3	0
Mariano Rivera	1	0	0.00	3	0	0	0	0	5.1	3	0	1	8
John Wetteland	0	1	14.54	3	0	0	0	0	4.1	8	7	2	5
Bob Wickman	0	0	0.00	3	0	0	0	0	3.0	5	0	0	3
TOTAL	2	3	5.94	19	5	0	0	0	50.0	63	33	25	41

GAME 1 AT NY OCT 3

SEA	000	101	202	6	9	0
NY	002	002	41X	9	13	0

Pitchers: Bosio, NELSON (6), Ayala (7), Risley (7), Wells (8) vs CONE, Wetteland (9)
Home Runs: Griffey-SEA (2), Boggs-NY, Sierra-NY
Attendance: 57,178

GAME 2 AT NY OCT 4

SEA	001	001	200	001	000	5	16	2
NY	000	012	100	001	002	7	11	0

Pitchers: Benes, Risley (6), Charlton (7), Nelson (11), BELCHER (12) vs Pettitte, Wickman (8), Wetteland (9), RIVERA (12)
Home Runs: Coleman-SEA, Griffey-SEA, Sierra-NY, Mattingly-NY, O'Neill-NY, Leyritz-NY
Attendance: 57,126

GAME 3 AT SEA OCT 6

NY	000	100	120	4	6	2
SEA	000	024	10X	7	7	0

Pitchers: McDOWELL, Howe (6), Wickman (6), Hitchcock (7), Rivera (7) vs JOHNSON, Risley (8), Charlton (8)
Home Runs: B.Williams-NY (2), Stanley-NY, T.Martinez-SEA
Attendance: 57,944

GAME 4 AT SEA OCT 7

NY	302	000	012	8	14	1
SEA	004	011	05X	11	16	0

Pitchers: Kamieniecki, Hitchcock (6), Wickman (7), WETTELAND (8), Howe (8) vs Bosio, Nelson (3), Belcher (7), CHARLTON (8), Ayala (9), Risley (9)
Home Runs: O'Neill-NY, E.Martinez-SEA (2), Griffey-SEA, Buhner-SEA
Attendance: 57,180

GAME 5 AT SEA OCT 8

NY	000	202	000	01	5	6	0
SEA	001	100	020	02	6	15	0

Pitchers: Cone, Rivera (8), McDOWELL (9) vs Benes, Charlton (7), JOHNSON (9)
Home Runs: O'Neill-NY, Cora-SEA, Griffey-SEA
Attendance: 57,411

Both the Braves and the Reds had moved through the National League's first-ever division series with ease, with Atlanta knocking off Colorado 3-1 and Cincinnati sweeping the Dodgers 3-0.

In Game One of the NLCS, a scant crowd of only 40,382 Riverfront Stadium patrons saw the Braves edge the Reds 2-1 in extra innings. Atlanta prevailed despite failing to move a runner past second base until the ninth inning, as the Reds' Pete Schourek held the Braves to four singles through eight. Atlanta broke through in the eleventh on Mike Devereaux's pinch-hit single, a feat which helped earn him NLCS MVP honors.

Game Two was another extra inning affair as Atlanta cracked the game open with four in the tenth to triumph 6-2. In that inning the Braves loaded the bases, scoring their first run on Mark Portugal's wild pitch. Javier Lopez followed with a three-run homer off the left-field foul screen. Game Three remained scoreless until the sixth, when catcher Charlie O'Brien homered to left off David Wells, scoring Fred McGriff and Mike Devereaux. Chipper Jones followed with a two-run homer to complete the Braves' scoring.

Game Four saw a 6-0 Atlanta win, completing the first National League postseason sweep since 1982. Steve Avery allowed just three singles, two of which failed to make it out of the infield. Mike Devereaux delivered the key blow, a three-run homer to left in the seventh. Atlanta, seeking its first Series win since 1957, would now face Cleveland, making its first Fall Classic appearance since 1954.

Atlanta Braves (E), 4;
Cincinnati Reds (C), 0

ATL (E)

PLAYER/POS	AVG	G	AB	R	H	2B	3B	HR	RB	BB	SO	SB
Steve Avery, p	.500	2	2	0	1	0	0	0	0	0	0	0
Rafael Belliard, ss	.273	4	11	1	3	0	0	0	0	0	3	0
Jeff Blauser, ss	.000	1	4	0	0	0	0	0	0	1	2	0
Brad Clontz, p	.000	1	0	0	0	0	0	0	0	0	0	0
Mike Devereaux, of	.308	4	13	2	4	1	0	1	5	1	2	0
Tom Glavine, p	.000	1	1	0	0	0	0	0	0	0	1	0
Marquis Grissom, of	.263	4	19	2	5	0	1	0	0	1	4	0
Chipper Jones, 3b	.438	4	16	3	7	0	0	1	3	3	1	1
David Justice, of	.273	3	11	1	3	0	0	0	1	2	1	0
Ryan Klesko, of-3	.000	4	7	0	0	0	0	0	0	3	4	0
Mark Lemke, 2b	.167	4	18	2	3	0	0	0	1	1	0	0
Javy Lopez, c	.357	3	14	2	5	1	0	1	3	0	1	0
Greg Maddux, p	.000	1	3	0	0	0	0	0	0	0	0	0
Fred McGriff, 1b	.438	4	16	5	7	4	0	0	3	3	0	0
Greg McMichael, p	.000	3	0	0	0	0	0	0	0	0	0	0
Mike Mordecai, ss-1	.000	2	2	0	0	0	0	0	0	0	1	0
Charlie O'Brien, c-1	.400	2	5	1	2	0	0	1	3	0	1	0
Alejandro Pena, p	.000	3	0	0	0	0	0	0	0	0	0	0
Luis Polonia, of-1	.500	3	2	0	1	0	0	0	1	0	0	0
Dwight Smith, ph	.000	2	2	0	0	0	0	0	0	0	0	0
John Smoltz, p	.333	1	3	0	1	0	0	0	0	0	1	1
Mark Wohlers, p	.000	4	0	0	0	0	0	0	0	0	0	0
TOTAL	.282		149	19	42	6	1	4	17	16	22	2

PITCHER	W	L	ERA	G	GS	CG	SV	SHO	IP	H	ER	BB	SO
Steve Avery	1	0	0.00	2	1	0	0	0	6.0	2	0	4	6
Brad Clontz	0	0	0.00	1	0	0	0	0	0.1	1	0	0	0
Tom Glavine	0	0	1.29	1	1	0	0	0	7.0	7	1	2	5
Greg Maddux	1	0	1.13	1	1	0	0	0	8.0	7	1	2	4
Greg McMichael	1	0	0.00	3	0	0	0	0	2.2	0	0	1	2
Alejandro Pena	0	0	0.00	3	0	0	0	0	3.0	2	0	1	4
John Smoltz	0	0	2.57	1	1	0	0	0	7.0	7	2	2	2
Mark Wohlers	1	0	1.80	4	0	0	0	0	5.0	2	1	0	8
TOTAL	4	0	1.15	16	4	0	1	0	39.0	28	5	12	31

CIN (C)

PLAYER/POS	AVG	G	AB	R	H	2B	3B	HR	RB	BB	SO	SB
Eric Anthony, ph	.000	2	1	0	0	0	0	0	0	1	1	0
Bret Boone, 2b	.214	4	14	1	3	0	0	0	0	1	2	0
Jeff Branson, 3b	.111	4	9	2	1	1	0	0	0	0	2	1
Jeff Brantley, p	.000	2	0	0	0	0	0	0	0	0	0	0
Dave Burba, p	.000	2	0	0	0	0	0	0	0	0	0	0
Hector Carrasco, p	.000	1	0	0	0	0	0	0	0	0	0	0
Mariano Duncan, 1b-1	.000	3	3	0	0	0	0	0	0	1	1	0
Ron Gant, of	.188	4	16	1	3	0	0	0	1	0	3	0
Lenny Harris, ph	1.000	3	2	0	2	0	0	0	1	0	0	1
Xavier Hernandez, p	.000	2	0	0	0	0	0	0	0	0	0	0
Thomas Howard, of-3	.250	4	8	0	2	1	0	0	1	2	0	0
Mike Jackson, p	.000	3	0	0	0	0	0	0	0	0	0	0
Barry Larkin, ss	.389	4	18	1	7	2	1	0	0	1	1	1
Darren Lewis, of	.000	2	1	0	0	0	0	0	0	0	0	0
Mark Lewis, 3b	.250	2	4	0	1	0	0	0	0	1	0	0
Hal Morris, 1b	.167	4	12	0	2	1	0	0	1	1	1	1
Mark Portugal, p	.000	1	0	0	0	0	0	0	0	0	0	0
Reggie Sanders, of	.125	4	16	0	2	0	0	0	0	2	10	0
Benito Santiago, c	.231	4	13	0	3	0	0	0	0	3	0	0
Pete Schourek, p	.000	2	5	0	0	0	0	0	0	0	4	0
John Smiley, p	.000	1	1	0	0	0	0	0	0	0	0	0
Eddie Taubensee, c-1	.500	2	2	0	1	0	0	0	0	0	0	0
Jerome Walton, of	.000	2	7	0	0	0	0	0	0	0	2	0
David Wells, p	.500	1	2	0	1	0	0	0	0	0	0	0
TOTAL	.209		134	5	28	5	1	0	4	12	31	4

PITCHER	W	L	ERA	G	GS	CG	SV	SHO	IP	H	ER	BB	SO
Jeff Brantley	0	0	0.00	2	0	0	0	0	2.2	0	0	2	1
Dave Burba	0	0	0.00	2	0	0	0	0	3.2	3	0	4	0
Hector Carrasco	0	0	0.00	1	0	0	0	0	1.1	1	0	0	3
Xavier Hernandez	0	0	27.00	1	0	0	0	0	0.2	3	2	0	0
Mike Jackson	0	1	23.14	3	0	0	0	0	2.1	5	6	4	1
Mark Portugal	0	1	36.00	1	0	0	0	0	1.0	3	4	1	0
Pete Schourek	0	1	1.26	2	2	0	0	0	14.1	14	2	3	13
John Smiley	0	0	3.60	1	1	0	0	0	5.0	5	2	0	1
David Wells	0	1	4.50	1	1	0	0	0	6.0	8	3	2	3
TOTAL	0	4	4.62	14	4	0	0	0	37.0	42	19	16	22

GAME 1 AT CIN OCT 10

ATL	000	000	001	01	2	7	0
CIN	000	100	000	00	1	8	0

Pitchers: Glavine, Pena (8), WOHLERS (9), Clontz (11), Avery (11), McMichael (11) vs Schourek, Brantley (9), JACKSON (11)
Attendance: 40,382

GAME 2 AT CIN OCT 11

ATL	100	100	000	4	6	11	1
CIN	000	020	000	0	2	9	1

Pitchers: Smoltz, Pena (8), McMICHAEL (9), Wohlers (10) vs Smiley, Burba (6), Jackson (8), Brantley (9), PORTUGAL (10)
Home Runs: Lopez-ATL
Attendance: 44,624

GAME 3 AT ATL OCT 13

CIN	000	000	011	2	8	0
ATL	000	003	20X	5	12	1

Pitchers: WELLS, Hernandez (7), Carrasco (7) vs MADDUX, Wohlers (9)
Home Runs: O'Brien-ATL, Jones-ATL
Attendance: 51,424

GAME 4 AT ATL OCT 14

CIN	000	000	000	0	3	1
ATL	001	000	50X	6	12	1

Pitchers: SCHOUREK, Jackson (7), Burba (7) vs AVERY, McMichael (7), Pena (8), Wohlers (9)
Home Runs: Devereaux-ATL
Attendance: 52,067

The Indians and Mariners faced each other after vastly different experiences in the first round of MLB's new postseason format.

Cleveland had romped against Boston, sweeping them 3-0. Seattle had engaged in a thrilling, exhausting series against New York, fraying their pitching—and probably their nerves—in the process.

Most observers expected the Tribe to take Game One. Seattle's rotation had been decimated in defeating the Yankees, and Mariners manager Lou Piniella had to start rookie Bob Wolcott rather than ace Randy Johnson. Wolcott gave up a game-tying seventh inning homer to Albert Belle, but otherwise Piniella had nothing to complain about. Seattle scored in the bottom of that frame and made the run hold up.

Cleveland stranded 10 runners in Game Two (making a total of 22 left on in the first two contests) but still triumphed 5-2. Manny Ramirez came into the game mired in a 1-for-16 postseason slump but went 4-for-4 with solo homers in the sixth and eighth innings.

Randy Johnson finally appeared in the series in Game Three but wasn't around for a decision in the eleven inning contest. The Mariners jumped off to a 2-0 lead thanks to two Indian errors, but at the end of eight the score was tied. In the top of the eleventh an intentional walk to Tino Martinez backfired as Jay Buhner followed with a three-run homer.

In Game Four Cleveland evened the series with a 7-0 triumph against an ineffective Andy Benes, aided by Eddie Murray's two-run first inning homer, Jim Thome's two-run third inning homer, and Omar Vizquel's run-scoring sixth inning double.

In Game Five Orel Hershiser ran his career postseason record to 7-0 as he struck out eight and walked only two. He needed help, however, leaving the game with a 3-2 lead which Paul Assenmacher and Jose Mesa skillfully protected.

In the final game, the Indians' Dennis Martinez defeated Randy Johnson 4-0. Through eight innings only one run had scored (an unearned one by Cleveland), but in that inning Mariners hopes unraveled. Johnson surrendered a lead-off double to Tony Pena, then an infield single to Kenny Lofton, who stole second.

Next came a wild pitch. Ruben Amaro (running for Pena) scored, but so did Lofton, motoring all the way past second, embarrassing Mariners catcher Dan Wilson. That play sealed the Mariners' doom. Carlos Baerga then homered, but it was an anticlimactic blow.

Cleveland Indians (C), 4; Seattle Mariners (W), 2

CLE (C)

PLAYER/POS	AVG	G	AB	R	H	2B	3B	HR	RB	BB	SO	SB
Sandy Alomar, c	.267	5	15	0	4	1	1	0	1	1	1	0
Ruben Amaro, dh-1	.000	3	1	1	0	0	0	0	0	0	0	0
Paul Assenmacher, p	.000	3	0	0	0	0	0	0	0	0	0	0
Carlos Baerga, 2b	.400	6	25	3	10	0	0	1	4	2	3	0
Albert Belle, of	.222	5	18	1	4	1	0	1	1	1	3	5
Alan Embree, p	.000	1	0	0	0	0	0	0	0	0	0	0
Alvaro Espinoza, 3b	.125	4	8	1	1	0	0	0	0	0	3	0
Orel Hershiser, p	.000	2	0	0	0	0	0	0	0	0	0	0
Ken Hill, p	.000	1	0	0	0	0	0	0	0	0	0	0
Wayne Kirby, of	.200	5	5	2	1	0	0	0	0	0	0	1
Kenny Lofton, of	.458	6	24	4	11	0	2	0	3	4	6	5
Dennis Martinez, p	.000	2	0	0	0	0	0	0	0	0	0	0
Jose Mesa, p	.000	4	0	0	0	0	0	0	0	0	0	0
Eddie Murray, dh	.250	6	24	2	6	1	0	1	3	2	3	0
Charles Nagy, p	.000	1	0	0	0	0	0	0	0	0	0	0
Chad Ogea, p	.000	1	0	0	0	0	0	0	0	0	0	0
Tony Pena, c	.333	4	6	1	2	1	0	0	0	1	0	0
Herb Perry, 1b	.000	3	8	0	0	0	0	0	0	1	3	0
Eric Plunk, p	.000	3	0	0	0	0	0	0	0	0	0	0
Jim Poole, p	.000	1	0	0	0	0	0	0	0	0	0	0
Manny Ramirez, of	.286	6	21	2	6	0	0	2	2	2	5	0
Paul Sorrento, 1b	.154	4	13	2	2	1	0	0	0	0	3	0
Julian Tavarez, p	.000	4	0	0	0	0	0	0	0	0	0	0
Jim Thome, 3b	.267	5	15	2	4	0	0	2	5	2	3	0
Omar Vizquel, ss	.087	6	23	2	2	1	0	0	2	5	2	3
TOTAL	.257		206	23	53	6	3	7	21	25	37	9

PITCHER	W	L	ERA	G	GS	CG	SV	SHO	IP	H	ER	BB	SO
Paul Assenmacher	0	0	0.00	3	0	0	0	0	1.1	0	0	1	2
Alan Embree	0	0	0.00	1	0	0	0	0	0.1	0	0	0	1
Orel Hershiser	2	0	1.29	2	2	0	0	0	14.0	9	2	3	15
Ken Hill	1	0	0.00	1	1	0	0	0	7.0	5	0	3	6
Dennis Martinez	1	1	2.03	2	2	0	0	0	13.1	10	3	3	7
Jose Mesa	0	0	2.25	4	0	0	1	0	4.0	3	1	1	1
Charles Nagy	0	0	1.13	1	1	0	0	0	8.0	5	1	0	6
Chad Ogea	0	0	0.00	1	0	0	0	0	0.2	1	0	0	2
Eric Plunk	0	0	9.00	3	0	0	0	0	2.0	1	2	3	2
Jim Poole	0	0	0.00	1	0	0	0	0	1.0	0	0	0	2
Julian Tavarez	0	1	2.70	4	0	0	0	0	3.1	3	1	1	2
TOTAL	4	2	1.64	23	6	0	1	0	55.0	37	10	15	46

SEA (W)

PLAYER/POS	AVG	G	AB	R	H	2B	3B	HR	RB	BB	SO	SB
Rich Amaral, ph	.000	2	2	0	0	0	0	0	0	0	1	0
Bobby Ayala, p	.000	2	0	0	0	0	0	0	0	0	0	0
Tim Belcher, p	.000	1	0	0	0	0	0	0	0	0	0	0
Andy Benes, p	.000	1	0	0	0	0	0	0	0	0	0	0
Mike Blowers, 3b	.222	6	18	1	4	0	0	1	2	0	4	0
Chris Bosio, p	.000	1	0	0	0	0	0	0	0	0	0	0
Jay Buhner, of	.304	6	23	5	7	2	0	3	5	2	8	0
Norm Charlton, p	.000	3	0	0	0	0	0	0	0	0	0	0
Vince Coleman, of-5	.100	6	20	0	2	0	0	0	0	2	6	4
Joey Cora, 2b	.174	6	23	3	4	1	0	0	0	1	0	2
Alex Diaz, of-3	.429	4	7	0	3	1	0	0	0	1	1	0
Felix Fermin, 2b-1,ss-1	.000	2	0	0	0	0	0	0	0	0	0	0
Ken Griffey, of	.333	6	21	2	7	2	0	1	2	4	4	2
Randy Johnson, p	.000	2	0	0	0	0	0	0	0	0	0	0
Tino Martinez, 1b	.136	6	22	1	3	0	0	0	0	3	7	0
Edgar Martinez, dh	.087	6	23	0	2	0	0	0	0	2	5	1
Jeff Nelson, p	.000	3	0	0	0	0	0	0	0	0	0	0
Bill Risley, p	.000	3	0	0	0	0	0	0	0	0	0	0
Alex Rodriguez, ph	.000	1	1	0	0	0	0	0	0	0	1	0
Luis Sojo, ss	.250	6	20	0	5	2	0	0	1	0	2	0
Doug Strange, 3b-2	.000	4	4	0	0	0	0	0	0	0	0	0
Bob Wells, p	.000	1	0	0	0	0	0	0	0	0	0	0
Chris Widger, c	.000	3	1	0	0	0	0	0	0	0	1	0
Dan Wilson, c	.000	6	16	0	0	0	0	0	0	0	4	0
Bob Wolcott, p	.000	1	0	0	0	0	0	0	0	0	0	0
TOTAL	.184		201	12	37	8	0	5	10	15	46	9

PITCHER	W	L	ERA	G	GS	CG	SV	SHO	IP	H	ER	BB	SO
Bobby Ayala	0	0	2.45	2	0	0	0	0	3.2	3	1	3	3
Tim Belcher	0	1	6.35	1	1	0	0	0	5.2	9	4	2	1
Andy Benes	0	1	23.14	1	1	0	0	0	2.1	6	6	2	3
Chris Bosio	0	1	3.38	1	1	0	0	0	5.1	7	2	2	3
Norm Charlton	1	0	0.00	3	0	0	1	0	6.0	1	0	1	5
Randy Johnson	0	1	2.35	2	2	0	0	0	15.1	12	4	2	13
Jeff Nelson	0	0	0.00	3	0	0	0	0	3.0	3	0	5	3
Bill Risley	0	0	0.00	3	0	0	0	0	2.2	2	0	1	2
Bob Wells	0	0	3.00	1	0	0	0	0	3.0	2	1	2	2
Bob Wolcott	1	0	2.57	1	1	0	0	0	7.0	8	2	5	2
TOTAL	2	4	3.33	18	6	0	1	0	54.0	53	20	25	37

After the game Cleveland celebrated and contemplated its first World Series appearance since 1954 ... but the nation watched the Seattle dugout, where Mariners second baseman Joey Cora wept uncontrollably.

GAME 1 AT SEA OCT 10

CLE	001	000	100	2	10 1
SEA	020	000	10X	3	7 0

Pitchers: MARTINEZ, Tavarez (7), Assenmacher (8), Plunk (8) vs WOLCOTT, Nelson (8), Charlton (8)
Home Runs: Belle-CLE, Blowers-SEA
Attendance: 57,065

GAME 2 AT SEA OCT 11

CLE	000	022	010	5	12 0
SEA	000	001	001	2	6 1

Pitchers: HERSHISER, Mesa (9) vs BELCHER, Ayala (6), Risley (9)
Home Runs: Ramirez-CLE (2), Griffey-SEA, Buhner-SEA
Attendance: 58,144

GAME 3 AT CLE OCT 13

SEA	011	000	000	03	5 9 1
CLE	000	100	010	00	2 4 2

Pitchers: Johnson, CHARLTON (9) vs Nagy, Mesa (9), TAVAREZ (9), Assenmacher (11), Plunk (11)
Home Runs: Buhner-SEA (2)
Attendance: 43,643

GAME 4 AT CLE OCT 14

SEA	000	000	000	0	6 1
CLE	312	001	00X	7	9 0

Pitchers: BENES, Wells (3), Ayala (6), Nelson (7), Risley (8) vs HILL, Poole (8), Ogea (9), Embree (9)
Home Runs: Murray-CLE, Thome-CLE
Attendance: 43,686

GAME 5 AT CLE OCT 15

SEA	001	010	000	2	5 2
CLE	100	002	00X	3	10 4

Pitchers: BOSIO, Nelson (6), Risley (7) vs HERSHISER, Tavarez (7), Assenmacher (7), Plunk (8), Mesa (9)
Home Runs: Thome-CLE
Attendance: 43,607

GAME 6 AT SEA OCT 17

CLE	000	010	030	4	8 0
SEA	000	000	000	0	4 1

Pitchers: MARTINEZ, Tavarez (8), Mesa (9) vs JOHNSON, Charlton (8)
Home Runs: Baerga-CLE
Attendance: 58,489

The Indians and Braves met for a rematch of their tussle in the 1948 World Series, but this time the transplanted Braves went home with the honors.

Game One quickly established that Atlanta's vaunted pitching staff was no myth. Perennial Cy Young Award winner Greg Maddux used just 95 pitches in shutting down the hard-hitting Indians. Only three runners reached against him, on opposite field singles by Kenny Lofton and Jim Thome, and on an error by Rafael Belliard. Cleveland starter Orel Hershiser tired in the seventh and walked two, leading to the second and third Atlanta runs and his first loss after seven straight postseason victories.

In Game Two Atlanta took a 2-0 series lead as catcher Javier Lopez anticipated a Dennis Martinez fastball on the outside part of the plate. He hammered it to straight-away center field for a two- run homer, shattering a 2-2 tie and providing the Braves with all the margin they would need for a 4-3 win. Earlier, Cleveland's Eddie Murray garnered a two-run homer of his own off starter Tom Glavine.

The Indians bats finally came alive in Game Three's 7-6 win. It looked like the Tribe would be facing a 3-0 deficit, as they trailed 6-5 in the bottom of the eighth. But in that inning Kenny Lofton (who reached base six times in the contest) scored the tying run on Sandy Alomar's first hit of the series. In the eleventh Murray singled off Alejandro Pena's first pitch to score pinch-runner Alvaro Espinoza with the winning run.

Atlanta's Ryan Klesko and Cleveland's Albert Belle traded solo sixth-inning homers in Game Four to set up a 1-1 tie going into the top of the seventh. Atlanta then scored three runs on Luis Polonia's run-scoring double and David Justice's two-out, two-RBI single to center to break the contest open and ultimately give Atlanta a 5-2 win.

The Tribe stayed alive in Game Five as Jim Thome singled in the go-ahead run in the sixth and provided a crucial insurance run with an eighth inning homer. Ryan Klesko nicked Jose Mesa for a two-run homer in the ninth—the third straight game in which he'd homered—but it wasn't enough.

With a 3-2 lead in the Series and Greg Maddux waiting to pitch Game Seven, the Braves had little to worry about in Game Six. Key to their victory were two players with something to prove: Tom Glavine, who had survived Atlanta's horrible days in the late 1980s, and David Justice, who was taking heat for comments he had made about Atlanta fans' lack of spirit. Glavine

allowed only a sixth inning single to Tony Pena, walked three and struck out eight. Justice brought home the game's only run with a sixth inning homer off reliever Jim Poole.

The Braves now had their first World Championship since 1957 and had become the first franchise to win the crown in three different cities—Boston, Milwaukee, and Atlanta.

Atlanta Braves (N,) 4; Cleveland Indians (A), 2

ATL (N)

PLAYER/POS	AVG	G	AB	R	H	2B	3B	HR	RB	BB	SO	SB
Steve Avery, pn	.000	1	0	0	0	0	0	0	0	0	0	0
Rafael Belliard, ss	.000	6	16	0	0	0	0	0	0	1	4	0
Pedro Borbon, p	.000	1	0	0	0	0	0	0	0	0	0	0
Brad Clontz, p	.000	2	0	0	0	0	0	0	0	0	0	0
Mike Devereaux, of-4,dh-1	.250	5	4	0	1	0	0	0	0	1	2	1	0
Tom Glavine, p	.000	2	4	0	0	0	0	0	0	0	1	2	0
Marquis Grissom, of	.360	6	25	3	9	1	0	0	1	1	3	3
Chipper Jones, 3b	.286	6	21	3	6	3	0	0	1	4	3	0
David Justice, of	.250	6	20	3	5	1	0	1	5	5	5	1	0
Ryan Klesko, of-3,dh-3	.313	6	16	4	5	0	0	3	4	3	4	0
Mark Lemke, 2b	.273	6	22	1	6	0	0	0	3	2	0
Javy Lopez, c	.176	6	17	1	3	2	0	1	3	1	1	0
Greg Maddux, p	.000	2	3	0	0	0	0	0	0	0	1	0
Fred McGriff, 1b	.261	6	23	5	6	2	0	2	3	3	7	1
Greg McMichael, p	.000	3	0	0	0	0	0	0	0	0	0	0
Kent Mercker, p	.000	1	0	0	0	0	0	0	0	0	0	0
Mike Mordecai, ss-2, dh-1	.333	3	3	0	1	0	0	0	0	0	1	0
Charlie O'Brien, c	.000	2	3	0	0	0	0	0	0	0	1	0
Alejandro Pena, p	.000	2	0	0	0	0	0	0	0	0	0	0
Luis Polonia, of-6	.286	6	14	3	4	1	0	1	4	1	3	1
Dwight Smith, ph	.500	3	2	0	1	0	0	0	0	1	0	0
John Smoltz, p	.000	1	0	0	0	0	0	0	0	0	0	0
Mark Wohlers, p	.000	4	0	0	0	0	0	0	0	0	0	0
TOTAL	.244		193	23	47	10	0	8	23	25	34	5

PITCHER	W	L	ERA	G	GS	CG	SV	SHO	IP	H	ER	BB	SO
Steve Avery	1	0	1.50	1	1	0	0	0	6.0	3	1	5	3
Pedro Borbon	0	0	0.00	1	0	0	1	0	1.0	0	0	0	2
Brad Clontz	0	0	2.70	2	0	0	0	0	3.1	2	1	0	2
Tom Glavine	2	0	1.29	2	2	0	0	0	14.0	4	2	6	11
Greg Maddux	1	1	2.25	2	2	1	0	0	16.0	9	4	3	8
Greg McMichael	0	0	2.70	3	0	0	0	0	3.1	3	1	2	2
Kent Mercker	0	0	4.50	1	0	0	0	0	2.0	1	1	2	2
Alejandro Pena	0	1	9.00	2	0	0	0	0	1.0	3	1	2	0
John Smoltz	0	0	15.43	1	1	0	0	0	2.1	6	4	2	4
Mark Wohlers	0	0	1.80	4	0	0	2	0	5.0	4	1	3	3
TOTAL	4	2	2.67	19	6	1	3	0	54.0	35	16	25	37

CLE (A)

PLAYER/POS	AVG	G	AB	R	H	2B	3B	HR	RB	BB	SO	SB
Sandy Alomar, c	.200	5	15	0	3	2	0	0	1	0	2	0
Ruben Amaro, of-1	.000	2	2	0	0	0	0	0	0	0	1	0
Paul Assenmacher, p	.000	4	0	0	0	0	0	0	0	0	0	0
Carlos Baerga, 2b	.192	6	26	1	5	2	0	0	4	1	1	0
Albert Belle, of	.235	6	17	4	4	0	0	2	4	7	5	0
Alan Embree, p	.000	4	0	0	0	0	0	0	0	0	0	0
Alvaro Espinoza, 3b-1	.500	2	2	1	1	0	0	0	0	0	0	0
Orel Hershiser, p	.000	2	2	0	0	0	0	0	0	0	1	0
Ken Hill, p	.000	2	0	0	0	0	0	0	0	0	0	0
Wayne Kirby, of-2	.000	3	1	0	0	0	0	0	0	0	0	0
Kenny Lofton, of	.200	6	25	6	5	1	0	0	3	1	6
Dennis Martinez, p	.000	2	3	0	0	0	0	0	0	0	1	0
Jose Mesa, p	.000	2	0	0	0	0	0	0	0	0	0	0
Eddie Murray, 1b-3,dh-3	.105	6	19	1	2	0	0	1	3	5	4	0
Charles Nagy, p	.000	1	0	0	0	0	0	0	0	0	0	0
Tony Pena, c	.167	2	6	0	1	0	0	0	0	0	0	0
Herb Perry, ph	.000	3	5	0	0	0	0	0	0	0	2	0
Jim Poole, p	.000	2	1	0	0	0	0	0	0	0	0	0
Manny Ramirez, of	.222	6	18	2	4	0	0	1	2	4	5	1
Paul Sorrento, 1b-3	.182	6	11	0	2	1	0	0	0	0	4	0
Julian Tavarez, p	.000	5	0	0	0	0	0	0	0	0	0	0
Jim Thome, 3b	.211	6	19	1	4	0	0	1	2	2	5	0
Omar Vizquel, ss	.174	6	23	3	4	0	1	0	1	3	5	1
TOTAL	.179		195	19	35	7	1	5	17	25	37	8

PITCHER	W	L	ERA	G	GS	CG	SV	SHO	IP	H	ER	BB	SO
Paul Assenmacher	0	0	6.75	4	0	0	0	0	1.1	1	1	3	3
Alan Embree	0	0	2.70	4	0	0	0	0	3.1	2	1	2	2
Orel Hershiser	1	1	2.57	2	2	0	0	0	14.0	8	4	4	13
Ken Hill	0	1	4.26	2	1	0	0	0	6.1	7	3	4	1
Dennis Martinez	0	1	3.48	2	2	0	0	0	10.1	12	4	8	5
Jose Mesa	1	0	4.50	2	0	0	1	0	4.0	5	2	1	4
Charles Nagy	0	0	6.43	1	1	0	0	0	7.0	8	5	1	4
Jim Poole	0	1	3.86	2	0	0	0	0	2.1	1	1	0	1
Julian Tavarez	0	0	0.00	5	0	0	0	0	4.1	3	0	2	1
TOTAL	2	4	3.57	24	6	0	1	0	53.0	47	21	25	34

GAME 1 AT ATL OCT 21

```
CLE   100 000 001    2 2 0
ATL   010 000 20X    3 3 2
```

Pitchers: HERSHISER, Assenmacher (7), Tavarez (7), Embree (8) vs MADDUX
Home Runs: McGriff-ATL
Attendance: 51,876

GAME 2 AT ATL OCT 22

```
CLE   020 000 100    3 6 2
ATL   002 002 00X    4 8 2
```

Pitchers: MARTINEZ, Embree (6), Poole (7), Tavarez (7), Wohlers (8)
McMichael (7), Pena (7), Wohlers (8)
Home Runs: Murray-CLE, Lopez-ATL
Attendance: 51,877

GAME 3 AT CLE OCT 24

```
ATL   100 001 130 00   6 12 1
CLE   202 000 110 01   7 12 2
```

Pitchers: Smoltz, Clontz (3), Mercker (5), McMichael (7), Wohlers (8), PENA (11) vs Nagy, Assenmacher (8), Tavarez (8), MESA (9)
Home Runs: McGriff-ATL, Klesko-ATL
Attendance: 43,584

GAME 4 AT CLE OCT 25

```
ATL   000 001 301    5 11 1
CLE   000 001 001    2 6 0
```

Pitchers: AVERY, McMichael (7), Wohlers (9), Borbon (9) vs HILL, Assenmacher (8), Tavarez (8), Embree (8)
Home Runs: Belle-CLE, Ramirez-CLE, Klesko-ATL
Attendance: 43,578

GAME 5 AT CLE OCT 26

```
ATL   000 110 002    4 7 0
CLE   200 002 01X    5 8 1
```

Pitchers: MADDUX, Clontz (8) vs HERSHISER, Mesa (9)
Home Runs: Belle-CLE, Thome-CLE, Polonia-ATL, Klesko-ATL
Attendance: 43,595

GAME 6 AT ATL OCT 28

```
CLE   000 000 000    0 1 1
ATL   000 001 00X    1 6 0
```

Pitchers: Martinez, POOLE (5), Hill (7), Embree (7), Tavarez (8), Assenmacher (8) vs GLAVINE, Wohlers (9)
Home Runs: Justice-ATL
Attendance: 51,875

The Braves became the first National League team to make five consecutive postseason appearances, but, its 96-66 record notwithstanding, 1996 was not Atlanta's strongest team. The Braves struggled in mid-September, but their opponents in the Division Series, the Dodgers, had really stumbled into the postseason. Los Angeles lost its last four regular-season games, but still captured the wild card. Dodger Stadium was abuzz when the Division Series began and the two starting pitchers, LA's Ramon Martinez and Atlanta's John Smoltz, were equal to the task. Martinez allowed just one run and three hits through eight innings while Smoltz pitched nine innings with only one run and four hits against him, although Mike Piazza's drive in the ninth was caught at the wall. Smoltz and the Braves caught the break they needed when Javier Lopez homered to right-center for a 2-1 lead. Reliever Mark Wohlers made it hold up with two strikeouts in the tenth inning.

Pitching was the name of the game again the next night. While Greg Maddux's four-year streak of Cy Young Awards would end in 1996, he reminded the country that his trophy collection was well-deserved. Maddux, however, was touched for unearned runs in the first and fourth innings on RBI by Piazza and Raul Mondesi as the Dodgers took a 2-1 lead into the seventh inning despite just three hits. Dodger starter Ismael Valdez limited the Braves to three hits as well through six innings, including a home run by Ryan Klesko, but that changed in a span of seven pitches in the seventh inning. Fred McGriff hit a line-drive home run to center field to tie the score. After Valdez recorded his fifth strikeout, Jermaine Dye hit the first pitch he saw over the left field wall for a 3-2 lead. Maddux cruised through the first seven innings on only 72 pitches, but he aggravated a hamstring injury and had to call it a day. Manager Bobby Cox sent Greg McMichael in to start the eighth and he retired the side in order. Wohlers followed suit in the ninth for the save.

A club-record crowd greeted the Braves at Fulton County Stadium for Game Three, but the fans fidgeted in their seats when Hideo Nomo struck out the first two Braves he faced. They were soon on their feet, however, when Chipper Jones singled and McGriff doubled him home. Nomo retired the first two batters he faced in the fourth inning, but he was on his way to the showers by the time the third out was recorded. Pitcher

Atlanta Braves (E), 3;
Los Angeles Dodgers (WC), 0

ATL (E)

PLAYER/POS	AVG	G	AB	R	H	2B	3B	HR	RB	BB	SO	SB
Rafael Belliard, ss	.000	3	0	0	0	0	0	0	0	0	0	0
Mike Bielecki, p	.000	1	0	0	0	0	0	0	0	0	0	0
Jeff Blauser, ss	.111	3	9	0	1	0	0	0	0	1	3	0
Jermaine Dye, of	.182	3	11	1	2	0	0	1	1	0	6	1
Tom Glavine, p	.500	1	2	1	1	1	0	0	0	0	0	0
Marquis Grissom, of	.083	3	12	2	1	0	0	0	0	1	2	1
Andruw Jones, of	.000	3	0	0	0	0	0	0	0	1	0	0
Chipper Jones, 3b	.222	3	9	2	2	0	0	1	2	3	4	1
Ryan Klesko, of	.125	3	8	1	1	0	0	1	1	3	4	1
Mark Lemke, 2b	.167	3	12	1	2	1	0	0	2	0	1	0
Javy Lopez, c	.286	2	7	1	2	0	0	1	1	1	0	1
Greg Maddux, p	.000	1	2	0	0	0	0	0	0	0	1	0
Fred McGriff, 1b	.333	3	9	1	3	1	0	1	3	2	1	0
Greg McMichael, p	.000	2	0	0	0	0	0	0	0	0	0	0
Terry Pendleton, ph	.000	1	1	0	0	0	0	0	0	0	1	0
Eddie Perez, c	.333	1	3	0	1	0	0	0	0	0	0	0
Luis Polonia, ph	.000	2	2	0	0	0	0	0	0	0	1	0
John Smoltz, p	.000	1	0	0	0	0	0	0	0	0	0	0
Mark Wohlers, p	.000	3	0	0	0	0	0	0	0	0	0	0
TOTAL	.180		89	10	16	3	0	5	10	12	24	5

PITCHER	W	L	ERA	G	GS	CG	SV	SHO	IP	H	ER	BB	SO
Mike Bielecki	0	0	0.00	1	0	0	0	0	0.2	0	0	1	1
Tom Glavine	1	0	1.35	1	1	0	0	0	6.2	5	1	3	7
Greg Maddux	1	0	0.00	1	1	0	0	0	7.0	3	0	0	7
Greg McMichael	0	0	6.75	2	0	0	0	0	1.1	1	1	1	3
John Smoltz	1	0	1.00	1	1	0	0	0	9.0	4	1	2	7
Mark Wohlers	0	0	0.00	3	0	0	2	0	3.1	1	0	0	4
TOTAL	3	0	0.96	9	3	0	2	0	28.0	14	3	7	29

LA (W)

PLAYER/POS	AVG	G	AB	R	H	2B	3B	HR	RB	BB	SO	SB
Billy Ashley, ph	.000	2	2	0	0	0	0	0	0	0	2	0
Pedro Astacio, p	.000	1	0	0	0	0	0	0	0	0	0	0
Tom Candiotti, p	.000	1	0	0	0	0	0	0	0	0	0	0
Juan Castro, 2b	.200	2	5	1	1	1	0	0	1	1	1	0
Dave Clark, ph	.000	2	2	0	0	0	0	0	0	0	2	0
Chad Curtis, of	.000	1	2	0	0	0	0	0	0	1	1	0
Delino DeShields, 2b	.000	2	4	0	0	0	0	0	0	0	1	0
Darren Dreifort, p	.000	1	0	0	0	0	0	0	0	0	0	0
Greg Gagne, ss	.273	3	11	2	3	1	0	0	0	0	5	0
Mark Guthrie, p	.000	1	0	0	0	0	0	0	0	0	0	0
Dave Hansen, ph	.000	2	2	0	0	0	0	0	0	0	0	0
Todd Hollandsworth, of	.333	3	12	1	4	3	0	0	1	0	3	0
Eric Karros, 1b	.000	3	9	0	0	0	0	0	0	2	3	0
Wayne Kirby, of	.125	3	8	1	1	0	0	0	0	2	1	0
Ramon Martinez, p	.000	1	3	0	0	0	0	0	0	0	2	0
Raul Mondesi, of	.182	3	11	0	2	2	0	0	1	0	4	0
Hideo Nomo, p	.000	1	1	0	0	0	0	0	0	0	1	0
Antonio Osuna, p	.000	2	0	0	0	0	0	0	0	0	0	0
Mike Piazza, c	.300	3	10	1	3	0	0	0	2	1	2	0
Scott Radinsky, p	.000	2	0	0	0	0	0	0	0	0	0	0
Ismael Valdes, p	.000	1	2	0	0	0	0	0	0	0	0	0
Tim Wallach, 3b	.000	3	11	0	0	0	0	0	0	0	1	0
Todd Worrell, p	.000	1	0	0	0	0	0	0	0	0	0	0
TOTAL	.147		95	5	14	7	0	0	5	7	29	0

PITCHER	W	L	ERA	G	GS	CG	SV	SHO	IP	H	ER	BB	SO
Pedro Astacio	0	0	0.00	1	0	0	0	0	1.2	0	0	0	1
Tom Candiotti	0	0	0.00	1	0	0	0	0	2.0	0	0	0	1
Darren Dreifort	0	0	0.00	1	0	0	0	0	0.2	0	0	0	0
Mark Guthrie	0	0	0.00	1	0	0	0	0	0.1	0	0	1	1
Ramon Martinez	0	0	1.13	1	1	0	0	0	8.0	3	1	3	6
Hideo Nomo	0	1	12.27	1	1	0	0	0	3.2	5	5	5	3
Antonio Osuna	0	1	4.50	2	0	0	0	0	2.0	3	1	1	4
Scott Radinsky	0	0	0.00	2	0	0	0	0	1.1	0	0	1	2
Ismael Valdes	0	1	4.26	1	1	0	0	0	6.1	5	3	0	5
Todd Worrell	0	0	0.00	1	0	0	0	0	1.0	0	0	1	1
TOTAL	0	3	3.33	12	3	0	0	0	27.0	16	10	12	24

Tom Glavine started the rally with a double and Marquis Grissom walked before Mark Lemke, who batted .167 in the three games, doubled home both runners. Jones followed with a two-run home run to give Atlanta a 5-0 lead, which seemed insurmountable considering that it had taken the Dodgers 43 innings to score their last five runs. To their credit, the Dodgers nicked Glavine for a run in the seventh inning and McMichael for another in the eighth, but Mike Bielecki and Wohlers allowed nothing more and the Braves had another opportunity to celebrate.

GAME ONE AT LA OCT 2

ATL	000 100 000	1	2	4	1
LA	000 010 000	0	1	5	0

Pitchers: SMOLTZ, Wohlers (10) vs Martinez, Radinsky (9), OSUNA (9)
Home Runs: Lopez-ATL
Attendance: 47,428

GAME TWO AT LA OCT 3

ATL	010 000 200	3	5	2
LA	100 100 000	2	3	0

Pitchers: MADDUX, McMichael (8), Wohlers (9) vs VALDES, Astacio (7), Worrell (9)
Home Runs: Klesko-ATL, McGriff-ATL, Dye-ATL
Attendance: 51,916

GAME THREE AT ATL OCT 5

LA	000 000 110	2	6	1
ATL	100 400 00X	5	7	0

Pitchers: NOMO, Guthrie (4), Candiotti (5), Radinsky (7), Osuna (8), Dreifort (8) vs GLAVINE, McMichael (7), Bielecki (8), Wohlers (8)
Home Runs: C.Jones-ATL
Attendance: 52,529

St. Louis finished 19 games under .500 in 1995, but with new manager Tony LaRussa and fourteen new players, the Cards of 1996 won 88 games and captured the NL Central by six games. San Diego's storybook season ended with a three-game sweep over the Dodgers to claim the NL West title with a 91-71 mark. The Cardinals took control of the Division Series at Busch Stadium when Gary Gaetti hit a three-run home run, his only hit of the series, to give the Cards a first-inning lead against Joey Hamilton. St. Louis made it hold up. Todd Stottlemyre, who entered the game with a postseason ERA of 7.50, allowed only a Rickey Henderson home run in 6⅔ innings. Then LaRussa's veteran bullpen of Rick Honeycutt and Dennis Eckersley, with forty years of major league experience between them, kept the Padres at bay. Eckersley made a nice play on a hard shot by Tony Gwynn with two runners on base in the ninth for the save.

Game Two was another well-played contest as the two teams matched each other run for run through the first seven and a half innings in front of a record crowd in St. Louis. Willie McGee singled in the first run of the game for the Cards in the third, but Ken Caminiti answered back with a home run to right field to tie the score at 1-1 in the top of the fifth. St. Louis rallied for three runs in the bottom of the frame when Ron Gant hit a bases-clearing double. The Padres scored twice in the sixth when Tony Gwynn singled in one run and a throwing error allowed another run to score. San Diego tied the game in the top of the eighth on a groundout by Steve Finley, but Tom Pagnozzi's line drive in the bottom of the inning ticked off the glove of reliever Trevor Hoffman and brought home the winning run. Eckersley retired the side in order in the ninth to make a winner of Honeycutt.

In San Diego's only other playoff appearance in 1984, the Padres dropped the first two games in Chicago and then won the last three at home for the pennant. The Padres were looking for that magic again in 1996 as they took a 4-1 lead after four innings against Cardinal starter Donovan Osborne. The Cards rallied to tie matters in the sixth to knock out Padre starter Andy Ashby. St. Louis pushed across a run in the seventh after the Padres misplayed a bunt, but Caminiti hit his second home run of the game—and third of the series—to tie the game in the eighth. San Diego had a chance to take the lead later in the inning, but right fielder Brian Jordan made a sensational diving catch to end the threat. With his shoulder aching

St. Louis Cardinals (C), 3; San Diego Padres (W), 0

STL (C)

PLAYER/POS	AVG	G	AB	R	H	2B	3B	HR	RB	BB	SO	SB
Luis Alicea, 2b	.182	3	11	1	2	2	0	0	0	1	4	0
Andy Benes, p	.500	1	2	1	1	0	0	0	0	0	1	0
Royce Clayton, ss	.333	2	6	1	2	0	0	0	0	3	1	0
Dennis Eckersley, p	.000	3	0	0	0	0	0	0	0	0	0	0
Gary Gaetti, 3b	.091	3	11	1	1	0	0	1	3	0	3	0
Mike Gallego, 2b-1,3b-1	.000	2	1	0	0	0	0	0	0	0	1	0
Ron Gant, of	.400	3	10	3	4	1	0	1	4	2	0	2
Rick Honeycutt, p	.000	3	1	0	0	0	0	0	0	0	1	0
Brian Jordan, of	.333	3	12	4	4	0	0	1	3	1	3	1
Ray Lankford, of	.500	1	2	1	1	0	0	0	0	1	0	0
John Mabry, 1b	.300	3	10	1	3	0	1	0	1	1	1	0
T. J. Mathews, p	.000	1	0	0	0	0	0	0	0	0	0	0
Willie McGee, of	.100	3	10	1	1	0	0	0	1	1	3	0
Miguel Mejia, pr	.000	1	0	0	0	0	0	0	0	0	0	0
Donovan Osborne, p	.000	1	1	0	0	0	0	0	0	0	0	0
Tom Pagnozzi, c	.273	3	11	0	3	0	0	0	2	1	3	0
Mark Petkovsek, p	.000	1	0	0	0	0	0	0	0	0	0	0
Ozzie Smith, ss-1	.333	2	3	1	1	0	0	0	0	0	2	0
Todd Stottlemyre, p	.000	1	2	0	0	0	0	0	0	0	2	0
Mark Sweeney, ph	1.000	1	1	0	1	0	0	0	0	0	0	0
TOTAL	.255		94	15	24	3	1	3	14	13	23	3

PITCHER	W	L	ERA	G	GS	CG	SV	SHO	IP	H	ER	BB	SO
Andy Benes	0	0	5.14	1	1	0	0	0	7.0	6	4	1	9
Dennis Eckersley	0	0	0.00	3	0	0	3	0	3.2	3	0	0	2
Rick Honeycutt	1	0	3.38	3	0	0	0	0	2.2	3	1	1	2
T. J. Mathews	1	0	0.00	1	0	0	0	0	1.0	1	0	0	2
Donovan Osborne	0	0	9.00	1	1	0	0	0	4.0	7	4	0	5
Mark Petkovsek	0	0	0.00	1	0	0	0	0	2.0	0	0	0	1
Todd Stottlemyre	1	0	1.35	1	1	0	0	0	6.2	5	1	2	7
TOTAL	3	0	3.33	11	3	0	3	0	27.0	25	10	4	28

SD (W)

PLAYER/POS	AVG	G	AB	R	H	2B	3B	HR	RB	BB	SO	SB
Andy Ashby, p	.000	1	1	0	0	0	0	0	0	0	1	0
Willie Blair, p.	.000	1	0	0	0	0	0	0	0	0	0	0
Doug Bochtler, p	.000	1	0	0	0	0	0	0	0	0	0	0
Ken Caminiti, 3b	.300	4	10	3	3	0	0	3	3	2	5	0
Archi Cianfrocco, 1b	.333	1	3	1	1	0	0	0	0	0	1	0
Steve Finley, of	.083	3	12	0	1	0	0	0	1	0	4	1
John Flaherty, c	.000	2	4	0	0	0	0	0	0	0	1	0
Chris Gomez, ss	.167	3	12	0	2	0	0	0	0	1	4	0
Tony Gwynn, of	.308	3	13	0	4	1	0	0	1	0	2	1
Chris Gwynn, ph	1.000	2	2	1	2	0	0	0	0	0	0	0
Joey Hamilton, p	.000	1	2	0	0	0	0	0	0	0	2	0
Rickey Henderson, of	.333	3	12	4	4	0	0	1	1	2	3	0
Trevor Hoffman, p	.000	2	0	0	0	0	0	0	0	0	0	0
Brian Johnson, c	.375	2	8	2	3	1	0	0	0	0	1	0
Wally Joyner, 1b	.111	3	9	0	1	0	0	0	0	1	2	0
Scott Livingstone, ph	.500	2	2	1	1	0	0	0	0	0	0	0
Luis Lopez, pr	.000	1	0	0	0	0	0	0	0	0	0	0
Jody Reed, 2b	.273	3	11	0	3	1	0	0	2	0	1	0
Scott Sanders, p	.000	1	1	0	0	0	0	0	0	0	0	0
Fernando Valenzuela, p	.000	1	0	0	0	0	0	0	0	0	0	0
Greg Vaughn, ph	.000	3	3	0	0	0	0	0	0	0	1	0
Dario Veras, p	.000	2	0	0	0	0	0	0	0	0	0	0
Tim Worrell, p	.000	2	0	0	0	0	0	0	0	0	0	0
TOTAL	.238		105	10	25	3	0	4	9	4	28	2

PITCHER	W	L	ERA	G	GS	CG	SV	SHO	IP	H	ER	BB	SO
Andy Ashby	0	0	6.75	1	1	0	0	0	5.1	7	4	1	5
Willie Blair	0	0	0.00	1	0	0	0	0	2.0	1	0	2	3
Doug Bochtler	0	1	27.00	1	0	0	0	0	0.1	0	1	2	0
Joey Hamilton	0	1	4.50	1	1	0	0	0	6.0	5	3	0	6
Trevor Hoffman	0	1	10.80	2	0	0	0	0	1.2	3	2	1	2
Scott Sanders	0	0	8.31	1	1	0	0	0	4.1	3	4	4	4
Fernando Valenzuela	0	0	0.00	1	0	0	0	0	0.2	0	0	2	0
Dario Veras	0	0	0.00	2	0	0	0	0	1.0	1	0	0	1
Tim Worrell	0	0	2.45	2	0	0	0	0	3.2	4	1	1	2
TOTAL	0	3	5.40	12	3	0	0	0	25.0	24	15	13	23

from the catch, Jordan crushed a home run to left off Hoffman for a 7-5 lead in the ninth. Eckersley made the sweep official by earning the save.

GAME ONE AT STL OCT 1

```
SD   000 001 000   1 8 1
STL  300 000 00X   3 6 0
```

Pitchers: HAMILTON, Blair (7) vs STOTTLEMYRE, Honeycutt (7), Eckersley (8)
Home Runs: Henderson-SD, Gaetti-STL
Attendance: 54,193

GAME TWO AT STL OCT 3

```
SD   000 012 010   4 6 0
STL  001 030 01X   5 5 1
```

Pitchers: Sanders, Veras (5), Worrell (6), BOCHTLER (8), Hoffman (8) vs An.Benes, HONEYCUTT (8), Eckersley (9)
Home Runs: Caminiti-SD
Attendance: 56,752

GAME THREE AT SD OCT 5

```
STL  100 003 102   7 13 1
SD   021 100 010   5 11 2
```

Pitchers: Osborne, Petkovsek (5), Honeycutt (7), MATHEWS (8), Eckersley (9) vs Ashby, Worrell (6), Valenzuela (8), Veras (8), HOFFMAN (9)
Home Runs: Gant-STL, Jordan-STL, Caminiti-SD (2)
Attendance: 53,899

The Rangers jumped out to a lead in all four games of the Division Series, but the difference was Yankee relief pitching—and Bernie Williams. The New York bullpen allowed just one earned run in 19⅔ innings of relief while Texas relievers failed to hold the lead in all three losses. Williams helped see to that. He hit three home runs in the series, including two in decisive Game Four. Juan Gonzalez hit five home runs and drove in nine runs for the Rangers, but the Yankees won by corralling the rest of the Texas bats in the series.

The series started with the Texas longball and the Ranger relievers stuck in the bullpen with nothing to do. John Burkett, a late-season acquisition, quieted the boisterous Yankee Stadium crowd with a complete-game effort and Gonzalez and Dean Palmer both homered off David Cone in the fifth inning for a 6-2 Ranger win. Texas jumped out to a 4-1 lead in Game Two against Andy Pettitte, courtesy of a pair of Gonzalez home runs, but the Rangers' failure to convert two tailor-made double-play grounders in the fourth inning gave the Yankees a key run. The Yankees tied it against the Texas bullpen and the Ranger defense gave New York the game when Palmer threw away Charlie Hayes's bunt in the twelfth inning to score Derek Jeter with the winner.

Williams homered to the opposite field in the top of the first inning and then reached over the fence to rob Rusty Greer of a home run in the bottom of the inning. Darren Oliver stole the show after that. In the first home postseason game in the history of the franchise, the southpaw gave the crowd plenty to cheer about as he held the Yankees to four hits through eight innings. Texas scored two runs off Jimmy Key as Gonzalez provided the expected power with a fourth-inning home run and the other run was set up when no one covered second base on a steal. Rangers manager Johnny Oates knew the shaky state of his bullpen, so he let Oliver start the ninth and yanked him only after the first two runners reached base. Mike Henneman allowed a game-tying sacrifice fly and surrendered a single by Mariano Duncan for a 3-2 Yankee lead. John Wetteland, on the other hand, retired the side in the ninth to give New York a two games to one lead.

The Rangers jumped out to a 4-0 lead the next afternoon in Game Four. Gonzalez, as usual, added a home run, but timely hits by Mickey Tettleton, Ivan Rodriguez, and Mark McLemore scored three more runs and ended the Yankees' streak of bullpen dominance. New York simply started a new streak.

New York Yankees (E), 3; Texas Rangers (W), 1

NY (E)

PLAYER/POS	AVG	G	AB	R	H	2B	3B	HR	RB	BB	SO	SB
Brian Boehringer, p	.000	2	0	0	0	0	0	0	0	0	0	0
Wade Boggs, 3b	.083	3	12	0	1	1	0	0	0	0	2	0
David Cone, p	.000	1	0	0	0	0	0	0	0	0	0	0
Mariano Duncan, 2b	.313	4	16	0	5	0	0	0	3	0	4	0
Cecil Fielder, dh	.364	3	11	2	4	0	0	1	4	1	2	0
Andy Fox, dh-1	.000	2	0	0	0	0	0	0	0	0	0	0
Joe Girardi, c	.222	4	9	1	2	0	0	0	0	1	4	1
Charlie Hayes, 3b-2	.200	3	5	0	1	0	0	0	1	0	0	0
Derek Jeter, ss	.412	4	17	2	7	1	0	0	1	0	2	0
Jimmy Key, p	.000	1	0	0	0	0	0	0	0	0	0	0
Jim Leyritz, c-1	.000	2	3	0	0	0	0	0	0	0	1	0
Graeme Lloyd, p	.000	2	0	0	0	0	0	0	0	0	0	0
Tino Martinez, 1b	.267	4	15	3	4	2	0	0	0	3	1	0
Jeff Nelson, p	.000	2	0	0	0	0	0	0	0	0	0	0
Paul O'Neill, of	.133	4	15	0	2	0	0	0	0	0	2	0
Andy Pettitte, p	.000	1	0	0	0	0	0	0	0	0	0	0
Tim Raines, of	.250	4	16	3	4	0	0	0	0	3	1	0
Mariano Rivera, p	.000	2	0	0	0	0	0	0	0	0	0	0
Ruben Rivera, of	.000	2	1	0	0	0	0	0	0	0	1	0
Kenny Rogers, p	.000	2	0	0	0	0	0	0	0	0	0	0
Luis Sojo, 2b	.000	2	0	0	0	0	0	0	0	0	0	0
Darryl Strawberry, dh	.000	2	5	0	0	0	0	0	0	0	2	0
Dave Weathers, p	.000	2	0	0	0	0	0	0	0	0	0	0
John Wetteland, p	.000	3	0	0	0	0	0	0	0	0	0	0
Bernie Williams, of	.467	4	15	5	7	0	0	3	5	2	1	0
TOTAL	.264		140	16	37	4	0	4	15	13	20	1

PITCHER	W	L	ERA	G	GS	CG	SV	SHO	IP	H	ER	BB	SO
Brian Boehringer	1	0	6.75	2	0	0	0	0	1.1	3	1	2	0
David Cone	0	1	9.00	1	1	0	0	0	6.0	8	6	2	8
Jimmy Key	0	0	3.60	1	1	0	0	0	5.0	5	2	1	3
Graeme Lloyd	0	0	0.00	2	0	0	0	0	1.0	1	0	0	0
Jeff Nelson	1	0	0.00	2	0	0	0	0	3.2	2	0	2	5
Andy Pettitte	0	0	5.68	1	1	0	0	0	6.1	4	4	6	3
Mariano Rivera	0	0	0.00	2	0	0	0	0	4.2	4	0	1	1
Kenny Rogers	0	0	9.00	2	1	0	0	0	2.0	5	2	2	1
Dave Weathers	1	0	0.00	2	0	0	0	0	5.0	1	0	0	5
John Wetteland	0	0	0.00	3	0	0	2	0	4.0	2	0	4	4
TOTAL	3	1	3.46	18	4	0	2	0	39.0	31	15	20	30

TEX (W)

PLAYER/POS	AVG	G	AB	R	H	2B	3B	HR	RB	BB	SO	SB
Damon Buford, pr	.000	2	0	0	0	0	0	0	0	0	0	0
John Burkett, p	.000	1	0	0	0	0	0	0	0	0	0	0
Will Clark, 1b	.125	4	16	1	2	0	0	0	0	3	2	0
Dennis Cook, p	.000	2	0	0	0	0	0	0	0	0	0	0
Kevin Elster, ss	.333	4	12	2	4	2	0	0	0	3	2	1
Rene Gonzales, ss	.000	1	0	0	0	0	0	0	0	0	0	0
Juan Gonzalez, of	.438	4	16	5	7	0	0	5	9	3	2	0
Rusty Greer, of	.125	4	16	2	2	0	0	0	0	3	3	0
Darryl Hamilton, of	.158	4	19	0	3	0	0	0	0	0	2	0
Mike Henneman, p	.000	3	0	0	0	0	0	0	0	0	0	0
Ken Hill, p	.000	1	0	0	0	0	0	0	0	0	0	0
Mark McLemore, 2b	.133	4	15	1	2	0	0	0	2	0	4	0
Warren Newson, ph	.000	2	1	0	0	0	0	0	0	1	0	0
Darren Oliver, p	.000	1	0	0	0	0	0	0	0	0	0	0
Dean Palmer, 3b	.211	4	19	3	4	1	0	1	2	0	5	0
Danny Patterson, p	.000	1	0	0	0	0	0	0	0	0	0	0
Roger Pavlik, p	.000	1	0	0	0	0	0	0	0	0	0	0
Ivan Rodriguez, c	.375	4	16	1	6	1	0	0	2	2	3	0
Jeff Russell, p	.000	2	0	0	0	0	0	0	0	0	0	0
Mike Stanton, p	.000	3	0	0	0	0	0	0	0	0	0	0
Mickey Tettleton, dh	.083	4	12	1	1	0	0	0	1	5	7	0
Ed Vosberg, p	.000	2	0	0	0	0	0	0	0	0	0	0
Bobby Witt, p	.000	1	0	0	0	0	0	0	0	0	0	0
TOTAL	.218		142	16	31	4	0	6	16	20	30	1

PITCHER	W	L	ERA	G	GS	CG	SV	SHO	IP	H	ER	BB	SO
John Burkett	1	0	2.00	1	1	1	0	0	9.0	10	2	1	7
Dennis Cook	0	0	0.00	2	0	0	0	0	1.1	0	0	1	0
Mike Henneman	0	0	0.00	3	0	0	0	0	1.0	1	0	1	1
Ken Hill	0	0	4.50	1	1	0	0	0	6.0	5	3	3	1
Darren Oliver	0	1	3.38	1	1	0	0	0	8.0	6	3	2	3
Danny Patterson	0	0	0.00	1	0	0	0	0	0.1	1	0	0	0
Roger Pavlik	0	1	6.75	1	0	0	0	0	2.2	4	2	0	1
Jeff Russell	0	0	3.00	2	0	0	0	0	3.0	3	1	0	1
Mike Stanton	0	1	2.70	3	0	0	0	0	3.1	2	1	3	3
Ed Vosberg	0	0	INF	1	0	0	0	0	0.0	1	0	0	0
Bobby Witt	0	0	8.10	1	1	0	0	0	3.1	4	3	2	3
TOTAL	1	3	3.55	17	4	1	0	0	38.0	37	15	13	20

David Weathers pitched three scoreless innings of relief and wound up with the win when Mariano Rivera and Wetteland followed suit. The Rangers, meanwhile, tried eight pitchers and still couldn't stop the Yankees. Cecil Fielder, Duncan, and Jeter each drove in runs in the fourth to cut the lead to 4-3. Switch-hitting Williams led off the fifth with a home run from the left side to tie the game and—after Fielder had given the Yankees the lead in the seventh—Williams clinched it with a homer from the right side in the ninth inning.

GAME ONE AT NY OCT 1

TEX	000 501 000	6	8	0
NY	100 100 000	2	19	0

Pitchers: BURKETT vs CONE, Lloyd (7), Weathers (8)
Home Runs: Gonzalez-TEX, Palmer-TEX
Attendance: 57,205

GAME TWO AT NY OCT 2

TEX	013 000 000 000	4	8	1
NY	010 100 110 001	5	8	0

Pitchers: Hill, Cook (7), Russell (8), STANTON (10), Henneman (12) vs Pettitte, Rivera (7), Wetteland (10), Lloyd (12), Nelson (12), Rogers (12), BOEHRINGER (12)
Home Runs: Gonzalez-TEX (2), Fielder-NY
Attendance: 57,156

GAME THREE AT TEX OCT 4

NY	100 000 002	3	7	1
TEX	000 110 000	2	6	1

Pitchers: Key, NELSON (6), Wetteland (9) vs OLIVER, Henneman (9), Stanton (9)
Home Runs: Williams-NY, Gonzalez-TEX
Attendance: 50,860

GAME FOUR AT TEX OCT 5

NY	000 310 101	6	12	1
TEX	022 000 000	4	9	0

Pitchers: Rogers, Boehringer (3), WEATHERS (4), Rivera (7), Wetteland (9) vs Witt, Patterson (4), Cook (4), PAVLIK (5), Vosberg (7), Russell (7), Stanton (8), Henneman (9)
Home Runs: Williams-NY (2), Gonzalez-TEX
Attendance: 50,066

An ugly spitting incident by Roberto Alomar overshadowed Baltimore's first trip to the postseason since 1983. Alomar spit at umpire John Hirschbeck during the last series of the regular season and that led the umpires to threaten to strike the postseason if Alomar was not suspended immediately. He was not suspended, the umpires (thanks to a court order) did not strike, and the fans both cheered Alomar (in Baltimore) and booed him (in Cleveland). But in the end, Alomar was the hero in the Orioles' unlikely win over the team with the best record in baseball. He singled in the ninth inning to tie Game Four and then homered in the twelfth to send the Orioles to the ALCS.

Alomar was not the only player to come through with a big home run. Brady Anderson, the poster boy for "Year of the Home Run" with 50 regular-season clouts, started the series with a home run to lead off Game One. The Orioles followed suit three more times, including a grand slam by Bobby Bonilla and two home runs by B.J. Surhoff, as the Orioles cruised to a 10-4 win. The Indians battled back from a 4-0 deficit to tie Game Two, but the difference was the way relief pitchers handled bases loaded situations in the eighth inning. In the top of the inning, the Indians had the bases loaded with no one out and the five-six-seven batters due up. Julio Franco hit a long sacrifice fly to tie the game, but reliever Armando Benitez came back to strike out Manny Ramirez and Sandy Alomar Jr. to end the threat. In the bottom of the eighth, the Orioles loaded the bases with none out and Indians reliever Paul Assenmacher got Surhoff to ground back to the mound. Assenmacher got the force out at home, but catcher Sandy Alomar's return throw to first bounced and could not be handled by Jeff Kent as Cal Ripken crossed the plate. The Indians argued that Surhoff ran on the inside route to the base and should have been ruled out automatically. This time, the umpires were on Baltimore's side and the O's went on to win, 7-4, to take a two games to none lead.

Relief pitching was again the difference in Game Three, but it was the Indians, not the Orioles who got the better of it at Jacobs Field. Jesse Orosco walked the bases loaded in the seventh inning and Benitez entered a 4-4 game with the chance to douse another Tribe rally. Albert Belle had a different view. Belle's grand slam broke the tie and shattered Baltimore's bid for a sweep. Game Four was an uncharacteristic pitcher's duel. Charles Nagy, who had been hit hard by the O's in the opener,

fanned 12 batters in six innings and four relievers held Baltimore to two runs through eight innings.

Cleveland closer Jose Mesa had a 3-2 lead and a chance to force Game Five, but Roberto Alomar came through with a single to tie the game in the ninth. Mesa faced Alomar again in the twelfth and he responded with a 402-foot home run to center for a 4-3 lead. Third baseman Todd Zeile, a converted catcher and a late-season pickup, made a great play on a bunt by Jose Vizcaino to get the first out in the bottom of the twelfth and reliever Randy Myers did the rest. The Orioles, who struck out a postseason-record 23 times in the game, still found a way to get the bat on the ball when it counted.

Baltimore Orioles (WC), 3; Cleveland Indians (C), 1

BAL (E)

PLAYER/POS	AVG	G	AB	R	H	2B	3B	HR	RB	BB	SO	SB
Manny Alexander, dh-1	.000	3	0	2	0	0	0	0	0	0	0	0
Roberto Alomar, 2b	.294	4	17	2	5	0	0	1	4	2	3	0
Brady Anderson, of	.294	4	17	3	5	0	0	2	4	2	3	0
Armando Benitez, p	.000	3	0	0	0	0	0	0	0	0	0	0
Bobby Bonilla, of	.200	4	15	4	3	0	0	2	5	4	6	0
Mike Devereaux, of-3	.000	4	1	0	0	0	0	0	0	0	0	0
Scott Erickson, p	.000	1	0	0	0	0	0	0	0	0	0	0
Chris Hoiles, c	.143	4	7	1	1	0	0	0	0	3	3	0
Pete Incaviglia, of	.200	2	5	1	1	0	0	0	0	0	4	0
Terry Mathews, p	.000	3	0	0	0	0	0	0	0	0	0	0
Eddie Murray, dh	.400	4	15	1	6	1	0	0	1	3	4	1
Mike Mussina, p	.000	1	0	0	0	0	0	0	0	0	0	0
Randy Myers, p	.000	3	0	0	0	0	0	0	0	0	0	0
Jesse Orosco, p	.000	4	0	0	0	0	0	0	0	0	0	0
Rafael Palmeiro, 1b	.176	4	17	4	3	1	0	1	2	1	6	0
Mark Parent, c	.200	4	5	0	1	0	0	0	0	0	2	0
Arthur Lee Rhodes, p	.000	2	0	0	0	0	0	0	0	0	0	0
Cal Ripken, ss	.444	4	18	2	8	3	0	0	2	0	3	0
B.J. Surhoff, of-3	.385	4	13	3	5	0	0	3	5	0	1	0
David Wells, p	.000	2	0	0	0	0	0	0	0	0	0	0
Todd Zeile, 3b	.263	4	19	2	5	1	0	0	2	5	0	
TOTAL	.289		149	25	43	6	0	9	23	17	40	1

PITCHER	W	L	ERA	G	GS	CG	SV	SHO	IP	H	ER	BB	SO
Armando Benitez	2	0	2.25	3	0	0	0	0	4.0	1	1	2	6
Scott Erickson	0	0	4.05	1	1	0	0	0	6.2	6	3	2	6
Terry Mathews	0	0	0.00	3	0	0	0	0	2.2	3	0	1	2
Mike Mussina	0	0	4.50	1	1	0	0	0	6.0	7	3	2	6
Randy Myers	0	0	0.00	3	0	0	2	0	3.0	0	0	0	3
Jesse Orosco	0	1	36.00	4	0	0	0	0	1.0	2	4	3	2
Arthur Lee Rhodes	0	0	9.00	2	0	0	0	0	1.0	1	1	1	1
David Wells	1	0	4.61	2	2	0	0	0	13.2	15	7	4	6
TOTAL	3	1	4.50	19	4	0	2	0	38.0	35	19	15	32

CLE (C)

PLAYER/POS	AVG	G	AB	R	H	2B	3B	HR	RB	BB	SO	SB
Sandy Alomar, c	.125	4	16	0	2	0	0	0	3	0	2	0
Paul Assenmacher, p	.000	3	0	0	0	0	0	0	0	0	0	0
Albert Belle, of	.200	4	15	2	3	0	0	2	6	3	2	1
Casey Candaele, dh-1	.000	2	0	1	0	0	0	0	0	1	0	0
Alan Embree, p	.000	3	0	0	0	0	0	0	0	0	0	0
Julio Franco, 1b-3,dh-1	.133	4	15	1	2	0	0	0	1	1	6	0
Brian Giles, ph	.000	1	1	0	0	0	0	0	0	0	1	0
Orel Hershiser, p	.000	1	0	0	0	0	0	0	0	0	0	0
Jeff Kent, 3b-2,1b-1, 2b-1	.125	4	8	2	1	1	0	0	0	0	0	0
Kenny Lofton, of	.167	4	18	3	3	0	0	0	1	2	3	5
Jack McDowell, p	.000	1	0	0	0	0	0	0	0	0	0	0
Jose Mesa, p	.000	2	0	0	0	0	0	0	0	0	0	0
Charles Nagy, p	.000	2	0	0	0	0	0	0	0	0	0	0
Chad Ogea, p	.000	1	0	0	0	0	0	0	0	0	0	0
Tony Pena, c	.000	1	0	0	0	0	0	0	0	0	0	0
Eric Plunk, p	.000	3	0	0	0	0	0	0	0	0	0	0
Manny Ramirez, of	.375	4	16	4	6	2	0	2	2	1	4	0
Kevin Seitzer, dh-3,1b-1	.294	4	17	1	5	1	0	0	4	2	4	1
Paul Shuey, p	.000	3	0	0	0	0	0	0	0	0	0	0
Julian Tavarez, p	.000	2	0	0	0	0	0	0	0	0	0	0
Jim Thome, 3b	.300	4	10	1	3	0	0	0	0	1	5	0
Jose Vizcaino, 2b	.333	3	12	1	4	2	0	0	0	1	1	0
Omar Vizquel, ss	.429	4	14	4	6	1	0	0	2	3	4	4
Nigel Wilson, ph	.000	1	1	0	0	0	0	0	0	0	0	0
TOTAL	.245		143	20	35	7	0	4	20	15	32	11

PITCHER	W	L	ERA	G	GS	CG	SV	SHO	IP	H	ER	BB	SO
Paul Assenmacher	1	0	0.00	3	0	0	0	0	1.2	0	0	1	2
Alan Embree	0	0	9.00	3	0	0	0	0	1.0	0	1	0	1
Orel Hershiser	0	0	5.40	1	1	0	0	0	5.0	7	3	3	3
Jack McDowell	0	0	6.35	1	1	0	0	0	5.2	6	4	1	5
Jose Mesa	0	1	3.86	2	0	0	0	0	4.2	8	2	0	7
Charles Nagy	0	1	7.15	2	2	0	0	0	11.1	15	9	5	13
Chad Ogea	0	0	0.00	1	0	0	0	0	0.1	0	0	0	0
Eric Plunk	0	1	6.75	3	0	0	0	0	4.0	1	3	2	6
Paul Shuey	0	0	9.00	3	0	0	0	0	2.0	5	2	2	2
Julian Tavarez	0	0	0.00	2	0	0	0	0	1.1	1	0	2	1
TOTAL	1	3	5.84	21	4	0	0	0	37.0	43	24	17	40

GAME ONE AT BAL OCT 1

CLE	010 200 100	4 10 0
BAL	112 005 10X	10 10 1

Pitchers: NAGY, Embree (6), Shuey (6), Tavarez (8) vs WELLS, Orosco (7), Mathews (7), Rhodes (8), Myers (9)
Home Runs: Ramirez-CLE, Anderson-BAL, Surhoff-BAL (2), Bonilla-BAL
Attendance: 47,644

GAME TWO AT BAL OCT 2

CLE	000 003 010	4 8 2
BAL	100 030 03X	7 9 0

Pitchers: Hershiser, PLUNK (6), Assenmacher (8), Tavarez (8) vs Erickson, Orosco (7), BENITEZ (8), Myers (9)
Home Runs: Belle-CLE, Anderson-BAL
Attendance: 48,970

GAME THREE AT CLE OCT 4

BAL	010 300 000	4 8 2
CLE	120 100 41X	9 10 0

Pitchers: Mussina, OROSCO (7), Benitez (7), Rhodes (8), Mathews (8) vs McDowell, Embree (6), Shuey (7), ASSENMACHER (7), Plunk (8), Mesa (9)
Home Runs: Surhoff-BAL, Ramirez-CLE, Belle-CLE
Attendance: 44,250

GAME FOUR AT CLE OCT 5

BAL	020 000 001 001	4 141
CLE	000 210 000 000	3 71

Pitchers: Wells, Mathews (8), Orosco (9), BENITEZ (10), Myers (12) vs Nagy, Embree (7), Shuey (7), Assenmacher (7), Plunk (8), MESA (9), Ogea (12)
Home Runs: Palmeiro-BAL, Bonilla-BAL, R.Alomar-BAL
Attendance: 44,280

The Cards and Braves last met in the NLCS in 1982—a 3-0 Cardinal sweep. Fourteen years later, the Cardinals were just as tough, but John Smoltz beat the Cards in the opener in Atlanta, 4-2. In Game Two, St. Louis turned the tables. Four-time Cy Young winner Greg Maddux was touched for three runs in the first three innings, but the Braves rallied to tie the game on a two-run home run by Marquis Grissom and a single by Ryan Klesko. After the Cards took a 4-3 lead in the seventh on a Ray Lankford sacrifice fly, Maddux fanned Ron Gant and intentionally walked Brian Jordan to pitch to Gary Gaetti. Gaetti hit the first pitch for a grand slam and finished the scoring at 8-3.

The Cards kept the pressure on in St. Louis. Gant hit a pair of home runs off Tom Glavine and Donovan Osborne pitched seven strong innings in Game Three. Dennis Eckersley came on in the ninth to earn his fourth save of the postseason in the 3-2 Cards win. The Braves came out hitting in Game Four and handed Denny Neagle a 3-0 lead on home runs by Klesko and Mark Lemke plus an RBI single by Dye. But the Cards came back. Neagle got the first two outs in the seventh, but John Mabry singled and Tom Pagnozzi walked and Neagle was suddenly in the dugout. Dmitri Young greeted reliever Greg McMichael with triple that plated two runs. Luis Alicea, followed with a walk and the Cards evened the score on an infield hit by Royce Clayton. In the eighth, Jordan lined a 2-1 pitch over the wall for a 4-3 lead.

The series' second part commenced in Game Five—and it was all Atlanta. The Braves had a 5-0 lead after half an inning and that was more than enough for John Smoltz. But they kept on hitting, collecting 22 hits and sending Stottlemyre to the showers in the second. McGriff and Javier Lopez added home runs in the 14-0 rout to send the series back to Atlanta. In Game Six, Maddux kept St. Louis off the scoreboard for 7⅔ innings. The only run the Cards got came on a wild pitch by Mark Wohlers, but he recovered to earn the save in the 3-1 win.

The Cards never even had a chance to do any damage against Glavine in Game Seven. Osborne allowed three runs on RBI by McGriff, Dye, and Andruw Jones, but the crushing blow came off the bat of Glavine. His line drive to left went for a three-run triple and a 6-0 lead. After one inning, the Braves had essentially won the pennant. Atlanta added nine more runs, including home runs by MVP Lopez and Andruw Jones, who, at nineteen, became the youngest player to hit a postseason round-

tripper. The Braves also became the first team to come back from a three games to one deficit to win the NLCS. From Game Five on, the Braves outscored the Cards, 32-1.

Atlanta Braves (E), 4; St. Louis Cardinals (C), 3

ATL (E)

PLAYER/POS	AVG	G	AB	R	H	2B	3B	HR	RB	BB	SO	SB
Steve Avery, p	.000	2	0	0	0	0	0	0	0	0	0	0
Rafael Belliard, ss	.667	4	6	0	4	0	0	0	0	2	0	0
Mike Bielecki, p	.000	3	0	0	0	0	0	0	0	0	0	0
Jeff Blauser, ss	.176	7	17	5	3	0	1	0	2	4	6	0
Brad Clontz, p	.000	1	0	0	0	0	0	0	0	0	0	0
Jermaine Dye, of	.214	7	28	2	6	1	0	0	4	1	7	0
Tom Glavine, p	.167	2	6	0	1	0	1	0	3	0	3	0
Marquis Grissom, of	.286	7	35	7	10	1	0	1	3	0	8	2
Andruw Jones, of	.222	5	9	3	2	0	0	1	3	3	2	0
Chipper Jones, 3b	.440	7	25	6	11	2	0	0	4	4	1	1
Ryan Klesko, of	.250	6	16	1	4	0	0	1	3	2	6	0
Mark Lemke, 2b	.444	7	27	4	12	2	0	1	5	3	2	0
Javy Lopez, c	.542	7	24	8	13	5	0	2	6	3	1	1
Greg Maddux, p	.000	2	4	0	0	0	0	0	0	0	2	0
Fred McGriff, 1b	.250	7	28	6	7	0	1	2	7	3	5	0
Greg McMichael, p	.000	3	0	0	0	0	0	0	0	0	0	0
Mike Mordecai, 2b-2, 3b-1	.250	4	4	1	1	0	0	0	0	0	1	0
Denny Neagle, p	.500	2	2	0	1	0	0	0	0	0	0	0
Terry Pendleton, 3b-2	.000	6	6	0	0	0	0	0	0	1	3	0
Eddie Perez, c	.000	4	1	0	0	0	0	0	0	1	0	0
Luis Polonia, ph	.000	3	3	0	0	0	0	0	0	0	0	0
John Smoltz, p	.286	2	7	1	2	0	0	0	1	0	3	0
Terrell Wade, p	.000	1	0	0	0	0	0	0	0	0	0	0
Mark Wohlers, p	.000	3	1	0	0	0	0	0	0	0	1	0
TOTAL	.309		249	44	77	11	3	8	43	25	51	4

PITCHER	W	L	ERA	G	GS	CG	SV	SHO	IP	H	ER	BB	SO
Steve Avery	0	0	0.00	2	0	0	0	0	2.0	2	0	1	1
Mike Bielecki	0	0	0.00	3	0	0	0	0	3.0	0	0	1	5
Brad Clontz	0	0	0.00	1	0	0	0	0	0.2	0	0	0	0
Tom Glavine	1	1	2.08	2	2	0	0	0	13.0	10	3	0	9
Greg Maddux	1	1	2.51	2	2	0	0	0	14.1	15	4	2	10
Greg McMichael	0	1	9.00	3	0	0	0	0	2.0	4	2	1	3
Denny Neagle	0	0	2.35	2	1	0	0	0	7.2	2	2	3	8
John Smoltz	2	0	1.20	2	2	0	0	0	15.0	12	3	3	12
Terrell Wade	0	0	0.00	1	0	0	0	0	0.1	0	0	0	1
Mark Wohlers	0	0	0.00	3	0	0	2	0	3.0	0	0	0	4
TOTAL	4	3	1.92	21	7	0	2	0	61.0	45	13	11	53

STL (C)

PLAYER/POS	AVG	G	AB	R	H	2B	3B	HR	RB	BB	SO	SB
Luis Alicea, 2b	.000	5	8	0	0	0	0	0	0	2	1	0
Alan Benes, p	.000	2	1	0	0	0	0	0	0	0	1	0
Andy Benes, p	.250	3	4	0	1	1	0	0	0	1	2	0
Royce Clayton, ss	.350	5	20	4	7	0	0	0	1	1	4	1
Dennis Eckersley, p	.000	3	0	0	0	0	0	0	0	0	0	0
Tony Fossas, p	.000	5	0	0	0	0	0	0	0	0	0	0
Gary Gaetti, 3b	.292	7	24	1	7	0	0	1	4	1	5	0
Mike Gallego, 2b-5,3b-2	.143	7	14	1	2	0	0	0	0	1	3	0
Ron Gant, of	.240	7	25	3	6	1	0	2	4	2	6	0
Rick Honeycutt, p	.000	5	0	0	0	0	0	0	0	0	0	0
Danny Jackson, p	.000	1	1	0	0	0	0	0	0	0	1	0
Brian Jordan, of	.240	7	25	3	6	1	1	1	2	1	3	0
Ray Lankford, of-3	.000	5	13	1	0	0	0	0	1	1	4	0
John Mabry, 1b-6,of-2	.261	7	23	1	6	0	0	0	0	0	6	0
T. J. Mathews, p	.000	2	0	0	0	0	0	0	0	0	0	0
Willie McGee, of-5	.333	6	15	0	5	0	0	0	0	0	1	0
Miguel Mejia, of-2	.000	3	1	1	0	0	0	0	0	0	0	1
Donovan Osborne, p	.000	2	3	0	0	0	0	0	0	0	3	0
Tom Pagnozzi, c	.158	7	19	1	3	1	0	0	1	1	4	0
Mark Petkovsek, p	.000	6	0	0	0	0	0	0	0	0	0	0
Danny Sheaffer, c	.000	2	3	0	0	0	0	0	0	0	1	0
Ozzie Smith, ss-2	.000	3	9	0	0	0	0	0	0	0	1	0
Todd Stottlemyre, p	.000	3	2	0	0	0	0	0	0	0	2	0
Mark Sweeney, of-2	.000	5	4	1	0	0	0	0	0	0	2	0
Dmitri Young, 1b-2	.286	4	7	1	2	0	1	0	2	0	2	0
TOTAL	.204		221	18	45	4	2	4	15	11	53	2

PITCHER	W	L	ERA	G	GS	CG	SV	SHO	IP	H	ER	BB	SO
Alan Benes	0	1	2.84	2	1	0	0	0	6.1	3	2	2	5
Andy Benes	0	0	5.28	3	2	0	0	0	15.1	19	9	3	9
Dennis Eckersley	1	0	0.00	3	0	0	1	0	3.1	2	0	0	4
Tony Fossas	0	0	2.08	5	0	0	0	0	4.1	1	1	3	1
Rick Honeycutt	0	0	9.00	5	0	0	0	0	4.0	5	4	3	3
Danny Jackson	0	0	9.00	1	0	0	0	0	3.0	7	3	3	0
T. J. Mathews	0	0	9.00	2	0	0	0	0	0.2	2	0	1	2
Donovan Osborne	1	1	9.39	2	2	0	0	0	7.2	12	8	4	6
Mark Petkovsek	0	1	7.36	6	0	0	0	0	7.1	11	6	3	7
Todd Stottlemyre	1	1	12.38	3	2	0	0	0	8.0	15	11	3	11
TOTAL	3	4	6.60	32	7	0	1	0	60.0	77	44	25	51

GAME ONE AT ATL OCT 9

STL	010	000	100	2	5 1
ATL	000	020	02X	4	9 0

Pitchers: An.Benes, PETKOVSEK (7), Fossas (8), Mathews (8) vs SMOLTZ, Wohlers (9)
Attendance: 48,686

GAME TWO AT ATL OCT 10

STL	102	000	500	8	11 2
ATL	002	001	000	3	5 2

Pitchers: STOTTLEMYRE, Petkovsek (7), Eckersley (8) vs MADDUX, McMichael (7), Neagle (8), Avery (9)
Home Runs: Gaetti-STL, Grissom-ATL
Attendance: 52,067

GAME THREE AT STL OCT 12

ATL	100	000	010	2	8 1
STL	200	001	00X	3	7 0

Pitchers: GLAVINE, Bielecki (7), McMichael (8) vs OSBORNE, Petkovsek (8), Honeycutt (9), Eckersley (9)
Home Runs: Gant-STL (2)
Attendance: 56,769

GAME FOUR AT STL OCT 13

ATL	010	002	000	3	9 1
STL	000	000	31X	4	5 0

Pitchers: Neagle, McMICHAEL (7), Wohlers (8) vs An.Benes, Fossas (6), Mathews (6), Al.Benes (6), Honeycutt (8), ECKERSLEY (9)
Home Runs: Klesko-ATL, Lemke-ATL, Jordan-STL
Attendance: 56,764

GAME FIVE AT STL OCT 14

ATL	520	310	012	14	22 0
STL	000	000	000	0	7 0

Pitchers: SMOLTZ, Bielecki (8), Wade (9), Clontz (9) vs STOTTLEMYRE, Jackson (2), Fossas (5), Petkovsek (7), Honeycutt (9)
Home Runs: Lopez-ATL, McGriff-ATL
Attendance: 56,782

GAME SIX AT ATL OCT 16

STL	000	000	010	1	6 1
ATL	010	010	01X	3	7 0

Pitchers: Al.BENES, Fossas (6), Petkovsek (6), Stottlemyre (9) vs MADDUX, Wohlers (8)
Attendance: 52,067

GAME SEVEN AT ATL OCT 17

STL	000	000	000	0	4 2
ATL	600	403	20X	15	17 0

Pitchers: OSBORNE, An.Benes (1), Petkovsek (6), Honeycutt (6), Fossas (8) vs GLAVINE, Bielecki (8), Avery (9)
Home Runs: Lopez-ATL, A.Jones-ATL, McGriff-ATL
Attendance: 52,067

The Yankees and the Orioles had gone a combined twenty-eight years without a pennant, but that was going to change in 1996—for one team at least. The Orioles had the early advantage in Game One on home runs from Brady Anderson and Rafael Palmeiro, but the Yankees cut the lead to 4-3 after seven. Derek Jeter led off the eighth with a long fly to right that Tony Tarasco seemed to have lined up at the wall, but fate—in the form of a twelve-year-old boy—intervened. Yankee fan Jeff Maier reached over the fence and knocked the ball into the stands. Right field umpire Rich Garcia ruled it a home run despite protests from several Orioles, including manager Davey Johnson, who was ejected. (Upon seeing a replay, Garcia admitted he made the wrong call, but AL president Gene Budig denied Baltimore's protest.) The Orioles got out of further trouble in the eighth, but Game One was tied at 4-4. With Randy Myers pitching in the bottom of the eleventh, Bernie Williams hit a 1-1 pitch deep to left to give the Yanks the improbable win.

Baltimore bounced back in Game Two. Orioles southpaw David Wells spotted the Yanks a pair of first inning runs but Wells improved to 10-1 at Yankee Stadium. Todd Zeile's two-run home run off David Cone tied the game in the third and Palmeiro's two-run shot off reliever Jeff Nelson gave Baltimore the lead in the seventh. In the seventh inning, with the O's leading 4-3, Jesse Orosco came in to get Tino Martinez to ground out to end another threat. The Orioles added a run in the eighth to go up 5-3, but Benitez retired Cecil Fielder and Tino Martinez with two on in the ninth to even the series at one game apiece.

The teams traveled to Camden Yards for the next three games, but the Yankees, who were 6-0 in Baltimore during the regular season, continued to treat the park like a home away from home. Zeile's two-run home run in the first looked like it might stand up as Mike Mussina was masterful through seven and two thirds. He never got that last out, though. The Yanks rallied to tie it in the eighth then Martinez followed with a double to left field and Williams stopped at third, but when Zeile's fake throw to second trickled away, Williams dashed home with the go-ahead run.

Darryl Strawberry took Game Four of the ALCS into his own hands. His solo home run in the second gave the Yanks a 3-1 lead and his two-run blast in the eighth capped off New York's 8-4 victory. Mariano Rivera bailed New York out of a bases-loaded, no-out jam

New York Yankees (E), 4; Baltimore Orioles (WC), 1

NY (E)

PLAYER/POS	AVG	G	AB	R	H	2B	3B	HR	RB	BB	SO	SB
Mike Aldrete, ph	.000	1	0	0	0	0	0	0	0	0	0	0
Wade Boggs, 3b	.133	3	15	1	2	0	0	0	0	1	3	0
David Cone, p	.000	1	0	0	0	0	0	0	0	0	0	0
Mariano Duncan, 2b	.200	4	15	0	3	2	0	0	0	0	3	0
Cecil Fielder, dh	.167	5	18	3	3	0	0	2	8	4	5	0
Andy Fox, dh	.000	2	0	0	0	0	0	0	0	0	0	0
Joe Girardi, c	.250	4	12	1	3	0	1	0	0	1	3	0
Charlie Hayes, 3b-2, dh-1	.143	4	7	0	1	0	0	0	0	2	2	0
Derek Jeter, ss	.417	5	24	5	10	2	0	1	1	0	5	2
Jimmy Key, p	.000	1	0	0	0	0	0	0	0	0	0	0
Jim Leyritz, c-2,of-1	.250	3	8	1	2	0	0	1	2	1	4	0
Graeme Lloyd, p	.000	2	0	0	0	0	0	0	0	0	0	0
Tino Martinez, 1b	.182	5	22	3	4	1	0	0	0	0	2	0
Jeff Nelson, p	.000	2	0	0	0	0	0	0	0	0	0	0
Paul O'Neill, of	.273	4	11	1	3	0	0	1	2	3	2	0
Andy Pettitte, p	.000	2	0	0	0	0	0	0	0	0	0	0
Tim Raines, of	.267	5	15	2	4	1	0	0	0	1	1	0
Mariano Rivera, p	.000	2	0	0	0	0	0	0	0	0	0	0
Kenny Rogers, p	.000	1	0	0	0	0	0	0	0	0	0	0
Luis Sojo, 2b	.200	3	5	0	1	0	0	0	0	0	1	0
Darryl Strawberry, of	.417	4	12	4	5	0	0	3	5	2	2	0
Dave Weathers, p	.000	2	0	0	0	0	0	0	0	0	0	0
John Wetteland, p	.000	4	0	0	0	0	0	0	0	0	0	0
Bernie Williams, of	.474	5	19	6	9	3	0	2	6	5	4	1
TOTAL	.273		183	27	50	9	1	10	24	20	37	3

PITCHER	W	L	ERA	G	GS	CG	SV	SHO	IP	H	ER	BB	SO
David Cone	0	0	3.00	1	1	0	0	0	6.0	5	2	5	5
Jimmy Key	1	0	2.25	1	1	0	0	0	8.0	3	2	1	5
Graeme Lloyd	0	0	0.00	2	0	0	0	0	1.2	0	0	0	1
Jeff Nelson	0	1	11.57	2	0	0	0	0	2.1	5	3	0	2
Andy Pettitte	1	0	3.60	2	2	0	0	0	15.0	10	6	5	7
Mariano Rivera	1	0	0.00	2	0	0	0	0	4.0	6	0	1	5
Kenny Rogers	0	0	12.00	1	1	0	0	0	3.0	5	4	2	3
Dave Weathers	1	0	0.00	2	0	0	0	0	3.0	3	0	0	0
John Wetteland	0	0	4.50	4	0	0	1	0	4.0	2	2	1	5
TOTAL	4	1	3.64	17	5	0	1	0	47.0	39	19	15	33

BAL (E)

PLAYER/POS	AVG	G	AB	R	H	2B	3B	HR	RB	BB	SO	SB
Roberto Alomar, 2b	.217	5	23	2	5	2	0	0	1	0	4	0
Brady Anderson, of	.190	5	21	5	4	1	0	1	1	3	5	0
Armando Benitez, p	.000	3	0	0	0	0	0	0	0	0	0	0
Bobby Bonilla, of	.050	5	20	1	1	0	0	1	2	1	4	0
Rocky Coppinger, p	.000	1	0	0	0	0	0	0	0	0	0	0
Mike Devereaux, of	.000	3	2	0	0	0	0	0	0	0	1	0
Scott Erickson, p	.000	2	0	0	0	0	0	0	0	0	0	0
Chris Hoiles, c	.167	4	12	1	2	0	0	1	2	1	3	0
Pete Incaviglia, dh	.500	1	2	1	1	0	0	0	0	0	0	0
Terry Mathews, p	.000	3	0	0	0	0	0	0	0	0	0	0
Alan Mills, p	.000	3	0	0	0	0	0	0	0	0	0	0
Eddie Murray, dh	.267	5	15	1	4	0	0	1	2	2	2	0
Mike Mussina, p	.000	1	0	0	0	0	0	0	0	0	0	0
Randy Myers, p	.000	3	0	0	0	0	0	0	0	0	0	0
Jesse Orosco, p	.000	4	0	0	0	0	0	0	0	0	0	0
Rafael Palmeiro, 1b	.235	5	17	4	4	0	0	2	4	4	4	0
Mark Parent, c	.167	2	6	0	1	0	0	0	0	0	2	0
Arthur Lee Rhodes, p	.000	3	0	0	0	0	0	0	0	0	0	0
Cal Ripken, ss	.250	5	20	1	5	1	0	0	0	1	4	0
B.J. Surhoff, of	.267	5	15	0	4	0	0	0	2	1	2	0
Tony Tarasco, of	.000	2	1	0	0	0	0	0	0	0	1	0
David Wells, p	.000	1	0	0	0	0	0	0	0	0	0	0
Todd Zeile, 3b	.364	5	22	3	8	0	0	3	5	2	1	0
TOTAL	.222		176	19	39	4	0	9	19	15	33	0

PITCHER	W	L	ERA	G	GS	CG	SV	SHO	IP	H	ER	BB	SO
Armando Benitez	0	0	7.71	3	0	0	1	0	2.1	3	2	3	2
Rocky Coppinger	0	1	8.44	1	1	0	0	0	5.1	6	5	1	3
Scott Erickson	0	1	2.38	2	2	0	0	0	11.1	14	3	4	8
Terry Mathews	0	0	0.00	3	0	0	0	0	2.1	0	0	2	3
Alan Mills	0	0	3.86	3	0	0	0	0	2.1	3	1	1	3
Mike Mussina	0	1	5.87	1	1	0	0	0	7.2	8	5	2	6
Randy Myers	0	1	2.25	3	0	0	0	0	4.0	4	1	3	2
Jesse Orosco	0	0	4.50	4	0	0	0	0	2.0	2	1	1	2
Arthur Lee Rhodes	0	0	0.00	3	0	0	0	0	2.0	2	0	0	2
David Wells	1	0	4.05	1	1	0	0	0	6.2	8	3	3	6
TOTAL	1	4	4.11	24	5	0	1	0	46.0	50	21	20	37

in the eighth and Wetteland retired the Orioles in order in the ninth.

The Yankees picked up where they left off the next afternoon. Jim Leyritz started the decisive third-inning rally with a home run off Scott Erickson. Jeter singled two batters later and Wade Boggs ended an 0-for-23 playoff skid with an infield hit to set the stage for the rally that put the Birds away for good. Series MVP Williams sent a tailor-made double-play grounder to Roberto Alomar, but the second baseman let it go through his legs. One out later, Fielder cleared the basepaths with a three-run home run for a 5-0 lead. Strawberry followed with a 446-foot drive that landed in the Yankee bullpen to tie the Yankees with the 1993 Blue Jays for the most home runs (10) in an LCS. Andy Pettitte and Wetteland held off Baltimore to bring the World Series back to Yankee Stadium for the first time since 1981 and send manager Joe Torre to the Fall Classic for the first time after a record 4,272 games as a player and manager.

The Braves were in their fourth World Series of the 1990s, while the Yankees had not been to the Series in fifteen years and hadn't won in eighteen.

New York looked disoriented in the opener, squandering opportunities early against John Smoltz, but it wasn't long before the Braves took advantage of Andy Pettitte. Nineteen-year-old Andruw Jones became the youngest player in series history to hit a homer in the second and an inning later joined Gene Tenace as the second player to homer his first two times up in the Series. It was 9-0 before Wade Boggs broke up the no-hit bid by Smoltz in the fifth. Things didn't get much better for the Yanks the next night. Greg Maddux handcuffed New York on six hits in eight innings as Fred McGriff drove in three runs against Jimmy Key. The Braves steamrolled N.Y. 16-1 in the first two games, and had outscored their postseason opposition 48-2 over their last five games.

Things changed in Atlanta. David Cone allowed just four hits through six and RBI singles by Bernie Williams and Darryl Strawberry gave the Yankees a 2-1 lead against Tom Glavine. The Yankees got insurance in the form of a two-run home run by Williams and an RBI single by Luis Sojo in the eighth. Mariano Rivera, Graeme Lloyd, and John Wetteland nailed down the 5-2 win. The Braves battered Kenny Rogers for five runs in two-plus innings in Game Four and Andruw Jones doubled off David Weathers for a 6-0 lead in the fifth. It looked like the Braves would take a three games to one lead for the second straight World Series, but right field umpire Tim Welke got in the way of Jermaine Dye and kept Derek Jeter's foul fly from being caught. Then Jeter singled; two hits, a walk and an error followed to cut Atlanta's lead in half. Closer Mark Wohlers came in to start the eighth and promptly gave up two hits. It looked like the Braves might escape when Mariano Duncan hit a double-play grounder to Rafael Belliard, but the shortstop botched it and only one out was recorded. Jim Leyritz then homered to tie the game. With runners on first and second in the tenth, Braves manager Bobby Cox opted to walk Williams to load the bases for Boggs. Steve Avery walked Boggs, to bring in the go-ahead run. Charlie Hayes hit a soft liner that Ryan Klesko lost in the lights and another run came in. The Yankees held on for the biggest comeback in the team's World Series history.

Things continued to go the Yankees' way in Game Five. New York won the last game ever at Fulton County Stadium because one of the N.L.'s best outfielders dropped a ball and two gimpy outfielders made great catches to preserve the 1-0 victory. The only run Smoltz allowed was set up when Grissom and Dye converged on the ball but it bounced off Grissom's glove; Fielder plated the run with a double. Andy Pettitte pitched brilliantly. Strawberry, playing despite a broken toe, crashed into the wall to take an extra-base hit away in the eighth and Paul O'Neill, nursing a torn hamstring, reached to his right to snag Luis Polonia's line drive to end the game with the tying run at third.

The Yankees, who went 8-0 on the road in the postseason, got good news on the only off-day of the Series. Manager Joe Torre's brother Frank, who won a World Series ring with the 1957 Braves, received a heart transplant after months of waiting for a donor. The good luck continued for Game Six. O'Neill doubled to start the third and Joe Girardi tripled him home; Jeter and Williams followed with RBI singles against Maddux. The Braves got a run when Dye walked with the bases loaded in the fourth, but Terry Pendleton grounded into a double play to end the threat. Key pitched into the sixth and Weathers, Lloyd, and Rivera got the Yanks to the ninth. Series MVP John Wetteland allowed a run but gained his fourth save of the Series when Mark Lemke popped up to Hayes in foul ground.

New York Yankees (A), 4; Atlanta Braves (N), 2

NY (A)

PLAYER/POS	AVG	G	AB	R	H	2B	3B	HR	RB	BB	SO	SB
Mike Aldrete, of-1	.000	2	1	0	0	0	0	0	0	0	0	0
Brian Boehringer, p	.000	2	0	0	0	0	0	0	0	0	0	0
Wade Boggs, 3b	.273	4	11	0	3	1	0	0	2	1	0	0
David Cone, p	.000	1	2	0	0	0	0	0	0	0	1	0
Mariano Duncan, 2b	.053	6	19	1	1	0	0	0	0	0	4	1
Cecil Fielder, 1b-3,dh-3	.391	6	23	1	9	2	0	0	2	2	2	0
Andy Fox, 2b-1,3b-1	.000	4	0	1	0	0	0	0	0	0	0	0
Joe Girardi, c	.200	4	10	1	2	0	1	0	1	1	2	0
Charlie Hayes, 3b-4, 1b-1	.188	5	16	2	3	0	0	0	1	1	5	0
Derek Jeter, ss	.250	6	20	5	5	0	0	0	1	4	6	1
Jimmy Key, p	.000	2	0	0	0	0	0	0	0	0	0	0
Jim Leyritz, c-3	.375	4	8	1	3	0	0	1	3	3	2	1
Graeme Lloyd, p	.000	4	1	0	0	0	0	0	0	0	0	0
Tino Martinez, 1b-5	.091	6	11	0	1	0	0	0	0	2	5	0
Jeff Nelson, p	.000	3	0	0	0	0	0	0	0	0	0	0
Paul O'Neill, of-4	.167	5	12	1	2	2	0	0	0	3	2	0
Andy Pettitte, p	.000	2	4	0	0	0	0	0	0	0	1	0
Tim Raines, of	.214	4	14	2	3	0	0	0	0	2	1	0
Mariano Rivera, p	.000	4	1	0	0	0	0	0	0	0	0	0
Kenny Rogers, p	1.000	1	1	0	1	0	0	0	0	0	0	0
Luis Sojo, 2b-3	.600	5	5	0	3	1	0	0	1	0	0	0
Darryl Strawberry, of	.188	5	16	3	3	0	0	1	4	1	6	0
Dave Weathers, p	.000	5	0	0	0	0	0	0	0	0	0	0
John Wetteland, p	.000	5	0	0	0	0	0	0	0	0	0	0
Bernie Williams, of	.167	6	24	3	4	0	0	1	4	3	6	1
TOTAL	.216		199	18	43	6	1	2	16	26	43	4

PITCHER	W	L	ERA	G	GS	CG	SV	SHO	IP	H	ER	BB	SO
Brian Boehringer	0	0	5.40	2	0	0	0	0	5.0	5	3	0	5
David Cone	1	0	1.50	1	1	0	0	0	6.0	4	1	4	3
Jimmy Key	1	1	3.97	2	2	0	0	0	11.1	15	5	5	1
Graeme Lloyd	1	0	0.00	4	0	0	0	0	2.2	0	0	0	4
Jeff Nelson	0	0	0.00	3	0	0	0	0	4.1	1	0	1	5
Andy Pettitte	1	1	5.91	2	2	0	0	0	10.2	11	7	4	5
Mariano Rivera	0	0	1.59	4	0	0	0	0	5.2	4	1	3	4
Kenny Rogers	0	0	22.50	1	1	0	0	0	2.0	5	5	2	0
Dave Weathers	0	0	3.00	3	0	0	0	0	3.0	2	1	3	3
John Wetteland	0	0	2.08	5	0	0	4	0	4.1	4	1	1	6
TOTAL	4	2	3.93	27	6	0	4	0	55.0	51	24	23	36

ATL (N)

PLAYER/POS	AVG	G	AB	R	H	2B	3B	HR	RB	BB	SO	SB
Steve Avery, p	.000	1	0	0	0	0	0	0	0	0	0	0
Rafael Belliard, ss-3	.000	4	0	0	0	0	0	0	0	0	0	0
Mike Bielecki, p	.000	2	1	0	0	0	0	0	0	0	0	0
Jeff Blauser, ss	.167	6	18	2	3	1	0	0	1	1	4	0
Brad Clontz, p	.000	3	0	0	0	0	0	0	0	0	0	0
Jermaine Dye, of	.118	5	17	0	2	0	0	0	1	1	1	0
Tom Glavine, p	.000	1	1	0	0	0	0	0	0	0	1	0
Marquis Grissom, of	.444	6	27	4	12	2	1	0	5	1	2	1
Andruw Jones, of	.400	6	20	4	8	1	0	2	6	3	6	1
Chipper Jones, 3b-6, ss-1	.286	6	21	3	6	3	0	0	3	4	2	1
Ryan Klesko, of-2, 1b-1,dh-1	.100	5	10	2	1	0	0	0	1	2	4	0
Mark Lemke, 2b	.231	6	26	2	6	1	0	0	2	0	3	0
Javy Lopez, c	.190	6	21	3	4	0	0	0	1	3	4	0
Greg Maddux, p	.000	2	0	0	0	0	0	0	0	0	0	0
Fred McGriff, 1b	.300	6	20	4	6	0	0	2	6	5	4	0
Greg McMichael, p	.000	2	0	0	0	0	0	0	0	0	0	0
Mike Mordecai, ph	.000	1	1	0	0	0	0	0	0	0	0	0
Denny Neagle, p	.000	2	1	0	0	0	0	0	0	0	0	0
Terry Pendleton, dh-2,3b-1	.222	4	9	1	2	1	0	0	2	1	0	0
Eddie Perez, c	.000	2	1	0	0	0	0	0	0	0	0	0
Luis Polonia, ph	.000	6	5	0	0	0	0	0	0	1	2	0
John Smoltz, p	.500	2	2	0	1	0	0	0	0	0	0	0
Terrell Wade, p	.000	2	0	0	0	0	0	0	0	0	1	0
Mark Wohlers, p	.000	4	0	0	0	0	0	0	0	0	0	0
TOTAL	.254		201	26	51	9	1	4	26	23	36	3

PITCHER	W	L	ERA	G	GS	CG	SV	SHO	IP	H	ER	BB	SO
Steve Avery	0	1	13.50	1	0	0	0	0	0.2	1	1	3	0
Mike Bielecki	0	0	0.00	2	0	0	0	0	3.0	0	0	3	6
Brad Clontz	0	0	0.00	3	0	0	0	0	1.2	1	0	1	2
Tom Glavine	0	1	1.29	1	1	0	0	0	7.0	4	1	3	8
Greg Maddux	1	1	1.72	2	2	0	0	0	15.2	14	3	1	5
Greg McMichael	0	0	27.00	2	0	0	0	0	1.0	5	3	0	1
Denny Neagle	0	0	3.00	2	0	0	0	0	6.0	5	2	4	3
John Smoltz	1	1	0.64	2	2	0	0	0	14.0	6	1	8	14
Terrell Wade	0	0	0.00	2	0	0	0	0	0.2	0	0	1	0
Mark Wohlers	0	0	6.23	4	0	0	0	0	4.1	7	3	2	4
TOTAL	2	4	2.33	21	6	0	0	0	54.0	43	14	26	43

GAME ONE AT NY OCT 20

ATL	026	013	000	12	13	0
NY	000	010	000	1	4	1

Pitchers: SMOLTZ, McMichael (7), Neagle (8), Wade (9), Clontz (9) vs PETTITTE, Boehringer (3), Weathers (6), Nelson (8), Wetteland (9)
Home Runs: A.Jones-ATL (2), McGriff-ATL
Attendance: 56,365

GAME TWO AT NY OCT 21

ATL	101	011	000	4	10	0
NY	000	000	000	0	7	1

Pitchers: MADDUX, Wohlers (9) vs KEY, Lloyd (7), Nelson (7), Rivera (9)
Attendance: 56,340

GAME THREE AT ATL OCT 22

NY	100	100	030	5	8	1
ATL	000	001	000	2	6	1

Pitchers: CONE, Rivera (7), Lloyd (8), Wetteland (9) vs GLAVINE, McMichael (8), Clontz (8), Bielecki (9)
Home Runs: Williams-NY
Attendance: 51,843

GAME FOUR AT ATL OCT 23

NY	000	003	030	2	8	12	0
ATL	041	010	000	0	6	9	2

Pitchers: Rogers, Boehringer (3), Weathers (5), Nelson (6), Rivera (8), LLOYD (9), Wetteland (10) vs Neagle, Wade (6), Bielecki (8), Wohlers (8), AVERY (10), Clontz (10)
Home Runs: Leyritz-NY, McGriff-ATL
Attendance: 51,881

GAME FIVE AT ATL OCT 24

NY	000	100	000	1	4	1
ATL	000	000	000	0	5	1

Pitchers: PETTITTE, Wetteland (9) vs SMOLTZ, Wohlers (9)
Attendance: 51,881

GAME SIX AT NY OCT 26

ATL	000	100	001	2	8	0
NY	003	000	00X	3	8	1

Pitchers: MADDUX, Wohlers (8) vs KEY, Weathers (6), Lloyd (6), Rivera (7), Wetteland (9)
Attendance: 56,375

## CHAPTER 14

Black Ball

Jules Tygiel

Fifty years have passed since what many have called the finest moment in the history of the national pastime—Jackie Robinson's shattering of the color barrier. Robinson's heroic triumph brought to an end six disgraceful decades of Jim Crow baseball. During that era, some of America's greatest ballplayers plied their trade on all-black teams, in Negro Leagues, on the playing fields of Latin America, and along the barnstorming frontier of the cities and towns of the United States, but never within the major and minor league realm of "organized baseball." When slowly and grudgingly given their chance in the years after 1947, blacks conclusively proved their competitive abilities on the diamond, but discrimination persisted as baseball executives continued to deny them the opportunity to display their talents in both managerial and front office positions.

Scattered evidence exists of blacks playing baseball in the antebellum period, but the first recorded black teams surfaced in Northern cities in the aftermath of the Civil War. In October 1867, the Uniques of Brooklyn hosted the Excelsiors of Philadelphia in a contest billed as the "championship of colored clubs." Before a large crowd of black and white spectators, the Excelsiors marched around the field behind a fife and drum corps before defeating the Uniques, 37–24. Two months later, a second Philadelphia squad, the Pythians, dispatched a representative to the inaugural meetings of the National Association of Base Ball Players, the first organized league. The nominating committee unanimously rejected the Pythian's application, barring "any club which may be composed of one or more colored persons." Using the impeccable logic of a racist society, the committee proclaimed, "If colored clubs were admitted there would be in all probability some division of feeling, whereas, by excluding them no injury could result to anyone." The Philadelphia Pythians, however, continued their quest for interracial competition. In 1869, they became the first black team to face an all-white squad, defeating the crosstown City Items, 27–17.

In 1876, athletic entrepreneurs in the nation's metropolitan centers established the National League which quickly came to represent the pinnacle of the sport. The new entity had no written policy regarding blacks, but precluded them nonetheless through a "gentleman's agreement" among the owners. In the smaller cities and towns of America, however, where under-funded teams and fragile minor league coalitions quickly appeared and faded, individual blacks found scattered opportunities to pursue baseball careers. During the next decade, at least two dozen black ballplayers sought to earn a living in this erratic professional baseball world.

Bud Fowler ranked among the best and most persistent of these trailblazers. Born John Jackson in upstate New York in 1858 and raised, ironically, in Cooperstown, Fowler first achieved recognition as a 20-year-old pitcher for a local team in Chelsea, Massachusetts. In April 1878, Fowler defeated the National League's Boston club, which included future Hall of Famers George Wright and Jim O' Rourke, 2–1, in an exhibition game, besting 40-game winner Tommy Bond. Later that season, Fowler hurled three games for the Lynn Live Oaks of the International Association, the nation's first minor league, and another for Worcester in the New England League. For the next six years, he toiled for a variety of independent and semi-professional teams in the United States and Canada. Despite a reputation as "one of the best pitchers on the continent," he failed to catch on with any major or minor league squads. In 1884, now appearing regularly as a second baseman, as well as a pitcher, Fowler joined Stillwater, Minnesota, in the Northwestern League. Over the next seven seasons, Fowler played for fourteen teams in nine leagues, seldom batting less than .300 for a season. In 1886, he led the Western League in triples. "He is one of the best general players in the country," reported *Sporting Life*, "and if he had a white face he would be playing with the best of them. . . Those who know, say there is no better second baseman in the country."

In 1886, however, a better second baseman did appear in the form of Frank Grant, perhaps the greatest black player of the nineteenth century. The light-skinned Grant, described as a "Spaniard" in the *Buffalo Express*, batted .325 for Meridien in the Eastern League. When that squad folded he joined Buffalo in the prestigious International Association and improved his average to .340, third best in the league.

Although not as talented as Fowler and Grant, barehand-catcher Moses Fleetwood Walker achieved the highest level of play of blacks of this era. The son of an Ohio physician, Fleet Walker had studied at Oberlin College, where in 1881 he and his younger brother Welday helped launch a varsity baseball team. For the next two years, the elder Walker played for the University of Michigan and in 1883 he appeared in 60 games for the pennant-winning Toledo squad in the Northwestern League. In 1884, Toledo entered the American Association, the National League's primary rival, and Walker became the first black major leaguer. In an age when many catchers caught barehanded and lacked chest protectors, Walker suffered frequent injuries and played little after a foul tip broke his rib in mid-July. Nonetheless, he batted .263 and pitcher Tony Mullane later called him "the best catcher I ever worked with." In July, Toledo briefly signed Walker's brother, Welday, who appeared in six games batting .182. The following year, Toledo dropped from the league, ending the Walkers' major league careers.

These early black players found limited acceptance among teammates, fans, and opponents. In Ontario, in 1881, Fowler's teammates forced him off the club. Walker found that Mullane and other pitchers preferred not to pitch to him. Although he acknowledged Walker's skills, Mullane confessed, "I disliked a Negro and whenever I had to pitch to him I used anything I wanted without looking at his signals." At Louisville in 1884, insults from Kentucky fans so rattled Walker that he made five errors in a game. In Richmond, after Walker had actually left the team due to injuries, the Toledo manager received a letter from "75 determined men" threatening "to mob Walker" and cause "much bloodshed" if the black catcher appeared. On August 10, 1883, Chicago White Stockings star and manager Cap Anson had threatened to cancel an exhibition game with Toledo if Walker played. The injured catcher had not been slated to start, but Toledo manager Charlie Morton defied Anson and inserted Walker into the lineup. The game proceeded without incident.

In 1887, Walker, Fowler, Grant, Higgins, Stovey, and three other blacks converged on the International League, a newly reorganized circuit in Canada and upstate New York, one notch below the major league level. At the same time, a new six-team entity, the League of Colored Baseball Clubs, won recognition under baseball's National Agreement, a mutual pact to honor player contracts among team owners. Thus, an air of optimism pervaded the start of the season. But 1887 would prove a fateful year for the future of blacks in baseball.

On May 6, the Colored League made its debut in Pittsburgh with "a grand street parade and a brass band concert." Twelve hundred spectators watched the hometown Keystones lose to the Gorhams of New York, 11–8. Within days, however, the new league began to flounder. The Boston franchise disbanded in Louisville on May 8, stranding its players in the Southern city. Three weeks later, league-founder Walter Brown formally announced the demise of the infant circuit.

Meanwhile, in the International League, black players found their numbers growing, but their status increasingly uncertain. Six of the 10 teams fielded blacks, prompting *Sporting Life* to wonder, "How far will this mania for engaging colored players go?" In Newark, fans marveled at the "colored battery" of Fleet Walker, dubbed the "coon catcher" by one Canadian newspaper, and "headstrong" pitcher George Stovey. Stovey, one of the greatest black pitchers of the nineteenth century, won 35 games, still an International League record. Frank Grant, in his second season as the Buffalo second baseman, led the league in batting average and home runs. Bud Fowler, one of two blacks on the Binghamton squad, compiled a .350 average through early July and stole 23 bases.

These athletes compiled their impressive statistics under the most adverse conditions. "I could not help pitying some of the poor black fellows that played in the International League," reported a white player. "Fowler used to play second base with the lower part of his legs encased in wooden guards. He knew that about every player that came down to second base on a steal had it in for him." Both Fowler and Grant, "would muff balls intentionally, so that [they] would not have to touch runners, fearing that they might injure [them]." In addition, "About half the pitchers try their best to hit these colored players when [they are] at bat." Grant, whose Buffalo teammates had refused to sit with him for a team portrait in 1886, reportedly saved himself from a "drubbing" at their hands in 1887, only by "the effective use of a club." In Toronto, fans chanted, "Kill the Nigger," at Grant, and a local newspaper headline declared, "THE COLORED PLAYERS DISTASTEFUL." In late June, Bud Fowler's Binghamton teammates refused to take the field unless the club removed him from the lineup. Soon after, on July 7, the Binghamton club submitted to the players' demands, releasing Fowler and a black teammate, a pitcher named Renfroe.

The most dramatic confrontations between black and white players occurred on the Syracuse squad, where a clique of refugees from the Southern League exacerbated racial tensions. In spring training, the club included a catcher named Dick Male, who, rumors had it, was a light-skinned black named Richard Johnson. Male charged "that the man calling him a Negro is himself a black liar," but when released after a poor preseason performance, he returned to his old club, Zanesville in the Ohio State League, and resumed his true identity as Richard Johnson. In May, Syracuse signed 19-year-old black pitcher Robert Higgins, angering the Southern clique. On May 25, Higgins appeared in his first International League game in Toronto. "THE SYRACUSE PLOTTERS," as a *Sporting News* headline called his teammates, undermined his debut. According to one account, they "seemed to want the Toronto team to knock Higgins out of the box, and time and again they fielded so badly that the home team were enabled to secure many hits after the side had been retired." "A disgusting exhibition," admonished the *Toronto World.* "They succeeded in running Male out of the club," reported a Newark paper, "and they will do the same with Higgins." One week later, two Syracuse players refused to pose for a team picture with Higgins. When manager "Ice Water" Joe Simmons suspended pitcher Doug Crothers for this incident, Crothers slugged the manager. Higgins miraculously recovered from his early travails and lack of support to post a 20–7 record.

On July 14, as the directors of the International League discussed the racial situation in Buffalo, the Newark Little Giants planned to send Stovey, their ace, to the mound in an exhibition game against the National League Chicago White Stockings. Once again manager Anson refused to field his squad if either Stovey or Walker appeared. Unlike 1883, Anson's will prevailed. On the same day, team owners, stating that "Many of the best players in the league are anxious to leave on account of the colored element," allowed current black players to remain, but voted by a six-to-four margin to reject all future contracts with blacks. The teams with black players all voted against the measure, but Binghamton, which had just released Fowler and Renfroe, swung the vote in favor of exclusion.

Events in 1887 continued to conspire against black

players. On September 11, the St. Louis Browns of the American Association refused to play a scheduled contest against the all-black Cuban Giants. "We are only doing what is right," they proclaimed. In November, the Buffalo and Syracuse teams unsuccessfully attempted to lift the International League ban on blacks. The Ohio State League, which had fielded three black players, also adopted a rule barring additional contracts with blacks, prompting Welday Walker, who had appeared in the league, to protest, "The law is a disgrace to the present age. . . There should be some broader cause—such as lack of ability, behavior and intelligence—for barring a player, rather than his color."

After 1887, only a handful of blacks appeared on integrated squads. Grant and Higgins returned to their original teams in 1888. Walker jumped from Newark to Syracuse. The following year, only Walker remained for one final season, the last black in the International League until 1946. Richard Johnson, the erstwhile Dick Male, reappeared in the Ohio State League in 1888 and in 1889 joined Springfield in the Central Interstate League, where he hit 14 triples, stole 45 bases, and scored 100 runs in 100 games. In 1890, Harrisburg in the Eastern Interstate League fielded two blacks, while Jamestown in the New York Penn League featured another. Bud Fowler and several other black players appeared in the Nebraska State League in 1892. Three years later, Adrian in the Michigan State League signed five blacks, including Fowler and pitcher George Wilson who posted a 29–4 record. Meanwhile Sol White, who later chronicled these events in his 1906 book, *The History of Colored Baseball*, played for Fort Wayne in the Western State League. In 1896, pitcher-outfielder Bert Jones joined Atchison in the Kansas State League where he played for three seasons before being forced out in 1898. Almost 50 years would pass before another black would appear on an interracial club in organized baseball.

While integrated teams grew rare, several leagues allowed entry to all black squads. In 1889, the Middle States League included the New York Gorhams and the Cuban Giants, the most famous black team of the age. The Giants posted a 55–17 record. In 1890, the alliance reorganized as the Eastern Interstate League and again included the Cuban Giants. Giants' star George Williams paced the circuit with a .391 batting average, while teammate Arthur Thomas slugged 26 doubles and 10 triples, both league-leading totals. The Eastern Interstate League folded in midseason, and in 1891 the Giants made one final minor league appearance in the Connecticut State League. When this circuit also disbanded, the brief entry of the Cuban Giants in organized baseball came to an end. In 1898, a team calling itself the Acme Colored Giants affiliated with Pennsylvania's Iron and Oil League, but won only eight of 49 games before dropping out, marking an ignoble conclusion to these early experiments in interracial play.

Overall, at least 70 blacks appeared in organized baseball in the late 19th century. About half played for all-black teams, the remainder for integrated clubs. Few lasted more than one season with the same team. By the 1890s, the pattern for black baseball that would prevail for the next half century had emerged. Blacks were relegated to "colored" teams playing most of their games on the barnstorming circuit, outside of any organized league structure. While exhibition contests allowed them to pit their skills against whites, they remained on the outskirts of baseball's mainstream, unheralded and unknown to most Americans.

As early as the 1880s and 1890s several all-black traveling squads had gained national reputations. The Cuban Giants, formed among the waiters of the Argyle Hotel to entertain guests in 1885, set the pattern and provided the recurrent nickname for these teams. Passing as Cubans, so as not to offend their white clientele, the Giants toured the East in a private railroad car playing amateur and professional opponents. In the 1890s, rivals like the Lincoln Giants from Nebraska, the Page Fence Giants from Michigan, and the Cuban X Giants in New York emerged. From the beginning these teams combined entertainment with their baseball to attract crowds. The Page Fence Giants, founded by Bud Fowler in 1895, would ride through the streets on bicycles to attract attention. In 1899, Fowler organized the All-American Black Tourists, who would arrive in full dress suits with opera hats and silk umbrellas. Their showmanship notwithstanding, the black teams of the 1890s included some of the best players in the nation. The Page Fence Giants won 118 of 154 games in 1895, with two of their losses coming against the major league Cincinnati Reds.

During the early years of the 20th century many blacks still harbored hopes of regaining access to organized baseball. Sol White wrote in 1906 that baseball, "should be taken seriously by the colored player. An honest effort of his great ability will open the avenue in the near future wherein he may walk hand-in-hand with the opposite race in the greatest of all American games—baseball." Rube Foster, the outstanding figure in black baseball from 1910-1926, stressed excellence because "we have to be ready when the time comes for integration."

But even clandestine efforts to bring in blacks met a harsh fate. In 1901, Baltimore Orioles Manager John McGraw attempted to pass second baseman Charlie Grant of the Columbia Giants off as an Indian named Chief Tokohama, until Chicago White Sox President Charles Comiskey exposed the ruse. In 1911, the Cincinnati Reds raised black hopes by signing two light-skinned Cubans, Armando Marsans and Rafael Almeida, prompting the *New York Age* to speculate, "Now that the first shock is over it would not be surprising to see a Cuban a few shades darker. . .breaking into the professional ranks. . .it would then be easier for colored players who are citizens of this country to get into fast company." But the Reds rushed to certify that Marsans and Almeida were "genuine Caucasians," and while light-skinned Cubans became a fixture in the majors, their darker brethren remained unwelcome. Over the years, tales circulated of United States blacks passing as Indians or Cubans, but no documented cases exist.

Although most blacks lived in the South, during the first two decades of the 20th century, the great black teams and players congregated in the metropolises and industrial cities of the North. Chicago emerged as the primary center of black baseball with teams like the Leland Giants and the Chicago American Giants. In New York, the Lincoln Giants, which boasted pitching stars Smokey Joe Williams and Cannonball Dick Redding, shortstop John Henry Lloyd and catcher Louis Santop, reigned supreme. Other top clubs of the era included the Philadelphia Giants, the Hilldale Club (also of Philadelphia), the Indianapolis ABC's and the Bacharach Giants of Atlantic City. Player contracts were nonexistent or nonbinding and stars jumped frequently from team to team. "Wherever the money was," recalled John Henry Lloyd, "that's where I was."

Fans and writers often compared the great black players of this era to their white counterparts. Lloyd, one of the outstanding shortstops and hitters of that or any era, came to be known as "The Black Wagner," after his white contemporary Honus Wagner, who called it an "honor" and a "privilege" to be compared to the gangling black infielder. A St. Louis sportswriter once said when asked who was the best player in baseball history, "If you mean in organized baseball, the answer would be Babe Ruth; but if you mean in all baseball. . .the answer would have to be a colored man named John Henry Lloyd." Pitcher "Rube" Foster earned his nickname by outpitching future Hall of Famer Rube Waddell, and Cuban Jose Mendez was called "The Black Matty" after Christy Mathewson.

The talents of Foster and Mendez notwithstanding, the greatest black pitcher of the early twentieth century was 6′5″ Smokey Joe Williams. Born in 1886, Williams spent a good part of his career pitching in his native Texas, unheralded until he joined the Leland Giants in 1909 at the age of 24. From 1912-1923 he won renown as a strikeout artist for Harlem's Lincoln Giants. Against major league competition Williams won six games, lost four, and tied two, including a three-hit 1–0 victory over the National League champion Philadelphia Phillies in 1915. In 1925, he signed with the Homestead Grays and although approaching his fortieth birthday, starred for seven more seasons. A 1952 poll to name the outstanding black pitcher of the half-century, placed Williams in first place, ahead of the legendary Satchel Paige.

Oscar Charleston ranks as the greatest outfielder of the 1910s and 1920s. With tremendous speed and a strong, accurate arm, Charleston was the quintessential centerfielder. During his 15-year career starting in 1915, Charleston hit for both power and average and may have been the most popular player of the 1920s. After he retired he managed the Philadelphia Stars, Brooklyn Brown Dodgers, and other clubs.

Several major stars of this era labored outside the usual channels of black baseball. In 1914, white Kansas City promoter J. L. Wilkinson organized the All-Nations team, which included whites, blacks, Indians, Asians, and Latin Americans. Pitchers John Donaldson, Jose Mendez, and Bill Drake and outfielder Cristobel Torriente played for the All-Nations team, described by one observer as "strong enough to give any major league team a nip-and-tuck battle." A black Army team from the 25th Infantry Unit in Nogales, Arizona, featured pitcher Bullet Joe Rogan and shortstop Dobie Moore. In 1920, when Wilkinson formed the famed Kansas City Monarchs, the players from the All-Nations and 25th Infantry teams formed the nucleus of his club. In 1921, the Monarchs challenged the minor league Kansas City Blues to a tournament for the city championship. The Blues won the series five games to three. In 1922, however, the Monarchs won five of six games to claim boasting honors

in Kansas City. One week later, they swept a doubleheader from the touring Babe Ruth All-Stars.

In the years after 1910, Andrew "Rube" Foster emerged as the dominant figure in black baseball. Like many of his white contemporaries, Foster rose through the ranks of the national pastime from star player to field manager to club owner. Born in Texas in 1879, Foster accepted an invitation to pitch for Chicago's Union Giants in 1902. "If you play the best clubs in the land, white clubs as you say," he told owner Frank Leland, "it will be a case of Greek meeting Greek. I fear nobody." By 1903, he was hurling for the Cuban X Giants against the Philadelphia Giants in a series billed as the "Colored Championship of the World." His four victories in a best of nine series clinched the title. The following year, he had switched sides and registered two of three wins for the Philadelphia Giants in a similar matchup, striking out 18 batters in one game and tossing a two-hitter in another. In 1907, he rejoined the Leland Giants and, in 1910, pitched for and managed a reconstituted team of that name to a 123–6 record.

As a pitcher, Foster had ranked among the nation's best; as a manager, his skills achieved legendary proportions. A master strategist and motivator, Foster's teams specialized in the bunt, the steal, and the hit-and-run, which came to characterize black baseball. Fans came to watch him sit on the bench giving signs with a wave of his ever-present pipe. He became the friend and confidant of major league managers like John McGraw. Over the years, Foster trained a generation of black managers, like Dave Malarcher, Biz Mackey, and Oscar Charleston in the subtleties of the game.

In 1911, Foster entered the ownership ranks, uniting with white saloon keeper John Schorling (the son-in-law of White Sox owner Charles Comiskey) to form the Chicago American Giants. With Schorling's financial backing, Foster's managerial acumen, a regular home field in Chicago, and high salaries, the American Giants attracted the best black players in the nation. Throughout the decade, whether barnstorming or hosting opponents in Chicago, the American Giants came to represent the pinnacle of black baseball.

By World War One, Foster dominated black baseball in Chicago and parts of the Midwest. In most other areas, however, white booking agents controlled access to stadiums, and as one newspaperman charged in 1917, "used circus methods to drag a bunch of our best citizens out, only to undergo humiliation . . . while [they sat] back and [grew] rich off a percentage of the proceeds." In the East, Nat Strong, the part owner of the Brooklyn Royal Giants, Philadelphia Giants, Cuban Stars, Cuban Giants, New York Black Yankees, and the renowned white semi-pro team, the Bushwicks, held a stranglehold on black competition. To break this monopoly and place the game more firmly under black control, Foster created the National Association of Professional Baseball Clubs, better known as the Negro National League, in 1920.

Foster's new organization marked the third attempt of the century to meld black teams into a viable league. In 1906, the International League of Independent Baseball Clubs, which had four black and two white teams, struggled through one season characterized by shifting and collapsing franchises. Four years later, Beauregard Moseley, secretary of Chicago's Leland Giants, attempted to form a National Negro Baseball League, but the association folded before a single game had been played.

The new Negro National League, which included the top teams from Chicago, St. Louis, Detroit, and other Midwestern cities, fared far better. At Foster's insistence, all clubs, with the exception of the Kansas City Monarchs, whom Foster reluctantly accepted, were controlled by blacks. J. L. Wilkinson, who owned the Monarchs, a major drawing card, had won the respect of his fellow owners and soon overcame Foster's reservations. He became the league secretary and Foster's trusted ally. Operating under the able guidance of Foster and Wilkinson, the league flourished during its early years. In 1923, it attracted 400,000 fans and accumulated $200,000 in gate receipts.

The success of the Negro National League inspired competitors. In 1923, booking agent Nat Strong formed an Eastern Colored League, with teams in New York, Brooklyn, Baltimore, New Jersey, and Philadelphia. With four of the six teams owned by whites, and Strong controlling an erratic schedule, the league had somewhat less legitimacy than Foster's circuit. Playing in larger population centers, however, the more affluent Eastern clubs successfully raided some of the top players of the Negro National League before the circuits negotiated an uneasy truce in 1924. Throughout the remainder of the decade, however, acrimony rather than harmony characterized interleague relations. A third association emerged in the South, where the stronger independent teams in major cities formed the Southern Negro League. While this group became a breeding ground for top players, the impoverished nature of its clientele, and the inability of clubs to bolster revenues with games against white squads, rendered them unable to prevent their best players from jumping to the higher paying Northern teams.

At their best the Negro Leagues of the 1920s were haphazard affairs. Since most clubs continued to rely on barnstorming for their primary livelihood, scheduling proved difficult. Teams played uneven numbers of games and especially in the Eastern circuit skipped official contests for more lucrative nonleague matchups. Several of the stronger independent teams, like the Homestead Grays, remained unaffiliated. Umpires were often incompetent and lacked authority to control conditions. Finally, players frequently jumped from one franchise to another, peddling their services to the highest bidder. In 1926, Foster grew ill, stripping the Negro National League of his vital leadership. Two years later, the Eastern Colored League disbanded and in 1931, less than a year after Foster's death, the Negro National League departed the scene, once again leaving black baseball with no organized structure.

With the collapse of Foster's Negro National League and the onset of the Great Depression, the always-borderline economics of operating a black baseball club grew more precarious. White booking agents, like Philadelphia's Eddie Gottlieb or Abe Saperstein of the Midwest, again reigned supreme. In the early 1930s, only the stronger independent clubs like the Homestead Grays or Kansas City Monarchs, novelty acts like the Cincinnati Clowns, or those teams backed by the "numbers kings" of the black ghettos could survive.

The Kansas City Monarchs emerged as the healthiest holdover from the old Negro National League. In 1929, owner Wilkinson had commissioned an Omaha, Nebraska, company to design a portable lighting system for night games. The equipment, consisting of a 250-horsepower motor and a 100-kilowatt generator, which illuminated lights atop telescoping poles 50 feet above the field, took about two hours to assemble. To pay for the innovation, Wilkinson mortgaged everything he owned and took in Kansas City businessman Tom Baird as a partner. But the gamble paid off. The novelty of night baseball allowed the Monarchs to play two and three games a day and made them the most popular touring club in the nation.

Meanwhile, in Pittsburgh, former basketball star Cumberland Posey, Jr. had forged the Homestead Grays into one of the best teams in America. Posey, the son of one of Pittsburgh's wealthiest black businessmen, had joined the Grays, then a sandlot team, as an outfielder in 1911. By the early 1920s he owned the club and began recruiting top national players to supplement local talent. In 1925, he signed 39-year-old Smokey Joe Williams, and the following year he lured Oscar Charleston, whom many consider the top black player of that era. Over the next several seasons Posey recruited Judy Johnson, Martin Dihigo, and Cool Papa Bell. In 1930, he added a catcher from the Pittsburgh sandlots named Josh Gibson, and in 1934 brought in first baseman Buck Leonard from North Carolina. Unwilling to subject himself to outside control, Posey preferred to remain free from league affiliations. Yet for two decades, the Homestead Grays reigned as one of the strongest teams in black baseball.

In the 1930s, Posey faced competition from crosstown rival Gus Greenlee, "Mr. Big" of Pittsburgh's North Side numbers rackets. Greenlee took over the Pittsburgh Crawfords, a local team, in 1930. Greenlee spent $100,000 to build a new stadium, and wooed established ballplayers with lavish salary offers. In 1931, he landed the colorful Satchel Paige, the hottest young pitcher in the land, and the following year raided the Grays, outbidding Posey for the services of Charleston, Johnson, and Gibson. In 1934, James "Cool Papa" Bell jumped the St. Louis Stars and brought his legendary speed to the Crawfords. With five future Hall of Famers, Greenlee had assembled one of the great squads of baseball history.

The emergence of Gus Greenlee marked a new era for black baseball, the reign of the numbers men. In an age of limited opportunities for blacks, many of the most talented northern black entrepreneurs turned to gambling and other illegal operations for their livelihood. Novelist Richard Wright explained, "They would have been steel tycoons, Wall Street brokers, auto moguls, had they been white." Like the political bosses of nineteenth century urban America, numbers operators provided an informal assistance network for needy patrons in the impoverished black communities and represented a major source of capital for black businesses. In city after city, the numbers barons, seeking an element of respectability or an outlet to shield gambling profits from the Internal Revenue Service or merely the thrill of sports ownership, came to dominate black baseball. In Harlem, second-generation Cuban immigrant Alex Pompez, a powerful figure in the Dutch Schultz mob, ran the Cuban Stars, while Ed "Soldier Boy" Semler controlled the Black Yankees. Abe

Manley of the Newark Eagles, Ed Bolden of the Philadelphia Stars, and Tom Wilson of the Baltimore Elite Giants all garnered their fortunes from the numbers game. Even Cum Posey, who had no connection with the rackets, had to bring in Homestead numbers banker Rufus "Sonnyman" Jackson as a partner and financier to stave off Greenlee's challenge.

In 1933, Greenlee unified the franchises owned by the numbers kings into a rejuvenated Negro National League. Under his leadership, writes Donn Rogosin, "The Negro National League meetings were enclaves of the most powerful black gangsters in the nation." This "unholy alliance" sustained black baseball in the Northeast through depression and war. Even the collapse of the Crawfords and demolition of Greenlee Stadium in 1939, failed to weaken the league which survived until the onset of integration. In 1937 a second circuit, the Negro American League was formed in the Midwest and South. Dominated by Wilkinson and the Kansas City Monarchs, the Negro American League relied less on numbers brokers, but more on white ownership for their financing.

The formation of the Negro American League encouraged the rejuvenation of an annual World Series, matching the champions of the two leagues. But the Negro League World Series never achieved the prominence of its white counterpart. The fact that league standings were often determined among teams playing uneven numbers of games diluted the notion of a champion. Furthermore, impoverished urban blacks could not sustain attendance at a prolonged series. As a result, the Negro League World Series always took a back seat to the annual East-West All-Star Game played in Chicago. The East-West Game, originated by Greenlee in 1933, quickly emerged as the centerpiece of black baseball. Fans chose the players in polls conducted by black newspapers. By 1939, leading candidates received as many as 500,000 votes. Large crowds of blacks and whites watched the finest Negro League stars, and the revenues divided among the teams often spelled the difference between profit and loss at the season's end.

By the 1930s and 1940s, black baseball had become an integral part of Northern ghetto life. With hundreds of employees and millions of dollars in revenue, the Negro Leagues, as Donn Rogosin notes, "may rank among the highest achievements of black enterprise during segregation." In addition, baseball provided an economic ripple effect, boosting business in hotels, cafes, restaurants and bars. In Kansas City and other towns, games became social events, as black citizens, recalls manager Buck O'Neil, "wore their finery." The Monarch Booster Club was a leading civic organization and the "Miss Monarch Bathing Beauty" pageant a popular event.

Black baseball also represented a source of pride for the black community. "The Monarchs was Kansas City's team," boasted bartender Jesse Fisher. "They made Kansas City the talk of the town all over the world." In several cities, white politicians routinely appeared at Opening Day games to curry favor with their often neglected black constituents. When Greenlee Field launched its operations in Pittsburgh, the mayor, city council, and county commissioners lined the field boxes. Negro League owners also played a role in the fight against segregation. In Newark, Effa Manley, who ran the Eagles with her husband Abe, served as treasurer of the New Jersey NAACP and belonged to the Citizen's League for Fair Play which fought for black employment opportunities. Manley sponsored a "Stop Lynching" fundraiser at one Eagles home game.

The impact of the Negro Leagues, however, ranged beyond the communities whose names the teams bore. Throughout the age of Jim Crow baseball, even in those years when a substantial league structure existed, official league games accounted for a relatively small part of the black baseball experience. Black teams would typically play over 200 games a year, only a third of which counted in the league standings. The vast majority of contests occurred on the "barnstorming" circuit, pitting black athletes against a broad array of professional and semi-professional competition, white and black, throughout the nation. In the pre-television era, traveling teams brought a higher level of baseball to fans in the towns and cities of America and allowed local talent to test their skills against the professionals. While some all-white teams, like the "House of David" also trod the barnstorming trail, itinerancy was the key to survival for black squads. The capital needed to finance a Negro League team existed primarily in Northern cities, but the overwhelming majority of blacks lived in the South.

"The schedule was a rugged one," recalled Roy Campanella of the Baltimore Elite Giants. "Rarely were we in the same city two days in a row. Mostly we played by day and traveled by night." After the Monarchs introduced night baseball, teams played both day and night appearing in two and sometimes three different ballparks on the same day. Teams traveled in buses—"our home, dressing room, dining room, and hotel"—or sandwiched into touring cars. "We had little time to waste on the road," states Quincy Trouppe, "so it was a rare treat when the cars would stop at times to let us stretch out and exercise for a few minutes." Most major hotels barred black guests, so even when the schedule allowed overnight stays, the athletes found themselves in less than comfortable accommodations. Large cities usually had better black hotels where ballplayers, entertainers, and other members of the black bourgeoisie congregated. On the road, however, Negro Leaguers more frequently were relegated to Jim Crow roadhouses, "continually under attack by bedbugs."

The black baseball experience extended beyond the confines of the United States and into Central America and the Caribbean. Negro Leaguers appeared regularly in the Cuban, Puerto Rican, Venezuelan, and Dominican winter leagues where they competed against black and white Latin stars and major leaguers as well. Some blacks, like Willie Wells and Ray Dandridge, jumped permanently to the Mexican League, where several also became successful managers of interracial teams. As Wells explained, "I am not faced by the racial problem. . . I've found freedom and democracy here, something I never found in the United States. . . In Mexico, I am a man."

In the United States, however, blacks often found themselves in more distasteful roles. To attract crowds throughout the nation and to keep fans interested in the frequently one-sided contests against amateur competition, some black clubs injected elements of clowning and showmanship into their pre-game and competitive performances. As early as the 1880s, comedy had characterized many barnstorming teams. Black baseball, even in its most serious form, tended to be flashier and less formal than white play. Against inferior teams, players often showboated and flaunted their superior skills. Pitcher Satchel Paige would call in his outfielders or guarantee to strike out the first six or nine batters to face him against semi-professional squads. In the late 1930s, Olympic star Jesse Owens traveled with the Monarchs, racing against horses in pre-game exhibitions.

Black teams, like the Tennessee Rats and Zulu Cannibals, thrived on their minstrel show reputations. The most famous of these franchises were the "Ethiopian Clowns." Originating in Miami in the 1930s, the Clowns later operated out of Cincinnati and then Indianapolis. Their antics included a "pepperball and shadowball" performance (later emulated by basketball's Harlem Globetrotters), and mid-game vaudeville routines by comics Spec Bebop, a dwarf, and King Tut. Players like Pepper Bassett, "the Rocking Chair Catcher" and "Goose" Tatum, a talented first baseman and natural comedian, enlivened the festivities. By the 1940s, the Clowns, through the effort of booking agent Syd Pollack, dominated the baseball comedy market. In 1943, their popularity won the Clowns entrance into the Negro Leagues, although other owners demanded they drop the demeaning "Ethiopian" nickname. Although never one of the better black teams, the Clowns greatly bolstered Negro League attendance.

Their popularity notwithstanding, the comedy teams reflected one of the worst elements of black baseball. The Clowns and Zulus perpetuated stereotypes drawn from Stepin Fetchit and Tarzan movies. "Negroes must realize the danger in insisting that ballplayers paint their faces and go through minstrel show revues before each ballgame," protested sportswriter Wendell Smith. Many black players resented the image that all were clowns. "Didn't nobody clown in our league but the Indianapolis Clowns," objected Piper Davis. "We played baseball."

Even without the clowning, black baseball offered a more freewheeling and, in many respects, more exciting brand of baseball than the major leagues. Since the 1920s, when Babe Ruth had revolutionized the game, the majors had pursued power strategies, emphasizing the home run above all else. Although the great sluggers of the Negro Leagues rivaled those in the National and American Leagues, they comprised but one element in the speed-dominated universe of "tricky baseball." Black teams emphasized the bunt, the stolen base, and the hit-and-run. "We played by the 'coonsbury' rules," boasted second baseman Newt Allen. "That's just any way you think you can win, any kind of play you think you could get by on." In games between white and black all-star teams, this style of play often confounded the major leaguers. Centerfielder James "Cool Papa" Bell personified this approach. Bell was so fast, marveled rival third baseman Judy Johnson, "You couldn't play back in your regular position or you'd never throw him out." In one game against a major league All-Star squad, Bell scored from first base on a sacrifice bunt! In center field, his great speed allowed him to lurk in the shallow reaches of the outfield, ranging great distances to make spectacular catches.

Negro League pitching also took on a peculiar caste. "Anything went in the Negro League," reported catcher Roy Campanella, "Spitballs, shineballs, emery balls; pitchers used any and all of them." Since league officials could not afford to replace the balls as frequently as in organized ball, scuffed and nicked baseballs remained in the game, giving pitchers great latitude for creative efforts. "I never knew what the ball would do once it left the pitcher's hand," recalled Campanella.

Since most rosters included only 14 to 18 men, Negro League players demonstrated a wide range of versatility. Each was required to fill in at a variety of positions. Star pitchers often found themselves in the outfield when not on the mound. Some won renown at more than one position. Ted "Double-Duty" Radcliffe often pitched in the first game of a doubleheader and caught in the second. Cuban Martin Dihigo, whom many rank as the greatest player of all time, excelled at every position. In 1938, in the Mexican League he led the league's pitchers with an 18–2 record and the league's hitters with a .387 average.

The manpower shortage offered opportunities for individuals to display their all-around talents, but it also limited the competitiveness of the black teams. While on a given day a Negro League franchise, featuring one of its top pitchers, might defeat a major league squad, most teams lacked the depth to compete on a regular basis. "The big leagues were strong in every position," remarks Radcliffe. "Most of the colored teams had a few stars but they weren't strong in every position."

While black teams may not have matched the top clubs in organized baseball, the individual stars of the 1930s and 1940s clearly ranked among the best of any age. Homestead Gray teammates Josh Gibson and Buck Leonard won renown as the Babe Ruth and Lou Gehrig of the Negro Leagues. The Grays discovered Gibson in 1929 as an 18-year-old catcher on the sandlots of Pittsburgh, where he had already earned a reputation for 500-foot home runs. For 17 years, he launched prodigious blasts off pitchers in the Negro Leagues, on the barnstorming tour, and in Latin America. As talented as any major league star, Gibson died in January 1947, at age 35, just three months before Jackie Robinson joined the Brooklyn Dodgers. Leonard, four-years older than Gibson, starred in both the Negro and Mexican Leagues as a sure-handed, power-hitting first baseman. The Newark Eagles in the early 1940s, boasted the "million dollar infield" of first baseman Mule Suttles, second baseman Dick Seay, shortstop Willie Wells, and third baseman Ray Dandridge. The acrobatic fielding skills of Seay, Wells and Dandridge led Roy Campanella to call this the greatest infield he ever saw.

Amidst the many talented Negro Leaguers of 1930s and 1940s, however, one long, lean figure came to personify black baseball to blacks and whites alike. Leroy "Satchel" Paige began his prolonged athletic odyssey in his hometown in 1924 as a 17-year-old pitcher with the semi-professional Mobile Tigers. He joined the Chattanooga Black Lookouts of the Negro Southern League in 1926. Two years later, the Lookouts sold his contract to the Birmingham Black Barons. By 1930, his explosive fastball, impeccable control, and eccentric mannerisms had made him a legend in the South. In 1932, Gus Greenlee brought Paige to the Pittsburgh Crawfords where the colorful pitcher embellished his reputation by winning 54 games in his first two years. Greenlee also began the practice of hiring out Paige to semi-professional clubs that needed a one-day box office boost.

For seven years Paige feuded with Greenlee, jumping the club when a better offer appeared, being banished "for life," and then returning. In the mid-1930s, in addition to his stints with the Crawfords, Paige won fame by boosting Bismarck, North Dakota, to the national semi-professional championships, hurling for the Dominican Republic at the behest of dictator Rafael Trujillo, in the Mexican League, and especially on the postseason barnstorming trail pitted against Dizzy Dean's Major League All-Stars. "That skinny old Satchel Paige with those long arms is my idea of the pitcher with the greatest stuff I ever saw," claimed the unusually immodest Dean.

Paige's appeal stemmed as much from his unusual persona as his pitching prowess. A born showman, Paige's lanky, lackadaisical presence evoked popular racial stereotypes of the age. "As undependable as a pair of second-hand suspenders," Paige often arrived late or failed to show. His names for his pitches (the "bee ball" which buzzed and all of a sudden, "be there"; the "jump ball"; and the "trouble ball") and his minstrel show one-liners enhanced the image. But on the mound, Paige invariably rose to the occasion against top competition or challenged inferior opponents by calling in the outfield or promising to strike out the side.

In 1938, a sore arm threatened to curtail Paige's career but the Kansas City Monarchs, hoping his reputation alone would draw fans, signed him for their traveling second team. On the road, Paige perfected a repertoire of curves and off-speed pitches, including his famous "hesitation" pitch. When his fastball returned in 1939, he became a better pitcher than ever. Promoted to the main Monarch club, Paige pitched the team to four consecutive Negro American League pennants. From 1941-1947, although officially still a Monarch, Paige spent far more time as an independent performer, hired out by Monarchs' owner J. L. Wilkinson to semi-pro and Negro League clubs. "He kept our league going," recalls Othello Renfroe. "Anytime a team got into trouble, it sent for Satchel to pitch." Paige also continued to hurl against major league All-Star teams. In the 1940s, the example of Satchel Paige, whose legend had spread into the white community, offered the most compelling argument for the desegregation of the National Pastime.

Paige's exploits against white players revealed a fundamental irony about baseball in the Jim Crow era. While organized baseball rigidly enforced its ban on black players within the major and minor leagues, opportunities abounded for black athletes to prove themselves against white competition along the unpoliced boundaries of the national pastime. During the 1930s, Western promoters sponsored tournaments for the best semi-professional teams in the nation. These squads often featured former and future major leaguers as well as top local talent. In 1934, the *Denver Post* tourney, "the little World Series of the West," invited the Kansas City Monarchs to compete for the $7,500 first prize. The Monarchs fought their way into the finals against the House of David team (also owned by J. L. Wilkinson) only to find themselves confronted on the mound by Paige, rented out to pitch this

one game. Paige outdueled Monarchs ace, Chet Brewer, 2–1. Black teams became a fixture in the Post series, emerging victorious for several consecutive years.

In 1935, the National Baseball Congress began an annual tournament in Wichita, Kansas. The competition attracted community squads heartily bankrolled by local business leaders. Neil Churchill, an auto dealer from Bismarck, North Dakota, recruited a half-dozen black stars, including Paige and Brewer, to represent the town in the Wichita competition. Bismarck naturally swept the series, and thereafter teams that were either integrated or all black routinely appeared in the National Baseball Congress invitational each year.

In an age in which the major leagues were confined to the East and Midwest, and television had yet to bring baseball into people's homes, postseason tours by big league stars offered yet another opportunity for black players to prove their equality on the diamond. Games pitting blacks against whites were popular features of the barnstorming circuit. Until the late 1920s, when Commissioner Kenesaw Mountain Landis limited postseason play to all-star squads, black teams frequently met and defeated major league clubs in postseason competition. During the next decade, matchups between the Babe Ruth or Dizzy Dean "All-Stars" and black players became frequent. In the autumns of 1934 and 1935, Dean's team traveled the nation accompanied by the "Satchel Paige All-Stars." In one memorable 1934 game, called by baseball executive Bill Veeck, "the greatest pitching battle I have ever seen," Paige bested Dean 1–0. Surviving records of interracial contests during the 1930s reveal that blacks won two-thirds of the games. "That's when we played the hardest," asserted Judy Johnson, "to let them know, and to let the public know, that we had the same talent they did and probably a little better at times."

The rivalries proved particularly keen on the West Coast where Monarchs co-owner Tom Baird organized the California Winter League, which included black teams, white major and minor league stars, and some of Mexico's top players. In 1940, pitcher Chet Brewer formed the Kansas City Royals, which each year fielded one of the best clubs on the coast. One year the Royals defeated the Hollywood Stars, who had won the Pacific Coast League championship, six straight times. In 1945, Brewer's team, including Jackie Robinson and Satchel Paige, regularly defeated major league competition.

The most famous of the interracial barnstorming tours occurred in 1946, when Cleveland Indian pitcher Bob Feller organized a major league All-Star Team, rented two Flying Tiger aircraft and hopped the nation accompanied by the Satchel Paige All-Stars. With Feller and Paige each pitching a few innings a day, the tour proved extremely lucrative for promoters and players alike and gave widespread publicity to the skills of the black athletes.

The World War Two years marked the heyday of the Negro Leagues. With black and white workers flooding into Northern industrial centers, relatively full employment, and a scarcity of available consumer goods, attendance at all sorts of entertainment events increased dramatically. In 1942, three million fans saw Negro League teams play, while the East-West game in 1943 attracted over 51,000 fans. "Even the white folks was coming out big," recalled Satchel Paige.

But World War Two also generated forces which would challenge the foundations of Jim Crow baseball. In the armed forces, baseball teams like the Black Bluejackets of the Great Lakes Naval Station team posted outstanding records against teams featuring white major leaguers. In 1945, a well-publicized tournament of teams in the European theatre featured top black players like Leon Day, Joe Green, and Willard Brown in the championship round. More significantly, the hypocrisy of blacks fighting for their country but unable to participate in the national pastime grew steadily more apparent. As wartime manpower shortages forced major league teams to rely on a 15-year-old pitcher, over-the-hill veterans, and one-armed Pete Gray, their refusal to sign black players seemed increasingly irrational. "How do you think I felt when I saw a one-armed outfielder?" moaned Chet Brewer. Pitcher Nate Moreland protested, "I can play in Mexico, but I have to fight for America where I can't play." Pickets at Yankee Stadium carried placards asking, "If we are able to stop bullets, why not balls?"

Amidst this heightened awareness, organized baseball repeatedly walked to the precipice of integration, but always failed to take the final leap. In 1942, Moreland and All-American football star Jackie Robinson requested a tryout at a White Sox training camp in Pasadena, California. Robinson, in particular, impressed White Sox manager Jimmy Dykes but nothing came of the event. Brooklyn Dodger manager Leo Durocher publicly stated his willingness to sign blacks, only to receive a stinging rebuke from Commissioner Landis. Landis again short-circuited integration talk the following year. At the annual baseball meetings, black leaders led by actor Paul Robeson gained the opportunity to address major league owners on the issue, but Landis ruled all further discussion out of order.

In 1943, several minor and major league teams were rumored close to signing black players. In California, where winter league play had demonstrated the potential of black players, several clubs considered integration. The Los Angeles Angels of the Pacific Coast League announced tryouts for three black players, but pressure from other league owners doomed the plan. Oakland owner Vince DeVicenzi ordered Manager Johnny Vergez to consider pitcher Chet Brewer, the most popular black player on the West Coast, for the Oaks. Vergez refused and the issue died. Two years later, Bakersfield, a Cleveland Indian farm team in the California League, offered Brewer a position as player-coach, but the parent club vetoed the plan.

At the major league level, Washington Senators owner Clark Griffith called sluggers Josh Gibson and Buck Leonard into his office and asked if they would like to play in the major leagues. They answered affirmatively, but never heard from Griffith again. In Pittsburgh, *Daily Worker* sports editor Nat Low pressured Pirate owner William Benswanger to arrange a tryout for catcher Roy Campanella and pitcher Dave Barnhill. At the last minute, Benswanger canceled the audition, citing "unnamed pressures." The most promising situation occurred in Philadelphia where young Bill Veeck had arranged to buy the Phillies. Veeck planned to stock the team with Negro League stars, whom he felt sure would guarantee Philadelphia the pennant. When Commissioner Landis learned of his plans, however, Veeck suddenly found his purchase blocked.

For more than two decades, the imperial Landis had reigned over baseball as an implacable foe of integration. While hypocritically denying the existence of any "rule, formal or informal, or any understanding—unwritten, subterranean, or sub-anything—against the signing of Negro players," Landis had stringently policed the color line. His death in 1944 removed a major barrier for integration advocates.

In April 1945, with World War Two entering its final months, the integration crusade gained momentum. On April 6, *People's Voice* sportswriter Joe Bostic appeared at the Brooklyn Dodger training camp at Bear Mountain, New York, with two Negro League players, Terris McDuffie and Dave "Showboat" Thomas, and demanded a tryout. An outraged, but outmaneuvered, Dodger President Branch Rickey allowed the pair to work out with the club. One week later, a more serious confrontation occurred in Boston. The Red Sox, under pressure from popular columnist Dave Egan and city councilman Isidore Muchnick, agreed to audition Sam Jethroe, the Negro League's leading hitter in 1944, second baseman Marvin Williams, and Kansas City Monarch shortstop Jackie Robinson, all top prospects in their mid-twenties. The Fenway Park tryout, however, proved little more than a formality and the players never again heard from the Red Sox.

The publicity surrounding these events, however, forced the major leagues to address the issue at its April meetings. At the urging of black sportswriter Sam Lacy, Leslie O'Connor, Landis's interim successor, established a Major League Committee on Baseball Integration in April 1945, to review the problem. In addition, the racial views of newly appointed Commissioner A. B. "Happy" Chandler came under close scrutiny. A former governor of the segregated state of Kentucky, Chandler nonetheless offered at least verbal support to the entry of blacks into organized ball. "If a black boy can make it on Okinawa and Guadalcanal, hell, he can make it in baseball," Chandler told black reporter Rick Roberts. Whether Chandler, however, unlike Landis, would reinforce his rhetoric with positive actions remained uncertain.

Unbeknownst to the integration advocates, baseball officials, and local politicians sand-dancing around the race issue, Branch Rickey, the president of the Brooklyn Dodgers, had already set in motion the events which would lead to the historic breakthrough.

Raised in rural Ohio in a strict Methodist family, Rickey, nicknamed by sportwriters "The Deacon" and "The Mahatma," had financed his way through college and law school playing and coaching baseball. His skills as a catcher merited two years in the major leagues. In 1913, he abandoned a fledgling law career to manage the St. Louis Browns, and in 1917 he began a 25-year relationship with the St. Louis Cardinals. Rickey served as the field manager of the Cardinals from 1919–1925, after which he became the club's vice-president and business manager. In the 1920s and 1930s, Rickey perfected the farm system, whereby a major league team controlled young, undeveloped players through a chain of minor league franchises. This innovation allowed the Cardinals to compete equally with richer teams in larger cities, generating pennants for the "Gas House Gang" and allowing the team to profitably sell off surplus talent.

Although Rickey later claimed that his desire to integrate baseball dated from 1904, when an Indiana hotel had denied lodgings to a black player on his college squad, he gave no indication of any interest in the race issue during his years in St. Louis. Perhaps this stemmed from the fact that St. Louis was a Southern city with firmly entrenched segregationist traditions. Throughout Rickey's reign with the Cardinals, blacks sat in Jim Crow sections at Sportsman's Park, a policy which he never openly challenged.

Nonetheless, in 1942, when Rickey left the Cardinals and assumed control of the Brooklyn Dodgers, he informed the Dodger ownership of his intentions to recruit black players in the near future. Rickey never clearly explained the motivations for this dramatic turnaround. At times Rickey cited moral considerations, stating, "I couldn't face my God much longer knowing that His black creatures are held separate and distinct from His white creatures in the game that has given me all I own." On other occasions, he eschewed the role of "crusader," proclaiming, "My selfish objective is to win baseball games. . .The Negroes will make us winners for years to come." Some observers saw financial reasons behind Rickey's actions, citing the lure of the growing black population in Northern cities and the prospects of increased attendance. Certainly, Brooklyn offered a more congenial atmosphere for integration than St. Louis. In all probability, a combination of these factors—geographic, moral, competitive, and financial—coupled with Rickey's desire for a broader role in history, impelled him to seek black players.

From 1942–1945, Rickey, a conservative, cautious, and conspiratorial man, moved slowly, studying the philosophical and sociological ramifications of integration and taking few people into his confidence. During the spring and summer of 1945, under the guise of creating a new black baseball circuit, the United States League, Rickey's scouts combed the nation and the Caribbean for black players. Rickey sought one player who would spearhead the breakthrough and several other potential stars who would follow in his wake. By August 1945, scouting reports and Rickey's own investigations pointed to one man as the ideal candidate for the struggle ahead—Kansas City Monarch shortstop Jackie Robinson.

In Robinson, Rickey had found a rare combination of athletic ability, competitive fire, intelligence, maturity, and poise. Born in Georgia and raised in Pasadena, California, Robinson had won fame at UCLA as the nation's greatest all-around athlete, earning All-America honors in football, establishing broad-jump records, and leading his basketball conference in scoring, all in addition to his baseball exploits. In 1942, he enlisted in the army where he attended officer's candidate school and became a lieutenant. Two years later, while stationed in Texas, Robinson's refusal to move to the back of a bus resulted in a court martial and ultimate acquittal. This incident demonstrated his commitment to the cause of equal rights. After his discharge from the army, Robinson joined the Monarchs and earned a starting spot in the 1945 East-West All-Star Game. Robinson's college education, experience in interracial athletics, and army career complemented his playing talents. But his fiery pride and temper seemed a potential obstacle to his success.

On August 28, 1945, Robinson met with Rickey at the latter's Brooklyn offices. Rickey revealed his bold plan to integrate organized baseball and challenged Robinson to accept the primary role. The Mahatma flamboyantly play-acted, assuming the role of racist players, fans and hotel clerks, impressing upon Robinson the need to "turn the other cheek" in the event of racial confrontations. By the end of the session, Robinson had signed a contract to play for the Montreal Royals in the International League, the top farm team in the Brooklyn system. Rickey promised that if Robinson's performance merited it, he would be promoted to the Dodgers.

Rickey intended to announce the Robinson signing along with that of several other black players, but political pressures stemming from the New York City fall elections forced him to abandon his original plans and, on October 23, 1945, to reveal the signing of Robinson alone. The announcement sent shock waves through the baseball establishment and placed Robinson into a spotlight that he would never relinquish. Numerous sports figures, from players to executives to reporters, predicted the ultimate failure of Rickey's "great experiment."

Robinson's first test came at spring training in Florida in 1946. Thrust into the deep South where Jim Crow reigned supreme, Robinson and black pitcher John Wright, whom Rickey had recruited to room with Robinson, were unable to room with their teammates and barred from playing in Jacksonville and other Florida cities. In addition, a shoulder injury hindered Robinson's performance, raising doubts about his abilities.

On April 18, 1946, at Roosevelt Stadium in Jersey City, Robinson became the first black to appear in modern Organized Baseball (excepting Jimmy Claxton, who passed as white in 1916 for the Oakland Oaks of the Pacific Coast League). In the process he staged one of the most remarkable performances under pressure in the history of the game. In Robinson's second at-bat, he hit a three-run home run. He followed this with three singles and two stolen bases, scoring a total of four runs. As the *New York Times* reported, "This would have been a big day for any man, but under the circumstances, it was a tremendous feat."

In many respects, 1946 proved a nightmare season for Robinson. Fans jeered him in Baltimore, and opposing players tormented him with insults. Pitchers made him a frequent target of brushback pitches and baserunners attempted to spike and maim him at second base. As the season drew to a close, Robinson hovered on the brink of a nervous breakdown. Through it all, however, Robinson remained a dominant force on the field. His .349 batting average and 113 runs-scored led the league and paced the Royals to the International League pennant. His presence inspired new attendance records throughout the circuit. In the Little World Series, which pitted Montreal against the Louisville Colonels of the American Association, Robinson braved the hostility of Kentucky fans and stroked game-winning hits in the final two games to give the Royals the championship.

Rickey's initiative and Robinson's dramatic success failed to inspire other team owners. In August, major league executives debated a controversial report discussing the "Race Question" which argued that integration would "lessen the value of several major league franchises." No other clubs moved to sign black players. Only four blacks, all in the Brooklyn system, joined Robinson in organized baseball in 1946. At Nashua, New Hampshire, in the New England League, the Dodger farm club fielded catcher Roy Campanella and pitcher Don Newcombe. The Nashua Dodgers won the league championship largely due to Campanella's hitting and Newcombe's hurling. In the small town of Trois Rivières in Quebec, pitchers John Wright and Roy Partlow, both of whom had appeared briefly with Robinson at Montreal, led a third Dodger farm team to the Canadian-American League crown. Nonetheless, at the start of the 1947 season, no additional black players appeared on major or minor league rosters.

Although Robinson's performance at Montreal merited promotion to the Dodgers, Robinson remained a Royal when he reported to spring training in 1947. Rickey hoped that the Brooklyn players themselves, when exposed to Robinson's talents, would request his addition to the team. He switched Robinson to first base, a weak spot on the Dodger squad, to make his case more compelling. Robinson compiled a .519 batting average against the major leaguers, but several Dodger players, instead of demanding his promotion, rebelled. Led by "Dixie" Walker, a group of mostly Southern Dodgers circulated a petition against Robinson. Rickey moved quickly to short-circuit the dissension, threatening to trade any athletes who opposed Robinson. In addition, the refusal of Pete Reiser, "Pee Wee" Reese and other Dodger stars to support the protestors, effectively squelched the petition drive. Finally, on April 10, just five days before the start of the 1947 season, Rickey officially announced that Robinson would join the Dodgers.

Throughout the early months of the 1947 campaign Robinson stoically endured crises and challenges. The Philadelphia Phillies, led by manager Ben Chapman, unleashed a barrage of verbal abuse against Robinson which horrified Dodger players and fans. The Benjamin Franklin Hotel in Philadelphia refused lodgings for Robinson and death threats appeared among his voluminous daily mail. In early May, rumors that the St. Louis Cardinals planned to strike rather than compete against Robinson prompted National League President Ford Frick to warn the players, "If you do this you will be suspended from the league." Opposing pitchers targeted Robinson's body at a record setting pace and an early season 0 for 20 batting drought led many to question his qualifications as a professional baseball player. "But for the fact that he is the first acknowledged Negro in major league history," observed a Cincinnati sportswriter, "he would have been benched a week ago."

Yet, as the season unfolded, Robinson converted doubters and enemies into admirers. By the end of June, a 21-game hitting streak had raised his batting average to .315 and propelled the Dodgers into first place. Robinson's daring baserunning, typical of Negro League play, evoked images of an "Ebony Ty Cobb." In city after city, record crowds flocked to experience Robinson's charismatic dynamism as five teams set new all-time season attendance marks. While periodic controversies erupted over baserunners who used their spikes "to make a pincushion

out of Robinson" at first base, Robinson won the acceptance and respect of teammates and opponents alike. In September, as the Dodgers coasted to the pennant, *The Sporting News* named Robinson the major league Rookie of the Year. To cap his triumphant season, Robinson became the first black player to appear in the World Series.

Robinson's success on the field and at the box office stimulated some movement on the part of other clubs to hire black players. In Cleveland Bill Veeck recruited 23-year-old Larry Doby, who jumped straight from the Negro League Newark Eagles to the Indians in July. Used sparingly, Doby batted a meager .156, casting doubts upon his future. The St. Louis Browns, seeking to boost flagging attendance, signed Willard Brown and Hank Thompson of the Kansas City Monarchs. When the turnstiles failed to respond, the Browns released both Brown and Thompson, although the latter had established himself as a top prospect. In the National League, the Dodgers signed Dan Bankhead to bolster the club's pitching down the stretch. On August 25, Bankhead, the first black pitcher to appear in the major leagues, surrendered eight runs in three innings but also slammed a home run in his initial at bat.

In addition to the five athletes who appeared in the major leagues, a handful of blacks surfaced in the minors. Campanella succeeded Robinson at Montreal, earning accolades as "the best catcher in the business." Newcombe returned to Nashua where he won 19 games. The independent Stamford Bombers of the Colonial League fielded six black players, and two blacks, including future major leaguer Chuck Harmon, played in the Canadian-American League. Veteran Negro League hurler Nate Moreland won 20 games in California's Class C Sunset League. For the most part, however, organized baseball continued to ignore the treasure trove of black talent submerged in the Negro Leagues. A full year would pass before additional major league teams would add black players to their chains.

In 1948, the integration focus shifted from the Dodgers, where Robinson now reigned at second base, to the Cleveland Indians. In spring training, Larry Doby, who had performed so dismally in 1947, unexpectedly won a starting berth in the Cleveland outfield. After an erratic early season stretch in which Doby alternated errors and strikeouts with tape-measure home runs, he batted .301 and became a key performer for the American League champion Indians. In July, Cleveland owner Bill Veeck added the legendary Satchel Paige to the team. Amidst charges that his signing had been a publicity stunt, the 42-year-old Paige won six out of seven decisions, including back-to-back shutouts, and posted a 2.47 earned run average. Standing-room-only crowds greeted him in Washington, Chicago, Boston, and even in Cleveland's mammoth Municipal Stadium. The Indians, after defeating the Boston Red Sox in a pennant playoff, won the World Series in six games with Doby's .318 average leading the club.

In 1947, the Dodgers had integrated and reached the World Series; in 1948, the Indians had duplicated and surpassed this achievement. Both teams had set all-time attendance records. Remarkably, as the 1948 season drew to a close, no other franchise had followed their lead. In the minor leagues, Roy Campanella became the first black in the American Association, stopping at St. Paul before permanently joining Robinson on the Dodgers. Newcombe and Bankhead each won more than 20 games for Brooklyn affiliates. The Dodgers also added fleet-footed Sam Jethroe to the Montreal roster, where he batted .322. The Indians also began to stockpile black talent, signing future major leaguers Al Smith, Dave Hoskins, and Orestes "Minnie" Minoso to minor league contracts. Several other blacks, including San Diego catcher John Ritchey, who broke the Pacific Coast League color line, played for independent teams.

In the interregnum between the 1948 and 1949 seasons four more teams—the Giants, Yankees, Braves, and Cubs—signed blacks to play in their farm systems, and 1949 would herald the beginning of widespread integration in the minor leagues. Blacks starred in all three Triple A leagues. In the Pacific Coast League, Luke Easter won acclaim as the "greatest natural hitter . . . since Ted Williams," amassing 25 home runs and 92 runs-batted-in in just 80 games before succumbing to a knee injury. Oakland's Artie Wilson led the league in hits, stolen bases, and batting average. In the International League, Jethroe scored 151 runs and stole 89 bases while Montreal teammate Dan Bankhead won 20 games for the second straight year. At Jersey City, Monte Irvin batted .373. The outstanding performer in the American Association was Ray Dandridge. Considered by many the greatest third baseman of all time, the acrobatic Dandridge, now in his late 30s, thrilled Minneapolis fans with his spectacular fielding, batting .364 in the process. Former Negro Leaguers turned in equally stellar performances at lower minor league levels as well.

In the major leagues, the spotlight again returned to Jackie Robinson. For three years, Robinson had honored his pledge to Branch Rickey "to turn the other cheek" and avoid confrontations. With his position in the majors firmly established, Robinson announced, "They better be prepared to be rough this year, because I'm going to be rough on them." The more combative Robinson produced his finest year, batting .342 and earning the Most Valuable Player Award. Complemented by teammates Newcombe and Campanella, Robinson led the Dodgers to another pennant.

By the end of the 1949 season, integration had achieved spectacular success at both the major and minor league level, but most teams moved "with all deliberate speed" in signing black players. The New York Giants joined the interracial ranks in 1949 when they promoted Monte Irvin and Hank Thompson. The following year, the Boston Braves purchased Jethroe from the Dodgers for $100,000 and installed him in the starting lineup. In 1951, the Chicago White Sox acquired Minnie Minoso in a trade with Cleveland, and Bill Veeck, who had acquired the hapless St. Louis Browns, brought back Satchel Paige for another major league stint. Yet, as late as August 1953, out of sixteen major league teams only these six fielded black players. Several teams displayed an interest in signing blacks but bypassed established Negro League stars who might have jumped directly to the majors, concentrating instead on younger prospects for the minor leagues. Still others like the Red Sox, Phillies, Cardinals, and Tigers continued to pursue a whites-only policy.

This failure to hire and promote blacks occurred amidst a continuing backdrop of outstanding performances by black players. The first generation of players from the Negro Leagues proved an extraordinary group. Jackie Robinson quickly established himself as one of the dominant stars in the national pastime, compiling a .311 batting average over his 10-year career while thrilling fans with his baserunning and clutch-hitting talents. Sportswriters called him, "the most dangerous man in baseball today." Campanella won accolades as the best catcher in the National League and won the Most Valuable Player Award in 1951, 1953, and 1955. Both Campanella and Robinson later won election to the Baseball Hall of Fame. Pitcher Don Newcombe averaged better than 20 wins a season during his first five full years with the Dodgers. In addition, from 1950-1953 Negro League graduates Sam Jethroe, Willie Mays, Joe Black, and Jim Gilliam each won the National League Rookie of the Year Award.

In the American League, where integration proceeded at a slower pace, several players compiled outstanding records. Larry Doby, while never achieving the superstar status many expected, nonetheless became a steady producer, twice leading the league in home runs and five times driving in more than 100 runs. His Cleveland teammate Luke Easter, who reached the majors in his mid-30s, slugged 86 home runs and drove in 300 runs in his brief three-season career. Satchel Paige, after a two-year stint with the Indians, joined the hapless St. Louis Browns from 1951-1953 and became one of the American League's best relief pitchers. On the Chicago White Sox, Minnie Minoso proved himself a consistent .300 hitter. Despite their relatively small numbers, teams with black players in both major leagues regularly finished high in the standings and only in 1950 did both pennant winners field all-white squads. In addition, the more aggressive stance of National League teams in recruiting black players gave that circuit a clear superiority in World Series and All-Star contests for more than two decades.

By the end of the 1953 season, the benefits of integration had grown apparent to all but the most recalcitrant of major league owners. In September, the Chicago Cubs purchased shortstop Ernie Banks from the Kansas City Monarchs and finally elevated longtime minor league standout Gene Baker. Connie Mack's Philadelphia Athletics ended their Jim Crow era by acquiring pitcher Bob Trice. At the start of the 1954 season, the Washington Senators, St. Louis Cardinals, Pittsburgh Pirates, and Cincinnati Reds all joined the interracial ranks. The sudden integration of six more clubs left only the Yankees, Tigers, Phillies, and Red Sox with all-white personnel. In addition, 1954 marked the debut of young Henry Aaron with the Braves and the return of Willie Mays, who had sparkled for the Giants in 1951, from military service.

The desegregation of organized baseball opened the way not only to blacks in the United States but to those in other parts of the Americas as well. Throughout the 20th century, baseball had imposed a curious double standard on Latin players, accepting those with light complexions but rejecting their darker countrymen. With the color barrier down, major league clubs found a wealth of talent in the Carribbean. Minnie Minoso, the "Cuban Comet" who integrated the Chicago White Sox, became the first of the great Latin stars. Over a 15-year career, Minoso compiled a .298 batting average. In 1954, slick-fielding Puerto Rican Vic Power launched his career with the Athletics. The following year, Roberto Clemente, the greatest of the Latin stars, debuted with the Pittsburgh Pirates. The proud Puerto Rican won four batting championships and amassed 3,000 hits en route to a .317 lifetime batting average. In the late 1950s, the San Francisco Giants revealed the previously ignored treasure trove that existed in the Dominican Republic. In 1958, Felipe Alou became the first of three Alou brothers to play for the Giants, and in 1960 the Giants unveiled pitcher Juan Marichal, "the Dominican Dandy," who won 243 games en route to the Hall of Fame.

Among the early Latin players were two sons of stars of the Jim Crow age. Perucho Cepeda, who had won renown as "The Bull" in his native Puerto Rico, had refused to play in the segregated Negro leagues. His son Orlando, dubbed "The Baby Bull," went on to star for the Giants and Cardinals. Luis Tiant, Sr., a standout performer in both Cuba and the Negro Leagues, lived to see Luis, Jr. win over 200 major league games and excel in the 1975 World Series.

As the major leagues moved slowly toward complete desegregation, throughout the nation blacks invaded the minor leagues. In the Northern and Western states, these athletes, a combination of youthful prospects and Negro League veterans, were greeted by a storm of insults, beanballs, and discrimination. "I learned more names than I thought we had," states Piper Davis of his treatment by fans in the Pacific Coast League. At least a half-dozen blacks had to be carried off the field on stretchers after being hit by pitches between 1949 and 1951. In city after city, blacks found hotels and restaurants unwilling to serve them. "At the same time when they signed blacks and Latins," argues John Roseboro about his Dodger employers, "they should have made sure they would be welcome." But neither the Dodgers nor other clubs provided any special assistance for their black farmhands. Despite these conditions, blacks compiled remarkable records in league after league. In the early 1950s, blacks overcame adversity and dominated the lists of batting leaders at the Triple A level and in many of the lower circuits as well.

In 1952, blacks began to appear on minor league clubs in the Jim Crow South. The Dallas Eagles of the Texas League, hoping to boost sagging attendance, signed former Homestead Gray pitcher Dave Hoskins to become the "Jackie Robinson of the Texas League." Hoskins took the Lone Star State by storm, attracting record crowds en route to a 22–10 record. The black pitcher posted a 2.12 earned run average and also finished third in the league in batting with a .328 mark. By 1955, every Texas League club except Shreveport fielded black players.

Hoskins' performance inspired other teams throughout the South to scramble for black players. In 1953, 19-year-old Henry Aaron desegregated the South Atlantic League, which included clubs in Florida, Atlanta, and Georgia, while Bill White appeared in the Carolina League. Playing for Jacksonville (a city which seven years earlier had barred Jackie Robinson), Aaron "led the league in everything but hotel accommodations." By 1954, when the United States Supreme Court issued its historic *Brown* v. *Board of Education* decision ordering school desegrega-

tion, blacks had appeared in most Southern minor leagues.

The integration of the South, however, did not proceed without incidents. Black players recall these years as "an ordeal" or a "sentence" and described the South as "enemy country" or a "hellhole." In 1953, the Cotton States League barred brothers Jim and Leander Tugerson from competing. The following year, Nat Peeples broke the color line in the Southern Association, but lasted only two weeks. For the remainder of the decade, the league adhered to a whites-only policy, a strategy which contributed to the collapse of the Southern Association in 1961. As resistance to the civil rights movement mounted in the 1950s, black players found themselves in increasingly hostile territory. Even in the pioneering Texas League, teams visiting Shreveport, Louisiana, in 1956 had to leave their black players at home due to stricter segregation laws.

In the face of these obstacles, young black stars like Aaron, Curt Flood, Frank Robinson, Bill White, and Leon Wagner overcame their frustrations "by taking it out on the ball." "What had started as a chance to test my baseball ability in a professional setting," wrote Curt Flood, "had become an obligation to test myself as a man." Throughout the 1950s, blacks appeared regularly among the league leaders of the Texas, South Atlantic, Carolina, and other circuits, advancing both their own careers and the cause of integration.

As these events unfolded in the South, the major leagues completed their long overdue integration process. In 1955, the Yankees, after denying charges of racism for almost a decade, finally promoted Elston Howard to the parent club. Two more years passed before the Phillies integrated, and not until 1958 did a black player don a Tiger uniform. Thus, at the start of the 1959 season, only the Boston Red Sox, who had yet to hire either black scouts or representatives in the Caribbean, retained their Jim Crow heritage. A storm of protest arose when the Red Sox cut black infielder Elijah "Pumpsie" Green just before Opening Day, but on July 21, 1959, 12 years and 107 days after Jackie Robinson's Dodger debut, Green won promotion to the Boston club, completing the cycle of major league integration.

While integration became a reality in organized baseball, the Negro Leagues gradually faded into oblivion. As early as 1947, Negro League attendance, especially in cities close to National League parks, dropped precipitously. "People wanted to go Brooklynites," recalls Monarch pitcher Hilton Smith. "Even if we were playing here in Kansas City, people wanted to go over to St. Louis to see Jackie." Negro League owners hoped to offset declining attendance by selling players to organized baseball, but major league teams paid what Effa Manley called "bargain basement" prices for all-star talent. In 1948, the Manleys' Newark Eagles and New York Black Yankees disbanded. The Homestead Grays severed all league connections and returned to its roots as a barnstorming unit. Without these teams, the Negro National League collapsed. A reorganized 10-team Negro American League, most of whose franchises were located in minor league cities, vowed to go on, but the spread of integration quickly thinned its ranks. By 1951, the league had dwindled to six teams. Two years later, only the Birmingham

Black Barons, Memphis Red Sox, Kansas City Monarchs, and Indianapolis Clowns remained.

For several years in the early 1950s, the Negro Leagues remained a breeding ground for young black talent. The New York Giants plucked Willie Mays from the roster of the Birmingham Black Barons, while the Boston Braves discovered Hank Aaron on the Indianapolis Clowns. The Kansas City Monarchs produced more than two dozen major leaguers, including Robinson, Paige, Banks, and Howard. But for most black players, the demise of the Negro Leagues had disastrous effects. "The livelihoods, the careers, the families of 400 Negro ballplayers are in jeopardy," complained Effa Manley in 1948, "because four players were successful in getting into the major leagues." The slow pace of integration left most in a state of limbo set adrift by their former teams, but still unwelcomed in organized baseball. Some players like Buck Leonard and Cool Papa Bell were too old to be considered, while others like Ray Dandridge and Piper Davis found themselves relegated to the minor leagues, where outstanding records failed to win them promotion.

Throughout the 1950s the Negro American League struggled to survive, recruiting teenagers and second-rate talent for the modest four-team loop. In 1963, Kansas City hosted the 30th and last East-West All-Star Game and the following year the famed Monarchs ceased touring the nation. By 1965, the Indianapolis Clowns remained as a last vestige of Jim Crow baseball. Utilizing white as well as black players, the Clowns continued for another decade. "We are all show now," explained their owner. "We clown, clown, clown."

But the legacy of the Negro Leagues remained. Robinson and other early black players introduced new elements of speed and "tricky baseball" into the major leagues, transforming and improving the quality of play. Since 1947, blacks have led the National League in stolen bases in all but two seasons. In the American League, a black or Latin baserunner has topped the league every year since 1951 with only two exceptions. Nor did this injection of speed come at the expense of power. In the 1950s and 1960s, Hank Aaron, Willie Mays, and Frank Robinson reigned as the greatest power hitters in baseball. Thus, by the 1960s, the national pastime more closely resembled the well-balanced offensive structure of the Negro Leagues than the unidimensional power-oriented attack that had typified the all-white majors.

The demise of the Negro Leagues and the decline of segregation in the majors, however, did not end discrimination. Conditions on and off the field, in spring training and in the executive suites, repeatedly reminded the black athletes of their second-class status. In the early 1950s, all-white teams taunted their black opponents with racial insults. Blacks like Jackie and Frank Robinson, Minnie Minoso and Luke Easter repeatedly appeared among the league leaders in being hit by pitches. While black superstars like Willie Mays had little difficulty ascending to the major leagues, players of only slightly above average talent found themselves buried for years in the minors. Many observers charged that teams had imposed quotas on the number of blacks they would field at one time.

In cities like St. Louis, Washington, D. C., and, later, Baltimore, black ballplayers could not stay at hotels with their teammates. In 1954, they achieved a breakthrough of sorts when the luxury Chase Hotel in St. Louis informed Jackie Robinson and other Dodger players that they could room there, but had to refrain from using the dining room or swimming pool or loitering in the lobby. Ten years later, the hotel had removed these restrictions, but still relegated black players, according to Hank Aaron, to rooms "looking out over some old building or some green pastures or a blank wall, so nobody can see us through a window."

Blacks faced even greater discrimination each year in spring training in Florida. While all spring training sites now accepted blacks, segregation statutes and local traditions forced them to live in all-black boarding houses far from the luxury air-conditioned hotels which accommodated white players. "The whole set-up is wrong," protested Jackie Robinson. "There is no reason why we shouldn't be able to live with our teammates." When teams traveled from place to place, blacks could not join their fellow players in restaurants. Instead they had to wait on the bus until someone brought their food out to them. Some teams attempted to reduce the problems faced by blacks. Several clubs moved to Arizona, where conditions were only moderately improved. The Dodgers built a special spring training camp at Vero Beach where players could live together. Most organizations, however, did very little to assist their black employees.

By the time that Jackie Robinson retired in 1956, conditions had barely improved. "After 10 years of traveling in the South," he charged, " I don't think advances have been fast enough. It's my belief that baseball itself hasn't done all it can to remedy the problems faced by . . . players." Over the next decade, a new generation of black players militantly demanded change. Cardinal stars Bill White, Curt Flood, and Bob Gibson protested against conditions in St. Petersburg, while Aaron and other black Braves demanded changes in Bradenton. In many instances, however, significant changes awaited passage of the Civil Rights Act of 1965 barring segregation in public facilities.

By 1960, Robinson, Campanella, Doby, and the cadre of Negro League veterans who had formed the vanguard of baseball integration had retired. In their wake, a second generation of black players, most of whom had never appeared in the Negro Leagues, made most Americans forget that Jim Crow baseball had ever existed, as they shattered longstanding "unbreakable" records. In 1962, black shortstop Maury Wills stole 104 bases, eclipsing Ty Cobb's 47-year-old stolen base mark. Twelve years later, outfielder Lou Brock stole 118 bases en route to breaking Cobb's career stolen-base record as well. In 1966, Frank Robinson, who had won the National League Most Valuable Player Award in 1961, became the first player to win that honor in both leagues when he led the Baltimore Orioles to the American League pennant. By the end of his career, Robinson had slugged 586 home runs; only Babe Ruth among players of the Jim Crow era had hit more. Both Ernie Banks and Willie McCovey also amassed more than 500 home runs during this era. On the pitcher's mound, the indomitable Bob Gibson proved himself one of the greatest strikeout pitchers in the game's history. Upon retirement, Gibson had amassed more strikeouts than anyone except Walter Johnson. Brock, Frank Robinson, Banks, McCovey, and Gibson all won election to the Hall of Fame in their first year of eligibility.

The greatness of these players notwithstanding, two other black players, Willie Mays and Hank Aaron, both of whom ironically had begun their careers in the Negro Leagues, reigned as the dominant stars of baseball in the 1950s and 1960s. Originally signed by the Birmingham Black Barons of the Negro American League, Mays had joined the New York Giants in midseason 1951, sparking their triumph in the most famous pennant race in history and winning the Rookie of the Year Award. After two years in the military, he returned in 1954 to bat a league-leading .345 and hit 41 home runs. The following year, he pounded 51 homers. A spectacular center fielder, Mays won widespread acclaim as the greatest all-around player in the history of the game. In 1969, he became only the second player in major league history to hit 600 home runs and took aim at Babe Ruth's legendary lifetime total of 714. Over the next four seasons, the aging Mays added 60 more homers before retiring, still well short of Ruth's record.

Unlike Mays, who had begun his career amidst the glare of the New York media, Hank Aaron had spent his career first in Milwaukee and later in Atlanta, far distant from the center of national publicity. Nonetheless, he steadily compiled record-threatening statistics in almost every offensive category. In 1972, at age 38, he surpassed Mays's home run total and set his sights on Ruth. Entering the 1973 season, he needed just 41 home runs to catch the Babe. Performing under tremendous pressure and fanfare, Aaron stroked 40 homers, leaving him just one shy of the record. He tied Ruth's mark with his first swing of the 1974 season. Three days later, on April 8, 1974, a nationwide television audience watched Aaron stroke home run number 715. Babe Ruth's "unreachable" record thus fell to a man whose career had started with the Indianapolis Clowns of the Negro Leagues. When Aaron retired in 1976, he boasted 755 home runs and held major league records for games played, at-bats, runs batted in and extra-base hits. He also ranked second to Ty Cobb in hits and runs scored.

By the 1970s, black players had become an accepted part of the baseball scene and regularly ranked among the most well-known symbols of the sport. Reggie Jackson, Willie Stargell, and Joe Morgan had succeeded Aaron, Mays, and the Robinsons as Hall of Fame caliber superstars. Yet three decades after Jackie Robinson had broken the color barrier, racism and discrimination remained a persistent problem for baseball. Several studies demonstrated that baseball management channeled blacks into positions thought to require less thinking and fewer leadership qualities. In 1968, blacks accounted for more than half of the major league outfielders, but only 20 percent of other position players. Black catchers were rare and fewer than one in 10 pitchers were black. By 1986, the disparity had grown greater. American-born blacks comprised 70 percent of all outfield positions but only 7 percent of all pitcher, second basemen, and third basemen positions. There were no American-born black catchers in the major leagues at the start of the 1986 season; the nineties, however, saw some progress with the appearance of Charles Johnson and Lenny Webster.

While superior black players had open access to the major leagues, those of average or slightly above average skills often found their paths blocked. "The Negro player may have to be better qualified than a white player to win the same position," argued Aaron Rosenblatt in 1967. "The undistinguished Negro player is less likely to play in the major leagues than the equally undistinguished white player." Rosenblatt demonstrated that black major leaguers on the whole batted 20 points higher than whites. As batting averages dropped, so did the proportion of blacks. This trend continued into the 1980s. A 1982 study revealed that 70 percent of all black non-pitchers were everyday starters, indicating a substantial bias against blacks who filled utility or pinch-hitting roles. Statistics compiled in 1986 showed a strikingly similar pattern.

The subtle nature of this on-the-field discrimination obscured it from public controversy. The failure of baseball to provide jobs for blacks in managerial and front office positions, however, became an increasing embarrassment. In the early years of integration, baseball executives bypassed the substantial pool of experienced Negro Leaguers from consideration for managerial and coaching positions. A handful of blacks, including Sam Bankhead, Nate Moreland, Marvin Williams, and Chet Brewer managed independent, predominantly all-black teams in the minor leagues. The first generation of black major leaguers fared no better. "We bring dollars into club treasuries when we play," exclaimed Larry Doby, "but when we stop playing, our dollars stop." No major league organization hired a black pilot at any level until 1961 when the Pittsburgh Pirates placed Gene Baker at the helm of their Batavia franchise. By the mid-1960s no blacks had managed in the majors and only two had held full-time major league coaching positions. The first black umpire did not appear in the majors until 1966, when Emmett Ashford appeared in the American League.

In the final years of his life, Jackie Robinson made repeated pleas for baseball to eliminate these lingering vestiges of Jim Crow. "I'd like to live to see a black manager," he stated before a national television audience at the 1972 World Series. Nine days later he died, his dream unfulfilled. In 1975, the Cleveland Indians hired Frank Robinson to be the first black major league manager. This precedent, however, opened few new doors. Robinson lasted two-and-a-half seasons with the Indians, later managed the San Francisco Giants for four years, and in 1988 was made manager of the Baltimore Orioles. Maury Wills and Larry Doby each had brief half-season stints as managers. After four decades of integration, only these three men had received major league managerial opportunities.

A similar situation existed in major league front offices. Only one black man, Bill Lucas of the Atlanta Braves, had served as a general manager. As late as 1982, a survey of 24 clubs (the Yankees and Red Sox refused to provide information) found that of 913 available white-collar baseball jobs, blacks held just 32 positions. Among 568 full-time major league scouts, only 15 were black. While many teams hired former players as announcers, few employed blacks in these roles. Five years later, conditions had not improved. Of the top 879 administrative positions in baseball only 17 were filled by blacks and 15 by Hispanics. Four teams in California—the Dodgers, Giants, Athletics, and Angels—accounted for almost two-thirds of the minority hiring. Ten out of 14 American League teams, and five of 12 National League franchises had no blacks in management positions.

These shortcomings came to haunt baseball in 1987. Commissioner Peter Ueberroth had dedicated the season to the commemoration of the fortieth anniversary of Jackie Robinson's major league debut. As the celebration began, Los Angeles Dodger general manager Al Campanis, who had played with Robinson at Montreal, appeared on ABC-TV's *Nightline*. When asked about the dearth of black managers, Campanis explained that blacks "may not have some of the necessities to be, let's say, a field manager or general manager." Campanis's statement, which surely reflected the thinking of many baseball executives, evoked a storm of protest, and precipitated his resignation. An embarrassed Ueberroth pledged to take action to bring more blacks into leadership positions and hired University of California sociologist Harry Edwards to facilitate the process. Fifty blacks and Latins with past or present connections to baseball created their own Minority Baseball Network to apprise blacks of employment opportunities and to lobby clubs to recruit more minorities for front office jobs.

When the controversy of 1987 had subsided, few franchises had taken significant steps to increase minority hiring. Several clubs added blacks to administrative positions, but none offered field or general manager positions to nonwhite candidates (although Bill White was named National League president). In 1988 Frank Robinson received his third chance to manage in the major leagues, this time with the Baltimore Orioles. At midseason 1989 Cito Gaston assumed the reins of the Toronto Blue Jays. When the squads managed by Robinson and Gaston had their initial confrontation, it marked, after 40 years of integration, the first time that two teams managed by black men had competed in a major league game. Fittingly, on the final weekend of the season, the Orioles and Blue Jays met face-to-face in a series to decide the championship of the American League Eastern Division. The spectacle offered a resounding rebuke to the shortsightedness and discrimination that continue to plague the national pastime.

By the 1993 season baseball seemed to have finally made some real progress in including minorities in its managerial ranks. The season saw five black and Hispanic field managers: Gaston, who after five years at the helm of the Blue Jays ranked as one of the most successful managers in baseball history, winning four divisional championships, two pennants and two world championships; Felipe Alou, who led the Montreal Expos to consecutive second place finishes; Dusty Baker, who became the winningest

rookie manager ever, when his San Francisco Giants won 103 games (after winning only 72 games the year before); Don Baylor, who would pilot the expansion Colorado Rockies into the playoffs in only their third year of existence in 1995; and Tony Perez, who started the season as the manager of the Cincinnati Reds.

Progress extended into other areas of hiring as well. By 1995, 27 percent of all coaches were black or latino. Minority hiring in the front office expanded to 17 percent in 1992, a level which held steady through 1994. The Houston Astros named Bob Watson their general manager, making him the second black man to assume these responsibilities. (Watson assumed the same position with the New York Yankees in 1996; under his stewardship the club won the World Championship.) Also in 1994, Leonard Coleman succeeded Bill White as National League vice-president.

These undeniable gains, however, occurred against a backdrop of continuing racial controversy. There are no American minority owners of major league clubs. All twenty-eight chief executive officers are white. Watson remains the sole minority general manager. Black stars still complain about unequal treatment of midlevel black players. In addition, the proportion of American-born black players in baseball's major leagues dropped from one in four in the late 1960s to only one in six in the late 1980s. In minor league and college baseball, important sources of major league talent, the percentage of African-Americans was even lower. Surveys indicated that African-Americans, who had flocked to major league ballparks in the 1950s, now accounted for one out of every fourteen fans.

Allegations that Cincinnati Reds owner Marge Schott had repeatedly used racial slurs (and that other owners had ignored these offenses) led to her suspension in 1993. When the Reds first hired, then unceremoniously fired, Perez as manager after a poor start, it appeared to some that the team had shamefully manipulated a local hero to evade charges of discrimination.

During the early 1990s baseball undertook several initiatives to improve its image among minorities. The major leagues embraced John Young's RBI ("Reviving Baseball in the Inner Cities") program, an effort to entice black youth away from other sports and back to the diamond. Attempts were also made to secure health benefits for surviving Negro League players and to gain Hall of Fame recognition for more stars from the Jim Crow era. Nonetheless, as baseball reached the fiftieth anniversary of the signing of Jackie Robinson, issues of race and discrimination remain as a persistent reminder of the legacy of the past and challenges of the present.

## CHAPTER 15

The Minor Leagues

Bob Hoie

The International Association, founded in 1877, is frequently described as the first minor league. For two major reasons it shouldn't be so regarded. First, it was barely a league. Structurally it resembled the old National Association—there was virtually no central authority, no limitation on the number or location of member teams, no set schedule, and haphazard umpire selection. The league was so loosely assembled in fact that some member teams competed at the same time for the championships of other organizations like the New England Association and the League Alliance. Second, the International Association was originally established as a rival to the National League and never officially recognized itself as being subordinate. It was generally acknowledged that several of its teams were as good as or better than some in the National League. Various off-the-field problems, administrative weaknesses, and a lack of solidarity and resolve on the part of the member clubs assured its subordinate status.

A strong case could be made for the 1879 Northwestern League as the first minor league—it had a preset schedule and had no pretensions of rivaling the National League, but the absence of league-appointed umpires led to frequent forfeits due to charges of biased "hometown" umpiring, and the league folded after only two months.

The Eastern Association was founded in 1881, but this was another loose alliance with no set schedule.

The first recognized minor league was another Northwestern League, this one organized on October 27, 1882. At that time they requested of the National League cooperation and reciprocity in protecting player contracts. This was necessary because independent clubs frequently lost their best players during the course of the season to the National League and later to the American Association clubs. In response to this request, the National League, American Association, and Northwestern League signed a "Tripartite Agreement" in March 1883. This agreement bound the clubs to honor the contracts of players on reserve lists, assured mutual recognition of expulsions and suspensions, established territorial rights, and created an arbitration committee to settle disputes. Minimum salaries were established and pegged at a higher level in the National League and American Association than in the Northwestern League or "any other parties to the agreement," thus by implication assigning a "major" and "minor" status to the leagues.

The Interstate Association was established early in 1883 and was quickly accepted as an "alliance" league by the American Association, becoming a junior partner of the Tripartite Agreement. Both the Northwestern and the Interstate opened their seasons on May 1, 1883. Each had a formal league organization, a schedule that was preset before the season opening, and a complement of umpires appointed and paid for by the league. Both leagues recognized and accepted their status as subordinate to the two "majors." In 1884 the Interstate Association reorganized as the Eastern League and became a fourth member of what now became known as the National Agreement.

In October 1885 a new National Agreement was adopted which made the National League and American Association the principal parties and removed from minor league clubs the protection of the reserve clause. Two years later the reserve clause was reinstated for the minors, but the major-minor league distinction had been formalized. Following the collapse of the American Association in 1892, another National Agreement for the first time established minor league classifications and gave major league clubs the right to draft minor league players at fixed prices.

While these events were taking place, organized baseball expanded dramatically, going from two minor leagues in 1883 to seventeen by 1888. Baseball was played throughout the country, of course, but organized ball was confined to the northeast quadrant of the United States in 1884; it expanded to the South in 1885, to Colorado and the upper Midwest in 1886, California in 1887, Texas in 1888, and the Pacific Northwest in 1890. So in the year that the American frontier was officially declared closed, organized baseball had extended to all corners of the country.

In 1887 an organization called the Negro Baseball League, fearing player raids by the still moderately integrated minors, sought and received protection under the National Agreement. The league was to play in eight cities that also had major league teams, but it folded in less than two weeks. This was unfortunately characteristic of the era. Many teams and leagues were underfinanced and were ultrasensitive to changes in the national or local economy. In addition, being unable or unwilling to pay the required fees for reserving their players, they lost their better ones at the close of the season—and those teams that even managed to finish the season could usually consider themselves lucky. During the nineteenth century, more than 40 percent of the leagues that started a season failed to finish it. There was, however, a solid core of support for minor league baseball. Regardless of how many leagues started each season—usually about fifteen but often as many as twenty—only eight to to ten usually finished; the rest failed. The 1890s were not a period of expansion nor of stability as throughout the decade nearly half of the leagues that started a season failed to finish it.

A depression in 1893 and the Spanish-American War in 1898 were significant factors, but a proliferation of "fly-by-night" operators played a role as well.

At the close of the 1900 season, the still minor American League withdrew from the National Agreement, announcing through that action its intention not to allow its players to be drafted and not to respect the reserve clause or territorial rights any longer.

In September 1901 the National League announced its intention to abrogate the National Agreement, contending that with the American League invading its cities and raiding its players the National League could not be expected to sit back and abide by restrictions which did not hinder its rival. Essentially this meant that the National, like the American, considered the players on minor league rosters "fair game."

In immediate reaction to this, the presidents of seven minor leagues met in Chicago on September 5, 1901, and in an act of self-protection they organized the National Association of Professional Baseball Leagues. On October 25 representatives of nine minor leagues met in New York and adopted a new "National Agreement." This new agreement established league classifications, roster and salary limits, and a draft system; it recognized reserve lists and created a Board of Arbitration which was given the power to suspend players, clubs, or officials for violations of the agreement. By the beginning of the 1902 season, the National Association included fifteen member leagues.

The American and National Leagues ratified a peace agreement early in 1903, and in late August the presidents of the two major leagues and the National Association drafted a National Agreement which was initially rejected by the minors. After some concessions were made by the majors, such as a prohibition on "farming," the plan was adopted in September. The agreement formalized relations between the majors and minors and established a National Commission to serve as a Board of Arbitration.

These agreements were necessary because the majors and minors were mutually dependent on each other. The majors needed the minors as a reliable source of talent, while the minors, many of whom relied on player sales to stay in business, needed assurances from the majors that they would recognize their property rights in players.

Despite this mutual dependence there was a basic buyer-seller conflict. The majors wanted to acquire players as cheaply as possible, while the minors wanted to sell them for as much as possible. This same conflict existed within the minors as well, with the highest-classification clubs wanting to buy cheaply from the lower minors and sell at high prices to the majors. Thus the National Agreement, the major-minor agreement, and the National Association itself were uneasy alliances of clubs and leagues with competing and often conflicting objectives, and the nearly annual revisions in draft rules and prices and limits on optional player assignments were required to maintain the equilibrium necessary to keep the alliance intact.

The majors favored an unlimited draft—i.e., any player on a minor league roster could be purchased for a fixed rate. As early as 1896, when Minneapolis of the Western League was decimated through what were in effect forced sales, it became clear that some limitations were necessary, so by 1905 only one player could be drafted from a club per year. The draft prices of top-classification minor leaguers went from $750 to $1,000 in 1905 and then to $2,500 in 1911. While these prices were not particularly low for average prospects in that era, they were well below the value of the best prospects in the minors; thus the draft or the threat of it served as an incentive for minor league clubs at all levels to sell their better players to major or higher-classification minor league clubs at competitive market prices. From the players' standpoint, the draft had the positive effect of allowing them eventually to advance to whatever levels their ability would take them. The lower-classification minor league clubs received lower draft prices for their players but seemed relatively satisfied with the system—after all, this was an era when the contracts of Tris Speaker, Rogers Hornsby, and Ty Cobb were sold to major league clubs for $400, $500, and $700 respectively.

On the other hand, many of the higher-classification minor league clubs had never really been satisfied with the draft. As early as 1908, this dissatisfaction nearly caused the two top minor leagues at that time—the American Association and the Eastern League—to go independent. Several of the top minor league clubs drew more fans annually than some major league clubs and represented substantial investments; their owners were understandably not happy with a system that forced the sale of their top players for below-market prices to the majors; in addition to the challenge to club stability and autonomy caused by the draft, the gap between the market value of the top prospects and the draft price widened throughout the 1910s.

Despite the rumblings of discontent, the establishment of the National Association ushered in a period of minor league expansion to a fairly stable core of thirty leagues. While there were still leagues that failed to finish the season, the failure rate was down to 10–15 percent. For some reason, in 1910 the minors reached a level never to be topped until the post–World War Two boom era—fifty-two leagues started the season and forty-four finished it. For the next five years more leagues folded, but each season generally closed with forty leagues operating. Then, for reasons that ranged from the automobile, movies, the war in Europe, and the Federal League War, the bottom started to drop out. Forty-three leagues started in the 1914 season, and by the end of the 1918 season only one was operating (ten leagues had started that year—one folded and eight suspended operations due to the war).

After the 1918 season, with most of the lower minors driven out of business, the National Association, for the first time dominated by the higher minors, adopted a resolution demanding that the majors relinquish the right of the draft and end the practice of "farming out" players. When the majors as expected rejected these demands, the National Association withdrew from the National Agreement. Pending a new major agreement, the majors and minors reached general agreement on property rights in players and territorial rights, and the National Commission ruled that the major league draft would be suspended. In addition the minors would not accept major league players on option, meaning that any players owned or controlled by major league clubs in excess of the active player roster limit would have to be sold or released to minor league clubs.

A. R. Tierney, president of two minor leagues and a leader in the fight to end the draft, said, "This means that the minor leagues will be able to build fences for themselves instead of for the major leagues." He predicted expansion of the minors and higher sale prices for the players. He was correct on both counts. With no players on option, the majors needed to buy more players from the minors, some of whom they had been forced to sell but now had to buy back at higher prices, and without the draft the minor league clubs could virtually name their own price. The minors expanded, as the leagues that had been driven out of business during the war now reentered the fold.

The reappearance of the low minors again shifted the balance of power within the minors. The higher minors had never been happy with the one-league, one-vote system in the National Association. Club owners were wary of having their investments affected by the vote of what they perceived as little more than "fly-by-night" operators, and on occasion they tried to change the arrangement. But just as the majors needed the minors, so the high minors needed the low minors. Thus the high minors always stopped short of enacting measures that might drive their underlings out of the Association.

As noted previously, many of the low minors needed the revenues they received from the draft to survive, and although the minor league draft still existed, it had ceased to be a dependable source of revenue as the combination of numerous prewar minor league failures and returning military veterans yielded more than enough talent to fill the higher minors' rosters. In addition, many of the low-minor clubs did not have the resources to scout for and sign enough players to remain competitive on the field and/or at the box office; thus they were dependent on receiving some players on option.

So while most of the higher minor leagues were prospering as never before under the new independence, by 1920 the low minors were ready to withdraw from the National Association if a new agreement with the majors restoring the draft was not adopted. In addition, some of the higher minor league clubs were upset that the "no-farming" rules were being circumvented by "gentleman's agreements" which enabled the major league clubs to "sell" a player to a minor league club and "buy" him back at the end of the season with little or no money actually changing hands.

On January 10, 1921, a new major-minor league agreement was signed which restored the major league draft with a top price of $5,000 but as a compromise gave individual minor leagues the right to be exempt from the draft; in addition major league clubs could option up to eight players for no more than two consecutive years, and a tax on player sales was instituted to help reduce the fake player transfers. Quickly the top three minors—the International League, Pacific Coast League, and the American Association—together with the Western and Three-I Leagues declared their exemption from the draft; this in turn prohibited them from drafting from the lower minors.

The prices the majors paid for top minor league players nearly doubled between 1919 and 1920, but they skyrocketed during the draft-exemption era. In 1921 the Giants paid $75,000 to San Francisco for Jimmy O'Connell; in 1922 the Giants paid $72,000 to Baltimore for Jack Bent-ley and the White Sox paid $100,000 to San Francisco for Willie Kamm. The majors clearly were not happy with this situation, and in 1922 they offered to raise the draft price to $7,500, but this failed to lure back the draft-exempt leagues. In early 1923 the majors, after considering but eventually rejecting the idea of a maximum purchase price of $25,000 for any minor league player and/or a boycott of draft-exempt leagues, declared that all players sent to the minors either by sale or option would be subject to the draft and increased the number of players who could be optioned to fifteen. Western League clubs immediately began accepting players on option under these conditions.

The prices for ballplayers remained high in 1923. Baltimore of the International League was reportedly offered $100,000 by Brooklyn for Joe Boley and sold Max Bishop to the Philadelphia A's for $50,000. Salt Lake sold Paul Strand to the A's for a reported $70,000, Louisville sold Earle Combs to the Yankees for $50,000, Toronto sold Red Wingo to the Tigers for $50,000 and Rochester sold Maurice Archdeacon to the White Sox for $50,000, but these were isolated cases. Baltimore, aided by five years of draft exemption, had built a powerhouse, but many of the higher-classification minor league clubs had not been nearly as successful and found that they needed to receive players on option to fill holes and remain competitive. Therefore at the close of the 1923 season all exempt leagues but the International agreed to the modified draft which exempted only those players who had come up through the minors. In 1924, after Baltimore sold Lefty Grove for $100,000 to the A's, the International League also fell into line.

The modified draft did nothing to reduce the prices paid for top minor league stars: Louisville sold Wayland Dean to the Giants for $72,000 in 1924, San Francisco sold Paul Waner and Hal Rhyne to Pittsburgh for $100,000 in 1925, and Baltimore continued selling star players to the majors for big prices—Tommy Thomas to the White Sox in 1925, Joe Boley to the A's in 1926, John Ogden to the Browns and George Earnshaw to the A's in 1927. In 1927 Portland (of the PCL) sold Billy Cissel to the White Sox for a package of cash and players worth over $100,000 and Oakland sold Lyn Lary and Jimmy Reese to the Yankees for $100,000. With prices like these, clubs could afford to lose an occasional Lefty O'Doul or Hack Wilson in the modified draft.

The major-minor agreement expired at the end of the 1927 season, with the National Association members deadlocked on the issue of the draft. The majors and minors were also at an impasse, so the modified draft continued and many of the higher minor league clubs continued to prosper, both through player sales and at the gate. The Los Angeles franchise and ballpark were valued at $2 million, but in the lower minors all was not well through the 1920s. Leagues were operating that never should have been admitted to the National Association—for example, the West Arkansas, which operated in 1924, was comprised of six towns within a 750-square-mile area that had a combined population of 16,000 and played just a 60-game schedule.

In 1929 the rift between the high and low minors widened as the low minors, rebuffed in their efforts to nullify the modified draft agreement, now attempted to impose their own draft exemption—essentially exempting from the draft any player with fewer than two seasons of organized baseball.

Early in 1931 the majors and minors finally adopted a new National Agreement, including a provision which eliminated the modified draft and granted to major league clubs greater control of talent through revised option and draft rules. The higher minors had originally objected, but the majors told them to accept the universal draft or they would no longer have any relations with them—in other words, major league teams would not sell or option players to or buy players from the American Association, the International League, or the Pacific Coast League. While such threats had been taken relatively lightly by the minors in the early days of the draft-exempt leagues, they were now taken seriously enough that in less than a month the three recalcitrant leagues capitulated to the majors' terms. In exchange for all this and largely to secure the support of the low minors, the majors agreed to sign only collegian amateurs, leaving all high-schoolers and sandlotters to the minors. Of course, by this time farm systems had developed to the point that most major league clubs could still sign noncollegian amateurs through their farm clubs.

Milwaukee had sold Fred Schulte to the Browns for a reported $100,000 in 1928, but this was the end of an era. There would be no more $100,000 minor leaguers; in fact there would be few if any minor leaguers sold for as much as $50,000 again. At the 1928 National Association Convention, president Mike Sexton wondered when the majors would own enough clubs to control the National Association. The farm system, an old idea now in the process of being perfected by Branch Rickey, had clearly begun to alter the way the minors operated, and despite the efforts of some—most notably Judge Landis—the trend couldn't be reversed.

The Great Depression caused a contraction of the minors in the early 1930s, but even though a near-record low of fourteen leagues opened the 1933 season, none of them folded. The minors then entered an era of unprecedented growth and stability, reaching forty-four leagues in 1940, with only two leagues failing to finish the season between 1933 and 1941. This can be attributed in part to the substantial involvement of the major leagues through outright ownership or regular infusions of money through working agreements, but there were obviously other factors at work. Judge Bramham, on becoming president of the National Association, instituted a number of reforms, many of which were aimed at getting rid of "fly-by-night" or "shoestring" operators. Minor league baseball was better promoted—they had established a public relations department in 1934—and the advent of night baseball was of incalculable value in generating attendance, which reached 20 million in 1940. Interestingly, that year 54 percent of the minor league clubs were not affiliated with any major league clubs compared to just 37 percent that operated independently in 1936.

World War Two caused the minors to drop to just ten leagues in 1944, but in the first postwar year it was up to forty-three, increasing to an all-time high of fifty-nine in 1949, and during that time no leagues folded. (In 1946 the Mexican National League, set up by organized baseball to compete with the outlaw Mexican League, is listed by the National Association as having folded during the season, but actually it only withdrew from the Association and continued to operate independently.)

According to a general consensus, it was the coming of television that caused the minors to begin to disintegrate. Between 1949 and 1963 the number of minor leagues dropped from fifty-nine to eighteen. Attendance decreased even more sharply, going from 40 million to less than 10 million over the same time period.

By 1963, the minors had become nothing more than a training ground for the majors—90 percent of the clubs were major league affiliates, and most of those that weren't were in the largely autonomous Mexican League. While television was commonly cited as the cause of the minors' contraction, some contended it was a natural response to overexpansion. Gerry Hirn, in an April 1954 *Baseball Digest* article, contended that while the number of minor leagues had dropped from fifty-nine to thirty-six, that was still too many and the minors would be stronger and more efficient if only sixteen to twenty leagues operated. Interestingly, in 1954 three leagues failed to finish the season, the most failures in peacetime since 1932; they remain the last United States–based minor leagues that failed to finish a season (the Inter-American League, which had a team in Miami but was largely based in the Caribbean, failed to finish the 1979 season—the only year it operated).

For reasons that aren't entirely clear, minor league baseball exploded in popularity in the 1980s. Attendance, which had remained stuck at 10–11 million through the 1960s and most of the 1970s, took off in the late 1970s, topping 20 million in 1987 for the first time since 1953. Louisville, which dropped out of organized ball after drawing just 116,000 in 1972, topped a million in 1983. Nashville, which dropped out in 1963 after drawing just 54,000 for the season, drew over half a million in 1980. Buffalo, which drew only 78,000 in 1969 and saw its franchise shifted to Winnipeg the following year, came back to set an all-time minor league attendance record with 1.1 million in 1988. The Louisville franchise, which didn't exist in 1981 (what became the Louisville franchise was at that time in Springfield, Illinois, drawing 120,000), sold for more than $4 million in 1987. In 1990 the far less successful Vancouver franchise sold to Japanese interests for $5.5 million. Minor league franchises that could be picked up in the early 1970s by anyone who would pay the outstanding debts were selling for several million dollars.

The high prices being paid for franchises may have precipitated the major-minor-league crisis of 1990, reminiscent of the battles earlier in the century. The Professional Baseball Agreement which binds the majors and minors was set to expire at the end of 1990. The majors, who under that agreement provided substantial financial support for the minors, proposed a reduction in those subsidies. The majors believed that the now financially healthy minor league clubs should assume a greater share of operational expenses. In addition, the majors wanted the Commissioner's office to have greater control over minor league affairs. The minors felt the majors were trying to usurp their autonomy and, to add injury to insult, charge them for the privilege. If there was no agreement, the majors threatened to place their entire farm systems in spring training complexes in Arizona and Florida. Some minor league operators threatened to go independent and even form a third major league.

In the end, however, the majority of minor league clubs capitulated, believing that they could not afford to operate without players supplied by the major league clubs. The majors would still pick up most of the minor league operators' expenses, but the new agreement (a) eliminated the minors' share of big-league TV revenue, (b) required that the minors pay a share of their ticket revenues to the majors, and (c) established minimum standards that must be met by minor league facilities by 1994 (subsequently extended to 1995). It was generally believed that these changes, by reducing minor league clubs' profits, might stabilize or reduce the value of franchises. However, in 1992 the Las Vegas franchise sold for a record $7 million and some unsuccessful Class A franchises were sold for well over a million dollars each. And the fans kept coming—in 1993 minor league attendance topped 30 million for the first time since 1950, and in 1993 Buffalo went over 1 million in attendance for the sixth consecutive year. In 1994 the Bisons just missed a seventh million-fan season due to two rainouts.

The positive trend of the past fifteen years is not unprecedented, but the minors have been riding a rollercoaster of success and failure over the past century— the Newark franchise which sold for a reported $600,000 during the depths of the Depression didn't even exist twenty years later. Even today the picture is not all positive: between 1987 and 1996 nearly 60 franchises were shifted, usually due to poor attendance. In the past few years these shifts have fueled large attendance increases as teams have moved from "dead" towns to virgin territories with spanking new state-of-the-art facilities. However, the supply of new towns with new ballparks seems to be diminishing and the big success stories of the 1980s have seen their attendance decline. In 1996 Buffalo still drew a robust 825,000 but that was down 300,000 from 1992; Louisville, once over a million, dropped to below half a million; and Nashville, which drew 550,000 as recently as 1990, was down to 300,000. Some clubs still draw less than a thousand a game; and it is generally believed that many clubs still substantially pad their attendance totals. So the current wave of success is somewhat deceptive and history tells us it won't last forever. However, regardless of fluctuations in popularity and economic viability, the minors have been and one can safely assume will continue to be the primary training ground for major league players.

The Players

Great players have passed through the minors, their careers frequently going in opposite directions and occasionally teaming up or crossing in unlikely locations such as Easton, Maryland, where in 1924 Jimmie Foxx broke into organized baseball as a catcher and the player-manager was Home Run Baker in his last season as an active player. There were many others: Rube Waddell and Red Faber with Minneapolis in 1911, young Waite Hoyt and ancient Jesse Burkett with Hartford in 1916, Dazzy Vance and Roger Bresnahan with Toledo in 1917, Chief Bender and Lefty Grove with Baltimore in 1923, and more recently Enos Slaughter and Billy Williams with Houston in 1960.

Former Negro Leaguers, their careers going in diametrical directions, Ray Dandridge and Willie Mays were teammates at Minneapolis in 1951 where another teammate was a seven-year minor league veteran, Hoyt Wilhelm. Wilhelm, a twenty-eight-year-old knuckleballer with a background that included three years in Class D ball and three more in the military service, at that time appeared to be a member of what in that era was a vast army of career minor leaguers, the best of whom held their own with the acknowledged major league greats passing through the minors, but who for a variety of reasons—some good, some not—would themselves spend the bulk of their careers in the minors.

For some of these players who were left behind, the DH rule came fifty years too late, because while they could hit both for average and power, they generally lacked speed or had defensive shortcomings. For others it is less clear what, if any, deficiencies kept them in the minors, but from these groups a few players emerged as true minor league greats whose impact on fans in minor league cities—Buzz Arlett in Oakland, Joe Hauser in Minneapolis, and Bunny Brief in Kansas City, to name a few—was as great as that of more renowned players in major league cities.

The greatest of the minor league players is generally acknowledged to be Buzz Arlett.

Arlett started his career as a right-handed spitball pitcher with the hometown Oakland Oaks in 1918 and went on to win 108 games, twice going over 25 wins in a season. The Detroit Tigers looked at him, but without the spitball, which he wouldn't be able to use in the majors, they did not consider him a prospect. After suffering arm trouble early in 1923, Buzz switched to the outfield. Although he had been nothing more than a fair-hitting pitcher, once becoming a regular he annually averaged nearly .360 with 30 homers and 140 RBIs through the rest of the 1920s, but early in his career as an outfielder a Cardinal scout labeled him "good hit, no field," and it stuck. Finally in 1931 he was purchased by the Phillies. The thirty-two-year-old switch-hitter batted .313 with 18 homers and 73 RBIs in a season when the National League introduced a "dead ball" in reaction to the hitting orgies of 1929–1930. However, at the end of the year Arlett was sent to Baltimore, where in 1932 he hit 4 homers in a game twice within a five-week period and led the league with 54 homers for the season, but he would never return to the majors. He spent another year with Baltimore, when he again won the home run title, a little over a month with Birmingham, and nearly three years with Minneapolis, where he had another home run championship. After a few games with Syracuse in 1937, Arlett's career was over.

In addition to his 108 wins, he hit 432 homers, a minor league record that held up until Hector Espino topped it in 1977. Arlett walked a lot, didn't strike out much, ran pretty well early in his career, had a .341 lifetime batting average—.350 after he became an outfielder—and was the only player to finish in the top five in home runs and slugging percentage in his only season in the majors. In addition, modern statistical analysis, including range factors, suggests he was nowhere near the defensive liability he was portrayed as being. He was big (6-4, 230) and gave the appearance of being lackadaisical, which apparently irritated some of his managers, but the evidence is strong that Arlett, despite nearly two decades spent in the minors, was a major-league-caliber player.

Ike Boone was another player whose hitting feats were not limited to the minors. Boone was a college teammate (at the University of Alabama) of Joe Sewell and Riggs Stephenson; his lifetime major league batting average was .319, and in his only two full seasons in the majors—1924-1925 with the Boston Red Sox—he hit .333 and .330, but due to alleged defensive deficiencies most of his career was spent in the minors. In 1929 with the Missions of San Francisco, Boone probably had the finest season any player has had in the minors. On the all-time minor league list of single-season accomplishments, his 553 total bases that year are first, his 323 hits are second, his 195 runs scored are tied for third, and his 218 RBIs are fourth. On the all-time Pacific Coast League list, his .407 average is second, and his 55 home runs are tied for fourth.

Boone's greatness wasn't confined to a single season; in four of his first eight years in the minors he hit over .400 (he was on his way to perhaps his greatest season in 1930, batting .448 with 22 homers and 96 RBIs when he was sold to Brooklyn in late June). His .402 average with San Antonio in 1923 is the highest in twentieth-century Texas League history; his .389 with New Orleans in 1921 is the fifth highest in the Southern Association; he also led the International League in batting twice. His .370 lifetime average is the minor league record for players with ten or more seasons. He had an exceptional arm, but limited range in the outfield. Although he hit 77 home runs in a season and a half with the Missions, he was not generally regarded as a power hitter. He was, however, a great pure hitter; in eleven of his fourteen seasons in the minors, he hit over .350, and there is no evidence that he couldn't hit major league pitching.

Smead Jolley was an atrocious outfielder. Stories of his defensive lapses are legion, and the statistical evidence suggests those stories are more than isolated anecdotes. Like Boone, Jolley had a powerful arm but no speed; like Arlett, he was big and awkward; and like both, he could hit—majors or minors. In the equivalent of three full major league seasons with the White Sox and Red Sox, he hit .305 and averaged 15 homers and 105 RBIs. He won six minor league batting championships—leading the Pacific Coast League in hitting three times (winning the Triple Crown with San Francisco in 1928) and the International League once. Twice he had over 300 hits in a season, and twice he drove in more than 180 runs. In the thirteen minor league seasons in which he played over 100 games, he had this run: .370, .372, .346, .397, .404, .387, .360, .372, .373, .350, .309, .373, .345. Perhaps because he spent nearly six years in the low minors, the first four as a pitcher, and had a somewhat nomadic career (he was with thirteen minor league teams), he has not always been ranked in the top echelon of minor league greats, yet he may have been the finest hitter of them all.

Minor league stars generally fit two stereotypes: one-dimensional players who could hit but could do nothing else well enough to stay in the majors—justly or not, Arlett, Boone, and Jolley were consigned to this group.

Then there are those who excelled in the minors but couldn't produce in the majors. Perhaps the classic example is Bunny Brief.

Brief, born Antonio Bordetski, may have been the most dominant power hitter in the minor leagues. In major league trials with the Browns, White Sox, and Pirates between 1912 and 1917, he was consistently unimpressive—in a combined 569 at-bats, he hit .223 with 5 homers, 59 RBIs, and nearly 100 strikeouts. In the minors, however, it was a different story. Although he hit 40 or more homers only twice and never had more than 42, he had eight league home run championships. Before going up to the majors, he led the Michigan State League twice; later he led the Pacific Coast League once and the American Association five times. He also led the Association in RBIs five times (four in succession), including a league-record 191 in 1921. He had a six-year stretch (1921–1926) with Kansas City and Milwaukee, where he averaged 90 extra-base hits, 151 RBIs, and a .351 average per season. Brief also drew a lot of walks. Early in his career he had excellent speed, and although he played most of his career at first base, he was the best defensive outfielder of the big minor league sluggers, with good range and an excellent arm—yet for reasons that remain unclear, Brief never played in a major league game after his twenty-fifth birthday.

Nick Cullop was another minor league great who never produced in the majors. He, like many of the great minor league sluggers, began his career as a pitcher. In trials with the Yankees, Senators, Indians, Dodgers, and Reds between 1926 and 1931 he totaled 490 at-bats, hit 11 homers, drove in 67 runs, hit .249, and struck out 128 times. He was the first farm-system minor league star, playing 1,450 games in the Cardinal chain from 1932 to 1944. In the minors, he hit 420 home runs and drove in 1,857 runs, ten times exceeding 100 in a season.

Cullop had good speed early in his career and was a good enough outfielder to play center field into the late 1920s, but he slowed up considerably in the 1930s. While it is not clear why Brief never did well in the majors, Cullop struck out a lot even in the minors and didn't walk much—suggesting that he had holes which could be and were pitched to effectively in the majors.

Ox Eckhardt was a great football star at the University of Texas who after graduation signed with both Austin of the Texas Association and the Cleveland Indians. The resulting dispute delayed his real professional debut for three years until he was twenty-six years old. Ox quickly made up for lost time, hitting .376 with a league leading 27 triples for Wichita and Amarillo in the Western League in 1928. That fall he played for the New York Giants of the NFL. His baseball contract had been acquired by the Detroit Tigers and although he was on their 40 man roster in 1929, 1930, and 1931 he never got into a game with the big club. In 1929 he was sent to Seattle, where he hit .354 and again led the league in triples. In 1930 he went to Beaumont, where he led the Texas League with a .379 average. In 1931 he was sold to the Missions, for whom he led the PCL with a .369 average. In the spring of 1932 he was with the Boston Braves—he played 8 games at the start of the season as a pinch hitter and was then sent back to the Missions, where over the next four seasons he hit .371, .414, .378, and .399, winning the batting title three times. He went to the Dodgers in 1936, lasted 16 games batting just .182, and was sent to Indianapolis, where he hit .353 and .341 over the next two years. He hit .321 with Toledo and Beaumont in 1938, .361 with Memphis in 1939, and after hitting .293 with Dallas in 1940, he retired with a minor league career batting average of .367 and the highest career average in organized baseball—.365. (Ty Cobb's minor league record drops his overall average to .3630; Ike Boone's major league record drops his organized-baseball average to .3629.) Eckhardt has the highest single-season and career batting average in the PCL, and ten times he hit over .350.

Unlike many of the minor league stars, Eckhardt did not want for opportunities to play in the majors—counting a trial with the Indians in 1925, he had six shots, but they resulted in his playing in just 24 major league games. The reasons for his failure to make it in the majors are not obscure. Despite being an exceptional athlete with good speed early in his career, he was a poor fielder with a weak arm and no power. Although he was 6-1, 190, the left-handed-hitting Eckhardt slapped the ball to left field. Reportedly managers tried to get him to pull the ball—an idea that should certainly have advanced his career in Detroit or Brooklyn—but it only served to foul up his swing, which he would rediscover after being returned to the minors.

A few minor league greats don't fit the stereotypes: Jigger Statz was the opposite of most—his strengths were speed and defense. Joe Hauser appeared to be on his way to a successful career in the majors, broke his leg, never regained his past form, and went to the minors, where he became the only player to have two 60-home-run seasons. Hector Espino spent virtually his entire career in Mexico, and while major league scouts believed he could hit in the majors, he apparently had no desire to leave his homeland.

Of the great minor league stars, Statz spent the most time in the majors—683 games—and the most time with one club: all of his eighteen minor league seasons were with Los Angeles. His 3,473 games in organized baseball were a record until broken by Hank Aaron in 1976.

Statz was a great fielder; virtually all of his contemporaries considered him the best or one of the best they had seen. Playing very shallow, he reminded many of Tris Speaker. The statistics offer strong support for his claim to greatness. In four full seasons in the majors, he led the league in chances-per-game once and was second the other three years. Between 1922 and 1932 in the majors and minors he had a stretch of ten seasons in which he played in at least 100 games and never finished lower than second in chances-per-game. He had excellent speed, but during most of his career with the Angels they were a hard-hitting club that did not feature the running game, but that changed in the mid-1930s, and in the three seasons following his thirty-sixth birthday he stole 157 bases. His game was not just limited to speed and defense. A classic leadoff man of his era—a good contact hitter, small and fast—he hit .285 in the majors and .315 in the minors, collecting over 2,300 runs, 4,000 hits, 700 doubles, and 500 stolen bases in his organized-baseball career.

On April 7, 1925, the day of Babe Ruth's "big belly-ache," Joe Hauser a twenty-six-year-old first baseman

beginning his fourth season with the Athletics, broke his leg in a non-contact play while fielding during a preseason game against the Phillies at Baker Bowl. He had a .304 average for his first three major league seasons and had hit 27 homers with 115 RBIs in 1924. The injury kept him out for the entire 1925 season. In 1926 he tried to come back but hit only .192. After an excellent season with Kansas City, he went back to the majors but didn't do much in stints with the Philadelphia A's and Indians. He went back to the minors and had 4½ remarkable seasons. In 1930 with Baltimore he set a professional record with 63 homers; then he dropped to 31 in 1931 but still led the league. In 1932 he went to Minneapolis, where he led the American Association in homers with 49. In 1933 he broke his own home run record with 69, and he was off to a great start in 1934—33 homers, 88 RBIs in 82 games—when he broke his kneecap, knocking him out for the season. He continued to play until 1942 but never came close to achieving the success he had in the early 1930s.

Hauser did not hit for a high average, and it has been suggested that he took enormous advantage of short right field fences in Baltimore and Minneapolis—no one would argue that point, since 50 of his 69 homers in 1933 came at home—but many greats played in Oriole and Nicollet Parks, and none came close to Hauser's two record-breaking seasons, which remain the two highest home run seasons in the high minors.

Hector Espino holds the minor league career home run record with 484, and all but 3 of those were hit in Mexico. At the end of the 1964 Mexican League season, the twenty-five-year-old first baseman, who had led the league with 46 homers and a .371 batting average, was sold by Monterrey to the St. Louis Cardinals' Jacksonville farm club. He hit .300 with those 3 homers in 100 at-bats and was invited to spring training by the Cards for 1965, but he never reported and was eventually returned to Monterrey. In the late 1960s, the California Angels coveted Espino, who had led the Mexican League in hitting in 1966–1968, but they were never able to consummate a deal. Espino was a legend in Mexico, but it has never been clear why he didn't try the majors—he has given conflicting answers. Possibly he enjoyed being a big fish in a small pond—it wasn't the money, since he never made more than $18,000 a year in Mexico. He was notorious for marching to his own drummer, occasionally leaving clubs for a midseason vacation, and perhaps he was unwilling to sacrifice that independence.

Espino could hit for power and average—he led the Mexican League in batting five times and home runs four times—and scouts said he could have done the same in the majors, but like many players he played too long. His power started a sharp decline after his thirty-third birthday, and he was virtually helpless at the plate during his last two or three seasons. Nevertheless he ranks as perhaps the greatest minor league player who never played in the majors.

Great players do not have to be distributed evenly among all positions or across all eras, but the emphasis being on great hitters, the result is a number of outfielder-first baseman-designated hitter types, most of whom played in the high-scoring 1920s and 1930s.

Ray French was perhaps the best middle infielder in the

minors. He spent twenty-eight years in the minors, most of it in the Pacific Coast League. He played 2,736 games at shortstop and was a brilliant fielder. In the fourteen seasons that he played more than 100 games at short, he led the league in chances-per-game seven times. He was not an outstanding hitter, but his fielding kept him around long enough for him to collect 3,254 hits—seventh on the all-time minor league list.

The two best nineteenth-century minor leaguers were first baseman Perry Werden and pitcher Willie Mains. Werden had good speed and power. He had several good years in the majors (twice leading the league in triples), won six minor league home run titles, including two seasons when he went over 40, and his .341 lifetime average was exceptionally high for that era.

Mains was the first minor league pitcher to win 300 games, reaching that figure early in 1905. A seven-time twenty-game winner, he was also an excellent hitter in an era when pitchers were frequently expected to take a shift in the outfield. Most of his career was in the New York State League, but in an interesting example of the mobility of players even in the game's early years, in 1892–1893 Mains had back-to-back seasons in Portland, Oregon, and Portland, Maine.

A highly productive but not great player who deserves mention is Spencer Harris, a little lefthanded-hitting outfielder who holds the minor league career records for runs, hits, doubles, total bases, and walks. He reached those levels primarily because he kept playing until he was forty-eight years old. He did lead the American Association in homers in 1928 while at Minneapolis, but he was aided enormously by the friendly right field fence at Nicollet Park. (He averaged 17 homers a year in ten seasons with Minneapolis but only 6 a year in his sixteen other minor league seasons.) He was never thought of as the top player on his many minor league clubs—just as a good solid player of the type that formed the backbone of the minors for so many years.

There have been few minor league pitching stars of the magnitude of the great hitters. Perhaps this is because pitching is a one-dimensional skill—no pitchers were kept in the minors because they couldn't hit or field. Many of the outstanding minor league pitchers stayed there because they didn't have great stuff. Bill Thomas, who won 383 games, and Hal Turpin, who won 271 without ever getting shots at the majors, had the same statistical profile—they struck out few, walked even less, and allowed a lot of hits.

Two pitchers that didn't fit that profile, however, were Joe Martina and Dick Barrett. Martina was a power pitcher who spent most of his career with Beaumont and with his hometown New Orleans Pelicans. He held the minor league career strikeout record until ageless George Brunet broke it while toiling in the Mexican League in 1981. Martina was a workhorse, pitching over 250 innings thirteen times and was a seven-time twenty-game winner. He got his first and only big league opportunity at age thirty-five with the world champion Washington Senators in 1924.

Kewpie Dick Barrett didn't really find himself until he joined Seattle of the PCL in 1935, ten years into his professional career. A little lefthander with less than pinpoint control (he holds the minor league record for

career bases on balls), he had good stuff and eight 20-win seasons.

Frank Shellenback is most frequently named as the greatest minor league pitcher. The Pacific Coast League career leader in wins with 295, Shellenback won 9 games with the White Sox as a nineteen-year-old rookie spitballer in 1918. After a poor start the following season, he was sent to Minneapolis. In February 1920 the baseball rules committee outlawed the spitball and other trick pitches. Each major league team was allowed to designate two spitball pitchers who would be able to continue using the pitch in the majors. Unfortunately for Shellenback, he was on the Vernon roster by this time and at age twenty-one would be consigned forever to pitching in the minors if he couldn't get by without the spitball. Throughout much of his career, articles would be written that usually declared that Shellenback would be a major league star if he was eligible to play there. He did have a great six-year stretch with Hollywood (1928–1933) when he went 142–59. He was a very popular player with the Stars as well as Vernon and a fine hitter with good power, but a review of his record suggests he was never as good as everyone thought he was—he led the PCL in wins twice but never led in another category. He had only five 20-win seasons.

Because of the spitball ban, Shellenback was viewed as a tragic figure, but he wasn't alone. Spitballer Paul Wachtel won 203 games in the Texas League after the ban, including five 20-win seasons. Rube Robinson won 148 games in the Southern Association, including two league-leading 26-win seasons. Wheeler Fuller, who never pitched in the majors, won 156 in the Eastern League after the ban.

Perhaps the greatest minor league pitcher was Tony Freitas, a little lefthander who spent all or part of fifteen seasons with Sacramento. He had great control, could get the strikeout, and had nine 20-win seasons (plus two 19-win seasons). If he hadn't lost three years to the military, he probably would have won 400 games in the minors. Freitas had an impressive major league debut, going 12–5 in less than a full season with the 1932 Philadelphia A's, but that was the last success he would have in the majors.

Four other pitchers worthy of mention are Sam Gibson, George Boehler, Bill Bailey, and George Brunet.

Gibson was an underappreciated pitcher who spent most of his career in the PCL—twelve years with San Francisco. He didn't make his organized-baseball debut until he was twenty-three years old. After two promising seasons with Detroit, he never had much success in the majors, but he was extremely effective in the minors. He had six 20-win seasons (plus three 19-win seasons) and, pitching in a high-scoring era, he had eight seasons where his ERA was below 3.00.

Boehler was a hard-throwing workhorse who spent most of his career in the Western League. Twice he pitched over 400 innings, six times over 300. Unfortunately he was terribly inconsistent: with Tulsa in 1921–1923 his seasonal win totals were 4–38–7. He was consistently ineffective in a number of major league trials.

Bailey had seven league-leading strikeout seasons in four different leagues (International, Texas, Southern, Western) but only three 20-win seasons. After a promising September debut with the Browns in 1907, he pitched over 200 games in the majors with five teams spread over fifteen years with no success.

Brunet pitched in organized ball for thirty-three years (1953-1985), and astonishingly he was a regular-rotation pitcher for all but the last year. When he was forty-eight years old, he had a 1.94 ERA pitching regularly in the Mexican League. He never won more than 17 games in a season, had only two 200-strikeout seasons (they were twenty-one years apart), but he had a credible major league career and holds the minor league career strikeout record.

The Teams

There have been a number of debates about the greatest minor league teams. The 1937 Newark Bears, the 1934 Los Angeles Angels, the 1920-1925 Ft. Worth Panthers, and the 1919-1925 Baltimore Orioles usually draw the most support. All were dominant teams with good players.

The Bears included Charlie Keller, Joe Gordon, George McQuinn, Atley Donald, and five other players who would go to the majors the following year. They won the International League pennant by 25½ games with a 109–41 record. The Angels included Frank Demaree, Jigger Statz, Gene Lillard, and Fay Thomas, and they compiled an astounding 137–50 record. The Panthers (or Cats) won six straight pennants and five Dixie Series. They were led by the home run hitting of Big Boy Kraft and a fine pitching staff that included spitballer Paul Wachtel and Joe Pate.

It is doubtful that any of the three could have competed successfully in the majors. It is occasionally claimed that the 1937 Newark Bears were the Yankee B team and could have finished second in the American League, or at least in the first division. But that ignores the talent that was in the majors. The Red Sox finished fifth in 1937 with a club that included Jimmie Foxx, Joe Cronin, Lefty Grove, Pinky Higgins, Doc Cramer, Ben Chapman, Jack Wilson, and Bobo Newsom, all of whom, it is safe to say, would have started for the Bears. The same is true of the Angels, whose pitching staff chose 1934 to have career years, and of the Cats, who played well as a team but had few players that were even considered minor league standouts.

The Orioles were a different story. Thanks to the draft exemption, Jack Dunn was able to assemble a powerhouse comprised of players ready and capable of playing in the majors. The 1922 team was probably the best minor league club ever assembled. It had Jack Bentley, Max Bishop, Fritz Maisel, and Joe Boley in the infield, and Otis Lawry, Merwyn Jacobson, and Jimmy Walsh in the outfield. The catcher was Lena Styles, and the pitchers were Lefty Grove, John Ogden, Tommy Thomas, Rube Parnham, and Harry Frank with Bentley occasionally seeing action on the mound.

Grove, Ogden, and Thomas combined for 60 wins and six years later would win a combined 56 games in the majors. Parnham, a free spirit who pitched when he wanted, was around long enough to win 16 (the following year he won 33). Frank won 22, but his career would soon be cut short by illness. Bentley hit .350 and won 13 games; he went to the Giants in 1923 as a pitcher but hit

.427. Bishop and Boley, who hit .261 and .343 respectively, went on to become the double-play combo with the 1929-1930 world champion Philadelphia A's. Styles was just twenty-two years old and hit .315, but that was his peak. Maisel (.306), Walsh (.327), Jacobson (.304), and Lawry (.333) had all played briefly and/or ineffectively in the majors but would all go on to have great careers in the International League. A twenty-year-old rookie utility player on the team was Dick Porter, who hit .279 and would have seven excellent seasons with the Orioles before going on to have several good years with the Indians.

As good as the Orioles were and as good as some of their players became, it is doubtful that even they could have finished in the first division of the American or National Leagues in 1922. Yet the strongest evidence of the attraction of minor league baseball and the hold it has long held on fans who were exposed to it is that those great Oriole, Bear, and Angel teams are far better known and more fondly remembered than hundreds of more talented second-division and higher major league clubs.

The Farm System

Farm teams are nearly as old as organized baseball. In 1884 the Boston Beaneaters of the National League owned a team called the Boston Reserves in the Massachusetts State Association. The Reserves, also called the Colts, were apparently intended to serve as a source of replacements for disabled members of the major league club. It has also been suggested that the farm team was a device to keep more players under contract and out of the hands of the Union Association that year. Whatever the origins of the idea, during the next decade a number of major league clubs operated such reserve teams, but they usually competed in local semipro leagues rather than in organized baseball and were viewed more as quick sources of replacements rather than as training grounds for players.

With John B. Day's joint ownership of the New York Gothams of the National League and the New York Metropolitans of the American Association as early as 1883 and with the proliferation of interlocking ownerships of major league clubs in the 1890s, it was only natural that some major and minor league clubs would come under joint ownership as well. The first instance of any significance, however, occurred when John T. Brush, owner of Cincinnati in the National League, entered the Indianapolis club in the newly formed Western League in 1894. While this was not the first case of joint major-minor league club ownership, Brush appears to have been the first to grasp the potential of such an arrangement. Indianapolis served as a place to develop talent that was not quite ready for the majors. The team gave Cincinnati an expanded roster as players were frequently shuffled to and from Indianapolis during the season; it also served as a source of profit because Indianapolis drew well at the gate, having become the dominant club in the Western League, with three pennants and two second-place finishes in five seasons (1895–1899). Indianapolis's success was aided in no small part by Brush's practice of drafting players from other Western League clubs and sending them to Indianapolis, thus simultaneously weakening the opposition and strengthening the Hoosiers. Efforts were made by the other Western League club owners to control "farming" or to modify the draft rules to stop Brush, but none were successful.

Perhaps copying Brush's strategy, in 1896 several National League clubs obtained minor league affiliates: Pittsburgh had Toronto, Boston had Wilkes-Barre, and Cleveland had Ft. Wayne. Philadelphia had a Philadelphia farm club in the Pennsylvania State League, and when that league folded, they shifted the junior club to the Atlantic Association. The New York Giants had the first farm "system," with the New York Mets in the Atlantic Association and Syracuse in the Eastern League.

When the National Agreement was adopted in 1903, it banned the "farming out" of players, but "farming" as defined in the agreement referred only to those efforts by major league clubs to exceed the limits on players who could be optioned through subterfuge—"fake transfers" such as loans or sell/buy-back arrangements with minor league clubs where title to a player was never surrendered.

The independent minor league operators saw farming as a curse for two reasons. First, it reduced their autonomy and potential revenue by placing more players under major league ownership, thus reducing the majors' need to buy or draft players from the minors. Second, clubs accepting players from the majors, either openly through options or secretly, might gain an unfair competitive advantage on the field. So while in 1905 the New York Giants' request to establish a working agreement with Bridgeport was validated by the National Commission, most of the legislation was focused on restricting farming, normally by limiting the number of players who could be optioned and the number of times each player could be optioned. For example, in 1904 a rule was adopted which required a player sent out on option to stay with the minor league club for the remainder of that season. In 1907 the rule was relaxed so that a major league club could option a player and recall him, but only once in a season. In 1911 a team could have no more than eight players out on option at one time.

Working agreements became quite common during this period. The major league club furnished the minor league club with its surplus players—youngsters in need of more experience or veterans past their prime who could still strengthen a minor league club—and/or cash. In return the major league club could obtain promising players from the minor league club. During this era the formal working agreement between major and minor league clubs was usually of short duration—a year or two at most—suggesting that major league clubs targeted certain minor league clubs that had two or three players they might be interested in and established a working agreement in order to get first claim on those that developed satisfactorily. There were also informal working agreements, generally based on friendships between major and minor league club operators, and it was usually through such arrangements that the "fake transfers" banned by the National Agreement took place. In the early 1900s, for example, there was substantial traffic in players between the White Sox and Milwaukee of the American Association and between the Dodgers and Baltimore in the Eastern League. (Brewer manager Joe Cantillon was a longtime friend of Charles Comiskey, and Brooklyn manager Ned Hanlon was also a minority owner of the Orioles.)

The most efficient and only legal method of circumventing the rules relating to major league control of players was through joint ownership of major and minor league clubs. By 1912 Charles W. Somers owned Cleveland and Toledo, and Charles Ebbets owned both Brooklyn and Newark. This enabled the Indians to hold title to sixty players and the Dodgers to sixty-one. In 1913 a National Commission confidential bulletin directed major league clubs to divest their interest in minor league clubs by January 1, 1914, but neither Somers nor Ebbets complied until several years later (in fact, Somers secretly acquired New Orleans in 1913). In 1921 the joint ownership of major and minor league clubs was again permitted, and the New National Agreement, although retaining option limits, dropped the antifarming provisions that had been in it since 1903.

In 1921 the Cardinals, who had already acquired an interest in Ft. Smith of the Western Association and Houston of the Texas League, acquired a half interest in Syracuse of the International League. This was the beginning of Branch Rickey's farm system, but initially it attracted little attention as it didn't appear to represent anything particularly new. Major league clubs had long been signing young talent directly off the sandlots and developing it in the minors. In 1910, for example, Cleveland signed Roger Peckinpaugh out of the Cleveland City League, gave him a brief trial, and then optioned him to New Haven and Portland in successive seasons before recalling him when he was deemed ready for the majors. This practice had developed to the point that Mike Sexton, president of the National Association, in 1921 spoke out against the fact that the majors and higher minors had preempted the low minors' traditional role of discovering and signing young talent.

As we have seen, major league clubs had occasionally owned minor league clubs, primarily to expand the number of players under their control, but these were always higher-classification clubs, where talent was refined rather than developed. Rickey's approach was original because he was the first to assemble a system of teams at various levels or classifications. This enabled him to sign young talent and, through a hierarchy of minor league clubs, to develop and retain continuous title to a large number of players, his theory being that out of quantity comes quality. It didn't take long for the system to begin producing talent—the Cards, who had never finished higher than third in this century, won the World Series in 1926 with a team that included future Hall of Famers Jim Bottomley and Chick Hafey as well as regulars Taylor Douthit, Tommy Thevenow, Les Bell, Ray Blades, Flint Rhem, and Art Reinhardt plus reserves Watty Holm, Jake Flowers, Spec Toporcher, Ernie Vick, and Bill Hallahan—all of whom were products of a farm system that was less than seven years old. In addition, Billy Southworth was acquired from the Giants for Heinie Mueller, another product of the Cardinal farm system.

During those seven years when the Cardinals were discovering, signing, and developing unprecedented quantities of players at little expense, the other major league clubs were essentially operating as they always had, signing some players out of the amateur ranks, optioning them out for seasoning, and buying top prospects from minor league clubs, even though the new draft rules were driving the prices of such players to unprecedented levels. For example, the Yankee team the Cardinals defeated in the 1926 World Series had just one home-grown player—Lou Gehrig, who was signed out of Columbia University in 1923 and optioned to Hartford until ready. Although this had been an inexpensive acquisition, the Yankees subsequently had purchased, for $50,000 each, Earle Combs from Louisville, Mark Koenig from St. Paul (with whom the Yankees had a working agreement), and Tony Lazzeri from Salt Lake. In 1925, the year the Pirates won the World Series, they acquired Paul Waner and Hal Rhyne from the San Francisco Seals for $100,000 and also signed Joe Cronin off the San Francisco sandlots for little more than train fare to his first assignment—Johnstown, Pennsylvania.

But the escalating prices of players and the success of the Cardinals finally encouraged other clubs to begin acquiring minor league clubs. Shortly after the Cardinals acquired the half interest in Syracuse in 1921, William Wrigley, owner of the Cubs, acquired Los Angeles of the Pacific Coast League, but he treated them virtually as separate investments. By 1927, however, major league acquisition of minor league clubs was causing concern in the minors. The first formal notice came late that year, when the American Association adopted a new Constitution which effectively prohibited major league ownership of its clubs (excluding Columbus, which was already owned by Cincinnati). At the National Association meeting in December 1928, Mike Sexton wondered aloud when the majors would own enough clubs to control the National Association. Early in 1929 major league clubs owned or controlled twenty-seven minor league clubs. At that point Judge Landis, who until then had been remarkably quiet on the issue of farm systems, opened fire. He began granting free agency to minor leaguers "covered up" by various major league organizations. Later in 1929, Landis denounced the farm system, and announced his intention of destroying it. In response, Sam Breadon, owner of the Cardinals, cited letters from seven minor leagues saying the farm system was beneficial to them. Interestingly, in 1921 Landis had said, "The object of organized baseball is to facilitate the development of skill among ball players." No one could seriously argue that this wasn't the purpose of the farm system, but by 1929 Landis was accusing Rickey and Breadon of "raping the minors," robbing smalltown America of its precious heritage of independent minor league baseball.

Through the 1930s Landis tried to make good on his threat to destroy the farm system, but since it was not contrary to baseball law, he had to pick at the edges—by levying fines against teams having an interest in more than one team in a minor league or by granting free agency to players who were "covered up" through violations of the option rules or "secret agreements." Attracting much attention in Landis's crusade was his granting of free agency to seventy-four Cardinal farmhands in 1938, and to ninety-one Detroit minor leaguers in 1940, but these shots were fired after the war was lost.

More important than the fireworks that erupted between Landis and Breadon at the 1929 major league meeting was Yankees owner Jacob Ruppert's declaration at the same meetings that no ball club could afford the prices being paid for minor league players; Ruppert added that he was "going to be forced into owning minor league clubs, and so is every other major league owner in this room." At the time he spoke, the Yankees had already purchased the Chambersburg club of the Class D Blue Ridge League. In November 1931 Ruppert purchased Newark of the International League for a reported $600,000 and soon thereafter hired Baltimore general manager George Weiss to develop a farm system. Thus the farm system, a concept that had been created largely out of necessity by Branch Rickey because the Cardinals didn't have the financial resources to compete with other clubs for top minor league prospects, had in less than a decade been embraced by the wealthiest club in baseball as being the most efficient method of acquiring talent. There would still be an occasional Joe DiMaggio or Ted Williams, signed by a minor league club and sold to the majors, but the major league club that didn't establish a farm system did so at its own peril—it cannot be coincidental that the eight teams which were the slowest to get on the bandwagon and had the thinnest farm systems in the 1930s—the Phillies, Athletics, Senators, White Sox, Giants, Cubs, Braves, and Pirates—were, aside from the Browns, the eight least successful teams in the 1940s. (The Browns and Reds established extensive farm systems in the 1930s, and overall they were the two most improved clubs of the 1940s.)

While several clubs caught on to what the Cardinals were doing, none could catch up as Rickey, taking advantage of the Depression, which had created a large pool of young men with few career options, signed players by the hundreds at tryout camps. Whereas during the 1920s the Cardinal system had only increased from three clubs to five, by 1936 it had expanded to twenty-eight teams— remarkable considering that there were only twenty-six minor leagues that year (the Cardinals had two teams each in the Nebraska State, Georgia-Florida, and Arkansas-Missouri Leagues). The Cardinal system finally topped out with thirty-three clubs in 1937—more than the two next-largest farm systems combined. Rickey's belief that out of quantity comes quality was proven on the field by the 1942 world champion Cardinals. Every player on the active roster, except for second-line pitchers Harry Gumbert and Whitey Moore, was a product of the Cardinal farm system, and Gumbert had been acquired in exchange for Cardinal farm graduate Bill McGee. In addition, the sale of players developed by the Cardinals kept the coffers full—in 1940–1941 alone, Johnny Mize, Joe Medwick, and Mickey Owen were exchanged to other clubs for $240,000 and nine players.

Thus from the perspective of the majors the farm system was a success, and the minors seemed to be flourishing—going from fourteen leagues in 1933 to forty-four by 1940. Sam Breadon, responding to another barrage of attacks by Landis in the late 1930s, claimed that the farm system had brought stability and strength to the minors, but there were other factors at work—the proliferation of night games, better promotion, and an influx of good young talent resulted in a per-club increase in attendance of 40 percent from 1937 to 1940. During that same period the portion of minor league clubs affiliated with the majors actually dropped from 61 to 46 percent. Rickey's theory that out of quantity comes quality might have had practical merit during a depression, or again immediately following World War Two when there was an influx of returning veterans. However, under normal circumstances huge farm systems were not cost-effective. While the minors were still expanding in the late 1930s, the Cardinals began pruning back their farm system of more than thirty teams; again while the minors were expanding in the late 1940s, farm systems were contracting—in 1948 there were six farm systems of twenty or more teams; by 1951 there were none. The portion of minor league teams affiliated with major league teams dropped from 62 percent in 1946 to 47 percent in 1951 as major league farm systems collectively dropped from 280 to 175 clubs and outright major league ownership of minor league clubs dropped from 125 to 75.

In 1950 there were 232 minor league teams not affiliated with the majors. This was the highest number of independent teams in organized baseball since the early teens. Nine of the fifty-eight leagues had no teams with major league affiliations, and more than a dozen others had only one or two affiliates. These leagues operated virtually outside the player-development chain, existing much as a semipro team or league does—to provide entertainment and reflect civic pride. Their only source of revenue was through the turnstiles, and just as forty years earlier automobiles and the movies helped drive out the marginal teams and leagues, now TV did the same. This can be clearly seen as the heavily populated Northeast, the first region to be heavily penetrated by television, suffered the first wave of league failures.

Over the next few years, attendance declined sharply, most of the independent clubs folded, and farm systems continued to contract. In 1956 the majors established a "stabilization fund" of $500,000 to aid clubs and leagues in lower classifications, but the free-fall of leagues, clubs, and attendance continued. In 1959 the majors discontinued the stabilization fund and established a fund of $1 million to finance a player-development and promotional program for the minors. In 1962 the majors and minors adopted the Player Development Plan that, by requiring each major league club to have five farm teams, would guarantee the operation of at least one-hundred minor league teams, which the majors felt was adequate for their player-development purposes. The plan also included the Player Development Contract under the terms of which the parent major league club became responsible for all spring training costs and all or most of the salaries of players, managers, and coaches. After major league expansion in 1969, major league clubs were only required to support four farm clubs each, but their financial support of each was increased. By 1976 there were only 106 minor league teams with major league affiliations, the lowest peacetime total since 1935. American League expansion the following year created the need for additional minor league affiliates, and in subsequent years major league clubs expanded their farm systems—all of them back up to a minimum of five clubs by 1984. With the dramatic increase in minor league attendance and the resulting increase in the value of franchises in the 1980s, a new Professional Baseball Agreement was ratified by the majors and minors in 1990 that required the minors to assume a greater share of operational expenses but the majors continued to pay the salaries and meal money of all uniformed personnel (including umpires). And farm systems continued to grow—by 1994 each major league club had at least six farm clubs and the number of minor league teams with major league affiliations was up to 195 (including 21 in the Dominican Rookie League), the highest total since 1950.

In 1928 Mike Sexton had asked how long it would be before the majors owned enough minor league clubs to control the National Association. Other than during World War Two, when the minors were severely constricted, major league clubs never have "owned" more than 28 percent of the minor league clubs; however, possibly as early as 1934, probably by 1935, and certainly by 1936, the majors through outright ownership, working agreements, or other interlocking devices "controlled" the National Association, and this situation was generally acknowledged throughout baseball by 1938.

Until about 1960 there was still some room in the National Association for independent clubs and career minor league players, but since then the minors have existed almost exclusively to develop talent for the majors. While this has dismayed many minor league fans and traditionalists, it should be remembered that the principal role of the minors within organized baseball has always been to develop talent for the majors, and to receive money in exchange. The farm system, which owed its success in no small part to the greed of some minor league operators, was merely a different device by which talent moved to the majors and money moved to the minors.

Minor Leagues

Year	Leagues Started	Didn't Finish	Year	Leagues Started	Didn't Finish	Year	Leagues Started	Didn't Finish	Year	Leagues Started	Didn't Finish	Year	Leagues Started	Didn't Finish	Year	Leagues Started	Didn't Finish
1883	2		1902	16	2	1921	26	1	1940	44	1	1959	21		1978	18	
1884	7	3	1903	19		1922	30	2	1941	41		1960	22		1979	18	1
1885	8	3	1904	23	3	1923	31	2	1942	31	5	1961	22		1980	17	
1886	11	3	1905	29	6	1924	29	3	1943	10	1	1962	20		1981	17	
1887	15	6	1906	33	5	1925	25	1	1944	10		1963	18		1982	17	
1888	17	9	1907	34	6	1926	29	4	1945	12		1964	20		1983	17	
1889	15	5	1908	39	8	1927	24		1946	43	1	1965	19		1984	17	
1890	18	9	1909	34	2	1928	30	3	1947	52		1966	19		1985	18	
1891	13	5	1910	52	8	1929	26	3	1948	58		1967	19		1986	17	
1892	14	10	1911	50	7	1930	23	2	1949	59		1968	21		1987	18	
1893	7	4	1912	45	6	1931	19	3	1950	58	1	1969	21		1988	19	
1894	8	2	1913	42	5	1932	19	6	1951	50	1	1970	20		1989	19	
1895	17	9	1914	43	7	1933	14		1952	43		1971	20		1990	19	
1896	15	8	1915	30	7	1934	20	1	1953	38		1972	19		1991	19	
1897	20	8	1916	25	3	1935	21		1954	36	3	1973	18		1992	19	
1898	20	11	1917	21	10	1936	26		1955	33		1974	18		1993	19	
1899	14	5	1918	10	9	1937	37		1956	28		1975	18		1994	19	
1900	15	6	1919	15	2	1938	37		1957	28		1976	20		1995	19	
1901	13	2	1920	22	1	1939	41		1958	24		1977	19		1996	19	

Minor League Clubs/Major League Affiliations

Year	Minor League Clubs	Affiliated with Majors	Owned by Majors	Year	Minor League Clubs	Affiliated with Majors	Owned by Majors	Year	Minor League Clubs	Affiliated with Majors	Owned by Majors
1936	184	115	38	1956	217	150	33	1976	148	106	24
1937	251	154	39	1957	200	153	32	1977	150	113	23
1938	267	163	48	1958	173	157	34	1978	156	118	24
1939	292	149	47	1959	150	132	30	1979	155	119	
1940	310	143	60	1960	152	126	18	1980	155	125	
1941	304	143	61	1961	147	129	21	1981	152	133	
1942	206	116	46	1962	134	121	22	1982	160	136	
1943	66	42	23	1963	130	114	22	1983	162	139	
1944	70	57	21	1964	136	108	19	1984	164	140	
1945	85	68	33	1965	136	110	28	1985	168	140	
1946	316	197	79	1966	138	116	32	1986	164	143	
1947	388	247	103	1967	141	118	36	1987	176	149	
1948	438	280	125	1968	152	119	39	1988	188	168	
1949	448	243	116	1969	155	128	46	1989	197	179	
1950	446	210	99	1970	153	120	39	1990	202	183	
1951	371	172	75	1971	155	127	45	1991	207	184	
1952	324	166	65	1972	148	125	49	1992	212	192	
1953	292	152	50	1973	147	117	38	1993	214	193	
1954	269	156	49	1974	145	113	27	1994	216	195	
1955	243	155	40	1975	137	109	26	1995	216	193	
								1996	218	198	

Major League Farm Systems
1936–1969

	36	37	38	39	40	41	42	43	44	45	46	47	48	49	50	51	52	53	54	55	56	57	58	59	60	61	62	63	64	65	66	67	68	69
Boston, AL	9	10	7	8	6	7	6	3	5	4	12	13	15	11	8	8	6	6	6	6	5	7	7	6	6	6	6	5	5	6	5	6	6	
Chicago, AL	5	4	10	8	6	5	5	0	0	17	12	15	9	8	8	6	8	8	6	6	6	6	6	6	6	5	5	5	6	6	6			
Cleveland, AL	5	7	13	16	9	8	9	8	3	3	11	18	20	20	16	12	10	8	9	9	8	7	5	6	5	4	4	4	5	5				
Detroit, AL	11	8	12	7	5	11	8	2	3	2	7	11	16	14	9	8	7	7	8	10	9	8	10	7	8	8	6	6	5	5	6	6		
New York, AL	11	15	15	15	14	12	9	5	5	5	15	22	24	22	15	14	10	11	9	10	11	10	10	8	7	7	6	5	7	7	7	6	6	
Phila.-K.C.-Oakland, AL	5	3	3	3	4	5	3	2	2	4	7	15	10	11	15	9	8	8	8	7	9	8	8	8	8	6	5	6	6	6	6	5		
St. Louis-Baltimore, AL	3	15	16	12	11	11	6	1	3	3	11	15	20	18	13	10	12	10	12	8	9	9	7	9	9	6	6	7	6	6	6	6		
Wash.-Minnesota, AL	1	5	2	8	4	6	3	1	2	2	5	7	12	9	10	6	8	7	8	7	6	8	7	7	6	8	8	8	8					
Milwaukee-Atlanta, NL	4	6	6	6	5	4	4	1	2	13	15	15	11	8	8	12	11	10	10	12	15	14	12	10	9	7	6	5	6	7	5	4		
Brkln.-Los Angeles, NL	5	14	14	11	18	14	10	4	7	9	21	25	26	26	22	19	17	15	15	16	14	13	12	12	12	11	9	7	8	6	6	6		
Chicago, NL	5	6	5	2	2	9	11	4	6	7	18	23	19	16	15	14	10	9	9	8	10	8	6	6	5	5	5	6	6	5	5			
Cincinnati, NL	16	10	10	10	8	8	5	2	1	3	4	8	11	10	7	4	6	7	9	9	11	11	8	8	6	5	5	4	5	5	5			
N.Y.-San Francisco, NL	2	11	4	5	6	7	3		5	8	16	19	22	19	18	14	13	9	9	10	10	10	12	9	8	7	7	6	6	6	6	5		
Philadelphia, NL	1	2	3	3	8	3	2	1	3	5	9	11	15	14	12	11	11	9	9	8	9	9	7	10	8	7	6	6	6	7	7	6		
Pittsburgh, NL	4	5	7	7	9	8	7	4	4	4	13	14	19	13	13	11	15	11	10	13	13	10	11	9	7	7	7	6	6	6	6	6		
St. Louis, NL	28	33	32	28	29	25	22	6	7	18	19	22	20	21	16	15	16	22	18	15	11	14	12	9	8	6	5	5	6	6	7	7	7	
L.A.-California, AL																											2	4	6	6	6	5	5	5
Washington, AL																											2	4	4	4	4	4	5	5
Houston, NL																											2	4	5	5	5	6	6	5
New York, NL																											3	4	5	4	4	6	6	5
Kansas City, AL																																		7
Seattle, AL																																		4
Montreal, NL																																		3
San Diego, NL																																		4

Annual Overall Minor League Pitching Percentage Leader (20 or more decisions)

Year	Player	Team (League)	W–L	Pct.	Overall W–L	Overall Pct.
1900	Willie Mains	Rome (N.Y. St.)	27–5	.844		
1901	Henry Allemang	Little Rock (So. Assn.)	20–4	.833		
1902	Louis Bruce	Toronto (Eastern)	18–2	.900		
1903	Ernest Nichols	Spokane (Pac. Nat.)	20–4	.833		
1904	Ed Craig	Springfield (Mo. Valley)	19–4	.826		
1905	Fred Steele	Oskaloosa (Iowa St.)	18–3	.857		
1906	Frank Dick	Marshalltown (Iowa St.)	18–3	.857		
1907	Harley Young	Wichita (West. Assn.)	29–4	.879		
1908	Harry Gaspar	Waterloo (Cent. Assn.)	32–4	.889		
1909	Ray Fisher	Hartford (Conn.)	24–5	.828		
1910	Cyrus Dahlgren	Superior (Minn.-Wis.)	22–3	.880		
1911	Howard Northrop	Reading (Inter.-St.)	27–4	.871		
1912	Larue Kirby	Traverse City (Mich. St.)	18–3	.857		
1913	Ralph Bell	Winona (Northern)	28–6	.824		
1914	Joe Chabek	Harrisburg (Tri-St.)	28–3	.903		
1915	Booth Hopper	Minneapolis (A.A.)	18–3	.857		
1916	Howard Ehmke	Syracuse (N.Y. St.)	31–7	.816		
1917	John Verbout	Wilkes-Barre (N.Y. St.)	26–7	.788		
1918	John Beckvermit	Binghamton (Int.)	17–4	.810		
1919	C. A. "Chief" Bender	Richmond (Va.)	29–2	.935		
1920	George Carmen	London (Mich.,-Ont.)	26–2	.926		
1921	Earl Keiser	Mitchell (Dakota)	20–2			
		Oakland (PCL)	3–0		23–2	.920
1922	Byrd Hodges	Joplin (West. Assn.)	26–3	.897		
1923	Emil Levsen	Cedar Rapids (Miss. Val.)	19–4	.826		
1924	Carl Dunagan	Dyersburg (Kitty)	19–2	.905		
1925	Lloyd Brown	Ardmore-Western Assn.	17–1	.944*		
1926	Frank Tubbs	Port Huron (Mich.-Ont.)	8–1			
		Port Huron (Mich. St.)	8–0			
		Oklahoma City (Western)	9–2		25–3	.893
1927	Ben Cantwell	Jacksonville (So'east.)	25–5	.833		
1928	Paul Fittery	Carrollton (Ga.-Ala.)	21–2	.913		
1929	Andrew Bednar	McCook (Neb. St.)	21–4	.840		
1930	Jim Cameron	McCook (Neb. St.)	19–2	.905		
1931	Lyle "Bud" Tinning	Minneapolis (A.A.)	1–2			
		Des Moines (West. Assn.)	24–2		25–4	.862
1932	Marvin Duke	Erie (Central)	23–4	.852		
1933	Al Piechota	Davenport (Miss. Val.)	19–4	.826		
1934	Fay Thomas	Los Angeles (PCL)	28–4	.875		
1935	Lloyd Sterling	Winnipeg (Northern)	24–2	.923		
1936	Bill Yocke	Akron (Mid. Atl.)	1–2			
		Norfolk (Piedmont)	18–1		19–3	.864
1937	Joe Kohlman	Salisbury (E. Shore)	25–1	.962		
1938	Paige Dennis	Thomasville (N.C. St.)	28–2	.933		
1939	Charles Wensloff	Joplin (West. Assn.)	26–4	.867		
1940	Arthur Cyrolewski	Johnson City (App.)	20–3	.870		

J. Merwin (Merv) Henley	La Crosse (Wis. St.)	20–3	.870		
1941 Frank Marino	Macon (Sally)	19–1	.950		
1942 Paul Minner	Elizabethton (App.)	18–2			
	Knoxville (So. Assn.)	1–0		19–2	.905
1943 Irvin Stein	Portsmouth (Piedmont)	24–6	.800		
1944 Pete Naktenis	Hartford (Eastern)	18–3	.857		
1945 Lewis Carpenter	Atlanta (So. Assn.)	22–2	.917		
1946 Bill Kennedy	Rocky Mount (C. Plain)	28–3	.903		
1947 Chris VanCuyk	Cambridge (E. Shore)	25–2	.926		
1948 Albert Tefft	Blackstone (Va.)	20–1	.952		
1949 Lynn Southworth	Thomasville (N.C. St.)	21–1	.955		
1950 Mike Hudak	Big Stone Gap (Mt. St.)	19–2	.905		
1951 Anderson Bush	Hagerstown (Int. St.)	22–3	.880		
1952 Russell Harris	Ozark (Ala.-Fla.)	27–3	.900		
1953 Steve Kraly	Binghamton (Eastern)	19–2	.905		
1954 Don Vaughn	Merryville-Morristown (Mt. St.)	11–1			
	Highpoint-Thomasville (Carolina)	0–0			
	Vidalia (Ga. St.)	9–1		20–2	.909
1955 Jim Grant	Keokuk (I-I-I)	19–3	.864		
1956 Francisco Ramirez	Mexico City Reds (Mex.)	20–3	.870		
1957 Bob Riesner	Alexandria (Evang.)	20–0			
	New Orleans (So. Assn.)	0–2		20–2	.909
1958 Jerry Walker	Knoxville (Sally)	18–4	.818		
Art Henriksen	St. Petersburg (Fla. St.)	17–3			
	New Orleans (So. Assn.)	0–1		18–4	.818
1959 Les Bass	Boise (Pioneer)	21–3	.875		
1960 Tom Haake	Grand Forks (Northern)	0–1			
	Dubuque (Midwest)	19–3		19–4	.826
1961 David Seeman	Selma (Ala.-Fla.)	17–3			
	Burlington (Carolina)	7–0		24–3	.889
1962 Bob Schmidt	Modesto (Calif.)	0–0			
	Jamestown (NYP)	17–3		17–3	.850
1963 Bob Lee	Batavia (NYP)	20–2			
	Asheville (Sally)	1–1		21–3	.875
1964 Ed Watt	Aberdeen (Northern)	14–1			
	Elmira (Eastern)	3–1		17–2	.895**
1965 Billy MacLeod	Pittsfield (Eastern)	18–0	1.000†		
1966 Bob Snow	Winston-Salem (Carolina)	20–2	.909		
1967 John Parker	Spartanburg (W. Car.)	17–3	.850		
1968 Pablo Montes De Oca	Campeche (Mex. S.E.)	21–4	.840		
1969 Don Eddy	Appleton (Midwest)	18–3	.857		
1970 Jim Flynn	Albuquerque (Texas)	19–4	.826		
1971 Rich Gossage	Appleton (Midwest)	18–2	.900		

1972 Andres Ayon	Saltillo (Mexican)	22–3	.880		
1973 Silvano Quezada	Tampico (Mexican)	22–2	.917		
1974 Bob Knepper	Fresno (Calif.)	20–5	.800		
1975 Jerry Garvin	Reno (Calif.)	17–5	.773		
1976 Enrique Romo	Mexico City Reds (Mexican)	20–4	.833		
1977 Mike Chris	Lakeland (Fla. St.)	18–5	.783		
1978 Tomas Armas	Saltillo (Mexican)	22–4	.846		
1979 Miguel Solis	Saltillo (Mexican)	25–5	.833		
1980 Gene Nelson	Ft. Lauderdale (Fla. St.)	20–3	.870		
1981 Ted Power	Albuquerque (PCL)	18–3	.857		
1982 Mike Warren	Stockton-Modesto (Calif.)	19–4	.826		
1983 Alfonso Pulido	Mexico City Reds (Mexican)	17–3	.850		
1984 Mike Bielecki	Hawaii (PCL)	19–3	.864		
1985 Eleazar Beltran	Tampico (Mexican)	18–3	.857		
1986 George Ferran	Shreveport (Texas)	16–1	.941‡		
1987 Bob Faron	Springfield (Midwest)	19–2	.905		
1988 Jimmy Rodgers	Myrtle Beach (So. Atl.)	18–4	.818		
1989 Royal Clayton	Albany (Eastern)	16–4	.800		
1989 Mercedes Esquer	Yucatan (Mexican)	16–4	.800		
1989 Walt Trice	Osceola (Fla. St.)	16–4	.800		
1990 Randy Marshall	Fayetteville (So. Atl.)	13–0			
	Lakeland (Fla. St.)	7–2			
1991 Jose Martinez	Columbus (So. Atl.)	20–4	.833		
1992 John Fritz	Quad Cities (Midwest)	20–4	.833		
1993 John Dettmer	Charlotte (Fla. St.)	16–3	.842		
Ryan Karp	Albany (Eastern)	0–0			
	Prince William (Carolina)	3–2			
	Greensboro (So. Atl.)	13–1	.842	16–3	****
1994 Francisco Montano	Monclova (Mexican)	19–1	.950		
1995 Rich Hunter	Piedmont (Sally)	10–2			
	Clearwater (Fla. St.)	6–0			
	Reading (Eastern)	3–0		19–2	.905
1996 Ted Silva	Charlotte (Fla. St.)	10–2			
	Tulsa (Texas)	7–2		17–4	.810

*Adding 2 losses to Brown's record giving him 20 decisions yields a .850 percent, better than John Schmutte, Johnstown Middle Atlantic, 19–4, .822
**Adding 1 loss to Watt's record, giving him 20 decisions, yields an .850 percentage, better than Dave Leonhard, Aberdeen (Northern), 16–4 .800
†Adding 2 losses to MacLeod's record, giving him 20 decisions, yields a .900 percentage, better than Dave Leonhard, Elmira (Eastern), 20–5 .800
****Adding Dettmer's and Karp's records giving them 20 decisions yields an .800 percentage, better than Urbano Lugo, Jalisco (Mexican) 17-5 .773.
‡Adding 3 losses to Ferran's record, giving him 20 decisions, yields an .800 percentage, better than Kevin Armstrong, Columbia (Sally), 17–5 .773.

Annual Overall Minor League Batting Leader (400 or more at-bats)

Year	Player	Team (League)	G	AB	R	H	2B	3B	HR	RBI	SB	AVG.
1900	Kitty Bransfield	Worcester (Eastern)	122	501	115*	186*	30	8	17	—	40	.371*
1901	Frank Huelsman	Shreveport (So. Assn.)	121*	487	98	191*	31	10	9	—	15	.392*
1902	Emil Frisk	Denver (Western)	123	450	89	168	22	22	14*	—	20	.373*
1903	Frank Huelsman	Spokane (Pac. Int.)	98	418	89	160	35	11	6	—	14	.392*
1904	Billy Hamilton	Haverhill (New Eng.)	113	408	113*	168*	32	8	0	—	74*	.412*
1905	Charlie Hemphill	St. Paul (A. A.)	145	560	122	204*	38	12	5	—	40	.364*
1906	Mike Welday	Des Moines (Western)	129	549	93	197	—	—	—	—	31	.359
1907	Ed Householder	Aberdeen (Northwest)	127	499	64	173	30*	19	9	—	19	.347*
1908	Ward Miller	Wausau (Wis.-Ill.)	124	408	91*	156*	—	—	—	—	—	.382*
1909	Harry Welch	Omaha (Western)	151	527	81	196*	41	15	7	—	51	.372*
1910	Dave Callahan	Eau Claire (Minn.-Wis.)	126	460	92*	168*	25	17*	2	—	52	.365*
1911	Frank Huelsman	Great Falls (U.A.)	135	516	117	212	48	15	17*	125*	25	.411*
1912	Charlie Johnson	Trenton (Tri-State)	109	400	86	161	31	5	14	—	22	.403*
1913	Frank Huelsman	Salt Lake City (U.A.)	122	473	123*	200*	36*	20*	22*	126*	16	.423*
1914	Joe Harris	Bay City (So. Michigan)	139	510	135	197*	39	22*	10	—	42	.386*
1915	Big Bill Kay	Binghamton (N.Y. St.)	125	447	98*	169*	22	25*	7	—	35	.378*
1916	Hank Butcher	Denver (Western)	145	541	116	204	31	20*	15	—	32	.377*
1917	Nap Lajoie	Toronto (Int.)	151	581	83	221*	39*	4	5	—	4	.380*
1918	Polly McLarry	Shreveport (Texas)	29	84	12	24	3	1	1	—	6	.286
		Binghamton (Int.)	103	335	51	129	26	7	4	—	15	.385*
		overall										.365
1919	Joe Wilhoit	Seattle (PCL)	17	67	8	11	1	0	0	—	3	.164
		Wichita (Western)	128	526	126*	222*	41	10	7	—	13	.422*
		overall										.393
1920	Merwyn Jacobson	Baltimore (Int.)	154*	581	161*	235*	35	16*	7	—	18	.404*
1921	Jack Lelivelt	Omaha (Western)	166	659	149	274*	70*	9	14	—	24	.416*
1922	Jack Schaefer	London (Mich.-Ont.)	100	407	79	167	27	21	9	—	9	.410*
1923	Moses Solomon	Hutchinson (So'west.)	134	527	143*	222*	40*	15	49*	—	12	.421*
1924	T. P. Osborne	Mt. Pleasant (E. Tex.)	101	396	93	171*	48	3	23	—	46*	.432*¹
1925	Paul Waner	San Francisco (PCL)	174	599	167	280	75*	7	11	130	8	.401*
1926	Bill Diester	Salina (So'west.)	106	428	110*	190*	33*	4	27	—	10	.444*
		Tulsa (Western)	11	44	5	15	4	0	0	—	0	.341
		overall										.434
1927	Elton Langford	Des Moines (Western)	149	611	132	250	47	28*	8	—	31	.409*
1928	Danny Boone	High Point (Piedmont)	128	468	123	196*	40	11	38*	131*	11	.419*
1929	Ed Kallina	Midland (W. Tex.)	94	367	126	159	28	7	44*	—	16	.433*
		Sherman (Lone Star)	17	64	22	22	—	—	6	—	1	.344
		overall										.420

Year	Player	Team (League)	G	AB	R	H	2B	3B	HR	RBI	SB	AVG
1930	Tony Antista	Bisbee (Arizona St.)	109*	444	127*	191*	36	16*	17	100	18	.430*
1931	Babe Phelps	Youngstown (Mid-Atl.)	115	436	71	178	29	9	15	88	9	.408*
1932	George Puccinelli	Rochester (Int.)	133	478	102	187	34	8	28	115	2	.391*
1933	Ox Eckhardt	Mission (PCL)	189*	760	145	315*	56	16	12	143	15	.414*
1934	Frank Demaree	Los Angeles (PCL)	186	702	190*	269*	51*	4	45*	173*	41	.383*
1935	Ox Eckhardt	Mission (PCL)	172	710	149	283*	40	11	2	114	8	.399*
1936	Cal Lahman	Jamestown (Northern)	127	466	154*	182*	30	9	48*	162*	20	.391*
1937	Earl (Red) Martin	Beckley (Mt. St.)	91	360	80	144	39*	14*	8	96*	7	.400*
		Scranton (NYP)	11	41	7	10	1	0	0	4	1	.244
											overall	.384
1938	Murray Franklin	Beckley (Mt. St.)	94	385	91	169	31	13*	26*	110	13	.439*²
1939	Joe Schmidt	Duluth (Northern)	120	440	114*	194*	29	9	31*	133*	17	.441*
1940	Ed Schweda	Lubbock (W. Tex.-N.M.)	114	469	142	198	39	15	11	118	7	.422*
1941	Lew Flick	Elizabethton (App.)	117	502*	127*	210*	37*	13	5	116*	20	.418*
1942	Don Manno	Welch (Mt. St.)	117	457	136*	174*	32	14*	34*	122*	23	.381*
1943	George Kell	Lancaster (Inter-St.)	138	555	120*	220*	33	23*	5	79	14	.396*
1944	Roland Gladu	Hartford (Eastern)	119	417	92	155	28	14	7	102	8	.372
1945	Arden (Cotton) McCaskey	Bristol (App.)	106	437	72	164*	26*	14*	2	96	5	.375*
1946	Walt Forwood	Carbondale (N. Atl.)	111	419	98	170*	43*	7	3	101	22	.406*
1947	Jim Prince	Midland (Longhorn)	108	415	111	178	31	6	34	141	4	.429*
		Lubbock (W. Tex.-N.M.)	12	37	7	10	3	0	1	12	0	.270
											overall	.416
1948	Hershel Martin	Albuquerque (W. Tex.-N.M.)	132	447	133	190	61*	6	18	128	5	.425*
1949	Bob Montag	Pawtucket (New Eng.)	125	454	139*	192*	36	18*	21*	91	43*	.423*
1950	Oscar Sierra	Hornell (Pony)	93	358	99	151	28	2	21	114	12	.422*
		Newport News (Piedmont)	15	45	5	13	1	0	0	5	0	.289
											overall	.407
1951	D. C. (Pud) Miller	Hickory (N.C. St.)	119	426	115	181	32	1	40*	136*	2	.425*
1952	Don Stafford	Salisbury (N.C. St.)	105	392	99	160	31	3	18	90	1	.408*³
1953	Russ Snyder	McAlester (Sooner St.)	138	556	137	240*	32	16	2	84	74*	.432*
1954	Neal Cobb	Crestview (Ala.-Fla.)	115	435	108	188	27	8	5	124	3	.432*
1955	Tom Jordan	Artesia (Longhorn)	136	543	116	221*	69*	2	28	159*	4	.407*
1956	Len Tucker	Pampa (So'west)	140	565	181*	228	40	13	51	181	47*	.404*
1957	Fran Boniar	Reno (Calif.)	110	443	102	193	33	15	11	138*	4	.436*
		Pueblo (Western)	11	37	5	9	1	0	0	7	3	.243
											overall	.421
1958	Neb Wilson	Ft. Walton Beach-Pensacola (Ala.-Fla.)	119	409	102*	162	38*	3	24*	106*	3	.396*
1959	Tom Hamilton	St. Petersburg (Fla. St.)	125	401	109	155	20	3	20*	96	3	.387*
1960	Al Pinkston	Mexico City Reds (Mexican)	138	567	110	225*	41	11	26	144*	4	.397*
1961	Al Pinkston	Veracruz (Mexican)	109	406	79	152	26*	4	13	86	4	.374*
1962	Ramiro Caballero	Guanajuato (Mex. Center)	113	423	123	175*	25	0	59*	170	3	.414*
1963	Vinicio Garcia	Monterrey (Mexican)	122	475	107*	175	36*	5	21	88	3	.368*
1964	Ramiro Caballero	Leon (Mex. Center)	121	460	135*	175*	29	1	35*	145*	3	.380*
1965	Alfonso Peciado	Guanajuato (Mex. Center)	130	529	103	224*	48*	14*	11	147	11	.423*
1966	Heriberto Vargas	Veracruz (Mexican)	7	14	0	3	0	0	0	0	0	.214
		Guanajuato (Mex. Center)	127	481	168*	214	33	1	55*	174*	3	.445*
											overall	.438
1967	Hilario Pena	Campeche (Mex. S.E.)	102	404	60	159	61	3	1	49	9	.394*
1968	Jim Hicks	Tulsa (PCL)	117	407	100*	149	32	7	23	85	14	.366*
1969	Bernie Carbo	Indianapolis (A.A.)	111	404	83	145	37	2	21	76	7	.359*
1970	Miguel Suarez	Tampico (Mex. Center)	126	460	105	181*	37*	4	14	101	15	.393*
1971	Téolindo Acosta	Puebla (Mexican)	133	441	75	173	22	11	7	71	17	.392*
1972	Don Anderson	Jalisco (Mexican)	130	445	76	161	31	2	8	68	0	.362*
1973	Hector Espino	Tampico (Mexican)	116	422	82	159	20	2	22	107*	3	.377*
1974	Téolindo Acosta	Puebla (Mexican)	122	464	93*	170*	17	6	2	43	20	.366*
1975	Gene Richards	Reno (Calif.)	134	501*	148*	191*	29	10	12	58	85*	.381*
1976	Pat Putnam	Asheville (W. Car.)	138	538	100	194*	33*	3	24*	142*	8	.361*
1977	Rudy Law	Lodi (California)	122	451	124	174	22	5	9	88	37	.386*
1978	Champ Summers	Indianapolis (A.A.)	132	462	98	170*	25	5	34*	124*	11	.368
1979	Jimmie Collins	Chihuahua (Mexican)	124	470	95	206*	35	10	6	60	33	.438*
1980	Jimmie Collins	Chihuahua (Mex. #1)	91	346	62	131	19	13	4	52	19	.379
		Saltillo (Mex. #2)	39	137	25	52*	8	3*	2	31*	5	.380
											overall	.379
1981	Kent Hrbek	Visalia (Calif.)	121	462	119	175	25	5	27	111	12	.379*
1982	Randy Ready	El Paso (Texas)	132	475	122*	178*	33	5	20	99	13	.375*
1983	Chris Smith	Phoenix (PCL)	123	449	88	170	31	5	21	102	4	.379*
1984	Jimmie Collins	Mexico City Reds-Cordoba (Mexican)	109	403	81	166	35	4	6	59	12	.412*
1985	Oswaldo Olivares	Aguas.-Campeche (Mexican)	110	441	85	175*	22	14*	5	49	20	.397*²
1986	Willie Aikens	Puebla (Mexican)	129	445	134	202*	38	3	46	154*	0	.454*
1987	Orlando Sanchez	Puebla (Mexican)	123	439	95	182	34	1	25	115	6	.415*
1988	Nelson Barrera	Mexico City Reds (Mexican)	129	460	90	171	26	0	31	124*	7	.372
1989	Willie Aikens	León (Mexican)	128	423	108*	167	40	1	37	131*	1	.395*
1990	Trench Davis	Saltillo (Mexican)	127	498	84	189*	33	4	5	50	20	.380
1991	Rich Renteria	Jalisco (Mexican)	104	382	90	169	30	6	24	106	17	.442*
		Indianapolis (A.A.)	20	72	6	17	5	0	1	5	0	.236
										overall		.410
1992	Raul Perez Tovar	Monclova (Mexican)	129	483	83	201	32	5	8	93	14	.416*
1993	Nelson Simmons	Jalisco (Mexican)	109	369	81	141	27	6	34	95	1	.382
		Palm Springs (California)	20	76	13	25	8	0	5	23	0	.329
1994	Brian Hunter	Tucson (PCL)	128	513	113*	191*	28	9	10	51	49*	.372*
1995	Adam Riggs	San Bernardino (Calif.)	134	542	111*	196*	39*	5	24	106	31	.362*
1996	Vladimer Guerrero	West Palm Beach (Fla. St.)	20	80	16	29	8	0	5	18	2	.363
		Harrisburg (Eastern)	118	417	84	150	32	8	19	78	17	.360*
		overall .360										

*Led league in category

[1]If charged with 400 at-bats, Osborne's average would be .428, higher than any player with 400 or more at-bats.
(George Rhinehardt, Greenville (Sally) G: 120, AB: 495, R: 110*, H: 200*, 2B: 45*, 3B: 18, HR: 8, RBI: 92, SB: 32*, AVG: .404*)

[2]If charged with 400 at-bats, Franklin's average would be .423, higher than any player with 400 or more at-bats.
(Butch Moran, Rogers (Ark.-Mo.) G: 105, AB: 406, R: 107, H: 159, 2B: 43*, 3B: 12, HR: 22*, RBI: 114, SB: 8, AVG: .392*)

[3]If charged with 400 at-bats, Stafford's average would be .400, higher than any player with 400 or more at-bats.
(Clint McCord, Clinton (Miss. Ohio Val.) G:119, AB: 482, R: 123, H: 189*, 2B: 40, 3B: 15, HR: 15, RBI: 109, SB: 20, AVG: .392*)

Minor League Career Records

Batters	Years	G	AB	R	H	2B	3B	HR	RBI	SB	AVG
Buzz Arlett	1918–37	2390	8001	1610	2726	598	107	432	1786	200	.341
Ike Boone	1920–37	1857	6807	1362	2521	477	128	215	1334	120	.370
Bunny Brief	1910–28	2426	8945	1776	2963	594	152	340	1776	247	.331
Nick Cullop	1920–44	2484	8571	1607	2670	523	147	420	1857	154	.312
Ox Eckhardt	1925–40	1926	7563	1275	2773	455	146	66	1037	140	.367
Hector Espino	1960–84	2500	8605	1597	2898	403	49	484	1678	54	.337
Ray French	1914–41	3278	12174	1769	3254	590	129	46	1029	363	.267
Spencer Harris	1921–48	3258	11377	2287	3617	743	150	258	1769	241	.318
Joe Hauser	1918–42	1854	6426	1430	1923	340	116	399	1353	109	.299
Smead Jolley	1922–41	2234	8300	1459	3043	640	77	336	1593	61	.367
Jigger Statz	1920–42	2790	10657	1996	3356	595	137	66	1044	466	.315
Perry Werden	1884–1908	1540	6234	1244	2125	392	87	171	—	350	.341

Pitchers	Years	G	IP	W	L	H	R	ER	BB	SO	ERA
Bill Bailey	1906–25	581	3730	242	219	3452	1572	612	1565	2375	2.87
Dick Barrett	1925–53	790	4964	325	257	4578	2176	1747	2099	2513	3.34
George Boehler	1911–30	562	3711	248	202	3421	1745	874	1464	2319	3.74
George Brunet	1953–85	669	4041	244	242	3761	1832	1466	1754	3175	3.27
Tony Freitas	1928–53	736	4905	342	238	5090	2073	1694	932	2324	3.11
Sam Gibson	1923–49	661	4469	307	200	4460	1860	1413	1073	2195	3.08
Willie Mains	1887–1906	551	4044	319	181	4442	2458	—	1225	1680	
Joe Martina	1910–31	833	5417	349	277	4950	2307	1355	1868	2770	3.22
Frank Shellenback	1917–38	638	4514	315	192	4922	2110	1775	1021	1742	3.55
Bill Thomas	1926–52	1016	5995	383	347	6721	3098	2211	1230	2204	3.71
Hal Turpin	1927–46	635	4084	271	203	4512	1917	1367	807	1254	3.28

Year	Number of Leagues	Number of Clubs	Regular Season Total Attendance
1947	52	388	37,815,753
1948	58	438	38,415,716
1949	59	448(6)	39,782,717
1950	58(1)	446(14)	32,960,733
1951	50(1)	371(13)	26,135,174
1952	43	324(5)	24,024,373
1953	38	292(4)	21,109,565
1954	36(3)	269(22)	18,674,503
1955	33	243(5)	18,203,889
1956	28	217(5)	16,402,953
1957	28	200(10)	14,875,346
1958	24	173	12,744,883
1959	21	150	11,622,581
1960	22	152	10,660,811
1961	22	147	9,766,505
1962	20	134	9,732,582
1963	18	130	9,749,381
1964	20	136	10,102,310
1965	19	136	10,029,518
1966	19	138	9,826,124
1967	19	141	9,940,660
1968	21	152	9,887,328
1969	21	155	9,993,615
1970	20	153	10,726,470
1971	20	155	11,134,084
1972	19	148	10,986,628
1973	18	147	10,828,828
1974	18	145	10,562,452
1975	18	137	11,021,848
1976	20	148(1)	11,324,947
1977	19	150	13,004,297
1978	18	156	13,012,727
1979	18(1)	155(6)	15,304,724
1980	17	155(14)	12,265,022
1981	17	152	16,178,790
1982	17	160	17,637,244
1983	17	162	18,599,190
1984	17	164	17,580,299
1985	17	168	18,380,000
1986	17	164	18,456,808
1987	18	176	20,215,564
1988	19	188	21,661,873
1989	19	197	23,103,593
1990	19	202	25,244,569
1991	19	207	26,590,096
1992	19	212	27,180,170
1993	19	214	30,022,761
1994	19	216	33,355,199
1995	22	216	33,126,934
1996	25	218	33,289,278

## CHAPTER 16

Baseball in Japan

Yoichi Nagata and John B. Holway

Hideo Nomo wins rookie of the year for the Dodgers and hurls a no-hitter. Sachio Kinugasa vaults into the limelight when Cal Ripken passes his world record for consecutive games played. Japan shocks the U.S. Olympic hopefuls, knocking them out of a silver medal, and possibly out of the gold as well.

It's time to take another, serious, look at the nation that gave us Sadaharu Oh and may in the not too distant future be playing America in a real November World Series. Already U.S. scouts are wistfully eyeing Japan, where, U.S. observers say, more Nomos are already blossoming, along with hitters equally as potent.

History

In earlier editions of *Total Baseball,* we focused on the development and key players of Japanese baseball's early years. We also placed what now seems undue emphasis on the performance of U.S. players in Japan, and the detailing of their statistical record. In this post-Nomo edition, however, we offer only a quick runthrough of the past, preferring to devote attention to the current state of baseball in Japan. And the statistical record is that of the Japanese Major Leagues and its best players, whatever their national origin.

Japanese baseball was born in the 1870s. Professor Horace Wilson is one of several credited with being the Abner Doubleday of Nippon. By 1908 Japanese teams beat the visiting University of Washington four games out of ten. The Chicago White Sox and New York Giants visited Japan in 1913. The nation's first pro team was formed in 1920. Casey Stengel's All Stars arrived in 1922 and Ty Cobb in 1928 arrived to teach his batting secrets. Three years later Cobb was followed by Lou Gehrig, Lefty Grove, Al Simmons, Frankie Frisch, and Lefty O'Doul.

In 1934 Ruth, Gehrig, Simmons, O'Doul, Jimmie Foxx, Charlie Gehringer, Earl Averill, and Lefty Gomez arrived. They won all their games handily—except one. An eighteen-year-old high schooler, Eiji Sawamura, whiffed Gehringer, Ruth, Gehrig, and Foxx in succession, losing 1-0. He was later killed in World War II. Japan's Cy Young Award is named the Sawamura Award.

Sawamura starred on the Tokyo Giants when Japan's first professional league was formed in 1936. The league lasted until the bombing of 1945. After World War II, General Douglas MacArthur encouraged the Japanese leagues to resume.

O'Doul brought his Pacific Coast League San Francisco Seals in 1949. The legendary Russian émigré, Vic Starffin, held them to one hit in eight innings before losing 1-0.

In 1951 O'Doul and Joe DiMaggio led a U.S. squad to Tokyo. The Japanese won their first victory over the Americans, beating Bobby Shantz, 3-1. DiMag hit his last homer during the tour.

U.S. teams continued the tradition every other year. In the spring of 1953 the Tokyo Giants visited Florida and won one out of five against big league clubs, beating the New York Giants, 9-7.

That fall an All-Star team of Bob Lemon, Robin Roberts, Yogi Berra, Enos Slaughter, Eddie Mathews, Hank Sauer, Harvey Kuenn, and others lost their first game, 5-4, to the fifth-place Japanese Orions but won their next 11.

That same year the New York Giants also visited Japan, winning 12 and losing one, with one tie. They came from behind to beat Masaichi Kaneda, 5-3. Then a little submarine-baller, Takumi Otomo, defeated Hoyt Wilhelm, 1-0, on an eighth-inning home run.

By 1956 the champion Dodgers dropped four games in Japan. In 1989, for the first time, Japan came out ahead of the Americans, beating the Los Angeles Dodgers nine games to eight. The following year they did it again, whipping an All Star team of Roger Clemens, Barry Bonds, Cecil Fielder, Roberto Alomar, Dave Stewart, etc. four games to three.

The Tokyo Giants

The Tokyo Giants, who play in the new Tokyo Dome, are the Yankees of Japan. Led by Sadaharu Oh and "Golden Boy" Shigeo Nagashima, they have won twenty-eight pennants in the last forty-seven years. In one stretch, 1965-1973, the heyday of Oh and Nagashima, they won nine straight Japan Series. Only one pro team in any country in any sport, Josh Gibson's 1937-45 Negro League Homestead Grays, has equaled that mark. Thanks to the immense publicity of their parent company, the Yomiuri newspaper and TV empire, the Giants are also by far the nation's favorite team.

Thanks to the Giants, their league, the Central, claims 31,000 fans per game, far above the rival Pacific League with 22,800. In the southern city of Fukuoka, the Hawks, managed by the immortal Oh, averaged 34,000 a game in their new retractable Fukuoka Dome.

For 1997 the Central League demanded a 140-game schedule, in place of the present 130 games, to increase its profits. The two leagues compromised on 135. In return, the Pacific demanded interleague play to cash in on the Giants' huge drawing power. However, the Central vetoed that idea.

Incidentally, the average Japanese player, including minor leaguers, made $253,000 in 1996.

Gaijin (Foreigners)

Foreign players who have starred in Japan include a long list of "U-Turn *Gaijin*" such as Cecil Fielder, Kevin Mitchell, Pete Incaviglia, Joe Pepitone, etc. They are often overpaid, come for a cup of coffee, earn reputations as whining, roughneck brawlers, and then go home, leaving a bad taste behind.

Some who stayed longer and left happy fans included sluggers Randy Bass, Leron Lee, and Greg "Boomer" Wells; Shane Mack, Warren Cromartie, George Altman, Steve Ontiveros, Jim Paciorek, Daryl Spencer, Julio Franco, and others. Franco has said he wants to return to Japan to finish his career.

In addition, Japan has imported stars from the Korean and Taiwan pro leagues. In 1996 several Latin players entered Japan by way of Taiwan. The biggest catch was Korean Sun Dong Yol, a five-time Korean strikeout king. His ERAs ranged from 1.70 to 0.78 before he switched to relief and led all Korean hurlers in saves. However, he had a disappointing injury-filled 1996 season in Japan.

In 1990 the Hiroshima Carp opened a baseball academy in the Dominican Republic, scouting for low-priced teenage talent in place of the often over-priced U.S. ex-big leaguers. Their biggest catch, pitcher Robinson Checo, had a fine debut in 1995 with 15-8, 2.74. However, he was plagued with injuries in '96 and jumped to the Boston Red Sox for the 1997 season.

1996: The Year of the Blue Wave

As the season opened, the big port city of Kobe was still rebuilding from the great earthquake of 1995 that killed more than 6,000 people and destroyed 100,000 homes. Many of the Blue Wave players lost their own homes.

A new team, formed in 1989, the Blue Wave was led by the young superstar, Ichiro. With his unorthodox stance—swinging his right, or lead, leg back behind his left leg before striding—the twenty-year old almost became Japan's first .400-hitter in 1994. He also has good speed and fair power, and ex-Ranger manager Bobby Valentine, who managed in Japan, hailed him as one of the ten best hitters in the world.

A quiet, retiring youngster, who seems more like a philosopher than a ballplayer, Ichiro has already gained the star status of a Babe Ruth. Like Madonna, Ichiro ("First son") doesn't use his last name, which is Suzuki. That's because he is in a TV-commercial battle against Nomo. Nomo endorses Toyota, Ichiro Nissan. To avoid a conflict with Suzuki cars, Ichiru decided to drop his last name.

After the '95 quake, the Waves donned uniforms with the words "Ganbaro, Kobe" ("Fight, Kobe") on their sleeves and won the '95 Pacific League pennant to lift the morale of the devastated city. However, in the Japan Series, Swallows manager Katsuya Nomura, the old-time slugging catcher, received a thorough computer study on Ichiro, showing that he couldn't hit high inside fastballs. Swallow pitchers tied him up, and the Blue Wave lost in five games.

They vowed to win it all for Kobe in 1996.

Batting clean-up was Troy Neel, ex-Oakland Athletic, who was almost fired for not hustling in 1995 after hitting .244 with 130 strikeouts. But he came to life in '96. Hideki Irabu, Japan's Nolan Ryan—who also wants to be its next Hideo Nomo—was the ace of the pitching staff. His fastball has been timed at 98 m.p.h. Manager Akira Ogi was a "magician" at juggling his lineup, especially his bullpen, using every man as a role-player.

Ichiro got off to a bad start, as everyone began pitching him high and tight, and the Blue Wave struggled in second place. Then Ichiro tried a new, open stance, and the hits began coming again. He won his third straight batting title and third straight MVP. Neel was tops in homers, RBI, and steals, Irabu (12-6) won his second ERA crown, and the Blue Wave surged to the pennant.

In the Central League, meanwhile, the famous Tokyo Giants were managed by Shigeo Nagashima, the most popular Japanese player of all time. They boasted several big stars. Pitching aces were three-time Sawamura Award winner Masaki Saito and former Dodger fireballer Balvino Galvez. On offense they had Shane Mack, the ex-Twin outfielder, and Hiromitsu Och-ai, who joined the 500-homer club during the season. Their main gun, however, was a husky twenty-two-year-old, Hideki Matsui, nicknamed "Godzilla" for his mammoth blasts. Matsui was a high school *sumo* wrestler, and his school couldn't build a fence high enough to contain his long drives. In his fourth year as a pro in 1996, Matsui, now weighing 198 pounds, abandoned his high leg kick and blossomed into a superstar.

Still, the Giants were staggering 11½ games behind Hiroshima by July 6, and Och-ai was sidelined with a broken finger. But Nagashima grimly predicted in English that his team was going to "make drama," and they did.

The Giants hurriedly called reliever Mario Brito from Taiwan and climbed back into the fight. Matsui took over for Och-ai. He blasted one ball that hit the roof of the Tokyo Dome and another that literally flew out of sight, an estimated 498 feet. On the next-to-last day of the season, Godzilla had slugged 38 homers in 130 games and was named MVP. He might have won the home run crown, but in the final game the Dragons walked him four straight times to preserve the title for their own Takeshi Yamasaki, who hit 39.

Balvez and Saito each won 16 games, tops in the league, and the Giants won the pennant on the next to the last day. That set up the Japan Series, which was billed as "Ichiro vs Godzilla." The two young stars compared thus:

	Age	Ht	Wt	BA	HR	HR/162 G
Ichiro	22	6'	165	.356	16	20
Matsui	22	6'2"	198	.314	38	47

Ichiro also stole 35 bases. In 1995 he had 49 steals and 25 homers. He hasn't missed a game in three years. Matsui, power, and Ichiro, finesse, are expected to lead Japan into the twenty-first century.

In the Series opener, Och-ai returned to the Giant lineup with three hits, but it was Ichiro's tenth-inning homer that won the game. The Kobe relievers shut down Matsui, but Neel produced three game-winning hits (his only three hits of the Series), and the Blue Wave overwhelmed the Giants in five games. Neel, the Series MVP, pumped his fist and led the crowd in shouts of "Gambaro, Kobe!"

U.S.-Japan Series

After their many onesided victories in the first half of the century, the Americans began to find out that they had to work harder to beat the bigger and improved Japanese. They can usually still win, but they now have to send their best players and take the games seriously in order to do it. Over the last decade, this is how the series has gone:

	U.S.	Japan	U.S. Players
1986	6	1	Ripken, Canseco, Sandberg, Murphy
1988	3	2	Hershiser, Puckett, Larkin, Molitor
1990	3	4	Bonds, Fielder, R. Johnson, Alomar, Barfield, R. Martinez, Stieb, Dibble, Thigpen, C. Finley, Stewart, Dibble
1992	7	1	Clemens, R.Johnson, Griffey Jr., Franco, Dunston, Dykstra, Finley, Stewart, Barfield, Montgomery, O. Smith, McDowell
1992	0	2	Los Angeles: Hershiser, Butler, Piazza, Offerman
1996	4	2	Nomo, Hentgen, Neagle, Gonzalez, Galarraga, Piazza, Bonds, Sheffield, Franco, Percival, C. Finley, Reynolds
Total	23	12	(No extra innings. This resulted in two ties in 1988, one in 1990 and two in '96.)

In 1990 Hideo Nomo defeated Rob Dibble 2-1, then lost 5-0 on a combined no-hitter by Randy Johnson and Chuck Finley. The 1996 series was another exciting one. Before crowds that averaged 45,000 a night, the games went like this:

	Winner	Score	Stadium
1.	Japan	6-5	Tokyo Dome
2.	U.S.	6-1	Tokyo Dome
3.	U.S.	4-2	Tokyo Dome
4.	U.S.	2-1	Seibu, Saitama
5.	tie	6-6	Fukuoka Dome
6.	U.S.	11-8	Koshien, Osaka
7.	Japan	8-6	Yokohama
8.	tie	8-8	Tokyo Dome

Japanese fans, who can see all Nomo's games on post-midnight TV, knew all the U.S. stars intimately. Nomo pitched for the American stars, but Japan's best gaijin—Troy Neel, Shane Mack, Alonzo Powell etc.—didn't play.

Game 1. Jet-lagged AL Cy Young winner Pat Hentgen (20-10) gave up a bases-loaded double to Central League home run champ Kazuhiro Kiyohara in the first inning. Ichiro had two hits, two walks, and a steal.

Game 2. Nomo packed the stadium and flashlights popped like fireworks as Ichiro, leading off, singled through his legs. But Nomo got the next man on a double play. In the third Nomo got Ichiro on a grounder and whiffed Godzilla Matsui on a forkball to complete three shutout innings with two hits.

Home runs: Andres Galarraga (NL home run champ), Julio Franco (who played in Japan in 1995), Juan Gonzalez, and Kiyohara (off Denny Neagle).

Game 3. Shane Reynolds and Chuck Finley overpowered the Central League All Stars, although Matsui slugged a Godzilla-sized home run. Ichiro injured his hip in a dugout accident and missed the next four games.

Game 4. Hentgen came back and survived a no-out two-on threat with Matsui up and the red-hot Kiyohara on deck, but Matsui hit into a double play. Ichiro continued to sit out games four, five, and six. Mike Piazza, a big hero as Nomo's catcher and as a star in Japanese TV commercials, tied the game with a homer, and Cal Ripken produced the game-winning hit in the seventh.

Game 5. Troy Percival preserved the tie by walking Matsui intentionally with the tying run on second.

Game 6. Nomo, an Osaka native, was blasted for four runs in four innings in his homecoming.

Game 7. Matsui smashed a grand slam off Shane Reynolds for the victory. "That's what happens when you hang a pitch," Reynolds shrugged. Steve Finley went two-for-two for the Americans.

Game 8. Piazza's homer gave the U.S. a 9-4 lead in the seventh, but the Japanese rallied for four runs in the last two frames.

The Next Nomo?

Several stars are trying to shake the rigid reserve clause that ties them to their Japanese teams. (Nomo was able to sign with the Dodgers because he had been injured and his team did not try to protect him.) Curiously, America has a very favorable balance of baseball trade with Japan, exporting much more than it imports. So far Japan has resisted most entreaties to open up its gates and let more baseball exports out.

Not every Japanese player wants to go. Stars are well paid and worshipped as heroes in their homeland. Still, others are anxious to make the jump.

Hard-throwing Katz Maeda, twenty-six, who dyes his hair alternately purple or yellow, threatened to quit the game if his team, the Lions, didn't let him go. After three very lackluster seasons, they did. He had a good winter in the Hawaiian League, then signed with the Yankees for $350,000. Another pitcher, Takayasu Kato, was released by the Marines because of knee problems and signed a minor league contract with the Red Sox.

An established star at twenty-seven, Shigetoshi Hasegawa of the Blue Wave weighs 163 pounds. He patterns himself after the Indians' Orel Hershiser, with a good breaking ball that he throws on the 2-0 or 3-1 count. Hasegawa has long wanted to go to America. He spent winters in Los Angeles with former Blue Wave pitching coach Jim Colburn, studying English and learning U.S. baseball. He says the higher stitches on American balls will make his breaking balls more effective. After an off-year in '96, when he was not a factor in the pennant drive, he might obtain a release from his team.

Hideki Irabu's fastball has been timed at 98 miles an hour, and he is, according to Valentine, the best of many excellent Japanese pitching prospects. (Bobby says every team has two or three hurlers who could make the major leagues.) Irabu, twenty-seven in 1996, weighs only 176 pounds, but he has worn out his videotape of Nolan Ryan. Like Ryan, Irabu at first had speed (1,000 strikeouts in his first 997 innings) but no control. However, by 1995 he had developed into an ERA champion while still fanning 239 men in 203 innings. Irabu eagerly wants to go to the United States. During the 1996 season he claimed he got the OK from GM Tatsuro Hiro-oka after much back-door negotiations. However, Hiro-oka was fired at the end of the season, and Irabu's fate is still undetermined.

Kazuhiro Sasaki has the best forkball and the most saves of any current pitcher in Japan. Even when Nomo was pitching there, Sasaki insisted that "I have the best forkball in Japan." Many observers believe Sasaki, at 6'4" and 210 pounds, is the best prospect to make it in the

United States. He was twenty-eight in 1996.

Many Japanese youngsters, including the then twenty-year-old Ichiro, have gotten experience and confidence in the Hawaiian Winter League. In 1994 Hawks second baseman Hiroki Kokubo blasted a pennant-clinching 400-foot homer in the final game and was named MVP. The next year he won the Pacific League home run title despite a 400-foot foul line in his home park, the Fukuoka Dome.

Mashi Murakami

Murakami, a hard-throwing reliever for the San Francisco Giants in 1964-65, was the first Japanese to play in the U.S. major leagues, and in any discussion of the next Nomo we inevitably recall the man who preceded Nomo to the U.S. major leagues. In his rookie year, Mashi struck out 15 men in 15 innings and posted a 1.80 ERA. The next year he whiffed 85 men in 74 innings, won four, lost one, and saved eight.

He became the darling of the San Francisco Nissei community and a favorite of his teammates, to whom he removed his cap and bowed after every good play.

Murakami had come to the States to get experience in the Giants' farm system; however, when the Giants wanted to keep him, his parent club demanded that he come home. Unfortunately, back in Japan he never did live up to expectations.

Olympics

Ever since baseball became an Olympic sport, Japan has been tough on the Americans, often beating some of the nation's top future stars out of gold and silver medals. The record:

	GOLD	SILVER	U.S. PLAYERS
1984	Japan	U.S.	W. Clark, McGwire, Mack, Larkin, Swift, Witt
1988	U.S.	Japan	Abbott, Benes, T.Martinez, Nagy, Ventura
1992	Cuba	Taiwan	Giambi
1996	Cuba	Japan	

In 1992, Japan won the bronze, the U.S. finished fourth. Taiwan's pitching star, Chien-fu Kuo-Lee, signed with the Tigers in Japan. In 1996 the U.S. thrashed Japan in their first meeting, 15-5, in a game called under the "mercy" rule. The semifinal rematch was supposed to be another easy triumph as the Americans kept their eyes on the final round against Cuba for the gold. Instead, Japan shocked the Americans by a score of 11-2. Masanori Sugiura, 28, a veteran of the '92 Games, gave up only two runs in six innings, while Japan smashed five homers and KO'd Kris Benson, the top pick in the U.S. draft. The loss forced the Americans to settle for the bronze.

Japanese stars to watch: power-hitting shortstop Tadahito Iguchi, and pitchers Takeo Kawamura and Hitoshi Ono. Slugging third baseman Kosuke Fukudome, nineteen, skipped the big leagues to sign with a company team.

Oh for Cooperstown

It's time someone said the obvious: Sadaharu Oh belongs in the Hall of Fame. No one may ever catch his world mark of 868 home runs. And remember two things:

1. Oh played only 130 games a year. If he had played 162, one could add 25 percent to his total, for a lifetime record of over 1,000.

2. He was walked so often that he never came to bat 500 times a year and often came up fewer than 300 times. Historically, the average U.S. home run champ has had 550 official at bats. Oh's best year per 550 at bats was 1974, when he hit 49 in only 385 trips. That's 67 per 550. Lifetime he averaged 48 per 550 at bats. Ruth also averaged 48; Hank Aaron, 30.

It's true that Japanese fences are shorter, about 280 feet down the line—but Ruth's targets were 257 feet in the Polo Grounds and 296 in Yankee Stadium. Japanese pitching in Oh's day was inferior to major league pitching in Ruth's day. But Babe saw more fastballs, Oh got more off-speed stuff. And the Japanese ball was not as lively.

Tom Seaver, who faced Oh in postseason tours, estimated that he could hit 35 homers a year in the U.S. major leagues. That's better than most of the hitters in Cooperstown have done.

Sachio Kinugasa: Japan's Lou Gehrig

The diminutive Japanese-American broke Lou Gehrig's consecutive-game record in 1987 and set a new world mark of 2,215. But not until 1996, when Cal Ripken finally caught him, did the world spotlight belatedly shift to him.

No one can argue that Kinugasa's mark was set in an inferior league: a game in Hiroshima is just as hard to play as a game in Baltimore. In fact, since Japanese teams play only 130 games a year, it took Kinugasa five years longer to set his mark than it took Gehrig and Ripken. Sachio had to play to the age of forty to do it, the two Americans were thirty-five.

Which is harder? Both Kinugasa and Ripken laughed and agreed the Japanese conditions were tougher.

Actually, Kinugasa almost made it 125 additional games. In 1972 he played the first 124 games, then missed one—the last one he would miss for fifteen years. Of course he wasn't even thinking of a record then. But if he had played that game, he would have finished with 2,340, and Ripken would still be chasing him as the 1997 season opened.

Ripken and Kinugasa share one thing in common—they both have red, white, and blue American blood coursing through their veins. Kinugasa's father was a black American GI.

Sachio ran up one mark that Cal (or Lou) will never catch—504 home runs. Pretty good for a little guy who stood four inches shorter than Cal and weighed sixty pounds less.

Cal and Sachio met on the field in Hiroshima in 1983, when the Orioles played the Hiroshima Carp. Baltimore hurler Mike Flanagan remembered the game well. "Kinugasa hit a double off me on an outside fastball on the 1-0 count," he said.

The Baseball Card Boom

The baseball card boom has hit Japan big-time. Virtually unknown until the 1960s, the first cards were snapped up by American GIs while the Japanese considered them valueless. By the 1980s American collectors came to Japan, scouring flea-markets and buying candy bars by the bag full, getting cards for next-to-nothing. It was reminiscent of the Japanese woodblock print craze of the 19th century, when U.S. and European collectors bought up now priceless prints and shipped them out of Japan to museums all over the world.

However, Nomo-mania woke the Japanese up, and in July 1996 more than 4,000 fans jammed into Tokyo's first big card show.

Batting Leaders

YEAR	CENTRAL LEAGUE		PACIFIC LEAGUE	
1950	Fumio Fujimura	.362	Hiroshi Oshita	.339
1951	Tetsuharu Kawakami	.377	Hiroshi Oshita	.383
1952	Michio Nishizawa	.353	Shigeya Iijima	.336
1953	Tetsuharu Kawakami	.347	Isami Okamoto	.318
1954	Wally Yonamine	.361	Larry Raines	.337
1955	Tetsuharu Kawakami	.338	Futoshi Nakanishi	.332
1956	Wally Yonamine	.338	Yasumitsu Toyoda	.325
1957	Wally Yonamine	.343	Kazuhiro Yamauchi	.331
1958	Kenjiro Tamiya	.320	Futoshi Nakanishi	.314
1959	Shigeo Nagashima	.334	Kohei Sugiyama	.323
1960	Shigeo Nagashima	.334	Kihachi Enomoto	.344
1961	Shigeo Nagashima	.353	Isao Harimoto	.336
1962	Katsuya Morinaga	.307	Jack Bloomfield	.374
1963	Shigeo Nagashima	.341	Jack Bloomfield	.335
1964	Shinichi Eto	.323	Yoshinori Hirose	.366
1965	Shinichi Eto	.336	Katsuya Nomura	.320
1966	Shigeo Nagashima	.344	Kihachi Enomoto	.351
1967	Toshio Naka	.343	Isao Harimoto	.336
1968	Sadaharu Oh	.326	Isao Harimoto	.336
1969	Sadaharu Oh	.345	Isao Harimoto	.333
			Yozo Nagafuchi	.333
1970	Sadaharu Oh	.325	Isao Harimoto	.383
1971	Shigeo Nagashima	.320	Shinichi Eto	.337
1972	Tsutomu Wakamatsu	.329	Isao Harimoto	.353
1973	Sadaharu Oh	.355	Hideji Kato	.337
1974	Sadaharu Oh	.332	Isao Harimoto	.340
1975	Koji Yamamoto	.319	Jinten Haku	.319
1976	Kenichi Yazawa	.354	Satoru Yoshioka	.309
1977	Tsutomu Wakamatsu	.358	Michiyo Arito	.329
1978	Jitsuo Mizutani	.348	Kyosuke Sasaki	.354
1979	Felix Millan	.346	Kideji Kahto	.364
1980	Kenichi Yazawa	.369	Leron Lee	.358
1981	Taira Fujita	.358	Hiromitsu Ochi-ai	.326
1982	Keiji Nagasaki	.351	Hiromitsu Ochi-ai	.325
1983	Akinobu Mayumi	.353	Hiromitsu Ochi-ai	.332
1984	Toshio Shinoz'ka	.334	Boomer Wells	.355
1985	Randy Bass	.350	Hiromitsu Ochi-ai	.367
1986	Randy Bass	.389*	Hiromitsu Ochi-ai	.360
1987	Toshio Shinozuka	.333	Hiromasa Arai	.366
	Kozo Shoda	.333		
1988	Kozo Shoda	.340	Hideaki Takazawa	.327
1989	Warren Cromartie	.378	Boomer Wells	.322
1990	Jim Paciorek	.326	Norifumi Nishimura	.338
1991	Atsuya Furuta	.339	Mitsuchika Hirai	.314
1992	Jack Howell	.331	Makoto Sasaki	.322
1993	Tom O'Malley	.329	Hatsush'ko Tsuji	.319
1994	Alonzo Powell	.324	Ichiro Suzuki	.385*
1995	Alonzo Powell	.355	Ichiro Suzuki	.342
1996	Alonzo Powell	.340	Ichiro Suzuki	.356

Home Run Leaders

YEAR	CENTRAL LEAGUE		PACIFIC LEAGUE	
1950	Makoto Kozuru	51	Kaoru Betto	43
1951	Noboru Aota	32	Hiroshi Osh'ta	26
1952	Satoru Sugiyama	27	Yasuhiro Fukami	25
1953	Fumio Fujimura	27	Futoshi Nakanishi	36
1954	Noboru Aota	31	Futoshi Nakanishi	31
1955	Yukihiko Machida	31	Futoshi Nakanishi	35
1956	Noboru Aota	25	Futoshi Nakanishi	29
1957	Takao Sato	22	Katsuya Nomura	30
	Noboru Aota	22		
1958	Shigeo Nagashima	29	Futoshi Nakanishi	23
1959	Takeshi Kuwata	31	Kazuhiro Yamauchi	25
	Toru Mori	31		
1960	Katsumi Fujimoto	22	Kazuhiro Yamauchi	32
1961	Shigeo Nagashima	28	Katsuya Nomura	29
			Masahiro Nakada	29
1962	Sadaharu Oh	38	Katsuya Nomura	44
1963	Sadaharu Oh	40	Katsuya Nomura	52*
1964	Sadaharu Oh	55*	Katsuya Nomura	41
1965	Sadaharu Oh	42	Katsuya Nomura	42
1966	Sadaharu Oh	48	Katsuya Nomura	34
1967	Sadaharu Oh	47	Katsuya Nomura	35
1968	Sadaharu Oh	49	Katsuya Nomura	38
1969	Sadaharu Oh	44	Tokuji Nagaike	41
1970	Sadaharu Oh	47	Katsuo Osugi	44
1971	Sadaharu Oh	39	Katsuo Osugi	41
1972	Sadaharu Oh	48	Tokuji Nagaike	41
1973	Sadaharu Oh	51	Tokuji Nagaike	43
1974	Sadaharu Oh	49	Clarence Jones	38
1975	Koichi Tabuchi	43	Masahiro Doi	34
1976	Sadaharu Oh	49	Clarence Jones	36
1977	Sadaharu Oh	50	Leron Lee	34
1978	Koji Yamamoto	44	Bobby Mitchell	36
1979	Masayuki Kakefu	48	Charlie Manuel	37
1980	Koji Yamamoto	44	Charlie Manuel	48
1981	Koji Yamamoto	43	Hiromitsu Kadota	44
			Tony Solaita	44
1982	Masayuki Kakefu	35	Hiromitsu Och-ai	32
	Yasunori Oshima	36		
1984	Masaru Uno	37	Boomer Wells	37
1985	Randy Bass	54	Hiromitsu Ochi-ai	50
1986	Randy Bass	47	Hiromitsu Ochi-ai	52*
1987	Rick Lancellotti	39	Koji Akiyama	43
1988	Carlos Ponce	33	Hiromitsu Kadota	44
1989	Larry Parrish	42	Ralph Bryant	49
1990	Hiromitsu Ochi-ai	34	Orestes Destrade	42
1991	Hiromitsu Ochi-ai	37	Orestes Destrade	39
1992	Jack Howell	38	Orestes Destrade	41
1993	Akira Eto	34	Ralph Bryant	42
1994	•Yasuaki Taihoh	38	Ralph Bryant	35
1995	Akira Eto	39	Hiroki Kokubo	28
1996	Takeshi Yamasaki	39	Troy Neel	32

•Taiwan   *League record

RBI Leaders

YEAR	CENTRAL LEAGUE		PACIFIC LEAGUE	
1950	Makoto Kozuru	161*	Kaoru Betto	105
1951	Noboru Aota	105	Tokuji Iida	87
1952	Michio Nishizawa	98	Tokuji Iida	86
1953	Fumio Fujimura	98	Futoshi Nakanishi	86
1954	Hiroyuki Watanabe	91	Kazuhiro Yamauchi	97
	Satoru Sugiyama	91		
1955	Tetsuharu Kawakami	79	Kazuhiro Yamauchi	99
1956	Toshio Miyamoto	69	Futoshi Nakanishi	95
1957	Toshio Miyamoto	78	Futoshi Nakanishi	100
1958	Shigeo Nagashima	92	Takao Katsuragi	85
1959	Toru Mori	87	Takao Katsuragi	95
1960	Katsumi Fujimoto	76	Kazuhiro Yamauchi	103
1961	Takeshi Kuwata	94	Kazuhiro Yamauchi	112
1962	Sadaharu Oh	85	Katsuya Nomura	104
1963	Shigeo Nagashima	112	Katsuya Nomura	135
1964	Sadaharu Oh	119	Katsuya Nomura	115
1965	Sadaharu Oh	104	Katsuya Nomura	110
1966	Sadaharu Oh	116	Katsuya Nomura	97
1967	Sadaharu Oh	108	Katsuya Nomura	100
1968	Shigeo Nagashima	125	George Altman	100
1969	Shigeo Nagashima	115	Atsushi Nagaike	101
1970	Shigeo Nagashima	105	Katsuo Osugi	129
1971	Sadaharu Oh	101	Hiromitsu Kadota	120
1972	Sadaharu Oh	120	Katsuo Osugi	101
			Katsuya Nomura	101
1973	Sadaharu Oh	114	AtsU.S.hi Nagaike	109
1974	Sadaharu Oh	107	AtsU.S.hi Naga-i-ke	96
1975	Sadaharu Oh	96	Hideji Kahto	97
1976	Sadaharu Oh	123	Hideji Kahto	82
1977	Sadaharu Oh	124	Leron Lee	109
1978	Sadaharu Oh	118	Bobby Marcano	94
1979	Koji Yamamoto	113	Hideji Kahto	104
1980	Koji Yamamoto	112	Charlie Manuel	129
1981	Koji Yamamoto	103	Tony Solaita	108
1982	Masayuki Kakefu	95	Hiromitsu Ochi-ai	99
1983	Tatsunori Hara	103	Jitsuo Mizutani	114
1984	Sachio Kinugasa	102	Boomer Wells	130
1985	Randy Bass	134	Hiromitsu Och-ai	146*
1986	Randy Bass	109	Hiromitsu Och-ai	116
1987	Carlos Ponce	98	Boomer Wells	119
1988	Carlos Ponce	102	Hiromitsu Kadota	125
1989	Hiromitsu Ochi-ai	116	Boomer Wells	124
1990	Hiromitsu Ochi-ai	102	Kazuhiko Ishimine	106
			Orestes Destrade	106
1991	Katsumi Hirosawa	102	Orestes Destrade	92
			Jim Traber	92
1992	Larry Sheets	100	Boomer Wells	97
1993	Katsumi Hirosawa	94	Ralph Bryant	107
	Bobby Rose	94		
1994	Yasuaki Taihoh	107	Hiro-o Ishii	111
1995	Akira Eto	106	Ichiro Suzuki	80
			Kiyoshi Hatsushiba	80
			Yukio Tanaka	80
1996	Luis Lopez	109	Troy Neel	111

Pitching Wins Leaders

YEAR	CENTRAL LEAGUE		PACIFIC LEAGUE	
1950	Shigeo Mada	39*	Jun Aramaki	26
1951	Shigeo Mada	28	Masaru Eto	24
1952	Takehiko Bessho	33	Masa-aki Noguchi	23
1953	Takumi Otomo	27	Tokuji Kawasaki	24
1954	Shigeru Sugishta	32	Motoji Taku	26
			Fumio Tanaka	26
1955	Ryohei Hasegawa	30	Motoji Taku	24
	Takumi Otomo	30		
1956	Takehiko Bessho	27	Masayoshi Miura	29
1957	Masaichi Kaneda	28	Kazuhisa Inao	35
1958	Masaichi Kaneda	31	Kazuhisa Inao	33
1959	Motoshi Fujita	27	Tadashi Sugiura	38
1960	Ritsuo Horimoto	29	Shoichi Ono	33
1961	Hiroshi Gondo	35	Kazuhisa Inao	42*
1962	Hiroshi Gondo	30	Masahiro Kubo	28
1963	Masaichi Kaneda	30	Kazuhisa Inao	28
1964	Gene Bacque	29	Masa-aki Koyama	30
1965	Minoru Murayama	25	Yukio Ozaki	27
1966	Minoru Murayama	24	Tetsuya Yoneda	25
1967	Kenjiro Ogawa	29	Masaaki Ikenaga	24
1968	Yutaka Enatsu	25	Mutsuo Minagawa	31
1969	Kazumi Takahashi	22	Keishi Suzuki	24
1970	Masaji Hiramatsu	25	Fumio Narita	25
1971	Masaji Hiramatsu	17	Masaaki Kitaru	24
1972	Tsuneo Horiuchi	26	Hisashi Yamada	20
			Tomohiro Kaneda	20
1973	Yutaka Enatsu	24	Fumio Narita	21
1974	Yukitsuru Matsumoto	20	Tomohiro Kaneda	16
	Motoyasu Kaneshige	20		
1975	Yoshiro Sotokoba	20	Osamu Higashio	23
1976	Kojiro Ikegaya	20	Hisashi Yamada	26
1977	Satoshi Takahashi	20	Keishi Suzuki	20
1978	Osamu Nomura	17	Keishi Suzuki	25
1979	Shigeru Kobayashi	22	Hisashi Yamada	21
1980	Suguru Egawa	16	Isamu Kida	22
1981	Suguru Egawa	20	Yutaro Imai	19
			Choji Murata	19
1982	Manabu Kitabeppu	20	Mikio Kudo	20
1983	Kazuhiko Endo	18	Osamu Higashio	18
			Kazuhiro Yamauchi	18
1984	Kazuhiko Endo	17	Yutaro Imai	21
1985	Tatsuo Komatsu	17	Yasunori Sahto	21
1986	Manabu Kitabeppu	18	Hisanobu Watanabe	16
1987	Tatsuo Komatsu	17	Yukihiko Yamaoki	19
1988	Kazuyuki Ono	18	Hisanobu Watanabe	15
	Akimitsu Ito	18	Yukihiro Nishizaki	15
			Hiroaki Matsuura	15
1989	Masaki Saito	20	Hideyuki Awano	19
	Takashi Nishimoto	20		
1990	Masaki Saito	20	Hideo Nomo	18
			Hisanobu Watanabe	18
1991	Shinji Sasaoka	17	Hideo Nomo	17
1992	Masaki Saito	17	Hideo Nomo	18
1993	Shinji Imanaka	17	Hideo Nomo	17
	Masahiro Yamamoto	17	Koji Noda	17
	Hiroki Nomura	17		
1994	Masahiro Yamamoto	19	Hideki Irabu	15
1995	Masaki Saito	18	Kip Gross	16
1996	Masaki Saito	16	Kip Gross	17
	Balvino Galvez	16		

Note: In the early years, managers overworked their pitchers. The result: astronomical victory totals and early burn-out. Now managers adopt a U.S.-style rotation. It is not clear how much the 130-game schedule affects victory totals, since Japanese teams have many rainouts, and the season lasts six months as the U.S. season does.

ERA Leaders

YEAR	CENTRAL LEAGUE		PACIFIC LEAGUE	
1950	Nobuo Oshima	2.03	Jun Aramaki	2.06
1951	Kiyoshi Matsuda	2.01	Susumu Yuki	2.08
1952	Tadashi Kajioka	1.71	Susumu Yuki	1.91
1953	Takumi Otomo	1.85	Tokuji Kawasaki	1.98
1954	Shigeru Sugishita	1.39	Motoji Kaku	1.58
1955	Takehiko Bessho	1.33	Takashi Nakagawa	2.08
1956	Shozo Watanabe	1.45	Kazuhisa Inao	1.06*
1957	Masaichi Kaneda	1.63	Kazuhisa Inao	1.37
1958	Masaichi Kaneda	1.30	Kazuhisa Inao	1.42
1959	Minoru Murayama	1.19	Tadashi Sugiura	1.40
1960	Noboru Akiyama	1.75	Shoichi Ono	1.98
1961	Hiroshi Gondo	1.70	Kazuhisa Inao	1.69
1962	Minoru Murayama	1.20	Osamu Kubota	2.21
1963	Minoru Kakimoto	1.70	Masahiro Kubo	2.36
1964	Gene Bacque	1.89	Yujiro Tsumajima	2.15
1965	Masaichi Kaneda	1.84	Kiyohiro Miura	1.57
1966	Tsuneo Horiuchi	1.39	Kazuhisa Inao	1.79
1967	Masatoshi Gondo	1.40	Mitsuhiro Adachi	1.75
1968	Yoshiro Sotokoba	1.94	Mutsuo Minagawa	1.61
1969	Yutaka Enatsu	1.81	Masa-aki Kitaru	1.72
1970	Minoru Murayama	0.98*	Michio Sahto	2.05
1971	Kazuhiro Fujimoto	1.71	Hisashi Yamada	2.37
1972	Takeshi Yasuda	2.08	Toshihiko Sei	2.36
1973	Takeshi Yasuda	2.02	Tetsuya Yoneda	2.47
1974	Shitoshi Sekimoto	2.28	Michio Sahto	1.91
1975	Sohachi Aniya	1.91	Choji Murata	2.20
1976	Takamasa Suzuki	2.98	Choji Murata	1.82
1977	Hisao Niura	2.32	Hisashi Yamada	2.28
1978	Hisao Niura	2.81	Keishi Suzuki	2.02
1979	Masaji Hiramatsu	2.39	Tetsuji Yamaguchi	2.49
1980	Hiromu Mistook	2.35	Isamu Kida	2.28
1981	Suguru Egawa	2.29	Noriaki Okabe	2.70
1982	Akio Saito	2.07	Satoshi Takahashi	1.84
1983	Osamu Fukuma	2.62	Osamu Higashio	2.92
1984	Seiji Kobayashi	2.20	Yutaro Imai	2.93
1985	Tatsuo Komatsu	2.65	Kimiyasu Kudo	2.76
1986	Manabu Kitabeppu	2.43	Yoshinori Sato	2.83
1987	Masumi Kuwata	2.17	Kimiyasu Kudo	2.41
1988	Yutaka Ono	1.70	Hirofumi Kono	2.38
1989	Masaki Saito	1.62	Choji Murata	2.50
1990	Masaki Saito	2.17	Hideo Nomo	2.91
1991	Shinji Sasaoka	2.44	Tomio Watanabe	2.35
1992	Koki Morita	2.05	Motoyuki Akahori	1.80
1993	Masahiro Yamamoto	2.05	Kimiyasu Kudo	2.06
1994	Genji Kaku	2.45	Hiroshi Shintani	2.91
1995	Terry Bross	2.33	Hideki Irabu	2.53
1996	Masaki Saito	2.36	Hideki Irabu	2.40

*League record

Most Valuable Players

YEAR	CENTRAL LEAGUE		PACIFIC LEAGUE	
1950	Makoto Kozuru	OF	Kaoru Betto	OF
1951	Tetsuharu Kawakami	1B	Kazuhito Yamamoto	2B
1952	Takehiko Bessho	P	Susumu Yuki	P
1953	Takumi Otomo	P	Isami Okamoto	2B
1954	Shigeru Shugishita	P	Hiroshi Oshita	OF
1955	Tetsuharu Kawakami	1B	Tokuji Iida	OF
1956	Takehiko Bessho	P	Futoshi Nakanishi	3B
1957	Wally Yonamine	OF	Kazuhisa Inao	P
1958	Motoshi Fujita	P	Kazuhisa Inao	P
1959	Motoshi Fujita	P	Tadashi Sugiura	P
1960	Noboru Akiyama	P	Kazuhiro Yamauchi	OF
1961	Shigeo Nagashima	3B	Katsuya Nomura	C
1962	Minoru Murayama	P	Isao Harimoto	OF
1963	Shigeo Nagashima	3B	Katsuya Nomura	C
1964	Sadaharu Oh	1B	Joe Stanka	P
1965	Sadaharu Oh	1B	Katsuya Nomura	C
1966	Shigeo Nagashima	3B	Katsuya Nomura	C
1967	Sadaharu Oh	1B	Mitsuhiro Adachi	P
1968	Shigeo Nagashima	3B	Tetsuya Yoneda	P
1969	Sadaharu Oh	1B	Tokuji Nagaike	OF
1970	Sadaharu Oh	1B	Masa-aki Kitaru	P
1971	Shigeo Nagashima	3B	Tokuji Nagaike	OF
1972	Tsuneo Horiuchi	P	Yutaka Fukumoto	OF
1973	Sadaharu Oh	1B	Katsuya Nomura	C
1974	Sadaharu Oh	1B	Tomohiro Kaneda	P
1975	Koji Yamamoto	OF	Hideji Kahto	1B
1976	Sadaharu Oh	1B	Hisashi Yamada	P
1977	Sadaharu Oh	1B	Hisashi Yamada	P
1978	Tsutomu Wakamatsu	OF	Hisashi Yamada	P
1979	Yutaka Enatsu	P	Charlie Manuel	OF
1980	Koji Yamamoto	OF	Isamu Kida	P
1981	Suguru Egawa	P	Yutaka Enatsu	P
1982	Takayoshi Nakao	C	Hiromitsu Ochi-ai	2B
1983	Tatsunori Hara	3B	Osamu Higashio	P
1984	Sachio Kinugasa	3B	Boomer Wells	1B
1985	Randy Bass	1B	Hiromitsu Ochi-ai	3B
1986	Manabu Kitabeppu	P	Hiromichi Ishige	SS
1987	Kazuhiro Yamakura	C	Osamu Higashio	P
1988	Genji Kaku	P	Hiromitsu Kadota	OF
1989	Warren Cromartie	OF	Ralph Bryant	OF
1990	Masaki Saito	P	Hideo Nomo	P
1991	Shinji Sasaoka	P	Taigen Kaku	P
1992	Jack Howell	3B	Takehiro Ishii	P
1993	Atsuya Furuta	C	Kimiyasu Kudo	P
1994	Masumi Kuwata	P	Ichiro Suzuki	OF
1995	Tom O'Malley	OF	Ichiro Suzuki	OF
1996	Hideki Matsui	OF	Ichiro Suzuki	OF

Home Runs

1.	Sadaharu Oh	868
2.	Katsuya Nomura	657
3.	Hiromitsu Kadota	567
4.	Koji Yamamoto	536
5.	*Hiromitsu Ochi-ai	505
6.	Isao Harimoto	504
7.	Sachio Kinugasa	504
8.	Katsuo Osugi	486
9.	Koichi Tabuchi	474
10.	Masahiro Doi	465

*Still active

RBI

1.	Sadaharu Oh	2170
2.	Katsuya Nomura	1988
3.	Hiromitsu Kadota	1678
4.	Isao Harimoto	
5.	Shigeo Nagashima	1522
6.	Katsuo Osugi	1507
7.	*Hiromitsu Ochi-ai	1503
8.	Koji Yamamoto	1475
9.	Sachio Kinugasa	1448
10.	Masahiro Doi	1400

Batting Average

1.	Leron Lee	.320
2.	Tsutomo Wakamatsu	.31918
3.	Isao Harimoto	.31915
4.	Boomer Wells	.317
5.	*Hiromitsu Ochi-ai	.315
6.	Tetsuharu Kawakami	.313
7.	Wally Yonamine	.311
8.	Leon Lee	.308
9.	Futoshi Nakanishi	.307
10.	Shigeo Nagashima	.305

Note: Leron and Leon Lee are brothers.

Hits

1.	Isao Harimoto	3085
2.	Katsuya Nomura	2901
3.	Sadaharu Oh	2786
4.	Hiromitsu Kadota	2566
5.	Sachio Kinugasa	2543
6.	Yutaka Fukumoto	2543
7.	Shigeo Nagashima	2471
8.	Masahiro Doi	2452
9.	Tetsuharu Kawakami	2351
10.	Koji Yamamoto	2339

In stolen bases, little Yutaka Fukumoto retired in 1988 with 1,065 stolen bases, the world record until Rickey Henderson broke it. He was caught 299 times for a .781 percent. Fukumoto also hit 208 homers and holds the Japanese record with 43 lead-off round-trippers.

Wins

		W-L	Pct
1.	Masaichi Kaneda	400-298	.573
2.	Tetsuya Yoneda	350-285	.551
3.	Masa-aki Koyama	320-232	.580
4.	Keishi Suzuki	317-238	.571
5.	Takehiko Bessho	310-178	.635
6.	Victor Starffin	303-176	.633
7.	Hisashi Yamada	284-166	.631
8.	Kazuhisa Inao	276-137	.668
9.	Takao Kajimoto	254-255	.499
10.	Osamu Higashio	251-247	.507

Note: Kaneda pitched most of his career with a last-place team and often won half their games. Inao had an amazing record until he ruined his arm from overwork and retired early.

Strikeouts

1.	Masaichi Kaneda	
2.	Tetsyya Yoneda	3388
3.	Masa-aki Koyama	3159
4.	Keishi Suzuki	3061
5.	Yutaka Enatsu	2987
6.	Takao Kajimoto	2945
7.	Kazahisa Inao	2574
8.	Choji Murata	2363
9.	Minoru Murayama	2271
10.	Shoichi Ono	2244

Kaneda pitched 5,527 innings. He held the world record until broken by Ryan.

ERA (2,000 IP)

1.	Hideo Fujimoto	1.90
2.	Jiro Noguchi	1.96
3.	Kazuhisa Inao	1.98
4.	Bozo Wakabayashi	1.99
5.	Victor Starffin	2.088
6.	Minoru Murayama	2.092
7.	Takehiko Bessho	2.18
8.	Jun Aramaki	2.30
9.	Shigeru Sugishita	2.33
10.	Masaichi Kaneda	2.34

Pennant Winners: Japan Pro-Baseball League

YEAR	TEAM	WON	LOST	PCT.
1936	FALL TOKYO GIANTS	18	9	—
1937	SPRING TOKYO GIANTS	41	13	.759
	FALL OSAKA TIGERS	39	9	.813
1938	SPRING OSAKA TIGERS	29	6	.829
	FALL TOKYO GIANTS	30	9	.769
1940	TOKYO GIANTS	76	28	.731
1941	TOKYO GIANTS	62	22	.738
1942	TOKYO GIANTS	73	27	.730
1943	TOKYO GIANTS	54	27	.667
1944	HANSHIN	27	6	.818
1945	Play Suspended			
1946	KINKI GREATRING	65	38	.631
1947	OSAKA TIGERS	79	37	.681
1948	NANKAI HAWKS	87	49	.640
1949	YOMIURI GIANTS	85	48	.639

Pennant Winners: Central League

YEAR	TEAM	WON	LOST	PCT.
1950	SHOCHIKU ROBINS	98	35	.737
1951	YOMIURI GIANTS	79	29	.731
1952	YOMIURI GIANTS	83	37	.692
1953	YOMIURI GIANTS	87	37	.702
1954	CHUNICHI DRAGONS	86	40	.683
1955	YOMIURI GIANTS	92	37	.713
1956	YOMIURI GIANTS	82	44	.646
1957	YOMIURI GIANTS	74	53	.581
1958	YOMIURI GIANTS	77	52	.596
1959	YOMIURI GIANTS	77	48	.612
1960	TAIYO WHALES	70	56	.554
1961	YOMIURI GIANTS	71	53	.569
1962	HANSHIN TIGERS	75	55	.577
1963	YOMIURI GIANTS	83	55	.601
1964	HANSHIN TIGERS	80	56	.588
1965	YOMIURI GIANTS	91	47	.659
1966	YOMIURI GIANTS	89	41	.685
1967	YOMIURI GIANTS	84	46	.646
1968	YOMIURI GIANTS	77	53	.592
1969	YOMIURI GIANTS	73	51	.589
1970	YOMIURI GIANTS	79	47	.627
1971	YOMIURI GIANTS	70	52	.574
1972	YOMIURI GIANTS	74	52	.587
1973	YOMIURI GIANTS	66	60	.524
1974	CHUNICHI DRAGONS	70	49	.588
1975	HIROSHIMA CARP	72	47	.605
1976	YOMIURI GIANTS	76	45	.628
1977	YOMIURI GIANTS	80	46	.635
1978	YAKULT SWALLOWS	68	46	.596
1979	HIROSHIMA CARP	67	50	.573
1980	HIROSHIMA CARP	73	44	.624
1981	YOMIURI GIANTS	73	48	.603
1982	CHUNICHI DRAGONS	64	47	.577
1983	YOMIURI GIANTS	72	50	.590
1984	HIROSHIMA CARP	75	45	.625

1985	HANSHIN TIGERS	74	49	.602
1986	HIROSHIMA CARP	73	46	.613
1987	YOMIURI GIANTS	76	43	.639
1988	CHUNICHI DRAGONS	79	46	.632
1989	YOMIURI GIANTS	84	44	.656
1990	YOMIURI GIANTS	88	42	.677
1991	HIROSHIMA CARP	74	56	.569
1992	YAKULT SWALLOWS	69	61	.531
1993	YAKULT SWALLOWS	80	50	.615
1994	YOMIURI GIANTS	70	60	.538
1995	YAKULT SWALLOWS	82	48	.631
1996	YOMIURI GIANTS	77	53	.592

Pennant Winners: Pacific League

YEAR	TEAM	WON	LOST	PCT.
1950	MAINICHI ORIONS	81	34	.704
1951	NANKAI HAWKS	72	24	.750
1952	NANKAI HAWKS	76	44	.633
1953	NANKAI HAWKS	71	48	.597
1954	NISHITETSU LIONS	90	47	.657
1955	NANKAI HAWKS	99	41	.707
1956	NISHITETSU LIONS	96	51	.646
1957	NISHITETSU LIONS	83	44	.648
1958	NISHITETSU LIONS	78	47	.619
1959	NANKAI HAWKS	88	42	.677
1960	DAIMAI ORIONS	82	48	.631
1961	NANKAI HAWKS	85	49	.629
1962	TOEI FLYERS	78	52	.600
1963	NISHITETSU LIONS	86	60	.589
1964	NANKAI HAWKS	84	63	.571
1965	NANKAI HAWKS	88	49	.642
1966	NANKAI HAWKS	79	51	.608
1967	HANKYU BRAVES	75	55	.577
1968	HANKYU BRAVES	80	50	.615
1969	HANKYU BRAVES	76	50	.603
1970	LOTTE ORIONS	80	47	.630
1971	HANKYU BRAVES	80	39	.672
1972	HANKYU BRAVES	80	48	.625
1973	1st HALF [†]NANKAI HAWKS	38	26	.594
	2nd HALF HANKYU BRAVES	43	19	.694
1974	1st HALF HANKYU BRAVES	36	23	.610
	2nd HALF [†]LOTTE ORIONS	38	23	.623
1975	1st HALF [†]HANKYU BRAVES	38	25	.603
	2nd HALF KINTETSU BUFFALOES	40	20	.667
1976	1st HALF HANKYU BRAVES	42	21	.667
	2nd HALF HANKYU BRAVES	37	24	.607
1977	1st HALF [†]HANKYU BRAVES	35	25	.583
	2nd HALF LOTTE ORIONS	33	24	.579
1978	1st HALF HANKYU BRAVES	44	20	.688
	2nd HALF HANKYU BRAVES	38	19	.667
1979	1st HALF [†]KINTETSU BUFFALOES	39	19	.672
	2nd HALF HANKYU BRAVES	36	23	.610
1980	1st HALF LOTTE ORIONS	33	25	.569
	2nd HALF [†]KINTETSU BUFFALOES	35	26	.574
1981	1st HALF LOTTE ORIONS	35	26	.574
	2nd HALF [†]NIPPON HAM FIGHTERS	37	23	.617

1982	1st HALF [†]SEIBU LIONS	36	27	.571
	2nd HALF NIPPON HAM FIGHTERS	35	23	.603
1983	SEIBU LIONS	86	40	.683
1984	HANKYU BRAVES	75	45	.625
1985	SEIBU LIONS	79	45	.637
1986	SEIBU LIONS	68	49	.581
1987	SEIBU LIONS	71	45	.612
1988	SEIBU LIONS	73	51	.589
1989	KINTETSU BUFFALOES	71	54	.568
1990	SEIBU LIONS	81	45	.643
1991	SEIBU LIONS	81	43	.653
1992	SEIBU LIONS	80	47	.630
1993	SEIBU LIONS	74	53	.581
1994	SEIBU LIONS	76	52	.594
1995	ORIX BLUE WAVE	82	47	.636
1996	ORIX BLUE WAVE	74	54	.597

[†]playoff winner

Japan Series

YEAR	TEAM/LEAGUE	WON	TEAM/LEAGUE	WON
1950	MAINICHI ORIONS, PL	4	SHOCHIKU ROBINS, CL	2
1951	YOMIURI GIANTS, CL	4	NANKAI HAWKS, PL	1
1952	YOMIURI GIANTS, CL	4	NANKAI HAWKS, PL	2
1953	YOMIURI GIANTS, CL	4	NANKAI HAWKS, PL	2 1 TIE
1954	CHUNICHI DRAGONS, CL	4	NISHITETSU LIONS, PL	3
1955	YOMIURI GIANTS, CL	4	NANKAI HAWKS, PL	3
1956	NISHITETSU LIONS, PL	4	YOMIURI GIANTS, CL	2
1957	NISHITETSU LIONS, PL	4	YOMIURI GIANTS, CL	0 1 TIE
1958	NISHITETSU LIONS, PL	4	YOMIURI GIANTS, CL	3
1959	NANKAI HAWKS, PL	4	YOMIURI GIANTS, CL	0
1960	TAIYO WHALES, CL	4	DAIMAI ORIONS, PL	0
1961	YOMIURI GIANTS, CL	4	NANKAI HAWKS, PL	2
1962	TOEI FLYERS, PL	4	HANSHIN TIGERS, CL	2 1 TIE
1963	YOMIURI GIANTS, CL	4	NISHITETSU LIONS, PL	3
1964	NANKAI HAWKS, PL	4	HANSHIN TIGERS	3
1965	YOMIURI GIANTS, CL	4	NANKAI HAWKS, PL	1
1966	YOMIURI GIANTS, CL	4	NANKAI HAWKS, PL	2
1967	YOMIURI GIANTS, CL	4	HANKYU BRAVES, PL	2
1968	YOMIURI GIANTS, CL	4	HANKYU BRAVES, PL	2
1969	YOMIURI GIANTS, CL	4	HANKYU BRAVES, PL	2
1970	YOMIURI GIANTS, CL	4	LOTTE ORIONS, PL	1
1971	YOMIURI GIANTS, CL	4	HANKYU BRAVES, PL	1
1972	YOMIURI GIANTS, CL	4	HANKYU BRAVES, PL	1
1973	YOMIURI GIANTS, CL	4	NANKAI HAWKS, PL	1
1974	LOTTE ORIONS, PL	4	CHUNICHI DRAGONS, CL	2
1975	HANKYU BRAVES, PL	4	HIROSHIMA CARP, CL	0 2 TIES
1976	HANKYU BRAVES, PL	4	YOMIURI GIANTS, CL	3
1977	HANKYU BRAVES, PL	4	YOMIURI GIANTS, CL	1
1978	YAKULT SWALLOWS, CL	4	HANKYU BRAVES, PL	3
1979	HIROSHIMA CARP, CL	4	KINTETSU BUFFALOES, PL	3
1980	HIROSHIMA CARP, CL	4	KINTETSU BUFFALOES, PL	3
1981	YOMIURI GIANTS, CL	4	NIPPON HAM FIGHTERS, PL	2
1982	SEIBU LIONS, PL	4	CHUNICHI DRAGONS, CL	2
1983	SEIBU LIONS, PL	4	YOMIURI GIANTS, CL	3
1984	HIROSHIMA CARP, CL	4	HANKYU BRAVES, PL	3
1985	HANSHIN TIGERS, CL	4	SEIBU LIONS, PL	2
1986	SEIBU LIONS, PL	4	HIROSHIMA CARP, CL	3 1 TIE
1987	SEIBU LIONS, PL	4	YOMIURI GIANTS, CL	2
1988	SEIBU LIONS, PL	4	CHUNICHI DRAGONS, CL	1
1989	YOMIURI GIANTS, CL	4	KINTETSU BUFFALOES, PL	3
1990	SEIBU LIONS, PL	4	YOMIURI GIANTS, CL	0
1991	SEIBU LIONS, PL	4	HIROSHIMA CARP, CL	3
1992	SEIBU LIONS, PL	4	YAKULT SWALLOWS, CL	3
1993	YAKULT SWALLOWS, CL	4	SEIBU LIONS, PL	3
1994	YOMIURI GIANTS, CL	4	SEIBU LIONS, PL	2
1995	YAKULT SWALLOWS	4	ORIX BLUE WAVE	1
1996	ORIX BLUE WAVE	4	YOMIURI GIANTS	1

Note on pronunciation. Vowels are the same as Spanish: A=ah, I=ee, U=oo, E=ay, O=oh. Y is a consonant or "ee," thus "kyo" and "ryo" are pronounced something like "keeo" and "reeo." U is usually not emphasized. Some combinations change a bit in actual speech. "Shita" comes out "sh'ta," and "hito" and "hiko" sound like "sh'to" and "sh'ko." G is always hard, as in "gh."

## CHAPTER 17

Baseball in the Caribbean

Rob Ruck

Soon after the World Series marks the season's end in the United States, baseball springs back to life in and around the Caribbean. There, to the beat of *salsa* and *merengue* and against a backdrop of palm trees and seasonal labor, some of the best baseball in the world is played each winter. While most of South America follows football and the British West Indies follows cricket, the rest of the Caribbean basin plays baseball—and has for the better part of a century.

Since baseball fever first infected Cuba in the 1870s, the game has infiltrated the sporting psyches of Mexico, Nicaragua, the Dominican Republic, Venezuela, Puerto Rico, Panama, and Colombia. Although tied to major league baseball in four of these countries through a set of winter leagues and as a source of fresh talent, Caribbean baseball is not simply an appendage of the game that is played in the United States. Rather, baseball has acquired an autonomous persona as the peoples of the region have made the game into their own national pastimes.

More than simply recreation or a display of grace and competence, baseball has catalyzed national consciousness and cohesion in the Caribbean basin. A critical part of the fabric of everyday life, the sport has also influenced how these societies have come to define themselves, their relations with each other, and their ties to the United States. "It's more than a game," Dominican winter league general manager Winston Llenas once remarked. "It's our passion. It's almost our way of life."

Pedro Julio Santana stands at his office window in what was once the colonial zone of Santo Domingo. A sportsman at the center of Dominican baseball's evolution earlier this century, he searches for words to describe how the game penetrated his country and the rest of the basin. Glancing below to the hulking walls of the first Catholic cathedral in the western hemisphere, Santana finds his metaphor. "It is much the same as that which happened with Christianity. Jesus could be compared to the North Americans, but the apostles were the ones that spread the faith, and the apostles of baseball were Cubans. Even though the Dominican Republic and Puerto Rico were occupied by the North Americans, the Cubans first brought baseball here, and to Mexico and Venezuela, too."

Caribbean baseball's first epicenter was Cuba, which had fallen into orbit around the United States by the late nineteenth century. Baseball arrived there last century, brought by sailors, students, and businessmen from the United States as well as by Cubans who had traveled

north. The U.S. military occupations that followed the 1898 conflict with Spain stimulated baseball's expansion there and across the basin. By the time the Good Neighbor Policy had supplanted the Big Stick in the 1930s, baseball was entrenched. Moreover, Cuban baseball had become the focal point of an international network that stretched from the Caribbean basin through the Negro Leagues.

What was likely the first ballgame in Cuba with local participation occurred in June 1866, when sailors of a U.S. ship taking on sugar invited Cuban longshoremen to play. *El Club Habana* (Havana) began two years later, crushing a team from Matanzas in the first organized contest of two Cuban teams.

Havana's victory over Matanzas featured two of Cuba's sporting pioneers, Esteban Bellan and Emilio Sabourín. Bellan became the first Latino in U.S. organized baseball, playing three seasons in the National Association (1871–1873). Sabourín, the A. G. Spalding of Cuban baseball, was the motivating force behind the *Liga de Beisbol Profesional Cubana,* whose inaugural tournament was won by Sabourín's reconstituted Havana club in 1878. Sabourín proselytized for his sport as well as for the cause of Cuban independence from Spain until his contribution of baseball revenues to the independence movement incurred the wrath of Spanish officials. They imprisoned Sabourín until his death and banned baseball in parts of their colony.

While initially a game of the more affluent and those with contact with the United States, baseball soon spread to all classes of Cuban society, both urban and rural. U.S. military occupations, support by companies and businessmen, and close ties to political elites would shape its subsequent development, much as these forces would elsewhere in the basin.

The game was organized on three overlapping levels in its early years. The first was an ad hoc player-organized, self-directed network of teams. The second involved clubs sponsored by businessmen, companies, and politicians who sought the promotional advantages of such patronage. The third level was that of professional (sometimes semiprofessional) baseball, which organized championships from 1878 until 1961, with a changing cast of teams and format. In some years, no tournaments were held, while in others both a summer and winter season took place. Havana, Almendares, Santa Clara, Cienfuegos, and Marianao were the league's mainstays.

Until the 1959 Cuban Revolution and the ensuing U.S. blockade, Cuba set the standard for Caribbean baseball. It sent the most players to the major and Negro leagues while its winter and summer tournaments featured the highest caliber of Latin ball and attracted players from both the States and the basin. Cuban players, radio broadcasts, and emigrants, in turn, became baseball's emissaries to the rest of the region.

In the Dominican Republic, Cubans who had migrated to escape the turmoil of the Ten Years' War (1868–1878) were the first to form teams. Young Dominicans emulated them and joined with compatriots who had studied in the United States to establish a self-organized matrix of teams and tournaments well in place before the U.S. Marines arrived in 1916 for their eight-year occupation. Santo Domingo's *Licey,* the oldest of the six professional Dominican clubs, formed in 1907, while the forerunners of San Pedro de Macoris's *Estrellas Orientales,* Santiago's *Aguilas Cibaeñas,* and Santo Domingo's other club, *Escogido,* took to the field soon afterward.

While Dominicans refer to these early decades as the romantic epoch of baseball, commercial forces were already at work there and across the basin. Teams occasionally recruited players with the lure of financial reward and soon began importing Cubans and Puerto Ricans for championship tournaments. Moreover, local clubs often induced talented players with payment in cash or work. North American oil companies in Venezuela, rum distilleries and tobacco manufacturers in Cuba, and sugar cane companies in Nicaragua, Puerto Rico, Cuba, and the Dominican Republic sponsored or assisted workplace teams for recreation and community entertainment, but with an industrial agenda, too—winning their workers' hearts and minds.

During these "Yankee years," between 1898 and 1933, when the Marines hit the beaches thirty-four times in ten different basin countries, they found baseball already implanted in Cuba, Puerto Rico, Nicaragua, Mexico, and the Dominican Republic. They never made it to Venezuela, but would have found baseball there, too, as early as the organization of the Caracas club in 1895. The occupations, though, helped to push the sport along. While Nicaraguans had played on their Atlantic coast since 1888, the nation's longest-running pro team, *Boer,* was founded by the U.S. consul in Managua. In the Dominican Republic, U.S. marines and sailors played ball to bolster morale; they were frequently challenged by Dominican teams, for whom these contests were both a test of sporting abilities and national character. Far more baseball was in evidence by the end of the U.S. stay on the island.

While Cubans and some other basin natives had broken into baseball in the States during the first half of the century, the center of gravity for Caribbean baseball remained a regional one. A "Have Glove—Will Travel" mentality soon took hold of basin baseball and its ablest practitioners made the rounds of national tournaments. A core of the finest black players from the States—then barred from major league play by the color line, as were most Latinos—joined them in Cuba, the Dominican Republic, Puerto Rico, Venezuela, and Mexico.

Caribbean baseball's apogee was probably reached in the summer of 1937 in the Dominican Republic during a national championship dedicated to the re-election of the then state-of-the-art dictator Rafael Trujillo. Top Dominican players were joined by the best Cuban, Puerto Rican, and Negro league talent that the Dominican peso could buy to form a three-team league. Santiago boasted the services of Martín Dihigo, Luís Tiant Sr., and Horacio Martínez; San Pedro de Macoris countered with Tetelo Vargas, Ramón Bragaña, and Cocaína García, while the eventual victor, *Ciudad Trujillo* (a merger of *Licey* and *Escogido* that represented the city Trujillo had renamed in his own honor) relied on future Hall of Famers Josh Gibson, Cool Papa Bell, and Satchel Paige, as well as Silvío García, Perucho Cepeda, and Sam Bankhead. Baseball on the island was the equal of that played anywhere that summer. These players barnstormed year-round, and many of them later played together as *Santa Clara* in Cuba and as *La Concordia* in Venezuela.

The proprietary interest taken by caudillos such as Trujillo or Nicaragua's Anastasio Somoza ensured baseball of its most-favored sport status and contributed to the growth of strong regional rivalries. Caribbean participation in the *Mundiales,* the world amateur baseball championships that began in 1938, and later the Caribbean Series of pro circuits, which started in 1949, reinforced the game's hegemony.

Latin ball was an opportunity for North American players to supplement their income and hone their skills in encounters that sometimes surpassed the caliber of major league play. However, it was also a threat to organized baseball in the States. Major league teams had played in Cuba before the turn of the century, and afterward Negro league squads as well as individual black and white pros journeyed south. The 1937 raids on the Negro leagues by Dominican teams destroyed the Pittsburgh Crawfords, and other Negro league squads frequently lost their best players and gate attractions to basin teams. From 1939 until the demise of independent black baseball a decade later, Venezuelan and Mexican franchises vied for Negro leaguers during the summer months, enticing Josh Gibson, Ray Dandridge, and other stars to jump their Negro league teams. They offered better pay and a different atmosphere. "Not only do I get more money playing here, but I live like a king," Willie Wells wrote to *Pittsburgh Courier* sportswriter Wendell Smith in 1939 to explain his switch from the Newark Eagles to Vera Cruz. "I am not faced with the racial problem. . . . I've found freedom and democracy here, something I never found in the United States. . . . Here, in Mexico, I am a man."

The major leagues were less vulnerable to such competition, but even they blanched when Mexican liquor mogul Jorge Pasquel sought major leaguers in addition to Negro leaguers to bolster the six-team summer Mexican League in 1946. Railroad workers from the States taught the game to their Mexican colleagues as early as the 1880s and a strong semipro league formed in the 1920s. In Sonora and Mexico City, the game felt the pull of baseball across the northern border, which Mexican and black teams frequently crossed. In the Yucatan, baseball pointed more toward the Caribbean, especially Cuba. Pasquel, pumping new capital into the league, persuaded Mickey Owen, Sal Maglie, and Max Lanier to desert their major league teams, prompting the latter to ban them. Pasquel also pursued Stan Musial, reportedly placing $50,000 on the bed in his spring training hotel room at a time when the Cardinals' outfielder was making but $13,000 a season. Other basin leagues also lost top players in the Mexican effort to upgrade. Pasquel's challenge, however, was blunted by organized baseball in the States, which tried to limit any competition for its players, and by the Mexican League's own logistical and financial difficulties. The challenge faded after the 1948 season. In the aftermath of the Mexican raids and with integration imminent, major league baseball began to sign accords with professional leagues throughout the basin, formalizing player movement and institutionalizing winter play.

That was especially important, for with the end of the color line in 1947 Latinos soon renewed their assault on major league ball. By the 1970s, the basin would constitute the freshest source of talent in the majors, especially important as the black community turned away from baseball as part of a general shift toward other sports in the United States. But Latin players—black and white—had played pro ball in the United States long before Jackie Robinson's historic debut.

Colombia's Luis Castro broke ground in baseball's modern era, after the creation of the National and American Leagues, but Cubans for the most part led the way. While Castro played only part of the 1902 season, Rafael Almeida and Armando Marsans spearheaded a Cuban invasion in 1911 that left its imprimatur on the game and numbered over thirty players before integration. Another ninety or so Cubans played major league ball after that divide.

The crucial factor controlling the entry of Cubans and other basin players into the major leagues was skin color. Barnstorming their way through black communities from the early century on, Cuban teams had become a mainstay of the Negro leagues that began in 1920. Popular draws, the Cuban Stars and the New York Cubans featured Latinos too dark to pass the color line into the majors. Playing most of their contests on the road, these Caribbean squads injected talent and a tropical allure to the game. Cubans Martín Dihigo, Alejandro Oms, Luís Tiant Sr., Orestes "Minnie" Miñoso, and Silvío García were joined by Dominicans Horacio Martínez and Tetelo Vargas, Puerto Rican Peruchin Cepeda, Panamanian Pat Scantlebury, and sometimes several black North Americans who passed for Cubans, on these pan-Caribbean aggregations. A few Cubans, such as Cristóbal Torriente, a powerful outfielder, and José de la Caridad Méndez, *"El Diamante Negro,"* who took a no-hitter into the ninth inning the first time he faced the barnstorming Cincinnati Reds, became mainstays of other Negro league franchises.

Lighter-skinned Cubans from that predominantly mixed island played on the other side of sport's racial boundary in the States, in the major leagues. Perhaps the greatest pre–Jackie Robinson Cuban major leaguer was Adolfo Luque, a pitcher whose twenty big league seasons were capped by a brilliant 27–8 record in 1923 and a winning relief stint of shutout ball in the seventh game of the 1933 World Series. Following that game, Clark Griffith, whose Washington Senators had lost the Series, decided to back a scouting exhibition to Cuba. He sent Joe Cambria.

"Papa Joe," as many still refer to Cambria, stocked the Senators with Cubans. Among his first signees was Roberto Estalella, from the sugarcane milltown that Hershey Chocolate operated in Cárdenas. The *Cincinnati Enquirer* had greeted the signings of Almeida and Marsans in 1911 with relief, introducing them as "two of the purest bars of Castilian soap to ever wash upon our shores," but the darker-hued Estalella was more controversial. No one challenged this indirect breaching of the color line, although it prompted Red Smith to write his classic column in which he suspected that "there was a Senegambian somewhere in the Cuban batpile where Senatorial lumber was seasoned."

The player regarded in the Caribbean as the best Cuban ever, and arguably the finest ballplayer of all time, never played major league ball. Martín Dihigo displayed his talents in Cuba, the United States, Mexico, Venezuela, and the Dominican Republic, and is enshrined in the Hall of Fame of three of these nations. Dihigo excelled at the plate, on the mound, and as a manager, but integration came too late for him. His bust at Havana's *Estadio Latinoamericano* reads simply, *El Immortal.*

The contradiction that some Cubans played in the majors and others in the Negro leagues was not lost upon blacks in the States or on Latin ballplayers. As early as Almeida's and Marsans' 1911 debut, the black press began to hope that black ballplayers would soon follow them into baseball's most exclusive league. And while Negro leaguers went south to adulation and greater pay, dark-skinned Latinos who came north encountered prejudice based on both skin color and nationality. As major leaguers such as Ty Cobb, Tris Speaker, and Carl Hubbell traveled south to play in winter ball, black North Americans and Latinos found that they could more than hold their own. These symbolic victories were appreciated both in the States and throughout the basin. North American blacks and the peoples of the region shared each other's athletes and appropriated each other's sporting heroes and symbols. If a proving ground was necessary to show that blacks could compete with whites, that the two could coexist on the same squad, or to dispel any other racial shibboleth, Caribbean baseball was just that.

Following integration, the more farsighted owners began scouring the islands for prospects. Soon a fresh wave of Latinos arrived in the majors, including three future Hall of Famers: Venezuela's Luís Aparicio, Puerto Rico's Roberto Clemente, and the Dominican Republic's Juan Marichal. They signaled, moreover, a shift away from Cuba as the primary spawning waters for Caribbean players.

With the 1959 Cuban Revolution and the subsequent deterioration of relations with the United States, Cuba fell out of organized baseball's system. The Havana Sugar Kings, an International League franchise affiliated with the Reds since 1954, were on their way to winning the Little World Series of the AAA minor leagues in 1959, just months after Fidel Castro came to power. The revolutionary government offered to underwrite the Sugar Kings' debts, and Castro sought to keep the franchise there, "even if I have to pitch," but the International League shipped the club to Jersey City during the 1960 season. Baseball in Cuba was cut off completely from baseball in the United States, and the movement of players and equipment halted. Cuba developed its own sporting goods industry and relied on the repatriated Dihigo, a political exile during the 1950s who had given money to Che Guevara and who now returned to help teach the game. Cuban baseball soon shed its commercial skin and sought instead to advance the social and political aims of the revolution. Cuba has remained *the* powerhouse in world amateur baseball ever since, but the island stopped producing new major leaguers. After the Zoilo Versalles, Tony Oliva, Tony Pérez generations passed out of baseball, the next set of Cubans to reach the majors were those who, while born on the island, had grown up in the United States.

The fulcrum of baseball power, meanwhile, shifted one island to the east, where the Dominican Republic shared Hispaniola with French-speaking, soccer-playing Haiti. After the star-studded 1937 season, pro ball in the Dominican Republic entered a fourteen-year hiatus. While an occasional tournament celebrated an event such as the nation's centennial, Dominican pros Horacio Martínez and Tetelo Vargas plied their trade in Cuba, Venezuela, or the United States. But several forces revitalized Dominican baseball in the 1940s, and after the reappearance of a professional league in 1951, these dynamics propelled over a hundred players to the major leagues.

The first catalyst was the birth of the *Mundial,* an international championship tournament for amateur baseball. After its inauguration in England in 1938, the *Mundial* moved to the Caribbean. Held in the basin throughout the 1940s, with Cuba hosting five consecutive tournaments, the *Mundial* had a decidedly Latin flavor and became the most important sporting competition in which these nations competed on something approximating equal footing, both with each other and with the United States. Basin nations won every championship from 1940 through 1972, with Cuba winning eleven out of eighteen times.

National aspirations and international rivalries sometimes were injected into the *Mundial.* An irate Anastasio Somoza fired the Nicaraguan manager in the midst of one and took to the dugout to direct the team himself. Nicaraguan national honor was restored by a victory over Cuba in the final game of the 1972 series, an event still celebrated as one of the Central American nation's greatest sporting exploits. The Dominican victory in 1948, coming just months after virtually the entire national championship team perished in a plane crash by the Río Verde, captivated the Republic and lent impetus to pro ball's rebirth there.

A second factor in Dominican baseball's rejuvenation was the creation of the *Dirección General de Deportes.* Modeled in part after the comparable Cuban agency, this government body organized regional and then national tournaments for amateur baseball (often with semiprofessional overtones) that gave further purpose to local, company, and armed forces support. Many of the Dominicans that entered the majors from the late 1950s on, including Marichal, Manuel Mota, and the three Rojas Alou brothers, played on these squads.

The final catalysts to Dominican ascendancy were bananas and sugarcane, and the concentrations of baseball fervor and expertise which they fostered. While the sugarcane milltowns of the southeast produce the most prospects today, the banana region along the northwest border with Haiti was instrumental in cultivating the first contingent of pros in the late 1950s. There the Grenada Company, a United Fruit Company subsidiary, began two teams for its workers and their sons in the 1940s. The squad won three national championships, and Juan

Marichal and Guayubín Olivo passed through its ranks to the majors.

Dominican sugarcane milltowns, like those in Cuba, had long spawned ballclubs. The six-month long *tiempo muerto,* or dead season, when the cane required minimal attention and most workers were unemployed, contributed to an intense sporting environment, first for cricket and ultimately for baseball. In the 1920s and '30s, *Central La Romana's Papagayo* team was an amateur powerhouse, and in the 1940s the milltowns in and around San Pedro de Macoris made their play. There the descendants of cricket-playing migrants from the British West Indies brought to cut cane and work in the mills displayed an aptitude for playing baseball and an approach to organizing the game that made San Pedro baseball's Mecca. Since Rico Carty's breakthrough in the 1960s, San Pedro has contributed about one-third of the Dominicans to play in the big leagues. The town currently sends more of its native sons to the majors on a per-capita basis than any town ever has. There is probably no other place on earth where the game is played as well and as widely.

Since the end of the color line, ballplayers from Cuba, the Dominican Republic, Venezuela, Puerto Rico, Panama, Nicaragua, Mexico, Colombia, and even the Bahamas have played major league ball. Although the Dominican Republic leads this basin contingent, substantial numbers of Puerto Ricans and Venezuelans are present, too. Mexico, despite a population that dwarfs the rest of the region combined and its well-developed pro leagues, sends few players to the majors. Unlike the other basin leagues, Mexican teams retain first rights to sign any native amateur. A major league club, therefore, must buy the contract from a player's Mexican club, usually for more than it costs to sign a prospect elsewhere in the region. This relationship, the summer Mexican league, and perhaps cultural factors, too, persuade native ballplayers to remain in Mexico.

Cuba opted out of this network after its revolution, and Nicaragua, whose eleven-year fling with the pro winter leagues ended in 1967, followed suit after its 1979 revolution. Panama and Colombia have also tried winter ball, but financial pressures made play sporadic.

The flow of players continues to run both north and south. Minor and major leaguers from the United States still play in the winter leagues, which presently operate in Venezuela, Puerto Rico, the Dominican Republic, and Mexico. In their heyday during the 1950s and '60s, these winter leagues featured major leaguers like Tommy Lasorda, Whitey Ford, and Willie Stargell. But as major league salaries soared in the 1970s and unfavorable rates of exchanges weakened basin economies, the winter leagues restricted the number of North American imports. Minor leaguers and inexperienced major leaguers have replaced them. For them, these leagues provide the chance to play in the winter months, developing the potential that might allow them to crack a big league roster. They also earn higher pay than they do in the minors, encounter competition from top Latino players, and are treated as demigods by the impassioned *fanáticos* of the winter game.

The winners of the winter leagues have met in a *Serie del Caribe* since 1949. Between 1949 and 1960, the pennant-winning squads of Cuba, Panama, Puerto Rico, and

Venezuela played in early February to determine a champion of the Caribbean. Cuba won over half of these tournaments, but after the revolution, the series was discontinued. When it resumed in 1970, Mexico and the Dominican Republic replaced Cuba and Panama. The current round-robin format sends the teams that win their postseason tournaments to the *Serie del Caribe* along with a number of reinforcements, including North Americans, from their defeated opponents. Willie Mays, Monte Irvin, Camilo Pasqual, Rico Carty, and Vic Pellot Power are among those who have starred in these postseason celebrations.

Winter ball has descended from its zenith of the 1950s and '60s largely due to economic dynamics beyond the control of the Caribbean franchises. Rising player and fuel costs, devalued currencies, and underdevelopment pushed many into deficits, with government subsidies often vital to their continuation. Government support, long a feature of basin baseball, helps to keep current the Dominican saying that there will never be political trouble during the baseball season, only afterward. But by the middle of the 1980s, fewer of the established Latin major leaguers suited up for the October-through-January campaign. The demands of the regular season, the threat of injury, and the relatively inconsequential pay of winter ball suggest that this trend will continue. The pattern, however, has given younger Latin ballplayers the chance to play before knowledgeable fans and against competition that is often at a major league level.

While winter ball in the late 1980s was troubled and other sports were making inroads, baseball remains *el rey de deportes* (the king of sports) throughout the basin. From the rocky hillsides and arid plains of northern Mexico through the canefields of the islands to the basin's southernmost flank in the Andes, baseball commands a fascination approaching reverence.

Baseball's significance derives from the role that it has played in the coming together of these societies in the twentieth century. Knitting a common cultural fabric, serving as a vent to social and political tensions, and offering a vehicle not only for individual mobility but collective social affirmation, baseball indeed has been more than a game. It has offered the citizens of the basin a chance to enter a ritual kinship embracing all fans and players. And while reflecting the progressive penetration of the United States in the region, baseball has been more than a cultural transmission belt for North American values. Beating each other and excelling in the major leagues and international competitions at a time when the Caribbean basin has encountered difficulties in asserting either its political or economic autonomy have been tremendous sources of pride. And that symbolic recognition has become a catalyst to national cohesion and consciousness for the region in its troubled evolution this century.

First Major Leaguers from Caribbean Basin Countries

Country	Player	Year	Team
Cuba	Esteban Bellan	1871	Troy Haymakers
	Rafael Almeida	1911	Cincinnati Reds
	Armando Marsans	1911	Cincinnati Reds
Colombia	Luis "Jud" Castro	1902	Philadelphia Athletics
Mexico	Baldomero "Mel" Almada	1933	Boston Red Sox
Venezuela	Alejandro Carrasquel	1939	Washington Senators
Puerto Rico	Hiram Bithorn	1942	Chicago Cubs
Panama	Héctor López	1955	Kansas City Athletics
	Humberto Robinson	1955	Milwaukee Braves
Dominican Republic	Osvaldo Virgil	1956	New York Giants
Virgin Islands	Joe Christopher	1959	Pittsburgh Pirates
Nicaragua	Dennis Martínez	1976	Baltimore Orioles
Honduras	Gerald Young	1987	Houston Astros
Curacao	Hensley Meulens	1990	New York Yankees
Belize	Chito Martinez	1991	Baltimore Orioles
Aruba	Gene Kingsale	1996	Baltimore Orioles

Serie del Caribe

Series	Year	Site	Winning Team/Country	Series	Year	Site	Winning Team/Country
I	1949	Cuba	Almendares/Cuba	XX	1977	Venezuela	Licey/Dominican Republic
II	1950	Puerto Rico	Carta Vieja/Panama	XXI	1978	Mexico	Mayagüez/Puerto Rico
III	1951	Venezuela	Santurce/Puerto Rico	XXII	1979	Puerto Rico	Magallanes/Venezuela
IV	1952	Panama	La Habana/Cuba	XXIII	1980	Dominican Republic	Licey/Dominican Republic
V	1953	Cuba	Santurce/Puerto Rico		1981	Not Held	
VI	1954	Puerto Rico	Caguas/Puerto Rico	XXIV	1982	Mexico	Caracas/Venezuela
VII	1955	Venezuela	Santurce/Puerto Rico	XXV	1983	Venezuela	Arecibo/Puerto Rico
VIII	1956	Panama	Cienfuegos/Cuba	XXVI	1984	Puerto Rico	Zulia/Venezuela
IX	1957	Cuba	Marianao/Cuba	XXVII	1985	Mexico	Licey/Dominican Republic
X	1958	Puerto Rico	Marianao/Cuba	XXVIII	1986	Venezuela	Mexicali/Mexico
XI	1959	Venezuela	Almendares/Cuba	XXIX	1987	Mexico	Caguas/Venezuela
XII	1960	Panama	Cienfuegos/Cuba	XXX	1988	Dominican Republic	Escogido/Dominican Republic
	1961–69	Not Held		XXXI	1989	Mazatlan	Zulia/Venezuela
XIII	1970	Venezuela	Magallanes/Venezuela	XXXII	1990	Miami	Escogido/Dominican Republic
XIV	1971	Puerto Rico	Licey/Dominican Republic	XXXIII	1991	Miami	Licey/Dominican Republic
XV	1972	Dominican Republic	Ponce/Puerto Rico	XXXIV	1992	Mexico	Mayagüez/Puerto Rico
XVI	1973	Venezuela	Licey/Dominican Republic	XXXV	1993	Mexico	Mayagüez/Puerto Rico
XVII	1974	Mexico	Caguas/Puerto Rico	XXXVI	1994	Mexico	Licey/Dominican Republic
XVIII	1975	Puerto Rico	Bayamón/Puerto Rico	XXXVII	1995	Puerto Rico	San Juan/Puerto Rico
XIX	1976	Dominican Republic	Hermosillo/Mexico	XXXVIII	1996	Dominican Republic	Culiacan/Mexico

Dominican League Statistics

Year	Champion	BA Leader	HR Leader	Most Games Won	Year	Champion	BA Leader	HR Leader	Most Games Won
1951	Licey	Luis Villodas .346	Pedro Formental 13	Guayuabín Olivo 10	1977–78	Aguilas	Omar Moreno .345	Dick Davis 8	Odell Jones Al Holland Mickey Mahler 7
1952	Aguilas	Luis Olmo .344	Alonzo Perry 11	Terry McDuffie 14	1978–79	Aguilas	Ted Cox .319	Bob Beall Dick Davis 7	Bo McLaughlin Mike Proly 9
1953	Licey	Tetelo Vargas .355	Alonzo Perry 11	Emilio Cueche 13	1979–80	Licey	Tony Peña .317	A. De Freitas Alberto Lois Leon Durham Samuel Mejía Pedro Guerrero Tied with 3	Jerry Hannahs 9
1954	Estrellas Orientales	Alonzo Perry .326	Bob Thurman 11	Carrao Bracho G. Olivo 8					
1955–56	Escogido*	Bob Wilson .333	Willie Kirkland 9	Fred Waters 11	1980–81	Escogido	Ken Landreaux .394	Tony Peña 7	Mario Soto M. Mahler 7
1956–57	Escogido	Osvaldo Virgil .312	Danny Kravitz 4	Pete Burnside 11	1981–82	Escogido	Pedro Hernandez .408	Dave Hostetler 9	Pasqual Pérez 10
1957–58	Escogido	Alonzo Perry .332	Dick Stuart 14	Fred Kipp 11	1982–83	Licey	César Geronimo .341	Howard Johnson 8	Pasqual Pérez 9
1958–59	Licey	Felipe Alou .351	Jim McDaniels 12	Bennie Daniels 12	1983–84	Licey	Miguel Diloné .343	Reggie Whittemore 12	Orel Hershiser Frank Wills 8
1959–60	Escogido	Felipe Alou .359	Frank Howard 9	Stan Williams 12	1984–85	Licey	Junior Noboa .327	Ralph Bryant 9	Tom Filer 8
1960–61	Escogido	Manuel Mota .344	Manuel Jiménez 13	Danilo Riva 13	1985–86	Aguilas	Tony Fernández .364	Tony Peña 9	Mickey Mahler 8
			J.V. Nicolás Victor Ramirez Felipe Alou N. Saviñón Tied with 4		1986–87	Aguilas	Stanley Javier .374	Ralph Bryant 13	Gibson Alba José Nuñez Eric Plunk Tied with 5
1961–62	Incomplete Season								
1962–63	Not Held				1987–88	Escogido	Stanley Javier .363	Mark Parent 10	José Bautista 8
1963–64	Licey	Manuel Mota .379	O. McFarlane 10	G. Olivo Steve Blass 9					
1964–65	Aguilas	Manuel Mota .364	O. McFarlane 8	Dick LeMay 8	1988–89	Licey	Julio Peguero .327	Domingo Michel 9	Melido Perez 8–3
1965–66	Season not organized by league				1989–90	Escogido	Angel González .403	Denny González 5	Mel Rojas Jeff Shaw Kevin Wickander Darren Holmes Tied with 6
1966–67	Aguilas	Mateo Alou .363	Winston Llenas Bob Robertson 10	Dock Ellis 9					
1967–68	Estrellas Orientales	Ricardo Carty .350	Bob Robertson 9	Silvano Quezada 11					
1968–69	Escogido	Mateo Alou .390	Nate Colbert 8	Jay Ritchie 9	1990–91	Licey	Hensley Meulens .338	Francisco Cabrera 8	Francesco De la Rosa 7
1969–70	Licey	Ralph Garr .387	Winston Llenas Byron Browne 9	G. Rounsaville 8	1991–92	Escogido	Luis Mercedes .333	Francisco Cabrera, Sammy Sosa, Geronimo Berroa, Kevin Koslofski, and Julian Yan tied with 4	José Nuñez 6
1970–71	Licey	Ralph Garr .457	César Cedeño 8	Rollie Fingers 9					
1971–72	Aguilas	Ralph Garr .388	Charlie Sands 10	Gene Garber 9					
1972–73	Licey	Von Joshua .358	Adrian Garrett 9	Pedro Borbón 9					
1973–74	Licey	Dave Parker .345	Ricardo Carty 9	Rick Waits 8	1992–93	Aguilas	Tom Marsh .318	Domingo Martinez 6	Efrain Valdez, Jose Martinez, Howard Farmer, and Rafael Valdez 5
1974–75	Aguilas	Bruce Bochte .352	Rafael Batista Bobby Darwin 8	James Richards 8					
1975–76	Aguilas	Wilbur Howard .341	Wilbur Howard John Hale Gary Alexander Larry Parrish G. Thomasson Bill Nahorodny Andre Thornton Tied with 4	Nino Espinosa Tom Dettore 8	1993–94	Licey	Alex Arias .371	Henry Rodriguez 6	Apolinar Garcia 6
					1994–95	Azucueros	Luis Mercedes .352	Domingo Martinez 11	Hipolito Pichardo, Julian Heredia 6
1976–77	Licey	Mario Guerrero .365	Pedro Guerrero Ike Hampton 6	Angel Torres 10	1995–96	Aguilas	Domingo Cedeno .419	Sherman Obando 7	Ramon Morel 5

* First year held in winter

Cuban League Statistics

Year	Champion	BA Leader	HR Leader	Most Games Won	Year	Champion	BA Leader	HR Leader	Most Games Won
1878–79	Habana Undefeated				1885	Habana	Pablo Ronquilla .350		
1879–80	Habana								
1880–81	Not held				1885–86	Habana Undefeated	Wenceslao Gálvez .345		Adolfo Luján 5–0
1882	Disputed: Fe and Habana								
1882–83	Habana				1887	Habana	R. Martínez .439		Adolfo Luján 5–0

Year	Champion	Batting Leader	Home Run Leader	Pitching Leader
1888	Fe	Antonio García .448		Francisco Hernández 10–2
1889	Habana	Francisco Salabarria .305		Adolfo Luján 10–3
1889–90	Habana	Antonio García .364		Miguel Prats 11–2
1890–91	Fe	Alfredo Crespo .375		Miguel Prats 9–4
1892	Habana	Antonio García .362		E. Hernández 4–1
1892–93	Matanzas	Antonio García .385		Francisco Hernández 4–1
1893–94	Almendares	Miguel Pratts .394		José Pastoriza 16–7
1894–95	Suspended due to War of Independence	Alfredo Arcaño .430		Enrique García 12–4
1897–98	Not finished			
1898	Habanista	Valentín González .394		José Romero 5–2
1900	San Francisco	Esteban Pratts .333		Luis Padrón 13–4
1901	Habana	Julián Castillo .454		Carlos Royer 12–3
1902	Habana Undefeated	Luis Padrón .463		Carlos Royer 17–0
1903	Habana	Julián Castillo .330		Cándido Fontanals 14–6
1904	Habana	Regino García .397		Carlos Royer 13–3
1905	Almendares	Regino García .305		Angel D'Meza 10–4
1905–6	Fe	Regino García .304		José Muñoz 8–1
1907	Almendares	Regino García .324		George Mack 4–2
1908	Almendares	Emilio Palomino .350		José Méndez 9–0
1908–9	Habana	Julián Castillo .315		José Méndez; L. Haggerman 15–6
1910	Almendares	Emilio Palomino .408		José Méndez 7–0
1910–11	Almendares	Preston Hill .365		José Méndez 11–2
1912	Habana	Emilio Palomino .440		José Junco 6–1
1913	Fe	Armando Marsans .400		Red Redding 7–2
1913–14	Almendares	Manuel Villa .351		José Méndez 10–0
1914–15	Habana	Cristóbal Torriente .387		José Acosta 5–1
1915–16	Almendares	Eustaquio Pedrosos .413		José Acosta 8–3
1917	Orientales	Adolfo Luque .355		José Acosta 2–1
1918–19	Habana	Manuel Cueto .344		José Acosta 16–10
1919–20	Almendares	Cristóbal Torriente .360		Emilio Palmero 5–1
1920–21	Habana	Pelayo Chacon .344	Cristóbal Torriente, M. González, B. Jiménez, M. Guerra Tied with 1	José "Cheo" Hernández 4–1
1921*	Habana	Bienvenido Jiménez .619	Manuel Cueto 1	Julio Leblanc 2–0
1922–23	Marianao	Bernardo Baró .401	Cristóbal Torriente 4	Lucas Boada 10–4
1923–24	Santa Clara	Oliver Marcells .393	Bienvenido Jiménez 4	Bill Holland 10–2
1924–25	Almendares	Manuel Cueto .364	Esteban Mantalvo 5	José Acosta 4–1
1925–26	Almendares	Johnny Wilson .430	J. H. Lloyd, Jud Wilson 3	César Alvarez 10–2
1926–27	Habana	Manuel Cueto .404	J. Hernández 4	Juan Olmo 3–0
1927–28	Habana	Johnny Wilson .424	Oscar Charleston 5	Oscar Levis 7–2
1928–29	Habana	Alejandro Oms .432	Cool Papa Bell 5	Adolfo Luque 9–2
1929–30	Cienfuegos	Alejandro Oms .380	Mule Suttles 7	Heliodoro "Yoyo" Diaz 13–3
1930–31*	Not finished	O. Charleston .373	Ernest Smith, José Fernández 1	Martin Dihigo 2–0
1931–32	Almendares	Rámon Cueto .400	Alejandro Oms, Ismael Morales 3	Juan Eckelson 5–1
1932–33	Tie: Habana Almendares	M. González .432	R. Estalella 3	Jésus Lorenzo 3–0
1933–34	No championship held			
1934–35	Almendares	Lázaro Salazar .407	Eleven tied with 1	Lázaro Salazar 6–1
1935–36	Santa Clara	Martín Dihigo .358	Willie Wells, Jacinto Roque 5	Martín Dihigo 11–2
1936–37	Marianao	Harry Williams .349	H. Andrews, R. Estalella 5	Raymond Brown 21–4
1937–38	Santa Clara	Sam Bankhead .366	Willie Wells, R. Estalella, Raymond Brown 4	Raymond Brown 12–5
1938–39	Santa Clara	Tony Castaños .371	Josh Gibson 11	Martín Dihigo 14–2
1939–40	Almendares	Tony Castaños .340	Mule Suttles 4	Rodolfo Fernández 7–4
1940–41	Habana	Lázaro Salazar .316	A. Crespo 3	Gilberto Torres 10–3
1941–42	Almendares	Silvío García .351		Macon Mayor, Agapito Mayor 6–2
1942–43	Almendares	A. Crespo .337	Roberto Ortiz, Saguita Hernández 2	Cocaina García 10–3
1943–44	Habana	Roberto Ortiz .337	Saguita Hernández 3	Martín Dihigo 8–1
1944–45	Almendares	Claro Duany .340	Claro Duany 3	Oliverio Ortiz 10–4
1945–46	Cienfuegos	L. Davenport .333	Dick Sisler 9	Adrián Zabala 9–3
1946–47	Almendares	Lou Klein .330	Roberto Ortiz 11	Cocaina García 10–3
1947–48	Habana	Harry Kimbro .346	Jesús Chanquilon Díaz 7	C. Marrero 12–2
1948–49	Almendares	A. Crespo .326	Monte Irvin 10	Octavio Rubert 8–1
1949–50	Almendares	P. Formental .336	Roberto Ortiz, Don Lenhardt 15	Octavio Rubert 5–1
1950–51	Habana	Silvío García .347	P. Formental, Bert Hass, Ed Mierkowitz, Charles Grant Tied with 8	Vincente López]7–3
1951–52	Habana	Bert Hass .323	P. Formental, James Basso 9	Joe Black 15–6
1952–53	Habana	Edmundo Amorós .373	Louis Klein 16	R. Alexander 10–3
1953–54	Almendares	Rocky Nelson .352	Earl Rapp, Rafael Noble 10	Cliff Fanning 13–4
1954–55	Almendares	Angel Scull .370	Rocky Nelson 13	Joe Hatten 13–5
1955–56	Cienfuegos	Forrest Jacobs .321	Ultus Alvarez 10	Pedro Ramos 13–5
1956–57	Marianao	Orestes Miñoso .312	Archie Wilson 11	Camilo Pascual 15–5
1957–58	Marianao	Milton Smith .320	Daniel Morejon, Norman Larker, B. Robinson, Frank Herrera 9	Billy O'Dell 7–2
1958–59	Almendares	Tony Taylor .303	Jim Baxes 9	Orlando Peña 13–5
1959–60	Cienfuegos	Octavio Rojas .322		
1960–61	Cienfuegos			

* Short season

Latin American Halls of Fame
Compiled by Eduardo Valero

Cooperstown's National Baseball Hall of Fame and the Canadian Baseball Hall of Fame are not the game's only Valhallas. Halls of Fame exist throughout Latin America, most notably in Cuba, Mexico, the Dominican Republic and Venezuela. They enshrine not only local favorites but also such major league Hall of Famers as Roberto Clemente, Juan Marichal, and Luis Aparicio and Negro League immortals such as Josh Gibson, Monte Irvin, Raymond Dandridge, and Martin Dihigo. Some Latin halls date back to 1939, the first year that the Baseball Hall of Fame opened in Cooperstown. Others are more recent, but all hold players worthy of our admiration.

Caribbean Baseball Series Hall of Fame

Willard Brown   Rico Carty   Hector Espino   Camilo Pascual

Players Selected for Cuban Baseball Hall of Fame
Selected in Cuba:

1939
Rafael Almeida
Luis (Anguilla) Bustamante
Antonio Maria (el Ingles) Garcia
Gervasio (Strike) Gonzalez
Adolfo Lujan
Armando Marsans
Jose de la Caridad Mendez
Carlos (Bebe) Royer
Cristobal Torriente

1940
Alfredo Arcano
Jose (Joseito) Munoz

1941
Regino (Mamelo) Garcia
Emilio Sabourin

1942
Alfredo (Pajaro) Cabrera
Agustin (Tinti) Molina

1943
Julian Castillo
Heliodoro (Jabuco) Hidalgo
Luis (Mulo) Padron

1944
Carlos Macia
Alejandro Oms

1945
Bernardo Baro
Roman Calzadilla
Valentin Dreke

Carlos (Chino) Moran
Juan Manuel Pastoriza

1946
Ricardo Cabaleiro
Wenceslao Galvez
Francisco A. Poyo
Arturo Valdes
Rogelio Valdes

1948
Juan Antiga
Jacinto Calvo
Nemesio Guillo
Rafael Hernandez
Antonio (Antonico) Mesa
Tomas (Italiano) Romanach

1949
Pelayo Chacon
Julio (El Cartero) Lopez
Eduardo Machado
Gonzalo Sanchez
Manuel Villa

1950
Manuel (Patato) Cueto
Rafael Figarola
Eustaquio Gutierrez
Eugenio Jimenez
Ricardo Martinez

1951
Alfredo Arango
Martin Dihigo
Bienvenido (Pata Joroba)

Jiminez
Jose (Joseito) Rodriguez
Jose Maria Teuma

1953
Moises Quintero
Juan Viola
Carlos Zaldo

1954
Emilio Palmero
Pablo Ronquillo

1955
Baldomero (Merito) Acosta
Miguel Angel Gonzalez

1956
Isidro Fabre
Emilio Palomino

1957
Adolfo Luque

1958
Jose (Acostica) Acosta
Lazaro Salazar

1959
Ramon Bragana
Armando Cabanas

1960
Tomas De la Cruz
Oscar Rodriguez

Selected in Miami in 1983:
Santos Amaro

Edmundo Amoros
Leonardo Cardenas
Antonio (Tony) Castano
Sandalio Consuegra
Alejandro Crespo
Rogelio Crespo
Heliodoro (Yoyo) Diaz
Pedro Dibut
Roberto Estalella
Jose Maria Fernandez
Rodolfo Fernandez
Andres Fleitas
Pedro Formental
Manuel (Cocaina) Garcia
Silvio Garcia
Fermin Guerra
Ramon (Paito) Herrera
Conrado Marrero
Agapito Mayor
Pablo (Champion) Mesa
Orestes Minoso
Guillermo (Willy) Mirando
Estaban (Mayari) Montalvo
Julio Moreno
Pedro (Tony) Oliva
Regino Otero
Roberto Ortiz
Agustin Parpetti
Camilo Pascual
Eustaquio (Bombin) Pedroso
Pedro Ramos

Napoleon Reyes
Hector Rodriguez
Octavio (Cuqui) Rojas
Antonio (Tony) Taylor
Luis Tiant Sr.
Zoilo Versalles

Selected in Miami in 1984:
Esteban Bellan
Miguel (Mike) Cuellar
Pedro (Preston) Gomez
Justo (Cando) Lopez
Julio Rojo
Adrian Zabala

Selected in Miami in 1985:
Lorenzo (Chiguitin) Cabrera
Miguel (Mike) Fornieles
Antonio (Tony) Gonzalez
Rafael Noble
Jose (Cheo) Olivares
Bartolo Portuondo
Basilio (Brujo) Rosell

Selected in Miami in 1986:
Pedro Arango
Jorge Comellas
Francisco (Cuco) Correa
Marcelino Guerra
Renée Monteagudo
Orlando Pena
Jose (Cheo) Ramos

The following executives, league presidents, umpires and journalists have also been elected to the Cuban Baseball Hall of Fame:

Executives:
Alfredo Suarez
Emilio de Armas
Mario Mendoza
Julio Sanguily
Roberto (Bobby) Maduro
Abel Linares
Julio Blanco Herrera
Miguel Suarez de Cardenas
Antonio (Tony) Pacheco
Rafael Inclan

Cuban League Presidents:
Leopoldo de Sola
Jose Antonio Lopez del Valle

Umpires:
Amado Maestri

Journalists:
Jose (Joe) Massaguer
Rafael Conte
Pedro Galiana
Bernardo (Llillo) Jimenez

Negro Leaguers Who Performed in Cuba:
Andrew (Rube) Foster – Pitcher
Preston Hill – Outfielder
John Henry Lloyd (Sam) – Infielder
Oscar Charleston – Outfielder
Oscar Lewis – Pitcher
William Julius (Judy) Johnson – Infielder
John (Jorocon) Wilson – Infielder
Charles (El Chino) Smith – Outfielder
Chaney Whitte – Outfielder

Baseball Players in the Dominican Republic Sports Hall of Fame

Andres J. (Grillo B) Baez	p–of	Enrique (Indio Bravo) Hernandez	p
Luis A. (Grillo C) Baez	of	Julian Javier*	2b
Rafael A. (Sonlly) Alvarado	of	Enrique Lantingua	c
Pedro A. (Grillo A) Baez	if	Diogenes Lara	2b
Rafael Batista*	1b	Winston Llenas*	if
Pedro Borbon*	p	Gustavo Lluvera	p
Manuel (Manolete) Caceres	p–of	Manuel Mallens (Lico)	p
Pedro J. Caratini	ss (Puerto Rican mgr.)	Juan Marichal*	p
Ricardo (Rico) Carty*	if–of	Aquiles Martinez	2b
Luis (Nino el Zurdo) Castro	p	Horacio Martinez	ss
Alcibiades Colon	of	Teodoro (Teddy) Martinez*	if–of
Ramon (Sijo) del Monte Consuegra	p	Fernando (Pita) Miranda	of
Ventura (Loro) Escalante	p	Manuel (Manny) Mota*	of
Arnulfo (Nino) Espinosa*	p	Diomedes (Guayubin) Olivo*	p
Juan Delfin (Braganita) Garcia	2b	Federico (Chichi) Olivo*	p
Cesar Geronimo*	of	Alfonso Perry	p–if
Rafael Emilio (Sijo) Gomez	p	Juan Manuel Ortiz Pina	c
Pedro Gonzalez*	if	Juan Buatista Perdomo	p–of
Rafael A. (Fellito) Guerra	p	Julio H. Pina	p
Manuel Henriquez	c	Miguel (Turco Pinto) Penales	p

Rafael (Mellizo) Puesan	p–if
Silvano Quesada	p
Danilo Rivas	p
Fernando (Minin) Rodriguez	of–if
Juan Bautista Rodriguez Cuevas	of
Luis Ernesto (Burrolote) Rodriguéz	p–c–if–of
Felipe Rojas Alou*	of–if
Jesus Rojas Alou*	of
Mateo Rojas Alou*	of
Mateo de la Rosa	1b
Miguel (Abejita) Ruiz	p
Pedro Alejandro San	p

Jose (Pepe Lucas) St. Clair	if
Luis (Guigui Lucas) St. Clair	c
Joaquien Suncar	p
Baldomero (Mero) Urena	p
Juan E. (Tetelo) Vargas	of–if
Rafael A. (Papito) Vargas	if
Rafael (Guagua) Vargas	c
Rene Velazquez	ss
Osvaldo (Ossie) Virgil Sr.*	if–of–c
Ramon E. (Tetelito) Vargas	of

*Played in Major Leagues

Members of the Hall of Fame of Mexican Professional Baseball

1939
Lucas Juarez "El Indio"
Antonio Delfin "Laniza"
Julio Molina "El Diamante Indio"
Leonardo "Najo" Alanis
Fernando Barradas "Cocuite"

1964
Angel Castro
Martin Dihigo
Epitacio "La Mala" Torres
Lazaro Salazar
Ramon Bragana
Genaro Casas

1972
Roberto "Beto" Avila
Jose Luis "Chige" Gomez
Baldomero "Melo" Almada
Alberto Romo Chavez
Jesus "Cochihuila" Valenzuela
Alejandro Aguilar Reyes
Jorge Pasquel
Ernesto Carmona
Roy Campanella
Joshua Gibson
Monte Irvin

1973
Daniel "La Coyota" Rios
Roberto Ortiz
Agustin Bejerano
Anuar Canavati
Lazaro Penagos

Manuel Oliveros

1974
No Members Elected

1975
Guilermo "Huevito" Alvarez
Luis Montes De Oca "Molinero"
Fernando M. Campos "Fray Kempis"

1976
Alfred Pinkston
Ramiro Cuevas
Agustin Verdo

1977
Santos Amaro
Guillermo "Memo" Garibay

1978
Felipe Montufar

1979
Basilio "Brujo" Rosell
Jesus "Chanquilon" Diaz

1980
Leonardo "Leo" Rodriguez
Eduardo "Lalo" Orvananos
Carlos Alberto Gonzalez
Ramon Montes De Oca

1981
Vinicio Garcia
Tomas Arroyo
Salvador Castro
Apolinar Pulido "Polin"

1982
Manuel Echevarria
Burnis "Wild Bill" Wright
Francisco "Panchillo" Ramirez
Horacio Lopez Diaz
Mario Ariosa

1983
Claudio Solano
Jose Bache
Ronaldo Camacho
Felipe Montemayor
Ing. Elejo Peralta Y D.C.
Rafael Reyes Najera "Kid Alto"

1984
Alfonso "La Tuza" Ramirez
Miguel "Becerril" Fernandez
Guillermo "Memo" Lopez
Manuel Gonzalez Caballero
Gabriel Atristain

1985
Porfirio "Chio" Martinez
Adolfo Luque
Miguel Sotelo

1986
Ruben Amaro
Moises "Moi" Camacho
Benjamin Valenzuela
Marcos Valdez "Bugarini"

1987
Manuel "Moro" Chavez

Jesus "Jessie" Flores
Guillermo "Memo" Luna
Raul Mendoza
Antonio Ramirez Muro
Juan Ley Fong

1988
Lino Donoso Galata
Horacio Pina
Arnulfo Rodriguez
Abel Francisco Cano
Hector Espino Gonzalez
Pedro Septien Orozco

1989
Raymond "Mamerto" Dandrige
Jose "Zacatillo" Guerrero
Teodoro Marical
Oscal "Rapido" Esquivel

1990
Alfredo "Yaqui" Rios
Ramon "Diablo" Montaya
Alfonso Robinson Bours
Amado Maestri
Tomas Morales

1991
Jaime Corella
Antonio Pollorena
Chara Mansur Julian
Agustin D. Valdez
Juan Lima Hernandez

1992
Benjamin "Cananea" Reyes

Vicente "Huevo" Romo
Jose Pena
Armando Rodriguez
Jorge Blanco

1993
Ramon Arano
Aurelio Lopez
Alfredo Ortiz
Rene Gonzalez
Oscar Rodriguez
Homobono Marquez
Humberto Galaz

1994
Celerino Sanchez
Miguel Suarez
Miguel "Pilo" Gaspar
Carlos Galina
Jaime Perez Avella

1995
Aurelio Rodriguez
William Berzunza
Arnoldo "Kiki" Castro
Rodolfo Alvarado

1996
Juan Manuel Ley Lopez
Orestes "Minnie" Minoso
Jorge "Sony" Alarcon Rubio
Jorge "Charolito" Orta
Cesar Diaz Perez

Puerto Rico Professional Baseball Hall of Fame

Jose (Pito) Alvarez de la Vega	p–if–of
Luis (Tite) Arroyo*	p
Carlos Bernier*	of
Raymond Brown	p–of
Pedro M. Caratini	if
Orlando Cepeda*	if–of
Pedro Cepeda	if–of
John "Buster" Clarkson	if
Francisco Coimbre	p–of
Roberto Clemente*	of
Ceferino (Cefo) Conde	p
Leon Day	p–of
Saturnino (Nino) Escalera*	if–of
Jose A. Figueroa	p–of
Josh Gibson	c
Ruben Gomez*	p
Juan Guilbe	p–if–of
Felix Mantilla*	if–of

Dr. Francisco Marquez	executive (club owner)
Jose M. Morales	c–if–dh
Emilio (Millito) Navarro	if–of
Luis R. Olmo*	if–of
Rafael Ortiz	p
Satchel Paige*	p
Atanasio "Tony" Perez*	if
Demetrio (Menchin) Pesante	if
Juan (Terin) Pizarro*	p
Victor (Pellot) Power*	if–of
Juan Sanchez	c–if–of
Carlos M. Santiago	if
Jose G. (Pantalones) Santiago*	p
George Scales	mgr-if
Jorge (Griffin) Tirado	c
Robert (Bob) Thurman*	p–of
Juan E. (Tetelo) Vargas	if–of
Luis Villodas	c
Artie Wilson*	ss

*Played in Major Leagues

Venezuela Sports Hall of Fame

Luis Aparicio, Jr.*	ss
Luis Aparicio Sr.	ss
Jose (Carrao) Bracho	p
Daniel Canonico	p
Alejandro Carrasquel*	p
Alfonso Carrasquel*	ss
David Concepcion*	ss
Emilio Cueche	p
Buadilio Diaz*	c
Victor Davalillo*	of–if

Luis (Camaleon) Garcia	if
Manuel (Cocaina) Garcia	p–of
Vidal Lopez	p–of
Ramon Monzant*	p
Andres Quintero	if–of
Jesus (Chucho) Ramos*	of
Benito (Juey) Torrens	if–of
Cesar Tovar*	if–of

* Played in Major Leagues

## CHAPTER 18

Baseball in Canada

Bruce L. Prentice and Merritt Clifton

Baseball as we know it—with three bases and home, nine players to a side, and three outs to an inning—has been played in Canada at least since 1860, when the existing teams in London, Hamilton, St. Thomas, and Woodstock, Ontario, all accepted the rules of the New York Game popularized by Henry Chadwick. This was the game played on June 19, 1846 between the New York and Knickerbocker clubs on the Elysian Fields of Hoboken, New Jersey.

But a game differing from early baseball mainly in having five bases was played in Beechville, Ontario, as early as June 4, 1838, according to witness Adam Ford, who described it in a letter to *Sporting Life* published on May 5, 1886. The game included at least two "greyheaded men" who "used to play when they were boys."

Thus the Canadian baseball tradition certainly predates Abner Doubleday's apocryphal invention of the game at Cooperstown in 1839, and may go back as far as the U.S. tradition. Indeed, in both nations, ancestors of baseball including cricket and rounders had been played since the early 1700s, and determining exactly where their derivatives ended and baseball began may be impossible.

Before the arrival of the New York Game, the southwestern Ontario teams played the Canadian Game, with five bases and eleven fielders. All eleven batters had to be retired to end an inning. Only after the New York rules were adopted did the game spread to the other provinces. By 1865 baseball had become so popular in Montreal that an ordinance was passed forbidding games in city parks as a menace to other users.

Baseball reached Manitoba no later than 1874, supplanting a local ancestor game called "bat," which had been played around the Red River Settlement as early as the 1840s. A professional three-team Manitoba League failed in 1886, but the game had firmly caught on by 1902, when the Great Northern Railway sponsored a Winnipeg entry in the professional North Dakota League.

Saskatchewan had semiprofessional baseball by 1887, when future provincial premier Walter Scott led a Regina team to two successive regional championships. Amateur baseball emerged in Alberta at about the same time, with games recorded as early as 1886.

By 1903 baseball was even played in the Yukon, where games attracted heavy gambling. Professional baseball debuted the same year in British Columbia, as twenty-year-old Hal Chase—"Prince Hal," the slick-fielding first baseman—starred for a Victoria entry in an otherwise Washington-based league.

While major league baseball came late to Canada,

Canadian entries in U.S.-based professional leagues won pennants as early as 1877, when the Tecumsehs of London, Ontario, led the International Association. The Tecumsehs reputedly declined a chance to join the two-year-old National League later that year, and disbanded from lack of fan support in early 1878. Ontario acquired another pennant winner in 1887, as Toronto began an only briefly interrupted eighty-year run as a mainstay of the International League, then called the Eastern League. Toronto either finished first during the regular season or won four-team playoffs fifteen times, with back-to-back winners in 1917-1918, 1956-1957, and 1965-1966.

Montreal's first Eastern League entry folded within weeks in 1890. While another Montreal club won the 1898 championship, the by then renamed International League didn't become lastingly situated there until 1928. Even then, Montreal's third entry struggled until it was acquired in 1935 by gas station magnate Charlie Trudeau, father of future Canadian prime minister Pierre Elliot Trudeau. Trudeau anchored the lineup with French-speaking Del Bissonnette and Quebec native Gus Dugas, who hit .327 with 191 homers in thirteen minor league seasons. Under manager Frank Shaughnessy, who became International League president in 1936 and originated the four-club playoff format many experts credit with saving minor league baseball, the Montreal Royals won the 1935 pennant.

Bought by the Brooklyn Dodgers in 1940, the Royals won either pennant or playoffs in ten of the next twenty years. Led by Quebecois Roland Gladu (12 homers, 105 RBIs, .338 batting average) and pitcher Jean Pierre Roy (25-11), the 1945 club was probably Montreal's favorite, but the 1946 Royals are best remembered: with them, second baseman Jackie Robinson (.349) broke the Organized Baseball color line that had prevailed since 1899, when Bill "Hippo" Galloway was released after playing five games for Woodstock, Ontario.

The color line had already been broken in Quebec by .392-hitting pitcher/outfielder Fred Wilson, who joined Granby of the then-outlaw Provincial League for the 1935 stretch run. The Provincial League had included a Montreal-based all-black entry, the Black Panthers, in 1936 and 1937; was all white again in 1940, during a one-year fling at Organized Baseball; and was reintegrated in 1946 by minor league hockey star Manny McIntyre, who signed with Sherbrooke only days after the Dodgers had signed Robinson and optioned him to Montreal.

The Provincial League was the longest-running of numerous native Canadian circuits, many of which owed ancestry to the work of longtime Canadian Pacific Railway sports representative Joseph Page, who helped set up teams and leagues wherever the trains stopped. A former semipro teammate of Tip O'Neill, Page was involved with O'Neill in assembling Montreal's 1898 International League pennant winner. He later enlisted former major league pitcher Jean Dubuc to help him organize the Eastern Canada League, a.k.a. the Ontario-Quebec-Vermont League, of 1922-1924. This was an ancestor of three leagues of note, each of which sent over 100 players to the majors—the Provincial, which had already come together for single seasons in 1894 and 1900; the Canadian-American League, which could claim descent from the short lived, Ontario-based Canadian League of 1885; and the outlaw Northern League that flourished in New York and Vermont from 1935 to 1952.

Reorganized a fourth time, the Provincial League grew steadily from 1935 to 1940, was interrupted by World War II, resumed play in 1944, collapsed in 1956 after a disastrous six-year return to Organized Baseball, and struggled on as an outlaw circuit in 1958-1971. Stars were plentiful, from Quebec native Sam LaRoque (1900) to Felix Mantilla (1969), but the zenith came in 1948-1949, as the league attracted black greats who were hoping to prove themselves against whites, displaced wartime major leaguers, and the so-called Mexican League Jumpers, who were barred from Organized Baseball in 1946-1950 after breaking their major league contracts in an ill-fated stand against the reserve clause. At least twenty-five major leaguers played in the Provincial League during those two years, among them Sal Maglie, Max Lanier, Vic Power, Gladu and Roy, and Negro League stars Dave Pope, Bus Clarkson, and Quincy Trouppe.

The less colorful Can-Am belonged to Organized Baseball from 1936 through 1951. Several of the Ontario teams continued as an outlaw league into the 1960s.

Page also helped promote the Western Canada League, which began play in 1907, continuing with frequent interruptions and occasional name changes into the late 1940s, when Edmonton and Calgary anchored the Big Four League. The Western Canada League's best year was probably 1921, when its stars included Babe Herman and Heinie Manush.

Canadian teams have also been part of the bygone Northern Copper Country League, which later became the Northern League; the Northwestern League and Western International League, which evolved into today's Northwest League; the Pacific Coast League; the American Association; the Eastern League; the New York-Pennsylvania League; and the Pioneer League.

As well as helping return blacks to Organized Baseball, Canada played a part in popularizing baseball in Japan, through the Asahis (Rising Suns), a team of Vancouver teenagers of Japanese descent (Niseis) formed in 1914. In 1921, twelve years after the first visit by a U.S. collegiate team and thirteen years before the first visit by U.S. major leaguers, the Asahis and a touring team from Seattle barnstormed Japan, playing both Japanese clubs and each other. The Asahis remained a power in Vancouver-area amateur baseball and heroes to the substantial British Columbia Nisei population for over twenty years.

Despite the many major leaguers who have played for Canadian teams, relatively few Canadian natives have made the majors—a reflection of short summers and a paucity of places to play since television killed the old town teams and outlaw leagues in the 1950s. (Only one high school baseball team exists in Quebec; none in several other provinces.) Of the ten Canadian provinces, only Newfoundland hasn't produced a major leaguer.

High school baseball programs have flourished in the Metro Toronto area since 1979, when four schools experimented with a short schedule. There are now close to seventy schools playing a spring schedule that culminates in a championship game played at the SkyDome, prior to a regular-season Blue Jays game. The winning team receives the "Blue Jays Cup."

College baseball was started in 1978, when Seneca College (near Toronto) joined the NJCAA, New York-Penn Conference, for five seasons and was the forerunner to the National Baseball Institute (NBI) located in British Columbia. This college program has produced Canadian major leaguers including outfielders Kevin Reimer and Larry Walker, plus lefthanded pitchers Steve Wilson and Dennis Boucher.

Seven players from the late 1800s are listed by most record books as having been born in the U.S., but are believed to have altered their birth records for various reasons, including the 1894 Alien Exemption Act, which barred Canadian athletes from U.S. employment. In addition, several players who were born abroad actually grew up in Canada, e.g., Hank Biasatti and Reno Bertoia, natives of Italy but raised in Windsor, Ontario, and Jimmy Archer, born in Ireland, raised in Toronto, and signed into Organized Baseball from an independent team in Manitoba.

Many of the best Canadian players actually grew up in the U.S., among them infielder Pete Ward, son of former Montreal hockey great Jim Ward, who learned baseball in Oregon; pitcher Dick Lines, born in Montreal but raised in Florida; pitcher Kirk McCaskill, born in Kapuskasing, Ontario, who grew up in Burlington, Vermont; and infielder Sherry Robertson, born in Montreal but raised in Washington, D.C. (as the nephew of Senators and Twins club owner Calvin Griffith, who was also born in Montreal but was brought to Washington in 1921 by Senators owner Clark Griffith, who married Calvin's aunt).

Pitcher Sheldon Burnside reversed that pattern. Born in South Bend, Indiana, Burnside grew up in Toronto.

The first Canadian-born major leaguer was first baseman Bill Phillips, who played for Cleveland, Brooklyn, and Kansas City, from 1879 to 1888. Born in St. John, New Brunswick, Phillips actually grew up in Chicago.

Among the 150 to follow Phillips are active players Rob Ducey, Larry Walker, Kevin Reimer, and Matt Stairs, as well as pitchers Steve Wilson, Kirk McCaskill, Dennis Boucher, Mike Gardiner, Vince Horsman, Paul Quantrill, and Rheal Cormier. While the number of players by position is roughly proportional to the numbers on major league rosters, pitchers have won the most distinction, perhaps because pitching skills can be developed more readily in short amateur seasons. Bob Emslie of Guelph, Ontario, was the first Canadian pitcher of note, and won more games in a big league season than any other Canadian, posting a 32-17 mark for the 1884 Baltimore Orioles. A poor start in 1885 sent him back to the minors, with a career major league record of just 44-44. Emslie returned to the majors, however, as an umpire, serving thirty-five years before retiring in 1926.

O'Neill, born at either Woodstock or Springfield, Ontario, in 1858, was the best Canadian hitter of his time or ever, batting .326 in a big-league career that ran from 1883 to 1892. Breaking into the majors with New York as a pitcher, O'Neill soon switched to the outfield. In 1886 he led the then-major league American Association in hits, doubles, triples, homers, runs scored, batting, and slugging. His batting average, at the time, was actually listed as .492, but 50 walks were counted as hits. Subtracting them, he still hit .435. Though O'Neill fell to .335 in 1887, he repeated as batting champion.

The best Canadian player of all was probably Ferguson Jenkins, a 6′5″ righthander from Chatham, Ontario, who compiled a 284-226 record over nineteen seasons from 1965 to 1983. At his peak, Jenkins, the only Canadian-born Hall of Famer won 20 games or more seven times in eight years. Noted for control, Jenkins fanned over three times as many batters as he walked—and led the NL with 273 whiffs in 1969, retiring ninth on the all-time strikeout list. He earned the 1971 NL Cy Young Award by leading the league in wins (24), innings pitched, and, for the third time each, starts and complete games. He also hit 6 homers that year, one behind the NL record for home runs by a pitcher.

Other Canadian pitchers of note include Russ Ford, John Hiller, Reggie Cleveland, Phil Marchildon, Dick Fowler, Claude Raymond, and Ron Taylor. Ford, whose older brother also made the big leagues briefly, won 26 games for the New York Highlanders in 1910, his first full season. Hiller saved a then-record 38 games in 1973 and won an AL record 17 games in relief the next year, but is best known for his comeback from a 1971 heart attack. Marchildon and Fowler were half of the Athletics' rotation during the 1940s. On September 9, 1945, Fowler became the only Canadian to hurl a no-hitter, beating the Browns 1-0 for his only victory that year after coming back from military service. Marchildon peaked with 19 wins in 1947. Raymond is remembered as the first native Quebecois to play for the Expos. Taylor relieved for two World Champions, the 1964 Cardinals and the 1969 Mets, then became team physician for the Toronto Blue Jays.

Other top Canadian hitters were George Selkirk and Jeff Heath. Selkirk, who replaced Babe Ruth in the Yankees' lineup in 1934, hit .290 over nine seasons, topping .300 five times and twice driving in more than 100 runs. He later served for ten years as general manager of the Washington Senators. Heath, who reputedly never lived up to his potential, averaged .293 over fourteen years, beginning in 1936, with 194 homers. His best years were 1938 (21-112-.343) and 1941 (24-123-.340.) In between he led a player revolt against Indians manager Oscar Vitt. In his final full year, Heath hit .319 with twenty-four homers, pacing the Braves to the 1948 NL pennant, but broke his leg sliding during the last week of the season, missing his only chance at a World Series.

Canadian managers have included Art Irwin, Freddie Lake, Moon Gibson, and Bill Watkins, who led the Detroit Wolverines to the 1887 NL pennant.

Catcher Nig Clarke, from Amhurstburg, Ontario, won a spot in the minor league record books on June 15, 1902, hitting eight homers for Corsicana of the Texas League in a 51-3 rout of Texarkana. Outfielder Jack Graney, of St. Thomas, Ontario, was reputedly the first major leaguer to wear a number, and was also both the first hitter to face Babe Ruth when the latter debuted as a pitcher, and the first ex-player to become a baseball broadcaster. Outfielder Glen Gorbous, of Drumheller, Alberta, made the *Guinness Book of Records* with the longest measured throw on record. Black pitcher Jimmy Claxton, of New Westminster, British Columbia, briefly broke the color line by passing as an alleged Native American with Oakland of the Pacific Coast League in 1916.

National League baseball finally came to Canada with the expansion Montreal Expos in 1969. Hoping to get off to a good start, the Expos drafted mainly veterans, including Maury Wills, who became the only player to appear with Montreal in both the majors and the minors. Wills was soon traded for another veteran, Ron Fairly, who had led the University of Alberta into the 1957 College World Series. A preseason swap of sluggers Donn Clendenon and Rusty Staub had to be rearranged when Clendenon quit rather than join the Astros. Clendenon eventually unretired and was swapped to the Mets. The affair was a milestone in the series of events that led to overturning the reserve clause in 1975. Although the Expos won both their first game and their home opener (on a home run by pitcher Dan McGinn), they finished last. No-hitters by Bill Stoneman in 1969 and 1972 were the club high points until 1973. Then, despite a 79-83 record, the Expos were in contention into the final week, paced by Ken Singleton, Ron Hunt, who set an all-time record by getting hit with pitches 50 times, rookie Steve Rogers, and reliever Mike Marshall, who saved 31 games and won 14 in 92 appearances.

Marshall was promptly traded to the Dodgers for Willie Davis, who staged a sit-down strike in center field before moving on. Singleton and pitcher Mike Torrez were sent to the Orioles a year later for former Cy Young Award winner Dave McNally and outfielder Rich Coggins. A thyroid ailment ended Coggins's career at age 25, while McNally played the 1975 season without a contract, then filed one of the two lawsuits that finally broke the reserve clause (Andy Messersmith of the Dodgers filed the other).

The Expos regrouped under new manager Dick Williams to win a club record 95 games in 1979. The arrival of young stars including Rogers, Andre Dawson, Gary Carter, Larry Parrish, Tim Raines, and Tim Wallach led management to bill the Expos as "The Team of the Eighties." The promise seemed real when the Expos won a playoff against the Phillies for the NL East title during the strike-shortened split season of 1981, and were leading the Dodgers 1-0 in the fifth inning of the final game of the NL Championship Series. But Rick Monday singled and scored the tying run, then won the game 2-1 with a two-out ninth inning homer off Rogers.

Toronto appeared ready to enter the National League in 1976 by purchasing the San Francisco Giants. When that deal fell through at the last minute, the American League admitted the Blue Jays as an expansion team in 1977. The Blue Jays drafted for the future, enduring six years in the cellar before winning 89 games to place fourth in 1983.

Good trades and a strong farm system loaded the lineup with sluggers George Bell, Jesse Barfield, Lloyd Moseby, and Willie Upshaw, plus hard-hitting infielders Tony Fernandez and Damaso Garcia, and produced a perennially strong pitching staff led by Dave Stieb and Jimmy Key. Ernie Whitt, an expansion draft selection, supplied power behind the plate through 1989. Winning 99 games and the AL East title in 1985, the Jays took a 3-1 lead in the Championship Series against Kansas City, but then dropped three games in a row to lose. The Jays disappointed their fans by dropping the ALCS again in 1989 and 1991, and losing the AL East lead in the last week of 1987 and 1990.

Perhaps those disappointments built character in Toronto. Then again, general manager Pat Gillick, nicknamed "Stand Pat" for his previous conservatism, might have turned the team around with the biggest trade of his career, sending first baseman Fred McGriff and shortstop Tony Fernandez to the San Diego Padres for outfielder Joe Carter and second baseman Roberto Alomar. McGriff was the Jays' top slugger, but Carter virtually duplicated his numbers; Fernandez, a former All Star, was the Jays' senior position player, but Alomar hit with more power, stole more bases, and was equally flashy on defense. Two costly free agent additions—Jack Morris, the pitching ace of the World Championship Minnesota club, and veteran designated hitter Dave Winfield—completed a $41 million roster, the most expensive in Canadian baseball history. Morris won 21 games; Winfield, at age forty-one, became the oldest player to knock in 100 runs.

A six-game victory over the Oakland Athletics in the Championship Series set up the first-ever genuinely international World Series, as Toronto met Atlanta. The Blue Jays split the first two games in Atlanta, took a pair at home, and then appeared to choke again, dropping the last game in Toronto and losing a 2-1 lead in the sixth Series game in the bottom of the ninth. But with the score still tied in the top of the eleventh, Winfield doubled home two runs. Reliever Mike Timlin held off one last Atlanta rally to preserve a 4-3 win. For the first time the World Championship of baseball belonged to a team from outside the U.S.—though to be sure, the Blue Jays had no native Canadian players, having unloaded reserve outfielder Rob Ducey midway through the season.

The 1993 team, shaken up by more Gillick moves, nonetheless picked up where the 1992 edition left off, leading the AL East virtually from start to finish as first baseman John Olerud, a .269 lifetime hitter, averaged .400 for more than half the season. Rolling over the Chicago White Sox in the ALCS, the Blue Jays took the World Championship for the second consecutive year on Joe Carter's bottom-of-the-ninth home run off the Phillies' Mitch Williams in the decisive sixth game.

While the Blue Jays struggled to turn near-success into glorious triumph, drawing more than 4 million fans a year, the Expos entered the 1990s just struggling. Discouraged by twenty-two years without a pennant, and by dropping fan support as the advertised "Team of the Eighties" aged and departed, founding owner Charles Bronfman sold the franchise—after a prolonged hunt for takers—to a group headed by club president Claude Brochu.

The 1991 Expos finished dead last, ending the unpromising campaign with a long unscheduled road trip after a fifty-ton block of concrete fell from the Olympic Stadium roof. The fifteen-year-old ballpark was closed for extensive repairs, while Brochu et al. contemplated relocating to either Buffalo or St. Petersburg.

But Felipe Alou, the first former Montreal player to manage the team, turned everything around after taking over in early 1992, leading the Expos to a 70-55 record in the last four months of the season. In 1993 Alou brought Montreal a club record of 97 victories. And 1994 promised to be Montreal's year, as the Expos held a six-game lead over Atlanta, the second-best team in baseball, when the August 12 strike stopped play. For the first time in several years, fans in other cities began to recognize the Expo regulars, notably the outfield of Moises Alou, Marquis Grissom, and Larry Walker, as well as All Star shortstop Wil Cordero and top starter Ken Hill.

Yet Alou couldn't keep the nucleus together. The Expos' financial fortunes declined in the mid-1990s with the Quebec economy, exacerbating the perennial loss of stars to free agency and trades intended to cut the payroll. Walker, Hill, and top reliever John Wetteland departed after 1994; Grissom and Cordero left, along with newly emergent .318-hitting third baseman Sean Berry, after the depleted Expos slumped to fifth in 1995.

By 1996, Alou's fifth season as manager, only son Moises, catcher Darrin Fletcher, and pitchers Jeff Fassero and Mel Rojas remained from 1992—but astute scouting and player development brought replacements for most of the missing. Obtained from the Red Sox, Rheal Cormier, 7-10, was the first-ever Quebecois native in the Expos' rotation. Rondell White, Grissom's replacement, hit over .290 for the second year in a row. Mark Grudzielanek, taking over shortstop, hit .306, with 99 runs scored, 201 hits, and 34 doubles, all club records for the position. Henry Rodriguez, written off by the Dodgers after repeated failures to hit major league pitching with authority, won the left field job by leading the National League in home runs for the first third of the season. He cooled off down the stretch, failing to homer from August 25 to September 12, but still ended up with 42 doubles, 103 RBI, and a team record 36 home runs, including a September 26 grand slam against Philadelphia that momentarily kept the Expos alive in the National League wild card playoff race.

Never seriously challenging the ever-powerful Braves in the National League East, the Expos had held a one-game lead in the wild card race despite losing eleven of sixteen games at the end of August, and recovered with six straight wins in early September—but lost ground thereafter as the Dodgers and Padres each surged in competition for the National League West title. The Expos' hopes were killed chiefly by John Smoltz of the Braves, who beat them with his own three-run homer on September 22, and beat them again on September 27, for his 24th and final victory.

The Blue Jays meanwhile staggered through the strike-shortened 1994 and 1995 campaigns, shedding stars from the championship seasons including Roberto Alomar and Paul Molitor, and didn't recover in 1996 despite the continuing consistent power of Carter, career highs of 36 homers and 101 RBI from third baseman Ed Sprague, and a 20-10 season from Cy Young Award winner Pat Hentgen.

Professional baseball enjoyed middecade success in prairie provinces, led by Winnipeg. Without a pro team since 1971, the city took instantly to the Goldeyes, of the independent Northern League, who won the 1994 league championship, and continued to play at a .621 clip through 1996, making the playoffs each year, paced by ex-major leaguers including former Expos Dann Bilardello (1994) and Terry Lee (1995), who missed the Northern League triple crown by just two home runs.

Edmonton, top farm club for the Oakland Athletics, won the 1996 Pacific Coast League championship, a decade after Vancouver became the only previous Canadian team to lead the PCL.

Lethbridge, struggling for years as an independent entry in the otherwise affiliated Pioneer League, also achieved a breakthrough championship in 1996, led by .424-hitting Kevin Sweeney. Also including a Blue Jays farm team at Medicine Hat, the Pioneer League was in the mid-1990s the only professional league other than the PCL with more than one Canadian representative.

At the amateur level, however, there were hints that the talent stream contributing to Canadian baseball success in the preceding several years might be thinning. The professional baseball draft, extended to Canadian players in 1991, tapped 145 Canadians through 1995, but just nine were selected in 1996. Team Canada, meanwhile, placed third behind the U.S. and Cuba at the Americas' Baseball Challenge tournament in Edmonton, and was eliminated from possible Olympic competition by Nicaragua.

Baseball Canada president Ron Rice was encouraged by the September 30 decision of the International Baseball Association to allow professionals and former professionals to compete in future international tournaments—which could enable Team Canada to get further help from former members who went on to pro ball but may now be again available. One example might be Quebecois ex-major leaguer Denis Boucher, 3-7 with a 9.60 ERA for Ottawa in 1996, but young enough at 28 to start over.

"Baseball Canada will be recruiting professionals and former professionals for Team Canada, beginning in 1997," Rice confirmed, but he didn't say who he had in mind.

[Thanks for research help to Eves Raja; Bill Humber; Donald Guay; and the Brome County Historical Society.]

## CHAPTER 19

Spring Training

Myles E. Friedman

Like the origins of baseball itself, the beginnings of spring training are veiled behind the mists of myth and legend. Throughout the 1930s and 1940s, baseball writers generally identified Cap Anson as the father of spring training. As evidence, reporters cited his Chicago White Stockings' 1886 trip to Hot Springs, Arkansas, as the crystallizing moment. Since Anson has been credited (incorrectly) by several writers as the greatest innovator of baseball in the nineteenth century, it may have been easy to overlook the journey Harry Wright's Philadelphia nine took that same year to Charleston and New Orleans.

In 1951, *The Sporting News* reported that the Boston Beaneaters, Honest John Morrill's National League outfit of 1884, should earn credit for a jaunt that year to New Orleans. Lee Allen's 1955 book, *The Hot Stove League,* reached even farther back, to 1870, and unearthed a preseason trip by Jimmy Wood's newly formed Chicago White Stockings. (Wood's men journeyed to New Orleans in an effort to steel themselves for a run at the Cincinnati Red Stockings, undefeated champions in 1869.) "The plan," wrote Allen, "worked so well that Chicago beat the Red Stockings not once, but twice. So in the years that immediately followed, many of the old National Association teams would winter at New Orleans and play games there."

Later, it was asserted that the Red Stockings themselves trained at New Orleans in 1870, though strictly speaking, they were into their season by the time they reached New Orleans, having already trounced the Louisville Eagle nine, 94-7, in Kentucky. Finally, some historians assert that in 1869 and possibly even before that, the New York Mutuals, who had recently come under the control of a new president, William "Boss" Tweed of Tammany Hall, put in a training session at New Orleans.

In fact, before the first major league was organized in 1871, baseball clubs often packed up in February for southern tours, though at the beginning with less emphasis on training and more on barnstorming. The famous Excelsior Base Ball Club of Brooklyn, led by Jim Creighton, made a "grand tour" in 1860, playing games as far south as Baltimore.

During the early years of major league baseball, the 1870s and '80s, it was hard enough to turn a profit without the additional burden of cold and ice. Weather played the largest role in directing itineraries southward, and big league squads leased locales in Charleston, Mobile, Macon, Savannah, Atlanta, Pensacola, and Jacksonville.

The outlays for training were incredibly modest by today's standards. In 1892, Wright's Phillies ran a spring training season from February 28 through March 29. Included were two weeks in Gainesville, Florida, and two weeks of barnstorming on the way back north; gate receipts for the whole exercise totaled nearly $700, leaving a net loss of $469.

In 1888 the Washington Nationals became the first club to train in Florida. It was not until 1914, however, that more than two teams would train in Florida during the same year. The idea of concentrating clubs in close proximity to each other for the purpose of exhibition play came not from the minds of baseball men, but from civic leaders and promoters of the sun belt.

Al Lang, a Pittsburgh businessman who had moved to St. Petersburg and later became its mayor, began wooing major league clubs in 1913. At first, Lang made the mistake of promising Barney Dreyfuss and his Pittsburgh Pirates beautiful scenery and excellent fishing if they were to shift to Florida from their long-time home in Hot Springs. Dreyfuss replied scornfully that he wasn't interested in giving his boys a good time for fishing and sitting; they were at training camp for hard work and the rougher environs of Arkansas were just fine for that.

Lang did entice Branch Rickey's St. Louis Browns to St. Petersburg for the 1914 season. A Browns' official had persuaded several of the town's citizens into agreeing to pay all the expenses for the Browns' retinue of fifty. Later, when Lang learned of the deal, he and public officials refused to pay any of the $6,500 bill. The Browns did not return the following spring.

Soon Lang drew the Boston Braves and New York Yankees to St. Petersburg. The Braves' requirement for relocating in 1922 was a new ballpark. Lang accommodated them with Waterfront Park and in 1925 lured the Yankees by extolling St. Petersburg's relatively chaste society—at least in comparison to New Orleans, the Bombers' long-time preseason home. (It didn't hurt Lang's pitch that manager Miller Huggins had recently bought a home in St. Pete.)

There were several semipermanent training sites before the 1920s, but they were the exceptions. The Pirates lasted at Hot Springs from the turn of the century until 1917, and John McGraw established a Giants camp at Marlin, Texas, that lasted eleven seasons. Marlin, the site of purportedly curative mineral baths like those at Hot Springs, was sufficiently remote for McGraw to keep his men in line. However, when spring training was delayed until mid-March in 1919 in the aftermath of World War I, McGraw opted for the convenience of Gainesville, Florida.

The land boom in the Sunshine State in the 1920s was

accompanied by a full-scale rush of baseball clubs. The Athletics, Braves, Browns, Dodgers, Yankees, Senators, Reds, and Phillies all set up long-term residences during the decade and most never left except during World War II, when long-distance travel was curtailed. One club that did leave was the Giants. In 1924, McGraw moved his outfit to Sarasota, but, after losing $100,000 in a land deal, he said goodbye to Florida; the Giants returned only after McGraw surrendered the reins.

Spring training sites were often determined by the personal holdings of owners or managers. The Cubs only became fixtures on Santa Catalina Island, twenty miles off the coast of Los Angeles, after Phil Wrigley, who owned Catalina, bought the Cubs in 1921. When the Tigers moved to Augusta, Georgia, in 1922, it was at the behest of their new manager, Ty Cobb, the Georgia Peach, who was part owner of the ballpark.

Bill Veeck, who bought the Indians in 1946, owned an Arizona ranch; hence the Indians' move to Tucson, where they stayed for forty-six years. The Yankees might still be in St. Petersburg but for owner Dan Topping's yacht and his desire to sail from a Fort Lauderdale mooring (though a promise to provide integrated housing in Fort Lauderdale may have been an equally forceful motivation).

The new congregation of clubs in Florida coincided with an unrelated phenomenon that changed spring training forever: Babe Ruth. When Ruth joined New York in 1920, his arrival had two immediate effects: (1) a nineteen-game barnstorming trip by the Giants and Red Sox—now without Ruth—became one of the worst spring training fiascoes of all time; and (2) Ruth generated tremendous interest for Yankee exhibitions. When the Yankees finally set up shop in St. Petersburg, spring training reached its zenith for ticket sales. In the spring after Ruth's record-setting 1927 season, 270,000 fans paid to see Yankee exhibition games, enabling Jacob Ruppert to clear an amazing profit of $60,000.

Naturally, other clubs wanted a piece of that action. By the mid-1930s only the Pirates, White Sox, Cubs, and Indians regularly trained outside Florida. Several teams split their spring between Florida and sites off-shore—Havana, San Juan, Bermuda, and the Dominican Republic; however, each returned to the mainland for games in Florida and a barnstorming jaunt north. Clubs sometimes scheduled more than 40 games before opening the regular season in mid-April.

World War II travel restrictions forced teams to train nearer home—north of the Potomac River and east of St. Louis. Clubs opened camps later and, from 1943 to 1945, lengthy barnstorming ventures were dropped.

After the War, the major leagues' passion for Florida continued, though with a harsh new aspect. In 1946 Branch Rickey brought Jackie Robinson to camp as a member of the Dodgers' Montreal farm club, thus beginning a twenty-year campaign to reverse racism. The Dodgers trained at Daytona Beach, a city which, though allowing Robinson to play in games, still enforced segregationist housing, dining, and travel codes. Robinson was barred from games in Sanford, Jacksonville, and Deland and other games were canceled. In 1947 Rickey moved his club to Cuba and Panama and only returned to Florida after making an inspired decision, one that would have an enduring impact on the game.

Rickey wanted to insulate his club from the hateful Jim Crow racial policies that prevailed in Florida and found the answer in a decommissioned naval base at Vero Beach. In 1948, the Dodgers would live, eat, train, and play at the club's new Dodgertown complex. In addition, the camp would encompass Brooklyn's entire minor league system, more than 400 players, giving Rickey the "baseball college" he had long wanted.

Other clubs encountered similar problems as they tried to integrate the game and, by 1953, five of the seven teams with black players on their rosters trained out west. Gradually most Florida communities, fearful of losing their lucrative spring showpiece, accepted the presence of blacks. But towns which played host to an occasional barnstorming game (and as such, were unaffected by the economic imperatives that worked on training camp cities), were slow to change.

In the spring of 1950, with fans eager to see Robinson, the Dodgers drew 232,000 on a tour north from Florida. But incidents of bigotry only worsened. By the late 1950s, racism throughout the region helped end the barnstorming circuits that had operated for nearly a century.

Like Florida, California offered great weather for training, and several teams had sampled West Coast training early in the century. Until 1924, however, there was never more than one per year. By 1932 four clubs trained in California (the Cubs, Pirates, Tigers, and Giants) and, for most of the next twenty years, the Orange League would remain four strong.

The directors of the Pacific Coast League ended spring training by major league teams in California by prohibiting games in PCL cities the week before the PCL season opened (about April 1). That meant that big-league teams had nearly three weeks to kill before their seasons opened. The last major league teams ensconced in California, the Orioles and the White Sox, pulled out after the 1953 season.

Arizona had had a spring training as early as 1929 when the Tigers trained in Phoenix, but eighteen years passed before another club trained in Arizona. In 1947, Horace Stoneham of the Giants and Bill Veeck of the Indians agreed to take their teams to Phoenix and Tucson, respectively. Those clubs, which had or would soon have black players on their rosters, may have stayed in Arizona because of eased race relations. Until 1993, when they moved to Winter Haven, Florida, the Indians (along with the Cubs, who arrived in 1952) formed the backbone of the Cactus League. By the 1969 expansion, seven teams were training in Arizona.

In 1951, the Giants and the Yankees engineered one of baseball's great trades. Yankee partner Del Webb was a Phoenix resident and was anxious to give his home town a close look at his championship squad. He prevailed upon Stoneham to switch training sites for one year and, for the last time, the Yankees trained away from Florida. Incidentally, the two met in the World Series that fall.

The next decisive stage in the evolution of spring training was a consequence of baseball's renaissance following the 1975 World Series. After struggling to compete with America's expanding entertainment marketplace in the 1960s and 1970s, baseball surged in popularity. Attendance in the two years following Carlton Fisk's World Series body-English homer jumped 19 percent, more than twice the growth during all the years since 1950. Then baseball really took off, reaching in 1994 a per-game figure (31,609) nearly twice that of 1975. The change was reflected in attendance at spring training games in Florida and Arizona, where games that were once attended by small crowds of scouts and locals were now attracting better than 2.5 million fans per year.

By 1977, renewed devotion to the game was evident throughout the Cactus League (eight teams) and Grapefruit Leagues (eighteen teams). Games which were once casual diversions became characterized by sold-out signs, scalpers, and ever-rising ticket prices. In 1990, *USA Today* began running box scores of spring games, providing a level of national coverage beyond the imaginings of earlier fans. Clubs began training in "complexes," following the example of Branch Rickey thirty years later.

By the late 1980s most teams played their spring training games in municipal ballparks or were seeking new ones, complete with practice fields for minor league camps and amenities rivaling major league ballparks. Even as the costs of luring a team to town or keeping it there escalated, cities in Arizona and Florida continued to compete for big league tenants. In 1937, $5,000 in cash was enough to lure Sam Breadon's St. Louis Cardinals to Daytona Beach. In 1994, Peoria, Arizona, invested $32 million into a stadium and compound for the Mariners and Padres.

Following Peoria's lead, other cities have put together packages designed to attract two clubs to one large facility. The Chicago White Sox and the expansion Arizona Diamondbacks are slated to share a new complex in Tuc-son in 1998, while the St. Louis Cardinals and Montreal Expos will move to a joint facility in Jupiter, Florida for the 1998 season.

Perhaps the most unwelcome change to affect spring training came in 1995 when replacement players were on hand for the first six weeks of the training season. Faced with the ongoing strike by the Major League Baseball Players Association, club owners opened training camps with minor-league and amateur replacements. Games were held, though drawing little interest from fans, until March 31, just before clubs broke camp to head north, when the strike ended. Regular players were quickly rushed to their training sites for a short training season before the April 26 regular season opener.

Much of spring training remains unchanged. Scribes and savants continue to debate the necessity of the six-week regimen of calisthenics and infield drills. Though professional to a fault, some ballplayers still arrive needing a concentrated cycle of weight reduction. And, despite it all, fans still look to the lengthening days of March for the renewal of hope and a new season in which past promises are at last fulfilled.

Spring Training Sites by Team Nickname

Records of spring training prior to 1900 are incomplete and unclear. While some teams went south as early as the 1860s, it is difficult to separate clubs that were barnstorming from clubs that were training. Future editions of *Total Baseball* will attempt to sort out the facts.

NATIONAL LEAGUE

Astros

1962-63 Apache Junction, Ariz.
1964-84 Cocoa Beach, Fla.
1985- Kissimmee, Fla.

Braves

1901 Norfolk, Va.
1902-04 Thomasville, Ga.
1905 Charleston, S.C.
1906 Jacksonville, Fla.
1907 Thomasville, Ga.
1908-12 Augusta, Ga.
1913 Athens, Ga.
1914-15 Macon, Ga.
1916-18 Miami, Fla.
1919-20 Columbus, Ga.
1921 Galveston, Tex.
1922-37 St. Petersburg, Fla.
1938-40 Bradenton, Fla.
1941 San Antonio, Tex.
1942 Sanford, Fla.
1943-44 Wallingford, Conn.
1945 Washington, D.C.
1946-47 Fort Lauderdale, Fla.
1948-62 Bradenton, Fla.
1963- West Palm Beach, Fla.

Cardinals

1901-02 St. Louis, Mo.
1903 Dallas, Tex.
1904 Houston, Tex.
1905 Marlin Springs, Tex.
1906-08 Houston, Tex.
1909-10 Little Rock, Ark.
1911 West Baden, Ind.
1912 Jackson, Miss.
1913 Columbus, Ga.
1914 St. Augustine, Fla.
1915-17 Hot Wells, Tex.
1918 San Antonio, Tex.
1919 St. Louis, Mo.
1920 Brownsville, Tex.
1921-22 Orange, Tex.
1923-24 Bradenton, Fla.

1925 Stockton, Cal.
1926 San Antonio, Tex.
1927-29 Avon Park, Fla.
1930-36 Bradenton, Fla.
1937 Daytona Beach, Fla.
1938-42 St. Petersburg, Fla.
1943-45 Cairo, Ill.
1946- St. Petersburg, Fla.

Cubs

1901-02 Champaign, Ill.
1903-04 Los Angeles, Cal.
1905 Santa Monica, Cal.
1906 Champaign, Ill.
1907 New Orleans, La.
1908 Vicksburg, Miss.
1909-10 Hot Springs, Ark.
1911-12 New Orleans, La.
1913-16 Tampa, Fla.
1917-21 Pasadena, Cal.
1922-42 Catalina Island, Cal.
1943-45 French Lick, Ind.
1946-47 Catalina Island, Cal.
1948-49 Los Angeles, Cal.
1950-51 Catalina Island, Cal.
1952-65 Mesa, Ariz.
1966 Long Beach, Cal.
1967-78 Scottsdale, Ariz.
1979- Mesa, Ariz.

Dodgers

1901 Charlotte, N.C.
1902-06 Columbia, S.C.
1907-09 Jacksonville, Fla.
1910-12 Hot Springs, Ark.
1913-14 Augusta, Ga.
1915-16 Daytona Beach, Fla.
1917-18 Hot Springs, Ark.
1919-20 Jacksonville, Fla.
1921 New Orleans, La.
1922 Jacksonville, Fla.
1923-32 Clearwater, Fla.
1933 Miami, Fla.
1934-35 Orlando, Fla.
1936-40 Clearwater, Fla.
1941-42 Havana, Cuba

1943-45 Bear Mountain, N.Y.
1946 Daytona Beach, Fla.
1947 Havana, Cuba
1948 Ciudad Trujillo, D.R.
1949- Vero Beach, Fla.

Expos

1969-72 West Palm Beach, Fla.
1973-80 Daytona Beach, Fla.
1981- West Palm Beach, Fla.

Giants

1901-02 N.Y., N.Y.
1903-05 Savannah, Ga.
1906 Memphis, Tenn.
1907 Los Angeles, Cal.
1908-18 Marlin Springs, Tex.
1919 Gainesville, Fla.
1920-23 San Antonio, Tex.
1924-27 Sarasota, Fla.
1928 Augusta, Ga.
1929-31 San Antonio, Tex.
1932-33 Los Angeles, Cal.
1934-35 Miami Beach, Fla.
1936 Pensacola, Fla.
1937 Havana, Cuba
1938-39 Baton Rouge, La.
1940 Winter Haven, Fla.
1941-42 Miami, Fla.
1943-45 Lakewood, N.J.
1946 Miami, Fla.
1947-50 Phoenix, Ariz.
1951 St. Petersburg, Fla.
1952-83 Phoenix, Ariz.
1984- Scottsdale, Ariz.

Marlins

1993 Cocoa, Fla.
1994- Viera, Fla.

Mets

1962-87 St. Petersburg, Fla.
1988- Port St. Lucie, Fla.

Padres

1969-93 Yuma, Ariz.
1994- Peoria, Ariz.

Phillies

1901 Philadelphia, Pa.
1902 Washington, N.C.
1903 Richmond, Va.
1904 Savannah, Ga.
1905 Augusta, Ga.
1906-08 Savannah, Ga.
1909-10 Southern Pines, N.C.
1911 Birmingham, Al.
1912 Hot Springs, Ark.
1913 Southern Pines, N.C.
1914 Wilmington, N.C.
1915-18 St. Petersburg, Fla.
1919 Charlotte, N.C.
1920 Birmingham, Al.
1921 Gainesville, Fla.
1922-24 Leesburg, Fla.
1925-27 Bradenton, Fla.
1928-37 Winter Haven, Fla.
1938 Biloxi, Miss.
1939 New Braunfels, Tex.
1940-42 Miami Beach, Fla.
1943 Hershey, Pa.
1944-45 Wilmington, Del.
1946 Miami Beach, Fla.
1947- Clearwater, Fla.

Pirates

1901-16 Hot Springs, Ark.
1917 Columbus, Ga.
1918 Jacksonville, Fla.
1919 Birmingham, Al.
1920-23 Hot Springs, Ark.
1924-34 Paso Robles, Cal.
1935 San Bernardino, Cal.
1936 San Antonio, Tex.
1937-42 San Bernardino, Cal.
1943-45 Muncie, Ind.
1946 San Bernardino, Cal.
1947 Miami Beach, Fla.
1948 Hollywood, Cal.

1949-52 San Bernardino, Cal.
1953 Havana, Cuba
1954 Fort Pierce, Fla.
1955-68 Fort Myers, Fla.
1969- Bradenton, Fla.

Reds
1901-02 Cincinnati, Oh.
1903 Augusta, Ga.
1904 Dallas, Tex.
1905 Jacksonville, Fla.
1906 San Antonio, Tex.
1907 Marlin Springs, Tex.
1908 St. Augustine, Tex.
1909 Atlanta, Ga.
1910-11 Hot Springs, Ark.
1912 Columbus, Ga.
1913 Mobile, Al.
1914-15 Alexandria, La.
1916-17 Shreveport, La.
1918 Montgomery, Al.
1919 Waxahachie, Tex.
1920 Miami, Fla.
1921 Cisco, Tex.
1922 Mineral Wells, Tex.
1923-30 Orlando, Fla.
1931-42 Tampa, Fla.
1943-45 Bloomington, Ind.
1946-87 Tampa, Fla.
1988- Plant City, Fla.

Rockies
1993- Tucson, Ariz.

AMERICAN LEAGUE

Angels
1961-92 Mesa/Palm Springs, Ariz./Cal.
1993 Mesa/Tempe, Ariz.

Athletics
1901 Philadelphia, Pa.
1902 Charlotte, N.C.
1903 Jacksonville, Fla.
1904 Spartanburg, S.C.
1905 Shreveport, La.
1906 Montgomery, Al.
1907 Dallas, Tex.
1908-09 New Orleans, La.
1910 Atlanta, Ga.
1911 Savannah, Ga.
1912-13 San Antonio, Tex.
1914-18 Jacksonville, Fla.
1919 Philadelphia, Pa.
1920-21 Lake Charles, La.
1922 Eagle Pass, Tex.
1923-24 Montgomery, Al.
1925-36 Fort Myers, Fla.
1937 Mexico City, Mex.
1938-39 Lake Charles, La.
1940-42 Anaheim, Cal.
1943 Wilmington, Del.
1944-45 Frederick, Md.
1946-62 West Palm Beach, Fla.
1963-68 Bradenton, Fla.
1969-78 Mesa, Ariz.
1979-83 Scottsdale, Ariz.
1984- Phoenix, Ariz.

Blue Jays
1977- Dunedin, Fla.

Brewers (Pilots)
1969-72 Tempe, Ariz.
1973-85 Sun City, Ariz.
1986- Chandler, Ariz.

Indians
1901 Cleveland, Oh.
1902-03 New Orleans, La.
1904 San Antonio, Tex.
1905-06 Atlanta, Ga.
1907-08 Macon, Ga.
1909 Mobile, Al.
1910-11 Alexandria, La.
1912 Mobile, Al.
1913 Pensacola, Fla.
1914 Athens, Ga.
1915 San Antonio, Tex.
1916-20 New Orleans, La.
1921-22 Dallas, Tex.
1923-27 Lakeland, Fla.
1928-39 New Orleans, La.
1940-41 Fort Myers, Fla.
1942 Clearwater, Fla.
1943-45 Lafayette, Ind.
1946 Clearwater, Fla.
1947-92 Tucson, Ariz.
1993- Winter Haven, Fla.

Mariners
1977-92 Tempe, Ariz.
1993- Peoria, Ariz.

Orioles (Browns)
1901 St. Louis, Mo.
1902 French Lick, Ind.
1903 Baton Rouge, La.
1904 Corsicana, Tex.
1905-06 Dallas, Tex.
1907 San Antonio, Tex.
1908 Shreveport, La.
1909-10 Houston, Tex.
1911 Hot Springs, Ark.
1912 Montgomery, Al.
1913 Waco, Tex.
1914 St. Petersburg, Fla.
1915 Houston, Tex.
1916-17 Palestine, Tex.
1918 Shreveport, La.
1919 San Antonio, Tex.
1920 Taylor, Al.
1921 Bogalusa, Al.
1922-24 Mobile, Al.
1925-27 Tarpon Springs, Fla.
1928-36 West Palm Beach, Fla.
1937-41 San Antonio, Tex.
1942 Deland, Fla.
1943-45 Cape Girardeau, Mo.
1946 Anaheim, Cal.
1947 Miami, Fla.
1948 San Bernardino, Cal.
1949-52 Burbank, Cal.
1953 San Bernardino, Cal.
1954 Yuma, Ariz.
1955 Daytona Beach, Fla.

1956-58 Scottsdale, Ariz.
1959-88 Miami, Fla.
1989-90 Miami/Sarasota, Fla.
1991 Sarasota, Fla.
1992-95 St. Petersburg/Sarasota, Fla.
1996- Ft. Lauderdale, Fla.

Rangers (Senators)
1961-86 Pompano Beach, Fla.
1987- Port Charlotte, Fla.

Red Sox
1901 Charlottesville, Va.
1902 Augusta, Ga.
1903-06 Macon, Ga.
1907-08 Little Rock, Ark.
1909-10 Hot Springs, Ark.
1911 Redondo Beach, Cal.
1912-18 Hot Springs, Ark.
1919 Tampa, Fla.
1920-23 Hot Springs, Ark.
1924 San Antonio, Tex.
1925-27 New Orleans, La.
1928-29 Bradenton, Fla.
1930-31 Pensacola, Fla.
1932 Savannah, Ga.
1933-42 Sarasota, Fla.
1943-44 Medford, Mass.
1945 Atlantic City, N.J.
1946-58 Sarasota, Fla.
1959-65 Scottsdale, Ariz.
1966-92 Winter Haven, Fla.
1993- Fort Myers, Fla.

Royals
1969-87 Fort Myers, Fla.
1988- Baseball City, Fla.

Tigers
1901 Detroit, Mich.
1902 Ypsilanti, Mich.
1903-04 Shreveport, La.
1905-07 Augusta, Ga.
1908 Hot Springs, Ark.
1909-10 San Antonio, Tex.
1911-12 Monroe, La.
1913-15 Gulfport, Miss.
1916-18 Waxahachie, Tex.
1919-20 Macon, Ga.
1921 San Antonio, Tex.
1922-26 Augusta, Ga.
1927-28 San Antonio, Tex.
1929 Phoenix, Ariz.
1930 Tampa, Fla.
1931 Sacramento, Cal.
1932 Palo Alto, Cal.
1933 San Antonio, Tex.
1934-42 Lakeland, Fla.
1943-45 Evansville, Ind.
1946- Lakeland, Fla.

Twins (Senators)
1901 Phoebus, Va.
1902-04 Washington, D.C.
1905 Hampton, Va.
1906 Charlottesville, Va.
1907-09 Galveston, Tex.

1910 Norfolk, Va.
1911 Atlanta, Ga.
1912-16 Charlottesville, Va.
1917 Atlanta, Ga.
1918-19 Augusta, Ga.
1920-29 Tampa, Fla.
1930-35 Biloxi, Miss.
1936-42 Orlando, Fla.
1943-45 College Park, Md.
1946-90 Orlando, Fla.
1991- Fort Myers, Fla.

White Sox
1901-02 Excelsior Springs, Mo.
1903 Mobile, Al.
1904 Marlin Springs, Tex.
1905-06 New Orleans, La.
1907 Mexico City, Mex.
1908 Los Angeles, Cal.
1909-10 San Francisco, Cal.
1911 Mineral Wells, Tex.
1912 Waco, Tex.
1913-15 Paso Robles, Cal.
1916-19 Mineral Wells, Tex.
1920 Waco, Tex.
1921 Waxahachie, Tex.
1922-23 Seguin, Tex.
1924 Winter Haven, Fla.
1925-28 Shreveport, La.
1929 Dallas, Tex.
1930-32 San Antonio, Tex.
1933-42 Pasadena, Cal.
1943-44 French Lick, Ind.
1945 Terre Haute, Ind.
1946-50 Pasadena, Cal.
1951 Pasadena/Palm Springs, Cal.
1952 Pasadena/El Centro, Cal.
1953 El Centro, Cal.
1954-59 Tampa, Fla.
1960- Sarasota, Fla.

Yankees
1901 Baltimore, Md.
1902 Savannah, Ga.
1903-04 Atlanta, Ga.
1905 Montgomery, Al.
1906 Birmingham, Al.
1907-08 Atlanta, Ga.
1909 Macon, Ga.
1910-11 Athens, Ga.
1912 Atlanta, Ga.
1913 Hamilton, Berm.
1914 Houston, Tex.
1915 Savannah, Ga.
1916-18 Macon, Ga.
1919-20 Jacksonville, Fla.
1921 Shreveport, La.
1922-24 New Orleans, La.
1925-42 St. Petersburg, Fla.
1943 Asbury Park, N.J.
1944-45 Atlantic City, N.J.
1946-50 St Petersburg, Fla.
1951 Phoenix, Ariz.
1952-61 St. Petersburg, Fla.
1962- Fort Lauderdale, Fla.
1996- Tampa, Fla.

## CHAPTER 20

Women in Baseball

Debra A. Shattuck

Women have been associated with baseball, either as players or spectators, since the game's dawn in the early nineteenth century. Even before baseball emerged in its final form, girls and young women sometimes played precursors of the game like One Old Cat, Town Ball, and Stoolball in Colonial America. As time passed, and the boys' amusement became serious business for grown men, baseball's reputation as a masculine domain was established. In 1865, one year before Charles Peverelly observed that baseball "has now become beyond question the leading feature of the outdoor sports of the United States," *Harper's Weekly* proclaimed: "There is no nobler or manlier game than base-ball." During the latter half of the nineteenth century, women's presence as spectators at baseball games was tolerated and sometimes encouraged. Eventually promoters of the game hosted regular "Ladies Days" to attract women fans who would bring in added gate receipts and, hopefully, have a calming effect on the sometimes unruly crowds. Many women were content with their role as spectators and moral uplifters, but others yearned for the opportunity to try their hand at the national pastime. Those who lived out their fantasy often had to endure verbal and written derision from observers anxious to preserve the baseball status quo.

For the most part, the negative attitude toward women baseball players continues to this day. Many still share the opinion of an editorialist who noted in The St. Louis *Globe-Democrat* in 1885 that "The female has no place in base ball, except to the degradation of the game." The criticisms notwithstanding, uncounted women have pursued their own field of dreams, contributing their unique chapter to baseball's rich heritage.

Many of the first women baseball players were college students. The secluded atmosphere of all-girl's schools enabled women to play the game without attracting too much attention. Students at Vassar College organized two baseball clubs as early as 1866. In 1879, according to Vassar alumna Sophia Foster Richardson, the Vassar girls organized at least seven baseball clubs. The private grounds of college campuses did not always protect female players from public criticism, however. In a speech to an alumnae association in 1896, Richardson recalled, "The public, so far as it knew of our playing, was shocked, but in our retired grounds, and protected from observation even in these grounds by sheltering trees, we continued to play in spite of a censorious public." Within a few years, however, the "censorious public" and "disapproving mothers" had succeeded in stifling the game at Vassar.

But Vassar was not the only college where women tried their hand at baseball. In a letter to her former classmates at Smith College, Minnie Stephens (class of 1883) reminisced about the baseball clubs they had organized at the school in 1880. Stephens described the enthusiasm of the players and the keen competition at games. She also related how the Victorian-style clothing of the day, generally a hindrance to sporting endeavors, had actually benefited one of the players during a heated contest, "One vicious batter drove a ball directly into the belt line of her opponent, and had it not been for the rigid steel corset clasp worn in those days, she would have been knocked out completely." Like the women at Vassar, baseball players at Smith College faced opposition which eventually forced them to give up the game for a number of years.

Women baseball players were not limited to college campuses. In Springfield, Illinois, three men organized a women's baseball club in 1875. They were confident that the novelty of women playing baseball would attract large crowds and fatten their bankroll. On September 11, 1875, the club's teams, labeled the "Blondes" and "Brunettes," played their first match. Newspapers heralded the event as the "first game of baseball ever played in public for gate money between feminine ball-tossers." The concept evidently caught on, for numerous other male entrepreneurs copied the idea and organized women's baseball teams. One group started the "Young Ladies' Baseball Club" in Philadelphia in 1883. These owners billed their team's games as entertainment spectacles, not serious competition, and they continually stressed the femininity and moral respectability of their players. A newspaper account of one of the club's first games relayed the management's claim that players were "selected with tender solicitude from 200 applicants, variety actresses and ballet girls being positively barred." Furthermore the article noted, "Only three of the lot had ever been on the stage, and they were in the strictly legitimate business."

The Young Ladies Baseball Club played its first game on August 18, 1883, at Pastime Park in Philadelphia. Despite the supposed "200 applicants," only sixteen girls were mustered to form the two teams for the contest; two young men rounded out the rosters. The game was played on a regulation-size diamond, but, as one observer wrote, it was too large for the women. "A ball thrown from pitcher to second base almost invariably fell short and was stopped on the roll. The throw from first to third base was an utter impossibility." Five hundred spectators witnessed the club's debut and were caught up in "uncontrollable laughter" much of the time. From a financial standpoint, however, the venture was a success. More than 1,500 fans turned out for the club's match at the Manhattan Athletic Club on September 23, 1883, where they "laughed themselves hungry and thirsty." Though one observer conceded that "four of the girls had become expert—for girls," it is obvious that "novelty" and not "ability" was the hallmark of women's baseball at the time.

Another novel group of women baseball players was the Bloomer Girls. Actually "Bloomer Girls" was a misnomer, since Bloomer Girls teams were composed of both men and women. Kansas City Bloomer Girls, New York Bloomer Girls, Texas Bloomer Girls, and Boston Bloomer Girls were just a few of the teams traveling from diamond to diamond in the late nineteenth and early twentieth centuries in search of fame and fortune. Despite the number of Bloomer Girl teams, they did not play each other and no formal league was set up. Instead, they journeyed from town to town, challenging men's amateur and semiprofessional teams. The Bloomer Girls teams relied on sideshow style appeal to draw fans and, not surprisingly, the bottom line was money. The manager of the Texas Bloomer Girls wrote to one prospective promoter in 1913, assuring him that the team's seven girls and four boys, "including the one-armed boy who plays center field," would draw enough fans to ensure the backer "three hundred dollars clear money" each week. A few of the male Bloomer Girls players like "Smoky Joe" Wood and Hall of Famer Rogers Hornsby went on to become successful big league ballplayers, but the future was not as bright for the female players who could not aspire to anything higher in the baseball world.

The Bloomer Girls teams were not the only option available to baseball-playing females around the turn of the century. Women's teams and mixed teams competed occasionally in "pickup" games. One such game took place in Kearsarge, New Hampshire, on August 7, 1903. An article in the Boston Herald the following day noted, "The teams were made up of young ladies gowned in white and young men decked out in girls' clothes, all New Englanders, guests at the hotel." On August 31, the newspaper announced an upcoming game at Forest Hills between the "Hickey and Clover clubs," each composed of five women and four men. One year later, in Flat Rock, Indiana, a group of women organized two baseball clubs, one consisting only of married players, the other only of single players.

While some women played on all-female or coed teams, others challenged social constraints of the day by playing on otherwise all-male teams. On June 12, 1903, the Cincinnati Enquirer printed an article about the efforts of a local woman, Miss M. E. Phelan, to get a job as center fielder with the all-male Flora Baseball Club of Indiana. Phelan wrote to the club's manager informing him, "I have played with a number of lady ball clubs and am considered the equal of the average country player." Whether the Flora club took Phelan up on her offer to play for them for "$60 per month and expenses" is unknown, but only four years later another Ohioan, Alta Weiss, became an overnight female baseball-playing sensation and, as one article put it, "perhaps the only girl in the United States to obtain [a] college education through skill as a baseball player."

Weiss, a native of Ragersville, Ohio, became a celebrity in the Cleveland area when she made her pitching debut with the all-male, semiprofessional Vermilion Independents on September 2, 1907. More than 1,200 fans attended the game in which Weiss pitched 5 innings, giving up only 4 hits and 1 run. By the time Weiss made her second appearance on September 8, she was already being heralded as the "Girl Wonder" in the press. According to the Vermilion News, so many fans wanted to see Weiss play that special trains had to be run to Vermilion from Cleveland and surrounding towns.

Weiss pitched 8 games for the Independents during their 1907 season. More than 13,000 fans saw the games, including a season high of 3,182, who witnessed her debut at Cleveland's League Park on October 2, 1907. At least a dozen newspapers covered her exploits. The following year her father bought a half-interest in a men's semiprofessional team which was known thereafter as the Weiss All-Stars. It was based in Cleveland and, with Alta as a drawing card, played for large crowds throughout Ohio and Kentucky.

Though Weiss was far and away the best-known woman baseball player in northern Ohio at this time, she was not the only one. On June 22, 1908, the Cleveland Press introduced fourteen-year-old Carita Masteller to the public. The paper reported that she had been playing baseball for eight or nine years and was as good as Weiss. That same month Weiss pitched against another female pitcher, Irma Gribble. The two dueled again in August. In another unique game, two sisters from Bellevue, Ohio, Irene and Ruth Basford, pitched for opposing men's teams.

Another well-known woman baseball player who played on men's teams was Rhode Islander Elizabeth Murphy. "Lizzie," as she liked to be called, played amateur and semiprofessional baseball from about 1915 to 1935 and was known as the "Queen of Baseball" throughout New England and eastern Canada. After playing for a number of amateur teams in Rhode Island, Murphy signed with the semiprofessional Providence Independents in 1918. A few years later she joined Ed Carr's All-Stars of Boston and earned quite a reputation for her skills as a first baseman.

In 1928, while Murphy was still impressing the fans in New England, fourteen-year-old Margaret Gisolo helped her Blanford, Indiana, American Legion boys' baseball team win county, district, sectional, and state championships. In seven tournament games she had 9 hits in 21 at-bats. She scored 10 putouts and 28 assists in the field, with no errors charged against her. A protest against her participation filed by opposing teams went all the way to the American Legion's National Americanism Commission, which referred it to the major league baseball commissioner, Judge Kenesaw Mountain Landis. Landis determined that American Legion rules did not specifically ban the participation of women and disallowed the protest.

Landis had to address a similar situation three years later when the "Barnum of Baseball," Chattanooga Lookouts manager Joe Engel, signed seventeen-year-old Jackie Mitchell to a contract with his Southern Association minor league team, thus making her the first female professional baseball player. Mitchell had been taught to pitch by major leaguer Dazzy Vance and had once struck out nine men in a row in an amateur game. She became an overnight celebrity on April 2, 1931, when she pitched in an exhibition game against the visiting New York Yankees—and struck out Babe Ruth and Lou Gehrig, back to back. Speculation continues as to whether Ruth and Gehrig were merely putting on a show or really trying to hit Mitchell's pitches. Mitchell contended that it was not a setup and that the only instructions to the Yankee players had been to try not to hit the ball straight through the pitcher's box. A number of Yankee players confirmed her story. Unfortunately Mitchell never had a chance to repeat her performance as a professional baseball player. A few days after her debut, Landis informed Engel that he had disallowed Mitchell's contract on the grounds that life in baseball was too strenuous for women. Organized baseball formalized the ban against women signing professional baseball contracts with men's teams on June 21, 1952; the ruling still stands.

The restriction on women playing professional baseball on men's teams did not prevent the formation of a women's professional baseball league, however. In 1943, with wartime manpower shortages threatening major league baseball, Chicago Cubs' owner Philip K. Wrigley decided to form a women's professional softball league which would play its games in the major league stadiums while the men were away at war. Within a year of its founding, the league modified its rules and the All-American Girls *Baseball* League (AAGBL) was born. The AAGBL made its debut in 1943, when four teams—the Rockford [Illinois] Peaches, the South Bend [Indiana] Blue Sox, the Racine [Wisconsin] Belles, and the Kenosha [Wisconsin] Comets—squared off during the League's 108-game schedule. Attendance that year was 176,000 fans, which, according to one contemporary, meant that the League was "drawing a higher percentage of the population [in league cities] than major league baseball ever did in its greatest attendance years." Attendance figures continued to rise year after year, reaching a peak in 1948, when the League's ten teams drew almost 1,000,000 fans. That same year, AAGBL teams drew more than 100,000 fans for a series of nine games in Puerto Rico.

Unlike women's teams of the past, the AAGBL relied on players' skills, not just their gender, to draw fans to the ballpark. The more than 500 women who played in the AAGBL during its twelve-year existence were top-notch athletes. Many were veterans of championship school, community, or industrial softball teams, and a few had even played on boys' or men's baseball teams. In addition, many of the AAGBL managers were experienced professional baseball players—some, like Bill Wambsganss (the only player ever to achieve an unassisted triple play in a World Series), Max Carey, Jimmie Foxx, and Dave Bancroft, were legends.

The AAGBL represented one of the only times in history that women baseball players received widespread moral and financial support. Once World War II ended, however, social pressures for women to leave nontradi-

tional jobs and return to household duties resumed. This fact, coupled with organizational problems and the rise of televised major league games, led to the demise of the AAGBL. Interest in the league all but disappeared until the 1980s, when a group of former players organized a players association and began lobbying to have the league honored in the National Baseball Hall of Fame. The popular media and serious scholars rediscovered the league and hundreds of articles about the AAGBL appeared in newspapers and magazines across the country. In October 1988, the Hall of Fame unveiled a permanent exhibit of AAGBL league memorabilia. In the summer of 1992, the AAGBL was further memorialized when it became the subject of the feature film, *A League of Their Own*.

Despite the newfound popularity of the AAGBL, modern-day women baseball players still face the same obstacles and criticisms endured by nineteenth century players. For the most part, organized teams and leagues remain closed to women. When Commissioner Ford Frick issued his ban against women players in 1952, his purpose was to prevent teams from using women players as publicity stunts. The end result of his edict was that even highly skilled women players (like those on the all-female team that tried, unsuccessfully, to gain admission to the men's Class A Florida State League in 1984) lost an important avenue for upward mobility and legitimacy in baseball. Women who challenge baseball's "men only" reputation rarely escape the experience unscathed. Julie Croteau, who gained notoriety in the late 1980s by playing first base for the St. Mary's (Maryland) College men's baseball team, earned school and conference honors yet still had to endure derisive comments from teammates. She left school in the middle of her junior year disillusioned with a system she believed treated women as inferior to men.

There is some indication, however, that the 1990s will see the gradual transformation of baseball from a strictly masculine pastime to a truly "national" pastime. Thanks to a series of court battles in the 1970s, generations of young girls have had the opportunity to play baseball on Little League teams. Many have resisted abandoning the game of their youth. A growing number of girls and women are finding opportunities to play baseball on newly organized municipal and professional teams. At least half a dozen cities, including Fort Wayne and Chicago, currently sponsor girls baseball leagues.

In 1994, the Coors Brewing Company fielded the Colorado Silver Bullets, a professional women's baseball team that plays men's teams.

If girls and women continue to enjoy opportunities to play baseball, the sport will undoubtedly lose its masculine reputation. The question is whether or not current opportunities for female players will last. If they don't, today's female baseball players may find themselves sidelined, once again, with "a league of their own," watching rather than directly experiencing the national pastime.

## CHAPTER 21

Baseball and the Law

Gary D. Hailey and Douglas R. Pappas

Like many other members of our litigation-happy society, baseball players and team owners have spent their fair share of time in the courtroom. Judges have been asked to decide lawsuits involving everything from a team's liability for fan injuries from foul balls and thrown bats to the legality of the decision to resume the infamous Yankees-Royals "Pine Tar Game" nearly a month after George Brett's home run had been ruled a game-ending out.

But the most significant baseball-related court cases were a series of mostly unsuccessful challenges to Organized Baseball's attempts to limit competition—especially from rivals like the Players League and the Federal League—for players' services. That litigation has reached the United States Supreme Court three times, and all three times that Court has ruled that baseball is not governed by the antitrust laws. The reasoning behind this holding may have been perfectly logical when the first of those cases was decided in 1922, but today it seems anachronistic.

From the game's earliest days, baseball owners have struggled to keep their expenses down by maintaining control over the players, who often decide that the grass (and the money) is greener in someone else's ballpark. In 1870 the National Association of Base Ball Players tried to stop "revolving," or contract jumping, by adopting a rule requiring players to give 60 days' notice before leaving one club for another. Tougher controls were agreed to after word leaked that A. G. Spalding and three other Boston Red Stockings stars had signed contracts in the middle of the 1875 season to play for Chicago in 1876. In 1879 the National League secretly agreed to allow each team owner to "reserve" his five best players at the end of the season; other owners were prohibited from bidding for the services of the reserved players. The owners also agreed not to sign any player who refused to play for the team that reserved him.

Forty-seven National Leaguers jumped to the American Association when that rival league commenced play in 1882, but virtually none of them were reserved players. During the 1882 season, the AA induced other NL players to promise to jump leagues in 1883, but the NL fought back to prevent these impending desertions. Charles Bennett, Detroit's star catcher, accepted $100 in exchange for his written promise to sign a contract with the AA's Pittsburgh team in 1883. Before Bennett signed that contract, Detroit offered him more money to stay in the NL. Pittsburgh got wind of what was happening and immediately filed suit in Federal court, seeking an injunction ordering Bennett to sign the Pittsburgh contract.

Bennett's lawyers offered a number of legal defenses, some rather narrow and technical. The court ruled in Bennett's favor[1] but did not issue a written opinion, so it is unclear just which of his attorneys' arguments were persuasive. But the court may have refused to enjoin Bennett's jump to Detroit simply because of the timing of the lawsuit. The Pittsburgh club would have suffered no real harm from Bennett's refusal to sign an 1883 contract until it had to play a game without him in the lineup. Its October 1882 lawsuit was, in a sense, premature because Bennett might have changed his mind and returned to Pittsburgh before the opening day of the 1883 season.

Shortstop Sam Wise followed in Bennett's footsteps, signing with the Cincinnati AA team but eventually jumping back to his NL team, the Boston Red Stockings, when they promised to increase his salary. Cincinnati persuaded an Ohio judge to order Wise not to play for Boston. But Cincinnati was unable to enforce the Ohio order in other states. Wise had to stay at home when the Red Stockings came to Cleveland, but was otherwise free to play for Boston.

The National League and American Association made peace in 1883 and signed the "National Agreement," which contained a strengthened reserve rule. The promoters of the Union Association hoped to capitalize on the players' resentment of the one-sided terms of their contracts with organized baseball, but the established leagues fought back hard by adopting the "Day Resolution," an agreement to blacklist any reserved player who jumped to a Union club. Star pitcher Tony Mullane, who jumped from the St. Louis Browns to the St. Louis Maroons of the new league, tried to return to the Browns after hearing about the Day Resolution. The Browns refused to welcome their prodigal back because they knew the Maroons would haul them into court if they did. The Toledo AA club wanted Mullane, but the National Agreement did not provide for player trades or sales. The Browns simply released Mullane outright, and Toledo signed him. The Union Association failed to persuade an Ohio Federal judge to order Mullane back to the Maroons.[2] After the demise of the upstart league at the end of the 1884 season, Toledo agreed to send Mullane back to the Browns, but the Cincinnati AA club—in flagrant violation of the National Agreement—signed the 35-game winner to a lucrative bonus contract. The Association's powers-that-be ultimately awarded Mullane to Cincinnati, but ordered him to sit out the 1885 season and give back part of his bonus.

Once the Union Association was dead and buried, Organized Baseball established a maximum annual player salary of $2,000. Owners soon found ways around this provision—in 1887, Boston paid superstar Mike "King" Kelly an additional $3,000 "for use of his picture." Their reduced bargaining leverage caused the players to form the National Brotherhood of Professional Base Ball Players under the leadership of John Montgomery Ward, the New York Giants shortstop who attended Columbia University law school in the off-season. Ward claimed that the reserve clause, the blacklist, and other intimidating provisions of the standard player contract were legally unenforceable. When the owners refused to scrap the salary cap or to agree not to sell or trade players without their consent, the brotherhood went on to form the Players League, which fielded eight teams in 1890. Over 80 National League players and almost 30 from the American Association—including future Hall of Famers Ward, Jake Beckley, Dan Brouthers, John Clarkson, Charles Comiskey, Roger Connor, Hugh Duffy, "Buck" Ewing, Tim Keefe, "King" Kelly, Connie Mack, "Orator Jim" O'Rourke, and "Old Hoss" Radbourn—signed up with the Players League.

Organized Baseball used every weapon at its disposal to strike back at this new rival. The owners told fans that the players were aligned with radical unionists. Boston reportedly gave pitcher Clarkson $10,000—five times the average 1889 salary—to desert the brotherhood, while Spalding offered King Kelly a blank check to play for the White Stockings. When propaganda and bankrolls failed, the established league fielded a team of lawyers at courthouses around the country.

The reserve rule was originally adopted by the parties to the National Agreement as a sort of gentlemen's agreement not to compete for their fellow owners' players. When the National League tried to enforce the reserve clause against the Players League, it got nowhere. A Federal court in New York City held that the Giants could not keep catcher Ewing from playing for their brotherhood rival because the reserve provisions in his 1889 contract were "merely a contract to make a contract" for 1890 "if the parties agree."[3] The reserve clause was valuable because it gave the Giants a "prior and exclusive" right to negotiate with Ewing that was enforceable against other clubs in Organized Baseball. But as a basis for an injunction preventing a player from taking the field for a Players League team, Ewing's contract was held "wholly nugatory" because it did not set forth in detail contract terms and conditions (including salary) for 1890. A party who seeks enforcement of a contract with vague or indefinite terms is really asking the court to fill in the blank spaces in that contract, which is something that courts are reluctant to do.

Other courts objected not only to the indefiniteness of player contracts but also to their one-sidedness, which they referred to as a "lack of mutuality." Owners could release players on ten days' notice, but the reserve clause purported to bind a player to one team for as long as the team wanted him. A New York state court judge expressed disgust at "the spectacle" of the Giants' attempt to enforce "a contract which binds [the player] for a series of years and [the team] for 10 days."[4] The National League spent $15,000 on lawyers' fees in New York alone fighting the Players League, but came away with nothing to show for it.

The Players League won the legal battles, but not the war—in fact, everyone lost money. Both sides agreed to Spalding's suggestion that some Players League teams be merged with existing NL and AA franchises and the rest be dissolved. After a bit of skirmishing over the rights to sign some of the returning Players League stars, the NL and AA merged their sixteen clubs into twelve after the 1891 season, and then signed a new National Agreement with the minor leagues. Players had little choice but to accept the terms offered by the "Baseball Trust," but a few rebelled. Amos Rusie won 22 games in 1895 and led the league in strikeouts, but Giants owner Andrew Freedman rewarded him by withholding $600 in fines from his paycheck. Rusie sat out 1896 and then sued the Giants when they invoked their reserve for 1897 as well. The case was settled before trial, with all the National League owners reportedly kicking in a portion of Rusie's $5,000 claim.

As usual the next baseball war set off a spate of contract jumping and legal skirmishes. Over half of the players who suited up for the American League's first season of play were ex-National Leaguers. The older league went to court to try to wrest back a number of their players, most notably Napoleon Lajoie. Lajoie signed a contract with the Phillies in 1900, but refused to be bound by the reserve clause and jumped to the Athletics before the 1901 season. The Pennsylvania Supreme Court held that the Phillies were entitled to an injunction barring the batting champ from playing for the A's.[5]

But that decision turned in part on two unusual factors. First, the Phillies' contract reserved Lajoie for only three years and stated what salary would be paid in each of those three years, so it was not simply "a contract to make a contract." Second, Lajoie was a star of the very highest order. Courts are reluctant to order someone to perform a contract for personal services, although they are not at all reluctant to order the defendant to pay monetary damages equal to the harm caused by his nonperformance. Only when the harm cannot be measured in dollars or the contract involves something unique or irreplaceable are injunctions or other nonmonetary remedies granted by a court. The Phillies may have been able to find equally talented replacements for many of their players, but Lajoie—who led the AL in hits, doubles, home runs, runs, RBIs, batting average, and slugging average in 1901—was a unique talent.

The Phillies' legal victory proved hollow. The A's quickly dealt Lajoie to Cleveland. Whenever Cleveland was scheduled to play in Philadelphia, Lajoie stayed far away. His old team's attempts to obtain an injunction from an Ohio court were not successful.

Other National League efforts to hold on to players also failed. Citing a Supreme Court case holding that a contract that could be abandoned on one year's notice was not enforceable, a Federal judge dismissed Brooklyn's suit against veteran catcher Deacon McGuire because the team could terminate his contract on only ten days' notice.[6] The judge also questioned whether McGuire's talents were so "unique and peculiar" that Brooklyn could not replace him. McGuire was a fine player, but he was no Nap Lajoie. A state judge in St. Louis went further in a case involving pitcher Jack Harper. Not only was the standard NL player contract lacking in mutuality, according to the court, but it also unreasonably restrained competition in violation of the Sherman Antitrust Act.[7]

After two years of rivalry, the National League agreed to recognize the American League as an equal. The two major leagues used blacklists and boycotts to bring "outlaw" minor leagues to their knees and keep control of players who had the audacity to hold out for higher salaries. When Ty Cobb refused to accept Detroit's 1913 salary offer, the Tigers suspended him. The impasse was broken only when two Georgia congressmen called for a Federal investigation. The threat of government action got Ty Cobb a raise, but the players in general benefited much more from Organized Baseball's war with the Federal League, which no doubt had the National and American Leagues muttering "Two's company, three's a crowd" when the 1914 season opened.

The established leagues didn't even try to use the courts to stop reserve jumpers from playing for the Federal League, but they did seek injunctions against a number of players who jumped, even though they had signed contracts for the upcoming season. The irrepressible Hal Chase signed a 1914 contract with the White Sox, but then moved on to the new league. Teams could release players they didn't want on ten days' notice, so Chase gave Chicago ten days' warning and shuffled off to the Buffalo Federals. A New York state judge agreed with Chase's reasoning and turned down Chicago's request that he order Chase to return.[8] Not only did the contract lack mutuality, said the judge, but Organized Baseball placed so many limits on the freedom of players that they were left in a state of *"quasi* peonage" that was "contrary to the spirit of American institutions and . . . contrary to the spirit of the Constitution of the United States." The court's opinion did contain some good news for Organized Baseball: while implying that baseball may have violated the common-law prohibition against monopolies, it ruled that baseball did not involve interstate commerce and, therefore, did not violate the Sherman Act.

The judges who heard cases involving contract jumpers occasionally showed real distaste for the whole nasty business. Phillies catcher Bill Killefer signed with the Chicago Federal League club for a substantial increase in salary, but re-signed with the Phillies only 12 days later when they topped Chicago's offer. When the Federals asked a Michigan federal judge to order Killefer not to play for Philadelphia, they were rudely received. Citing the opinions in the Ewing, Ward, and McGuire cases, Judge Sessions noted that the right of reservation in the Phillies' 1913 contract with Killefer did not bind him for the 1914 season because it was indefinite and lacked mutuality.[9] But he refused to enforce Chicago's contract because it came into court with "unclean hands." Killefer was under a moral, although not a legal obligation to play for Philadelphia in 1914, but Chicago persuaded him to repudiate that obligation. Both teams had "acted wrongfully and in bad faith," and the judge refused to lift a finger to help either one of them. He also let Killefer know what he thought of him, calling him "a person upon whose pledged word little or no reliance can be placed, and who, for gain to himself, neither scruples nor hesitates to disregard and violate his express engagements and agreements." Chicago appealed the decision but was unsuccessful. The Sixth Circuit Court of Appeals agreed with Judge Sessions that none of the parties to these underhanded dealings was deserving of any assistance from the courts.[10]

Knowing that they could not outlast their better-financed rivals, the Federal League owners filed an antitrust suit against Organized Baseball in Chicago on January 5, 1915. They asked Federal Judge Kenesaw Mountain Landis, who had a reputation as a committed trustbuster, to declare the National Agreement's reserve and blacklisting provisions to be unreasonable and illegal restraints on competition. The trial was completed that month, but the Federal League's hopes for a quick verdict in their favor were in vain. The future baseball commissioner pondered the evidence all through the 1915 season, which resulted in another healthy dose of red ink for team owners. After waiting almost a year for Judge Landis to make up his mind, the rival leagues cut a deal. Organized Baseball bought some of the Federal League's player contracts and stadiums—in reality, they were buying peace—and the Federals dropped the antitrust suit.

The final deal satisfied everyone except AL president Ban Johnson, who preferred to fight to the death rather than pay his enemies a nickel of tribute, and the Baltimore Federal League club, which wanted to buy an existing major league franchise and move it to Baltimore. Angered by Brooklyn owner Ebbets's scornful description of their city as "one of the worst minor league towns in this country," the Baltimore owners pledged $50,000 to finance a new antitrust suit against Organized Baseball and the Federal League owners who had sold the league out for a few pieces of silver. When the Department of Justice refused to investigate, Baltimore filed its complaint in Federal district court in Washington, D.C., in 1917.

The testimony given at the trial, which didn't begin until March 1919, left little doubt that Organized Baseball's team owners had agreed to use the reserve clause and blacklisting to maintain tight control over the supply of players and paid the Federal League to go out of business in order to protect their monopoly over professional baseball. The judge's directions to the jury virtually directed a verdict for the plaintiffs. The Baltimore club won $254,000 in damages.

Organized Baseball's lawyers immediately appealed the decision. They contended that baseball was not commerce because it involved "personal effort not related to [the] production" of material goods. If baseball did not involve interstate commerce, it was not subject to the Sherman Act or any other Federal law. The court of appeals heard oral arguments on October 15, 1920, only three days after the final game of the World Series was played between the Cleveland Indians and the Brooklyn Dodgers. Only a few weeks later, it overturned the lower court's decision in favor of Baltimore.[11] The appellate court first noted that

The transportation in interstate commerce of the players and the paraphernalia used by them was but an incident to the main purpose of the appellants, namely the production of the game. It was for it they were in business—not for the purpose of transferring players, balls, and uniforms . . .

. . . So here, baseball is not commerce, though some of its incidents may be. Suppose a law firm in the city of Washington sends its members to points in different states to try

lawsuits; they would travel, and probably carry briefs and records, in interstate commerce. Could it be correctly said that the firm, in the trial of the lawsuits, was engaged in trade and commerce? Or, take the case of a lecture bureau, which employs persons to deliver lectures before Chautauqua gatherings at points in different states. It would be necessary for the lecturers to travel in interstate commerce, in order that they might fulfill their engagements; but would it not be an unreasonable stretch of the ordinary meaning of the words to say that the bureau was engaged in trade or commerce?

The court of appeals then cited with approval cases holding that those who produce theatrical exhibitions, practice medicine, or launder clothes are not engaged in commerce.

The Baltimore club tried to persuade the United States Supreme Court to reinstate the original verdict in its favor. But Justice Oliver Wendell Holmes, writing for a unanimous Court, upheld the decision of the court of appeals.[12]

Exhibitions of base ball . . . are purely state affairs. It is true that, in order to attain for the exhibitions the great popularity that they have achieved, competitions must be arranged between clubs from different cities and States. But the fact that in order to give the exhibitions the League must induce free persons to cross state lines and arrange and pay for their doing so is not enough to change the character of the business. . . . [T]he transport is a mere incident, not the essential thing. That to which it is incident, the exhibition, although made for money would not be called trade or commerce in the commonly accepted use of those words. As it is put by the defendants, personal effort, not related to production, is not a subject of commerce. That which in its consummation is not commerce does not become commerce among the States because the transportation that we have mentioned takes place. To repeat the illustrations given by the Court below, a firm of lawyers sending out a member to argue a case, or the Chautauqua lecture bureau sending out lecturers, does not engage in such commerce because the lawyer or lecturer goes to another State.

Only a year later, the Court ruled that a company that presented vaudeville shows in cities around the country was, unlike major league baseball, engaged in interstate commerce.[13] Justice Holmes explained the different outcomes in the two cases by pointing to the difference in "the degree of interstate activity" in baseball games and vaudeville shows.

The next challenge to Organized Baseball's hegemony came a quarter century later from Don Jorge Pasqual, the millionaire organizer of the Mexican League, who lured eighteen major leaguers south of the border in 1946. In August of that year, the owners amended their Rule 15 to provide that any player who jumped to the new league would be ineligible to return to Organized Baseball for five years. The Cubs' general manager, who proposed the amendment, said that the prospect of being blacklisted for five years "will do a lot more to discourage Stan Musial from going to Mexico next winter than any suits we may file on the reserve clause."

The Rule 15 blacklist stemmed the southward flow of players. Commissioner A. B. "Happy" Chandler refused to reinstate the players who returned to the states in 1947. Catcher Mickey Owen was reduced to managing a semi-pro club in Winner, South Dakota, while several other Mexican League refugees signed with Cuban and Canadian clubs.

When blacklisted outfielder Danny Gardella filed an antitrust complaint against Organized Baseball, a Federal district judge in New York noted the "clear trend toward a broader conception of what constitutes interstate commerce" than had existed when *Federal Baseball Club of Baltimore* was decided over twenty-five years earlier, but felt bound to follow the Supreme Court's decision in that case.[14] But in February 1949 a Federal court of appeals voted 2–1 to reverse the district court's dismissal of Gardella's complaint.[15] Judge Learned Hand distinguished *Federal Baseball* by emphasizing the importance to modern-day baseball of interstate radio and television broadcasts of major league games. Judge Frank's separate opinion strongly condemned the reserve system.

For the "reserve clause," as has been observed, results in something resembling peonage of the baseball player. . . . Although many courts have refused to enforce the "reserve" clause, yet severe and practically efficacious extra-legal penalties are imposed for violation. The most extreme of these penalties is the blacklisting of the player so that no club in Organized Baseball will hire him. . . . The violator may perhaps become a . . . bartender or a street-sweeper, but his chances of ever again playing baseball are exceedingly slim.

Gardella's victory was not a final one; it simply allowed him the opportunity to prove his allegations in a trial. Former Cardinals Fred Martin, Max Lanier, and Lou Klein filed a separate suit, and all four players asked the district court to order their immediate reinstatement pending the outcome of the trials, but the court declined to do so.[16] Faced with the prospect of spending the 1949 season in a courtroom rather than on a baseball field, the players were receptive to baseball's offer to settle the case. Commissioner Chandler later characterized his reinstatement of the four "good kids" who had "said they were sorry" for jumping their reserves as inspired by his desire to "temper justice with mercy." But the court of appeals decision—and Judge Frank's sentiments in particular—no doubt had an effect too. Gardella, who had been working as a hospital orderly after returning from Mexico, was reportedly given $60,000 to drop his case.

Subsequent litigation and congressional inquiries kept baseball's attorneys busy in the 1950s. Organized Baseball was the defendant in eight pending antitrust suits when it sought relief from Congress in 1951. At its behest three separate bills that would have granted all professional sports leagues a complete exemption from the antitrust laws were introduced in the House of Representatives that year. After lengthy hearings, Congressman Emanuel Celler's Subcommittee on the Study of Monopoly Power recommended that the bills not be passed, and none of them were. The Celler Subcommittee did not favor blanket antitrust immunity, but it did conclude that professional baseball could not operate successfully without some form of the reserve clause.[17]

After the Gardella decision, Organized Baseball's lawyers and the Subcommittee assumed that *Federal Baseball* was no longer good law. But the Supreme Court surprised them in 1953 in *Toolson* v. *New York Yankees*.[18] When Yankee farmhand George Toolson was placed on the ineligible list for refusing to accept a demotion to a lower-classification team, he sued the Yankees. A California Federal judge dismissed the case before trial on the basis of *Federal Baseball*. "If [that] case is, as Judge Frank intimates [in his *Gardella* opinion], an 'impotent zombi,'" the judge wrote, "I feel that it is not my duty to so find but that the Supreme Court should so declare."[19] The Ninth Circuit Court of Appeals agreed,[20] and the Supreme Court reaffirmed *Federal Baseball* with two Justices dissenting, in a one-paragraph opinion.

In Federal Baseball . . . *this Court held that . . . professional baseball . . . was not within the scope of the Federal antitrust laws. Congress has had the ruling under consideration but has not seen fit to bring such business under these laws by legislation having prospective effect. . . . The present cases ask us to overrule the prior decision, and, with retrospective effect, hold the [antitrust laws] applicable. We think that if there are evils in this field which now warrant application to it of the antitrust laws it should be by legislation. Without re-examination of the underlying issues, the judgments below are affirmed on the authority of* Federal Baseball . . .

The Court's conclusion that "Congress has had the ruling under consideration but has not seen fit to bring [baseball] under [the antitrust] laws by legislation" is questionable. The Celler Subcommittee report concluded that given the *Gardella* decision and cases subsequent to *Federal Baseball*, which took a broader view of what constituted interstate commerce, "it may be seriously doubted whether baseball should now be regarded as exempt from the antitrust laws." If Congress assumed that baseball was subject to the antitrust laws, its failure to act on bills granting an antitrust exemption was evidence that it did not intend baseball to be exempt—which was just the opposite of what the Court said in *Toolson*.

The next few years saw the Supreme Court hold that professional boxing and football did not share baseball's antitrust immunity. In *Radovich* v. *National Football League*,[21] the Court expressly limited the reach of the *Federal Baseball* precedent to baseball. Three justices dissented from this decision "to put baseball in a class by itself."

Another flurry of congressional activity followed. In 1957 the House Antitrust Subcommittee held fifteen days of hearings on seven different bills, some of which would have exempted all professional sports from antitrust liability. Congressman Celler introduced a bill exempting only those acts that were "reasonably necessary" to maintaining competitive balance and the integrity of sports, but the full House voted to give professional sports leagues a broader although not unlimited exemption. A Senate committee held more hearings in 1958—Casey Stengel, Mickey Mantle, Ted Williams, and Stan Musial testified the day after the All-Star Game was played in nearby Baltimore—but the full Senate never considered

the bill. In a 1959 report to the membership, the Major League Baseball Players Association's lawyers said, "There does not seem any doubt that Congress will eventually pass a law concerning Baseball's right to continue its reserve clause," but Congress never came any closer to passing comprehensive sports antitrust legislation. Bills were introduced year after year—attempts to organize a third major league, franchise moves, and the CBS purchase of the Yankees inspired some of the legislative proposals—but none was enacted.

In 1972 the U.S. Supreme Court upheld *Federal Baseball* once more in *Flood* v. *Kuhn*.[22] When the Cardinals traded Curt Flood to the Phillies after the 1969 season, Flood refused to go. "I am [not] a piece of property to be bought and sold irrespective of my wishes," he wrote to Commissioner Bowie Kuhn. Although Flood had not signed a contract for the 1970 season, Kuhn refused to declare him a free agent, so Flood filed suit, hiring former Supreme Court Justice and Secretary of Labor Arthur Goldberg to represent him. The lower court dismissed his case, and, by a 5-3 vote, the Supreme Court upheld its dismissal.

After opening with an overview of baseball history so effusively unjudicial that two members of the majority refused to join it, Justice Harry Blackmun's opinion recognized that, *Federal Baseball* notwithstanding, "Professional baseball is a business and it is engaged in interstate commerce," and that subsequent decisions had applied the antitrust laws to the NFL and professional boxing. Justice Blackmun referred to baseball's antitrust immunity as an "exception," an "anomaly," and an "aberration," but concluded that after fifty years, any change must come from Congress:

The Court has emphasized that since 1922 baseball, with full and continuing congressional awareness, has been allowed to develop and to expand unhindered by Federal legislative action. Remedial legislation has been introduced repeatedly in Congress but none has ever been enacted. The Court, accordingly, has concluded that Congress as yet has had no intention to subject baseball's reserve system to the reach of the antitrust statutes. . . . If there is any inconsistency or illogic in all this, it is an inconsistency and illogic of long standing that is to be remedied by the Congress and not by this Court.

The dissenting Justices responded that "[t]he unbroken silence of Congress should not prevent us from correcting our own mistakes," but to date neither the Court nor Congress has done so. Major League Baseball has relied upon *Federal Baseball* and *Flood* to rebuff a variety of antitrust claims, including umpires' allegations that they were illegally dismissed for union activity[23] and a minor league team's challenge to the rules governing player assignment and franchise location.[24] After *Flood*, however, baseball's antitrust status faded into the background for two decades as free agency created new legal problems.

On December 23, 1975, an arbitration panel issued a decision which shook baseball to its foundations by rejecting the owners' interpretation of the reserve clause. The reserve clause, contained in every player's contract, stated that if the player and club hadn't agreed to terms by

March 1, "the Club shall have the right by written notice to the Player ... to renew this contract for one year on the same terms."[25] The owners read the reserve clause as creating another identical contract with the same right of renewal, thereby giving the club a perpetual option on the player's services. However, arbitrator Peter Seitz agreed with the players that this language created only a one-year right of renewal, after which the club had no further claim to the player. The arbitrator's decision allowed pitcher Andy Messersmith, who had played without a written contract in 1975, to sell his services to the highest bidder: Messersmith, who had earned $115,000 with the Dodgers in 1975, soon signed a three- year, $1 million contract with the Atlanta Braves.

The owners attacked the panel's decision in court but could not overcome the strong Federal policy favoring arbitration of labor disputes. The courts "do not sit as an appellate tribunal to review the merits of the arbitrator's decision"; rather, they ask only whether a reasonable arbitrator could have reached that result. A century of owners' control over the labor market ended when the Court of Appeals affirmed the arbitrators' decision with the words, "We cannot say that [the reserve clause and related provisions] are not susceptible of the construction given them by the panel. Accordingly, the award must be sustained."[26] The era of free agency had begun.

In 1976, as players and owners adjusted to the new rules, Braves owner Ted Turner ran afoul of Commissioner Kuhn by announcing he would outbid anyone for the Giants' Gary Matthews when Matthews became a free agent. Kuhn suspended Turner for one year for tampering and revoked the Braves' first-round choice in the 1977 amateur draft. A Federal court upheld Turner's suspension, citing a clause in the Major League Agreement which empowered the Commissioner "to investigate . . . any act . . . not in the best interests of the national game of Baseball" and "to determine . . . what punitive action is appropriate . . . ."[27] However, the court restored the Braves' draft pick, limiting the Commissioner to those punitive sanctions expressly made available to him by the Major League Agreement.[28] Although the Commissioner had "all the attributes of a benevolent but absolute despot and all the disciplinary powers of the proverbial pater familias,"[29] the Major League Agreement which established his authority also limited its exercise.

No team was more affected by free agency than the Oakland A's, whose talented roster had won three of the past four World Series and five straight division championships. Concluding that he couldn't afford the enormous salaries his stars would command in the open market, A's owner Charles O. Finley decided to sell their contracts to wealthier clubs before they could leave as free agents. In June 1976, Finley sold Joe Rudi and Rollie Fingers to the Boston Red Sox for $2 million and Vida Blue to the New York Yankees for $1.5 million, but Commissioner Bowie Kuhn quickly nullified the transactions as "inconsistent with the best interests of baseball, the integrity of the game, and the maintenance of public confidence in it."

A Federal judge rejected Finley's argument that Kuhn had exceeded his authority, pointing to the Commissioner's power to invalidate acts "not in the best interests of Baseball" and a provision in the Major League Agreement through which the club owners agreed to be bound by the Commissioner's decisions and to "waive such right of recourse to the courts as would otherwise have existed in their favor."[30] This decision was upheld on appeal,[31] the appeals court noting that the "waiver of recourse" provision quoted above kept Finley from going to court to challenge Kuhn's ruling unless he could show that the Major League Agreement was inconsistent with state or Federal law or that the procedures followed by Kuhn "failed to follow the basic rudiments of due process of law."[32]

Pete Rose's 1989 lawsuit against A. Bartlett Giamatti relied on just that argument—that Rose was being denied the right to a fair hearing by an unbiased decisionmaker. When Rose asked a state court judge in his home town of Cincinnati to enjoin the Commissioner from holding a hearing on charges that Rose had bet on baseball games, he claimed that Giamatti had already decided he was guilty. Giamatti's lawyers filed a motion to remove the case to Federal court. In most cases, state courts have jurisdiction if one or both of the parties to the lawsuit are citizens of that state; if the plaintiff and defendant are citizens of different states, Federal courts usually have jurisdiction to hear the case. Because Rose was a citizen of Ohio and Giamatti was a citizen of New York, Giamatti was able to remove the case from the Ohio court—which might favor Ohioans over New Yorkers—to a Federal court.[33] After losing that legal skirmish, Rose withdrew his lawsuit and agreed to be suspended indefinitely from baseball, so the courts never ruled on the merits of Rose's claim that the Commissioner was not treating him fairly.

Some twenty years after *Flood v. Kuhn* was decided, baseball's antitrust exemption came under attack once again. Commissioner Fay Vincent was shown the door by unhappy team owners in 1992. There was widespread speculation that the owners might lock the players out of spring training in 1993 in order to gain the upper hand in their negotiations with the MLBPA, and some owners allegedly were worried that Vincent would use the Commissioner's traditional authority to take action in the "best interests of baseball."

The mere existence of a Commissioner—in theory, an independent arbiter who could be trusted to do the right thing and keep the owners in line when they tried to go too far—had helped to deflect attacks on baseball's antitrust exemption. So when Congress held hearings on a bill to repeal the exemption in 1993, the owners promised to name a new Commissioner by the end of that year.

But baseball had no Commissioner when the 1994 season ended. With negotiations on a new collective bargaining agreement headed for a major meltdown, Senator Howard Metzenbaum of Ohio—a parking-lot tycoon who had once owned a piece of the Cleveland Indians—introduced yet another bill to repeal baseball's antitrust exemption. Despite support from Senator Connie Mack III (the grandson of the legendary owner/manager) and Congressman Jim Bunning (who won 224 major league games), the Metzenbaum bill failed to get out of committee. After the players struck on August 12, 1994, there was another attempt to repeal the antitrust exemption, but Congress adjourned without taking action on it.

Those who supported the proposals to repeal baseball's antitrust exemption touted repeal as a remedy for baseball's chronic labor-management woes. But in reality, overturning *Federal Baseball* would have done nothing of the kind.

That's because labor-management issues are never subject to the antitrust laws in the first place. As long as a collective bargaining relationship exists, the antitrust laws do not apply—and that's true not only for baseball, but also for the steel industry and any other business. That's why you never hear about the UAW bringing an antitrust suit against GM, Ford, and Chrysler. If a union doesn't prevail at the bargaining table, it can file an unfair labor practice complaint with the National Labor Relations Board, or it can go on strike—but it can't file an antitrust suit. So even if Curt Flood had been successful in persuading the Supreme Court to overrule *Federal Baseball* the owners still would have an absolute defense to antitrust suits brought by the MLBPA (and vice versa).

Baseball's owners are not immune to charges that they are guilty of violating the Federal labor laws. When employees decide to join a union, those laws provide that an employer must bargain with the union before it changes wages or terms of employment. Only if the employer and the union cannot reach an agreement—or, to use labor law terminology, if an "impasse" is reached—can the employer unilaterally make changes.

After months of fruitless negotiations, the owners declared in late December 1994 that they and the union were at an impasse and unilaterally imposed the salary cap that the MLBPA had refused to accept. The MLBPA promptly filed a complaint with the National Labor Relations Board, alleging that the owners acted prematurely. If anything, "impasse" seems too mild a term to describe the deadlock that then existed between owners and players, but the NLRB let it be known that they believed that the owners had acted before a legal state of impasse existed.

The owners backtracked somewhat, and negotiations resumed. Even President Clinton tried to broker a deal. But the MLBPA—led by Donald Fehr, who someone once said was born without a "yes" gene in his body—and the owners—who were planning to open the season with so-called "replacement" players—stuck to their guns. Once again, believing that they were at an impasse, the owners announced they were no longer bound by the old collective bargaining provisions on free agency and salary arbitration.

Only a couple of days before the 1995 season was scheduled to open, Judge Sonia Sotomayor sided with the NLRB and the union and ordered the owners to restore the *status quo*. The owners could have locked out the players and continued to fight the MLBPA and NLRB in court, but they soon decided to throw in the towel. The replacement players were sent home, and the 1995 season belatedly got under way.

But that season and the next came and went without the owners and the players' union reaching agreement on a new collective bargaining pact, and it began to look like Judge Sotomayor might once again be called on to decide if the impasse in fact had become an impasse for legal purposes. After the owners voted down, by a count of 18-12 against, the concord reached by their own negotiator, Randy Levine, a 1997 season season of continued discord and impending doom seemed probable. But on November 26, 1997 the owners reversed their stand by an astonishing vote of 26-4 in favor of accepting the very proposal they

had rejected two weeks earlier.

Peace seemed assured until the millennium. Yet if another labor-management war does break out, at any point after that, you can expect to hear MLBPA officials (who probably know better) and assorted members of the U.S. Congress (who probably don't) blame it on baseball's antitrust exemption.

So even if Congress finally voted to overturn the *Federal Baseball* decision, the only way the players could bring antitrust suit against the owners would be to dissolve, or "decertify" their union—when there's no union, there can be no collective bargaining relationship. That's what the NFL players did a few years ago when they were unable to persuade their league's owners to liberalize restrictive free-agency rules. But there is little chance that the baseball players will ever choose to decertify the MLBPA.

If repealing baseball's antitrust exemption would do nothing to cure baseball's labor-management woes, exactly what effect would a repeal have? For one thing, you could expect to see a lot more baseball teams pulling up stakes and moving to cities offering them sweetheart stadium deals or similar incentives. The Oakland Raiders won their antitrust suit against the NFL when the league tried to stop them from moving to Los Angeles, where they stayed for only a few years before moving back to Oakland. Since then, several football teams have moved to greener pastures, and you can expect to see more teams moving in the years to come.

If baseball lost its antitrust exemption, Bud Selig and his brethren could do little to stop renegade baseball owners from following in the footsteps of the St. Louis (now Arizona) Cardinals, Los Angeles (now St. Louis) Rams, Cleveland Browns (now the Baltimore Ravens), and other NFL teams who have opted for relocation. Whether that's a good thing or a bad thing depends, of course, on whether you live in a city in danger of losing a team or a city that's trying to attract one.

[1]*Allegheny Base-ball Club* v. *Bennett*, 14 Fed. 257 (C.C.W.D. Pa., 1882).
[2]*St. Louis Athletic Ass'n* v. *Mullane*, No. 3642 (C.C.S.D. Ohio, May 13, 1884). Reprinted in *Sporting Life*, May 21, 1884, p.2, col.1.
[3]*Metropolitan Exhibition Co.* v. *Ewing*, 42 Fed. 198 (C.C.S.D. N.Y. 1890).
[4]*Metropolitan Exhibition Co.* v. *Ward*, 9 N.Y.S. 779 (Sup. Ct., New York Co. 1890).
[5]*Philadelphia Base Ball Club* v. *Lajoie*, 51 Atl. 973 (Pa. S. Ct. 1902).
[6]*Brooklyn Baseball Club* v. *McGuire*, 116 Fed. 783 (C.C.E.D. Pa. 1902).
[7]*American Base Ball & Athletic Exhibition Co. of St. Louis* v. *Harper*, 54 Cent. L.J. 449 (St. Louis Cir. Ct. 1902).
[8]*American League Baseball Club of Chicago* v. *Chase*, 86 Misc. 441, 149 N.Y. Supp. 6 (Sup. Ct. 1914).
[9]*Weeghman* v. *Killefer*, 214 Fed. 168 (W.D. Mich. 1914).
[10]*Weeghman* v. *Killefer*, 215 Fed. 289 (6th Cir. 1914).
[11]*National League of Professional Baseball Clubs* v. *Federal Baseball Club of Baltimore*, 269 Fed. 681 (D.C. Cir. 1921).
[12]*Federal Baseball Club of Baltimore* v. *National League of Professional Baseball Clubs*, 259 U.S. 200 (1922).
[13]*Hart* v. *Keith Vaudeville Exchange*, 262 U.S. 271 (1923).
[14]*Gardella* v. *Chandler*, 79 F.Supp. 260 (S.D.N.Y. 1948).
[15]*Gardella* v. *Chandler*, 172 F.2d 402 (2d Cir. 1949).
[16]*Martin* v. *Chandler*, 174 F.2d 917 (2d. Cir. 1949); *Gardella* v. *Chandler*, 174 F.2d 919 (2d. Cir. 1949).
[17]H.R. Rep. 2002, 82d Cong., 2d Sess. 228–32 (1952).
[18]346 U.S. 356 (1953).
[19]*Toolson* v. *New York Yankees*, 101 F.Supp. 93 (S.D. Cal. 1951).
[20]200 F.2d 198 (9th Cir. 1952).
[21]358 U.S. 445 (1957).
[22]407 U.S. 258 (1972).
[23]*Salerno* v. *American League*, 429 F.2d 1003 (2d Cir. 1970).
[24]*Professional Baseball Schools and Clubs, Inc.* v. *Kuhn*, 693 F.2d 1085 (11th Cir. 1982).
[25]Player Contract, P 10(a).
[26]*Kansas City Royals Baseball Corp.* v. *Major League Baseball Players Association*, 532 F.2d 615 (8th Cir. 1976).
[27]Major League Agreement, Art. I, Sec. 2.
[28]*Atlanta National League Baseball Club* v. *Kuhn*, 432 F. Supp. 1213 (N.D. Ga. 1977).
[29]*Milwaukee American Ass'n* v. *Landis*, 49 F.2d 298 (N.D. Ill. 1931).
[30]Id. at Art. VII, Sec. 2.
[31]*Charles O. Finley & Co.* v. *Kuhn*, 569 F.2d 527 (7th Cir. 1978).
[32]Id. at 544.
[33]*Rose* v. *Giamatti*, 721 F. Supp. 906 (1989).

CHAPTER 22

The Amateur Draft

Allan Simpson

The year was 1964. Baseball was at a crossroads. By buying up the game's best amateur talent, the New York Yankees and some of the game's wealthier clubs were threatening to make a mockery of competitive balance, one of the game's time-honored virtues. The more they spent, the more successful they became.

To keep pace with the Yankees, who had won nine of the last ten American League pennants and fourteen of sixteen, some of the smaller-market teams were committing financial suicide. The fledgling Los Angeles Angels opened owner Gene Autry's saddlebags that year and paid untested outfielder Rick Reichardt a record $205,000 bonus—at the time, more than the annual salary of most major leaguers.

The more everyone willfully misspent on raw, unproven amateur prospects, the less there was to prop up a sagging player-development system. Once vibrant and self-sustaining with 460 teams in 1949, the minor leagues were rotting at the core. They had decayed fifteen years later to a dangerously low 121 clubs, all of which were dependent on major league subsidization for survival.

By overspending on amateur talent and then underspending to develop it, baseball was playing its own version of Catch-22. The game's future well-being was at stake.

Not coincidentally, 1964 was the year baseball's high-ranking officers instituted a much-debated, much-awaited draft of amateur players. It would become effective in 1965 and become the primary means by which amateurs would infiltrate the professional ranks.

The draft's purpose was twofold: to stop the upward spiral of bonuses and to more evenly distribute talent. It was a reactionary measure to the Reichardt signing and the Yankees' decade of dominance. During the next 32 years, some 41,500 players would be selected in baseball's annual draft. No one—in 1964 dollars—would again approach the lavish signing bonus Reichardt received until all aspects of cost containment went out the window in the early- and mid-1990s. And no team in the draft era would ever dominate the game as the Yankees did. From 1978 to 1987, 10 different teams would win the World Series. "Since the draft, there have been no particular dynasties," said Roland Hemond, Angels farm director in 1964 and Baltimore's general manager 30 years later. "That's given every indication that the draft has worked, giving more clubs the opportunity to build."

In 1936, the year the National Football League adopted its draft, the Cleveland Indians signed 17-year-old Iowa farmboy Bob Feller to a contact. The price? One dollar.

Players yearned then for the opportunity to play professional baseball, and were happy just for the chance. There was little competition among clubs for a player's services, no matter how talented he was.

By 1942, America's efforts in World War II siphoned off much of the available talent. The supply of players suddenly became limited. Competition drove the Detroit Tigers to sign outfielder Dick Wakefield to an unprecedented bonus of $52,000. Suddenly, the rush was on.

By the end of World War II, baseball had entered a new era, a golden era. Interest in the game fanned like wildfire. Minor league teams sprung up all over and competition for players became fierce. Teams had to offer bonuses to remain in the game.

At the 1946 Winter Meetings, baseball made its first effort to curtail escalating bonuses by instituting a bonus rule. An agreement between the two major leagues and the National Association (the governing body for the minor leagues) designated a bonus player as anyone signed to a contract that exceeded a fixed level. Teams were fined if they paid out an amount that exceeded an imposed limit.

For the next two decades, major league officials wrestled with problems stemming from reckless spending and the competition for new recruits. Various solutions were proposed. None worked. Almost all were revised annually or simply thrown out.

They tried several variations of the bonus rule, but that rule was legislated out in 1957 mainly because teams were openly cheating and regularly found ways to circumvent it.

"We'd pass a bonus rule and by the time we got out of the room," Detroit general manager Jim Campbell said, "we already figured out how to skin the cat. There was no way to really police it."

It also didn't help that few high-priced bonus babies reached the major leagues. Pittsburgh made 18-year-old lefthander Paul Pettit the game's first $100,000 bonus player in 1950, but it proved a foolhardy investment. The sore-armed Pettit won only one game in the big leagues.

Beginning in 1958, baseball tried a first-year rule that required teams to retain bonus babies on major league rosters in each of their first two full seasons, or expose them to waivers. But that didn't work either. Opponents said it was anti-development, that too many young players were forced to play in the big leagues before they were ready. Bonuses continued to escalate. In 1957, the Milwaukee Braves spent a record $120,000 for power-hitting outfielder Dave Nicholson, then topped that a few months later by handing $125,000 to shortstop Denis Menke.

At the 1959 Winter Meetings, a proposal introducing a draft of amateur talent was made, but it proved to be five years before its time and was defeated.

In 1960, the Chicago Cubs inked pitcher-outfielder Danny Murphy, 17, to a record $130,000 bonus and immediately placed him in the big leagues. A year later, shortstop Bob Bailey was awarded $175,000 by Pittsburgh. At least six teams that year shelled out the largest bonus in club history. The heavy spending of 1961 sent ripples throughout baseball.

"Maybe we have to be saved from ourselves," Braves general manager John McHale said. "I think it's unfortunate that this is the system. A club like ours must be competitive. To achieve this, we must get ballplayers. If you're not prepared to pay, well, you just stand by and watch somebody else sign 'em.

"No, I don't know how to stop it. We've tried all kinds of ways, including several bonus rules. But nothing has worked. If a draft system similar to that used by football and basketball would hold up under our justice system, maybe that would be the answer.

"Certainly it would be a much healthier situation if the money that's paid for these tremendous bonuses could be channeled back into baseball. But right now it's as simple as this: If you want the kids, you've got to pay. We want 'em."

From 1958-63, an estimated $45 million was spent on bonuses and first-year player salaries.

In 1964, bonus payments continued to go through the roof. Led by Rick Reichardt's lavish deal, a record $7 million-plus was paid out that year to amateur players, more than was spent on major league salaries. Teams such as the New York Yankees and Los Angeles Dodgers were buying up much of the talent in sight, and were prospering.

The timing was right for a systematic change to the conventional means of procuring talent.

By 1964, all the other major team sports in the United States deployed a draft to equally distribute amateur talent. Football introduced the concept in 1936, basketball followed in 1947 and hockey adopted a draft in 1963. But baseball officials were reluctant to follow suit.

It was argued that a draft would penalize the industrious teams and be a form of socialism. Others opposed the draft for legal reasons. Baseball, unlike the other professional sports, had operated under an anti-trust exemption since Supreme Court Justice Oliver Wendell Holmes bestowed favorable treatment for baseball in 1922. There was concern that a draft, which would restrict a player's freedom and bargaining power, would jeopardize baseball's special judicial standing.

The game's hierarchy also feared that Congress would take an adverse stance on the premise that a baseball draft would deal primarily with high school players, or minors.

Football had no such concerns. At the time, most football players were of majority age and had options available to them. Players could consider three professional leagues—the NFL, American Football League and Canadian Football League—to market their talents. Baseball had no such options.

Opponents of a draft, however, were in the minority. Teams like the Dodgers and Yankees opposed it not on legal principle, but more for selfish reasons.

"There was some concern whether or not governmental interference would happen, whether some of the players and their representatives would challenge it," said Lee MacPhail, Orioles general manager in 1964 and mastermind of the powerful Yankees teams of the '50s and early '60s. "But some clubs preferred things go on as they were, if they felt they were getting more than their fair share. They didn't want to change that.

"In the 10 years I was farm director of the Yankees (1949-58), we won nine pennants and won the World Series five years in a row. Kids wanted to sign with the Yankees, the most glamorous team in baseball at the time. If two or three teams were after them, and one was the Yankees, we generally had the inside track."

Baseball adopted its draft at the 1964 Winter Meetings. "The free agent draft will help solve our biggest problem: player procurement and development," Cleveland general manager Gabe Paul said. "It'll help equalize our teams. We have to do something to give the weaker teams greater incentive.

"Football has gone ahead unafraid of legal obstacles and they had more obstacles when they instituted their draft than we do now. They have benefited by our mistakes. It's about time for us to profit by their experience."

Baseball's new free-agent draft would function in a manner similar to football and basketball. All eligible talent would be placed in a common pool with every team selecting from it in turn. When a team picked a player, it would gain exclusive rights to negotiate with him. The baseball draft, however, introduced several notable differences. First, three drafts would be held each year instead of one. A summer meeting would be held around June 1, a winter session around Jan. 15. A third draft, limited to American Legion players not eligible to sign until Sept. 1, would be held in late summer. The Legion phase lasted only one year and the winter session was phased out in 1986.

The new amateur draft, officially known as the Rule IV draft, initially was open to permanent residents of the United States only, with a focus on high school graduates and college players who had attained sophomore standing or age 21. The college rule was amended two years later to include players of junior class standing. By 1990, players from Canada, Puerto Rico and other U.S. territories had become subject to selection.

A full international draft remained the subject of debate through 1996. Whereas a football team retained permanent negotiating rights to a draftee, a baseball clubs' rights terminated 15 days before the next draft session. If a player didn't sign by then, he went back into a special "secondary" pool for the next time he was eligible to be selected. The secondary phase of the draft was eliminated in 1987.

One of the immediate benefits of a free-agent draft, most clubs agreed, would be an improved game at the major league level. No longer would clubs be forced to clutter their 25-man rosters with green, untested youngsters. In 1964, major league teams had been forced to protect 77 first-year players on their winter rosters.

While most of the emphasis in the early years of the draft was on raw high school talent, a gradual transition took place in the mid-'70s. College players became more and more attractive to scouts as college programs around the country took on a new commitment to fielding competitive teams.

In 1977, for the first time, more college players than high school players were selected, a trend that has never reversed itself. By 1981, the swing to college talent was so pronounced that the ratio of players entering the professional ranks from college programs as compared to high schools was nearly 5 to 1.

No matter what the source of talent, the baseball draft remained, at best, an inexact science. The success rate for first-round picks reaching the big leagues—even for a game or two—was no more than two in three, as compared to a near-100 percent success rate for first-round picks in football and basketball.

"Picking high school and college kids is the most unscientific, inexact of all the evaluations of talent," said Syd Thrift, former Pirates and Yankees general manager. "The reason is these kids are the furthest from the major leagues."

Unlike in football and basketball, whose drafts deal with more finished products, the best players drafted in baseball, even the top college players, invariably need to develop and refine their skills for several seasons in the minor leagues.

In the draft's first 32 years, only 18 players went directly to the major leagues. Of that total, 14 had to backtrack to the minor leagues for additional seasoning.

"In football and basketball," Baltimore general manager Pat Gillick said, "they're drafting guys after they've spent three or four years in what is the equivalent of our farm system. The caliber of play in college baseball is not equivalent to that of basketball and football. "It's not a very exact science. No matter how much testing you do, you never really know how a young guy's going to react to a pro situation until he plays in one."

Even a former No. 1 overall pick acknowledged how hit-and-miss the baseball draft can be.

"The draft is, at best, a shot in the dark," said Bill Almon, the top selection in 1974 by the San Diego Padres. "That's the reason they draft so many players."

Boston Red Sox scout Joe Stephenson might have said it best, when describing how inexact and unpredictable the baseball draft can be. "We belong to the 4-H club," Stephenson said. "You hope you find a prospect. You hope you get him in the draft. You hope you can sign him. And you hope he can play."

To point out what a crapshoot the baseball draft can be, 1979 provided graphic evidence. Seattle took first baseman Al Chambers with the No. 1 overall pick that year, and he enjoyed only a cup of coffee in the big leagues. Minnesota spent its first-round pick on outfielder Kevin Brandt, whose career was such a washout that he played in only 40 minor-league games. Meanwhile, the Dodgers quietly claimed pitcher Orel Hershiser in the 17th round and the Yankees plucked first baseman Don Mattingly in the 19th round.

Several other potential Hall of Famers were late-round finds. For example, second baseman Ryne Sandberg went in the 20th round to Philadelphia in 1978.

Catcher Mike Piazza was one of the great finds of all. He was a 62nd-round pick of Los Angeles in 1988, yet went on to become a star with the Dodgers. Players such as Kevin Mitchell and Bobby Bonilla, who went on to become impact players in the big leagues, weren't drafted at all.

Astute drafting, though, was largely responsible for a series of mini-dynasties of the draft era. Oakland laid the foundation to World Series championship teams from 1972-74 by selecting Rick Monday, Sal Bando, Gene Tenace and Reggie Jackson in 1965-66, the first two drafts.

The Dodgers had a contending team for much of the 1970s because of a 1968 draft that produced 15 future big leaguers, including Bill Buckner, Ron Cey, Steve Garvey and Dave Lopes. The Mets became a force in the mid to late '80s because of accurate drafting in the early '80s: They landed Darryl Strawberry (1980) and Dwight Gooden (1982) with first-round picks.

In the same 1987-90 period that the Chicago White Sox chose pitcher Jack McDowell, third baseman Robin Ventura, first baseman Frank Thomas and pitcher Alex Fernandez with consecutive first-round picks, the corresponding first-round picks for the Dodgers were pitchers Dan Opperman, Bill Bene, Kiki Jones and Ron Walden—none of whom reached the big leagues.

The Atlanta Braves became a World Series regular in the 1990s because of astute drafting. Third baseman Chipper Jones was the first pick in 1990—Atlanta's reward for finishing last in 1989. The nucleus of the team's celebrated pitching staff was acquired through the draft. Since its inception, the draft largely has achieved its two underlying goals. Payments to untried amateur players have, except in the '90s, been kept in line, while new meaning has been given to competitive balance.

Monday, the No. 1 selection in the first draft, received a signing bonus from Kansas City of $104,000, little more than half what Reichardt received in his landmark deal of 1964.

It wasn't until Detroit signed outfielder Kirk Gibson in 1978 and the Mets signed Strawberry two years later that players began to approach, in real dollars, the bonus Reichardt received. By then, inflation had reduced those figures to a fraction of Reichardt's windfall package. As late as 1987, Seattle paid a mere $160,000 to sign Ken Griffey Jr., the first overall pick.

It was only in 1988 and 1989—when Baltimore signed No. 1 overall pick Ben McDonald to an $800,000 three-year major league contract that provided for a $350,000 bonus, and Toronto later went to $575,000 for first baseman John Olerud—that players regularly topped the $200,000 barrier. By then, the financial well-being of the game was on such solid footing that spending lavishly on amateurs wasn't as dangerous as it was in 1964 when the draft was implemented.

In the early 1990s, however, the financial infrastructure of baseball took a quantum leap into uncharted waters. Not only were major league players paid annual salaries that often topped $5-6 million, but bonus payments to draft picks also went off the board.

Atlanta refused to select Arlington, Texas, high school pitcher Todd Van Poppel with the first selection in 1990 because of his insistence on attending the University of Texas. Undeterred, Oakland swooped in and drafted Van Poppel with its first-round pick. He was signed to a record $1.2 million, three-year major league contract that provided for a $500,000 bonus.

A year after, the Yankees stunned the baseball world by signing pitcher Brien Taylor to a whopping $1.55 bonus—more than double the previous record. Average bonus payments to first-round picks began to escalate appreciably, rising from $355,000 in 1991, to $482,000 in 1992, to $611,000 in 1993, to $790,000 in 1994.

In 1994, with a strike looming, the average first-round bonus reached $796,000 with five players receiving bonuses of $1 million or more. No. 1 pick Paul Wilson tied Taylor's record bonus by signing with the Mets for $1.55 million. Within weeks, that record was broken when the Florida Marlins coughed up $1.6 million to entice short-stop Josh Booty away from a promising football career at Louisiana State University.

Booty's record bonus held up until 1996, when all hell broke loose. The entire process of signing amateur players went off the chart in January of that year when the Marlins outbid every major league team for the rights to Cuban defector Livan Hernandez, 20, who was signed to a four-year major league contract that provided a record $2.5 million bonus. Several more Cubans went on to sign lucrative, seven-figure bonuses in the next few months.

The wave of Cuban defectors was fueled by Oakland's signing of righthander Ariel Prieto in the 1995 draft. Prieto, 29, had escaped Cuba months earlier and made himself eligible for the draft by pitching for a team in the independent Western League. He was selected fifth overall by Oakland and signed to a contact that provided a $1.2 million bonus. The draft's restrictive nature caused future Cuban defectors to take up residency in a foreign country that had diplomatic relations with the United States, but wasn't subject to the draft. As such, the Cubans would be free to sign on the open market. As expected, bonuses to Cubans rose appreciably.

Soon, means of circumventing the draft greatly impacted the draft itself and turned the whole player procurement process upside down. No longer would foreign players be the only ones to benefit from a free-market system.

Prior to 1996, major league teams rarely followed draft rules as outlined in the Professional Baseball Agreement, specifically as they pertained to Rule IV (e). That provision required teams to tender formal, uniform contract offers to draft picks within 15 days of their selection.

At the behest of agents, seven players—six first-round picks and a third-rounder—challenged that rule in 1996. Three elected not to follow through with grievance procedures, but four did and were declared free agents by Major League Baseball.

Free to offer their services to all 30 major league clubs, the four were wined and dined extensively and in the end signed the four largest bonuses ever awarded amateur prospects—not just draft picks. First baseman Travis Lee, who had been drafted second overall by Minnesota, signed a stunning $10 million package with the expansion Arizona Diamondbacks. Soon thereafter, righthander John Patterson (5th, Expos) signed with the Diamondbacks for $6.075 million and lefthander Bobby Seay (12th, White Sox) signed with the expansion Tampa Bay Devil Rays for $3 million.

The fourth player, righthander Matt White (7th, Giants), completed the once-in-a-lifetime windfall by agreeing to terms with the Tampa Bay Devil Rays for $10.2 million. Almost certainly, teams would close that loophole in the future.

Meanwhile, righthander Kris Benson became a mere footnote in draft history. Pittsburgh selected the Clemson righthander with the first overall pick in the 1996 draft and while he signed with the Pirates for a record bonus of $2 million, his figure became almost pocket change compared to some of the deals signed by his fellow members of the Draft Class of '96.

The unsettling effects of 1996 and other developments notwithstanding, adoption of the draft in 1964 proved to be a blessing for baseball. It was the root that enabled the game to grow and prosper.

"It's been an unqualified success," Lee MacPhail said. "Certainly, it's evened competition. It's given teams that have a difficult time competing for free-agent talent a fair share, or even more than a fair share. Close races in all divisions today goes back to the free-agent draft. If you didn't have it today, it would be a disaster."

Top 10 Draft Picks 1965-1996

Players are listed in the order in which they were drafted. Those who did not reach the major leagues are listed with the highest minor league classification they attained as of October 1996. DNP signifies that the draft pick did not play in Organized Baseball, or has not as of this edition of TOTAL BASEBALL.

Year/ Selection Number	Player	Team	Position — Highest Minor League Reached	Year/ Selection Number	Player	Team	Position — Highest Minor League Reached	Year/ Selection Number	Player	Team	Position — Highest Minor League Reached
1965				**1966**				**1967**			
1	Rick Monday	A's	OF	1	Steve Chilcott	Mets	C - AAA	1	Ron Blomberg	Yankees	1B
2	Les Rohr	Mets	P	2	Reggie Jackson	A's	OF	2	Terry Hughes	Cubs	SS
3	Joe Coleman	Senators	P	3	Wayne Twitchell	Astros	P	3	Mike Garman	Red Sox	P
4	Alex Barrett	Astros	SS - AAA	4	Ken Brett	Red Sox	P-OF	4	Jon Matlack	Mets	P
5	Billy Conigliaro	Red Sox	OF	5	Dean Burk	Cubs	P - AAA	5	John Jones	Senators	C - A
6	Rick James	Cubs	P	6	Tom Grieve	Senators	OF	6	John Mayberry	Astros	1B
7	Ray Fosse	Indians	C	7	Leron Lee	Cardinals	OF	7	Brian Bickerton	A's	P - AAA
8	John Wyatt	Dodgers	SS - A	8	Jim De Neff	Angels	SS - AAA	8	Wayne Simpson	Reds	P
9	Eddie Leon	Twins	SS	9	Mike Biko	Phillies	P - A	9	Mike Nunn	Angel	C - AAA
10	Doug Dickerson	Pirates	OF - A	10	Jim Lyttle	Yankees	OF	10	Ted Simmons	Cardinals	C

Year/Selection Number	Player	Team	Position — Highest Minor League Reached
1968			
1	Tim Foli	Mets	SS
2	Pete Broberg	A's	P
3	Marty Cott	Astros	C - AAA
4	Thurman Munson	Yankees	C
5	Bobby Valentine	Dodgers	OF
6	Robert Weaver	Indians	SS - AA
7	Curtis Moore	Braves	OF - AAA
8	Donnie Castle	Senators	P-OF
9	Dick Sharon	Pirates	OF
10	Junior Kennedy	Orioles	SS
1969			
1	Jeff Burroughs	Senators	OF
2	J.R. Richard	Astros	P
3	Ted Nicholson	White Sox	3B - A
4	Randy Sterling	Mets	P
5	Alan Bannister	Angels	SS
6	Mike Anderson	Phillies	1B
7	Paul Ray Powell	Twins	OF
8	Terry McDermot	Dodgers	C
9	Don Stanhouse	A's	SS
10	Bob May	Pirates	P - A
1970			
1	Mike Ivie	Padres	C
2	Steve Dunning	Indians	P
3	Barry Foote	Expos	C
4	Darrell Porter	Brewers	C
5	Mike Martin	Phillies	P - AAA
6	Lee Richard	White Sox	SS
7	Randy Scarberry	Astros	P
8	Rex Goodson	Royals	C - AA
9	Jim Haller	Dodgers	P - AAA
10	Paul Dade	Angels	3B-OF
1971			
1	Denny Goodwin	White Sox	C
2	Jay Franklin	Padres	P
3	Tom Bianco	Brewers	SS
4	Condredge Holloway	Expos	SS - DNP
5	Roy Branch	Royals	P
6	Roy Thomas	Phillies	P
7	Roger Quiroga	Senators	P - A
8	Ed Kurpiel	Cardinals	1B-P - AAA
9	David Sloan	Indians	P - AA
10	Taylor Duncan	Braves	SS
1972			
1	Dave Roberts	Padres	3B
2	Rick Manning	Indians	SS
3	Larry Christenson	Phillies	P
4	Roy Howell	Rangers	3B
5	Bobby Goodman	Expos	C - AAA
6	Danny Thomas	Brewers	1B
7	Larry Payne	Reds	P - AAA
8	Dick Ruthven	Twins	P
9	Steve Englishbey	Astros	OF - AA
10	Dave Chalk	Angels	3B
1973			
1	David Clyde	Rangers	P
2	John Stearns	Phillies	C
3	Robin Yount	Brewers	SS
4	Dave Winfield	Padres	P-OF
5	Glenn Tufts	Indians	1B-P - AA
6	Johnnie LeMaster	Giants	SS
7	Billy Taylor	Angels	OF - A
8	Gary Roenicke	Expos	SS
9	Lew Olsen	Royals	P-AAA
10	Pat Rockett	Braves	SS

Year/Selection Number	Player	Team	Position — Highest Minor League Reached
1974			
1	Bill Almon	Padres	SS
2	Tommy Boggs	Rangers	P
3	Lonnie Smith	Phillies	OF
4	Tom Brennan	Indians	P
5	Dale Murphy	Braves	C
6	Butch Edge	Brewers	P
7	Scot Thompson	Cubs	OF
8	Larry Monroe	White Sox	P
9	Ron Sorey	Expos	3B - A
10	Mike Miley	Angels	SS
1975			
1	Danny Goodwin	Angels	C
2	Mike Lentz	Padres	P
3	Les Filkins	Tigers	OF - AAA
4	Brian Rosinski	Cubs	OF - AAA
5	Rich O'Keefe	Brewers	OF- AAA
6	Butch Benton	Mets	C - AAA
7	Rick Cerone	Indians	C
8	Ted Barnickle	Giants	P - AAA
9	Clint Hurdle	Royals	OF
10	Art Miles	Expos	SS - A
1976			
1	Floyd Bannister	Astros	P
2	Pat Underwood	Tigers	P
3	Ken Smith	Braves	3B
4	Bill Bordley	Brewers	P
5	Bob Owchinko	Padres	P
6	Ken Landreaux	Angels	OF
7	Herm Segelke	Cubs	P
8	Steve Trout	White Sox	P
9	Bob James	Expos	P
10	Jamie Allen	Twins	P
1977			
1	Harold Baines	White Sox	1B-OF
2	Bill Gullikson	Expos	P
3	Paul Molitor	Brewers	SS
4	Tim Cole	Braves	P - AAA
5	Kevin Richards	Tigers	P - AA
6	Terry Kennedy	Cardinals	C
7	Richard Dotson	Angels	P
8	Brian Greer	Padres	OF
9	David Hibner	Rangers	SS - A
10	Craig Landis	Giants	SS - AAA
1978			
1	Bob Horner	Braves	3B
2	Lloyd Moseby	Blue Jays	1B
3	Hubie Brooks	Mets	SS
4	Mike Morgan	A's	P
5	Andy Hawkins	Padres	P
6	Tito Nanni	Mariners	OF-1B - AAA
7	Bob Cummings	Giants	C - AA
8	Nick Hernandez	Brewers	C - A
9	Glen Franklin	Expos	SS - AAA
10	Phil Lansford	Indians	3B - A
1979			
1	Al Chambers	Mariners	OF
2	Tim Leary	Mets	P
3	Jay Schroeder	Blue Jays	C - A
4	Brad Komminsk	Braves	OF
5	Juan Bustabad	A's	SS - AAA
6	Andy Van Slyke	Cardinals	OF
7	Jon Bohnet	Indians	P
8	John Mizerock	Astros	C
9	Steve Buechele	White Sox	SS
10	Tim Wallach	Expos	1B

Year/Selection Number	Player	Team	Position — Highest Minor League Reached
1980			
1	Darryl Strawberry	Mets	OF
2	Gary Harris	Blue Jays	SS - AA
3	Ken Dayley	Braves	P
4	Mike King	A's	P - AAA
5	Jeff Pyburn	Padres	OF - AAA
6	Darnell Coles	Mariners	SS
7	Jay Reid	Giants	1B
8	Cecil Espy	White Sox	OF
9	Ross Jones	Dodgers	SS
10	Kelly Gruber	Indians	SS
1981			
1	Mike Moore	Mariners	P
2	Joe Carter	Cubs	OF
3	Dick Schofield	Angels	SS
4	Terry Blocker	Mets	OF
5	Matt Williams	Blue Jays	P
6	Kevin McReynolds	Padres	OF
7	Daryl Boston	White Sox	OF
8	Bobby Meacham	Cardinals	SS
9	Ron Darling	Rangers	P
10	Mark Grant	Giants	P
1982			
1	Shawon Dunston	Cubs	SS
2	Augie Schmidt	Blue Jays	SS - AAA
3	Jimmy Jones	Padres	P
4	Bryan Oelkers	Twins	P
5	Dwight Gooden	Mets	P
6	Spike Owen	Mariners	SS
7	Sam Khalifa	Pirates	SS
8	Bob Kipper	Angels	P
9	Duane Ward	Braves	P
10	John Morris	Royals	OF
1983			
1	Tim Belcher	Twins	P
2	Kurt Stillwell	Reds	SS
3	Jeff Kunkel	Rangers	SS
4	Eddie Williams	Mets	3B
5	Stan Hilton	A's	P - AAA
6	Jackie Davidson	Cubs	P - AAA
7	Darrel Ackerfields	Mariners	P
8	Robbie Wine	Astros	C
9	Matt Stark	Blue Jays	C
10	Ray Hayward	Padres	P
1984			
1	Shawn Abner	Mets	OF
2	Billy Swift	Mariners	P
3	Drew Hall	Cubs	P
4	Cory Snyder	Indians	AA
5	Pat Pacillo	Reds	P
6	Erik Pappas	Angels	C - AA
7	Mike Dunne	Cardinals	P
8	Jay Bell	Twins	SS
9	Alan Cockrell	Giants	OF
10	Mark McGwire	A's	1B
1985			
1	B.J. Surhoff	Brewers	SS
2	Will Clark	Giants	1B
3	Bobby Witt	Rangers	P
4	Barry Larkin	Reds	SS
5	Kurt Brown	White Sox	C - AA
6	Barry Bonds	Pirates	OF
7	Mike Campbell	Mariners	P
8	Pete Incaviglia	Expos	OF
9	Mike Poehl	Indians	P - AA
10	Chris Gwynn	Dodgers	OF

Year/ Selection Number	Player	Team	Position — Highest Minor League Reached
1986			
1	Jeff King	Pirates	3B
2	Greg Swindell	Indians	P
3	Matt Williams	Giants	SS
4	Kevin Brown	Rangers	P
5	Kent Mercker	Braves	P
6	Gary Sheffield	Brewers	SS
7	Brad Brink	Phillies	P
8	Patrick Lennon	Mariners	SS
9	Derrick May	Cubs	OF
10	Derek Parks	Twins	C
1987			
1	Ken Griffey, Jr.	Mariners	OF
2	Mark Merchant	Pirates	OF - AAA
3	Willie Banks	Twins	P
4	Mike Harkey	Cubs	P
5	Jack McDowell	White Sox	P
6	Derek Lilliquist	Braves	P
7	Chris Myers	Orioles	P - AA
8	Dan Opperman	Dodgers	P - AAA
9	Kevin Appier	Royals	P
10	Kevin Garner	Padres	P-OF - AAA
1988			
1	Andy Benes	Padres	P
2	Mark Lewis	Indians	SS
3	Steve Avery	Braves	P
4	Greg Olson	Orioles	P
5	Bill Bene	Dodgers	P - AAA
6	Monty Fariss	Rangers	SS
7	Willie Ansley	Astros	OF - AAA
8	Jim Abbott	Angels	P
9	Ty Griffin	Cubs	2B - AA
10	Robin Ventura	White Sox	3B
1989			
1	Ben McDonald	Orioles	P
2	Tyler Houston	Braves	C
3	Roger Salkeld	Mariners	P
4	Jeff Jackson	Phillies	OF - AA
5	Donald Harris	Rangers	OF
6	Paul Coleman	Cardinals	OF - AA
7	Frank Thomas	White Sox	1B
8	Earl Cunningham	Cubs	OF - A
9	Kyle Abbott	Angels	P
10	Charles Johnson	Expos	C

Year/ Selection Number	Player	Team	Position — Highest Minor League Reached
1990			
1	Chipper Jones	Braves	SS
2	Tony Clark	Tigers	1B
3	Mike Lieberthal	Phillies	C
4	Alex Fernandez	White Sox	P
5	Kurt Miller	Pirates	P
6	Marc Newfield	Mariners	1B-OF
7	Dan Wilson	Reds	C
8	Tim Costo	Indians	SS
9	Ron Walden	Dodgers	P - A
10	Carl Everett	Yankees	OF
1991			
1	Brien Taylor	Yankees	P - AA
2	Mike Kelly	Braves	OF
3	David McCarty	Twins	1B
4	Dmitri Young	Cardinals	3B
5	Kenny Henderson	Brewers	P - A
6	John Burke	Astros	P
7	Joe Vitiello	Royals	1B
8	Joey Hamilton	Padres	P
9	Mark Smith	Orioles	OF
10	Tyler Green	Phillies	P
1992			
1	Phil Nevin	Astros	3B
2	Paul Shuey	Indians	P
3	B.J. Wallace	Expos	P - AA
4	Jeffrey Hammonds	Orioles	OF
5	Chad Mottola	Reds	OF
6	Derek Jeter	Yankees	SS
7	Calvin Murray	Giants	OF - AAA
8	Pete Janicki	Angels	P - AAA
9	Preston Wilson	Mets	3B - A
10	Michael Tucker	Royals	SS
1993			
1	Alex Rodriguez	Mariners	SS
2	Darren Dreifort	Dodgers	P
3	Brian Anderson	Angels	P
4	Wayne Gomes	Phillies	P - AA
5	Jeff Granger	Royals	P
6	Steve Soderstrom	Giants	P
7	Trot Nixon	Red Sox	OF
8	Kirk Presley	Mets	P - A
9	Matt Brunson	Tigers	SS - A
10	Brooks Kieschnick	Cubs	1B-OF

Year/ Selection Number	Player	Team	Position — Highest Minor League Reached
1994			
1	Paul Wilson	Mets	P
2	Ben Grieve	A's	OF - AA
3	Dustin Hermanson	Padres	P
4	Antone Williamson	Brewers	3B - AAA
5	Josh Booty	Marlins	SS
6	McKay Christensen	Angels	OF - A
7	Doug Million	Rockies	P - AA
8	Todd Walker	Twins	2B
9	C.J. Nitkowski	Reds	P
10	Jaret Wright	Indians	P - A
1995			
1	Darin Erstad	Angels	Majors
2	Ben Davis	Padres	A
3	Jose Cruz Jr.	Mariners	AAA
4	Kerry Wood	Cubs	A
5	Ariel Prieto	Athletics	Majors
6	Jaime Jones	Marlins	A
7	Jonathan Johnson	Rangers	AA
8	Todd Helton	Rockies	AAA
9	Geoff Jenkins	Brewers	AA
10	Chad Hermansen	Pirates	A
1996			
1	Kris Benson	Pirates	DNP
2	Travis Lee	Twins	DNP
3	Braden Looper	Cardinals	DNP
4	Bill Koch	Blue Jays	DNP
5	John Patterson	Expos	DNP
6	Seth Greisinger	Tigers	DNP
7	Matt White	Giants	DNP
8	Chad Green	Brewers	Rookie
9	Mark Kotsay	Marlins	A
10	Eric Chavez	Athletics	DNP

## CHAPTER 23

Baseball Reporting

Jack Lang

If baseball really was invented by Abner Doubleday at Cooperstown, N.Y., in 1839, we have only the findings of the Mills Commission to support the theory. That commission, formed in 1905, relied heavily on the rambling recollections of an old mining engineer named Abner Graves to reach the conclusion that Doubleday indeed "devised the first scheme for playing baseball." Graves's testimonies were later found to be chock full of inaccuracies.

There can be no dispute, however, as to when the art of writing about baseball began. In the mid-1850s William Trotter Porter gave a decided lift to the game with extensive coverage in his publication *Spirit of the Times*. Until Porter's reports began appearing regularly, baseball in America was ignored in most publications.

John Rickards Betts of Tulane University, in his *American Quarterly* paper "Sporting Journalism in Nineteenth-Century America," credits Porter with being the greatest "antebellum sports editor" in America. On December 10, 1831, he published the first copy of *Spirit of the Times*. It was, for a time, the country's leading sports journal. But while it reported on racing, prize fighting, and even cricket, it did not devote space to baseball until the 1850s.

When he did start reporting on baseball, Porter is credited with having given it the title of "the national game" and also with having printed the first box scores (although this claim is questionable) and "dope" stories.

Shortly thereafter, Frank Queen and Harrison Trent founded the *New York Clipper*, which devoted even more space to baseball. One reason was the addition to the staff of Henry Chadwick, who had begun his career as a journalist in 1844 by contributing to the *Long Island Star*. Chadwick, who had played baseball briefly in his youth, was a devotee of the game and wrote of it voluminously.

Alfred H. Spink, in his book *The National Game,* published in 1910, credits William Cauldwell, editor of the *New York Mercury,* as being the first man to write about baseball for a daily newspaper. Spink's authority for this assertion is a gentleman named William M. Rankin, one of the nation's leading reporters on sports in the late 1880s. Rankin, who was the official scorer for the Mutual Club, also wrote extensively for such New York papers as the *Times, Tribune, World, Mail,* and *Express.* He was considered one of the game's leading authorities. According to Rankin, Cauldwell was writing about baseball by 1853. But Cauldwell found the work of editing his newspaper and writing about baseball too exhausting, and he soon hired Chadwick to write on baseball for the *Mercury.* It was not long before Henry Chadwick became the leading baseball authority in America.

If weekly and daily publications were slow to catch on to the popularity of baseball, they caught up in the late 1880s. Magazines like *The Police Gazette* and *Sporting Life* devoted considerable space to the game. Soon editors of daily newspapers recognized the interest in baseball. James Gordon Bennett, one of the world's most respected newspapermen, who was editor of the *New York Tribune,* was one of the first to increase coverage of the game.

In time every newspaper in America devoted a full page to sports . . . focusing on baseball. Charles Dana of the *New York Sun* and Joseph Pulitzer of the *New York World* are recognized as pioneers in the creation of entire sports departments. By the 1890s, most newspapers in America had created a sports staff. It was in the final decade of the nineteenth century that sports writing began to develop as a full-time occupation on the nation's newspapers.

At the time of his death in 1908, Chadwick was clearly established as the nation's leading baseball authority. Chadwick, who even in his youth had been honored with the nickname "Father Chadwick" for his role in the development of baseball, was such a busy writer that the history of his various affiliations is in conflict. He is credited in some publications as having worked for the *Brooklyn Eagle* in 1856 and the *New York Clipper* in 1857. In others, Chadwick is reported to have written for the *Mercury* before any of the others, or for both at the same time.

Whatever his affiliations, Chadwick was the most prolific of the early-day baseball writers, and eventually he abandoned daily reporting of the game to concentrate on weekly roundups and books about the game.

Chadwick originated what is known today as *The Baseball Guide,* published by *The Sporting News.* He wrote and edited the first baseball guide in 1860, the *Beadle's Dime Base Ball Player.* Later he edited the *DeWitt's Guide* from 1869 to 1880 and, finally, *Spalding's Baseball Guide* from 1881 until his death.

Chadwick's involvement in the game was more than just writing of it. He was instrumental in changing several rules, is credited with having perfected the box score, and was most concerned about drinking, gambling, and rowdyism at ballparks. He led campaigns to clean up the game. Baseball officials of the day heeded his advice.

As early as 1868, Chadwick wrote the first hardcover book in America devoted strictly to baseball. Appropriately, it was titled: *The Game of Base Ball.*

Chadwick's writings on the game led to honors that would be unheard of in the modern era. In 1894, the National League elected Henry an honorary member and two years later voted him a lifetime pension of $600 a year. If a major league today awarded a baseball writer a pension, it would result in an investigation.

Honors continued for Chadwick thirty years after his death. In 1938, one year before the Hall of Fame opened, Chadwick was elected to the Cooperstown shrine as one of the great contributors to the game along with Alexander Cartwright. It was the same year that Grover Cleveland Alexander was elected. Although baseball writers are now honored with the J.G. Taylor Spink Award and scrolls in their honor are mounted in the Hall of Fame Library, Chadwick is the only former baseball writer with a bronze plaque in the main hall, alongside those of Babe Ruth, Ty Cobb, Joe DiMaggio, Cy Young, Mickey Mantle, Ted Williams, and others.

Another early-day baseball writer who earned great respect from the leaders of the game was Timothy H. Murnane, known as the Silver King. When Murnane died in 1917, he was so highly regarded that the American League paid for and erected a huge marble tombstone over his grave in Old Calvary Cemetery in Roslindale, Massachusetts.

The tombstone cites Murnane as a "pioneer of baseball . . . champion of its integrity . . . gifted and fearless writer."

Murnane was a baseball player who turned to writing after his playing days were over. He founded the *Boston Referee* in 1885, and his writings attracted the editors of the *Boston Globe,* who in 1888 hired him as their baseball writer, a job he held until his death. In his thirty years as baseball editor of the *Globe,* he was one of the most influential writers in the country and even found time to serve as president of the New England League for twenty-four years.

Upon his death, it was learned that Murnane left only a small estate to his widow. Immediately, a benefit all-star game was scheduled between great players of the American League and the Boston Red Sox with all proceeds to go to Murnane's widow.

On September 17, 1917, 17,119 Boston fans attended the game which included a pregame show featuring Ziegfeld Follies stars Will Rogers and Fanny Brice. The all-star team included such names as Grover Cleveland Alexander, Walter Johnson, Johnny Evers, Wally Schang, Shoeless Joe Jackson, Buck Weaver, Stuffy McInnis, Eddie Collins, Ty Cobb, and Tris Speaker. Heavyweight boxing champion John L. Sullivan coached first base and Babe Ruth pitched the first six innings for Boston.

All appeared without pay. That was evidence of the esteem in which Murnane was held.

Until the creation of full-time sports staffs in the late 1890s, writing about baseball was, in many cities, a hit-and-miss affair. In many areas, the reports of games were turned in by club secretaries or part-time correspondents. It was often less-than-objective reporting.

With the advent of full-time sports reporters and sports editors in the early 1890s, especially in New York, other major cities suddenly followed suit. This resulted in localized styles of writing and language familiar to the areas. John Rickards Betts describes it in his *American Quarterly* article on nineteenth-century journalism: "The most important developments in sporting journalism outside New York were taking place on the Chicago newspapers. Charles Seymour of the *Herald,* Finley Peter Dunne of the *News* and a reporter for the *Times* were creators of a novel style among baseball writers, a style based on picturesque jargon, lively humor and grotesque exaggeration."

Hugh Fullerton, who was one of the great turn-of-the-century baseball writers in Chicago, noted that "the style of reporting baseball changed all over the country."

In New York and Boston the style of baseball writing emphasized expert knowledge of the game. In Chicago and other western cities, the style involved more humor and cynicism. Often the final score of the game was secondary. Reporters described games with a great flourish and seemed intent on capturing readers' interest with their individual writing styles. Here is the way one *Chicago Times* writer reported a Chicago Cubs game on September 26, 1888:

"The ninth inning of yesterday's ball game was a marvel of beauty. To describe it one needs a big stretch of canvas, a white-wash brush, a pan of green paint, and an artist's hand. Words are hardly expressive enough . . . Mr. Schoeneck is a large secretion of fat around considerable bone and muscle, and he knocked the ball out of the diamond and puffed down to first base . . . Immediately after which Mr. Buckley bunted the ball and went to first, his fatness moving to second.

"The inning had not been particularly gorgeous up to this moment, but with the hitting of a fly by Mr. Hines it took on a resplendent and glorious aspect, for Mr. Van Altren [Van Haltren] got under the fly, gauged it with his blue eye, and muffed it beautifully. When the ball reached Capt. Anson it had lost much of its virulence and was bounding gently long, smiling the while. But if it had not been for a chunk of lava fresh from the earth it could not have had more fun with Capt. Anson, for it rollicked out of his hands and into them again and all over his person, blithely tapped him in the face, and danced away. Indeed, it was a beautiful error, that one of Anson's—a regular sunset error flushed and radiant with shadings of purple and a mellow border.

"Mr. Van Altren picked it up and looked about irresolutely. He was debating whether he should sacrifice skill to art, and being a young man of no high culture in this respect, he esteemed art as naught, but hurled the ball to the plate to catch Mr. Hines. But art was triumphant for all, for Mr. Van Altren's irresolution had been fatal. The ball came to the plate a second after Mr. Hines crossed safe, and Mr. Raphael, Mr. M. Angelo, and Mr. Turner will have to take a seat near the door."

A reporter describing a game in that manner today would not be assigned to cover the next day's game. But it was in that style that games were recorded around the turn of the century. A baseball writer, covering a game at three o'clock in the afternoon, had until three o'clock in the morning to write his story. This enabled many to write what some journalists later referred to as "fabulous narratives." Writers were bent on influencing the readers with their imaginative use of the language in long, descriptive phrases. Space in newspapers was plentiful, and baseball writers frequently used two and three columns to describe a single game. It gave writers an opportunity to develop their own style in an effort to capture the imagination of the readers.

Nowhere was this more evident than in Chicago, where such writers as Sy Sanborn, Ring Lardner, Hugh Fullerton, and Charles Dryden were winning over readers with their often humorous accounts of baseball games. Lardner came out of South Bend, Indiana, and covered the Chicago Cubs for the *Inter-Ocean,* the *Examiner* and later the *Tribune.* Eventually he abandoned daily baseball writing and made his mark as an author of short stories, many with a baseball theme. *You Know Me Al* and "Alibi Ike" are two of his baseball classics.

Fullerton was considered the most remarkable forecaster of his day, and his predictions on the outcome of games were sought in every major league city. When he died at age seventy-two in 1946, he was hailed in his obituaries as "the game's original dopester." But for all the expertise and humor that he brought to his readers, Fullerton is best remembered in journalistic circles as the writer most responsible for exposing the Chicago White Sox for throwing the 1919 World Series.

Prior to the 1919 Series, the fearless forecaster had predicted an easy victory for the Sox against Cincinnati. But early in the Series Fullerton was convinced that the Sox were not giving it their best effort. In his summary of the Series after Chicago lost, Fullerton suggested as much. But he was not about to let go of it there. Fullerton went to New York, where he followed up leads that tied some of the White Sox to gamblers. The *New York Evening World* published a toned-down version of his theory, and Fullerton was criticized by members of his own craft. But his persistence continued until he convinced American League president Ban Johnson to investigate the matter. Using much of the information Fullerton supplied, Johnson brought the investigation to a head late in the 1920 season. The result was a trial in which eight players were found innocent. But the same eight were later banned from organized baseball for life by Judge Kenesaw Mountain Landis, the newly appointed commissioner of baseball. Fullerton's investigative reporting was responsible for the findings of the commissioner.

Fullerton was a baseball purist, and his Ten Commandments of Sports were widely published. They read:

1. *Thou shalt not quit.*
2. *Thou shalt not alibi.*
3. *Thou shalt not gloat over winning.*
4. *Thou shalt not sulk over losing.*
5. *Thou shalt not take unfair advantage.*
6. *Thou shalt not ask odds thou art not willing to give.*
7. *Thou shalt always be willing to give the benefit of doubt.*
8. *Thou shalt not underestimate an opponent or overestimate thyself.*
9. *Remember that the game is the thing and he who thinks otherwise is no true sportsman.*
10. *Honor the game thou playest; he who plays the game straight and hard wins even when he loses.*

It was common at the turn of the century for baseball writers to begin their stories with a few lines of verse. Grantland Rice, who came out of Nashville, where he had been sports editor of the *Tennessean,* to join the staff of the *Cleveland Plain Dealer,* was perhaps the most widely known writer in this style. His poetic jingles were read throughout the American League and many attempted to copy his style.

Rice did not remain long in Cleveland. He longed for the South and returned there. But then he returned North to New York, where his syndicated column appeared throughout the country. Rice actually was better known for his football writing than he was for his baseball work.

Besides Rice, another leading baseball writer of the early twentieth century who frequently began his stories with a few lines of verse was Franklin Pierce Adams, who wrote under the byline of "F.P.A." He wrote what is known as "Baseball's Sad Lexicon" during a New York Giants-Chicago Cubs series in 1908. Quoted to this day, it read in part:

Ruthlessly pricking our gonfalon bubble,
Making a Giant hit into a double,
Words that are weighty with nothing but trouble,
Tinker to Evers to Chance.

That verse, as much as their actual records on the field, is credited with leading to the induction of the Chicago Cubs' infield trio into the Hall of Fame.

Charles Dryden, born in 1857, moved about as much as any baseball writer in the late 1890s and into the 1900s. He covered the California League for the *San Francisco Examiner* and then moved to the *New York American* and on again to Philadelphia with the *North American.* But in 1905 he was offered what was then considered the highest salary paid a baseball writer and moved to the *Chicago Examiner.* The salary was reported to be $100 weekly.

It was in Chicago that Dryden gained fame with his nicknames for the baseball people he wrote about. He called Charles Comiskey, the White Sox owner, "the Old Roman". He termed the light-hitting White Sox the "Hitless Wonders." Chicago Cubs' manager Frank Chance was dubbed "the Peerless Leader." It was also Dryden who coined the phrase about the hapless Washington Senators: "Washington . . . first in war, first in peace and last in the American League."

Dryden was a charter member of the Baseball Writers Association of America (BBWAA), which was formed officially in 1908. It was an association born of necessity when baseball writing in the early years of the twentieth century was attracting some of the nation's outstanding young writers and baseball itself was dominating the sports pages. Only the baseball owners failed to recognize the importance of this feisty band of scribes. They were treated—or mistreated—as a necessary evil.

At the 1908 playoff game between the Chicago Cubs and the New York Giants at New York's Polo Grounds, Hugh Fullerton arrived to find actor Louis Mann in his seat. This was not uncommon. Giants manager John McGraw loved to hobnob with Broadway actors and often told them to sit in the press box. When Fullerton asked Mann to vacate the seat, Mann refused. No Giants official would order him to move. At first Fullerton attempted to write his story sitting on Mann's lap, but eventually he sat on a box in the aisle next to him and covered the entire game from that seat.

Baseball writers continued to suffer mistreatment during the Chicago Cubs-Detroit Tigers World Series that followed. The writers covering the Series were outraged at the treatment accorded them. In Chicago, out-of-town writers were placed in the back row of the grandstand. In

Detroit, the writers were compelled to climb a ladder to the roof of the first base pavilion, where they were forced to write in the rain and snow that hampered the Series. Finally, unwilling to endure these conditions another year, the writers decided to organize. At the request of Jack Ryder of Cincinnati and Henry Edwards of Cleveland, Joseph S. Jackson, sports editor of the *Detroit Free Press,* arranged a meeting room in the Hotel Ponchartrain on the morning of the final game. That was October 14, 1908. Present at that first meeting, the founding fathers of the Baseball Writers Association of America, were: Tim Murnane and Paul Shannon, Boston; Charles Hughes, Hugh Keough, Malcolm McLean, Hugh Fullerton, Bill Phelon, and Sy Sanborn, Chicago; Ed Bang and Henry Edwards, Cleveland; Jack Ryder and Charles Zuber, Cincinnati; J.W. McConaughy and Sid Mercer, New York; William Weart, Philadelphia; George Moreland, Pittsburgh; Joseph Jackson and Joseph Smith, Detroit; James Crusinberry, Hal Lanigan, W.G. Murphy, and J.B. Sheridan, St. Louis; and Ed Grillo, Washington.

Joseph Jackson was appointed temporary chairman and Sy Sanborn, secretary. Tim Murnane was appointed treasurer, and he passed the hat to collect $1 dues from each of the founding fathers.

A more formal meeting was held in New York in December 1908 at the annual winter meetings of the two leagues. Fullerton, Edwards, and Weart, who had been appointed in Detroit to draw up a constitution, listed four items as the main objective of the BBWAA. They were:

1. *To encourage a square deal in baseball.*
2. *To simplify the rules in scoring baseball games and promote uniformity in scoring.*
3. *To secure better facilities for reporting baseball games and better regulation of the scorers' boxes during both championship seasons and World Series at the parks of the American and National League Clubs, hereinafter to be designated the major leagues.*
4. *To bring together into a closer bond of friendship the writers of baseball throughout the United States and Canada.*

The organization was enthusiastically endorsed from the start by both leagues. Promise of full support was received by league presidents, who appointed the local representatives of chapters in each city to serve as custodians of the league press boxes.

Immediately conditions improved throughout baseball. No longer did writers have the problem of outsiders occupying seats in the press box. Interlopers were immediately escorted out by park security men upon orders of the local BBWAA representative. The writers had the backing of the league to police their own work area.

By 1910-11, the baseball writing fraternity was accepting into its ranks some of the bright young writers of that era—men who would go on to greater heights in the field of literature. Covering the Giants in New York that year were men like Grantland Rice, Damon Runyon, Heywood Broun, and Fred Lieb. Rice later became recognized as the dean of America's sportswriters; Runyon became the chronicler of Broadway night life and the characters who inhabited the Great White Way, while Broun went on to the editorial side of newspapers and founded the Newspaper Guild of America. Lieb was a prolific writer who was one of baseball's leading biographers.

Elsewhere in the country, other fine young writers were honing their skills covering baseball. Some of the greats who were regular beat writers in those days were Red Smith, Frank Graham, John Kieran, J. Roy Stockton, Warren Brown, John Carmichael, Shirley Povich, John Drebinger, and Tom Meany.

There was a coterie of writers in that era whose names were synonymous with baseball for the simple reason that they covered baseball from the first day of spring training until the final out of the World Series. A writer assigned to the Tigers or Cardinals or Pirates or any other club stayed with that team the entire season, traveled to the cities in each league, and made every road trip. Writers associated with one club were almost as well known as the players they wrote about.

Baseball coverage did not vary until after World War II. It was standard practice up to then for the writers on morning newspapers to wait until the end of the game and write on who won or lost, and how. The final score might not appear until well down into the story, but the reporter was writing up the details of the game. Writers for afternoon papers also often sat in the press box after the game and wrote their versions, with considerable editorial opinion and second-guessing. Talking to ballplayers after the game was not considered a necessity. Occasionally, but not always, writers did visit the clubhouses after games for some conversation and verification with ballplayers.

The style of writing changed after World War II. The need to know was of primary importance, and reporters for afternoon papers made it a habit to get down to the clubhouse after a game for what was then known as "the second-day angle." The afternoon papers of the next day had to offer the readers something they had not learned in their morning paper.

But starting in 1946 and in the years that followed, a change in the style of covering a baseball game was evident—especially in New York. No longer did the writers on afternoon papers have the ballplayers to themselves after a game. Dick Young was an enterprising young baseball writer for the *New York Daily News,* a morning newspaper. Because of the multiple editions of his newspaper, he had the time to visit the clubhouse and "pick up quotes" or find out why certain plays had occurred.

Young changed the style of baseball reporting with his hustle, and ever since he arrived, the work of the morning newspaper reporter has not been the same. No beat reporter nowadays would dare turn in a story unless it had clubhouse quotes. Editors demand it.

Along with the enterprise of Dick Young came radio and the television age. Fans were now able to listen to and watch games at home. What they wanted in their papers the next day was inside stuff from the players and managers. For reporters working night games with deadlines approaching, the job of writing baseball was no longer the sinecure it had been in the first four decades of the century.

Picture the baseball writer of the 1930s. All games started around 3 PM. There was no need for a pregame story, since most newspapers did not go to press until around midnight. A baseball writer in that era was finished working around 6 or 7 PM and was free again until game time the next day.

The baseball beat writer's job was always considered the glamour assignment on any sports staff. Baseball writers were envied for what was considered an easy lifestyle: spring training in some warm climate around the middle of February and then a ballgame every afternoon for six months followed by the World Series. From mid-October until mid-February, the baseball writer had a relative vacation, covering only signings, trades, and trivial matters.

Today's baseball writer, what with virtually every game being played at night and early editions at all papers, finds himself working around the clock. The average writer covering baseball today, especially for a morning newspaper, will find himself writing three or four stories in a single day. He also works year-round, covering labor-management issues.

Night games and travel have also made it difficult for the modern-day writer. Before plane travel, all clubs moved from city to city by train, and the writers traveled with them. Trains left around midnight and arrived early the next morning in the team's next city. At least there was a night of rest and time to fraternize with the ballplayers. Today, teams fly out right after a game, and writers find it impossible to catch the team plane. They most often travel alone.

The result is that fewer writers remain on the baseball beat for any length of time. The travel, the long hours, and the night games have made it an arduous task. Before the age of television, it was quite common for a writer to remain on the beat for twenty to thirty years. Today, a writer feels "burned out" after just a few years.

Despite the changes in baseball writing, the BBWAA retains the prestige it earned shortly after being founded in 1908. Much of this is due to the organization's annual awards and its responsibility for voting on the Hall of Fame.

The major awards the BBWAA votes on each year are the Most Valuable Player, the Cy Young Award, the Rookie of the Year, the Manager of the Year, and the Hall of Fame, since the Cooperstown shrine's creation in 1936. (For a detailed discussion and the annual balloting for these awards, see Bill Deane's essay in this volume.)

Of all the responsibilities of the Baseball Writers Association, none is taken more seriously than voting for the Hall of Fame. The idea for a baseball Hall of Fame was first discussed in 1935 to celebrate the hundredth anniversary of baseball in 1939. The National Baseball Centennial Commission was formed. Ford Frick, then the National League president, was the moving force behind the creation of the Hall of Fame and the decision to name Cooperstown as the site for the museum. That same year, the Baseball Writers Association was asked by the Commission to vote for players to be elected to the Hall of Fame and inducted officially when the Hall opened in 1939.

The BBWAA has been charged with that responsibility ever since. Another group, known as the Veterans Committee, also votes on players, former executives, managers, and umpires.

Baseball, especially in recent years, has been the most written-about sport in America. No longer is it a sport covered solely by the beat writers for newspapers. It is a game that captures the imagination of authors, a fact born out by the Hall of Fame Library. By the middle of 1990, the library contained approximately 25,000 books about baseball.

By the end of 1990 the library was unable to handle the volume of books and magazine and newspaper articles that were being written about the game. Under the directorship of Hall of Fame Chairman Edward Stack, an expansion to the library was undertaken. The completely refurbished library opened late in 1993 and included over 30,000 books. In addition, the written words of the game on file at the library include copies of the *New York Clipper* from the 1850s, *Sporting Life,* and *The Sporting News.*

So important have the contributions of the Baseball Writers Association of America been to the Hall of Fame that in 1962, the Hall decided to honor the outstanding writers with an award and a place of honor in the library. The award was named in honor of J. G. Taylor Spink, former publisher of *The Sporting News.* Since 1962, over 40 writers have had their names enshrined in the writers' wing of the Hall, among them Damon Runyon, Ring Lardner, Grantland Rice, and Dick Young.

Leonard Koppett, the 1993 honoree, noted in his Cooperstown acceptance speech: "The daily baseball writer has played an indispensable role in the creation, growth and maintenance of baseball's popularity. Its commercial success, as well as its place in American culture, have been based on daily newspaper accounts, from Henry B. Chadwick down through Red Smith.

"Even today, when radio and television have surpassed newspapers in impact, it is the daily baseball coverage from which all other media get their information about what they decide to emphasize. And even the call-in talk shows, which set so much of the news agenda, exist only because callers form opinions from what they read about that they cannot see."

One major change in baseball writing and reporting in the 1970s was the need for each paper to have a reporter focus on the labor angle in the game. Writers like Murray Chass of the *New York Times* and Jerome Holtzman of the *Chicago Tribune* devoted much of their attention to reporting the struggles between the Players Association and the club owners. Writing about the labor front has become a full-time job and both men, former beat writers, now concentrate almost exclusively on these off-the-field activities.

Another innovation in baseball writing in the 1970s was the advent of the "notes and quotes" columns which began appearing in Sunday newspapers in most major league cities. These columns began with beat writers picking up notes and gossip during the week and saving them all for a juicy Sunday column of tidbits. They became as popular as the Broadway gossip columns and soon every paper of any size was running a "notes and quotes" feature. Dick Young of the *New York Daily News* was one of the early innovators of this style of reporting with his popular "Clubhouse Confidential." Peter Gammons of the *Boston Globe* soon concentrated on collecting gossip from other writers around the leagues. The *Globe* devotes an entire page to Gammons's writings.

Baseball writers who became tired of the daily beat found a way in the 1990s to keep writing baseball. They convinced editors that a "National Baseball Writer" was needed. These writers spend their time writing about baseball events of national interest such as a big series between two contending teams, a player on a hitting streak about to set a record, a pitcher with a scoreless streak going . . . anything that is of national interest aside from the doings of the local club. Today, virtually every newspaper had a beat writer covering that city's club plus a national baseball writer focusing on the overall baseball scene.

Baseball is a sport that has inspired political columnists like George Will and Pulitzer Prize-winning authors such as James Michener and David Halberstam to publish books about the game. No sport in America is covered more extensively or comprehensively than baseball. It all begins with the game and the beat writers who cover it.

## CHAPTER 24

Phantom Ballplayers

Clifford S. Kachline

Garbage in, garbage out is an expression that gained currency with the advent of the computer age. The logic behind the catch phrase, however, prevailed long before the electronic marvels came into being. Baseball, in fact, has had its own version of the maxim almost since the game's earliest days, largely as a consequence of recordkeepers who sometimes unwittingly entered erroneous data into the record books.

Numerous examples of the garbage in, garbage out principle have been discovered in baseball's statistical archives through the years. But statistics aren't the only area where the phenomenon has shown up. Another involves what researchers of the sport refer to as "phantoms"—players credited with having performed in the major leagues but who in reality never did appear in a big league game.

Phantoms are hardly a recent phenomenon. They have existed almost as long as boxscores have been published. Some were the product of misunderstandings by—or misinformation given to—official scorers or the parties who compiled the boxscores. A few of these crept into the leagues' official records. Others were created by mistakes on the part of telegraph operators or by typographical errors and appeared only in newspaper boxscores.

Little if any attention was paid to the situation until the 1950s. The original edition of The Official Encyclopedia of Baseball, published by A. S. Barnes and Co. in 1951, provided fans for the first time with a supposedly complete alphabetical tabulation of every man who ever played in the majors, together with his basic yearly big league stats. The publication stimulated the interest of the sport's researchers. When editors Hy Turkin and S. C. Thompson deleted the names of some players—most of whom were previously shown as having a one-game career—from subsequent revised editions, the matter of phantoms started to become a source of fascination.

Who really were the "impostors" that were listed in earlier editions? What had prompted the editors to include them in the first place? And what evidence had been found to prove conclusively that they never played in the big leagues?

The introduction of The Baseball Encyclopedia by the Macmillan Publishing Company in 1969 focused additional attention on the subject. In compiling data for that publication, David Neft and his crew of Information Concepts, Inc. researchers continued the process of purging phantoms from the records. Since then, further investigation by Neft, Pete Palmer, Bill Haber, Al Kermisch, and others has led to the expunging of several more players.

In many instances confirming the status of a phantom was a complicated chore. The task sometimes was made more difficult because the player's name was included in the official league statistics. In other cases, especially those involving nineteenth-century performers, the fact that official league records no longer exist compounded the problem because it made it impossible to determine who was credited by the official scorer and/or league statistician with appearing in the game or games in question. (The American League's official game-by-game player sheets of 1901–1904 reportedly were destroyed by fire decades ago, while the official National League data also vanished for the pre-1902 period except for the 1899 season.)

An example of a phantom who appears in the league records is Albert W. Olsen. For thirty-five years he was carried in the Encyclopedias and shown as participating in one game—as a pinch hitter—for the Boston Red Sox in 1943. Olsen did train with the Red Sox that spring, but he was shipped to San Diego of the Pacific Coast League before opening day and spent the entire season in the minors. In addition, it was his exploits as a lefthanded pitcher, not as a hitter, that originally attracted the Red Sox.

Nevertheless, American League records list Olsen as playing for Boston in a game in Chicago on May 16, 1943. Newspaper boxscores credited him with drawing a walk while batting for pitcher Dick Newsome and subsequently stealing a base. However, research has confirmed that the Red Sox pinch-hitter on that occasion definitely was not Olsen. Instead, it may have been outfielder Leon Culberson, who had just been called up from Louisville of the American Association, or possibly another Boston rookie outfielder, Johnny Lazor.

And why is there still uncertainty as to who the pinch-hitter really was? How could this mistake have occurred? First off, the exchange of roster data among major league teams during that period was quite limited. Consequently scorecards often contained the same player names and uniform numbers for the visiting team, especially early in the season, as the team listed in spring training. For example, the scorecard for a Red Sox–Senators game in Washington approximately a week before the incident in question showed Olsen on Boston's roster with uniform number 14, even though he was pitching for San Diego. Second, it's unlikely there were phone lines from the pressbox to the dugouts in those days, and in the absence of being able to call down to check on the identity of a player, the media and official scorers relied on outdated roster information.

Several years ago researchers felt they had cleared up the Olsen mystery upon discovering that one Boston newspaper identified the pinch-hitter as "Culbeson." This seemed to settle the matter. After all, Culberson had joined the team that day and was installed as the Red Sox' leadoff batter in the second half of the afternoon doubleheader, collecting a single and triple in five at-bats. But the mystery was revived when Ed Walton, a Red Sox historian, discussed the situation with Culberson at a Red Sox Old Timers affair in 1986. According to Walton, Culberson contended he did not pinch-hit in the twin-bill opener, but rather made his debut in the second game. He added that manager Joe Cronin said he wanted the young newcomer to sit beside him (Cronin) through the first game to get a feel of the big leagues. However, the records reveal Cronin played third base during the entire first game. All of which raises the questions: Was Culberson's memory playing tricks on him and was he indeed the pinch-hitter listed as Olsen? Or was it Lazor, who is shown as wearing uniform number 14 later in the year but who was batting a mere .136 (3 for 22) at the time? Because the passage of time makes memories hazy and also because the incident was of no particular significance, the mystery may never be solved.

A manager's pique led to a phantom known as J. A. Costello getting into the early *Encyclopedias*. Curiously, the incident also took place in Chicago and likewise involved a player's big league debut. It occurred in the morning half of a holiday bill between Cleveland and the White Sox on July 4, 1912. Late in the contest, Indians' Manager Harry Davis, still burning over an umpire's decision, sent the newcomer into the game to replace center fielder Joe Birmingham and instructed him to announce himself to umpire Gene Hart as "Costello."

In reality, the player was Kenneth Nash, who had only recently joined Cleveland from Boston University law school. He subsequently appeared in ten additional games with Cleveland that season under his correct surname, mostly as a shortstop, and then played with the St. Louis Cardinals for part of 1914. Nash later became a prominent state representative, state senator, and judge in his home state of Massachusetts.

The 1903 official National League records contain a phantom who long baffled researchers. Among the Pittsburgh player sheets is one headed "George Gray" with entries for two games as an outfielder—on May 28 and May 31. Four years earlier the Pirates had a pitcher named George "Chummy" Gray, and it's possible the scorer or league statistician remembered him while filling in the player's first name. When the first *Official Encyclopedia* appeared in 1951, the player was identified as William (rather than George) Gray, a native of Pittsburgh.

It turns out that the two George (or William) Gray entries properly belonged to not one, but two different players. The Pirates' left fielder in the May 28 game really was Romer Carl "Reddy" Grey, younger brother of novelist Zane Grey. He had been obtained on loan from the Worcester club of the Eastern League to fill in that afternoon in the final game of a series in Boston.

On the other hand, while boxscores in Cincinnati newspapers listed the Pittsburgh left fielder for the May 31 game in Cincinnati as "Gray," the player actually was Ernest Diehl, a Cincinnati sandlotter who had been re-cruited by the injury-riddled Pirates. The game represented Diehl's first appearance in the major leagues and his only game that season, but he played 12 more games with Pittsburgh the following year. It should be noted that ever since the original Turkin/Thompson tome, the *Encyclopedias* have credited Diehl with playing one game with Pittsburgh in 1903, but until recent years they also carried William Gray with two games.

A majority of baseball's phantoms were the product of typographical errors—instances where a linotypist or a typesetter mistakenly included one or more incorrect letters in a name, or where a printer inserted a correction line in the wrong place. In compiling data for the *Encyclopedias,* the authors/researchers relied not only on the so-called official league records but also combed boxscores published in *The Sporting News, Sporting Life, The New York Clipper,* and various local newspapers. In the process they occasionally came upon what appeared to be a previously unlisted "new" player who, in the final analysis, proved to be someone else. Even today, misspellings of this type in newspapers can cause great befuddlement.

A classic illustration of a phantom who was created by a typographical error is the player carried in the early *Encyclopedias* as John P. Morgan. He was listed as appearing in one game as a third baseman with the Philadelphia Athletics in 1916. A study of A's boxscores for the season disclosed the source of the mix-up: It was *The Sporting News*'s boxscore of the August 3 game at Cleveland. (*Sporting Life* had dropped boxscores by this time.) The Philadelphia half of *TSN*'s box has "Morgan, 2b," while on the same line in Cleveland's half is "Gandil, 1b."

Careful examination reveals the Morgan/Gandil type slug was a correction line that the printer inserted in the wrong place. It was intended for the Washington-at-Cleveland boxscore of the previous day (August 2) in which the Senators' second baseman, Harry Morgan, appeared on the same line as Chick Gandil and contained the identical AB-H-PO-A-E figures given for each player in the misaligned August 2 line.

This explanation may well leave you, the reader, with several questions, to wit: (1) Who did play third for the A's that day, and was he properly credited in the official records? (2) Why did the *Encyclopedia* compilers show Morgan as a third baseman instead of a second baseman? (3) How did they come up with "John P." for the impostor's name?

The answers are: (1) Lee McElwee and, yes, he was credited with this game; (2) because veteran Nap Lajoie played the entire game at his usual second base position for the A's, the researcher who made this "discovery" apparently assumed it should have read "Morgan, 3b" rather than "2b"; (3) an infielder named John P. Morgan was active in the minor leagues that season, and the *Encyclopedia* editors probably figured the A's had given him a trial. Numerous other phantoms were similarly tagged with the first names of then-current minor leaguers.

Typos involving misspelled names led to a number of one-game phantoms. Two examples will serve to demonstrate the point. They are John H. Carlock (1912, Cleveland) and a player listed simply as Deniens (no first name given) with the 1914 Chicago Federals. *Sporting Life* had "Carlock, ph" for Cleveland in an August 24, 1912, game at Boston, but Cleveland newspapers and *The Sporting News* reported the pinch-hitter was Fred Carisch, a reserve catcher with the Indians. Official AL records also credit Carisch with that appearance. "Deniens, c" turned out to be Clem Clemens, a catcher in 13 games with the 1914 ChiFeds. One can readily visualize how handwritten names "Carisch" and "Clemens" could have been misinterpreted by a telegrapher or linotypist for "Carlock" and "Deniens."

The origins of some other phantoms are more mysterious. Take the case of Lou Proctor. The *Encyclopedias* credited him with one appearance with the 1912 St. Louis Browns. *The Sporting News* and *Sporting Life,* which may have obtained their boxscores from the same source, show "Proctor, ph" and "Procter, pi," respectively, in a May 13 game at Boston. However, a Boston newspaper referred to the pinch hitter as Albert "Pete" Compton, a catcher with the Browns that season (whose real first name was, of all things, Anna). While AL records contain no reference to Proctor, they unfortunately also fail to include the May 13 appearance among Compton's 100 games. Rumor has it that Proctor was a prankish Western Union telegrapher who inserted his own name as a pinch hitter.

The presence on one team of two players with the same or an almost similar surname can lead to problems. The Washington Senators figured in three such mixups. Ironically, in one instance research by Kermisch has established that a player long labeled a phantom was, in fact, the real McCoy. The player in question was Charles C. Conway. In 1911 the Senators had both Conway, a rookie outfielder up from Youngstown (Ohio-Pennsylvania League), and William "Wid" Conroy, veteran infielder-outfielder, on their spring roster. When the season began, Conroy was idled by a stone bruise of the foot. Meantime, Conway appeared in two games during opening week, finishing up in right field on April 15 and starting at that position three days later, before the Senators returned him to Youngstown. Unfortunately, *Sporting Life* and *The Sporting News* each showed "Conroy" as the replacement in the first contest, but both had "Conway, rf" in their April 18 boxscore. Although the early *Encyclopedias* listed Conway and credited him with playing two games, the Macmillan compilers dropped his name 20 years ago on the erroneous premise that it was the veteran Conroy who participated in the April 15-18 games. Actually, Conway didn't make the first of his 106 appearances that year until April 27.

An equally confusing puzzle centered on a 1914 Washington pitcher known as Barron or Barton. The early *Encyclopedias* carried both John J. Barron (later changed to Frank John Barron) and Carroll R. "Buck" Barton and credited each with pitching in one game for the '14 Senators. Actually only one pitcher was involved (and just one appearance), but which pitcher was it? Player contract data of the period reveal that Washington signed Carroll R. Barton in 1913 and retained rights to him while he pitched for Newport News (Virginia League) that season and again in 1914. During the same two years John J. Barron was pitching in the New England League. To complicate matters further, Washington signed Frank J. Barron in 1914 and shipped him to Newport News, where he became a teammate of Barton. While Barron posted a dismal 1-3 record, Barton was a 16-game winner.

So who was the 1914 Washington pitcher? The American League player records contain an entry headed "Barron" with data for an August 18 game, and boxscores of the contest likewise have "Barron" pitching one inning—the ninth—for the Senators against the visiting St. Louis Browns. The player's correct identity was confirmed when, shortly before his death in 1964, Frank Barron disclosed in an interview that while still studying for his law degree at West Virginia University he was signed by Clark Griffith in 1914, was assigned to Newport News and later pitched one inning for Washington before resuming his law studies.

The third Washington mix-up relates to a 1944 player identified in the *Encyclopedias* as Armando Viera Valdes. Official AL records contain a sheet for Armand (without the final "o") Valdes and note that he made a pinch-hitting appearance for the Senators in a May 3 game at Boston, but Richard Topp's research has disclosed that the pinch hitter was Rogelio "Roy" Valdes, a fellow Cuban but no relative of Armando.

With many major leaguers lost to military service in 1944, scout Joe Cambria lined up several Cubans to fill voids on the Senators' roster. Early in the year he signed an outfielder who was listed in the 1944 *American League Red Book* as Armand (without the "o") Valdes. Several weeks thereafter—too late for inclusion in the *Red Book*—Cambria signed Rogelio Valdes, a catcher. Both spent the early weeks of the season with Washington (each was later optioned to Williamsport of the Eastern League), and presumably the official scorer and/or league statistician picked up the incorrect first name from the Senator roster in the *AL Red Book*.

As in the case of Charles Conway, another player once regarded as a phantom has turned out to be a legitimate athlete after all. The Turkin-Thompson tomes listed him as William Krouse, a second baseman in one game with Cincinnati in 1901. Compilers of the Macmillan encyclopedia decided he was an imposter and dropped him, crediting his appearance to Bill Fox, the Reds' regular keystoner. However, research has revealed that the "Krouse, 2b" for Cincinnati in the July 27, 1901 game at Chicago was a recently-released minor leaguer whose correct name was Charles "Famous" Krause. Krause, who was on his way home to Detroit at the time, was given a chance with the Reds because Fox was sidelined with a split finger, but the "famous" newcomer performed so poorly that, not only was his name misspelled in the record, he was dumped after that one appearance.

Recent research has revealed that one player long listed as a phantom—Ivan Bigler, who was shown in one boxscore at first base with the 1917 St. Louis Browns when George Sisler actually played there that day—really did make an appearance with the Browns as a pinch runner on May 6 that season, and thus he's been restored to the all-time list of major leaguers.

The accompanying table lists the phantoms who have been eliminated from the all-time roster of major league players since the first Turkin/Thompson *Official Encyclopedia* of 1951. In the absence of an official clearinghouse for such data, no claim is made that the list is complete. Where it is available, brief information on the reason for the deletion of the player is given. Unfortunately, documentation by Turkin/Thompson and the ICI group that compiled the 1969 *Encyclopedia* disappeared years ago.

With today's sophisticated technology and record-keeping procedures, the margin for error in the identification of players—and in the official statistics—has been reduced considerably. Still, a slipup that occurred in the 1984 official American League averages (Alvaro Espinoza was omitted completely, even though he appeared in one game with Minnesota) emphasizes that mistakes still are possible.

A factor that poses the potential for error is the increasing frequency in recent years of teams having two or more players with an identical surname—and who often perform at the same position. In 1992 and 1993, for instance, the Los Angeles pitching staff included brothers Ramon and Pedro J. Martinez as well as Kip and Kevin Gross, who are not related. Meantime, San Diego unveiled pitcher Pedro A. Martinez in '93. Following that season, the Dodgers swapped Pedro J. Martinez to Montreal, where he succeeded another Martinez—Dennis—on the Expos' pitching staff when the latter signed with Cleveland as a free agent. But lo and behold, the situation was further muddied in 1994 when San Diego added a second pitching Martinez—Jose. This meant there were five Martinezes pitching in the majors at the same time, including Pedro J. with Montreal and Pedro A. with San Diego.

Besides the Dodgers, four other teams had a pair of pitchers of the same surname in 1993. They were: Houston—Todd and Doug Jones; Philadelphia— Mitch and Mike Williams; Cleveland—Matt and Curt Young; and San Diego—Gene and Greg W. Harris (not to be confused with Boston pitcher Greg A. Harris). In addition, Philadelphia also had Tommy Greene and Tyler Green on its staff at one point.

To add to the confusion, the Phillies swapped relief ace Mitch Williams to Houston after the '93 World Series, and he teamed on the Astros' mound corps briefly in 1994 with Brian Williams. The '94 season also found several other teams fielding players with the identical surname who played the same position. The most confusing situation involved Baltimore. At one time or another the Orioles had three outfielders named Smith—Lonnie, Mark, and Dwight—as well as relief ace Lee Smith. An early-season Atlanta-Cincinnati trade sent Roberto Kelly to the Braves, where he joined Mike Kelly, likewise an outfielder, while Deion Sanders went to the Reds and teamed in the outfield with Reggie Sanders. Other 1993-94 teammates sharing a common surname and position included Bernie and Gerald Williams, outfielders with the New York Yankees, and infielders Edgar and Tino Martinez of Seattle, who normally manned third base and first base, respectively, but on occasion in the past performed at the opposite corner.

Couple these potential mixups with the typographical errors that still show up in newspaper boxscores, and you can see that the days of *"garbage in, garbage out"* are likely to continue.

Tabulation of Phantoms

Allen, Robert. 1919 Philadelphia AL, 9 games as OF. Pseudonym used by Alvah C. "Rowdy" Elliott, long-time minor leaguer.

Baldwin,——. 1907 Boston NL, 1 game as C. One of James C. Ball's 10 games.

Barton, Carroll R. 1914 Washington AL, 1 game as P. Same as game credited to Frank J. Barron.

Boylan,——. 1887 Philadelphia NL, 1 game as 2B. One of Charles J. Bastian's 60 games.

Carlock, John H. 1912 Cleveland AL, 1 game as PH. Typographical error; one of Frederick B. Carisch's 25 games.

Christman, H. B. 1888 Kansas City AA, 1 game as C. Documentation behind deletion no longer available.

Costello, J. A. 1912 Cleveland AL, 1 game as OF. One of 11 games played by Kenneth L. Nash, who used pseudonym in debut.

Davis, Thomas J. 1890 Cleveland NL, 1 game as OF. One of George Stacey Davis' 136 games.

Davis,——. 1903 Chicago NL, 1 game as OF. Documentation behind deletion no longer available.

Deniens,——. 1914 Chicago FL, 1 game as C. Typographical error; one of Clement L. Clemens' 13 games.

Drennan, K. John. 1904 Detroit AL, 1 game as 1B. Typographical error; one of William "Wild Bill" Donovan's 46 games.

Dresser, Edward. 1898 Brooklyn NL, 1 game as SS. Typographical error; one of Jack Dunn's 51 games.

Dugan, E. 1884 Kansas City UA, 3 games as OF. Same player as William H. Dugan, who played 9 games with Richmond AA the same year.

Gray, William. 1903 Pittsburgh NL, 2 games as OF. One game belongs to Romer C. Grey; other game belongs to Ernest G. Diehl.

Kerns, Daniel P. 1920 Philadelphia AL, 1 game as PH. Pseudonym used by Edward "Ted" Kearns, later a 1B with 1924–25 Chicago NL.

King, Frederick. 1901 Milwaukee AL, 1 game as C. Game belongs to John A. Butler, later with St. Louis and Brooklyn NL, who used pseudonym in debut.

Lane,——. 1901 Boston NL, 1 game as 3B. Typographical error; one of Bobby Lowe's 129 games.

Mares,——. 1894 Louisville NL, 1 games as OF. Documentation behind deletion no longer available.

McCauley, William. 1884 St. Louis AA, 1 game as C. Game belongs to James A. McCauley, who also played in 1885–1886.

Meddlebrook,——. 1884 Baltimore UA, 1 game as OF. Documentation behind deletion no longer available.

Merson,——. 1914 Brooklyn FL, 1 game as PH. Typographical error; one of George J. Anderson's 98 games.

Miller, Bert. 1897 Philadelphia NL, 3 games as 2B. Games belong to Frank A. Miller, formerly listed as Frederick Miller, who also played one game each with Washington NL and St. Louis NL in 1892.

Miller, Henry D. 1892 Chicago NL, 4 games as P. Games belong to Harry DeMiller, who was erroneously listed for 1 game as 3B with 1892 St. Louis NL.

Moore, Guy W. 1922 St. Louis NL, 1 game as OF. Documentation behind deletion no longer available.

Morgan, John P. 1916 Philadelphia AL, 1 game as 3B. Typographical error; one of Leland S. McElwee's 54 games.

Olsen, Albert W. 1943 Boston AL, 1 game as PH. Appearance apparently belongs to either Leon Culberson or Johnny Lazor.

Pratt, Thomas J. 1884 Baltimore AA, 1 game as OF. Documentation behind deletion no longer available.

Proctor, Lou. 1912 St. Louis AL, 1 game as PH. Game belongs to Anna S. "Pete" Compton, who played in 103 games that season.

Ritchie,——. 1910 St. Louis NL, 1 game as PH. Documentation behind deletion no longer available.

Schauer,——. 1890 Columbus AA, 1 game as 1B. Documentation behind deletion no longer available.

Seymour, Thomas. 1882 Pittsburgh AA, 1 game as P. Player's correct name was Jacob Semer.

Sheehan, Timothy. 1884 Washington UA, 1 game as OF. One of seven games belonging to player known as John A. Ryan, whose real name was Daniel Sheehan.

Smith, Charles H. "Pacer." 1877 Chicago/Cincinnati NL, 34 games as 2B-OF-C. Record belongs to Harry W. Smith, who also played 1 game with 1889 Louisville AA.

Smith, E. J. 1890 Buffalo PL, 1 game as 1B. One of John Irwin's 77 games.

Strands, Lewis. 1915 Chicago FL, 1 game as 2B. One of John J. Farrell's 70 games.

Thayer, Edward L. 1876 New York NL, 1 game as 2B. Player's correct name was George T. Fair.

Turbot,——. 1902 St. Louis NL, 1 game as OF. Documentation behind deletion no longer available.

Valdes, Armando V. 1944 Washington AL, 1 game as PH. Game belongs to a different player, Rogelio "Roy" Valdes.

Young, David. 1895 St. Louis NL, 1 game as 3B. Documentation behind deletion no longer available.

## CHAPTER 25

Casey at the Bat:
A Ballad of the Republic

Donald Hall

A century ago, on June 3, 1888, a twenty-five-year-old Harvard graduate, one-poem poet Ernest Lawrence Thayer, published "Casey at the Bat" in the pages of the San Francisco *Examiner*. I suppose it's the most popular poem in our country's history, if not exactly in its literature. Martin Gardner collected twenty-five sequels and parodies to print in his prodigy of scholarship, *The Annotated Casey at the Bat* (1967; rev. 1984). Will the next Casey bat clean-up in a St. Petersburg Over-Ninety Softball League? Perhaps, instead, we will hear of a transparent Casey on an Elysian diamond, shade swinging the shadow of a bat while wraith pitcher uncoils phantom ball—or spheroid, I should say.

The author of this people's poem was raised in Worcester, Massachusetts: gentleman and scholar, son of a mill owner. At Harvard he combined scholastic and social eminence, not always feasible on the banks of the Charles. A bright student of William James in philosophy, he graduated magna cum laude and delivered the Ivy Oration at graduation. On the other hand, he was editor of the *Lampoon*, for which traditional requirements are more social than literary; he belonged to Fly, a club of decent majesty. It is perhaps not coincidence, considering Victorian Boston's social prejudices, that Thayer's vainglorious mock hero carries an Irish name.

After his lofty graduation, Thayer drifted about in Europe. One of his Harvard acquaintances had been young William Randolph Hearst, business manager of the *Lampoon*, expelled from Harvard for various pranks while Thayer was pulling a magna. The disgraced young Hearst was rewarded by his father with editorship of the San Francisco *Examiner*, where he offered Thayer work as humorous columnist. By the time "Casey" appeared, Thayer had left California to return to Worcester, where he later managed a mill for his father and studied philosophy in his spare time.

He received five dollars for "Casey" and never claimed reward for its hundreds of further printings. By all accounts, "Casey's" author found his notoriety problematic. As with all famous nineteenth-century recitation pieces— "The Night Before Christmas," "Backward Turn Backward O Time in Thy Flight"—other poets claimed authorship, which annoyed Thayer first because he *did* write it, and second because he wasn't especially proud of it. There was the additional annoyance that old ballplayers

continually asserted themselves the *original* Casey of the ballad: Thayer insisted that he made the poem up. The author of "Casey at the Bat" died in Santa Barbara in 1940 without ever doing another notable thing.

The poem's biography is richer than the poet's: At first "Casey" blushed unseen, wasting its sweetness on the desert air, until an accident blossomed it into eminence. In New York, DeWolf Hopper, a young star of comic opera, was acting in *Prince Methusalem*. On August 15, 1888, management invited players from the New York Giants and the Chicago White Stockings to attend a performance, and Hopper gave thought to finding a special bit that he might perform in the ballplayers' honor. His friend the novelist Archibald Clavering Gunter, recently returned from San Francisco, showed him a clipping from the San Francisco *Examiner*.

In Hopper's autobiography, he noted that when "[I] dropped my voice to B-flat, below low C, at the 'multitude was awed,' I remember seeing Buck Ewing's gallant mustachios give a single nervous twitch." Apparently Hopper's recitation left everyone in the house twitching with joy, and not only the Giants' hirsute catcher. For the rest of his life, Hopper repeated his performance by demand, no matter what part he sang or played, doomed to recite the poem (five minutes and forty seconds) an estimated ten thousand times before his death in 1935. As word spread from Broadway, the poem was reprinted in newspapers across the country, clipped out, memorized, and performed for the millions who would never hear De Wolf Hopper. Eventually the ballad was set to music, made into silent movies, and animated into cartoons; radio broadcast it, there were recordings by Hopper and others, and William Schuman wrote an opera called *The Mighty Casey* [premiere 1953].

When he first recited the poem, Hopper had no notion who had written it. Thayer had signed it "Phin.," abbreviating his college nickname of Phinny. Editors reprinted the poem anonymously or made up a name that sounded reasonable. When Hopper played Worcester early in the 1890s, he met the retiring Thayer—and poet recited poem for actor, as Hopper later reported, without a trace of elocutionary ability.

There are things in any society that *we always knew*. We do not remember when we first heard about Ground Hog Day or Thirty Days Hath September. Who remembers first hearing "Casey at the Bat"? Although I cannot remember my original exposure, I remember many splendid renditions from early in my life by the great ham actor of my childhood. My New Hampshire grandfather, Wesley Wells, was locally renowned for his powers of recitation—for speaking pieces, as we called it. He farmed bad soil in central New Hampshire: eight Holsteins, fifty sheep, a hundred chickens. In the tie-up for milking, morning and night, he leaned his bald head into warm Holstein ribs and recited poems with me for audience; he kept time as his hands pulled blue milk from long teats. When he got to the best part, he let go the nozzles, leaned back in his milking chair, spread his arms wide and opened his mouth in a great O, the taught gestures of elocution. He spellbound me as he set the line out on the warm cowy air: "But there is no joy in Mudville—mighty Casey has struck out!" The old barn (with its whitewash over rough boards, with its spider webs and straw, with its patched harness and homemade ladders and pitchforks shiny from decades of hand labor) paused in its shadowy hugeness and applauded again the ringing failure of the hero.

If he had not recited it for me lately, I reminded him. He recited a hundred other poems also, a few from Whittier and Longfellow, but mostly from newspapers by poets without names. I don't suppose he knew "Ernest Lawrence Thayer" or the history of the poem, but "Casey" itself was as solid as the rocks of his fields. The word that left Broadway and traveled was: *This poem is good to say out loud*. Earlier, the same news traveled about Edgar Allan Poe's "The Raven" and Bret Harte's "The Heathen Chinee." Public schooling once consisted largely of group memorization and recitation. The New England Primer taught theology and the alphabet together: "In Adam's fall / We sinnèd all" through "Zacchaeus he / Did climb a tree / His Lord to see." Less obviously the Primer instilled pleasures of rhyme and oral performance. When we decided fifty and sixty years ago that rote memorization was bad teaching, we threw out not only the multiplication table but also "Barbara Frietchie." Recitation of verse was turned over to experts.

Earlier, for two hundred years at least, recitation and performance took center stage in the one-room schools; but it did not end there. At schools, recitation as performance—not merely to retain information—climbed toward competitive speaking, elimination and reward on Prize Speaking Day, when the athletes of elocution recited in contest before judges. The same athletes did not stop when school stopped, and recitation exfoliated into the adult world as a major form of entertainment. Hamlets and cities alike formed clubs meeting weekly for mutual entertainment that variously included singing, playing the violin and the piano, recitation, and political debate. In the country towns and villages, which couldn't afford to hire Mr. Hopper to entertain them (nor earlier Mr. Emerson to instruct and inspire them), citizens made their own Lyceums and Chautauquas. In my grandfather's South Danbury, New Hampshire, young people founded the South Danbury Debating and Oratorical Society. Twice a month they met for programs that began with musical offerings and recitations, paused for coffee and doughnuts, and concluded with a political debate. "Resolved:

That the United States should Cease from Territorial Expansion."

While recitation thrived, the recitable poem became a way of entertaining ideas and each other, of exposing or exercising public concerns. Poetry in the United States was briefly a public art. But after the Great War came cars, radios, and John Dewey; recitation departed, and poets have been blamed ever since for losing their audience. The blame is unfair, because the connection between poetry and a mass audience was brief, nor did it work for all poetry. John Donne never had a great audience; neither did George Herbert nor Andrew Marvell, nor in America Walt Whitman or Emily Dickinson. These poets made poems with a fineness of language that required sophisticated reading.

All the same, *some* nineteenth-century poets wrote poems both popular and fine—without being as popular as baseball or as fine as Gerard Manley Hopkins. This moment was the fragile age of elocution. Many poets turned in one direction to talk to the people, and in another to talk to the ages. Longfellow's best work—the *Divine Comedy* sonnets, "The Jewish Cemetery at Newport"—is dense, sophisticated, adult poetry of the second order. But in his nationalistic fervor he also wrote epics of the Republic's prehistory like *Evangeline*, or lyrics of the common life like "The Village Blacksmith." Making these poems, he made recitation pieces; without intending to, he wrote poems for children and for entertainment. When Whittier made "Barbara Frietchie" in his abolitionist passion, he made willy-nilly a patriotic poem for schoolkids to recite. Meantime Walt Whitman—who had notions about poetry for the people—went relatively unread as he went unrecited. Mind you, he showed he could turn his hand to the recitation piece: "O Captain My Captain" is poetically inferior to "Casey."

The twin phenomena of recitation and the popular poem thrived in England at the same time, and Macaulay's *The Lays of Ancient Rome* turned up in American school readers and on prize-speaking days. The public Tennyson, laureate not melancholic, wrote verses often memorized for performance; lyrical Wordsworth and bouncy Browning served as well. There were many English sources, even for "Casey at the Bat": Thayer remembered reading W.S. Gilbert's *Bab Ballads* before composing "Casey."

At my school in the 1930s we memorized American poets: Whitman for "O Captain My Captain," Joaquin Miller's "Columbus," something by James Whitcomb Riley. The trajectory of the recitation piece, of which "Casey" is a late honorable example, began its descent early. James Whitcomb Riley scored hits with "Little Orphant Annie" and others, but Riley was mostly hokum. Then there was Eugene Field, whose "Little Boy Blue" is gross sentimentality accomplished with skill; then there is Ella Wheeler Wilcox; then there is Edgar Lee Guest. [The Canadian Robert Service is a late recitable anomaly.] Vachel Lindsay and Carl Sandburg were themselves performers who did not give rise to performance in others; they led from recitation toward the poetry reading. There are poets today as sentimental and popular as Edgar Guest, but they write free verse and no one recites them.

The tradition of recitation survives only in backwaters, like Danbury, New Hampshire. If you come on Prize

Speaking Day and sit in the school cafeteria-gymnasium-assembly, a miniature elocutionist may break your heart reciting "Little Boy Blue," or you may watch a rawboned young outfielder, straight out of central casting, begin: "The outlook wasn't brilliant for the Mudville nine that day. . ."

Among the thousands of pieces memorized and recited, few survive. Why "Casey at the Bat"? For a hundred years this mock heroic ballad has lurked alive at the edges of American consciousness. It has endured past the culture that spawned it. When an artifact like this old clownish poem persists for a century, surviving not only its moment but its natural elocutionary habitat, there must be reasons. There must be public reasons for public endurance.

We might as well ask: Why has baseball survived? Neither the Black Sox scandal nor the Crash nor two World Wars nor the National Football League have ended the game of baseball. Every year more people buy tickets to sit in wooden seats over a diamond of grass—or in plastic seats over plastic grass, as may be. We need to ask: *Has* baseball survived? Casey's game pitted town against town with five thousand neighbors watching. Maybe the descendant of Casey's game is industrial league softball played under the lights by teams wearing rainbow acrylics. These days when we speak of baseball we mostly mean the Major Leagues, millionaire's hardball, where our box seats place us half a mile from the symmetrical petro-chemical field. Do we watch the game that Mudville watched?

Yes.

As "Casey at the Bat" survives the culture of recitation, the game's shape and import survive its intimate origins. Not without *change*: If the five thousand ghosts of the Mudville crowd, drinking a Mississippi of blood to turn solid, reconstituted themselves on a Friday night at Three Rivers Stadium to witness combat between Cincinnati's team and Pittsburgh's, they would gape in spiritual astonishment at the zircon light of a distant diamond under the velvet darkness, at the pool-table green of imitation grass, at amenities of Lite, at the wave, at the skin color of many players, at tight uniforms, and at a scoreboard that shows moving pictures of what just happened.

But in their ectoplasmic witness they would also observe the template of an unaltered game. They would watch a third baseman move to his right, a second baseman flip underhand to a shortstop pivoting toward first for the double play, and an outfielder charge a line drive while setting himself to throw. Above all, they would see a pitcher facing a batter late in the game with men on base. They would see a cleanup man approaching the batter's box with defiance curling his lip. "Casey at the Bat" survives—to begin with—because it crystallizes baseball's moment, the medallion carved at the center of the game, where pitcher and batter confront each other.

There are other reasons, literary and historical. When a poem is so popular, one needs to quote Mallarmé again, and observe that poems are made of words. "Casey's" language is a small, consistent, comic triumph of irony. The diction is mock heroic, big words for small occasions: When a few fans go home in the ninth inning, they depart not in discouragement but "in deep despair." The

remaining five thousand illustrate a learned illusion: In his *Essay on Man*, Alexander Pope wrote that, "Hope springs eternal in the human breast. . ." and Thayer of course knew the source of his saw; but Pope, like Shakespeare, is largely composed of book titles and proverbs: Thayer uses Pope not as literary allusion but as appeal to common knowledge by way of common elevated sentiment.

Elevation is fundamental: Despite the flicker of hope, the crowd is a "grim multitude"—a language appropriate to Milton's hell—and if the hero is mocked, hero worshippers are twice mocked. Thayer's poetic similes are Homeric—as if Achilles faced Hector instead of Casey the pitcher; or if Casey is not quite Achilles, at least he is Ajax. Imagery of noise, loud in Homer and his echo Virgil, rouses Thayer to exalted moments: A yell "rumbled through the valley, it rattled in the dell; / It knocked upon the mountain and recoiled upon the flat. . ." This yell is cousin to the "roar / Like the beating of the stormwaves on a stern and distant shore." It is noise again when Thayer's crowd reacts to a called strike: "'Fraud!' cried the maddened thousands, and echo answered fraud. . ." These days at Fenway Park the bleacherites divide themselves for a rhythmic double chant, but they do not say "Fraud." When they feel polite they cry "less filling" and echo answers "tastes great."

Possibly crowds were not chanting "Fraud" in the late 1880s either. It was a major form of Victorian humor to elevate diction over circumstance. Mr. Micawber soared with paraphrastic euphemism to admit that he was in debt; W. C. Fields was an orotund low-comedy grandson. For a hundred years it was witty or amusing to call kissing osculation, and to refer to a house as a domicile. If somebody missed our tone, we sounded pompous, but usually people understood us: When we enjoyed something common or vulgar (like baseball) we could show a humorous affection for it, yet retain our superiority by calling the ball a spheroid.

This habit of language has not entirely disappeared, but more and more it looks like an anglophile or academic *tic*. The late poet and renowned advocate of baseball, Marianne Moore, always talked this way, never more than when she spoke of the game. When she identified the Giants' pitcher, "Mr. Mathewson," she noted: "I've read his instructive book on the art of pitching, and it's a pleasure to note how unerringly his execution supports his theories." Another St. Louis poet was T. S. Eliot, born the same year as "Casey," and, like Moore, expert in the humor of a polysyllabic synonym. Eliot is the most eminent poet influenced by "Casey at the Bat." *Old Possum's Book of Practical Cats* includes "Growltiger's Last Stand," conflation of Custer and Casey, written in metrical homage and in allusion: "Oh there was joy in Wapping when the news flew through the land. . ." Growltiger is a vicious fellow, racist or at least nationalist ("But most to Cats of foreign race his hatred has been vowed"), and loathed by felines of an Asian provenance. Absorbed in romantic adventure he is surrounded by a "fierce Mongolian horde," captured, and made to walk the plank.

The author of *Four Quartets* and "The Love Song of J. Alfred Prufrock" grew up in the age of recitation; we could be certain that he knew "Casey" even if "Growltiger" were not written in homage. Like many poets he could write high or low, wide or narrow; unlike some poets, when he wrote for children he recognized that he was doing it.

Mockery is "Casey's" point, with humor to soften it. After the crowd (which is us), the great Casey himself takes the brunt of our laughter. His name is the poem's mantra, repeated twenty-two times, often twice in a line: As he puffs with vainglory, "Defiance gleamed in Casey's eye, a sneer curled Casey's lip." The hero's role is written in the script of gesture. After five stanzas of requisite exposition, we catch sight of the rumored Casey in the sixth stanza: "There was ease in Casey's manner. . ." By this phrase we are captured and the double-naming locks us in: "There was pride in Casey's bearing and a smile on Casey's face." We know the smile's message, and we know how Casey doffs his cap. Casey is Godlike: "With a smile of Christian charity. . ." he "stilled the rising tumult"; if we remember that this metaphoric storm occurs at sea ("the beating of the stormwaves"), we may understand that Casey's charity earns its adjective.

And every time we hear "Casey at the Bat," the hero strikes out. We require this failure.

Not all of us. My grandfather, who was sanguine, always regretted that Casey struck out. He memorized the sequels and tried them all, especially "The Volunteer." In Clarence P. MacDonald's poem, printed in the San Francisco *Examiner* in 1908, the home team plays with no bench; behind in the game, it loses its catcher to an injury, and the captain calls for a substitute from the stands: A gray-headed volunteer finishes the game as catcher and his home run wins the game in the ninth. Besieged by teammates and fans to reveal his identity, the weeping stranger proclaims: "I'm mighty Casey who struck out just twenty years ago."

Wonderful.

But it won't do. None of the triumphant sequels will do. None show the flair of Thayer's ballad, its vigorous bumpety septameter and mostly well-earned rhymes, or its consistently overplayed language. Most important, none celebrate failure: Casey must strike out: Casey's failure makes the poem.

When Thayer first published "Casey at the Bat" in 1888, it bore a subtitle seldom reprinted: "A Ballad of the Republic." Once we lived in heroic times: once—and then again. When we suffer wars and undertake explorations we require heroes, and Jeb Stuart must gallop behind Union lines, Lindbergh fly the Atlantic, Davey Crockett enter the wilderness alone, Washington endure Valley Forge, the *Merrimack* attack the *Monitor*, Neil Armstrong step on the moon, and U.S. stand for Ulysses S., Unconditional Surrender, *and* the United States.

The Civil War, which ripped the country apart, began the work of stitching it together again. (One small agent of integrity was baseball, as blue and gray troops played the game at rest and even in prison camps, even North against South, as legend tells us.) For five years North and South lived through the triumphs and disasters of heroes. Although nameless boys charged stone walls blazing with rifle fire, we concentrated our attention on heroic leaders, from dandified cavalrymen to dignified generals. Sons born to veterans, late in the sixties and early in the seventies, were christened Forrest, Jackson, Sherman, Grant, Lee, Bedford, Beauregard. . .

But hero worship is dangerous and needs correction, especially in a democracy if we will remain democratic. To survive hero worship we mock our heroes; if we don't, we become their victims. Odysseus came home to slay the suitors; Ulysses S. allowed them to fatten on our larder: Heroic governance became disaster as the triumphant General Grant turned into the ruinous President. Many other heroes struck out. When the romantic vainglorious George Custer, with his shoulder-length hair, made combat with Crazy Horse and Sitting Bull in 1876, Growltiger walked the plank. Affluence and corruption, defeat and corruption bred irony. Violence of reconstruction and violence of anti-reconstruction eventually encouraged detachment from crowd passion.

Whatever young Thayer had in mind as he wrote his "Ballad of the Republic," 1888 was of course a Presidential year. We elected the mighty Benjamin Harrison President, a former officer of the Union Army, who took the job in a deal and installed as Secretary of State the notorious James G. Blaine. De Tocqueville stands behind this poem as much as Homer does. Democracies choose figures to vote in and out of office—to argue over, to ridicule: We do not want gods or kings—that's why we crossed the ocean west—but human beings, fallible like us.

We pretend to forgive failure; really we celebrate it. Bonehead Merkle lives forever and Bill Mazeroski's home run fades in memory. We fail, we all fail, we fail all our lives. The best hitters fail, two out of three at bats. If from time to time we succeed, our success is only prelude to further failure—and success's light makes failure darker still. Triumph's pleasures are intense but brief; failure remains with us forever, a featherbed, a mothering nurturing common humanity. With Casey we all strike out. Although Bill Buckner won a thousand games with his line drives and brilliant fielding, he will endure in our memories in the ninth inning of the sixth game of a World Series, one out to go, as the ball inexplicably, ineluctably, and eternally rolls between his legs.

Casey at the Bat

A Ballad of the Republic, Sung in the Year 1888

The outlook wasn't brilliant for the Mudville nine that
day;
The score stood four to two with but one inning more to
play.
And then when Cooney died at first, and Barrows did the
same,
A sickly silence fell upon the patrons of the game.

A straggling few got up to go in deep despair. The rest
Clung to that hope which springs eternal in the human
breast;
They thought if only Casey could but get a whack at
that—
We'd put up even money now with Casey at the bat.

But Flynn preceded Casey, as did also Jimmy Blake,
And the former was a lulu and the latter was a cake;
So upon that stricken multitude grim melancholy sat,
For there seemed but little chance of Casey's getting to
the bat.

But Flynn let drive a single, to the wonderment of all,
And Blake, the much despis-ed, tore the cover off the ball;
And when the dust had lifted, and the men saw what had
occurred,
There was Johnnie safe at second and Flynn a-hugging
third.

Then from 5,000 throats and more there rose a lusty yell;
It rumbled through the valley, it rattled in the dell;
It knocked upon the mountain and recoiled upon the flat,
For Casey, mighty Casey, was advancing to the bat.

There was ease in Casey's manner as he stepped into his
place;
There was pride in Casey's bearing and a smile on
Casey's face.
And when, responding to the cheers, he lightly doffed his
hat,
No stranger in the crowd could doubt 'twas Casey at the
bat.

Ten thousand eyes were on him as he rubbed his hands
with dirt;
Five thousand tongues applauded when he wiped them on
his shirt.
Then while the writhing pitcher ground the ball into his
hip,

Defiance gleamed in Casey's eye, a sneer curled Casey's
lip.

And now the leather-covered sphere came hurtling
through the air,
And Casey stood a-watching it in haughty grandeur there.
Close by the sturdy batsman the ball unheeded sped—
"That ain't my style," said Casey. "Strike one," the um-
pire said.

From the benches, black with people, there went up a
muffled roar,
Like the beating of the storm-waves on a stern and distant
shore.
"Kill him! Kill the umpire!" shouted some one on the
stand;
And it's likely they'd have killed him had not Casey
raised his hand.

With a smile of Christian charity great Casey's visage
shone;
He stilled the rising tumult; he bade the game go on;
He signaled to the pitcher, and once more the spheroid
flew;
But Casey still ignored it, and the umpire said, "Strike
two."
"Fraud!" cried the maddened thousands, and echo answered fraud;
But one scornful look from Casey and the audience was
awed.
They saw his face grow stern and cold, they saw his
muscles strain,
And they knew that Casey wouldn't let that ball go by
again.

The sneer is gone from Casey's lip, his teeth are clenched
in hate;
He pounds with cruel violence his bat upon the plate.
And now the pitcher holds the ball, and now he lets it go,
And now the air is shattered by the force of Casey's blow.

Oh, somewhere in this favored land the sun is shining
bright;
The band is playing somewhere, and somewhere hearts
are light,
And somewhere men are laughing, and somewhere children shout;
But there is no joy in Mudville—mighty Casey has struck
out.

Ernest Lawrence Thayer

## CHAPTER 26

Take Me Out to the Ball Game

Warner Fusselle

On a sunshiny September Saturday in Chicago, around 4 o'clock, a portly, grandfatherly man with white hair and thick, dark-rimmed glasses, wearing a light-colored, short-sleeved shirt with buttoned-down collar, beige sweater vest, and tan trousers, stood up, grabbed a microphone, and started to sway.

"All right! Let me hear you. A one, a two, a three! *Take me out to the ball game. Take me out with the crowd. Buy me some peanuts and Cracker Jack. I don't care if I never get back. Oh, it's root, root, root, for the [what's the name of that team?] . . . If they don't win it's a shame. For it's one, two, three strikes you're out, at the old ball game.* Hey!"

Harry Caray, the voice of the Chicago Cubs, had just led a gathering of 32,043 people at Wrigley Field in the singing of baseball's greatest song—"Take Me Out to the Ball Game." It was the seventh-inning stretch, and the Cubs led the Cardinals, 6-4, in a meaningless late-season game in 1988. Both teams were 20 games out of first place; nevertheless, everyone stood, waved, and cheered as they eyed the WGN broadcast booth overlooking the Friendly Confines.

The Chicago Pied Piper led the singing of those wearing Cubs blue and Cardinals red. There were young, and there were old, all waving their baseball caps. There were toddlers hanging on to their fathers. There were mothers who glowed, holding up their babies who cooed in wonderment.

Harry worked the crowd, holding a microphone with a blue wind screen in his left hand, while waving and encouraging the world of baseball fans standing below with his right hand. It was a special moment. From the first chord on the ballpark organ to Harry's exclamatory "Hey" at the end, "Take Me Out to the Ball Game" took less than a minute—only fifty-one seconds to be exact. However, it was an eventful minute, a happy minute, the happiest minute in all of sports.

Harry Caray has sung "Take Me Out to the Ballgame" to hometown fans during the seventh-inning stretch since 1976. That was the year Bill Veeck bought the White Sox. Harry had been the voice of the Sox since 1971 and had always sung baseball's beloved chorus whenever the organist played it. He had the perfect explanation, "I would always sing it, because I think it's the only song I knew the words to." However, no one except Harry's broadcast partner and a couple of others had heard it.

When Harry broadcast the White Sox games on TV, Bill Veeck noticed that the fans within earshot of Caray's booth would always sing along. One day Veeck had a microphone secretly installed in the broadcast booth, and the rest is history.

Harry joined the Cubs in 1982, where "Take Me Out to the Ball Game" elevated the word "Cubbies" into modern, respectable usage. Harry needed two syllables to replace "home team," so it just had to be "root, root, root for the Cub-bies" instead of Cubs. Lifelong Cub fan Mike Royko, Chicago's most famous columnist, had detested the term "Cubbies" for years, but Harry Caray and "Take Me Out to the Ball Game" prevailed.

In the Beginning

"Take Me Out to the Ball Game" was neither the first baseball song nor the first hit baseball song. Fifty years earlier, in 1858, "The Base Ball Polka" was written by an amateur player on the Niagara Base Ball Club of Buffalo, and the "Home Run Polka" followed nine years later. Neither song had words, nor were they recorded since sound recording wouldn't become a reality until 1877; however, they were available to the public in the form of sheet music.

Baseball's first hit song was "Slide, Kelly, Slide," published in 1889. The Kelly in verse spoofed the baseball star of the day, Michael "King" Kelly. King Kelly stole 208 bases for Boston of the National League from 1887 to 1889. He was King of the Diamond, a nineteenth century combination of Babe Ruth and Ty Cobb. Kelly even batted with a Cobb-like split grip and had once hit .388. His speed and daring made him the darling of the day. He developed the hook slide, and his base-stealing prowess encouraged the cheers of "Slide, Kelly, Slide." In 1893, "Slide, Kelly, Slide" became the first known baseball recording when it was issued on an Edison cylinder.

"Slide, Kelly, Slide" actually lampooned King Kelly and made fun of another buffoonish Kelly, but the two were linked in comedic fun. Even though "Slide, Kelly, Slide" remained a baseball standard even after the King's premature death in 1894, its success was scant compared with that of a sensational new song written in 1908.

Manhattan Transfer

"Take Me Out to the Ball Game" was written in fifteen minutes on a piece of scrap paper by vaudeville entertainer and songwriter Jack Norworth as he rode the (oxymoronic) elevated subway train toward the tip of Manhattan in New York City.

Norworth, who wrote 2,500 songs including "Shine On, Harvest Moon," had never seen a big league baseball game. His inspiration was a poster, prominently displayed on the brand new subway, which invited fans to take in a baseball game at the Polo Grounds. After he wrote the lyrics, his longtime friend, Albert Von Tilzer (who had also never attended a baseball game) composed the music. Von Tilzer was also the manager of the York Music Company, which published "Take Me Out to the Ball Game."

Norworth decided to debut "Take Me Out to the Ball Game" on stage at the Amphion Theater in Brooklyn. "It didn't go over," he later said, "because I was fumbling for the lyrics, and I did it deadpanned."

Three weeks later, Norworth, who had conceived the song as a romantic ballad, decided to try again. Booked as the closing act at Hammerstein's Victoria Theater in New York, the top vaudeville house in the country, he decided to liven up "Take Me Out to the Ball Game" in hopes of better results.

When the day came for the big show, Norworth was forced to change his plans. "I couldn't sing my own song, because every act ahead of me used it." The song was already on its way to becoming a nationwide hit thanks to the nickelodeon, an early-day movie house that charged a nickel for admission. Some of the more popular nickelodeons had started using illustrated songs, pictured on a set of slides, between the several short silent films that made up a typical program in the first decade of the century. "Take Me Out to the Ball Game" was played by the resident pianist and accompanied by pictorial slides that also displayed the words, for the audience to sing along.

A slide at the outset pictured the cover of the sheet music (on which "Take Me Out to the Ball Game" was prophetically named "The Sensational Base Ball Song") and other slides told the story of one afternoon in the life of Katie Casey, the heroine of "Take Me Out to the Ball Game." She and her beau, portrayed by models, were photographed going to the ball game at the Polo Grounds, and a final slide showed the lyrics of the chorus and invited the audience to "All join in."

The song caught on in the midst of one of baseball's greatest two-league pennant races; six teams were battling for the 1908 pennants a mere two days before the season ended. The effect of these races, which involved both Chicago teams as well as clubs in Cleveland, Detroit, New York, and Pittsburgh, was to make baseball front-page news across the country and promote Norworth's song.

Several recordings of "Take Me Out to the Ball Game" were made in 1908. Edward Meeker performed it on an Edison two-minute roll, an early phonograph record shaped like a cylinder. Frank Lambert's 1908 recording was available on a ten-inch, single-faced Zon-O-Phone record, and the Haydn Quartet recorded "Take Me Out to the Ball Game" on a Victor ten-inch single-faced record.

The Denver Nightingale

Harry MacDonough sang with the Haydn Quartet at first, but later the quartet re-recorded the song with vaudevil-lian and baseball fanatic Billy Murray. Murray, who was the number one recording artist of all time in terms of records made, was known as "The Denver Nightingale." He made more than 6,000 recordings between 1897 and 1943. Moreover, he knew and befriended all the Yankees (known as the Highlanders until 1913) and even practiced with them.

In 1906, Murray had recorded "It's Great at a Base Ball Game." On October 24, 1908, he performed "Take Me Out to the Ball Game" and immediately became identified with the song. His recorded version was easily the most popular of his many recordings.

Norworth's success encouraged many other songwriters to try their hand at diamond ditties. George M. Cohan wrote "Take Your Girl to the Ball Game" and the "Connie Mack Song." Cohan's failure, after Jack Norworth's success, caused him to alibi, "I didn't write mine soon enough." Norworth's response? "Or good enough."

In 1913, Irving Berlin composed the music to the baseball novelty song "Jake! Jake! The Yiddisher Ball Player." Then in 1925, he wrote "I Know a Foul Ball." John Philip Sousa penned "The National Game March," but none of the big names came close to the success that Norworth enjoyed. Yet, while "Take Me Out to the Ball Game" is one of the three most frequently sung compositions in the United States (only "Happy Birthday" and "The Star Spangled Banner" top it), the song everyone sings today is just the chorus of the tune.

Katie Casey to Nelly Kelly

The song actually begins, "Katie Casey was baseball mad." Katie Casey was such a big baseball fan that when her beau suggested they take in a show, Miss Kate expressed her preference for baseball.

> *Katie Casey was base ball mad,*
> *Had the fever and had it bad;*
> *Just to root for the home town crew,*
> *Ev'ry sou Katie blew.*
> *On a Saturday, her young beau*
> *Called to see if she'd like to go,*
> *To see a show but Miss Kate said,*
> *"No, I'll tell you what you can do."*
>
> *"Take me out to the ball game,*
> *Take me out with the crowd.*
> *Buy me some peanuts and cracker jack,*
> *I don't care if I never get back,*
> *Let me root, root, root, for the home team,*
> *If they don't win it's a shame.*
> *For it's one, two, three strikes, you're out,*
> *At the old ball game."*
>
> *Katie Casey saw all the games,*
> *Knew the players by their first names;*
> *Told the umpire he was wrong,*
> *All along good and strong.*
> *When the score was just two to two,*
> *Katie Casey knew what to do,*
> *Just to cheer up the boys she knew,*
> *She made the gang sing this song:*
> *(REPEAT CHORUS)*

Despite the song's success, Jack Norworth decided to change some of the words. In 1927, he changed Katie Casey to Nelly Kelly (and thus secured a new copyright).

Nelly Kelly loved baseball games,
Knew the players, knew all their names,
You could see her there ev'ry day,
Shout "Hurray," when they'd play.
Her boy friend by the name of Joe
Said, "To Coney Isle, dear, let's go,"
Then Nelly started to fret and pout,
And to him I heard her shout.

"Take me out to the ball game,
Take me out with the crowd,
Buy me some peanuts and crackerjack,
I don't care if I never get back.
Let me root root root for the home team,
If they don't win it's a shame,
For it's one two three strikes, you're out
At the old ball game."

Nelly Kelly was sure some fan,
She would root just like any man,
Told the umpire he was wrong,
All along, good and strong.
When the score was just two to two,
Nelly Kelly knew what to do,
Just to cheer up the boys she knew,
She made the gang sing this song.
(REPEAT CHORUS)

The original copyright of "Take Me Out to the Ball Game" expired in 1936. The renewed copyright had a new subtitle, "The Famous Baseball Song." Not only had the word "baseball" become one word instead of two, "sensational" was updated to "famous." That would change again in 1949 to "Official," as in "The Official Baseball Song."

The Aftermath of the Hit

After his success with "Take Me Out to the Ball Game," Von Tilzer, previously known as Albert Gumm, tried again but failed with other baseball tunes. In 1909 he wrote the music for "Did He Run?" This song satirized Fred Merkle's Boner in the famous 1908 pennant race involving the Giants and Cubs. The chorus began,

Did he run?
Did he run to second,
As he should that day.
Or did Mr. Merkle semi-circle away?

Albert also wrote "Back to the Bleachers for Mine" and "I Want to Go to the Ball Game." His brother Harry, who wrote "Wait Till the Sun Shines, Nellie," also tried to write a baseball hit without success. He was 0-for-2 with "My Old Man Is Baseball Mad" in 1910 and "The Baseball Glide" in 1911.

Norworth, too, tried his hand at more baseball music but failed. With his wife Nora Bayes, a musical comedy star, he wrote "Let's Get the Umpire's Goat." Often criticized for writing a baseball song even though he had never seen a game, he had the perfect response: "A friend of mine, Harry Williams, wrote 'In the Shade of the Old Apple Tree,' and he never saw an apple tree."

Finally, however, Jack did get to see his first major league game. Some say he saw his first game in 1916 at Ebbets Field in Brooklyn where he root, root, rooted like crazy for the hometown, pennant-winning Robins. Other historians push the date to somewhere in the 1940s, when the Robins-turned-Dodgers supposedly had a special day for Jack at Ebbets Field on June 27, 1940.

Whenever it was, Norworth became fascinated with what he saw and later pioneered Little League Baseball in California. The Cracker Jack Company even honored him with a trophy, the Jack Norworth Award, which was given to deserving Little Leaguers. In 1958, on the fiftieth anniversary of his creation of "Take Me Out to the Ball Game," Norworth was honored in Los Angeles and was presented with a gold lifetime pass which would enable him to see any major league game. Norworth, proud of his accomplishment, said, "It has kept me eating for fifty years."

He died September 1, 1959, at age eighty, but almost every ballpark features "Take Me Out to the Ball Game" during the seventh-inning stretch. One notable exception is the Toronto Blue Jays, who have used a fan-participation song since 1979 called "OK Blue Jays," which has become the team's theme song. At Busch Stadium in St. Louis, Norworth's composition was for a time replaced by the Budweiser beer jingle, "Here Comes the King."

Oriole Park at Camden Yards in Baltimore is also an exception, but only sometimes. There, the fans get to choose their favorite song for that day's game from a list of four choices; however, the fans' applause usually selects "Take Me Out to the Ball Game," with John Denver's "Thank God I'm a Country Boy" a close second.

"Take Me Out to the Ball Game" has been called by some an American folk song. Children learn it right after their nursery rhymes, and soldiers sing it during world wars. Music boxes play it, and so do doorbell chimes. Baseball's most popular song has even been played in wedding processions, and, in 1955, *Variety* gave the song its stamp of approval by naming "Take Me Out to the Ball Game" one of the ten greatest popular songs of the last fifty years.

## CHAPTER 27

Fantasy Baseball

Don L. Daglow, Jack Kavanagh, and Garth Chouteau

Young baseball fans lie in bed at night and dream of playing baseball in the big leagues. Old boys—that is, grownups—imagine that they may yet manage their hometown teams. Table-top board games, dice baseball, and the computer have allowed us to live out both fantasies by recreating game situations and allowing us to experiment, rewarding us with different results based on the strategic wisdom of our decisions.

Table Baseball—A World Apart

Baseball simulations have been around longer than Organized Baseball. The first professional league, the National Association, was formed in 1871. The first table baseball game had been patented in 1868. In 1994, baseball simulations took the place of the real thing when major league baseball shut down. Rotisserie type leagues—for which team owners drafted and traded major-league players and conducted their season's play based on real-life performances—could not feed off daily boxscores. However, table gamers rolled dice, shuffled cards, flicked spinners or, in the digital simulations, tapped keyboards or clicked mouse buttons.

The undisputed Father of Table Baseball was Francis C. Sebring, whose board game, Parlour Baseball, was described in an 1866 issue of *Frank Leslie's Illustrated Newspaper.* The game was patented in 1868 (patent No. 74154). The diagram shows it was a mechanical game. One player sent a coin plateward by a spring mechanism while another swung a swiveled bat. The coin, when struck, would end up in a slot, designated an out or a hit. This simple approach was continued in dozens of mechanical games, on tabletops and in pinball arcades, which miniaturized the real game.

However, games played with dice, cards, or spinners have dominated the home baseball game area. These approaches provide greater options and more variable outcomes. Thousands of such games were invented. Most probably remained the private passion of a fan who created his own game to play on his own table. Inventing a simulation of baseball is simple. Baseball itself can be viewed as being transferred from a board game to a playing field. The ancient Hindu game of Pachesi (parcheesi) starts the player at home base and returns him there after he has circled the bases. That's what the play action of baseball amounts to.

As in more complicated board games, the trip around the bases can be made more elaborate and difficult, but the goal is the same: to score more times than your opponents.

However, for the first sixty-plus years of table baseball, a problem existed. The players in the lineup did not perform the way they did in actual baseball play. Babe Ruth was no more likely to hit a home run than the weakest hitting infielder. Even worse, the good glove work of the infielder was not reflected in the play of the table game. Pitchers had no traits of superiority nor were any of them easier to hit than others. You could write Walter Johnson's name in the lineup but a pitcher with any other name was as likely to strike out batters.

The first breakthrough to real life came when Clifford A. Van Beek of Green Bay, Wisconsin, marketed *National Pastime* in 1931. He had patented his game in 1923 and was issued No. 1,536,639 in 1925. Although it was advertised in the 1931 issues of *Baseball Magazine,* the fledgling game succumbed to the Great Depression and was not seen again until *APBA* was marketed in 1951. The APBA game imitated *National Pastime* and, as its followers grew into cultlike devotees, its inventor, J. Richard Seitz, allowed them to believe he was the one who had mastered a way to imitate the baseball performances of actual players.

Actually, a game with a different approach, *All-Star Baseball,* marketed by CADACO and designed by a real-life baseball player, Ethan Allen, had appeared in 1941. Seitz had contributed a primitive method of ranking pitchers to his upgrading of the *National Pastime* game. Allen, a .300 hitting outfielder in the National League, did not bother (all pitchers might have looked alike to him). At any rate, in *All-Star Baseball,* the spinner was influenced only by the batter's tendencies. Babe Ruth would hit more home runs than the weak-hitting shortstop because the space for HRs was larger on his player disc. Alas, Allen had not built in a way for the glove man to justify his place on the team. Seitz had tackled that with a grading system. Seitz also widened the play variations by borrowing another idea from the past. Although it was not a real life game, like the one that appeared in the early 1930s, purportedly the brainstorm of pitcher Danny MacFayden, it provided different play charts according to the base/out situation.

The *APBA* game was challenged by *Strat-O-Matic,* also using dice and cards, and its own closely guarded method of rating players. Both games found acceptance and survive to the present. Many other games came and went, but a few had enduring value beyond their playability because, unlike *APBA* and *Strat-O-Matic,* they did not conceal their codes. They revealed the process of rating players for batting, for power factors, for defense, and for pitching effectiveness as well as strikeout and walks. At least one of these is still marketed, *Extra Innings,* by Big League Game Company of Duluth, Minnesota.

Which game is best? It is whichever game satisfies the particular player. The cost of advertising and, particularly, the requirement of royalty payments to Major League Baseball Properties and the Major League Baseball Players Association for the use of the names of the teams and the players, drove most small competitors from the market. *ABPA* and *Strat-O-Matic* have been able to pass the costs along to their loyal followers.

Before It Was a Business

We often hear that before the excesses of Charlie Finley and the beginning of the age of free agency in the mid-1970s, "Baseball was a game, not just a business." The same is true of the computer baseball simulations of that too-soon ancient era. As we'll discuss later in this article, however, the consumers of computer baseball simulations are arguably more fortunate than the observers of the real thing, because baseball on the computer just keeps getting better and better.

In 1959, George R. Lindsey published an article in the Operations Research Journal titled "Statistical Data Useful for the Operation of a Baseball Team." Laboriously tracking each detail of hundreds of games by traditional paper and pencil methods, Lindsey and his father demonstrated that, on average, the traditional righty-lefty matchup did indeed benefit the hitter (by some 15 percentage points). They also established that teams did indeed plan wisely when, with the bases loaded in the early innings, they played the infield back for the double play.

It was also in 1959 that the first baseball model was written on a computer to try to answer the same questions posed by the Lindseys, as R. E. Trueman built a mathematical analysis of 5,000 games to answer these key strategic questions. By 1973 the power of computers had grown to the point where R. Allen Freeze of the University of British Columbia ran a 200,000-game simulation to determine the best batting order for a baseball team, which turned out to be the good-hitting leadoff and powerful cleanup hitter order enshrined in baseball tradition. In those years in the early 1970s the computer had helped lay the foundation for the invention of sabermetrics and the work of Dick Cramer, Bill James, Pete Palmer, John Thorn and many others who deserve mention in such a list.

The computer baseball simulations written before 1970 were, by necessity, focused on a study of the overall averages of baseball, analyzing which strategy produces the best results most often in a given situation. Created on "batch" machines that read computer cards punched with holes to encode their programs and data, they operated without intervention by any user, following the programmer's instructions and recording the results until the designated number of games had been replayed. On such archaic computers it was not uncommon to make a mistake in a baseball simulation program, then face a very unhappy computer operator when (for example) a Giants-Dodgers grudge match accidentally forgot to stop playing

after nine innings, and a thousand batters later had printed several hundred pages of text narrating the action.

In the early 1970s there were no video games. Pong was not yet a word unless preceded by Ping. Pac Man had yet to munch his first dot. The invention of economical time-sharing machines in the late 1960s opened up a new possibility for baseball on computers: the potential for the simulation to become interactive, to actually become a game. These machines, with their ability to serve many users at once, were immediately popular with colleges, and it is on such campuses where the evolution of today's computer games, including computer baseball simulations, began.

The Digital Equipment Corp. (DEC) PDP-10 computer was the choice of many colleges, and it made super-complex baseball formulas simple to calculate. These same DEC machines, which filled a room the size of a two-car garage, influenced many young programmers, including Microsoft founder Bill Gates, who started his computing career on the machine often referred to simply as the "10".

The big sky-blue DECs had 32,000 bytes of RAM (memory), shared by more than thirty users at a time, quickly "swapping" one program into the computer's memory for a few tenths of a second before kicking it out and bringing in the next program. It was the technical equivalent of watching a class of 35 students reciting 35 different poems over 35 different telephones, with each poet getting to speak one word at a time before yielding the floor to the next person. Under such a system no one would finish a poem very quickly, and the computer was likewise slow: to search a list of 200 names for a single player took almost a minute during peak usage times.

By contrast, only twenty-five years of technology later, today's typical new home computer may have 16,000,000 bytes of memory. In one human generation we took what would have filled 500 two-car garages and made it small enough to fit on the top of your desk. The search through 200 names now happens so quickly that to the naked eye it appears to be instantaneous.

Of course, back in 1971 the huge, slow PDP-10 raced through calculations like the proverbial roadrunner compared to the process of figuring out complex equations by hand and slide rule. Don Daglow, a student at Pomona College in Claremont, California, thought he could create a more sophisticated baseball simulation using these "new" computers. With Daglow's simulation, players could watch the play-by-play account of any game as it was rattled off on the same kind of teletype printer from which Red Barber, Ernie Harwell, and Mel Allen used to report the results of road games on the radio. By the following year, users could sit at the computer and make basic managerial decisions such as inserting a pinch hitter, walking the batter, or warming up a reliever in the bullpen. No one realized it at the time, but it was the first computer baseball simulation game, the first time a human manager could match wits against a computer in a mathematically defined environment.

Where the pioneering work of such computer simulation innovators as Trueman, Freeze, and Palmer was focused on the scientific analysis of baseball and its strategy (and the debunking of some of its myths), that first game in 1971-72 emphasized a different power of the computer:

interaction. Its designer and players were driven to create the program by a fantasy, a consuming desire to somehow be a part of the game. No one ever dreamed that within just a few short years this hobby would become Big Business.

1978-83: The First Great Video Game War

In the early and mid-1970s, a series of coin-operated, arcade-style machines entertained people by showing squares and lines on a TV screen, and allowed users to move the lines or squares to play a game. The most famous of these was *Pong,* where two lines controlled by plastic knobs knocked a square "ball" back and forth across the screen. Home versions followed , consoles that plugged into a TV set and allowed consumers to play *Pong* in their living rooms. Atari, the manufacturer of *Pong,* improved on this concept by creating a console that played different games on interchangeable cartridges, and which could display images in a variety of colors. By the late 1970s the "Atari VCS" was a huge hit in American toy stores, followed by Intellivision and Colecovision.

Baseball video games of the late 1970s and early 1980s were arcade contests, where the screen showed the outline of a baseball field, and single-color player silhouettes were drawn in at each position. Everything had to be controlled by a human being; the games had no "artificial (computerized) intelligence." One user pressed a button to choose a fast or slow pitch, and perhaps another button to select if the pitch would be straigh or if it would curve. The player controlling the batter pressed a button to swing the bat. Once the ball was in the air, a joystick or "control disk" was used by each player to direct the lead runner and the fielder closest to the ball. Though primitive by today's standards, some of these games sold over 2 million copies, big hits by the standards of any entertainment medium.

With the technology evolving rapidly, the "second generation" of baseball video games arrived almost on top of the first. By 1982, these new versions could show the game on TV in a format similar to an actual TV broadcast, from a center field camera, with insets in the corners to show the runner on first dancing off the bag.

With this level of realism, it became practical for the first time in video games to spend the extra money to license the names and stats of real major league players, so that a computer figure that represented Dale Murphy or Andre Dawson really would hit more home runs, while Nolan Ryan's fastball would be greased lightning on the screen. In turn, this assignment of an identity to each player enabled other elements of actual baseball to enter the videogame arena: to have pitchers tire and pinch hitters and runners enter the game, meaning much more real baseball strategy came into users' living rooms.

The first game to achieve this new level of realism was Mattel's *World Series Baseball,* and it delivered two other important firsts as well. Don Daglow, now serving as director of game design for Mattel Electronics, designed the project, working with programmer Eddie Dombrower. So it's not surprising that *World Series Baseball* was the first baseball simulation in a video game, meaning that it went beyond arcade-style play and gave users control over many of the strategic decisions that occur in any baseball contest. It was also the first to use the television-camera-style display format.

By 1983, too many games crowded the shelves, and fast-buck publishers went bankrupt right and left. Unable to return games to the defunct manufacturers, toy stores sold them off at bargain prices on huge discount tables. Soon parents and kids balked at paying $35 for one new game when they could buy seven $5 games for the same price. The final blow was the arriv al of inexpensive home computers such as the Commodore 64 and Atari 800, which not only played games but could be used for word processing and educational software.

One by one, the major firms folded their video game divisions, laid off their staffs and struggled to save whatever was left of their companies. Atari split into two separate units that were sold to different investors; Mattel Electronics went from 1,800 people to five in fifteen months; Coleco ultimately disappeared entirely into bankruptcy. When Mattel's *World Series Baseball* shipped in 1983 this market disaster was operating at full force, and few copies were ever actually sold.

1982-94: The Home Computer Comes of Age

When the Apple II home computer was first introduced in 1977, it seemed to be yet another in a line of devices marketed in small quantities to techie wizards by fellow computer nerds who assembled the devices in the family garage.

But the Apple II was not just another techie toy. Instead its introduction heralded a defining moment in personal computers, when the prior generation of machines (led by the 1975 release of the MITS Altair 8800, by many definitions the first PC) slipped into obscurity, while the next wave—the Tandy TRS-80, Commodore PET and the Atari 800—pushed on to a whole new level of public acceptance.

The earliest major baseball simulation on home computers was the Apple II game simply called *Computer Baseball,* published by Strategic Simulations Inc. (SSI) in 1981. Although its designers were not familiar with sabermetrics, it was nonetheless a reasonably accurate simulation that pitted great teams from history against each other and allowed the user to manage either or both teams. Harnessing the 48K of memory in the Apple II (versus 4K to 8K for video game cartridges of the time), *Computer Baseball* nevertheless ignored the flashy graphics, displaying an outline of a stadium while describing the action in text. The ball's location was displayed on the stadium diagram, giving some added inspiration to the user's imagination.

By 1982 the Commodore 64 home computer had challenged the Apple II, offering many of the same capabilities in a cheaper plastic case for much less money ($850 for a complete system, vs. about twice that much for a somewhat more powerful contemporary Apple IIe). To the layman, only the much- slower disk drives represented a clear difference between the machines, and the Commodores sold in the millions.

Apple soon focused its efforts on the new Macintosh line, and Mattel and Atari were slow to introduce their planned new computers. In 1983-84, the height of the Commodore 64's success, its sales wave helped push the first generation video games over the brink of disaster. After all, as the Commodore TV commercials warned, why buy your child a video game when the kid next door is using a Commodore 64 to prepare for the college courses and jobs of the next century?

Ironically, these less expensive home computers often turned out to be used primarily as game machines, and the computer game business grew into a real industry as Commodore sales boomed. Electronic Arts (EA) Inc., founded in 1982 by Trip Hawkins, pushed lasting play value, simple interfaces, and graphic quality. Video games seemed simplistic by comparison, and began to fade from prominence.

In 1984 this trend caught up with *Computer Baseball,* as the first version of *Micro League Baseball* arrived to take the baseball simulation crown. Micro League Sports Inc., creators of *Micro League,* published versions for a variety of different computers, featuring better graphics than earlier games. The graphics now told the story so well that text narration was omitted, and only the names and stats of the batter and the pitcher were displayed. Interestingly, as the following ten years saw an ever-escalating arms race of flashy graphics between competing games, the original *Computer Baseball* style of text-plus-graphics display also continued to be used by some designers, who lacked the big budgets necessary to include lifelike animations and photorealistic backgrounds.

Action-only games, which ignored stats and played as arcade style contests, also flourished during the early 1980s on home computers. Scott Orr's Gamestar Inc. produced *Star League Baseball* as part of its line of sports games, and no other baseball game of that era, including all the simulations, sold as well.

In the mid-1980s Gamestar was sold to Activision, while Accolade (then led by Activision co-founder Alan Miller) introduced the first *Hardball* game, designed by Bob Whitehead. Although Intellivision *World Series Baseball* was the first game to show the pitches from one angle and the fielding action from another, *Hardball* was the first to do so on home computers, and its graphics were larger and its textures more detailed than prior games. Replacing *Star League* as the leading action baseball game, *Hardball* and its sequels have been major products for almost a decade, outselling any other series of computer baseball games.

In 1985 the time had come when the newest personal computers (then the Amiga and the IBM PC) could support a hybrid game, one which was both an accurate simulation and a competitive graphic display of baseball. Daglow, by then a producer at Electronic Arts, believed that such a game would sell best if anchored by the name of a famous baseball personality, particularly since the new machines could support sophisticated software imitating the strategy of an individual manager. Earl Weaver, then newly (and temporarily) retired as Orioles manager, was the unanimous choice as the game's standard-bearer, while Eddie Dombrower again signed on to do the programming. Over the next several years EA published versions of *Earl Weaver Baseball* for the Amiga, the PC, and the Macintosh.

Utilizing a split-screen approach that showed a closeup of the batter and pitcher alongside a picture of the field, *Weaver Baseball* changed the face of all succeeding simulations due to its many innovations. First of all was the feature of Weaver himself. Daglow and his team of designers worked closely with the Orioles manager, trying to boil his "God bless the three run homer" philosophy down into the key factors he used to make managerial decisions. Once the original "electronic Earl Weaver" had been built, its tendencies were compared against those that Weaver himself showed in real games and the model was fine-tuned.

Also important was the game's ability to schedule and simulate a complete season of 162 games and keep records of all the simulated stats, although to play such a full schedule game by game (at half an hour per contest) would take several months. All prior games had required the user to plan out a schedule, play the games, keep the stats, and figure out who were the league leaders. Weaver automated this process, and for all its relative slowness it was a huge improvement over paper-and-pencil record-keeping. It was also the first game to support trading players from one team to another. Although its sales numbers did not equal those of the arcade-oriented *Hardball,* Weaver earned a Gold Disk (the software equivalent of a Gold Record) and was honored with a place in *Computer Gaming World* magazine's Computer Game Hall of Fame. Today, more than ten years after its release, *Earl Weaver Baseball* and its sequels are still considered by many avid gamers to be the best baseball simulations ever devised.

The introduction of *Earl Weaver Baseball* put pressure on both well-ensconced leaders, *Hardball* and *Micro League Baseball,* and the late 1980s saw a "battle of the versions" as all three games maneuvered for position. Activision's *Pete Rose Baseball* and Epyx's *Sporting News Baseball,* each of which also combined stats with graphics, also joined the fray briefly. The venerable board games *Strat-O-Matic Baseball, Pursue the Pennant* and *APBA* all introduced text-only, then text-with-graphics versions of their best-selling products, and by 1990 baseball fans had a broad choice of computer games to simulate the national pastime.

Not wanting to be typecast as "all action and no simulation," Accolade's *Hardball II,* designed by Distinctive Software in Canada, included a core of basic baseball stats to add solid simulation to the game. In *Hardball III* Accolade introduced the first "VGA graphics" baseball game to PCs, with higher resolution graphics that showed off the power of what was then a new graphic format. *Micro League Baseball II* and *III* added more stats to refine its simulation and a feature that allowed users to draft players onto teams, and *Micro League IV* tried adding miniature videos to its display to keep up on the graphics front. Eyeing *Hardball's* still-better sales numbers, *Weaver II* experimented with a "multiple camera" TV broadcast style display that showed the action from behind the fielders and allowed users to choose between several different angles for the display. Although the game was not as popular as its predecessor, *Weaver II* (as well as Activision's *Pete Rose Baseball*) did break new ground in the use of 3D displays.

In 1990 Daglow, having founded Stormfront Studios Inc., an independent game development house, began working on *Tony LaRussa Baseball.* Like the original *Weaver* seven years before, LaRussa sought to out-do

Hardball as an action game while taking the top rung of the simulation game category as well. The game was also specifically designed to present a balance between sabermetrics and traditional baseball stats, trying to appeal to both the hard core, well-informed baseball fan and the casual player who wanted to learn more about the sport.

Daglow and the company's design team spent many hours learning how to simulate LaRussa's managerial style. Major League Baseball's winningest active manager was generous with his time and determined to get things right; in many ways, the *LaRussa Baseball* series incorporates more "real baseball knowledge" than any game before or since. When the first *Tony LaRussa Baseball* was introduced for the IBM PC in the fall of 1991, it shipped within weeks of *Earl Weaver Baseball II*. Both products did well, dividing the market between them. While the latter product was maintaining a legacy of sorts, the former was breaking new ground.

For years, baseball games that allowed users to control the fielding had suffered from a basic problem: it was hard to catch a fly or popup on the TV screen just by watching the tiny white circle that was the ball and the tiny black circle that was its shadow. Even experienced players often missed routine flies, undermining the enjoyment of many games.

For *LaRussa,* Stormfront realized that some better kind of signal was needed for where to catch the ball. Knowing that computers are good at quickly drawing basic geometric shapes, the programmers created a shaded circle on the field to show where the ball was going to land. When the ball was high in the air the circle would be large, and as it fell the circle would shrink and then disappear as the ball hit the ground. The math was not easy to perfect (especially when the circle's location started shifting in the wind), but the process was refined until it worked. This single innovation drew more attention from the press than all the years of work perfecting the baseball simulation, and all computer baseball products and video games now use some form of fly ball "fielding target."

Accolade countered in the spring of 1992 with *Hardball III,* which again took top honors among action games. Although less sophisticated as a simulation than *Weaver* or *LaRussa, Hardball III* was nevertheless a solid basic-stat-based game. Stormfront in turn countered in the spring of 1993 with *LaRussa II,* which added higher quality graphics and even more league play and simulation features to the model. It also delivered an arcade mode which further enabled users to immerse themselves in the experience.

1989-94: The Second Great Video Game War

Japanese game makers Nintendo and Sega first started showing their new video game consoles at trade shows in the United States in the mid-1980s, and by 1987 Nintendo's "NES" unit in particular was selling very well to its young audience. Some of the first baseball games for Nintendo, Japanese-designed by companies such as Jaleco, already included the stats of American major leaguers and used batter power ratings, runners' speed, and pitchers' control abilities to influence play. Although rather simple by comparison with the PC simulations,

these cartridges accomplished a very important goal: they got the mainstream of video game playing kids interested in the names and stats of real players in the game.

Soon after, the Sega Genesis appeared, a more powerful videogame system than the original Nintendo NES. One of the first Genesis games was Sega's *Tommy Lasorda Baseball,* which featured a unique "blimp view" after the ball was hit, displaying the action looking straight down on top of the heads of the players. Stores began to believe that video games were really back, and stocked both Sega and Nintendo cartridges more deeply as their popularity continued to grow.

These early 1990s cartridges were very different from those programmed only a decade before. An early Intellivision video game contained 4,000 characters of computer code and graphics. When LaRussa Baseball '95 was introduced for the Sega Genesis in 1994, the game shipped on a cartridge that held the equivalent of 2,000,000 characters of information, an increase of 500 times over the size of the earlier game.

That size, of course, made these new video game platforms potential new battlegrounds for the creators of baseball simulations. Some games, like *Cal Ripken Baseball, Ken Griffey Baseball, Nolan Ryan Baseball* and *Roger Clemens Baseball* used famous players and flashy graphics to appeal to the younger audiences who buy video games, while also including basic player stats and baseball simulation. Sega's 1992 *Sports Talk Baseball* featured the voice of veteran broadcaster Lon Simmons, and Accolade's *Hardball III* for Sega and PC featured network broadcaster Al Michaels, but the digitized voices used too much precious cartridge space and were dropped from later versions until CD-ROMs replaced cartridges in the mid-1990s.

And the "arms race" of computer baseball simulations continues to spiral upwards: where the room-sized PDP-10 replayed a season at the rate of five seconds per game in 1971, the desk-sized PC in 1996 used twenty times as many variables for every batter and pitcher, yet still played each complete game in less than a quarter of a second. In the past year, computer baseball simulation designers have begun harnessing this additional power through the latest in graphics technology—real 3D displays. Providing a richer, more immersive experience, 3D graphics are the future of virtually all computer and videogame entertainment; it's expected that nearly all "next-generation" computer baseball games will use this technology.

The Waves of New Technology . . . and What We Cannot Simulate

The advent of the compact disk has already impacted the sports simulation market through products such as *LaRussa Baseball 3* and *Hardball 5.* Many games now offer modem play, where users in different cities can play against each other over telephone lines, and in 1994 the Prodigy service debuted *Baseball Manager,* a unique fantasy game in which subscribers across the country compete in fantasy leagues where the computer actually plays out every game between teams whose rosters the users build via drafting and trades.

But for all our new technology, there are still parts of

baseball that we cannot simulate, and different schools of thought on what "baseball simulations" ought to be. For example, one game designer who was not himself a baseball fan tried to develop a game by listening carefully to the opinions of coworkers who were baseball experts. He concluded that he could create the best baseball simulation ever . . . by making sure all the statistics from the simulated games came out exactly the same as those from real life! If a player had a .280 batting average in real life and his simulated average was bel ow .280, he would get a hit the next time up, guaranteed, whether the pitcher was Roger Clemens or a converted peanut vendor. If a player who hit 30 round-trippers in real life had 30 home runs on August 20 of the simulated season, he could not hit a homer the rest of the season lest he make the game "inaccurate." Fortunately, the publisher's management listened to the customer complaints and the next year the design was altered to allow nonidentical results.

Ironically, the same interaction by the user that makes baseball games fun to play on the computer can also play havoc with the "accuracy" of the simulation. At the simplest level, the user might change the 1996 Yankees' usual lineup, batting Derek Jeter, Bernie Williams, and Darryl Strawberry 1-2-3 to see if this will work better than Joe Torre's alignment. This is the whole idea of computer games—to allow people to play with the system and see what happens—but after users make such changes they sometimes complain about the resulting inaccuracy of the final standings in the product!

For those games where the user is also given the chance to control the pitching, hitting, and fielding, even greater chaos can break loose. You can pitch fastball after fastball right down the pipe to Willie Mays or Babe Ruth on every at bat, and watch the home run totals mount. Take the starter who pitched eight tough innings last night and force him to start to day's 1:00 P.M. game, then duck as the line drives scream in all directions. These are the moments when simulation takes a back seat to fun, and that fun is part of the charm of what makes people buy the games.

At one National SABR Convention presentation, a researcher had replayed a recent season ten times on a leading baseball simulation to see how often the real life pennant winners duplicated their feat. The average was about six times out of ten, but one pennant winner only won two of the ten simulated seasons, while the second place team won five times. Although even the best baseball simulation is not a magical tool to predict the future or precisely duplicate the past, as long-time students of baseball these results seemed intuitively reasonable to us. Yet several members of the audience politely indicated their skepticism about the scholar's methodology.

The skeptics missed one key point about real baseball in their assumption that the real winners would never sink so low as to win only two of ten identically-weighted seasons. After a 162-game season, very often the pennant contending teams' results in wins and losses are so close as to be almost identical. The decade f rom 1970-79, for example, is an era remembered for many pennant races that were over in July as teams built big leads and ran away from the competition. Nevertheless, in that ten year span, 22.5 percent of the division races were decided by two games or less, 30 percent of the League Champion-

ship Series went for what was then the complete five games, and five out of the ten Wo rld Series, a full 50 percent, went the maximum seven games. The difference between the performance of the champion and that of the second place team in baseball is often perilously thin.

Let's take one of those season races in which the pennant was decided by a margin of two games. What does it take to swing the margin of victory to the other side? On May 11, a first base ump misses a tough call in deep right field in the top of the ninth, ruling that the outfielder trapped a line drive when the TV replay clearly shows he caught it. The runner ends up at second and scores on a sacrifice fly two batters later, winning the game. On August 10 the runner on third tries to go home after a bad throw from short dribbles out of the first baseman's glove and into foul territory. The game started at 5:00 P.M. to align with the TV schedule, and the shadow from the top of the stadium lies between first and home. When the first baseman pegs his throw to the plate, the changing light and the white shirts of the crowd throw off the catcher, and he drops the ball as the runner slides in safely. Once again the game is lost.

And on that pair of cosmic events the pennant is decided. An ump guesses wrong on a tough, no-win call, and a catcher loses a ball in the crowd. As a result, all the baseball encyclopedias for all time will proclaim the losing team's clear inferiority, because they came in second.

Observers occasionally remark that computer simulations are inherently inaccurate, because if you turn on the computer and play a game at 10:00 in the morning you will get a different result than if you turn it on at noon. In our mythical two-game margin above, however, the same thing is true. If the contestants ignore the TV schedule and start at 7:30, the sun has set in the ninth inning and the catcher sees the ball pegged from foul territory to the plate. If the game starts at 1:05, the afternoon breeze that springs up carries that deep fly ball in the top of the seventh and makes it a three run homer. If star shortstop John Smith doesn't have to wake up early that morning for a 12:15 start time, he doesn't have a fight with his wife and slam the front door on his throwing hand, putting him on the DL for the remainder of the season.

Just as the Weather Service can simulate what thunderstorms and heat waves are likely to do in the next three days, we can simulate what baseball players and teams are likely to do over the course of a season. But human beings and the weather have a lot in common when it comes to unpredictability, and it is these kinds of factors that no computer will ever be able to predict. Will right fielder John Doe's new baby keep him up at night and reduce his performance, or will his sense of satisfaction and happiness at being a new dad raise his average? These are not the studies of statistical experts but of psychologists, and our inscrutable human individuality should keep that part of baseball sacrosanct for the foreseeable future.

The Convergence of Simulation and Reality

In the past year or so, a multitude of new baseball simulations have appeared, from both veteran and rookie software developers. As competition gets even more fierce, and the technology for creating and enjoying computer baseball simulations continues apace, fans can (and do) expect greater leaps in the evolution of such products. With the ability of the computer to simulate a full 162-game season well-established, and the speed of the computer itself constantly accelerating, recent enhancements have focused primarily on two areas: the presentation of the on-field action, and the "big picture," control of one or more teams over a longer period of decades or even centuries of simulated seasons.

When it comes to realism on the field, today's games, whether console (videogame) or PC-based, simply blow away the top games of a decade ago. Surround-sound quality audio with play-by-play and color commentators describing the action while the PA announcer introduces the next batter; umpires making calls, peanut vendors hawking their wares, and hecklers screaming at the visiting team's superstar; crisp, accurate sound effects like doubles bouncing off the wall, bats "clattering" to the ground as the batter dashes out of the box, and the "smack" of horsehide settling into a fielder's glove. Not to mention crowds that cheer lustily for a home team dinger and groan mightily when the local favorite's drive is caught on the warning track, then sing along to a rousing organ rendition of "Hit the Road, Jack," when the visitors' starter is yanked in the sixth.

Advances in 3D graphics and animation will soon enable gamers to choose from a variety of "custom bodies" to more accurately represent individual players' physiques, batter stances, pitching motions, etc. Already, the on-field figures are often amazingly realistic, with real team logos on their jerseys, correct jersey numbers, and in at least one case, real player photos applied to their virtual counterparts' faces. While these improvements are almost entirely cosmetic, there's no disputing the added visual realism they provide.

Greater computing power also means a greater attention to subtle detail in today's (and tomorrow's) crop of games: realistic weather allows for cloudy, foggy, rainy, even snowy on-field conditions, as well as night games. Often, these are user-controlled, down to wind speed and direction, exact humidity and temperature, and so forth. Add to this the ability to play in precisely modeled, beautifully rendered facsimiles of any of the twenty-eight current stadiums, and you've got yourself a ballgame; even interleague play is a snap.

For the more statistically and/or strategically-minded fan, new features abound. How about head-to-head and situational stats, taken from the real world and applied to every batter-pitcher confrontation? Want an idea how Tony Gwynn fares against Greg Maddux in night games on the road in July, with runners in scoring position? No problem. Games like *Tony LaRussa Baseball* and Front Page Sports's *Baseball Pro '96* even let you assume the role of general manager. Controlling a team over many seasons offers a very different perspective, in which gamers worry about trade deadlines, salary caps, free agency, minor league prospects and the like.

Few things in life are certain, let alone in the frantic, fast-paced computer industry. But computer baseball simulations are sure to go on evolving and improving for years to come, as the power and sophistication of home PCs increase quickly and prices continue to fall. While it's easy to sympathize with fans of real-world baseball who yearn for the days when it was "just a game," fans of computer baseball can always take comfort in looking forward, not backward, for a Golden Age.

## CHAPTER 28

Reel Baseball

Bob Carroll and Rob Edelman

None of the very first movies shown to a paying audience in the United States featured pitchers and catchers, fielders making acrobatic plays and runners barreling into home plate. Some of their titles were *Sea Waves, Umbrella Dance, Butterfly Dance, Kaiser Wilhelm Reviewing His Troops,* and *A Boxing Bout.* They were among the dozen short films screened on April 23, 1896 as part of a vaudeville program at Koster and Bial's Music Hall in New York City.

But baseball, that all-American of sports, shortly would make its way onto movie screens. The Koster and Bial's program was presented by Thomas Alva Edison, inventor of the phonograph and lightbulb and one of the key figures in the development of early motion picture technology. It was Edison who produced the first official baseball movie: *The Ball Game* (1898), in which an amateur Newark, New Jersey nine battles an unnamed rival.

Since then, baseball has found its way into countless celluloid comedies and mysteries, musicals and dramas. It also has come to be a symbol for America. In the Academy Award-winning *The Best Years of Our Lives* (1946), three returning World War II veterans drive past their town's ballyard in a taxi that is dropping them at their respective residences, and the talk turns to the fortunes of the local nine. Before they have arrived at their doorsteps and greeted their relatives, they now officially are home.

However, the earliest baseball movies with plots were, as most other movies of the period, one or two reels in length. Many were melodramatic, and predated the Black Sox Scandal as their scenarios involved attempts to pay off players to throw games. A typical entry is *His Last Game* (1909), in which gamblers try but fail to bribe a ballplayer. Others were comedies: for example, in 1917 came a series of humorous "Mudville" comedy shorts. Some even featured the travails of fans. *How the Office Boy Saw the Ball Game* (1906) and *How Jones Saw the Baseball Game* (1907) chart the plight of employees scheming to skip out of work and attend a game. Real-life ballplayers appeared on screen in *Hal Chase's Home Fun* (1911) and *Home Run Baker's Double* (1914), *The Baseball Bug* (1911, featuring Chief Bender, Jack Coombs and Rube Oldring) and *Baseball's Peerless Leader* (1913), with Frank Chance.

The first feature-length baseball movie came in 1915 with *Right Off the Bat.* And with it came the first baseball hero-turned-movie actor: Mike Donlin, an outfielder who hit .333 in a twelve-year major league career (which ended the year before his screen debut). *Right Off the Bat* is the earliest example of one of the most venerable of all baseball film genres: the biography, in which a real-life ballplayer's on- and off-the-field heroics are chronicled, with liberal doses of fiction interspersed with fact. Donlin plays himself in *Right Off the Bat,* and the scenario follows his rise to baseball prominence. Throughout the 1920s and early '30s, until his death in 1933, Donlin played supporting roles in feature films (with baseball and nonbaseball themes). Also appearing as himself in *Right Off the Bat* is John McGraw (who may be seen in another early feature, 1917's *One Touch of Nature,* the story of a junior at Yale who becomes the New York Giants' rookie second baseman).

Almost seventy years before being depicted by director Ron Shelton in *Cobb,* Tyrus Raymond Cobb starred in a baseball movie: *Somewhere in Georgia* (1916). Like *Right Off the Bat, Somewhere in Georgia* is an attempt to mythicize a baseball hero. Cobb is cast as a bank clerk who ends up playing for the Detroit Tigers as he thwarts some villains and captures the heart of the heroine. Nowhere in evidence is there the smallest hint of Cobb's legendary contentiousness.

And nowhere to be found in *Headin' Home* (1920) is the real personality or history of its star, Babe Ruth. The Bambino plays a character who is meant to be autobiographical: a humble, mother-adoring small town lad who whittles his own bats out of wood. During the silent era, the Babe was to star in one other feature, *Babe Comes Home* (1927), and appear in a cameo in *Speedy* (1928), a Harold Lloyd comedy. His most notable screen role, however, came in the Lou Gehrig biography *The Pride of the Yankees* (1942).

Other baseball features were made during the twentieth century's second decade, most conspicuously the comedy *The Pinch Hitter* (1917) and the comedy-drama *The Busher* (1919), the latter easily the most entertaining of the first baseball features. Both starred Charles Ray, then at his peak playing rural clodhoppers who in the course of the story would come to maturity. In *The Busher,* Ray is cast as a talented small-town pitcher who is humbled after his ego becomes oversized upon his making the majors. In *The Pinch Hitter,* he is a shy farm boy who goes off to college and becomes a baseball hero.

From the time of *Right Off the Bat* and *The Busher* to the present, baseball has been a constant reference point in movies. However, not all of the films related to baseball have come out of Hollywood. In addition to baseball as a theme within a scenario, there have been baseball documentaries, which spotlight footage of real ballplayers in action or feature interviews and narration in which the individuals and incidents portrayed are placed within a historical context; and baseball instructionals, which are fashioned as teaching tools for those learning to play the game and understand its rules.

Documentaries

The primary footage included in baseball documentaries is of real-life ballplayers swinging bats, running the bases and making catches. Some simply are compilations of filmed events. While their footage is of historical interest today, much of it was shot strictly for profit-making purposes, to be marketed and sold to the public. In 1908 Essanay, a motion picture production and distribution company, commenced filming the World Series. High points of games were edited into one and two-reel films which were shown in movie theaters. The title tells all in *The Giants-White Sox World Tour* (1914), a celluloid record of an around-the-world trip undertaken during the winter of 1913-1914. Later on, countless baseball-related events were filmed and included in newsreels: visual records of the era's news which were produced prior to the popularity of television, and projected in movie theaters.

Today, the best of this early material which survives, along with footage culled from television broadcasts of ballgames, has been recycled into visual histories of the game. For example, in 1979, Major League Baseball (MLB) put together a film with a self explanatory title: *75 Years of World Series Memories.* For star-gazers, films and videos of All-Star Games are available from MLB from 1962 on, although another rare-film vendor offers earlier All-Star highlights. MLB also has marketed individual films and videos which highlight each World Series from 1943 to the present. The earliest, featuring the New York Yankees walloping the St. Louis Cardinals in five games, is in black-and-white and runs 30 minutes. Fifteen years later, when the Yankees edged the Milwaukee Braves in seven games, Major League Baseball began shooting the Series in color. But it wasn't until 1984 that the Series highlights were expanded to a full 60 minutes.

Major league teams produce short films and videos offering pennant race highlights. The purpose of these promos is not so much to relive the previous season as to help sell tickets for the upcoming one. Therefore, the footage is always upbeat. The local heroes exude spirit against overwhelming odds. While they may have finished last for the third season in a row, the mood is consistently cheerful as the near future is certain to be chock-filled with first place finishes and World Series victories. Fortunately for the makers of highlight films, even the most inept team will produce enough stellar plays over its approximately 500 hours of game-time to fill a 30-minute video.

In recent years, compilations of baseball clips have been marketed on video, under such titles as *Baseball's Greatest Moments, The 50 Greatest Home Runs in Baseball History,* and *MLB Unbelievable Bloopers and Great Plays.* Just about every top star of the modern era as well as a number of earlier luminaries has his own personal-highlight video. In fact, it seems as if, each week, an altogether new baseball video is offered for sale via television commercial.

Some baseball compilations are sublime. One such title

is *When It Was a Game* (1991), which along with a sequel, *When It Was a Game II,* was produced for HBO. *When It Was a Game* consists of home movies, filmed by players and fans between 1934 and 1957, and includes eye-popping images of the era's top stars. There are glimpses of what baseball looked like after many of its players went off to World War II, and peeks at extinct pre-expansion ballparks. Plus, there are some incredible images of the 1938 World Series, featuring the New York Yankees and Chicago Cubs. This is the earliest known color footage taken of the fall classic. Indeed, each image in *When It Was a Game* is in color, and this is what makes the program extra-special.

Easily the most famous of the baseball documentaries fashioned as a commentary on the game is *Baseball,* the much-ballyhooed, eighteen-hour epic which first aired on PBS in 1994. The film, while generally enjoyable, was not without controversy. Fans of baseball west of New York and Boston complained that *Baseball* was hampered by an Eastern bias. Other fans observed that Burns devoted too much footage to celebrity talking heads and not enough to the living legends and ordinary baseball figures. If one star emerged from *Baseball,* it was Buck O'Neil, the octogenarian Negro Leaguer whose warmth and perceptiveness transformed him into a national celebrity.

However, Ken Burns's *Baseball* is not the lone baseball documentary. Hundreds have been made over the decades, too numerous to cite here. A typically illuminating one, featuring conversations with players from the past, is *The Glory of Their Times* (1977), produced for PBS and based on Lawrence Ritter's classic book. In interviewing players from the 1898-1916 era, Ritter initiated the genre of oral baseball history, and many of the men with whom he spoke in the early 1960s still were alive when this film was produced. Another similar, equally excellent film is *The Boys of Summer* (1983), based on the Roger Kahn book, which spotlights Brooklyn Dodger stars of the 1950s.

Instructionals

"Instructional" films employ real ballplayers, coaches and managers to explain to the uninitiated how real ballplayers fire fastballs, belt home runs, or make letter-perfect pegs to nail runners attempting to take extra bases. These films date from the silent era. Technically, *Babe Ruth, How He Makes His Home Runs,* a 1920 one-reeler, qualifies as an instructional; the Bambino is shown swinging a bat in practice and in game action. The real point, however, was to give fans unable to get to the Polo Grounds (where the Yankees then played) or any other American League ballpark a chance to see baseball's newest hero "up close and personal." In 1932, the Bambino also appeared in several short films in the "Babe Ruth Baseball Series," which mixed athletic instruction with slim plots.

Lew Fonseca, while serving as manager of the Chicago White Sox between 1932 and 1934, experimented with using film to detect flaws in his players' techniques. (Considering that the Sox never rose above sixth place under his tutelage, he must have shot a lot of film.) Despite such worthy efforts as *Play Ball, Son!,* a 1946 three-reeler that showed viewers how to play the game position by position, instructionals were not an important part of baseball films until the advent of home video.

Today, a Little Leaguer can relax in his or her living room and be tutored in batting by Charley Lau (in *The Art of Hitting .300*) and Tony Gwynn (*King of Swing*); in baserunning by Maury Wills (*Baserunning Basics*); in fielding by Ozzie Smith (*Let's Play Baseball*); and in pitching by Mel Stottlemyre (*Pitching for Kids*). A young wannabe major leaguer can learn *George Brett's Secrets of Baseball,* or be taught by *Do-It-Better Baseball* or *Little League's Official How-to-Play Baseball.*

A parent seeking to improve a child's play will find plenty of instructionals, but the key is to select the one that teaches at the appropriate level for the student. Just as a fourth grader would be overwhelmed by a course in calculus, a baseball beginner will not be ready for a video meant to fine-tune the skills of a more advanced player. Similarly, that already-skilled player will quickly become bored with a video dealing only in the basics. Most instructionals list a range of ages for which they are designed, but the buyer should still ask if his or her youngster plays above or below others in that age range.

For example, *Baseball Tips for All Ages,* with Mickey Mantle, Whitey Ford, and Phil Rizzuto, is one of many excellent instructionals for beginners. It includes information on proper equipment, warming up, and safety. On the other hand, *Play Ball with Mickey Mantle,* featuring Gary Carter and Tom Seaver, is designed for more advanced students. Another important point is that children are more impressed by current players than with greats of the past. No matter how much you may worship Al Kaline, your child is more likely to pay attention to Ken Griffey, Jr.

Movie Movies

The term "baseball movies" usually connotes neither documentaries nor instructionals but fictional scenarios with actors playing ballplayers. Some are among the classics of all sports movies: *Bull Durham,* say, or *Field of Dreams,* or *The Bad News Bears.* Others make up the dregs of the genre: the original *Babe Ruth Story,* starring William Bendix, or the more recent *Ed,* or *The Bad News Bears in Breaking Training* and *The Bad News Bears Go to Japan.*

Ballfields and bleachers may be the settings of these and all of the other baseball movies, but most of the time we are supposed to focus on whether the hero will get the girl or foil the villain or be party to some heroic act—like belting a ninth-inning game-winning homer. The focus of the scenario is on characterization and plot, not baseball as a game.

However, there are certain constants in baseball films. Many of the older ones feature renditions of "Take Me Out to the Ball Game" over the opening credits. Many depict heroes who are youthful outsiders. Early on, they are refused spots on the sandlots by older, louder, tougher kids, but eventually prove to be destined for Hall-of-Fame-caliber careers. Some of the more intelligent baseball films—*Bull Durham* is the best of the lot—spotlight aging ballyard warriors and contrast them to talented young turks in desperate need of seasoning.

Ironically, several of the greatest baseball sequences appear in films whose content is otherwise completely unrelated to the sport. One such example is *Woman of the Year* (1942), a comedy about the evolving relationship between Sam Craig (Spencer Tracy), a sportswriter, and Tess Harding (Katharine Hepburn), a newspaper columnist. The film was released just as America had entered World War II and Tess, who admits that she knows nothing of sports, would have baseball prohibited for the duration. Sam vehemently protests that baseball is synonymous with America. The country is at war to protect all things American. So what would be the purpose of banning on the homefront the very thing that brave young soldiers are defending on foreign battlefields? This sequence is a consummate illustration of baseball employed as a metaphor for patriotism and Americanism. Additionally, Sam attempts to explain baseball to Tess during a visit to Yankee Stadium, in a sequence that is genuinely funny—and far more memorable than most found in the more generic baseball comedies.

Trivia buffs can endlessly cite the errors and inconsistencies in baseball films. The relationship between Lou Gehrig and Babe Ruth constantly varies from screen biography to screen biography. In *The Pride of the Yankees,* Gehrig's consecutive games-played streak ends when he is taken out of a game, not when he fails to appear in one. One of the more notorious and well-publicized gaffes of recent years occurs in *Field of Dreams* (1989), in which Shoeless Joe Jackson (Ray Liotta) bats righthanded and throws lefthanded. Sticklers can cite all the physically awkward actors cast as ballplayers, from over-aged and athletically inept Gary Cooper as Lou Gehrig in *The Pride of the Yankees* to gangly Anthony Perkins as Jimmy Piersall in *Fear Strikes Out* (1957) and narrow-shouldered Robert Young as a fireballing St. Louis Cardinals rookie hurler in *Death on the Diamond* (1934).

But only a confirmed nitpicker would let an occasional lapse ruin an otherwise enjoyable film. Despite its gaffes, *The Pride of the Yankees* remains a warmhearted love story. *Field of Dreams* expertly captures the game's nostalgia. *Fear Strikes Out* is an effective psychological portrait. *Death on the Diamond,* however, would be a lightweight, contrived murder mystery even if Dizzy Dean had replaced Young.

Admittedly, the most intrinsically exciting baseball movies just may be those World Series compilation films featuring Carlton Fisk willing his fly ball to stay fair in the 1975 Series, or Mookie Wilson's grounder eluding the glove of Bill Buckner in 1986. But no documentary can convey an altogether different type of passion, one that is found in fictional (or fictionalized) stories which deal with individuals and their baseball dreams.

Angels, Rhubarbs and Whatever Lola Wants

Among the most entertaining of all older baseball films is a trio of 1930s spoofs starring wide-mouthed comic Joe E. Brown. They are *Fireman, Save My Child* (1932), *Elmer the Great* (1933), and *Alibi Ike* (1935), the latter two based on the writings of sportswriter Ring Lardner. Unlike most of his acting peers, Brown was an excellent athlete who truly loved and understood the game of baseball. His is a likable screen presence, and he actually looked like a ballplayer even when winding up to pitch like some lunatic windmill. Buster Keaton is another comic who genuinely enjoyed the game. He incorporated baseball into two of his silent-era comedies, *College* (1927) and *The Cameraman* (1928), and made the sport the focus of a two-reeler, *One Run Elmer* (1935).

Comedy and fantasy are combined in a series of still-entertaining films from the late 1940s and early 1950s. The first is *It Happens Every Spring* (1949), without a doubt the best-ever title for a baseball movie. Ray Milland plays a chemistry professor who concocts a substance which has the peculiar ability to avoid wood. He becomes an unhittable pitcher by rubbing it on baseballs just before tossing them in the direction of hitters. For once, an actor's awkward throwing style works to the movie's advantage; this character is supposed to be neither pitcher nor athlete.

Paul Douglas, a former professional football player and radio sportscaster, nearly steals *It Happens Every Spring* as Milland's catcher. He also is quite funny in the original *Angels in the Outfield* (1951), far superior to the 1994 remake, in which he plays the hard-headed, hard-hearted, hard-cursing manager. The scenario chronicles how his team, the ever-incompetent Pittsburgh Pirates, is helped to a pennant by angels. Another sweetly likable comedy-fantasy is *Rhubarb* (1951), about a cat which inherits the Brooklyn baseball club.

Well down in the second division of the genre is *Roogie's Bump* (1954), in which a mysterious bump on his arm allows a little boy to throw a fearsome fastball and eventually play for the Brooklyn Dodgers. This scenario is reworked far more successfully in *Rookie of the Year* (1993), in which a fractured arm allows another youngster to toss a ball at 100 miles per hour, and hurl for the Chicago Cubs.

While the fantasy element is less apparent in *The Kid from Left Field* (1953), the scenario is structured around a gimmick—a nine-year-old becomes the manager of a major league team—with the result another diverting illustration of Hollywood escapism. The film was innocuously remade in 1979 as a television movie. It also predates the scenario of the decidedly minor league *Little Big League* (1994), in which a twelve-year-old inherits the Minnesota Twins and resolves to manage the team. Arguably the funniest of the comedies of this period is *Kill the Umpire* (1950), starring William Bendix—two years past his disastrous turn as Babe Ruth in *The Babe Ruth Story*—as a former ballplayer and maniacal fan who is forced to become the baseball lover's mortal enemy: an umpire.

Comedy unites with song in the baseball musical. The two best-known baseball song-and-dance fests are *Take Me Out to the Ball Game* (1949) and *Damn Yankees* (1958). The first is a lesser but still enjoyable MGM musical featuring Gene Kelly, Frank Sinatra, and Jules Munshin as a singing and dancing turn-of-the-century Tinker-to-Evers-to-Chance-like threesome. The second is the screen version of the long-running Broadway show about a middle-aged Washington Senators fan/New York Yankees hater who sells his soul to the devilish Mr. Applegate (Ray Walston) and is transformed into Joe Hardy (Tab Hunter), the phenom who will lead the lowly Washingtonians to the pennant. Applegate is aided by the ravishing Lola (Gwen Verdon), and the screen *Damn Yankees* remains a charming union of baseball and sex and an effective allegory about childhood fantasies contrasted to life's real priorities.

However, *Take Me Out to the Ball Game* and *Damn Yankees* are not the sole baseball musicals. *They Learned About Women* (1930) predates *Take Me Out to the Ball Game* as a story of ballplayers who tour the vaudeville circuit in the off-season. The stars are the real-life vaudeville team of Gus Van and Joseph T. Schenck, and the film is a harmonious early talkie crammed with songs and comedy routines.

Several of the more light-hearted baseball films involve children. *The Great American Pastime* (1956) is a by-the-numbers comedy featuring Tom Ewell as a suburban dad who coaches his son's Little League team. Two others are unintentionally hilarious: *The Kid from Cleveland* (1949), in which the previous year's world champions save the title character (Rusty Tamblyn) from juvenile delinquency; and *Safe at Home!* (1962), in which Mickey Mantle and Roger Maris, the previous year's home run sensations, rescue a Little Leaguer who brags that he can get them to attend his league's banquet. While it is fun to see the M-and-M boys (not to mention Whitey Ford and Ralph Houk) on screen, they were no threat to Gregory Peck or Jack Lemmon come Academy Awards night.

Baseball Biopics

The first sound-era baseball biography came in 1942, with the release of *The Pride of the Yankees,* starring Gary Cooper as doomed superstar Lou Gehrig. Despite Cooper's athletic ineptitude, he and Teresa Wright (as Eleanor Gehrig) give winning performances in what essentially is more of a love story than a baseball drama. In fact, a made-for-TV retelling of the Gehrig story, *A Love Affair: The Eleanor and Lou Gehrig Story* (1978), featured not a single scene of baseball action. Back in 1938, Gehrig himself had starred in *Rawhide,* a B-Western in which the Iron Horse traded his Yankee pinstripes for chaps and a cowboy hat. In several scenes—most notably when he thwarts a villain by instinctively belting a ball through a window—you know you are watching a poised, skilled athlete rather than an actor impersonating one.

The next baseball biography is probably the worst baseball movie ever made: *The Babe Ruth Story* (1948). Paul Douglas originally was slated for the role, but poor William Bendix ended up being sent up to bat as the Bambino. Bendix was one of Hollywood's finest character actors, as adept at playing comedy (in the aforementioned *Kill the Umpire)* and drama (in a series of films starring his friend Alan Ladd). Bendix also was perfectly cast in such war films as *Guadalcanal Diary* (1943), playing the stereotypical GI from Brooklyn whose every other thought is of his beloved "Bums." But the forty-two-year-old actor looks ridiculous impersonating the Babe, especially as a teenager, and the character as written is so honorable and heroic that it is unplayable. St. Babe absentmindedly misses a game to take an injured puppy to a hospital. He is unjustly chastised by his manager, Miller Huggins. He bashes a long spring training home run, at which point a young invalid, who is supposed to be crippled for life, rises to his feet in awe. The Babe belts his legendary "called" home run in the 1932 World Series because he had vowed to do so for a sick child. He passes on a job as manager of the Yankees' minor league affiliate in Newark solely to prevent the team's present skipper from being fired. Finally, the fatally ill Babe agrees to take an experimental serum because it "might help other people." (Less than a month before his death from cancer in August, 1948, the real Bambino appeared at the premiere of *The Babe Ruth Story,* but left the theater well before the finale.)

The story of Babe Ruth has been told twice more: in *Babe Ruth* (1991), a made-for-television movie starring Stephen Lang, and *The Babe* (1992), a theatrical feature with John Goodman. The latter differs from *The Babe Ruth Story* in that its subject is depicted far more realistically. For one thing, his first marriage, which is completely ignored in *The Babe Ruth Story,* is a major part of *The Babe.* The film offers a warts-and-all characterization of its subject, chronicling the incidents in his life, the idiosyncrasies of his character, and his conquests and frustrations.

However, the bulk of baseball biographies was produced during the late 1940s and early 1950s. *The Stratton Story* (1949) stars James Stewart as pitcher Monty Stratton, who lost his leg in a hunting accident but came back to pitch in the Texas League. As in the Gehrig movies the emphasis is on romance, with June Allyson playing Stratton's ever-supportive, girl-next-door wife.

No baseball movie ever had a lead more believable on the diamond than *The Jackie Robinson Story* (1950), simply because Jackie played himself. He was believable in his dramatic scenes, too, helped by Ruby Dee as his wife Rachel. Today, *The Jackie Robinson Story* serves as a compelling and valuable chronicle of its time, as the scenario clearly and soberly depicts the ballplayer's struggles as he becomes the first twentieth-century African American to play in the major leagues.

The Pride of St. Louis (1952), starring Dan Dailey as Dizzy Dean, and *The Winning Team* (1952), with Ronald Reagan as Grover Cleveland Alexander, feature remarkably similar scenarios. In each, a gifted young hurler emerges from backwoods America to perform Hall of Fame heroics on the ballfield. Once his career has crested, he sinks to a nadir as he pities himself and abuses alcohol, only to find redemption at the finale. While not strictly a biography, *Big Leaguer* (1953) is worth citing as it depicts a real-life former major leaguer: John B. "Hans" Lobert (Edward G. Robinson), who operates a Florida-based tryout camp for New York Giant wannabes.

Joining *The Babe* as the other major 1990s biography is *Cobb* (1994), starring Tommy Lee Jones and directed by Ron Shelton. The scenario focuses not on the Georgia Peach's on-field heroics but on his infamous belligerence and his relationship with sportswriter Al Stump (Robert Wuhl), hired to author the aged ballplayer's highly fictionalized life story. Like *The Pride of the Yankees* and *Fear Strikes Out,* the primary emphasis is not on sports, as *Cobb* acutely examines the cult of celebrity in America.

From the 1970s to the present, the majority of baseball biographies have been made-for-television movies. *It's Good to Be Alive* (1974), the story of Roy Campanella's struggle after a near-fatal automobile accident left him paralyzed, benefits from a touching performance by Paul Winfield as the former Dodger catcher. The perceptive, sobering *One in a Million: The Ron LeFlore Story* (1978) casts LeVar Burton in the title role of the outfielder who went from doing hard time in prison to swiping bases for the Detroit Tigers. *Don't Look Back: The Story of Leroy "Satchel" Paige* (1981) is an acceptable biography starring Louis Gossett, Jr. *A Winner Never Quits* (1986) is the inspiring story of Pete Gray (Keith Carradine), the one-armed outfielder who played for the St. Louis Browns during World War II.

The title tells all in *The Court-Martial of Jackie Robinson* (1990), a solid and revealing drama which focuses on Robinson's refusal to move to the rear of an army bus while stationed at Camp Hood in Texas during World War II. *Soul of the Game* (1996) is the generally effective, occasionally poignant story of three Negro Leaguers—Satchel Paige (Delroy Lindo), Josh Gibson (Mykelti Williamson), and Jackie Robinson (Blair Underwood)— in the mid-1940s, as the Brooklyn Dodgers' Branch Rickey was setting his plan in motion to integrate baseball. (The Paige-Gibson relationship was fictionalized in *The Bingo Long Traveling All-Stars & Motor Kings* (1976), with Billy Dee Williams playing the Paige character and James Earl Jones cast in the Gibson role. While entertaining, *Bingo Long* ultimately is a lightweight concoction rather than a realistic depiction of Negro League baseball.)

The final made-for-television biography does not involve a ballplayer. *Aunt Mary* (1979) is the heartfelt account of Mary Dobkin (Jean Stapleton), a dedicated fan and welfare recipient. The scenario charts how she comes to coach a sandlot team in the Baltimore slums during the 1950s.

The Golden Age of Baseball Movies

While the best baseball movies—*Bull Durham* and *Field of Dreams, The Bad News Bears* and *Bang the Drum Slowly*—have been released from the 1970s onward, it is a misnomer to declare that there were no good baseball films from earlier decades. In addition to the films commended above, even such an obscure feature as *The Battling Orioles* (1924), a slapstick in which the rowdy nineteenth-century Baltimore Orioles have aged into terminally tired stuffed shirts, is not without its moments of genuine mirth. So is *The Heckler* (1940), a two-reeler starring Charley Chase as a boorish fan. (*The Heckler* is a reworking of another comedy short, 1932's *The Loudmouth,* and was remade in 1946 as *Mr. Noisy.*)

At the same time, quite a few recent baseball movies have been something less than home runs. *The Slugger's Wife* (1985), *Brewster's Millions* (1985), *Stealing Home* (1988), *Trading Hearts* (1988), and *Night Game* (1989) are strictly second division. Despite its popularity, *Major League* (1989), the chronicle of a how a dreadful Cleveland Indians' team outmaneuvers its scheming new owner and becomes a pennant winner, is an insipid, minor league comedy—and its sequel is no improvement. *Ed* (1996), about a ballplaying chimpanzee, doesn't even make good kitsch; it rivals *The Babe Ruth Story* in the worst-ever department. *The Fan* (1996) is not only a bad movie: in its unashamedly cynical characterizations of a Barry Bonds-like ballplayer (Wesley Snipes) and the murderous fan (Robert De Niro) who idolizes him, it exudes distaste for ballplayers and fans alike.

The Golden Age of Baseball Movies dawns with *Bang the Drum Slowly* (1973), based on the Mark Harris novel and easily the best baseball drama made to date. It is the heartrending, supremely humanistic tale of a star pitcher (Michael Moriarty) and his relationship with a none-too-bright lug of a reserve catcher (Robert De Niro) who is terminally ill. *The Bad News Bears* (1976) is a genuinely funny comedy about a beer-guzzling ex-minor leaguer (Walter Matthau, in training for his role almost two decades later as one of the *Grumpy Old Men)* who comes to coach a thoroughly inept Little League team—which improves considerably when a girl (Tatum O'Neal) becomes its pitcher. Unfortunately, just about every child-related baseball film to come in the wake of *The Bad News Bears* has been mindlessly (if not insultingly) unfunny. One exception is *Rookie of the Year;* another is *The Sandlot* (1993), a sweet reminiscence about a gang of kids playing sandlot ball in the summer of 1962.

Two films fit into the "divided-camp" category. *The Natural* (1984), adapted from the Bernard Malamud novel, is an attempt at an adult baseball fable which ends up veering markedly from its source material and, to some critics, wallowing in simplicity and sentimentality; others have declared it a mythic poem superior to its literary source. It is the story of Roy Hobbs (Robert Redford), who might have been the greatest slugger ever had he not been shot and nearly killed by a mysterious woman in black. Sixteen years later, he becomes a middle-aged rookie who belts tape-measure dingers with "Wonderboy," his trusty bat. Regardless of how one regarded *The Natural,* it was a significant film in that its box-office success spurred production of other movies with baseball themes. *Mr. Baseball* (1992), a comedy about an ex-major leaguer (Tom Selleck) playing in Japan, offers some insight into Eastern-versus-Western philosophies, and while some are mystified by its brand of humor, others find it hilarious.

Two little-known movies about life in the minor leagues during the 1950s are effective as odes to their era, to baseball, and to the integrity of the game: *Pastime* (1991), with William Russ as an aging pitcher who befriends a young African-American rookie (Glenn Plummer); and *Long Gone* (1987), a made-for-TV feature starring William L. Petersen as a player-manager who refuses to barter his soul in order to appease his avaricious bosses.

One of the more intelligent baseball films of recent years is *Eight Men Out* (1988), John Sayles's chronicle of the Black Sox Scandal. Unlike most baseball movies set in the past, *Eight Men Out* in no way romanticizes its characters. *A League of Their Own* (1992) entertainingly recreates the first year of the All American Girls Professional Baseball League, which featured women players. The league was launched during World War II, and folded in 1954, and the scenario champions a woman's right to determine her own destiny.

Bull Durham (1988) arguably is the greatest baseball movie ever. It was made by Ron Shelton, a five-year veteran of minor league ball, and it is an at-once supremely funny and deeply knowing ode to baseball in the sticks. Kevin Costner has never been better, as Crash Davis, a career minor leaguer who truly respects the game

but languishes in the obscurity of the bushes. Tim Robbins plays Ebby Calvin "Nuke" LaLoosh, a fireballing young hurler with "a million-dollar arm, but a five-cent head." As Crash is assigned to tutor the youngster, *Bull Durham* becomes the prototype of all baseball films which contrast aging ballplayers whose baseball dreams were never quite realized and young hotshots whose natural ability alone will propel them to the majors. Finally, the scenario features the baseball fan to end all baseball fans: Annie Savoy (Susan Sarandon), whose "church of baseball" monologue as the film opens is a classic, poetic delineation of the game's appeal. (A group of prototypical Baby Boomer baseball fans may be found in 1991's *City Slickers,* whose best days have been spent in ballparks. And during the Vietnam era, the sole communication with their fathers centered around a shared love of baseball.)

Finally, *Field of Dreams* is the ultimate union of baseball and poetry, with the sport serving as a seed from which springs the wonder of life. *Field of Dreams,* based on W.P. Kinsella's novel Shoeless Joe, is the saga of an Iowa farmer named Ray Kinsella (Kevin Costner) who constructs a ballyard in his cornfield after being told by a mysterious voice that, "If you build it, they will come." Soon enough, the spirits of Shoeless Joe Jackson, other Black Soxers, and other baseball legends are frolicking in the infield.

The fantasy sequence in which the farmer comes to play catch with his now-young and rejuvenated father is nothing short of magical. So is the character of Old Doc Graham (Burt Lancaster), who decades earlier, as "Moonlight" Graham, played in a lone game for the New York Giants. (Back in 1905, a real ballplayer by this name did indeed play one game for the Giants.) While his baseball dreams were thwarted, Doc Graham nonetheless lived a happy and productive life as a small-town doctor.

In the 1990s, professional baseball has faced a series of controversies that have tested the patience of fans. A bit of dialogue from *Field of Dreams* sustained many of us. It is spoken to Ray Kinsella by Terence Mann (James Earl Jones), a reclusive writer who becomes a part of Kinsella's design to "build it":

"The one constant through all the years, Ray, has been baseball. Baseball has marked the time. This field, this game, is a part of our past, Ray. It reminds us of all that once was good, and that could be again."

Baseball Filmography

The list below includes feature films which include baseball in a major portion of their scenarios, and selected feature films in which real ballplayers appear as actors (such as Rawhide, *a B-Western starring Lou Gehrig).*

Right Off the Bat (1915) Arrow Film Corp., B&W, 5 reels. Dir.: Hugh Reticker. Cast: Mike Donlin, John J. McGraw, Claire Mersereau.

Casey at the Bat (1916) Fine Arts Film Co., B&W, 5 reels. Dir.: Lloyd Ingraham. Cast: DeWolf Hopper, Kate Toncray.

Somewhere in Georgia (1916) Sunbeam Motion Picture Corp., B&W, 6 reels. Dir.: George Ridgwell. Cast: Ty Cobb, Elsie MacLeod.

The Pinch Hitter (1917) New York Motion Picture Corp., B&W 5 reels. Dir.: Victor L. Schertzinger. Cast: Charles Ray, Sylvia Bremer.

One Touch of Nature (1917) Thomas A. Edison, Inc., B&W, 5 reels. Dir.: Edward H. Griffith. Cast: John Drew Bennett, Viola Cain, John J. McGraw.

The Busher (1919) Thomas H. Ince Corp., B&W, 5 reels. Dir.: Jerome Storm. Cast: Charles Ray, Colleen Moore, John Gilbert.

Headin' Home (1920) Kessel & Baumann Yankee Photo Corp., B&W, 5 reels. Dir.: Lawrence Windom. Cast: Babe Ruth, Ruth Taylor.

As the World Rolls On (1921) Andlauer Productions Elk Photo Plays, B&W, 7 reels. Dir.: W.A. Andlauer. Cast: Jack Johnson, Blanche Thompson.

Trifling with Honor (1923) Universal Pictures, B&W, 8 reels. Dir.: Harry A. Pollard. Cast: Rockliffe Fellowes, Fritzi Ridgeway.

Hit and Run (1924) Universal Pictures, B&W, 6 reels. Dir.: Edward Sedgwick. Cast: Hoot Gibson, Marion Harlan, Cyril Ring, Mike Donlin.

Life's Greatest Game (1924) Emory Johnson Productions, B&W, 8 reels. Dir.: Emory Johnson. Cast: Tom Santschi, Johnnie Walker, Jane Thomas.

The Battling Orioles (1924) Hal E. Roach Studios, B&W, 6 reels. Dir.: Ted Wilde, Fred Guiol. Cast: Glenn Tryon, Blanche Mahaffey.

The Pinch Hitter (1925) Associated Exhibitors, B&W, 7 reels. Dir.: Joseph Henabery. Cast: Glenn Hunter, Constance Bennett.

Play Ball (1925) Pathe Exchange, B&W, 10 chapter serial, 2 reels per chapter. Dir.: Spencer G. Bennet. Cast: Allene Ray, Walter Miller, John McGraw and the New York Giants.

The New Klondike (1926) Famous Players-Lasky Paramount Pictures, B&W, 8 reels. Dir.: Lewis Milestone. Cast: Thomas Meighan, Lila Lee, Paul Kelly.

Out of the West (1926) R-C Pictures, B&W, 5 reels. Dir.: Robert De Lacy. Cast: Tom Tyler, Bernice Welch, Frankie Darrow.

Babe Comes Home (1927) First National Pictures, B&W, 6 reels. Dir.: Ted Wilde. Cast: Babe Ruth, Anna Q. Nilsson, Louise Fazenda.

The Bush Leaguer (1927) Warner Bros., B&W, 7 reels. Dir.: Howard Bretherton. Cast: Monte Blue, Clyde Cook, Leila Hyams, William Demarest.

Casey at the Bat (1927) Famous Players-Lasky Paramount Pictures, B&W, 6 reels. Dir.: Monte Brice. Cast: Wallace Beery, Ford Sterling, ZaSu Pitts, Sterling Holloway.

Catch-as-Catch-Can (1927) Gotham Productions, B&W, 5 reels. Dir.: Charles Hutchinson. Cast: William Fairbanks, Jack Richardson, Rose Blossom.

College (1927) Buster Keaton Productions United Artists, B&W, 6 reels. Dir.: James W. Horne. Cast: Buster Keaton, Anne Cornwall, Flora Bramley, Harold Goodwin, University of Southern California Baseball Team.

Slide, Kelly, Slide (1927) Metro-Goldwyn-Mayer, B&W, 8 reels. Dir.: Edward Sedgwick. Cast: William Haines, Sally O'Neil, Harry Carey, Karl Dane, Junior Coghlan, Warner Richmond, Paul Kelly, Guinn "Big Boy" Williams, Mike Donlin, Bob Meusel, Irish Meusel, Tony Lazzeri.

The Cameraman (1928) Metro-Goldwyn-Mayer, B&W, 8 reels. Dir.: Edward Sedgwick. Cast: Buster Keaton, Marceline Day, Harry Gribbon, Harold Goodwin.

Speedy (1928) Harold Lloyd Corp. Paramount Famous Lasky Corp., B&W, 8 reels. Dir.: Ted Wilde. Cast: Harold Lloyd, Ann Christy, Babe Ruth.

Warming Up (1928) Paramount Famous Lasky Corp., B&W, 8 reels. Dir.: Fred Newmeyer. Cast: Richard Dix, Jean Arthur, Roscoe Karns, Mike Donlin.

Fast Company (1929) Paramount Famous Lasky Corp., B&W, 8 reels. Dir.: A. Edward Sutherland. Cast: Jack Oakie, Evelyn Brent, Skeets Gallagher, Irish Meusel, Arnold "Jigger" Statz.

Hot Curves (1930) Tiffany Productions, B&W, 9 reels. Dir.: Norman Taurog. Cast: Benny Rubin, Rex Lease, Alice Day, Pert Kelton, Mike Donlin.

They Learned About Women (1930) Metro-Goldwyn-Mayer, B&W, 11 reels. Dir.: Jack Conway, Sam Wood. Cast: Joseph T. Schenck, Gus Van, Bessie Love, Mary Doran, Benny Rubin.

Fireman, Save My Child (1932) First National and Vitaphone, B&W, 67 min. Dir.: Lloyd Bacon. Cast: Joe E. Brown, Evalyn Knapp, Lillian Bond, Guy Kibbee.

Elmer the Great (1933) First National and Vitaphone, B&W, 74 min. Dir.: Mervyn LeRoy. Cast: Joe E. Brown, Patricia Ellis, Frank McHugh, Claire Dodd, Preston S. Foster, Sterling Holloway.

Death on the Diamond (1934) Metro-Goldwyn-Mayer, B&W, 69 min. Dir.: Edward Sedgwick. Cast: Robert Young, Madge Evans, Nat Pendleton, Ted Healy, C. Henry Gordon, Paul Kelly, Mickey Rooney.

Alibi Ike (1935) Warner Brothers and Vitaphone, B&W, 73 min. Dir.: Ray Enright. Cast: Joe E. Brown, Olivia de Havilland, Roscoe Karns, William Frawley.

Swell-Head (1935) Columbia Pictures, B&W, 62 min. Dir.: Ben Stoloff. Cast: Wallace Ford, Dickie Moore, Barbara Kent, J. Farrell MacDonald, Mike Donlin.

The Adventures of Frank Merriwell (1936) Universal Pictures, B&W, 12-chapter serial, 2 reels per chapter. Dir.: Cliff Smith. Cast: Don Briggs, Jean Rogers, John King.

Girls Can Play (1937) Columbia Pictures, B&W, 6 reels. Dir.: Lambert Hillyer. Cast: Jacqueline Wells (Julie Bishop), Charles Quigley, Rita Hayworth.

Manhattan Merry-Go-Round (1937) Republic Pictures, B&W, 82 min., D.: Charles F. Reisner. Cast: Phil Regan, Leo Carillo, Ann Dvorak, James Gleason, Joe DiMaggio.

Rawhide (1938) Principal Productions, Inc. Twentieth Century-Fox, B&W, 60 min. Dir.: Ray Taylor. Cast: Smith Ballew, Lou Gehrig, Evalyn Knapp.

Brother Rat (1938) Warner Bros., B&W, 90 min. Dir.: William Keighley. Cast: Priscilla Lane, Wayne Morris, Johnnie Davis, Jane Bryan, Eddie Albert, Ronald Reagan, Jane Wyman.

Woman of the Year (1942) Metro-Goldwyn-Mayer, B&W, 1112 m., Dir.: George Stevens. Cast: Spencer Tracy, Katharine Hepburn, Fay Bainter, Reginald Owen, Minor Watson, William Bendix.

The Pride of the Yankees (1942) The Samuel Goldwyn Company RKO-Radio, B&W, 128 min. Dir.: Sam Wood. Cast: Gary Cooper, Teresa Wright, Walter Brennan, Dan Duryea, Babe Ruth, Elsa Jansen, Ludwig Stossel, Bill Dickey, Bob Meusel, Mark Koenig, Bill Stern.

It Happened in Flatbush (1942) Twentieth Century-Fox, B&W, 80 min. D.: Ray McCarey. Cast: Lloyd Nolan, Carol Landis, Sara Allgood, William Frawley, Robert Armstrong, Jane Darwell.

Ladies' Day (1943) RKO-Radio, B&W, 62 min. Dir.: Leslie Goodwins. Cast: Lupe Velez, Eddie Albert, Patsy Kelly, Max Baer.

Whistling in Brooklyn (1943) Metro-Goldwyn-Mayer, B&W, 87 min. D.: S. Sylvan Simon. Cast: Red Skelton, Ann Rutherford, Jean Rogers, Rags Ragland, Ray Collins, William Frawley, Sam Levene, Leo Durocher and The Brooklyn Dodgers.

The Naughty Nineties (1945) Universal Pictures, B&W, 76 min. Dir.: Jean Yarbrough. Cast: Bud Abbott, Lou Costello, Alan Curtis, Rita Johnson.

Make Mine Music (1946) Walt Disney Productions RKO-Radio, Color, 75 min. "Casey at the Bat" directed by Clyde Geronimi, narrated by Jerry Colonna.

The Babe Ruth Story (1948) Allied Artists, B&W, 106 min. Dir.: Roy Del Ruth. Cast: William Bendix, Claire Trevor, Charles Bickford, Sam Levene, William Frawley, Mark Koenig, Harry Wismer, Mel Allen, H.V. Kaltenborn, Knox Manning.

It Happens Every Spring (1949) Twentieth Century-Fox, B&W, 87 min. Dir.: Lloyd Bacon. Cast: Ray Milland, Jean Peters, Paul Douglas, Ed Begley, Ted de Corsia, Ray Collins, Jessie Royce Landis, Alan Hale, Jr.

The Kid from Cleveland (1949) Republic Pictures, B&W, 89 min. Dir.: Herbert Kline. Cast: George Brent, Lynn Bari, Rusty Tamblyn, John Berardino, Bill Veeck, The Cleveland Indians.

The Stratton Story (1949) Metro-Goldwyn-Mayer, B&W, 106 min. Dir.: Sam Wood. Cast: James Stewart, June Allyson, Frank Morgan, Agnes Moorehead, Bill Williams, Gene Bearden, Jimmy Dykes, Mervyn "Spec" Shea, Bill Dickey.

Take Me Out to the Ball Game (1949) Metro-Goldwyn-Mayer, Color, 93 min. Dir.: Busby Berkeley. Cast: Gene Kelly, Frank Sinatra, Esther Williams, Jules Munshin, Betty Garrett, Edward Arnold.

The Jackie Robinson Story (1950) Jewell Pictures Corp. Eagle-Lion Films, B&W, 77 min. Dir.: Alfred E. Green. Cast: Jackie Robinson, Ruby Dee, Minor Watson, Louise Beavers, Richard Lane, Kenny Washington.

Kill the Umpire (1950) Columbia Pictures, B&W, 78 min. Dir.: Lloyd Bacon. Cast: William Bendix, Una Merkel, Ray Collins, William Frawley, Gloria Henry, Tom D'Andrea, Alan Hale, Jr.

Angels in the Outfield (1951) Metro-Goldwyn-Mayer, B&W, 99 min. Dir.: Clarence Brown. Cast: Paul Douglas, Janet Leigh, Donna Corcoran, Keenan Wynn, Lewis Stone, Spring Byington, Bruce Bennett, Ellen Corby, Joe DiMaggio, Bing Crosby, Ty Cobb, Harry Ruby.

Rhubarb (1951) Paramount Pictures, B&W, 94 min. Dir.: Arthur Lubin. Cast: Ray Milland, Jan Sterling, Gene Lockhart, William Frawley, Elsie Holmes, Leonard Nimoy.

The Pride of St. Louis (1952) Twentieth Century-Fox, B&W, 93 min. Dir.: Harmon Jones. Cast: Dan Dailey, Joanne Dru, Richard Hylton, Richard Crenna, Chet Huntley.

The Winning Team (1952) Warner Bros., B&W, 98 min. Dir.: Lewis Seiler. Cast: Doris Day, Ronald Reagan, Frank Lovejoy, Eve Miller, Bob Lemon, Gerry Priddy, Peanuts Lowery, George (Catfish) Metkovich, Irving (Irv) Noren, Hank Sauer, Al Zarilla, Gene Mauch.

Big Leaguer (1953) Metro-Goldwyn-Mayer, B&W, 70 min. Dir.: Robert Aldrich. Cast: Edward G. Robinson, Vera Ellen, Jeff Richards, Richard Jaeckel, William Campbell, Carl Hubbell, Al Campanis, Bob Tricolor, Tony Ravish.

The Kid from Left Field (1953) Twentieth Century-Fox, B&W, 80 min. Dir.: Harmon Jones. Cast: Dan Dailey, Anne Bancroft, Billy Chapin, Lloyd Bridges, Ray Collins, Richard Egan, Fess Parker, John Berardino, John "Beans" Reardon.

Roogie's Bump (1954) Republic Pictures, B&W, 71 min. Dir.: Harold Young. Cast: Robert Marriot, Ruth Warrick, Olive Blackeney, Robert Simon, Roy Campanella, Billy Loes, Carl Erskine, Russ Meyer.

Three Stripes in the Sun (1955) Columbia Pictures, B&W, 93 min. Dir.: Richard Murphy. Cast: Aldo Ray, Phil Carey, Dick York, Mitsuko Kimura, Chuck Connors.

The Great American Pastime (1956) Metro-Goldwyn-Mayer, B&W, 89 min. Dir.: Herman Hoffman. Cast: Tom Ewell, Anne Francis, Ann Miller, Dean Jones.

I'll Buy You (1956) Shochiku, B&W, 113 min. Dir.: Masaki Kobayashi. Cast: Keiji Sata, Keiko Kishi, Minoru Oki.

Fear Strikes Out (1957) Paramount Pictures, B&W, 100 min. Dir.: Robert Mulligan. Cast: Anthony Perkins, Karl Malden, Norma Moore, Adam Williams, Perry Wilson.

Damn Yankees (1958) Warner Bros., Color, 110 min. Dir.: George Abbott, Stanley Donen. Cast: Tab Hunter, Gwen Verdon, Ray Walston, Russ Brown, Shannon Bolin, Robert Shafer, Rae Allen, Nathaniel Frey, Jimmie Komack, Jean Stapleton, Bob Fosse.

The Geisha Boy (1958) Paramount Pictures, Color, 95 min. Dir.: Frank Tashlin. Cast: Jerry Lewis, Marie McDonald, Sessue Hayakawa, Suzanne Pleshette, The Los Angeles Dodgers.

Safe at Home! (1962) Naud-Hamilburg Productions Columbia Pictures, B&W, 83 min. Dir.: Walter Doniger. Cast: Mickey Mantle, Roger Maris, William Frawley, Patricia Barry, Don Collier, Bryan Russell, Ralph Houk, Whitey Ford.

That Touch of Mink (1962) Granley Company-Arwin Productions-Nob Hill Productions Universal-International, Color, 99 min. Dir.: Delbert Mann. Cast: Cary Grant, Doris Day, Gig Young, Audrey Meadows, Mickey Mantle, Roger Maris, Yogi Berra, Art Passarella.

The Ceremony (1971) Sozosha-Atg Shibata Org., Color, 122 min., Dir: Nagisa Oshima. Cast: Kenzo Kawarazaki, Atsuko Kaku, Atsuo Nakamura.

One-Legged Ace (1971) Katsu Productions Daiei, Color, 100 min., Dir.: Kazuo Ikehiro.

Bang the Drum Slowly (1973) Paramount Pictures, Color, 97 min. Dir.: John Hancock. Cast: Michael Moriarty, Robert De Niro, Vincent Gardenia, Phil Foster, Ann Wedgeworth, Tom Ligon.

It's Good to Be Alive (1974, made for TV) Metromedia Producers Corporation/ Larry Harman Pictures CBS, Color, 100 min. Dir.: Michael Landon. Cast: Paul Winfield, Louis Gossett Jr., Ruby Dee, Ramon Bieri.

The Bad News Bears (1976) Paramount Pictures, Color, 102 min. Dir.: Michael Ritchie. Cast: Walter Matthau, Tatum O'Neal, Vic Morrow, Joyce Van Patten, Ben Piazza, Jackie Earle Haley.

The Bingo Long Traveling All-Stars & Motor Kings (1976) Motown Production/Pan Arts Enterprises Universal Pictures, Color, 110 minutes. Dir.: John Badham. Cast: Billy Dee Williams, James Earl Jones, Richard Pryor, Stan Shaw, Ted Ross, Leon Wagner, Emmett Ashford.

The Bad News Bears in Breaking Training (1977) Paramount Pictures, Color, 100 min. Dir.: Michael Pressman. Cast: William Devane, Clifton James, Jackie Earle Haley, Jimmy Baio, Bob Watson, Enos Cabell, Roger Metzger, J.R. Richard, Joe Ferguson, Ken Forsch, Cesar Cedeno, Bill Virdon.

Just the Beginning (1977) Yung Bang Films, Color, 105 min. Dir.: Jung In Yup. Cast: Jin Yoo Young, Ha Myoung Jung, Kang Ju Hee.

Murder at the World Series (1977, made for TV) ABC Circle Films ABC, Color, 100 min. Dir.: Andrew V. McLaglen. Cast: Lynda Day George, Murray Hamilton, Karen Valentine, Gerald S. O'Loughlin, Michael Parks, Janet Leigh, Hugh O'Brian.

The Bad News Bears Go to Japan (1978) Paramount Pictures, Color, 91 min. Dir.: John Berry. Cast: Tony Curtis, Jackie Earle Haley, Tomasaburo Wakayama.

A Boy Called Third Base (1978) Gentosha and ATG, Color, 102 min. Dir.: Yoichi Higashi. Cast: Toshiyuki Nagashima, Tsuguaki Yoshida, Aiko Morishita.

Goodbye, Franklin High (1978) Cal-Am Productions, Color, 94 min. Dir.: Mike MacFarland. Cast: Lane Caudell, Julie Adams, William Windom.

Here Come the Tigers (1978) Filmways Pictures American International, Color, 90 min. Dir.: Sean S. Cunningham. Cast: Richard Lincoln, James Zvanut, Samantha Grey.

A Love Affair: The Eleanor and Lou Gehrig Story (1978, made for TV) Charles Fries Productions/Stonehenge Productions ABC, Color, 100 min. Dir.: Fielder Cook. Cast: Blythe Danner, Edward Herrmann, Patricia Neal, Gerald S. O'Laughlin, Ramon Bieri, Jane Wyatt, Georgia Engel, Michael Lerner.

One in a Million: The Ron LeFlore Story (1978, made for TV) Roger Gimbel Productions/EMI Television CBS, Color, 100 min. Dir.: William A. Grahame. Cast: LeVar Burton, Madge Sinclair, Paul Benjamin, James Luisi, Billy Martin, Larry B. Scott, Al Kaline, Norm Cash, Jim Northrup, Bill Freehan.

Aunt Mary (1979, made for TV) Henry Jaffe Enterprises CBS, Color, 100 min. Dir.: Peter Werner. Cast: Jean Stapleton, Martin Balsam, Harold Gould, Dolph Sweet, Ernie Harwell.

The Kid from Left Field (1979, made for TV) Gary Coleman Productions/ Deena Silver Kramer's Movie Company NBC, Color, 100 min. Dir.: Adell Aldrich. Cast: Gary Coleman, Robert Guillaume, Gary Collins, Ed McMahon, Tab Hunter.

The Comeback Kid (1980, made for TV) ABC Circle Films ABC, Color, 100 min. Dir.: Peter Levin. Cast: John Ritter, Susan Dey, Doug McKeon, James Gregory, Patrick Swayze.

Squeeze Play (1980) Troma, Color, 92 minutes. Dir.: Samuel Weil. Cast: Jim Harris, Jenni Hetrick, Rick Gitlin.

Don't Look Back: The Story of Leroy "Satchel" Paige (1981, made for TV) TBA Productions; Satie Productions; Triseme ABC, Color, 100 min. Dir.: Richard A. Colla. Cast: Louis Gossett Jr., Beverly Todd, Cleavon Little, Ernie Barnes, Clifton Davis, John Beradino, Ossie Davis, Satchel Paige, Bubba Phillips.

Chasing Dreams (1982) Nascent Productions Prism Entertainment Corp., Color, 96 min. Dir.: Therese Conte. Cast: David G. Brown, John Fife, Jim Shane, Kevin Costner.

Million Dollar Infield (1982, made for TV) CBS Entertainment CBS, Color, 100 min. Dir.: Hal Cooper. Cast: Bonnie Bedelia, Robert Costanzo, Rob Reiner, Christopher Guest, Bruno Kirby, Mel Allen.

Zapped! (1982) Embassy Pictures, Color, 96 min. Dir.: Robert J. Rosenthal. Cast: Scott Baio, Willie Aames, Heather Thomas.

Blue Skies Again (1983) Lantana Production Warner Bros., Color, 96 min. Dir.: Richard Michaels. Cast: Harry Hamlin, Mimi Rogers, Robyn Barto, Kenneth McMillan, Dana Elcar, Andy Garcia.

Tiger Town (1983, made for TV) Walt Disney Productions The Disney Channel, Color, 76 min. Dir.: Alan Shapiro. Cast: Roy Scheider, Justin Henry, Ron McLarty, Sparky Anderson, Ernie Harwell.

Max Dugan Returns (1983), Twentieth Century-Fox, Color, 98 min. D.: Herbert Ross. Cast: Marsha Mason, Jason Robards, Donald Sutherland, Matthew Broderick, Charlie Lau.

The Natural (1984) Tri-Star-Delphi II Tri-Star Pictures, Color, 134 min. Dir.: Barry Levinson. Cast: Robert Redford, Robert Duvall, Glenn Close, Kim Basinger, Wilford Brimley, Barbara Hershey, Robert Prosky, Richard Farnsworth, Darren McGavin, Joe Don Baker, Michael Madsen, Sibbi Sisti.

A Soldier's Story (1984) Columbia Pictures, Color, 102 min. Dir.: Norman Jewison. Cast: Howard E. Rollins, Jr., Adolph Caesar, Art Evans, David Alan Grier, David Harris, Larry Riley, Denzel Washington.

The Slugger's Wife (1985) Rastar Columbia Pictures, Color, 105 min. Dir.: Hal Ashby. Cast: Michael O'Keefe, Rebecca De Mornay, Martin Ritt, Randy Quaid, Cleavant Derricks, Mark Fidrych, Al Hrobosky, Ted Turner, Pete Van Wieren, Ernie Johnson, Skip Caray, Nick Charles.

Brewster's Millions (1985) Universal Pictures, Color, 97 min., Dir: Walter Hill. Cast: Richard Pryor, John Candy, Lonette McKee, Stephen Collins, Jerry Orbach, Pat Hingle, Tovah Feldshuh, Hume Cronyn, Rick Moranis.

MacArthur's Children (1985) Orion Classics, Color, 115 min., Dir.: Masahiro Shinoda. Cast: Takaya Yamuchi, Yoshiyuki Omuri, Shiori Sakura.

Insignificance (1985) Zenith Productions Island Alive, Color, 105 min. Dir.: Nicolas Roeg. Cast: Gary Busey, Michael Emil, Theresa Russell, Will Sampson, Tony Curtis.

A Winner Never Quits (1986, made for TV) Blatt/Singer Production Columbia Pictures ABC, Color, 100 min. Dir.: Mel Damski. Cast: Keith Carradine, Huckleberry Fox, Mare Winningham, Dennis Weaver, Ed O'Neill, Dana Delaney.

Long Gone (1987, made for TV) Landsburg Company HBO, Color, 110 min. Dir.: Martin Davidson. Cast: William L. Petersen, Virginia Madsen, Dermot Mulroney, Larry Riley.

Amazing Grace and Chuck (1987) Turnstar Production Tri-Star Pictures/Rastar, Color, 115 min., Dir.: Mike Newell. Cast: Gregory Peck, William L. Petersen, Joshua Zuehlke, Alex English, Jamie Lee Curtis.

Bull Durham (1988) Mount Company Orion Pictures, Color, 115 min. Dir.: Ron Shelton. Cast: Kevin Costner, Susan Sarandon, Tim Robbins, Trey Wilson, Robert Wuhl, Max Patkin.

Eight Men Out (1988) Orion Pictures, Color, 115 min. Dir.: John Sayles. Cast: John Cusack, David Strathairn, D.B. Sweeney, Michael Rooker, Charlie Sheen, John Sayles, Studs Terkel, Michael Lerner, Christopher Lloyd.

Stealing Home (1988) Mount Company Warner Bros., Color, 98 min. Dir.: John Sayles. Cast: Mark Harmon, Jodie Foster, Blair Brown, Jonathan Silverman, Harold Ramis.

Naked Gun: From the Files of Police Squad (1988) Paramount Pictures, Color, 85 min. Dir.: David Zucker. Cast: Leslie Nielsen, George Kennedy, Priscilla Presley, Ricardo Montalban, O.J. Simpson, Reggie Jackson, Jay Johnstone, Hank Robinson, Joe West, Curt Gowdy, Jim Palmer, Tim McCarver, Dick Vitale, Mel Allen, Dick Enberg.

Trading Hearts (1988) The Vista Organization Cineworld Enterprises/IVE, Color, 88 min. D.: Neil Leifer. Cast: Raul Julia, Beverly D'Angelo, Jenny Lewis, Frank DeFord, Ed Koch.

Field of Dreams (1989) Gordon Company Production Universal Pictures, Color, 107 min. Dir.: Phil Alden Robinson. Cast: Kevin Costner, Amy Madigan, Gaby Hoffman, James Earl Jones, Ray Liotta, Burt Lancaster, Timothy Busfield.

Major League (1989) Morgan Creek/Mirage Production Paramount Pictures, Color, 106 min. Dir.: David Ward. Cast: Tom Berenger, Charlie Sheen, Corbin Bernsen, Margaret Whitton, Rene Russo, James Gammon, Bob Uecker, Wesley Snipes, Dennis Haysbert, Steve Yeager, Pete Vukovich.

Night Game (1989) Epic Productions Trans World Entertainment, Color, 95 min., D.: Peter Masterson. Cast: Roy Scheider, Karen Young, Richard Bradford.

The Court-Martial of Jackie Robinson (1990, made for TV) Von Zerneck-Sertner Films; Turner Pictures TNT, Color, 100 min. Dir.: Larry Peerce. Cast: Andre Braugher, Ruby Dee, Stan Shaw, Kasi Lemmons, Daniel Stern, Bruce Dern, Paul Dooley.

Babe Ruth (1991, made for TV) Lyttle Productions NBC, Color, 100 min. Dir.: Mark Tinker. Cast: Stephen Lang, Bruce Weitz, Donald Moffat, Lisa Zane, Pete Rose, John Anderson.

Pastime (1991) Bullpen Ltd./Open Road Productions Miramax, Color, 95 min. Dir.: Robin B. Armstrong. Cast: William Russ, Glenn Plummer, Noble Willingham, Jeffrey Tambor, Scott Plank, Dierdre O'Connell, Duke Snider, Don Newcombe, Ernie Banks, Bill Mazeroski, Harmon Killebrew, Bob Feller.

Talent for the Game (1991) Paramount Pictures, Color, 91 min. Dir.: Robert M. Young. Cast: Edward James Olmos, Lorraine Bracco, Jeffrey Corbett, Jamey Sheridan, Terry Kinney, Bobby Tolan, Derrel Thomas, Lenny Randle, Todd Cruz, John D'Aquisto, Phil Lombardi, Lee Lacy, Rudy Law, Steve Ontiveros.

City Slickers (1991) Castle Rock Entertainment/Nelson Entertainment/A Face Production Columbia Pictures, Color, 112 min. Dir.: Ron Underwood. Cast: Billy Crystal, Daniel Stern, Bruno Kirby, Patricia Wettig, Helen Slater, Jack Palance, Josh Mostel, David Paymer.

The Babe (1992) Waterhorse/Finnegan-Pinchuk Universal Pictures, Color, 113 min. Dir.: Arthur Hiller. Cast: John Goodman, Kelly McGillis, Trini Alvarado, Bruce Boxleitner, Peter Donat, James Cromwell, J.C. Quinn, Joe Ragno, Richard Tyson.

The Comrades of Summer (1992, made for TV) Grossbart Barnett Productions HBO, Color, 108 min. Dir.: Tommy Lee Wallace. Cast: Joe Mantegna, Natalya Negoda, Mark Rolston, Michael Lerner, Jim Lampley.

A League of Their Own (1992) Parkway Production Columbia Pictures, Color, 124 min. Dir.: Penny Marshall. Cast: Tom Hanks, Geena Davis, Lori Petty, Madonna, Rosie O'Donnell, Megan Cavanagh, David Strathairn, Garry Marshall, Jon Lovitz, Bill Pullman.

Mr. Baseball (1992) Outlaw Production Universal Pictures, Color, 100 min. Dir.: Fred Schepisi. Cast: Tom Selleck, Ken Takakura, Aya Takanashi, Dennis Haysbert, Toshi Shioya, Tim McCarver, Sean McDonough, Greg Goossen, Frank Thomas.

Cooperstown (1993, made for TV) Brandman Productions, Inc./Ambler Television TNT Screenworks, Color, 90 min. Dir.: Charles Haid. Cast: Alan Arkin, Graham Greene, Hope Lange, Josh Charles, Ed Begley Jr., Maria Pitillo, Ann Wedgeworth, Paul Dooley, Charles Haid, Ernie Harwell.

The Sandlot (1993) Island World Twentieth Century-Fox, Color, 101 min. Dir.: David Mickey Evans. Cast: Tom Guiry, Mike Vitar, Patrick Renna, Chauncy Leopardi, James Earl Jones, Art LaFleur.

Rookie of the Year (1993) Twentieth Century-Fox, Color, 103 min. Dir.: Daniel Stern. Cast: Thomas Ian Nicholas, Gary Busey, Albert Hall, Amy Morton, John Candy, Eddie Bracken, Daniel Stern, Barry Bonds, Bobby Bonilla, Pedro Guerrero, Tim Stoddard.

The Man from Left Field (1993) Burt Reynolds Productions, Inc. CBS, Color, 100 min. Dir.: Burt Reynolds. Burt Reynolds, Reba McEntire, Derek Baxter, Sean Dunne, Billy Gardner III.

The Scout (1994) Ruddy Morgan Twentieth Century-Fox, Color, 101 min. Dir.: Michael Ritchie. Cast: Albert Brooks, Brendan Fraser, Dianne Wiest, Lane Smith, Anne Twomey, Michael Rapaport, Ken Brett, Bob Costas, Roy Firestone, Steve Garvey, Keith Hernandez, Tom Kelly, Tim McCarver, Bobby Murcer, Brett Saberhagen, Bob Sheppard, Ozzie Smith, Reggie Smith, George Steinbrenner III.

Angels in the Outfield (1994) Walt Disney Pictures/Caravan Pictures Buena Vista, Color, 102 min. Dir.: William Dear. Cast: Danny Glover, Brenda Fricker, Tony Danza, Christopher Lloyd, Ben Johnson, Jay O. Sanders, Joseph Gordon-Levitt, Dermot Mulroney, Taylor Negron, Tony Longo, Matthew McConaughy, Mitchell Page, Carney Lansford.

Major League II (1994) Morgan Creek Warner Bros., Color, 104 min. Dir.: David S. Ward. Cast: Charlie Sheen, Tom Berenger, Corbin Bernsen, Dennis Haysbert, James Gammon, Bob Uecker, Margaret Whitton, Randy Quaid, Steve Yeager, Kevin Hickey, Jay Leno.

Little Big League (1994) Castle Rock Entertainment Columbia Pictures, Color, 119 min. Dir.: Andrew Scheinman. Cast: Luke Edwards, Timothy Busfield, John Ashton, Ashley Crow, Kevin Dunn, Jason Robards, Jonathan Silverman, Dennis Farina, Leon "Bull" Durham, Kevin Elster, Ken Griffey, Jr., Lou Pinella, Mickey Tettleton, Ivan Rodriguez, Sandy Alomar, Jr., Eric Anthony, Carlos Baerga, Alex Fernandez, Randy Johnson, Wally Joyner, Dave Magadan, Lenny Webster, Paul O'Neill, Rafael Palmeiro, Dean Palmer, Tim Raines, Chris Berman.

Cobb (1994) Regency Enterprises/Alcor Films Warner Bros., Color, 128 min. Dir.: Ron Shelton. Cast: Tommy Lee Jones, Robert Wuhl, Lolita Davidovich, Lou Myers, Tyler Logan Cobb, Roger Clemens, Jay Tibbs, Ernie Harwell.

The Wormkillers' Last Spring (1994) Clear Gate Films, Color, 94 min. Dir.: Tom Dempsey. Cast: Tom Nowicki, Billy Gillespie, Tracy Roberts.

Past the Bleachers (1995) Signboard Hill Prods. Inc. ABC, Color, 100 min. Dir.: Michael Switzer. Cast: Richard Dean Anderson, Barnard Hughes, Glynnis O'Connor, Ken Jenkins, Grayson Fricke, Noah Fleiss.

Ed (1996) Longview Entertainment Universal Pictures, Color, 94 min. Dir.: Bill Couturie. Cast: Matt LeBlanc, Doren Fein, Jayne Brook, Bill Cobbs, Jack Warden, Charlie Schlatter, Mike McGlone, Tommy Lasorda.

Soul of the Game (1996, made for TV) Gary Hoffman Productions HBO, Color, 105 min. Dir.: Kevin Rodney Sullivan. Cast: Delroy Lindo, Mykelti Williamson, Blair Underwood, Edward Herrmann, R. Lee Ermey, Salli Richardson, Gina Ravera, Obba Babatunde.

The Fan (1996) Mandalay Entertainment/Sony Pictures Entertainment Tri-Star, Color, 120 min. Dir.: Tony Scott. Cast: Robert De Niro, Wesley Snipes, Ellen Barkin, John Leguizamo, Benicio Del Toro, Patti D'Arbanville-Quinn, Chris Mulkey, Andrew J. Ferchland, John Kruk.

## CHAPTER 29

Fans and Concessions

Paul Adomites

Called "kranks" or "bugs" during the early days of professional baseball, the followers of the sport were allegedly given the name of "fans" by Ted Sullivan, manager of the St. Louis Browns in 1883. Although some say the word came from "fanatic," etymologist Peter Tamony has stated it probably derived from "fancier,"—i.e., one who fancies the sport.

Famous Fans

Along with heroic athletes and staunch umpires, baseball has had a large number of fans who also achieved celebrity status. In the first modern World Series in 1903, the Boston "Royal Rooters" were headed by the tall, bulky bartender Mike McGreevy, whose stature as ultimate authority on all baseball matters earned him the sobriquet of "'Nuf Ced." The Rooters sang parodies of popular songs with new lyrics uncomplimentary to Boston's opponents: "Tessie, why do I love you madly?" became "Honus [Wagner], why do you hit so badly?" for example. When Boston triumphed in the Series, at least one Pirate gave the Rooters credit. Tommy Leach noted, "It was that damn song."

'Nuf Ced and the Rooters also had an effect on the 1912 World Series, although an opposite one. When a 6–6 tie in the second game, called on account of darkness after 10 innings, sent the Series back to Boston for an additional game, the Rooters expected they would keep the rights to the seats they had for Games Two, Three, and Five. But a clerk wasn't thinking; he sold the Rooters' seats for Game Seven.

The game was nearly ready to begin when 'Nuf Ced and his gang (five hundred strong), including Boston Mayor John Fitzgerald (whose daughter would bear future President John Fitzgerald Kennedy) marched onto the field and toward their seats, only to discover other people sitting there. The Rooters took to the field in protest. Today it would have been called a riot. It took mounted police more than a half hour to clear the crowd from the field. Meanwhile, Boston starting pitcher Smokey Joe Wood, who had stopped his warmups while the police rounded up the Royal Rooters, cooled off, and was ineffective.

But before 'Nuf Ced and the Royal Rooters, many teams had fans who earned fame, usually through lung power. In the 1890s, Frank B. Wood of the grizzled countenance and loud voice became a minor celebrity at the Polo Grounds for his editorial "Well well well."

The 1940s and '50s were the era of three of the most famous female fans. One, Mary Ott of St. Louis, had a "neigh . . . known to cause stampedes in Kansas City stockyards"; Lollie Hopkins, a prim Bostonian, used a megaphone to cheer for both sides when they played well; the legendary Hilda Chester toted two large cowbells and displayed a banner saying "Hilda is here" to make her voice heard in Ebbets Field for years.

Ebbets Field featured another famous fan in the late 1930s who did more than just root. Jack Pierce used to buy ten seats, a bottle of Scotch, balloons and the gas to blow them up, all to salute Dodgers' shortstop Cookie Lavagetto. Pierce's dedication was so complete that he continued his gaseous act even in 1942, when Cookie was in the Army.

Legendary lungs could be found in nearly every big league town. In the 1930s, the Kessler Brothers, Bull and Eddie, of Philadelphia, would sit "on opposite sides of the grandstand and conduct what practically amounted to a private conversation across the diamond." In Pittsburgh, Bruce McAllister's screeching could be heard at every game and over the radio, too. Detroit's Patsy O'Toole was hailed as the "All-American earache."

Then there were the fans of dedication, not just noise. Some fans received press mention because they routinely took road trips with their favorite team. Others made a point of never missing a World Series, spring training, or All-Star Game, thereby meriting recognition. Still others built extensive (and expensive) "museums" or libraries.

The Royal Rooters tradition of fan groups—sitting together, leading cheers, and heckling the opposition—also had counterparts in most towns. In St. Louis it was the Ice Wagon Boys, in Chicago the Stockyards Boys, and in Pittsburgh the Steel Puddlers. But group cheering was less popular during the thirties and forties until it reappeared in the form of Wrigley Field's Bleacher Bums, who have inspired their own literature, including an Off-Broadway play. Active in the 1960s, dormant in the '70s, and resuscitated in the '80s, the Bleacher Bums were described tongue-in-cheek as "almost on a par with the old Brooklyn Dodger fans, but with more taste."

Fandom once created an on-the-field star. In 1902, Bill Armour, manager of the pitching-short Cleveland team, was told by a Philadelphia ticket-taker that a talented young pitcher was in the stands. Given a quick tryout and just as quickly signed, Charlie Smith won the game and went on to a ten-year big league career.

Worthy of special mention are the Brooklyn Dodger fans of today who still cannot mention the name of Walter O'Malley without a curse, and the St. Louis Browns Fan Club, active today four decades after their team's demise.

Many people who achieved celebrity status in other fields were famous fans, too. Poetess Marianne Moore's love of the game was legendary. Composer Charles Ives wrote a piano piece called "Some Southpaw Pitching." Broadway, music, and film stars, including DeWolf Hopper, Harry Ruby, George M. Cohan, Jack White, and Pearl Bailey were avid fans, along with many politicians, especially Presidents Taft, Eisenhower, and Nixon, and Speaker of the House Uncle Joe Cannon. Of course, many pols used fandom to garner favor; it was never certain whether they attended because they truly loved the game or whether they simply loved being seen in public.

Being Rowdy

The color that fun-loving fans add to a game turns, however, when fans interfere with the on-the-field action. Baseball kranks were causing trouble from the beginning. As early as 1857, there were eight incidents of bad fan behavior altering a game's result.

In fact, in the game that many call the first great American professional game (the Cincinnati Red Stockings vs. the Brooklyn Atlantics, June 14, 1870), a Brooklyn fan is said to have jumped on the back of Red Stockings' outfielder Cal McVey as he tried to field a ball in the eleventh inning. Brooklyn won the game 8–7, ending Cincinnati's 84-game winning streak.

Through the 1890s, a fan attacking the umpire or an opposing player was considered a social gaffe, but hardly a criminal offense. There are several instances cited of umpires being mobbed, seriously injured, or two-fistedly turning on their attackers. Pop bottles were the commonest weapons for umpire abuse, and a record of a woman serving time for tossing a bottle at an ump was not described in the outraged tone one might expect.

Fans could harm the game even without maiming the umpires or attacking opponents. In the 1880s, tossing straw hats on the field to acknowledge a good play was common. However, cleaning up the skimmers often delayed the proceedings. In 1892, a Chicago crowd "cheered madly as Anson's men thrashed the whey out of Louisville." The exuberant fans demonstrated their joy by tossing a deluge of seat cushions on the field. Manager Cap Anson pleaded with them to stop, but to no avail. Chicago lost in a forfeit.

In 1911, William Phelon described a different kind of fan behavior. "Out at Kansas City, the crowd had a custom, once, that was all its own. Whenever the multitude couldn't see the wisdom of a decision, they arose, marched down onto the field, and advanced upon the umpire. They never offered harm or discourtesy to that official, but simply asked him, with all courtesy, to tell them the rules governing that one decision. The umpire would tell them, and then with a chorus of thanks, they would turn, march back to their seats, and let the game go on."

But two major factors changed the sentiment about what made a baseball outing fun. The first was the gradual elimination of ballpark gambling, which altered behavior both off and on the field. Another was the increased presence of women at the parks.

Legend has it that Ladies Day began in 1889 in Cincinnati because the women wanted to see handsome Tony Mullane pitch. However, the New York Knickerbockers had established a regular Ladies Day by 1867. The Athletics and Orioles did the same in 1883, Brooklyn in 1885. *The Sporting News* pointed out in 1886 that when women are present, the men become less excited and exercise "more choice in their selection of adjectives."

By the turn of the century, baseball was less a rowdy afternoon for gamblers and toughs, and much more of a family enterprise. The newer parks of the century were larger, too, making it harder for the fans to interfere.

But they still managed. A rain of snowballs from the stands in April 1907 led to forfeiture of the Giants' Opening Day game to the Phillies. The same year, some thought the pop-bottle hit taken by umpire Billy Evans would be fatal. (Evans did survive, though, and his teenaged assailant was fined $100.) This kind of behavior was hardly unexpected; a popular song of the teens was "Let's Get the Umpire's Goat."

On May 15, 1912, Ty Cobb leaped into the stands to beat up a fan who was harassing him—a fan described in the press as a "helpless cripple." Cobb's suspension for this act led his teammates to walk out the following day, and the locally recruited "substitutes" took a 24–2 licking from the Athletics before Cobb's reinstatement.

After Yankee center fielder Whitey Witt was struck by a pop bottle in 1922, the leagues cracked down on bottle throwing, and seriously. Ban Johnson offered a $1,000 reward to find the culprit. However, he received so many versions of what happened that he finally settled on $100 cash, railroad fare, and a World Series ticket to someone who claimed that "Witt stepped on the neck of a bottle and caused it to jump up and hit him on the head." The stricter enforcement (and public relations efforts of paper cup manufacturers) did the trick.

Fan violence was minimal in the 1920s. By the '30s, things had re-soured. In the seventh game of the 1934 World Series, Cardinal left fielder Joe Medwick slid hard into third baseman Marv Owen. When Medwick took his defensive position the next inning, the Tiger fans showered him with fruit. Four times he was forced off the field. (Allegedly the concessionaire was increasing the price of an apple each time.) Finally Commissioner Landis ordered both Medwick and Owen out of the game. Owen later admitted that he overreacted (the score was 7–0 at the time) and probably helped to incite the crowd.

In 1940 umpire George Magerkurth was attacked in Ebbets Field by a Frank Germano. The story goes that the attacker, looking toward a sentence of six months at hard labor, commented, "I'll be out in time for Opening Day."

The Cleveland Indians of 1940 earned the nickname of "Cry Babies" for their public dissatisfaction with manager Ossie Vitt. Fans demonstrated their displeasure by hurling baby bottles. The changing tables were turned, however, when Cleveland fans pelted the Detroit Tigers' Hank Greenberg with fruit in a critical series at the end of that year.

In 1941, a sportswriter, reflecting on "Fifty Years of Being a Baseball Fan," said that night baseball and broadcasting had resulted in a "marked increase in the baseball intelligence of the fans . . . Perhaps this increased knowledge is responsible for one marked change for the better I have noticed over these fifty years—the improvement in sportsmanship of the fans."

His perception held true throughout the 1950s and '60s. But the 1970s were the noisiest years of fan violence since the early days of professional baseball. Unlike the literal "Kill the umpire" cries of the 1870s and '80s, however, the violence of the 1970s was undirected and mindless. Fans turned on each other, on the players, on the fields themselves. "Celebrations" after winning playoff or World Series games became orgies of destruction that spilled out of the ballparks into city streets.

Several ballpark promotions to boost attendance resulted in hometeam forfeits when fans got out of hand, most memorably a riot during a "10-cent Beer Night" at Cleveland in 1974. At Chicago's Comiskey Park in 1979, a "Disco Demolition" record-burning event began rowdy and got worse. The second game scheduled for that night was canceled and forfeited to Detroit.

An incident in the 1973 National League Championship Series in New York's Shea Stadium paralleled the Medwick/Owen spat. Pete Rose slid hard into Mets' shortstop Bud Harrelson; ballplayer fisticuffs resulted; the fans got into the act when Rose took his place in left field the next inning. Their garbage and abuse actually drove the Reds from the field. It took a peace delegation— Yogi Berra, Tom Seaver, Cleon Jones, Rusty Staub and Willie Mays (a legend on his last legs)—to walk to the outfield and settle the crowd.

All in all, the 1970s had nearly forty "noteworthy" examples of bad fan behavior, with 1974 and 1979 being the worst years. The nation's sportswriters were unable to offer viable reasons. One national columnist interviewed a medical nutritionist who said additives in the ballpark food were the culprit, another lay the blame at the feet of the Watergate scandal ("Richard Nixon loves baseball and used to come out to the ballpark. No more. Wonder why?").

The situation stayed consistently grim for the first few years of the 1980s. Detroit owner Jim Campbell closed the bleachers after fourteen fans were arrested for fighting during a 1980 contest. On the day that Pittsburgh paid tribute to Willie Stargell, the noble heart of its "family" team, a battery nearly struck Pirate right fielder Dave Parker, and Parker and Pittsburgh were never on speaking terms again. During a 1981 playoff game, a Yankee fan jumped from the stands and attacked umpire Mike Reilly.

Since then, baseball teams have taken strong steps to prevent the ugliness that fan rowdiness can become. Tightening of alcohol sales—smaller cups, limited quantities per sale, closing of beer sales after a specified inning—have shown success. In every park, security is emphasized. The massive troubles of the 1970s have not reoccurred.

Curiously, more incidents occurred of ballplayers going after fans than fans attacking ballplayers. Twice in 1981 Reggie Smith felt the need to slug a heckler. In 1985 Rick Miller of the California Angels felt he had to leap into the Anaheim stands to protect his wife and son from harassment. Three stars showed thin skins in 1991: Albert Belle of the Indians, a recovering alcoholic, threw a ball at (and hit) a Cleveland fan who had loudly invited him to a beer party. Cincinnati reliever Rob Dibble hurled a ball into the stands after a game, injuring an unsuspecting fan. And Oakland's Jose Canseco charged the stands after a New York fan who had overzealously reminded him of his late exit the night before from Madonna's apartment. (We learned later that Jose was only giving Madonna batting tips for her upcoming role in *A League of Their Own*.)

Gambling

One of the major factors that changed baseball from crude entertainment to "the National Pastime" was the eradication of gambling from the game. In the early days, betting at ballparks was widespread, with a double effect. First, the atmosphere in the crowd was rowdy and vulgar; people with money at stake behave differently from people who are there merely for the pleasure of seeing a game well played.

The second effect was more damaging to the game's health. Ballplayers themselves were bettors, and "hippodroming," or throwing games, was common.

Despite fines and bans and the inclusion of anti-gambling statutes in the league bylaws, gambling remained a large part of the game. Along with the notorious Hal Chase, figures as "respectable" as John McGraw, Ty Cobb, Joe Wood, Buck Herzog, and Tris Speaker had their names linked to game fixing. Every year the *Spalding Baseball Guide* railed against gambling evils in its introduction.

From the 1870s through the early 1900s, the baseball pools were the most popular form of gambling. Similar to today's football pools, a pool bettor simply picked the team that would win the most games or score the most or fewest runs in the week, rather than bet on a team to win a particular game. Although certainly less harmful than direct game betting, these pools still offered the gamblers great chances to win money by "involving" players or managers.

The betting was substantial. According to Professor Harold Seymour, one such pool in Pittsburgh ranged over the entire East Coast and Canada, offering prizes of $1,000 a week. (The average per capita income annually was less than $550.) Another pool earned its managers from $30,000 to $50,000 a week. A 1911 estimate said that in the city of New Haven alone, 40,000 factory workers and boys held pool tickets costing $10,000.

Baseball understood the danger and kept responding, in fits and starts, to the problem. On August 5, 1908, the *New York Evening Telegram* said, "Efforts to stamp out gambling in baseball will immediately be made by the American League." (Interestingly, this followed by two days a spurious announcement in the *New York American*: "Bookmaking on baseball games in Chicago has not been profitable, and bookmakers announced they are going out of the business . . . 'The baseball "fan" is too wise. He knows too much about the game,' said one disgusted bookmaker.")

The effort to eliminate betting continued throughout the 1910s. *New York Times,* 1913: "Gamblers ejected from game"; 1914, "Gambling pools barred"; 1915, "Arrests for gambling." By 1919, the *Times* could state "Gambling stopped at all ball parks."

But it wasn't until 1920, the year of the Black Sox Scandal, that the action to eradicate gambling took hold. That year six people were arrested for gambling in Boston, four at the Polo Grounds, forty-seven in Chicago, five more in New York, ten at a Pacific Coast League game.

The uproar over a gambling-run World Series had finally been too much for baseball and its fans to take.

Today baseball is still heavily gambled; Las Vegas estimates of legal baseball gambling place it at around thirty million dollars a year, about a third of that wagered on pro football. But with major league baseball playing 2,000 games a year and pro football one-tenth as many, the difference per game is substantial. When less is wagered, less can be won, which means less incentive for someone to attempt to "swing the odds."

Attendance

Before the National League was founded in 1876, baseball already had recorded single-game attendances as high as 40,000. In 1876, the patent of Bright's self-registering turnstile helped keep baseball body counts, although formal data were not regularly available until the turn of the century.

1880s. According to baseball historian Bill James, "Systematic data [were] not available. [But] attendance grew rapidly during this period."

- 1884. The first "bargain bill" doubleheader was held by Cleveland.
- 1889. The White Stockings drew 216,802 at home.

1890s. The average per game according to Bill James, was 2,000–3,000. He described overall attendance during this period as "Awful, and declining," reporting that "In 1890 . . . the Players' League drew 981,000 fans, the National League 814,000."

- The first promotion and advertising occurred: streetcar billing, signboards, handbills, window hangers, posters, boys on streets giving out handbills. Cincinnati ran paid ads in local papers (including the German-language one).
- Baseball cards were introduced as advertisements.
- "Children's Days" with 10¢ admission were popular, and women were admitted free on Ladies Days.
- 1891. "Base Ball Day" in Chicago let all amateur teams in uniform in free.

1900s. Total attendance was 50 million—4,100 per game.
- 1908. "Take Me Out to the Ball Game" was introduced.
- 1909. The first concrete and steel stadiums were built.
- Old Timers Days began, along with "days" to honor individual players.

1910s. Total attendance was 56 million—4,500 per game. James: "Essentially a decade of no growth." Seymour: "A prodigious $100 billion increase in national wealth brightened the first two decades of the century." The effects included suburbs with trolley lines and stadiums as the population moved from the country to the city.

Sunday baseball, which had disappeared with the demise of the American Association in 1891, was finally permitted by state and local legislatures. By 1918 it was legal in Cleveland, Detroit, and Washington. New York voted it in the following year. (Boston didn't allow it till 1929; the state of Pennsylvania, the final holdout, did not until 1933.)

- 1912. "Foreign-born spectators from seventeen different countries were observed at a game in New York." (*Spalding Baseball Guide*). Blacks also were becoming avid fans.
- 1913. In Brooklyn, the first Honor Roll Day was held.
- 1917. Scorecard winning numbers become common.
- 1917. The first "Knothole Gang" was organized in St. Louis.
- Ladies Day, which had been abolished by the National League in 1909, resurfaced eight years later.

1920s. Total attendance, 93 million—7,500 per game. The Yankees exceeded a million almost every year. Average club attendance rose 50 percent over what it had been the decade before. Seymour states that even though 1920–1930 showed the largest single-decade rise in American population ever (17 million), baseball attendance rose at an even faster rate.

- 1921. Pittsburgh, August 5. The first baseball broadcast occurred, over KDKA radio with Harold Arlin. The World Series (Giants vs. Yankees) was also broadcast that year.
- 1925. Philip K. Wrigley allowed all Cubs game to be aired every day.

1930s. Total attendance, 81 million—6,600 per game. The first night baseball game was held in 1880, at Nantasket Beach, Massachusetts. Amateur players from two local department stores performed in a promotion for the light company; the event has since been celebrated in a General Electric television commercial. Described as having "innumerable" errors because of lights, the first effort was not successful. Three years later, a game in Fort Wayne, Indiana, was.

Night baseball was first embraced on the minor league level. By 1934, fifteen of nineteen minor leagues had at least one lighted park. On May 24, 1935, Cincinnati owner Larry MacPhail hosted the first major league night game, at Crosley Field. A total of 20,422 attended, President Franklin D. Roosevelt threw the switch from the White House. Ford Frick, then the National League president, threw out the first ball, and the Reds defeated the Dodgers 2–1.

In 1938, when MacPhail moved to Brooklyn, so did lights. The first Brooklyn night game, on June 15, was Johnny Vander Meer's second successive no-hitter. The first American League team to play night games was Philadelphia, in 1939. By 1940, seventy major league night games were scheduled. The only parks without lights that year were Washington, which added them the next year; Yankee Stadium and Braves Field (which added them in 1946); Fenway Park (1947); Detroit (1948); and Chicago's Wrigley Field (1988). The first World Series game to be played at night happened on October 13, 1971, when the Pirates beat the Orioles at Three Rivers Stadium.

- 1930. Major league attendance in 1930 was 10,132,272—the highest of any season between 1901 and 1945.

- 1931. Players' numbers became official practice in the AL.
- 1935. Night baseball was introduced.
- 1939. All teams broadcast their games on radio.
- August 26, 1939. The first TV broadcast was made.

1940s. Total attendance, 135 million—11,000 per game.

James describes 1946 as "the Great Leap Forward"—1946 attendance was 18.5 million, 71 percent above the previous high. He lists as reasons the advent of night baseball, a return to economic normalcy after World War II, and great pennant races.

1950s. Total attendance, 165 million—13,500 per game.
- 1951. The first nationally televised World Series game occurred.

David Voigt says, "In the years after the war, baseball crowds became predominantly family gatherings, united by the ethic of 'togetherness' in their fun-seeking. Television pushed the trend by bombarding families with ball games in the summertime."

1960s. Total attendance, 224 million—14,000 per game.
- Bill Veeck added players' names to their uniforms in 1960.
- Major League Baseball expanded (after changing only two locations in fifty-seven years previously), adding eight new teams.

1970s. Total attendance, 330 million—16,561 per game.
- 1976. Free agency was instated by an arbitrator's decree.
- 1977. Cable television began to have an impact on viewing.
- 1978. Dodgers are first team with single-season attendance of more than 3 million.

1980s. Total attendance, about 512 million, or 24,300 per game.
- 1981. A strike by players eliminated as many as fifty-nine games of the season for some teams.
- 1982. Braves take name of "America's Team" for themselves.
- 1984. Cal Griffith sells the Twins.
- 1985. Players' strike settled in two days by Commissioner Ueberroth.
- 1986. For the first time, all twenty-six teams pass 1 million mark in attendance.
- 1988. Night baseball comes to Wrigley Field.
- 1989. Toronto's new SkyDome opens.

1990–1996. Total attendance, about 398 million, or 27,900 per game.
- 1991. New Comiskey Park opens in Chicago.
- 1991. Toronto is first club to draw 4 million fans.
- 1992. Oriole Park at Camden Yards opens in Baltimore.
- 1992. Second overall attendance drop since 1989, attributed to bad teams in New York and Los Angeles.
- 1994. Strike cancels World Series.
- 1995. Wild Card introduced.

Concessions

Food and beverages have been a big part of the fun at a baseball game from the beginning. In 1859, New Orleans ballclubs pitched "commodious tents for the ladies . . . under the umbrageous branches of fine old live oaks" to shelter their delicate skin from the sun as they enjoyed refreshments as well as the local baseball rivalry.

In the first decade of professional baseball, you could find an array of food: peanuts, soft drinks, crackerjacks, ice cream, cherry pie, cheese, chocolates, planked onions, and even tripe. Vendors moved through the crowd hawking sandwiches, soda water, and chewing gum. By 1871 the Olympics of Washington, D.C., had anticipated the "stadium clubs" of today's parks when they opened a first-class restaurant at the park.

Ballpark concession stands as we have come to know them can be traced to 1875, from which time we have a photo of the Boston team posed in front of their grandstand clearly showing large painted signs saying SODA and REFRESHMENTS. During his tenure as owner of the Chicago team, Albert Spalding himself encouraged concession stands, rather than hawkers moving throughout the crowd. The ChiFeds of 1914 lay claim to the earliest permanent concession *stand* in Wrigley Field.

Along with various sorts of munchies, ballparks sold beer and hard liquor, too. In his *Baseball: The Early Years,* Harold Seymour lists how many beer and whiskey glasses the typical ballpark bar stocked. But in 1880, the always image-conscious National League tried to eliminate ballpark drinking, and the result was the second major professional league, the American Association.

The four-year-old National League was trying to civilize its image, fighting the coarsening effect of gambling and promoting the calming influence of female attendance. As part of this effort, in 1880 the league passed a law forbidding gambling and the sale of alcohol at the ballparks. Unfortunately the Cincinnati team had a long tradition of beer and whiskey sales; they were averaging $3,000 a season of concession income. Breweries and distilleries were two of the largest industries in the city. So rather than face the financial damage of a no-beer ballpark, Cincinnati quit the league and was the leader in starting the Association, which detractors unsurprisingly called "The Beer and Whiskey League." The *New York World,* with perfect big city parochialism, charged that Cincinnati was a place to "watch for flying mugs . . . cheap sports and toughs" gathered behind home plate. Meanwhile, the New York Giants had a bar in full view of the field.

Although the major league American Association folded after ten years, and the attempt to eliminate gambling continued for twenty more, baseball and beer have always remained linked.

Ballpark food and drink and scorecards can be traced back to the 1850s and sixties, but it wasn't till the 1880s that one man turned these concepts into enterprise: the first professional concessionaire and the first concession empire. Harry M. Stevens, a British immigrant, went to a baseball game in Columbus, Ohio, one afternoon (so the story goes). Realizing that there was no way to identify the players, Stevens sought out the owner and for $500 obtained the right to publish and sell a program. (Scorecards predate this anecdote by twenty years, but they were usually very modest items, with little or no advertising. It took Stevens to see the potential for profits.) "Scorecard Harry" sold the programs himself, calling out the now famous slogan "You can't tell the players without a scorecard."

The scorecard idea had an intriguing spinoff. Although the ballplayers had no numbers on their uniforms, they were given numbers on the scorecards. Then, as each player came to bat, his number was placed on the scoreboard. A scandal occurred when people brought old scorecards into the park, or bought "counterfeit" ones from "illegal" scorecard vendors outside. The teams were forced to change the scorecard numbers often.

Harry M. Stevens didn't stop with scorecards. An ambitious promoter, he started selling food: hard-boiled eggs, sandwiches, even coconut custard pies. He expanded his business into Wheeling, Pittsburgh, Toledo, and Milwaukee. A conversation with New York Giants manager John Montgomery Ward in Pittsburgh in 1893 led to Harry's landing the Polo Grounds concession. Before long the Stevens empire used its New York connection to include contracts with Madison Square Garden, hotels, and racetracks.

Stevens was always the innovator. On a cold day in the Polo Grounds in 1901, ice cream wasn't selling, but Harry had an idea. He sent an assistant out for frankfurters (locally called "dachshund sausages"), which were sold in the neighborhood German groceries, heated the sausages in hot water, and put them in long buns so the fans could hold and eat them. The vendors shouted out what made these inventions so special: "Get 'em while they're hot! Get your red hots here!"

Sports cartoonist Thomas A. "Tad" Dorgan, looking for an idea that day, drew a sketch of waiters serving talking frankfurters ("You're not so hot!" "Bologna!"). Some say Dorgan couldn't remember how to spell "dachshund"; others say his spelling problem was with "frankfurter." For whatever reason, he coined the term "hot dogs" instead. Baseball food has never been the same. To this day, hot dogs, soda pop, and beer are the three biggest-selling items in every major league park.

Stevens continued to bring new ideas to his business. Realizing that fans might not purchase soda pop because raising their heads to drink might make them miss some of the game action, Harry came up with the idea of selling the soda with a straw. Now even the most devoted fan could quench his or her thirst and never miss a single pitch.

During the early decades of the century, only scattered figures are available, but they mention profits of several thousand dollars a year for the average club. By 1929, *Baseball Magazine* was saying that concession "receipts at Wrigley Field soar far above $100,000 a year." The same article stated that money from gate sales created 87.6 percent of the major leagues' gross profit, and concessions 5.5 percent.

Today selling food at the ballparks, stadiums, and racetracks of America is big business. Since Harry M. Stevens, many companies have entered the field. At the most basic level, professional concessionaires provide and prepare all the food for the ballgames, hire and train their employees, and then agree to pay the contractee a percentage of their gross. (The few absolute exceptions are those teams which act as their own concessionaire, subcontracting specialized

stands for specific food items to outside companies—Kentucky Fried Chicken, Burger King, etc.)

The contract to provide concession services may be with the baseball team, or it may be with the stadium authority, or it may be with the city or municipality that owns the stadium. Everyone gets a share; the main contractee gets the most. For example, some concessionaires pay as much as 52 percent of their receipts back to the contractee. If the baseball team signed the contract, it could receive 47 percent of that 52 percent, and give the rest to the other partners. Or the club could receive 24 or 25 percent (which is about average).

But few baseball teams own their ballparks; most share the facility with pro football or other teams. So the football team could receive a certain percentage of the gross, the baseball team another, the stadium authority another. In certain *categories* the percentage can vary; the baseball club may get a bigger percentage of soft drink sales than the football team, which might get more for hot drink sales; the city may take the lion's share of the concessionaire income and allot only a certain percentage to the teams, or vice versa.

With only a handful of major concessionaires (Harry M. Stevens, ARA Services, Ogden Allied, Sportservice, and a few others), and with contracts that typically run for fifteen to eighteen years (some for thirty), the competition is fierce.

The growth of fast food restaurants has changed the kinds of food available in ballparks, by making certain kinds of packaging acceptable. Because fans have become more demanding and the American palate is changing, concessionaires experiment, sometimes adding as many as twenty new menu items per year. For some reason soft ice cream is a hit in air-conditioned Houston, while windy Comiskey is selling a lot of cold deli sandwiches and funnel cakes. Cleveland is trying onion rings. Oriole Park at Camden Yards brags about its Maryland crab cakes ("made here fresh daily") and crab soup. Sausage varieties way past the humble hot dog (Italian, Polish, brat– and knockwursts) have proliferated. And in Toronto's SkyDome, the number two selling item in the park is the Big Mac, according to their chief concessionaire, McDonald's. But despite all the innovations, baseball fans remain traditionalists at heart.

In addition, the modern stadiums of today are echoing the earlier days, with their "cafes" and restaurants offering more serious fare before, during, and after the game. Homer Rose, longtime employee of the Harry M. Stevens Company, and grandson of Harry himself, said, "At first it was peanuts, ice cream cones, lemonade, and bottled soft drinks. Now in the dining rooms and private boxes we're serving shrimp salads and full-course dinners." The Stevens Company alone runs restaurants at dozens of racetracks and stadiums.

One more change is becoming apparent—beer, a ballpark staple since the beginning, is again less easy to obtain. Concern about drunk driving has resulted in every team selling beer in smaller servings, allowing fewer servings to be sold to one person at one time, having special no-alcohol sections, and stopping sales after a certain time in the game. So far, no one has raised a serious voice about banning all alcohol sales at the ballpark.

## CHAPTER 30

Baseball Collecting

Barry Halper and Bill Madden

In the early 1970s baseball began to take on a new dimension—one that would transform the hobby of a dedicated few into a national phenomenon and, incidentally, a multimillion dollar industry.

The game's first century did not produce many collectors of baseball memorabilia. Oh, sure, there were a few baseball cards as early as the 1860s and extensive sets by the 1880s; even in the game's infancy there was always that legion of autograph-seekers waiting outside the players' gate at any given ballpark. But the cards were seldom saved (as evidenced by the scarcity today of early cards, even those produced in great quantities in the 1950s) and the autographs were a fancy of one's idol-worshiping days. There were no prices attached to such mementos of youthful infatuation, just as there was no business of collecting.

But then, in 1967, a man by the name of Jefferson Burdick published *The American Card Catalog*—a guide listing the origin, description, and estimated value of every card (baseball or otherwise) ever printed. It was a monumental volume, which took years of painstaking research. What his catalog did was to transform the informal and undocumented hobby of baseball card collecting into the more elevated and established rank of stamp and coin collecting. Prices and values, scarcity and condition—these commercial considerations, once they were applied to cards, quickly moved into just about anything associated with baseball: autographs, bats, balls, uniforms, photos, press pins, chinaware, publications, you name it.

Cards

Despite the growing interest in other memorabilia, cards remain at the center of the baseball collecting hobby. The most extensive early card set (it remains one of the largest ever issued, with 520 players in 1 to 17 variants each) was the Old Judge Cigarette Brand series of 1887 to 1889. Catalogued by Burdick as N172, these insert cards were photographs mounted on board, in the same manner as the cartes de visite that were popular in the 1860s. In terms of interest today, however, the most popular early baseball card set was the 1909-11 tobacco issue, No. T206 in the Burdick volume. These 523 cards, approximately 2¼ by 1½ inches, were inserted in packages of Sweet Caporal, Piedmont, Sovereign, Cycle, and other cigarette brands of the American Tobacco Company.

Included in the T206 set are two of the most valuable cards in the history of collecting: the Honus Wagner and the Eddie Plank. Both cards are rare for different reasons. According to legend, Wagner, a nonsmoker, became incensed when he discovered that his picture on a card was being used to promote smoking, and he ordered that the card be removed from the T206 set. (Evidently he had a change of heart years later, as he is depicted in the 1948 Leaf Gum card set with chewing tobacco packed in his jaw.) Today, no more than 25 T206 Wagner cards are said to be in existence. The Plank card is equally rare, a result of an accidental fire in 1909 that destroyed the printing plates.

Burdick, acknowledging the scarcity of both cards, listed the Wagner card's value at $50 and the Plank card at $10. The remainder of the T206 cards are listed at 10 cents apiece. Today, the common T206 lists at $100 mint. The Plank lists at about $25,000, while the Wagner card sold for $451,000 at auction in 1991 and again for $640,500 at auction in September 1996.

Allen & Ginters, Turkey Reds and Old Judges

Besides the T206s, the most popular early lithographed tobacco cards then and now are the 1887-88 Allen & Ginters (N28, N29, and N43) and the 1911 T3 Turkey Reds. The Allen & Ginters maintain their value and popularity because of their beauty. They are the same size as the T206s, but the N28 and N29 series are magnificent watercolor paintings of baseball players printed on glossy stock. The N28 is generally considered the first of the tobacco card baseball sets and includes 10 players, among them Hall of Famers Cap Anson, John Clarkson, Charles Comiskey, King Kelly, John Montgomery Ward, and Tim Keefe. The N29, or second series, adds six players, among them Hall of Famer Buck Ewing. The Anson card is the most expensive today, listing at $2,000 mint. Burdick listed the average Allen & Ginter card at 10 cents.

The T3s are classified as cabinet cards because they measure a much larger 5¾ by 8 inches in size and were obtained by sending in coupons found in Turkey Red, Fez, and Old Mill brand cigarettes. They are also beautiful cards, depicting players in full-color portraits. One hundred of the 126 athletes in the Turkey Red set are baseball players, and the cards average $250 for common cards and considerably more for Hall of Famers (Ty Cobb lists at $5,000). In 1967 Burdick listed the price of T3s at $1 apiece. The N172 Old Judge cards were sepia toned, 1½ by 2½ inch blank backed cards issued by the Goodwin Co. of N.Y. from 1887-1890. The set of 565 major and minor league players from that era included all the prominent Hall of Famers, Harry Wright, John Clarkson, Buck Ewing, John Montgomery Ward, King Kelly, Roger Connor, Ed Delahanty et al. The average value of the Old Judge common players is $150 with the Hall of Famers ranging from $500-$1,200. At a September 1996 auction, however, an assorted cache of 219 Old Judges sold for $40,250.

Gum and Candy Replaces Tobacco

In the 1930s tobacco companies gave way to gum and confectionery companies as the prime dispensers of baseball cards. The most prominent was the Goudey Gum Company, which issued significant sets from 1933 to 1941. These cards, like all the gum/confectionery cards of the 1930-50 era, measured 2½ by 3¼ inches. The most popular of all the Goudey sets is its initial 1933 effort, which was comprised of 240 cards, including one of the rarest of all, No. 106, Napoleon Lajoie. The Lajoie card was inadvertently omitted from the original 1933 Goudey set, and when collectors inquired about the absence of card No. 106, the company offered it as a premium the following year. The few Lajoie cards that exist today contain the 1934 Goudey card design. Burdick listed the common R319 1933 Goudeys at 20 cents apiece and the Lajoie at $1. Today, the common cards list at $50, the numerous Hall of Famers in the set at $150/$250 and above, and the Lajoie at $30,000.

In 1939 Gum Inc. of Boston entered the baseball card field, issuing the first of its three Play Ball sets. The 1939 and 1940 Play Ball sets were sepia-toned cards, while the 1941 set used color. The 72-card 1941 Play Ball set is the most popular of the sets, listing at $10,000 in mint condition. It also features the first color cards of Joe DiMaggio (mint today $2,500) and Ted Williams ($1,750).

World War II prompted a shutdown of the baseball card industry, and it did not resume production until 1948, when the Chicago-based Leaf Company issued its 168-card set of colorized photo cards with gum. The Leaf set, which contains a number of less-distributed cards, lists at $13,000 in mint condition today. The DiMaggio and Babe Ruth cards list at $1,800 and $2,200 respectively, and the Satchel Paige, because it is his rookie card, $2,400.

In 1950 the Bowman Gum Company of Philadelphia replaced Leaf as the premier baseball card manufacturer. Bowman maintained that position until 1952, when the Topps Gum Company of Brooklyn began making inroads into the burgeoning industry. Topps began modestly with two 52-card sets in 1951, as well as a pair of now highly valuable premium sets called Connie Mack and Current All-Stars. The company broke historical ground in 1952 when it issued a 407-card set.

The 1952 Topps remains the Holy Grail of modern-day card sets for collectors, if only because of the difficulty in completing it. Cards Nos. 311 to 407 were issued late in the year by Topps and only in the New York area and Canada. Because of this they are more difficult to find. Burdick listed the 1952 Topps from 1 to 310 at 10 cents apiece and 311 to 407 at 30 cents in 1967.

Making the final series even more valuable is the fact that Topps included many of the game's superstars of that year, including Mickey Mantle, Jackie Robinson, Pee Wee Reese, Eddie Mathews, and Roy Campanella. All of them list today at over $1,000 mint. The Mantle card, No. 311, at $18,000, is considered the jewel of all modern-day baseball cards. The 311 to 407 commons list at $220 apiece.

When Burdick published his *American Card Catalog,* baseball card collecting was limited to just that-collecting. It was not until the mid-1970s when card values began to be known nationwide that baseball card shows and flea markets began to crop up across the country. Prior to then, only a small network of serious baseball card collectors existed: Frank Nagy of Detroit, Buck Barker of St. Louis and myself [Barry Halper] among them. Cards were never sold within this network, although on many occasions the trading would branch into other collections, trading an autograph for a suitable card or cards.

All in all, in 1972, there were about ten card dealers who would meet once a month in New York on Friday nights. No money ever changed hands. It was strictly trading.

A couple of years later, however, the hobby began to grow and groups of dealers began organizing annual or biannual baseball card conventions in church basements around New York and other large cities. These conventions aroused the public interest in baseball cards, rekindling the childhood memories of many whose cards had long since been thrown away. As the demand for old cards increased and prices began to rise, the church basement card shows evolved into bigger productions held in hotels, convention centers, and ballparks.

As an added attraction for the larger baseball card shows, promoters began bringing in old-time and current ballplayers to sign autographs at a modest price. Gradually this has developed into spectacular baseball card/autograph shows in which as many as 10 or 12 Hall of Famers can be found signing autographs at upwards of $10 per item.

Autographs

For the longest time, baseball autographs were something to be personally treasured but not necessarily valued. No one, for instance, put a value on a Babe Ruth autograph even twenty years after the Babe's death. For one thing, a Ruth autograph was still one of the most common of all Hall of Famer autographs, simply because the Babe signed willingly for everyone he came in contact with. A Lou Gehrig, by contrast, was not nearly as common, although until the advent of the autograph-collecting boom—which occurred at the same time the baseball card boom hit in the mid 1970s—collectors paid little notice.

Today Ruth, because of who he was and what he is to baseball, remains one of the most sought-after and high-priced baseball autographs. Of living players, Joe DiMaggio is still commanding top dollar on the autograph circuit, with Mickey Mantle and Willie Mays close behind. But as autograph collectors will testify, it is turn-of-the-century Hall of Famers such as Pud Galvin, Tommy McCarthy, King Kelly, John Clarkson, Roger Connor, Candy Cummings, and Cap Anson whose signatures command the highest prices. These players have been dead for more than 60 years, and their autographs are scarcer than a Ruth, Gehrig, or Ty Cobb.

Perhaps the best way to sum up the modern-day baseball autograph craze is to recall an incident at the New York Yankees' annual Old Timer's Day game in 1980. All the Yankee living legends, from Joe DiMaggio to Mickey Mantle, Yogi Berra, and Whitey Ford, were on hand for the occasion and were besieged throughout the day for autographs. Reggie Jackson, the Yankees' star right fielder at the time, was expressing dismay at all the autograph seekers around him. "I don't understand all this idolatry," Jackson told the assembled writers. The next day in the New York *Daily News* coverage of the Old Timer's Day festivities was a picture of Reggie Jackson getting an autograph on a baseball from Joe DiMaggio.

World Series Press Pins

Press pins from the World Series, All-Star Game, and Hall of Fame induction ceremonies are the only baseball collectibles separated from the players. The pins have nothing to do with the games, other than their being displayed on the coats of attending sportswriters, and they cannot be autographed. Nevertheless, in conjunction with the baseball collecting boom of the 1970s and 1980s, press pins are now among the most sought-after and highly valued of memorabilia.

The origin of the baseball press pin dates back to 1911. According to legend, New York Giants Manager John McGraw had invited several of his cronies to attend the hotly contested games of September 1908. Because of the scarcity of tickets, McGraw assigned his friends seats in the press box, where they became rowdy, distracting members of the working press. The Baseball Writers Association of America was formed as a result of this unwelcome intrusion into their working domain, and the new union issued press pins in order to establish proper identity for the World Series. No one was permitted into the press boxes without a press pin.

As years went on, press accreditation for the World Series became far more sophisticated, but press pins continued to be a tradition. Each World Series team designed its own pin for the games in its ballpark, and though most sportswriters kept their pins through the years, they didn't view them as valuable memorabilia. It was not until the early 1970s, when collectors began to realize how genuinely scarce old press pins were (due to limited distribution and the fact that so many of them were thrown away through the years), that they became a prized baseball collectible.

The earliest press pins are now valued at upwards of $10,000 apiece. But even the press pins from the 1940s, '50s, and '60s have considerable value. The most valued of all World Series pins is that of the 1956 Brooklyn Dodgers, primarily because it isn't a pin but a tie clasp. The Dodgers chose to break tradition that year and issue tie clasps with a blue Brooklyn cap affixed to them. Probably because the tie clasps were actually worn by the writers long after the Series was over, many of them disappeared. Today the Brooklyn Dodgers 1956 World Series tie clasp has commanded as much as $2,000 in collectors' markets as opposed to the $300 value established for the 1956 New York Yankees World Series press pin.

All-Star Game Press Pins

In 1937 baseball extended its press-pin tradition to the All-Star Game, and those pins have also risen greatly in value. No press pins were issued prior to 1937 because the All-Star Game's creator and founder, sportswriter Arch Ward, had envisioned his "gala" as being a one-time event. The prices of All-Star press pins vary greatly, based primarily on the issuing city. One of the rarest All-Star press pins is the 1948 pin issued by the host St. Louis Browns. It is a beautiful pin depicting the white Brownies cap with the brown bill and gold piping. It is dated 1948 and lists for upwards of $3,500.

Hall of Fame Press Pins

The Hall of Fame joined the press-pin field in 1982. Beginning that year, the Hall of Fame issued commemorative press pins listing the names of each year's inductees. Because a limited number of media personnel cover the Hall of Fame ceremonies, the distribution of the pins is believed to be about one-tenth that of the World Series pins. The Hall of Fame pins have quickly shot past their contemporary World Series and All-Star pins in value. The first Hall of Fame pin in 1982, engraved with the names of inductees Hank Aaron, Happy Chandler, Frank Robinson, and Travis Jackson, was going for $650 in the collectors' market.

"Phantom" Pins

In the early years of press pins the Dieges & Clust Company of John Street in New York was the primary manufacturer. In 1946 the Balfour Company of Attleboro, Massachusetts, assumed the contract from Major League Baseball to produce the pins. The company remains the primary producer of pins and rings for the World Series and All-Star Game, although some teams have, in the interest of cost-cutting, sought local companies to produce their pins.

The advent of the playoff system also caused economic problems for contending clubs that were compelled to commission press pins. It had long been the custom of clubs to date the pins for each year's World Series. In many cases, however, the club wouldn't advance to the Series and the press pins produced were rendered unusable for any future Series. These so-called "phantom" pins, such as the 1951 Brooklyn Dodgers (who lost in a playoff to the Giants on Bobby Thomson's historic home run), the 1938 Pittsburgh Pirates (victims of Chicago Cub Gabby Hartnett's "homer in the gloamin' "), or the 1949 Cardinals are harder to come by and as valuable as the "official" Series press pins of those years.

As John Scarpellini, Balfour's longtime representative to baseball recalled, "The elimination of the dating of the pins came about when Dick O'Connell, general manager of the Red Sox, was asked by us about the kind of press pin he wanted designed for the 1975 World Series. Instead of committing himself, O'Connell opened up a closet door in his office and produced what had to be nearly 50,000 press pins. 'Look at these,' he said. 'They're all dated and therefore no good to us. I've got all these pins, which we've paid for, and we can't do anything with them.'

"After that, we came up with the idea of labeling the pins with the phrase 'Our Second World Series' or whatever number that particular World Series was for that particular team. That way, if the club was beaten out in the playoffs, but had already had to produce their pins, they could just put them away in a vault and use them whenever they made it."

Uniforms

In the entire spectrum of baseball collecting no item is more personal than a uniform. Unfortunately, collecting uniforms from modern-day players has become a risky venture because of the increase in counterfeits on the market. Modern-day doubleknits are so easy to manufacture that it is difficult to tell a counterfeit from the authentic article.

The source for legitimate modern-day uniforms is generally the clubhouse man for the major league ballclubs. This has created a serious problem for Major League Baseball. Officials are aware of how little clubhouse men are paid and how easily they can become prey for dealers in baseball memorabilia.

In some cases the players themselves can be sources for uniforms. Pete Rose, for example, reportedly had a deal with the Cincinnati Reds that he be given 25 or more uniforms during the course of the season to do with as he wished. During the game in which Rose tied Ty Cobb's all-time hits record, he wore a different jersey for each at bat. Presumably, Rose sold each jersey to a different collector.

Similarly, Gaylord Perry, in winning his 300th game against the New York Yankees, wore two different Seattle Mariner uniforms. The reason I know that is that Perry had promised his uniform from that game to me. But a couple of days before he pitched, I got a call from the visiting clubhouse man in Baltimore, who was also a dealer in memorabilia. The clubhouse man offered me Perry's Seattle uniform from his 300th-win game. It seems that Gaylord had decided that two uniforms were better than one when it came to maximizing his profit on 300 wins, and he decided to make a change after four innings. I wound up having to make separate deals with both Perry and the clubhouse man from Baltimore in order to have what was surely the uniform in which Perry won his 300th game.

The values of modern-day players' uniforms vary greatly. Naturally, the uniforms players wore performing historic feats such as Rose's 4,192nd hit are of considerably more value than an everyday game-worn uniform. In the uniform-collecting hobby of the 1990s, common players' uniforms were selling in the $400-$600 range, star-quality players' from 1,500 to $1,500, and superstar/Hall of Fame-caliber players' (the Ripkens, Ozzie Smiths) from $3,000 up.

Old-Time Uniforms

Old-time uniforms are a far more challenging hobby, one that has been the most satisfying and exciting aspect of my collecting career. Why? Because I never believed so many of these old uniforms, particularly the ones from the pre-1900 Hall of Fame players, could still exist. And exist in such remarkable condition! Through the years, I have managed to amass approximately 1,000 uniforms, which I have stored on a dry cleaner conveyer belt that is computerized to stop at whichever uniform number I punch in. Included among these are uniforms of every Hall of Famer who played or managed, and even some minor league uniforms of Hall of Fame executives (such as longtime Yankee business manager Ed Barrow) who never wore a major league uniform.

As one might expect, values for the oldest, turn-of-the-century uniforms far exceed those for any of the more recent Hall of Famers of the 1930s to the present day. Uniforms worn by Babe Ruth, Lou Gehrig, and Ty Cobb have been appraised in excess of $100,000. The uniforms of such Hall of Famers as Pud Galvin (Buffalo, 1879), John Clarkson (Saginaw, 1883), King Kelly (NY Giants, 1893), Charles Comiskey (Cincinnati, 1893), Hoss Radbourn (Boston, 1886), Roger Connor (NY Giants, 1893), Joe McGinnity (NY Giants, 1904), and Cy Young (Boston, 1903) are worth much more.

The existence of these uniforms only adds to and rounds out the lore and history of baseball. How they were uncovered after all these years—the treasure hunt—is the most fulfilling aspect of collecting baseballiana.

It was during a conversation I once had with Pete Sheehy, the venerable New York Yankee clubhouse man from the days of Ruth in the '20s right up until the Don Mattingly-Dave Winfield Yankees of the '80s, that I got my most valuable tip in regard to uniform collecting. I asked Sheehy: "Pete, where are all the Pete Sheehys of yesterday? The clubhouse men who kept a vigil over all the old uniforms?"

Not surprisingly, in his days as Yankee clubhouse man, Sheehy did become friends with the clubhouse men from other clubs and they would correspond frequently. Most of his contemporaries had died when I talked to him about this, but he kept track of many of their relatives.

One person Sheehy put me in contact with was a man from Coxsackie, New York, who, Sheehy thought, was in possession of most of the old Yankee uniforms from 1927, the year of Murderers' Row. Sure enough, upon getting in touch with the man, I was able to acquire the 1927 Yankee uniforms of Ruth, Gehrig, Earle Combs, Waite Hoyt, Bob Meusel, Mark Koenig, Bob Shawkey, and about a half dozen others. Sheehy also put me in contact with the relatives of the equipment manager at Columbia University during the early '20s when Gehrig played there. It was through that contact that I was able to uncover Gehrig's Columbia uniform and the first uniform he ever wore as a professional, with Hartford. He had played there under the assumed name of Lewis in 1921 to protect his amateur standing at Columbia; that name is sewn into the bottom flap of the shirt.

All the uniforms from that pre-1920s period are identified by the players' names sewn somewhere on them since numbers did not come into existence until 1929. The

Yankees that year introduced numbers on the backs of their uniforms in the order in which the players appeared in the batting order.

Another valuable source of old uniforms was Dick Bartell, the pepperpot New York Giants and Detroit Tigers shortstop of the 1930s and '40s. Bartell put me in touch with Ollie O'Mara, an old ballplayer, then in his 80s, who lived in Reno, Nevada. O'Mara had had a brief major league career with the Brooklyn Dodgers from 1914 to 1919, a team that was managed by Hall of Famer Wilbert Robinson. Apparently O'Mara had maintained a close friendship with Robinson. That is the only explanation I can offer for the fact that he had in his possession the 1894 Baltimore Orioles uniforms of Robinson, Joe Kelley, Wee Willie Keeler, Dan Brouthers, and Hughie Jennings—Hall of Famers all. O'Mara never did tell me how he got the uniforms or why he had kept them all those years in near-perfect condition. In 1989 he went to his grave with that secret, but baseball historians can be forever grateful that he preserved so much of the game's valuable past.

Bats, Balls, and Books

Until recently vintage bats, balls, gloves, and other gear were a neglected area for collectors. One could find an antique glove or ball in a thrift store or flea market for only a few dollars. Without an autograph or major league player "association," the items were not viewed as desirable. The same could be said of baseball books and photos, although scorecards, guides (Spalding, Reach, Beadle, and so on), yearbooks, and programs-especially World Series programs-did attract collectors before the baseball-card boom in the 1980s.

A handful of early-baseball enthusiasts picked up as many of these antique items as possible, from club constitutions of the amateur era to thick-handled bats with "mushroom" knobs, from gold-painted trophy balls of the 1860s to sepia-toned photographs of unknown teams. This type of memorabilia has increased in value over the years but not as spectacularly as, for example, the cards of the 1950s. Where a 1952 Mickey Mantle card might fetch $25,000, a rare 1868 book by Henry Chadwick might bring only $5,000. However, as card prices continued to soar, sophisticated collectors and devoted fans who have been made nervous by the explosive speculation of the 1980s are beginning to see relative safety in the pursuit of older collectibles, where the market is driven more by true scarcity than widespread demand. Prices may go up or down with general economic conditions, but the lure of baseball and its collectibles remains constant.

The History of Major League Baseball Statistics

John Thorn, Pete Palmer, and Joseph M. Wayman

Part Two, the statistical section of *Total Baseball*, presents the record of major league contests played from 1871 through 1996—all 164,867 of them. It details the accomplishments of the game's 2,237 teams and 14,611 players so completely and accurately that Major League Baseball has authorized *Total Baseball* to be the official encyclopedia of the game, its authentic historical record.

Total Baseball won critical acclaim and a devoted following not only for its breadth and depth of information but also for its pioneering "sabermetric" stats that offered alternative, unofficial measures of player performance. Yet for all its innovation, *Total Baseball* has stood squarely in the tradition of baseball record keeping; it is—like each new spring of our national pastime—a link in a long, long chain. As the New York Knickerbockers' game of 150 years ago lives on in the game of today, so is this volume enriched by the labors of statisticians from Henry Chadwick to Ernie Lanigan, from S.C. Thompson and Seymour Siwoff to David Neft and Bill James.

How we came from the Knickerbockers' primitive accounting of outs and runs to the vast array of statistics available today is an interesting process, in which Major League Baseball's role has been central. Through its evolving scoring rules and procedures, its judicious endorsement of new measures, and its continuing mission to set the record straight, the Commissioner's Office and its official scorers have provided fans with a wealth of statistical data unmatched by any other sport—perhaps any other human activity—on earth.

Here is how we who love baseball came to this fortunate estate, and how we at *Total Baseball* created what is now the official historical record.

The Origins, 1845-1875

Baseball and stats were a tandem from the very Eden of the game. The first box score appeared in the *New York Morning News* on October 22, 1845, less than a month after Alexander Cartwright and his Knickerbocker teammates codified the first set of rules. Why did these early players and scribes measure individual performance rather than simply count the score? In part to imitate the custom of cricket; yet the larger explanation is that the numbers served to legitimize men's concern with a boys'

pastime. The pioneers of baseball reporting—William Cauldwell of the *Sunday Mercury*, William Porter of *Spirit of the Times*, the unknown annalist at the *News*, and later Henry Chadwick—may indeed have reflected that if they did not cloak the game in the "importance" of statistics, it might not seem worthwhile for adults to read about, let alone play. Statistics elevated baseball from other boys' field games of the 1840s and '50s to make it somehow systematic and serious, like business; despite baseball's essential simplicity, it was laced with intricate detail that suited it perfectly to quantification.

In the development of baseball statistics, no man is more important than Father Chadwick. Born in England in 1824, he came to these shores at age thirteen steeped in the tradition of cricket. In his teens he played the English game and in his twenties he reported on it for a variety of newspapers, including the *Long Island Star* and the *New York Times*. In the early 1840s, before the Knickerbocker rules eliminated the practice of retiring a base runner by throwing the ball at him rather than to the base, Chadwick occasionally played baseball too, but he was not favorably impressed, having received "some hard hits in the ribs." Not until 1856, by which time he had been a cricket reporter for a decade, were Chadwick's eyes opened to the possibilities in the American game, which had improved dramatically since his youth. In 1868 he recalled, "On returning from the early close of a cricket match on Fox Hill, I chanced to go through the Elysian Fields during the progress of a contest between the noted Eagle and Gotham clubs. The game was being sharply played on both sides, and I watched it with deeper interest than any previous ball game between clubs that I had seen. It was not long before I was struck with the idea that baseball was just the game for a national sport for Americans . . . as much so as cricket in England. At the time I refer to I had been reporting cricket for years, and, in my method of taking notes of contests, I had a plan peculiarly my own. It was not long, therefore, after I had become interested in baseball, before I began to invent a method of giving detailed reports of leading contests at baseball . . . ."

Thus Chadwick's cricket background was largely the impetus to his method of scoring a baseball game, the format of his early box scores, and the copious if primitive statistics that appeared in his year-end summaries in the *New York Clipper*, Beadle's *Dime Base-Ball Player*, and other publications.

Actually, cricket had begun to shape baseball statistics even before Chadwick's conversion. The first box score reported on two categories, outs and runs: outs, or "hands out," counted both unsuccessful times at bat and outs run into on the basepaths; "runs" were runs scored, not those driven in. The reason for not recording hits in the early years, when coverage of baseball matches appeared alongside reports of cricket matches, was that, unlike baseball, cricket had no such category as the successful hit which did not produce a run. To reach "base" in cricket is to run to the opposite wicket, which tallies a run; if you hit the ball and do not score a run, you have been put out.

Cricket box scores were virtual play-by-plays, a fact made possible by the lesser number of possible events. This play-by-play aspect was applied to a baseball box score as early as 1856; interestingly, despite the abundance of detail, hits were not accounted, nor did they appear in Chadwick's own box scores until 1867. The batting champion as declared by Chadwick, whose computations were immediately and universally accepted as "official," was the man with the highest average of runs per game. An inverse though imprecise measure of batting quality was outs per game. After 1863, when a fair ball caught on one bounce was no longer an out, fielding leaders were those with the greatest total of fly catches, assists, and "foul bounds" (fouls caught on one bounce). Pitching effectiveness was based purely on control, with the leader recognized as the one whose delivery offered the most opportunities for outs at first base and led to the fewest passed balls.

In a sense, Chadwick's measuring of baseball as if it were cricket can be viewed as correct: when you strip the game to its basic elements, those that determine victory or defeat, outs and runs are indeed all that count in the end. No individual statistic is meaningful to the team unless it relates directly to the scoring of runs.

Early player stats were of the most primitive kind, the counting kind. They'd tell you how many runs, or outs, or fly catches had occurred—later, how many hits or total bases. Counting is the most basic of all statistical processes; the next step up is averaging, and Chadwick was the first to put this into practice.

As professionalism infiltrated the game, teams began to bid for star-caliber players. Stars were known not by their stats but by their style until 1865, when Chadwick began to record in the *Clipper* a form of batting average taken from the cricket pages—runs per game. Two years later, in his newly founded baseball weekly, *The Ball Players' Chronicle*, he began to record not only average runs and outs per game, but also home runs, total bases, total bases per game—and hits per game. The averages were expressed not with decimal places but in the standard cricket format of the "average and over." Thus a batter with 23 hits in 6 games would have an average expressed not as 3.83 but as "3–5"—an average of 3 with an overage, or remainder, of 5. Another innovation was to remove from the individual accounting all bases gained through errors. Runs scored by a team, beginning in 1867, were divided between those scored after a man reached base on a clean hit and those arising from a runner's having reached base on an error. This was a clear precursor of the modern earned run average.

By the end of the decade Chadwick was recording total bases and home runs, but he placed little stock in either, as conscious attempts at slugging violated his cricket-bred image of "form." Just as cricket aficionados watch the game for the many opportunities for fine fielding it affords, so was baseball from its inception perceived as a fielders' sport. The original Knickerbocker rules of 1845, in fact, specified that a ball hit out of the field—in fair territory or foul—was a foul ball! "Long hits are showy," Chadwick wrote in the *Clipper* in 1868, "but they do not pay in the long run. Sharp grounders insuring the first-base certain, and sometimes the second-base easily, are worth all the hits made for home-runs which players strive for."

Chadwick prevailed, and the batting average used from that year on is the same as that used today except in its denominator, where at bats replaced games in 1876. Moreover, Chadwick created a measure in the 1860s that divided total bases by games played; change that denominator to at bats and you have today's slugging average—which, incidentally, was not accepted by the National League as an official statistic until 1923 and by the American until 1946.

Chadwick's "total bases average" represent the game's first attempt at a weighted average—an average in which the elements collected together in the numerator or the denominator are recognized numerically as being unequal. In this instance, a single is the unweighted unit, the double is weighted by a factor of two, the triple by three, and the home run by four. Statistically, this is a distinct leap forward from, first, counting, and next, averaging. The weighted average is in fact the cornerstone of today's statistical innovations, or sabermetrics.

The 1870s gave rise to some new batting stats and to the first attempt to quantify thoroughly the other principal facets of the game, pitching and fielding. Although the *Clipper* recorded base hits and total bases as early as 1868, a significant wrinkle was added in 1870 when at bats were listed as well. This was a critical introduction because it permitted the improvement of the batting average, first introduced in its current form by H.A. Dobson of Washington, D.C., in the *Dime Base-Ball Player* of 1872, and first computed "officially"—that is, for the newly created National League—in 1876, the lone year in which bases on balls were figured as outs. Since then the batting average has not changed, except for 1887, when bases on balls were counted as *hits*. In accord with previously created Major League Baseball policy, *Total Baseball* counts a walk as neither an out nor a hit for all years since 1871.

The objections to the batting average are well known, but to date have not disturbed its place as the most popular measure of hitting ability. First of all, the batting average makes no distinction between the single, the double, the triple, and the home run, treating all as the same unit. This objection had been addressed in 1868 by Chadwick's total bases average. Second, the batting average gives no indication of the effect of that base hit—that is, its value to the team. Third, the batting average does not take into account those occasions when first base is reached via a walk, hit batsman, or error. This last point was addressed at a surprisingly early date, too: in 1879 the National League adopted as an official statistic a forerunner of the on base percentage; it was called "reached first base," which included times reached by error as well as base on balls and base hits. (Being hit by a pitch did not give the batter first base until the ensuing decade.)

The Flowering, 1876-1920

Ever since the Civil War, serial guides like *Beadle* and *DeWitt* and sporting columns like those in the *Clipper* had carried year-end tabulations of batting, fielding, and pitching exploits, varying from year to year with the brainstorms of Chadwick or other demon compilers like New York's M.J. Kelly or Philadelphia's Al Wright. But the year 1876 was special. It was significant not only for the founding of the National League and the official debut of the batting average in its current form, it was also the Centennial of the United States, which was marked by a giant exposition in Philadelphia celebrating the mechanical marvels of the day. American ingenuity reigned, and technology was seen as the new handmaiden of democracy. Baseball, that mirror of American life, reflected the fervor for things scientific with an explosion of statistics far more complex than those seen before, particularly in the previously neglected areas of pitching and fielding. The increasingly minute statistical examination of the game met a responsive audience, one primed to view complexity as a measure of worth.

In 1876 the number of "official" offensive stats tabulated at season's end—i.e., in any of the publications inspired by Chadwick or Albert Spalding—was six: games, at bats, runs, hits, runs per game, and batting average. (And as with all the various guides until 1941, the stats of men who played in fewer than a specified minimum number of games were not noted.) Of these six, only runs and runs per game were common in the 1860s, while that decade's tabulation of total bases vanished. The number of official offensive stats a hundred years later? Twenty. (Today the number is twenty-one, with the addition of on base percentage).

The number of "official" pitching categories in 1876 was eleven, and there were some modernistic surprises, such as earned run average, hits allowed, hits per game, and opponents' batting average. Strikeouts were not recorded, for Chadwick saw them strictly as a sign of poor batting rather than good pitching (his view had such an impact that pitcher strikeouts were not kept officially until 1889). The number of official pitching stats today? Twenty-four.

The number of fielding categories in 1876 was six. One hundred years later it was still six (with the exception of the catcher, who gets a seventh: passed balls), dramatizing how the game, which originated as a showcase for fielders, had changed. The fielding stats of 1876 lumped "battery errors" with fielding errors, so that wild pitches and passed balls—in some years, even walks—diminished one's fielding percentage. This practice continued until 1887, but in *Total Baseball* battery errors are not included in fielding stats. Battery-mates' fielding stats were boosted by the awarding of an assist to the pitcher on strikeouts. This practice lasted until 1889, but is not reflected in *Total Baseball*.

The custom in 1876, as it is now, was to combine putouts, assists, and errors to form a "percentage of chances accepted," or what is today known as fielding average or fielding percentage. A "missing link" variant, devised by Al Wright in 1875, was to form averages by dividing the putouts by the number of games to yield a "putout average"; dividing the assists similarly to arrive at an "assist average"; and dividing putouts plus assists by games to get "fielding average." These averages took no account of errors. (Wright's "fielding average" was reborn a century later as Bill James's "range factor.")

The public's appetite for new statistics was not sated by the outburst of 1876. New measures were introduced in dizzying profusion in the remaining years of the century. Some of these did not catch on and were soon dropped for all time, like the meaningless "total bases run," while others fizzled only to reappear with new vigor in the twentieth century. These include (a) the above-mentioned "reached first base," which resurfaced in the early 1950s in an unofficial, improved form called on base percentage and became an official stat more than thirty years later, and (b) an 1860s stat, earned run average, which was periodically revived before dropping from sight in the 1880s, only to return triumphant to the NL in 1912 and the AL in 1913. (In 1913 Ban Johnson not only proclaimed the ERA official but became so enamored with it that he also instructed American League scorers to compile no official won-lost records. This state of affairs lasted for seven years, 1913-1919, but *Total Baseball* does record wins and losses by pitchers in those years, in accordance with the understood scoring practices of the time.)

Another stat that was "sent back to the minors" before its eventual adoption as an official stat in 1920 was the run batted in. Introduced by a Buffalo newspaper in 1879, the stat was picked up the following year by the *Chicago Tribune* and even became an official NL stat for the opening months of 1891. By season's end it had faded as most NL scorers declined to account for it in their summaries (the American Association, however, recorded it all year long). Ernie Lanigan picked up the RBI baton with his reports to the *New York Press* from 1907 through 1919, and he did not figure RBI for men who played in fewer than ten games, or club totals for traded players. For *Total Baseball* we have placed much reliance upon the source material donated by Information Concepts, Inc. (ICI) to the National Baseball Library in Cooperstown following publication of *The Baseball Encyclopedia* which it developed for publication by Macmillan in 1969. David Neft also kindly supplied us with his unpublished RBI data for the previously missing National League seasons of 1880-1885. The John Tattersall collection of nineteenth century game accounts and box scores was valuable for uncovering RBI as well. (For a detailed accounting of the sources employed for this official historical record of Major League Baseball, see the conclusion of the essay.)

Other statistics introduced officially before the turn of the century were stolen bases (though not caught stealing); doubles, triples, and homers; and sacrifice bunts (though an at-bat was charged from 1889 through 1893). Pitcher strikeouts, bases on balls, and the hit-by-pitch also appeared before 1900, but hit-by-pitch stats were not kept for batters on a systematic basis until 1917 in the NL and 1920 in the AL. Through newspaper research, we have filled in HBP data from 1884 through 1916 in the National League; the Players League of 1890; the American Association of 1882-1891; from 1901 through 1919 in the American League, and the 1914-1915 Federal League.

Hit into double play—including line outs as well as an groundouts—was an erratically recorded stat in the nineteenth century, but separate stats for groundouts into double plays have been kept by the leagues only since 1933 in the NL and 1939 in the AL. Batters' strikeouts were reported unofficially in 1891, but not as a league stat until 1910 in the NL and 1913 in the AL. Innings pitched were not kept until 1908 in the AL and 1903 in the NL. You can see what a patchwork quilt the records of Major League Baseball were in its early years.

Stolen bases were awarded not only for clean steals but also for extra bases taken through daring, from the first year in which totals were kept, 1886, until 1898. Because the figures reported in the guides were grossly inflated (such as Harry Stovey's ostensible 156 steals in 1888), the figures in *Total Baseball* reflect game-by-game research and refiguring. Caught-stealing (CS) figures are available on a very sketchy basis in some of the later years of the century, as some newspapers carried the data in the box scores of hometown games. From 1912 on, Lanigan recorded CS in box scores of the *New York Press*, but the leagues did not keep the figure officially until 1920. The AL has tabulated CS from that year to the present, excepting 1927, which members of the Society for American Baseball Research reconstructed from newspaper box scores. National League caught-stealing data exists for 1920-1925, and for 1951 to the present.

The new century added little in the way of new official statistics—ERA, RBI, and slugging average are better regarded as revivals despite their respective adoption dates of 1912, 1920, and 1923. But back in 1908 there was a classic case of a statistic rushing in to fill a void, as Phillies' manager Billy Murray observed that his outfielder Sherry Magee had the happy facility of providing a long fly ball whenever presented with a situation of a man on third and fewer than two outs. Taking up the cudgels on his player's behalf, Murray protested to the National League office that it was unfair to charge Magee with an unsuccessful time at bat when he was in fact succeeding, doing precisely what the situation demanded. (More recent stats—the save and the late lamented game-winning run batted in, or GWRBI—have followed from this sort of perception that something important was occurring on the field yet had no verifiable reality because it was not being measured.)

A signal event took place in 1912: the publication by *Baseball Magazine* editor John Lawres of *Who's Who in Baseball,* a small book that became the first to provide career statistics and personal facts for a group of players. Although thoroughly inadequate by today's standards—its only tabulations were games, batting average, and fielding average (even for pitchers, who were given no pitching records!)—*Who's Who* was a groundbreaking work. It gave rise to a much-expanded format in 1916 and inspired two other significant encyclopedic works: in 1914, George Moreland's self-published opus called *Balldom* (grandiosely subtitled "The Britannica of Baseball,") and Ernest J. Lanigan's *Baseball Cyclopedia*, also sponsored by *Baseball Magazine*, which debuted in 1922 and was updated annually through 1933.

The Golden Age, 1920-1968

There have been other new statistical tabulations in this century, but generally of the counting sort: complete games (NL 1910, AL 1922), games started (AL 1926, NL 1938), games finished (NL 1920, AL 1926). And there were sacrifice bunts allowed (NL 1913, AL 1921), intentional bases on balls (only since 1955), and, in the next period, saves (1969) and game-winning RBI (1980). The only new average since slugging average was adopted in 1923 has been the on base percentage, adopted in 1985. The ICI group computed saves for prior years. Another such stat that failed to survive, alas, was stolen bases off pitchers, which the American League recorded only in 1920-1924; it has been recorded on an unofficial basis since the 1980s by the Elias Sports Bureau and Baseball Workshop. The only new fielding measure was team double plays, added to the AL list in 1912 and the NL in 1919. Other new and more interesting stats appeared in the 1940s and '50s but have not yet gained the official stamp of approval, such as Ted Oliver's Weighted Rating System, Alfred P. Berry's Average Bases Allowed (opponents' slugging average), and Branch Rickey and Allan Roth's Isolated Power. (See the ensuing essay, "Sabermetrics" for more about these unorthodox measures, some of which have gained wide acceptance and may, like the on base percentage, one day be embraced by Major League Baseball.)

This period of baseball's history may have fielded its most dazzling array of stars, but strategically and statistically it was rather dim. There was some excitement, however, in baseball record keeping. First came *Daguerreotypes*, issued by *The Sporting News* in 1934, featuring the playing records of many retired players both celebrated and obscure; most if not all of these statistical and biographical profiles originally appeared in the pages of TSN. Although its number of statistical categories was fewer than one might have wished, *Daguerreotypes* was very useful and, through its several editions ably edited by Paul MacFarlane, long-lived.

In 1940 came *The Sporting News's Baseball Register*, which supplied full records for active players, managers, coaches, and umpires, plus a grab bag of former stars. Since the expansion of the major leagues from sixteen teams to twenty-eight, the Register has only accommodated contemporary players and managers, but it remains a valuable source.

Then in 1951 came the first true encyclopedia of baseball, the claims of Moreland and Lanigan notwithstanding. Compiled by Hy Turkin and S.C. Thompson, *The Official Encyclopedia of Baseball* was published by the A.S. Barnes Company. Its 620 pages contained a wealth of features such as manager and umpire rosters, historical essays, playing tips, a bibliography, and much more. But the heart of the volume and the key to its subsequent success was a register of nearly nine thousand men who had played one or more games at the major league level from 1871 through 1949 (the 1950 record of players appearing in ten games or more was tacked on to the end). In this register, Turkin/Thompson also offered birth and death data and what today seems fairly limited statistical information but by previous standards was a veritable cornucopia: year, club, league, position, games, and batting average or won-lost record. A landmark volume that did much to inspire this one, the Barnes encyclopedia endured through ten revised editions, the last being published in 1979, ten years after the initial appearance of Macmillan's *The Baseball Encyclopedia.*

The Barnes encyclopedia went a long way toward making the study of baseball history and records a respectable pursuit, just as a century earlier the statistical accounting of a boys' game had helped to make baseball a sport for grown men. The researchers' ranks expanded to include such men as Bob Davids, who in 1971, aided by other experts like Cliff Kachline, Bill Haber, Ray Nemec, John Pardon, and Joe Simenic, would create SABR, the Society for American Baseball Research (pronounced "saber"). Formerly the lonely pursuit of a handful of "nuts" like S.C. Thompson, baseball research and sabermetrics—a neologism coined in honor of SABR, signifying the statistical analysis of the game's records— would become the pastime of thousands.

An article in *Life* magazine by Branch Rickey on August 2, 1954, gave further impetus to the study of baseball statistics, but not just to set the historical record straight. Indeed, this article may be viewed as the opening shot of the sabermetric assault of the 1980s. In "Goodby to Some Old Baseball Ideas," Rickey, with the aid of some new mathematical tools supplied by Dodger statistician Allan Roth, sought to puncture some long-held conceptions about how the game was divided among its elements (batting, baserunning, pitching, fielding), who was best at playing it, and what caused one team to win and another to lose. This is a pretty fair statement of what sabermetrics is about.

Rickey attacked the batting average and proposed in its place the on base percentage, but the most important thing Rickey did for baseball statistics was to strip the game and its stats to their pre-1876 essentials and start again, this time remembering that individual stats came into being as an attempt to apportion the players' contributions to achieving a team victory.

Rickey and Roth devised a formula to measure a team's efficiency in turning its offensive and defensive statistics into runs, and thus wins. They realized, and had confirmed for them by mathematicians at the Massachusetts Institute of Technology, that just as the team which scores more runs in a game gets the win, so a team which over the course of a season scores more runs than it allows should win more games than it loses—and by an extent correlated to its run differential. From this startlingly simple (or rather, seemingly simple) observation of 1954 flowed: first, the trailblazing but little noted work of George Lindsey in the 1950s and early 1960s, when he developed a model for run-scoring probability from the twenty-four combinations of outs and bases occupied; the development of "percentage baseball" stats and strategies by Earnshaw Cook in the 1960s; the play-by-play analysis of complete seasons by the Mills brothers, Eldon and Harlan, in 1969-1970; the recording and analysis of situational statistics by the Elias Sports Bureau for use by Major League Baseball and its clubs; and, over the next two decades, the statistical and historical works of many sabermetricians.

The Computer Age, 1969-

Despite the death of Turkin in 1957 and Thompson ten years later, their encyclopedia remained the dominant book of baseball statistics, although many fans were frustrated with the fragmentary records it presented. As Frank V. Phelps wrote in the 1987 edition of *The National Pastime,* "Gaps and obvious errors in official averages, the lack of many early records, difficulty in securing the records of players who appeared in only a few games, and frustrating discrepancies among existing guides and registers had long since created a desire for an ultimate, complete, correct set of major league records. But it wasn't until the mid-1960s that the development of sophisticated computers which could absorb, retain, order, and output huge amounts of data finally made a project feasible."

Beginning in 1967, a battalion of researchers commanded by David Neft foraged through the official records and newspaper box scores to provide freshly compiled figures for those who had no ERAs, RBI, slugging averages, saves, and all manner of wonderful things. The material which finally appeared in the tome was entered into a data bank, and the book was the first to be typeset entirely by computer, now a common practice. Published in 1969, *The Baseball Encyclopedia* was a milestone in computer technology, but as indispensable as the computer were the old-fashioned scrapbooks and files of Lee Allen and John Tattersall. The result was a mammoth ledger book of the major leagues more thorough than any that had appeared before.

The ICI group not only found new data to correct old inaccuracies but also applied new yardsticks to men who had gone to their graves never having heard of an RBI or a save. The ICI research that went into *The Baseball Encyclopedia* of 1969 created new stars, launching several previously underappreciated heroes of old into the Hall of Fame. Sam Thompson, Addie Joss, Roger Connor, Amos Rusie—their phenomenal level of play was hidden simply because statisticians back then were not recording the particular numbers which would show them off to best advantage. If sabermetrics consists of finding things in the existing data that were not seen before, or in collecting that data which makes possible the application of new statistics to old performances, the first edition of *The Baseball Encyclopedia* was a monument in the course of sabermetrics.

However, its subsequent editions declined from that standard, dropping valuable data, altering figures for star players in a misguided homage to tradition, and making a shambles of individual/team balance in the totals.

The seventh edition was issued in 1988 and, like the five that preceded it, was less accurate than the classic first issue. The eighth edition, published in 1990, corrected many of the errors in the seventh but retained many once-contested errors that historians had long since expunged from the record, while changing other statistics in a manner at variance with Major League Baseball's standards and with a rationale that remains unclear. For the ninth edition, Major League Baseball distanced itself from the both the product and its database.

Even when *The Baseball Encyclopedia* had been launched back in 1969, the ICI findings raised the hackles of traditionalists, prompting the formation by Major League Baseball of a Special Baseball Records Committee. Its members ruled upon such matters as whether, for the historical record, bases on balls should be counted as hits (as they were in 1887), outs (as they were in 1876), or neither (as has been the practice in all other years); or whether "sudden-death" home runs—thirty-seven game-winning blows with men on base that they identified as having occurred in the bottom half of the ninth or an extra inning—would be credited as homers or, in the practice before 1920, would count for only as many bases as were needed to push across the winning run. In the latter controversy, committee members first decided to count the disputed blows as homers, but then, when complaints arose that Babe Ruth's famous total of 714 would change to 715, they reversed themselves. They also decided that the National Association of 1871-1875 was not a major league, while the Federal League, Union Association, and Players League were; and they ruled on several other issues, all of which were published in the Appendix to *The Baseball Encyclopedia.*

Because earlier editions of *Total Baseball* enjoyed neither the privilege nor the responsibility of official Major League Baseball status, the editors committed themselves to the *process* of history—its research, reporting, and interpretation—rather than to its product. History is not static and unchanging. Our course then as now seemed unassailable: publish the best-documented data and remain humbly amenable to subsequent revision in the light of new evidence. (This is not very different from the placard in the Baseball Hall of Fame, which states that although later studies have called into question the accuracy of information on the plaques, the facts as engraved were believed to be accurate at the time.)

However, it must be acknowledged that we paid little mind to the consequences of our findings and reasoned judgments, such as the stripping of a batting championship from Ty Cobb in 1910 or Bobby Avila in 1954. For the fourth, landmark edition of *Total Baseball*, our challenge was to devise a more historically sensitive framework that would permit us to incorporate the best modern research while continuing to honor the judgments of the past.

Total Baseball abided by the Special Baseball Records Committee's decision on game-ending homers—not to preserve Ruth's total, but because there were many more such homers before 1920 than the thirty-seven the committee identified, and the disputes surrounding some of them are now beyond settling.

Like Turkin/Thompson and all previous record books, and in accordance with the view of most historians, we rejected the committee's position that the National Association was not a major league. We committed fully to the creation of a full statistical record of that trailblazing circuit, and hope one day soon to integrate the NA and NL records of such players as Al Spalding, Cap Anson, George Wright, and all the others who played in the professional league between 1871 and 1875. For now, we provide NA stats within the Player and Pitcher Registers, but total them separately from those of the NL (or, in a rare case, the American Association, a major league from 1882 through 1891).

We also differed from the committee's ruling on awarding pitchers wins and losses in the years before 1920. Not finding any official scoring rule or practice for that time, they chose to apply 1950 guidelines to decisions awarded in 1876-1920. This well-intentioned decision produced substantial alterations in the records of such hurlers as Cy Young, Christy Mathewson, Grover Alexander, and others. In the ensuing years, the notable research of Frank Williams (reported in "All the Record Books Are Wrong," *The National Pastime*, 1982) revealed that there was indeed a pattern and a rationale for the way decisions were awarded in those days; the data in *Total Baseball* conforms with his meticulously substantiated findings.

More involved, and perhaps of most direct interest to fans and media, are the subjects of (a) statistical discrepancies between the official record presented in *Total Baseball* and the figures published in other reference works, or memorialized on Hall of Fame plaques, and (b) the implications of corrected data for the awarding of batting championships. We will address those questions, as well as the larger ones of transcription accuracy and ledger balance, in the "Issues and Answers" section of this essay.

Let's resume our chronicle of how Major League Baseball and others have kept the record of the game. Besides the debut of *The Baseball Encyclopedia* (and the Miracle Mets and the centennial of professional baseball), there were two other interesting baseball developments in 1969. The first and less celebrated was a research project launched by Eldon and Harlan Mills that, like the ICI effort, could not have been contemplated without the computer. The Mills brothers tracked the entire major league seasons of 1969 and 1970 on a play-by-play basis. Then they applied to that record the probabilities of winning which derived from each possible outcome of a plate appearance, as determined by a computer simulation incorporating nearly eight thousand possibilities. What, for example, was the visiting team's chance of winning the game before the first pitch was thrown? Fifty percent, if we are pitting two theoretical teams of equal or unknown ability on a neutral site. If the first man fails to get on base, the chances of the visiting team winning are reduced to 49.8 percent; should he hit a double, the visiting team's chance of victory is raised to 55.9 percent, as determined by the probabilistic simulation. Every possible situation—combining half-inning, score, men on base, and men out—was tested by the simulator to arrive at "Win Points."

The Millses' purpose was to determine the clutch value of, say, hitting a homer with two men on and one man out in the bottom of the ninth, with the team trailing by two runs, the situation Bobby Thomson faced in the climactic National League game of 1951—oddly, the rookie year of the first modern computer. (That home run gained for him 1,472 Win Points; had it come with no one on in the eighth inning of a game in which his team led 4-0, the homer would have been worth only 12 Win Points.) What the Mills brothers were attempting to do was to evaluate not only the *what* of a performance, which traditional statistics indicate, but the *when*, or clutch factor, which no measure to that time could provide.

This project, detailed in a small book issued in 1970 called *Player Win Averages*, proceeded from the same impulse that led to other measures of clutch performance:

the game winning RBI, introduced as an official Major League Baseball stat in 1980 and scrapped in 1989; the measures of batting performance in late-inning and men-on-base situations first published by Seymour Siwoff, Steve Hirdt, and Peter Hirdt of the Elias Sports Bureau in 1985; and the historically complete indexes of clutch hitting and clutch pitching developed for the first edition of this book.

The other noteworthy baseball event of 1969 was the official adoption by the major leagues of the save, the stat associated with relief pitching, the game's most significant strategic development since the advent of the gopher ball. Now shown in the papers on a daily basis, saves were not officially recorded at all until 1960; it was at the instigation of Jerome Holtzman of the *Chicago Sun-Times*, with the cooperation of *The Sporting News*, that this statistic was finally accepted. (Although Pat McDonough, a founding member of SABR, had developed a similar stat in 1924 which he called "games finished by relief hurlers"; its first appearance in print came in the *New York Telegram* three years later.) The need for the save arose because relievers operated at a disadvantage when it came to picking up wins. The bullpen specialists were a new breed, and as their role increased, the need emerged to identify excellence, as it had long ago for batters, starting pitchers, and fielders.

The save's prime statistical drawback is that there is no negative to counteract the positive, no stat for saves blown (except, all too often, a victory for the "fireman"); unofficial attempts to develop such a stat have accelerated in recent years, and now are part of the formula for the Fireman of the Year award.

August 10, 1971, marked another milestone, the founding in Cooperstown of SABR, the group in whose annual publications most of today's sabermetricians cut their analytical teeth. Its statistical analysis research committee, headed for more than a decade by Pete Palmer, has served as a sounding board for the inventive approaches of such men as Dallas Adams, Dick Cramer, Steve Mann, Craig Wright, Gary Gillette, and Bill James.

Developments of the ensuing decade include the previously mentioned adoption of the game-winning RBI (GWRBI) in 1980; it rewarded the batter who drove in a run to give his club a lead that it never relinquished. This stat was pilloried in the press from its introduction; Major League Baseball finally gave up on it before the 1989 season. In 1985 on base percentage was made official, thirty-one years after its introduction to the general baseball public by Rickey and Roth.

Situational stats, unofficial but widely reported and employed, have been the specialty of the Elias Sports Bureau, the Baseball Workshop, and Stats, Inc.—performance in day games vs. night, grass vs. artificial turf, lefty vs. righty, day game following night, bases-loaded situations, and so on. When the data is drawn from a large enough sample, these stats can be provocative and meaningful; they represent the wave of the future in baseball, and are fast becoming useful analytical tools for review of the past—Elias has recorded situational data systematically since 1975, Baseball Workshop since 1984.

Total Baseball

The next major event in the history of baseball record keeping has been *Total Baseball*. Founded upon a unique historical database that Pete Palmer has cultivated for decades—in the tradition of baseball archivists like S.C. Thompson, Bradshaw Swales, Leonard Gettelson, and John Tattersall—*Total Baseball* is the third-generation encyclopedia of the game. Just as the advent of the Macmillan/ICI encyclopedia supplanted Turkin/ Thompson, the standard for two decades, *Total Baseball* has taken advantage of new technology and new research, notably by members of the Society for American Baseball Research, to present data more accurate than ever before, and more of it. There are, of course, the traditional stats one would expect in a baseball reference work; there are many of the more revealing sabermetric stats (discussed in detail in the essay that follows this); there are stats never published before their appearance in this book. And as you have seen in Part One, there is a recognition that baseball history and knowledge resides not only in its numbers.

Issues and Answers: Sources of Baseball Statistics

There are six major sources for baseball statistical research, and thus for the official statistics that comprise *Total Baseball*. By far the most significant one is the official Major League Baseball records kept by the leagues, published in the baseball guides, and maintained on microfilm at the Baseball Hall of Fame in Cooperstown and in the league offices. These records cover the years since 1903 for the National League and 1905 for the American League. Any source data before these years were lost.

The second major source is the computer printouts prepared by ICI for *The Baseball Encyclopedia* in 1969. These cover the NL for 1891-1902, the AL for 1901-05, the Federal League for 1914-15, plus all the nineteenth-century leagues (1882-91 American Association, 1884 Union Association, and the 1890 Players League). These records, obtained from newspaper box scores, were turned over to the Baseball Hall of Fame and made public by agreement with its resident historian Lee Allen, who permitted ICI to use his voluminous player demographic files.

The third source is John Tattersall's newspaper box-score research for the NL of 1876-90. Since Tattersall had done such careful work, day-by-day computer printouts were never generated for this period. Any day-by-day records created by John have been lost, but what has survived is a batting and fielding summary and a pitching summary for each club each year listing many categories. This collection, now owned by SABR, also includes the home run log, which lists every home run ever hit from 1871 to date, the date, teams, game location, batter, pitcher, inning, men on base, and other notes. This has been computerized by SABR and is maintained by David Vincent. John Tattersall, Bob McConnell, and Pete Palmer have discovered over a hundred errors in the homer data from the various accepted sources, either ICI research or guide data.

The fourth source for baseball statistics is a box score collection accumulated by Michael Stagno, covering the National Association of 1871-1875, which was also purchased by SABR. Preliminary basic data was calculated by Stagno. Bob Richardson of Boston and Bob Tiemann of St. Louis have accumulated complete totals in all categories from this data with the exception of caught stealing data.

The fifth source is additional work done by the ICI researchers for the 1969 edition, covering data that were not kept officially during the years since 1903 for the NL and 1905 for the AL. Examples of this data are runs batted in before 1920, extra base hits in the AL for 1905 and 1906, double plays by fielders before 1920 NL and 1923 AL, pitching data except wins and losses for the AL for 1905-07, earned runs for pitchers before 1912 NL and 1913 AL, complete games before 1913 NL and 1926 AL, games started before 1926 AL and 1938 NL, and saves before 1969. Any day-by-day records from this source have been lost, but the season totals have survived.

The sixth source is newspaper box score research to pick up additional categories not covered by the first five sources. Examples of this are hit by pitch for batters before 1917 NL and 1920 AL (by Alex Haas, Tattersall, Palmer, and many others), triple plays by fielders before 1928 AL and 1930 NL (mainly by Jim Smith), home runs allowed by pitchers before 1950 AL and 1952 NL (again by Tattersall). Frank Williams carefully researched AL pitching records for 1901-1919, when the league records were particularly sloppy. *Total Baseball* has day-by-day sheets for most of this data, with the rest residing in the Tattersall collection.

Issues and Answers: Discrepancies

The original data for record books and Hall of Fame plaques, before the 1969 ICI research, were mostly obtained from two sources, the Spalding and Reach annual guides and two *Sporting News* publications: the *Baseball Register* (published yearly 1940-date), which often contained records of oldtimers, and *Daguerreotypes* (published every so often from 1951 to date), which had records of all Hall of Famers and many other notable players. This research was done from guides and newspapers by Paul Rickart, Leonard Gettelson, and Paul MacFarlane.

When the 1969 encyclopedia came out, there were many small differences in player stats when compared to the traditional data. However, since any records used to generate guide data in the early years were lost, the new data appeared to be more reliable. In addition, many more categories were given, like extra base hits, runs batted in, pitcher innings, hits and earned runs allowed, and fielder double plays. Also included in the new data were club splits for traded players and information on those who played in fewer than fifteen games.

In addition to the previously mentioned retroactive scoring decisions of the Special Baseball Records Committee, it ruled to include in the averages many games that were thrown out before, particularly in 1877, 1879, and 1899. Also included were the NL's tie games of five or more innings in 1878 through 1884 (thirty-eight of them)

previously uncounted. Before 1912 in the NL pinch hitters and defensive replacements were included in the official game sheets, but the players were not credited with a game played. The committee decided to add these in, too.

Our research has uncovered a great many small errors and a few major ones in the official statistics. This was done by comparing individual totals to team totals, and by rechecking the addition on the player sheets. Most of these errors were in the American League, particularly before 1920, for which the record keeping was very sloppy. The NL has been much better over the years. For example, from 1910 to date, they took the sum of all the batter and fielder stats for each team, compared them to the sum of the team stats, and resolved almost all the differences. The AL did not start doing this until 1973 when the record keeping was first computerized. The NL went to computers in 1981.

For example, up through 1935, most AL clubs are not in agreement in player sums and team figures for at bats and hits. The differences are usually small, less than 10. (We have corrected the larger discrepancies of those years, but the smaller ones are yet to be resolved.) For 1905 to 1920, the team totals are further removed from the sum of the players, so that *The Baseball Encyclopedia* and *Total Baseball* have replaced the team totals with the sum of the players. We corrected all the post-1935 cases of team at-bat and hit totals not agreeing, but have not yet begun work on the previous years.

An interesting quirk in the way records are kept—and another reminder, as if one needed it, that baseball record keeping remains subject to error and controversy—occurred as recently as the strike-shortened season of 1981. The American League rule was to round off the innings pitched at the end of the season, although the weekly reports showed thirds of innings. Baltimore's Sammy Stewart had 29 earned runs in 112⅓ innings, while Oakland's Steve McCatty had 48 in 185⅔ innings. This gave Stewart the ERA title, 2.323 to 2.327. But when the innings were rounded off, McCatty won, 2.32 to 2.33. McCatty got the title, but the next year both leagues decided to count thirds of innings.

Issues and Answers: Hall of Famers

The data reported by the ICI group in the first edition of *The Baseball Encyclopedia* upset many people in baseball, for their numbers were different from those traditionally accepted; in subsequent editions, many of the prominent players' statistics were fudged back to their traditional values. Yet 1969 had hardly been the first time corrections had been made to official data. In 1929 Grover Cleveland Alexander won his 373rd game, breaking Christy Mathewson's National League record, then thought to be 372. He never won another game. A number of years later, Joseph Reichler found a game in which, by the rules of that time, Matty should have gotten the win, this game taking place on May 21, 1902. The official record was changed and Matty pulled into a tie with Alex. The problem was that no one checked all of Mathewson's other games to see how many times he received a win under the old rules that wouldn't have been credited that way today. When ICI did its original research in 1968, it found Matty had only 367 wins total by today's rules, while Alexander had 374. (Further research, notably by Frank Williams, has restored Alexander and Mathewson to a tie at 373 wins.)

In another celebrated example of record-book flip-flops, when the American League was formed in 1901, Nap Lajoie was credited with a .422 average, with 220 hits in 543 at bats. After a number of years, someone noticed that if you take these at bats and hits, the average comes out only to .405, so his average was changed. (Turkin/Thompson gave Nap a mark of .409 in its first edition.) Later in the 1950s, John Tattersall had his doubts and decided to go through his newspaper collection of box scores. He found 229 hits for Lajoie, not 220—the error had been in the figure for hits, not in the figure for batting average. Thus his average was restored to .422, which happened to be the highest in American League history. Then ICI research in this area came up with a .426 mark (232 for 544, based on newspaper accounts), which was published in the first edition, then trimmed back to .422 in subsequent editions. The .426 figure is the one this book uses, because the day-by-day source data for the American League of 1901 has been lost.

Lajoie seemed to be involved in a number of controversies. ICI research found four more hits for him in 1902, raising his average from .369 to .378. Later editions of *The Baseball Encyclopedia* have changed Lajoie's stats back to the old values; we have not.

In 1910 there was a very close batting race between Cobb and Lajoie. At the end of the season, most people thought Nap had won, based on his getting seven hits in a doubleheader on the final day of the season. There was talk that the opposing Browns had let him get a number of bunts by playing back, so that the hated Cobb would lose. However, the AL office went over their figures and gave Cobb the title, .385 to .384. Nearly eighty years later, Palmer discovered a critical error: a game in which Cobb had two hits in three at bats had been entered twice. This was found because Sam Crawford had 14 games on his official sheet for the homestand yet the Tigers had only played 13. It turned out that Detroit played a doubleheader on September 24, but the second game inadvertently was inserted in the official sheets as being played on September 25. Later, this second game of the 24th, which appeared to have been missing, was put in the scoresheets again. The League Office discovered this mistake soon after its official announcement that Cobb had won the batting title, because the double entry was corrected for all the other Detroit players. However, Ban Johnson had made a big deal out of how carefully his people had checked the figures in order to settle the controversy, so the AL kept quiet about the gaffe, leaving Cobb the winner.

Appeals to Commissioner Kuhn in 1981 to set the matter straight officially were to no avail, because that would not only have changed the outcome of the 1910 batting race, it would also have altered Cobb's lifetime hit total, then being pursued to massive media attention by Pete Rose. Kuhn's statement read, in part, "The passage of seventy years, in our judgment . . . constitutes a certain statute of limitation as to recognizing any changes in the records with confidence of the accuracy of such changes . . . . Since a variety of questions have been raised through the years about the accuracy of the statistics of that period, the only way to make changes with confidence would be for a complete and thorough review of all team and individual statistics. That is not practical." It may not have not been practical, but we have embarked upon such a course, and Major League Baseball has dedicated itself to that ongoing process.

Asked at the time how we would have resolved the dispute over the 1910 batting race, we responded in this way: remove Cobb's two redundant hits and alter his batting average accordingly, effectively dropping it beneath Lajoie's, and correct his lifetime hit total as well; however, retain Cobb's batting championship, for two reasons—one, because Lajoie's flurry of bunt hits were highly suspect, and two, because Cobb was awarded the title *in his day*, and awards should be permanent, not contingent. Furthermore, a reasonable case can be made that Ban Johnson, if he had believed that Lajoie's tainted hits would have been sufficient to produce a batting championship, would have nullified them; after all, he did banish from baseball the Browns' manager who had instructed his rookie third baseman to play exceptionally deep.

It is this singular event in baseball history that supplied a model for how *Total Baseball* and Major League Baseball developed a policy for incorporating new research finds into the historical record without revoking long-held personal championships. Player records may be changed upon the evidence of historical error, but league awards and titles are forever.

Here is what happened in the now celebrated Honus Wagner case in the 1990 edition of *The Baseball Encyclopedia*, over which Major League Baseball and the Macmillan publishing firm became estranged. The Macmillan editor noticed that previous edition figures for Wagner did not agree with the data presented in the first edition in 1969. He assumed that the data had been corrupted over the years, and thus returned the 1897-1900 data to the original figures, costing Wagner 12 hits. However, the editor did not restore the 1901-02 data, which would have resulted in Wagner losing three more hits. The outcome was that Wagner had a total of 3415 hits in the 1969 edition, 3430 in the 1988 edition (the traditional figure) and 3418 in the 1990 edition (also in 1993). One of the problems with the Macmillan newspaper research was that it did not count protested games in the player data. Although the games were thrown out of the standings, the player stats *did* count in the league compilations at the time, which should be the criterion for inclusion. (Protested games were included in the official records through 1909, then omitted 1910-1919, and were made once again part of the official records in 1920. When our review of these protested games prior to 1909 is completed, the individual stats will be added to our figures.)

Wagner was involved in three of these protested games. There were about twenty-five of them altogether in the nineteenth century. However, the newspaper research did show up additional differences in player stats beyond those from the protested games.

When checking the plaques for the Hall of Fame players, we found about forty players with differences from the *Total Baseball* data. Most were nineteenth century players with small differences due to discrepancies between the old guide figures and the later newspaper research. Some had to do with rule changes from the 1969 Special Baseball Records Committee, such as not counting walks as hits in 1887. For the twentieth century, there were a number of differences due to official errors, mostly in the area of pitcher won-lost marks in the 1901-1919 American League period. There were only a few outright errors on the plaques (see below for Anson, Clarkson, Hamilton, McCarthy, McGinnity, and Nichols). Exact differences can be found by comparing *Daguerreotypes* (which often agrees with the plaques) with *Total Baseball*.

Below is a guide to variances between the plaques and the official record of Major League Baseball embodied in *Total Baseball* (TB).

Nineteenth Century Hall of Famers:

Cap Anson   *Plaque*, *four batting titles;* **TB**, *three*
In 1879, Anson appears to have been the beneficiary of 20 extra hits, either by error or, as is commonly believed, a civic-minded Chicago official scorer. This error was found by John Tattersall in his review of newspaper box scores. In addition he (and we) incorporated the player records of four Chicago tie games, of which Anson played in two. His traditional mark of .407 was really only .317, and is so recorded in this volume; however, although a modern accounting would result in an 1879 batting title for Paul Hines, with .357, we credit the *championship* that year to Anson, as an instance of the official Major League Baseball policy cited above.

The singular season of 1887 presents a different case. Following the long-standing directive of the Special Baseball Records Committee, we do not count walks as hits, the practice which had been the sole basis of Anson's fourth batting championship. The modern computation reveals Sam Thompson to have had the highest batting average, and in this instance we withdraw the fourth batting title from Anson. Note that only for this year, in which walks were aberrationally recorded as hits, and 1876, when they were aberrationally recorded as outs, will we overturn the scoring practice of the time in favor of a modern reinterpretation of who was the batting leader.

Jake Beckley   *Plaque*, *.309 lifetime, also for fielding at first base, 2368 games, 23696 putouts, 25000 chances;* **TB**, *.308, 2377, 23709, 25024*
These are about as close as you can get when comparing several sources prior to 1900.

Dan Brouthers   *Plaque*, *.419 average in 1887;* **TB**, *.338*
This average is inflated by the aforementioned scoring practice of 1887; even if we elected to keep that practice in effect, Brouthers' walks would have lifted him to .426.

John Clarkson   *Plaque*, *175 losses, 2013 strikeouts, 4514 innings;* **TB**, *178, 1978, 4536*
The major difference in strikeouts occurred in 1886, where the guide had 340 and we counted only 313. We recorded two additional losses in 1894, in accordance

with the scoring rules of the day. Reviewing our sources, we counted 27 more innings in 1887. His plaque bore a clear error concerning his wins in 1888. He had 33 and did not lead the league, although the plaque says 49. This was a confusion with the 49 Clarkson did win in 1889, which was also listed.

Roger Connor   *Plaque*, *hit .300 twelve times;* **TB**, *eleven*
If we counted walks as hits in 1887, we would also have twelve times.

Ed Delahanty   *Plaque*, *hit. 408 in 1899;* **TB**, *.410*
The correction is a product of newspaper research.

Hugh Duffy   *Plaque*, *hit .438 in 1894;* **TB**, *.440*
This was the highest average all-time. The 1895 guide has 236 hits while the newspaper count is 237; both had 539 at bats. Since no backup data has survived for the guide, there is no way to determine where the difference might be.

Jim Galvin   *Plaque*, *365-311 won-lost;* **TB**, *360-308*
The plaque data includes a 4-2 mark in the 1875 NA, which has been denied major league status by the Special Baseball Records Committee. There are other smaller differences.

Billy Hamilton   *Plaque*, *196 runs in 1894, 115 stolen bases and .338 batting average in 1891, 937 stolen bases total, 1893-1895 batting averages of .395,.399 .393, ten times scoring 100 runs;* **TB**, *192 runs in '94, 111 steals and .340 batting average in '91, 912 lifetime steals, 1893-1895 batting averages of .380, .404, .389, eleven times scoring 100 runs*
Whether Hamilton scored 196 runs or 192, he still holds the all-time record. There were small differences in stolen bases in several years. We speculate that when the folks at Cooperstown counted Hamilton's seasons of scoring 100 or more runs, they overlooked his 1889 A.A. accomplishment.

Hughie Jennings   *Plaque*, *once hit .397;* **TB**, *.401 in 1896*
The guide had 208 hits in 523 at bats, which actually computes to .398, although .397 was shown. The newspaper research showed 209 for 521.

Tim Keefe   *Plaque*, *346 wins;* **TB**, *342*
Daguerreotypes currently also has 342.

Joe Kelley   *Plaque*, *.391 in 1894;* **TB**, *.393*
Newspaper box score research pointed up discrepancies in the figures recorded in the guides.

King Kelly   *Plaque*, *.394 average in 1887;* **TB**, *.322*
We do not count walks as hits; if we did, Kelly would have a mark of .393.

Tommy McCarthy   *Plaque*, *1268 games, 109 stolen bases in 1888, 53 assists in 1893;* **TB**, *1275 games, 93 steals, 28 assists*
Newspaper research found the early stolen base figures to be inflated, especially for the American Association. His

53 assists in 1893 included many at second base and shortstop. However, he did have 44 in the outfield in 1888, fourth best all-time.

Kid Nichols **Plaque**, *360-202 won-lost, 30 wins in 1895;* **TB** *361-208, 26*
Daguerreotypes now has 361-208 as we do, including 26 wins in 1895. Nichols for years had been credited with winning 30 or more games from 1891 through 1897, but it has been conclusively shown that he had only 26 in 1895. The Spalding guide showed games pitched (which was usually interpreted to be decisions) and percentage. They had 44 and .681 which would give a mark of 30-14. The 1942 *Baseball Register* showed him 30-15. ICI's *The Baseball Encyclopedia* had him at 26-16 in 42 complete games and 0-0 in 5 relief appearances. Ironically, the corrected figures give him 30 wins in 1898, for seven seasons of 30 victories or more—total, but not consecutive.

Amos Rusie **Plaque**, *led in shutouts five times;* **TB**, *4*
Rusie pitched 7 innings of a 9-inning shutout on July 5, 1897. Taking this shutout away, in accordance with current scoring rules (there were no official rules for crediting shutouts until 1951), gave him 2 shutouts instead of 3 that year.

Sam Thompson **Plaque**, *.336 lifetime, hit .400 twice;* **TB**, *.331, once*
If walks counted as hits, we would have him at .407 in 1887 and .334 lifetime.

John Ward **Plaque**, *158-102 won-lost, 2151 hits;* **TB**, *164-102, 2105*
Walks in 1887 accounted for 29 of the now "missing" hits. An additional 18 came from the 1890 Players League, for which newspaper research offered a lower total than the league figures. Other discrepancies were spread out over several years. We spotted 3 extra wins in 1879 and again in 1883.

Twentieth Century Hall of Famers

Luke Appling **Plaque**, *11,569 chances accepted at shortstop;* **TB**, *11,616*
There was an addition error for his putouts in 1940. He had 307, not 257. *Daguerreotypes* had 11,566, not 11,569.

Jack Chesbro **Plaque**, *192-128 won-lost;* **TB**, *198-132*
Daguerreotypes now has 198-128. The 1947 *Baseball Register*—only one year after Jack's election and the creation of his plaque—had 197-127. Still under review are two other games for which it has been argued that Chesbro should have received wins.

Ty Cobb **Plaque**, *4191 hits;* **TB**, *4189*
See above for discussion of the doubly entered 2-for-3 game. But that is not the whole story of how Cobb's lifetime hit total fell by two, nor of how he comes to retain his twelve batting titles. Modern research of the official day-by-day sheets revealed that Cobb had two games in

1906—on April 22 and 23—in which he went 1-for-8 that were not entered on his sheet. Additionally, there was a game on July 12, 1912 (the first game of a doubleheader) in which Cobb had a run which was entered in his hit column. (If this had indeed been a hit, he would have had a 34-game hitting streak. It was really only 23 games.) Finally, under today's rules, Cobb would not have won the batting title in 1914, because he didn't have enough plate appearances (or at bats). However, he did win it under the rules of the day, as he won the 1910 title, and that is what counts.

Eddie Collins **Plaque**, *3313 hits;* **TB**, *3315*
Collins picked up two hits in 1920 in a game for which his stats were switched with those of Buck Weaver.

Stan Coveleski **Plaque**, *214-141 won-lost, 2.88 ERA;* **TB**, *215-142, 2.89 Daguerreotypes* has 215-141. The 1942 *Baseball Register* has 216-142. Our ERA includes 1912, when Stan had a 3.43 era in 21 innings. The beginning of official status for ERA in the AL was 1913.

Sam Crawford **Plaque**, *2505 games, 2964 hits, 312 triples;* **TB**, *2517, 2961, 309*
Crawford's games played vary from the plaque largely because of the practice of not counting pinch-hit apperaances as games played. His ICI sheets reveal 5 additional games in 1900 and 7 in 1901. Also, he loses a triple in each of three seasons (1899, 1902, 1904) before the survival of official sheets; newspaper research does not support the Guide figures. And finally, Crawford lost 3 hits in 1900 through a recount of box score data, and 5 more in 1901. He gained back 3 in 1903 and 2 in 1904.

Red Faber **Plaque**, *253-211 won-lost, 3.13 era;* **TB**, *254-213, 3.*
15 Faber was credited with one win less than he actually recorded in 1916, one of the years in which the American League, at Ban Johnson's behest, posted no official data in this category. For 1915, we add a loss that clearly was overlooked on the official AL sheet, and for 1926 we add another loss that somehow was not posted when the Guide figures were released. The ERA variance is purely mathematical; it had been computed incorrectly.

Elmer Flick **Plaque**, *.378 in 1900;* **TB**, *.367*
The guide had 207 hits in 547 at bats, while the newspaper research showed 200 in 545.

Harry Heilmann **Plaque**, *2146 games;* **TB**, *2148*
Daguerreotypes has 2145 games. Heilmann appeared in 69 games in 1914, not 66. For 1912-14 the official AL averages did not count a game for any player who had all zeros in his entry. These would be pinch-runners or late-inning defensive replacements. There were a total of over 400 such uncounted appearances in this category altogether.

Walter Johnson **Plaque**, *414 wins;* **TB**, *417*
This research was done by Frank Williams and detailed minutely in his previously cited essay in *The National Pastime* of 1982. Walter had a 16-game winning streak in 1912, but one of the games (August 5) was not marked as

a win on his sheet. In 1911, wins were incorrectly marked as losses on June 27 and July 9. For the AL before 1920, there were about twenty or thirty errors in awarding wins and losses in the official statistics each year.

Heinie Manush   *Plaque, 2009 games;* **TB**, *2008*
His games were added incorrectly on the 1927 American League official sheet.

Joe McGinnity   *Plaque, won 20 seven times;* **TB**, *eight*
This looks like an error made by the Hall of Fame. He won 20 in 1902 between two leagues, as shown in the 1941 *Baseball Register* (McGinnity was elected in 1946).

Herb Pennock   *Plaque, 161 losses;* **TB**, *162*
Daguerreotypes agrees with 162 losses. The 1941 *Baseball Register* had 161.

Eppa Rixey   *Plaque, 4494 innings;* **TB**, *4494 2/3*
Official stats rounded innings pitched until 1982. *Total Baseball* records thirds of innings pitched in all seasons.

Red Ruffing   *Plaque, led in shutouts 1938 and 1939;* **TB**, *1939 only*
Lefty Gomez had 4 shutouts in 1938, not 3. This included a rain-shortened complete game on July 15. Ruffing had 3. Also, the comment on the plaque about making the all-star team in 1937-38-39 applies to the *Sporting News* All-Star team, not the All-Star Game team.

Tris Speaker   *Plaque, .344 lifetime;* **TB**, *.345*
There was an addition error on his official sheet for 1911. He had 500 at bats, not 510.

Pie Traynor   *Plaque, one of few players with 200 hits in a season;* **TB**, *of course, many players have had 200 or more hits in a season*

Zack Wheat   *Plaque, 2318 games for Brooklyn, 2406 total;* **TB**, *2322 for Brooklyn, 2410 total*
There were four unrecorded games in 1911 in which Wheat appeared only as a pinch hitter.

Issues and Answers: League Batting Leaders

Until the fourth edition of *Total Baseball*, Major League Baseball had established no official historical record, despite its product endorsement of several statistical compendiums over the years. As a result, writers, historians, statisticians, and fans were offered a choice amongst differing annual league batting leaders, depending on the major record book favored. Those most favored by recent chroniclers have been *Total Baseball* and *The Baseball Encyclopedia* because they had all player and club records.

There are two recognized record summary tomes which feature leaders in various statistical categories, lifetime or single-season: *The Book of Baseball Records* (Elias Sports Bureau Inc.) and *The Complete Baseball Record Book* (*The Sporting News*). Though both are respected works, and both organizations have had long, and often times official, relationships with Organized Baseball, neither record book enjoys official status, and discrepancies exist between the two.

There was *no* official batting championship rule until 1950. *Total Baseball* and *The Baseball Encyclopedia* remedied this oversight by formulating—independently—their own guidelines for the many years of omission, each based on their own concepts of fairness and equality.

In previous editions, *Total Baseball* established the following criteria for batting championships: 1876-1956, qualification by having plate appearances equal to 3.1 per game times the number of scheduled games, thus conforming to the Major League Baseball practice since 1957. The batting championship criteria for *The Baseball Encyclopedia* over the years have been: 1876-1919, games played equal to at least 60 percent of games the team scheduled; 1920-1949, at least 100 games played, based on acceptance of the unofficial but universally assumed rule requiring appearance in at least 100 games; and 1950-present, the various changing official rule definitions.

In a policy shift endorsed by Major League Baseball, *Total Baseball* identifies league batting champions according to the practice of the time, in each league, and each champion will have his seasonal batting average recorded in boldface in his entry in the Player Register. However, as noted above in the discussion of the 1910 AL batting race, in the Annual Record section of this volume, we record the highest batting averages in each league season as correctly calculated, although not necessarily in descending order.

The history of the official batting championship rule is as follows: (1) 1950-1951, 400 official times at bat; (2) 1952-1954, 400 official times at bat or, if less than 400 times at bat and by adding enough imaginary hitless at bats so as to total 400, "he still would have the highest batting average in his league, he shall be the champion batter"; (3) 1955-1956, 400 official times at bat; (4) 1957-1966, 3.1 plate appearances per game times number of scheduled games, equaling 477 in a 154-game schedule and 502 in a 162-game schedule; and it's 502 plate appearances; and (5) 1967-present, 3.1 plate appearances per scheduled game, except that "if there is any player whose average would be the highest if he were charged with the required number of plate appearances or official at bats, then that player shall be awarded the batting championship."

In the strike-shortened season of 1972, a 156-game standard prevailed instead of the 162 scheduled games. In the strike seasons of 1981 and 1994, the rule of 3.1 plate appearances per game was applied to the number of games played by each team, rather than to those scheduled.

The early record tomes, the *Spalding Record Book* and *The Sporting News Record Book*, placed Jake Stenzel (NL) in the lead for 1893 and Nap Lajoie (AL) on top in 1905. Both Stenzel and Lajoie were the leaders during the life of the Spalding volumes, 1908-1924, and in the *Sporting News* volume from its debut in 1921 until 1929, when Hugh Duffy replaced Stenzel and 1930, when Elmer Flick supplanted Lajoie. The reasoning behind the *Sporting News* switches was that both Stenzel and Lajoie failed to meet the unwritten criterion of a representative number of games—Stenzel had played in only 60 games and Lajoie in 65, not even half of their club's scheduled games. Otherwise the early record books' leaders were those endorsed by the leagues.

The Spalding Record Book in its 1917 edition made two important batting championship changes, both on the basis of mathematical errors which their editors had noted. To that time, Dan Brouthers had been tied with Cupid Childs for the highest batting average in 1892, but had been awarded the title based on his having played in more games, which was the tie-breaking guideline of the day. In 1917, however, Childs went to the front on the basis of extended batting average (calculating to extra decimal places beyond the thousandths that comprise conventional reporting of batting averages). Next, Lajoie's average of .422 in 1901 was reduced in 1917 because of a *Reach Guide* typo in the hit column to a .405 figure. The Spalding management (the once independent Reach company had long since been acquired by Spalding) should have known that in 1892, the criterion for awarding a batting championship was indeed games played, not extended batting average, and that in 1901 they would have found Lajoie's correct (as then calculated) average in any number of newspapers. Lajoie's .422 average was restored in 1954 in response to John Tattersall's research, but Childs remained, until this writing, ahead of Brouthers in the NL's *Green Book*. (In this fifth edition of *Total Baseball*, Brouthers is credited as the champion because he played in more games, which was the criterion of the time—not because modern research has lowered Childs' batting average from .335 to .317.)

During its formative years, 1876-1919, the National League omitted any mention of batting championship criteria in its published rules. Certainly, this should have been addressed before 1920. Still, batting championships were tacitly acknowledged by the league, with guidelines drawn primarily from the comments of Henry Chadwick.

From 1876 to ca. 1888, the criterion was understood to be the best seasonal performance; as expressed by Chadwick in the *Spalding Guide* of 1887, "an average rating of a player should be on a season's work." Seasonal leadership may be deduced when the league's recognized champion was not listed first in the official averages. His preeminence was based on a representative number of games played over the season in which he excelled, as opposed to the nominal leader's handful of games.

The yardstick between 1889 and 1919 was playing in at least 100 games. In the 1890 *Spalding Guide* Chadwick wrote: "With the object in view of equalizing the averages and placing the names of the batsmen who have played in 100 games or over, are given the front rank, while those who have played in 50 games and over occupy second place, and those in 25 games and over third place, and so on."

The American League rules in its early years, 1901-1919, omitted any batting championship language. In honoring Cobb as its 1914 bat champ, the AL was undoubtedly proceeding from the guideline of best seasonal performance.

As discussed in the "Sources of Baseball Statistics" section of this essay, *Total Baseball* relies upon newspaper research and other data for the years before 1903 in the NL and 1905 in the AL. For subsequent seasons, the official league day-by-day sheets are available for study. The record summary books issued by Elias and *Sporting News* accept all the batting leaders recognized in the yearly Guides (Spalding, Reach, etc.). These champions are also accepted in today's league publications (AL *Red Book* and NL *Green Book*). Henceforward, *Total Baseball* recognizes the same champions, with the exception of 1892, discussed above, and 1887, when walks were counted as hits.

For students of the game, Joe Wayman documented the variances among the record books and encyclopedias and highlighted particularly those traditional batting champions whom previous editions of *Total Baseball* had toppled from the pinnacle. Even though most of these champions have been rethroned, the following thumbnail account of the debatable batting leaders will serve to explain the seeming anomaly of a batting champion whose average is lower than that of a rival.

OFFICIAL   TB (eds. 1-5)

			G	AB	H	BA		G	AB	H	BA
1878 NL	Dalrymple	60	267	95	.356	Hines	62	257	92	.358
1879 NL	Anson	49	221	90	.407	Hines	85	409	146	.357
1884 NL	O'Rourke	104	448	197	.350	Kelly	108	452	160	.354
1887 NL	Anson	122	532	224	.421	Thompson	127	545	203	.372
1892 NL	Brouthers	152	588	197	.335	Brouthers	152	588	197	.335
1892 NL	Childs	144	552	185	.335					
1893 NL	Duffy	131	537	203	.378	Hamilton	82	355	135	.380
1910 AL	Cobb	140	509	196	.385	Lajoie	159	591	227	.384
1914 AL	Cobb	97	345	127	.368	Collins	152	526	181	.344
1926 NL	Hargrave	105	326	115	.353	Waner,P.	144	536	180	.336
1932 AL	Alexander	124	392	144	.367	Foxx	154	585	213	.364
1938 AL	Foxx	149	565	197	.349	Foxx	149	565	197	.349
1940 NL	Garms	103	358	127	.355	Hack	149	603	191	.317
1942 NL	Lombardi	105	309	102	.330	Slaughter	152	591	188	.318
1954 AL	Avila	143	555	189	.341	Williams	117	386	133	.345
1981 NL	Madlock	83	279	95	.341	Rose	107	431	140	.325

*Thompson becomes the official batting champion with a .372 average in accordance with the decision of the Special Baseball Records Committee not to count walks as hits. Anson would be a .347 hitter without the benefit of his walks.

1878: Abner Dalrymple captured the NL's batting title. Modern record tomes (*The Baseball Encyclopedia* and *Total Baseball*) list Paul Hines in the top spot. The NL in 1878 did not include tie games in its official averages, while today's record tomes count them. Thus, by counting tie games, Hines emerges with the higher average, but does not take away Dalrymple's championship.

1879: Cap Anson, the day's recognized batting champion, has been challenged by the moderns (*The Baseball Encyclopedia*, *Total Baseball*, *The Sports Encyclopedia: Baseball*, and *The National League Story*, Lee Allen) as to whether his .407 average is legitimate. In fact, the average was disputed as early as the 1880 DeWitt Guide, the averages for which were compiled by William Stevens of the *Boston Herald*, and *Balldom* (1914), compiled by George Moreland. *Total Baseball* keeps the title with Anson in recognition of the league action at the time, but reports his batting average correctly in the Player Register and in the Annual Record's listing of top batting averages in the 1879 NL.

1884: The official batting champion remains Orator Jim O'Rourke. Newspaper box scores, game accounts, and the results of tie games elevate King Kelly to a higher average. Tie games were not included in the official averages at the time, and how to handle them today remains a matter of controversy. No matter how we treat Kelly's 2-for-4 in his only tie-game appearance (August 11), his average is higher than O'Rourke's.

1887: In only this season, bases on balls counted as hits. One month into the season, the American Association wanted to scrap the absurd rule, but the NL would not consent. *Total Baseball* gives the championship to Sam Thompson. Without his 60 walks registering as hits, Anson batted .347.

1892: Brouthers and Childs were honored as co-champions at .335, as discussed above. Childs had the higher extended average, .3351, against Brouthers' .3350 mark. By the day's reasoning, however, Brouthers is the leader. As Chadwick noted in the *Spalding Guide*, "the lead in all cases of tie scores in base hits belongs by right to the batsman who has played in the greatest number of games, and in this case Brouthers batted in 152 games to Child's 144." Childs's statistics, as compiled by ICI from newspapers, yield a batting average of .317, placing him third.

1893: Billy Hamilton's average was higher than Duffy's, and he would have met modern criteria for plate appearances. The NL, however, honored Duffy because he appeared in at least 100 games, which was expected of the leading players of that day. The title is thus accorded to him.

1910: Cobb is the champion, for reasons discussed amply above.

1914: Cobb, due to his proven hitting excellence, was awarded the championship because, in all reasoned probability, he would have been the leader over the full season. Consider, also, that the batting championship for the Chalmers car in 1910 for position players was based on 350 at bats. Cobb would have easily captured the hit crown on a mythical 100 game requirement, even though he was three games shy.

1926: Bubbles Hargrave topped three other questionable contenders—those not credited with at least 400 at bats. All qualified for the title, though, based on the period's acceptance of appearance in at least 100 games. In Hargrave's favor was his position—catcher. Over the years, catchers were considered somewhat differently when it came to handing out awards, because of the demands of their position. In fact, in order for a catcher to qualify for the fielding championship at his position, he need only have appeared in at least 77 games. Hargrave caught in 93 games.

1932: Dale Alexander had the games and at bats to satisfy the AL as to his claim. If the 400 at bat rule had been on the books, Alexander no doubt would have been inserted into the lineup until he secured eight additional at bats. If Jimmie Foxx were today recognized as champion, he would have the first of two consecutive Triple Crowns.

1938: Foxx was the AL leader—no ifs, ands, or buts about it. The AL had a rule in 1938 requiring the batting " . . . winner to be at least 400 times at bat." (*Reach Guide*, 1939) Taffy Wright is the trivia-question champion, batting .350 in 100 games.

1940: Debs Garms raised a few eyebrows as a come-from-nowhere champion. If enough imaginary at bats to reach 400 were to be added to Garms' total, his adjusted average would still be one point higher than that of Stan Hack, the runnerup.

1942: Ernie Lombardi was the recognized NL batting king. As a *Sporting News* headline advised, "Ernie's 105 contests suffice to qualify him for a second title." The announcement called attention to the "inquiries" which had been made regarding a Lombardi award since the AL had put in place a 400 at bat requirement. Bill James noted that the NL announced a "meritorious 400 at bat" requirement after the problematic Garms award two years earlier. NL President Frick, however, contended there was no specific bat rule and catchers, because of their demanding position, deserved special consideration. The catcher's fielding championship by this time was based on 100 games, lessening the Frick contention. Frick may have had in mind the prior, 77-game catching requirement for fielding leadership. Thus, Frick's reasoning could have been to create a proportion: 77 games for catchers is to 100 games for position players what 77 percent of 400 at bats (308) for catchers is to 400 at bats for position players.

1954: Ted Williams, the batter with the highest average in the AL, did not meet the official qualifications to claim the title. The 1954 official Rule 10.17 spelled out the champion as one who, with at least 400 at bats, or with fewer than 400 at bats plus enough imaginary ones to equal 400, has the higher average. Under the official rules definition, Bobby Avila is the batting leader. During the closing weeks of the campaign, Williams was aware of the rule but continued to be selective of pitches, rather than swing at those outside the strike zone simply in order to reach the required 400 at bats. Williams' extended average based on adding imaginary at bats to his 386 is a .331 figure.

1981: Bill Madlock is the official batting champion by the rules of the day. Due to the strike-shortened season, the games a team played, rather than the scheduled games, were the basis for individual championships. Pittsburgh, Madlock's club, played 103 games. Thus, $103 \times 3.1 = 319$ plate appearances to qualify for the batting championship. Madlock topped the required 319 PA's by one, with 279 at bats, 4 sacrifice flies, 34 bases on balls, 3 hit by pitch, and no sacrifice hits or interference calls. *Total Baseball* awarded the title to Pete Rose in editions 1 and 2, based on average games played per team, then corrected the procedure in its third edition.

The record of the four defunct major leagues show only the American Association had batting champions not agreeing with *Total Baseball* champions. This happened twice: in the 1884 AA, the official winner was Dude Esterbrook though his teammate Dave Orr actually batted 50 points higher; and in 1886 AA, the champ was officially Orr though Guy Hecker's recomputed average nips him by a point. (Pete Browning also surpassed Orr and was listed as champion in earlier editions of *Total Baseball*, for which a guideline of 3.1 plate appearances per game was employed throughout.)

A Little Help from Our Friends

The computer has made possible the rapid analysis of mountains of raw baseball data. But as invaluable as the computer has been in producing and cross-checking the statistical data for *Total Baseball*, the editors owe more to the people who have contributed their time, their expertise, their love of the game, and their passion for getting things right. These individuals are listed below, or in the Acknowledgements, or in the table at the end of the book that enumerates those readers of the first three editions who helped us improve the accuracy of *Total Baseball* this time around. A collective debt is owed to the Society for American Baseball Research and the National Baseball Library.

The six principal sources of the statistics herein were discussed earlier. Supplemental sources were:

- For work on the Stagno Collection of NA data, 1871-75, SABR's nineteenth-century research committee, headed successively by John Thorn and Mark Rucker, Bob Tiemann, Bob Richardson, and Fred Ivor-Campbell. New for the fifth edition are strikeouts for 1874-75 and incomplete stolen bases and caught stealing for all years, as well as fielding for all years.
- For batters hit by pitch, 1884-1896 AA/NL/PL, 1909-1916 NL, 1909-1919 AL, research from newspapers by Alex Haas, Pete Palmer, John Schwartz, Bob Davids, John Tattersall, Lyle Spatz, Herb Goldman, Keith Carlson, Tom Chase, Ed Luteran, Frank Phelps, and others. (Note: research continues for the 1897-1908 period, but the data is, at this writing, about 95 percent complete.)
- For home runs allowed by pitchers, 1876-1950 AL/NL, the Tattersall Collection, aided by Bob McConnell.
- For runs batted in, 1903-1919 NL, 1905-1919 AL, ICI research.
- For runs batted in, 1880-1885 NL and 1882-87, 1890 AA, David Neft.
- For pitcher saves (except 1901-1919 AL) 1876-1968 NL/AA/UA/PL/AL, ICI research.
- For stolen bases, 1886 NL, Spalding *Baseball Guide*.
- For wins and losses for pitchers, 1876-1900 NL/AA/PL, and for wins, losses, games started, complete games, shutouts, saves, 1901-1919 AL, and complete pitching data, 1892, research from newspapers and official sheets by Frank Williams.

- For shutouts, 1876-1939, Joe Wayman.
- For biographical data, the biographical research committee of SABR, notably Richard Topp, Bill Carle.
- For caught-stealing data, 1914-1916 AL, 1915-1916 NL, Ernie Lanigan, courtesy of Bob Davids.
- For home/away data, 1876-1891 NL/AA/UA/PL, Bob McConnell.
- For game scores, 1876-1884 NL/AA/UA, Bob Tiemann.
- For game scores, 1885-1891 NL/AA/PL, Richard Topp.
- For runs and homers home/away, 1980s NL/AL, Bill Carr.

Missing data includes:

- Hit batters: 1897-1908, scattered data, especially for New York and Cincinnati.
- Caught stealing: 1886-1914, 1916 (players with fewer than 20 steals), 1917-1919, 1926-1950 NL; 1886-1891 AA; 1890 PL; 1901-1913, 1916 (players with fewer than 20 steals), 1917-1919, 1914-15 FL.
- Sacrifice hits: 1927-1930 (fly balls advancing runners to any base counted as sacrifice hits).
- Sacrifice flies: 1908-1930, 1939.
- Runs batted in, 1882-1884 AA; 1884 UA. Partial data is shown for 1884-84. For 1885-87 and 1890, about 10% of the data is estimated.
- Strikeouts for batters: 1882-1888, 1890 AA; 1884 UA; 1897-1909 NL; 1901-1912 AL. (Team batting strikeouts are presented for 1897-1902 NL and 1901-1904 AL.)

Incomplete data for those years up to 1903 NL and 1905 AL are available from the ICI computer printouts at the National Baseball Library. Additional research could turn up more data. If your research or sharp eye should detect errors or gaps in *Total Baseball*, please write us in care of the publisher (or alternatively, simply e-mail us at dpiet@totalsportsonline.com) and we'll be delighted to improve our data and credit your catch in the next edition.

Sabermetrics

Pete Palmer and John Thorn

Sabermetrics may be a new coinage for the statistical analysis of baseball but it is not a new phenomenon. Henry Chadwick, in the antebellum period, was as much a sabermetrician as Allan Roth or Bill James: he saw as clearly as they that because the object of the game is to win, runs are the best measure of player performance, just as they are of team performance at the end of a game.

After many decades in which this fundamental truth was lost (amid the general worship of false idols like batting average and pitcher won-lost percentage), today's sabermetricians have come around full circle to the game as it was originally understood. And what's remarkable about this is that in order to return to the primordial simplicity of the 1840s, '50s, and '60s, when runs and outs were all that went into the box score, they have relied upon computer simulations and higher mathematics. In other words, with the new statistics, simplicity emerges from complexity; what baseball statistics have offered for the last hundred years or so has been, despite the appearance of simplicity, in fact extremely complex.

For the veteran fan as well as for Major League Baseball, new ideas, new statistics, and new discoveries that dispute long-held verities (Ty Cobb's hit total, Hoss Radbourn's number of victories in 1884, etc.) may represent a challenge to tradition and thus a threat to the very soul of baseball, its pride in anachronism. Bernard Malamud wrote, "The whole history of baseball has the quality of mythology." The editors of *Total Baseball* relish the game's myths, from Abner Doubleday to the sacrifice bunt, and believe that in setting the record straight or turning conventional wisdom on its head, they are adding to the fan's enjoyment of the rich texture of the game. If you are one of the skeptics—like Earl Weaver, who once said, "There's no such thing as a new statistic"—please permit us to make the case for sabermetrics. (Much of the material in this section is adapted from our 1984 study, *The Hidden Game of Baseball*.)

What's in a Number?

On April 27, 1983, the Montreal Expos came to bat in the bottom of the eighth inning trailing the Houston Astros 4-2. First up to face pitcher Nolan Ryan was Tim Blackwell, a lifetime .228 hitter who had struck out in his first time at bat. At this routine juncture of this commonplace game, Ryan stared down at Blackwell, but his invisible—yet, for all that, more substantial—opponent was a man who had died the month before Ryan was born, a man about whom Ryan knew nothing, he confessed, except his statistical line. For at this moment of his glorious big-league career, Ryan had accumulated a total of 3,507 strikeouts, only one short of the mark Walter Johnson had set over twenty-one seasons, from 1907 to 1927. Long thought invulnerable, Johnson's record was in imminent danger of falling, in 1983, not only to Ryan but also to Steve Carlton and Gaylord Perry.

Ryan fanned Blackwell and then froze the next batter, pinch hitter Brad Mills, with a 1-and-2 curveball. The pinnacle was his. Johnson had been baseball's all-time strikeout leader since 1921, when he surpassed Cy Young. Ryan would hold that title for just a few weeks, then would be overtaken by Carlton, only to display an incredible finishing kick and finish at 5,714 in 1994. But at the time that Ryan topped Johnson, baseball savants scurried to assess the meaning of 3,509 for both the deposed King of K and the new.

In the aftermath of Ryan's feat, some writers pointed out that he only needed sixteen full seasons, plus fractions of two others, in which to record 3,509 strikeouts while Johnson needed twenty-one, or that Johnson pitched over 2,500 more innings than Ryan. Coming into the 1983 season, Ryan had fanned 9.44 men per nine innings, while Johnson was way down the list at 5.33. And Ryan had allowed fewer hits per nine innings than Johnson, or, for that matter, anyone in the history of the game. So, it would seem 3,509 was not just one batter better than Johnson, but rather was mere confirmation for the masses of a superiority that was clear to the cognoscenti years before.

However, other writers introduced mitigating factors on Johnson's behalf, much as Ruth found supporters as the home run king even after Aaron hit number 715. These champions of the old order cited Johnson's won-lost record of 417-279 and earned run average of 2.17 while scoffing at Ryan's mark, entering 1983, of 205-186 with an ERA of 3.11. This tack led to further argument in print, bringing in the quality of the teams each man pitched for and against, the resiliency of the ball, the attitudes of the batters in each era toward the strikeout, the advent of night ball, integration, expansion, the designated hitter, the overall talent pool, competition from other professional sports . . . and on down into the black hole of subjectivism.

Why were so many things dragged into that discussion? Because the underlying question about 3,509 was: does this total make Ryan better than Johnson, or even a better strikeout pitcher than Johnson? At the least, does it make him a great pitcher? In our drive to identify excellence on the baseball field (or off it), we inevitably look to the numbers as a means of encapsulating and comprehending experience. This quantifying habit is at the heart of baseball's hidden game, the one ceaselessly played by Ryan and Johnson and Ruth and Aaron—and, thanks to baseball's voluminous records, more than 14,600 other players—in a stadium bounded only by the imagination.

What's in a number? The answer to "How Many?" and sometimes a great deal more. In this case, 3,509 men had come to the plate against Ryan and failed to put the ball in play, one more man than Johnson had returned to the dugout, cursing. So what's the big deal? That Ryan was .0002849 faster, scarier, tougher—better—than Johnson? An absolute number like 3,509, or 714 (the home-run record once thought invulnerable, too), or 4,191 (the erroneous hit total of Ty Cobb that Pete Rose finally surpassed) does not resound with meaning unless it is placed into some context that will give it life.

Baseball statistics are not the instruments of vivisection, taking the life out of the game in order to examine it; rather, statistics are themselves the vital part of baseball, the only tangible and imperishable remains of contests played yesterday or a hundred years ago. Baseball may be loved without statistics, but it cannot be understood without them. As the statistics reflect more accurately the reality of what happened on the field, greater understanding leads to a deeper love and appreciation of this great game—which is, essentially, the case for sabermetrics and the reason for *Total Baseball.*

The Linear Weights System

In 1982, Milwaukee's Robin Yount had the year of his life, batting .331 with 29 homers, 114 RBIs and 129 runs scored; he led the American League in hits, doubles, total bases, and slugging percentage, while finishing just one point behind the league leader in batting average. First of the two times in his career, he was voted the Most Valuable Player in the American League, being named first on all but one of the twenty-eight ballots cast by the baseball writers.

Over in the other league, Mike Schmidt of the Phillies was having an off year, batting only .280 with 35 homers and 87 RBIs; the previous year, when he was awarded the MVP, in only 102 games played he had totaled 31 homers and 91 RBIs. He did lead the league once again in 1982 in slugging percentage, and he did win the Gold Glove at third base for the seventh straight year, yet in the MVP balloting none of the ballots listed him higher than fourth; ten ballots were cast without listing him at all.

For Yount, 1982 was a crowning achievement; for Schmidt, a disappointment: that was the verdict reached by the baseball writers and conventional baseball statistics. Yet in terms of actual performance, as determined by the number of runs contributed, Schmidt's "off year" was scarcely different from Yount's. With the bat, Yount accounted for 59 park-adjusted runs beyond what an average batter might have contributed; Schmidt, 45. Through base stealing, Yount added 2; Schmidt none. With the glove, Yount was 4 runs below league average at his position, shortstop; Schmidt was 19 above average at third base. Total runs contributed: Yount 57, Schmidt 64.

(Because Yount's batting so far exceeded that of other shortstops, while third base provided several heavy hitters, Yount contributed 7.0 extra wins to his Brewers; Schmidt contributed 6.1 to the Phillies.) Both men had outstanding seasons, the best in their respective leagues, and both outstripped the second-best player by about the same margin.

Viewing player (and team) performance through this sort of prism frequently produces such illuminating results. Cecil Fielder had a wonderful year in 1990, with his 51 homers, 132 RBIs, and league-leading figures in slugging average and extra-base hits. But how did he convince any writer voting for MVP that he had a better year than Rickey Henderson? In *Total Baseball,* you could look it up: Fielder contributed 4.2 extra wins to his team (wins that an average player would not), which was the fourth-best figure in the American League that year; Henderson was responsible for a whopping 8.2, not only the top mark in 1990 but also, at the time, the second-best mark in the AL since Mickey Mantle's epic seasons of 1956-57!

This is the kind of analysis of player performance possible with a variety of sabermetric measures, not just the Linear Weights System. The common ingredient of most of the new, as yet unofficial statistics is their creators' recognition of the relationship between runs and wins. These newly calculated measures are not official statistics of Major League Baseball, but they are constructed from the raw data of the official record. Some of the new measures may one day be officially embraced, as the on base percentage became an official stat three decades after its introduction. Because of fan interest, we include them in the Player and Pitcher Registers that follow, alongside the officially tabulated numbers.

Runs and Wins

George Lindsey, in an article in *Operations Research* in 1963, was the first to assign run values to the various offensive events which lead to runs: Runs = (.41)1B + (.82)2B + (1.06)3B + (1.42)HR. He based these values on recorded play-by-play data and basic probability theory. Unlike Earnshaw Cook, who in the following year assigned run values on the basis of the sum of the individual scoring probabilities—that is, the *direct* run potential of the hit or walk plus those of the baserunners set in motion—Lindsey recognized that a substantial part of the run value of any non-out is that it *brings another man to the plate.* This additional batter has a one-in-three chance of reaching base and thus bringing another man to the plate with the same chance, as do the batters to follow. The *indirect* run potential of these batters cannot be ignored.

Steve Mann's Run Productivity Average (RPA) assigned these values based on observation of some 12,000 plate appearances: RPA = (.51)1B + (.82)2B + (1.38)3B + (2.63)HR + (.25)BB + (.15)SB − (.25)CS, all divided by plate appearances, then plus .016. His values were denominated in terms of the number of runs and RBIs each event produced. Bill James, at about the same time, came up with a similar formula, since shunned, with values based on runs plus RBIs *minus home runs.* The drawbacks to the approaches of Mann and James were the drawbacks of the RBI, which gives the entire credit for producing a run to the man who plates it, and of the run scored, which gives credit only to the man who touches home, no matter how he came to do so. For example, with no outs, a man reaches first on an error; the next batter hits a double, placing runners on second and third; the following batter taps a roller to short and is thrown out at first, with the run scoring from third. The man who produced the out is given the credit for producing a run, while the man who started the sequence by reaching first on an error is likewise credited with a run. The man who hit the double, which was surely the key event in the sequence which produced the run, and the only one reflecting batting skill, receives no credit whatsoever. In this regard, any formula based on "Runs Produced" (whether R + RBI or R + RBI − HR) is philosophically inferior to the formula Lindsey proposed, despite his failure to account for walks, steals, and other events.

The run values in the Linear Weights formula for identifying batters' real contribution are derived from Pete Palmer's 1978 computer simulation of all major-league games played since 1901. All the data available concerning the frequencies of the various events was collected; following a test run, these were tabulated. Unmeasured quantities, such as the probability of a man going from first to third on a single vs. that of his advancing only one base, were assigned values based on play-by-play analysis of over 100 World Series contests. The goal was to get all the measured quantities very nearly equal to the league statistics; then the simulation would provide run values of each event in terms of net runs produced above average. Expressing the values in those terms would give a meaningful base line to individual performances, because if you are told that a player contributed 87 runs you don't know what that signifies unless you know the average level of run contribution in that year: 87 may sound like a lot, but if the norm was 80, then you know the player contributed only 7 runs beyond average.

The values obtained from the simulation are remarkably similar from one era to the next, confounding expectations that the home run would prove more valuable today than in the dead-ball era, or that the steal was once a primary offensive weapon. These values are expressed in beyond-average runs.

Run Values of Various Events, by Periods

Event	Period			
	1901–20	1921–40	1941–60	1961–77
home run	1.36	1.40	1.42	1.42
triple	1.02	1.05	1.03	1.00
double	.82	.83	.80	.77
single	.46	.50	.47	.45
walk/HBP	.32	.35	.35	.33
stolen base	.20	.22	.19	.19
caught stealing	−.33	−.39	−.36	−.32
out*	−.24	−.30	−.27	−.25

*An out is considered to be a hitless at bat and its value is set so that the sum of all events times their frequency is zero, thus establishing zero as the base line, or norm, for performance.

In the years since this simulation was conducted, statistician Dave Smith ("Maury Wills and the Value of the Stolen Base," *Baseball Research Journal,* 1980) convinced Pete to adjust the values of the stolen base and caught stealing because of their situation-dependent,

elective nature: attempts are apt to occur more frequently in close games, where they would be worth more than if they were distributed randomly the way an event like a single or a home run would be. Pete revised the value for the steal upward to .30 runs, while for the caught stealing it becomes -.60 runs.

Just as these run values change marginally with changing conditions of play, they differ slightly up and down the batting order (a homer is not worth as much to the leadoff hitter as it is to the fifth-place batter; a walk is worth more for the man batting second than for the man batting eighth); however, these differences have been averaged out in the figures above. For evaluating runs contributed by any batter at any time, there is no better method than Batting Runs, the Linear Weights formula derived from the computer simulation which is the basis of the table above.

The Formula

Runs = (.47)1B + (.78)2B + (1.09)3B + (1.40)HR + (.33)(BB + HB) + (.30)SB − (.60)CS − (.25)(AB − H) − .50(OOB).

The events not included in the formula that you might have thought to see are sacrifices, sacrifice hits, grounded into double plays, and reached on error. The last is not known for most years and in the official statistics is indistinguishable from outs on base (OOB). The sacrifice has essentially canceling values, trading an out for an advanced base which, often as not, leaves the team in a situation with poorer run potential than it had before the sacrifice. The sacrifice fly has dubious run value because it is entirely dependent upon a situation not under the batter's control: while a single or a walk always has a potential run value, a long fly does not, unless a man happens to be poised at third base (whether it is achieved by accident or design is open to question, as well, but that is beside the point—getting hit by a pitch is not a product of intent, either). Last, the grounded into double play is to a far greater extent a function of one's place in the batting order than it is of poor speed or failure in the clutch, and thus it does not find a home in a formula applicable to all batters. It is no accident that Henry Aaron, who ran well for most of his long career and wasn't too bad in the clutch, hit into more DP's than anyone else, nor that Roberto Clemente, Al Kaline, and Frank Robinson, who fit the same description, are also among the ten "worst" in this department. If a .230-hitting American League shortstop doesn't hit into many twin killings, it's not because of adept bat handling or blazing speed but because he bats ninth.

The Linear Weights formula for batters may be long, but it calls for only addition, subtraction, and multiplication and thus is as simple as the slugging average, whose incorrect weights (1, 2, 3, and 4) it revises and expands upon. Each event has a value and a frequency, just as in slugging average, yet—as in no batting statistic you have ever seen—outs are treated as offensive events with a run value of their own (albeit a negative one), a truth so obvious it somehow escaped notice. Just as the run potential for a team in a given half inning is boosted by a man reaching base, it is diminished by a man being retired; not only has he failed to change the situation on the bases but he has deprived his team of the services of a man further down the order who might have come up in this half inning, either with men on base and/or with scores already in.

What Batting Runs does is to take every offensive event and treat it in terms of its impact upon the team—an average team, so that a man does not benefit in his individual record for having the good fortune to bat cleanup with the Giants or suffer for batting seventh with the Marlins. The relationship of individual performance to team play is stated poorly or not at all in conventional baseball statistics. In Batting Runs it is crystal clear: the linear progression, the sum of the various offensive events, when weighted by their accurately predicted run values, will total the runs contributed by that batter or that team beyond the league average.

Recognizing that some dedicated readers of *Total Baseball* will wish to keep track of batting performance by computing Batting Runs themselves over the course of a season, and that they may be frustrated by the difficulty of calculating the "At Bats-Hits" factor for the league, which is necessary to determine the negative value of an out, we advise that using a fixed value of -.25 for outs will tend to work quite well if you wish to include pitcher batting performance, and a fixed value of -.27 will serve if you wish to delete it. Actually, any fixed value will suffice in midseason; it's only when all the numbers are in and you care to compare this year's results with last year's (or with those of the 1927 Yankees) that more precision is desirable. At that point the value of the out may be calculated by the ambitious among you, but ideally, the sporting press will provide accurate Batting Runs figures. Who, after all, calculates ERA for himself?

Batting Runs and Production

For those to whom calculation is anathema, or at the least no pleasure, Batting Runs has a "shadow stat" that tracks its accuracy to a remarkable degree and is a breeze to calculate: Production, which consists simply of On Base Percentage plus Slugging Average. While it is not expressed in runs and thus lacks the philosophical appeal of Batting Runs, the standard deviation of its most complete version is 20.4 runs compared to the 19.8 of Batting Runs. In other words, the correlation between Batting Runs and Production over the course of an average team season is 99.7 percent.

However, as an average or ratio, Production measures the *rate* of batting success (efficiency), while Batting Runs measures the *amount* of success. For example, a batter who goes 2-for-5 with a walk in one game, those 2 hits being doubles, will have an On Base Percentage of .500 and a Slugging Average of .800; his Production will be 1.30 or, as stated for convenience in *Total Baseball*, 130. Another batter, who in 162 games gets 200 hits and 100 walks in 500 at bats, with 400 total bases, will have an identical OBP, SLG, and PRO. Which player has contributed more to his team? Clearly, longevity, or amount of production, is no less important than rate of production.

To cite a specific instance in which Production and

Batting Runs differ, take George Brett's remarkable 1980 season in which he batted .390, had 298 total bases, 75 bases through walks or HBP, and 118 RBIs—all in only 117 games played. In the table of all-time single-season leaders in Production, the Kansas City third baseman ranks 48th when his PRO of 1.124 is normalized to the league average and adjusted for home-park effects. Yet in the table of park adjusted Batting Runs, Brett's season ranks only 96th all-time because he missed 45 games, in which his team derived no benefit from his high rate of performance. (Had Brett played 162 games and continued to perform at the same level, his Batting Runs would have been not 64 but 88.6, the 21st best mark in history.)

Because PRO is not expressed in runs, it is less versatile than Batting Runs. For just as runs are proportional to the events that form them, so are they proportional to wins and losses. This statement, a truism today, was a novelty in 1954 when Rickey and Roth first stated the correlation between run differentials and team standings. But they did not take the next step, to recognize that not only a team's standing but even its won-lost record could be predicted from the run totals.

"The initial published attempt on this subject," Palmer wrote in the 1982 issue of the SABR annual *The National Pastime,* "was Earnshaw Cook's *Percentage Baseball,* in 1964. Examining major-league results from 1950 through 1960 he found winning percentage equal to .484 times runs scored divided by runs allowed. . . . Arnold Soolman, in an unpublished paper which received some media attention, looked at results from 1901 through 1970 and came up with winning percentage equal to .102 times runs scored per game minus .103 times runs allowed per game plus .505. . . . Bill James, in the *Baseball Abstract,* developed winning percentage equal to runs scored raised to the power x, divided by the sum of runs scored and runs allowed, each raised to the power x. Originally, x was equal to two but then better results were obtained when a value of 1.83 was used. . . .

"My work showed that as a rough rule of thumb, each additional ten runs scored (or ten less runs allowed) produced one extra win, essentially the same as the Soolman study. However, breaking the teams into groups showed that high-scoring teams needed more runs to produce a win. This runs-per-win factor I determined to be ten times the square root of the average number of runs scored per inning by both teams. Thus in normal play, when 4.5 runs per game are scored by each club, each team scores .5 runs per inning—totaling one run, the square root of which is one, times ten."

Note that when we refer to the need for approximately ten additional runs scored (or ten fewer allowed) to provide a team with an additional win, we do not mean that it takes ten runs to win any given game. Obviously, in a specific case, a one-run margin is all that is required; but statistics are designed for the long haul, not the short.

What does this have to do with Batting Runs? Remembering that Batting Runs are expressed not simply in runs but in beyond-average runs, the conversion from a batter's Linear Weights runs to his wins is a snap: simply divide Batting Runs by the number of runs it takes to gain an extra win in a given year. Taking the exploits of Babe Ruth in 1927, we see that through batting alone he contributed 100.7 runs, or 9.56 wins, since in the American

League in 1927 it took 10.53 runs to produce an additional win. If every other player on the Yankees had performed at the league average, the New York record should have been 87-67; if each of the seven other batters had performed only half as well as Ruth and had added five extra wins (discounting reserves, pitchers, fielders, and stealers, whom we shall presume for this discussion to have been average), the Yankees would have gained another 35 wins (7 × 5) to finish with a won-lost mark of 122-32.

Stolen Base Runs

The Linear Weights formula for batters contains a factor for base stealers, expressed in runs. How do you judge the effectiveness of a base stealer? Conventional baseball statistics will lead you to the conclusion that whoever has the most steals is the best thief; that is the sole criterion for *The Sporting News* annual "Golden Shoe Award" in each league. How often the man with the most steals may have been thrown out is of no concern.

An article in the 1981 *Baseball Research Journal* by Bob Davids offered something more sophisticated yet utterly simple: a stolen base percentage, which is simply stolen bases divided by attempts. The best stolen base average of all time, insofar as we know and based on a minimum of 30 attempts, is Max Carey's in 1922 when he stole 51 bases in 53 attempts. The most times caught stealing in the course of a season was Ty Cobb's 38 in 1915, until 1982 when Rickey Henderson was nabbed 42 times. But the best method yet devised, and the one that is pleasingly simple, is to apply the Linear Weights method to get Stolen Base Runs. One multiplies the steals by their run value of .30 and the failed attempts by -.60, and adds the two products. The implication for such men as Ty Cobb, Rickey Henderson, and Vince Coleman is clear: it takes a fabulous stealing performance to produce as many as ten extra runs—i.e., one extra win—for the team.

In 1915 Ty Cobb, when he established the modern stolen base record of 96, can be seen to have contributed to his team 28.8 runs, while his 38 foiled larcenies cost 22.8. Thus Cobb, for all his whirling-dervish activity, accounted for only 6 non-par runs—not even a single win. Whoa! You mean that not a single one of Cobb's steals produced a victory? That is not what is being said: the fact is that while the gain from the stolen base is entirely visible—an extra base which may be followed by a hit that would otherwise not have produced a run—the cost of the caught stealing is entirely invisible, or conjectural, except with the aid of statistics. How many big innings did Cobb run his team out of? How many batters reached base in ensuing innings who might, in an earlier inning, have had their contributions count for runs? What Stolen Base Runs indicate are that, on balance, not on a specific-case basis, the stolen base is at best a dubious method of increasing a team's run production.

Now let's take a look at what Henderson did. His record 130 stolen bases in 1982 produced 39 runs for his team. His 42 failed attempts took away 25.2 possible runs. Net effect: approximately 14 runs, or one and a half wins, a performance nearly three times as good as Cobb's. In 1983, stealing 22 fewer bases, he was even better, ac-

counting for 21.0 runs. However, the all-time best stealing record is that of Maury Wills in 1962, when he stole 104 bases and was caught only 13 times. Wills's 104 stolen bases produced 31.2 runs; his 13 failed attempts cost only 7.8. So, his baserunning contribution was 23.4, or a little over two wins.

Fielding Runs

As mentioned earlier, in 1954 when Branch Rickey and Allan Roth came up with their "efficiency formula" for run scoring and run prevention, the defensive half of the equation was divided into five segments, the last of which was fielding, to which they assigned a mathematical value of zero. "There is nothing on earth," Rickey declared, "anyone can do with fielding."

Since then many have tried, with mixed results, to improve upon the mere toting up of raw data—putouts, assists, errors, double plays. In the second edition of *Total Baseball,* we improved upon the Fielding Runs formula by calculating innings played at each position, plate appearances for all players on the team, and then rating each fielder based on his chances per inning. Where previously all outfield positions had been grouped together, we now rate left fielders against left fielders, center fielders against center fielders, and right fielders against right fielders; we also revised thoroughly the formula for catchers, which retains the highest degree of subjectivism because their primary defensive contribution comes not with the glove but through calling the pitches.

More on this complex subject in the Glossary.

Pitching Runs

Determining the run contributions of pitchers is much easier than determining those of fielders or batters, though not quite so simple as that of base stealers. Actual runs allowed are known, as are innings pitched. Let's assume that a pitcher is responsible only for earned runs. Then why, we hear some of you asking, is the ERA not measure enough of his ability? Because it tells only the pitcher's *rate* of efficiency, not his actual benefit to the team. In a league with an ERA of 3.50, a starter who throws 300 innings with an ERA of 2.50 must be worth twice as much to his team as a starter with the same ERA who appears in only 150 innings. Through Pitching Runs, we seek to determine the number of beyond-average runs a pitcher saved—the number he prevented from scoring that an average pitcher would have allowed.

The formula for Earned Run Average is:

$$\text{ERA} = (\text{Earned Runs} \times 9)/\text{Innings Pitched}$$

The number of average, or par, runs for a pitcher, which is represented by a Pitching Runs figure of zero, is equal to:

$$(\text{League ERA} \times \text{IP})/9$$

If the league ERA is 4.21 (as the National League's was in 1994) and a pitcher's ERA is also 4.21, he will by definition have held batters in check at the league average no matter how many innings he pitched. If, however, his ERA was 1.56 and he hurled 202 innings (as Greg Maddux did for the Braves in '94), he will have saved a certain number of runs that an average pitcher might have allowed in his place; to find that number we employ the Pitching Runs formula:

Pitcher's Runs = Innings Pitched × (League ERA/9) − ER

This represents the difference between the number of earned runs allowed at the league average for the innings pitched and the actual earned runs allowed. For the case of Maddux, we get

$$\text{Runs} = 202 \times (4.21/9) - 35 = 59.5$$

Maddux was 59.5 runs better than the average National League pitcher in 1994, and had he been transported to an average NL team—that mythical entity that scores as many runs as it allows while winning 81 and losing 81—he would have made that team's mark 87-75. (Actually, in the strike shortened 112 game season of 1994, an average team would have been 56-56, and the addition of Maddux would have made that team's record 62-50.) An alternative way to calculate pitchers' Linear Weights, useful with oldtimers for whom you may have the ERA but not the number of earned runs allowed, is to use the pitcher's ERA, subtracted from the league's ERA, multiplying by the innings pitched, then dividing by nine. In Maddux's case, this approach would look like:

$$(4.21 - 1.56) \times 202/9 = 59.5$$

The two parts of performance—efficiency and durability—are incorporated into all Linear Weights measures. If you are performing at a better than average clip, the more regularly you do so, the more your team will benefit and thus the higher your Linear Weights measure. If you are stealing bases nine times out of ten, your team will benefit more from sixty attempts than from forty; if you are batting at an above average clip, it's better to play in 160 games than 110; if you're allowing one earned run per game less than the average pitcher, your LWTS will increase with innings pitched.

Linear Weights in Practice

Having formulas for pitching, fielding, baserunning, and batting, we can assess the run-scoring contribution of every individual who has ever played the game, and thus the number of wins that he has contributed in a given season or over his career. The number of runs required to produce an additional win has varied over the years between 9 and 11 runs, with a very few league seasons outside those parameters.

Limited by conventional baseball statistics, one might, in 1990, have uttered something like, "Barry Bonds hit .293 with 33 homers and 114 RBIs—the guy must have been worth 10 extra wins to Pittsburgh all by himself!" Or: "The White Sox are only one pitcher away from winning the division." Or: "The Yankees are only three players away from being a contender." Or, "Letting Darryl Strawberry get away was the worst thing the Mets ever did; they'll be a second-division club for a decade." With Linear Weights, these statements, or rather the concerns they reflect, can be approached with some data and with some degree of objectivity. First: Barry Bonds had a fine

year in 1990, but to have contributed 10 wins by himself he would have had to account for nearly 100 Linear Weights runs, a mark that up till then had been attained by only three men in major-league history. In fact, Bonds contributed 6.5 wins in '90, though he did post 9.0 wins in 1992.

As to the White Sox, they finished 94-68 in 1990, while their Linear Weights projected them to finish at 81-81. The Athletics, who won the AL West at 103-59, actually projected to finish 96-66. So, the Sox management might have asked, how to close ground on the Athletics? Could one pitcher—like Bob Welch, for whom they bid in the free-agent bazaar—make the difference? To do so, he would have to contribute about 150 Pitching Runs, a feat no pitcher has ever accomplished. In 1990, pitching for Oakland—and remember, the Linear Weights formula is divorced from considerations of batter support—Welch contributed 20.7 park-adjusted Pitching Runs. So presuming that he pitched as well for the White Sox as he did for the Athletics, or even slightly better, he would not be enough to "win" Chicago the flag on paper; Chicago would need help from other quarters.

Regarding the other statements, you get the picture: sabermetric analyses like the ones above will tend to puncture fantasies.

Park Factor

A central issue for sabermetricians is the network of illusion created by home-park dimensions, atmospheric conditions, and visibility for batters. How many home runs would Matt Williams hit if he played half his games in Fenway Park? Will the Boston Red Sox and Chicago Cubs keep "failing" to put together solid pitching staffs—or has their pitching been adequate all along? Why had the American League leaders in triples so often worn a Royals uniform? One's home park has a powerful effect on a player or pitcher's record, elevating some good players to greatness and denying the spotlight to some outstanding performers.

It should be understood that the average player does better at home regardless of the park—familiarity breeds success. Individuals bat and pitch at a rate 10 percent higher at home, on average. But parks don't create performance; they only affect it. For example, a lefthanded hitter at Fenway can do very well indeed, as Wade Boggs did, by learning to take the outside pitch to left field. Likewise, a righthanded batter can make the friendly Green Monster into his nemesis by trying to pull every pitch.

For hard luck in some parks, it is tough to top the record of Mark McGwire, who has had the misfortune to call the Oakland Coliseum home. Through 1996, his lifetime Production, normalized to league average but not adjusted for park effects, was twenty-eighth best on the all time list of those playing in 1,000 games. Had he played his home games instead in Fenway Park, his PRO would have projected to the eighth best of all time. Had he even played in an average hitters' park—which is what PRO+ measures—his record would show itself to be the twelfth best ever.

If we desire to remove the silver spoon or the millstone

that a home park can be, and measure individual ability alone, we must create a statistical balancer that diminishes the individual batting marks created in parks like Fenway and augments those created in Oakland. Pete Palmer developed an adjustment that enables us, for the first time, to measure a player's accomplishments apart from the influence of his home park.

Parks differ in so many ways that it may be hard to imagine how their differences can be quantified. The most obvious way in which they differ is in their dimensions, from home plate to the outfield walls, and from the base lines to the stands. The older arenas—Fenway Park, Wrigley Field, Tiger Stadium—tend to favor hitters in both regards, with reachable fences and little room to pursue a foul pop. Yet two parks can have nearly equal dimensions, like Pittsburgh's Three Rivers Stadium and Atlanta's Fulton County Stadium, yet have highly dissimilar impacts upon hitters because of climate (balls travel farther in hot weather), elevation (travel farther as altitude increases), and playing surface (travel faster and truer on artificial turf). Still another factor is how well batters think they see the ball; Shea Stadium is notorious as a cause of complaints.

And perhaps more important than any of the objective park characteristics, suggested Robert Kingsley in a 1980 study of why so many homers were hit in Atlanta, is the attitude of the players, the way that the park changes their view of how the game must be played in order to win. Every team that comes into Atlanta in August knows that the ball is going to fly and, whether it is a team designed for power or not, it plays ball there as if it were the 1927 Yankees. In their own home park the Astros might peck and scratch for runs, but in Atlanta they will put the steal and hit-and-run in mothballs. Conversely, a team which comes into the Astrodome and plays for the big inning will generally get what it deserves—a loss. The successful team is one that can play its game at home—the game for which the team was constructed—yet is flexible enough to adapt when on the road. How to quantify attitude?

Rather than try to assign a numerical value to each of the six or more variables that might go into establishing an estimator of home park impact, we looked to the single measure in which all these variables are reflected—runs. After all, why would we assign one value to dimensions, another to climate, and so on, except to identify their impact on scoring? If a stadium is a "hitters' park," it stands to reason that more runs would be scored there than in a park perceived as neutral, just as a "pitchers' park" could be expected to depress scoring.

The full and lengthy explanation for the computation of the Park Factor is left to the Glossary, where hardy readers might consider taking a peek right now. For most of us, though, it will be enough to understand that the Park Factor consists mainly of the team's home-road ratio of runs allowed, compared to the league's home-road ratio.

Relativity

Sabermetric statistics can be marvelous tools for cross-era comparisons, enabling us to determine if baseball's history is truly a seamless web or if its seams are real enough, but are camouflaged by traditional statistics.

If Batter A presented himself to you for approval with these statistics—.330 batting average, 16 home runs, 107 RBIs—what would your reaction be? You'd like to have him on your team, right? And what to make of Batter B, who presents these numbers—.257 batting average, 14 home runs, 53 RBIs? Not bad for a middle infielder with a good glove, you say, but otherwise undistinguished? In fact, the "impressive" figures of Batter A represent the average performance of a National League outfielder in 1930, while the "blah" figures of Batter B are those of the average American League outfielder of 1968: the former has more than twice the RBIs of the latter, along with a batting average 73 points higher, yet the two performed at identical levels, and an argument could be made that Batter B was superior.

In a similar comparison involving those two years of extremes, Bill Terry led the National League in 1930 with a BA of .401, a mark surpassed by Ted Williams in 1941 but not equaled since; Carl Yastrzemski led the American League of 1968 with a performance that oldtimers held to be a disgrace, a lowly BA of .301, the worst ever to win a batting championship. Terry's mark was achieved at a time when most pitchers had only two pitches, a fastball and a curve, and not enough confidence in the latter to throw it when behind in the count at 2-0 or 3-1. The parks were smaller; there was no night ball; the game was segregated racially; and a team played 22 games with each of its seven rivals, none farther west of the Mississippi than St. Louis. Moreover, 1930 was the year in which National League officials, attempting to match the popularity of the slugging American League, juiced the ball to such an extent that the entire league batted .312 (if you remove pitcher batting). In other words, the average nonpitcher in the NL of 1930 batted higher than the AL leader in 1968! When Yaz hit .301, pitchers dominated the game and the average American League nonpitcher hit .238. How to compare Terry and Yaz, who played under such different conditions thirty-eight years apart?

You could view Terry's .401 in relation to his league's BA of .312, concluding that Memphis Bill was a better hitter (by BA alone, which despite its previously cited deficiencies remains the most comfortable stat by which to introduce this technique) by 28.5 percent. You could compare Yaz's .301 to his league's BA of .238 and conclude that he was a better than average hitter by 26.5 percent. A mere 2 percentage points separate the men—had they both played in the National League of 1983, when the league average was .255, the Terry of 1930 might have hit .328, the Yaz of 1968, .323. (A further refinement of this method would be to delete Terry's at bats and hits from his league's, and those of Yastrzemski from his league's, so that the batters are not in effect compared with themselves. This, however, necessitates the use of at bats and hits rather than simply the averages and does not significantly alter the results.)

Why do we need relative measures? Basically, for the same reason we need statistics altogether, to compare, to interpret, and to comprehend, but in a more reasonable and accurate manner when the disparity of the data sources makes the use of absolute, unadjusted numbers illogical. If the analysis involves data produced under widely varying conditions, such as a sample including performances twenty, fifty, or a hundred years apart, any comparison will be meaningless without dragging in a series of rather complex historical understandings to modify the analysis—and in a highly subjective, unreliable manner.

Until the 1970s, when David Shoebotham ("Relative Batting Averages," *Baseball Research Journal,* 1976) and Merritt Clifton ("Relative Baseball," *Samisdat,* 1979) introduced the relativist approach, all baseball stats were absolute. And for cross-era comparison, that favorite Hot Stove League activity, absolute stats were absolutely useless, generating plenty of heat and precious little light. What the theory of relativity, baseball-style, does beautifully is to eliminate the need for bringing historical baggage to statistical analysis. The normalized or relative versions of any statistic—batting average, Production, ERA, slugging average, you name it; even homers or strikeouts, though there are problems with these—will be greater than 1.00 for all above-average performers (1.41, for example, means 41 percent better than average in the given category) while relative statistics less than 1.00 will indicate a below average level of play (0.88 means 12 percent below the norm).

It is as simple as can be. So Early Wynn had a 3.20 ERA in 1950? What does that mean? Well, the league ERA was 4.58, so Wynn did very well indeed. His normalized ERA thus was 143, a mark better than that earned by Tom Seaver in 1968, when he had an absolute ERA a full run lower at 2.20.

We cannot employ a Relative Won-Lost record, for the league average is every year the same: .500. (A logical corollary is that one cannot fruitfully use relative measures of any sort for a single season's analysis, as all like figures will be compared to the same league average. The numbers may be changed into normalized form, but the players' rankings will be unchanged: the top ten in batting average in 1990, for example, will retain their ranks in Relative Batting Average.)

Relativism in baseball echoes not only Einstein but also Shakespeare, whose words in *Hamlet* might be modified to read "There is nothing either good or bad, but context makes it so." No longer must we accept arbitrary assessments of performance or regard with awe such old-time figures as Hugh Duffy's BA of .440 in 1894 (not the accomplishment that Rod Carew's .388 was in 1977) or George Sisler's .407 in 1920 (not as good as Roberto Clemente's .357 in 1967). Conversely, a "mediocre" per-

formance of recent years, such as Bobby Murcer's .292 of 1972, for instance, stacks up as the equal of Eddie Collins' .360 in 1923, while Charlie Grimm's seemingly solid .298 in 1929 compares unfavorably to Mike Cubbage's .260 in 1976.

Relativism redefines our understanding not only of particular accomplishments but also of baseball history itself. We see that the men who batted .400 with numbing regularity in the 1890s and 1920s were not supermen (would you swap Wade Boggs for Tuck Turner? Tony Gwynn for Tip O'Neill?) anymore than the sub-2.00 ERA pitchers of the late 1960s were superhuman (Gary Peters, Bob Bolin, Dave McNally, et al.). Absolute figures lie. Are hitters today worse because none has hit .400 since 1941? Or are they superior because a Dave Kingman could average nearly 30 homers a year while Cap Anson only averaged 4? Are infielders better today because they make fewer errors than their counterparts of 50, 75, or 100 years ago? Do modern outfielders have limp-noodle arms because their assist totals pale before those registered in the early decades of the 1900s? Is baseball improving or declining, and has its rise or fall been steady? One can spit absolute stats on the hot stove all winter long and get no closer to the answer, but with relative statistics, the issues are clarified.

The Future

The most exciting frontier for sabermetrics is in situational stats, the type employed by The Baseball Workshop, The Elias Sports Bureau, and Stats, Inc. As the years go by and their data bases grow, the sampling sizes of the data will enlarge and their figures for day vs. night, left vs. right, and so on, will be statistically meaningful as well as statistically correct. Cross-era comparison remains a subject of intense interest, and the debate over average-player skill rages on. Fielding stats, as discussed, also provide fertile ground for invention.

Fantasy baseball aficionados seem caught up in the competition and dealmaking (as well as player evaluation), but some of the newsletters provide sound analysis and trend-spotting tips. It would not be surprising if Rotisserie-type leagues and digital game designers compete with SABR to furnish the best sabermetricians of the 1990s.

The Player Register

The Player Register consists of the central batting, baserunning, and fielding statistics of every man who has batted in major league play since 1871, excepting those men who were primarily pitchers. A pitcher's complete batting record, however, is included for those pitchers who also, over the course of their careers, played in 100 or more games at another position—including pinch hitter—or played in more than half of their total major league games at a position other than pitcher, or played more games at a position other than pitcher in at least one year. (Pitcher batting is also expressed in Batting Wins in the Pitcher Batting column of the Pitcher Register.)

The players are listed alphabetically by surname and, when more than one player bears the name, alphabetically by *given* name—not by "use name," by which we mean the name that may have been applied to him during his playing career. This is the standard method of alphabetizing used in other biographical reference works, and in the case of baseball it makes it easier to find a lesser-known player with a common surname like Smith or Johnson. This method also jibes with that employed in the Annual Record where, for example, Charles "Old Hoss" Radbourn is shown not as the puzzling O. Radbourn or H. Radbourn, as some reference books have it, but as C. Radbourn. On the whole, we have been conservative in ascribing nicknames, doing so only when the player was in fact known by that name during his playing days.

Each page of the Player Register is topped at the corner by a finding aid: in capital letters, the surname of, first, the player whose entry heads up the page and, second, the player whose entry concludes it. Another finding aid is the use of boldface numerals to indicate a league-leading total in those categories in which a player is truly attempting to excel (no boldface is given to the "leaders" in batter strikeouts, times caught stealing, at bats, or games played). An additional finding aid is an asterisk alongside the team for which a player appeared in postseason competition. Additional symbols denote All Star Game selection and/or play; these appear to the right of the team/league column. Condensed type appears occasionally throughout this section; it has no special significance but is designed simply to accommodate unusually wide figures, such as the 4.000 slugging average of a man who, in his only at bat of the year, hit a home run.

The record for each man who played in more than one season is given in a line for each season, plus a career total line. If he played for more than one team in a given year, his totals for each team are stated on separate lines. And if the teams for which he played in his "traded year" are in the same league, then his full record is stated in both separate and combined fashion. (In the odd case of a man playing for three or more clubs in one year, with some of these clubs being in the same league, the combined total line will reflect only his play in that one league.) Also in this edition, we include position data in the "Yr" line for traded players. A man who played in only one year will have no additional career total line, since it would be identical to his seasonal listing.

Batting records for the National Association are included in The Player Register because the editors, like most baseball historians, regard it as a major league, inasmuch as it was the only professional league of its day and supplied the National League of 1876 with most of its players. In this edition of *Total Baseball*, we benefit from the SABR research project referred to in the Introduction to the Annual Record—which to date has produced extra-base hits, corrected averages, walks, and some stolen bases, strikeouts, and other data heretofore unavailable. Unless Major League Baseball reverses the position it adopted in 1969 and restores the NA to offical major-league status, we will continue the practice of carrying separate totals lines for the National Association years rather than integrating them into the career marks of those players whose major league tenures began before 1876 and concluded in that year or later.

Gaps remain elsewhere in the official record of baseball and in the ongoing process of sabermetric reconstruction. The reader will note occasional blank elements in biographical lines, or in single-season columns; these are not typographical lapses but signs that the information does not exist or has not yet been found. In the totals lines of many players, an underlined figure indicates that the total reflects partial data, such as caught stealing for a man whose career covers the National League of 1918–1930 (during which this data was available only for 1920–1925), or batter strikeouts for a man whose career spanned both sides of the year 1909.

For a discussion of which data is missing for particular years, see "The History of Major League Baseball Statistics." Here is a quick summation of the missing data:

Hit batters, 1897–1908 NL/AL, 5 percent missing;
Caught stealing, 1886–1914, 1916 for players with fewer than 20 stolen bases, 1917–1919, 1926–1950 NL; 1886–1891 AA; 1890 PL; 1901–1913, 1916 for players with fewer than 20 stolen bases, 1917–1919 AL (1927 data, missing from the first edition, is now 90 percent complete); 1914–15 FL;
Sacrifice hit, 1908–1930, 1939 (in these years fly balls scoring runners counted as sacrifice hits, and in 1927–1930 fly balls advancing runners to any base

counted as sacrifices);

   Sacrifice fly, 1908–1930, 1939 (counted but inseparable from sacrifice hits), 1940–1953 (not counted);

   Runs batted in, 1882–1887, 1890 AA; 1884 UA;

   Strikeouts for batters, 1882–1884, 1890 AA; 1884 UA; 1897–1909 NL; 1901-1912 AL.

For a key to the team and league abbreviations used in the Player Register, flip to the last page of this volume. For a guide to the other procedures and abbreviations employed in the Player Register, review the comments on the prodigiously extended playing record below.

Looking at the biographical line for any player, we see first his use name in full capitals, then his given name and nickname (and any other name he may have used or been born with, such as the matronymic of a Latin American

YEAR	TM/L	G	AB	R	H	2B	3B	HR	RBI	BB	SO	AVG	OBP	SLG	PRO+	BR/A	SB	CS	SBR	FA	FR	G/POS	TPR
■ **KID DE LEON**		Ponce de Leon, Juan "Castilian Kid" (also played in 1874 as Kid Madrid)																					
		b: 3/13/1460, Madrid, Spain d: 2/25/1963, St. Augustine, Fl. BR/TR, 5'11", 173 lbs. Deb: 5/21/1874 FMUCH																					
1874	Bos-n	52	277	73	94	7	4	1	14	2	4	.339	.342	.400	111	4	2	0	1	.892	3	*2-52	0.2
1875	Wes-n	2	3	1	1	0	0	0	1	0	0	.333	.333	.333	95	0	0	0	0	.500	0	/S-2	0.0
1883	Bal-a	28	121	12	33	2	1	1	8			.273	.318	.331	101	1				.901	0	C-16,O-10/S-2	0.0
1884	Was-U	86	371	75	107	12	5	1	11			.288	.309	.356	127	5	0			.913	0	1-62,O-15/C-8	0.9
	KC-U	1	4	1	0	0	0	0	0			.000	.000	.000	97	0				1.000	0	/1-1	0.0
	Yr	87	375	76	107	12	5	1	11			.287	.308	.355	126	-0	0			.914	0	1-63,O-15/C-8	0.9
1890	Cin-P	1	1	1	1	0	0	0	1	0		1.000	1.000	4.000	700	1	0			.000	0	/2-1	0.0
1908	Phi-N	1	0	0	0	0	0	0	0	0		—	—	—		0	0			.000	0	/R-1	0.0
	Phi-A	9	31	5	9	3	0	0	2	0		.290	.290	.387	113	0				.899	-1	/3-8	0.0
1909	Phi-A	148	541	73	165	27	19	4	85	26		.305	.343	.447	146	26	20			.920	-5	*3-141	3.0
1910	Phi-A	146	561	83	159	25	15	2	74	34		.283	.329	.392	123	13	21			.934	3	*3-144	2.4
1911	Phi-A	148	592	96	198	40	4	11	115	50		.334	.379	.505	157	38	38			.912	-8	*3-147	3.3
1912	Phi-A	149	577	110	200	40	21	10	130	50		.347	.404	.541	171	50	40			.930	9	*3-149	5.4
1913	Phi-A	149	564	116	190	34	9	12	117	63	31	.337	.413	.493	171	48	34			.927	7	*3-148	6.1
1914	Phi-A	150	570	84	182	23	10	9	89	53	37	.319	.380	.442	151	33	19	20	-6	.929	8	*3-150	4.1
1915	Nwk-F	2	8	5	4	2	1	1	4	0	2	.500	.500	1.38	304	3	0			.977	1	/3-2	0.1
1916	NY-A	100	360	46	97	23	2	10	52	36	30	.269	.344	.428	130	12	15			.931	3	3-98	2.1
1917	NY-A	146	553	57	156	24	2	6	71	48	27	.282	.345	.365	109	6	18			.940	11	*3-145	2.7
1918	NY-A	126	504	65	154	24	5	6	62	38	13	.306	.357	.409	138	20	8			.943	11	*3-122	3.4
1939	*NY-A☆	141	567	70	166	22	1	10	83	44	18	.293	.346	.388	100	-0	13			.944	-2	*3-140	0.9
1941	*NY-A★	94	330	46	97	16	2	9	71	26	12	.294	.353	.436	98	-2	8	5	-1	.955	13	3-92	1.6
1942	*NY-A†	69	234	30	65	12	3	7	36	15	14	.278	.327	.444	98	-2	1	3	-2	.940	-8	3-67	-0.4
Total	2 n	54	280	74	95	7	4	1	15	2	4	.339	.348	.404	110	4	/2	0	1	.892	3	*2-52/S-2	0.2
Total	17	1694	6489	981	1983	329	100	100	992	502	184	.306	.354	.446	130	246	235	28		.938	41	*3-1409,1-126/CSO2R	45.1

player). His date and place of birth follow "b" and his date and place of death follow "d." Years through 1900 are expressed fully, in four digits, and years after 1900 are expressed in their last two digits.

Then comes the player's manner of batting and throwing, abbreviated for a lefthanded batter who throws right as BL/TR (a switch-hitter would be shown as BB for "bats both" and a switch thrower as TB for "throws both").

Next, and for most players last, is the player's debut date in the major leagues, all of which are reported now.

Some players continue in major league baseball after their playing days are through, as managers, coaches, or even umpires. A player whose biographical line concludes with an M can be located in the Manager Roster; one whose line bears a C will be listed in the Coach Roster; and one with a U occupies a place in the Umpire Roster. (In the last case we have placed a U on the biographical line only for those players who umpired in at least six games in a year, for in the nineteenth century—and especially in the years of the National Association—literally hundreds of players were pressed into service as umpires for a game or two. It would be misleading to accord such players the same code we give to Bob Emslie or Babe Pinelli.) The select few who have been enshrined in the Baseball Hall of Fame at Cooperstown, NY, are noted with an H. They are also listed in the Hall of Fame Roster found toward the end of Bill Deane's "Awards and Honors" essay. Also in *Total Baseball* since the fourth edition is an F on this line to denote family connection—father-son-grandfather or brother.

The explanations for the statistical column heads follow; for more technical information about formulas and calculations, see the Glossary. The vertical rules in the column-header line separate the stats into seven logical groupings: year, team, league; fundamental counting stats for batters; hits and plate appearances broken out into their component counting stats; basic calculated averages; sabermetric figures of more complex calculation; base-running stats; fielding stats and Total Player Rating.

Absent from the Player Register in recent editions are some statistics present in the original: production as a raw, unadjusted figure (still available by simply adding OBP plus SLG, as well as in the Annual Record and Leaders sections); Park Factor for batters (still available from the Annual Record); Clutch Hitting Index, newly developed for *Total Baseball* but which we have judged to be of lesser interest and value than the more established sabermetric measures (like PRO, however, it is still present in the Annual Record and Leaders sections); and Total Average, a popular stat but one that is mirrored by Runs Created and Batting Runs, both of which are more accurate (TA is present in the Annual Record and Leaders sections). By deleting these statistics from the Register we have improved legibility, particularly by adding to the margin in the gutter of the book, and reduced some redundancy.

New to the fifth edition was additional hit-by-pitch data for batters in the 1897-1908 period, which is reflected in their on base percentages. We have also made an upward adjustment to overall league performance in the Federal League of 1914-15 and the Union Association of 1884 (thus lowering individual ratings), because while both leagues are regarded as major leagues, there can be no doubt that their caliber of play was not equivalent to that in the rival leagues of those years. Suffice it to say here that league at bats were reduced to 80 percent for the UA and 90 percent for the FL. A full explanation of the adjustment procedure may be found in the Glossary, under "League Performance."

New to the fifth edition are RBI for the American Association for 1885-87 and 1890 with data for some players in 1882-1884. Also added are RBI and strikeouts, stolen bases and caught stealing (incomplete) and fielding data for the National Association.

YEAR   Year of play (when a space in the column is blank, this indicates that the man has played for two or more clubs in the last year stated in the column; if those clubs were in the same league, then the man will also have a combined total line, beginning with the abbreviation "Yr" placed in the TEAM/L column)

Yr   Year's totals for play with two or more clubs in same league (see comments for YEAR)

*   Denotes postseason play, World Series or League Championship Series

TM/L   Team and League (see comments for YEAR)

★   Named to All Star Game, played

☆   Named to All Star Game, did not play

†   Named to All Star Game, replaced because of injury

G   Games

AB   At-bats

R   Runs

H   Hits (Bases on balls were counted as hits by scorers in 1887, but in *Total Baseball* they are not figured as times at bat, nor as hits.)

2B   Doubles

3B   Triples

HR   Home Runs

RBI   Runs Batted In

BB   Bases on Balls (Bases on balls were counted as outs by scorers in 1876, but in *Total Baseball* they are not figured as times at bat nor as outs.)

SO   Strikeouts

AVG   Batting Average (Figured as hits over at-bats; mathematically meaningless averages created through a division by zero are rendered as dashes; see Kid De Leon's entry for 1908 with Pit-N. League leaders in this category, as in others in the Player Register, are noted by bold type. However, some boldface leaders in batting average will have lower marks than other batters who are not credited with having won a championship; for a full explanation of the reasoning for this anomaly, see "The History of Major League Baseball Statistics."

OBP   On Base Percentage (See comments for AVG)

SLG   Slugging Average (See comments for AVG, and

note the use of condensed type to express Kid De Leon's maximum SLG in 1890.)

PRO+   Production Plus, or Adjusted Production (On Base Percentage plus Slugging Average, normalized to league average and adjusted for home-park factor.) See comments for /A.

BR/A   Batting Runs (Linear Weights measure of runs contributed beyond what a league-average batter or team might have contributed, defined as zero. Occasionally the curious figure of -0 will appear in this column, or in the columns of other Linear Weights measures of batting, baserunning, fielding, and the TPR. This "negative zero" figure signifies a run contribution that falls below the league average, but to so small a degree that it cannot be said to have cost the team a run. The "/A" signifies that the measure has been adjusted for home-park factor and normalized to league average. A mark of 100 is a league-average performance. Pitcher batting is removed from all league batting statistics before normalization, for a variety of reasons expanded upon in the Glossary. Three-year averages are employed for batting park factors. If a team moved or the park changed dramatically, then two-year averages are employed; if the park was used for only one year, then of course only that run-scoring data is used.)

SB   Stolen Bases (for 1886 to the present, plus new data for the NA years, 1871-75.)

CS   Caught Stealing (Available 1915, 1916 for players with 20 or more stolen bases, 1920–1925, 1951–date NL; 1914–1915, 1916 for players with 20 or more stolen bases, 1920 to date AL with scattered data still missing from 1927.)

SBA   Stolen Base Average (Stolen bases divided by attempts; availability dependent upon CS as shown above.)

SBR   Stolen Base Runs (This is a Linear Weights measure of runs contributed *beyond* what a league-average base stealer might have gained, defined as zero and calculated on the basis of a 66.7 percent success rate, which computer simulations have shown to be the break-even point beyond which stolen bases have positive run value to the team; see the general introduction to Part Two and the Glossary. The presence of a figure in the SBR column in the Player Register is dependent upon the availability of CS as shown above. Lifetime Stolen Base Runs are not totaled where data is incomplete, but seasonal SBRs are reflected in the seasonal Total Player Ratings, which in turn are added to form the lifetime Total Player Rating.)

FA   Fielding Average, often called Fielding Percentage as well (putouts plus assists divided by putouts plus assists plus errors, here calculated only for the position at which a man played the most games in a season or career.)

FR   Fielding Runs (The Linear Weights measure of

runs saved *beyond* what a league-average player at that position might have saved, defined as zero; this stat is calculated to take account of the particular demands of the different positions; see Glossary for formulas, and note new method for the positional adjustment.)

G/POS Positions played (This is a ranking from left to right by frequency of the positions played in the field or at designated hitter. An asterisk to the left of the position indicates, generally, that in a given year the man played about two-thirds of his team's scheduled games at that position; more precisely, it is figured at 20 games in 1871, 30 in 1872, 35 in 1873, 40 in 1874, and 50 in 1875; two-thirds of the scheduled games in 1876-1900, and 100 or more games since. When a slash separates positions, the man played those positions listed to the left of the slash in 10 or more games and the positions to the right of the slash in fewer than 10 games. If there is no slash, he played all positions listed in 10 or more games. For the lifetime line, the asterisk signifies 1,000 games and the slash marks a dividing point of 100 games. A player's POS column will list him as a pinch runner or pinch hitter in only those years in which he appeared at no other position. New to the fourth edition were listings of the number of games played at the individual's two most common positions. New to the fifth edition are games played at the third and fourth positions when space permits. The positions and their abbreviations are)

1: First base	P: Pitcher
2: Second base	D: Designated hitter
S: Shortstop	R: Runner (pinch)
3: Third base	H: Hitter (pinch)
O: Outfield	M: Manager (playing)
C: Catcher	

TPR Total Player Rating (This is the sum of a player's Adjusted Batting Runs, Fielding Runs, and Base Stealing Runs, minus his positional adjustment, all divided by the Runs Per Win factor for that year—generally around 10, historically in the 9–11 range. For more information on the formula and the Runs Per Win concept, see the general introduction to the statistical section and the Glossary. In the lifetime line, the TPR is the sum of the seasonal TPRs. For men who were primarily pitchers but whose extent of play at other positions warrants a listing in the Player Register as well as the Pitcher Register, the TPR may be listed as 0.0; this signifies that their batting records are summed up in the Total Pitcher Index [TPI] column of the Pitcher Register.) Note that the TPR (and the TPI, Total Pitcher Index) from the fourth edition on will differ from those in earlier volumes, for four reasons which are explained in greater detail in the Glossary. (1) A

broader and more sophisticated computation of the positional adjustment to Batting Runs has improved the accuracy and reasonableness of the method, by which the TPR of those who play skill positions like shortstop and second base tend to be boosted and the TPR of the sluggers who customarily play first base and left field are generally diminished. (2) Because games in left, center, and right fields are now available for all outfielders, center fielders no longer need be compared to an average of the regular center fielders and now may be set against all the men who played center, thus tending to elevate their Fielding Runs. (3) Because Hit Batsmen data is now available for the 1903–1908 period, plus considerable data for the years 1897–1902, men like Frank Chance, who was hit over 100 times in his career, increase their Batter Ratings perceptibly. (4) And for players who were both batters and pitchers, the method of allocating Wins between TPR and TPI (Total Pitcher Index) was improved. Previously, if a pitcher pitched in over half his games, all his batting was included with his pitcher rating (TPI); if he pitched in less than half his games, his Batting Wins were thrown over to his batter rating (TPR), with his TPI including only his Pitching Wins and Pitcher Defense. The new method prorates batting proportionally with the number of games pitched. In addition, fielding ratings at nonpitching positions for players who pitched in over half their games, previously omitted, are now part of the Total Baseball Ranking. In any case, the TPR values of batter-pitchers should remain about the same. Thus in 1918, Babe Ruth now has a batter rating of 2.6 Wins and a pitcher rating of 2.9 (total 5.5). In some previous editions his marks used to be 4.1 and 1.0, respectively, or 5.1 overall, with none of his batting counted in with his pitching record even though he pitched 20 of 95 games. The large jump in his pitcher rating is because now his pitcher batting is compared against average batting for pitchers.

Total For players whose careers include play in the National Association as well as other major leagues, two totals are given, as described above and as illustrated in Kid De Leon's record, where the record of his years in the National Association is shown alongside the notation "Total 2 n," where *2* stands for the number of years totaled and *n* stands for National Association. For players whose careers began in 1876 or later, the lifetime record is shown alongside the notation "Total x," where *x* stands for the number of post-1875 years totaled. Note the underlined entries in the record for Kid De Leon, reflecting the partial data for RBI, batter strikeouts, stolen bases, and times caught stealing.

YEAR	TM/L	G	AB	R	H	2B	3B	HR	RBI	BB	SO	AVG	OBP	SLG	PRO+	BR/A	SB	CS	SBR	FA	FR	G/POS	TPR

■ HANK AARON
Aaron, Henry Louis "Hammerin' Hank" b: 2/5/34, Mobile, Ala. BR/TR, 6', 180 lbs. Deb: 4/13/54 FH

YEAR	TM/L	G	AB	R	H	2B	3B	HR	RBI	BB	SO	AVG	OBP	SLG	PRO+	BR/A	SB	CS	SBR	FA	FR	G/POS	TPR
1954	Mil-N	122	468	58	131	27	6	13	69	28	39	.280	.325	.447	105	1	2	2	-1	.970	-2	*O-116	-0.6
1955	Mil-N★	153	602	105	189	37	9	27	106	49	61	.314	.369	.540	144	36	3	1	0	.967	6	*O-126,2-27	3.8
1956	Mil-N★	153	609	106	200	34	14	26	92	37	54	.328	.369	.558	154	43	2	4	-2	.962	10	*O-152	4.4
1957	*Mil-N★	151	615	118	198	27	6	44	132	57	58	.322	.379	.600	170	58	1	1	-0	.983	2	*O-150	5.0
1958	*Mil-N★	153	601	109	196	34	4	30	95	59	49	.326	.387	.546	157	47	4	1	1	.984	2	*O-153	4.1
1959	Mil-N★	154	629	116	223	46	7	39	123	51	54	.355	.406	.636	188	75	8	0	2	.982	-2	*O-152/3-5	6.6
1960	Mil-N★	153	590	102	172	20	11	40	126	60	63	.292	.359	.566	160	46	16	7	1	.982	9	*O-153/2-2	4.8
1961	Mil-N★	155	603	115	197	39	10	34	120	56	64	.327	.386	.594	165	54	21	9	1	.982	12	*O-154/3-2	5.6
1962	Mil-N★	156	592	127	191	28	6	45	128	66	73	.323	.393	.618	171	58	15	7	0	.980	8	*O-153/1-1	5.5
1963	Mil-N★	161	631	121	201	29	4	44	130	78	94	.319	.394	.586	180	64	31	5	6	.979	-1	*O-161	6.5
1964	Mil-N★	145	570	103	187	30	2	24	95	62	46	.328	.393	.514	152	40	22	4	4	.983	11	*O-139,2-11	5.1
1965	Mil-N★	150	570	109	181	40	1	32	89	60	81	.318	.384	.560	161	45	24	4	5	.987	10	*O-148	5.5
1966	Atl-N★	158	603	117	168	23	1	44	127	76	96	.279	.360	.539	144	35	21	3	5	.988	5	*O-158/2-2	4.3
1967	Atl-N★	155	600	113	184	37	3	39	109	63	97	.307	.373	.573	169	52	17	6	2	.979	12	*O-152/2-1	6.1
1968	Atl-N★	160	606	84	174	33	4	29	86	64	62	.287	.356	.498	154	39	28	5	5	.991	14	*O-151,1-14	5.5
1969	*Atl-N★	147	547	100	164	30	3	44	97	87	47	.300	.398	.607	177	56	9	10	-3	.982	6	*O-144/1-4	5.2
1970	Atl-N★	150	516	103	154	26	1	38	118	74	63	.298	.389	.574	146	33	9	3	1	.977	5	*O-125,1-11	3.2
1971	Atl-N★	139	495	95	162	22	3	47	118	71	58	.327	.414	.669	190	58	1	1	-0	.996	-8	1-71,O-60	4.2
1972	Atl-N★	129	449	75	119	10	0	34	77	92	55	.265	.391	.514	142	27	4	0	1	.987	1	*1-109,O-15	1.9
1973	Atl-N★	120	392	84	118	12	1	40	96	68	51	.301	.406	.643	173	39	1	1	-0	.977	2	*O-105	3.7
1974	Atl-N★	112	340	47	91	16	0	20	69	39	29	.268	.343	.491	126	11	1	0	0	.986	-4	O-89	0.3
1975	Mil-A★	137	465	45	109	16	2	12	60	70	51	.234	.336	.355	95	-2	0	1	-1	1.000	-0	D-128/O-3	-0.7
1976	Mil-A	85	271	22	62	8	0	10	35	35	38	.229	.317	.369	102	1	0	1	-1	1.000	-0	D-74/O-1	-0.2
Total	23	3298	12364	2174	3771	624	98	755	2297	1402	1383	.305	.377	.555	156	914	240	73	28	.980	101	*O-2760,1-210,D/23	89.8

■ TOMMIE AARON
Aaron, Tommie Lee b: 8/5/39, Mobile, Ala. d: 8/16/84, Atlanta, Ga. BR/TR, 6'1", 200 lbs. Deb: 4/10/62 FC

YEAR	TM/L	G	AB	R	H	2B	3B	HR	RBI	BB	SO	AVG	OBP	SLG	PRO+	BR/A	SB	CS	SBR	FA	FR	G/POS	TPR
1962	Mil-N	141	334	54	77	20	2	8	38	41	58	.231	.315	.374	86	-7	6	0	2	.989	2	*1-110,O-42/2-1,3-1	-0.8
1963	Mil-N	72	135	6	27	6	1	1	15	11	27	.200	.260	.281	57	-8	0	3	-2	1.000	-6	1-45,O-14/2-6,3-1	-1.8
1965	Mil-N	8	16	1	3	0	0	0	1	1	2	.188	.235	.188	21	-2	0	0	0	.961	-1	/1-6	-0.2
1968	Atl-N	98	283	21	69	10	3	1	25	21	37	.244	.296	.311	82	-6	3	4	-2	.942	-4	O-62,1-28/3-1	-1.9
1969	*Atl-N	49	60	13	15	2	0	1	5	6	6	.250	.318	.333	82	-1	0	1	-1	1.000	1	1-16/O-8	-0.2
1970	Atl-N	44	63	3	13	2	0	2	7	3	10	.206	.242	.333	50	-5	0	0	0	.955	-2	1-16,O-12	-0.8
1971	Atl-N	25	53	4	12	2	0	0	3	3	5	.226	.268	.264	48	-4	0	0	0	.974	2	1-11/3-7	-0.2
Total	7	437	944	102	216	42	6	13	94	86	145	.229	.293	.327	75	-31	9	8	-5	.990	-7	1-232,O-138/3-10,2	-5.9

■ JOHN ABADIE
Abadie, John b: 11/4/1854, Philadelphia, Pa. d: 5/17/05, Pemberton, N.J. BR/TR, 6', 192 lbs. Deb: 6/10/1875

YEAR	TM/L	G	AB	R	H	2B	3B	HR	RBI	BB	SO	AVG	OBP	SLG	PRO+	BR/A	SB	CS	SBR	FA	FR	G/POS	TPR
1875	Cen-n	11	45	3	10	0	0	0	4	0	3	.222	.222	.222	60	-2	1	0	0	.912	-0	1-11	-0.1
	Atl-n	1	4	1	1	0	0	0	0	0	0	.250	.250	.250	85	-0	0	0	0	.875	-0	/1-1	0.0
	Yr	12	49	4	11	0	0	0	4	0	3	.224	.224	.224	62	-2	1	0	0	.910	-1	1-12	-0.1

■ ED ABBATICCHIO
Abbaticchio, Edward James "Batty" b: 4/15/1877, Latrobe, Pa. d: 1/6/57, Ft.Lauderdale, Fla. BR/TR, 5'11", 170 lbs. Deb: 9/4/1897

YEAR	TM/L	G	AB	R	H	2B	3B	HR	RBI	BB	SO	AVG	OBP	SLG	PRO+	BR/A	SB	CS	SBR	FA	FR	G/POS	TPR
1897	Phi-N	3	10	0	3	0	0	0	0	1		.300	.364	.300	78	-0	0			.875	-2	/2-3	-0.2
1898	Phi-N	25	92	9	21	4	0	0	14	7		.228	.290	.272	64	-4	4			.818	-13	3-20/2-4,O-1	-1.6
1903	Bos-N	136	489	61	111	18	5	1	46	52		.227	.306	.290	73	-16	23			.934	3	*2-116,S-17	-0.7
1904	Bos-N	154	579	76	148	18	10	3	54	40		.256	.309	.337	103	2	24			.915	2	*S-154	0.9
1905	Bos-N	153	610	70	170	25	12	3	41	35		.279	.326	.374	111	7	30			.919	-12	*S-152/O-1	-0.2
1907	Pit-N	147	496	63	130	14	7	2	82	65		.262	.357	.331	114	10	35			.951	-23	*2-147	-1.6
1908	Pit-N	146	500	43	125	16	7	1	61	58		.250	.336	.316	108	7	22			.969	-12	*2-144	-0.8
1909	*Pit-N	36	87	13	20	0	0	1	16	19		.230	.368	.264	89	-0	2			.966	2	S-18/2-4,O-1	0.2
1910	Pit-N	3	3	0	0	0	0	0	0	0		.000	.000	.000	-95	-1	0			.500	-0	/S-1	-0.1
	Bos-N	52	178	20	44	4	2	0	10	12	16	.247	.295	.292	68	-7	2			.910	-3	S-46/2-1	-0.9
	Yr	55	181	20	44	4	2	0	10	12	16	.243	.290	.287	66	-8	2			.907	-4	S-47/2-1	-1.0
Total	9	855	3044	355	772	99	43	11	324	289	16	.254	.325	.325	98	-4	142			.949	-59	2-419,S-388/3-20,O	-5.0

■ CHARLIE ABBEY
Abbey, Charles S. b: 10/14/1866, Falls City, Neb. d: 4/27/26, San Francisco, Cal. BL, 5'8.5", 169 lbs. Deb: 8/16/1893

YEAR	TM/L	G	AB	R	H	2B	3B	HR	RBI	BB	SO	AVG	OBP	SLG	PRO+	BR/A	SB	CS	SBR	FA	FR	G/POS	TPR
1893	Was-N	31	116	11	30	1	4	0	12	12	6	.259	.333	.336	80	-3	9			.937	3	O-31	-0.2
1894	Was-N	129	523	95	164	26	18	7	101	58	38	.314	.389	.472	110	9	31			.909	14	*O-129	1.0
1895	Was-N	132	511	102	141	14	10	8	84	43	41	.276	.340	.389	89	-9	28			.903	10	*O-132	-0.8
1896	Was-N	79	301	47	79	12	4	0	49	27	20	.262	.331	.352	80	-9	16			.879	-6	O-78/P-1	-1.8
1897	Was-N	80	300	52	78	14	8	4	34	27		.260	.329	.390	90	-5	9			.946	2	O-80	-0.8
Total	5	451	1751	307	492	67	46	19	280	167	105	.281	.351	.404	94	-17	93			.910	21	O-450/P-1	-2.6

■ FRED ABBOTT
Abbott, Harry Frederick (b: Harry Frederick Winbigler) b: 10/22/1874, Versailles, Ohio d: 6/11/35, Los Angeles, Cal. BR/TR, 5'10", 180 lbs. Deb: 4/25/03

YEAR	TM/L	G	AB	R	H	2B	3B	HR	RBI	BB	SO	AVG	OBP	SLG	PRO+	BR/A	SB	CS	SBR	FA	FR	G/POS	TPR
1903	Cle-A	77	255	25	60	11	3	1	25	7		.235	.270	.314	76	-8	8			.958	9	C-71/1-3	0.8
1904	Cle-A	41	130	14	22	4	2	0	12	6		.169	.206	.231	38	-9	2			.953	-3	C-33/1-7	-1.0
1905	Phi-A	42	128	9	25	6	1	0	12	6		.195	.248	.258	53	-8	4			.954	-0	C-34/1-5	-0.5
Total	3	160	513	48	107	21	6	1	49	19		.209	.248	.279	61	-24	14			.956	6	C-138/1-15	-0.7

■ KURT ABBOTT
Abbott, Kurt Thomas b: 6/2/69, Zanesville, Ohio BR/TR, 6', 170 lbs. Deb: 9/8/93

YEAR	TM/L	G	AB	R	H	2B	3B	HR	RBI	BB	SO	AVG	OBP	SLG	PRO+	BR/A	SB	CS	SBR	FA	FR	G/POS	TPR
1993	Oak-A	20	61	11	15	1	0	3	9	3	20	.246	.281	.410	89	-1	2	0	1	.971	1	O-13/S-6,2-2	0.1
1994	Fla-N	101	345	41	86	17	3	9	33	16	98	.249	.292	.394	75	-13	3	0	1	.966	-8	S-99	-1.2
1995	Fla-N	120	420	60	107	18	7	17	60	36	110	.255	.321	.452	101	-1	4	3	-1	.959	-11	*S-115	-0.2
1996	Fla-N	109	320	37	81	18	7	8	33	22	99	.253	.305	.428	95	-3	3	3	-1	.969	2	S-44,3-33,2-20	0.2
Total	4	350	1146	149	289	54	17	37	135	77	327	.252	.307	.426	91	-19	12	6	0	.963	-16	S-264/3-33,2-22,O	-1.1

■ ODY ABBOTT
Abbott, Ody Cleon b: 9/5/1888, New Eagle, Pa. d: 4/13/33, Washington, D.C. BR/TR, 6'2", 180 lbs. Deb: 9/10/10

YEAR	TM/L	G	AB	R	H	2B	3B	HR	RBI	BB	SO	AVG	OBP	SLG	PRO+	BR/A	SB	CS	SBR	FA	FR	G/POS	TPR
1910	StL-N	22	70	2	13	2	1	0	6	6	20	.186	.250	.243	46	-5	3			.982	1	O-21	-0.5

■ DAVE ABERCROMBIE
Abercrombie, David b: 5/6/1840, Falkirk, Scotland d: 9/2/16, Baltimore, Md. Deb: 10/21/1871

YEAR	TM/L	G	AB	R	H	2B	3B	HR	RBI	BB	SO	AVG	OBP	SLG	PRO+	BR/A	SB	CS	SBR	FA	FR	G/POS	TPR
1871	Tro-n	4	14	0	0	0	0	0	0	0	0	.000	.000	.000	-99	-1	0	0	0	.667	-0	/S-1	-0.1

■ CLIFF ABERSON
Aberson, Clifford Alexander "Kif" b: 8/28/21, Chicago, Ill. d: 6/23/73, Vallejo, Cal. BR/TR, 6', 200 lbs. Deb: 7/18/47

YEAR	TM/L	G	AB	R	H	2B	3B	HR	RBI	BB	SO	AVG	OBP	SLG	PRO+	BR/A	SB	CS	SBR	FA	FR	G/POS	TPR
1947	Chi-N	47	140	24	39	6	3	4	20	20	32	.279	.369	.450	121	4	0			.920	-1	O-40	0.1
1948	Chi-N	12	32	1	6	1	0	1	6	5	10	.188	.297	.313	68	-1	0			.867	-1	/O-8	-0.3
1949	Chi-N	4	7	0	0	0	0	0	0	0	2	.000	.000	.000	-99	-2	0			1.000	0	/O-1	-0.2
Total	3	63	179	25	45	7	3	5	26	25	44	.251	.343	.408	103	1	0			.913	-2	/O-49	-0.4

■ SHAWN ABNER
Abner, Shawn Wesley b: 6/17/66, Hamilton, Ohio BR/TR, 6'1", 190 lbs. Deb: 9/8/87

YEAR	TM/L	G	AB	R	H	2B	3B	HR	RBI	BB	SO	AVG	OBP	SLG	PRO+	BR/A	SB	CS	SBR	FA	FR	G/POS	TPR
1987	SD-N	16	47	5	13	4	1	2	7	2	8	.277	.306	.511	116	1	1	0	0	.926	1	O-14	0.1
1988	SD-N	37	83	6	15	3	0	2	5	4	19	.181	.227	.289	48	-6	0	1	-1	.982	-4	O-35	-1.2
1989	SD-N	57	102	13	18	4	2	2	14	5	20	.176	.215	.353	39	-8	1	0	0	1.000	0	O-51	-1.9
1990	SD-N	91	184	17	45	9	0	1	15	9	28	.245	.287	.310	64	-9	2	3	-1	.991	-7	O-62	-1.9
1991	SD-N	53	115	15	19	4	1	1	5	7	25	.165	.220	.243	29	-11	0	0	0	1.000	1	O-39	-1.1
	Cal-A	41	101	12	23	6	0	1	4	4	17	.228	.257	.366	71	-4	1	2	-1	1.000	1	O-38/D-3	-0.7
1992	Chi-A	97	208	21	58	10	1	2	16	12	35	.279	.327	.351	91	-2	5	1	0	1.000	-13	O-94/D-1	-1.8
Total	6	392	840	89	191	39	4	11	71	43	153	.227	.271	.323	65	-40	6	8	-3	.993	-32	O-333/D-4	-8.5

■ CAL ABRAMS
Abrams, Calvin Ross b: 3/2/24, Philadelphia, Pa. BL/TL, 5'11", 195 lbs. Deb: 4/20/49

YEAR	TM/L	G	AB	R	H	2B	3B	HR	RBI	BB	SO	AVG	OBP	SLG	PRO+	BR/A	SB	CS	SBR	FA	FR	G/POS	TPR
1949	Bro-N	8	24	6	2	1	0	0	0	7	6	.083	.290	.125	15	-3	1			.833	-1	/O-7	-0.4
1950	Bro-N	38	44	5	9	2	0	1	4	5	13	.205	.340	.227	51	-3	0			1.000	-3	O-15	-0.6

YEAR	TM/L	G	AB	R	H	2B	3B	HR	RBI	BB	SO	AVG	OBP	SLG	PRO+	BR/A	SB	CS	SBR	FA	FR	G/POS	TPR
1951	Bro-N	67	150	27	42	8	0	3	19	36	26	.280	.419	.393	118	6	3	2	-0	.944	-1	O-34	0.3
1952	Bro-N	10	10	1	2	0	0	0	0	2	4	.200	.333	.200	51	-1	0	0	0	.000	-0	/O-1	-0.1
	Cin-N	71	158	23	44	9	2	2	13	19	25	.278	.356	.399	109	2	1	0	0	1.000	-5	O-46	-0.4
	Yr	81	168	24	46	9	2	2	13	21	29	.274	.354	.387	106	2	1	0	0	1.000	-5	O-47	-0.5
1953	Pit-N	119	448	66	128	10	6	15	43	58	70	.286	.368	.435	109	7	4	4	-1	.973	5	*O-112	0.6
1954	Pit-N	17	42	6	6	1	0	0	3	3	7	.143	.308	.214	39	-4	0	0	0	1.000	0	O-13	-0.4
	Bal-A	115	423	67	124	22	7	6	25	72	67	.293	.401	.421	135	23	1	4	-2	.977	4	*O-115	2.0
1955	Bal-A	118	309	56	75	12	3	6	32	89	69	.243	.416	.359	118	14	2	8	-4	.985	-13	O-96/1-4	-0.8
1956	Chi-A	4	3	0	0	0	0	0	0	2	1	.333	.600	.333	150	1	0	0	0	1.000	-0	/O-2	0.0
Total	8	567	1611	257	433	64	19	32	138	304	290	.269	.387	.392	113	42	12	18		.977	-14	O-441/1-4	0.2

■ BOB ABREU
Abreu, Bob Kelly b:3/11/74, Aragua, Venez. BL/TR, 6', 160 lbs. Deb: 9/1/96

YEAR	TM/L	G	AB	R	H	2B	3B	HR	RBI	BB	SO	AVG	OBP	SLG	PRO+	BR/A	SB	CS	SBR	FA	FR	G/POS	TPR
1996	Hou-N	15	22	1	5	1	0	0	1	2	3	.227	.292	.273	55	-1	0	0	0	1.000	-1	/O-7	-0.3

■ JOE ABREU
Abreu, Joseph Lawrence b:5/24/13, Oakland, Cal. d:3/17/93, Hayward, Cal. BR/TR, 5'8", 160 lbs. Deb: 4/23/42

YEAR	TM/L	G	AB	R	H	2B	3B	HR	RBI	BB	SO	AVG	OBP	SLG	PRO+	BR/A	SB	CS	SBR	FA	FR	G/POS	TPR
1942	Cin-N	9	28	4	6	1	0	1	3	4	4	.214	.313	.357	96	-1				.941	-1	/3-6,2-2	-0.1

■ BILL ABSTEIN
Abstein, William Henry "Big Bill" b:2/2/1883, St.Louis, Mo. d:4/8/40, St.Louis, Mo. BR/TR, 6', 185 lbs. Deb: 9/25/06

YEAR	TM/L	G	AB	R	H	2B	3B	HR	RBI	BB	SO	AVG	OBP	SLG	PRO+	BR/A	SB	CS	SBR	FA	FR	G/POS	TPR
1906	Pit-N	8	20	2	4	0	0	0		3	0	.200	.200	.200	24	-2	2			.769	-2	/2-3,O-2	-0.4
1909	*Pit-N	137	512	51	133	20	10	1	70	27		.260	.302	.344	93	-6	16			.982	-5	*1-135	-1.4
1910	StL-N	25	87	1	13	2	0	0	3	2		.149	.169	.172	7	-9	3			.963	2	1-23	-0.9
Total	3	170	619	54	150	22	10	1	76	29		.242	.281	.315	80	-18	21			.979	-5	1-158/2-3,O-2	-2.7

■ MERITO ACOSTA
Acosta, Baldomero Pedro (Fernandez) b:5/19/1896, Bauta, Cuba d:11/17/63, Miami, Fla. BL/TL, 5'7", 140 lbs. Deb: 6/15/13 F

YEAR	TM/L	G	AB	R	H	2B	3B	HR	RBI	BB	SO	AVG	OBP	SLG	PRO+	BR/A	SB	CS	SBR	FA	FR	G/POS	TPR
1913	Was-A	12	20	3	6	0	1	0	1	4	2	.300	.417	.400	136	1	2			.714	-0	/O-9	-0.2
1914	Was-A	39	74	10	19	2	2	0	4	11	18	.257	.353	.338	104	1	3	4	-2	.857	-2	O-25	-0.4
1915	Was-A	72	163	20	34	4	1	0	18	28	15	.209	.338	.245	73	-4	8	4	0	.963	-4	O-53	-1.1
1916	Was-A	5	8	0	1	0	0	0	0	2	0	.125	.300	.125	28	-1	0			1.000	1	/O-4	0.0
1918	Was-A	3	2	0	0	0	0	0	0	0	1	.000	.000	.000	-99	-0	0			.000	0	H	-0.1
	Phi-N	49	169	23	51	3	3	0	14	18	10	.302	.369	.355	117	4	4			.944	-3	O-45	-0.2
	Yr	52	171	23	51	3	3	0	14	18	11	.298	.365	.351	115	3	4			.944	-3	O-45	-0.3
Total	5	180	436	56	111	9	7	0	37	63	46	.255	.354	.307	97	0	17	8		.933	-11	O-136	-2.0

■ JIMMY ADAIR
Adair, James Aubrey "Choppy" b:1/25/07, Waxahachie, Tex. d:12/9/82, Dallas, Tex. BR/TR, 5'10.5", 154 lbs. Deb: 8/24/31 C

YEAR	TM/L	G	AB	R	H	2B	3B	HR	RBI	BB	SO	AVG	OBP	SLG	PRO+	BR/A	SB	CS	SBR	FA	FR	G/POS	TPR
1931	Chi-N	18	76	9	21	3	1	0	3	1	8	.276	.286	.342	67	-4	1			.948	-1	S-18	-0.3

■ JERRY ADAIR
Adair, Kenneth Jerry b:12/17/36, Sand Springs, Okla. d:5/31/87, Tulsa, Okla. BR/TR, 6', 175 lbs. Deb: 9/2/58 C

YEAR	TM/L	G	AB	R	H	2B	3B	HR	RBI	BB	SO	AVG	OBP	SLG	PRO+	BR/A	SB	CS	SBR	FA	FR	G/POS	TPR
1958	Bal-A	11	19	1	2	0	0	0	0	1	7	.105	.150	.105	-30	-3	0	0	0	.967	2	S-10/2-1	-0.1
1959	Bal-A	12	35	3	11	0	0	0	2	1	5	.314	.333	.371	95	-0	0	0	0	.932	-4	2-11/S-1	-0.3
1960	Bal-A	3	5	1	1	0	0	1	1	0	0	.200	.200	.800	159	0	0	0	0	1.000	0	/2-3	0.1
1961	Bal-A	133	386	41	102	21	1	9	30	35	51	.264	.329	.394	95	-3	5	2	0	.987	-1	*2-107,S-27/3-2	0.8
1962	Bal-A	139	538	67	153	29	4	11	48	27	77	.284	.321	.414	103	-0	7	7	-2	.969	-10	*S-113,2-34/3-1	0.1
1963	Bal-A	109	382	34	87	21	3	6	30	9	51	.228	.249	.346	67	-18	3	3	-1	.985	-0	*2-103	-1.0
1964	Bal-A	155	569	56	141	20	3	9	47	28	72	.248	.284	.341	73	-21	3	2	-0	.994	9	*2-153	0.0
1965	Bal-A	157	582	51	151	26	3	7	66	35	65	.259	.304	.351	84	-13	6	4	-1	.986	12	*2-157	1.4
1966	Bal-A	17	52	3	15	1	0	0	3	4	13	.288	.339	.308	89	-1	0	0	0	.969	-1	2-13	-0.1
	Chi-A	105	370	27	90	18	2	4	36	17	44	.243	.278	.335	81	-10	3	2	-0	.975	-2	S-75,2-50	-0.4
	Yr	122	422	30	105	19	2	4	39	21	52	.249	.286	.332	82	-11	3	2	-0	.975	-3	S-75,2-63	-0.5
1967	Chi-A	28	98	6	20	4	0	0	9	4	17	.204	.243	.245	46	-7	0	1	-1	.985	-0	2-27	-0.6
	*Bos-A	89	316	41	92	13	1	3	26	13	35	.291	.323	.367	96	-2	1	4	-2	.952	-8	3-35,S-30,2-23	-1.0
	Yr	117	414	47	112	17	1	3	35	17	52	.271	.304	.338	85	-8	1	5	-3	.976	-9	2-50,3-35,S-30	-1.6
1968	Bos-A	74	208	18	45	1	0	2	12	9	28	.216	.252	.250	49	-13	0	0	0	.976	-5	S-46,2-12/3-7,1-1	-1.6
1969	KC-A	126	432	29	108	9	1	5	48	20	36	.250	.281	.310	67	-20	1	3	-2	.984	-22	*2-109/S-8,3-1	-3.6
1970	KC-A	7	27	0	4	0	0	0	1	5	3	.148	.281	.148	22	-3	0	1	-1	1.000	2	2-7	-0.1
Total	13	1165	4019	378	1022	163	19	57	366	208	499	.254	.294	.347	80	-112	29	29	-9	.985	-30	2-810,S-310/3-46,1	-6.4

■ SPARKY ADAMS
Adams, Earl John b:8/26/1894, Zerbe, Pa. d:2/24/89, Pottsville, Pa. BR/TR, 5'5.5", 151 lbs. Deb: 9/18/22

YEAR	TM/L	G	AB	R	H	2B	3B	HR	RBI	BB	SO	AVG	OBP	SLG	PRO+	BR/A	SB	CS	SBR	FA	FR	G/POS	TPR
1922	Chi-N	11	44	5	11	0	1	0	3	4	3	.250	.313	.295	56	-3	1	2	-1	.914	-4	2-11	-0.7
1923	Chi-N	95	311	40	90	12	0	4	35	26	10	.289	.346	.367	88	-5	20	19	-5	.935	-6	S-79/O-1	-0.9
1924	Chi-N	117	418	66	117	11	5	1	27	40	20	.280	.344	.337	83	-9	15	17	-6	.941	-8	S-88,2-19	-1.3
1925	Chi-N	149	627	95	180	29	8	2	48	44	15	.287	.341	.368	80	-18	26	12	1	.983	28	*2-144/S-5	1.3
1926	Chi-N	154	624	95	193	35	0	0	39	52	27	.309	.367	.375	99	1	27			.965	17	*2-136,3-19/S-2	2.2
1927	Chi-N	146	647	100	189	17	7	0	49	24	26	.292	.335	.340	81	-17	26			.994	-1	2-60,3-53,S-40	-0.8
1928	Pit-N	135	539	91	149	14	6	0	38	64	18	.276	.357	.325	76	-16	8			.971	-11	*2-107,S-27/O-1	-2.1
1929	Pit-N	74	196	37	51	8	1	0	11	15	5	.260	.316	.311	55	-14	3			.901	-15	S-30,2-20,3-15/O-2	-2.3
1930	*StL-N	137	570	98	179	36	9	0	55	45	27	.314	.365	.409	84	-14	7			.966	-13	*3-104,2-25/S-7	-1.7
1931	*StL-N	143	608	97	178	46	5	1	40	42	24	.293	.340	.390	92	-7	16			.963	-12	*3-138/S-6	-1.0
1932	StL-N	31	127	22	35	3	1	0	13	14	5	.276	.352	.315	79	-3	0			.931	-4	3-30	-0.5
1933	StL-N	8	30	1	5	1	0	0	0	1	3	.167	.219	.200	19	-3	0			.955	-2	/S-5,3-3	-0.5
	Cin-N	137	538	59	141	21	1	1	22	44	30	.262	.320	.310	82	-12	3			.963	-3	*3-132/S-8	-0.6
	Yr	145	568	60	146	22	1	1	22	45	33	.257	.315	.305	78	-15	3			.959	-5	3-135,S-13	-1.1
1934	Cin-N	87	278	38	70	16	1	0	14	20	10	.252	.307	.317	69	-12	3			.955	-3	3-38,2-29	-1.1
Total	13	1424	5557	844	1588	249	48	9	394	453	223	.286	.343	.353	82	-131	154	50		.974	-37	2-551,3-532,S/O	-10.0

■ BUSTER ADAMS
Adams, Elvin Clark b:6/24/15, Trinidad, Col. d:9/1/90, Rancho Mirage, Cal. BR/TR, 6', 180 lbs. Deb: 4/27/39

YEAR	TM/L	G	AB	R	H	2B	3B	HR	RBI	BB	SO	AVG	OBP	SLG	PRO+	BR/A	SB	CS	SBR	FA	FR	G/POS	TPR
1939	StL-N	2	1	1	0	0	0	0	0	0	0	.000	.000	.000	-94	-0	0			.000	0	H	0.0
1943	StL-N	8	11	1	1	1	0	0	1	4	4	.091	.333	.182	48	-1	0			1.000	-1	/O-6	-0.2
	Phi-N	111	418	48	107	14	7	4	38	39	67	.256	.319	.352	98	-2	2			.984	3	*O-107	-0.5
	Yr	119	429	49	108	15	7	4	39	43	71	.252	.320	.347	96	-3	2			.984	2	*O-113	-0.7
1944	Phi-N	151	584	86	165	35	3	17	64	74	74	.283	.370	.440	132	25	2			.979	11	*O-151	2.8
1945	Phi-N	14	56	6	13	3	1	2	5	8	5	.232	.295	.429	103	-0	0			1.000	-1	O-14	-0.2
	StL-N	140	578	98	169	26	0	20	101	57	75	.292	.359	.441	119	14	3			.978	1	*O-140	0.7
	Yr	154	634	104	182	29	1	22	109	62	80	.287	.353	.440	117	14	3			.979	0	*O-154	0.5
1946	StL-N	81	173	21	32	6	0	5	22	29	27	.185	.312	.306	73	-6	3			.990	-9	O-58	-1.8
1947	Phi-N	69	182	21	45	11	1	2	15	29	31	.247	.341	.352	88	-3	2			.954	-4	O-51	-0.9
Total	6	576	2003	282	532	96	12	50	249	234	281	.266	.346	.400	110	27	12			.979	0	O-527	-0.1

■ GEORGE ADAMS
Adams, George b: Grafton, Mass. BR/TR, 5'6", 175 lbs. Deb: 6/14/1879

YEAR	TM/L	G	AB	R	H	2B	3B	HR	RBI	BB	SO	AVG	OBP	SLG	PRO+	BR/A	SB	CS	SBR	FA	FR	G/POS	TPR
1879	Syr-N	4	13	0	3	0	0	0	0	0	1	.231	.286	.231	82	-0				1.000	-1	/O-2,1-2	-0.1

■ GLENN ADAMS
Adams, Glenn Charles b:10/4/47, Northbridge, Mass. BL/TR, 6', 185 lbs. Deb: 5/4/75

YEAR	TM/L	G	AB	R	H	2B	3B	HR	RBI	BB	SO	AVG	OBP	SLG	PRO+	BR/A	SB	CS	SBR	FA	FR	G/POS	TPR
1975	SF-N	61	90	10	27	2	1	4	15	11	25	.300	.382	.478	132	4	1	0	0	.941	-3	O-25	0.1
1976	SF-N	69	74	2	18	4	0	0	3	1	12	.243	.253	.297	54	-5	1	0	0	1.000	-0	O-6	-0.7
1977	Min-A	95	269	32	91	17	0	6	49	18	30	.338	.380	.468	132	12	0	2	-1	.969	-4	D-47,O-44	0.4
1978	Min-A	116	310	27	80	18	1	7	35	17	32	.258	.297	.390	90	-5	0	1	-1	1.000	-1	*D-101/O-5	-1.0
1979	Min-A	119	326	34	98	13	1	8	50	25	21	.301	.356	.420	104	-2	2	1	-1	.958	-8	D-55,O-53	-1.0
1980	Min-A	99	262	32	75	11	0	6	38	15	26	.286	.325	.412	94	-3	2	4	-2	.947	-3	D-81,O-12	-1.0
1981	Min-A	72	220	13	46	10	0	2	24	20	26	.209	.275	.282	57	-12	0	1	-1	.000	0	D-62	-1.6
1982	Tor-A	30	66	2	17	4	0	1	6	3	11	.258	.300	.364	74	-2	0	0	0	.000	0	D-27	-0.7
Total	8	661	1617	152	452	79	3	34	225	111	183	.280	.327	.398	96	-9	6	10	-4	.959	-20	D-373,O-145	-5.1

YEAR	TM/L	G	AB	R	H	2B	3B	HR	RBI	BB	SO	AVG	OBP	SLG	PRO+	BR/A	SB	CS	SBR	FA	FR	G/POS	TPR
■ **DOUG ADAMS**	Adams, Harold Douglas b: 1/27/43, Blue River, Wis. BL/TR, 6'3", 185 lbs. Deb: 9/8/69																						
1969	Chi-A	8	14	1	3	0	0	0	1	1	3	.214	.267	.214	34	-1	0	0	0	1.000	-1	/C-4	-0.2
■ **HERB ADAMS**	Adams, Herbert Loren b: 4/14/28, Hollywood, Cal. BL/TL, 5'9", 160 lbs. Deb: 9/17/48																						
1948	Chi-A	5	11	1	3	1	0	0	0	1	1	.273	.333	.364	88	-0	0	0	0	1.000	2	/O-4	0.1
1949	Chi-A	56	208	26	61	5	3	0	16	9	16	.293	.323	.346	79	-7	1	2	-1	.975	-0	O-48	-1.0
1950	Chi-A	34	118	12	24	2	3	0	2	12	7	.203	.288	.271	45	-10	3	0	1	.978	-1	O-33	-1.1
Total	3	95	337	39	88	8	6	0	18	22	24	.261	.310	.320	67	-17	4	2	0	.978	0	/O-85	-2.0
■ **JIM ADAMS**	Adams, James J. b: 1868, E.St.Louis, Ill. TR , Deb: 4/21/1890																						
1890	StL-a	1	4	0	1	0	0	0	0	0	0	.250	.250	.250	42	-0	0			1.000	-1	/C-1	-0.1
■ **BERT ADAMS**	Adams, John Bertram b: 6/21/1891, Wharton, Tex. d: 6/24/40, Los Angeles, Cal. BB/TR, 6'1", 185 lbs. Deb: 8/30/10																						
1910	Cle-A	5	13	1	3	0	0	0	0	0		.231	.231	.231	44	-1	0			.964	3	/C-5	0.3
1911	Cle-A	2	5	0	1	0	0	0	1	0		.200	.333	.200	50	-0	0			.900	-1	/C-2	-0.1
1912	Cle-A	20	54	5	11	2	1	0	6	4		.204	.259	.278	52	-4	0			.942	2	C-20	0.0
1915	Phi-N	24	27	1	3	0	0	0	2	2	3	.111	.172	.111	-13	-4	0			.974	-4	C-23/1-1	-0.8
1916	Phi-N	11	13	2	3	0	0	0	1	0	3	.231	.231	.231	40	-1	0			.929	1	C-11	0.0
1917	Phi-N	43	107	4	22	4	1	1	7	0	20	.206	.206	.290	49	-7	0			.994	1	C-38/1-1	-0.4
1918	Phi-N	84	227	10	40	4	0	0	12	10	26	.176	.214	.194	23	-21	5			.976	-1	C-76	-1.8
1919	Phi-N	78	232	14	54	7	2	1	16	7	27	.233	.252	.293	59	-12	4			.966	-2	C-73/1-1	-0.9
Total	8	267	678	37	137	17	4	2	45	23	79	.202	.229	.248	42	-48	9			.970	-2	C-248/1-3	-3.7
■ **DICK ADAMS**	Adams, Richard Leroy b: 4/8/20, Tuolumne, Cal. BR/TL, 6', 185 lbs. Deb: 5/20/47 F																						
1947	Phi-A	37	89	9	18	2	3	2	11	2	18	.202	.220	.360	58	-6	0	0	0	.995	0	1-24/O-3	-0.6
■ **RICKY ADAMS**	Adams, Ricky Lee b: 1/21/59, Upland, Cal. BR/TR, 6'2", 180 lbs. Deb: 9/15/82																						
1982	Cal-A	8	14	1	2	0	0	0	2	1	5	.143	.200	.143	-4	-2	1	0	0	.947	-1	/S-8	-0.2
1983	Cal-A	58	112	22	28	2	0	2	6	5	12	.250	.300	.321	72	-4	1	1	-0	.960	22	S-38,3-16/2-4	1.9
1985	SF-N	54	121	12	23	3	1	0	15	6	23	.190	.228	.281	44	-9	1	1	-0	.964	3	S-25,3-16/2-6	-0.5
Total	3	120	247	35	53	5	1	4	16	10	37	.215	.260	.291	54	-16	3	2	-0	.961	24	/S-71,3-32,2-10	1.2
■ **BOBBY ADAMS**	Adams, Robert Henry b: 12/14/21, Tuolumne, Cal. BR/TR, 5'10", 170 lbs. Deb: 4/16/46 FC																						
1946	Cin-N	94	311	35	76	13	3	4	24	18	32	.244	.292	.344	83	-8	16			.967	24	2-74/O-2,3-1	2.2
1947	Cin-N	81	217	39	59	11	2	4	20	25	23	.272	.358	.396	101	1	9			.967	14	2-69	1.8
1948	Cin-N	87	262	33	78	20	1	1	21	25	23	.298	.361	.408	112	4	6			.965	-12	2-64/3-7	-0.4
1949	Cin-N	107	277	32	70	16	2	0	25	26	36	.253	.317	.325	72	-11	4			.984	-9	2-63,3-14	-1.7
1950	Cin-N	115	348	57	98	21	8	3	26	43	29	.282	.361	.414	103	2	7			.981	-9	2-53,3-42	-1.2
1951	Cin-N	125	403	57	107	12	5	5	24	43	40	.266	.338	.357	86	-7	4	10	-5	.956	-10	3-60,2-42/O-1	-2.1
1952	Cin-N	154	637	85	180	25	4	6	48	49	67	.283	.334	.363	93	-6	11	9	-2	.962	9	*3-154	-0.2
1953	Cin-N	150	607	99	167	14	6	8	49	58	67	.275	.338	.357	81	-16	3	2	-0	.951	8	*3-150	-1.1
1954	Cin-N	110	390	69	105	25	6	3	23	55	46	.269	.364	.387	93	-3	2	5	-2	.951	1	3-93/2-2	-0.6
1955	Cin-N	64	150	23	41	11	2	2	20	20	21	.273	.370	.413	102	1	2	0	1	.969	3	3-42/2-5	0.5
	Chi-A	28	21	8	2	0	1	0	3	4	4	.095	.240	.190	16	-3	0	0	0	.933	5	/3-9,2-1	0.3
1956	Bal-A	41	111	19	25	6	1	0	7	25	15	.225	.368	.297	84	-2	1	1	-0	.984	-6	3-24,2-18	-0.6
1957	Chi-N	60	187	21	47	10	2	1	10	17	27	.251	.320	.342	79	-5	0	3	-2	.949	-8	3-47/2-1	-1.4
1958	Chi-N	62	96	14	27	4	0	4	6	15	15	.281	.324	.406	93	-1	2	0	1	.961	-2	1-11/3-9,2-7	-0.2
1959	Chi-N	3	2	0	0	0	0	0	0	0	1	.000	.000	.000	-99	-1	0	0	0	.667	-1	/1-1	-0.1
Total	14	1281	4019	591	1082	188	49	37	303	414	447	.269	.340	.368	90	-54	67	30		.955	10	3-652,2-399/1-12,O	-4.2
■ **BOB ADAMS**	Adams, Robert Melvin b: 1/6/52, Pittsburgh, Pa. BR/TR, 6'2", 200 lbs. Deb: 7/10/77																						
1977	Det-A	15	24	2	6	1	0	2	2	0	5	.250	.250	.542	103	-0	0	0	0	1.000	-0	/1-2,C-1	0.0
■ **MIKE ADAMS**	Adams, Robert Michael b: 7/24/48, Cincinnati, Ohio BR/TR, 5'9", 180 lbs. Deb: 9/10/72 F																						
1972	Min-A	3	6	0	2	0	0	0	0	0	1	.333	.333	.333	94	-0	0	0	0	1.000	-0	/O-1	0.0
1973	Min-A	55	66	21	14	2	0	3	6	17	18	.212	.381	.379	110	2	2	1	0	.978	-1	O-24/D-2	0.0
1976	Chi-N	25	29	1	4	2	0	0	2	8	7	.138	.342	.207	54	-1	0	0	0	1.000	-3	/O-4,3-3,2-1	-0.5
1977	Chi-N	2	2	0	0	0	0	0	0	0	1	.000	.000	.000	-90	-1	0	0	0	.000	-1	/O-2	-0.1
1978	Oak-A	15	15	5	3	1	0	0	1	7	2	.200	.455	.267	113	1	0	0	0	1.000	-1	/2-6,3-3,D-3	0.1
Total	5	100	118	27	23	5	0	3	9	32	29	.195	.375	.314	93	1	2	1	0	.980	-5	/O-31,2-7,3-6,D-5	-0.5
■ **SPENCER ADAMS**	Adams, Spencer Dewey b: 6/21/1898, Layton, Utah d: 11/24/70, Salt Lake City, Ut BL/TR, 5'9", 158 lbs. Deb: 5/8/23																						
1923	Pit-N	25	56	11	14	0	1	0	4	6	6	.250	.323	.286	60	-3	2	1	0	.879	-6	2-11/S-6	-0.8
1925	*Was-A	39	55	11	15	4	1	0	4	5	4	.273	.338	.382	83	-2	1	1	-0	.941	-2	2-15/S-8,3-3	-0.3
1926	*NY-A	28	25	7	3	1	0	0	1	3	7	.120	.214	.160	-1	-4	1	0	0	1.000	4	/2-4,3-1	0.1
1927	StL-A	88	259	32	69	11	3	0	29	24	33	.266	.333	.332	71	-11	1	8	-5	.948	1	2-54,3-28	-1.1
Total	4	180	395	61	101	16	5	0	38	38	50	.256	.324	.322	66	-19	5	10	-5	.944	-3	/2-84,3-32,S-14	-2.1
■ **JOE ADCOCK**	Adcock, Joseph Wilbur b: 10/30/27, Coushatta, La. BR/TR, 6'4", 220 lbs. Deb: 4/23/50 M																						
1950	Cin-N	102	372	46	109	16	6	8	55	24	24	.293	.336	.406	94	-4	2			.968	6	O-75,1-24	-0.2
1951	Cin-N	113	395	40	96	16	4	10	47	24	29	.243	.288	.380	77	-14	1	2	-1	.983	-0	*O-107	-1.8
1952	Cin-N	117	378	43	105	22	4	13	52	23	38	.278	.321	.460	115	6	1	4	-2	.985	-4	O-85,1-17	0.4
1953	Mil-N	157	590	71	168	33	6	18	80	42	82	.285	.334	.453	110	6	3	2	-0	.991	-4	*1-157	-0.5
1954	Mil-N	133	500	73	154	27	5	23	87	44	58	.308	.367	.520	137	25	1	4	-2	.995	-11	*1-133	0.5
1955	Mil-N	84	288	40	76	14	0	15	45	31	44	.264	.340	.469	118	7	0	2	-1	.990	-5	1-78	-0.4
1956	Mil-N	137	454	76	132	23	1	38	103	32	86	.291	.339	.597	**154**	31	1	0	0	**.995**	-6	*1-129	1.8
1957	*Mil-N	65	209	31	60	13	2	12	38	20	51	.287	.352	.541	146	13	0	0	0	.996	-3	1-56	0.6
1958	*Mil-N	105	320	40	88	15	1	19	54	21	63	.275	.322	.506	125	9	0	0	0	.989	-1	1-71,O-22	0.3
1959	Mil-N	115	404	53	118	19	2	25	76	32	77	.292	.344	.535	141	21	0	0	0	.998	10	1-89,O-21	2.5
1960	Mil-N★	138	514	55	153	21	4	25	91	46	86	.298	.357	.500	142	28	2	2	-1	**.993**	3	*1-136	1.9
1961	Mil-N	152	562	77	160	20	0	35	108	59	94	.285	.355	.507	133	25	2	1	0	**.993**	-5	*1-148	0.8
1962	Mil-N	121	391	48	97	12	1	29	78	50	91	.248	.335	.506	126	13	2	2	-1	**.997**	-4	*1-112	0.3
1963	Cle-A	97	283	28	71	7	1	13	49	30	53	.251	.323	.420	107	3	1	2	-1	.995	-4	1-78	-0.6
1964	LA-A	118	366	39	98	13	0	21	64	48	61	.268	.353	.475	142	20	0	2	-1	.993	-5	*1-105	1.0
1965	Cal-A	122	349	30	84	14	0	14	47	37	74	.241	.315	.401	104	2	0	2	-1	.997	1	1-97	-0.9
1966	Cal-A	83	231	33	63	10	3	18	48	31	48	.273	.359	.576	168	20	2	2	-1	.997	-0	1-71	1.6
Total	17	1959	6606	823	1832	295	35	336	1122	594	1059	.277	.339	.485	125	210	20	25		.994	-28	*1-1501,O-310	7.3
■ **BOB ADDIS**	Addis, Robert Gordon b: 11/6/25, Mineral, Ohio BL/TR, 6', 175 lbs. Deb: 9/1/50																						
1950	Bos-N	16	28	7	7	1	0	0	2	3	5	.250	.323	.286	66	-1	1			1.000	-2	/O-7	-0.3
1951	Bos-N	85	199	23	55	7	1	2	24	9	10	.276	.308	.327	76	-7	3	2	-0	.982	-0	O-46	-0.9
1952	Chi-N	93	292	38	86	13	2	1	20	23	30	.295	.346	.363	96	-1	4	4	-1	.988	-2	O-79	-0.8
1953	Chi-N	10	12	2	2	1	0	0	1	2	0	.167	.286	.250	40	-1	0	0	0	1.000	1	/O-3	0.0
	Pit-N	4	3	0	0	0	0	0	0	1	2	.000	.000	.000	-99	-1	0	0	0	.000	0	H	-0.1
	Yr	14	15	2	2	1	0	0	1	3	2	.133	.235	.200	15	-2	0	0	0	1.000	1	/O-3	-0.1
Total	4	208	534	70	150	22	2	2	47	37	47	.281	.327	.341	84	-12	8	6		.986	-3	O-135	-2.1
■ **JIM ADDUCI**	Adduci, James David b: 8/9/59, Chicago, Ill. BL/TL, 6'5", 200 lbs. Deb: 9/12/83																						
1983	StL-N	10	20	1	1	0	0	0	0	1	6	.050	.095	.050	-59	-4	0	0	0	1.000	0	/1-6,O-1	-0.5
1986	Mil-A	3	11	2	1	1	0	0	0	0	4	.091	.167	.182	-5	-2	0	0	0	1.000	0	/1-3	-0.2
1988	Mil-A	44	94	8	25	1	0	1	15	0	15	.266	.266	.383	79	-3	1	1		.969	-4	O-24,D-10/1-3	-0.8

YEAR	TM/L	G	AB	R	H	2B	3B	HR	RBI	BB	SO	AVG	OBP	SLG	PRO+	BR/A	SB	CS	SBR	FA	FR	G/POS	TPR
1989	Phi-N	13	19	1	7	1	0	0	0	0	4	.368	.368	.421	125	1	0	0	0	1.000	0	/1-4,O-1	0.1
Total	4	70	144	11	34	8	1	1	15	2	27	.236	.247	.326	58	-8	0	1	-1	.969	-3	/O-26,1-16,D-10	-1.4

■ BOB ADDY
Addy, Robert Edward "Magnet" b: 2/1845, Rochester, N.Y. d: 4/9/10, Pocatello, Idaho BL/TL, 5'8", 160 lbs. Deb: 5/6/1871 M

YEAR	TM/L	G	AB	R	H	2B	3B	HR	RBI	BB	SO	AVG	OBP	SLG	PRO+	BR/A	SB	CS	SBR	FA	FR	G/POS	TPR
1871	Rok-n	25	118	30	32	6	0	0	13	4	0	.271	.295	.322	81	-2	8	1	2	.768	1	*2-22/S-3	-0.1
1873	Phi-n	10	51	12	16	1	0	0	10	2	0	.314	.340	.333	97	-0	0	1	-1	.855	-4	2-10	-0.4
	Bos-n	31	152	37	54	5	2	1	36	1	0	.355	.359	.434	124	3	2	3	-1	.750	-2	O-31	0.1
	Yr	41	203	49	70	6	2	1	46	3	0	.345	.354	.409	118	3	2	4	-2	.750	-5	O-31,2-10	-0.3
1874	Har-n	50	213	25	51	9	2	0	23	1	0	.239	.243	.300	70	-8	4	2	0	.846	2	*2-45/3-5,S-1	-0.6
1875	Phi-n	69	310	60	80	8	4	0	43	0	2	.258	.258	.310	93	-3	16	8	0	.761	-0	*O-68/2-2,M	-0.2
1876	Chi-N	32	142	36	40	4	1	0	16	5	0	.282	.306	.324	98	-1				.800	0	O-32	-0.1
1877	Cin-N	57	245	27	68	2	3	0	31	6	5	.278	.295	.310	102	1				.805	5	*O-57/M	0.3
Total	4 n	185	844	164	233	29	8	1	125	8	2	.276	.283	.333	92	-10	30	15	4	.758	-2	/O-99,2-79,3-5,S-4	-1.2
Total	2	89	387	63	108	6	4	0	47	11	5	.279	.299	.315	100	0				.803	5	/O-89	0.2

■ MORRIE ADERHOLT
Aderholt, Morris Woodrow b: 9/13/15, Mt.Olive, N.C. d: 3/18/55, Sarasota, Fla. BL/TR, 6'1", 188 lbs. Deb: 9/13/39

YEAR	TM/L	G	AB	R	H	2B	3B	HR	RBI	BB	SO	AVG	OBP	SLG	PRO+	BR/A	SB	CS	SBR	FA	FR	G/POS	TPR
1939	Was-A	7	25	5	5	1	0	0	4	2	6	.200	.259	.320	51	-2	0	1	-1	.872	0	/2-7	-0.2
1940	Was-A	1	2	0	0	0	0	0	0	0	0	.000	.000	.000	-99	-1	0	0	0	1.000	0	/2-1	0.0
1941	Was-A	11	14	3	2	0	0	0	1	1	3	.143	.200	.143	-8	-2	0	0	0	.818	1	/2-2,3-1	-0.2
1944	Bro-N	17	59	9	16	2	3	0	10	4	4	.271	.317	.407	105	0	0			.871	-1	O-13	-0.1
1945	Bro-N	39	60	4	13	1	0	0	6	3	10	.217	.254	.233	36	-5	0			1.000	-2	O-8	-0.8
	Bos-N	31	102	15	34	4	0	2	11	9	6	.333	.387	.431	127	4	3			.984	0	O-24/2-1	0.3
	Yr	70	162	19	47	5	0	2	17	12	16	.290	.339	.358	94	-1	3			.985	-2	O-32/2-1	-0.5
Total	5	106	262	36	70	7	3	3	32	19	29	.267	.317	.351	85	-6	3	1	1	.949	-2	/O-45,2-11,3-1	-1.0

■ DICK ADKINS
Adkins, Richard Earl b: 3/3/20, Electra, Tex. d: 9/12/55, Electra, Tex. BR/TR, 5'10", 165 lbs. Deb: 9/19/42

YEAR	TM/L	G	AB	R	H	2B	3B	HR	RBI	BB	SO	AVG	OBP	SLG	PRO+	BR/A	SB	CS	SBR	FA	FR	G/POS	TPR
1942	Phi-A	3	7	2	1	0	0	0	2	1	1	.143	.333	.143	37	-0	0	0	0	.875	-1	/S-3	-0.2

■ HENRY ADKINSON
Adkinson, Henry Magee b: 9/1/1874, Chicago, Ill. d: 5/1/23, Salt Lake City, Ut. Deb: 9/25/1895

YEAR	TM/L	G	AB	R	H	2B	3B	HR	RBI	BB	SO	AVG	OBP	SLG	PRO+	BR/A	SB	CS	SBR	FA	FR	G/POS	TPR
1895	StL-N	1	5	1	2	0	0	0	0	0	0	.400	.400	.400	108	-0				.667	-0	/O-1	0.0

■ DAVE ADLESH
Adlesh, David George b: 7/15/43, Long Beach, Cal. BR/TR, 6', 187 lbs. Deb: 5/12/63

YEAR	TM/L	G	AB	R	H	2B	3B	HR	RBI	BB	SO	AVG	OBP	SLG	PRO+	BR/A	SB	CS	SBR	FA	FR	G/POS	TPR
1963	Hou-N	6	8	0	0	0	0	0	0	0	4	.000	.000	.000	-99	-2	0	0	0	.889	-2	/C-6	-0.4
1964	Hou-N	3	10	0	2	0	0	0	0	0	5	.200	.200	.200	14	-1	0	0	0	1.000	-1	/C-3	-0.2
1965	Hou-N	15	34	2	5	1	0	0	3	2	12	.147	.194	.176	13	-4	0	0	0	1.000	-1	C-13	-0.5
1966	Hou-N	3	6	0	0	0	0	0	0	0	4	.000	.000	.000	-99	-2	0	0	0	1.000	1	/C-1	-0.1
1967	Hou-N	39	94	4	17	1	0	1	4	11	28	.181	.267	.223	43	-7	0	0	0	.995	-3	C-31	-0.9
1968	Hou-N	40	104	3	19	1	1	0	4	5	27	.183	.227	.212	33	-8	0	0	0	.990	-3	C-36	-1.0
Total	6	106	256	9	43	3	1	1	11	18	80	.168	.228	.199	26	-24	0	0	0	.992	-8	/C-90	-3.1

■ TROY AFENIR
Afenir, Michael Troy b: 9/21/63, Escondido, Cal. BR/TR, 6'4", 185 lbs. Deb: 9/14/87

YEAR	TM/L	G	AB	R	H	2B	3B	HR	RBI	BB	SO	AVG	OBP	SLG	PRO+	BR/A	SB	CS	SBR	FA	FR	G/POS	TPR
1987	Hou-N	10	20	1	6	1	0	0	1	0	12	.300	.300	.350	74	-1	0	0	0	.974	-1	C-10	-0.1
1990	Oak-A	14	14	0	2	0	0	0	2	0	6	.143	.143	.143	-21	-2	0	0	0	1.000	-1	C-12/D-1	-0.3
1991	Oak-A	5	11	0	1	0	0	0	0	0	2	.091	.091	.091	-53	-2	0	0	0	1.000	1	/C-4,D-1	-0.1
1992	Cin-N	16	34	3	6	1	2	0	4	5	12	.176	.282	.324	69	-1	0	0	0	1.000	-3	C-15	-0.4
Total	4	45	79	4	15	2	2	0	7	5	32	.190	.238	.266	40	-7	0	0	0	.992	-4	/C-41,D-2	-0.9

■ TOMMIE AGEE
Agee, Tommie Lee b: 8/9/42, Magnolia, Ala. BR/TR, 5'11", 195 lbs. Deb: 9/14/62

YEAR	TM/L	G	AB	R	H	2B	3B	HR	RBI	BB	SO	AVG	OBP	SLG	PRO+	BR/A	SB	CS	SBR	FA	FR	G/POS	TPR
1962	Cle-A	5	14	0	3	0	0	0	2	0	4	.214	.214	.214	16	-2	0	0	0	1.000	-0	/O-3	-0.2
1963	Cle-A	13	27	3	4	1	0	1	3	2	9	.148	.207	.296	39	-2	0	0	0	1.000	-1	O-13	-0.4
1964	Cle-A	13	12	0	2	0	0	0	0	0	3	.167	.167	.167	-7	-2	0	0	0	1.000	0	O-12	-0.6
1965	Cle-A	10	19	2	3	1	0	0	3	2	6	.158	.238	.211	30	-2	0	1	-1	1.000	-2	/O-9	-0.5
1966	Chi-A★	160	629	98	172	27	8	22	86	41	127	.273	.328	.447	129	21	44	18	2	.982	11	*O-159	2.9
1967	Chi-A★	158	529	73	124	26	2	14	52	44	129	.234	.303	.371	102	0	28	10	2	.969	2	*O-152	-0.3
1968	NY-N	132	368	30	80	12	3	5	17	15	103	.217	.256	.307	68	-15	13	8	-1	.978	-10	*O-127	-3.6
1969	*NY-N	149	565	97	153	23	4	26	76	59	137	.271	.343	.464	121	15	12	9	-2	.986	6	*O-146	1.1
1970	NY-N	153	636	107	182	30	7	24	75	55	156	.286	.345	.469	115	12	31	15	0	.967	13	*O-150	1.7
1971	NY-N	113	425	58	121	19	0	14	50	50	84	.285	.363	.428	125	14	28	6	5	.978	5	*O-107	1.9
1972	NY-N	114	422	52	96	23	0	13	47	53	92	.227	.319	.374	99	-0	8	9	-3	.962	6	*O-109	-0.3
1973	Hou-N	83	204	30	48	5	2	8	15	16	55	.235	.294	.397	90	-3	2	5	-2	.983	-4	O-67	-1.3
	StL-N	26	62	8	11	3	1	3	7	5	13	.177	.239	.403	75	-2	1	0	0	.981	1	O-19	-0.2
	Yr	109	266	38	59	8	3	11	22	21	68	.222	.281	.398	87	-6	3	5	0	.982	-3	O-86	-1.5
Total	12	1129	3912	558	999	170	27	130	433	342	918	.255	.321	.412	108	35	167	81	2	.975	22	*O-1073	0.2

■ HARRY AGGANIS
Agganis, Harry "The Golden Greek" b: 4/20/29, Lynn, Mass. d: 6/27/55, Cambridge, Mass. BL/TL, 6'2", 200 lbs. Deb: 4/13/54

YEAR	TM/L	G	AB	R	H	2B	3B	HR	RBI	BB	SO	AVG	OBP	SLG	PRO+	BR/A	SB	CS	SBR	FA	FR	G/POS	TPR
1954	Bos-A	132	434	54	109	13	8	11	57	47	57	.251	.324	.394	86	-9	6	3	0	.990	7	*1-119	-0.8
1955	Bos-A	25	83	11	26	10	1	0	10	10	10	.313	.387	.458	116	2	2	0	1	.987	0	1-20	0.1
Total	2	157	517	65	135	23	9	11	67	57	67	.261	.334	.404	91	-7	8	3	1	.989	7	1-139	-0.7

■ JOE AGLER
Agler, Joseph Abram b: 6/12/1887, Coshocton, Ohio d: 4/26/71, Massillon, Ohio BL/TL, 5'11", 165 lbs. Deb: 10/1/12

YEAR	TM/L	G	AB	R	H	2B	3B	HR	RBI	BB	SO	AVG	OBP	SLG	PRO+	BR/A	SB	CS	SBR	FA	FR	G/POS	TPR
1912	Was-A	2	1	0	0	0	0	0	0	0	0	.000	.000	.000	-99	-0	0			.000	0	/1-1	0.0
1914	Buf-F	135	463	82	126	17	6	0	20	77	78	.272	.376	.335	93	-8	21			.985	5	1-76,O-54	-0.8
1915	Buf-F	25	73	11	13	1	2	0	2	20	14	.178	.355	.247	69	-3	2			.973	2	O-20/1-1	-0.7
	Bal-F	72	214	28	46	4	2	0	14	34	38	.215	.325	.252	62	-13	15			.981	5	1-58/O-4,2-3	-1.1
	Yr	97	287	39	59	5	4	0	16	54	52	.206	.333	.251	64	-16	17			.981	3	1-59,O-24/2-3	-1.8
Total	3	234	751	121	185	22	10	0	36	131	130	.246	.359	.302	81	-25	38			.983	7	1-136/O-78,2-3	-2.6

■ SAM AGNEW
Agnew, Samuel Lester "Slam" b: 4/12/1887, Farmington, Mo. d: 7/19/51, Sonoma, Cal. BR/TR, 5'11", 185 lbs. Deb: 4/10/13

YEAR	TM/L	G	AB	R	H	2B	3B	HR	RBI	BB	SO	AVG	OBP	SLG	PRO+	BR/A	SB	CS	SBR	FA	FR	G/POS	TPR
1913	StL-A	105	307	27	64	9	5	2	24	20	49	.208	.272	.290	66	-14	11			.952	2	*C-103	-0.3
1914	StL-A	115	311	22	66	5	4	0	16	24	63	.212	.279	.254	63	-14	10	8	-2	.961	3	*C-115	-0.5
1915	StL-A	104	295	18	60	4	2	0	19	12	36	.203	.247	.231	45	-21	5	2	0	.934	5	*C-102	-0.8
1916	Bos-A	40	67	4	14	2	1	0	7	6	4	.209	.293	.269	69	-3				.952	0	C-38	0.8
1917	Bos-A	85	260	17	54	6	2	0	16	19	30	.208	.267	.246	57	-13	2			.965	-10	C-85	-1.9
1918	*Bos-A	72	199	11	33	8	0	0	6	11	26	.166	.241	.206	29	-17	0			.965	11	C-72	-0.2
1919	Was-A	42	98	6	23	7	0	0	10	10	8	.235	.312	.306	74	-3	1			.974	5	C-36	0.7
Total	7	563	1537	105	314	41	14	2	98	102	216	.204	.265	.253	56	-85	29	10		.955	26	C-551	-2.2

■ LUIS AGUAYO
Aguayo, Luis (Muriel) b: 3/13/59, Vega Baja, P.R. BR/TR, 5'9", 185 lbs. Deb: 4/19/80

YEAR	TM/L	G	AB	R	H	2B	3B	HR	RBI	BB	SO	AVG	OBP	SLG	PRO+	BR/A	SB	CS	SBR	FA	FR	G/POS	TPR
1980	Phi-N	20	47	7	13	1	2	1	8	2	3	.277	.306	.447	102	-0	1	1	-0	.962	1	2-14/S-5	0.2
1981	*Phi-N	45	84	11	18	4	0	1	7	6	15	.214	.283	.298	62	-4	1	0	0	.938	-4	S-21/3-3	-0.7
1982	Phi-N	50	56	11	15	1	2	3	7	5	7	.268	.339	.518	133	2	1	1	-0	.966	5	2-21,S-15/3-5	0.6
1983	Phi-N	2	4	1	1	0	0	0	1	2	2	.250	.400	.250	85	-0	0	0	0	1.000	-2	/S-2	-0.2
1984	Phi-N	58	72	15	20	4	0	3	11	8	16	.278	.350	.458	123	2	0	0	0	.909	-8	3-14,2-12,S-10	1.0
1985	Phi-N	91	165	27	46	7	5	6	21	22	26	.279	.383	.467	133	8	1	0	0	.957	-5	S-60,2-17/3-7	1.6
1986	Phi-N	62	133	17	28	4	3	8	21	8	26	.211	.271	.361	70	-6	1	1	-0	.967	-7	2-31,S-20/3-1	-1.1
1987	Phi-N	94	209	25	43	9	1	12	21	15	56	.206	.275	.431	81	-7	0	0	0	.971	-9	S-78/2-6,3-2	-1.1
1988	Phi-N	49	97	9	24	3	0	5	13	12	17	.247	.336	.371	101	0	2	0	1	.967	-4	S-27,3-13/2-2	0.5
	NY-A	50	140	12	35	4	0	7	13	7	34	.250	.291	.343	77	-2	0	1	-0	.961	-3	3-33,2-13/S-6	-0.7
1989	Cle-A	47	97	7	17	4	1	1	8	7	19	.175	.245	.268	44	-7	0	0	0	.950	-1	3-19,S-15,2-10/D-2	-0.1
Total	10	568	1104	142	260	43	10	37	109	94	220	.236	.307	.393	91	-16	7	5	-1	.960	-2	S-259,2-147/3-97,D	-0.0

YEAR	TM/L	G	AB	R	H	2B	3B	HR	RBI	BB	SO	AVG	OBP	SLG	PRO+	BR/A	SB	CS	SBR	FA	FR	G/POS	TPR

■ CHARLIE AHEARN   Ahearn, Charles   b: Troy, N.Y.   Deb: 6/19/1880

| 1880 | Tro-N | 1 | 4 | 1 | 1 | 0 | 0 | 0 | 0 | 0 | 0 | .250 | .250 | .250 | 67 | -0 | | | | .778 | -0 | /C-1 | 0.0 |

■ WILLIE AIKENS   Aikens, Willie Mays   b: 10/14/54, Seneca, S.C.   BL/TR, 6'3", 220 lbs.   Deb: 5/17/77

1977	Cal-A	42	91	5	18	4	0	0	6	10	23	.198	.277	.242	45	-7	1	2	-1	.971	0	1-13,D-13	-0.9
1979	Cal-A	116	379	59	106	18	0	21	81	61	79	.280	.381	.493	138	21	1	3	-2	.996	-2	1-55,D-51	1.3
1980	*KC-A	151	543	70	151	24	0	20	98	64	88	.278	.362	.433	116	13	1	0	0	.990	-9	*1-138,D-13	-0.4
1981	*KC-A	101	349	45	93	16	0	17	53	62	47	.266	.382	.458	142	21	0	0	0	.992	-5	1-99	1.0
1982	KC-A	134	466	50	131	29	1	17	74	45	70	.281	.348	.457	119	12	0	1	-1	.994	-3	*1-128	0.1
1983	KC-A	125	410	49	124	26	1	23	72	45	75	.302	.374	.539	148	26	0	0	0	.989	-5	*1-112/D-6	1.5
1984	Tor-A	93	234	21	48	7	0	11	26	29	56	.205	.298	.376	82	-6	0	0	0	1.000	0	D-81/1-2	-0.8
1985	Tor-A	12	20	2	4	1	0	0	5	3	6	.200	.304	.400	89	-0	0	0	0	.000	0	D-11	-0.1
Total	8	774	2492	301	675	125	2	110	415	319	444	.271	.358	.455	123	80	3	6	-3	.991	-24	1-547,D-175	1.7

■ DANNY AINGE   Ainge, Daniel Ray   b: 3/17/59, Eugene, Ore.   BR/TR, 6'4", 175 lbs.   Deb: 5/21/79

1979	Tor-A	87	308	26	73	7	1	2	19	12	58	.237	.270	.286	50	-22	1	0	0	.977	-4	2-86/D-1	-1.9
1980	Tor-A	38	111	11	27	6	1	0	4	2	29	.243	.263	.315	55	-7	3	0	1	.986	2	O-29/3-3,2-1,D-2	-0.5
1981	Tor-A	86	246	20	46	6	2	0	14	23	41	.187	.259	.228	39	-19	8	5	-1	.949	1	3-77/S-6,O-4,2-2,D	-2.1
Total	3	211	665	57	146	19	4	2	37	37	128	.220	.265	.269	47	-48	12	5	1	.977	-1	/2-89,3-80,O-33,SD	-4.5

■ EDDIE AINSMITH   Ainsmith, Edward Wilbur "Dorf"   b: 2/4/1892, Cambridge, Mass.   d: 9/6/81, Ft.Lauderdale, Fla   BR/TR, 5'11", 180 lbs.   Deb: 8/9/10

1910	Was-A	33	104	4	20	1	2	0		9	6	.192	.236	.240	52	-6	0			.963	-4	C-30	-0.8
1911	Was-A	61	149	12	33	2	3	0	14	10		.221	.275	.275	55	-9	5			.952	0	C-47	-0.5
1912	Was-A	61	186	22	42	7	2	0	22	14		.226	.280	.285	61	-10	4			.958	15	C-59	1.1
1913	Was-A	84	229	26	49	4	4	2	20	12	41	.214	.262	.293	61	-12	17			.967	6	C-79/P-1	0.0
1914	Was-A	62	151	11	34	7	0	0	13	9	28	.225	.273	.272	61	-7	8	5	-1	.969	4	C-51	0.4
1915	Was-A	47	120	13	24	4	2	0	6	10	18	.200	.267	.267	59	-6	7	4	-0	.988	6	C-42	0.2
1916	Was-A	51	100	11	17	4	0	0	8	8	14	.170	.231	.210	33	-8	3			.959	13	C-46	0.7
1917	Was-A	125	350	38	67	17	4	0	42	40	48	.191	.280	.263	66	-14	16			.971	15	*C-119	1.1
1918	Was-A	96	292	22	62	10	9	0	20	29	44	.212	.283	.308	80	-8	6			.975	8	C-89	0.8
1919	Det-A	114	364	42	99	17	12	3	32	45	30	.272	.354	.409	117	8	9			.962	-11	*C-106	0.7
1920	Det-A	69	186	19	43	5	3	1	19	14	19	.231	.285	.306	58	-11	4	3	-1	.955	-2	C-61/1-1	-1.1
1921	Det-A	35	98	6	27	5	2	0	12	13	7	.276	.360	.367	87	-2	1	0	0	.947	-4	C-34	-0.3
	StL-N	27	62	5	18	0	1	0	5	3	4	.290	.323	.323	73	-2	0	0	0	.956	1	*C-23/1-1	0.0
1922	StL-N	119	379	46	111	14	4	13	59	28	43	.293	.343	.454	109	4	2	3	-1	.963	-2	*C-116	0.6
1923	StL-N	82	263	22	56	11	6	3	34	22	19	.213	.276	.335	62	-15	4	0	1	.980	-8	C-80	-1.8
	Bro-N	2	10	0	2	0	0	0	2	0	0	.200	.200	.200	6	-1	0	1	-1	1.000	1	/C-2	-0.1
	Yr	84	273	22	58	11	6	3	36	22	19	.212	.274	.330	60	-17	4	1	0	.981	-7	C-82	-1.9
1924	NY-N	10	5	0	3	0	0	0	0	0	0	.600	.600	.600	229	0	0	0	0	1.000	-0	/C-9	0.1
Total	15	1078	3048	299	707	108	54	22	317	263	315	.232	.296	.324	76	-100	86	16		.966	41	C-993/1-2,P-1	1.1

■ GEORGE AITON   Aiton, George Wilson   b: 12/29/1890, Kingman, Kan.   d: 8/16/76, Van Nuys, Cal.   BB/TR, 5'11.5", 175 lbs.   Deb: 6/29/12

| 1912 | StL-A | 10 | 17 | 1 | 4 | 0 | 0 | 0 | 1 | 4 | | .235 | .381 | .235 | 80 | -0 | 0 | | | .917 | -0 | /O-7 | -0.1 |

■ JOHN AKE   Ake, John Leckie   b: 8/29/1861, Altoona, Pa.   d: 5/11/1887, LaCrosse, Wis.   BR/TR, 6'1", 180 lbs.   Deb: 5/12/1884

| 1884 | Bal-a | 13 | 52 | 1 | 10 | 0 | 1 | 0 | | 2 | 0 | .192 | .208 | .231 | 41 | -3 | | | | .677 | -3 | /3-9,O-3,S-1 | -0.6 |

■ BILL AKERS   Akers, William G. "Bump"   b: 12/25/04, Chattanooga, Tenn.   d: 4/13/62, Chattanooga, Tenn.   BR/TR, 5'11", 178 lbs.   Deb: 9/8/29

1929	Det-A	24	83	15	22	4	1	1	9	10	9	.265	.351	.373	86	-2	2	0	1	.935	-9	S-24	-0.6
1930	Det-A	85	233	36	65	8	5	9	40	36	34	.279	.375	.472	111	4	5	5	-2	.944	9	S-49,3-26	1.6
1931	Det-A	29	66	5	13	2	2	0	3	7	6	.197	.274	.288	46	-5	0	1	-1	.935	-2	S-21/2-2	-0.6
1932	Bos-N	36	93	8	24	3	1	1	17	10	15	.258	.330	.344	85	-2	0	0	0	.927	-5	3-20/2-5,S-5	-0.5
Total	4	174	475	64	124	17	9	11	69	63	64	.261	.349	.404	93	-4	7	6		.936	-6	/S-99,3-46,2-7	-0.1

■ GUS ALBERTS   Alberts, Augustus Peter   b: 1861, Reading, Pa.   d: 5/7/12, Idaho Springs, Colo   BR/TR, 5'6.5", 180 lbs.   Deb: 5/1/1884

1884	Pit-a	2	5	1	1	0	0	0		0		.200	.200	.200	30	-0				.500	-1	/S-2	-0.2
	Was-U	4	16	4	4	0	0	0		0	4	.250	.400	.250	105	-0				.870	2	/S-4	0.2
1888	Cle-a	102	364	51	75	10	6	1	48	41		.206	.299	.275	87	-4	26			.862	4	S-53,3-49	0.3
1891	Mil-a	12	41	6	4	0	0	0	2	5		.098	.260	.098	2	-6	1			.814	-3	3-12	-0.7
Total	3	120	426	62	84	10	6	1	50	52	5	.197	.298	.256	76	-10	27			.880	2	/3-61,S-59	-0.4

■ BUTCH ALBERTS   Alberts, Francis Burt   b: 5/4/50, Williamsport, Pa.   BR/TR, 6'2", 205 lbs.   Deb: 9/7/78

| 1978 | Tor-A | 6 | 18 | 1 | 5 | 1 | 0 | 0 | 0 | 0 | 2 | .278 | .278 | .333 | 70 | -1 | 0 | 0 | 0 | .000 | 0 | /D-4 | -0.1 |

■ JACK ALBRIGHT   Albright, Harold John   b: 6/30/21, St.Petersburg, Fla.   d: 7/22/91, San Diego, Cal.   BR/TR, 5'9", 175 lbs.   Deb: 5/19/47

| 1947 | Phi-N | 41 | 99 | 9 | 23 | 4 | 0 | 2 | 10 | 5 | 11 | .232 | .303 | .333 | 71 | -4 | 1 | | | .943 | 3 | S-33 | 0.0 |

■ LUIS ALCARAZ   Alcaraz, Angel Luis (Acosta)   b: 6/20/41, Humacao, P.R.   BR/TR, 5'9", 165 lbs.   Deb: 9/13/67

1967	LA-N	17	60	1	14	1	0	0	3	1	13	.233	.246	.250	46	-4	1	1	-0	.990	9	2-17	0.5
1968	LA-N	41	106	4	16	1	0	2	5	9	23	.151	.217	.217	33	-9	1	1	-0	.979	3	2-20,3-13/S-1	-0.5
1969	KC-A	22	79	15	20	2	1	2	7	7	9	.253	.314	.342	83	-2	0	0	0	.988	-5	2-19/3-2,S-1	-0.5
1970	KC-A	35	120	10	20	5	1	1	14	4	13	.167	.194	.250	21	-13	0	0	0	.993	-8	2-31	-2.0
Total	4	115	365	30	70	9	2	4	29	21	58	.192	.236	.260	43	-28	2	2	-1	.988	-1	/2-87,3-15,S-2	-2.5

■ SCOTTY ALCOCK   Alcock, John Forbes   b: 11/29/1885, Wooster, Ohio   d: 1/30/73, Wooster, Ohio   BR/TR, 5'9.5", 160 lbs.   Deb: 4/19/14

| 1914 | Chi-A | 54 | 156 | 12 | 27 | 4 | 2 | 0 | 7 | 14 | | .173 | .213 | .224 | 32 | -13 | 4 | 2 | 0 | .905 | 4 | 3-48/2-1 | -0.9 |

■ MIKE ALDRETE   Aldrete, Michael Peter   b: 1/29/61, Carmel, Cal.   BL/TL, 5'11", 185 lbs.   Deb: 5/28/86

1986	SF-N	84	216	27	54	18	0	2	25	33	34	.250	.355	.389	110	4	1	3	-2	1.000	3	1-37,O-31	0.2
1987	*SF-N	126	357	50	116	18	2	9	51	43	50	.325	.398	.462	133	18	6	0	2	.986	-2	O-79,1-33	1.4
1988	SF-N	139	389	44	104	15	0	3	50	56	65	.267	.360	.329	103	-4	6	5	-1	.982	-7	*O-115,1-10	-0.9
1989	Mon-N	76	136	12	30	8	0	1	12	19	30	.221	.321	.316	81	-3	1	3	-2	.980	-3	O-37,1-10	-0.9
1990	Mon-N	96	161	22	39	7	1	1	18	37	31	.242	.387	.317	100	2	1	1	-1	.982	-4	O-38,1-18	-0.4
1991	SD-N	12	15	2	0	0	0	0	1	3	4	.000	.167	.000	-48	-3	0	1	-1	1.000	0	/O-5	-0.4
	Cle-A	85	183	22	48	6	1	1	19	36	37	.262	.384	.322	97	1	1	2	-1	.994	-3	1-47,O-16/D-7	-0.5
1993	Oak-A	95	255	40	68	13	1	10	33	34	45	.267	.353	.443	120	7	1	1	0	.995	-3	1-59,O-20/D-6	0.0
1994	Oak-A	76	178	23	43	5	0	4	18	20	35	.242	.318	.337	76	-6	2	0	1	1.000	0	O-35,1-27/D-1	-1.5
1995	Oak-A	60	125	18	34	8	0	4	21	19	23	.272	.372	.432	115	3	0	0	0	.989	-6	1-35,O-16	-0.5
	Cal-A	18	24	1	6	0	0	0	3	0	9	.250	.250	.250	31	-2	0	0	0	1.000	1	/O-2,1-1,D-2	-0.1
	Yr	78	149	19	40	8	0	4	24	19	31	.268	.355	.403	101	0	0	0	0	.989	-5	1-36,O-18/D-2	-0.7
1996	Cal-A	31	40	5	6	0	0	3	8	5	14	.150	.244	.400	60	-3	0	0	0	.750	-3	/O-6,1-1,D-6	-0.4
	*NY-A	32	68	11	17	6	0	1	9	9	15	.250	.338	.456	96	-1	0	1	-1	1.000	-3	/O-9,1-8,P-1,D-9	-0.5
	Yr	63	108	16	23	6	0	6	20	14	19	.213	.303	.435	84	-3	0	1	-1	.917	-5	O-15,D-15/1-9,P-1	-0.9
Total	10	930	2147	277	565	104	9	41	271	314	381	.263	.358	.377	104	20	19	18	-5	.983	-36	O-409,1-286/D-31,P	-4.6

■ CHUCK ALENO   Aleno, Charles   b: 2/19/17, St.Louis, Mo.   BR/TR, 6'1.5", 215 lbs.   Deb: 5/15/41

1941	Cin-N	54	169	23	41	8	11	1	16	16		.243	.289	.337	76	-6	3			.975	-4	3-40/1-2	-0.9
1942	Cin-N	7	14	1	2	1	0	0	2	1	0	.143	.294	.214	50	-0	1			.727	1	/3-2,2-1	0.1
1943	Cin-N	7	10	0	3	0	0	0	1	2	1	.300	.417	.300	110	0	0			1.000	0	/O-2	0.0
1944	Cin-N	50	127	10	21	3	1	1	15	15	15	.165	.259	.213	35	-11	0			.952	-4	3-42/1-3,S-3	-1.5
Total	4	118	320	34	67	11	3	2	34	34	35	.209	.281	.281	60	-17	3			.954	-7	/3-84,1-5,S-3,O2	-2.3

YEAR	TM/L	G	AB	R	H	2B	3B	HR	RBI	BB	SO	AVG	OBP	SLG	PRO+	BR/A	SB	CS	SBR	FA	FR	G/POS	TPR

■ **DALE ALEXANDER**   Alexander, David Dale "Moose"   b: 4/26/03, Greeneville, Tenn.   d: 3/2/79, Greeneville, Tenn.   BR/TR, 6'3", 210 lbs.   Deb: 4/16/29

1929	Det-A	155	626	110	**215**	43	15	25	137	56	63	.343	.397	.580	148	42	5	9	-4	.988	-4	*1-155	1.7
1930	Det-A	154	602	86	196	33	8	20	135	42	56	.326	.372	.507	118	15	6	5	-1	.985	-7	*1-154	-0.7
1931	Det-A	135	517	75	168	47	3	3	87	64	35	.325	.401	.445	118	15	5	8	-3	.987	-8	*1-126/O-4	-0.8
1932	Det-A	23	16	0	4	0	0	0	4	6	2	.250	.455	.250	84	0	0	0	0	1.000	-0	/1-2	0.0
	Bos-A	101	376	58	140	27	3	8	56	55	19	.372	.454	.524	157	34	4	5	-2	.992	2	*1-101	2.4
	Yr	124	392	58	144	27	3	8	60	61	21	**.367**	.454	.513	152	33	4	5	-2	.992	2	*1-103	2.4
1933	Bos-A	94	313	40	88	14	1	5	40	25	22	.281	.336	.380	90	-5	0	1	-1	.992	3	1-79	-0.9
Total	5	662	2450	369	811	164	30	61	459	248	197	.331	.394	.497	128	102	20	28	-11	.988	-14	1-617/O-4	1.7

■ **GARY ALEXANDER**   Alexander, Gary Wayne   b: 3/27/53, Los Angeles, Cal.   BR/TR, 6'2", 200 lbs.   Deb: 9/12/75

1975	SF-N	3	3	1	0	0	0	0	0	1	2	.000	.250	.000	-25	-0	0	0	0	1.000	-1	/C-2	-0.1
1976	SF-N	23	73	12	13	1	1	2	7	10	16	.178	.277	.301	62	-4	1	0	0	.964	-4	C-23	-0.7
1977	SF-N	51	119	17	36	4	2	5	20	20	33	.303	.411	.496	143	8	3	1	0	.968	-8	C-33/O-1	0.1
1978	Oak-A	58	174	18	36	6	1	10	22	22	66	.207	.299	.425	107	1	0	3	-2	1.000	0	D-45/O-6,C-1,1-1	-0.2
	Cle-A	90	324	39	76	14	3	17	62	35	100	.235	.311	.454	114	5	0	2	-1	.983	-9	C-66,D-25	-0.5
	Yr	148	498	57	112	20	4	27	84	57	166	.225	.307	.444	112	6	0	5	-3	.983	-9	D-70,C-67/O-6,1-1	-0.7
1979	Cle-A	110	358	54	82	9	2	15	54	46	100	.229	.319	.391	90	-5	4	2	0	.961	-21	C-91,D-13/O-2	-2.3
1980	Cle-A	76	178	22	40	7	1	5	31	17	52	.225	.292	.360	77	-6	0	4	-2	.971	-2	D-40,C-13/O-2	-1.1
1981	Pit-N	21	47	6	10	4	1	1	6	3	12	.213	.260	.404	84	-1	0	0	0	.964	1	/1-9,O-8	-0.1
Total	7	432	1276	169	293	45	11	55	202	154	381	.230	.315	.411	99	-3	8	12	-5	.969	-42	C-229,D-123/O-19,1	-4.9

■ **HUGH ALEXANDER**   Alexander, Hugh   b: 7/10/17, Buffalo, Mo.   BR/TR, 6', 190 lbs.   Deb: 8/15/37

1937	Cle-A	7	11	0	1	0	0	0	0	0	5	.091	.091	.091	-54	-3	1	0	0	.667	-2	/O-3	-0.4

■ **MANNY ALEXANDER**   Alexander, Manuel De Jesus (b: Manuel De Jesus (Alexander))   b: 3/20/71, San Pedro De Macoris, D.R.   BR/TR, 5'10", 150 lbs.   Deb: 9/18/92

1992	Bal-A	4	5	1	1	0	0	0	0	0	3	.200	.200	.200	12	-1	0	0	0	1.000	1	/S-3	0.0
1993	Bal-A	3	0	1	0	0	0	0	0	0	0	—	—	—		0	0	0	0	.000	0	/R	0.0
1995	Bal-A	94	242	35	57	9	1	3	23	20	30	.236	.299	.318	60	-14	11	4	1	.971	-4	2-81/S-7,3-2,D-1	-1.3
1996	*Bal-A	54	68	6	7	0	0	0	4	3	27	.103	.141	.103	-38	-14	3	3	-1	.940	7	S-21/2-7,3-7,OPD	-0.7
Total	4	155	315	43	65	9	1	3	27	23	60	.206	.265	.270	38	-29	14	7	0	.972	3	/2-88,S-31,3-9,ODP	-2.0

■ **MATT ALEXANDER**   Alexander, Matthew   b: 1/30/47, Shreveport, La.   BB/TR, 5'11", 169 lbs.   Deb: 8/23/73

1973	Chi-N	12	5	4	1	0	0	0	1	1	1	.200	.333	.200	48	-0	2	0	1	1.000	-1	/O-3	-0.1
1974	Chi-N	45	54	15	11	2	1	0	0	12	12	.204	.358	.278	76	-1	8	4	0	.921	-2	3-19/O-4,2-2	-0.3
1975	Oak-A	63	10	16	1	0	0	0	1	0	5	.100	.182	.100	-19	-2	17	10	-1	1.000	-3	D-17,O-11/2-3,3-2	-0.6
1976	Oak-A	61	30	16	1	0	0	0	0	0	5	.033	.033	.033	-84	-7	20	7	2	1.000	-7	O-23,D-19	-1.4
1977	Oak-A	90	42	24	10	1	0	0	2	4	6	.238	.304	.262	57	-2	26	14	-1	1.000	-11	O-31,S-12/2-4,3D	-1.4
1978	Pit-N	7	0	2	0	0	0	0	0	0	0	—	—	—		0	4	1	1	1.000	0	R	0.0
1979	*Pit-N	44	13	16	7	0	1	0	0	0	1	.538	.538	.692	223	2	13	1	3	1.000	-3	O-11/S-1	0.2
1980	Pit-N	37	3	13	1	1	0	0	0	0	1	.333	.333	.667	170	0	10	3	1	1.000	-1	/O-4,2-1	0.1
1981	Pit-N	15	11	5	4	0	0	0	1	0	0	.364	.364	.364	104	0	3	2	-0	1.000	-1	/O-6	-0.2
Total	9	374	168	111	36	4	2	0	4	18	26	.214	.294	.262	56	-10	103	42	6	1.000	-29	/O-93,D-37,3-22,S2	-3.7

■ **WALT ALEXANDER**   Alexander, Walter Ernest   b: 3/5/1891, Atlanta, Ga.   d: 12/29/78, Fort Worth, Tex.   BR/TR, 5'10.5", 165 lbs.   Deb: 6/21/12

1912	StL-A	37	97	5	17	4	0	0	5	8		.175	.245	.216	34	-8	1			.969	-3	C-37	-0.8
1913	StL-A	43	110	5	15	2	1	0	7	4	36	.136	.174	.173	2	-14	1			.947	4	C-43	-0.8
1915	StL-A	1	1	0	0	0	0	0	0	0	0	.000	.000	.000	-99	-0	0			.000	0	/C-1	0.0
	NY-A	25	68	7	17	4	0	1	5	13	16	.250	.370	.353	117	2	2	1	0	.967	9	C-24	1.3
	Yr	26	69	7	17	4	0	1	5	13	16	.246	.366	.348	114	2	2	1	0	.967	9	C-25	1.3
1916	NY-A	36	78	8	20	6	1	0	3	13	20	.256	.376	.359	118	2	0			.960	2	C-27	0.6
1917	NY-A	20	51	1	7	2	1	0	4	4	11	.137	.200	.216	27	-5	1			.951	0	C-20	-0.4
Total	5	162	405	26	76	18	3	1	24	42	83	.188	.271	.254	56	-23	5	1		.959	11	C-152	-0.1

■ **NIN ALEXANDER**   Alexander, William Henry   b: 11/24/1858, Pana, Ill.   d: 12/22/33, Pana, Ill.   BR/TR, 5'4.5", 163 lbs.   Deb: 6/7/1884

1884	KC-U	19	65	2	9	0	0	0		1		.138	.152	.138	-13	-11				.907	-2	C-17/S-2,O-2	-1.0
	StL-a	1	4	0	0	0	0	0		0		.000	.000	.000	-97	-1				.667	-0	/C-1,O-1	-0.1
Total	1	20	69	2	9	0	0	0		1	19	.130	.143	.130	-19	-12				.895	-2	/C-18,O-3,S-2	-1.1

■ **EDGARDO ALFONZO**   Alfonzo, Edgardo Antonio   b: 8/11/73, Santa Teresa, Venez.   BR/TR, 5'11", 185 lbs.   Deb: 4/26/95

1995	NY-N	101	335	26	93	13	5	4	41	12	37	.278	.305	.382	82	-9	1	1	-0	.962	-6	3-58,2-29/S-6	-1.4
1996	NY-N	123	368	36	96	15	2	4	40	25	56	.261	.308	.345	77	-13	2	0	1	.974	-2	2-66,3-36,S-15	-0.9
Total	2	224	703	62	189	28	7	8	81	37	93	.269	.306	.363	80	-22	3	1	0	.977	-8	/2-95,3-94,S-21	-2.3

■ **LUIS ALICEA**   Alicea, Luis Rene (De Jesus)   b: 7/29/65, Santurce, P.R.   BB/TR, 5'9", 165 lbs.   Deb: 4/23/88

1988	StL-N	93	297	20	63	10	4	1	24	25	32	.212	.278	.283	61	-15	1	1	-0	.970	4	2-91	-0.9
1991	StL-N	56	68	5	13	3	0	0	0	8	19	.191	.276	.235	45	-5	0	1	-1	1.000	-1	2-11/3-2,S-1	-0.7
1992	StL-N	85	265	26	65	9	11	2	32	27	40	.245	.324	.385	103	1	2	5	-2	.989	2	2-75/S-4	0.2
1993	StL-N	115	362	50	101	19	3	3	46	47	54	.279	.368	.373	101	2	11	1	3	.978	2	2-96/O-4,3-1	0.9
1994	StL-N	88	205	32	57	12	5	5	29	30	38	.278	.378	.459	119	6	4	0	2	.986	4	2-53/O-2	1.0
1995	*Bos-A	132	419	64	113	20	3	6	44	63	61	.270	.374	.375	93	-3	13	10	-2	.977	12	*2-132	1.5
1996	*StL-N	129	380	54	98	26	3	5	42	52	78	.258	.355	.382	94	-2	11	3	2	.957	-22	*2-125	-1.5
Total	7	698	1996	251	510	99	29	22	217	252	322	.256	.346	.367	92	-15	42	26	-3	.975	3	2-583/O-6,S-5,3-3	0.5

■ **ANDY ALLANSON**   Allanson, Andrew Neal   b: 12/22/61, Richmond, Va.   BR/TR, 6'5", 225 lbs.   Deb: 4/7/86

1986	Cle-A	101	293	30	66	7	3	1	29	14	36	.225	.263	.280	49	-21	10	1	2	.960	-7	C-99	-2.0
1987	Cle-A	50	154	17	41	6	0	3	16	9	30	.266	.307	.364	76	-5	1	1	-0	.986	-7	C-50	-0.9
1988	Cle-A	133	434	44	114	11	0	5	50	25	63	.263	.307	.323	75	-14	5	9	-4	.986	1	*C-133	-0.8
1989	Cle-A	111	323	30	75	9	1	3	17	23	47	.232	.291	.294	64	-15	4	4	-1	.986	3	*C-111	-0.7
1991	Det-A	60	151	10	35	10	0	1	16	7	31	.232	.266	.318	60	-8	0	1	-1	.979	6	C-56/1-2,D-1	-0.1
1992	Mil-A	9	25	6	8	1	0	0	2	1	2	.320	.346	.360	100	-0	3	1	0	.943	-2	/C-9	-0.1
1993	SF-N	13	24	3	4	1	0	0	2	1	2	.167	.200	.208	10	-3	0	0	0	1.000	-1	/C-8,1-2	-0.4
1995	Cal-A	35	82	5	14	3	0	3	25	5	12	.171	.244	.317	45	-7	0	1	-1	.994	6	C-35	0.0
Total	8	512	1486	145	357	48	4	16	140	87	223	.240	.286	.310	64	-74	23	18	-6	.980	-1	C-501/1-4,D-1	-5.0

■ **NICK ALLEN**   Allen, Artemus Ward   b: 9/14/1888, Norton, Kan.   d: 10/16/39, Hines, Ill.   BR/TR, 6', 180 lbs.   Deb: 5/1/14

1914	Buf-F	32	63	3	15	1	0	0	4	3	12	.238	.273	.254	43	-6	3			.969	2	C-26	-0.3
1915	Buf-F	84	215	14	44	7	1	0	17	18	34	.205	.269	.247	45	-19	4			.956	7	C-80	-0.7
1916	Chi-N	5	16	1	1	0	0	0	1	0	3	.063	.063	.063	-56	-3	0			.958	-1	/C-4	-0.4
1918	Cin-N	37	96	6	25	2	0	0	5	4	7	.260	.297	.323	91	-1	0			.950	8	C-31	0.9
1919	Cin-N	15	25	7	8	1	0	0	5	2	6	.320	.393	.400	142	1	0			.958	3	C-12	0.5
1920	Cin-N	43	85	10	23	1	0	0	4	6	11	.271	.340	.329	94	-0	0			.961	6	C-36	0.8
Total	6	216	500	41	116	13	1	0	36	33	73	.232	.288	.278	62	-28	8	0		.958	25	C-189	0.8

■ **BERNIE ALLEN**   Allen, Bernard Keith   b: 4/16/39, E.Liverpool, O.   BL/TR, 6', 185 lbs.   Deb: 4/10/62

1962	Min-A	159	573	79	154	27	7	12	64	62	82	.269	.340	.403	96	-3	0	1	-1	.983	-17	*2-158	-0.4
1963	Min-A	139	421	52	101	20	1	9	43	38	52	.240	.340	.356	83	-10	0	0	-0	.976	-24	*2-128	-2.5
1964	Min-A	74	243	28	52	8	1	6	20	33	30	.214	.310	.329	78	-7	1	2	-1	.979	-11	2-71	-1.4
1965	Min-A	19	39	2	9	2	0	0	6	6	12	.231	.333	.282	73	-1	0	0	0	1.000	-2	2-10/3-1	-0.2
1966	Min-A	101	319	34	76	18	1	5	30	26	40	.238	.300	.348	80	-8	2	3	-1	.974	-7	2-89/3-2	-1.1
1967	Was-A	87	254	13	49	3	1	8	18	18	43	.193	.246	.256	56	-16	1	1	-1	.990	19	2-75	0.7

YEAR	TM/L	G	AB	R	H	2B	3B	HR	RBI	BB	SO	AVG	OBP	SLG	PRO+	BR/A	SB	CS	SBR	FA	FR	G/POS	TPR
1968	Was-A	120	373	31	90	12	4	6	40	28	35	.241	.301	.343	98	-1	2	0	1	**.991**	5	*2-110/3-2	1.1
1969	Was-A	122	365	33	90	17	4	9	45	50	35	.247	.337	.389	108	4	5	4	-1	.974	3	*2-110/3-6	1.5
1970	Was-A	104	261	31	61	7	1	8	29	43	21	.234	.342	.360	99	0	0	2	-1	.969	-11	2-80,3-12	0.4
1971	Was-A	97	229	18	61	11	1	4	22	33	27	.266	.359	.376	115	5	2	1	0	.961	-11	2-41,3-34	-0.4
1972	NY-A	84	220	26	50	9	0	9	21	23	42	.227	.300	.391	108	2	0	1	-1	.940	2	3-44,2-20	0.1
1973	NY-A	17	57	5	13	3	0	0	4	5	5	.228	.290	.281	64	-3	0	0	0	.985	0	2-13/D-2	-0.2
	Mon-N	16	50	5	9	1	0	2	9	5	6	.180	.255	.320	56	-3	0	0	0	.970	-1	/2-9,3-8	-0.4
Total	12	1139	3404	357	815	140	21	73	351	370	424	.239	.315	.357	91	-41	13	16	-6	.980	-47	2-914,3-109/D-2	-2.8

■ JACK ALLEN
Allen, Cyrus Alban   b: 10/2/1855, Woodstock, Ill.   d: 4/21/15, Girard, Pa.   BR/TR, 160 lbs.   Deb: 5/1/1879

YEAR	TM/L	G	AB	R	H	2B	3B	HR	RBI	BB	SO	AVG	OBP	SLG	PRO+	BR/A	SB	CS	SBR	FA	FR	G/POS	TPR
1879	Syr-N	11	48	7	9	2	1	0	3	1	5	.188	.204	.271	62	-2				.655	-6	/3-8,O-3	-0.7
	Cle-N	16	60	7	7	1	1	0	4	1	9	.117	.131	.167	-3	-6				.845	3	3-14/O-2	-0.3
	Yr	27	108	14	16	3	2	0	7	2	14	.148	.164	.213	24	-8				.790	-3	3-22/O-5	-1.0

■ ETHAN ALLEN
Allen, Ethan Nathan   b: 1/1/04, Cincinnati, Ohio   d: 9/15/93, Brookings, Ore.   BR/TR, 6'1", 180 lbs.   Deb: 6/21/26

YEAR	TM/L	G	AB	R	H	2B	3B	HR	RBI	BB	SO	AVG	OBP	SLG	PRO+	BR/A	SB	CS	SBR	FA	FR	G/POS	TPR
1926	Cin-N	18	13	3	4	1	0	0	0	0	3	.308	.308	.385	88	-0				1.000	-3	/O-9	-0.3
1927	Cin-N	111	359	54	106	26	4	2	20	14	23	.295	.325	.407	98	-2	12			.988	-2	O-98	-1.0
1928	Cin-N	129	485	55	148	30	7	1	62	27	29	.305	.343	.402	96	-4	6			.981	3	*O-129	-1.0
1929	Cin-N	143	538	69	157	27	11	6	64	20	21	.292	.317	.416	84	-16	21			**.988**	-10	*O-137	-3.2
1930	Cin-N	21	46	10	10	1	0	3	7	5	2	.217	.294	.435	77	-2	1			.969	-4	O-15	-0.4
	NY-N	76	238	48	73	9	2	7	31	12	23	.307	.340	.450	91	-4	5			.985	-4	O-62	-1.1
	Yr	97	284	58	83	10	2	10	38	17	25	.292	.332	.447	89	-6	6			.981	-6	O-77	-1.5
1931	NY-N	94	298	58	98	18	2	5	43	15	15	.329	.363	.453	121	8	6			.975	-7	O-77	-0.3
1932	NY-N	54	103	13	18	6	2	1	7	1	12	.175	.198	.301	33	-10				.957	-4	O-24	-1.5
1933	StL-N	91	261	25	63	7	3	0	36	13	22	.241	.280	.291	60	-13	3			.984	8	O-67	-0.9
1934	Phi-N	145	581	87	192	**42**	4	10	85	33	47	.330	.370	.468	108	6	6			.978	9	*O-145	0.8
1935	Phi-N	156	645	90	198	46	1	8	63	43	54	.307	.351	.419	96	-4	5			.980	17	*O-156	0.6
1936	Phi-N	30	125	21	37	3	1	1	9	4	8	.296	.318	.360	75	-5	4			.954	-0	O-30	-0.6
	Chi-N	91	373	47	110	18	6	3	39	13	30	.295	.322	.399	91	-5	12			.980	-2	O-89	-1.1
	Yr	121	498	68	147	21	7	4	48	17	38	.295	.321	.390	87	-10	16			.972	-3	*O-119	-1.7
1937	StL-A	103	320	39	101	18	1	0	31	21	17	.316	.360	.378	86	-7	3	4	-2	.980	-1	O-78	-1.1
1938	StL-A	19	33	4	10	3	1	0	4	2	4	.303	.343	.455	98	-0	0	0	0	1.000	-1	/O-7	-0.2
Total	13	1281	4418	623	1325	255	45	47	501	223	310	.300	.336	.410	92	-58	84			.981	-0	*O-1123	-11.3

■ SLED ALLEN
Allen, Fletcher Manson   b: 8/23/1886, West Plains, Mo.   d: 10/16/59, Lubbock, Tex.   BR/TR, 6'1", 180 lbs.   Deb: 5/4/10

YEAR	TM/L	G	AB	R	H	2B	3B	HR	RBI	BB	SO	AVG	OBP	SLG	PRO+	BR/A	SB	CS	SBR	FA	FR	G/POS	TPR
1910	StL-A	14	23	3	3	1	0	0	1	1	1	.130	.231	.174	29	-2	0			.903	-6	C-12/1-1	-0.8

■ HANK ALLEN
Allen, Harold Andrew   b: 7/23/40, Wampum, Pa.   BR/TR, 6', 190 lbs.   Deb: 9/9/66   F

YEAR	TM/L	G	AB	R	H	2B	3B	HR	RBI	BB	SO	AVG	OBP	SLG	PRO+	BR/A	SB	CS	SBR	FA	FR	G/POS	TPR
1966	Was-A	9	31	2	12	0	0	1	6	3	6	.387	.441	.484	167	3	0	0	0	.917	0	/O-9	0.2
1967	Was-A	116	292	34	68	8	4	3	17	13	53	.233	.266	.318	75	-10	3	4	-2	.980	-21	O-99	-4.1
1968	Was-A	68	128	16	28	2	2	1	9	7	16	.219	.265	.289	70	-5	0	0	0	.895	-8	O-25,3-16,2-11	-1.5
1969	Was-A	109	271	42	75	9	3	1	17	13	28	.277	.312	.343	88	-5	12	3	2	.933	-17	O-91/3-6,2-3	-2.5
1970	Was-A	22	38	3	8	2	0	0	4	5	9	.211	.302	.263	60	-2	0	0	0	1.000	-0	O-17	-0.6
	Mil-A	28	61	4	14	4	0	0	4	7	5	.230	.309	.295	67	-3	0	0	-1	1.000	-1	O-14/2-5,1-4	-0.5
	Yr	50	99	7	22	6	0	0	8	12	14	.222	.306	.283	65	-5	0	0	-1	1.000	-4	O-31/2-5,1-4	-1.1
1972	Chi-A	9	21	1	3	0	0	0	0	0	2	.143	.143	.143	-15	-3	0	0	0	.905	3	/3-6	0.0
1973	Chi-A	28	39	2	4	2	0	0	0	1	9	.103	.125	.154	-21	-6	0	1	-1	1.000	-0	/3-9,1-8,O-5,C-1,2	-0.8
Total	7	389	881	104	212	27	9	6	57	49	128	.241	.282	.312	74	-31	15	9	-1	.957	-48	O-260/3-37,2-20,1C	-9.8

■ HEZEKIAH ALLEN
Allen, Hezekiah "Ki"   b: 2/25/1863, Westport, Conn.   d: 9/21/16, Saugatuck, Conn.   5'11", 160 lbs.   Deb: 5/16/1884

YEAR	TM/L	G	AB	R	H	2B	3B	HR	RBI	BB	SO	AVG	OBP	SLG	PRO+	BR/A	SB	CS	SBR	FA	FR	G/POS	TPR
1884	Phi-N	1	3	0	2	0	0	0	0	0	0	.667	.667	.667	337	1				1.000	-1	/C-1	0.0

■ HAM ALLEN
Allen, Homer S.   b: 8/1854, Hamden, Conn.   d: 1/7/1892, Hamden, Conn.   Deb: 4/27/1872

YEAR	TM/L	G	AB	R	H	2B	3B	HR	RBI	BB	SO	AVG	OBP	SLG	PRO+	BR/A	SB	CS	SBR	FA	FR	G/POS	TPR
1872	Man-n	16	66	8	18	1	0	0	7	0	1	.273	.273	.288	77	-1	0	0	0	.750	6	/O-9,S-8	0.3

■ HORACE ALLEN
Allen, Horace Tanner "Pug"   b: 6/11/1899, DeLand, Fla.   d: 7/5/81, Canton, N.C.   BL/TR, 6', 187 lbs.   Deb: 6/15/19

YEAR	TM/L	G	AB	R	H	2B	3B	HR	RBI	BB	SO	AVG	OBP	SLG	PRO+	BR/A	SB	CS	SBR	FA	FR	G/POS	TPR
1919	Bro-N	4	7	0	0	0	0	0	0	0	2	.000	.000	.000	-98	-2	0			1.000	0	/O-2	-0.2

■ JAMIE ALLEN
Allen, James Bradley   b: 5/29/58, Yakima, Wash.   BR/TR, 6', 205 lbs.   Deb: 5/1/83

YEAR	TM/L	G	AB	R	H	2B	3B	HR	RBI	BB	SO	AVG	OBP	SLG	PRO+	BR/A	SB	CS	SBR	FA	FR	G/POS	TPR
1983	Sea-A	86	273	23	61	10	4	0	21	33	52	.223	.309	.304	67	-12	6	5	-1	.959	-6	3-82/D-2	-2.0

■ PETE ALLEN
Allen, Jesse Hall   b: 5/1/1868, Columbiana, Ohio   d: 4/16/46, Philadelphia, Pa.   BR/TR, 5'8.5", 185 lbs.   Deb: 8/4/1893

YEAR	TM/L	G	AB	R	H	2B	3B	HR	RBI	BB	SO	AVG	OBP	SLG	PRO+	BR/A	SB	CS	SBR	FA	FR	G/POS	TPR
1893	Cle-N	1	4	0	0	0	0	0	0	0	0	.000	.000	.000	-94	-1				1.000	-1	/C-1	-0.2

■ KIM ALLEN
Allen, Kim Bryant   b: 4/5/53, Fontana, Cal.   BR/TR, 5'11", 175 lbs.   Deb: 9/2/80

YEAR	TM/L	G	AB	R	H	2B	3B	HR	RBI	BB	SO	AVG	OBP	SLG	PRO+	BR/A	SB	CS	SBR	FA	FR	G/POS	TPR
1980	Sea-A	23	51	9	12	3	0	0	3	8	3	.235	.350	.294	78	-1	10	3	1	.970	-2	2-15/O-4,S-1	-0.2
1981	Sea-A	19	3	1	0	0	0	0	0	0	0	.000	.000	.000	-96	-1	2	1	0	.000	-1	/2-2,O-2,D-2	-0.2
Total	2	42	54	10	12	3	0	0	3	8	5	.222	.333	.278	69	-2	12	4	1	.970	-4	/2-17,O-6,D-2,S-1	-0.4

■ MYRON ALLEN
Allen, Myron Smith "Zeke"   b: 3/22/1854, Kingston, N.Y.   d: 3/8/24, Kingston, N.Y.   BR/TR, 5'8", 150 lbs.   Deb: 7/19/1883

YEAR	TM/L	G	AB	R	H	2B	3B	HR	RBI	BB	SO	AVG	OBP	SLG	PRO+	BR/A	SB	CS	SBR	FA	FR	G/POS	TPR
1883	NY-N	1	4	0	0	0	0	0	1	0	2	.000	.000	.000	-99	-1				1.000	-0	/P-1	0.0
1886	Bos-N	1	3	0	0	0	0	0	0	0		.000	.000	.000	-99	-1				1.000	-0	/2-1	-0.1
1887	Cle-a	117	463	66	128	22	10	4	77	36		.276	.335	.393	106	3	26			.894	8	*O-115/3-3,S-2,P-2	0.8
1888	KC-a	37	136	23	29	6	4	0	10	9		.213	.267	.316	81	-3	4			.931	7	O-35/P-2	0.2
Total	4	156	606	89	157	28	14	4	88	45	3	.259	.317	.371	99	-2	30			.903	15	O-150/P-5,3-3,S2	0.9

■ DICK ALLEN
Allen, Richard Anthony   b: 3/8/42, Wampum, Pa.   BR/TR, 5'11", 190 lbs.   Deb: 9/3/63   F

YEAR	TM/L	G	AB	R	H	2B	3B	HR	RBI	BB	SO	AVG	OBP	SLG	PRO+	BR/A	SB	CS	SBR	FA	FR	G/POS	TPR
1963	Phi-N	10	24	6	7	2	1	0	2	0	5	.292	.292	.458	114	0	0	0	0	.833	-1	/O-7,3-1	-0.1
1964	Phi-N	162	632	**125**	201	38	**13**	29	91	67	138	.318	.383	.557	163	52	3	4	-2	.921	7	*3-162	5.8
1965	Phi-N★	161	619	93	187	31	14	20	85	74	150	.302	.378	.494	146	38	15	2	3	.943	-2	3-160/S-2	3.7
1966	Phi-N★	141	524	112	166	25	10	40	110	68	136	.317	.398	**.632**	181	57	10	6	-1	.967	-8	3-91,O-47	4.5
1967	Phi-N★	122	463	89	142	31	10	23	77	75	117	.307	**.404**	.566	173	45	20	5	3	.908	-6	*3-121/2-1,S-1	4.4
1968	Phi-N	152	521	87	137	17	9	33	90	74	161	.263	.356	.520	160	38	7	7	-2	.973	-5	*O-139,3-10	2.7
1969	Phi-N	118	438	79	126	23	3	32	89	64	144	.288	.378	.573	168	38	9	3	1	.985	-9	*1-117	2.1
1970	StL-N★	122	459	88	128	17	5	34	101	71	118	.279	.378	.560	145	28	4	4	-1	.993	-12	1-79,3-38/O-3	0.9
1971	LA-N	155	549	82	162	24	1	23	90	93	100	.295	.398	.468	154	41	8	1	2	.918	-3	3-67,O-60,1-28	3.1
1972	Chi-A★	148	506	90	156	28	5	**37**	**113**	**99**	126	.308	**.422**	**.603**	**199**	**64**	19	8	1	.995	-4	1-143/3-2	5.4
1973	Chi-A†	72	250	39	79	20	3	16	41	33	51	.316	.398	.612	175	24	7	2	1	.994	0	1-67/2-2,D-1	2.0
1974	Chi-A★	128	462	84	139	23	1	**32**	88	57	80	.301	.379	**.563**	164	37	7	1	2	.986	-11	*1-125/2-1,D-1	2.0
1975	Phi-N	119	416	54	97	21	3	12	62	58	109	.233	.330	.385	94	-3	11	2	2	.982	-1	*1-113	-1.0
1976	*Phi-N	85	298	52	80	16	1	15	49	37	63	.268	.349	.480	130	11	11	4	1	.989	-3	1-85	0.3
1977	Oak-A	54	171	19	41	4	0	5	31	24	36	.240	.337	.351	89	-2	1	3	2	.984	2	1-50/D-1	-0.5
Total	15	1749	6332	1099	1848	320	79	351	1119	894	1556	.292	.381	.534	156	469	133	52	9	.989	-62	1-807,3-652,O/2DS	35.3

■ BOB ALLEN
Allen, Robert (b: Alvah Charles Elliott)   b: 10/13/1894, Muscoda, Wis.   d: 12/18/75, Naperville, Ill.   BR/TR, 5'10", 180 lbs.   Deb: 8/20/19

YEAR	TM/L	G	AB	R	H	2B	3B	HR	RBI	BB	SO	AVG	OBP	SLG	PRO+	BR/A	SB	CS	SBR	FA	FR	G/POS	TPR
1919	Phi-A	9	22	3	3	1	0	0	3	7		.136	.269	.182	27	-2	0			.889	-2	/O-6	-0.5

■ BOB ALLEN
Allen, Robert Gilman   b: 7/10/1867, Marion, Ohio   d: 5/14/43, Little Rock, Ark.   BR/TR, 5'11", 175 lbs.   Deb: 4/19/1890   M

YEAR	TM/L	G	AB	R	H	2B	3B	HR	RBI	BB	SO	AVG	OBP	SLG	PRO+	BR/A	SB	CS	SBR	FA	FR	G/POS	TPR
1890	Phi-N	133	456	69	103	15	11	2	57	87	54	.226	.356	.320	95	-0	13			.924	**39**	*S-133/M	4.0
1891	Phi-N	118	438	46	97	7	4	1	51	43	64	.221	.291	.250	60	-22	12			.896	13	*S-118	-0.2
1892	Phi-N	152	563	77	128	20	14	2	64	61	60	.227	.304	.323	90	-7	15			.919	18	*S-152	1.6
1893	Phi-N	124	471	86	126	19	12	8	90	71	40	.268	.369	.410	107	5	8			.919	18	*S-124	2.4

YEAR	TM/L	G	AB	R	H	2B	3B	HR	RBI	BB	SO	AVG	OBP	SLG	PRO+	BR/A	SB	CS	SBR	FA	FR	G/POS	TPR
1894	Phi-N	40	149	26	38	10	3	0	19	17	11	.255	.335	.362	70	-7	4			.915	-2	S-40	-0.6
1897	Bos-N	34	119	33	38	5	0	1	24	18		.319	.409	.387	104	1	1			.924	8	S-32/O-1,2-1	0.8
1900	Cin-N	5	15	0	2	1	0	0	1	0		.133	.188	.200	7	-2	0			.864	-0	/S-5,M	-0.2
Total	7	606	2211	337	532	77	44	14	306	297	209	.241	.334	.334	88	-33	53			.915	93	S-604/2-1,O-1	7.8

■ ROD ALLEN   Allen, Roderick Bernet b: 10/5/59, Los Angeles, Cal. BR/TR, 6'1", 185 lbs. Deb: 4/7/83

YEAR	TM/L	G	AB	R	H	2B	3B	HR	RBI	BB	SO	AVG	OBP	SLG	PRO+	BR/A	SB	CS	SBR	FA	FR	G/POS	TPR
1983	Sea-A	11	12	1	2	0	0	0	0	0	1	.167	.167	.167	-8	-2	0	0	0	1.000	0	/O-2,D-3	-0.2
1984	Det-A	15	27	6	8	1	0	0	3	2	8	.296	.367	.333	96	-0	1	0	0	1.000	-0	D-11/O-2	0.0
1988	Cle-A	5	11	1	1	1	0	0	0	0	2	.091	.091	.182	-25	-2	0	0	0	.000	0	/D-4	-0.2
Total	3	31	50	8	11	2	0	0	3	2	11	.220	.264	.260	45	-4	1	0	0	1.000	-0	/D-18,O-4	-0.4

■ RON ALLEN   Allen, Ronald Frederick b: 12/23/43, Wampum, Pa. BB/TR, 6'3", 205 lbs. Deb: 8/11/72 F

YEAR	TM/L	G	AB	R	H	2B	3B	HR	RBI	BB	SO	AVG	OBP	SLG	PRO+	BR/A	SB	CS	SBR	FA	FR	G/POS	TPR
1972	StL-N	7	11	2	1	0	0	0	1	1	5	.091	.286	.364	84	-0	0	0	0	.968	-0	/1-5	-0.1

■ GARY ALLENSON   Allenson, Gary Martin b: 2/4/55, Culver City, Cal. BR/TR, 5'11", 185 lbs. Deb: 4/8/79 C

YEAR	TM/L	G	AB	R	H	2B	3B	HR	RBI	BB	SO	AVG	OBP	SLG	PRO+	BR/A	SB	CS	SBR	FA	FR	G/POS	TPR
1979	Bos-A	108	241	27	49	10	2	3	22	20	42	.203	.267	.299	50	-17	1	1	-0	.980	9	*C-104/3-3	-0.6
1980	Bos-A	36	70	9	25	6	0	0	10	13	11	.357	.458	.443	141	5	2	2	-1	.981	4	C-24/3-5,D-6	0.9
1981	Bos-A	47	139	23	31	8	0	5	25	23	33	.223	.337	.388	102	1	0	0	0	.969	1	C-47	0.3
1982	Bos-A	92	264	25	54	11	0	6	33	38	39	.205	.307	.314	67	-11	0	3	-2	.992	8	C-91	-0.2
1983	Bos-A	84	230	19	53	11	0	3	30	27	43	.230	.317	.317	70	-9	0	1	-1	.984	4	C-84	-0.2
1984	Bos-A	35	83	9	19	2	0	2	8	9	14	.229	.304	.325	71	-3	0	0	0	.987	0	C-35	-0.2
1985	Tor-A	14	34	2	4	1	0	0	3	0	10	.118	.118	.147	-27	-6	0	0	0	1.000	-2	C-14	-0.7
Total	7	416	1061	114	235	49	2	19	131	130	192	.221	.309	.325	71	-41	3	7	-3	.984	25	C-399/3-8,D-6	-0.7

■ JERMAINE ALLENSWORTH   Allensworth, Jermaine Lamont b: 1/11/72, Anderson, Ind. BR/TR, 6', 189 lbs. Deb: 7/23/96

YEAR	TM/L	G	AB	R	H	2B	3B	HR	RBI	BB	SO	AVG	OBP	SLG	PRO+	BR/A	SB	CS	SBR	FA	FR	G/POS	TPR
1996	Pit-N	61	229	32	60	9	3	4	31	23	50	.262	.340	.380	87	-4	11	6	-0	.979	4	O-61	-0.2

■ GENE ALLEY   Alley, Leonard Eugene b: 7/10/40, Richmond, Va. BR/TR, 6', 165 lbs. Deb: 9/4/63

YEAR	TM/L	G	AB	R	H	2B	3B	HR	RBI	BB	SO	AVG	OBP	SLG	PRO+	BR/A	SB	CS	SBR	FA	FR	G/POS	TPR
1963	Pit-N	17	51	3	11	1	0	0	2	2	12	.216	.245	.235	39	-4	0	1	-1	.947	1	/3-7,2-4,S-4	-0.3
1964	Pit-N	81	209	30	44	3	1	6	13	21	56	.211	.289	.321	72	-8	0	1	-1	.966	24	S-61/3-3,2-1	2.0
1965	Pit-N	153	500	47	126	21	6	5	47	32	82	.252	.302	.348	82	-12	7	2	1	.968	**30**	*S-110,2-40/3-1	3.0
1966	Pit-N	147	579	88	173	28	10	7	43	27	83	.299	.336	.418	108	6	8	8	-2	.979	13	*S-143	3.1
1967	Pit-N★	152	550	59	158	25	7	6	55	36	70	.287	.339	.391	108	6	10	5	0	.967	8	*S-146	3.0
1968	Pit-N†	133	474	48	116	20	2	4	39	39	78	.245	.309	.321	91	-5	13	5	1	.974	26	*S-109,2-24	3.8
1969	Pit-N	82	285	28	70	3	2	8	32	19	48	.246	.295	.354	83	-7	4	0	1	.977	7	2-53,S-25/3-5	0.8
1970	*Pit-N	121	426	46	104	16	5	8	41	31	70	.244	.300	.362	78	-14	7	3	0	.975	34	*S-108/2-8,3-2	3.2
1971	*Pit-N	114	348	38	79	8	7	6	28	35	43	.227	.298	.342	81	-9	9	2	2	.958	-16	*S-108/3-1	-1.1
1972	*Pit-N	119	347	30	86	12	2	3	36	38	52	.248	.322	.320	85	-6	4	3	-1	.970	-5	*S-114/3-4	0.3
1973	Pit-N	76	158	25	32	3	2	2	8	20	28	.203	.292	.285	62	-8	1	0	0	.981	4	S-49/3-8	0.2
Total	11	1195	3927	442	999	140	44	55	342	300	622	.254	.312	.354	88	-62	63	30	1	.970	125	S-977,2-130/3-31	18.0

■ GAIR ALLIE   Allie, Gair Roosevelt b: 10/28/31, Statesville, N.C. BR/TR, 6'1", 190 lbs. Deb: 4/13/54

YEAR	TM/L	G	AB	R	H	2B	3B	HR	RBI	BB	SO	AVG	OBP	SLG	PRO+	BR/A	SB	CS	SBR	FA	FR	G/POS	TPR
1954	Pit-N	121	418	38	83	8	6	3	30	56	84	.199	.296	.268	49	-31	1	1	-0	.952	-16	S-95,3-19	-4.0

■ BOB ALLIETTA   Allietta, Robert George b: 5/1/52, New Bedford, Mass. BR/TR, 6', 190 lbs. Deb: 5/6/75

YEAR	TM/L	G	AB	R	H	2B	3B	HR	RBI	BB	SO	AVG	OBP	SLG	PRO+	BR/A	SB	CS	SBR	FA	FR	G/POS	TPR
1975	Cal-A	21	45	4	8	1	0	1	2	1	6	.178	.196	.267	32	-4	0	0	0	1.000	2	C-21	-0.2

■ ANDY ALLISON   Allison, Andrew K. b: 1848, New York, N.Y. 5'10", 150 lbs. Deb: 5/7/1872

YEAR	TM/L	G	AB	R	H	2B	3B	HR	RBI	BB	SO	AVG	OBP	SLG	PRO+	BR/A	SB	CS	SBR	FA	FR	G/POS	TPR
1872	Eck-n	24	93	11	15	3	0	0	9	0	3	.161	.161	.194	10	-8	0	0	0	.913	-2	1-22/O-1,M	-0.6

■ ART ALLISON   Allison, Arthur Algernon b: 1/29/1849, Philadelphia, Pa. d: 2/25/16, Washington, D.C. 5'8", 150 lbs. Deb: 5/4/1871 F

YEAR	TM/L	G	AB	R	H	2B	3B	HR	RBI	BB	SO	AVG	OBP	SLG	PRO+	BR/A	SB	CS	SBR	FA	FR	G/POS	TPR
1871	Cle-n	29	137	28	40	4	5	0	19	2	5	.292	.302	.394	104	1	3	1	0	.885	1	*O-29/2-2	0.3
1872	Cle-n	19	87	13	23	4	0	0	8	0	2	.264	.264	.310	81	-2	0	0	0	.804	0	O-19	0.0
1873	Res-n	23	99	12	32	2	0	0	11	0	0	.323	.323	.343	106	1	0	0	0	.848	1	O-21/1-3,C-1	0.0
1875	Was-n	26	112	18	24	3	1	0	3	1	2	.214	.221	.259	69	-3	6	0	2	.924	-3	1-23/O-3,C-1	-0.4
	Har-n	40	175	26	42	4	1	1	19	0	3	.240	.240	.291	80	-4	1	2	-1	.785	-2	O-37/2-2,C-1,1-1	-0.1
	Yr	66	287	44	66	7	2	1	22	1	5	.230	.233	.279	76	-7	7	2	1	.800	1	O-40,1-24/C-2,2-2	-0.5
1876	Lou-N	31	130	9	27	2	1	0	10	2	6	.208	.220	.238	45	-9				.789	6	O-23/1-8	-0.3
Total	4 n	137	610	97	161	17	7	1	60	3	12	.264	.268	.320	88	-6	10	3	1	.833	1	O-109/1-27,2-4,C-3	-0.2

■ DOUG ALLISON   Allison, Douglas L. b: 7/1845, Philadelphia, Pa. d: 12/19/16, Washington, D.C. BR/TR, 5'10.5", 160 lbs. Deb: 5/5/1871 F

YEAR	TM/L	G	AB	R	H	2B	3B	HR	RBI	BB	SO	AVG	OBP	SLG	PRO+	BR/A	SB	CS	SBR	FA	FR	G/POS	TPR
1871	Oly-n	27	133	28	44	10	2	2	27	0	2	.331	.331	.481	137	7	1	1	-0	.806	-3	*C-27	0.2
1872	Tro-n	23	115	23	35	4	2	0	20	1	3	.304	.310	.374	108	1	1	1	-0	.897	6	C-22/S-1	0.4
	Eck-n	18	79	18	27	2	1	0	5	1	2	.342	.350	.392	151	6	0	0	0	.837	-8	C-18	-0.2
	Yr	41	194	41	62	6	3	0	25	2	5	.320	.327	.381	124	6	1	1	-0	.874	-2	C-40/S-1	0.2
1873	Res-n	19	83	11	24	5	0	0	8	0	0	.289	.289	.349	96	0	0	0	0	.810	-0	C-18/O-3,M	-0.2
	Mut-n	11	48	6	10	0	0	0	3	1	0	.208	.224	.208	30	-4	0	0	0	.868	1	C-11/O-1	-0.2
	Yr	30	131	17	34	5	0	0	11	1	0	.260	.265	.298	71	-4	0	0	0	.837	1	C-29/O-4	-0.2
1874	Mut-n	65	318	60	90	5	7	0	28	6	5	.283	.296	.336	99	-1	1	0	0	.800	-5	*O-47,C-34/2-1	-0.3
1875	Har-n	61	269	38	67	7	0	0	21	6	3	.249	.265	.275	84	-5	2	0	1	**.896**	17	*C-59/1-2,O-2	1.3
1876	Har-N	44	163	19	43	4	0	0	15	3	9	.264	.277	.288	82	-4				**.881**	11	C-40/O-6	0.7
1877	Har-N	29	115	14	17	0	2	0	6	3	7	.148	.169	.165	7	-11				.896	2	C-29	-0.8
1878	Pro-N	19	76	9	22	2	0	0	7	1	8	.289	.299	.316	102	0				.911	0	C-19/P-1	0.0
1879	Pro-N	1	5	0	0	0	0	0	0	0	1	.000	.000	.000	-99	-1				.833	0	/C-1	-0.1
1883	Bal-a	1	3	2	2	0	0	0	0	0	0	.667	.667	.667	321	1				.000	-1	/O-1,C-1	0.0
Total	5 n	224	1045	192	297	35	10	2	112	15	15	.284	.294	.343	101	3	5	2	0	.858	9	C-189/O-53,1-2,2S	1.2
Total	5	94	362	44	84	8	0	0	28	7	25	.232	.247	.254	63	-15				.892	12	/C-90,O-7,P-1	-0.2

■ MILO ALLISON   Allison, Milo Henry b: 10/16/1890, Elk Rapids, Mich. d: 6/18/57, Kenosha, Wis. BL/TR, 6', 163 lbs. Deb: 9/26/13

YEAR	TM/L	G	AB	R	H	2B	3B	HR	RBI	BB	SO	AVG	OBP	SLG	PRO+	BR/A	SB	CS	SBR	FA	FR	G/POS	TPR
1913	Chi-N	2	6	1	2	0	0	0	0	0	1	.333	.333	.333	90	-0	1			1.000	0	/O-1	0.0
1914	Chi-N	1	1	0	1	0	0	0	0	0	0	1.000	1.000	1.000	497	0	0			.000	0	H	0.0
1916	Cle-A	14	18	10	5	0	0	0	0	6	1	.278	.458	.278	115	1	0			1.000	-1	/O-5	0.0
1917	Cle-A	32	35	4	5	0	0	0	0	9	7	.143	.318	.143	38	-2	3			1.000	-3	O-11	-0.6
Total	4	49	60	15	13	0	0	0	0	15	9	.217	.373	.217	74	-1	4			1.000	-4	/O-17	-0.6

■ BILL ALLISON   Allison, William Andrew b: 9/18/1848, Philadelphia, Pa. d: 6/12/23, Deb: 5/21/1872

YEAR	TM/L	G	AB	R	H	2B	3B	HR	RBI	BB	SO	AVG	OBP	SLG	PRO+	BR/A	SB	CS	SBR	FA	FR	G/POS	TPR
1872	Eck-n	5	19	5	3	0	0	0	1	0	1	.158	.158	.158	-3	-2	0	0	0	.923	-2	/1-2,O-2,2-1	-0.2

■ BOB ALLISON   Allison, William Robert b: 7/11/34, Raytown, Mo. d: 4/9/95, Rio Verde, Ariz. BR/TR, 6'4", 220 lbs. Deb: 9/16/58

YEAR	TM/L	G	AB	R	H	2B	3B	HR	RBI	BB	SO	AVG	OBP	SLG	PRO+	BR/A	SB	CS	SBR	FA	FR	G/POS	TPR
1958	Was-A	11	35	1	7	1	0	0	4	2	9	.200	.243	.229	31	-3	0	2	-1	1.000	-0	O-11	-0.5
1959	Was-A☆	150	570	83	149	18	**9**	30	85	60	92	.261	.334	.482	122	15	13	8	-1	.974	-2	*O-149	0.5
1960	Was-A	144	501	79	126	30	3	15	69	92	94	.251	.370	.413	113	11	11	9	-2	.965	9	*O-140/1-4	1.1
1961	Min-A	159	556	83	136	21	3	29	105	103	100	.245	.367	.450	111	10	2	7	-4	.975	7	*O-150,1-18	0.4
1962	Min-A	149	519	102	138	24	8	29	102	84	115	.266	.372	.511	130	22	8	5	-1	.977	7	*O-147	2.1
1963	Min-A★	148	527	**99**	143	25	4	35	91	90	109	.271	.381	.533	**150**	37	4	4	1	.971	11	*O-147	4.2
1964	Min-A★	149	492	90	141	27	4	32	86	92	99	.287	.406	.553	163	44	10	1	2	.986	-4	1-93,O-61	3.8
1965	*Min-A	135	438	71	102	14	5	23	78	73	114	.233	.345	.445	118	11	10	2	2	.972	11	*O-122/1-3	1.9
1966	Min-A	70	168	34	37	6	1	8	19	30	34	.220	.348	.411	110	3	6	0	0	.967	-1	O-56	0.2
1967	Min-A	153	496	73	128	21	6	24	75	74	114	.258	.357	.470	132	20	6	4	-1	.978	-1	*O-145	1.3
1968	Min-A	145	469	63	116	16	8	22	52	52	98	.247	.325	.456	128	15	9	7	1	.966	-4	*O-117,1-17	0.4
1969	*Min-A	81	189	18	43	8	2	8	27	39	39	.228	.358	.418	107	2	2	4	-2	1.000	-3	O-58/1-3	-0.6

YEAR	TM/L	G	AB	R	H	2B	3B	HR	RBI	BB	SO	AVG	OBP	SLG	PRO+	BR/A	SB	CS	SBR	FA	FR	G/POS	TPR
1970	*Min-A	47	72	15	15	5	0	1	7	14	20	.208	.345	.319	83	-1	1	0	0	1.000	-3	O-17/1-7	-0.5
Total	13	1541	5032	811	1281	216	53	256	796	795	1033	.255	.360	.471	126	186	84	50	-5	.975	27	*O-1320,1-145	14.3

■ BEAU ALLRED
Allred, Dale Le Beau b: 6/4/65, Mesa, Ariz. BL/TL, 6', 190 lbs. Deb: 9/7/89

YEAR	TM/L	G	AB	R	H	2B	3B	HR	RBI	BB	SO	AVG	OBP	SLG	PRO+	BR/A	SB	CS	SBR	FA	FR	G/POS	TPR
1989	Cle-A	13	24	0	6	3	0	1	2	2	10	.250	.308	.375	90	-0	0	0	0	1.000	1	/O-5,D-2	0.1
1990	Cle-A	4	16	2	3	1	0	1	2	2	3	.188	.278	.438	98	-0	0	0	0	.833	-1	/O-4	-0.1
1991	Cle-A	48	125	17	29	3	0	3	12	25	35	.232	.343	.328	92	-0	2	2	-1	.972	2	O-42/D-1	0.0
Total	3	65	165	19	38	7	0	4	15	29	48	.230	.349	.345	93	-1	2	2	-1	.969	2	/O-51,D-3	0.0

■ MEL ALMADA
Almada, Baldomero Melo (Quiros) b: 2/7/13, Huatabampo, Mexico d: 8/13/88, Hermosillo, Mexico BL/TL, 6', 170 lbs. Deb: 9/8/33

YEAR	TM/L	G	AB	R	H	2B	3B	HR	RBI	BB	SO	AVG	OBP	SLG	PRO+	BR/A	SB	CS	SBR	FA	FR	G/POS	TPR
1933	Bos-A	14	44	11	15	0	0	1	3	11	3	.341	.473	.409	137	3	3	1	0	1.000	-0	O-13	0.2
1934	Bos-A	23	90	7	21	2	1	0	10	6	8	.233	.281	.278	42	-8	3	2	-0	.985	4	O-23	-0.5
1935	Bos-A	151	607	85	176	27	9	3	59	55	34	.290	.350	.379	83	-15	20	9	1	.968	-0	*O-149/1-3	-2.0
1936	Bos-A	96	320	40	81	16	4	1	21	24	15	.253	.305	.338	55	-23	2	4	-2	.987	-2	O-81	-2.7
1937	Bos-A	32	110	17	26	6	2	1	9	15	6	.236	.328	.355	69	-5	0	1	-1	.927	-6	O-27/1-4	-1.2
	Was-A	100	433	74	134	21	4	4	33	38	21	.309	.365	.404	98	-1	12	4	1	.964	14	*O-100	1.0
	Yr	132	543	91	160	27	6	5	42	53	27	.295	.357	.394	91	-7	12	5	1	.960	9	*O-127/1-4	-0.2
1938	Was-A	47	197	24	48	7	4	1	15	8	16	.244	.277	.335	56	-14	4	1	1	.968	5	O-47	-0.9
	StL-A	102	436	77	149	22	2	3	37	38	22	.342	.398	.422	106	5	9	5	-0	.966	-1	*O-101	0.1
	Yr	149	633	101	197	29	6	4	52	46	38	.311	.362	.395	92	-8	13	6	0	.967	4	*O-148	-0.8
1939	StL-A	42	134	17	32	1	2	1	7	10	8	.239	.292	.291	48	-10	1	0	0	.987	-3	O-34	-1.3
	Bro-N	39	112	11	24	4	0	0	3	9	7	.214	.273	.250	40	-9	2	2		.977	2	O-32	-0.9
Total	7	646	2483	363	706	107	27	15	197	214	150	.284	.342	.367	79	-78	56	27		.970	13	O-607/1-7	-8.2

■ RAFAEL ALMEIDA
Almeida, Rafael D. "Mike" b: 7/30/1887, Havana, Cuba d: 3/68, Havana, Cuba BR/TR, 5'9", 164 lbs. Deb: 7/4/11

YEAR	TM/L	G	AB	R	H	2B	3B	HR	RBI	BB	SO	AVG	OBP	SLG	PRO+	BR/A	SB	CS	SBR	FA	FR	G/POS	TPR
1911	Cin-N	36	96	9	30	1	0	0	15	9	16	.313	.383	.385	120	3	3			.890	-2	3-27/2-1,S-1	0.1
1912	Cin-N	16	59	9	13	4	3	0	10	5	8	.220	.281	.390	85	-2	0			.891	2	3-15	-0.3
1913	Cin-N	50	130	14	34	8	3	3	21	11	16	.262	.324	.392	104	0	4			.919	-1	3-37/O-3,S-2,2-1	0.5
Total	3	102	285	32	77	13	6	3	46	25	40	.270	.335	.389	106	2	7			.904	0	/3-79,O-3,S-3,2-2	0.3

■ BILL ALMON
Almon, William Francis b: 11/21/52, Providence, R.I. BR/TR, 6'3", 190 lbs. Deb: 9/2/74

YEAR	TM/L	G	AB	R	H	2B	3B	HR	RBI	BB	SO	AVG	OBP	SLG	PRO+	BR/A	SB	CS	SBR	FA	FR	G/POS	TPR
1974	SD-N	16	38	4	12	1	0	0	3	2	9	.316	.350	.342	98	-0	1	0	0	.915	-2	S-14	0.0
1975	SD-N	6	10	0	4	0	0	0	0	0	1	.400	.400	.400	131	0	0	0	0	1.000	1	/S-2	0.1
1976	SD-N	14	57	6	14	3	0	1	6	2	9	.246	.271	.351	82	-2	3	1	0	.962	1	S-14	0.2
1977	SD-N	155	613	75	160	18	11	2	43	37	114	.261	.303	.336	79	-20	20	9	1	.954	18	*S-155	1.6
1978	SD-N	138	405	39	102	19	2	0	21	33	74	.252	.308	.309	79	-12	17	5	2	.933	0	*3-114,S-15/2-7	-1.1
1979	SD-N	100	198	20	45	3	0	1	8	21	49	.227	.301	.258	59	-11	6	5	-1	.985	16	2-61,S-25/O-1	0.8
1980	Mon-N	18	38	2	10	1	1	0	3	1	5	.263	.282	.342	73	-1	2	0	0	.911	-2	S-12/2-1	-0.3
	NY-N	48	112	13	19	3	2	0	4	8	27	.170	.225	.232	29	-11	2	0	1	.967	9	S-22,2-18/3-9	0.1
	Yr	66	150	15	29	4	3	0	7	9	32	.193	.239	.260	40	-12	2	0	1	.948	5	S-34,2-19/3-9	-0.2
1981	Chi-A	103	349	46	105	10	2	4	41	21	60	.301	.344	.375	109	4	16	6	1	.969	14	*S-103	3.1
1982	Chi-A	111	308	40	79	10	4	4	26	25	49	.256	.314	.354	83	-7	10	8	-2	.949	20	*S-108/D-1	1.9
1983	Oak-A	143	451	45	120	29	1	4	63	26	61	.266	.309	.361	89	-7	26	8	3	.941	-31	S-52,3-40,10/2D	-3.5
1984	Oak-A	106	211	24	47	11	0	7	16	10	42	.223	.258	.374	78	-7	5	7	-3	1.000	-9	O-48,1-44,D/3CS	-2.2
1985	Pit-N	88	244	33	66	17	0	6	29	22	61	.270	.333	.414	109	3	10	7	-1	.987	-22	S-43,O-32/1-7,3-7	-1.9
1986	Pit-N	102	196	29	43	7	2	2	27	30	38	.219	.323	.383	92	-2	11	4	1	.983	-13	O-54,3-28,S-19,/1-4	-1.5
1987	Pit-N	19	20	5	4	1	0	0	1	1	5	.200	.238	.250	29	-2	0	0	0	.944	1	/S-4,O-2,3-1	-0.1
	NY-N	49	54	8	13	3	0	0	4	8	16	.241	.339	.296	74	-2	1	0	0	.972	-3	S-22,2-10/1-2,O-1	-0.3
	Yr	68	74	13	17	4	0	0	5	9	21	.230	.313	.284	62	-4	1	0	0	.963	-2	S-26,2-10/O-3,13	-0.5
1988	Phi-N	20	26	1	3	0	0	0	1	0	11	.115	.207	.192	15	-3	0	0	0	.944	1	/3-9,S-5,1-1	-0.2
Total	15	1236	3330	390	846	138	25	36	296	250	636	.254	.307	.343	83	-81	128	60		.956	-29	S-616,3-212,O2/1DC	-3.4

■ ROBERTO ALOMAR
Alomar, Roberto (Velazquez) b: 2/5/68, Ponce, P.R. BB/TR, 6', 184 lbs. Deb: 4/22/88 F

YEAR	TM/L	G	AB	R	H	2B	3B	HR	RBI	BB	SO	AVG	OBP	SLG	PRO+	BR/A	SB	CS	SBR	FA	FR	G/POS	TPR
1988	SD-N	143	545	84	145	24	6	9	41	47	83	.266	.328	.382	105	3	24	6	4	.980	17	*2-143	3.1
1989	SD-N	158	623	82	184	27	1	7	56	53	76	.295	.352	.376	108	7	42	17	2	.967	5	*2-157	2.1
1990	SD-N★	147	586	80	168	27	5	6	60	48	72	.287	.343	.381	98	-1	24	7	3	.976	-2	*2-137/S-5	0.4
1991	*Tor-A★	161	637	88	188	41	11	9	69	57	86	.295	.357	.436	114	12	53	11	9	.981	-22	*2-160	0.2
1992	*Tor-A★	152	571	105	177	27	8	8	76	87	52	.310	.406	.427	128	25	49	9	9	.993	-24	*2-150/D-1	1.3
1993	*Tor-A★	153	589	109	192	35	6	17	93	80	67	.326	.411	.492	141	36	55	15	8	.980	-7	*2-150	4.0
1994	Tor-A★	107	392	78	120	25	4	8	38	51	41	.306	.389	.452	115	10	19	8	1	.991	-4	*2-106	1.1
1995	Tor-A★	130	517	71	155	24	7	13	66	47	45	.300	.358	.449	109	7	30	3	7	**.994**	-5	*2-128	1.6
1996	*Bal-A★	153	588	132	193	43	4	22	94	90	65	.328	.418	.527	139	37	17	6	2	.985	13	*2-141,D-10	5.4
Total	9	1304	5048	829	1522	273	52	99	593	560	587	.302	.374	.435	118	136	313	82	45	.982	-29	*2-1272/D-11,S-5	19.2

■ SANDY ALOMAR
Alomar, Santos Jr. (Velazquez) b: 6/18/66, Salinas, P.R. BR/TR, 6'5", 200 lbs. Deb: 9/30/88 F

YEAR	TM/L	G	AB	R	H	2B	3B	HR	RBI	BB	SO	AVG	OBP	SLG	PRO+	BR/A	SB	CS	SBR	FA	FR	G/POS	TPR
1988	SD-N	1	1	0	0	0	0	0	0	0	0	.000	.000	.000	-99	-0	0	0	0	.000	0	H	0.0
1989	SD-N	7	19	1	4	1	0	1	6	3	3	.211	.318	.421	110	0	0	0	0	1.000	-0	/C-6	0.0
1990	Cle-A★	132	445	60	129	26	2	9	66	25	46	.290	.331	.418	109	4	4	1	1	.981	-13	*C-129	0.0
1991	Cle-A★	51	184	10	40	9	0	0	7	8	24	.217	.265	.266	47	-13	0	4	-2	.987	-4	C-46/D-4	-1.1
1992	Cle-A★	89	299	22	75	16	0	2	26	13	32	.251	.293	.324	74	-11	3	3	-1	.996	-4	C-88/D-1	-1.1
1993	Cle-A	64	215	24	58	7	1	6	32	11	28	.270	.323	.395	92	-3	3	1	0	.984	-12	C-64	-1.0
1994	Cle-A	80	292	44	84	15	1	14	43	25	31	.288	.348	.490	113	5	8	4	0	.996	-1	C-78	0.9
1995	*Cle-A	66	203	32	61	6	0	10	35	7	26	.300	.333	.478	106	1	3	1	0	.995	1	C-61	0.6
1996	*Cle-A★	127	418	53	110	23	0	11	50	19	42	.263	.300	.397	74	-17	1	0	-1	.988	2	*C-124/1-1	-0.6
Total	9	617	2076	246	561	103	4	53	265	111	233	.270	.315	.400	90	-34	22	14	-2	.989	-25	C-596/D-5,1-1	-2.3

■ SANDY ALOMAR
Alomar, Santos Sr. (Conde) b: 10/19/43, Salinas, P.R. BB/TR, 5'9", 155 lbs. Deb: 9/15/64 FC

YEAR	TM/L	G	AB	R	H	2B	3B	HR	RBI	BB	SO	AVG	OBP	SLG	PRO+	BR/A	SB	CS	SBR	FA	FR	G/POS	TPR
1964	Mil-N	19	53	3	13	1	0	0	0	0	11	.245	.245	.264	43	-4	1	0	0	.967	8	S-19	0.6
1965	Mil-N	67	108	16	26	1	1	0	8	4	12	.241	.268	.269	51	-7	12	5	1	.964	14	S-39,2-19	1.0
1966	Atl-N	31	44	4	4	1	0	0	2	1	10	.091	.111	.114	-37	-8	0	0	0	.981	3	2-21/S-5	-0.4
1967	NY-N	15	22	1	0	0	0	0	0	0	6	.000	.000	.000	-99	-6	0	0	0	1.000	2	S-10/3-3,2-2	-0.3
	Chi-A	12	15	4	3	0	0	0	0	2	0	.200	.294	.200	50	-1	2	0	1	.952	2	/S-8,2-2	0.2
1968	Chi-A	133	363	41	92	8	2	0	12	20	42	.253	.294	.287	76	-11	21	8	2	.958	-16	2-99,3-27/S-9,O-1	-2.2
1969	Chi-A	22	58	8	13	2	0	0	4	4	6	.224	.274	.259	47	-4	2	0	1	.980	3	2-22	0.1
	Cal-A	134	559	60	140	10	2	1	30	36	48	.250	.296	.281	65	-26	18	3	4	.969	-10	*2-134	-2.2
	Yr	156	617	68	153	12	2	1	34	40	54	.248	.294	.279	63	-31	20	3	4	.970	-7	*2-156	-2.1
1970	Cal-A★	162	672	82	169	18	2	2	36	49	65	.251	.303	.293	68	-30	35	12	3	.979	9	*2-153,S-10/3-1	-0.3
1971	Cal-A	162	689	77	179	24	3	4	42	41	60	.260	.301	.321	82	-18	39	10	6	.989	21	*2-137,S-28	2.6
1972	Cal-A	155	610	65	146	20	3	1	25	47	55	.239	.294	.282	78	-17	20	12	-1	.977	3	*2-154/S-4	-0.7
1973	Cal-A	136	470	45	112	7	1	0	28	34	44	.238	.290	.257	60	-25	25	10	2	.979	-4	*2-110,S-31	-2.2
1974	Cal-A	46	54	12	12	0	1	0	1	2	8	.222	.250	.259	44	-4	1	1	0	.977	9	S-19,2-15/3-5,OD	0.7
	NY-A	76	279	35	75	8	0	1	27	14	25	.269	.304	.308	78	-8	6	4	-1	.977	-12	2-76	-1.8
	Yr	122	333	47	87	8	1	1	28	16	33	.261	.295	.300	74	-11	8	4	0	.976	-3	2-91,S-19/3-5,OD	-1.1
1975	NY-A	151	489	61	117	18	4	2	39	26	58	.239	.278	.305	66	-23	28	6	5	**.985**	-12	*2-150/S-1	-2.3
1976	*NY-A	67	163	20	39	4	0	1	10	13	12	.239	.295	.282	70	-6	12	7	-1	.970	-5	2-38/S-6,3,3,1-1,O	-0.8
1977	Tex-A	69	83	21	22	3	0	1	11	8	13	.265	.337	.337	84	-2	5	3	-1	.973	13	D-26,2-18/S-6,O13	1.0
1978	Tex-A	60	49	8	13	1	0	0	3	8	8	.265	.293	.265	34	-3	0	0	0			/1-9,2-6,3,3-5,O,6,O13	-0.6
Total	15	1481	4760	558	1168	126	19	13	282	302	482	.245	.291	.288	68	-201	227	80	20	.977	31	*2-1156,S-197/3D1O	-6.9

■ FELIPE ALOU
Alou, Felipe Rojas (b: Felipe Rojas (Alou)) b: 5/12/35, Haina, D.R. BR/TR, 6', 195 lbs. Deb: 6/8/58 FMC

YEAR	TM/L	G	AB	R	H	2B	3B	HR	RBI	BB	SO	AVG	OBP	SLG	PRO+	BR/A	SB	CS	SBR	FA	FR	G/POS	TPR
1958	SF-N	75	182	21	46	9	2	4	16	19	34	.253	.327	.390	91	-2	4	2	0	.985	-3	O-70	-0.8

YEAR	TM/L	G	AB	R	H	2B	3B	HR	RBI	BB	SO	AVG	OBP	SLG	PRO+	BR/A	SB	CS	SBR	FA	FR	G/POS	TPR
1959	SF-N	95	247	38	68	13	2	10	33	17	38	.275	.322	.466	109	2	5	3	-0	.974	-6	O-69	-0.7
1960	SF-N	106	322	48	85	17	3	8	44	16	42	.264	.303	.410	99	-2	10	2	2	.958	-4	O-95	-0.8
1961	SF-N	132	415	59	120	19	0	18	52	26	41	.289	.334	.465	113	7	11	4	1	.990	-4	*O-122	-0.2
1962	*SF-N★	154	561	96	177	30	3	25	98	33	66	.316	.359	.513	133	24	10	7	-1	.971	-2	*O-150	1.3
1963	SF-N	157	565	75	159	31	9	20	82	27	87	.281	.321	.474	127	18	11	2	2	.986	0	*O-153	1.3
1964	Mil-N	121	415	60	105	26	3	9	51	30	41	.253	.310	.395	96	-2	5	2	0	.975	-1	O-92,1-18	-0.9
1965	Mil-N	143	555	80	165	29	2	23	78	31	63	.297	.340	.481	128	19	8	4	0	.980	-4	O-91,1-69/3-2,S-1	0.8
1966	Atl-N☆	154	666	122	218	32	6	31	74	24	51	.327	.362	.533	143	36	5	7	-3	.988	1	1-90,O-79/3-3,S-1	2.7
1967	Atl-N	140	574	76	157	26	3	15	43	32	50	.274	.320	.408	108	5	6	5	-1	.993	-11	1-85,O-56	-1.7
1968	Atl-N★	160	662	72	210	37	5	11	57	48	56	.317	.367	.438	140	32	12	11	-3	.980	8	*O-158	3.2
1969	*Atl-N	123	476	54	134	13	1	5	32	23	23	.282	.320	.345	86	-9	4	6	-2	.989	3	*O-116	-1.6
1970	Oak-A	154	575	70	156	25	3	8	55	32	31	.271	.311	.367	89	-10	10	5	0	.977	-3	*O-145/1-1	-2.1
1971	Oak-A	2	8	0	2	1	0	0	0	0	1	.250	.250	.375	77	-0	0	0	0	1.000	1	/O-2	0.0
	NY-A	131	461	52	133	20	6	8	69	32	24	.289	.337	.410	118	9	5	5	-2	.985	-12	O-80,1-42	-1.3
	Yr	133	469	52	135	21	6	8	69	32	25	.288	.336	.409	117	9	5	5	-2	.986	-11	O-82,1-42	-1.3
1972	NY-A	120	324	33	90	18	1	6	37	22	27	.278	.328	.395	118	6	1	0	0	.990	1	1-95,O-15	0.1
1973	NY-A	93	280	25	66	12	0	4	27	9	25	.236	.260	.321	65	-14	0	1	-1	.988	-1	1-67,O-22	-2.1
	Mon-N	19	48	4	10	1	0	1	4	2	4	.208	.240	.292	45	-4	0	1	-1	1.000	-1	O-15/1-1	-0.4
1974	Mil-A	3	3	0	0	0	0	0	0	0	2	.000	.000	.000	-99	-1	0	0	0	1.000	-1	/O-1	-0.2
Total	17	2082	7339	985	2101	359	49	206	852	423	706	.286	.330	.433	114	114	107	67	-8	.979	-37	*O-1531,1-468/3-5,S	-3.4

■ JESUS ALOU
Alou, Jesus Maria Rojas (b: Jesus Maria Rojas (Alou))   b: 3/24/42, Haina, D.R.   BR/TR, 6'2", 195 lbs.   Deb: 9/10/63   FC

YEAR	TM/L	G	AB	R	H	2B	3B	HR	RBI	BB	SO	AVG	OBP	SLG	PRO+	BR/A	SB	CS	SBR	FA	FR	G/POS	TPR
1963	SF-N	16	24	3	6	1	0	0	5	0	3	.250	.280	.292	66	-1	0	0	-1	.875	-4	O-12	-0.6
1964	SF-N	115	376	42	103	11	0	3	28	13	35	.274	.305	.327	77	-11	6	6	-2	.973	-1	*O-108	-1.9
1965	SF-N	143	543	76	162	19	4	9	52	13	40	.298	.318	.398	98	-3	8	5	-1	.980	1	*O-136	-0.9
1966	SF-N	110	370	41	96	13	1	1	20	9	22	.259	.281	.308	62	-19	5	5	-2	.967	-5	*O-100	-3.2
1967	SF-N	129	510	55	149	15	4	5	30	14	39	.292	.316	.367	96	-3	1	7	-4	.948	-6	*O-123	-2.1
1968	SF-N	120	419	26	110	15	4	0	39	9	23	.263	.280	.317	79	-11	1	4	-2	.989	0	*O-105	-2.1
1969	Hou-N	115	452	49	112	19	4	5	34	15	30	.248	.278	.341	74	-17	4	6	-2	.928	-0	*O-112	-2.8
1970	Hou-N	117	458	59	140	27	3	1	44	21	15	.306	.338	.384	97	-3	3	2	-0	.962	-7	*O-108	-1.5
1971	Hou-N	122	433	41	121	21	4	2	40	13	17	.279	.307	.360	91	-6	3	7	-3	.983	6	*O-109	-0.9
1972	Hou-N	52	93	8	29	4	1	0	11	7	5	.312	.366	.376	114	2	0	2	-1	.970	-3	O-23	-0.3
1973	Hou-N	28	55	7	13	2	0	1	8	1	6	.236	.276	.327	67	-3	0	0	0	.941	-3	O-14	-0.6
	*Oak-A	36	108	10	33	3	0	1	11	2	6	.306	.318	.361	96	-1	0	0	0	1.000	-0	O-21/D-6	-0.2
1974	*Oak-A	96	220	13	59	8	0	2	15	5	9	.268	.291	.332	84	-5	0	0	-1	1.000	-1	D-41,O-25	-0.8
1975	NY-N	62	102	9	27	3	0	0	11	4	5	.265	.299	.294	68	-5	0	0	-1	.963	-1	O-20	-0.7
1978	Hou-N	77	139	7	45	1	2	1	19	6	5	.324	.352	.417	123	4	0	0	0	.976	-2	O-28	0.1
1979	Hou-N	42	43	3	11	4	0	0	10	6	7	.256	.347	.349	96	-0	0	0	0	1.000	-1	/O-6,1-1	-0.1
Total	15	1380	4345	448	1216	170	26	32	377	138	267	.280	.307	.353	87	-83	31	46	-18	.968	-26	*O-1050/D-47,1-1	-18.6

■ MATTY ALOU
Alou, Mateo Rojas (b: Mateo Rojas (Alou))   b: 12/22/38, Haina, D.R.   BL/TL, 5'9", 160 lbs.   Deb: 9/26/60   F

YEAR	TM/L	G	AB	R	H	2B	3B	HR	RBI	BB	SO	AVG	OBP	SLG	PRO+	BR/A	SB	CS	SBR	FA	FR	G/POS	TPR
1960	SF-N	4	3	1	1	0	0	0	0	0	0	.333	.333	.333	88	-0	0	0	0	1.000	-0	/O-1	0.0
1961	SF-N	81	200	38	62	7	2	6	24	15	18	.310	.358	.455	118	5	3	2	-0	.978	-4	O-58	-0.2
1962	*SF-N	78	195	28	57	8	1	3	14	14	19	.292	.349	.390	100	0	3	1	-0	.976	-6	O-57	-0.8
1963	SF-N	63	76	4	11	1	0	0	2	2	13	.145	.177	.158	-3	-10	0	1	-1	.952	-1	O-20	-1.6
1964	SF-N	110	250	28	66	4	2	1	14	11	25	.264	.303	.308	71	-9	5	3	-0	.976	-9	O-80	-2.2
1965	SF-N	117	324	37	75	12	2	2	18	17	28	.231	.274	.299	60	-17	10	2	-2	.986	4	*O-103/P-1	-1.6
1966	Pit-N	141	535	86	183	18	9	2	27	24	44	**.342**	.375	.421	121	15	23	15	-2	.972	-1	*O-136	0.6
1967	Pit-N	139	550	87	186	21	7	2	28	24	42	.338	.372	.413	124	17	16	10	-1	.989	-3	*O-134/1-1	0.7
1968	Pit-N★	146	558	59	185	28	4	0	52	27	26	.332	.365	.396	130	21	20	18	-10	.984	-2	*O-144	1.1
1969	Pit-N★	162	698	105	**231**	41	6	1	48	42	35	.331	.371	.411	121	19	22	8	2	.977	5	*O-162	1.7
1970	*Pit-N	155	677	97	201	21	8	1	47	30	18	.297	.331	.356	86	-14	19	11	-1	.975	5	*O-153	-1.8
1971	StL-N	149	609	85	192	28	6	7	74	34	27	.315	.355	.415	113	10	19	10	-0	.981	-0	O-94,1-57	-0.1
1972	StL-N	108	404	46	127	17	2	3	31	24	23	.314	.354	.389	112	6	11	4	-1	.988	-2	1-66,O-39	-0.2
	*Oak-A	32	121	11	34	5	0	1	16	11	12	.281	.346	.347	112	2	2	1	0	1.000	-2	O-32/1-1	-0.2
1973	NY-A	123	497	59	147	22	1	2	28	30	43	.296	.340	.356	100	-0	0	5	2	.974	-4	O-85,1-40/D-1	-1.1
	StL-N	11	11	1	3	0	0	0	1	1	0	.273	.333	.273	70	-0	0	0	0	1.000	0	/1-1,O-1	0.0
1974	SD-N	48	81	8	16	3	0	0	3	5	6	.198	.244	.235	36	-7	0	0	0	.947	-2	O-13/1-2	-1.0
Total	15	1667	5789	780	1777	236	50	31	427	311	377	.307	.346	.381	105	35	156	80	-1	.979	-23	*O-1312,1-168/D-1,P	-6.7

■ MOISES ALOU
Alou, Moises Rojas (b: Moises Rojas)   b: 7/3/66, Atlanta, Ga.   BR/TR, 6'3", 185 lbs.   Deb: 7/26/90   F

YEAR	TM/L	G	AB	R	H	2B	3B	HR	RBI	BB	SO	AVG	OBP	SLG	PRO+	BR/A	SB	CS	SBR	FA	FR	G/POS	TPR
1990	Pit-N	2	5	0	1	0	0	0	0	0	1	.200	.200	.200	11	-1	0	0	0	1.000	-0	/O-2	-0.1
	Mon-N	14	15	4	3	0	1	0	0	0	3	.200	.200	.333	46	-1	0	0	0	1.000	-0	/O-5	-0.1
	Yr	16	20	4	4	0	1	0	0	0	4	.200	.200	.300	37	-2	0	0	0	1.000	-0	/O-7	-0.2
1992	Mon-N	115	341	53	96	28	2	9	56	25	46	.282	.332	.455	122	9	16	2	4	.978	-3	*O-100	0.8
1993	Mon-N	136	482	70	138	29	6	18	85	38	53	.286	.345	.483	114	9	17	6	2	.985	-1	*O-136	0.7
1994	Mon-N★	107	422	81	143	31	5	22	78	42	63	.339	.401	.592	153	32	7	6	-2	.986	4	*O-106	3.1
1995	Mon-N	93	344	48	94	22	0	14	58	29	56	.273	.346	.459	106	3	4	3	-1	.981	-0	O-92	-0.1
1996	Mon-N	143	540	87	152	28	2	21	96	49	83	.281	.343	.457	106	4	9	4	0	.989	-1	*O-142	0.0
Total	6	610	2149	343	627	138	16	84	373	183	304	.292	.353	.488	119	55	53	21	3	.984	-1	O-583	4.3

■ WHITEY ALPERMAN
Alperman, Charles Augustus   b: 11/11/1879, Etna, Pa.   d: 12/25/42, Pittsburgh, Pa.   BR/TR, 5'10", 180 lbs.   Deb: 4/13/06

YEAR	TM/L	G	AB	R	H	2B	3B	HR	RBI	BB	SO	AVG	OBP	SLG	PRO+	BR/A	SB	CS	SBR	FA	FR	G/POS	TPR
1906	Bro-N	128	441	38	111	15	7	3	46	6		.252	.284	.338	102	-2	13			.940	2	*2-103,S-24/3-1	0.2
1907	Bro-N	141	558	44	130	23	**16**	2	39	13		.233	.266	.342	98	-5	5			.953	14	*2-115,3-14,S-12	0.9
1908	Bro-N	70	213	17	42	3	1	1	15	9		.197	.253	.235	58	-10	2			.934	-5	2-42/3-9,O-5,S-2	-1.8
1909	Bro-N	111	420	35	104	19	12	1	41	2		.248	.262	.357	95	-6	7			.931	8	*2-108	0.0
Total	4	450	1632	134	387	60	36	7	141	30		.237	.268	.331	93	-23	27			.941	19	2-368/S-38,3-24,O-5	-0.7

■ TOM ALSTON
Alston, Thomas Edison   b: 1/31/26, Greensboro, N.C.   d: 12/30/93, Winston-Salem, N.C.   BL/TR, 6'5", 210 lbs.   Deb: 4/13/54

YEAR	TM/L	G	AB	R	H	2B	3B	HR	RBI	BB	SO	AVG	OBP	SLG	PRO+	BR/A	SB	CS	SBR	FA	FR	G/POS	TPR
1954	StL-N	66	244	28	60	14	2	4	34	24	41	.246	.319	.369	78	-8	3	5	-2	.989	10	1-65	-0.3
1955	StL-N	13	8	0	1	0	0	0	0	0	0	.125	.125	.125	-33	-2	0	0	0	1.000	0	/1-7	-0.1
1956	StL-N	3	2	0	0	0	0	0	0	0	0	.000	.000	.000	-99	-1	0	0	0	1.000	0	/1-3	0.0
1957	StL-N	9	17	2	5	1	0	0	2	1	5	.294	.333	.353	83	-0	0	0	0	.947	-1	/1-6	-0.2
Total	4	91	271	30	66	15	2	4	36	25	46	.244	.312	.358	74	-10	3	5	-2	.987	9	/1-81	-0.6

■ WALTER ALSTON
Alston, Walter Emmons "Smokey"   b: 12/1/11, Venice, Ohio   d: 10/1/84, Oxford, Ohio   BR/TR, 6'2", 195 lbs.   Deb: 9/27/36   MH

YEAR	TM/L	G	AB	R	H	2B	3B	HR	RBI	BB	SO	AVG	OBP	SLG	PRO+	BR/A	SB	CS	SBR	FA	FR	G/POS	TPR
1936	StL-N	1	1	0	0	0	0	0	0	0	1	.000	.000	.000	-99	-0				.500	-0	/1-1	-0.1

■ DELL ALSTON
Alston, Wendell   b: 9/22/52, Valhalla, N.Y.   BL/TR, 6', 180 lbs.   Deb: 5/17/77

YEAR	TM/L	G	AB	R	H	2B	3B	HR	RBI	BB	SO	AVG	OBP	SLG	PRO+	BR/A	SB	CS	SBR	FA	FR	G/POS	TPR
1977	NY-A	22	40	10	13	4	0	1	4	3	4	.325	.372	.500	137	2	3	3	-1	1.000	0	D-10/O-2	0.1
1978	NY-A	3	3	0	0	0	0	0	0	0	2	.000	.000	.000	-99	-1	0	0	0			H	
	Oak-A	58	173	17	36	2	0	1	9	10	21	.208	.251	.237	40	-14	11	10	-3	.956	-5	O-50/1-9,D-3	-2.5
	Yr	61	176	17	36	2	0	1	10	10	23	.205	.247	.233	38	-15	11	10	-3	.956	-5	O-50/1-9,D-3	-2.6
1979	Cle-A	54	62	10	18	2	0	2	12	10	10	.290	.389	.403	114	2	4	4	-1	.969	-5	O-30/D-7	-0.5
1980	Cle-A	52	54	11	12	3	2	0	1	8	10	.222	.311	.315	72	-2	2	4	-2	.947	-4	O-26/D-6	-0.8
Total	4	189	332	48	79	7	4	3	35	28	44	.238	.301	.310	71	-13	20	21	-7	.957	-14	O-108/D-26,1-9	-3.8

■ JESSE ALTENBURG
Altenburg, Jesse Howard   b: 1/2/1893, Ashley, Mich.   d: 3/12/73, Lansing, Mich.   BL/TR, 5'9", 158 lbs.   Deb: 9/19/16

YEAR	TM/L	G	AB	R	H	2B	3B	HR	RBI	BB	SO	AVG	OBP	SLG	PRO+	BR/A	SB	CS	SBR	FA	FR	G/POS	TPR
1916	Pit-N	8	14	2	6	1	1	0	3	1	1	.429	.467	.643	237	2	0			1.000	-2	/O-8	0.0
1917	Pit-N	11	17	1	3	0	0	0	3	0	4	.176	.176	.176	8	-2	0			1.000	-1	/O-4	-0.3
Total	2	19	31	3	9	1	1	0	3	1	5	.290	.313	.387	112	0	0			1.000	-3	/O-12	-0.3

YEAR	TM/L	G	AB	R	H	2B	3B	HR	RBI	BB	SO	AVG	OBP	SLG	PRO+	BR/A	SB	CS	SBR	FA	FR	G/POS	TPR

■ DAVE ALTIZER
Altizer, David Tilden "Filipino" b: 11/6/1876, Pearl, Ill. d: 5/14/64, Pleasant Hill, Ill BL/TR, 5'10.5", 160 lbs. Deb: 5/29/06

YEAR	TM/L	G	AB	R	H	2B	3B	HR	RBI	BB	SO	AVG	OBP	SLG	PRO+	BR/A	SB	CS	SBR	FA	FR	G/POS	TPR
1906	Was-A	115	433	56	111	9	5	1	27	35		.256	.324	.307	103	2	37			.931	-20	*S-113/O-2	-1.6
1907	Was-A	147	540	60	145	15	5	2	42	34		.269	.319	.326	115	8	38			.923	-2	S-80,1-50,O-17	0.7
1908	Was-A	67	205	19	46	1	1	0	18	13		.224	.274	.239	73	-6	8			.959	-3	2-38,3-16/1-4,S-1	-1.0
	Cle-A	29	89	11	19	1	2	0	5	7		.213	.278	.270	78	-2	7			.952	4	O-24/S-3	0.1
	Yr	96	294	30	65	2	3	0	23	20		.221	.275	.248	75	-8	15			.959	1	2-38,O-24,3-16/1S	-0.9
1909	Chi-A	116	382	47	89	6	7	1	20	39		.233	.330	.293	101	2	27			.949	8	O-61,1-46	0.8
1910	Cin-N	3	10	3	6	0	0	0	0	3		.600	.692	.600	290	3	0			.933	-2	/S-3	0.2
1911	Cin-N	37	75	8	17	4	1	0	4	9	5	.227	.318	.307	78	-2	2			.907	1	S-23/1-1,2-1,0-1	-0.3
Total	6	514	1734	204	433	36	21	4	116	140	5	.250	.318	.302	101	6	119			.925	-14	S-223,O-105,1/23	-0.8

■ GEORGE ALTMAN
Altman, George Lee b: 3/20/33, Goldsboro, N.C. BL/TR, 6'4", 200 lbs. Deb: 4/11/59

YEAR	TM/L	G	AB	R	H	2B	3B	HR	RBI	BB	SO	AVG	OBP	SLG	PRO+	BR/A	SB	CS	SBR	FA	FR	G/POS	TPR
1959	Chi-N	135	420	54	103	14	4	12	47	34	80	.245	.312	.383	85	-9	1	0	0	.990	4	*O-121	-1.1
1960	Chi-N	119	334	50	89	16	4	13	51	32	67	.266	.332	.455	114	6	4	3	-1	.993	-5	O-79,1-21	-0.4
1961	Chi-N★	138	518	77	157	28	**12**	27	96	40	92	.303	.358	.560	137	26	6	2	1	.978	5	*O-130/1-3	1.9
1962	Chi-N★	147	534	74	170	27	5	22	74	62	89	.318	.394	.511	136	28	19	7	2	.972	-0	*O-129,1-16	2.0
1963	StL-N	135	464	62	127	18	7	9	47	47	93	.274	.343	.401	104	3	13	4	2	.979	2	*O-124	0.1
1964	NY-N	124	422	48	97	14	1	9	47	18	70	.230	.263	.332	68	-19	4	2	0	.968	13	*O-109	-1.2
1965	Chi-N	90	196	24	46	7	1	4	23	19	36	.235	.302	.342	79	-5	3	2	-0	.943	-3	O-45/1-2	-1.1
1966	Chi-N	88	185	19	41	6	0	5	17	14	37	.222	.276	.335	68	-8	2	2	-1	.958	-3	O-42/1-4	-1.4
1967	Chi-N	15	18	1	2	2	0	0	1	2	8	.111	.200	.222	20	-2	0	0	0	1.000	-1	/O-4,1-1	-0.4
Total	9	991	3091	409	832	132	34	101	403	268	572	.269	.331	.432	105	19	52	22	2	.977	7	O-783/1-47	-1.7

■ JOE ALTOBELLI
Altobelli, Joseph Salvatore b: 5/26/32, Detroit, Mich. BL/TL, 6', 185 lbs. Deb: 4/14/55 MC

YEAR	TM/L	G	AB	R	H	2B	3B	HR	RBI	BB	SO	AVG	OBP	SLG	PRO+	BR/A	SB	CS	SBR	FA	FR	G/POS	TPR
1955	Cle-A	42	75	8	15	3	0	2	5	5	14	.200	.259	.320	53	-5	0	1	-1	.992	-1	1-40	-0.8
1957	Cle-A	83	87	9	18	3	2	0	9	5	14	.207	.258	.287	49	-6	3	2	-0	.994	-0	1-56/O-7	-0.8
1961	Min-A	41	95	10	21	2	1	3	14	13	14	.221	.315	.358	75	-3	0	0	0	.951	-1	O-25/1-2	-0.7
Total	3	166	257	27	54	8	3	5	28	23	42	.210	.280	.323	60	-15	3	3	-1	.993	-3	/1-98,O-32	-2.3

■ NICK ALTROCK
Altrock, Nicholas b: 9/15/1876, Cincinnati, Ohio d: 1/20/65, Washington, D.C. BB/TL, 5'10", 197 lbs. Deb: 7/14/1898 C

YEAR	TM/L	G	AB	R	H	2B	3B	HR	RBI	BB	SO	AVG	OBP	SLG	PRO+	BR/A	SB	CS	SBR	FA	FR	G/POS	TPR
1898	Lou-N	11	29	4	7	0	0	0	2	2		.241	.313	.241	60	-1	1			1.000	2	P-11	0.0
1902	Bos-A	3	8	0	0	0	0	0	0	0		.000	.000	.000	-97	-2	0			.818	1	/P-3	0.0
1903	Bos-A	1	3	0	2	0	0	0	0	1		.667	.750	.667	311	1	0			1.000	1	/P-1	0.0
	Chi-A	13	30	6	9	0	0	0	3	3		.300	.364	.300	105	0	1			.935	3	P-12	0.0
	Yr	14	33	6	11	0	0	0	3	4		.333	.405	.333	128	1	1			.944	3	P-13	0.0
1904	Chi-A	41	111	13	22	1	0	1	8	4		.198	.239	.234	52	-6	0			.969	4	P-38/1-1	0.0
1905	Chi-A	40	112	8	14	1	0	0	5	6		.125	.190	.134	3	-12	0			.988	8	P-38/1-1	0.0
1906	*Chi-A	38	100	4	16	0	0	0	3	8		.160	.222	.180	27	-8	2			.970	4	P-38/1-1	0.0
1907	Chi-A	30	72	7	13	2	0	0	2	3		.181	.234	.222	47	-5	0			.958	5	P-30	0.0
1908	Chi-A	23	49	6	10	2	0	0	3	0		.204	.235	.245	57	-2	1			.967	5	P-23	0.0
1909	Chi-A	1	3	0	0	0	0	0	0	0		.000	.000	.000	-99	-1	0			1.000	-0	/P-1	0.0
	Was-A	12	19	2	1	0	0	0	0	1		.053	.143	.053	-40	-3	0			.905	-0	/P-9,O-3	-0.2
	Yr	13	22	2	1	0	0	0	0	1		.045	.125	.045	-48	-4	0			.920	-0	/P-10/O-3	-0.2
1912	Was-A	1	1	0	0	0	0	0	0	0		.000	.000	.000	-99	-0	0			.000	-0	/P-1,1-1	0.0
1913	Was-A	4	1	0	0	0	0	0	0	0		.000	.000	.000	-98	-0	0			.833	-0	/P-4	0.0
1914	Was-A	1	0	0	0					—		—	—	—			0			.000	-0	/P-1	0.0
1915	Was-A	1	1	0	0	0	0	0	0	0		.000	.000	.000	-98	-0	0			.000	-0	/P-1	0.0
1918	Was-A	5	8	1	1	0	0	1	0			.125	.125	.500	90	-0	2			.917	-0	/P-5,1-1	0.0
1919	Was-A	1	0	0	0												0			.000	-0	/P-1	0.0
1924	Was-A	1	1	1	1	0	1	0	0			1.000	1.000	3.000	935	1	0	0	0	.667	0	/P-1	0.0
1929	Was-A	1	1	0	1	0	0	0	0			1.000	1.000	1.000	413	0	0	0	0	.000	-0	/O-1	0.0
1931	Was-A	1	0	0	0					—			1.000	—	182	-0	0	0	1	-1	.000	0	H	0.0
1933	Was-A	1	1	0	0	0	0	0	0	1		.000	.000	.000	-99	-0	0	0	0	.000	-0	H	0.0
Total	19	230	550	52	97	9	1	2	27	29	0	.176	.232	.207	39	-38	5	1		.964	33	P-218/1-5,O-4	-0.2

■ GEORGE ALUSIK
Alusik, George Joseph b: 2/11/35, Ashley, Pa. BR/TR, 6'3.5", 175 lbs. Deb: 9/11/58

YEAR	TM/L	G	AB	R	H	2B	3B	HR	RBI	BB	SO	AVG	OBP	SLG	PRO+	BR/A	SB	CS	SBR	FA	FR	G/POS	TPR
1958	Det-A	2	2	0	0	0	0	0	0	0	1	.000	.000	.000	-93	-1	0	0	0	1.000	-0	/O-1	-0.1
1961	Det-A	15	14	0	2	0	0	0	2	1	4	.143	.200	.143	-6	-2	0	0	0	.000	-0	/O-1	-0.3
1962	Det-A	2	2	0	0	0	0	0	0	0	0	.000	.000	.000	-97	-1	0	0	0	.000	-0	H	-0.1
	KC-A	90	209	29	57	10	1	11	35	16	29	.273	.327	.488	111	3	1	1	-0	.968	-3	O-50/1-1	-0.3
	Yr	92	211	29	57	10	1	11	35	16	29	.270	.325	.483	109	2	1	1	-0	.968	-3	O-50/1-1	-0.4
1963	KC-A	87	221	28	59	11	0	9	37	26	33	.267	.347	.439	112	4	0	1	-1	1.000	0	O-63	-0.3
1964	KC-A	102	204	18	49	10	1	3	19	30	36	.240	.343	.343	89	-2	0	0	0	.984	-4	O-44,1-12	-0.9
Total	5	298	652	75	167	31	2	23	93	73	103	.256	.335	.416	101	1	1	2	-1	.985	-10	O-159/1-13	-2.0

■ LUIS ALVARADO
Alvarado, Luis Cesar (Martinez) b: 1/15/49, Lajas, P.R. BR/TR, 5'9", 162 lbs. Deb: 9/13/68

YEAR	TM/L	G	AB	R	H	2B	3B	HR	RBI	BB	SO	AVG	OBP	SLG	PRO+	BR/A	SB	CS	SBR	FA	FR	G/POS	TPR
1968	Bos-A	11	46	3	6	0	0	0	1	1	11	.130	.167	.174	3	-5	0	0	0	.976	-4	S-11	-0.9
1969	Bos-A	6	5	0	0	0	0	0	0	0	2	.000	.000	.000	-95	-1	0	1	-1	1.000	2	/S-5	0.0
1970	Bos-A	59	183	19	41	11	0	1	10	9	30	.224	.260	.301	51	-12	1	2	-1	.929	5	3-29,S-27	-0.6
1971	Chi-A	99	264	22	57	14	1	0	8	11	34	.216	.247	.277	47	-19	1	2	-1	.959	15	S-71,2-16	-0.3
1972	Chi-A	103	254	30	54	4	1	4	29	13	36	.213	.254	.283	58	-13	2	2	-1	.957	7	S-81,2-16/3-2	-0.3
1973	Chi-A	80	203	21	47	7	2	0	20	4	20	.232	.250	.286	49	-14	6	2	1	.980	5	2-45,S-18,3-10/D-1	-0.5
1974	Chi-A	8	10	1	1	0	0	0	0	0	1	.100	.100	.100	-41	-2	0	0	0	.667	-1	/S-4,2-1,3-1	0.0
	StL-N	17	36	3	5	0	0	0	1	2	6	.139	.184	.194	6	-5	0	0	0	.980	-2	S-17	-0.5
	Cle-A	61	114	12	25	2	0	0	12	6	14	.219	.258	.237	44	-8	1	1	-0	.972	11	2-46/S-7,D-3	0.4
1976	StL-N	16	42	5	12	0	0	0	3	3	6	.286	.333	.310	82	-1	0	0	0	.936	-9	2-16	-1.0
1977	NY-N	1	2	0	0	0	0	0	0	0	0	.000	.000	.000	-99	-1	0	0	0	1.000	0	/2-1	0.0
	Det-A	2	1	0	0	0	0	0	0	0	0	.000	.000	.000	-95	-0	0	0	0	.000	0	/3-2	0.0
Total	9	463	1160	116	248	43	4	5	84	49	160	.214	.248	.271	47	-81	11	10	-3	.957	26	S-241,2-141/3-44,D	-3.3

■ ORLANDO ALVAREZ
Alvarez, Jesus Manuel Orlando (Monge) b: 2/28/52, Rio Grande, P.R. BR/TR, 6', 165 lbs. Deb: 9/1/73

YEAR	TM/L	G	AB	R	H	2B	3B	HR	RBI	BB	SO	AVG	OBP	SLG	PRO+	BR/A	SB	CS	SBR	FA	FR	G/POS	TPR
1973	LA-N	4	4	0	1	0	0	0	0	0	1	.250	.250	.500	108	-0	0	0	0	.000	0	H	0.0
1974	LA-N	2	1	0	0	0	0	0	0	0	0	.000	.000	.000	-99	-0	0	0	0	1.000	-0	/O-1	0.0
1975	LA-N	4	4	0	0	0	0	0	0	0	0	.000	.000	.000	-99	-1	0	0	0	.000	-0	H	-0.1
1976	Cal-A	15	42	4	7	1	0	2	8	0	3	.167	.167	.333	47	-3	0	0	0	1.000	-1	O-11/D-2	-0.5
Total	4	25	51	4	8	1	0	2	8	0	5	.157	.157	.314	36	-4	0	0	0	1.000	-2	/O-12,D-2	-0.6

■ OSSIE ALVAREZ
Alvarez, Oswaldo (Gonzalez) b: 10/19/33, Matanzas, Cuba BR/TR, 5'10", 165 lbs. Deb: 4/19/58

YEAR	TM/L	G	AB	R	H	2B	3B	HR	RBI	BB	SO	AVG	OBP	SLG	PRO+	BR/A	SB	CS	SBR	FA	FR	G/POS	TPR
1958	Was-A	87	196	20	41	3	0	0	5	16	26	.209	.269	.224	38	-16	1	1	-0	.968	12	S-64,2-14/3-3	0.0
1959	Det-A	8	2	0	1	0	0	0	0	0	1	.500	.500	.500	166	0	0	0	0	.000	-0	H	0.0
Total	2	95	198	20	42	3	0	0	5	16	27	.212	.271	.227	39	-16	1	1	-0	.968	12	/S-64,2-14,3-3	0.0

■ ROGELIO ALVAREZ
Alvarez, Rogelio (Hernandez) b: 4/18/38, Pinar Del Rio, Cuba BR/TR, 5'11", 183 lbs. Deb: 9/18/60

YEAR	TM/L	G	AB	R	H	2B	3B	HR	RBI	BB	SO	AVG	OBP	SLG	PRO+	BR/A	SB	CS	SBR	FA	FR	G/POS	TPR
1960	Cin-N	3	9	1	1	0	0	0	0	0	3	.111	.111	.111	-38	-2	0	0	0	1.000	-1	/1-2	-0.3
1962	Cin-N	14	28	1	6	0	0	0	2	1	10	.214	.241	.214	23	-3	0	0	0	.973	1	1-13	-0.4
Total	2	17	37	2	7	0	0	0	2	1	13	.189	.211	.189	8	-5	0	0	0	.979	-1	/1-15	-0.7

■ MAX ALVIS
Alvis, Roy Maxwell b: 2/2/38, Jasper, Tex. BR/TR, 5'11", 187 lbs. Deb: 9/11/62

YEAR	TM/L	G	AB	R	H	2B	3B	HR	RBI	BB	SO	AVG	OBP	SLG	PRO+	BR/A	SB	CS	SBR	FA	FR	G/POS	TPR
1962	Cle-A	12	51	1	11	2	0	0	3	2	13	.216	.245	.255	36	-5	3	1	0	.935	-4	3-12	-0.8
1963	Cle-A	158	602	81	165	32	7	22	67	36	109	.274	.326	.460	118	13	9	7	-2	.942	-5	*3-158	0.7
1964	Cle-A	107	381	51	96	14	3	18	53	29	77	.252	.315	.446	110	4	5	5	-2	.955	-7	*3-105	-0.6

YEAR	TM/L	G	AB	R	H	2B	3B	HR	RBI	BB	SO	AVG	OBP	SLG	PRO+	BR/A	SB	CS	SBR	FA	FR	G/POS	TPR
1965	Cle-A★	159	604	88	149	24	2	21	61	47	121	.247	.311	.397	99	-2	12	8	-1	.958	-19	*3-156	-2.7
1966	Cle-A★	157	596	67	146	22	3	17	55	50	98	.245	.306	.378	95	-4	4	7	-3	.958	-6	*3-157	-1.8
1967	Cle-A★	161	637	66	163	23	4	21	70	38	107	.256	.302	.403	106	3	3	10	-5	.965	-8	*3-161	-1.3
1968	Cle-A	131	452	38	101	17	3	8	37	41	91	.223	.294	.327	89	-6	5	5	-2	.960	-17	*3-128	-2.8
1969	Cle-A	66	191	13	43	6	0	1	15	14	26	.225	.278	.272	53	-12	1	1	-0	.973	-2	3-58/S-1	-1.5
1970	Mil-A	62	115	16	21	2	0	3	12	5	20	.183	.217	.278	35	-10	1	2	-1	.909	2	3-36	-1.0
Total	9	1013	3629	421	895	142	22	111	373	262	662	.247	.304	.390	97	-19	43	46	-15	.956	-64	3-971/S-1	-11.8

■ BILLY ALVORD
Alvord, William Charles "Uncle Bill"   b: 8/1863, St.Louis, Mo.   5'10", 187 lbs.   Deb: 4/30/1885

YEAR	TM/L	G	AB	R	H	2B	3B	HR	RBI	BB	SO	AVG	OBP	SLG	PRO+	BR/A	SB	CS	SBR	FA	FR	G/POS	TPR
1885	StL-N	2	5	0	0	0	0	0	0	1	2	.000	.167	.000	-45	-1				.714	-1	/3-2	-0.1
1889	KC-a	50	186	23	43	8	9	0	18	10	35	.231	.270	.371	77	-7	3			.877	5	3-34/S-8,2-8	0.0
1890	Tol-a	116	495	69	135	13	16	2	52	22		.273	.304	.376	97	-5	21			.872	4	*3-116	0.3
1891	Cle-N	13	59	7	17	2	2	1	7	0	7	.288	.300	.441	110	0	0			.814	-2	3-13	-0.1
	Was-a	81	312	29	73	8	3	0	30	11	38	.234	.260	.279	57	-19	3			.862	17	3-81	0.2
1893	Cle-N	3	12	2	2	0	0	0	2	0	1	.167	.167	.167	-11	-2	0			.875	-2	/3-3	-0.3
Total	5	265	1069	129	270	31	30	3	109	44	83	.253	.283	.346	81	-33	27			.865	22	3-249/2-8,S-8	0.0

■ BRANT ALYEA
Alyea, Garrabrant Ryerson   b: 12/8/40, Passaic, N.J.   BR/TR, 6'3", 215 lbs.   Deb: 9/11/65

YEAR	TM/L	G	AB	R	H	2B	3B	HR	RBI	BB	SO	AVG	OBP	SLG	PRO+	BR/A	SB	CS	SBR	FA	FR	G/POS	TPR
1965	Was-A	8	13	3	3	0	0	2	6	1	4	.231	.286	.692	171	1	0	0	0	1.000	-1	/1-3,O-1	0.0
1968	Was-A	53	150	18	40	11	1	6	23	10	39	.267	.317	.473	141	7	0	0	0	1.000	1	O-39	0.6
1969	Was-A	104	237	29	59	4	0	11	40	34	67	.249	.346	.405	115	5	1	3	-2	.938	-7	O-69/1-3	-0.8
1970	*Min-A	94	258	34	75	12	1	16	61	28	51	.291	.367	.531	143	3	3	3	-1	.980	-5	O-75	0.5
1971	Min-A	79	158	13	28	4	0	2	15	24	38	.177	.290	.241	50	-10	1	1	-0	.962	-6	O-48	-2.0
1972	Oak-A	20	31	3	6	1	0	1	2	3	5	.194	.265	.323	78	-1	0	0	0	1.000	3	/O-8	0.2
	StL-N	13	19	0	3	1	0	0	1	0	6	.158	.158	.211	4	-2	0	0	0	1.000	1	/O-3	-0.2
Total	6	371	866	100	214	33	2	38	148	100	210	.247	.329	.421	113	14	5	7	-3	.972	-15	O-243/1-6	-1.7

■ JOEY AMALFITANO
Amalfitano, John Joseph   b: 1/23/34, San Pedro, Cal.   BR/TR, 5'11", 180 lbs.   Deb: 5/3/54   MC

YEAR	TM/L	G	AB	R	H	2B	3B	HR	RBI	BB	SO	AVG	OBP	SLG	PRO+	BR/A	SB	CS	SBR	FA	FR	G/POS	TPR
1954	NY-N	9	5	2	0	0	0	0	0	0	4	.000	.000	.000	-99	-1	0	0	0	1.000	2	/3-4,2-1	0.1
1955	NY-N	36	22	8	5	1	1	0	1	2	2	.227	.292	.364	72	-1	0	0	0	.957	10	/S-5,3-2	0.9
1960	SF-N	106	328	47	91	15	3	1	27	26	31	.277	.336	.351	94	-3	2	3	-1	.935	3	3-63,2-33/S-3,O-1	0.1
1961	SF-N	109	384	64	98	11	4	2	23	44	59	.255	.332	.320	77	-12	7	4	-0	.970	-22	2-95/3-6	-2.4
1962	Hou-N	117	380	44	90	12	5	1	27	45	43	.237	.319	.303	73	-14	4	4	-1	.967	2	*2-110/3-5	-0.3
1963	SF-N	54	137	11	24	3	0	1	7	12	18	.175	.247	.219	36	-11	2	6	-3	.980	-3	2-37/3-7	-1.6
1964	Chi-N	100	324	51	78	19	6	4	27	40	42	.241	.333	.373	95	-1	2	7	-4	.964	2	2-86/1-1,S-1	0.4
1965	Chi-N	67	96	13	26	4	0	1	8	12	14	.271	.364	.313	90	-1	2	2	-1	.989	5	2-24/S-4	0.5
1966	Chi-N	41	38	8	6	2	0	0	3	4	10	.158	.238	.211	26	-4	0	0	0	.977	1	2-12/3-3,S-2	-0.2
1967	Chi-N	4	1	0	0	0	0	0	0	0	1	.000	.000	.000	-96	-0	0	0	0	.000	0	H	0.0
Total	10	643	1715	248	418	67	19	9	123	185	224	.244	.322	.321	78	-48	19	26	-10	.970	0	2-398/3-90,S-15,10	-2.5

■ RICH AMARAL
Amaral, Richard Louis   b: 4/1/62, Visalia, Cal.   BR/TR, 6', 175 lbs.   Deb: 5/27/91

YEAR	TM/L	G	AB	R	H	2B	3B	HR	RBI	BB	SO	AVG	OBP	SLG	PRO+	BR/A	SB	CS	SBR	FA	FR	G/POS	TPR
1991	Sea-A	14	16	2	1	0	0	0	0	1	5	.063	.167	.063	-34	-3	0	0	0	1.000	4	/2-5,3-2,S-2,1-1,D	0.1
1992	Sea-A	35	100	9	24	3	0	1	7	5	16	.240	.276	.300	61	-5	4	2	0	.955	4	3-17,S-17/O-3,12	-0.3
1993	Sea-A	110	373	53	108	24	1	1	44	33	54	.290	.352	.367	92	-3	19	11	-1	.975	10	2-77,3-19,S-14,/1D	0.8
1994	Sea-A	77	228	37	60	10	2	4	18	24	28	.263	.336	.377	82	-6	5	1	1	.943	-12	2-42,O-16/S-7,1D	-1.4
1995	*Sea-A	90	238	45	67	14	2	2	19	21	33	.282	.342	.382	87	-4	21	2	5	.992	-7	O-73/D-1	-0.8
1996	Sea-A	118	312	69	91	11	3	1	29	47	55	.292	.393	.356	92	-2	25	6	4	1.000	-5	O-91,2-15,1-10,/3D	-0.4
Total	6	444	1267	215	351	62	8	9	117	131	191	.277	.350	.360	86	-23	74	22	9	.994	-9	O-183,2-140/S3D1	-2.0

■ RUBEN AMARO
Amaro, Ruben Jr.   b: 2/12/65, Philadelphia, Pa.   BB/TR, 5'10", 170 lbs.   Deb: 6/8/91   F

YEAR	TM/L	G	AB	R	H	2B	3B	HR	RBI	BB	SO	AVG	OBP	SLG	PRO+	BR/A	SB	CS	SBR	FA	FR	G/POS	TPR
1991	Cal-A	10	23	0	5	1	0	0	2	3	3	.217	.308	.261	59	-1	0	0	0	1.000	-2	/O-5,2-4,D-1	-0.4
1992	Phi-N	126	374	43	82	15	6	7	34	37	54	.219	.305	.348	65	-7	11	5	0	.992	0	*O-113	-1.0
1993	Phi-N	25	48	7	16	2	2	1	6	6	5	.333	.407	.521	149	3	0	0	0	.963	-2	O-16	0.2
1994	Cle-A	26	23	5	5	1	0	2	5	2	3	.217	.280	.522	100	-0	2	1	0	.909	-4	O-12/D-3	-0.4
1995	*Cle-A	28	60	5	12	3	0	1	7	4	6	.200	.273	.300	48	-5	1	3	-2	1.000	-4	O-22/D-3	-1.0
1996	Phi-N	61	117	14	37	10	0	2	9	9	18	.316	.380	.453	115	3	0	0	0	1.000	-4	O-35/1-1	-0.2
Total	6	276	645	74	157	32	8	13	69	61	89	.243	.322	.378	92	-7	14	9	-1	.989	-16	O-203/D-7,2-4,1-1	-2.8

■ RUBEN AMARO
Amaro, Ruben Sr. (Mora)   b: 1/6/36, Veracruz, Mexico   BR/TR, 5'11", 170 lbs.   Deb: 6/29/58   FC

YEAR	TM/L	G	AB	R	H	2B	3B	HR	RBI	BB	SO	AVG	OBP	SLG	PRO+	BR/A	SB	CS	SBR	FA	FR	G/POS	TPR
1958	StL-N	40	76	8	17	2	0	0	5		8	.224	.272	.276	44	-6	0	1	-1	.948	3	S-36/2-1	-0.2
1960	Phi-N	92	264	25	61	9	1	0	16	21	32	.231	.293	.273	56	-16	0	1	-1	.965	-8	S-92	-1.9
1961	Phi-N	135	381	34	98	14	9	1	32	53	59	.257	.351	.349	88	-5	1	0	-1	.970	14	*S-132/1-3,2-1	1.9
1962	Phi-N	79	226	24	55	10	0	0	19	30	28	.243	.335	.288	71	-8	5	2	0	.968	0	S-78/1-1	0.5
1963	Phi-N	115	217	25	47	9	2	2	19	19	31	.217	.280	.304	69	-9	0	1	-1	.950	2	S-63,3-45/1-5	-0.5
1964	Phi-N	129	299	31	79	11	0	4	34	16	37	.264	.308	.341	84	-6	1	6	-3	.971	-4	S-79,1-58/2-3,3O	-1.0
1965	Phi-N	118	184	26	39	7	0	0	15	27	22	.212	.316	.250	63	-8	1	1	-0	.990	-3	1-60,S-60/2-6	-0.9
1966	NY-A	14	23	0	5	0	0	0	3	0	2	.217	.217	.217	26	-2	0	0	0	.977	5	S-14	0.4
1967	NY-A	130	417	31	93	12	0	1	17	43	49	.223	.297	.259	68	-16	3	2	0	.973	9	*S-123/3-3,1-2	0.5
1968	NY-A	47	41	3	5	1	0	0	0	6	6	.122	.280	.146	33	-3	0	0	0	.962	0	S-23,1-22	-0.3
1969	Cal-A	41	27	4	6	0	0	0	1	4	6	.222	.323	.222	58	-1	0	0	0	1.000	0	1-18/2-9,S-5,3-2	-0.1
Total	11	940	2155	211	505	75	13	8	156	227	280	.234	.310	.292	70	-81	11	14	-5	.967	24	S-705,1-169/32O	-1.6

■ WAYNE AMBLER
Ambler, Wayne Harper   b: 11/8/15, Abington, Pa.   BR/TR, 5'8.5", 165 lbs.   Deb: 6/4/37

YEAR	TM/L	G	AB	R	H	2B	3B	HR	RBI	BB	SO	AVG	OBP	SLG	PRO+	BR/A	SB	CS	SBR	FA	FR	G/POS	TPR
1937	Phi-A	56	162	3	35	5	0	0	11	13	8	.216	.274	.247	33	-17	1	0	0	.955	-4	2-56	-1.6
1938	Phi-A	120	393	42	92	21	2	0	38	48	31	.234	.317	.298	56	-26	2	1	0	.942	-19	*S-116/2-4	-3.3
1939	Phi-A	95	227	15	48	13	0	0	24	22	25	.211	.281	.269	42	-20	1	0	0	.954	-3	S-77,2-19	-1.5
Total	3	271	782	60	175	39	2	0	73	83	64	.224	.298	.279	47	-63	4	1	1	.946	-26	S-193/2-79	-6.4

■ ED AMELUNG
Amelung, Edward Allen   b: 4/13/59, Fullerton, Cal.   BL/TL, 5'11", 180 lbs.   Deb: 7/28/84

YEAR	TM/L	G	AB	R	H	2B	3B	HR	RBI	BB	SO	AVG	OBP	SLG	PRO+	BR/A	SB	CS	SBR	FA	FR	G/POS	TPR
1984	LA-N	34	46	7	10	0	0	0	4	2	4	.217	.250	.217	33	-4	3	2	-0	1.000	-3	O-23	-0.8
1986	LA-N	8	11	0	1	0	0	0	0	2	4	.091	.091	.091	-53	-2	0	0	0	1.000	-1	/O-4	-0.3
Total	2	42	57	7	11	0	0	0	4	4	8	.193	.220	.193	17	-6	3	2	-0	1.000	-4	/O-27	-1.1

■ SANDY AMOROS
Amoros, Edmundo (Isasi)   b: 1/30/30, Havana, Cuba   d: 6/27/92, Miami, Fla.   BL/TL, 5'7.5", 170 lbs.   Deb: 8/22/52

YEAR	TM/L	G	AB	R	H	2B	3B	HR	RBI	BB	SO	AVG	OBP	SLG	PRO+	BR/A	SB	CS	SBR	FA	FR	G/POS	TPR
1952	*Bro-N	20	44	10	11	3	1	0	3	5	14	.250	.327	.364	90	-1	1	0	0	1.000	-3	O-10	-0.4
1954	Bro-N	79	263	44	72	18	6	9	34	31	24	.274	.353	.490	113	5	1	4	-2	.987	5	O-70	0.4
1955	*Bro-N	119	388	59	96	16	7	10	51	55	45	.247	.350	.402	96	-1	10	5	0	.972	-1	*O-109	-0.7
1956	*Bro-N	114	292	53	76	11	8	16	58	59	51	.260	.386	.517	130	13	3	4	-2	.955	-10	O-86	-0.3
1957	Bro-N	106	238	40	66	7	1	7	26	46	42	.277	.401	.403	107	4	3	2	-1	.984	-1	O-66	0.0
1959	LA-N	5	5	1	1	0	0	0	1	0	1	.200	.200	.200	6	-1	0	0	0	.000	0	H	-0.1
1960	LA-N	9	14	1	2	0	0	0	0	2	5	.143	.294	.143	23	-1	0	0	0	1.000	-0	/O-3	-0.1
	Det-A	65	67	7	10	0	0	0	7	12	10	.149	.278	.194	29	-6	0	0	0	1.000	-1	O-10	-0.8
Total	7	517	1311	215	334	55	23	43	180	211	189	.255	.363	.430	105	12	18	15	-4	.976	-11	O-354	-2.0

■ ALF ANDERSON
Anderson, Alfred Walton   b: 1/28/14, Gainesville, Ga.   d: 6/23/85, Albany, Ga.   BR/TR, 5'11", 165 lbs.   Deb: 4/20/41

YEAR	TM/L	G	AB	R	H	2B	3B	HR	RBI	BB	SO	AVG	OBP	SLG	PRO+	BR/A	SB	CS	SBR	FA	FR	G/POS	TPR
1941	Pit-N	70	223	32	48	7	2	1	10	14	30	.215	.265	.278	53	-14	2			.931	-6	S-58	-1.7
1942	Pit-N	54	166	24	45	4	1	0	7	18	19	.271	.342	.307	89	-2	4			.942	-15	S-48	-1.6
1946	Pit-N	2	1	0	0	0	0	0	0	1	0	.000	.500	.000	47	0	0			.000	0	H	0.0
Total	3	126	390	56	93	11	3	1	17	33	49	.238	.300	.290	68	-16	6			.936	-21	S-106	-3.3

■ ANDY ANDERSON
Anderson, Andy Holm   b: 11/13/22, Bremerton, Wash.   d: 7/18/82, Seattle, Wash.   BR/TR, 5'11", 172 lbs.   Deb: 5/10/48

YEAR	TM/L	G	AB	R	H	2B	3B	HR	RBI	BB	SO	AVG	OBP	SLG	PRO+	BR/A	SB	CS	SBR	FA	FR	G/POS	TPR
1948	StL-A	51	87	13	24	5	1	1	12	8	15	.276	.337	.391	91	-1	0	0	0	.917	-2	2-21,S-10/1-2	-0.2

YEAR	TM/L	G	AB	R	H	2B	3B	HR	RBI	BB	SO	AVG	OBP	SLG	PRO+	BR/A	SB	CS	SBR	FA	FR	G/POS	TPR
1949	StL-A	71	136	10	17	3	0	1	5	14	21	.125	.207	.169	-0	-20	0	1	-1	.957	-7	S-44/2-8,3-8	-2.5
Total	2	122	223	23	41	8	1	2	17	22	36	.184	.257	.256	35	-21	0	1	-1	.946	-9	/S-54,2-29,3-8,1-2	-2.7

■ BRADY ANDERSON
Anderson, Brady Kevin b: 1/18/64, Silver Spring, Md. BL/TL, 6'1", 170 lbs. Deb: 4/4/88

YEAR	TM/L	G	AB	R	H	2B	3B	HR	RBI	BB	SO	AVG	OBP	SLG	PRO+	BR/A	SB	CS	SBR	FA	FR	G/POS	TPR
1988	Bos-A	41	148	14	34	5	3	0	12	15	35	.230	.317	.304	72	-5	4	2	0	.989	2	O-41	-0.5
	Bal-A	53	177	17	35	8	1	1	9	8	40	.198	.232	.271	42	-14	6	4	-1	.981	5	O-49	-1.1
	Yr	94	325	31	69	13	4	1	21	23	75	.212	.273	.286	57	-19	10	6	-1	.984	7	O-90	-1.6
1989	Bal-A	94	266	44	55	12	2	4	16	43	45	.207	.324	.312	82	-5	16	4	2	.985	-2	O-79/D-8	-0.7
1990	Bal-A	89	234	24	54	5	2	3	24	31	46	.231	.333	.308	83	-4	15	2	3	.987	2	O-63,D-11	0.0
1991	Bal-A	113	256	40	59	12	3	2	27	38	44	.230	.341	.324	89	-3	12	5	1	.981	-15	*O-101/D-2	-1.9
1992	Bal-A★	159	623	100	169	28	10	21	80	98	98	.271	.378	.449	128	25	53	16	6	.980	14	*O-158	4.2
1993	Bal-A	142	560	87	147	36	8	13	66	82	99	.262	.367	.425	108	7	24	12	0	.993	2	*O-140/D-2	0.7
1994	Bal-A	111	453	78	119	25	5	12	48	57	75	.263	.358	.419	95	-3	31	1	9	.996	-0	*O-109	0.2
1995	Bal-A	143	554	108	145	33	10	16	64	87	111	.262	.372	.444	109	9	26	7	4	.989	-16	*O-142	-0.7
1996	*Bal-A★	149	579	117	172	37	5	50	110	76	106	.297	.399	.637	158	51	21	8	2	.992	6	*O-143/D-2	4.9
Total	9	1094	3850	629	989	201	49	122	456	535	699	.257	.359	.430	109	59	208	61	26	.988	-2	*O-1025/D-25	5.1

■ DAVE ANDERSON
Anderson, David Carter b: 8/1/60, Louisville, Ky. BR/TR, 6'2", 185 lbs. Deb: 5/8/83

YEAR	TM/L	G	AB	R	H	2B	3B	HR	RBI	BB	SO	AVG	OBP	SLG	PRO+	BR/A	SB	CS	SBR	FA	FR	G/POS	TPR
1983	LA-N	61	115	12	19	4	2	1	2	12	15	.165	.244	.261	40	-9	3	6	0	.969	3	S-53/3-1	-0.3
1984	LA-N	121	374	51	94	16	2	3	34	45	55	.251	.335	.329	88	-5	15	5	2	.965	19	*S-111,3-11	2.6
1985	*LA-N	77	221	24	44	6	0	4	18	35	42	.199	.311	.281	69	-8	5	4	-1	.957	17	3-51,S-25/2-2	1.0
1986	LA-N	92	216	31	53	9	0	1	15	22	39	.245	.315	.301	76	-7	5	1	1	.976	9	3-51,S-34/2-5	0.5
1987	LA-N	108	265	32	62	12	3	1	13	24	43	.234	.300	.313	64	-13	9	5	-0	.977	6	S-65,3-35/2-5	-0.4
1988	*LA-N	116	285	31	71	10	2	2	20	32	45	.249	.327	.319	89	-3	4	2	0	.986	14	S-82,3-12,2-11	1.8
1989	LA-N	87	140	15	32	2	0	1	14	17	26	.229	.312	.264	67	-5	2	0	1	.990	0	S-33,3-18/2-7	-0.3
1990	SF-N	60	100	14	35	5	1	1	6	3	20	.350	.369	.450	129	4	1	2	-1	1.000	-6	S-29,2-13/1-3,3-2	-0.2
1991	SF-N	100	226	24	56	5	4	2	13	12	35	.248	.286	.314	71	-9	2	4	-2	.956	-10	S-63,1-16,3-11/2-6	-1.9
1992	LA-N	51	84	10	24	4	0	3	4	9	11	.286	.348	.440	115	1	0	4	-2	.974	2	3-26/S-7	0.1
Total	10	873	2026	244	490	73	12	19	143	206	331	.242	.313	.318	79	-56	49	30	-3	.970	54	S-502,3-218/2-49,1	2.9

■ DWAIN ANDERSON
Anderson, Dwain Cleaven b: 11/23/47, Oakland, Cal. BR/TR, 5'11", 165 lbs. Deb: 9/3/71

YEAR	TM/L	G	AB	R	H	2B	3B	HR	RBI	BB	SO	AVG	OBP	SLG	PRO+	BR/A	SB	CS	SBR	FA	FR	G/POS	TPR
1971	Oak-A	16	37	3	10	2	1	0	2	5	9	.270	.372	.378	115	1	0	1	-1	.968	-1	S-10/2-5,3-1	0.1
1972	Oak-A	3	7	2	0	0	0	0	0	1	4	.000	.125	.000	-64	-1	0	0	0	1.000	-0	/S-1,3-1	-0.2
	StL-N	57	135	12	36	4	1	1	8	8	23	.267	.313	.333	85	-3	0	1	-1	.952	-3	S-43,3-13/2-1	-0.3
1973	StL-N	18	17	5	2	0	0	0	0	4	4	.118	.286	.118	16	-2	0	0	0	.500	-3	/S-3,O-2	-0.4
	SD-N	53	107	11	13	0	0	0	3	14	29	.121	.223	.121	-2	-15	0	1	0	.932	3	S-39/3-6	-0.8
	Yr	71	124	16	15	0	0	0	3	18	33	.121	.232	.121	1	-16	0	1	0	.919	1	S-42/3-6,O-2	-1.2
1974	Cle-A	2	3	0	1	0	0	0	0	0	1	.333	.333	.333	93	-0	0	0	0	1.000	-1	/2-1	-0.1
Total	4	149	306	33	62	6	2	1	14	32	70	.203	.282	.245	52	-20	2	2	-1	.940	-4	/S-96,3-21,2-7,O-2	-1.7

■ GOAT ANDERSON
Anderson, Edward John b: 1/13/1880, Cleveland, Ohio d: 3/15/23, South Bend, Ind. BL/TR, Deb: 4/11/07

YEAR	TM/L	G	AB	R	H	2B	3B	HR	RBI	BB	SO	AVG	OBP	SLG	PRO+	BR/A	SB	CS	SBR	FA	FR	G/POS	TPR
1907	Pit-N	127	413	73	85	3	1	1	28	80		.206	.343	.225	77	-6	27			.953	-1	*O-117/2-5	-1.3

■ FERRELL ANDERSON
Anderson, Ferrell Jack "Andy" b: 1/9/18, Maple City, Mo. d: 3/12/78, Joplin, Mo. BR/TR, 6'1", 200 lbs. Deb: 4/16/46

YEAR	TM/L	G	AB	R	H	2B	3B	HR	RBI	BB	SO	AVG	OBP	SLG	PRO+	BR/A	SB	CS	SBR	FA	FR	G/POS	TPR
1946	Bro-N	79	199	19	51	10	0	2	14	18	21	.256	.330	.337	89	-3	1			.964	-2	C-70	-0.2
1953	StL-N	18	35	1	10	2	0	0	1	0	4	.286	.286	.343	63	-2	0	0	0	1.000	-1	C-12	-0.3
Total	2	97	234	20	61	12	0	2	15	18	25	.261	.324	.338	85	-5	1	0		.968	-3	/C-82	-0.5

■ GARRET ANDERSON
Anderson, Garret Joseph b: 6/30/72, Los Angeles, Cal. BL/TL, 6'3", 190 lbs. Deb: 7/27/94

YEAR	TM/L	G	AB	R	H	2B	3B	HR	RBI	BB	SO	AVG	OBP	SLG	PRO+	BR/A	SB	CS	SBR	FA	FR	G/POS	TPR
1994	Cal-A	5	13	0	5	0	0	0	1	0	2	.385	.385	.385	98	-0	0	0	0	1.000	0	/O-4	0.0
1995	Cal-A	106	374	50	120	19	1	16	69	19	65	.321	.355	.505	122	11	6	2	1	.978	7	*O-100/D-1	1.5
1996	Cal-A	150	607	79	173	33	2	12	72	27	84	.285	.315	.405	82	-18	7	9	-3	.979	6	*O-146/D-1	-1.7
Total	3	261	994	129	298	52	3	28	142	46	151	.300	.331	.443	97	-7	13	11	-2	.979	13	O-250/D-2	-0.2

■ GEORGE ANDERSON
Anderson, George Jendrus "Andy" (Born George Andrew Jendrus) b: 9/26/1889, Cleveland, Ohio d: 5/28/62, Cleveland, Ohio BL/TR, 5'8.5", 160 lbs. Deb: 5/26/14

YEAR	TM/L	G	AB	R	H	2B	3B	HR	RBI	BB	SO	AVG	OBP	SLG	PRO+	BR/A	SB	CS	SBR	FA	FR	G/POS	TPR
1914	Bro-F	98	364	58	115	13	3	3	24	31	50	.316	.376	.393	110	1	16			.946	4	O-92	0.0
1915	Bro-F	136	511	70	135	23	9	2	39	52	54	.264	.342	.356	97	-9	20			.956	-8	*O-134	-2.5
1918	StL-N	35	132	20	39	4	5	0	6	15	7	.295	.380	.402	143	7	0			.956	-1	O-35	0.4
Total	3	269	1007	148	289	40	17	5	69	98	111	.287	.359	.375	108	-1	36			.952	-5	O-261	-2.1

■ SPARKY ANDERSON
Anderson, George Lee b: 2/22/34, Bridgewater, S.Dak BR/TR, 5'9", 170 lbs. Deb: 4/10/59 MC

YEAR	TM/L	G	AB	R	H	2B	3B	HR	RBI	BB	SO	AVG	OBP	SLG	PRO+	BR/A	SB	CS	SBR	FA	FR	G/POS	TPR
1959	Phi-N	152	477	42	104	9	3	0	34	42	53	.218	.283	.249	43	-38	6	9	-4	.984	3	*2-152	-2.9

■ HAL ANDERSON
Anderson, Harold b: 2/10/04, St.Louis, Mo. d: 5/1/74, St.Louis, Mo. BR/TR, 5'11", 160 lbs. Deb: 4/12/32

YEAR	TM/L	G	AB	R	H	2B	3B	HR	RBI	BB	SO	AVG	OBP	SLG	PRO+	BR/A	SB	CS	SBR	FA	FR	G/POS	TPR
1932	Chi-A	9	32	4	8	0	0	0	2	0	1	.250	.250	.250	32	-3	0	1	-1	1.000	0	/O-9	-0.4

■ HARRY ANDERSON
Anderson, Harry Walter b: 9/10/31, North East, Md. BL/TR, 6'3", 210 lbs. Deb: 4/18/57

YEAR	TM/L	G	AB	R	H	2B	3B	HR	RBI	BB	SO	AVG	OBP	SLG	PRO+	BR/A	SB	CS	SBR	FA	FR	G/POS	TPR
1957	Phi-N	118	400	53	107	15	4	17	56	36	61	.268	.337	.452	113	7	2	3	-1	.986	4	*O-109	0.4
1958	Phi-N	140	515	80	155	34	6	23	97	59	95	.301	.376	.524	137	27	0	2	-1	.975	-2	O-87,1-49	1.7
1959	Phi-N	142	508	50	122	28	6	14	63	43	95	.240	.306	.402	85	-12	1	1	-0	.980	18	*O-137	0.0
1960	Phi-N	38	93	10	23	2	0	5	12	10	19	.247	.333	.430	107	1	0	0	0	1.000	-1	O-16,1-12	-0.2
	Cin-N	42	66	6	11	3	0	1	9	11	20	.167	.286	.258	49	-4	0	0	0	.990	-1	1-15/O-4	-0.7
	Yr	80	159	16	34	5	0	6	21	21	39	.214	.313	.358	82	-4	0	0	0	.989	-2	1-27,O-20	-0.9
1961	Cin-N	4	4	0	1	0	0	0	1	0	1	.250	.250	.250	33	-0	0	0	0	.000	0	H	0.0
Total	5	484	1586	199	419	82	16	60	242	159	291	.264	.337	.450	109	18	3	6	-3	.982	19	O-353/1-76	1.2

■ JIM ANDERSON
Anderson, James Lea b: 2/23/57, Los Angeles, Cal. BR/TR, 6', 170 lbs. Deb: 7/2/78

YEAR	TM/L	G	AB	R	H	2B	3B	HR	RBI	BB	SO	AVG	OBP	SLG	PRO+	BR/A	SB	CS	SBR	FA	FR	G/POS	TPR
1978	Cal-A	48	108	6	21	7	0	0	7	11	16	.194	.269	.259	51	-7	0	0	0	.955	3	S-47/2-1	0.0
1979	*Cal-A	96	234	33	58	13	1	3	23	17	31	.248	.302	.350	78	-7	3	2	-0	.949	-1	S-82,3-10/2-6,C-3	-0.2
1980	Sea-A	116	317	46	72	7	0	8	30	27	39	.227	.294	.325	69	-14	2	4	-2	.958	3	S-65,3-33/2-2,CD	-0.6
1981	Sea-A	70	162	12	33	7	0	2	19	17	29	.204	.283	.284	61	-8	3	5	-2	.947	4	S-68/3-2	-0.1
1983	Tex-A	50	102	8	22	1	1	0	6	5	8	.216	.252	.245	38	-9	1	2	-1	.962	5	S-27,2-17/3-3,OCD	-0.2
1984	Tex-A	39	47	2	5	0	0	0	1	4	7	.106	.176	.106	-19	-8	0	0	0	.989	10	S-31/3-6,2-1	-0.0
Total	6	419	970	107	211	35	2	13	86	81	130	.218	.281	.298	60	-52	9	13	-5	.955	24	S-320/3-54,2DCO	-0.7

■ JOHN ANDERSON
Anderson, John Joseph "Honest John" b: 12/14/1873, Sarpsborg, Norway d: 7/23/49, Worcester, Mass. BB/TR, 6'2", 180 lbs. Deb: 9/8/1894

YEAR	TM/L	G	AB	R	H	2B	3B	HR	RBI	BB	SO	AVG	OBP	SLG	PRO+	BR/A	SB	CS	SBR	FA	FR	G/POS	TPR
1894	Bro-N	17	63	14	19	1	3	1	19	3	3	.302	.333	.460	97	-1	7			.778	-5	O-16/3-1	-0.5
1895	Bro-N	102	419	76	120	11	14	9	87	12	29	.286	.314	.444	102	-1	24			.882	-6	*O-101	-1.2
1896	Bro-N	108	430	70	135	23	17	1	55	18	23	.314	.344	.453	116	8	37			.942	-3	O-68,1-42	0.0
1897	Bro-N	117	492	93	160	28	12	4	85	17		.325	.357	.455	120	12	29			.936	0	*O-115/1-3	0.3
1898	Bro-N	6	21	1	3	2	0	0	2	1		.143	.217	.238	31	-2	0			1.000	0	/O-5	-0.2
	Was-N	110	430	70	131	28	18	9	71	23		.305	.357	.516	150	24	18			.948	-1	O-93,1-17	2.4
	Bro-N	19	69	11	19	3	4	0	8	5		.275	.333	.435	120	1	2			.966	-1	O-17/1-2	0.0
	Yr	135	520	82	153	33	**22**	9	81	29		.294	.348	**.494**	141	24	20			.952	8	*O-115,1-19	2.2
1899	Bro-N	117	439	65	118	18	7	4	92	7		.269	.317	.369	86	-10	25			.933	-4	O-76,1-41	-1.7
1901	Mil-A	138	576	90	190	46	7	8	99	24		.330	.360	.476	137	26	35			**.982**	5	*1-125,O-13	2.6
1902	StL-A	126	524	60	149	29	6	4	85	21		.284	.316	.385	95	-5	16			.985	-9	*1-126/O-3	-1.6
1903	StL-A	138	550	65	156	34	8	2	78	23		.284	.312	.385	111	6	16			.986	4	*1-133/O-7	0.8
1904	NY-A	143	558	62	155	27	12	3	82	23		.278	.313	.385	115	9	20			.956	-0	*O-112,1-33	0.1
1905	NY-A	32	99	12	23	1	2	0	14	8		.232	.296	.283	75	-3	9			.900	-2	O-22/1-3	-0.6
	Was-A	101	400	50	116	21	6	1	38	22		.290	.330	.380	130	12	22			.960	0	O-97/1-4	0.8

YEAR	TM/L	G	AB	R	H	2B	3B	HR	RBI	BB	SO	AVG	OBP	SLG	PRO+	BR/A	SB	CS	SBR	FA	FR	G/POS	TPR
	Yr	133	499	62	139	24	7	1	52	30		.279	.323	.361	117	9	31			.949	-2	*O-119/1-7	0.2
1906	Was-A	151	583	62	158	25	4	3	70	19		.271	.296	.343	105	1	**39**			.953	5	*O-151	-0.2
1907	Was-A	87	333	33	96	12	4	0	44	34		.288	.359	.348	136	14	19			.983	-1	1-61,O-26	1.2
1908	Chi-A	123	355	36	93	17	1	0	47	30		.262	.321	.315	109	4	21			.963	-6	O-87/1-9	-0.6
Total	14	1635	6341	870	1841	328	124	49	976	310	55	.290	.329	.404			96			.939	-13	*O-1009,1-599/3-1	1.6

■ KENT ANDERSON

Anderson, Kent McKay b: 8/12/63, Florence, S.C. BR/TR, 6'1", 180 lbs. Deb: 4/15/89 F

YEAR	TM/L	G	AB	R	H	2B	3B	HR	RBI	BB	SO	AVG	OBP	SLG	PRO+	BR/A	SB	CS	SBR	FA	FR	G/POS	TPR
1989	Cal-A	86	223	27	51	6	1	0	17	17	42	.229	.286	.265	57	-12	1	2	-1	.972	14	S-70/2-7,3-5,O-2,D	0.6
1990	Cal-A	49	143	16	44	6	1	1	5	13	19	.308	.369	.385	113	3	0	2	-1	.964	13	S-28,3-16/2-5	1.6
Total	2	135	366	43	95	12	2	1	22	30	61	.260	.319	.311	79	-9	1	4	-2	.969	27	/S-98,3-21,2-12,OD	2.2

■ MIKE ANDERSON

Anderson, Michael Allen b: 6/22/51, Florence, S.C. BR/TR, 6'2", 200 lbs. Deb: 9/2/71 F

YEAR	TM/L	G	AB	R	H	2B	3B	HR	RBI	BB	SO	AVG	OBP	SLG	PRO+	BR/A	SB	CS	SBR	FA	FR	G/POS	TPR
1971	Phi-N	26	89	11	22	5	1	2	5	13	28	.247	.343	.393	108	1	0	0	0	.986	2	O-26	0.2
1972	Phi-N	36	103	8	20	5	1	2	9	19	36	.194	.320	.320	80	-2	1	0	0	.987	4	O-35	0.0
1973	Phi-N	87	193	32	49	9	1	9	28	19	53	.254	.324	.451	110	2	0	3	-2	.981	-6	O-67	-0.8
1974	Phi-N	145	395	35	99	22	2	5	34	37	75	.251	.315	.354	83	-9	2	1	0	.980	4	*O-133/1-1	-1.0
1975	Phi-N	115	247	24	64	10	3	4	28	17	66	.259	.312	.372	86	-5	1	2	-1	.977	-10	*O-105/1-3	-1.9
1976	StL-N	86	199	17	58	8	1	1	12	26	30	.291	.376	.357	108	3	1	1	-0	.982	1	O-58/1-5	0.1
1977	StL-N	94	154	18	34	4	1	4	17	14	31	.221	.309	.338	68	-7	2	3	-1	.980	-10	O-77	-2.0
1978	Bal-A	53	32	2	3	0	1	0	3	3	10	.094	.171	.156	-8	-5	0	0	0	.962	-15	O-47	-2.1
1979	Phi-N	79	78	12	18	4	0	1	2	13	14	.231	.341	.321	79	-2	2	1	-1	.973	-13	O-70/P-1	-1.8
Total	9	721	1490	159	367	67	11	28	134	161	343	.246	.321	.362	88	-24	8	12	-5	.980	-44	O-618/1-9,P-1	-9.3

■ ERNIE ANDRES

Andres, Ernest Henry "Junie" b: 1/11/18, Jeffersonville, Ind. BR/TR, 6'1", 200 lbs. Deb: 4/16/46

YEAR	TM/L	G	AB	R	H	2B	3B	HR	RBI	BB	SO	AVG	OBP	SLG	PRO+	BR/A	SB	CS	SBR	FA	FR	G/POS	TPR
1946	Bos-A	15	41	0	4	2	0	0	1	3	5	.098	.159	.146	-14	-6	0	0	0	1.000	1	3-15	-0.5

■ KIM ANDREW

Andrew, Kim Darrell b: 11/14/53, Glendale, Cal. BR/TR, 5'10", 160 lbs. Deb: 4/16/75

YEAR	TM/L	G	AB	R	H	2B	3B	HR	RBI	BB	SO	AVG	OBP	SLG	PRO+	BR/A	SB	CS	SBR	FA	FR	G/POS	TPR
1975	Bos-A	2	2	0	1	0	0	0	0	0	0	.500	.500	.500	169	0	0	0	0	1.000	-0	/2-2	0.0

■ SHANE ANDREWS

Andrews, Darrell Shane b: 8/28/71, Dallas, Tex. BR/TR, 6'1", 215 lbs. Deb: 4/26/95

YEAR	TM/L	G	AB	R	H	2B	3B	HR	RBI	BB	SO	AVG	OBP	SLG	PRO+	BR/A	SB	CS	SBR	FA	FR	G/POS	TPR
1995	Mon-N	84	220	27	47	10	1	8	31	17	68	.214	.273	.377	67	-11	1	1	-0	.973	2	3-51,1-29	-1.2
1996	Mon-N	127	375	43	85	15	2	19	64	35	119	.227	.296	.429	86	-9	3	1	0	.955	21	*3-123	1.2
Total	2	211	595	70	132	25	3	27	95	52	187	.222	.288	.410	79	-20	4	2	0	.960	23	3-174/1-29	0.0

■ FRED ANDREWS

Andrews, Fred b: 5/4/52, Lafayette, La. BR/TR, 5'8", 163 lbs. Deb: 9/26/76

YEAR	TM/L	G	AB	R	H	2B	3B	HR	RBI	BB	SO	AVG	OBP	SLG	PRO+	BR/A	SB	CS	SBR	FA	FR	G/POS	TPR
1976	Phi-N	4	6	1	4	0	1	0	2	0	0	.667	.778	.667	304	2	1	1	-0	1.000	-1	/2-4	0.2
1977	Phi-N	12	23	3	4	0	1	0		2	5	.174	.208	.261	24	-2	1	0	0	1.000	3	/2-7	0.1
Total	2	16	29	4	8	0	1	0	2	3	5	.276	.364	.345	90	-0	2	1	-0	1.000	2	/2-11	0.3

■ ED ANDREWS

Andrews, George Edward b: 4/5/1859, Painesville, Ohio d: 8/12/34, W.Palm Beach, Fla. BR/TR, 5'8", 160 lbs. Deb: 5/1/1884 U

YEAR	TM/L	G	AB	R	H	2B	3B	HR	RBI	BB	SO	AVG	OBP	SLG	PRO+	BR/A	SB	CS	SBR	FA	FR	G/POS	TPR
1884	Phi-N	109	420	74	93	21	2	0	23	9	42	.221	.238	.281	66	-16				.891	-22	*2-109	-3.2
1885	Phi-N	103	421	77	112	15	3	0	23	22	25	.266	.318	.316	108	4				.921	-0	*O-99/2-5	0.2
1886	Phi-N	107	437	93	109	15	4	2	28	31	35	.249	.299	.316	86	-7	**56**			.903	4	*O-104/2-3	-0.5
1887	Phi-N	104	464	110	151	19	7	4	67	21	21	.325	.359	.422	110	5	57			.902	-4	*O-99/2-7,1-1	-0.1
1888	Phi-N	124	528	75	126	14	4	3	44	21	41	.239	.272	.297	77	-14	35			.903	-4	*O-124	-2.2
1889	Phi-N	10	39	10	11	1	0	0	7	2	4	.282	.317	.308	69	-2	7			.808	-1	/O-9,2-1	-0.5
	Ind-N	40	173	32	53	11	0	0	22	5	10	.306	.330	.370	94	-2	7			.885	-3	O-40/2-1	-0.5
	Yr	50	212	42	64	12	0	0	29	7	14	.302	.327	.358	89	-4	14			.867	-4	O-49/2-2	-0.7
1890	Bro-P	94	395	84	100	14	2	3	38	40	32	.253	.323	.322	68	-19	21			.912	1	*O-94	-1.7
1891	Cin-a	83	356	47	75	7	4	0	26	33	35	.211	.279	.253	48	-26	22			.961	17	O-83	-1.0
Total	8	774	3233	602	830	117	26	12	278	194	245	.257	.301	.320	82	-76	205			.912	-13	O-652,2-126/1-1	-9.2

■ JIM ANDREWS

Andrews, James Pratt b: 6/5/1865, Shelburne Falls, Mass. d: 12/27/07, Chicago, Ill. Deb: 4/19/1890

YEAR	TM/L	G	AB	R	H	2B	3B	HR	RBI	BB	SO	AVG	OBP	SLG	PRO+	BR/A	SB	CS	SBR	FA	FR	G/POS	TPR
1890	Chi-N	53	202	32	38	4	2	3	17	23	41	.188	.278	.272	58	-11	11			.900	1	O-53	-1.1

■ MIKE ANDREWS

Andrews, Michael Jay b: 7/9/43, Los Angeles, Cal. BR/TR, 6'3", 195 lbs. Deb: 9/18/66 F

YEAR	TM/L	G	AB	R	H	2B	3B	HR	RBI	BB	SO	AVG	OBP	SLG	PRO+	BR/A	SB	CS	SBR	FA	FR	G/POS	TPR
1966	Bos-A	5	18	1	3	0	0	0	0	0	2	.167	.167	.167	-4	-2	0	0	0	1.000	2	/2-5	0.0
1967	*Bos-A	142	494	79	130	20	0	8	40	62	72	.263	.348	.352	99	1	7	7	-2	.976	-6	*2-139/S-6	0.2
1968	Bos-A	147	536	77	145	22	1	7	45	81	57	.271	.369	.354	113	11	3	8	-4	.976	-4	*2-139/S-4,3-1	2.0
1969	Bos-A★	121	464	79	136	26	2	15	59	71	53	.293	.393	.455	129	20	1	1	-0	.972	5	*2-148	3.6
1970	Bos-A	151	589	91	149	28	1	17	65	81	63	.253	.346	.390	96	-2	3	2	-1	.973	-30	*2-148	-2.0
1971	Chi-A	109	330	45	93	16	0	12	47	67	36	.282	.405	.439	135	18	3	5	-2	.956	-3	2-76,1-25	1.8
1972	Chi-A	148	505	58	111	18	4	7	50	70	78	.220	.317	.297	82	-9	2	2	-1	.973	-14	*2-145/1-5	-1.9
1973	Chi-A	52	159	10	32	9	0	1	10	23	28	.201	.302	.258	57	-9	0	1	-1	1.000	3	D-30/1-9,2-6,3-5	-1.4
	*Oak-A	18	21	1	4	1	0	0	0	3	1	.190	.292	.238	53	-1	0	0	0	.944	1	/2-9,D-2	-0.2
	Yr	70	180	11	36	10	0	1	10	26	29	.200	.301	.256	57	-10	0	1	-1	.974	-4	D-32,2-15/1-9,3-5	-1.6
Total	8	893	3116	441	803	140	4	66	316	458	390	.258	.356	.369	104	26	18	25	-10	.973	-49	2-787/1-39,D-32,S3	2.1

■ ROB ANDREWS

Andrews, Robert Patrick b: 12/11/52, Santa Monica, Cal. BR/TR, 6', 185 lbs. Deb: 4/7/75 F

YEAR	TM/L	G	AB	R	H	2B	3B	HR	RBI	BB	SO	AVG	OBP	SLG	PRO+	BR/A	SB	CS	SBR	FA	FR	G/POS	TPR
1975	Hou-N	103	277	29	66	5	4	0	19	31	34	.238	.315	.285	73	-10	12	5	1	.982	7	2-94/S-6	0.2
1976	Hou-N	109	410	42	105	8	5	0	23	33	27	.256	.312	.300	81	-11	7	3	0	.977	8	*2-107/S-3	0.5
1977	SF-N	127	436	60	115	11	3	0	25	56	33	.264	.348	.303	76	-12	5	6	-2	.964	-12	*2-115	-1.9
1978	SF-N	79	177	21	39	3	1	0	11	20	18	.220	.299	.288	67	-8	5	1	1	.977	9	2-62/S-1	0.6
1979	SF-N	75	154	22	40	3	2	0	13	8	9	.260	.296	.318	73	-6	4	1	1	.956	4	2-53/3-3	0.1
Total	5	493	1454	174	365	30	15	0	91	148	121	.251	.320	.298	76	-47	33	16	0	.972	15	2-431/S-10,3-3	-0.5

■ STAN ANDREWS

Andrews, Stanley Joseph "Polo" (b: Stanley Joseph Andruskewicz)
b: 4/17/17, Lynn, Mass. d: 6/10/95, Bradenton, Fla. BR/TR, 5'11", 178 lbs. Deb: 6/11/39

YEAR	TM/L	G	AB	R	H	2B	3B	HR	RBI	BB	SO	AVG	OBP	SLG	PRO+	BR/A	SB	CS	SBR	FA	FR	G/POS	TPR
1939	Bos-N	13	26	1	6	0	0	0	1	2		.231	.259	.231	35	-2	0			.857	-2	C-10	-0.4
1940	Bos-N	19	33	1	6	0	0	0	2	0	3	.182	.182	.182	1	-4	1			.944	-1	C-14	-0.5
1944	Bro-N	4	8	1	1	0	0	0	0	1		.125	.222	.125	-1	-1	0			1.000	-0	/C-4	-0.1
1945	Bro-N	21	49	5	8	0	0	0	2	5	4	.163	.255	.204	29	-5	0			.948	2	C-21	-0.2
	Phi-N	13	33	3	11	2	0	1	6	1	5	.333	.353	.485	135	1	0			.950	-1	C-12	0.1
	Yr	34	82	8	19	2	1	1	8	6	9	.232	.292	.317	70	-3	0			.949	1	C-33	-0.1
Total	4	70	149	11	32	2	1	1	12	8	16	.215	.259	.262	46	-11	2			.938	-1	/C-61	-1.1

■ WALLY ANDREWS

Andrews, William Walter b: 9/18/1859, Philadelphia, Pa. d: 1/20/40, Indianapolis, Ind. BR/TR, 6'3", 170 lbs. Deb: 5/22/1884

YEAR	TM/L	G	AB	R	H	2B	3B	HR	RBI	BB	SO	AVG	OBP	SLG	PRO+	BR/A	SB	CS	SBR	FA	FR	G/POS	TPR
1884	Lou-a	14	49	10	10	5	1	0	8	4		.204	.264	.347	102	0				.950	-1	/1-9,3-0,1,S-1	-0.1
1888	Lou-a	26	93	12	18	6	3	0	6	13		.194	.292	.323	99	0	5			.997	2	1-26	-0.1
Total	2	40	142	22	28	11	4	0	14	17		.197	.283	.331	100	0	5			.985	0	/1-35,3-3,S-1,0-1	-0.2

■ FRED ANDRUS

Andrus, Frederick Hotham b: 8/23/1850, Washington, Mich. d: 11/10/37, Detroit, Mich. BR/TR, 6'2", 185 lbs. Deb: 7/25/1876

YEAR	TM/L	G	AB	R	H	2B	3B	HR	RBI	BB	SO	AVG	OBP	SLG	PRO+	BR/A	SB	CS	SBR	FA	FR	G/POS	TPR
1876	Chi-N	8	36	6	11	3	0	0	2	0	5	.306	.306	.389	116	0				.714	-3	/O-8	-0.3
1884	Chi-N	1	5	3	1	0	0	0	0	0		.200	.333	.200	67	-0				1.000	-0	/P-1	0.0
Total	2	9	41	9	12	3	0	0	2	1	5	.293	.310	.366	110	0				.714	-3	/O-8,P-1	-0.3

■ BILL ANDRUS

Andrus, William Morgan "Andy" b: 7/25/07, Beaumont, Tex. d: 3/12/82, Washington, D.C. BR/TR, 6', 185 lbs. Deb: 9/19/31

YEAR	TM/L	G	AB	R	H	2B	3B	HR	RBI	BB	SO	AVG	OBP	SLG	PRO+	BR/A	SB	CS	SBR	FA	FR	G/POS	TPR
1931	Was-A	3	7	0	0	0	0	0	0	0	1	.000	.000	.000	-99	-2	0	0	0	.750	-0	/3-2	-0.2
1937	Phi-N	3	2	0	0	0	0	0	0	0	0	.000	.000	.000	-93	-1	0	0	0	.000	-0	/3-1	-0.1
Total	2	6	9	0	0	0	0	0	0	0	1	.000	.000	.000			0	0	0			/3-3	-0.3

■ WIMAN ANDRUS

Andrus, William Wiman b: 10/14/1858, Orono, Ontario, Can. d: 6/17/35, Miles City, Mont. 5'6.5", 155 lbs. Deb: 9/15/1885

YEAR	TM/L	G	AB	R	H	2B	3B	HR	RBI	BB	SO	AVG	OBP	SLG	PRO+	BR/A	SB	CS	SBR	FA	FR	G/POS	TPR
1885	Pro-N	1	4	0	0	0	0	0	0	0	1	.000	.000	.000	-99	-1				1.000	1	/3-1	0.0

YEAR	TM/L	G	AB	R	H	2B	3B	HR	RBI	BB	SO	AVG	OBP	SLG	PRO+	BR/A	SB	CS	SBR	FA	FR	G/POS	TPR
■ TOM ANGLEY	Angley, Thomas Samuel b: 10/2/04, Baltimore, Md. d: 10/26/52, Wichita, Kan. BL/TR, 5'8", 190 lbs. Deb: 4/23/29																						
1929	Chi-N	5	16	1	4	1	0	0	6	2	2	.250	.333	.313	61	-1	0			.968	1	/C-5	0.1
■ PAT ANKENMAN	Ankenman, Frederick Norman b: 12/23/12, Houston, Tex. d: 1/13/89, Houston, Tex. BR/TR, 5'4", 125 lbs. Deb: 4/16/36																						
1936	StL-N	1	3	0	0	0	0	0	0	0	3	.000	.000	.000	-99	-1	0			.600	-1	/S-1	-0.2
1943	Bro-N	1	2	1	1	0	0	0	0	0	0	.500	.500	.500	189	0	0			1.000	1	/S-1	0.1
1944	Bro-N	13	24	1	6	1	0	0	3	0	2	.250	.250	.292	53	-2	0			.971	-2	2-11/S-2	-0.1
Total	3	15	29	2	7	1	0	0	3	0	5	.241	.241	.276	46	-2	0			.800	-1	/2-11,S-4	-0.2
■ BILL ANNIS	Annis, William Perley b: 3/8/1857, Stoneham, Mass. d: 6/10/23, Kennebunkport, Me BR, 5'7", 150 lbs. Deb: 5/1/1884																						
1884	Bos-N	27	96	17	17	2	0	0	3	0	8	.177	.177	.198	18	-9				.897	-3	O-27	-1.2
■ CAP ANSON	Anson, Adrian Constantine b: 4/11/1852, Marshalltown, Iowa d: 4/14/22, Chicago, Ill. BR/TR, 6', 227 lbs. Deb: 5/6/1871 MH																						
1871	Rok-n	25	120	29	39	11	3	0	16	2	1	.325	.336	.467	134	6	6	2	1	.763	2	*3-20/C-5,2-2,1O	0.4
1872	Ath-n	46	217	60	90	10	7	0	50	16	3	.415	.455	.525	200	26	6	6	-2	.752	-10	*3-46	0.8
1873	Ath-n	52	254	53	101	9	2	0	36	5	1	.398	.409	.449	144	12	0	2	-1	.923	-4	1-36,3-11/C-3,2O	0.5
1874	Ath-n	55	259	51	87	8	3	0	37	4	1	.336	.346	.390	125	5	6	0	2	.936	-6	1-24,3-20/O-8,SC	0.1
1875	Ath-n	69	326	84	106	15	3	0	58	4	2	.325	.333	.390	135	8	11	6	-0	.922	12	1-32,O-25,C-13/3M	1.7
1876	Chi-N	66	309	63	110	9	7	2	59	12	8	.356	.380	.450	157	16				.849	13	*3-66/C-2	2.6
1877	Chi-N	59	255	52	86	19	1	0	32	9	3	.337	.360	.420	129	7				.883	8	*3-40,C-31	1.5
1878	Chi-N	60	261	55	89	12	2	0	40	13	1	.341	.372	.402	145	12				.825	-8	*O-48/2-9,3-3,C-3	0.2
1879	Chi-N	51	227	40	72	20	1	0	34	2	2	.317	.323	.414	133	7				.975	0	1-51/M	0.5
1880	Chi-N	86	356	54	120	24	1	1	74	14	12	.337	.362	.419	154	19				.978	0	*1-81/3-9,S-1,2M	1.2
1881	Chi-N	84	343	67	137	21	7	1	82	26	4	.399	.442	.510	189	35				.975	7	*1-84/C-2,S-1,M	3.1
1882	Chi-N	82	348	69	126	29	8	1	83	20	7	.362	.397	.500	177	29				.949	-1	*1-82/C-1,M	1.7
1883	Chi-N	98	413	70	127	36	5	0	68	18	9	.308	.336	.419	121	9				.964	5	*1-98/P-2,O-1,CM	0.2
1884	Chi-N	112	475	108	159	30	3	21	102	29	13	.335	.373	.543	170	35				.956	-0	*1-112/C-3,S-1,PM	2.0
1885	*Chi-N	112	464	100	144	35	7	7	108	14	13	.310	.357	.461	142	18				.958	-4	*1-112/C-1,M	0.0
1886	*Chi-N	125	504	117	187	35	11	10	147	55	19	.371	.433	.544	170	39	29			.963	9	*1-125,C-12,M	3.0
1887	Chi-N	122	472	107	164	33	13	7	102	60	18	.347	.422	.517	141	24	27			.973	10	*1-122/C-1,M	1.8
1888	Chi-N	134	515	101	177	20	12	12	84	47	24	.344	.400	.499	139	41	28			.986	9	*1-134,M	3.6
1889	Chi-N	134	518	100	161	32	7	7	117	86	19	.311	.414	.440	132	24	27			.982	9	*1-134,M	2.1
1890	Chi-N	139	504	95	157	14	5	7	107	113	23	.312	.443	.401	141	33	29			.978	0	*1-135/C-3,2-2,M	2.3
1891	Chi-N	136	540	81	157	24	8	8	120	75	29	.291	.378	.409	129	21	17			.981	8	*1-136/C-2,M	2.0
1892	Chi-N	146	559	62	152	25	9	1	74	67	30	.272	.354	.354	113	10	13			.973	-5	*1-146/M	-0.2
1893	Chi-N	103	398	70	125	24	2	0	91	68	12	.314	.415	.384	115	12	13			.981	-4	*1-101/M	0.4
1894	Chi-N	83	340	82	132	28	4	5	99	40	15	.388	.457	.538	132	17	18			.990	3	1-82/2-1,M	1.6
1895	Chi-N	122	474	87	159	23	6	2	91	55	23	.335	.408	.422	107	6	12			.985	-1	*1-122/M	0.6
1896	Chi-N	108	402	72	133	18	5	2	90	49	10	.331	.407	.400	109	7	24			.983	-1	*1-98,C-10,M	0.7
1897	Chi-N	114	424	67	121	17	3	3	75	60		.285	.379	.361	92	-3	11			.975	1	*1-103,C-11,M	0.5
Total	5 n	247	1176	277	423	53	18	0	197	31	8	.360	.376	.435	146	56	29	16	-1	.765	-6	3-102/1-93,OCS2	3.5
Total	22	2276	9101	1719	2995	528	124	97	1879	952	294	.329	.395	.446	138	417	247			.974	57	*1-2058,3-118/CO2PS	30.8
■ ERIC ANTHONY	Anthony, Eric Todd b: 11/8/67, San Diego, Cal. BL/TL, 6'2", 195 lbs. Deb: 7/29/89																						
1989	Hou-N	25	61	7	11	2	0	4	7	9	16	.180	.286	.410	100	-0	0	0	0	1.000	-1	O-21	-0.1
1990	Hou-N	84	239	26	46	8	0	10	29	29	78	.192	.285	.351	76	-8	5	0	2	.970	-1	O-71	-1.1
1991	Hou-N	39	118	11	18	6	0	1	7	12	41	.153	.231	.229	31	-11	1	0	0	.986	3	O-37	-0.9
1992	Hou-N	137	440	45	105	15	1	19	80	38	98	.239	.301	.407	103	0	5	4	-1	.973	-6	*O-115	-1.0
1993	Hou-N	145	486	70	121	19	4	15	66	49	99	.249	.320	.397	94	-5	3	5	-2	.988	-7	*O-131	-1.7
1994	Sea-A	79	262	31	62	14	1	10	30	23	66	.237	.298	.412	79	-9	6	2	1	.985	-1	O-71/D-4	-1.1
1995	*Cin-N	47	134	19	36	6	0	5	23	13	30	.269	.333	.425	99	-0	2	1	0	1.000	-1	O-24,1-17	-0.3
1996	Cin-N	47	123	22	30	6	0	8	13	22	36	.244	.359	.488	121	4	0	0	0	.949	-5	O-37	-0.3
	Col-N	32	62	10	15	2	0	4	9	10	20	.242	.347	.468	87	-2	0	1	-1	1.000	4	O-19	-0.5
	Yr	79	185	32	45	8	0	12	22	32	56	.243	.355	.481	106	1	0	1	-1	.967	-8	O-56	-0.8
Total	8	635	1925	241	444	78	6	76	264	205	473	.231	.306	.396	90	-31	22	14	-2	.981	-25	O-526/1-17,D-4	-7.0
■ JOE ANTOLICK	Antolick, Joseph b: 4/11/16, Hokendauqua, Pa. BR/TR, 6', 185 lbs. Deb: 9/20/44																						
1944	Phi-N	4	6	1	2	0	0	0	0	1	0	.333	.429	.333	120	0	0			1.000	1	/C-3	0.1
■ JOHN ANTONELLI	Antonelli, John Lawrence b: 7/15/15, Memphis, Tenn. d: 4/18/90, Memphis, Tenn. BR/TR, 5'10.5", 165 lbs. Deb: 9/16/44																						
1944	StL-N	8	21	1	4	1	0	0	4	0	4	.190	.190	.238	20	-2	0			1.000	1	/1-3,3,3-2,2-2	-0.1
1945	StL-N	2	3	0	0	0	0	0	0	1	0	.000	.000	.000	-98	-1	0			.667	-0	/3-1	-0.1
	Phi-N	125	504	50	129	27	2	1	28	24	24	.256	.292	.323	73	-19	1			.959	-9	*3-108,2-23/1-1,S-1	-2.5
	Yr	127	507	50	129	27	2	1	28	25	24	.254	.291	.321	72	-20	1			.957	-9	*3-109,2-23/1-1,S-1	-2.6
Total	2	135	528	50	133	28	2	1	29	24	29	.252	.287	.318	70	-22	1			.958	-8	3-112/2-25,1-4,S-1	-2.7
■ BILL ANTONELLO	Antonello, William James b: 5/19/27, Brooklyn, N.Y. d: 3/4/93, Fridley, Minn. BR/TR, 5'11", 185 lbs. Deb: 4/30/53																						
1953	Bro-N	40	43	9	7	1	1	1	5	6	11	.163	.200	.302	28	-5	0	0	0	.964	-6	O-25	-1.0
■ LUIS APARICIO	Aparicio, Luis Ernesto (Montiel) b: 4/29/34, Maracaibo, Venez. BR/TR, 5'9", 160 lbs. Deb: 4/17/56 H																						
1956	Chi-A	152	533	69	142	19	6	3	56	34	63	.266	.312	.341	71	-23	21	4	4	.954	0	*S-152	-0.6
1957	Chi-A	143	575	82	148	22	6	3	41	52	55	.257	.319	.332	78	-17	28	8	4	.972	-13	*S-142	-1.4
1958	Chi-A★	145	557	76	148	20	9	2	40	35	38	.266	.310	.345	82	-14	29	6	5	.973	9	*S-145	1.3
1959	*Chi-A★	152	612	98	157	18	5	6	51	53	40	.257	.319	.332	80	-16	56	13	9	.970	-4	*S-152	0.2
1960	Chi-A★	153	600	86	166	20	7	2	61	43	39	.277	.326	.343	82	-15	51	8	11	.979	30	*S-153	3.8
1961	Chi-A	156	625	90	170	24	4	6	45	38	33	.272	.315	.352	79	-19	53	13	8	.962	6	*S-156	0.8
1962	Chi-A★	153	581	72	140	23	5	7	40	32	36	.241	.282	.342	65	-29	31	12	2	.973	10	*S-152	-0.5
1963	Bal-A★	146	601	73	150	18	5	5	45	36	35	.250	.294	.331	78	-18	40	6	8	.983	-5	*S-145	1.5
1964	Bal-A†	146	578	93	154	20	3	10	37	49	51	.266	.327	.363	92	-4	57	17	7	.979	3	*S-145	1.5
1965	Bal-A	144	564	67	127	20	10	8	40	46	56	.225	.287	.339	76	-18	26	7	4	.971	7	*S-141	-0.2
1966	*Bal-A	151	659	97	182	25	6	6	41	33	42	.276	.312	.366	95	-5	25	11	1	.978	10	*S-151	2.2
1967	Bal-A	134	546	55	127	22	5	4	31	29	44	.233	.273	.313	73	-19	18	5	2	.957	-20	*S-131	-2.6
1968	Chi-A	155	622	55	164	24	4	4	36	33	43	.264	.303	.334	92	-7	17	11	-2	.977	25	*S-154	3.7
1969	Chi-A	156	599	77	168	24	5	5	51	66	29	.280	.354	.362	96	-2	24	4	5	.976	29	*S-154	5.1
1970	Chi-A★	146	552	86	173	29	3	5	43	53	34	.313	.375	.404	110	9	8	3	1	.976	18	*S-146	4.6
1971	Bos-A★	125	491	56	114	23	0	4	45	35	43	.232	.286	.303	63	-24	6	3	-1	.971	-18	*S-121	-2.9
1972	Bos-A†	110	436	47	112	26	3	3	39	26	28	.257	.302	.351	89	-6	3	3	-1	.968	-17	*S-109	-1.0
1973	Bos-A	132	499	56	135	17	1	0	49	43	33	.271	.328	.309	76	-15	13	3	-1	.966	-17	*S-132	-1.2
Total	18	2599	10230	1335	2677	394	92	83	791	736	742	.262	.313	.343	82	-245	506	136	70	.972	51	*S-2581	12.4
■ LUKE APPLING	Appling, Lucius Benjamin b: 4/2/07, High Point, N.C. d: 1/3/91, Cumming, Ga. BR/TR, 5'10", 183 lbs. Deb: 9/10/30 MCH																						
1930	Chi-A	6	26	2	8	2	0	0	2	0	0	.308	.308	.385	77	-1	2	0	1	.879	-1	/S-6	-0.1
1931	Chi-A	96	297	36	69	13	4	1	28	29	27	.232	.303	.313	66	-15	9	2	2	.900	-6	S-76/2-1	-1.1
1932	Chi-A	139	489	66	134	20	10	3	63	40	36	.274	.329	.374	87	-10	9	8	-2	.929	18	S-85,2-30,3-14	1.4
1933	Chi-A	151	612	90	197	36	10	6	85	56	29	.322	.379	.443	122	19	6	11	-5	.939	11	*S-151	3.4
1934	Chi-A	118	452	75	137	28	6	2	61	59	27	.303	.384	.405	100	2	3	1	0	.945	-9	*S-110/2-8	0.0
1935	Chi-A	153	525	94	161	28	6	1	71	122	40	.307	.437	.389	112	17	12	6	0	.958	21	*S-153	4.3
1936	Chi-A★	138	526	111	204	31	7	6	128	85	25	.388	.474	.508	137	36	10	6	-1	.951	15	*S-137	5.1
1937	Chi-A	154	574	98	182	42	8	4	77	86	28	.317	.407	.439	113	15	18	10	-1	.944	14	*S-154	3.5
1938	Chi-A	81	294	41	89	14	0	0	44	42	17	.303	.392	.350	85	-5	1	3	-2	.953	1	S-78	0.1
1939	Chi-A☆	148	516	82	162	16	6	0	56	105	37	.314	.430	.368	103	3	16	9	-1	.951	-2	*S-148	1.8

YEAR	TM/L	G	AB	R	H	2B	3B	HR	RBI	BB	SO	AVG	OBP	SLG	PRO+	BR/A	SB	CS	SBR	FA	FR	G/POS	TPR
1940	Chi-A★	150	566	96	197	27	13	0	79	69	35	.348	.420	.442	122	22	3	5	-2	.953	-2	*S-150	2.9
1941	Chi-A☆	154	592	93	186	26	8	1	57	82	32	.314	.399	.390	111	13	12	8	-1	.948	0	*S-154	2.2
1942	Chi-A	142	543	78	142	26	4	3	53	63	23	.262	.342	.341	94	-3	17	5	2	.948	-7	*S-141	0.1
1943	Chi-A☆	155	585	63	192	33	2	3	80	90	29	**.328**	**.419**	.407	142	35	27	8	3	.957	7	*S-155	6.0
1945	Chi-A	18	57	12	21	2	2	1	10	12	7	.368	.478	.526	197	8	1	0	0	.930	-1	S-17	0.9
1946	Chi-A★	149	582	59	180	27	5	1	55	71	41	.309	.384	.378	118	16	6	4	-1	.951	-1	*S-149	3.2
1947	Chi-A★	139	503	67	154	29	0	8	49	64	28	.306	.386	.412	126	19	8	6	-1	.949	-7	*S-129/3-2	1.8
1948	Chi-A	139	497	63	156	16	2	0	47	94	35	.314	.423	.354	112	14	10	4	1	.943	12	3-72,S-64	2.9
1949	Chi-A	142	492	82	148	21	5	5	58	121	24	.301	.439	.394	125	25	7	12	-5	.964	-1	*S-141	2.8
1950	Chi-A	50	128	11	30	3	4	0	13	12	8	.234	.300	.320	61	-8	2	0	1	.967	0	S-20,1-13/2-1	-0.5
Total	20	2422	8856	1319	2749	440	102	45	1116	1302	528	.310	.399	.398	113	207	179	108	-11	.948	73	*S-2218/3-88,2-40,1	40.7

■ ANGEL ARAGON
Aragon, Angel (Valdes) "Pete" b: 8/2/1890, Havana, Cuba d: 1/24/52, New York, N.Y. BR/TR, 5'5", 150 lbs. Deb: 8/20/14 F

YEAR	TM/L	G	AB	R	H	2B	3B	HR	RBI	BB	SO	AVG	OBP	SLG	PRO+	BR/A	SB	CS	SBR	FA	FR	G/POS	TPR
1914	NY-A	6	7	1	1	0	0	0	0	1	2	.143	.333	.143	44	-0	0			.000	-1	/O-1	-0.1
1916	NY-A	12	24	1	5	0	0	0	3	2	2	.208	.269	.208	43	-2	2			.864	1	/3-8,O-2	0.0
1917	NY-A	14	45	2	3	1	0	0	2	0	6	.067	.106	.089	-40	-8	0			.933	1	/O-6,3-4,S-2	-0.8
Total	3	32	76	4	9	1	0	0	5	5	6	.118	.183	.132	-4	-10	2			.921	1	/3-12,O-9,S-2	-0.9

■ JACK ARAGON
Aragon, Angel Valdes (Reyes) b: 11/20/15, Havana, Cuba d: 4/4/88, Clearwater, Fla. BR/TR, 5'10", 176 lbs. Deb: 8/13/41 F

YEAR	TM/L	G	AB	R	H	2B	3B	HR	RBI	BB	SO	AVG	OBP	SLG	PRO+	BR/A	SB	CS	SBR	FA	FR	G/POS	TPR
1941	NY-N	1	0	0	0	0	0	0	0	0	0						0	0		.000	0	R	0.0

■ MAURICE ARCHDEACON
Archdeacon, Maurice John "Flash" b: 12/14/1898, St.Louis, Mo. d: 9/5/54, St.Louis, Mo. BL/TL, 5'8", 153 lbs. Deb: 9/17/23

YEAR	TM/L	G	AB	R	H	2B	3B	HR	RBI	BB	SO	AVG	OBP	SLG	PRO+	BR/A	SB	CS	SBR	FA	FR	G/POS	TPR
1923	Chi-A	22	87	23	35	5	1	0	4	6	8	.402	.441	.483	145	6	2	3	-1	.918	-2	O-20	0.1
1924	Chi-A	95	288	59	92	9	3	0	25	40	30	.319	.410	.372	106	5	11	7	-1	.958	-5	O-77	-0.5
1925	Chi-A	10	9	2	1	0	0	0	0	2	1	.111	.273	.111	0	-1	0	0	0	1.000	-0	/O-1	-0.1
Total	3	127	384	84	128	14	4	0	29	48	39	.333	.413	.391	112	9	13	10	-2	.950	-7	/O-98	-0.5

■ JIMMY ARCHER
Archer, James Patrick b: 5/13/1883, Dublin, Ireland d: 3/29/58, Milwaukee, Wis. BR/TR, 5'10", 168 lbs. Deb: 9/6/04

YEAR	TM/L	G	AB	R	H	2B	3B	HR	RBI	BB	SO	AVG	OBP	SLG	PRO+	BR/A	SB	CS	SBR	FA	FR	G/POS	TPR
1904	Pit-N	7	20	1	3	0	0	0	1	0		.150	.150	.150	-7	-2	0			.919	0	/C-7,O-1	-0.2
1907	*Det-A	18	42	6	5	0	0	0	0	4		.119	.196	.119	1	-5	0			.975	2	C-17/2-1	-0.1
1909	Chi-N	80	261	31	60	9	2	1	30	12		.230	.266	.291	71	-10	5			.960	-4	C-80	-0.7
1910	*Chi-N	98	313	36	81	17	6	2	41	14	49	.259	.293	.371	94	-4	6			.970	3	C-49,1-40	0.4
1911	Chi-N	116	387	41	98	18	5	4	41	18	43	.253	.288	.357	80	-12	5			.977	-1	*C-102,1-10/2-1	-0.3
1912	Chi-N	120	385	35	109	20	1	6	58	22	36	.283	.330	.387	96	-3	7			.966	-5	*C-118	0.3
1913	Chi-N	111	368	38	98	14	7	2	44	19	27	.266	.311	.359	91	-5	4			.969	-3	*C-103/1-8	0.1
1914	Chi-N	79	248	17	64	9	2	0	19	9	9	.258	.284	.310	77	-8	1			.973	5	C-76	0.4
1915	Chi-N	97	309	21	75	11	5	1	27	11	38	.243	.273	.320	79	-9	5	6	-2	.977	-3	C-88/1-4	-0.6
1916	Chi-N	77	205	11	45	6	2	1	30	12	24	.220	.269	.283	63	-9	3			.979	-3	C-61/3-1	-0.9
1917	Chi-N	2	2	0	0	0	0	0	0	0	1	.000	.000	.000	-93	-0	0			.000	0	H	-0.1
1918	Pit-N	24	58	4	9	1	2	0	3	1	6	.155	.197	.241	32	-5	0			.989	5	C-21/1-1	0.1
	Bro-N	9	22	3	6	0	1	0	0	1	5	.273	.304	.364	104	-0	0			.968	1	/C-7	0.1
	Cin-N	9	26	2	7	1	0	0	2	1	3	.269	.296	.308	86	-0	0			1.000	1	/C-7,1-1	0.1
	Yr	42	106	9	22	2	3	0	5	3	14	.208	.243	.283	59	-5	0			.987	7	C-35/1-2	0.3
Total	12	847	2646	246	660	106	33	17	296	124	241	.249	.288	.334	80	-72	36	6		.971	-0	C-736/1-64,2-2,3O	-1.4

■ GEORGE ARCHIE
Archie, George Albert b: 4/27/14, Nashville, Tenn. BR/TR, 6', 170 lbs. Deb: 9/14/38

YEAR	TM/L	G	AB	R	H	2B	3B	HR	RBI	BB	SO	AVG	OBP	SLG	PRO+	BR/A	SB	CS	SBR	FA	FR	G/POS	TPR
1938	Det-A	3	2	1	0	0	0	0	0	1		.000	.000	.000	-95	-1	0			.000	0	H	-0.1
1941	Was-A	105	379	45	102	20	4	3	48	30	42	.269	.324	.367	87	-8	8	4	0	.936	-4	3-73,1-23	-1.2
	StL-A	9	29	3	11	3	0	0	5	7	3	.379	.500	.483	156	3	2	0	1	.975	0	/1-8	0.3
	Yr	114	408	48	113	23	4	3	53	37	45	.277	.339	.375	92	-5	10	4	1	.936	-4	3-73,1-31	-0.9
1946	StL-A	4	11	1	2	1	0	0	0	0	1	.182	.182	.273	25	-1	0	0	0	1.000	0	/1-3	-0.1
Total	3	121	421	50	115	24	4	3	53	37	47	.273	.333	.371	90	-7	10	4	1	.988	-2	/3-73,1-34	-0.9

■ JOSE ARCIA
Arcia, Jose Raimundo (Orta) b: 8/22/43, Havana, Cuba BR/TR, 6'3", 170 lbs. Deb: 4/10/68

YEAR	TM/L	G	AB	R	H	2B	3B	HR	RBI	BB	SO	AVG	OBP	SLG	PRO+	BR/A	SB	CS	SBR	FA	FR	G/POS	TPR
1968	Chi-N	59	84	15	16	4	0	1	8	3	24	.190	.218	.274	44	-6	0	0	0	1.000	-2	O-17,2-10/S-7,3-1	-0.9
1969	SD-N	120	302	35	65	11	3	0	10	14	47	.215	.255	.272	49	-21	14	7	0	.977	5	2-68,S-37/3-8,O1	-1.0
1970	SD-N	114	229	28	51	9	3	0	17	12	36	.223	.282	.288	55	-15	3	6	-3	.955	10	S-67,2-20/3-9,O-7	-0.1
Total	3	293	615	78	132	24	6	1	35	29	107	.215	.260	.278	51	-41	17	13	-3	.950	13	S-111/2-98,O-28,31	-2.0

■ DAN ARDELL
Ardell, Daniel Miers b: 5/27/41, Seattle, Wash. BL/TL, 6'2", 190 lbs. Deb: 9/14/61

YEAR	TM/L	G	AB	R	H	2B	3B	HR	RBI	BB	SO	AVG	OBP	SLG	PRO+	BR/A	SB	CS	SBR	FA	FR	G/POS	TPR
1961	LA-A	7	4	1	1	0	0	0	0	1	2	.250	.400	.250	70	-0	0	0	0	1.000	-0	/1-1	0.0

■ JOE ARDNER
Ardner, Joseph A. "Old Hoss" b: 2/27/1858, Mt.Vernon, Ohio d: 9/15/35, Cleveland, Ohio BR/TR, 160 lbs. Deb: 5/1/1884

YEAR	TM/L	G	AB	R	H	2B	3B	HR	RBI	BB	SO	AVG	OBP	SLG	PRO+	BR/A	SB	CS	SBR	FA	FR	G/POS	TPR
1884	Cle-N	26	92	6	16	1	0	4	4	1	24	.174	.183	.207	21	-8				.866	-5	2-25/3-1	-1.1
1890	Cle-N	84	323	28	72	13	1	0	35	17	40	.223	.266	.269	57	-18	9			.920	-6	2-84	-1.7
Total	2	110	415	34	88	14	2	0	39	18	64	.212	.248	.255	50	-26	9			.908	-11	2-109/3-1	-2.8

■ HANK ARFT
Arft, Henry Irven "Bow Wow" b: 1/28/22, Manchester, Mo. BL/TL, 5'10.5", 190 lbs. Deb: 7/27/48

YEAR	TM/L	G	AB	R	H	2B	3B	HR	RBI	BB	SO	AVG	OBP	SLG	PRO+	BR/A	SB	CS	SBR	FA	FR	G/POS	TPR
1948	StL-A	69	248	25	59	10	3	5	38	45	43	.238	.355	.363	89	-3	1	2	-1	.995	-1	1-69	-0.5
1949	StL-A	6	5	1	1	1	0	0	2	0	1	.200	.200	.400	55	-0	0	0	0	.000	0	H	-0.0
1950	StL-A	98	280	45	75	16	4	1	32	46	48	.268	.375	.364	87	-5	3	2	-0	.995	-1	1-84	-0.5
1951	StL-A	112	345	44	90	16	5	7	42	41	34	.261	.339	.397	96	-2	4	6	-2	.989	8	1-97	-0.1
1952	StL-A	15	28	1	4	3	1	0	4	5	7	.143	.273	.321	63	-1	0	0	0	.985	-0	1-10	-0.2
Total	5	300	906	116	229	46	13	13	118	137	133	.253	.352	.375	90	-12	8	10	-4	.992	8	1-260	-1.3

■ ALEX ARIAS
Arias, Alejandro b: 11/20/67, New York, N.Y. BR/TR, 6'3", 185 lbs. Deb: 5/12/92

YEAR	TM/L	G	AB	R	H	2B	3B	HR	RBI	BB	SO	AVG	OBP	SLG	PRO+	BR/A	SB	CS	SBR	FA	FR	G/POS	TPR
1992	Chi-N	32	99	14	29	6	0	0	7	11	13	.293	.375	.354	105	1	0	0	0	.967	-4	S-30	-0.1
1993	Fla-N	96	249	27	67	5	1	2	20	27	18	.269	.348	.321	76	-7	1	1	-0	.987	-9	2-30,3-22,S-18	-1.4
1994	Fla-N	59	113	4	27	5	0	0	15	9	19	.239	.301	.283	52	-8	0	1	-1	.985	-5	S-20,3-15	-1.2
1995	Fla-N	94	216	22	58	9	2	3	26	22	20	.269	.342	.370	87	-4	1	0	0	.947	-5	S-36,3-21/2-6	-0.5
1996	Fla-N	100	224	27	62	11	2	3	26	17	28	.277	.336	.384	93	-2	2	0	1	.956	1	3-59,S-20/1-1,2-1	0.1
Total	5	381	901	94	243	36	5	8	94	86	98	.270	.341	.347	83	-20	4	2	-1	.961	-22	S-124,3-117/2-37,1	-3.1

■ GEORGE ARIAS
Arias, George Alberto b: 3/12/72, Tucson, Ariz. BR/TR, 5'11", 190 lbs. Deb: 4/2/96

YEAR	TM/L	G	AB	R	H	2B	3B	HR	RBI	BB	SO	AVG	OBP	SLG	PRO+	BR/A	SB	CS	SBR	FA	FR	G/POS	TPR
1996	Cal-A	84	252	19	60	8	1	6	28	16	50	.238	.284	.349	60	-16	2	0	1	.960	28	3-83/D-1	1.2

■ BUZZ ARLETT
Arlett, Russell Loris b: 1/3/1899, Elmhurst, Cal. d: 5/16/64, Minneapolis, Minn. BB/TR, 6'3.5", 225 lbs. Deb: 4/14/31

YEAR	TM/L	G	AB	R	H	2B	3B	HR	RBI	BB	SO	AVG	OBP	SLG	PRO+	BR/A	SB	CS	SBR	FA	FR	G/POS	TPR
1931	Phi-N	121	418	65	131	26	7	18	72	45	39	.313	.387	.538	135	20	3			.955	1	O-94,1-13	1.4

■ TONY ARMAS
Armas, Antonio Rafael (Machado) b: 7/2/53, Anzoategui, Venez. BR/TR, 6'1", 200 lbs. Deb: 9/6/76 F

YEAR	TM/L	G	AB	R	H	2B	3B	HR	RBI	BB	SO	AVG	OBP	SLG	PRO+	BR/A	SB	CS	SBR	FA	FR	G/POS	TPR
1976	Pit-N	4	6	0	2	0	0	0	0	0	2	.333	.333	.333	89	-0	0	0	0	1.000	-0	/O-2	0.0
1977	Oak-A	118	363	26	87	8	2	13	53	20	99	.240	.279	.380	79	-12	1	2	-1	.981	9	O-112/S-1	-0.7
1978	Oak-A	91	239	17	51	6	1	2	13	10	62	.213	.251	.272	50	-16	1	2	-1	.991	-0	O-85/D-3	-1.8
1979	Oak-A	80	278	29	69	9	3	11	34	16	67	.248	.292	.421	95	-3	1	0	0	.976	1	O-80	0.1
1980	Oak-A	158	628	87	175	18	8	35	109	29	128	.279	.313	.500	128	19	5	3	-0	.975	18	*O-158	3.1
1981	*Oak-A★	109	440	51	115	24	3	**22**	76	19	115	.261	.295	.480	126	11	5	1	1	.993	12	*O-109	2.1
1982	Oak-A	138	536	58	125	19	2	28	89	33	128	.233	.279	.433	96	-5	2	4	-1	.983	-1	*O-135/D-1	0.2
1983	Bos-A	145	574	77	125	23	2	36	107	29	131	.218	.254	.453	85	-14	0	1	-1	.985	-6	*O-116,D-27	-1.3
1984	Bos-A☆	157	639	107	171	29	5	**43**	**123**	32	156	.268	.304	.531	120	14	1	3	-2	.974	-0	*O-126,D-31	0.9
1985	Bos-A	103	385	40	102	17	5	23	64	19	91	.265	.301	.514	114	5	0	0	0	.983	-7	O-79,D-19	-0.5
1986	*Bos-A	121	425	40	112	21	4	11	58	24	77	.264	.306	.409	92	-5	0	1	0	.969	-13	*O-117/D-1	-2.4
1987	Cal-A	28	81	8	16	3	1	3	9	1	11	.198	.207	.370	51	-6	0	1	0	1.000	-4	O-27	-1.0

YEAR	TM/L	G	AB	R	H	2B	3B	HR	RBI	BB	SO	AVG	OBP	SLG	PRO+	BR/A	SB	CS	SBR	FA	FR	G/POS	TPR
1988	Cal-A	120	368	42	100	20	2	13	49	22	87	.272	.313	.443	112	5	1	3	-2	.986	-9	*O-113/D-5	-0.9
1989	Cal-A	60	202	22	52	7	1	11	30	7	48	.257	.282	.465	109	1	0	0	0	.990	2	O-47/1-2,D-6	0.2
Total	14	1432	5164	614	1302	204	39	251	815	260	1201	.252	.290	.453	103	-7	18	20	-7	.981	38	*O-1306/D-93,1-2,S	-2.0

■ MARCOS ARMAS
Armas, Marcos Rafael (Ruiz)   b: 8/5/69, Puerto Piritu, Venez.   BR/TR, 6'5", 195 lbs.   Deb: 5/25/93   F

YEAR	TM/L	G	AB	R	H	2B	3B	HR	RBI	BB	SO	AVG	OBP	SLG	PRO+	BR/A	SB	CS	SBR	FA	FR	G/POS	TPR
1993	Oak-A	15	31	7	6	2	0	1	1	1	12	.194	.242	.355	62	-2	1	0	0	1.000	0	1-12/O-1,D-2	-0.2

■ ED ARMBRISTER
Armbrister, Edison Rosanda   b: 7/4/48, Nassau, Bahamas   BR/TR, 5'11", 160 lbs.   Deb: 8/31/73

YEAR	TM/L	G	AB	R	H	2B	3B	HR	RBI	BB	SO	AVG	OBP	SLG	PRO+	BR/A	SB	CS	SBR	FA	FR	G/POS	TPR
1973	*Cin-N	18	37	5	8	3	1	1	5	2	8	.216	.256	.432	92	-1	0	0	0	.917	-2	O-14	-0.3
1974	Cin-N	9	7	0	2	0	0	0	0	1	1	.286	.375	.286	88	-0	0	0	0	1.000	-1	/O-4	-0.2
1975	*Cin-N	59	65	9	12	1	0	0	2	5	19	.185	.254	.200	27	-6	3	1	0	.867	-7	O-19	-1.4
1976	*Cin-N	73	78	20	23	7	1	2	7	6	22	.295	.345	.462	124	2	7	3	0	.972	-4	O-32	-0.2
1977	Cin-N	65	78	12	20	4	3	1	5	10	21	.256	.341	.423	102	0	5	6	-2	.903	-3	O-27	-0.5
Total	5	224	265	46	65	11	6	4	19	24	71	.245	.310	.377	88	-5	15	10	-2	.925	-17	/O-96	-2.6

■ CHARLIE ARMBRUSTER
Armbruster, Charles A.   b: 8/30/1880, Cincinnati, Ohio   d: 10/7/64, Grants Pass, Ore.   BR/TR, 5'9", 180 lbs.   Deb: 7/17/05

YEAR	TM/L	G	AB	R	H	2B	3B	HR	RBI	BB	SO	AVG	OBP	SLG	PRO+	BR/A	SB	CS	SBR	FA	FR	G/POS	TPR
1905	Bos-A	35	91	13	18	4	0	0	6	18		.198	.336	.242	83	-1	3			.944	-1	C-35	-0.4
1906	Bos-A	72	201	9	29	6	1	0	6	25		.144	.242	.184	34	-15	2			.955	1	C-66/1-1	-0.8
1907	Bos-A	23	60	2	6	1	0	0	6	8		.100	.206	.117	-3	-6	1			.935	2	C-21	-0.3
	Chi-A	1	3	0	0	0	0	0	0	1		.000	.250	.000	-20	-0	0			1.000	1	/C-1	0.0
	Yr	24	63	2	6	1	0	0	6	9		.095	.208	.111	2	-7	1			.940	3	C-22	-0.3
Total	3	131	355	24	53	11	1	0	12	52		.149	.262	.186	42	-22	6			.949	-2	C-123/1-1	-1.5

■ HARRY ARMBRUSTER
Armbruster, Henry "Army"   b: 3/20/1882, Cincinnati, Ohio   d: 12/10/53, Cincinnati, Ohio   BL/TL, 5'10", 190 lbs.   Deb: 4/30/06

YEAR	TM/L	G	AB	R	H	2B	3B	HR	RBI	BB	SO	AVG	OBP	SLG	PRO+	BR/A	SB	CS	SBR	FA	FR	G/POS	TPR
1906	Phi-A	91	265	40	63	6	3	2	24	43		.238	.353	.306	103	3	13			.971	0	O-74	0.0

■ GEORGE ARMSTRONG
Armstrong, Noble George "Dodo"   b: 6/3/24, Orange, N.J.   d: 7/24/93, Orange, N.J.   BR/TR, 5'10", 190 lbs.   Deb: 4/26/46

YEAR	TM/L	G	AB	R	H	2B	3B	HR	RBI	BB	SO	AVG	OBP	SLG	PRO+	BR/A	SB	CS	SBR	FA	FR	G/POS	TPR
1946	Phi-A	8	6	0	1	1	0	0	1	1		.167	.286	.333	73	-0	0	0	0	1.000	1	/C-4	0.0

■ SAM ARMSTRONG
Armstrong, Samuel   b: 1850, Baltimore, Md.   6'2", 160 lbs.   Deb: 6/26/1871

YEAR	TM/L	G	AB	R	H	2B	3B	HR	RBI	BB	SO	AVG	OBP	SLG	PRO+	BR/A	SB	CS	SBR	FA	FR	G/POS	TPR
1871	Kek-n	12	49	9	11	2	1	0	5	0	1	.224	.224	.306	50	-3	0	1	-1	.816	2	O-12	-0.1

■ HARRY ARNDT
Arndt, Harry J.   b: 2/12/1879, South Bend, Ind.   d: 3/25/21, South Bend, Ind.   TR ,   Deb: 7/2/02

YEAR	TM/L	G	AB	R	H	2B	3B	HR	RBI	BB	SO	AVG	OBP	SLG	PRO+	BR/A	SB	CS	SBR	FA	FR	G/POS	TPR
1902	Det-A	10	34	4	5	0	1	0	7	6		.147	.275	.206	34	-3	0			.958	0	O-10/1-1	-0.3
	Bal-A	68	248	41	63	7	4	2	28	35		.254	.355	.339	89	-3	9			.872	1	0-62/2-4,3-2,S-1	-0.6
	Yr	78	282	45	68	7	5	2	35	41		.241	.346	.323	83	-5	9			.885	1	0-72/2-4,3-2,1-1,S	-0.9
1905	StL-N	113	415	40	101	11	6	2	36	24		.243	.290	.313	82	-10	13			.951	-14	2-90/O-9,3-7,S-5	-2.4
1906	StL-N	69	256	30	69	7	9	2	26	19		.270	.320	.391	127	7	5			.965	12	3-65/1-1,O-1	2.2
1907	StL-N	11	32	3	6	1	0	0	2	1		.188	.212	.219	36	-2	0			1.000	0	/1-4,3-3	-0.3
Total	4	271	985	118	244	26	20	6	99	85		.248	.312	.333	91	-11	27			.952	-1	/2-94,O-82,3-77,S1	-1.4

■ LARRY ARNDT
Arndt, Larry Wayne   b: 2/25/63, Fremont, Ohio   BR/TR, 6'1", 195 lbs.   Deb: 6/6/89

YEAR	TM/L	G	AB	R	H	2B	3B	HR	RBI	BB	SO	AVG	OBP	SLG	PRO+	BR/A	SB	CS	SBR	FA	FR	G/POS	TPR
1989	Oak-A	2	6	1	1	0	0	0	0	0	1	.167	.167	.167	-6	-1	0	0	0	1.000	0	/1-1,3-1	-0.1

■ CHRIS ARNOLD
Arnold, Christopher Paul   b: 11/6/47, Long Beach, Cal.   BR/TR, 5'10", 160 lbs.   Deb: 9/7/71

YEAR	TM/L	G	AB	R	H	2B	3B	HR	RBI	BB	SO	AVG	OBP	SLG	PRO+	BR/A	SB	CS	SBR	FA	FR	G/POS	TPR
1971	SF-N	6	13	2	3	0	1	0	3	1	2	.231	.286	.462	110	-1	0	0	0	.917	-1	/2-3	-0.1
1972	SF-N	51	84	8	19	3	1	1	4	8	12	.226	.293	.321	74	-3	0	1	-1	.970	3	3-17/2-7,S-4	0.0
1973	SF-N	49	54	7	16	2	0	1	13	8	11	.296	.387	.389	111	1	0	0	0	.944	-5	/C-9,2-1,3-1	-0.4
1974	SF-N	78	174	22	42	7	3	1	26	15	27	.241	.305	.333	75	-6	1	1	-0	.974	-6	2-31/3-7,S-1	-1.1
1975	SF-N	29	41	4	8	0	0	0	4	5	8	.195	.267	.195	28	-4	0	0	0	.923	1	/2-4,O-4	-0.4
1976	SF-N	60	69	4	15	0	0	1	1	6	16	.217	.280	.246	49	-4	0	0	0	1.000	3	/2-8,3-4,1-1,S-1	-0.1
Total	6	273	435	47	103	12	5	4	51	42	76	.237	.305	.315	72	-16	1	2	-1	.971	-5	/2-54,3-29,C-9,SO1	-2.1

■ BILLY ARNOLD
Arnold, Willis S.   b: 3/2/1851, Middletown, Conn.   d: 1/17/1899, Albany, N.Y.   Deb: 4/26/1872

YEAR	TM/L	G	AB	R	H	2B	3B	HR	RBI	BB	SO	AVG	OBP	SLG	PRO+	BR/A	SB	CS	SBR	FA	FR	G/POS	TPR
1872	Man-n	2	7	2	1	0	0	0	0	0	0	.143	.143	.143	-13	-1	0	0	0	1.000	-0	/O-2	-0.1

■ MORRIE ARNOVICH
Arnovich, Morris "Snooker"   b: 11/16/10, Superior, Wis.   d: 7/20/59, Superior, Wis.   BR/TR, 5'10", 168 lbs.   Deb: 9/14/36

YEAR	TM/L	G	AB	R	H	2B	3B	HR	RBI	BB	SO	AVG	OBP	SLG	PRO+	BR/A	SB	CS	SBR	FA	FR	G/POS	TPR
1936	Phi-N	13	48	4	15	3	0	1	7	1	3	.313	.353	.438	102	0	0			1.000	0	O-13	0.2
1937	Phi-N	117	410	60	119	27	4	10	60	34	32	.290	.349	.449	107	3	5			.972	7	*O-107	0.6
1938	Phi-N	139	502	47	138	29	0	4	72	42	37	.275	.333	.357	92	-5	2			.983	17	*O-133	0.8
1939	Phi-N☆	134	491	68	159	25	2	5	67	58	28	.324	.397	.413	122	17	7			.983	15	*O-132	2.7
1940	Phi-N	39	141	13	28	2	1	0	12	14	15	.199	.276	.227	42	-11	0			.959	3	O-37	-1.0
	*Cin-N	62	211	17	60	10	2	0	21	13	10	.284	.326	.351	86	-4	1			1.000	2	O-60	-0.5
	Yr	101	352	30	88	12	3	0	33	27	25	.250	.305	.301	68	-15	1			.983	4	O-97	-1.5
1941	NY-N	85	207	25	58	13	2	2	22	23	14	.280	.352	.377	103	1	2			.982	-4	O-61	-0.6
1946	NY-N	1	3	0	0	0	0	0	0	0	0	.000	.000	.000	-99	-1	0			1.000	-0	/O-1	-0.1
Total	7	590	2013	234	577	104	12	22	261	185	139	.287	.350	.383	100	0	17			.981	42	O-544	2.1

■ TUG ARUNDEL
Arundel, John Thomas   b: 6/30/1862, Romulus, N.Y.   d: 9/5/12, Auburn, N.Y.   Deb: 5/23/1882

YEAR	TM/L	G	AB	R	H	2B	3B	HR	RBI	BB	SO	AVG	OBP	SLG	PRO+	BR/A	SB	CS	SBR	FA	FR	G/POS	TPR
1882	Phi-a	1	5	0	0	0	0	0		0		.000	.000	.000	-90	-1				.800	-0	/C-1	-0.1
1884	Tol-a	15	47	6	4	0	0	0		3		.085	.140	.085	-24	-6				.946	8	C-15	0.3
1887	Ind-N	43	157	13	31	4	0	0	13	8	12	.197	.241	.223	31	-14	8			.865	-3	C-42/O-2,1-1	-1.4
1888	Was-N	17	51	2	10	0	1	0	3	5	10	.196	.268	.235	65	-2	1			.840	-7	C-17	-0.8
Total	4	76	260	21	45	4	1	0	16	16	22	.173	.224	.196	25	-23	9			.882	-4	/C-75,O-2,1-1	-2.0

■ RANDY ASADOOR
Asadoor, Randall Carl   b: 10/20/62, Fresno, Cal.   BR/TR, 6'1", 185 lbs.   Deb: 9/14/86

YEAR	TM/L	G	AB	R	H	2B	3B	HR	RBI	BB	SO	AVG	OBP	SLG	PRO+	BR/A	SB	CS	SBR	FA	FR	G/POS	TPR
1986	SD-N	15	55	9	20	5	0	0	7	3	13	.364	.397	.455	137	3	1	2	-1	.889	-1	3-15/2-2	0.2

■ JIM ASBELL
Asbell, James Marion "Big Train"   b: 6/22/14, Dallas, Tex.   d: 7/6/67, San Mateo, Cal.   BR/TR, 6', 195 lbs.   Deb: 5/8/38

YEAR	TM/L	G	AB	R	H	2B	3B	HR	RBI	BB	SO	AVG	OBP	SLG	PRO+	BR/A	SB	CS	SBR	FA	FR	G/POS	TPR
1938	Chi-N	17	33	6	6	2	0	3	9	3	9	.182	.250	.242	35	-4	0			1.000	-1	O-10	-0.4

■ CASPER ASBJORNSON
Asbjornson, Robert Anthony (Name Changed To Asby)   b: 6/19/09, Concord, Mass.   d: 1/21/70, Williamsport, Pa.   BR/TR, 6'1", 196 lbs.   Deb: 9/17/28

YEAR	TM/L	G	AB	R	H	2B	3B	HR	RBI	BB	SO	AVG	OBP	SLG	PRO+	BR/A	SB	CS	SBR	FA	FR	G/POS	TPR
1928	Bos-A	6	16	0	3	1	0	0	1	1	1	.188	.235	.250	28	-2	0	0	0	.917	-2	/C-6	-0.3
1929	Bos-A	17	29	1	3	0	0	0	0	1	1	.103	.133	.103	-39	-6	0	0	0	.897	-3	C-15	-0.7
1931	Cin-N	45	118	13	36	7	1	0	22	7	23	.305	.349	.381	102	0	0			.981	0	C-31	0.2
1932	Cin-N	29	58	5	10	2	0	1	4	0	15	.172	.186	.259	19	-7	0			.961	0	C-16	-0.6
Total	4	97	221	19	52	10	1	1	27	9	45	.235	.272	.303	56	-14	0			.960	-5	/C-68	-1.4

■ RICHIE ASHBURN
Ashburn, Don Richard "Whitey"   b: 3/19/27, Tilden, Neb.   BL/TR, 5'10", 170 lbs.   Deb: 4/20/48   H

YEAR	TM/L	G	AB	R	H	2B	3B	HR	RBI	BB	SO	AVG	OBP	SLG	PRO+	BR/A	SB	CS	SBR	FA	FR	G/POS	TPR
1948	Phi-N★	117	463	78	154	17	4	2	40	60	22	.333	.410	.400	122	17	**32**			.981	**18**	*O-116	2.8
1949	Phi-N	154	662	84	188	18	11	1	37	58	38	.284	.343	.349	88	-10	9			.980	**25**	*O-154	0.6
1950	*Phi-N	151	594	84	180	25	**14**	2	41	63	32	.303	.372	.402	105	6	14			.988	8	*O-147	0.7
1951	Phi-N★	154	643	92	**221**	31	5	4	63	50	37	.344	.393	.426	122	21	29	6	5	.988	**32**	*O-154	5.2
1952	Phi-N	154	613	93	173	31	6	1	42	75	30	.282	.362	.357	101	3	16	11	-2	.980	15	*O-154	1.1
1953	Phi-N★	156	622	110	**205**	25	9	2	57	61	35	.330	.394	.408	110	12	14	6	1	.990	**26**	*O-156	3.1
1954	Phi-N	153	559	111	175	16	8	1	**125**	46		.313	**.442**	.376	116	22	11	8	2	.984	17	*O-153	4.0
1955	Phi-N	140	533	91	180	32	9	3	42	105	36	**.338**	**.449**	.448	142	39	12	10	-2	.983	11	*O-140	3.0
1956	Phi-N	154	628	94	190	26	8	3	50	79	45	.303	.384	.384	110	12	10	1	2	.983	4	*O-154	3.2
1957	Phi-N	156	626	93	186	26	8	0	33	**94**	44	.297	.392	.364	108	12	13	10	2	.987	**32**	*O-156	3.7
1958	Phi-N☆	152	615	98	**215**	24	**13**	2	33	**97**	48	**.350**	**.441**	.441	136	38	30	12	2	.984	22	*O-152	5.3
1959	Phi-N	153	564	86	150	16	2	1	20	79	42	.266	.362	.307	79	-13	9	11	-4	.971	5	*O-149	-2.0
1960	Chi-N	151	547	99	159	16	5	0	40	**116**	50	.291	**.416**	.338	110	15	16	4	2	.976	1	*O-146	1.2

YEAR	TM/L	G	AB	R	H	2B	3B	HR	RBI	BB	SO	AVG	OBP	SLG	PRO+	BR/A	SB	CS	SBR	FA	FR	G/POS	TPR
1961	Chi-N	109	307	49	79	7	4	0	19	55	27	.257	.375	.306	83	-5	7	6	-2	.978	-7	O-76	-1.8
1962	NY-N★	135	389	60	119	7	3	7	28	81	39	.306	.426	.393	119	15	12	7	-1	.975	-4	O-97/2-2	0.5
Total	15	2189	8365	1322	2574	317	109	29	586	1198	571	.308	.397	.382	111	184	234	92		.983	227	*O-2104/2-2	30.2

■ ALAN ASHBY
Ashby, Alan Dean   b: 7/8/51, Long Beach, Cal.   BB/TR, 6'2", 190 lbs.   Deb: 7/3/73

YEAR	TM/L	G	AB	R	H	2B	3B	HR	RBI	BB	SO	AVG	OBP	SLG	PRO+	BR/A	SB	CS	SBR	FA	FR	G/POS	TPR
1973	Cle-A	11	29	4	5	1	0	1	3	2	11	.172	.226	.310	49	-2	0	0	0	.978	-2	C-11	-0.4
1974	Cle-A	10	7	1	1	0	0	0	0	1	2	.143	.250	.143	15	-1	0	0	0	1.000	0	/C-9	0.0
1975	Cle-A	90	254	32	57	10	1	5	32	30	42	.224	.309	.331	81	-6	3	2	-0	.990	3	C-87/1-2,3-1,D-1	0.0
1976	Cle-A	89	247	26	59	5	1	4	32	27	49	.239	.314	.316	86	-4	0	2	-1	.987	6	C-86/1-2,3-1	0.3
1977	Tor-A	124	396	25	83	16	3	2	29	50	51	.210	.301	.280	59	-22	0	2	-1	.984	-7	*C-124	-2.6
1978	Tor-A	81	264	27	69	15	0	9	29	28	32	.261	.334	.420	109	3	1	1	-0	.986	-7	C-81	-0.3
1979	Hou-N	108	336	25	68	15	2	2	35	26	70	.202	.264	.277	51	-24	0	0	0	.987	-1	*C-105	-2.2
1980	*Hou-N	116	352	30	90	19	2	3	48	35	40	.256	.323	.347	94	-3	0	0	0	.991	2	*C-114	0.3
1981	*Hou-N	83	255	20	69	13	0	4	33	35	33	.271	.359	.369	112	5	0	0	0	.982	7	C-81	1.4
1982	Hou-N	100	339	40	87	14	2	12	49	27	53	.257	.313	.416	111	3	2	0	1	.977	-5	C-95	0.3
1983	Hou-N	87	275	31	63	18	1	8	34	31	38	.229	.307	.389	98	-2	0	0	0	.974	-13	C-85	-1.1
1984	Hou-N	66	191	16	50	7	0	4	27	20	22	.262	.335	.361	103	1	0	0	0	.986	-3	C-63	0.1
1985	Hou-N	65	189	20	53	8	0	8	25	24	27	.280	.364	.450	130	8	0	0	0	.978	-0	C-60	1.1
1986	*Hou-N	120	315	24	81	15	0	7	38	39	56	.257	.339	.371	98	-0	1	0	0	.985	-4	*C-103	0.2
1987	Hou-N	125	386	53	111	16	0	14	63	50	52	.288	.371	.438	118	10	0	1	-1	.993	-4	*C-110	1.4
1988	Hou-N	73	227	19	54	10	0	7	33	29	36	.238	.324	.374	104	1	0	0	0	.991	-10	C-66	-0.4
1989	Hou-N	22	61	4	10	1	0	1	3	7	16	.164	.261	.213	38	-5	0	0	0	1.000	-3	C-19	-0.7
Total	17	1370	4123	397	1010	183	13	90	513	461	622	.245	.323	.361	93	-37	7	10	-4	.986	-41	*C-1299/1-4,3-2,D-1	-2.6

■ TUCKER ASHFORD
Ashford, Thomas Steven   b: 12/4/54, Memphis, Tenn.   BR/TR, 6'1", 195 lbs.   Deb: 9/21/76

YEAR	TM/L	G	AB	R	H	2B	3B	HR	RBI	BB	SO	AVG	OBP	SLG	PRO+	BR/A	SB	CS	SBR	FA	FR	G/POS	TPR
1976	SD-N	4	5	0	3	1	0	0	1	0	1	.600	.667	.800	343	2	2	0	1	1.000	0	/3-1	0.3
1977	SD-N	81	249	25	54	18	0	3	24	21	35	.217	.280	.325	69	-12	2	3	-1	.937	2	3-74,S-10/2-4	-1.1
1978	SD-N	75	155	11	38	11	0	3	26	14	31	.245	.308	.374	97	-1	1	0	0	.917	-16	3-32,2-18,1-14	-1.8
1980	Tex-A	15	32	2	4	0	0	0	3	3	3	.125	.200	.125	-9	-5	0	0	0	.943	3	3-12/S-2	-0.2
1981	NY-A	3	0	0	0	0	0	0	0	0	0	—	—	—	—	0	0	0	0	.000	0	/2-2	0.0
1983	NY-N	35	56	3	10	1	0	2	7	4	4	.179	.270	.214	36	-5	0	0	0	.957	-1	3-15,2-13/C-1	-0.6
1984	KC-A	9	13	1	2	1	0	0	1	2	1	.154	.214	.231	23	-1	0	0	0	.909	0	/3-9	-0.1
Total	7	222	510	42	111	31	1	6	55	47	75	.218	.285	.318	70	-22	5	3	-0	.936	-12	3-143/2-37,1-14,SC	-3.5

■ BILLY ASHLEY
Ashley, Billy Manual   b: 7/11/70, Trenton, Mich.   BR/TR, 6'7", 220 lbs.   Deb: 9/1/92

YEAR	TM/L	G	AB	R	H	2B	3B	HR	RBI	BB	SO	AVG	OBP	SLG	PRO+	BR/A	SB	CS	SBR	FA	FR	G/POS	TPR
1992	LA-N	29	95	6	21	5	0	2	6	5	34	.221	.260	.337	69	-4	0	0	0	.857	-3	O-27	-0.8
1993	LA-N	14	37	0	9	0	0	0	2	2	11	.243	.282	.243	45	-3	0	0	0	1.000	0	/O-11	-0.3
1994	LA-N	2	6	0	2	1	0	0	0	0	2	.333	.333	.500	121	0	0	0	0	1.000	-0	/O-2	0.0
1995	*LA-N	81	215	17	51	5	0	8	27	25	88	.237	.322	.372	91	-5	0	0	0	.972	-1	O-69	-0.5
1996	*LA-N	71	110	18	22	2	1	9	25	21	44	.200	.333	.482	122	3	0	0	0	.952	-4	O-38	-0.1
Total	5	197	463	41	105	13	1	19	58	53	179	.227	.310	.382	91	-7	0	0	0	.947	-7	O-147	-1.7

■ TOM ASMUSSEN
Asmussen, Thomas William   b: 9/26/1876, Chicago, Ill.   d: 8/21/63, Arlington Heights, Ill.   TR,   Deb: 8/10/07

YEAR	TM/L	G	AB	R	H	2B	3B	HR	RBI	BB	SO	AVG	OBP	SLG	PRO+	BR/A	SB	CS	SBR	FA	FR	G/POS	TPR
1907	Bos-N	2	5	0	0	0	0	0	0	0		.000	.000	.000	-99	-1	0			1.000	-1	/C-2	-0.3

■ KEN ASPROMONTE
Aspromonte, Kenneth Joseph   b: 9/22/31, Brooklyn, N.Y.   BR/TR, 6', 180 lbs.   Deb: 9/2/57   FM

YEAR	TM/L	G	AB	R	H	2B	3B	HR	RBI	BB	SO	AVG	OBP	SLG	PRO+	BR/A	SB	CS	SBR	FA	FR	G/POS	TPR
1957	Bos-A	24	78	9	21	5	0	0	4	17	10	.269	.400	.333	97	1	0	1	-1	.965	-3	2-24	-0.1
1958	Bos-A	6	16	0	2	0	0	0	0	3	1	.125	.263	.125	10	-2	0	0	0	.952	-3	/2-6	-0.5
	Was-A	92	253	15	57	9	1	5	27	25	28	.225	.297	.328	73	-9	1	1	-0	.964	3	2-72,3-11/S-1	-0.2
	Yr	98	269	15	59	9	1	5	27	28	29	.219	.295	.316	69	-11	1	1	-0	.963	-0	2-78,3-11/S-1	-0.7
1959	Was-A	70	225	31	55	12	0	2	14	26	39	.244	.323	.324	79	-6	2	1	0	.960	-10	2-52,S-12/1-1,0-1	-1.1
1960	Was-A	4	3	0	0	0	0	0	0	0	1	.000	.000	.000	-99	-1	0	0	0	.000	0	H	-0.1
	Cle-A	117	459	65	133	20	1	10	48	53	32	.290	.364	.403	111	8	4	1	1	.976	-12	2-80,3-36	0.4
	Yr	121	462	65	133	20	1	10	48	53	33	.288	.364	.400	107	7	4	1	1	.976	-12	2-80,3-36	0.3
1961	LA-A	66	238	29	53	10	0	2	14	33	21	.223	.322	.290	58	-14	0	0	0	.970	18	2-62	1.1
	Cle-A	22	70	5	16	6	1	0	5	6	3	.229	.289	.343	70	-3	0	0	0	.963	-2	2-21	-0.3
	Yr	88	308	34	69	16	1	2	19	39	24	.224	.315	.302	61	-17	0	0	0	.969	17	2-83	0.8
1962	Cle-A	20	28	4	4	2	0	0	1	6	5	.143	.294	.214	41	-2	0	0	0	1.000	-1	/2-6,3-3	-0.3
	Mil-N	34	79	11	23	2	0	0	7	6	6	.291	.349	.316	82	-2	0	1	-1	1.000	-0	2-12/3-6	-0.1
1963	Chi-N	20	34	2	5	3	0	0	4	4	4	.147	.237	.235	35	-3	0	0	0	.951	3	/2-7,1-2	0.1
Total	7	475	1483	171	369	69	3	19	124	179	149	.249	.332	.338	82	-33	7	5	-1	.969	-7	2-342/3-56,S-13,10	-1.1

■ BOB ASPROMONTE
Aspromonte, Robert Thomas   b: 6/19/38, Brooklyn, N.Y.   BR/TR, 6'2", 185 lbs.   Deb: 9/19/56   F

YEAR	TM/L	G	AB	R	H	2B	3B	HR	RBI	BB	SO	AVG	OBP	SLG	PRO+	BR/A	SB	CS	SBR	FA	FR	G/POS	TPR
1956	Bro-N	1	1	0	0	0	0	0	0	0	1	.000	.000	.000	-93	-0	0	0	0	.000	0	H	0.0
1960	LA-N	21	55	1	10	1	0	1	6	0	6	.182	.196	.255	21	-6	1	0	0	.933	-2	S-15/3-4	-0.7
1961	LA-N	47	58	7	14	3	0	0	2	4	12	.241	.290	.293	51	-4	0	0	0	.917	0	/3-9,S-4,2-2	-0.3
1962	Hou-N	149	534	59	142	18	4	11	59	46	54	.266	.333	.376	97	-2	4	5	-2	.967	1	*3-142,S-11/2-1	-0.1
1963	Hou-N	136	468	42	100	9	5	8	49	40	57	.214	.277	.306	72	-17	3	1	0	.938	-14	*3-131/1-1	-3.6
1964	Hou-N	157	553	51	155	20	3	12	69	35	54	.280	.332	.392	109	6	6	7	-2	.973	-15	*3-155	-1.4
1965	Hou-N	152	578	53	152	15	2	5	52	38	54	.263	.312	.322	85	-12	2	2	-1	.962	-4	*3-146/1-6,S-4	-1.7
1966	Hou-N	152	560	55	141	16	3	8	52	35	63	.252	.298	.334	81	-15	0	4	-2	.962	-11	*3-149/1-2,S-2	-3.3
1967	Hou-N	137	486	51	143	24	5	6	58	45	44	.294	.356	.401	121	13	2	2	-1	.963	-4	*3-133	0.8
1968	Hou-N	124	409	25	92	9	2	1	46	35	57	.225	.289	.264	68	-15	1	0	0	.973	-6	3-75,0-36/1-1,S-1	-1.9
1969	*Atl-N	82	198	16	50	8	1	3	24	13	19	.253	.305	.348	82	-5	0	1	-1	.975	-6	0-24,3-23,S-18/2-2	-1.1
1970	Atl-N	62	127	5	27	3	0	0	7	13	13	.213	.286	.236	39	-11	0	0	0	.938	-1	3-30/S-4,1-1,0-1	-1.1
1971	NY-N	104	342	21	77	9	1	5	33	29	25	.225	.286	.301	67	-15	0	0	0	.965	-5	3-97	-2.3
Total	13	1324	4369	386	1103	135	26	60	457	333	459	.252	.310	.336	86	-84	19	24	-8	.960	-57	*3-1094/O-61,S12	-16.9

■ BRIAN ASSELSTINE
Asselstine, Brian Hanly   b: 9/23/53, Santa Barbara, Cal   BL/TR, 6'1", 175 lbs.   Deb: 9/14/76

YEAR	TM/L	G	AB	R	H	2B	3B	HR	RBI	BB	SO	AVG	OBP	SLG	PRO+	BR/A	SB	CS	SBR	FA	FR	G/POS	TPR
1976	Atl-N	11	33	2	7	0	0	1	3	1	2	.212	.235	.303	49	-2	0	0	0	1.000	-1	/O-9	-0.3
1977	Atl-N	83	124	12	26	6	0	4	17	9	10	.210	.263	.355	57	-8	1	0	0	.983	-2	O-35	-1.1
1978	Atl-N	39	103	11	28	3	3	2	13	11	16	.272	.353	.417	103	0	2	1	0	.968	-5	O-35	-0.7
1979	Atl-N	8	10	1	1	0	0	0	0	1	2	.100	.182	.100	-20	-2	0	0	0	1.000	0	/O-1	-0.2
1980	Atl-N	87	218	18	62	13	1	3	25	11	37	.284	.322	.394	96	-2	1	3	-2	.962	-9	O-61	-1.5
1981	Atl-N	56	86	8	22	5	0	2	10	5	7	.256	.297	.384	90	-1	1	0	0	.958	-1	O-16	-0.3
Total	6	284	574	52	146	27	4	12	68	38	74	.254	.304	.378	83	-14	5	4	-1	.971	-19	O-157	-4.1

■ JOE ASTROTH
Astroth, Joseph Henry   b: 9/1/22, East Alton, Ill.   BR/TR, 5'9", 187 lbs.   Deb: 8/13/45

YEAR	TM/L	G	AB	R	H	2B	3B	HR	RBI	BB	SO	AVG	OBP	SLG	PRO+	BR/A	SB	CS	SBR	FA	FR	G/POS	TPR
1945	Phi-A	10	17	1	1	0	0	0	0	0	1	.059	.111	.059	-50	-3	0	0	0	.857	-0	/C-8	-0.3
1946	Phi-A	4	7	0	1	0	0	0	0	0	1	.143	.143	.143	-20	-1	0	0	0	.889	-0	/C-4	-0.1
1949	Phi-A	55	148	18	36	4	1	0	12	21	13	.243	.337	.284	67	-7	1	0	0	.979	2	C-44	-0.2
1950	Phi-A	39	110	11	36	3	1	1	18	18	3	.327	.422	.400	113	3	0	0	0	.985	-6	C-38	-0.1
1951	Phi-A	64	187	30	46	10	2	2	19	18	13	.246	.312	.353	78	-6	0	1	-1	.992	4	C-57	-0.1
1952	Phi-A	104	337	24	84	7	2	1	36	25	27	.249	.305	.291	62	-17	2	2	-0	.992	-5	*C-102	-1.8
1953	Phi-A	82	260	28	77	15	2	3	24	27	12	.296	.367	.404	104	2	0	1	-1	.987	7	C-79	1.2
1954	Phi-A	77	226	22	50	8	1	4	23	21	19	.221	.296	.279	58	-13	0	0	0	.988	-2	C-71	-1.2
1955	KC-A	101	274	29	69	4	1	3	23	47	33	.252	.373	.328	89	-2	1	0	0	.989	-4	*C-100	-0.4
1956	KC-A	8	13	0	1	0	0	0	0	0	1	.077	.077	.077	-59	-3	0	0	0	1.000	2	/C-8	-0.1
Total	10	544	1579	163	401	51	10	13	156	177	124	.254	.334	.324	77	-47	6	6	-2	.987	-2	C-511	-3.1

YEAR	TM/L	G	AB	R	H	2B	3B	HR	RBI	BB	SO	AVG	OBP	SLG	PRO+	BR/A	SB	CS	SBR	FA	FR	G/POS	TPR

■ CHARLIE ATHERTON Atherton, Charles Morgan Herbert "Prexy"
b: 10/19/1873, New Brunswick, N.J d: 12/19/34, Vienna, Austria BR/TR, 5'10", 160 lbs. Deb: 5/30/1899

| 1899 | Was-N | 65 | 242 | 28 | 60 | 5 | 6 | 0 | 23 | 21 | | .248 | .313 | .318 | 74 | -9 | 2 | | | .890 | -6 | 3-63/O-1 | -1.3 |

■ ED ATKINSON Atkinson, Edward b: 1851, Baltimore, Md. Deb: 10/22/1873

| 1873 | Was-n | 2 | 8 | 2 | 0 | 0 | 0 | 0 | 0 | 0 | 0 | .000 | .000 | .000 | -99 | -2 | 0 | 0 | 0 | 1.000 | -0 | /O-2 | -0.2 |

■ LEFTY ATKINSON Atkinson, Hubert Burley b: 6/4/04, Chicago, Ill. d: 2/12/61, Chicago, Ill. BL/TL, 5'6.5", 149 lbs. Deb: 8/5/27

| 1927 | Was-A | 1 | 1 | 1 | 0 | 0 | 0 | 0 | 0 | 0 | 0 | .000 | .000 | .000 | -99 | -0 | 0 | 0 | 0 | .000 | 0 | H | 0.0 |

■ DICK ATTREAU Attreau, Richard Gilbert b: 4/8/1897, Chicago, Ill. d: 7/5/64, Chicago, Ill. BL/TL, 6', 160 lbs. Deb: 9/14/26

1926	Phi-N	17	61	9	14	1	1	0	5	6	5	.230	.299	.279	53	-4	0			.989	-1	1-17	-0.6
1927	Phi-N	44	83	17	17	1	1	1	11	14	18	.205	.320	.277	60	-4	1			.989	-2	1-26	-0.7
Total	2	61	144	26	31	2	2	1	16	20	23	.215	.311	.278	57	-8	1			.989	-3	/1-43	-1.3

■ TOBY ATWELL Atwell, Maurice Dailey b: 3/8/24, Leesburg, Va. BL/TR, 5'9.5", 185 lbs. Deb: 4/15/52

1952	Chi-N☆	107	362	36	105	16	3	2	31	40	22	.290	.362	.367	102	2	2	1	0	.977	-7	*C-101	0.0
1953	Chi-N	24	74	10	17	2	0	1	8	13	7	.230	.345	.297	68	-3	0	0	0	.940	1	C-24	-0.1
	Pit-N	53	139	11	34	6	0	0	17	20	12	.245	.352	.288	70	-5	0	0	0	.967	-3	C-45	-0.6
	Yr	77	213	21	51	8	0	1	25	33	19	.239	.349	.291	69	-8	0	0	0	.957	-2	C-69	-0.7
1954	Pit-N	96	287	36	83	8	4	3	26	43	21	.289	.387	.376	101	2	2	3	-1	.990	-2	C-88	0.3
1955	Pit-N	71	207	21	44	8	0	1	18	40	16	.213	.343	.266	65	-9	0	1	-1	.992	6	C-67	-0.2
1956	Pit-N	12	18	0	2	0	0	0	3	1	5	.111	.158	.111	-27	-3	0	0	0	1.000	1	/C-9	-0.2
	Mil-N	15	30	2	5	1	0	2	7	4	1	.167	.265	.400	80	-1	0	0	0	1.000	-1	C-10	-0.1
	Yr	27	48	2	7	1	0	2	10	5	6	.146	.226	.292	40	-4	0	0	0	1.000	0	C-19	-0.3
Total	5	378	1117	116	290	41	7	9	110	161	84	.260	.357	.333	86	-17	4	5	-2	.980	-5	C-344	-0.9

■ BILL ATWOOD Atwood, William Franklin b: 9/25/11, Rome, Ga. d: 9/14/93, Snyder, Tex. BR/TR, 5'11.5", 190 lbs. Deb: 4/15/36

1936	Phi-N	71	192	21	58	9	2	2	29	11	15	.302	.346	.401	92	-2	0			.972	-1	C-53	-0.1
1937	Phi-N	87	279	27	68	15	1	2	32	30	27	.244	.317	.326	69	-12	3			.968	-15	C-80	-2.2
1938	Phi-N	102	281	27	55	8	1	3	28	25	26	.196	.261	.263	46	-21	0			.969	0	C-94	-1.6
1939	Phi-N	4	6	0	0	0	0	0	0	1	2	.000	.250	.000	-29	-1	1			1.000	-0	/C-2	-0.1
1940	Phi-N	78	203	7	39	9	0	0	22	25	18	.192	.284	.236	47	-14	0			.989	1	C-69	-0.9
Total	5	342	961	82	220	41	4	7	112	93	89	.229	.299	.302	63	-50	4			.974	-14	C-298	-4.9

■ JAKE ATZ Atz, John Jacob (b: John Jacob Zimmerman) b: 7/1/1879, Washington, D.C. d: 5/22/45, New Orleans, La. BR/TR, 5'9.5", 160 lbs. Deb: 9/24/02

1902	Was-A	3	10	1	1	0	0	0		0		.100	.100	.100	-44	-2	0			1.000	0	/2-3	-0.1
1907	Chi-A	4	8	0	1	0	0	0	0	0		.125	.125	.125	-21	-1	0			1.000	1	/3-2,O-1	0.0
1908	Chi-A	83	206	24	40	3	0	0	27	31		.194	.311	.209	71	-5	9			.936	-3	2-46,S-18/3-1	-0.9
1909	Chi-A	119	381	39	90	18	3	0	22	38		.236	.309	.299	96	-1	14			.954	-7	*2-114/O-3,S-1	-1.2
Total	4	209	605	64	132	21	3	0	49	69		.218	.304	.263	83	-9	23			.949	-8	2-163/S-19,O-4,3-3	-2.2

■ HARRY AUBREY Aubrey, Harry Herbert "Chub" b: 7/5/1880, St.Joseph, Mo. d: 9/18/53, Baltimore, Md. TR , Deb: 4/22/03

| 1903 | Bos-N | 96 | 325 | 26 | 69 | 8 | 2 | 0 | 27 | 18 | | .212 | .264 | .249 | 49 | -22 | 7 | | | .868 | -10 | S-94/2-1,O-1 | -2.7 |

■ RICH AUDE Aude, Richard Thomas b: 7/13/71, Van Nuys, Cal. BR/TR, 6'5", 180 lbs. Deb: 9/9/93

1993	Pit-N	13	26	1	3	1	0	0	4	1	7	.115	.148	.154	-19	-4	0	0	0	1.000	-1	/1-7,O-1	-0.6
1995	Pit-N	42	109	10	27	8	0	2	19	6	20	.248	.287	.376	72	-5	1	2	-1	.996	-3	1-32	-1.1
1996	Pit-N	7	16	0	4	0	0	0	1	0	8	.250	.250	.250	31	-2	0	0	0	.969	0	/1-4	-0.2
Total	3	62	151	11	34	9	0	2	24	7	35	.225	.259	.325	52	-11	1	2	-1	.994	-4	/1-43,O-1	-1.9

■ RICK AUERBACH Auerbach, Frederick Steven b: 2/15/50, Woodland Hills, Cal BR/TR, 6', 165 lbs. Deb: 4/13/71

1971	Mil-A	79	236	22	48	10	4	1	9	20	40	.203	.271	.258	51	-15	3	2	-0	.963	-10	S-78	-1.7
1972	Mil-A	153	554	50	121	16	3	2	30	43	62	.218	.277	.269	64	-24	24	8	2	.959	-21	*S-153	-2.5
1973	Mil-A	6	10	2	1	1	0	0	0	0	1	.100	.100	.200	-18	-2	0	1	-1	.833	0	/S-2	-0.2
1974	*LA-N	45	73	12	25	0	0	1	4	8	9	.342	.407	.384	127	3	4	2	0	.950	-3	S-19,2-16/3-3	0.6
1975	LA-N	85	170	18	38	9	0	0	12	18	22	.224	.298	.276	63	-8	3	2	-0	.960	-17	S-81/2-1,3-1	-2.1
1976	LA-N	36	47	7	6	0	0	0	1	6	6	.128	.226	.128	2	-6	0	1	-1	.943	11	S-12/3-8,2-7	0.6
1977	Cin-N	33	45	5	7	2	0	0	3	4	7	.156	.224	.200	15	-5	0	0	0	.976	4	2-19,S-12	0.2
1978	Cin-N	63	55	17	18	6	0	1	5	7	12	.327	.413	.545	166	5	2	0	0	.971	10	S-26,2-10/3-3	1.7
1979	*Cin-N	62	100	17	21	8	1	1	12	14	19	.210	.307	.340	76	-3	5	2	0	.933	-1	3-18,S-16/2-3	-0.3
1980	Cin-N	24	33	5	11	1	1	0	4	3	5	.333	.389	.515	150	2	0	3	-2	1.000	1	/S-3,3-3,2-1	0.0
1981	Sea-A	38	84	12	13	3	0	1	6	4	15	.155	.202	.226	22	-8	1	1	-0	.979	3	S-38	-0.3
Total	11	624	1407	167	309	56	5	9	86	127	199	.220	.287	.286	65	-62	36	21	-2	.960	-16	S-440/2-57,3-36	-4.0

■ DAVE AUGUSTINE Augustine, David Ralph b: 11/28/49, Follansbee, W.Va. BR/TR, 6'2", 174 lbs. Deb: 9/3/73

1973	Pit-N	11	7	1	2	1	0	0	0	0	1	.286	.286	.429	98	-0	0	0	0	1.000	-2	/O-9	-0.2
1974	Pit-N	18	22	3	4	0	0	0	0	0	5	.182	.182	.182	2	-3	0	1	-1	1.000	1	O-11	-0.3
Total	2	29	29	4	6	1	0	0	0	0	6	.207	.207	.241	26	-3	0	1	-1	1.000	-2	/O-20	-0.5

■ TEX AULDS Aulds, Leycester Doyle b: 12/28/20, Farmerville, La. BR/TR, 6'2", 185 lbs. Deb: 5/25/47

| 1947 | Bos-A | 3 | 4 | 0 | 1 | 0 | 0 | 0 | 0 | 0 | | .250 | .250 | .250 | 37 | | 0 | 0 | 0 | 1.000 | 0 | /C-3 | 0.0 |

■ DOUG AULT Ault, Douglas Reagan b: 3/9/50, Beaumont, Tex. BR/TL, 6'3", 200 lbs. Deb: 9/9/76

1976	Tex-A	9	20	0	6	1	0	0	1	3		.300	.333	.350	98	-0	0	0	0	1.000	-1	/1-4,D-3	-0.1
1977	Tor-A	129	445	44	109	22	3	11	64	39	68	.245	.311	.382	87	-8	4	4	-1	.987	7	*1-122/D-4	-1.0
1978	Tor-A	54	104	10	25	1	1	3	7	17	14	.240	.352	.356	98	-0	0	0	0	.979	-2	1-25/O-7,D-5	-0.3
1980	Tor-A	64	144	12	28	5	1	3	15	14	23	.194	.275	.306	56	-9	0	1	-1	1.000	3	1-32,D-21/O-1	-0.8
Total	4	256	713	66	168	29	5	17	86	71	108	.236	.311	.362	82	-17	4	5	-2	.988	8	1-183/D-33,O-8	-2.2

■ RICH AURILIA Aurilia, Richard Santo b: 9/2/71, Brooklyn, N.Y. BR/TR, 6', 170 lbs. Deb: 9/6/95

1995	SF-N	9	19	4	9	3	0	2	4	1	2	.474	.500	.947	280	5	1	0	0	1.000	1	/S-6	0.6
1996	SF-N	105	318	27	76	7	1	3	26	25	52	.239	.297	.296	59	-19	4	1	1	.973	-4	S-93,2-11	-1.4
Total	2	114	337	31	85	10	1	5	30	26	54	.252	.308	.332	72	-14	5	1	1	.974	-2	/S-99,2-11	-0.8

■ BRAD AUSMUS Ausmus, Bradley David b: 4/14/69, New Haven, Conn. BR/TR, 5'11", 185 lbs. Deb: 7/28/93

1993	SD-N	49	160	18	41	8	1	5	12	6	28	.256	.283	.412	82	-5	2	0	1	.975	5	C-49	0.4
1994	SD-N	101	327	45	82	12	1	7	24	30	63	.251	.316	.358	77	-11	5	1	1	.991	2	C-99/1-1	-0.2
1995	SD-N	103	328	44	96	16	4	5	34	31	56	.293	.357	.412	106	3	16	5	2	.992	1	*C-100/1-1	1.2
1996	SD-N	50	149	16	27	4	0	1	13	13	27	.181	.261	.228	32	-15	1	4	-2	.982	2	C-46	-1.2
	Det-A	75	226	30	56	12	0	4	22	26	45	.248	.331	.354	74	-9	3	4	-2	.992	1	C-73	-0.4
Total	4	378	1190	153	302	52	6	22	105	106	219	.254	.319	.363	80	-36	27	14	-0	.988	11	C-367/1-2	-0.2

■ HENRY AUSTIN Austin, Henry C. b: 1844, Brooklyn, N.Y. d: 9/3/1895, Amityville, N.Y. Deb: 4/28/1873

| 1873 | Res-n | 23 | 101 | 10 | 25 | 3 | 3 | 0 | 11 | 0 | 4 | .248 | .248 | .337 | 78 | -2 | 0 | 0 | 0 | .722 | -0 | O-23 | -0.1 |

■ JIMMY AUSTIN Austin, James Philip "Pepper" b: 12/8/1879, Swansea, Wales d: 3/6/65, Laguna Beach, Cal. BB/TR, 5'7.5", 155 lbs. Deb: 4/19/09 MC

1909	NY-A	136	437	37	101	11	5	1	39	32		.231	.285	.286	80	-10	30			.928	13	*3-111,S-23/2-1	0.8
1910	NY-A	133	432	46	94	11	4	2	36	47		.218	.305	.275	77	-11	22			.942	4	*3-133	-0.4
1911	StL-A	148	541	84	141	25	11	2	45	69		.261	.351	.359	102	3	26			.931	16	*3-148	2.0
1912	StL-A	149	536	57	135	14	8	2	44	38		.252	.306	.319	82	-13	28			.911	-1	*3-149	-1.4
1913	StL-A	142	489	56	130	18	6	1	42	45	51	.266	.338	.339	101	1	37			**.944**	7	*3-142,M	1.0
1914	StL-A	130	466	55	111	16	4	0	30	40	59	.238	.300	.290	80	-12	20	23	-8	.935	1	*3-127	-1.6

YEAR	TM/L	G	AB	R	H	2B	3B	HR	RBI	BB	SO	AVG	OBP	SLG	PRO+	BR/A	SB	CS	SBR	FA	FR	G/POS	TPR
1915	StL-A	141	477	61	127	6	6	1	30	64	60	.266	.355	.310	103	4	18	15	-4	.917	10	*3-141	1.6
1916	StL-A	129	411	55	85	15	6	1	28	74	59	.207	.333	.280	89	-3	19			.939	-7	*3-124	-0.6
1917	StL-A	127	455	61	109	18	8	0	19	50	46	.240	.319	.314	97	-1	13			.947	3	*3-121/S-6	0.4
1918	StL-A	110	367	42	97	14	4	0	20	53	32	.264	.359	.324	109	6	18			.939	-1	S-57,3-48,M	-0.8
1919	StL-A	106	396	54	94	9	9	1	21	42	31	.237	.314	.313	74	-13	8			.939	7	3-98	-0.3
1920	StL-A	83	280	38	76	11	3	1	32	31	15	.271	.352	.343	82	-6	2	4	-2	.943	2	3-75	-0.2
1921	StL-A	27	66	8	18	2	1	0	2	4	7	.273	.324	.333	64	-4	2	1	0	.938	-3	S-14/2-6,3-2	-0.5
1922	StL-A	15	31	6	9	3	1	0	1	3	2	.290	.353	.452	105	0	0	0	0	.957	-3	/3-9,2-2	-0.2
1923	StL-A	1	0	0	0	0	0	0	0	0	0	—	—	—	—	0	0	0	0	.000	0	/M	0.0
1925	StL-A	1	1	0	0	0	0	0	0	0	0	.000	.000	.000	-95	-0	0	0	0	1.000	0	/3-1	0.0
1926	StL-A	1	2	1	1	1	0	0	1	0	0	.500	.500	1.000	272	0	1	0	0	1.000	0	/3-1	0.1
1929	StL-A	1	1	0	0	0	0	0	0	0	0	.000	.000	.000	-96	-0	0	0	0	1.000	1	/3-1	0.0
Total	18	1580	5388	661	1328	174	76	13	390	592	363	.246	.326	.314	90	-60	244	43		.933	32	*3-1431,S-100/2-9	-0.1

■ CHICK AUTRY
Autry, Martin Gordon b: 3/5/03, Martindale, Tex. d: 1/26/50, Savannah, Ga. BR/TR, 6', 180 lbs. Deb: 4/20/24

YEAR	TM/L	G	AB	R	H	2B	3B	HR	RBI	BB	SO	AVG	OBP	SLG	PRO+	BR/A	SB	CS	SBR	FA	FR	G/POS	TPR
1924	NY-A	2	0	1	0	0	0	0	0	0	0	—	1.000	—	172	0	0	0	0	1.000	-0	/C-2	0.0
1926	Cle-A	3	7	1	1	0	0	0	0	1	0	.143	.250	.143	4	-1	0	0	0	1.000	-0	/C-3	-0.1
1927	Cle-A	16	43	5	11	4	1	0	7	0	6	.256	.256	.395	66	-2	0	0	0	.933	2	C-14	0.1
1928	Cle-A	22	60	6	18	6	1	1	9	1	7	.300	.311	.483	105	-0	0	0	0	.972	0	C-18	0.2
1929	Chi-A	43	96	7	20	6	0	1	12	1	8	.208	.224	.302	35	-10	0	0	0	.940	-4	C-30	-1.1
1930	Chi-A	34	71	1	18	1	1	0	5	4	8	.254	.293	.296	52	-5	0	0	0	.992	8	C-29	0.4
Total	6	120	277	21	68	17	3	2	33	7	29	.245	.269	.350	59	-18	0	0	0	.965	5	/C-96	-0.5

■ CHICK AUTRY
Autry, William Askew b: 1/2/1885, Humboldt, Tenn. d: 1/16/76, Santa Rosa, Cal. BL/TL, 5'11", 168 lbs. Deb: 9/18/07

YEAR	TM/L	G	AB	R	H	2B	3B	HR	RBI	BB	SO	AVG	OBP	SLG	PRO+	BR/A	SB	CS	SBR	FA	FR	G/POS	TPR
1907	Cin-N	7	25	3	5	0	0	0		0	1	.200	.231	.200	34	-2	0			.929	-1	/O-7	-0.4
1909	Cin-N	9	33	3	6	2	0	0		4	2	.182	.229	.242	46	-2	1			.956	0	/1-9	-0.2
	Bos-N	65	199	16	39	4	0	0		13	21	.196	.279	.216	51	-11	5			.994	5	1-61/O-4	-0.7
	Yr	74	232	19	45	6	0	0		17	23	.194	.272	.220	51	-13	6			.989	5	1-70/O-4	-0.9
Total	2	81	257	22	50	6	0	0		17	24	.195	.269	.218	49	-15	6			.968	4	/1-70,O-11	-1.3

■ EARL AVERILL
Averill, Earl Douglas b: 9/9/31, Cleveland, Ohio BR/TR, 5'10", 190 lbs. Deb: 4/19/56 F

YEAR	TM/L	G	AB	R	H	2B	3B	HR	RBI	BB	SO	AVG	OBP	SLG	PRO+	BR/A	SB	CS	SBR	FA	FR	G/POS	TPR
1956	Cle-A	42	93	12	22	6	0	3	14	14	25	.237	.343	.398	93	-1	0	1	-1	.994	3	C-34	0.2
1958	Cle-A	17	55	2	10	1	0	2	7	4	7	.182	.250	.309	54	-4	1	0	0	.863	0	3-17	-0.3
1959	Chi-N	74	186	20	44	10	0	10	34	15	39	.237	.300	.452	98	-1	0	1	-0	.963	3	C-32,3-13/O-5,2-2	0.3
1960	Chi-N	52	102	14	24	4	0	1	13	11	16	.235	.316	.304	71	-4	1	1	-0	.979	-9	C-34/3-1,O-1	-1.2
	Chi-A	10	14	2	3	0	0	0	2	4	2	.214	.389	.214	68	-0	0			1.000	2	/C-5	0.0
1961	LA-A	115	323	56	86	9	0	21	59	62	70	.266	.388	.489	119	9	1	0	0	.991	-7	C-88/O-9,2-1	0.7
1962	LA-A	92	187	21	41	9	0	4	22	43	47	.219	.368	.332	93	-0	0	1	0	1.000	-4	O-49/C-6	-0.6
1963	Phi-N	47	71	8	19	2	0	3	8	9	14	.268	.350	.423	123	2	0	0	0	.966	1	C-20/O-8,1-1,3-1	0.3
Total	7	449	1031	137	249	41	0	44	159	162	220	.242	.349	.409	101	1	3	3	-1	.984	-11	C-219/O-72,3-32,21	-0.4

■ EARL AVERILL
Averill, Howard Earl "Rock" b: 5/21/02, Snohomish, Wash. d: 8/16/83, Everett, Wash. BL/TR, 5'9.5", 172 lbs. Deb: 4/16/29 FH

YEAR	TM/L	G	AB	R	H	2B	3B	HR	RBI	BB	SO	AVG	OBP	SLG	PRO+	BR/A	SB	CS	SBR	FA	FR	G/POS	TPR
1929	Cle-A	151	597	110	198	43	13	18	96	63	53	.332	.398	.538	134	29	13	13	-4	.966	-4	*O-151	1.1
1930	Cle-A	139	534	102	181	33	8	19	119	56	48	.339	.404	.537	131	25	10	7	-1	.949	2	*O-134	1.5
1931	Cle-A	155	627	140	209	36	10	32	143	68	38	.333	.404	.576	147	41	9	9	-3	.976	0	*O-155	2.5
1932	Cle-A	153	631	116	198	37	14	32	124	75	40	.314	.392	.569	137	33	5	8	-3	.964	0	*O-153	1.9
1933	Cle-A★	151	599	83	180	39	16	11	92	54	29	.301	.363	.474	115	12	3	1	0	.971	2	*O-149	0.6
1934	Cle-A★	154	598	128	187	48	6	31	113	99	44	.313	.414	.569	119	44	5	3	0	.970	9	*O-154	4.2
1935	Cle-A†	140	563	109	162	34	13	19	79	70	58	.288	.368	.496	119	15	8	4	0	.982	0	*O-150	0.7
1936	Cle-A★	152	614	136	**232**	39	**15**	28	126	65	35	.378	.438	.627	159	55	3	3	-1	.969	-4	*O-156	3.9
1937	Cle-A★	156	609	121	182	33	11	21	92	88	65	.299	.387	.493	119	18	5	3	-1	.976	-8	*O-156	0.4
1938	Cle-A★	134	482	101	159	27	15	14	93	81	48	.330	.429	.535	143	34	5	2	0	.975	5	*O-131	3.2
1939	Cle-A	24	55	8	15	8	0	1	7	6	12	.273	.344	.473	111	1	0	1	-1	1.000	-0	O-11	-0.3
	Det-A	87	309	58	81	20	6	10	58	43	30	.262	.354	.463	100	0	4	2	0	.976	-5	O-80	-0.8
	Yr	111	364	66	96	28	6	11	65	49	42	.264	.353	.464	102	0	4	3	-1	.977	-7	O-91	-1.1
1940	*Det-A	64	118	10	33	4	1	2	20	5	14	.280	.309	.381	71	-5	0			.962	-5	O-22	-1.1
1941	Bos-N	8	17	2	2	0	0	0	2	1	4	.118	.211	.118	-6	-2	0			1.000	1	/O-4	-0.2
Total	13	1668	6353	1224	2019	401	128	238	1164	774	518	.318	.395	.534	132	296	70	57		.970	-8	*O-1589	17.6

■ BOBBY AVILA
Avila, Roberto Francisco (Gonzales) b: 4/2/24, Veracruz, Mexico BR/TR, 5'10", 175 lbs. Deb: 4/30/49

YEAR	TM/L	G	AB	R	H	2B	3B	HR	RBI	BB	SO	AVG	OBP	SLG	PRO+	BR/A	SB	CS	SBR	FA	FR	G/POS	TPR
1949	Cle-A	31	14	3	3	1	0	0	3	1	2	.214	.267	.214	29	-0	0	0	0	1.000	4	/2-5	0.2
1950	Cle-A	80	201	39	60	10	2	1	21	29	17	.299	.390	.383	102	1	5	0	2	.983	-5	2-62/S-2	0.0
1951	Cle-A	141	542	76	165	21	3	10	58	60	31	.304	.374	.410	118	14	14	8	-1	.982	-1	*2-136	1.9
1952	Cle-A★	150	597	102	179	26	**11**	7	45	67	36	.300	.371	.415	127	21	12	10	-2	.966	-18	*2-149	0.9
1953	Cle-A	141	559	85	160	22	3	8	55	58	27	.286	.355	.379	101	1	10	8	-2	**.986**	13	*2-140	2.1
1954	*Cle-A★	143	555	112	189	27	2	15	67	59	31	**.341**	.405	.477	139	30	3	6	-2	.976	8	*2-141/S-7	4.7
1955	Cle-A★	141	537	83	146	22	4	13	61	82	47	.272	.370	.400	103	4	1	4	-0	.982	-3	*2-141	1.0
1956	Cle-A	138	513	74	115	14	2	10	54	70	68	.224	.323	.318	68	-23	17	4	3	.977	-10	*2-135	-1.8
1957	Cle-A	129	463	60	124	19	3	5	48	46	47	.268	.335	.354	89	-6	2	4	-0	.983	-15	*2-107,3-16	-1.5
1958	Cle-A	113	375	54	95	21	3	6	30	55	45	.253	.350	.365	100	1	5	7	-3	.986	-21	2-82,3-33	-1.7
1959	Bal-A	20	47	1	8	0	0	0		4	5	.170	.235	.170	14	-6	0	0	0	1.000	-4	O-10/2-8,3-1	-1.0
	Bos-N	22	45	7	11	0	0	3	6	6	11	.244	.333	.444	107	0	0	0	0	.975	-2	2-11	-0.1
	Yr	42	92	8	19	0	0	3	6	10	16	.207	.284	.304	61	-5	0	0	0	.967	-6	2-19,O-10/3-1	-1.1
	Mil-N	51	172	29	41	3	3	2	19	24	31	.238	.332	.331	44	0	3	3	1	.967	-12	2-51	-1.1
Total	11	1300	4620	725	1296	185	35	80	467	561	399	.281	.360	.388	104	34	78	52	-8	.979	-64	*2-1168/3-50,O-10,S	3.6

■ RAMON AVILES
Aviles, Ramon Antonio (Miranda) b: 1/22/52, Manati, P.R. BR/TR, 5'9", 155 lbs. Deb: 7/10/77

YEAR	TM/L	G	AB	R	H	2B	3B	HR	RBI	BB	SO	AVG	OBP	SLG	PRO+	BR/A	SB	CS	SBR	FA	FR	G/POS	TPR
1977	Bos-A	1	0	0	0	0	0	0	0	0	0	—	—	—	—	-0	0	0	0	1.000	0	/2-1	0.0
1979	Phi-N	27	61	7	17	2	0	0	12	8	6	.279	.371	.311	86	-1	0	0	0	.977	-7	2-27	-0.7
1980	*Phi-N	51	101	12	28	6	0	2	9	10	9	.277	.342	.396	100	-0	0	0	0	.944	-7	S-29,2-15	-0.4
1981	*Phi-N	38	28	2	6	1	0	0	3	3	5	.214	.290	.250	52	-2	0	0	0	1.000	4	2-20,3-13/S-5	0.3
Total	4	117	190	21	51	9	0	2	24	21	22	.268	.344	.347	88	-2	0	0	0	.971	-10	/2-63,S-34,3-13	-0.8

■ BENNY AYALA
Ayala, Benigno (Felix) b: 2/7/51, Yauco, P.R. BR/TR, 6'1", 185 lbs. Deb: 8/27/74

YEAR	TM/L	G	AB	R	H	2B	3B	HR	RBI	BB	SO	AVG	OBP	SLG	PRO+	BR/A	SB	CS	SBR	FA	FR	G/POS	TPR
1974	NY-N	23	68	9	16	1	0	2	8	7	17	.235	.316	.338	84	-1	0	0	0	.927	0	O-20	-0.2
1976	NY-N	22	26	2	3	2	0	0	2	2	6	.115	.179	.231	16	-3	0	1	-1	.889	-1	/O-7	-0.5
1977	StL-N	1	3	0	1	0	0	0	0	0	1	.333	.333	.333	81	-0	0	0	0	1.000	2	/O-1	0.2
1979	*Bal-A	42	86	15	22	5	0	6	13	6	9	.256	.304	.523	123	4	0	0	0	.974	-3	O-24,D-10	-0.2
1980	Bal-A	76	170	28	45	8	1	10	33	19	21	.265	.339	.500	128	6	0	0	0	1.000	-2	D-41,O-19	0.2
1981	Bal-A	44	86	12	24	2	0	3	13	11	9	.279	.367	.407	123	3	1	0	0	1.000	-0	D-27/O-4	0.1
1982	Bal-A	64	128	17	39	6	0	4	25	14	24	.305	.381	.492	123	3	1	1	0	.972	-5	O-25,D-17/1-3	-0.2
1983	*Bal-A	47	104	12	23	7	0	4	19	10	18	.221	.283	.404	88	-2	0	0	0	.953	-3	O-24,D-11	-0.6
1984	Bal-A	60	118	9	25	6	0	4	24	14	24	.212	.262	.364	73	-5	1	1	-0	1.000	-4	D-34,O-13	-1.0
1985	Cle-A	46	76	10	19	7	0	2	14	6	17	.250	.307	.421	92	-1	0	2	-2	.917	-4	O-20/D-3	-0.7
Total	10	425	865	114	217	42	1	38	145	71	136	.251	.309	.434	104	2	2	4	-2	.958	-19	O-157,D-143/1-3	-2.7

■ DICK AYLWARD
Aylward, Richard John "Dandy" b: 6/4/25, Baltimore, Md. d: 6/11/83, Spring Valley, Cal. BR/TR, 6', 190 lbs. Deb: 5/1/53

YEAR	TM/L	G	AB	R	H	2B	3B	HR	RBI	BB	SO	AVG	OBP	SLG	PRO+	BR/A	SB	CS	SBR	FA	FR	G/POS	TPR
1953	Cle-A	4	3	0	0	0	0	0	0	0	1	.000	.000	.000	-99	-1	0	0	0	1.000	-0	/C-4	-0.1

■ JOE AYRAULT
Ayrault, Joseph Allen b: 10/8/71, Rochester, Mich. BR/TR, 6'3", 190 lbs. Deb: 9/1/96

YEAR	TM/L	G	AB	R	H	2B	3B	HR	RBI	BB	SO	AVG	OBP	SLG	PRO+	BR/A	SB	CS	SBR	FA	FR	G/POS	TPR
1996	Atl-N	7	5	0	1	0	0	0	0	0	1	.200	.333	.200	43	-0	0	0	0	1.000	0	/C-7	0.0

YEAR	TM/L	G	AB	R	H	2B	3B	HR	RBI	BB	SO	AVG	OBP	SLG	PRO+	BR/A	SB	CS	SBR	FA	FR	G/POS	TPR

■ JOE AZCUE   Azcue, Jose Joaquin (Lopez) b: 8/18/39, Cienfuegos, Cuba BR/TR, 6', 200 lbs. Deb: 8/3/60

YEAR	TM/L	G	AB	R	H	2B	3B	HR	RBI	BB	SO	AVG	OBP	SLG	PRO+	BR/A	SB	CS	SBR	FA	FR	G/POS	TPR
1960	Cin-N	14	31	1	3	0	0	0	3	2	6	.097	.152	.097	-30	-5	0	1	-1	1.000	5	C-14	0.0
1962	KC-A	72	223	18	51	9	1	2	25	17	27	.229	.292	.305	58	-13	1	0	0	.985	3	C-70	-0.7
1963	KC-A	2	4	0	0	0	0	0	0	0	1	.000	.000	.000	-95	-1	0	0	0	1.000	0	/C-1	-0.1
	Cle-A	94	320	26	91	16	0	14	46	15	46	.284	.316	.466	117	6	1	1	-0	.992	5	C-91	1.4
	Yr	96	324	26	91	16	0	14	46	15	47	.281	.313	.460	114	5	1	1	-0	.992	5	C-92	1.3
1964	Cle-A	83	271	20	74	9	1	4	34	16	38	.273	.318	.358	88	-4	0	2	-1	.993	-0	C-76	-0.2
1965	Cle-A	111	335	16	77	7	0	2	35	27	54	.230	.293	.269	60	-17	2	1	0	.994	-1	*C-108	-1.3
1966	Cle-A	98	302	22	83	10	1	9	37	20	22	.275	.324	.404	108	3	0	2	-1	.989	-8	C-97	-0.1
1967	Cle-A	86	295	33	74	12	5	11	34	22	35	.251	.309	.437	117	5	0	3	-2	.999	5	C-86	1.5
1968	Cle-A★	115	357	23	100	10	0	4	42	28	33	.280	.332	.342	106	3	1	1	-0	.996	11	C-97	2.2
1969	Cle-A	7	24	1	7	0	0	1	1	4	3	.292	.393	.417	122	1	0	0	0	.980	2	/C-6	0.3
	Bos-A	19	51	7	11	2	0	0	3	4	5	.216	.273	.255	46	-4	0	0	0	.981	3	C-19	0.0
	Cal-A	80	248	15	54	6	0	1	19	27	28	.218	.300	.254	59	-13	0	1	-1	.992	5	C-80	-0.5
	Yr	106	323	23	72	8	0	2	23	35	36	.223	.303	.266	62	-16	0	1	-1	.989	9	*C-105	-0.2
1970	Cal-A	114	351	19	85	13	1	2	25	24	40	.242	.294	.302	67	-16	0	1	-0	.991	-5	*C-112	-1.7
1972	Cal-A	3	2	0	0	0	0	0	0	0	1	.000	.000	.000	-99	-1	0	0	0	1.000	1	/C-2	0.0
	Mil-A	11	14	0	2	0	0	0	0	1	5	.143	.200	.143	3	-2	0	0	0	1.000	2	/C-9	0.0
	Yr	14	16	0	2	0	0	0	0	1	6	.125	.176	.125	-10	-2	0	0	0	1.000	2	C-11	0.0
Total	11	909	2828	201	712	94	9	50	304	207	344	.252	.307	.344	85	-58	5	12	-6	.992	26	C-868	0.8

■ OSCAR AZOCAR   Azocar, Oscar Gregorio (Azocar) b: 2/21/65, Soro, Venez. BL/TL, 6'1", 170 lbs. Deb: 7/17/90

YEAR	TM/L	G	AB	R	H	2B	3B	HR	RBI	BB	SO	AVG	OBP	SLG	PRO+	BR/A	SB	CS	SBR	FA	FR	G/POS	TPR
1990	NY-A	65	214	18	53	8	0	5	19	2	15	.248	.258	.355	70	-9	7	0	2	.991	-9	O-57/D-1	-0.9
1991	SD-N	38	57	5	14	2	0	0	9	1	9	.246	.271	.281	54	-3	2	0	1	.875	-3	O-13/1-1	-0.6
1992	SD-N	99	168	15	32	6	0	0	8	9	12	.190	.232	.226	30	-15	1	0	0	.942	-1	O-37	-1.8
Total	3	202	439	38	99	16	0	5	36	12	36	.226	.249	.296	52	-28	10	0	3	.964	-4	O-107/1-1,D-1	-3.3

■ CHARLIE BABB   Babb, Charles Amos b: 2/20/1873, Milwaukie, Ore. d: 3/20/54, Portland, Ore. BB/TR, 5'10", 165 lbs. Deb: 4/17/03

YEAR	TM/L	G	AB	R	H	2B	3B	HR	RBI	BB	SO	AVG	OBP	SLG	PRO+	BR/A	SB	CS	SBR	FA	FR	G/POS	TPR
1903	NY-N	121	424	68	105	15	8	0	46	45		.248	.350	.321	88	-5	22			.912	-2	*S-113/3-8	-0.1
1904	Bro-N	151	521	49	138	18	3	0	53	53		.265	.345	.311	106	6	34			.927	-3	*S-151	0.7
1905	Bro-N	75	235	27	44	8	2	0	17	27		.187	.303	.238	67	-8	10			.923	-2	S-36,1-31/3-5,2-2	-1.1
Total	3	347	1180	144	287	41	13	0	116	125		.243	.339	.300	92	-7	66			.921	-7	S-300/1-31,3-13,2-2	-0.5

■ LOREN BABE   Babe, Loren Rolland "Bee Bee" b: 1/11/28, Pisgah, Iowa d: 2/14/84, Omaha, Neb. BL/TR, 5'10", 180 lbs. Deb: 8/19/52 C

YEAR	TM/L	G	AB	R	H	2B	3B	HR	RBI	BB	SO	AVG	OBP	SLG	PRO+	BR/A	SB	CS	SBR	FA	FR	G/POS	TPR
1952	NY-A	12	21	1	2	1	0	0	4	4	4	.095	.240	.143	9	-3	1	0	0	.909	3	/3-9	-0.1
1953	NY-A	5	18	2	6	1	0	2	6	0	2	.333	.333	.722	185	2	0	0	0	.920	3	/3-5	0.5
	Phi-A	103	343	34	77	16	2	0	20	35	20	.224	.300	.283	56	-21	0	1	-1	.950	5	3-93/S-1	-2.2
	Yr	108	361	36	83	17	2	2	26	35	22	.230	.302	.305	62	-19	0	1	-1	.948	5	3-98/S-1	-1.7
Total	2	120	382	37	85	18	2	2	26	39	26	.223	.298	.296	59	-21	1	1	-0	.946	6	3-107/S-1	-1.8

■ CHARLIE BABINGTON   Babington, Charles Percy b: 5/4/1895, Cranston, R.I. d: 3/22/57, Providence, R.I. BR/TR, 6', 170 lbs. Deb: 7/20/15

YEAR	TM/L	G	AB	R	H	2B	3B	HR	RBI	BB	SO	AVG	OBP	SLG	PRO+	BR/A	SB	CS	SBR	FA	FR	G/POS	TPR
1915	NY-N	28	33	5	8	3	1	0	2	0	4	.242	.265	.394	104	-0	1			.909	-5	O-12/1-1	-0.6

■ SHOOTY BABITT   Babitt, Mack Neal b: 3/9/59, Oakland, Cal. BR/TR, 5'8", 174 lbs. Deb: 4/9/81

YEAR	TM/L	G	AB	R	H	2B	3B	HR	RBI	BB	SO	AVG	OBP	SLG	PRO+	BR/A	SB	CS	SBR	FA	FR	G/POS	TPR
1981	Oak-A	54	156	10	40	1	3	0	14	13	13	.256	.314	.301	82	-4	5	4	-1	.972	-17	2-52	-2.0

■ WALLY BACKMAN   Backman, Walter Wayne b: 9/22/59, Hillsboro, Ore. BB/TR, 5'9", 160 lbs. Deb: 9/2/80

YEAR	TM/L	G	AB	R	H	2B	3B	HR	RBI	BB	SO	AVG	OBP	SLG	PRO+	BR/A	SB	CS	SBR	FA	FR	G/POS	TPR
1980	NY-N	27	93	12	30	1	1	0	9	11	14	.323	.400	.355	115	3	2	3	-1	1.000	-10	2-20/S-8	-0.7
1981	NY-N	26	36	5	10	2	0	0	4	7	7	.278	.350	.333	96	-0	1	0	0	.946	-3	2-11/3-1	-0.3
1982	NY-N	96	261	37	71	13	2	3	22	49	47	.272	.387	.372	114	7	8	7	-2	.964	-13	2-88/3-6,S-1	-0.5
1983	NY-N	26	42	6	7	0	1	0	3	2	8	.167	.205	.214	16	-5	0	0	0	1.000	-2	2-14/3-2	-0.7
1984	NY-N	128	436	68	122	19	2	1	26	56	63	.280	.362	.339	99	2	32	9	4	.981	-12	*2-115/S-8	-0.2
1985	NY-N	145	520	77	142	24	5	1	38	36	72	.273	.321	.344	88	-8	30	12	2	.989	-9	*2-140/S-1	-1.2
1986	*NY-N	124	387	67	124	18	2	1	27	36	32	.320	.378	.385	114	8	13	7	-0	.966	-3	*2-113	0.9
1987	NY-N	94	300	43	75	6	1	1	23	25	43	.250	.308	.287	62	-16	11	3	2	.983	-7	2-87	-1.8
1988	*NY-N	99	294	44	89	12	0	0	17	41	49	.303	.390	.344	118	9	9	5	0	.989	-9	2-92	0.3
1989	Min-A	87	299	33	69	9	2	1	26	32	45	.231	.307	.284	63	-14	1	1	-0	.982	-22	2-84/D-1	-3.5
1990	*Pit-N	104	315	62	92	21	3	2	28	42	53	.292	.377	.397	118	9	6	3	0	.920	-19	3-71,2-15	-1.0
1991	Phi-N	94	185	20	45	12	0	0	15	30	30	.243	.349	.308	87	-2	3	2	-0	.981	-15	2-36,3-20	-1.7
1992	Phi-N	42	48	6	13	1	0	0	6	6	9	.271	.352	.292	84	-1	1	0	0	.968	-0	2-10/3-2	0.0
1993	Sea-A	10	29	2	4	0	0	0	1	0	8	.138	.167	.138	-17	-5	0	0	0	.857	-1	/3-9,2-1	-0.5
Total	14	1102	3245	482	893	138	19	10	240	371	480	.275	.350	.339	94	-13	117	52	4	.980	-125	2-826,3-111/S-18,D	-10.9

■ EDDIE BACON   Bacon, Edgar Suter b: 4/8/1895, Franklin Co., Ky. d: 10/2/63, Louisville, Ky. Deb: 8/13/17

YEAR	TM/L	G	AB	R	H	2B	3B	HR	RBI	BB	SO	AVG	OBP	SLG	PRO+	BR/A	SB	CS	SBR	FA	FR	G/POS	TPR
1917	Phi-A	4	6	1	3	1	0	0	2	0	1	.500	.500	.667	259	1	0			1.000	1	/P-1	0.0

■ ART BADER   Bader, Arthur Herman b: 9/21/1886, St.Louis, Mo. d: 4/5/57, St.Louis, Mo. BR/TR, 5'10", 170 lbs. Deb: 8/2/04

YEAR	TM/L	G	AB	R	H	2B	3B	HR	RBI	BB	SO	AVG	OBP	SLG	PRO+	BR/A	SB	CS	SBR	FA	FR	G/POS	TPR
1904	StL-A	2	3	0	0	0	0	0	0	1		.000	.250	.000	-19	-0	0			1.000	1	/O-1	0.0

■ RED BADGRO   Badgro, Morris Hiram b: 12/1/02, Orillia, Wash. BL/TR, 6', 190 lbs. Deb: 6/20/29

YEAR	TM/L	G	AB	R	H	2B	3B	HR	RBI	BB	SO	AVG	OBP	SLG	PRO+	BR/A	SB	CS	SBR	FA	FR	G/POS	TPR
1929	StL-A	54	148	27	42	12	0	1	18	11	15	.284	.342	.385	84	-4	1	0	0	.983	-4	O-37	-0.9
1930	StL-A	89	234	30	56	18	3	1	27	13	27	.239	.285	.355	59	-15	3	5	-2	.952	0	O-61	-1.9
Total	2	143	382	57	98	30	3	2	45	24	42	.257	.307	.366	69	-19	4	5	-2	.962	-4	/O-98	-2.8

■ CARLOS BAERGA   Baerga, Carlos Obed (Ortiz) b: 11/4/68, Santurce, P.R. BB/TR, 5'11", 165 lbs. Deb: 4/14/90

YEAR	TM/L	G	AB	R	H	2B	3B	HR	RBI	BB	SO	AVG	OBP	SLG	PRO+	BR/A	SB	CS	SBR	FA	FR	G/POS	TPR
1990	Cle-A	108	312	46	81	17	2	7	47	16	57	.260	.304	.394	94	-3	0	2	-1	.944	-9	3-50,S-48/2-8	-1.2
1991	Cle-A	158	593	80	171	28	2	11	69	48	74	.288	.348	.398	105	4	3	2	-0	.944	11	3-89,2-75/S-2	1.7
1992	Cle-A★	161	657	92	205	32	1	20	105	35	76	.312	.359	.455	129	24	10	2	2	.979	8	*2-160/D-1	3.8
1993	Cle-A★	154	624	105	200	28	6	21	114	34	68	.321	.361	.486	126	21	15	4	2	.979	8	*2-150/D-4	3.4
1994	Cle-A	103	442	81	139	32	2	19	80	10	45	.314	.338	.525	118	10	8	2	1	.973	6	*2-102/D-1	2.3
1995	*Cle-A★	135	557	87	175	28	2	15	90	35	31	.314	.358	.452	108	6	11	2	2	.973	12	*2-134/D-1	2.6
1996	Cle-A	100	424	54	113	25	0	10	55	16	25	.267	.304	.396	75	-17	1	1	-0	.971	-3	*2-100	-1.2
	NY-N	26	83	5	16	3	0	2	11	5	2	.193	.256	.301	50	-6	0	0	0	.990	-5	1-16/3-6,2-1	-1.2
Total	7	945	3692	550	1100	193	15	105	571	199	378	.298	.342	.444	109	38	48	15	5	.974	32	2-730,3-145/S1D	10.2

■ JOSE BAEZ   Baez, Jose Antonio (b: Jose Antonio Mota (Baez)) b: 12/31/53, San Cristobal, D.R. BR/TR, 5'8", 160 lbs. Deb: 4/6/77

YEAR	TM/L	G	AB	R	H	2B	3B	HR	RBI	BB	SO	AVG	OBP	SLG	PRO+	BR/A	SB	CS	SBR	FA	FR	G/POS	TPR
1977	Sea-A	91	305	39	79	14	1	1	17	19	20	.259	.305	.321	71	-12	6	1	1	.973	9	2-77/3-1,D-3	0.3
1978	Sea-A	23	50	8	8	0	1	0	2	6	7	.160	.250	.200	28	-5	1	0	1	.978	12	2-14/3-3,D-1	0.9
Total	2	114	355	47	87	14	2	1	19	25	27	.245	.297	.304	65	-17	7	1	2	.974	21	/2-91,D-4,3-4	1.2

■ KEVIN BAEZ   Baez, Kevin Richard b: 1/10/67, Brooklyn, N.Y. BR/TR, 6', 160 lbs. Deb: 9/3/90

YEAR	TM/L	G	AB	R	H	2B	3B	HR	RBI	BB	SO	AVG	OBP	SLG	PRO+	BR/A	SB	CS	SBR	FA	FR	G/POS	TPR
1990	NY-N	5	12	0	2	1	0	0	0	0	0	.167	.167	.250	13	-1	0	0	0	1.000	0	/S-4	-0.1
1992	NY-N	6	13	0	2	0	0	0	0	0	0	.154	.154	.154	-13	-2	0	0	0	.889	1	/S-5	-0.1
1993	NY-N	52	126	10	23	9	0	0	7	13	17	.183	.259	.254	38	-11	0	0	0	.967	-5	S-52	-1.2
Total	3	63	151	10	27	10	0	0	7	13	17	.179	.244	.245	33	-14	0	0	0	.962	-4	/S-61	-1.4

■ JEFF BAGWELL   Bagwell, Jeffery Robert b: 5/27/68, Boston, Mass. BR/TR, 6', 195 lbs. Deb: 4/8/91

YEAR	TM/L	G	AB	R	H	2B	3B	HR	RBI	BB	SO	AVG	OBP	SLG	PRO+	BR/A	SB	CS	SBR	FA	FR	G/POS	TPR
1991	Hou-N	156	554	79	163	26	4	15	82	75	116	.294	.391	.437	141	32	7	4	-0	.991	-1	*1-155	2.1
1992	Hou-N	162	586	87	160	34	6	18	96	84	97	.273	.375	.444	137	31	10	6	-1	.995	7	*1-159	2.7
1993	Hou-N	142	535	76	171	37	4	20	88	62	73	.320	.393	.516	146	35	13	4	2	.993	6	*1-140	3.1
1994	Hou-N★	110	400	**104**	147	32	2	39	**116**	65	65	.368	**.461**	**.750**	220	71	15	4	2	.991	17	*1-109/O-1	**7.6**
1995	Hou-N	114	448	88	130	29	0	21	87	79	102	.290	.403	.496	145	32	12	5	1	.994	18	*1-114	3.8

YEAR	TM/L	G	AB	R	H	2B	3B	HR	RBI	BB	SO	AVG	OBP	SLG	PRO+	BR/A	SB	CS	SBR	FA	FR	G/POS	TPR
1996	Hou-N★	162	568	111	179	**48**	2	31	120	135	114	.315	.454	.570	185	78	21	7	2	.989	8	*1-162	6.8
Total	6	846	3091	545	950	206	18	144	589	500	567	.307	.412	.525	161	279	78	30	5	.992	54	1-839/O-1	26.1

■ BILL BAGWELL
Bagwell, William Mallory "Big Bill" b: 2/24/1896, Choudrant, La. d: 10/5/76, Choudrant, La. BL/TL, 6'1", 175 lbs. Deb: 4/17/23

YEAR	TM/L	G	AB	R	H	2B	3B	HR	RBI	BB	SO	AVG	OBP	SLG	PRO+	BR/A	SB	CS	SBR	FA	FR	G/POS	TPR
1923	Bos-N	56	93	8	27	4	2	2	10	6	12	.290	.333	.441	107	1	0	0	0	1.000	-3	O-22	-0.3
1925	Phi-A	36	50	4	15	2	1	0	10	2	2	.300	.327	.380	74	-2	0	0	0	.667	-2	/O-4	-0.4
Total	2	92	143	12	42	6	3	2	20	8	14	.294	.331	.420	95	-2	0	0	0	.973	-5	/O-26	-0.7

■ FRANK BAHRET
Bahret, Frank J. b: Poughkeepsie, N.Y. 6'1", 184 lbs. Deb: 4/17/1884

YEAR	TM/L	G	AB	R	H	2B	3B	HR	RBI	BB	SO	AVG	OBP	SLG	PRO+	BR/A	SB	CS	SBR	FA	FR	G/POS	TPR
1884	Bal-U	2	8	0	0	0	0	0	0	0	0	.000	.000	.000	-91	-2				1.000	0	/O-2	-0.2

■ GENE BAILEY
Bailey, Arthur Eugene b: 11/25/1893, Pearsall, Tex. d: 11/14/73, Houston, Tex. BR/TR, 5'8", 160 lbs. Deb: 9/10/17

YEAR	TM/L	G	AB	R	H	2B	3B	HR	RBI	BB	SO	AVG	OBP	SLG	PRO+	BR/A	SB	CS	SBR	FA	FR	G/POS	TPR
1917	Phi-A	5	12	1	1	0	0	0	0	1	1	.083	.154	.083	-28	-2	0			.833	-1	/O-4	-0.4
1919	Bos-N	4	6	0	2	0	0	0	1	0	2	.333	.333	.333	105	0	1			1.000	0	/O-3	0.0
1920	Bos-N	13	24	2	2	0	0	0	0	3	3	.083	.185	.083	-22	-0	1		-1	.929	-2	/O-8	-0.8
	Bos-A	46	135	14	31	2	0	0	5	9	15	.230	.283	.244	42	-11	2	7	-4	.986	-4	O-40	-2.1
1923	Bro-N	127	411	71	109	11	7	1	42	43	34	.265	.343	.333	81	-10	9	7	-2	.959	2	*O-100/1-5	-1.5
1924	Bro-N	18	46	7	11	3	0	1	7	6	7	.239	.340	.370	93	-0	1	0	0	1.000	1	O-17	0.0
Total	5	213	634	95	156	16	7	2	52	63	61	.246	.321	.303	69	-27	13	15		.965	-5	O-172/1-5	-4.8

■ FRED BAILEY
Bailey, Frederick Middleton "Penny" b: 8/16/1895, Mt.Hope, W.Va. d: 8/16/72, Huntington, W.Va. BL/TL, 5'11", 150 lbs. Deb: 8/19/16

YEAR	TM/L	G	AB	R	H	2B	3B	HR	RBI	BB	SO	AVG	OBP	SLG	PRO+	BR/A	SB	CS	SBR	FA	FR	G/POS	TPR
1916	Bos-N	6	10	0	1	0	0	0	1	0	3	.100	.100	.100	-40	-2	0			1.000	0	/O-2	-0.2
1917	Bos-N	50	110	9	21	2	1	1	5	9	25	.191	.270	.255	65	-4	3			.962	-1	O-27	-0.8
1918	Bos-N	4	4	1	1	0	0	0	0	1	1	.250	.250	.250	55	-0	0			.000	0	H	0.0
Total	3	60	124	10	23	2	1	1	6	9	29	.185	.257	.242	57	-6	3			.963	-2	O-29	-1.0

■ BILL BAILEY
Bailey, Harry Lewis b: 11/19/1881, Shawnee, Ohio d: 10/27/67, Seattle, Wash. BL/TR, 5'10.5", 170 lbs. Deb: 4/21/11

YEAR	TM/L	G	AB	R	H	2B	3B	HR	RBI	BB	SO	AVG	OBP	SLG	PRO+	BR/A	SB	CS	SBR	FA	FR	G/POS	TPR
1911	NY-A	5	9	1	1	0	0	0	0	0	0	.111	.111	.111	-36	-2	0			.000	0	/O-2,3-1	-0.1

■ MARK BAILEY
Bailey, John Mark b: 11/4/61, Springfield, Mo. BB/TR, 6'5", 195 lbs. Deb: 4/27/84

YEAR	TM/L	G	AB	R	H	2B	3B	HR	RBI	BB	SO	AVG	OBP	SLG	PRO+	BR/A	SB	CS	SBR	FA	FR	G/POS	TPR
1984	Hou-N	108	344	38	73	16	1	9	34	53	71	.212	.321	.343	93	-3	0	1	-1	.983	-2	*C-108	0.0
1985	Hou-N	114	332	47	88	14	0	10	45	67	70	.265	.390	.398	124	14	0	2	-1	.979	-10	*C-110/1-2	0.8
1986	Hou-N	57	153	9	27	5	0	4	15	28	45	.176	.304	.288	66	-7	1	1	-0	.989	-0	C-53/1-1	-0.3
1987	Hou-N	35	64	5	13	1	0	0	3	10	21	.203	.311	.219	45	-5	1	0	0	.985	-0	C-27	-0.4
1988	Hou-N	8	23	1	3	0	0	0	0	5	6	.130	.286	.130	24	-2	0	1	-1	.981	-1	/C-8	-0.3
1990	SF-N	5	7	1	1	0	0	0	3	0	2	.143	.143	.571	90	-0	0	0	0	1.000	-1	/C-1	-0.1
1992	SF-N	13	26	0	4	1	0	0	1	3	7	.154	.241	.192	26	-3	0	0	0	.983	-1	/C-7	-0.3
Total	7	340	949	101	209	37	1	24	101	166	222	.220	.338	.337	93	-5	2	5	-3	.983	-13	C-314/1-3	-0.6

■ ED BAILEY
Bailey, Lonas Edgar b: 4/15/31, Strawberry Plains, Tenn. BL/TR, 6'2", 205 lbs. Deb: 9/26/53 F

YEAR	TM/L	G	AB	R	H	2B	3B	HR	RBI	BB	SO	AVG	OBP	SLG	PRO+	BR/A	SB	CS	SBR	FA	FR	G/POS	TPR
1953	Cin-N	2	8	1	3	1	0	0	1	1	3	.375	.444	.500	145	1	0	0	0	1.000	-1	/C-2	0.0
1954	Cin-N	73	183	21	36	2	3	9	20	35	34	.197	.326	.388	83	-5	1	0	0	.973	-12	C-61	-1.4
1955	Cin-N	21	39	3	8	1	1	1	4	4	10	.205	.326	.359	77	-1	0	0	0	.962	3	C-11	0.2
1956	Cin-N★	118	383	58	115	8	2	28	75	52	50	.300	.388	.551	140	22	2	0	1	.984	4	*C-106	3.1
1957	Cin-N★	122	391	54	102	15	2	20	48	73	69	.261	.380	.463	117	11	5	3	0	.991	-12	*C-115	0.3
1958	Cin-N	112	360	39	90	23	1	11	59	47	61	.250	.338	.411	92	-4	2	2	-1	.988	-4	C-99	-0.3
1959	Cin-N	121	379	43	100	13	0	12	40	62	53	.264	.370	.393	101	2	0	1	0	.990	2	*C-117	1.1
1960	Cin-N★	133	441	52	115	19	3	13	67	59	70	.261	.351	.406	105	2	4	1	0	.990	-13	*C-129	-0.1
1961	Cin-N	12	43	4	13	4	0	0	2	3	5	.302	.348	.395	95	-0	0	0	0	.967	-4	C-12	-0.2
	SF-N☆	107	340	39	81	9	1	13	51	42	41	.238	.329	.385	92	-4	1	5	-3	.985	-1	*C-103/O-1	-0.4
	Yr	119	383	43	94	13	1	13	53	45	46	.245	.331	.386	93	-4	1	5	-3	.984	-5	*C-115/O-1	-0.6
1962	*SF-N	96	254	32	59	9	1	17	45	42	42	.232	.354	.476	123	8	1	1	0	.987	-5	C-75	0.6
1963	SF-N★	105	308	41	81	8	0	21	68	50	64	.263	.368	.494	147	19	0	6	-4	.987	-9	C-88	2.0
1964	Mil-N	95	271	30	71	10	1	5	34	34	39	.262	.346	.362	99	-3	1	2	0	.982	-10	C-80	-0.5
1965	SF-N	24	28	1	3	0	0	0	3	6	7	.107	.265	.107	9	-3	0	0	0	1.000	3	C-12/1-2	0.2
	Chi-N	66	150	13	38	6	0	5	23	34	28	.253	.391	.393	119	5	0	1	-1	.981	-5	C-54/1-3	0.2
	Yr	90	178	14	41	6	0	5	26	40	35	.230	.372	.348	102	2	0	1	-1	.984	-2	C-66/1-5	0.2
1966	Cal-A	5	3	0	0	0	0	0	0	0	0	.000	.250	.000	-22	-0	0	0	0	.000	0	H	-0.2
Total	14	1212	3581	432	915	128	15	155	540	545	577	.256	.358	.429	110	56	17	18	-6	.986	-54	*C-1064/1-5,O-1	4.6

■ BOB BAILEY
Bailey, Robert Sherwood b: 10/13/42, Long Beach, Cal. BR/TR, 6', 188 lbs. Deb: 9/14/62

YEAR	TM/L	G	AB	R	H	2B	3B	HR	RBI	BB	SO	AVG	OBP	SLG	PRO+	BR/A	SB	CS	SBR	FA	FR	G/POS	TPR
1962	Pit-N	14	42	6	7	2	1	0	6	6	10	.167	.271	.262	44	-3	1	1	-0	.921	0	3-12	-0.3
1963	Pit-N	154	570	60	130	15	3	12	45	58	98	.228	.305	.328	82	-13	10	9	-2	.933	6	*3-153/S-3	-1.0
1964	Pit-N	143	530	73	149	26	3	11	51	44	78	.281	.337	.404	108	6	10	8	-2	.943	6	*3-105,O-35/S-2	0.8
1965	Pit-N	159	626	87	160	28	3	11	49	70	93	.256	.330	.363	95	-3	10	14	-5	.939	-8	*3-142,O-28	-3.2
1966	Pit-N	126	380	51	106	19	3	13	46	47	65	.279	.361	.447	123	13	5	3	-5	.956	-0	3-96,O-20	1.0
1967	LA-N	116	322	21	73	8	2	4	28	40	50	.227	.314	.301	84	-6	5	5	-2	.941	0	3-65,O-27/1-4,S-1	-1.0
1968	LA-N	105	322	24	73	9	3	3	39	38	69	.227	.310	.348	105	2	1	2	-1	.953	-4	3-90/S-1,O-1	-0.2
1969	Mon-N	111	358	46	95	16	6	9	53	40	76	.265	.341	.419	111	5	3	3	-1	.992	1	4-85,O-12/3-1	0.1
1970	Mon-N	131	352	77	101	19	3	28	84	72	70	.287	.409	.597	166	34	5	3	-2	.953	-13	3-48,O-44,1-18	1.7
1971	Mon-N	157	545	65	137	21	4	14	83	97	105	.251	.364	.382	111	11	13	7	-0	**.960**	-15	*3-120,O-51/1-9	-0.8
1972	Mon-N	143	489	55	114	10	4	16	57	59	112	.233	.317	.368	92	-5	6	7	-2	.938	-8	*3-134/O-5,1-3	-1.7
1973	Mon-N	151	513	77	140	25	4	26	86	88	99	.273	.380	.489	134	25	5	3	-3	.956	-5	*3-146/O-2	1.7
1974	Mon-N	152	507	69	142	20	2	20	73	100	107	.280	.400	.446	129	23	4	7	-3	.974	-16	O-78,3-68	0.0
1975	Mon-N	106	227	23	62	5	0	5	30	46	34	.273	.398	.361	107	4	4	4	-1	.979	-5	O-61/3-3	-0.4
1976	Cin-N	69	124	17	37	6	1	6	26	19	26	.298	.379	.508	107	7	0	0	0	.974	-5	O-31,3-10	0.2
1977	Cin-N	49	79	9	20	2	1	2	11	12	10	.253	.352	.380	94	-0	1	1	-0	.975	-1	1-19/O-3	-0.2
	Bos-A	2	2	0	0	0	0	0	0	0	1	.000	.000	.000	-90	-1	0	0	0	.000	0	H	-0.1
1978	Bos-A	43	92	9	16	4	0	3	9	19	19	.191	.333	.351	84	-2	1	0	0	.953	-3	D-34/3-1,O-1	-0.3
Total	17	1931	6082	772	1564	234	43	189	773	852	1126	.257	.350	.403	111	97	85	83	-24	.946	-71	*3-1194,O-399,1/DS	-3.7

■ BOB BAILOR
Bailor, Robert Michael b: 7/10/51, Connellsville, Pa. BR/TR, 5'11", 170 lbs. Deb: 9/6/75 C

YEAR	TM/L	G	AB	R	H	2B	3B	HR	RBI	BB	SO	AVG	OBP	SLG	PRO+	BR/A	SB	CS	SBR	FA	FR	G/POS	TPR
1975	Bal-A	5	7	0	1	0	0	0	0	1	0	.143	.250	.143	14	-1	0	0	0	1.000	2	/S-2,2-1	0.1
1976	Bal-A	9	6	2	2	0	1	0	0	0	1	.333	.333	.667	200	1	0	1	-1	.000	-0	/S-1,D-1	0.4
1977	Tor-A	122	496	62	154	21	5	5	32	17	26	.310	.336	.403	99	-1	15	6	1	.988	1	O-63,S-53/D-7	0.4
1978	Tor-A	154	621	74	164	29	7	1	52	38	21	.264	.312	.338	81	-16	5	6	-2	.964	15	*O-125,3-28/S-4	-0.8
1979	Tor-A	130	414	50	95	11	5	1	38	36	27	.229	.300	.287	59	-23	14	8	-1	.987	1	*O-118/3-9,D-1	-2.7
1980	Tor-A	117	347	44	82	14	2	1	16	36	33	.236	.312	.297	65	-16	12	8	-1	.991	12	O-98,S-12,3/P2D	-0.5
1981	NY-N	51	81	11	23	3	1	0	8	11	12	.284	.356	.346	101	0	2	0	1	.955	9	S-22,2-13,O-13/3-1	-0.2
1982	NY-N	110	376	44	104	14	1	0	31	20	31	.277	.317	.319	79	-10	6	6	3	.984	-19	S-60,2-56,3-21/O-4	-2.1
1983	NY-N	118	340	33	85	8	0	1	30	20	23	.250	.294	.282	61	-18	18	3	4	.969	-8	S-75,2-50,3-11/O-3	-1.8
1984	LA-N	65	131	11	36	4	0	0	8	8	11	.275	.317	.305	76	-4	3	1	0	.944	10	2-23,3-17,S-16	0.8
1985	*LA-N	74	118	8	29	3	1	0	11	8	14	.246	.312	.305	58	-7	3	1	0	.962	15	3-45,2-16/S-5,O-1	0.9
Total	11	955	2937	339	775	107	23	9	222	187	164	.264	.312	.325	76	-95	90	36	5	.980	26	O-425,S-250,23/DP	-5.8

■ HAROLD BAINES
Baines, Harold Douglass b: 3/15/59, Easton, Md. BL/TL, 6'2", 195 lbs. Deb: 4/10/80

YEAR	TM/L	G	AB	R	H	2B	3B	HR	RBI	BB	SO	AVG	OBP	SLG	PRO+	BR/A	SB	CS	SBR	FA	FR	G/POS	TPR
1980	Chi-A	141	491	55	125	23	6	13	49	19	65	.255	.284	.405	87	-11	2	4	-2	.963	-7	*O-137/D-1	-2.4
1981	Chi-A	82	280	42	80	11	7	10	41	12	41	.286	.320	.482	131	10	6	2	1	.985	-0	O-80/D-1	0.8
1982	Chi-A	161	608	89	165	29	8	25	105	49	95	.271	.326	.469	115	11	10	3	1	.980	2	*O-161	1.0
1983	*Chi-A	156	596	76	167	33	2	20	99	49	85	.280	.336	.443	108	6	7	5	-1	.973	0	*O-155	0.1
1984	Chi-A	147	569	72	173	28	10	29	94	54	75	.304	.364	**.541**	141	30	1	2	0	.981	-5	*O-147	2.5
1985	Chi-A★	160	640	86	198	29	3	22	113	42	89	.309	.353	.467	118	15	1	1	-0	.994	7	*O-159/D-1	1.6

YEAR	TM/L	G	AB	R	H	2B	3B	HR	RBI	BB	SO	AVG	OBP	SLG	PRO+	BR/A	SB	CS	SBR	FA	FR	G/POS	TPR
1986	Chi-A★	145	570	72	169	29	2	21	88	38	89	.296	.343	.465	114	10	2	1	0	.984	12	*O-141/D-3	1.7
1987	Chi-A★	132	505	59	148	26	4	20	93	46	82	.293	.353	.479	115	11	0	0	0	1.000	-1	*D-117/O-8	0.6
1988	Chi-A	158	599	55	166	39	1	13	81	67	109	.277	.351	.411	113	11	0	0	0	.882	-1	*D-147/O-9	0.6
1989	Chi-A★	96	333	55	107	20	1	13	56	60	52	.321	.426	.505	165	31	0	1	-1	.981	-0	D-70,O-25	2.8
	Tex-A	50	172	18	49	9	0	3	16	13	27	.285	.335	.390	102	0	0	2	-1	.667	-0	D-46/O-1	-0.2
	Yr	146	505	73	156	29	1	16	72	73	79	.309	.397	.465	144	31	0	3	-2	.964	-1	*D-116,O-26	2.6
1990	Tex-A	103	321	41	93	10	1	13	44	47	63	.290	.380	.449	131	14	0	1	-1	.833	0	D-95/O-2	1.1
	*Oak-A	32	94	11	25	5	0	3	21	20	17	.266	.395	.415	132	5	0	2	-1	.000	0	D-30	0.3
	Yr	135	415	52	118	15	1	16	65	67	80	.284	.384	.441	131	19	0	3	-2	.833	-1	*D-125/O-2	1.4
1991	Oak-A★	141	488	76	144	25	1	20	90	72	67	.295	.387	.473	145	31	0	1	-1	.923	-2	*D-125/O-12	2.3
1992	*Oak-A	140	478	58	121	18	0	16	76	59	61	.253	.335	.391	109	5	1	3	-2	.964	-5	*D-116,O-23	-0.5
1993	Bal-A	118	416	64	130	22	0	20	78	57	51	.313	.395	.510	136	21	0	0	0	.000		*D-116	1.6
1994	Bal-A	94	326	44	96	12	1	16	54	30	49	.294	.356	.485	109	4	0	0	0	.000		D-91	-0.1
1995	Bal-A	127	385	60	115	19	1	24	63	70	45	.299	.407	.540	142	25	0	2	-1	.000		*D-122	1.4
1996	Chi-A	143	495	80	154	29	0	22	95	73	62	.311	.401	.503	134	27	3	1	0	.000		*D-141	1.6
Total	17	2326	8366	1113	2425	416	48	323	1356	877	1225	.290	.358	.467	122	256	33	31	-9	.978	6	*D-1222,O-1060	16.8

■ AL BAIRD   Baird, Albert Wells b: 6/2/1895, Cleburne, Tex. d: 11/27/76, Shreveport, La. BR/TR, 5'9", 160 lbs. Deb: 9/10/17

YEAR	TM/L	G	AB	R	H	2B	3B	HR	RBI	BB	SO	AVG	OBP	SLG	PRO+	BR/A	SB	CS	SBR	FA	FR	G/POS	TPR
1917	NY-N	10	24	1	7	0	0	0	4	2	2	.292	.346	.292	100	0	2			1.000	2	/2-7,S-3	0.2
1919	NY-N	38	83	8	20	1	0	0	5	5	9	.241	.284	.253	63	-4	3			.898	8	2-24/S-9,3-5	0.6
Total	2	48	107	9	27	1	0	0	9	7	11	.252	.298	.262	71	-4	5			.921	10	/2-31,S-12,3-5	0.8

■ DOUG BAIRD   Baird, Howard Douglas b: 9/27/1891, St.Charles, Mo. d: 6/13/67, Thomasville, Ga. BR/TR, 5'9.5", 148 lbs. Deb: 4/18/15

YEAR	TM/L	G	AB	R	H	2B	3B	HR	RBI	BB	SO	AVG	OBP	SLG	PRO+	BR/A	SB	CS	SBR	FA	FR	G/POS	TPR
1915	Pit-N	145	512	49	112	26	12	1	53	37	88	.219	.277	.322	82	-12	29	12	2	.939	-1	*3-120,O-20/2-3	-0.8
1916	Pit-N	128	430	41	93	10	7	1	28	24	49	.216	.263	.279	66	-18	20	16	-4	.933	-5	3-80,2-29,O-16	-2.7
1917	Pit-N	43	135	17	35	6	1	0	18	20	19	.259	.355	.319	104	1	8			.935	-4	3-41/2-2	-0.2
	StL-N	104	364	38	92	19	12	0	24	23	52	.253	.301	.371	108	3	18			.941	13	*3-103/O-2	2.0
	Yr	147	499	55	127	25	13	0	42	43	71	.255	.316	.357	107	4	26			.940	9	*3-144/2-2,O-2	1.8
1918	StL-N	82	316	41	78	12	8	2	25	25	42	.247	.304	.354	104	1	25			.967	16	3-81/S-1,O-1	2.0
1919	Phi-N	66	242	33	61	13	3	2	30	22	28	.252	.317	.355	95	-1	13			.950	11	3-66	1.3
	StL-N	16	33	4	7	0	1	0	4	2	3	.212	.257	.273	63	-2	2			.773	-4	/3-8,2-1,O-1	-0.6
	Bro-N	20	60	6	11	0	1	0	8	1	10	.183	.197	.217	24	-6	3			1.000	1	3-17	-0.4
	Yr	102	335	43	79	13	5	2	42	25	41	.236	.291	.322	81	-8	18			.946	8	3-91/2-1,O-1	0.3
1920	Bro-N	6	6	1	2	0	0	0	1	2	1	.333	.556	.333	154	1	0	0	0	.800	-0	/3-2	0.1
	NY-N	7	8	0	1	0	0	0	0	1	3	.125	.222	.125	1	-1	0	0	0	1.000	2	/3-4	0.1
	Yr	13	14	1	3	0	0	0	1	3	4	.214	.389	.214	76	-0	0	0	0	.929	1	/3-6	0.2
Total	6	617	2106	230	492	86	45	6	191	157	295	.234	.291	.326	89	-33	118	28		.944	28	3-522/O-40,2-35,S-1	0.8

■ CHARLIE BAKER   Baker, Charles A. b: 1/15/1856, Sterling, Mass. d: 1/15/37, Manchester, N.H.   Deb: 8/1/1884

YEAR	TM/L	G	AB	R	H	2B	3B	HR	RBI	BB	SO	AVG	OBP	SLG	PRO+	BR/A	SB	CS	SBR	FA	FR	G/POS	TPR
1884	CP-U	15	57	5	8	2	0	1			0	.140	.140	.228	10	-8				.722	-1	O-11/S-3,2-1	-0.8

■ CHUCK BAKER   Baker, Charles Joseph b: 12/6/52, Seattle, Wash. BR/TR, 5'11", 180 lbs. Deb: 4/7/78

YEAR	TM/L	G	AB	R	H	2B	3B	HR	RBI	BB	SO	AVG	OBP	SLG	PRO+	BR/A	SB	CS	SBR	FA	FR	G/POS	TPR
1978	SD-N	44	58	8	12	1	0	0	3	2	15	.207	.233	.224	31	-5	0	0	0	.952	14	2-24,S-12	1.0
1980	SD-N	9	22	0	3	1	0	0	0	0	4	.136	.136	.182	-13	-3	0	0	0	.963	2	/S-8	-0.1
1981	Min-A	40	66	6	12	0	3	0	6	1	8	.182	.194	.273	31	-6	0	0	0	.969	7	S-31/2-3,3-1,D-1	0.3
Total	3	93	146	14	27	2	3	0	9	3	27	.185	.201	.240	25	-15	0	0	0	.962	22	/S-51,2-27,D-1,3-1	1.2

■ DAVE BAKER   Baker, David Glenn b: 11/25/57, Lacona, Iowa BL/TR, 6', 185 lbs. Deb: 9/12/82 F

YEAR	TM/L	G	AB	R	H	2B	3B	HR	RBI	BB	SO	AVG	OBP	SLG	PRO+	BR/A	SB	CS	SBR	FA	FR	G/POS	TPR
1982	Tor-A	9	20	3	5	1	0	0	2	3	3	.250	.400	.300	88	-0	0	0	0	.808	1	/3-8	0.0

■ DEL BAKER   Baker, Delmer David b: 5/3/1892, Sherwood, Ore. d: 9/11/73, San Antonio, Tex. BR/TR, 5'11.5", 176 lbs. Deb: 4/16/14 MC

YEAR	TM/L	G	AB	R	H	2B	3B	HR	RBI	BB	SO	AVG	OBP	SLG	PRO+	BR/A	SB	CS	SBR	FA	FR	G/POS	TPR
1914	Det-A	44	70	4	15	2	1	0	1	6	9	.214	.276	.271	63	-3	0	2	-1	.920	-6	C-38	-0.9
1915	Det-A	68	134	16	33	3	3	0	15	15	15	.246	.327	.313	87	-2	3	1	0	.940	-5	C-61	-0.3
1916	Det-A	61	98	7	15	4	0	0	6	11	8	.153	.245	.194	31	-8	2			.975	-2	C-59	-0.9
Total	3	173	302	27	63	9	4	0	22	32	32	.209	.289	.265	63	-13	5	3		.948	-12	C-158	-2.1

■ DOUG BAKER   Baker, Douglas Lee b: 4/3/61, Fullerton, Cal. BB/TR, 5'9", 165 lbs. Deb: 7/2/84 F

YEAR	TM/L	G	AB	R	H	2B	3B	HR	RBI	BB	SO	AVG	OBP	SLG	PRO+	BR/A	SB	CS	SBR	FA	FR	G/POS	TPR
1984	*Det-A	43	108	15	20	4	1	0	12	7	22	.185	.241	.241	34	-10	3	0	1	.969	2	S-39/2-5,D-1	-0.4
1985	Det-A	15	27	4	5	1	0	0	1	0	9	.185	.185	.222	11	-3	0	0	0	.960	-3	S-12/2-1	-0.5
1986	Det-A	13	24	1	3	1	0	0	0	2	7	.125	.192	.167	-1	-3	0	0	0	.970	2	S-10/2-2,D-1	-0.1
1987	Det-A	8	1	0	0	0	0	0	0	0	1	.000	.000	.000	-99	-0	0	0	0	1.000		/S-6,2-1,3-1	0.2
1988	Min-A	11	7	1	0	0	0	0	0	0	5	.000	.000	.000	-97	-0	0	0	0	1.000	1	/S-9,2-1,3-1	0.0
1989	Min-A	43	78	17	23	5	1	0	9	9	18	.295	.382	.385	109	1	0	0	0	.982	5	2-25,S-19/D-1	0.1
1990	Min-A	3	1	0	0	0	0	0	0	0	0	.000	.000	.000	-94	-0	0	0	0	1.000		/2-3	0.0
Total	7	136	246	38	51	11	2	0	22	18	62	.207	.270	.268	49	-17	3	0	1	.973	5	/S-95,2-38,D-3,3-2	-0.7

■ GENE BAKER   Baker, Eugene Walter b: 6/15/25, Davenport, Iowa BR/TR, 6'1", 170 lbs. Deb: 9/20/53 C

YEAR	TM/L	G	AB	R	H	2B	3B	HR	RBI	BB	SO	AVG	OBP	SLG	PRO+	BR/A	SB	CS	SBR	FA	FR	G/POS	TPR
1953	Chi-N	7	22	1	5	0	0	0		1	4	.227	.261	.273	39	-2	1	0	0	.917	-3	/2-6	-0.4
1954	Chi-N	135	541	68	149	32	5	13	61	47	55	.275	.336	.425	96	-4	4	5	-2	.967	-3	*2-134	0.0
1955	Chi-N★	154	609	82	163	29	7	11	52	49	57	.268	.324	.392	89	-10	9	7	-2	.967	7	*2-154	0.8
1956	Chi-N	140	546	65	141	23	3	12	57	39	54	.258	.311	.377	85	-12	3	4	-1	.969	17	*2-140	1.7
1957	Chi-N	12	44	4	11	3	1	1	10	6	3	.250	.353	.432	111	1	0	0	0	.867	-4	3-12	-0.3
	Pit-N	111	365	36	97	19	4	2	36	29	29	.266	.322	.356	84	-8	3	2	-0	.955	-4	3-60,S-28,2-13	-0.8
	Yr	123	409	40	108	22	5	3	46	35	32	.264	.325	.364	87	-7	3	2	-0	.942	-3	3-72,S-28,2-13	-1.1
1958	Pit-N	29	56	3	14	2	1	0	7	8	6	.250	.344	.321	80	-1	0	0	0	1.000	-1	3-11/2-3	-0.2
1960	*Pit-N	33	37	5	9	0	0	0	3	2	9	.243	.282	.243	45	-3	0	0	0	1.000	2	/3-7,2-1	-0.1
1961	Pit-N	9	10	1	1	0	0	0	0	3	2	.100	.308	.100	15	-1	0	0	0	1.000	1	/3-3	0.0
Total	8	630	2230	265	590	109	21	39	227	184	219	.265	.323	.385	88	-40	21	17	-4	.968	12	2-451/3-93,S-28	0.7

■ FLOYD BAKER   Baker, Floyd Wilson b: 10/10/16, Luray, Va. BL/TR, 5'9", 160 lbs. Deb: 5/4/43 C

YEAR	TM/L	G	AB	R	H	2B	3B	HR	RBI	BB	SO	AVG	OBP	SLG	PRO+	BR/A	SB	CS	SBR	FA	FR	G/POS	TPR
1943	StL-A	22	46	5	8	2	0	0	4	6	4	.174	.269	.217	42	-3	0	1	-1	.961	0	S-10/3-1	-0.3
1944	*StL-A	44	97	10	17	3	0	0	5	11	5	.175	.259	.206	32	-8	2	0	1	.979	-3	2-17,S-16	-1.0
1945	Chi-A	82	208	22	52	8	0	0	19	23	12	.250	.325	.288	81	-5	3	2	-0	.971	2	3-58,2-11	-0.2
1946	Chi-A	9	24	2	6	1	0	0	3	2	3	.250	.308	.292	71	-1	0	0	0	.962	0	/3-6	0.1
1947	Chi-A	105	371	61	98	12	3	0	22	66	28	.264	.375	.313	96	1	9	7	-2	.980	18	*3-101/2-1,S-1	1.9
1948	Chi-A	104	335	47	72	9	0	0	18	73	26	.215	.359	.257	68	-12	4	10	-5	.961	4	3-71,2-18/S-1	-0.4
1949	Chi-A	125	388	38	101	15	4	1	40	84	32	.260	.392	.327	94	1	3	1	0	**.977**	12	*3-122/S-3,2-1	1.1
1950	Chi-A	83	186	26	59	7	0	0	11	32	10	.317	.417	.355	102	3	1	1	-0	.987	3	3-53/2-3,O-2	0.4
1951	Chi-A	82	133	24	35	6	1	0	14	25	12	.263	.380	.323	93	-0	1	1	-1	.924	-3	3-44/2-5,S-3	-0.2
1952	Was-A	79	263	27	69	8	0	0	33	30	17	.262	.342	.293	81	-6	1	0	0	.994	-16	2-68/S-7,3-1	-1.9
1953	Was-A	9	7	0	0	0	0	0	0	1	0	.000	.222	.000	-37	-1	0	0	0	.000	0	/3-1	-0.2
	Bos-A	81	172	22	47	4	2	0	24	24	10	.273	.365	.320	82	-3	1	0	-1	.963	1	3-37,2-16	-0.4
	Yr	90	179	22	47	4	2	0	24	25	10	.263	.359	.307	78	-5	1	0	-1	.952	1	3-38,2-16	-0.6
1954	Bos-A	21	20	1	4	0	0	0	1	3	0	.200	.304	.200	32	-1	0	0	0	.889	1	/3-7,2-1	-0.1
	Phi-N	23	22	0	5	0	0	0	0	5	4	.227	.370	.227	60	-1	0	0	0	1.000	4	/3-7,2-2	0.3
1955	Phi-N	6	2	2	0	0	0	0	0	0	0	.000	.000	.000	-99	-0	0	0	0	1.000	1	/3-1	-0.1
Total	13	874	2280	285	573	76	13	1	196	382	165	.251	.360	.297	82	-41	23	25	-8	.971	34	3-510,2-143/S-41,O-1	-1.0

■ FRANK BAKER   Baker, Frank b: 1/11/44, Bartow, Fla. BL/TR, 5'10", 180 lbs. Deb: 7/27/69

YEAR	TM/L	G	AB	R	H	2B	3B	HR	RBI	BB	SO	AVG	OBP	SLG	PRO+	BR/A	SB	CS	SBR	FA	FR	G/POS	TPR
1969	Cle-A	52	172	21	44	5	3	3	15	14	34	.256	.316	.372	89	-3	2	1	0	.950	1	O-46	-0.5
1971	Cle-A	73	181	18	38	12	1	1	23	12	34	.210	.263	.304	55	-11	1	3	-2	.985	-6	O-51	-2.3
Total	2	125	353	39	82	17	4	4	38	26	68	.232	.289	.337	71	-14	3	4	-2	.966	-6	/O-97	-2.8

YEAR	TM/L	G	AB	R	H	2B	3B	HR	RBI	BB	SO	AVG	OBP	SLG	PRO+	BR/A	SB	CS	SBR	FA	FR	G/POS	TPR

■ FRANK BAKER
Baker, Frank Watts b: 10/29/46, Meridian, Miss. BL/TR, 6'2", 178 lbs. Deb: 8/9/70

YEAR	TM/L	G	AB	R	H	2B	3B	HR	RBI	BB	SO	AVG	OBP	SLG	PRO+	BR/A	SB	CS	SBR	FA	FR	G/POS	TPR
1970	NY-A	35	117	6	27	4	1	0	11	14	26	.231	.323	.282	72	-4	1	2	-1	.973	4	S-35	0.3
1971	NY-A	43	79	9	11	2	0	0	2	16	22	.139	.284	.165	32	-7	3	0	1	.949	11	S-38	0.9
1973	*Bal-A	44	63	10	12	1	2	1	11	7	7	.190	.271	.317	66	-3	0	0	0	.964	4	S-32/2-7,1-1,3-1	0.3
1974	*Bal-A	24	29	3	5	1	0	0	0	3	5	.172	.250	.207	34	-2	0	0	0	.842	2	S-17/2-3,3-1	0.0
Total	4	146	288	28	55	8	3	1	24	40	60	.191	.294	.250	56	-16	4	2	0	.953	20	S-122/2-10,3-2,1-1	1.5

■ GEORGE BAKER
Baker, George F. b: 1859, St.Louis, Mo. Deb: 5/24/1883

YEAR	TM/L	G	AB	R	H	2B	3B	HR	RBI	BB	SO	AVG	OBP	SLG	PRO+	BR/A	SB	CS	SBR	FA	FR	G/POS	TPR
1883	Bal-a	7	22	0	5	0	0	0				.227	.227	.227	45	-1				.667	-3	/S-4,C-3,O-1	-0.3
1884	StL-U	80	317	39	52	6	0	0		5		.164	.177	.183	9	-44				.897	16	C-68/2-4,O-4,3-3,S	-1.9
1885	StL-N	38	131	5	16	0	0	0	5	9	28	.122	.179	.122	-1	-14				.865	-11	C-32/3-3,O-2,2-1	-2.1
1886	KC-N	1	4	1	1	0	0	0	0	0	1	.250	.250	.250	49	-0	0			.889	-0	/C-1	0.0
Total	4	126	474	45	74	6	0	0	5	14	29	.156	.180	.169	8	-60	0			.887	3	C-104/O-7,3-6,S2	-4.3

■ HOWARD BAKER
Baker, Howard Francis b: 3/1/1888, Bridgeport, Conn. d: 1/16/64, Bridgeport, Conn. BR/TR, 5'11", 175 lbs. Deb: 8/11/12

YEAR	TM/L	G	AB	R	H	2B	3B	HR	RBI	BB	SO	AVG	OBP	SLG	PRO+	BR/A	SB	CS	SBR	FA	FR	G/POS	TPR
1912	Cle-A	11	30	1	5	0	0	0	2		5	.167	.286	.167	29	-3	0			.964	-1	3-10	-0.4
1914	Chi-A	15	47	4	13	1	1	0	5	3	8	.277	.320	.340	100	-0	2	1	0	.879	-4	3-15	-0.5
1915	Chi-A	2	2	0	0	0	0	0	0	0	0	.000	.000	.000	-97	-0	0			.000	0	H	-0.1
	NY-N	1	3	0	0	0	0	0	0	0	0	.000	.000	.000	-99	-1	0			1.000	0	/3-1	-0.1
Total	3	29	82	5	18	1	1	0	7	8	10	.220	.289	.256	61	-4	2		1	.922	-6	/3-26	-1.1

■ JACK BAKER
Baker, Jack Edward b: 5/4/50, Birmingham, Ala. BR/TR, 6'5", 225 lbs. Deb: 9/11/76

YEAR	TM/L	G	AB	R	H	2B	3B	HR	RBI	BB	SO	AVG	OBP	SLG	PRO+	BR/A	SB	CS	SBR	FA	FR	G/POS	TPR
1976	Bos-A	12	23	1	3	0	0	1	2	1	5	.130	.167	.261	21	-2	0	0	0	.981	-0	/1-8,D-1	-0.3
1977	Bos-A	2	3	0	0	0	0	0	0	0	1	.000	.000	.000	-90	-1	0	0	0	.857	0	/1-1	-0.1
Total	2	14	26	1	3	0	0	1	2	1	6	.115	.148	.231	8	-3	0	0	0	.966	-0	/1-9,D-1	-0.4

■ JESSE BAKER
Baker, Jesse (b: Michael Myron Silverman) b: 3/4/1895, Cleveland, Ohio d: 7/29/76, W.Los Angeles, Cal. BR/TR, 5'4", 140 lbs. Deb: 9/14/19

YEAR	TM/L	G	AB	R	H	2B	3B	HR	RBI	BB	SO	AVG	OBP	SLG	PRO+	BR/A	SB	CS	SBR	FA	FR	G/POS	TPR
1919	Was-A	1	0	0	0	0	0	0	0			1						0	0		1.000	0	/S-1	0.0

■ FRANK BAKER
Baker, John Franklin "Home Run" b: 3/13/1886, Trappe, Md. d: 6/28/63, Trappe, Md. BL/TR, 5'11", 173 lbs. Deb: 9/21/08 H

YEAR	TM/L	G	AB	R	H	2B	3B	HR	RBI	BB	SO	AVG	OBP	SLG	PRO+	BR/A	SB	CS	SBR	FA	FR	G/POS	TPR
1908	Phi-A	9	31	5	9	3	0	0				.290	.290	.387	112	-0				1.000	2	/3-9	0.3
1909	Phi-A	148	541	73	165	27	**19**	4	85	26		.305	.343	.447	146	25	20			.920	-9	*3-146	2.5
1910	*Phi-A	146	561	83	159	25	15	2	74	34		.283	.329	.392	127	15	21			.920	6	*3-146	2.7
1911	*Phi-A	148	592	96	198	42	14	**11**	115	40		.334	.379	.508	149	35	38			**.942**	-1	*3-148	3.6
1912	Phi-A	149	577	116	200	40	21	**10**	**130**	50		.347	.404	.541	176	54	40			.941	10	*3-149	6.3
1913	*Phi-A	149	564	116	190	34	9	**12**	**117**	63	31	.337	.413	.493	169	48	34			.942	8	*3-149	6.1
1914	*Phi-A	150	570	84	182	23	10	**9**	89	53	37	.319	.380	.442	153	35	19	20	-6	.955	10	*3-149	4.7
1916	NY-A	100	360	46	97	23	2	10	52	36	30	.269	.344	.428	129	11	15			.940	2	3-96	1.8
1917	NY-A	146	553	57	156	24	2	6	71	48	27	.282	.345	.365	116	10	18			.949	11	*3-146	2.6
1918	NY-A	126	504	65	154	24	5	6	62	38	13	.306	.357	.409	128	15	8			**.972**	11	*3-126	3.2
1919	NY-A	141	567	70	166	22	1	10	83	44	18	.293	.346	.388	105	3	13			.955	-2	*3-141	0.7
1921	*NY-A	94	330	46	97	16	2	9	71	26	12	.294	.353	.436	98	-2	8	5	-1	.959	-2	3-83	0.2
1922	*NY-A	69	234	30	65	12	3	7	36	15	14	.278	.327	.444	97	-2	1	3	-2	.962	-10	3-60	-0.9
Total	13	1575	5984	887	1838	315	103	96	987	473	182	.307	.363	.442	136	250	235	28		.943	36	*3-1548	33.8

■ DUSTY BAKER
Baker, Johnnie B b: 6/15/49, Riverside, Cal. BR/TR, 6'2", 187 lbs. Deb: 9/7/68 MC

YEAR	TM/L	G	AB	R	H	2B	3B	HR	RBI	BB	SO	AVG	OBP	SLG	PRO+	BR/A	SB	CS	SBR	FA	FR	G/POS	TPR
1968	Atl-N	6	5	0	2	0	0	0	0	0	1	.400	.400	.400	140	0	0	0	0	.000	-1	/O-3	-0.1
1969	Atl-N	3	7	0	0	0	0	0	0	0	3	.000	.000	.000	-99	-2	0	0	0	1.000	-1	/O-3	-0.3
1970	Atl-N	13	24	3	7	0	0	0	4	2	4	.292	.346	.292	69	-1	0	0	0	.800	-2	O-11	-0.3
1971	Atl-N	29	62	2	14	2	0	0	4	1	14	.226	.238	.258	38	-5	0	1	-1	1.000	-2	O-18	-0.9
1972	Atl-N	127	446	62	143	27	2	17	76	45	68	.321	.388	.504	139	23	4	7	-3	.989	-1	*O-123	1.7
1973	Atl-N	159	604	101	174	29	4	21	99	67	72	.288	.364	.454	116	14	24	3	5	.983	10	*O-156	2.3
1974	Atl-N	149	574	80	147	35	0	20	69	71	87	.256	.339	.422	107	5	18	7	1	.981	-18	*O-148	-1.9
1975	Atl-N	142	494	63	129	18	2	19	72	67	57	.261	.349	.421	109	6	12	7	-1	.990	-7	*O-136	-2.1
1976	LA-N	112	384	36	93	13	0	4	39	31	54	.242	.300	.307	74	-13	2	4	-2	.996	-1	*O-106	-2.1
1977	*LA-N	153	533	86	155	26	1	30	86	58	89	.291	.367	.512	134	25	2	6	-3	.987	-4	*O-152	1.2
1978	*LA-N	149	522	62	137	24	1	11	66	47	66	.262	.327	.375	96	-3	12	3	-2	.985	5	*O-145	-0.2
1979	LA-N	151	554	86	152	29	1	23	88	56	70	.274	.342	.455	117	12	11	4	1	.990	13	*O-150	2.0
1980	LA-N	153	579	80	170	26	4	29	97	43	66	.294	.346	.503	137	26	12	10	-2	.991	6	*O-151	2.5
1981	*LA-N★	103	400	48	128	17	3	9	49	29	43	.320	.367	.445	134	17	10	7	-1	.990	-1	*O-101	1.5
1982	LA-N★	147	570	80	171	19	1	23	88	56	62	.300	.366	.458	132	24	17	10	-1	.975	-7	*O-144	1.3
1983	*LA-N	149	531	71	138	25	1	15	73	72	59	.260	.350	.395	107	8	6	7	1	.981	-1	*O-143	0.2
1984	SF-N	100	243	31	71	7	2	3	32	42	47	.292	.392	.374	120	8	4	1	0	.974	-1	O-62	0.7
1985	Oak-A	111	343	48	92	15	1	14	52	50	47	.268	.361	.440	128	14	2	1	0	.993	-5	1-58,O-35,D-13	0.4
1986	Oak-A	83	242	25	58	8	0	4	19	27	37	.240	.316	.322	80	-6	0	1	-1	1.000	-3	O-55,D-15/1-3	-1.2
Total	19	2039	7117	964	1981	320	23	242	1013	762	926	.278	.342	.432	116	149	137	73	25	.985	-2	*O-1842/1-61,D-28	7.5

■ KIRTLEY BAKER
Baker, Kirtley "Whitey" b: 6/24/1869, Aurora, Ind. d: 4/15/27, Covington, Ky. BR/TR, 5'9", 160 lbs. Deb: 5/7/1890

YEAR	TM/L	G	AB	R	H	2B	3B	HR	RBI	BB	SO	AVG	OBP	SLG	PRO+	BR/A	SB	CS	SBR	FA	FR	G/POS	TPR
1890	Pit-N	26	68	6	10	0	0	0	0	10	6	.147	.275	.147	27	-6	1			.878	-0	P-25	0.0
1893	Bal-N	19	57	9	17	1	1	0	6	8	6	.298	.385	.351	94	-0	1			.930	5	P-15/O-3	0.2
1894	Bal-N	2	4	0	0	0	0	0	0	0	1	.000	.000	.000	-96	-1	0			1.000	1	/O-1,P-1	0.0
1898	Was-N	6	18	3	5	0	1	0	3		3	.278	.381	.389	121	1	0			1.000	-1	/P-6	0.0
1899	Was-N	12	19	1	3	0	0	0	1		1	.158	.200	.158	-1	-3	0			.862	2	P-11	0.0
Total	5	65	166	19	35	1	2	0	10	22	13	.211	.311	.241	57	-9	2			.895	7	/P-58,O-4	0.2

■ PHIL BAKER
Baker, Philip b: 9/19/1856, Philadelphia, Pa. d: 6/4/40, Washington, D.C. BL/TL, 5'8", 152 lbs. Deb: 5/1/1883

YEAR	TM/L	G	AB	R	H	2B	3B	HR	RBI	BB	SO	AVG	OBP	SLG	PRO+	BR/A	SB	CS	SBR	FA	FR	G/POS	TPR
1883	Bal-a	28	121	22	33	2	1	1	8			.273	.318	.331	106	1				.883	-7	C-19,O-14/S-1	-0.4
1884	Was-U	86	371	75	107	12	5	1		11		.288	.309	.356	106	-9				.955	-10	1-39,O-32,C-27	-1.9
1886	Was-N	81	325	37	72	6	5	1	34	20	32	.222	.267	.280	70	-11	16			.967	-7	1-56,O-21/C-4	-2.3
Total	3	195	817	134	212	20	11	3	34	39	32	.259	.293	.322	91	-19	16			.963	-23	/1-95,O-67,C-50,S-1	-4.6

■ TRACY BAKER
Baker, Tracy Lee b: 11/7/1891, Pendleton, Ore. d: 3/14/75, Placerville, Cal. BR/TR, 6'1", 180 lbs. Deb: 6/19/11

YEAR	TM/L	G	AB	R	H	2B	3B	HR	RBI	BB	SO	AVG	OBP	SLG	PRO+	BR/A	SB	CS	SBR	FA	FR	G/POS	TPR
1911	Bos-A	1	0	0	0	0	0	0	0	0							0			1.000	-0	/1-1	0.0

■ BILL BAKER
Baker, William Presley b: 2/22/11, Paw Creek, N.C. BR/TR, 6', 200 lbs. Deb: 5/4/40 C

YEAR	TM/L	G	AB	R	H	2B	3B	HR	RBI	BB	SO	AVG	OBP	SLG	PRO+	BR/A	SB	CS	SBR	FA	FR	G/POS	TPR
1940	*Cin-N	27	69	5	15	0	1	0	7	4	8	.217	.260	.261	44	-5	2			1.000	4	C-24	0.0
1941	Cin-N	2	1	0	0	0	0	0	0	1	1	.000	.500	.000	49	0	0			1.000	0	/C-1	0.0
	Pit-N	35	67	5	15	3	0	0	6	11	0	.224	.333	.269	71	-2	0			.967	0	C-33	0.0
	Yr	37	68	5	15	3	0	0	6	12	1	.221	.338	.265	71	-2	0			.967	0	C-34	0.0
1942	Pit-N	18	17	1	2	0	0	0	2	1	0	.118	.167	.118	-16	-2	0			1.000	1	C-11	-0.1
1943	Pit-N	63	172	12	47	6	3	1	26	22	6	.273	.365	.360	106	2	3			.979	0	C-56	0.6
1946	Pit-N	53	113	7	27	4	0	1	8	12	6	.239	.312	.301	72	-4	0			.965	-6	C-41/1-1	-0.9
1948	StL-N	45	119	13	35	10	1	0	15	15	7	.294	.373	.395	102	1	1			.994	-1	C-36	0.2
1949	StL-N	20	30	2	4	1	0	0	2	5	1	.133	.188	.167	-4	-4	0			1.000	-2	C-10	-0.6
Total	7	263	588	45	145	25	5	2	68	68	30	.247	.328	.316	79	-15	6			.983	-3	C-212/1-1	-0.8

■ JOHN BALAZ
Balaz, John Lawrence b: 11/24/50, Toronto, Ont., Can. BR/TR, 6'3", 180 lbs. Deb: 9/10/74

YEAR	TM/L	G	AB	R	H	2B	3B	HR	RBI	BB	SO	AVG	OBP	SLG	PRO+	BR/A	SB	CS	SBR	FA	FR	G/POS	TPR
1974	Cal-A	14	42	4	10	0	0	1	5	2	10	.238	.289	.310	76	-1	0	0	0	1.000	-1	O-12	-0.3
1975	Cal-A	45	120	10	29	8	1	1	10	5	25	.242	.272	.350	80	-4	0	0	0	1.000	-0	/O-27,D-11	-0.5
Total	2	59	162	14	39	8	1	2	15	7	35	.241	.286	.340	79	-5	0	0	0	1.000	-1	/O-39,D-11	-0.8

YEAR	TM/L	G	AB	R	H	2B	3B	HR	RBI	BB	SO	AVG	OBP	SLG	PRO+	BR/A	SB	CS	SBR	FA	FR	G/POS	TPR
■ **STEVE BALBONI**			Balboni, Stephen Charles		b: 1/16/57, Brockton, Mass.				BR/TR, 6'3", 225 lbs.		Deb: 4/22/81												
1981	NY-A	4	7	2	2	1	1	0	2	1	4	.286	.375	.714	211	1	0	0	0	1.000	0	/1-3,D-1	0.1
1982	NY-A	33	107	8	20	2	1	2	4	6	34	.187	.230	.280	40	-9	0	0	0	.990	-1	1-26/D-5	-1.1
1983	NY-A	32	86	8	20	2	0	5	17	8	23	.233	.298	.430	101	-0	0	0	0	.984	-1	1-23/D-4	-0.2
1984	*KC-A	126	438	58	107	23	2	28	77	45	139	.244	.320	.498	122	11	0	0	0	.987	-5	*1-125/D-1	-0.1
1985	*KC-A	160	600	74	146	28	2	36	88	52	166	.243	.309	.477	111	7	1	1	-0	.993	-8	*1-160	-1.1
1986	KC-A	138	512	54	117	25	1	29	88	43	146	.229	.290	.451	96	-5	0	0	0	.987	-6	*1-137	-2.0
1987	KC-A	121	386	44	80	11	1	24	60	34	97	.207	.275	.427	80	-12	0	0	0	.989	-1	1-55,D-52	-1.6
1988	KC-A	21	63	2	9	2	0	2	5	1	20	.143	.156	.270	17	-7	0	0	0	.980	-1	1-13/D-6	-0.9
	Sea-A	97	350	44	88	15	1	21	61	23	67	.251	.299	.480	110	3	0	1	-1	.994	-1	D-56,1-40	-0.4
	Yr	118	413	46	97	17	1	23	66	24	87	.235	.279	.448	96	-4	0	1	-1	.991	-2	D-62,1-53	-1.3
1989	NY-A	110	300	33	71	12	2	17	59	25	67	.237	.302	.460	113	4	0	0	0	.994	-2	D-82,1-20	-0.1
1990	NY-A	116	266	24	51	6	0	17	34	35	91	.192	.293	.406	93	-3	0	0	0	.984	-3	D-72,1-28	-1.0
1993	Tex-A	2	5	0	3	0	0	0	1	0	2	.600	.600	.600	233	1	0	0	0	.000	0	/D-2	0.1
Total	11	960	3120	351	714	127	11	181	495	273	856	.229	.295	.451	100	-9	1	2	-1	.989	-26	1-630,D-281	-8.3
■ **BOBBY BALCENA**			Balcena, Robert Rudolph		b: 8/1/25, San Pedro, Cal.			d: 1/4/90, San Pedro, Cal.		BR/TL, 5'7", 160 lbs.		Deb: 9/16/56											
1956	Cin-N	7	2	2	0	0	0	0	0	1	.000	.000	.000	-94	-1	0	0	0	1.000	-1	/O-2	-0.1	
■ **LADY BALDWIN**			Baldwin, Charles Busted		b: 4/8/1859, Oramel, N.Y.			d: 3/7/37, Hastings, Mich.		BL/TL, 5'11", 160 lbs.		Deb: 9/30/1884											
1884	Mil-U	7	27	6	6	3	0	0		0		.222	.222	.333	122	-2				.778	0	/O-5,P-2	-0.1
1885	Det-N	31	124	12	30	6	3	0	18	6	22	.242	.277	.339	98	-0				.879	1	P-21,O-12	-0.1
1886	Det-N	57	204	25	41	6	3	0	25	18	44	.201	.266	.260	59	-10	3			.969	3	P-56/O-2	0.0
1887	*Det-N	24	85	15	23	0	1	0	7	10	6	.271	.354	.294	79	-2	4			.926	1	P-24	0.0
1888	Det-N	6	23	5	6	0	0	0	3	3	3	.261	.346	.261	96	0				1.000	-0	/P-6,O-1	0.0
1890	Bro-N	2	3	1	0	0	0	0	0	1	1	.000	.250	.000	-25	-0	0			.625	0	/P-2	0.0
	Buf-P	7	28	4	8	1	0	0	2	2	1	.286	.333	.321	82	-1	0			1.000	-0	/P-7	0.0
Total	6	134	494	68	114	16	7	0	55	40	77	.231	.290	.291	76	-15	7			.934	6	P-118/O-20	-0.2
■ **KID BALDWIN**			Baldwin, Clarence Geoghan		b: 11/1/1864, Newport, Ky.			d: 7/10/1897, Cincinnati, Ohio		BR/TR, 5'6", 147 lbs.		Deb: 7/27/1884											
1884	KC-U	50	191	19	37	6	3	0			4	.194	.210	.257	47	-18				.885	1	C-44,O-10/2-1,3-1	-1.3
	CP-U	1	1	0	1	0	0	0				1.000	1.000	1.000	511	-0				1.000	0	/C-1	0.0
	Yr	51	192	19	38	6	3	0			4	.198	.214	.260	49	-18				.885	0	C-45,O-10/2-1,3-1	-1.3
1885	Cin-a	34	126	9	17	1	0	1	8	3		.135	.155	.167	2	-14				.863	-2	C-25/O-6,2-2,P-2,3	-1.3
1886	Cin-a	87	315	41	72	8	7	3	32	8		.229	.252	.327	78	-9	12			.891	-6	C-71,3-13/O-6	-0.8
1887	Cin-a	96	388	46	98	15	10	1	57	6		.253	.271	.351	71	-17	13			.874	-2	*C-96/O-2	-0.8
1888	Cin-a	67	271	27	59	11	3	1	25	3		.218	.235	.292	65	-12	4			.918	-2	C-65/O-2,1-1	-0.7
1889	Cin-a	60	223	34	55	14	2	1	34	5	32	.247	.273	.341	72	-9	7			.912	2	C-55/O-4,3-1,1-1	-0.2
1890	Cin-N	22	72	5	11	0	0	0	10	3	6	.153	.187	.153	-1	-9	2			.902	3	C-20/O-2	-0.4
	Phi-a	24	90	5	21	1	2	0	12	4		.233	.274	.289	67	-4	2			.887	1	C-19/3-5	-0.1
Total	7	441	1677	186	371	56	27	7	178	36	38	.221	.243	.299	61	-93	40			.893	-6	C-396/O-32,321P	-5.5
■ **FRANK BALDWIN**			Baldwin, Frank De Witt		b: 12/25/28, High Bridge, N.J.			BR/TR, 5'11", 195 lbs.		Deb: 4/22/53												
1953	Cin-N	16	20	0	2	0	0	0	1	9	.100	.143	.100	-35	-4	0	0	0	1.000	-1	/C-6	-0.5	
■ **HENRY BALDWIN**			Baldwin, Henry Clay "Ted"		b: 6/13/1894, Chadds Ford, Pa.			d: 2/24/64, West Chester, Pa.		BR/TR, 5'11", 180 lbs.		Deb: 5/22/27											
1927	Phi-N	6	16	1	5	1	0	0	1	2	.313	.353	.313	78	-0				.857	-2	/S-3,3-2	-0.2	
■ **JEFF BALDWIN**			Baldwin, Jeffrey Allen		b: 9/5/65, Milford, Del.			BL/TL, 6'1", 180 lbs.		Deb: 5/22/90												
1990	Hou-N	7	8	1	0	0	0	0	0	1	2	.000	.111	.000	-69	-2	0	0	0	1.000	-1	/O-3	-0.3
■ **REGGIE BALDWIN**			Baldwin, Reginald Conrad		b: 8/19/54, River Rouge, Mich.			BR/TR, 6'1", 195 lbs.		Deb: 5/25/78											
1978	Hou-N	38	67	5	17	5	0	1	11	3	3	.254	.286	.373	89	-1	0	0	0	.955	-1	C-17	-0.2
1979	Hou-N	14	20	0	4	1	0	0	1	0	1	.200	.200	.250	23	-2	0	0	0	1.000	-1	/C-3,1-1	-0.3
Total	2	52	87	5	21	6	0	1	12	3	4	.241	.267	.345	74	-4	0	0	0	.956	-2	/C-20,1-1	-0.5
■ **BILLY BALDWIN**			Baldwin, Robert Harvey		b: 6/9/51, Tazewell, Va.			BL/TL, 6', 175 lbs.		Deb: 7/29/75											
1975	Det-A	30	95	8	21	3	0	4	8	5	14	.221	.260	.379	75	-3	2	1	0	.983	2	O-25/D-1	-0.3
1976	NY-N	9	22	4	6	1	1	1	5	1	2	.273	.304	.545	146	1	0	0	0	.929	1	/O-5	0.2
Total	2	39	117	12	27	4	1	5	13	6	16	.231	.268	.410	87	-2	2	1	0	.972	3	/O-30,D-1	-0.1
■ **MIKE BALENTI**			Balenti, Michael Richard		b: 7/3/1886, Calumet, Okla.			d: 8/4/55, Altus, Okla.		BR/TR, 5'11", 175 lbs.		Deb: 7/19/11											
1911	Cin-N	8	8	2	2	0	0	0		0	1	.250	.250	.250	42	-1	3			.857	0	/S-2,O-1	0.0
1913	StL-A	70	211	17	38	2	4	0	11	6	32	.180	.206	.227	28	-20	3			.923	1	S-56/O-8	-1.6
Total	2	78	219	19	40	2	4	0	11	6	33	.183	.208	.228	28	-21	6			.922	1	/S-58,O-9	-1.6
■ **LEE BALES**			Bales, Wesley Owen		b: 12/4/44, Los Angeles, Cal.			BB/TR, 5'10.5", 165 lbs.		Deb: 8/7/66											
1966	Atl-N	12	16	4	1	0	0	0	0	0	5	.063	.063	.063	-64	-3	0	0	0	1.000	3	/2-7,3-3	0.0
1967	Hou-N	19	27	4	3	0	0	0	2	8	7	.111	.314	.111	28	-2	1	1	-0	.944	-2	/2-6,S-1	-0.4
Total	2	31	43	8	4	0	0	0	2	8	12	.093	.235	.093	-3	-6	1	1	-0	.978	1	/2-13,3-3,S-1	-0.4
■ **ART BALL**			Ball, Arthur Clark		b: 4/1876, Kentucky			d: 12/26/15, Chicago, Ill.		TR , 168 lbs.		Deb: 8/1/1894											
1894	StL-N	1	3	0	1	0	0	0	0	1	.333	.333	.333	61	-0	0		.667	-1	/2-1	-0.1		
1898	Bal-N	32	81	7	15	2	0	0	8	7		.185	.258	.210	34	-7	2		.906	9	3-15,S-14/2-2,O-1	0.2	
Total	2	33	84	7	16	2	0	0	8	7	1	.190	.261	.214	35	-7	2		.929	8	/3-15,S-14,2-3,O-1	0.1	
■ **NEAL BALL**			Ball, Cornelius		b: 4/22/1881, Grand Haven, Mich.			d: 10/15/57, Bridgeport, Conn.		BR/TR, 5'7", 145 lbs.		Deb: 9/12/07											
1907	NY-A	15	44	5	9	1	1	0	4	1		.205	.222	.273	53	-2	1			.817	-3	S-11/2-5	-0.6
1908	NY-A	132	446	34	110	16	2	0	38	21		.247	.284	.291	86	-7	32			.898	-6	*S-130/2-1	-1.3
1909	NY-A	8	29	5	6	1	1	0	3	3		.207	.281	.310	86	-0	2			.917	-3	/2-8	-0.5
	Cle-A	96	324	29	83	13	2	1	25	17		.256	.295	.318	90	-4	17			.914	-11	S-95	-1.5
	Yr	104	353	34	89	14	3	1	28	20		.252	.294	.317	90	-5	19			.914	-14	S-95/2-8	-2.0
1910	Cle-A	53	119	13	25	3	1	0	12	9		.210	.266	.252	61	-5	4			.927	-2	S-27/2-6,0-6,3-3	-0.7
1911	Cle-A	116	412	45	122	14	9	3	45	27		.296	.339	.364	104	1	21			.945	6	2-94,3-17/S-1	0.5
1912	Cle-A	40	132	12	30	6	1	0	14	9		.227	.277	.273	55	-8	7			.938	2	2-37	-0.7
	*Bos-A	18	45	10	9	2	0	0	6	3		.200	.250	.244	40	-4	5			.927	-4	2-17	-0.7
	Yr	58	177	22	39	6	1	0	20	12		.220	.270	.266	51	-11	12			.936	-3	2-54	-1.5
1913	Bos-A	23	58	9	10	2	0	0	4	9	13	.172	.294	.207	46	-4	3			.902	1	2-10/S-7,3-1	-0.5
Total	7	501	1609	162	404	56	17	4	151	99	13	.251	.296	.314	83	-34	92			.902	-25	S-271,2-178/3-21,O	-6.1
■ **JIM BALL**			Ball, James Chandler		b: 2/22/1884, Harford Co., Md.			d: 4/7/63, Glendale, Cal.		BR/TR, 5'11", 175 lbs.		Deb: 9/21/07											
1907	Bos-N	10	36	3	6	2	0	0	3	2		.167	.211	.222	36	-3	0			.963	-2	C-10	-0.4
1908	Bos-N	6	15	1	1	0	0	0	0	1		.067	.125	.067	-39	-2	0			.917	-1	/C-6	-0.3
Total	2	16	51	4	7	2	0	0	3	3		.137	.185	.176	14	-5	0			.949	-2	/C-16	-0.7
■ **PELHAM BALLENGER**			Ballenger, Pelham Ashby		b: 2/6/1894, Gilreath Mill, S.C.			d: 12/8/48, Greenville County, S.C.		BR/TR, 5'11", 160 lbs.		Deb: 5/7/28											
1928	Was-A	3	9	0	1	0	0	0	0	0	1	.111	.111	.111	-42	-2	0	0	0	1.000	1	/3-3	0.0
■ **HAL BAMBERGER**			Bamberger, Harold Earl "Dutch"		b: 10/29/24, Lebanon, Pa.			BL/TR, 6', 173 lbs.		Deb: 9/15/48												
1948	NY-N	7	12	0	1	0	0	0	0	0	2	.083	.154	.083	-34	-2	0	0	0	1.000	-0	/O-3	-0.3
■ **STUD BANCKER**			Bancker, John		b: Philadelphia, Pa.			Deb: 4/21/1875															
1875	NH-n	19	72	3	11	0	0	0		0	3	.153	.153	.153	7	-6	1	0	0	.796	-4	C-14/2-4,3-3,S-1,1	-0.9

YEAR	TM/L	G	AB	R	H	2B	3B	HR	RBI	BB	SO	AVG	OBP	SLG	PRO+	BR/A	SB	CS	SBR	FA	FR	G/POS	TPR

■ DAVE BANCROFT   Bancroft, David James "Beauty"   b: 4/20/1891, Sioux City, Iowa   d: 10/9/72, Superior, Wis.   BB/TR, 5'9.5", 160 lbs.   Deb: 4/14/15   MCH

1915	*Phi-N	153	563	85	143	18	2	7	30	77	62	.254	.346	.330	104	5	15	27	-12	.928	5	*S-153	1.1
1916	Phi-N	142	477	53	101	10	0	3	33	74	57	.212	.323	.252	75	-11	15			.933	25	*S-142	2.4
1917	Phi-N	127	478	56	116	22	5	4	43	44	42	.243	.307	.335	93	-4	14			.936	28	*S-120/2-3,O-2	3.3
1918	Phi-N	125	499	69	132	19	4	0	26	54	36	.265	.338	.319	94	-2	11			.928	18	*S-125	2.4
1919	Phi-N	92	335	45	91	13	7	0	25	31	30	.272	.333	.352	99	0	8			.951	10	S-88	1.7
1920	Phi-N	42	171	23	51	7	2	0	5	9	12	.298	.337	.363	96	-1	1	7	-4	.981	9	S-42	0.9
	NY-N	108	442	79	132	29	7	0	31	33	32	.299	.349	.396	115	8	7	5	-1	.946	30	*S-108	4.8
	Yr	150	613	102	183	36	9	0	36	42	44	.299	.346	.387	109	7	8	12	-5	.955	39	*S-150	5.7
1921	*NY-N	153	606	121	193	26	15	6	67	66	23	.318	.389	.441	119	18	17	10	-1	.960	17	*S-153	4.8
1922	*NY-N	156	651	117	209	41	5	4	60	79	27	.321	.397	.418	109	12	16	11	-2	.941	22	*S-156	4.5
1923	*NY-N	107	444	80	135	33	3	1	31	62	23	.304	.391	.399	110	9	8	7	-2	.936	21	S-96,2-11	3.6
1924	Bos-N	79	319	49	89	11	1	2	21	37	24	.279	.356	.339	91	-3	4	4	-1	.961	-5	S-79,M	-0.1
1925	Bos-N	128	479	75	153	29	8	2	49	64	22	.319	.400	.426	122	18	7	4	-0	.945	10	*S-125,M	3.8
1926	Bos-N	127	453	70	141	18	6	1	44	64	29	.311	.399	.384	122	17	3			.956	-3	*S-123/3-2,M	2.7
1927	Bos-N	111	375	44	91	13	4	1	31	43	36	.243	.322	.307	75	-13	5			.939	6	*S-104/3-1,M	0.4
1928	Bro-N	149	515	47	127	19	5	0	51	59	20	.247	.326	.303	66	-24	7			.948	4	*S-149	-0.3
1929	Bro-N	104	358	35	99	11	3	1	44	29	11	.277	.331	.332	66	-19	7			.955	-0	*S-102	-0.6
1930	NY-N	10	17	0	1	1	0	0	0	2	1	.059	.158	.118	-33	-4				.966	1	/S-8	-0.2
Total	16	1913	7182	1048	2004	320	77	32	591	827	487	.279	.355	.358	98	8	145	75		.944	198	*S-1873/2-14,3-3,O	35.2

■ CHRIS BANDO   Bando, Christopher Michael   b: 2/4/56, Cleveland, Ohio   BB/TR, 6', 195 lbs.   Deb: 8/13/81   FC

1981	Cle-A	21	47	3	10	3	0	0	6	2	2	.213	.245	.277	51	-3	0	0	0	.967	-2	C-15/D-2	-0.5
1982	Cle-A	66	184	13	39	6	1	3	16	24	30	.212	.303	.304	68	-8	0	0	0	.990	-6	C-63/3-2	-1.2
1983	Cle-A	48	121	15	31	3	0	4	15	15	19	.256	.338	.380	94	-1	0	1	-1	.995	-2	C-43	-0.2
1984	Cle-A	75	220	38	64	11	0	12	41	33	35	.291	.383	.505	141	13	1	2	-1	.982	-4	C-63/1-1,3-1,D-1	1.1
1985	Cle-A	73	173	11	24	4	1	0	13	22	21	.139	.236	.173	14	-20	0	1	-1	.986	-3	C-67	-2.1
1986	Cle-A	92	254	28	68	9	0	2	26	22	49	.268	.329	.327	81	-6	0	1	-1	.990	-10	C-86	-1.2
1987	Cle-A	89	211	20	46	9	0	5	16	12	28	.218	.260	.332	55	-14	0	0	0	.990	-2	C-86	-1.1
1988	Cle-A	32	72	6	9	1	0	1	8	8	12	.125	.222	.181	14	-8	0	0	0	.979	1	C-32	-0.6
	Det-A	1	0	0	0	0	0	0	0	0	0	—	—	—			0	0	0	.000	0	/C-1	0.0
	Yr	33	72	6	9	1	0	1	8	8	12	.125	.222	.181	14	-8	0	0	0	.979	1	C-33	-0.6
1989	Oak-A	1	2	0	1	0	0	0	1	0	1	.500	.500	.500	189	0	0	0	0	1.000	1	/C-1	0.1
Total	9	498	1284	134	292	46	2	27	142	138	197	.227	.303	.329	73	-47	1	5	-3	.987	-28	C-457/3-3,D-3,1-1	-5.7

■ SAL BANDO   Bando, Salvatore Leonard   b: 2/13/44, Cleveland, O.   BR/TR, 6', 205 lbs.   Deb: 9/3/66   FC

1966	KC-A	11	24	5	7	1	1	0	1	1	3	.292	.320	.417	113	0	0	0	0	.933	4	/3-7	0.5
1967	KC-A	47	130	11	25	3	2	0	6	16	24	.192	.295	.246	64	-5	1	0	0	.959	8	3-44	0.3
1968	Oak-A	162	605	67	152	25	5	9	67	51	78	.251	.317	.354	108	5	13	4	2	.964	-12	*3-162/O-1	-0.5
1969	Oak-A★	162	609	106	171	25	3	31	113	111	82	.281	.401	.484	153	47	1	4	-2	.954	-13	*3-162	3.3
1970	Oak-A	155	502	93	132	20	2	20	75	118	88	.263	.409	.430	137	31	6	10	-4	.954	-22	*3-152	0.4
1971	*Oak-A	153	538	75	146	23	1	24	94	86	55	.271	.380	.452	137	28	7	3	-3	.971	-17	*3-153	0.8
1972	*Oak-A★	152	535	64	126	20	3	15	77	78	55	.236	.342	.368	118	13	3	1	0	.960	6	*3-151/2-1	2.0
1973	*Oak-A★	162	592	97	170	32	3	29	98	82	84	.287	.378	.498	153	41	4	2	0	.949	-23	*3-159/D-3	1.8
1974	*Oak-A†	146	498	84	121	21	2	22	103	86	74	.243	.360	.426	134	24	2	3	-1	.946	-13	*3-141/D-3	0.8
1975	*Oak-A	160	562	64	129	24	1	15	78	87	80	.230	.338	.356	98	1	7	1	2	.967	-16	*3-160	-1.4
1976	Oak-A	158	550	75	132	18	2	27	84	76	74	.240	.337	.427	128	19	20	6	2	.962	-5	*3-155/S-5,D-2	1.7
1977	Mil-A	159	580	65	145	27	3	17	82	75	89	.250	.339	.395	99	0	4	2	0	.966	-2	*3-135,D-24/2-1,S-1	-0.3
1978	Mil-A	152	540	85	154	20	6	17	78	72	54	.285	.375	.439	128	22	3	2	-0	.968	12	*3-134,D-12/1-5	3.1
1979	Mil-A	130	476	57	117	14	3	9	43	57	42	.246	.330	.345	82	-11	2	0	1	.963	-9	*3-109,D-19/1-4,P2	-2.0
1980	Mil-A	78	254	28	50	12	1	5	31	29	35	.197	.282	.311	64	-13	5	3	-0	.934	-4	3-57,D-15/1-7	-1.9
1981	*Mil-A	32	65	10	13	4	0	2	9	6	3	.200	.268	.354	82	-2	1	1	0	.967	0	3-15/1-9,D-2	-0.2
Total	16	2019	7060	982	1790	289	38	242	1039	1031	923	.254	.346	.408	120	200	75	46	-5	.959	-104	*3-1896/D-80,1S2PO	8.4

■ JEFF BANISTER   Banister, Jeffery Todd   b: 1/15/65, Weatherford, Okla.   BR/TR, 6'2", 200 lbs.   Deb: 7/23/91

| 1991 | Pit-N | 1 | 1 | 0 | 1 | 0 | 0 | 0 | 0 | 0 | 0 | 1.000 | 1.000 | 1.000 | 471 | 0 | 0 | 0 | 0 | .000 | 0 | /H | 0.0 |

■ BRIAN BANKS   Banks, Brian Glen   b: 9/28/70, Mesa, Ariz.   BB/TR, 6'3", 200 lbs.   Deb: 9/9/96

| 1996 | Mil-A | 4 | 7 | 2 | 4 | 2 | 0 | 1 | 2 | 1 | 2 | .571 | .625 | 1.286 | 347 | 3 | 0 | 0 | 0 | 1.000 | -1 | /O-3,1-1 | 0.1 |

■ ERNIE BANKS   Banks, Ernest   b: 1/31/31, Dallas, Tex.   BR/TR, 6'1", 180 lbs.   Deb: 9/17/53   CH

1953	Chi-N	10	35	3	11	1	1	2	6	4	5	.314	.385	.571	142	2	0	0	0	.981	3	S-10	0.5
1954	Chi-N	154	593	70	163	19	7	19	79	40	50	.275	.328	.427	94	-6	6	10	-4	.959	-1	*S-154	0.1
1955	Chi-N★	154	596	98	176	29	9	44	117	45	72	.295	.347	.596	145	35	9	3	1	.972	5	*S-154	5.3
1956	Chi-N☆	139	538	82	160	25	8	28	85	52	62	.297	.359	.530	137	27	6	9	-4	.962	-16	*S-139	2.0
1957	Chi-N★	156	594	113	169	34	6	43	102	70	85	.285	.363	.579	150	40	8	4	0	.975	-17	*S-100,3-58	3.5
1958	Chi-N★	154	617	119	193	23	11	47	129	52	87	.313	.370	.614	157	48	4	4	-1	.960	-2	*S-154	5.7
1959	Chi-N★	155	589	97	179	25	6	45	143	64	72	.304	.379	.596	156	46	2	4	-2	.985	6	*S-154	6.2
1960	Chi-N★	156	597	94	162	32	7	41	117	71	69	.271	.353	.554	145	36	1	3	-2	.977	11	*S-156	5.8
1961	Chi-N	138	511	75	142	22	4	29	80	54	75	.278	.349	.507	122	15	1	2	-1	.965	13	*S-104,O-23/1-7	3.3
1962	Chi-N	154	610	87	164	20	6	37	104	30	71	.269	.311	.503	110	6	5	1	1	.993	0	*1-149/3-3	-0.3
1963	Chi-N	130	432	41	98	20	1	18	64	39	73	.227	.297	.403	94	-7	0	3	-2	.993	-2	*1-125	-1.4
1964	Chi-N	157	591	67	156	29	6	23	95	36	84	.264	.310	.450	107	-1	1	1	-1	.994	11	*1-157	0.8
1965	Chi-N★	163	612	79	162	25	3	28	106	55	64	.265	.331	.453	116	12	3	5	-2	.992	-7	*1-162	-0.7
1966	Chi-N	141	511	52	139	23	7	15	75	29	59	.272	.317	.432	105	3	0	0	0	.992	2	*1-130/3-8	-0.5
1967	Chi-N	151	573	68	158	26	4	23	95	27	93	.276	.312	.455	107	7	2	2	-1	.993	1	*1-147	-0.2
1968	Chi-N	150	552	71	136	27	0	32	83	27	67	.246	.288	.469	116	9	2	0	1	.996	-1	*1-147	-0.4
1969	Chi-N★	155	565	60	143	19	2	23	106	42	101	.253	.310	.416	91	-8	0	0	0	.997	1	*1-153	-2.1
1970	Chi-N	72	222	25	56	6	2	12	44	20	33	.252	.317	.459	94	-3	0	0	0	.993	-2	1-62	-1.0
1971	Chi-N	39	83	4	16	2	0	3	6	6	14	.193	.247	.325	53	-5	0	0	0	1.000	1	1-20	-0.7
Total	19	2528	9421	1305	2583	407	90	512	1636	763	1236	.274	.333	.500	122	262	50	53	-17	.994	4	*1-1259,S-1125/3O	25.9

■ GEORGE BANKS   Banks, George Edward   b: 9/24/38, Pacolet Mills, S.C.   d: 3/1/85, Spartanburg, S.C.   BR/TR, 5'11", 185 lbs.   Deb: 4/15/62

1962	Min-A	63	103	22	26	0	2	4	15	21	27	.252	.384	.408	109	2	0	0	0	.962	-3	O-17/3-6	-0.1
1963	Min-A	25	71	5	11	4	0	3	9	8	21	.155	.259	.338	65	-3	0	0	0	.910	3	3-21	-0.2
1964	Min-A	1	1	0	0	0	0	0	0	0	1	.000	.000	.000	-99	-0	0	0	0	.000	0	H	0.0
	Cle-A	9	17	6	5	1	0	2	3	6	6	.294	.478	.706	226	3	0	0	0	1.000	-1	/O-3,2-1,3-1	0.3
	Yr	10	18	6	5	1	0	2	3	6	7	.278	.458	.667	210	3	0	0	0	1.000	-1	/O-3,2-1,3-1	0.3
1965	Cle-A	4	5	0	1	1	0	0	0	1	3	.200	.333	.400	107	0	0	0	0	1.000	0	/3-1	0.0
1966	Cle-A	4	4	0	1	0	0	1	0	1	1	.250	.250	.250	40	-1	0	0	0	1.000	0	/3-1	0.0
Total	5	106	201	33	44	6	2	9	27	37	59	.219	.346	.403	102	1	0	0	0	.919	-1	/3-29,O-20,2-1	0.0

■ EVERETT BANKSTON   Bankston, Wilborn Everett   b: 5/25/1893, Barnesville, Ga.   d: 2/26/70, Griffin, Ga.   BL/TR, 5'11", 180 lbs.   Deb: 8/15/15

| 1915 | Phi-A | 11 | 36 | 6 | 5 | 1 | 1 | 0 | 2 | 1 | | .139 | .205 | .306 | 55 | -2 | 1 | | | .882 | -1 | /O-8 | -0.3 |

■ JIM BANNING   Banning, James M.   b: 1866, New York, N.Y.   BL/TR, 5'6", 150 lbs.   Deb: 9/27/1888

1888	Was-N	1	0	0	0	0	0	0	0	0		—	—	—			0	0		1.000	-0	/C-1	0.0
1889	Was-N	2	1	0	0	0	0	0	0	0		.000	.000	.000	-99	-0	0			1.000	1	/C-2	0.1
Total	2	3	1	0	0	0	0	0	0	0		.000	.000	.000	-99	-0	0			1.000	1	/C-3	0.1

YEAR	TM/L	G	AB	R	H	2B	3B	HR	RBI	BB	SO	AVG	OBP	SLG	PRO+	BR/A	SB	CS	SBR	FA	FR	G/POS	TPR

■ ALAN BANNISTER   Bannister, Alan   b: 9/3/51, Montebello, Cal.   BR/TR, 5'11", 175 lbs.   Deb: 7/13/74

YEAR	TM/L	G	AB	R	H	2B	3B	HR	RBI	BB	SO	AVG	OBP	SLG	PRO+	BR/A	SB	CS	SBR	FA	FR	G/POS	TPR
1974	Phi-N	26	25	4	3	0	0	0	1	3	7	.120	.241	.120	3	-3	0	0	0	1.000	-2	/O-8,S-2	-0.5
1975	Phi-N	24	61	10	16	3	1	0	0	1	9	.262	.274	.344	68	-3	2	2	-1	1.000	1	O-18/2-1,S-1	-0.3
1976	Chi-A	73	145	19	36	6	2	0	8	14	21	.248	.319	.317	86	-2	12	4	1	.988	-2	O-43,S-14/2-4,3D	-0.4
1977	Chi-A	139	560	87	154	20	3	3	57	54	49	.275	.341	.338	86	-10	4	3	-1	.936	-34	*S-133/2-3,O-3	-2.9
1978	Chi-A	49	107	16	24	3	2	0	8	11	12	.224	.303	.290	67	-5	3	3	-1	1.000	-3	D-19,O-15/S-8,2-2	-0.9
1979	Chi-A	136	506	71	144	28	8	2	55	43	40	.285	.344	.383	96	-2	22	6	3	.963	-24	2-65,O-47,3-12/,1D	-2.1
1980	Chi-A	45	130	16	25	6	0	0	9	12	16	.192	.261	.238	38	-11	5	2	0	1.000	-2	O-23,3-17	-1.4
	Cle-A	81	262	41	86	17	4	1	32	28	25	.328	.393	.435	126	10	9	2	2	.968	-17	2-41,O-40/3-3,S-2	-0.4
	Yr	126	392	57	111	23	4	1	41	40	41	.283	.350	.370	97	-1	14	4	2	.981	-19	O-63,2-41,3-20/S-2	-1.8
1981	Cle-A	68	232	36	61	11	1	1	17	16	19	.263	.310	.332	86	-4	16	2	4	.986	-14	O-35,2-30/1-2,S-1	-1.4
1982	Cle-A	101	348	40	93	16	1	4	41	42	41	.267	.348	.353	94	-2	18	5	2	.991	-11	O-55,2-48/S-2,3D	-1.0
1983	Cle-A	117	377	51	100	25	4	5	43	31	43	.265	.326	.393	93	-4	6	6	0	.969	-14	O-91,2-27/1-3,D-3	-2.1
1984	Hou-N	9	20	2	4	2	0	0	0	2	2	.200	.273	.300	65	-1	0	0	0	.947	-1	/S-4,O-1	-0.2
	Tex-A	47	112	20	33	2	1	2	9	21	17	.295	.410	.384	118	4	3	0	1	.959	-1	2-25/O-3,1-1,3-1,D	-0.7
1985	Tex-A	57	122	17	32	4	1	1	6	14	17	.262	.338	.336	84	-2	8	2	1	1.000	-2	D-21,O-14,2-10/31	-0.4
Total	12	972	3007	430	811	143	28	19	288	292	318	.270	.337	.355	90	-35	108	37	10	.983	-138	O-396,2-256,S/D31	-14.8

■ JIMMY BANNON   Bannon, James Henry "Foxy Grandpa"   b: 5/5/1871, Amesbury, Mass.   d: 3/24/48, Glen Rock, N.J.   BR/TR, 5'5", 160 lbs.   Deb: 6/15/1893   F

YEAR	TM/L	G	AB	R	H	2B	3B	HR	RBI	BB	SO	AVG	OBP	SLG	PRO+	BR/A	SB	CS	SBR	FA	FR	G/POS	TPR
1893	StL-N	26	107	9	36	3	4	0	15	4	5	.336	.366	.439	113	2	8			.795	-6	O-24/S-2,P-1	-0.4
1894	Bos-N	128	494	130	166	29	10	13	114	62	42	.336	.414	.514	114	9	47			.873	18	*O-128/P-1	1.4
1895	Bos-N	123	489	101	171	35	5	6	74	54	31	.350	.420	.479	122	15	28			.879	10	O-122/P-1	1.3
1896	Bos-N	89	343	52	86	9	5	0	50	32	23	.251	.316	.306	61	-20	16			.901	-1	O-76/2-6,S-5,3-3	-2.2
Total	4	366	1433	292	459	76	24	19	253	152	101	.320	.390	.447	105	5	99			.877	22	O-350/S-7,2-6,3P	0.1

■ TOM BANNON   Bannon, Thomas Edward "Ward Six"   b: 5/8/1869, Amesbury, Mass.   d: 1/26/50, Lynn, Mass.   BR/TR, 5'8", 175 lbs.   Deb: 5/10/1895   F

YEAR	TM/L	G	AB	R	H	2B	3B	HR	RBI	BB	SO	AVG	OBP	SLG	PRO+	BR/A	SB	CS	SBR	FA	FR	G/POS	TPR
1895	NY-N	37	159	33	43	6	2	0	8	7	8	.270	.301	.333	65	-9	20			.894	2	O-21,1-16	-0.7
1896	NY-N	2	7	1	1	1	0	0	1	0	1	.143	.250	.286	42	-1	0			.500	-1	/O-2	-0.2
Total	2	39	166	34	44	7	2	0	8	8	9	.265	.299	.331	64	-9	20			.878	1	/O-23,1-16	-0.9

■ WALTER BARBARE   Barbare, Walter Lawrence "Dinty"   b: 8/11/1891, Greenville, S.C.   d: 10/28/65, Greenville, S.C.   BR/TR, 6', 162 lbs.   Deb: 9/17/14

YEAR	TM/L	G	AB	R	H	2B	3B	HR	RBI	BB	SO	AVG	OBP	SLG	PRO+	BR/A	SB	CS	SBR	FA	FR	G/POS	TPR
1914	Cle-A	15	52	6	16	2	2	0	5	2	5	.308	.345	.423	126	1	1	4	-2	.933	0	3-14/S-1	0.0
1915	Cle-A	77	246	15	47	3	1	0	11	10	27	.191	.235	.211	33	-21	6	5	-1	.960	7	3-68/1-1	-1.3
1916	Cle-A	13	48	3	11	1	0	0	3	4	9	.229	.288	.250	58	-2	0			.977	1	3-12	-0.1
1918	Bos-A	13	29	2	5	0	0	0	2	0	1	.172	.172	.276	36	-2	1			.826	-4	3-11/S-1	-0.7
1919	Pit-N	85	293	34	80	11	5	1	34	18	18	.273	.317	.355	98	-1	11			.961	-7	3-80/2-1	-0.5
1920	Pit-N	57	186	9	51	5	2	0	12	9	11	.274	.308	.323	79	-5	5	3	0	.923	-5	S-34,2-12/3-5	-0.8
1921	Bos-N	134	550	66	166	22	7	0	49	24	28	.302	.331	.367	89	-9	11	4	1	.957	-17	*S-121/2-8,3-2	-1.3
1922	Bos-N	106	373	38	86	5	4	0	40	21	22	.231	.272	.265	41	-33	2	0	1	.966	2	2-45,3-38/1-14	-2.5
Total	8	500	1777	173	462	52	21	1	156	88	121	.260	.297	.315	71	-72	37	16		.959	-21	3-230,S-157/2-66,1	-7.2

■ RED BARBARY   Barbary, Donald Odell   b: 6/20/20, Simpsonville, S.C   BR/TR, 6'3", 190 lbs.   Deb: 5/22/43

YEAR	TM/L	G	AB	R	H	2B	3B	HR	RBI	BB	SO	AVG	OBP	SLG	PRO+	BR/A	SB	CS	SBR	FA	FR	G/POS	TPR
1943	Was-A	1	1	0	0	0	0	0	0	0	0	.000	.000	.000	-99	-0	0	0	0	.000	0	H	0.0

■ JAP BARBEAU   Barbeau, William Joseph   b: 6/10/1882, New York, N.Y.   d: 9/10/69, Milwaukee, Wis.   BR/TR, 5'5", 140 lbs.   Deb: 9/27/05

YEAR	TM/L	G	AB	R	H	2B	3B	HR	RBI	BB	SO	AVG	OBP	SLG	PRO+	BR/A	SB	CS	SBR	FA	FR	G/POS	TPR
1905	Cle-A	11	37	1	10	1	0	0	2	1		.270	.289	.351	102	0	1			.905	1	2-11	0.1
1906	Cle-A	42	129	8	25	5	3	0	12	9		.194	.257	.279	69	-5	5			.830	-7	3-32/S-6	-1.2
1909	Pit-N	91	350	60	77	16	3	0	25	37		.220	.302	.283	75	-10	19			.891	-19	3-85	-3.0
	StL-N	48	175	23	44	3	0	0	5	28		.251	.370	.269	105	3	14			.901	-10	3-47	-0.6
	Yr	139	525	83	121	19	3	0	30	65		.230	.326	.278	85	-7	33			.895	-29	*3-132	-3.6
1910	StL-N	7	21	4	4	0	1	0	2	3		.190	.292	.286	71	-1	0			.917	2	/3-6,2-1	0.2
Total	4	199	712	96	160	25	8	0	46	78	3	.225	.311	.282	82	-12	39			.884	-33	3-170/2-12,S-6	-4.5

■ DAVE BARBEE   Barbee, David Monroe   b: 5/7/05, Greensboro, N.C.   d: 7/1/68, Albemarle, N.C.   BR/TR, 5'11.5", 178 lbs.   Deb: 7/29/26

YEAR	TM/L	G	AB	R	H	2B	3B	HR	RBI	BB	SO	AVG	OBP	SLG	PRO+	BR/A	SB	CS	SBR	FA	FR	G/POS	TPR
1926	Phi-A	19	47	7	8	1	1	1	5	2	4	.170	.220	.298	32	-5	0	0	0	1.000	0	O-10	-0.5
1932	Pit-N	97	327	37	84	22	6	5	55	18	38	.257	.300	.407	89	-6	1			.975	4	O-78	-0.7
Total	2	116	374	44	92	23	7	6	60	20	42	.246	.290	.393	82	-11	1	0		.977	4	/O-88	-1.2

■ CHARLIE BARBER   Barber, Charles D.   b: 1854, Philadelphia, Pa.   d: 11/23/10, Philadelphia, Pa.   BR/TR,   Deb: 4/17/1884

YEAR	TM/L	G	AB	R	H	2B	3B	HR	RBI	BB	SO	AVG	OBP	SLG	PRO+	BR/A	SB	CS	SBR	FA	FR	G/POS	TPR
1884	Cin-U	55	204	38	41	1	4	0		11		.201	.242	.245	44	-20				.837	4	3-55	-1.4

■ TURNER BARBER   Barber, Tyrus Turner   b: 7/9/1893, Lavinia, Tenn.   d: 10/20/68, Milan, Tenn.   BL/TR, 5'11", 170 lbs.   Deb: 8/19/15

YEAR	TM/L	G	AB	R	H	2B	3B	HR	RBI	BB	SO	AVG	OBP	SLG	PRO+	BR/A	SB	CS	SBR	FA	FR	G/POS	TPR
1915	Was-A	20	53	9	16	1	1	0	6	6	7	.302	.383	.358	120	1	0	3	-2	.952	-2	O-19	-0.3
1916	Was-A	15	33	3	7	0	1	1	5	2	3	.212	.257	.364	87	-1	0			.833	-3	O-10	-0.4
1917	Chi-N	7	28	2	6	1	0	0	2	2	8	.214	.267	.250	55	-1	1			1.000	1	/O-7	-0.1
1918	*Chi-N	55	123	11	29	3	2	0	10	9	16	.236	.293	.293	77	-3	3			.940	-8	O-27/1-4	-1.4
1919	Chi-N	76	230	26	72	9	4	0	21	14	17	.313	.355	.387	122	6	7			.949	-4	O-68	-0.3
1920	Chi-N	94	340	27	90	10	5	0	50	9	26	.265	.290	.324	74	-12	5	6	-2	.988	-7	1-69,O-17/2-2	-2.5
1921	Chi-N	127	452	73	142	14	4	1	54	41	24	.314	.379	.369	99	1	5	9	-4	.970	2	*O-123	-1.0
1922	Chi-N	84	226	35	70	7	4	0	29	30	9	.310	.391	.376	97	0	7	4	-0	.953	-6	O-47,1-16	-0.9
1923	Bro-N	13	46	3	10	2	0	0	8	2	2	.217	.250	.261	36	-4	0	1	-1	1.000	1	O-12	-0.7
Total	9	491	1531	189	442	47	21	2	185	115	112	.289	.343	.351	93	-12	28	23		.959	-29	O-330/1-89,2-2	-7.6

■ BRET BARBERIE   Barberie, Bret Edward   b: 8/16/67, Long Beach, Cal.   BB/TR, 5'11", 185 lbs.   Deb: 6/16/91

YEAR	TM/L	G	AB	R	H	2B	3B	HR	RBI	BB	SO	AVG	OBP	SLG	PRO+	BR/A	SB	CS	SBR	FA	FR	G/POS	TPR
1991	Mon-N	57	136	16	48	12	2	2	18	20	22	.353	.443	.515	171	14	0	0		.931	-2	S-19,2-10,3-10/1-1	1.4
1992	Mon-N	111	285	26	66	11	0	1	24	47	62	.232	.356	.281	83	-4	9	5	-0	.932	5	3-63,2-26/S-1	0.2
1993	Fla-N	99	375	45	104	16	2	5	33	33	58	.277	.347	.371	87	-6	2	4	-2	.982	11	2-97	0.6
1994	Fla-N	107	372	40	112	20	2	5	31	23	65	.301	.356	.406	95	-2	2	6	-2	.975	10	*2-106	1.3
1995	Bal-A	90	237	32	57	14	0	2	25	36	50	.241	.355	.325	77	-7	3	3	-1	.977	-4	2-74/3-3,D-5	-0.7
1996	Chi-N	15	29	4	1	0	0	1	2	5	11	.034	.176	.138	-15	-5	0	1	-1	1.000	-3	/2-6,3-2,S-1	-0.8
Total	6	479	1434	163	388	73	6	16	133	164	268	.271	.358	.363	92	-10	16	13	-3	.980	17	2-319/3-78,S-21,D1	2.0

■ JIM BARBIERI   Barbieri, James Patrick   b: 9/15/41, Schenectady, N.Y.   BL/TR, 5'7", 155 lbs.   Deb: 7/5/66

YEAR	TM/L	G	AB	R	H	2B	3B	HR	RBI	BB	SO	AVG	OBP	SLG	PRO+	BR/A	SB	CS	SBR	FA	FR	G/POS	TPR
1966	*LA-N	39	64	9	18	3	0	0	9	9	7	.280	.352	.341	102	0	2	0	1	.939	0	O-20	0.1

■ GEORGE BARCLAY   Barclay, George Oliver "Deerfoot"   b: 5/16/1876, Millville, Pa.   d: 4/3/09, Philadelphia, Pa.   TR, 5'10", 162 lbs.   Deb: 4/17/02

YEAR	TM/L	G	AB	R	H	2B	3B	HR	RBI	BB	SO	AVG	OBP	SLG	PRO+	BR/A	SB	CS	SBR	FA	FR	G/POS	TPR
1902	StL-N	137	543	79	163	14	2	3	53	31		.300	.345	.350	119	12	30			.904	-7	*O-137	-0.5
1903	StL-N	108	419	37	104	10	8	0	42	15		.248	.278	.310	70	-18	12			.901	-8	*O-107	-3.1
1904	StL-N	103	375	41	75	7	4	1	28	12		.200	.237	.248	52	-22	14			.947	-6	*O-103	-3.6
	Bos-N	24	93	5	21	3	1	0	10	2		.226	.258	.280	68	-4	3			.935	-3	O-24	-0.9
	Yr	127	468	46	96	10	5	1	38	14		.205	.241	.254	55	-25	17			.945	-9	*O-127	-4.5
1905	Bos-N	29	108	5	19	1	0	0	7	2		.176	.205	.185	17	-11	2			.854	-5	O-28	-1.8
Total	4	401	1538	167	382	35	15	4	140	62		.248	.286	.298	79	-42	61			.911	-29	O-399	-9.9

■ JESSE BARFIELD   Barfield, Jesse Lee   b: 10/29/59, Joliet, Ill.   BR/TR, 6'1", 205 lbs.   Deb: 9/3/81

YEAR	TM/L	G	AB	R	H	2B	3B	HR	RBI	BB	SO	AVG	OBP	SLG	PRO+	BR/A	SB	CS	SBR	FA	FR	G/POS	TPR
1981	Tor-A	25	95	7	22	3	2	2	9	4	19	.232	.270	.368	77	-3	4	3	-1	1.000	5	O-25	0.1
1982	Tor-A	139	394	54	97	13	2	18	58	42	79	.246	.323	.426	95	-3	1	4	-2	.963	-6	*O-137/D-1	-1.4
1983	Tor-A	128	388	58	98	13	3	27	68	22	110	.253	.300	.510	111	4	2	2	0	.980	4	*O-120/D-5	0.3
1984	Tor-A	110	320	51	91	14	1	14	49	35	81	.284	.354	.466	122	9	8	2	1	.952	6	O-88/D-9	1.4
1985	*Tor-A	155	539	94	156	34	9	27	84	66	143	.289	.371	.536	141	30	22	8	3	.989	22	*O-154	4.8
1986	Tor-A★	158	589	107	170	35	2	**40**	108	69	146	.289	.371	.559	145	36	8	6	-1	.992	21	*O-157	**4.8**
1987	Tor-A	159	590	89	155	14	3	28	84	58	141	.263	.332	.458	104	3	3	5	-2	.992	16	*O-158	1.2

YEAR	TM/L	G	AB	R	H	2B	3B	HR	RBI	BB	SO	AVG	OBP	SLG	PRO+	BR/A	SB	CS	SBR	FA	FR	G/POS	TPR
1988	Tor-A	137	468	62	114	21	5	18	56	41	108	.244	.306	.425	102	0	7	3	0	.988	13	*O-136/D-1	0.9
1989	Tor-A	21	80	8	16	4	0	5	11	5	28	.200	.256	.438	94	-1	0	2	-1	.979	3	O-21	0.0
	NY-A	129	441	71	106	19	1	18	56	82	122	.240	.362	.410	119	13	5	3	0	.972	9	*O-129	1.9
	Yr	150	521	79	122	23	1	23	67	87	150	.234	.347	.415	115	12	5	5	-2	.973	12	*O-150	1.9
1990	NY-A	153	476	69	117	21	2	25	78	82	150	.246	.362	.456	127	18	4	3	-1	.973	9	*O-151	2.3
1991	NY-A	84	284	37	64	12	0	17	48	36	80	.225	.313	.447	107	2	1	0	0	1.000	11	O-81	1.2
1992	NY-A	30	95	8	13	2	0	2	7	9	27	.137	.212	.221	21	-10	1	1	-0	.966	0	O-30	-1.1
Total	12	1428	4759	715	1219	216	30	241	716	551	1234	.256	.338	.466	116	99	66	47	-8	.980	114	*O-1387/D-16	16.4

■ AL BARKER   Barker, Alfred L   b: 1/18/1839, Rockford, Ill.   d: 9/15/12, Rockford, Ill.   Deb: 6/1/1871

YEAR	TM/L	G	AB	R	H	2B	3B	HR	RBI	BB	SO	AVG	OBP	SLG	PRO+	BR/A	SB	CS	SBR	FA	FR	G/POS	TPR
1871	Rok-n	1	4	0	1	0	0	0	0	0		.250	.400	.250	97	0	0	0	0	1.000	-0	/O-1	0.0

■ RAY BARKER   Barker, Raymond Herrell "Buddy"   b: 3/12/36, Martinsburg, W.Va.   BL/TR, 6', 192 lbs.   Deb: 9/13/60

YEAR	TM/L	G	AB	R	H	2B	3B	HR	RBI	BB	SO	AVG	OBP	SLG	PRO+	BR/A	SB	CS	SBR	FA	FR	G/POS	TPR
1960	Bal-A	5	6	0	0	0	0	0	0	0	3	.000	.000	.000	-99	-2	0	0	0	.000	-0	/O-1	-0.2
1965	Cle-A	11	6	0	0	0	0	0	0	2	2	.000	.250	.000	-22	-1	0	0	0	1.000	-0	/1-3	-0.1
	NY-A	98	205	21	52	11	0	7	31	20	46	.254	.329	.410	109	2	1	0	0	.991	6	1-61/3-3	0.7
	Yr	109	211	21	52	11	0	7	31	22	48	.246	.326	.398	105	1	1	0	0	.991	6	1-64/3-3	0.6
1966	NY-A	61	75	11	14	5	0	3	13	4	20	.187	.228	.373	72	-3	0	0	0	.987	5	1-47	0.1
1967	NY-A	17	26	2	2	0	0	0	0	3	5	.077	.172	.077	-25	-4	0	0	0	.961	1	1-13	-0.4
Total	4	192	318	34	68	16	0	10	44	29	76	.214	.286	.358	84	-7	1	0	0	.987	12	1-124/3-3,O-1	0.1

■ RED BARKLEY   Barkley, John Duncan   b: 9/19/13, Childress, Tex.   BR/TR, 5'11", 160 lbs.   Deb: 9/2/37

YEAR	TM/L	G	AB	R	H	2B	3B	HR	RBI	BB	SO	AVG	OBP	SLG	PRO+	BR/A	SB	CS	SBR	FA	FR	G/POS	TPR
1937	StL-A	31	101	9	27	6	0	0	14	14	17	.267	.357	.327	92	-4	1	0	0	.969	-4	2-31	-0.5
1939	Bos-N	12	11	1	0	0	0	0	0	1	2	.000	.083	.000	-82	-3	0	0	0	.842	4	/S-7,3-4	0.1
1943	Bro-N	20	51	6	16	3	0	0	7	4	7	.314	.364	.373	113	1	1	1		.894	-3	S-18	-0.1
Total	3	63	163	16	43	9	0	0	21	19	26	.264	.341	.319	75	-6	2	0		.882	-3	/2-31,S-25,3-4	-0.5

■ SAM BARKLEY   Barkley, Samuel E   b: 5/24/1858, Wheeling, W.Va.   d: 4/20/12, Wheeling, W.Va.   BR/TR, 5'11.5", 180 lbs.   Deb: 5/1/1884   M

YEAR	TM/L	G	AB	R	H	2B	3B	HR	RBI	BB	SO	AVG	OBP	SLG	PRO+	BR/A	SB	CS	SBR	FA	FR	G/POS	TPR
1884	Tol-a	104	435	71	133	**39**	9	1		22		.306	.342	.444	149	22				.930	25	*2-103/C-2	**4.4**
1885	*StL-a	106	418	67	112	18	10	3	53	25		.268	.312	.380	113	5				.921	15	*2-96,1-11	1.9
1886	Pit-a	122	478	77	127	31	8	1	69	58		.266	.345	.370	125	15	22			.936	-4	*2-112/O-8,1-2	1.3
1887	Pit-N	89	340	44	76	10	4	1	35	30	24	.224	.294	.285	66	-15	6			.979	-5	1-53,2-36	-2.0
1888	KC-a	116	482	67	104	21	6	4	51	26		.216	.262	.309	78	-14	15			.938	-7	*2-116/M	-1.6
1889	KC-a	45	176	36	50	6	2	0	23	15	20	.284	.340	.341	89	-3	8			.923	-12	2-41/1-4	-1.1
Total	6	582	2329	362	602	125	39	10	231	176	<u>44</u>	.258	.314	.359	105	10	51			.929	12	2-504/1-70,O-8,C-2	2.9

■ TOM BARLOW   Barlow, Thomas H.   Deb: 5/2/1872

YEAR	TM/L	G	AB	R	H	2B	3B	HR	RBI	BB	SO	AVG	OBP	SLG	PRO+	BR/A	SB	CS	SBR	FA	FR	G/POS	TPR
1872	Atl-n	37	171	34	53	1	0	0	10	3	2	.310	.322	.316	83	-7	7	5	-1	.761	-8	*C-36/S-4,3-1	-1.2
1873	Atl-n	55	271	48	74	0	2	1	14	4	0	.273	.284	.299	82	-4	3	3	-1	.762	-15	*C-55/2-1,S-1	-1.4
1874	Har-n	32	156	37	46	4	1	0	10	0	2	.295	.295	.333	96	-1	9	2	2	.819	8	S-32	0.5
1875	NH-n	1	5	1	1	0	0	0	0	0	0	.200	.200	.200	45	-0	0	0	0	.800	0	/S-1	0.0
	Atl-n	1	4	0	0	0	0	0	0	0	0	.000	.000	.000	-99	-1	0	0	0	.500	-2	/2-1	-0.2
	Yr	2	9	1	1	0	0	0	0	0	0	.111	.111	.111	-26	-1	0	0	0	.800	-1	/S-1,2-1	-0.2
Total	4 n	126	607	120	174	5	3	1	34	7	4	.287	.295	.310	84	-13	19	10	-0	.762	-17	/C-91,S-38,2-2,3-1	-2.3

■ BRUCE BARMES   Barmes, Bruce Raymond "Squeaky"   b: 10/23/29, Vincennes, Ind.   BL/TR, 5'8", 165 lbs.   Deb: 9/13/53

YEAR	TM/L	G	AB	R	H	2B	3B	HR	RBI	BB	SO	AVG	OBP	SLG	PRO+	BR/A	SB	CS	SBR	FA	FR	G/POS	TPR
1953	Was-A	5	5	1	1	0	0	0	0	0	0	.200	.200	.200	1		0	0	0	1.000	0	/O-1	-0.1

■ BABE BARNA   Barna, Herbert Paul   b: 3/2/15, Clarksburg, W.Va.   d: 5/18/72, Charleston, W.Va.   BL/TR, 6'2", 210 lbs.   Deb: 9/16/37

YEAR	TM/L	G	AB	R	H	2B	3B	HR	RBI	BB	SO	AVG	OBP	SLG	PRO+	BR/A	SB	CS	SBR	FA	FR	G/POS	TPR
1937	Phi-A	14	36	10	14	2	0	2	9	2	6	.389	.421	.611	159	3	1	0	0	.800	-2	/O-9,1-1	0.1
1938	Phi-A	9	30	4	4	0	0	0	2	3	5	.133	.212	.133	-12	-5	0	0	0	.917	-1	/O-7	-0.6
1941	NY-N	10	42	5	9	3	0	1	5	2	6	.214	.250	.357	68	-2	0			1.000	1	O-10	-0.2
1942	NY-N	104	331	39	85	8	7	6	58	38	48	.257	.333	.378	107	3	3			.983	-5	O-89	-0.7
1943	NY-N	40	113	11	23	5	1	1	12	16	9	.204	.302	.292	72	-4	3			.984	-1	O-31	-0.7
	Bos-A	30	112	19	19	4	1	2	10	15	24	.170	.268	.277	58	-6	2	1	0	.940	-4	O-29	-1.3
Total	5	207	664	88	154	22	9	12	96	76	98	.232	.311	.346	88	-11	9	1		.969	-13	O-175/1-1	-3.4

■ RED BARNES   Barnes, Emile Deering   b: 12/25/03, Suggsville, Ala.   d: 7/3/59, Mobile, Ala.   BL/TR, 5'10.5", 158 lbs.   Deb: 9/29/27

YEAR	TM/L	G	AB	R	H	2B	3B	HR	RBI	BB	SO	AVG	OBP	SLG	PRO+	BR/A	SB	CS	SBR	FA	FR	G/POS	TPR
1927	Was-A	3	11	5	4	1	0	0	0	1	3	.364	.417	.455	127	0	0	0	0	1.000	0	/O-3	0.0
1928	Was-A	114	417	82	127	22	15	6	51	55	38	.305	.391	.472	127	17	7	3	0	.978	8	*O-104	1.3
1929	Was-A	72	130	16	26	5	2	1	15	13	12	.200	.273	.292	45	-11	1	0	0	.877	-6	O-30	-1.7
1930	Was-A	12	12	1	2	1	0	0	0	3	1	.167	.167	.250	4	-2	0	0	0	.000	0	H	-0.2
	Chi-A	85	266	48	66	12	7	1	31	26	20	.248	.317	.357	73	-11	4	2	0	.939	-0	O-72	-1.4
	Yr	97	278	49	68	13	7	1	31	29	23	.245	.311	.353	70	-13	4	2	0	.939	-0	O-72	-1.6
Total	4	286	836	152	225	41	24	8	97	95	76	.269	.347	.404	95	-6	12	5	1	.953	-2	O-209	-2.0

■ EPPIE BARNES   Barnes, Everett Duane   b: 12/1/1900, Ossining, N.Y.   d: 11/17/80, Mineola, N.Y.   BL/TL, 5'9", 175 lbs.   Deb: 9/25/23

YEAR	TM/L	G	AB	R	H	2B	3B	HR	RBI	BB	SO	AVG	OBP	SLG	PRO+	BR/A	SB	CS	SBR	FA	FR	G/POS	TPR
1923	Pit-N	2	2	0	1	0	0	0	0	0	1	.500	.500	.500	161	0	0	0	0	1.000	0	/1-1	0.0
1924	Pit-N	2	5	0	0	0	0	0	0	0	0	.000	.000	.000	-98	-1	0	0	0	1.000	0	/1-1	-0.1
Total	2	4	7	0	1	0	0	0	0	0	1	.143	.143	.143	-23	-1	0	0	0	1.000	0	/1-2	-0.1

■ HONEY BARNES   Barnes, John Francis   b: 1/29/1900, Fulton, N.Y.   d: 6/18/81, Lockport, N.Y.   BL/TR, 5'10", 175 lbs.   Deb: 4/20/26

YEAR	TM/L	G	AB	R	H	2B	3B	HR	RBI	BB	SO	AVG	OBP	SLG	PRO+	BR/A	SB	CS	SBR	FA	FR	G/POS	TPR
1926	NY-A	1	0	0	0	0	0	0	0	1	0	—	1.000	—	179	0	0	0	0	.000	0	/C-1	0.0

■ LUTE BARNES   Barnes, Luther Owens   b: 4/28/47, Forest City, Iowa   BR/TR, 5'10", 160 lbs.   Deb: 8/6/72

YEAR	TM/L	G	AB	R	H	2B	3B	HR	RBI	BB	SO	AVG	OBP	SLG	PRO+	BR/A	SB	CS	SBR	FA	FR	G/POS	TPR
1972	NY-N	24	72	5	17	2	2	0	6	6	4	.236	.295	.319	76	-2	0	1	-1	.959	1	2-14/S-6	-0.1
1973	NY-N	3	2	2	1	0	0	0	1	0	1	.500	.500	.500	181	0	0	0	0	.000	0	H	0.0
Total	2	27	74	7	18	2	2	0	7	6	5	.243	.300	.324	79	-2	0	1	-1	.959	1	/2-14,S-6	-0.1

■ ROSS BARNES   Barnes, Roscoe Charles   b: 5/8/1850, Mount Morris, N.Y.   d: 2/5/15, Chicago, Ill.   BR/TR, 5'8.5", 145 lbs.   Deb: 5/5/1871   U

YEAR	TM/L	G	AB	R	H	2B	3B	HR	RBI	BB	SO	AVG	OBP	SLG	PRO+	BR/A	SB	CS	SBR	FA	FR	G/POS	TPR
1871	Bos-n	31	157	**66**	63	10	9	0	34	13	1	.401	.447	.580	186	17	11	6	-0	.873	13	2-16,S-15	1.8
1872	Bos-n	45	229	81	**99**	**28**	2	1	44	9	4	**.432**	.454	**.585**	206	27	12	2	**2**	**.901**	25	*2-45	3.4
1873	Bos-n	60	322	**125**	137	29	8	2	62	**18**	2	**.425**	.456	**.584**	191	33	13	4	2	.852	20	*2-47,3-13	3.4
1874	Bos-n	51	259	72	88	12	4	0	41	8	2	.340	.360	.417	140	10	8	7	-2	**.856**	19	*2-51/O-1	1.9
1875	Bos-n	78	393	115	143	20	4	1	58	7	3	.364	**.375**	.443	177	28	29	6	**5**	.877	**19**	*2-76/O-3,S-2	4.3
1876	Chi-N	66	322	126	138	21	14	1	59	**20**	8	**.429**	**.462**	**.590**	222	39				**.910**	5	*2-66/P-1	3.7
1877	Chi-N	22	92	16	25	1	0	0	5	7	4	.272	.323	.283	83	-2				.838	-3	2-22	-0.9
1879	Cin-N	77	323	55	86	9	2	1	30	16	25	.266	.301	.316	109	4				.864	-1	*S-61,2-16	0.7
1881	Bos-N	69	295	42	80	14	1	0	17	16	16	.271	.309	.325	104	2				.854	-0	*S-63/2-7	0.6
Total	5 n	265	1360	459	530	99	27	4	239	55	12	.390	.413	.511	180	115	73	25	7	.871	97	2-235/S-17,3-13,O-4	14.8
Total	4	234	1032	239	329	45	17	2	111	59	53	.319	.356	.401	143	43				.859	-5	S-124,2-111/P-1	4.1

■ SAM BARNES   Barnes, Samuel Thomas   b: 12/18/1899, Suggsville, Ala.   d: 2/19/81, Montgomery, Ala.   BL/TR, 5'8", 150 lbs.   Deb: 9/14/21

YEAR	TM/L	G	AB	R	H	2B	3B	HR	RBI	BB	SO	AVG	OBP	SLG	PRO+	BR/A	SB	CS	SBR	FA	FR	G/POS	TPR
1921	Det-A	7	11	2	2	1	0	0	0	2	1	.182	.357	.273	63	-1	0	0	0	.944	2	/2-2	0.1

■ BILL BARNES   Barnes, William H.   b: Indianapolis, Ind.   Deb: 9/27/1884

YEAR	TM/L	G	AB	R	H	2B	3B	HR	RBI	BB	SO	AVG	OBP	SLG	PRO+	BR/A	SB	CS	SBR	FA	FR	G/POS	TPR
1884	StP-U	8	30	2	6	1	0	0		0		.200	.200	.233	57	-4				.727	-2	/O-8	-0.5

■ SKEETER BARNES   Barnes, William Henry   b: 3/3/57, Cincinnati, Ohio   BR/TR, 5'10", 180 lbs.   Deb: 9/6/83

YEAR	TM/L	G	AB	R	H	2B	3B	HR	RBI	BB	SO	AVG	OBP	SLG	PRO+	BR/A	SB	CS	SBR	FA	FR	G/POS	TPR
1983	Cin-N	15	34	5	7	1	0	1	4	7	3	.206	.372	.294	84	-0	2	2	-1	1.000	-0	/1-7,3-7	-0.2
1984	Cin-N	32	42	5	5	0	0	1	3	4	6	.119	.196	.190	8	-5	0	0	0	1.000	0	3-11/O-3	-0.5
1985	Mon-N	19	26	0	4	0	0	0	0	0	5	.154	.154	.192	-4	-4	0	0	0	1.000	1	/3-4,O-3,1-1	-0.3
1987	StL-N	4	4	1	1	0	0	1	3	0	0	.250	.250	1.000	208	1	0	0	0	.000	0	/3-1	0.1

YEAR	TM/L	G	AB	R	H	2B	3B	HR	RBI	BB	SO	AVG	OBP	SLG	PRO+	BR/A	SB	CS	SBR	FA	FR	G/POS	TPR
1989	Cin-N	5	3	1	0	0	0	0	0	0	0	.000	.000	.000	-97	-1	0	1	-1	.000	0	H	-0.2
1991	Det-A	75	159	28	46	13	2	5	17	9	24	.289	.327	.491	121	4	10	7	-1	1.000	0	O-33,3-17/1-9,2D	0.1
1992	Det-A	95	165	27	45	8	1	3	25	10	18	.273	.322	.388	97	-1	3	1	0	.919	2	3-39,1-17,O-15,2D	0.1
1993	Det-A	84	160	24	45	8	1	2	27	11	19	.281	.327	.381	90	-2	5	5	-2	.984	1	1-27,O-18,3D2/S	-0.5
1994	Det-A	24	21	4	6	0	0	1	4	0	2	.286	.286	.429	81	-1	1	0	-1	1.000	-1	1-15/O-4,D-1	-0.2
Total	9	353	614	95	159	30	4	14	83	41	74	.259	.310	.389	90	-9	20	18	-5	.938	1	/3-92,O-76,1D2S	-1.6

■ ED BARNEY
Barney, Edmund J.   b: 1/23/1890, Amery, Wis.   d: 10/4/67, Rice Lake, Wis.   BL/TR, 5'10.5", 178 lbs.   Deb: 7/22/15

YEAR	TM/L	G	AB	R	H	2B	3B	HR	RBI	BB	SO	AVG	OBP	SLG	PRO+	BR/A	SB	CS	SBR	FA	FR	G/POS	TPR
1915	NY-A	11	36	1	7	0	0	0	8	3	6	.194	.256	.194	35	-3	2	1	0	1.000	-0	O-10	-0.4
	Pit-N	32	99	16	27	1	2	0	5	11	12	.273	.363	.323	110	2	7	3	0	.972	2	O-26	0.3
1916	Pit-N	45	137	16	27	4	0	0	9	23	15	.197	.313	.226	66	-4	8			.964	5	O-40	-0.2
Total	2	88	272	33	61	5	2	0	22	37	33	.224	.324	.257	78	-5	17	4		.971	7	/O-76	-0.3

■ CLYDE BARNHART
Barnhart, Clyde Lee "Pooch"   b: 12/29/1895, Buck Valley, Pa.   d: 1/21/80, Hagerstown, Md.   BR/TR, 5'10", 155 lbs.   Deb: 9/22/20   F

YEAR	TM/L	G	AB	R	H	2B	3B	HR	RBI	BB	SO	AVG	OBP	SLG	PRO+	BR/A	SB	CS	SBR	FA	FR	G/POS	TPR
1920	Pit-N	12	46	5	15	4	2	0	5	1	2	.326	.340	.500	135	2	1	0	0	.971	0	3-12	0.3
1921	Pit-N	124	449	66	116	15	13	3	62	32	36	.258	.312	.370	78	-15	3	3	-1	.956	-19	*3-118	-2.6
1922	Pit-N	75	209	30	69	7	5	1	38	25	7	.330	.402	.426	112	7	3	2	-0	.918	-12	3-30,O-26	-0.7
1923	Pit-N	114	327	60	106	25	13	9	72	47	21	.324	.409	.563	151	24	5	7	-3	.985	3	O-92	1.8
1924	Pit-N	102	344	49	95	6	11	3	51	30	17	.276	.338	.384	91	-4	8	4	0	.970	2	O-88	-0.8
1925	*Pit-N	142	539	85	175	32	11	4	114	59	25	.325	.391	.447	106	6	9	5	-0	.962	1	*O-138	-0.2
1926	Pit-N	76	203	26	39	3	0	0	10	23	13	.192	.278	.207	30	-19	1			.991	6	O-61	-2.7
1927	*Pit-N	108	360	65	115	23	4	3	54	37	19	.319	.384	.431	110	6	2			.978	4	O-94	0.4
1928	Pit-N	61	196	18	58	6	2	4	30	11	9	.296	.333	.408	89	-3	3			.971	-2	O-48/3-1	-0.8
Total	9	814	2673	404	788	121	61	27	436	265	149	.295	.360	.416	100		35	21		.973	-27	O-547,3-161	-5.3

■ VIC BARNHART
Barnhart, Victor Dee   b: 9/1/22, Hagerstown, Md.   BR/TR, 6', 188 lbs.   Deb: 10/1/44   F

YEAR	TM/L	G	AB	R	H	2B	3B	HR	RBI	BB	SO	AVG	OBP	SLG	PRO+	BR/A	SB	CS	SBR	FA	FR	G/POS	TPR
1944	Pit-N	1	2	0	1	0	0	0	0	1	1	.500	.667	.500	222	0				.889	1	/S-1	0.2
1945	Pit-N	71	201	21	54	7	0	0	19	9	11	.269	.300	.303	65	-9	2			.928	8	S-60/3-4	-0.6
1946	Pit-N	2	1	0	0	0	0	0	0	0	0	.000	.000	.000	-98	-0	0			.000	0	H	0.0
Total	3	74	204	21	55	7	0	0	19	10	12	.270	.304	.304	67	-9	2			.927	9	/S-61,3-4	0.4

■ BILLY BARNIE
Barnie, William Harrison "Bald Billy"   b: 1/26/1853, New York, N.Y.   d: 7/15/1900, Hartford, Conn.   5'7", 157 lbs.   Deb: 5/7/1874   MU

YEAR	TM/L	G	AB	R	H	2B	3B	HR	RBI	BB	SO	AVG	OBP	SLG	PRO+	BR/A	SB	CS	SBR	FA	FR	G/POS	TPR
1874	Har-n	45	190	21	35	4	2	0	19	1	13	.184	.188	.226	31	-15	2	1	-1	.725	-6	C-29,O-29/S-1	-1.6
1875	Wes-n	10	36	3	4	1	0	0	2	0	3	.111	.111	.139	-13	-4	0	0	0	.889	-4	/O-7,C-3	-0.3
	Mut-n	9	34	1	5	0	0	0	1	1	0	.147	.171	.147	11	-3	0	0	0	.750	-4	/C-6,O-3	-0.6
	Yr	19	70	4	9	1	0	0	3	1	3	.129	.141	.143	-1	-7	0	0	0	.857	-3	O-10/C-9	-0.9
1883	Bal-a	17	55	7	11	2	0	0		0	2	.200	.228	.200	38	-4				.846	-2	C-13/O-6,S-1,M	-0.4
1886	Bal-a	2	6	0	0	0	0	0	0	1		.000	.143	.000	-55	-2	0			.000	-1	/O-1,C-1	-0.2
Total	2 n	64	260	25	44	5	2	0	22	2	16	.169	.176	.204	23	-22	2	2	-1	.690	-9	/O-39,C-38,S-1	-2.5
Total	2	19	61	7	11	2	0	0	0	3		.180	.219	.180	29	-5	0			.848	-3	/C-14,O-7,S-1	-0.6

■ DICK BARONE
Barone, Richard Anthony   b: 10/13/32, San Jose, Cal.   BR/TR, 5'9", 165 lbs.   Deb: 9/22/60

YEAR	TM/L	G	AB	R	H	2B	3B	HR	RBI	BB	SO	AVG	OBP	SLG	PRO+	BR/A	SB	CS	SBR	FA	FR	G/POS	TPR
1960	Pit-N	3	6	0	0	0	0	0	0	0	1	.000	.000	.000	-99	-2	0	0	0	.875	-0	/S-2	-0.2

■ SCOTTY BARR
Barr, Hyder Edward   b: 10/6/1886, Bristol, Tenn.   d: 12/2/34, Ft. Worth, Tex.   BR/TR, 6', 175 lbs.   Deb: 8/22/08

YEAR	TM/L	G	AB	R	H	2B	3B	HR	RBI	BB	SO	AVG	OBP	SLG	PRO+	BR/A	SB	CS	SBR	FA	FR	G/POS	TPR
1908	Phi-A	19	56	4	8	2	0	0	1	3		.143	.200	.179	22	-5	0			.923	-7	2-11/3-4,1-2,O-2	-1.4
1909	Phi-A	22	51	5	4	1	0	0	1	11		.078	.254	.098	12	-5	2			.947	-1	O-15/1-7	-0.7
Total	2	41	107	9	12	3	0	0	2	14		.112	.228	.140	17	-9	2			.947	-8	/O-17,2-11,1-9,3-4	-2.1

■ CUNO BARRAGAN
Barragan, Facundo Anthony   b: 6/20/32, Sacramento, Cal.   BR/TR, 5'11", 180 lbs.   Deb: 9/1/61

YEAR	TM/L	G	AB	R	H	2B	3B	HR	RBI	BB	SO	AVG	OBP	SLG	PRO+	BR/A	SB	CS	SBR	FA	FR	G/POS	TPR
1961	Chi-N	10	28	3	6	0	0	1	2	2	7	.214	.267	.321	54	-2	0	0	0	1.000	-1	C-10	-0.3
1962	Chi-N	58	134	11	27	6	1	0	12	21	28	.201	.310	.261	53	-8	0	2	-1	.971	-7	C-55	-1.5
1963	Chi-N	1	1	0	0	0	0	0	0	0	0	.000	.000	.000	-95	-0	0	0	0	1.000	-0	/C-1	0.0
Total	3	69	163	14	33	6	1	1	14	23	36	.202	.301	.270	53	-11	0	2	-1	.975	-8	/C-66	-1.8

■ GERMAN BARRANCA
Barranca, German (Costales)   b: 10/19/56, Veracruz, Mex.   BL/TR, 6', 160 lbs.   Deb: 9/2/79

YEAR	TM/L	G	AB	R	H	2B	3B	HR	RBI	BB	SO	AVG	OBP	SLG	PRO+	BR/A	SB	CS	SBR	FA	FR	G/POS	TPR
1979	KC-A	5	5	3	3	1	0	0	0	0	0	.600	.600	.800	269	1	3	1	0	1.000	3	/2-1,3-1,D-1	0.4
1980	KC-A	7	0	3	0	0	0	0	0	0	0	—	—	—	—	-0	0	0	0	.000	0	/R	0.0
1981	Cin-N	9	6	2	2	0	0	0	1	0	0	.333	.333	.333	88	-0	0	0	0	.000	0	/H	0.0
1982	Cin-N	46	51	11	13	1	3	0	2	5	9	.255	.283	.392	85	-1	2	0	0	.824	-1	/2-6	-0.2
Total	4	67	62	19	18	2	3	0	3	5	9	.290	.313	.419	101	-1	5	1	0	.893	2	/2-7,D-1,3-1	0.2

■ BARRETT
Barrett   b: Brooklyn, N.Y.   Deb: 9/18/1872

YEAR	TM/L	G	AB	R	H	2B	3B	HR	RBI	BB	SO	AVG	OBP	SLG	PRO+	BR/A	SB	CS	SBR	FA	FR	G/POS	TPR
1872	Atl-n	8	34	7	7	1	0	0	2	0	1	.206	.206	.235	30	-3	1	0	0	.808	-0	/O-8	-0.2

■ JIMMY BARRETT
Barrett, James Erigena   b: 3/28/1875, Athol, Mass.   d: 10/24/21, Detroit, Mich.   BL/TR, 5'9", 170 lbs.   Deb: 9/13/1899

YEAR	TM/L	G	AB	R	H	2B	3B	HR	RBI	BB	SO	AVG	OBP	SLG	PRO+	BR/A	SB	CS	SBR	FA	FR	G/POS	TPR
1899	Cin-N	26	92	30	34	2	4	0	10	18		.370	.477	.478	160	9	4			.936	-2	O-26	0.4
1900	Cin-N	137	545	114	172	11	7	5	42	72		.316	.400	.389	121	19	44			.929	4	*O-137	1.2
1901	Det-A	135	542	110	159	16	9	4	65	76		.293	.385	.378	107	8	26			.940	15	*O-135	1.1
1902	Det-A	136	509	93	154	19	6	4	44	74		.303	.397	.387	116	14	24			.961	6	*O-136	1.2
1903	Det-A	136	517	95	163	13	10	2	31	**74**		.315	**.407**	.391	144	32	27			.955	7	*O-136	3.2
1904	Det-A	162	624	83	167	10	5	0	31	**79**		.268	.353	.300	111	12	15			.971	12	*O-162	1.6
1905	Det-A	20	67	2	17	1	0	0	3	5		.254	.324	.269	88	-1	0			1.000	1	O-18	-0.5
1906	Cin-N	5	12	1	0	0	0	0	0	2		.000	.143	.000	-53	-2	0			1.000	0	/O-4	-0.3
1907	Bos-A	106	390	52	95	11	6	1	28	38		.244	.314	.310	100	1	3			.966	3	O-99	0.1
1908	Bos-A	3	8	0	1	0	0	0	1	1		.125	.222	.125	13	-1	0			1.000	-1	/O-2	-0.2
Total	10	866	3306	580	962	83	47	16	255	440		.291	.379	.359	117	91	143			.954	44	O-855	7.8

■ JOHNNY BARRETT
Barrett, John Joseph "Jack"   b: 12/18/15, Lowell, Mass.   d: 8/17/74, Seabrook Beach, N.H.   BL/TL, 5'10.5", 170 lbs.   Deb: 4/14/42

YEAR	TM/L	G	AB	R	H	2B	3B	HR	RBI	BB	SO	AVG	OBP	SLG	PRO+	BR/A	SB	CS	SBR	FA	FR	G/POS	TPR
1942	Pit-N	111	332	56	82	11	6	0	26	48	32	.247	.347	.316	92	-1	10			.973	6	O-94	0.0
1943	Pit-N	130	290	41	67	12	3	1	32	32	23	.231	.316	.303	77	-8	5			.988	-11	O-99	-2.5
1944	Pit-N	149	568	99	153	24	**19**	7	83	86	56	.269	.366	.415	115	13	**28**			.972	-1	*O-147	0.4
1945	Pit-N	142	507	97	130	29	4	15	67	79	68	.256	.357	.418	111	8	25			.976	-2	*O-132	-0.1
1946	Pit-N	32	71	7	12	3	0	0	6	8	11	.169	.253	.211	32	-6	1			.919	-3	O-21	-1.1
	Bos-N	24	43	3	10	3	0	0	6	12	1	.233	.400	.302	100	1	0			.962	-3	O-17	-0.3
	Yr	56	114	10	22	6	0	0	12	20	12	.193	.313	.246	59	-6	1			.937	-6	O-38	-1.4
Total	5	588	1811	303	454	82	32	23	220	265	201	.251	.349	.369	100		69			.954	-15	O-510	-3.6

■ MARTY BARRETT
Barrett, Martin F.   b: 11/1860, Port Henry, N.Y.   d: 1/29/10, Holyoke, Mass.   BR/TR, 5'9", 170 lbs.   Deb: 6/24/1884

YEAR	TM/L	G	AB	R	H	2B	3B	HR	RBI	BB	SO	AVG	OBP	SLG	PRO+	BR/A	SB	CS	SBR	FA	FR	G/POS	TPR
1884	Bos-N	3	6	0	0	0	0	0	0	0	4	.000	.000	.000	-99	-2				.900	-1	/C-3	-0.2
	Ind-a	5	13	1	1	1	0	0		0	1	.077	.143	.154	-3	-1				.808	-3	/C-4,O-1	-0.4
Total	1	8	19	1	1	1	0	0	0	1	4	.053	.100	.105	-3	-3				.833	-4	/C-7,O-1	-0.6

■ MARTY BARRETT
Barrett, Martin Glenn   b: 6/23/58, Arcadia, Cal.   BR/TR, 5'10", 176 lbs.   Deb: 9/6/82   F

YEAR	TM/L	G	AB	R	H	2B	3B	HR	RBI	BB	SO	AVG	OBP	SLG	PRO+	BR/A	SB	CS	SBR	FA	FR	G/POS	TPR
1982	Bos-A	8	18	0	1	0	0	0	0	0	1	.056	.056	.056	-66	-4	0	0	0	1.000	5	/2-7	0.1
1983	Bos-A	33	44	7	10	1	1	0	2	3	1	.227	.277	.295	54	-3	0	0	0	.984	4	2-23/D-5	0.2
1984	Bos-A	139	475	56	144	23	0	3	45	42	25	.303	.361	.383	101	-2	5	3	-0	**.987**	4	*2-136	0.6
1985	Bos-A	156	534	59	142	26	0	5	56	56	50	.266	.338	.343	84	-11	7	5	-1	.987	15	*2-155	0.5
1986	*Bos-A	158	625	94	179	39	4	4	60	65	31	.286	.355	.381	100	1	15	7	0	.982	-3	*2-158	0.5
1987	Bos-A	137	559	72	164	23	1	3	43	51	38	.293	.354	.351	85	-10	15	2	3	**.988**	**32**	*2-137	3.0
1988	*Bos-A	150	612	83	173	28	1	1	65	40	35	.283	.334	.337	85	-12	11	2	0	.990	2	*2-137	-0.3
1989	Bos-A	86	336	31	86	18	0	1	27	32	12	.256	.324	.318	77	-10	4	1	1	.975	2	2-80/D-4	-0.6

YEAR	TM/L	G	AB	R	H	2B	3B	HR	RBI	BB	SO	AVG	OBP	SLG	PRO+	BR/A	SB	CS	SBR	FA	FR	G/POS	TPR
1990	*Bos-A	62	159	15	36	4	0	0	13	15	13	.226	.297	.252	53	-10	4	0	1	.992	9	2-60/3-1,D-1	0.1
1991	SD-N	12	16	1	3	1	0	0	3	0	3	.188	.235	.438	83	-0	0	0	0	1.000	1	/2-2,3-2	0.0
Total	10	941	3378	418	938	163	9	18	314	304	209	.278	.340	.347	86	-57	57	21	5	.986	66	2-908/D-10,3-3	4.4

■ BOB BARRETT
Barrett, Robert Schley "Jumbo" b: 1/27/1899, Atlanta, Ga. d: 1/18/82, Atlanta, Ga. BR/TR, 5'11", 175 lbs. Deb: 4/30/23

YEAR	TM/L	G	AB	R	H	2B	3B	HR	RBI	BB	SO	AVG	OBP	SLG	PRO+	BR/A	SB	CS	SBR	FA	FR	G/POS	TPR
1923	Chi-N	3	3	0	1	0	0	0	0	0	0	.333	.333	.333	76	-0	0	0	0	.000	0	H	0.0
1924	Chi-N	54	133	12	32	2	3	5	21	7	29	.241	.279	.414	82	-4	1	0	0	.943	-1	2-25,1-10/3-8	-0.5
1925	Chi-N	14	32	1	10	1	0	0	7	1	4	.313	.333	.344	72	-1	1	2	-1	1.000	-3	/3-6,2-4	-0.5
	Bro-N	1	1	0	0	0	0	0	1	0	0	.000	.000	.000	-99	-0	0	0	0	.000	0	H	0.0
	Yr	15	33	1	10	1	0	0	8	1	4	.303	.324	.333	67	-1	1	2	-1	1.000	-3	/3-6,2-4	-0.5
1927	Bro-N	99	355	29	92	10	2	5	38	14	22	.259	.289	.341	68	-17	1			.920	-8	3-96	-2.0
1929	Bos-A	68	126	15	34	10	0	0	19	10	6	.270	.324	.349	75	-5	3	1	0	.938	6	3-34/1-4,2-2,0-1	0.2
Total	5	239	650	57	169	23	5	10	86	32	61	.260	.296	.357	72	-27	6	3		.924	-6	3-144/2-31,1-14,O-1	-2.8

■ TOM BARRETT
Barrett, Thomas Loren b: 4/2/60, San Fernando, Cal. BB/TR, 5'9", 157 lbs. Deb: 7/2/88 F

YEAR	TM/L	G	AB	R	H	2B	3B	HR	RBI	BB	SO	AVG	OBP	SLG	PRO+	BR/A	SB	CS	SBR	FA	FR	G/POS	TPR
1988	Phi-N	36	54	5	11	1	0	0	3	7	8	.204	.306	.222	53	-3	0	0	0	.959	2	2-10	-0.1
1989	Phi-N	14	27	3	6	0	0	0	1	1	7	.222	.250	.222	36	-3	0	0	0	.978	4	/2-9	0.2
1992	Bos-A	4	3	1	0	0	0	0	0	2	0	.000	.400	.000	19	-0	0	0	0	1.000	1	/2-2	0.0
Total	3	54	84	9	17	1	0	0	4	10	15	.202	.295	.214	47	-5	0	0	0	.970	7	/2-21	0.1

■ BILL BARRETT
Barrett, William b: Washington, D.C. Deb: 7/8/1871

YEAR	TM/L	G	AB	R	H	2B	3B	HR	RBI	BB	SO	AVG	OBP	SLG	PRO+	BR/A	SB	CS	SBR	FA	FR	G/POS	TPR
1871	Kek-n	1	5	1	1	1	0	0	1	0	0	.200	.200	.400	66	-0	0	0	0	1.000	1	/C-1,3-1	0.0
1872	Oly-n	1	4	0	0	0	0	0	0	0	0	.000	.000	.000	-99	-1	0	0	0	.400	-1	/C-1	-0.2
1873	Bal-n	1	4	0	1	0	0	0	0	0	0	.250	.250	.250	49	-0	0	1	-1	.667	-1	/S-1,O-1	-0.1
Total	3 n	3	13	1	2	1	0	0	1	0	0	.154	.154	.231	12	-1	0	1	-1	.769	-1	/C-2,O-1,S,1,3-1	-0.3

■ BILL BARRETT
Barrett, William Joseph "Whispering Bill" b: 5/28/1900, Cambridge, Mass. d: 1/26/51, Cambridge, Mass. BR/TR, 6', 175 lbs. Deb: 5/13/21

YEAR	TM/L	G	AB	R	H	2B	3B	HR	RBI	BB	SO	AVG	OBP	SLG	PRO+	BR/A	SB	CS	SBR	FA	FR	G/POS	TPR
1921	Phi-A	14	30	3	7	2	1	0	3	0	5	.233	.233	.367	51	-2	0	0	0	.925	2	/S-8,P-4,3-2,1-1	0.1
1923	Chi-A	44	162	17	44	7	2	2	23	9	24	.272	.310	.377	81	-5	12	3	2	.940	0	O-40/3-1	-0.5
1924	Chi-A	119	406	52	110	18	5	2	56	30	38	.271	.326	.355	78	-14	15	10	-2	.904	-15	S-77,O-28/3-8	-2.2
1925	Chi-A	81	245	44	89	23	3	3	40	24	27	.363	.420	.518	145	16	5	6	-2	.943	-7	2-41,O-27/S-4,3-4	0.7
1926	Chi-A	111	368	46	113	31	4	6	61	25	26	.307	.353	.462	115	6	9	7	-2	.969	-6	*O-102/1-2	-0.7
1927	Chi-A	147	556	62	159	35	9	4	83	52	46	.286	.347	.403	96	-4	20	13	-2	.963	7	*O-147	-0.8
1928	Chi-A	76	235	34	65	11	2	3	26	14	30	.277	.320	.379	84	-6	8	3	1	.988	-5	O-37,2-25	-1.1
1929	Chi-A	3	1	0	0	0	0	0	0	2	0	.000	.667	.000	87	0	0	0	0	.000	0	H	0.0
	Bos-A	111	370	57	100	23	4	3	35	51	38	.270	.363	.378	93	-3	11	8	-2	.974	4	*O-109/3-1	-0.7
	Yr	114	371	57	100	23	4	3	35	53	38	.270	.365	.377	94	-2	11	8	-2	.974	4	*O-109/3-1	-0.7
1930	Bos-A	6	18	3	3	1	0	0	1	1	3	.167	.211	.222	10	-2	0	0	0	1.000	-1	/O-5	-0.4
	Was-A	6	4	0	0	0	0	0	0	1	2	.000	.200	.000	-44	-1	0	0	0	1.000	-0	/O-1	-0.1
	Yr	12	22	3	3	1	0	0	1	2	5	.136	.208	.182	-0	-3	0	0	0	1.000	-1	/O-6	-0.5
Total	9	718	2395	318	690	151	30	23	328	209	239	.288	.347	.405	97	-14	80	50	-6	.964	-21	O-496/S-89,23P1	-5.7

■ JOSE BARRIOS
Barrios, Jose Manuel b: 6/26/57, New York, N.Y. BR/TR, 6'4", 195 lbs. Deb: 4/23/82

YEAR	TM/L	G	AB	R	H	2B	3B	HR	RBI	BB	SO	AVG	OBP	SLG	PRO+	BR/A	SB	CS	SBR	FA	FR	G/POS	TPR
1982	SF-N	10	19	2	3	0	0	0	0	1	4	.158	.200	.158	1	-2	0	0	0	1.000	-1	/1-7	-0.4

■ TONY BARRON
Barron, Anthony Dirk b: 8/17/66, Portland, Ore. BR/TR, 6', 185 lbs. Deb: 6/2/96

YEAR	TM/L	G	AB	R	H	2B	3B	HR	RBI	BB	SO	AVG	OBP	SLG	PRO+	BR/A	SB	CS	SBR	FA	FR	G/POS	TPR
1996	Mon-N	1	1	0	0	0	0	0	0	0	1	.000	.000	.000	-98	-0	0	0	0	.000	0	/H	0.0

■ RED BARRON
Barron, David Irenus b: 6/21/1900, Clarksville, Ga. d: 10/4/82, Atlanta, Ga. BR/TR, 5'11.5", 185 lbs. Deb: 6/10/29

YEAR	TM/L	G	AB	R	H	2B	3B	HR	RBI	BB	SO	AVG	OBP	SLG	PRO+	BR/A	SB	CS	SBR	FA	FR	G/POS	TPR
1929	Bos-N	10	21	3	4	1	0	0	0	1	1	.190	.227	.238	16	-3	2			.929	1	/O-6	-0.2

■ FRANK BARROWS
Barrows, Franklin L. b: 10/22/1846, Hudson, Ohio d: 2/6/22, Fitchburg, Mass. Deb: 5/20/1871

YEAR	TM/L	G	AB	R	H	2B	3B	HR	RBI	BB	SO	AVG	OBP	SLG	PRO+	BR/A	SB	CS	SBR	FA	FR	G/POS	TPR
1871	Bos-n	18	86	13	13	2	1	0	11	0	0	.151	.151	.198	-1	-11	1	0	0	.829	-2	O-17/2-1	-0.8

■ CUKE BARROWS
Barrows, Roland b: 10/20/1883, Gray, Maine d: 2/10/55, Gorham, Maine BL/TR, 5'8", 158 lbs. Deb: 9/18/09

YEAR	TM/L	G	AB	R	H	2B	3B	HR	RBI	BB	SO	AVG	OBP	SLG	PRO+	BR/A	SB	CS	SBR	FA	FR	G/POS	TPR
1909	Chi-A	5	20	1	3	0	0	0	0	0		.150	.190	.150	8	-2	0			.923	2	/O-5	-0.1
1910	Chi-A	6	20	0	4	0	0	0	1	3		.200	.304	.200	61	-1	0			.875	-1	/O-6	-0.3
1911	Chi-A	13	46	5	9	2	0	0	4	7		.196	.315	.239	57	-2	2			1.000	0	O-13	-0.5
1912	Chi-A	8	13	0	3	0	0	0	2	2		.231	.333	.231	64	-0	1			1.000	-0	/O-3	-0.1
Total	4	32	99	6	19	2	0	0	9	12		.192	.292	.212	50	-6	3			.950	2	/O-27	-1.0

■ JEFF BARRY
Barry, Jeffrey Finas b: 9/22/69, Medford, Ore. BB/TR, 6'1", 190 lbs. Deb: 6/9/95

YEAR	TM/L	G	AB	R	H	2B	3B	HR	RBI	BB	SO	AVG	OBP	SLG	PRO+	BR/A	SB	CS	SBR	FA	FR	G/POS	TPR
1995	NY-N	15	15	2	2	1	0	0	0	1	8	.133	.188	.200	2	-2	0	0	0	1.000	-0	/O-2	-0.2

■ SHAD BARRY
Barry, John C. b: 10/27/1878, Newburgh, N.Y. d: 11/27/36, Los Angeles, Cal. BR/TR, Deb: 5/30/1899

YEAR	TM/L	G	AB	R	H	2B	3B	HR	RBI	BB	SO	AVG	OBP	SLG	PRO+	BR/A	SB	CS	SBR	FA	FR	G/POS	TPR
1899	Was-N	78	247	31	71	7	5	1	33	12		.287	.328	.368	92	-3	11			.946	-16	O-23,1-22,S-13,3/2	-1.7
1900	Bos-N	81	254	40	66	10	7	1	37	13		.260	.301	.366	74	-10	9			.956	-16	O-24,S-18,2-16,1/3	-2.4
1901	Bos-N	11	40	3	7	2	0	0	6	2		.175	.233	.225	30	-4	1			.926	-0	O-11	-0.5
	Phi-N	67	252	35	62	10	0	1	22	15		.246	.294	.298	70	-10	13			.903	-13	2-35,3-16,O-13,/S-1	-2.1
	Yr	78	292	38	69	12	0	1	28	17		.236	.285	.288	64	-13	14			.903	-13	2-35,O-24,3-16,/S-1	-2.6
1902	Phi-N	138	543	65	156	20	6	3	58	44		.287	.343	.363	118	11	14			.939	-5	*O-137/1-1	-0.4
1903	Phi-N	138	550	75	152	24	5	1	60	30		.276	.321	.344	92	-6	26			.970	-2	*O-107,1-30/3-1	-1.5
1904	Phi-N	35	122	15	25	2	0	0	3	11		.205	.281	.221	58	-6	2			.979	13	O-32/3-1	0.6
	Chi-N	73	263	29	69	7	2	1	26	17		.262	.310	.316	93	-2	12			.917	-1	O-30,1-18,3-16,/S2	-0.5
	Yr	108	385	44	94	9	2	1	29	28		.244	.300	.286	82	-8	14			.955	12	O-62,1-18,3-17,/S2	0.1
1905	Chi-N	27	104	10	22	2	0	0	10	5		.212	.255	.231	43	-7	5			.982	1	1-26	-0.8
	Cin-N	125	494	90	160	11	12	3	56	33		.324	.372	.401	118	9	16			.982	-7	*1-124/O-2	-0.2
	Yr	152	598	100	182	13	12	1	66	38		.304	.352	.371	105	3	21			.982	-7	*1-150/O-2	-1.0
1906	Cin-N	73	279	38	80	10	5	1	33	26		.287	.354	.369	120	7	11			.993	1	1-43,O-30	0.5
	StL-N	62	237	26	59	9	0	0	12	15		.249	.299	.295	89	-3	6			.930	-7	O-35,1-21/3-6	-1.3
	Yr	135	516	64	139	19	6	1	45	41		.269	.329	.335	107	4	17			.922	-6	O-65,1-64/3-6	-0.8
1907	StL-N	81	294	30	73	5	2	0	19	28		.248	.320	.279	91	-2	4			.963	-6	O-81	-1.4
1908	StL-N	74	268	24	61	8	1	0	11	19		.228	.286	.265	80	-6	9			.967	-1	O-69/S-2	-1.1
	NY-N	37	67	5	10	1	1	0	5	9		.149	.260	.194	43	-4	1			.971	-6	O-31	-1.3
	Yr	111	335	29	71	9	2	0	16	28		.212	.281	.251	71	-10	10			.968	-7	*O-100/S-2	-2.4
Total	10	1100	4014	516	1073	128	47	10	391	279		.267	.321	.330	94	-37	140			.955	-65	O-625,1-295/23S	-14.1

■ JACK BARRY
Barry, John Joseph b: 4/26/1887, Meriden, Conn. d: 4/23/61, Shrewsbury, Mass. BR/TR, 5'9", 158 lbs. Deb: 7/13/08 M

YEAR	TM/L	G	AB	R	H	2B	3B	HR	RBI	BB	SO	AVG	OBP	SLG	PRO+	BR/A	SB	CS	SBR	FA	FR	G/POS	TPR
1908	Phi-A	40	135	13	30	4	3	0	8	10		.222	.291	.296	85	-2	5			.966	-11	2-20,S-14/3-3	-1.5
1909	Phi-A	124	409	56	88	11	2	1	23	44		.215	.307	.259	77	-9	17			.927	-31	*S-124	-4.4
1910	*Phi-A	145	487	64	126	19	5	3	60	52		.259	.336	.337	112	8	14			.916	-22	*S-145	-1.0
1911	*Phi-A	127	442	73	117	18	7	1	63	38		.265	.333	.344	90	-6	30			.944	-5	*S-127	-0.4
1912	Phi-A	140	483	75	126	19	9	0	55	47		.261	.335	.337	96	-3	22			.925	-1	*S-139	0.3
1913	*Phi-A	134	455	62	125	20	6	3	85	44	32	.275	.349	.365	111	7	15			.953	-8	*S-134	1.2
1914	*Phi-A	140	467	57	113	12	0	0	42	53	34	.242	.324	.268	81	-9	22	13	-1	.947	5	*S-140	0.6
1915	Phi-A	54	194	16	43	6	2	0	15	15	9	.222	.284	.273	69	-8	6	5	-1	.952	-4	S-54	-1.0
	*Bos-A	78	248	30	65	13	2	0	26	24	11	.262	.342	.331	104	2	0			.962	-4	2-78	-0.2
	Yr	132	442	46	108	19	4	0	41	39	20	.244	.317	.305	89	-6	6			.962	-9	2-78,S-54	-1.2
1916	Bos-A	94	330	28	67	6	1	0	20	17	24	.203	.277	.227	52	-19	8			.974	2	2-94	-1.6
1917	Bos-A	116	388	45	83	9	0	2	30	47	27	.214	.305	.253	71	-12	12			.974	-11	*2-116,M	-1.9
1919	Bos-A	31	108	13	26	5	1	0	2	5	5	.241	.293	.306	72	-4	0			.922	-7	2-31	-1.0
Total	11	1223	4146	532	1009	142	38	10	429	396	142	.243	.321	.303	88	-54	153	18		.935	-105	S-877,2-339/3-3	-10.9

YEAR	TM/L	G	AB	R	H	2B	3B	HR	RBI	BB	SO	AVG	OBP	SLG	PRO+	BR/A	SB	CS	SBR	FA	FR	G/POS	TPR

■ RICH BARRY   Barry, Richard Donovan   b: 9/12/40, Berkeley, Cal.   BR/TR, 6'4", 205 lbs.   Deb: 7/4/69

| 1969 | Phi-N | 20 | 32 | 4 | 6 | 1 | 0 | 0 | 5 | 6 | | .188 | .316 | .219 | 54 | -2 | 0 | 0 | 0 | .938 | -0 | /O-9 | -0.2 |

■ KIMERA BARTEE   Bartee, Kimera Anotchi   b: 7/21/72, Omaha, Neb.   BR/TR, 6', 175 lbs.   Deb: 4/3/96

| 1996 | Det-A | 110 | 217 | 32 | 55 | 6 | 1 | 1 | 14 | 17 | 77 | .253 | .308 | .304 | 56 | -14 | 20 | 10 | | .991 | -5 | O-99/D-2 | -2.0 |

■ DICK BARTELL   Bartell, Richard William "Rowdy Richard"   b: 11/22/07, Chicago, Ill.   d: 8/4/95, Almeda, Cal.   BR/TR, 5'9", 160 lbs.   Deb: 10/2/27   C

1927	Pit-N	1	2	0	0	0	0	0				.000	.500	.000	41	0	0			1.000	0	/S-1	0.0
1928	Pit-N	72	233	27	71	8	4	1	36	21	18	.305	.377	.386	96	-1	4			.974	2	2-39,S-27/3-1	0.5
1929	Pit-N	143	610	101	184	40	13	2	57	40	29	.302	.347	.420	87	-13	11			.953	4	S-74,2-70	0.3
1930	Pit-N	129	475	69	152	32	13	4	75	39	34	.320	.378	.467	102	2	8			.941	6	*S-126	1.9
1931	Phi-N	135	554	88	160	43	7	0	34	27	38	.289	.325	.392	85	-12	6			.948	3	*S-133/2-3	0.5
1932	Phi-N	154	614	118	189	48	7	1	53	64	47	.308	.379	.414	101	2	8			.963	10	*S-154	2.5
1933	Phi-N★	152	587	78	159	25	5	1	37	56	46	.271	.340	.336	83	-12	6			.951	9	*S-152	0.8
1934	Phi-N	146	604	102	187	30	4	0	37	64	59	.310	.384	.373	91	-6	13			.954	14	*S-146	1.6
1935	NY-N	137	539	60	141	28	4	14	53	37	52	.262	.316	.406	94	-5	5			.954	10	*S-137	1.2
1936	*NY-N	145	510	71	152	31	3	8	42	40	36	.298	.355	.418	109	6	6			.956	**45**	*S-144	**5.7**
1937	*NY-N★	128	516	91	158	38	2	14	62	40	38	.306	.367	.469	124	17	5			.958	**38**	*S-128	6.1
1938	NY-N	127	481	67	126	26	1	9	49	55	60	.262	.347	.376	98	-0	4			.952	22	*S-127	3.2
1939	Chi-N	105	336	37	80	24	2	3	34	42	25	.238	.335	.348	82	-8	6			.943	-5	*S-101/3-1	-0.4
1940	*Det-A	139	528	76	123	24	3	7	53	76	53	.233	.335	.330	67	-26	12	2	2	.953	12	*S-139	0.0
1941	Det-A	5	12	0	2	1	0	0	1	2	2	.167	.333	.250	51	-1	0	1	-1	.920	1	/S-5	0.0
	NY-N	104	373	44	113	20	0	5	35	52	29	.303	.394	.397	121	12	6			.959	-10	3-84,S-21	0.5
1942	NY-N	90	316	53	77	10	3	5	24	44	34	.244	.351	.342	102	2	4			.965	1	3-52,S-31	0.6
1943	NY-N	99	337	48	91	14	0	5	28	47	27	.270	.371	.356	110	6	5			.980	18	3-54,S-33	2.9
1946	NY-N	5	2	0	0	0	0	0	0	0	0	.000	.000	.000	-99	-1	0			1.000	1	/3-4,2-2	0.0
Total	18	2016	7629	1130	2165	442	71	79	710	748	627	.284	.355	.391	96	-36	109	3		.953	178	*S-1679,3-196,2-114	27.9

■ TONY BARTIROME   Bartirome, Anthony Joseph   b: 5/9/32, Pittsburgh, Pa.   BL/TL, 5'10", 155 lbs.   Deb: 4/19/52   C

| 1952 | Pit-N | 124 | 355 | 32 | 78 | 10 | 3 | 0 | 16 | 26 | 37 | .220 | .273 | .265 | 48 | -25 | 3 | 3 | -1 | .989 | 2 | *1-118 | -2.8 |

■ BOYD BARTLEY   Bartley, Boyd Owen   b: 2/11/20, Chicago, Ill.   BR/TR, 5'8.5", 165 lbs.   Deb: 5/30/43

| 1943 | Bro-N | 9 | 21 | 0 | 1 | 0 | 0 | 0 | 1 | 1 | 3 | .048 | .091 | .048 | -59 | -4 | 0 | | | .897 | 2 | /S-9 | -0.2 |

■ IRV BARTLING   Bartling, Henry Irving   b: 6/27/14, Bay City, Mich.   d: 6/12/73, Westland, Mich.   BR/TR, 6', 175 lbs.   Deb: 9/8/38

| 1938 | Phi-A | 14 | 46 | 5 | 8 | 1 | 0 | 0 | 5 | 3 | 7 | .174 | .224 | .239 | 17 | -6 | 0 | 0 | 0 | .914 | -3 | S-13/3-1 | -0.7 |

■ HARRY BARTON   Barton, Harry Lamb   b: 1/20/1875, Chester, Pa.   d: 1/25/55, Upland, Pa.   BR/TR, 5'6.5", 155 lbs.   Deb: 4/15/05

| 1905 | Phi-A | 29 | 60 | 5 | 10 | 2 | 1 | 0 | 3 | 3 | | .167 | .206 | .233 | 39 | -4 | 2 | | | .954 | -5 | C-13/1-2,3-2,O-1 | -1.0 |

■ BOB BARTON   Barton, Robert Wilbur   b: 7/30/41, Norwood, O.   BR/TR, 6', 175 lbs.   Deb: 9/17/65

1965	SF-N	4	7	1	4	0	0	0	1	0	0	.571	.571	.571	217	1	0	0	0	1.000	1	/C-2	0.2
1966	SF-N	43	91	1	16	2	1	0	3	5	5	.176	.219	.220	22	-9	0	0	0	.994	7	C-39	-0.1
1967	SF-N	7	19	0	4	0	0	0	1	0	2	.211	.250	.211	34	-2	0	0	0	1.000	1	/C-7	-0.1
1968	SF-N	46	92	4	24	2	0	0	5	7	18	.261	.313	.283	80	-2	0	0	0	.995	12	C-45	1.3
1969	SF-N	49	106	5	18	2	0	1	9	9	19	.170	.241	.189	22	-11	0	0	0	.985	1	C-49	-0.9
1970	SD-N	61	188	15	41	6	0	4	16	15	37	.218	.279	.314	61	-11	1	1	-0	.995	7	C-59	-0.1
1971	SD-N	121	376	23	94	17	2	5	23	35	49	.250	.317	.346	94	-3	0	5	-3	.981	14	*C-119	1.2
1972	SD-N	29	88	2	17	1	0	0	9	2	19	.193	.211	.205	20	-9	2	0	1	.989	1	C-29	-0.7
1973	Cin-N	3	1	0	0	0	0	0	0	0	0	.000	.500	.000	52	0	0	0	0	1.000	1	/C-2	0.1
1974	SD-N	30	81	4	19	1	0	0	7	13	19	.235	.340	.247	69	-3	0	0	0	.981	10	C-29	0.8
Total	10	393	1049	54	237	31	3	9	66	87	168	.226	.288	.287	65	-49	3	6	-3	.987	53	C-380	1.7

■ VINCE BARTON   Barton, Vincent David   b: 2/1/08, Edmonton, Alberta, Canada   d: 9/13/73, Toronto, Ont., Can   BL/TR, 6', 180 lbs.   Deb: 7/17/31

1931	Chi-N	66	239	45	57	10	1	13	50	21	40	.238	.323	.452	104	1	1			.964	-4	O-61	-0.7
1932	Chi-N	36	134	19	30	2	3	3	15	8	22	.224	.273	.351	67	-6	0			1.000	-2	O-34	-1.0
Total	2	102	373	64	87	12	4	16	65	29	62	.233	.306	.416	91	-6	1			.976	-6	/O-95	-1.7

■ DAVE BARTOSCH   Bartosch, David Robert   b: 3/24/17, St.Louis, Mo.   BR/TR, 6'1", 190 lbs.   Deb: 4/28/45

| 1945 | StL-N | 24 | 47 | 9 | 12 | 1 | 0 | 0 | 6 | 3 | | .255 | .340 | .277 | 71 | -2 | | | | .964 | 1 | O-11 | -0.2 |

■ MONTY BASGALL   Basgall, Romanus   b: 2/8/22, Pfeifer, Kan.   BR/TR, 5'10.5", 175 lbs.   Deb: 4/19/48   C

1948	Pit-N	38	51	12	11	1	0	2	6	3	5	.216	.259	.353	63	-3	0			1.000	6	2-22	0.3
1949	Pit-N	107	308	25	67	9	1	2	26	31	32	.218	.291	.273	51	-21	1			.972	-7	2-98/3-3	-2.4
1951	Pit-N	55	153	15	32	5	2	0	9	12	14	.209	.271	.268	44	-12	0	0	0	.969	11	2-55	0.1
Total	3	200	512	52	110	15	3	4	41	46	51	.215	.282	.279	50	-36	1	0		.973	9	2-175/3-3	-2.0

■ AL BASHANG   Bashang, Albert C.   b: 8/22/1888, Cincinnati, Ohio   d: 6/23/67, Cincinnati, Ohio   BB/TR, 5'8", 150 lbs.   Deb: 7/30/12

1912	Det-A	6	12	3	1	0	0	0	0	3		.083	.267	.083	2	-1	0			1.000	-1	/O-6	-0.3
1918	Bro-N	2	5	0	1	0	0	0	0	0	0	.200	.200	.200	22	-0	0			1.000	0	/O-1	-0.1
Total	2	8	17	3	2	0	0	0	0	3	0	.118	.250	.118	8	-2	0			1.000	-1	/O-7	-0.3

■ WALT BASHORE   Bashore, Walter Franklin (b: Walter Franklin Beshore)   b: 10/6/09, Harrisburg, Pa.   d: 9/26/84, Sebring, Fla.   BR/TR, 6', 170 lbs.   Deb: 7/14/36

| 1936 | Phi-N | 10 | 10 | 1 | 2 | 0 | 0 | 0 | 0 | 1 | 3 | .200 | .273 | .200 | 26 | -1 | 0 | | | 1.000 | -3 | /O-6,3-1 | -0.4 |

■ EDDIE BASINSKI   Basinski, Edwin Frank "Bazooka" or "Fiddler"   b: 11/4/22, Buffalo, N.Y.   BR/TR, 6'1", 172 lbs.   Deb: 5/20/44

1944	Bro-N	39	105	13	27	4	1	0	9	6	10	.257	.310	.314	77	-3	1			.960	-2	2-37/S-3	-0.3
1945	Bro-N	108	336	30	88	9	4	0	33	11	33	.262	.293	.313	69	-15	0			.926	-10	*S-101/2-6	-1.7
1947	Pit-N	56	161	15	32	6	2	4	17	18	27	.199	.279	.335	61	-9	0			.972	-1	2-56	-0.8
Total	3	203	602	58	147	19	7	4	59	35	70	.244	.292	.319	68	-27	1			.925	-13	S-104/2-99	-2.8

■ JOHN BASS   Bass, John E.   b: 1850, Baltimore, Md.   5'6", 150 lbs.   Deb: 5/4/1871

1871	Cle-n	22	89	18	27	1	**10**	3	18	3	4	.303	.326	.640	179	9	0	1	-1	.779	-6	*S-22/C-1	0.2
1872	Atl-n	2	7	0	1	1	0	0	1	0	0	.143	.143	.286	24	-1	0	0	0	.500	0	/O-2	-0.1
1877	Har-N	1	4	1	1	0	0	0	0	0	0	.250	.250	.250	65	-0				.000	0	/O-1	-0.1
Total	2 n	24	96	18	28	2	10	3	19	3	4	.292	.313	.615	166	8	0	1	-1	.779	-7	/S-22,O-2,C-1	0.1

■ KEVIN BASS   Bass, Kevin Charles   b: 5/12/59, Redwood City, Cal.   BB/TR, 6', 183 lbs.   Deb: 4/9/82

1982	Mil-A	18	9	4	0	0	0	0	0	0	1	.000	.100	.000	-74	-2	0	0	0	1.000	-5	O-14/D-2	-0.8
	Hou-N	12	24	2	1	0	0	0	1	0	8	.042	.042	.042	-83	-6	0	0	0	.917	-1	/O-7	-0.8
1983	Hou-N	88	195	25	46	7	3	2	18	6	27	.236	.259	.333	67	-10	2	2	0	.945	-6	O-52	-1.9
1984	Hou-N	121	331	33	86	17	5	2	29	6	57	.260	.279	.360	84	-9	5	5	-2	.975	-2	O-81	-1.5
1985	Hou-N	150	539	72	145	27	5	16	68	31	63	.269	.316	.427	109	4	19	8	1	**.997**	6	*O-141	0.8
1986	*Hou-N★	157	591	83	184	33	5	20	79	38	72	.311	.359	.486	134	26	22	13	-1	.984	5	*O-155	2.4
1987	Hou-N	157	592	83	168	31	5	19	85	53	77	.284	.347	.449	113	10	21	8	2	.987	10	*O-155	1.6
1988	Hou-N	157	541	57	138	27	2	14	72	42	65	.255	.316	.390	106	3	31	6	6	.979	2	*O-147	0.7
1989	Hou-N	87	313	42	94	19	4	5	44	29	44	.300	.362	.435	131	12	11	4	1	.985	9	O-84	2.1
1990	SF-N	61	214	25	54	7	1	7	32	14	26	.252	.304	.402	96	-2	2	4	-1	.968	-3	O-55	-0.9
1991	SF-N	124	361	43	84	10	4	10	40	36	56	.233	.309	.366	92	-4	7	4	-0	.977	-1	*O-101	-0.8
1992	SF-N	89	265	25	71	11	3	7	30	16	53	.268	.312	.411	108	1	7	7	-2	.983	-5	O-72	-0.7
	NY-N	46	137	15	37	12	2	2	9	7	17	.270	.306	.431	108	1	7	2	1	.987	-1	O-39	0.2
	Yr	135	402	40	108	23	5	9	39	23	70	.269	.310	.418	109	3	14	9	-1	.985	-5	*O-111	-0.5

YEAR	TM/L	G	AB	R	H	2B	3B	HR	RBI	BB	SO	AVG	OBP	SLG	PRO+	BR/A	SB	CS	SBR	FA	FR	G/POS	TPR
1993	Hou-N	111	229	31	65	18	0	3	37	26	31	.284	.359	.402	107	3	7	1	2	.989	-7	O-64	-0.3
1994	Hou-N	82	203	37	63	15	1	6	35	28	24	.310	.397	.483	135	11	2	3	-1	.977	-4	O-57	0.5
1995	Bal-A	111	295	32	72	12	0	5	32	24	47	.244	.305	.336	66	-15	8	8	-2	.984	-5	O-77,D-19	-2.4
Total	14	1571	4839	609	1308	248	40	118	611	357	668	.270	.325	.411	106	25	151	73	2	.982	-10	*O-1301/D-21	-1.8

■ RANDY BASS
Bass, Randy William b: 3/13/54, Lawton, Okla. BL/TR, 6'1", 210 lbs. Deb: 9/3/77

YEAR	TM/L	G	AB	R	H	2B	3B	HR	RBI	BB	SO	AVG	OBP	SLG	PRO+	BR/A	SB	CS	SBR	FA	FR	G/POS	TPR
1977	Min-A	9	19	0	2	0	0	0	0	0	5	.105	.105	.105	-43	-4	0	0	0	.000	0	/D-6	-0.4
1978	KC-A	2	2	0	0	0	0	0	0	0	0	.000	.000	.000	-97	-1	0	0	0	.000	0	H	-0.1
1979	Mon-N	2	1	0	0	0	0	0	0	0	0	.000	.000	.000	-99	-0	0	0	0	1.000	-0	/1-1	0.0
1980	SD-N	19	49	5	14	0	1	3	8	7	7	.286	.386	.510	157	4	0	0	0	.985	-1	1-15	0.2
1981	SD-N	69	176	13	37	4	1	4	20	20	20	.210	.294	.313	78	-5	0	1	-1	.993	2	1-50	-0.7
1982	SD-N	13	30	1	6	0	0	1	8	2	4	.200	.273	.300	63	-2	0	0	0	1.000	-1	/1-9	-0.3
	Tex-A	16	48	5	10	2	0	1	6	1	7	.208	.240	.313	53	-2	0	0	-1	1.000	-0	/1-6,D-7	-0.4
Total	6	130	325	24	69	6	2	9	42	30	51	.212	.287	.326	76	-11	0	1	-1	.993	-0	/1-81,D-13	-1.7

■ DOC BASS
Bass, William Capers (also played one game in 1918 under name of Johnson)
b: 12/4/1899, Macon, Ga. d: 1/12/70, Macon, Ga. BL/TL, 5'10", 165 lbs. Deb: 7/29/18

YEAR	TM/L	G	AB	R	H	2B	3B	HR	RBI	BB	SO	AVG	OBP	SLG	PRO+	BR/A	SB	CS	SBR	FA	FR	G/POS	TPR
1918	Bos-N	2	1	1	1	0	0	0	0	0	0	1.000	1.000	1.000	533	0		1		.000	0	/H	0.1

■ CHARLEY BASSETT
Bassett, Charles Edwin b: 2/9/1863, Central Falls, R.I. d: 5/28/42, Pawtucket, R.I. BR/TR, 5'10", 150 lbs. Deb: 7/22/1884

YEAR	TM/L	G	AB	R	H	2B	3B	HR	RBI	BB	SO	AVG	OBP	SLG	PRO+	BR/A	SB	CS	SBR	FA	FR	G/POS	TPR
1884	Pro-N	27	79	10	11	2	1	0	6	4	15	.139	.181	.190	17	-7				.815	0	3-13/S-7,O-2,2-1	-0.6
1885	Pro-N	82	285	21	41	8	2	0	16	19	60	.144	.197	.186	26	-22				.900	5	2-39,S-23,3-20,/C-1	-1.4
1886	KC-N	90	342	41	89	19	8	2	32	36	43	.260	.331	.380	109	3	6			.886	8	S-82/3-8	1.0
1887	Ind-N	119	452	41	104	14	6	1	47	25	31	.230	.278	.294	61	-23	25			.931	16	*2-119	-0.3
1888	Ind-N	128	481	58	116	20	3	2	60	32	41	.241	.297	.308	91	-4	24			.922	-16	*2-128	-1.5
1889	Ind-N	127	477	64	117	12	5	4	68	37	38	.245	.304	.317	72	-19	15			.937	11	*2-127	-0.1
1890	NY-N	100	410	52	98	13	8	0	54	29	25	.239	.300	.310	78	-12	14			.952	12	*2-100	0.5
1891	NY-N	130	524	60	136	19	8	4	68	36	29	.260	.312	.349	96	-3	16			.908	8	*3-121/2-9	1.0
1892	NY-N	35	130	9	27	2	3	0	16	6	11	.208	.254	.269	59	-7	0			.938	9	2-30/3-5	0.3
	Lou-N	79	313	36	67	5	5	2	35	15	19	.214	.250	.281	66	-14	16			.861	-0	3-73/2-6	-1.1
	Yr	114	443	45	94	7	8	2	51	21	30	.212	.251	.278	64	-20	16			.858	9	3-78,2-36	-0.8
Total	9	917	3493	392	806	114	49	15	402	239	312	.231	.285	.304	76	-108	116			.932	53	2-559,3-240,S/OC	-2.2

■ JOHNNY BASSLER
Bassler, John Landis b: 6/3/1895, Mechanics Grove, Pa. d: 6/29/79, Santa Monica, Cal BL/TR, 5'9", 170 lbs. Deb: 7/11/13 C

YEAR	TM/L	G	AB	R	H	2B	3B	HR	RBI	BB	SO	AVG	OBP	SLG	PRO+	BR/A	SB	CS	SBR	FA	FR	G/POS	TPR
1913	Cle-A	1	2	0	0	0	0	0	0	0	0	.000	.000	.000	-97	-0	0			.500	-1	/C-1	-0.2
1914	Cle-A	43	77	5	14	1	1	0	6	15	11	.182	.323	.221	61	-3	3	2	-0	.946	-1	C-25/3-1,O-1	-0.2
1921	Det-A	119	388	37	119	18	5	0	56	58	16	.307	.401	.379	101	3	2	1	0	.975	-1	*C-114	1.1
1922	Det-A	121	372	41	120	14	0	0	41	62	12	.323	.422	.360	109	9	2	1	0	.980	-3	*C-118	1.2
1923	Det-A	135	383	45	114	12	3	0	49	76	13	.298	.414	.345	103	6	2	4	0	.988	12	*C-128	2.3
1924	Det-A	124	379	43	131	20	3	1	68	62	11	.346	.441	.422	125	18	2	1	0	.979	-4	*C-122	2.1
1925	Det-A	121	344	40	96	19	3	0	52	74	6	.279	.408	.352	96	2	1	1	-0	.983	-8	*C-118	0.0
1926	Det-A	66	174	20	53	8	1	0	22	45	6	.305	.447	.362	111	6	0	0	0	1.000	6	C-63	1.2
1927	Det-A	81	200	19	57	7	0	0	24	45	9	.285	.416	.320	92	0	1	0	0	.974	-2	C-67	0.3
Total	9	811	2319	250	704	99	16	1	318	437	81	.304	.416	.361	104	42	13	8		.980	-1	C-756/O-1,3-1	7.8

■ CHARLIE BASTIAN
Bastian, Charles J. b: 7/4/1860, Philadelphia, Pa. d: 1/18/32, Pennsauken, N.J. BR/TR, 5'6.5", 145 lbs. Deb: 8/18/1884

YEAR	TM/L	G	AB	R	H	2B	3B	HR	RBI	BB	SO	AVG	OBP	SLG	PRO+	BR/A	SB	CS	SBR	FA	FR	G/POS	TPR
1884	Wil-U	17	60	6	12	1	3	2		6	3	.200	.238	.417	92	-3				.907	10	2-16/P-1,S-1	0.7
	KC-U	11	46	6	9	3	0	1		4		.196	.260	.326	88	-2				.950	-1	2-11	-0.2
	Yr	28	106	12	21	4	3	3		7		.198	.248	.377	90	-5				.923	10	2-27/P-1,S-1	0.5
1885	Phi-N	103	389	63	65	11	5	4	29	35	82	.167	.236	.252	59	-17				.890	6	S-103	-0.8
1886	Phi-N	105	373	46	81	9	11	3	38	33	73	.217	.281	.316	81	-9	29			.945	-5	*2-87,S-10/3-8	-0.9
1887	Phi-N	60	221	33	47	11	1	1	21	19	29	.213	.284	.285	55	-14	11			.921	-13	2-39,S-18/3-4	-2.2
1888	Phi-N	80	275	30	53	4	1	1	17	27	41	.193	.282	.225	60	-12	12			.945	12	2-65,S-14/3-1	-0.9
1889	Chi-N	46	155	19	21	0	0	0	10	25	46	.135	.256	.135	10	-18	1			.919	6	S-45/2-1	-0.9
1890	Chi-P	80	283	38	54	10	5	0	29	33	37	.191	.287	.261	45	-23	4			.880	-10	S-64,2-12/3-4	-2.3
1891	Cin-a	1	4	0	0	0	0	0	0	0	0	.000	.000	.000	-92	-1	0			1.000	1	/2-1	0.0
	Phi-N	1	0	0	0	0	0	0	0	0	0	—	—	—			0			1.000	0	/S-1	0.0
Total	8	504	1806	241	342	49	26	11	144	179	308	.189	.268	.264	57	-97	57			.892	7	S-243,2-232/3-30,P	-6.3

■ EMIL BATCH
Batch, Emil "Heinie" or "Ace" b: 1/21/1880, Brooklyn, N.Y. d: 8/23/26, Brooklyn, N.Y. BR/TR, 5'7", 170 lbs. Deb: 9/13/04

YEAR	TM/L	G	AB	R	H	2B	3B	HR	RBI	BB	SO	AVG	OBP	SLG	PRO+	BR/A	SB	CS	SBR	FA	FR	G/POS	TPR
1904	Bro-N	28	94	9	24	1	2	2	7	1	6	.255	.271	.372	100	-1	6			.880	-2	3-28	-0.1
1905	Bro-N	145	568	64	143	20	11	5	49	26		.252	.285	.352	96	-5	21			.887	-8	*3-145	-0.9
1906	Bro-N	59	203	23	52	7	6	0	11	15		.256	.311	.350	115	3	3			.964	1	O-50/3-2	0.1
1907	Bro-N	116	388	38	96	10	3	0	31	23		.247	.291	.289	89	-6	7			.937	-3	*O-102/3-2,2-1,S-1	-1.4
Total	4	348	1253	134	315	38	22	7	98	65		.251	.290	.334	98	-9	37			.886	-12	3-177,O-152/S-1,2-1	-2.3

■ JOHN BATEMAN
Bateman, John Alvin b: 7/21/42, Killeen, Tex. BR/TR, 6'3", 220 lbs. Deb: 4/19/63

YEAR	TM/L	G	AB	R	H	2B	3B	HR	RBI	BB	SO	AVG	OBP	SLG	PRO+	BR/A	SB	CS	SBR	FA	FR	G/POS	TPR
1963	Hou-N	128	404	23	85	8	6	10	59	13	103	.210	.251	.334	71	-16	0	0		.971	2	*C-115	-1.1
1964	Hou-N	74	221	18	42	8	0	5	19	17	48	.190	.251	.294	56	-13	0	1	-1	.987	6	C-72	-0.5
1965	Hou-N	45	142	15	28	3	1	7	14	12	37	.197	.260	.380	83	-4	0	1	-1	.985	0	C-39	-0.2
1966	Hou-N	131	433	39	121	24	3	17	70	20	74	.279	.319	.467	123	12	0	0	0	.981	-0	*C-121	2.1
1967	Hou-N	76	252	16	48	9	0	4	17	17	53	.190	.247	.250	44	-18	0	0		.989	1	C-71	-1.4
1968	Hou-N	111	350	28	87	19	0	4	33	23	46	.249	.301	.337	93	-3	1	1	-0	.985	-0	*C-108	0.1
1969	Mon-N	74	235	16	49	4	0	8	19	12	44	.209	.250	.328	60	-13	0	2	-1	.985	-0	C-66	-1.2
1970	Mon-N	139	520	51	123	21	5	15	68	28	94	.237	.277	.383	75	-20	8	4	0	.983	-1	*C-137	-1.5
1971	Mon-N	139	492	34	119	17	3	10	56	19	87	.242	.276	.350	76	-17	1	0	0	.985	-9	*C-137	-2.2
1972	Mon-N	18	29	0	7	1	0	0	3	4	4	.241	.313	.276	67	-1	0	0	0	1.000	-2	/C-7	-0.3
	Phi-N	82	252	10	56	9	0	3	17	9	39	.222	.249	.294	54	-16	0	1	-1	.972	1	C-80	-1.4
	Yr	100	281	10	63	10	0	3	20	11	43	.224	.256	.292	54	-17	0	1	-1	.973	-1	C-87	-1.7
Total	10	1017	3330	250	765	123	18	81	375	172	610	.230	.273	.350	77	-111	10	10	-3	.982	-2	C-953	-7.6

■ CHARLIE BATES
Bates, Charles William b: 9/17/07, Philadelphia, Pa. d: 1/29/80, Topeka, Kan. BR/TR, 5'10", 165 lbs. Deb: 9/22/27

YEAR	TM/L	G	AB	R	H	2B	3B	HR	RBI	BB	SO	AVG	OBP	SLG	PRO+	BR/A	SB	CS	SBR	FA	FR	G/POS	TPR
1927	Phi-A	9	38	5	9	2	2	0	2	3	5	.237	.293	.395	73	-2	3	1	0	.857	-0	/O-9	-0.2

■ DEL BATES
Bates, Delbert Oakley b: 6/12/40, Seattle, Wash. BL/TR, 6'2", 195 lbs. Deb: 5/6/70

YEAR	TM/L	G	AB	R	H	2B	3B	HR	RBI	BB	SO	AVG	OBP	SLG	PRO+	BR/A	SB	CS	SBR	FA	FR	G/POS	TPR
1970	Phi-N	22	60	1	8	2	0	1	6	6	15	.133	.257	.167	16	-7	0	1	-1	.992	-4	C-20	-1.1

■ BUD BATES
Bates, Hubert Edgar b: 3/16/12, Los Angeles, Cal. d: 4/29/87, Long Beach, Cal. BR/TR, 6', 165 lbs. Deb: 9/16/39

YEAR	TM/L	G	AB	R	H	2B	3B	HR	RBI	BB	SO	AVG	OBP	SLG	PRO+	BR/A	SB	CS	SBR	FA	FR	G/POS	TPR
1939	Phi-N	15	58	8	15	2	0	1	2	2	8	.259	.283	.345	70	-3	1			.978	3	O-14	-0.1

■ JASON BATES
Bates, Jason Charles b: 1/5/71, Downey, Cal. BB/TR, 5'11", 170 lbs. Deb: 4/26/95

YEAR	TM/L	G	AB	R	H	2B	3B	HR	RBI	BB	SO	AVG	OBP	SLG	PRO+	BR/A	SB	CS	SBR	FA	FR	G/POS	TPR
1995	*Col-N	116	322	42	86	17	4	8	46	42	70	.267	.355	.419	80	-11	3	6	-3	.991	10	2-82,S-20,3-15	0.1
1996	Col-N	88	160	19	33	8	1	1	9	23	34	.206	.314	.287	47	-13	2	1	0	.978	0	2-37,S-18,3-12	-1.1
Total	2	204	482	61	119	25	5	9	55	65	104	.247	.341	.376	69	-24	5	7	-3	.987	10	2-119/S-38,3-27	-1.0

■ JOHNNY BATES
Bates, John William b: 8/21/1882, Steubenville, Ohio d: 2/10/49, Steubenville, Ohio BL/TL, 5'7", 168 lbs. Deb: 4/12/06

YEAR	TM/L	G	AB	R	H	2B	3B	HR	RBI	BB	SO	AVG	OBP	SLG	PRO+	BR/A	SB	CS	SBR	FA	FR	G/POS	TPR
1906	Bos-N	140	504	52	127	21	5	6	54	36		.252	.315	.349	110	5	9			.958	-10	*O-140	-1.3
1907	Bos-N	126	447	52	116	18	12	2	49	39		.260	.329	.367	118	9	11			.979	-2	*O-120	-0.6
1908	Bos-N	127	445	48	115	14	6	1	29	35		.258	.315	.324	106	3	25			.948	-4	*O-117	-0.6
1909	Bos-N	63	236	27	68	15	3	1	23	20		.288	.354	.390	125	7	15			.945	5	O-60	1.0
	Phi-N	77	266	43	78	11	1	1	15	28		.293	.363	.353	122	7	22			.959	-2	*O-73	0.3
	Yr	140	502	70	146	26	4	2	38	48		.291	.360	.371	123	14	37			.952	3	*O-133	1.3

YEAR	TM/L	G	AB	R	H	2B	3B	HR	RBI	BB	SO	AVG	OBP	SLG	PRO+	BR/A	SB	CS	SBR	FA	FR	G/POS	TPR
1910	Phi-N	135	498	91	152	26	11	3	61	61	49	.305	.385	.420	130	20	31			.954	12	*O-131	2.6
1911	Cin-N	148	518	89	151	24	13	1	61	103	59	.292	.415	.394	131	28	33			.966	5	*O-147	2.5
1912	Cin-N	81	239	45	69	12	7	1	29	47	16	.289	.406	.410	127	11	10			.950	7	O-65	1.4
1913	Cin-N	131	407	63	113	13	7	6	51	67	30	.278	.387	.388	122	15	21			.946	4	*O-111	1.4
1914	Cin-N	58	155	29	39	7	5	2	15	28	17	.252	.380	.400	128	6	4			.913	-6	O-54	-0.2
	Chi-N	9	8	2	1	0	0	0	1	1	1	.125	.300	.125	28	-1	0			1.000	-0	/O-3	-0.1
	Yr	67	163	31	40	7	5	2	16	29	18	.245	.376	.387	124	6	4			.917	-6	O-57	-0.3
	Bal-F	59	190	24	58	6	3	1	29	38	18	.305	.429	.384	119	5	6			.950	-0	O-59	0.1
Total	9	1154	3913	565	1087	167	73	25	417	503	<u>190</u>	.278	.367	.377	121	114	187			.955	9	*O-1080	7.3

■ RAY BATES
Bates, Raymond   b: 2/8/1890, Paterson, N.J.   d: 8/15/70, Tucson, Ariz.   BR/TR, 6', 165 lbs.   Deb: 5/31/13

YEAR	TM/L	G	AB	R	H	2B	3B	HR	RBI	BB	SO	AVG	OBP	SLG	PRO+	BR/A	SB	CS	SBR	FA	FR	G/POS	TPR
1913	Cle-A	27	30	4	5	1	0	0	4	3	9	.167	.265	.300	63	-1	3			.905	-0	3-12/O-2	-0.2
1917	Phi-A	127	485	47	115	20	7	2	66	21	39	.237	.277	.320	83	-12	12			.933	6	*3-124	-0.4
Total	2	154	515	51	120	20	9	2	70	24	48	.233	.277	.318	82	-13	15			.932	6	3-136/O-2	-0.6

■ BILLY BATES
Bates, William Derrick   b: 12/7/63, Houston, Tex.   BL/TR, 5'7", 155 lbs.   Deb: 8/17/89

YEAR	TM/L	G	AB	R	H	2B	3B	HR	RBI	BB	SO	AVG	OBP	SLG	PRO+	BR/A	SB	CS	SBR	FA	FR	G/POS	TPR
1989	Mil-A	7	14	3	3	0	0	0	0	0	1	.214	.214	.214	21	-1	2	0	1	.938	4	/2-7	0.3
1990	Mil-A	14	29	6	3	1	0	0	2	4	7	.103	.212	.138	-0	-4	4	0	1	.962	3	2-14	0.0
	*Cin-N	8	5	2	0	0	0	0	0	0	2	.000	.000	.000	-96	-1	2	1	0	1.000	0	/2-1	-0.1
Total	2	29	48	11	6	1	0	0	2	4	10	.125	.192	.146	-4	-7	8	1	2	.953	7	/2-22	0.2

■ BILL BATHE
Bathe, William David   b: 10/14/60, Downey, Cal.   BR/TR, 6'2", 200 lbs.   Deb: 4/12/86

YEAR	TM/L	G	AB	R	H	2B	3B	HR	RBI	BB	SO	AVG	OBP	SLG	PRO+	BR/A	SB	CS	SBR	FA	FR	G/POS	TPR
1986	Oak-A	39	103	9	19	3	0	5	11	2	20	.184	.208	.359	55	-7	0	0	0	.991	1	C-39	-0.4
1989	*SF-N	30	32	3	9	1	0	0	6	0	7	.281	.281	.313	72	-1	0	0	0	1.000	-1	/C-7	-0.2
1990	SF-N	52	48	3	11	0	1	3	12	7	12	.229	.327	.458	118	1	0	0	0	1.000	-1	/C-8	0.0
Total	3	121	183	15	39	4	1	8	29	9	39	.213	.254	.377	75	-7	0	0	0	.992	-1	/C-54	-0.6

■ TONY BATISTA
Batista, Leocadio Francisco   b: 12/9/73, Puerto Plata, D.R.   BR/TR, 6', 180 lbs.   Deb: 6/3/96

YEAR	TM/L	G	AB	R	H	2B	3B	HR	RBI	BB	SO	AVG	OBP	SLG	PRO+	BR/A	SB	CS	SBR	FA	FR	G/POS	TPR
1996	Oak-A	74	238	38	71	10	2	6	25	19	49	.298	.353	.433	101	0	7	3	0	.988	10	2-52,3-18/S-4,D-4	1.2

■ RAFAEL BATISTA
Batista, Rafael (Sanchez)   b: 10/20/47, San Pedro De Macoris, D.R.   BL/TL, 6'1", 195 lbs.   Deb: 6/17/73

YEAR	TM/L	G	AB	R	H	2B	3B	HR	RBI	BB	SO	AVG	OBP	SLG	PRO+	BR/A	SB	CS	SBR	FA	FR	G/POS	TPR
1973	Hou-N	12	15	2	4	0	0	0	2	1	6	.267	.313	.267	62	-1	0	0	0	1.000	-0	/1-8	-0.1
1975	Hou-N	10	10	0	3	1	0	0	0	0	4	.300	.300	.400	100	-0	0	0	0	.000	0	H	0.0
Total	2	22	25	2	7	1	0	0	2	1	10	.280	.308	.320	76	-1	0	0	0	1.000	0	/1-8	-0.1

■ KEVIN BATISTE
Batiste, Kevin Wade   b: 10/21/66, Galveston, Tex.   BR/TR, 6'2", 175 lbs.   Deb: 6/13/89

YEAR	TM/L	G	AB	R	H	2B	3B	HR	RBI	BB	SO	AVG	OBP	SLG	PRO+	BR/A	SB	CS	SBR	FA	FR	G/POS	TPR
1989	Tor-A	6	8	1	2	0	0	0	0	0	5	.250	.250	.250	42	-1	0	0	0	1.000	-1	/O-5	-0.1

■ KIM BATISTE
Batiste, Kimothy Emil   b: 3/15/68, New Orleans, La.   BR/TR, 6', 175 lbs.   Deb: 9/8/91

YEAR	TM/L	G	AB	R	H	2B	3B	HR	RBI	BB	SO	AVG	OBP	SLG	PRO+	BR/A	SB	CS	SBR	FA	FR	G/POS	TPR
1991	Phi-N	10	27	2	6	0	0	1	1	8	.222	.222	.222	34	-2	0	1	-1	.970	1	/S-7	-0.1
1992	Phi-N	44	136	9	28	4	1	1	10	4	18	.206	.229	.257	37	-11	0	0	0	.922	-8	S-41	-1.9
1993	*Phi-N	79	156	14	44	7	1	5	29	3	29	.282	.300	.436	95	-2	0	1	0	.956	13	3-58,S-24	1.2
1994	Phi-N	64	209	17	49	6	1	1	13	1	32	.234	.242	.278	34	-20	1	1	-0	.919	2	3-42,S-17	-1.7
1996	SF-N	54	130	17	27	6	0	3	11	5	33	.208	.237	.323	48	-10	3	3	-1	.847	13	3-25/S-7	-1.4
Total	5	251	658	59	154	23	1	10	64	14	120	.234	.252	.318	52	-45	4	6	-2	.908	5	3-125/S-96	-3.9

■ BILL BATSCH
Batsch, William McKinley   b: 5/18/1892, Mingo Junction, O.   d: 12/31/63, Canton, Ohio   BR/TR, 5'10.5", 168 lbs.   Deb: 9/9/16

YEAR	TM/L	G	AB	R	H	2B	3B	HR	RBI	BB	SO	AVG	OBP	SLG	PRO+	BR/A	SB	CS	SBR	FA	FR	G/POS	TPR
1916	Pit-N	1	0	0	0	0	0	0	0	1	0	—	1.000	—	218	0	0			.000	0	H	0.0

■ LARRY BATTAM
Battam, Lawrence J.   b: 5/1/1878, Brooklyn, N.Y.   d: 1/27/38, Brooklyn, N.Y.   5'11",   Deb: 9/28/1895

YEAR	TM/L	G	AB	R	H	2B	3B	HR	RBI	BB	SO	AVG	OBP	SLG	PRO+	BR/A	SB	CS	SBR	FA	FR	G/POS	TPR
1895	NY-N	2	4	0	1	0	0	0	0	2	1	.250	.500	.250	99	0	0			.667	-1	/3-2	0.0

■ GEORGE BATTEN
Batten, George Burnett   b: 10/7/1891, Haddonfield, N.J.   d: 8/4/72, New Port Richey, Fla.   BR/TR, 5'11", 165 lbs.   Deb: 9/28/12

YEAR	TM/L	G	AB	R	H	2B	3B	HR	RBI	BB	SO	AVG	OBP	SLG	PRO+	BR/A	SB	CS	SBR	FA	FR	G/POS	TPR
1912	NY-A	1	3	0	0	0	0	0	0	0	0	.000	.000	.000	-94	-1	0			1.000	-1	/2-1	-0.1

■ EARL BATTEY
Battey, Earl Jesse   b: 1/5/35, Los Angeles, Cal.   BR/TR, 6'1", 205 lbs.   Deb: 9/10/55

YEAR	TM/L	G	AB	R	H	2B	3B	HR	RBI	BB	SO	AVG	OBP	SLG	PRO+	BR/A	SB	CS	SBR	FA	FR	G/POS	TPR
1955	Chi-A	5	7	1	2	0	0	0	0	1	1	.286	.444	.286	97	0	0	0	0	1.000	2	/C-5	0.2
1956	Chi-A	4	4	1	1	0	0	0	0	1	1	.250	.400	.250	74	-0	0	0	0	.800	-1	/C-3	-0.1
1957	Chi-A	48	115	12	20	2	3	3	6	11	38	.174	.246	.322	54	-8	0	2	-1	.989	6	C-43	-0.2
1958	Chi-A	68	168	24	38	8	0	8	26	24	34	.226	.330	.417	106	1	1	0	0	.988	2	C-49	0.6
1959	Chi-A	26	64	9	14	1	2	2	7	8	13	.219	.306	.391	91	-1	0	0	0	.990	4	C-20	0.4
1960	Was-A	137	466	49	126	24	2	15	60	48	68	.270	.349	.427	110	6	4	5	-2	.982	5	*C-136	1.8
1961	Min-A	133	460	70	139	24	1	17	55	53	66	.302	.378	.470	118	12	3	3	-1	.993	7	*C-131	2.4
1962	Min-A★	148	522	58	146	20	3	11	57	57	48	.280	.351	.393	96	-2	0	0	0	.991	6	*C-147	1.0
1963	Min-A★	147	508	64	145	17	1	26	84	61	75	.285	.371	.476	133	23	0	0	0	.994	1	*C-146	3.1
1964	Min-A	131	405	33	110	17	1	12	52	51	49	.272	.354	.407	111	7	1	1	-0	.990	-5	*C-125	0.7
1965	*Min-A★	131	394	36	117	22	2	6	60	50	35	.297	.379	.409	119	11	0	0	0	.986	-8	*C-128	1.0
1966	Min-A★	115	364	30	93	12	1	4	34	43	30	.255	.339	.327	87	-5	4	1	1	.995	6	*C-113	0.9
1967	Min-A	48	109	6	18	3	1	0	8	13	24	.165	.254	.211	36	-8	0	0	0	.987	-2	C-41	-1.0
Total	13	1141	3586	393	969	150	17	104	449	421	470	.270	.351	.409	106	37	13	12	-3	.990	23	*C-1087	10.8

■ JOE BATTIN
Battin, Joseph V.   b: 11/11/1851, Philadelphia, Pa.   d: 12/10/37, Akron, Ohio   BR/TR,   Deb: 8/11/1871   MU

YEAR	TM/L	G	AB	R	H	2B	3B	HR	RBI	BB	SO	AVG	OBP	SLG	PRO+	BR/A	SB	CS	SBR	FA	FR	G/POS	TPR
1871	Cle-n	1	3	0	0				0	1	0	.000	.250	.000	-21	-0	0	0	0	1.000	-0	/O-1	0.0
1873	Ath-n	1	5	4	3	0	0	0	2	1	0	.600	.667	.600	260	1	0	0	0	.667	0	/O-1	0.1
1874	Ath-n	51	226	40	52	11	1	0	27	1	7	.230	.233	.288	61	-11	3	2	-0	.813	5	*2-41/O-7,S-5	-0.6
1875	StL-n	67	284	31	71	6	3	0	33	0	6	.250	.250	.292	97	0	15	3	3	.861	14	*2-62/3-6,C-2,O-1	1.3
1876	StL-N	64	283	34	85	11	4	0	46	6	6	.300	.315	.367	134	10				.867	14	*3-63/2-1	2.2
1877	StL-N	57	226	29	45	3	7	1	22	6	17	.199	.220	.288	62	-9				.823	-3	3-32,2-21/O-5,P-1	-0.9
1882	Pit-a	34	133	13	28	5	1	1		3		.211	.228	.286	76	-3				.876	21	3-34	1.7
1883	Pit-a	98	388	42	83	9	6	1		11		.214	.236	.276	67	-13				.891	29	*3-98/P-2,M	1.3
1884	Pit-a	43	158	10	28	1	2	0		3		.177	.198	.209	32	-12				.919	8	3-43,M	-0.3
	CP-U	18	69	8	13	2	0	0		0		.188	.188	.217	23	-8				.908	11	3-18,M	0.2
	Bal-U	17	59	3	6	1	0	0		0		.102	.102	.119	-30	-11				.813	2	3-17	-0.8
	Yr	35	128	11	19	3	0	0		0		.148	.148	.172	-3	-20				.868	13	3-35	-0.6
1890	Syr-a	29	119	15	25	2	1	0	13	8		.210	.260	.244	54	-7	8			.794	-4	3-29	-0.9
Total	4 n	120	518	75	126	17	4	0	62	3	13	.243	.248	.292	80	-10	18	5	2	.842	19	2-103/O-10,3-6,SC	0.8
Total	6	360	1435	153	313	34	21	3	<u>81</u>	37	<u>23</u>	.218	.238	.277	67	-53	8			.870	77	3-334/2-22,O-5,P-3	2.5

■ ALLEN BATTLE
Battle, Allen Zelmo   b: 11/29/68, Grantham, N.C.   BR/TR, 6', 170 lbs.   Deb: 4/26/95

YEAR	TM/L	G	AB	R	H	2B	3B	HR	RBI	BB	SO	AVG	OBP	SLG	PRO+	BR/A	SB	CS	SBR	FA	FR	G/POS	TPR
1995	StL-N	61	118	13	32	5	0	0	2	15	26	.271	.358	.314	79	-3	3	3	-1	.984	-2	O-32	-0.6
1996	Oak-A	47	130	20	25	3	0	1	5	17	26	.192	.295	.238	39	-12	10	2	1	.988	-6	O-47	-1.6
Total	2	108	248	33	57	8	0	1	7	32	52	.230	.325	.274	58	-15	13	5	1	.986	-8	/O-79	-2.2

■ HOWARD BATTLE
Battle, Howard Dion   b: 3/25/72, Biloxi, Miss.   BR/TR, 6', 210 lbs.   Deb: 9/5/95

YEAR	TM/L	G	AB	R	H	2B	3B	HR	RBI	BB	SO	AVG	OBP	SLG	PRO+	BR/A	SB	CS	SBR	FA	FR	G/POS	TPR
1995	Tor-A	9	15	0	3	0	0	0	0	4	8	.200	.368	.200	53	-1	1	0	0	1.000	0	/3-6,D-1	0.0
1996	Phi-N	5	5	0	0	0	0	0	0	0	2	.000	.000	.000	-97	-1	0	0	0	.000	0	/3-1	-0.1
Total	2	14	20	0	3	0	0	0	0	4	10	.150	.292	.150	20	-2	1	0	0	1.000	0	/3-7,D-1	-0.1

■ JIM BATTLE
Battle, James Milton   b: 3/26/01, Bailey, Tex.   d: 9/30/65, Chico, Cal.   BR/TR, 6'1", 170 lbs.   Deb: 9/9/27

YEAR	TM/L	G	AB	R	H	2B	3B	HR	RBI	BB	SO	AVG	OBP	SLG	PRO+	BR/A	SB	CS	SBR	FA	FR	G/POS	TPR
1927	Chi-A	6	8	1	3	0	1	0	0	0	0	.375	.375	.625	160	1	0	0	0	.900	-1	/3-4,S-2	0.0

■ MATT BATTS
Batts, Matthew Daniel   b: 10/16/21, San Antonio, Tex.   BR/TR, 5'11", 200 lbs.   Deb: 9/10/47

YEAR	TM/L	G	AB	R	H	2B	3B	HR	RBI	BB	SO	AVG	OBP	SLG	PRO+	BR/A	SB	CS	SBR	FA	FR	G/POS	TPR
1947	Bos-A	7	16	3	8	1	0	1	5	1	1	.500	.529	.750	236	3	0	0	0	1.000	-1	/C-6	0.2

YEAR	TM/L	G	AB	R	H	2B	3B	HR	RBI	BB	SO	AVG	OBP	SLG	PRO+	BR/A	SB	CS	SBR	FA	FR	G/POS	TPR
1948	Bos-A	46	118	13	37	12	0	1	24	15	9	.314	.391	.441	115	3	0	0	0	.986	-1	C-41	0.4
1949	Bos-A	60	157	23	38	9	1	3	31	25	22	.242	.350	.369	84	-4	1	0	0	.977	3	C-50	0.1
1950	Bos-A	75	238	27	65	15	3	4	34	18	19	.273	.327	.412	80	-8	0	0	0	.994	3	C-73	-0.2
1951	Bos-A	11	29	1	4	1	0	0	2	1	2	.138	.167	.172	-8	-4	0	0	0	.975	-0	C-11	-0.4
	StL-A	79	248	26	75	17	1	5	31	21	21	.302	.357	.440	111	3	2	0	1	.960	-8	C-64	-0.4
	Yr	90	277	27	79	18	1	5	33	22	23	.285	.338	.412	98	-1	2	0	1	.962	-9	C-75	-0.6
1952	Det-A	56	173	11	41	4	1	3	13	14	22	.237	.298	.324	72	-7	1	0	0	.983	3	C-55	-0.1
1953	Det-A	116	374	38	104	24	3	6	43	24	36	.278	.322	.406	97	-3	2	3	-1	.986	-14	*C-103	-1.3
1954	Det-A	12	21	1	6	1	0	0	5	2	4	.286	.348	.333	89	-0	0	0	0	.967	1	/C-8	0.1
	Chi-A	55	158	16	36	7	1	3	19	17	15	.228	.303	.342	74	-6	0	1	-1	.992	7	C-42	0.1
	Yr	67	179	17	42	8	1	3	24	19	19	.235	.308	.341	76	-6	0	1	-1	.989	8	C-50	0.3
1955	Cin-N	26	71	4	18	4	1	0	13	6	11	.254	.293	.338	63	-4	0	0	0	.986	-1	C-21	-0.4
1956	Cin-N	3	2	0	0	0	0	0	0	1	1	.000	.333	.000	89	-0	0	0	0	.000	0	H	0.0
Total	10	546	1605	163	432	95	11	26	220	143	163	.269	.330	.391	89	-27	6	4	-1	.983	-10	C-474	-1.6

■ HANK BAUER
Bauer, Henry Albert   b: 7/31/22, E.St.Louis, Ill.   BR/TR, 6', 192 lbs.   Deb: 9/6/48   MC

YEAR	TM/L	G	AB	R	H	2B	3B	HR	RBI	BB	SO	AVG	OBP	SLG	PRO+	BR/A	SB	CS	SBR	FA	FR	G/POS	TPR
1948	NY-A	19	50	6	9	1	1	1	9	6	13	.180	.268	.300	51	-4	1	0	0	.964	-1	O-14	-0.5
1949	*NY-A	103	301	56	82	6	6	10	45	37	42	.272	.354	.432	107	2	2	2	-1	.977	-9	O-95	-1.1
1950	*NY-A	113	415	72	133	16	2	13	70	35	41	.320	.380	.463	118	11	2	3	-1	.987	-1	*O-110	0.4
1951	*NY-A	118	348	53	103	19	3	10	54	42	39	.296	.373	.454	128	13	5	2	0	.990	-5	*O-107	0.5
1952	*NY-A★	141	553	86	162	31	6	17	74	50	61	.293	.355	.463	134	23	6	7	-2	.984	3	*O-139	1.8
1953	*NY-A★	133	437	77	133	20	6	10	57	59	45	.304	.394	.446	131	20	2	3	-1	.992	0	*O-126	1.5
1954	NY-A★	114	377	73	111	16	5	12	54	40	42	.294	.362	.459	128	14	4	4	-1	.989	-6	*O-108	0.2
1955	*NY-A	139	492	97	137	20	5	20	53	56	65	.278	.362	.461	122	14	8	4	0	.981	4	*O-133/C-1	1.2
1956	*NY-A	147	539	96	130	18	7	26	84	59	72	.241	.318	.445	103	-1	4	2	0	.969	-8	*O-146	-1.6
1957	*NY-A	137	479	70	124	22	9	18	65	42	64	.259	.324	.455	112	6	7	2	1	.986	-7	*O-135	-0.8
1958	*NY-A	128	452	62	121	22	6	12	50	32	56	.268	.318	.423	106	2	3	2	-0	.980	-9	*O-123	-1.3
1959	NY-A	114	341	44	81	20	0	9	39	33	54	.238	.309	.375	90	-5	4	2	0	.972	-13	*O-111	-2.3
1960	KC-A	95	255	30	70	15	0	3	31	21	36	.275	.332	.369	89	-4	1	0	0	.978	-6	O-67	-1.3
1961	KC-A	43	106	11	28	3	1	3	18	9	8	.264	.322	.396	89	-2	1	0	0	.958	-7	O-35,M	-1.0
Total	14	1544	5145	833	1424	229	57	164	703	521	638	.277	.347	.439	114	90	50	33	-5	.982	-65	*O-1449/C-1	-4.3

■ PADDY BAUMANN
Baumann, Charles John   b: 12/20/1885, Indianapolis, Ind.   d: 11/20/69, Indianapolis, Ind.   BR/TR, 5'9", 160 lbs.   Deb: 8/10/11

YEAR	TM/L	G	AB	R	H	2B	3B	HR	RBI	BB	SO	AVG	OBP	SLG	PRO+	BR/A	SB	CS	SBR	FA	FR	G/POS	TPR
1911	Det-A	26	94	8	24	2	4	0	11	6		.255	.307	.362	82	-3	1			.956	6	2-23/O-3	0.2
1912	Det-A	16	42	3	11	1	0	0	7	6		.262	.354	.286	86	-0	4			.786	-2	/3-6,2-5,O-2	-0.2
1913	Det-A	50	191	31	57	7	4	1	22	16	18	.298	.353	.393	120	4	4			.943	-7	2-49	-0.4
1914	Det-A	3	11	1	0	0	0	0	2	1		.000	.154	.000	-52	-2	0			1.000	-1	/2-3	-0.4
1915	NY-A	76	219	30	64	13	1	2	28	28	32	.292	.380	.388	130	9	9	10	-3	.978	-2	2-43,3-19/O-1	0.5
1916	NY-A	79	237	35	68	5	3	1	25	19	16	.287	.352	.346	108	2	10			.958	-7	O-28,3-26/2-9	-0.6
1917	NY-A	49	110	10	24	2	1	0	8	4	3	.218	.246	.255	52	-7	2			.941	-12	2-18/O-7,3-1	-2.1
Total	7	299	904	118	248	30	13	4	101	81	76	.274	.340	.350	103	4	30	10		.953	-26	2-150/3-52,O-41	-3.0

■ JIM BAUMER
Baumer, James Sloan   b: 1/29/31, Tulsa, Okla.   d: 7/8/96, Paoli, Pa.   BR/TR, 6'2", 185 lbs.   Deb: 9/14/49

YEAR	TM/L	G	AB	R	H	2B	3B	HR	RBI	BB	SO	AVG	OBP	SLG	PRO+	BR/A	SB	CS	SBR	FA	FR	G/POS	TPR
1949	Chi-A	8	10	2	4	1	0	0	2	1		.400	.571	.700	243	2	0	0	0	.938	1	/S-7	0.3
1961	Cin-N	10	24	0	3	0	0	0	0	9		.125	.125	.125	-33	-4	0	0	0	1.000	-0	/2-9	-0.4
Total	2	18	34	2	7	1	0	0	2	2	10	.206	.289	.294	55	-2	0	0	0	1.000	1	/2-9,S-7	-0.1

■ JOHN BAUMGARTNER
Baumgartner, John Edward   b: 5/29/31, Birmingham, Ala.   BR/TR, 6'1", 190 lbs.   Deb: 4/14/53

YEAR	TM/L	G	AB	R	H	2B	3B	HR	RBI	BB	SO	AVG	OBP	SLG	PRO+	BR/A	SB	CS	SBR	FA	FR	G/POS	TPR
1953	Det-A	7	27	3	5	0	0	0	2	0	5	.185	.185	.185	0	-4	0	0	0	.913	-1	/3-7	-0.5

■ FRANK BAUMHOLTZ
Baumholtz, Frank Conrad   b: 10/7/18, Midvale, Ohio   BL/TL, 5'10.5", 175 lbs.   Deb: 4/15/47

YEAR	TM/L	G	AB	R	H	2B	3B	HR	RBI	BB	SO	AVG	OBP	SLG	PRO+	BR/A	SB	CS	SBR	FA	FR	G/POS	TPR
1947	Cin-N	151	643	96	182	32	9	5	45	56	53	.283	.341	.384	93	-7	6			.977	-5	*O-150	-1.9
1948	Cin-N	128	415	57	123	19	5	4	30	27	32	.296	.344	.395	103	1	8			.987	3	*O-110	-0.2
1949	Cin-N	27	81	12	19	5	3	1	8	6	8	.235	.295	.407	86	-2	0			.964	-2	O-20	-0.1
	Chi-N	58	164	15	37	4	2	1	15	9	21	.226	.270	.293	52	-11	2			.986	-4	O-43	-1.8
	Yr	85	245	27	56	9	5	2	23	15	29	.229	.279	.331	64	-13	2			.976	-3	O-63	-1.9
1951	Chi-N	146	560	62	159	28	10	2	50	49	36	.284	.346	.380	94	-5	5	4	-1	.975	-7	*O-140	-1.7
1952	Chi-N	103	409	59	133	17	4	4	35	27	27	.325	.371	.416	116	9	5	7	-3	.974	3	*O-101	0.5
1953	Chi-N	133	520	75	159	36	7	3	25	42	36	.306	.359	.419	100	0	3	3	-1	.980	-3	*O-130	-0.8
1954	Chi-N	90	303	38	90	12	6	4	28	20	15	.297	.343	.416	95	-2	1	3	-2	.988	-10	O-71	-1.6
1955	Chi-N	105	280	23	81	12	5	1	27	16	24	.289	.330	.379	88	-5	0	1	-1	.993	2	O-63	-0.6
1956	Phi-N	76	100	13	27	0	0	0	9	6	6	.270	.318	.270	61	-5	0	2	-1	.962	-0	O-15	-0.8
1957	Phi-N	2	2	0	0	0	0	0	0	0	0	.000	.000	.000	-99	-1	0	0	0	.000	0	H	-0.1
Total	10	1019	3477	450	1010	165	51	25	272	258	258	.290	.342	.389	95	-27	30	20		.980	-20	O-843	-9.1

■ DANNY BAUTISTA
Bautista, Daniel (Alcantara)   b: 5/24/72, Santo Domingo, D.R.   BR/TR, 5'11", 170 lbs.   Deb: 9/15/93

YEAR	TM/L	G	AB	R	H	2B	3B	HR	RBI	BB	SO	AVG	OBP	SLG	PRO+	BR/A	SB	CS	SBR	FA	FR	G/POS	TPR
1993	Det-A	17	61	6	19	0	1	1	9	1	10	.311	.323	.410	96	-1	3	1	0	1.000	1	O-16/D-1	0.1
1994	Det-A	31	99	12	23	4	1	4	15	3	18	.232	.255	.414	68	-5	1	2	-1	1.000	1	O-30/D-1	-0.7
1995	Det-A	89	271	28	55	9	0	7	27	12	68	.203	.237	.314	42	-24	4	1	1	.988	1	O-86/D-1	-2.3
1996	Det-A	25	64	12	16	2	0	2	8	9	15	.250	.342	.375	82	-2	1	2	-1	.974	-2	O-22/D-1	-0.5
	Atl-N	17	20	1	3	0	0	0	1	2	5	.150	.261	.150	11	-3	0	0	0	1.000	-3	O-14	-0.6
Total	4	179	515	59	116	18	1	14	60	27	116	.225	.265	.346	57	-34	9	6	-1	.991	-5	O-168/D-4	-4.0

■ JIM BAXES
Baxes, Dimitrios Speros   b: 7/5/28, San Francisco, Cal   BR/TR, 6'1", 190 lbs.   Deb: 4/11/59   F

YEAR	TM/L	G	AB	R	H	2B	3B	HR	RBI	BB	SO	AVG	OBP	SLG	PRO+	BR/A	SB	CS	SBR	FA	FR	G/POS	TPR
1959	LA-N	11	33	4	10	1	0	2	5	4	7	.303	.395	.515	130	2	1	0	0	.952	7	3-10	0.8
	Cle-A	77	247	35	59	11	0	15	34	21	47	.239	.299	.466	111	2	0	1	-1	.956	-13	2-48,3-22	-0.8
Total	1	88	280	39	69	12	0	17	39	25	54	.246	.310	.471	113	4	1	1	-0	.931	-7	/2-48,3-32	0.0

■ MIKE BAXES
Baxes, Michael   b: 12/18/30, San Francisco, Cal   BR/TR, 5'10", 175 lbs.   Deb: 4/17/56   F

YEAR	TM/L	G	AB	R	H	2B	3B	HR	RBI	BB	SO	AVG	OBP	SLG	PRO+	BR/A	SB	CS	SBR	FA	FR	G/POS	TPR
1956	KC-A	73	106	9	24	3	1	0	5	18	15	.226	.339	.302	70	-4	0	1	-1	.944	4	S-62/2-1	0.2
1958	KC-A	73	231	31	49	10	1	0	8	21	24	.212	.286	.264	52	-15	1	6	-3	.969	-4	2-61/S-4	-1.9
Total	2	146	337	40	73	13	2	1	13	39	39	.217	.303	.276	58	-19	1	7	-4	.946	-0	/S-66,2-62	-1.7

■ JOHN BAXTER
Baxter, John Morris   b: 7/27/1876, Chippewa Falls, Wis.   d: 8/7/26, Portland, Ore.   BR/TR, 6'3",   Deb: 4/19/07

YEAR	TM/L	G	AB	R	H	2B	3B	HR	RBI	BB	SO	AVG	OBP	SLG	PRO+	BR/A	SB	CS	SBR	FA	FR	G/POS	TPR
1907	StL-N	6	21	1	4	0	0	0	0	0		.190	.190	.190	20	-2	0			.921	-1	/1-6	-0.3

■ HARRY BAY
Bay, Harry Elbert "Deerfoot"   b: 1/17/1878, Pontiac, Ill.   d: 3/20/52, Peoria, Ill.   BL/TL, 5'8", 138 lbs.   Deb: 7/23/01

YEAR	TM/L	G	AB	R	H	2B	3B	HR	RBI	BB	SO	AVG	OBP	SLG	PRO+	BR/A	SB	CS	SBR	FA	FR	G/POS	TPR
1901	Cin-N	41	157	25	33	1	2	1	3	13		.210	.275	.261	60	-8	1			.953	-1	O-40	-1.1
1902	Cin-N	6	16	3	6	0	0	0	1	2		.375	.474	.375	148	1	0			.778	3	/O-3	0.1
	Cle-A	108	455	71	132	10	5	0	23	36		.290	.343	.334	92	-4	22			**.973**	4	*O-107	-0.7
1903	Cle-A	140	579	94	169	15	12	1	35	29		.292	.329	.364	110	7	**45**			.950	-3	*O-140	-0.5
1904	Cle-A	132	506	69	122	12	9	3	36	43		.241	.307	.318	99	-0	**38**			**.987**	7	*O-132	0.0
1905	Cle-A	144	552	90	166	18	10	0	22	36		.301	.349	.370	126	16	36			.970	0	*O-144	1.0
1906	Cle-A	68	280	47	77	8	5	0	14	26		.275	.337	.325	109	3	17			.979	5	O-68	-0.3
1907	Cle-A	34	95	14	17	1	1	0	7	10		.179	.271	.211	53	-5	7			.968	1	O-31	-0.6
1908	Cle-A	2										—	—	—						.000	0	R	0.0
Total	8	675	2640	413	722	65	42	5	141	195		.273	.328	.336	103	11	169			.968	6	O-665	-2.1

■ DICK BAYLESS
Bayless, Harry Owen   b: 9/6/1883, Joplin, Mo.   d: 12/16/20, Santa Rita, N.Mex.   BL/TR, 5'9", 178 lbs.   Deb: 9/9/08

YEAR	TM/L	G	AB	R	H	2B	3B	HR	RBI	BB	SO	AVG	OBP	SLG	PRO+	BR/A	SB	CS	SBR	FA	FR	G/POS	TPR
1908	Cin-N	19	71	7	16	1	0	1	3	6		.225	.304	.282	90	-1	0			.946	3	O-19	0.1

YEAR	TM/L	G	AB	R	H	2B	3B	HR	RBI	BB	SO	AVG	OBP	SLG	PRO+	BR/A	SB	CS	SBR	FA	FR	G/POS	TPR

■ DON BAYLOR   Baylor, Don Edward   b: 6/28/49, Austin, Tex.   BR/TR, 6'1", 195 lbs.   Deb: 9/18/70   MC

YEAR	TM/L	G	AB	R	H	2B	3B	HR	RBI	BB	SO	AVG	OBP	SLG	PRO+	BR/A	SB	CS	SBR	FA	FR	G/POS	TPR
1970	Bal-A	8	17	4	4	0	0	0	4	2	3	.235	.316	.235	54	-1	1	1	-0	1.000	0	/O-6	-0.2
1971	Bal-A	1	2	0	0	0	0	0	0	0	1	.000	.600	.000	83	0	0	0	0	1.000	0	/O-1	0.1
1972	Bal-A	102	320	33	81	13	3	11	38	29	50	.253	.332	.416	118	7	24	8	6	.975	-9	O-84/1-9	0.1
1973	*Bal-A	118	405	64	116	20	4	11	51	35	48	.286	.362	.437	125	14	32	9	4	.981	-1	*O-110/1-6,D-1	1.2
1974	*Bal-A	137	489	66	133	22	4	10	59	44	56	.272	.343	.382	112	8	29	12	2	.978	-17	*O-129/1-8,D-1	-1.4
1975	Bal-A	145	524	79	148	21	6	25	76	53	64	.282	.363	.489	148	32	32	17	-1	.982	-2	*O-135/1-2,D-7	2.4
1976	Oak-A	157	595	85	147	25	1	15	68	58	72	.247	.334	.368	110	8	52	12	8	.981	-9	O-76,1-69,D-23	0.0
1977	Cal-A	154	561	87	141	27	0	25	75	62	76	.251	.339	.433	113	10	26	12	1	.966	-1	O-77,D-61,1-18	0.3
1978	Cal-A	158	591	103	151	26	0	34	99	56	71	.255	.338	.472	131	23	22	9	1	.974	-2	*D-102,O-39,1-17	1.7
1979	*Cal-A★	162	628	**120**	186	33	3	36	**139**	71	51	.296	.377	.530	147	41	22	12	-1	.976	2	O-97,D-65/1-1	3.4
1980	Cal-A	90	340	39	85	12	2	5	51	24	32	.250	.320	.341	83	-7	6	6	-2	.969	3	O-54,D-36	-1.0
1981	Cal-A	103	377	52	90	18	1	17	66	42	51	.239	.326	.427	116	7	3	3	-1	1.000	1	D-97/1-4,O-1	0.4
1982	*Cal-A	157	608	80	160	24	1	24	93	57	69	.263	.333	.424	106	5	10	4	1	.000	0	*D-155	0.0
1983	NY-A	144	534	82	162	33	3	21	85	40	53	.303	.366	.494	139	28	17	7	1	.000	-1	*D-136/O-5,1-1	2.3
1984	NY-A	134	493	84	129	29	1	27	89	38	68	.262	.343	.489	132	21	1	1	-0	.889	-1	*D-127/O-5	1.6
1985	NY-A	142	477	70	110	24	1	23	91	52	90	.231	.336	.430	111	8	0	4	-2	.000	0	*D-140	0.3
1986	*Bos-A	160	585	93	139	23	1	31	94	62	111	.238	.346	.439	112	10	3	5	-2	.986	-1	*D-143,1-13/O-3	0.4
1987	Bos-A	108	339	64	81	8	0	16	57	40	47	.239	.360	.404	100	1	5	2	0	.000	0	D-97	-0.1
	*Min-N	20	49	3	14	1	0	0	6	5	12	.286	.397	.306	87	-0	0	1	-1	.000	0	D-14	-0.1
	Yr	128	388	67	95	9	0	16	63	45	59	.245	.364	.392	98	1	5	3	-0	.000	0	*D-111	-0.2
1988	*Oak-A	92	264	28	58	7	0	7	34	34	44	.220	.335	.326	89	-3	0	1	-1	.000	0	D-80	-0.5
Total	19	2292	8198	1236	2135	366	28	338	1276	805	1069	.260	.346	.436	119	212	285	120	14	.977	-37	*D-1285,O-822,1-148	10.9

■ JACK BEACH   Beach, Stonewall Jackson   b: 1862, Alexandria, Va.   d: 7/23/1896, Alexandria, Va.   Deb: 5/1/1884

YEAR	TM/L	G	AB	R	H	2B	3B	HR	RBI	BB	SO	AVG	OBP	SLG	PRO+	BR/A	SB	CS	SBR	FA	FR	G/POS	TPR
1884	Was-a	8	31	3	3	2	0	0		0		.097	.097	.161	-20	-4				.667	-1	/O-8	-0.5

■ JOHNNY BEALL   Beall, John Woolf   b: 3/12/1882, Beltsville, Md.   d: 6/14/26, Beltsville, Md.   BL/TR, 6', 180 lbs.   Deb: 4/17/13

YEAR	TM/L	G	AB	R	H	2B	3B	HR	RBI	BB	SO	AVG	OBP	SLG	PRO+	BR/A	SB	CS	SBR	FA	FR	G/POS	TPR
1913	Cle-A	6	6	0	1	0	0	0	1	0	2	.167	.167	.167	-2	-1	0			.000	0	H	-0.1
	Chi-A	17	60	10	16	0	1	2	3	0	0	.267	.279	.400	99	-1	1			.953	1	O-17	-0.1
	Yr	23	66	10	17	0	1	2	4	0	2	.258	.269	.379	89	-1	1			.953	1	O-17	-0.2
1915	Cin-N	10	34	3	8	1	0	0	3	5	10	.235	.350	.265	86	-0	0	1	-1	.960	1	O-10	0.0
1916	Cin-N	6	21	3	7	2	0	1	4	3	7	.333	.417	.571	207	3	1			1.000	1	/O-6	0.4
1918	StL-N	19	49	2	11	1	0	0	6	3	6	.224	.269	.245	59	-2	0			1.000	-1	/O-18	-0.5
Total	4	58	170	18	43	4	1	3	17	11	25	.253	.306	.341	95	-1	2	1		.972	2	/O-51	-0.3

■ BOB BEALL   Beall, Robert Brooks   b: 4/24/48, Portland, Ore.   BB/TL, 5'11", 180 lbs.   Deb: 5/12/75

YEAR	TM/L	G	AB	R	H	2B	3B	HR	RBI	BB	SO	AVG	OBP	SLG	PRO+	BR/A	SB	CS	SBR	FA	FR	G/POS	TPR
1975	Atl-N	20	31	2	7	1	0	1	6	9	9	.226	.351	.290	77	-1	0	0	0	.984	-0	/1-8	-0.1
1978	Atl-N	108	185	29	45	8	0	1	16	36	27	.243	.369	.303	81	-3	4	5	-2	.987	-1	1-40/O-8	-0.9
1979	Atl-N	17	15	1	2	2	0	0	1	3	4	.133	.278	.267	46	-1	0	0	0	1.000	0	/1-3	-0.1
1980	Pit-N	3	3	0	0	0	0	0	0	0	1	.000	.000	.000	-99	-1	0	0	0	.000	0	/H	-0.1
Total	4	148	234	32	54	12	0	1	18	45	41	.231	.357	.295	76	-6	4	5	-2	.987	-1	/1-51,O-8	-1.2

■ TOMMY BEALS   Beals, Thomas L. (a.k.a. W.Thomas in 1871-1873)   b: 8/1850, New York   d: 10/2/15, San Francisco, Cal.   BR , 5'5", 144 lbs.   Deb: 7/27/1871

YEAR	TM/L	G	AB	R	H	2B	3B	HR	RBI	BB	SO	AVG	OBP	SLG	PRO+	BR/A	SB	CS	SBR	FA	FR	G/POS	TPR
1871	Oly-n	10	36	6	7	0	0	0	1	2	0	.194	.237	.194	27	-3	2	0	1	.778	3	/O-8,2-2	0.0
1872	Oly-n	9	36	6	11	1	1	0	5	1	1	.306	.324	.389	125	1	0	0	0	.853	1	2-5,S-2,O-2	0.1
1873	Was-n	37	169	35	46	9	5	0	24	1	1	.272	.276	.385	97	-0	1	0	0	.871	7	2-26,C-13/O-1	0.4
1874	Bos-n	19	97	20	19	3	4	0	17	0	2	.196	.196	.309	56	-5	0	1	-1	.849	-2	2-12/O-9	-0.6
1875	Bos-n	35	155	38	41	2	6	0	16	3	1	.265	.278	.355	114	2	0	0	0	.867	1	O-30/2-8	0.3
1880	Chi-N	13	46	4	7	0	0	0	3	1	6	.152	.170	.152	10	-4				.889	-6	O-10/2-3	-1.0
Total	5 n	110	493	105	124	15	16	0	63	7	5	.252	.262	.347	90	-5	4	1	1	.864	10	/2-53,O-50,C-13,S-2	0.2

■ CHARLIE BEAMON   Beamon, Charles Alfonzo Jr.   b: 12/4/53, Oakland, Cal.   BL/TL, 6'1", 183 lbs.   Deb: 9/11/78   F

YEAR	TM/L	G	AB	R	H	2B	3B	HR	RBI	BB	SO	AVG	OBP	SLG	PRO+	BR/A	SB	CS	SBR	FA	FR	G/POS	TPR
1978	Sea-A	10	11	2	2	0	0	0	0	1	1	.182	.250	.182	23	-1	0	0	0	1.000	1	/1-2,D-6	0.0
1979	Sea-A	27	25	5	5	1	0	0	0	5	5	.200	.200	.240	18	-3	1	0	0	1.000	1	/1-7,O-2,D-5	-0.3
1981	Tor-A	8	15	1	3	1	0	0	2	2	2	.200	.294	.267	59	-1	0	0	0	1.000	-0	/D-4,1-1	-0.1
Total	3	45	51	8	10	2	0	0	2	8	8	.196	.241	.235	32	-5	1	0	0	1.000	1	/D-15,1-10,O-2	-0.4

■ TREY BEAMON   Beamon, Clifford   b: 2/11/74, Dallas, Tex.   BL/TR, 6'3", 195 lbs.   Deb: 8/4/96

YEAR	TM/L	G	AB	R	H	2B	3B	HR	RBI	BB	SO	AVG	OBP	SLG	PRO+	BR/A	SB	CS	SBR	FA	FR	G/POS	TPR
1996	Pit-N	24	51	7	11	2	0	0	6	4	6	.216	.273	.255	39	-4	1	1	-0	.960	2	O-14	-0.6

■ JOE BEAN   Bean, Joseph William   b: 3/18/1874, Boston, Mass.   d: 2/15/61, Atlanta, Ga.   BR/TR, 5'8", 138 lbs.   Deb: 4/28/02

YEAR	TM/L	G	AB	R	H	2B	3B	HR	RBI	BB	SO	AVG	OBP	SLG	PRO+	BR/A	SB	CS	SBR	FA	FR	G/POS	TPR
1902	NY-N	48	176	13	39	2	1	0	5	5		.222	.247	.244	52	-10	9			.889	-9	S-48	-1.7

■ BILL BEAN   Bean, William Daro   b: 5/11/64, Santa Ana, Cal.   BL/TL, 6' ", 185 lbs.   Deb: 4/25/87

YEAR	TM/L	G	AB	R	H	2B	3B	HR	RBI	BB	SO	AVG	OBP	SLG	PRO+	BR/A	SB	CS	SBR	FA	FR	G/POS	TPR
1987	Det-A	26	66	6	17	2	0	0	4	5	11	.258	.310	.288	63	-3	1	1	-0	1.000	0	O-24	-0.4
1988	Det-A	10	11	2	2	0	1	0	0	0	3	.182	.182	.364	51	-1	0	0	0	1.000	-1	/O-4,1-2,D-1	-0.2
1989	Det-A	9	11	0	0	0	0	0	0	0	3	.000	.214	.000	-36	-2	0	0	0	.833	-3	/O-6,1-2	-0.5
	LA-N	51	71	7	14	4	0	0	3	4	10	.197	.250	.254	45	-5	0	2	-1	1.000	-9	O-44	-1.7
1993	SD-N	88	177	19	46	9	0	5	32	6	29	.260	.292	.395	81	-5	2	4	-2	.987	-7	O-54,1-12	-1.6
1994	SD-N	84	135	9	29	5	1	0	14	7	25	.215	.254	.267	37	-13	0	1	-1	1.000	-5	O-39,1-16	-1.9
1995	SD-N	4	7	1	0	0	0	0	1	1	4	.000	.125	.000	-66	-2	0	0	0	.750	-1	/O-4	-0.3
Total	6	272	478	42	108	20	2	5	53	25	84	.226	.270	.308	55	-31	3	8	-4	.988	-25	O-175/1-32,D-1	-6.6

■ BILLY BEANE   Beane, William Lamar   b: 3/29/62, Orlando, Fla.   BR/TR, 6'4", 195 lbs.   Deb: 9/13/84

YEAR	TM/L	G	AB	R	H	2B	3B	HR	RBI	BB	SO	AVG	OBP	SLG	PRO+	BR/A	SB	CS	SBR	FA	FR	G/POS	TPR
1984	NY-N	5	10	0	1	0	0	0	0	0	2	.100	.100	.100	-44	-2	0	1		1.000	-2	/O-5	-0.4
1985	NY-N	8	8	0	2	1	0	0	1	0	3	.250	.250	.375	74	-0	0	0	0	1.000	-1	/O-2	-0.1
1986	Min-A	80	183	20	39	6	0	3	15	11	54	.213	.258	.295	49	-13	2	3	-1	1.000	-5	O-67/D-5	-2.0
1987	Min-A	12	15	1	4	2	0	0	1	0	6	.267	.267	.400	71	-1	0	0	0	1.000	-1	/O-7	-0.2
1988	Det-A	6	6	1	1	0	0	0	0	0	2	.167	.167	.167	-7	-1	0	0	0	1.000	0	/O-6	-0.3
1989	Oak-A	37	79	8	19	5	0	0	11	0	13	.241	.241	.304	54	-5	3	1	0	1.000	-2	O-25/1-4,C-3,1-D	-0.7
Total	6	148	301	30	66	14	0	6	28	11	80	.219	.247	.296	48	-22	5	5	-2	1.000	-11	O-112/D-9,1-4,3C	-3.7

■ TED BEARD   Beard, Cramer Theodore   b: 1/7/21, Woodsboro, Md.   BL/TL, 5'8", 165 lbs.   Deb: 9/5/48

YEAR	TM/L	G	AB	R	H	2B	3B	HR	RBI	BB	SO	AVG	OBP	SLG	PRO+	BR/A	SB	CS	SBR	FA	FR	G/POS	TPR
1948	Pit-N	25	81	15	16	1	3	0	7	12	18	.198	.316	.284	62	-4	5			1.000	2	O-22	-0.4
1949	Pit-N	14	24	1	2	0	0	0	1	2	2	.083	.154	.083	-34	-5	0			.900	-3	O-10	-0.8
1950	Pit-N	61	177	32	41	6	2	4	12	27	45	.232	.333	.356	79	-5	3			.983	2	O-49	-0.5
1951	Pit-N	22	48	7	9	1	0	1	3	6	14	.188	.291	.271	51	-3	0	0	1	1.000	-2	O-15	-0.5
1952	Pit-N	15	44	5	8	2	1	0	3	7	9	.182	.294	.273	57	-2	2	0	1	1.000	0	O-13	-0.2
1957	Chi-A	38	78	15	16	1	0	0	7	18	14	.205	.354	.218	59	-3	3	2	-0	.974	-1	O-28	-0.6
1958	Chi-A	19	22	5	2	0	0	1	2	6	5	.091	.286	.227	44	-2	3	0	1	1.000	-4	O-15	-0.5
Total	7	194	474	80	94	11	6	6	35	78	107	.198	.315	.285	61	-25	16	2		.987	-5	O-152	-3.5

■ OLLIE BEARD   Beard, Oliver Perry   b: 5/2/1862, Lexington, Ky.   d: 5/28/29, Cincinnati, Ohio   BR/TR, 5'11", 180 lbs.   Deb: 4/17/1889

YEAR	TM/L	G	AB	R	H	2B	3B	HR	RBI	BB	SO	AVG	OBP	SLG	PRO+	BR/A	SB	CS	SBR	FA	FR	G/POS	TPR
1889	Cin-a	141	558	96	159	13	14	1	77	35	39	.285	.328	.364	94	-6	36			.896	20	*S-141	1.8
1890	Cin-N	122	492	64	132	17	15	3	72	44	13	.268	.331	.382	108	-4	30			.897	1	*S-113/3-9	1.0
1891	Lou-a	68	257	35	62	4	5	0	24	33	9	.241	.330	.296	80	-6	7			.879	7	3-61/S-7	0.3
Total	3	331	1307	195	353	34	34	4	173	112	61	.270	.330	.357	97	-8	73			.896	28	S-261/3-70	3.1

■ LEW BEASLEY   Beasley, Lewis Paige   b: 8/27/48, Sparta, Va.   BL/TR, 5'10", 172 lbs.   Deb: 5/21/77

YEAR	TM/L	G	AB	R	H	2B	3B	HR	RBI	BB	SO	AVG	OBP	SLG	PRO+	BR/A	SB	CS	SBR	FA	FR	G/POS	TPR
1977	Tex-A	25	32	5	7	1	0	0	3	2	2	.219	.265	.250	41	-3	1	1	-0	.833	-6	O-18/S-1,D-1	-0.9

YEAR	TM/L	G	AB	R	H	2B	3B	HR	RBI	BB	SO	AVG	OBP	SLG	PRO+	BR/A	SB	CS	SBR	FA	FR	G/POS	TPR
■ DAVE BEATLE						Beatle, David b: 1861, New York, N.Y. 6'2", 200 lbs. Deb: 6/17/1884																	
1884	Det-N	1	3	0	0	0	0	0	0	0	2	.000	.000	.000	-99	-1				.500	-1	/O-1,C-1	-0.1
■ DESMOND BEATTY						Beatty, Aloysius Desmond "Desperate" b: 4/7/1893, Baltimore, Md. d: 10/6/69, Norway, Maine BR/TR, 5'8.5", 158 lbs. Deb: 9/28/14																	
1914	NY-N	2	3	0	0	0	0	0	1	0	0	.000	.000	.000	-99	-1		0		.400	-1	/S-1,3-1	-0.1
■ JIM BEAUCHAMP						Beauchamp, James Edward b: 8/21/39, Vinita, Okla. BR/TR, 6'2", 205 lbs. Deb: 9/22/63 C																	
1963	StL-N	4	3	0	0	0	0	0	0	0	2	.000	.000	.000	-91	-1	0	0	0	.000	0	H	-0.1
1964	Hou-N	23	55	6	9	2	0	2	4	5	16	.164	.246	.309	58	-3	0	2	-1	.913	-1	O-15/1-2	-0.5
1965	Hou-N	24	53	5	10	1	0	0	4	5	11	.189	.259	.208	36	-4	0	2	-1	1.000	2	/O-9,1-3	-0.5
	Mil-N	4	3	0	0	0	0	0	0	1	1	.000	.250	.000	-23	-0	0	1	-1	1.000	-0	/1-2	-0.1
	Yr	28	56	5	10	1	0	0	4	6	12	.179	.258	.196	32	-5	0	3	-2	1.000	1	/O-9,1-5	-0.6
1967	Atl-N	4	3	0	0	0	0	0	1	0	0	.000	.000	.000	-99	-1	0	0	0	.000	0	H	-0.1
1968	Cin-N	31	57	10	15	2	0	2	14	4	19	.263	.311	.404	107	1	0	0	0	1.000	-0	O-13/1-1	0.0
1969	Cin-N	43	60	8	15	1	0	1	8	5	13	.250	.308	.317	71	-2	0	0	0	1.000	-2	/O-9,1-3	-0.5
1970	Hou-N	31	26	3	5	0	0	1	4	3	7	.192	.276	.308	59	-2	0	1	-1	1.000	-4	O-16	-0.7
	StL-N	44	58	8	15	2	0	1	6	8	11	.259	.348	.345	85	-1	2	1	0	1.000	-1	O-10/1-5	-0.1
	Yr	75	84	11	20	2	0	2	10	11	18	.238	.326	.333	78	-3	2	2	-1	1.000	-4	O-26/1-5	-0.8
1971	StL-N	77	162	24	38	8	3	2	16	9	26	.235	.279	.358	76	-5	3	1	0	.982	-2	1-44/O-1	-1.1
1972	NY-N	58	120	10	29	1	0	5	19	7	33	.242	.289	.375	90	-2	0	0	0	.979	-3	1-35/O-5	-0.8
1973	*NY-N	50	61	5	17	1	1	0	14	7	11	.279	.353	.328	91	-1	0	0	0	.969	-1	1-11	-0.2
Total	10	393	661	79	153	18	4	14	90	54	150	.231	.292	.334	76	-22	6	5	-1	.980	-11	1-106/O-78	-4.7
■ GINGER BEAUMONT						Beaumont, Clarence Howeth b: 7/23/1876, Rochester, Wis. d: 4/10/56, Burlington, Wis. BL/TR, 5'8", 190 lbs. Deb: 4/21/1899																	
1899	Pit-N	111	437	90	154	15	8	3	38	41		.352	.416	.444	137	23	31			.924	6	*O-100/1-2	1.9
1900	*Pit-N	138	567	105	158	14	9	5	50	40		.279	.331	.362	90	-8	27			.944	-12	*O-138	-2.8
1901	Pit-N	133	558	120	185	14	5	8	72	44		.332	.382	.418	128	20	36			.943	-5	*O-133	0.5
1902	Pit-N	130	541	100	**193**	21	6	6	67	39		**.357**	.404	.418	148	31	33			.975	0	*O-130	2.3
1903	*Pit-N	141	613	**137**	**209**	30	6	7	68	44		.341	.390	.444	133	25	23			.948	-7	*O-141	0.9
1904	Pit-N	153	615	97	**185**	12	12	3	54	34		.301	.338	.374	117	11	28			.968	-4	O-97	0.9
1905	Pit-N	103	384	60	126	12	8	3	40	22		.328	.365	.424	131	14	21			.972	-0	O-78	-1.2
1906	Pit-N	80	310	48	82	9	3	2	32	19		.265	.311	.332	96	-2	1			.945	-5	*O-149	3.2
1907	Bos-N	150	580	67	**187**	19	14	4	62	37		.322	.366	.424	148	30	25			.962	5	*O-149	3.2
1908	Bos-N	125	476	66	127	20	6	2	52	42		.267	.328	.347	117	9	13			.965	-1	*O-121	0.4
1909	Bos-N	123	407	35	107	11	4	0	60	35		.263	.321	.310	92	-4	12			.969	1	*O-111	-0.8
1910	*Chi-N	76	172	30	46	5	1	2	22	28	14	.267	.373	.343	110	3	4			.957	-4	O-56	-0.3
Total	12	1463	5660	955	1759	182	82	39	617	425	14	.311	.362	.393	122	151	254			.956	-25	*O-1407/1-2	4.7
■ E. P. BEAVENS						Beavens, E. P. (a.k.a. E. P. Bevens) b: 1848, Troy, N.Y. TR, 5'8", 138 lbs. Deb: 5/9/1871																	
1871	Tro-n	3	15	7	6	0	0	0	5	0	0	.400	.400	.400	129	1	2	0	1	.818	1	/2-3	0.1
1872	Atl-n	10	43	6	9	2	0	0	2	1	0	.209	.227	.256	41	-4	0	0	0	.683	-5	2-10/S-1,O-1	-0.7
Total	2 n	13	58	13	15	2	0	0	7	1	0	.259	.271	.293	62	-3	2	0	1	.720	-4	/2-13,O-1,S-1	-0.6
■ BUCK BECANNON						Becannon, James Melvin b: 8/22/1859, New York, N.Y. d: 11/5/23, New York, N.Y. 5'10", 165 lbs. Deb: 10/15/1884																	
1884	*NY-a	1	3	0	0	0	0	0		0	0	.000	.000	.000	-99	-1				1.000	0	/P-1	0.0
1885	NY-a	10	33	3	10	0	0	0		2	1	.303	.343	.303	114	-1				.947	0	P-10	0.0
1887	NY-N	1	5	0	0	0	0	0	0	0	2	.000	.000	.000	-99	-1	0			.667	-0	/3-1	-0.2
Total	3	12	41	3	10	0	0	0	2	1	2	.244	.279	.244	99	-1	0			.952	0	/P-11,3-1	-0.2
■ GEORGE BECHTEL						Bechtel, George A. b: 1848, Philadelphia, Pa. 5'11", 165 lbs. Deb: 5/20/1871																	
1871	Ath-n	20	94	24	33	9	1	1	21	2	2	.351	.365	.500	147	6	4	0	1	.821	0	O-15/P-3,3-3	0.4
1872	Mut-n	51	248	60	74	11	2	0	41	6	3	.298	.315	.359	114	6	9	1	2	.823	-0	*O-50/1-1	0.7
1873	Phi-n	53	258	53	63	12	1	1	40	9	1	.244	.270	.310	69	-10	2	1	0	.853	8	*O-52/P-3	0.0
1874	Phi-n	32	151	29	42	4	5	1	34	2	1	.278	.288	.391	111	1	0	0	0	.731	-3	O-28/P-6	0.0
1875	Cen-n	14	61	12	17	5	0	0	7	1	1	.279	.290	.361	136	2	0	0	0	.791	-1	P-14	0.0
	Ath-n	35	164	33	46	6	2	0	20	1	3	.280	.285	.341	105	-1	2	0	1	.810	1	O-31/P-4	0.2
	Yr	49	225	45	63	11	2	0	27	2	4	.280	.286	.347	113	2	2	0	1	.810	0	O-31,P-18	0.2
1876	Lou-N	14	55	2	10	1	0	0	2	0	1	.182	.182	.200	23	-5				.882	-2	O-14	-0.6
	NY-N	2	10	2	3	0	0	0	0	0	0	.300	.300	.300	115	-0				.429	-1	/O-2	-0.1
	Yr	16	65	4	13	1	0	0	2	0	1	.200	.200	.215	34	-5				.750	-3	O-16	-0.7
Total	5 n	205	976	211	275	47	11	3	163	21	11	.282	.297	.362	104	4	17	2	4	.816	5	O-176/P-30,3-3,1-1	1.3
■ CLYDE BECK						Beck, Clyde Eugene "Jersey" b: 1/6/1900, Bassett, Cal. d: 7/15/88, Temple City, Cal. BR/TR, 5'10", 176 lbs. Deb: 5/19/26																	
1926	Chi-N	30	81	10	16	0	0	1	4	7	15	.198	.261	.235	34	-7	0			.993	12	2-30	0.5
1927	Chi-N	117	391	44	101	20	5	2	44	43	37	.258	.332	.350	83	-9	0			.969	22	2-99,3-17/S-1	1.7
1928	Chi-N	131	483	72	124	18	4	3	52	58	58	.257	.341	.329	77	-15	3			.958	-1	3-87,S-47/2-1	-0.6
1929	Chi-N	54	190	28	40	7	0	0	9	19	24	.211	.282	.247	32	-20	3			.978	5	3-33,S-14	-1.1
1930	Chi-N	83	244	32	52	7	0	6	34	36	32	.213	.314	.316	53	-19	2			.953	0	S-57,2-24/3-2	-1.1
1931	Cin-N	53	136	17	21	4	2	0	19	21	14	.154	.272	.213	34	-12	1			.960	-2	3-38/S-6	-1.2
Total	6	468	1525	203	354	56	11	12	162	184	180	.232	.317	.307	63	-83	9			.959	36	3-177,2-154,S-125	-1.8
■ ERVE BECK						Beck, Ervin Thomas "Dutch" b: 7/19/1878, Toledo, Ohio d: 12/23/16, Toledo, Ohio BR/TR, 5'10", 168 lbs. Deb: 9/19/1899																	
1899	Bro-N	8	24	2	4	2	0	0	2	0		.167	.167	.250	13	-3	0			.931	-2	/2-6,S-2	-0.4
1901	Cle-A	135	539	78	156	26	8	6	79	23		.289	.320	.401	103	1	7			.927	-11	*2-132	-0.4
1902	Cin-N	48	187	19	57	10	3	1	20	3		.305	.319	.406	113	2	2			.936	-5	2-32/1-6,O-6	-0.3
	Det-A	41	162	23	48	4	0	2	22	4		.296	.313	.358	84	-4	3			.971	1	1-36/O-5	-0.3
Total	3	232	912	122	265	42	11	9	123	30		.291	.315	.390	99	-4	12			.929	-16	2-170/1-42,O-11,S-2	-1.4
■ FRANK BECK						Beck, Frank J. (b: Frank J. Hengstebeck) b: 4/29/1860, Poughkeepsie, N.Y. d: 2/8/41, Detroit, Mich. TR, 5'9", 141 lbs. Deb: 5/2/1884																	
1884	Pit-a	3	12	1	4	1	0	0		0		.333	.333	.417	141	0				1.000	0	/P-3	0.0
	Bal-U	5	20	1	2	1	0	0		0		.100	.100	.150	-23	-4				.500	-1	/O-4,P-2	-0.4
Total	1	8	32	2	6	2	0	0		0		.188	.188	.250	33	-4				1.000	-1	/P-5,O-4	-0.4
■ FRED BECK						Beck, Frederick Thomas b: 11/17/1886, Havana, Ill. d: 3/12/62, Havana, Ill. BL/TL, 6'1", 180 lbs. Deb: 4/14/09																	
1909	Bos-N	96	334	20	66	5	6	2	27	17		.198	.245	.266	56	-18	5			.966	4	O-57,1-33	-1.8
1910	Bos-N	154	571	52	157	32	9	**10**	64	19	55	.275	.307	.415	105	-0	8			.963	2	*O-134,1-19	-0.5
1911	Cin-N	41	87	7	16	1	2	2	20	1	13	.184	.193	.310	41	-7	2			1.000	-2	O-16/1-6	-1.0
	Phi-N	66	210	26	59	8	3	3	25	17	21	.281	.346	.390	105	1	3			.957	-5	O-61	-0.8
	Yr	107	297	33	75	9	5	5	45	18	34	.253	.304	.367	88	-6	5			.966	-7	O-77/1-6	-1.8
1914	Chi-F	157	555	51	155	23	4	11	77	44	66	.279	.341	.395	106	-9	9			.982	-13	*1-157	-2.3
1915	Chi-F	121	373	35	83	9	3	5	38	24	38	.223	.277	.303	67	-24	4			.992	-6	*1-117	-3.6
Total	5	635	2130	191	536	78	27	33	251	122	**193**	.252	.301	.360	89	-54	31			.984	-20	1-332,O-268	-10.0
■ ZINN BECK						Beck, Zinn Bertram b: 9/30/1885, Steubenville, O. d: 3/19/81, W.Palm Beach, Fla. BR/TR, 5'10.5", 160 lbs. Deb: 9/14/13																	
1913	StL-N	10	30	4	5	1	0	0	2	4	10	.167	.265	.200	34	-2	1			.833	1	/S-5,3-5	-0.2
1914	StL-N	137	457	42	106	15	11	3	45	28	32	.232	.282	.333	84	-11	14			.935	10	*3-122,S-16	0.5
1915	StL-N	70	223	21	52	9	4	0	15	12	31	.233	.282	.309	79	-6	6	10	-5	.935	-2	3-62/S-4,2-2	-0.9
1916	StL-N	62	184	8	41	7	1	0	10	14	21	.223	.281	.272	71	-6	3			.910	-6	3-52/1-1,2-1	-1.3
1918	NY-A	11	8	0	0	0	0	0	1	0	1	.000	.000	.000	-98	-2	0			1.000	0	/1-5,3-1	-0.2
Total	5	290	902	75	204	32	16	3	73	58	95	.226	.279	.307	76	-27	21	10	-5	.932	5	3-242/S-25,1-6,2-3	-2.1

YEAR	TM/L	G	AB	R	H	2B	3B	HR	RBI	BB	SO	AVG	OBP	SLG	PRO+	BR/A	SB	CS	SBR	FA	FR	G/POS	TPR
■ HEINIE BECKENDORF				Beckendorf, Henry Ward b: 6/15/1884, New York, N.Y. d: 9/15/49, Jackson Heights, N.Y. BR/TR, 5'9", 174 lbs. Deb: 4/16/09																				
1909	Det-A	15	27	1	7	1	0	0	1	2		.259	.310	.296	88	-0	0			.957	-0	C-15	0.0
1910	Det-A	3	7	0	3	0	0	0	2	1		.429	.500	.429	179	1	0			.909	-1	/C-2	0.0
	Was-A	37	103	8	15	1	0	0	10	5		.146	.207	.155	14	-10	0			.991	-0	C-36	-0.7
	Yr	40	110	8	18	1	0	0	12	6		.164	.227	.173	26	-9	0			.988	-0	C-38	-0.7
Total	2	55	137	9	25	2	0	0	13	8		.182	.243	.197	39	-10	0			.983	-1	/C-53	-0.7
■ BEALS BECKER				Becker, David Beals b: 7/5/1886, ElDorado, Kan. d: 8/16/43, Huntington Park, Cal. BL/TL, 5'9", 170 lbs. Deb: 4/19/08																				
1908	Pit-N	20	65	4	10	0	1	0	0	2		.154	.191	.185	20	-6	2			1.000	-1	O-17	-0.8
	Bos-N	43	171	13	47	3	1	0	7	7		.275	.303	.304	96	-1	7			.941	-4	O-43	-0.8
	Yr	63	236	17	57	3	2	0	7	9		.242	.272	.271	74	-7	9			.958	-5	O-60	-1.6
1909	Bos-N	152	562	60	138	15	6	6	24	47		.246	.305	.326	91	-7	21			.932	-2	*O-152	-1.6
1910	NY-N	80	126	18	36	2	4	3	24	14	25	.286	.357	.437	131	5	11			.972	-3	O-45/1-1	0.1
1911	*NY-N	88	172	28	45	11	1	1	20	26	22	.262	.359	.355	97	-0	19			.975	-5	O-55	-0.7
1912	*NY-N	125	402	66	106	18	8	6	58	54	35	.264	.354	.393	101	1	30			.958	-1	*O-117	-0.5
1913	Cin-N	30	108	11	32	5	3	0	14	6	12	.296	.333	.398	109	1	0			.971	2	O-28	0.2
	Phi-N	88	306	53	99	19	10	9	44	22	30	.324	.369	.539	151	19	11			.983	-2	O-77/1-1	1.4
	Yr	118	414	64	131	24	13	9	58	28	42	.316	.360	.502	140	20	11			.980	0	*O-105/1-1	1.6
1914	Phi-N	138	514	76	167	25	5	9	66	37	59	.325	.370	.446	133	20	16			.947	9	*O-126	2.4
1915	*Phi-N	112	338	38	83	16	4	11	35	26	48	.246	.301	.414	114	4	12	15	-5	.943	-8	O-98	-1.5
Total	8	876	2764	367	763	114	43	45	292	241	231	.276	.335	.397	112	35	129	15		.955	-13	O-758/1-2	-1.8
■ HEINZ BECKER				Becker, Heinz Reinhard "Dutch" b: 8/26/15, Berlin, Germany d: 11/11/91, Dallas, Tex. BB/TR, 6'2", 200 lbs. Deb: 4/21/43																				
1943	Chi-N	24	69	5	10	0	0	2	9	6		.145	.244	.145	14	-7	0			.983	1	1-18	-0.8
1945	*Chi-N	67	133	25	38	8	2	2	27	17	16	.286	.375	.421	124	4	0			1.000	-2	1-28	0.1
1946	Chi-N	9	7	0	2	0	0	0	1	1		.286	.375	.286	91	-0	0			.000	0	H	0.0
	Cle-A	50	147	15	44	10	1	0	17	23	18	.299	.401	.381	127	6	1	0	0	.995	0	1-44	0.5
1947	Cle-A	2	2	0	0	0	0	0	0	0	1	.000	.000	.000	-99	-1	0	0	0	.000	0	H	-0.1
Total	4	152	358	45	94	18	3	6	54	50	42	.263	.359	.346	102	3	1	0		.994	0	/1-90	-0.3
■ JOE BECKER				Becker, Joseph Edward b: 6/25/08, St.Louis, Mo. BR/TR, 6'1", 180 lbs. Deb: 5/10/36 C																				
1936	Cle-A	22	50	5	9	3	1	1	11	5	4	.180	.255	.340	45	-5	0	0	0	.977	-4	C-15	-0.8
1937	Cle-A	18	33	3	11	2	1	0	2	3	4	.333	.405	.455	116	1	0	0	0	.949	-1	C-12	0.1
Total	2	40	83	8	20	5	2	1	13	8	8	.241	.315	.386	73	-4	0	0	0	.964	-5	/C-27	-0.7
■ MARTY BECKER				Becker, Martin Henry b: 12/25/1893, Tiffin, Ohio d: 9/25/57, Cincinnati, Ohio BB/TL, 5'8.5", 155 lbs. Deb: 9/8/15																				
1915	NY-N	17	52	5	13	2	0	0	3	2	9	.250	.278	.288	76	-2	3			.917	0	O-16	-0.1
■ RICH BECKER				Becker, Richard Godhard b: 2/1/72, Aurora, Ill. BB/TR, 5'10", 180 lbs. Deb: 9/10/93																				
1993	Min-A	3	7	3	2	2	0	0	5	4		.286	.583	.571	211	2	1	1	-0	.875	-0	/O-3	0.1
1994	Min-A	28	98	12	26	0	1	0	8	13	25	.265	.351	.327	76	-3	6	1	1	.989	5	O-26/D-1	0.3
1995	Min-A	106	392	45	93	15	1	2	33	34	95	.237	.305	.296	57	-24	8	9	-3	.986	13	*O-105	-1.7
1996	Min-A	148	525	92	153	31	4	12	71	68	118	.291	.375	.434	102	3	19	5	3	.993	24	*O-146	2.3
Total	4	285	1022	152	274	51	5	15	112	120	242	.268	.348	.372	84	-23	34	16	1	.989	42	O-280/D-1	1.0
■ GLENN BECKERT				Beckert, Glenn Alfred b: 10/12/40, Pittsburgh, Pa. BR/TR, 6'1", 190 lbs. Deb: 4/12/65																				
1965	Chi-N	154	614	73	147	21	3	8	30	28	52	.239	.276	.298	60	-32	6	8	-3	.973	9	*2-153	-1.3
1966	Chi-N	153	656	73	188	23	7	1	59	26	36	.287	.318	.348	84	-14	10	4	1	.970	-20	*2-152/S-1	-2.4
1967	Chi-N	146	597	91	167	32	5	5	40	30	25	.280	.314	.369	91	-8	10	3	1	.968	4	*2-144	0.8
1968	Chi-N	155	643	98	189	28	4	4	37	31	20	.294	.328	.369	102	1	8	4	0	.977	6	*2-155	1.9
1969	Chi-N★	131	543	69	158	22	1	1	37	24	24	.291	.328	.341	78	-16	6	0	2	.965	6	*2-129	0.3
1970	Chi-N★	143	591	99	170	15	6	3	36	32	22	.288	.324	.349	72	-24	4	1	1	.970	10	*2-138/O-1	-0.2
1971	Chi-N★	131	530	80	181	18	5	2	42	24	24	.342	.370	.406	104	3	3	2	-0	.986	-3	*2-129	1.1
1972	Chi-N★	120	474	51	128	22	2	3	43	23	17	.270	.307	.344	76	-15	2	1	0	.976	11	*2-118	0.3
1973	Chi-N	114	372	38	95	13	0	0	29	30	15	.255	.314	.290	64	-17	0	2	-1	.984	-12	2-88	-2.7
1974	SD-N	64	172	11	44	1	0	0	7	11	8	.256	.301	.262	61	-9	0	0	0	.938	-17	2-36/3-1	-2.6
1975	SD-N	9	16	2	6	1	0	0	1	0	1	.375	.412	.438	145	1	0	0	0	1.000	1	/3-4	0.0
Total	11	1320	5208	685	1473	196	31	22	360	260	243	.283	.319	.345	81	-129	49	25	-0	.973	-7	*2-1242/3-5,O-1,S-1	-4.8
■ JAKE BECKLEY				Beckley, Jacob Peter "Eagle Eye" b: 8/4/1867, Hannibal, Mo. d: 6/25/18, Kansas City, Mo. BL/TL, 5'10", 200 lbs. Deb: 6/20/1888 H																				
1888	Pit-N	71	283	35	97	15	3	0	27	7	22	.343	.363	.417	160	18	20			.979	-3	1-71	0.9
1889	Pit-N	123	522	91	157	24	10	9	97	29	29	.301	.345	.437	130	19	11			.982	2	*1-122/O-1	1.1
1890	Pit-P	121	516	109	167	38	22	9	120	42	32	.324	.381	.535	156	39	18			.976	-0	*1-121	2.5
1891	Pit-N	133	554	94	162	20	19	4	73	44	46	.292	.353	.419	128	18	13			.982	13	*1-133	2.1
1892	Pit-N	151	614	102	145	21	19	10	96	31	44	.236	.288	.381	102	-2	30			.978	21	*1-151	1.0
1893	Pit-N	131	542	108	164	32	19	5	106	54	26	.303	.386	.459	127	20	15			.986	11	*1-131	2.2
1894	Pit-N	131	533	121	183	36	18	7	120	43	16	.343	.412	.518	124	21	21			.978	5	*1-131	2.0
1895	Pit-N	129	530	104	174	31	19	5	110	24	20	.328	.381	.487	130	22	20			.978	-7	*1-129	1.5
1896	Pit-N	59	217	44	55	7	5	3	32	22	28	.253	.349	.373	94	-1	8			.982	-1	1-56/O-3,2-1	-0.1
	NY-N	46	182	37	55	8	4	5	38	9	7	.302	.352	.473	120	4	11			.982	-1	1-45/O-2	0.3
	Yr	105	399	81	110	15	9	8	70	31	35	.276	.351	.419	106	3	19			.982	-2	*1-101/O-5,2-1	0.2
1897	NY-N	17	68	8	17	2	3	1	11	2		.250	.301	.412	90	-1	2			.973	1	1-17	0.1
	Cin-N	97	365	76	126	17	9	7	76	18		.345	.395	.499	127	12	23			.979	-3	1-97	0.8
	Yr	114	433	84	143	19	12	8	87	20		.330	.380	.485	121	11	25			.978	-1	1-114	0.9
1898	Cin-N	118	459	86	135	20	12	4	72	28		.294	.348	.416	111	4	6			.983	-1	*1-118	0.3
1899	Cin-N	134	513	87	171	27	16	3	99	40		.333	.393	.466	133	22	23			.986	5	*1-134	2.5
1900	Cin-N	141	558	98	190	26	10	2	94	40		.341	.389	.434	130	23	23			.980	6	*1-140	2.5
1901	Cin-N	140	580	78	178	36	13	3	79	28		.307	.346	.429	133	22	4			.977	-4	*1-140	1.6
1902	Cin-N	129	531	82	175	23	7	5	69	34		.330	.377	.427	135	20	15			.983	-3	*1-129/P-1	1.5
1903	Cin-N	120	459	85	150	29	10	2	81	42		.327	.384	.447	123	12	23			.976	4	*1-119	1.3
1904	StL-N	142	551	72	179	22	9	1	67	35		.325	.375	.403	147	30	17			.988	-12	*1-142	1.6
1905	StL-N	134	514	48	147	20	10	1	57	30		.286	.333	.370	113	7	12			.982	-8	*1-134	-0.5
1906	StL-N	87	320	29	79	16	6	0	44	13		.247	.283	.353	96	-3	3			.987	-4	1-85	-1.1
1907	StL-N	32	115	6	24	3	0	0	7	1		.209	.222	.235	45	-8	0			.988	-2	1-32	-0.7
Total	20	2386	9526	1600	2930	473	243	86	1575	616	270	.308	.361	.435	125	299	315			.981	19	*1-2377/O-6,P-1,2-1	22.9
■ JULIO BECQUER				Becquer, Julio (Villegas) b: 12/20/31, Havana, Cuba BL/TL, 5'11.5", 178 lbs. Deb: 9/13/55																				
1955	Was-A	10	14	1	3	0	1	0	1	0	1	.214	.214	.214	16	-2	0	0	0	1.000	1	/1-2	-0.1
1957	Was-A	105	186	14	42	6	2	2	22	10	29	.226	.269	.312	59	-11	3	3	-1	1.000	1	1-43	-1.4
1958	Was-A	86	164	10	39	3	0	0	12	8	21	.238	.273	.256	47	-12	1	1	0	.994	6	1-42/O-1	-1.0
1959	Was-A	108	220	20	59	12	5	1	26	9	17	.268	.297	.382	85	-5	3	1	0	.990	2	1-53	-0.6
1960	Was-A	110	298	41	75	15	7	4	35	12	35	.252	.283	.389	81	-9	1	3	-2	.989	-3	1-77/P-1	-1.9
1961	LA-A	11	8	0	0	0	0	0	0	1	5	.000	.111	.000	-61	-2	0	0	0	1.000	0	/1-5	-0.2
	Min-A	57	84	13	20	1	2	5	18	2	12	.238	.256	.476	86	-2	1	0	-1	1.000	-1	1-18/O-5,P-1	-0.4
	Yr	68	92	13	20	1	2	5	18	3	17	.217	.242	.435	72	-4	1	0	-1	1.000	-1	1-23/O-5,P-1	-0.6
1963	Min-A	1	0	1	0	0	0	0	0	0	0	—	—	—		0	0	0	0	.000	0	H	0.0
Total	7	488	974	100	238	37	16	12	114	41	120	.244	.277	.352	70	-42	8	11	-4	.993	5	1-240/O-6,P-2	-5.6
■ HOWIE BEDELL				Bedell, Howard William b: 9/29/35, Clearfield, Pa. BL/TR, 6'1", 185 lbs. Deb: 4/10/62 C																				
1962	Mil-N	58	138	15	27	1	2	0	2	11	22	.196	.255	.232	33	-13	1	0	0	.955	-3	O-45	-1.8

YEAR	TM/L	G	AB	R	H	2B	3B	HR	RBI	BB	SO	AVG	OBP	SLG	PRO+	BR/A	SB	CS	SBR	FA	FR	G/POS	TPR
1968	Phi-N	9	7	0	1	0	0	0	1	1	0	.143	.250	.143	20	-1	0	0	0	.000	0	H	-0.1
Total	2	67	145	15	28	1	2	0	3	12	22	.193	.255	.228	32	-14	1	0	0	.955	-3	/O-45	-1.9

■ GENE BEDFORD   Bedford, William Eugene b: 12/2/1896, Dallas, Tex. d: 10/6/77, San Antonio, Tex. BB/TR, 5'8", 170 lbs. Deb: 6/25/25

YEAR	TM/L	G	AB	R	H	2B	3B	HR	RBI	BB	SO	AVG	OBP	SLG	PRO+	BR/A	SB	CS	SBR	FA	FR	G/POS	TPR
1925	Cle-A	2	3	1	0	0	0	0	0	1	.000	.000	.000	-99	-1	0	0	0	1.000	-1	/2-2	-0.2

■ ED BEECHER   Beecher, Edward "Scrap Iron" b: 5/1876, Indiana   Deb: 9/26/1897

YEAR	TM/L	G	AB	R	H	2B	3B	HR	RBI	BB	SO	AVG	OBP	SLG	PRO+	BR/A	SB	CS	SBR	FA	FR	G/POS	TPR
1897	StL-N	3	12	1	4	0	0	0	1	0	.333	.333	.333	78	-0	1	1.000	-0	/O-3	-0.1
1898	Cle-N	8	25	1	5	2	0	0	1	0	.200	.200	.280	38	-2	0	.846	-2	/O-8	-0.4
Total	2	11	37	2	9	2	0	0	1	0	.243	.243	.297	51	-3	1	.895	-2	/O-11	-0.5

■ ED BEECHER   Beecher, Edward Harry b: 7/2/1860, Guilford, Conn. d: 9/12/35, Hartford, Conn. BL/TL, 5'10", 185 lbs. Deb: 6/28/1887

YEAR	TM/L	G	AB	R	H	2B	3B	HR	RBI	BB	SO	AVG	OBP	SLG	PRO+	BR/A	SB	CS	SBR	FA	FR	G/POS	TPR
1887	Pit-N	41	169	15	41	8	0	2	22	7	8	.243	.281	.325	72	-6	8	.915	5	O-41	-0.2
1889	Was-N	42	179	20	53	9	0	0	30	5	4	.296	.319	.346	91	-2	3	.861	-1	O-39/1-3	-0.4
1890	Buf-P	126	536	69	159	22	10	3	90	29	23	.297	.341	.392	104	3	14	.810	-5	*O-126/P-1	-0.5
1891	Was-a	58	235	35	57	11	3	2	28	27	9	.243	.333	.340	97	-1	17	.824	3	O-58	0.1
	Phi-a	16	71	9	15	2	4	0	7	3	4	.211	.243	.352	68	-4	7	1.000	-1	O-16	-0.4
	Yr	74	306	44	72	13	7	2	35	30	13	.235	.314	.343	91	-4	24	.845	2	O-74	-0.3
Total	4	283	1190	148	325	52	17	7	177	71	48	.273	.322	.363	94	-10	49	.843	1	O-280/1-3,P-1	-1.4

■ JODIE BEELER   Beeler, Joseph Sam b: 11/26/21, Dallas, Tex. BR/TR, 6', 170 lbs. Deb: 9/21/44

YEAR	TM/L	G	AB	R	H	2B	3B	HR	RBI	BB	SO	AVG	OBP	SLG	PRO+	BR/A	SB	CS	SBR	FA	FR	G/POS	TPR
1944	Cin-N	3	3	0	0	0	0	0	0	0	0	.000	.000	.000	-99	-1	0		-1	/2-1,3-1	-0.2

■ GENE BEGLEY   Begley, Eugene T. b: 6/7/1861, Brooklyn, N.Y. Deb: 9/11/1886

YEAR	TM/L	G	AB	R	H	2B	3B	HR	RBI	BB	SO	AVG	OBP	SLG	PRO+	BR/A	SB	CS	SBR	FA	FR	G/POS	TPR
1886	NY-N	5	16	1	2	0	0	0	1	3	.125	.176	.125	-7	-2	1	.864	-1	/C-3,O-2	-0.2

■ JIM BEGLEY   Begley, James Lawrence "Imp" b: 9/19/02, San Francisco, Cal. d: 2/20/57, San Francisco, Cal BR/TR, 5'6", 145 lbs. Deb: 5/28/24

YEAR	TM/L	G	AB	R	H	2B	3B	HR	RBI	BB	SO	AVG	OBP	SLG	PRO+	BR/A	SB	CS	SBR	FA	FR	G/POS	TPR
1924	Cin-N	2	5	1	1	0	0	0	2	0	.200	.429	.200	75	-0	0	0	0	.933	1	/2-2	0.1

■ STEVE BEHEL   Behel, Stephen Arnold Douglas b: 11/6/1860, Earlville, Ill. d: 2/15/45, Los Angeles, Cal. Deb: 9/27/1884

YEAR	TM/L	G	AB	R	H	2B	3B	HR	RBI	BB	SO	AVG	OBP	SLG	PRO+	BR/A	SB	CS	SBR	FA	FR	G/POS	TPR
1884	Mil-U	9	33	5	8	1	0	0	3	.242	.306	.273	141	-1	1.000	-1	/O-9	-0.1
1886	NY-a	59	224	32	46	5	2	0	17	22	.205	.279	.246	68	-7	16	.858	-4	O-59	-1.1
Total	2	68	257	37	54	6	2	0	17	25	.210	.283	.249	73	-8	16	.865	-5	/O-68	-1.2

■ OLLIE BEJMA   Bejma, Alojzy Frank b: 9/12/07, South Bend, Ind. d: 1/3/95, South Bend, Ind. BR/TR, 5'10", 165 lbs. Deb: 4/24/34

YEAR	TM/L	G	AB	R	H	2B	3B	HR	RBI	BB	SO	AVG	OBP	SLG	PRO+	BR/A	SB	CS	SBR	FA	FR	G/POS	TPR
1934	StL-A	95	262	39	71	16	3	2	29	40	36	.271	.376	.378	87	-4	3	2	-0	.952	-12	S-32,2-14,3-13,/O-9	-1.3
1935	StL-A	64	198	18	38	8	2	2	26	27	21	.192	.289	.283	46	-16	1	0	0	.952	-4	2-47/S-8,3-2	-1.5
1936	StL-A	67	139	19	36	2	3	2	18	27	21	.259	.380	.360	81	-3	0	0	0	.963	-12	2-32/3-7,S-1	-1.2
1939	Chi-A	90	307	52	77	9	3	8	44	36	27	.251	.331	.378	79	-10	1	3	-2	.981	-14	2-81/S-1,3-1	-2.0
Total	4	316	906	128	222	35	11	14	117	130	105	.245	.343	.354	75	-34	5	5	-2	.967	-42	2-174/S-42,3-23,0-9	-6.0

■ MARK BELANGER   Belanger, Mark Henry b: 6/8/44, Pittsfield, Mass. BR/TR, 6'1", 170 lbs. Deb: 8/7/65

YEAR	TM/L	G	AB	R	H	2B	3B	HR	RBI	BB	SO	AVG	OBP	SLG	PRO+	BR/A	SB	CS	SBR	FA	FR	G/POS	TPR
1965	Bal-A	11	3	1	1	0	0	0	0	0	0	.333	.333	.333	88	-0	0	1	-1	1.000	1	/S-4	0.0
1966	Bal-A	8	19	2	3	1	0	0	0	0	3	.158	.158	.211	5	-2	0	0	0	1.000	4	/S-6	0.2
1967	Bal-A	69	184	19	32	5	0	1	10	12	46	.174	.224	.217	31	-16	6	1	1	.952	7	S-38,2-26/3-2	-0.4
1968	Bal-A	145	472	40	98	13	0	2	21	40	114	.208	.275	.248	59	-22	10	1	2	.969	12	*S-145	0.8
1969	*Bal-A	150	530	76	152	17	4	2	50	53	54	.287	.354	.345	95	-2	14	6	1	.968	-10	*S-148	0.5
1970	*Bal-A	145	459	53	100	6	5	1	36	52	65	.218	.304	.259	56	-26	13	2	3	.970	8	*S-143	-0.1
1971	*Bal-A	150	500	67	133	19	4	0	35	73	48	.266	.367	.320	97	1	10	8	-2	.978	0	*S-149	2.0
1972	Bal-A	113	285	36	53	9	1	2	16	18	53	.186	.239	.246	43	-20	6	2	0	.975	21	*S-105	1.4
1973	*Bal-A	154	470	60	106	15	1	0	27	49	54	.226	.305	.262	61	-23	13	6	0	.971	3	*S-154	0.0
1974	*Bal-A	155	493	54	111	14	4	5	36	51	69	.225	.300	.300	75	-15	17	7	1	**.984**	9	*S-155	1.6
1975	Bal-A	152	442	44	100	11	1	3	27	36	53	.226	.286	.276	63	-21	16	4	2	.978	**28**	*S-152	2.5
1976	Bal-A★	153	522	66	141	22	2	1	40	51	64	.270	.337	.326	101	1	27	17	-2	.982	16	*S-153	3.6
1977	Bal-A	144	402	39	83	13	4	2	30	43	68	.206	.288	.274	58	-23	15	8	-0	**.985**	21	*S-142	1.1
1978	Bal-A	135	348	39	74	13	0	0	16	40	53	.213	.305	.250	61	-17	6	6	-2	**.985**	34	*S-134	3.0
1979	*Bal-A	101	198	28	33	6	2	0	9	29	33	.167	.276	.217	36	-17	5	1	1	.990	3	S-98	-0.6
1980	Bal-A	113	268	37	61	7	3	0	22	12	25	.228	.261	.276	48	-19	6	3	0	.975	-1	*S-109	-1.1
1981	Bal-A	64	139	9	23	3	2	1	10	12	25	.165	.242	.237	39	-11	2	1	0	.973	5	S-63	-0.2
1982	LA-N	54	50	6	12	1	0	0	4	5	10	.240	.309	.260	62	-2	1	0	0	.953	8	S-44/2-1	0.7
Total	18	2016	5784	676	1316	175	33	20	389	576	839	.228	.302	.280	68	-234	167	75	5	.977	167	*S-1942/2-27,3-2	15.0

■ WAYNE BELARDI   Belardi, Carroll Wayne b: 9/5/30, St.Helena, Cal. d: 10/21/93, Santa Cruz, Cal. BL/TL, 6'1", 185 lbs. Deb: 4/18/50

YEAR	TM/L	G	AB	R	H	2B	3B	HR	RBI	BB	SO	AVG	OBP	SLG	PRO+	BR/A	SB	CS	SBR	FA	FR	G/POS	TPR
1950	Bro-N	10	10	0	0	0	0	0	0	0	4	.000	.000	.000	-98	-3	0	1.000	-0	/1-1	-0.3
1951	Bro-N	3	3	1	1	0	1	0	0	0	2	.333	.333	1.000	240	1	0	0	0	.000	-0	H	0.1
1953	*Bro-N	69	163	19	39	3	2	11	34	16	40	.239	.311	.485	101	-0	0	0	0	.984	-0	1-38	-0.2
1954	Bro-N	11	9	0	2	0	0	0	1	2	3	.222	.364	.222	55	-0	0	0	0	.000	-0	H	0.0
	Det-A	88	250	27	58	7	1	11	24	33	34	.232	.333	.400	102	0	1	0	0	.988	2	1-79	-0.1
1955	Det-A	3	3	0	0	0	0	0	0	0	1	.000	.000	.000	-99	-1	0	.000	-0	H	-0.1
1956	Det-A	79	154	24	43	3	1	6	15	15	13	.279	.373	.429	111	3	0	0	0	.988	-1	1-31/O-2	0.3
Total	6	263	592	71	143	13	5	28	74	66	97	.242	.332	.422	100	-1	1	0	0	.987	0	1-149/O-2	-0.6

■ KEVIN BELCHER   Belcher, Kevin Donnell b: 8/8/67, Waco, Tex. BR/TR, 6', 170 lbs. Deb: 9/3/90

YEAR	TM/L	G	AB	R	H	2B	3B	HR	RBI	BB	SO	AVG	OBP	SLG	PRO+	BR/A	SB	CS	SBR	FA	FR	G/POS	TPR
1990	Tex-A	16	15	4	2	1	0	0	2	6	.133	.235	.200	23	-2	0	0	0	1.000	-2	/O-9	-0.3

■ IRA BELDEN   Belden, Ira Allison b: 4/16/1874, Cleveland, Ohio d: 7/15/16, Lakewood, Ohio BL/TR, 5'11", 175 lbs. Deb: 9/17/1897

YEAR	TM/L	G	AB	R	H	2B	3B	HR	RBI	BB	SO	AVG	OBP	SLG	PRO+	BR/A	SB	CS	SBR	FA	FR	G/POS	TPR
1897	Cle-N	8	30	5	8	0	2	0	4	2	.267	.333	.400	88	-1	0	1.000	2	/O-8	0.0

■ TIM BELK   Belk, Timothy William b: 4/6/70, Cincinnati, Ohio BR/TR, 6'3", 200 lbs. Deb: 6/25/96

YEAR	TM/L	G	AB	R	H	2B	3B	HR	RBI	BB	SO	AVG	OBP	SLG	PRO+	BR/A	SB	CS	SBR	FA	FR	G/POS	TPR
1996	Cin-N	7	15	2	3	0	0	0	0	1	2	.200	.250	.200	21	-2	0	0	0	1.000	-1	/1-6	-0.3

■ CHARLIE BELL   Bell, Charles C. b: 8/12/1868, Cincinnati, Ohio d: 2/7/37, Cincinnati, Ohio TR, Deb: 10/13/1889 F

YEAR	TM/L	G	AB	R	H	2B	3B	HR	RBI	BB	SO	AVG	OBP	SLG	PRO+	BR/A	SB	CS	SBR	FA	FR	G/POS	TPR
1889	KC-a	2	6	1	1	1	0	0	3	2	.167	.375	.333	97	0	0	.000	-0	/O-1,P-1	-0.1
1891	Lou-a	10	28	3	1	0	0	0	6	8	.036	.206	.036	-31	-5	0	.783	-2	P-10	0.0
	Cin-a	1	4	1	2	0	0	0	1	0	.500	.500	.500	171	0	0	1.000	0	/P-1	0.0
	Yr	11	32	4	3	0	0	0	7	8	.094	.237	.094	-5	-4	0	.815	-1	P-11	0.0
Total	2	13	38	5	4	1	0	0	4	8	10	.105	.261	.132	13	-4	0	.844	-1	/P-12,O-1	-0.1

■ BUDDY BELL   Bell, David Gus b: 8/27/51, Pittsburgh, Pa. BR/TR, 6'2", 185 lbs. Deb: 4/15/72 FMC

YEAR	TM/L	G	AB	R	H	2B	3B	HR	RBI	BB	SO	AVG	OBP	SLG	PRO+	BR/A	SB	CS	SBR	FA	FR	G/POS	TPR
1972	Cle-A	132	466	49	119	21	1	9	36	34	29	.255	.310	.363	96	-2	5	6	-2	.990	7	*O-123/3-6	-0.3
1973	Cle-A★	156	631	86	169	23	7	14	59	49	47	.268	.323	.393	100	-1	7	15	-7	.958	24	*3-154/O-2	1.6
1974	Cle-A	116	423	51	111	15	1	7	46	35	29	.262	.323	.352	95	-3	1	3	-2	.963	4	*3-115/D-1	-0.1
1975	Cle-A	153	553	66	150	20	4	10	59	51	72	.271	.334	.376	100	0	6	5	-1	.950	-3	*3-153	-0.5
1976	Cle-A	159	604	75	170	26	2	7	60	44	49	.281	.332	.366	105	4	3	8	-4	.956	5	*3-158/1-2	0.4
1977	Cle-A	129	479	64	140	23	4	11	64	45	63	.292	.354	.426	115	10	1	8	-5	.960	13	*3-118,O-11	1.6
1978	Cle-A	142	556	71	157	27	8	6	62	39	43	.282	.329	.392	103	2	1	3	-2	.970	28	*3-139/D-1	2.7
1979	Tex-A	162	670	89	200	42	3	18	101	30	45	.299	.331	.451	110	7	5	4	-1	.969	12	*3-147,S-33	2.0
1980	Tex-A★	129	490	76	161	24	4	17	83	40	39	.329	.379	.498	143	28	3	1	0	**.981**	22	*3-120/S-3	4.7
1981	Tex-A★	97	360	44	106	16	1	10	64	42	30	.294	.373	.428	137	18	3	5	-1	.961	**30**	3-96/S-1	4.6
1982	Tex-A★	148	537	62	159	27	2	13	70	70	50	.296	.379	.426	127	22	5	4	-1	**.976**	**34**	*3-145/S-4	5.1
1983	Tex-A	156	618	75	171	35	3	14	66	50	48	.277	.335	.411	106	5	3	4	-1	.967	16	*3-154	1.6
1984	Tex-A★	148	553	88	174	36	5	11	83	63	54	.315	.388	.458	129	23	2	1	0	.958	21	*3-147	4.1
1985	Tex-A	84	313	33	74	13	3	4	32	33	21	.236	.311	.335	76	-10	3	2	-0	.942	13	3-83	0.2

YEAR	TM/L	G	AB	R	H	2B	3B	HR	RBI	BB	SO	AVG	OBP	SLG	PRO+	BR/A	SB	CS	SBR	FA	FR	G/POS	TPR
1985	Cin-N	67	247	28	54	15	2	6	36	34	27	.219	.313	.368	86	-5	0	1	-1	.946	-9	3-67	-1.6
1986	Cin-N	155	568	89	158	29	3	20	75	73	49	.278	.365	.445	117	14	2	8	-4	.975	1	*3-151/2-1	0.9
1987	Cin-N	143	522	74	148	19	2	17	70	71	39	.284	.370	.425	105	6	4	1	1	.979	-17	*3-142	-1.3
1988	Cin-N	21	54	3	10	0	0	0	3	7	3	.185	.279	.185	34	-4	0	0	0	.968	0	3-13/1-2	-0.5
	Hou-N	74	269	24	68	10	1	7	37	19	29	.253	.302	.375	97	-2	1	1	-0	.924	-11	3-66/1-7	-1.6
	Yr	95	323	27	78	10	1	7	40	26	32	.241	.298	.344	86	-6	1	1	-0	.931	-11	3-79/1-9	-2.1
1989	Tex-A	34	82	4	15	4	0	0	3	7	10	.183	.247	.232	35	-7	0	0	0	1.000	5	D-22/3-9,1-1	-0.7
Total	18	2405	8995	1151	2514	425	56	201	1106	836	776	.279	.343	.406	108	105	55	79	-31	.964	191	*3-2183,O-136/SD12	22.9

■ DAVID BELL

Bell, David Michael b: 9/14/72, Cincinnati, Ohio BR/TR, 5'10", 170 lbs. Deb: 5/3/95 F

YEAR	TM/L	G	AB	R	H	2B	3B	HR	RBI	BB	SO	AVG	OBP	SLG	PRO+	BR/A	SB	CS	SBR	FA	FR	G/POS	TPR
1995	Cle-A	2	2	0	0	0	0	0	0	0	0	.000	.000	.000	-99	-1	0	0	0	1.000	0	/3-2	0.0
	StL-N	39	144	13	36	7	2	2	19	4	25	.250	.280	.368	69	-7	1	2	-1	.967	-3	2-37/3-3	-0.8
1996	StL-N	62	145	12	31	6	0	1	9	10	22	.214	.269	.276	44	-12	1	1	-0	.953	9	3-45,2-20/S-1	-0.2
Total	2	103	291	25	67	13	2	3	28	14	47	.230	.273	.320	55	-19	2	3	-1	.973	7	/2-57,3-50,S-1	-1.0

■ GUS BELL

Bell, David Russell b: 11/15/28, Louisville, Ky. d: 5/7/95, Montgomery, Ohio BL/TR, 6'2", 196 lbs. Deb: 5/30/50 F

YEAR	TM/L	G	AB	R	H	2B	3B	HR	RBI	BB	SO	AVG	OBP	SLG	PRO+	BR/A	SB	CS	SBR	FA	FR	G/POS	TPR
1950	Pit-N	111	422	62	119	22	11	8	53	28	46	.282	.333	.443	99	-2	4			.977	6	*O-104	0.0
1951	Pit-N	149	600	80	167	27	**12**	16	89	42	41	.278	.330	.443	103	1	1	4	-2	.986	3	*O-145	-0.3
1952	Pit-N	131	468	53	117	21	5	16	59	36	72	.250	.306	.419	97	-4	1	4	-2	.972	-7	*O-123	-1.8
1953	Cin-N★	151	610	102	183	37	5	30	105	48	72	.300	.354	.525	124	20	0	2	-1	.977	14	*O-151	2.5
1954	Cin-N★	153	619	104	185	38	7	17	101	48	58	.299	.353	.465	108	7	5	3	-0	.986	2	*O-153	0.1
1955	Cin-N	154	610	88	188	30	6	27	104	54	57	.308	.364	.510	122	18	4	1	-0	.987	-8	*O-154	0.2
1956	Cin-N★	150	603	82	176	31	6	29	84	50	66	.292	.349	.501	117	14	6	2	1	.986	-7	*O-149	-0.1
1957	Cin-N★	121	510	65	149	20	3	13	61	30	54	.292	.335	.420	95	-4	0	1	-1	.988	0	*O-121	-1.2
1958	Cin-N	112	385	42	97	16	2	10	46	36	40	.252	.318	.382	80	-11	2	3	-1	**.996**	-2	*O-107	-2.0
1959	Cin-N	148	580	59	170	27	2	19	115	29	40	.293	.329	.445	101	-0	2	3	-1	**.996**	7	*O-145	-0.2
1960	Cin-N	143	515	65	135	19	5	12	62	29	40	.262	.303	.388	86	-11	4	3	-1	.988	0	*O-131	-1.8
1961	*Cin-N	103	235	27	60	10	1	3	33	18	21	.255	.308	.345	72	-9	1	1	-0	.991	-6	O-75	-1.9
1962	NY-N	30	101	8	15	2	0	1	6	10	7	.149	.225	.198	14	-12	1	1	-0	.979	4	O-26	-1.1
	Mil-N	79	214	28	61	11	3	5	24	12	17	.285	.323	.435	104	1	0	0	0	.987	-3	O-58	-0.6
	Yr	109	315	36	76	13	3	6	30	22	24	.241	.291	.359	74	-12	1	1	-0	.984	0	O-84	-1.7
1963	Mil-N	3	3	0	1	0	0	0	0	0	0	.333	.333	.333	94	-0	0	0	0	.000	0	H	0.0
1964	Mil-N	3	3	0	0	0	0	0	0	0	0	.000	.000	.000	-99	-1	0	0	0	.000	0	H	-0.1
Total	15	1741	6478	865	1823	311	66	206	942	470	636	.281	.333	.445	102	7	30	<u>31</u>		.985	2	*O-1642	-8.3

■ DEREK BELL

Bell, Derek Nathaniel b: 12/11/68, Tampa, Fla. BR/TR, 6'2", 200 lbs. Deb: 6/28/91

YEAR	TM/L	G	AB	R	H	2B	3B	HR	RBI	BB	SO	AVG	OBP	SLG	PRO+	BR/A	SB	CS	SBR	FA	FR	G/POS	TPR
1991	Tor-A	18	28	5	4	0	0	1	6	1	14	.143	.314	.143	30	-2	3	2	-0	.889	-2	O-13	-0.6
1992	*Tor-A	61	161	23	39	6	3	2	15	15	34	.242	.326	.354	86	-3	7	2	1	1.000	-1	O-56/D-1	-0.4
1993	SD-N	150	542	73	142	19	1	21	72	23	122	.262	.307	.417	90	-9	26	5	5	.976	6	*O-125,3-19	0.0
1994	SD-N	108	434	54	135	20	0	14	54	29	68	.311	.356	.454	112	7	24	8	2	.962	-0	*O-108	0.7
1995	Hou-N	112	452	63	151	21	2	8	86	33	71	.334	.389	.442	128	18	27	9	3	.963	1	*O-110	1.9
1996	Hou-N	158	627	84	165	40	2	17	113	40	123	.263	.316	.418	100	-2	29	3	7	.977	9	*O-157	0.9
Total	6	607	2244	302	636	106	9	62	341	146	443	.283	.337	.422	104	9	116	29	17	.972	13	O-569/3-19,D-1	2.5

■ FERN BELL

Bell, Fernando Jerome Lee (b: Fern Oran Bell) "Danny" b: 1/21/13, Ada, Okla. BR/TR, 6', 180 lbs. Deb: 4/17/39

YEAR	TM/L	G	AB	R	H	2B	3B	HR	RBI	BB	SO	AVG	OBP	SLG	PRO+	BR/A	SB	CS	SBR	FA	FR	G/POS	TPR
1939	Pit-N	83	262	44	75	5	8	2	34	42	18	.286	.385	.389	110	5	5			.975	0	O-67/3-1	0.3
1940	Pit-N	6	3	0	0	0	0	0	0	1	1	.000	.250	.000	-26	-0	0			.000	0	H	-0.1
Total	2	89	265	44	75	5	8	2	35	43	19	.283	.383	.385	109	5	5			.975	0	/O-67,3-1	0.2

■ FRANK BELL

Bell, Frank Gustav b: 1863, Cincinnati, Ohio d: 4/14/1891, Cincinnati, Ohio 6', Deb: 7/7/1885 F

YEAR	TM/L	G	AB	R	H	2B	3B	HR	RBI	BB	SO	AVG	OBP	SLG	PRO+	BR/A	SB	CS	SBR	FA	FR	G/POS	TPR
1885	Bro-a	10	29	5	5	0	1	0	2	0	6	.172	.200	.241	39	-2				.739	-2	/C-5,O-4,3-2	-0.3

■ GEORGE BELL

Bell, George Antonio (Mathey) b: 10/21/59, San Pedro De Macoris, D.R. BR/TR, 6'1", 190 lbs. Deb: 4/9/81 F

YEAR	TM/L	G	AB	R	H	2B	3B	HR	RBI	BB	SO	AVG	OBP	SLG	PRO+	BR/A	SB	CS	SBR	FA	FR	G/POS	TPR
1981	Tor-A	60	163	19	38	2	1	5	12	5	27	.233	.256	.350	69	-7	3	1	-0	.969	1	O-44/D-8	-0.8
1983	Tor-A	39	112	5	30	5	4	2	17	4	17	.268	.305	.438	96	-1	1	1	-0	.954	-2	O-34/D-2	-0.4
1984	Tor-A	159	606	85	177	39	4	26	87	24	86	.292	.328	.498	121	15	11	2	2	.971	-1	*O-147/3-3,D-7	1.1
1985	*Tor-A	157	607	87	167	28	6	28	95	43	90	.275	.331	.479	116	12	21	6	3	.968	8	*O-157/3-2	1.7
1986	Tor-A	159	641	101	198	38	6	31	108	41	62	.309	.352	.532	133	27	7	8	-3	.966	8	*O-147,D-11/3-2	2.5
1987	Tor-A★	156	610	111	188	32	4	47	**134**	39	75	.308	.357	.605	146	37	5	1	1	.960	0	*O-148/2-1,3-1,D-7	3.2
1988	Tor-A	156	614	78	165	27	5	24	99	34	66	.269	.308	.446	108	4	4	2	0	.946	-4	*O-149/D-7	-0.8
1989	*Tor-A	153	613	88	182	41	2	18	104	33	60	.297	.337	.458	124	18	4	3	-1	.963	-4	*O-134,D-19	-0.8
1990	Tor-A★	142	562	67	149	25	0	21	86	32	80	.265	.308	.422	100	1	3	2	-0	.979	4	*O-106,D-36	-0.2
1991	Chi-N★	149	558	63	159	27	0	25	86	32	62	.285	.328	.468	116	10	2	6	-3	.962	-5	*O-146	-0.1
1992	Chi-A	155	627	74	160	27	0	25	112	31	97	.255	.297	.418	99	-3	5	2	-3	.964	-2	*D-140,O-15	-1.0
1993	Chi-A	102	410	36	89	17	2	13	64	13	49	.217	.248	.363	64	-23	1	1	-0	.000	0	*D-102	-2.7
Total	12	1587	6123	814	1702	308	34	265	1002	331	771	.278	.320	.469	113	88	67	36	-2	.964	-0	*O-1227,D-339/3-8,2	3.4

■ JAY BELL

Bell, Jay Stuart b: 12/11/65, Eglin A.F.B., Fla. BR/TR, 6'1", 180 lbs. Deb: 9/29/86

YEAR	TM/L	G	AB	R	H	2B	3B	HR	RBI	BB	SO	AVG	OBP	SLG	PRO+	BR/A	SB	CS	SBR	FA	FR	G/POS	TPR
1986	Cle-A	5	14	3	5	0	1	0	4	2	3	.357	.438	.714	211	2	0	0	0	.778	-0	/2-2,D-2	0.2
1987	Cle-A	38	125	14	27	9	1	2	13	8	31	.216	.269	.352	62	-7	2	0	1	.947	3	S-38	-0.1
1988	Cle-A	73	211	23	46	5	1	2	21	21	53	.218	.292	.280	59	-11	4	2	0	.965	-13	S-72/D-1	-1.9
1989	Pit-N	78	271	33	70	13	3	2	27	19	47	.258	.309	.351	91	-3	5	3	-0	.968	-15	S-78	-1.3
1990	*Pit-N	159	583	93	148	28	7	7	52	65	109	.254	.332	.362	94	-4	10	6	-1	.970	-3	*S-159	0.6
1991	*Pit-N	157	608	96	164	32	8	16	67	52	99	.270	.331	.428	114	10	10	6	-1	.968	8	*S-156	3.0
1992	*Pit-N	159	632	87	167	36	6	9	55	55	103	.264	.327	.383	102	1	7	5	-1	.973	17	*S-159	3.0
1993	Pit-N★	154	604	102	187	32	9	9	51	77	122	.310	.393	.437	122	22	16	10	-1	**.986**	26	*S-154	5.7
1994	Pit-N	110	424	68	117	35	4	9	45	49	82	.276	.355	.441	105	3	2	0	1	.973	19	*S-110	3.2
1995	Pit-N	138	530	79	139	28	4	13	55	55	110	.262	.336	.404	92	-6	2	5	-2	.978	9	*S-136/3-3	1.1
1996	Pit-N	151	527	65	132	29	3	13	71	54	108	.250	.326	.391	85	-11	2	5	-1	**.986**	13	*S-151	1.4
Total	11	1222	4529	663	1202	249	46	83	461	457	867	.265	.337	.396		-4	64	41	-5	.974	62	*S-1213/3-3,D-3,2-2	14.9

■ RUDY BELL

Bell, John (b: Rudolph Fred Baerwald) b: 1/1/1881, Wausau, Wis. d: 7/28/55, Albuquerque, N.Mex. BR/TR, 5'8.5", 158 lbs. Deb: 9/16/07

YEAR	TM/L	G	AB	R	H	2B	3B	HR	RBI	BB	SO	AVG	OBP	SLG	PRO+	BR/A	SB	CS	SBR	FA	FR	G/POS	TPR
1907	NY-A	17	52	4	11	2	1	0	3	3	3	.212	.268	.288	72	-2	4			.897	-1	O-17	-0.4

■ JUAN BELL

Bell, Juan (Mathey) b: 3/29/68, San Pedro De Macoris, D.R. BR/TR, 5'11", 172 lbs. Deb: 9/6/89 F

YEAR	TM/L	G	AB	R	H	2B	3B	HR	RBI	BB	SO	AVG	OBP	SLG	PRO+	BR/A	SB	CS	SBR	FA	FR	G/POS	TPR
1989	Bal-A	8	4	2	0	0	0	0	0	0	1	.000	.000	.000	-99	-1	1	0	0	1.000	2	/2-2,S-2,D-4	0.1
1990	Bal-A	5	2	1	0	0	0	0	0	0	0	.000	.000	.000	-99	-1	0	0	0	1.000	0	/S-1,D-1	0.0
1991	Bal-A	100	209	26	36	9	2	1	15	8	51	.172	.203	.249	25	-22	5	0	0	.973	-1	2-77,S-15/O-1,D-4	-2.1
1992	Phi-N	46	147	12	30	3	1	1	8	18	29	.204	.295	.259	58	-8	5	0	2	.972	4	S-46	0.1
1993	Phi-N	24	65	5	13	6	1	0	7	5	12	.200	.268	.323	58	-4	0	1	-1	.909	-3	S-22	-0.1
	Mil-A	91	286	42	67	6	2	5	29	36	64	.234	.322	.322	75	-10	6	6	-2	.983	2	2-47,S-40/O-3,D-2	-0.5
1994	Mon-N	38	97	12	27	4	0	2	10	15	21	.278	.375	.381	97	2	6	0	1	.991	-2	2-25/3-3,S-1	0.1
1995	Bos-A	17	26	7	4	2	0	1	2	3	1	.154	.214	.346	41	-2	0	0	0	.857	4	/S-6,2-5,3-1	0.2
Total	7	329	836	107	177	30	6	10	71	84	189	.212	.286	.298	60	-47	16	7	1	.981	13	2-156,S-133/D3O	-2.2

■ KEVIN BELL

Bell, Kevin Robert b: 7/13/55, Los Angeles, Cal. BR/TR, 6', 195 lbs. Deb: 6/16/76

YEAR	TM/L	G	AB	R	H	2B	3B	HR	RBI	BB	SO	AVG	OBP	SLG	PRO+	BR/A	SB	CS	SBR	FA	FR	G/POS	TPR
1976	Chi-A	68	230	24	57	7	6	5	20	18	56	.248	.305	.396	104	0	2	1	0	.970	3	3-67/D-1	0.3
1977	Chi-A	9	28	4	5	1	0	1	6	3	8	.179	.258	.321	57	-2	0	0	0	.909	0	/S-5,3-4,O-1	-0.1
1978	Chi-A	54	68	9	13	0	0	1	6	3	12	.191	.257	.279	50	-5	1	0	-1	.946	11	3-52/D-1	0.7
1979	Chi-A	70	200	20	49	8	1	4	22	15	43	.245	.298	.355	75	-7	0	2	-2	.923	12	3-68/S-2	0.3
1980	Chi-A	92	191	16	34	5	2	1	11	29	37	.178	.286	.241	46	-14	3	5	-2	.925	7	3-83/S-3,D-3	-0.8

YEAR	TM/L	G	AB	R	H	2B	3B	HR	RBI	BB	SO	AVG	OBP	SLG	PRO+	BR/A	SB	CS	SBR	FA	FR	G/POS	TPR
1982	Oak-A	4	9	1	3	1	0	0	0	0	2	.333	.333	.444	117	0	0	0	0	.857	0	/3-3,D-1	0.0
Total	6	297	726	74	161	22	9	13	64	70	165	.222	.292	.331	73	-26	5	5	-2	.940	33	3-277/S-10,D-6,O-1	0.4

■ LES BELL
Bell, Lester Rowland   b: 12/14/01, Harrisburg, Pa.   d: 12/26/85, Hershey, Pa.   BR/TR, 5'11", 165 lbs.   Deb: 9/18/23

YEAR	TM/L	G	AB	R	H	2B	3B	HR	RBI	BB	SO	AVG	OBP	SLG	PRO+	BR/A	SB	CS	SBR	FA	FR	G/POS	TPR
1923	StL-N	15	51	5	19	2	1	0	9	9	7	.373	.467	.451	146	4	1	0	0	.917	-1	S-15	0.4
1924	StL-N	17	57	5	14	3	2	1	5	3	7	.246	.295	.421	91	-1	0	0	0	.905	-4	S-17	-0.3
1925	StL-N	153	586	80	167	29	9	11	88	43	47	.285	.334	.422	89	-10	4	5	-2	.924	-1	*3-153/S-1	-0.2
1926	*StL-N	155	581	85	189	33	14	17	100	54	62	.325	.383	.518	135	27	9			.950	-22	*3-155	1.5
1927	StL-N	115	390	48	101	26	6	9	65	34	63	.259	.320	.426	95	-4	5			.904	-14	*3-100,S-10	-1.3
1928	Bos-N	153	591	58	164	36	7	10	91	40	45	.277	.323	.413	96	-6	1			.948	5	*3-153	0.8
1929	Bos-N	139	483	59	144	23	5	9	72	50	42	.298	.364	.422	98	-1	1			.953	-20	*3-127/2-1,S-1	-1.5
1930	Chi-N	74	248	35	69	15	4	5	47	24	27	.278	.342	.431	85	-6	1			.948	-0	3-70/1-2	-0.3
1931	Chi-N	75	252	30	71	17	1	4	32	19	22	.282	.332	.405	95	-2	0			.944	4	3-70	0.6
Total	9	896	3239	404	938	184	49	66	509	276	322	.290	.348	.438	102	1	25	5		.939	-53	3-828/S-44,1-2,2-1	-0.3

■ MIKE BELL
Bell, Michael Allen   b: 4/22/68, Lewiston, N.Y.   BL/TL, 6'1", 175 lbs.   Deb: 5/2/90

YEAR	TM/L	G	AB	R	H	2B	3B	HR	RBI	BB	SO	AVG	OBP	SLG	PRO+	BR/A	SB	CS	SBR	FA	FR	G/POS	TPR
1990	Atl-N	36	45	8	11	5	1	1	5	2	9	.244	.292	.467	99	-0	0	1	-1	.981	1	1-24	-0.1
1991	Atl-N	17	30	4	4	0	0	1	1	2	7	.133	.188	.233	17	-3	1	0	0	.975	-0	1-14	-0.4
Total	2	53	75	12	15	5	1	2	6	4	16	.200	.250	.373	67	-4	1	1	-0	.979	1	/1-38	-0.5

■ BEAU BELL
Bell, Roy Chester   b: 8/20/07, Bellville, Tex.   d: 9/14/77, College Station, Tex.   BR/TR, 6'2", 185 lbs.   Deb: 4/16/35

YEAR	TM/L	G	AB	R	H	2B	3B	HR	RBI	BB	SO	AVG	OBP	SLG	PRO+	BR/A	SB	CS	SBR	FA	FR	G/POS	TPR
1935	StL-A	76	220	20	55	8	2	3	17	16	16	.250	.304	.345	65	-12	1	1	-0	.918	-5	O-37,1-15/3-3	-1.9
1936	StL-A	155	616	100	212	40	12	11	123	60	55	.344	.403	.502	119	18	4	1	1	.974	-2	*O-142,1-17	0.8
1937	StL-A☆	156	642	82	218	51	8	14	117	53	54	.340	.391	.509	124	23	2	2	-1	.984	5	*O-131,1-26/3-2	1.6
1938	StL-A	147	526	91	138	35	3	13	84	71	46	.262	.350	.414	91	-8	1	3	-2	.979	4	*O-132/1-4	-0.9
1939	StL-A	11	32	4	7	1	0	1	5	4	3	.219	.324	.344	69	-1	0	0	-0	1.000	-0	/O-9	-0.2
	Det-A	54	134	14	32	4	2	0	24	24	16	.239	.358	.299	65	-7	0	1	-1	1.000	-0	O-37	-0.7
	Yr	65	166	18	39	5	2	1	29	28	19	.235	.352	.307	66	-8	0	1	-1	1.000	1	O-46	-0.9
1940	Cle-A	120	444	55	124	22	2	4	58	34	41	.279	.332	.365	83	-11	2	2	-0	.971	-2	O-97,1-14	-1.9
1941	Cle-A	48	104	12	20	4	3	0	9	10	8	.192	.270	.288	50	-8	1	2	-1	1.000	-3	O-14,1-10	-1.3
Total	7	767	2718	378	806	165	32	46	437	272	239	.297	.362	.432	99	-6	11	12	-4	.976	-5	O-599/1-86,3-5	-4.5

■ TERRY BELL
Bell, Terence William   b: 10/27/62, Dayton, Ohio   BR/TR, 6', 195 lbs.   Deb: 9/3/86

YEAR	TM/L	G	AB	R	H	2B	3B	HR	RBI	BB	SO	AVG	OBP	SLG	PRO+	BR/A	SB	CS	SBR	FA	FR	G/POS	TPR
1986	KC-A	8	3	0	0	0	0	0	0	2	1	.000	.400	.000	20	-0	0	0	0	1.000	-0	/C-8	0.0
1987	Atl-N	1	1	0	0	0	0	0	0	0	0	.000	.000	.000	-95	-0	0	0	0	.000	-0	/H	0.0
Total	2	9	4	0	0	0	0	0	0	2	1	.000	.333	.000	-0	-0	0	0	0	1.000	-0	/C-8	0.0

■ ZEKE BELLA
Bella, John   b: 8/23/30, Greenwich, Conn.   BR/TL, 5'11", 185 lbs.   Deb: 9/11/57

YEAR	TM/L	G	AB	R	H	2B	3B	HR	RBI	BB	SO	AVG	OBP	SLG	PRO+	BR/A	SB	CS	SBR	FA	FR	G/POS	TPR
1957	NY-A	5	10	1	1	0	0	0	1	2	1	.100	.182	.100	-21	-2	0	0	0	1.000	1	/O-4	-0.1
1959	KC-A	47	82	10	17	2	1	1	9	9	14	.207	.293	.293	60	-4	0	0	0	1.000	-3	O-25/1-1	-0.9
Total	2	52	92	10	18	2	1	1	9	10	16	.196	.282	.272	52	-6	0	0	0	1.000	-3	/O-29,1-1	-1.0

■ STEVE BELLAN
Bellan, Esteban Enrique   b: 1850, Cuba   d: 8/8/32, Havana, Cuba   5'6", 154 lbs.   Deb: 5/9/1871

YEAR	TM/L	G	AB	R	H	2B	3B	HR	RBI	BB	SO	AVG	OBP	SLG	PRO+	BR/A	SB	CS	SBR	FA	FR	G/POS	TPR
1871	Tro-n	29	128	26	32	3	3	0	23	9	2	.250	.299	.320	77	-4	4	4	-1	.713	-2	*3-28/S-1	-0.6
1872	Tro-n	23	114	22	30	4	0	0	16	0	0	.263	.263	.298	71	-4	1	0	0	.673	-6	/S-9,3-8,O-6	-0.7
1873	Mut-n	8	32	4	7	2	0	0	3	2	0	.219	.265	.281	63	-1	0	0	0	.488	-5	/3-7,2-3	-0.5
Total	3 n	60	274	52	69	9	3	0	42	11	2	.252	.281	.307	73	-9	5	4	-1	.671	-14	/3-43,S-10,O-6,2-3	-1.8

■ ALBERT BELLE
Belle, Albert Jojuan "Joey"   b: 8/25/66, Shreveport, La.   BR/TR, 6'1", 190 lbs.   Deb: 7/15/89

YEAR	TM/L	G	AB	R	H	2B	3B	HR	RBI	BB	SO	AVG	OBP	SLG	PRO+	BR/A	SB	CS	SBR	FA	FR	G/POS	TPR
1989	Cle-A	62	218	22	49	8	4	7	37	12	55	.225	.272	.394	84	-5	2	2	-1	.979	1	O-44,D-17	-0.7
1990	Cle-A	9	23	1	4	0	0	1	3	1	6	.174	.208	.304	42	-2	0	0	0	.000	-0	/O-1,D-6	-0.2
1991	Cle-A	123	461	60	130	31	2	28	95	25	99	.282	.326	.540	134	19	3	1	0	.952	-4	O-89,D-32	1.9
1992	Cle-A	153	585	81	152	23	1	34	112	52	128	.260	.324	.477	124	16	8	2	1	.969	-4	*D-100,O-52	1.0
1993	Cle-A★	159	594	93	172	36	3	38	129	76	96	.290	.378	.552	147	39	23	12	6	.986	19	*O-104/D-2	5.2
1994	Cle-A★	106	412	90	147	35	2	36	101	58	71	.357	.442	.714	191	56	9	6	-1	.973	3	*O-104/D-2	5.0
1995	*Cle-A★	143	546	121	173	52	1	50	126	73	80	.317	.403	.690	175	59	5	2	0	.981	8	*O-142/D-1	5.8
1996	*Cle-A★	158	602	124	187	38	3	48	148	99	87	.311	.414	.623	157	54	11	0	3	.970	7	*O-152/D-6	5.3
Total	8	913	3441	592	1014	223	16	242	751	396	622	.295	.374	.580	150	235	61	25	3	.974	36	O-734,D-173	23.3

■ RAFAEL BELLIARD
Belliard, Rafael Leonidas (Matias)   b: 10/24/61, Pueblo Nuevo, D.R.   BR/TR, 5'6", 160 lbs.   Deb: 9/6/82

YEAR	TM/L	G	AB	R	H	2B	3B	HR	RBI	BB	SO	AVG	OBP	SLG	PRO+	BR/A	SB	CS	SBR	FA	FR	G/POS	TPR
1982	Pit-N	9	2	3	1	0	0	0	0	0	0	.500	.500	.500	175	0	1	0	0	1.000	1	/S-4	0.2
1983	Pit-N	4	1	1	0	0	0	0	0	0	1	.000	.000	.000	-98	-0	0	0	0	1.000	1	/S-3	0.1
1984	Pit-N	20	22	3	5	0	0	0	0	1	5	.227	.227	.227	28	-2	4	1	1	.889	1	S-12/2-1	0.0
1985	Pit-N	17	20	1	4	0	0	0	1	0	2	.200	.200	.200	12	-2	0	0	0	.947	6	S-12	0.4
1986	Pit-N	117	309	33	72	5	2	0	31	26	54	.233	.299	.262	55	-18	12	2	2	.970	13	S-96,2-23	0.5
1987	Pit-N	81	203	26	42	4	3	1	15	20	25	.207	.288	.271	49	-15	5	1	1	.979	6	S-71/2-7	-0.3
1988	Pit-N	122	286	28	61	0	4	0	11	26	47	.213	.288	.241	54	-16	7	1	2	.977	-12	*S-117/2-3	-2.0
1989	Pit-N	67	154	10	33	4	0	0	8	8	22	.214	.253	.240	43	-11	5	2	0	.978	7	S-40,2-20/3-6	-0.2
1990	Pit-N	47	54	10	11	3	0	0	6	5	13	.204	.283	.259	52	-3	1	2	-1	1.000	5	2-21,S-10/3-5	0.1
1991	*Atl-N	149	353	36	88	9	2	0	27	22	63	.249	.296	.286	61	-18	3	1	0	.967	26	*S-145	1.7
1992	*Atl-N	144	285	20	60	6	1	0	14	14	43	.211	.255	.239	38	-23	0	1	-1	.969	27	*S-139/2-1	1.0
1993	*Atl-N	91	79	6	18	5	0	0	6	4	13	.228	.291	.291	56	-5	0	1	0	1.000	20	S-58,2-24	1.6
1994	Atl-N	46	120	9	29	1	0	0	9	2	29	.242	.246	.317	50	-9	0	2	-1	.984	-5	S-26,2-18	-1.2
1995	*Atl-N	75	180	12	40	7	1	0	6	6	28	.222	.255	.244	32	-18	2	2	-1	.992	13	S-40,2-32	-0.1
1996	*Atl-N	87	142	9	24	7	0	0	3	2	15	.169	.181	.218	4	-19	3	1	0	.983	23	S-63,2-15	0.7
Total	15	1076	2210	207	488	52	14	1	138	135	366	.221	.273	.258	46	-160	43	16	3	.973	132	S-836,2-165/3-11	2.5

■ JACK BELLMAN
Bellman, John Hutchins "Happy Jack"   b: 3/4/1864, Taylorsville, Ky.   d: 12/8/31, Louisville, Ky.   Deb: 4/23/1889

YEAR	TM/L	G	AB	R	H	2B	3B	HR	RBI	BB	SO	AVG	OBP	SLG	PRO+	BR/A	SB	CS	SBR	FA	FR	G/POS	TPR
1889	StL-a	1	2	1	1	0	0	0	0	1	0	.500	.667	.500	207	0	0			1.000	-0	/C-1	0.0

■ ROB BELLOIR
Belloir, Robert Edward   b: 7/13/48, Heidelberg, W.Ger.   BR/TR, 5'10", 155 lbs.   Deb: 8/2/75

YEAR	TM/L	G	AB	R	H	2B	3B	HR	RBI	BB	SO	AVG	OBP	SLG	PRO+	BR/A	SB	CS	SBR	FA	FR	G/POS	TPR
1975	Atl-N	43	105	11	23	2	1	0	9	7	8	.219	.268	.257	45	-8	0	0	0	.922	-2	S-38/2-1	-0.7
1976	Atl-N	30	60	5	12	2	0	0	4	5	7	.200	.262	.233	39	-5	0	0	0	.929	-1	S-12,3-10/2-5	-0.5
1977	Atl-N	6	1	2	0	0	0	0	0	0	0	.000	.000	.000	-89	-0	0	0	0	1.000	1	/S-3	0.1
1978	Atl-N	2	1	0	1	0	0	0	0	0	0	1.000	1.000	2.000	647	1	0	0	0	1.000	-0	/S-1,3-1	0.1
Total	4	81	167	18	36	5	1	0	13	12	15	.216	.268	.257	45	-12	0	0	0	.924	-3	/S-54,3-11,2-6	-1.0

■ ESTEBAN BELTRE
Beltre, Esteban (Valera)   b: 12/26/67, Ingenio Quisqueya, D.R.   BR/TR, 5'10", 155 lbs.   Deb: 9/3/91

YEAR	TM/L	G	AB	R	H	2B	3B	HR	RBI	BB	SO	AVG	OBP	SLG	PRO+	BR/A	SB	CS	SBR	FA	FR	G/POS	TPR
1991	Chi-A	8	6	0	1	0	0	0	0	1	1	.167	.286	.167	29	-1	0	0	0	1.000	-1	/S-8	-0.1
1992	Chi-A	49	110	21	21	2	0	1	10	3	18	.191	.212	.236	26	-11	0	1	0	.924	-1	S-43/D-4	-0.9
1994	Tex-A	48	131	12	37	5	0	0	12	16	25	.282	.361	.321	78	-4	2	5	-2	.961	8	S-41/3-5,2-1	0.5
1995	Tex-A	54	92	7	20	8	0	0	7	4	15	.217	.250	.304	42	-8	0	0	0	.969	3	S-36,2-15/3-1	-0.3
1996	Bos-A	27	62	6	16	2	0	0	6	4	14	.258	.302	.290	49	-5	1	0	0	1.000	-1	3-13/2-8,S-6,D-1	-0.4
Total	5	186	401	46	95	17	0	1	35	28	73	.237	.287	.287	51	-28	5	5	-2	.951	9	S-134/2-24,3-19,D-5	-1.2

■ HARRY BEMIS
Bemis, Harry Parker   b: 2/1/1874, Farmington, N.H.   d: 5/23/47, Cleveland, Ohio   BR/TR, 5'6.5", 155 lbs.   Deb: 4/23/02

YEAR	TM/L	G	AB	R	H	2B	3B	HR	RBI	BB	SO	AVG	OBP	SLG	PRO+	BR/A	SB	CS	SBR	FA	FR	G/POS	TPR
1902	Cle-A	93	317	42	99	12	7	1	29	19		.312	.366	.404	118	8	3			.964	6	C-87/O-2,2-1	2.2
1903	Cle-A	92	314	31	82	20	3	1	41	8		.261	.295	.354	96	-2	5			.988	-7	C-74,1-10/2-1	-0.2
1904	Cle-A	97	336	35	76	11	6	0	25	8		.226	.259	.295	76	-10	6			.958	-9	C-79,1-13/2-1	-0.4
1905	Cle-A	70	226	27	66	13	3	0	28	13		.292	.344	.376	127	7	3			.972	-6	C-58/2-4,3-2,1-1	0.8
1906	Cle-A	93	297	28	82	13	2	0	30	14		.276	.311	.374	116	4	4			.963	-10	C-81	0.3
1907	Cle-A	65	172	12	43	7	0	0	19	7		.250	.283	.291	82	-4	5			.957	-8	C-51/1-2	-0.8

YEAR	TM/L	G	AB	R	H	2B	3B	HR	RBI	BB	SO	AVG	OBP	SLG	PRO+	BR/A	SB	CS	SBR	FA	FR	G/POS	TPR
1908	Cle-A	91	277	23	62	9	1	0	33	7		.224	.253	.264	68	-10	14			.964	-6	C-76/1-2	-1.1
1909	Cle-A	42	123	4	23	2	3	0	13	0		.187	.194	.252	39	-9	2			.971	-0	C-36	-0.7
1910	Cle-A	61	167	12	36	5	1	1	16	5		.216	.238	.275	60	-8	3			.961	-4	C-46	-0.9
Total	9	704	2229	214	569	92	29	5	234	79		.255	.292	.329	92	-24	49			.966	-37	C-588/1-28,2-7,3O	-0.8

■ MARVIN BENARD
Benard, Marvin Larry   b: 1/20/71, Bluefields, Nic.   BL/TL, 5'10", 180 lbs.   Deb: 9/5/95

YEAR	TM/L	G	AB	R	H	2B	3B	HR	RBI	BB	SO	AVG	OBP	SLG	PRO+	BR/A	SB	CS	SBR	FA	FR	G/POS	TPR
1995	SF-N	13	34	5	13	2	0	1	4	1	7	.382	.400	.529	147	2	1	0	0	1.000	1	/O-7	0.3
1996	SF-N	135	488	89	121	17	4	5	27	59	84	.248	.334	.330	79	-14	25	11	1	.984	5	*O-132	-1.1
Total	2	148	522	94	134	19	4	6	31	60	91	.257	.338	.343	84	-11	26	11	1	.985	5	O-139	-0.8

■ FREDDIE BENAVIDES
Benavides, Alfredo   b: 4/7/66, Laredo, Tex.   BR/TR, 6'2", 180 lbs.   Deb: 5/14/91

YEAR	TM/L	G	AB	R	H	2B	3B	HR	RBI	BB	SO	AVG	OBP	SLG	PRO+	BR/A	SB	CS	SBR	FA	FR	G/POS	TPR
1991	Cin-N	24	63	11	18	1	0	0	3	1	15	.286	.308	.302	69	-3	1	0	0	.974	3	S-20/2-3	0.2
1992	Cin-N	74	173	14	40	10	1	1	17	10	34	.231	.277	.318	66	-8	0	1	-1	1.000	4	2-37,S-34/3-1	-0.3
1993	Col-N	74	213	20	61	10	3	3	26	6	27	.286	.306	.404	76	-8	3	2	-0	.937	5	S-48,2-19/3-5,1-1	-0.7
1994	Mon-N	47	85	8	16	5	1	0	6	3	15	.188	.225	.271	28	-9	0	0	0	.976	-5	2-36/3-5,1-3,S-3	-1.3
Total	4	219	534	53	135	26	5	4	52	20	91	.253	.284	.343	65	-27	4	3	-1	.948	-0	S-105/2-95,3-11,1-4	-2.1

■ JOHNNY BENCH
Bench, Johnny Lee   b: 12/7/47, Oklahoma City, Okla.   BR/TR, 6'1", 208 lbs.   Deb: 8/28/67   H

YEAR	TM/L	G	AB	R	H	2B	3B	HR	RBI	BB	SO	AVG	OBP	SLG	PRO+	BR/A	SB	CS	SBR	FA	FR	G/POS	TPR
1967	Cin-N	26	86	7	14	3	1	1	6	5	19	.163	.209	.256	29	-8	0	1	-1	.995	5	C-26	-0.2
1968	Cin-N★	154	564	67	155	40	2	15	82	31	96	.275	.315	.433	115	9	1	5	-3	.991	7	*C-154	2.6
1969	Cin-N★	148	532	83	156	23	1	26	90	49	86	.293	.357	.487	128	19	6	6	-2	.992	-3	*C-147	2.3
1970	*Cin-N★	158	605	97	177	35	4	**45**	**148**	54	102	.293	.351	.587	146	35	5	2	0	.986	4	*C-139,O-24,1-12/3	4.5
1971	*Cin-N★	149	562	80	134	19	2	27	61	49	83	.238	.300	.423	105	1	2	1	0	.988	4	*C-141,1-12,O-12/3	1.1
1972	*Cin-N★	147	538	87	145	22	2	**40**	**125**	100	84	.270	.386	.541	**171**	**51**	6	6	-2	.992	-5	*C-129,O-17/1-7,3-4	5.1
1973	*Cin-N★	152	557	83	141	17	3	25	104	83	83	.253	.350	.429	121	16	4	1	1	.995	-3	*C-134,O-23/1-4,3-1	1.9
1974	Cin-N★	160	621	108	174	38	2	33	**129**	80	90	.280	.365	.507	144	35	5	4	-1	.993	-5	*C-137,3-36/1-5	3.6
1975	*Cin-N★	142	530	83	150	39	1	28	110	65	108	.283	.363	.519	140	27	11	0	3	.989	0	*C-121,O-19/1-9	3.9
1976	*Cin-N★	135	465	62	109	24	1	16	74	81	95	.234	.350	.394	108	7	13	2	3	**.997**	-3	*C-128/O-5,1-1	1.0
1977	*Cin-N★	142	494	67	136	34	2	31	109	58	95	.275	.353	.540	133	22	2	4	-2	.987	-13	*C-135/O-8,1-4,3-1	1.1
1978	Cin-N†	120	393	52	102	17	1	23	73	50	83	.260	.345	.483	129	14	4	2	0	.989	-9	*C-107,1-11/O-2	0.8
1979	*Cin-N†	130	464	73	128	19	0	22	80	67	73	.276	.367	.459	123	16	4	2	0	.986	-7	*C-126/1-2	1.4
1980	*Cin-N★	114	360	52	90	12	0	24	68	41	64	.250	.330	.483	124	11	4	2	0	.991	-17	*C-105	-0.3
1981	Cin-N	52	178	14	55	8	0	8	25	17	21	.309	.369	.489	139	9	0	2	-1	.983	-2	1-38/C-7	0.4
1982	Cin-N	119	399	44	103	16	0	13	38	37	58	.258	.321	.396	98	-2	1	2	-1	.917	-17	*3-107/1-8,C-1	-2.4
1983	Cin-N★	110	310	32	79	15	2	12	54	24	38	.255	.308	.432	100	-1	0	1	-1	.933	-12	3-42,1-32/C-5,O-1	-1.7
Total	17	2158	7658	1091	2048	381	24	389	1376	891	1278	.267	.345	.476	127	261	68	43	-5	.990	-80	*C-1742,3-195,1O	24.3

■ ART BENEDICT
Benedict, Arthur Melville   b: 3/31/1862, Cornwall Twsp., Ill.   d: 1/20/48, Denver, Colo.   BR/TR,   Deb: 5/14/1883

YEAR	TM/L	G	AB	R	H	2B	3B	HR	RBI	BB	SO	AVG	OBP	SLG	PRO+	BR/A	SB	CS	SBR	FA	FR	G/POS	TPR
1883	Phi-N	3	15	3	4	1	0	0	4	0	4	.267	.267	.333	89	-0				.571	-5	/2-3	-0.4

■ BRUCE BENEDICT
Benedict, Bruce Edwin   b: 8/18/55, Birmingham, Ala.   BR/TR, 6'1", 190 lbs.   Deb: 8/18/78

YEAR	TM/L	G	AB	R	H	2B	3B	HR	RBI	BB	SO	AVG	OBP	SLG	PRO+	BR/A	SB	CS	SBR	FA	FR	G/POS	TPR
1978	Atl-N	22	52	3	13	2	0	1	6	6		.250	.328	.288	66	-2	0	0	0	.990	2	C-22	0.0
1979	Atl-N	76	204	14	46	11	0	0	15	33	18	.225	.333	.279	64	-9	1	3	-2	.984	1	C-76	-0.8
1980	Atl-N	120	359	18	91	14	1	2	34	28	36	.253	.309	.315	72	-13	3	3	-1	.988	3	*C-120	-0.7
1981	Atl-N★	90	295	26	78	12	1	5	35	33	21	.264	.344	.363	98	-0	1	1	-0	.986	6	C-90	1.0
1982	*Atl-N	118	386	34	95	11	1	3	44	37	40	.246	.317	.303	71	-14	4	4	-1	**.993**	2	*C-118	-0.9
1983	Atl-N★	134	423	43	126	13	1	2	43	61	24	.298	.388	.348	98	2	3	5	-2	.992	9	*C-134	1.5
1984	Atl-N	95	300	26	67	8	1	4	25	34	25	.223	.304	.297	65	-13	1	2	-1	.991	1	C-95	-1.0
1985	Atl-N	70	208	12	42	6	0	0	20	22	12	.202	.281	.231	42	-16	0	1	-0	.989	-2	C-70	-1.6
1986	Atl-N	64	160	11	36	10	1	0	13	15	10	.225	.299	.300	62	-8	0	0	0	.993	-3	C-57	-0.8
1987	Atl-N	37	95	4	14	1	0	1	5	17	15	.147	.277	.189	25	-10	0	1	-1	.989	4	C-35	-0.5
1988	Atl-N	90	236	11	57	7	0	0	19	19	26	.242	.298	.271	61	-11	0	0	-1	.989	8	C-89	0.0
1989	Atl-N	66	160	12	31	3	1	0	6	23	18	.194	.299	.231	52	-9	0	0	-1	.995	16	C-65	1.0
Total	12	982	2878	214	696	98	6	18	260	328	251	.242	.322	.299	71	-104	12	20	-8	.990	47	C-971	-2.8

■ JOE BENES
Benes, Joseph Anthony "Bananas"   b: 1/8/01, Long Island City, N.Y.   d: 3/7/75, Elmhurst, N.Y.   BR/TR, 5'8.5", 158 lbs.   Deb: 5/9/31

YEAR	TM/L	G	AB	R	H	2B	3B	HR	RBI	BB	SO	AVG	OBP	SLG	PRO+	BR/A	SB	CS	SBR	FA	FR	G/POS	TPR
1931	StL-N	10	12	1	2	0	0	0	2	1		.167	.333	.167	37	-1	0			1.000	1	/S-6,2-2,3-1	0.0

■ BENNY BENGOUGH
Bengough, Bernard Oliver   b: 7/27/1898, Niagara Falls, N.Y.   d: 12/22/68, Philadelphia, Pa.   BR/TR, 5'7.5", 168 lbs.   Deb: 5/18/23   C

YEAR	TM/L	G	AB	R	H	2B	3B	HR	RBI	BB	SO	AVG	OBP	SLG	PRO+	BR/A	SB	CS	SBR	FA	FR	G/POS	TPR
1923	NY-A	19	53	1	7	2	0	0	3	4	2	.132	.193	.170	-4	-8	0			.973	1	C-19	-0.7
1924	NY-A	11	16	4	5	1	1	0	3	2	0	.313	.389	.500	128	1	0	0	0	1.000	0	C-11	0.4
1925	NY-A	95	283	17	73	14	2	0	23	19	9	.258	.305	.322	60	-18	0	2	-1	**.993**	6	C-94	-0.8
1926	NY-A	36	84	9	32	6	0	0	14	7	4	.381	.435	.452	134	4	1	0	0	.973	8	C-35	1.4
1927	*NY-A	31	85	6	21	3	3	0	10	4	4	.247	.281	.353	66	-5	0	3	-2	.986	12	C-30	0.6
1928	*NY-A	58	161	12	43	3	1	0	9	7	8	.267	.302	.298	60	-9	0	0	0	.992	6	C-58	0.1
1929	NY-A	23	62	5	12	2	1	0	7	0	2	.194	.194	.258	16	-8	0	0	0	.982	-5	C-23	-1.1
1930	NY-A	44	102	10	24	4	2	0	12	3	8	.235	.257	.314	46	-9	1	0	0	.990	9	C-44	0.3
1931	StL-A	40	140	6	35	4	1	0	14	6	5	.250	.271	.293	46	-11	0	3	-2	.986	-1	C-37	-1.1
1932	StL-A	54	139	13	35	7	1	0	15	12	4	.252	.311	.317	60	-8	0	1	-1	.989	-1	C-47	0.0
Total	10	411	1125	83	287	46	12	0	108	62	45	.255	.295	.317	59	-70	2	9	-5	.988	45	C-398	-0.9

■ JUAN BENIQUEZ
Beniquez, Juan Jose (Torres)   b: 5/13/50, San Sebastian, P.R.   BR/TR, 5'11", 165 lbs.   Deb: 9/4/71

YEAR	TM/L	G	AB	R	H	2B	3B	HR	RBI	BB	SO	AVG	OBP	SLG	PRO+	BR/A	SB	CS	SBR	FA	FR	G/POS	TPR
1971	Bos-A	16	57	8	17	2	0	4	4	3	4	.298	.333	.333	83	-1	3	1	0	.895	-8	S-15	-0.7
1972	Bos-A	33	99	10	24	4	1	1	8	7	11	.242	.292	.333	81	-2	2	0	1	.900	5	S-27	0.7
1974	Bos-A	106	389	60	104	14	3	5	33	25	61	.267	.313	.357	86	-7	19	11	-1	.978	2	O-97/D-4	-1.1
1975	*Bos-A	78	254	43	74	14	4	2	17	25	26	.291	.359	.402	106	2	7	10	-4	.991	0	O-44,D-20,3-14	-0.3
1976	Tex-A	145	478	49	122	14	4	0	33	39	56	.255	.315	.301	79	-12	17	6	-2	.986	20	*O-141/2-1	0.5
1977	Tex-A	123	424	56	114	19	6	10	50	43	43	.269	.338	.413	102	1	26	18	-3	.988	7	*O-123	0.0
1978	Tex-A	127	473	61	123	17	3	11	50	20	59	.260	.294	.338	88	-9	10	12	-4	.972	-0	*O-126	-2.0
1979	NY-A	62	142	19	36	6	1	4	17	9	17	.254	.307	.394	90	-2	3	3	-3	.981	-6	O-60/3-3	-1.0
1980	Sea-A	70	237	26	54	10	0	6	21	17	25	.228	.280	.346	70	-10	2	1	-1	.957	1	O-65/D-1	-1.3
1981	Cal-A	58	166	18	30	9	0	5	13	15	16	.181	.253	.265	49	-11	2	1	-0	.959	-7	O-55/D-1	-2.0
1982	*Cal-A	112	196	25	52	11	2	3	24	15	21	.265	.321	.388	93	-2	3	0	0	.983	-27	*O-107	-2.9
1983	Cal-A	92	315	44	96	15	1	3	34	15	29	.305	.344	.381	100	0	4	0	1	.968	-8	O-84/D-6	-1.0
1984	Cal-A	110	354	60	119	17	4	8	39	18	43	.336	.373	.452	128	13	9	4	-0	.971	-12	O-98	-0.3
1985	Cal-A	132	411	54	125	13	4	6	34	34	46	.304	.364	.418	114	9	4	3	-1	1.000	-15	O-71,1-46,D-14/3S	-1.1
1986	Bal-A	113	343	48	103	15	0	6	36	40	49	.300	.378	.397	113	7	2	4	-1	.963	-6	O-54,3-25,D-16,1-14	-0.3
1987	KC-A	57	174	14	41	7	0	3	26	11	26	.236	.285	.328	60	-10	0	0	0	1.000	-6	O-22,D-15/1-6,3-6	-1.5
	Tor-A	39	81	6	23	5	1	5	21	5	13	.284	.333	.556	127	3	0	1	-2	.875	-2	D-15/O-7,1-2	0.0
	Yr	96	255	20	64	12	1	8	47	16	39	.251	.300	.400	82	-7	0	1	-2	.976	-6	D-30,O-29/1-8,3-6	-1.5
1988	Tor-A	27	58	9	17	2	0	1	8	8	6	.293	.379	.379	112	1	0	0	0	.000	0	D-19/O-1	0.0
Total	17	1500	4651	610	1274	190	30	79	476	349	551	.274	.329	.379	95	-29	104	76	-14	.977	-60	*O-1155,D-111/13S2	-14.3

■ YAMIL BENITEZ
Benitez, Yamil Antonio   b: 10/5/72, San Juan, P.R.   BR/TR, 6'2", 180 lbs.   Deb: 9/16/95

YEAR	TM/L	G	AB	R	H	2B	3B	HR	RBI	BB	SO	AVG	OBP	SLG	PRO+	BR/A	SB	CS	SBR	FA	FR	G/POS	TPR
1995	Mon-N	14	39	8	15	2	1	2	7	1	7	.385	.400	.641	163	3	0	2	-1	.950	-2	O-14	0.0
1996	Mon-N	11	12	0	2	0	0	0	2	0	4	.167	.167	.167	-11	-2	0	0	0	.500	-1	/O-4	-0.3
Total	2	25	51	8	17	2	1	2	9	1	11	.333	.346	.529	123	1	0	2	-1	.909	-3	/O-18	-0.3

■ STAN BENJAMIN
Benjamin, Alfred Stanley   b: 5/20/14, Framingham, Mass.   BR/TR, 6'2", 194 lbs.   Deb: 9/16/39

YEAR	TM/L	G	AB	R	H	2B	3B	HR	RBI	BB	SO	AVG	OBP	SLG	PRO+	BR/A	SB	CS	SBR	FA	FR	G/POS	TPR
1939	Phi-N	12	50	4	7	2	1	0	1	2	6	.140	.157	.220	0	-7	1			.867	-0	/O-7,3-5	-0.8
1940	Phi-N	8	9	1	2	0	0	0	1	1	1	.222	.300	.222	48	-1	0			1.000	1	/O-2	0.0
1941	Phi-N	129	480	47	113	20	7	3	27	20	81	.235	.266	.325	68	-22	17			.980	-4	*O-110/1-8,2-2,3-1	-3.4

YEAR	TM/L	G	AB	R	H	2B	3B	HR	RBI	BB	SO	AVG	OBP	SLG	PRO+	BR/A	SB	CS	SBR	FA	FR	G/POS	TPR
1942	Phi-N	78	210	24	47	8	3	2	8	10	27	.224	.262	.319	73	-8	5			.976	-3	O-45,1-15	-1.4
1945	Cle-A	14	21	1	7	2	0	0	3	0	0	.333	.333	.429	126	1	0	1	-1	1.000	2	/O-4	0.1
Total	5	241	770	77	176	32	11	5	41	32	115	.229	.260	.318	66	-37	23	1		.975	-5	O-168/1-23,3-6,2-2	-5.5

■ MIKE BENJAMIN
Benjamin, Michael Paul b: 11/22/65, Euclid, Ohio BR/TR, 6'3", 195 lbs. Deb: 7/7/89

YEAR	TM/L	G	AB	R	H	2B	3B	HR	RBI	BB	SO	AVG	OBP	SLG	PRO+	BR/A	SB	CS	SBR	FA	FR	G/POS	TPR
1989	SF-N	14	6	0	1	0	0	0	0	0	1	.167	.167	.167	-5	-1	0	0	0	1.000	2	/S-8	0.1
1990	SF-N	22	56	7	12	3	1	2	3	7	10	.214	.254	.411	83	-2	1	0	0	.988	5	S-21	0.5
1991	SF-N	54	106	12	13	3	0	2	8	7	26	.123	.191	.208	13	-13	3	0	1	.984	16	S-51/3-1	0.7
1992	SF-N	40	75	4	13	2	1	1	3	4	15	.173	.215	.267	38	-6	1	0	0	.991	5	S-33/3-2	0.0
1993	SF-N	63	146	22	29	7	0	4	16	9	23	.199	.264	.329	59	-9	0	0	0	.991	20	2-23,S-23,3-16	1.2
1994	SF-N	38	62	9	16	5	1	1	9	5	16	.258	.343	.419	102	0	5	0	2	.968	9	S-18,2-10/3-5	1.2
1995	SF-N	68	186	19	41	6	0	3	12	8	51	.220	.256	.301	48	-14	11	1	3	.964	3	3-43,S-16/2-8	-0.8
1996	Phi-N	35	103	13	23	5	1	4	13	12	21	.223	.316	.408	87	-2	3	1	0	.954	-2	S-31/2-1	-0.1
Total	8	334	740	92	148	31	4	17	64	48	163	.200	.260	.322	57	-46	24	2	6	.979	57	S-201/3-67,2-42	2.8

■ IKE BENNERS
Benners, Isaac B. b: 6/7/1856, Philadelphia, Pa. d: 4/18/32, Philadelphia, Pa. BL, 175 lbs. Deb: 5/1/1884

YEAR	TM/L	G	AB	R	H	2B	3B	HR	RBI	BB	SO	AVG	OBP	SLG	PRO+	BR/A	SB	CS	SBR	FA	FR	G/POS	TPR
1884	Bro-a	49	189	25	38	11	5	1	7			.201	.237	.328	82	-4				.815	-5	O-49	-0.9
	Wil-U	6	22	0	1	0	0	0	1			.045	.087	.045	-57	-5				.750	-5	/O-6	-0.5
Total	1	55	211	25	39	11	5	1	8			.185	.222	.299	66	-9				.806	-5	/O-55	-1.4

■ CHARLIE BENNETT
Bennett, Charles Wesley b: 11/21/1854, New Castle, Pa. d: 2/24/27, Detroit, Mich. BR/TR, 5'11", 180 lbs. Deb: 5/1/1878

YEAR	TM/L	G	AB	R	H	2B	3B	HR	RBI	BB	SO	AVG	OBP	SLG	PRO+	BR/A	SB	CS	SBR	FA	FR	G/POS	TPR
1878	Mil-N	49	184	16	45	9	0	1	12	10	26	.245	.284	.310	89	-2				.831	-13	C-35,O-20	-1.5
1880	Wor-N	51	193	20	44	9	3	0	18	10	30	.228	.266	.306	86	-3				.913	-0	C-46/O-6	-0.3
1881	Det-N	76	299	44	90	18	7	7	64	18	37	.301	.340	.478	149	16				.962	18	*C-70/3-5,O-3	3.3
1882	Det-N	84	342	43	103	16	10	5	51	20	33	.301	.340	.450	151	19				.945	7	*C-65,3-11/2-7,S1	2.5
1883	Det-N	92	371	56	113	34	7	5	55	26	59	.305	.350	.474	155	25				.944	-3	*C-72,2-15/O-12	2.3
1884	Det-N	90	341	37	90	18	6	3	40	36	40	.264	.334	.378	132	14				.917	-5	*C-80/O-5,S-4,321	1.4
1885	Det-N	91	349	49	94	24	13	5	60	47	37	.269	.356	.456	161	24				.919	-1	C-62,O-19,3-10	2.6
1886	Det-N	72	235	37	57	13	5	4	34	48	29	.243	.371	.391	128	10	4			.955	12	C-69/O-4,S-1	2.6
1887	*Det-N	46	160	26	39	6	5	3	20	30	22	.244	.363	.400	108	2	7			.951	2	C-45/O-1,1-1	0.7
1888	Det-N	74	258	32	68	12	4	5	29	31	40	.264	.347	.399	138	12	4			.966	7	C-73/1-1	2.5
1889	Bos-N	82	247	42	57	8	2	4	28	21	43	.231	.296	.328	70	-11	7			.955	12	C-82	0.6
1890	Bos-N	85	281	59	60	17	2	3	40	72	56	.214	.377	.320	96	1	6			.959	10	C-85	1.6
1891	Bos-N	75	256	35	55	9	3	5	39	42	61	.215	.332	.332	84	-6	3			.960	14	C-75	1.3
1892	*Bos-N	35	114	19	23	4	0	1	16	27	23	.202	.355	.263	80	-2	6			.948	1	C-35	0.2
1893	Bos-N	60	191	34	40	8	0	4	27	40	36	.209	.352	.304	69	-8	5			.953	-3	C-60	-0.6
Total	15	1062	3821	549	978	203	67	55	533	478	572	.256	.340	.387	118	90	42			.942	57	C-954/O-70,32S1	19.2

■ GARY BENNETT
Bennett, Gary David b: 4/17/72, Waukegan, Ill. BR/TR, 6', 190 lbs. Deb: 9/24/95

YEAR	TM/L	G	AB	R	H	2B	3B	HR	RBI	BB	SO	AVG	OBP	SLG	PRO+	BR/A	SB	CS	SBR	FA	FR	G/POS	TPR
1995	Phi-N	1	1	0	0	0	0	0	0	0	1	.000	.000	.000	-99	-0	0	0	0	.000	0	-0,-0	0.0
1996	Phi-N	6	16	0	4	0	0	0	1	2	6	.250	.333	.250	55	-1	0	0	0	1.000	3	/C-5	0.2
Total	2	7	17	0	4	0	0	0	1	2	7	.235	.316	.235	47	-1	0	0	0	1.000	3	/C-5	0.2

■ HERSCHEL BENNETT
Bennett, Herschel Emmett b: 9/21/1896, Elwood, Mo. d: 9/9/64, Springfield, Mo. BL/TR, 5'9.5", 160 lbs. Deb: 4/19/23

YEAR	TM/L	G	AB	R	H	2B	3B	HR	RBI	BB	SO	AVG	OBP	SLG	PRO+	BR/A	SB	CS	SBR	FA	FR	G/POS	TPR
1923	StL-A	5	4	0	0	0	0	0	0	0	1	.000	.200	.000	-42	-1				1.000	-0	/O-1	-0.1
1924	StL-A	41	94	16	31	4	3	1	11	3	6	.330	.364	.468	107	1	1	0		.966	-4	O-21	-0.4
1925	StL-A	93	298	46	83	11	6	2	37	18	16	.279	.324	.376	73	-13	4	10	-5	.916	-2	O-73	-2.2
1926	StL-A	80	225	33	60	14	2	1	26	22	21	.267	.337	.360	78	-7	2	1	0	.950	3	O-50	-0.8
1927	StL-A	93	256	40	68	12	2	3	30	14	21	.266	.311	.363	72	-11	6	2	1	.946	1	O-55	-1.2
Total	5	312	877	135	242	41	13	7	104	58	65	.276	.327	.376	77	-31	13	13	-4	.937	-1	O-200	-4.7

■ FRED BENNETT
Bennett, James Fred "Red" b: 3/15/02, Atkins, Ark. d: 5/12/57, Atkins, Ark. BR/TR, 5'9", 185 lbs. Deb: 4/13/28

YEAR	TM/L	G	AB	R	H	2B	3B	HR	RBI	BB	SO	AVG	OBP	SLG	PRO+	BR/A	SB	CS	SBR	FA	FR	G/POS	TPR
1928	StL-A	7	8	0	2	1	0	0	0	0	2	.250	.250	.375	60	-0	0	0	0	1.000	0	/O-1	-0.1
1931	Pit-N	32	89	6	25	5	0	1	7	7	4	.281	.333	.371	90	-1	0	0	0	.951	-2	O-21	-0.5
Total	2	39	97	6	27	6	0	1	7	7	6	.278	.327	.371	87	-2	0	0	0	.953	-2	O-22	-0.6

■ JOE BENNETT
Bennett, Joseph Rosenblum b: 7/2/1900, New York, N.Y. d: 7/11/87, Morro Bay, Cal. BR/TR, 5'9", 168 lbs. Deb: 7/5/23

YEAR	TM/L	G	AB	R	H	2B	3B	HR	RBI	BB	SO	AVG	OBP	SLG	PRO+	BR/A	SB	CS	SBR	FA	FR	G/POS	TPR
1923	Phi-N	1	0	0	0	0	0	0	0	0	0	—	—	—		0	0	0	0	1.000	0	/3-1	0.0

■ PUG BENNETT
Bennett, Justin Titus b: 2/20/1874, Ponca, Neb. d: 9/12/35, Kirkland, Wash. BR/TR, 5'11", 165 lbs. Deb: 4/12/06

YEAR	TM/L	G	AB	R	H	2B	3B	HR	RBI	BB	SO	AVG	OBP	SLG	PRO+	BR/A	SB	CS	SBR	FA	FR	G/POS	TPR
1906	StL-N	153	595	66	156	16	7	1	34	56		.262	.334	.318	108	6	20			.948	-7	*2-153	0.0
1907	StL-N	87	324	20	72	8	2	0	21	21		.222	.272	.259	69	-12	7			.939	-16	2-83/3-3	-3.4
Total	2	240	919	86	228	24	9	1	55	77		.248	.312	.297	94	-6	27			.945	-23	2-236/3-3	-3.4

■ VERN BENSON
Benson, Vernon Adair b: 9/19/24, Granite Quarry, N.C. BL/TR, 5'11", 180 lbs. Deb: 7/31/43 MC

YEAR	TM/L	G	AB	R	H	2B	3B	HR	RBI	BB	SO	AVG	OBP	SLG	PRO+	BR/A	SB	CS	SBR	FA	FR	G/POS	TPR
1943	Phi-A	2	2	0	0	0	0	0	0	0	0	.000	.000	.000	-99	-1	0	0	0	.000	-0	H	-0.1
1946	Phi-A	7	5	1	0	0	0	0	0	0	1	.000	.167	.000	-51	-1	0	0	0	1.000	-0	/O-2	-0.1
1951	StL-N	13	46	8	12	3	1	1	7	6	8	.261	.346	.435	108	1	0	0	0	.950	1	/3-9,O-4	0.1
1952	StL-N	20	47	6	9	2	0	2	5	5	9	.191	.269	.362	73	-2	0	0	0	.889	-1	3-15	-0.3
1953	StL-N	13	4	2	0	0	0	0	0	2		.000	.200	.000	-42	-1	0	0	0	.000	-0	H	-0.1
Total	5	55	104	17	21	5	1	3	12	13	22	.202	.291	.356	75	-4	0	0	0	.911	-0	/3-24,O-6	-0.5

■ JACK BENTLEY
Bentley, John Needles b: 3/8/1895, Sandy Spring, Md. d: 10/24/69, Olney, Md. BL/TL, 5'11.5", 200 lbs. Deb: 9/6/13

YEAR	TM/L	G	AB	R	H	2B	3B	HR	RBI	BB	SO	AVG	OBP	SLG	PRO+	BR/A	SB	CS	SBR	FA	FR	G/POS	TPR
1913	Was-A	3	3	0	0	0	0	0	0	0	0	.000	.000	.000	-98	-1	0			1.000	-1	/P-3	0.0
1914	Was-A	30	40	7	11	2	0	0	4	0	5	.275	.275	.325	77	-1	0			.930	-1	P-30	0.0
1915	Was-A	4	2	0	0	0	0	0	0	0	0	.000	.000	.000	-98	-0	0			.750	-0	/P-4	0.0
1916	Was-A	2	0	0	0	0	0	0	0	0	0	—	—	—		0	0			1.000	0	/P-2	0.0
1923	*NY-N	52	89	9	38	6	2	1	14	3	4	.427	.446	.573	169	9	0			.977	-1	P-31	0.0
1924	*NY-N	46	98	12	26	5	1	0	13	4	13	.265	.287	.337	68	-5	0			.930	-2	P-28/O-3,1-1	-0.1
1925	NY-N	64	99	10	30	5	2	3	18	9	11	.303	.361	.485	119	3	0			.993	-1	1-56/P-7	-1.6
1926	Phi-N	75	240	19	62	12	3	2	27	5	4	.258	.273	.358	66	-12	0			.993	-1	1-56/P-8	-1.6
	NY-N	3	4	0	1	0	0	0	0	0	1	.250	.250	.250	35	-0	0			.000	-0	/P-1	0.0
	Yr	78	244	19	63	12	3	2	27	5	4	.258	.273	.357	65	-13	0	0		.993	-1	1-56/P-8	-1.6
1927	NY-N	9	9	1	2	0	0	0	1	2	1	.222	.300	.556	125	-0	0			.750	-0	/P-4,1-2	0.0
Total	9	287	584	58	170	30	8	7	71	21	39	.291	.316	.406	91	-8	0	0		.949	-6	P-138/1-59,O-3	-1.7

■ BUTCH BENTON
Benton, Alfred Lee b: 8/24/57, Tampa, Fla. BR/TR, 6'1", 190 lbs. Deb: 9/14/78

YEAR	TM/L	G	AB	R	H	2B	3B	HR	RBI	BB	SO	AVG	OBP	SLG	PRO+	BR/A	SB	CS	SBR	FA	FR	G/POS	TPR
1978	NY-N	4	4	1	2	0	0	0	0	0	0	.500	.600	.500	218	1	0	0	0	1.000	0	/C-1	0.1
1980	NY-N	12	21	0	1	0	0	0	0	2	4	.048	.167	.048	-39	-4	0	0	0	.935	-1	/C-8	-0.5
1982	Chi-N	4	7	0	1	0	0	0	1	0	1	.143	.143	.143	-19	-1	0	0	0	1.000	0	/C-4	0.1
1985	Cle-A	31	67	5	12	4	0	0	7	3	9	.179	.214	.239	24	-7	0	0	0	.957	-3	C-26	-0.9
Total	4	51	99	6	16	4	0	0	10	5	14	.162	.217	.202	16	-11	0	0	0	.959	-2	/C-39	-1.2

■ RABBIT BENTON
Benton, Stanley W. "Stan" b: 9/29/01, Cannel City, Ky. d: 6/7/84, Mesquite, Tex. BR/TR, 5'7", 150 lbs. Deb: 9/13/22

YEAR	TM/L	G	AB	R	H	2B	3B	HR	RBI	BB	SO	AVG	OBP	SLG	PRO+	BR/A	SB	CS	SBR	FA	FR	G/POS	TPR
1922	Phi-N	6	19	1	4	1	0	0	3	2	1	.211	.286	.263	39	-2	0	0	0	.889	0	/2-5	-0.1

■ TODD BENZINGER
Benzinger, Todd Eric b: 2/11/63, Dayton, Ky. BB/TR, 6'1", 185 lbs. Deb: 6/21/87

YEAR	TM/L	G	AB	R	H	2B	3B	HR	RBI	BB	SO	AVG	OBP	SLG	PRO+	BR/A	SB	CS	SBR	FA	FR	G/POS	TPR
1987	Bos-A	73	223	36	62	11	1	8	43	22	41	.278	.344	.444	105	2	5	4	-1	.987	8	O-61/1-2	0.7
1988	*Bos-A	120	405	47	103	28	1	13	70	20	82	.254	.294	.425	95	-4	2	3	-1	.991	-4	1-85,O-48/D-1	-1.6
1989	Cin-N	161	628	79	154	28	3	17	76	44	120	.245	.297	.381	89	-10	3	7	-3	.995	-13	*1-158	-4.2
1990	*Cin-N	118	376	35	95	14	2	5	46	19	69	.253	.296	.340	71	-15	3	4	-2	.992	-1	1-95,O-10	-2.6
1991	Cin-N	51	123	10	23	3	2	1	11	10	20	.187	.248	.268	43	-9	2	0	1	.986	-1	1-21,O-15	-1.2

YEAR	TM/L	G	AB	R	H	2B	3B	HR	RBI	BB	SO	AVG	OBP	SLG	PRO+	BR/A	SB	CS	SBR	FA	FR	G/POS	TPR
	KC-A	78	293	29	86	15	3	2	40	17	46	.294	.339	.386	99	-0	2	6	-3	.996	-5	1-75/D-1	-1.3
1992	LA-N	121	293	24	70	16	2	4	31	15	54	.239	.276	.348	77	-10	2	4	-2	.989	0	O-51,1-42	-1.5
1993	SF-N	86	177	25	51	7	2	6	26	13	35	.288	.337	.452	112	3	0	0	0	1.000	-4	1-40/O-7,3-1	-0.4
1994	SF-N	107	328	32	87	13	2	9	31	17	84	.265	.305	.399	86	-8	2	1	0	.994	-4	1-99	-2.0
1995	SF-N	9	10	2	2	0	0	1	2	2	3	.200	.333	.500	120	0	0	0	0	1.000	-1	/1-5	-0.1
Total	9	924	2856	316	733	135	18	66	376	181	552	.257	.304	.386	88	-51	21	29	-11	.994	-25	1-622,O-192/D-2,3-1	-14.2

■ JOHNNY BERARDINO
Berardino, John "Bernie" b: 5/1/17, Los Angeles, Cal. d: 5/19/96, Los Angeles, Cal. BR/TR, 6', 180 lbs. Deb: 4/22/39

YEAR	TM/L	G	AB	R	H	2B	3B	HR	RBI	BB	SO	AVG	OBP	SLG	PRO+	BR/A	SB	CS	SBR	FA	FR	G/POS	TPR
1939	StL-A	126	468	42	120	24	5	5	58	37	36	.256	.314	.361	71	-21	6	2	1	.958	4	*2-114/3-8,S-2	-1.0
1940	StL-A	142	523	71	135	31	4	16	85	32	46	.258	.301	.424	84	-14	6	8	-3	.939	13	*S-112,2-13/3-9	0.6
1941	StL-A	128	469	48	127	30	4	5	89	41	27	.271	.332	.384	86	-10	3	5	-2	.954	-14	*S-123/3-1	-1.6
1942	StL-A	29	74	11	21	6	0	1	10	4	7	.284	.329	.405	104	0	3	1	0	.950	0	/S-6,3-6,1-5,2-4	0.1
1946	StL-A	144	582	70	154	29	5	5	68	34	58	.265	.306	.357	81	-16	2	4	-2	.972	-2	*2-143	-1.0
1947	StL-A	90	306	29	80	22	1	1	20	44	26	.261	.358	.350	95	-1	6	5	-1	.977	-9	2-86	-0.5
1948	Cle-A	66	147	19	28	5	1	2	10	27	16	.190	.328	.279	64	-7	0	1	-1	.988	4	2-20,1-18,S-12/3-3	-0.3
1949	Cle-A	50	116	11	23	6	1	0	13	14	14	.198	.295	.267	50	-8	0	1	-1	.935	-1	3-25/2-8,S-3	-1.0
1950	Cle-A	4	5	1	2	0	0	0	3	1	0	.400	.500	.400	137	0	0	0	0	1.000	1	/2-1,3-1	0.1
	Pit-N	40	131	12	27	3	1	1	12	19	11	.206	.307	.267	51	-9	0			.964	3	2-36/3-3	-0.5
1951	StL-A	39	119	13	27	7	1	0	13	17	18	.227	.324	.303	68	-5	1	1	-0	.917	-7	3-31/2-2,1-1,O-1	-1.2
1952	Cle-A	35	32	5	3	0	0	0	2	10	8	.094	.310	.094	17	-3	0	1	-1	.960	2	/2-8,S-8,3-4,1-2	-0.2
	Pit-N	19	56	2	8	4	0	0	4	4	5	.143	.200	.214	14	-7	0	0	0	.960	6	2-18	0.1
Total	11	912	3028	334	755	167	23	36	387	284	268	.249	.316	.355	77	-101	27	29		.968	1	2-453,S-266/310	-6.4

■ LOU BERBERET
Berberet, Louis Joseph b: 11/20/29, Long Beach, Cal. BL/TR, 5'11", 212 lbs. Deb: 9/17/54

YEAR	TM/L	G	AB	R	H	2B	3B	HR	RBI	BB	SO	AVG	OBP	SLG	PRO+	BR/A	SB	CS	SBR	FA	FR	G/POS	TPR
1954	NY-A	5	5	1	2	0	0	0	3	1	1	.400	.500	.400	154	0	0	0	0	1.000	1	/C-3	0.2
1955	NY-A	2	5	1	2	0	0	0	2	1	0	.400	.500	.400	147	0	0	0	0	1.000	1	/C-1	0.1
1956	Was-A	95	207	25	54	6	3	4	27	46	33	.261	.402	.377	107	4	0	0	0	.997	-1	C-59	0.6
1957	Was-A	99	264	24	69	11	2	7	36	41	38	.261	.365	.398	110	4	0	1	-1	**1.000**	-3	C-77	0.5
1958	Was-A	5	6	0	1	0	0	0	0	4	1	.167	.500	.167	94	0	0	0	0	.917	-1	/C-2	0.0
	Bos-A	57	167	11	35	5	3	2	18	31	32	.210	.337	.311	74	-5	0	2	-1	.984	-6	C-49	-0.9
	Yr	62	173	11	36	5	3	2	18	35	33	.208	.344	.306	76	-5	0	2	-1	.981	-5	C-51	-0.8
1959	Det-A	100	338	38	73	8	2	13	44	35	59	.216	.290	.367	75	-12	0	0	0	.989	-11	C-95	-1.8
1960	Det-A	85	232	18	45	4	0	1	21	41	31	.194	.318	.276	60	-12	2	0	1	.993	-0	C-81	-0.7
Total	7	448	1224	118	281	34	10	31	153	200	195	.230	.341	.350	86	-19	2	3		.992	-17	C-367	-2.0

■ MOE BERG
Berg, Morris b: 3/2/02, New York, N.Y. d: 5/29/72, Belleville, N.J. BR/TR, 6'1", 185 lbs. Deb: 7/4/23 C

YEAR	TM/L	G	AB	R	H	2B	3B	HR	RBI	BB	SO	AVG	OBP	SLG	PRO+	BR/A	SB	CS	SBR	FA	FR	G/POS	TPR
1923	Bro-N	49	129	9	24	3	2	0	6	2	5	.186	.198	.240	16	-16	1	0		.906	-6	S-47/2-1	-1.8
1926	Chi-A	41	113	4	25	6	2	0	7	6	9	.221	.261	.274	41	-10	2	0	-1	.948	6	S-31/2-2,3-1	-0.3
1927	Chi-A	35	69	4	17	4	0	0	4	4	10	.246	.288	.304	55	-5	0	0	0	.952	-4	2-11,C-10/S-6,3-3	-0.7
1928	Chi-A	76	224	25	55	16	0	0	29	14	25	.246	.302	.317	64	-12	2	1	0	.990	5	C-73	-0.1
1929	Chi-A	107	352	32	101	7	0	0	47	17	16	.287	.323	.307	64	-18	5	1	1	.982	-3	*C-106	-1.0
1930	Chi-A	20	61	4	7	3	0	0	7	1	5	.115	.129	.164	-27	-12	0	0	0	.986	-1	C-20	-1.0
1931	Cle-A	10	13	1	1	1	0	0	1	0	1	.077	.143	.154	-21	-2	0	0	0	.889	-1	/C-8	-0.2
1932	Was-A	75	195	16	46	8	1	1	26	8	13	.236	.266	.303	48	-15	1	1	-0	1.000	7	C-75	-0.5
1933	Was-A	40	65	8	12	4	0	0	5	3	5	.185	.232	.323	46	-5	0	0	0	1.000	3	C-35	-0.2
1934	Was-A	33	86	5	21	4	0	0	6	6	4	.244	.301	.291	55	-6	0	0	0	.988	-4	C-31	-0.8
	Cle-A	29	97	4	25	3	1	0	9	1	7	.258	.265	.309	47	-8	0	0	0	.980	5	C-28	-0.1
	Yr	62	183	9	46	7	1	0	15	7	11	.251	.283	.301	51	-13	0	0	0	.983	1	C-59	-0.9
1935	Bos-A	38	98	13	28	5	0	2	12	5	3	.286	.320	.398	79	-3	0	0	0	.991	2	C-37	0.0
1936	Bos-A	39	125	9	30	4	1	0	19	2	6	.240	.264	.288	34	-13	0	0	0	.986	12	C-39	0.0
1937	Bos-A	47	141	13	36	3	1	0	20	5	4	.255	.281	.291	43	-12	0	0	0	.979	3	C-47	-0.7
1938	Bos-A	10	12	0	4	0	0	0	0	0	1	.333	.333	.333	64	-1	0	0	0	1.000	1	/C-7,1-1	0.0
1939	Bos-A	14	33	3	9	1	0	1	5	2	3	.273	.314	.394	77	-1	0	0	0	.965	4	C-13	0.3
Total	15	663	1813	150	441	71	6	6	206	78	117	.243	.278	.299	49	-140	11	5	0	.986	29	C-529/S-84,2-14,31	-7.1

■ AUGIE BERGAMO
Bergamo, August Samuel b: 2/14/17, Detroit, Mich. d: 8/19/74, Grosse Pointe, Mich. BL/TL, 5'9", 165 lbs. Deb: 4/25/44

YEAR	TM/L	G	AB	R	H	2B	3B	HR	RBI	BB	SO	AVG	OBP	SLG	PRO+	BR/A	SB	CS	SBR	FA	FR	G/POS	TPR
1944	*StL-N	80	192	35	55	6	3	2	19	35	23	.286	.399	.380	118	6	0			.988	-7	O-50/1-2	-0.4
1945	StL-N	94	304	51	96	17	2	3	44	43	21	.316	.401	.414	124	11	0			.969	-1	O-77/1-2	0.6
Total	2	174	496	86	151	23	5	5	63	78	44	.304	.400	.401	122	17	0			.975	-9	O-127/1-4	0.2

■ MARTY BERGEN
Bergen, Martin b: 10/25/1871, N.Brookfield, Mass d: 1/19/1900, N.Brookfield, Mass TR, 5'10", 170 lbs. Deb: 4/17/1896 F

YEAR	TM/L	G	AB	R	H	2B	3B	HR	RBI	BB	SO	AVG	OBP	SLG	PRO+	BR/A	SB	CS	SBR	FA	FR	G/POS	TPR
1896	Bos-N	65	245	39	66	6	4	4	37	11	22	.269	.309	.376	75	-10	6			.920	6	C-63/1-1	0.2
1897	*Bos-N	87	327	47	81	11	3	2	45	18		.248	.295	.318	58	-21	5			.963	4	C-85/O-1	-0.6
1898	Bos-N	120	446	62	125	16	5	3	60	13		.280	.302	.359	85	-11	9			.962	2	*C-117/1-2	0.2
1899	Bos-N	72	260	32	67	11	3	1	34	10		.258	.290	.335	65	-14	4			.955	3	C-72	-0.5
Total	4	344	1278	180	339	44	15	10	176	52	22	.265	.299	.347	72	-56	24			.954	15	C-337/1-3,O-1	-0.7

■ BILL BERGEN
Bergen, William Aloysius b: 6/13/1878, N.Brookfield, Mass. d: 12/19/43, Worcester, Mass. BR/TR, 6', 184 lbs. Deb: 5/6/01 F

YEAR	TM/L	G	AB	R	H	2B	3B	HR	RBI	BB	SO	AVG	OBP	SLG	PRO+	BR/A	SB	CS	SBR	FA	FR	G/POS	TPR
1901	Cin-N	87	308	15	55	6	4	1	17	8		.179	.199	.234	27	-29	4			.970	-4	C-87	-2.4
1902	Cin-N	89	322	19	58	8	3	0	36	14		.180	.214	.224	32	-26	2			.959	17	C-89	0.0
1903	Cin-N	58	207	21	47	4	2	0	19	7		.227	.252	.266	43	-16	2			.980	2	C-58	-0.8
1904	Bro-N	96	329	17	60	4	2	0	12	9		.182	.204	.207	28	-28	3			.959	14	C-93/1-1	-0.4
1905	Bro-N	79	247	12	47	3	2	0	22	7		.190	.213	.219	31	-21	4			.954	12	C-76	-0.3
1906	Bro-N	103	353	9	56	3	2	0	19	7		.159	.175	.184	13	-37	4			.977	6	*C-103	-2.3
1907	Bro-N	51	138	2	22	3	0	0	14	1		.159	.165	.181	9	-15	1			.968	3	C-51	-1.0
1908	Bro-N	99	302	8	53	8	2	0	15	5		.175	.189	.215	30	-24	1			**.989**	16	C-99	0.0
1909	Bro-N	112	346	16	48	1	1	0	15	10		.139	.163	.156	-1	-41	2			.976	22	*C-112	-1.1
1910	Bro-N	89	249	11	40	2	1	0	14	6	39	.161	.180	.177	4	-31	0			.981	18	C-89	-0.5
1911	Bro-N	84	227	8	30	3	1	0	10	14	42	.132	.183	.154	-6	-32	2			**.981**	15	C-84	-1.0
Total	11	947	3028	138	516	45	21	2	193	88	81	.170	.194	.201	20	-301	23			.972	119	C-941/1-1	-9.8

■ CLARENCE BERGER
Berger, Clarence Edward b: 11/1/1894, E.Cleveland, Ohio d: 6/30/59, Washington, D.C. BL/TR, 6', 185 lbs. Deb: 9/23/14

YEAR	TM/L	G	AB	R	H	2B	3B	HR	RBI	BB	SO	AVG	OBP	SLG	PRO+	BR/A	SB	CS	SBR	FA	FR	G/POS	TPR
1914	Pit-N	6	13	2	1	0	0	0	0	0		.077	.143	.077	-36	-2	0			1.000	-2	/O-5	-0.5

■ JOHNNY BERGER
Berger, John Henne b: 8/27/01, Philadelphia, Pa. d: 5/7/79, Lake Charles, La. BR/TR, 5'9", 165 lbs. Deb: 4/20/22

YEAR	TM/L	G	AB	R	H	2B	3B	HR	RBI	BB	SO	AVG	OBP	SLG	PRO+	BR/A	SB	CS	SBR	FA	FR	G/POS	TPR
1922	Phi-A	2	1	0	1	0	0	0	0	0	0	1.000	1.000	1.000	412	0	1	0	0	1.000	1	/C-2	0.1
1927	Was-A	9	15	1	4	0	0	0	1	2	3	.267	.353	.267	63	-1	0	0	0	.926	0	/C-9	0.0
Total	2	11	16	1	5	0	0	0	1	2	3	.313	.389	.313	85	-0	1	0	0	.935	1	/C-11	0.1

■ TUN BERGER
Berger, John Henry b: 12/6/1867, Pittsburgh, Pa. d: 6/10/07, Pittsburgh, Pa. TR, 204 lbs. Deb: 5/9/1890

YEAR	TM/L	G	AB	R	H	2B	3B	HR	RBI	BB	SO	AVG	OBP	SLG	PRO+	BR/A	SB	CS	SBR	FA	FR	G/POS	TPR
1890	Pit-N	104	391	64	104	18	6	0	40	35	23	.266	.337	.332	108	5	11			.912	-7	O-41,S-33,C-21,/23	0.1
1891	Pit-N	43	134	15	32	2	1	0	14	12	10	.239	.315	.291	79	-3	4			.920	-13	C-18,2-17/S-6,0-2	-1.2
1892	Was-N	26	97	9	14	2	0	0	3	7	9	.144	.210	.186	20	-9	3			.872	-11	S-18/C-9	-1.8
Total	3	173	622	88	150	22	6	1	57	54	42	.241	.313	.301	87	-8	18			.837	-30	/S-57,C-48,O-43,23	-2.9

■ JOE BERGER
Berger, Joseph August "Fats" b: 12/20/1886, St.Louis, Mo. d: 3/5/56, Rock Island, Ill. BR/TR, 5'10.5", 170 lbs. Deb: 4/11/13

YEAR	TM/L	G	AB	R	H	2B	3B	HR	RBI	BB	SO	AVG	OBP	SLG	PRO+	BR/A	SB	CS	SBR	FA	FR	G/POS	TPR
1913	Chi-A	79	223	27	48	7	2	0	20	36	28	.215	.330	.287	82	-4	5			.959	3	2-71/S-4,3-1	-0.2
1914	Chi-A	48	148	11	23	2	1	0	3	13	9	.155	.224	.189	25	-14	2	8	-4	.922	-2	S-28,2-12/3-7	-2.0
Total	2	127	371	38	71	9	3	2	23	49	37	.191	.289	.248	60	-18	7	8		.956	1	/2-83,S-32,3-8	-2.2

■ BOZE BERGER
Berger, Louis William b: 5/13/10, Baltimore, Md. d: 11/3/92, Bethesda, Md. BR/TR, 6'2", 180 lbs. Deb: 8/17/32

YEAR	TM/L	G	AB	R	H	2B	3B	HR	RBI	BB	SO	AVG	OBP	SLG	PRO+	BR/A	SB	CS	SBR	FA	FR	G/POS	TPR
1932	Cle-A	1	1	0	0	0	0	0	0	0	1	.000	.000	.000	-94	-0	0	0	0	1.000	1	/S-1	0.1

YEAR	TM/L	G	AB	R	H	2B	3B	HR	RBI	BB	SO	AVG	OBP	SLG	PRO+	BR/A	SB	CS	SBR	FA	FR	G/POS	TPR
1935	Cle-A	124	461	62	119	27	5	5	43	34	97	.258	.310	.371	74	-19	7	5	-1	.964	13	*2-120/S-3,1-2,3-1	0.2
1936	Cle-A	28	52	1	9	2	0	0	3	1	14	.173	.189	.212	-1	-8	0	0	0	.959	4	/1-8,2-8,3-7,S-2	-0.4
1937	Chi-A	52	130	19	31	5	0	5	13	15	24	.238	.322	.392	79	-5	1	1	-0	.931	-1	3-40/2-1,S-1	-0.4
1938	Chi-A	118	470	60	102	15	3	3	36	43	80	.217	.284	.281	41	-43	4	1	1	.946	-10	S-67,2-42/3-9	-4.1
1939	Bos-A	20	30	4	9	2	0	0	2	1	10	.300	.323	.367	73	-1	0	0	0	.947	1	S-10/3-5,2-2	0.0
Total	6	343	1144	146	270	51	8	13	97	94	226	.236	.296	.329	57	-77	12	7	-1	.954	9	*2-173/S-84,3-62,1	-4.6

■ WALLY BERGER
Berger, Walter Antone b: 10/10/05, Chicago, Ill. d: 11/30/88, Redondo Beach, Cal BR/TR, 6'2", 198 lbs. Deb: 4/15/30

YEAR	TM/L	G	AB	R	H	2B	3B	HR	RBI	BB	SO	AVG	OBP	SLG	PRO+	BR/A	SB	CS	SBR	FA	FR	G/POS	TPR
1930	Bos-N	151	555	98	172	27	14	38	119	54	69	.310	.375	.614	139	31	3			.966	4	*O-145	2.2
1931	Bos-N	156	617	94	199	44	8	19	84	55	70	.323	.380	.512	143	36	13			.977	11	*O-156/1-1	3.5
1932	Bos-N	145	602	90	185	34	6	17	73	33	66	.307	.346	.468	121	16	5			**.993**	5	*O-134,1-11	1.2
1933	Bos-N★	137	528	84	165	37	8	27	106	41	77	.313	.365	.566	**177**	49	2			.977	4	*O-136	4.7
1934	Bos-N★	150	615	92	183	35	4	34	121	49	65	.298	.352	.546	148	38	2			.978	1	*O-150	3.1
1935	Bos-N★	150	589	91	174	39	4	34	130	50	80	.295	.355	.548	151	39	3			.965	9	*O-149	4.0
1936	Bos-N☆	138	534	88	154	23	3	25	91	53	84	.288	.361	.483	134	24	1			.966	7	*O-133	2.5
1937	Bos-N	30	113	14	31	9	1	5	22	11	33	.274	.344	.504	140	6	0			1.000	-2	O-28	0.3
	*NY-N	59	199	40	58	11	2	12	43	18	30	.291	.359	.548	141	11	3			.965	-2	O-52	0.7
	Yr	89	312	54	89	20	3	17	65	29	63	.285	.354	.532	141	16	3			.976	-4	O-80	1.0
1938	NY-N	16	32	5	6	0	0	0	4	2	4	.188	.235	.188	17	-4	0			1.000	1	/O-9	-0.3
	Cin-N	99	407	74	125	23	4	16	56	29	44	.307	.356	.501	137	19	2			.966	-3	O-98	1.3
	Yr	115	439	79	131	23	4	16	60	31	48	.298	.347	.478	128	15	2			.970	-2	O-107	1.0
1939	*Cin-N	97	329	36	85	15	1	14	44	36	63	.258	.341	.438	107	3	1			.970	-8	O-95	-0.8
1940	Cin-N	2	2	0	0	0	0	0	0	0	1	.000	.000	.000	-99	-1	0			.000	0	H	-0.1
	Phi-N	20	41	3	13	2	0	1	5	4	8	.317	.378	.439	130	2	1			.947	-2	O-11/1-1	-0.1
	Yr	22	43	3	13	2	0	1	5	4	9	.302	.362	.419	119	1	1			.947	-2	O-11/1-1	-0.2
Total	11	1350	5163	809	1550	299	59	242	898	435	694	.300	.359	.522	140	269	36			.974	26	*O-1296/1-13	22.2

■ JOHN BERGH
Bergh, John Baptist b: 10/8/1857, Boston, Mass. d: 4/16/1883, Boston, Mass. Deb: 8/5/1876

YEAR	TM/L	G	AB	R	H	2B	3B	HR	RBI	BB	SO	AVG	OBP	SLG	PRO+	BR/A	SB	CS	SBR	FA	FR	G/POS	TPR
1876	Phi-N	1	4	0	0	0	0	0	0	0	2	.000	.000	.000	-99	-1				1.000	-0	/O-1,C-1	-0.1
1880	Bos-N	11	40	2	8	3	0	0	0	2	5	.200	.238	.275	76	-1				.844	-3	C-11	-0.4
Total	2	12	44	2	8	3	0	0	0	2	7	.182	.217	.250	59	-2				.841	-4	/C-12,O-1	-0.5

■ MARTY BERGHAMMER
Berghammer, Martin Andrew "Pepper" b: 6/18/1888, Elliott, Pa. d: 12/21/57, Pittsburgh, Pa. BL/TR, 5'9", 172 lbs. Deb: 9/8/11

YEAR	TM/L	G	AB	R	H	2B	3B	HR	RBI	BB	SO	AVG	OBP	SLG	PRO+	BR/A	SB	CS	SBR	FA	FR	G/POS	TPR
1911	Chi-A	2	5	0	0	0	0	0	0	0	0	.000	.167	.000	-54	-1	0			1.000	-0	/2-2	-0.1
1913	Cin-N	74	188	25	41	4	1	1	13	10	29	.218	.269	.266	53	-11	16			.909	5	S-54,2-13	-0.3
1914	Cin-N	77	112	15	25	2	0	0	6	10	18	.223	.287	.241	56	-6	4			.906	7	S-33,2-13	0.2
1915	Pit-F	132	469	96	114	10	6	0	33	83	44	.243	.371	.286	88	-10	26			.943	-16	*S-132	-1.6
Total	4	285	774	136	180	16	7	1	52	103	91	.233	.335	.275	75	-28	46			.931	5	S-219/2-28	-1.8

■ AL BERGMAN
Bergman, Alfred Henry "Dutch" b: 9/27/1890, Peru, Ind. d: 6/20/61, Fort Wayne, Ind. BR/TR, 5'7", 155 lbs. Deb: 8/29/16

YEAR	TM/L	G	AB	R	H	2B	3B	HR	RBI	BB	SO	AVG	OBP	SLG	PRO+	BR/A	SB	CS	SBR	FA	FR	G/POS	TPR
1916	Cle-A	8	14	2	3	0	1	0	3	2	4	.214	.313	.357	95	-0	0			.889	-2	/2-3	-0.2

■ DAVE BERGMAN
Bergman, David Bruce b: 6/6/53, Evanston, Ill. BL/TL, 6'1.5", 185 lbs. Deb: 8/26/75

YEAR	TM/L	G	AB	R	H	2B	3B	HR	RBI	BB	SO	AVG	OBP	SLG	PRO+	BR/A	SB	CS	SBR	FA	FR	G/POS	TPR
1975	NY-A	7	17	0	0	0	0	0	0	0	4	.000	.105	.000	-69	-4	0	0	0	.917	0	/O-6	-0.4
1977	NY-A	5	4	1	1	0	0	0	1	0	0	.250	.250	.250	37	-0	0	0	0	1.000	-1	/O-3,1-2	-0.1
1978	Hou-N	104	186	15	43	5	1	0	12	39	32	.231	.364	.269	86	-2	2	0	1	.993	-2	1-66,O-29	-0.6
1979	Hou-N	13	15	4	6	0	0	1	2	0	3	.400	.400	.600	179	1	0	0	0	1.000	-0	/1-4	0.1
1980	*Hou-N	90	78	12	20	6	1	0	10	10	10	.256	.341	.359	104	0	1	0	1	.995	2	1-59/O-5	0.2
1981	Hou-N	6	6	1	1	0	0	1	1	0	0	.167	.167	.667	134	0	0	0	0	1.000	-0	/1-1	0.1
	SF-N	63	145	16	37	9	0	3	13	19	18	.255	.341	.379	106	1	2	0	1	.992	-1	1-33,O-15	0.1
	Yr	69	151	17	38	9	0	4	14	19	18	.252	.335	.391	108	2	2	0	1	.992	1	1-34,O-15	0.2
1982	SF-N	100	121	22	33	3	1	4	18	18	11	.273	.367	.413	118	3	2	0	1	.991	-1	1-69/O-6	0.4
1983	SF-N	90	140	16	40	4	1	6	24	24	21	.286	.394	.457	140	8	2	1	0	.994	1	1-50/O-6	0.9
1984	*Det-A	120	271	42	74	8	5	7	44	33	40	.273	.358	.417	115	6	3	4	-2	.989	8	*1-114/O-2	0.8
1985	Det-A	69	140	8	25	2	0	3	7	14	15	.179	.253	.257	41	-11	0	0	0	.991	-1	1-44/O-1,D-5	-1.2
1986	Det-A	65	130	14	30	6	1	1	9	21	16	.231	.338	.315	79	-3	0	0	-0	.986	2	1-41/O-2,D-8	-0.3
1987	*Det-A	91	172	25	47	7	3	6	22	30	23	.273	.384	.453	127	7	1	0	-1	.992	-1	1-65/O-7,D-7	0.3
1988	Det-A	116	289	37	85	14	0	5	35	38	34	.294	.376	.394	121	9	0	1	-1	.990	-0	1-64,D-30,O-13	0.3
1989	Det-A	137	385	38	103	13	1	7	37	44	44	.268	.346	.361	102	2	1	3	-2	.993	5	*1-123/O-1,D-7	-0.3
1990	Det-A	100	205	21	57	10	1	2	26	33	17	.278	.378	.366	108	4	3	2	-0	.995	-3	D-51,1-27/O-5	-0.3
1991	Det-A	86	194	23	46	10	1	7	29	35	40	.237	.354	.407	108	3	1	4	-1	.997	-1	1-49,D-13/O-4	-0.1
1992	Det-A	87	181	17	42	3	0	1	10	20	19	.232	.308	.265	62	-9	0	1	-0	.986	-2	1-55,D-12/O-1	-1.4
Total	17	1349	2679	312	690	100	16	54	289	380	347	.258	.351	.367	102	17	19	14	-3	.992	10	1-866,D-133,O-106	-1.5

■ FRANK BERKELBACH
Berkelbach, Francis P. b: Philadelphia, Pa. 6', 182 lbs. Deb: 7/4/1884

YEAR	TM/L	G	AB	R	H	2B	3B	HR	RBI	BB	SO	AVG	OBP	SLG	PRO+	BR/A	SB	CS	SBR	FA	FR	G/POS	TPR
1884	Cin-a	6	25	3	6	1	0	0	3	0	3	.240	.296	.320	96	-0				.667	-2	/O-6	-0.2

■ NATE BERKENSTOCK
Berkenstock, Nathan b: 1831, Pennsylvania d: 2/23/1900, Philadelphia, Pa. Deb: 10/30/1871

YEAR	TM/L	G	AB	R	H	2B	3B	HR	RBI	BB	SO	AVG	OBP	SLG	PRO+	BR/A	SB	CS	SBR	FA	FR	G/POS	TPR
1871	Ath-n	1	4	0	0	0	0	0	0	0	3	.000	.000	.000	-99	-1	0	0	0	1.000	0	/O-1	0.0

■ BOB BERMAN
Berman, Robert Leon b: 1/24/1899, New York, N.Y. d: 8/2/88, Bridgeport, Conn. BR/TR, 5'8", 147 lbs. Deb: 6/4/18

YEAR	TM/L	G	AB	R	H	2B	3B	HR	RBI	BB	SO	AVG	OBP	SLG	PRO+	BR/A	SB	CS	SBR	FA	FR	G/POS	TPR
1918	Was-A	2	0	0	0	0	0	0	0	0	0	—	—	—	—	—	0			1.000	0	/C-1	0.0

■ CURT BERNARD
Bernard, Curtis Henry b: 2/18/1878, Parkersburg, W.Va. d: 4/10/55, Culver City, Cal. BL/TR, 5'10", 150 lbs. Deb: 9/17/00

YEAR	TM/L	G	AB	R	H	2B	3B	HR	RBI	BB	SO	AVG	OBP	SLG	PRO+	BR/A	SB	CS	SBR	FA	FR	G/POS	TPR
1900	NY-N	20	71	9	18	2	0	0	8	6		.254	.329	.282	73	-2	1			.929	-2	O-19/S-1	-0.6
1901	NY-N	23	76	11	17	0	2	0	6	7		.224	.289	.276	67	-3	2			.800	-1	O-15/2-4,S-2,3-1	-0.5
Total	2	43	147	20	35	2	2	0	14	13		.238	.309	.279	70	-5	3			.857	-3	/O-34,2-4,S-3,3-1	-1.1

■ TONY BERNAZARD
Bernazard, Antonio (Garcia) b: 8/24/56, Caguas, P.R. BB/TR, 5'9", 160 lbs. Deb: 7/13/79

YEAR	TM/L	G	AB	R	H	2B	3B	HR	RBI	BB	SO	AVG	OBP	SLG	PRO+	BR/A	SB	CS	SBR	FA	FR	G/POS	TPR
1979	Mon-N	22	40	11	12	2	0	1	8	15	12	.300	.500	.425	156	5	1	2	-1	.982	-1	2-14	0.3
1980	Mon-N	82	183	26	41	7	1	5	18	17	41	.224	.290	.355	79	-5	9	2	2	.976	2	2-39,S-22	0.2
1981	Chi-A	106	384	53	106	14	4	6	34	54	66	.276	.368	.380	118	11	4	4	-1	.987	-1	*2-104/S-1	1.6
1982	Chi-A	137	540	90	138	25	9	11	56	67	88	.256	.340	.396	101	2	11	0	3	.985	25	*2-137	3.7
1983	Chi-A	59	233	30	61	16	2	2	26	17	45	.262	.312	.373	85	-5	2	1	0	.976	-2	2-59	-0.4
	Sea-A	80	300	35	80	18	1	6	30	38	52	.267	.353	.393	101	1	21	8	2	.971	1	2-79	0.7
	Yr	139	533	65	141	34	3	8	56	55	97	.265	.336	.385	94	-4	23	9	2	.973	-1	2-138	0.3
1984	Cle-A	140	439	44	97	15	4	2	38	64	70	.221	.293	.287	60	-23	20	13	-2	.971	-11	*2-136/D-1	-3.1
1985	Cle-A	153	500	73	137	26	3	11	59	69	72	.274	.363	.404	111	9	17	9	-0	.978	-29	*2-147/S-1	-1.5
1986	Cle-A	146	562	88	169	28	4	17	73	53	77	.301	.367	.456	125	19	17	8	0	.979	1	*2-146	2.6
1987	Cle-A	79	293	39	70	12	1	11	30	25	49	.239	.301	.399	89	-8	7	4	-0	.983	-16	2-78	-1.9
	Oak-A	61	214	34	57	14	1	3	19	30	30	.266	.357	.383	103	2	4	1	-1	.953	-18	2-59/D-3	-1.5
	Yr	140	507	73	127	26	2	14	49	55	79	.250	.325	.393	91	-6	11	5	-2	.971	-34	2-137/D-3	-3.4
1991	Det-A	6	12	0	2	0	0	0	0	0	2	.167	.167	.167	-7	-0	0	0	0	.900	1	/2-2,D-2	0.0
Total	10	1071	3700	523	970	177	30	75	391	428	606	.255	.343	.381	100	6	113	55	1	.978	-48	2-1000/S-24,D-6	0.7

■ JUAN BERNHARDT
Bernhardt, Juan Ramon (Coradin) b: 8/31/53, San Pedro De Macoris, D.R. BR/TR, 5'11", 160 lbs. Deb: 7/10/76

YEAR	TM/L	G	AB	R	H	2B	3B	HR	RBI	BB	SO	AVG	OBP	SLG	PRO+	BR/A	SB	CS	SBR	FA	FR	G/POS	TPR
1976	NY-A	10	21	1	4	1	0	0	2	0	2	.190	.190	.238	25	-2	0	0	0	.800	-1	/O-4,3-1,D-2	-0.3
1977	Sea-A	89	305	32	74	9	2	7	30	5	26	.243	.260	.354	66	-15	2	3	-1	.982	-1	D-54,3-21/1-8	-1.9
1978	Sea-A	54	165	13	38	9	0	2	12	9	10	.230	.274	.327	67	-7	1	4	-0	.989	-0	1-25,3-22/D-2	-1.0
1979	Sea-A	1	1	0	1	0	0	0	0	0	0	1.000	1.000	1.000	434	0	0	0	-0	.000	0	/H	0.0
Total	4	154	492	46	117	19	2	9	43	14	40	.238	.263	.339	66	-24	3	4	-2	.965	-2	/D-58,3-44,1-33,O-4	-3.2

YEAR	TM/L	G	AB	R	H	2B	3B	HR	RBI	BB	SO	AVG	OBP	SLG	PRO+	BR/A	SB	CS	SBR	FA	FR	G/POS	TPR

■ CARLOS BERNIER   Bernier, Carlos (Rodriguez)   b: 1/28/27, Juana Diaz, P.R.   d: 4/6/89, Juana Diaz, P.R.   BR/TR, 5'9", 180 lbs.   Deb: 4/22/53

YEAR	TM/L	G	AB	R	H	2B	3B	HR	RBI	BB	SO	AVG	OBP	SLG	PRO+	BR/A	SB	CS	SBR	FA	FR	G/POS	TPR
1953	Pit-N	105	310	48	66	7	8	3	31	51	53	.213	.332	.316	70	-12	15	14	-4	.970	5	O-86	-1.4

■ JOHNNY BERO   Bero, John George   b: 12/22/22, Gary, W.Va.   d: 5/11/85, Gardena, Cal.   BL/TR, 6', 170 lbs.   Deb: 9/26/48

YEAR	TM/L	G	AB	R	H	2B	3B	HR	RBI	BB	SO	AVG	OBP	SLG	PRO+	BR/A	SB	CS	SBR	FA	FR	G/POS	TPR
1948	Det-A	4	9	2	0	0	0	0	0	1	1	.000	.100	.000	-70	-2	0	0	0	1.000	-1	/2-2	-0.3
1951	StL-A	61	160	24	34	5	0	5	17	26	30	.213	.323	.338	76	-5	1	1	-0	.954	-9	S-55/2-1	-1.1
Total	2	65	169	26	34	5	0	5	17	27	31	.201	.311	.320	69	-7	1	1	-0	1.000	-10	/S-55,2-3	-1.4

■ DALE BERRA   Berra, Dale Anthony   b: 12/13/56, Ridgewood, N.J.   BR/TR, 6', 190 lbs.   Deb: 8/22/77   F

YEAR	TM/L	G	AB	R	H	2B	3B	HR	RBI	BB	SO	AVG	OBP	SLG	PRO+	BR/A	SB	CS	SBR	FA	FR	G/POS	TPR
1977	Pit-N	17	40	0	7	1	0	0	3	1	8	.175	.195	.200	6	-5	0	0	0	.973	3	3-14	-0.3
1978	Pit-N	56	135	16	28	2	0	6	14	13	20	.207	.287	.356	75	-5	3	1	0	.908	1	3-55/S-2	-0.4
1979	Pit-N	44	123	11	26	5	0	3	15	11	17	.211	.276	.325	61	-7	0	0	0	.940	1	S-22,3-22	-0.5
1980	Pit-N	93	245	21	54	8	2	6	31	16	52	.220	.271	.343	69	-11	2	0	1	.968	2	3-48,S-45/2-4	-0.5
1981	Pit-N	81	232	21	56	12	0	2	27	17	34	.241	.302	.319	74	-8	11	1	3	.976	-2	3-42,S-30,2-18	-0.1
1982	Pit-N	156	529	64	139	25	5	10	61	33	83	.263	.311	.386	91	-7	6	6	-2	.961	-2	*S-153/3-6	0.3
1983	Pit-N	161	537	51	135	25	1	10	52	61	84	.251	.328	.358	88	-8	8	5	-1	.963	16	*S-161	2.3
1984	Pit-N	136	450	31	100	16	0	9	52	34	78	.222	.278	.318	67	-20	1	3	-2	.955	-5	*S-135/3-1	-1.1
1985	NY-A	48	109	8	25	5	1	1	8	7	20	.229	.276	.321	64	-5	1	1	-0	.917	4	3-41/S-6	-0.2
1986	NY-A	42	108	10	25	7	0	2	13	9	14	.231	.297	.352	77	-4	0	0	0	.972	-1	S-19,3-18/D-4	-0.5
1987	Hou-N	19	45	3	8	3	0	0	2	8	12	.178	.302	.244	49	-3	0	0	0	.963	-3	S-18/2-3	-0.5
Total	11	853	2553	236	603	109	9	49	278	210	422	.236	.297	.344	76	-83	32	17	-1	.959	21	S-591,3-247/2-25,D	-1.3

■ YOGI BERRA   Berra, Lawrence Peter   b: 5/12/25, St.Louis, Mo.   BL/TR, 5'8", 194 lbs.   Deb: 9/22/46   FMCH

YEAR	TM/L	G	AB	R	H	2B	3B	HR	RBI	BB	SO	AVG	OBP	SLG	PRO+	BR/A	SB	CS	SBR	FA	FR	G/POS	TPR
1946	NY-A	7	22	3	8	1	0	2	4	1	1	.364	.391	.682	193	2	0	0	0	1.000	2	/C-6	0.5
1947	*NY-A	83	293	41	82	15	3	11	54	13	12	.280	.310	.464	115	3	0	1	-1	.972	-6	C-51,O-24	-0.1
1948	NY-A☆	125	469	70	143	24	10	14	98	25	24	.305	.341	.488	120	10	3	3	-1	.979	-9	C-71,O-50	0.2
1949	*NY-A★	116	415	59	115	20	2	20	91	22	25	.277	.323	.480	111	2	2	1	0	.989	11	*C-109	1.9
1950	*NY-A★	151	597	116	192	30	6	28	124	55	12	.322	.383	.533	136	29	4	2	0	.985	1	*C-148	3.4
1951	*NY-A★	141	547	92	161	19	4	27	88	44	20	.294	.350	.492	131	20	5	4	-1	.984	5	*C-141	3.3
1952	*NY-A★	142	534	97	146	17	1	30	98	66	24	.273	.358	.478	130	26	2	3	-1	.992	2	*C-140	3.5
1953	*NY-A★	137	503	80	149	23	5	27	108	50	32	.296	.363	.523	142	27	0	3	-2	.986	3	*C-133	3.4
1954	*NY-A★	151	584	88	179	28	6	22	125	56	29	.307	.371	.488	139	29	0	1	-1	.990	0	*C-149/3-1	3.6
1955	*NY-A★	147	541	84	147	20	3	27	108	60	20	.272	.352	.470	121	14	1	0	-0	.984	-0	*C-145	1.9
1956	*NY-A★	140	521	93	155	29	2	30	105	65	29	.298	.381	.534	144	31	3	2	-0	.986	7	*C-135/O-1	4.2
1957	*NY-A★	134	482	74	121	14	2	24	82	57	24	.251	.331	.438	110	6	1	2	-1	.995	16	*C-121/O-6	2.6
1958	*NY-A★	122	433	60	115	17	3	22	90	35	35	.266	.323	.471	120	10	3	0	1	**1.000**	6	C-88,O-21/1-2	2.1
1959	*NY-A★	131	472	64	134	25	1	19	69	43	38	.284	.349	.462	125	15	1	2	-1	.997	7	*C-116/O-7	2.8
1960	*NY-A★	120	359	46	99	14	1	15	62	38	23	.276	.350	.446	120	10	2	1	-0	.989	-10	C-63,O-36	0.2
1961	*NY-A★	119	395	62	107	11	0	22	61	35	28	.271	.330	.466	117	8	2	0	0	.988	3	O-87,C-15	0.7
1962	*NY-A★	86	232	25	52	8	0	10	35	24	18	.224	.302	.388	87	-5	0	1	-1	.990	8	C-31,O-28	0.2
1963	*NY-A	64	147	20	43	6	0	8	28	15	17	.293	.362	.497	139	8	1	0	0	.988	8	C-35	1.8
1965	NY-N	4	9	1	2	0	0	0	0	0	0	.222	.222	.222	27	-1	0	0	0	.941	1	/C-2	0.0
Total	19	2120	7555	1175	2150	321	49	358	1430	704	414	.285	.350	.482	126	245	30	26	-7	.989	57	*C-1699,O-260/1-2,3	36.2

■ DENNIS BERRAN   Berran, Dennis Martin   b: 10/8/1887, Merrimac, Mass.   d: 4/28/43, Boston, Mass.   BL/TL,   Deb: 8/11/12

YEAR	TM/L	G	AB	R	H	2B	3B	HR	RBI	BB	SO	AVG	OBP	SLG	PRO+	BR/A	SB	CS	SBR	FA	FR	G/POS	TPR
1912	Chi-A	2	4	1	1	0	0	0	0	0		.250	.250	.250	44	-0	0			1.000	-1	/O-2	-0.1

■ RAY BERRES   Berres, Raymond Frederick   b: 8/31/07, Kenosha, Wis.   BR/TR, 5'9", 170 lbs.   Deb: 4/24/34   C

YEAR	TM/L	G	AB	R	H	2B	3B	HR	RBI	BB	SO	AVG	OBP	SLG	PRO+	BR/A	SB	CS	SBR	FA	FR	G/POS	TPR
1934	Bro-N	39	79	7	17	3	0	1	3	1	16	.215	.225	.266	32	-8	0			.969	-2	C-37	-0.8
1936	Bro-N	105	267	16	64	10	1	1	13	14	35	.240	.280	.296	55	-17	1			.988	23	*C-105	0.9
1937	Pit-N	2	6	0	1	0	0	0	0	0	0	.167	.167	.167	-9	-1	0			1.000	1	/C-2	0.0
1938	Pit-N	40	100	7	23	2	0	0	6	8	10	.230	.287	.250	48	-7	0			.993	4	C-40	-0.1
1939	Pit-N	81	231	22	53	6	1	0	16	11	25	.229	.267	.264	44	-18	1			.993	-2	C-80	-1.7
1940	Pit-N	21	32	2	6	0	0	0	2	1	1	.188	.212	.188	11	-4	0			.980	3	C-21	-0.1
	Bos-N	85	229	12	44	4	1	0	14	18	19	.192	.251	.218	32	-21	0			.981	3	C-85	-1.5
	Yr	106	261	14	50	4	1	0	16	19	20	.192	.246	.215	29	-25	0			.981	3	*C-106	-1.6
1941	Bos-N	120	279	21	56	10	0	1	19	17	20	.201	.247	.247	41	-22	2			**.995**	9	*C-120	-0.6
1942	NY-N	12	32	0	6	0	0	0	1	2	3	.188	.235	.188	24	-3	0			.973	2	C-12	-0.4
1943	NY-N	20	28	1	4	1	0	0	0	2	1	.143	.172	.179	1	-4	0			.981	-0	C-17	0.1
1944	NY-N	16	17	4	8	0	0	1	2	1	0	.471	.526	.647	230	4	0			1.000	0	C-12	0.0
1945	NY-N	20	30	4	5	0	0	0	2	3	1	.167	.219	.167	8	-4	0			1.000	1	C-20	-0.2
Total	11	561	1330	96	287	37	3	5	78	76	134	.216	.260	.255	43	-105	4			.989	40	C-551	-4.0

■ GERONIMO BERROA   Berroa, Geronimo Emiliano Letta (b: Geronimo Emiliano Letta (Berroa))   b: 3/18/65, Santo Domingo, D.R.   BR/TR, 6', 165 lbs.   Deb: 4/5/89

YEAR	TM/L	G	AB	R	H	2B	3B	HR	RBI	BB	SO	AVG	OBP	SLG	PRO+	BR/A	SB	CS	SBR	FA	FR	G/POS	TPR
1989	Atl-N	81	136	7	36	4	0	2	9	7	32	.265	.301	.338	80	-4	0	1	-1	.971	1	O-34	-0.4
1990	Atl-N	7	4	0	0	0	0	0	0	1	1	.000	.200	.000	-38	-1	0	0	0	1.000	1	/O-3	-0.0
1992	Cin-N	13	15	2	4	1	0	0	0	2	1	.267	.389	.333	103	0	0	1	-1	1.000	0	/O-3	0.0
1993	Fla-N	14	34	3	4	1	0	0	0	2	7	.118	.167	.147	-14	-5	0	0	0	.833	-1	/O-9	-0.7
1994	Oak-A	96	340	55	104	18	2	13	65	41	62	.306	.385	.485	134	18	7	2	1	1.000	1	D-44,O-42/1-9	1.4
1995	Oak-A	141	546	87	152	22	3	22	88	63	98	.278	.354	.451	114	11	7	4	-0	.971	2	D-72,O-71	0.5
1996	Oak-A	153	586	101	170	32	1	36	106	47	122	.290	.347	.532	123	18	0	3	-2	.980	-7	D-91,O-61	0.1
Total	7	505	1661	255	470	78	6	73	268	163	323	.283	.350	.469	115	37	14	11	-2	.975	-5	O-223,D-207/1-9	0.7

■ KEN BERRY   Berry, Allen Kent   b: 5/10/41, Kansas City, Mo.   BR/TR, 5'11", 180 lbs.   Deb: 9/9/62

YEAR	TM/L	G	AB	R	H	2B	3B	HR	RBI	BB	SO	AVG	OBP	SLG	PRO+	BR/A	SB	CS	SBR	FA	FR	G/POS	TPR
1962	Chi-A	3	6	2	2	0	0	0	0	0	0	.333	.333	.333	80	-0	0	0	0	1.000	1	/O-2	0.0
1963	Chi-A	4	5	2	1	0	0	0	0	1	1	.200	.333	.200	55	-0	0	0	0	.857	-0	/O-2,2-1	0.0
1964	Chi-A	12	32	4	12	1	0	1	4	5	3	.375	.459	.500	171	3	0	1	0	1.000	-3	O-12	0.0
1965	Chi-A	157	472	51	103	17	4	12	42	28	96	.218	.269	.347	79	-15	4	2	0	.980	3	*O-156	-1.9
1966	Chi-A	147	443	50	120	20	2	8	34	28	63	.271	.317	.379	106	2	7	10	-4	.991	-9	*O-141	-1.8
1967	Chi-A★	147	485	49	117	14	4	7	41	46	68	.241	.311	.330	93	-7	4	5	-2	.992	-15	*O-143	-3.1
1968	Chi-A	153	504	49	127	21	2	7	32	25	64	.252	.289	.343	90	-7	6	6	-2	.981	4	*O-151	-1.5
1969	Chi-A	130	297	25	69	12	4	2	18	24	50	.232	.296	.327	71	-12	1	2	-1	**1.000**	-5	*O-120	-2.3
1970	Chi-A	141	463	45	128	12	2	7	50	43	61	.276	.346	.356	90	-5	6	4	-1	.988	6	*O-138	-0.6
1971	Cal-A	111	298	29	66	17	3	2	22	18	33	.221	.273	.309	69	-13	4	4	-0	.988	-3	*O-101	-1.6
1972	Cal-A	119	409	41	118	15	5	3	39	35	47	.289	.348	.377	122	11	5	3	-0	**1.000**	14	*O-116	2.2
1973	Cal-A	136	415	48	118	11	2	3	36	26	50	.284	.328	.342	96	-3	1	6	-3	**.997**	-3	*O-129	-0.8
1974	Mil-A	98	267	21	64	9	2	1	24	18	26	.240	.295	.300	72	-10	0	3	-2	.995	-3	O-82,D-13	-1.7
1975	Cle-A	25	46	6	8	1	0	0	1	1	7	.200	.238	.225	31	-4	0	1	-0	.926	-2	O-18/D-5	-0.7
Total	14	1383	4136	422	1053	150	23	58	343	298	569	.255	.309	.344	90	-56	45	46	-14	.988	-5	*O-1311/D-18,2-1	-13.8

■ CHARLIE BERRY   Berry, Charles Francis   b: 10/18/02, Phillipsburg, N.J.   d: 9/6/72, Evanston, Ill.   BR/TR, 6', 185 lbs.   Deb: 6/15/25   FUC

YEAR	TM/L	G	AB	R	H	2B	3B	HR	RBI	BB	SO	AVG	OBP	SLG	PRO+	BR/A	SB	CS	SBR	FA	FR	G/POS	TPR
1925	Phi-A	10	14	1	3	1	0	0	0	0	2	.214	.214	.286	24	-2	0			.900	-1	/C-4	-0.2
1928	Bos-A	80	177	18	46	7	3	1	19	21	19	.260	.342	.350	84	-4	1	1	-0	.959	-9	C-63	-0.9
1929	Bos-A	77	207	19	50	11	4	1	21	15	29	.242	.302	.348	69	-10	2	4	-2	.983	3	C-72	-0.3
1930	Bos-A	88	256	31	74	9	6	6	35	16	22	.289	.331	.441	98	-2	2	0	1	.988	7	C-85	1.2
1931	Bos-A	111	357	41	101	16	2	6	49	29	38	.283	.337	.389	96	-3	4	0	1	.985	-3	*C-102	0.2
1932	Bos-A	10	32	0	6	3	0	0	1	2	1	.188	.257	.281	40	-3	0	0	0	1.000	-1	C-10	-0.3
	Chi-A	72	226	33	69	15	6	4	31	21	23	.305	.364	.478	124	7	3	0	1	.981	-2	C-70	1.0
	Yr	82	258	33	75	18	6	4	37	24	25	.291	.351	.453	114	4	3	0	1	.977	-2	C-80	0.7
1933	Chi-A	86	271	25	69	18	2	1	28	17	16	.255	.301	.328	70	-12	3	0	2	.987	-8	C-83	-1.5
1934	Phi-A	99	269	14	72	10	2	0	34	22	23	.268	.323	.320	62	-12	0	0	0	.987	-0	C-99	-0.8

YEAR	TM/L	G	AB	R	H	2B	3B	HR	RBI	BB	SO	AVG	OBP	SLG	PRO+	BR/A	SB	CS	SBR	FA	FR	G/POS	TPR
1935	Phi-A	62	190	14	48	7	3	3	29	10	20	.253	.290	.368	70	-9	0	0	0	.987	-1	C-56	-0.7
1936	Phi-A	13	17	0	1	1	0	0	1	6	2	.059	.304	.118	8	-2	0	0	0	.971	1	C-12	-0.1
1938	Phi-A	1	2	0	0	0	0	0	0	0	0	.000	.000	.000	-99	-1	0	0	0	1.000	0	/C-1	0.0
Total	11	709	2018	196	539	88	29	23	256	160	196	.267	.322	.374	83	-52	13	5	1	.982	-12	C-657	-2.4

■ CHARLIE BERRY Berry, Charles Joseph b: 9/6/1860, Elizabeth, N.J. d: 1/22/40, Phillipsburg, N.J. BR/TR, 5'11", 175 lbs. Deb: 4/30/1884 F

YEAR	TM/L	G	AB	R	H	2B	3B	HR	RBI	BB	SO	AVG	OBP	SLG	PRO+	BR/A	SB	CS	SBR	FA	FR	G/POS	TPR
1884	Alt-U	7	25	2	6	0	0	0			0	.240	.240	.240	45	-2				.862	-4	/2-7	-0.8
	KC-U	29	118	15	29	6	1	1	29			.246	.252	.339	89	-5				.887	3	2-22/O-8,3-1	-0.2
	CP-U	7	27	4	3	2	0	0			0	.111	.111	.185	-12	-4				.833	1	/2-7	-0.3
	Yr	43	170	21	38	8	1	1			1	.224	.228	.300	64	-13				.871	-3	2-36/O-8,3-1	-1.3

■ CLAUDE BERRY Berry, Claude Elzy "Admiral" b: 2/14/1880, Losantville, Ind. d: 2/1/74, Richmond, Ind. BR/TR, 5'7", 165 lbs. Deb: 4/22/04

YEAR	TM/L	G	AB	R	H	2B	3B	HR	RBI	BB	SO	AVG	OBP	SLG	PRO+	BR/A	SB	CS	SBR	FA	FR	G/POS	TPR
1904	Chi-A	3	1	1	0	0	0	0	0	1		.000	.500	.000	68	0	0			1.000	0	/C-3	0.1
1906	Phi-A	10	30	2	7	0	0	0	2	2		.233	.281	.233	60	-1	1			.938	6	C-10	0.5
1907	Phi-A	8	19	2	4	2	0	0	1	2		.211	.286	.316	90	-0				.944	-2	/C-8	-0.2
1914	Pit-F	124	411	35	98	18	9	2	36	26	50	.238	.284	.341	70	-25	6			.970	1	*C-122	-1.4
1915	Pit-F	100	292	32	56	11	1	1	26	29	42	.192	.269	.247	46	-25	7			.980	-0	C-99	-2.0
Total	5	245	753	72	165	31	10	3	65	60	92	.219	.279	.299	61	-52	14			.971	4	C-242	-3.0

■ NEIL BERRY Berry, Cornelius John b: 1/11/22, Kalamazoo, Mich. BR/TR, 5'10", 170 lbs. Deb: 4/20/48

YEAR	TM/L	G	AB	R	H	2B	3B	HR	RBI	BB	SO	AVG	OBP	SLG	PRO+	BR/A	SB	CS	SBR	FA	FR	G/POS	TPR
1948	Det-A	87	256	46	68	8	1	0	16	37	23	.266	.358	.305	75	-8	1	3	-2	.930	4	S-41,2-26	-0.2
1949	Det-A	109	329	38	78	9	1	0	18	27	24	.237	.299	.271	51	-23	4	2	0	.970	-0	2-95/S-4	-1.9
1950	Det-A	39	40	9	10	1	0	0	7	6	11	.250	.348	.275	59	-2	0	0	0	.944	2	S-12/2-2,3-1	0.1
1951	Det-A	67	157	17	36	5	2	0	9	10	15	.229	.287	.287	52	-11	4	2	0	.944	8	S-38,2-10/3-7	-0.3
1952	Det-A	73	189	22	43	4	3	0	13	22	19	.228	.311	.280	65	-9	1	3	-2	.965	-0	S-66/3-2	-0.3
1953	StL-A	57	99	14	28	1	2	0	11	9	10	.283	.343	.333	82	-2	1	2	-1	.825	-1	3-18,2-15/S-6	-0.4
	Chi-A	5	8	1	1	0	0	0	0	0	1	.125	.222	.125	-4	-1	0	0	0	1.000	2	/2-3	0.1
	Yr	62	107	15	29	1	2	0	11	10	11	.271	.333	.318	75	-4	1	2	-1	.825	-1	3-18,2-18/S-6	-0.3
1954	Bal-A	5	9	1	1	0	0	0	0	1	2	.111	.200	.111	-14	-1	0	0	0	1.000	-0	/S-5	-0.1
Total	7	442	1087	148	265	28	9	0	74	113	105	.244	.317	.286	62	-58	11	12	-4	.949	19	S-172,2-151/3-28	-2.7

■ JOE BERRY Berry, Joseph Howard Jr. "Nig" b: 12/31/1894, Philadelphia, Pa. d: 4/29/76, Philadelphia, Pa. BB/TR, 5'10.5", 159 lbs. Deb: 7/18/21 F

YEAR	TM/L	G	AB	R	H	2B	3B	HR	RBI	BB	SO	AVG	OBP	SLG	PRO+	BR/A	SB	CS	SBR	FA	FR	G/POS	TPR
1921	NY-N	9	6	0	2	0	1	0	2	1	1	.333	.429	.667	185	1	0	0	0	.875	0	/2-7	0.1
1922	NY-N	6	0	0	0	0	0	0	0	0	0	—	—	—		0	0	0	0	.000	0	R	0.0
Total	2	15	6	0	2	0	1	0	2	1	1	.333	.429	.667	185	1	0	0	0	.875	0	/2-7	0.1

■ JOE BERRY Berry, Joseph Howard Sr. "Hodge" b: 9/10/1872, Wheeling, W.Va. d: 3/13/61, Allenwood, N.J. BB/TR, 5'9", 172 lbs. Deb: 9/4/02 F

YEAR	TM/L	G	AB	R	H	2B	3B	HR	RBI	BB	SO	AVG	OBP	SLG	PRO+	BR/A	SB	CS	SBR	FA	FR	G/POS	TPR
1902	Phi-N	1	4	0	1	0	0	0	1		1	.250	.400	.250	101	-1				1.000	-1	/C-1	-0.1

■ SEAN BERRY Berry, Sean Robert b: 3/22/66, Santa Monica, Cal. BR/TR, 5'11", 200 lbs. Deb: 9/17/90

YEAR	TM/L	G	AB	R	H	2B	3B	HR	RBI	BB	SO	AVG	OBP	SLG	PRO+	BR/A	SB	CS	SBR	FA	FR	G/POS	TPR
1990	KC-A	8	23	2	5	1	1	0	4	2	5	.217	.280	.348	76	-1	0	0	0	.944	1	/3-8	0.0
1991	KC-A	31	60	5	8	3	0	0	4	5	23	.133	.212	.183	10	-7	0	0	0	.970	8	3-30	0.1
1992	Mon-N	24	57	5	19	1	0	1	4	1	11	.333	.345	.404	112	1	2	1	0	.879	-3	3-20	-0.2
1993	Mon-N	122	299	50	78	15	2	14	49	41	70	.261	.354	.465	112	5	12	2	2	.936	5	3-96	1.3
1994	Mon-N	103	320	43	89	19	2	11	41	32	50	.278	.349	.453	106	3	14	0	4	.938	-2	*3-100	0.5
1995	Mon-N	103	314	38	100	22	1	14	55	25	53	.318	.372	.529	130	13	3	8	-4	.947	6	3-83/1-3	1.4
1996	Hou-N	132	431	55	121	38	1	17	95	23	58	.281	.330	.492	125	13	12	6	0	.922	-5	*3-110	0.7
Total	7	523	1504	198	420	99	7	57	249	129	270	.279	.343	.468	113	26	43	17	3	.936	9	3-447/1-3	3.8

■ TOM BERRY Berry, Thomas Haney b: 12/31/1842, Chester, Pa. d: 6/6/15, Chester, Pa. 5'6", 140 lbs. Deb: 9/2/1871

YEAR	TM/L	G	AB	R	H	2B	3B	HR	RBI	BB	SO	AVG	OBP	SLG	PRO+	BR/A	SB	CS	SBR	FA	FR	G/POS	TPR
1871	Ath-n	1	4	0	1	0	0	0	0	0	0	.250	.250	.250	45	-0	0	0	0	.000	-1	/O-1	0.0

■ DAMON BERRYHILL Berryhill, Damon Scott b: 12/3/63, South Laguna, Cal. BB/TR, 6'", 210 lbs. Deb: 9/5/87

YEAR	TM/L	G	AB	R	H	2B	3B	HR	RBI	BB	SO	AVG	OBP	SLG	PRO+	BR/A	SB	CS	SBR	FA	FR	G/POS	TPR
1987	Chi-N	12	28	2	5	1	0	0	3		5	.179	.258	.214	26	-3	0	1	-1	.909	-4	C-11	-0.7
1988	Chi-N	95	309	19	80	19	1	7	38	17	56	.259	.298	.395	93	-3	1	0	0	.982	-8	C-90	0.0
1989	Chi-N	91	334	37	86	13	0	5	41	16	54	.257	.295	.341	76	-11	0	0	0	.992	-12	C-89	-1.8
1990	Chi-N	17	53	6	10	4	0	1	9	5	14	.189	.259	.321	54	-3	0	0	0	.978	-3	C-15	-0.5
1991	Chi-N	62	159	13	30	7	0	5	14	11	41	.189	.246	.327	57	-9	1	2	-1	.967	-6	C-48	-1.5
	Atl-N	1	1	0	0	0	0	0	0	0	1	.000	.000	.000	-94	-0	0	0	0	1.000	0	/C-1	0.0
	Yr	63	160	13	30	7	0	5	14	11	42	.188	.244	.325	56	-10	1	2	-1	.967	-6	C-49	-1.5
1992	*Atl-N	101	307	21	70	16	1	10	43	17	67	.228	.271	.384	79	-9	0	2	-1	.998	-8	C-84	-1.5
1993	*Atl-N	115	335	24	82	18	2	8	43	21	64	.245	.293	.382	78	-11	0	0	0	.990	8	*C-105	0.2
1994	Bos-A	82	255	30	67	17	2	6	34	19	59	.263	.314	.416	92	-7	0	1	-1	.995	-1	C-67/D-6	-0.5
1995	Cin-N	34	82	5	15	3	0	2	6	10	19	.183	.272	.293	49	-6	0	0	0	.988	2	C-29/1-1	-0.3
Total	9	610	1863	158	445	98	6	44	234	119	380	.239	.287	.369	76	-64	3	6	-3	.988	-27	C-539/D-6,1-1	-6.6

■ HARRY BERTE Berte, Harry Thomas b: 5/10/1872, Covington, Ky. d: 5/6/52, Los Angeles, Cal. TR, Deb: 9/17/03

YEAR	TM/L	G	AB	R	H	2B	3B	HR	RBI	BB	SO	AVG	OBP	SLG	PRO+	BR/A	SB	CS	SBR	FA	FR	G/POS	TPR
1903	StL-N	4	15	1	5	0	0	0	1	1		.333	.375	.333	106	0	0			.778	-4	/2-3,S-1	-0.4

■ DICK BERTELL Bertell, Richard George b: 11/21/35, Oak Park, Ill. BR/TR, 6'0.5", 200 lbs. Deb: 9/22/60

YEAR	TM/L	G	AB	R	H	2B	3B	HR	RBI	BB	SO	AVG	OBP	SLG	PRO+	BR/A	SB	CS	SBR	FA	FR	G/POS	TPR
1960	Chi-N	5	15	0	2	0	0	0	2	3	1	.133	.278	.133	17	-2	0	0	0	1.000	-1	/C-5	-0.3
1961	Chi-N	92	267	20	73	7	1	2	33	15	33	.273	.312	.330	70	-11	0	0	0	.982	4	C-90	-0.4
1962	Chi-N	77	215	19	65	6	2	2	18	13	30	.302	.345	.377	90	-3	0	1	-1	.986	-13	C-76	-1.4
1963	Chi-N	100	322	15	75	7	2	2	14	24	41	.233	.286	.286	62	-15	0	2	-1	.988	16	C-99	0.4
1964	Chi-N	112	353	29	84	11	3	4	35	33	67	.238	.307	.320	74	-12	1	0	-0	.981	-5	*C-110	-1.2
1965	Chi-N	34	84	6	18	2	0	0	7	11	10	.214	.305	.238	54	-5	0	0	0	.981	-4	C-34	-0.1
	SF-N	22	48	1	9	1	0	0	3	7	5	.188	.291	.208	42	-3	0	0	0	.992	2	C-22	-0.1
	Yr	56	132	7	27	3	0	0	10	18	15	.205	.302	.227	50	-8	0	0	0	.986	5	C-56	-0.2
1967	Chi-N	2	6	1	1	0	0	0	0	0	1	.167	.167	.500	80	-0	0	0	0	1.000	0	/C-2	0.0
Total	7	444	1310	91	327	34	9	10	112	106	188	.250	.307	.312	70	-51	2	4	-2	.985	7	C-438	-3.1

■ HARRY BERTHRONG Berthrong, Henry W. b: 1/1/1844, Mumford, N.Y. d: 4/28/28, Chelsea, Mass. TR, 5'6.5", 140 lbs. Deb: 5/5/1871

YEAR	TM/L	G	AB	R	H	2B	3B	HR	RBI	BB	SO	AVG	OBP	SLG	PRO+	BR/A	SB	CS	SBR	FA	FR	G/POS	TPR
1871	Oly-n	17	73	17	17	1	1	0	8	4	2	.233	.273	.274	61	-3	3	1	0	.806	-3	O-12/2-5,C-1	-0.4

■ RENO BERTOIA Bertoia, Reno Peter b: 1/8/35, St.Vito Udine, Italy BR/TR, 5'11.5", 185 lbs. Deb: 9/22/53

YEAR	TM/L	G	AB	R	H	2B	3B	HR	RBI	BB	SO	AVG	OBP	SLG	PRO+	BR/A	SB	CS	SBR	FA	FR	G/POS	TPR
1953	Det-A	1	1	0	0	0	0	0	0	0	1	.000	.000	.000	-99	-0	0	0	0	.500	-0	/2-1	-0.1
1954	Det-A	54	37	13	6	2	0	1	2	5	9	.162	.262	.297	54	-2	1	0	0	.969	17	2-15/3-8,S-3	1.5
1955	Det-A	38	68	13	14	2	1	1	10	5	11	.206	.260	.309	54	-5	0	0	0	.923	7	3-14/2-6,S-5	0.2
1956	Det-A	22	66	7	12	2	0	1	5	6	12	.182	.260	.258	37	-6	0	0	0	.982	10	2-18/3-2	0.2
1957	Det-A	97	295	28	81	16	2	4	28	19	43	.275	.327	.383	91	-4	2	3	-1	.953	-19	3-83/S-7,2-2	-2.3
1958	Det-A	86	240	28	56	6	0	6	27	20	35	.233	.298	.333	68	-10	4	4	0	.950	4	3-68/S-5,O-1	-0.5
1959	Was-A	90	308	33	73	10	0	9	29	28	48	.237	.305	.347	79	-9	2	5	-2	.971	-11	2-71/3-5,S-1	-1.7
1960	Was-A	121	460	44	122	17	7	4	45	26	58	.265	.316	.359	83	-11	3	5	-2	.961	-0	*3-112,2-21	-1.4
1961	Min-A	35	104	17	22	2	0	1	8	20	12	.212	.339	.260	59	-5	0	0	0	.900	-5	3-32	-1.1
	KC-A	39	120	12	29	2	0	2	13	9	15	.242	.295	.258	48	-9	1	0	0	.942	5	3-29/2-6	-0.3
	Det-A	24	46	6	10	1	0	1	4	3	8	.217	.265	.304	50	-3	2	0	1	.931	0	3-13/2-7,S-1	-0.3
	Yr	98	270	35	61	5	0	4	25	32	35	.226	.308	.267	53	-17	3	0	1	.923	-1	3-74,2-13/S-1	-1.6
1962	Det-A	5	3	0	0	0	0	0	0	1	2	.000	.250	.000	-8	-1	0	0	0	1.000	0	2-1,S-1,3-1	0.0
Total	10	612	1745	204	425	60	10	27	171	142	252	.244	.306	.336	73	-65	16	15	-4	.949	7	3-367,2-148/S-23,O	-5.4

■ BOB BESCHER Bescher, Robert Henry b: 2/25/1884, London, Ohio d: 11/29/42, London, Ohio BB/TL, 6'1", 200 lbs. Deb: 9/5/08

YEAR	TM/L	G	AB	R	H	2B	3B	HR	RBI	BB	SO	AVG	OBP	SLG	PRO+	BR/A	SB	CS	SBR	FA	FR	G/POS	TPR
1908	Cin-N	32	114	16	31	5	5	0	17	9		.272	.336	.404	140	5	10			1.000	4	O-32	0.8

YEAR	TM/L	G	AB	R	H	2B	3B	HR	RBI	BB	SO	AVG	OBP	SLG	PRO+	BR/A	SB	CS	SBR	FA	FR	G/POS	TPR
1909	Cin-N	124	446	73	107	17	6	1	34	56		.240	.335	.312	102	3	**54**			.953	-0	*O-117	-0.3
1910	Cin-N	150	589	95	147	20	10	4	48	81	75	.250	.344	.338	104	4	**70**			.947	2	*O-150	-0.2
1911	Cin-N	153	599	106	165	32	10	1	45	102	78	.275	.385	.367	115	16	**81**			.954	-8	*O-153	0.0
1912	Cin-N	145	548	**120**	154	29	11	4	38	83	61	.281	.381	.396	116	15	**67**			.963	4	*O-143	1.1
1913	Cin-N	141	511	86	132	22	11	1	37	**94**	68	.258	.377	.350	109	10	38			.968	4	*O-138	0.8
1914	NY-N	135	512	82	138	23	4	6	35	45	48	.270	.336	.365	112	7	36			.960	9	*O-126	1.1
1915	StL-N	130	486	71	128	15	7	4	34	52	53	.263	.342	.348	109	6	27	19	-3	.971	-1	*O-129	-0.6
1916	StL-N	151	561	78	132	24	8	6	43	60	50	.235	.316	.339	102	2	39	12	5	.953	0	*O-151	-0.2
1917	StL-N	42	110	10	17	1	1	1	8	20	13	.155	.290	.209	56	-5	3			.984	-3	O-32	-1.1
1918	Cle-A	25	60	12	20	2	1	0	6	17	5	.333	.487	.400	153	5	3			.969	-0	O-17	0.4
Total	11	1228	4536	749	1171	190	74	28	345	619	451	.258	.353	.351	109	68	428	31		.960	9	*O-1188	1.8

■ BESTICK
Bestick   b: New York, N.Y.   Deb: 6/10/1872

YEAR	TM/L	G	AB	R	H	2B	3B	HR	RBI	BB	SO	AVG	OBP	SLG	PRO+	BR/A	SB	CS	SBR	FA	FR	G/POS	TPR
1872	Eck-n	4	14	0	4	0	0	0	1	0	0	.286	.286	.286	90	0	0	0	0	.773	-2	/C-4	-0.1

■ JIM BESWICK
Beswick, James William   b: 2/12/58, Wilkinsburg, Pa.   BB/TR, 6'1", 180 lbs.   Deb: 8/9/78

YEAR	TM/L	G	AB	R	H	2B	3B	HR	RBI	BB	SO	AVG	OBP	SLG	PRO+	BR/A	SB	CS	SBR	FA	FR	G/POS	TPR
1978	SD-N	17	20	2	1	0	0	0	0	1	7	.050	.095	.050	-63	-4	0	0	0	1.000	-1	/O-6	-0.6

■ FRANK BETCHER
Betcher, Franklin Lyle (b: Franklin Lyle Bettger)
b: 2/15/1888, Philadelphia, Pa.   d: 11/27/81, Wynnewood, Pa.   BB/TR, 5'11", 173 lbs.   Deb: 5/21/10

YEAR	TM/L	G	AB	R	H	2B	3B	HR	RBI	BB	SO	AVG	OBP	SLG	PRO+	BR/A	SB	CS	SBR	FA	FR	G/POS	TPR
1910	StL-N	35	89	7	18	2	0	0	7	8		.202	.276	.225	48	-6	1			.928		S-12/3-7,2-6,O-2	-0.5

■ BILL BETHEA
Bethea, William Lamar "Spot"   b: 1/1/42, Houston, Tex.   BR/TR, 6', 175 lbs.   Deb: 9/13/64

YEAR	TM/L	G	AB	R	H	2B	3B	HR	RBI	BB	SO	AVG	OBP	SLG	PRO+	BR/A	SB	CS	SBR	FA	FR	G/POS	TPR
1964	Min-A	10	30	4	5	1	0	0	2	4	4	.167	.265	.200	31	-3	0	0	0	1.000	-1	/2-7,S-3	-0.3

■ LARRY BETTENCOURT
Bettencourt, Lawrence Joseph   b: 9/22/05, Newark, Cal.   d: 9/15/78, New Orleans, La.   BR/TR, 5'11", 195 lbs.   Deb: 6/2/28

YEAR	TM/L	G	AB	R	H	2B	3B	HR	RBI	BB	SO	AVG	OBP	SLG	PRO+	BR/A	SB	CS	SBR	FA	FR	G/POS	TPR
1928	StL-A	67	159	30	45	9	4	4	24	22	19	.283	.377	.465	117	4	2	1	0	.946	-11	3-41/O-2,C-1	-0.4
1931	StL-A	74	206	27	53	9	2	3	26	31	35	.257	.357	.364	87	-3	4	3	-1	.963	-2	O-58	-0.9
1932	StL-A	27	30	4	4	1	0	1	3	7	6	.133	.297	.267	45	-2	1	0	0	1.000	-0	/O-4,3-2	-0.2
Total	3	168	395	61	102	19	6	8	53	60	60	.258	.360	.397	95	-2	7	4	-0	.966	-13	/O-64,3-43,C-1	-1.5

■ BRUNO BETZEL
Betzel, Christian Frederick Albert John Henry David
b: 12/6/1894, Chattanooga, Ohio   d: 2/7/65, W.Hollywood, Fla.   BR/TR, 5'9", 158 lbs.   Deb: 9/3/14

YEAR	TM/L	G	AB	R	H	2B	3B	HR	RBI	BB	SO	AVG	OBP	SLG	PRO+	BR/A	SB	CS	SBR	FA	FR	G/POS	TPR
1914	StL-N	7	9	2	0	0	0	0	0	1	1	.000	.100	.000	-70	-2	0			1.000	2	/2-4,3-1	0.0
1915	StL-N	117	367	42	92	12	4	0	27	18	48	.251	.291	.305	80	-9	10	13	-5	.937	-2	*3-105/2-3,S-2	-0.5
1916	StL-N	142	510	49	119	15	11	1	37	39	77	.233	.288	.312	85	-10	22	16	-3	.960	28	*2-113,3-33/O-7	2.3
1917	StL-N	106	328	24	71	4	3	1	17	20	47	.216	.266	.256	62	-15	9			.962	12	2-75,O-23/3-4	-0.1
1918	StL-N	76	230	18	51	6	7	0	13	12	16	.222	.260	.309	76	-7	8			.914	-2	3-34,O-21,2-10	-1.0
Total	5	448	1444	135	333	37	25	2	94	90	189	.231	.278	.295	76	-42	49	29		.956	46	2-205,3-177/O-51,S	0.7

■ KURT BEVACQUA
Bevacqua, Kurt Anthony   b: 1/23/47, Miami Beach, Fla.   BR/TR, 6'1", 185 lbs.   Deb: 6/22/71

YEAR	TM/L	G	AB	R	H	2B	3B	HR	RBI	BB	SO	AVG	OBP	SLG	PRO+	BR/A	SB	CS	SBR	FA	FR	G/POS	TPR
1971	Cle-A	55	137	9	28	3	1	3	13	4	28	.204	.227	.307	46	-10	0	0	0	.971	-9	2-36/O-5,3-3,S-2	-1.8
1972	Cle-A	19	35	2	4	0	0	1	1	3	10	.114	.184	.200	14	-4	0	0	0	.900	-1	O-11/3-1	-0.6
1973	KC-A	99	276	39	71	8	3	2	40	25	42	.257	.321	.330	78	-8	2	3	-1	.935	-11	3-40,2-16,D-16,O/1	-2.1
1974	Pit-N	18	35	1	4	1	0	0	0	2	9	.114	.162	.143	-15	-5	0	0	0	.955	-1	/3-8,O-1	-0.6
	KC-A	39	90	10	19	0	0	0	3	9	20	.211	.290	.211	43	-6	1	1	-0	.987	-4	1-14,3-13/2-7,SD	-1.1
1975	Mil-A	104	258	30	59	14	0	2	24	26	45	.229	.302	.306	72	-9	3	4	-2	.948	1	3-60,2-32/S-5,1D	-0.8
1976	Mil-A	12	7	3	1	0	0	0	0	0	0	.143	.143	.143	-17	-1	0	0	0	1.000	2	/2-2,D-3	0.1
1977	Tex-A	39	96	13	32	7	2	5	28	6	13	.333	.373	.604	159	7	0	1	-1	1.000	-7	O-14,3-11/1-5,2D	0.0
1978	Tex-A	90	248	21	55	12	0	6	30	18	31	.222	.274	.343	72	-10	1	2	-1	.877	-4	3-49,D-16,2-13,1/1-1	-1.6
1979	SD-N	114	297	23	75	12	4	1	34	38	25	.253	.337	.330	88	-4	2	5	-2	.954	-5	3-64,2-16/1-8,O-8	-1.2
1980	SD-N	62	71	4	19	6	1	0	12	6	1	.268	.325	.380	102	0	1	1	-0	.929	-3	3-13/O-4,2,1-1	-0.4
	Pit-N	22	43	1	7	1	0	0	4	6	7	.163	.280	.186	32	-4	0	0	0	.958	0	/3-9,1-2	-0.4
	Yr	84	114	5	26	7	1	0	16	12	8	.228	.307	.307	75	-4	1	1	-0	.947	-3	3-22/O-4,1-3,2-2	-0.8
1981	Pit-N	29	27	2	7	1	0	1	4	2	6	.259	.355	.407	112	0	0	0	0	.941	1	/2-4,3-2	0.2
1982	SD-N	64	123	15	31	9	0	2	24	17	22	.252	.343	.325	93	-1	2	0	1	.989	-3	1-30/O-3,3-1	-0.4
1983	SD-N	74	156	17	38	7	0	2	24	18	33	.244	.322	.327	83	-3	0	3	-2	.995	-1	1-27,3-12,O-12	-0.8
1984	*SD-N	59	80	7	16	3	0	1	9	14	19	.200	.326	.275	71	-3	0	0	0	1.000	-2	1-20,3-10/O-3	-0.5
1985	SD-N	71	138	17	33	6	0	3	25	25	17	.239	.356	.348	99	1	0	0	0	.946	-2	3-33/1-9,O-1	-0.2
Total	15	970	2117	214	499	90	11	27	275	221	329	.236	.309	.327	78	-59	12	20	-8	.938	-46	3-329,2-133,1/ODS	-12.2

■ HAL BEVAN
Bevan, Joseph Harold   b: 11/15/30, New Orleans, La.   d: 10/5/68, New Orleans, La.   BR/TR, 6'2", 198 lbs.   Deb: 4/24/52

YEAR	TM/L	G	AB	R	H	2B	3B	HR	RBI	BB	SO	AVG	OBP	SLG	PRO+	BR/A	SB	CS	SBR	FA	FR	G/POS	TPR
1952	Bos-A	1	1	0	0	0	0	0	0	0	0	.000	.000	.000	-93	-0	0	0	0	.000	0	/3-1	0.0
	Phi-A	8	17	1	6	0	0	0	4	0	0	.353	.353	.353	91	-0	2	0	1	1.000	0	/3-6	0.1
	Yr	9	18	1	6	0	0	0	4	0	0	.333	.333	.333	81	-0	2	0	1	1.000	1	/3-7	0.1
1955	KC-A	3	3	0	0	0	0	0	0	0	1	.000	.000	.000	-99	-0	0	0	0	1.000	0	/3-1	-0.1
1961	Cin-N	3	3	1	1	0	0	1	1	0	2	.333	.333	1.333	311	1	0	0	0	.000	0	H	0.1
Total	3	15	24	2	7	0	0	1	5	0	3	.292	.292	.417	89	-0	2	0	1	1.000	1	/3-8	0.1

■ MONTE BEVILLE
Beville, Henry Monte   b: 2/24/1875, Dublin, Ind.   d: 1/24/55, Grand Rapids, Mich   BL/TR, 5'11", 180 lbs.   Deb: 4/24/03

YEAR	TM/L	G	AB	R	H	2B	3B	HR	RBI	BB	SO	AVG	OBP	SLG	PRO+	BR/A	SB	CS	SBR	FA	FR	G/POS	TPR
1903	NY-A	82	258	23	50	14	1	0	29	16		.194	.252	.256	49	-16	4			.960	-11	C-75/1-3	-2.0
1904	NY-A	9	22	2	6	2	0	0	2	2		.273	.333	.364	115	0	0			.906	-2	/1-4,C-3	-0.1
	Det-A	54	174	14	36	5	1	0	13	8		.207	.250	.247	59	-8	2			.957	-3	C-30,1-24	-1.0
	Yr	63	196	16	42	7	1	0	15	10		.214	.260	.260	66	-8	2			.950	-5	C-33,1-28	-1.1
Total	2	145	454	39	92	21	2	0	44	26		.203	.255	.258	56	-23	6			.957	-16	C-108/1-31	-3.1

■ BUDDY BIANCALANA
Biancalana, Roland Americo   b: 2/2/60, Larkspur, Cal.   BB/TR, 5'11", 160 lbs.   Deb: 9/12/82

YEAR	TM/L	G	AB	R	H	2B	3B	HR	RBI	BB	SO	AVG	OBP	SLG	PRO+	BR/A	SB	CS	SBR	FA	FR	G/POS	TPR
1982	KC-A	3	2	0	1	0	0	0	0	0	0	.500	.667	1.500	474	1	0	0	0	1.000	3	/S-3	0.3
1983	KC-A	6	15	2	3	0	0	0	0	0	7	.200	.200	.200	10	-2	1	0	0	.914	4	/S-6	0.3
1984	*KC-A	66	134	18	26	6	1	2	9	6	44	.194	.229	.299	44	-10	1	2	-1	.946	6	S-33,2-29/D-1	-0.2
1985	*KC-A	81	138	21	26	5	1	1	6	17	34	.188	.277	.261	48	-10	4	4	-2	.961	11	S-74/2-4,D-2	0.1
1986	KC-A	100	190	24	46	8	2	0	8	15	50	.242	.298	.337	71	-8	5	1	1	.946	2	S-89,2-12	0.1
1987	KC-A	37	47	4	10	1	0	1	7	1	10	.213	.229	.298	37	-6	0	0	0	.886	-3	S-22,2-12/D-1	0.1
	Hou-N	18	24	1	1	0	0	0	1	1	12	.042	.080	.042	-69	-6	0	0	0	.889	-1	S-16/2-3	-0.6
Total	6	311	550	70	113	16	5	6	30	41	157	.205	.261	.293	50	-38	8	7	-2	.945	28	S-243/2-60,D-4	0.3

■ TOMMY BIANCO
Bianco, Thomas Anthony   b: 12/16/52, Rockville Centre, N.Y.   BB/TR, 5'11", 190 lbs.   Deb: 5/28/75

YEAR	TM/L	G	AB	R	H	2B	3B	HR	RBI	BB	SO	AVG	OBP	SLG	PRO+	BR/A	SB	CS	SBR	FA	FR	G/POS	TPR
1975	Mil-A	18	34	6	6	1	0	0	3	3	7	.176	.263	.206	34	-3	0	0	0	.941	-1	/3-7,1-5,D-2	-0.4

■ HANK BIASATTI
Biasatti, Henry Arcado   b: 1/14/22, Beano, Italy   d: 4/20/96, Dearborn, Mich.   BL/TL, 5'11", 175 lbs.   Deb: 4/23/49

YEAR	TM/L	G	AB	R	H	2B	3B	HR	RBI	BB	SO	AVG	OBP	SLG	PRO+	BR/A	SB	CS	SBR	FA	FR	G/POS	TPR
1949	Phi-A	21	24	6	2	0	0	0	2	8	5	.083	.313	.167	30	-2	0	0	0	.979	-1	/1-8	-0.3

■ DANTE BICHETTE
Bichette, Alphonse Dante   b: 11/18/63, W.Palm Beach, Fla.   BR/TR, 6'3", 215 lbs.   Deb: 9/5/88

YEAR	TM/L	G	AB	R	H	2B	3B	HR	RBI	BB	SO	AVG	OBP	SLG	PRO+	BR/A	SB	CS	SBR	FA	FR	G/POS	TPR
1988	Cal-A	21	46	1	12	2	0	0	8	0	7	.261	.261	.304	59	-3	0	0	0	.979	-2	O-21	-0.5
1989	Cal-A	48	138	13	29	7	0	3	15	6	24	.210	.243	.326	60	-8	3	0	1	.990	6	O-40/D-1	-0.2
1990	Cal-A	109	349	40	89	15	1	15	53	16	79	.255	.293	.433	103	-0	5	2	0	.965	-4	*O-105	-0.7
1991	Mil-A	134	445	53	106	18	3	15	59	22	107	.238	.276	.393	85	-11	14	8	-1	.976	11	*O-127/3-1	-0.4
1992	Mil-A	112	387	37	111	27	2	5	41	16	74	.287	.320	.406	104	1	18	7	1	.990	-2	*O-101/D-4	-0.1
1993	Col-N	141	538	93	167	43	5	21	89	28	99	.310	.353	.526	113	8	14	8	-1	.973	13	*O-137	1.7
1994	Col-N★	116	484	74	147	33	2	27	95	19	70	.304	.335	.548	107	3	21	8	2	.991	-6	*O-116	0.6
1995	*Col-N★	139	579	102	**197**	38	2	**40**	**128**	22	96	.340	.369	**.620**	120	12	13	9	-2	.986	-6	*O-136	0.0

YEAR	TM/L	G	AB	R	H	2B	3B	HR	RBI	BB	SO	AVG	OBP	SLG	PRO+	BR/A	SB	CS	SBR	FA	FR	G/POS	TPR
1996	Col-N★	159	633	114	198	39	3	31	141	45	105	.313	.364	.531	103	-3	31	12	2	.967	-7	*O-156	-1.2
Total	9	979	3599	527	1056	222	18	157	629	174	661	.293	.331	.496	105	-1	119	54	3	.978	12	O-939/D-5,3-1	-0.8

■ OSCAR BIELASKI
Bielaski, Oscar b: 3/21/1847, Washington, D.C. d: 11/8/11, Washington, D.C. BR/TR, 5'10.5", 170 lbs. Deb: 4/24/1872

YEAR	TM/L	G	AB	R	H	2B	3B	HR	RBI	BB	SO	AVG	OBP	SLG	PRO+	BR/A	SB	CS	SBR	FA	FR	G/POS	TPR
1872	Nat-n	10	46	13	9	0	0	0	3	0	0	.196	.196	.196	18	-5	0	0		.737	-1	O-10	-0.4
1873	Was-n	38	173	35	49	3	2	0	23	4	5	.283	.299	.324	88	-2	0	1	-1	.772	4	*O-38	0.2
1874	Bal-n	43	187	24	45	0	0	0	8	2	4	.241	.246	.241	58	-8	3	1	0	.807	5	*O-42/1-1,2-1	-0.2
1875	Chi-n	51	201	21	48	1	0	0	11	2	5	.239	.246	.244	70	-6	5	5	-2	.748	-2	*O-51	-0.6
1876	Chi-n	32	139	24	29	3	0	0	10	2	3	.209	.220	.230	45	-9				.763	-2	O-32	-1.0
Total	4 n	142	607	93	151	4	2	0	45	8	14	.249	.259	.262	67	-21	8	7	-2	.771	8	O-141/2-1,1-1	-1.0

■ LOU BIERBAUER
Bierbauer, Louis W. b: 9/28/1865, Erie, Pa. d: 1/31/26, Erie, Pa. BL/TR, 5'8", 140 lbs. Deb: 4/17/1886

YEAR	TM/L	G	AB	R	H	2B	3B	HR	RBI	BB	SO	AVG	OBP	SLG	PRO+	BR/A	SB	CS	SBR	FA	FR	G/POS	TPR
1886	Phi-a	137	522	56	118	17	5	2	47	21		.226	.256	.289	70	-19	19			.910	-3	*2-133/C-4,S-2,P-2	-1.4
1887	Phi-a	126	530	74	144	19	7	1	82	13		.272	.289	.340	75	-19	40			.921	-8	*2-126/P-1	-2.0
1888	Phi-a	134	535	83	143	20	9	0	80	25		.267	.301	.338	105	2	34			.916	22	*2-121,3-13/P-1	2.7
1889	Phi-a	130	549	80	167	27	7	7	105	29	30	.304	.344	.417	118	11	17			.941	37	*2-130/C-1	4.5
1890	Bro-P	133	589	128	180	31	11	7	99	40	15	.306	.350	.431	102	-3	16			.931	25	*2-133	2.4
1891	Pit-N	121	500	60	103	13	6	1	47	28	19	.206	.252	.262	51	-32	12			.929	-2	*2-121	-2.5
1892	Pit-N	152	649	81	153	20	9	8	65	25	29	.236	.264	.331	79	-19	11			.921	-19	*2-152	1.4
1893	Pit-N	128	528	84	150	19	11	0	94	36	12	.284	.335	.384	93	-7	11			.959	16	*2-128	0.9
1894	Pit-N	130	525	86	159	19	13	3	107	26	9	.303	.337	.406	79	-19	19			.938	9	*2-130	-0.3
1895	Pit-N	117	466	53	120	13	11	0	69	19	8	.258	.290	.333	64	-26	18			.946	14	*2-117	-0.5
1896	Pit-N	59	258	33	74	10	6	0	39	5	7	.287	.300	.372	80	-9	7			.966	12	2-59	0.6
1897	StL-N	12	46	1	10	0	0	0	1	0		.217	.217	.217	15	-6	2			.921	-2	2-12	-0.7
1898	StL-N	4	9	0	0	0	0	0	0	1		.000	.100	.000	-69	-2	0			.429	-1	/2-2,S-1,3-1	-0.3
Total	13	1383	5706	819	1521	208	95	33	835	268	129	.267	.301	.354	83	-148	206			.935	150	*2-1364/3-14,CPS	4.8

■ CHARLIE BIERMAN
Bierman, Charles S. b: 1845, Hoboken, N.J. d: 8/4/1879, Hoboken, N.J. 6', 180 lbs. Deb: 6/21/1871

YEAR	TM/L	G	AB	R	H	2B	3B	HR	RBI	BB	SO	AVG	OBP	SLG	PRO+	BR/A	SB	CS	SBR	FA	FR	G/POS	TPR
1871	Kek-n	1	2	0	0	0	0	0	1	0		.000	.333	.000	6	-0	0			.818	-0	/1-1	0.0

■ CARSON BIGBEE
Bigbee, Carson Lee "Skeeter" b: 3/31/1895, Waterloo, Ore. d: 10/17/64, Portland, Ore. BL/TR, 5'9", 157 lbs. Deb: 8/25/16 F

YEAR	TM/L	G	AB	R	H	2B	3B	HR	RBI	BB	SO	AVG	OBP	SLG	PRO+	BR/A	SB	CS	SBR	FA	FR	G/POS	TPR
1916	Pit-N	43	164	17	41	3	6	0	3	7	14	.250	.285	.341	91	-2	8			.946	-5	2-23,O-19/3-1	-0.8
1917	Pit-N	133	469	46	112	11	6	0	21	37	16	.239	.301	.288	78	-11	19			.961	-3	*O-107,2-16/S-2	-2.2
1918	Pit-N	92	310	47	79	11	3	1	19	42	10	.255	.344	.319	99	1	19			.958	0	O-92	-0.4
1919	Pit-N	125	478	61	132	11	4	2	27	37	26	.276	.332	.328	95	-2	31			.971	18	*O-124	0.8
1920	Pit-N	137	550	78	154	19	15	4	32	45	28	.280	.341	.391	106	5	31	15	0	.971	6	*O-133	0.1
1921	Pit-N	147	632	100	204	23	17	3	42	41	19	.323	.364	.427	106	6	21	20	-6	.977	16	*O-146	0.5
1922	Pit-N	150	614	113	215	29	15	5	99	56	13	.350	.405	.471	124	23	24	15	-2	.956	17	*O-150	2.5
1923	Pit-N	123	499	79	149	18	7	0	54	43	15	.299	.355	.363	88	-8	10	9	-2	.990	10	*O-122	-0.8
1924	Pit-N	89	282	42	74	4	1	0	15	26	12	.262	.331	.284	65	-13	15	7	0	.943	0	O-75	-1.7
1925	*Pit-N	66	126	31	30	7	0	0	8	7	8	.238	.278	.294	43	-11	2	2	-1	.942	-6	O-42	-1.8
1926	Pit-N	42	68	15	15	3	1	0	5	3	2	.221	.264	.382	69	-3	2			.966	-3	O-21	-0.7
Total	11	1147	4192	629	1205	139	75	17	324	344	161	.287	.345	.369	96	-16	182	68		.966	50	*O-1031/2-39,S-2,3	-4.5

■ LYLE BIGBEE
Bigbee, Lyle Randolph "Al" b: 8/22/1893, Sweet Home, Ore. d: 8/5/42, Portland, Ore. BL/TR, 6', 180 lbs. Deb: 4/15/20 F

YEAR	TM/L	G	AB	R	H	2B	3B	HR	RBI	BB	SO	AVG	OBP	SLG	PRO+	BR/A	SB	CS	SBR	FA	FR	G/POS	TPR
1920	Phi-A	38	75	5	14	2	0	1	8	9	12	.187	.282	.253	42	-6	1	0		.857	-2	O-13,P-12	-0.7
1921	Pit-N	5	2	0	0	0	0	0	0	0	1	.000	.000	.000	-97	-1	0	0	0	1.000	-0	/P-5	0.0
Total	2	43	77	5	14	2	0	1	8	9	13	.182	.276	.247	39	-7	1	0	0	1.000	-0	/P-17,O-13	-0.7

■ ELLIOT BIGELOW
Bigelow, Elliot Allardice "Babe" or "Gilly" b: 10/13/1897, Tarpon Springs, Fla. d: 8/10/33, Tampa, Fla. BL/TL, 5'11", 185 lbs. Deb: 4/18/29

YEAR	TM/L	G	AB	R	H	2B	3B	HR	RBI	BB	SO	AVG	OBP	SLG	PRO+	BR/A	SB	CS	SBR	FA	FR	G/POS	TPR
1929	Bos-A	100	211	23	60	16	0	1	26	23	18	.284	.357	.374	91	-2	1	4	-2	.944	-10	O-59	-1.7

■ CRAIG BIGGIO
Biggio, Craig Alan b: 12/14/65, Smithtown, N.Y. BR/TR, 5'11", 185 lbs. Deb: 6/26/88

YEAR	TM/L	G	AB	R	H	2B	3B	HR	RBI	BB	SO	AVG	OBP	SLG	PRO+	BR/A	SB	CS	SBR	FA	FR	G/POS	TPR
1988	Hou-N	50	123	14	26	6	1	3	5	7	29	.211	.254	.350	74	-5	6	1	1	.991	16	C-50	1.6
1989	Hou-N	134	443	64	114	21	2	13	60	49	64	.257	.339	.402	115	9	21	3	5	.990	-6	*C-125/O-5	1.5
1990	Hou-N	150	555	53	153	24	2	4	42	53	79	.276	.342	.348	93	-4	25	11	1	.985	-7	*C-113,O-50	-0.5
1991	Hou-N	149	546	79	161	23	4	4	46	53	71	.295	.358	.374	113	10	19	6	2	.990	-14	*C-139/2-3,O-2	0.6
1992	Hou-N★	162	613	96	170	32	3	6	39	94	95	.277	.380	.369	118	18	38	15	2	.984	-21	*2-161	0.4
1993	Hou-N	155	610	98	175	41	5	21	64	77	93	.287	.376	.474	130	27	15	17	-6	.982	-2	*2-155	2.4
1994	Hou-N	114	437	88	153	**44**	5	6	56	62	58	.318	.412	.483	139	28	**39**	4	9	.988	-5	*2-113	3.6
1995	Hou-N★	141	553	**123**	167	30	2	22	77	80	85	.302	.411	.483	145	39	33	8	5	.986	-9	*2-141	4.8
1996	Hou-N★	162	605	113	174	24	4	15	75	75	72	.288	.390	.415	124	24	25	7	3	.988	-2	*2-162	3.5
Total	9	1217	4485	728	1279	245	28	94	464	550	646	.285	.374	.415	121	146	221	72	23	.985	-44	2-735,C-427/O-57	17.9

■ PETE BIGLER
Bigler, Ivan Edward b: 12/13/1892, Bradford, Ohio d: 4/1/75, Coldwater, Mich. BR/TR, 5'9", 150 lbs. Deb: 5/6/17

YEAR	TM/L	G	AB	R	H	2B	3B	HR	RBI	BB	SO	AVG	OBP	SLG	PRO+	BR/A	SB	CS	SBR	FA	FR	G/POS	TPR
1917	StL-A	1	0	0	0	0	0	0	0	0	0									.000	0	/R	0.0

■ GEORGE BIGNELL
Bignell, George William b: 7/18/1858, Taunton, Mass. d: 1/16/25, Providence, R.I. 5'9", 160 lbs. Deb: 9/27/1884

YEAR	TM/L	G	AB	R	H	2B	3B	HR	RBI	BB	SO	AVG	OBP	SLG	PRO+	BR/A	SB	CS	SBR	FA	FR	G/POS	TPR
1884	Mil-U	4	9	4	2	0	0	0		0	1	.222	.300	.222	112	-0				.951	3	/C-4	0.3

■ LARRY BIITTNER
Biittner, Lawrence David b: 7/27/45, Pocahontas, Ia. BL/TL, 6'2", 205 lbs. Deb: 7/17/70

YEAR	TM/L	G	AB	R	H	2B	3B	HR	RBI	BB	SO	AVG	OBP	SLG	PRO+	BR/A	SB	CS	SBR	FA	FR	G/POS	TPR
1970	Was-A	2	2	0	0	0	0	0	0	0	0	.000	.000	.000	-99	-1	0	0	0	.000	0	H	-0.1
1971	Was-A	66	171	12	44	4	1	0	16	16	20	.257	.324	.292	80	-4	1	0	0	.940	-0	O-41/1-3	-0.7
1972	Tex-A	137	382	34	99	18	1	3	31	29	37	.259	.315	.335	98	-2	1	3	-2	.991	-1	1-65,O-65	-1.2
1973	Tex-A	83	258	19	65	8	2	1	12	20	21	.252	.308	.310	78	-8	0	0	0	.980	1	O-57,1-20/D-3	-1.0
1974	Mon-N	18	26	2	7	1	0	0	3	0	2	.269	.269	.308	58	-1	0	0	0	1.000	0	/O-4	-0.1
1975	Mon-N	121	346	34	109	13	5	3	28	34	33	.315	.376	.408	113	6	0	0	0	.972	0	O-93	0.3
1976	Mon-N	11	32	2	6	1	0	0	1	0	3	.188	.188	.219	14	-4	0	0	0	.947	1	/O-7	-0.3
	Chi-N	78	192	21	47	13	1	0	17	10	6	.245	.286	.323	66	-9	0	2	-1	.985	4	1-33,O-24	-0.9
	Yr	89	224	23	53	14	1	0	18	10	9	.237	.272	.308	59	-12	0	2	-1	.985	5	1-33,O-31	-1.2
1977	Chi-N	138	493	74	147	28	1	12	62	35	36	.298	.346	.432	97	-3	1	1	0	.987	6	1-80,O-52/P-1	-0.3
1978	Chi-N	120	343	32	88	15	1	4	50	23	27	.257	.305	.341	72	-13	0	1	-1	.987	5	1-62,O-29	-1.3
1979	Chi-N	111	272	35	79	13	3	3	50	21	23	.290	.341	.393	91	-3	1	1	0	.925	-6	O-44,1-32	-1.3
1980	Chi-N	127	273	21	68	12	2	1	34	18	33	.249	.300	.319	68	-12	1	1	-2	.996	1	1-41,O-38	-1.6
1981	Cin-N	42	61	2	13	4	0	0	8	4	1	.213	.262	.279	52	-4	0	0	0	1.000	1	/1-8,O-3	0.2
1982	Cin-N	97	184	18	57	9	2	4	29	17	16	.310	.373	.413	118	5	0	0	0	.978	-2	O-31,1-15	0.2
1983	Tex-A	66	116	5	32	5	1	0	18	9	16	.276	.328	.336	85	-2	1	0	0	.987	2	1-22/O-2,D-9	-0.1
Total	14	1217	3151	310	861	144	20	29	354	236	287	.273	.326	.359	87	-53	10	12	-4	.970	14	O-490,1-381/D-12,P	-8.7

■ DANN BILARDELLO
Bilardello, Dann James b: 5/26/59, Santa Cruz, Cal. BR/TR, 6', 190 lbs. Deb: 4/11/83

YEAR	TM/L	G	AB	R	H	2B	3B	HR	RBI	BB	SO	AVG	OBP	SLG	PRO+	BR/A	SB	CS	SBR	FA	FR	G/POS	TPR
1983	Cin-N	109	298	27	71	18	0	9	38	15	49	.238	.277	.389	80	-9	2	1	0	.991	-1	*C-105	-0.7
1984	Cin-N	68	182	16	38	7	0	5	10	19	34	.209	.287	.280	57	-10	0	1	-1	.992	1	C-68	-0.7
1985	Cin-N	42	102	6	17	0	0	1	9	4	15	.167	.206	.196	12	-12	0	0	0	.986	8	C-42	-0.2
1986	Mon-N	79	191	12	37	5	0	4	17	14	32	.194	.249	.283	47	-14	1	0	0	.982	2	C-77	-0.9
1989	Pit-N	33	80	11	18	6	0	2	8	2	18	.225	.244	.375	77	-3	1	2	-1	.970	5	C-33	0.3
1990	Pit-N	19	37	1	2	0	0	0	3	4	10	.054	.146	.054	-44	-7	0	0	0	1.000	3	C-19	-0.4
1991	SD-N	15	26	3	7	1	0	1	6	4	4	.269	.345	.423	111	0	0	0	0	1.000	6	C-13	0.6
1992	SD-N	17	33	2	4	1	0	0	1	4	9	.121	.216	.152	6	-4	0	0	0	1.000	5	C-14	0.2
Total	8	382	949	79	194	39	0	22	91	65	170	.204	.258	.305	55	-59	4	4	-1	.988	28	C-371	-1.8

YEAR	TM/L	G	AB	R	H	2B	3B	HR	RBI	BB	SO	AVG	OBP	SLG	PRO+	BR/A	SB	CS	SBR	FA	FR	G/POS	TPR

■ STEVE BILKO   Bilko, Stephen Thomas   b: 11/13/28, Nanticoke, Pa.   d: 3/7/78, Wilkes-Barre, Pa.   BR/TR, 6'1", 230 lbs.   Deb: 9/22/49

1949	StL-N	6	17	3	5	2	0	0	2	5	6	.294	.455	.412	128	1	0			1.000	0	/1-5	0.1
1950	StL-N	10	33	1	6	1	0	0	2	4	10	.182	.270	.212	27	-3	0			.989	0	/1-9	-0.3
1951	StL-N	21	72	5	16	4	0	2	12	9	10	.222	.309	.361	79	-2	0	0	0	.984	-0	1-19	-0.3
1952	StL-N	20	72	7	19	6	1	1	6	4	15	.264	.303	.417	97	-1	0	0	0	.995	4	1-20	0.3
1953	StL-N	154	570	72	143	23	3	21	84	70	125	.251	.334	.412	93	-6	0	1	-1	.991	7	*1-154	-0.5
1954	StL-N	8	14	1	2	0	0	0	1	3	1	.143	.294	.143	18	-2	0	0	0	1.000	2	/1-6	-0.1
	Chi-N	47	92	11	22	8	1	4	12	11	24	.239	.327	.478	104	0	0	0	0	1.000	6	1-22	0.5
	Yr	55	106	12	24	8	1	4	13	14	25	.226	.317	.434	92	-1	0	0	0	1.000	8	1-28	0.5
1958	Cin-N	31	87	12	23	4	2	4	17	10	20	.264	.340	.494	111	1	0	0	0	.995	-1	1-21	-0.1
	LA-N	47	101	13	21	1	2	7	18	8	37	.208	.266	.465	86	-3	0	0	0	.995	2	1-25	-0.2
	Yr	78	188	25	44	5	4	11	35	18	57	.234	.301	.479	98	-1	0	0	0	.995	-1	1-46	-0.3
1960	Det-A	78	222	20	46	11	2	9	25	27	31	.207	.293	.396	82	-6	0	1	-1	.991	-1	1-62	-1.1
1961	LA-A	114	294	49	82	16	1	20	59	58	81	.279	.398	.544	134	14	1	1	-0	.989	3	1-86/O-3	1.0
1962	LA-A	64	164	26	47	9	1	8	38	25	35	.287	.387	.500	141	10	1	1	-0	.995	-1	1-50	0.6
Total	10	600	1738	220	432	85	13	76	276	234	395	.249	.339	.444	103	5	2	4		.992	22	1-479/O-3	0.6

■ JOSH BILLINGS   Billings, John Augustus   b: 11/30/1891, Grantville, Kan.   d: 12/30/81, Santa Monica, Cal.   BR/TR, 5'11", 165 lbs.   Deb: 9/9/13

1913	Cle-A	1	3	0	0	0	0	0	0	0	3	.000	.000	.000	-97	-1	0			.857	0	/C-1	0.0
1914	Cle-A	11	8	2	2	1	0	0	0	1	1	.250	.333	.375	109	0	1			.813	2	/C-3	0.3
1915	Cle-A	8	21	2	4	1	0	0	1	0	6	.190	.190	.238	28	-2	1			1.000	-1	/C-7,O-1	-0.3
1916	Cle-A	22	31	2	5	0	0	0	1	1	11	.161	.212	.161	12	-3	0			.981	3	C-12	0.0
1917	Cle-A	66	129	8	23	0	0	0	9	8	21	.178	.243	.233	42	-9	2			.974	2	C-48	-0.4
1918	Cle-A	2	3	0	1	0	0	0	0	0	0	.333	.333	.333	92	0	0			1.000	-0	/C-1	0.0
1919	StL-A	38	76	9	15	1	1	0	3	1	12	.197	.218	.237	27	-7	0			.982	5	C-26/1-1	-0.1
1920	StL-A	66	155	19	43	5	2	0	11	11	10	.277	.353	.335	81	-4	1	0	0	.967	-5	C-40	-0.6
1921	StL-A	20	46	2	10	1	0	0	4	0	7	.217	.217	.217	11	-6	0	0	0	.982	2	C-12	-0.4
1922	StL-A	5	7	0	3	1	0	0	1	0	0	.429	.429	.571	153	1	0			1.000	0	/C-3	0.1
1923	StL-A	4	9	0	0	0	0	0	0	0	2	.000	.000	.000	-95	-3	0			.917	0	/C-4	-0.2
Total	11	243	488	44	106	12	5	0	29	23	73	.217	.268	.262	47	-35	5	0		.970	7	C-157/1-1,O-1	-1.6

■ DICK BILLINGS   Billings, Richard Arlin   b: 12/4/42, Detroit, Mich.   BR/TR, 6'1", 195 lbs.   Deb: 9/11/68

1968	Was-A	12	33	3	6	1	0	0	3	5	13	.182	.289	.303	82	-1	0	0	0	.929	0	/O-8,3-4	-0.1
1969	Was-A	27	37	3	5	0	0	0	6	8	5	.135	.256	.135	13	-4	0	1	-1	1.000	0	/O-6,3-1	-0.5
1970	Was-A	11	24	3	6	2	0	1	1	2	3	.250	.308	.458	114	0	0	0	0	1.000	-2	/C-8	-0.1
1971	Was-A	116	349	32	86	14	0	6	48	21	54	.246	.299	.338	85	-8	2	5	-2	.992	5	C-62,O-32/3-2	-1.3
1972	Tex-A	133	469	41	119	15	1	5	58	29	77	.254	.300	.322	89	-7	1	5	-3	.981	-5	C-92/O-41/3-5,1-1	-1.5
1973	Tex-A	81	280	17	50	11	0	3	32	20	43	.179	.238	.250	39	-23	1	1	-0	.975	-19	C-72/O-4,1-3,D-2	-4.1
1974	Tex-A	16	31	2	7	1	0	0	4	6	6	.226	.314	.258	68	-1	2	0	1	1.000	1	C-13/O-1,D-1	0.1
	StL-N	1	5	0	1	0	0	0	0	0	0	.200	.200	.200	12	-1	0	0	0	1.000	0	/C-1	0.0
1975	StL-N	3	3	0	0	0	0	0	0	0	2	.000	.000	.000	-97	-1	0			.000	0	H	-0.1
Total	8	400	1231	101	280	44	1	16	142	87	207	.227	.283	.304	73	-45	6	12	-5	.984	-27	C-248/O-92,3-12,1D	-7.6

■ GEORGE BINKS   Binks, George Alvin "Bingo" (b: George Alvin Binkowski)   b: 7/11/16, Chicago, Ill.   BL/TL, 6', 175 lbs.   Deb: 9/23/44

1944	Was-A	5	12	0	3	0	0	0	0	1	1	.250	.250	.250	45	-1	0	0	0	1.000	-1	/O-3	-0.2
1945	Was-A	145	550	62	153	32	6	6	81	34	52	.278	.324	.391	117	8	11	7	-1	.977	4	*O-128,1-20	0.4
1946	Was-A	65	134	13	26	3	0	0	12	6	16	.194	.229	.216	26	-13	1	0		1.000	0	O-28	-1.5
1947	Phi-A	104	333	33	86	19	4	2	34	23	36	.258	.308	.357	83	-8	8	2	1	.965	1	O-75,1-13	-1.1
1948	Phi-A	17	41	2	4	1	0	0	2	2	9	.098	.140	.122	-30	-8	0	0	0	1.000	0	O-14	-1.0
	StL-A	15	23	2	5	0	0	0	1	2	1	.217	.280	.217	32	-2	0	0	0	1.000	1	/O-5,1-4	-0.4
	Yr	32	64	4	9	1	0	0	3	4	10	.141	.191	.156	-7	-10	0	0	0	1.000	0	O-19/1-4	-1.4
Total	5	351	1093	112	277	55	10	8	130	67	108	.253	.299	.344	86	-24	21	9	1	.977	1	O-253/1-37	-3.8

■ STEVE BIRAS   Biras, Stephen Alexander   b: 2/26/22, E.St.Louis, Ill.   d: 4/21/65, St.Louis, Mo.   BR/TR, 5'11", 185 lbs.   Deb: 9/15/44

1944	Cle-A	2	2	0	2	0	0	0	0	0	0	1.000	1.000	1.000	491	1	0	0	0	.667	0	/2-1	0.1

■ JUD BIRCHALL   Birchall, Adoniram Judson   b: 1858, Germantown, Pa.   d: 12/22/1887, Philadelphia, Pa.   Deb: 5/2/1882

1882	Phi-a	75	338	65	89	12	1	0	27	8		.263	.280	.305	87	-7				.860	0	*O-74/2-1	-0.6
1883	Phi-a	96	448	95	108	10	1	1	24	20		.241	.274	.275	71	-16				.809	6	*O-96	-1.0
1884	Phi-a	54	221	36	57	2	2	0		4		.258	.287	.285	82	-5				.838	3	O-52/3-2	-0.2
Total	3	225	1007	196	254	24	4	1	51	32		.252	.279	.287	79	-27				.832	9	O-222/3-2,2-1	-1.8

■ FRANK BIRD   Bird, Frank Zepherin "Dodo"   b: 3/10/1869, Spencer, Mass.   d: 5/20/58, Worcester, Mass.   BR/TR, 5'10", 195 lbs.   Deb: 4/16/1892

1892	StL-N	17	50	9	10	3	1	1	6	11		.200	.286	.360	100	-0	2			.920	-4	C-17	-0.3

■ GEORGE BIRD   Bird, George Raymond   b: 6/23/1850, Stillman Valley, Ill.   d: 11/9/40, Rockford, Ill.   BR/TR, 5'9", 150 lbs.   Deb: 5/6/1871

1871	Rok-n	25	106	19	28	2	5	0	13	3	2	.264	.284	.377	92	-1	1	0	0	.756	-5	*O-25	-0.2

■ DAVE BIRDSALL   Birdsall, David Solomon   b: 7/16/1838, New York, N.Y.   d: 12/30/1896, Boston, Mass.   BR/TR, 5'9", 126 lbs.   Deb: 5/5/1871

1871	Bos-n	29	152	51	46	3	3	0	24	4	4	.303	.321	.362	90	-2	6	0	2	.769	-1	*O-27/C-7	0.0
1872	Bos-n	16	76	11	16	3	0	0	15	1	0	.211	.221	.250	42	-5	0	2	-1	.838	1	C-12/O-8	-0.4
1873	Bos-n	3	12	4	1	0	0	0	1	0	0	.083	.083	.083	-46	-2	0	0	0	.200	-1	/O-3	-0.3
Total	3 n	48	240	66	63	6	3	0	40	5	4	.262	.278	.313	70	-10	6	2	1	.720	-1	/O-38,C-19	-0.7

■ JOE BIRMINGHAM   Birmingham, Joseph Leo "Dode"   b: 8/6/1884, Elmira, N.Y.   d: 4/24/46, Tampico, Mexico   BR/TR, 5'10", 185 lbs.   Deb: 9/12/06   M

1906	Cle-A	10	40	5	11	2	1	0	6	1		.275	.293	.375	110	0	2			1.000	1	/O-9,3-1	0.1
1907	Cle-A	137	476	55	112	10	9	1	33	16		.235	.265	.300	79	-12	23			.949	13	*O-133/S-3	-0.5
1908	Cle-A	122	413	32	88	10	1	2	38	19		.213	.253	.257	65	-16	15			.957	6	*O-121/S-1	-1.7
1909	Cle-A	100	343	29	99	10	5	1	38	19		.289	.333	.356	113	5	12			.948	4	O-98	0.6
1910	Cle-A	104	367	41	84	11	2	0	35	23		.229	.284	.270	72	-12	18			.961	14	*O-103/3-1	-0.3
1911	Cle-A	125	447	55	136	18	5	2	51	15		.304	.334	.380	98	-3	16			.973	8	*O-102,3-16	0.0
1912	Cle-A	107	369	49	94	19	3	1	45	26		.255	.311	.331	81	-10	15			.952	5	O-96/1-9,M	-1.0
1913	Cle-A	47	131	16	37	6	2	0	15	8	22	.282	.324	.366	99	-1	7			.974	-3	O-36,M	-0.5
1914	Cle-A	19	47	2	6	2	0	0	4	2	5	.128	.163	.128	-12	-6	0	1	-1	1.000	-2	O-14,M	-1.1
Total	9	771	2633	284	667	89	27	7	265	129	27	.253	.294	.316	84	-55	108	1		.958	46	O-712/3-18,1-9,S-4	-4.4

■ JOHN BISCHOFF   Bischoff, John George "Smiley"   b: 10/28/1894, Granite City, Ill.   d: 12/28/81, Granite City, Ill.   BR/TR, 5'7", 165 lbs.   Deb: 4/18/25

1925	Chi-A	7	11	1	1	0	0	0	0	1	1	.091	.167	.091	-35	-2	0	0	0	1.000	-0	/C-4	-0.2
	Bos-A	41	133	13	37	9	1	1	16	6	11	.278	.309	.383	75	-6	1	2	0	.952	-2	/C-40	-0.7
	Yr	48	144	14	38	9	1	1	16	7	16	.264	.298	.361	67	-8	1	2	0	.955	-2	C-44	-0.9
1926	Bos-A	59	127	6	33	11	2	0	19	15	16	.260	.343	.378	91	-2	1	3	-2	.974	-1	C-46	-0.3
Total	2	107	271	20	71	20	3	1	35	22	32	.262	.320	.369	78	-10	2	5	-2	.964	-4	/C-90	-1.1

■ FRANK BISHOP   Bishop, Frank H.   b: 9/21/1860, Belvidere, Ill.   d: 6/18/29, Chicago, Ill.   Deb: 5/27/1884

1884	CP-U	4	16	1	3	1	0	0		0		.188	.188	.250	32	-2				.667	-2	/3-3,S-1	-0.3

■ MAX BISHOP   Bishop, Max Frederick "Tilly" or "Camera Eye"   b: 9/5/1899, Waynesboro, Pa.   d: 2/24/62, Waynesboro, Pa.   BL/TR, 5'8.5", 165 lbs.   Deb: 4/15/24

1924	Phi-A	91	294	52	75	13	2	2	21	54	30	.255	.380	.333	84	-5	4	3	-1	.969	6	2-80	0.1
1925	Phi-A	105	368	66	103	18	4	3	27	87	37	.280	.420	.383	98	5	9	4		.957	2	*2-104	0.5
1926	Phi-A	122	400	77	106	20	2	0	33	116	41	.265	.431	.325	94	4	4	5	-2	**.987**	0	*2-119	0.5
1927	Phi-A	117	372	80	103	15	1	6	22	105	28	.277	.442	.323	95	5	8	6	-1	.967	3	*2-106	1.0
1928	Phi-A	126	472	104	149	27	5	6	50	97	36	.316	.432	.432	125	23	9	9	-3	**.978**	-11	*2-125	1.2

YEAR	TM/L	G	AB	R	H	2B	3B	HR	RBI	BB	SO	AVG	OBP	SLG	PRO+	BR/A	SB	CS	SBR	FA	FR	G/POS	TPR
1929	*Phi-A	129	475	102	110	19	6	3	36	**128**	44	.232	.398	.316	83	-6	1	4	-2	.970	-26	*2-129	-2.7
1930	*Phi-A	130	441	117	111	27	6	10	38	128	60	.252	.426	.408	108	11	3	2	-0	.976	-6	*2-127	1.1
1931	*Phi-A	130	497	115	146	30	4	5	37	112	51	.294	.426	.400	111	14	3	1	0	.984	-0	*2-130	2.1
1932	Phi-A	114	409	89	104	24	2	5	37	110	43	.254	.412	.359	98	4	2	2	-1	**.988**	-9	*2-106	0.0
1933	Phi-A	117	391	80	115	27	1	4	42	106	46	.294	.446	.399	124	21	1	5	-3	.975	-13	*2-113	1.1
1934	Bos-A	97	253	65	66	13	1	1	22	82	22	.261	.445	.332	96	4	3	2	-0	.990	0	2-57,1-15	0.5
1935	Bos-A	60	122	19	28	3	1	1	14	28	14	.230	.377	.295	71	-4	0	2	-1	.978	-5	2-34,1-11/S-2	-0.8
Total	12	1338	4494	966	1216	236	35	41	379	1153	452	.271	.423	.366	102	72	43	50	-17	.976	-56	*2-1230/1-26,S-2	4.6

■ MIKE BISHOP
Bishop, Michael David b: 11/5/58, Santa Maria, Cal. BR/TR, 6'2", 188 lbs. Deb: 4/16/83

YEAR	TM/L	G	AB	R	H	2B	3B	HR	RBI	BB	SO	AVG	OBP	SLG	PRO+	BR/A	SB	CS	SBR	FA	FR	G/POS	TPR
1983	NY-N	3	8	2	1	0	0	0	3	4		.125	.364	.250	74	-0	0	0	0	.944	-0	/C-3	0.0

■ RIVINGTON BISLAND
Bisland, Rivington Martin b: 2/17/1890, New York, N.Y. d: 1/11/73, Salzburg, Austria BR/TR, 5'9", 155 lbs. Deb: 9/13/12

YEAR	TM/L	G	AB	R	H	2B	3B	HR	RBI	BB	SO	AVG	OBP	SLG	PRO+	BR/A	SB	CS	SBR	FA	FR	G/POS	TPR
1912	Pit-N	1	1	0	0	0	0	0	0	0	0	.000	.000	.000	-99	-0				.000	0	H	0.0
1913	StL-A	12	44	3	6	0	0	0	3	2	5	.136	.191	.136	-4	-6				.963	-5	S-12	-1.1
1914	Cle-A	18	57	9	6	1	0	0	2	6	2	.105	.190	.123	-5	-7	2	5	-2	.962	-0	S-15/3-1	-1.0
Total	3	31	102	12	12	1	0	0	5	8	7	.118	.189	.127	-6	-13	2	5		.962	-5	/S-27,3-1	-2.1

■ DEL BISSONETTE
Bissonette, Delphia Louis b: 9/6/1899, Winthrop, Me. d: 6/9/72, Augusta, Maine BL/TL, 5'11", 180 lbs. Deb: 4/11/28 MC

YEAR	TM/L	G	AB	R	H	2B	3B	HR	RBI	BB	SO	AVG	OBP	SLG	PRO+	BR/A	SB	CS	SBR	FA	FR	G/POS	TPR
1928	Bro-N	155	587	90	188	30	13	25	106	70	75	.320	.396	.543	145	38	5			.987	-4	*1-155	2.0
1929	Bro-N	116	431	68	121	28	10	12	75	46	58	.281	.351	.476	105	2	2			.987	-9	*1-113	-1.7
1930	Bro-N	146	572	90	192	33	13	16	113	56	66	.336	.396	.523	121	20	4			.987	-9	*1-146	-0.3
1931	Bro-N	152	587	90	170	19	14	12	87	59	53	.290	.354	.431	111	9	4			.990	-7	*1-152	-1.2
1933	Bro-N	35	114	9	28	7	0	1	10	2	17	.246	.259	.333	71	-5	2			.988	0	1-32	-0.8
Total	5	604	2291	359	699	117	50	66	391	233	269	.305	.371	.486	119	64	17			.988	-28	1-598	-2.0

■ RED BITTMAN
Bittman, Henry Peter b: 7/22/1862, Cincinnati, Ohio d: 11/8/29, Cincinnati, Ohio Deb: 10/10/1889

YEAR	TM/L	G	AB	R	H	2B	3B	HR	RBI	BB	SO	AVG	OBP	SLG	PRO+	BR/A	SB	CS	SBR	FA	FR	G/POS	TPR
1889	KC-a	4	14	2	4	0	0	0	2	1	1	.286	.333	.286	73	-1	1			1.000	1	/2-4	0.1

■ GEORGE BJORKMAN
Bjorkman, George Anton b: 8/26/56, Ontario, Cal. BR/TR, 6'2", 190 lbs. Deb: 7/10/83

YEAR	TM/L	G	AB	R	H	2B	3B	HR	RBI	BB	SO	AVG	OBP	SLG	PRO+	BR/A	SB	CS	SBR	FA	FR	G/POS	TPR
1983	Hou-N	29	75	8	17	4	0	2	14	16	29	.227	.370	.360	110	2	0	0	0	.993	-3	C-29	0.0

■ JOHN BLACK
Black, John Falcnor "Jack" (b: John Falcnor Haddow) b: 2/23/1890, Covington, Ky. d: 3/20/62, Rutherford, N.J. BR/TR, 6'1", 185 lbs. Deb: 6/20/11

YEAR	TM/L	G	AB	R	H	2B	3B	HR	RBI	BB	SO	AVG	OBP	SLG	PRO+	BR/A	SB	CS	SBR	FA	FR	G/POS	TPR
1911	StL-A	54	186	13	28	1	0	0		7	10	.151	.202	.172	5	-24	4			.972	0	1-54	-2.4

■ BILL BLACK
Black, John William "Jigger" b: 8/12/1899, Philadelphia, Pa. d: 1/14/68, Philadelphia, Pa. BL/TR, 5'11", 168 lbs. Deb: 5/4/24

YEAR	TM/L	G	AB	R	H	2B	3B	HR	RBI	BB	SO	AVG	OBP	SLG	PRO+	BR/A	SB	CS	SBR	FA	FR	G/POS	TPR
1924	Chi-A	6	5	0	1	0	0	0	0	0	0	.200	.200	.200	3	-1	0	0	0	.000	0	/2-1	-0.1

■ BOB BLACK
Black, Robert Benjamin b: 12/10/1862, Cincinnati, Ohio d: 3/21/33, Sioux City, Iowa 5'5.5", 155 lbs. Deb: 8/19/1884

YEAR	TM/L	G	AB	R	H	2B	3B	HR	RBI	BB	SO	AVG	OBP	SLG	PRO+	BR/A	SB	CS	SBR	FA	FR	G/POS	TPR
1884	KC-U	38	146	25	36	14	2	1		10		.247	.295	.390	122	-1				.784	-1	O-19,P-16/2-6,S-1	-0.3

■ ETHAN BLACKABY
Blackaby, Ethan Allen b: 7/24/40, Cincinnati, O. BL/TL, 5'11", 190 lbs. Deb: 9/6/62

YEAR	TM/L	G	AB	R	H	2B	3B	HR	RBI	BB	SO	AVG	OBP	SLG	PRO+	BR/A	SB	CS	SBR	FA	FR	G/POS	TPR
1962	Mil-N	6	13	0	2	1	0	0	1	0	8	.154	.214	.231	20	-1	0	0	0	1.000	-1	/O-3	-0.2
1964	Mil-N	9	12	0	1	0	0	0	1	1	2	.083	.154	.083	-31	-2	0	0	0	.500	-2	/O-5	-0.4
Total	2	15	25	0	3	1	0	0	1	2	10	.120	.185	.160	-4	-4	0	0	0	.800	-2	/O-8	-0.6

■ EARL BLACKBURN
Blackburn, Earl Stuart b: 11/1/1892, Leesville, Ohio d: 8/3/66, Mansfield, Ohio BR/TR, 5'11", 180 lbs. Deb: 9/17/12

YEAR	TM/L	G	AB	R	H	2B	3B	HR	RBI	BB	SO	AVG	OBP	SLG	PRO+	BR/A	SB	CS	SBR	FA	FR	G/POS	TPR
1912	Pit-N	1	0	0	0	0	0	0	0	0	0	—	—	—		0	0			1.000	0	/C-1	0.0
	Cin-N	1	0	0	0	0	0	0	0	1	0	—	1.000	—	191	0	0			1.000	0	/C-1	0.1
	Yr	2	0	0	0	0	0	0	0	1	0	—	1.000	—	190	0	0			1.000	0	/C-2	0.1
1913	Cin-N	17	27	1	7	0	0	0	3	2	5	.259	.310	.259	64	-1	2			.848	-1	C-12	-0.2
1915	Bos-N	3	6	0	1	0	0	0	0	2	0	.167	.375	.167	70	-0				1.000	-0	/C-3	0.0
1916	Bos-N	47	110	12	30	4	4	0	7	9	21	.273	.328	.382	123	3	2			.972	-1	C-44	0.5
1917	Chi-N	2	2	0	0	0	0	0	0	0	0	.000	.000	.000	-93	-0				.000	0	H	-0.1
Total	5	71	145	13	38	4	4	0	10	14	27	.262	.327	.345	107	1	4			.954	-2	/C-61	0.3

■ LENA BLACKBURNE
Blackburne, Russell Aubrey "Slats" b: 10/23/1886, Clifton Heights, Pa. d: 2/29/68, Riverside, N.J. BR/TR, 5'11", 160 lbs. Deb: 4/14/10 MC

YEAR	TM/L	G	AB	R	H	2B	3B	HR	RBI	BB	SO	AVG	OBP	SLG	PRO+	BR/A	SB	CS	SBR	FA	FR	G/POS	TPR
1910	Chi-A	75	242	16	42	3	1	0	10		19	.174	.245	.194	39	-16	4			.911	19	S-74	0.6
1912	Chi-A	5	1	0	0	0	0	0	0		1	.000	.500	.000	48	-0	1			.800	1	/S-4,3-1	0.1
1914	Chi-A	144	474	52	105	10	5	1	35	66	58	.222	.324	.270	80	-9	25	15	-1	.963	1	*2-143	-1.2
1915	Chi-A	96	283	33	61	9	1	0	25	35	34	.216	.304	.240	61	-13	13	11	-3	.949	-10	3-83/S-9	-2.4
1918	Cin-N	125	435	34	99	8	10	1	45	25	30	.228	.271	.299	75	-14	6			.938	10	*S-125	0.2
1919	Bos-N	31	80	5	21	3	1	0	4	6	7	.262	.322	.325	99	-0	3			.948	3	3-24/1-1,2-1,S-1	0.5
	Phi-N	72	291	32	58	10	5	2	19	10	22	.199	.228	.289	51	-18	5			.933	8	3-72/1-1	-1.0
	Yr	103	371	37	79	13	6	2	23	16	29	.213	.249	.296	61	-18	5			.937	11	3-96/1-2,2-1,S-1	-0.5
1927	Chi-A	1	1	1	1	0	0	0	0	1	0	1.000	1.000	1.000	431	0	0	0	0	.000	0	H	0.0
1929	Chi-A	1	0	0	0	0	0	0	0	0	0	.000	.000	.000		0	0	0	0	.000	0	/P-1,M	0.0
Total	8	550	1807	173	387	39	23	4	139	162	151	.214	.284	.268	67	-69	54	26		.927	30	S-213,3-180,2/1P	-3.2

■ GEORGE BLACKERBY
Blackerby, George Franklin b: 11/10/03, Luther, Okla. d: 5/30/87, Wichita Falls, Tex. BR/TR, 6'1", 176 lbs. Deb: 8/10/28

YEAR	TM/L	G	AB	R	H	2B	3B	HR	RBI	BB	SO	AVG	OBP	SLG	PRO+	BR/A	SB	CS	SBR	FA	FR	G/POS	TPR
1928	Chi-A	30	83	8	21	0	0	0	12	4	10	.253	.287	.253	44	-7	2	1	0	.953	-1	O-20	-0.9

■ FRED BLACKWELL
Blackwell, Fredrick William "Blacky" b: 9/7/1891, Bowling Green, Ky. d: 12/8/75, Morgantown, Ky. BL/TR, 5'11.5", 160 lbs. Deb: 9/25/17

YEAR	TM/L	G	AB	R	H	2B	3B	HR	RBI	BB	SO	AVG	OBP	SLG	PRO+	BR/A	SB	CS	SBR	FA	FR	G/POS	TPR
1917	Pit-N	3	10	1	2	0	0	0	0	0	3	.200	.200	.200	22	-1	0			1.000	0	/C-3	-0.1
1918	Pit-N	8	13	1	2	0	0	0	4	3	4	.154	.313	.154	42	-1	0			.926	0	/C-8	0.0
1919	Pit-N	24	65	3	14	3	0	0	6	3	9	.215	.261	.262	55	-4	0			.964	-0	C-22	-0.2
Total	3	35	88	5	18	3	0	0	10	6	16	.205	.263	.239	50	-5	0			.961	-0	/C-33	-0.3

■ TIM BLACKWELL
Blackwell, Timothy P b: 8/19/52, San Diego, Cal. BB/TR, 5'11", 180 lbs. Deb: 7/3/74

YEAR	TM/L	G	AB	R	H	2B	3B	HR	RBI	BB	SO	AVG	OBP	SLG	PRO+	BR/A	SB	CS	SBR	FA	FR	G/POS	TPR
1974	Bos-A	44	122	9	30	1	1	0	8	10	21	.246	.308	.270	63	-5	1	1	-0	.971	2	C-44	-0.2
1975	Bos-A	59	132	15	26	3	2	0	6	19	13	.197	.303	.250	53	-8	0	0	0	.984	8	C-57/D-2	0.2
1976	Phi-N	4	8	0	2	0	0	0	0	1	0	.250	.250	.250	41	-1	0	0	0	1.000	1	/C-4	0.0
1977	Phi-N	1	0	1	0	0	0	0	0	0	0	—	—	—	—	0	0	0	0	1.000	0	/C-1	0.0
	Mon-N	16	22	3	2	1	0	0	2	0	7	.091	.167	.136	-18	-4	0	0	0	.925	-1	C-14	-0.4
	Yr	17	22	4	2	1	0	0	2	0	7	.091	.167	.136	-18	-4	0	0	0	.929	-1	C-15	-0.4
1978	Chi-N	49	103	8	23	3	0	0	7	23	17	.223	.370	.252	68	-3	0	0	0	.987	7	C-49	0.5
1979	Chi-N	63	122	8	20	3	1	0	12	32	25	.164	.342	.205	48	-8	0	0	0	.975	1	C-63	-0.5
1980	Chi-N	103	320	24	87	16	4	5	30	41	62	.272	.355	.394	101	1	0	1	-1	.982	17	*C-103	2.2
1981	Chi-N	58	158	21	37	10	2	1	11	23	23	.234	.331	.342	87	-2				.993	2	C-56	0.1
1982	Mon-N	23	42	2	8	1	0	0	3	6	11	.190	.244	.286	47	-3	0	0	0	.985	2	C-18	-0.1
1983	Mon-N	6	15	0	3	1	0	0	2	1	3	.200	.250	.267	43	-1	0	0	0	.935	1	/C-5	-0.1
Total	10	426	1044	91	238	40	11	6	80	154	183	.228	.329	.305	73	-34	3	5	-1	.981	40	C-414/D-2	1.7

■ RAY BLADES
Blades, Francis Raymond b: 8/6/1896, Mt.Vernon, Ill. d: 5/18/79, Lincoln, Ill. BR/TR, 5'7.5", 163 lbs. Deb: 8/19/22 MC

YEAR	TM/L	G	AB	R	H	2B	3B	HR	RBI	BB	SO	AVG	OBP	SLG	PRO+	BR/A	SB	CS	SBR	FA	FR	G/POS	TPR
1922	StL-N	37	130	27	39	2	4	3	21	25	21	.300	.418	.446	132	8	3	3	-1	.931	-1	O-29/S-4,3-1	0.4
1923	StL-N	98	317	48	78	21	5	5	44	37	46	.246	.342	.391	95	-2	4			.967	6	O-83/3-4	-0.1
1924	StL-N	131	456	86	142	21	13	11	68	35	38	.311	.373	.487	131	19	7	9		.956	-3	*O-109/2-7,3-7	0.7
1925	StL-N	122	462	112	158	37	8	12	57	59	47	.342	.423	.535	140	29	6	8		.979	11	*O-114/3-1	2.7
1926	StL-N	107	416	81	127	17	12	8	43	62	67	.305	.409	.462	129	19	6			.980	4	*O-105	1.6
1927	StL-N	61	180	33	57	8	5	2	29	28	22	.317	.414	.450	127	8	3			.914	-13	O-50	-0.8
1928	*StL-L	51	85	9	20	7	1	1	19	20	26	.235	.393	.376	100	1	0			.972	-2	O-19	-0.2
1930	*StL-N	45	101	26	40	6	2	4	29	21	15	.396	.504	.614	163	12	1			.957	-3	O-32	0.6

YEAR	TM/L	G	AB	R	H	2B	3B	HR	RBI	BB	SO	AVG	OBP	SLG	PRO+	BR/A	SB	CS	SBR	FA	FR	G/POS	TPR
1931	*StL-N	35	67	10	19	4	0	1	5	10	7	.284	.392	.388	106	1			1	.871	-4	O-20	-0.4
1932	StL-N	80	201	35	46	10	1	3	29	34	31	.229	.340	.333	80	-5			2	.975	-5	O-62/3-1	-1.3
Total	10	767	2415	467	726	133	51	50	340	331	310	.301	.395	.460	123	90	33	22		.963	-10	O-623/3-14,2-7,S-4	3.2

■ **RICK BLADT**   Bladt, Richard Alan b: 12/9/46, Santa Cruz, Cal. BR/TR, 6'1", 160 lbs. Deb: 6/15/69

YEAR	TM/L	G	AB	R	H	2B	3B	HR	RBI	BB	SO	AVG	OBP	SLG	PRO+	BR/A	SB	CS	SBR	FA	FR	G/POS	TPR
1969	Chi-N	10	13	1	2	0	0	0	1	0	5	.154	.154	.154	-12	-2	0	0	0	1.000	0	/O-7	-0.2
1975	NY-A	52	117	13	26	3	1	1	11	11	8	.222	.295	.291	67	-5	6	2	1	.973	-2	O-51	-0.8
Total	2	62	130	14	28	3	1	1	12	11	13	.215	.282	.277	58	-7	6	2	1	.976	-2	/O-58	-1.0

■ **RAE BLAEMIRE**   Blaemire, Rae Bertrum b: 2/8/11, Gary, Ind. d: 12/23/75, Champaign, Ill. BR/TR, 6', 178 lbs. Deb: 9/13/41

YEAR	TM/L	G	AB	R	H	2B	3B	HR	RBI	BB	SO	AVG	OBP	SLG	PRO+	BR/A	SB	CS	SBR	FA	FR	G/POS	TPR
1941	NY-N	2	5	0	2	0	0	0	0	0	0	.400	.400	.400	123	0	0			1.000	-0	/C-2	0.0

■ **FOOTSIE BLAIR**   Blair, Clarence Vick b: 7/13/1900, Enterprise, Okla. d: 7/1/82, Texarkana, Tex. BL/TR, 6'1", 180 lbs. Deb: 4/28/29

YEAR	TM/L	G	AB	R	H	2B	3B	HR	RBI	BB	SO	AVG	OBP	SLG	PRO+	BR/A	SB	CS	SBR	FA	FR	G/POS	TPR
1929	*Chi-N	26	72	10	23	5	0	1	8	3	4	.319	.347	.431	91	-1	1			.897	1	/3-8,1-7,2-2	0.0
1930	Chi-N	134	578	97	158	24	12	6	59	20	58	.273	.306	.388	66	-33	9			.958	8	*2-115,3-13	-1.6
1931	Chi-N	86	240	31	62	19	4	3	29	14	26	.258	.302	.408	88	-5	1			.956	-6	2-44,1-23/3-1	-0.9
Total	3	246	890	138	243	48	16	10	96	37	88	.273	.308	.397	73	-39	11			.958	4	2-161/1-30,3-22	-2.5

■ **BUDDY BLAIR**   Blair, Louis Nathan b: 9/10/10, Columbia, Miss. d: 6/7/96, Monroe, La. BL/TR, 6', 186 lbs. Deb: 4/14/42

YEAR	TM/L	G	AB	R	H	2B	3B	HR	RBI	BB	SO	AVG	OBP	SLG	PRO+	BR/A	SB	CS	SBR	FA	FR	G/POS	TPR
1942	Phi-A	137	484	48	135	26	8	5	66	30	30	.279	.325	.397	103	0	1	6	-3	.931	-7	*3-126	-0.8

■ **PAUL BLAIR**   Blair, Paul L D b: 2/1/44, Cushing, Okla. BR/TR, 6', 171 lbs. Deb: 9/9/64

YEAR	TM/L	G	AB	R	H	2B	3B	HR	RBI	BB	SO	AVG	OBP	SLG	PRO+	BR/A	SB	CS	SBR	FA	FR	G/POS	TPR
1964	Bal-A	8	1	0	0	0	0	0	0	0	1	.000	.000	.000	-99	-0	0	1	-1	1.000	-2	/O-6	-0.3
1965	Bal-A	119	364	49	85	19	2	5	25	32	52	.234	.303	.338	80	-9	8	5	-1	.992	3	*O-116	-1.3
1966	*Bal-A	133	303	35	84	20	2	6	33	15	36	.277	.311	.416	109	2	5	6	-2	.990	-11	*O-127	-1.5
1967	Bal-A	151	552	72	162	27	**12**	11	64	50	68	.293	.357	.446	137	25	8	6	-1	.985	21	*O-146	4.1
1968	Bal-A	141	421	48	89	22	1	7	38	37	60	.211	.278	.318	80	-10	4	2	0	.993	-7	*O-132/3-1	-1.8
1969	*Bal-A★	150	625	102	178	32	5	26	76	40	72	.285	.330	.477	122	15	20	6	2	.988	25	*O-150	3.5
1970	*Bal-A	133	480	79	128	24	2	18	65	56	93	.267	.347	.438	114	9	24	11	1	.990	19	*O-128/3-1	2.3
1971	*Bal-A	141	516	75	135	24	8	10	44	32	94	.262	.306	.397	99	-3	14	11	-2	.991	2	*O-138	-1.0
1972	Bal-A	142	477	47	111	20	8	8	49	25	78	.233	.271	.358	84	-11	7	8	-3	.991	9	*O-139	-1.2
1973	*Bal-A★	146	500	73	140	25	3	10	64	43	72	.280	.337	.402	108	5	18	8	1	.990	7	*O-144/D-1	0.7
1974	*Bal-A	151	552	77	144	27	4	17	62	43	59	.261	.317	.417	113	7	27	9	3	.985	7	*O-151	1.2
1975	Bal-A	140	440	51	96	13	4	5	31	25	82	.218	.260	.300	62	-23	17	11	-2	.991	-1	*O-138/1-1,D-1	-3.3
1976	Bal-A	145	375	29	74	16	0	3	16	22	49	.197	.246	.264	52	-23	15	6	1	.979	-8	*O-139/D-1	-3.6
1977	*NY-A	83	164	20	43	9	3	4	25	9	16	.262	.309	.396	91	-2	3	2	-0	.969	-12	O-79/D-1	-1.7
1978	*NY-A	75	125	10	22	5	0	2	13	9	17	.176	.231	.264	40	-10	1	1	-0	.989	-15	O-64/2-5,S-4,3-3	-2.8
1979	NY-A	2	5	0	1	0	0	0	0	0	1	.200	.200	.200	4	-0	0	0	0	1.000	0	/O-2	0.0
	Cin-N	75	140	7	21	4	1	2	15	11	27	.150	.212	.236	22	-15	0	0	0	.992	-10	O-67	-2.8
1980	NY-A	12	2	2	0	0	0	0	0	0	0	.000	.000	.000	-99	-1	0	0	0	1.000	-4	O-12	-0.5
Total	17	1947	6042	776	1513	282	55	134	620	449	877	.250	.305	.382	96	-45	171	93	-5	.988	29	*O-1878/2-5,3SD1	-10.0

■ **WALTER BLAIR**   Blair, Walter Allen "Heavy" b: 10/13/1883, Landrus, Pa. d: 8/20/48, Lewisburg, Pa. BR/TR, 6', 185 lbs. Deb: 9/17/07 M

YEAR	TM/L	G	AB	R	H	2B	3B	HR	RBI	BB	SO	AVG	OBP	SLG	PRO+	BR/A	SB	CS	SBR	FA	FR	G/POS	TPR
1907	NY-A	7	22	1	4	0	0	0	1	2		.182	.250	.182	35	-2	0			.922	1	/C-7	0.1
1908	NY-A	76	211	9	40	5	1	1	13	11		.190	.237	.237	53	-11	0			.956	-14	C-60/O-9,1-3	-2.3
1909	NY-A	42	110	5	23	2	2	0	11	7		.209	.269	.264	68	-4	2			.964	-8	C-42	-1.0
1910	NY-A	6	22	2	5	0	1	0	2	0		.227	.227	.318	67	-1	0			.970	-2	/C-6	-0.3
1911	NY-A	85	222	18	43	9	2	0	26	16		.194	.257	.252	40	-18	2			.970	4	C-84/1-1	-0.7
1914	Buf-F	128	378	22	92	11	2	0	33	32	64	.243	.304	.283	59	-27	6			.984	5	*C-128	-1.2
1915	Buf-F	98	290	23	65	15	3	2	20	18	32	.224	.274	.317	65	-19	4			**.981**	5	C-97,M	-0.7
Total	7	442	1255	80	272	42	11	3	106	86	96	.217	.272	.275	56	-81	18			.974	-9	C-424/O-9,1-4	-6.1

■ **HARRY BLAKE**   Blake, Harry Cooper b: 6/16/1874, Portsmouth, Ohio d: 10/14/19, Chicago, Ill. BR/TR, 5'7", 165 lbs. Deb: 7/7/1894

YEAR	TM/L	G	AB	R	H	2B	3B	HR	RBI	BB	SO	AVG	OBP	SLG	PRO+	BR/A	SB	CS	SBR	FA	FR	G/POS	TPR
1894	Cle-N	73	296	51	78	15	4	1	51	30	22	.264	.335	.351	63	-19	1			.932	2	O-73	-1.6
1895	*Cle-N	84	315	50	87	10	1	3	45	30	33	.276	.341	.343	72	-14	11			.898	-2	O-83	-1.8
1896	Cle-N	104	383	66	92	12	5	1	43	46	30	.240	.322	.305	62	-21	10			.944	2	*O-103/S-1	-2.4
1897	Cle-N	32	117	17	30	3	1	1	15	12		.256	.331	.325	70	-5	5			.989	4	O-32	-0.3
1898	Cle-N	136	474	65	116	18	7	0	58	69		.245	.342	.312	89	-5	12			.952	7	*O-136/1-2	-0.7
1899	StL-N	97	292	50	70	9	4	2	41	43		.240	.341	.318	80	-7	16			.979	-2	O-87/2-4,S-1,1-1,C	-1.3
Total	6	526	1877	299	473	67	22	8	253	230	85	.252	.336	.324	73	-71	55			.948	12	O-514/2-4,1-3,SC	-8.1

■ **LINC BLAKELY**   Blakely, Lincoln Howard b: 2/12/12, Oakland, Cal. d: 9/28/76, Oakland, Cal. BR/TR, 6', 180 lbs. Deb: 4/29/34

YEAR	TM/L	G	AB	R	H	2B	3B	HR	RBI	BB	SO	AVG	OBP	SLG	PRO+	BR/A	SB	CS	SBR	FA	FR	G/POS	TPR
1934	Cin-N	34	102	11	23	1	1	0	10	5	14	.225	.269	.255	42	-8	1			.987	3	O-28	-0.6

■ **BOB BLAKISTON**   Blakiston, Robert J. (b: Robert J. Blackstone)
b: 10/2/1855, San Francisco, Cal. d: 12/25/18, San Francisco, Cal 5'8.5", 180 lbs. Deb: 5/2/1882

YEAR	TM/L	G	AB	R	H	2B	3B	HR	RBI	BB	SO	AVG	OBP	SLG	PRO+	BR/A	SB	CS	SBR	FA	FR	G/POS	TPR
1882	Phi-a	72	281	40	64	4	1	0	20	9		.228	.252	.249	62	-12				.855	0	O-38,3-34/2-1	-1.1
1883	Phi-a	44	167	26	41	3	3	0	26	9		.246	.284	.299	82	-4				.857	-4	O-37/1-6,3-5	-0.7
1884	Phi-a	32	128	21	33	6	0	0		11		.258	.336	.305	104	1				.902	2	O-28/3-2,1-1,2-1,S	0.2
	Ind-a	6	18	0	4	1	0	0		1		.222	.263	.278	79	-0				.884	-1	/1-5,O-1	-0.1
	Yr	38	146	21	37	7	0	0		12		.253	.327	.301	101	0				.902	1	O-29/1-6,3-2,2-1,S	0.1
Total	3	154	594	87	142	14	4	0	46	30		.239	.280	.276	77	-16				.872	-2	O-104/3-41,1-12,2S	-1.7

■ **JOHNNY BLANCHARD**   Blanchard, John Edwin b: 2/26/33, Minneapolis, Minn. BL/TR, 6'1", 198 lbs. Deb: 9/25/55

YEAR	TM/L	G	AB	R	H	2B	3B	HR	RBI	BB	SO	AVG	OBP	SLG	PRO+	BR/A	SB	CS	SBR	FA	FR	G/POS	TPR
1955	NY-A	1	3	0	0	0	0	0	0	1	0	.000	.250	.000	-29	-1	0	0	0	1.000	0	/C-1	0.0
1959	NY-A	49	59	6	10	1	0	2	4	7	12	.169	.258	.288	51	-4	1	0	0	.963	-2	C-12/O-8,1-1	-0.6
1960	*NY-A	53	99	8	24	3	1	4	14	6	17	.242	.292	.414	94	-1	1	0	0	.988	10	C-28	0.9
1961	*NY-A	93	243	38	74	10	1	21	54	27	28	.305	.383	.613	170	23	1	0	0	.990	-2	C-48,O-15	2.3
1962	*NY-A	93	246	33	57	7	0	13	39	28	32	.232	.313	.419	98	-1	1	0	0	.987	-7	O-47,C-15/1-2	-1.1
1963	*NY-A	76	218	22	49	4	0	16	45	26	30	.225	.307	.463	114	3	0	0	0	.987	-9	O-64	-0.9
1964	*NY-A	77	161	18	41	8	0	7	28	24	24	.255	.351	.435	115	4	1	0	0	.984	-3	C-25,O-14/1-3	0.1
1965	NY-A	12	34	1	5	1	0	1	3	7	3	.147	.293	.265	60	-2	0	0	0	.961	-1	C-12	-0.2
	KC-A	52	120	10	24	2	0	2	11	8	16	.200	.256	.267	49	-8	0	0	0	1.000	-10	O-20,C-14	-2.0
	Yr	64	154	11	29	3	0	3	14	15	19	.188	.265	.266	52	-10	0	0	0	.971	-11	C-26,O-20	-2.2
	Mil-N	10	10	1	1	0	0	1	2	2	1	.100	.250	.400	79	-0	0	0	0	.000	-0	/O-1	-0.1
Total	8	516	1193	137	285	36	2	67	200	136	163	.239	.320	.441	109	13	0	0	1	.987	-25	O-169,C-155/1-6	-1.6

■ **DAMASO BLANCO**   Blanco, Damaso (Caripe) b: 12/11/41, Curiepe, Venez. BR/TR, 5'10", 165 lbs. Deb: 5/26/72

YEAR	TM/L	G	AB	R	H	2B	3B	HR	RBI	BB	SO	AVG	OBP	SLG	PRO+	BR/A	SB	CS	SBR	FA	FR	G/POS	TPR
1972	SF-N	39	20	5	7	1	0	0	2	1	3	.350	.458	.400	144	1	2	1	0	.889	6	3-19/S-8,2-3	0.8
1973	SF-N	28	12	4	0	0	0	0	0	1	3	.000	.077	.000	-74	-3	0	2	0	1.000	3	/3-7,S-5,2-3	-0.1
1974	SF-N	5	1	0	0	0	0	0	0	0	0	.000	.000	.000	-96	-0	1	0	0	.000	0	H	0.0
Total	3	72	33	9	7	1	0	0	2	2	6	.212	.316	.242	58	-2	3	3	0	.929	8	/3-26,S-13,2-6	0.7

■ **OSSIE BLANCO**   Blanco, Oswaldo Carlos (Diaz) b: 9/8/45, Caracas, Venez. BR/TR, 6', 185 lbs. Deb: 5/26/70

YEAR	TM/L	G	AB	R	H	2B	3B	HR	RBI	BB	SO	AVG	OBP	SLG	PRO+	BR/A	SB	CS	SBR	FA	FR	G/POS	TPR
1970	Chi-A	34	66	4	13	0	0	0	8	3	14	.197	.232	.197	19	-7	0	1	0	.993	-1	1-22/O-1	-1.0
1974	Cle-A	18	36	1	7	0	0	1	2	7	4	.194	.326	.194	53	-2	0	3	-2	.992	-1	1-16/D-1	-0.6
Total	2	52	102	5	20	0	0	1	10	10	18	.196	.268	.196	31	-9	0	4	-2	.993	-2	/1-38,D-1,O-1	-1.6

■ **COONIE BLANK**   Blank, Frank Ignatz b: 10/18/1892, St.Louis, Mo. d: 12/8/61, St.Louis, Mo. BR/TR, 5'11", 165 lbs. Deb: 8/15/09

YEAR	TM/L	G	AB	R	H	2B	3B	HR	RBI	BB	SO	AVG	OBP	SLG	PRO+	BR/A	SB	CS	SBR	FA	FR	G/POS	TPR
1909	StL-N	1	2	0	0	0	0	0	0	0		.000	.000	.000	-99	-0	0			1.000	-0	/C-1	-0.1

■ **CLIFF BLANKENSHIP**   Blankenship, Clifford Douglas b: 4/10/1880, Columbus, Ga. d: 4/26/56, Oakland, Cal. BR/TR, 5'10.5", 165 lbs. Deb: 4/17/05

YEAR	TM/L	G	AB	R	H	2B	3B	HR	RBI	BB	SO	AVG	OBP	SLG	PRO+	BR/A	SB	CS	SBR	FA	FR	G/POS	TPR
1905	Cin-N	19	56	8	11	1	1	0	7	4		.196	.250	.250	44	-4	1			.960	-2	1-15	-0.7

YEAR	TM/L	G	AB	R	H	2B	3B	HR	RBI	BB	SO	AVG	OBP	SLG	PRO+	BR/A	SB	CS	SBR	FA	FR	G/POS	TPR
1907	Was-A	37	102	4	23	2	0	0	6	3		.225	.248	.245	62	-5	3			.991	0	C-22/1-9	-0.3
1909	Was-A	39	60	4	15	1	0	0	9	0		.250	.250	.267	66	-3	2			.907	-9	C-17/O-4	-1.2
Total	3	95	218	16	49	4	1	0	22	7		.225	.249	.252	58	-11	6			.964	-11	/C-39,1-24,O-4	-2.2

■ LANCE BLANKENSHIP
Blankenship, Lance Robert b: 12/6/63, Portland, Ore. BR/TR, 6', 190 lbs. Deb: 9/4/88

YEAR	TM/L	G	AB	R	H	2B	3B	HR	RBI	BB	SO	AVG	OBP	SLG	PRO+	BR/A	SB	CS	SBR	FA	FR	G/POS	TPR
1988	Oak-A	10	3	1	0	0	0	0	0	0	1	.000	.000	.000	-99	-1	0	1	-1	1.000	0	/2-4,D-4	-0.1
1989	*Oak-A	58	125	22	29	5	1	1	4	8	31	.232	.278	.312	68	-5	5	1	1	1.000	0	O-25,2-24,D-10	-1.1
1990	*Oak-A	86	136	18	26	3	0	0	10	20	23	.191	.295	.213	46	-9	3	1	0	.947	-2	3-28,O-28,2-20,/1D	-1.1
1991	Oak-A	90	185	33	46	8	0	3	21	23	42	.249	.341	.341	95	-1	12	3	2	.983	8	2-45,O-28,3-14,/D-6	0.9
1992	*Oak-A	123	349	59	84	24	1	3	34	82	57	.241	.394	.341	113	11	21	7	2	.992	-3	2-78,O-51/1-7,D-3	1.1
1993	Oak-A	94	252	43	48	8	1	2	23	67	64	.190	.364	.254	74	-6	13	5	1	.994	4	O-66,2-19/1-6,SD	-0.2
Total	6	461	1050	176	233	48	3	9	92	200	218	.222	.352	.299	86	-11	54	18	5	.987	10	O-198,2-190/3D1S	0.5

■ LARVELL BLANKS
Blanks, Larvell b: 1/28/50, Del Rio, Tex. BR/TR, 5'8", 167 lbs. Deb: 7/19/72

YEAR	TM/L	G	AB	R	H	2B	3B	HR	RBI	BB	SO	AVG	OBP	SLG	PRO+	BR/A	SB	CS	SBR	FA	FR	G/POS	TPR
1972	Atl-N	33	85	10	28	5	0	1	7	7	12	.329	.380	.424	117	2	0	0	0	1.000	6	2-18/S-4,3-2	1.0
1973	Atl-N	17	18	1	4	0	0	0	0	1	3	.222	.263	.222	33	-2	0	0	0	.000	-3	/3-3,2-2,S-2	-0.4
1974	Atl-N	3	8	0	2	0	0	0	1	0		.250	.250	.250	38	-1	0	0	0	.889	-0	/S-2	-0.1
1975	Atl-N	141	471	49	110	13	3	3	38	38	43	.234	.294	.293	61	-25	4	3	-1	.960	-12	*S-129,2-12	-2.5
1976	Cle-A	104	328	45	92	8	7	5	41	30	31	.280	.341	.393	116	6	1	2	-1	.977	-20	S-56,2-46/3-2,D-3	-0.6
1977	Cle-A	105	322	43	92	10	4	6	38	19	37	.286	.327	.398	100	-1	3	0	1	.960	-25	S-66,3-18,2-12/D-6	-1.8
1978	Cle-A	70	193	19	49	10	0	2	20	10	16	.254	.291	.337	77	-6	0	0	0	.926	-10	S-43,2-17/3-3,D-1	-1.0
1979	Tex-A	68	120	13	24	5	0	1	15	11	9	.200	.267	.267	45	-9	0	0	0	.972	-10	S-49,2-16/D-1	-1.5
1980	Atl-N	88	221	23	45	6	0	2	12	16	27	.204	.257	.258	43	-17	1	2	-1	.947	7	S-56,3-43/2-1	-0.8
Total	9	629	1766	203	446	57	14	20	172	132	178	.253	.306	.335	78	-51	9	7	-2	.957	-66	S-407,2-124/3-71,D	-7.7

■ DON BLASINGAME
Blasingame, Don Lee b: 3/16/32, Corinth, Miss. BL/TR, 5'10", 165 lbs. Deb: 9/20/55

YEAR	TM/L	G	AB	R	H	2B	3B	HR	RBI	BB	SO	AVG	OBP	SLG	PRO+	BR/A	SB	CS	SBR	FA	FR	G/POS	TPR
1955	StL-N	5	16	4	6	1	0	0	0	0	6	.375	.545	.438	165	2	1	1	-0	.955	2	/2-3,S-2	0.4
1956	StL-N	150	587	94	153	22	7	0	27	72	52	.261	.344	.322	81	-14	8	8	-2	.986	22	2-98,S-49/3-2	1.8
1957	StL-N	154	650	108	176	25	7	8	58	71	49	.271	.343	.368	89	-8	21	9	1	.984	26	*2-154	3.1
1958	StL-N★	143	547	71	150	19	10	2	36	57	47	.274	.344	.356	83	-12	20	5	3	.964	-1	*2-137	-0.1
1959	StL-N	150	615	90	178	26	7	1	24	67	42	.289	.361	.359	87	-9	15	15	-5	.979	21	*2-150	1.8
1960	SF-N	136	523	72	123	12	8	2	31	49	53	.235	.303	.300	70	-21	14	2	3	.979	-13	*2-133	-1.9
1961	SF-N	3	1	1	0	0	0	0	0	2	1	.000	.667	.000	100	0	0	0	0	.000	0	H	0.0
	*Cin-N	123	450	59	100	18	4	1	21	39	38	.222	.287	.287	52	-30	4	3	-1	.972	-19	*2-116	-3.8
	Yr	126	451	60	100	18	4	1	21	41	39	.222	.289	.286	53	-30	4	3	-1	.972	-19	*2-116	-3.8
1962	Cin-N	141	494	77	139	9	7	2	35	63	44	.281	.365	.340	88	-6	4	3	-1	.976	-10	*2-137	-0.2
1963	Cin-N	18	31	4	5	0	0	0	7	5		.161	.316	.226	57	-1	0	0	0	.974	2	2-11/3-2	-0.1
	Was-A	69	254	29	65	10	2	2	12	24	18	.256	.320	.335	84	-5	3	2	-0	.991	1	2-64	0.2
1964	Was-A	143	506	56	135	17	2	1	34	40	44	.267	.321	.314	78	-14	5	5	-1	.977	-30	*2-135	-3.6
1965	Was-A	129	403	47	90	8	8	1	18	35	45	.223	.289	.290	66	-18	5	4	-1	.984	1	*2-110	-1.0
1966	Was-A	68	200	18	43	9	1	0	11	18	21	.215	.280	.275	61	-10	2	1	0	.984	-1	2-58/S-1	-0.8
	KC-A	12	19	1	3	0	0	0	1	2	3	.158	.238	.158	17	-2	0	1	-1	1.000	-2	/2-4	-0.3
	Yr	80	219	19	46	9	1	0	12	20	24	.210	.276	.265	57	-12	2	2	-1	.985	-2	2-62/S-1	-1.1
Total	12	1444	5296	731	1366	178	62	21	308	552	462	.258	.330	.327	78	-149	105	60	-4	.979	-3	*2-1310/S-52,3-4	-4.5

■ JOHNNY BLATNIK
Blatnik, John Louis b: 3/10/21, Bridgeport, Ohio BR/TR, 6', 195 lbs. Deb: 4/21/48

YEAR	TM/L	G	AB	R	H	2B	3B	HR	RBI	BB	SO	AVG	OBP	SLG	PRO+	BR/A	SB	CS	SBR	FA	FR	G/POS	TPR
1948	Phi-N	121	415	56	108	27	8	6	45	31	77	.260	.315	.407	96	-4	3			.946	-1	*O-105	-1.0
1949	Phi-N	6	8	3	1	0	0	0	4	1		.125	.417	.125	53	-0	0			1.000	-0	/O-2	-0.1
1950	Phi-N	4	4	0	1	0	0	0	0	2	3	.250	.500	.250	106	0	0			1.000	0	/O-1	0.0
	StL-N	7	20	0	3	0	0	0	1	3	2	.150	.261	.150	11	-3	0			.875	-2	/O-7	-0.5
	Yr	11	24	0	4	0	0	0	1	5	5	.167	.345	.167	29	-2	0			.900	-2	/O-8	-0.5
Total	3	138	447	59	113	27	8	6	46	40	83	.253	.317	.389	91	-6	3			.945	-3	O-115	-1.6

■ BUDDY BLATTNER
Blattner, Robert Garnett b: 2/8/20, St.Louis, Mo. BR/TR, 6'0.5", 180 lbs. Deb: 4/18/42

YEAR	TM/L	G	AB	R	H	2B	3B	HR	RBI	BB	SO	AVG	OBP	SLG	PRO+	BR/A	SB	CS	SBR	FA	FR	G/POS	TPR
1942	StL-N	19	23	3	1	0	0	0	1	3	6	.043	.185	.043	-29	-4	0			.900	-0	S-13/2-3	-0.4
1946	NY-N	126	420	63	107	18	6	11	49	56	52	.255	.351	.405	113	8	12			.976	1	*2-114/1-1	1.7
1947	NY-N	55	153	28	40	9	2	0	13	21	19	.261	.351	.346	85	-3	4			.947	-3	2-34,3-11	-0.4
1948	NY-N	8	20	3	4	1	0	0	0	3	2	.200	.304	.250	51	-1	2			1.000	2	/2-7	0.1
1949	Phi-N	64	97	15	24	6	0	5	21	19	17	.247	.371	.464	126	4	0			.981	-10	2-15,3-12/S-1	-0.6
Total	5	272	713	112	176	34	8	16	84	102	96	.247	.347	.384	102	4	18			.971	-11	2-173/3-23,S-14,1-1	0.4

■ JEFF BLAUSER
Blauser, Jeffrey Michael b: 11/8/65, Los Gatos, Cal. BR/TR, 6'1", 180 lbs. Deb: 7/5/87

YEAR	TM/L	G	AB	R	H	2B	3B	HR	RBI	BB	SO	AVG	OBP	SLG	PRO+	BR/A	SB	CS	SBR	FA	FR	G/POS	TPR
1987	Atl-N	51	165	11	40	6	3	2	15	18	34	.242	.328	.352	76	-5	7	3	0	.962	10	S-50	0.9
1988	Atl-N	18	67	7	16	3	1	2	7	2	11	.239	.271	.403	87	-1	0	1	-1	.967	3	/2-9,S-8	0.2
1989	Atl-N	142	456	63	123	24	2	12	46	38	101	.270	.327	.410	107	3	5	2	0	.929	-17	3-78,2-39,S-30/O-2	-1.0
1990	Atl-N	115	386	46	104	24	3	8	39	35	70	.269	.338	.409	99	-1	3	5	-2	.961	-3	S-93,2-14/3-9,O-1	0.2
1991	*Atl-N	129	352	49	91	14	3	11	54	54	59	.259	.360	.409	109	5	5	6	-2	.948	-36	S-85,2-32,3-18	-2.9
1992	*Atl-N	123	343	61	90	19	3	14	46	46	82	.262	.356	.458	122	10	5	5	-2	.968	-47	*S-106,2-21/3-1	-3.5
1993	*Atl-N★	161	597	110	182	29	2	15	73	85	109	.305	.405	.436	124	24	16	6	1	.970	-23	*S-161	1.5
1994	*Atl-N	96	380	56	98	21	4	6	45	38	64	.258	.333	.382	84	-9	1	3	-2	.970	3	S-96	0.1
1995	*Atl-N	115	431	60	91	16	2	12	31	57	107	.211	.320	.341	72	-17	8	5	-1	.970	-1	*S-115	-0.7
1996	*Atl-N	83	265	48	65	14	1	10	35	40	54	.245	.357	.419	98	-0	6	0	2	.926	-22	S-79	-1.3
Total	10	1033	3442	511	900	170	24	92	391	413	691	.261	.350	.405	101	11	56	36	-5	.962	-132	S-823,2-115,3/O	-6.5

■ MARV BLAYLOCK
Blaylock, Marvin Edward b: 9/30/29, Ft.Smith, Ark. d: 10/23/93, Conway, Ark. BL/TL, 6'1.5", 175 lbs. Deb: 9/26/50

YEAR	TM/L	G	AB	R	H	2B	3B	HR	RBI	BB	SO	AVG	OBP	SLG	PRO+	BR/A	SB	CS	SBR	FA	FR	G/POS	TPR
1950	NY-N	1	1	0	0	0	0	0	0	0		.000	.000	.000	-99	-0	0			.000	0	H	0.0
1955	Phi-N	113	259	30	54	7	7	3	24	31	43	.208	.296	.324	66	-13	6	1	1	.991	3	1-77/O-6	-1.2
1956	Phi-N	136	460	61	117	14	8	10	50	50	86	.254	.330	.385	93	-4	5	1	1	.992	-5	*1-124/O-1	-1.7
1957	Phi-N	37	26	5	4	0	0	2	4	3	8	.154	.313	.385	89	-0	0	0	0	1.000	0	1-12/O-1	0.0
Total	4	287	746	96	175	21	15	15	78	84	137	.235	.317	.363	83	-18	11	2	2	.992	-2	1-213/O-8	-2.9

■ CURT BLEFARY
Blefary, Curtis Le Roy b: 7/5/43, Brooklyn, N.Y. BL/TR, 6'2", 195 lbs. Deb: 4/14/65

YEAR	TM/L	G	AB	R	H	2B	3B	HR	RBI	BB	SO	AVG	OBP	SLG	PRO+	BR/A	SB	CS	SBR	FA	FR	G/POS	TPR
1965	Bal-A	144	462	72	120	23	4	22	70	88	73	.260	.382	.470	138	25	4	2	0	.979	2	*O-136	2.3
1966	*Bal-A	131	419	73	107	14	3	23	64	73	56	.255	.373	.468	142	25	1	4	-2	.976	-3	*O-109,1-20	1.5
1967	Bal-A	155	554	69	134	19	5	22	81	73	94	.242	.339	.413	122	16	4	4	-1	.968	13	*O-103,1-52	2.2
1968	Bal-A	137	451	50	90	8	1	15	39	65	66	.200	.306	.322	90	-4	6	3	0	.962	-9	O-92,C-40,1-12	-1.8
1969	Hou-N	155	542	66	137	26	7	12	67	77	79	.253	.350	.393	110	8	7	2	-2	.987	6	*1-152/O-1	0.0
1970	NY-A	99	269	34	57	6	0	9	37	43	37	.212	.327	.335	87	-4	1	3	-2	.972	-11	O-79/1-6	-2.1
1971	NY-A	21	36	4	7	1	0	1	2	3	5	.194	.256	.306	62	-2	0	0	0	.875	-1	/O-6,1-4	-0.4
	*Oak-A	50	101	15	22	2	0	5	12	15	15	.218	.325	.386	103	0	0	0	0	.975	-5	C-14,O-14/3-5,2-2	-0.5
	Yr	71	137	19	29	3	0	6	14	18	20	.212	.308	.365	93	-1	0	0	0	.958	-5	O-20,C-14/3-5,12	-0.9
1972	Oak-A	8	11	1	5	2	0	1	0	1	1	.455	.455	.636	234	2	0	0	0	.000	-0	/1-1,2-1,O-1	-1.0
	SD-N	74	102	10	20	3	0	3	9	19	18	.196	.322	.314	88	-1	0	0	0	.982	-8	C-12/1-6,3-3,O-3	-1.0
Total	8	974	2947	394	699	104	20	112	382	456	444	.237	.345	.400	115	65	24	24	-7	.972	-15	O-544,1-253/C32	0.3

■ IKE BLESSITT
Blessitt, Isaiah b: 9/30/49, Detroit, Mich. BR/TR, 5'11", 185 lbs. Deb: 9/7/72

YEAR	TM/L	G	AB	R	H	2B	3B	HR	RBI	BB	SO	AVG	OBP	SLG	PRO+	BR/A	SB	CS	SBR	FA	FR	G/POS	TPR
1972	Det-A	4	4	0	0	0	0	0	0	0	0	.000	.000	.000	-97	-1	0			1.000	-0	/O-1	-0.2

■ NED BLIGH
Bligh, Edwin Forrest b: 6/30/1864, Brooklyn, N.Y. d: 4/18/1892, Brooklyn, N.Y. BR/TR, 5'11", 172 lbs. Deb: 6/26/1886

YEAR	TM/L	G	AB	R	H	2B	3B	HR	RBI	BB	SO	AVG	OBP	SLG	PRO+	BR/A	SB	CS	SBR	FA	FR	G/POS	TPR
1886	Bal-a	3	9	0	0	0	0	0	0	1		.000	.100	.000	-69	-2				.833	-2	/C-3	-0.3
1888	Cin-a	3	5	0	0	0	0	0	0	0		.000	.000	.000	-95	-1				1.000	-1	/C-2,O-1	-0.2
1889	Col-a	28	93	6	13	1	1	0	5	4	14	.140	.200	.172	7	-11	2			.927	-3	C-28	-1.0

YEAR	TM/L	G	AB	R	H	2B	3B	HR	RBI	BB	SO	AVG	OBP	SLG	PRO+	BR/A	SB	CS	SBR	FA	FR	G/POS	TPR
1890	Col-a	8	29	2	6	2	0	0	5	2		.207	.258	.276	62	-1	0			.933	2	/C-8	0.1
	*Lou-a	24	73	9	15	0	0	1	9	9		.205	.293	.247	60	-3	1			.921	-0	C-24	-0.2
	Yr	32	102	11	21	2	0	1	14	11		.206	.283	.255	61	-5	1			.925	1	C-32	-0.1
Total	4	66	209	17	34	3	1	1	19	16	14	.163	.232	.201	28	-19	3			.923	-5	/C-65,O-1	-1.6

■ ELMER BLISS   Bliss, Elmer Ward b: 3/9/1875, Penfield, Pa. d: 3/18/62, Bradford, Pa. BL/TR, 6′, 180 lbs. Deb: 9/28/03

YEAR	TM/L	G	AB	R	H	2B	3B	HR	RBI	BB	SO	AVG	OBP	SLG	PRO+	BR/A	SB	CS	SBR	FA	FR	G/POS	TPR
1903	NY-A	1	3	0	0	0	0	0	0	0		.000	.000	.000	-94	-1	0			.000	-0	/P-1	0.0
1904	NY-A	1	1	0	0	0	0	0	0	0		.000	.000	.000	-96	-0	0			.000	-0	/O-1	-0.1
Total	2	2	4	0	0	0	0	0	0	0		.000	.000	.000	-94	-1	0			—	-1	/O-1,P-1	-0.1

■ FRANK BLISS   Bliss, Frank Eugene b: 12/10/1852, Chicago, Ill. d: 1/8/29, Nashville, Tenn. Deb: 6/20/1878

YEAR	TM/L	G	AB	R	H	2B	3B	HR	RBI	BB	SO	AVG	OBP	SLG	PRO+	BR/A	SB	CS	SBR	FA	FR	G/POS	TPR
1878	Mil-N	2	8	1	1	0	0	0	0	0	0	.125	.125	.125	-17	-1				1.000	-0	/3-1,C-1	-0.1

■ JACK BLISS   Bliss, John Joseph Albert b: 1/9/1882, Vancouver, Wash. d: 10/23/68, Temple City, Cal. BR/TR, 5′9″, 185 lbs. Deb: 5/10/08

YEAR	TM/L	G	AB	R	H	2B	3B	HR	RBI	BB	SO	AVG	OBP	SLG	PRO+	BR/A	SB	CS	SBR	FA	FR	G/POS	TPR
1908	StL-N	44	136	9	29	4	0	1	5	8		.213	.267	.265	73	-4	3			.992	5	C-43	0.5
1909	StL-N	35	113	12	25	2	1	1	8	12		.221	.307	.283	89	-3	1			.951	1	C-32	0.3
1910	StL-N	16	33	2	2	0	0	0	3	4	8	.061	.162	.061	-36	-6	0			.980	-1	C-13	-0.7
1911	StL-N	97	258	36	59	6	4	1	27	42	25	.229	.341	.295	81	-5	5			.952	-9	C-84/S-1	-0.7
1912	StL-N	49	114	11	28	3	1	0	18	19	14	.246	.372	.289	84	-1	3			.973	-6	C-41	-0.3
Total	5	241	654	70	143	15	6	3	61	85	47	.219	.318	.274	76	-18	13			.966	-10	C-213/S-1	-0.9

■ BRUNO BLOCK   Block, James John (b: James John Blochowicz) b: 3/13/1885, Wisconsin Rapids, Wis. d: 8/6/37, S.Milwaukee, Wis. BR/TR, 5′9″, 185 lbs. Deb: 8/5/07

YEAR	TM/L	G	AB	R	H	2B	3B	HR	RBI	BB	SO	AVG	OBP	SLG	PRO+	BR/A	SB	CS	SBR	FA	FR	G/POS	TPR
1907	Was-A	24	57	3	8	1	1	0	2	2		.140	.169	.211	23	-5	0			.949	-6	C-21	-1.1
1910	Chi-A	55	152	12	32	1	1	0	9	13		.211	.273	.230	60	-7	3			.964	1	C-47	-0.2
1911	Chi-A	39	115	11	35	6	1	1	18	6		.304	.339	.400	109	1	0			.972	-3	C-38	0.2
1912	Chi-A	46	136	8	35	5	6	0	26	7		.257	.294	.382	96	-2	1			.980	2	C-46	0.4
1914	Chi-F	44	105	8	21	4	1	0	14	11	17	.200	.276	.257	49	-9	1			.966	0	C-34	-0.7
Total	5	208	565	42	131	18	10	1	69	39	17	.232	.281	.304	74	-22	5			.969	-5	C-186	-1.4

■ CY BLOCK   Block, Seymour b: 5/4/19, Brooklyn, N.Y. BR/TR, 6′, 180 lbs. Deb: 9/7/42

YEAR	TM/L	G	AB	R	H	2B	3B	HR	RBI	BB	SO	AVG	OBP	SLG	PRO+	BR/A	SB	CS	SBR	FA	FR	G/POS	TPR
1942	Chi-N	9	33	6	12	1	1	0	4	3	3	.364	.417	.455	161	3	2			.917	-2	/3-8,2-1	0.0
1945	*Chi-N	2	7	1	1	0	0	0	1	0	0	.143	.143	.143	-21	-1	0			1.000	1	/2-1,3-1	0.0
1946	Chi-N	6	13	2	3	0	0	0	0	4	0	.231	.412	.231	86	0	0			1.000	1	/3-4	0.1
Total	3	17	53	9	16	1	1	0	5	7	3	.302	.383	.358	118	1	2			.947	-0	/3-13,2-2	0.1

■ TERRY BLOCKER   Blocker, Terry Fennell b: 8/18/59, Columbia, S.C. BL/TL, 6′2″, 195 lbs. Deb: 4/11/85

YEAR	TM/L	G	AB	R	H	2B	3B	HR	RBI	BB	SO	AVG	OBP	SLG	PRO+	BR/A	SB	CS	SBR	FA	FR	G/POS	TPR
1985	NY-N	18	15	1	1	0	0	0	0	1	2	.067	.125	.067	-46	-3	0	0	0	1.000	-1	/O-5	-0.4
1988	Atl-N	66	198	13	42	4	2	2	10	10	20	.212	.250	.283	50	-13	1	1	-0	.994	4	O-61	-1.2
1989	Atl-N	26	31	1	7	1	0	0	1	1	5	.226	.250	.258	44	-2	1	0	0	1.000	-2	/O-8,P-1	-0.4
Total	3	110	244	15	50	5	2	2	11	12	27	.205	.242	.266	44	-18	2	1	0	.994	1	/O-74,P-1	-2.0

■ WES BLOGG   Blogg, Wesley Collins b: 1855, Norfolk, Va. d: 3/10/1897, Baltimore, Md. Deb: 6/20/1883

YEAR	TM/L	G	AB	R	H	2B	3B	HR	RBI	BB	SO	AVG	OBP	SLG	PRO+	BR/A	SB	CS	SBR	FA	FR	G/POS	TPR
1883	Pit-a	9	34	0	5	0	0	0				.147	.147	.147	-5	-4				.881	-1	/C-6,O-3	-0.4

■ RON BLOMBERG   Blomberg, Ronald Mark "Boomer" b: 8/23/48, Atlanta, Ga. BL/TR, 6′1″, 205 lbs. Deb: 9/10/69

YEAR	TM/L	G	AB	R	H	2B	3B	HR	RBI	BB	SO	AVG	OBP	SLG	PRO+	BR/A	SB	CS	SBR	FA	FR	G/POS	TPR
1969	NY-A	4	6	0	3	0	0	0	0	1	1	.500	.571	.500	210	1	0	0	0	1.000	-0	/O-2	0.1
1971	NY-A	64	199	30	64	6	2	7	31	14	23	.322	.366	.477	146	11	2	4	-2	.970	-5	O-57	0.2
1972	NY-A	107	299	36	80	22	1	14	49	38	26	.268	.356	.488	155	20	0	2	-1	.985	-8	1-95	0.4
1973	NY-A	100	301	45	99	13	1	12	57	34	25	.329	.397	.498	156	22	2	1		.980	1	D-55,1-41	1.9
1974	NY-A	90	264	39	82	11	2	10	48	29	33	.311	.383	.481	150	17	1	0		1.000	0	D-58,O-19	1.5
1975	NY-A	34	106	18	27	8	2	4	17	13	10	.255	.336	.481	131	4	0	0		1.000	0	D-27/O-1	0.3
1976	NY-A	1	2	0	0	0	0	0	0	0	0	.000	.000	.000	-99	-0	0	0		.000	0	/D-1	-0.1
1978	Chi-A	61	156	16	36	7	0	5	22	11	16	.231	.281	.372	81	-4	0	0	0	.986	-1	D-36/1-7	-0.7
Total	8	461	1333	184	391	67	8	52	224	140	134	.293	.363	.473	142	70	6	7	-2	.983	-14	D-177,1-143/O-79	3.6

■ JOE BLONG   Blong, Joseph Myles b: 9/17/1853, St.Louis, Mo. d: 9/16/1892, St.Louis, Mo. BR/TR, Deb: 5/4/1875

YEAR	TM/L	G	AB	R	H	2B	3B	HR	RBI	BB	SO	AVG	OBP	SLG	PRO+	BR/A	SB	CS	SBR	FA	FR	G/POS	TPR
1875	RS-n	16	68	3	10	2	0	0	5	0	7	.147	.147	.176	13	-5	1	0	0	.927	3	P-15/O-4	-0.1
1876	StL-N	62	264	30	62	7	4	0	30	2	9	.235	.241	.292	81	-5				.895	1	*O-62/P-1	-0.4
1877	StL-N	58	218	17	47	8	3	0	13	4	22	.216	.230	.280	63	-9				.835	-3	*O-40,P-25	-0.8
Total	2	120	482	47	109	15	7	0	43	6	31	.226	.236	.286	72	-13				.867	-2	O-102/P-26	-1.2

■ JIMMY BLOODWORTH   Bloodworth, James Henry b: 7/26/17, Tallahassee, Fla. BR/TR, 5′11″, 180 lbs. Deb: 9/14/37

YEAR	TM/L	G	AB	R	H	2B	3B	HR	RBI	BB	SO	AVG	OBP	SLG	PRO+	BR/A	SB	CS	SBR	FA	FR	G/POS	TPR
1937	Was-A	15	50	3	11	0	0	0	8	5	8	.220	.291	.300	51	-4	0	1	-1	.946	-1	2-14	-0.4
1939	Was-A	83	318	34	92	24	1	4	40	10	26	.289	.313	.409	90	-7	3	1	0	.972	14	2-73/O-5	1.1
1940	Was-A	119	469	47	115	17	8	11	70	16	71	.245	.272	.386	73	-21	3	1	0	.978	13	2-96,1-17/3-6	-0.3
1941	Was-A	142	506	59	124	24	3	7	66	41	58	.245	.303	.346	75	-20	1	1	-0	.971	35	*2-132/3-6,S-1	2.3
1942	Det-A	137	533	62	129	23	1	13	57	35	63	.242	.295	.362	78	-17	2	8	-4	.972	10	*2-134/S-2	-0.3
1943	Det-A	129	474	41	114	23	4	6	52	29	59	.241	.289	.344	79	-14	4	7	-3	.972	17	*2-129	0.8
1946	Det-A	76	249	25	61	8	1	5	36	12	26	.245	.285	.345	71	-10	3	3	-1	.974	-1	2-71	-0.7
1947	Pit-N	88	316	27	79	9	0	7	48	16	39	.250	.290	.345	66	-16	1			.979	-14	2-87	-2.4
1949	Cin-N	134	452	40	118	27	1	9	59	27	36	.261	.304	.385	83	-12	1			.981	-3	2-92,1-23/3-8	-1.2
1950	Cin-N	4	14	1	3	1	0	0	1	2	0	.214	.313	.286	58	-1	0			1.000	-3	/2-4	-0.4
	*Phi-N	54	96	6	22	2	0	0	13	6	12	.229	.275	.250	40	-8	0			1.000	-2	2-27/1-7,3-2	-0.9
	Yr	58	110	7	25	3	0	0	14	8	12	.227	.280	.255	42	-9	0			1.000	-5	2-31/1-7,3-2	-1.3
1951	Phi-N	21	42	2	6	0	0	0	1	3	9	.143	.200	.143	-6	-6	1	0	0	1.000	-1	2-8,1-6	-0.7
Total	11	1002	3519	347	874	160	20	62	451	202	407	.248	.292	.358	74	-136	19	22		.975	64	2-867/1-53,3-22,OS	-3.1

■ BUD BLOOMFIELD   Bloomfield, Clyde Stalcup b: 1/5/36, Oklahoma City, Okla. BR/TR, 5′11.5″, 175 lbs. Deb: 9/25/63

YEAR	TM/L	G	AB	R	H	2B	3B	HR	RBI	BB	SO	AVG	OBP	SLG	PRO+	BR/A	SB	CS	SBR	FA	FR	G/POS	TPR
1963	StL-N	1	0	0	0	0	0	0	0	0	0	—	—	—			0	0	0	.000	0	/3-1	0.0
1964	Min-A	7	7	1	1	0	0	0	0	0	0	.143	.143	.143	-20	-1	0	0	0	1.000	0	/2-3,S-2	0.0
Total	2	8	7	1	1	0	0	0	0	0	0	.143	.143	.143	-20	-1	0	0	0	1.000	0	/2-3,S-2,3-1	0.0

■ GREG BLOSSER   Blosser, Gregory Brent b: 6/26/71, Manatee, Fla. BL/TL, 6′3″, 200 lbs. Deb: 9/5/93

YEAR	TM/L	G	AB	R	H	2B	3B	HR	RBI	BB	SO	AVG	OBP	SLG	PRO+	BR/A	SB	CS	SBR	FA	FR	G/POS	TPR
1993	Bos-A	17	28	1	2	1	0	0	1	2	7	.071	.133	.107	-33	-5	1	0	0	1.000	-1	/O-9,D-1	-0.6
1994	Bos-A	5	11	2	1	0	0	0	1	4	4	.091	.333	.091	16	-1	0	0	0	.727	-0	/O-3,D-1	-0.1
Total	2	22	39	3	3	1	0	0	2	6	11	.077	.200	.103	-16	-7	1	0	0	.870	-1	/O-12,D-2	-0.7

■ JACK BLOTT   Blott, John Leonard b: 8/24/02, Girard, Ohio d: 6/11/64, Ann Arbor, Mich. BR/TR, 6′, 210 lbs. Deb: 7/30/24

YEAR	TM/L	G	AB	R	H	2B	3B	HR	RBI	BB	SO	AVG	OBP	SLG	PRO+	BR/A	SB	CS	SBR	FA	FR	G/POS	TPR
1924	Cin-N	2	1	0	0	0	0	0	0	0	0	.000	.000	.000	-99	-0	0	0	0	1.000	-0	/C-1	0.0

■ MIKE BLOWERS   Blowers, Michael Roy b: 4/24/65, Wurzburg, Germany BR/TR, 6′2″, 190 lbs. Deb: 9/1/89

YEAR	TM/L	G	AB	R	H	2B	3B	HR	RBI	BB	SO	AVG	OBP	SLG	PRO+	BR/A	SB	CS	SBR	FA	FR	G/POS	TPR
1989	NY-A	13	38	2	10	0	0	3	3	13		.263	.317	.263	66	-2	0	0	0	.852	-3	3-13	-0.4
1990	NY-A	48	144	16	27	4	0	5	21	12	50	.188	.255	.319	59	-8	1	0	0	.899	-3	3-45/D-2	-1.6
1991	NY-A	15	35	3	7	0	1	1	1	3	9	.200	.282	.286	57	-2	0	0	0	.870	-3	3-14	-0.5
1992	Sea-A	31	73	7	14	3	0	1	2	6	20	.192	.253	.274	47	-5	0	0	0	.984	6	3-29/1-3	0.0
1993	Sea-A	127	379	55	106	23	3	15	57	44	98	.280	.358	.475	120	10	1	5	-3	.951	12	*3-117/O-2,C-1,1D	2.0
1994	Sea-A	85	270	37	78	13	0	9	49	25	60	.289	.351	.437	100	-0	2	1	-1	.939	10	3-48,1-20/O-9,D-9	0.7
1995	*Sea-A	134	439	59	113	24	1	23	96	53	128	.257	.337	.474	107	4	2	1	0	.947	-13	*3-126/1-7,O-5	-0.9
1996	LA-N	92	317	31	84	19	2	6	38	37	77	.265	.344	.394	103	5	0	0	0	.951	-20	3-90/1-6,S-1	-1.9
Total	8	545	1695	210	439	86	6	60	267	184	449	.259	.333	.420	100	-2	6	8	0	.942	-19	3-482/1-37,ODSC	-2.6

YEAR	TM/L	G	AB	R	H	2B	3B	HR	RBI	BB	SO	AVG	OBP	SLG	PRO+	BR/A	SB	CS	SBR	FA	FR	G/POS	TPR

■ BERT BLUE   Blue, Bird Wayne   b: 12/9/1877, Bettsville, Ohio   d: 9/2/29, Detroit, Mich.   BR/TR, 6'3", 200 lbs.   Deb: 6/15/08

1908	StL-A	11	24	2	9	1	2	0	1	3		.375	.444	.583	232	3	0			.942	1	/C-8	0.5
	Phi-A	6	18	2	3	0	0	0	1	0		.167	.167	.167	8	-2	0			1.000	1	/C-6	0.0
	Yr	17	42	4	12	1	2	0	2	3		.286	.333	.405	136	2	0			.967	2	C-14	0.5

■ LU BLUE   Blue, Luzerne Atwell   b: 3/5/1897, Washington, D.C.   d: 7/28/58, Alexandria, Va.   BB/TL, 5'10", 165 lbs.   Deb: 4/14/21

1921	Det-A	153	585	103	180	33	11	5	75	103	47	.308	.416	.427	117	19	13	17	-6	.990	-7	*1-152	0.2
1922	Det-A	145	584	131	175	31	9	6	45	82	48	.300	.392	.414	114	15	8	5	-1	.991	0	*1-144	0.8
1923	Det-A	129	504	100	143	27	7	1	46	96	40	.284	.402	.371	106	10	10	11	-4	.992	5	*1-129	0.3
1924	Det-A	108	395	81	123	26	7	2	53	64	26	.311	.413	.428	119	14	9	4	0	.986	3	*1-108	1.0
1925	Det-A	150	532	91	163	18	9	3	94	83	29	.306	.403	.391	104	7	19	5	3	.988	0	*1-148	0.1
1926	Det-A	128	429	92	123	24	14	1	52	90	18	.287	.413	.415	115	13	13	7	-0	.985	-5	*1-109/O-1	0.1
1927	Det-A	112	365	71	95	17	9	1	42	71	28	.260	.384	.364	94	-1	13	7	-0	.984	-2	*1-104	-0.9
1928	StL-A	154	549	116	154	32	11	14	80	105	43	.281	.400	.455	120	19	12	7	-1	.989	2	*1-154	0.7
1929	StL-A	151	573	111	168	40	10	6	61	126	32	.293	.422	.429	115	19	12	6	0	.994	-3	*1-151	0.1
1930	StL-A	117	425	85	100	27	5	4	42	81	44	.235	.363	.351	79	-12	12	7	-1	.987	0	*1-111	-2.1
1931	Chi-A	155	589	119	179	23	15	1	62	127	60	.304	.430	.399	126	31	13	3	2	.990	-3	*1-155	1.5
1932	Chi-A	112	373	51	93	21	2	0	43	64	21	.249	.364	.316	83	-7	17	6	2	.986	9	*1-105	-0.4
1933	Bro-N	1	1	0	0	0	0	0	0	0	0	.000	.000	.000	-99	-0	0			1.000	-0	/1-1	0.0
Total	13	1615	5904	1151	1696	319	109	44	695	1092	436	.287	.402	.401	109	126	151	85		.989	1	*1-1571/O-1	1.4

■ OSSIE BLUEGE   Bluege, Oswald Louis   b: 10/24/1900, Chicago, Ill.   d: 10/14/85, Edina, Minn.   BR/TR, 5'11", 162 lbs.   Deb: 4/24/22   FMC

1922	Was-A	19	61	5	12	1	0	0	2	7	7	.197	.300	.213	37	-5	1			.925	-3	3-17/S-2	-0.7
1923	Was-A	109	379	48	93	15	7	2	42	48	53	.245	.343	.338	84	-8	5	3	-0	.936	4	*3-106/2-4	0.4
1924	*Was-A	117	402	59	113	15	4	2	49	39	36	.281	.358	.353	86	-7	7	5	-1	.943	-12	*3-102,2-10/S-4	-1.1
1925	*Was-A	145	522	77	150	27	4	4	79	59	56	.287	.362	.377	89	-8	16	15	-4	.953	1	*3-144/S-4	-0.1
1926	Was-A	139	487	69	132	19	8	3	65	70	46	.271	.368	.361	93	-3	12	9	-2	.952	-19	*3-134/S-8	-1.5
1927	Was-A	146	503	71	138	21	10	1	66	57	47	.274	.354	.362	87	-9	15	5	2	.961	15	*3-146	1.4
1928	Was-A	146	518	78	154	33	7	2	75	46	27	.297	.364	.400	101	1	18	6	2	.960	12	*3-144/2-1	2.2
1929	Was-A	64	220	35	65	6	0	5	31	19	15	.295	.354	.391	91	-3	6	4	-1	.967	2	3-35,2-14,S-10	0.2
1930	Was-A	134	476	64	138	27	7	3	69	51	40	.290	.368	.395	93	-4	15	8	-0	.964	-1	*3-134	0.3
1931	Was-A	152	570	82	155	25	7	8	98	50	39	.272	.336	.382	88	-10	16	10	-1	**.960**	-5	*3-152/S-1	-0.7
1932	Was-A	149	507	64	131	22	4	5	64	83	41	.258	.367	.347	87	-7	9	7	-2	.970	6	*3-149	0.8
1933	*Was-A	140	501	63	131	14	0	6	71	55	34	.261	.338	.325	77	-15	6	7	-2	.965	-8	*3-138	-1.6
1934	Was-A	99	285	39	70	9	2	0	11	23	15	.246	.306	.291	57	-18	2	1	-0	.950	-3	3-41,S-30/2-5,O-5	-0.6
1935	Was-A★	100	320	44	84	14	3	0	34	37	21	.262	.341	.325	75	-11	2	2	-1	.967	1	S-58,3-25/2-4	-0.6
1936	Was-A	90	319	43	92	12	1	1	55	38	16	.288	.373	.342	83	-2	5	3	-0	.993	2	2-52,S-23,3-15	-0.1
1937	Was-A	42	127	12	36	4	2	1	13	19	9	.283	.355	.370	87	-2	1	1	-0	.952	2	S-28/1-2,3-2	0.1
1938	Was-A	58	184	25	48	12	1	0	21	21	11	.261	.340	.337	75	-7	3	1	0	.990	1	2-38,S-10/1-1,3-1	-0.3
1939	Was-A	18	59	5	9	0	0	0	3	7	2	.153	.242	.153	3	-9	1			.989	1	1-11/2-2,S-2,3-2	-0.8
Total	18	1867	6440	883	1751	276	67	43	848	723	515	.272	.352	.356	85	-131	140	87	-10	.957	4	*3-1487,S-180,2/10	-2.7

■ OTTO BLUEGE   Bluege, Otto Adam "Squeaky"   b: 7/20/09, Chicago, Ill.   d: 6/28/77, Chicago, Ill.   BR/TR, 5'10", 154 lbs.   Deb: 4/12/32   F

1932	Cin-N	1	0	0	0	0	0	0	0	0	0	—	—	—			0			.000	0	R	0.0
1933	Cin-N	108	291	17	62	6	2	0	18	26	29	.213	.278	.247	52	-18	0			.937	-9	S-95,2-10/3-1	-2.2
Total	2	109	291	18	62	6	2	0	18	26	29	.213	.278	.247	52	-18	0			.937	-9	/S-95,2-10,3-1	-2.2

■ RED BLUHM   Bluhm, Harvey Fred   b: 6/27/1894, Cleveland, Ohio   d: 5/7/52, Flint, Mich.   BR/TR, 5'11", 165 lbs.   Deb: 7/3/18

1918	Bos-A	1	1	0	0	0	0	0	0	0	0	.000	.000	.000	-99	-0	0			.000	0	H	0.0

■ CHET BOAK   Boak, Chester Robert   b: 6/19/35, New Castle, Pa.   d: 11/28/83, Emporium, Pa.   BR/TR, 6', 180 lbs.   Deb: 9/18/60

1960	KC-A	5	13	1	2	0	0	0	1	0		.154	.214	.154	0	-2	0	0	0	.957	1	/2-5	-0.1
1961	Was-A	5	7	0	0	0	0	0	0	1	1	.000	.125	.000	-64	-2	1	0	0	1.000	-1	/2-1	-0.2
Total	2	10	20	1	2	0	0	0	1	1	3	.100	.182	.100	-22	-3	1	0	0	.962	0	/2-6	-0.3

■ FREDERICK BOARDMAN   Boardman, Frederick   Deb: 8/29/1874

1874	Bal-n	1	4	0	1	0	0	0	0			.250	.250	.250	61	-0	0	0	0	.000	-0	/O-1	0.0

■ RANDY BOBB   Bobb, Mark Randall   b: 1/1/48, Los Angeles, Cal.   d: 6/13/82, Carnelian Bay, Cal   BR/TR, 6'1", 185 lbs.   Deb: 8/15/68

1968	Chi-N	7	8	0	1	0	0	0	0	1		.125	.222	.125	6	-1	0	0	0	1.000	0	/C-7	-0.1
1969	Chi-N	3	2	0	0	0	0	0	0	0	0	.000	.000	.000	-89	-0	0	0	0	1.000	0	/C-2	0.0
Total	2	10	10	0	1	0	0	0	0	1	3	.100	.182	.100	-14	-1	0	0	0	1.000	0	/C-9	-0.1

■ JOHN BOCCABELLA   Boccabella, John Dominic   b: 6/29/41, San Francisco, Cal   BR/TR, 6'1", 200 lbs.   Deb: 9/2/63

1963	Chi-N	24	74	7	14	4	1	1	5	6	21	.189	.250	.311	57	-4	0	1	-1	.996	-1	1-24	-0.7
1964	Chi-N	9	23	4	9	2	1	0	6	0	3	.391	.391	.565	159	2	0	0	-1	1.000	-1	/1-5,O-2	0.1
1965	Chi-N	6	12	2	4	0	0	2	4	1	2	.333	.385	.833	227	2	0	0	-0	1.000	-0	/1-2,O-1	0.2
1966	Chi-N	75	206	22	47	9	0	6	25	14	39	.228	.277	.359	74	-7	0	1	-1	.981	-1	O-33,1-30/C-5	-1.0
1967	Chi-N	25	35	4	6	0	0	1	8	3	7	.171	.256	.257	45	-2	0	0	-1	1.000	-1	/O-9,1-3,C-1	-0.4
1968	Chi-N	7	14	0	1	0	0	0	1	2	2	.071	.188	.071	-19	-2	0	0	-0	1.000	1	/C-4,O-1	-0.3
1969	Mon-N	40	86	4	9	2	0	1	6	6	30	.105	.172	.163	-6	-12	0	1	-1	.993	1	C-32	-1.1
1970	Mon-N	61	145	18	39	3	1	5	17	11	24	.269	.321	.407	94	-2	0	1	-1	.993	10	1-33,C-24/3-1	0.6
1971	Mon-N	74	177	15	39	11	0	3	15	14	26	.220	.281	.333	73	-6	0	1	-1	.979	-1	C-37,1-37/3-2	-1.0
1972	Mon-N	83	207	14	47	8	1	1	19	9	29	.227	.263	.290	56	-12	1	2	-1	.983	8	C-73/1-7,3-1	-0.4
1973	Mon-N	118	403	25	94	13	2	6	46	26	57	.233	.281	.318	63	-20	1	1	-0	.980	1	*C-117/1-1	-1.5
1974	SF-N	29	80	6	11	3	0	0	5	4	6	.138	.179	.175	-1	-11	0	0	0	.991	-0	C-26	-1.3
Total	12	551	1462	117	320	56	5	26	148	96	246	.219	.269	.317	62	-76	3	7	-3	.984	14	C-319,1-142/O-46,3	-6.8

■ MILT BOCEK   Bocek, Milton Frank   b: 7/16/12, Chicago, Ill.   BR/TR, 6'1", 185 lbs.   Deb: 9/3/33

1933	Chi-A	11	22	3	8	1	0	1	3	4	6	.364	.462	.545	173	2	0	0	0	1.000	-2	/O-6	0.0
1934	Chi-A	19	38	3	8	1	0	0	3	5	5	.211	.302	.237	39	-3	0	0	0	1.000	2	O-10	-0.1
Total	2	30	60	6	16	2	0	1	6	9	11	.267	.362	.350	86	-1	0	0	0	1.000	1	/O-16	-0.1

■ BRUCE BOCHTE   Bochte, Bruce Anton   b: 11/12/50, Pasadena, Cal.   BL/TL, 6'3", 200 lbs.   Deb: 7/19/74

1974	Cal-A	57	196	24	53	4	1	5	26	18	23	.270	.335	.378	111	3	6	3	-0	.985	-4	O-39,1-24	-0.4
1975	Cal-A	107	375	41	107	19	3	6	48	45	43	.285	.365	.376	118	10	3	4	-2	.987	-7	*1-105/D-1	-0.5
1976	Cal-A	146	466	53	120	17	1	4	49	64	53	.258	.350	.311	101	3	4	5	-2	.988	-2	O-86,1-59/D-1	-0.9
1977	Cal-A	25	100	12	29	6	4	2	8	7	4	.290	.336	.390	101	0	3	2	-0	1.000	0	O-24/D-1	0.1
	Cle-A	112	392	52	119	19	1	5	43	40	38	.304	.368	.395	112	7	3	2	-0	.966	5	O-76,1-36/D-1	0.7
	Yr	137	492	64	148	23	1	7	51	47	42	.301	.362	.394	110	7	6	4	-1	.974	7	*O-100,1-36/D-2	0.8
1978	Sea-A	140	486	58	128	25	3	11	55	60	47	.263	.346	.395	108	6	3	4	-2	.984	-4	O-91,D-43/1-1	-0.5
1979	Sea-A★	150	554	81	175	38	6	16	100	67	64	.316	.392	.493	134	28	2	2	-1	.991	5	*1-147	2.2
1980	Sea-A	148	520	69	156	34	4	13	78	72	81	.300	.385	.456	128	22	2	3	-1	.996	6	*1-133,D-11	1.8
1981	Sea-A	99	335	39	87	16	0	6	30	47	53	.260	.354	.361	102	2	1	3	-2	.995	-5	1-82,O-14/D-1	-0.9
1982	Sea-A	144	509	58	151	21	0	12	70	67	71	.297	.382	.409	114	12	8	5	-1	.988	-5	O-99,1-34/D-12	0.1
1984	Oak-A	148	469	58	124	23	0	5	52	52	59	.264	.338	.345	96	-2	3	2	-0	.993	-13	*1-144/D-2	-2.6
1985	Oak-A	137	424	48	125	14	1	6	60	49	58	.295	.368	.439	129	17	3	1	-0	.990	-9	*1-128	0.2
1986	Oak-A	125	407	57	104	13	2	6	43	66	68	.256	.358	.337	98	1	3	4	-2	.991	2	1-115/D-1	-0.6
Total	12	1538	5233	643	1478	250	21	100	658	653	662	.282	.363	.396	114	109	43	41	-12	.992	-30	*1-1008,O-429/D-74	-1.3

YEAR	TM/L	G	AB	R	H	2B	3B	HR	RBI	BB	SO	AVG	OBP	SLG	PRO+	BR/A	SB	CS	SBR	FA	FR	G/POS	TPR

■ BRUCE BOCHY
Bochy, Bruce Douglas   b: 4/16/55, Landes De Bussac, France   BR/TR, 6'4", 210 lbs.   Deb: 7/19/78   MC

1978	Hou-N	54	154	8	41	8	0	3	15	11	35	.266	.315	.377	100	-1	0	0	0	.974	3	C-53	0.3
1979	Hou-N	56	129	11	28	4	0	1	6	13	35	.217	.294	.271	59	-7	0	0	0	.970	-1	C-55	-0.7
1980	*Hou-N	22	22	0	4	1	0	0	0	5	7	.182	.357	.227	72	-1	0	0	0	1.000	-2	C-10/1-1	-0.3
1982	NY-N	17	49	4	15	4	0	2	8	4	6	.306	.358	.510	141	3	0	0	0	.961	4	C-16/1-1	0.7
1983	SD-N	23	42	2	9	1	0	3	0	0	9	.214	.214	.286	39	-4	0	0	0	1.000	2	C-11	-0.2
1984	*SD-N	37	92	10	21	5	1	4	15	3	21	.228	.253	.435	90	-2	0	1	-1	.988	5	C-36	0.4
1985	SD-N	48	112	16	30	2	0	6	13	6	30	.268	.305	.446	109	1	0	0	0	.988	1	C-46	0.3
1986	SD-N	63	127	16	32	9	0	8	22	14	23	.252	.326	.512	130	5	1	0	0	.991	3	C-48	1.0
1987	SD-N	38	75	8	12	3	0	2	11	11	21	.160	.267	.280	47	-6	0	1	-1	.962	-4	C-23	-0.9
Total	9	358	802	75	192	37	2	26	93	67	177	.239	.300	.388	92	-12	1	4		.979	9	C-298/1-2	0.6

■ EDDIE BOCKMAN
Bockman, Joseph Edward   b: 7/26/20, Santa Ana, Cal.   BR/TR, 5'9", 175 lbs.   Deb: 9/11/46

1946	NY-A	4	12	2	1	0	0	0	1	4		.083	.154	.167	-10	-2	0	0	0	.933	1	/3-4	0.0
1947	Cle-A	46	66	8	17	2	1	1	14	5	17	.258	.310	.394	97	-1	0	0	0	.946	9	3-12/2-4,S-1,O-1	0.8
1948	Pit-N	70	176	23	42	7	1	4	23	17	35	.239	.309	.358	79	-5	2			.962	8	3-51/2-1	0.2
1949	Pit-N	79	220	21	49	6	1	6	19	23	31	.223	.296	.341	69	-10	3			.959	6	3-68/2-5	-0.5
Total	4	199	474	54	109	16	4	11	56	46	87	.230	.299	.350	74	-18	5	0		.958	24	3-135/2-10,O-1,S-1	0.5

■ PING BODIE
Bodie, Frank Stephan (b: Francesco Stephano Pezzolo)
b: 10/8/1887, San Francisco, Cal.   d: 12/17/61, San Francisco, Cal   BR/TR, 5'8", 195 lbs.   Deb: 4/22/11

1911	Chi-A	145	551	75	159	27	13	4	97	49		.289	.348	.407	114	9	14			.969	7	*O-128,2-16	0.9
1912	Chi-A	138	472	58	139	24	5	5	72	43		.294	.358	.407	123	13	12			.969	-12	*O-130	-0.6
1913	Chi-A	127	406	39	107	14	8	8	48	35	57	.264	.325	.397	112	4	5			.968	-5	*O-119	-0.6
1914	Chi-A	107	327	21	75	9	5	3	29	21	35	.229	.278	.315	79	-9	12	11	-3	.959	-2	O-95	-2.1
1917	Phi-A	148	557	51	162	28	11	7	74	53	40	.291	.356	.418	138	24	13			.963	5	*O-145/1-1	2.2
1918	NY-A	91	324	36	83	12	6	3	46	27	24	.256	.319	.358	102	-0	6			.971	4	O-90	-0.1
1919	NY-A	134	475	45	132	27	8	6	59	36	46	.278	.334	.406	107	3	15			.959	-8	*O-134	-1.5
1920	NY-A	129	471	63	139	26	12	7	79	40	30	.295	.350	.446	106	3	6	14	-7	.968	-10	O-129	-2.2
1921	NY-A	31	81	5	14	2	1	0	8	2	8	.172	.242	.241	23	-10	0	1	-1	.944	-6	O-25	-1.8
Total	9	1050	3670	393	1011	169	72	43	516	312	240	.275	.335	.396	110	36	83	26		.963	-27	O-995/2-16,1-1	-5.8

■ TONY BOECKEL
Boeckel, Norman Doxie   b: 8/25/1892, Los Angeles, Cal.   d: 2/16/24, Torrey Pines, Cal.   BR/TR, 5'10.5", 175 lbs.   Deb: 7/23/17

1917	Pit-N	64	219	16	58	11	4	0	23	8	31	.265	.297	.324	87	-4	6			.935	-4	3-62	-0.7
1919	Pit-N	45	152	18	38	9	2	0	16	18	20	.250	.333	.336	97	0	11			.930	-8	3-45	-0.7
	Bos-N	95	365	42	91	11	5	1	26	35	13	.249	.317	.315	94	-2	10			.960	-4	3-93	-0.2
	Yr	140	517	60	129	20	7	1	42	53	33	.250	.322	.321	95	-2	21			.951	-12	*3-138	-0.9
1920	Bos-N	153	582	70	156	28	5	3	62	38	50	.268	.314	.349	94	-5	18	15	-4	.936	-7	*3-149/S-3,2-1	-0.8
1921	Bos-N	153	592	93	185	20	13	10	84	52	41	.313	.370	.441	120	17	20	15	-3	.933	-12	*3-153	1.2
1922	Bos-N	119	402	61	116	19	6	6	47	35	32	.289	.349	.410	99	-1	14	8	-1	.952	-11	3-106	-0.4
1923	Bos-N	148	568	72	169	32	4	7	79	51	31	.298	.357	.405	105	4	11	8	-2	.939	-10	*3-147/S-1	0.6
Total	6	777	2880	372	813	130	36	27	337	237	218	.282	.339	.381	102	10	90	46		.941	-55	3-755/S-4,2-1	-1.0

■ LEN BOEHMER
Boehmer, Leonard Joseph Stephen   b: 6/28/41, Flinthill, Mo.   BR/TR, 6'1", 192 lbs.   Deb: 6/18/67

1967	Cin-N	2	3	0	0	0	0	0	0	0	0	.000	.000	.000	-90	-1	0	0	0	1.000	-0	/2-1	-0.1
1969	NY-A	45	108	5	19	4	0	0	7	8	10	.176	.233	.213	26	-11	0	1	-1	.995	1	1-21/3-8,2-1,S-1	-1.2
1971	NY-A	3	5	0	0	0	0	0	0	0	0	.000	.000	.000	-99	-1	0	0	0	1.000	-0	/3-1	-0.2
Total	3	50	116	5	19	4	0	0	7	8	10	.164	.218	.198	18	-13	0	1	-1	.933	1	/1-21,3-9,2-2,S-1	-1.5

■ TIM BOGAR
Bogar, Timothy Paul   b: 10/28/66, Indianapolis, Ind.   BR/TR, 6'2", 198 lbs.   Deb: 4/21/93

1993	NY-N	78	205	19	50	13	0	3	25	14	29	.244	.302	.351	75	-7	0	1	-1	.972	15	S-66/3-7,2-6	1.1
1994	NY-N	50	52	5	8	0	0	2	5	4	11	.154	.214	.269	25	-6	1	0	0	.909	8	3-22,1-14/S-7,2O	0.2
1995	NY-N	78	145	17	42	7	0	1	21	9	25	.290	.331	.359	85	-3	1	0	0	.971	1	S-27,3-25,1-10/2O	-0.1
1996	NY-N	91	89	17	19	4	0	0	6	8	20	.213	.293	.258	50	-6	1	3	-2	1.000	8	1-32,3-25,S-19,2-8	0.0
Total	4	297	491	58	119	24	0	6	57	35	85	.242	.299	.328	68	-23	3	4	-2	.977	32	S-119/3-79,1-56,2O	1.2

■ TERRY BOGENER
Bogener, Terry Wayne   b: 9/28/55, Hannibal, Mo.   BL/TL, 6', 193 lbs.   Deb: 6/14/82

1982	Tex-A	24	60	6	13	2	1	1	4	4	8	.217	.288	.333	74	-2	2	0	1	1.000	-4	O-16/D-4	-0.5

■ WADE BOGGS
Boggs, Wade Anthony   b: 6/15/58, Omaha, Neb.   BL/TR, 6'2", 197 lbs.   Deb: 4/10/82

1982	Bos-A	104	338	51	118	14	1	5	44	35	21	.349	.410	.441	126	13	1	0	0	.994	18	1-49,3-44/O-1,D-3	2.8
1983	Bos-A	153	582	100	210	44	7	5	74	92	36	**.361**	.449	.486	147	41	3	3	-1	.947	8	*3-153	4.5
1984	Bos-A	158	625	109	203	31	4	6	55	89	44	.325	.409	.416	123	23	3	2	-0	.959	21	*3-156/D-2	4.2
1985	Bos-A★	161	653	107	**240**	42	3	8	78	96	61	.368	.452	.478	149	49	2	3	-1	.965	8	*3-161	5.3
1986	*Bos-A★	149	580	107	207	47	2	8	71	**105**	44	.357	.455	.486	156	51	0	4	-2	.953	-1	*3-149	4.3
1987	Bos-A★	147	551	108	200	40	6	24	89	105	48	.363	.467	.588	173	63	1	3	-2	.965	3	*3-145/1-1,D-1	**5.8**
1988	*Bos-A★	155	584	**128**	214	**45**	6	5	58	**125**	34	.366	.480	.490	165	60	2	3	-1	.971	-5	*3-151/D-3	5.3
1989	Bos-A★	156	621	**113**	205	**51**	7	3	54	107	51	.330	**.434**	.449	141	39	2	6	-3	.958	-4	*3-152/D-3	3.3
1990	*Bos-A★	155	619	89	187	44	5	6	63	87	68	.302	.389	.418	120	19	0	0	0	.946	-22	*3-152/D-3	-0.2
1991	Bos-A★	144	546	93	181	42	2	8	51	89	32	.332	.423	.460	138	32	1	2	-1	.968	-1	*3-140	3.2
1992	Bos-A★	143	514	62	133	22	4	7	50	74	31	.259	.356	.358	94	-2	1	3	-2	.952	-1	*3-117,D-21	-0.5
1993	NY-A★	143	560	83	169	26	1	2	59	74	49	.302	.383	.363	105	7	0	1	-1	**.970**	20	*3-134/D-8	2.6
1994	NY-A★	97	366	61	125	19	1	11	55	61	29	.342	.433	.489	144	27	2	1	0	.962	13	3-93/1-4	3.6
1995	*NY-A★	126	460	76	149	22	4	5	63	74	50	.324	.418	.422	120	17	1	1	-0	**.981**	-6	*3-117/1-9	1.0
1996	*NY-A★	132	501	80	156	29	2	2	41	67	32	.311	.393	.389	97	0	1	2	-1	.974	-6	*3-123/D-4	-0.6
Total	15	2123	8100	1367	2697	518	55	105	905	1280	630	.333	.425	.449	134	440	20	32	-13	.962	47	*3-1987/1-63,D-48,O	44.6

■ CHARLIE BOHN
Bohn, Charles   b: 1857, Cleveland, Ohio   d: 8/1/03, Cleveland, Ohio   BR/TR, 5'9", 165 lbs.   Deb: 6/20/1882

1882	Lou-a	4	13	0	2	0	0	0		0		.154	.154	.154	4	-1				.667	1	/O-2,P-2	0.0

■ SAM BOHNE
Bohne, Samuel Arthur (b: Samuel Arthur Cohen)   b: 10/22/1896, San Francisco, Cal   d: 5/23/77, Palo Alto, Cal.   BR/TR, 5'8.5", 175 lbs.   Deb: 9/9/16

1916	StL-N	14	38	3	9	0	0	0	4	6		.237	.310	.237	69	-1	3			.870	-4	S-14	-0.5
1921	Cin-N	153	613	98	175	28	16	3	44	54	38	.285	.347	.398	101	1	26	22	-5	.973	6	*2-102,3-53	1.0
1922	Cin-N	112	383	53	105	14	5	3	51	39	18	.274	.344	.360	83	-9	13	8	-1	.958	11	2-85,S-20	0.5
1923	Cin-N	139	539	77	136	18	10	3	47	48	37	.252	.316	.340	74	-20	16	19	-7	.975	5	2-96,3-35/S-9,1-1	-1.6
1924	Cin-N	100	349	42	89	15	9	4	46	18	24	.255	.293	.384	81	-10	9	6	-1	.941	-8	2-48,S-40,3-12	-1.5
1925	Cin-N	73	214	24	55	9	2	4	24	14	14	.257	.303	.336	65	-12	6	4	-1	.933	-8	S-49,2-10/O-4,13	-1.4
1926	Cin-N	25	54	6	11	0	2	0	5	4	8	.204	.259	.278	46	-4	1			.931	-3	S-20	-0.5
	Bro-N	47	125	4	25	3	2	1	11	12	9	.200	.270	.280	49	-9	1			.965	11	2-31,3-15	0.3
	Yr	72	179	12	36	3	4	1	16	16	17	.201	.267	.279	48	-13	2			.965	8	2-31,S-20,3-15	-0.2
Total	7	663	2315	309	605	87	45	16	228	193	154	.261	.321	.359	81	-64	75	59		.966	11	2-372,S-152,3/O1	-3.7

■ BRUCE BOISCLAIR
Boisclair, Bruce Armand   b: 12/9/52, Putnam, Conn.   BL/TL, 6'2", 190 lbs.   Deb: 9/11/74

1974	NY-N	7	12	0	3	1	0	0	1	1		.250	.308	.333	81	-0	1			.923	1	/O-5	0.1
1976	NY-N	110	286	42	82	13	3	2	13	28	55	.287	.350	.374	112	4	9	5	-0	.981	-6	O-87	-0.5
1977	NY-N	127	307	41	90	21	1	4	44	31	57	.293	.360	.407	110	5	6	4	-1	.959	-9	O-91/1-9	-0.8
1978	NY-N	107	214	24	48	7	1	4	15	23	43	.224	.300	.322	77	-7	3	1	-1	.983	5	O-69/1-1	-1.6
1979	NY-N	59	98	7	18	5	1	0	4	3	28	.184	.216	.255	29	-10	0	2	-1	1.000	-2	O-24/1-1	-1.5
Total	5	410	917	114	241	47	6	10	77	86	183	.263	.327	.360	95	-8	18	14	-3	.975	-6	O-276/1-11	-4.3

■ BOB BOKEN
Boken, Robert Anthony   b: 2/23/08, Maryville, Ill.   d: 10/6/88, Las Vegas, Nev.   BR/TR, 6'2", 165 lbs.   Deb: 4/25/33

1933	Was-A	55	133	19	37	5	2	3	26	9	16	.278	.324	.414	92	-1	0	0	0	.969	-2	2-31,3-19,S-10	-0.1

YEAR	TM/L	G	AB	R	H	2B	3B	HR	RBI	BB	SO	AVG	OBP	SLG	PRO+	BR/A	SB	CS	SBR	FA	FR	G/POS	TPR
1934	Was-A	11	27	5	6	1	1	0	6	3	1	.222	.300	.333	66	-1	2	0	1	.864	1	/3-6,2-1	0.1
	Chi-A	81	297	30	70	9	1	3	40	15	32	.236	.277	.303	47	-24	2	1	0	.929	-10	2-57,S-22	-2.7
	Yr	92	324	35	76	10	2	3	46	18	33	.235	.277	.306	49	-25	4	1	1	.929	-9	2-58,S-22/3-6	-2.6
Total	2	147	457	54	113	15	4	6	72	27	49	.247	.291	.337	62	-26	4	1	1	.941	-11	/2-89,S-32,3-25	-2.7

■ BOLAND   Boland   Deb: 9/4/1875

| 1875 | Atl-n | 1 | 4 | 0 | 0 | 0 | 0 | 0 | 0 | 0 | 0 | .000 | .000 | .000 | -99 | -1 | 0 | 0 | 0 | .750 | -0 | /3-1 | -0.1 |

■ ED BOLAND   Boland, Edward John   b: 4/18/08, Long Island City, N.Y.   d: 2/5/93, Clearwater, Fla.   BL/TL, 5'10", 165 lbs.   Deb: 9/18/34

1934	Phi-N	8	30	2	9	1	1	0	5	0	2	.300	.300	.400	76	-1	1			.778	-2	/O-7	-0.3
1935	Phi-N	30	47	5	10	0	0	0	4	4	6	.213	.275	.213	30	-5	1			.833	-3	O-10	-0.7
1944	Was-A	19	59	4	16	4	0	0	14	0	6	.271	.271	.339	77	-2	0	0	0	.889	-1	O-14	-0.4
Total	3	57	136	11	35	5	1	0	23	4	14	.257	.279	.309	59	-8	2	0	2	.852	-5	/O-31	-1.4

■ CHARLIE BOLD   Bold, Charles Dickens "Dutch"   b: 10/27/1894, Karlskrona, Sweden   d: 7/29/78, Chelsea, Mass.   BR/TR, 6'2", 185 lbs.   Deb: 8/24/14

| 1914 | StL-A | 2 | 1 | 0 | 0 | 0 | 0 | 0 | 0 | 0 | 0 | .000 | .000 | .000 | -99 | -0 | 0 | | | .500 | -0 | /1-1 | -0.1 |

■ CARL BOLES   Boles, Carl Theodore   b: 10/31/34, Center Point, Ark.   BR/TR, 5'11", 185 lbs.   Deb: 8/2/62

| 1962 | SF-N | 19 | 24 | 4 | 9 | 0 | 0 | 0 | 1 | 0 | 6 | .375 | .375 | .375 | 104 | 0 | 0 | 0 | 0 | .833 | -1 | /O-7 | -0.2 |

■ JOE BOLEY   Boley, John Peter (b: John Peter Bolinsky)   b: 7/19/1896, Mahanoy City, Pa.   d: 12/30/62, Mahanoy City, Pa.   BR/TR, 5'11", 170 lbs.   Deb: 4/12/27

1927	Phi-A	118	370	49	115	18	8	1	52	26	14	.311	.361	.411	95	-3	8	5	-1	.951	-11	*S-114	-0.3
1928	Phi-A	132	425	49	112	20	3	0	49	32	11	.264	.317	.325	67	-20	5	1	1	.949	-17	*S-132	-2.1
1929	*Phi-A	91	303	36	76	17	6	2	47	24	16	.251	.310	.366	71	-14	1	0	0	.963	-10	S-88/3-1	-1.2
1930	*Phi-A	121	420	41	116	22	2	4	55	32	26	.276	.335	.367	74	-16	0	0	0	**.970**	-7	*S-120	-0.9
1931	*Phi-A	67	224	26	51	9	3	0	20	15	13	.228	.282	.295	49	-17	1	1	-0	.954	-13	S-62/2-1	-2.3
1932	Phi-A	10	34	2	7	2	0	0	4	1	4	.206	.229	.265	26	-4	0	1	-1	.897	-7	S-10	-1.0
	Cle-A	1	4	0	1	0	0	0	0	0	0	.250	.250	.250	28	-0	0	0	0	.000	0	/S-1	0.0
	Yr	11	38	2	8	2	0	0	4	1	4	.211	.231	.263	27	-4	0	1	-1	.897	-7	S-11	-1.0
Total	6	540	1780	203	478	88	22	7	227	130	84	.269	.323	.354	72	-74	15	8	-0	.957	-64	S-527/2-1,3-1	-7.8

■ JIM BOLGER   Bolger, James Cyril "Dutch"   b: 2/23/32, Cincinnati, Ohio   BR/TR, 6'2", 180 lbs.   Deb: 6/24/50

1950	Cin-N	2	1	0	0	0	0	0	0	0	0	.000	.000	.000	-99	-0	0			.000	-1	/O-2	-0.1
1951	Cin-N	2	0	0	0	0	0	0	0	0	0	—	—	—	—	0	1	0	0	1.000	0	R	0.0
1954	Cin-N	5	3	1	1	0	0	0	0	0	1	.333	.333	.333	72	-0	0	0	0	.000	-1	/O-2	-0.1
1955	Chi-N	64	160	19	33	5	4	0	7	9	17	.206	.257	.287	45	-13	2	2	-1	.955	-3	O-51	-1.8
1957	Chi-N	112	273	28	75	4	1	5	29	10	36	.275	.308	.352	78	-9	0	1	-1	.987	2	O-63/3-3	-1.1
1958	Chi-N	84	120	15	27	4	1	1	11	9	20	.225	.285	.300	56	-8	0	1	-1	.940	-6	O-37	-1.5
1959	Cle-A	8	5	7	0	0	0	0	0	0	1	.000	.125	.000	-65	-2	0	0	0	.000	0	H	-0.2
	Phi-N	35	48	1	4	1	0	0	1	3	8	.083	.137	.104	-34	-9	0	0	0	.938	-1	/O-9	-1.0
Total	7	312	612	65	140	14	6	6	48	32	83	.229	.274	.301	54	-40	3	4		.966	-9	O-164/3-3	-5.8

■ FRANK BOLICK   Bolick, Frank Charles   b: 6/28/66, Ashland, Pa.   BB/TR, 5'10", 180 lbs.   Deb: 4/5/93

| 1993 | Mon-N | 95 | 213 | 25 | 45 | 13 | 0 | 4 | 24 | 23 | 37 | .211 | .300 | .329 | 65 | -10 | 1 | 0 | 0 | .992 | 3 | 1-51,3-24 | -1.1 |

■ FRANK BOLLING   Bolling, Frank Elmore   b: 11/16/31, Mobile, Ala.   BR/TR, 6'1", 175 lbs.   Deb: 4/13/54   F

1954	Det-A	117	368	46	87	15	2	6	38	36	51	.236	.304	.337	77	-12	3	5	-2	.974	-29	*2-113	-3.8
1956	Det-A	102	366	53	103	21	7	7	45	42	51	.281	.359	.434	108	4	6	2	1	.978	-15	*2-102	-0.2
1957	Det-A	146	576	72	149	27	6	15	40	57	64	.259	.328	.405	96	-3	4	9	-4	.980	-3	*2-146	0.2
1958	Det-A	154	610	91	164	25	4	14	75	54	54	.269	.332	.392	92	-7	6	4	1	**.985**	8	*2-154	1.2
1959	Det-A	127	459	56	122	18	3	13	55	45	37	.266	.341	.403	98	-1	2	2	-1	.987	-1	*2-126	0.7
1960	Det-A	139	536	64	136	20	4	9	59	40	48	.254	.305	.356	77	-18	7	4	-0	.978	-5	*2-138	-0.9
1961	Mil-N★	148	585	86	153	16	4	15	56	57	62	.262	.330	.379	93	-6	7	3	0	**.988**	1	*2-148	1.1
1962	Mil-N★	122	406	45	110	17	4	9	43	35	45	.271	.335	.399	99	-1	2	2	-1	**.989**	-9	*2-119	0.1
1963	Mil-N	142	542	73	132	18	2	5	43	41	47	.244	.300	.312	77	-15	2	1	0	.981	-5	*2-141	-0.8
1964	Mil-N	120	352	35	70	11	1	5	34	21	44	.199	.248	.278	48	-24	0	1	-1	**.985**	-9	*2-117	-2.7
1965	Mil-N	148	535	55	141	26	3	7	50	24	41	.264	.295	.363	84	-12	0	4	-2	.976	-16	*2-147	-1.9
1966	Atl-N	75	227	16	48	7	1	3	23	10	22	.211	.248	.256	40	-18	1	1	-0	.983	-15	2-67	-3.2
Total	12	1540	5562	692	1415	221	40	106	556	462	558	.254	.315	.366	85	-114	40	38	-11	.982	-98	*2-1518	-10.2

■ JACK BOLLING   Bolling, John Edward   b: 2/20/17, Mobile, Ala.   BL/TL, 5'11", 168 lbs.   Deb: 6/10/39

1939	Phi-N	69	211	27	61	11	0	3	13	11	10	.289	.324	.384	92	-3	6			.982	2	1-48	-0.6
1944	Bro-N	56	131	21	46	14	1	1	25	14	4	.351	.418	.496	159	10	0			.991	1	1-27	1.0
Total	2	125	342	48	107	25	1	4	38	25	14	.313	.361	.427	118	8	6			.985	3	/1-75	0.4

■ MILT BOLLING   Bolling, Milton Joseph   b: 8/9/30, Mississippi City, Miss.   BR/TR, 6'1", 180 lbs.   Deb: 9/10/52   F

1952	Bos-A	11	36	4	8	1	0	1	3	3	5	.222	.282	.333	66	-2	0	1	-1	.984	6	S-11	0.4
1953	Bos-A	109	323	30	85	12	1	5	28	23	41	.263	.318	.353	77	-11	1	4	-2	.956	5	*S-109	-0.1
1954	Bos-A	113	370	42	92	20	3	6	36	47	55	.249	.340	.368	84	-8	2	4	-2	.946	15	*S-107/3-5	1.5
1955	Bos-A	6	5	0	1	0	0	0	0	0	0	.200	.200	.200	7	-1	0	0	0	.800	-1	/S-2	-0.1
1956	Bos-A	45	118	19	25	3	2	5	8	18	20	.212	.321	.347	68	-6	0	1	-1	.947	-8	S-26,3-11/2-1	-1.2
1957	Bos-A	1	1	0	0	0	0	0	0	0	0	.000	.000	.000	-95	-0	0	0	0	.000	0	H	0.0
	Was-A	91	277	29	63	12	1	4	19	18	59	.227	.279	.321	64	-14	2	2	-1	.982	8	2-53,S-37/3-1	-0.1
	Yr	92	278	29	63	12	1	4	19	18	59	.227	.279	.320	64	-14	2	2	-1	.982	8	2-53,S-37/3-1	-0.1
1958	Det-A	13	31	3	6	2	0	0	5	2	8	.194	.306	.258	53	-2	0	0	0	.946	2	S-13/2-1,3-1	0.1
Total	7	400	1161	127	280	50	7	19	94	114	188	.241	.314	.345	74	-43	5	12	-6	.952	28	S-305/2-55,3-18	0.5

■ DON BOLLWEG   Bollweg, Donald Raymond   b: 2/12/21, Wheaton, Ill.   d: 5/26/96, Wheaton, Ill.   BL/TL, 6'1", 190 lbs.   Deb: 9/28/50

1950	StL-N	4	11	0	2	0	0	0	1	1	1	.182	.250	.182	15	-1	0			1.000	-1	/1-4	-0.2
1951	StL-N	6	9	1	1	1	0	0	2	0	2	.111	.111	.222	-13	-1	0	0	0	.941	1	/1-2	-0.2
1953	*NY-A	70	155	24	46	6	4	6	24	21	31	.297	.384	.503	143	9	0	0	0	.983	-4	1-43	0.4
1954	Phi-A	103	268	35	60	15	3	5	24	35	33	.224	.320	.358	85	-5	1	0	0	.978	2	1-71	-0.7
1955	KC-A	12	9	1	1	0	0	0	2	3	1	.111	.333	.111	23	-1	0	0	0	1.000	-0	/1-3	-0.1
Total	5	195	452	62	110	22	7	11	53	60	68	.243	.337	.396	100	0	2	0	0	.980	-3	1-123	-0.8

■ CECIL BOLTON   Bolton, Cecil Glenford "Glenn"   b: 2/13/04, Booneville, Miss.   d: 8/25/93, Jackson, Miss.   BL/TR, 6'4", 195 lbs.   Deb: 9/21/28

| 1928 | Cle-A | 4 | 13 | 1 | 2 | 0 | 2 | 0 | 2 | 2 | 2 | .154 | .267 | .462 | 87 | -0 | 0 | | | .955 | -1 | /1-4 | -0.2 |

■ CLIFF BOLTON   Bolton, William Clifton   b: 4/10/07, High Point, N.C.   d: 4/21/79, Lexington, N.C.   BL/TR, 5'9", 160 lbs.   Deb: 4/20/31

1931	Was-A	23	43	3	11	0	1	0	6	1	5	.256	.273	.326	56	-3	0			.947	-6	C-13	-0.7
1933	*Was-A	33	39	4	16	1	1	0	6	3	1	.410	.500	.462	164	4	0	0	0	.889	-2	/C-9,O-1	0.3
1934	Was-A	42	148	12	40	9	7	1	17	11	9	.270	.321	.365	80	-5	2	0	1	.981	-9	C-39	-0.5
1935	Was-A	110	375	47	114	18	11	2	55	58	13	.304	.399	.427	117	11	0	1	-1	.971	-23	*C-106	-0.6
1936	Was-A	86	289	41	84	18	4	2	51	25	12	.291	.349	.401	90	-5	0	0	0	.979	-3	C-83	-0.4
1937	Det-A	27	57	6	15	2	0	1	9	1	2	.263	.354	.351	76	-2	0	0	0	.982	0	C-13	-0.1
1941	Was-A	14	11	0	0	0	0	0	0	1	0	.000	.083	.000	-80	-3	0	0	0	1.000	0	/C-3	-0.3
Total	7	335	962	113	280	49	18	6	143	110	50	.291	.366	.398	98	-2	3	3	-1	.974	-36	C-266/O-1	-2.3

■ TOMMY BOND   Bond, Thomas Henry   b: 4/2/1856, Granard, Ireland   d: 1/24/41, Boston, Mass.   BR/TR, 5'7.5", 160 lbs.   Deb: 5/5/1874   MU

1874	Atl-n	55	245	25	54	10	1	0	20	0	0	.220	.224	.269	65	-8	0	0	0	.841	-5	*P-55	0.0
1875	Har-n	72	289	32	77	11	3	0	33	0	5	.266	.266	.325	99	-1	5	1	1	.905	8	P-40,O-29/1-4,2-3	0.3
1876	Har-N	45	182	18	50	8	0	0	21	0	4	.275	.275	.319	90	-3				.887	5	P-45	0.0

YEAR	TM/L	G	AB	R	H	2B	3B	HR	RBI	BB	SO	AVG	OBP	SLG	PRO+	BR/A	SB	CS	SBR	FA	FR	G/POS	TPR
1877	Bos-N	61	259	32	59	4	3	0	30	1	15	.228	.231	.266	54	-14				.937	3	*P-58/O-3	-0.1
1878	Bos-N	59	236	22	50	4	1	0	23	0	9	.212	.212	.237	44	-15				.941	1	*P-59/O-2	-0.1
1879	Bos-N	65	257	35	62	3	1	0	21	6	8	.241	.259	.261	70	-8				**.957**	5	*P-64/O-5,1-1	-0.2
1880	Bos-N	76	282	27	62	4	1	0	24	8	14	.220	.241	.241	66	-9				.940	13	*P-63,O-26/3-1,1-1	0.0
1881	Bos-N	3	10	0	2	0	0	0	0	0	0	.200	.200	.200	27	-1				1.000	1	/P-3	0.0
1882	Wor-N	8	30	1	4	0	0	0	2	2	3	.133	.188	.133	5	-3				.714	-3	/O-8,P-2,M	-0.5
1884	Bos-U	37	162	21	48	8	0	0			4	.296	.313	.346	101	-4				.863	1	P-23,O-17/3-1	-0.4
	Ind-a	7	23	0	3	1	1	0				.130	.130	.261	25	-2				.700	-2	/P-5,O-2	-0.1
Total	2 n	127	534	57	131	21	4	0	53	1	10	.245	.247	.300	84	-9	5	1	1	.867	17	P-95,O-29,1-4,2-3	0.3
Total	8	361	1441	156	340	32	7	0	121	21	53	.236	.247	.268	66	-59				.927	24	P-322/O-63,3-2,1-2	-1.4

■ WALT BOND
Bond, Walter Franklin b: 10/19/37, Denmark, Tenn. d: 9/14/67, Houston, Tex. BL/TL, 6'7", 228 lbs. Deb: 4/19/60

YEAR	TM/L	G	AB	R	H	2B	3B	HR	RBI	BB	SO	AVG	OBP	SLG	PRO+	BR/A	SB	CS	SBR	FA	FR	G/POS	TPR
1960	Cle-A	40	131	19	29	2	1	5	18	13	14	.221	.306	.366	84	-3	4	1	1	1.000	2	O-36	-0.2
1961	Cle-A	38	52	7	9	1	1	2	7	6	10	.173	.271	.346	65	-3	1	0	0	1.000	-1	O-12	-0.4
1962	Cle-A	12	50	10	19	3	0	6	17	4	9	.380	.426	.800	228	9	1	0	0	1.000	-0	O-12	0.8
1964	Hou-N	148	543	63	138	16	7	20	85	38	90	.254	.312	.420	110	6	2	2	-1	.989	-8	1-76,O-71	-0.9
1965	Hou-N	117	407	46	107	17	5	7	47	42	51	.263	.339	.366	106	3	2	1	0	.983	-5	1-74,O-38	-0.7
1967	Min-A	10	16	4	5	1	0	1	5	3	1	.313	.421	.563	174	2	0	0	0	.875	0	/O-3	0.2
Total	6	365	1199	149	307	40	14	41	179	106	175	.256	.325	.410	110	14	10	4	1	.974	-11	O-172,1-150	-1.2

■ BARRY BONDS
Bonds, Barry Lamar b: 7/24/64, Riverside, Cal. BL/TL, 6'1", 185 lbs. Deb: 5/30/86 F

YEAR	TM/L	G	AB	R	H	2B	3B	HR	RBI	BB	SO	AVG	OBP	SLG	PRO+	BR/A	SB	CS	SBR	FA	FR	G/POS	TPR
1986	Pit-N	113	413	72	92	26	3	16	48	65	102	.223	.331	.416	102	2	36	7	7	.983	15	*O-110	2.0
1987	Pit-N	150	551	99	144	34	9	25	59	54	88	.261	.331	.492	114	9	32	10	4	.986	20	*O-145	2.7
1988	Pit-N	144	538	97	152	30	5	24	58	72	82	.283	.369	.491	147	33	17	11	-2	.980	5	*O-136	3.4
1989	Pit-N	159	580	96	144	34	6	19	58	93	93	.248	.353	.426	126	21	32	10	4	.984	20	*O-156	4.2
1990	*Pit-N★	151	519	104	156	32	3	33	114	93	83	.301	.410	**.565**	172	53	52	13	5	.983	15	*O-150	7.2
1991	*Pit-N★	153	510	95	149	28	5	25	116	107	73	.292	**.419**	.514	163	47	43	13	5	.991	14	*O-150	6.4
1992	*Pit-N★	140	473	**109**	147	36	5	34	103	**127**	69	.311	**.461**	**.624**	207	73	39	8	7	.991	11	*O-139	9.2
1993	SF-N★	159	539	129	181	38	4	**46**	**123**	126	79	.336	**.463**	**.677**	207	87	29	12	2	.984	5	*O-157	8.8
1994	SF-N★	112	391	89	122	18	1	37	81	74	43	.312	.429	.647	184	50	29	9	3	.986	8	*O-112	5.6
1995	SF-N★	144	506	109	149	30	7	33	104	**120**	83	.294	.434	.577	169	55	31	10	3	.980	15	*O-143	6.7
1996	SF-N★	158	517	122	159	27	3	42	129	**151**	76	.308	.465	.615	190	76	40	7	**8**	.980	10	*O-152	8.5
Total	11	1583	5537	1121	1595	333	51	334	993	1082	871	.288	.407	.548	162	506	380	110	48	.984	138	*O-1550	64.7

■ BOBBY BONDS
Bonds, Bobby Lee b: 3/15/46, Riverside, Cal. BR/TR, 6'1", 190 lbs. Deb: 6/25/68 FC

YEAR	TM/L	G	AB	R	H	2B	3B	HR	RBI	BB	SO	AVG	OBP	SLG	PRO+	BR/A	SB	CS	SBR	FA	FR	G/POS	TPR
1968	SF-N	81	55	95	78	10	5	9	35	38	84	.254	.338	.407	123	9	16	7	1	.978	-3	O-80	0.3
1969	SF-N	158	622	120	161	25	6	32	90	81	187	.259	.353	.473	132	26	45	4	11	.978	-0	*O-155	2.9
1970	SF-N	157	663	134	200	36	10	26	78	77	189	.302	.376	.504	135	32	48	10	8	.969	7	*O-157	3.8
1971	*SF-N★	155	619	110	178	32	4	33	102	62	137	.288	.357	.512	146	35	26	8	3	**.994**	9	*O-154	3.5
1972	SF-N	153	626	118	162	29	5	26	80	60	137	.259	.329	.446	116	12	44	6	10	.978	11	*O-153	2.7
1973	SF-N★	160	643	**131**	182	34	4	39	96	87	148	.283	.372	.530	141	35	43	17	3	.970	9	*O-158	4.1
1974	SF-N	150	567	97	145	22	8	21	71	95	134	.256	.366	.434	118	15	41	11	6	.966	7	*O-148	2.1
1975	NY-A	145	529	93	143	26	3	32	85	89	137	.270	.378	.512	152	37	30	17	1	.987	7	*O-129,D-12	3.7
1976	Cal-A	99	378	48	100	10	5	10	54	41	90	.265	.341	.386	120	10	30	15	0	.977	5	O-98/D-1	1.1
1977	Cal-A	158	592	103	156	23	9	37	115	74	141	.264	.347	.520	138	30	41	18	2	.986	5	*O-140,D-18	3.0
1978	Chi-A	26	90	8	25	4	0	2	8	10	10	.278	.350	.389	107	1	6	2	1	.956	1	O-22/D-3	0.1
	Tex-A	130	475	85	126	15	4	29	82	69	110	.265	.361	.497	139	24	37	20	-1	.970	5	*O-111,D-18	2.3
	Yr	156	565	93	151	19	4	31	90	79	120	.267	.359	.480	133	25	43	22	-0	.968	5	*O-133,D-21	2.4
1979	Cle-A	146	538	93	148	24	1	25	85	74	135	.275	.371	.463	123	18	34	23	4	.979	11	*O-116,D-29	1.9
1980	StL-N	86	231	37	47	5	3	5	24	33	74	.203	.308	.316	72	-8	15	5	2	.967	-5	O-70	-1.5
1981	Chi-N	45	163	26	35	7	1	6	19	24	48	.215	.323	.380	95	-1	5	6	-2	.982	-0	O-45	-0.5
Total	14	1849	7043	1258	1886	302	66	332	1024	914	1757	.268	.356	.471	129	276	461	169	37	.977	61	*O-1736/D-81	29.5

■ GEORGE BONE
Bone, George Drummond b: 8/28/1876, New Haven, Conn. d: 5/26/18, West Haven, Conn. BB/TR, 5'7", 152 lbs. Deb: 9/18/01

YEAR	TM/L	G	AB	R	H	2B	3B	HR	RBI	BB	SO	AVG	OBP	SLG	PRO+	BR/A	SB	CS	SBR	FA	FR	G/POS	TPR
1901	Mil-A	12	43	6	13	2	0	0	6	4		.302	.362	.349	103	0				.869	-2	S-12	-0.1

■ NINO BONGIOVANNI
Bongiovanni, Anthony Thomas b: 12/21/11, Pikes Peak, La. BL/TL, 5'10", 175 lbs. Deb: 4/23/38

YEAR	TM/L	G	AB	R	H	2B	3B	HR	RBI	BB	SO	AVG	OBP	SLG	PRO+	BR/A	SB	CS	SBR	FA	FR	G/POS	TPR
1938	Cin-N	2	7	0	2	1	0	0	0	0	0	.286	.286	.429	97	-0	0			1.000	0	/O-2	0.0
1939	*Cin-N	66	159	17	41	6	0	0	16	9	8	.258	.298	.296	60	-9	0			.989	1	O-39	-0.9
Total	2	68	166	17	43	7	0	0	16	9	8	.259	.297	.301	61	-9	0			.990	1	/O-41	-0.9

■ JUAN BONILLA
Bonilla, Juan Guillermo b: 2/12/55, Santurce, P.R. BR/TR, 5'9", 170 lbs. Deb: 4/9/81

YEAR	TM/L	G	AB	R	H	2B	3B	HR	RBI	BB	SO	AVG	OBP	SLG	PRO+	BR/A	SB	CS	SBR	FA	FR	G/POS	TPR
1981	SD-N	99	369	30	107	13	2	1	25	25	23	.290	.338	.344	101	0	4	9	-4	.976	-11	2-97	-1.0
1982	SD-N	45	182	21	51	6	2	0	8	11	15	.280	.325	.335	90	-3	0	1	-1	.975	-8	2-45	-0.9
1983	SD-N	152	556	55	132	17	4	4	45	50	40	.237	.304	.304	71	-21	3	0	1	.986	-15	*2-149	-3.0
1985	NY-A	8	16	0	2	1	0	0	2	0	3	.125	.125	.188	-16	-3	0	0	0	.955	0	/2-7	-0.1
1986	Bal-A	102	284	33	69	10	1	1	18	25	21	.243	.311	.296	67	-12	0	0	0	.981	-9	2-70,3-33/D-2	-2.0
1987	NY-A	23	55	6	14	3	0	1	3	5	6	.255	.317	.364	81	-2	0	0	0	.965	1	2-22/3-1,D-1	-0.1
Total	6	429	1462	145	375	50	9	7	101	116	108	.256	.315	.317	79	-40	7	10	-4	.980	-41	2-390/3-34,D-3	-7.0

■ BOBBY BONILLA
Bonilla, Roberto Martin Antonio b: 2/23/63, Bronx, N.Y. BB/TR, 6'3", 230 lbs. Deb: 4/9/86

YEAR	TM/L	G	AB	R	H	2B	3B	HR	RBI	BB	SO	AVG	OBP	SLG	PRO+	BR/A	SB	CS	SBR	FA	FR	G/POS	TPR
1986	Chi-A	75	234	27	63	10	2	2	26	33	49	.269	.362	.355	93	-1	4	1	1	.989	-1	O-43,1-30	-0.5
	Pit-N	63	192	28	46	6	2	1	17	29	39	.240	.342	.307	79	-5	4	4	-1	.974	-7	O-51/1-4,3-4	-1.6
1987	Pit-N	141	466	58	140	33	3	15	77	39	64	.300	.357	.481	119	12	3	5	-2	.932	-20	3-89,O-46/1-6	-1.2
1988	Pit-N★	159	584	87	160	32	7	24	100	85	82	.274	.370	.476	143	34	3	5	-2	.935	-1	*3-159	3.1
1989	Pit-N★	163	616	96	173	37	10	24	86	76	93	.281	.361	.490	146	36	8	8	-2	.929	6	*3-156/1-8,O-1	4.3
1990	*Pit-N★	160	625	112	175	39	7	32	120	45	103	.280	.329	.518	135	26	4	3	-1	.961	-3	*O-149,3-14/1-3	2.0
1991	*Pit-N★	157	577	102	174	**44**	6	18	100	90	67	.302	.398	.492	151	41	2	4	-2	.989	3	*O-104,3-67/1-4	4.1
1992	NY-N	128	438	62	109	23	0	19	70	66	73	.249	.349	.432	121	13	4	3	-1	.992	7	*O-121/1-6	1.8
1993	NY-N★	139	502	81	133	21	3	34	87	72	96	.265	.357	.522	133	23	3	3	-1	.969	-2	O-85,3-52/1-6	1.8
1994	NY-N	108	403	60	117	24	1	20	67	55	101	.290	.376	.504	128	17	1	3	-2	.942	3	*3-107	1.8
1995	NY-N★	80	317	49	103	12	4	18	53	31	48	.325	.387	.599	160	27	0	3	-2	.882	-8	3-46,O-31,1-10	1.5
	Bal-A	61	237	47	79	12	4	10	46	23	31	.333	.395	.544	139	13	0	2	-1	.971	-5	O-39,3-24	1.1
1996	*Bal-A	159	595	107	171	27	5	28	116	75	85	.287	.372	.491	117	16	1	5	-2	.975	-2	*O-108,D-44/1-9,3-4	0.5
Total	11	1593	5786	916	1643	333	54	245	965	719	931	.284	.365	.487	131	251	37	47	-17	.977	-23	O-778,3-722/1-86,D	18.6

■ LUTHER BONIN
Bonin, Ernest Luther "Bonnie" b: 1/13/1888, Greenhill, Ind. d: 1/3/65, Sycamore, Ohio BL/TL, 5'9.5", 178 lbs. Deb: 4/13/13

YEAR	TM/L	G	AB	R	H	2B	3B	HR	RBI	BB	SO	AVG	OBP	SLG	PRO+	BR/A	SB	CS	SBR	FA	FR	G/POS	TPR
1913	StL-A	1	1	0	0	0	0	0	0	0	0	.000	.000	.000	-99	-0	0			.000	0	H	0.0
1914	Buf-F	20	76	6	14	4	1	0	4	7	11	.184	.253	.263	40	-8	3			.970	1	O-20	-0.9
Total	2	21	77	6	14	4	1	0	4	7	11	.182	.250	.260	38	-8	3			.970	1	/O-20	-0.9

■ BARRY BONNELL
Bonnell, Robert Barry b: 10/27/53, Clermont County, O. BR/TR, 6'3", 200 lbs. Deb: 5/4/77

YEAR	TM/L	G	AB	R	H	2B	3B	HR	RBI	BB	SO	AVG	OBP	SLG	PRO+	BR/A	SB	CS	SBR	FA	FR	G/POS	TPR
1977	Atl-N	100	360	41	108	11	0	1	45	37	32	.300	.368	.339	81	-8	7	5	-1	.989	8	O-75,3-32	-0.4
1978	Atl-N	117	304	36	73	11	3	1	16	20	30	.240	.287	.306	59	-17	12	6	0	.984	-9	*O-105,3-15	-3.1
1979	Atl-N	127	375	47	97	20	3	12	45	26	55	.259	.312	.424	92	-5	8	7	-2	.983	-15	*O-124/3-1	-2.7
1980	Tor-A	130	463	55	124	22	4	13	56	37	59	.268	.325	.417	97	-2	3	4	-2	.973	6	*O-122/D-3	-0.3
1981	Tor-A	66	227	21	50	7	4	4	28	12	25	.220	.262	.339	68	-10	4	3	-1	.975	2	O-66	-1.1
1982	Tor-A	140	437	59	128	26	3	6	49	32	51	.293	.345	.407	97	-2	14	2	3	.979	-18	*O-125/3-9,D-6	-2.0
1983	Tor-A	137	397	49	120	21	3	10	54	33	52	.318	.373	.469	121	9	8	5	-2	.986	-13	*O-117/3-4,D-1	-0.5
1984	Sea-A	110	363	42	96	15	4	8	48	25	51	.264	.315	.394	96	-2	5	5	-2	.994	-11	O-94,3-10/1-5,D-8	-1.6
1985	Sea-A	48	111	9	27	8	1	1	10	6	19	.243	.282	.342	70	-5	1	2	-1	.976	-1	O-22/1-5,D-2	-0.7

YEAR	TM/L	G	AB	R	H	2B	3B	HR	RBI	BB	SO	AVG	OBP	SLG	PRO+	BR/A	SB	CS	SBR	FA	FR	G/POS	TPR
1986	Sea-A	17	51	4	10	2	0	0	4	1	13	.196	.212	.235	21	-6	0	1	-1	.941	1	/O-9,1-8,D-2	-0.6
Total	10	976	3068	363	833	143	24	56	355	229	387	.272	.325	.389	89	-45	64	39	-4	.982	-51	O-859/3-71,D-22,1	-13.0

■ FRANK BONNER
Bonner, Frank J b: 8/20/1869, Lowell, Mass. d: 12/31/05, Kansas City, Mo. BR/TR, 5'7.5", 169 lbs. Deb: 4/26/1894

YEAR	TM/L	G	AB	R	H	2B	3B	HR	RBI	BB	SO	AVG	OBP	SLG	PRO+	BR/A	SB	CS	SBR	FA	FR	G/POS	TPR
1894	*Bal-N	33	118	27	38	10	2	0	24	17	5	.322	.412	.441	101	0	12			.904	-15	2-27/O-4,3-2,S-1	-1.0
1895	Bal-N	11	42	9	14	1	1	0	7	5	1	.333	.404	.405	106	0	4			.742	-5	3-11	-0.4
	StL-N	15	59	3	8	0	1	1	8	1	8	.136	.164	.220	-1	-9	2			.656	-5	3-10/O-5,C-1	-1.2
	Yr	26	101	12	22	1	2	1	15	6	9	.218	.269	.297	46	-9	6			.698	-10	3-21/O-5,C-1	-1.6
1896	Bro-N	9	34	8	6	2	0	0	5	2	8	.176	.263	.235	34	-3	1			.915	-1	/2-9	-0.3
1899	Was-N	85	347	41	95	20	4	2	44	18		.274	.313	.372	89	-7	6			.940	2	2-85	0.0
1902	Cle-A	34	132	14	37	6	0	0	14	5		.280	.312	.326	80	-4	1			.907	-10	2-34	-1.2
	Phi-A	11	44	2	8	0	0	0	3	0		.182	.200	.182	6	-6	0			.937	-1	2-11	-0.6
	Yr	45	176	16	45	6	0	0	17	5		.256	.284	.290	61	-9	1			.915	-12	2-45	-1.8
1903	Bos-N	48	173	11	38	5	0	1	10	7		.220	.262	.266	53	-11	2			.957	-6	2-24,S-22	-1.2
Total	6	246	949	115	244	44	8	4	115	55	22	.257	.305	.333	73	-38	28			.931	-39	2-190/S-23,3-23,OC	-5.9

■ BOBBY BONNER
Bonner, Robert Averill b: 8/12/56, Uvalde, Tex. BR/TR, 6', 185 lbs. Deb: 9/12/80

YEAR	TM/L	G	AB	R	H	2B	3B	HR	RBI	BB	SO	AVG	OBP	SLG	PRO+	BR/A	SB	CS	SBR	FA	FR	G/POS	TPR
1980	Bal-A	4	4	1	0	0	0	0	0	0	0	.000	.000	.000	-99	-1	0	0	0	.889	1	/S-3	0.0
1981	Bal-A	10	27	6	8	2	0	0	2	1	4	.296	.321	.370	99	-0	1	0	0	.976	1	/S-9	0.2
1982	Bal-A	41	77	8	13	3	1	0	5	3	12	.169	.200	.234	19	-9	0	0	0	.959	-5	S-38/2-3	-1.2
1983	Bal-A	6	0	0	0	0	0	0	0	0	0				—	0	0	0	0	1.000	-0	/2-5,D-1	0.0
Total	4	61	108	15	21	5	1	0	4	4	16	.194	.223	.259	34	-10	1	0	0	.960	-4	/S-50,2-8,D-1	-1.0

■ ZEKE BONURA
Bonura, Henry John b: 9/20/08, New Orleans, La. d: 3/9/87, New Orleans, La. BR/TR, 6', 210 lbs. Deb: 4/17/34

YEAR	TM/L	G	AB	R	H	2B	3B	HR	RBI	BB	SO	AVG	OBP	SLG	PRO+	BR/A	SB	CS	SBR	FA	FR	G/POS	TPR
1934	Chi-A	127	510	86	154	35	4	27	110	64	31	.302	.380	.545	132	22	0	2	-1	**.996**	5	*1-127	1.4
1935	Chi-A	138	550	107	162	34	4	21	92	57	28	.295	.364	.485	115	11	4	0	1	.994	2	*1-138	-0.1
1936	Chi-A	148	587	120	194	39	7	12	138	94	29	.330	.426	.482	119	27	4	2	0	**.996**	12	*1-146	1.6
1937	Chi-A	116	447	79	154	41	2	19	100	49	24	.345	.412	.573	146	30	5	1	1	.989	-2	*1-115	1.5
1938	Was-A	137	540	72	156	27	3	22	114	44	29	.289	.346	.472	111	6	2	0	1	**.993**	3	*1-129	-0.6
1939	NY-N	123	455	75	146	26	6	11	85	46	22	.321	.388	.477	130	20	1			.992	5	*1-122	1.2
1940	Was-A	79	311	41	85	16	3	3	45	40	13	.273	.358	.373	96	-1	2			.982	-4	1-79	-1.2
	Chi-N	49	182	20	48	14	0	2	20	10	4	.264	.302	.407	96	-2	1			.991	5	1-44	-0.1
Total	7	917	3582	600	1099	232	29	119	704	404	180	.307	.380	.487	121	106	19	7		.992	27	1-900	3.7

■ EVERETT BOOE
Booe, Everett Little b: 9/28/1891, Mocksville, N.C. d: 5/21/69, Kenedy, Tex. BL/TR, 5'8.5", 165 lbs. Deb: 4/13/13

YEAR	TM/L	G	AB	R	H	2B	3B	HR	RBI	BB	SO	AVG	OBP	SLG	PRO+	BR/A	SB	CS	SBR	FA	FR	G/POS	TPR
1913	Pit-N	29	80	9	16	0	2	0	2	6	9	.200	.256	.250	47	-6	2			1.000	-1	O-22	-0.8
1914	Ind-F	20	31	5	7	1	0	0	6	7	6	.226	.368	.258	65	-2	4			.778	-2	/O-5,S-3	-0.3
	Buf-F	76	241	29	54	9	2	0	14	21	50	.224	.289	.278	54	-19	8			.959	-4	O-58/S-8,3-2,2-1	-2.6
	Yr	96	272	34	61	10	2	0	20	28	56	.224	.299	.276	55	-21	12			.944	-5	O-63,S-11,3-2,2-1	-2.9
Total	2	125	352	43	77	10	4	0	22	34	65	.219	.289	.270	54	-26	14			.959	-6	/O-85,S-11,3-2,2-1	-3.7

■ BUDDY BOOKER
Booker, Richard Lee b: 5/28/42, Lynchburg, Va. BL/TR, 5'10", 170 lbs. Deb: 6/4/66

YEAR	TM/L	G	AB	R	H	2B	3B	HR	RBI	BB	SO	AVG	OBP	SLG	PRO+	BR/A	SB	CS	SBR	FA	FR	G/POS	TPR
1966	Cle-A	18	28	6	6	1	0	2	6	1	2	.214	.267	.464	105	0	0	0	0	.964	-5	C-12	-0.5
1968	Chi-A	5	5	0	0	0	0	0	0	1	2	.000	.167	.000	-46	-1	0	0	0	1.000	-1	/C-3	-0.2
Total	2	23	33	6	6	1	0	2	6	2	4	.182	.250	.394	82	-1	0	0	0	.967	-6	/C-15	-0.7

■ ROD BOOKER
Booker, Roderick Stewart b: 9/4/58, Los Angeles, Cal. BL/TR, 6' ", 175 lbs. Deb: 4/29/87

YEAR	TM/L	G	AB	R	H	2B	3B	HR	RBI	BB	SO	AVG	OBP	SLG	PRO+	BR/A	SB	CS	SBR	FA	FR	G/POS	TPR
1987	StL-N	44	47	9	13	1	1	0	8	7	7	.277	.370	.340	88	-1	2	0	1	.960	3	2-18/3-4,S-1	0.4
1988	StL-N	18	35	6	12	3	0	0	3	4	3	.343	.410	.429	140	2	2	2	-1	.889	-3	3-13/2-1	-0.1
1989	StL-N	10	8	1	2	0	0	0	0	1	.250	.250	.250	42	-1	0	0	0	.867	2	/2-5,3-1	0.2
1990	Phi-N	73	131	19	29	5	2	0	10	15	26	.221	.301	.290	64	-6	3	1	0	.976	-6	S-27,2-23,3-10	-1.0
1991	Phi-N	28	53	3	12	1	0	0	7	1	7	.226	.241	.245	37	-4	0	0	0	1.000	-2	S-20/3-3	-0.6
Total	5	173	274	38	68	10	3	0	28	27	44	.248	.316	.307	72	-10	7	3	0	.985	-5	/S-48,2-47,3-31	-1.1

■ AL BOOL
Bool, Albert J. b: 8/24/1897, Lincoln, Neb. d: 9/27/81, Lincoln, Neb. BR/TR, 5'11", 180 lbs. Deb: 9/29/28

YEAR	TM/L	G	AB	R	H	2B	3B	HR	RBI	BB	SO	AVG	OBP	SLG	PRO+	BR/A	SB	CS	SBR	FA	FR	G/POS	TPR
1928	Was-A	2	7	0	1	0	0	0	1	0	0	.143	.143	.143	-25	-1	0	0	0	1.000	0	/C-2	-0.1
1930	Pit-N	78	216	30	56	12	4	7	46	25	29	.259	.336	.449	87	-5	0			.967	-1	C-65	0.0
1931	Bos-N	49	85	5	16	1	0	0	6	9	13	.188	.266	.200	28	-8	0			.989	-2	C-37	-0.9
Total	3	129	308	35	73	13	4	7	53	34	42	.237	.313	.373	71	-15	0			.973	-2	C-104	-1.0

■ BRET BOONE
Boone, Bret Robert b: 4/6/69, ElCajon, Cal. BR/TR, 5'10", 180 lbs. Deb: 8/19/92 F

YEAR	TM/L	G	AB	R	H	2B	3B	HR	RBI	BB	SO	AVG	OBP	SLG	PRO+	BR/A	SB	CS	SBR	FA	FR	G/POS	TPR
1992	Sea-A	33	129	15	25	4	0	4	15	4	34	.194	.224	.318	50	-9	1	1	-0	.965	-0	2-32/3-6	-0.9
1993	Sea-A	76	271	31	68	12	2	12	38	17	52	.251	.305	.443	97	-2	2	3	-1	.991	-9	2-74/D-1	-1.0
1994	Cin-N	108	381	59	122	25	2	12	68	24	74	.320	.373	.491	124	13	3	4	-2	.974	-17	*2-106/3-2	-0.1
1995	*Cin-N	138	513	63	137	34	2	15	68	41	84	.267	.329	.429	98	-2	5	1	1	**.994**	-16	*2-138	-0.8
1996	Cin-N	142	520	56	121	21	3	12	69	31	100	.233	.280	.354	66	-26	3	2	-0	**.991**	4	*2-141	-1.4
Total	5	497	1814	224	473	96	9	55	258	117	344	.261	.313	.415	91	-27	14	11	-2	.987	-39	2-491/3-8,D-1	-4.2

■ IKE BOONE
Boone, Isaac Morgan b: 2/17/1897, Samantha, Ala. d: 8/1/58, Northport, Ala. BL/TR, 6', 195 lbs. Deb: 4/22/22 F

YEAR	TM/L	G	AB	R	H	2B	3B	HR	RBI	BB	SO	AVG	OBP	SLG	PRO+	BR/A	SB	CS	SBR	FA	FR	G/POS	TPR
1922	NY-N	2	2	0	1	0	0	0	0	0	1	.500	.500	.500	157	0	0	0	0	.000	0	H	0.0
1923	Bos-A	5	15	1	4	0	1	0	2	1	0	.267	.313	.400	86	-0	0	1	-1	.929	0	/O-4	-0.1
1924	Bos-A	128	487	72	164	31	4	13	98	54	32	.337	.404	.497	131	22	2	2	-1	.976	-7	*O-124	0.6
1925	Bos-A	133	476	79	157	34	5	9	68	60	19	.330	.406	.479	124	18	1	4	-2	.941	-7	*O-118	0.1
1927	Chi-A	29	53	10	12	4	0	1	11	3	4	.226	.268	.358	63	-3	0	0	0	1.000	0	O-11	-0.6
1930	Bro-N	40	101	13	30	9	1	3	13	14	8	.297	.383	.495	111	2	0			.960	-2	O-27	-0.1
1931	Bro-N	6	5	0	1	0	0	0	0	1	1	.200	.333	.200	47	-0	0			.000	0	H	-0.1
1932	Bro-N	13	21	2	3	1	0	0	2	5	2	.143	.308	.190	38	-2	0			1.000	-1	/O-8	-0.3
Total	8	356	1160	177	372	79	11	26	194	138	67	.321	.394	.475	121	37	3	7		.960	-18	O-292	-0.4

■ LUKE BOONE
Boone, Lute Joseph "Danny" b: 5/6/1890, Pittsburgh, Pa. d: 7/29/82, Pittsburgh, Pa. BR/TR, 5'9", 160 lbs. Deb: 9/9/13

YEAR	TM/L	G	AB	R	H	2B	3B	HR	RBI	BB	SO	AVG	OBP	SLG	PRO+	BR/A	SB	CS	SBR	FA	FR	G/POS	TPR
1913	NY-A	6	12	3	4	0	0	0	1	3	1	.333	.467	.333	134	1	0			.857	-1	/S-4	0.0
1914	NY-A	106	370	34	82	8	2	0	21	31	41	.222	.285	.254	63	-17	10	18	-8	.960	23	2-90/3-9,O-1	-0.3
1915	NY-A	130	431	44	88	12	2	5	43	41	53	.204	.285	.276	68	-17	14	17	-6	.965	**21**	*2-115,S-11/3-4	0.0
1916	NY-A	46	124	14	23	4	0	1	8	10	17	.185	.250	.242	47	-8	7			.973	7	3-25,S-12/2-8	0.1
1918	Pit-N	27	91	7	18	3	0	0	3	6	9	.198	.263	.231	49	-5	1			.921	-0	S-26/2-1	-0.5
Total	5	315	1028	102	215	27	4	6	76	91	111	.209	.282	.261	63	-46	32	35		.964	50	2-214/S-53,3-38,O-1	-0.7

■ RAY BOONE
Boone, Raymond Otis "Ike" b: 7/27/23, San Diego, Cal. BR/TR, 6'1", 188 lbs. Deb: 9/3/48 F

YEAR	TM/L	G	AB	R	H	2B	3B	HR	RBI	BB	SO	AVG	OBP	SLG	PRO+	BR/A	SB	CS	SBR	FA	FR	G/POS	TPR
1948	*Cle-A	6	5	2	2	1	0	0	1	0	1	.400	.400	.600	168	0	0	0	0	.889	1	/S-4	0.2
1949	Cle-A	86	258	39	65	4	4	4	26	38	17	.252	.352	.345	87	-5	0	2	-1	.947	3	S-76	0.1
1950	Cle-A	109	365	53	110	14	6	7	58	56	27	.301	.397	.430	116	10	4	3	-1	.945	-9	*S-102	0.7
1951	Cle-A	151	544	65	127	14	1	12	51	48	36	.233	.302	.329	75	-21	1	3	-1	.957	-7	*S-151	-1.7
1952	Cle-A	103	316	57	83	8	2	7	45	53	33	.263	.372	.367	113	7	0	3	-1	.941	-10	S-96/3-2,2-1	0.3
1953	Cle-A	34	112	21	27	1	2	4	21	24	21	.241	.375	.393	110	2	1	0	1	.952	-1	S-31	0.3
	Det-A	101	385	73	120	16	6	22	93	48	47	.312	.395	.556	156	30	2	3	-1	.958	1	3-97/S-3	2.8
	Yr	135	497	94	147	17	8	26	114	72	68	.296	.390	.519	146	32	3	3	-1	.958	0	3-97,S-34	3.1
1954	Det-A★	148	543	76	160	19	7	20	85	71	53	.295	.378	.466	133	24	1	1	0	.964	2	*3-148/S-1	2.3
1955	Det-A	135	500	61	142	22	7	20	**116**	50	49	.284	.350	.476	123	14	0			.953	-5	*3-126	0.8
1956	Det-A★	131	481	77	148	24	6	25	81	77	46	.308	.406	.518	142	30	0	0	0	.959	-7	*3-130	2.5
1957	Det-A	129	462	48	126	25	3	12	65	57	47	.273	.356	.418	108	6	0	1	-0	.990	-10	*1-117/3-4	-1.2
1958	Det-A	39	114	16	27	4	1	6	20	14	13	.237	.326	.447	103	1	0	0	0	.988	-1	1-32	-0.4
	Chi-A	77	246	25	60	12	1	7	41	18	33	.244	.298	.386	89	-4	1	1	0	.986	-2	1-63	-1.1

YEAR	TM/L	G	AB	R	H	2B	3B	HR	RBI	BB	SO	AVG	OBP	SLG	PRO+	BR/A	SB	CS	SBR	FA	FR	G/POS	TPR
	Yr	116	360	41	87	16	2	13	61	32	46	.242	.307	.406	93	-4	1	3	-2	.986	-3	1-95	-1.5
1959	Chi-A	9	21	3	5	0	0	1	5	7	5	.238	.429	.381	126	1	1	0	0	.955	0	/1-6	0.1
	KC-A	61	132	19	36	6	0	2	12	27	17	.273	.396	.364	108	3	1	0	1	.983	1	1-38/3-3	0.2
	Yr	70	153	22	41	6	0	3	17	34	22	.268	.401	.366	111	4	2	0	1	.980	1	1-44/3-3	0.3
	Mil-N	13	15	3	3	0	0	1	2	4	2	.200	.368	.400	114	0	0	0	0	1.000	-0	/1-3	0.0
1960	Mil-N	7	12	3	3	1	0	0	4	5	1	.250	.471	.333	135	1	0	0	0	1.000	-0	/1-4	0.1
	Bos-A	34	78	6	16	1	0	1	11	11	15	.205	.303	.256	51	-5	0	0	0	.994	-0	1-22	-0.7
Total	13	1373	4589	645	1260	162	46	151	737	608	463	.275	.363	.429	115	95	21	19	-5	.958	-46	3-510,S-464,1/2	5.3

■ BOB BOONE
Boone, Robert Raymond b: 11/19/47, San Diego, Cal. BR/TR, 6'2", 202 lbs. Deb: 9/10/72 FMC

YEAR	TM/L	G	AB	R	H	2B	3B	HR	RBI	BB	SO	AVG	OBP	SLG	PRO+	BR/A	SB	CS	SBR	FA	FR	G/POS	TPR
1972	Phi-N	16	51	4	14	1	0	1	4	5	7	.275	.339	.353	95	-0	1	0	0	.936	-6	C-14	-0.6
1973	Phi-N	145	521	42	136	20	2	10	61	41	36	.261	.315	.365	86	-10	3	4	-2	.990	6	*C-145	0.0
1974	Phi-N	146	488	41	118	24	3	3	52	35	29	.242	.298	.322	70	-20	3	1	0	.976	-7	*C-146	-2.0
1975	Phi-N	97	289	28	71	14	2	2	20	32	14	.246	.323	.329	78	-8	1	3	-2	.990	1	C-92/3-3	-0.6
1976	*Phi-N★	121	361	40	98	18	2	4	54	45	44	.271	.354	.366	101	2	2	5	-2	.993	-9	*C-108/1-4	-0.8
1977	*Phi-N	132	440	55	125	26	4	11	66	42	54	.284	.349	.436	105	3	5	5	-2	.989	3	*C-131/3-2	0.8
1978	*Phi-N★	132	435	48	123	18	4	12	62	46	37	.283	.353	.425	115	9	2	5	-2	**.991**	-9	*C-129/1-3,O-1	0.0
1979	Phi-N★	119	398	38	114	21	3	9	58	49	33	.286	.367	.422	111	7	1	4	-2	.988	-12	*C-117/3-2	-0.3
1980	*Phi-N	141	480	34	110	23	1	9	55	48	41	.229	.301	.338	74	-17	3	4	-2	.979	5	*C-138	-0.9
1981	*Phi-N	76	227	19	48	7	0	4	24	22	16	.211	.281	.295	61	-12	2	2	-1	.985	-2	C-75	-1.3
1982	*Cal-A	143	472	42	121	17	0	7	58	39	34	.256	.313	.337	79	-14	0	2	-1	.989	7	*C-143	-0.2
1983	Cal-A★	142	468	46	120	18	0	9	52	24	42	.256	.293	.353	77	-15	4	3	-1	.980	4	*C-142	-0.5
1984	Cal-A	139	450	33	91	16	1	3	32	25	45	.202	.244	.262	40	-36	3	3	-1	.984	7	*C-137	-2.4
1985	Cal-A	150	460	37	114	17	0	5	55	37	35	.248	.308	.317	72	-17	1	2	-1	.987	5	*C-147	-0.6
1986	*Cal-A	144	442	48	98	12	2	7	49	43	30	.222	.291	.305	63	-22	1	0	0	.988	12	*C-144	-0.1
1987	Cal-A	128	389	42	94	18	0	3	33	35	36	.242	.306	.311	66	-18	0	2	-1	.983	5	*C-127/D-1	-1.1
1988	Cal-A	122	352	38	104	17	0	5	39	29	26	.295	.352	.386	110	5	2	2	-1	.986	-6	*C-121	0.6
1989	KC-A	131	405	33	111	13	2	1	43	49	37	.274	.355	.323	93	-2	3	2	-0	.991	4	*C-129	0.9
1990	KC-A	40	117	11	28	3	0	0	9	17	12	.239	.336	.265	71	-4	1	1	-0	.985	2	C-40	0.0
Total	19	2264	7245	679	1838	303	26	105	826	663	608	.254	.318	.346	82	-170	38	50	-19	.986	6	*C-2225/1-7,3-7,DO	-9.1

■ BOOTH
Booth Deb: 5/1/1875

YEAR	TM/L	G	AB	R	H	2B	3B	HR	RBI	BB	SO	AVG	OBP	SLG	PRO+	BR/A	SB	CS	SBR	FA	FR	G/POS	TPR
1875	NH-n	1	2	0	0	0	0	0		0	1	.000	.000	.000	-99	-0	0	0	0	.500	-0	/S-1	-0.1

■ AMOS BOOTH
Booth, Amos Smith "Darling" b: 9/14/1853, Cincinnati, O. d: 7/1/21, Miamisburg, Ohio BR/TR, 5'9", 159 lbs. Deb: 4/25/1876

YEAR	TM/L	G	AB	R	H	2B	3B	HR	RBI	BB	SO	AVG	OBP	SLG	PRO+	BR/A	SB	CS	SBR	FA	FR	G/POS	TPR
1876	Cin-N	63	272	31	71	3	0	0	14	9	11	.261	.285	.272	101	2				.760	-18	3-24,C-24,S-22,OP	-1.3
1877	Cin-N	44	157	16	27	2	1	0	13	12	10	.172	.231	.197	41	-9				.853	-5	S-13,C-12,P2/3O	-0.9
1880	Cin-N	1	2	0	0	0	0	0	0	0	0	.000	.000	.000	-99	-0				.000	0	/3-1	-0.1
1882	Bal-a	1	3	0	0	0	0	0		0	0	.000	.000	.000	-99	-1				1.000	0	/3-1	-0.1
	Lou-a	1	4	0	0	0	0	0		0	0	.000	.000	.000	-99	-1				1.000	-1	/2-1	-0.1
	Yr	2	7	0	0	0	0	0		0	0	.000	.000	.000	-99	-1				1.000	-1	/3-1,2-1	-0.2
Total	4	110	438	47	98	5	1	0	27	21	21	.224	.259	.240	73	-9				.746	-24	/C-36,S-35,3P2O	-2.4

■ EDDIE BOOTH
Booth, Edward H. b: Brooklyn, N.Y. Deb: 4/26/1872

YEAR	TM/L	G	AB	R	H	2B	3B	HR	RBI	BB	SO	AVG	OBP	SLG	PRO+	BR/A	SB	CS	SBR	FA	FR	G/POS	TPR
1872	Man-n	24	117	25	38	4	2	0	12	0	1	.325	.325	.393	127	4	0	0	0	.764	-2	2-20/O-4	0.2
	Atl-n	15	62	11	19	4	0	0	8	0	0	.306	.306	.371	92	-2	0	2	-1	.792	1	O-14/2-1	-0.1
	Yr	39	179	36	57	8	2	0	20	0	1	.318	.318	.385	112	2	0	2	-1	.769	2	2-21,O-18	0.1
1873	Res-n	18	72	11	21	3	2	0	4	0	2	.292	.292	.389	109	1	0	0	0	.848	-3	O-17/2-1	-0.1
	Atl-n	16	69	8	14	3	1	0	8	0	0	.203	.236	.275	58	-3	0	1	-1	.788	1	O-16	-0.1
	Yr	34	141	19	35	6	3	0	12	3	2	.248	.264	.333	84	-2	0	1	-1	.818	-2	O-33/2-1	-0.2
1874	Atl-n	44	185	24	47	4	3	1	16	3	3	.254	.266	.324	100	1	0	0	0	.809	-9	*O-44/2-1	-0.6
1875	Mut-n	68	281	33	56	3	4	0	18	0	2	.199	.199	.238	49	-15	4	3	-1	.827	-1	*O-63/2-8	-1.3
1876	NY-N	57	228	17	49	2	1	0	7	2	4	.215	.222	.232	55	-8				.764	-5	*O-53/2-5,P-1	-1.2
Total	4 n	185	786	112	195	21	12	1	66	6	8	.248	.254	.309	82	-13	4	6	-2	.820	-11	O-158/2-31	-2.0

■ JOSH BOOTY
Booty, Joshua Gibson b: 4/29/75, Starkville, Miss. BR/TR, 6'3", 210 lbs. Deb: 9/24/96

YEAR	TM/L	G	AB	R	H	2B	3B	HR	RBI	BB	SO	AVG	OBP	SLG	PRO+	BR/A	SB	CS	SBR	FA	FR	G/POS	TPR
1996	Fla-N	2	2	1	1	0	0	0	0	0	0	.500	.500	.500	172	0	0	0	0	.000	0	/3-1	0.0

■ FRENCHY BORDAGARAY
Bordagaray, Stanley George b: 1/3/10, Coalinga, Cal. BR/TR, 5'7.5", 175 lbs. Deb: 4/17/34

YEAR	TM/L	G	AB	R	H	2B	3B	HR	RBI	BB	SO	AVG	OBP	SLG	PRO+	BR/A	SB	CS	SBR	FA	FR	G/POS	TPR
1934	Chi-A	29	87	12	28	3	1	0	2	3	8	.322	.344	.379	84	-2	4	2	-1	.938	-1	O-17	-0.4
1935	Bro-N	120	422	69	119	19	6	1	39	17	29	.282	.319	.363	85	-9	18			.980	1	*O-105	-1.2
1936	Bro-N	125	372	63	117	21	3	4	31	17	42	.315	.346	.419	104	2	12			.991	0	O-92,2-11/3-6	-0.1
1937	StL-N	96	300	43	88	11	4	1	37	15	25	.293	.331	.367	88	-5	11			.942	-9	3-50,O-28	-1.4
1938	StL-N	81	156	19	44	5	1	0	21	8	9	.282	.325	.327	76	-5	2			.959	0	O-29/3-4	-0.6
1939	*Cin-N	63	122	19	24	5	1	0	12	9	10	.197	.252	.254	36	-11	3			1.000	-6	O-43/2-2	-1.8
1941	*NY-A	36	73	10	19	1	0	0	4	6	8	.260	.325	.274	61	-4	1	0	0	.967	-3	O-19	-0.7
1942	Bro-N	48	58	11	14	2	0	0	5	3	3	.241	.279	.276	62	-3	2			1.000	-4	O-17	-0.7
1943	Bro-N	89	268	47	81	18	2	0	19	30	15	.302	.379	.384	120	3	8			.989	-15	O-53,3-25	-0.9
1944	Bro-N	130	501	85	141	26	4	6	51	36	22	.281	.331	.385	103	1	3			.945	-20	3-98,O-25	-2.0
1945	Bro-N	113	273	32	70	9	6	2	49	29	15	.256	.328	.355	91	-4	7			.886	-11	3-57,O-22	-1.4
Total	11	930	2632	410	745	120	28	14	270	173	186	.283	.331	.366	91	-32	66	2		.982	-66	O-450,3-240/2-13	-11.2

■ PAT BORDERS
Borders, Patrick Lance b: 5/14/63, Columbus, Ohio BR/TR, 6'2", 190 lbs. Deb: 4/6/88

YEAR	TM/L	G	AB	R	H	2B	3B	HR	RBI	BB	SO	AVG	OBP	SLG	PRO+	BR/A	SB	CS	SBR	FA	FR	G/POS	TPR
1988	Tor-A	56	154	15	42	6	3	5	21	3	24	.273	.287	.448	102	-0	0	0	0	.973	2	C-43/2-1,3-1,D-7	0.4
1989	*Tor-A	94	241	22	62	11	1	3	29	11	45	.257	.292	.349	81	-6	2	1	0	.980	0	C-68,D-18	-0.4
1990	Tor-A	125	346	36	99	24	2	15	49	18	57	.286	.321	.497	123	9	0	1	-1	.993	7	*C-115/D-1	1.5
1991	*Tor-A	105	291	22	71	17	0	5	36	11	45	.244	.274	.354	70	-13	0	0	0	.993	13	*C-102	0.5
1992	*Tor-A	138	480	47	116	26	2	13	53	33	75	.242	.293	.385	85	-11	1	1	-0	.991	5	*C-137	0.2
1993	*Tor-A	138	488	38	124	30	0	9	55	20	66	.254	.286	.371	75	-19	2	2	-1	.986	5	*C-138	-0.7
1994	Tor-A	85	295	24	73	13	1	3	26	15	50	.247	.284	.329	57	-19	1	1	-0	.988	7	C-85	-0.6
1995	KC-A	52	143	14	33	8	1	4	13	7	22	.231	.267	.385	66	-8	0	0	0	1.000	-2	C-45/D-3	-0.7
	Hou-N	11	35	1	4	0	0	0	2	7	11	.114	.162	.114	-27	-6	0	0	0	.987	1	C-11	-0.5
1996	StL-N	26	69	3	22	3	0	0	4	1	14	.319	.329	.362	82	-2	0	1	-1	.984	3	C-17/1-1	0.2
	Cal-A	19	57	6	13	3	0	2	8	3	11	.228	.267	.386	64	-3	0	1	-1	.984	4	C-19	0.1
	Chi-A	31	94	6	26	1	0	3	6	4	18	.277	.313	.383	79	-3	0	0	0	.982	-2	C-30/D-1	-0.3
	Yr	50	151	12	39	4	0	5	14	8	29	.258	.296	.384	73	-7	0	1	-1	.983	2	C-49/D-1	-0.2
Total	9	880	2693	234	685	142	10	62	300	129	434	.254	.290	.384	80	-81	6	8	-3	.988	36	C-810/D-30,1-1,32	-0.3

■ MIKE BORDICK
Bordick, Michael Todd b: 7/21/65, Marquette, Mich. BR/TR, 5'11", 170 lbs. Deb: 4/11/90

YEAR	TM/L	G	AB	R	H	2B	3B	HR	RBI	BB	SO	AVG	OBP	SLG	PRO+	BR/A	SB	CS	SBR	FA	FR	G/POS	TPR
1990	*Oak-A	25	14	0	1	0	0	0	0	1	4	.071	.133	.071	-43	-3	0	0	0	1.000	-0	3-10/S-9,2-7	-0.3
1991	Oak-A	90	235	21	56	5	1	0	21	14	37	.238	.290	.268	59	-13	3	4	-2	.972	-4	S-84/2-5,3-1	-1.2
1992	*Oak-A	154	504	62	151	19	4	3	48	40	59	.300	.362	.371	111	8	12	6	0	.987	8	2-95,S-70	2.3
1993	Oak-A	159	546	60	136	21	2	3	48	60	58	.249	.335	.310	80	-14	10	10	-3	.982	-16	*S-159/2-1	-1.9
1994	Oak-A	114	391	38	99	18	4	2	37	38	44	.253	.324	.335	77	-13	7	2	1	.974	-2	*S-112/2-4	-0.3
1995	Oak-A	126	428	46	113	13	0	8	44	35	48	.264	.327	.350	81	-12	11	3	2	.983	7	*S-126/D-1	0.7
1996	Oak-A	155	525	46	126	18	4	5	54	39	59	.240	.310	.318	62	-31	5	3	1	.979	13	*S-155	-0.6
Total	7	823	2643	273	682	94	15	21	252	240	309	.258	.327	.329	79	-77	48	31	-4	.978	5	S-715,2-112/3-11,D	-1.3

■ GLENN BORGMANN
Borgmann, Glenn Dennis b: 5/25/50, Paterson, N.J. BR/TR, 6'4", 210 lbs. Deb: 7/1/72

YEAR	TM/L	G	AB	R	H	2B	3B	HR	RBI	BB	SO	AVG	OBP	SLG	PRO+	BR/A	SB	CS	SBR	FA	FR	G/POS	TPR
1972	Min-A	56	175	11	41	6	0	3	14	25	25	.234	.330	.309	86	-2	0	0	0	.965	-1	C-56	-0.1
1973	Min-A	12	34	7	9	2	0	0	9	6	10	.265	.375	.324	95	0	0	0	0	1.000	-2	C-12	-0.2

YEAR	TM/L	G	AB	R	H	2B	3B	HR	RBI	BB	SO	AVG	OBP	SLG	PRO+	BR/A	SB	CS	SBR	FA	FR	G/POS	TPR
1974	Min-A	128	345	33	87	8	1	3	45	39	44	.252	.330	.307	82	-7	2	1	0	**.997**	-2	*C-128	-0.4
1975	Min-A	125	352	34	73	15	2	2	33	47	59	.207	.304	.278	65	-15	0	1	-1	.989	-2	*C-125	-1.4
1976	Min-A	24	65	10	16	3	0	1	6	19	7	.246	.417	.338	120	3	1	1	-0	.976	2	C-24	0.5
1977	Min-A	17	43	12	11	1	0	2	7	11	9	.256	.407	.419	128	2	0	0	0	1.000	2	C-17	0.4
1978	Min-A	49	123	16	26	4	1	3	15	18	17	.211	.312	.333	80	-3	0	0	0	.990	5	C-46/D-1	0.3
1979	Min-A	31	70	4	14	3	0	0	8	12	11	.200	.317	.243	52	-4	1	0	0	.993	7	C-31	0.4
1980	Chi-A	32	87	10	19	2	0	2	14	14	9	.218	.327	.310	76	-3	0	0	0	1.000	2	C-32	0.0
Total	9	474	1294	137	296	42	4	16	151	191	191	.229	.329	.304	79	-30	4	3	-1	.989	10	C-471/D-1	-0.5

■ BOB BORKOWSKI
Borkowski, Robert Vilarian b: 1/27/26, Dayton, Ohio BR/TR, 6', 182 lbs. Deb: 4/22/50

YEAR	TM/L	G	AB	R	H	2B	3B	HR	RBI	BB	SO	AVG	OBP	SLG	PRO+	BR/A	SB	CS	SBR	FA	FR	G/POS	TPR
1950	Chi-N	85	256	27	70	7	4	4	29	16	30	.273	.319	.379	84	-6	1			.975	1	O-65/1-1	-0.8
1951	Chi-N	58	89	9	14	1	0	0	10	3	16	.157	.185	.169	-4	-13	0	0	0	.933	-4	O-25	-1.8
1952	Cin-N	126	377	42	95	11	4	4	24	26	53	.252	.300	.334	76	-13	1	3	-2	.991	-6	*O-103/1-5	-2.5
1953	Cin-N	94	249	32	67	11	1	7	29	21	41	.269	.328	.406	89	-4	0	1	-1	.982	-7	O-67/1-2	-1.3
1954	Cin-N	73	162	13	43	12	1	1	19	8	18	.265	.304	.370	73	-7	0	2	-1	1.000	0	O-36/1-3	-0.9
1955	Cin-N	25	18	1	3	1	0	0	1	1	2	.167	.211	.222	14	-2	0	0	0	1.000	-4	O-11/1-1	-0.6
	Bro-N	9	19	2	2	0	0	0		1	6	.105	.150	.105	-30	-4	0	0	0	1.000	-3	/O-9	-0.6
	Yr	34	37	3	5	1	0	0	1	2	8	.135	.179	.162	-8	-6	0	0	0	1.000	-6	O-20/1-1	-1.2
Total	6	470	1170	126	294	43	10	16	112	76	166	.251	.299	.346	71	-48	2	6		.982	-22	O-316/1-12	-8.5

■ RED BOROM
Borom, Edward Jones b: 10/30/15, Spartanburg, S.C. BL/TR, 5'11", 180 lbs. Deb: 4/23/44

YEAR	TM/L	G	AB	R	H	2B	3B	HR	RBI	BB	SO	AVG	OBP	SLG	PRO+	BR/A	SB	CS	SBR	FA	FR	G/POS	TPR
1944	Det-A	7	14	1	1	0	0	0	1	2	2	.071	.188	.071	-23	-2	0	0	0	.950	1	/2-4,S-1	-0.1
1945	*Det-A	55	130	19	35	4	0	0	9	7	8	.269	.307	.300	72	-5	4	2	0	.966	5	2-28/3-4,S-2	0.2
Total	2	62	144	20	36	4	0	0	10	9	10	.250	.294	.278	62	-7	4	2	0	.964	6	/2-32,3-4,S-3	0.1

■ STEVE BOROS
Boros, Stephen b: 9/3/36, Flint, Mich. BR/TR, 6', 185 lbs. Deb: 6/19/57 MC

YEAR	TM/L	G	AB	R	H	2B	3B	HR	RBI	BB	SO	AVG	OBP	SLG	PRO+	BR/A	SB	CS	SBR	FA	FR	G/POS	TPR
1957	Det-A	24	41	4	6	1	0	0	2	1	8	.146	.167	.171	-7	-6	0	0	0	.906	3	/3-9,S-5	-0.3
1958	Det-A	6	2	0	0	0	0	0	0	0	0	.000	.000	.000	-93	-1	0	0	0	1.000	0	/2-1	0.0
1961	Det-A	116	396	51	107	18	2	5	62	68	42	.270	.388	.364	99	3	4	2	0	.953	-21	*3-116	-1.7
1962	Det-A	116	356	46	81	14	1	16	47	53	62	.228	.333	.407	95	-3	3	1	0	.931	-15	*3-105/2-6	-1.6
1963	Chi-A	41	90	9	19	5	1	3	7	12	19	.211	.304	.389	93	-1	0	2	-1	.975	-3	1-14,O-11	-0.6
1964	Cin-N	117	370	31	95	12	3	2	31	47	43	.257	.344	.322	86	-5	4	1	1	.961	-4	*3-114	-0.3
1965	Cin-N	2	0	0	0	0	0	0	0	0	0	—	—	—	—	0	0	0	0	1.000	0	/3-2	0.0
Total	7	422	1255	141	308	50	7	26	149	181	174	.245	.346	.359	90	-13	11	6	-0	.948	-31	3-346/1-14,O-11,2S	-4.5

■ BABE BORTON
Borton, William Baker b: 8/14/1888, Marion, Ill. d: 7/29/54, Berkeley, Cal. BL/TL, 6', 178 lbs. Deb: 9/2/12

YEAR	TM/L	G	AB	R	H	2B	3B	HR	RBI	BB	SO	AVG	OBP	SLG	PRO+	BR/A	SB	CS	SBR	FA	FR	G/POS	TPR
1912	Chi-A	31	105	15	39	3	1	0	17	8		.371	.416	.419	143	6	1			.997	0	1-30	0.6
1913	Chi-A	28	80	9	22	5	0	0	13	23	5	.275	.442	.338	130	5	1			.991	-2	1-26	0.3
	NY-A	33	108	8	14	2	0	0	11	18	19	.130	.260	.148	20	-10	1			.978	4	1-33	-0.7
	Yr	61	188	17	36	7	0	0	24	41	24	.191	.342	.229	68	-5	2			.984	3	1-59	-0.4
1915	StL-F	159	549	**97**	157	20	14	3	83	**92**	64	.286	.395	.390	115	7	17			.993	-10	*1-159	-0.7
1916	StL-A	66	98	10	22	2	1	1	12	19	13	.224	.350	.306	102	1	1			.991	-1	1-22	-0.1
Total	4	317	940	139	254	31	17	4	136	160	101	.270	.381	.352	108	9	21			.991	-8	1-270	-0.6

■ DON BOSCH
Bosch, Donald John b: 7/15/42, San Francisco, Cal. BB/TR, 5'10", 160 lbs. Deb: 9/19/66

YEAR	TM/L	G	AB	R	H	2B	3B	HR	RBI	BB	SO	AVG	OBP	SLG	PRO+	BR/A	SB	CS	SBR	FA	FR	G/POS	TPR
1966	Pit-N	3	2	0	0	0	0	0	0	0	0	.000	.000	.000	-99	-1	0	0	0	.000	-0	/O-1	-0.1
1967	NY-N	44	93	7	13	0	1	0	2	5	24	.140	.184	.161	-0	-12	3	1	0	1.000	-4	O-39	-1.9
1968	NY-N	50	111	14	19	1	0	3	7	9	33	.171	.233	.261	48	-7	0	2	-1	.974	2	O-33	-0.9
1969	Mon-N	49	112	13	20	5	0	1	4	8	20	.179	.233	.250	35	-10	1	0	0	.964	-3	O-32	-1.4
Total	4	146	318	34	52	6	1	4	13	22	77	.164	.218	.226	28	-29	4	3	-1	.979	-5	O-105	-4.3

■ RICK BOSETTI
Bosetti, Richard Alan b: 8/5/53, Redding, Cal. BR/TR, 5'11", 185 lbs. Deb: 9/9/76

YEAR	TM/L	G	AB	R	H	2B	3B	HR	RBI	BB	SO	AVG	OBP	SLG	PRO+	BR/A	SB	CS	SBR	FA	FR	G/POS	TPR
1976	Phi-N	13	18	6	5	1	0	0	0	1	3	.278	.316	.333	82	-0	0	0	1	1.000	0	/O-6	0.0
1977	StL-N	41	69	12	16	0	0	0	3	6	11	.232	.303	.232	47	-5	4	4	-1	1.000	-4	O-35	-1.1
1978	Tor-A	136	568	61	147	25	5	5	42	30	65	.259	.300	.347	80	-16	6	10	-4	.986	25	*O-135	-0.1
1979	Tor-A	162	619	59	161	35	2	8	65	22	70	.260	.289	.362	73	-24	13	12	-3	.974	17	*O-162	-1.7
1980	Tor-A	53	188	24	40	7	1	4	18	15	29	.213	.278	.324	62	-10	4	6	-2	.985	-1	O-51	-1.6
1981	Tor-A	25	47	5	11	2	0	0	4	2	6	.234	.265	.277	53	-3	0	2	-1	1.000	-2	O-19/D-1	-0.7
	*Oak-A	9	19	4	2	0	0		1	3	3	.105	.227	.105	-2	-2	0	0	0	1.000	-0	/O-5,D-2	-0.3
	Yr	34	66	9	13	2	0	0	5	5	9	.197	.254	.227	38	-5	0	2	-1	1.000	-2	O-24/D-3	-1.0
1982	Oak-A	6	15	1	3	0	0	0	0	0	1	.200	.200	.200	11	-2	0	0	0	1.000	1	/O-6	-0.1
Total	7	445	1543	172	385	70	8	17	133	79	188	.250	.290	.338	71	-62	30	34	-11	.982	37	O-419/D-3	-5.6

■ THAD BOSLEY
Bosley, Thaddis b: 9/17/56, Oceanside, Cal. BL/TL, 6'3", 175 lbs. Deb: 6/29/77

YEAR	TM/L	G	AB	R	H	2B	3B	HR	RBI	BB	SO	AVG	OBP	SLG	PRO+	BR/A	SB	CS	SBR	FA	FR	G/POS	TPR
1977	Cal-A	58	212	19	63	10	2	0	19	16	32	.297	.349	.363	98	-0	5	4	-1	.963	1	O-55	-0.3
1978	Chi-A	66	219	25	59	5	1	2	13	13	32	.269	.310	.329	79	-6	12	11	-3	.975	0	O-64	-1.2
1979	Chi-A	36	77	13	24	1	1	1	8	9	14	.312	.384	.390	109	1	4	1	1	.967	1	O-28/D-1	0.2
1980	Chi-A	70	147	12	33	2	0	2	14	10	27	.224	.274	.279	52	-10	3	2	-0	.966	1	O-52	-1.8
1981	*Mil-A	42	105	11	24	2	0	0	3	6	13	.229	.270	.248	53	-6	3	1	0	.966	-6	O-37/D-1	-1.4
1982	Sea-A	22	46	3	8	1	0	0	2	4	7	.174	.240	.196	21	-5	3	1	0	1.000	-5	O-19	-1.1
1983	Chi-N	43	72	12	21	4	1	2	12	10	12	.292	.378	.458	125	3	1	1	1	.976	-2	O-20	0.0
1984	*Chi-N	55	98	17	29	2	2	2	14	13	22	.296	.378	.418	113	2	5	1	1	.976	-4	O-33	-0.2
1985	Chi-N	108	180	25	59	6	3	7	27	20	29	.328	.395	.511	137	9	5	1	1	.988	-7	O-55	0.2
1986	Chi-N	87	120	15	33	4	1	9	18	24	24	.275	.370	.350	92	-1	5	1	1	.969	-10	O-41	-1.0
1987	KC-A	80	140	13	39	6	1	1	16	9	26	.279	.322	.357	78	-4	0	0	0	.966	-6	O-28,D-13	-1.1
1988	KC-A	15	21	1	4	0	0	0	2	0	2	.190	.190	.190	28	-2	0	0	0	1.000	-0	/O-6,D-4	-0.4
	Cal-A	35	75	9	21	5	0	0	9	8	18	.280	.333	.347	93	-1	1	1	0	.965	-1	O-26/D-2	-0.6
	Yr	50	96	10	25	5	0	0	11	8	20	.260	.317	.313	78	-3	1	1	0	.967	-3	O-32/D-6	-0.6
1989	Tex-A	37	40	5	9	2	0	1	9	3	11	.225	.279	.350	75	-1	2	0	1	1.000	-3	/O-8,D-5	-0.1
1990	Tex-A	30	29	3	4	0	0	0	1	3	4	.138	.242	.241	36	-3	1	0	0	1.000	-3	/O-9,D-4	-0.5
Total	14	784	1581	183	430	50	12	20	158	143	275	.272	.333	.357	89	-24	47	24	-0	.972	-48	O-481/D-30	-8.9

■ HARLEY BOSS
Boss, Elmer Harley "Lefty" b: 11/19/08, Hodge, La. d: 5/15/64, Nashville, Tenn. BL/TL, 5'11.5", 185 lbs. Deb: 7/19/28

YEAR	TM/L	G	AB	R	H	2B	3B	HR	RBI	BB	SO	AVG	OBP	SLG	PRO+	BR/A	SB	CS	SBR	FA	FR	G/POS	TPR
1928	Was-A	12	12	1	3	0	0	0	2	3	1	.250	.400	.250	75	-1	0	0	0	.970	-1	/1-5	-0.1
1929	Was-A	28	66	9	18	2	1	0	6	2	6	.273	.294	.333	61	-4	0	0	0	.977	1	1-18	-0.5
1930	Was-A	3	3	0	0	0	0	0	0	0	0	.000	.000	.000	-99	-1	0	0	0	1.000	-0	/1-1	-0.1
1933	Cle-A	112	438	54	118	17	7	1	53	25	27	.269	.310	.347	71	-19	2	5	0	.994	6	*1-110	-2.5
Total	4	155	519	64	139	19	8	1	61	30	34	.268	.309	.341	69	-24	2	5	0	.992	5	1-134	-3.2

■ HENRY BOSTICK
Bostick, Henry Landers (b: Henry Lipschitz) b: 1/12/1895, Boston, Mass. d: 9/16/68, Denver, Colo. BR/TR, Deb: 5/18/15

YEAR	TM/L	G	AB	R	H	2B	3B	HR	RBI	BB	SO	AVG	OBP	SLG	PRO+	BR/A	SB	CS	SBR	FA	FR	G/POS	TPR
1915	Phi-A	2	7	0	0	0	0	0	0	1		.000	.125	.000	-65	-1				.970	-1	/3-2	-0.3

■ LYMAN BOSTOCK
Bostock, Lyman Wesley b: 11/22/50, Birmingham, Ala. d: 9/23/78, Gary, Ind. BL/TR, 6'1", 180 lbs. Deb: 4/8/75

YEAR	TM/L	G	AB	R	H	2B	3B	HR	RBI	BB	SO	AVG	OBP	SLG	PRO+	BR/A	SB	CS	SBR	FA	FR	G/POS	TPR
1975	Min-A	98	369	52	104	21	5	0	29	28	42	.282	.332	.366	96	-2	2	3	-1	.985	-3	O-92/D-1	-1.0
1976	Min-A	128	474	75	153	21	9	4	60	33	37	.323	.368	.430	131	18	12	6	0	.988	6	*O-124	1.9
1977	Min-A	153	593	104	199	36	12	14	90	51	59	.336	.394	.508	146	38	16	7	1	.989	4	*O-149	3.5
1978	Cal-A	147	568	74	168	24	4	5	71	59	36	.296	.364	.379	113	11	15	12	-3	.989	11	*O-146/D-1	1.3
Total	4	526	2004	305	624	102	30	23	250	171	174	.311	.368	.427	124	64	45	28	-3	.988	18	O-511/D-2	5.7

■ DARYL BOSTON
Boston, Daryl Lamont b: 1/4/63, Cincinnati, Ohio BL/TL, 6'3", 193 lbs. Deb: 5/13/84

YEAR	TM/L	G	AB	R	H	2B	3B	HR	RBI	BB	SO	AVG	OBP	SLG	PRO+	BR/A	SB	CS	SBR	FA	FR	G/POS	TPR
1984	Chi-A	35	83	8	14	3	1	0	3	4	20	.169	.207	.229	20	-9	6	0	2	.910	-6	O-34/D-1	-1.4
1985	Chi-A	95	232	20	53	13	1	3	15	14	44	.228	.272	.332	62	-12	8	6	-1	.989	-6	O-93/D-2	-2.1

YEAR	TM/L	G	AB	R	H	2B	3B	HR	RBI	BB	SO	AVG	OBP	SLG	PRO+	BR/A	SB	CS	SBR	FA	FR	G/POS	TPR
1986	Chi-A	56	199	29	53	11	3	5	22	21	33	.266	.336	.427	103	1	9	5	-0	.969	5	O-53/D-1	0.3
1987	Chi-A	103	337	51	87	21	2	10	29	25	68	.258	.309	.421	89	-6	12	6	0	.991	-0	O-92/D-5	-0.8
1988	Chi-A	105	281	37	61	12	2	15	31	21	44	.217	.272	.434	95	-3	9	3	1	.951	-3	O-85/D-5	-0.7
1989	Chi-A	101	218	34	55	3	4	5	23	24	31	.252	.326	.372	99	-0	7	2	1	.971	-7	O-75/D-9	-0.8
1990	Chi-A	5	1	0	0	0	0	0	0	0	0	.000	.000	.000	-99	-0	1	0	0	.000	-0	/O-1,D-3	0.0
	NY-N	115	366	65	100	21	2	12	45	28	50	.273	.328	.440	110	4	18	7	1	.986	-5	*O-109	-0.2
1991	NY-N	137	255	40	70	16	4	4	21	30	42	.275	.351	.416	116	5	15	8	-0	.981	-17	*O-115	-1.4
1992	NY-N	130	289	37	72	14	2	11	35	38	60	.249	.342	.426	118	7	12	6	0	.993	-6	O-95	0.0
1993	Col-N	124	291	46	76	15	1	14	40	26	57	.261	.326	.464	93	-4	6	3	-3	.985	-6	O-79	-1.5
1994	NY-A	52	77	11	14	2	0	4	14	6	20	.182	.250	.364	58	-5	0	1	-1	1.000	-4	O-16/D-9	-0.9
Total	11	1058	2629	378	655	131	22	83	278	237	469	.249	.313	.410	95	-23	98	50	-1	.977	-54	O-847/D-35	-9.5

■ KEN BOSWELL
Boswell, Kenneth George b: 2/23/46, Austin, Tex. BL/TR, 6′, 172 lbs. Deb: 9/18/67

YEAR	TM/L	G	AB	R	H	2B	3B	HR	RBI	BB	SO	AVG	OBP	SLG	PRO+	BR/A	SB	CS	SBR	FA	FR	G/POS	TPR
1967	NY-N	11	40	2	9	3	0	1	4	1	5	.225	.244	.375	76	-1	0	0	0	.971	2	/2-6,3-4	0.1
1968	NY-N	75	284	37	74	7	2	4	11	16	27	.261	.302	.342	93	-3	7	2	1	.965	-1	2-69	0.1
1969	*NY-N	102	362	48	101	14	7	3	32	36	47	.279	.348	.381	102	1	7	3	0	.959	-15	2-96	-0.7
1970	NY-N	105	351	32	89	13	2	5	44	41	32	.254	.335	.345	82	-8	5	4	-1	.996	-15	*2-101	-1.6
1971	NY-N	116	392	46	107	20	1	5	40	36	31	.273	.337	.367	101	1	5	2	0	.973	-29	*2-109	-2.1
1972	NY-N	100	355	35	75	9	1	9	33	32	35	.211	.276	.318	70	-14	2	2	-1	.990	-31	2-94	-4.5
1973	*NY-N	76	110	12	25	2	1	2	14	12	11	.227	.303	.318	74	-4	0	1	-1	.973	0	3-17/2-3	-0.4
1974	NY-N	96	222	19	48	6	1	2	15	19	24	.216	.278	.279	57	-13	0	1	-1	1.000	7	2-28,3-20/O-7	-0.6
1975	Hou-N	86	178	16	43	8	2	0	21	30	12	.242	.354	.309	92	-1	0	3	-2	.991	-10	2-31,3-23	-1.2
1976	Hou-N	91	126	12	33	8	1	0	18	8	8	.262	.306	.341	92	-2	1	0	0	.933	-5	3-16/2-3,O-1	-0.7
1977	Hou-N	72	97	7	21	1	1	0	12	10	12	.216	.290	.247	50	-7	0	0	0	1.000	-3	2-26/3-2	-0.9
Total	11	930	2517	266	625	91	19	31	244	240	239	.248	.316	.337	85	-51	27	17	-2	.979	-100	2-566/3-82,O-8	-12.5

■ JOHN BOTTARINI
Bottarini, John Charles b: 9/14/08, Crockett, Cal. d: 10/8/76, Jemez Springs, N.Mex. BR/TR, 6′, 190 lbs. Deb: 4/22/37

YEAR	TM/L	G	AB	R	H	2B	3B	HR	RBI	BB	SO	AVG	OBP	SLG	PRO+	BR/A	SB	CS	SBR	FA	FR	G/POS	TPR
1937	Chi-N	26	40	3	11	3	0	1	7	5	10	.275	.370	.425	111	1	0	0	0	1.000	1	C-18/O-1	0.2

■ JIM BOTTOMLEY
Bottomley, James Leroy "Sunny Jim" b: 4/23/1900, Oglesby, Ill. d: 12/11/59, St.Louis, Mo. BL/TL, 6′, 180 lbs. Deb: 8/18/22 MCH

YEAR	TM/L	G	AB	R	H	2B	3B	HR	RBI	BB	SO	AVG	OBP	SLG	PRO+	BR/A	SB	CS	SBR	FA	FR	G/POS	TPR
1922	StL-N	37	151	29	49	8	5	5	35	6	13	.325	.358	.543	136	7	3			.986	-3	1-34	0.3
1923	StL-N	134	523	79	194	34	14	8	94	45	44	.371	.425	.535	155	42	4	6	-2	.986	-12	*1-130	1.9
1924	StL-N	137	528	87	167	31	12	14	111	35	35	.316	.382	.500	131	21	5	4	-1	.982	-12	*1-133/2-1	0.0
1925	StL-N	153	619	92	**227**	**44**	12	21	128	47	36	.367	.413	.578	147	42	4			.987	-4	*1-153	2.6
1926	*StL-N	154	603	98	180	**40**	14	19	**120**	58	52	.299	.364	.506	127	21	4			.989	-15	*1-154	-0.3
1927	StL-N	152	574	95	174	31	15	19	124	74	49	.303	.387	.509	134	28	8			.989	-11	*1-152	0.6
1928	*StL-N	149	576	123	187	42	**20**	**31**	**136**	71	54	.325	.402	.628	163	50	10			.987	-14	*1-148	2.2
1929	StL-N	146	560	108	176	31	12	29	137	70	54	.314	.391	.568	133	28	3			.991	-6	*1-145	0.7
1930	*StL-N	131	487	92	148	33	7	15	97	44	36	.304	.388	.493	102	1	5			.990	-14	*1-124	-2.2
1931	*StL-N	108	382	73	133	34	5	9	75	34	24	.348	.403	.534	144	23	3			.987	-3	1-93	1.1
1932	StL-N	91	311	45	92	16	3	11	48	25	32	.296	.350	.473	115	6	2			.986	-3	1-74	-0.2
1933	Cin-N	145	549	57	137	23	9	13	83	42	28	.250	.311	.395	102	1	3			.991	-9	*1-145	-2.3
1934	Cin-N	142	556	72	158	31	11	11	78	33	40	.284	.324	.439	105	2	1			.989	-4	*1-139	-1.3
1935	Cin-N	107	399	44	103	21	1	1	49	18	24	.258	.294	.323	68	-18	3			.992	-3	1-97	-3.1
1936	StL-A	140	544	72	162	39	11	12	95	44	55	.298	.354	.476	100	-2	0	0	0	.992	-10	*1-140	-2.2
1937	StL-A	65	109	11	26	7	0	1	12	18	15	.239	.346	.330	71	-5	1	0	0	.995	1	1-24,M	-0.5
Total	16	1991	7471	1177	2313	465	151	219	1422	664	591	.310	.369	.500	124	247	58	15		.988	-120	*1-1885/2-1	-2.7

■ ED BOUCHEE
Bouchee, Edward Francis b: 3/7/33, Livingston, Mont. BL/TL, 6′1″, 205 lbs. Deb: 9/19/56

YEAR	TM/L	G	AB	R	H	2B	3B	HR	RBI	BB	SO	AVG	OBP	SLG	PRO+	BR/A	SB	CS	SBR	FA	FR	G/POS	TPR
1956	Phi-N	9	22	0	6	2	0	0	1	5	6	.273	.407	.364	112	1	0	0	0	1.000	-0	/1-6	0.0
1957	Phi-N	154	574	78	168	35	8	17	76	84	91	.293	.396	.470	136	32	1	0	0	.988	4	*1-154	2.7
1958	Phi-N	89	334	55	86	19	5	9	39	51	74	.257	.356	.425	107	4	1	0	0	.993	-0	1-89	-0.1
1959	Phi-N	136	499	75	142	29	4	15	74	70	74	.285	.378	.449	117	14	0	4	-2	.986	-0	*1-134	0.2
1960	Phi-N	22	65	1	17	4	0	0	8	9	11	.262	.360	.323	89	-1	0	0	0	.994	1	1-22	-0.1
	Chi-N	98	299	33	71	11	1	5	44	45	51	.237	.341	.331	86	-5	2	0	1	.991	-0	1-80	-1.1
	Yr	120	364	34	88	15	1	5	52	54	62	.242	.344	.330	86	-5	2	0	1	.992	1	1-102	-1.2
1961	Chi-N	112	319	49	79	12	3	12	38	58	77	.248	.372	.417	108	5	1	4	-2	.983	1	*1-107	-0.4
1962	NY-N	50	87	7	14	2	0	3	10	18	17	.161	.305	.287	59	-5	0	0	0	.976	4	1-19	-0.2
Total	7	670	2199	298	583	114	21	61	290	340	401	.265	.370	.419	112	46	3	8	-4	.988	9	1-611	1.0

■ AL BOUCHER
Boucher, Alexander Francis "Bo" b: 11/13/1881, Franklin, Mass. d: 6/23/74, Torrance, Cal. BR/TR, 5′8.5″, 156 lbs. Deb: 4/16/14

YEAR	TM/L	G	AB	R	H	2B	3B	HR	RBI	BB	SO	AVG	OBP	SLG	PRO+	BR/A	SB	CS	SBR	FA	FR	G/POS	TPR
1914	StL-F	147	516	62	119	26	4	2	49	52	88	.231	.304	.308	64	-34	13			.916	-4	*3-147	-3.4

■ MEDRIC BOUCHER
Boucher, Medric Charles Francis b: 3/12/1886, St.Louis, Mo. d: 3/12/74, Martinez, Cal. BR/TR, 5′10″, 165 lbs. Deb: 5/20/14

YEAR	TM/L	G	AB	R	H	2B	3B	HR	RBI	BB	SO	AVG	OBP	SLG	PRO+	BR/A	SB	CS	SBR	FA	FR	G/POS	TPR
1914	Bal-F	16	16	2	5	1	0	2	2	1	1	.313	.353	.500	127	0	0			.950	0	/C-7,1-1,O-1	0.1
	Pit-F	1	1	0	0	0	0	0	0	0	0	.000	.000	.000	-99	-0	0			.000	0	H	0.0
	Yr	17	17	2	5	1	0	2	2	1	1	.294	.333	.471	114	-0	0			.950	0	/C-7,1-1,O-1	0.1

■ LOU BOUDREAU
Boudreau, Louis b: 7/17/17, Harvey, Ill. BR/TR, 5′11″, 185 lbs. Deb: 9/9/38 MH

YEAR	TM/L	G	AB	R	H	2B	3B	HR	RBI	BB	SO	AVG	OBP	SLG	PRO+	BR/A	SB	CS	SBR	FA	FR	G/POS	TPR
1938	Cle-A	1	1	0	0	0	0	0	0	1	0	.000	.000	.000	36	0	0	0	0	.000	0	/3-1	0.0
1939	Cle-A	53	225	42	58	15	4	0	19	28	24	.258	.340	.360	82	-6	2	1	0	.953	8	S-53	0.6
1940	Cle-A★	155	627	97	185	46	10	9	101	73	39	.295	.370	.443	113	13	6	3	0	**.968**	12	*S-155	3.5
1941	Cle-A★	148	579	95	149	**45**	8	10	56	85	57	.257	.355	.415	108	7	9	4	0	**.966**	13	*S-147	3.1
1942	Cle-A★	147	506	57	143	18	10	2	58	75	39	.283	.379	.370	118	15	7	16	-8	.965	-0	*S-146,M	1.6
1943	Cle-A☆	152	539	69	154	32	7	3	67	90	31	.286	.388	.388	135	27	4	7	-3	**.970**	28	*S-152/C-1,M	6.7
1944	Cle-A☆	150	584	91	191	**45**	5	3	67	73	39	**.327**	.406	.437	146	37	11	3	2	**.978**	26	*S-149/C-1,M	7.8
1945	Cle-A†	97	345	50	106	24	5	3	48	35	20	.307	.374	.409	133	14	0	4	-2	.983	12	S-97,M	2.2
1946	Cle-A	140	515	51	151	30	6	6	62	40	14	.293	.345	.410	118	11	6	7	-2	**.970**	16	*S-139,M	3.4
1947	Cle-A★	150	538	79	165	**45**	3	4	67	67	10	.307	.388	.424	129	22	1	0	0	**.982**	17	*S-148,M	4.8
1948	*Cle-A★	152	560	116	199	34	6	18	106	98	9	.355	.453	.534	166	56	3	2	-0	**.975**	21	*S-151/C-1,M	6.9
1949	Cle-A	134	475	53	135	20	5	4	60	70	10	.284	.381	.364	100	2	0	1	-1	.982	5	S-88,3-38/1-6,2M	1.1
1950	Cle-A	81	260	23	70	13	2	1	29	31	5	.269	.349	.346	81	-7	1	2	-1	.986	0	S-61/1-8,2-2,3-2,M	-0.3
1951	Bos-A	82	273	37	73	18	1	5	47	30	12	.267	.353	.396	93	-3	1	0	0	.951	-1	S-52,3-15/1-2	-0.1
1952	Bos-A	4	2	1	0	0	0	0	2	0	0	.000	.000	.000	-93	-1	0	0	0	1.000	-0	/S-1,3-1,M	-0.1
Total	15	1646	6029	861	1779	385	66	68	789	796	309	.295	.380	.415	121	187	51	50	-15	.973	134	*S-1539/3-57,12C	41.3

■ CHRIS BOURJOS
Bourjos, Christopher b: 10/16/57, Chicago, Ill. BR/TR, 6′, 185 lbs. Deb: 8/31/80

YEAR	TM/L	G	AB	R	H	2B	3B	HR	RBI	BB	SO	AVG	OBP	SLG	PRO+	BR/A	SB	CS	SBR	FA	FR	G/POS	TPR
1980	SF-N	13	22	4	5	1	0	1	2	2	7	.227	.292	.409	96	-0	0	0	0	1.000	-1	/O-6	-0.2

■ RAFAEL BOURNIGAL
Bournigal, Rafael Antonio (Pelletier) b: 5/12/66, Azua, D.R. BR/TR, 5′11″, 160 lbs. Deb: 9/1/92

YEAR	TM/L	G	AB	R	H	2B	3B	HR	RBI	BB	SO	AVG	OBP	SLG	PRO+	BR/A	SB	CS	SBR	FA	FR	G/POS	TPR
1992	LA-N	10	20	1	3	1	0	0	1	2	1	.150	.227	.200	22	-2	0	0	0	.967	2	/S-9	0.1
1993	LA-N	8	18	0	9	1	0	0	3	0	2	.500	.500	.556	193	2	0	0	0	1.000	1	/2-4,S-4	0.3
1994	LA-N	40	116	12	26	3	1	0	11	9	5	.224	.291	.267	50	-8	0	0	0	.981	0	S-40	-0.5
1996	Oak-A	88	252	33	61	14	2	0	18	16	19	.242	.290	.313	55	-18	4	3	-1	.993	4	2-64,S-23	-0.9
Total	4	146	406	36	99	19	3	0	32	26	28	.244	.296	.305	58	-26	4	3	-1	.984	7	/S-76,2-68	-1.0

■ PAT BOURQUE
Bourque, Patrick Daniel b: 3/23/47, Worcester, Mass. BL/TL, 6′, 210 lbs. Deb: 9/6/71

YEAR	TM/L	G	AB	R	H	2B	3B	HR	RBI	BB	SO	AVG	OBP	SLG	PRO+	BR/A	SB	CS	SBR	FA	FR	G/POS	TPR
1971	Chi-N	14	37	3	7	0	1	1	3	3	9	.189	.250	.324	54	-2	0	0	0	.957	2	1-11	-0.1
1972	Chi-N	11	27	3	7	1	0	0	5	2	7	.259	.310	.296	66	-1	0	0	0	1.000	1	/1-7	-0.1
1973	Chi-N	57	139	11	29	6	0	7	20	16	21	.209	.299	.403	86	-3	1	1	-0	.986	5	1-38	0.0
	*Oak-A	23	42	8	8	4	1	2	9	15	10	.190	.404	.476	155	4	0	0	0	1.000	-1	D-15/1-5	0.3
1974	Oak-A	73	96	6	22	4	0	1	16	15	20	.229	.333	.302	90	-1	0	2	-1	.988	-1	1-39/D-8	-0.4

YEAR	TM/L	G	AB	R	H	2B	3B	HR	RBI	BB	SO	AVG	OBP	SLG	PRO+	BR/A	SB	CS	SBR	FA	FR	G/POS	TPR
	Min-A	23	64	5	14	2	0	1	8	7	11	.219	.296	.297	69	-2	0	0	0	.987	3	1-21	-0.1
	Yr	96	160	11	36	6	0	2	24	22	31	.225	.319	.300	82	-3	0	2	-1	.988	2	1-60/D-8	-0.5
Total	4	201	405	36	87	17	2	12	61	58	73	.215	.316	.356	87	-6	1	3	-2	.985	11	1-121/D-23	-0.4

■ LARRY BOWA
Bowa, Lawrence Robert b: 12/6/45, Sacramento, Cal. BB/TR, 5'10", 155 lbs. Deb: 4/7/70 MC

YEAR	TM/L	G	AB	R	H	2B	3B	HR	RBI	BB	SO	AVG	OBP	SLG	PRO+	BR/A	SB	CS	SBR	FA	FR	G/POS	TPR
1970	Phi-N	145	547	50	137	17	6	0	34	21	48	.250	.278	.303	57	-34	24	13	-1	.979	-21	*S-143/2-1	-3.9
1971	Phi-N	159	650	74	162	18	5	0	25	36	51	.249	.294	.292	66	-28	28	11	2	.987	10	*S-157	0.5
1972	Phi-N	152	579	67	145	11	13	1	31	32	51	.250	.292	.320	72	-22	17	9	-0	.987	5	*S-150	0.4
1973	Phi-N	122	446	42	94	11	3	0	23	24	31	.211	.253	.249	38	-37	10	6	1	.979	-0	*S-122	-2.3
1974	Phi-N★	162	669	97	184	19	10	1	36	23	52	.275	.300	.338	75	-23	39	11	5	.984	-16	*S-162	-1.4
1975	Phi-N★	136	583	79	178	18	9	2	38	24	32	.305	.335	.377	94	-6	24	6	4	.962	-12	*S-135	0.1
1976	*Phi-N★	156	624	71	155	15	9	0	49	32	31	.248	.285	.301	65	-29	30	8	4	.975	-14	*S-156	-2.2
1977	*Phi-N	154	624	93	175	19	3	4	41	32	32	.280	.316	.340	73	-24	32	3	8	.983	1	*S-154	0.3
1978	Phi-N★	156	654	78	192	31	5	3	43	24	40	.294	.320	.370	91	-9	27	5	5	.986	2	*S-156	1.9
1979	Phi-N★	147	539	74	130	17	11	0	31	61	32	.241	.319	.314	71	-20	20	9	1	.991	-12	*S-146	-1.6
1980	*Phi-N	147	540	57	144	16	4	2	39	24	28	.267	.302	.322	70	-21	21	6	3	.975	-13	*S-147	-1.6
1981	*Phi-N	103	360	34	102	14	3	0	31	26	17	.283	.332	.339	87	-6	16	7	1	.975	-10	*S-102	-0.5
1982	Chi-N	142	499	50	123	15	7	0	29	39	38	.246	.302	.305	68	-21	8	3	1	.973	-30	*S-140	-3.9
1983	Chi-N	147	499	73	133	20	5	2	43	35	30	.267	.315	.339	77	-15	7	3	0	.984	15	*S-145	1.5
1984	*Chi-N	133	391	33	87	14	2	0	17	28	24	.223	.274	.269	49	-26	10	4	1	.974	7	*S-132	-0.8
1985	Chi-N	72	195	13	48	6	4	0	13	11	20	.246	.286	.318	62	-10	5	1	1	.970	12	S-66	0.8
	NY-N	14	19	2	2	1	0	0	2	2	2	.105	.190	.158	-2	-3	0	0	0	.882	1	/S-9,2-4	-0.2
	Yr	86	214	15	50	7	4	0	15	13	22	.234	.278	.304	57	-12	5	1	1	.965	12	S-75/2-4	0.6
Total	16	2247	8418	987	2191	262	99	15	525	474	569	.260	.301	.320	71	-333	318	105	32	.980	-75	*S-2222/2-5	-12.9

■ BENNY BOWCOCK
Bowcock, Benjamin James b: 10/28/1879, Fall River, Mass. d: 6/16/61, New Bedford, Mass BR/TR, 5'7", 150 lbs. Deb: 9/18/03

YEAR	TM/L	G	AB	R	H	2B	3B	HR	RBI	BB	SO	AVG	OBP	SLG	PRO+	BR/A	SB	CS	SBR	FA	FR	G/POS	TPR
1903	StL-A	14	50	7	16	3	1	1	10	3		.320	.358	.480	154	3	1			.885	-7	2-14	-0.3

■ TIM BOWDEN
Bowden, David Timon b: 8/15/1891, McDonough, Ga. d: 10/25/49, Emory, Ga. BL/TR, 5'10", 175 lbs. Deb: 9/17/14

YEAR	TM/L	G	AB	R	H	2B	3B	HR	RBI	BB	SO	AVG	OBP	SLG	PRO+	BR/A	SB	CS	SBR	FA	FR	G/POS	TPR
1914	StL-A	7	9	0	2	0	0	0	0	1	6	.222	.300	.222	60	-0	0			1.000	-1	/O-4	-0.2

■ CHICK BOWEN
Bowen, Emmons Joseph b: 7/26/1897, New Haven, Conn. d: 8/9/48, New Haven, Conn. BR/TR, 5'7", 165 lbs. Deb: 9/15/19

YEAR	TM/L	G	AB	R	H	2B	3B	HR	RBI	BB	SO	AVG	OBP	SLG	PRO+	BR/A	SB	CS	SBR	FA	FR	G/POS	TPR
1919	NY-N	3	5	0	1	0	0	0	1	1	2	.200	.333	.200	63	-0	0			1.000	-0	/O-2	-0.1

■ SAM BOWEN
Bowen, Samuel Thomas b: 9/18/52, Brunswick, Ga. BR/TR, 5'9", 170 lbs. Deb: 8/25/77

YEAR	TM/L	G	AB	R	H	2B	3B	HR	RBI	BB	SO	AVG	OBP	SLG	PRO+	BR/A	SB	CS	SBR	FA	FR	G/POS	TPR
1977	Bos-A	3	2	0	0	0	0	0	0	0	2	.000	.000	.000	-90	-1	0	0	0	1.000	-1	/O-3	-0.1
1978	Bos-A	6	7	3	1	0	0	1	1	1	2	.143	.250	.571	112	0	0	0	0	1.000	-2	/O-4	-0.2
1980	Bos-A	7	13	0	2	0	0	0	0	2	3	.154	.267	.154	17	-1	1	0	0	1.000	1	/O-6	0.0
Total	3	16	22	3	3	0	0	1	1	3	7	.136	.240	.273	38	-2	1	0	0	1.000	-1	/O-13	-0.3

■ SAM BOWENS
Bowens, Samuel Edward b: 3/23/39, Wilmington, N.C. BR/TR, 6'1.5", 195 lbs. Deb: 9/7/63

YEAR	TM/L	G	AB	R	H	2B	3B	HR	RBI	BB	SO	AVG	OBP	SLG	PRO+	BR/A	SB	CS	SBR	FA	FR	G/POS	TPR
1963	Bal-A	15	48	8	16	3	1	1	9	4	5	.333	.385	.500	151	3	1	1	-0	.952	-1	O-13	0.1
1964	Bal-A	139	501	58	132	25	2	22	71	42	99	.263	.325	.453	114	9	4	3	-1	.981	-0	*O-135	0.2
1965	Bal-A	84	203	16	33	4	1	7	20	10	41	.163	.202	.296	39	-17	7	1	2	.982	-2	O-68	-2.1
1966	Bal-A	89	243	26	51	9	1	6	20	17	52	.210	.275	.329	74	-8	9	3	1	.960	-3	O-68	-1.1
1967	Bal-A	62	120	13	22	2	1	5	12	11	43	.183	.258	.342	76	-4	3	4	-2	.977	-2	O-32	-0.9
1968	Was-A	57	115	14	22	4	0	4	7	11	39	.191	.262	.330	81	-3	0	0	0	.957	-1	O-27	-0.6
1969	Was-A	33	57	6	11	1	0	0	4	5	14	.193	.258	.211	34	-5	1	1	-0	.971	-5	O-30	-1.2
Total	7	479	1287	141	287	48	6	45	143	100	293	.223	.284	.375	87	-25	25	13	-0	.974	-12	O-373	-5.6

■ FRANK BOWERMAN
Bowerman, Frank Eugene "Mike" b: 12/5/1868, Romeo, Mich. d: 11/30/48, Romeo, Mich. BR/TR, 6'2", 190 lbs. Deb: 8/24/1895 M

YEAR	TM/L	G	AB	R	H	2B	3B	HR	RBI	BB	SO	AVG	OBP	SLG	PRO+	BR/A	SB	CS	SBR	FA	FR	G/POS	TPR
1895	Bal-N	1	1	0	0	0	0	0	0	0	0	.000	.000	.000	-97	-0	0			1.000	0	/C-1	0.0
1896	Bal-N	4	16	0	2	0	0	0	4	1	0	.125	.176	.125	-20	-3	0			.900	0	/C-3,1-1	-0.2
1897	*Bal-N	38	130	16	41	5	0	1	21	1		.315	.331	.377	86	-3	3			.948	3	C-36	0.3
1898	Bal-N	5	16	5	7	1	0	0	1	2		.438	.526	.500	191	2	1			.950	-0	/C-4	0.2
	Pit-N	69	241	17	66	6	3	0	29	7		.274	.297	.324	79	-7	4			.946	5	C-59/1-9	0.3
	Yr	74	257	22	73	7	3	0	30	9		.284	.313	.335	87	-5	5			.946	5	C-63/1-9	0.5
1899	Pit-N	109	424	49	110	16	10	3	53	11		.259	.286	.366	79	-15	10			.948	12	C-79,1-28	0.3
1900	NY-N	80	270	25	65	5	3	1	42	6		.241	.268	.293	57	-16	10			.929	14	C-75/S-2	0.4
1901	NY-N	59	191	20	38	5	3	0	14	7		.199	.235	.257	44	-14	3			.950	13	C-46/2-3,S-3,3-1	0.4
1902	NY-N	107	367	38	93	14	6	0	26	13		.253	.279	.324	87	-7	12			.956	2	C-98/1-3	0.5
1903	NY-N	64	210	22	58	6	2	1	31	6		.276	.302	.338	80	-6	5			.977	0	C-55/1-4,O-1	0.5
1904	NY-N	93	289	38	67	11	4	2	27	16		.232	.288	.318	84	-6	7			.977	3	C-79/1-9,2-2,P-1	0.6
1905	NY-N	98	297	37	80	8	1	3	41	12		.269	.302	.333	93	-3	6			.982	-3	C-72,1-17/2-1	0.0
1906	NY-N	103	285	23	65	7	3	1	42	15		.228	.274	.284	72	-10	5			.984	4	C-67,1-20	-0.1
1907	NY-N	96	311	31	81	8	2	0	32	17		.260	.309	.299	88	-4	11			.990	-5	C-62,1-29	-0.5
1908	Bos-N	86	254	16	58	8	1	1	25	13		.228	.274	.280	78	-7	4			.971	-3	C-63,1-11	-0.5
1909	Bos-N	33	99	6	21	2	0	0	4	2		.212	.228	.232	41	-7	0			.928	1	C-27,M	-0.4
Total	15	1045	3401	343	852	102	38	13	392	129	0	.251	.287	.314	77	-105	81			.963	47	C-826,1-132/2S3PO	1.3

■ BRENT BOWERS
Bowers, Brent Raymond b: 5/2/71, Bridgeview, Ill. BL/TR, 6'3", 200 lbs. Deb: 8/16/96

YEAR	TM/L	G	AB	R	H	2B	3B	HR	RBI	BB	SO	AVG	OBP	SLG	PRO+	BR/A	SB	CS	SBR	FA	FR	G/POS	TPR
1996	Bal-A	21	39	6	12	2	0	0	3	0	7	.308	.308	.359	69	-2	0	0	0	1.000	-3	O-21	-0.4

■ BILLY BOWERS
Bowers, Grover Bill b: 3/25/23, Parkin, Ark. BL/TR, 5'9.5", 176 lbs. Deb: 4/24/49

YEAR	TM/L	G	AB	R	H	2B	3B	HR	RBI	BB	SO	AVG	OBP	SLG	PRO+	BR/A	SB	CS	SBR	FA	FR	G/POS	TPR
1949	Chi-A	26	78	5	15	2	1	0	6	4	5	.192	.232	.244	27	-9	1	1	-0	.980	0	O-20	-1.0

■ STEW BOWERS
Bowers, Stewart Cole "Doc" b: 2/26/15, New Freedom, Pa. BB/TR, 6', 170 lbs. Deb: 8/5/35

YEAR	TM/L	G	AB	R	H	2B	3B	HR	RBI	BB	SO	AVG	OBP	SLG	PRO+	BR/A	SB	CS	SBR	FA	FR	G/POS	TPR
1935	Bos-A	11	5	1	1	0	0	0	0	1	2	.200	.333	.200	38	-0	0	0	0	.875	0	P-10	0.0
1936	Bos-A	6	0	1	0	0	0	0	0	0	0	—	—	—	—	0	0	0	0	.000	-0	/P-5	0.0
1937	Bos-A	1	0	1	0	0	0	0	0	0	0	—	—	—	—	0	0	0	0	.000	0	R	0.0
Total	3	18	5	3	1	0	0	0	0	1	2	.200	.333	.200	38	-0	0	0	0	.875	-0	/P-15	0.0

■ FRANK BOWES
Bowes, Frank M. b: 1865, Bath, N.Y. d: 1/21/1895, New York, N.Y. TR, 5'9", 160 lbs. Deb: 4/17/1890

YEAR	TM/L	G	AB	R	H	2B	3B	HR	RBI	BB	SO	AVG	OBP	SLG	PRO+	BR/A	SB	CS	SBR	FA	FR	G/POS	TPR
1890	Bro-a	61	232	28	51	5	2	0	24	7		.220	.246	.259	50	-15	11			.813	-9	C-25,O-19,3-13,/1S	-2.0

■ JIM BOWIE
Bowie, Jim b: 2/17/65, Tokyo, Japan BL/TL, 6', 205 lbs. Deb: 8/3/94

YEAR	TM/L	G	AB	R	H	2B	3B	HR	RBI	BB	SO	AVG	OBP	SLG	PRO+	BR/A	SB	CS	SBR	FA	FR	G/POS	TPR
1994	Oak-A	6	14	0	3	0	0	0	2	0	0	.214	.214	.214	12	-2	0	0	0	1.000	0	/1-6	-0.2

■ WELDON BOWLIN
Bowlin, Lois Weldon "Hoss" b: 12/10/40, Paragould, Ark. BR/TR, 5'9", 155 lbs. Deb: 9/16/67

YEAR	TM/L	G	AB	R	H	2B	3B	HR	RBI	BB	SO	AVG	OBP	SLG	PRO+	BR/A	SB	CS	SBR	FA	FR	G/POS	TPR
1967	KC-A	2	5	0	1	0	0	0	0	0	1	.200	.200	.200	19	-0	0	0	0	1.000	0	/3-2	0.0

■ STEVE BOWLING
Bowling, Stephen Shaddon b: 6/26/52, Tulsa, Okla. BR/TR, 6', 185 lbs. Deb: 9/7/76

YEAR	TM/L	G	AB	R	H	2B	3B	HR	RBI	BB	SO	AVG	OBP	SLG	PRO+	BR/A	SB	CS	SBR	FA	FR	G/POS	TPR
1976	Mil-A	14	42	4	7	2	0	0	2	2	5	.167	.205	.214	23	-4	0	0	0	.975	1	O-13/D-1	-0.3
1977	Tor-A	89	194	19	40	8	1	1	13	37	42	.206	.338	.273	67	-8	2	3	-1	.987	-0	O-87	-1.2
Total	2	103	236	23	47	10	1	1	15	39	47	.199	.313	.263	60	-12	2	3	-1	.985	1	O-100/D-1	-1.5

■ ELMER BOWMAN
Bowman, Elmari Wilhelm "Big Bow" b: 3/19/1897, Proctor, Vt. d: 12/17/85, Los Angeles, Cal. BR/TR, 6'0.5", 193 lbs. Deb: 8/3/20

YEAR	TM/L	G	AB	R	H	2B	3B	HR	RBI	BB	SO	AVG	OBP	SLG	PRO+	BR/A	SB	CS	SBR	FA	FR	G/POS	TPR
1920	Was-A	2	1	0	0	0	0	0	0	0	0	.000	.500	.000	42	-0	0			.000	0	H	0.0

■ ERNIE BOWMAN
Bowman, Ernest Ferrell b: 7/28/35, Johnson City, Tenn. BR/TR, 5'10", 160 lbs. Deb: 4/12/61

YEAR	TM/L	G	AB	R	H	2B	3B	HR	RBI	BB	SO	AVG	OBP	SLG	PRO+	BR/A	SB	CS	SBR	FA	FR	G/POS	TPR
1961	SF-N	38	38	10	8	0	0	2	2	1	8	.211	.231	.316	45	-3	2	0	1	.885	3	2-13,S-12/3-7	0.1
1962	*SF-N	46	42	9	8	1	0	1	4	1	10	.190	.227	.286	37	-4	0	1	-1	1.000	3	2-17,3-11,S-10	-0.1

YEAR	TM/L	G	AB	R	H	2B	3B	HR	RBI	BB	SO	AVG	OBP	SLG	PRO+	BR/A	SB	CS	SBR	FA	FR	G/POS	TPR
1963	SF-N	81	125	10	23	3	0	0	4	0	15	.184	.184	.208	13	-14	1	2	-1	.952	4	S-40,2-26,3-12	-1.0
Total	3	165	205	29	39	4	2	1	10	2	33	.190	.202	.244	24	-21	3	3	-1	.950	9	/S-62,2-56,3-30	-1.0

◼ JOE BOWMAN
Bowman, Joseph Emil b: 6/17/10, Kansas City, Kan. d: 11/22/90, Kansas City, Mo. BL/TR, 6'2", 190 lbs. Deb: 4/18/32

YEAR	TM/L	G	AB	R	H	2B	3B	HR	RBI	BB	SO	AVG	OBP	SLG	PRO+	BR/A	SB	CS	SBR	FA	FR	G/POS	TPR
1932	Phi-A	7	1	0	1	0	0	0	0	0	0	1.000	1.000	1.000	405	0	0	0	0	.875	1	/P-7	0.0
1934	NY-N	31	29	4	5	0	1	0	4	2	3	.172	.226	.241	26	-3	0			1.000	-0	P-30	0.0
1935	Phi-N	49	67	6	13	1	1	1	7	4	7	.194	.239	.284	36	-6	1			.947	-1	P-33/O-1	0.0
1936	Phi-N	44	77	9	15	1	0	0	6	6	14	.195	.253	.208	23	-8	0			.886	-2	P-40	0.0
1937	Pit-N	35	47	3	10	1	0	0	4	5	9	.213	.288	.234	43	-4	0			1.000	0	P-30	0.0
1938	Pit-N	18	21	5	7	0	1	0	1	1	3	.333	.364	.429	116	0	0			.909	-1	P-17	0.0
1939	Pit-N	70	96	9	33	8	1	0	18	5	9	.344	.382	.448	124	5	0			1.000	0	P-37	0.0
1940	Pit-N	57	90	11	22	5	1	1	14	14	14	.244	.352	.356	96	-0	0			.981	-0	P-32	0.0
1941	Pit-N	22	31	4	8	1	0	0	1	1	2	.258	.281	.290	61	-2	0			1.000	-0	P-18	0.0
1944	Bos-A	59	100	7	20	5	2	0	16	5	19	.200	.238	.290	51	-7	1	0	0	.935	-2	P-26	0.0
1945	Bos-A	9	9	0	2	0	0	0	1	1	1	.222	.300	.222	51	-1	0	0	0	1.000	-0	/P-3	0.0
	Cin-N	29	71	4	5	2	1	0	3	2	9	.070	.096	.127	-39	-13	1			.927	-2	P-25	0.0
Total	11	430	639	62	141	24	8	2	75	46	90	.221	.275	.293	55	-39	3	0		.958	-8	P-298/O-1	0.0

◼ BOB BOWMAN
Bowman, Robert Leroy b: 5/10/31, Laytonville, Cal. BR/TR, 6'1", 195 lbs. Deb: 4/16/55

YEAR	TM/L	G	AB	R	H	2B	3B	HR	RBI	BB	SO	AVG	OBP	SLG	PRO+	BR/A	SB	CS	SBR	FA	FR	G/POS	TPR
1955	Phi-N	3	3	0	0	0	0	0	0	0	0	.000	.000	.000	-99	-1	0	0	0	1.000	-0	/O-2	-0.1
1956	Phi-N	6	16	2	3	0	1	0	1	2	0	.188	.188	.500	78	-1	0	0	0	.833	-1	/O-5	-0.2
1957	Phi-N	99	237	31	63	8	2	6	23	27	50	.266	.356	.392	104	2	0	0	0	.929	-2	O-81	-0.4
1958	Phi-N	91	184	31	53	11	2	8	24	16	30	.288	.345	.500	122	5	0	1	-1	.988	-6	O-57	-0.3
1959	Phi-N	57	79	7	10	0	0	2	5	5	23	.127	.179	.203	1	-11	0	0	0	1.000	-1	O-20/P-5	-1.2
Total	5	256	519	71	129	19	5	17	54	48	109	.249	.319	.403	93	-5	0	1	-1	.955	-10	O-165/P-5	-2.2

◼ BILL BOWMAN
Bowman, William George b: 1869, Chicago, Ill. d: 4/6/18, Arlington Heights, Ill. 5'11", 180 lbs. Deb: 6/18/1891

YEAR	TM/L	G	AB	R	H	2B	3B	HR	RBI	BB	SO	AVG	OBP	SLG	PRO+	BR/A	SB	CS	SBR	FA	FR	G/POS	TPR
1891	Chi-N	15	45	2	4	1	0	0	5	5	9	.089	.196	.111	-10	-6	0			.915	-5	C-15	-0.9

◼ RED BOWSER
Bowser, James Harvey b: 9/20/1881, Freeport, Pa. d: 5/22/43, Moundsville, W.Va. Deb: 9/13/10

YEAR	TM/L	G	AB	R	H	2B	3B	HR	RBI	BB	SO	AVG	OBP	SLG	PRO+	BR/A	SB	CS	SBR	FA	FR	G/POS	TPR
1910	Chi-A	1	2	0	0	0	0	0	0	0	0	.000	.000	.000	-99	-0	0			.000	0	/O-1	-0.1

◼ FRANK BOYD
Boyd, Frank Jay b: 4/2/1868, West Middletown, Pa d: 12/16/37, Oil City, Pa. BR/TR, Deb: 5/18/1893

YEAR	TM/L	G	AB	R	H	2B	3B	HR	RBI	BB	SO	AVG	OBP	SLG	PRO+	BR/A	SB	CS	SBR	FA	FR	G/POS	TPR
1893	Cle-N	2	5	3	1	0	1	0	3	1	0	.200	.333	.400	89	-0	0			1.000	-0	/C-2	0.0

◼ JAKE BOYD
Boyd, Jacob Henry b: 1/19/1874, Martinsburg, W.Va. d: 8/12/32, Gettysburg, Pa. TL, 160 lbs. Deb: 9/20/1894

YEAR	TM/L	G	AB	R	H	2B	3B	HR	RBI	BB	SO	AVG	OBP	SLG	PRO+	BR/A	SB	CS	SBR	FA	FR	G/POS	TPR
1894	Was-N	6	21	1	3	0	0	0	1	1	4	.143	.182	.143	-22	-4	2			.833	1	/O-3,P-3	-0.2
1895	Was-N	51	157	29	42	5	1	1	16	20	28	.268	.375	.331	84	-3	2			.786	-14	O-21,P-14,2-10/S3	-1.4
1896	Was-N	4	13	1	1	0	0	0	1	1	1	.077	.200	.077	-25	-2	0			.909	1	/P-4	0.0
Total	3	61	191	31	46	5	1	1	18	22	33	.241	.344	.293	65	-9	4			.794	-12	/O-24,P-21,2-10,S3	-1.6

◼ BOB BOYD
Boyd, Robert Richard "The Rope" b: 10/1/25, Potts Camp, Miss. BL/TL, 5'10", 170 lbs. Deb: 9/8/51

YEAR	TM/L	G	AB	R	H	2B	3B	HR	RBI	BB	SO	AVG	OBP	SLG	PRO+	BR/A	SB	CS	SBR	FA	FR	G/POS	TPR
1951	Chi-A	12	18	3	3	0	1	0	4	3	3	.167	.286	.278	54	-1	0	0	0	1.000	-1	/1-6	-0.2
1953	Chi-A	55	165	20	49	6	2	3	23	13	11	.297	.352	.412	103	0	1	4	-2	1.000	-2	1-29,O-16	-0.5
1954	Chi-A	29	56	10	10	3	0	0	5	4	3	.179	.233	.232	27	-6	2	0	1	.955	-1	O-13,1-12	-0.7
1956	Bal-A	70	225	28	70	8	3	2	11	30	14	.311	.395	.400	119	7	0	5	-3	.990	-7	1-60/O-8	-0.7
1957	Bal-A	141	485	73	154	16	8	4	34	55	31	.318	.389	.408	126	18	2	4	-2	.991	-3	*1-132/O-1	0.6
1958	Bal-A	125	401	58	124	21	5	7	36	25	24	.309	.353	.439	123	11	1	1	-0	.994	0	1-99	0.4
1959	Bal-A	128	415	42	110	20	2	3	41	29	14	.265	.315	.345	83	-10	3	1	0	.985	-9	*1-109	-2.6
1960	Bal-A	71	82	9	26	5	2	0	9	6	5	.317	.364	.427	114	2	0	0	0	1.000	-0	1-17	0.1
1961	KC-A	26	48	7	11	2	0	0	9	1	2	.229	.245	.271	37	-4	0	2	-1	1.000	-1	/1-8	-0.7
	Mil-N	36	41	3	10	0	0	0	7	1	5	.244	.262	.244	38	-1	0	0	0	1.000	1	/1-3	-0.3
Total	9	693	1936	253	567	81	23	19	175	167	114	.293	.351	.388	105	14	9	17	-8	.991	-24	1-475/O-38	-4.6

◼ BILL BOYD
Boyd, William J. b: 12/22/1852, New York, N.Y. d: 9/30/12, Jamaica, N.Y. Deb: 4/22/1872 MU

YEAR	TM/L	G	AB	R	H	2B	3B	HR	RBI	BB	SO	AVG	OBP	SLG	PRO+	BR/A	SB	CS	SBR	FA	FR	G/POS	TPR
1872	Mut-n	35	165	26	44	6	1	1	32	6	7	.267	.292	.333	98	1	4	2	0	.730	-11	*3-34/O-1	-0.9
1873	Atl-n	50	228	31	63	5	4	1	31	2	2	.276	.283	.346	96	1	1	1	-0	.716	1	*O-43/3-8	0.2
1874	Har-n	26	117	22	41	8	4	0	20	1	2	.350	.356	.487	160	7	1	0	0	.664	-8	3-25/O-1	-0.1
1875	Atl-n	36	151	14	44	11	0	1	10	1	0	.291	.296	.384	154	9	0	0	0	.774	-5	2-15,O-12/3-9,1PSM	0.3
Total	4 n	147	661	93	192	30	9	3	93	10	11	.290	.301	.377	120	17	6	3	0	.704	-23	/3-76,O-57,21SP	-0.4

◼ CLETE BOYER
Boyer, Cletis Leroy b: 2/9/37, Cassville, Mo. BR/TR, 6', 182 lbs. Deb: 6/5/55 FC

YEAR	TM/L	G	AB	R	H	2B	3B	HR	RBI	BB	SO	AVG	OBP	SLG	PRO+	BR/A	SB	CS	SBR	FA	FR	G/POS	TPR
1955	KC-A	47	79	3	19	1	0	0	6	3	17	.241	.268	.253	40	-7	0	0	0	.963	6	S-12,3-11,2-10	0.0
1956	KC-A	67	129	15	28	3	1	1	4	11	24	.217	.284	.279	49	-10	1	1	-0	.971	18	2-51/3-7	1.0
1957	KC-A	10	0	0	0	0	0	0	0	0	0	—	—	—	0	0	0	0	0	.000	0	/2-1,3-1	0.0
1959	NY-A	47	114	4	20	2	0	0	3	6	23	.175	.217	.193	14	-13	1	0	0	.990	5	S-26,3-16	-0.6
1960	*NY-A	124	393	54	95	20	1	14	46	23	85	.242	.289	.405	90	-7	2	3	-1	.967	28	3-99,S-33	2.0
1961	*NY-A	148	504	61	113	19	5	11	55	63	83	.224	.313	.347	80	-14	1	3	-2	.967	30	*3-141,S-12/O-1	1.6
1962	*NY-A	158	566	85	154	24	1	18	68	51	106	.272	.335	.413	104	2	3	2	-0	.964	36	*3-157	4.0
1963	*NY-A	152	557	59	140	20	3	12	54	33	91	.251	.296	.363	84	-13	3	4	-2	.954	22	*3-141/S-9,2-1	1.1
1964	NY-A	147	510	43	111	10	5	8	52	36	93	.218	.271	.304	59	-29	6	1	1	.968	19	*3-123,S-21	-0.9
1965	NY-A	148	514	69	129	23	6	18	58	39	79	.251	.306	.424	106	3	4	1	1	.968	26	*3-147/S-2	2.7
1966	NY-A	144	500	59	120	22	4	14	57	46	48	.240	.307	.384	101	-0	6	0	2	.966	20	3-85,S-59	2.7
1967	Atl-N	154	572	63	140	18	3	26	96	39	81	.245	.295	.423	105	1	6	3	0	.970	5	*3-150/S-6	0.6
1968	Atl-N	71	273	19	62	7	2	4	17	16	32	.227	.271	.315	75	-8	2	1	0	.981	-3	3-69	-0.9
1969	*Atl-N	144	496	57	124	16	1	14	57	55	87	.250	.330	.371	96	-3	3	7	-3	.965	3	*3-141	-0.3
1970	Atl-N	134	475	44	117	14	1	16	62	41	71	.246	.308	.381	79	-15	2	5	-2	.954	12	*3-126/S-5	-0.6
1971	Atl-N	30	98	10	24	1	0	6	19	8	11	.245	.302	.439	101	-0	0	0	0	.961	5	3-25/S-1	0.2
Total	16	1725	5780	645	1396	200	33	162	654	470	931	.242	.301	.372	87	-112	41	28	-5	.965	233	*3-1439,S-186/2O	12.6

◼ KEN BOYER
Boyer, Kenton Lloyd b: 5/20/31, Liberty, Mo. d: 9/7/82, St.Louis, Mo. BR/TR, 6'2", 200 lbs. Deb: 4/12/55 FMC

YEAR	TM/L	G	AB	R	H	2B	3B	HR	RBI	BB	SO	AVG	OBP	SLG	PRO+	BR/A	SB	CS	SBR	FA	FR	G/POS	TPR
1955	StL-N	147	530	78	140	27	2	18	62	37	67	.264	.313	.425	94	-6	22	17	-4	.952	4	*3-139,S-18	-0.5
1956	StL-N★	150	595	91	182	30	2	26	98	38	65	.306	.349	.494	123	18	8	3	1	.961	9	*3-149	3.0
1957	StL-N	142	544	79	144	18	3	19	62	44	77	.265	.321	.414	94	-5	12	8	-1	.996	4	*O-105,3-41	-0.7
1958	StL-N	150	570	101	175	21	9	23	90	49	53	.307	.365	.496	121	16	11	6	-0	.962	23	*3-144/O-6,S-1	4.0
1959	StL-N★	149	563	86	174	18	5	28	94	67	77	.309	.384	.508	127	22	12	6	0	.956	14	*3-143,S-12	3.6
1960	StL-N★	151	552	95	168	26	10	32	97	56	77	.304	.373	.562	139	29	8	7	-2	.959	13	*3-146	4.0
1961	StL-N	153	589	109	194	26	11	24	95	68	91	.329	.400	.533	132	27	6	3	0	.951	13	*3-153	4.1
1962	StL-N★	160	611	92	178	27	5	24	98	75	104	.291	.370	.470	113	11	12	7	-1	.956	4	*3-160	1.6
1963	StL-N★	159	617	86	176	28	2	24	111	70	90	.285	.360	.454	121	18	1	0	0	.925	-13	*3-159	0.5
1964	*StL-N★	162	628	100	185	30	10	24	**119**	70	85	.295	.367	.489	128	23	3	5	-2	.951	9	*3-162	2.3
1965	StL-N	144	535	71	139	18	2	13	75	57	73	.260	.332	.374	90	-6	2	7	-4	**.968**	-11	*3-143	-2.6
1966	NY-N	136	496	62	132	28	2	14	61	30	64	.266	.308	.415	101	-0	4	3	-1	.951	11	*3-130/1-2	0.7
1967	NY-N	56	166	17	39	7	2	3	13	26	22	.235	.339	.355	100	1	2	1	0	.949	-2	3-44/1-8	-0.3
	Chi-A	57	180	17	47	5	1	4	21	7	25	.261	.289	.367	96	-2	0	1	-1	.957	1	3-33,1-18	-0.3
1968	Chi-A	10	24	0	3	0	0	0	1	6	6	.125	.160	.125	-3	-3	0	0	0	.900	-1	/3-5,1-1	0.0
	LA-N	83	221	20	60	7	2	6	41	16	34	.271	.324	.403	127	6	0	2	-1	.922	-4	3-34,1-32	0.0
1969	LA-N	25	34	0	7	2	0	0	4	2	5	.206	.250	.265	48	-2	0	0	0	.971	-0	/1-4	-0.3
Total	15	2034	7455	1104	2143	318	68	282	1141	713	1017	.287	.351	.462	115	147	105	77	-15	.952	69	*3-1785,O-111/1S	18.6

◼ DOE BOYLAND
Boyland, Dorian Scott b: 1/6/55, Chicago, Ill. BL/TL, 6'4", 200 lbs. Deb: 9/4/78

YEAR	TM/L	G	AB	R	H	2B	3B	HR	RBI	BB	SO	AVG	OBP	SLG	PRO+	BR/A	SB	CS	SBR	FA	FR	G/POS	TPR
1978	Pit-N	6	8	1	2	0	0	0	1	0	1	.250	.250	.250	38	-1	0	0	0	1.000	-0	/1-1	-0.1

YEAR	TM/L	G	AB	R	H	2B	3B	HR	RBI	BB	SO	AVG	OBP	SLG	PRO+	BR/A	SB	CS	SBR	FA	FR	G/POS	TPR
1979	Pit-N	4	3	0	0	0	0	0	0	0	2	.000	.000	.000	-96	-1	0	0	0	.000	0	/H	-0.1
1981	Pit-N	11	8	0	0	0	0	0	0	1	3	.000	.111	.000	-64	-2	0	0	0	.000	0	/H	-0.2
Total	3	21	19	1	2	0	0	0	1	1	6	.105	.150	.105	-26	-3	0	0	0	1.000	-0	/1-1	-0.4

■ **EDDIE BOYLE**   Boyle, Edward J. b: 5/8/1874, Cincinnati, Ohio d: 2/9/41, Cincinnati, Ohio BR/TR, 6'3", 200 lbs. Deb: 4/17/1896 F

1896	Lou-N	3	9	0	0	0	0	0	2	0	2	.000	.182	.000	-52	-2	0			.938	1	/C-3	-0.1
	Pit-N	2	5	0	0	0	0	0	0	0	1	.000	.000	.000	-99	-1	0			.833	-0	/C-2	-0.1
	Yr	5	14	0	0	0	0	0	2	0	3	.000	.125	.000	-68	-3	0			.909	0	/C-5	-0.2

■ **HENRY BOYLE**   Boyle, Henry J. "Handsome Henry" b: 9/20/1860, Philadelphia, Pa. d: 5/25/32, Philadelphia, Pa. TR,   Deb: 7/9/1884

1884	StL-U	65	262	41	68	10	3	4		9		.260	.284	.366	93	-10				.885	5	O-43,P-19/3-4,S21	-0.2
1885	StL-N	72	258	24	52	9	1	1	21	13	38	.202	.240	.256	64	-10				.907	-4	P-42,O-31/2-2	-0.7
1886	StL-N	30	108	8	27	2	2	1	13	5	19	.250	.283	.333	93	-1	0			.852	1	P-25/O-6	0.0
1887	Ind-N	41	141	17	27	9	1	2	13	9	18	.191	.250	.312	57	-8	2			.912	-5	P-38/O-4	-0.2
1888	Ind-N	37	125	13	18	2	0	1	6	6	31	.144	.189	.184	19	-11	1			.933	3	P-37/1-1	0.0
1889	Ind-N	46	155	17	38	10	0	1	17	9	23	.245	.291	.329	72	-6	4			.958	-5	P-46/3-1	0.0
Total	6	291	1049	120	230	42	7	10	70	51	129	.219	.258	.301	69	-47	7			.912	-5	P-207/O-84,3-5,21S	-1.1

■ **JIM BOYLE**   Boyle, James John b: 1/19/04, Cincinnati, Ohio d: 12/24/58, Cincinnati, Ohio BR/TR, 6', 180 lbs. Deb: 6/20/26 F

1926	NY-N	1	0	0	0	0	0	0	0	0	0	—	—	—			0	0		.000	0	/C-1	0.0

■ **JACK BOYLE**   Boyle, John Anthony "Honest Jack" b: 3/22/1866, Cincinnati, Ohio d: 1/7/13, Cincinnati, Ohio BR/TR, 6'4", 190 lbs. Deb: 10/8/1886 F

1886	Cin-a	1	5	0	1	0	0	0		0		.200	.200	.200	25	-0	0			.769	-0	/C-1	0.0
1887	*StL-a	88	350	48	66	3	1	2	41	20		.189	.237	.220	25	-37	7			**.897**	-11	C-86/O-2,1-2,3-1	-3.3
1888	*StL-a	71	257	33	62	8	1	1	23	13		.241	.286	.292	77	-8	11			**.932**	14	C-70/O-1	1.1
1889	StL-a	99	347	54	85	11	5	3	42	21	42	.245	.301	.331	71	-16	5			.947	5	C-80,3-12/O-5,12	-0.3
1890	Chi-P	100	369	56	96	9	5	1	49	44	29	.260	.347	.320	76	-13	11			.940	-4	C-50,3-30,S-16,1/O	-0.9
1891	StL-a	123	439	78	123	18	8	5	79	47	36	.280	.365	.392	101	-3	19			.936	-14	C-91,S-26/3-8,021	-0.7
1892	NY-N	120	436	52	80	8	8	0	32	36	41	.183	.252	.239	49	-27	10			.922	14	C-79,1-40/O-2,S-2	-0.8
1893	Phi-N	116	504	105	144	29	9	4	81	41	30	.286	.341	.403	100	-1	22			.988	6	*1-112/C-6,2-2	0.2
1894	Phi-N	114	495	98	149	21	10	4	88	45	26	.301	.363	.408	88	-10	21			.983	-5	*1-114/3-1,2-1	-0.6
1895	Phi-N	133	565	90	143	17	4	0	67	35	23	.253	.302	.297	55	-38	13			.973	-6	*1-133	-3.4
1896	Phi-N	40	145	17	43	4	1	1	28	6	7	.297	.346	.359	87	-3	5			.920	-7	C-28,1-12	-0.5
1897	Phi-N	75	288	37	73	9	1	2	36	19		.253	.306	.313	65	-15	3			.962	-9	C-50,1-24	-1.5
1898	Phi-N	6	22	0	2	0	1	0	3	1		.091	.130	.182	-11	-3	0			.919	-0	/1-4,C-3	-0.3
Total	13	1086	4222	668	1067	137	54	23	569	328	234	.253	.315	.327	72	-174	125			.929	-10	C-544,1-455/3SO2	-11.0

■ **JACK BOYLE**   Boyle, John Bellew b: 7/9/1889, Morris, Ill. d: 4/3/71, Ft.Lauderdale, Fla. BL/TR, 5'11.5", 165 lbs. Deb: 6/28/12

1912	Phi-N	15	25	4	7	1	0	0	1	2	5	.280	.308	.320	67	-1	0			.905	5	/3-6,S-2	0.4

■ **BUZZ BOYLE**   Boyle, Ralph Francis b: 2/9/08, Cincinnati, Ohio d: 11/12/78, Cincinnati, Ohio BL/TL, 5'11.5", 170 lbs. Deb: 9/11/29 F

1929	Bos-N	17	57	8	15	2	1	1	2	6	11	.263	.333	.386	81	-2	2			1.000	-0	O-17	-0.3
1930	Bos-N	1	1	0	0	0	0	0	0	0	1	.000	.000	.000	-99	-0	0			.000	-1	/O-1	-0.1
1933	Bro-N	93	338	38	101	13	4	0	31	16	24	.299	.331	.361	102	0	7			.975	-6	O-90	-1.1
1934	Bro-N	128	472	88	144	26	10	7	48	51	44	.305	.376	.447	126	18	8			.970	11	*O-121	2.3
1935	Bro-N	127	475	51	129	17	9	4	44	43	45	.272	.332	.371	90	-6	7			.963	3	*O-124	-0.8
Total	5	366	1343	185	389	58	24	12	125	116	125	.290	.347	.395	105	10	24			.970	6	O-353	-0.0

■ **GIBBY BRACK**   Brack, Gilbert Herman b: 3/29/08, Chicago, Ill. d: 1/20/60, Greenville, Tex. BR/TR, 5'9", 170 lbs. Deb: 4/23/37

1937	Bro-N	112	372	60	102	27	5	5	38	44	93	.274	.351	.435	111	5	9			.969	1	*O-101	0.3
1938	Bro-N	40	56	10	12	2	1	1	6	4	14	.214	.267	.339	64	-3	1			1.000	2	O-13	-0.1
	Phi-N	72	282	40	81	20	4	4	28	18	30	.287	.332	.429	111	3	2			.964	-2	O-68	-0.1
	Yr	112	338	50	93	22	5	5	34	22	44	.275	.321	.414	102	-0	3			.969	-0	O-81	-0.2
1939	Phi-N	91	270	40	78	21	4	6	41	26	49	.289	.351	.463	121	7	1			.959	-4	O-48,1-19	-0.1
Total	3	315	980	150	273	70	18	16	113	92	186	.279	.341	.436	111	13	13			.967	-4	O-230/1-19	0.0

■ **BUDDY BRADFORD**   Bradford, Charles William b: 7/25/44, Mobile, Ala. BR/TR, 5'11", 191 lbs. Deb: 9/9/66

1966	Chi-A	14	28	3	4	0	0	0	2	6	.143	.200	.143	0	-4	0	0	0	.833	-3	/O-9	-0.7
1967	Chi-A	24	20	6	2	1	0	0	1	1	7	.100	.143	.150	-14	-3	1	0	0	.900	4	O-14	-0.8
1968	Chi-A	103	281	32	61	11	0	5	24	23	67	.217	.281	.310	78	-7	8	4	0	.965	-12	O-99	-2.7
1969	Chi-A	93	273	36	70	8	2	11	27	34	75	.256	.342	.421	109	3	5	2	0	.961	-13	O-88	-1.5
1970	Chi-A	32	91	8	17	3	0	2	8	10	30	.187	.267	.286	51	-6	1	2	-1	.979	-4	O-27	-1.3
	Cle-A	75	163	25	32	6	1	7	23	21	43	.196	.292	.374	79	-5	0	1	-1	.984	-4	O-64/3-1	-1.3
	Yr	107	254	33	49	9	1	9	31	31	73	.193	.283	.343	69	-11	1	3	-2	.982	-8	O-91/3-1	-2.6
1971	Cle-A	20	38	4	6	2	1	0	3	6	10	.158	.273	.263	48	-3	0	1	0	.930	-0	O-18	-0.4
	Cin-N	79	100	17	20	3	0	2	12	14	23	.200	.316	.290	74	-3	4	2	0	.986	-13	O-66	-1.9
1972	Chi-A	35	48	13	13	2	0	2	8	4	13	.271	.340	.438	127	2	3	2	-0	1.000	-5	O-28	-0.5
1973	Chi-A	53	168	24	40	3	1	5	15	17	43	.238	.316	.411	100	-0	4	5	-2	.992	-5	O-51	0.0
1974	Chi-A	39	96	16	32	3	0	5	10	13	11	.333	.418	.510	162	8	1	2	-1	.980	-3	O-32/D-1	0.3
1975	Chi-A	25	58	8	9	3	1	2	15	8	22	.155	.290	.345	78	-2	3	2	-0	.966	-2	O-18/D-4	-0.4
	StL-N	50	81	12	22	1	0	4	15	12	24	.272	.366	.432	117	2	1	1	-0	.935	-1	O-25	-0.1
1976	Chi-A	55	160	20	35	5	2	4	14	19	37	.219	.309	.350	92	-1	6	0	2	.978	-3	O-48/D-3	-0.5
Total	11	697	1605	224	363	50	8	52	175	184	411	.226	.313	.364	91	-19	36	24	-4	.971	-64	O-587/D-8,3-1	-11.8

■ **VIC BRADFORD**   Bradford, Henry Victor b: 3/5/15, Brownsville, Tenn. BR/TR, 6'2", 190 lbs. Deb: 5/1/43

1943	NY-N	6	5	1	1	0	0	0	1	1	1	.200	.333	.200	55	-0	0			1.000	0	/O-1	0.0

■ **AL BRADLEY**   Bradley, Al 5'10", 185 lbs. Deb: 5/21/1884

1884	Was-U	1	3	0	0	0	0	0		2		.000	.400	.000	32	-0				1.000	0	/O-1	0.0

■ **GEORGE BRADLEY**   Bradley, George Washington "Grin" b: 7/13/1852, Reading, Pa. d: 10/2/31, Philadelphia, Pa. BR/TR, 5'10.5", 175 lbs. Deb: 5/4/1875

1875	StL-n	60	254	28	62	7	3	0	24	1	19	.244	.247	.295	96	0	3	3	-1	.896	-2	*P-60/S-2,2-1,0-1	-0.5
1876	StL-N	64	265	29	66	7	6	0	28	3	12	.249	.257	.321	97	-0				.919	1	*P-64	0.0
1877	Chi-N	55	214	31	52	7	3	0	12	6	19	.243	.264	.304	70	-8				**.950**	-2	*P-50,3-16/1-3,0-1	-0.3
1879	Tro-N	63	251	36	62	9	5	0	23	1	20	.247	.250	.323	93	-1				.867	5	P-54/3-5,1-3,0-1,S	0.2
1880	Pro-N	82	309	32	70	7	6	0	23	5	38	.227	.239	.288	80	-6				.858	19	*3-57,P-28/O-7,1-2	1.5
1881	Det-N	1	4	0	0	0	0	0	0	0	0	.000	.000	.000	-96	-1				.667	-1	/S-1	-0.2
	Cle-N	60	241	21	60	10	1	2	18	4	25	.249	.261	.324	88	-3				.865	-9	3-48/P-6,S-6,0-1	-0.9
	Yr	61	245	21	60	10	1	2	18	4	25	.245	.257	.318	84	-4				.865	-10	3-48/S-7,P-6,0-1	-1.1
1882	Cle-N	30	115	16	21	5	1	0	6	4	16	.183	.210	.226	41	-7				.897	-3	P-18/O-9,1-6	-0.5
1883	Cle-N	4	16	0	5	0	1	0	1	0	1	.313	.313	.438	126	0				.792	-0	/S-4	0.0
	Phi-a	76	312	47	73	8	5	1	36	8		.234	.253	.301	72	-11				.779	3	3-44,P-26,O-11/1-2	-0.3
1884	Cin-U	58	226	31	43	4	7	0		7		.190	.215	.270	43	-23				.912	-0	P-41,O-16/S-5,1-2	-0.9
1886	Phi-a	13	48	1	4	0	0	0	1	1		.083	.102	.125	-29	-7	2			.849	-5	S-13	-0.5
1888	Bal-a	1	3	0	0	0	0	0		0		.000	.000	.000	-99	-1	0			.600	-1	/S-1	-0.1
Total	10	507	2004	244	456	57	35	3	148	39	131	.228	.242	.295	72	-69	2	0		.896	22	P-287,3-170/OS1	-1.9

■ **GEORGE BRADLEY**   Bradley, George Washington b: 4/1/14, Greenwood, Ark. d: 10/19/82, Lawrenceburg, Tenn. BR/TR, 6'1.5", 185 lbs. Deb: 4/28/46

1946	StL-A	4	12	2	2	1	0	0	1	1	3	.167	.167	.250	15	-1	0			1.000	-1	/O-3	-0.2

■ **HUGH BRADLEY**   Bradley, Hugh Frederick "Corns" b: 5/23/1885, Grafton, Mass. d: 1/26/49, Worcester, Mass. BR/TR, 5'10", 175 lbs. Deb: 4/25/10

1910	Bos-A	32	83	8	14	6	2	0	7	5		.169	.216	.289	57	-5	2			.995	-2	1-21/C-3,O-1	-0.7

YEAR	TM/L	G	AB	R	H	2B	3B	HR	RBI	BB	SO	AVG	OBP	SLG	PRO+	BR/A	SB	CS	SBR	FA	FR	G/POS	TPR
1911	Bos-A	12	41	9	13	2	0	1	4	2		.317	.364	.439	125	1	1			.993	1	1-12	0.2
1912	Bos-A	40	137	16	26	11	1	1	19	15		.190	.275	.307	63	-7	3			.989	0	1-40	-0.8
1914	Pit-F	118	427	41	131	20	6	0	61	27	27	.307	.359	.382	103	-4	7			.990	-0	*1-118	-0.8
1915	Pit-F	26	66	3	18	4	1	0	6	4	5	.273	.314	.364	91	-2	2			.952	-3	O-15	-0.6
	Bro-F	37	126	7	31	3	2	0	18	4	9	.246	.269	.302	61	-9	6			.996	2	1-26/O-7,C-1	-0.8
	New-F	12	33	0	5	0	0	0	2	3	3	.152	.243	.152	13	-4	2			.986	-2	/1-8	-0.7
	Yr	75	225	10	54	7	3	0	26	10	17	.240	.278	.298	63	-15	10			.994	-2	1-34,O-22/C-1	-2.1
Total	5	277	913	84	238	46	12	2	117	59	44	.261	.314	.344	84	-30	23			.991	-3	1-225/O-23,C-4	-4.2

■ **JACK BRADLEY**   Bradley, John Thomas   b: 9/20/1893, Denver, Colo.   d: 3/18/69, Tulsa, Okla.   BR/TR, 5'11", 175 lbs.   Deb: 6/18/16

YEAR	TM/L	G	AB	R	H	2B	3B	HR	RBI	BB	SO	AVG	OBP	SLG	PRO+	BR/A	SB	CS	SBR	FA	FR	G/POS	TPR
1916	Cle-A	2	3	0	0	0	0	0	0	0	1	.000	.000	.000	-94	-1	0			1.000	-0	/C-1	-0.1

■ **MARK BRADLEY**   Bradley, Mark Allen   b: 12/3/56, Elizabethtown, Ky.   BR/TR, 6'1", 180 lbs.   Deb: 9/3/81

YEAR	TM/L	G	AB	R	H	2B	3B	HR	RBI	BB	SO	AVG	OBP	SLG	PRO+	BR/A	SB	CS	SBR	FA	FR	G/POS	TPR
1981	LA-N	9	6	2	1	1	0	0	0	0	1	.167	.167	.333	41	-1	0	0	0	1.000	-1	/O-6	-0.2
1982	LA-N	8	3	1	1	0	0	0	0	0	0	.333	.333	.333	89	-0	0	0	0	1.000	-1	/O-3	-0.1
1983	NY-N	73	104	10	21	4	0	3	5	11	35	.202	.278	.327	68	-5	4	2	0	1.000	-5	O-35	-1.1
Total	3	90	113	13	23	5	0	3	5	11	36	.204	.274	.327	67	-5	4	2	0	1.000	-7	/O-44	-1.4

■ **PHIL BRADLEY**   Bradley, Philip Poole   b: 3/11/59, Bloomington, Ind.   BR/TR, 6', 185 lbs.   Deb: 9/2/83

YEAR	TM/L	G	AB	R	H	2B	3B	HR	RBI	BB	SO	AVG	OBP	SLG	PRO+	BR/A	SB	CS	SBR	FA	FR	G/POS	TPR
1983	Sea-A	23	67	8	18	2	0	0	5	8	5	.269	.347	.299	77	-2	3	1	0	.974	-6	O-21/D-1	-0.8
1984	Sea-A	124	322	49	97	12	4	0	24	34	61	.301	.373	.363	106	4	21	8	2	.992	-11	*O-117/D-3	-0.8
1985	Sea-A★	159	641	100	192	33	8	26	88	55	129	.300	.366	.498	133	29	22	9	1	.986	6	*O-159	3.0
1986	Sea-A	143	526	88	163	27	4	12	50	77	134	.310	.406	.445	130	25	21	12	-1	.996	1	*O-140	2.1
1987	Sea-A	158	603	101	179	38	10	14	67	84	119	.297	.390	.463	119	18	40	10	6	.983	1	*O-158	1.9
1988	Phi-N	154	569	77	150	30	5	11	56	54	106	.264	.344	.392	109	7	11	9	-2	.990	9	*O-153	1.0
1989	Bal-A	144	545	83	151	23	10	11	55	70	103	.277	.367	.417	124	19	20	6	2	.990	-2	*O-140/D-2	1.5
1990	Bal-A	72	289	39	78	9	1	4	26	30	35	.270	.353	.349	100	1	10	4	1	.987	2	O-70/D-2	0.2
	Chi-A	45	133	20	30	5	1	0	5	20	26	.226	.344	.278	78	-3	7	3	0	.973	-4	O-38/D-7	-0.8
	Yr	117	422	59	108	14	2	4	31	50	61	.256	.350	.327	93	-2	17	7	1	.982	-2	*O-108/D-9	-0.6
Total	8	1022	3695	565	1058	179	43	78	376	432	718	.286	.371	.421	118	99	155	62	9	.988	-3	O-996/D-15	7.3

■ **SCOTT BRADLEY**   Bradley, Scott William   b: 3/22/60, Glen Ridge, N.J.   BL/TR, 5'11", 185 lbs.   Deb: 9/9/84

YEAR	TM/L	G	AB	R	H	2B	3B	HR	RBI	BB	SO	AVG	OBP	SLG	PRO+	BR/A	SB	CS	SBR	FA	FR	G/POS	TPR
1984	NY-A	9	21	3	6	1	0	0	2	1	1	.286	.318	.333	84	-1	0	0	0	1.000	-1	/O-5,C-3	-0.1
1985	NY-A	19	49	4	8	2	1	0	1	1	5	.163	.196	.245	20	-5	0	0	0	.923	-1	/C-3,D-9	-0.6
1986	Chi-A	9	21	3	6	0	0	0	0	1	0	.286	.375	.286	81	-0	0	2	-1	.000	-0	/O-1,D-6	-0.2
	Sea-A	68	199	17	60	8	3	5	28	12	7	.302	.347	.447	113	3	1	0	0	.990	-13	C-59/D-3	-0.6
	Yr	77	220	20	66	8	3	5	28	13	7	.300	.350	.432	110	3	1	2	-1	.990	-14	C-59/D-9,O-1	-0.8
1987	Sea-A	102	342	34	95	15	1	5	43	15	18	.278	.314	.371	77	-11	0	1	-1	.983	-6	C-82/3-8,O-2,D-6	-1.3
1988	Sea-A	103	335	45	86	17	1	4	33	17	16	.257	.297	.349	77	-11	1	1	-0	.991	4	C-85/O-4,3-3,1-2	-0.1
1989	Sea-A	103	270	21	74	16	0	3	37	21	23	.274	.329	.367	93	-3	1	1	-0	.993	1	C-70/1-2,O-1,D-6	0.4
1990	Sea-A	101	233	11	52	9	0	1	28	15	20	.223	.270	.275	52	-15	1	1	-1	.995	1	C-63/3-5,1-1,D-6	-1.2
1991	Sea-A	83	172	10	35	7	0	0	11	19	19	.203	.283	.244	47	-12	0	0	0	.993	-5	C-65/3-4,1-1,D-2	-1.4
1992	Sea-A	2	1	0	0	0	0	0	0	1	1	.000	.500	.000	51	-0	0	0	0	1.000	-1	/C-1	0.1
	Cin-N	5	5	1	2	0	0	0	1	0	1	.400	.500	.400	154	0	0	0	0	1.000	-1	/C-2	0.0
Total	9	604	1648	149	424	75	6	18	184	104	110	.257	.306	.343	76	-54	3	6	-3	.990	-19	C-433/D-38,3-20,01	-5.0

■ **BILL BRADLEY**   Bradley, William Joseph   b: 2/13/1878, Cleveland, Ohio   d: 3/11/54, Cleveland, Ohio   BR/TR, 6', 185 lbs.   Deb: 8/26/1899   M

YEAR	TM/L	G	AB	R	H	2B	3B	HR	RBI	BB	SO	AVG	OBP	SLG	PRO+	BR/A	SB	CS	SBR	FA	FR	G/POS	TPR
1899	Chi-N	35	129	26	40	6	1	2	18	12		.310	.378	.419	122	4	4			.884	-3	3-30/S-5	0.1
1900	Chi-N	122	444	63	125	21	8	5	49	27		.282	.330	.399	104	1	14			.882	17	*3-106,1-15	1.7
1901	Cle-A	133	516	95	151	28	13	1	55	26		.293	.336	.403	109	5	15			**.930**	10	*3-133/P-1	1.5
1902	Cle-A	137	550	104	187	39	12	11	77	27		.340	.375	.515	151	35	11			.923	12	*3-137	4.4
1903	Cle-A	136	536	101	168	36	22	6	68	25		.313	.348	.496	154	33	21			.924	12	*3-136	4.7
1904	Cle-A	154	609	94	183	32	8	5	83	26		.300	.334	.404	134	24	23			**.955**	9	*3-154	3.9
1905	Cle-A	146	541	63	145	34	6	0	51	27		.268	.321	.353	112	7	22			**.945**	13	*3-146,M	2.7
1906	Cle-A	82	302	32	83	16	2	0	25	18		.275	.324	.361	116	5	13			.966	4	3-82	1.3
1907	Cle-A	139	498	48	111	20	1	0	34	35		.223	.286	.267	76	-13	20			**.938**	5	*3-139	-0.4
1908	Cle-A	148	548	70	133	24	7	1	46	29		.243	.297	.318	99	-1	18			.939	-31	*3-118,S-30	-3.2
1909	Cle-A	95	334	30	62	6	3	0	22	19		.186	.236	.222	43	-22	8			.957	-11	3-87/1-3,2-3	-3.4
1910	Cle-A	61	214	12	42	3	0	0	12	10		.196	.236	.210	39	-15	6			.956	-1	3-61	-1.6
1914	Bro-F	7	6	1	3	0	0	0	3	0		.500	.500	.667	218	1	0			.000	0	HM	0.1
1915	KC-F	66	203	15	38	9	1	0	9	18		.187	.225	.241	33	-22	6			.949	-6	3-61	-2.9
Total	14	1461	5430	754	1471	275	84	33	552	290	18	.271	.317	.371	108	40	181			.933	28	*3-1390/S-35,12P	8.9

■ **DALLAS BRADSHAW**   Bradshaw, Dallas Carl "Windy"   b: 11/23/1895, Wolf Creek, Ill.   d: 12/11/39, Herrin, Ill.   BL/TR, 5'7", 145 lbs.   Deb: 6/5/17

YEAR	TM/L	G	AB	R	H	2B	3B	HR	RBI	BB	SO	AVG	OBP	SLG	PRO+	BR/A	SB	CS	SBR	FA	FR	G/POS	TPR
1917	Phi-A	2	4	0	0	0	0	0	0	0	1	.000	.000	.000	-99	-1	0					/2-1	0.0

■ **GEORGE BRADSHAW**   Bradshaw, George Thomas   b: 9/12/24, Salisbury, N.C.   d: 11/4/94, Hendersonville, N.C.   BR/TR, 6'2", 185 lbs.   Deb: 8/10/52

YEAR	TM/L	G	AB	R	H	2B	3B	HR	RBI	BB	SO	AVG	OBP	SLG	PRO+	BR/A	SB	CS	SBR	FA	FR	G/POS	TPR
1952	Was-A	10	23	3	5	2	0	0	6	1	2	.217	.280	.304	65	-1	0	0	0	.917	-3	/C-9	-0.4

■ **TERRY BRADSHAW**   Bradshaw, Terry Leon   b: 2/3/69, Franklin, Va.   BL/TR, 6', 180 lbs.   Deb: 5/4/95

YEAR	TM/L	G	AB	R	H	2B	3B	HR	RBI	BB	SO	AVG	OBP	SLG	PRO+	BR/A	SB	CS	SBR	FA	FR	G/POS	TPR
1995	StL-N	19	44	6	10	1	0	2	2	10		.227	.261	.295	46	-3	1	2	-1	.952	1	O-10	-0.4
1996	StL-N	15	21	4	7	1	0	0	3	3	2	.333	.417	.381	112	1	0	1	-1	1.000	-2	/O-7	-0.2
Total	2	34	65	10	17	2	1	0	5	5	12	.262	.314	.323	69	-3	1	3	-2	.960	-2	/O-17	-0.6

■ **BRADY**   Brady   Deb: 9/25/1875

YEAR	TM/L	G	AB	R	H	2B	3B	HR	RBI	BB	SO	AVG	OBP	SLG	PRO+	BR/A	SB	CS	SBR	FA	FR	G/POS	TPR
1875	Chi-n	1	4	1	1	0	1	0		0	0	.250	.250	.750	231	1	0	0		.625	1	/O-1	0.1

■ **BRIAN BRADY**   Brady, Brian Phelan   b: 7/11/62, Elmhurst, N.Y.   BL/TL, 5'11", 185 lbs.   Deb: 4/16/89

YEAR	TM/L	G	AB	R	H	2B	3B	HR	RBI	BB	SO	AVG	OBP	SLG	PRO+	BR/A	SB	CS	SBR	FA	FR	G/POS	TPR
1989	Cal-A	2	2	0	1	1	0	0	1	0	0	.500	.500	1.000	319	1	0	0		.000	-0	/O-1	0.0

■ **CLIFF BRADY**   Brady, Clifford Francis   b: 3/6/1897, St.Louis, Mo.   d: 9/25/74, Belleville, Ill.   BR/TR, 5'5.5", 140 lbs.   Deb: 8/8/20

YEAR	TM/L	G	AB	R	H	2B	3B	HR	RBI	BB	SO	AVG	OBP	SLG	PRO+	BR/A	SB	CS	SBR	FA	FR	G/POS	TPR
1920	Bos-A	53	180	16	41	5	1	0	12	13	12	.228	.284	.267	48	-13	1	1	-1	.974	17	2-53	0.5

■ **BOB BRADY**   Brady, Robert Jay   b: 11/8/22, Lewistown, Pa.   d: 4/22/96, Manchester, Conn.   BL/TR, 6'1", 175 lbs.   Deb: 8/24/46

YEAR	TM/L	G	AB	R	H	2B	3B	HR	RBI	BB	SO	AVG	OBP	SLG	PRO+	BR/A	SB	CS	SBR	FA	FR	G/POS	TPR
1946	Bos-N	3	5	0	1	0	0	0	0	1	1	.200	.333	.200	52	-0	0			.857	0	/C-1	0.0
1947	Bos-N	1	1	0	0	0	0	0	0	0	0	.000	.000	.000	-99	-0	0			.000	0	H	0.0
Total	2	4	6	0	1	0	0	0	0	1	1	.167	.286	.167	29	-1	0			.857	0	/C-1	0.0

■ **STEVE BRADY**   Brady, Stephen A.   b: 7/14/1851, Worcester, Mass.   d: 11/1/17, Hartford, Conn.   5'9.5", 165 lbs.   Deb: 7/23/1874

YEAR	TM/L	G	AB	R	H	2B	3B	HR	RBI	BB	SO	AVG	OBP	SLG	PRO+	BR/A	SB	CS	SBR	FA	FR	G/POS	TPR
1874	Har-n	27	118	19	37	5	1	0	14	2	10	.314	.325	.373	117	2	1	2	-1	.662	-10	3-16,O-11/S-1	-0.7
1875	Was-n	21	91	7	13	0	0	0	3	0	4	.143	.143	.143	-0	-9	5	0	2	.815	-6	2-18/O-2,C-1,1-1	-1.2
	Har-n	1	4	0	0	0	0	0	0	0	0	.000	.000	.000	-95	-0	0	0	0	1.000	1	/O-1	0.0
	Yr	22	95	7	13	0	0	0	3	0	5	.137	.137	.137	-5	-9	5	0	2	.815	-5	2-18/O-3,C-1,1-1	-1.2
1883	NY-a	97	432	69	117	12	2	0		11		.271	.289	.322	94	-4				.961	3	*1-81,O-16	-0.8
1884	*NY-a	112	485	102	122	11	3	1		21		.252	.283	.293	90	-5				.918	1	*O-110/1-5,2-1	-0.5
1885	NY-a	108	434	60	128	14	5	0	58	25		.295	.342	.371	136	19				.879	-6	*O-105/1-4,2-3,3-1	0.9
1886	NY-a	124	466	56	112	8	5	0	39	35		.240	.298	.279	85	-7	16			.830	-5	*O-123/1-1	-1.3
Total	2 n	49	213	26	50	5	1	0	17	2	15	.235	.242	.268	68	-8	6	2	1	.703	-15	/2-18,3-16,O1CS	-1.7
Total	4	441	1817	287	479	45	19	4	97	92		.264	.302	.316	100	3	16			.875	-6	O-354/1-91,2-3,3-1	-1.7

■ **DOUG BRADY**   Brady, Stephen Douglas   b: 11/23/69, Jacksonville, Ill.   BB/TR, 5'11", 165 lbs.   Deb: 9/5/95

YEAR	TM/L	G	AB	R	H	2B	3B	HR	RBI	BB	SO	AVG	OBP	SLG	PRO+	BR/A	SB	CS	SBR	FA	FR	G/POS	TPR
1995	Chi-A	12	21	4	4	1	0	0	3	2	4	.190	.261	.238	32	-2	0	1	-1	1.000	6	/2-6,D-3	0.3

YEAR	TM/L	G	AB	R	H	2B	3B	HR	RBI	BB	SO	AVG	OBP	SLG	PRO+	BR/A	SB	CS	SBR	FA	FR	G/POS	TPR

■ **BOBBY BRAGAN**   Bragan, Robert Randall "Nig"   b: 10/30/17, Birmingham, Ala.   BR/TR, 5'10.5", 175 lbs.   Deb: 4/16/40   MC

YEAR	TM/L	G	AB	R	H	2B	3B	HR	RBI	BB	SO	AVG	OBP	SLG	PRO+	BR/A	SB	CS	SBR	FA	FR	G/POS	TPR
1940	Phi-N	132	474	36	105	14	1	7	44	28	34	.222	.265	.300	58	-28	2			.936	1	*S-132/3-2	-1.7
1941	Phi-N	154	557	37	140	19	3	4	69	26	29	.251	.285	.318	72	-22	7			.944	-7	*S-154/2-2,3-1	-1.8
1942	Phi-N	109	335	17	73	12	2	2	15	20	21	.218	.264	.284	63	-16	0			.939	9	S-78,C-22/2-4,3-3	-0.1
1943	Bro-N	74	220	17	58	7	2	2	24	15	16	.264	.311	.341	88	-4	0			.973	4	C-57,3-12	0.5
1944	Bro-N	94	266	26	71	8	4	0	17	13	14	.267	.304	.327	79	-8	2			.954	-0	S-51,C-35/3-6,2-1	-0.3
1947	*Bro-N	25	36	3	7	2	0	0	3	7	3	.194	.326	.250	53	-2	1			1.000	4	C-21	0.2
1948	Bro-N	9	12	0	2	0	0	0	0	0	2	.167	.167	.167	9	-2	0			1.000	-0	/C-5	-0.2
Total	7	597	1900	136	456	62	12	15	172	110	117	.240	.282	.309	69	-82	12			.941	10	S-415,C-140/3-24,2	-3.4

■ **DARREN BRAGG**   Bragg, Darren William   b: 9/7/69, Waterbury, Conn.   BL/TR, 5'9", 180 lbs.   Deb: 4/12/94

YEAR	TM/L	G	AB	R	H	2B	3B	HR	RBI	BB	SO	AVG	OBP	SLG	PRO+	BR/A	SB	CS	SBR	FA	FR	G/POS	TPR
1994	Sea-A	8	19	4	3	1	0	0	2	5		.158	.238	.211	17	-2	0	0	0	1.000	-1	/O-3,D-3	-0.3
1995	Sea-A	52	145	20	34	5	1	3	12	18	37	.234	.335	.345	77	-5	9	0	3	.989	4	O-47/D-2	0.1
1996	Sea-A	69	195	36	53	12	1	7	25	33	35	.272	.383	.451	110	4	8	5	-1	.992	1	O-63	0.2
	Bos-A	58	222	38	56	14	1	3	22	36	39	.252	.362	.365	82	-5	6	4	-1	.986	-5	O-58	-1.2
	Yr	127	417	74	109	26	2	10	47	69	74	.261	.371	.405	95	-2	14	9	-1	.989	-4	*O-121	-1.0
Total	3	187	581	98	146	32	3	13	61	89	116	.251	.358	.384	88	-6	23	9	2	.989	-1	O-171/D-5	-1.2

■ **GLENN BRAGGS**   Braggs, Glenn Erick   b: 10/17/62, San Bernardino, Cal.   BR/TR, 6'3", 210 lbs.   Deb: 7/18/86

YEAR	TM/L	G	AB	R	H	2B	3B	HR	RBI	BB	SO	AVG	OBP	SLG	PRO+	BR/A	SB	CS	SBR	FA	FR	G/POS	TPR
1986	Mil-A	58	215	19	51	8	2	4	18	11	47	.237	.278	.349	67	-10	1	1	-0	.910	1	O-56/D-2	-1.1
1987	Mil-A	132	505	67	136	28	7	13	77	47	96	.269	.336	.430	98	-1	12	5	1	.972	14	*O-123/D-8	0.9
1988	Mil-A	72	272	30	71	14	0	10	42	14	60	.261	.309	.423	102	0	6	4	-1	.978	4	O-54/D-18	0.1
1989	Mil-A	144	514	77	127	12	3	15	66	42	111	.247	.309	.370	91	-6	17	5	2	.972	-0	*O-132,D-13	-0.8
1990	Mil-A	37	113	17	28	5	0	3	13	12	21	.248	.336	.372	98	-0	5	3	-0	.965	2	O-32/D-2	0.1
	*Cin-N	72	201	22	60	9	1	6	28	26	43	.299	.387	.443	122	7	3	4	-1	.968	6	O-60	1.0
1991	Cin-N	85	250	36	65	10	0	11	39	23	46	.260	.327	.432	108	2	11	3	2	.966	-2	O-74	0.0
1992	Cin-N	92	266	40	63	16	3	8	38	36	48	.237	.332	.410	106	2	3	1	0	.946	-9	O-79	-0.8
Total	7	692	2336	308	601	102	16	70	321	211	472	.257	.325	.405	98	-6	58	26	2	.963	16	O-610/D-43	-0.6

■ **DAVE BRAIN**   Brain, David Leonard   b: 1/24/1879, Hereford, England   d: 5/25/59, Los Angeles, Cal.   BR/TR, 5'10", 170 lbs.   Deb: 4/24/01

YEAR	TM/L	G	AB	R	H	2B	3B	HR	RBI	BB	SO	AVG	OBP	SLG	PRO+	BR/A	SB	CS	SBR	FA	FR	G/POS	TPR
1901	Chi-A	5	20	2	7	1	0	0	5	1		.350	.381	.400	120	1	0			.909	1	/2-5	0.1
1903	StL-N	119	464	44	107	8	15	1	60	25		.231	.270	.319	70	-20	21			.908	10	S-72,3-46	-0.6
1904	StL-N	127	488	57	130	24	12	7	72	17		.266	.291	.408	120	8	18			.927	3	S-59,3-30,O-19,2/1	1.4
1905	StL-N	44	158	11	36	4	5	1	17	8		.228	.269	.335	82	-4	4			.910	-9	S-29/3-6,O-6	-1.3
	Pit-N	85	307	31	79	17	6	3	46	15		.257	.296	.381	99	-2	8			.923	6	3-78/S-4	0.7
	Yr	129	465	42	115	21	11	4	63	23		.247	.287	.366	93	-6	12			.929	-3	3-84,S-33/O-6	-0.6
1906	Bos-N	139	525	43	131	19	5	5	45	29		.250	.293	.333	98	-3	11			.917	26	*3-139	2.9
1907	Bos-N	133	509	60	142	24	9	**10**	56	29		.279	.324	.420	134	17	10			.916	25	*3-130/O-3	5.0
1908	Cin-N	16	55	4	6	0	0	0	1	8		.109	.222	.109	7	-5	0			.947	-1	O-16	-0.8
	NY-N	11	17	2	3	0	0	0	0	2		.176	.263	.176	39	-1	1			.867	-3	/2-3,O-3,3-2,S-1	-0.4
	Yr	27	72	6	9	0	0	0	2	10		.125	.232	.125	14	-7	1			.947	-3	O-19/2-3,3-2,S-1	-1.2
Total	7	679	2543	254	641	97	52	27	303	134		.252	.292	.363	101	-10	73			.913	58	3-431,S-165/O21	7.0

■ **ASA BRAINARD**   Brainard, Asa "Count"   b: 1841, Albany, N.Y.   d: 12/29/1888, Denver, Colo.   TR, 5'8.5", 150 lbs.   Deb: 5/5/1871

YEAR	TM/L	G	AB	R	H	2B	3B	HR	RBI	BB	SO	AVG	OBP	SLG	PRO+	BR/A	SB	CS	SBR	FA	FR	G/POS	TPR
1871	Oly-n	30	134	24	30	4	0	0	21	7	2	.224	.262	.254	52	-7	4	0	1	.852	-3	*P-30	0.0
1872	Oly-n	9	43	8	16	3	0	0	6	0	0	.372	.372	.442	157	3	0	0	0	.625	-1	/P-9	0.0
	Man-n	6	25	2	5	0	0	0	0	1	0	.200	.231	.200	36	-2	0	0	0	.682	-3	/2-4,P-2,O-1	-0.3
	Yr	15	68	10	21	3	0	0	6	1	0	.309	.319	.353	112	0	0	0	0	.667	-4	P-11/2-4,O-1	-0.3
1873	Bal-n	16	69	18	18	1	0	0	8	2	0	.261	.261	.275	60	-3	0	0	0	.800	-2	P-14/O-2,2-1	-0.1
1874	Bal-n	47	196	19	47	3	0	0	8	2	3	.240	.247	.255	62	-8	0	3	-2	.782	-8	P-30,2-20/O-3	-0.8
Total	4 n	108	467	71	116	11	0	0	43	10	7	.248	.264	.272	66	-17	4	3	-1	.796	-17	/P-85,2-25,O-6	-1.2

■ **FRED BRAINERD**   Brainerd, Frederick F.   b: 2/17/1892, Champaign, Ill.   d: 4/17/59, Galveston, Tex.   BR/TR, 6', 176 lbs.   Deb: 10/6/14

YEAR	TM/L	G	AB	R	H	2B	3B	HR	RBI	BB	SO	AVG	OBP	SLG	PRO+	BR/A	SB	CS	SBR	FA	FR	G/POS	TPR
1914	NY-N	2	5	1	1	0	0	0	0	1	0	.200	.333	.200	62	-0	0			.923	1	/2-2	0.1
1915	NY-N	91	249	31	50	7	2	1	21	21	44	.201	.266	.257	62	-11	6	7	-2	.988	7	1-43,3-15/S-9,2O	-0.8
1916	NY-N	2	7	0	0	0	0	0	0	0	0	.000	.000	.000	-99	-2	0			.625	-1	/3-2	-0.3
Total	3	95	261	32	51	7	2	1	21	22	44	.195	.261	.249	58	-13	6	7		.857	7	/1-43,3-17,S-9,2O	-1.0

■ **ART BRAMHALL**   Bramhall, Arthur Washington   b: 2/22/09, Oak Park, Ill.   d: 9/4/85, Madison, Wis.   BR/TR, 5'11", 170 lbs.   Deb: 4/18/35

YEAR	TM/L	G	AB	R	H	2B	3B	HR	RBI	BB	SO	AVG	OBP	SLG	PRO+	BR/A	SB	CS	SBR	FA	FR	G/POS	TPR
1935	Phi-N	2	1	0	0	0	0	0	0	0	0	.000	.000	.000	-91	-0	0			1.000	1	/S-1,3-1	0.0

■ **AL BRANCATO**   Brancato, Albert "Bronk"   b: 5/29/19, Philadelphia, Pa.   BR/TR, 5'9.5", 188 lbs.   Deb: 9/7/39

YEAR	TM/L	G	AB	R	H	2B	3B	HR	RBI	BB	SO	AVG	OBP	SLG	PRO+	BR/A	SB	CS	SBR	FA	FR	G/POS	TPR
1939	Phi-A	21	68	12	14	5	1	0	8	8	4	.206	.299	.324	60	-4	1	0	0	.939	-1	3-20/S-1	-0.5
1940	Phi-A	107	298	42	57	11	2	1	23	28	36	.191	.265	.252	36	-29	3	1	0	.949	0	S-80,3-25	-2.1
1941	Phi-A	144	530	60	124	20	9	2	49	59	49	.234	.311	.317	68	-24	1	5	-3	.915	-19	*S-139/3-7	-3.5
1945	Phi-A	10	34	3	4	1	0	0	1	0	3	.118	.143	.147	-16	-5	0			.959	-1	S-10	-0.6
Total	4	282	930	117	199	37	11	4	80	96	92	.214	.290	.290	54	-62	5	6	-2	.927	-21	S-230/3-52	-6.7

■ **RON BRAND**   Brand, Ronald George   b: 1/13/40, Los Angeles, Cal.   BR/TR, 5'8", 170 lbs.   Deb: 5/26/63

YEAR	TM/L	G	AB	R	H	2B	3B	HR	RBI	BB	SO	AVG	OBP	SLG	PRO+	BR/A	SB	CS	SBR	FA	FR	G/POS	TPR
1963	Pit-N	46	66	8	19	2	0	1	7	10	11	.288	.390	.364	118	2	0	0	0	.968	9	C-33/2-2,3-2	1.2
1965	Hou-N	117	391	27	92	6	3	2	37	19	34	.235	.281	.281	63	-19	10	5	0	.988	-7	*C-102/3-6,O-5	-2.3
1966	Hou-N	56	123	12	30	2	0	0	10	9	13	.244	.306	.260	64	-6	0	2	-1	.986	-5	C-25/2-9,O-3,3-1	-1.1
1967	Hou-N	84	215	22	52	4	1	0	18	23	17	.242	.321	.288	78	-6	5	4	0	.998	-3	C-67/2-1,O-1	-0.4
1968	Hou-N	43	81	7	13	2	0	0	4	9	11	.160	.261	.185	36	-6	1	1	-0	1.000	-1	C-29/3-1,O-1	-0.2
1969	Mon-N	103	287	19	74	12	0	2	20	30	19	.258	.330	.300	77	-8	2	3	-1	.985	-8	C-84/O-2	-1.3
1970	Mon-N	72	126	10	30	3	0	0	9	9	16	.238	.289	.302	59	-7	2	5	0	.952	-7	S-19,3-12/C-9,O2	-1.3
1971	Mon-N	47	56	3	12	0	0	1	0	3	5	.214	.254	.214	34	-5	1	1	-0	.957	-3	S-22/3-4,O-4,C-1,2	-0.1
Total	8	568	1345	108	322	34	7	3	106	112	126	.239	.305	.282	68	-55	20	13	-2	.988	-16	C-350/S-41,3-26,O2	-5.5

■ **JACKIE BRANDT**   Brandt, John George   b: 4/28/34, Omaha, Neb.   BR/TR, 5'11", 170 lbs.   Deb: 4/21/56

YEAR	TM/L	G	AB	R	H	2B	3B	HR	RBI	BB	SO	AVG	OBP	SLG	PRO+	BR/A	SB	CS	SBR	FA	FR	G/POS	TPR
1956	StL-N	27	42	9	12	3	0	1	3	4	5	.286	.362	.429	111	1	0	1	-1	1.000	-3	O-26	-0.4
	NY-N	98	351	45	105	16	8	11	47	17	31	.299	.332	.484	116	7	3	4	-2	.989	-6	O-96	-0.5
	Yr	125	393	54	117	19	8	12	50	21	36	.298	.335	.478	116	8	3	5	-2	.990	-9	*O-122	-0.9
1958	SF-N	18	52	7	13	1	0	0	3	6	5	.250	.328	.269	62	-3	1	0	0	1.000	-0	O-14	-0.3
1959	SF-N	137	429	63	116	16	5	12	57	35	69	.270	.325	.415	98	-2	11	4	1	.984	-7	*O-116,3-18/1-3,2-1	-1.0
1960	Bal-A	145	511	73	130	24	6	15	65	47	69	.254	.321	.413	98	-2	5	3	-0	.983	-10	*O-142/3-2,1-1	-2.0
1961	Bal-A★	139	516	93	153	18	7	16	72	62	51	.297	.373	.444	122	16	10	2	-1	.974	-16	*O-136/3-1	-0.6
1962	Bal-A	143	505	76	129	29	5	19	75	55	64	.255	.333	.446	115	9	3	4	-2	.976	9	*O-138/3-2	1.1
1963	Bal-A	142	451	49	112	15	5	11	61	34	85	.248	.301	.404	99	-2	4	3	-1	.986	-7	*O-134/3-1	-1.8
1964	Bal-A	137	523	64	127	25	1	13	47	45	104	.243	.306	.369	87	-9	1	4	-1	.981	16	*O-134	-0.2
1965	Bal-A	96	243	35	59	7	0	8	24	21	40	.243	.303	.412	99	-1	1	2	-1	.961	-6	O-84	-1.1
1966	Phi-N	82	164	16	41	6	1	1	15	17	36	.250	.320	.317	78	-4	0	2	-1	.988	-12	O-71	-2.1
1967	Phi-N	16	19	1	2	1	0	0	1	0	6	.105	.105	.158	-25	-3	0	1	-0	1.000	-1	/O-3	-0.4
	Hou-N	41	89	7	21	4	1	1	15	8	15	.236	.299	.337	85	-2	2	1	-1	.991	-2	1-14/O-6,3-1	-0.6
	Yr	57	108	8	23	5	1	1	16	8	15	.213	.267	.306	65	-5	2	2	-1	.991	-3	1-14/O-9,3-1	-1.0
Total	11	1221	3895	540	1020	175	37	112	485	351	574	.262	.325	.412	102	5	45	30	-4	.980	-46	*O-1100/3-25,1-18,2	-10.2

■ **OTIS BRANNAN**   Brannan, Otis Owen   b: 3/13/1899, Greenbrier, Ark.   d: 6/6/67, Little Rock, Ark.   BL/TR, 5'9", 160 lbs.   Deb: 4/11/28

YEAR	TM/L	G	AB	R	H	2B	3B	HR	RBI	BB	SO	AVG	OBP	SLG	PRO+	BR/A	SB	CS	SBR	FA	FR	G/POS	TPR
1928	StL-A	135	483	68	118	18	3	10	66	60	19	.244	.333	.356	79	-15	3	9	-5	.964	-8	*2-135	-2.3
1929	StL-A	23	51	4	15	1	0	1	8	4	4	.294	.345	.373	82	-1	0	0	0	.975	-1	2-19	-0.2
Total	2	158	534	72	133	19	3	11	74	64	23	.249	.338	.358	79	-16	3	9	-5	.966	-9	2-154	-2.5

YEAR	TM/L	G	AB	R	H	2B	3B	HR	RBI	BB	SO	AVG	OBP	SLG	PRO+	BR/A	SB	CS	SBR	FA	FR	G/POS	TPR

■ **MIKE BRANNOCK**   Brannock, Michael J.   b: 1853, Guelph, Ont., Canada   5'8", 162 lbs.   Deb: 10/21/1871

YEAR	TM/L	G	AB	R	H	2B	3B	HR	RBI	BB	SO	AVG	OBP	SLG	PRO+	BR/A	SB	CS	SBR	FA	FR	G/POS	TPR
1871	Chi-n	3	14	2	1	0	0	0	0	0	0	.071	.071	.071	-53	-3	0	0	0	.500	-2	/3-3	-0.4
1875	Chi-n	2	9	2	1	0	0	0	0	0	0	.111	.111	.111	-22	-1	2	0	1	.500	-2	/3-2	-0.2
Total	2 n	5	23	4	2	0	0	0	0	0	0	.087	.087	.087	-43	-4	2	0	1	.500	-4	/3-5	-0.6

■ **DUD BRANOM**   Branom, Edgar Dudley   b: 11/30/1897, Sulphur Springs, Tex.   d: 2/4/80, Sun City, Ariz.   BL/TL, 6'1", 190 lbs.   Deb: 4/12/27

YEAR	TM/L	G	AB	R	H	2B	3B	HR	RBI	BB	SO	AVG	OBP	SLG	PRO+	BR/A	SB	CS	SBR	FA	FR	G/POS	TPR
1927	Phi-A	30	94	8	22	1	0	0	13	2	5	.234	.250	.245	27	-10	2	1	0	.973	-0	1-26	-1.1

■ **KITTY BRANSFIELD**   Bransfield, William Edward   b: 1/7/1875, Worcester, Mass.   d: 5/1/47, Worcester, Mass.   BR/TR, 5'11", 207 lbs.   Deb: 8/22/1898 U

YEAR	TM/L	G	AB	R	H	2B	3B	HR	RBI	BB	SO	AVG	OBP	SLG	PRO+	BR/A	SB	CS	SBR	FA	FR	G/POS	TPR
1898	Bos-N	5	9	2	2	0	1	0	1	0		.222	.222	.444	85	-0	0			.889	-1	/C-4,1-1	-0.1
1901	Pit-N	139	566	92	167	26	16	0	91	29		.295	.335	.398	109	5	23			.981	-10	*1-139	-0.7
1902	Pit-N	102	413	49	126	21	8	0	69	17		.305	.336	.395	121	8	23			.984	-6	*1-101	0.1
1903	*Pit-N	127	505	69	134	23	7	2	57	33		.265	.314	.350	87	-10	13			.981	6	*1-127	-0.6
1904	Pit-N	139	520	47	116	17	9	0	60	22		.223	.259	.290	68	-21	11			.981	-3	*1-139	-2.9
1905	Phi-N	151	580	55	150	23	9	3	76	27		.259	.294	.345	93	-7	27			.985	-1	*1-151	-1.3
1906	Phi-N	140	524	47	144	28	5	1	60	16		.275	.300	.353	104	-1	12			.980	-2	*1-139	-0.7
1907	Phi-N	94	348	25	81	15	2	0	38	14		.233	.262	.287	73	-12	8			.978	-3	1-92	-2.0
1908	Phi-N	144	527	53	160	25	7	3	71	23		.304	.335	.395	128	15	30			.986	-1	*1-143	1.3
1909	Phi-N	140	527	47	154	27	6	1	59	18		.292	.319	.372	114	6	17			**.989**	7	*1-138	1.3
1910	Phi-N	123	427	39	102	17	4	3	52	20	34	.239	.275	.319	71	-18	10			.982	-4	*1-110	-2.4
1911	Phi-N	23	43	4	11	1	1	0	3	0	5	.256	.256	.326	61	-2	1			.987	0	/1-8	-0.2
	Chi-N	3	10	0	4	2	0	0	0	2	2	.400	.500	.600	207	2	0			1.000	-0	/1-3	0.1
	Yr	26	53	4	15	3	1	0	3	2	7	.283	.309	.377	91	-1	1			.991	0	1-11	-0.1
Total	12	1330	4999	529	1351	225	75	13	637	221	41	.270	.304	.353	97	-35	175			.983	-18	*1-1291/C-4	-8.1

■ **JEFF BRANSON**   Branson, Jeffery Glenn   b: 1/26/67, Waynesboro, Miss.   BL/TR, 6', 180 lbs.   Deb: 4/12/92

YEAR	TM/L	G	AB	R	H	2B	3B	HR	RBI	BB	SO	AVG	OBP	SLG	PRO+	BR/A	SB	CS	SBR	FA	FR	G/POS	TPR
1992	Cin-N	72	115	12	34	7	1	0	15	5	16	.296	.325	.374	95	-1	0	1	-1	.946	2	2-33/3-8,S-1	0.1
1993	Cin-N	125	381	40	92	15	1	3	22	19	73	.241	.278	.310	57	-23	4	1	1	.978	5	S-59,2-45,3-14/1-1	-1.3
1994	Cin-N	58	109	18	31	4	1	6	16	5	16	.284	.316	.505	110	1	0	0	0	.980	-1	2-19,3-18/S-8,1-2	-0.2
1995	*Cin-N	122	331	43	86	18	2	12	45	44	69	.260	.350	.435	106	3	2	1	0	.971	**22**	3-98,S-32/2-6,1-1	2.6
1996	Cin-N	129	311	34	76	16	4	9	37	31	67	.244	.315	.408	90	-5	2	0	1	.932	2	3-64,S-38,2-31	0.0
Total	5	506	1247	147	319	60	9	30	135	104	241	.256	.315	.391	87	-25	8	3	1	.958	26	3-202,S-138,2/1	1.2

■ **MARSHALL BRANT**   Brant, Marshall Lee   b: 9/17/55, Garberville, Cal.   BR/TR, 6'5", 185 lbs.   Deb: 10/1/80

YEAR	TM/L	G	AB	R	H	2B	3B	HR	RBI	BB	SO	AVG	OBP	SLG	PRO+	BR/A	SB	CS	SBR	FA	FR	G/POS	TPR
1980	NY-A	3	6	0	0	0	0	0	0	0	3	.000	.000	.000	-99	-2	0	0	0	1.000	0	/1-2,D-1	-0.1
1983	Oak-A	5	14	2	2	0	0	0	2	0	3	.143	.143	.143	-22	-2	0	0	0	.905	-1	/1-3,D-1	-0.4
Total	2	8	20	2	2	0	0	0	2	0	6	.100	.100	.100	-47	-4	0	0	0	.935	-1	/1-5,D-2	-0.5

■ **MICKEY BRANTLEY**   Brantley, Michael Charles   b: 6/17/61, Catskill, N.Y.   BR/TR, 5'10", 180 lbs.   Deb: 8/9/86

YEAR	TM/L	G	AB	R	H	2B	3B	HR	RBI	BB	SO	AVG	OBP	SLG	PRO+	BR/A	SB	CS	SBR	FA	FR	G/POS	TPR
1986	Sea-A	27	102	12	20	3	2	5	7	10	21	.196	.268	.353	67	-5	1	1	-0	.983	0	O-25	-0.6
1987	Sea-A	92	351	52	106	23	2	14	54	24	44	.302	.347	.499	115	7	13	4	2	.982	-6	O-82/D-8	-0.1
1988	Sea-A	149	577	76	152	25	4	15	56	26	64	.263	.298	.399	89	-10	18	7	1	.982	-5	*O-147/D-2	-1.8
1989	Sea-A	34	108	14	17	5	0	0	8	7	7	.157	.209	.204	16	-12	2	2	-1	1.000	1	O-23/D-7	-1.2
Total	4	302	1138	154	295	56	8	32	125	67	136	.259	.302	.407	89	-20	34	14	2	.984	-9	O-277/D-17	-3.7

■ **ROY BRASHEAR**   Brashear, Roy Parks   b: 1/3/1874, Ashtabula, Ohio   d: 4/20/51, Los Angeles, Cal.   BR/TR, 5'11", 205 lbs.   Deb: 4/25/02 F

YEAR	TM/L	G	AB	R	H	2B	3B	HR	RBI	BB	SO	AVG	OBP	SLG	PRO+	BR/A	SB	CS	SBR	FA	FR	G/POS	TPR
1902	StL-N	110	388	36	107	8	2	1	40	32		.276	.333	.314	104	2	9			.980	-9	1-67,2-21,0-16,S-3	-0.8
1903	Phi-N	20	75	9	17	3	0	0	4	6		.227	.284	.267	59	-4	2			.918	-4	2-18/1-2	-0.7
Total	2	130	463	45	124	11	2	1	44	38		.268	.325	.307	96	-2	11			.978	-13	/1-69,2-39,0-16,S-3	-1.5

■ **JOE BRATCHER**   Bratcher, Joseph Warlick "Goobers"   b: 7/22/1898, Grand Saline, Tex.   d: 10/13/77, Fort Worth, Tex.   BL/TR, 5'8.5", 140 lbs.   Deb: 8/26/24

YEAR	TM/L	G	AB	R	H	2B	3B	HR	RBI	BB	SO	AVG	OBP	SLG	PRO+	BR/A	SB	CS	SBR	FA	FR	G/POS	TPR
1924	StL-N	4	1	1	0	0	0	0	0	0	0	.000	.000	.000	-99	-0	0	0	0	.000	-1	/O-1	-0.1

■ **FRED BRATSCHI**   Bratschi, Frederick Oscar "Fritz"   b: 1/16/1892, Alliance, Ohio   d: 1/10/62, Massillon, Ohio   BR/TR, 5'10", 170 lbs.   Deb: 7/24/21

YEAR	TM/L	G	AB	R	H	2B	3B	HR	RBI	BB	SO	AVG	OBP	SLG	PRO+	BR/A	SB	CS	SBR	FA	FR	G/POS	TPR
1921	Chi-A	16	28	0	8	1	0	0	3	0	2	.286	.286	.321	55	-2	0	0	0	1.000	1	/O-5	-0.1
1926	Bos-A	72	167	12	46	10	1	0	19	14	15	.275	.335	.347	81	-5	0	1	-1	.949	-7	O-37	-1.4
1927	Bos-A	1	1	0	0	0	0	0	0	0	0	.000	.000	.000	-99	-0	0	0	0	.000	0	H	0.0
Total	3	89	196	12	54	11	1	0	22	14	17	.276	.327	.342	76	-7	0	1	-1	.956	-6	/O-42	-1.5

■ **STEVE BRAUN**   Braun, Stephen Russell   b: 5/8/48, Trenton, N.J.   BL/TR, 5'10", 180 lbs.   Deb: 4/6/71 C

YEAR	TM/L	G	AB	R	H	2B	3B	HR	RBI	BB	SO	AVG	OBP	SLG	PRO+	BR/A	SB	CS	SBR	FA	FR	G/POS	TPR
1971	Min-A	128	343	51	87	12	2	5	35	48	50	.254	.354	.344	95	-1	8	3	1	.933	-13	3-73,2-28,S-10/O-2	-1.1
1972	Min-A	121	402	40	116	21	0	2	50	45	38	.289	.363	.356	109	6	4	5	-2	.970	-12	3-74,2-20,S-11/O-9	-0.8
1973	Min-A	115	361	46	102	28	5	6	42	74	48	.283	.409	.438	133	19	4	3	-1	.941	-11	*3-102/O-6	0.7
1974	Min-A	129	453	53	127	12	1	8	40	56	51	.280	.362	.364	106	5	4	4	-1	.964	2	*O-108,3-17	0.1
1975	Min-A	136	453	70	137	18	3	11	45	66	53	.302	.392	.428	130	20	0	2	-1	.971	-3	*O-106/1-9,3-2,2D	1.2
1976	Min-A	122	417	73	120	12	3	3	61	67	43	.288	.388	.353	115	11	12	4	1	.971	-3	D-71,O-32,3-16	0.6
1977	Sea-A	139	451	51	106	19	1	5	31	80	59	.235	.353	.315	84	-7	8	3	1	.975	5	*O-100,D-32/3-1	-0.6
1978	Sea-A	32	74	11	17	4	0	3	15	9	5	.230	.313	.405	101	0	1	0	0	1.000	1	D-14/O-4	-0.1
	*KC-A	64	137	16	36	10	1	0	14	28	16	.263	.388	.350	106	2	3	2	-0	.964	0	O-33,3-11	-0.5
	Yr	96	211	27	53	14	1	3	29	37	21	.251	.363	.370	105	3	4	2	0	.967	-6	O-37,D-14,3-11	-0.6
1979	KC-A	58	116	15	31	2	0	4	10	22	11	.267	.384	.388	107	2	0	0	0	1.000	1	O-18,D-11/3-2	-0.7
1980	KC-A	14	23	0	1	0	0	0	1	2	2	.043	.120	.043	-53	-5	0	0	0	1.000	1	/O-5,D-1	-0.7
	Tor-A	37	55	4	15	2	0	1	9	8	5	.273	.365	.364	96	-0	0	0	0	1.000	0	D-13/3-1	0.0
	Yr	51	78	4	16	2	0	1	10	10	7	.205	.295	.269	54	-5	0	0	0	1.000	-2	D-14/O-5,3-1	-0.7
1981	StL-N	44	46	9	9	2	1	0	2	15	7	.196	.393	.283	92	0	1	0	0	1.000	0	O-12/3-1	0.0
1982	*StL-N	58	62	6	17	4	0	1	11	10	10	.274	.384	.339	103	1	0	0	0	1.000	-5	/O-8,3-5	-0.4
1983	StL-N	78	92	8	25	2	1	3	7	21	7	.272	.407	.413	128	4	0	1	-1	1.000	-2	O-22/3-4	-0.2
1984	StL-N	98	67	6	27	4	1	1	16	17	17	.276	.383	.327	104	3	1	0	0	1.000	-2	O-19/3-1	-0.4
1985	*StL-N	64	67	7	16	4	0	1	6	10	9	.239	.346	.343	94	-0	0	0	0	1.000	-2	O-14	-0.7
Total	15	1425	3650	466	989	155	19	52	388	579	433	.271	.373	.367	108	60	45	27	-3	.973	-57	O-498,3-310,D/2S1	-2.2

■ **ANGEL BRAVO**   Bravo, Angel Alfonso (Urdaneta)   b: 8/4/42, Maracaibo, Venez.   BL/TL, 5'8", 150 lbs.   Deb: 6/6/69

YEAR	TM/L	G	AB	R	H	2B	3B	HR	RBI	BB	SO	AVG	OBP	SLG	PRO+	BR/A	SB	CS	SBR	FA	FR	G/POS	TPR
1969	Chi-A	27	90	10	26	3	2	3	5	5		.289	.319	.411	98	-0	2	0	1	.978	-4	O-25	-0.6
1970	*Cin-N	65	65	10	18	1	1	0	3	9	13	.277	.365	.323	86	-1	0	1	-1	.947	-5	O-22	-0.7
1971	Cin-N	5	5	0	1	0	0	0	0	1		.200	.200	.200	14	-1	0	0	0	.000	0	H	-0.1
	SD-N	52	58	6	9	2	0	0	6	8	12	.155	.269	.190	34	-5	0	1	-1	.833	-3	/O-9	-0.9
	Yr	57	63	6	10	2	0	0	6	8	13	.159	.264	.190	33	-5	0	1	-1	.833	-3	/O-9	-1.0
Total	3	149	218	26	54	7	3	1	12	20	31	.248	.317	.321	77	-7	2	2	-1	.957	-12	/O-56	-2.3

■ **BUSTER BRAY**   Bray, Clarence Wilbur   b: 4/1/13, Birmingham, Ala.   d: 9/4/82, Evansville, Ind.   BL/TL, 6', 170 lbs.   Deb: 4/18/41

YEAR	TM/L	G	AB	R	H	2B	3B	HR	RBI	BB	SO	AVG	OBP	SLG	PRO+	BR/A	SB	CS	SBR	FA	FR	G/POS	TPR
1941	Bos-N	4	11	2	1	1	0	0	1	1	2	.091	.167	.182	-2	-2	0			1.000	-0	/O-3	-0.2

■ **FRANK BRAZILL**   Brazill, Frank Leo   b: 8/11/1899, Spangler, Pa.   d: 11/3/76, Oakland, Cal.   BL/TR, 5'11.5", 175 lbs.   Deb: 4/13/21

YEAR	TM/L	G	AB	R	H	2B	3B	HR	RBI	BB	SO	AVG	OBP	SLG	PRO+	BR/A	SB	CS	SBR	FA	FR	G/POS	TPR
1921	Phi-A	66	177	17	48	3	1	0	19	23	21	.271	.361	.299	70	-7	2	4	-2	.984	-1	1-36/3-9	-1.0
1922	Phi-A	6	13	0	1	0	1	0	1	0	1	.077	.077	.077	-58	-3	0	0	0	.750	-2	/3-2	-0.5
Total	2	72	190	17	49	3	2	0	20	23	22	.258	.344	.284	62	-10	2	4	-2	.892	-2	/1-36,3-11	-1.5

■ **SID BREAM**   Bream, Sidney Eugene   b: 8/3/60, Carlisle, Pa.   BL/TL, 6'4", 220 lbs.   Deb: 9/1/83

YEAR	TM/L	G	AB	R	H	2B	3B	HR	RBI	BB	SO	AVG	OBP	SLG	PRO+	BR/A	SB	CS	SBR	FA	FR	G/POS	TPR
1983	LA-N	15	11	1	2	0	0	0	2	2	2	.182	.308	.182	39	-1	0	0	0	1.000	-0	/1-4	-0.1
1984	LA-N	27	49	2	9	3	0	0	6	6	9	.184	.273	.245	47	-3	1	0	0	1.000	2	1-14	-0.2
1985	LA-N	24	53	4	7	0	0	3	6	7	10	.132	.233	.302	50	-4	0	0	0	.994	1	1-16	-0.3
	Pit-N	26	95	14	27	7	0	3	15	11	14	.284	.358	.453	127	3	2	-1		.992	2	1-25	0.2

YEAR	TM/L	G	AB	R	H	2B	3B	HR	RBI	BB	SO	AVG	OBP	SLG	PRO+	BR/A	SB	CS	SBR	FA	FR	G/POS	TPR
	Yr	50	148	18	34	7	0	6	21	18	24	.230	.313	.399	100	-0	0	2	-1	.993	4	1-41	-0.1
1986	Pit-N	154	522	73	140	37	5	16	77	60	73	.268	.345	.450	115	10	13	7	-0	.989	23	*1-153/O-2	2.3
1987	Pit-N	149	516	64	142	25	3	13	65	49	69	.275	.338	.411	97	-3	9	8	-2	.988	11	*1-144	-0.4
1988	Pit-N	148	462	50	122	37	0	10	65	47	64	.264	.333	.409	114	8	9	9	-3	.995	21	*1-138	1.7
1989	Pit-N	19	36	3	8	3	0	0	4	12	10	.222	.417	.306	113	2	0	4	-2	.992	-0	1-13	-0.2
1990	*Pit-N	147	389	39	105	23	2	15	67	48	65	.270	.353	.455	125	13	8	4	0	.993	10	*1-142	1.5
1991	*Atl-N	91	265	32	67	12	0	11	45	25	31	.253	.317	.423	100	-0	0	3	-2	.996	-0	1-85	-0.7
1992	*Atl-N	125	372	30	97	25	1	10	61	46	51	.261	.344	.414	107	4	6	0	2	.989	-3	*1-120	-0.5
1993	*Atl-N	117	277	33	72	14	1	9	35	31	43	.260	.334	.415	98	-1	4	2	0	.996	5	1-90	-0.1
1994	Hou-N	46	61	7	21	5	0	0	7	9	9	.344	.429	.426	131	3	0	1	-1	.986	2	1-10	0.4
Total	12	1088	3108	351	819	191	12	90	455	353	450	.264	.340	.420	107	32	50	40	-9	.992	74	1-954/O-2	3.6

■ JIM BREAZEALE
Breazeale, James Leo b: 10/3/49, Houston, Tex. BL/TR, 6'2", 210 lbs. Deb: 9/13/69

YEAR	TM/L	G	AB	R	H	2B	3B	HR	RBI	BB	SO	AVG	OBP	SLG	PRO+	BR/A	SB	CS	SBR	FA	FR	G/POS	TPR
1969	Atl-N	2	1	1	0	0	0	0	0	0	2	.000	.667	.000	101	0	0	0	0	.833	-0	/1-1	0.0
1971	Atl-N	10	21	1	4	0	0	1	3	0	3	.190	.190	.333	43	-2	0	0	0	1.000	-0	/1-4	-0.2
1972	Atl-N	52	85	10	21	2	0	5	17	6	12	.247	.297	.447	100	-0	0	1	-1	1.000	-2	1-16/3-1	-0.4
1978	Chi-A	25	72	8	15	3	0	3	13	8	10	.208	.287	.375	84	-2	0	0	0	.992	-3	1-19/D-4	-0.5
Total	4	89	179	20	40	5	0	9	33	16	25	.223	.287	.402	88	-3	0	1	-1	.993	-5	/1-40,D-4,3-1	-1.1

■ BRENT BREDE
Brede, Brent David b: 9/13/71, Belleville, Ill. BL/TL, 6'4", 190 lbs. Deb: 9/8/96

YEAR	TM/L	G	AB	R	H	2B	3B	HR	RBI	BB	SO	AVG	OBP	SLG	PRO+	BR/A	SB	CS	SBR	FA	FR	G/POS	TPR
1996	Min-A	10	20	2	6	0	1	0	2	1	5	.300	.333	.400	83	-1	0	0	0	1.000	0	/O-7	0.0

■ DANNY BREEDEN
Breeden, Danny Richard b: 6/27/42, Albany, Ga. BR/TR, 5'11.5", 185 lbs. Deb: 7/24/69 F

YEAR	TM/L	G	AB	R	H	2B	3B	HR	RBI	BB	SO	AVG	OBP	SLG	PRO+	BR/A	SB	CS	SBR	FA	FR	G/POS	TPR
1969	Cin-N	3	8	0	1	0	0	0	1	0	3	.125	.125	.125	-28	-1	0	0	0	.941	0	/C-3	-0.1
1971	Chi-N	25	65	3	10	1	0	0	4	9	18	.154	.267	.169	23	-6	0	0	0	.975	4	C-25	-0.2
Total	2	28	73	3	11	1	0	0	5	9	21	.151	.253	.164	18	-8	0	0	0	.972	5	/C-28	-0.3

■ HAL BREEDEN
Breeden, Harold Noel b: 6/28/44, Albany, Ga. BR/TL, 6'2", 200 lbs. Deb: 4/7/71 F

YEAR	TM/L	G	AB	R	H	2B	3B	HR	RBI	BB	SO	AVG	OBP	SLG	PRO+	BR/A	SB	CS	SBR	FA	FR	G/POS	TPR
1971	Chi-N	23	36	1	5	1	0	1	2	2	7	.139	.184	.250	19	-4	0	0	0	.982	1	/1-8	-0.3
1972	Mon-N	42	87	6	20	2	0	3	10	7	15	.230	.287	.356	80	-2	0	0	0	.994	1	1-26/O-1	-0.6
1973	Mon-N	105	258	36	71	10	6	15	43	29	45	.275	.353	.535	138	12	0	1	-1	.991	3	1-66	1.1
1974	Mon-N	79	190	14	47	13	0	2	20	24	35	.247	.332	.347	85	-3	0	1	-1	.987	1	1-56	-0.7
1975	Mon-N	24	37	4	5	2	0	0	1	7	5	.135	.273	.189	29	-3	0	0	0	.989	-0	1-12	-0.2
Total	5	273	608	61	148	28	6	21	76	69	107	.243	.323	.413	99	-1	0	2	-1	.990	4	1-168/O-1	-1.0

■ MARV BREEDING
Breeding, Marvin Eugene b: 3/8/34, Decatur, Ala. BR/TR, 6', 175 lbs. Deb: 4/19/60

YEAR	TM/L	G	AB	R	H	2B	3B	HR	RBI	BB	SO	AVG	OBP	SLG	PRO+	BR/A	SB	CS	SBR	FA	FR	G/POS	TPR
1960	Bal-A	152	551	69	147	25	2	8	43	35	80	.267	.314	.336	77	-18	10	4	1	.977	5	*2-152	0.2
1961	Bal-A	90	244	32	51	8	0	1	16	14	33	.209	.252	.254	37	-22	5	2	0	.970	7	2-80	-0.8
1962	Bal-A	95	240	27	59	10	1	2	18	8	41	.246	.273	.321	63	-13	2	2	-1	.977	21	2-73/S-1,3-1	1.3
1963	Was-A	58	197	20	54	7	2	1	14	7	21	.274	.299	.345	80	-5	1	1	-0	.914	-9	3-29,2-22/S-2	-1.3
	LA-N	20	36	6	6	0	0	0	1	2	5	.167	.211	.167	11	-4	1	0	0	.972	-4	2-17/S-1,3-1	-0.8
Total	4	415	1268	154	317	50	5	7	92	66	180	.250	.289	.314	65	-63	19	9	0	.975	20	2-344/3-31,S-4	-1.4

■ HERB BREMER
Bremer, Herbert Frederick b: 10/26/13, Chicago, Ill. d: 11/28/79, Columbus, Ga. BR/TR, 6', 195 lbs. Deb: 9/16/37

YEAR	TM/L	G	AB	R	H	2B	3B	HR	RBI	BB	SO	AVG	OBP	SLG	PRO+	BR/A	SB	CS	SBR	FA	FR	G/POS	TPR
1937	StL-N	11	33	2	7	1	0	0	3	2	4	.212	.257	.242	36	-3	0			.979	-0	C-10	-0.3
1938	StL-N	50	151	14	33	5	1	2	14	9	36	.219	.262	.305	53	-10	1			.977	3	C-50	-0.5
1939	StL-N	9	9	0	1	0	0	0	1	0	2	.111	.111	.111	-38	-2	0			1.000	1	/C-8	-0.1
Total	3	70	193	16	41	6	1	2	18	11	42	.212	.255	.285	45	-15	1			.979	3	/C-68	-0.9

■ SAM BRENEGAN
Brenegan, Olaf Selmar b: 9/1/1890, Galesville, Wis. d: 4/20/56, Galesville, Wis. BL/TR, 6'2", 185 lbs. Deb: 4/24/14

YEAR	TM/L	G	AB	R	H	2B	3B	HR	RBI	BB	SO	AVG	OBP	SLG	PRO+	BR/A	SB	CS	SBR	FA	FR	G/POS	TPR
1914	Pit-N	1	0	0	0	0	0	0	0	0	0	—	—	—		0	0			.000	-0	/C-1	0.0

■ BOB BRENLY
Brenly, Robert Earl b: 2/25/54, Coshocton, Ohio BR/TR, 6'2", 210 lbs. Deb: 8/14/81 C

YEAR	TM/L	G	AB	R	H	2B	3B	HR	RBI	BB	SO	AVG	OBP	SLG	PRO+	BR/A	SB	CS	SBR	FA	FR	G/POS	TPR
1981	SF-N	19	45	5	15	2	1	1	4	6	4	.333	.423	.489	161	4	0	1	-1	.964	-4	C-14/3-3,O-1	0.0
1982	SF-N	65	180	26	51	4	1	4	15	18	26	.283	.352	.383	106	2	6	2	1	.961	0	C-61/3-1	0.5
1983	SF-N	104	281	36	63	12	2	7	34	37	48	.224	.319	.356	89	-4	10	7	-1	.983	1	C-90,1-10/O-2	-0.1
1984	SF-N★	145	506	74	147	28	0	20	80	48	52	.291	.355	.464	133	21	6	9	-4	.986	-18	*C-127,1-22/O-3	0.5
1985	SF-N	133	440	41	97	16	1	19	56	57	62	.220	.313	.391	100	-0	1	4	-2	.984	-7	*C-110,3-17,1-10	-0.4
1986	SF-N	149	472	60	116	26	0	16	62	74	97	.246	.352	.403	113	9	10	6	-1	.995	-7	*C-101,3-45,1-19	0.6
1987	*SF-N	123	375	55	100	19	1	18	51	54	85	.267	.353	.467	121	11	10	7	-1	.988	9	*C-108/1-6,3-2	2.5
1988	SF-N	73	206	13	39	7	0	5	22	20	40	.189	.268	.296	64	-10	1	2	-1	.984	-4	C-69	-1.1
1989	Tor-A	48	88	9	15	3	1	1	6	10	17	.170	.255	.261	47	-6	1	0	0	.975	2	D-28,C-13/1-5	-0.5
	SF-N	12	22	2	4	2	0	0	3	1	7	.182	.217	.273	40	-2	0	0	0	1.000	1	C-12	-0.1
Total	9	871	2615	321	647	119	7	91	333	318	438	.247	.336	.403	107	25	45	38	-9	.987	-26	C-705/1-72,3-68,DO	1.9

■ JIM BRENNAN
Brennan, James Augustus (b: John Gottlieb Dorn) b: 1862, St.Louis, Mo. d: 10/18/04, Philadelphia, Pa. Deb: 4/20/1884

YEAR	TM/L	G	AB	R	H	2B	3B	HR	RBI	BB	SO	AVG	OBP	SLG	PRO+	BR/A	SB	CS	SBR	FA	FR	G/POS	TPR
1884	StL-U	56	231	38	50	6	1	0		12		.216	.255	.251	52	-20				.891	-2	C-33,O-16/3-7,S-1	-1.8
1885	StL-N	3	10	0	1	0	0	0	1	1	1	.100	.182	.100	-7	-1				.750	-1	/O-2,3-1	-0.2
1888	KC-a	34	118	5	20	2	0	0	6	3		.169	.203	.186	24	-10	3			.884	-3	C-25/O-5,3-5	-1.0
1889	Phi-a	31	113	12	25	4	0	0	15	10	15	.221	.285	.257	55	-6	1			.818	-4	C-13/O-7,2-7,3-4	-0.8
1890	Cle-P	59	233	32	59	3	7	0	26	13	29	.253	.304	.326	74	-9	8			.845	-4	C-42,3-14/O-6	-0.7
Total	5	183	705	87	155	15	8	0	48	39	45	.220	.267	.264	55	-46	12			.869	-15	C-113/O-36,3-31,2S	-4.5

■ BILL BRENZEL
Brenzel, William Richard b: 3/3/10, Oakland, Cal. d: 6/12/79, Oakland, Cal. BR/TR, 5'10", 173 lbs. Deb: 4/13/32

YEAR	TM/L	G	AB	R	H	2B	3B	HR	RBI	BB	SO	AVG	OBP	SLG	PRO+	BR/A	SB	CS	SBR	FA	FR	G/POS	TPR
1932	Pit-N	9	24	0	1	1	0	0	2	0	4	.042	.042	.083	-69	-6	0			1.000	2	/C-9	-0.3
1934	Cle-A	15	51	4	11	3	0	0	3	2	1	.216	.245	.275	33	-5	0	0	0	1.000	3	C-15	-0.2
1935	Cle-A	52	142	12	31	5	1	0	14	6	10	.218	.250	.268	33	-14	2	2	-1	.975	-7	C-51	-1.8
Total	3	76	217	16	43	9	1	0	19	8	15	.198	.227	.249	23	-25	2	2		.985	-2	/C-75	-2.3

■ ROGER BRESNAHAN
Bresnahan, Roger Philip "The Duke Of Tralee"
b: 6/11/1879, Toledo, Ohio d: 12/4/44, Toledo, Ohio BR/TR, 5'9", 200 lbs. Deb: 8/27/1897 MCH

YEAR	TM/L	G	AB	R	H	2B	3B	HR	RBI	BB	SO	AVG	OBP	SLG	PRO+	BR/A	SB	CS	SBR	FA	FR	G/POS	TPR
1897	Was-N	6	16	1	6	0	0	0				.375	.412	.375	109	0				1.000	-1	/P-6,O-1	0.0
1900	Chi-N	2	2	0	0	0	0	0	0	0		.000	.000	.000	-99	-1	0			.000	-0	/C-1	-0.1
1901	Bal-A	86	295	40	79	9	9	1	32	23		.268	.323	.369	88	-5	10			.919	-19	C-69/O-8,3-4,P-2,2	-1.6
1902	Bal-A	65	235	30	64	8	6	4	34	21		.272	.337	.409	102	0	12			.880	-7	3-30,C-22,O-15	-0.5
	NY-N	51	178	16	51	9	3	1	22	16		.287	.352	.388	129	6	6			.946	0	O-27,C-16/1-4,S3	0.7
1903	NY-N	113	406	87	142	30	8	4	55	61		.350	.443	.493	160	34	34			.965	0	O-84,1-13,C-11/3-4	2.8
1904	NY-N	109	402	81	114	22	7	5	33	58		.284	.381	.410	138	20	13			.954	0	O-93,1-10/S-4,23	1.5
1905	*NY-N	104	331	58	100	18	3	0	46	50		.302	.411	.359	132	16	11			.970	-1	C-87/O-8	2.5
1906	NY-N	124	405	69	114	22	4	0	43	81		.281	.419	.356	139	25	25			.974	5	C-82,O-40	3.9
1907	NY-N	110	328	57	83	9	7	4	38	61		.253	.380	.360	128	13	15			.986	-7	C-95/1-6,O-2,3-1	1.7
1908	NY-N	140	449	70	127	25	3	1	54	83		.283	.401	.359	136	23	14			.985	-18	*C-139	2.1
1909	StL-N	72	234	27	57	4	1	0	23	46		.244	.370	.269	105	5	11			.960	-6	C-59/2-9,3-1,M	0.3
1910	StL-N	88	234	35	65	15	0	0	27	55	17	.278	.419	.368	135	14	13			.961	-9	C-77/O-2,P-1,M	1.2
1911	StL-N	81	227	22	63	17	8	3	41	45	19	.278	.404	.463	146	15	4			.968	-2	C-77/2-2,M	2.0
1912	StL-N	48	108	8	36	7	2	1	15	14	9	.333	.419	.463	145	7	4			.974	7	C-28,M	-0.5
1913	Chi-N	69	162	20	37	8	1	2	21	21	11	.228	.324	.302	79	-4	7			.963	-5	C-58	-0.5
1914	Chi-N	101	248	42	69	10	4	0	24	49	20	.278	.401	.351	125	11	14			.978	-3	C-85,2-14/O-1	1.5
1915	Chi-N	77	221	19	45	8	1	0	19	29	23	.204	.296	.262	70	-7	19	3	4	.982	3	C-68,M	0.5
Total	17	1446	4481	682	1252	218	71	26	530	714	99	.279	.386	.377	126	172	212	3		.971	-63	C-974,O-281/312PS	19.7

YEAR	TM/L	G	AB	R	H	2B	3B	HR	RBI	BB	SO	AVG	OBP	SLG	PRO+	BR/A	SB	CS	SBR	FA	FR	G/POS	TPR

■ RUBE BRESSLER
Bressler, Raymond Bloom b: 10/23/1894, Coder, Pa. d: 11/7/66, Cincinnati, Ohio BR/TL, 6′, 187 lbs. Deb: 4/24/14

YEAR	TM/L	G	AB	R	H	2B	3B	HR	RBI	BB	SO	AVG	OBP	SLG	PRO+	BR/A	SB	CS	SBR	FA	FR	G/POS	TPR
1914	Phi-A	29	51	6	11	1	1	0	4	6	7	.216	.310	.275	79	-1	0			.941	-2	P-29	0.0
1915	Phi-A	33	55	9	8	0	1	1	4	9	13	.145	.277	.236	56	-3	0			.900	0	P-32	0.0
1916	Phi-A	4	5	1	1	0	1	0	1	0	0	.200	.200	.600	147	0	0			1.000	-0	/P-4	0.0
1917	Cin-N	3	5	0	1	0	0	0	0	0	2	.200	.200	.200	24	-0	0			1.000	-0	/P-2	0.0
1918	Cin-N	23	62	10	17	5	0	0	6	5	5	.274	.328	.355	110	1	0			.982	2	P-17/O-3	-0.1
1919	Cin-N	61	165	22	34	3	4	2	17	23	15	.206	.311	.309	89	-2	2			.965	1	O-48,P-13	-0.5
1920	Cin-N	21	30	4	8	1	0	0	3	1	4	.267	.290	.300	71	-1	1	0	0	1.000	-1	P-10/O-3,1-2	-0.2
1921	Cin-N	109	323	41	99	18	6	1	54	39	20	.307	.385	.409	115	8	5	5	-2	.953	-6	O-85/1-6	-0.6
1922	Cin-N	52	53	7	14	0	2	0	8	4	4	.264	.316	.340	70	-2	1	0	0	1.000	-2	/1-3,O-2	-0.4
1923	Cin-N	54	119	25	33	3	1	0	18	20	4	.277	.399	.319	93	0	3	1	0	.983	-3	1-22/O-6	-0.3
1924	Cin-N	115	383	41	133	14	13	4	49	22	20	.347	.389	.483	134	18	9	10	-3	.990	-5	1-50,O-49	1.3
1925	Cin-N	97	319	43	111	17	6	4	61	40	16	.348	.424	.476	133	17	9	5	-0	.982	-3	1-52,O-38	0.8
1926	Cin-N	86	297	58	106	15	9	1	51	37	20	.357	.433	.478	149	22	3			.970	-4	O-80/1-4	1.3
1927	Cin-N	124	467	43	136	14	8	3	77	32	22	.291	.338	.375	94	-4	4			.972	7	*O-120	-0.5
1928	Bro-N	145	501	78	148	29	13	4	70	80	33	.295	.398	.429	118	16	2			**.985**	-6	*O-137	0.1
1929	Bro-N	136	456	72	145	22	8	9	77	67	27	.318	.406	.461	117	14	4			.954	3	*O-122	0.8
1930	Bro-N	109	335	53	100	12	8	3	52	51	19	.299	.394	.409	96	-0	4			.995	6	O-90/1-7	0.0
1931	Bro-N	67	153	22	43	4	5	0	26	11	10	.281	.329	.373	89	-2	0			.982	-4	O-35/1-1	-0.9
1932	Phi-N	27	83	9	19	6	1	0	6	2	5	.229	.247	.325	47	-6	0			1.000	3	O-18	-0.4
	StL-N	10	19	0	3	0	0	0	2	0	1	.158	.158	.158	-14	-3	0			1.000	0	/O-4	-0.3
	Yr	37	102	9	22	6	1	0	8	2	6	.216	.231	.294	37	-9	0			1.000	3	O-22	-0.7
Total	19	1305	3881	544	1170	164	87	32	586	449	246	.301	.378	.413	110	71	47	21		.971	-4	O-840,1-147,P-107	0.1

■ EDDIE BRESSOUD
Bressoud, Edward Francis b: 5/2/32, Los Angeles, Cal. BR/TR, 6′1″, 175 lbs. Deb: 6/14/56

YEAR	TM/L	G	AB	R	H	2B	3B	HR	RBI	BB	SO	AVG	OBP	SLG	PRO+	BR/A	SB	CS	SBR	FA	FR	G/POS	TPR
1956	NY-N	49	163	15	37	4	2	0	9	12	20	.227	.284	.276	52	-11	1	0	0	.950	-9	S-48	-1.7
1957	NY-N	49	127	11	34	2	2	5	10	4	19	.268	.301	.433	94	-1	0	1	-1	.940	1	S-33,3-12	0.2
1958	SF-N	66	137	19	36	5	3	0	8	14	22	.263	.331	.343	81	-4	0	1	-1	.966	-2	2-57/3-6,S-4	-0.3
1959	SF-N	104	315	36	79	17	2	9	26	28	55	.251	.312	.403	91	-5	0	0	-0	.974	-5	S-92/1-1,2-1,3-1	-0.4
1960	SF-N	116	386	37	87	19	6	9	43	35	72	.225	.293	.376	87	-8	1	2	-1	.960	6	*S-115	0.6
1961	SF-N	59	114	14	24	6	0	3	11	11	23	.211	.280	.342	66	-6	1	1	-0	.964	4	S-34/3-3,2-1	-1.3
1962	Bos-A	153	599	79	166	40	9	14	68	46	118	.277	.331	.444	103	1	2	3	-1	.965	25	*S-153	3.8
1963	Bos-A	140	497	61	129	23	6	20	60	52	93	.260	.332	.451	113	9	1	1	-0	.962	-9	*S-137	0.9
1964	Bos-A☆	158	566	86	166	41	3	15	55	72	99	.293	.374	.456	123	19	1	1	-0	.972	-14	*S-158	1.7
1965	Bos-A	107	296	29	67	11	1	8	25	29	77	.226	.298	.351	79	-8	0	1	-0	.963	-5	S-86/3-2,O-1	-0.9
1966	NY-N	133	405	48	91	15	5	10	49	47	107	.225	.307	.360	87	-7	0	2	-1	.960	8	S-94,3-32/1-9,2-7	0.7
1967	*StL-N	52	67	8	9	1	1	1	9	1	18	.134	.237	.224	33	-6	0	0	0	.929	-4	S-48/3-1	-0.9
Total	12	1186	3672	443	925	184	40	94	365	359	723	.252	.321	.401	96	-26	9	13	-5	.963	-19	*S-1002/2-66,310	2.4

■ JIM BRETON
Breton, John Frederick b: 7/15/1891, Chicago, Ill. d: 5/30/73, Beloit, Wis. BR/TR, 5′10.5″, 178 lbs. Deb: 8/25/13

YEAR	TM/L	G	AB	R	H	2B	3B	HR	RBI	BB	SO	AVG	OBP	SLG	PRO+	BR/A	SB	CS	SBR	FA	FR	G/POS	TPR
1913	Chi-A	12	30	1	5	1	1	0	2	2	5	.167	.194	.267	35	-3	0			.938	3	/S-7,3-3	0.0
1914	Chi-A	81	231	21	49	7	2	0	24	24	42	.212	.292	.260	67	-9	9	6	-1	.910	3	3-79	-0.5
1915	Chi-A	16	36	3	5	1	0	0	1	5	9	.139	.262	.167	27	-3	2	1	0	.882	-2	3-14/2-1,S-1	-0.5
Total	3	109	297	25	59	9	3	0	27	30	56	.199	.279	.249	59	-15	11	7		.906	4	/3-96,S-8,2-1	-1.0

■ GEORGE BRETT
Brett, George Howard b: 5/15/53, Glen Dale, W.Va. BL/TR, 6′, 200 lbs. Deb: 8/2/73 F

YEAR	TM/L	G	AB	R	H	2B	3B	HR	RBI	BB	SO	AVG	OBP	SLG	PRO+	BR/A	SB	CS	SBR	FA	FR	G/POS	TPR
1973	KC-A	13	40	2	5	2	0	0	0	0	5	.125	.125	.175	-15	-6	0	0	0	.974	3	3-13	-0.3
1974	KC-A	133	457	49	129	21	5	2	47	21	38	.282	.314	.363	89	-7	8	5	-1	.948	-9	*3-132/S-1	-1.9
1975	KC-A	159	634	84	**195**	35	**13**	11	89	46	49	.308	.356	.456	125	19	13	10	-2	.949	-6	*3-159/S-1	1.1
1976	*KC-A★	159	645	94	**215**	34	**14**	7	67	49	36	**.333**	.381	.462	145	35	21	11	-0	.948	-6	*3-157/S-4	4.0
1977	*KC-A★	139	564	105	176	32	13	22	88	55	24	.312	.375	.532	143	33	14	12	-3	.957	17	*3-135/S-1,D-3	4.4
1978	*KC-A★	128	510	79	150	**45**	8	9	62	39	35	.294	.345	.467	123	14	23	7	3	.961	5	*3-128/S-1	2.1
1979	*KC-A★	154	645	119	**212**	42	**20**	23	107	51	36	.329	.378	.563	147	40	17	10	-1	.944	13	*3-149/1-8,D-1	4.9
1980	*KC-A†	117	449	87	175	33	9	24	118	58	22	**.390**	**.461**	**.664**	203	64	15	6	1	.955	4	*3-112/1-1	6.4
1981	*KC-A★	89	347	42	109	27	7	6	43	27	23	.314	.365	.484	144	19	14	6	1	.946	-9	3-88	0.9
1982	KC-A★	144	552	101	166	32	9	21	82	71	51	.301	.381	.505	141	32	6	1	1	.959	-6	*3-134,O-12	2.3
1983	KC-A★	123	464	90	144	38	2	25	93	57	39	.310	.387	**.563**	157	36	0	1	-1	.919	-25	*3-102,1-14,O-13/D	0.8
1984	*KC-A★	104	377	42	107	21	3	13	69	38	37	.284	.349	.459	121	10	0	2	-1	.949	-4	*3-101	0.4
1985	*KC-A★	155	550	108	184	38	5	30	112	103	49	.335	.442	**.585**	178	63	9	1	2	.967	12	*3-152/D-1	7.2
1986	KC-A†	124	441	70	128	28	4	16	73	80	45	.290	.404	.481	137	25	1	2	-1	.952	-2	*3-115/S-2,D-7	1.9
1987	KC-A	115	427	71	124	18	2	22	78	72	47	.290	.394	.496	131	21	6	3	0	.993	-9	1-83,D-21,3-11	0.8
1988	KC-A★	157	589	90	180	42	3	24	103	82	51	.306	.393	.509	149	40	14	3	2	.992	-9	*1-124,D-33/S-1	2.2
1989	KC-A	124	457	67	129	26	3	12	80	59	47	.282	.368	.431	125	16	14	4	2	.998	4	*1-104,D-17/O-2	1.3
1990	KC-A	142	544	82	179	**45**	7	14	87	56	63	**.329**	.392	.515	154	39	9	2	1	.993	-1	*1-102,D-32/O-9,3-1	3.0
1991	KC-A	131	505	77	129	40	2	10	61	58	75	.255	.332	.402	102	1	2	0	1	.989	-1	*D-118,1-10	-0.5
1992	KC-A	152	592	55	169	35	5	7	61	35	69	.285	.332	.397	101	-0	8	6	-1	.987	0	*D-132,1-15/3-3	-0.7
1993	KC-A	145	560	69	149	31	3	19	75	39	67	.266	.317	.434	94	-6	7	5	-1	1.000	0	*D-140	-1.3
Total	21	2707	10349	1583	3154	665	137	317	1595	1096	908	.305	.373	.487	135	488	201	97	2	.951	-17	*3-1692,D-506,1/OS	39.0

■ TONY BREWER
Brewer, Anthony Bruce b: 11/25/57, Shreveport, La. BR/TR, 5′11″, 190 lbs. Deb: 8/1/84 F

YEAR	TM/L	G	AB	R	H	2B	3B	HR	RBI	BB	SO	AVG	OBP	SLG	PRO+	BR/A	SB	CS	SBR	FA	FR	G/POS	TPR
1984	LA-N	24	37	3	4	1	0	1	4	4	9	.108	.195	.216	16	-4	1	0	0	1.000	-2	O-10	-0.6

■ MIKE BREWER
Brewer, Michael Quinn b: 10/24/59, Coushatta, La. BR/TR, 6′5″, 190 lbs. Deb: 6/11/86 F

YEAR	TM/L	G	AB	R	H	2B	3B	HR	RBI	BB	SO	AVG	OBP	SLG	PRO+	BR/A	SB	CS	SBR	FA	FR	G/POS	TPR
1986	KC-A	12	18	0	3	1	0	0	6	2	6	.167	.250	.222	29	-2	0	1	-1	1.000	-2	/O-9,D-1	-0.4

■ ROD BREWER
Brewer, Rodney Lee b: 2/24/66, Eustis, Fla. BL/TL, 6′3″, 210 lbs. Deb: 9/5/90

YEAR	TM/L	G	AB	R	H	2B	3B	HR	RBI	BB	SO	AVG	OBP	SLG	PRO+	BR/A	SB	CS	SBR	FA	FR	G/POS	TPR
1990	StL-N	14	25	4	6	1	0	0	2	0	4	.240	.240	.280	42	-2	0	0	0	.981	1	/1-9	-0.2
1991	StL-N	19	13	0	1	0	0	0	1	0	5	.077	.077	.077	-56	-3	0	0	0	1.000	-0	1-15/O-3	-0.3
1992	StL-N	29	103	11	31	6	0	0	10	8	12	.301	.357	.359	107	1	1	1	-1	1.000	1	1-27/O-4	-0.1
1993	StL-N	110	147	15	42	8	0	2	20	17	26	.286	.364	.381	102	1	1	0	0	.960	-6	O-33,1-32/P-1	-0.6
Total	4	172	288	30	80	15	0	2	33	25	47	.278	.340	.351	92	-3	1	1	-0	.995	-4	/1-83,O-40,P-1	-1.2

■ CHARLIE BREWSTER
Brewster, Charles Lawrence b: 12/27/16, Marthaville, La. BR/TR, 5′8.5″, 175 lbs. Deb: 5/2/43

YEAR	TM/L	G	AB	R	H	2B	3B	HR	RBI	BB	SO	AVG	OBP	SLG	PRO+	BR/A	SB	CS	SBR	FA	FR	G/POS	TPR
1943	Cin-N	7	8	0	1	0	0	0	0	0	1	.125	.125	.125	-28	-1	0			1.000	-0	/2-2	-0.1
	Phi-N	49	159	13	35	2	0	0	12	10	19	.220	.275	.233	49	-10	1			.901	-20	S-46	-3.0
	Yr	56	167	13	36	2	0	0	12	10	20	.216	.268	.228	45	-12	1			.901	-20	S-46/2-2	-3.1
1944	Chi-N	10	44	4	11	2	0	0	2	5	7	.250	.327	.295	76	-1	0			.903		S-10	-0.1
1946	Cle-A	3	2	0	0	0	0	0	0	1	1	.000	.333	.000	-1	-0	0			1.000	0	/S-1	0.0
Total	3	69	213	17	47	4	0	0	14	16	28	.221	.281	.239	52	-13	1	0		.902	-20	/S-57,2-2	-3.1

■ FRITZ BRICKELL
Brickell, Fritz Darrell b: 3/19/35, Wichita, Kan. d: 10/15/65, Wichita, Kan. BR/TR, 5′5.5″, 157 lbs. Deb: 4/30/58

YEAR	TM/L	G	AB	R	H	2B	3B	HR	RBI	BB	SO	AVG	OBP	SLG	PRO+	BR/A	SB	CS	SBR	FA	FR	G/POS	TPR
1958	NY-A	2	0	0	0	0	0	0	0	0	0	—	—	—	—		0	0	0	1.000	0	/2-2	0.0
1959	NY-A	18	39	4	10	1	0	1	4	1	9	.256	.275	.359	75	-1	0	0	0	.925	0	S-15/2-3	0.0
1961	LA-A	21	49	3	6	0	0	0	3	6	9	.122	.218	.122	-6	-5	0	0	0	.901	0	S-17	-0.6
Total	3	41	88	7	16	1	0	1	7	7	19	.182	.242	.227	26	-9	0	0	0	.911	0	/S-32,2-5	-0.6

■ FRED BRICKELL
Brickell, George Frederick b: 11/9/06, Saffordville, Kan. d: 4/8/61, Wichita, Kan. BL/TR, 5′7″, 160 lbs. Deb: 8/19/26 F

YEAR	TM/L	G	AB	R	H	2B	3B	HR	RBI	BB	SO	AVG	OBP	SLG	PRO+	BR/A	SB	CS	SBR	FA	FR	G/POS	TPR
1926	Pit-N	24	55	11	19	3	1	0	4	3	6	.345	.400	.436	119	2	0			.920	-0	O-14	0.1
1927	*Pit-N	32	21	6	6	1	0	1	4	4	0	.286	.318	.476	103	0	0			1.000	-1	/O-3	0.0
1928	Pit-N	81	202	34	65	4	3	0	41	20	18	.322	.383	.426	107	2	0			.958	1	O-50	0.1
1929	Pit-N	60	118	13	37	4	2	0	17	7	12	.314	.352	.381	80	-4	3			1.000	0	O-27	-0.5

YEAR	TM/L	G	AB	R	H	2B	3B	HR	RBI	BB	SO	AVG	OBP	SLG	PRO+	BR/A	SB	CS	SBR	FA	FR	G/POS	TPR
1930	Pit-N	68	219	36	65	9	3	1	14	15	20	.297	.342	.379	74	-9	3			.951	-4	O-61	-1.5
	Phi-N	53	240	33	59	12	6	0	17	13	21	.246	.290	.346	49	-20	1			.963	5	O-53	-1.7
	Yr	121	459	69	124	21	9	1	31	28	41	.270	.315	.362	61	-29	4			.958	0	*O-114	-3.2
1931	Phi-N	130	514	77	130	14	5	1	31	42	39	.253	.316	.305	63	-26	5			.978	4	*O-122	-3.1
1932	Phi-N	45	66	9	22	6	1	0	2	4	5	.333	.389	.455	112	1	2			.935	-0	O-12	0.1
1933	Phi-N	8	13	2	4	1	1	0	1	1	0	.308	.357	.538	136	1	0			1.000	1	/O-4	0.1
Total	8	501	1448	221	407	54	23	6	131	106	121	.281	.335	.363	75	-53	19			.967	5	O-346	-6.5

■ GEORGE BRICKLEY

Brickley, George Vincent b: 7/19/1894, Everett, Mass. d: 2/23/47, Everett, Mass. BR/TR, 5'9", 180 lbs. Deb: 9/26/13

YEAR	TM/L	G	AB	R	H	2B	3B	HR	RBI	BB	SO	AVG	OBP	SLG	PRO+	BR/A	SB	CS	SBR	FA	FR	G/POS	TPR
1913	Phi-A	5	12	0	2	0	1	0	0	0	4	.167	.231	.333	66	-1	0			1.000	-1	/O-4	-0.2

■ JIM BRIDEWESER

Brideweser, James Ehrenfeld b: 2/13/27, Lancaster, Ohio d: 8/25/89, El Toro, Cal. BR/TR, 6', 165 lbs. Deb: 9/29/51

YEAR	TM/L	G	AB	R	H	2B	3B	HR	RBI	BB	SO	AVG	OBP	SLG	PRO+	BR/A	SB	CS	SBR	FA	FR	G/POS	TPR
1951	NY-A	2	8	1	3	0	0	0	0	0	1	.375	.375	.375	107	0	0	0	0	.818	0	/S-2	0.0
1952	NY-A	42	38	12	10	0	0	0	2	3	5	.263	.317	.263	67	-2	0	0	0	.935	2	S-22/2-4,3-1	0.1
1953	NY-A	7	3	3	3	0	1	0	3	1	0	1.000	1.000	1.667	631	2	0	0	0	.833	0	/S-3	0.3
1954	Bal-A	73	204	18	54	7	2	0	12	15	27	.265	.318	.319	81	-6	1	1	-0	.944	-12	S-48,2-19	-1.4
1955	Chi-A	34	58	6	12	3	2	0	4	3	7	.207	.246	.328	52	-4	0	0	0	.949	6	S-26/3-3,2-2	0.3
1956	Chi-A	10	11	0	2	1	0	0	1	0	3	.182	.250	.273	37	-1	0	0	0	.938	0	S-10	-0.1
	Det-A	70	156	23	34	4	0	0	10	20	19	.218	.307	.244	47	-12	3	1	0	.987	14	S-32,2-31/3-4	0.6
	Yr	80	167	23	36	5	0	0	11	20	22	.216	.303	.246	46	-13	3	1	0	.979	14	S-42,2-31/3-4	0.5
1957	Bal-A	91	142	16	38	7	1	1	18	21	15	.268	.362	.352	102	1	2	0	1	.943	5	S-74/3-3,2-1	1.1
Total	7	329	620	79	156	22	6	1	50	63	77	.252	.323	.311	75	-21	6	3	1	.946	15	S-217/2-57,3-11	0.9

■ ROCKY BRIDGES

Bridges, Everett Lamar b: 8/7/27, Refugio, Tex. BR/TR, 5'8", 175 lbs. Deb: 4/17/51 C

YEAR	TM/L	G	AB	R	H	2B	3B	HR	RBI	BB	SO	AVG	OBP	SLG	PRO+	BR/A	SB	CS	SBR	FA	FR	G/POS	TPR
1951	Bro-N	63	134	13	34	7	0	1	15	10	10	.254	.306	.328	69	-6	0	0	-0	.871	3	3-40,2-10/S-9	-0.2
1952	Bro-N	51	56	9	11	3	0	0	2	7	9	.196	.286	.250	49	-4	0	1	-1	.986	12	2-24,S-13/3-6	0.8
1953	Cin-N	122	432	52	98	13	2	1	21	37	42	.227	.288	.273	47	-33	6	3	0	.976	11	*2-115/S-6,3-3	-1.6
1954	Cin-N	53	52	4	12	1	0	0	2	7	7	.231	.322	.250	50	-4	0	1	-1	1.000	11	S-20,2-19,3-13	0.7
1955	Cin-N	95	168	20	48	4	0	1	18	15	19	.286	.344	.327	75	-6	1	1	-0	.965	7	3-59,S-26/2-9	0.1
1956	Cin-N	71	19	9	4	0	0	0	1	4	3	.211	.348	.211	52	-1	1	2	-1	.966	8	3-51/2-8,S-7,O-1	0.6
1957	Cin-N	5	1	0	0	0	0	0	0	1	1	.000	.500	.000	46	0	0	0	0	1.000	-1	/2-2,S-1,3-1	-0.1
	Was-A	120	391	40	89	17	2	3	47	40	32	.228	.303	.304	67	-17	2	2	-1	.971	**29**	*S-108,2-14/3-1	2.2
1958	Was-A☆	116	377	38	99	14	3	5	28	27	32	.263	.317	.355	86	-7	0	3	-2	.976	3	*S-112/2-3,3-3	0.4
1959	Det-A	116	381	38	102	16	3	3	35	30	35	.268	.323	.349	80	-10	1	2	-1	.952	-6	*S-110/2-5	-0.7
1960	Det-A	10	5	0	1	0	0	0	0	0	0	.200	.200	.200	8	-1	0	0	0	1.000	0	/3-7,S-3	0.2
	Cle-A	10	27	1	9	0	0	0	3	1	2	.333	.357	.333	91	-0	0	0	0	1.000	3	/S-7,3-3	0.3
	Yr	20	32	1	10	0	0	0	3	1	2	.313	.333	.313	76	-1	0	0	0	1.000	6	3-10,S-10	0.5
	StL-N	3	0	0	0	0	0	0	0	0	0	—	—	—	—	0	0	0	0	1.000	1	/2-3	0.1
1961	LA-A	84	229	20	55	5	1	2	5	26	37	.240	.320	.297	59	-13	1	0	0	.988	12	2-58,S-25/3-4	0.8
Total	11	919	2272	245	562	80	11	16	187	205	229	.247	.312	.313	67	-102	10	15	-6	.968	95	S-447,2-270,3/O	3.2

■ AL BRIDWELL

Bridwell, Albert Henry b: 1/4/1884, Friendship, Ohio d: 1/23/69, Portsmouth, Ohio BL/TR, 5'9", 170 lbs. Deb: 4/16/05

YEAR	TM/L	G	AB	R	H	2B	3B	HR	RBI	BB	SO	AVG	OBP	SLG	PRO+	BR/A	SB	CS	SBR	FA	FR	G/POS	TPR
1905	Cin-N	82	254	17	64	3	1	0	17	19		.252	.309	.272	66	-11	8			.944	0	3-43,O-18/2-7,S1	-1.0
1906	Bos-N	120	459	41	104	9	1	0	22	44		.227	.297	.251	73	-14	6			.930	17	*S-119/O-1	0.8
1907	Bos-N	140	509	49	111	8	2	0	26	61		.218	.309	.242	73	-13	17			**.942**	7	*S-140	-0.4
1908	NY-N	147	467	53	133	14	1	0	46	52		.285	.364	.319	113	9	20			.933	11	*S-147	2.6
1909	NY-N	145	476	59	140	11	5	0	55	67		.294	.386	.338	123	16	32			.940	2	*S-145	2.3
1910	NY-N	142	492	74	136	15	7	0	48	73	23	.276	.374	.335	107	7	14			.946	6	*S-141	2.0
1911	NY-N	76	263	28	71	10	1	0	31	33	10	.270	.358	.316	86	-4	8			.917	6	S-76	0.7
	Bos-N	51	182	29	53	5	0	0	10	33	8	.291	.403	.319	95	0	2			.950	-11	S-51	-0.7
	Yr	127	445	57	124	15	1	0	41	66	18	.279	.377	.317	90	-3	10			.929	-5	*S-127	0.0
1912	Bos-N	31	106	6	25	5	1	0	14	5	5	.236	.270	.302	55	-7	2			.936	-6	S-31	-1.0
1913	Chi-N	136	405	35	97	6	6	1	37	74	28	.240	.358	.291	86	-4	12			.948	2	*S-136	1.1
1914	StL-F	117	381	46	90	6	5	1	33	71	18	.236	.359	.286	73	-17	9			.944	-11	*S-103,2-11	-2.1
1915	StL-F	65	175	20	40	3	2	0	9	25	6	.229	.328	.269	65	-10	6			.952	1	2-42,3-15/1-1	-0.8
Total	11	1252	4169	457	1064	95	32	2	348	557	98	.255	.347	.295	89	-45	136			.939	23	*S-1094/2-60,3O1	3.5

■ BUNNY BRIEF

Brief, Anthony Vincent (b: Anthony John Grzeszkowski) b: 7/3/1892, Remus, Mich. d: 2/10/63, Milwaukee, Wis. BR/TR, 6', 185 lbs. Deb: 9/22/12

YEAR	TM/L	G	AB	R	H	2B	3B	HR	RBI	BB	SO	AVG	OBP	SLG	PRO+	BR/A	SB	CS	SBR	FA	FR	G/POS	TPR
1912	StL-A	15	42	9	13	3	0	0	5	6		.310	.408	.381	131	2	3			.826	-1	/O-9,1-4	0.1
1913	StL-A	85	258	24	56	11	6	1	26	21	46	.217	.284	.318	78	-8	3			.986	-1	1-62/O-8	-1.1
1915	Chi-A	48	154	13	33	6	2	2	17	16	28	.214	.305	.318	84	-3	8	6	-1	.986	-2	1-46	-0.8
1917	Pit-N	36	115	15	25	5	1	2	11	15	21	.217	.308	.330	96	-0	4			.988	2	1-34	-0.0
Total	4	184	569	61	127	25	9	5	59	58	95	.223	.306	.325	87	-9	17	6		.987	-2	1-146/O-17	-1.8

■ CHARLIE BRIGGS

Briggs, Charles R. b: 1861, Batavia, Ill. 5'7", 170 lbs. Deb: 5/2/1884

YEAR	TM/L	G	AB	R	H	2B	3B	HR	RBI	BB	SO	AVG	OBP	SLG	PRO+	BR/A	SB	CS	SBR	FA	FR	G/POS	TPR
1884	CP-U	49	182	29	31	8	2	1		11		.170	.218	.253	42	-18				.814	-5	O-37,2-12/S-2	-2.1

■ DAN BRIGGS

Briggs, Dan Lee b: 11/18/52, Scotia, Cal. BL/TL, 6', 180 lbs. Deb: 9/10/75

YEAR	TM/L	G	AB	R	H	2B	3B	HR	RBI	BB	SO	AVG	OBP	SLG	PRO+	BR/A	SB	CS	SBR	FA	FR	G/POS	TPR
1975	Cal-A	13	31	3	7	1	0	1	3	2	6	.226	.273	.355	82	-1	0	2	-1	.953	-1	/1-6,O-5,D-2	-0.4
1976	Cal-A	77	248	19	53	13	2	1	14	13	47	.214	.256	.294	65	-12	0	3	-2	.993	-0	1-44,O-40/D-1	-1.9
1977	Cal-A	59	74	6	12	2	0	1	4	8	14	.162	.244	.230	31	-7	0	0	0	.993	0	1-45,O-13	-0.8
1978	Cle-A	15	49	4	8	0	1	1	1	4	9	.163	.226	.265	38	-4	0	0	0	1.000	2	O-15	-0.3
1979	SD-N	104	227	34	47	4	3	8	30	18	45	.207	.280	.357	77	-8	2	1	0	.986	-1	1-50,O-44	-1.2
1981	Mon-N	9	11	0	1	0	0	0	0	0	3	.091	.091	.091	-48	-2	0	1	-1	1.000	-1	/1-3,O-3	-0.4
1982	Chi-N	48	48	1	6	0	0	1	0	9	9	.125	.143	.125	-24	-8	0	0	0	.875	-2	O-10/1-4	-1.0
Total	7	325	688	67	134	20	6	12	53	45	133	.195	.251	.294	56	-42	2	7	-4	.989	-2	1-152,O-130/D-3	-6.0

■ GRANT BRIGGS

Briggs, Grant b: 3/16/1865, Pittsburgh, Pa. d: 5/31/28, Pittsburgh, Pa. 5'11", 170 lbs. Deb: 4/17/1890

YEAR	TM/L	G	AB	R	H	2B	3B	HR	RBI	BB	SO	AVG	OBP	SLG	PRO+	BR/A	SB	CS	SBR	FA	FR	G/POS	TPR
1890	Syr-a	86	316	44	57	6	5	0	21	16		.180	.222	.231	37	-25	7			.928	-4	C-46,O-33/3-5,S-4	-2.3
1891	Lou-a	1	4	0	1	0	0	0	0	0	0	.250	.250	.250	44	-0	0			1.000	-0	/C-1	0.0
1892	StL-N	22	55	2	4	1	0	0	1	5	16	.073	.164	.091	-24	-8	2			.902	-11	C-15/O-8	-1.8
1895	Lou-N	1	3	0	0	0	0	0	0	0		.000	.000	.000	-99	-1	0			1.000	-1	/C-1	-0.2
Total	4	110	378	46	62	7	5	0	22	21	17	.164	.212	.209	27	-35	9			.925	-15	/C-63,O-41,3-5,S-4	-4.3

■ JOHNNY BRIGGS

Briggs, John Edward b: 3/10/44, Paterson, N.J. BL/TL, 6'1", 195 lbs. Deb: 4/17/64

YEAR	TM/L	G	AB	R	H	2B	3B	HR	RBI	BB	SO	AVG	OBP	SLG	PRO+	BR/A	SB	CS	SBR	FA	FR	G/POS	TPR
1964	Phi-N	61	66	16	17	2	0	1	6	9	12	.258	.347	.333	94	-0	1	1	-0	.957	-2	O-19/1-1	-0.3
1965	Phi-N	93	229	47	54	9	4	4	23	42	44	.236	.354	.362	104	3	3	2	-0	.982	-3	O-66	-0.4
1966	Phi-N	81	255	43	72	13	5	10	23	41	55	.282	.382	.490	140	15	3	2	-0	.977	-4	O-69	0.7
1967	Phi-N	106	332	47	77	12	4	9	30	41	61	.232	.316	.373	96	-2	3	5	-2	.979	-2	O-94	-1.1
1968	Phi-N	110	338	36	86	13	1	7	31	58	72	.254	.365	.361	119	10	8	5	-1	.968	-3	O-65,1-36	0.1
1969	Phi-N	124	361	51	86	20	3	12	46	64	78	.238	.353	.410	116	9	9	6	-1	.971	-9	*O-108/1-2	0.2
1970	Phi-N	110	341	43	92	15	7	9	47	39	65	.270	.345	.434	110	5	5	4	-1	.980	6	O-95	0.5
1971	Phi-N	10	22	3	4	1	0	0	3	6	2	.182	.357	.227	69	-1	0	0	0	.846	-1	/O-8	-0.2
	Mil-A	125	375	51	99	11	1	21	59	71	79	.264	.383	.467	141	22	1	2	-1	.958	1	O-65,1-60	1.5
1972	Mil-A	135	418	58	111	14	1	21	65	54	67	.266	.351	.455	141	21	1	2	-1	.980	-2	*O-106,1-28	1.3
1973	Mil-A	142	488	78	120	20	7	18	57	87	83	.246	.362	.426	124	17	15	9	-1	.968	-7	*O-137/D-1	1.7
1974	Mil-A	154	554	72	140	30	4	13	73	71	102	.253	.338	.428	120	14	9	7	-2	.973	5	*O-149/D-2	1.2
1975	Mil-A	28	74	12	22	1	0	5	5	20	13	.297	.447	.432	149	6	0	0	0	.962	2	O-21/D-1	0.6
	Min-A	87	264	44	61	9	2	7	39	60	41	.231	.373	.360	106	5	6	6	-0	.983	7	1-49,O-35/D-2	1.4
	Yr	115	338	56	83	10	2	10	44	80	54	.246	.390	.376	116	11	6	6	-1	.983	9	O-56,1-49/D-3	1.4
Total	12	1366	4117	601	1041	170	43	139	507	663	785	.253	.357	.416	121	123	64	49	-10	.973	12	*O-1037,1-176/D-6	6.6

YEAR	TM/L	G	AB	R	H	2B	3B	HR	RBI	BB	SO	AVG	OBP	SLG	PRO+	BR/A	SB	CS	SBR	FA	FR	G/POS	TPR

■ HARRY BRIGHT   Bright, Harry James   b: 9/22/29, Kansas City, Mo.   BR/TR, 6', 190 lbs.   Deb: 8/7/58

1958	Pit-N	15	24	4	6	1	0	1	3	1	6	.250	.280	.417	84	-1	0	0	0	1.000	0	/3-7	0.0
1959	Pit-N	40	48	4	12	1	0	3	8	5	10	.250	.321	.458	105	0	0	0	0	1.000	-2	/O-4,3-3,2-1	-0.2
1960	Pit-N	4	4	0	0	0	0	0	0	0	2	.000	.000	.000	-99	-1	0	0	0	.000	0	H	-0.1
1961	Was-A	72	183	20	44	6	0	4	21	19	23	.240	.312	.339	75	-7	0	2	-1	.928	7	3-40/C-8,2-1	0.0
1962	Was-A	113	392	55	107	15	4	17	67	26	51	.273	.321	.462	109	3	2	1	0	.989	-1	1-99/C-3,3-1	-0.4
1963	Cin-N	1	1	0	0	0	0	0	0	0	1	.000	.000	.000	-97	-0	0	0	0	1.000	0	/1-1	0.0
	*NY-A	60	157	15	37	7	0	7	23	13	31	.236	.298	.414	98	-1	0	0	0	.985	-5	1-35,3-12	-0.7
1964	NY-A	4	5	0	1	0	0	0	0	1	1	.200	.333	.200	52	-0	0	0	0	1.000	0	/1-2	-0.1
1965	Chi-N	27	25	1	7	1	0	0	4	0	8	.280	.280	.320	67	-1	0	0	0	.000	0	H	-0.1
Total	8	336	839	99	214	31	4	32	126	65	133	.255	.311	.416	96	-7	2	3	-1	.988	-1	1-137/3-63,C-11,02	-1.6

■ GREG BRILEY   Briley, Gregory "Peewee"   b: 5/24/65, Greenville, N.C.   BL/TR, 5'9", 175 lbs.   Deb: 6/27/88

1988	Sea-A	13	36	6	9	2	0	1	4	5	6	.250	.341	.389	100	0	0	1	-1	.929	-2	O-11	-0.3
1989	Sea-A	115	394	52	105	22	4	13	52	39	82	.266	.340	.442	115	7	11	5	0	.958	-5	*O-105,2-10/D-2	0.1
1990	Sea-A	125	337	40	83	18	2	5	29	37	48	.246	.323	.356	89	-5	16	4	2	.989	-4	*O-107/D-4	-0.9
1991	Sea-A	139	381	39	99	17	3	2	26	27	51	.260	.309	.336	78	-11	23	11	0	.980	-17	*O-125/2-1,3-1,D-2	-3.0
1992	Sea-A	86	200	18	55	10	0	5	12	4	31	.275	.293	.400	92	-3	9	2	0	.967	-9	O-42,D-12/2-4,3-4	-1.1
1993	Fla-N	120	170	17	33	6	0	3	12	12	42	.194	.251	.282	40	-14	6	2	1	.986	-12	O-67	-2.7
Total	6	598	1518	172	384	75	9	29	135	124	260	.253	.313	.372	88	-26	65	25	4	.975	-48	O-457/D-20,2-15,3-5	-7.9

■ BILL BRINKER   Brinker, William Hutchinson "Dode"   b: 8/30/1883, Warrensburg, Mo.   d: 2/5/65, Arcadia, Cal.   BB/TR, 6'1", 190 lbs.   Deb: 4/24/12

1912	Phi-N	9	18	1	4	1	0	0	2	2	3	.222	.300	.278	55	-1	0			.778	-1	/3-2,O-2	-0.2

■ CHUCK BRINKMAN   Brinkman, Charles Ernest   b: 9/16/44, Cincinnati, O.   BR/TR, 6'1", 185 lbs.   Deb: 7/10/69 F

1969	Chi-A	14	15	2	1	0	0	0	0	1	5	.067	.125	.067	-43	-3	0	0	0	1.000	1	C-14	-0.2
1970	Chi-A	9	20	4	5	1	0	0	0	3	3	.250	.348	.300	77	-1	0	0	0	.974	1	/C-9	0.1
1971	Chi-A	15	20	0	4	0	0	0	1	3	5	.200	.304	.200	44	-1	0	0	0	1.000	2	C-14	0.1
1972	Chi-A	35	52	1	7	0	0	0	0	4	7	.135	.196	.135	-0	-6	0	0	0	.985	7	C-33	0.2
1973	Chi-A	63	139	13	26	6	0	1	10	11	37	.187	.252	.252	41	-11	0	0	0	.987	10	C-63	0.1
1974	Chi-A	8	14	1	2	0	0	0	0	1	3	.143	.200	.143	-0	-2	0	0	0	1.000	-1	/C-8	-0.3
	Pit-N	4	7	1	1	0	0	0	1	0	0	.143	.143	.143	-21	-1	0	0	0	1.000	0	/C-4	-0.1
Total	6	148	267	22	46	7	0	1	12	23	60	.172	.241	.210	28	-25	0	0	0	.988	20	C-145	-0.2

■ ED BRINKMAN   Brinkman, Edwin Albert   b: 12/8/41, Cincinnati, O.   BR/TR, 6', 170 lbs.   Deb: 9/6/61 FC

1961	Was-A	4	11	0	1	0	0	0	0	1	1	.091	.167	.091	-30	-2	0	0	0	.889	4	/3-3	-0.2
1962	Was-A	54	133	8	22	7	1	0	4	11	28	.165	.229	.233	25	-14	1	0	0	.942	2	S-38,3-10	-1.0
1963	Was-A	145	514	44	117	20	3	7	45	31	86	.228	.277	.319	67	-23	5	3	-0	.950	7	*S-143	-0.7
1964	Was-A	132	447	54	100	20	3	8	34	26	99	.224	.273	.336	68	-20	2	2	-1	.969	-3	*S-125	-1.5
1965	Was-A	154	444	35	82	13	2	5	35	38	82	.185	.252	.257	46	-32	1	2	-1	.964	6	*S-150	-2.1
1966	Was-A	158	582	42	133	18	9	7	48	29	105	.229	.265	.326	70	-24	7	9	-3	.965	12	*S-158	-0.1
1967	Was-A	109	320	21	60	9	2	1	18	24	58	.188	.253	.237	47	-21	1	3	-2	**.979**	14	*S-109	0.0
1968	Was-A	77	193	12	36	3	0	0	6	19	31	.187	.259	.202	43	-13	0	0	0	.967	3	S-74/2-2,O-1	-0.5
1969	Was-A	151	576	71	153	18	5	2	43	50	42	.266	.330	.325	88	-9	2	2	-1	.976	15	*S-150	2.3
1970	Was-A	158	625	63	164	17	2	1	40	60	41	.262	.332	.301	79	-16	8	9	-3	.974	31	*S-157	3.2
1971	Det-A	159	527	40	120	18	2	1	37	44	54	.228	.296	.275	60	-27	1	4	-2	.980	12	*S-159	0.3
1972	*Det-A	156	516	42	105	19	1	6	49	38	51	.203	.262	.279	59	-26	0	0	0	**.990**	-1	*S-156	-0.2
1973	Det-A★	162	515	55	122	16	4	7	40	34	79	.237	.285	.324	67	-23	0	1	-1	.968	-13	*S-162	-1.7
1974	Det-A	153	502	55	111	15	3	14	54	29	71	.221	.268	.347	73	-19	2	0	1	.972	13	*S-151/3-2	1.5
1975	StL-N	28	75	6	18	4	0	1	6	7	10	.240	.313	.333	77	-2	0	0	0	.948	-3	S-24	0.0
	Tex-A	1	2	0	0	0	0	0	0	0	1	.000	.000	.000	-99	-1	0	0	0	1.000	0	/3-1	-0.1
	NY-A	44	63	2	11	4	1	0	2	3	6	.175	.224	.270	40	-5	0	0	0	.933	-3	S-39/2-3,3-3	-0.6
	Yr	45	65	2	11	4	1	0	2	3	7	.169	.217	.262	35	-6	0	0	0	.933	-3	S-39/3-4,2-3	-0.7
Total	15	1845	6045	550	1355	201	38	60	461	444	845	.224	.282	.300	65	-276	30	35	-12	.970	94	*S-1795/3-19,2-5,O	-1.4

■ LEON BRINKOPF   Brinkopf, Leon Clarence   b: 10/20/26, Cape Girardeau, Mo   BR/TR, 5'11.5", 185 lbs.   Deb: 4/18/52

1952	Chi-N	9	22	1	4	0	0	0	2	4	5	.182	.308	.182	38	-2	0	0	0	.955	-2	/S-6	-0.4

■ FATTY BRIODY   Briody, Charles F. "Alderman"   b: 8/13/1858, Lansingburg, N.Y.   d: 6/22/03, Chicago, Ill.   TR, 5'8.5", 190 lbs.   Deb: 6/16/1880

1880	Tro-N	1	4	0	0	0	0	0	0	0		.000	.000	.000	-95	-1				.700	-1	/C-1	-0.2
1882	Cle-N	53	194	30	50	13	0	0	13	9	13	.258	.291	.325	100	0				.902	2	C-53	0.3
1883	Cle-N	40	145	23	34	5	1	0	10	3	13	.234	.250	.283	62	-6				.900	4	C-33/2-4,1-2,3-1	-0.1
1884	Cle-N	43	148	17	25	6	0	1	12	6	19	.169	.201	.230	34	-11				.922	10	C-42/O-1	0.2
	Cin-U	22	89	11	30	2	2	0		1		.337	.344	.404	117	-1				.943	17	C-22	1.5
1885	StL-N	62	215	14	42	9	0	1	17	12	23	.195	.238	.251	62	-8				.893	-9	C-60/O-1,3-1,2-1	-1.2
1886	KC-N	56	215	14	51	10	3	0	29	3	35	.237	.248	.312	65	-10	0			.919	2	C-54/O-2,1-1	-0.2
1887	Det-N	33	128	24	29	6	1	1	26	9	10	.227	.283	.313	63	-7	6			.907	6	C-33	0.2
1888	KC-a	13	48	1	10	1	0	0	8	1		.208	.224	.229	43	-3	0			.896	4	C-13	-0.5
Total	8	323	1186	134	271	52	7	3	115	44	113	.228	.257	.292	68	-47	6			.910	25	C-311/2-5,O-4,13	0.0

■ GEORGE BRISTOW   Bristow, George T.   b: 5/1870, Paw Paw, Ill.   TR ,   Deb: 4/15/1899

1899	Cle-N	3	8	1	1	1	0	0	0	0		.125	.222	.250	32	-1	0			1.000	0	/O-3	-0.1

■ BERNARDO BRITO   Brito, Bernardo   b: 12/4/63, San Cristobal, D.R.   BR/TR, 6'1", 190 lbs.   Deb: 9/15/92

1992	Min-A	8	14	1	2	1	0	0	2	0	4	.143	.143	.214	-1	-2	0	1	-1	.750	-1	/O-3,D-1	-0.4
1993	Min-A	27	54	8	13	2	0	4	9	1	20	.241	.255	.500	97	-1	0	0	0	1.000	-1	O-10/D-7	-0.2
1995	Min-A	5	5	1	1	0	0	1	1	0	3	.200	.333	.800	183	1	0	0	0	.000	0	/D-3	0.0
Total	3	40	73	10	16	3	0	5	12	1	27	.219	.240	.466	85	-2	0	1	-1	.941	-2	/O-13,D-11	-0.6

■ JORGE BRITO   Brito, Jorge Manuel (Uceta)   b: 6/22/66, Moncion, D.R.   BR/TR, 6'1", 190 lbs.   Deb: 4/30/95

1995	Col-N	18	51	5	11	3	0	0	7	2	17	.216	.259	.275	32	-5	1	0	0	.991	5	C-18	0.1
1996	Col-N	8	14	1	1	0	0	0	0	1	8	.071	.235	.071	-11	-2	0	0	0	1.000	1	/C-8	0.2
Total	2	26	65	6	12	3	0	0	7	3	25	.185	.254	.231	22	-8	1	0	0	.994	4	/C-26	0.3

■ TILSON BRITO   Brito, Tilson Manuel (Jiminez)   b: 5/28/72, Santo Domingo, D.R.   BR/TR, 6', 175 lbs.   Deb: 4/1/96

1996	Tor-A	26	80	10	19	7	0	1	10	10	18	.237	.344	.363	79	-1	1	1	-0	.956	-1	2-18/S-5,D-2	-0.2

■ GUS BRITTAIN   Brittain, August Schuster   b: 11/29/09, Wilmington, N.C.   d: 2/16/74, Wilmington, N.C.   BR/TR, 5'10", 192 lbs.   Deb: 7/22/37

1937	Cin-N	3	6	0	1	0	0	0	0	0	3	.167	.167	.167	-10	-1	0			1.000	-0	/C-1	-0.1

■ GIL BRITTON   Britton, Stephen Gilbert   b: 9/21/1891, Parsons, Kan.   d: 6/20/83, Parsons, Kan.   BR/TR, 5'10", 160 lbs.   Deb: 9/20/13

1913	Pit-N	3	12	0	0	0	0	0	0	0	2	.000	.000	.000	-99	-3	0			.824	-1	/S-3	-0.4

■ GREG BROCK   Brock, Gregory Allen   b: 6/14/57, McMinnville, Ore.   BL/TR, 6'3", 205 lbs.   Deb: 9/1/82

1982	LA-N	18	17	1	2	1	0	0	1	1	5	.118	.167	.176	-4	-2	0	0	0	1.000	-0	/1-3	-0.3
1983	*LA-N	146	455	64	102	14	2	20	66	83	81	.224	.345	.396	105	5	5	1	1	.991	5	*1-140	0.3
1984	LA-N	88	271	33	61	6	0	14	34	39	37	.225	.323	.402	104	1	8	0	2	.995	7	1-83	0.7
1985	*LA-N	129	438	64	110	19	0	21	66	54	72	.251	.333	.438	118	10	4	2	0	.996	-1	*1-122	0.4
1986	LA-N	115	325	33	76	13	0	16	52	37	60	.234	.312	.422	108	2	2	5	-2	.996	12	1-99	0.6
1987	Mil-A	141	532	81	159	29	3	13	85	57	63	.299	.373	.438	111	10	5	4	-1	.993	4	*1-141	0.2
1988	Mil-A	115	364	50	77	16	1	6	50	63	48	.212	.333	.310	81	-8	6	2	1	.993	9	*1-114/D-1	-0.7
1989	Mil-A	107	373	40	99	16	0	12	52	43	49	.265	.346	.405	112	6	6	1	1	.995	-5	*1-100/D-7	-0.5

YEAR	TM/L	G	AB	R	H	2B	3B	HR	RBI	BB	SO	AVG	OBP	SLG	PRO+	BR/A	SB	CS	SBR	FA	FR	G/POS	TPR
1990	Mil-A	123	367	42	91	23	0	7	50	43	45	.248	.330	.368	96	-2	4	2	0	.995	-4	*1-115	-1.4
1991	Mil-A	31	60	9	17	4	0	1	6	14	9	.283	.419	.400	131	3	1	1	-0	1.000	-1	1-25	0.1
Total	10	1013	3202	420	794	141	6	110	462	434	469	.248	.340	.399	105	25	41	18	2	.994	29	1-942/D-8	-0.6

■ JOHN BROCK
Brock, John Roy   b: 10/16/1896, Hamilton, Ill.   d: 10/27/51, Clayton, Mo.   BR/TR, 5'6.5", 165 lbs.   Deb: 8/10/17

YEAR	TM/L	G	AB	R	H	2B	3B	HR	RBI	BB	SO	AVG	OBP	SLG	PRO+	BR/A	SB	CS	SBR	FA	FR	G/POS	TPR
1917	StL-N	7	15	4	6	1	0	0	2	0	2	.400	.400	.467	170	1	2			.944	-1	/C-4	0.1
1918	StL-N	27	52	9	11	2	0	0	4	3	10	.212	.255	.250	56	-3	5			.951	-2	C-18/O-1	-0.4
Total	2	34	67	13	17	3	0	0	6	3	12	.254	.286	.299	81	-2	7			.949	-2	/C-22,O-1	-0.3

■ LOU BROCK
Brock, Louis Clark   b: 6/18/39, ElDorado, Ark.   BL/TL, 5'11.5", 170 lbs.   Deb: 9/10/61   H

YEAR	TM/L	G	AB	R	H	2B	3B	HR	RBI	BB	SO	AVG	OBP	SLG	PRO+	BR/A	SB	CS	SBR	FA	FR	G/POS	TPR
1961	Chi-N	4	11	1	1	0	0	0	0	1	3	.091	.167	.091	-29	-2	0	0	0	.750	-1	/O-3	-0.3
1962	Chi-N	123	434	73	114	24	7	9	35	35	96	.263	.322	.412	92	-5	16	7	1	.965	2	*O-106	-1.0
1963	Chi-N	148	547	79	141	19	11	9	37	31	122	.258	.302	.382	91	-7	24	12	0	.973	13	*O-140	-0.1
1964	Chi-N	52	215	30	54	9	2	2	14	13	40	.251	.300	.340	77	-7	10	3	1	.959	2	O-52	-0.6
	*StL-N	103	419	81	146	21	9	12	44	27	87	.348	.391	.527	143	23	33	15	1	.949	6	*O-102	2.6
	Yr	155	634	111	200	30	11	14	58	40	127	.315	.360	.464	121	17	43	18	2	.953	8	*O-154	2.0
1965	StL-N	155	631	107	182	35	8	16	69	45	116	.288	.345	.445	110	8	63	27	3	.959	8	*O-153	1.3
1966	StL-N	156	643	94	183	24	12	15	46	31	134	.285	.321	.429	106	4	74	18	11	.936	3	*O-154	1.2
1967	*StL-N★	159	689	113	206	32	12	21	76	24	109	.299	.328	.472	128	22	52	18	5	.956	7	*O-157	2.7
1968	*StL-N	159	660	92	184	46	14	6	51	46	124	.279	.329	.418	125	18	62	12	11	.952	6	*O-156	3.1
1969	StL-N	157	655	97	195	33	10	12	47	50	115	.298	.349	.434	118	14	53	14	8	.949	5	*O-157	1.8
1970	StL-N	155	664	114	202	29	5	13	57	60	99	.304	.363	.422	107	7	51	15	6	.962	3	*O-152	0.8
1971	StL-N★	157	640	126	200	37	7	7	61	76	107	.313	.386	.425	125	23	64	19	8	.951	-1	*O-157	2.3
1972	StL-N☆	153	621	81	193	26	8	3	42	47	93	.311	.360	.393	115	12	63	18	8	.952	-4	*O-149	1.1
1973	StL-N	160	650	110	193	29	8	7	63	71	112	.297	.366	.398	112	12	70	20	9	.963	1	*O-153	1.5
1974	StL-N★	153	635	105	194	25	7	3	48	61	88	.306	.368	.381	111	10	118	33	16	.967	2	*O-152	2.2
1975	StL-N★	136	528	78	163	27	6	3	47	38	64	.309	.359	.400	106	5	56	16	7	.966	1	*O-128	0.7
1976	StL-N	133	498	73	150	24	5	4	67	35	75	.301	.348	.394	109	6	56	19	5	.983	0	*O-123	0.7
1977	StL-N	141	489	69	133	22	6	2	46	30	74	.272	.317	.354	81	-13	35	24	-4	.954	-11	*O-130	-3.4
1978	StL-N	92	298	31	66	9	0	0	12	17	29	.221	.263	.252	45	-22	17	5	2	.975	-6	O-79	-3.1
1979	StL-N★	120	405	56	123	15	4	5	38	23	43	.304	.346	.398	101	1	21	12	-1	.958	-3	O-98	-0.8
Total	19	2616	10332	1610	3023	486	141	149	900	761	1730	.293	.344	.410	109	110	938	307	97	.959	32	*O-2507	12.7

■ MATT BRODERICK
Broderick, Matthew Thomas   b: 12/1/1877, Lattimer, Pa.   d: 2/26/40, Freeland, Pa.   BR/TR, 5'6.5", 135 lbs.   Deb: 5/1/03

YEAR	TM/L	G	AB	R	H	2B	3B	HR	RBI	BB	SO	AVG	OBP	SLG	PRO+	BR/A	SB	CS	SBR	FA	FR	G/POS	TPR
1903	Bro-N	2	2	0	0	0	0	0	0	0	0	.000	.000	.000	-99	-1	0			1.000	0	/2-1	0.0

■ STEVE BRODIE
Brodie, Walter Scott   b: 9/11/1868, Warrenton, Va.   d: 10/30/35, Baltimore, Md.   BL/TR, 5'11", 180 lbs.   Deb: 4/21/1890

YEAR	TM/L	G	AB	R	H	2B	3B	HR	RBI	BB	SO	AVG	OBP	SLG	PRO+	BR/A	SB	CS	SBR	FA	FR	G/POS	TPR
1890	Bos-N	132	514	77	152	19	9	0	67	66	20	.296	.387	.368	111	8	29			.953	3	*O-132	0.6
1891	Bos-N	133	523	84	136	13	6	2	78	63	39	.260	.331	.319	85	-11	25			.951	10	*O-133	-0.4
1892	StL-N	154	602	85	152	10	9	4	60	52	31	.252	.316	.319	97	-2	28			.943	3	*O-137,2-16/3-2	0.1
1893	StL-N	107	469	71	149	16	8	2	79	33	16	.318	.376	.399	106	4	41			.951	9	*O-107	0.6
	Bal-N	25	97	18	35	7	2	0	19	12	2	.361	.446	.474	142	6	8			.963	-3	O-25	0.2
	Yr	132	566	89	184	23	10	2	98	45	18	.325	.389	.412	112	10	49			.953	6	*O-132	0.8
1894	*Bal-N	129	573	134	210	25	11	3	113	18		.366	.399	.464	103	1	42			.950	-6	*O-129	-1.0
1895	*Bal-N	131	528	85	184	27	10	2	134	26	15	.348	.394	.449	114	10	35			.965	5	*O-131	0.4
1896	*Bal-N	132	516	98	153	19	11	2	87	36	17	.297	.363	.388	97	-2	25			.972	11	*O-132	-0.2
1897	Pit-N	100	370	47	108	7	12	2	53	25		.292	.348	.392	99	-1	11			.983	-0	*O-100	-0.7
1898	Pit-N	42	156	15	41	5	0	0	21	6		.263	.303	.295	73	-6	3			.958	3	O-42	-0.5
	Bal-N	23	98	12	30	3	2	0	19	5		.306	.346	.378	105	0	3			.923	3	O-23	0.1
	Yr	65	254	27	71	8	2	0	40	11		.280	.320	.327	86	-5	6			.946	6	O-65	-0.4
1899	Bal-N	137	531	82	164	26	1	3	87	31		.309	.373	.379	101	1	19			.979	1	*O-137	-0.8
1901	Bal-A	83	306	41	95	6	6	2	41	25		.310	.378	.389	108	4	9			.963	-3	O-83	-0.5
1902	NY-N	109	416	37	117	8	2	3	42	22		.281	.327	.332	104	2	11			.953	7	*O-109	0.1
Total	12	1437	5699	886	1726	191	89	25	900	420	_148_	.303	.364	.381	102	15	289			.959	48	*O-1420/2-16,3-2	-2.0

■ RICO BROGNA
Brogna, Rico Joseph   b: 4/18/70, Turners Falls, Mass.   BL/TL, 6'2", 202 lbs.   Deb: 8/8/92

YEAR	TM/L	G	AB	R	H	2B	3B	HR	RBI	BB	SO	AVG	OBP	SLG	PRO+	BR/A	SB	CS	SBR	FA	FR	G/POS	TPR
1992	Det-A	9	26	3	5	1	0	1	3	3	5	.192	.276	.346	73	-1	0	0	0	.982	1	/1-8,D-2	-0.1
1994	NY-N	39	131	16	46	11	2	7	20	6	29	.351	.380	.626	158	10	1	0	0	.997	2	1-35	0.9
1995	NY-N	134	495	72	143	27	2	22	76	39	111	.289	.343	.485	119	12	0	0	0	.998	5	*1-131	0.6
1996	NY-N	55	188	18	48	10	1	7	30	19	50	.255	.324	.431	104	0	0	0	0	.996	-2	1-52	-0.6
Total	4	237	840	109	242	49	5	37	129	67	195	.288	.342	.490	121	22	1	0	0	.997	6	1-226/D-2	0.8

■ JACK BROHAMER
Brohamer, John Anthony   b: 2/26/50, Maywood, Cal.   BL/TR, 5'10", 165 lbs.   Deb: 4/18/72

YEAR	TM/L	G	AB	R	H	2B	3B	HR	RBI	BB	SO	AVG	OBP	SLG	PRO+	BR/A	SB	CS	SBR	FA	FR	G/POS	TPR
1972	Cle-A	136	527	49	123	13	2	5	35	27	46	.233	.272	.294	66	-22	3	2	-0	.977	6	*2-132/3-1	-1.1
1973	Cle-A	102	300	29	66	12	1	4	29	32	23	.220	.295	.307	69	-12	0	2	-1	.971	17	2-97	0.8
1974	Cle-A	101	315	33	85	11	1	2	30	26	22	.270	.331	.330	92	-3	2	1	0	.987	-4	2-99	-0.3
1975	Cle-A	69	217	15	53	5	0	6	16	14	14	.244	.290	.350	80	-6	2	2	-1	.976	4	2-66	0.0
1976	Chi-A	119	354	33	89	12	2	7	40	44	28	.251	.336	.356	103	2	1	3	-2	.984	18	*2-117/3-1	2.7
1977	Chi-A	59	152	26	39	10	3	2	20	21	8	.257	.351	.401	105	1	0	0	0	.923	-3	3-38,2-18/D-1	0.4
1978	Bos-A	81	244	34	57	14	1	1	25	25	13	.234	.305	.311	67	-11	1	3	-2	.974	-3	3-30,D-25,2-23	-1.6
1979	Bos-A	64	192	25	51	7	1	1	11	15	15	.266	.319	.328	71	-8	0	3	-2	.982	-0	2-36,3-22	-0.8
1980	Bos-A	21	57	5	18	2	0	1	6	4	3	.316	.361	.404	104	0	0	0	0	.900	-1	3-13/2-4,D-3	-0.1
	Cle-A	53	142	13	32	5	1	1	15	14	6	.225	.295	.296	62	-7	0	1	-1	.979	-4	2-47/D-1	-0.9
	Yr	74	199	18	50	7	1	2	21	18	9	.251	.309	.327	74	-7	0	1	-1	.981	-5	2-51,3-13/D-4	-1.0
Total	9	805	2500	262	613	91	12	30	227	222	178	.245	.309	.327	79	-65	9	17	-8	.979	33	2-639,3-105/D-30	-0.9

■ HERMAN BRONKIE
Bronkie, Herman Charles "Dutch"   b: 3/31/1885, S.Manchester, Conn   d: 5/27/68, Somers, Conn.   BR/TR, 5'9", 165 lbs.   Deb: 9/20/10

YEAR	TM/L	G	AB	R	H	2B	3B	HR	RBI	BB	SO	AVG	OBP	SLG	PRO+	BR/A	SB	CS	SBR	FA	FR	G/POS	TPR
1910	Cle-A	5	9	1	2	0	0	0	0	0	0	.222	.300	.222	63	-0	1			.625	-1	/3-3,S-1	-0.2
1911	Cle-A	2	6	0	1	0	0	0	0	0	0	.167	.167	.167	-7	-1	0			1.000	-1	/3-2	-0.2
1912	Cle-A	6	16	1	0	0	0	0	0	1	0	.000	.059	.000	-80	-4	0			.917	2	/3-6	-0.1
1914	Chi-N	1	1	1	1	1	0	0	1	0	0	1.000	1.000	2.000	786	1	0			.000	-0	/3-1	0.0
1918	StL-N	18	68	7	15	3	0	1	7	2	4	.221	.243	.309	70	-3	0			.984	1	3-18	-0.4
1919	StL-N	67	196	23	50	6	4	0	14	23	23	.255	.336	.327	84	-4	2			.939	4	3-34,2-16/1-2	0.2
1922	StL-A	23	64	5	18	4	1	0	2	6	7	.281	.343	.375	84	-1	0	2	-1	.917	-0	3-18	-0.2
Total	7	122	360	40	87	14	5	1	24	33	_34_	.242	.307	.317	75	-12	3	_2_		.931	2	/3-82,2-16,1-2,S-1	-0.9

■ TOM BROOKENS
Brookens, Thomas Dale   b: 8/10/53, Chambersburg, Pa.   BR/TR, 5'10", 170 lbs.   Deb: 7/10/79

YEAR	TM/L	G	AB	R	H	2B	3B	HR	RBI	BB	SO	AVG	OBP	SLG	PRO+	BR/A	SB	CS	SBR	FA	FR	G/POS	TPR
1979	Det-A	60	190	23	50	5	2	4	21	11	40	.263	.310	.374	81	-5	10	3	1	.945	12	3-42,2-19/D-1	0.8
1980	Det-A	151	509	64	140	25	9	10	66	32	71	.275	.319	.418	98	-2	13	11	-3	.931	4	*3-138/2-9,S-1,D-1	-0.3
1981	Det-A	71	239	19	58	10	1	4	25	14	43	.243	.290	.343	79	-7	5	3	-0	.952	-4	3-71	-1.3
1982	Det-A	140	398	40	92	15	3	9	58	27	63	.231	.280	.352	72	-16	5	9	-4	.939	10	*3-113,2-26/S-9,0-1	-1.1
1983	Det-A	138	332	50	71	13	3	6	32	29	46	.214	.281	.325	68	-15	10	4	1	.928	-3	*3-103,S-30,2-10/D	-0.9
1984	*Det-A	113	224	32	55	11	4	5	26	19	38	.246	.307	.397	94	-2	6	6	-2	.969	20	3-68,S-28,2-26/D-1	1.8
1985	Det-A	156	485	54	115	34	6	7	47	27	78	.237	.277	.375	77	-16	14	5	1	.943	3	*3-151/S-8,2-3,CD	-1.4
1986	Det-A	98	281	42	76	11	2	3	25	20	42	.270	.321	.356	84	-6	11	8	-2	.955	2	3-35,2-31/S-14,D/O	-0.5
1987	*Det-A	143	444	59	107	15	3	13	59	33	63	.241	.296	.376	80	-13	7	4	-0	.954	2	*3-122,S-16,2-11	-1.1
1988	Det-A	136	441	62	107	23	5	5	38	44	74	.243	.316	.351	90	-6	4	4	-1	.952	-3	*3-136/S-3,2-1	-1.1
1989	NY-A	66	168	14	38	6	0	4	14	11	27	.226	.274	.333	71	-7	1	3	-2	.926	-4	3-51/S-7,2-5,O-3,D	-1.2
1990	Cle-A	64	154	18	41	7	2	1	20	14	25	.266	.327	.357	92	-2	0	0	0	.923	4	3-35,2-21/S-3,1D	0.3
Total	12	1336	3865	477	950	175	40	71	431	281	605	.246	.299	.367	83	-97	86	60	-10	.943	49	*3-1065,2-162,S/DO1C	-6.0

YEAR	TM/L	G	AB	R	H	2B	3B	HR	RBI	BB	SO	AVG	OBP	SLG	PRO+	BR/A	SB	CS	SBR	FA	FR	G/POS	TPR

■ HARRY BROOKS
Brooks, Harry Frank   b: 11/30/1865, Philadelphia, Pa.   d: 12/5/45, Philadelphia, Pa.   Deb: 7/24/1886

| 1886 | NY-a | 1 | 1 | 0 | 0 | 0 | 0 | 0 | 0 | 0 | 0 | .000 | .000 | .000 | -99 | -0 | 0 | | | .500 | -1 | /O-1,P-1 | 0.0 |

■ HUBIE BROOKS
Brooks, Hubert   b: 9/24/56, Los Angeles, Cal.   BR/TR, 6', 200 lbs.   Deb: 9/4/80

1980	NY-N	24	81	8	25	2	1	1	10	5	9	.309	.364	.395	115	2	1	1	-0	.966	-1	3-23	0.0
1981	NY-N	98	358	34	110	21	2	4	38	23	65	.307	.351	.411	117	7	9	5	-0	.924	-2	3-93/O-3,S-1	0.3
1982	NY-N	126	457	40	114	21	2	2	40	28	76	.249	.300	.317	73	-16	6	3	0	.931	-8	*3-126	-2.9
1983	NY-N	150	586	53	147	18	4	5	58	24	96	.251	.285	.321	68	-26	6	4	-1	.950	3	*3-145/2-7	-2.7
1984	NY-N	153	561	61	159	23	2	16	73	48	79	.283	.342	.417	114	10	6	5	-1	.929	-18	*3-129,S-26	-0.9
1985	Mon-N	156	605	67	163	34	7	13	100	34	79	.269	.314	.413	108	4	6	9	-4	.958	-34	*S-155	-2.0
1986	Mon-N★	80	306	50	104	18	5	14	58	25	60	.340	.393	.569	164	25	4	2	0	.958	-14	S-80	2.0
1987	Mon-N★	112	430	57	113	22	3	14	72	24	72	.263	.303	.426	88	-9	4	3	-1	.953	-26	*S-109	-2.7
1988	Mon-N	151	588	61	164	35	2	20	90	35	108	.279	.321	.447	113	8	7	3	0	.968	-2	*O-149	0.3
1989	Mon-N	148	542	56	145	30	1	14	70	39	108	.268	.321	.404	105	2	6	11	-5	.964	-2	*O-140	-0.8
1990	LA-N	153	568	74	151	28	1	20	91	33	108	.266	.313	.424	104	1	2	5	-2	.964	-3	*O-150	-0.8
1991	NY-N	103	357	48	85	11	1	16	50	44	62	.238	.327	.409	106	3	3	1	0	.972	-1	*O-100	0.0
1992	Cal-A	82	306	28	66	13	0	8	36	12	46	.216	.248	.337	62	-16	3	3	-1	.986	-0	D-70/1-6	-2.1
1993	KC-A	75	168	14	48	12	0	1	24	11	27	.286	.333	.375	85	-4	0	1	-1	.966	-3	O-40/1-3,D-9	-0.8
1994	KC-A	34	61	5	14	2	0	1	14	2	10	.230	.254	.311	43	-5	1	0	0	1.000	-0	D-19/1-4	-0.6
Total	15	1645	5974	656	1608	290	31	149	824	387	1005	.269	.318	.403	100	-13	64	56	-14	.966	-112	O-582,3-516,S/D12	-13.7

■ JERRY BROOKS
Brooks, Jerome Edward   b: 3/23/67, Syracuse, N.Y.   BR/TR, 6', 195 lbs.   Deb: 9/6/93

1993	LA-N	9	9	2	2	1	0	1	1	0	2	.222	.222	.667	135	0	0	0	0	.000	-1	/O-2	-0.1
1996	Fla-N	8	5	2	2	0	1	0	3	1	1	.400	.571	.800	267	1	0	0	0	1.000	-1	/O-2,1-1	0.1
Total	2	17	14	4	4	1	1	1	4	1	3	.286	.375	.714	192	2	0	0	0	1.000	-1	/O-4,1-1	0.0

■ MANDY BROOKS
Brooks, Jonathan Joseph (b: Jonathan Joseph Brozek)   b: 8/18/1897, Milwaukee, Wis.   d: 6/17/62, Kirkwood, Mo.   BR/TR, 5'9", 165 lbs.   Deb: 5/30/25

1925	Chi-N	90	349	55	98	25	7	14	72	19	28	.281	.322	.513	108	2	10	3	1	.977	5	O-89	0.2
1926	Chi-N	26	48	7	9	1	0	1	6	5	5	.188	.278	.271	48	-4	0			1.000	-2	O-18	-0.7
Total	2	116	397	62	107	26	7	15	78	24	33	.270	.316	.484	101	-2	10	3		.979	2	O-107	-0.5

■ BOBBY BROOKS
Brooks, Robert   b: 11/1/45, Los Angeles, Cal.   d: 10/11/94, Harbor City, Cal.   BR/TR, 5'8.5", 165 lbs.   Deb: 9/1/69

1969	Oak-A	29	79	13	19	5	0	3	10	20	24	.241	.400	.418	135	5	0	2	-1	1.000	0	O-21	0.3
1970	Oak-A	7	18	2	6	0	0	2	5	1	7	.333	.368	.722	201	2	0	1	-1	1.000	-1	/O-5	0.0
1972	Oak-A	15	39	4	7	0	0	0	5	8	8	.179	.319	.179	54	-2	0	1	-1	.930	2	/O-1	-0.1
1973	Cal-A	4	7	0	1	0	0	0	0	0	3	.143	.143	.143	-21	-1	0	0	0	.000	-0	/O-1	-0.2
Total	4	55	143	19	33	6	0	5	20	29	42	.231	.364	.378	116	4	0	4	-2	.964	1	/O-38	0.0

■ SCOTT BROSIUS
Brosius, Scott David   b: 8/15/66, Hillsboro, Ore.   BR/TR, 6'1", 185 lbs.   Deb: 8/7/91

1991	Oak-A	36	68	9	16	5	0	2	4	3	11	.235	.268	.397	86	-2	3	1	0	1.000	-4	2-18,O-13/3-7,D-1	-0.2
1992	Oak-A	38	87	13	19	2	0	4	13	3	13	.218	.261	.379	82	-3	3	0	1	1.000	-8	O-20,3-12/1-3,SD	-1.1
1993	Oak-A	70	213	26	53	10	1	6	25	14	37	.249	.298	.390	89	-4	6	0	2	.991	-2	O-46,1-11,3-10/,SD	-0.5
1994	Oak-A	96	324	31	77	14	1	14	49	24	51	.238	.294	.417	88	-7	2	6	-3	.946	-4	3-93/O-7,1-1	-1.4
1995	Oak-A	123	389	69	102	19	2	17	46	41	67	.262	.345	.452	111	6	4	2	0	.918	-9	3-60,O-49,1/2SD	-0.5
1996	Oak-A	114	428	73	130	25	0	22	71	59	85	.304	.397	.516	134	23	7	2	1	.969	15	*3-109,1-10/O-4	3.4
Total	6	477	1509	221	397	75	4	65	208	144	270	.263	.335	.447	108	13	25	11	1	.954	-9	3-291,O-139/12SD	-0.3

■ SIG BROSKIE
Broskie, Sigmund Theodore "Chops"   b: 3/23/11, Iselin, Pa.   d: 5/17/75, Canton, Ohio   BR/TR, 5'11.5", 200 lbs.   Deb: 9/11/40

| 1940 | Bos-N | 11 | 22 | 1 | 6 | 1 | 0 | 0 | 4 | 1 | 2 | .273 | .304 | .318 | 76 | -1 | 0 | | | .935 | 0 | C-11 | 0.0 |

■ TONY BROTTEM
Brottem, Anton Christian   b: 4/30/1892, Halstad, Minn.   d: 8/5/29, Chicago, Ill.   BR/TR, 6'0.5", 176 lbs.   Deb: 4/17/16

1916	StL-N	26	33	3	6	1	0	0	4	3	10	.182	.250	.212	43	-2	1			.900	-1	C-15/O-2	-0.3
1918	StL-N	2	4	0	0	0	0	0	1	0	0	.000	.200	.000	-39	-1	0			1.000	1	/1-2	0.0
1921	Was-A	4	7	1	1	0	0	0	0	2	1	.143	.333	.143	26	-1	0	0	0	1.000	1	/C-4	0.1
	Pit-N	30	91	6	22	2	0	0	9	3	11	.242	.266	.264	40	-8	0	1	-1	.983	-2	C-29	-0.9
Total	3	62	135	10	29	3	0	0	13	9	22	.215	.264	.237	38	-11	1	1		.977	-1	/C-48,1-2,O-2	-1.1

■ CAL BROUGHTON
Broughton, Cecil Calvert   b: 12/28/1860, Magnolia, Wis.   d: 3/15/39, Evansville, Wis.   BR/TR,   Deb: 5/2/1883

1883	Cle-N	4	10	2	2	0	0	0		0	1	.200	.333	.200	68	-0				.950	-0	/C-4	0.0
	Bal-a	9	32	1	6	0	0	0		0	1	.188	.212	.188	29	-2				.825	-3	/C-8,O-1	-0.3
1884	Mil-U	11	39	5	12	5	0	0	0	0	0	.308	.308	.436	227	2				.937	-1	/C-7,O-5	0.2
1885	StL-a	4	17	1	1	0	0	0		0	1	.059	.059	.059	-60	-3				.889	-1	/C-4	-0.4
	NY-a	11	41	1	6	1	0	0	1	1		.146	.167	.171	7	-4				.860	-2	C-11	-0.4
	Yr	15	58	2	7	1	0	0	1	1		.121	.136	.138	-14	-7				.867	-3	C-15	-0.8
1888	Det-N	1	4	0	0	0	0	0	0	0	0	.000	.000	.000	-99	-1	0			1.000	1	/C-1	0.0
Total	4	40	143	10	27	6	0	0	3	4	2	.189	.211	.231	44	-8	0			.887	-5	/C-35,O-6	-0.9

■ MARK BROUHARD
Brouhard, Mark Steven   b: 5/22/56, Burbank, Cal.   BR/TR, 6'1", 210 lbs.   Deb: 4/12/80

1980	Mil-A	45	125	17	29	6	0	5	16	7	24	.232	.278	.400	86	-3	1	0	0	.964	0	D-21,O-12,1-10	-0.4
1981	Mil-A	60	186	19	51	6	3	2	20	7	41	.274	.308	.371	100	-1	1	1	-0	.990	1	O-51/D-7	-0.1
1982	*Mil-A	40	108	16	29	4	1	4	10	9	17	.269	.336	.435	117	2	0	3	-2	.986	2	O-30/D-7	0.2
1983	Mil-A	56	185	25	51	10	1	7	23	9	39	.276	.316	.454	118	4	0	4	-2	.991	2	O-42,D-11	0.2
1984	Mil-A	66	197	20	47	7	0	6	22	16	36	.239	.302	.365	87	-4	0	3	-2	.983	-14	O-52/D-8	-0.3
1985	Mil-A	37	108	11	28	7	2	1	13	5	26	.259	.298	.389	87	-1	0			.964	1	O-29/D-1	-0.6
Total	6	304	909	108	235	40	7	25	104	53	183	.259	.307	.400	99	-3	2	11	-6	.983	7	O-216/D-55,1-10	-1.0

■ ART BROUTHERS
Brouthers, Arthur H.   b: 11/25/1882, Montgomery, Ala.   d: 9/28/59, Charleston, S.C.   TR, 6'1",   Deb: 4/14/06

| 1906 | Phi-A | 37 | 144 | 18 | 30 | 5 | 1 | 0 | 14 | 5 | | .208 | .240 | .257 | 54 | -8 | 4 | | | .900 | -5 | 3-35/2-1 | -1.2 |

■ DAN BROUTHERS
Brouthers, Dennis Joseph "Big Dan"   b: 5/8/1858, Sylvan Lake, N.Y.   d: 8/2/32, E.Orange, N.J.   BL/TL, 6'2", 207 lbs.   Deb: 6/23/1879   H

1879	Tro-N	39	168	17	46	12	1	4	17	1	18	.274	.278	.429	138	7				.926	-5	1-37/P-3	0.1
1880	Tro-N	3	12	0	2	0	0	0	1	1	0	.167	.231	.167	35	-1				.893	-1	/1-3	-0.2
1881	Buf-N	65	270	60	86	19	8	**8**	45	18	22	.319	.361	**.541**	182	25				.797	-5	O-35,1-30	1.5
1882	Buf-N	84	351	71	**129**	23	11	6	63	21	7	**.368**	**.403**	.547	198	37				**.974**	1	*1-84	2.6
1883	Buf-N	98	425	85	**159**	41	**17**	3	**97**	16	17	**.374**	**.397**	.572	186	42				.961	2	*1-97/3-1,P-1	2.9
1884	Buf-N	94	398	82	130	22	15	14	79	33	20	.327	.378	**.563**	186	38				.964	0	*1-93/3-1	2.4
1885	Buf-N	98	407	87	146	32	11	7	59	34	10	.359	.408	.543	199	43				.975	-2	*1-98	2.7
1886	Det-N	121	489	139	181	**40**	15	**11**	72	66	16	.370	.445	.581	204	62	21			.968	-8	*1-121	3.5
1887	*Det-N	123	500	**153**	169	**36**	20	12	101	71	9	.338	**.426**	.562	167	46	34			.969	-4	*1-123	2.4
1888	Det-N	129	522	118	160	**33**	11	9	66	68	13	.307	.399	.464	174	47	34			.971	-2	*1-129	3.2
1889	Bos-N	126	485	105	181	26	9	7	118	66	6	**.373**	.462	.507	161	42	22			.974	1	*1-126	2.9
1890	Bos-P	123	460	117	152	36	9	1	97	99	17	.330	**.466**	.454	137	29	28			.963	2	*1-123	2.0
1891	Bos-a	130	486	117	170	26	19	5	109	87	20	**.350**	**.471**	**.512**	184	59	31			.978	-7	*1-130	3.8
1892	Bro-N	152	588	121	**197**	30	20	5	**124**	84	30	**.335**	.432	.480	182	62	31			.982	12	*1-152	**6.1**
1893	Bro-N	77	282	57	95	21	11	2	59	52	10	**.337**	.450	.511	163	28	9			.986	3	1-77	2.4
1894	*Bal-N	123	525	137	182	39	23	9	128	67	9	.347	.425	.560	130	24	38			.976	-3	*1-123	1.8
1895	Bal-N	5	23	2	6	2	0	0	5	1	1	.261	.292	.348	63	-1	0			1.000	0	/1-5	-0.1
	Lou-N	24	97	13	30	10	1	2	15	11	2	.309	.380	.495	133	5	1			.953	-2	1-24	0.1
	Yr	29	120	15	36	12	1	2	20	12	3	.300	.364	.467	119	3	1			.960	-2	1-29	0.1
1896	Phi-N	57	218	42	75	13	3	1	41	44	11	.344	.462	.445	141	16	7			.983	-3	1-57	1.2

YEAR	TM/L	G	AB	R	H	2B	3B	HR	RBI	BB	SO	AVG	OBP	SLG	PRO+	BR/A	SB	CS	SBR	FA	FR	G/POS	TPR
1904	NY-N	2	5	0	0	0	0	0	0	0	0	.000	.000	.000	-96	-1	0			1.000	-0	/1-1	-0.2
Total	19	1673	6711	1523	2296	460	205	106	1296	840	238	.342	.423	.519	170	609	256			.971	-18	*1-1633/O-35,P-4,3	41.2

■ **JOE BROVIA**   Brovia, Joseph John "Ox" b: 2/18/22, Davenport, Cal. d: 8/15/94, Santa Cruz, Cal. BL/TR, 6'3", 195 lbs. Deb: 7/3/55

YEAR	TM/L	G	AB	R	H	2B	3B	HR	RBI	BB	SO	AVG	OBP	SLG	PRO+	BR/A	SB	CS	SBR	FA	FR	G/POS	TPR
1955	Cin-N	21	18	0	2	0	0	0	4	1	6	.111	.158	.111	25	-3	0	0	0	.000	0	H	-0.3

■ **FRANK BROWER**   Brower, Frank Willard "Turkeyfoot" b: 3/26/1893, Gainesville, Va. d: 11/20/60, Baltimore, Md. BL/TR, 6'2", 180 lbs. Deb: 8/14/20

YEAR	TM/L	G	AB	R	H	2B	3B	HR	RBI	BB	SO	AVG	OBP	SLG	PRO+	BR/A	SB	CS	SBR	FA	FR	G/POS	TPR
1920	Was-A	36	119	21	37	7	1	1	13	9	11	.311	.374	.429	115	3	1	1	-0	.900	-4	O-20/1-9,3-1	0.1
1921	Was-A	83	203	31	53	12	3	1	35	18	7	.261	.330	.365	81	-6	1	1	-0	.917	3	O-46/1-4	-0.6
1922	Was-A	139	471	61	138	20	6	9	71	52	25	.293	.375	.414	112	9	8	6	-1	.978	-4	*O-121/1-7	-0.4
1923	Cle-A	126	397	77	113	25	8	16	66	62	32	.285	.392	.509	136	21	6	5	-1	.988	-3	*1-112/O-4	1.1
1924	Cle-A	66	107	16	30	10	1	3	20	27	9	.280	.434	.477	133	6	1	1	-0	.990	-1	1-26/P-4,O-3	0.3
Total	5	450	1297	206	371	74	20	30	205	168	84	.286	.379	.443	117	33	17	14	-3	.952	-4	O-194,1-158/P-4,3-1	0.5

■ **LOUIS BROWER**   Brower, Louis Lester b: 7/1/1900, Cincinnati, Ohio d: 3/4/94, Tyler, Tex. BR/TR, 5'10", 155 lbs. Deb: 6/13/31

YEAR	TM/L	G	AB	R	H	2B	3B	HR	RBI	BB	SO	AVG	OBP	SLG	PRO+	BR/A	SB	CS	SBR	FA	FR	G/POS	TPR
1931	Det-A	21	62	3	10	1	0	0	6	8	5	.161	.278	.177	21	-7	1	0	0	.886	-7	S-20/2-2	-1.1

■ **BOB BROWER**   Brower, Robert Richard b: 1/10/60, Jamaica, N.Y. BR/TR, 5'11", 185 lbs. Deb: 9/3/86

YEAR	TM/L	G	AB	R	H	2B	3B	HR	RBI	BB	SO	AVG	OBP	SLG	PRO+	BR/A	SB	CS	SBR	FA	FR	G/POS	TPR
1986	Tex-A	21	9	3	1	0	0	0	0	0	3	.111	.111	.222	-12	-1	1	2	-1	1.000	-5	O-17/D-1	-0.8
1987	Tex-A	127	303	63	79	10	3	14	46	36	66	.261	.339	.452	107	3	15	9	-1	.964	-13	*O-106/D-7	-1.3
1988	Tex-A	82	201	29	45	7	0	1	11	27	38	.224	.316	.274	65	-9	10	5	0	.972	-7	O-59,D-13	-1.8
1989	NY-A	26	69	9	16	3	0	2	3	6	11	.232	.293	.362	85	-2	3	1	0	.970	2	O-25/D-1	0.1
Total	4	256	582	104	141	21	3	17	60	69	118	.242	.323	.376	89	-9	29	17	-2	.968	-24	O-207/D-22	-3.8

■ **BROWN**   Brown Deb: 7/29/1874

YEAR	TM/L	G	AB	R	H	2B	3B	HR	RBI	BB	SO	AVG	OBP	SLG	PRO+	BR/A	SB	CS	SBR	FA	FR	G/POS	TPR
1874	Bal-n	2	9	0	0	0	0	0	0	0	0	.000	.000	.000	-99	-2	0	0		.727	-1	/S-2	-0.2

■ **BRANT BROWN**   Brown, Brant Michael b: 6/22/71, Porterville, Cal. BL/TL, 6'3", 220 lbs. Deb: 6/15/96

YEAR	TM/L	G	AB	R	H	2B	3B	HR	RBI	BB	SO	AVG	OBP	SLG	PRO+	BR/A	SB	CS	SBR	FA	FR	G/POS	TPR
1996	Chi-N	29	69	11	21	1	0	5	9	2	17	.304	.333	.536	123	2	3	3	-1	1.000	3	1-18	0.3

■ **CURTIS BROWN**   Brown, Curtis b: 9/14/45, Sacramento, Cal. BR/TR, 5'11", 180 lbs. Deb: 5/27/73 F

YEAR	TM/L	G	AB	R	H	2B	3B	HR	RBI	BB	SO	AVG	OBP	SLG	PRO+	BR/A	SB	CS	SBR	FA	FR	G/POS	TPR
1973	Mon-N	1	4	0	0	0	0	0	0	0	0	.000	.000	.000	-97	-1	0	0	0	1.000	4	/O-1	-0.1

■ **DARRELL BROWN**   Brown, Darrell Wayne b: 10/29/55, Oklahoma City, Okla BB/TR, 6', 184 lbs. Deb: 4/11/81

YEAR	TM/L	G	AB	R	H	2B	3B	HR	RBI	BB	SO	AVG	OBP	SLG	PRO+	BR/A	SB	CS	SBR	FA	FR	G/POS	TPR
1981	Det-A	16	4	4	1	0	0	0	0	0	1	.250	.250	.250	43	-0	1	0	0	1.000	-2	/O-6,D-4	-0.2
1982	Oak-A	8	18	2	6	0	0	0	3	1	2	.333	.368	.444	128	1	1	0	0	1.000	-1	/O-7,D-1	0.0
1983	Min-A	91	309	40	84	6	2	0	22	10	28	.272	.294	.304	64	-15	3	3	-1	.995	-4	O-81/D-3	-2.2
1984	Min-A	95	260	36	71	9	4	0	19	14	16	.273	.310	.342	77	-8	4	1	1	.993	4	O-55/D-13	-0.5
Total	4	210	591	82	162	15	6	1	44	25	47	.274	.305	.325	71	-23	9	4	0	.994	-3	O-149/D-21	-2.9

■ **DELOS BROWN**   Brown, Delos Hight b: 10/4/1892, Anna, Ill. d: 12/21/64, Carbondale, Ill. BR/TR, 5'9", 160 lbs. Deb: 6/12/14

YEAR	TM/L	G	AB	R	H	2B	3B	HR	RBI	BB	SO	AVG	OBP	SLG	PRO+	BR/A	SB	CS	SBR	FA	FR	G/POS	TPR
1914	Chi-A	1	1	0	0	0	0	0	0	0	1	.000	.000	.000	-99	-0	0			.000	0	H	0.0

■ **DRUMMOND BROWN**   Brown, Drummond Nicol b: 1/31/1885, Los Angeles, Cal. d: 1/27/27, Parkville, Mo. BR/TR, 6', 180 lbs. Deb: 4/25/13

YEAR	TM/L	G	AB	R	H	2B	3B	HR	RBI	BB	SO	AVG	OBP	SLG	PRO+	BR/A	SB	CS	SBR	FA	FR	G/POS	TPR
1913	Bos-N	15	34	3	11	1	0	1	2	2	9	.324	.361	.441	126	1	0			.960	-4	C-12	-0.2
1914	KC-F	31	58	4	11	0	0	0	5	7	6	.190	.277	.241	44	-6	1			.954	5	C-23/1-2	0.1
1915	KC-F	77	227	13	55	10	1	1	26	12	23	.242	.289	.308	71	-13	3			.961	-2	C-65/1-1	-1.1
Total	3	123	319	20	77	14	1	2	33	21	38	.241	.294	.310	72	-17	4			.960	-2	C-100/1-3	-1.2

■ **ED BROWN**   Brown, Edward P. b: Chicago, Ill. TR, 178 lbs. Deb: 8/19/1882

YEAR	TM/L	G	AB	R	H	2B	3B	HR	RBI	BB	SO	AVG	OBP	SLG	PRO+	BR/A	SB	CS	SBR	FA	FR	G/POS	TPR
1882	StL-a	17	60	4	11	0	0	0		4		.183	.234	.183	41	-4				.808	-2	O-15/2-2,P-1	-0.5
1884	Tol-a	42	153	13	27	3	0	0		2		.176	.187	.196	24	-13				.815	-8	3-40/O-2,C-1,P-1	-1.9
Total	2	59	213	17	38	3	0	0		6		.178	.201	.192	29	-16				.815	-11	/3-40,O-17,P-2,2C	-2.4

■ **EDDIE BROWN**   Brown, Edward William "Glass Arm Eddie" b: 7/17/1891, Milligan, Neb. d: 9/10/56, Vallejo, Cal. BR/TR, 6'3", 190 lbs. Deb: 9/26/20

YEAR	TM/L	G	AB	R	H	2B	3B	HR	RBI	BB	SO	AVG	OBP	SLG	PRO+	BR/A	SB	CS	SBR	FA	FR	G/POS	TPR
1920	NY-N	3	8	1	1	0	0	0	0	0	3	.125	.125	.250	6	-1	0	0	0	1.000	0	/O-2	-0.1
1921	NY-N	70	128	16	36	6	2	0	12	4	11	.281	.324	.359	80	-4	1	0	0	.956	-3	O-30	-0.8
1924	Bro-N	114	455	56	140	30	4	5	78	26	15	.308	.345	.424	108	5	3	5	-2	.975	2	*O-114	-0.3
1925	Bro-N	153	618	88	189	39	11	5	99	22	18	.306	.332	.429	95	-6	3	4	-2	.972	8	*O-153	-0.9
1926	Bos-N	153	612	71	**201**	31	8	2	84	23	20	.328	.355	.415	117	12	5			.965	8	*O-153	1.0
1927	Bos-N	155	558	64	171	35	6	2	75	28	20	.306	.340	.401	106	3	11			.980	3	*O-150/1-1	-0.4
1928	Bos-N	142	523	45	140	28	2	2	59	24	22	.268	.305	.340	72	-22	6			.960	-4	*O-129/1-1	-3.5
Total	7	790	2902	341	878	170	33	16	407	127	109	.303	.334	.400	99	-14	29	9		.970	13	O-731/1-2	-5.0

■ **RANDY BROWN**   Brown, Edwin Randolph b: 8/29/44, Leesburg, Fla. BL/TR, 5'7", 170 lbs. Deb: 9/11/69

YEAR	TM/L	G	AB	R	H	2B	3B	HR	RBI	BB	SO	AVG	OBP	SLG	PRO+	BR/A	SB	CS	SBR	FA	FR	G/POS	TPR
1969	Cal-A	13	25	3	4	1	0	0	0	6	1	.160	.323	.200	52	-1	0	0	0	1.000	-1	C-10/O-1	-0.2
1970	Cal-A	5	4	0	0	0	0	0	0	0	0	.000	.000	.000	-99	-1	0	0	0	1.000	-0	/C-5	-0.1
Total	2	18	29	3	4	1	0	0	0	6	1	.138	.286	.172	32	-1	0	0	0	1.000	-1	/C-15,O-1	-0.3

■ **FRED BROWN**   Brown, Fred Herbert b: 4/12/1879, Ossipee, N.H. d: 2/3/55, Somersworth, N.H. BR/TR, 5'10.5", 190 lbs. Deb: 5/4/01

YEAR	TM/L	G	AB	R	H	2B	3B	HR	RBI	BB	SO	AVG	OBP	SLG	PRO+	BR/A	SB	CS	SBR	FA	FR	G/POS	TPR
1901	Bos-N	7	14	1	2	0	0	0	2	0		.143	.143	.143	-16	-2	0			1.000	0	/O-5	-0.2
1902	Bos-N	2	6	1	2	1	0	0	0	0		.333	.333	.500	155	0	0			1.000	0	/O-2	0.0
Total	2	9	20	2	4	1	0	0	2	0		.200	.200	.250	30	-2	0			1.000	0	/O-7	-0.2

■ **IKE BROWN**   Brown, Isaac b: 4/13/42, Memphis, Tenn. BR/TR, 6'1", 205 lbs. Deb: 6/17/69

YEAR	TM/L	G	AB	R	H	2B	3B	HR	RBI	BB	SO	AVG	OBP	SLG	PRO+	BR/A	SB	CS	SBR	FA	FR	G/POS	TPR
1969	Det-A	70	170	24	39	4	3	5	12	26	43	.229	.338	.376	96	-1	2	3	-1	.962	-6	2-45,3-12/O-3,S-1	-0.5
1970	Det-A	56	94	17	27	5	0	4	15	13	26	.287	.380	.468	132	4	0	0	0	.935	-3	2-23/O-4,3-1	0.3
1971	Det-A	59	110	20	28	1	0	8	19	19	25	.255	.364	.482	133	5	0	1	-1	1.000	-1	1-17/O-9,2-8,3-4,S	0.2
1972	*Det-A	51	84	12	21	3	0	2	10	17	23	.250	.376	.357	115	2	1	2	-1	1.000	3	O-22,1-13/2-3,3S	0.3
1973	Det-A	42	76	12	22	2	1	1	9	15	13	.289	.407	.382	115	2	0	1	-1	.983	-2	1-21,O-12/3-2,D-2	-0.2
1974	Det-A	2	2	0	0	0	0	0	0	0	0	.000	.000	.000	-97	-0	0	0	0	1.000	0	/3-2	0.0
Total	6	280	536	85	137	15	4	20	65	90	130	.256	.366	.410	115	13	3	7	-3	.956	-9	/2-79,1-51,O3SD	0.1

■ **JIM BROWN**   Brown, James Donaldson "Don" or "Moose" b: 3/31/1897, Laurel, Md. BR/TR, 6', 178 lbs. Deb: 9/13/15

YEAR	TM/L	G	AB	R	H	2B	3B	HR	RBI	BB	SO	AVG	OBP	SLG	PRO+	BR/A	SB	CS	SBR	FA	FR	G/POS	TPR
1915	StL-N	1	2	0	1	0	0	0	0	2	1	.500	.750	.500	281	1	0			1.000	-0	/O-1	0.1
1916	Phi-A	14	42	6	10	2	1	0	5	4	9	.238	.304	.405	119	1	0			.895	-1	O-12	-0.1
Total	2	15	44	6	11	2	1	0	5	6	10	.250	.340	.409	131	2	0			.900	-2	/O-13	0.0

■ **JIMMY BROWN**   Brown, James Roberson b: 4/25/10, Jamesville, N.C. d: 12/29/77, Bath, N.C. BB/TR, 5'8.5", 165 lbs. Deb: 4/23/37 C

YEAR	TM/L	G	AB	R	H	2B	3B	HR	RBI	BB	SO	AVG	OBP	SLG	PRO+	BR/A	SB	CS	SBR	FA	FR	G/POS	TPR
1937	StL-N	138	525	86	145	20	9	2	53	27	29	.276	.313	.360	81	-15	10			.964	-14	*2-112,S-25/3-1	-1.9
1938	StL-N	108	382	50	115	12	6	0	38	27	9	.301	.350	.364	91	-4	7			.968	1	2-49,S-30,3-24	-0.1
1939	StL-N	147	645	88	192	31	8	3	51	32	18	.298	.335	.384	87	-12	7			.957	-5	*S-104,2-50	-0.5
1940	StL-N	107	454	56	127	17	4	0	30	24	15	.280	.317	.335	76	-15	9			.977	-22	2-48,3-41,S-28	-3.2
1941	StL-N	132	549	81	168	28	3	6	56	45	22	.306	.363	.406	109	7	2			.965	3	*3-123,2-11	1.3
1942	*StL-N★	145	606	75	155	28	4	1	71	52	11	.256	.315	.320	80	-15	9			.970	-12	2-82,3-66,S-12	-2.3
1943	StL-N	34	110	6	20	4	0	0	8	6	5	.182	.224	.255	37	-9	0			.978	2	2-19/3-9,S-6	-1.3
1946	Pit-N	79	241	23	58	6	0	0	12	18	5	.241	.293	.266	58	-13	3			.960	-2	S-30,2-21/3-9	-1.3
Total	8	890	3512	465	980	146	42	9	319	231	110	.279	.326	.352	84	-76	39			.968	-50	2-392,3-273,S-235	-8.3

■ **JIM BROWN**   Brown, James W. H. b: 12/12/1860, Clinton Co., Pa. d: 4/6/08, Williamsport, Pa. Deb: 4/17/1884

YEAR	TM/L	G	AB	R	H	2B	3B	HR	RBI	BB	SO	AVG	OBP	SLG	PRO+	BR/A	SB	CS	SBR	FA	FR	G/POS	TPR
1884	Alt-U	21	88	12	22	2	2	1		1		.250	.258	.352	82	-5				.615	-3	O-14,P-11	-0.6
	NY-N	1	4	0	0	0	0	0		0	1	.000	.000	.000	-98	-1				.333	-0	/P-1	0.0
	StP-U	6	16	5	5	4	0	0		1		.313	.353	.563	320	3				.706	0	/P-6,1-1,O-1	0.0

YEAR	TM/L	G	AB	R	H	2B	3B	HR	RBI	BB	SO	AVG	OBP	SLG	PRO+	BR/A	SB	CS	SBR	FA	FR	G/POS	TPR
1886	Phi-a	1	3	0	0	0	0	0	0	0		.000	.000	.000	-99	-1	0			1.000	-0	/P-1	0.0
Total	2	29	110	17	27	6	2	1	0	2	1	.245	.259	.364	92	-3	0			.741	-4	/P-19,O-15,1-1	-0.6

■ JARVIS BROWN   Brown, Jarvis Ardel   b: 3/26/67, Waukegan, Ill.   BR/TR, 5'7", 165 lbs.   Deb: 7/2/91

YEAR	TM/L	G	AB	R	H	2B	3B	HR	RBI	BB	SO	AVG	OBP	SLG	PRO+	BR/A	SB	CS	SBR	FA	FR	G/POS	TPR
1991	*Min-A	38	37	10	8	0	0	0	0	2	8	.216	.256	.216	31	-3	7	1	2	.955	-11	O-32/D-4	-1.3
1992	Min-A	35	15	8	1	0	0	0	0	2	4	.067	.222	.067	-15	-2	2	2	-1	.952	-10	O-31/D-2	-1.4
1993	SD-N	47	133	21	31	9	2	0	8	15	26	.233	.338	.331	78	-4	3	3	-1	.982	2	O-43	-0.4
1994	Atl-N	17	15	3	2	1	0	1	1	0	2	.133	.133	.400	31	-2	0	0	0	1.000	-2	/O-9	-0.3
1995	Bal-A	18	27	2	4	1	0	0	1	7	9	.148	.324	.185	36	-2	1	1	-0	1.000	-5	O-17	-0.7
Total	5	155	227	44	46	11	2	1	10	26	49	.203	.304	.282	57	-13	13	7	-0	.978	-26	O-132/D-6	-4.1

■ JAKE BROWN   Brown, Jerald Ray   b: 3/22/48, Sumrall, Miss.   d: 12/18/81, Houston, Tex.   BR/TR, 6'2", 200 lbs.   Deb: 5/17/75

YEAR	TM/L	G	AB	R	H	2B	3B	HR	RBI	BB	SO	AVG	OBP	SLG	PRO+	BR/A	SB	CS	SBR	FA	FR	G/POS	TPR
1975	SF-N	41	43	6	9	3	0	0	3	1	3	.209	.292	.279	57	-2	0	0	0	.857	-3	O-14	-0.6

■ CHRIS BROWN   Brown, John Christopher   b: 8/15/61, Jackson, Miss.   BR/TR, 6'2", 210 lbs.   Deb: 9/3/84

YEAR	TM/L	G	AB	R	H	2B	3B	HR	RBI	BB	SO	AVG	OBP	SLG	PRO+	BR/A	SB	CS	SBR	FA	FR	G/POS	TPR
1984	SF-N	23	84	6	24	7	1	1	11	9	19	.286	.362	.405	119	2	2	1	0	.900	-2	3-23	0.0
1985	SF-N	131	432	50	117	20	3	16	61	38	78	.271	.345	.442	125	14	2	3	-1	**.971**	5	*3-120	1.7
1986	SF-N★	116	416	57	132	16	3	7	49	33	43	.317	.380	.421	127	16	13	9	-2	.933	-14	*3-111/S-2	-0.2
1987	SF-N	38	132	17	32	6	0	6	17	9	16	.242	.306	.424	95	-1	1	3	-2	.905	-2	3-37/S-1	-0.5
	SD-N	44	155	17	36	3	0	6	23	11	30	.232	.296	.368	77	-5	3	1	0	.942	-4	3-43	-0.9
	Yr	82	287	34	68	9	0	12	40	20	46	.237	.300	.394	86	-7	4	4	-1	.923	-6	3-80/S-1	-1.4
1988	SD-N	80	247	14	58	6	0	2	19	19	49	.235	.297	.283	69	-10	0	0	0	.949	5	3-72	-0.6
1989	Det-A	17	57	3	11	3	0	0	4	1	17	.193	.207	.246	28	-6	0	0	0	.909	-1	3-17	-0.7
Total	6	449	1523	164	410	61	6	38	184	120	252	.269	.335	.392	105	9	21	17	-4	.943	-13	3-423/S-3	-1.2

■ LINDSAY BROWN   Brown, John Lindsay "Red"   b: 7/22/11, Mason, Tex.   d: 1/1/67, San Antonio, Tex.   BR/TR, 5'10", 160 lbs.   Deb: 7/13/37

YEAR	TM/L	G	AB	R	H	2B	3B	HR	RBI	BB	SO	AVG	OBP	SLG	PRO+	BR/A	SB	CS	SBR	FA	FR	G/POS	TPR
1937	Bro-N	48	115	16	31	3	1	0	6	3	17	.270	.288	.313	62	-6	1			.937	6	S-45	0.3

■ JOE BROWN   Brown, Joseph E.   b: 4/4/1859, Warren, Pa.   d: 6/28/1888, Warren, Pa.   5'10", 162 lbs.   Deb: 8/16/1884

YEAR	TM/L	G	AB	R	H	2B	3B	HR	RBI	BB	SO	AVG	OBP	SLG	PRO+	BR/A	SB	CS	SBR	FA	FR	G/POS	TPR
1884	Chi-N	15	61	6	13	1	0	0	3	0	15	.213	.213	.230	36	-5				.750	-3	/O-9,P-7,1-1,C-1	-0.5
1885	Bal-a	5	19	2	3	0	0	0	0	0		.158	.158	.158	-0	-2				1.000	0	/P-4,2-1	0.0
Total	2	20	80	8	16	1	0	0	3	0	15	.200	.200	.213	28	-7				.895	-3	/P-11,O-9,2-1,C1	-0.5

■ KEVIN BROWN   Brown, Kevin Lee   b: 4/21/73, Valparaiso, Ind.   BR/TR, 6'2", 200 lbs.   Deb: 9/12/96

YEAR	TM/L	G	AB	R	H	2B	3B	HR	RBI	BB	SO	AVG	OBP	SLG	PRO+	BR/A	SB	CS	SBR	FA	FR	G/POS	TPR
1996	Tex-A	3	4	1	0	0	0	0	0	3	0	.000	.429	.000	20	-0	0	0	0	1.000	1	/C-2,D-1	0.1

■ LARRY BROWN   Brown, Larry Leslie   b: 3/1/40, Shinnston, W.Va.   BR/TR, 5'11", 165 lbs.   Deb: 7/6/63   F

YEAR	TM/L	G	AB	R	H	2B	3B	HR	RBI	BB	SO	AVG	OBP	SLG	PRO+	BR/A	SB	CS	SBR	FA	FR	G/POS	TPR
1963	Cle-A	74	247	28	63	6	0	5	18	22	27	.255	.319	.340	85	-5	4	3	-1	.938	-8	S-46,2-27	-0.9
1964	Cle-A	115	335	33	77	12	1	12	40	24	55	.230	.285	.379	84	-8	1	2	-1	.981	11	*2-103/S-4	1.0
1965	Cle-A	124	438	52	111	22	2	8	40	38	62	.253	.316	.368	93	-4	5	7	-3	.977	3	S-95,2-26	0.5
1966	Cle-A	105	340	29	78	12	0	3	17	36	58	.229	.309	.291	73	-11	0	1	-1	.961	-4	S-90,2-10	-0.7
1967	Cle-A	152	485	38	110	16	2	7	37	53	62	.227	.311	.311	84	-9	4	4	-1	.967	1	*S-150	0.6
1968	Cle-A	154	495	43	116	18	3	6	35	43	46	.234	.302	.319	90	-6	1	1	-0	.966	-14	*S-154	-0.6
1969	Cle-A	132	469	48	112	10	2	4	24	44	43	.239	.305	.294	66	-21	5	3	-0	.959	-17	*S-101,3-29/2-5	-2.8
1970	Cle-A	72	155	17	40	5	2	0	15	20	14	.258	.343	.316	79	-4	1	0	0	.950	-2	S-27,3-17,2-16	-0.2
1971	Cle-A	13	50	4	11	1	0	0	5	3	3	.220	.264	.240	44	-4	0	0	0	.980	-6	S-13	-0.9
	Oak-A	70	189	14	37	2	1	1	9	7	19	.196	.228	.233	31	-17	1	2	-1	.959	4	S-31,2-23,3-10	-1.1
	Yr	83	239	18	48	3	1	1	14	10	22	.201	.239	.234	35	-21	1	2	-1	.965	-2	S-44,2-23,3-10	-2.0
1972	Oak-A	47	142	11	26	2	0	0	4	13	8	.183	.252	.197	37	-11	0	0	0	.974	-8	2-46/3-1	-1.9
1973	*Bal-A	17	28	4	7	0	0	1	5	5	4	.250	.364	.357	104	0	0	0	0	.880	-2	3-15/2-1	-0.2
1974	Tex-A	54	76	10	15	2	0	0	4	6	13	.197	.282	.224	48	-5	0	0	0	.931	8	3-47/2-8,S-1	0.3
Total	12	1129	3449	331	803	108	13	47	254	317	414	.233	.301	.313	76	-103	22	23	-7	.964	-34	S-712,2-265,3-119	-6.9

■ LEON BROWN   Brown, Leon   b: 11/16/49, Sacramento, Cal.   BR/TR, 6', 185 lbs.   Deb: 5/19/76   F

YEAR	TM/L	G	AB	R	H	2B	3B	HR	RBI	BB	SO	AVG	OBP	SLG	PRO+	BR/A	SB	CS	SBR	FA	FR	G/POS	TPR
1976	NY-N	64	70	11	15	3	0	0	4	4	4	.214	.257	.257	49	-5	2	4	-2	1.000	-18	O-43	-2.7

■ LEW BROWN   Brown, Lewis J. "Blower"   b: 2/1/1858, Leominster, Mass.   d: 1/16/1889, Boston, Mass.   BR/TR, 5'10.5", 185 lbs.   Deb: 6/17/1876

YEAR	TM/L	G	AB	R	H	2B	3B	HR	RBI	BB	SO	AVG	OBP	SLG	PRO+	BR/A	SB	CS	SBR	FA	FR	G/POS	TPR
1876	Bos-N	45	195	23	41	6	2	2	21	3	22	.210	.222	.333	82	-4				.856	-2	C-45/O-1	-0.4
1877	Bos-N	58	221	27	56	12	8	1	31	6	33	.253	.273	.394	104	0				.897	15	*C-55/1-4	1.6
1878	Pro-N	58	243	44	74	21	6	1	43	7	37	.305	.324	.453	153	13				.880	3	*C-45,1-15/O-1,P-1	1.5
1879	Pro-N	53	229	23	59	13	4	2	38	4	24	.258	.270	.376	112	3				.847	-4	C-48/O-6	0.0
	Chi-N	6	21	2	6	1	0	0	3	1	4	.286	.318	.333	109	0				.974	0	/1-6	0.0
	Yr	59	250	25	65	14	4	2	41	5	28	.260	.275	.372	112	3				.847	-4	C-48/O-6,1-6	0.0
1881	Det-N	27	108	16	26	3	1	3	14	3	16	.241	.261	.370	93	-1				.959	-1	1-27	-0.4
	Pro-N	18	75	9	18	3	1	0	10	4	13	.240	.278	.307	85	-1				.833	-4	O-13/1-5	-0.5
	Yr	45	183	25	44	6	2	3	24	7	29	.240	.268	.344	90	-2				.960	-4	1-32,O-13	-0.9
1883	Bos-N	14	54	5	13	4	1	0	9	3	6	.241	.281	.352	89	-1				.943	-2	1-14	-0.3
	Lou-a	14	60	6	11	2	1	0		1		.183	.197	.250	46	-3				.891	-2	1-14/C-1	-0.6
1884	Bos-U	85	325	50	75	18	3	1		13		.231	.260	.314	74	-20				.914	13	C-54,1-33/O-2,P-1	-0.5
Total	7	378	1531	205	379	83	31	10	169	45	155	.248	.269	.362	99	-13				.884	17	C-248,1-118/O-23,P	0.4

■ MARTY BROWN   Brown, Marty Leo   b: 1/23/63, Lawton, Okla.   BR/TR, 6'1", 190 lbs.   Deb: 9/4/88

YEAR	TM/L	G	AB	R	H	2B	3B	HR	RBI	BB	SO	AVG	OBP	SLG	PRO+	BR/A	SB	CS	SBR	FA	FR	G/POS	TPR
1988	Cin-N	10	16	0	3	1	0	0	2	1	2	.188	.235	.250	38	-1	0	1	-1	1.000	1	/3-8	-0.1
1989	Cin-N	16	30	2	5	1	0	0	4	4	9	.167	.265	.200	34	-3	0	0	0	.913	2	3-11	-0.1
1990	Bal-A	9	15	1	3	0	0	0	0	1	7	.200	.250	.200	28	-1	0	0	0	1.000	0	/2-3,3-2,D-4	-0.1
Total	3	35	61	3	11	2	0	0	6	6	18	.180	.254	.213	34	-5	0	1	-1	.943	3	/3-21,D-4,2-3	-0.3

■ MIKE BROWN   Brown, Michael Charles   b: 12/29/59, San Francisco, Cal.   BR/TR, 6'2", 195 lbs.   Deb: 7/21/83

YEAR	TM/L	G	AB	R	H	2B	3B	HR	RBI	BB	SO	AVG	OBP	SLG	PRO+	BR/A	SB	CS	SBR	FA	FR	G/POS	TPR
1983	Cal-A	31	104	12	24	5	1	3	9	7	20	.231	.279	.385	81	-3	1	0	0	.949	-2	O-31	-0.5
1984	Cal-A	62	148	19	42	8	3	7	22	13	23	.284	.342	.520	136	7	0	2	-1	.968	-6	O-44/D-3	-0.1
1985	Cal-A	60	153	23	41	9	1	4	20	7	21	.268	.304	.418	96	-1	0	1	-1	1.000	-3	O-48/D-7	-0.5
	Pit-N	57	205	29	68	18	2	5	33	22	27	.332	.396	.512	154	15	2	2	-1	.938	-2	O-56	1.0
1986	Pit-N	87	243	18	53	7	4	2	26	27	32	.218	.296	.296	62	-12	2	3	-1	.973	-4	O-71	-2.1
1988	Cal-A	18	50	4	11	2	0	0	3	1	12	.220	.235	.260	40	-4	0	0	0	.946	-1	O-18	-0.5
Total	5	315	903	105	239	49	7	23	113	77	135	.265	.323	.411	102	2	5	8	-4	.964	-17	O-268/D-10	-2.7

■ OLIVER BROWN   Brown, Oliver S.   b: 1849, Brooklyn, N.Y.   d: 9/23/32, Brooklyn, N.Y.   Deb: 8/1/1872

YEAR	TM/L	G	AB	R	H	2B	3B	HR	RBI	BB	SO	AVG	OBP	SLG	PRO+	BR/A	SB	CS	SBR	FA	FR	G/POS	TPR
1872	Atl-n	4	15	0	2	0	0	0	0	0	1	.133	.133	.133	-15	-2	0	0	0	.889	0	/O-4	-0.1
1875	Atl-n	3	10	0	0	0	0	0	0	0	0	.000	.000	.000	-99	-2	0	0	0	.833	-1	/1-2,O-2	-0.2
Total	2 n	7	25	0	2	0	0	0	0	0	1	.080	.080	.080	-46	-4	0	0	0	.846	-1	/O-6,1-2	-0.3

■ OLLIE BROWN   Brown, Ollie Lee "Downtown"   b: 2/11/44, Tuscaloosa, Ala.   BR/TR, 6'3", 200 lbs.   Deb: 9/10/65   F

YEAR	TM/L	G	AB	R	H	2B	3B	HR	RBI	BB	SO	AVG	OBP	SLG	PRO+	BR/A	SB	CS	SBR	FA	FR	G/POS	TPR
1965	SF-N	6	10	0	2	1	0	0	0	0	2	.200	.200	.300	38	-1	0	0	0	1.000	-1	/O-4	-0.2
1966	SF-N	115	348	32	81	7	1	7	33	33	66	.233	.304	.319	71	-13	2	5	-2	.978	-7	O-114	-2.9
1967	SF-N	120	412	44	110	12	1	13	53	25	65	.267	.315	.396	104	1	2	5	-2	.985	-6	*O-115	-1.3
1968	SF-N	40	95	7	22	4	0	0	11	3	23	.232	.270	.274	64	-4	1	0	0	1.000	-7	O-35	-1.5
1969	SD-N	151	568	76	150	18	3	20	61	44	97	.264	.320	.412	108	4	10	6	-1	.976	7	*O-148	0.2
1970	SD-N	139	534	79	156	34	2	23	89	34	78	.292	.335	.489	123	14	5	3	-0	.964	7	*O-137	1.3
1971	SD-N	145	484	36	132	16	2	9	55	52	74	.273	.347	.362	108	6	3	3	-1	.982	5	*O-134	0.3
1972	SD-N	23	70	3	12	2	0	1	6	3	6	.171	.227	.200	24	-7	0	0	0	1.000	1	O-17	-0.8
	Oak-A	20	54	5	13	1	0	1	4	6	14	.241	.317	.315	93	-0	1	2	-1	1.000	1	O-16	-0.4
	Mil-A	66	179	21	50	8	0	3	25	17	24	.279	.345	.374	116	4	0	2	-1	.992	7	O-56/3-1	0.8

YEAR	TM/L	G	AB	R	H	2B	3B	HR	RBI	BB	SO	AVG	OBP	SLG	PRO+	BR/A	SB	CS	SBR	FA	FR	G/POS	TPR
	Yr	86	233	26	63	9	0	4	29	23	38	.270	.339	.361	111	3	1	3	-2	.994	5	O-72/3-1	0.4
1973	Mil-A	97	296	28	83	10	1	7	32	33	53	.280	.356	.392	113	6	4	1	1	1.000	-1	D-82/O-4	0.3
1974	Hou-N	27	69	8	15	1	0	3	6	4	15	.217	.260	.362	76	-3	0	0	0	1.000	-4	O-20	-0.4
	Phi-N	43	99	11	24	5	2	4	13	6	20	.242	.286	.455	101	-1	0	1	-1	.921	-5	O-33	-0.8
	Yr	70	168	19	39	6	2	7	19	10	35	.232	.275	.417	91	-3	0	1	-1	.961	-6	O-53	-1.2
1975	Phi-N	84	145	19	44	12	0	6	26	15	29	.303	.369	.510	137	7	1	1	-0	1.000	-14	O-63	-0.9
1976	*Phi-N	92	209	30	53	10	1	5	30	33	33	.254	.355	.383	106	2	2	1	0	.949	-6	O-75	-0.6
1977	*Phi-N	53	70	5	17	3	1	1	13	4	14	.243	.284	.357	68	-3	1	1	-0	1.000	-4	O-21	-0.8
Total	13	1221	3642	404	964	144	11	102	454	314	616	.265	.326	.394	103	11	30	27	-7	.977	-29	O-992/D-82,3-1	-7.7

■ **OSCAR BROWN**   Brown, Oscar Lee   b: 2/8/46, Long Beach, Cal.   BR/TR, 6', 175 lbs.   Deb: 9/3/69   F

1969	Atl-N	7	4	2	1	0	0	0	0	0	1	.250	.250	.250	40	-0	0	0	0	1.000	-1	/O-3	-0.1
1970	Atl-N	28	47	6	18	2	1	1	7	7	7	.383	.473	.532	159	4	0	2	-1	.960	-5	O-25	-0.2
1971	Atl-N	27	43	4	9	4	0	0	5	3	8	.209	.261	.302	56	-3	0	0	-1	1.000	-2	O-15	-0.5
1972	Atl-N	76	164	19	37	5	1	3	16	4	29	.226	.244	.323	55	-10	0	2	-1	.899	-4	O-59	-1.8
1973	Atl-N	22	58	3	12	3	0	0	0	3	10	.207	.246	.259	37	-5	0	0	0	1.000	-2	O-13	-0.4
Total	5	160	316	34	77	14	2	4	28	17	55	.244	.284	.339	68	-13	0	4	-2	.939	-10	O-115	-3.0

■ **DICK BROWN**   Brown, Richard Ernest   b: 1/17/35, Shinnston, W.Va.   d: 4/17/70, Baltimore, Md.   BR/TR, 6'3", 190 lbs.   Deb: 6/20/57   F

1957	Cle-A	34	114	10	30	4	0	4	22	4	23	.263	.288	.404	88	-2	1	1	-0	.986	1	C-33	0.0
1958	Cle-A	68	173	20	41	5	0	7	20	14	27	.237	.305	.387	91	-2	1	0	0	.987	6	C-62	0.6
1959	Cle-A	48	141	15	31	7	0	5	16	11	39	.220	.290	.376	85	-3	0	0	0	.996	4	C-48	0.3
1960	Chi-A	16	43	4	7	0	0	3	5	3	11	.163	.217	.372	57	-3	0	0	0	.986	3	C-14	0.1
1961	Det-A	93	308	32	82	12	2	16	45	22	57	.266	.315	.474	105	1	0	2	-1	.990	-1	C-91	0.4
1962	Det-A	134	431	40	104	12	0	12	40	21	66	.241	.280	.353	67	-21	0	1	-1	.994	3	*C-132	-1.4
1963	Bal-A	59	171	13	42	7	0	2	13	15	35	.246	.310	.322	80	-4	1	0	0	.986	6	C-58	0.3
1964	Bal-A	88	230	24	59	6	0	8	32	12	45	.257	.296	.387	89	-4	2	0	1	.988	4	C-84	0.3
1965	Bal-A	96	255	17	59	9	1	5	30	17	53	.231	.282	.333	73	-9	2	2	-1	.983	10	C-92	0.4
Total	9	636	1866	175	455	62	3	62	223	119	356	.244	.293	.380	83	-49	7	6	-2	.989	35	C-614	1.0

■ **BOBBY BROWN**   Brown, Robert William "Doc"   b: 10/25/24, Seattle, Wash.   BL/TR, 6'1", 180 lbs.   Deb: 9/22/46

1946	NY-A	7	24	1	8	1	0	0	1	4	0	.333	.429	.375	124	1	0	0	0	1.000	-4	/S-5,3-2	-0.2
1947	*NY-A	69	150	21	45	6	1	1	18	21	9	.300	.390	.373	114	4	0	2	-1	.932	-11	3-27,S-11/O-3	-0.9
1948	*NY-A	113	363	62	109	19	5	3	48	48	16	.300	.383	.405	111	6	0	1	-1	.946	-18	3-41,S-26,2-17,/O-4	-1.0
1949	*NY-A	104	343	61	97	14	4	6	61	38	18	.283	.359	.399	101	-0	4	3	-1	.949	-5	3-86/O-3	-0.6
1950	*NY-A	95	277	33	74	4	2	4	37	39	18	.267	.360	.339	82	-7	3	1	0	.958	-4	3-82	0.0
1951	*NY-A	103	313	44	84	15	2	6	51	47	18	.268	.369	.387	108	5	1	1	-0	.955	-5	3-90	-0.1
1952	NY-A	29	89	6	22	4	0	1	14	9	6	.247	.323	.303	80	-2	1	1	-0	.894	3	3-24	0.0
1954	NY-A	28	60	5	13	1	0	1	7	8	3	.217	.309	.283	65	-3	0	1	-1	1.000	-0	3-17	-0.4
Total	8	548	1619	233	452	62	14	22	237	214	88	.279	.367	.376	100	4	9	10	-3	.948	-43	3-369/S-42,2-17,O	-4.2

■ **BOBBY BROWN**   Brown, Rogers Lee   b: 5/24/54, Norfolk, Va.   BB/TR, 6'1", 205 lbs.   Deb: 4/5/79

1979	Tor-A	4	10	1	0	0	0	0	2	1	0	.000	.167	.000	-50	-2	0	0	0	1.000	-0	/O-4	-0.2
	NY-A	30	68	7	17	3	1	0	3	2	17	.250	.271	.324	61	-4	2	1	0	.949	-3	O-27/D-1	-0.8
	Yr	34	78	8	17	3	1	0	3	4	18	.218	.256	.282	46	-6	2	1	0	.955	-3	O-31/D-1	-1.0
1980	*NY-A	137	412	65	107	12	5	14	47	29	82	.260	.308	.415	98	-2	27	8	3	.972	-5	*O-131/D-1	-0.4
1981	*NY-A	31	62	5	14	1	0	0	6	5	15	.226	.284	.242	53	-4	4	2	0	.949	-2	O-29/D-2	-0.6
1982	Sea-A	79	245	29	59	7	1	4	17	17	32	.241	.290	.327	67	-11	28	6	5	.968	3	O-68/D-3	-0.5
1983	SD-N	57	225	40	60	5	3	5	22	23	38	.267	.335	.382	102	0	27	9	3	.963	-1	O-54	-0.5
1984	*SD-N	85	171	28	43	7	2	3	29	11	33	.251	.297	.368	86	-4	16	4	2	.971	-2	O-53	-0.5
1985	SD-N	79	84	8	13	3	0	0	6	5	20	.155	.202	.190	11	-10	6	4	0	1.000	-7	O-28	-1.9
Total	7	502	1277	183	313	38	12	26	130	94	238	.245	.297	.355	80	-36	110	34	13	.968	-13	O-394/D-7	-4.9

■ **SAM BROWN**   Brown, Samuel Wakefield   b: 5/21/1878, Webster, Pa.   d: 11/8/31, Mount Pleasant, Pa.   BR/TR,   Deb: 4/21/06

1906	Bos-N	71	231	12	48	6	1	0	20	13		.208	.262	.242	59	-11	4			.970	-1	C-35,O-13,3-12,/12	-0.9
1907	Bos-N	70	208	17	40	6	0	0	14	12		.192	.256	.221	48	-12	0			.970	7	C-63/1-2	0.0
Total	2	141	439	29	88	12	1	0	34	25		.200	.256	.232	54	-24	4			.970	7	/C-98,O-13,3-12,12	-0.9

■ **TOMMY BROWN**   Brown, Thomas Michael "Buckshot"   b: 12/6/27, Brooklyn, N.Y.   BR/TR, 6'1", 170 lbs.   Deb: 8/3/44

1944	Bro-N	46	146	17	24	4	0	0	8	8	17	.164	.208	.192	13	-17	0			.925	-9	S-46	-2.4
1945	Bro-N	57	196	13	48	3	4	2	19	6	16	.245	.267	.332	66	-10	3			.918	-4	S-55/O-1	-1.0
1947	Bro-N	15	34	3	8	1	0	0	2	1	6	.235	.257	.265	37	-3	0			1.000	2	/3-6,O-3,S-1	-0.1
1948	Bro-N	54	145	18	35	4	0	2	20	7	17	.241	.281	.310	58	-9	1			.936	-1	3-43/1-1	-1.0
1949	*Bro-N	41	89	14	27	2	0	3	18	6	8	.303	.347	.427	102	0	0			.931	-2	O-27	-0.3
1950	Bro-N	48	86	15	25	2	1	8	20	11	9	.291	.378	.616	153	6	0			.917	0	O-16	0.6
1951	Bro-N	11	25	2	4	2	0	0	1	2	4	.160	.222	.240	24	-3	0	0	0	.909	-2	/O-5	-0.3
	Phi-N	78	196	24	43	2	1	10	32	15	21	.219	.278	.393	80	-6	1	2	-1	.966	-12	O-32,2-14,1-12,/3-1	-2.0
	Yr	89	221	26	47	4	1	10	33	17	25	.213	.272	.376	73	-9	1	2	-1	.957	-11	O-37,2-14,1-12,/3-1	-2.3
1952	Phi-N	18	25	2	4	1	0	1	2	4	3	.160	.276	.320	65	-1	0	0	0	1.000	-1	/1-3,O-3	-0.2
	Chi-N	61	200	24	64	11	0	3	24	12	24	.320	.358	.420	114	3	1	2	-1	.911	-19	S-39,2-10/1-5	-1.4
	Yr	79	225	26	68	12	0	4	26	16	27	.302	.344	.409	109	2	1	2	-1	.911	-20	S-39,2-10/1-8,O-3	-1.6
1953	Chi-N	65	138	19	27	7	1	2	13	13	17	.196	.279	.304	72	-10	1	0	0	.903	-6	S-25/O-6	-1.4
Total	9	494	1280	151	309	39	7	31	159	85	142	.241	.292	.355	74	-48	7	4		.916	-52	S-166/O-93,3-50,21	-9.5

■ **TOM BROWN**   Brown, Thomas Tarlton   b: 9/21/1860, Liverpool, England   d: 10/25/27, Washington, D.C.   BL/TR, 5'10", 168 lbs.   Deb: 7/6/1882   MU

1882	Bal-a	45	181	30	55	5	2	1	23	6		.304	.326	.370	146	9				.728	-0	O-45/P-2	0.8
1883	Col-a	97	420	69	115	12	7	5	32	20		.274	.307	.371	127	14				.808	-1	*O-96/P-3	1.1
1884	Col-a	107	451	93	123	9	11	4	32	24		.273	.315	.375	135	18				.847	-6	*O-107/P-4	1.0
1885	Pit-a	108	437	81	134	16	12	4	68	34		.307	.366	.426	152	26				.828	-3	*O-108/P-2	1.9
1886	Pit-a	115	460	106	131	11	11	1	51	56		.285	.365	.363	129	17	30			.837	6	*O-115/P-1	1.8
1887	Pit-N	47	192	30	47	3	4	0	6	11	40	.245	.289	.302	69	-8	12			.870	5	O-47	-0.3
	Ind-N	36	140	20	25	3	0	2	9	8	25	.179	.239	.243	32	-13	13			.813	-2	O-36	-1.3
	Yr	83	332	50	72	6	4	2	15	19	65	.217	.263	.277	53	-21	25			.851	3	O-83	-1.6
1888	Bos-N	107	420	62	104	10	7	3	49	30	68	.248	.299	.369	110	4	46			.896	-3	*O-107	-0.1
1889	Bos-N	90	362	93	84	10	5	2	24	59	56	.232	.341	.304	76	-11	63			.901	3	O-90	-0.9
1890	Bos-P	128	543	146	149	23	14	4	61	86	84	.274	.377	.390	98	-2	79			.911	8	*O-128	-0.2
1891	Bos-a	137	589	**177**	**189**	30	**21**	5	72	70	96	.321	.397	.469	150	37	**106**			.878	-10	*O-137	1.9
1892	Lou-N	153	660	105	150	16	8	2	45	47	94	.227	.284	.285	78	-17	78			.919	19	*O-153	-0.5
1893	Lou-N	122	529	104	127	15	7	5	54	56	63	.240	.319	.323	77	-17	**66**			.929	27	*O-122	0.3
1894	Lou-N	129	536	122	136	22	14	6	57	60	73	.254	.332	.397	81	-18	66			.912	3	*O-129	-1.9
1895	StL-N	83	350	72	76	11	4	1	31	48	44	.217	.315	.280	55	-23	34			.950	8	O-83	-1.7
	Was-N	34	134	25	32	8	3	2	16	18	16	.239	.329	.388	86	-3	8			.909	-7	O-34	-1.0
	Yr	117	484	97	108	19	7	3	47	66	60	.223	.319	.310	63	-26	42			.942	1	*O-117	-2.7
1896	Was-N	116	435	87	128	17	6	2	59	58	49	.294	.385	.375	101	3	28			.928	-5	*O-116	-1.0
1897	Was-N	116	469	91	137	17	2	5	45	52		.292	.364	.369	94	-3	25			.928	1	*O-115/M	-0.9
1898	Was-N	16	55	8	9	1	0	0	2	5		.164	.233	.182	19	-6	3			.925	0	O-15/M	-0.6
Total	17	1786	7363	1521	1951	239	138	64	736	748	708	.265	.337	.361	101	8	657			.890	39	*O-1783/P-12	-1.6

■ **TOM BROWN**   Brown, Thomas William   b: 12/12/40, Laureldale, Pa.   BB/TL, 6'1", 190 lbs.   Deb: 4/8/63

1963	Was-A	61	116	8	17	4	0	1	4	11	45	.147	.227	.207	23	-12	2	1	0	1.000	-2	O-16,1-14	-1.6

YEAR	TM/L	G	AB	R	H	2B	3B	HR	RBI	BB	SO	AVG	OBP	SLG	PRO+	BR/A	SB	CS	SBR	FA	FR	G/POS	TPR

■ WILLARD BROWN
Brown, Willard "Big Bill" or "California"
b: 1866, San Francisco, Cal.   d: 12/20/1897, San Francisco, Cal   BR/TR, 6'2", 190 lbs.   Deb: 5/10/1887

YEAR	TM/L	G	AB	R	H	2B	3B	HR	RBI	BB	SO	AVG	OBP	SLG	PRO+	BR/A	SB	CS	SBR	FA	FR	G/POS	TPR
1887	NY-N	49	170	17	37	3	2	0	25	10	15	.218	.273	.259	51	-11	10			.914	-0	C-46/3-3,O-2	-0.6
1888	*NY-N	20	59	4	16	1	0	0	6	1	8	.271	.283	.288	84	-1	1			.893	3	C-20	0.3
1889	*NY-N	40	139	16	36	10	0	1	29	9	9	.259	.318	.353	87	-3	6			.846	-5	C-37/O-3	-0.5
1890	NY-P	60	230	47	64	8	4	4	43	13	13	.278	.320	.400	84	-7	5			.900	-5	C-34,0-13/1-9,32	-0.8
1891	Phi-N	115	441	62	107	20	4	0	50	34	35	.243	.303	.306	75	-14	7			**.989**	5	*1-97,C-19/O-2	-1.2
1893	Bal-N	7	32	5	4	3	0	0	5	1	3	.125	.152	.219	-2	-5	0			.985	-0	/1-7	-0.5
	Lou-N	111	461	80	140	23	7	1	85	50	32	.304	.373	.390	112	9	9			.989	-2	*1-111/C-1	0.3
	Yr	118	493	85	144	26	7	1	90	51	35	.292	.360	.379	104	3	9			**.988**	-2	*1-118/C-1	-0.2
1894	Lou-N	13	48	5	10	2	0	0	9	5	7	.208	.283	.250	32	-5	1			.977	4	1-13	-0.1
	StL-N	3	9	0	1	0	0	0	0	0	2	.111	.111	.111	-46	-2	0			1.000	0	/1-3	-0.1
	Yr	16	57	5	11	2	0	0	9	5	9	.193	.258	.228	19	-8	1			.982	4	1-16	-0.2
Total	7	418	1589	236	415	70	17	6	252	123	124	.261	.319	.338	82	-40	39			.987	-0	1-240,C-157/O32	-3.2

■ WILLARD BROWN
Brown, Willard Jessie   b: 6/26/15, Shreveport, La.   d: 8/8/96, Houston, Tex.   BR/TR, 5'11.5", 200 lbs.   Deb: 7/19/47

YEAR	TM/L	G	AB	R	H	2B	3B	HR	RBI	BB	SO	AVG	OBP	SLG	PRO+	BR/A	SB	CS	SBR	FA	FR	G/POS	TPR
1947	StL-A	21	67	4	12	3	0	1	6	0	7	.179	.179	.269	23	-7	2	2	-1	1.000	0	O-18	-0.9

■ GATES BROWN
Brown, William James   b: 5/2/39, Crestline, O.   BL/TR, 5'11", 220 lbs.   Deb: 6/19/63   C

YEAR	TM/L	G	AB	R	H	2B	3B	HR	RBI	BB	SO	AVG	OBP	SLG	PRO+	BR/A	SB	CS	SBR	FA	FR	G/POS	TPR
1963	Det-A	55	82	16	22	3	1	2	14	8	13	.268	.341	.402	104	1	2	1	0	1.000	4	O-16	0.3
1964	Det-A	123	426	65	116	22	6	15	54	31	53	.272	.328	.458	114	7	11	4	1	.981	8	*O-106	1.1
1965	Det-A	96	227	33	58	14	2	10	43	17	33	.256	.307	.467	115	4	6	0	2	.973	2	O-56	0.6
1966	Det-A	88	169	27	45	5	1	7	27	18	19	.266	.344	.432	119	4	3	0	1	.980	-3	O-43	0.1
1967	Det-A	51	91	17	17	1	1	2	9	13	15	.187	.288	.286	68	-3	0	0	0	1.000	-2	O-20	-0.6
1968	*Det-A	67	92	15	34	7	2	6	15	12	4	.370	.442	.685	231	14	0	0	0	1.000	-1	O-17/1-1	1.4
1969	Det-A	60	93	13	19	1	2	1	6	5	17	.204	.253	.290	49	-6	0	0	0	.906	-1	O-14	-0.7
1970	Det-A	81	124	18	28	3	0	3	24	20	14	.226	.338	.323	82	-2	0	0	0	.950	-1	O-26	-0.5
1971	Det-A	82	195	37	66	3	2	11	29	21	17	.338	.408	.549	163	16	4	2	0	.986	-6	O-56	0.9
1972	*Det-A	103	252	33	58	5	0	10	31	26	28	.230	.307	.369	97	-1	3	0	1	.977	2	O-72	-0.1
1973	Det-A	125	377	48	89	11	1	12	50	52	41	.236	.330	.366	90	-5	1	1	-0	1.000	-1	*D-119/O-2	-0.9
1974	Det-A	73	99	7	24	2	0	4	17	10	15	.242	.312	.384	96	-1	0	0	0	.000	0	D-13	-0.1
1975	Det-A	47	35	1	6	2	0	1	3	9	6	.171	.356	.314	87	-0	0	0	0	.000	0	H	-0.1
Total	13	1051	2262	330	582	78	19	84	322	242	275	.257	.333	.420	109	27	30	8	4	.977	3	O-428,D-132/1-1	1.4

■ BILL BROWN
Brown, William Verna "Verna"   b: 7/8/1893, Coleman, Tex.   d: 5/13/65, Lubbock, Tex.   BL/TL, 5'8", 185 lbs.   Deb: 8/15/12

YEAR	TM/L	G	AB	R	H	2B	3B	HR	RBI	BB	SO	AVG	OBP	SLG	PRO+	BR/A	SB	CS	SBR	FA	FR	G/POS	TPR
1912	StL-A	9	20	0	4	0	0	0	1	0		.200	.200	.200	15	-2	0			.909	-2	/O-7	-0.4

■ BYRON BROWNE
Browne, Byron Ellis   b: 12/27/42, St.Joseph, Mo.   BR/TR, 6'2", 200 lbs.   Deb: 9/9/65

YEAR	TM/L	G	AB	R	H	2B	3B	HR	RBI	BB	SO	AVG	OBP	SLG	PRO+	BR/A	SB	CS	SBR	FA	FR	G/POS	TPR
1965	Chi-N	4	6	0	0	0	0	0	0	0	2	.000	.000	.000	-98	-2	0	0	0	.667	-1	/O-4	-0.3
1966	Chi-N	120	419	46	102	15	7	16	51	40	143	.243	.317	.427	103	2	3	3	-1	.967	-4	*O-114	-0.9
1967	Chi-N	10	19	3	3	2	0	0	2	4	5	.158	.304	.263	61	-1	1	1	-0	1.000	-1	/O-8	-0.3
1968	Hou-N	10	13	0	3	0	0	0	1	4	6	.231	.412	.231	99	0	0	0	0	1.000	2	/O-2	0.2
1969	StL-N	22	53	9	12	0	1	1	7	11	14	.226	.359	.321	92	-0	0	0	0	1.000	3	O-16	0.2
1970	Phi-N	104	270	29	67	17	2	10	36	33	72	.248	.330	.437	107	2	2	-1		.975	-2	O-88	-0.5
1971	Phi-N	58	68	5	14	3	0	3	5	8	23	.206	.289	.382	89	-1	0	0	0	1.000	-8	O-30	-1.1
1972	Phi-N	21	21	2	4	0	0	0	0	1	8	.190	.227	.190	19	-2	0	0	0	1.000	-3	O-9	-0.6
Total	8	349	869	94	205	37	10	30	102	101	273	.236	.319	.405	98	-2	5	6	-2	.973	-16	O-271	-3.3

■ EARL BROWNE
Browne, Earl James "Snitz"   b: 3/5/11, Louisville, Ky.   d: 1/12/93, Whittier, Cal.   BL/TL, 6', 175 lbs.   Deb: 9/12/35

YEAR	TM/L	G	AB	R	H	2B	3B	HR	RBI	BB	SO	AVG	OBP	SLG	PRO+	BR/A	SB	CS	SBR	FA	FR	G/POS	TPR
1935	Pit-N	9	32	6	8	2	0	0	6	2	8	.250	.294	.313	61	-2	0			1.000	0	/1-9	-0.3
1936	Pit-N	8	23	7	7	1	2	0	3	1	4	.304	.333	.522	124	1	0			1.000	0	/O-4,1-1	0.1
1937	Phi-N	105	332	42	97	19	3	6	52	21	41	.292	.342	.422	98	-1	4			.980	1	O-54,1-23	-0.5
1938	Phi-N	21	74	4	19	4	0	0	8	5	11	.257	.304	.311	71	-3	0			.978	-0	1-16/O-2	-0.5
Total	4	143	461	59	131	26	5	6	69	29	64	.284	.332	.401	93	-5	4			.983	1	/O-60,1-49	-1.2

■ GEORGE BROWNE
Browne, George Edward   b: 1/12/1876, Richmond, Va.   d: 12/9/20, Hyde Park, N.Y.   BL/TR, 5'10.5", 160 lbs.   Deb: 9/27/01

YEAR	TM/L	G	AB	R	H	2B	3B	HR	RBI	BB	SO	AVG	OBP	SLG	PRO+	BR/A	SB	CS	SBR	FA	FR	G/POS	TPR
1901	Phi-N	8	26	2	5	1	0	0	4	0	1	.192	.250	.231	39	-2	2			1.000	-1	/O-8	-0.4
1902	Phi-N	70	281	41	73	7	1	0	26	16		.260	.304	.292	84	-5	11			.910	8	O-70	-0.3
	NY-N	53	216	30	69	9	5	0	14	9		.319	.355	.407	136	8	13			.895	-0	O-53	0.5
	Yr	123	497	71	142	16	6	0	40	25		.286	.326	.342	106	3	24			.904	7	O-123	0.2
1903	NY-N	141	591	105	185	20	3	6	45	43		.313	.364	.372	106	4	27			.918	-4	O-141	-0.8
1904	NY-N	150	596	99	169	16	5	4	39	39		.284	.332	.347	105	3	24			.925	-5	*O-149	-1.2
1905	*NY-N	127	536	95	157	16	14	4	43	20		.293	.321	.397	111	5	26			.915	-9	*O-127	-1.0
1906	NY-N	122	477	61	126	16	0	0	38	27		.264	.304	.302	87	-8	32			.934	-5	O-121	-2.1
1907	NY-N	127	458	54	119	11	10	5	37	31		.260	.308	.360	106	2	15			.941	-9	O-121	-1.4
1908	Bos-N	138	536	61	122	10	6	1	34	36		.228	.276	.274	77	-14	17			.950	4	O-138	-1.9
1909	Chi-N	12	39	7	8	0	1	0	1	5		.205	.295	.256	70	-1	3			.944	-2	O-12	-0.4
	Was-A	103	393	40	107	15	5	1	16	17		.272	.308	.344	111	3	13			.935	-2	O-101	-0.4
1910	Was-A	7	22	1	4	0	0	0	0	1		.182	.217	.182	26	-2	0			.667	-2	/O-5	-0.4
	Chi-A	30	112	17	27	4	1	0	4	12		.241	.315	.295	95	-0	5			.952	-4	O-29	-0.6
	Yr	37	134	18	31	4	1	0	4	13		.231	.299	.276	84	-2	5			.917	-5	/O-34	-1.0
1911	Bro-N	8	12	1	4	0	0	0	2	1	1	.333	.385	.333	106	0	2			1.000	-0	/O-2	0.0
1912	Phi-N	5	5	0	1	0	0	0	0	0	0	.200	.333	.200	45	-0	0			.000	0	H	0.0
Total	12	1102	4300	614	1176	119	55	18	303	259	1	.273	.318	.339	100	-8	190			.927	-32	*O-1077	-10.4

■ JERRY BROWNE
Browne, Jerome Austin   b: 2/13/66, Christiansted, V.I.   BB/TR, 5'10", 170 lbs.   Deb: 9/6/86

YEAR	TM/L	G	AB	R	H	2B	3B	HR	RBI	BB	SO	AVG	OBP	SLG	PRO+	BR/A	SB	CS	SBR	FA	FR	G/POS	TPR
1986	Tex-A	12	24	6	10	2	0	0	3	1		.417	.440	.500	151	2	0	2	-1	.923	-1	/2-8	0.0
1987	Tex-A	132	454	63	123	16	6	1	38	61	50	.271	.360	.339	87	-7	27	17	-2	.980	-17	*2-130/D-1	-1.9
1988	Tex-A	73	214	26	49	9	2	1	17	25	32	.229	.310	.304	71	-8	7	5	-1	.958	-25	2-70/D-1	-3.2
1989	Cle-A	153	598	83	179	31	4	5	45	68	64	.299	.372	.390	113	12	14	6	1	.979	-48	*2-151/D-2	-3.1
1990	Cle-A	140	513	92	137	26	5	6	50	72	46	.267	.359	.372	105	6	12	7	-1	.985	-21	*2-139	-1.3
1991	Cle-A	107	290	28	66	5	2	1	29	27	29	.228	.296	.259	57	-16	2	4	-2	.964	-10	2-47,O-17,3-15/D-7	-2.7
1992	*Oak-A	111	324	43	93	12	2	3	40	40	40	.287	.372	.364	113	7	3	3	-1	.965	-1	3-58,O-43,2-19/SD	-0.6
1993	Oak-A	76	260	27	65	13	0	2	19	22	17	.250	.309	.323	74	-9	4	0	1	.985	-4	O-56,3-13/2-3,1-2	-1.3
1994	Fla-N	101	329	42	97	17	4	3	30	52	23	.295	.394	.398	104	4	3	0	1	.931	-7	3-62,O-30,2-15	-0.2
1995	Fla-N	77	184	21	47	4	0	1	17	25	20	.255	.348	.293	71	-7	1	1	-0	.959	6	O-29,2-27/3-7	-0.4
Total	10	982	3190	431	866	135	25	23	288	393	325	.271	.354	.351	94	-16	73	45	-5	.977	-138	2-609,O-175,3/D1S	-14.4

■ PIDGE BROWNE
Browne, Prentice Almont   b: 3/21/29, Peekskill, N.Y.   BL/TL, 6'1", 190 lbs.   Deb: 4/13/62

YEAR	TM/L	G	AB	R	H	2B	3B	HR	RBI	BB	SO	AVG	OBP	SLG	PRO+	BR/A	SB	CS	SBR	FA	FR	G/POS	TPR
1962	Hou-N	65	100	8	21	4	2	1	10	13	9	.210	.301	.320	72	-4	0	0	0	.983	1	1-26	-0.4

■ PETE BROWNING
Browning, Louis Rogers "The Gladiator"   b: 6/17/1861, Louisville, Ky.   d: 9/10/05, Louisville, Ky.   BR/TR, 6', 180 lbs.   Deb: 5/2/1882

YEAR	TM/L	G	AB	R	H	2B	3B	HR	RBI	BB	SO	AVG	OBP	SLG	PRO+	BR/A	SB	CS	SBR	FA	FR	G/POS	TPR
1882	Lou-a	69	288	67	109	17	3	5		26		.378	.430	.510	229	40				.890	12	2-42,S-18,3-13	4.7
1883	Lou-a	84	358	95	121	15	9	4		23		.338	.378	.464	183	34				.861	-8	O-48,S-26,3-10/21	2.3
1884	Lou-a	103	447	101	150	33	4	4	47	13		.336	.357	.472	176	36				.806	-9	3-52,O-24,1-23/2P	2.1
1885	Lou-a	112	481	98	174	34	10	9	73	25		.362	.393	.530	190	47				.900	5	*O-112	4.3
1886	Lou-a	112	467	86	159	29	6	2	68	30		.340	.389	.441	151	25	26			.791	-10	*O-112	1.1
1887	Lou-a	134	547	137	220	35	16	4	118	55		.402	.464	.547	178	58	103			.868	-3	*O-134	4.2
1888	Lou-a	99	383	58	120	22	8	3	72	37		.313	.380	.436	164	28	36			.888	-1	*O-99	2.2
1889	Lou-a	83	324	39	83	19	5	2	32	34	30	.256	.327	.364	98	-1	21			.882	-3	*O-83	-0.5
1890	Cle-P	118	493	112	184	**40**	8	5	93	75	36	**.373**	.459	.517	**175**	57	35			.893	4	*O-118	4.5

YEAR	TM/L	G	AB	R	H	2B	3B	HR	RBI	BB	SO	AVG	OBP	SLG	PRO+	BR/A	SB	CS	SBR	FA	FR	G/POS	TPR
1891	Pit-N	50	203	35	59	14	1	4	28	27	31	.291	.377	.429	138	10	4			.904	5	O-50	1.2
	Cin-N	55	216	29	74	10	3	0	33	24	23	.343	.413	.417	141	12	12			.924	-1	O-55	0.8
	Yr	105	419	64	133	24	4	4	61	51	54	.317	.395	.422	139	22	16			.913	5	*O-105	2.0
1892	Lou-N	21	77	10	19	4	0	0	4	12	7	.247	.348	.299	104	1	5			.911	-1	O-21	-0.1
	Cin-N	83	307	47	93	12	5	3	52	40	25	.303	.383	.404	140	16	8			.917	-2	O-82/1-2	0.9
	Yr	104	384	57	112	16	5	3	56	52	32	.292	.376	.383	133	17	13			.916	-3	O-103/1-2	0.8
1893	Lou-N	57	220	38	78	11	3	1	37	44	15	.355	.466	.445	155	21	8			.881	-3	O-57	1.2
1894	StL-N	2	7	1	1	0	0	0	0	0	0	.143	.143	.143	-31	-1	0			1.000	-0	/O-2	-0.2
	Bro-N	1	2	1	2	0	0	0	2	1	0	1.000	1.000	1.000	413	1	0			1.000	-0	/O-1	0.1
	Yr	3	9	2	3	0	0	0	2	1	0	.333	.400	.333	80	-0	0			1.000	-1	/O-3	-0.1
Total	13	1183	4820	954	1646	295	85	46	659	466	167	.341	.403	.467	164	384	258			.883	-16	O-998/3-75,2S1P	28.8

■ BILL BRUBAKER
Brubaker, Wilbur Lee b: 11/7/10, Cleveland, Ohio d: 4/2/78, Laguna Hills, Cal. BR/TR, 6'2", 185 lbs. Deb: 9/8/32 F

YEAR	TM/L	G	AB	R	H	2B	3B	HR	RBI	BB	SO	AVG	OBP	SLG	PRO+	BR/A	SB	CS	SBR	FA	FR	G/POS	TPR
1932	Pit-N	7	24	3	10	3	0	0	4	3	4	.417	.481	.542	178	3	1			.909	-0	/3-7	0.3
1933	Pit-N	2	2	0	0	0	0	0	0	0	0	.000	.000	.000	-99	-1	0			1.000	-0	/3-1	0.0
1934	Pit-N	3	6	0	2	0	0	0	1	1	0	.333	.429	.500	144	0	0			1.000	1	/3-3	0.1
1935	Pit-N	6	11	1	0	0	0	0	0	2	5	.000	.154	.000	-53	-2	0			.889	-0	/3-5	-0.3
1936	Pit-N	145	554	77	160	27	4	6	102	50	96	.289	.352	.384	96	-2	5			.940	-15	*3-145	-1.2
1937	Pit-N	120	413	57	105	20	4	6	48	47	51	.254	.335	.420	90	-5	2			.952	1	*3-115/S-3,1-1	0.0
1938	Pit-N	45	112	18	33	5	0	3	19	9	14	.295	.347	.420	109	1	2			.875	-1	3-18/1-9,S-3,0-1	0.0
1939	Pit-N	100	345	41	80	23	1	7	43	29	51	.232	.297	.365	78	-11	3			.950	10	2-65,3-32/S-1	0.2
1940	Pit-N	38	78	8	15	3	1	0	7	8	16	.192	.267	.256	45	-6	0			.955	6	3-19/S-8,1-4	0.0
1943	Bos-N	13	19	3	8	3	0	1	1	2	2	.421	.476	.579	207	3	0			.778	-1	/3-5,1-3	0.2
Total	10	479	1564	208	413	85	10	22	225	151	239	.264	.333	.373	90	-20	13			.938	2	3-350/2-65,1-17,SO	-0.7

■ LOU BRUCE
Bruce, Louis R. b: 1/16/1877, St.Regis, N.Y. d: 2/9/68, Ilion, N.Y. BL/TR, 5'5", 145 lbs. Deb: 6/22/04

YEAR	TM/L	G	AB	R	H	2B	3B	HR	RBI	BB	SO	AVG	OBP	SLG	PRO+	BR/A	SB	CS	SBR	FA	FR	G/POS	TPR
1904	Phi-A	30	101	9	27	3	0	0		8	5	.267	.302	.297	85	-2	2			.969	-2	O-25/P-2,2-1,3-1	-0.6

■ EARLE BRUCKER
Brucker, Earle Francis Jr. b: 8/29/25, Los Angeles, Cal. BL/TR, 6'2", 210 lbs. Deb: 10/2/48 F

YEAR	TM/L	G	AB	R	H	2B	3B	HR	RBI	BB	SO	AVG	OBP	SLG	PRO+	BR/A	SB	CS	SBR	FA	FR	G/POS	TPR
1948	Phi-A	2	6	0	1	1	0	0	0	1	1	.167	.286	.333	64	-0	0	0	0	1.000	-0	/C-2	-0.1

■ EARLE BRUCKER
Brucker, Earle Francis Sr. b: 5/6/01, Albany, N.Y. d: 5/8/81, San Diego, Cal. BR/TR, 5'11", 175 lbs. Deb: 4/19/37 FMC

YEAR	TM/L	G	AB	R	H	2B	3B	HR	RBI	BB	SO	AVG	OBP	SLG	PRO+	BR/A	SB	CS	SBR	FA	FR	G/POS	TPR
1937	Phi-A	102	317	40	82	16	5	6	37	48	30	.259	.356	.397	91	-4	1	2	-1	.971	-6	C-92	-0.6
1938	Phi-A	53	171	26	64	21	1	3	35	19	16	.374	.437	.561	152	14	1	1	-0	.986	-2	C-44/1-1	1.3
1939	Phi-A	62	172	18	50	15	1	3	31	24	16	.291	.381	.442	112	3	0	1	-1	1.000	-5	C-47	0.0
1940	Phi-A	23	46	3	9	1	1	0	2	6	3	.196	.288	.261	44	-0	0	0	0	.966	2	C-13	-0.1
1943	Phi-A	1	1	0	0	0	0	0	0	0	0	.000	.000	.000	-99	-0	0	0	0	.000	0	H	0.0
Total	5	241	707	87	205	53	8	12	105	97	65	.290	.376	.438	108	9	2	4	-2	.980	-11	C-196/1-1	0.6

■ J. T. BRUETT
Bruett, Joseph Timothy b: 10/8/67, Milwaukee, Wis. BL/TL, 5'11", 175 lbs. Deb: 6/3/92

YEAR	TM/L	G	AB	R	H	2B	3B	HR	RBI	BB	SO	AVG	OBP	SLG	PRO+	BR/A	SB	CS	SBR	FA	FR	G/POS	TPR
1992	Min-A	56	76	7	19	4	0	0	2	6	12	.250	.313	.303	71	-3	6	3	0	.979	-12	O-45/D-3	-1.6
1993	Min-A	17	20	2	5	2	0	0	1	1	4	.250	.318	.350	79	-1	0	0	0	.857	-4	O-13	-0.5
Total	2	73	96	9	24	6	0	0	3	7	16	.250	.314	.313	73	-3	6	3	0	.952	-16	/O-58,D-3	-2.1

■ FRANK BRUGGY
Bruggy, Frank Leo b: 5/4/1891, Elizabeth, N.J. d: 4/5/59, Elizabeth, N.J. BR/TR, 5'11", 195 lbs. Deb: 4/13/21

YEAR	TM/L	G	AB	R	H	2B	3B	HR	RBI	BB	SO	AVG	OBP	SLG	PRO+	BR/A	SB	CS	SBR	FA	FR	G/POS	TPR
1921	Phi-N	96	277	28	86	11	2	5	28	23	37	.310	.370	.419	100	1	6	2	1	.953	-9	C-86/1-2	-0.3
1922	Phi-A	53	111	10	31	7	0	0	9	6	11	.279	.322	.342	71	-5	1	2	-1	.925	-2	C-31	-0.6
1923	Phi-A	54	105	4	22	3	0	1	6	4	9	.210	.245	.267	34	-10	1	1	-0	.950	-1	C-34/1-5	-0.9
1924	Phi-A	50	113	9	30	6	0	0	8	8	15	.265	.314	.319	63	-6	4	0	1	.928	-8	C-44	-1.0
1925	Cin-N	6	14	2	3	0	0	0	1	2	0	.214	.313	.214	38	-1	0	0	0	.870	-1	/C-6	-0.1
Total	5	259	620	53	172	27	2	6	52	43	72	.277	.329	.356	76	-22	12	5	1	.941	-18	C-201/1-7	-2.9

■ JACOB BRUMFIELD
Brumfield, Jacob Donnell b: 5/27/65, Bogalusa, La. BR/TR, 6', 170 lbs. Deb: 4/6/92

YEAR	TM/L	G	AB	R	H	2B	3B	HR	RBI	BB	SO	AVG	OBP	SLG	PRO+	BR/A	SB	CS	SBR	FA	FR	G/POS	TPR
1992	Cin-N	24	30	6	4	0	0	0	2	2	4	.133	.212	.133	-0	-4	6	0	2	1.000	-2	O-16	-0.4
1993	Cin-N	103	272	40	73	17	3	6	23	21	47	.268	.323	.419	97	-2	20	8	1	.978	-5	O-96/2-4	-0.7
1994	Cin-N	68	122	36	38	10	2	4	11	15	18	.311	.387	.525	136	7	6	3	0	.987	-3	O-43	0.3
1995	Pit-N	116	402	64	109	23	4	4	26	37	71	.271	.340	.368	85	-8	22	12	-1	.969	7	*O-104	-0.5
1996	Pit-N	29	80	11	20	9	0	2	8	5	17	.250	.294	.438	87	-2	3	1	0	.946	-2	O-22	-0.4
	Tor-N	90	308	52	79	19	2	12	52	24	58	.256	.318	.448	90	-5	12	3	2	.982	-3	O-83/D-5	-0.8
Total	5	430	1214	209	323	78	9	28	122	104	215	.266	.330	.414	92	-14	69	27	5	.976	-9	O-364/D-5,2-4	-2.5

■ MIKE BRUMLEY
Brumley, Anthony Michael b: 4/9/63, Oklahoma City, Okla. BB/TR, 5'10", 165 lbs. Deb: 6/16/87 F

YEAR	TM/L	G	AB	R	H	2B	3B	HR	RBI	BB	SO	AVG	OBP	SLG	PRO+	BR/A	SB	CS	SBR	FA	FR	G/POS	TPR
1987	Chi-N	39	104	8	21	2	2	1	9	10	30	.202	.278	.288	49	-7	8	1	2	.965	4	S-34/2-1	0.0
1989	Det-A	92	212	33	42	5	2	1	11	14	45	.198	.251	.255	44	-16	8	4	0	.980	-8	S-42,2-24,3-11,/OD	-2.1
1990	Sea-A	62	147	19	33	5	4	0	9	10	22	.224	.274	.313	63	-7	2	0	1	.983	-1	S-47/2-6,3-3,0-2,D	-0.5
1991	Bos-A	63	118	16	25	5	0	0	5	10	22	.212	.273	.254	45	-9	2	0	1	.950	15	S-31,3-17/2-7,0D	0.8
1992	Bos-A	2	1	0	0	0	0	0	0	0	0	.000	.000	.000	-94	-0	0	0	0	.000	0	/H	0.0
1993	Hou-N	8	10	1	3	0	0	0	2	1	3	.300	.364	.300	83	-0	0	1	-1	.000	0	/3-1,S-1,O-1	-0.2
1994	Oak-A	11	25	0	6	0	0	0	2	1	8	.240	.269	.240	36	-2	0	0	0	.929	-3	/2-4,3-4,0-3,S-1	-0.5
1995	Hou-N	18	18	1	1	0	0	1	0	0	6	.056	.056	.222	-33	-4	1	0	0	1.000	-1	/S-3,0-3,1-1,3-1	-0.4
Total	8	295	635	78	131	17	8	3	38	46	136	.206	.262	.272	47	-46	20	6	2	.972	5	S-159/2-42,3OD1	-2.9

■ MIKE BRUMLEY
Brumley, Tony Mike b: 7/10/38, Granite, Okla. BL/TR, 5'10", 195 lbs. Deb: 4/18/64 F

YEAR	TM/L	G	AB	R	H	2B	3B	HR	RBI	BB	SO	AVG	OBP	SLG	PRO+	BR/A	SB	CS	SBR	FA	FR	G/POS	TPR
1964	Was-A	136	426	36	104	19	2	4	35	40	54	.244	.310	.312	74	-14	1	1	-0	.991	-13	*C-132	-2.3
1965	Was-A	79	216	15	45	4	0	3	15	20	33	.208	.282	.269	58	-12	1	1	-0	.990	2	C-66	-0.8
1966	Was-A	9	18	1	2	1	0	0	0	0	2	.111	.111	.167	-22	-3	0	0	0	1.000	-1	/C-7	-0.4
Total	3	224	660	52	151	24	2	5	50	60	89	.229	.296	.294	67	-29	2	2	-1	.991	-12	C-205	-3.5

■ GLENN BRUMMER
Brummer, Glenn Edward b: 11/23/54, Olney, Ill. BR/TR, 6', 200 lbs. Deb: 5/25/81

YEAR	TM/L	G	AB	R	H	2B	3B	HR	RBI	BB	SO	AVG	OBP	SLG	PRO+	BR/A	SB	CS	SBR	FA	FR	G/POS	TPR
1981	StL-N	21	30	2	6	1	0	0	2	1	3	.200	.226	.233		-3	0	0	0	1.000	2	C-19	-0.1
1982	*StL-N	35	64	4	15	4	0	0	8	0	12	.234	.234	.297	47	-5	2	0	1	.970	3	C-32	0.0
1983	StL-N	45	87	7	24	7	0	0	9	10	11	.276	.351	.356	96	-0	1	3	-2	.978	5	C-41	0.0
1984	StL-N	28	58	3	12	1	0	0	3	3	7	.207	.246	.259	43	-4	0	0	0	.973	4	C-26	0.0
1985	Tex-A	49	108	7	30	3	0	1	5	11	22	.278	.355	.315	84	-2	1	5	-3	.989	-4	C-47/O-1,D-1	-0.7
Total	5	178	347	23	87	16	0	1	27	25	54	.251	.305	.305	70	-14	4	8	-4	.981	10	C-165/D-1,O-1	-0.8

■ TOM BRUNANSKY
Brunansky, Thomas Andrew b: 8/20/60, Covina, Cal. BR/TR, 6'4", 211 lbs. Deb: 4/9/81

YEAR	TM/L	G	AB	R	H	2B	3B	HR	RBI	BB	SO	AVG	OBP	SLG	PRO+	BR/A	SB	CS	SBR	FA	FR	G/POS	TPR
1981	Cal-A	11	33	7	5	0	0	3	6	8	10	.152	.317	.424	112	1	1	0	0	.938	3	O-11	0.3
1982	Min-A	127	463	77	126	30	1	20	46	71	101	.272	.378	.471	128	19	1	2	-1	.986	13	*O-127	2.7
1983	Min-A	151	542	70	123	24	5	28	82	61	95	.227	.310	.445	101	0	2	5	-2	.985	18	*O-146/D-4	1.1
1984	Min-A	155	567	75	144	21	0	32	85	57	94	.254	.322	.460	109	5	4	5	-2	.984	5	*O-153/D-1	0.4
1985	Min-A★	157	567	71	137	28	4	27	90	71	86	.242	.326	.448	103	2	5	3	-0	.984	5	*O-155	0.4
1986	Min-A	157	593	69	152	28	1	23	75	53	98	.256	.318	.423	97	-3	12	4	1	.982	8	*O-152/D-2	0.1
1987	*Min-A	155	532	83	138	22	2	32	85	74	104	.259	.354	.489	116	12	11	11	-3	.990	-2	*O-138,D-17	0.2
1988	Min-A	14	49	5	9	1	0	1	6	7	11	.184	.286	.265	54	-3	1	2	-1	.864	9	O-13/D-1	-0.7
	StL-N	143	523	69	128	22	4	22	79	79	82	.245	.348	.428	121	15	16	6	1	**.996**	4	*O-143	1.7
1989	StL-N	158	556	67	133	29	3	20	85	59	107	.239	.314	.410	102	1	5	9	-4	.977	-5	*O-155/1-1	-0.3
1990	StL-N	19	57	5	9	3	0	1	2	12	10	.158	.314	.263	60	-3	0	0	0	.950	1	O-17	-0.2
	*Bos-A	129	461	61	123	24	5	15	71	54	105	.267	.347	.438	113	8	5	10	-5	.982	10	*O-121/D-7	1.0
1991	Bos-A	142	459	54	105	24	1	16	70	49	72	.229	.307	.390	87	-9	1	2	-1	.989	3	*O-137/D-1	-1.0
1992	Bos-A	138	458	47	122	31	3	15	74	66	96	.266	.359	.445	116	10	2	5	-2	.980	3	O-92,1-28,D-17	0.7
1993	Mil-A	80	224	20	41	7	3	6	29	25	59	.183	.265	.321	58	-14	3	4	-2	.987	1	O-71/D-6	-1.6

YEAR	TM/L	G	AB	R	H	2B	3B	HR	RBI	BB	SO	AVG	OBP	SLG	PRO+	BR/A	SB	CS	SBR	FA	FR	G/POS	TPR
1994	Mil-A	16	28	2	6	2	0	0	0	1	9	.214	.241	.286	34	-3	0	0	0	1.000	-3	/O-6,1-2,D-2	-0.5
	Bos-A	48	177	22	42	10	1	10	34	23	48	.237	.325	.475	98	-1	0	2	-1	.989	-3	O-42/1-5,D-3	-0.6
	Yr	64	205	24	48	12	1	10	34	24	57	.234	.314	.449	90	-4	0	2	-1	.989	-5	O-48/1-7,D-5	-1.1
Total	14	1800	6289	804	1543	306	33	271	919	770	1187	.245	.331	.434	105	39	69	70	-21	.984	65	*O-1679/D-61,1-36	3.5

■ ARLO BRUNSBERG
Brunsberg, Arlo Adolph   b: 8/15/40, Fertile, Minn.   BL/TR, 6', 195 lbs.   Deb: 9/23/66

YEAR	TM/L	G	AB	R	H	2B	3B	HR	RBI	BB	SO	AVG	OBP	SLG	PRO+	BR/A	SB	CS	SBR	FA	FR	G/POS	TPR
1966	Det-A	2	3	1	1	1	0	0	0	0	0	.333	.500	.667	227	1	0	0	0	1.000	-1	/C-2	0.0

■ BOB BRUSH
Brush, Robert   b: 3/8/1875, Osage, Iowa   d: 4/2/44, San Bernardino, Cal.   Deb: 4/20/07

YEAR	TM/L	G	AB	R	H	2B	3B	HR	RBI	BB	SO	AVG	OBP	SLG	PRO+	BR/A	SB	CS	SBR	FA	FR	G/POS	TPR
1907	Bos-N	2	2	0	0	0	0	0	0	0	0	.000	.000	.000	-99	-0				1.000	-0	/1-1	-0.1

■ BILL BRUTON
Bruton, William Haron   b: 12/22/25, Panola, Ala.   d: 12/5/95, Marshalltown, Del.   BL/TR, 6'0.5", 169 lbs.   Deb: 4/13/53

YEAR	TM/L	G	AB	R	H	2B	3B	HR	RBI	BB	SO	AVG	OBP	SLG	PRO+	BR/A	SB	CS	SBR	FA	FR	G/POS	TPR
1953	Mil-N	151	613	82	153	18	14	1	41	44	100	.250	.306	.330	70	-27	**26**	11	1	.979	8	*O-150	-2.3
1954	Mil-N	142	567	89	161	20	7	4	30	40	78	.284	.336	.365	88	-11	**34**	13	2	.981	1	*O-141	-1.3
1955	Mil-N	149	636	106	175	30	12	9	47	43	72	.275	.325	.403	97	-4	**25**	11	1	.968	15	*O-149	0.4
1956	Mil-N	147	525	73	143	23	**15**	8	56	26	63	.272	.308	.419	99	-3	8	6	-1	.969	4	*O-145	-0.9
1957	Mil-N	79	306	41	85	16	9	5	30	19	35	.278	.322	.438	110	3	11	4	1	.981	1	O-79	0.0
1958	*Mil-N	100	325	47	91	11	3	3	28	27	37	.280	.339	.360	93	-4	4	1	1	.977	-7	O-96	-1.4
1959	Mil-N	133	478	72	138	22	6	6	41	35	54	.289	.339	.397	104	1	13	5	1	.991	4	*O-133	0.0
1960	Mil-N	151	629	**112**	180	27	**13**	12	54	41	97	.286	.332	.428	115	10	22	13	-1	.986	4	*O-149	0.5
1961	Det-A	160	596	99	153	15	5	17	63	61	66	.257	.329	.384	87	-11	22	6	3	.988	12	*O-155	-0.5
1962	Det-A	147	561	90	156	27	5	16	74	55	67	.278	.348	.430	104	3	14	7	0	.983	19	*O-145	1.4
1963	Det-A	145	524	84	134	21	8	8	48	59	70	.256	.331	.372	93	-4	14	7	0	.991	10	*O-138	-0.1
1964	Det-A	106	296	42	82	11	5	5	33	32	54	.277	.348	.399	105	3	14	5	1	.987	-1	O-81	0.0
Total	12	1610	6056	937	1651	241	102	94	545	482	793	.273	.329	.393	96	-43	207	89	9	.981	68	*O-1561	-4.2

■ ED BRUYETTE
Bruyette, Edward T.   b: 8/31/1874, Manawa, Wis.   d: 8/5/40, Peshastin, Wash.   BL/TR, 5'10", 170 lbs.   Deb: 8/6/01

YEAR	TM/L	G	AB	R	H	2B	3B	HR	RBI	BB	SO	AVG	OBP	SLG	PRO+	BR/A	SB	CS	SBR	FA	FR	G/POS	TPR
1901	Mil-A	26	82	7	15	3	0	0	4	12		.183	.295	.220	46	-5	1			.778	-6	O-21/2-3,S-1,3-1	-1.2

■ BILLY BRYAN
Bryan, William Ronald   b: 12/4/38, Morgan, Ga.   BL/TR, 6'4", 200 lbs.   Deb: 9/12/61

YEAR	TM/L	G	AB	R	H	2B	3B	HR	RBI	BB	SO	AVG	OBP	SLG	PRO+	BR/A	SB	CS	SBR	FA	FR	G/POS	TPR
1961	KC-A	9	19	2	3	0	0	1	2	2	7	.158	.238	.316	46	-2	0	0	0	1.000	-2	/C-4	-0.3
1962	KC-A	25	74	5	11	2	1	2	7	5	32	.149	.203	.284	28	-8	0	0	0	.976	-3	C-22	-1.0
1963	KC-A	24	65	11	11	1	1	3	7	9	22	.169	.270	.354	69	-3	0	0	0	.981	5	C-24	0.3
1964	KC-A	93	220	19	53	9	2	13	36	16	69	.241	.292	.477	107	1	0	0	0	.991	-9	C-65	-0.6
1965	KC-A	108	325	36	82	11	5	14	51	29	87	.252	.317	.446	116	6	0	0	0	.984	-6	C-95	-0.6
1966	KC-A	32	76	0	10	4	0	0	7	6	17	.132	.195	.184	10	-9	0	0	0	.965	-1	C-21/1-3	-1.0
	NY-A	27	69	5	15	2	0	4	5	5	19	.217	.270	.420	99	-0	0	0	0	.988	-0	C-14/1-3	0.0
	Yr	59	145	5	25	6	0	4	12	11	36	.172	.231	.297	52	-9	0	0	0	.975	-2	C-35/1-6	-1.0
1967	NY-A	16	12	1	2	0	0	1	2	5	3	.167	.412	.417	151	1	0	0	0	1.000	1	/C-1	0.2
1968	Was-A	40	108	7	22	3	0	3	8	14	27	.204	.301	.315	90	-1	0	1	-1	.983	-4	C-28	-0.4
Total	8	374	968	86	209	32	9	41	125	91	283	.216	.285	.395	91	-14	0	1	-1	.984	-18	C-274/1-6	-2.2

■ DEREK BRYANT
Bryant, Derek Roszell   b: 10/9/51, Lexington, Ky.   BR/TR, 5'11", 185 lbs.   Deb: 4/24/79

YEAR	TM/L	G	AB	R	H	2B	3B	HR	RBI	BB	SO	AVG	OBP	SLG	PRO+	BR/A	SB	CS	SBR	FA	FR	G/POS	TPR
1979	Oak-A	39	106	8	19	3	1	0	13	10	10	.179	.250	.217	29	-11	0	0	0	1.000	-2	O-33/D-2	-1.3

■ DON BRYANT
Bryant, Donald Ray   b: 7/13/41, Jasper, Fla.   BR/TR, 6'5", 200 lbs.   Deb: 7/17/66   C

YEAR	TM/L	G	AB	R	H	2B	3B	HR	RBI	BB	SO	AVG	OBP	SLG	PRO+	BR/A	SB	CS	SBR	FA	FR	G/POS	TPR
1966	Chi-N	13	26	2	8	2	0	0	4	1	4	.308	.357	.385	105	0	1	0	0	.978	0	C-10	0.1
1969	Hou-N	31	59	2	11	1	0	1	6	4	13	.186	.250	.254	42	-5	0	0	0	.993	3	C-28	-0.1
1970	Hou-N	15	24	2	5	0	0	0	3	1	8	.208	.240	.208	22	-3	0	0	0	.957	-0	C-13	-0.3
Total	3	59	109	6	24	3	0	1	13	6	25	.220	.274	.275	53	-7	1	0	0	.983	3	/C-51	-0.3

■ GEORGE BRYANT
Bryant, George F.   b: 2/10/1857, Bridgeport, Conn.   d: 6/12/07, Boston, Mass.   Deb: 8/6/1885

YEAR	TM/L	G	AB	R	H	2B	3B	HR	RBI	BB	SO	AVG	OBP	SLG	PRO+	BR/A	SB	CS	SBR	FA	FR	G/POS	TPR
1885	Det-N	1	4	0	0	0	0	0	1	0	2	.000	.000	.000	-99	-1				1.000	-1	/2-1	-0.2

■ RALPH BRYANT
Bryant, Ralph Wendell   b: 5/20/61, Fort Gaines, Ga.   BL/TR, 6'2", 200 lbs.   Deb: 9/8/85

YEAR	TM/L	G	AB	R	H	2B	3B	HR	RBI	BB	SO	AVG	OBP	SLG	PRO+	BR/A	SB	CS	SBR	FA	FR	G/POS	TPR
1985	LA-N	6	6	0	2	0	0	0	0	0	2	.333	.333	.333	90	-0	0	0	0	.000	-1	/O-3	-0.1
1986	LA-N	27	75	15	19	4	2	6	13	5	25	.253	.309	.600	156	5	0	1	-1	.953	-1	O-26	0.3
1987	LA-N	46	69	7	17	2	1	2	10	10	24	.246	.350	.391	99	-0	2	1	0	.917	-3	O-19	-0.4
Total	3	79	150	22	38	6	3	8	24	15	51	.253	.329	.493	125	5	2	2	-1	.940	-5	/O-48	-0.2

■ STEVE BRYE
Brye, Stephen Robert   b: 2/4/49, Alameda, Cal.   BR/TR, 6', 190 lbs.   Deb: 9/3/70

YEAR	TM/L	G	AB	R	H	2B	3B	HR	RBI	BB	SO	AVG	OBP	SLG	PRO+	BR/A	SB	CS	SBR	FA	FR	G/POS	TPR
1970	Min-A	9	11	1	2	1	0	0	0	2	4	.182	.308	.273	60	-1	0	0	0	1.000	-2	/O-6	-0.2
1971	Min-A	28	107	10	24	1	0	3	11	7	15	.224	.272	.318	65	-5	3	1	0	.966	1	O-28	-0.6
1972	Min-A	100	253	18	61	9	3	0	12	17	38	.241	.292	.300	73	-8	3	1	0	.994	2	O-93	-1.0
1973	Min-A	92	278	39	73	9	5	6	33	35	43	.263	.345	.396	104	2	3	5	-2	.986	1	O-87/D-1	-0.3
1974	Min-A	135	488	52	138	32	1	2	41	22	59	.283	.320	.365	94	-4	1	3	-2	**.997**	1	*O-129	-1.1
1975	Min-A	86	246	41	62	13	1	9	34	21	37	.252	.316	.423	106	1	2	1	0	.983	-3	O-72/D-6	-0.4
1976	Min-A	87	258	33	68	11	0	2	23	13	31	.264	.299	.329	82	-6	1	2	-1	.987	-13	O-78/D-3	-2.4
1977	Mil-A	94	241	27	60	14	3	7	28	16	39	.249	.298	.419	93	-3	1	0	0	1.000	-1	O-83/D-6	-0.6
1978	Pit-N	66	115	16	27	7	0	1	9	11	10	.235	.307	.322	73	-4	2	1	0	.983	-6	O-47	-1.2
Total	9	697	1997	237	515	97	13	30	193	144	276	.258	.311	.365	90	-29	16	14	-4	.991	-19	O-623/D-16	-7.8

■ HAL BUBSER
Bubser, Harold Fred   b: 9/28/1895, Chicago, Ill.   d: 6/22/59, Melrose Park, Ill   BR/TR, 5'11", 170 lbs.   Deb: 4/15/22

YEAR	TM/L	G	AB	R	H	2B	3B	HR	RBI	BB	SO	AVG	OBP	SLG	PRO+	BR/A	SB	CS	SBR	FA	FR	G/POS	TPR
1922	Chi-A	3	3	0	0	0	0	0	0	0	2	.000	.000	.000	-99	-1	0	0	0	.000	0	H	-0.1

■ JOHNNY BUCHA
Bucha, John George   b: 1/22/25, Allentown, Pa.   d: 4/28/96, Bethlehem, Pa.   BR/TR, 5'11", 190 lbs.   Deb: 5/2/48

YEAR	TM/L	G	AB	R	H	2B	3B	HR	RBI	BB	SO	AVG	OBP	SLG	PRO+	BR/A	SB	CS	SBR	FA	FR	G/POS	TPR
1948	StL-N	2	1	0	0	0	0	0	0	1	0	.000	.500	.000	43	0	0			1.000	-0	/C-1	0.0
1950	StL-N	22	36	1	5	1	0	0	1	4	7	.139	.225	.167	5	-5	0			.959	0	C-17	-0.5
1953	Det-A	60	158	17	35	9	0	1	14	20	14	.222	.309	.297	65	-8	1	1	-0	.984	-4	C-56	-1.0
Total	3	84	195	18	40	10	0	1	15	25	21	.205	.295	.272	53	-12	1	1		.980	-4	/C-74	-1.5

■ JERRY BUCHEK
Buchek, Gerald Peter   b: 5/9/42, St.Louis, Mo.   BR/TR, 5'11", 185 lbs.   Deb: 6/30/61

YEAR	TM/L	G	AB	R	H	2B	3B	HR	RBI	BB	SO	AVG	OBP	SLG	PRO+	BR/A	SB	CS	SBR	FA	FR	G/POS	TPR
1961	StL-N	31	90	6	12	2	0	0	9	0	28	.133	.152	.156	-16	-15	0	0	0	.912	-6	S-31	-1.9
1963	StL-N	3	4	0	1	0	0	0	0	0	2	.250	.250	.250	41	-0	0	0	0	1.000	0	/S-1	0.0
1964	*StL-N	35	30	7	6	0	2	0	1	3	11	.200	.273	.333	64	-1	0	0	0	.929	7	S-20/2-9,3-1	0.6
1965	StL-N	55	166	17	41	8	3	3	21	13	46	.247	.302	.386	84	-4	1	0	0	.994	10	2-33,S-18/3-1	1.1
1966	StL-N	100	284	23	67	10	4	4	25	23	71	.236	.293	.342	75	-9	0	5	-3	.974	-13	2-49,S-48/3-4	-2.0
1967	NY-N	124	411	35	97	11	2	14	41	26	101	.236	.285	.375	89	-7	3	5	-2	.977	4	2-95,3-17/S-9	0.1
1968	NY-N	73	192	8	35	4	0	1	11	10	52	.182	.234	.219	36	-15	1	1	-0	.935	-1	3-37,2-12/O-9	-1.8
Total	7	421	1177	96	259	35	11	22	108	75	312	.220	.271	.325	67	-51	5	11	-5	.978	2	2-198,S-127/3-60,O	-3.9

■ JIM BUCHER
Bucher, James Quinter   b: 3/11/11, Manassas, Va.   BL/TR, 5'11", 170 lbs.   Deb: 4/18/34

YEAR	TM/L	G	AB	R	H	2B	3B	HR	RBI	BB	SO	AVG	OBP	SLG	PRO+	BR/A	SB	CS	SBR	FA	FR	G/POS	TPR
1934	Bro-N	47	84	12	19	5	2	0	8	4	7	.226	.261	.333	61	-5	1			.920	-1	2-20/3-6	-0.5
1935	Bro-N	123	473	72	143	22	1	7	58	10	33	.302	.337	.397	93	-6	4			.950	-1	2-41,3-39,O-37	-1.4
1936	Bro-N	110	370	49	93	12	8	2	41	29	27	.251	.306	.343	74	-14	5			.910	-8	3-39,2-32,O-30	-2.0
1937	Bro-N	125	380	44	96	11	2	4	37	20	18	.253	.295	.324	67	-18	5			.951	-14	2-49,3-43/O-6	-2.7
1938	StL-N	17	57	7	13	5	1	0	2	6	3	.228	.254	.316	53	-4	0			.955	-4	2-14/3-1	-0.7
1944	Bos-A	80	277	39	76	9	4	4	31	19	13	.274	.326	.365	98	-1	3	3	-1	.958	-9	3-44,2-21	-1.0
1945	Bos-A	52	151	19	34	4	1	0	11	13	12	.225	.264	.291	60	-8	3	3	-2	.940	-2	3-32/2-2	-1.1
Total	7	554	1792	242	474	66	19	17	193	91	113	.265	.302	.351	78	-55	19	6		.939	-48	3-204,2-179/O-73	-9.4

■ KEVIN BUCKLEY
Buckley, Kevin John   b: 1/16/59, Quincy, Mass.   BR/TR, 6'1", 200 lbs.   Deb: 9/4/84

YEAR	TM/L	G	AB	R	H	2B	3B	HR	RBI	BB	SO	AVG	OBP	SLG	PRO+	BR/A	SB	CS	SBR	FA	FR	G/POS	TPR
1984	Tex-A	5	7	1	2	1	0	0	0	2	4	.286	.444	.429	138	0	0	0	0	.000	0	/D-3	0.0

YEAR	TM/L	G	AB	R	H	2B	3B	HR	RBI	BB	SO	AVG	OBP	SLG	PRO+	BR/A	SB	CS	SBR	FA	FR	G/POS	TPR

■ DICK BUCKLEY   Buckley, Richard D.   b: 9/21/1858, Troy, N.Y.   d: 12/12/29, Pittsburgh, Pa.   TR, 5'10", 195 lbs.   Deb: 4/20/1888

YEAR	TM/L	G	AB	R	H	2B	3B	HR	RBI	BB	SO	AVG	OBP	SLG	PRO+	BR/A	SB	CS	SBR	FA	FR	G/POS	TPR
1888	Ind-N	71	260	28	71	9	3	5	22	6	24	.273	.289	.388	112	3	4			.898	-21	C-51,3-22/O-1,1-1	-1.3
1889	Ind-N	68	260	35	67	11	0	8	41	15	32	.258	.301	.392	91	-5	5			.877	-21	C-55,3-12/O-1,1-1	-1.8
1890	NY-N	70	266	39	68	11	0	2	26	23	35	.256	.324	.320	88	-4	3			.931	9	C-62/3-8	1.0
1891	NY-N	75	253	23	55	9	1	4	31	11	30	.217	.258	.308	67	-11	3			.958	19	C-74/3-1	1.2
1892	StL-N	121	410	43	93	17	4	5	52	22	34	.227	.275	.324	85	-9	7			.937	-5	*C-119/1-2	-0.5
1893	StL-N	9	23	2	4	1	0	0	1	0	0	.174	.174	.217	4	-3	0			.914	1	/C-9	-0.1
1894	StL-N	29	89	5	16	1	2	1	3	6	3	.180	.240	.270	23	-12	1			.936	2	C-27/1-1	-0.6
	Phi-N	43	160	18	47	7	3	1	26	6	13	.294	.327	.394	75	-7	0			.966	3	C-42/1-1	0.0
	Yr	72	249	23	63	8	5	2	29	12	16	.253	.295	.349	56	-19	1			.954	4	C-69/1-2	-0.6
1895	Phi-N	38	112	20	28	6	1	0	14	9	17	.250	.333	.321	69	-5	2			.919	6	C-38	0.3
Total	8	524	1833	213	449	72	14	26	216	98	188	.245	.291	.342	81	-53	25			.931	-7	C-477/3-43,1-6,O-2	-1.8

■ BILL BUCKNER   Buckner, William Joseph   b: 12/14/49, Vallejo, Cal.   BL/TL, 6', 185 lbs.   Deb: 9/21/69   C

YEAR	TM/L	G	AB	R	H	2B	3B	HR	RBI	BB	SO	AVG	OBP	SLG	PRO+	BR/A	SB	CS	SBR	FA	FR	G/POS	TPR
1969	LA-N	1	1	0	0	0	0	0	0	0	0	.000	.000	.000	-99	-0	0	0	0	.000	0	H	0.0
1970	LA-N	28	68	6	13	3	1	0	4	3	7	.191	.225	.265	32	-7	0	1	-1	1.000	1	O-20/1-1	-0.7
1971	LA-N	108	358	37	99	15	1	5	41	11	18	.277	.307	.366	96	-3	4	1	1	.994	2	O-86,1-11	-0.6
1972	LA-N	105	383	47	122	14	3	5	37	17	13	.319	.349	.410	118	8	10	3	1	.992	-3	O-61,1-35	0.1
1973	LA-N	140	575	68	158	20	0	8	46	17	34	.275	.299	.351	83	-15	12	2	2	.998	-3	1-93,O-48	-2.6
1974	*LA-N	145	580	83	182	30	3	7	58	30	24	.314	.352	.412	118	12	31	13	2	.976	-3	*O-137/1-6	0.4
1975	LA-N	92	288	30	70	11	2	6	31	17	15	.243	.290	.358	82	-8	8	3	1	.986	2	O-72	-0.9
1976	LA-N	154	642	76	193	28	4	7	60	26	26	.301	.329	.389	105	2	28	9	3	.985	7	*O-153/1-1	0.6
1977	Chi-N	122	426	40	121	27	0	11	60	21	23	.284	.319	.425	88	-8	7	5	-1	.990	-0	1-99	-1.5
1978	Chi-N	117	446	47	144	26	1	5	74	18	17	.323	.349	.419	102	-0	7	5	-1	.995	8	*1-105	0.1
1979	Chi-N	149	591	72	168	34	7	14	66	30	28	.284	.321	.437	96	-5	9	4	0	.995	18	*1-140	0.5
1980	Chi-N	145	578	69	187	41	3	10	68	30	18	**.324**	.357	.457	117	12	1	2	-1	.993	8	1-94,O-50	1.2
1981	Chi-N★	106	421	45	131	**35**	3	10	75	26	16	.311	.353	.480	129	14	5	2	0	.984	1	*1-105	1.0
1982	Chi-N	161	657	93	201	34	5	15	105	36	26	.306	.347	.441	116	13	15	5	2	.993	16	*1-161	2.2
1983	Chi-N	153	626	79	175	**38**	6	16	66	25	30	.280	.313	.436	101	-2	12	4	1	.992	21	*1-144,O-15	1.2
1984	Chi-N	21	43	3	9	0	0	0	2	1	1	.209	.244	.209	26	-4	0	0	0	1.000	2	/1-7,O-2	-0.3
	Bos-A	114	439	51	122	21	2	11	67	24	38	.278	.323	.410	97	-2	2	2	-1	.986	5	*1-113	-0.6
1985	Bos-A	162	673	89	201	46	3	16	110	30	36	.299	.330	.447	106	4	18	4	3	.992	25	*1-162	2.2
1986	*Bos-A	153	629	73	168	39	2	18	102	40	25	.267	.315	.421	98	-3	6	4	-1	.989	20	*1-138,D-15	0.6
1987	Bos-A	75	286	23	78	6	1	2	42	13	19	.273	.304	.322	65	-14	1	3	-2	.991	3	1-74	-1.7
	Cal-A	57	183	16	56	12	1	3	32	9	7	.306	.339	.432	106	1	0	0	0	1.000	-0	D-39/1-5	0.0
	Yr	132	469	39	134	18	2	5	74	22	26	.286	.318	.365	80	-13	1	3	-1	.992	4	1-79,D-39	-1.7
1988	Cal-A	19	43	1	9	0	0	0	9	4	0	.209	.277	.209	39	-3	0	0	1	1.000	0	D-11/1-1	-0.3
	KC-A	89	242	18	62	14	0	3	34	13	19	.256	.294	.351	79	-7	3	1	0	.994	0	D-42,1-21	-1.0
	Yr	108	285	19	71	14	0	3	43	17	19	.249	.291	.330	73	-10	5	1	1	.994	0	D-53,1-22	-1.3
1989	KC-A	79	176	7	38	4	1	1	16	6	11	.216	.242	.267	43	-13	1	0	0	.985	-0	1-24,D-19	-1.6
1990	Bos-A	22	43	4	8	0	0	1	3	3	2	.186	.239	.256	37	-4	0	0	0	1.000	-0	1-15	-0.5
Total	22	2517	9397	1077	2715	498	49	174	1208	450	453	.289	.324	.408	99	-31	183	73	11	.992	127	*1-1555,O-644,D-126	-2.2

■ MARK BUDASKA   Budaska, Mark David   b: 12/27/52, Sharon, Pa.   BB/TL, 6', 180 lbs.   Deb: 6/6/78

YEAR	TM/L	G	AB	R	H	2B	3B	HR	RBI	BB	SO	AVG	OBP	SLG	PRO+	BR/A	SB	CS	SBR	FA	FR	G/POS	TPR
1978	Oak-A	4	4	0	1	1	0	0	1	2	.250	.400	.500	160	0	0	0	0	.500	-1	/O-2	-0.1
1981	Oak-A	9	32	3	5	1	0	2	4	10	.156	.250	.188	29	-3	0	1	-1	.000	0	/D-9	-0.4
Total	2	13	36	3	6	2	0	2	5	12	.167	.268	.222	44	-3	0	1	-1	.500	-1	/D-9,O-2	-0.5

■ BUDD   Budd   b: Cleveland, Ohio   Deb: 9/10/1890

YEAR	TM/L	G	AB	R	H	2B	3B	HR	RBI	BB	SO	AVG	OBP	SLG	PRO+	BR/A	SB	CS	SBR	FA	FR	G/POS	TPR
1890	Cle-P	1	4	0	0	0	0	0	0	3	.000	.000	.000	-99	-1	0			1.000	-0	/O-1	-0.1

■ DON BUDDIN   Buddin, Donald Thomas   b: 5/5/34, Turbeville, S.C.   BR/TR, 5'11", 178 lbs.   Deb: 4/17/56

YEAR	TM/L	G	AB	R	H	2B	3B	HR	RBI	BB	SO	AVG	OBP	SLG	PRO+	BR/A	SB	CS	SBR	FA	FR	G/POS	TPR
1956	Bos-A	114	377	49	90	24	0	5	37	65	62	.239	.357	.342	76	-12	2	0	1	.953	14	*S-113	1.1
1958	Bos-A	136	497	74	118	25	2	12	43	82	106	.237	.350	.368	92	-4	0	4	-2	.958	15	*S-136	2.1
1959	Bos-A	151	485	75	117	24	1	10	53	92	99	.241	.368	.357	95	0	6	1	1	.949	-17	*S-150	-0.3
1960	Bos-A	124	428	62	105	21	5	6	36	62	59	.245	.342	.360	87	-7	4	2	0	.951	-5	*S-124	-0.2
1961	Bos-A	115	339	58	89	22	3	6	42	72	45	.263	.395	.398	110	8	2	1	0	.956	-1	*S-109	1.5
1962	Hou-N	40	80	10	13	4	1	2	10	17	17	.162	.316	.313	75	-3	0	0	0	.952	3	S-27/3-9	0.2
	Det-A	31	83	14	19	3	0	0	4	20	16	.229	.385	.265	76	-2	1	0	0	.978	-2	S-19/2-5,3-2	-0.2
Total	6	711	2289	342	551	123	12	41	225	410	404	.241	.360	.359	90	-19	15	8	-0	.954	7	S-678/3-11,2-5	4.2

■ STEVE BUECHELE   Buechele, Steven Bernard   b: 9/26/61, Lancaster, Cal.   BR/TR, 6'2", 190 lbs.   Deb: 7/19/85

YEAR	TM/L	G	AB	R	H	2B	3B	HR	RBI	BB	SO	AVG	OBP	SLG	PRO+	BR/A	SB	CS	SBR	FA	FR	G/POS	TPR
1985	Tex-A	69	219	22	48	6	3	6	21	14	38	.219	.272	.356	70	-10	3	2	-0	.969	6	3-69/2-1	-0.4
1986	Tex-A	153	461	54	112	19	2	18	54	35	98	.243	.303	.410	90	-7	5	8	-3	.968	19	*3-137,2-33/O-2	0.6
1987	Tex-A	136	363	45	86	20	0	13	50	28	66	.237	.293	.399	81	-11	2	2	-1	.964	3	*3-123,2-18/O-2	-0.9
1988	Tex-A	155	503	68	126	21	4	16	58	65	79	.250	.342	.404	105	4	2	4	-2	.962	8	*3-153/2-2	0.7
1989	Tex-A	155	486	60	114	22	2	16	59	36	107	.235	.294	.387	89	-8	1	3	-1	.969	15	*3-145,2-18/S-1,D-1	0.7
1990	Tex-A	91	251	30	54	10	0	7	30	27	63	.215	.296	.339	77	-8	1	0	0	.966	6	3-88/2-4	-0.1
1991	Tex-A	121	416	58	111	17	2	18	66	39	69	.267	.337	.447	117	9	0	4	-2	**.991**	20	*3-111,2-13/S-4	2.7
	*Pit-N	31	114	16	28	5	1	4	19	10	28	.246	.317	.412	105	1	0	1	-1	.956	3	3-31	0.3
1992	Pit-N	80	285	27	71	14	1	8	43	34	61	.249	.333	.389	105	2	0	2	-1	.957	6	3-80	0.8
	Chi-N	65	239	25	66	9	3	1	21	18	44	.276	.340	.351	94	-2	1	1	-0	.960	-2	3-63/2-2	-0.5
	Yr	145	524	52	137	23	4	9	64	52	105	.261	.336	.372	100	1	1	3	-2	.958	4	*3-143/2-2	0.3
1993	Chi-N	133	460	53	125	27	2	15	65	48	87	.272	.347	.437	110	6	1	1	-0	**.975**	1	*3-129/1-6	0.7
1994	Chi-N	104	339	33	82	11	1	14	52	39	80	.242	.327	.404	91	-5	1	0	0	.974	-10	3-99/1-6,2-1	-1.4
1995	Chi-N	32	106	10	20	2	0	1	9	11	19	.189	.265	.236	34	-10	0	0	0	.942	0	3-32	-1.0
	Tex-A	9	24	0	3	0	0	0	4	3	.125	.250	.125	1	-3	0	0	0	1.000	-0	/3-9	-0.3
Total	11	1334	4266	501	1046	183	21	137	547	408	842	.245	.317	.394	94	-41	17	28	-12	.968	75	*3-1269/2-92,1SOD	2.2

■ CHARLIE BUELOW   Buelow, Charles John   b: 1/12/1877, Dubuque, Iowa   d: 5/4/51, Dubuque, Iowa   BR/TR,   Deb: 6/1/01

YEAR	TM/L	G	AB	R	H	2B	3B	HR	RBI	BB	SO	AVG	OBP	SLG	PRO+	BR/A	SB	CS	SBR	FA	FR	G/POS	TPR
1901	NY-N	22	72	3	8	4	0	0	4	2	.111	.147	.167	-10	-10	0			.853	3	3-17/2-2	-0.7

■ FRITZ BUELOW   Buelow, Frederick William Alexander   b: 2/13/1876, Berlin, Germany   d: 12/27/33, Detroit, Mich.   BR/TR, 5'10.5", 170 lbs.   Deb: 9/28/1899

YEAR	TM/L	G	AB	R	H	2B	3B	HR	RBI	BB	SO	AVG	OBP	SLG	PRO+	BR/A	SB	CS	SBR	FA	FR	G/POS	TPR
1899	StL-N	7	15	4	7	0	2	0	2	2	.467	.556	.733	247	3	0			1.000	-2	/C-4,O-2	0.1
1900	StL-N	6	17	2	4	0	0	0	3	0	.235	.235	.235	30	-2	0			.864	-1	/C-4,O-1	-0.2
1901	Det-A	70	231	28	52	5	5	2	29	11	.225	.269	.316	59	-13	2			.967	5	C-69	-0.2
1902	Det-A	66	224	23	50	5	2	2	29	9	.223	.256	.290	50	-15	4			.927	-1	C-63/1-2	-0.8
1903	Det-A	63	192	24	41	3	6	1	13	6	.214	.249	.307	68	-8	4			.961	1	C-60/1-2	-0.1
1904	Det-A	42	136	6	15	1	1	0	5	8	.110	.160	.132	-7	-16	2			.975	1	C-42	-1.3
	Cle-A	42	119	11	21	4	1	0	5	11	.176	.252	.227	52	-6	2			.979	1	C-42	-0.1
	Yr	84	255	17	36	5	2	0	10	19	.141	.204	.176	21	-22	4			.977	1	C-84	-1.4
1905	Cle-A	75	239	11	41	4	1	1	18	6	.172	.198	.209	29	-19	7			.960	-7	C-60/O-8,1-3,3-2	-2.2
1906	Cle-A	34	86	7	14	2	0	0	8	9	.163	.250	.186	38	-6	0			.938	3	C-33/1-1	-0.1
1907	StL-A	26	75	9	11	0	7	1	.147	.220	.160	21	-6	0			.983	1	C-25	-0.4
Total	9	431	1334	125	256	25	18	6	112	69	.192	.238	.251	46	-89	20			.960	1	C-402/O-11,1-8,3-2	-5.3

■ ART BUES   Bues, Arthur Frederick   b: 3/3/1888, Milwaukee, Wis.   d: 11/7/54, Whitefish Bay, Wis.   BR/TR, 5'11", 184 lbs.   Deb: 4/17/13

YEAR	TM/L	G	AB	R	H	2B	3B	HR	RBI	BB	SO	AVG	OBP	SLG	PRO+	BR/A	SB	CS	SBR	FA	FR	G/POS	TPR
1913	Bos-N	2	1	0	0	0	0	0	0	0	1	.000	.000	.000	-98	-0	0			.000	0	/2-1,3-1	0.0
1914	Chi-N	14	45	3	10	1	1	0	4	5	6	.222	.300	.289	76	-1	1			.968	-2	3-12	-0.4
Total	2	16	46	3	10	1	1	0	4	5	7	.217	.294	.283	72	-2	1			.968	-2	/3-13,2-1	-0.4

YEAR	TM/L	G	AB	R	H	2B	3B	HR	RBI	BB	SO	AVG	OBP	SLG	PRO+	BR/A	SB	CS	SBR	FA	FR	G/POS	TPR

■ **CHARLIE BUFFINTON** Buffinton, Charles G. b: 6/14/1861, Fall River, Mass. d: 9/23/07, Fall River, Mass. BR/TR, 6′1″, 180 lbs. Deb: 5/17/1882 M

1882	Bos-N	15	50	5	13	1	0	0	4	2	3	.260	.288	.280	83	-1				.615	-1	/O-7,P-5,1-4	-0.2
1883	Bos-N	86	341	28	81	8	3	1	26	6	24	.238	.251	.287	62	-16				.756	-7	O-51,P-43/1-2	-1.4
1884	Bos-N	87	352	48	94	18	3	1	39	16	12	.267	.299	.344	102	1				.946	-1	P-67,O-13,1-11	-0.5
1885	Bos-N	82	338	26	81	12	3	1	33	3	26	.240	.246	.302	79	-8				.912	-0	P-51,O-18,1-15	-1.1
1886	Bos-N	44	176	27	51	4	1	1	30	6	12	.290	.313	.341	103	1	3			.968	-6	1-19,P-18/O-9	-0.7
1887	Phi-N	66	269	34	72	12	1	1	46	11	3	.268	.299	.331	71	-11	8			.931	2	P-40,O-22,1-10	-0.9
1888	Phi-N	46	160	14	29	4	1	0	12	7	5	.181	.216	.219	37	-11	1			.939	9	P-46/O-1	0.0
1889	Phi-N	47	154	16	32	2	0	0	21	9	5	.208	.256	.221	31	-15	0			.916	1	P-47/O-1	0.0
1890	Phi-P	42	150	24	41	3	2	1	24	9	4	.273	.319	.340	74	-6	1			.864	0	P-36/O-5,1-3,M	-0.1
1891	Bos-a	58	181	16	34	2	1	1	16	19	15	.188	.269	.227	43	-13	0			.934	3	P-48,O-10/1-4	-0.5
1892	Bal-N	13	43	7	15	1	1	0	4	3	6	.349	.391	.419	141	2	1			.892	2	P-13	0.0
Total	11	586	2214	245	543	67	16	7	255	91	114	.245	.276	.299	72	-78	14			.916	2	P-414,O-137/1-68	-5.4

■ **DAMON BUFORD** Buford, Damon Jackson b: 6/12/70, Baltimore, Md. BR/TR, 5′10″, 170 lbs. Deb: 5/4/93 F

1993	Bal-A	53	79	18	18	5	0	2	9	9	19	.228	.315	.367	79	-2	2	2	-1	.984	-1	O-30,D-17	-0.5
1994	Bal-A	4	2	2	1	0	0	0	0	0	0	.500	.500	.500	151	0	0	0	0	.000	-0	/O-1,D-1	0.0
1995	Bal-A	24	32	6	2	0	0	0	2	6	7	.063	.211	.063	-24	-6	3	1	0	1.000	-2	O-24	-0.8
	NY-N	44	136	24	32	5	0	4	12	19	28	.235	.350	.360	91	-1	7	7	-2	.972	-1	O-39	-0.5
1996	*Tex-A	90	145	30	41	9	0	6	20	15	34	.283	.350	.469	98	-1	8	5	-1	1.000	-15	O-80	-1.6
Total	4	215	394	80	94	19	0	12	43	49	89	.239	.332	.378	82	-10	20	15	-3	.989	-20	O-174/D-18	-3.4

■ **DON BUFORD** Buford, Donald Alvin b: 2/2/37, Linden, Tex. BB/TR, 5′8″, 165 lbs. Deb: 9/14/63 FC

1963	Chi-A	12	42	9	12	1	2	0	5	5	7	.286	.362	.405	116	1	1	0	0	.955	-5	/3-9,2-2	-0.3
1964	Chi-A	135	442	62	116	14	6	4	30	46	62	.262	.339	.348	94	-3	12	7	-1	.968	-16	2-92,3-37	-1.3
1965	Chi-A	155	586	93	166	22	5	10	47	67	76	.283	.361	.389	120	17	17	7	1	.981	5	*2-139,3-41	3.3
1966	Chi-A	163	607	85	148	26	7	8	52	69	71	.244	.324	.349	100	1	51	22	2	.939	1	*3-133,2-37,O-11	0.4
1967	Chi-A	156	535	61	129	10	9	4	32	65	51	.241	.324	.316	93	-3	34	21	-2	.948	4	*3-121,2-51/O-1	0.0
1968	Bal-A	130	426	65	120	13	4	15	46	57	46	.282	.372	.437	144	24	27	12	1	1.000	-6	O-65,2-58/3-2	2.0
1969	*Bal-A	144	554	99	161	31	3	11	64	96	62	.291	.400	.417	128	24	19	18	-5	.983	-4	*O-128,2-10/3-6	0.9
1970	*Bal-A	144	504	99	137	15	2	17	66	109	55	.272	.409	.411	125	23	16	8	0	.987	6	*O-130/2-3,3-3	2.3
1971	*Bal-A★	122	449	99	130	19	4	19	54	89	62	.290	.415	.477	153	35	15	7	0	.987	-1	*O-115	3.5
1972	Bal-A	125	408	46	84	9	5	5	22	69	83	.206	.326	.267	76	-9	8	3	1	.989	-1	*O-105	-1.6
Total	10	1286	4553	718	1203	157	44	93	418	672	575	.264	.364	.379	115	109	200	105	-3	.988	-15	O-555,2-392,3-352	9.2

■ **JAY BUHNER** Buhner, Jay Campbell b: 8/13/64, Louisville, Ky. BR/TR, 6′3″, 205 lbs. Deb: 9/11/87

1987	NY-A	7	22	0	5	2	0	1	1	1	6	.227	.261	.318	53	-2	0	1	0	1.000	0	/O-7	-0.2
1988	NY-A	25	69	8	13	0	0	3	13	3	25	.188	.253	.319	60	-4	0	0	0	.964	1	O-22	-0.4
	Sea-A	60	192	28	43	13	1	10	25	25	68	.224	.323	.458	111	3	1	1	-0	.993	9	O-59	1.0
	Yr	85	261	36	56	13	1	13	38	28	93	.215	.305	.421	98	-1	1	1	-0	.985	10	O-81	0.6
1989	Sea-A	58	204	27	56	15	1	9	33	19	55	.275	.342	.490	128	7	1	4	-2	.966	3	O-57	0.4
1990	Sea-A	51	163	16	45	12	0	7	33	17	50	.276	.359	.479	131	7	2	2	-1	.966	-4	O-40,D-10	0.1
1991	Sea-A	137	406	64	99	14	4	27	77	53	117	.244	.340	.498	128	15	0	1	-1	.981	6	*O-131	1.7
1992	Sea-A	152	543	69	132	16	3	25	79	71	146	.243	.337	.422	111	8	0	6	-4	.994	11	*O-150	1.2
1993	Sea-A	158	563	91	153	28	3	27	98	100	144	.272	.383	.476	128	24	2	5	-2	.978	-2	*O-148,D-10	1.5
1994	Sea-A	101	358	74	100	23	4	21	68	66	63	.279	.399	.542	137	21	0	1	-1	.990	6	O-96/D-4	2.2
1995	*Sea-A	126	470	86	123	23	0	40	121	60	120	.262	.347	.566	131	19	0	1	-1	.989	-3	*O-120/D-4	1.1
1996	Sea-A★	150	564	107	153	29	0	44	138	84	159	.271	.374	.557	132	27	0	1	-1	.989	-0	*O-142/D-8	2.0
Total	10	1025	3554	570	922	175	16	213	686	499	953	.259	.357	.497	125	124	6	22	-11	.985	24	O-972/D-36	10.6

■ **HARRY BUKER** Buker, Henry L. "Happy" b: 1859, Chicago, Ill. d: 8/10/1899, Chicago, Ill. Deb: 6/11/1884

1884	Det-N	30	111	5	15	1	0	0	3	4	15	.135	.165	.144	-2	-12				.867	1	S-19,O-11	-1.0

■ **GEORGE BULLARD** Bullard, George Donald "Curly" b: 10/24/28, Lynn, Mass. BR/TR, 5′9.5″, 165 lbs. Deb: 9/17/54

1954	Det-A	4	1	0	0	0	0	0	0	0	0	.000	.000	.000	-99	-0	0	0	0	.800	1	/S-1	0.1

■ **SIM BULLAS** Bullas, Simeon Edward b: 4/10/1861, Cleveland, Ohio d: 1/14/08, Cleveland, Ohio 5′7.5″, 150 lbs. Deb: 5/2/1884

1884	Tol-a	13	45	4	4	0	1	0		1		.089	.109	.133	-21	-6				.909	-6	C-12/O-2	-1.0

■ **SCOTT BULLETT** Bullett, Scott Douglas b: 12/25/68, Martinsburg, W.Va. BB/TL, 6′2″, 200 lbs. Deb: 9/3/91

1991	Pit-N	11	4	2	0	0	0	0	0	0	3	.000	.200	.000	-40	-1	1	1	-0	1.000	-1	/O-3	-0.2
1993	Pit-N	23	55	2	11	0	2	0	4	3	15	.200	.241	.273	37	-5	3	2	-0	1.000	-2	O-19	-0.7
1995	Chi-N	104	150	19	41	5	3	3	22	12	30	.273	.331	.460	108	1	8	3	1	.968	-11	O-64	-1.0
1996	Chi-N	109	165	26	35	5	0	3	16	10	54	.212	.257	.297	45	-13	7	3	0	.986	-8	O-58	-2.1
Total	4	247	374	49	87	10	6	6	42	25	102	.233	.284	.356	68	-18	19	9	0	.983	-22	O-144	-4.0

■ **BUD BULLING** Bulling, Terry Charles "Terry" b: 12/15/52, Lynwood, Cal. BR/TR, 6′1″, 200 lbs. Deb: 7/3/77

1977	Min-A	15	32	2	5	1	0	0	5	5	5	.156	.270	.188	28	-2	0	0	0	.952	-0	C-10/D-3	-0.3
1981	Sea-A	62	154	15	38	3	0	2	15	21	20	.247	.341	.305	84	-2	0	0	0	.977	-3	C-62	-0.3
1982	Sea-A	56	154	17	34	7	0	1	8	19	16	.221	.306	.286	62	-8	2	1	0	.991	7	C-56	0.1
1983	Sea-A	5	5	0	0	0	0	0	0	0	0	.000	.000	.000	-96	-1	0	0	0	1.000	1	/C-5	0.0
Total	4	138	345	34	77	11	0	3	28	45	41	.223	.315	.281	66	-14	2	1	0	.983	6	C-133/D-3	-0.5

■ **ERIC BULLOCK** Bullock, Eric Gerald b: 2/16/60, Los Angeles, Cal. BL/TL, 5′11″, 185 lbs. Deb: 8/26/85

1985	Hou-N	18	25	3	7	2	0	0	2	4	4	.280	.308	.360	89	-0	0	1	-1	.750	-2	/O-7	-0.3
1986	Hou-N	6	21	0	1	0	0	0	1	0	5	.048	.048	.048	-76	-5	2	0	1	.875	-1	/O-6	-0.6
1988	Min-A	16	17	3	5	0	0	0	3	3	1	.294	.400	.294	95	-0	1	0	0	.875	-1	/O-4,D-2	-0.1
1989	Phi-N	6	4	1	0	0	0	0	0	0	2	.000	.000	.000	-99	-1	0	0	0	1.000	-1	/O-3	-0.2
1990	Mon-N	4	2	0	1	0	0	0	0	0	0	.500	.500	.500	183	0	0	0	0	.000	-0	/H	0.0
1991	Mon-N	73	72	6	16	4	0	1	6	9	13	.222	.309	.319	78	-2	6	1	1	1.000	-1	/O-9,1-3	-0.2
1992	Mon-N	8	5	0	0	0	0	0	0	0	0	.000	.000	.000	-99	-1	0	0	0	.000	-0	/H	-0.2
Total	7	131	146	13	30	6	0	1	12	13	23	.205	.270	.267	52	-9	9	2	2	.892	-5	/O-29,1-3,D-2	-1.6

■ **AL BUMBRY** Bumbry, Alonza Benjamin (b: Alonza Benjamin Bumbrey) b: 4/21/47, Fredericksburg, Va. BL/TR, 5′8″, 175 lbs. Deb: 9/5/72 C

1972	Bal-A	9	11	5	4	0	0	0	2	1	1	.364	.364	.545	164	1	1	1	-0	1.000	-0	/O-2	0.1
1973	*Bal-A	110	356	73	120	15	11	7	34	34	49	.337	.399	.500	153	25	23	10	1	.978	-10	O-86/D-7	1.2
1974	*Bal-A	94	270	35	63	10	3	1	19	21	46	.233	.291	.304	74	-9	12	4	1	.953	-1	O-67/D-7	-1.2
1975	Bal-A	114	349	47	94	19	4	2	32	32	81	.269	.338	.364	105	2	16	3	3	1.000	-2	D-48,O-39/3-1	0.1
1976	Bal-A	133	450	71	113	15	7	9	36	43	76	.251	.318	.376	109	4	42	10	7	.989	-12	*O-116,D-10	-0.6
1977	Bal-A	133	518	74	164	31	3	4	41	45	88	.317	.373	.411	121	16	19	8	1	.991	-10	*O-130	0.1
1978	Bal-A	33	114	21	27	4	2	2	6	17	15	.237	.346	.368	108	2	5	3	-0	.985	-2	O-28	-0.2
1979	*Bal-A	148	569	80	162	29	1	7	49	59	74	.285	.338	.376	96	-3	37	12	4	.982	-3	*O-146	-0.8
1980	Bal-A★	160	645	118	205	29	9	9	53	78	75	.318	.394	.432	128	27	44	11	7	.990	15	*O-160	4.2
1981	Bal-A	101	392	61	107	18	2	1	27	51	51	.273	.360	.337	102	3	22	15	-2	.992	4	*O-100	0.1
1982	Bal-A	150	562	77	147	20	4	5	40	44	77	.262	.315	.338	80	-15	10	5	0	.986	8	*O-147/D-1	-1.1
1983	*Bal-A	124	378	63	104	14	4	3	31	31	33	.275	.330	.357	91	-4	12	5	1	.988	-11	*O-104,D-11	-0.9
1984	Bal-A	119	344	47	93	12	1	3	24	25	35	.270	.320	.337	84	-7	9	5	-0	.988	-6	O-99/D-9	-1.7
1985	SD-N	68	95	6	19	3	0	1	10	7	9	.200	.255	.263	46	-7	2	0	1	.939	-2	O-17	-0.9
Total	14	1496	5053	778	1422	220	52	54	402	471	709	.281	.345	.378	104	33	254	92	21	.986	-31	*O-1241/D-93,3-1	-2.5

YEAR	TM/L	G	AB	R	H	2B	3B	HR	RBI	BB	SO	AVG	OBP	SLG	PRO+	BR/A	SB	CS	SBR	FA	FR	G/POS	TPR

■ JOSH BUNCE
Bunce, Joshua   b: 5/10/1847, Brooklyn, N.Y.   d: 4/28/12, Brooklyn, N.Y.   Deb: 8/27/1877

YEAR	TM/L	G	AB	R	H	2B	3B	HR	RBI	BB	SO	AVG	OBP	SLG	PRO+	BR/A	SB	CS	SBR	FA	FR	G/POS	TPR
1877	Har-N	1	4	0	0	0	0	0	0	0	0	.000	.000	.000	-99	-1				1.000	-0	/O-1	-0.1

■ NELSON BURBRINK
Burbrink, Nelson Edward   b: 12/28/21, Cincinnati, Ohio   BR/TR, 5'10", 195 lbs.   Deb: 6/5/55

YEAR	TM/L	G	AB	R	H	2B	3B	HR	RBI	BB	SO	AVG	OBP	SLG	PRO+	BR/A	SB	CS	SBR	FA	FR	G/POS	TPR
1955	StL-N	58	170	11	47	8	1	0	15	14	13	.276	.335	.335	79	-5	1	1	-0	.979	-1	C-55	-0.4

■ AL BURCH
Burch, Albert William   b: 10/7/1883, Albany, N.Y.   d: 10/5/26, Brooklyn, N.Y.   BL/TR, 5'8.5", 160 lbs.   Deb: 6/19/06

YEAR	TM/L	G	AB	R	H	2B	3B	HR	RBI	BB	SO	AVG	OBP	SLG	PRO+	BR/A	SB	CS	SBR	FA	FR	G/POS	TPR
1906	StL-N	91	335	40	89	5	1	0	11	37		.266	.339	.287	99	1	15			.934	1	O-91	-0.3
1907	StL-N	48	154	18	35	3	1	0	5	17		.227	.304	.260	79	-3	7			.922	0	O-48	-0.6
	Bro-N	40	120	12	35	2	2	0	12	11		.292	.351	.342	127	4	5			.890	2	O-36/2-1	0.5
	Yr	88	274	30	70	5	3	0	17	28		.255	.325	.296	100	0	12			.908	2	O-84/2-1	-0.1
1908	Bro-N	123	456	45	111	8	4	2	18	33		.243	.294	.292	91	-5	15			.971	13	*O-116	0.3
1909	Bro-N	152	601	80	163	20	6	1	30	51		.271	.329	.329	108	5	38			.955	6	*O-151/1-1	0.5
1910	Bro-N	103	352	41	83	8	3	1	20	22	30	.236	.281	.284	67	-16	13			.957	-1	O-70,1-13	-2.1
1911	Bro-N	54	167	18	38	2	3	0	7	15	22	.228	.291	.275	61	-9	3			.972	2	O-43/2-3	-0.9
Total	6	611	2185	254	554	48	20	4	103	186	52	.254	.312	.299	91	-23	96			.950	22	O-555/1-14,2-4	-2.6

■ ERNIE BURCH
Burch, Earnest W.   b: 1856, Dekalb Co., Ill.   BL ,   Deb: 8/15/1884

YEAR	TM/L	G	AB	R	H	2B	3B	HR	RBI	BB	SO	AVG	OBP	SLG	PRO+	BR/A	SB	CS	SBR	FA	FR	G/POS	TPR
1884	Cle-N	32	124	9	26	4	0	0	7	5	24	.210	.240	.242	50	-7				.899	4	O-32	-0.3
1886	Bro-a	113	456	78	119	22	6	2	72	39		.261	.321	.349	109	4	16			.884	-13	*O-113	-1.0
1887	Bro-a	49	188	47	55	4	4	2	26	29		.293	.395	.388	118	6	15			.899	1	O-49	0.4
Total	3	194	768	134	200	30	10	4	105	73	24	.260	.328	.341	102	3	31			.891	-8	O-194	-0.9

■ BOB BURDA
Burda, Edward Robert   b: 7/16/38, St.Louis, Mo.   BL/TL, 5'11", 180 lbs.   Deb: 8/25/62

YEAR	TM/L	G	AB	R	H	2B	3B	HR	RBI	BB	SO	AVG	OBP	SLG	PRO+	BR/A	SB	CS	SBR	FA	FR	G/POS	TPR
1962	StL-N	7	14	0	1	0	0	0	0	3	1	.071	.235	.071	-12	-2	1	0	0	.917	-0	/O-6	-0.2
1965	SF-N	31	27	0	3	0	0	0	5	5	6	.111	.250	.111	6	-3	0	0	0	.969	-1	1-11/O-1	-0.4
1966	SF-N	37	43	3	7	3	0	0	2	2	5	.163	.200	.233	19	-5	0	0	0	1.000	-1	/1-7,O-4	-0.6
1969	SF-N	97	161	20	37	8	0	6	27	21	12	.230	.319	.391	100	-0	0	1	-1	.995	-1	1-45/O-19	-0.4
1970	SF-N	28	23	1	6	0	0	0	3	5	2	.261	.414	.261	86	-0	0	0	0	.933	-1	/1-8,O-1	-0.1
	Mil-A	78	222	19	55	9	0	4	20	16	17	.248	.307	.342	78	-7	1	0	0	.987	-7	O-64/1-7	-1.8
1971	StL-N	65	71	6	21	0	0	1	12	10	11	.296	.390	.338	104	1	0	0	0	1.000	0	1-13/O-1	0.0
1972	Bos-A	45	73	4	12	1	0	0	9	8	11	.164	.247	.260	48	-5	0	0	0	.992	-0	1-15/O-1	-0.7
Total	7	388	634	53	142	21	0	13	78	70	65	.224	.306	.319	74	-21	2	1	0	.992	-11	1-106/O-97	-4.2

■ JACK BURDOCK
Burdock, John Joseph "Black Jack"   b: 4/1852, Brooklyn, N.Y.   d: 11/27/31, Brooklyn, N.Y.   BR/TR, 5'9.5", 158 lbs.   Deb: 5/2/1872   MU

YEAR	TM/L	G	AB	R	H	2B	3B	HR	RBI	BB	SO	AVG	OBP	SLG	PRO+	BR/A	SB	CS	SBR	FA	FR	G/POS	TPR
1872	Atl-n	37	174	26	46	3	0	0	15	1	1	.264	.269	.282	59	-12	0	1	-1	.738	-4	*S-36/C-4,2-2	-1.1
1873	Atl-n	55	245	56	62	7	1	2	36	7	4	.253	.274	.314	83	-3	3	1	0	.816	1	2-55/C-2	-0.4
1874	Mut-n	61	273	45	75	11	4	1	27	1	5	.275	.277	.355	98	-1	4	0	1	**.820**	8	*3-60/O-3	0.6
1875	Har-n	74	350	72	103	12	5	0	35	3	13	.294	.300	.357	121	6	20	11	-1	**.895**	-4	*2-73/3-2,C-1	0.0
1876	Har-N	69	309	66	80	9	1	0	23	13	16	.259	.289	.294	87	-5				.895	1	*2-69/3-1	-0.4
1877	Har-N	58	277	35	72	6	0	0	9	2	16	.260	.265	.282	81	-5				**.903**	7	*2-55/3-3	0.3
1878	Bos-N	60	246	37	64	12	6	0	25	3	17	.260	.269	.358	97	-2				**.918**	21	*2-60	2.2
1879	Bos-N	84	359	64	86	10	3	0	36	9	28	.240	.258	.284	77	-9				.911	10	*2-84	0.6
1880	Bos-N	86	356	58	90	17	4	2	35	8	26	.253	.269	.340	108	3				**.923**	12	*2-86	1.9
1881	Bos-N	73	282	36	67	12	4	1	24	7	18	.238	.256	.319	84	-5				.911	-11	*2-72/S-1	-1.2
1882	Bos-N	83	319	36	76	6	7	0	27	9	24	.238	.259	.301	79	-7				**.932**	3	*2-83	-0.2
1883	Bos-N	96	400	80	132	27	6	5	88	14	35	.330	.353	.475	145	20				.921	-1	*2-96/M	1.8
1884	Bos-N	87	361	65	97	14	4	6	49	15	52	.269	.298	.380	112	5				**.922**	1	*2-87/3-1	0.7
1885	Bos-N	45	169	18	24	5	0	0	7	8	18	.142	.181	.172	15	-15				.917	-4	2-45	-1.7
1886	Bos-N	59	221	26	48	6	1	0	25	11	27	.217	.254	.253	57	-11	3			.904	-8	2-59	-1.5
1887	Bos-N	65	237	36	61	6	0	0	29	18	22	.257	.320	.283	69	-9	19			.882	-19	2-65	-2.3
1888	Bos-N	22	79	5	16	4	0	0	4	2	5	.203	.232	.203	39	-5	1			.903	0	2-22	-0.4
	Bro-a	70	246	15	30	1	2	1	8	8		.122	.166	.154	3	-26	9			.904	2	2-70	-2.1
1891	Bro-N	3	12	1	1	0	0	0	1	1	1	.083	.154	.083	-31	-2	0			1.000	-1	/2-3	-0.2
Total	4 n	227	1042	199	286	33	10	3	113	12	23	.274	.283	.334	94	-10	27	13	0	.858	1	2-130/3-62,S-36,CO	-0.9
Total	14	960	3873	578	944	131	40	15	390	128	305	.244	.270	.310	83	-74	32			.912	13	2-956/3-5,S-1	-2.5

■ JOE BURG
Burg, Joseph Peter   b: 6/4/1882, Chicago, Ill.   d: 4/28/69, Joliet, Ill.   BR/TR, 5'10", 150 lbs.   Deb: 9/26/10

YEAR	TM/L	G	AB	R	H	2B	3B	HR	RBI	BB	SO	AVG	OBP	SLG	PRO+	BR/A	SB	CS	SBR	FA	FR	G/POS	TPR
1910	Bos-N	13	46	7	15	0	1	0	10	7	12	.326	.415	.370	124	2	5			.867	3	3-12/S-1	0.5

■ SMOKY BURGESS
Burgess, Forrest Harrill   b: 2/6/27, Caroleen, N.C.   d: 9/15/91, Asheville, N.C.   BL/TR, 5'8", 187 lbs.   Deb: 4/19/49

YEAR	TM/L	G	AB	R	H	2B	3B	HR	RBI	BB	SO	AVG	OBP	SLG	PRO+	BR/A	SB	CS	SBR	FA	FR	G/POS	TPR
1949	Chi-N	46	56	4	15	0	0	1	12	4	4	.268	.317	.321	73	-2	0			1.000	0	/C-8	-0.1
1951	Chi-N	94	219	21	55	4	2	2	20	21	12	.251	.317	.315	69	-9	2	0	1	.980	-3	C-64	-0.9
1952	Phi-N	110	371	49	110	27	2	6	56	49	21	.296	.380	.429	125	14	3	1	0	.978	-6	*C-104	1.4
1953	Phi-N	102	312	31	91	17	5	4	36	37	17	.292	.370	.417	105	3	3	2	-0	**.993**	-8	C-95	-0.1
1954	Phi-N★	108	345	41	127	27	5	4	46	42	11	.368	.437	.510	146	25	1	5	-3	.975	-8	C-91	1.8
1955	Phi-N	7	21	4	4	2	0	1		3	1	.190	.292	.429	90	-0				1.000	1	/C-6	0.0
	Cin-N★	116	421	67	129	15	3	20	77	47	35	.306	.377	.499	123	14	1	1	-0	.986	-9	*C-107	0.8
	Yr	123	442	71	133	17	3	21	78	50	36	.301	.373	.495	122	14	1	1	-0	.987	-9	*C-113	0.8
1956	Cin-N	90	229	28	63	10	0	12	39	26	18	.275	.349	.476	112	4	0	1	-1	1.000	-2	C-55	0.3
1957	Cin-N	90	205	29	58	14	1	14	39	24	16	.283	.358	.566	134	9	0	0	0	.988	-5	C-45	0.6
1958	Cin-N	99	251	28	71	12	1	6	31	22	20	.283	.343	.410	93	-2	0	0	0	.988	-8	C-58	0.5
1959	Pit-N★	114	377	41	112	28	5	11	59	31	16	.297	.354	.485	122	11	0	0	0	.984	-17	*C-101	0.0
1960	*Pit-N★	110	337	33	99	13	0	7	46	30	12	.294	.360	.412	110	5	0	1	-1	**.994**	7	C-89	1.1
1961	Pit-N★	100	323	37	98	17	3	12	52	30	16	.303	.366	.486	123	11	0	0	0	**.991**	-14	C-92	0.2
1962	Pit-N	103	360	38	118	19	2	13	61	31	19	.328	.381	.500	134	17	0	1	0	.988	-11	*C-101	0.9
1963	Pit-N	91	264	20	74	10	1	6	37	24	14	.280	.343	.394	111	4	0	1	0	.990	-11	C-72	-0.6
1964	Pit-N☆	68	171	9	42	7	1	3	17	13	14	.246	.303	.310	73	-6	2	1	0	.992	-8	C-44	-1.2
	Chi-A	7	5	1	1	0	0	1	1	2	0	.200	.429	.800	239	1	0	0	0	.000	0	H	0.1
1965	Chi-A	80	77	2	22	4	0	0	11	7	7	.286	.356	.416	132	1	0	0	0	1.000	-0	/C-5	0.4
1966	Chi-A	79	67	0	21	5	0	0	15	11	8	.313	.418	.388	143	4	0	0	0	1.000	-0	/C-2	0.5
1967	Chi-A	77	60	2	8	1	0	1	2	11	6	.133	.307	.250	69	-2	0	0	0	.000	0	H	-0.2
Total	18	1691	4471	485	1318	230	33	126	673	477	270	.295	.364	.446	116	104	13	14		.988	-96	*C-1139	5.5

■ TOM BURGESS
Burgess, Thomas Roland "Tim"   b: 9/1/27, London, Ont., Can.   BL/TL, 6', 180 lbs.   Deb: 4/17/54   C

YEAR	TM/L	G	AB	R	H	2B	3B	HR	RBI	BB	SO	AVG	OBP	SLG	PRO+	BR/A	SB	CS	SBR	FA	FR	G/POS	TPR
1954	StL-N	17	21	2	1	1	0	0	1	3	9	.048	.167	.095	-29	-4	0	0	0	.750	-1	/O-4	-0.6
1962	LA-A	87	143	17	28	7	1	2	13	36	20	.196	.358	.301	82	-2	2	0	1	.997	-3	1-35/O-2	-0.6
Total	2	104	164	19	29	8	1	2	14	39	29	.177	.335	.274	67	-6	2	0	1	.857	-4	/1-35,O-6	-1.2

■ BILL BURGO
Burgo, William Ross   b: 11/5/19, Johnstown, Pa.   d: 10/19/88, Morgan City, La.   BR/TR, 5'8", 185 lbs.   Deb: 9/22/43

YEAR	TM/L	G	AB	R	H	2B	3B	HR	RBI	BB	SO	AVG	OBP	SLG	PRO+	BR/A	SB	CS	SBR	FA	FR	G/POS	TPR
1943	Phi-A	17	70	12	26	4	2	1	9	4	1	.371	.421	.529	178	7	0	2	-1	.979	2	O-17	0.7
1944	Phi-A	27	88	6	21	2	0	1	3	7	3	.239	.316	.295	76	-3	1	3	-2	.955	2	O-22	-0.3
Total	2	44	158	18	47	6	2	2	12	11	4	.297	.362	.399	121	4	1	5	-3	.965	4	/O-39	0.4

■ BILL BURICH
Burich, William Max   b: 5/29/18, Calumet, Mich.   BR/TR, 6', 180 lbs.   Deb: 4/15/42

YEAR	TM/L	G	AB	R	H	2B	3B	HR	RBI	BB	SO	AVG	OBP	SLG	PRO+	BR/A	SB	CS	SBR	FA	FR	G/POS	TPR
1942	Phi-N	25	80	3	23	1	0	0	7	6	13	.287	.337	.300	92	-1	2			.917	-5	S-19/3-3	-0.5
1946	Phi-N	2	1	1	0	0	0	0	0	0	0	.000	.000	.000	-99	-0				.000	0	/3-1	0.0
Total	2	27	81	4	23	1	0	0	7	6	13	.284	.333	.296	89	-1	2			1.000	-5	/S-19,3-4	-0.5

■ MACK BURK
Burk, Mack Edwin   b: 4/21/35, Nacogdoches, Tex.   BR/TR, 6'4", 180 lbs.   Deb: 5/25/56

YEAR	TM/L	G	AB	R	H	2B	3B	HR	RBI	BB	SO	AVG	OBP	SLG	PRO+	BR/A	SB	CS	SBR	FA	FR	G/POS	TPR
1956	Phi-N	15	1	3	1	0	0	0	0	0	0	1.000	1.000	1.000	449	0	0	0	0	1.000	0	/C-1	0.1

YEAR	TM/L	G	AB	R	H	2B	3B	HR	RBI	BB	SO	AVG	OBP	SLG	PRO+	BR/A	SB	CS	SBR	FA	FR	G/POS	TPR
1958	Phi-N	1	1	0	0	0	0	0	0	0	1	.000	.000	.000	-99	-0	0	0	0	.000	0	H	0.0
Total	2	16	2	3	1	0	0	0	0	0	1	.500	.500	.500			0	0	0	.500	0	/C-1	0.1

■ CHRIS BURKAM   Burkam, Chauncey De Pew   b: 10/13/1892, Benton Harbor, Mich.   d: 5/9/64, Kalamazoo, Mich.   BL/TR, 5'11", 175 lbs.   Deb: 6/24/15

YEAR	TM/L	G	AB	R	H	2B	3B	HR	RBI	BB	SO	AVG	OBP	SLG	PRO+	BR/A	SB	CS	SBR	FA	FR	G/POS	TPR
1915	StL-A	1	1	0	0	0	0	0	0	0	0	.000	.000	.000	-99	-0	0			.000	0	H	0.0

■ DAN BURKE   Burke, Daniel L.   b: 10/25/1868, Abington, Mass.   d: 3/20/33, Taunton, Mass.   BR/TR, 5'10", 190 lbs.   Deb: 4/18/1890

YEAR	TM/L	G	AB	R	H	2B	3B	HR	RBI	BB	SO	AVG	OBP	SLG	PRO+	BR/A	SB	CS	SBR	FA	FR	G/POS	TPR
1890	Roc-a	32	102	14	22	1	0	0	9	17		.216	.333	.225	70	-3	2			.944	-5	O-29/C-4,1-2	-0.7
	Syr-a	9	20	1	0	0	0	0	0	5		.000	.231	.000	-35	-3	0			.900	3	/C-9	0.0
	Yr	41	122	15	22	1	0	0	9	22		.180	.315	.189	53	-6	2			.944	-2	O-29,C-13/1-2	-0.7
1892	Bos-N	1	4	0	0	0	0	0	0	0	2	.000	.000	.000	-92	-1	0			.900	1	/C-1	0.0
Total	2	42	126	15	22	1	0	0	9	22	2	.175	.307	.183	48	-7	2			.892	-2	/O-29,C-14,1-2	-0.7

■ EDDIE BURKE   Burke, Edward D.   b: 10/6/1866, Northumberland, Pa.   d: 11/26/07, Utica, N.Y.   BL/TR, 5'6", 161 lbs.   Deb: 4/19/1890

YEAR	TM/L	G	AB	R	H	2B	3B	HR	RBI	BB	SO	AVG	OBP	SLG	PRO+	BR/A	SB	CS	SBR	FA	FR	G/POS	TPR
1890	Phi-N	100	430	85	113	16	11	4	50	49	40	.263	.349	.379	109	5	38			.904	4	*O-96/2-4	0.5
	Pit-N	31	124	17	26	5	2	1	7	14	9	.210	.295	.306	85	-2	6			.911	1	O-31	-0.2
	Yr	131	554	102	139	21	13	5	57	63	49	.251	.337	.363	105	4	44			.906	4	*O-127/2-4	0.3
1891	Mil-a	35	144	31	34	9	0	2	21	12	19	.236	.337	.340	78	-6	7			.918	3	O-35	-0.4
1892	Cin-N	15	41	6	6	1	0	0	4	9	4	.146	.300	.171	44	-2	2			1.000	0	O-14/3-1	-0.5
	NY-N	89	363	81	94	10	5	6	41	46	37	.259	.350	.364	118	9	42			.857	-3	2-59,O-30	0.5
	Yr	104	404	87	100	11	5	6	45	55	41	.248	.345	.344	110	6	44			.857	-6	2-59,O-44/3-1	0.0
1893	NY-N	135	537	122	150	23	10	9	80	51	32	.279	.369	.410	106	5	54			.912	-2	*O-135	0.0
1894	*NY-N	136	566	121	172	23	11	4	77	37	35	.304	.357	.405	84	-15	34			.933	-4	*O-136	-2.2
1895	NY-N	39	167	38	43	6	2	1	12	7	9	.257	.299	.335	65	-9	14			.914	2	O-39	-0.8
	Cin-N	56	228	52	61	8	6	1	25	22	14	.268	.343	.368	80	-7	19			.899	2	O-56	-0.8
	Yr	95	395	90	104	14	8	2	37	29	23	.263	.325	.354	74	-16	33			.905	4	O-95	-1.6
1896	Cin-N	122	521	120	177	24	9	1	52	41	29	.340	.392	.426	108	6	53			.935	3	*O-122	-0.1
1897	Cin-N	95	387	71	103	17	1	1	41	29		.266	.327	.323	67	-19	22			.940	7	*O-95	-1.6
Total	8	853	3508	744	979	142	57	30	410	317	228	.279	.352	.378	93	-37	291			.921	14	O-789/2-63,3-1	-5.6

■ FRANK BURKE   Burke, Frank Aloysius   b: 2/16/1880, Carbon Co., Pa.   d: 9/17/46, Los Angeles, Cal.   TR ,   Deb: 9/14/06

YEAR	TM/L	G	AB	R	H	2B	3B	HR	RBI	BB	SO	AVG	OBP	SLG	PRO+	BR/A	SB	CS	SBR	FA	FR	G/POS	TPR
1906	NY-N	8	9	2	3	1	1	0	1	1		.333	.400	.667	227	1	1			.667	-2	/O-4	0.0
1907	Bos-N	43	129	6	23	0	1	0	8	11		.178	.243	.194	37	-9	3			.955	-4	O-36	-1.6
Total	2	51	138	8	26	1	2	0	9	12		.188	.253	.225	50	-8	4			.942	-5	/O-40	-1.6

■ GLENN BURKE   Burke, Glenn Lawrence   b: 11/16/52, Oakland, Cal.   d: 5/30/95, San Leandro, Cal.   BR/TR, 6', 195 lbs.   Deb: 4/9/76

YEAR	TM/L	G	AB	R	H	2B	3B	HR	RBI	BB	SO	AVG	OBP	SLG	PRO+	BR/A	SB	CS	SBR	FA	FR	G/POS	TPR
1976	LA-N	25	46	9	11	2	0	0	5	3	8	.239	.300	.283	67	-2	3	2	-0	.971	-3	O-20	-0.7
1977	*LA-N	83	169	16	43	8	0	1	13	5	22	.254	.280	.320	61	-9	13	5	1	.971	-15	O-74	-2.6
1978	LA-N	16	19	2	4	0	0	0	2	0	4	.211	.211	.211	18	-2	1	0	0	1.000	-5	O-15	-0.7
	Oak-A	78	200	19	47	6	1	1	14	10	26	.235	.271	.290	61	-11	15	8	-0	.987	-4	O-67/1-1,D-2	-1.8
1979	Oak-A	23	89	4	19	2	1	0	4	4	10	.213	.247	.258	39	-8	3	1	0	1.000	-4	O-23	-0.7
Total	4	225	523	50	124	18	2	2	38	22	70	.237	.271	.291	56	-32	35	16	1	.983	-26	O-199/D-2,1-1	-6.5

■ JIMMY BURKE   Burke, James Timothy "Sunset Jimmy"   b: 10/12/1874, St.Louis, Mo.   d: 3/26/42, St.Louis, Mo.   BR/TR, 5'7", 160 lbs.   Deb: 10/6/1898   MC

YEAR	TM/L	G	AB	R	H	2B	3B	HR	RBI	BB	SO	AVG	OBP	SLG	PRO+	BR/A	SB	CS	SBR	FA	FR	G/POS	TPR
1898	Cle-N	13	38	1	4	1	0	0	1	2		.105	.150	.132	-19	-6	0			.853	-4	3-13	-1.0
1899	StL-N	2	6	1	2	0	0	0	0	1		.333	.429	.333	108	0	0			.923	1	/2-2	0.1
1901	Mil-A	64	233	24	48	8	0	0	26	17		.206	.266	.240	43	-17	6			.860	-7	3-64	-2.2
	Chi-A	42	148	20	39	5	0	0	21	12		.264	.327	.297	76	-4	11			.867	-2	S-31,3-11	-0.3
	Yr	106	381	44	87	13	0	0	47	29		.228	.290	.262	56	-22	17			.859	-9	3-75,S-31	-2.5
	Pit-N	14	51	4	10	0	0	0	4	4		.196	.268	.196	35	-4	0			.877	3	3-14	-0.1
1902	Pit-N	60	203	24	60	12	2	0	26	17		.296	.359	.374	122	5	9			.895	-5	2-27,O-18/3-9,S-4	0.1
1903	StL-N	115	431	55	123	13	3	0	42	23		.285	.326	.329	90	-6	28			.911	6	3-93,2-15/O-5	0.2
1904	StL-N	118	406	37	92	10	3	0	37	15		.227	.271	.266	69	-15	17			.897	-7	*3-118	-2.0
1905	StL-N	122	431	34	97	9	5	1	30	21		.225	.275	.276	67	-18	15			.924	3	*3-122,M	-1.1
Total	7	550	1947	200	475	58	13	1	187	112		.244	.295	.289	73	-65	87			.899	-12	3-444/2-44,S-35,O	-6.3

■ JOHN BURKE   Burke, John Patrick   b: 1/27/1877, Hazleton, Pa.   d: 8/4/50, Jersey City, N.J.   BR/TR,   Deb: 6/27/02

YEAR	TM/L	G	AB	R	H	2B	3B	HR	RBI	BB	SO	AVG	OBP	SLG	PRO+	BR/A	SB	CS	SBR	FA	FR	G/POS	TPR
1902	NY-N	4	13	0	2	0	0	0		0		.154	.154	.154	-5	-2	0			1.000	-0	/P-2,O-2	-0.1

■ JOE BURKE   Burke, Joseph A.   b: Cincinnati, Ohio   5'7", 160 lbs.   Deb: 9/26/1890

YEAR	TM/L	G	AB	R	H	2B	3B	HR	RBI	BB	SO	AVG	OBP	SLG	PRO+	BR/A	SB	CS	SBR	FA	FR	G/POS	TPR
1890	StL-a	2	6	3	4	0	0	0	2	1		.667	.750	.667	278	2	0			.750	-0	/3-2	0.1
1891	Cin-a	1	4	0	1	0	0	0	1	0	2	.250	.250	.250	40	-0	1			1.000	1	/2-1	0.1
Total	2	3	10	3	5	0	0	0	3	1	2	.500	.583	.500	192	1	0			.750	1	/3-2,2-1	0.2

■ LEO BURKE   Burke, Leo Patrick   b: 5/6/34, Hagerstown, Md.   BR/TR, 5'10", 190 lbs.   Deb: 9/7/58

YEAR	TM/L	G	AB	R	H	2B	3B	HR	RBI	BB	SO	AVG	OBP	SLG	PRO+	BR/A	SB	CS	SBR	FA	FR	G/POS	TPR
1958	Bal-A	7	11	4	5	1	0	1	4	1	2	.455	.500	.818	271	2	0	0	0	1.000	-2	/O-3,3-1	0.1
1959	Bal-A	5	10	1	2	0	0	0	1	0	5	.200	.273	.200	33	-1	0	0	0	1.000	-2	/2-2,3-2	-0.3
1961	LA-A	6	5	0	0	0	0	0	0	0	1	.000	.000	.000	-90	-1	0	0	0	.000	0	H	-0.1
1962	LA-A	19	64	8	17	1	0	4	14	5	11	.266	.329	.469	115	1	0	0	0	.958	-1	O-12/3-4,S-1	0.0
1963	StL-N	30	49	6	10	2	1	1	5	4	12	.204	.264	.347	68	-2	0	0	0	1.000	0	O-11/3-5	-0.5
	Chi-N	27	49	4	9	0	0	2	7	4	13	.184	.245	.306	55	-3	0	1	-1	.925	3	2-10/1-4	0.0
	Yr	57	98	10	19	2	1	3	12	8	25	.194	.255	.327	61	-5	0	1	-1	1.000	1	O-11,2-10/3-5,1-4	-0.5
1964	Chi-N	59	103	11	27	3	1	1	14	7	31	.262	.315	.340	81	-2	0	0	0	1.000	-2	O-18/2-5,3-4,1-2,C	-0.5
1965	Chi-N	12	10	0	2	0	0	0	0	0	4	.200	.200	.200	13	-1	0	0	0	1.000	-0	/C-2,O-1	-0.1
Total	7	165	301	33	72	7	2	9	45	21	79	.239	.295	.365	81	-7	0	1	-1	.985	-6	/O-45,2-17,31CS	-1.4

■ LES BURKE   Burke, Leslie Kingston "Buck"   b: 12/18/02, Lynn, Mass.   d: 5/6/75, Danvers, Mass.   BL/TR, 5'9", 168 lbs.   Deb: 5/2/23

YEAR	TM/L	G	AB	R	H	2B	3B	HR	RBI	BB	SO	AVG	OBP	SLG	PRO+	BR/A	SB	CS	SBR	FA	FR	G/POS	TPR
1923	Det-A	7	10	2	1	0	0	0	2	0	1	.100	.100	.100	-48	-2	0	0	0	.500	-1	/3-2,2-1	-0.3
1924	Det-A	72	241	30	61	10	4	0	17	22	20	.253	.321	.328	69	-11	2	4	-2	.957	-6	2-58/S-6	-1.7
1925	Det-A	77	180	32	52	6	3	0	24	17	8	.289	.357	.356	82	-4	4	1	1	.962	2	2-52	-0.2
1926	Det-A	38	75	9	17	1	0	0	4	7	3	.227	.301	.240	42	-6	1	2	-1	.942	4	2-15/3-7,S-1	-0.2
Total	4	194	506	73	131	17	7	0	47	46	32	.259	.327	.320	67	-24	7	7	-2	.958	-1	2-126/3-9,S-7	-2.4

■ MIKE BURKE   Burke, Michael E.   b: Cincinnati, Ohio   d: 6/9/1889, Albany, N.Y.   BR/TR, 6', 190 lbs.   Deb: 5/1/1879

YEAR	TM/L	G	AB	R	H	2B	3B	HR	RBI	BB	SO	AVG	OBP	SLG	PRO+	BR/A	SB	CS	SBR	FA	FR	G/POS	TPR
1879	Cin-N	28	117	13	26	3	0	0	8	2	5	.222	.235	.248	63	-4				.786	-8	S-19/O-5,3-5	-1.0

■ PAT BURKE   Burke, Patrick Edward   b: 5/13/01, St.Louis, Mo.   d: 7/7/65, St.Louis, Mo.   BR/TR, 5'10.5", 170 lbs.   Deb: 9/23/24

YEAR	TM/L	G	AB	R	H	2B	3B	HR	RBI	BB	SO	AVG	OBP	SLG	PRO+	BR/A	SB	CS	SBR	FA	FR	G/POS	TPR
1924	StL-A	1	3	0	0	0	0	0	1	0	0	.000	.000	.000	-94	-1	0	0	0	.000	0	/3-1	-0.1

■ JESSE BURKETT   Burkett, Jesse Cail "Crab"   b: 12/4/1868, Wheeling, W.Va.   d: 5/27/53, Worcester, Mass.   BL/TL, 5'8", 155 lbs.   Deb: 4/22/1890   CH

YEAR	TM/L	G	AB	R	H	2B	3B	HR	RBI	BB	SO	AVG	OBP	SLG	PRO+	BR/A	SB	CS	SBR	FA	FR	G/POS	TPR
1890	NY-N	101	401	67	124	23	13	4	60	33	52	.309	.366	.461	140	19	14			.824	3	O-90,P-21	1.3
1891	Cle-N	40	167	29	45	7	4	0	13	23	19	.269	.358	.359	105	1	1			.892	3	O-40	-0.3
1892	*Cle-N	145	608	119	167	15	14	6	66	67	59	.275	.348	.375	114	9	36			.904	3	O-145	0.5
1893	Cle-N	125	511	145	178	25	15	6	82	98	23	.348	.459	.491	144	35	39			.849	-8	*O-125	1.7
1894	Cle-N	125	523	138	187	27	14	8	94	84	27	.358	.447	.509	125	23	28			.915	-4	*O-125/P-1	0.8
1895	*Cle-N	131	550	153	**225**	22	13	5	83	74	31	**.409**	.486	.524	152	45	41			.884	-3	*O-131	2.5
1896	*Cle-N	133	586	160	**240**	27	16	6	72	49	19	**.410**	.461	.541	155	46	34			.926	2	*O-133	2.7
1897	Cle-N	127	517	129	198	28	7	2	60	76		.383	.468	.476	142	35	28			.949	-2	*O-127	2.0
1898	Cle-N	150	624	114	213	18	9	0	42	69		.341	.415	.399	135	32	19			.938	-8	*O-150	1.2
1899	StL-N	141	558	116	221	17	8	7	70	48		.396	.463	.500	160	48	25			.938	-3	*O-140/2-1	3.1
1900	StL-N	141	559	88	203	11	5	7	68	62		.363	.429	.474	150	40	32			.934	-4	*O-141	3.0
1901	StL-N	142	601	**142**	**226**	20	15	10	75	59		**.376**	**.440**	.509	**184**	**66**	27			.923	-1	*O-142	5.2

YEAR	TM/L	G	AB	R	H	2B	3B	HR	RBI	BB	SO	AVG	OBP	SLG	PRO+	BR/A	SB	CS	SBR	FA	FR	G/POS	TPR
1902	StL-A	138	553	97	169	29	9	5	52	71		.306	.390	.418	126	22	23			.924	6	*O-137/P-1,S-1,3-1	1.7
1903	StL-A	132	515	73	151	20	7	3	40	52		.293	.361	.377	125	17	17			.941	-4	*O-132	0.5
1904	StL-A	147	575	72	156	15	10	2	27	78		.271	.363	.343	132	24	12			.942	5	*O-147	2.3
1905	Bos-A	148	573	78	147	12	13	4	47	67		.257	.339	.344	115	11	13			.929	-2	*O-148	0.3
Total	16	2066	8421	1720	2850	320	182	75	952	1029	230	.338	.415	.446	140	474	389			.917	-19	*O-2053/P-23,3S2	28.5

■ ELLIS BURKS
Burks, Ellis Rena b: 9/11/64, Vicksburg, Miss. BR/TR, 6'2", 200 lbs. Deb: 4/30/87

YEAR	TM/L	G	AB	R	H	2B	3B	HR	RBI	BB	SO	AVG	OBP	SLG	PRO+	BR/A	SB	CS	SBR	FA	FR	G/POS	TPR
1987	Bos-A	133	558	94	152	30	2	20	59	41	98	.272	.324	.441	98	-3	27	6	5	.988	14	*O-132/D-1	1.1
1988	*Bos-A	144	540	93	159	37	5	18	92	62	89	.294	.370	.481	131	22	25	9	2	.977	12	*O-142/D-2	3.2
1989	Bos-A	97	399	73	121	19	6	12	61	36	52	.303	.368	.471	127	14	21	5	3	.977	7	O-95/D-1	2.2
1990	*Bos-A†	152	588	89	174	33	8	21	89	48	82	.296	.350	.486	126	19	9	11	-4	.994	2	*O-143/D-6	1.3
1991	Bos-A	130	474	56	119	33	3	14	56	39	81	.251	.316	.422	97	-3	6	11	-5	.993	-3	*O-126/D-2	-1.3
1992	Bos-A	66	235	35	60	8	3	8	30	25	48	.255	.330	.417	101	0	5	2	0	.984	-7	O-63/D-1	-0.8
1993	*Chi-A	146	499	75	137	24	4	17	74	60	97	.275	.357	.441	116	11	6	9	-4	.982	0	*O-146	0.5
1994	Col-N	42	149	33	48	8	3	13	24	16	39	.322	.388	.678	147	9	3	1	0	.964	-2	O-39	0.6
1995	*Col-N	103	278	41	74	10	6	14	49	39	72	.266	.361	.496	96	-4	7	3	0	.970	-4	O-80	-1.0
1996	Col-N★	156	613	142	211	45	8	40	128	61	114	.344	.409	.639	133	24	32	6	6	.983	1	*O-152	2.6
Total	10	1169	4333	731	1255	247	48	177	662	427	772	.290	.357	.491	118	91	141	63	5	.983	20	*O-1118/D-13	8.4

■ RICK BURLESON
Burleson, Richard Paul "Rooster" b: 4/29/51, Lynwood, Cal. BR/TR, 5'10", 165 lbs. Deb: 5/4/74 C

YEAR	TM/L	G	AB	R	H	2B	3B	HR	RBI	BB	SO	AVG	OBP	SLG	PRO+	BR/A	SB	CS	SBR	FA	FR	G/POS	TPR
1974	Bos-A	114	384	36	109	22	0	4	44	21	34	.284	.324	.372	93	-4	3	3	-1	.957	-5	S-88,2-31/3-2	0.2
1975	*Bos-A	158	580	66	146	25	1	6	62	45	44	.252	.309	.329	74	-20	8	5	-1	.963	-1	*S-158	-0.4
1976	Bos-A	152	540	75	157	27	1	7	42	60	37	.291	.367	.383	107	5	14	9	-1	.957	-7	*S-152	1.7
1977	Bos-A★	154	663	80	194	36	7	3	52	47	69	.293	.341	.382	87	-12	13	12	-3	.970	12	*S-154	1.4
1978	Bos-A†	145	626	75	155	32	5	5	49	40	71	.248	.297	.339	71	-25	8	8	-2	.981	19	*S-144	1.1
1979	Bos-A★	153	627	93	174	32	5	5	60	35	54	.278	.319	.368	80	-18	9	5	-0	.980	22	*S-153	2.0
1980	Bos-A	155	644	89	179	29	2	8	51	62	51	.278	.343	.366	90	-8	12	13	-4	.974	26	*S-155	3.1
1981	Cal-A★	109	430	53	126	17	1	5	33	42	38	.293	.360	.372	111	7	4	6	-2	.979	21	*S-109	3.8
1982	Cal-A	11	45	4	7	1	0	0	2	6	3	.156	.255	.178	21	-5	0	0	0	.986	7	S-11	0.4
1983	Cal-A	33	119	22	34	7	0	0	11	12	12	.286	.351	.345	93	-1	0	2	-1	.969	-0	S-31	0.1
1984	Cal-A	7	4	2	0	0	0	0	0	2	0	.000	.000	.000	-99	-1	0	0	0	.000	0	/H	-0.1
1986	*Cal-A	93	271	35	77	14	0	5	29	33	32	.284	.364	.391	107	3	1	3	-2	.984	-7	D-38,S-37/2-6,3-4	-0.3
1987	Bal-A	62	206	26	43	14	1	2	14	17	30	.209	.279	.316	59	-12	0	2	-1	.977	-1	2-55/D-7	-1.2
Total	13	1346	5139	656	1401	256	23	50	449	420	477	.273	.331	.361	87	-89	72	68	-19	.971	86	*S-1192/2-92,D-45,3	11.8

■ HERCULES BURNETT
Burnett, Hercules H. b: 8/13/1865, Louisville, Ky. d: 10/4/36, Louisville, Ky. BR, 177 lbs. Deb: 6/26/1888

YEAR	TM/L	G	AB	R	H	2B	3B	HR	RBI	BB	SO	AVG	OBP	SLG	PRO+	BR/A	SB	CS	SBR	FA	FR	G/POS	TPR
1888	Lou-a	1	4	1	0	0	0	0	0	1		.000	.200	.000	-34	-1	1			.667	-0	/O-1	-0.1
1895	Lou-N	5	17	6	7	0	1	2	3	2	2	.412	.474	.882	261	4	2			.769	-0	/O-4,1-1	0.3
Total	2	6	21	7	7	0	1	2	3	3	2	.333	.417	.714	211	3	3			.750	-1	/O-5,1-1	0.2

■ JOHNNY BURNETT
Burnett, John Henderson b: 11/1/04, Bartow, Fla. d: 8/13/59, Tampa, Fla. BL/TR, 5'11", 175 lbs. Deb: 5/7/27

YEAR	TM/L	G	AB	R	H	2B	3B	HR	RBI	BB	SO	AVG	OBP	SLG	PRO+	BR/A	SB	CS	SBR	FA	FR	G/POS	TPR
1927	Cle-A	17	8	5	0	0	0	0	0	0	3	.000	.000	.000	-99	-2	1	0	0	.833	2	/2-2	0.0
1928	Cle-A	3	10	3	5	0	0	0	1	0	1	.500	.500	.500	162	-0	0	0	0	.867	0	/S-2	0.1
1929	Cle-A	19	33	2	5	1	0	0	2	1	2	.152	.200	.182	-1	-5	0	0	0	.923	6	S-10/2-8	0.1
1930	Cle-A	54	170	28	53	13	0	0	20	17	8	.312	.388	.388	91	-2	2	2	-1	.973	-5	3-27,S-19	-0.3
1931	Cle-A	111	427	85	128	25	5	1	52	39	25	.300	.360	.389	92	-5	5	2	0	.938	-15	S-63,2-35,3-21,/O-1	-1.0
1932	Cle-A	129	512	81	152	23	5	4	53	46	27	.297	.359	.385	87	-9	2	5	-2	.946	-22	*S-103,2-26	-2.2
1933	Cle-A	83	261	39	71	11	2	1	29	23	14	.272	.333	.341	76	-9	3	2	-0	.938	-5	S-41,2-17,3-12	-0.9
1934	Cle-A	72	208	28	61	11	2	3	30	18	11	.293	.352	.409	94	-2	1	1	-0	.981	-8	3-42/S-9,2-3,0-2	-0.7
1935	StL-A	70	206	17	46	10	1	0	26	19	16	.223	.289	.282	46	-17	1	0	0	.939	-6	3-31,S-18,2-12	-1.8
Total	9	558	1835	288	521	94	15	9	213	163	107	.284	.345	.366	81	-50	15	12	-3	.935	-53	S-265,3-133,2/O	-6.7

■ JACK BURNETT
Burnett, John P. b: 12/2/1889, Missouri d: 9/8/29, Taft, Cal. Deb: 7/2/07

YEAR	TM/L	G	AB	R	H	2B	3B	HR	RBI	BB	SO	AVG	OBP	SLG	PRO+	BR/A	SB	CS	SBR	FA	FR	G/POS	TPR
1907	StL-N	59	206	18	49	9	2	0		8		.238	.296	.316	95	-2	5			.955	-4	O-59	-1.0

■ JEROMY BURNITZ
Burnitz, Jeromy Neal b: 4/15/69, Westminster, Cal. BL/TR, 6', 190 lbs. Deb: 6/21/93

YEAR	TM/L	G	AB	R	H	2B	3B	HR	RBI	BB	SO	AVG	OBP	SLG	PRO+	BR/A	SB	CS	SBR	FA	FR	G/POS	TPR
1993	NY-N	86	263	49	64	10	6	13	38	38	66	.243	.341	.475	117	6	3	6	-3	.977	2	O-79	0.4
1994	NY-N	45	143	26	34	4	0	3	15	23	45	.238	.347	.329	78	-4	1	1	-0	.970	-5	O-42	-1.0
1995	Cle-A	9	7	4	4	1	0	0	0	0	0	.571	.571	.714	229	1	0	0	0	1.000	-1	/O-6,D-2	0.1
1996	Cle-A	71	128	30	36	10	0	2	26	25	31	.281	.406	.523	133	7	2	1	0	1.000	-1	O-30,D-15	0.1
	Mil-A	23	72	8	17	4	2	2	14	8	16	.236	.329	.375	73	-3	2	0	1	.976	-2	O-22	-0.4
	Yr	94	200	38	53	14	2	4	40	33	47	.265	.380	.470	112	4	4	1	1	.988	-6	O-52,D-15	-0.3
Total	4	234	613	117	155	29	6	25	93	94	158	.253	.358	.442	107	8	8	8	-2	.979	-8	O-179/D-17	-0.8

■ C.B. BURNS
Burns, Charles Birmingham b: 5/15/1879, Bay View, Md. d: 6/6/68, Havre De Grace, Md BR/TR, 6', 175 lbs. Deb: 8/19/02

YEAR	TM/L	G	AB	R	H	2B	3B	HR	RBI	BB	SO	AVG	OBP	SLG	PRO+	BR/A	SB	CS	SBR	FA	FR	G/POS	TPR
1902	Bal-A	1	1	0	1	0	0	0	0	0		1.000	1.000	1.000	436	0	0			.000	0	H	0.0

■ ED BURNS
Burns, Edward James b: 10/31/1888, San Francisco, Cal d: 6/1/42, Monterey, Cal. BR/TR, 5'6", 165 lbs. Deb: 6/25/12

YEAR	TM/L	G	AB	R	H	2B	3B	HR	RBI	BB	SO	AVG	OBP	SLG	PRO+	BR/A	SB	CS	SBR	FA	FR	G/POS	TPR
1912	StL-N	1	1	0	0	0	0	0	1	0	0	.000	.000	.000	-99	-0	0			.000	0	/C-1	0.0
1913	Phi-N	17	30	3	6	3	0	0	3	6	3	.200	.351	.300	83	-0	2			.980	-4	C-15	-0.4
1914	Phi-N	70	139	8	36	3	4	0	16	20	12	.259	.352	.338	99	0	5			.947	-2	C-55	0.2
1915	*Phi-N	67	174	11	42	5	0	0	16	20	12	.241	.327	.270	81	-3	1			.981	-6	C-62	-0.5
1916	Phi-N	78	219	14	51	8	1	0	14	16	18	.233	.294	.279	74	-6	3			.981	-12	C-75/S-1,O-1	-1.5
1917	Phi-N	20	49	2	10	2	0	0	6	1	5	.204	.220	.224	35	-4	2			.971	-1	C-15	-0.5
1918	Phi-N	68	184	10	38	1	1	0	9	20	9	.207	.288	.223	53	-10	1			.981	-4	C-68	-1.0
Total	7	321	796	48	183	21	6	0	65	83	59	.230	.308	.271	73	-23	14			.974	-29	C-291/O-1,S-1	-3.7

■ GEORGE BURNS
Burns, George Henry "Tioga George" b: 1/31/1893, Niles, Ohio d: 1/7/78, Kirkland, Wash. BR/TR, 6'1.5", 180 lbs. Deb: 4/14/14

YEAR	TM/L	G	AB	R	H	2B	3B	HR	RBI	BB	SO	AVG	OBP	SLG	PRO+	BR/A	SB	CS	SBR	FA	FR	G/POS	TPR
1914	Det-A	137	478	55	139	22	5	5	57	32	56	.291	.351	.389	119	10	23	13	-1	.982	-5	*1-137	0.1
1915	Det-A	105	392	49	99	18	3	5	50	22	51	.253	.301	.352	91	-6	9	3	-1	.986	-4	*1-104	-1.3
1916	Det-A	135	479	60	137	22	6	4	73	22	30	.286	.327	.382	109	3	12			.985	-10	*1-124	-1.3
1917	Det-A	119	407	42	92	14	10	1	40	15	33	.226	.264	.317	77	-13	3			.990	-4	*1-104	-2.3
1918	Phi-A	130	505	61	178	22	9	6	70	23	25	.352	.390	.467	157	32	8			.983	6	*1-128/O-2	3.6
1919	Phi-A	126	470	63	139	29	9	8	57	19	18	.296	.339	.447	118	9	15			.980	2	1-86,O-34	0.7
1920	Phi-A	22	60	1	14	3	0	1	7	6	7	.233	.313	.333	71	-3	4	0	1	.958	1	O-13	-0.2
	*Cle-A	44	56	7	15	4	1	0	13	4	3	.268	.339	.375	86	-1	1	0	0	.979	1	1-12/O-1	0.0
	Yr	66	116	8	29	7	1	1	20	10	10	.250	.326	.353	78	-4	5	0	2	.958	1	O-14,1-12	-0.2
1921	Cle-A	84	244	52	88	22	4	0	49	13	19	.361	.398	.480	121	7	3	1	0	.990	2	1-73	0.7
1922	Bos-A	147	558	71	171	32	5	12	73	20	28	.306	.341	.446	104	1	8	2	1	.987	-1	*1-140	-0.4
1923	Bos-A	146	551	91	181	47	5	7	82	45	33	.328	.386	.470	124	18	9	7	-2	.990	-1	*1-146	0.8
1924	Cle-A	129	462	64	143	37	5	4	68	29	27	.310	.350	.437	106	3	14	5	1	.987	8	*1-127	0.5
1925	Cle-A	127	488	69	164	41	4	6	79	24	24	.336	.371	.473	112	7	16	11	-2	.989	-7	*1-126	-0.2
1926	Cle-A	151	603	97	216	64	3	4	114	28	33	.358	.394	.494	129	24	13	7	-0	.988	1	*1-151	1.5
1927	Cle-A	140	549	84	175	51	7	7	78	42	27	.319	.375	.435	109	7	13	11	-3	.990	3	*1-139	-0.2
1928	Cle-A	82	209	29	52	12	1	5	30	17	11	.249	.323	.388	85	-5	2	3	-0	.984	2	1-53	-0.8
	NY-A	4	4	1	2	0	0	0	0	0	1	.500	.500	.500	169	0	0	0	0	1.000	-0	/1-2	0.0
	Yr	86	213	30	54	12	1	5	30	17	12	.254	.326	.390	87	-4	2	3	-0	.985	2	1-55	-0.8
1929	NY-A	9	9	0	0	0	0	0	0	0	4	.000	.000	.000	-99	-3	0	0	0	.000	0	H	-0.3
	*Phi-A	29	49	5	13	5	0	1	11	2	3	.265	.294	.429	81	-2	1	0	0	1.000	-0	1-19	-0.2
	Yr	38	58	5	13	5	0	1	11	2	7	.224	.250	.362	55	-4	1	0	0	1.000	-0	1-19	-0.5
Total	16	1866	6573	901	2018	444	72	72	951	363	433	.307	.354	.429	112	91	154	63		.987	0	*1-1671/O-50	0.7

YEAR	TM/L	G	AB	R	H	2B	3B	HR	RBI	BB	SO	AVG	OBP	SLG	PRO+	BR/A	SB	CS	SBR	FA	FR	G/POS	TPR

■ GEORGE BURNS
Burns, George Joseph b: 11/24/1889, Utica, N.Y. d: 8/15/66, Gloversville, N.Y. BR/TR, 5'7", 160 lbs. Deb: 10/3/11 C

YEAR	TM/L	G	AB	R	H	2B	3B	HR	RBI	BB	SO	AVG	OBP	SLG	PRO+	BR/A	SB	CS	SBR	FA	FR	G/POS	TPR
1911	NY-N	6	17	2	1	0	0	0	0	1	0	.059	.111	.059	-50	-3	0			1.000	-2	/O-6	-0.5
1912	NY-N	29	51	11	15	4	0	0	3	8	8	.294	.400	.373	109	1	7			1.000	-4	O-23	-0.4
1913	*NY-N	150	605	81	173	37	4	2	54	58	74	.286	.352	.370	106	5	40			.963	7	*O-150	0.5
1914	NY-N	154	561	**100**	170	35	10	3	60	89	53	.303	.403	.417	149	38	62			.950	8	*O-154	4.1
1915	NY-N	155	622	83	169	27	14	3	51	56	57	.272	.333	.375	121	15	27	20	-4	.960	-6	*O-155	-0.3
1916	NY-N	155	623	**105**	174	24	8	5	41	63	47	.279	.346	.368	126	19	37	26	-5	.962	3	*O-155	1.1
1917	*NY-N	152	597	103	180	25	13	5	45	**75**	55	.302	.380	.412	148	35	40			.974	5	*O-152	3.5
1918	NY-N	119	465	80	135	22	6	4	51	43	37	.290	.354	.389	129	16	40			.965	9	*O-119	2.0
1919	NY-N	139	534	**86**	162	30	9	2	46	**82**	37	.303	**.396**	.404	142	31	**40**			**.990**	1	*O-139	2.5
1920	NY-N	154	631	**115**	181	35	9	6	46	**76**	48	.287	.365	.399	121	19	22	22	-7	.983	1	*O-154	0.2
1921	*NY-N	149	605	111	181	28	9	4	61	**80**	24	.299	.386	.395	107	9	19	20	-6	.972	3	*O-149/3-1	-0.5
1922	Cin-N	156	631	104	180	20	10	1	53	78	38	.285	.366	.353	88	-9	30	23	-5	.976	6	*O-156	-1.8
1923	Cin-N	154	614	99	168	27	13	3	45	**101**	46	.274	.376	.375	101	4	12	14	-5	.960	-1	*O-154	-1.2
1924	Cin-N	93	336	43	86	19	2	2	33	29	21	.256	.315	.342	77	-11	3	6	-3	.963	1	O-90	-1.8
1925	Phi-N	88	349	65	102	29	1	1	22	33	20	.292	.353	.390	82	-9	4	8	-4	.990	0	O-88	-1.7
Total	15	1853	7241	1188	2077	362	108	41	611	872	565	.287	.366	.384	115	161	383	_139_		.970	32	*O-1844/3-1	5.7

■ JIM BURNS
Burns, James M. b: Quincy, Ill. 5'7", 168 lbs. Deb: 9/25/1888

YEAR	TM/L	G	AB	R	H	2B	3B	HR	RBI	BB	SO	AVG	OBP	SLG	PRO+	BR/A	SB	CS	SBR	FA	FR	G/POS	TPR
1888	KC-a	15	66	13	20	0	0	0		4	1	.303	.343	.303	101	-0	6			.853	2	O-15	0.1
1889	KC-a	134	579	103	176	23	11	5	97	20	68	.304	.335	.408	105	-0	56			.913	-7	*O-134/3-1	-0.9
1891	Was-a	20	82	15	26	6	0	0	10	6	10	.317	.378	.390	125	3	2			.771	-4	O-20/S-1	-0.1
Total	3	169	727	131	222	29	11	5	111	27	_78_	.305	.341	.396	107	3	64			.897	-9	O-169/S-1,3-1	-0.9

■ JACK BURNS
Burns, John Irving "Slug" b: 8/31/07, Cambridge, Mass. d: 4/18/75, Brighton, Mass. BL/TL, 5'10.5", 175 lbs. Deb: 9/17/30 C

YEAR	TM/L	G	AB	R	H	2B	3B	HR	RBI	BB	SO	AVG	OBP	SLG	PRO+	BR/A	SB	CS	SBR	FA	FR	G/POS	TPR
1930	StL-A	8	30	5	9	3	0	2	5	5	5	.300	.400	.400	100	0	0	0	0	1.000	1	/1-8	0.0
1931	StL-A	144	570	75	148	27	7	4	70	42	58	.260	.312	.353	72	-24	19	12	-2	.993	18	*1-143	-1.9
1932	StL-A	150	617	111	188	33	8	11	70	61	43	.305	.368	.438	102	2	17	11	-2	.992	4	*1-150	-0.7
1933	StL-A	144	556	89	160	43	4	7	71	56	51	.288	.353	.417	97	-3	11	11	-3	.992	5	*1-143	-1.6
1934	StL-A	154	612	86	157	28	8	13	73	62	47	.257	.327	.392	78	-22	9	3	1	.992	-0	*1-154	-3.2
1935	StL-A	143	549	77	157	28	1	5	67	68	49	.286	.366	.368	86	-10	3	2	-0	.992	-8	*1-141	-3.1
1936	StL-A	9	14	2	3	1	0	0	1	3	1	.214	.353	.286	58	-1	0	0	0	1.000	0	/1-2	-0.1
	Det-A	138	558	96	158	36	3	4	63	79	45	.283	.375	.380	87	-10	4	8	-4	.994	1	*1-138	-2.3
	Yr	147	572	98	161	37	3	4	64	82	46	.281	.374	.378	86	-11	4	8	-4	.994	1	*1-140	-2.4
Total	7	890	3506	541	980	199	31	44	417	376	299	.280	.351	.392	87	-67	63	47	-9	.992	19	1-879	-12.9

■ JACK BURNS
Burns, John Joseph b: 5/13/1880, Avoca, Pa. d: 6/24/57, Waterford, Conn. BR/TR, 5'10", 160 lbs. Deb: 9/11/03

YEAR	TM/L	G	AB	R	H	2B	3B	HR	RBI	BB	SO	AVG	OBP	SLG	PRO+	BR/A	SB	CS	SBR	FA	FR	G/POS	TPR
1903	Det-A	11	37	2	10	0	0	0	3		1	.270	.325	.270	82	-1	0			.981	1	2-11	0.0
1904	Det-A	4	16	3	2	0	0	0	1		1	.125	.176	.125	-4	-2	1			.952	-1	/2-4	-0.4
Total	2	15	53	5	12	0	0	0	4		2	.226	.281	.226	57	-3	1			.973	-0	/2-15	-0.4

■ JOE BURNS
Burns, Joseph Francis b: 3/26/1889, Ipswich, Mass. d: 7/12/87, Beverly, Mass. BL/TL, 5'11", 170 lbs. Deb: 6/19/10

YEAR	TM/L	G	AB	R	H	2B	3B	HR	RBI	BB	SO	AVG	OBP	SLG	PRO+	BR/A	SB	CS	SBR	FA	FR	G/POS	TPR
1910	Cin-N	1	1	0	1	0	0	0	0	0		1.000	1.000	1.000	506	0	1			.000	0	H	0.1
1913	Det-A	4	13	0	5	0	0	0	1	2	4	.385	.500	.385	162	1	0			1.000	-1	/O-4	0.1
Total	2	5	14	0	6	0	0	0	1	2	4	.429	.529	.429	184	2	1			1.000	-1	/O-4	0.2

■ JOE BURNS
Burns, Joseph Francis b: 2/25/1900, Trenton, N.J. d: 1/7/86, Trenton, N.J. BR/TR, 6', 175 lbs. Deb: 4/18/24

YEAR	TM/L	G	AB	R	H	2B	3B	HR	RBI	BB	SO	AVG	OBP	SLG	PRO+	BR/A	SB	CS	SBR	FA	FR	G/POS	TPR
1924	Chi-A	8	19	1	2	0	0	0	0		2	.105	.105	.105	-47	-4	0	0	0	.933	-2	/C-6	-0.6

■ JOE BURNS
Burns, Joseph James b: 6/17/16, Bryn Mawr, Pa. d: 6/24/74, Bryn Mawr, Pa. BR/TR, 5'10.5", 175 lbs. Deb: 4/24/43

YEAR	TM/L	G	AB	R	H	2B	3B	HR	RBI	BB	SO	AVG	OBP	SLG	PRO+	BR/A	SB	CS	SBR	FA	FR	G/POS	TPR
1943	Bos-N	52	135	12	28	3	0	1	5	8	25	.207	.262	.252	49	-9	2			.933	-1	3-34/O-4	-1.0
1944	Phi-A	28	75	5	18	2	0	1	6	3	17	.240	.278	.307	68	-3	0	1	-1	.919	-8	3-17/2-9	-1.2
1945	Phi-A	31	90	7	23	1	1	0	3	4	17	.256	.287	.289	68	-4	0	1	-1	1.000	-4	O-19/3-5,1-1	-1.0
Total	3	111	300	24	69	6	1	2	16	16	50	.230	.274	.277	60	-16	2	_2_		.920	-12	/3-56,O-23,2-9,1-1	-3.2

■ PAT BURNS
Burns, Patrick Deb: 8/11/1884

YEAR	TM/L	G	AB	R	H	2B	3B	HR	RBI	BB	SO	AVG	OBP	SLG	PRO+	BR/A	SB	CS	SBR	FA	FR	G/POS	TPR
1884	Bal-a	6	25	3	5	2	1	0			3	.200	.286	.360	105	0				.953	-1	/1-6	-0.1
	Bal-U	1	4	0	2	0	0	0			0	.500	.500	.500	185	0				.917	-0	/1-1	0.0
Total	1	7	29	3	7	2	1	0			3	.241	.313	.379	117	0				.947	-1	/1-7	-0.1

■ DICK BURNS
Burns, Richard Simon b: 12/26/1863, Holyoke, Mass. d: 11/16/37, Holyoke, Mass. BL/TL, 5'7", 140 lbs. Deb: 5/3/1883

YEAR	TM/L	G	AB	R	H	2B	3B	HR	RBI	BB	SO	AVG	OBP	SLG	PRO+	BR/A	SB	CS	SBR	FA	FR	G/POS	TPR
1883	Det-N	37	140	11	26	7	1	0	5	2	22	.186	.197	.250	36	-10				.758	-6	O-24,P-17	-1.0
1884	Cin-U	79	350	84	107	17	**12**	4		5		.306	.315	.457	122	-2				.827	-3	O-44,P-40/S-2	-0.5
1885	StL-N	14	54	2	12	2	1	0	4	3	8	.222	.263	.296	86	-1				.682	-3	O-14/P-1	-0.5
Total	3	130	544	97	145	26	14	4	_9_	10	_30_	.267	.280	.388	98	-13				.785	-12	/O-82,P-58,S-2	-2.0

■ TOM BURNS
Burns, Thomas Everett b: 3/30/1857, Honesdale, Pa. d: 3/19/02, Jersey City, N.J. BR/TR, 5'7", 152 lbs. Deb: 5/1/1880 MU

YEAR	TM/L	G	AB	R	H	2B	3B	HR	RBI	BB	SO	AVG	OBP	SLG	PRO+	BR/A	SB	CS	SBR	FA	FR	G/POS	TPR
1880	Chi-N	85	333	47	103	17	3	0	43	12	23	.309	.333	.378	133	10				.864	-24	*S-79/3-9,C-2,P-1	-0.9
1881	Chi-N	84	342	41	95	20	3	4	42	14	22	.278	.306	.389	112	4				.870	-5	2-43,S-41	0.4
1882	Chi-N	84	355	55	88	23	6	0	48	15	28	.248	.278	.346	95	-3				.911	0	2-43,S-41	0.0
1883	Chi-N	97	405	69	119	37	7	2	67	13	31	.294	.316	.435	118	7				.872	-1	*S-79,2-19/O-1	0.7
1884	Chi-N	83	343	54	84	14	2	7	44	13	50	.245	.272	.359	89	-6				.838	-2	*S-80/3-3	-0.6
1885	*Chi-N	111	445	82	121	23	9	7	71	16	48	.272	.297	.411	111	1				.844	-5	*S-111/2-1	0.1
1886	*Chi-N	112	445	64	123	18	10	3	65	14	40	.276	.298	.382	92	-8	15			.890	13	*3-112	0.7
1887	Chi-N	115	424	57	112	20	10	3	60	34	32	.264	.320	.380	83	-13	32			.872	21	*3-107/O-8	0.9
1888	Chi-N	134	483	60	115	16	3	7	70	26	49	.238	.281	.306	81	-11	34			.905	17	*3-134	0.8
1889	Chi-N	136	525	64	127	27	6	4	66	32	57	.242	.288	.339	71	-23	18			.880	3	*3-136	-1.3
1890	Chi-N	139	538	86	149	17	6	5	86	57	45	.277	.348	.359	102	1	44			.898	2	*3-139	0.7
1891	Chi-N	59	243	36	55	8	1	1	17	21	21	.226	.288	.280	66	-11	18			.892	-2	3-53/S-4,O-2	-0.9
1892	Pit-N	12	39	7	8	0	0	0	4	3	8	.205	.262	.205	41	-3	1			.690	-5	/3-8,O-3,M	-0.7
Total	13	1251	4920	722	1299	236	69	39	683	270	454	.264	.303	.364	95	-53	162			.886	16	3-704,S-474/2OCP	-0.1

■ OYSTER BURNS
Burns, Thomas P. b: 9/6/1864, Philadelphia, Pa. d: 11/11/28, Brooklyn, N.Y. BR/TR, 5'8", 183 lbs. Deb: 8/18/1884

YEAR	TM/L	G	AB	R	H	2B	3B	HR	RBI	BB	SO	AVG	OBP	SLG	PRO+	BR/A	SB	CS	SBR	FA	FR	G/POS	TPR
1884	Wil-U	2	7	0	1	0	1	0		1		.143	.250	.429	99	-0				.778	-0	/S-2	0.0
	Bal-a	35	131	34	39	2	6	6	23	7		.298	.348	.542	179	11				.826	-5	O-24,2-10/P-2,3-1	0.5
1885	Bal-a	78	321	47	74	11	6	5	37	16		.231	.280	.349	99	-0				.908	-0	O-45,P-15,S/321	-0.1
1887	Bal-a	140	551	122	188	33	**19**	9	99	63		.341	.414	.594	169	53	58			.841	-19	*S-98,3-42/P-3,2-1	2.8
1888	Bal-a	79	325	54	97	18	9	4	42	24		.298	.349	.446	158	20	23			.855	-5	O-56,S-23/P-5,32	1.3
	Bro-a	52	204	40	58	9	6	2	25	14		.284	.339	.417	142	9	21			.851	-13	S-36,O-14/2-3	-0.3
	Yr	131	529	94	155	27	15	6	67	38		.293	.345	.435	152	30	44			.847	-18	O-70,S-59/P-5,23	1.0
1889	*Bro-a	131	504	105	153	19	13	5	100	68	26	.304	.391	.423	131	22	32			.920	-8	*O-113,S-19	1.0
1890	*Bro-N	119	472	102	134	22	12	**13**	**128**	51	42	.284	.359	.464	139	21	21			.941	-3	*O-116/3-3	1.3
1891	Bro-N	123	470	75	134	24	13	4	83	53	30	.285	.358	.417	126	15	21			.922	0	*O-113/S-6,3-5	1.2
1892	Bro-N	141	542	88	171	27	18	4	96	65	42	.315	.395	.454	163	42	33			.937	-13	*O-129/3-7,S-5	2.2
1893	Bro-N	109	415	68	112	22	6	7	60	36	16	.270	.334	.412	103	-0	14			.932	-1	*O-108/S-1	-0.5
1894	Bro-N	125	505	106	179	32	14	5	107	44	16	.354	.409	.503	128	23	30			.949	-6	*O-125	0.9
1895	Bro-N	20	76	7	14	1	0	1	7	8	2	.184	.271	.211	27	-8	0			.918	1	O-19	-0.7
	NY-N	33	114	21	35	5	3	1	25	14	6	.307	.388	.430	113	3	10			.870	-5	O-32/1-1	-0.3
	Yr	53	190	28	49	6	3	2	32	22	8	.258	.341	.342	80	-5	10			.893	-3	O-51/1-1	-1.0
Total	11	1187	4637	869	1389	224	129	65	_832_	464	_182_	.300	.368	.446	135	210	263			.920	-73	O-894,S-200/3P21	9.3

YEAR	TM/L	G	AB	R	H	2B	3B	HR	RBI	BB	SO	AVG	OBP	SLG	PRO+	BR/A	SB	CS	SBR	FA	FR	G/POS	TPR

■ ALEX BURR Burr, Alexander Thomson b: 11/1/1893, Chicago, Ill. d: 10/12/18, Cazaux, France BR/TR, 6'3.5", 190 lbs. Deb: 4/21/14

| 1914 | NY-A | 1 | 0 | 0 | 0 | 0 | 0 | 0 | 0 | 0 | 0 | — | — | — | — | | 0 | 0 | | .000 | -1 | /O-1 | -0.1 |

■ BUSTER BURRELL Burrell, Frank Andrew b: 12/22/1866, Weymouth, Mass. d: 5/8/62, Weymouth, Mass. BR/TR, 5'10", 165 lbs. Deb: 8/1/1891

1891	NY-N	15	53	1	5	0	0	1	3	12	.094	.158	.094	-27	-8	2			.856	-5	C-15/O-1	-1.2
1895	Bro-N	12	28	7	4	0	0	1	5	4	3	.143	.250	.250	32	-3	0			.838	-2	C-12	-0.3
1896	Bro-N	62	206	19	62	11	3	0	23	15	13	.301	.348	.383	98	-1	1			.928	-9	C-60	-0.3
1897	Bro-N	33	103	15	25	2	0	2	18	10		.243	.310	.320	70	-4	1			.884	-4	C-27/1-4	-0.5
Total	4	122	390	42	96	13	3	3	47	32	28	.246	.305	.318	70	-16	4			.896	-19	C-114/1-4,O-1	-2.3

■ LARRY BURRIGHT Burright, Larry Allen "Possum" b: 7/10/37, Roseville, Ill. BR/TR, 5'11", 170 lbs. Deb: 4/12/62

1962	LA-N	115	249	35	51	6	5	4	30	21	67	.205	.267	.317	60	-15	4	3	-1	.962	14	*2-109/S-1	0.6
1963	NY-N	41	100	9	22	2	1	0	3	8	25	.220	.291	.260	59	-5	1	0	0	.946	12	S-19,2-15/3-1	1.0
1964	NY-N	3	7	0	0	0	0	0	0	0	0	.000	.000	.000	-99	-2	0	0	0	1.000	4	/2-3	0.3
Total	3	159	356	44	73	8	6	4	33	29	92	.205	.269	.295	56	-22	5	3	-0	.964	30	2-127/S-20,3-1	1.9

■ PAUL BURRIS Burris, Paul Robert b: 7/21/23, Hickory, N.C. BR/TR, 6', 190 lbs. Deb: 10/2/48

1948	Bos-N	2	4	0	2	0	0	0	0	0	0	.500	.500	.500	174	0	0			1.000	1	/C-2	0.1
1950	Bos-N	10	23	1	4	1	0	0	3	1	2	.174	.208	.217	13	-3	0			1.000	1	/C-8	-0.1
1952	Bos-N	55	168	14	37	4	0	2	21	7	19	.220	.256	.280	50	-12	0	0	0	1.000	-4	C-50	-1.4
1953	Mil-N	2	1	0	0	0	0	0	0	0	0	.000	.000	.000	-99	-0	0	0	0	1.000	-0	/C-2	0.0
Total	4	69	196	15	43	5	0	2	24	8	21	.219	.254	.276	47	-14	0	0	0	1.000	-2	/C-62	-1.4

■ HENRY BURROUGHS Burroughs, Henry F. b: 1845, Detroit, Mich. 5'8", 147 lbs. Deb: 5/5/1871

1871	Oly-n	12	63	11	15	2	3	1	14	1	1	.238	.250	.413	91	-0	0	0		.706	-2	/O-8,3-5,2-1	-0.2
1872	Oly-n	2	7	1	1	0	0	0	0	1	0	.143	.250	.143	25	-1	0	0		.625	0	/O-2	0.0
Total	2 n	14	70	12	16	2	3	1	14	2	1	.229	.250	.386	85	-1	0	0		.680	-2	/O-10,3-5,2-1	-0.2

■ JEFF BURROUGHS Burroughs, Jeffrey Alan b: 3/7/51, Long Beach, Cal. BR/TR, 6'1", 200 lbs. Deb: 7/20/70

1970	Was-A	6	12	1	2	0	0	0	1	2	5	.167	.286	.167	29	-1	0	0	0	1.000	-0	/O-3	-0.1
1971	Was-A	59	181	20	42	9	0	5	25	22	55	.232	.319	.365	99	-1	1	0	0	.966	-5	O-50	-0.8
1972	Tex-A	22	65	4	12	1	0	1	3	5	22	.185	.243	.246	48	-4	0	2	-1	.935	-1	O-19/1-1	-0.8
1973	Tex-A	151	526	71	147	17	1	30	85	67	88	.279	.362	.487	143	29	0	0	0	.975	13	*O-148/1-3,D-1	3.5
1974	Tex-A★	152	554	84	167	33	2	25	**118**	91	104	.301	.405	.504	164	48	2	3	-1	.972	-8	*O-150/1-2,D-1	3.3
1975	Tex-A	152	585	81	132	20	0	29	94	79	155	.226	.319	.409	105	3	4	4	-1	.966	-8	*O-148/D-3	-1.3
1976	Tex-A	158	604	71	143	22	2	18	86	69	93	.237	.317	.369	98	-1	0	0	0	.987	-2	*O-155/D-3	-1.0
1977	Atl-N	154	579	91	157	19	1	41	114	86	126	.271	.365	.520	120	16	4	1	1	.974	-4	*O-154	0.6
1978	Atl-N☆	153	488	72	147	30	6	23	77	**117**	92	.301	**.436**	.529	151	38	1	2	-1	.975	-0	*O-146	3.2
1979	Atl-N	116	397	49	89	14	1	11	47	73	75	.224	.349	.348	84	-7	2	2	-1	.963	-1	*O-110	-1.3
1980	Atl-N	99	278	35	73	14	0	13	51	35	57	.263	.349	.453	118	7	1	1	-0	.977	-4	O-73	0.0
1981	Sea-A	89	319	32	81	13	1	10	41	41	64	.254	.339	.395	107	3	0	1	-1	.985	-9	O-87/D-1	-1.0
1982	Oak-A	113	285	42	79	13	2	16	48	45	61	.277	.376	.505	146	18	1	3	-2	.981	-5	D-48,O-34	0.9
1983	Oak-A	121	401	43	108	15	1	10	56	47	79	.269	.346	.387	108	5	0	2	-1	1.000	5	*D-114	-0.1
1984	Oak-A	58	71	5	15	1	0	2	8	18	23	.211	.371	.310	97	1	0	0	0	1.000	-2	D-23/O-4	-0.2
1985	*Tor-A	86	191	19	49	9	3	4	28	34	36	.257	.369	.429	115	5	0	1	0	1.000	0	D-75	0.3
Total	16	1689	5536	720	1443	230	20	240	882	831	1135	.261	.359	.439	120	159	16	22	-8	.974	-36	*O-1281,D-269/1-6	5.2

■ DICK BURRUS Burrus, Maurice Lennon b: 1/29/1898, Hatteras, N.C. d: 2/2/72, Elizabeth City, N.C BL/TL, 5'11", 175 lbs. Deb: 6/23/19

1919	Phi-A	70	194	17	50	3	4	0	8	9	25	.258	.294	.314	70	-8	2			.986	-4	1-38,O-10	-1.5
1920	Phi-A	71	135	11	25	8	0	0	10	5	7	.185	.225	.244	24	-15	0	3	-2	.989	-2	1-31/O-2	-1.9
1925	Bos-N	152	588	82	200	41	4	5	87	51	29	.340	.396	.449	126	24	8	9	-3	**.990**	-4	*1-151	1.2
1926	Bos-N	131	486	59	131	21	5	3	61	37	16	.270	.324	.335	85	-11	4			.991	12	*1-128	-0.6
1927	Bos-N	72	220	22	70	8	3	0	32	17	10	.318	.370	.382	110	3	3			.972	1	1-61	0.1
1928	Bos-N	64	137	15	37	6	0	3	13	19	8	.270	.367	.380	101	1	1			.977	-2	1-32	-0.4
Total	6	560	1760	206	513	87	12	11	211	138	95	.291	.347	.373	97	-6	18	12		.986	7	1-441/O-12	-3.1

■ FRANK BURT Burt, Frank J. b: Camden, N.J. Deb: 5/2/1882

| 1882 | Bal-a | 10 | 36 | 2 | 4 | 2 | 1 | 0 | | 1 | | .111 | .135 | .222 | 20 | -3 | | | | .815 | -1 | O-10 | -0.3 |

■ ELLIS BURTON Burton, Ellis Narrington b: 8/12/36, Los Angeles, Cal. BB/TR, 5'11", 165 lbs. Deb: 9/18/58

1958	StL-N	8	30	5	7	0	1	2	4	4	8	.233	.324	.500	110	0	0	1	-1	1.000	-0	/O-7	-0.1
1960	StL-N	29	28	5	6	1	0	0	2	4	14	.214	.313	.250	52	-2	0	2	-1	1.000	-7	O-23	-1.1
1963	Cle-A	26	31	6	6	3	0	1	4	4	4	.194	.286	.387	87	-1	0	0	0	1.000	-6	O-16	-0.5
	Chi-N	93	322	45	74	16	1	12	41	36	59	.230	.315	.398	98	-1	6	3	0	.975	-9	O-90	-1.5
1964	Chi-N	42	105	12	20	3	2	2	7	17	22	.190	.303	.314	71	-4	4	0	1	.981	-4	O-29	-0.9
1965	Chi-N	17	40	6	7	1	0	0	1	0	10	.175	.195	.200	11	-5	1	0	0	1.000	-5	O-12	-0.5
Total	5	215	556	79	120	24	4	17	59	65	117	.216	.304	.365	85	-11	11	6	-0	.981	-24	O-177	-4.6

■ JIM BUSBY Busby, James Franklin b: 1/8/27, Kenedy, Tex. d: 7/8/96, Augusta, Ga. BR/TR, 6'1", 175 lbs. Deb: 4/23/50 C

1950	Chi-A	18	48	5	10	0	0	0	4	1	5	.208	.224	.208	12	-6	0	2	-1	.964	-1	O-12	-0.8
1951	Chi-A★	143	477	59	135	15	2	5	68	40	46	.283	.344	.354	91	-6	26	11	-1	.982	3	*O-139	-0.6
1952	Chi-A	16	39	5	5	0	0	0	0	2	7	.128	.171	.128	-16	-6	0	2	-1	1.000	-0	O-16	-0.9
	Was-A	129	512	58	125	24	4	2	47	22	48	.244	.281	.318	69	-23	5	6	-2	.993	14	*O-128	-1.8
	Yr	145	551	63	130	24	4	2	47	24	55	.236	.273	.305	62	-29	5	8	-3	.994	13	*O-144	-2.7
1953	Was-A	150	586	68	183	28	7	6	82	38	45	.312	.358	.415	111	8	13	6	0	.988	**19**	*O-150	2.1
1954	Was-A	155	628	83	187	24	7	7	80	43	56	.298	.346	.389	107	4	17	2	4	.988	12	*O-155	1.4
1955	Was-A	47	191	23	44	6	2	6	14	13	22	.230	.279	.377	79	-7	3	3	-1	.993	-2	O-47	-0.5
	Chi-A	99	337	38	82	13	4	1	27	25	37	.243	.296	.315	62	-18	7	3	0	.984	2	O-99	-2.0
	Yr	146	528	61	126	19	6	7	41	38	59	.239	.290	.337	68	-25	12	3	2	.987	5	*O-146	-2.5
1956	Cle-A	135	494	72	116	17	3	12	50	43	47	.235	.301	.354	71	-22	8	3	1	.989	5	*O-133	-2.3
1957	Cle-A	30	74	9	14	2	1	2	4	1	8	.189	.200	.324	41	-6	0	1	-1	.978	-3	O-26	-1.2
	Bal-A	86	288	31	72	10	1	3	19	23	36	.250	.305	.323	77	-10	6	3	0	.984	10	O-85	-0.5
	Yr	116	362	40	86	12	2	5	23	24	44	.238	.285	.323	69	-16	6	4	-1	.983	6	*O-111	-1.7
1958	Bal-A	113	215	32	51	7	2	3	19	24	37	.237	.322	.330	84	-4	6	4	-1	**.995**	-9	*O-103/3-1	-1.7
1959	Bos-A	61	102	16	23	8	0	1	5	5	18	.225	.269	.333	61	-6	6	0	1	.980	-6	O-34	-1.3
1960	Bos-A	1	0	0	0	0	0	0	0	0	0	—	—	—	—	0	0	0	0	.000	0	/O-1	0.0
	Bal-A	79	159	25	41	7	1	0	12	19	14	.258	.341	.314	79	-4	2	3	-1	.985	-5	O-71	-1.3
	Yr	80	159	25	41	7	1	0	12	19	14	.258	.341	.314	79	-4	2	3	-1	.985	-6	O-72	-1.3
1961	Bal-A	75	89	15	23	3	1	0	6	8	10	.258	.320	.315	73	-3	2	1	-1	.987	-16	O-71	-2.1
1962	Hou-N	15	11	2	2	0	0	0	1	2	1	.182	.308	.182	38	-1	0	1	-1	1.000	-4	O-10/C-1	-0.5
Total	13	1352	4250	541	1113	162	35	48	438	310	439	.262	.316	.350	82	-110	97	48	0	.988	22	*O-1280/C-1,3-1	-14.0

■ PAUL BUSBY Busby, Paul Miller "Red" b: 8/25/18, Waynesboro, Miss. BL/TR, 6'1", 175 lbs. Deb: 9/14/41

1941	Phi-N	10	16	3	5	0	0	0	2	0	1	.313	.313	.313	79	-0	0			1.000	-1	/O-3	-0.1
1943	Phi-N	26	40	13	10	1	0	0	5	2	1	.250	.286	.275	65	-2	2			1.000	0	O-10	-0.2
Total	2	36	56	16	15	1	0	0	7	2	2	.268	.293	.286	69	-2	2			1.000	-1	/O-13	-0.3

■ ED BUSCH Busch, Edgar John b: 11/16/17, Lebanon, Ill. d: 1/17/87, St.Clair Co., Ill. BR/TR, 5'10", 175 lbs. Deb: 9/30/43

| 1943 | Phi-A | 4 | 17 | 2 | 5 | 0 | 0 | 0 | 0 | 0 | 0 | .294 | .368 | .294 | 95 | -0 | 0 | 1 | -1 | .941 | -3 | /S-4 | -0.3 |
| 1944 | Phi-A | 140 | 484 | 41 | 131 | 18 | 3 | 0 | 40 | 29 | 22 | .271 | .313 | .306 | 78 | -14 | 5 | 3 | 0 | .940 | -30 | *S-111,2-27/3-4 | -3.6 |

YEAR	TM/L	G	AB	R	H	2B	3B	HR	RBI	BB	SO	AVG	OBP	SLG	PRO+	BR/A	SB	CS	SBR	FA	FR	G/POS	TPR
1945	Phi-A	126	416	37	104	10	3	0	35	32	9	.250	.305	.288	73	-14	2	3	-1	.952	1	*S-116/2-2,3-2,1-1	-0.6
Total	3	270	917	80	240	21	6	0	75	62	28	.262	.311	.298	76	-28	7	7	-2	.946	-32	S-231/2-29,3-6,1-1	-4.5

■ MIKE BUSCH
Busch, Michael Anthony b: 7/7/68, Davenport, Iowa BR/TR, 6'5", 249 lbs. Deb: 8/30/95

YEAR	TM/L	G	AB	R	H	2B	3B	HR	RBI	BB	SO	AVG	OBP	SLG	PRO+	BR/A	SB	CS	SBR	FA	FR	G/POS	TPR
1995	LA-N	13	17	3	4	0	0	3	6	0	7	.235	.235	.765	165	1	0	0	0	.875	-1	3-10/1-2	0.1
1996	LA-N	38	83	8	18	4	0	4	17	5	33	.217	.261	.410	80	-3	0	0	0	.932	-4	3-23/1-1	-0.7
Total	2	51	100	11	22	4	0	7	23	5	40	.220	.257	.470	95	-2	0	0	0	.923	-4	/3-33,1-3	-0.6

■ DONIE BUSH
Bush, Owen Joseph b: 10/8/1887, Indianapolis, Ind. d: 3/28/72, Indianapolis, Ind. BB/TR, 5'6", 140 lbs. Deb: 9/18/08 M

YEAR	TM/L	G	AB	R	H	2B	3B	HR	RBI	BB	SO	AVG	OBP	SLG	PRO+	BR/A	SB	CS	SBR	FA	FR	G/POS	TPR
1908	Det-A	20	68	13	20	1	1	0	4	7		.294	.360	.338	122	2	2			.938	-4	S-20	-0.2
1909	*Det-A	157	532	114	145	18	2	0	33	**88**		.273	.380	.314	114	13	53			.925	4	*S-157	2.3
1910	Det-A	142	496	90	130	13	4	3	34	**78**		.262	.365	.323	108	7	49			**.940**	9	*S-141/3-1	2.4
1911	Det-A	150	561	126	130	18	5	1	36	**98**		.232	.349	.287	74	-16	40			.925	17	*S-150	1.0
1912	Det-A	144	511	107	118	14	8	2	38	**117**		.231	.377	.301	98	5	35			.929	29	*S-144	4.6
1913	Det-A	153	597	98	150	19	10	1	40	80	32	.251	.344	.322	96	-1	44			.938	2	*S-153	1.6
1914	Det-A	157	596	97	150	18	4	0	32	**112**	44	.252	.373	.295	98	4	35	26	-5	.944	**34**	*S-157	5.0
1915	Det-A	155	561	99	128	12	8	1	44	118	44	.228	.364	.283	89	-2	35	27	-6	.937	9	*S-155	1.4
1916	Det-A	145	550	73	124	5	9	0	34	75	42	.225	.319	.267	74	-16	19			.954	-15	*S-144	-2.6
1917	Det-A	147	581	**112**	163	18	3	0	24	80	40	.281	.370	.322	111	11	34			.932	-18	*S-147	0.0
1918	Det-A	128	500	74	117	10	3	0	22	79	31	.234	.340	.266	86	-5	9			.931	-20	*S-128	-2.2
1919	Det-A	129	509	82	124	11	6	0	26	75	36	.244	.343	.289	80	-11	22			.943	-12	*S-129	-1.5
1920	Det-A	141	506	85	133	18	5	1	33	73	32	.263	.357	.324	83	-9	15	7	0	.938	-17	*S-140	-1.4
1921	Det-A	104	402	72	113	6	5	0	27	45	23	.281	.355	.321	74	-14	8	11	-4	.949	-5	S-81,2-23	-1.4
	Was-A	23	84	15	18	1	0	0	2	12	4	.214	.313	.226	41	-7	2	2	-1	.932	-4	S-21	-1.0
	Yr	127	486	87	131	7	5	0	29	57	27	.270	.347	.305	69	-21	10	13	-5	.946	-9	*S-102,2-23	-2.4
1922	Was-A	41	134	17	32	4	1	0	7	21	7	.239	.342	.284	68	-6	1	1	-0	.957	-2	3-37/2-1	-0.5
1923	Was-A	10	22	6	9	0	0	0	0		1	.409	.409	.409	122	1	1	1	-0	.813	-2	/3-5,2-2,M	-0.1
Total	16	1946	7210	1280	1804	186	74	9	436	1158	346	.250	.356	.300	91	-42	404	75		.936	9	*S-1867/3-43,2-26	7.4

■ RANDY BUSH
Bush, Robert Randall b: 10/5/58, Dover, Del. BL/TL, 6'1", 186 lbs. Deb: 5/1/82

YEAR	TM/L	G	AB	R	H	2B	3B	HR	RBI	BB	SO	AVG	OBP	SLG	PRO+	BR/A	SB	CS	SBR	FA	FR	G/POS	TPR
1982	Min-A	55	119	13	29	6	1	4	13	8	28	.244	.308	.412	93	-1	0	0		1.000	-1	D-26/O-6	-0.4
1983	Min-A	124	373	43	93	24	3	11	56	34	51	.249	.324	.418	99	-1	0	1	-1	1.000	1	*D-103/1-3	-0.5
1984	Min-A	113	311	46	69	17	1	11	43	31	60	.222	.301	.389	85	-7	1	2	-1	1.000	-0	D-89/1-2	-1.0
1985	Min-A	97	234	26	56	13	3	10	35	24	30	.239	.323	.449	103	1	3	0	1	.969	-6	O-41,D-28/1-1	-0.6
1986	Min-A	130	357	50	96	19	7	7	45	39	63	.269	.348	.420	105	3	5	3	-0	.977	-7	*O-102/1-3,D-6	-0.7
1987	*Min-A	122	293	46	74	10	2	11	46	43	49	.253	.354	.413	99	0	10	3	1	.982	-8	*O-75/1-9,D-9	-0.9
1988	Min-A	136	394	51	103	20	3	14	51	54	49	.261	.369	.434	120	12	8	6	-1	.979	-6	*O-109/1-6,D-7	0.2
1989	Min-A	141	391	60	103	17	4	14	54	48	73	.263	.348	.435	112	6	5	8	-3	.986	-9	*O-109,1-25/D-5	-1.0
1990	Min-A	73	181	17	44	8	1	6	18	21	27	.243	.341	.387	97	-0	0	3	-2	1.000	-6	O-32,D-29/1-6	-0.6
1991	*Min-A	93	165	21	50	10	1	6	23	24	25	.303	.401	.485	137	9	0	2	-1	1.000	-5	O-38,1-12,D-10	0.2
1992	Min-A	100	182	14	39	8	1	2	22	11	37	.214	.267	.302	57	-11	1	1	-0	1.000	-3	O-24,D-24/1-8	-1.6
1993	Min-A	35	45	1	7	2	0	0	3	7	13	.156	.269	.200	28	-4	0	0	0	1.000	-1	/1-4,O-1,D-5	-0.5
Total	12	1219	3045	388	763	154	26	96	409	348	505	.251	.337	.413	101	7	33	29	-8	.983	-48	O-537,D-341/1-79	-7.4

■ DOC BUSHONG
Bushong, Albert John b: 9/15/1856, Philadelphia, Pa. d: 8/19/08, Brooklyn, N.Y. BR/TR, 5'11", 165 lbs. Deb: 7/19/1875

YEAR	TM/L	G	AB	R	H	2B	3B	HR	RBI	BB	SO	AVG	OBP	SLG	PRO+	BR/A	SB	CS	SBR	FA	FR	G/POS	TPR
1875	Atl-n	1	5	0	3	0	0	0				.600	.600	1.000	511	2	0	0		.800	-0	/C-1	0.1
1876	Phi-N	5	21	4	1	0	0	0	1	0	0	.048	.048	.048	-69	-4				.769	-1	/C-5	-0.4
1880	Wor-N	41	146	13	25	3	0	0	19	1	16	.171	.177	.192	23	-12				.918	16	C-40/O-1,3-1	0.5
1881	Wor-N	76	275	35	64	7	4	0	21	21	23	.233	.287	.287	77	-7				.918	11	*C-76	0.6
1882	Wor-N	69	253	20	40	4	1	1	15	5	17	.158	.174	.194	18	-23				.897	-3	*C-69	-2.1
1883	Cle-N	63	215	15	37	5	0	0	9	7	19	.172	.198	.195	21	-20				.909	15	C-63	-0.1
1884	Cle-N	62	203	24	48	6	1	0	10	17	11	.236	.295	.276	78	-5				.886	0	C-62/O-1	0.1
1885	*StL-a	85	300	42	80	13	5	0	21	11		.267	.297	.343	97	-2				.932	14	*C-85/3-1	1.7
1886	*StL-a	107	386	56	86	8	0	1	31	31		.223	.281	.251	64	-16	12			**.942**	16	*C-106/1-1	1.0
1887	*StL-a	53	201	35	51	4	0	0	26	11		.254	.299	.274	55	-13	14			.927	7	C-52/O-2,3-2	-0.2
1888	Bro-a	69	253	23	53	5	1	0	16	5		.209	.231	.237	50	-14	9			.915	-7	C-69	-1.4
1889	*Bro-a	25	84	15	13	1	0	0	8	9	7	.155	.237	.167	16	-9	2			.894	-1	C-25	-0.7
1890	*Bro-N	16	55	5	13	2	0	0	7	6	4	.236	.311	.273	70	-2	2			.913	-1	C-15/O-2	-0.2
Total	12	671	2392	287	511	58	12	2	184	124	97	.214	.254	.250	55	-127	39	0		.916	66	C-667/O-6,3-4,1-1	-1.2

■ JOE BUSKEY
Buskey, Joseph Henry "Jazzbow" b: 12/18/02, Cumberland, Md. d: 4/11/49, Cumberland, Md. BR/TR, 5'10", 175 lbs. Deb: 4/19/26

YEAR	TM/L	G	AB	R	H	2B	3B	HR	RBI	BB	SO	AVG	OBP	SLG	PRO+	BR/A	SB	CS	SBR	FA	FR	G/POS	TPR
1926	Phi-N	5	8	1	0	0	0	0	0	1	1	.000	.111	.000	-65	-2	0	0	0	.810	-0	/S-5	-0.2

■ MIKE BUSKEY
Buskey, Michael Thomas b: 1/13/49, San Francisco, Cal. BR/TR, 5'11", 160 lbs. Deb: 9/2/77

YEAR	TM/L	G	AB	R	H	2B	3B	HR	RBI	BB	SO	AVG	OBP	SLG	PRO+	BR/A	SB	CS	SBR	FA	FR	G/POS	TPR
1977	Phi-N	6	7	1	2	0	1	0	1	0	1	.286	.375	.571	143	0	0	0	0	.882	-0	/S-6	0.2

■ RAY BUSSE
Busse, Raymond Edward b: 9/25/48, Daytona Beach, Fla. BR/TR, 6'4", 175 lbs. Deb: 7/24/71

YEAR	TM/L	G	AB	R	H	2B	3B	HR	RBI	BB	SO	AVG	OBP	SLG	PRO+	BR/A	SB	CS	SBR	FA	FR	G/POS	TPR
1971	Hou-N	10	34	2	5	3	0	0	4	2	9	.147	.194	.235	22	-4	0	0	0	.929	-2	/S-5,3-3	-0.6
1973	StL-N	24	70	6	10	4	2	2	5	5	21	.143	.200	.343	48	-5	0	1	-1	.898	-2	S-23	-0.6
	Hou-N	15	17	1	1	0	0	0	0	1	12	.059	.111	.059	-52	-3	0	0	0	1.000	-1	/S-5,3-3	-0.2
	Yr	39	87	7	11	4	2	2	5	6	33	.126	.183	.287	28	-9	0	1	-1	.906	-1	S-28/3-3	-0.8
1974	Hou-N	19	34	3	7	1	0	0	3	0	12	.206	.270	.235	44	-3	0	0	0	.864	-0	/3-8	-0.3
Total	3	68	155	12	23	8	2	2	9	11	54	.148	.205	.265	31	-15	0	1	-1	.908	-3	/S-33,3-14	-1.7

■ HANK BUTCHER
Butcher, Henry Joseph b: 7/12/1886, Chicago, Ill. d: 12/28/79, Hazel Crest, Ill. BR/TR, 5'10", 180 lbs. Deb: 7/8/11

YEAR	TM/L	G	AB	R	H	2B	3B	HR	RBI	BB	SO	AVG	OBP	SLG	PRO+	BR/A	SB	CS	SBR	FA	FR	G/POS	TPR
1911	Cle-A	38	133	21	32	7	3	1	11	11		.241	.303	.361	84	-3	9			.984	0	O-34	-0.5
1912	Cle-A	26	82	9	16	4	1	1	10	6		.195	.250	.305	57	-5	1			.920	1	O-21	-0.5
Total	2	64	215	30	48	11	4	2	21	17		.223	.283	.340	74	-8	10			.956	2	/O-55	-1.0

■ SAL BUTERA
Butera, Salvatore Philip b: 9/25/52, Richmond Hill, N.Y BR/TR, 6', 190 lbs. Deb: 4/10/80

YEAR	TM/L	G	AB	R	H	2B	3B	HR	RBI	BB	SO	AVG	OBP	SLG	PRO+	BR/A	SB	CS	SBR	FA	FR	G/POS	TPR
1980	Min-A	34	85	4	23	1	0	0	2	3	6	.271	.303	.282	57	-5	0	0	0	.950	-5	C-32/D-2	-0.5
1981	Min-A	62	167	13	40	7	1	0	18	22	14	.240	.328	.293	75	-5	0	0	0	.970	5	C-59/1-1,D-1	0.2
1982	Min-A	54	126	9	32	2	0	0	8	17	12	.254	.347	.270	70	-4	0	0	0	.988	6	C-53	0.3
1983	Det-A	4	5	1	1	0	0	0	0	1	0	.200	.200	.200	11	-1	0	0	0	.929	1	/C-4	0.1
1984	Mon-N	3	3	0	0	0	0	0	0	1	0	.000	.250	.000	-26	-0	0	0	0	1.000	1	/C-2	0.0
1985	Mon-N	67	120	11	24	1	0	3	12	13	12	.200	.284	.283	63	-6	0	0	0	.984	0	C-66/P-1	-0.4
1986	Cin-N	56	113	14	27	6	1	2	16	21	10	.239	.358	.363	95	-0	0	0	0	.979	1	C-53/P-1	0.3
1987	Cin-N	5	11	1	2	0	0	1	2	1	6	.182	.250	.455	78	-0	0	0	0	.920	1	/C-5	0.1
	*Min-A	51	111	7	19	5	0	1	12	7	16	.171	.220	.243	22	-13	0	0	0	.983	-1	C-51	-0.9
1988	Tor-A	23	60	3	14	2	1	0	6	1	9	.233	.246	.350	65	-3	0	0	0	.991	5	C-23	0.1
Total	9	359	801	63	182	24	3	7	76	86	85	.227	.304	.295	65	-37	0	0	0	.978	17	C-348/D-3,P-2,1-1	-0.7

■ ED BUTKA
Butka, Edward Luke "Babe" b: 1/7/16, Canonsburg, Pa. BR/TR, 6'3", 193 lbs. Deb: 9/26/43

YEAR	TM/L	G	AB	R	H	2B	3B	HR	RBI	BB	SO	AVG	OBP	SLG	PRO+	BR/A	SB	CS	SBR	FA	FR	G/POS	TPR
1943	Was-A	3	9	0	3	1	0	0	0	0	3	.333	.333	.444	132	0	0	0	0	1.000	1	/1-3	0.1
1944	Was-A	15	41	1	8	1	0	0	2	5	11	.195	.233	.220	31	-4	0	0	0	.972	0	1-14	-0.5
Total	2	18	50	1	11	2	0	0	2	5	14	.220	.250	.260	48	-3	0	0	0	.977	1	/1-17	-0.4

■ ART BUTLER
Butler, Arthur Edward (b: Arthur Edward Bouthillier) b: 12/19/1887, Fall River, Mass. d: 10/7/84, Fall River, Mass. BR/TR, 5'9", 160 lbs. Deb: 4/14/11

YEAR	TM/L	G	AB	R	H	2B	3B	HR	RBI	BB	SO	AVG	OBP	SLG	PRO+	BR/A	SB	CS	SBR	FA	FR	G/POS	TPR
1911	Bos-N	27	68	11	12	2	0	0	6	6		.176	.263	.206	30	-6	0			.930	-3	3-14/2-4,S-1	-1.0
1912	Pit-N	43	154	19	42	4	2	1	17	15	13	.273	.337	.344	88	-2	2			.960	-22	2-43	-2.6
1913	Pit-N	82	214	40	60	9	3	0	20	32	14	.280	.379	.350	114	5	9			.919	-12	2-28,S-26/3-2,O-2	-0.5

YEAR	TM/L	G	AB	R	H	2B	3B	HR	RBI	BB	SO	AVG	OBP	SLG	PRO+	BR/A	SB	CS	SBR	FA	FR	G/POS	TPR
1914	StL-N	86	274	29	55	12	3	1	24	39	23	.201	.311	.277	76	-7	14			.927	-19	S-83/O-1	-2.1
1915	StL-N	130	469	73	119	12	5	1	31	47	34	.254	.323	.307	91	-4	26	14	-1	.916	-34	*S-125/2-2	-3.2
1916	StL-N	86	110	9	23	5	0	0	7	12	12	.209	.256	.255	57	-6	3			.882	-6	O-15/2-8,S-1,3-1	-1.4
Total	6	454	1289	181	311	44	13	3	101	146	102	.241	.323	.303	85	-20	54	14		.919	-96	S-236/2-85,O-18,3	-10.8

■ BRETT BUTLER
Butler, Brett Morgan   b: 6/15/57, Los Angeles, Cal.   BL/TL, 5'10", 160 lbs.   Deb: 8/20/81

YEAR	TM/L	G	AB	R	H	2B	3B	HR	RBI	BB	SO	AVG	OBP	SLG	PRO+	BR/A	SB	CS	SBR	FA	FR	G/POS	TPR
1981	Atl-N	40	126	17	32	2	3	0	4	19	17	.254	.352	.317	89	-1	9	1	2	.987	-2	O-37	-0.2
1982	*Atl-N	89	240	35	52	2	0	0	7	25	35	.217	.291	.225	44	-17	21	8	2	1.000	-10	O-77	-2.9
1983	Atl-N	151	549	84	154	21	**13**	5	37	54	56	.281	.347	.393	98	-1	39	23	-2	.987	6	*O-143	-0.2
1984	Cle-A	159	602	108	162	25	9	3	49	86	62	.269	.364	.355	98	2	52	22	2	.991	15	*O-156	1.4
1985	Cle-A	152	591	106	184	28	14	5	50	63	42	.311	.379	.431	122	19	47	20	2	**.998**	22	*O-150/D-1	3.7
1986	Cle-A	161	587	92	163	17	**14**	4	51	70	65	.278	.359	.375	102	3	32	15	1	.993	9	*O-159	0.7
1987	Cle-A	137	522	91	154	25	8	9	41	91	55	.295	.401	.425	119	18	33	16	0	.990	15	*O-136	2.7
1988	SF-N	157	568	**109**	163	27	9	6	43	97	64	.287	.395	.398	134	29	43	20	1	.988	6	*O-155	3.4
1989	*SF-N	154	594	100	168	22	4	4	36	59	69	.283	.351	.354	105	5	31	16	-0	.986	14	*O-152	1.6
1990	SF-N	160	622	108	**192**	20	9	3	44	90	62	.309	.401	.384	122	23	51	19	4	.986	7	*O-159	3.0
1991	LA-N★	161	615	**112**	182	13	5	2	38	**108**	79	.296	.402	.343	114	18	38	28	-5	**1.000**	12	*O-161	2.1
1992	LA-N	157	553	86	171	14	11	3	39	95	67	.309	.413	.391	131	28	41	21	-0	.995	2	*O-155	2.8
1993	LA-N	156	607	80	181	21	10	1	42	86	69	.298	.390	.371	111	14	39	19	0	**1.000**	5	*O-155	1.3
1994	LA-N	111	417	79	131	13	**9**	8	33	68	52	.314	.413	.446	133	23	27	8	3	.993	5	*O-111	2.7
1995	NY-N	90	367	54	114	13	7	1	25	43	52	.311	.383	.392	108	6	21	7	2	.995	6	O-90	1.1
	*LA-N	39	146	24	40	5	2	0	13	24	9	.274	.376	.336	98	1	11	1	3	.987	-1	O-38	0.1
	Yr	129	513	78	154	18	**9**	1	38	67	51	.300	.381	.376	106	7	32	8	5	.993	4	O-128	1.2
1996	LA-N	34	131	22	35	1	1	0	8	9	22	.267	.319	.290	68	-6	8	3	1	.987	1	O-34	-0.5
Total	16	2108	7837	1307	2278	269	128	54	560	1087	867	.291	.380	.378	111	162	543	247	15	.992	110	*O-2068/D-1	22.8

■ FRANK BUTLER
Butler, Frank Dean "Stuffy" or "Goldbrick"   b: 7/18/1860, Savannah, Ga.   d: 7/10/45, Jacksonville, Fla   BL/TL,   Deb: 7/30/1895

YEAR	TM/L	G	AB	R	H	2B	3B	HR	RBI	BB	SO	AVG	OBP	SLG	PRO+	BR/A	SB	CS	SBR	FA	FR	G/POS	TPR
1895	NY-N	5	22	5	6	1	0	0	2	1	1	.273	.304	.318	62	-1	1			1.000	-1	/O-5	-0.2

■ KID BUTLER
Butler, Frank Edward   b: 5/1861, Boston, Mass.   d: 4/9/21, S.Boston, Mass.   5'6", 140 lbs.   Deb: 5/20/1884

YEAR	TM/L	G	AB	R	H	2B	3B	HR	RBI	BB	SO	AVG	OBP	SLG	PRO+	BR/A	SB	CS	SBR	FA	FR	G/POS	TPR
1884	Bos-U	71	255	36	43	15	0	0			12	.169	.206	.227	32	-29				.810	-6	O-53,2-12/S-6,3-2	-3.2

■ JOHN BUTLER
Butler, John Albert (a.k.a. Frederick King In 1901)   b: 7/26/1879, Boston, Mass.   d: 2/2/50, Boston, Mass.   BR/TR, 5'7", 170 lbs.   Deb: 9/28/01

YEAR	TM/L	G	AB	R	H	2B	3B	HR	RBI	BB	SO	AVG	OBP	SLG	PRO+	BR/A	SB	CS	SBR	FA	FR	G/POS	TPR
1901	Mil-A	1	3	0	0	0	0	0		0	1	.000	.250	.000	-28	-0	0			1.000	-1	/C-1	-0.1
1904	StL-N	12	37	0	6	1	0	0	1		4	.162	.262	.189	42	-2	0			.968	-2	C-12	-0.4
1906	Bro-N	1	0	0	0	0	0	0	0	0		—	—	—	—	-0	0			1.000	0	/C-1	0.0
1907	Bro-N	30	79	6	10	1	0	0	2		9	.127	.216	.139	12	-8	0			.946	-5	C-28/O-1	-1.2
Total	4	44	119	6	16	2	0	0		3	14	.134	.231	.151	21	-11	0			.953	-8	/C-42,O-1	-1.7

■ JOHNNY BUTLER
Butler, John Stephen "Trolley Line"   b: 3/20/1893, Fall River, Kan.   d: 4/29/67, Seal Beach, Cal.   BR/TR, 6', 175 lbs.   Deb: 4/18/26   C

YEAR	TM/L	G	AB	R	H	2B	3B	HR	RBI	BB	SO	AVG	OBP	SLG	PRO+	BR/A	SB	CS	SBR	FA	FR	G/POS	TPR
1926	Bro-N	147	501	54	135	27	5	1	68	54	44	.269	.346	.349	89	-6	6			.949	-7	*S-102,3-42/2-8	0.0
1927	Bro-N	149	521	39	124	13	6	2	57	34	33	.238	.292	.298	58	-31	9			.959	-2	S-90,3-60	-2.0
1928	Chi-N	62	174	17	47	7	0	0	16	19	7	.270	.352	.310	75	-5	2			.950	10	3-59/S-2	0.7
1929	StL-N	17	55	5	9	1	1	0	5	4	5	.164	.220	.218	9	-8	0			.964	1	/3-9,S-8	-0.5
Total	4	375	1251	115	315	48	12	3	146	111	89	.252	.320	.317	70	-51	17			.954	2	S-202,3-170/2-8	-1.8

■ DICK BUTLER
Butler, Richard H.   b: Brooklyn, N.Y.   Deb: 6/16/1897

YEAR	TM/L	G	AB	R	H	2B	3B	HR	RBI	BB	SO	AVG	OBP	SLG	PRO+	BR/A	SB	CS	SBR	FA	FR	G/POS	TPR
1897	Lou-N	10	38	3	7	0	0	0	2		0	.184	.184	.184	-3	-6	1			.818	-2	C-10	-0.6
1899	Was-N	12	36	4	10	0	1	0	1		2	.278	.316	.333	79	-1	1			.892	-3	C-11	-0.3
Total	2	22	74	7	17	0	1	0	3		2	.230	.250	.257	37	-7	2			.852	-6	/C-21	-0.9

■ ROB BUTLER
Butler, Robert Frank John   b: 4/10/70, E.York, Ont., Can.   BL/TL, 5'11", 185 lbs.   Deb: 6/12/93

YEAR	TM/L	G	AB	R	H	2B	3B	HR	RBI	BB	SO	AVG	OBP	SLG	PRO+	BR/A	SB	CS	SBR	FA	FR	G/POS	TPR
1993	*Tor-A	17	48	8	13	4	0	0	2	7	12	.271	.375	.354	97	-0	2	2	-1	.970	-0	O-16	-0.1
1994	Tor-A	41	74	13	13	0	1	0	5	7	8	.176	.256	.203	20	-9	0	1	-1	.977	-5	O-31/D-1	-1.4
Total	2	58	122	21	26	4	1	0	7	14	20	.213	.304	.262	50	-9	2	3	-1	.974	-5	/O-47,D-1	-1.5

■ BILL BUTLER
Butler, William J.   b: 1861, New Orleans, La.   Deb: 6/29/1884

YEAR	TM/L	G	AB	R	H	2B	3B	HR	RBI	BB	SO	AVG	OBP	SLG	PRO+	BR/A	SB	CS	SBR	FA	FR	G/POS	TPR
1884	Ind-a	9	31	7	7	3	2	0			1	.226	.250	.452	128	1				.700	-2	/O-9	-0.1

■ KID BUTLER
Butler, Willis Everett   b: 8/9/1887, Franklin, Pa.   d: 2/22/64, Richmond, Cal.   BR/TR, 5'11", 155 lbs.   Deb: 4/30/07

YEAR	TM/L	G	AB	R	H	2B	3B	HR	RBI	BB	SO	AVG	OBP	SLG	PRO+	BR/A	SB	CS	SBR	FA	FR	G/POS	TPR
1907	StL-A	20	59	4	13	2	0	0	4			.220	.246	.254	60	-3	1			.940	-1	2-11/3-5,S-1	-0.4

■ FRANK BUTTERY
Buttery, Frank   b: 5/13/1851, Silvermine, Conn.   d: 12/16/02, Silvermine, Conn.   Deb: 4/26/1872

YEAR	TM/L	G	AB	R	H	2B	3B	HR	RBI	BB	SO	AVG	OBP	SLG	PRO+	BR/A	SB	CS	SBR	FA	FR	G/POS	TPR
1872	Man-n	18	93	19	24	0	0	0	0		2	.258	.258	.258	63	-3	0	0	0	.600	-2	/O-8,P-7,3-5	-0.2

■ JOE BUZAS
Buzas, Joseph John   b: 10/2/19, Alpha, N.J.   BR/TR, 6'1", 180 lbs.   Deb: 4/17/45

YEAR	TM/L	G	AB	R	H	2B	3B	HR	RBI	BB	SO	AVG	OBP	SLG	PRO+	BR/A	SB	CS	SBR	FA	FR	G/POS	TPR
1945	NY-A	30	65	8	17	2	1	0	6	2	5	.262	.284	.323	73	-2	2	0	1	.898	-3	S-12	-0.4

■ BURLEY BYERS
Byers, Burley (b: Christopher A. Bayer)   b: 12/19/1875, Louisville, Ky.   d: 5/30/33, Louisville, Ky.   175 lbs.   Deb: 6/17/1899

YEAR	TM/L	G	AB	R	H	2B	3B	HR	RBI	BB	SO	AVG	OBP	SLG	PRO+	BR/A	SB	CS	SBR	FA	FR	G/POS	TPR
1899	Lou-N	1	3	0	0	0	0	0	0		0	.000	.000	.000	-99	-1	0			.600	-1	/S-1	-0.2

■ BILL BYERS
Byers, James William   b: 10/3/1877, Bridgeton, Ind.   d: 9/8/48, Baltimore, Md.   BR/TR, 5'7",   Deb: 4/15/04

YEAR	TM/L	G	AB	R	H	2B	3B	HR	RBI	BB	SO	AVG	OBP	SLG	PRO+	BR/A	SB	CS	SBR	FA	FR	G/POS	TPR
1904	StL-N	19	60	3	13	0	0	0	4		1	.217	.230	.217	40	-4	0			.971	-1	C-16/1-1	-0.4

■ RANDY BYERS
Byers, Randell Parker   b: 10/2/64, Bridgeton, N.J.   BL/TR, 6'2", 180 lbs.   Deb: 9/7/87

YEAR	TM/L	G	AB	R	H	2B	3B	HR	RBI	BB	SO	AVG	OBP	SLG	PRO+	BR/A	SB	CS	SBR	FA	FR	G/POS	TPR
1987	SD-N	10	16	1	5	0	0	0	1	1	5	.313	.353	.375	96	0	1	0	0	1.000	0	/O-5	0.0
1988	SD-N	11	10	0	2	1	0	0	1	0	5	.200	.200	.300	42	-1	0	0	0	.000	-1	/O-2	-0.2
Total	2	21	26	1	7	2	0	0	1	1	10	.269	.296	.346	77	-1	1	0	0	1.000	-1	/O-7	-0.2

■ JIM BYRD
Byrd, James Edward   b: 10/3/68, Wewahitchka, Fla.   BR/TR, 6'1", 185 lbs.   Deb: 5/31/93

YEAR	TM/L	G	AB	R	H	2B	3B	HR	RBI	BB	SO	AVG	OBP	SLG	PRO+	BR/A	SB	CS	SBR	FA	FR	G/POS	TPR
1993	Bos-A	2	0	0	0	0	0	0	0	0	0	—	—	—	—		0	0	0	.000	0	/R	0.0

■ SAMMY BYRD
Byrd, Samuel Dewey "Babe Ruth's Legs"   b: 10/15/07, Bremen, Ga.   d: 5/11/81, Mesa, Ariz.   BR/TR, 5'10.5", 175 lbs.   Deb: 5/11/29

YEAR	TM/L	G	AB	R	H	2B	3B	HR	RBI	BB	SO	AVG	OBP	SLG	PRO+	BR/A	SB	CS	SBR	FA	FR	G/POS	TPR
1929	NY-A	62	170	32	53	12	0	5	28	28	18	.312	.409	.471	135	10	1	4	-2	.950	0	O-54	0.4
1930	NY-A	92	218	46	62	12	2	6	31	30	18	.284	.371	.440	110	4	5	1	1	.992	-12	O-85	-1.0
1931	NY-A	115	248	51	67	18	3	6	32	29	28	.270	.349	.395	101	0	5	0	-1	.974	-13	O-88	-1.4
1932	*NY-A	105	209	49	62	12	1	8	30	30	20	.297	.385	.478	129	9	1	2	-1	.964	-18	O-91	-1.2
1933	NY-A	85	107	26	30	6	1	2	11	15	12	.280	.369	.411	113	2	0	1	-1	.987	-16	O-71	-1.5
1934	NY-A	106	191	32	47	8	0	3	23	18	22	.246	.318	.335	73	-8	1	2	-1	**.988**	-13	*O-104	-2.3
1935	Cin-N	121	416	51	109	25	4	9	52	37	51	.262	.322	.406	97	-2	4			.970	3	*O-115	-0.4
1936	Cin-N	59	141	17	35	8	2	0	13	11	11	.248	.303	.348	80	-4	0			.989	-1	O-37	-0.6
Total	8	745	1700	304	465	101	10	38	220	198	178	.274	.350	.412	104	11	17	10		.975	-71	O-645	-8.0

■ BOBBY BYRNE
Byrne, Robert Matthew   b: 12/31/1884, St.Louis, Mo.   d: 12/31/64, Wayne, Pa.   BR/TR, 5'7.5", 145 lbs.   Deb: 4/11/07

YEAR	TM/L	G	AB	R	H	2B	3B	HR	RBI	BB	SO	AVG	OBP	SLG	PRO+	BR/A	SB	CS	SBR	FA	FR	G/POS	TPR
1907	StL-N	149	559	55	143	11	5	0	29	35		.256	.307	.293	91	-6	21			.920	22	*3-148/S-1	2.3
1908	StL-N	127	439	27	84	7	1	0	14	23		.191	.238	.212	46	-27	16			.925	9	*3-122/S-4	-1.6
1909	StL-N	105	421	61	90	13	6	1	33	46		.214	.302	.280	86	-6	21			.922	17	*3-105	1.6
	*Pit-N	46	168	31	43	6	0	0	7	32		.256	.387	.315	109	4	8			.987	6	3-46	1.2
	Yr	151	589	92	133	19	8	1	40	78		.226	.327	.290	93	-2	29			.939	23	*3-151	2.8
1910	Pit-N	148	602	101	**178**	**43**	12	6	52	46	27	.296	.366	.417	121	15	36			.929	-7	*3-148	-0.5
1911	Pit-N	153	598	96	155	24	17	2	52	67	41	.259	.342	.366	95	-4	23			.930	-3	*3-152	-0.5
1912	Pit-N	130	528	99	152	31	11	3	35	54	40	.288	.358	.405	110	7	20			**.948**	-23	*3-130	-1.5
1913	Pit-N	113	448	54	121	22	0	1	47	29	28	.270	.326	.326	89	-7	10			.940	-9	*3-110	-1.5

YEAR	TM/L	G	AB	R	H	2B	3B	HR	RBI	BB	SO	AVG	OBP	SLG	PRO+	BR/A	SB	CS	SBR	FA	FR	G/POS	TPR
	Phi-N	19	58	9	13	1	0	1	4	5	3	.224	.308	.293	69	-2	2			.963	3	3-15	0.1
	Yr	132	506	63	134	23	0	2	51	34	31	.265	.320	.322	86	-9	12			.943	-7	*3-125	-1.4
1914	Phi-N	126	467	61	127	12	1	0	26	45	44	.272	.339	.302	85	-7	9			.934	-3	*2-101,3-22	-1.1
1915	*Phi-N	105	387	50	81	6	4	0	21	39	28	.209	.290	.245	62	-16	4	12	-6	**.969**	-7	*3-105	-2.8
1916	Phi-N	48	141	22	33	10	1	0	9	14	7	.234	.308	.319	89	-2	6			.933	3	3-40	0.3
1917	Phi-N	13	14	1	5	0	0	0	0	1	2	.357	.400	.357	128	0	0			1.000	-1	/3-4	-0.1
	Chi-A	1	1	0	0	0	0	0	0	0	0	.000	.000	.000	-98	-0	0			1.000	0	/2-1	0.0
Total	11	1283	4831	667	1225	186	60	10	329	456	220	.254	.324	.323	91	-51	176	12		.934	6	*3-1147,2-102/S-5	-2.3

■ **JIM BYRNES**   Byrnes, James Joseph b: 1/5/1880, San Francisco, Cal. d: 7/31/41, San Francisco, Cal BR/TR, 5'9", 150 lbs. Deb: 4/19/06

YEAR	TM/L	G	AB	R	H	2B	3B	HR	RBI	BB	SO	AVG	OBP	SLG	PRO+	BR/A	SB	CS	SBR	FA	FR	G/POS	TPR
1906	Phi-A	10	23	2	4	0	1	0	0	1		.174	.174	.261	34	-2	0			.889	-0	/C-9	-0.1

■ **MILT BYRNES**   Byrnes, Milton John "Skippy" b: 11/15/16, St.Louis, Mo. d: 2/1/79, St.Louis, Mo. BL/TL, 5'10.5", 170 lbs. Deb: 4/21/43

YEAR	TM/L	G	AB	R	H	2B	3B	HR	RBI	BB	SO	AVG	OBP	SLG	PRO+	BR/A	SB	CS	SBR	FA	FR	G/POS	TPR
1943	StL-A	129	429	58	120	28	7	4	50	53	49	.280	.362	.406	122	12	1	4	-2	**.997**	8	*O-114	1.3
1944	*StL-A	128	407	63	120	20	4	4	45	68	50	.295	.396	.393	119	12	1	7	-4	.976	-6	*O-122	-0.3
1945	StL-A	133	442	53	110	29	4	8	59	78	84	.249	.363	.387	112	8	1	3	-2	.988	5	*O-125/1-2	0.6
Total	3	390	1278	174	350	77	15	16	154	199	183	.274	.373	.395	117	33	3	14	-8	.987	8	O-361/1-2	1.6

■ **PUTSY CABALLERO**   Caballero, Ralph Joseph b: 11/5/27, New Orleans, La. BR/TR, 5'10", 170 lbs. Deb: 9/14/44

YEAR	TM/L	G	AB	R	H	2B	3B	HR	RBI	BB	SO	AVG	OBP	SLG	PRO+	BR/A	SB	CS	SBR	FA	FR	G/POS	TPR
1944	Phi-N	4	4	0	0	0	0	0	0	0	1	.000	.000	.000	-99	-1	0			.889	2	/3-2	0.1
1945	Phi-N	9	1	1	0	0	0	0	0	1	0	.000	.000	.000	-99	-0	0			.857	2	/3-5	0.1
1947	Phi-N	2	7	2	1	0	0	0	0	0	0	.143	.250	.143	7	-1	0			1.000	-0	/2-2,3-1	-0.1
1948	Phi-N	113	351	33	86	12	1	0	19	24	18	.245	.293	.285	58	-20	7			.962	6	3-79,2-23	-1.4
1949	Phi-N	29	68	8	19	3	0	0	3	0	3	.279	.279	.324	63	-4	0			.981	4	2-21/S-1	0.1
1950	*Phi-N	46	24	12	4	0	0	0	0	2	2	.167	.231	.167	7	-3	1			.950	6	/2-5,3-4,S-2	0.3
1951	Phi-N	84	161	15	30	3	2	1	11	12	7	.186	.243	.248	33	-15	1	2	-1	.985	9	2-54/3-3,S-1	-0.5
1952	Phi-N	35	42	10	10	3	0	0	6	2	3	.238	.273	.310	62	-2	1	0	0	.857	2	/S-8,2-7,3-7	0.1
Total	8	322	658	81	150	21	3	1	40	41	34	.228	.273	.274	49	-47	10	2		.968	31	2-112,3-101/S-12	-1.3

■ **ENOS CABELL**   Cabell, Enos Milton b: 10/8/49, Fort Riley, Kan. BR/TR, 6'5", 185 lbs. Deb: 9/17/72

YEAR	TM/L	G	AB	R	H	2B	3B	HR	RBI	BB	SO	AVG	OBP	SLG	PRO+	BR/A	SB	CS	SBR	FA	FR	G/POS	TPR
1972	Bal-A	3	5	0	0	0	0	0	1	0	0	.000	.000	.000	-97	-1	0	0	0	1.000	-0	/1-1	-0.2
1973	Bal-A	32	47	12	10	2	0	1	3	3	7	.213	.260	.319	63	-2	1	3	-2	.991	-1	1-23/3-1	-0.6
1974	*Bal-A	80	174	24	42	4	2	3	17	7	20	.241	.271	.339	77	-6	5	3	-0	.995	2	1-28,0-22,3-19/2D	-0.6
1975	Hou-N	117	348	43	92	17	6	2	43	18	53	.264	.306	.365	92	-5	12	3	2	.973	-0	O-67,1-25,3-22	-0.7
1976	Hou-N	144	586	85	160	13	7	2	43	29	79	.273	.310	.329	89	-10	35	8	6	.958	-9	*3-143/1-3	-1.5
1977	Hou-N	150	625	101	176	36	7	16	68	27	55	.282	.315	.438	109	4	42	22	-1	.948	-6	*3-144/1-8,S-1	-1.4
1978	Hou-N	162	660	92	195	31	8	7	71	22	80	.295	.323	.398	109	4	33	15	1	.958	-16	*3-153,1-14/S-1	-1.4
1979	Hou-N	155	603	60	164	30	5	6	67	21	68	.272	.300	.352	90	-14	37	18	0	.957	-23	*3-132,1-51	-4.1
1980	*Hou-N	152	604	69	167	23	8	2	55	26	84	.276	.307	.351	90	-10	21	13	-2	.927	-20	*3-150/1-1	-3.6
1981	SF-N	96	396	41	101	20	1	2	36	10	47	.255	.275	.326	71	-16	7		-2	.987	-1	1-69,3-22	-2.6
1982	Det-A	125	464	45	121	17	3	2	37	15	48	.261	.285	.323	67	-21	15	6	1	.992	-8	1-83,3-59/O-3	-3.3
1983	Det-A	121	392	62	122	23	5	5	46	16	41	.311	.340	.434	114	7	4	8	-4	.997	7	*1-106/3-4,S-1,D-8	0.4
1984	Hou-N	127	436	52	135	17	3	8	44	21	47	.310	.343	.417	121	10	8	11	-4	.993	-1	*1-112	-0.1
1985	Hou-N	60	143	20	35	8	1	2	14	16	15	.245	.321	.357	92	-1	3	1	0	.994	-1	1-49	-0.5
	*LA-N	57	192	20	56	11	0	2	22	14	21	.292	.340	.349	96	-1	6	2	1	.920	-2	3-32,1-21/O-4	-0.4
	Yr	117	335	40	91	19	1	2	36	30	36	.272	.332	.352	94	-3	9	3	1	.993	-3	1-70,3-32/O-4	-0.9
1986	LA-N	107	277	27	71	11	0	2	29	14	26	.256	.297	.318	75	-10	10	4	1	.987	0	1-61,O-16/3-7	-1.4
Total	15	1688	5952	753	1647	263	56	60	596	259	691	.277	.309	.370	93	-74	238	124	-3	.944	-77	3-888,1-655,O/DS2	-21.0

■ **AL CABRERA**   Cabrera, Alfredo A. b: 1883, Canary Islands d: Havana, Cuba TR Deb: 5/16/13

YEAR	TM/L	G	AB	R	H	2B	3B	HR	RBI	BB	SO	AVG	OBP	SLG	PRO+	BR/A	SB	CS	SBR	FA	FR	G/POS	TPR
1913	StL-N	1	2	0	0	0	0	0	0	0	0	.000	.000	.000	-99	-1	0			.000	0	/S-1	-0.1

■ **FRANCISCO CABRERA**   Cabrera, Francisco (Paulino) b: 10/10/66, Santo Domingo, D.R. BR/TR, 6'4", 195 lbs. Deb: 7/24/89

YEAR	TM/L	G	AB	R	H	2B	3B	HR	RBI	BB	SO	AVG	OBP	SLG	PRO+	BR/A	SB	CS	SBR	FA	FR	G/POS	TPR
1989	Tor-A	3	12	1	2	1	0	0	0	0	3	.167	.231	.250	36	-1	0	0	0	.000	0	/D-3	-0.1
	Atl-N	4	14	0	3	2	0	0	0	0	3	.214	.214	.357	59	-1	0	0	0	1.000	-1	/1-2,C-1	-0.2
1990	Atl-N	63	137	14	38	5	1	7	25	5	21	.277	.303	.482	106	1	1	0	0	.990	-2	1-48/C-3	-0.3
1991	*Atl-N	44	95	7	23	6	0	4	23	6	20	.242	.287	.432	94	-1	1	1	-0	.987	-3	C-17,1-14	-0.4
1992	*Atl-N	12	10	2	3	0	0	2	3	1	1	.300	.364	.900	233	2	0	0	0	.000	0	/C-1	0.2
1993	*Atl-N	70	83	8	20	3	0	4	11	8	21	.241	.308	.422	92	-1	0	0	0	1.000	1	1-12/C-2	-0.0
Total	5	196	351	32	89	17	1	17	62	21	69	.254	.296	.453	99	-2	2	1	0	.989	-3	/1-76,C-24,D-3	-0.8

■ **CRAIG CACEK**   Cacek, Craig Thomas b: 9/10/54, Hollywood, Cal. BR/TR, 6'1", 200 lbs. Deb: 6/18/77

YEAR	TM/L	G	AB	R	H	2B	3B	HR	RBI	BB	SO	AVG	OBP	SLG	PRO+	BR/A	SB	CS	SBR	FA	FR	G/POS	TPR
1977	Hou-N	7	20	0	1	0	0	0	1	1	3	.050	.095	.050	-66	-5	0	0	0	.981	-1	/1-6	-0.6

■ **EDGAR CACERES**   Caceres, Edgar F. b: 6/6/64, Barquisimeto, Venez. BB/TR, 6'1", 170 lbs. Deb: 6/8/95

YEAR	TM/L	G	AB	R	H	2B	3B	HR	RBI	BB	SO	AVG	OBP	SLG	PRO+	BR/A	SB	CS	SBR	FA	FR	G/POS	TPR
1995	KC-A	55	117	13	28	6	2	1	17	8	15	.239	.294	.350	66	-6	2	2	-1	.992	1	2-36/S-8,1-6,3-3,D	-0.4

■ **CHARLIE CADY**   Cady, Charles B. b: 12/1865, Chicago, Ill. d: 6/7/09, Kankakee, Ill. 5'11", 180 lbs. Deb: 9/5/1883

YEAR	TM/L	G	AB	R	H	2B	3B	HR	RBI	BB	SO	AVG	OBP	SLG	PRO+	BR/A	SB	CS	SBR	FA	FR	G/POS	TPR
1883	Cle-N	3	11	0	0	0	0	0	0	1	5	.000	.083	.000	-73	-2				1.000	-1	/O-2,P-1	-0.2
1884	CP-U	6	20	4	2	1	1	0		0	1	.100	.143	.250	17	-3				.909	-0	/P-4,O-2	-0.1
	KC-U	2	3	0	0	0	0	0		0	0	.000	.000	.000	-99	-1				.600	-2	/C-1,2-1	-0.2
	Yr	8	23	4	2	1	1	0		0	1	.087	.125	.217	2	-4				.909	-2	/P-4,O-2,C-1,2-1	-0.3
Total	2	11	34	4	2	1	1	0	0	2	5	.059	.111	.147	-23	-6				.917	-3	/P-5,O-4,2-1,C-1	-0.5

■ **HICK CADY**   Cady, Forrest Leroy b: 1/26/1886, Bishop Hill, Ill. d: 3/3/46, Cedar Rapids, Iowa BR/TR, 6'2", 179 lbs. Deb: 4/26/12

YEAR	TM/L	G	AB	R	H	2B	3B	HR	RBI	BB	SO	AVG	OBP	SLG	PRO+	BR/A	SB	CS	SBR	FA	FR	G/POS	TPR
1912	*Bos-A	47	135	19	35	13	2	0	9	10		.259	.324	.385	98	-1	0			.990	11	C-43/1-4	1.4
1913	Bos-A	40	96	10	24	5	2	0	6	5	14	.250	.294	.344	84	-2	1			.992	8	C-39	0.9
1914	Bos-A	61	159	14	41	6	1	0	8	12	22	.258	.310	.308	86	-3	2	1	0	.971	-3	C-58	-0.1
1915	*Bos-A	78	205	25	57	10	2	0	17	19	25	.278	.342	.346	109	2	0	2	-1	.980	-2	C-77	0.5
1916	*Bos-A	78	162	5	31	6	3	0	13	15	16	.191	.264	.265	59	-8	0			.967	-13	C-63/1-3	-2.0
1917	Bos-A	17	46	4	7	1	2	1	6	2	6	.152	.170	.217	18	-5	0			.959	1	C-14	-1.0
1919	Phi-N	34	98	6	21	6	1	0	19	4	8	.214	.252	.306	63	-5	1			.984	-7	C-29	-1.0
Total	7	355	901	83	216	47	11	1	74	66	91	.240	.297	.320	82	-21	4	3		.979	-4	C-323/1-7	-0.6

■ **TOM CAFEGO**   Cafego, Thomas b: 8/21/11, Whipple, W.Va. d: 10/29/61, Detroit, Mich. BL/TR, 5'10", 160 lbs. Deb: 9/3/37

YEAR	TM/L	G	AB	R	H	2B	3B	HR	RBI	BB	SO	AVG	OBP	SLG	PRO+	BR/A	SB	CS	SBR	FA	FR	G/POS	TPR
1937	StL-A	4	4	1	0	0	0	0	0	0	1	.000	.000	.000	-99	-1	0	0	0	.500	-1	/O-1	-0.2

■ **JOE CAFFIE**   Caffie, Joseph Clifford "Rabbit" b: 2/14/31, Ramer, Ala. BL/TR, 5'10.5", 180 lbs. Deb: 9/13/56

YEAR	TM/L	G	AB	R	H	2B	3B	HR	RBI	BB	SO	AVG	OBP	SLG	PRO+	BR/A	SB	CS	SBR	FA	FR	G/POS	TPR
1956	Cle-A	12	38	7	13	0	0	1	4		8	.342	.432	.342	104	1	3	2	-0	1.000	1	O-10	0.1
1957	Cle-A	32	89	14	24	2	1	3	10	4	11	.270	.301	.416	95	-1	0	1	-1	.976	-0	O-19	-0.3
Total	2	44	127	21	37	2	1	3	11	5	11	.291	.343	.394	99	-0	3	3	-1	.984	1	/O-29	-0.2

■ **BEN CAFFYN**   Caffyn, Benjamin Thomas b: 2/10/1880, Peoria, Ill. d: 11/22/42, Peoria, Ill. BL/TL, Deb: 8/21/06

YEAR	TM/L	G	AB	R	H	2B	3B	HR	RBI	BB	SO	AVG	OBP	SLG	PRO+	BR/A	SB	CS	SBR	FA	FR	G/POS	TPR
1906	Cle-A	30	103	16	20	4	0	0	3		12	.194	.291	.233	65	-4	2			.909	-4	O-29	-1.0

■ **WAYNE CAGE**   Cage, Wayne Levell b: 11/23/51, Monroe, La. BL/TL, 6'4", 205 lbs. Deb: 4/22/78

YEAR	TM/L	G	AB	R	H	2B	3B	HR	RBI	BB	SO	AVG	OBP	SLG	PRO+	BR/A	SB	CS	SBR	FA	FR	G/POS	TPR
1978	Cle-A	36	98	11	24	6	1	3	13	9	28	.245	.308	.449	112	-1	2	2	1	.988	1	D-20,1-11	0.0
1979	Cle-A	29	56	6	13	2	0	1	6	5	16	.232	.295	.321	66	-3	0	2	-1	1.000	1	/1-7,D-9	-0.4
Total	2	65	154	17	37	8	1	4	19	14	44	.240	.304	.403	94	-2	1	4	-0	.992	2	/D-29,1-18	-0.4

■ **JOHN CAHILL**   Cahill, John Patrick Parnell "Patsy" b: 4/30/1865, San Francisco, Cal d: 10/31/01, Pleasanton, Cal. BR/TR, 5'7.5", 168 lbs. Deb: 5/31/1884

YEAR	TM/L	G	AB	R	H	2B	3B	HR	RBI	BB	SO	AVG	OBP	SLG	PRO+	BR/A	SB	CS	SBR	FA	FR	G/POS	TPR
1884	Col-a	59	210	28	46	3	3	0		6		.219	.248	.262	72	-6				.843	-0	O-56/S-5,P-2	-0.6
1886	StL-N	125	463	43	92	17	6	1	32	9	79	.199	.214	.268	49	-28	16			.866	2	*O-124/P-2,S-1,3-1	-2.7

YEAR	TM/L	G	AB	R	H	2B	3B	HR	RBI	BB	SO	AVG	OBP	SLG	PRO+	BR/A	SB	CS	SBR	FA	FR	G/POS	TPR
1887	Ind-N	68	263	22	54	4	3	0	26	9	5	.205	.234	.243	34	-23	34			.826	-6	O-56/3-9,P-6,S-1	-2.4
Total	3	252	936	93	192	24	12	1	58	24	84	.205	.227	.260	49	-57	50			.851	-5	O-236/3-10,P-10,S-7	-5.7

■ TOM CAHILL   Cahill, Thomas H.   b: 10/1868, Fall River, Mass.   d: 12/25/1894, Scranton, Pa.   Deb: 4/9/1891

YEAR	TM/L	G	AB	R	H	2B	3B	HR	RBI	BB	SO	AVG	OBP	SLG	PRO+	BR/A	SB	CS	SBR	FA	FR	G/POS	TPR
1891	Lou-a	120	433	70	111	18	7	3	47	41	51	.256	.329	.351	96	-3	39			.931	-3	C-56,S-49,O-12/23	0.2

■ BOB CAIN   Cain, Robert Max "Sugar"   b: 10/16/24, Longford, Kan.   BL/TL, 6', 165 lbs.   Deb: 9/18/49

YEAR	TM/L	G	AB	R	H	2B	3B	HR	RBI	BB	SO	AVG	OBP	SLG	PRO+	BR/A	SB	CS	SBR	FA	FR	G/POS	TPR
1949	Chi-A	6	3	0	0	0	0	0	0	0	1	.000	.000	.000	-99	-1	0	0	0	1.000	-0	/P-6	0.0
1950	Chi-A	35	61	7	12	2	0	0	2	3	15	.197	.234	.230	20	-7	0	0	0	.974	0	P-34	0.0
1951	Chi-A	4	9	1	3	1	0	0	0	0	3	.333	.333	.444	111	0	0	0	0	1.000	-0	/P-4	0.0
	Det-A	35	53	9	13	3	0	0	9	6	9	.245	.322	.302	69	-2	0	0	0	.972	0	P-35	0.0
	Yr	39	62	10	16	4	0	0	9	6	12	.258	.324	.323	75	-2	0	0	0	.975	-0	P-39	0.0
1952	StL-A	35	58	7	8	0	1	0	1	4	14	.138	.194	.172	2	-8	0	0	0	.966	-2	P-29	0.0
1953	StL-A	34	30	3	6	2	0	0	2	1	3	.200	.226	.267	32	-3	0	0	0	1.000	-0	P-32	0.0
1954	Chi-A	1	0	1	0	0	0	0	0	0	0	—	—	—			0			.000	0	R	0.0
Total	6	150	214	28	42	8	1	0	14	14	45	.196	.246	.243	31	-21	0	0	0	.975	-4	P-140	0.0

■ MIGUEL CAIRO   Cairo, Miguel Jesus   b: 5/4/74, Anaco, Venez.   BR/TR, 6', 160 lbs.   Deb: 4/17/96

YEAR	TM/L	G	AB	R	H	2B	3B	HR	RBI	BB	SO	AVG	OBP	SLG	PRO+	BR/A	SB	CS	SBR	FA	FR	G/POS	TPR
1996	Tor-A	9	27	5	6	2	0	0	1	2	9	.222	.300	.296	51	-2	0	0	0	1.000	0	/2-9	-0.1

■ GEORGE CAITHAMER   Caithamer, George Theodore "Sidel"   b: 7/22/10, Chicago, Ill.   d: 6/1/54, Chicago, Ill.   BR/TR, 5'7.5", 160 lbs.   Deb: 9/17/34

YEAR	TM/L	G	AB	R	H	2B	3B	HR	RBI	BB	SO	AVG	OBP	SLG	PRO+	BR/A	SB	CS	SBR	FA	FR	G/POS	TPR
1934	Chi-A	5	19	1	6	1	0	0	3	1	5	.316	.350	.368	83	-0	0	0	0	.958	-1	/C-5	-0.1

■ IVAN CALDERON   Calderon, Ivan (Perez)   b: 3/19/62, Fajardo, P.R.   BR/TR, 6'1", 220 lbs.   Deb: 8/10/84

YEAR	TM/L	G	AB	R	H	2B	3B	HR	RBI	BB	SO	AVG	OBP	SLG	PRO+	BR/A	SB	CS	SBR	FA	FR	G/POS	TPR
1984	Sea-A	11	24	2	5	1	0	0	2	1	5	.208	.269	.375	77	-1	1	0	0	1.000	-1	O-11	-0.1
1985	Sea-A	67	210	37	60	16	4	8	28	19	45	.286	.351	.514	132	9	4	2	0	.981	1	O-53/1-2,D-3	0.8
1986	Sea-A	37	131	13	31	5	0	2	13	6	33	.237	.275	.321	61	-7	3	1	0	.937	-1	O-32	-0.9
	Chi-A	13	33	3	10	2	1	0	2	3	6	.303	.361	.424	109	-0	3	0	0	.900	-0	/O-5,D-6	0.0
	Yr	50	164	16	41	7	1	2	15	9	39	.250	.293	.341	71	-7	3	1	0	.932	-1	O-37/D-6	-0.9
1987	Chi-A	144	542	93	159	38	2	28	83	60	109	.293	.365	.526	129	22	10	5	0	.984	5	*O-139/D-3	2.2
1988	Chi-A	73	264	40	56	14	0	14	35	34	66	.212	.302	.424	101	-0	4	4	-1	.954	2	O-67/D-3	-0.2
1989	Chi-A	157	622	83	178	34	9	14	87	43	94	.286	.335	.442	119	14	7	1	2	.978	-0	*O-103,D-36,1-26	1.0
1990	Chi-A	158	607	85	166	44	2	14	74	51	79	.273	.331	.422	111	8	32	16	0	.975	4	*O-130,D-27/1-2	0.8
1991	Mon-N★	134	470	69	141	22	3	19	75	53	64	.300	.375	.481	141	26	31	16	-0	.974	5	*O-122/1-4	2.8
1992	Mon-N	48	170	19	45	14	2	3	24	14	22	.265	.324	.424	111	2	1	2	-1	.988	-0	O-46	0.1
1993	Bos-A	73	213	25	47	8	2	1	19	21	28	.221	.294	.291	54	-14	4	2	0	1.000	-1	O-47,D-19	-1.6
	Chi-A	9	26	1	3	2	0	0	3	0	5	.115	.115	.192	-19	-4	0	0	0	.000	0	/D-6	-0.5
	Yr	82	239	26	50	10	2	1	22	21	33	.209	.276	.326	47	-18	4	2	0	1.000	-1	O-47,D-19/H-6	-2.1
Total	10	924	3312	470	901	200	25	104	444	306	556	.272	.336	.442	113	55	97	49	-0	.976	15	O-755,D-103/1-34	4.4

■ SAM CALDERONE   Calderone, Samuel Francis   b: 2/6/26, Beverly, N.J.   BR/TR, 5'10.5", 185 lbs.   Deb: 4/19/50

YEAR	TM/L	G	AB	R	H	2B	3B	HR	RBI	BB	SO	AVG	OBP	SLG	PRO+	BR/A	SB	CS	SBR	FA	FR	G/POS	TPR
1950	NY-N	34	67	9	20	1	0	1	12	2	5	.299	.319	.358	77	-2				.972	-4	C-33	-0.5
1953	NY-N	35	45	4	10	2	0	0	8	1	4	.222	.239	.267	31	-5	0	0	0	.966	-1	C-31	-0.4
1954	Mil-N	22	29	3	11	2	0	0	5	4	4	.379	.455	.448	146	2	0	0	0	1.000	3	C-16	0.5
Total	3	91	141	16	41	5	0	1	25	7	13	.291	.324	.348	76	-5	0	0	0	.978	-2	/C-80	-0.4

■ BRUCE CALDWELL   Caldwell, Bruce   b: 2/8/06, Ashton, R.I.   d: 2/15/59, West Haven, Conn.   BR/TR, 6', 195 lbs.   Deb: 6/30/28

YEAR	TM/L	G	AB	R	H	2B	3B	HR	RBI	BB	SO	AVG	OBP	SLG	PRO+	BR/A	SB	CS	SBR	FA	FR	G/POS	TPR
1928	Cle-A	18	27	2	6	1	1	0	3	2	2	.222	.300	.333	66	-1	1	0	0	1.000	-2	O-10/1-1	-0.3
1932	Bro-N	7	11	2	1	0	0	0	2	2	2	.091	.231	.091	-10	-2	0			.875	-1	/1-6	-0.3
Total	2	25	38	4	7	1	1	0	5	4	4	.184	.279	.263	44	-3	1	0		.900	-3	/O-10,1-7	-0.6

■ RAY CALDWELL   Caldwell, Raymond Benjamin "Rube" or "Sum"   b: 4/26/1888, Corydon, Pa.   d: 8/17/67, Salamanca, N.Y.   BL/TR, 6'2", 190 lbs.   Deb: 9/9/10

YEAR	TM/L	G	AB	R	H	2B	3B	HR	RBI	BB	SO	AVG	OBP	SLG	PRO+	BR/A	SB	CS	SBR	FA	FR	G/POS	TPR
1910	NY-A	6	6	0	0	0	0	0	0	0	0	.000	.000	.000	-95	-1	0			1.000	-0	/P-6	0.0
1911	NY-A	59	147	14	40	4	1	0	17	11		.272	.323	.313	73	-5	5			.953	-2	P-41,O-11	-0.1
1912	NY-A	44	76	18	18	1	2	0	6	5		.237	.284	.303	64	-4	4			.938	1	P-30/O-1	0.0
1913	NY-A	59	97	10	28	3	2	0	11	3	15	.289	.310	.361	96	-1	3			**1.000**	-1	P-27/O-3	-0.1
1914	NY-A	59	113	9	22	4	0	0	10	7	24	.195	.248	.230	44	-8	2	1	0	.967	-4	P-31/1-6	-0.3
1915	NY-A	72	144	27	35	4	1	4	20	9	32	.243	.288	.368	96	-2	4	3	-1	**.988**	-3	P-36	0.0
1916	NY-A	45	93	6	19	2	0	0	4	2	17	.204	.221	.226	34	-8	1			.960	-1	P-21/O-2	0.0
1917	NY-A	63	124	12	32	6	1	2	12	16	16	.258	.343	.371	117	3	2			.973	-3	P-32/O-8	-0.2
1918	NY-A	65	151	14	44	10	0	1	18	13	23	.291	.352	.377	117	3	2			.977	-2	P-24/O-19	0.1
1919	Bos-A	38	48	5	13	1	1	0	6	0	9	.271	.271	.333	73	-2	0			.950	-2	P-18/O-6	-0.1
	Cle-A	6	23	4	8	4	0	0	2	0	4	.348	.348	.522	134	1	0			.900	-1	/P-6	0.0
	Yr	39	71	9	21	5	1	0	6	0	13	.296	.296	.394	97	-1	0			.933	-3	P-24/O-6	-0.1
1920	*Cle-A	41	89	17	19	3	0	0	7	10	13	.213	.300	.247	45	-7	0	2	-1	.917	-3	P-34	0.0
1921	Cle-A	38	53	2	11	4	0	1	2	5	5	.208	.236	.340	45	-5	0	0	0	.930	-0	P-37	0.0
Total	12	590	1164	138	289	46	8	8	114	78	158	.248	.297	.322	78	-36	23	6		.960	-20	P-343/O-46,1-6	-0.7

■ JACK CALHOUN   Calhoun, John Charles "Red"   b: 12/14/1879, Pittsburgh, Pa.   d: 2/27/47, Cincinnati, Ohio   BR/TR, 6', 185 lbs.   Deb: 6/27/02

YEAR	TM/L	G	AB	R	H	2B	3B	HR	RBI	BB	SO	AVG	OBP	SLG	PRO+	BR/A	SB	CS	SBR	FA	FR	G/POS	TPR
1902	StL-N	20	64	3	10	2	1	0	8	8		.156	.260	.219	50	-4	1			.972	-2	3-12/1-5,O-1	-0.6

■ BILL CALHOUN   Calhoun, William Davitte "Mary"   b: 6/23/1890, Rockmart, Ga.   d: 1/28/55, Sandersville, Ga.   BL/TL, 6', 180 lbs.   Deb: 4/24/13

YEAR	TM/L	G	AB	R	H	2B	3B	HR	RBI	BB	SO	AVG	OBP	SLG	PRO+	BR/A	SB	CS	SBR	FA	FR	G/POS	TPR
1913	Bos-N	6	13	0	1	0	0	0	0	0	3	.077	.077	.077	-55	-3	0			.970	-1	/1-3	-0.3

■ MARTY CALLAGHAN   Callaghan, Martin Francis   b: 6/9/1900, Norwood, Mass.   d: 6/23/75, Norfolk, Mass.   BL/TL, 5'10", 157 lbs.   Deb: 4/13/22

YEAR	TM/L	G	AB	R	H	2B	3B	HR	RBI	BB	SO	AVG	OBP	SLG	PRO+	BR/A	SB	CS	SBR	FA	FR	G/POS	TPR
1922	Chi-N	74	175	31	45	7	4	0	20	17	17	.257	.326	.343	71	-7	2	3	-1	.946	-9	O-53	-2.0
1923	Chi-N	61	129	18	29	1	3	0	14	8	18	.225	.275	.279	47	-10	2	5	-2	.969	-4	O-38	-1.7
1928	Cin-N	81	238	29	69	11	4	0	24	27	10	.290	.362	.370	93	-2	5			.980	-4	O-69	-1.0
1930	Cin-N	79	225	28	62	9	2	0	16	19	25	.276	.335	.333	66	-12	1			.986	3	O-54	-1.2
Total	4	295	767	106	205	28	13	0	74	71	70	.267	.332	.338	72	-31	10	8		.973	-14	O-214	-5.9

■ DAVE CALLAHAN   Callahan, David Joseph   b: 7/20/1888, Ottawa, Ill.   d: 10/28/69, Ottawa, Ill.   BL/TR, 5'10", 165 lbs.   Deb: 9/14/10

YEAR	TM/L	G	AB	R	H	2B	3B	HR	RBI	BB	SO	AVG	OBP	SLG	PRO+	BR/A	SB	CS	SBR	FA	FR	G/POS	TPR
1910	Cle-A	13	44	6	8	1	0	0	2	4		.182	.265	.205	47	-3	5			1.000	0	O-12	-0.3
1911	Cle-A	6	16	1	4	0	1	0	0	1		.250	.294	.375	85	-0	0			1.000	0	/O-4	0.0
Total	2	19	60	7	12	1	1	0	2	5		.200	.273	.250	58	-3	5			1.000	1	/O-16	-0.3

■ ED CALLAHAN   Callahan, Edward Joseph   b: 12/11/1857, Boston, Mass.   d: 2/5/47, New York, N.Y.   Deb: 7/19/1884

YEAR	TM/L	G	AB	R	H	2B	3B	HR	RBI	BB	SO	AVG	OBP	SLG	PRO+	BR/A	SB	CS	SBR	FA	FR	G/POS	TPR
1884	StL-U	1	3	0	0	0	0	0		0		.000	.000	.000	-97	-1				1.000	0	/O-1	0.0
	KC-U	3	11	0	4	0	0	0		0		.364	.364	.364	139	0				.800	1	/S-3	0.1
	Bos-U	4	13	2	5	0	0	0		0		.385	.429	.385	151	1				.750	-1	/O-4	0.0
	Yr	8	27	2	9	0	0	0		1		.333	.357	.333	117	-0				.778	0	/O-5,S-3	0.1

■ NIXEY CALLAHAN   Callahan, James Joseph   b: 3/18/1874, Fitchburg, Mass.   d: 10/4/34, Boston, Mass.   BR/TR, 5'10.5", 180 lbs.   Deb: 5/12/1894   M

YEAR	TM/L	G	AB	R	H	2B	3B	HR	RBI	BB	SO	AVG	OBP	SLG	PRO+	BR/A	SB	CS	SBR	FA	FR	G/POS	TPR
1894	Phi-N	9	21	4	5	0	0	0	0	0	7	.238	.238	.238	16	-3	0			.923	1	/P-9	0.0
1897	Chi-N	94	360	60	105	18	6	3	47	10		.292	.320	.400	86	-9	12			.918	5	2-30,P-23,O-21,S/3	-0.3
1898	Chi-N	43	164	27	43	7	5	0	22	4		.262	.280	.366	85	-4	3			.947	-2	P-31/O-9,S-1,2-1,1	-0.4
1899	Chi-N	47	150	21	39	4	3	0	19	6		.260	.306	.327	76	-5	9			.904	3	P-35/O-9,S-2,2-1	-0.3
1900	Chi-N	32	115	16	27	3	2	0	9	6		.235	.273	.296	59	-7	6			.975	6	P-32	0.0
1901	Chi-A	45	118	15	39	7	3	1	19	10		.331	.383	.466	138	6	10			.944	4	P-27/3-6,2-2	0.0
1902	Chi-A	70	218	27	51	9	2	2	34			.234	.261	.284	53	-14	4			.941	2	P-35,O-23/S-1	-1.0
1903	Chi-A	118	439	47	128	26	5	2	56	20		.292	.324	.387	118	9	24			.895	-6	*3-102/O-8,P-3,M	0.3
1904	Chi-A	132	482	66	126	23	2	0	54	39		.261	.318	.317	105	4	29			.977	-17	*O-104,2-28,M	-2.0

YEAR	TM/L	G	AB	R	H	2B	3B	HR	RBI	BB	SO	AVG	OBP	SLG	PRO+	BR/A	SB	CS	SBR	FA	FR	G/POS	TPR
1905	Chi-A	96	345	50	94	18	6	1	43	29		.272	.336	.368	128	11	26			.956	-8	O-93	-0.1
1911	Chi-A	120	466	64	131	13	5	3	60	15		.281	.306	.350	86	-11	45			.963	-9	*O-114	-2.6
1912	Chi-A	111	408	45	111	9	7	1	52	12		.272	.298	.336	84	-10	19			.939	-16	*O-107,M	-3.1
1913	Chi-A	6	9	0	2	0	0	0	1	2		.222	.222	.222	30	-1	0			1.000	-0	/O-1,M	-0.1
Total	13	923	3295	442	901	135	46	11	394	159	9	.273	.311	.352	94	-34	186			.953	-36	O-489,P-195,3/2S1	-9.6

■ JIM CALLAHAN

Callahan, James Timothy "Red" (b: James Timothy Callaghan) b: 1/12/1879, Allegheny Co., Pa. d: 3/9/68, Carnegie, Pa. BR/TR, 5'9", 145 lbs. Deb: 5/25/02

YEAR	TM/L	G	AB	R	H	2B	3B	HR	RBI	BB	SO	AVG	OBP	SLG	PRO+	BR/A	SB	CS	SBR	FA	FR	G/POS	TPR
1902	NY-N	1	4	0	0	0	0	0	0	1		.000	.200	.000	-38	-1	0			.000	-0	/O-1	-0.1

■ LEO CALLAHAN

Callahan, Leo David b: 8/9/1890, Jamaica Plain, Mass d: 5/2/82, Erie, Pa. BL/TL, 5'8", 142 lbs. Deb: 4/9/13

YEAR	TM/L	G	AB	R	H	2B	3B	HR	RBI	BB	SO	AVG	OBP	SLG	PRO+	BR/A	SB	CS	SBR	FA	FR	G/POS	TPR
1913	Bro-N	33	41	6	7	3	1	0	3	4	5	.171	.244	.293	52	-3	0			.857	-2	/O-8	-0.5
1919	Phi-N	81	235	26	54	14	4	1	9	29	19	.230	.317	.336	90	-2	5			.950	1	O-58	-0.6
Total	2	114	276	32	61	17	5	1	12	33	24	.221	.306	.330	84	-5	5			.941	-1	/O-66	-1.1

■ PAT CALLAHAN

Callahan, Patrick Henry b: 10/15/1866, Cleveland, Ohio d: 2/4/40, Louisville, Ky. Deb: 5/1/1884

YEAR	TM/L	G	AB	R	H	2B	3B	HR	RBI	BB	SO	AVG	OBP	SLG	PRO+	BR/A	SB	CS	SBR	FA	FR	G/POS	TPR
1884	Ind-a	61	258	38	67	8	5	2		8		.260	.282	.353	109	2				.812	-7	3-61	-0.4

■ WESLEY CALLAHAN

Callahan, Wesley Leroy b: 7/3/1888, Lyons, Ind. d: 9/13/53, Dayton, Ohio BR/TR, 5'7.5", 155 lbs. Deb: 9/7/13

YEAR	TM/L	G	AB	R	H	2B	3B	HR	RBI	BB	SO	AVG	OBP	SLG	PRO+	BR/A	SB	CS	SBR	FA	FR	G/POS	TPR
1913	StL-N	7	14	0	4	0	0	0	1	2	2	.286	.375	.286	91	-0	1			.920	1	/S-6	0.1

■ FRANK CALLAWAY

Callaway, Frank Burnett b: 2/26/1898, Knoxville, Tenn. d: 8/21/87, Knoxville, Tenn. BR/TR, 6', 170 lbs. Deb: 9/17/21

YEAR	TM/L	G	AB	R	H	2B	3B	HR	RBI	BB	SO	AVG	OBP	SLG	PRO+	BR/A	SB	CS	SBR	FA	FR	G/POS	TPR
1921	Phi-A	14	50	7	12	1	1	0	4	2	11	.240	.283	.300	49	-4	1	0	0	.878	-5	S-14	-0.7
1922	Phi-A	29	48	5	13	0	2	0	4	0	13	.271	.271	.354	60	-3	0	0	0	.880	1	2-11/3-5,S-4	-0.1
Total	2	43	98	12	25	1	3	0	8	2	24	.255	.277	.327	54	-7	1	0	0	.889	-4	/S-18,2-11,3-5	-0.8

■ JOHNNY CALLISON

Callison, John Wesley b: 3/12/39, Qualls, Okla. BL/TR, 5'10", 175 lbs. Deb: 9/9/58

YEAR	TM/L	G	AB	R	H	2B	3B	HR	RBI	BB	SO	AVG	OBP	SLG	PRO+	BR/A	SB	CS	SBR	FA	FR	G/POS	TPR
1958	Chi-A	18	64	10	19	4	2	1	12	6	14	.297	.357	.469	128	1	1	0	0	.976	3	O-18	0.4
1959	Chi-A	49	104	12	18	3	0	3	12	13	20	.173	.271	.288	54	-7	0	1	-1	.983	-3	O-41	-1.2
1960	Phi-N	99	288	36	75	11	5	9	30	45	70	.260	.360	.427	114	7	0	4	-2	.989	1	O-86	0.1
1961	Phi-N	138	455	74	121	20	11	9	47	69	76	.266	.366	.418	109	7	10	4	1	.967	5	*O-124	0.6
1962	Phi-N★	157	603	107	181	26	**10**	23	83	54	96	.300	.363	.491	131	25	8	3	1	.980	23	*O-152	3.9
1963	Phi-N	157	626	96	178	36	11	26	78	50	111	.284	.339	.502	140	31	8	3	1	.994	23	*O-157	4.8
1964	Phi-N★	162	654	101	179	30	10	31	104	36	95	.274	.318	.492	126	20	6	3	0	.988	19	*O-162	3.3
1965	Phi-N☆	160	619	93	162	25	**16**	32	101	57	117	.262	.330	.509	135	26	6	5	-1	.982	19	*O-159	3.8
1966	Phi-N	155	612	93	169	**40**	7	11	55	55	83	.276	.340	.418	109	8	8	8	-2	.990	6	*O-154	0.4
1967	Phi-N	149	556	62	145	30	5	14	64	55	63	.261	.331	.408	109	7	6	12	-5	.977	9	*O-147	0.3
1968	Phi-N	121	398	46	97	18	4	14	40	42	70	.244	.321	.415	119	9	4	3	-1	**1.000**	2	*O-109	0.6
1969	Phi-N	134	495	66	131	29	5	16	64	49	73	.265	.335	.440	119	11	2	1	0	.990	16	*O-129	2.0
1970	Chi-N	147	477	65	126	23	2	19	68	60	63	.264	.350	.440	98	-2	7	2	1	.973	-0	*O-144	-0.8
1971	Chi-N	103	290	27	61	12	1	8	38	36	55	.210	.302	.341	71	-11	2	4	-3	.982	-3	O-89	-1.9
1972	NY-A	92	275	28	71	10	0	9	34	18	34	.258	.304	.393	110	2	3	0	1	.992	-3	O-74	-0.3
1973	NY-A	45	136	10	24	4	0	1	10	4	24	.176	.200	.228	21	-14	1	1	-0	.960	-2	/O-32,D-10	-1.9
Total	16	1886	6652	926	1757	321	89	226	840	650	1064	.264	.333	.441	114	121	74	51	-8	.984	113	*O-1777/D-10	14.1

■ JACK CALVO

Calvo, Jacinto (Gonzalez) (Born Jacinto Del Calvo) b: 6/11/1894, Havana, Cuba d: 6/15/65, Miami, Fla. BL/TL, 5'10", 156 lbs. Deb: 5/9/13

YEAR	TM/L	G	AB	R	H	2B	3B	HR	RBI	BB	SO	AVG	OBP	SLG	PRO+	BR/A	SB	CS	SBR	FA	FR	G/POS	TPR
1913	Was-A	17	33	5	8	0	1	2	1	4		.242	.265	.333	73	-1	0	0	0	.900	-2	O-13	-0.4
1920	Was-A	17	23	5	1	0	1	0	2	2	2	.043	.120	.130	-35	-5	0	0	0	1.000	-4	O-10	-0.9
Total	2	34	56	10	9	0	1	1	4	3	6	.161	.203	.250	27	-6	0	0	0	.938	-6	/O-23	-1.3

■ HANK CAMELLI

Camelli, Henry Richard b: 12/12/14, Gloucester, Mass. d: 7/14/96, Wellesley, Mass. BR/TR, 5'11", 190 lbs. Deb: 10/3/43

YEAR	TM/L	G	AB	R	H	2B	3B	HR	RBI	BB	SO	AVG	OBP	SLG	PRO+	BR/A	SB	CS	SBR	FA	FR	G/POS	TPR
1943	Pit-N	1	3	1	0	0	0	0	0	0	1	.000	.250	.000	-24	-0	0			1.000	0	/C-1	0.0
1944	Pit-N	63	125	14	37	5	1	0	10	18	12	.296	.385	.376	110	2	0			.959	4	C-61	0.8
1945	Pit-N	1	2	0	0	0	0	0	0	1	0	.000	.333	.000	-3	-0	0			1.000	-0	/C-1	0.0
1946	Pit-N	42	96	8	20	2	0	0	5	8	9	.208	.269	.271	52	-6	0			.971	4	C-39	-0.1
1947	Bos-N	52	150	10	29	8	1	1	11	18	18	.193	.280	.280	50	-11	0			.977	6	C-51	-0.2
Total	5	159	376	33	86	15	2	1	26	46	39	.229	.313	.306	70	-15	0			.970	14	C-153	0.5

■ JACK CAMERON

Cameron, John William "Happy Jack" b: 9/1884, Nova Scotia, Can. d: 8/17/51, Boston, Mass. Deb: 9/13/06

YEAR	TM/L	G	AB	R	H	2B	3B	HR	RBI	BB	SO	AVG	OBP	SLG	PRO+	BR/A	SB	CS	SBR	FA	FR	G/POS	TPR
1906	Bos-N	18	61	3	11	0	0	0	2	8		.180	.206	.180	21	-6	1			.852	-2	O-16/P-2	-0.8

■ MIKE CAMERON

Cameron, Michael Terrance b: 1/8/73, LaGrange, Ga. BR/TR, 6'1", 170 lbs. Deb: 8/27/95

YEAR	TM/L	G	AB	R	H	2B	3B	HR	RBI	BB	SO	AVG	OBP	SLG	PRO+	BR/A	SB	CS	SBR	FA	FR	G/POS	TPR
1995	Chi-A	28	38	4	7	2	0	1	2	3	15	.184	.244	.316	46	-3	0	0	0	1.000	-4	O-28	-0.7
1996	Chi-A	11	11	1	1	0	0	0	0	1	3	.091	.167	.091	-34	-2	0	1	-1	1.000	-3	/O-8,D-2	-0.6
Total	2	39	49	5	8	2	0	1	2	4	18	.163	.226	.265	28	-5	0	1	-1	1.000	-7	/O-36,D-2	-1.3

■ DOLPH CAMILLI

Camilli, Adolph Louis b: 4/23/07, San Francisco, Cal BL/TL, 5'10", 185 lbs. Deb: 9/9/33 F

YEAR	TM/L	G	AB	R	H	2B	3B	HR	RBI	BB	SO	AVG	OBP	SLG	PRO+	BR/A	SB	CS	SBR	FA	FR	G/POS	TPR
1933	Chi-N	16	58	8	13	2	1	2	7	4	11	.224	.274	.397	90	-1	3			.994	2	1-16	-0.1
1934	Chi-N	32	120	17	33	8	0	4	19	5	25	.275	.315	.442	102	-0	1			.988	2	1-32	-0.1
	Phi-N	102	378	52	100	20	3	12	68	48	69	.265	.350	.429	95	-3	3			.985	-4	*1-102	-1.5
	Yr	134	498	69	133	28	3	16	87	53	94	.267	.342	.432	96	-3	4			.986	-2	*1-134	-1.6
1935	Phi-N	156	602	88	157	23	5	25	83	65	113	.261	.336	.440	97	-4	9			.987	-1	*1-156	-2.2
1936	Phi-N	151	530	106	167	29	13	28	102	116	84	.315	.441	.577	156	45	5			.988	-10	*1-150	2.0
1937	Phi-N	131	475	101	161	23	7	27	80	90	82	.339	**.446**	.587	165	45	6			**.994**	4	*1-131	3.3
1938	Bro-N	146	509	106	128	25	11	24	100	**119**	101	.251	.393	.485	137	29	6			.995	4	*1-145	1.2
1939	Bro-N★	157	565	105	164	30	12	26	104	**110**	107	.290	.409	.524	144	38	1			.990	10	*1-157	3.0
1940	Bro-N	142	512	92	147	29	13	23	96	89	83	.287	.397	.529	145	32	9			.992	-4	*1-140	1.5
1941	*Bro-N†	149	529	92	151	29	6	**34**	120	104	115	.285	.407	.556	162	**45**	3			.989	3	*1-148	3.7
1942	Bro-N	150	524	89	132	23	7	26	109	97	85	.252	.372	.471	144	30	10			.992	-1	*1-150	2.2
1943	Bro-N	95	353	56	87	15	6	6	43	65	48	.246	.365	.374	113	8	2			.992	-1	1-95	0.2
1945	Bos-A	63	198	24	42	5	2	2	19	35	38	.212	.330	.288	78	-4	2	0	1	.991	2	1-54	-0.6
Total	12	1490	5353	936	1482	261	86	239	950	947	961	.277	.388	.492	134	260	60	0		.990	1	*1-1476	12.6

■ DOUG CAMILLI

Camilli, Douglas Joseph b: 9/22/36, Philadelphia, Pa. BR/TR, 5'11", 195 lbs. Deb: 9/25/60 FC

YEAR	TM/L	G	AB	R	H	2B	3B	HR	RBI	BB	SO	AVG	OBP	SLG	PRO+	BR/A	SB	CS	SBR	FA	FR	G/POS	TPR
1960	LA-N	6	24	4	8	2	0	1	3	1	4	.333	.385	.542	141	1	0	0	0	.980	0	/C-6	0.2
1961	LA-N	13	30	3	4	0	0	3	4	1	7	.133	.161	.433	47	-2	0	0	0	.986	2	C-12	0.0
1962	LA-N	45	88	16	25	5	2	4	22	12	21	.284	.370	.523	145	5	0	0	0	.983	-5	C-39	0.1
1963	LA-N	49	117	9	19	1	1	3	10	11	22	.162	.234	.265	47	-8	0	0	0	.977	8	C-47	0.1
1964	LA-N	50	123	1	22	3	0	0	10	8	19	.179	.229	.203	25	-12	0	0	0	.990	8	C-46	-0.2
1965	Was-A	75	193	13	37	6	1	3	18	16	34	.192	.257	.280	53	-12	0	1	0	.980	1	C-59	-0.9
1966	Was-A	44	107	5	22	4	0	3	8	3	19	.206	.234	.299	53	-7	0	0	0	.990	4	C-39	-0.1
1967	Was-A	30	82	5	15	1	0	2	5	4	16	.183	.221	.268	46	-6	0	0	0	.993	0	C-24	-0.5
1969	Was-A	1	3	0	1	0	0	0	0	0	1	.333	.333	.333	92	-0	0	0	0	1.000	-0	/C-1	0.0
Total	9	313	767	56	153	22	4	18	80	56	146	.199	.257	.309	61	-41	0	0	0	.984	19	C-273	-1.3

■ LOU CAMILLI

Camilli, Louis Steven b: 9/24/46, ElPaso, Tex. BB/TR, 5'10", 170 lbs. Deb: 8/9/69

YEAR	TM/L	G	AB	R	H	2B	3B	HR	RBI	BB	SO	AVG	OBP	SLG	PRO+	BR/A	SB	CS	SBR	FA	FR	G/POS	TPR
1969	Cle-A	13	14	0	0	0	0	0	0	0	3	.000	.000	.000	-97	-4	0	0	0	1.000	3	3-13	0.0
1970	Cle-A	16	15	1	0	0	0	0	0	2	2	.000	.118	.000	-62	-3	0	0	0	1.000	-1	/S-3,2-2,3-1	-0.4
1971	Cle-A	39	81	5	16	2	0	0	3	6	15	.198	.270	.222	37	-6	0	0	0	.938	1	S-23,2-16	-0.4
1972	Cle-A	39	41	2	6	2	0	0	0	5	3	.146	.255	.195	19	-4	0	0	0	1.000	-2	/S-8,2-2	-0.6
Total	4	107	151	7	22	4	0	0	3	13	23	.146	.213	.172	9	-18	0	0	0	.951	2	/S-34,2-20,3-14	-1.4

YEAR	TM/L	G	AB	R	H	2B	3B	HR	RBI	BB	SO	AVG	OBP	SLG	PRO+	BR/A	SB	CS	SBR	FA	FR	G/POS	TPR

■ KEN CAMINITI   Caminiti, Kenneth Gene b: 4/21/63, Hanford, Cal.   BB/TR, 6', 200 lbs.   Deb: 7/16/87

YEAR	TM/L	G	AB	R	H	2B	3B	HR	RBI	BB	SO	AVG	OBP	SLG	PRO+	BR/A	SB	CS	SBR	FA	FR	G/POS	TPR
1987	Hou-N	63	203	10	50	7	1	3	23	12	44	.246	.288	.335	67	-10	0	0	0	.949	3	3-61	-0.7
1988	Hou-N	30	83	5	15	2	0	1	7	5	18	.181	.227	.241	36	-7	0	0	0	.948	-1	3-28	-0.8
1989	Hou-N	161	585	71	149	31	3	10	72	51	93	.255	.318	.369	99	-1	4	1	1	.954	13	*3-160	1.4
1990	Hou-N	153	541	52	131	20	2	4	51	48	97	.242	.304	.309	71	-21	9	4	0	.945	-11	*3-149	-3.2
1991	Hou-N	152	574	65	145	30	3	13	80	46	85	.253	.314	.383	101	-1	4	5	-2	.948	8	*3-152	0.6
1992	Hou-N	135	506	68	149	31	2	13	62	44	68	.294	.352	.441	129	18	10	4	1	.966	-9	*3-129	1.0
1993	Hou-N	143	543	75	142	31	0	13	75	49	88	.262	.323	.390	93	-6	8	5	-1	.942	5	*3-143	-0.1
1994	Hou-N★	111	406	63	115	28	2	18	75	43	71	.283	.355	.495	125	14	4	3	-1	**.969**	2	*3-108	1.5
1995	SD-N	143	526	74	159	33	0	26	94	69	94	.302	.384	.513	139	30	12	5	1	.936	10	*3-143	3.8
1996	*SD-N★	146	546	109	178	37	2	40	130	78	99	.326	.408	.621	177	61	11	5	0	.954	12	*3-145	7.0
Total	10	1237	4513	592	1233	250	15	141	669	445	757	.273	.341	.429	113	77	62	32	-1	.951	33	*3-1218	10.5

■ HOWIE CAMP   Camp, Howard Lee "Red" b: 7/1/1893, Munford, Ala.   d: 5/8/60, Eastaboga, Ala.   BL/TR, 5'9", 169 lbs.   Deb: 9/19/17

YEAR	TM/L	G	AB	R	H	2B	3B	HR	RBI	BB	SO	AVG	OBP	SLG	PRO+	BR/A	SB	CS	SBR	FA	FR	G/POS	TPR
1917	NY-A	5	21	3	6	1	0	0	0	1	2	.286	.318	.333	98	-0	0			.857	1	/O-5	0.0

■ LEW CAMP   Camp, Llewellyn Robert b: 2/22/1868, Columbus, Ohio   d: 10/1/48, Omaha, Neb.   BL/TR, 6', 175 lbs.   Deb: 8/26/1892 F

YEAR	TM/L	G	AB	R	H	2B	3B	HR	RBI	BB	SO	AVG	OBP	SLG	PRO+	BR/A	SB	CS	SBR	FA	FR	G/POS	TPR
1892	StL-N	42	145	19	30	3	1	2	13	17	27	.207	.294	.283	79	-3	12			.780	-16	3-39/O-3	-1.7
1893	Chi-N	38	156	37	41	7	7	2	17	19	19	.263	.347	.436	109	1	30			.847	-10	3-16,O-11/2-9,S-3	-0.7
1894	Chi-N	8	33	1	6	2	0	0	1	1	6	.182	.206	.242	7	-5	0			.830	-3	/2-8	-0.6
Total	3	88	334	57	77	12	8	4	31	37	52	.231	.311	.350	85	-7	42			.801	-28	/3-55,2-17,O-14,S-3	-3.0

■ ROY CAMPANELLA   Campanella, Roy b: 11/19/21, Philadelphia, Pa.   d: 6/26/93, Woodland Hills, Cal.   BR/TR, 5'8", 200 lbs.   Deb: 4/20/48 H

YEAR	TM/L	G	AB	R	H	2B	3B	HR	RBI	BB	SO	AVG	OBP	SLG	PRO+	BR/A	SB	CS	SBR	FA	FR	G/POS	TPR
1948	Bro-N	83	279	32	72	11	3	9	45	36	45	.258	.345	.416	102	1	3			.981	10	C-78	1.6
1949	*Bro-N★	130	436	65	125	22	2	22	82	67	36	.287	.385	.498	130	19	3			.985	-5	*C-127	3.0
1950	Bro-N★	126	437	70	123	19	3	31	89	55	51	.281	.364	.551	134	21	1			.985	-4	*C-123	2.1
1951	Bro-N★	143	505	90	164	33	1	33	108	53	51	.325	.393	.590	158	40	1	2	-1	.986	9	*C-140	5.2
1952	*Bro-N★	128	468	73	126	18	1	22	97	57	59	.269	.352	.453	120	13	8	4	0	**.994**	-7	*C-122	1.3
1953	*Bro-N★	144	519	103	162	26	3	41	**142**	67	58	.312	.395	.611	154	40	4	2	0	.989	3	*C-140	4.7
1954	Bro-N★	111	397	43	82	14	3	19	51	42	49	.207	.286	.401	74	-17	1	4	-2	.989	-3	*C-111	-1.6
1955	*Bro-N†	123	446	81	142	20	1	32	107	56	41	.318	.402	.583	153	34	2	3	-1	.992	1	*C-121	3.8
1956	*Bro-N★	124	388	39	85	6	1	20	73	66	61	.219	.334	.394	88	-6	1	0		.985	3	*C-121	0.3
1957	Bro-N	103	330	31	80	9	0	13	62	34	50	.242	.321	.388	81	-9	1	0		**.993**	16	*C-100	1.2
Total	10	1215	4205	627	1161	178	18	242	856	533	501	.276	.362	.500	123	136	25	<u>15</u>		.988	33	*C-1183	21.6

■ BERT CAMPANERIS   Campaneris, Dagoberto (Blanco) "Campy" (b: Dagoberto Campanaria (Blanco))   b: 3/9/42, Pueblo Nuevo, Cuba   BR/TR, 5'10", 160 lbs.   Deb: 7/23/64

YEAR	TM/L	G	AB	R	H	2B	3B	HR	RBI	BB	SO	AVG	OBP	SLG	PRO+	BR/A	SB	CS	SBR	FA	FR	G/POS	TPR
1964	KC-A	67	269	27	69	14	3	4	22	15	41	.257	.306	.375	86	-5	10	2	2	.981	-6	S-38,O-27/3-6	-0.9
1965	KC-A	144	578	67	156	23	**12**	6	42	41	71	.270	.328	.382	103	2	**51**	19	4	.938	-14	*S-109,O-39/PC123	-0.3
1966	KC-A	142	573	82	153	29	10	5	42	25	72	.267	.303	.379	98	-3	**52**	10	10	.971	-17	*S-138	0.3
1967	KC-A	147	601	85	149	29	4	3	32	36	82	.248	.298	.331	89	-9	**55**	16	7	.954	-19	*S-145	-0.8
1968	Oak-A★	159	642	87	**177**	25	9	4	38	50	69	.276	.332	.361	116	11	**62**	22	5	.956	1	*S-155/O-3	3.8
1969	Oak-A	135	547	71	142	15	2	2	25	30	62	.260	.303	.305	74	-20	62	8	14	.967	-5	*S-125	0.2
1970	Oak-A	147	603	97	168	28	4	22	64	36	73	.279	.323	.448	115	9	**42**	10	7	.973	-10	*S-143	2.4
1971	Oak-A	134	569	80	143	18	4	5	47	29	64	.251	.290	.323	75	-20	34	7	6	.960	-5	*S-133	-0.1
1972	*Oak-A☆	149	625	85	150	25	2	8	32	32	88	.240	.279	.325	84	-15	**52**	14	7	.977	7	*S-148	2.3
1973	*Oak-A★	151	601	89	150	17	6	4	46	50	79	.250	.311	.318	82	-14	34	10	4	.969	-7	*S-149	0.2
1974	*Oak-A★	134	527	77	153	18	8	2	41	47	81	.290	.348	.366	113	9	34	15	1	.966	-9	*S-133/D-1	1.9
1975	*Oak-A★	137	509	69	135	15	4	4	46	50	71	.265	.339	.330	92	-4	24	12	0	.962	-31	*S-137	-2.1
1976	Oak-A	149	536	67	137	14	1	1	52	63	80	.256	.337	.291	89	-5	54	12	**9**	.969	-6	*S-149	1.6
1977	Tex-A★	150	552	77	140	19	7	5	46	47	86	.254	.317	.341	78	-16	27	20	-4	.968	18	*S-149	1.4
1978	Tex-A	98	269	30	50	5	3	1	17	20	36	.186	.247	.238	37	-22	22	4	4	.954	4	S-89/D-4	-0.4
1979	Tex-A	8	9	1	1	0	0	0	0	1	3	.111	.200	.111	-14	-1	1	0	0	.962	4	/S-8	0.3
	*Cal-A	85	239	27	56	4	4	0	15	19	32	.234	.290	.285	59	-13	12	4	1	.957	4	S-82/D-1	0.0
	Yr	93	248	29	57	4	4	0	15	20	35	.230	.293	.278	57	-15	13	4	2	.957	7	S-90/D-1	0.3
1980	Cal-A	77	210	32	53	8	1	2	18	14	33	.252	.302	.329	75	-7	10	5	0	.957	-5	S-64/2-1,D-2	-0.6
1981	Cal-A	55	82	11	21	2	1	1	10	5	10	.256	.299	.341	84	-2	5	2	0	.900	-2	3-45/S-3,2-2	-0.4
1983	NY-A	60	143	19	46	5	0	0	11	8	9	.322	.358	.357	101	0	6	7	-2	.964	-3	2-32,3-24	-0.4
Total	19	2328	8684	1181	2249	313	86	79	646	618	1142	.259	.313	.342	89	-127	649	199	75	.964	-102	*S-2097/3-76,O2D1CP	8.4

■ AL CAMPANIS   Campanis, Alexander Sebastian (b: Alessandro Campani) b: 11/2/16, Kos, Dodecanese Islands   BB/TR, 6', 185 lbs.   Deb: 9/23/43 F

YEAR	TM/L	G	AB	R	H	2B	3B	HR	RBI	BB	SO	AVG	OBP	SLG	PRO+	BR/A	SB	CS	SBR	FA	FR	G/POS	TPR
1943	Bro-N	7	20	3	2	0	0	0	0	4	5	.100	.250	.100	3	-2	0			1.000	4	/2-7	0.2

■ JIM CAMPANIS   Campanis, James Alexander b: 2/9/44, New York, N.Y.   BR/TR, 6', 195 lbs.   Deb: 9/20/66 F

YEAR	TM/L	G	AB	R	H	2B	3B	HR	RBI	BB	SO	AVG	OBP	SLG	PRO+	BR/A	SB	CS	SBR	FA	FR	G/POS	TPR
1966	LA-N	1	1	0	0	0	0	0	0	0	0	.000	.000	.000	-99	-0	0	0	0	1.000	0	/C-1	0.0
1967	LA-N	41	62	3	10	1	0	2	5	9	14	.161	.268	.274	60	-3	0	0	0	.990	-0	C-23	-0.3
1968	LA-N	4	11	0	1	0	0	0	1	0	2	.091	.167	.091	-23	-2	0	0	0	.960	1	/C-4	0.0
1969	KC-A	30	83	4	13	5	0	0	5	5	19	.157	.205	.217	18	-9	0	0	0	.982	3	C-26	-0.5
1970	KC-A	31	54	6	7	0	0	2	4	4	14	.130	.203	.241	22	-6	0	0	0	.986	1	C-13/O-1	-0.5
1973	Pit-N	6	6	0	1	0	0	0	0	0	0	.167	.167	.167	-8	-1	0	0	0	.000	0	H	-0.1
Total	6	113	217	13	32	6	0	4	19	18	49	.147	.219	.230	27	-21	0	0	0	.983	5	/C-67,O-1	-1.4

■ COUNT CAMPAU   Campau, Charles Columbus b: 10/17/1863, Detroit, Mich.   d: 4/3/38, New Orleans, La.   BL/TR, 5'11", 160 lbs.   Deb: 7/7/1888 M

YEAR	TM/L	G	AB	R	H	2B	3B	HR	RBI	BB	SO	AVG	OBP	SLG	PRO+	BR/A	SB	CS	SBR	FA	FR	G/POS	TPR
1888	Det-N	70	251	28	51	5	3	1	18	19	36	.203	.259	.259	66	-9	27			.933	-4	O-70	-1.5
1890	StL-a	75	314	68	101	9	12	**9**	75	26		.322	.374	.513	141	12	36			.934	-3	O-74/3-1,1-1,M	1.1
1894	Was-N	2	7	1	1	0	0	0	0	1	4	.143	.250	.143	-3	-1	0			1.000	-0	/O-2	-0.1
Total	3	147	572	97	153	14	15	10	93	46	<u>40</u>	.267	.322	.397	109	1	63			.934	-1	O-146/1-1,3-1	-0.5

■ VIN CAMPBELL   Campbell, Arthur Vincent b: 1/30/1888, St.Louis, Mo.   d: 11/16/69, Towson, Md.   BL/TR, 6', 185 lbs.   Deb: 6/6/08

YEAR	TM/L	G	AB	R	H	2B	3B	HR	RBI	BB	SO	AVG	OBP	SLG	PRO+	BR/A	SB	CS	SBR	FA	FR	G/POS	TPR
1908	Chi-N	1	1	0	0	0	0	0	0	0	0	.000	.000	.000	-96	-0	0			.000	0	H	0.0
1910	Pit-N	97	282	42	92	9	5	4	21	26	23	.326	.391	.436	133	12	17			.895	-4	O-74	0.4
1911	Pit-N	30	93	12	29	3	1	0	8	7		.312	.366	.366	101	0	6			.923	-3	O-21	-0.3
1912	Bos-N	145	624	102	185	32	9	3	48	32	44	.296	.334	.391	96	-5	19			.938	-5	O-144	-1.2
1914	Ind-F	134	544	92	173	23	11	7	44	37	47	.318	.368	.439	108	-2	26			.925	-5	*O-132	-1.4
1915	New-F	127	525	78	163	18	10	1	44	29	35	.310	.352	.389	115	1	24			.947	-5	*O-126	-1.1
Total	6	546	2069	326	642	85	36	15	167	132	<u>156</u>	.310	.357	.408	109	6	92			.929	-17	O-497	-3.6

■ BRUCE CAMPBELL   Campbell, Bruce Douglas b: 10/20/09, Chicago, Ill.   d: 6/17/95, Ft.Myers Beach, Fla.   BL/TR, 6'1", 185 lbs.   Deb: 9/12/30

YEAR	TM/L	G	AB	R	H	2B	3B	HR	RBI	BB	SO	AVG	OBP	SLG	PRO+	BR/A	SB	CS	SBR	FA	FR	G/POS	TPR
1930	Chi-A	5	10	4	5	1	1	0	5	1	2	.500	.545	.800	245	2	0	0	0	1.000	-0	/O-4	0.2
1931	Chi-A	4	17	4	7	2	0	2	5	0	4	.412	.444	.882	256	4	0	0	0	.900	-0	/O-4	0.3
1932	Chi-A	7	18	3	4	1	0	0	2	2	2	.222	.222	.278	31	-2	0	1	-1	1.000	-0	/O-8	-0.3
	StL-A	139	593	83	169	35	11	14	85	40	102	.285	.336	.452	97	-5	7	5	-1	.935	6	*O-139	-0.8
	Yr	146	611	86	173	36	11	14	87	40	104	.283	.333	.447	95	-6	7	6	-2	.935	5	*O-143	-1.1
1933	StL-A	148	567	87	157	38	8	16	106	69	77	.277	.357	.457	108	5	10	4	1	.950	-1	*O-144	-1.1
1934	StL-A	138	481	62	134	25	6	9	74	51	64	.279	.350	.412	88	-9	5	4	-1	.935	3	*O-123	-1.1
1935	Cle-A	80	308	56	100	26	3	6	54	31	33	.325	.390	.497	126	11	2	1	0	.992	-5	O-75	0.3
1936	Cle-A	76	312	35	64	13	3	6	35	19	29	.372	.440	.497	150	14	2	1	0	.960	-4	O-47	0.7
1937	Cle-A	134	448	82	135	42	11	4	61	67	49	.301	.392	.471	116	12	4	5	-2	.978	-2	O-122	0.4
1938	Cle-A	133	511	90	148	27	12	12	72	53	57	.290	.360	.460	106	3	11	7	-1	.967	-0	O-122	-0.1
1939	Cle-A	130	450	84	129	23	13	8	72	67	48	.287	.383	.449	116	12	7	5	-1	.942	-5	O-115	-0.3
1940	*Det-A	103	297	56	84	15	5	8	44	45	28	.283	.381	.448	104	2	5	7	-4	.959	-2	O-74	-0.7

YEAR	TM/L	G	AB	R	H	2B	3B	HR	RBI	BB	SO	AVG	OBP	SLG	PRO+	BR/A	SB	CS	SBR	FA	FR	G/POS	TPR
1941	Det-A	141	512	72	141	28	10	15	93	68	67	.275	.364	.457	105	3	3	3	-1	.976	-8	*O-133	-1.3
1942	Was-A	122	378	41	105	17	5	5	63	37	34	.278	.344	.389	107	3	0	6	-4	.955	-1	O-87	-0.6
Total	13	1360	4762	759	1382	295	87	106	766	548	584	.290	.367	.455	108	55	53	50	-14	.956	-19	*O-1194	-3.0

■ **SOUP CAMPBELL**   Campbell, Clarence   b: 3/7/15, Sparta, Va.   BL/TR, 6'1", 188 lbs.   Deb: 4/21/40

1940	Cle-A	35	62	8	14	1	0	0	2	7	12	.226	.304	.242	45	-5	0	0	0	1.000	-2	O-16	-0.7
1941	Cle-A	104	328	36	82	10	4	3	35	31	21	.250	.317	.332	75	-12	1	9	-5	.981	2	O-78	-1.9
Total	2	139	390	44	96	11	4	3	37	38	33	.246	.315	.318	70	-17	1	9	-5	.984	0	/O-94	-2.6

■ **DAVE CAMPBELL**   Campbell, David Wilson   b: 1/14/42, Manistee, Mich.   BR/TR, 6', 185 lbs.   Deb: 9/17/67

1967	Det-A	2	2	0	0	0	0	0	0	0	1	.000	.000	.000	-97	-0	0	0	0	.500	-0	/1-1	-0.1
1968	Det-A	9	8	1	1	0	0	1	2	1	3	.125	.222	.500	111	0	0	0	0	1.000	0	/2-5	0.1
1969	Det-A	32	39	4	4	1	0	0	2	4	15	.103	.205	.128	-5	-5	0	1	-1	.967	-2	1-13/2-5,3-1	-0.8
1970	SD-N	154	581	71	127	28	2	12	40	40	115	.219	.270	.336	64	-32	18	6	2	.974	12	*2-153	-0.6
1971	SD-N	108	365	38	83	14	2	7	29	37	75	.227	.299	.334	85	-8	9	6	-1	.968	-2	2-69,3-40/S-4,1O	-0.6
1972	SD-N	33	100	6	24	5	0	0	3	11	12	.240	.315	.290	79	-3	0	4	-2	.988	4	3-31/2-1	-0.1
1973	SD-N	33	98	2	22	3	0	0	8	7	15	.224	.276	.255	52	-6	1	1	-0	.979	-1	2-27/1-3,3-2	-0.7
	StL-N	13	21	1	0	0	0	0	1	1	6	.000	.045	.000	-87	-5	0	0	0	.933	-3	/2-6	-0.8
	Hou-N	9	15	1	4	2	0	0	2	0	4	.267	.267	.400	83	-0	0	0	0	1.000	0	/3-5,1-2,O-1	0.1
	Yr	55	134	4	26	5	0	0	11	8	25	.194	.239	.231	33	-12	1	1	-0	.975	-2	2-33/3-7,1-5,O-1	-1.4
1974	Hou-N	35	23	4	2	1	0	0	2	1	8	.087	.125	.130	-30	-4	1	0	0	.895	5	/2-9,1-6,3-2,O-1	0.2
Total	8	428	1252	128	267	54	4	20	89	102	254	.213	.274	.311	64	-64	29	18	-2	.971	16	2-275/3-81,1-27,OS	-3.3

■ **JIM CAMPBELL**   Campbell, James Robert   b: 6/24/37, Palo Alto, Cal.   BR/TR, 6', 190 lbs.   Deb: 7/17/62

1962	Hou-N	27	86	6	19	4	0	3	6	6	23	.221	.272	.372	77	-3	0	0	0	.970	6	C-25	0.4
1963	Hou-N	55	158	9	35	3	0	4	19	10	40	.222	.268	.316	72	-6	0	0	0	.979	-2	C-42	-0.7
Total	2	82	244	15	54	7	0	7	25	16	63	.221	.269	.336	74	-9	0	0	0	.975	4	/C-67	-0.3

■ **JIM CAMPBELL**   Campbell, James Robert   b: 1/10/43, Hartsville, S.C.   BL/TR, 6', 205 lbs.   Deb: 4/11/70

1970	StL-N	13	13	0	3	0	0	0	1	0	3	.231	.231	.231	24	-1	0	0	0	.000	0	H	-0.1

■ **JOE CAMPBELL**   Campbell, Joseph Earl   b: 3/10/44, Louisville, Ky.   BR/TR, 6'1", 175 lbs.   Deb: 5/3/67

1967	Chi-N	1	3	0	0	0	0	0	0	0	3	.000	.000	.000	-96	-1	0	0	0	.000	-0	/O-1	-0.1

■ **MARC CAMPBELL**   Campbell, Marc Thaddeus   b: 11/29/1884, Punxsutawney, Pa.   d: 2/13/46, New Bethlehem, Pa.   BL/TR, 5'10", 155 lbs.   Deb: 9/30/07

1907	Pit-N	2	4	0	1	0	0	0	1	1		.250	.400	.250	102	-0				.889	0	/S-2	0.0

■ **MAT CAMPBELL**   Campbell, Mathew   b: 1850, Ireland   Deb: 4/28/1873   F

1873	Res-n	21	83	9	12	0	0	0	3	3	6	.145	.174	.145	-5	-10	1	0		.927	-2	1-18/S-3,O-1	-0.8

■ **PAUL CAMPBELL**   Campbell, Paul McLaughlin   b: 9/1/17, Paw Creek, N.C.   BL/TL, 5'10", 185 lbs.   Deb: 4/15/41

1941	Bos-A	1	0	0	0	0	0	0	0	0	0	—	—	—	—	—	0	0	0	.000	0	R	—
1942	Bos-A	26	15	4	1	0	0	0	0	1	5	.067	.125	.067	-44	-3	1	0	0	1.000	-2	/O-4	-0.5
1946	*Bos-A	28	26	3	3	1	0	0	0	2	7	.115	.179	.154	-6	-4	0	0	0	1.000	-0	/1-5	-0.4
1948	Det-A	59	83	15	22	1	1	1	11	1	10	.265	.274	.337	60	-5	0	0	0	.969	3	1-27	-0.2
1949	Det-A	87	255	38	71	15	4	3	30	24	32	.278	.343	.404	97	-2	3	3	-1	.988	-1	1-74	-0.6
1950	Det-A	3	1	1	0	0	0	0	0	0	0	.000	.000	.000	-97	-0	0	0	0	.000	0	H	0.0
Total	6	204	380	61	97	17	5	4	41	28	54	.255	.308	.358	76	-14	4	3	-1	.984	-2	1-106/O-4	-1.7

■ **RON CAMPBELL**   Campbell, Ronald Thomas   b: 4/5/40, Chattanooga, Tenn.   BR/TR, 6'1", 180 lbs.   Deb: 9/1/64

1964	Chi-N	26	92	7	25	6	1	1	10	1	21	.272	.280	.391	83	-2	0	1	-1	.941	14	2-26	1.3
1965	Chi-N	2	2	0	0	0	0	0	0	0	0	.000	.000	.000	-98	-1	0	0	0	.000	0	H	-0.1
1966	Chi-N	24	60	4	13	1	0	0	4	6	5	.217	.288	.233	46	-4	1	1	-0	.980	4	S-11/3-7	0.0
Total	3	52	154	11	38	7	1	1	14	7	26	.247	.280	.325	67	-7	1	2	-1	.941	18	/2-26,S-11,3-7	1.2

■ **SAM CAMPBELL**   Campbell, Samuel   b: Philadelphia, Pa.   Deb: 10/11/1890

1890	Phi-a	2	5	0	0	0	0	0	0	0	1	.000	.167	.000	-52	-1				.833	-2	/2-2	-0.3

■ **GILLY CAMPBELL**   Campbell, William Gilthorpe   b: 2/13/08, Kansas City, Kan.   d: 2/21/73, Los Angeles, Cal.   BL/TR, 5'7.5", 182 lbs.   Deb: 4/25/33

1933	Chi-N	46	89	11	25	3	1	1	9	7	4	.281	.347	.371	105	1	0			.949	-2	C-20	0.0
1935	Cin-N	88	218	26	56	7	0	3	30	42	7	.257	.379	.330	95	1	3			.986	0	C-66/1-5,O-1	0.3
1936	Cin-N	89	235	28	63	13	1	1	40	43	14	.268	.384	.345	104	3	2			.984	6	C-71/1-1	1.2
1937	Cin-N	18	40	3	11	2	0	0	2	5	1	.275	.356	.325	90	-0				.967	-1	C-17	0.0
1938	Bro-N	54	126	10	31	5	0	0	11	19	9	.246	.354	.286	76	-3	0			.958	-0	C-44	-0.1
Total	5	295	708	78	186	30	2	5	92	116	35	.263	.371	.332	96	1	5			.975	4	C-218/1-6,O-1	1.4

■ **FRANK CAMPOS**   Campos, Francisco Jose (Lopez)   b: 5/11/24, Havana, Cuba   BL/TL, 5'11", 180 lbs.   Deb: 9/11/51

1951	Was-A	8	26	4	11	3	1	0	3	0	1	.423	.423	.615	182	2	0	0	0	1.000	-2	/O-7	0.1
1952	Was-A	53	112	9	29	6	1	0	9	1	13	.259	.278	.330	71	-5	0	0	0	.978	-2	O-23	-0.8
1953	Was-A	10	9	0	1	0	0	0	1	1	0	.111	.200	.111	-14	-1	0	0	0	.000	0	H	-0.1
Total	3	71	147	13	41	9	2	0	13	2	14	.279	.298	.367	86	-4	0	0	0	.981	-4	/O-30	-0.8

■ **SIL CAMPUSANO**   Campusano, Silvestre (Diaz)   b: 12/31/65, Santo Domingo, D.R.   BR/TR, 6', 175 lbs.   Deb: 4/4/88

1988	Tor-A	73	142	14	31	10	2	2	12	9	33	.218	.284	.359	78	-4	0	0	0	.934	-10	O-69/D-2	-1.6
1990	Phi-N	66	85	10	18	1	1	2	9	6	16	.212	.272	.318	62	-5	1	0	0	.976	-13	O-47	-1.9
1991	Phi-N	15	35	2	4	0	0	1	2	1	10	.114	.139	.200	-6	-5	0	0	0	1.000	0	O-15	-0.6
Total	3	154	262	26	53	11	3	5	23	16	59	.202	.261	.324	62	-14	1	0	0	.953	-24	O-131/D-2	-4.1

■ **GEORGE CANALE**   Canale, George Anthony   b: 8/11/65, Memphis, Tenn.   BL/TR, 6'1", 190 lbs.   Deb: 9/3/89

1989	Mil-A	13	26	5	5	2	0	2	3	3	6	.192	.250	.346	67	-1	0	1	-1	.989	-0	1-11	-0.3
1990	Mil-A	10	13	4	1	1	0	0	2	7	8	.077	.200	.154	0	-2	0	1	-1	1.000	1	/1-6,D-3	-0.2
1991	Mil-A	21	34	6	6	1	0	3	10	8	6	.176	.333	.500	130	1	0	0	0	.983	3	1-19	0.3
Total	3	44	73	15	12	4	0	4	13	12	15	.164	.282	.384	85	-2	0	2	-1	.988	3	/1-36,D-3	-0.2

■ **WILLIE CANATE**   Canate, Emisael William (Librada)   b: 12/11/71, Maracaibo, Venez.   BR/TR, 6', 170 lbs.   Deb: 4/16/93

1993	*Tor-A	38	47	12	10	0	0	1	3	6	15	.213	.315	.277	60	-2	1	1	-0	1.000	-4	O-31/D-1	-0.7

■ **JIM CANAVAN**   Canavan, James Edward   b: 11/26/1866, New Bedford, Mass.   d: 5/27/49, New Bedford, Mass.   BR/TR, 5'8", 160 lbs.   Deb: 4/8/1891

1891	Cin-a	101	426	74	97	13	14	7	66	27	44	.228	.282	.373	80	-16	21			.860	-11	*S-101	-1.8
	Mil-a	35	142	33	38	2	4	3	21	16	10	.268	.342	.401	94	-3	7			.864	-2	2-24,S-11	-0.3
	Yr	136	568	107	135	15	18	10	87	43	54	.238	.297	.380	84	-19	28			.860	-13	*S-112,2-24	-2.1
1892	Chi-N	118	439	48	73	10	11	0	32	48	48	.166	.248	.239	47	-28	33			.923	-2	*2-112/O-4,S-2	-2.7
1893	Cin-N	121	461	65	104	13	7	5	64	51	20	.226	.305	.317	64	-25	31			.931	-1	*O-117/2-5,3-1	-2.6
1894	Cin-N	101	356	77	97	16	9	13	70	62	25	.272	.380	.478	102	-0	13			.904	-2	*O-95/S-3,3-2,21	-0.7
1897	Bro-N	63	240	25	52	9	3	2	34	26		.217	.299	.304	63	-13	9			.909	-21	2-63	-2.7
Total	5	539	2064	322	461	63	48	30	287	230	147	.223	.304	.344	74	-86	114			.920	-40	O-216,2-205,S/31	-10.8

■ **CASEY CANDAELE**   Candaele, Casey Todd   b: 1/12/61, Lompoc, Cal.   BB/TR, 5'9", 165 lbs.   Deb: 6/5/86

1986	Mon-N	30	104	9	24	4	1	0	6	5	15	.231	.266	.288	53	-7	3	5	-2	.983	-2	2-24/3-4	-1.0
1987	Mon-N	138	449	62	122	23	4	1	23	38	28	.272	.331	.347	78	-14	7	10	-4	.985	-1	2-68,O-67,S-25,/1-1	-1.7
1988	Mon-N	36	116	9	20	5	1	0	4	10	11	.172	.238	.233	34	-10	1	0	0	.988	1	2-35	-0.9
	Hou-N	21	31	2	5	3	0	1	1	1	6	.161	.188	.258	28	-3	0	1	-1	1.000	1	2-10/O-5,3-1	-0.3
	Yr	57	147	11	25	8	1	0	5	11	17	.170	.228	.238	33	-13	1	1	-0	.990	2	2-45/O-5,3-1	-1.1

YEAR	TM/L	G	AB	R	H	2B	3B	HR	RBI	BB	SO	AVG	OBP	SLG	PRO+	BR/A	SB	CS	SBR	FA	FR	G/POS	TPR
1990	Hou-N	130	262	30	75	8	6	3	22	31	42	.286	.364	.397	112	5	7	5	-1	1.000	-14	O-58,2-49,S-13,/3-1	-1.0
1991	Hou-N	151	461	44	121	20	7	4	50	40	49	.262	.321	.362	97	-2	9	3	1	.982	5	*2-109,O-26,3-11	0.6
1992	Hou-N	135	320	19	68	12	1	1	18	24	36	.213	.274	.266	56	-19	7	1	2	.968	-5	S-65,3-29,O-21,/2-9	-2.0
1993	Hou-N	75	121	18	29	8	0	1	7	10	14	.240	.298	.331	70	-5	2	3	-1	1.000	-6	2-19,O-17,S-14,/3-4	-1.2
1996	*Cle-A	24	44	8	11	2	0	1	4	1	9	.250	.267	.364	57	-3	0	0	0	1.000	7	2-11/3-3,S-1	0.4
Total	8	740	1908	201	475	85	20	11	135	160	210	.249	.309	.332	78	-57	36	28	-6	.986	-13	2-334,O-194,S/31	-7.0

■ JOHN CANGELOSI
Cangelosi, John Anthony b: 3/10/63, Brooklyn, N.Y. BB/TL, 5'8", 150 lbs. Deb: 6/3/85

YEAR	TM/L	G	AB	R	H	2B	3B	HR	RBI	BB	SO	AVG	OBP	SLG	PRO+	BR/A	SB	CS	SBR	FA	FR	G/POS	TPR
1985	Chi-A	5	2	2	0	0	0	0	0	0	1	.000	.333	.000	1	-0	0	0	0	1.000	-2	/O-3,D-2	-0.2
1986	Chi-A	137	438	65	103	16	3	2	32	71	61	.235	.351	.299	77	-12	50	17	5	.969	-5	*O-129/D-3	-1.6
1987	Pit-N	104	182	44	50	8	3	4	18	46	33	.275	.429	.418	125	9	21	6	3	.962	-4	O-47	0.7
1988	Pit-N	75	118	18	30	4	1	0	8	17	16	.254	.353	.305	92	-1	9	4	0	.963	-2	O-24/P-1	-0.3
1989	Pit-N	112	160	18	35	4	2	0	9	35	20	.219	.369	.269	88	-0	11	8	-2	.973	-6	O-46	-1.0
1990	Pit-N	58	76	13	15	2	0	0	1	11	12	.197	.307	.224	50	-5	7	2	1	1.000	-1	O-12	-0.5
1992	Tex-A	73	85	12	16	2	0	1	6	18	16	.188	.330	.247	66	-3	6	5	-1	.964	-13	O-65/D-6	-1.9
1994	NY-N	62	111	14	28	4	0	0	4	19	20	.252	.371	.288	76	-3	5	1	1	1.000	-6	O-50	-0.9
1995	Hou-N	90	201	46	64	5	2	2	18	48	42	.318	.458	.393	137	15	21	5	3	.950	-4	O-59/P-1	1.3
1996	Hou-N	108	262	49	69	11	4	1	16	44	41	.263	.379	.347	103	3	17	9	-0	.975	-4	O-78	-0.3
Total	10	824	1635	281	410	56	15	10	112	309	262	.251	.378	.322	94	3	147	57	10	.970	-45	O-513/D-11,P-2	-4.7

■ JAY CANIZARO
Canizaro, Jason Kyle b: 7/4/73, Beaumont, Tex. BR/TR, 5'9", 170 lbs. Deb: 4/28/96

YEAR	TM/L	G	AB	R	H	2B	3B	HR	RBI	BB	SO	AVG	OBP	SLG	PRO+	BR/A	SB	CS	SBR	FA	FR	G/POS	TPR
1996	SF-N	43	120	11	24	4	1	2	8	9	38	.200	.262	.300	50	-9	0	2	-1	.972	0	2-35/S-7	-0.8

■ RIP CANNELL
Cannell, Virgin Wirt b: 1/23/1880, S.Bridgton, Maine d: 8/26/48, Bridgton, Maine BL/TR, 5'10.5", 180 lbs. Deb: 4/14/04

YEAR	TM/L	G	AB	R	H	2B	3B	HR	RBI	BB	SO	AVG	OBP	SLG	PRO+	BR/A	SB	CS	SBR	FA	FR	G/POS	TPR
1904	Bos-N	100	346	32	81	5	1	0	18	23		.234	.286	.254	70	-12	10			.897	-11	O-93	-3.0
1905	Bos-N	154	567	52	140	14	4	0	36	51		.247	.311	.286	80	-13	17			.935	-8	*O-154	-3.0
Total	2	254	913	84	221	19	5	0	54	74		.242	.302	.274	76	-25	27			.923	-19	O-247	-6.0

■ CHRIS CANNIZZARO
Cannizzaro, Christopher John b: 5/3/38, Oakland, Cal. BR/TR, 6', 190 lbs. Deb: 4/17/60 C

YEAR	TM/L	G	AB	R	H	2B	3B	HR	RBI	BB	SO	AVG	OBP	SLG	PRO+	BR/A	SB	CS	SBR	FA	FR	G/POS	TPR
1960	StL-N	7	9	0	2	0	0	0	1	1	3	.222	.300	.222	42	-1	0	0	0	1.000	1	/C-6	0.1
1961	StL-N	6	2	0	1	0	0	0	0	0	0	.500	.500	.500	151	0	0	0	0	1.000	1	/C-5	0.1
1962	NY-N	59	133	9	32	2	1	0	9	19	26	.241	.340	.271	65	-6	1	1	-0	.973	2	C-56/O-1	-0.3
1963	NY-N	16	33	4	8	1	0	0	4	1	8	.242	.265	.273	54	-2	0	0	0	1.000	-1	C-15	-0.2
1964	NY-N	60	164	11	51	10	0	0	10	14	28	.311	.369	.372	112	3	0	5	-3	.988	5	C-53	0.4
1965	NY-N	114	251	17	46	8	2	0	7	28	60	.183	.270	.231	44	-18	0	2	-1	.977	12	*C-112	-0.3
1968	Pit-N	25	58	5	14	2	1	0	7	9	13	.241	.343	.397	123	2	0	0	0	.976	-0	C-25	0.3
1969	SD-N☆	134	418	23	92	14	3	4	33	42	81	.220	.291	.297	68	-18	0	1	-1	.988	-14	*C-132	-2.7
1970	SD-N	111	341	27	95	13	5	4	42	48	49	.279	.369	.378	105	4	2	7	-4	.980	-16	*C-110	-1.0
1971	SD-N	21	63	2	12	1	0	1	8	11	10	.190	.320	.254	69	-2	0	0	0	.992	-2	C-19	-0.3
	Chi-N	71	197	18	42	8	1	5	23	28	24	.213	.314	.340	74	-7	0	0	0	.983	-11	C-70	-1.6
	Yr	92	260	20	54	9	1	6	31	39	34	.208	.316	.319	73	-9	0	0	0	.985	-12	C-89	-1.9
1972	LA-N	73	200	14	48	6	0	2	18	31	38	.240	.342	.300	86	-3	0	1	-1	.983	-8	C-72	-0.9
1973	LA-N	17	21	0	4	0	0	0	3	3	3	.190	.292	.190	38	-2	0	0	0	1.000	6	C-13	-0.2
1974	SD-N	26	60	2	11	1	0	0	5	6	11	.183	.258	.200	31	-6	0	0	0	.979	5	C-26	0.0
Total	13	740	1950	132	458	66	12	18	169	241	354	.235	.321	.309	77	-55	3	17	-9	.983	-28	C-714/O-1	-6.6

■ JOE CANNON
Cannon, Joseph Jerome b: 7/13/53, Camp Lejeune, N.C. BL/TR, 6'3", 193 lbs. Deb: 9/22/77

YEAR	TM/L	G	AB	R	H	2B	3B	HR	RBI	BB	SO	AVG	OBP	SLG	PRO+	BR/A	SB	CS	SBR	FA	FR	G/POS	TPR
1977	Hou-N	9	17	3	2	2	0	0	1	0	3	.118	.118	.235	-9	-3	1	1	-0	1.000	0	/O-3	-0.3
1978	Hou-N	8	18	1	4	0	0	0	1	0	1	.222	.222	.222	26	-2	0	1	-1	.778	-1	/O-5	-0.4
1979	Tor-A	61	142	14	30	1	1	1	5	1	34	.211	.217	.254	26	-15	12	2	2	1.000	-4	O-50	-1.8
1980	Tor-A	70	50	16	4	0	0	0	4	0	14	.080	.098	.080	-48	-10	2	2	-1	.968	-10	O-33/D-1	-2.2
Total	4	148	227	34	40	3	1	1	11	1	54	.176	.183	.211	7	-29	15	6	1	.977	-15	/O-91,D-1	-4.7

■ JOSE CANSECO
Canseco, Jose (Capas) b: 7/2/64, Havana, Cuba BR/TR, 6'3", 240 lbs. Deb: 9/2/85 F

YEAR	TM/L	G	AB	R	H	2B	3B	HR	RBI	BB	SO	AVG	OBP	SLG	PRO+	BR/A	SB	CS	SBR	FA	FR	G/POS	TPR
1985	Oak-A	29	96	16	29	3	0	5	13	4	31	.302	.330	.490	130	3	1	1	-0	.951	-0	O-26	0.2
1986	Oak-A☆	157	600	85	144	29	1	33	117	65	175	.240	.322	.457	118	13	15	7	0	.958	-3	*O-155/D-1	0.5
1987	Oak-A	159	630	81	162	35	3	31	113	50	157	.257	.314	.470	111	8	15	3	3	.975	11	*O-130,D-30	1.5
1988	*Oak-A★	158	610	120	187	34	0	**42**	**124**	78	128	.307	.394	**.569**	**172**	59	40	16	2	.978	8	*O-144,D-13	**6.4**
1989	*Oak-A†	65	227	40	61	9	1	17	57	23	69	.269	.341	.542	151	14	6	3	0	.976	4	O-56/D-5	1.6
1990	*Oak-A★	131	481	83	132	14	2	37	101	72	158	.274	.375	.543	160	38	19	10	-0	.995	5	O-88,D-43	4.0
1991	Oak-A	154	572	115	152	32	1	**44**	122	78	152	.266	.363	.556	159	45	26	6	4	.965	-3	*O-131,D-24	4.2
1992	Oak-A†	97	366	66	90	11	0	22	72	48	104	.246	.338	.456	127	13	5	7	-3	.988	4	O-77,D-20	1.2
	Tex-A	22	73	8	17	4	0	4	15	15	24	.233	.385	.452	139	4	1	0	0	.970	1	O-13/D-8	0.5
	Yr	119	439	74	107	15	0	26	87	63	128	.244	.346	.456	129	17	6	7	-2	.985	5	O-90,D-28	1.7
1993	Tex-A	60	231	30	59	14	1	10	46	16	62	.255	.312	.455	107	1	6	6	-2	.970	1	O-49/P-1	1.7
1994	Tex-A	111	429	88	121	19	2	31	90	69	114	.282	.388	.552	139	25	15	8	-0	.000	0	*D-111	1.7
1995	*Bos-A	102	396	64	121	25	1	24	81	42	93	.306	.382	.556	136	20	4	0	1	1.000	-0	*D-101/O-1	1.3
1996	Bos-A	96	360	68	104	22	1	28	82	63	82	.289	.403	.589	142	23	3	1	0	1.000	-1	D-84,O-11	1.5
Total	12	1341	5071	864	1379	251	13	328	1033	623	1349	.272	.359	.521	139	268	156	68	6	.974	27	O-881,D-440/P-1	24.6

■ OZZIE CANSECO
Canseco, Osvaldo (Capas) b: 7/2/64, Havana, Cuba BR/TR, 6'2", 220 lbs. Deb: 7/18/90 F

YEAR	TM/L	G	AB	R	H	2B	3B	HR	RBI	BB	SO	AVG	OBP	SLG	PRO+	BR/A	SB	CS	SBR	FA	FR	G/POS	TPR
1990	Oak-A	9	19	1	2	1	0	0	1	0	10	.105	.150	.158	-14	-3	0	0	0	1.000	-0	/O-2,D-4	-0.3
1992	StL-N	9	29	7	8	5	0	0	3	7	4	.276	.417	.448	150	2	0	0	0	.889	-2	/O-8	0.0
1993	StL-N	6	17	0	3	0	0	0	0	1	3	.176	.222	.176	8	-2	0	0	0	.500	-2	/O-5	-0.5
Total	3	24	65	8	13	6	0	0	4	9	17	.200	.297	.292	67	-3	0	0	0	.857	-4	/O-15,D-4	-0.8

■ BART CANTZ
Cantz, Bartholomew L. b: 1/29/1860, Philadelphia, Pa. d: 2/12/43, Philadelphia, Pa. Deb: 7/25/1888

YEAR	TM/L	G	AB	R	H	2B	3B	HR	RBI	BB	SO	AVG	OBP	SLG	PRO+	BR/A	SB	CS	SBR	FA	FR	G/POS	TPR
1888	Bal-a	37	126	7	21	2	1	0	9	2		.167	.180	.198	22	-11	0			.904	-9	C-33/O-4	-1.6
1889	Bal-a	20	69	6	12	2	0	0	8	4	14	.174	.219	.203	20	-7	2			.860	-7	C-18/O-2	-1.1
1890	Phi-a	5	22	1	1	0	0	0		0	1	.045	.045	.045	-75	-5	0			.893	-3	/C-5	-0.6
Total	3	62	217	14	34	4	1	0	18	6	14	.157	.179	.184	11	-23	2			.890	-19	/C-56,O-6	-3.3

■ NICK CAPRA
Capra, Nick Lee b: 3/8/58, Denver, Colo. BR/TR, 5'8", 165 lbs. Deb: 9/6/82

YEAR	TM/L	G	AB	R	H	2B	3B	HR	RBI	BB	SO	AVG	OBP	SLG	PRO+	BR/A	SB	CS	SBR	FA	FR	G/POS	TPR
1982	Tex-A	13	15	2	4	0	0	0	1	3	4	.267	.421	.467	151	1	2	1	0	1.000	-0	/O-9	0.2
1983	Tex-A	8	2	2	0	0	0	0	0	1	0	.000	.000	.000	-99	-1	0	0	0	.000	-2	/O-4	-0.2
1985	Tex-A	8	8	1	1	0	0	0	0	0	2	.125	.125	.125	-31	-1	0	0	0	1.000	-1	/O-8	-0.3
1988	KC-A	14	29	3	4	1	0	0	2	3	3	.138	.194	.172	3	-4	1	0	0	1.000	-2	O-11/D-1	-0.6
1991	Tex-A	2	0	1	0	0	0	0	0	1	0	—	1.000	—	205	-0	0	0	0	1.000	-0	/O-2	0.0
Total	5	45	54	9	9	1	0	0	3	8	9	.167	.262	.241	41	-5	3	1	0	1.000	-5	/O-34,D-1	-0.9

■ PAT CAPRI
Capri, Patrick Nicholas b: 11/27/18, New York, N.Y. d: 6/14/89, New York, N.Y. BR/TR, 6'0.5", 170 lbs. Deb: 7/16/44

YEAR	TM/L	G	AB	R	H	2B	3B	HR	RBI	BB	SO	AVG	OBP	SLG	PRO+	BR/A	SB	CS	SBR	FA	FR	G/POS	TPR
1944	Bos-N	7	1	0	0	0	0	0	0	0	1	.000	.000	.000	-96	-0	0			1.000	1	/2-1	0.1

■ RALPH CAPRON
Capron, Ralph Earl b: 6/16/1889, Minneapolis, Minn d: 9/19/80, Los Angeles, Cal. BL/TR, 5'11.5", 165 lbs. Deb: 4/25/12

YEAR	TM/L	G	AB	R	H	2B	3B	HR	RBI	BB	SO	AVG	OBP	SLG	PRO+	BR/A	SB	CS	SBR	FA	FR	G/POS	TPR
1912	Pit-N	1	0	0	0	0	0	0	0	0	0	—	—	—	—					.000	0	R	0.0
1913	Phi-N	2	1	0	0	0	0	0	0	0	0	.000	.000	.000	-96	-0				.000	-1	/O-1	-0.1
Total	2	3	1	1	0	0	0	0	0	0	0	.000	.000	.000	-96					—	-1	/O-1	-0.1

■ RAMON CARABALLO
Caraballo, Ramon (Sanchez) b: 5/23/69, Rio San Juan, D.R. BB/TR, 5'7", 150 lbs. Deb: 9/9/93

YEAR	TM/L	G	AB	R	H	2B	3B	HR	RBI	BB	SO	AVG	OBP	SLG	PRO+	BR/A	SB	CS	SBR	FA	FR	G/POS	TPR
1993	Atl-N	6	0	0	0	0	0	0	0	0	0	—	—	—	—		0	0	0	1.000	2	/2-5	0.2
1995	StL-N	34	99	10	20	4	1	2	3	6	33	.202	.269	.323	55	-7	3	2	-0	.956	-1	2-24	-0.7
Total	2	40	99	10	20	4	1	2	3	6	33	.202	.269	.323	55	-7	3	2	-0	.958	1	/2-29	-0.5

YEAR	TM/L	G	AB	R	H	2B	3B	HR	RBI	BB	SO	AVG	OBP	SLG	PRO+	BR/A	SB	CS	SBR	FA	FR	G/POS	TPR

■ JOHN CARBINE   Carbine, John C.   b: 10/12/1855, Syracuse, N.Y.   d: 9/11/15, Chicago, Ill.   6′, 187 lbs.   Deb: 5/8/1875

| 1875 | Wes-n | 10 | 36 | 0 | 3 | 0 | 0 | 0 | 2 | 0 | 1 | .083 | .083 | .083 | -40 | -5 | 0 | 0 | 0 | .950 | 1 | 1-10 | -0.4 |
| 1876 | Lou-N | 7 | 25 | 3 | 4 | 0 | 0 | 0 | 1 | 0 | 0 | .160 | .160 | .160 | 6 | -3 | | | | .878 | -0 | /1-6,O-1 | -0.3 |

■ BERNIE CARBO   Carbo, Bernardo   b: 8/5/47, Detroit, Mich.   BL/TR, 6′, 175 lbs.   Deb: 9/2/69

1969	Cin-N	4	3	0	0	0	0	0	0	0	1	.000	.000	.000	-95	-1	0	0	0	.000	0	H	-0.1
1970	*Cin-N	125	365	54	113	19	3	21	63	94	77	.310	.456	.551	168	40	10	4	1	.979	0	*O-119	3.5
1971	Cin-N	106	310	33	68	20	1	5	20	54	56	.219	.339	.339	94	-1	2	1	0	.982	2	O-90	-0.3
1972	Cin-N	19	21	2	3	0	0	0	0	6	3	.143	.357	.143	50	-1	0	0	0	1.000	0	/O-4	-0.1
	StL-N	99	302	42	78	13	1	7	34	57	56	.258	.385	.377	119	10	0	1	-1	.967	8	O-92/3-1	1.4
	Yr	118	323	44	81	13	1	7	34	63	59	.251	.383	.362	115	9	0	1	-1	.969	8	O-96/3-1	1.3
1973	StL-N	111	308	42	88	18	0	8	40	58	52	.286	.401	.422	128	14	2	0	1	.978	3	O-94	1.4
1974	Bos-A	117	338	40	84	20	0	12	61	58	90	.249	.365	.414	116	8	4	3	-1	.994	-1	O-87,D-15	0.3
1975	*Bos-A	107	319	64	82	21	3	15	50	83	69	.257	.412	.483	140	20	2	4	-2	.976	-1	O-85,D-13	1.4
1976	Bos-A	17	55	5	13	4	0	2	6	8	17	.236	.333	.418	106	0	1	0	0	1.000	-0	D-15/O-1	0.0
	Mil-A	69	183	20	43	7	0	3	15	33	55	.235	.352	.322	100	1	1	2	-1	1.000	4	O-33,D-24	0.2
	Yr	86	238	25	56	11	0	5	21	41	72	.235	.348	.345	102	2	2	2	-1	1.000	3	D-39,O-34	0.2
1977	Bos-A	86	228	36	66	6	1	15	34	47	72	.289	.411	.522	136	12	1	2	-1	.951	2	O-67/D-7	1.1
1978	Bos-A	17	46	7	12	3	0	1	6	8	8	.261	.370	.391	103	0	1	1	-0	1.000	1	/O-9,D-8	0.1
	Cle-A	60	174	21	50	8	0	4	16	20	31	.287	.364	.402	117	4	1	0	0	1.000	-2	D-49/O-4	0.1
	Yr	77	220	28	62	11	0	5	22	28	39	.282	.365	.400	113	5	2	1	0	1.000	-0	D-57,O-13	0.2
1979	StL-N	52	64	6	18	1	0	3	12	10	22	.281	.378	.438	121	2	1	0	0	1.000	-5	O-17	-0.3
1980	StL-N	14	11	0	2	0	0	0	0	1	0	.182	.250	.182	22	-1	0	0	0	.000	0	H	-0.2
	Pit-N	7	6	0	2	0	0	0	1	1	1	.333	.429	.333	114	0	0	0	0	.000	0	/H	0.0
	Yr	21	17	0	4	0	0	0	1	2	1	.235	.316	.235	55	-1	0	0	0	.000	0	-0	-0.2
Total	12	1010	2733	372	722	140	9	96	358	538	611	.264	.389	.427	125	109	26	18	-3	.978	12	O-702,D-131/3-1	8.5

■ JOSE CARDENAL   Cardenal, Jose Rosario Domec (b: Jose Rosario Domec (Cardenal))   b: 10/7/43, Matanzas, Cuba   BR/TR, 5′10″, 150 lbs.   Deb: 4/14/63   C

1963	SF-N	9	5	1	1	0	0	0	2	1	1	.200	.333	.200	58	-0	1	0	0	.000	-1	/O-2	-0.2
1964	SF-N	20	15	3	0	0	0	0	0	2	3	.000	.118	.000	-62	-3	2	0	1	.909	-3	O-16	-0.6
1965	Cal-A	134	512	58	128	23	2	11	57	27	72	.250	.290	.367	87	-10	37	17	1	.964	0	*O-129/3-2,2-1	-0.5
1966	Cal-A	154	561	67	155	15	3	16	48	34	69	.276	.322	.399	109	5	24	11	1	.992	12	O-146	1.2
1967	Cal-A	108	381	40	90	13	5	6	27	15	63	.236	.269	.344	83	-9	10	5	0	.986	0	*O-101	-1.6
1968	Cle-A	157	583	78	150	21	7	7	44	39	74	.257	.306	.353	101	-0	40	18	1	.974	13	*O-153	0.6
1969	Cle-A	146	557	75	143	26	3	11	45	49	58	.257	.317	.373	89	-8	36	6	7	.982	11	*O-142/3-5	0.2
1970	StL-N	148	552	73	162	32	6	10	74	34	65	.293	.348	.428	104	3	26	9	2	.969	-0	*O-134	-0.2
1971	StL-N	89	301	37	73	13	2	4	7	48	29	.243	.309	.379	90	-4	12	3	2	.969	7	O-83	0.1
	Mil-A	53	198	20	51	10	0	3	32	13	20	.258	.307	.354	88	-4	9	5	-0	.979	7	O-52	0.0
1972	Chi-N	143	533	96	155	24	6	17	70	55	58	.291	.358	.454	117	12	25	14	-1	.971	-9	*O-137	-0.5
1973	Chi-N	145	522	80	158	33	2	11	68	58	62	.303	.378	.437	116	13	19	7	2	.980	-3	*O-142	-0.5
1974	Chi-N	143	542	75	159	35	3	13	72	56	67	.293	.361	.441	118	13	23	9	2	.965	-8	*O-137	1.7
1975	Chi-N	154	574	85	182	30	2	9	68	77	50	.317	.402	.423	124	21	34	12	3	.976	12	*O-151	3.0
1976	Chi-N	136	521	64	156	25	2	8	47	32	39	.299	.341	.401	101	0	23	14	-2	.981	7	*O-128	0.0
1977	Chi-N	100	226	33	54	12	1	3	18	28	30	.239	.325	.341	71	-9	5	4	-1	.989	-6	O-62/2-1,S-1	-1.9
1978	*Phi-N	87	201	27	50	12	0	4	33	23	16	.249	.326	.368	93	-2	2	3	-1	.990	-9	1-50,O-13	-1.5
1979	Phi-N	29	48	4	10	3	0	0	9	8	8	.208	.321	.271	62	-2	1	0	0	1.000	-3	O-12/1-1	-0.6
	NY-N	11	37	8	11	4	0	2	4	6	3	.297	.409	.568	170	4	1	0	0	1.000	-1	/O-9,1-2	0.2
	Yr	40	85	12	21	7	0	2	13	14	11	.247	.360	.400	106	1	2	0	0	1.000	-4	O-21/1-3	-0.4
1980	NY-N	26	42	4	7	1	0	0	4	4	4	.167	.271	.190	32	-4	0	1	-1	1.000	-0	O-6,1-5	-0.5
	*KC-A	25	53	8	18	2	0	5	5	5	5	.340	.397	.377	112	1	0	0	0	.970	-3	O-23	-0.2
Total	18	2017	6964	936	1913	333	46	138	775	608	807	.275	.335	.395	102	16	329	139	15	.976	48	*O-1778/1-58,32S	-0.9

■ LEO CARDENAS   Cardenas, Leonardo Lazaro (Alfonso) "Chico"   b: 12/17/38, Matanzas, Cuba   BR/TR, 5′10″, 163 lbs.   Deb: 7/25/60

1960	Cin-N	48	142	13	33	2	4	1	12	6	32	.232	.264	.324	59	-8	0	0	0	.958	5	S-47	0.2
1961	*Cin-N	74	198	23	61	18	1	5	24	15	39	.308	.357	.485	119	5	1	0	0	.973	-5	S-63	0.5
1962	*Cin-N	153	589	77	173	31	4	10	60	39	99	.294	.343	.411	98	-2	2	5	-2	.972	-7	*S-149	0.3
1963	Cin-N	158	565	42	133	22	4	7	48	23	101	.235	.270	.326	69	-23	3	5	-2	**.972**	-7	*S-157	-1.9
1964	Cin-N★	163	597	61	150	32	2	9	69	41	110	.251	.302	.357	82	-14	4	4	-1	.960	-10	*S-163	-1.5
1965	Cin-N★	156	557	65	160	25	11	11	57	60	100	.287	.358	.431	113	10	1	4	-2	.975	-1	*S-155	1.9
1966	Cin-N★	160	568	59	145	25	4	20	81	45	87	.255	.311	.419	93	-6	9	4	0	**.980**	-15	*S-160	-0.5
1967	Cin-N	108	379	30	97	14	3	2	21	34	77	.256	.320	.325	76	-11	0	4	-2	.971	-10	*S-108	-1.3
1968	Cin-N★	137	452	45	106	13	2	7	41	36	83	.235	.294	.319	79	-11	2	1	0	.955	-23	*S-136	-2.3
1969	*Min-A	160	578	67	162	24	4	10	70	66	96	.280	.358	.388	106	6	5	6	-2	.965	**34**	*S-160	5.6
1970	*Min-A	160	588	67	146	34	4	11	65	42	101	.247	.301	.374	84	-14	2	5	-2	.978	3	*S-160	0.6
1971	Min-A☆	153	554	59	146	25	4	18	75	51	69	.264	.327	.421	107	4	3	3	-1	**.985**	-0	*S-153	2.4
1972	Cal-A	150	551	25	123	11	2	6	42	35	73	.223	.272	.283	69	-22	1	2	-1	.970	3	*S-150	-1.9
1973	Cle-A	72	195	9	42	4	0	0	12	13	42	.215	.264	.236	41	-15	1	4	-2	.964	-8	S-67/3-5	-1.9
1974	Tex-A	34	92	5	25	3	0	0	7	3	14	.272	.287	.304	72	-3	0	1	0	1.000	2	3-21,S-10/D-4	-0.1
1975	Tex-A	55	102	15	24	2	0	1	5	14	12	.235	.328	.284	75	-3	0	0	0	.956	11	3-43/S-5,2-3	0.8
Total	16	1941	6707	662	1725	285	49	118	689	522	1135	.257	.313	.367	88	-107	39	48	-17	.971	-22	*S-1843/3-69,D-4,2	2.9

■ ROD CAREW   Carew, Rodney Cline   b: 10/1/45, Gatun, C.Z.   BL/TR, 6′, 182 lbs.   Deb: 4/11/67   CH

1967	Min-A★	137	514	66	150	22	7	8	51	37	91	.292	.342	.409	112	7	5	9	-4	.976	-10	*2-134	0.2
1968	Min-A★	127	461	46	126	27	2	1	42	26	71	.273	.314	.347	95	-3	12	4	1	.968	-14	*2-117/S-4	-1.0
1969	*Min-A★	123	458	79	152	30	4	8	56	37	72	**.332**	.386	.467	135	21	19	8	1	.970	-17	*2-118	1.5
1970	*Min-A†	51	191	27	70	12	3	4	28	11	28	.366	.407	.524	153	13	4	6	-2	.961	-11	2-45/1-1	0.3
1971	Min-A★	147	577	88	177	16	10	2	48	45	81	.307	.358	.380	106	5	6	7	-2	.976	-25	*2-142/3-2	-1.2
1972	Min-A★	142	535	61	170	21	6	0	51	43	60	**.318**	.371	.379	118	13	12	6	0	.978	-0	*2-139	2.3
1973	Min-A★	149	580	98	**203**	30	**11**	6	62	62	55	**.350**	.415	.471	143	35	41	16	3	.984	7	*2-147	**5.3**
1974	Min-A★	153	599	86	**218**	30	5	3	55	74	49	**.364**	**.435**	.446	149	41	38	16	2	.960	9	*2-148	**6.0**
1975	Min-A★	143	535	89	192	24	4	14	80	64	40	**.359**	**.428**	.497	159	43	35	9	5	.973	-2	*2-123,1-14/D-2	5.7
1976	Min-A★	156	605	97	200	29	12	9	90	67	52	.331	.398	.463	149	38	49	22	2	.989	-2	*1-152/2-7	2.8
1977	Min-A★	155	616	**128**	**239**	38	**16**	14	100	69	55	**.388**	**.452**	.570	**179**	**69**	23	13	-1	.994	6	*1-151/2-4,D-1	**6.3**
1978	Min-A★	152	564	85	188	26	10	5	70	78	62	**.333**	**.415**	.441	138	32	27	7	4	.989	1	*1-148/2-4,O-1	2.8
1979	*Cal-A†	110	409	78	130	15	3	4	44	73	46	.318	.421	.391	125	19	18	8	1	.988	-7	*1-103/D-6	0.6
1980	Cal-A★	144	540	74	179	34	7	3	59	59	38	.331	.398	.437	132	25	23	15	-2	.994	-4	*1-103,D-32	1.1
1981	Cal-A★	93	364	57	111	17	1	2	21	45	45	.305	.381	.374	118	10	16	9	-1	.995	-1	1-90/D-2	0.4
1982	*Cal-A†	138	523	88	167	25	5	3	44	67	49	.319	.399	.403	121	18	10	17	-7	.992	-1	*1-134	0.5
1983	Cal-A★	129	472	66	160	24	2	2	44	57	48	.339	.411	.411	128	21	6	7	-2	.994	-9	1-89,D-24/2-2	0.3
1984	Cal-A	93	329	42	97	8	1	3	31	40	39	.295	.371	.353	102	3	4	3	-1	.981	-4	1-83/D-1	-0.2
1985	Cal-A	127	443	69	124	17	3	2	39	64	47	.280	.372	.345	99	2	5	5	-2	.994	-8	1-116	-1.5
Total	19	2469	9315	1424	3053	445	112	92	1015	1018	1028	.328	.395	.429	131	411	353	187	-6	.991	-85	*1-1184,2-1130/DS30	31.7

■ ANDY CAREY   Carey, Andrew Arthur   b: 10/18/31, Oakland, Cal.   BR/TR, 6′1″, 195 lbs.   Deb: 5/2/52

1952	NY-A	16	40	6	6	0	0	0	1	3	10	.150	.209	.150	1	-5	0	0	0	.889	-1	3-14/S-1	-0.7
1953	NY-A	51	81	14	26	5	0	4	9	3	9	.321	.389	.531	152	6	2	1	0	.988	8	3-40/S-2,2-1	1.4
1954	NY-A	122	411	60	124	14	6	8	65	43	38	.302	.377	.423	123	13	5	5	-2	.967	17	*3-120	2.7
1955	*NY-A	135	510	73	131	19	**11**	7	47	46	48	.257	.317	.378	88	-10	3	3	-1	.954	14	*3-135	0.2
1956	*NY-A	132	422	54	100	18	2	7	50	45	53	.237	.313	.339	75	-16	9	6	-1	.947	-4	*3-131	-1.8
1957	*NY-A	85	247	30	63	6	5	6	33	15	42	.255	.311	.393	92	-3	2	2	-1	.977	3	3-81	0.1

YEAR	TM/L	G	AB	R	H	2B	3B	HR	RBI	BB	SO	AVG	OBP	SLG	PRO+	BR/A	SB	CS	SBR	FA	FR	G/POS	TPR
1958	*NY-A	102	315	39	90	19	4	12	45	34	43	.286	.366	.486	137	16	1	2	-1	.961	10	3-99	2.6
1959	NY-A	41	101	11	26	1	0	3	9	7	17	.257	.306	.356	84	-2	1	1	-0	.916	2	3-34	-0.1
1960	NY-A	4	3	1	1	0	0	0	1	0	1	.333	.333	.333	86	-0	0	0	0	1.000	-1	/3-2,O-1	-0.1
	KC-A	102	343	30	80	14	4	12	53	26	52	.233	.289	.402	84	-9	0	0	0	.975	-0	3-91	-0.9
	Yr	106	346	31	81	14	4	12	54	26	53	.234	.290	.402	85	-9	0	0	0	.975	-1	3-93/O-1	-1.0
1961	KC-A	39	123	20	30	6	2	3	11	15	23	.244	.336	.398	94	-1	0	0	0	.944	-1	3-39	-0.2
	Chi-A	56	143	21	38	12	3	0	14	11	24	.266	.327	.392	93	-2	0	1	-1	.961	-5	3-54	-0.7
	Yr	95	266	41	68	18	5	3	25	26	47	.256	.331	.395	93	-3	0	1	-1	.953	-6	3-93	-0.9
1962	LA-N	53	111	12	26	5	1	2	13	16	23	.234	.336	.351	90	-1	0	0	0	.932	1	3-42	0.0
Total	11	938	2850	371	741	119	38	64	350	268	389	.260	.329	.396	97	-15	23	21	-6	.958	45	3-882/S-3,O-1,2-1	2.5

■ SCOOPS CAREY

Carey, George C. b: 12/4/1870, Pittsburgh, Pa. d: 12/17/16, E.Liverpool, Ohio BR/TR, 175 lbs. Deb: 4/26/1895

YEAR	TM/L	G	AB	R	H	2B	3B	HR	RBI	BB	SO	AVG	OBP	SLG	PRO+	BR/A	SB	CS	SBR	FA	FR	G/POS	TPR
1895	*Bal-N	123	490	59	128	21	6	1	75	27	32	.261	.305	.335	63	-28	2			.987	-6	*1-123/O-1,S-1,3-1	-2.6
1898	Lou-N	8	32	1	6	1	1	0	1	1		.188	.212	.281	42	-3	0			.961	0	/1-8	-0.2
1902	Was-A	120	452	46	142	35	11	0	60	20		.314	.350	.440	117	9	3			.989	4	*1-120	1.0
1903	Was-A	48	183	8	37	3	2	0	23	4		.202	.223	.240	38	-14	0			.977	-3	1-47	-1.8
Total	4	299	1157	114	313	60	20	1	159	52	32	.271	.308	.360	80	-35	5			.986	-6	1-298/3-1,S-1,O-1	-3.6

■ MAX CAREY

Carey, Max George "Scoops" (b: Maximilian Carnarius)
b: 1/11/1890, Terre Haute, Ind. d: 5/30/76, Miami, Fla. BB/TR, 5'11.5", 170 lbs. Deb: 10/3/10 MCH

YEAR	TM/L	G	AB	R	H	2B	3B	HR	RBI	BB	SO	AVG	OBP	SLG	PRO+	BR/A	SB	CS	SBR	FA	FR	G/POS	TPR
1910	Pit-N	2	6	2	3	0	1	0	2	2	1	.500	.625	.833	307	2	0			1.000	2	/O-2	0.3
1911	Pit-N	129	427	77	110	15	10	5	43	44	75	.258	.337	.375	95	-3	27			.975	7	*O-122	-0.3
1912	Pit-N	150	587	114	177	23	8	5	66	61	79	.302	.372	.394	111	10	45			.968	9	*O-150	1.0
1913	Pit-N	154	620	99	172	23	10	5	49	55	67	.277	.339	.371	107	6	61			.961	15	*O-154	1.3
1914	Pit-N	156	593	76	144	25	17	1	31	59	56	.243	.313	.347	101	-0	38			.966	11	*O-154	0.3
1915	Pit-N	140	564	76	143	26	5	3	27	57	58	.254	.326	.333	101	2	36	17	1	.982	13	*O-139	0.9
1916	Pit-N	154	599	90	158	23	11	7	42	59	58	.264	.337	.374	117	13	63	19	8	.983	30	*O-154	4.6
1917	Pit-N	155	588	82	174	21	12	1	51	58	38	.296	.369	.378	125	19	46			.979	25	*O-153	3.9
1918	Pit-N	126	468	70	128	14	6	3	48	62	25	.274	.363	.348	113	10	58			.958	19	*O-126	2.3
1919	Pit-N	66	244	41	75	10	2	0	9	25	24	.307	.376	.365	119	6	18			.947	2	O-63	0.4
1920	Pit-N	130	485	74	140	18	4	1	35	59	31	.289	.369	.348	104	5	52	10	10	.967	1	*O-129	0.6
1921	Pit-N	140	521	85	161	34	4	7	56	70	30	.309	.395	.430	115	14	37	12	4	.957	16	*O-139	2.3
1922	Pit-N	155	629	140	207	28	12	10	70	80	26	.329	.408	.459	122	23	51	2	14	.969	19	*O-155	4.1
1923	Pit-N	153	610	120	188	32	19	6	63	73	28	.308	.388	.452	119	18	51	8	11	.962	20	*O-153	3.6
1924	Pit-N	149	599	113	178	30	9	5	55	58	17	.297	.366	.417	108	7	49	13	7	.965	9	*O-149	1.3
1925	*Pit-N	133	542	109	186	39	13	5	44	66	19	.343	.408	.491	123	20	46	11	7	.950	9	*O-130	2.6
1926	Pit-N	86	324	46	72	14	5	0	28	30	14	.222	.288	.296	55	-21	10			.943	4	O-82	-2.2
	Bro-N	27	100	18	26	3	1	0	7	8	5	.260	.315	.310	70	-4	0			.933	-1	O-27	-0.7
	Yr	113	424	64	98	17	6	0	35	38	19	.231	.294	.300	58	-25	10			.941	3	*O-109	-2.9
1927	Bro-N	144	538	70	143	30	10	1	54	64	18	.266	.345	.364	90	-7	32			.970	6	*O-141	-1.0
1928	Bro-N	108	296	41	73	11	0	2	19	47	24	.247	.354	.304	74	-9	18			.986	-12	O-95	-2.7
1929	Bro-N	19	23	2	7	0	0	1	3	2	4	.304	.407	.304	81	-0	0			1.000	-1	/O-4	-0.1
Total	20	2476	9363	1545	2665	419	159	70	800	1040	695	.285	.361	.386	107	109	738	92		.966	198	*O-2421	22.6

■ PAUL CAREY

Carey, Paul Stephan b: 1/8/68, Boston, Mass. BL/TR, 6'4", 215 lbs. Deb: 5/25/93

YEAR	TM/L	G	AB	R	H	2B	3B	HR	RBI	BB	SO	AVG	OBP	SLG	PRO+	BR/A	SB	CS	SBR	FA	FR	G/POS	TPR
1993	Bal-A	18	47	1	10	1	0	3	5	14	.213	.288	.234	41	-4	0	0	0	.970	-2	/1-9,D-5	-0.6

■ ROGER CAREY

Carey, Roger J. Deb: 7/9/1887

YEAR	TM/L	G	AB	R	H	2B	3B	HR	RBI	BB	SO	AVG	OBP	SLG	PRO+	BR/A	SB	CS	SBR	FA	FR	G/POS	TPR
1887	NY-N	1	4	0	0	0	0	0	2	0	1	.000	.000	.000	-99	-1	0			.800	1	/2-1	0.0

■ TOM CAREY

Carey, Thomas Francis Aloysius "Scoops" b: 10/11/06, Hoboken, N.J. d: 2/21/70, Rochester, N.Y. BR/TR, 5'8.5", 170 lbs. Deb: 7/19/35 C

YEAR	TM/L	G	AB	R	H	2B	3B	HR	RBI	BB	SO	AVG	OBP	SLG	PRO+	BR/A	SB	CS	SBR	FA	FR	G/POS	TPR
1935	StL-A	76	296	29	86	18	4	0	42	13	11	.291	.320	.378	77	-11	0	2	-1	.961	-1	2-76	-0.6
1936	StL-A	134	488	58	133	27	6	1	57	27	25	.273	.315	.359	64	-28	2	1	0	.967	-2	*2-128/S-1	-1.8
1937	StL-A	130	487	54	134	24	1	1	40	21	26	.275	.306	.335	61	-29	1	2	-1	.983	2	2-87,S-44/3-1	-1.8
1939	Bos-A	54	161	17	39	6	2	0	20	3	9	.242	.265	.304	44	-14	0	0	0	1.000	6	2-35,S-10	-0.6
1940	Bos-A	43	62	4	20	4	0	0	7	2	1	.323	.344	.387	86	-1	0	0	0	.953	5	S-20/2-4,3-4	0.4
1941	Bos-A	25	21	7	4	0	0	0	0	0	0	.190	.190	.190	1	-3	0	0	0	1.000	4	/2-9,S-8,3-1	0.1
1942	Bos-A	1	1	0	1	0	0	0	0	0	0	1.000	1.000	1.000	448	0	0	0	0	1.000	-0	/2-1	0.0
1946	Bos-A	3	5	0	1	0	0	0	1	0	1	.200	.200	.200	11	-1	0	0	0	.900	1	/2-3	0.1
Total	8	466	1521	169	418	79	13	2	167	66	73	.275	.308	.348	63	-87	3	5	-2	.973	17	2-343/S-83,3-6	-4.2

■ TOM CAREY

Carey, Thomas John (b: J. J. Norton) b: 1849, Brooklyn, N.Y. d: 2/13/1899, Los Angeles, Cal. BR/TR, 5'8", 145 lbs. Deb: 5/4/1871 M

YEAR	TM/L	G	AB	R	H	2B	3B	HR	RBI	BB	SO	AVG	OBP	SLG	PRO+	BR/A	SB	CS	SBR	FA	FR	G/POS	TPR
1871	Kek-n	19	87	16	20	0	0	0	10	2	1	.230	.247	.253	43	-6	5	0	2	.857	0	2-19	-0.4
1872	Bal-n	42	198	42	57	7	0	2	27	0	2	.288	.288	.354	92	-3	4	1	1	.815	-12	2-29/S-9,3-3,O-3,1	-1.1
1873	Bal-n	56	290	76	97	19	3	1	55	1	2	.334	.337	.431	127	9	1	3	-2	.845	-2	*2-54/3-4,S-3,M	0.1
1874	Mut-n	64	286	56	82	10	3	1	39	2	4	.287	.292	.353	103	0	3	0	1	.776	-17	*S-51,2-13,M	-1.5
1875	Har-n	86	382	63	101	6	2	0	38	1	3	.264	.266	.291	89	-5	13	3	2	.844	-13	*S-86/2-1	-1.7
1876	Har-N	68	289	51	78	7	0	0	26	3	4	.270	.277	.294	84	-6				.882	-1	*S-68	-0.7
1877	Har-N	60	274	38	70	3	2	1	20	0	9	.255	.255	.292	81	-5				.826	-6	*S-60	-0.9
1878	Pro-N	61	253	33	60	10	3	0	24	0	14	.237	.237	.300	76	-7				.874	1	*S-61	-0.2
1879	Cle-N	80	335	30	80	14	1	0	32	5	20	.239	.250	.287	77	-8				.864	-3	*S-80	-0.6
Total	5 n	267	1243	253	357	44	8	4	169	6	12	.287	.291	.345	98	-6	26	7	4	.814	-44	S-149,2-116/3-7,O1	-4.6
Total	4	269	1151	152	288	34	6	1	102	8	47	.250	.255	.293	79	-26				.862	-9	S-269	-2.4

■ BOBBY CARGO

Cargo, Robert J. b: 10/1868, Pittsburgh, Pa. d: 4/27/04, Atlanta, Ga. BR/TR, Deb: 10/6/1892

YEAR	TM/L	G	AB	R	H	2B	3B	HR	RBI	BB	SO	AVG	OBP	SLG	PRO+	BR/A	SB	CS	SBR	FA	FR	G/POS	TPR
1892	Pit-N	2	4	0	1	0	0	0	0	0	0	.250	.250	.250	51	-0	0			.636	1	/S-2	0.0

■ FRED CARISCH

Carisch, Frederick Behlmer b: 11/14/1881, Fountain City, Wis. d: 4/19/77, San Gabriel, Cal. BR/TR, 5'10.5", 174 lbs. Deb: 8/31/03 C

YEAR	TM/L	G	AB	R	H	2B	3B	HR	RBI	BB	SO	AVG	OBP	SLG	PRO+	BR/A	SB	CS	SBR	FA	FR	G/POS	TPR
1903	Pit-N	5	18	4	6	4	0	1	5	0		.333	.333	.722	192	2	0			.969	1	/C-4	0.3
1904	Pit-N	37	125	9	31	3	1	0	8	9		.248	.299	.288	79	-3	3			.984	2	C-22,1-14	0.1
1905	Pit-N	32	107	7	22	0	3	0	8	2		.206	.227	.262	44	-8	1			.973	2	C-30	-0.3
1906	Pit-N	4	12	0	1	0	0	0	0	1		.083	.154	.083	-25	-2	1			.909	-0	/C-4	-0.2
1912	Cle-A	24	69	4	19	3	1	0	5	1		.275	.286	.348	78	-2	3			.952	6	C-23	0.6
1913	Cle-A	82	222	11	48	8	2	0	26	21	19	.216	.287	.252	56	-12	6			.971	13	C-79	-0.1
1914	Cle-A	40	102	8	22	3	2	0	5	12	18	.216	.298	.284	72	-3	2	2	-1	.962	0	C-38	-0.1
1923	Det-A	2	0	0	0	0	0	0	0	0	0	—	—	—	—	0	0	0	0	1.000	-0	/C-2	0.0
Total	8	226	655	43	149	17	9	1	57	46	37	.227	.280	.285	66	-28	16	2		.968	24	C-202/1-14	1.2

■ FRED CARL

Carl, Frederick E. b: 9/8/1858, Baltimore, Md. d: 5/4/19, Washington, D.C. BL/TL, 5'6", 158 lbs. Deb: 7/25/1889

YEAR	TM/L	G	AB	R	H	2B	3B	HR	RBI	BB	SO	AVG	OBP	SLG	PRO+	BR/A	SB	CS	SBR	FA	FR	G/POS	TPR
1889	Lou-a	25	99	13	20	2	2	0	13	16	22	.202	.313	.263	66	-4	0			.735	0	O-18/2-6,3-1	-0.3

■ LEW CARL

Carl, Lewis b: Baltimore, Md. Deb: 9/9/1874

YEAR	TM/L	G	AB	R	H	2B	3B	HR	RBI	BB	SO	AVG	OBP	SLG	PRO+	BR/A	SB	CS	SBR	FA	FR	G/POS	TPR
1874	Bal-n	1	3	0	0	0	0	0	0	0	0	.000	.000	.000	-99	-1	0	0	0	.250	-1	/C-1	-0.1

■ JIM CARLETON

Carleton, James b: 1849, New York 5'8", 155 lbs. Deb: 5/4/1871

YEAR	TM/L	G	AB	R	H	2B	3B	HR	RBI	BB	SO	AVG	OBP	SLG	PRO+	BR/A	SB	CS	SBR	FA	FR	G/POS	TPR
1871	Cle-n	29	127	31	32	8	1	0	18	8	3	.252	.296	.331	85	-1	2	1	0	.898	-3	*1-29	-0.2
1872	Cle-n	7	38	8	12	1	0	0	4	1	0	.316	.333	.342	114	1	1	0	0	.956	2	/1-7	0.2
Total	2 n	36	165	39	44	9	1	0	22	9	3	.267	.305	.333	91	1	3	1	0	.908	-1	/1-36	0.0

■ JIM CARLIN

Carlin, James Arthur b: 2/23/18, Wylam, Ala. BR/TR, 5'11", 165 lbs. Deb: 7/26/41

YEAR	TM/L	G	AB	R	H	2B	3B	HR	RBI	BB	SO	AVG	OBP	SLG	PRO+	BR/A	SB	CS	SBR	FA	FR	G/POS	TPR
1941	Phi-N	16	21	2	3	1	3	0	1	2	3	.143	.250	.333	66	-1	0			1.000	-5	/O-9,3-2	-0.7

YEAR	TM/L	G	AB	R	H	2B	3B	HR	RBI	BB	SO	AVG	OBP	SLG	PRO+	BR/A	SB	CS	SBR	FA	FR	G/POS	TPR

■ WALTER CARLISLE   Carlisle, Walter G. "Rosy" b: 7/6/1883, Yorkshire, England   d: 5/27/45, Los Angeles, Cal.   BB/TR, 5'9", 154 lbs.   Deb: 5/8/08

| 1908 | Bos-A | 3 | 10 | 0 | 1 | 0 | 0 | 0 | 0 | 1 | | .100 | .182 | .100 | -8 | -1 | 1 | | | 1.000 | 1 | /O-3 | -0.1 |

■ SWEDE CARLSTROM   Carlstrom, Albin Oscar b: 10/26/1886, Elizabeth, N.J.   d: 4/28/35, Elizabeth, N.J.   BR/TR, 6', 167 lbs.   Deb: 9/13/11

| 1911 | Bos-A | 2 | 6 | 0 | 1 | 0 | 0 | 0 | 0 | 0 | 0 | .167 | .167 | .167 | -7 | -1 | 0 | | | 1.000 | 0 | /S-2 | 0.0 |

■ CLEO CARLYLE   Carlyle, Hiram Cleo b: 9/7/02, Fairburn, Ga.   d: 11/12/67, Los Angeles, Cal.   BL/TR, 6', 170 lbs.   Deb: 5/16/27 F

| 1927 | Bos-A | 95 | 278 | 31 | 65 | 12 | 8 | 1 | 28 | 36 | 40 | .234 | .324 | .345 | 75 | -10 | 4 | 4 | -1 | .965 | -7 | O-83 | -2.2 |

■ ROY CARLYLE   Carlyle, Roy Edward "Dizzy" b: 12/10/1900, Buford, Ga.   d: 11/22/56, Norcross, Ga.   BL/TR, 6'2.5", 195 lbs.   Deb: 4/16/25 F

1925	Was-A	1	1	0	0	0	0	0	0	0	1	.000	.000	.000	-99	-2	0	0	0	.000	0	H	0.0
	Bos-A	93	276	36	90	20	3	7	49	16	28	.326	.365	.496	117	6	1	1	-0	.909	-6	O-67	-0.4
	Yr	94	277	36	90	20	3	7	49	16	29	.325	.364	.495	116	5	1	1	-0	.909	-6	O-67	-0.4
1926	Bos-A	45	165	22	47	6	2	2	16	4	18	.285	.310	.382	82	-5	0	0	0	.904	-4	O-38	-1.1
	NY-A	35	52	3	20	5	1	0	11	4	9	.385	.439	.519	151	4	0	0	0	.941	-3	O-15	0.0
	Yr	80	217	25	67	11	3	2	27	8	27	.309	.342	.415	99	-1	0	0	0	.911	-7	O-53	-1.1
Total	2	174	494	61	157	31	6	9	76	24	56	.318	.354	.460	109	4	1	1	-0	.910	-12	O-120	-1.5

■ GEORGE CARMAN   Carman, George Wartman b: 3/29/1866, Philadelphia, Pa.   d: 6/16/29, Lancaster, Pa.   Deb: 9/4/1890

| 1890 | Phi-a | 28 | 97 | 9 | 17 | 2 | 0 | 0 | 7 | 8 | | .175 | .245 | .196 | 31 | -8 | 5 | | | .767 | -9 | S-15,O-10/2-2,3-1 | -1.5 |

■ DUKE CARMEL   Carmel, Leon James b: 4/23/37, New York, N.Y.   BL/TL, 6'3", 202 lbs.   Deb: 9/10/59

1959	StL-N	10	23	2	3	1	0	0	3	1	6	.130	.167	.174	-9	-4	0	1	-1	1.000	-3	O-10	-0.7
1960	StL-N	4	3	0	0	0	0	0	0	1	1	.000	.250	.000	-23	-0	1	1	-0	1.000	-0	1-2,O-1	-0.1
1963	StL-N	57	44	9	10	1	0	1	2	9	11	.227	.358	.318	88	-0	0	0	0	.974	-7	O-38/1-1	-0.8
	NY-N	47	149	11	35	5	3	3	18	16	37	.235	.309	.369	93	-1	2	2	-1	.980	-1	O-21,1-18	-0.5
	Yr	104	193	20	45	6	3	4	20	25	48	.233	.321	.358	90	-2	2	2	-1	.977	-7	O-59,1-19	-1.3
1965	NY-A	6	8	0	0	0	0	0	0	0	5	.000	.000	.000	-99	-2	0	0	0	1.000	0	/1-2	-0.2
Total	4	124	227	22	48	7	3	4	23	27	60	.211	.295	.322	73	-8	3	4	-2	.981	-10	/O-70,1-23	-2.3

■ EDDIE CARNETT   Carnett, Edwin Elliott "Lefty" b: 10/21/16, Springfield, Mo.   BL/TL, 6', 185 lbs.   Deb: 4/19/41

1941	Bos-N	2	0	0	0	0	0	0	0	0	0	—	—	—	—	0	0			.000	0	/P-2	0.0
1944	Chi-A	126	457	51	126	18	8	1	60	26	35	.276	.322	.357	95	-4	5	2	0	.949	-8	O-88,1-25/P-2	-1.8
1945	Cle-A	30	73	5	16	7	0	0	7	2	9	.219	.250	.315	66	-4	0	1	-1	.971	-0	O-16/P-2	-0.6
Total	3	158	530	56	142	25	8	1	67	28	44	.268	.312	.351	91	-7	5	3		.952	-8	O-104/1-25,P-6	-2.4

■ JOHN CARNEY   Carney, John Joseph "Handsome Jack" b: 11/10/1866, Salem, Mass.   d: 10/19/25, Litchfield, N.H.   BR/TR, 5'10.5", 175 lbs.   Deb: 4/24/1889

1889	Was-N	69	273	25	63	7	0	1	29	14	14	.231	.271	.267	54	-17	12			.957	-7	1-53,O-16	-2.4
1890	Buf-P	28	107	11	29	3	0	0	13	7	14	.271	.333	.299	76	-3	2			.972	-2	1-24/O-4	-0.5
	Cle-P	25	89	15	31	5	3	0	21	14	5	.348	.442	.472	157	8	6			.857	-3	O-19/1-6	0.3
	Yr	53	196	26	60	8	3	0	34	21	19	.306	.385	.378	113	5	8			.969	-6	1-30,O-23	-0.2
1891	Cin-a	99	367	47	102	10	8	3	43	35	18	.278	.346	.373	97	-4	15			.974	1	1-99	-0.7
	Mil-a	31	110	22	33	5	2	3	23	13	8	.300	.389	.464	120	1	5			.986	4	1-31	0.3
	Yr	130	477	69	135	15	10	6	66	48	26	.283	.346	.394	103	-2	20			.977	5	*1-130	-0.4
Total	3	252	946	120	258	30	13	7	129	83	59	.273	.338	.354	92	-14	40			.971	-8	1-213/O-39	-3.0

■ PAT CARNEY   Carney, Patrick Joseph "Doc" b: 8/7/1876, Holyoke, Mass.   d: 1/9/53, Worcester, Mass.   BL/TL, 6', 200 lbs.   Deb: 9/20/01

1901	Bos-N	13	55	6	16	2	0	0	6	3		.291	.339	.364	95	-0	0			.933	-3	O-13	-0.4
1902	Bos-N	137	522	75	141	17	4	2	65	42		.270	.339	.330	105	4	27			.930	-9	*O-137/P-2	-1.4
1903	Bos-N	110	392	37	94	12	4	1	49	28		.240	.297	.298	73	-14	10			.953	-6	O-92,P-10/1-1	-2.3
1904	Bos-N	78	279	24	57	5	2	0	11	12		.204	.240	.237	49	-17	6			.953	-2	O-71/P-4,1-1	-2.4
Total	4	338	1248	142	308	36	11	3	131	85		.247	.304	.300	82	-27	43			.942	-20	O-313/P-16,1-2	-6.5

■ BILL CARNEY   Carney, William John b: 3/25/1874, St.Paul, Minn.   d: 7/31/38, Hopkins, Minn.   BB/TR, 5'10", Deb: 8/22/04

| 1904 | Chi-N | 2 | 7 | 0 | 0 | 0 | 0 | 0 | 0 | 1 | | .000 | .125 | .000 | -60 | -1 | 0 | | | 1.000 | 0 | /O-2 | -0.2 |

■ HICK CARPENTER   Carpenter, Warren William b: 8/16/1855, Grafton, Mass.   d: 4/18/37, San Diego, Cal.   BR/TL, 5'11", 186 lbs.   Deb: 5/1/1879

1879	Syr-N	65	261	30	53	6	0	0	2	15		.203	.209	.226	49	-13				.948	-4	1-34,3-18,O-11,/2-3	-1.7
1880	Cin-N	77	300	32	72	6	4	0	23	2	15	.240	.245	.287	80	-6				.853	-1	*3-67/1-9,S-1	-0.5
1881	Wor-N	83	347	40	75	12	2	2	31	3	19	.216	.223	.280	54	-19				.848	3	*3-83	-1.4
1882	Cin-a	80	351	78	**120**	15	5	1	67	10		.342	.360	.422	154	18				**.835**	-1	3-80	1.7
1883	Cin-a	95	435	99	130	18	4	3	40	19		.299	.328	.379	120	8				.870	-6	3-95	0.2
1884	Cin-a	108	474	80	121	16	4	2	60	6		.255	.271	.323	89	-7				.881	-9	3-108/O-1	-1.4
1885	Cin-a	112	473	89	131	12	8	1	61	9		.277	.295	.349	101	-1				.860	-3	3-112	-0.5
1886	Cin-a	111	458	67	101	8	5	2	61	18		.221	.262	.273	66	-19	8			.841	-6	3-111	-2.0
1887	Cin-a	127	498	70	124	12	6	1	50	19		.249	.282	.303	62	-27	44			.846	-13	3-127	-3.0
1888	Cin-a	136	551	68	147	14	5	3	67	5		.267	.280	.327	89	-9	59			.866	-12	3-136	-1.7
1889	Cin-a	123	486	67	127	23	6	0	63	18	41	.261	.293	.333	76	-17	47			.835	-25	*3-121/1-2	-3.3
1892	StL-N	1	3	0	1	0	0	0	0	1	1	.333	.500	.333	161	0	0			.714	0	/3-1	0.0
Total	12	1118	4637	720	1202	142	47	18	543	112	91	.259	.281	.322	86	-92	158			.853	-80	*3-1059/1-45,O2S	-13.6

■ CHARLIE CARR   Carr, Charles Carbitt b: 12/27/1876, Coatesville, Pa.   d: 11/25/32, Memphis, Tenn.   BR/TR, 6'2", 195 lbs.   Deb: 9/15/1898

1898	Was-N	20	73	6	14	2	0	0	4	2		.192	.213	.219	24	-7	2			.950	-2	1-20	-0.9
1901	Phi-A	2	8	0	1	0	0	0	0	0		.125	.125	.125	-29	-1	0			.926	0	/1-2	-0.1
1903	Det-A	135	548	59	154	23	11	2	59	10		.281	.296	.374	103	0	10			.982	12	*1-135	1.1
1904	Det-A	92	360	29	77	13	3	0	40	14		.214	.245	.267	64	-15	4			.983	16	1-92	-0.1
	Cle-A	32	120	9	27	5	1	0	7	4		.225	.250	.283	69	-4	0			.973	-0	1-32	-0.6
	Yr	124	480	38	104	18	4	0	47	18		.217	.246	.271	65	-20	6			.980	16	*1-124	-0.7
1905	Cle-A	89	306	29	72	12	4	1	31	13		.235	.266	.310	82	-7	12			.991	-2	1-87	-1.3
1906	Cin-N	22	94	9	18	2	3	0	10	2		.191	.216	.277	51	-6	0			.983	1	1-22	-0.6
1914	Ind-F	115	441	44	129	11	10	3	69	26	47	.293	.333	.383	86	-15	19			**.991**	4	*1-115	-1.8
Total	7	507	1950	185	492	68	32	6	240	71	47	.252	.280	.329	81	-56	49			.984	26	1-505	-4.3

■ CHUCK CARR   Carr, Charles Lee Glenn b: 8/10/67, San Bernardino, Cal.   BB/TR, 5'10", 155 lbs.   Deb: 4/28/90

1990	NY-N	4	2	0	0	0	0	0	0	0	2	.000	.000	.000	-99	-1	1	0	0	.000	-0	/O-1	-0.1
1991	NY-N	12	11	1	2	0	0	0	0	0	2	.182	.182	.182	3	-1	1	0	0	1.000	-0	/O-9	-0.3
1992	StL-N	22	64	8	14	3	0	0	3	6	6	.219	.315	.266	68	-2	10	2	2	1.000	-1	O-19	-0.2
1993	Fla-N	142	551	75	147	19	2	4	41	49	74	.267	.329	.330	73	-20	**58**	22	4	.985	16	*O-139	-0.3
1994	Fla-N	106	433	61	114	19	2	2	30	22	71	.263	.307	.330	64	-22	32	8	5	.980	10	*O-104	-1.0
1995	Fla-N	105	308	54	70	20	0	2	20	46	49	.227	.331	.312	71	-12	25	11	1	.987	5	*O-103	-0.9
1996	Mil-A	27	106	18	29	6	1	1	11	6	21	.274	.313	.377	69	-5	5	4	-1	1.000	5	O-27	-0.2
Total	7	418	1475	217	376	67	5	9	106	132	225	.255	.320	.325	69	-64	132	47	11	.986	32	O-402	-3.0

■ LEW CARR   Carr, Lewis Smith b: 8/15/1872, Union Springs, N.Y.   d: 6/15/54, Moravia, N.Y.   BR/TR, 6'2", 200 lbs.   Deb: 7/4/01

| 1901 | Pit-N | 9 | 28 | 2 | 7 | 1 | 0 | 2 | 4 | 2 | | .250 | .344 | .357 | 102 | 0 | 0 | | | .886 | -5 | /S-9,3-1 | -0.4 |

■ CHICO CARRASQUEL   Carrasquel, Alfonso (Colon) b: 1/23/28, Caracas, Venez.   BR/TR, 6', 170 lbs.   Deb: 4/18/50

1950	Chi-A	141	524	72	148	21	5	4	46	66	46	.282	.368	.365	91	-6	0	2	-1	.961	11	*S-141	1.4
1951	Chi-A★	147	538	41	142	22	4	2	58	46	39	.264	.325	.331	79	-16	14	4	2	**.975**	13	*S-147	0.9
1952	Chi-A	100	359	36	89	7	4	1	42	33	27	.248	.315	.298	71	-14	2	2	-1	.964	-16	S-99	-2.4
1953	Chi-A★	149	552	72	154	30	4	3	47	38	47	.279	.330	.359	83	-13	5	3	-0	.976	3	*S-149	0.1
1954	Chi-A★	155	620	106	158	28	3	12	62	85	67	.255	.349	.368	93	-4	7	6	-2	**.975**	11	*S-155	1.9

YEAR	TM/L	G	AB	R	H	2B	3B	HR	RBI	BB	SO	AVG	OBP	SLG	PRO+	BR/A	SB	CS	SBR	FA	FR	G/POS	TPR
1955	Chi-A★	145	523	83	134	11	2	11	52	61	59	.256	.338	.348	83	-12	1	1	-0	.973	0	*S-144	0.0
1956	Cle-A	141	474	60	115	15	1	7	48	52	61	.243	.325	.323	70	-20	0	4	-2	.967	-25	*S-141/3-1	-3.6
1957	Cle-A	125	392	37	108	14	1	8	57	41	53	.276	.356	.378	102	2	0	2	-1	.960	-5	*S-122	0.7
1958	Cle-A	49	156	14	40	6	0	2	21	14	12	.256	.318	.333	81	-4	0	0	0	.931	-19	S-32,3-14	-2.1
	KC-A	59	160	19	34	5	1	2	13	21	15	.213	.304	.294	64	-8	0	1	-1	.976	-6	3-32,S-22	-1.3
	Yr	108	316	33	74	11	1	4	34	35	27	.234	.311	.313	72	-12	0	1	-1	.947	-25	S-54,3-46	-3.4
1959	Bal-A	114	346	28	77	13	0	4	28	34	41	.223	.294	.295	64	-17	2	3	-1	.970	-14	S-89,2-22/3-2,1-1	-2.4
Total	10	1325	4644	568	1199	172	25	55	474	491	467	.258	.334	.342	82	-111	31	28	-8	.969	-47	*S-1241/3-49,2-22,1	-6.8

■ CAM CARREON
Carreon, Camilo b: 8/6/37, Colton, Cal. d: 9/2/87, Tucson, Ariz. BR/TR, 6', 198 lbs. Deb: 9/27/59 F

YEAR	TM/L	G	AB	R	H	2B	3B	HR	RBI	BB	SO	AVG	OBP	SLG	PRO+	BR/A	SB	CS	SBR	FA	FR	G/POS	TPR
1959	Chi-A	1	1	0	0	0	0	0	0	0	0	.000	.000	.000	-99	-0	0	0	0	1.000	0	/C-1	0.0
1960	Chi-A	8	17	2	4	0	0	0	2	1	3	.235	.278	.235	41	-1	0	0	0	1.000	0	/C-7	-0.1
1961	Chi-A	78	229	32	62	5	1	4	27	21	24	.271	.332	.354	85	-5	0	1	-1	.995	9	C-71	0.7
1962	Chi-A	106	313	31	80	19	1	4	37	33	37	.256	.329	.361	86	-6	0	1	-1	.995	8	C-93	0.5
1963	Chi-A	101	270	28	74	10	1	2	35	23	32	.274	.333	.341	91	-3	1	1	-0	.987	6	C-92	0.0
1964	Chi-A	37	95	12	26	5	0	0	4	7	13	.274	.330	.326	86	-2	0	0	0	.987	-4	C-34	-0.5
1965	Cle-A	19	52	6	12	2	1	1	7	9	6	.231	.344	.365	101	0	1	1	-0	1.000	0	C-19	0.1
1966	Bal-A	4	9	2	2	2	0	0	2	3	2	.222	.417	.444	150	1	0	0	0	1.000	0	/C-3	0.1
Total	8	354	986	113	260	43	4	11	114	97	117	.264	.331	.349	87	-16	3	4	-2	.993	14	C-320	0.8

■ MARK CARREON
Carreon, Mark Steven b: 7/19/63, Chicago, Ill. BR/TL, 6', 194 lbs. Deb: 9/8/87 F

YEAR	TM/L	G	AB	R	H	2B	3B	HR	RBI	BB	SO	AVG	OBP	SLG	PRO+	BR/A	SB	CS	SBR	FA	FR	G/POS	TPR
1987	NY-N	9	12	0	3	0	0	0	1	1	1	.250	.308	.250	53	-1	0	1	-1	.800	-1	/O-5	-0.3
1988	NY-N	7	9	5	5	1	0	1	2	1	1	.556	.636	1.111	413	4	0	0	0	1.000	-1	/O-4	0.3
1989	NY-N	68	133	20	41	6	0	6	16	12	17	.308	.370	.489	151	8	2	3	-1	.983	-3	O-39	0.4
1990	NY-N	82	188	30	47	12	0	10	26	15	29	.250	.312	.473	113	3	1	0	0	1.000	-8	O-60	-0.7
1991	NY-N	106	254	18	66	6	0	4	21	12	26	.260	.299	.331	77	-8	2	1	0	.971	-12	O-77	-2.2
1992	Det-A	101	336	34	78	11	1	10	41	22	57	.232	.281	.360	78	-11	3	1	0	.979	2	O-83,D-13	-1.1
1993	SF-N	78	150	22	49	9	1	7	33	13	16	.327	.384	.540	149	10	1	0	0	.943	-7	O-41/1-3	0.3
1994	SF-N	51	100	8	27	4	0	3	20	7	20	.270	.330	.400	94	-1	0	0	0	.978	-5	O-33	-0.6
1995	SF-N	117	396	53	119	24	0	17	65	23	37	.301	.345	.490	121	11	0	1	-1	.993	-10	1-81,O-22	-0.8
1996	SF-N	81	292	40	76	22	3	9	51	22	33	.260	.319	.449	104	1	2	3	-1	.986	-6	1-73/O-5	-1.3
	Cle-A	38	142	16	46	12	0	2	14	11	9	.324	.385	.451	110	3	1	1	-0	.994	-2	1-34/O-5,D-2	-0.3
Total	10	738	2012	246	557	108	5	69	289	140	246	.277	.330	.438	108	18	12	11	-3	.974	-53	O-374,1-191/D-15	-6.3

■ BILL CARRIGAN
Carrigan, William Francis "Rough" b: 10/22/1883, Lewiston, Me. d: 7/8/69, Lewiston, Me. BR/TR, 5'9", 175 lbs. Deb: 7/7/06 M

YEAR	TM/L	G	AB	R	H	2B	3B	HR	RBI	BB	SO	AVG	OBP	SLG	PRO+	BR/A	SB	CS	SBR	FA	FR	G/POS	TPR
1906	Bos-A	37	109	5	23	0	0	0	10	5		.211	.252	.211	45	-7	3			.940	-2	C-35	-0.5
1908	Bos-A	57	149	13	35	5	2	0	14	3		.235	.255	.295	77	-4	1			.955	6	C-47/1-3	0.6
1909	Bos-A	94	280	25	83	13	2	1	36	17		.296	.341	.368	121	6	2			.972	1	C-77/1-8	1.6
1910	Bos-A	114	342	36	85	11	1	3	53	23		.249	.307	.313	92	-3	10			.962	-21	*C-110	-1.6
1911	Bos-A	72	232	29	67	6	1	1	30	26		.289	.373	.336	99	1	5			.972	-1	C-62/1-6	0.6
1912	*Bos-A	87	266	34	70	7	1	0	24	38		.263	.359	.297	84	-4	7			**.970**	-12	C-87	-0.7
1913	Bos-A	87	256	17	62	5	5	0	28	27	26	.242	.319	.340	91	-3	6			.979	-8	C-82,M	-0.4
1914	Bos-A	82	178	18	45	5	1	0	22	40	18	.253	.395	.309	112	5	1	2	-1	**.984**	3	C-78,M	1.5
1915	*Bos-A	46	95	10	19	3	0	0	7	16	12	.200	.321	.232	68	-3	0			.975	8	C-44,M	0.8
1916	*Bos-A	33	63	7	17	2	1	0	11	11	3	.270	.378	.333	113	2	2			1.000	5	C-27,M	1.0
Total	10	709	1970	194	506	67	14	6	235	206	59	.257	.334	.314	94	-11	37	2		.971	-18	C-649/1-17	2.9

■ MATIAS CARRILLO
Carrillo, Matias (Garcia) b: 2/24/63, Los Mochis, Mexico BL/TL, 5'11", 190 lbs. Deb: 5/23/91

YEAR	TM/L	G	AB	R	H	2B	3B	HR	RBI	BB	SO	AVG	OBP	SLG	PRO+	BR/A	SB	CS	SBR	FA	FR	G/POS	TPR
1991	Mil-A	3	0	0	0	0	0	0	0	0	0	—	—	—		0	0	0	0	.000	-1	/O-3	-0.1
1993	Fla-N	24	55	4	14	6	0	0	3	1	7	.255	.281	.364	67	-3	0	0	0	1.000	-3	O-16	-0.6
1994	Fla-N	80	136	13	34	7	0	0	9	9	31	.250	.297	.301	55	-9	3	3	-1	.982	-7	O-49	-1.8
Total	3	107	191	17	48	13	0	0	12	10	38	.251	.292	.319	58	-11	3	3	-1	.987	-12	/O-68	-2.5

■ DIXIE CARROLL
Carroll, Dorsey Lee b: 5/9/1891, Paducah, Ky. d: 10/13/84, Jacksonville, Fla BL/TR, 5'11", 165 lbs. Deb: 9/12/19

YEAR	TM/L	G	AB	R	H	2B	3B	HR	RBI	BB	SO	AVG	OBP	SLG	PRO+	BR/A	SB	CS	SBR	FA	FR	G/POS	TPR
1919	Bos-N	15	49	10	13	3	1	0	7	7	1	.265	.379	.367	130	2	5			.921	2	O-13	0.3

■ CHICK CARROLL
Carroll, Edward b: 1868, Arkansas d: 7/13/08, Chicago, Ill. Deb: 4/17/1884

YEAR	TM/L	G	AB	R	H	2B	3B	HR	RBI	BB	SO	AVG	OBP	SLG	PRO+	BR/A	SB	CS	SBR	FA	FR	G/POS	TPR
1884	Was-U	4	16	1	4	0	0	0		0		.250	.250	.250	54	-1				.500	-1	/O-4	-0.2

■ FRED CARROLL
Carroll, Frederick Herbert b: 7/2/1864, Sacramento, Cal. d: 11/7/04, San Rafael, Cal. BR/TR, 5'11", 185 lbs. Deb: 5/1/1884

YEAR	TM/L	G	AB	R	H	2B	3B	HR	RBI	BB	SO	AVG	OBP	SLG	PRO+	BR/A	SB	CS	SBR	FA	FR	G/POS	TPR
1884	Col-a	69	252	46	70	13	5	6		13		.278	.326	.440	161	17				.944	16	C-54,O-15	3.3
1885	Pit-a	71	280	45	75	13	8	0	30	7		.268	.298	.371	112	3				.926	4	C-60,O-12	1.1
1886	Pit-a	122	486	92	140	28	11	5	64	52		.288	.362	.422	146	26	20			.921	11	C-70,O-27,1-25/S-1	3.6
1887	Pit-N	102	421	71	138	24	15	6	54	36	21	.328	.383	.499	152	30	23			.833	-12	O-46,C-40,1-17/S-1	1.7
1888	Pit-N	97	366	62	91	14	5	2	48	32	31	.249	.326	.331	119	10	18			.897	-11	C-54,O-38/1-5,3-1	0.2
1889	Pit-N	91	318	80	105	21	11	2	51	85	26	.330	**.486**	.484	**190**	48	19			.930	-13	C-43,O-41/1-7,3-1	3.2
1890	Pit-P	111	416	95	124	20	7	2	71	75	22	.298	.404	.394	128	23	35			.856	-17	C-56,O-49/1-7	0.7
1891	Pit-N	91	353	55	77	13	4	4	48	48	36	.218	.315	.312	85	-6	22			.915	6	O-91	-0.3
Total	8	754	2892	546	820	146	66	27	366	348	136	.284	.370	.408	137	151	137			.913	-16	C-377,O-319/13S	13.5

■ SCRAPPY CARROLL
Carroll, John E. b: 8/27/1860, Buffalo, N.Y. d: 11/14/42, Buffalo, N.Y. 5'7.5", Deb: 9/27/1884

YEAR	TM/L	G	AB	R	H	2B	3B	HR	RBI	BB	SO	AVG	OBP	SLG	PRO+	BR/A	SB	CS	SBR	FA	FR	G/POS	TPR
1884	StP-U	9	31	3	3	1	0	0				.097	.152	.129	-26	-7				.824	3	/O-8,3-2	-0.4
1885	Buf-N	13	40	1	3	0	0	0	1	2	8	.075	.119	.075	-35	-6				.917	1	O-13	-0.5
1887	Cle-a	57	216	30	43	5	1	0	19	15		.199	.264	.231	40	-17	19			.843	-5	O-54/3-2,2-1	-1.9
Total	3	79	287	34	49	6	1	0	20	19	8	.171	.232	.199	26	-30	19			.853	-2	/O-75,3-5,2-1	-2.8

■ PAT CARROLL
Carroll, Patrick b: 3/1853, Philadelphia, Pa. d: 2/14/16, Philadelphia, Pa. Deb: 5/10/1884

YEAR	TM/L	G	AB	R	H	2B	3B	HR	RBI	BB	SO	AVG	OBP	SLG	PRO+	BR/A	SB	CS	SBR	FA	FR	G/POS	TPR
1884	Alt-U	11	49	4	13	1	0	0	1			.265	.280	.286	71	-3				.920	-4	/C-8,O-3	-0.5
	Phi-U	5	19	1	3	1	0	0				.158	.158	.211	12	-3				.839	3	/C-5	-0.0
	Yr	16	68	5	16	2	0	0	1			.235	.246	.265	56	-6				.877	-1	C-13/O-3	-0.5

■ DOC CARROLL
Carroll, Ralph Arthur "Red" b: 12/28/1891, Worcester, Mass. d: 6/27/83, Worcester, Mass. BR/TR, 6', 170 lbs. Deb: 6/27/16

YEAR	TM/L	G	AB	R	H	2B	3B	HR	RBI	BB	SO	AVG	OBP	SLG	PRO+	BR/A	SB	CS	SBR	FA	FR	G/POS	TPR
1916	Phi-A	10	22	1	2	0	0	0	0	1	8	.091	.167	.091	-24	-3	0			.942	0	C-10	-0.3

■ CLIFF CARROLL
Carroll, Samuel Clifford b: 10/18/1859, Clays Grove, Iowa d: 6/12/23, Portland, Ore. BB/TR, 5'8", 163 lbs. Deb: 8/3/1882

YEAR	TM/L	G	AB	R	H	2B	3B	HR	RBI	BB	SO	AVG	OBP	SLG	PRO+	BR/A	SB	CS	SBR	FA	FR	G/POS	TPR
1882	Pro-N	10	41	4	5	0	0	0	1			.122	.122	.122	-21	-5				1.000	1	O-10	-0.4
1883	Pro-N	58	238	37	63	12	3	1	20	4	28	.265	.277	.353	87	-4				.902	5	O-58	0.0
1884	*Pro-N	113	452	90	118	16	4	3	54	29	39	.261	.306	.334	104	3				.904	2	*O-113	0.2
1885	Pro-N	104	426	62	99	12	3	1	40	29	29	.232	.283	.329	86	-6				.886	4	*O-104	-0.5
1886	Was-N	111	433	73	99	11	4	2	22	44	26	.229	.300	.296	87	-5	31			.862	-1	*O-111	-0.8
1887	Was-N	103	420	79	104	17	4	4	37	17	30	.248	.291	.336	78	-12	40			.902	1	*O-103	-1.1
1888	Pit-N	5	20	1	0	0	0	0	0	0	0	.000	.000	.000	-99	-5	2			.667	-1	/O-5	-0.6
1890	Chi-N	136	582	134	166	16	6	7	65	53	34	.285	.352	.369	106	4	34			.936	15	*O-136	1.2
1891	Chi-N	130	515	87	132	20	8	7	80	50	42	.256	.340	.367	106	4	31			.915	-5	*O-130	-0.4
1892	StL-N	101	407	82	111	19	8	4	49	47	22	.273	.363	.376	130	16	30			.901	4	*O-101	1.4
1893	Bos-N	120	438	80	98	7	5	2	54	88	28	.224	.360	.276	65	-21	29			.917	2	*O-120	-2.1
Total	11	991	3972	729	995	125	47	31	423	361	290	.251	.320	.329	93	-31	197			.905	25	O-991	-3.1

■ TOM CARROLL
Carroll, Thomas Edward b: 9/17/36, Jamaica, N.Y. BR/TR, 6'3", 186 lbs. Deb: 5/7/55

YEAR	TM/L	G	AB	R	H	2B	3B	HR	RBI	BB	SO	AVG	OBP	SLG	PRO+	BR/A	SB	CS	SBR	FA	FR	G/POS	TPR
1955	*NY-A	14	6	3	2	0	0	0	0	0	2	.333	.333	.333	81	-0	0	0	0	.875	2	/S-4	0.2
1956	NY-A	36	17	11	6	0	0	0	0	3	1	.353	.389	.353	100	0	1	0	0	.857	5	3-11/S-1	0.5

YEAR	TM/L	G	AB	R	H	2B	3B	HR	RBI	BB	SO	AVG	OBP	SLG	PRO+	BR/A	SB	CS	SBR	FA	FR	G/POS	TPR
1959	KC-A	14	7	1	1	0	0	0	1	0	1	.143	.143	.143	-21	-1	0	0	0	1.000	4	/S-9,3-3	0.3
Total	3	64	30	15	9	0	0	0	1	1	6	.300	.323	.300	69	-1	1	0	0	.813	11	/3-14,S-14	1.0

■ KID CARSEY   Carsey, Wilfred b: 10/22/1870, New York, N.Y. d: 3/29/60, Miami, Fla. BL/TR, 5'7", 168 lbs. Deb: 4/8/1891

YEAR	TM/L	G	AB	R	H	2B	3B	HR	RBI	BB	SO	AVG	OBP	SLG	PRO+	BR/A	SB	CS	SBR	FA	FR	G/POS	TPR
1891	Was-a	61	187	25	28	5	2	0	15	19	38	.150	.236	.198	25	-18	2			.922	5	P-54/O-7,S-2	-0.2
1892	Phi-N	44	131	8	20	2	1	1	10	9	24	.153	.207	.206	25	-12	1			.888	2	P-43/O-2	-0.1
1893	Phi-N	39	145	12	27	1	1	0	10	5	14	.186	.229	.207	16	-18	2			.925	2	P-39	0.0
1894	Phi-N	35	125	30	34	2	2	0	18	16	11	.272	.359	.320	67	-6	3			.937	2	P-35	0.0
1895	Phi-N	44	141	24	41	2	0	0	20	15	12	.291	.363	.305	73	-5	2			.878	-1	P-44	0.0
1896	Phi-N	27	81	13	18	2	2	0	7	11	12	.222	.315	.296	62	-4	1			.908	1	P-27	0.0
1897	Phi-N	4	13	1	3	0	0	0	1	0	0	.231	.231	.231	23	-1	0			1.000	-0	/P-4	0.0
	StL-N	13	43	2	13	2	2	0	5	1		.302	.318	.442	101	-0	1			.917	1	P-12	0.0
	Yr	17	56	3	16	2	2	0	6	1		.286	.298	.393	83	-2	1			.930	1	P-16	0.0
1898	StL-N	38	105	8	21	0	1	1	10	10		.200	.270	.248	47	-7	3			.935	-6	P-20,2-10/O-8	-1.0
1899	Cle-N	11	36	5	10	0	0	0	4	3		.278	.333	.278	74	-1	0			.879	3	P-10/S-1	0.1
	Was-N	4	11	1	0	0	0	0	0	0		.000	.000	.000	-99	-3	0			.923	1	/P-4	0.0
	NY-N	5	18	2	6	1	0	0	1	2		.333	.400	.389	121	1	2			.667	-1	/3-3,S-2	0.0
	Yr	20	65	8	16	1	0	0	5	5		.246	.300	.262	57	-4	2			.891	3	P-14/S-3,3-3	0.1
1901	Bro-N	2	2	0	0	0	0	0	0	0		.000	.000	.000	-97	-0	0			1.000	-0	/P-2	0.0
Total	10	327	1038	131	221	17	11	2	101	91	111	.213	.281	.256	47	-76	17			.911	7	P-294/O-17,2-10,S3	-1.2

■ KIT CARSON   Carson, Walter Lloyd b: 11/15/12, Colton, Cal. d: 6/21/83, Long Beach, Cal. BL/TL, 6', 180 lbs. Deb: 7/21/34

YEAR	TM/L	G	AB	R	H	2B	3B	HR	RBI	BB	SO	AVG	OBP	SLG	PRO+	BR/A	SB	CS	SBR	FA	FR	G/POS	TPR
1934	Cle-A	5	18	4	5	2	1	0	1	2	3	.278	.350	.500	115	0	0	0	0	1.000	-1	/O-4	-0.1
1935	Cle-A	16	22	1	5	2	0	0	1	2	6	.227	.292	.318	57	-1	0	1	-1	1.000	-0	/O-4	-0.2
Total	2	21	40	5	10	4	1	0	2	4	9	.250	.318	.400	83	-1	0	1	-1	1.000	-2	/O-8	-0.3

■ FRANK CARSWELL   Carswell, Frank Willis "Tex" or "Wheels" b: 11/6/19, Palestine, Tex. BR/TR, 6', 195 lbs. Deb: 4/17/53

YEAR	TM/L	G	AB	R	H	2B	3B	HR	RBI	BB	SO	AVG	OBP	SLG	PRO+	BR/A	SB	CS	SBR	FA	FR	G/POS	TPR
1953	Det-A	16	15	2	4	0	0	0	3	1	1	.267	.389	.267	81	-0	0	0	0	1.000	-1	/O-3	-0.1

■ GARY CARTER   Carter, Gary Edmund b: 4/8/54, Culver City, Cal. BR/TR, 6'2", 215 lbs. Deb: 9/16/74

YEAR	TM/L	G	AB	R	H	2B	3B	HR	RBI	BB	SO	AVG	OBP	SLG	PRO+	BR/A	SB	CS	SBR	FA	FR	G/POS	TPR
1974	Mon-N	9	27	5	11	0	1	6	1	2	.407	.429	.593	174	2	2	0	1	1.000	-1	/C-6,O-2	0.3
1975	Mon-N★	144	503	58	136	20	1	17	68	72	83	.270	.363	.416	111	8	5	2	0	.974	-16	O-92,C-66/3-1	-0.8
1976	Mon-N	91	311	31	68	8	1	6	38	30	43	.219	.289	.309	67	-13	0	2	-1	.994	3	C-60,O-36	-1.2
1977	Mon-N	154	522	86	148	29	2	31	84	58	103	.284	.361	.525	138	27	5	5	-2	.990	3	*C-146/O-1	3.3
1978	Mon-N	157	533	76	136	27	1	20	72	62	70	.255	.338	.422	113	9	10	6	-1	.989	10	*C-152/1-1	2.3
1979	Mon-N★	141	505	74	143	26	5	22	75	40	62	.283	.342	.485	124	15	3	2	-0	.989	13	*C-138	3.4
1980	Mon-N★	154	549	76	145	25	5	29	101	58	78	.264	.336	.486	127	18	3	2	-0	.993	14	*C-149	3.9
1981	*Mon-N★	100	374	48	94	20	2	16	68	35	35	.251	.317	.444	113	5	1	5	-3	.993	2	*C-100/1-1	0.9
1982	Mon-N★	154	557	91	163	32	1	29	97	78	64	.293	.385	.510	146	35	2	5	-2	.991	14	*C-153	5.4
1983	Mon-N★	145	541	63	146	37	3	17	79	51	57	.270	.341	.444	116	11	1	1	-0	.995	10	*C-144/1-1	2.8
1984	Mon-N★	159	596	75	175	32	1	27	**106**	64	57	.294	.368	.487	145	34	2	2	-1	.993	-5	*C-143,1-25	3.5
1985	NY-N†	149	555	83	156	17	1	32	100	69	46	.281	.365	.488	141	30	1	1	-0	.992	5	*C-143/1-6,O-1	4.3
1986	*NY-N★	132	490	81	125	14	2	24	105	62	63	.255	.346	.439	118	12	1	0	-0	.991	6	*C-122/1-9,O-4,3-1	2.7
1987	NY-N★	139	523	55	123	18	2	20	83	42	73	.235	.293	.392	84	-14	0	0	-0	.991	-0	*C-135/1-4,O-1	-0.5
1988	*NY-N★	130	455	39	110	16	2	11	46	34	52	.242	.304	.358	94	-4	0	2	-1	.990	-3	*C-119,1-10/3-1	-1.0
1989	NY-N	50	153	14	28	8	0	2	15	12	15	.183	.242	.275	50	-10	0	0	-0	.980	-2	C-47/1-1	-1.0
1990	SF-N	92	244	24	62	10	0	9	27	25	31	.254	.326	.406	104	1	1	1	-0	.992	-3	C-80/1-3	0.1
1991	LA-N	101	248	22	61	14	0	6	26	22	26	.246	.325	.375	98	-0	2	2	-1	.988	5	C-68,1-10	0.6
1992	Mon-N	95	285	24	62	18	1	5	29	33	37	.218	.303	.340	83	-6	0	4	-2	.989	1	C-85/1-5	-0.4
Total	19	2296	7971	1025	2092	371	31	324	1225	848	997	.262	.338	.439	116	159	39	42	-14	.991	54	*C-2056,O-137/13	29.6

■ HOWIE CARTER   Carter, John Howard b: 10/13/04, New York, N.Y. d: 7/24/91, New York, N.Y. BR/TR, 5'10", 154 lbs. Deb: 6/21/26

YEAR	TM/L	G	AB	R	H	2B	3B	HR	RBI	BB	SO	AVG	OBP	SLG	PRO+	BR/A	SB	CS	SBR	FA	FR	G/POS	TPR
1926	Cin-N	5	1	0	0	0	0	0	0	0	0	.000	.000	.000	-99	-0	0			1.000	0	/2-3,S-1	0.0

■ JOE CARTER   Carter, Joseph Chris b: 3/7/60, Oklahoma City, Okla. BR/TR, 6'3", 215 lbs. Deb: 7/30/83

YEAR	TM/L	G	AB	R	H	2B	3B	HR	RBI	BB	SO	AVG	OBP	SLG	PRO+	BR/A	SB	CS	SBR	FA	FR	G/POS	TPR
1983	Chi-A	23	51	6	9	1	1	0	1	0	21	.176	.176	.235	13	-6	1	0	0	1.000	-2	O-16	-0.8
1984	Cle-A	66	244	32	67	6	1	13	41	11	48	.275	.309	.467	109	2	2	4	-2	.956	1	O-59/1-7	-0.1
1985	Cle-A	143	489	64	128	27	0	15	59	25	74	.262	.300	.409	93	-6	24	6	4	.983	-1	*O-135,1-11/2-1,3D	-0.8
1986	Cle-A	162	663	108	200	36	9	29	**121**	32	95	.302	.339	.514	130	25	29	7	5	.976	-6	*O-104,1-70	1.5
1987	Cle-A	149	588	83	155	27	2	32	106	27	105	.264	.306	.480	103	1	31	6	6	.983	-8	1-84,O-62/D-5	-0.9
1988	Cle-A	157	621	85	168	36	6	27	98	35	82	.271	.317	.478	116	11	27	5	5	.985	14	*O-156	2.5
1989	Cle-A	162	651	84	158	32	4	35	105	39	112	.243	.292	.465	109	4	13	5	1	.978	-1	*O-146,1-11/D-8	-0.1
1990	SD-N	162	634	79	147	27	1	24	115	48	93	.232	.293	.391	86	-14	22	6	3	.988	9	*O-150,1-14	-0.7
1991	*Tor-A★	162	638	89	174	42	3	33	108	49	112	.273	.334	.503	124	18	20	9	1	.974	3	*O-151,D-11	1.8
1992	*Tor-A★	158	622	97	164	30	7	34	119	36	109	.264	.315	.498	119	13	12	5	1	.971	6	*O-129,D-24/1-4	1.5
1993	*Tor-A★	155	603	92	153	33	5	33	121	47	113	.254	.317	.489	113	8	8	3	1	.974	-1	*O-151/D-3	0.6
1994	Tor-A★	111	435	70	118	25	2	27	103	33	64	.271	.326	.524	114	7	11	0	3	.991	0	*O-110/D-1	0.7
1995	Tor-A	139	558	70	141	23	0	25	76	37	87	.253	.303	.428	88	-12	12	1	3	.975	3	*O-128/1-7,D-5	-1.0
1996	Tor-A★	157	625	84	158	35	7	30	107	44	106	.253	.309	.475	94	-9	7	6	-2	.961	-12	*O-115,1-41,D-15	-2.7
Total	14	1906	7422	1043	1940	380	48	357	1280	463	1221	.261	.312	.470	107	43	219	63	28	.977	6	*O-1612,1-249/D32	1.5

■ BLACKIE CARTER   Carter, Otis Leonard b: 9/30/02, Langley, S.C. d: 9/10/76, Greenville, S.C. BR/TR, 5'10", 175 lbs. Deb: 10/3/25

YEAR	TM/L	G	AB	R	H	2B	3B	HR	RBI	BB	SO	AVG	OBP	SLG	PRO+	BR/A	SB	CS	SBR	FA	FR	G/POS	TPR
1925	NY-N	1	4	0	0	0	0	0	0	0	1	.000	.000	.000	-99	-1	0	0	0	1.000	1	/O-1	-0.1
1926	NY-N	5	17	4	4	1	0	1	1	1	0	.235	.278	.471	100	-0	0			.917	0	/O-4	-0.0
Total	2	6	21	4	4	1	0	1	1	1	1	.190	.227	.381	61	-1	0	0	0	.929	1	/O-5	-0.1

■ STEVE CARTER   Carter, Steven Jerome b: 12/3/64, Charlottesville, Va. BL/TR, 6'4", 201 lbs. Deb: 4/16/89

YEAR	TM/L	G	AB	R	H	2B	3B	HR	RBI	BB	SO	AVG	OBP	SLG	PRO+	BR/A	SB	CS	SBR	FA	FR	G/POS	TPR
1989	Pit-N	9	16	2	2	1	0	1	3	2	5	.125	.222	.375	70	-1	0	0	0	1.000	-1	/O-5	-0.2
1990	Pit-N	5	5	0	1	0	0	0	0	1	1	.200	.200	.200	11	-0	0	0	0	1.000	-1	/O-3	-0.2
Total	2	14	21	2	3	1	0	1	3	2	6	.143	.217	.333	56	-1	0	0	0	1.000	-2	/O-8	-0.4

■ ED CARTWRIGHT   Cartwright, Edward Charles "Jumbo" b: 10/6/1859, Johnstown, Pa. d: 9/3/33, St.Petersburg, Fla BR/TR, 5'10", 220 lbs. Deb: 7/10/1890

YEAR	TM/L	G	AB	R	H	2B	3B	HR	RBI	BB	SO	AVG	OBP	SLG	PRO+	BR/A	SB	CS	SBR	FA	FR	G/POS	TPR
1890	StL-a	75	300	70	90	12	4	8	60	29		.300	.367	.447	123	5	26			.976	-1	1-75	0.0
1894	Was-N	132	507	88	149	35	13	12	106	57	43	.294	.374	.485	109	6	31			.973	-2	*1-132	0.4
1895	Was-N	122	472	95	156	34	17	3	90	54	41	.331	.400	.494	131	22	50			.984	14	*1-122	3.1
1896	Was-N	133	499	76	138	15	10	1	62	54	44	.277	.350	.353	85	-10	28			.978	-9	*1-133	-0.7
1897	Was-N	33	124	19	29	4	0	0	15	8		.234	.286	.266	46	-10	9			.963	1	1-33	-0.6
Total	5	495	1902	348	562	100	44	24	333	202	128	.295	.368	.432	106	14	144			.977	13	1-495	2.2

■ RICO CARTY   Carty, Ricardo Adolfo Jacobo (b: Ricardo Adolfo Jacobo (Carty)) b: 9/1/39, San Pedro De Macoris, D.R. BR/TR, 6'3", 200 lbs. Deb: 9/15/63

YEAR	TM/L	G	AB	R	H	2B	3B	HR	RBI	BB	SO	AVG	OBP	SLG	PRO+	BR/A	SB	CS	SBR	FA	FR	G/POS	TPR
1963	Mil-N	2	2	0	0	0	0	0	0	0	0	.000	.000	.000	-99	-1	0			.000	0	H	-0.1
1964	Mil-N	133	455	72	150	28	4	22	88	43	78	.330	.391	.554	162	37	1	2	-1	.978	1	*O-121	3.3
1965	Mil-N	83	271	37	84	18	1	10	35	17	44	.310	.357	.494	136	12	1	4	-2	.958	1	O-73	0.8
1966	Atl-N	151	521	73	170	25	2	15	76	60	74	.326	.396	.468	137	28	4	6	-2	.971	5	*O-126,C-17/1-2,3-1	2.7
1967	Atl-N	134	444	41	113	16	2	15	64	49	70	.255	.330	.401	110	6	4	3	-1	.959	4	*O-112/1-9	0.3
1969	*Atl-N	104	304	47	104	16	0	16	58	32	28	.342	.409	.549	164	26	0	2	-1	.952	-3	*O-79	1.8
1970	Atl-N★	136	478	84	175	23	3	25	101	77	46	**.366**	**.456**	.584	167	48	1	2	-1	.974	3	*O-133	4.2
1972	Atl-N	86	271	31	75	12	2	6	29	44	33	.277	.378	.402	111	5	0	1	-0	.979	-1	O-78	0.1
1973	Tex-A	86	306	24	71	12	0	3	33	36	29	.232	.315	.301	77	-9	2	2	-1	1.000	0	O-53,D-31	-1.3
	Chi-N	22	70	4	15	4	0	0	6	6	10	.214	.276	.257	45	-5	0	0	-0	.947	-0	O-19	-0.7
	Oak-A	7	8	1	2	1	0	0	3	2	1	.250	.400	.750	230	1	0	0	0	.000	0	/D-2	0.1
1974	Cle-A	33	91	6	33	5	0	1	16	5	9	.363	.396	.451	144	5	0	0	-2	.985	-2	D-14/1-8	0.3

YEAR	TM/L	G	AB	R	H	2B	3B	HR	RBI	BB	SO	AVG	OBP	SLG	PRO+	BR/A	SB	CS	SBR	FA	FR	G/POS	TPR
1975	Cle-A	118	383	57	118	19	1	18	64	45	31	.308	.384	.504	149	25	2	2	-1	.990	-1	D-72,1-26,O-12	2.0
1976	Cle-A	152	552	67	171	34	0	13	83	67	45	.310	.384	.442	143	31	1	1	-0	1.000	-2	*D-137,1-12/O-1	2.5
1977	Cle-A	127	461	50	129	23	1	15	80	56	51	.280	.358	.432	118	12	1	2	-1	1.000	1	*D-123/1-2	0.8
1978	Tor-A	104	387	51	110	16	0	20	68	36	41	.284	.345	.481	127	13	1	1	-0	.000	0	*D-101	1.0
	Oak-A	41	141	19	39	5	1	11	31	21	16	.277	.370	.560	167	12	0	0	0	.000	0	D-41	1.1
	Yr	145	528	70	149	21	1	31	99	57	57	.282	.352	.502	138	25	1	1	-0	.667	0	*D-142	2.1
1979	Tor-A	132	461	48	118	26	0	12	55	46	45	.256	.325	.390	91	-6	3	1	0	.000	0	*D-129	-1.0
Total	15	1651	5606	712	1677	278	17	204	890	642	663	.299	.372	.464	132	240	21	26	-9	.970	3	O-807,D-650/1C3	17.9

■ BOB CARUTHERS
Caruthers, Robert Lee "Parisian Bob" b: 1/5/1864, Memphis, Tenn. d: 8/5/11, Peoria, Ill. BL/TR, 5'7", 138 lbs. Deb: 9/7/1884 MU

YEAR	TM/L	G	AB	R	H	2B	3B	HR	RBI	BB	SO	AVG	OBP	SLG	PRO+	BR/A	SB	CS	SBR	FA	FR	G/POS	TPR
1884	StL-a	23	82	15	22	2	0	2		4		.268	.302	.366	113	1				.750	-6	O-16,P-13	-0.4
1885	*StL-a	60	222	37	50	10	2	1	12	20		.225	.289	.302	83	-4				.902	-0	P-53/O-7	-0.1
1886	*StL-a	87	317	91	106	21	14	4	61	64		.334	.448	.527	196	37	26			.897	-6	P-44,O-43/2-2	1.1
1887	*StL-a	98	364	102	130	23	11	8	73	66		.357	.463	.547	164	31	49			.903	9	O-54,P-39/1-7	1.5
1888	Bro-a	94	335	58	77	10	5	5	53	45		.230	.328	.334	113	6	23			.899	1	O-51,P-44	0.1
1889	*Bro-a	59	172	45	43	8	3	2	31	44	17	.250	.408	.366	121	7	9			.968	0	P-56/O-3,1-2	-0.1
1890	*Bro-N	71	238	46	63	7	4	1	29	47	18	.265	.397	.340	115	7	13			.860	-4	O-39,P-37	-0.4
1891	Bro-N	56	171	24	48	5	3	2	23	25	13	.281	.372	.380	120	5	4			.940	-3	P-38,O-17/2-1	-0.2
1892	StL-N	143	513	76	142	16	8	3	69	86	29	.277	.386	.357	131	24	24			.892	-11	*O-122,P-16/2-6,1M	0.6
1893	Chi-N	1	3	0	0	0	0	0	0	0	1	.000	.000	.000	-99	-1	0			1.000	-0	/O-1	-0.1
	Cin-N	13	48	14	14	2	0	1	8	16	1	.292	.477	.396	130	3	3			.857	-1	O-13	0.1
	Yr	14	51	14	14	2	0	1	8	16	2	.275	.456	.373	119	3	3			.862	-1	O-14	0.1
Total	10	705	2465	508	695	104	50	29	359	417	79	.282	.391	.400	135	117	152			.875	-22	O-366,P-340/1-13,2	2.1

■ PAUL CASANOVA
Casanova, Paulino (Ortiz) b: 12/21/41, Colon, Matanzas, Cuba BR/TR, 6'4", 200 lbs. Deb: 9/18/65

YEAR	TM/L	G	AB	R	H	2B	3B	HR	RBI	BB	SO	AVG	OBP	SLG	PRO+	BR/A	SB	CS	SBR	FA	FR	G/POS	TPR
1965	Was-A	5	13	2	4	1	0	1		1	3	.308	.357	.385	112	0	0	0	0	.938	-2	/C-4	-0.2
1966	Was-A	122	429	45	109	16	5	13	44	14	78	.254	.279	.406	95	-4	1	2	-1	.981	-10	*C-119	-0.8
1967	Was-A☆	141	528	47	131	19	1	9	53	17	65	.248	.274	.339	84	-13	1	1	-0	.984	-5	*C-137	-1.1
1968	Was-A	96	322	19	63	6	0	4	25	7	52	.196	.213	.252	42	-23	0	1	-1	.989	-6	C-92	-3.2
1969	Was-A	124	379	26	82	9	2	4	37	18	52	.216	.257	.282	54	-25	0	0	0	.992	-6	*C-122	-2.6
1970	Was-A	104	328	25	75	17	3	6	30	10	47	.229	.254	.354	69	-15	0	0	0	.988	-1	*C-100	-1.2
1971	Was-A	94	311	19	63	9	1	5	26	14	52	.203	.239	.286	51	-21	0	3	-2	.985	-4	C-83	-2.7
1972	Atl-N	49	136	8	28	3	0	2	10	4	28	.206	.229	.272	38	-11	0	1	-1	.975	-6	C-43	-1.8
1973	Atl-N	82	236	18	51	7	0	7	18	11	36	.216	.244	.335	58	-14	0	2	-1	.977	6	C-78	-0.7
1974	Atl-N	42	104	5	21	0	0	0	8	5	17	.202	.239	.202	23	-11	0	0	0	.986	-1	C-33	-1.1
Total	10	859	2786	214	627	87	12	50	252	101	430	.225	.254	.319	64	-137	2	10	-5	.985	-38	C-811	-15.4

■ RAUL CASANOVA
Casanova, Raul b: 8/23/72, Humacao, P.R. BB/TR, 6', 192 lbs. Deb: 5/24/96

YEAR	TM/L	G	AB	R	H	2B	3B	HR	RBI	BB	SO	AVG	OBP	SLG	PRO+	BR/A	SB	CS	SBR	FA	FR	G/POS	TPR
1996	Det-A	25	85	6	16	1	0	4	9	6	18	.188	.242	.341	45	-7	0	0	0	.978	-4	C-22/D-3	-0.9

■ GEORGE CASE
Case, George Washington b: 11/11/15, Trenton, N.J. d: 1/23/89, Trenton, N.J. BR/TR, 6', 183 lbs. Deb: 9/8/37 C

YEAR	TM/L	G	AB	R	H	2B	3B	HR	RBI	BB	SO	AVG	OBP	SLG	PRO+	BR/A	SB	CS	SBR	FA	FR	G/POS	TPR
1937	Was-A	22	90	14	26	6	2	0	11	3	5	.289	.312	.400	82	-3	2	1	0	.945	-0	O-22	-0.4
1938	Was-A	107	433	69	132	27	3	2	40	39	28	.305	.362	.395	96	-3	11	6	0	.964	-4	*O-101	-0.9
1939	Was-A☆	128	530	103	160	20	7	2	35	56	36	.302	.369	.377	98	-0	51	17	5	.955	3	*O-123	0.3
1940	Was-A	154	656	109	192	29	5	5	56	52	39	.293	.349	.375	94	-6	35	10	5	.970	1	*O-154	-0.8
1941	Was-A	153	649	95	176	32	8	2	53	51	37	.271	.325	.354	84	-16	33	9	5	.975	15	*O-151	-0.6
1942	Was-A	125	513	101	164	26	2	5	43	44	30	.320	.377	.407	122	15	44	6	10	.951	-2	*O-120	1.7
1943	Was-A★	141	613	102	180	36	5	0	52	41	27	.294	.341	.374	113	8	61	14	10	.985	1	*O-140	1.3
1944	Was-A	119	464	63	116	14	2	2	32	49	22	.250	.326	.302	83	-9	49	18	4	.970	-5	*O-114	-0.6
1945	Was-A†	123	504	72	148	19	5	1	31	49	27	.294	.360	.357	118	12	30	16	-1	.979	13	*O-123	1.8
1946	Cle-A	118	484	46	109	23	4	1	22	34	38	.225	.280	.295	65	-24	28	11	2	.983	-4	*O-118	-3.4
1947	Was-A	36	80	11	12	1	0	0	2	8	8	.150	.227	.162	10	-10	5	1	0	.963	0	O-21	-1.0
Total	11	1226	5016	785	1415	233	43	21	377	426	297	.282	.341	.358	95	-36	349	109	39	.970	30	*O-1187	-2.6

■ DENNIS CASEY
Casey, Dennis Patrick b: 3/30/1858, Binghamton, N.Y. d: 1/19/09, Binghamton, N.Y. BL/TR, 5'9", 164 lbs. Deb: 8/18/1884 F

YEAR	TM/L	G	AB	R	H	2B	3B	HR	RBI	BB	SO	AVG	OBP	SLG	PRO+	BR/A	SB	CS	SBR	FA	FR	G/POS	TPR
1884	Wil-U	2	8	1	2	1	0	0		0		.250	.250	.375	85	-0				1.000	-0	/O-2	0.0
	Bal-a	37	149	20	37	7	4	3		5		.248	.273	.409	115	2				.898	-1	O-37	0.1
1885	Bal-a	63	264	50	76	10	5	3	29	21		.288	.347	.398	137	12				.821	-5	O-63	0.4
Total	2	102	421	71	115	18	9	6	29	26		.273	.320	.401	128	13				.847	-6	O-102	0.5

■ DOC CASEY
Casey, James Patrick b: 3/15/1870, Lawrence, Mass. d: 12/31/36, Detroit, Mich. BB/TR, 5'6", 157 lbs. Deb: 9/14/1898

YEAR	TM/L	G	AB	R	H	2B	3B	HR	RBI	BB	SO	AVG	OBP	SLG	PRO+	BR/A	SB	CS	SBR	FA	FR	G/POS	TPR
1898	Was-N	28	112	13	31	2	0	0	15	3		.277	.302	.295	71	-4	15			.893	-3	3-22/S-4,C-3	-0.6
1899	Was-N	9	34	3	4	2	0	0	2	2		.118	.167	.176	-6	-5	1			.853	-1	/3-9	-0.5
	Bro-N	134	525	75	141	14	8	1	43	25		.269	.313	.331	75	-19	27			.892	-19	*3-134	-3.3
	Yr	143	559	78	145	16	8	1	45	27		.259	.304	.322	70	-24	28			.889	-20	*3-143	-3.8
1900	Bro-N	1	3	0	1	0	0	0	0	1		.333	.500	.333	125	0	0			1.000	-0	/3-1	0.0
1901	Det-A	128	540	105	153	16	9	2	46	32		.283	.335	.357	88	-9	34			.887	5	*3-127	-0.2
1902	Det-A	132	520	69	142	18	7	3	55	44		.273	.338	.352	90	-7	22			.904	2	*3-132	-0.4
1903	Chi-N	112	435	56	126	8	3	1	40	19		.290	.324	.329	89	-7	11			.915	-19	*3-112	-2.4
1904	Chi-N	136	548	71	147	20	4	1	43	18		.268	.300	.325	93	-6	21			.911	-10	*3-134/C-2	-1.2
1905	Chi-N	144	526	66	122	21	10	1	56	41		.232	.295	.316	79	-14	22			.949	-9	*3-142/S-1	-1.9
1906	Bro-N	149	571	71	133	17	6	0	34	52		.233	.306	.291	93	-4	22			.919	-17	*3-149	-1.8
1907	Bro-N	141	527	55	122	19	3	0	19	34		.231	.282	.279	82	-12	16			.955	-6	*3-138	-1.6
Total	10	1114	4341	584	1122	137	52	9	354	270		.258	.310	.320	85	-86	191			.915	-77	*3-1100/C-5,S-5	-13.9

■ JOE CASEY
Casey, Joseph Felix b: 8/15/1887, Boston, Mass. d: 6/2/66, Melrose, Mass. BR/TR, 5'9", 180 lbs. Deb: 10/1/09

YEAR	TM/L	G	AB	R	H	2B	3B	HR	RBI	BB	SO	AVG	OBP	SLG	PRO+	BR/A	SB	CS	SBR	FA	FR	G/POS	TPR
1909	Det-A	3	5	1	0	0	0	0		1		.000	.167	.000	-45	-1	0			1.000	2	/C-3	0.1
1910	Det-A	23	62	3	12	3	0	0	2	2		.194	.231	.242	45	-4	4			.964	5	C-22	0.4
1911	Det-A	15	33	2	5	0	0	0	3	3		.152	.222	.152	5	-3	0			.956	-3	C-12/O-3	-0.6
1918	Was-A	9	17	3	4	0	0	0	2	2		.235	.316	.235	68	-1	1			1.000	2	/C-8	0.2
Total	4	50	117	9	21	3	0	0	7	8	2	.179	.238	.205	32	-10	1			.970	6	/C-45,O-3	0.1

■ BOB CASEY
Casey, Orrin Robinson b: 1/26/1859, Adolphustown, Ontario, Canada d: 11/28/36, Syracuse, N.Y. 5'11", 190 lbs. Deb: 7/17/1882

YEAR	TM/L	G	AB	R	H	2B	3B	HR	RBI	BB	SO	AVG	OBP	SLG	PRO+	BR/A	SB	CS	SBR	FA	FR	G/POS	TPR
1882	Det-N	9	39	5	9	2	1	1	7	0	15	.231	.231	.410	101	-0				.667	-5	/3-8,2-1	-0.4

■ DAVE CASH
Cash, David b: 6/11/48, Utica, N.Y. BR/TR, 5'11", 175 lbs. Deb: 9/13/69 C

YEAR	TM/L	G	AB	R	H	2B	3B	HR	RBI	BB	SO	AVG	OBP	SLG	PRO+	BR/A	SB	CS	SBR	FA	FR	G/POS	TPR
1969	Pit-N	18	61	8	17	3	1	0	4	9	9	.279	.371	.361	108	1	2	0	1	.990	5	2-17	0.8
1970	*Pit-N	64	210	30	66	7	6	1	28	17	25	.314	.368	.419	113	4	5	2	0	.974	9	2-55	1.4
1971	*Pit-N	123	478	79	138	17	4	2	34	16	33	.289	.351	.354	101	1	13	5	1	.987	6	*2-105,3-24/S-3	1.7
1972	*Pit-N	99	425	58	120	22	4	3	30	22	31	.282	.318	.374	98	-2	9	9	-3	.992	28	2-97	3.0
1973	Pit-N	116	436	59	118	21	2	2	31	38	36	.271	.329	.342	88	-7	2	5	-2	.979	6	2-92,3-17	0.2
1974	Phi-N★	162	687	89	206	26	11	2	58	46	33	.300	.352	.378	100	0	20	8	1	.977	29	*2-162	4.0
1975	Phi-N★	162	699	111	213	40	3	4	57	56	34	.305	.360	.388	103	4	13	6	0	.981	9	*2-162	2.3
1976	*Phi-N★	160	666	92	189	19	12	1	56	54	13	.284	.339	.345	92	-6	10	12	-4	.988	-2	*2-158	-0.2
1977	Mon-N	153	650	91	188	42	7	0	43	52	33	.289	.344	.375	96	-4	21	12	-1	.986	-11	*2-153	-0.5
1978	Mon-N	159	658	66	166	23	3	3	43	37	29	.252	.292	.315	70	-27	12	6	0	.986	-30	*2-159	-4.9
1979	Mon-N	76	187	24	60	11	1	2	19	12	13	.321	.382	.422	114	4	7	5	0	.971	-6	2-47	0.0
1980	SD-N	130	397	25	90	14	2	1	23	35	21	.227	.289	.280	63	-20	6	5	-1	.987	4	*2-123	-1.1
Total	12	1422	5554	732	1571	243	56	21	426	424	309	.283	.336	.358	93	-51	120	74	-8	.984	43	*2-1330/3-41,S-3	6.7

■ NORM CASH
Cash, Norman Dalton b: 11/10/34, Justiceburg, Tex. d: 10/12/86, Beaver Island, Mich. BL/TL, 6', 190 lbs. Deb: 6/18/58

YEAR	TM/L	G	AB	R	H	2B	3B	HR	RBI	BB	SO	AVG	OBP	SLG	PRO+	BR/A	SB	CS	SBR	FA	FR	G/POS	TPR
1958	Chi-A	13	8	2	2	0	0	0	0	0	1	.250	.250	.250	39	-1	0	0	0	1.000	-1	/O-4	-0.2

YEAR	TM/L	G	AB	R	H	2B	3B	HR	RBI	BB	SO	AVG	OBP	SLG	PRO+	BR/A	SB	CS	SBR	FA	FR	G/POS	TPR
1959	*Chi-A	58	104	16	25	0	1	4	16	18	9	.240	.378	.375	109	2	1	1	-0	.984	-1	1-31	-0.1
1960	Det-A	121	353	64	101	16	3	18	63	65	58	.286	.406	.501	140	22	4	2	0	.991	-2	1-99/O-4	1.3
1961	Det-A★	159	535	119	**193**	22	8	41	132	124	85	**.361**	**.488**	.662	198	82	11	5	0	.992	5	*1-157	7.1
1962	Det-A	148	507	94	123	16	2	39	89	104	82	.243	.385	.513	134	27	6	3	0	.992	7	*1-146/O-3	2.4
1963	Det-A	147	493	67	133	19	1	26	79	89	76	.270	.388	.471	135	26	2	3	-1	.994	2	*1-142	2.1
1964	Det-A	144	479	63	123	15	5	23	83	70	66	.257	.355	.453	121	15	2	1	0	**.997**	4	*1-137	1.3
1965	Det-A	142	467	79	124	23	1	30	82	77	62	.266	.374	.512	147	30	6	6	-2	.992	5	*1-139	2.8
1966	Det-A★	160	603	98	168	18	3	32	93	66	91	.279	.354	.478	133	26	2	1	0	.988	4	*1-158	2.0
1967	Det-A	152	488	64	118	16	5	22	72	81	100	.242	.354	.430	127	18	3	2	0	**.995**	9	*1-146	2.0
1968	*Det-A	127	411	50	108	15	1	25	63	39	70	.263	.331	.487	141	19	1	1	-0	.992	9	*1-117	2.2
1969	Det-A	142	483	81	135	15	4	22	74	63	80	.280	.370	.464	126	17	2	1	0	.994	8	*1-134	1.3
1970	Det-A	130	370	58	96	18	2	15	53	72	58	.259	.387	.441	127	16	0	1	-1	.989	2	*1-114	0.8
1971	Det-A★	135	452	72	128	10	3	32	91	59	86	.283	.375	.531	148	28	1	0	0	.992	-0	*1-131	1.8
1972	*Det-A	137	440	51	114	16	0	22	61	50	64	.259	.340	.445	128	15	0	2	-1	.993	-0	*1-134	0.3
1973	Det-A	121	363	51	95	19	0	19	40	47	73	.262	.359	.471	124	11	0	0	0	.991	2	*1-114/D-3	0.6
1974	Det-A	53	149	17	34	3	2	7	12	19	30	.228	.327	.416	109	2	1	1	0	.985	-1	1-44	-0.2
Total	17	2089	6705	1046	1820	241	41	377	1103	1043	1091	.271	.374	.488	138	355	43	30	-5	.992	50	*1-1943/O-11,D-3	27.5

■ RON CASH

Cash, Ronald Forrest   b: 11/20/49, Atlanta, Ga.   BR/TR, 6', 180 lbs.   Deb: 9/4/73

YEAR	TM/L	G	AB	R	H	2B	3B	HR	RBI	BB	SO	AVG	OBP	SLG	PRO+	BR/A	SB	CS	SBR	FA	FR	G/POS	TPR
1973	Det-A	14	39	8	16	1	1	0	6	5	5	.410	.477	.487	161	3	0	0	0	.900	-2	/O-7,3-6	0.1
1974	Det-A	20	62	6	14	2	0	0	5	0	11	.226	.226	.258	38	-5	0	1	-1	.979	-1	1-15,3/4	-0.8
Total	2	34	101	14	30	3	1	0	11	5	16	.297	.330	.347	89	-2	0	1	-1	.950	-3	/1-15,3-10,O-7	-0.7

■ ED CASKIN

Caskin, Edward James   b: 12/30/1851, Danvers, Mass.   d: 10/9/24, Danvers, Mass.   BR/TR, 5'9.5", 165 lbs.   Deb: 5/1/1879

YEAR	TM/L	G	AB	R	H	2B	3B	HR	RBI	BB	SO	AVG	OBP	SLG	PRO+	BR/A	SB	CS	SBR	FA	FR	G/POS	TPR
1879	Tro-N	70	304	32	78	13	2	0	21	2	14	.257	.261	.313	95	-1				.902	6	S-42,C-22/2-6	0.8
1880	Tro-N	82	333	36	75	5	4	0	28	7	24	.225	.241	.264	68	-12				.885	7	*S-82/C-2	0.1
1881	Tro-N	63	234	33	53	7	1	0	21	13	29	.226	.267	.265	65	-9				.906	1	*S-63	-0.5
1883	NY-N	95	383	47	91	11	2	1	40	14	25	.238	.264	.285	68	-14				.855	-5	*S-81,2-13/C-1	-1.5
1884	NY-N	100	351	49	81	11	1	1	40	34	55	.231	.299	.276	80	-7				.883	5	*S-96/C-6	-0.1
1885	StL-N	71	262	31	47	3	0	0	12	12	22	.179	.215	.191	34	-18				.884	-4	3-69/C-2,S-1	-1.9
1886	NY-N	1	4	1	2	0	0	0	1	0	0	.500	.500	.500	203	0	0			1.000	-1	/S-1	-0.1
Total	7	482	1871	229	427	50	10	2	163	82	170	.228	.261	.269	70	-61				.883	9	S-366/3-69,C-33,2	-3.1

■ HARRY CASSADY

Cassady, Harry Delbert (b: Harry Delbert Cassaday)   b: 7/20/1880, Bellflower, Ill.   d: 4/19/69, Fresno, Cal.   BL/TL, 5'8", 145 lbs.   Deb: 8/8/04

YEAR	TM/L	G	AB	R	H	2B	3B	HR	RBI	BB	SO	AVG	OBP	SLG	PRO+	BR/A	SB	CS	SBR	FA	FR	G/POS	TPR
1904	Pit-N	12	44	8	9	0	0	0	3	2		.205	.239	.205	36	-3	2			.867	-1	O-12	-0.5
1905	Was-A	10	30	1	4	0	0	0	4	0		.133	.133	.133	-16	-4	0			1.000	0	/O-9	-0.4
Total	2	22	74	9	13	0	0	0	4	2		.176	.197	.176	17	-7	2			.933	-1	/O-21	-0.9

■ JOHN CASSIDY

Cassidy, John P.   b: 1857, Brooklyn, N.Y.   d: 7/2/1891, Brooklyn, N.Y.   BR/TL, 5'8", 168 lbs.   Deb: 4/24/1875

YEAR	TM/L	G	AB	R	H	2B	3B	HR	RBI	BB	SO	AVG	OBP	SLG	PRO+	BR/A	SB	CS	SBR	FA	FR	G/POS	TPR
1875	Atl-n	41	166	14	29	3	2	1	6	0	4	.175	.175	.235	47	-7	0	0	0	.782	-8	P-30,O-12,1-10/2-2	-1.0
	NH-n	6	22	3	3	1	0	0	1	0	1	.136	.136	.182	11	-2	0	1	-1	.988	1	/1-6	-0.2
	Yr	47	188	17	32	4	2	1	7	0	5	.170	.170	.229	43	-9	0	1	-1	.782	-8	P-30,1-16,O-12/2-2	-1.2
1876	Har-N	12	47	6	13	2	0	0	8	1	0	.277	.292	.319	95	-0				1.000	1	/O-8,1-4	0.0
1877	Har-N	60	251	43	95	10	5	0	27	3	3	.378	.386	.458	184	24				.722	-5	*O-58/P-2	1.4
1878	Chi-N	60	256	33	68	7	1	0	29	9	11	.266	.291	.301	89	-4				.810	2	*O-60/C-1	0.2
1879	Tro-N	9	37	4	7	1	0	0	1	2	4	.189	.231	.216	52	-2				.889	-2	/O-8,1-2	-0.4
1880	Tro-N	83	352	40	89	14	8	0	29	12	34	.253	.277	.338	102	0				.880	-2	*O-82/2-1	-0.4
1881	Tro-N	85	370	57	82	13	3	1	11	18	21	.222	.258	.281	66	-15				.872	-9	*O-84/S-1	-2.4
1882	Tro-N	29	121	14	21	3	1	0	9	3	16	.174	.194	.215	32	-9				.778	-9	O-16,3-13	-1.6
1883	Pro-N	89	366	46	87	16	5	0	42	9	38	.238	.256	.309	69	-14				.864	1	*O-88/2-1,1-1	-1.6
1884	Bro-a	106	433	57	109	11	6	2	19			.252	.286	.319	96	-2				.847	-8	*O-101/3-4,S-1	-1.1
1885	Bro-a	54	221	36	47	6	2	1	28	8		.213	.250	.271	64	-9				.852	-7	O-54	-1.6
Total	10	587	2454	336	618	83	31	4	184	84	127	.252	.278	.316	89	-30				.845	-31	O-559/3-17,1S2PC	-7.1

■ JOE CASSIDY

Cassidy, Joseph Phillip   b: 2/8/1883, Chester, Pa.   d: 3/25/06, Chester, Pa.   BR/TR,   Deb: 4/18/04

YEAR	TM/L	G	AB	R	H	2B	3B	HR	RBI	BB	SO	AVG	OBP	SLG	PRO+	BR/A	SB	CS	SBR	FA	FR	G/POS	TPR
1904	Was-A	152	581	63	140	12	**19**	1	33	15		.241	.265	.332	90	-9	17			.937	12	S-99,O-32,3-23	0.6
1905	Was-A	151	576	67	124	16	4	1	43	25		.215	.250	.262	65	-24	23			.934	**34**	*S-151	1.5
Total	2	303	1157	130	264	28	23	2	76	40		.228	.258	.297	78	-32	40			.935	46	S-250/O-32,3-23	2.1

■ PETE CASSIDY

Cassidy, Peter Francis   b: 4/8/1873, Wilmington, Del.   d: 7/9/29, Wilmington, Del.   BR/TR, 5'10", 165 lbs.   Deb: 4/18/1896

YEAR	TM/L	G	AB	R	H	2B	3B	HR	RBI	BB	SO	AVG	OBP	SLG	PRO+	BR/A	SB	CS	SBR	FA	FR	G/POS	TPR
1896	Lou-N	49	184	16	39	1	1	0	12	7	7	.212	.256	.228	29	-19	5			.973	-7	1-38,S-11	-2.2
1899	Bro-N	6	20	2	3	1	0	0	4	1		.150	.261	.200	27	-2	1			1.000	-4	/3-3,S-2	-0.5
	Was-N	46	178	21	56	13	0	3	32	9		.315	.365	.438	121	5	5			.970	-2	1-37/3-6,S-3	0.3
	Yr	52	198	23	59	14	0	3	36	10		.298	.353	.414	111	3	6			.970	-5	1-37/3-9,S-5	-0.2
Total	2	101	382	39	98	15	1	3	48	17	7	.257	.307	.325	72	-16	11			.972	-13	/1-75,S-16,3-9	-2.4

■ JACK CASSINI

Cassini, Jack Dempsey "Gabby" or "Scat"   b: 10/26/19, Dearborn, Mich.   BR/TR, 5'10", 175 lbs.   Deb: 4/19/49

YEAR	TM/L	G	AB	R	H	2B	3B	HR	RBI	BB	SO	AVG	OBP	SLG	PRO+	BR/A	SB	CS	SBR	FA	FR	G/POS	TPR
1949	Pit-N	8	0	3	0	0	0	0	0	0	0	—	—	—	—		0	0		.000	0	R	0.0

■ PEDRO CASTELLANO

Castellano, Pedro Orlando (Arrieta)   b: 3/11/70, Lara, Venez.   BR/TR, 6'1", 175 lbs.   Deb: 5/30/93

YEAR	TM/L	G	AB	R	H	2B	3B	HR	RBI	BB	SO	AVG	OBP	SLG	PRO+	BR/A	SB	CS	SBR	FA	FR	G/POS	TPR
1993	Col-N	34	71	12	13	2	0	3	8	8	16	.183	.266	.338	52	-5	1	1	-0	.909	-1	3-13,1-10/S-5,2-4	-0.7
1995	Col-N	4	5	0	0	0	0	0	0	2	3	.000	.286	.000	-13	-1	0	0	0	1.000	-1	/3-3	-0.2
1996	Col-N	13	17	1	2	0	0	0	2	3	6	.118	.286	.118	9	-2	0	0	0	1.000	1	/2-3,3-1,O-1	-0.2
Total	3	51	93	13	15	2	0	3	9	13	25	.161	.271	.280	39	-8	1	1	-0	.917	-2	/3-17,1-10,2-7,SO	-1.1

■ JIM CASTIGLIA

Castiglia, James Vincent   b: 9/30/18, Passaic, N.J.   BL/TR, 5'11", 200 lbs.   Deb: 4/14/42

YEAR	TM/L	G	AB	R	H	2B	3B	HR	RBI	BB	SO	AVG	OBP	SLG	PRO+	BR/A	SB	CS	SBR	FA	FR	G/POS	TPR
1942	Phi-A	16	18	2	7	0	0	0	2	1	3	.389	.421	.389	129	1				.875	-1	/C-3	0.0

■ PETE CASTIGLIONE

Castiglione, Peter Paul   b: 2/13/21, Greenwich, Conn.   BR/TR, 5'11", 175 lbs.   Deb: 9/10/47

YEAR	TM/L	G	AB	R	H	2B	3B	HR	RBI	BB	SO	AVG	OBP	SLG	PRO+	BR/A	SB	CS	SBR	FA	FR	G/POS	TPR
1947	Pit-N	13	50	6	14	0	0	0	1	2	5	.280	.308	.280	55	-3	0			.970	1	S-13	-0.1
1948	Pit-N	4	2	0	0	0	0	0	0	0	0	.000	.000	.000	-98	-1	1			1.000	0	/S-1	0.0
1949	Pit-N	118	448	57	120	20	2	6	43	20	43	.268	.299	.362	74	-17	2			.957	-1	3-98,S-17/O-2	-1.9
1950	Pit-N	94	263	29	67	10	3	3	22	23	23	.255	.317	.350	73	-10	1			.970	-17	3-35,S-29/2-9,1-3	-2.6
1951	Pit-N	132	482	62	126	19	4	7	42	34	28	.261	.311	.361	78	-15	2	2	-1	.957	4	3-99,S-28	-1.1
1952	Pit-N	67	214	27	57	9	1	4	18	17	8	.266	.323	.374	90	-3	3	3	-1	.951	4	3-57/1-1,O-1	0.1
1953	Pit-N	45	159	14	33	2	1	4	21	5	14	.208	.236	.308	41	-14	1	1	-0	.978	4	3-43	-1.1
	StL-N	67	52	9	9	2	0	0	3	2	5	.173	.204	.212	9	-7	0			.967	8	3-51/2-9,S-3	0.1
	Yr	112	211	23	42	4	1	4	24	7	19	.199	.228	.284	33	-21	1	1	-0	.976	12	3-94/2-9,S-3	-1.0
1954	StL-N	5	0	1	0	0	0	0	0	0	0	—	—	—	—		0	0		.000	0	/3-5	0.0
Total	8	545	1670	205	426	62	11	24	150	103	126	.255	.300	.349	71	-70	10	6		.960	4	3-388/S-91,2-18,10	-6.6

■ VINNY CASTILLA

Castilla, Vinicio (Soria)   b: 7/4/67, Oaxaca, Mexico   BR/TR, 6'1", 175 lbs.   Deb: 9/1/91

YEAR	TM/L	G	AB	R	H	2B	3B	HR	RBI	BB	SO	AVG	OBP	SLG	PRO+	BR/A	SB	CS	SBR	FA	FR	G/POS	TPR
1991	Atl-N	12	5	1	1	0	0	0	0	0	2	.200	.200	.200	12	-1	0	0	0	1.000	1	S-12	0.1
1992	Atl-N	9	16	1	4	1	0	0	1	1	4	.250	.294	.313	79	-0	0	0	0	.875	0	/3-4,S-4	0.0
1993	Col-N	105	337	36	86	9	7	9	30	13	45	.255	.287	.404	71	-15	2	5	-2	.975	8	*S-104	-0.2
1994	Col-N	52	130	16	43	11	1	3	18	7	23	.331	.365	.500	105	1	2	1	0	.984	0	S-18,2-14/3-9,1-2	0.2
1995	*Col-N★	139	527	82	163	34	2	32	90	30	87	.309	.351	.564	106	-0	2	4	0	.958	-7	*3-137/S-5	-1.1
1996	Col-N	160	629	97	191	34	0	40	113	35	88	.304	.345	.548	102	-4	7	2	1	.960	28	*3-160	2.4
Total	6	477	1644	233	488	89	10	84	252	86	249	.297	.336	.516	97	-19	13	16	-6	.959	31	3-310,S-143/2-14,1	1.4

YEAR	TM/L	G	AB	R	H	2B	3B	HR	RBI	BB	SO	AVG	OBP	SLG	PRO+	BR/A	SB	CS	SBR	FA	FR	G/POS	TPR

■ ALBERTO CASTILLO   Castillo, Alberto Terrero b: 2/10/70, San Juan De La Maguana, D.R. BR/TR, 6′, 185 lbs. Deb: 5/28/95

1995	NY-N	13	29	2	3	0	0	0	0	3	9	.103	.212	.103	-14	-5	1	0	0	.974	4	C-12	0.0
1996	NY-N	6	11	1	4	0	0	0	0	0	4	.364	.364	.364	99	-0	0	0	0	1.000	1	/C-6	0.1
Total	2	19	40	3	7	0	0	0	0	3	13	.175	.250	.175	15	-5	1	0	0	.980	5	/C-18	0.1

■ TONY CASTILLO   Castillo, Anthony b: 6/14/57, San Jose, Cal. BR/TR, 6′4″, 190 lbs. Deb: 9/22/78

1978	SD-N	5	8	0	1	0	0	0	1	0	2	.125	.125	.125	-33	-1	0	0	0	.950	1	/C-5	0.0

■ BRAULIO CASTILLO   Castillo, Braulio Robinson Medrano (b: Braulio Robinson Medrano (Castillo)) b: 5/13/68, Elias Pina, D.R. BR/TR, 6′, 160 lbs. Deb: 8/18/91

1991	Phi-N	28	52	3	9	3	0	0	2	1	15	.173	.189	.231	18	-6	1	1	-0	.977	-2	O-26	-0.9
1992	Phi-N	28	76	12	15	3	1	2	7	4	15	.197	.237	.342	62	-4	1	0	0	.956	-2	O-24	-0.6
Total	2	56	128	15	24	6	1	2	9	5	30	.188	.218	.297	44	-10	2	1	0	.966	-4	/O-50	-1.5

■ MANNY CASTILLO   Castillo, Esteban Manuel Antonio (Cabrera) b: 4/1/57, Santo Domingo, D.R. BB/TR, 5′9″, 160 lbs. Deb: 9/1/80

1980	KC-A	7	10	1	2	0	0	0	0	0	0	.200	.200	.200	10	-1	0	0	0	1.000	2	/3-3,2-1,D-2	0.0
1982	Sea-A	138	506	49	130	29	1	3	49	22	35	.257	.291	.336	70	-21	2	8	-4	.938	-24	*3-130/2-9	-5.3
1983	Sea-A	91	203	13	42	6	3	0	24	7	20	.207	.237	.266	37	-17	1	1	-0	.971	8	3-55,1-11/2-5,PD	-1.1
Total	3	236	719	63	174	35	4	3	73	29	55	.242	.274	.314	59	-40	3	9	-5	.949	-15	3-188/2-15,1-11,DP	-6.4

■ JUAN CASTILLO   Castillo, Juan (Bryas) b: 1/25/62, San Pedro De Macoris, D.R. BB/TR, 5′11″, 162 lbs. Deb: 4/12/86

1986	Mil-A	26	54	6	9	0	1	0	5	5	12	.167	.250	.204	24	-6	1	1	-0	1.000	5	2-17/S-4,3-2,0-1,D	-0.1
1987	Mil-A	116	321	44	72	11	4	3	28	33	76	.224	.303	.312	62	-17	15	7	0	.973	-6	2-97,S-13/3-7	-1.7
1988	Mil-A	54	90	10	20	0	0	0	2	3	14	.222	.247	.222	32	-8	2	0	1	.932	7	2-18,3-17,S-13/OD	0.0
1989	Mil-A	3	4	0	0	0	0	0	3	0	2	.000	.000	.000	-99	-1	0	0	0	1.000	1	/2-3	0.0
Total	4	199	469	60	101	11	5	3	38	41	104	.215	.284	.279	51	-32	18	8	1	.972	6	2-135/S-30,3-26,DO	-1.8

■ LUIS CASTILLO   Castillo, Luis Antonio (Donato) b: 9/12/75, San Pedro De Macoris, D.R. BB/TR, 5′11″, 145 lbs. Deb: 8/8/96

1996	Fla-N	41	164	26	43	2	1	1	8	14	46	.262	.320	.305	69	-7	17	4	3	.986	1	2-41	-0.1

■ MARTY CASTILLO   Castillo, Martin Horace b: 1/16/57, Long Beach, Cal. BR/TR, 6′1″, 190 lbs. Deb: 8/19/81

1981	Det-A	6	8	1	1	0	0	0	0	0	0	.125	.125	.125	-27	-1	0	0	0	1.000	0	/3-4,C-1,O-1	0.1
1982	Det-A	1	0	0	0	0	0	0	0	0	0	—	—	—	—	0	0	0	0	1.000	-0	/C-1	0.0
1983	Det-A	67	119	10	23	4	0	2	10	7	22	.193	.238	.277	42	-9	2	0	1	.990	4	3-58,C-10	-0.5
1984	*Det-A	70	141	16	33	5	2	4	17	10	33	.234	.285	.383	83	-3	1	0	0	.970	-2	C-36,3-33/D-1	0.0
1985	Det-A	57	84	4	10	2	0	2	5	2	19	.119	.140	.214	-5	-12	0	2	-1	.977	7	C-32,3-25	-0.5
Total	5	201	352	31	67	11	2	8	32	19	76	.190	.232	.301	46	-26	3	2	-0	.978	15	3-120/C-80,D-1,O-1	-0.9

■ CARMEN CASTILLO   Castillo, Monte Carmelo b: 6/8/58, San Pedro De Macoris, D.R. BR/TR, 6′1″, 190 lbs. Deb: 7/17/82

1982	Cle-A	47	120	11	25	4	0	2	11	6	17	.208	.258	.292	51	-8	0	0	0	.978	-3	O-43/D-2	-1.2
1983	Cle-A	23	36	9	10	2	1	1	3	4	6	.278	.366	.472	124	1	1	1	-0	.929	-1	O-19/D-1	0.0
1984	Cle-A	87	211	36	55	9	2	10	36	21	32	.261	.333	.464	116	4	1	3	-2	.933	-6	O-70/D-5	-0.5
1985	Cle-A	67	184	27	45	5	1	11	25	11	40	.245	.298	.462	105	1	3	0	1	.953	-2	O-51/D-9	-0.2
1986	Cle-A	85	205	34	57	9	0	8	32	9	48	.278	.312	.439	103	0	2	1	0	.939	-2	O-37,D-35	-0.3
1987	Cle-A	89	220	27	55	17	0	11	31	16	52	.250	.301	.477	101	-0	1	1	-0	1.000	-1	D-43,O-23	-0.3
1988	Cle-A	66	176	12	48	8	0	4	14	5	31	.273	.297	.386	87	-3	6	2	1	.933	-6	O-45/D-9	-1.0
1989	Min-A	94	218	23	56	13	3	8	33	15	40	.257	.308	.454	105	1	1	2	-1	.976	-3	O-67,D-16	-0.5
1990	Min-A	64	137	11	30	4	0	0	12	3	23	.219	.241	.248	35	-12	0	1	-1	.923	-5	D-35,O-21	-1.9
1991	Min-A	9	12	0	2	0	0	0	0	0	2	.167	.231	.333	52	-1	0	0	0	1.000	-1	/O-4,D-2	-0.2
Total	10	631	1519	190	383	71	8	55	197	90	291	.252	.300	.418	93	-18	15	11	-2	.953	-30	O-380,D-154	-6.1

■ JOHN CASTINO   Castino, John Anthony b: 10/23/54, Evanston, Ill. BR/TR, 5′11″, 175 lbs. Deb: 4/6/79

1979	Min-A	148	393	49	112	13	8	5	52	27	72	.285	.333	.397	92	-5	5	2	0	.963	18	*3-143/S-5	1.3
1980	Min-A	150	546	67	165	17	7	13	64	29	67	.302	.337	.430	101	-0	7	5	-1	.961	28	*3-138,S-18	2.6
1981	Min-A	101	381	41	102	13	9	6	36	18	52	.268	.303	.396	94	-4	4	5	-2	.975	11	3-98/2-4	0.4
1982	Min-A	117	410	48	99	12	6	6	37	36	51	.241	.306	.344	76	-13	2	5	-2	.995	4	2-96,3-21/O-6,D-1	-0.8
1983	Min-A	142	563	83	156	30	4	11	57	62	54	.277	.350	.403	103	3	4	2	0	.990	7	*2-132/3-8,D-1	1.6
1984	Min-A	8	27	5	12	1	0	0	3	5	2	.444	.531	.481	174	3	0	0	0	1.000	-1	/3-8	0.2
Total	6	666	2320	293	646	86	34	41	249	177	298	.278	.331	.398	95	-16	22	19	-5	.967	67	3-416,2-232/SOD	5.3

■ VINCE CASTINO   Castino, Vincent Charles b: 10/11/17, Willisville, Ill. d: 3/6/67, Sacramento, Cal. BR/TR, 5′9″, 175 lbs. Deb: 6/24/43

1943	Chi-A	33	101	14	23	1	0	2	16	12	11	.228	.310	.297	78	-3	0	0	0	.971	-9	C-30	-1.1
1944	Chi-A	29	78	8	18	5	0	0	3	10	13	.231	.326	.295	79	-2	0	1	-1	.990	1	C-26	0.0
1945	Chi-A	26	36	2	8	1	0	0	4	3	7	.222	.282	.250	56	-2	0	0	0	.951	-2	C-25	-0.4
Total	3	88	215	24	49	7	0	2	23	25	31	.228	.311	.288	75	-7	0	1	-1	.976	-11	/C-81	-1.5

■ DON CASTLE   Castle, Donald Hardy b: 2/1/50, Kokomo, Ind. BL/TL, 6′1″, 205 lbs. Deb: 9/11/73

1973	Tex-A	4	13	0	4	1	0	0	2	1	3	.308	.357	.385	114	0	0	0	0	.000	0	/D-3	0.0

■ JOHN CASTLE   Castle, John Francis b: 6/1/1883, Honey Brook, Pa. d: 4/13/29, Philadelphia, Pa. 5′10.5″, Deb: 4/30/10

1910	Phi-N	3	4	1	1	0	0	0	0	0		.250	.250	.250	44	-0	1			.000	-1	/O-2	-0.1

■ FOSTER CASTLEMAN   Castleman, Foster Ephraim b: 1/1/31, Nashville, Tenn. BR/TR, 6′, 175 lbs. Deb: 8/4/54

1954	NY-N	13	12	0	3	0	0	0	1	0	3	.250	.308	.250	47	-1	0	0	0	.000	0	/3-2	-0.1
1955	NY-N	15	28	3	6	1	0	2	4	2	4	.214	.267	.464	89	-1	0	0	0	1.000	-3	/2-6,3-1	-0.3
1956	NY-N	124	385	33	87	16	3	14	45	15	50	.226	.259	.392	72	-16	2	1	0	.947	7	*3-107/S-2,2-1	-0.9
1957	NY-N	18	37	7	6	2	0	1	2	0	8	.162	.205	.297	33	-4	0	1	-1	.867	-2	/3-7,2-1,S-1	-0.6
1958	Bal-A	98	200	15	34	5	0	3	14	16	34	.170	.240	.240	35	-18	2	0	1	.964	-19	S-91/2-4,3-4,0-1	-3.2
Total	5	268	662	58	136	24	3	20	65	35	99	.205	.252	.341	60	-39	4	1	1	.944	-17	3-121/S-94,2-12,O-1	-5.1

■ JUAN CASTRO   Castro, Juan Gabriel b: 6/20/72, Los Mochis, Mex. BR/TR, 5′10″, 165 lbs. Deb: 9/2/95

1995	LA-N	11	4	0	1	0	0	0	0	1	1	.250	.400	.250	84	-0	0	0	0	1.000	2	/3-7,S-4	0.2
1996	*LA-N	70	132	16	26	5	3	0	5	10	27	.197	.254	.280	44	-11	1	0	0	.982	-4	S-30,3-23/2-9,0-1	-1.2
Total	2	81	136	16	27	5	3	0	5	11	28	.199	.259	.279	46	-11	1	0	0	.983	-1	/S-34,3-30,2-9,0-1	-1.0

■ LUIS CASTRO   Castro, Luis Manuel "Jud" b: 1877, Colombia d: Venezuela BR/TR, 5′7″, Deb: 4/23/02

1902	Phi-A	42	143	18	35	8	1	1	15	4		.245	.265	.336	63	-8	2			.918	-15	2-36/O-3,S-1	-2.0

■ DANNY CATER   Cater, Danny Anderson b: 2/25/40, Austin, Tex. BR/TR, 5′11.5″, 180 lbs. Deb: 4/14/64

1964	Phi-N	60	152	13	45	9	1	4	13	7	15	.296	.327	.388	102	0	1	0	0	.981	-1	O-39/1-7,3-1	-0.2
1965	Chi-A	142	514	74	139	18	4	14	55	33	65	.270	.318	.403	110	5	3	3	-1	.978	-9	*O-127,3-11/1-3	-1.2
1966	Chi-A	21	60	3	11	1	0	0	6	0	10	.183	.197	.233	25	-6	3	1	0	.909	-3	O-18	-1.1
	KC-A	116	425	47	124	16	3	7	52	28	37	.292	.337	.393	113	6	1	4	-2	.994	-5	1-53,3-42,O-22	-0.6
	Yr	137	485	50	135	17	4	7	56	28	47	.278	.320	.373	102	1	4	5	-2	.994	-8	1-53,3-42,O-40	-1.7
1967	KC-A	142	529	55	143	17	4	6	46	34	56	.270	.319	.340	98	-2	4	5	-3	.916	-15	3-56,O-55,1-44	-2.6
1968	Oak-A	147	504	53	146	28	3	6	62	35	43	.290	.338	.393	127	15	8	7	-2	.995	-4	*1-121,O-20/2-1	-0.1
1969	Oak-A	152	584	64	153	24	2	10	76	28	40	.262	.296	.361	87	-12	1	4	-2	.992	6	*1-132,O-20/2-4	-2.0
1970	NY-A	155	582	64	175	26	5	6	76	34	44	.301	.341	.393	108	5	2	0	-4	.992	-4	*1-131,3-42/O-7	-1.0
1971	NY-A	121	428	39	118	16	5	4	50	19	25	.276	.310	.364	96	-4	0	3	-2	.995	8	1-78,3-52	-0.4
1972	Bos-A	92	317	32	75	19	1	8	39	15	33	.237	.270	.372	87	-4	0	0	0	.993	6	1-90	-0.9
1973	Bos-A	63	195	20	61	12	0	1	24	10	22	.313	.350	.390	102	0	0	0	0	.997	1	1-37,3-21/D-3	0.0
1974	Bos-A	56	126	14	31	5	0	5	20	10	13	.246	.312	.405	98	-1	1	0	0	1.000	1	1-23,D-14	-0.1

YEAR	TM/L	G	AB	R	H	2B	3B	HR	RBI	BB	SO	AVG	OBP	SLG	PRO+	BR/A	SB	CS	SBR	FA	FR	G/POS	TPR
1975	StL-N	22	35	3	8	2	0	0	2	1	3	.229	.250	.286	47	-3	0	0	0	.981	0	1-12	-0.3
Total	12	1289	4451	491	1229	191	29	66	519	254	406	.276	.318	.377	102	-1	26	30	-10	.994	-20	1-731,O-308,3/D2	-10.5

■ ELI CATES Cates, Eli Eldo b: 1/26/1877, Greens Fork, Ind. d: 5/29/64, Anderson, Ind. BR/TR, 5'9.5", 175 lbs. Deb: 4/20/08

YEAR	TM/L	G	AB	R	H	2B	3B	HR	RBI	BB	SO	AVG	OBP	SLG	PRO+	BR/A	SB	CS	SBR	FA	FR	G/POS	TPR
1908	Was-A	40	59	5	11	1	1	0	3	6		.186	.273	.237	72	-2	0			.907	-0	P-19/2-3	-0.2

■ TED CATHER Cather, Theodore Physick b: 5/20/1889, Chester, Pa. d: 4/9/45, Elkton, Md. BR/TR, 5'10.5", 178 lbs. Deb: 9/23/12

YEAR	TM/L	G	AB	R	H	2B	3B	HR	RBI	BB	SO	AVG	OBP	SLG	PRO+	BR/A	SB	CS	SBR	FA	FR	G/POS	TPR
1912	StL-N	5	19	4	8	1	1	0	2	0	4	.421	.421	.579	176	2	1			.944	2	/O-5	0.3
1913	StL-N	67	183	16	39	8	4	0	12	9	24	.213	.250	.301	58	-11	7			.915	-7	O-57/P-1,1-1	-2.1
1914	StL-N	39	99	11	27	7	0	0	13	3	15	.273	.294	.343	90	-2	4			.981	0	O-28	-0.3
	*Bos-N	50	145	19	43	11	2	0	27	7	28	.297	.338	.400	120	3	7			.953	-9	O-48	-0.8
	Yr	89	244	30	70	18	2	0	40	10	43	.287	.320	.377	108	1	11			.966	-9	O-76	-1.1
1915	Bos-N	40	102	10	21	3	1	2	18	15	19	.206	.319	.314	96	-0	2	4	-2	.902	-7	O-32	-1.2
Total	4	201	548	60	138	30	8	2	72	34	90	.252	.300	.347	91	-7	21	4		.938	-21	O-170/1-1,P-1	-4.1

■ HOWDY CATON Caton, James Howard "Buster" b: 7/16/1896, Zanesville, Ohio d: 1/8/48, Zanesville, Ohio BR/TR, 5'6", 165 lbs. Deb: 9/17/17

YEAR	TM/L	G	AB	R	H	2B	3B	HR	RBI	BB	SO	AVG	OBP	SLG	PRO+	BR/A	SB	CS	SBR	FA	FR	G/POS	TPR
1917	Pit-N	14	57	6	12	1	2	0	4	6	7	.211	.286	.298	77	-2	0			.895	-2	S-14	-0.4
1918	Pit-N	80	303	37	71	5	7	0	17	32	16	.234	.312	.297	83	-5	12			.928	-7	S-79	-1.0
1919	Pit-N	39	102	13	18	1	2	0	5	12	10	.176	.263	.225	46	-6	2			.927	-11	S-17,3-14/O-1	-1.8
1920	Pit-N	98	352	29	83	11	5	0	27	33	19	.236	.305	.295	71	-13	4	9	-4	.929	-22	S-96	-3.4
Total	4	231	814	85	184	18	16	0	53	83	52	.226	.301	.287	72	-26	18	9		.926	-43	S-206/3-14,O-1	-6.6

■ TOM CATTERSON Catterson, Thomas Henry b: 8/25/1884, Warwick, R.I. d: 2/5/20, Portland, Maine BL/TL, 5'10", 170 lbs. Deb: 9/19/08

YEAR	TM/L	G	AB	R	H	2B	3B	HR	RBI	BB	SO	AVG	OBP	SLG	PRO+	BR/A	SB	CS	SBR	FA	FR	G/POS	TPR
1908	Bro-N	19	68	5	13	1	1	1	2	5		.191	.257	.279	74	-2	0			.976	0	O-18	-0.3
1909	Bro-N	9	18	0	4	0	0	0	1	3		.222	.333	.222	75	-0	0			.833	-2	/O-6	-0.3
Total	2	28	86	5	17	1	1	1	3	8		.198	.274	.267	75	-2	0			.957	-2	/O-24	-0.6

■ JAKE CAULFIELD Caulfield, John Joseph b: 11/23/17, Los Angeles, Cal. d: 12/16/86, San Francisco, Cal BR/TR, 5'11", 170 lbs. Deb: 4/24/46

YEAR	TM/L	G	AB	R	H	2B	3B	HR	RBI	BB	SO	AVG	OBP	SLG	PRO+	BR/A	SB	CS	SBR	FA	FR	G/POS	TPR
1946	Phi-A	44	94	13	26	8	0	0	10	4	11	.277	.306	.362	87	-2	0	0	0	.929	-6	S-31/3-1	-0.7

■ WAYNE CAUSEY Causey, James Wayne b: 12/26/36, Ruston, La. BL/TR, 5'10.5", 175 lbs. Deb: 6/5/55

YEAR	TM/L	G	AB	R	H	2B	3B	HR	RBI	BB	SO	AVG	OBP	SLG	PRO+	BR/A	SB	CS	SBR	FA	FR	G/POS	TPR
1955	Bal-A	68	175	14	34	2	1	1	9	17	25	.194	.269	.234	39	-15	0	1	-1	.912	-8	3-55/2-7,S-1	-2.4
1956	Bal-A	53	88	7	15	1	1	1	4	8	23	.170	.240	.227	26	-10	0	0	0	.980	-6	3-30/2-7	-0.7
1957	Bal-A	14	10	2	2	0	0	0	1	5	2	.200	.500	.200	105	1	0	0	0	.960	3	/2-6,3-5	0.4
1961	KC-A	104	312	37	86	14	1	8	49	37	28	.276	.352	.404	100	0	0	0	0	.955	20	3-88,S-11/2-9	2.2
1962	KC-A	117	305	40	77	14	1	4	38	41	30	.252	.345	.344	82	-7	2	0	1	.953	-2	S-51,3-26/2-9	0.1
1963	KC-A	139	554	72	155	32	4	8	44	56	54	.280	.346	.395	101	2	4	2	0	.978	5	*S-135/3-2	1.7
1964	KC-A	157	604	82	170	31	4	8	49	88	65	.281	.379	.386	110	12	0	1	-1	.967	-1	*S-131,2-17/3-9	2.2
1965	KC-A	144	513	48	134	17	3	8	34	61	48	.261	.342	.343	97	-1	1	3	-2	.972	-19	S-62/2-45,3-35	-1.5
1966	KC-A	28	79	1	18	0	0	0	5	7	6	.228	.291	.228	53	-5	1	1	0	.871	-6	3-15,S-10	-1.0
	Chi-A	78	164	23	40	8	2	0	13	24	13	.244	.340	.317	97	-0	2	0	1	.980	-16	2-60/S-1,3-1	-1.3
	Yr	106	243	24	58	8	2	0	18	31	19	.239	.325	.288	83	-5	3	0	1	.980	-21	2-60,3-16,S-11	-2.3
1967	Chi-A	124	292	21	66	10	3	1	28	32	35	.226	.305	.291	80	-7	2	5	-2	.978	-8	2-96/S-2	-1.4
1968	Chi-A	59	100	8	18	2	0	0	7	14	7	.180	.287	.200	49	-6	0	0	0	.971	-13	2-41	-2.0
	Cal-A	4	11	0	0	0	0	0	0	0	1	.000	.000	.000	-99	-3	0	0	0	1.000	1	/2-4	-0.2
	Yr	63	111	8	18	2	0	0	7	14	8	.162	.262	.180	36	-8	0	0	0	.975	-13	2-45	-2.2
	Atl-N	16	37	2	4	0	1	0	4	0	4	.108	.108	.243	3	-4	0	0	0	1.000	-4	/2-6,S-2,3-2	-1.0
Total	11	1105	3244	357	819	130	26	35	285	390	341	.252	.335	.341	89	-42	12	12	-4	.969	-42	S-406,2-307,3-268	-4.9

■ JOHN CAVANAUGH Cavanaugh, John J. b: 6/5/1900, Scranton, Pa. d: 1/14/61, New Brunswick, N.J BR/TR, 5'9", 158 lbs. Deb: 7/7/19

YEAR	TM/L	G	AB	R	H	2B	3B	HR	RBI	BB	SO	AVG	OBP	SLG	PRO+	BR/A	SB	CS	SBR	FA	FR	G/POS	TPR
1919	Phi-N	1	1	0	0	0	0	0	0	0	1	.000	.000	.000	-93	-0	0			.000	0	/3-1	0.0

■ PHIL CAVARRETTA Cavarretta, Philip Joseph b: 7/19/16, Chicago, Ill. BL/TL, 5'11.5", 175 lbs. Deb: 9/16/34 MC

YEAR	TM/L	G	AB	R	H	2B	3B	HR	RBI	BB	SO	AVG	OBP	SLG	PRO+	BR/A	SB	CS	SBR	FA	FR	G/POS	TPR
1934	Chi-N	7	21	5	8	0	1	1	6	2	3	.381	.435	.619	182	2	1			1.000	1	/1-5	0.3
1935	*Chi-N	146	589	85	162	28	12	8	82	39	61	.275	.322	.404	93	-6	4			.986	2	*1-145	-2.0
1936	Chi-N	124	458	55	125	18	1	9	56	17	36	.273	.306	.376	81	-13	8			.987	-2	*1-115	-2.6
1937	Chi-N	106	329	43	94	18	7	5	56	32	35	.286	.349	.429	106	2	7			.972	-1	O-55,1-43	-0.5
1938	*Chi-N	92	268	29	64	11	4	1	28	14	27	.239	.287	.321	65	-13	4			.962	-7	O-52,1-28	-2.4
1939	Chi-N	22	55	4	15	3	1	0	4	3	3	.273	.322	.364	82	-1	2			.991	1	1-13/O-1	-0.4
1940	Chi-N	65	193	34	54	11	4	2	22	31	18	.280	.388	.409	122	7	3			.991	-1	1-52	0.1
1941	Chi-N	107	346	46	99	18	4	6	40	53	28	.286	.384	.413	129	15	2			.992	-8	O-66,1-33	0.1
1942	Chi-N	136	482	59	130	28	4	3	54	71	42	.270	.365	.363	118	13	7			.989	6	O-70,1-61	1.2
1943	Chi-N	143	530	93	154	27	9	8	73	75	42	.291	.382	.421	134	24	3			.987	-11	*1-134/O-7	0.6
1944	Chi-N★	152	614	106	**197**	35	15	5	82	67	42	.321	.390	.451	137	31	4			.992	-7	*1-139/O-13	1.6
1945	*Chi-N†	132	498	94	177	34	10	6	97	81	34	**.355**	**.449**	.500	167	49	5			.993	1	*1-120,O-11	3.8
1946	Chi-N★	139	510	89	150	28	10	8	78	88	54	.294	.401	.435	140	30	2			.967	1	O-86,1-51	2.4
1947	Chi-N★	127	459	56	144	22	5	2	63	58	35	.314	.391	.397	114	11	2			.977	-0	*O-100,1-24	0.4
1948	Chi-N	111	334	41	93	16	5	3	40	35	29	.278	.349	.383	102	1	4			.998	1	1-41,O-40	-0.1
1949	Chi-N	105	360	46	106	22	4	8	49	45	31	.294	.374	.444	122	12	1			.993	9	1-70,O-25	1.8
1950	Chi-N	82	256	49	70	11	1	10	31	40	31	.273	.376	.441	115	6	1			.986	-1	1-67/O-3	0.4
1951	Chi-N	89	206	24	64	7	1	6	28	27	28	.311	.393	.442	122	7	0	0	0	.994	4	1-53,M	0.8
1952	Chi-N	41	63	7	15	1	1	3	9	9	8	.238	.333	.333	84	-1	1	0	0	.991	1	1-13,M	-0.1
1953	Chi-N	27	21	3	6	3	0	0	3	6	4	.286	.444	.429	126	1	0	0	0	.000	0	HM	0.1
1954	Chi-A	71	158	21	50	6	0	3	24	26	12	.316	.419	.411	124	7	4	0	1	.993	-4	1-44/O-9	0.2
1955	Chi-A	4	6	1	0	0	0	0	0	0	1	.000	.000	.000	-97	-0	0	0	0	1.000	-0	/1-3	-0.1
Total	22	2030	6754	990	1977	347	99	95	920	820	598	.293	.372	.416	118	182	65	0		.990	-21	*1-1254,O-538	5.6

■ IKE CAVENEY Caveney, James Christopher b: 12/10/1894, San Francisco, Cal d: 7/6/49, San Francisco, Cal BR/TR, 5'9", 168 lbs. Deb: 4/12/22

YEAR	TM/L	G	AB	R	H	2B	3B	HR	RBI	BB	SO	AVG	OBP	SLG	PRO+	BR/A	SB	CS	SBR	FA	FR	G/POS	TPR
1922	Cin-N	118	394	41	94	12	9	3	54	29	33	.239	.301	.338	66	-21	6	6	-2	.934	-6	*S-118	-1.6
1923	Cin-N	138	488	58	135	21	9	4	63	26	41	.277	.315	.381	84	-12	5	4	-1	.942	-0	*S-138	0.0
1924	Cin-N	95	337	36	92	19	1	4	32	14	21	.273	.310	.371	83	-9	2	3	-1	.924	3	S-90/2-5	0.3
1925	Cin-N	115	358	38	89	9	5	2	47	28	31	.249	.303	.318	60	-21	2	0	1	.941	9	S-111	-0.1
Total	4	466	1577	173	410	61	24	13	196	97	126	.260	.307	.354	74	-63	15	13	-3	.936	6	S-457/2-5	-1.4

■ ANDUJAR CEDENO Cedeno, Andujar (Donastorg) b: 8/21/69, LaRomana, D.R. BR/TR, 6'1", 170 lbs. Deb: 9/2/90 F

YEAR	TM/L	G	AB	R	H	2B	3B	HR	RBI	BB	SO	AVG	OBP	SLG	PRO+	BR/A	SB	CS	SBR	FA	FR	G/POS	TPR
1990	Hou-N	7	8	0	0	0	0	0	0	0	5	.000	.000	.000	-99	-2	0	0	0	.833	-0	/S-3	-0.3
1991	Hou-N	67	251	27	61	13	2	9	36	9	74	.243	.272	.418	97	-3	4	3	-1	.930	-14	S-66	-1.3
1992	Hou-N	71	220	15	38	13	2	2	13	14	71	.173	.232	.277	46	-16	2	1	0	.959	-2	S-70	-1.5
1993	Hou-N	149	505	69	143	24	4	11	56	48	97	.283	.349	.412	107	5	9	7	-2	.955	-25	*S-149/3-1	-1.1
1994	Hou-N	98	342	38	90	26	4	9	49	29	79	.263	.335	.418	100	-1	1	1	-0	.947	1	S-95	0.8
1995	SD-N	120	390	42	82	16	2	6	31	28	92	.210	.272	.308	54	-26	5	3	-0	.965	-7	*S-116/3-1	-2.3
1996	SD-N	49	154	10	36	2	1	3	18	9	32	.234	.280	.318	60	-9	3	2	0	.946	4	S-47/3-2	-0.2
	Det-N	52	179	19	35	4	2	7	20	4	37	.196	.213	.358	41	-17	2	1	0	.951	3	S-51/3-1	-1.3
	Hou-N	3	2	1	0	0	0	0	0	2	1	.000	.500	.000	51	0	0	0	0	1.000	3	/S-2,3-1	0.3
Total	7	616	2051	221	485	98	13	47	223	143	488	.236	.293	.366	78	-69	26	17	-2	.952	-43	S-599/3-6	-6.9

■ CESAR CEDENO Cedeno, Cesar (Encarnacion) b: 2/25/51, Santo Domingo, D.R. BR/TR, 6'2", 195 lbs. Deb: 6/20/70

YEAR	TM/L	G	AB	R	H	2B	3B	HR	RBI	BB	SO	AVG	OBP	SLG	PRO+	BR/A	SB	CS	SBR	FA	FR	G/POS	TPR
1970	Hou-N	90	355	46	110	21	4	7	42	15	57	.310	.341	.451	115	6	17	4	3	.968	-2	O-90	0.7
1971	Hou-N	161	611	85	161	**40**	6	10	81	25	102	.264	.296	.398	97	-5	20	9	1	.989	-2	*O-157/1-2	-1.5
1972	Hou-N★	139	559	103	179	**39**	8	22	82	56	62	.320	.387	.537	163	45	55	21	4	.981	11	*O-137	**5.6**
1973	Hou-N	139	525	86	168	35	2	25	70	41	79	.320	.377	.537	151	34	56	15	8	.981	15	*O-136	5.3
1974	Hou-N★	160	610	95	164	29	5	26	102	64	103	.269	.342	.461	129	21	57	17	7	.993	21	*O-157	4.3

YEAR	TM/L	G	AB	R	H	2B	3B	HR	RBI	BB	SO	AVG	OBP	SLG	PRO+	BR/A	SB	CS	SBR	FA	FR	G/POS	TPR
1975	Hou-N	131	500	93	144	31	3	13	63	62	52	.288	.374	.440	135	24	50	17	5	.982	4	*O-131	2.8
1976	Hou-N★	150	575	89	171	26	5	18	83	55	51	.297	.360	.454	143	30	58	15	8	.990	10	*O-146	4.4
1977	Hou-N	141	530	92	148	36	8	14	71	47	50	.279	.350	.457	126	18	61	14	10	.997	12	*O-137	3.4
1978	Hou-N	50	192	31	54	8	2	7	23	15	24	.281	.333	.453	127	6	23	2	6	.987	8	O-50	1.8
1979	Hou-N	132	470	57	123	27	4	6	54	64	52	.262	.354	.374	105	4	30	13	1	.981	-5	1-91,O-40	-0.7
1980	*Hou-N	137	499	71	154	32	8	10	73	66	72	.309	.390	.465	150	34	48	15	5	.977	8	*O-136	4.3
1981	*Hou-N	82	306	42	83	19	0	5	34	24	31	.271	.326	.382	106	2	12	7	-1	.991	-1	1-46,O-34	-0.4
1982	Cin-N	138	492	52	142	35	1	8	57	41	41	.289	.348	.413	110	6	16	11	-2	.990	4	*O-131/1-1	0.5
1983	Cin-N	98	332	40	77	16	0	9	39	33	53	.232	.307	.361	82	-8	13	9	-2	.993	2	O-73,1-17	-1.2
1984	Cin-N	110	380	59	105	24	2	10	47	25	54	.276	.323	.429	105	2	19	3	4	.980	-2	O-77,1-44	-0.1
1985	Cin-N	83	220	24	53	12	0	3	30	19	35	.241	.310	.336	77	-7	9	5	-0	.990	-1	O-53,1-34	-1.0
	*StL-N	28	76	14	33	4	1	6	19	5	7	.434	.469	.750	238	13	5	1	1	.993	-4	1-23/O-2	1.0
	Yr	111	296	38	86	16	1	9	49	24	42	.291	.350	.443	116	6	14	6	1	.993	-4	1-57,O-55	0.0
1986	LA-N	37	78	5	18	2	1	2	9	4	11	.231	.294	.282	64	-1	1	1	-0	.944	-4	O-31	-1.0
Total	17	2006	7310	1084	2087	436	60	199	976	664	938	.285	.350	.443	124	221	550	179	58	.985	79	*O-1718,1-258	28.3

■ DOMINGO CEDENO

Cedeno, Domingo Antonio (Donastorg) b: 11/4/68, LaRomana, D.R. BB/TR, 6', 170 lbs. Deb: 5/19/93 F

YEAR	TM/L	G	AB	R	H	2B	3B	HR	RBI	BB	SO	AVG	OBP	SLG	PRO+	BR/A	SB	CS	SBR	FA	FR	G/POS	TPR
1993	Tor-A	15	46	5	8	0	0	0	7	1	10	.174	.191	.174	-1	-6	0	1	0	.973	-3	S-10/2-5	-0.8
1994	Tor-A	47	97	14	19	2	3	0	10	10	31	.196	.271	.278	42	-8	1	2	-1	.935	-3	2-28/S-8,3-6,0-1	-1.1
1995	Tor-A	51	161	18	38	6	1	4	14	10	35	.236	.289	.360	68	-8	0	1	-1	.980	-4	S-30,2-20/3-1	-0.1
1996	Tor-A	77	282	44	79	10	2	2	17	15	60	.280	.321	.351	69	-13	5	3	-0	.969	-2	2-62/3-6,S-5	-1.0
	Chi-A	12	19	2	3	2	0	0	3	0	4	.158	.158	.263	4	-3	1	0	0	.000	-1	/2-2,S-2,D-1	-0.3
	Yr	89	301	46	82	12	2	2	20	15	64	.272	.311	.346	66	-16	6	3	0	.969	-3	2-64/S-7,3-6,D-1	-1.3
Total	4	202	605	83	147	20	6	6	51	36	140	.243	.290	.326	58	-39	8	6	-1	.969	-4	2-117/S-55,3-13,DO	-3.3

■ ROGER CEDENO

Cedeno, Roger Leandro b: 8/16/74, Valencia, Venez. BB/TR, 6'1", 165 lbs. Deb: 6/20/95

YEAR	TM/L	G	AB	R	H	2B	3B	HR	RBI	BB	SO	AVG	OBP	SLG	PRO+	BR/A	SB	CS	SBR	FA	FR	G/POS	TPR
1995	LA-N	40	42	4	10	2	0	0	3	3	10	.238	.289	.286	57	-3	1	0	0	.977	-5	O-36	-0.8
1996	LA-N	86	211	26	52	11	1	2	18	24	47	.246	.336	.336	82	-5	5	1	1	.983	-5	O-71	-1.1
Total	2	126	253	30	62	13	1	2	21	27	57	.245	.320	.328	78	-8	6	1	1	.982	-10	O-107	-1.9

■ ORLANDO CEPEDA

Cepeda, Orlando Manuel (Penne) "Baby Bull" or "Cha Cha" b: 9/17/37, Ponce, P.R. BR/TR, 6'2", 210 lbs. Deb: 4/15/58 C

YEAR	TM/L	G	AB	R	H	2B	3B	HR	RBI	BB	SO	AVG	OBP	SLG	PRO+	BR/A	SB	CS	SBR	FA	FR	G/POS	TPR
1958	SF-N	148	603	88	188	38	4	25	96	29	84	.312	.346	.512	126	20	15	11	-2	.989	-5	*1-147	0.6
1959	SF-N★	151	605	92	192	35	4	27	105	33	100	.317	.358	.522	134	27	23	9	2	.984	-8	*1-122,O-44/3-4	1.2
1960	SF-N	151	569	81	169	36	3	24	96	34	91	.297	.345	.497	135	25	15	6	1	.983	0	O-91,1-63	1.7
1961	SF-N★	152	585	105	182	28	4	46	142	39	91	.311	.363	.609	158	45	12	8	-1	.997	-3	1-81,O-80	3.0
1962	*SF-N★	162	625	105	191	26	1	35	114	37	97	.306	.350	.518	132	26	10	4	1	.991	-8	*1-160/O-2	0.8
1963	SF-N☆	156	579	100	183	33	4	34	97	37	70	.316	.367	.563	166	47	8	7	0	.985	-8	*1-150/O-3	3.4
1964	SF-N★	142	529	75	161	27	2	31	97	43	83	.304	.366	.539	148	33	9	4	0	.986	-4	*1-139/O-1	2.4
1965	SF-N	33	34	1	6	1	0	1	5	3	9	.176	.243	.294	49	-2	0	0	0	1.000	-0	/1-4,O-2	-0.3
1966	SF-N	19	49	5	14	2	0	3	15	4	11	.286	.352	.510	132	2	0	1	-1	.778	-3	/O-8,1-6	-0.2
	StL-N	123	452	65	137	24	0	17	58	34	68	.303	.369	.469	130	19	9	8	-2	.989	-6	*1-120	0.2
	Yr	142	501	70	151	26	0	20	73	38	79	.301	.367	.473	130	21	9	9	-3	.990	-9	*1-126/O-8	0.0
1967	*StL-N★	151	563	91	183	37	0	25	111	62	75	.325	.403	.524	166	49	11	2	2	.993	-0	*1-151	4.4
1968	*StL-N	157	600	71	149	26	2	16	73	43	96	.248	.308	.378	107	4	8	6	-1	.988	-5	*1-154	-1.6
1969	*Atl-N	154	573	74	147	28	2	22	88	55	76	.257	.327	.428	109	6	12	5	1	.994	3	*1-153	-0.3
1970	Atl-N	148	567	87	173	33	0	34	111	47	75	.305	.368	.543	133	25	6	5	-1	.992	3	*1-148	1.3
1971	Atl-N	71	250	31	69	10	1	14	44	22	29	.276	.335	.492	124	7	3	6	-3	.992	2	1-63	0.1
1972	Atl-N	28	84	6	25	3	0	4	9	7	17	.298	.352	.476	122	2	0	0	0	1.000	-1	1-22	0.1
	Oak-A	3	3	0	0	0	0	0	0	0	0	.000	.000	.000	-99	-1	0	0	0	.000	0	H	-0.1
1973	Bos-A	142	550	51	159	25	0	20	86	50	81	.289	.352	.444	116	11	0	2	-1	.000	0	*D-142	0.6
1974	KC-A	33	107	3	23	5	0	1	18	6	15	.215	.282	.290	61	-5	1	0	0	.000	0	D-26	-0.6
Total	17	2124	7927	1131	2351	417	27	379	1365	588	1169	.297	.353	.499	133	338	142	80	-5	.990	-39	*1-1683,O-231,D/3	16.7

■ ED CERMAK

Cermak, Edward Hugo b: 3/10/1882, Cleveland, Ohio d: 11/22/11, Cleveland, Ohio BR/TR, 5'11", 170 lbs. Deb: 9/9/01

YEAR	TM/L	G	AB	R	H	2B	3B	HR	RBI	BB	SO	AVG	OBP	SLG	PRO+	BR/A	SB	CS	SBR	FA	FR	G/POS	TPR
1901	Cle-A	1	4	0	0	0	0	0	0	0	0	.000	.000	.000	-99	-1	0			1.000	1	/O-1	0.0

■ RICK CERONE

Cerone, Richard Aldo b: 5/19/54, Newark, N.J. BR/TR, 5'11", 192 lbs. Deb: 8/17/75

YEAR	TM/L	G	AB	R	H	2B	3B	HR	RBI	BB	SO	AVG	OBP	SLG	PRO+	BR/A	SB	CS	SBR	FA	FR	G/POS	TPR
1975	Cle-A	7	12	1	3	1	0	0	1	1	0	.250	.308	.333	81	-0	0	0	0	1.000	-1	/C-7	-0.1
1976	Cle-A	7	16	1	2	0	0	0	1	0	2	.125	.125	.125	-27	-3	0	0	0	.963	0	/C-6,D-1	-0.2
1977	Tor-A	31	100	7	20	4	0	1	10	6	12	.200	.245	.270	40	-8	0	0	0	.994	-2	C-31	-0.9
1978	Tor-A	88	282	25	63	8	2	3	20	23	32	.223	.284	.298	63	-14	0	3	-2	.992	-0	C-84/D-2	-1.5
1979	Tor-A	136	469	47	112	27	4	7	61	37	40	.239	.296	.358	75	-17	1	4	-2	.980	-8	*C-136	-2.2
1980	*NY-A	147	519	70	144	30	4	14	85	32	56	.277	.327	.432	108	4	1	3	-2	.990	-6	*C-147	1.4
1981	*NY-A	71	234	23	57	13	2	2	21	12	24	.244	.280	.342	80	-7	0	2	-1	.992	-6	C-69	-1.2
1982	NY-A	89	300	29	68	10	0	5	28	19	27	.227	.275	.310	61	-16	0	2	-1	.989	-8	C-89	-2.2
1983	NY-A	80	246	18	54	7	0	2	22	15	29	.220	.267	.272	51	-17	0	0	0	.991	-0	C-78/3-1	-1.4
1984	NY-A	38	120	8	25	3	0	2	13	9	15	.208	.269	.283	55	-7	1	0	0	.996	3	C-38	-0.2
1985	Atl-N	96	282	15	61	9	0	3	25	29	25	.216	.292	.280	57	-6	0	3	-2	.986	-8	C-91	-2.2
1986	Mil-A	68	216	22	56	14	0	4	18	15	28	.259	.310	.380	84	-5	1	1	-0	.991	7	C-68	0.6
1987	NY-A	113	284	28	69	12	1	4	23	30	46	.243	.324	.335	76	-9	0	1	-1	.998	4	*C-111/P-2,1-2	0.1
1988	Bos-A	84	264	31	71	13	1	3	27	20	32	.269	.328	.360	89	-4	0	0	0	1.000	-5	C-83/D-1	-0.3
1989	Bos-A	102	296	28	72	16	1	4	48	34	40	.243	.325	.345	84	-6	0	1	-0	.984	-3	C-97/O-1,D-1	0.1
1990	NY-A	49	139	12	42	6	0	2	11	5	13	.302	.326	.388	99	-1	0	0	0	.995	-3	C-35/2-1,D-6	-0.2
1991	NY-N	90	227	18	62	13	0	2	16	30	24	.273	.360	.357	103	-1	1	1	-0	.987	-2	C-81	0.4
1992	Mon-N	33	63	10	17	4	1	1	9	7	3	.270	.313	.381	97	-0	1	2	-1	1.000	1	C-28	-0.2
Total	18	1329	4069	393	998	190	15	59	436	320	450	.245	.304	.343	78	-123	6	22	-11	.990	-19	*C-1279/D-11,1P2O3	-10.0

■ BOB CERV

Cerv, Robert Henry b: 5/5/26, Weston, Neb. BR/TR, 6', 202 lbs. Deb: 8/1/51

YEAR	TM/L	G	AB	R	H	2B	3B	HR	RBI	BB	SO	AVG	OBP	SLG	PRO+	BR/A	SB	CS	SBR	FA	FR	G/POS	TPR
1951	NY-A	12	28	4	6	1	0	0	2	4	6	.214	.313	.250	55	-2	0	0	0	.875	-1	/O-9	-0.3
1952	NY-A	36	87	11	21	3	2	1	8	9	22	.241	.313	.356	91	-1	0	1	-1	1.000	-2	O-27	-0.5
1953	NY-A	8	6	0	0	0	0	0	1	0	1	.000	.143	.000	-61	-1	0	0	0	.000	0	H	-0.1
1954	NY-A	56	100	14	26	6	0	5	13	11	17	.260	.333	.470	122	3	0	2	-1	.897	-5	O-24	-0.4
1955	*NY-A	55	85	17	29	4	2	3	7	16	13	.341	.411	.541	157	7	4	0	1	1.000	-4	O-20	0.4
1956	*NY-A	54	115	16	35	5	6	3	25	18	13	.304	.398	.530	148	8	0	1	-1	.984	-4	O-44	0.2
1957	KC-A	124	345	35	94	14	2	11	44	20	57	.272	.314	.420	97	-2	1	1	0	.964	-7	O-89	-1.5
1958	KC-A★	141	515	93	157	20	7	38	104	50	82	.305	.372	.592	158	39	3	3	-1	.985	20	*O-136	5.1
1959	KC-A	125	463	61	132	22	4	20	87	35	87	.285	.339	.479	120	11	3	2	-0	.980	5	*O-119	1.1
1960	KC-A	23	78	14	20	1	1	6	12	10	12	.256	.341	.526	130	3	0	0	0	.977	3	O-21	0.5
	*NY-A	87	216	32	54	11	1	8	28	30	36	.250	.349	.421	114	4	0	0	0	.982	3	O-51/1-3	1.0
	Yr	110	294	46	74	12	2	14	40	40	53	.252	.347	.449	119	7	0	0	0	.980	6	O-72/1-3	1.0
1961	LA-A	18	57	3	9	3	0	2	6	1	8	.158	.172	.316	25	-6	0	0	0	.944	-2	O-15	-1.0
	NY-A	57	118	17	32	5	2	4	20	12	17	.271	.344	.483	125	4	1	0	0	.983	1	O-30/1-3	0.4
	Yr	75	175	20	41	8	1	8	26	13	25	.234	.291	.429	91	-3	1	0	0	.974	-1	O-45/1-3	-0.6
1962	NY-A	14	17	1	2	1	0	0	3	0	3	.118	.250	.176	18	-2	0	0	0	1.000	-0	/O-3	-0.3
	Hou-N	19	44	4	7	1	0	1	6	7	4	.226	.237	.419	89	-1	0	0	0	.833	0	/O-6	-0.1
Total	12	829	2261	320	624	96	26	105	374	212	392	.276	.343	.481	122	63	12	10	-2	.976	8	O-594/1-6	4.0

■ RON CEY

Cey, Ronald Charles b: 2/15/48, Tacoma, Wash. BR/TR, 5'10", 185 lbs. Deb: 9/3/71

YEAR	TM/L	G	AB	R	H	2B	3B	HR	RBI	BB	SO	AVG	OBP	SLG	PRO+	BR/A	SB	CS	SBR	FA	FR	G/POS	TPR
1971	LA-N	2	2	0	0	0	0	0	0	0	2	.000	.000	.000	-99	-1	0	0	0	.000	0	H	-0.1
1972	LA-N	11	37	3	10	1	0	1	3	7	10	.270	.400	.378	125	2	0	0	0	.900	-2	3-11	-0.1
1973	LA-N	152	507	60	124	18	4	15	80	74	77	.245	.343	.385	106	5	1	1	-0	.961	16	*3-146	2.1

YEAR	TM/L	G	AB	R	H	2B	3B	HR	RBI	BB	SO	AVG	OBP	SLG	PRO+	BR/A	SB	CS	SBR	FA	FR	G/POS	TPR
1974	*LA-N★	159	577	88	151	20	2	18	97	76	68	.262	.355	.397	115	12	1	1	-0	.959	17	*3-158	2.9
1975	*LA-N★	158	566	72	160	29	2	25	101	78	74	.283	.376	.473	141	31	5	2	-0	.960	-4	*3-158	2.8
1976	LA-N★	145	502	69	139	18	3	23	80	89	74	.277	.389	.462	144	31	0	4	-2	.965	11	*3-144	4.1
1977	*LA-N★	153	564	77	136	22	3	30	110	93	106	.241	.351	.450	114	11	3	4	-2	.964	17	*3-153	2.5
1978	*LA-N★	159	555	84	150	32	0	23	84	96	96	.270	.384	.452	134	28	2	5	-2	.966	5	*3-158	2.9
1979	LA-N★	150	487	77	137	20	1	28	81	86	85	.281	.391	.499	143	31	3	3	-1	**.977**	-1	*3-150	2.9
1980	LA-N	157	551	81	140	25	0	28	77	69	92	.254	.342	.452	122	16	2	2	-1	.972	7	*3-157	2.1
1981	*LA-N	85	312	42	90	15	2	13	50	40	55	.288	.375	.474	145	18	0	2	-1	.941	7	3-84	2.4
1982	LA-N	150	556	62	141	23	1	24	79	57	99	.254	.327	.428	113	8	3	2	-0	.963	11	*3-149	1.6
1983	Chi-N	159	581	73	160	33	1	24	90	62	85	.275	.350	.460	117	13	0	0	-0	.955	-21	*3-157	-1.0
1984	*Chi-N	146	505	71	121	27	0	25	97	61	108	.240	.329	.442	105	3	3	2	-0	**.967**	-20	*3-144	-2.0
1985	Chi-N	145	500	64	116	18	2	22	63	58	106	.232	.317	.408	91	-6	1	1	-0	.943	-7	*3-140	-1.7
1986	Chi-N	97	256	42	70	21	0	13	36	44	66	.273	.386	.508	134	12	0	0	-0	.952	-6	3-77	0.5
1987	Oak-A	45	104	12	23	6	0	4	11	22	32	.221	.362	.394	108	2	0	0	0	.982	-1	D-30/1-7,3-3	0.0
Total	17	2073	7162	977	1868	328	21	316	1139	1012	1235	.261	.357	.445	121	216	24	29	-10	.961	30	*3-1989/D-30,1-7	21.9

■ ELIO CHACON
Chacon, Elio (Rodriguez) b: 10/26/36, Caracas, Venez. d: 4/24/92, Caracas, Venez. BR/TR, 5'9", 160 lbs. Deb: 4/20/60

YEAR	TM/L	G	AB	R	H	2B	3B	HR	RBI	BB	SO	AVG	OBP	SLG	PRO+	BR/A	SB	CS	SBR	FA	FR	G/POS	TPR
1960	Cin-N	49	116	14	21	1	0	0	7	14	23	.181	.275	.190	29	-11	7	1	2	.980	5	2-43/O-2	-0.1
1961	*Cin-N	61	132	26	35	4	2	2	5	21	22	.265	.374	.371	97	0	1	4	-2	.989	0	2-42/O-7	0.2
1962	NY-N	118	368	49	87	10	3	2	27	76	64	.236	.369	.296	80	-7	12	7	-1	.961	-3	*S-110/2-2,3-1	-0.1
Total	3	228	616	89	143	15	5	4	39	111	109	.232	.353	.292	74	-18	20	12	-1	.985	3	S-110/2-87,O-9,3-1	0.0

■ CHET CHADBOURNE
Chadbourne, Chester James "Pop" b: 10/28/1884, Parkman, Me. d: 6/21/43, Los Angeles, Cal. BL/TR, 5'9", 170 lbs. Deb: 9/17/06

YEAR	TM/L	G	AB	R	H	2B	3B	HR	RBI	BB	SO	AVG	OBP	SLG	PRO+	BR/A	SB	CS	SBR	FA	FR	G/POS	TPR
1906	Bos-A	11	43	7	13	1	0	0	3	3		.302	.348	.326	111	1	1			.926	3	2-11/S-1	0.4
1907	Bos-A	10	38	0	11	0	0	0	1	7		.289	.400	.289	121	1	1			1.000	-0	O-10	0.1
1914	KC-F	147	581	92	161	22	8	1	37	69	49	.277	.359	.348	97	-10	42			.965	9	*O-146	-0.8
1915	KC-F	152	587	75	133	16	9	1	35	62	29	.227	.307	.290	71	-31	29			**.979**	4	*O-152	-4.1
1918	Bos-N	27	104	9	27	2	1	0	6	5	5	.260	.300	.298	86	-2	5			.925	-3	O-27	-0.7
Total	5	347	1353	183	345	41	18	2	82	146	83	.255	.333	.316	86	-41	78			.969	10	O-335/2-11,S-1	-5.1

■ DAVE CHALK
Chalk, David Lee b: 8/30/50, Del Rio, Tex. BR/TR, 5'10", 175 lbs. Deb: 9/4/73

YEAR	TM/L	G	AB	R	H	2B	3B	HR	RBI	BB	SO	AVG	OBP	SLG	PRO+	BR/A	SB	CS	SBR	FA	FR	G/POS	TPR
1973	Cal-A	24	69	14	16	2	0	0	6	9	13	.232	.329	.261	74	-2	0	0	0	.962	2	S-22	0.2
1974	Cal-A★	133	465	44	117	9	3	5	31	30	57	.252	.307	.316	84	-10	10	10	-3	.938	-2	S-99,3-38	-0.2
1975	Cal-A☆	149	513	59	140	24	2	3	56	66	49	.273	.358	.345	107	7	6	9	-4	.976	6	*3-149	0.9
1976	Cal-A	142	438	39	95	14	1	0	33	49	62	.217	.310	.253	71	-14	0	0	0	.971	6	*S-102,3-49	0.1
1977	Cal-A	149	519	58	144	27	2	3	45	52	69	.277	.349	.355	96	-1	12	8	-1	.948	-3	*3-141/2-7,S-4	-0.6
1978	Cal-A	135	470	42	119	12	0	1	34	38	34	.253	.318	.285	74	-15	5	8	-3	.955	-20	S-97,2-29,3-22/D-1	-2.6
1979	Tex-A	9	8	0	2	0	0	0	0	0	0	.250	.250	.250	36	-1	0	0	0	1.000	1	/S-3,2-1,D-2	-0.1
	Oak-A	66	212	15	47	6	0	2	13	29	14	.222	.318	.278	66	-9	2	1	0	.988	-18	2-37,S-16,3-16	-2.3
	Yr	75	220	15	49	6	0	2	13	29	14	.223	.316	.277	65	-10	2	1	0	.988	-18	2-38,S-19,3-16/D-2	-2.4
1980	*KC-A	69	167	19	42	10	1	1	20	18	27	.251	.332	.341	84	-3	1	1	0	.964	-3	3-33,2-17/S-1,D-6	-0.7
1981	KC-A	27	49	2	11	3	0	0	5	4	2	.224	.283	.286	65	-2	0	1	-1	.955	-2	3-14,2-10/S-1	-0.2
Total	9	903	2910	292	733	107	9	15	243	295	327	.252	.328	.310	85	-52	36	38	-12	.962	-34	3-462,S-345,2/D	-5.7

■ JOE CHAMBERLAIN
Chamberlain, Joseph Jeremiah b: 5/10/10, San Francisco, Cal d: 1/28/83, San Francisco, Cal. BR/TR, 6'1", 175 lbs. Deb: 4/17/34

YEAR	TM/L	G	AB	R	H	2B	3B	HR	RBI	BB	SO	AVG	OBP	SLG	PRO+	BR/A	SB	CS	SBR	FA	FR	G/POS	TPR
1934	Chi-A	43	141	13	34	5	1	2	17	6	38	.241	.272	.333	54	-10	1	1	-0	.896	-6	S-26,3-14/2-1	-1.4

■ WES CHAMBERLAIN
Chamberlain, Wesley Polk b: 4/13/66, Chicago, Ill. BR/TR, 6'2", 210 lbs. Deb: 8/31/90

YEAR	TM/L	G	AB	R	H	2B	3B	HR	RBI	BB	SO	AVG	OBP	SLG	PRO+	BR/A	SB	CS	SBR	FA	FR	G/POS	TPR
1990	Phi-N	18	46	9	13	3	0	2	4	1	9	.283	.298	.478	110	0	4	0	1	.958	-1	O-10	0.1
1991	Phi-N	101	383	51	92	16	3	13	50	31	73	.240	.300	.399	96	-3	9	4	0	.985	5	O-98	0.0
1992	Phi-N	76	275	26	71	18	0	9	41	10	55	.258	.287	.422	99	-2	4	0	1	.971	-5	O-73	-0.3
1993	*Phi-N	96	284	34	80	20	2	12	45	17	51	.282	.325	.493	117	6	2	1	0	.993	5	O-76	0.9
1994	Phi-N	24	69	7	19	5	0	2	6	3	12	.275	.306	.435	88	-1	0	0	0	1.000	1	O-18	-0.1
	Bos-A	51	164	13	42	9	1	4	20	12	38	.256	.307	.396	76	-6	0	2	-1	1.000	4	O-34,D-12	-0.5
1995	Bos-A	19	42	4	5	1	0	1	1	3	11	.119	.178	.214	1	-6	1	0	0	.955	-3	O-12/D-5	-0.6
Total	6	385	1263	144	322	72	6	43	167	77	249	.255	.300	.424	99	-13	20	7	2	.984	12	O-321/D-17	-0.5

■ AL CHAMBERS
Chambers, Albert Eugene b: 3/24/61, Harrisburg, Pa. BL/TL, 6'4", 217 lbs. Deb: 7/23/83

YEAR	TM/L	G	AB	R	H	2B	3B	HR	RBI	BB	SO	AVG	OBP	SLG	PRO+	BR/A	SB	CS	SBR	FA	FR	G/POS	TPR
1983	Sea-A	31	67	11	14	3	0	1	7	18	20	.209	.376	.299	85	1	0	1	-1	1.000	-1	D-22/O-3	-0.3
1984	Sea-A	22	49	4	11	1	0	1	4	3	12	.224	.269	.306	60	-3	2	1	0	.947	-2	O-13/D-1	-0.5
1985	Sea-A	4	4	0	0	0	0	0	0	0	2	.000	.000	.000	-99	-1	0	0	0	.000	0	/H	-0.1
Total	3	57	120	15	25	4	0	2	11	21	34	.208	.326	.292	71	-4	2	2	-1	.955	-3	/D-23,O-16	-0.9

■ CHRIS CHAMBLISS
Chambliss, Carroll Christopher b: 12/26/48, Dayton, O. BL/TR, 6'1", 215 lbs. Deb: 5/28/71 C

YEAR	TM/L	G	AB	R	H	2B	3B	HR	RBI	BB	SO	AVG	OBP	SLG	PRO+	BR/A	SB	CS	SBR	FA	FR	G/POS	TPR
1971	Cle-A	111	415	49	114	20	4	9	48	40	83	.275	.341	.407	102	1	2	0	1	.992	-5	*1-108	-1.4
1972	Cle-A	121	466	51	136	27	2	6	44	26	63	.292	.329	.397	112	6	3	4	-2	.993	-6	*1-119	-1.3
1973	Cle-A	155	572	70	156	30	2	11	53	58	76	.273	.343	.390	104	3	4	8	-4	.991	-7	*1-154	-0.6
1974	Cle-A	17	67	8	22	4	0	0	7	5	5	.328	.375	.388	121	2	0	1	0	.982	-2	1-17	-0.2
	NY-A	110	400	38	97	16	4	6	43	23	43	.243	.284	.343	81	-11	0	4	0	.992	7	*1-106	-1.1
	Yr	127	467	46	119	20	5	6	50	28	48	.255	.297	.349	87	-9	0	5	0	.990	5	*1-123	-1.3
1975	NY-A	150	562	66	171	38	4	9	72	29	50	.304	.340	.434	119	12	0	1	-1	.991	-1	*1-147	0.5
1976	*NY-A★	156	641	79	188	32	6	17	96	27	80	.293	.325	.441	124	16	1	0	0	.994	-2	*1-155/D-1	0.4
1977	*NY-A	157	600	90	172	32	6	17	90	45	73	.287	.338	.445	113	10	4	0	1	.989	-5	*1-157	-0.3
1978	*NY-A	162	625	81	171	26	3	12	90	41	60	.274	.323	.382	100	-1	2	1	0	**.997**	-5	*1-155/D-7	-0.6
1979	NY-A	149	554	61	155	27	3	18	63	34	53	.280	.327	.437	106	4	3	2	0	.995	-1	*1-134,D-16	-0.5
1980	Atl-N	158	602	83	170	37	2	18	72	49	73	.282	.340	.440	113	9	7	3	0	.993	-2	*1-158	-0.2
1981	Atl-N	107	404	44	110	25	2	8	51	44	41	.272	.345	.403	109	5	4	1	1	.997	7	*1-107	0.7
1982	*Atl-N	157	534	57	144	25	2	20	86	57	57	.270	.340	.436	111	8	5	2	0	.993	14	*1-151	1.5
1983	Atl-N	131	447	59	125	24	3	20	78	63	68	.280	.369	.481	124	15	2	7	-4	.996	0	*1-126	0.5
1984	Atl-N	135	389	47	100	14	0	9	44	58	54	.257	.355	.362	95	-1	1	2	-1	.993	-2	*1-109	-0.7
1985	Atl-N	101	170	16	40	7	0	3	21	18	22	.235	.309	.329	74	-6	0	0	0	.997	2	1-39	-0.6
1986	Atl-N	97	122	13	38	8	0	2	14	15	24	.311	.387	.426	117	3	0	2	-1	.993	-2	1-20	-0.1
1988	NY-A	1	1	0	0	0	0	0	0	0	1	.000	.000	.000	-99	-0	0	0	0	.000	0	/H	0.0
Total	17	2175	7571	912	2109	392	42	185	972	632	926	.279	.336	.415	108	75	40	35	-9	.993	25	*1-1962/D-24	-4.0

■ MIKE CHAMPION
Champion, Robert Michael b: 2/10/55, Montgomery, Ala. BR/TR, 6', 185 lbs. Deb: 9/14/76

YEAR	TM/L	G	AB	R	H	2B	3B	HR	RBI	BB	SO	AVG	OBP	SLG	PRO+	BR/A	SB	CS	SBR	FA	FR	G/POS	TPR
1976	SD-N	11	38	4	9	2	0	1	2	1	3	.237	.256	.368	82	-1	0	0	0	.940	-4	2-11	-0.5
1977	SD-N	150	507	35	116	14	6	1	43	27	85	.229	.271	.286	55	-34	3	3	-1	.974	-26	*2-149	-5.3
1978	SD-N	32	53	3	12	0	0	0	4	5	13	.226	.293	.302	72	-2	0	0	0	.932	2	2-20/3-4	0.1
Total	3	193	598	42	137	16	6	2	49	33	101	.229	.272	.293	58	-37	3	3	-1	.968	-28	2-180/3-4	-5.7

■ FRANK CHANCE
Chance, Frank Leroy "Husk" or "The Peerless Leader"
b: 9/9/1877, Fresno, Cal. d: 9/15/24, Los Angeles, Cal. BR/TR, 6', 190 lbs. Deb: 4/29/1898 MH

YEAR	TM/L	G	AB	R	H	2B	3B	HR	RBI	BB	SO	AVG	OBP	SLG	PRO+	BR/A	SB	CS	SBR	FA	FR	G/POS	TPR
1898	Chi-N	53	147	32	41	1	3	1	14	7		.279	.338	.367	102	0	7			.950	-5	C-33,O-17/1-3	-0.4
1899	Chi-N	64	192	37	55	6	2	1	22	15		.286	.351	.354	96	-1	10			.950	-2	C-57/O-1,1-1	0.2
1900	Chi-N	56	149	26	44	9	3	0	13	15		.295	.413	.396	129	8	8			.932	-1	O-51/1-1	1.0
1901	Chi-N	69	241	38	67	12	4	0	36	29		.278	.376	.361	119	8	27			.932	-5	O-51,C-13/1-6	0.0
1902	Chi-N	75	240	39	69	9	4	1	31	35		.287	.396	.371	141	14	27			.969	-4	*1-38,C-29/O-4	1.2
1903	Chi-N	125	441	83	144	24	10	2	81	78		.327	.439	.490	155	37	**67**			.972	-5	*1-121/C-2	3.0
1904	Chi-N	124	451	89	140	16	10	6	49	36		.310	.382	.430	150	27	42			.990	12	*1-123/C-1	3.7
1905	Chi-N	118	392	92	124	16	12	2	70	78		.316	**.450**	.434	157	34	38			.990	2	*1-115,M	3.3

YEAR	TM/L	G	AB	R	H	2B	3B	HR	RBI	BB	SO	AVG	OBP	SLG	PRO+	BR/A	SB	CS	SBR	FA	FR	G/POS	TPR
1906	*Chi-N	136	474	**103**	151	24	10	3	71	70		.319	.419	.430	156	34	**57**			.989	-1	*1-136,M	3.2
1907	*Chi-N	111	382	58	112	19	2	1	49	51		.293	.395	.361	129	15	35			**.992**	7	*1-109,M	2.2
1908	*Chi-N	129	452	65	123	27	4	2	55	37		.272	.338	.363	119	10	27			.989	4	*1-126,M	1.3
1909	Chi-N	93	324	53	88	16	4	0	46	30		.272	.341	.346	110	4	29			.994	-2	1-92,M	0.2
1910	Chi-N	88	295	54	88	12	8	0	36	37	15	.298	.395	.393	131	13	16			.996	-2	1-87,M	1.2
1911	Chi-N	31	88	23	21	6	3	1	17	25	13	.239	.432	.409	136	6	9			.990	-2	1-29,M	0.4
1912	Chi-N	2	5	2	1	0	0	0	0	3	0	.200	.500	.200	96	0	1			1.000	-0	/1-2,M	0.0
1913	NY-A	12	24	3	5	0	0	0	6	8	1	.208	.406	.208	81	0	1			1.000	1	/1-7,M	0.0
1914	NY-A	1	0	0	0	0	0	0	0	0	0	—	—	—	—	0	0			1.000	-0	/1-1,M	0.0
Total	17	1287	4297	797	1273	200	79	20	596	554	<u>29</u>	.296	.394	.394	135	208	401			.987	-1	1-997,C-186/O-73	20.5

■ BOB CHANCE
Chance, Robert   b: 9/10/40, Statesboro, Ga.   BL/TR, 6'2", 219 lbs.   Deb: 9/4/63

1963	Cle-A	16	52	5	15	4	0	2	7	1	10	.288	.302	.481	116	1	0	1	-1	.909	-2	O-14	-0.2
1964	Cle-A	120	390	45	109	16	1	14	75	40	101	.279	.351	.433	118	9	3	3	-1	.988	-12	1-81,O-31	-0.9
1965	Was-A	72	199	20	51	9	0	4	14	18	44	.256	.318	.362	94	-2	0	1	-1	.988	-2	1-48/O-3	-0.7
1966	Was-A	37	57	1	10	3	0	1	8	2	23	.175	.203	.281	38	-5	0	0	0	.974	-2	1-13	-0.7
1967	Was-A	27	42	5	9	2	0	3	7	7	13	.214	.340	.476	144	2	0	0	0	1.000	-0	1-10	0.2
1969	Cal-A	5	7	0	1	0	0	0	1	0	4	.143	.143	.143	-21	-1	0	0	0	.909	-0	/1-1	-0.2
Total	6	277	747	76	195	34	1	24	112	68	195	.261	.326	.406	106	5	3	5	-2	.987	-18	1-153/O-48	-2.5

■ DARREL CHANEY
Chaney, Darrel Lee   b: 3/9/48, Hammond, Ind.   BB/TR, 6'1", 190 lbs.   Deb: 4/11/69

1969	Cin-N	93	209	21	40	5	2	0	15	24	75	.191	.278	.234	43	-16	1	0	0	.947	-12	S-91	-2.2
1970	*Cin-N	57	95	7	22	3	0	1	4	3	26	.232	.263	.295	49	-7	1	1	-0	.941	5	S-30,2-18/3-3	0.0
1971	Cin-N	10	24	2	3	0	0	0	1	1	3	.125	.160	.125	-19	-4	0	1	-1	1.000	-1	/S-7,2-1,3-1	-0.4
1972	*Cin-N	83	196	29	49	7	2	2	19	29	28	.250	.347	.337	101	1	1	3	-2	.963	-7	S-64,2-12,3-10	-0.1
1973	*Cin-N	105	227	27	41	7	1	0	14	26	50	.181	.268	.220	39	-19	4	3	-1	.964	12	S-75,2-14,3-12	0.1
1974	*Cin-N	117	135	27	27	6	1	2	16	26	33	.200	.329	.304	79	-3	1	2	-1	.952	17	3-81,2-38,S-12	1.5
1975	*Cin-N	71	160	18	35	6	2	0	26	14	38	.219	.282	.294	59	-9	3	0	1	.961	17	S-34,2-23,3-13	1.2
1976	Atl-N	153	496	42	125	20	8	1	50	54	92	.252	.327	.331	82	-11	5	7	-3	.950	-0	*S-151/2-1,3-1	0.4
1977	Atl-N	74	209	22	42	7	2	3	15	17	44	.201	.261	.297	44	-17	0	0	0	.979	4	S-41,2-24	-0.7
1978	Atl-N	89	245	27	55	9	1	3	20	25	48	.224	.296	.306	62	-12	1	0	0	.976	-6	S-77/3-8,2-1	-1.0
1979	Atl-N	63	117	15	19	5	0	0	10	19	34	.162	.279	.205	32	-11	2	1	0	.945	-3	S-39/2-5,3-4,C-1	-1.1
Total	11	915	2113	237	458	75	17	14	190	238	471	.217	.297	.288	61	-107	19	18	-5	.959	26	S-621,2-137,3/C	-2.3

■ LES CHANNELL
Channell, Lester Clark "Goat" or "Gint"   b: 3/3/1886, Crestline, Ohio   d: 5/8/54, Denver, Colo.   BL/TL, 6', 180 lbs.   Deb: 5/11/10

1910	NY-A	6	19	3	6	1	0	0	3	2		.316	.381	.316	112	0	2			1.000	-1	/O-6	-0.1
1914	NY-A	1	1	0	1	0	0	0	0	0		1.000	1.000	2.000	803	1	0			.000	0	H	0.1
Total	2	7	20	3	7	1	0	0	3	2	<u>0</u>	.350	.409	.400	145	1	2			1.000	-1	/O-6	0.0

■ CHARLIE CHANT
Chant, Charles Joseph   b: 8/7/51, Bell, Cal.   BR/TR, 6', 190 lbs.   Deb: 9/12/75

1975	Oak-A	5	5	1	0	0	0	0	0	0	0	.000	.000	.000	-99	-1	0	0	0	1.000	-2	/O-5,D-1	-0.3
1976	StL-N	15	14	0	2	0	0	0	0	0	4	.143	.143	.143	-19	-2	0	0	0	1.000	-2	O-14	-0.5
Total	2	20	19	1	2	0	0	0	0	0	4	.105	.105	.105	-40	-3	0	0	0	1.000	-4	/O-19,D-1	-0.8

■ ED CHAPLIN
Chaplin, Bert Edgar (b: Bert Edgar Chapman)   b: 9/25/1893, Pelzer, S.C.   d: 8/15/78, Sanford, Fla.   BL/TR, 5'7", 158 lbs.   Deb: 9/4/20

1920	Bos-A	4	5	2	1	0	0	0	1	4	1	.200	.556	.400	163	1	0	0	0	.900	-1	/C-2	0.1
1921	Bos-A	3	2	0	0	0	0	0	0	0	1	.000	.000	.000	-99	-1	0	0	0	1.000	0	/C-1	0.0
1922	Bos-A	28	69	8	13	1	1	0	6	9	9	.188	.282	.232	35	-6	2	1	0	.960	-3	C-21	-0.8
Total	3	35	76	10	14	2	1	0	7	13	11	.184	.303	.237	43	-6	2	1	0	.953	-3	/C-24	-0.7

■ CALVIN CHAPMAN
Chapman, Calvin Louis   b: 12/20/10, Courtland, Miss.   d: 4/1/83, Batesville, Miss.   BL/TR, 5'9", 160 lbs.   Deb: 9/10/35

1935	Cin-N	15	53	6	18	1	0	0	3	4	5	.340	.386	.358	105	1	2			.949	-3	S-12/2-4	-0.1
1936	Cin-N	96	219	35	54	7	3	1	22	16	19	.247	.301	.320	72	-9	5			.961	-14	O-31,2-23/3-1	-2.2
Total	2	111	272	41	72	8	3	1	25	20	24	.265	.317	.327	78	-8	7			.968	-16	/O-31,2-27,S-12,3-1	-2.3

■ GLENN CHAPMAN
Chapman, Glenn Justice "Pete"   b: 1/21/06, Cambridge City, Ind.   d: 11/5/88, Richmond, Ind.   BR/TR, 5'11.5", 170 lbs.   Deb: 4/18/34

1934	Bro-N	67	93	19	26	5	1	0	10	7	19	.280	.330	.387	96	-1	1			1.000	-7	O-40,2-14	-0.8

■ HARRY CHAPMAN
Chapman, Harry E.   b: 10/26/1887, Severance, Kan.   d: 10/21/18, Nevada, Mo.   BR/TR, 5'11", 160 lbs.   Deb: 10/6/12

1912	Chi-N	1	4	1	1	0	0	1	0	0		.250	.250	.750	169	0	1			1.000	1	/C-1	0.1
1913	Cin-N	2	2	0	1	0	0	0	0	0		.500	.500	.500	187	0	0			.000	0	H	0.0
1914	StL-F	64	181	16	38	2	1	0	14	13	27	.210	.270	.232	36	-19	2			.973	-4	C-51/1-1,2-1,O-1	-1.9
1915	StL-F	62	186	19	37	6	1	0	29	22	24	.199	.284	.280	56	-14	4			.989	8	C-53	-0.2
1916	StL-A	18	31	2	3	0	0	0	2	0	5	.097	.152	.097	-27	-5	0			.981	2	C-14	-0.2
Total	5	147	404	38	80	8	5	1	44	37	57	.198	.269	.250	43	-37	7			.982	7	C-119/O-1,2-1,1-1	-2.2

■ JACK CHAPMAN
Chapman, John Curtis "Death To Flying Things"   b: 5/8/1843, Brooklyn, N.Y.   d: 6/10/16, Brooklyn, N.Y.   TR, 5'11", 170 lbs.   Deb: 5/5/1874   M

1874	Atl-n	53	242	32	64	10	2	0	25	4	11	.264	.276	.322	103	3	2	1	0	.741	2	*O-53/1-1	0.5
1875	StL-n	43	195	28	44	5	3	0	30	1	7	.226	.230	.282	84	-2	4	1	1	.733	-3	O-43/1-1	-0.4
1876	Lou-N	17	67	4	16	1	0	0	5	1	3	.239	.250	.254	58	-4				.750	-4	O-17/3-1,M	-0.7
Total	2 n	96	437	60	108	15	5	0	55	5	18	.247	.256	.304	95	1	6	2	1	.738	-1	/O-96,1-2	0.1

■ JOHN CHAPMAN
Chapman, John Joseph   b: 10/15/1899, Centralia, Pa.   d: 11/3/53, Philadelphia, Pa.   BR/TR, 5'10.5", 175 lbs.   Deb: 6/28/24

1924	Phi-A	19	71	7	20	4	1	0	7	4	8	.282	.329	.366	78	-2	0	0	0	.958	-10	S-19	-1.0

■ KELVIN CHAPMAN
Chapman, Kelvin Keith   b: 6/2/56, Willits, Cal.   BR/TR, 5'11", 173 lbs.   Deb: 4/5/79

1979	NY-N	35	80	7	12	1	2	0	4	5	15	.150	.200	.213	13	-10	0	0	0	.980	-4	2-22/3-1	-1.3
1984	NY-N	75	197	27	57	13	4	3	23	19	30	.289	.358	.401	115	4	8	7	-2	.979	1	2-57/3-3	0.5
1985	NY-N	62	144	16	25	3	0	0	7	9	15	.174	.232	.194	21	-15	5	4	-1	.970	-6	2-48/3-1	-2.2
Total	3	172	421	50	94	17	2	3	34	33	60	.223	.286	.295	64	-21	13	11	-3	.976	-9	2-127/3-5	-3.0

■ RAY CHAPMAN
Chapman, Raymond Johnson   b: 1/15/1891, Beaver Dam, Ky.   d: 8/17/20, New York, N.Y.   BR/TR, 5'10", 170 lbs.   Deb: 8/30/12

1912	Cle-A	31	109	29	34	6	3	0	19	10		.312	.375	.422	124	3	10			.904	-14	S-31	-0.4
1913	Cle-A	141	508	78	131	19	7	3	39	46	51	.258	.322	.341	91	-6	29			.936	-9	*S-138/O-1	-0.2
1914	Cle-A	106	375	59	103	16	10	2	42	48	48	.275	.358	.387	119	9	24	9		.913	-15	S-72,2-33	0.2
1915	Cle-A	154	570	101	154	14	17	3	67	70	82	.270	.353	.370	114	10	36	15	2	.944	9	*S-154	3.4
1916	Cle-A	109	346	50	80	10	5	0	27	50	46	.231	.330	.289	81	-7	21	14	2	.935	13	S-52,3-36,2-16	0.9
1917	Cle-A	156	563	98	170	28	13	2	36	61	65	.302	.370	.409	128	18	52			.938	**24**	*S-156	5.4
1918	Cle-A	128	446	**84**	119	19	8	1	32	84	46	.267	.390	.352	113	10	30			.936	6	*S-128/O-1	2.4
1919	Cle-A	115	433	75	130	23	10	3	53	31	38	.300	.351	.420	109	4	18			.944	-0	*S-115	1.2
1920	Cle-A	111	435	97	132	27	8	3	49	52	38	.303	.380	.423	109	6	13	9	-2	.959	12	*S-111	2.5
Total	9	1051	3785	671	1053	162	81	17	364	452	414	.278	.358	.377	110	48	233	<u>47</u>		.939	30	S-957/2-49,3-36,O-2	15.4

■ SAM CHAPMAN
Chapman, Samuel Blake   b: 4/11/16, Tiburon, Cal.   BR/TR, 6'1", 190 lbs.   Deb: 5/16/38

1938	Phi-A	114	406	60	105	17	7	11	63	56	94	.259	.353	.461	105	2	3	4	-2	.952	-2	*O-110	-0.4
1939	Phi-A	140	498	74	134	24	6	15	64	51	62	.269	.338	.432	98	-3	11	4	1	.955	4	*O-117,1-19	-0.3
1940	Phi-A	134	508	88	140	26	3	23	75	46	96	.276	.337	.474	110	6	2	6	-3	.963	4	*O-129	0.0
1941	Phi-A	143	552	97	178	29	9	25	106	47	49	.322	.378	.543	145	33	6	9	-4	.967	14	*O-141	3.4
1945	Phi-A	9	30	3	6	2	0	1	2	4		.200	.250	.267	50	-2	0	0	0	1.000	-1	/O-8	-0.4
1946	Phi-A★	146	545	77	142	22	5	20	67	54	66	.261	.327	.429	111	6	1	3	-2	.970	10	*O-145	0.8
1947	Phi-A	149	551	84	139	18	5	14	83	65	70	.252	.331	.379	95	-4	3	4	-2	.987	12	*O-146	-0.2
1948	Phi-A	123	445	58	115	18	6	13	70	55	50	.258	.341	.413	100	-1	6	1	1	.982	7	*O-118	0.1

YEAR	TM/L	G	AB	R	H	2B	3B	HR	RBI	BB	SO	AVG	OBP	SLG	PRO+	BR/A	SB	CS	SBR	FA	FR	G/POS	TPR
1949	Phi-A	154	589	89	164	24	4	24	108	80	68	.278	.367	.455	121	16	3	4	-2	.979	11	*O-154	1.7
1950	Phi-A	144	553	93	139	20	6	23	95	68	79	.251	.338	.434	98	-4	3	3	-1	.978	10	*O-140	0.0
1951	Phi-A	18	65	7	11	1	0	0	5	12	12	.169	.299	.185	32	-6	0	0	0	.957	-1	O-17	-0.7
	Cle-A	94	246	24	56	9	1	6	36	27	32	.228	.304	.346	80	-8	3	0	1	.985	-18	O-84/1-1	-2.7
	Yr	112	311	31	67	10	1	6	41	39	44	.215	.303	.312	69	-14	3	0	1	.978	-19	*O-101/1-1	-3.4
Total	11	1368	4988	754	1329	210	52	180	773	562	682	.266	.342	.438	107	34	41	38	-11	.972	53	*O-1309/1-20	1.3

■ BEN CHAPMAN
Chapman, William Benjamin   b: 12/25/08, Nashville, Tenn.   d: 7/7/93, Hoover, Ala.   BR/TR, 6', 190 lbs.   Deb: 4/15/30   MC

YEAR	TM/L	G	AB	R	H	2B	3B	HR	RBI	BB	SO	AVG	OBP	SLG	PRO+	BR/A	SB	CS	SBR	FA	FR	G/POS	TPR
1930	NY-A	138	513	74	162	31	10	10	81	43	58	.316	.371	.474	118	13	14	6	1	.912	-6	3-91,2-45	1.4
1931	NY-A	149	600	120	189	28	11	17	122	75	77	.315	.396	.483	138	33	**61**	23	**5**	.963	8	*O-137,2-11	3.5
1932	*NY-A	151	581	101	174	41	15	10	107	71	55	.299	.381	.473	126	23	**38**	18	1	.949	5	*O-150	1.1
1933	NY-A★	147	565	112	176	36	4	9	98	72	45	.312	.393	.437	127	24	**27**	18	-3	.975	11	*O-147	2.3
1934	NY-A★	149	588	82	181	21	**13**	5	86	67	68	.308	.381	.413	113	12	26	16	-2	.967	8	*O-149	1.1
1935	NY-A★	140	553	118	160	38	8	9	74	61	39	.289	.361	.430	110	8	17	10	1	.964	17	*O-138	1.7
1936	NY-A	36	139	19	37	14	3	1	21	15	20	.266	.338	.432	92	-2	1	2	-1	.965	2	O-36	-0.2
	Was-A★	97	401	91	133	36	7	4	60	69	18	.332	.431	.486	133	24	19	7	2	.959	4	O-97	2.2
	Yr	133	540	110	170	50	10	5	81	84	38	.315	.408	.472	123	21	20	9	1	.961	5	*O-133	2.0
1937	Was-A	35	130	23	34	7	1	0	12	26	7	.262	.385	.331	86	-2	8	0	2	.957	-1	O-32	-0.2
	Bos-A	113	423	76	130	23	11	7	57	57	35	.307	.391	.463	110	7	27	12	1	.985	9	*O-112/S-1	1.2
	Yr	148	553	99	164	30	12	7	69	83	42	.297	.389	.432	105	6	**35**	12	**3**	.978	7	*O-144/S-1	1.0
1938	Bos-A	127	480	92	163	40	8	6	80	65	33	.340	.418	.494	122	17	13	6	0	.966	6	*O-126/3-1	1.8
1939	Cle-A	149	545	101	158	31	9	6	82	87	30	.290	.390	.413	109	10	18	6	2	.971	-4	*O-146	0.3
1940	Cle-A	143	548	82	157	40	6	4	50	78	45	.286	.377	.403	105	7	13	7	-0	.964	2	*O-140	0.0
1941	Was-A	28	110	9	28	6	0	1	10	10	6	.255	.317	.336	76	-4	2	2	-1	.983	1	O-26	-0.5
	Chi-A	57	190	26	43	9	1	2	19	19	14	.226	.297	.316	63	-10	2	2	-1	.992	1	O-49	-1.3
	Yr	85	300	35	71	15	1	3	29	29	20	.237	.304	.323	68	-14	4	4	-1	.989	2	O-75	-1.8
1944	Bro-N	20	38	11	14	4	0	0	11	5	4	.368	.442	.474	161	3	1			.900	-2	P-11	0.0
1945	Bro-N	13	22	2	3	0	0	0	3	2	1	.136	.208	.136	-3	-3	0			.938	1	P-10	0.0
	Phi-N	24	51	4	16	2	0	0	4	2	1	.314	.340	.353	95	-0	0			.933	-3	O-10/3-4,P-3,M	-0.4
	Yr	37	73	6	19	2	0	0	7	4	2	.260	.299	.288	65	-3	0			.941	-3	P-13,O-10/3-4	-0.4
1946	Phi-N	1	1	0	0	0	0	0	0	0	0	.000	.000	.000	-99	-0				.000	0	/P-1,M	0.0
Total	15	1717	6478	1144	1958	407	107	90	977	824	556	.302	.383	.440	115	159	287	135		.967	50	*O-1495/3-96,2PS	14.0

■ FRED CHAPMAN
Chapman, William Fred "Chappie"   b: 7/17/16, Liberty, S.C.   BR/TR, 6'1", 185 lbs.   Deb: 9/15/39

YEAR	TM/L	G	AB	R	H	2B	3B	HR	RBI	BB	SO	AVG	OBP	SLG	PRO+	BR/A	SB	CS	SBR	FA	FR	G/POS	TPR
1939	Phi-A	15	49	5	14	1	1	0	1	1	3	.286	.300	.347	66	-3	1	0	0	.899	-4	S-15	-0.4
1940	Phi-A	26	69	6	11	1	0	0	4	6	10	.159	.227	.174	6	-10	1	1	-0	.862	-5	S-25	-1.3
1941	Phi-A	35	69	1	11	1	0	0	4	4	15	.159	.205	.174	1	-10	1	2	-1	.917	-2	S-28/3-2,2-1	-1.1
Total	3	76	187	12	36	3	1	0	9	11	28	.193	.237	.219	20	-22	3	3	-1	.889	-11	/S-68,3-2,2-1	-2.8

■ HARRY CHAPPAS
Chappas, Harry Perry   b: 10/26/57, Mt.Rainier, Md.   BB/TR, 5'3", 150 lbs.   Deb: 9/7/78

YEAR	TM/L	G	AB	R	H	2B	3B	HR	RBI	BB	SO	AVG	OBP	SLG	PRO+	BR/A	SB	CS	SBR	FA	FR	G/POS	TPR
1978	Chi-A	20	75	11	20	1	0	0	6	6	11	.267	.329	.280	72	-3	1	2	-1	1.000	0	S-20	-0.1
1979	Chi-A	26	59	9	17	1	0	1	4	5	5	.288	.354	.356	92	-0	1	1	-0	.929	3	S-23	0.3
1980	Chi-A	26	50	6	8	2	0	0	2	4	10	.160	.236	.200	21	-5	0	2	-1	.981	-2	S-19/2-1,D-2	-0.6
Total	3	72	184	26	45	4	0	1	12	15	26	.245	.312	.283	65	-8	2	5	-2	.967	1	/S-62,D-2,2-1	-0.4

■ LARRY CHAPPELL
Chappell, La Verne Ashford   b: 2/19/1890, McClusky, Ill.   d: 11/8/18, San Francisco, Cal.   BL/TR, 6', 186 lbs.   Deb: 7/18/13

YEAR	TM/L	G	AB	R	H	2B	3B	HR	RBI	BB	SO	AVG	OBP	SLG	PRO+	BR/A	SB	CS	SBR	FA	FR	G/POS	TPR
1913	Chi-A	60	208	20	48	8	1	0	15	18	22	.231	.295	.279	69	-8	7			.952	-1	O-59	-1.3
1914	Chi-A	21	39	3	9	0	0	0	1	4	11	.231	.302	.231	61	-2	0			.929	-2	I/O-9	-0.4
1915	Chi-A	1	1	0	0	0	0	0	0	0	0	.000	.000	.000	-97	-0	0			.000	0	H	0.0
1916	Cle-A	3	2	0	0	0	0	0	0	1	0	.000	.333	.000	1	-0	1			.000	0	H	0.0
	Bos-N	20	53	4	12	1	1	0	9	2	8	.226	.268	.283	72	-2	0			.957	-2	O-14	-0.5
1917	Bos-N	4	2	0	0	0	0	0	1	0	1	.000	.000	.000	-99	-0	0			.000	-1	/O-1	-0.1
Total	5	109	305	27	69	9	2	0	26	25	42	.226	.289	.269	66	-13	9			.951	-5	/O-83	-2.3

■ JOE CHARBONEAU
Charboneau, Joseph   b: 6/17/55, Belvidere, Ill.   BR/TR, 6'2", 205 lbs.   Deb: 4/11/80

YEAR	TM/L	G	AB	R	H	2B	3B	HR	RBI	BB	SO	AVG	OBP	SLG	PRO+	BR/A	SB	CS	SBR	FA	FR	G/POS	TPR
1980	Cle-A	131	453	76	131	17	2	23	87	49	70	.289	.362	.488	130	18	2	4	-2	.963	1	O-67,D-57	1.3
1981	Cle-A	48	138	14	29	1	4	4	18	7	22	.210	.248	.362	75	-5	1	0	0	.963	-2	O-27,D-14	-0.8
1982	Cle-A	22	56	7	12	2	1	2	9	5	7	.214	.290	.393	86	-1	0	0	0	.955	-3	O-18/D-1	-0.5
Total	3	201	647	97	172	20	7	29	114	61	99	.266	.333	.453	115	12	3	4	-2	.962	-4	O-112/D-72	-0.0

■ ED CHARLES
Charles, Edwin Douglas   b: 4/29/33, Daytona Beach, Fla.   BR/TR, 5'10", 170 lbs.   Deb: 4/11/62

YEAR	TM/L	G	AB	R	H	2B	3B	HR	RBI	BB	SO	AVG	OBP	SLG	PRO+	BR/A	SB	CS	SBR	FA	FR	G/POS	TPR
1962	KC-A	147	535	81	154	24	7	17	74	54	70	.288	.358	.454	111	9	20	4	4	.964	4	*3-140/2-2	1.8
1963	KC-A	158	603	82	161	28	2	15	79	58	79	.267	.336	.395	99	-1	15	8	-0	.949	-8	*3-158	-0.9
1964	KC-A	150	557	69	134	25	2	16	63	64	92	.241	.323	.379	92	-6	12	7	-1	.954	-15	*3-147	-2.4
1965	KC-A	134	480	55	129	19	7	8	56	44	72	.269	.335	.387	106	4	13	4	2	.971	-1	*3-128/2-1,S-1	0.2
1966	KC-A	118	385	52	110	18	5	9	42	30	53	.286	.337	.444	127	12	12	5	1	.963	-6	*3-104/1-1,O-1	0.5
1967	KC-A	19	61	5	15	1	0	0	5	12	13	.246	.378	.262	95	0	1	0	0	.966	-0	3-18	0.1
	NY-N	101	323	32	77	13	2	3	31	24	58	.238	.305	.319	80	-8	4	1	1	.944	9	3-89	0.0
1968	NY-N	117	369	41	102	11	1	15	53	28	57	.276	.331	.434	127	12	5	4	-1	.954	9	*3-106/1-2	1.3
1969	*NY-N	61	169	21	35	8	1	3	18	18	31	.207	.287	.320	68	-7	4	2	0	.946	-0	3-52	-0.8
Total	8	1005	3482	438	917	147	30	86	421	332	525	.263	.332	.397	103	16	86	35	5	.957	-15	3-942/1-3,2-3,0S	-0.2

■ CHAPPY CHARLES
Charles, Raymond (b: Charles Shuh Achenbach)   b: 3/25/1881, Phillipsburg, N.J.   d: 8/4/59, Bethlehem, Pa.   BR/TR, 5'11", 175 lbs.   Deb: 4/15/08

YEAR	TM/L	G	AB	R	H	2B	3B	HR	RBI	BB	SO	AVG	OBP	SLG	PRO+	BR/A	SB	CS	SBR	FA	FR	G/POS	TPR
1908	StL-N	121	454	39	93	14	3	1	17	19		.205	.238	.256	61	-21	15			.921	-12	2-65,S-31,3-23	-3.9
1909	StL-N	99	339	33	80	7	3	0	29	31		.236	.309	.274	87	-5	7			.918	-2	2-71,S-26/3-2	-0.8
	Cin-N	13	43	3	11	2	0	0	5	4		.256	.319	.302	94	-0	2			.932	-3	2-10/S-3	-0.4
	Yr	112	382	36	91	9	3	0	34	35		.238	.310	.277	87	-5	9			.920	-4	2-81,S-29/3-2	-1.2
1910	Cin-N	4	15	1	2	0	1	0	0	0	1	.133	.133	.267	17	-2	0			.818	-2	/S-4	-0.3
Total	3	237	851	76	186	23	7	1	51	54	1	.219	.270	.266	72	-28	24			.920	-18	2-146/S-64,3-25	-5.4

■ MIKE CHARTAK
Chartak, Michael George "Shotgun"   b: 4/28/16, Brooklyn, N.Y.   d: 7/25/67, Cedar Rapids, Ia.   BL/TL, 6'2", 180 lbs.   Deb: 9/13/40

YEAR	TM/L	G	AB	R	H	2B	3B	HR	RBI	BB	SO	AVG	OBP	SLG	PRO+	BR/A	SB	CS	SBR	FA	FR	G/POS	TPR
1940	NY-A	11	15	2	2	1	0	0	3	5	5	.133	.350	.200	49	-1	0	0	0	1.000	-1	/O-3	-0.2
1942	NY-A	5	5	0	0	0	0	0	0	0	0	.000	.000	.000	-99	-1	0	0	0	.000	0	H	-0.1
	Was-A	24	92	11	20	4	2	1	8	14	16	.217	.321	.337	86	-2	0	1	-1	.926	-0	O-24	-0.6
	StL-A	73	237	37	59	11	2	9	43	40	27	.249	.362	.426	119	7	3	3	-1	.974	7	O-64	1.0
	Yr	102	334	48	79	15	4	10	51	54	43	.237	.346	.395	107	4	3	4	-2	.962	7	O-88	0.5
1943	StL-A	108	344	38	88	16	2	10	37	39	55	.256	.333	.401	112	5	1	3	-2	.970	-4	O-77,1-18	-0.5
1944	*StL-A	35	72	8	17	2	1	1	7	6	9	.236	.304	.333	77	-2	0	0	0	1.000	4	1-12/O-7	-0.3
Total	4	256	765	96	186	34	7	21	98	104	112	.243	.337	.388	105	5	4	7	-3	.967	3	O-175/1-30	-0.5

■ HAL CHASE
Chase, Harold Homer "Prince Hal"   b: 2/13/1883, Los Gatos, Cal.   d: 5/18/47, Colusa, Cal.   BR/TL, 6', 175 lbs.   Deb: 4/14/05   M

YEAR	TM/L	G	AB	R	H	2B	3B	HR	RBI	BB	SO	AVG	OBP	SLG	PRO+	BR/A	SB	CS	SBR	FA	FR	G/POS	TPR
1905	NY-A	128	465	60	116	16	6	3	49	15		.249	.277	.329	83	-11	22			.976	-9	*1-124/S-2,2-1	-2.7
1906	NY-A	151	597	84	193	23	10	0	76	13		.323	.341	.395	118	10	28			.980	-3	*1-150/2-1	0.3
1907	NY-A	125	498	72	143	23	3	2	68	19		.287	.315	.357	106	1	32			.973	0	*1-121/O-4	-0.2
1908	NY-A	106	405	50	104	11	3	1	36	15		.257	.285	.306	91	-5	27			.980	-4	1-98/2-3,O-3,3-1,P	-1.2
1909	NY-A	118	474	60	134	17	3	4	63	20		.283	.317	.357	112	5	25			.978	-2	*1-118/S-1	0.2
1910	NY-A	130	524	67	152	20	5	3	73	16		.290	.312	.365	106	1	40			.981	-4	*1-130,M	-0.4
1911	NY-A	133	527	82	166	32	7	3	62	21		.315	.342	.419	105	1	36			.974	-2	*1-124/O-7,2-2,M	-0.6
1912	NY-A	131	522	61	143	21	9	4	58	17		.274	.299	.372	86	-12	33			.979	-2	*1-122/2-7	-1.6
1913	NY-A	39	146	15	31	2	4	0	9	11	13	.212	.268	.281	60	-8	5			.982	-5	1-29/2-5,O-5	-1.4

YEAR	TM/L	G	AB	R	H	2B	3B	HR	RBI	BB	SO	AVG	OBP	SLG	PRO+	BR/A	SB	CS	SBR	FA	FR	G/POS	TPR
	Chi-A	102	384	49	110	11	10	2	39	16	41	.286	.320	.383	107	1	9			.976	1	*1-102	0.1
	Yr	141	530	64	141	13	14	2	48	27	54	.266	.305	.355	94	-7	14			.977	-4	*1-131/2-5,O-5	-1.3
1914	Chi-A	58	206	27	55	10	5	0	20	23	19	.267	.343	.364	114	4	9	4	0	.981	2	1-58	0.5
	Buf-F	75	291	43	101	19	9	3	48	6	31	.347	.365	.505	133	7	10			.980	-1	1-73	0.5
1915	Buf-F	145	567	85	165	31	10	**17**	89	20	50	.291	.316	.471	118	1	23			.983	0	*1-143/O-1	-0.3
1916	Cin-N	142	542	66	**184**	29	12	4	82	19	48	**.339**	.363	.459	**155**	**32**	22	11	0	.986	-7	1-98,O-25,2-16	2.3
1917	Cin-N	152	602	71	167	28	15	4	86	15	49	.277	.296	.394	115	7	21			.983	-3	*1-151	-0.1
1918	Cin-N	74	259	30	78	12	6	2	38	13	15	.301	.339	.417	133	9	5			.980	-2	1-67/O-2	0.5
1919	NY-N	110	408	58	116	17	7	5	45	17	40	.284	.318	.397	115	6	16			.984	-1	*1-107	0.1
Total	15	1919	7417	980	2158	322	124	57	941	276	306	.291	.319	.391	110	51	363	15		.980	-42	*1-1815/O-47,2SP3	-3.6

■ BUSTER CHATHAM
Chatham, Charles L   b: 12/25/01, West, Tex.   d: 12/15/75, Waco, Tex.   BR/TR, 5'5", 150 lbs.   Deb: 6/1/30

YEAR	TM/L	G	AB	R	H	2B	3B	HR	RBI	BB	SO	AVG	OBP	SLG	PRO+	BR/A	SB	CS	SBR	FA	FR	G/POS	TPR
1930	Bos-N	112	404	48	108	20	11	5	56	37	41	.267	.332	.408	80	-13	8			.920	-14	3-92,S-17	-1.8
1931	Bos-N	17	44	4	10	1	0	1	3	6	6	.227	.320	.318	75	-1	0			.762	-6	/S-6,3-6	-0.6
Total	2	129	448	52	118	21	11	6	59	43	47	.263	.331	.400	80	-15	8			.924	-20	/3-98,S-23	-2.4

■ JIM CHATTERTON
Chatterton, James M.   b: 10/14/1864, Brooklyn, N.Y.   d: 12/15/44, Tewksbury, Mass.   Deb: 6/7/1884

YEAR	TM/L	G	AB	R	H	2B	3B	HR	RBI	BB	SO	AVG	OBP	SLG	PRO+	BR/A	SB	CS	SBR	FA	FR	G/POS	TPR
1884	KC-U	4	15	4	2	1	0	0			2	.133	.235	.200	38	-2				1.000	0	/O-2,1-2,P-1	-0.1

■ OSSIE CHAVARRIA
Chavarria, Osvaldo (Quijano)   b: 8/5/40, Colon, Panama   BR/TR, 5'11", 155 lbs.   Deb: 4/14/66

YEAR	TM/L	G	AB	R	H	2B	3B	HR	RBI	BB	SO	AVG	OBP	SLG	PRO+	BR/A	SB	CS	SBR	FA	FR	G/POS	TPR
1966	KC-A	86	191	26	46	10	0	2	10	18	43	.241	.306	.325	84	-4	3	2	-0	.939	-5	O-26,S-23,2-14,/13	-0.8
1967	KC-A	38	59	2	6	2	0	0	4	7	16	.102	.209	.136	4	-7	1	0	0	1.000	2	2-17/3-7,O-3,S-2	-0.4
Total	2	124	250	28	52	12	0	2	14	25	59	.208	.283	.280	65	-11	4	2	0	.990	-2	/2-31,O-29,S-25,31	-1.2

■ RAUL CHAVEZ
Chavez, Raul Alexander   b: 3/18/73, Valencia, Venez.   BR/TR, 5'11", 175 lbs.   Deb: 8/30/96

YEAR	TM/L	G	AB	R	H	2B	3B	HR	RBI	BB	SO	AVG	OBP	SLG	PRO+	BR/A	SB	CS	SBR	FA	FR	G/POS	TPR
1996	Mon-N	4	5	1	1	0	0	0	0	0	1	.200	.333	.200	44	-0	1	0	0	1.000	1	/C-3	0.1

■ HARRY CHEEK
Cheek, Harry G.   b: 1879, Sedalia, Mo.   d: 6/25/56, Paramas, N.J.   TR ,   Deb: 5/12/10

YEAR	TM/L	G	AB	R	H	2B	3B	HR	RBI	BB	SO	AVG	OBP	SLG	PRO+	BR/A	SB	CS	SBR	FA	FR	G/POS	TPR
1910	Phi-N	2	4	1	2	1	0	0	0	0	0	.500	.500	.750	255	1	0			1.000	-1	/C-2	0.0

■ PAUL CHERVINKO
Chervinko, Paul   b: 7/28/10, Trauger, Pa.   d: 6/3/76, Danville, Ill.   BR/TR, 5'8", 185 lbs.   Deb: 5/30/37

YEAR	TM/L	G	AB	R	H	2B	3B	HR	RBI	BB	SO	AVG	OBP	SLG	PRO+	BR/A	SB	CS	SBR	FA	FR	G/POS	TPR
1937	Bro-N	30	48	1	7	0	1	0	2	3	16	.146	.196	.188	5	-6	0			1.000	0	C-26	-0.5
1938	Bro-N	12	27	0	4	0	0	0	3	2	0	.148	.207	.148	-1	-4	0			.974	0	C-12	-0.3
Total	2	42	75	1	11	0	1	0	5	5	16	.147	.200	.173	3	-10	0			.990	1	/C-38	-0.8

■ CUPID CHILDS
Childs, Clarence Algernon   b: 8/14/1867, Calvert Co., Md.   d: 11/8/12, Baltimore, Md.   BL/TR, 5'8", 185 lbs.   Deb: 4/23/1888

YEAR	TM/L	G	AB	R	H	2B	3B	HR	RBI	BB	SO	AVG	OBP	SLG	PRO+	BR/A	SB	CS	SBR	FA	FR	G/POS	TPR
1888	Phi-N	2	4	0	0	0	0	0	0	0	0	.000	.000	.000	-95	-1	0			.857	3	/2-2	-0.1
1890	Syr-a	126	493	109	170	**33**	14	2	89	72		.345	.434	.481	189	**59**	56			.928	12	*2-125/S-1	**6.7**
1891	Cle-N	141	551	120	155	21	12	2	83	97	32	.281	.395	.374	119	17	39			.910	-12	*2-141	1.0
1892	*Cle-N	145	558	**136**	177	14	11	3	53	117	20	.317	**.443**	.398	149	40	26			.938	-6	*2-145	3.4
1893	Cle-N	124	485	145	158	19	10	3	65	120	12	.326	.463	.425	129	26	23			.926	10	*2-123	3.1
1894	Cle-N	118	479	143	169	21	12	2	52	107	11	.353	.475	.459	122	23	17			.916	-3	*2-118	1.9
1895	*Cle-N	119	462	96	133	15	3	4	90	74	24	.288	.393	.359	90	-5	20			.921	10	*2-119	0.9
1896	*Cle-N	132	498	106	177	24	9	1	106	100	18	.355	.467	.446	134	30	25			.942	42	*2-132	6.6
1897	Cle-N	114	444	105	150	15	9	1	61	74		.338	.435	.419	119	15	25			.944	17	*2-114	3.2
1898	Cle-N	110	413	90	119	9	4	1	31	69		.288	.395	.337	112	10	9			.931	9	*2-110	2.4
1899	StL-N	125	464	73	123	11	11	1	48	74		.265	.369	.343	93	-2	11			.934	-12	*2-125	-0.6
1900	Chi-N	137	531	67	128	14	5	0	44	57		.241	.323	.286	71	-19	15			.935	16	*2-137	0.3
1901	Chi-N	63	236	24	61	9	0	0	21	30		.258	.359	.297	95	0	3			.939	9	2-63	1.2
Total	13	1456	5618	1214	1720	205	100	20	743	991	117	.306	.416	.389	119	194	269			.930	92	*2-1454/S-1	30.0

■ PETE CHILDS
Childs, Peter Pierre   b: 11/15/1871, Philadelphia, Pa.   d: 2/15/22, Philadelphia, Pa.   TR ,   Deb: 4/24/01

YEAR	TM/L	G	AB	R	H	2B	3B	HR	RBI	BB	SO	AVG	OBP	SLG	PRO+	BR/A	SB	CS	SBR	FA	FR	G/POS	TPR
1901	StL-N	29	79	12	21	1	0	0	8	14		.266	.389	.278	100	1	0			.907	-7	2-19/O-2,S-1	-0.4
	Chi-N	60	210	23	48	5	1	0	14	26		.229	.319	.262	72	-6	4			.959	13	2-60	0.9
	Yr	89	289	35	69	6	1	0	22	40		.239	.339	.266	80	-5	4			.947	6	2-79/O-2,S-1	0.5
1902	Phi-N	123	403	25	78	5	0	0	25	34		.194	.256	.206	43	-26	6			.945	-9	*2-123	-3.3
Total	2	212	692	60	147	11	1	0	47	74		.212	.292	.231	59	-31	10			.946	-3	2-202/O-2,S-1	-2.8

■ PEARCE CHILES
Chiles, Pearce Nuget "What's The Use"   b: 5/28/1867, Deepwater, Mo.   BR/TR, 5'11", 185 lbs.   Deb: 4/18/1899

YEAR	TM/L	G	AB	R	H	2B	3B	HR	RBI	BB	SO	AVG	OBP	SLG	PRO+	BR/A	SB	CS	SBR	FA	FR	G/POS	TPR
1899	Phi-N	97	338	57	108	28	7	2	76	16		.320	.352	.462	127	10	6			.944	-15	O-46,1-25,2-16	-0.6
1900	Phi-N	33	111	13	24	6	2	1	23	6		.216	.256	.333	63	-6	4			.987	-3	1-16,2-12/O-3	-0.8
Total	2	130	449	70	132	34	9	3	99	22		.294	.328	.430	111	4	10			.947	-18	/O-49,1-41,2-28	-1.4

■ RICH CHILES
Chiles, Richard Francis   b: 11/22/49, Sacramento, Cal.   BL/TL, 5'11", 170 lbs.   Deb: 4/20/71

YEAR	TM/L	G	AB	R	H	2B	3B	HR	RBI	BB	SO	AVG	OBP	SLG	PRO+	BR/A	SB	CS	SBR	FA	FR	G/POS	TPR
1971	Hou-N	67	119	12	27	5	1	2	15	6	20	.227	.270	.336	73	-5	0	1	-1	1.000	-3	O-27	-1.0
1972	Hou-N	9	11	0	3	1	0	0	2	1	1	.273	.364	.364	100	0	0	0	0	1.000	-2	/O-2	0.0
1973	NY-N	8	25	2	3	2	0	0	1	0	2	.120	.120	.200	-13	-4	0	0	0	1.000	2	/O-8	-0.2
1976	Hou-N	5	4	1	2	1	0	0	0	0	0	.500	.500	.750	276	1	0	0	0	1.000	-0	/O-1	0.1
1977	Min-A	108	261	31	69	16	1	3	36	23	17	.264	.329	.368	91	-3	0	1	-1	.946	-2	D-61,O-22	-0.8
1978	Min-A	87	198	22	53	12	0	1	22	20	25	.268	.341	.343	91	-2	1	2	-1	.965	-2	O-61/D-8	-0.7
Total	6	284	618	68	157	37	2	6	76	50	65	.254	.315	.350	85	-13	1	4	-2	.972	-5	O-121/D-69	-2.6

■ DINO CHIOZZA
Chiozza, Dino Joseph "Dynamo"   b: 6/30/12, Memphis, Tenn.   d: 4/23/72, Memphis, Tenn.   BL/TR, 6', 170 lbs.   Deb: 7/14/35   F

YEAR	TM/L	G	AB	R	H	2B	3B	HR	RBI	BB	SO	AVG	OBP	SLG	PRO+	BR/A	SB	CS	SBR	FA	FR	G/POS	TPR
1935	Phi-N	2	0	1	0	0	0	0	0	0	0	—	—	—			0	0		1.000	-0	/S-2	0.0

■ LOU CHIOZZA
Chiozza, Louis Peo   b: 5/17/10, Tallulah, La.   d: 2/28/71, Memphis, Tenn.   BL/TR, 6', 172 lbs.   Deb: 4/17/34   F

YEAR	TM/L	G	AB	R	H	2B	3B	HR	RBI	BB	SO	AVG	OBP	SLG	PRO+	BR/A	SB	CS	SBR	FA	FR	G/POS	TPR
1934	Phi-N	134	484	66	147	28	5	0	44	34	35	.304	.357	.382	86	-9	9			.938	-24	2-85,3-26,O-17	-2.7
1935	Phi-N	124	472	71	134	26	6	3	47	33	44	.284	.333	.383	84	-11	6			.947	3	*2-120/3-2	0.1
1936	Phi-N	144	572	83	170	32	6	1	48	37	39	.297	.346	.379	87	-11	17			.972	1	O-90,2-33,3-26	-1.1
1937	*NY-N	117	439	49	102	11	2	4	29	20	30	.232	.266	.294	51	-30	6			.939	2	3-93,O-12/2-2	-2.6
1938	NY-N	57	179	15	42	7	3	0	17	12	7	.235	.283	.346	72	-7	5			.944	-8	2-34,O-16/3-1	-1.4
1939	NY-N	40	142	19	38	3	1	3	12	9	10	.268	.311	.366	81	-4	3			.915	-3	3-30/S-8	-0.6
Total	6	616	2288	303	633	107	22	14	197	145	165	.277	.324	.361	78	-72	45			.943	-30	2-274,3-178,O/S	-8.3

■ WALT CHIPPLE
Chipple, Walter John (b: Walter John Chlipala)   b: 9/26/18, Utica, N.Y.   d: 6/8/88, Tonawanda, N.Y.   BR/TR, 6'0.5", 168 lbs.   Deb: 4/17/45

YEAR	TM/L	G	AB	R	H	2B	3B	HR	RBI	BB	SO	AVG	OBP	SLG	PRO+	BR/A	SB	CS	SBR	FA	FR	G/POS	TPR
1945	Was-A	18	44	4	6	0	0	0	5	5	6	.136	.224	.136	6	-5	0	1	-1	.978	3	O-13	-0.4

■ TOM CHISM
Chism, Thomas Raymond   b: 5/9/55, Chester, Pa.   BL/TL, 6'1", 195 lbs.   Deb: 9/13/79

YEAR	TM/L	G	AB	R	H	2B	3B	HR	RBI	BB	SO	AVG	OBP	SLG	PRO+	BR/A	SB	CS	SBR	FA	FR	G/POS	TPR
1979	Bal-A	6	3	0	0	0	0	0	0	0	0	.000	.000	.000	-99	-1	0	0	0	1.000	-0	/1-4	-0.1

■ HARRY CHITI
Chiti, Harry   b: 11/16/32, Kincaid, Ill.   BR/TR, 6'3", 225 lbs.   Deb: 9/27/50

YEAR	TM/L	G	AB	R	H	2B	3B	HR	RBI	BB	SO	AVG	OBP	SLG	PRO+	BR/A	SB	CS	SBR	FA	FR	G/POS	TPR
1950	Chi-N	3	6	0	2	0	0	0	0	0	0	.333	.333	.333	77	-0	0			1.000	-1	/C-1	-0.1
1951	Chi-N	9	31	1	11	2	0	0	5	2	2	.355	.394	.419	117	1	0			.913	0	/C-8	0.1
1952	Chi-N	32	113	14	31	5	0	5	13	5	8	.274	.305	.451	106	0	0	1	-1	.984	6	C-32	0.7
1955	Chi-N	113	338	24	78	6	1	11	41	26	68	.231	.286	.352	68	-16	0	0	0	.984	4	*C-113	-1.2
1956	Chi-N	72	203	17	43	6	4	4	18	19	36	.212	.283	.340	68	-10	0	0	0	.981	2	C-67	-0.5
1958	KC-A	103	295	32	79	11	3	9	44	15	48	.268	.316	.417	98	-1	3	4	-2	.987	3	C-83	0.6
1959	KC-A	55	162	20	44	11	1	5	25	17	26	.272	.344	.444	113	3	0	1	-1	.988	2	C-47	0.7
1960	KC-A	58	190	16	42	7	0	5	28	14	33	.221	.288	.337	68	-9	1	0	-0	.983	-1	C-52	-0.6
	Det-A	37	104	9	17	0	0	2	5	12	12	.163	.237	.221	24	-11	0	3	-2	.984	1	C-36	-1.0
	Yr	95	294	25	59	7	0	7	33	26	45	.201	.270	.296	52	-20	1	3	-2	.984	1	C-88	-1.6
1961	Det-A	5	12	0	1	0	0	0	0	1	2	.083	.154	.083	-34	-2	0	0	0	1.000	1	/C-5	-0.1

YEAR	TM/L	G	AB	R	H	2B	3B	HR	RBI	BB	SO	AVG	OBP	SLG	PRO+	BR/A	SB	CS	SBR	FA	FR	G/POS	TPR
1962	NY-N	15	41	2	8	1	0	0	0	1	8	.195	.233	.220	22	-4	0	0	0	.971	-1	C-14	-0.5
Total	10	502	1495	135	356	49	9	41	179	115	242	.238	.296	.365	77	-50	4	7		.983	13	C-458	-1.9

■ FELIX CHOUINARD
Chouinard, Felix George   b: 10/5/1887, Hines, Ill.   d: 4/28/55, Hines, Ill.   BR/TR, 5'7", 150 lbs.   Deb: 9/11/10

YEAR	TM/L	G	AB	R	H	2B	3B	HR	RBI	BB	SO	AVG	OBP	SLG	PRO+	BR/A	SB	CS	SBR	FA	FR	G/POS	TPR
1910	Chi-A	24	82	6	16	3	2	0	9	8		.195	.275	.280	77	-2	4			.962	4	O-23/2-1	0.1
1911	Chi-A	14	17	3	3	0	0	0	8	0		.176	.176	.176	-2	-2	0			.857	1	/2-4,O-4	-0.1
1914	Pit-F	9	30	2	9	1	0	1	3	0	4	.300	.300	.433	99	-1	1			.917	-0	/2-4,O-3,S-1	-0.1
	Bro-F	32	79	7	20	1	2	0	8	4	13	.253	.289	.316	65	-5	3			.929	-1	O-20	-0.7
	Bal-F	5	9	3	4	0	0	0	1	0	1	.444	.444	.444	138	0	0			1.000	-0	/O-2	0.0
	Yr	46	118	12	33	2	2	1	12	4	18	.280	.303	.356	79	-5	4			.941	-1	O-25/2-4,S-1	-0.8
1915	Bro-F	4	4	1	2	0	0	0	2	0		.500	.500	.500	183	0	0			1.000	-1	/O-2	0.0
Total	4	88	221	22	54	5	4	1	23	12	18	.244	.286	.317	75	-10	8			.948	4	/O-54,2-9,S-1	-0.8

■ HARRY CHOZEN
Chozen, Harry   b: 9/27/15, Winnebago, Minn.   d: 9/16/94, Houston, Tex.   BR/TR, 5'9.5", 190 lbs.   Deb: 9/21/37

YEAR	TM/L	G	AB	R	H	2B	3B	HR	RBI	BB	SO	AVG	OBP	SLG	PRO+	BR/A	SB	CS	SBR	FA	FR	G/POS	TPR
1937	Cin-N	1	4	0	1	0	0	0	0	0	0	.250	.250	.250	38	-0	0			.833	-0	/C-1	-0.1

■ NEIL CHRISLEY
Chrisley, Barbra O'Neil   b: 12/16/31, Calhoun Falls, S.C   BL/TR, 6'3", 187 lbs.   Deb: 4/15/57

YEAR	TM/L	G	AB	R	H	2B	3B	HR	RBI	BB	SO	AVG	OBP	SLG	PRO+	BR/A	SB	CS	SBR	FA	FR	G/POS	TPR
1957	Was-A	26	51	6	8	2	1	0	3	7	7	.157	.259	.235	36	-4	0	0	0	.810	-1	O-11	-0.6
1958	Was-A	105	233	19	50	7	4	5	26	16	18	.215	.265	.343	67	-11	1	3	-2	.992	1	O-69/3-1	-1.6
1959	Det-A	65	106	7	14	3	0	6	11	12	10	.132	.227	.330	48	-8	0	0	0	1.000	-2	O-21	-1.1
1960	Det-A	96	220	27	56	10	3	5	24	19	26	.255	.317	.395	89	-4	2	0	1	.981	2	O-47/1-2	-0.3
1961	Mil-N	10	9	1	2	0	0	0	0	2	0	.222	.300	.222	44	-1	0	0	0	.000	-0	H	-0.1
Total	5	302	619	60	130	22	8	16	64	55	62	.210	.277	.349	69	-28	3	3	-1	.975	-0	O-148/1-2,3-1	-3.7

■ LLOYD CHRISTENBURY
Christenbury, Lloyd Reid "Low"   b: 10/19/1893, Mecklenburg Co., N.C.   d: 12/13/44, Birmingham, Ala.   BL/TR, 5'7", 165 lbs.   Deb: 9/20/19

YEAR	TM/L	G	AB	R	H	2B	3B	HR	RBI	BB	SO	AVG	OBP	SLG	PRO+	BR/A	SB	CS	SBR	FA	FR	G/POS	TPR
1919	Bos-N	7	31	5	9	1	0	0	4	2	2	.290	.333	.323	102	0	0			.941	1	/O-7	0.1
1920	Bos-N	65	106	17	22	2	2	0	14	13	12	.208	.300	.264	66	-4	0	1	-1	.895	-7	O-14/S-7,2-6,3-2	-1.2
1921	Bos-N	62	125	34	44	6	2	3	16	21	7	.352	.449	.504	161	12	3	4	-2	.914	-13	2-32/S-2,3-2	-0.1
1922	Bos-N	71	152	22	38	5	2	1	13	18	11	.250	.337	.329	76	-5	2	4	-2	.946	0	O-32/2-5,3-2	-0.8
Total	4	205	414	78	113	14	6	4	47	54	32	.273	.362	.365	101	3	5	9		.936	-18	/O-53,2-43,S-9,3-6	-2.0

■ BRUCE CHRISTENSEN
Christensen, Bruce Ray   b: 2/22/48, Madison, Wis.   BL/TR, 5'11", 160 lbs.   Deb: 7/17/71

YEAR	TM/L	G	AB	R	H	2B	3B	HR	RBI	BB	SO	AVG	OBP	SLG	PRO+	BR/A	SB	CS	SBR	FA	FR	G/POS	TPR
1971	Cal-A	29	63	4	17	1	0	0	3	6	5	.270	.333	.286	83	-1	0	1	-1	.988	2	S-24	0.3

■ JOHN CHRISTENSEN
Christensen, John Lawrence   b: 9/5/60, Downey, Cal.   BR/TR, 6'3", 205 lbs.   Deb: 9/13/84

YEAR	TM/L	G	AB	R	H	2B	3B	HR	RBI	BB	SO	AVG	OBP	SLG	PRO+	BR/A	SB	CS	SBR	FA	FR	G/POS	TPR
1984	NY-N	5	11	2	3	2	0	0	3	1	2	.273	.333	.455	121	0	0	1	-1	.500	-2	/O-5	-0.2
1985	NY-N	51	113	10	21	4	1	3	13	19	23	.186	.303	.319	76	-3	1	2	-1	.956	-6	O-38	-1.2
1987	Sea-A	53	132	19	32	6	1	2	12	12	28	.242	.306	.348	69	-6	2	0	1	1.000	-5	O-43/D-8	-0.8
1988	Min-A	23	38	5	10	4	0	0	5	3	5	.263	.349	.368	98	0	0	0	0	1.000	-3	O-17/D-1	-0.3
Total	4	132	294	36	66	16	2	5	33	35	58	.224	.311	.344	77	-9	3	3	-1	.977	-13	O-103/D-9	-2.5

■ CUCKOO CHRISTENSEN
Christensen, Walter Niels "Seacap"   b: 10/24/1899, San Francisco, Cal   d: 12/20/84, Menlo Park, Cal.   BL/TL, 5'6.5", 156 lbs.   Deb: 4/13/26

YEAR	TM/L	G	AB	R	H	2B	3B	HR	RBI	BB	SO	AVG	OBP	SLG	PRO+	BR/A	SB	CS	SBR	FA	FR	G/POS	TPR
1926	Cin-N	114	329	41	115	15	7	0	41	40	18	.350	.426	.438	136	19	8			.978	-10	O-93	0.3
1927	Cin-N	57	185	25	47	6	0	0	16	20	16	.254	.330	.286	68	-8	4			.957	-3	O-50	-1.4
Total	2	171	514	66	162	21	7	0	57	60	34	.315	.392	.383	112	11	12			.970	-13	O-143	-1.1

■ BOB CHRISTIAN
Christian, Robert Charles   b: 10/17/45, Chicago, Ill.   d: 2/20/74, San Diego, Cal.   BR/TR, 5'10", 180 lbs.   Deb: 9/2/68

YEAR	TM/L	G	AB	R	H	2B	3B	HR	RBI	BB	SO	AVG	OBP	SLG	PRO+	BR/A	SB	CS	SBR	FA	FR	G/POS	TPR
1968	Det-A	3	3	0	1	1	0	0	0	0	0	.333	.333	.667	191	0	0	0	0	1.000	-0	/1-1,O-1	0.0
1969	Chi-A	39	129	11	28	4	0	3	16	10	19	.217	.279	.318	63	-6	3	0	1	.958	-0	O-38	-0.8
1970	Chi-A	12	15	3	4	0	1	0	3	1	4	.267	.313	.467	108	0	0	0	0	1.000	-1	/O-4	-0.1
Total	3	54	147	14	33	5	0	4	19	11	23	.224	.283	.340	70	-6	3	0	1	.959	-1	/O-43,1-1	-0.9

■ MARK CHRISTMAN
Christman, Marquette Joseph   b: 10/21/13, Maplewood, Mo.   d: 10/9/76, St.Louis, Mo.   BR/TR, 5'11", 180 lbs.   Deb: 4/20/38

YEAR	TM/L	G	AB	R	H	2B	3B	HR	RBI	BB	SO	AVG	OBP	SLG	PRO+	BR/A	SB	CS	SBR	FA	FR	G/POS	TPR
1938	Det-A	95	318	35	79	6	4	1	44	27	21	.248	.307	.302	50	-24	5	2	0	.983	9	3-69,S-21	-1.2
1939	Det-A	6	16	0	4	2	0	0	0	0	2	.250	.250	.375	54	-1	0	0	0	.900	-1	/3-5	-0.2
	StL-A	79	222	27	48	6	3	0	20	20	10	.216	.281	.270	41	-20	2	1	0	.960	21	S-64/2-1	0.6
	Yr	85	238	27	52	8	3	0	20	20	12	.218	.279	.277	42	-21	2	1	0	.960	20	S-64/3-5,2-1	0.4
1943	StL-A	98	336	31	91	11	5	2	35	19	19	.271	.318	.351	94	-3	0	3	-2	.991	-0	3-37,S-24,1-20,2-14	-0.4
1944	*StL-A	148	547	56	148	25	1	6	83	47	37	.271	.332	.353	90	-7	5	2	0	.972	4	*3-145/1-3	-0.1
1945	StL-A	78	289	32	80	7	4	4	34	19	14	.277	.328	.370	90	-1	1	0	0	.973	-3	3-77	-0.2
1946	StL-A	128	458	40	118	22	2	1	41	22	29	.258	.295	.321	68	-20	0	2	-1	.975	9	3-77,S-47	-0.8
1947	Was-A	110	374	27	83	15	2	1	33	32	16	.222	.287	.281	60	-21	4	4	-1	.978	-10	*S-106/2-1	-2.7
1948	Was-A	120	409	38	106	17	2	1	40	25	19	.259	.303	.318	67	-20	0	3	-2	.969	-32	*S-102/3-9,2-3	-4.8
1949	Was-A	49	112	8	24	2	0	3	18	8	7	.214	.273	.313	56	-8	0	0	0	.967	3	3-23/1-6,S-4,2-1	-0.3
Total	9	911	3081	294	781	113	23	19	348	219	179	.253	.306	.324	71	-125	17	17	-5	.975	-0	3-442,S-368/1-29,2	-10.3

■ STEVE CHRISTMAS
Christmas, Stephen Randall   b: 12/9/57, Orlando, Fla.   BL/TR, 6', 190 lbs.   Deb: 9/1/83

YEAR	TM/L	G	AB	R	H	2B	3B	HR	RBI	BB	SO	AVG	OBP	SLG	PRO+	BR/A	SB	CS	SBR	FA	FR	G/POS	TPR
1983	Cin-N	9	17	0	1	0	0	0	0	1	3	.059	.111	.059	-50	-3	0	0	0	1.000	-0	/C-7	-0.4
1984	Chi-A	12	11	1	4	1	0	1	4	0	2	.364	.364	.727	185	1	0	0	0	1.000	-0	/C-1	0.1
1986	Chi-N	3	9	0	1	1	0	0	1	0	2	.111	.111	.222	-10	-0	0	0	0	1.000	-0	/C-1,1-1	-0.2
Total	3	24	37	1	6	2	0	1	7	1	6	.162	.184	.297	30	-4	0	0	0	1.000	-0	/C-9,1-1	-0.5

■ JOE CHRISTOPHER
Christopher, Joseph O'Neal   b: 12/13/35, Frederiksted, V.I.   BR/TR, 5'10", 176 lbs.   Deb: 5/26/59

YEAR	TM/L	G	AB	R	H	2B	3B	HR	RBI	BB	SO	AVG	OBP	SLG	PRO+	BR/A	SB	CS	SBR	FA	FR	G/POS	TPR
1959	Pit-N	15	12	6	0	0	0	0	0	1	4	.000	.077	.000	-78	-3	0	0	0	1.000	-3	/O-9	-0.6
1960	*Pit-N	50	56	21	13	2	0	1	3	5	8	.232	.295	.321	68	-2	1	0	0	1.000	-2	O-17	-0.5
1961	Pit-N	76	186	25	49	7	3	0	14	18	24	.263	.328	.333	76	-6	6	4	-1	.978	-2	O-55	-1.1
1962	NY-N	119	271	36	66	10	2	6	32	35	42	.244	.339	.362	87	-4	11	3	2	.972	-9	O-94	-1.6
1963	NY-N	64	149	19	33	5	1	1	8	13	21	.221	.287	.289	68	-6	1	3	-2	.983	-5	O-45	-1.5
1964	NY-N	154	543	78	163	26	8	16	76	48	92	.300	.363	.466	135	25	6	5	-1	.974	-1	*O-145	1.8
1965	NY-N	148	437	38	109	18	3	5	40	35	82	.249	.314	.339	87	-7	4	4	-1	.989	-3	*O-112	-1.8
1966	Bos-A	12	13	1	1	0	0	0	0	0	2	.077	.077	.077	-15	-2	0	0	0	1.000	-1	/O-2	-0.4
Total	8	638	1667	224	434	68	17	29	173	157	277	.260	.331	.374	96	-6	29	19	-3	.979	-24	O-479	-5.6

■ LOYD CHRISTOPHER
Christopher, Loyd Eugene   b: 12/31/19, Richmond, Cal.   d: 9/5/91, Richmond, Cal.   BR/TR, 6'2", 190 lbs.   Deb: 4/20/45   F

YEAR	TM/L	G	AB	R	H	2B	3B	HR	RBI	BB	SO	AVG	OBP	SLG	PRO+	BR/A	SB	CS	SBR	FA	FR	G/POS	TPR
1945	Bos-A	8	14	4	4	0	0	0	4	3	2	.286	.412	.286	101	0	0	0	0	1.000	-1	/O-3	-0.1
	Chi-N	1	0	0	0	0	0	0	0	0	0	—	—	—	—	—	0			.000	-0	/O-1	0.0
1947	Chi-A	7	23	1	5	0	1	0	0	2	4	.217	.280	.304	65	-1	0	1	-1	1.000	-0	/O-7	-0.1
Total	2	16	37	5	9	0	1	0	4	5	6	.243	.333	.297	80	-1	0	1		1.000	-0	/O-11	-0.2

■ HI CHURCH
Church, Hiram Lincoln   b: 11/23/1863, Central Square, N.Y.   d: 2/23/26, Jacksonville, Fla.   Deb: 8/23/1890

YEAR	TM/L	G	AB	R	H	2B	3B	HR	RBI	BB	SO	AVG	OBP	SLG	PRO+	BR/A	SB	CS	SBR	FA	FR	G/POS	TPR
1890	Bro-a	3	9	1	1	0	0	0	0	0	0	.111	.111	.111	-36	-2	0			1.000	-1	/O-3	-0.3

■ JOHN CHURRY
Churry, John   b: 11/26/1900, Johnstown, Pa.   d: 2/8/70, Zanesville, Ohio   BR/TR, 5'9", 172 lbs.   Deb: 5/24/24

YEAR	TM/L	G	AB	R	H	2B	3B	HR	RBI	BB	SO	AVG	OBP	SLG	PRO+	BR/A	SB	CS	SBR	FA	FR	G/POS	TPR
1924	Chi-N	6	7	0	1	1	0	0	0	2	0	.143	.333	.286	67	-0	0			1.000	0	/C-3	0.0
1925	Chi-N	3	6	1	3	0	0	0	0	3	0	.500	.500	.500	154	0	0			1.000	0	/C-3	0.0
1926	Chi-N	2	4	0	0	0	0	0	0	1	2	.000	.200	.000	-42	-1	0			1.000	0	/C-3	-0.1
1927	Chi-N	1	1	0	1	0	0	0	0	0	0	1.000	1.000	1.000	436	0	0			1.000	0	/C-1	0.1
Total	4	12	18	1	5	1	0	0	0	6	2	.278	.381	.333	89	-0	0			1.000	0	/C-8	0.0

■ LARRY CIAFFONE
Ciaffone, Lawrence Thomas "Symphony Larry"   b: 8/17/24, Brooklyn, N.Y.   d: 12/14/91, Brooklyn, N.Y.   BR/TR, 5'9.5", 185 lbs.   Deb: 4/17/51

YEAR	TM/L	G	AB	R	H	2B	3B	HR	RBI	BB	SO	AVG	OBP	SLG	PRO+	BR/A	SB	CS	SBR	FA	FR	G/POS	TPR
1951	StL-N	5	5	0	0	0	0	0	0	1	2	.000	.167	.000	-51	-1	0	0	0	1.000	-0	/O-1	-0.1

YEAR	TM/L	G	AB	R	H	2B	3B	HR	RBI	BB	SO	AVG	OBP	SLG	PRO+	BR/A	SB	CS	SBR	FA	FR	G/POS	TPR

■ ARCHI CIANFROCCO   Cianfrocco, Angelo Dominic   b: 10/6/66, Rome, N.Y.   BR/TR, 6'5", 200 lbs.   Deb: 4/8/92

YEAR	TM/L	G	AB	R	H	2B	3B	HR	RBI	BB	SO	AVG	OBP	SLG	PRO+	BR/A	SB	CS	SBR	FA	FR	G/POS	TPR
1992	Mon-N	86	232	25	56	5	2	6	30	11	66	.241	.279	.358	80	-7	3	0	1	.993	1	1-56,3-19/O-5	-0.8
1993	Mon-N	12	17	3	4	1	0	1	1	0	5	.235	.235	.471	80	-1	0	0		1.000	-0	1-11	-0.1
	SD-N	84	279	27	68	10	2	11	47	17	64	.244	.294	.412	85	-7	2	0	1	.932	-5	3-64,1-31	-1.3
	Yr	96	296	30	72	11	2	12	48	17	69	.243	.291	.416	85	-7	2	0	1	.932	-6	3-64,1-42	-1.4
1994	SD-N	59	146	9	32	8	0	4	13	3	39	.219	.255	.356	59	-9	2	0	1	.920	2	3-37,1-16/S-1	-0.7
1995	SD-N	51	118	22	31	7	0	5	31	11	28	.263	.336	.449	109	1	0	2	-1	1.000	-2	1-30,S-15/O-7,23	-0.1
1996	*SD-N	79	192	21	54	13	3	2	32	8	56	.281	.317	.411	95	-2	1	0	0	1.000	-8	1-33,3-11,S/O2C	-1.1
Total	5	371	984	107	245	44	7	29	154	50	258	.249	.293	.396	85	-24	8	2	1	.996	-12	1-177,3-134/SO2C	-4.1

■ DARRYL CIAS   Cias, Darryl Richard   b: 4/23/57, New York, N.Y.   BR/TR, 5'11", 190 lbs.   Deb: 4/27/83

YEAR	TM/L	G	AB	R	H	2B	3B	HR	RBI	BB	SO	AVG	OBP	SLG	PRO+	BR/A	SB	CS	SBR	FA	FR	G/POS	TPR
1983	Oak-A	19	18	1	6	1	0	0	1	2	4	.333	.400	.389	126	1	1	0	0	.967	-0	C-19	0.1

■ JOE CICERO   Cicero, Joseph Francis "Dode"   b: 11/18/10, Atlantic City, N.J   d: 3/30/83, Clearwater, Fla.   BR/TR, 5'8", 167 lbs.   Deb: 9/20/29

YEAR	TM/L	G	AB	R	H	2B	3B	HR	RBI	BB	SO	AVG	OBP	SLG	PRO+	BR/A	SB	CS	SBR	FA	FR	G/POS	TPR
1929	Bos-A	10	32	6	10	2	1	0	4	0	2	.313	.313	.500	108	0	0	0	0	1.000	-1	/O-7	-0.1
1930	Bos-A	18	30	5	5	1	2	0	4	1	5	.167	.194	.333	32	-3	0	0	0	.000	-2	/O-5,3-2	-0.5
1945	Phi-A	12	19	3	3	0	0	0	0	1	6	.158	.238	.158	16	-2	0	0	0	1.000	-2	/O-7	-0.5
Total	3	40	81	14	18	3	4	0	8	2	13	.222	.250	.358	60	-5	0	0	0	1.000	-4	/O-19,3-2	-1.1

■ TED CIESLAK   Cieslak, Thaddeus Walter   b: 11/22/16, Milwaukee, Wis.   BR/TR, 5'10", 175 lbs.   Deb: 4/18/44

YEAR	TM/L	G	AB	R	H	2B	3B	HR	RBI	BB	SO	AVG	OBP	SLG	PRO+	BR/A	SB	CS	SBR	FA	FR	G/POS	TPR
1944	Phi-N	85	220	18	54	10	0	0	11	21	17	.245	.314	.318	81	-5	1			.877	-15	3-48/O-5	-2.1

■ AL CIHOCKI   Cihocki, Albert Joseph   b: 5/7/24, Nanticoke, Pa.   BR/TR, 5'11", 185 lbs.   Deb: 4/17/45

YEAR	TM/L	G	AB	R	H	2B	3B	HR	RBI	BB	SO	AVG	OBP	SLG	PRO+	BR/A	SB	CS	SBR	FA	FR	G/POS	TPR
1945	Cle-A	92	283	21	60	9	3	0	24	11	48	.212	.241	.265	49	-19	2	1	0	.946	1	S-41,3-29,2-23	-1.5

■ ED CIHOCKI   Cihocki, Edward Joseph "Cy"   b: 5/9/07, Wilmington, Del.   d: 11/9/87, Newark, Del.   BR/TR, 5'8", 163 lbs.   Deb: 5/29/32

YEAR	TM/L	G	AB	R	H	2B	3B	HR	RBI	BB	SO	AVG	OBP	SLG	PRO+	BR/A	SB	CS	SBR	FA	FR	G/POS	TPR
1932	Phi-A	1	1	0	0	0	0	0	0	0	0	.000	.000	.000	-97	-0	0	0	0	.000	0	H	0.0
1933	Phi-A	33	97	6	14	2	3	0	9	7	16	.144	.202	.227	13	-12	0	0	0	.904	-2	S-28/2-1,3-1	-1.3
Total	2	34	98	6	14	2	3	0	9	7	16	.143	.200	.224	12	-13	0	0	0	.904	-2	/S-28,3-1,2-1	-1.3

■ GINO CIMOLI   Cimoli, Gino Nicholas   b: 12/18/29, San Francisco, Cal.   BR/TR, 6'2", 200 lbs.   Deb: 4/19/56

YEAR	TM/L	G	AB	R	H	2B	3B	HR	RBI	BB	SO	AVG	OBP	SLG	PRO+	BR/A	SB	CS	SBR	FA	FR	G/POS	TPR
1956	*Bro-N	73	36	3	4	1	0	4	1	8		.111	.135	.139	-24	-6	1	0	0	.946	-18	O-62	-2.6
1957	Bro-N★	142	532	88	156	22	5	10	57	39	86	.293	.346	.410	93	-5	3	1	0	.979	-3	*O-138	-1.5
1958	LA-N	109	325	35	80	6	3	9	27	18	49	.246	.292	.366	71	-14	3	3	-1	.974	-8	*O-104	-2.8
1959	StL-N	143	519	61	145	40	7	8	72	37	83	.279	.330	.430	94	-5	7	0	2	.979	-5	*O-141	-0.5
1960	*Pit-N	101	307	36	82	14	4	0	28	32	43	.267	.338	.339	85	-5	1	0	0	.964	-7	O-91	-1.7
1961	Pit-N	21	67	4	20	3	1	0	6	2	13	.299	.319	.373	83	-2	0	0	0	.971	-0	O-19	-0.3
	Mil-N	37	117	12	23	5	0	3	4	11	15	.197	.266	.316	57	-8	1	0	0	.985	-3	O-31	-1.2
	Yr	58	184	16	43	8	1	3	10	13	28	.234	.284	.337	67	-9	1	0	0	.980	-3	O-50	-1.5
1962	KC-A	152	550	67	151	20	**15**	10	71	40	89	.275	.326	.420	95	-5	2	1	0	.968	-9	*O-147	-2.2
1963	KC-A	145	529	56	139	19	11	4	48	39	72	.263	.316	.363	85	-10	3	1	0	.985	-2	*O-136	-1.6
1964	KC-A	4	9	1	0	0	0	0	0	0	1	.000	.000	.000	-97	-2	0	0	0	1.000	-0	/O-4	-0.3
	Bal-A	38	58	6	8	3	2	0	3	2	13	.138	.167	.259	16	-7	0	0	0	.893	-9	O-35	-1.7
	Yr	42	67	7	8	3	2	0	3	2	14	.119	.145	.224	1	-9	0	0	0	.912	-9	O-39	-2.0
1965	Cal-A	4	5	1	0	0	0	0	0	0	1	.000	.000	.000	-99	-1	0	0	0	1.000	0	/O-1	-0.1
Total	10	969	3054	370	808	133	48	44	321	221	474	.265	.317	.383	84	-70	21	6	3	.974	-50	O-909	-16.5

■ FRANK CIPRIANI   Cipriani, Frank Dominick   b: 4/14/41, Buffalo, N.Y.   BR/TR, 6', 180 lbs.   Deb: 9/8/61

YEAR	TM/L	G	AB	R	H	2B	3B	HR	RBI	BB	SO	AVG	OBP	SLG	PRO+	BR/A	SB	CS	SBR	FA	FR	G/POS	TPR
1961	KC-A	13	36	2	9	0	0	0	2	4		.250	.289	.250	45	-3	0	0	0	1.000	-1	O-11	-0.4

■ JEFF CIRILLO   Cirillo, Jeffrey Howard   b: 9/23/69, Pasadena, Cal.   BR/TR, 6'2", 190 lbs.   Deb: 5/11/94

YEAR	TM/L	G	AB	R	H	2B	3B	HR	RBI	BB	SO	AVG	OBP	SLG	PRO+	BR/A	SB	CS	SBR	FA	FR	G/POS	TPR
1994	Mil-A	39	126	17	30	9	0	3	12	11	16	.238	.309	.381	73	-5	0	1	-1	.965	-1	3-37/2-1	-0.7
1995	Mil-A	125	328	57	91	19	4	9	39	47	42	.277	.375	.442	106	3	7	2	1	.938	15	*3-108,2-25/1-3,S-2	1.9
1996	Mil-A	158	566	101	184	46	5	15	83	58	69	.325	.395	.504	118	16	4	9	-4	.950	-11	*3-154/1-2,2-1,D-3	0.1
Total	3	322	1020	175	305	74	9	27	134	116	127	.299	.378	.469	109	15	11	12	-4	.948	3	3-299/2-27,1-5,DS	1.3

■ GEORGE CISAR   Cisar, George Joseph   b: 8/25/12, Chicago, Ill.   BR/TR, 6', 175 lbs.   Deb: 9/9/37

YEAR	TM/L	G	AB	R	H	2B	3B	HR	RBI	BB	SO	AVG	OBP	SLG	PRO+	BR/A	SB	CS	SBR	FA	FR	G/POS	TPR
1937	Bro-N	20	29	8	6	0	0	0	4	2	6	.207	.258	.207	27	-3	3			1.000	-3	O-13	-0.6

■ BILL CISSELL   Cissell, Chalmer William   b: 1/3/04, Perryville, Mo.   d: 3/15/49, Chicago, Ill.   BR/TR, 5'11", 170 lbs.   Deb: 4/11/28

YEAR	TM/L	G	AB	R	H	2B	3B	HR	RBI	BB	SO	AVG	OBP	SLG	PRO+	BR/A	SB	CS	SBR	FA	FR	G/POS	TPR
1928	Chi-A	125	443	66	116	22	3	1	60	29	41	.260	.307	.330	68	-21	18	6	2	.938	-2	*S-123	-0.6
1929	Chi-A	152	618	83	173	27	12	5	62	28	53	.280	.312	.387	80	-20	25	17	-3	.937	-3	*S-152	-0.7
1930	Chi-A	141	562	82	152	28	6	2	48	28	32	.270	.307	.363	72	-25	16	9	-1	.948	-11	*2-107,3-24,S-10	-2.6
1931	Chi-A	109	409	42	90	13	5	1	46	16	26	.220	.256	.284	44	-34	18	6	0	.944	-10	S-83,2-23/3-1	-3.1
1932	Chi-A	12	43	7	11	1	1	1	5	1	0	.256	.273	.395	76	-2	0	0	0	.928	4	S-12	-0.1
	Cle-A	131	541	78	173	35	6	6	93	28	25	.320	.354	.440	98	-3	18	15	-4	.964	11	*2-129/S-6	1.1
	Yr	143	584	85	184	36	7	7	98	29	25	.315	.349	.437	97	-4	18	15	-4	.964	11	2-129,S-18	1.0
1933	Cle-A	112	409	53	94	21	3	6	33	31	29	.230	.284	.340	62	-23	6	6	-2	.947	-7	2-62,S-46/3-1	-2.5
1934	Bos-A	102	416	71	111	13	4	4	44	28	23	.267	.315	.346	66	-22	11	4		.959	-4	2-96/S-7,3-2	-1.8
1937	Phi-A	34	117	15	31	7	0	1	14	17	10	.265	.358	.350	81	-3	0	0	0	.962	3	2-33	0.2
1938	NY-N	38	149	19	40	6	0	2	18	6	11	.268	.297	.349	76	-5	1			.977	9	2-33/3-6	0.6
Total	9	956	3707	516	990	173	43	29	423	212	250	.267	.308	.360	73	-158	113	63		.958	-14	2-483,S-439/3-34	-9.5

■ MOOSE CLABAUGH   Clabaugh, John William   b: 11/13/01, Albany, Mo.   d: 7/11/84, Tucson, Ariz.   BL/TR, 6', 185 lbs.   Deb: 8/30/26

YEAR	TM/L	G	AB	R	H	2B	3B	HR	RBI	BB	SO	AVG	OBP	SLG	PRO+	BR/A	SB	CS	SBR	FA	FR	G/POS	TPR
1926	Bro-N	11	14	2	1	0	0	0	1	0	5	.071	.133	.143	-26	-3	0			.600	-1	/O-2	-0.3

■ BOBBY CLACK   Clack, Robert S. "Gentlemanly Bob" (b: Robert S. Clark)   b: 6/1850, England   d: 10/22/33, Danvers, Mass.   BR/TR, 5'9", 153 lbs.   Deb: 5/13/1874

YEAR	TM/L	G	AB	R	H	2B	3B	HR	RBI	BB	SO	AVG	OBP	SLG	PRO+	BR/A	SB	CS	SBR	FA	FR	G/POS	TPR
1874	Atl-n	33	135	22	23	1	0	0	13	4	2	.170	.194	.178	23	-10	0	0	0	.779	-1	O-31/1-2	-0.8
1875	Atl-n	17	59	1	6	0	0	0	1	0	3	.102	.102	.102	-33	-7	0	0	0	.867	5	O-17/1-1	-0.4
1876	Cin-N	32	118	10	19	0	1	0	5	1	12	.161	.195	.178	29	-8				.736	0	O-17/2-8,1-5,3-3,P	-0.7
Total	2 n	50	194	23	29	1	1	0	14	4	5	.149	.167	.155	7	-17	0	0	0	.811	5	/O-48,1-3	-1.2

■ DANNY CLAIRE   Claire, David Matthew   b: 11/17/1897, Ludington, Mich.   d: 1/7/56, Las Vegas, Nev.   BR/TR, 5'8", 164 lbs.   Deb: 9/17/20

YEAR	TM/L	G	AB	R	H	2B	3B	HR	RBI	BB	SO	AVG	OBP	SLG	PRO+	BR/A	SB	CS	SBR	FA	FR	G/POS	TPR
1920	Det-A	3	7	1	1	0	0	0	0	0	0	.143	.143	.143	-25	-1	0	0	0	.800	-0	/S-3	-0.2

■ AL CLANCY   Clancy, Albert Harrison   b: 8/14/1888, Santa Fe, N.Mex.   d: 10/17/51, Las Cruces, N.Mex.   BR/TR, 5'10.5", 175 lbs.   Deb: 6/20/11

YEAR	TM/L	G	AB	R	H	2B	3B	HR	RBI	BB	SO	AVG	OBP	SLG	PRO+	BR/A	SB	CS	SBR	FA	FR	G/POS	TPR
1911	StL-A	3	5	0	0	0	0	0	0	0		.000	.167	.000	-54	-1	0			.800	-1	/3-2	-0.1

■ BUD CLANCY   Clancy, John William   b: 9/15/1900, Odell, Ill.   d: 9/26/68, Ottumwa, Iowa   BL/TL, 6', 170 lbs.   Deb: 8/29/24

YEAR	TM/L	G	AB	R	H	2B	3B	HR	RBI	BB	SO	AVG	OBP	SLG	PRO+	BR/A	SB	CS	SBR	FA	FR	G/POS	TPR
1924	Chi-A	13	35	5	9	1	0	0	6	3	2	.257	.316	.286	58	-2	3	2	-0	.947	-2	/1-8	-0.4
1925	Chi-A	4	3	0	0	0	0	0	0	0	0	.000	.000	.000	-34	-1	0	0	0	.000	0	H	-0.1
1926	Chi-A	12	38	3	13	2	0	0	7	1	1	.342	.375	.500	131	2	0	0	0	.991	1	1-10	0.1
1927	Chi-A	130	464	46	139	21	2	0	53	24	24	.300	.337	.373	86	-10	4	3	-1	.991	0	*1-123	-1.8
1928	Chi-A	130	487	64	132	19	11	2	37	42	25	.271	.331	.368	85	-11	6	9	-4	.991	5	*1-128	-2.1
1929	Chi-A	92	290	36	82	14	6	3	45	16	19	.283	.320	.403	86	-7	3	1		.991	0	1-74	-1.1
1930	Chi-A	68	234	28	57	8	3	0	27	12	18	.244	.286	.342	61	-14	3	1	0	.995	-3	1-60	-2.2
1932	Bro-N	53	196	14	60	4	0	1	26	6	13	.306	.327	.342	83	-5	0			.996	3	1-53	-0.6
1934	Phi-N	20	49	8	12	0	1	0	7	6	4	.245	.339	.306	65	-2	0			1.000	-1	1-10	-0.4
Total	9	522	1796	204	504	69	26	12	198	111	106	.281	.325	.368	81	-50	19	16		.992	4	1-466	-8.6

■ BILL CLANCY   Clancy, William Edward   b: 4/12/1879, Redfield, N.Y.   d: 2/10/48, Oriskany, N.Y.   BR/TR, 6'2", 180 lbs.   Deb: 4/14/05

YEAR	TM/L	G	AB	R	H	2B	3B	HR	RBI	BB	SO	AVG	OBP	SLG	PRO+	BR/A	SB	CS	SBR	FA	FR	G/POS	TPR
1905	Pit-N	56	227	23	52	11	3	2	34	4		.229	.246	.330	69	-10	3			.983	-4	1-52/O-4	-1.6

YEAR	TM/L	G	AB	R	H	2B	3B	HR	RBI	BB	SO	AVG	OBP	SLG	PRO+	BR/A	SB	CS	SBR	FA	FR	G/POS	TPR

■ UKE CLANTON   Clanton, Eucal "Cat"   b: 2/19/1898, Powell, Mo.   d: 2/24/60, Antlers, Okla.   BL/TL, 5'8", 165 lbs.   Deb: 9/21/22

1922	Cle-A	1	1	0	0	0	0	0	0	0	1	.000	.000	.000	-99	-0	0	0	0	.500	-0	/1-1	-0.1

■ AARON CLAPP   Clapp, Aaron Bronson   b: 7/1856, Ithaca, N.Y.   d: 1/13/14, Sayre, Pa.   TR , 5'8", 175 lbs.   Deb: 5/1/1879   F

1879	Tro-N	36	146	24	39	9	3	0	18	6	10	.267	.296	.370	126	4				.935	-4	1-25,O-11	0.0

■ JOHN CLAPP   Clapp, John Edgar   b: 7/17/1851, Ithaca, N.Y.   d: 12/18/04, Ithaca, N.Y.   BR/TR, 5'7", 194 lbs.   Deb: 4/26/1872   FM

1872	Man-n	19	97	28	28	6	1	1	10	1	0	.289	.296	.402	120	3	2	1	0	.860	-1	C-19/S-2,O-1,M	0.1
1873	Ath-n	45	204	36	62	10	2	1	28	2	1	.304	.311	.387	99	-2	4	5	-2	**.908**	3	*C-43/S-6,2-1,0-1	-0.1
1874	Ath-n	39	165	46	48	7	4	3	20	1	1	.291	.295	.436	121	2	2	0	1	.861	7	C-27,O-15/S-1	0.9
1875	Ath-n	60	292	65	77	8	7	0	39	7	1	.264	.281	.339	103	-1	9	5	-0	.874	18	*C-60	1.6
1876	StL-N	64	298	60	91	4	2	0	29	8	2	.305	.324	.332	125	9				.874	9	*C-61/O-4,2-1	1.7
1877	StL-N	60	255	47	81	6	6	0	34	8	6	.318	.338	.388	135	11				.887	-6	*C-53,O-10/1-1	0.5
1878	Ind-N	63	263	42	80	10	2	0	29	13	8	.304	.337	.357	148	15				.890	-7	*0-44,1-12/C-9,S2M	0.5
1879	Buf-N	70	292	47	77	12	5	1	36	11	11	.264	.290	.349	107	2				.906	-9	*C-63/O-7,M	-0.5
1880	Cin-N	80	323	33	91	16	4	1	20	21	10	.282	.326	.365	135	12				.897	17	*C-73,O-10,M	2.9
1881	Cle-N	68	261	47	66	12	2	0	25	**35**	6	.253	.341	.314	113	6				.890	-5	C-48,O-21,M	0.3
1883	NY-N	20	73	6	13	0	0	0	5	5	4	.178	.231	.178	27	-6				.895	5	C-16/O-5,M	0.0
Total	4 n	163	758	175	215	31	14	5	97	11	4	.284	.294	.381	107	2	17	11	-2	.878	27	C-149/O-17,S-2,1-1	2.5
Total	7	425	1765	282	499	60	21	2	178	101	47	.283	.322	.344	122	48				.892	4	C-323,O-101/1S2	5.4

■ DENNY CLARE   Clare, Dennis J.   b: 1/1853, Brooklyn, N.Y.   d: 11/26/28, Brooklyn, N.Y.   Deb: 9/14/1872

1872	Atl-n	2	7	1	1	0	0	0	1	0	0	.143	.143	.143	-10	-1	0	0	0	.857	-3	/2-2,S-1	-0.3

■ DOUG CLAREY   Clarey, Douglas William   b: 4/20/54, Los Angeles, Cal.   BR/TR, 6', 180 lbs.   Deb: 4/20/76

1976	StL-N	9	4	2	1	0	0	1	2	0	1	.250	.250	1.000	240	1	0	0	0	1.000	0	/2-7	0.1

■ ALLIE CLARK   Clark, Alfred Aloysius   b: 6/16/23, S.Amboy, N.J.   BR/TR, 6', 185 lbs.   Deb: 8/5/47

1947	*NY-A	24	67	9	25	5	0	1	14	5	2	.373	.417	.493	154	5	0	0	0	1.000	0	O-16	0.4
1948	*Cle-A	81	271	43	84	5	2	9	38	23	13	.310	.364	.443	117	6	0	2	-1	.982	-6	O-65/3-5,1-1	-0.5
1949	Cle-A	35	74	8	13	4	0	1	9	4	7	.176	.218	.270	29	-8	0	0	0	1.000	-4	O-17/1-1	-1.3
1950	Cle-A	59	163	19	35	6	1	6	21	11	10	.215	.264	.374	64	-10	0	1	-1	.987	-3	O-41	-1.4
1951	Cle-A	3	10	3	3	2	0	1	3	1	2	.300	.364	.800	221	1	0	0	0	1.000	-1	/O-3	0.1
	Phi-A	56	161	20	40	10	1	4	22	15	7	.248	.320	.398	91	-2	2	0	1	.984	-1	O-32,3-10	-0.4
	Yr	59	171	23	43	12	1	5	25	16	9	.251	.323	.421	98	-1	2	0	1	.985	-1	O-35,3-10	-0.3
1952	Phi-A	71	186	23	51	12	0	7	29	10	19	.274	.315	.452	105	-0	0	1	0	.988	-5	O-48/1-2	-0.6
1953	Phi-A	20	74	6	15	4	0	3	13	3	5	.203	.234	.378	61	-5	0	0	0	1.000	-0	O-19	-0.6
	Chi-A	9	15	0	1	0	0	0	0	0	5	.067	.067	.067	-62	-3	0	0	0	1.000	-0	/1-1,O-1	-0.4
	Yr	29	89	6	16	4	0	3	13	3	10	.180	.207	.326	40	-8	0	0	0	1.000	-1	O-20/1-1	-1.0
Total	7	358	1021	131	267	48	4	32	149	72	70	.262	.312	.410	92	-16	2	5	-2	.988	-19	O-242/3-15,1-5	-4.7

■ DAD CLARK   Clark, Alfred Robert "Fred"   b: 7/16/1873, San Francisco, Cal.   d: 7/26/56, Ogden, Utah   BL/TL, 5'11", 170 lbs.   Deb: 7/3/02

1902	Chi-N	12	43	1	8	1	0	0	2	4		.186	.255	.209	45	-3	1			.938	-1	1-12	-0.5

■ TONY CLARK   Clark, Anthony Christopher   b: 6/15/72, Newton, Kan.   BB/TR, 6'7", 240 lbs.   Deb: 9/3/95

1995	Det-A	27	101	10	24	5	1	3	11	8	30	.238	.294	.396	78	-4	0	0	0	.985	-1	1-27	-0.6
1996	Det-A	100	376	56	94	14	0	27	72	29	127	.250	.304	.503	100	-2	0	1	-1	.993	-2	1-86,D-12	-1.3
Total	2	127	477	66	118	19	1	30	83	37	157	.247	.302	.480	95	-6	0	1	-1	.991	-3	1-113/D-12	-1.9

■ EARL CLARK   Clark, Bailey Earl   b: 11/6/07, Washington, D.C.   d: 1/16/38, Washington, D.C.   BR/TR, 5'10", 160 lbs.   Deb: 8/17/27

1927	Bos-N	13	44	6	12	1	0	0	3	2	4	.273	.304	.295	66	-2	0			1.000	-1	O-13	-0.3
1928	Bos-N	28	112	18	34	9	1	0	10	4	8	.304	.339	.402	98	-1	0			.987	-1	O-27	-0.3
1929	Bos-N	84	279	43	88	13	3	1	30	12	30	.315	.346	.394	86	-6	6			.978	4	O-74	-0.6
1930	Bos-N	82	233	29	69	11	3	3	28	7	22	.296	.320	.408	77	-9	3			.977	-1	O-63	-1.1
1931	Bos-N	16	50	8	11	2	0	0	4	7	4	.220	.316	.260	58	-3	1			.970	-1	O-14	-0.3
1932	Bos-N	50	44	11	11	2	0	0	4	2	5	.250	.283	.295	58	-3	1			1.000	-2	O-16	-0.5
1933	Bos-N	7	23	3	8	1	0	1	4	3	2	.348	.400	.391	138	1	0			1.000	1	/O-6	0.0
1934	StL-A	13	41	4	7	2	0	0	1	3	1	.171	.190	.220	5	-6	0	0	0	1.000	1	/O-9	-0.5
Total	8	293	826	122	240	41	7	4	81	37	79	.291	.324	.372	78	-28	11	0		.981	-0	O-222	-3.6

■ DANNY CLARK   Clark, Daniel Curran   b: 1/18/1894, Meridian, Miss.   d: 5/23/37, Meridian, Miss.   BL/TR, 5'9", 167 lbs.   Deb: 4/12/22

1922	Det-A	83	185	31	54	11	3	3	26	15	11	.292	.345	.432	105	1	1	0	0	.945	-6	2-38/O-5,3-1	-0.4
1924	Bos-A	104	325	36	90	23	3	2	54	51	19	.277	.378	.385	97	-0	4	7	-3	.943	-6	3-94	-0.2
1927	StL-N	58	72	8	17	2	0	0	13	8	7	.236	.313	.319	67	-3	0			.929	1	/O-9	-0.3
Total	3	245	582	75	161	36	8	5	93	74	37	.277	.360	.392	96	-3	5	7		.943	-11	/3-95,2-38,O-14	-0.9

■ DAVE CLARK   Clark, David Earl   b: 9/3/62, Tupelo, Miss.   BL/TR, 6'2", 200 lbs.   Deb: 9/3/86

1986	Cle-A	18	58	10	16	1	0	3	9	7	11	.276	.354	.448	119	2	1	0	0	1.000	1	O-10/D-7	0.2
1987	Cle-A	29	87	11	18	5	0	3	12	2	24	.207	.225	.368	53	-6	1	0	0	1.000	0	O-13,D-12	-0.6
1988	Cle-A	63	156	11	41	4	1	3	18	17	28	.263	.335	.359	92	-1	0	2	-1	.947	-4	D-27,O-23	-0.8
1989	Cle-A	102	253	21	60	12	0	8	29	30	63	.237	.318	.379	94	-2	0	2	-1	.964	-5	D-55,O-24	-1.0
1990	Chi-N	84	171	22	47	4	2	5	20	8	40	.275	.307	.409	89	-3	7	1	2	1.000	-2	O-39	-0.5
1991	KC-A	11	10	1	2	0	0	0	1	1	1	.200	.273	.200	33	-1	0	0	0	.000	-0	/O-1,D-1	-0.1
1992	Pit-N	23	33	3	7	0	0	2	7	6	8	.212	.333	.394	106	-1	0	0	0	1.000	-1	O-8	-0.1
1993	Pit-N	110	277	43	75	11	2	11	46	38	58	.271	.361	.444	114	6	1	0	0	.957	-11	O-91	-0.6
1994	Pit-N	86	223	37	66	11	1	10	46	22	48	.296	.359	.489	117	5	2	2	-1	.974	2	O-57	0.5
1995	Pit-N	77	196	30	55	6	0	4	24	24	38	.281	.362	.372	92	-1	3	3	-1	.961	-3	O-61	-0.7
1996	Pit-N	92	211	28	58	12	2	8	35	31	51	.275	.368	.464	114	5	2	1	0	.988	-4	O-61	-0.1
	*LA-N	15	15	0	3	0	0	0	1	3	2	.200	.333	.200	49	-1	0	0	0	.000	-0	/O-1	-0.1
	Yr	107	226	28	61	12	2	8	36	34	53	.270	.365	.447	111	4	2	1	0	.988	-4	O-62	-0.2
Total	11	710	1690	217	448	66	8	57	248	189	372	.265	.340	.415	101	2	17	11	-2	.973	-28	O-386,D-102	-3.9

■ GLEN CLARK   Clark, Glen Ester   b: 3/7/41, Austin, Tex.   BB/TR, 6'1", 190 lbs.   Deb: 6/3/67

1967	Atl-N	4	4	0	0	0	0	0	0	0	1	.000	.000	.000	-99	-1	0	0	0	.000	0	H	-0.1

■ PEP CLARK   Clark, Harry   b: 3/20/1883, Union City, Ohio   d: 6/8/65, Milwaukee, Wis.   BR/TR, 5'7.5", 175 lbs.   Deb: 9/11/03

1903	Chi-A	15	65	7	20	4	2	0	9	2		.308	.338	.431	135	3	5			.877	-0	3-15	0.2

■ JACK CLARK   Clark, Jack Anthony   b: 11/10/55, New Brighton, Pa.   BR/TR, 6'2", 205 lbs.   Deb: 9/12/75

1975	SF-N	8	17	3	4	0	0	0	2	1	2	.235	.278	.235	42	-1	1	0	0	1.000	-0	/O-3,3-2	-0.2
1976	SF-N	26	102	14	23	6	2	2	10	8	18	.225	.282	.382	85	-2	6	2	1	.987	1	O-26	-0.2
1977	SF-N	136	413	64	104	17	4	13	51	49	73	.252	.334	.407	98	-1	12	4	1	.975	7	*O-114	0.3
1978	SF-N★	156	592	90	181	46	8	25	98	50	72	.306	.363	.537	155	40	15	11	-2	.982	14	*O-152	4.7
1979	SF-N★	143	527	84	144	25	2	26	86	63	95	.273	.352	.476	133	22	11	8	-2	.982	5	*O-140/3-2	2.0
1980	SF-N	127	437	77	124	20	8	22	82	74	52	.284	.390	.517	155	33	2	5	-2	.967	1	*O-120	2.8
1981	SF-N	99	385	60	103	19	2	17	53	45	45	.268	.346	.460	129	14	1	1	-0	.981	12	O-98	2.4
1982	SF-N	157	563	90	154	30	3	27	103	90	91	.274	.375	.481	138	30	6	9	-4	.980	1	*O-155	2.6
1983	SF-N	135	492	82	132	25	0	20	66	74	79	.268	.365	.441	126	18	5	3	-0	.967	14	*O-133/1-2	2.8
1984	SF-N	57	203	33	65	9	1	11	44	43	29	.320	.439	.537	179	23	1	1	-0	.980	-0	O-54/1-4	0.7
1985	*StL-N★	126	442	71	124	26	3	22	87	83	88	.281	.397	.502	151	32	1	4	-2	.988	-11	*1-121,O-12	1.3
1986	StL-N	65	232	34	55	12	1	9	23	45	61	.237	.363	.422	117	6	1	1	-0	.995	-7	1-64	-0.5
1987	*StL-N★	131	419	93	120	23	1	35	106	**136**	139	.286	**.461**	**.597**	**174**	52	1	2	-1	.989	-8	*1-126/O-1	3.3

YEAR	TM/L	G	AB	R	H	2B	3B	HR	RBI	BB	SO	AVG	OBP	SLG	PRO+	BR/A	SB	CS	SBR	FA	FR	G/POS	TPR
1988	NY-A	150	496	81	120	14	0	27	93	113	141	.242	.385	.433	130	24	3	2	-0	.951	-1	*D-112,O-19,1-10	1.9
1989	SD-N	142	455	76	110	19	1	26	94	**132**	145	.242	.413	.459	149	36	6	2	1	.988	1	*1-131,O-12	2.8
1990	SD-N	115	334	59	89	12	1	25	62	**104**	91	.266	.443	.533	166	36	4	3	-1	.994	-3	*1-110	2.5
1991	Bos-A	140	481	75	120	18	1	28	87	96	133	.249	.378	.466	126	19	0	2	-1	.000		*D-135	1.2
1992	Bos-A	81	257	32	54	11	0	5	33	56	87	.210	.356	.311	83	-4	1	1	-0	.992	-1	D-64,1-13	0.3
Total	18	1994	6847	1118	1826	332	39	340	1180	1262	1441	.267	.383	.476	138	377	77	61	-14	.978	27	*O-1039,1-581,D/3	31.1

■ **JIM CLARK**   Clark, James (b: James Petrosky) b: 9/21/27, Baggaley, Pa.   BR/TR, 5'9", 150 lbs.   Deb: 8/17/48

YEAR	TM/L	G	AB	R	H	2B	3B	HR	RBI	BB	SO	AVG	OBP	SLG	PRO+	BR/A	SB	CS	SBR	FA	FR	G/POS	TPR
1948	Was-A	9	12	1	3	0	0	0	0	0	2	.250	.250	.250	34	-1	0	0	0	1.000	-0	/S-1,3-1	-0.1

■ **JIM CLARK**   Clark, James Edward b: 4/30/47, Kansas City, Kan.   BR/TR, 6'1", 190 lbs.   Deb: 7/16/71

YEAR	TM/L	G	AB	R	H	2B	3B	HR	RBI	BB	SO	AVG	OBP	SLG	PRO+	BR/A	SB	CS	SBR	FA	FR	G/POS	TPR
1971	Cle-A	13	18	2	3	0	0	0		2	7	.167	.250	.278	45	-1	0	0	0	1.000	-0	/O-3,1-1	-0.1

■ **JIM CLARK**   Clark, James Francis b: 12/26/1887, Brooklyn, N.Y. d: 3/20/69, Beaumont, Tex.   BR/TR, 5'11", 175 lbs.   Deb: 9/2/11

YEAR	TM/L	G	AB	R	H	2B	3B	HR	RBI	BB	SO	AVG	OBP	SLG	PRO+	BR/A	SB	CS	SBR	FA	FR	G/POS	TPR
1911	StL-N	14	18	2	3	0	1	0	3	3	4	.167	.286	.278	60	-1	2			1.000	-3	/O-8	-0.4
1912	StL-N	2	1	0	0	0	0	0	0	0	1	.000	.000	.000	-99	-0	0			.000	-0	H	0.0
Total	2	16	19	2	3	0	1	0	3	3	5	.158	.273	.263	51	-1	2			1.000	-3	/O-8	-0.4

■ **JERALD CLARK**   Clark, Jerald Dwayne b: 8/10/63, Crockett, Tex.   BR/TR, 6'4", 189 lbs.   Deb: 9/19/88   F

YEAR	TM/L	G	AB	R	H	2B	3B	HR	RBI	BB	SO	AVG	OBP	SLG	PRO+	BR/A	SB	CS	SBR	FA	FR	G/POS	TPR
1988	SD-N	6	15	0	3	1	0	0	3	0	4	.200	.200	.267	33	-1	0	0	0	1.000	1	/O-4	0.0
1989	SD-N	17	41	5	8	2	0	1	7	3	9	.195	.250	.317	61	-2	0	1	-1	.947	-1	O-14	-0.4
1990	SD-N	53	101	12	27	4	1	5	11	5	24	.267	.302	.475	109	1	0	0	0	.994	-1	1-15,O-13	-0.1
1991	SD-N	118	369	26	84	16	0	10	47	31	90	.228	.298	.352	80	-10	2	1	0	.994	-3	O-96,1-16	-1.7
1992	SD-N	146	496	45	120	22	6	12	58	22	97	.242	.280	.383	85	-12	3	0	1	.990	12	*O-134,1-11	-0.1
1993	Col-N	140	478	65	135	26	6	13	67	20	60	.282	.325	.444	89	-9	9	6	-1	.966	2	O-96,1-37	-1.3
1995	Min-A	36	109	17	37	8	3	3	15	2	11	.339	.357	.550	132	4	3	0	1	1.000	-2	O-23,1-11/D-3	0.3
Total	7	516	1609	170	414	79	16	44	208	83	295	.257	.302	.408	89	-29	17	8	0	.983	9	O-380/1-90,D-3	-3.3

■ **CAP CLARK**   Clark, John Carrol b: 9/19/06, Snow Camp, N.C. d: 2/16/57, Fayetteville, N.C.   BL/TR, 5'11", 180 lbs.   Deb: 4/23/38

YEAR	TM/L	G	AB	R	H	2B	3B	HR	RBI	BB	SO	AVG	OBP	SLG	PRO+	BR/A	SB	CS	SBR	FA	FR	G/POS	TPR
1938	Phi-N	52	74	11	19	1	0	1	4	9	10	.257	.337	.297	78	-2	0			.936	-3	C-29	-0.4

■ **MEL CLARK**   Clark, Melvin Earl b: 7/7/26, Letart, W.Va.   BR/TR, 6', 180 lbs.   Deb: 9/11/51

YEAR	TM/L	G	AB	R	H	2B	3B	HR	RBI	BB	SO	AVG	OBP	SLG	PRO+	BR/A	SB	CS	SBR	FA	FR	G/POS	TPR
1951	Phi-N	10	31	2	10	1	0	1	3	0	3	.323	.323	.452	108	0	0	1	-1	1.000	-1	/O-7	-0.1
1952	Phi-N	47	155	20	52	6	4	1	15	6	13	.335	.364	.445	125	5	2	1	0	1.000	4	O-38/3-1	0.7
1953	Phi-N	60	198	31	59	10	4	0	19	11	17	.298	.338	.389	89	-3	1	0	0	.991	-1	O-51	-0.3
1954	Phi-N	83	233	26	56	9	7	1	24	7	21	.240	.292	.352	67	-12	0	-1	-1	.961	2	O-63	-1.2
1955	Phi-N	10	32	3	5	3	0	0	1	3	4	.156	.229	.250	27	-3	0		1	1.000	3	/O-8	-0.1
1957	Det-A	5	7	0	0	0	0	0	0	0	3	.000	.000	.000	-97	-2	0	0		1.000	0	/O-2	-0.2
Total	6	215	656	82	182	29	15	3	63	37	61	.277	.318	.381	85	-15	3	3	-1	.983	10	O-169/3-1	-1.2

■ **SPIDER CLARK**   Clark, Owen F. b: 9/16/1867, Brooklyn, N.Y. d: 2/8/1892, Brooklyn, N.Y.   TR, 5'10", 150 lbs.   Deb: 5/2/1889

YEAR	TM/L	G	AB	R	H	2B	3B	HR	RBI	BB	SO	AVG	OBP	SLG	PRO+	BR/A	SB	CS	SBR	FA	FR	G/POS	TPR
1889	Was-N	38	145	19	37	7	3	2	22	6	18	.255	.285	.393	94	-2	8			.887	6	C-14,S-13/O-9,32	0.5
1890	Buf-P	69	260	45	69	11	1	1	25	20	16	.265	.325	.327	81	-6	8			.938	-4	O-34,C-14,2/13SP	-0.8
Total	2	107	405	64	106	18	4	3	47	26	34	.262	.311	.351	86	-8	16			.952	2	/O-43,C-28,2S13P	-0.3

■ **PHIL CLARK**   Clark, Phillip Benjamin b: 5/6/68, Crockett, Tex.   BR/TR, 6', 180 lbs.   Deb: 5/27/92   F

YEAR	TM/L	G	AB	R	H	2B	3B	HR	RBI	BB	SO	AVG	OBP	SLG	PRO+	BR/A	SB	CS	SBR	FA	FR	G/POS	TPR
1992	Det-A	23	54	3	22	4	0	1	5	2	9	.407	.467	.537	179	6	1	0	0	.931	-1	O-13/D-7	0.5
1993	SD-N	102	240	33	75	17	0	9	33	8	31	.313	.348	.496	121	6	2	0	1	.963	7	O-36,1-24,C-11/3-5	1.2
1994	SD-N	61	149	14	32	6	0	5	20	5	17	.215	.255	.356	59	-10	1	2	-1	.992	-2	1-24,O-17/C-5,3-1	-1.4
1995	SD-N	75	97	12	21	3	0	2	7	8	18	.216	.283	.309	58	-6	0	2	-1	1.000	-8	O-34/1-2	-1.5
1996	Bos-A	3	3	0	0	0	0	0	0	0	1	.000	.000	.000	-97	-1	0	0	0	1.000	0	/1-1,3-1,D-1	-0.1
Total	5	264	543	62	150	30	0	17	65	27	65	.276	.321	.425	97	-4	4	4	-1	.951	-3	O-100/1-51,C-16,D3	-1.3

■ **BOBBY CLARK**   Clark, Robert Cale b: 6/13/55, Sacramento, Cal.   BR/TR, 6', 190 lbs.   Deb: 8/21/79

YEAR	TM/L	G	AB	R	H	2B	3B	HR	RBI	BB	SO	AVG	OBP	SLG	PRO+	BR/A	SB	CS	SBR	FA	FR	G/POS	TPR
1979	*Cal-A	19	54	8	16	2	2	1	5	5	11	.296	.356	.463	123	2	1	1	-0	.978	2	O-19	0.3
1980	Cal-A	78	261	26	60	10	1	5	23	11	42	.230	.266	.333	65	-13	0	1	-1	.982	8	O-77	-0.9
1981	Cal-A	34	88	12	22	2	1	4	19	7	18	.250	.305	.432	110	1	0	0	0	1.000	0	O-34	0.0
1982	*Cal-A	102	90	11	19	1	0	2	8	0	29	.211	.211	.289	36	-8	1	0	0	1.000	-29	*O-102	-3.8
1983	Cal-A	76	212	17	49	9	1	5	21	9	45	.231	.262	.354	68	-10	1	1	0	1.000	-11	O-72/3-1,D-2	-2.2
1984	Mil-A	58	169	17	44	7	2	2	16	16	35	.260	.328	.361	94	-1	1	5	-3	.981	-10	O-56	-1.6
1985	Mil-A	29	93	6	21	3	0	0	7	8	19	.226	.280	.258	49	-6	1	1	-0	1.000	-7	O-27	-0.7
Total	7	396	967	97	231	34	7	19	100	55	199	.239	.282	.347	74	-36	4	8	-4	.990	-39	O-387/D-2,3-1	-8.9

■ **BOB CLARK**   Clark, Robert H. b: 3/18/1863, Covington, Ky. d: 8/21/19, Covington, Ky.   BR/TR, 5'10", 175 lbs.   Deb: 4/17/1886

YEAR	TM/L	G	AB	R	H	2B	3B	HR	RBI	BB	SO	AVG	OBP	SLG	PRO+	BR/A	SB	CS	SBR	FA	FR	G/POS	TPR
1886	Bro-a	71	269	37	58	8	0	0	26	17		.216	.262	.260	63	-12	14			.864	-13	C-44,O-17,S-12	-1.7
1887	Bro-a	48	177	24	47	3	1	0	18	7		.266	.297	.294	64	-9	15			.871	-1	C-45/O-3	-0.5
1888	Bro-a	45	150	23	36	5	3	1	20	9		.240	.292	.333	100	-0	11			.884	-2	C-36/O-8,1-1	0.1
1889	*Bro-a	53	182	32	50	5	2	0	22	26	7	.275	.368	.324	98	0	18			.870	7	C-53	1.0
1890	*Bro-N	43	151	24	33	3	0	1	15	15	8	.219	.306	.278	70	-5	10			.836	-14	C-42/O-1	-1.4
1891	Cin-N	16	54	2	6	0	0	0	3	6	9	.111	.213	.111	-5	-7	3			.868	-5	C-16	-1.0
1893	Lou-N	12	28	3	3	1	0	0	3	5	5	.107	.242	.143	4	-4	0			.947	-2	C-10/O-1,S-1	-0.4
Total	7	288	1011	145	233	25	11	1	107	85	<u>29</u>	.230	.296	.280	71	-36	71			.867	-30	C-246/O-30,S-13,1-1	-3.9

■ **RON CLARK**   Clark, Ronald Bruce b: 1/14/43, Ft.Worth, Tex.   BR/TR, 5'10", 175 lbs.   Deb: 9/11/66   C

YEAR	TM/L	G	AB	R	H	2B	3B	HR	RBI	BB	SO	AVG	OBP	SLG	PRO+	BR/A	SB	CS	SBR	FA	FR	G/POS	TPR
1966	Min-A	5	1	1	1	0	0	0	1	0		1.000	1.000	1.000	448	0	0	0	0	.000	0	/3-1	0.0
1967	Min-A	20	60	7	10	3	1	2	11	4	9	.167	.219	.350	61	-3	0	0	0	.891	-1	3-16	-0.5
1968	Min-A	104	227	14	42	5	1	1	13	16	44	.185	.245	.229	42	-16	3	2	-0	.932	-8	3-52,S-43,2-10	-2.2
1969	Min-A	8	8	0	1	0	0	0	0	0	1	.125	.125	.125	-29	-1	0	0	0	1.000	-1	/3-2	0.0
	Sea-A	57	163	9	32	5	0	0	12	13	29	.196	.260	.227	38	-13	1	0	0	.966	-9	S-38,3-15/2-5,1-1	-1.9
	Yr	62	171	9	33	5	0	0	12	13	29	.193	.254	.222	35	-15	1	0	0	.966	-10	S-38,3-17/2-5,1-1	-2.1
1971	Oak-A	2	1	0	0	0	0	0	0	0	1	.000	.500	.000	53	0	0	0	0	.000	0	H	0.1
1972	Oak-A	14	15	1	4	2	0	0	1	2	4	.267	.353	.400	130	0	0	0	0	1.000	0	2-11/3-3	0.1
	Mil-A	22	54	8	10	1	1	2	5	5	11	.185	.254	.352	81	-1	0	0	0	.963	5	2-11,3-10	0.5
	Yr	36	69	9	14	3	1	2	6	7	15	.203	.276	.362	92	-1	0	0	0	.974	6	2-22,3-13	0.6
1975	Phi-N	1	1	0	0	0	0	0	0	0	0	.000	.000	.000	-96	-0	0	0	0			H	0.0
Total	7	230	530	40	100	16	3	5	43	41	98	.189	.251	.258	49	-34	4	2	-0	.904	-13	/3-99,S-81,2-37,1-1	-4.2

■ **ROY CLARK**   Clark, Roy Elliott "Pepper" b: 5/11/1874, New Haven, Conn. d: 11/1/25, Bridgeport, Conn.   BL/TL, 5'8", 170 lbs.   Deb: 4/19/02

YEAR	TM/L	G	AB	R	H	2B	3B	HR	RBI	BB	SO	AVG	OBP	SLG	PRO+	BR/A	SB	CS	SBR	FA	FR	G/POS	TPR
1902	NY-N	21	76	4	11	1	0	0	3	1		.145	.156	.158	-3	-9	5			.962	-3	O-20	-1.4

■ **WILL CLARK**   Clark, William Nuschler b: 3/13/64, New Orleans, La.   BL/TL, 6'2", 190 lbs.   Deb: 4/8/86

YEAR	TM/L	G	AB	R	H	2B	3B	HR	RBI	BB	SO	AVG	OBP	SLG	PRO+	BR/A	SB	CS	SBR	FA	FR	G/POS	TPR
1986	SF-N	111	408	66	117	27	2	11	41	34	76	.287	.346	.444	122	11	4	7	-3	.989	-2	*1-102	0.0
1987	*SF-N	150	529	89	163	29	5	35	91	49	98	.308	.372	.580	155	40	5	17	-9	.991	2	*1-139	2.3
1988	SF-N★	162	575	102	162	31	6	29	109	**100**	129	.282	.392	.508	163	**49**	9	1	2	.993	-3	*1-158	3.8
1989	*SF-N★	159	588	**104**	196	38	9	23	111	74	103	.333	.412	.546	177	59	8	3	1	.994	0	*1-158	5.0
1990	SF-N★	154	600	91	177	25	5	19	95	62	97	.295	.364	.448	127	22	8	2	1	.992	-1	*1-153	1.2
1991	SF-N★	148	565	84	170	32	7	29	116	51	91	.301	.361	**.536**	154	38	4	2	0	**.997**	3	*1-144	3.3
1992	SF-N	144	513	69	154	40	1	16	73	73	82	.300	.392	.476	153	37	12	2	1	.993	-0	*1-141	0.0
1993	SF-N	132	491	82	139	27	2	14	73	63	60	.283	.371	.432	118	14	2	2	0	.988	3	*1-129	0.0
1994	Tex-A★	110	389	73	128	24	2	13	80	71	50	.329	.436	.501	141	27	5	1	1	.990	1	*1-107/D-1	1.7
1995	Tex-A	123	454	85	137	27	3	16	92	68	50	.302	.397	.480	124	18	2	5	1	.994	-0	*1-122/D-1	0.4

YEAR	TM/L	G	AB	R	H	2B	3B	HR	RBI	BB	SO	AVG	OBP	SLG	PRO+	BR/A	SB	CS	SBR	FA	FR	G/POS	TPR
1996	*Tex-A	117	436	69	124	25	1	13	72	64	67	.284	.382	.436	99	1	2	1	0	.996	-2	*1-117	-1.1
Total	11	1510	5548	914	1667	325	43	218	953	709	920	.300	.384	.492	140	315	59	44	-9	.993	-2	*1-1470/D-2	19.4

■ WILLIE CLARK
Clark, William Otis "Wee Willie" b: 8/16/1872, Pittsburgh, Pa. d: 11/13/32, Pittsburgh, Pa. BL, Deb: 6/20/1895

YEAR	TM/L	G	AB	R	H	2B	3B	HR	RBI	BB	SO	AVG	OBP	SLG	PRO+	BR/A	SB	CS	SBR	FA	FR	G/POS	TPR
1895	NY-N	23	88	9	23	3	2	0	16	5	6	.261	.301	.341	67	-5	1			.974	1	1-23	-0.3
1896	NY-N	72	247	38	72	12	4	0	33	15	12	.291	.352	.372	94	-2	8			.975	-4	1-65	-0.5
1897	NY-N	116	431	63	122	17	12	1	75	37		.283	.352	.385	97	-2	18			.984	2	*1-107/O-7,3-1	0.1
1898	Pit-N	57	209	29	64	9	7	1	31	22		.306	.368	.431	134	9	0			.984	1	1-57	0.9
1899	Pit-N	80	298	49	85	13	10	0	44	35		.285	.379	.396	113	6	11			.989	1	1-78	0.7
Total	5	348	1273	188	366	54	35	2	199	114	18	.288	.359	.390	104	7	38			.983	0	1-330/O-7,3-1	0.9

■ BILL CLARK
Clark, William Winfield b: 4/11/1875, Circleville, Ohio d: 4/15/59, Los Angeles, Cal. BR/TR, 5'10", 175 lbs. Deb: 7/12/1897

YEAR	TM/L	G	AB	R	H	2B	3B	HR	RBI	BB	SO	AVG	OBP	SLG	PRO+	BR/A	SB	CS	SBR	FA	FR	G/POS	TPR
1897	Lou-N	4	16	2	3	0	0	0	2	1		.188	.235	.188	13	-2	1			.810	-2	/2-3,3-1	-0.3

■ ARTIE CLARKE
Clarke, Arthur Franklin b: 5/6/1865, Providence, R.I. d: 11/14/49, Brookline, Mass. BR/TR, 5'8", 155 lbs. Deb: 4/19/1890

YEAR	TM/L	G	AB	R	H	2B	3B	HR	RBI	BB	SO	AVG	OBP	SLG	PRO+	BR/A	SB	CS	SBR	FA	FR	G/POS	TPR
1890	NY-N	101	395	55	89	12	8	0	49	32	38	.225	.290	.296	71	-15	44			.908	-3	C-36,O-33,3-16,2/S	-1.3
1891	NY-N	48	174	17	33	2	2	0	21	15	16	.190	.254	.224	41	-13	5			.916	-12	C-42/3-5,O-2	-1.9
Total	2	149	569	72	122	14	10	0	70	47	54	.214	.279	.274	62	-28	49			.912	-15	/C-78,O-35,3-21,2S	-3.2

■ FRED CLARKE
Clarke, Fred Clifford "Cap" b: 10/3/1872, Winterset, Iowa d: 8/14/60, Winfield, Kan. BL/TR, 5'10.5", 165 lbs. Deb: 6/30/1894 FMCH

YEAR	TM/L	G	AB	R	H	2B	3B	HR	RBI	BB	SO	AVG	OBP	SLG	PRO+	BR/A	SB	CS	SBR	FA	FR	G/POS	TPR
1894	Lou-N	75	310	54	83	11	7	7	48	25	27	.268	.330	.416	85	-9	25			.885	4	O-75	-0.8
1895	Lou-N	132	550	96	191	21	5	4	82	34	24	.347	.396	.425	119	17	40			.881	11	*O-132	1.4
1896	Lou-N	131	517	96	168	15	18	9	79	43	34	.325	.392	.476	133	25	34			.908	0	*O-131	1.2
1897	Lou-N	128	518	120	202	30	13	6	67	45		.390	.462	.533	**168**	**53**	57			.926	6	*O-127,M	4.2
1898	Lou-N	149	599	116	184	23	12	3	47	48		.307	.373	.401	124	19	40			.940	6	*O-149,M	1.3
1899	Lou-N	148	602	122	206	23	9	5	70	49		.342	.406	.435	131	27	49			.964	1	*O-144/S-3,M	1.5
1900	Pit-N	106	399	84	110	15	12	3	32	51		.276	.368	.396	110	6	21			.944	3	*O-104,M	0.1
1901	Pit-N	129	527	118	171	24	15	6	60	51		.324	.395	.461	143	30	23			.970	2	*O-127/S-1,3-1,M	2.1
1902	Pit-N	113	459	103	145	27	14	2	53	51		.316	.401	.449	156	32	29			.958	-1	*O-113,M	2.5
1903	*Pit-N	104	427	88	150	**32**	15	5	70	41		.351	.414	**.532**	164	34	21			.962	-8	*O-101/S-2,M	1.9
1904	Pit-N	72	278	51	85	7	11	0	25	22		.306	.367	.410	136	12	11			.979	0	O-70,M	0.8
1905	Pit-N	141	525	95	157	18	15	2	51	55		.299	.368	.402	126	17	24			.976	4	*O-137,M	1.5
1906	Pit-N	118	417	69	129	14	**13**	1	39	40		.309	.383	.412	138	18	18			.974	6	*O-110,M	2.0
1907	Pit-N	148	501	97	145	18	13	2	59	68		.289	.383	.389	140	25	37			.987	6	*O-144,M	2.9
1908	Pit-N	151	551	83	146	18	15	2	53	65		.265	.349	.363	127	18	24			.973	10	*O-151,M	2.5
1909	*Pit-N	152	550	97	158	16	11	3	68	**80**		.287	.384	.373	124	18	31			**.987**	7	*O-152,M	2.1
1910	Pit-N	123	429	57	113	23	9	2	63	53	23	.263	.350	.373	105	2	12			.967	3	*O-118,M	1.9
1911	Pit-N	110	392	73	127	25	13	5	49	53	27	.324	.407	.492	146	24	10			.970	0	*O-101,M	1.9
1913	Pit-N	9	13	0	1	1	0	0	0	0	0	.077	.077	.154	-37	-2	0			1.000	-1	/O-2,M	-0.3
1914	Pit-N	2	2	0	0	0	0	0	0	0	0	.000	.000	.000	-99	-0	0			.000		HM	-0.1
1915	Pit-N	1	2	0	1	0	0	0	0	0	0	.500	.500	.500	206	0	0			.000	-1	/O-1,M	0.0
Total	21	2242	8568	1619	2672	361	220	67	1015	874	135	.312	.386	.429	132	366	506			.952	59	*O-2189/S-6,3-1	28.7

■ HARRY CLARKE
Clarke, Harry Corson b: 1861, d: 3/3/23, Long Beach, Cal. Deb: 8/28/1889

YEAR	TM/L	G	AB	R	H	2B	3B	HR	RBI	BB	SO	AVG	OBP	SLG	PRO+	BR/A	SB	CS	SBR	FA	FR	G/POS	TPR
1889	Was-N	1	3	0	0	0	0	0	0	0	1	.000	.000	.000	-99	-1	0			1.000	1	/O-1	0.0

■ HENRY CLARKE
Clarke, Henry Tefft b: 8/28/1875, Bellevue, Neb. d: 3/28/50, Colorado Springs, Colo. BR/TR, Deb: 6/26/1897

YEAR	TM/L	G	AB	R	H	2B	3B	HR	RBI	BB	SO	AVG	OBP	SLG	PRO+	BR/A	SB	CS	SBR	FA	FR	G/POS	TPR
1897	Cle-N	7	25	3	7	0	0	0	3	2		.280	.333	.280	60	-1	0			.714	-1	/P-5,O-2	-0.1
1898	Chi-N	2	4	0	1	0	0	0	0	1		.250	.400	.250	87	0	0			.000	-1	/O-1,P-1	-0.1
Total	2	9	29	3	8	0	0	0	3	3		.276	.344	.276	64	-1	0			.750	-2	/P-6,O-3	-0.2

■ HORACE CLARKE
Clarke, Horace Meredith b: 6/2/40, Frederiksted, St.Croix, V.I. BB/TR, 5'9", 178 lbs. Deb: 5/13/65

YEAR	TM/L	G	AB	R	H	2B	3B	HR	RBI	BB	SO	AVG	OBP	SLG	PRO+	BR/A	SB	CS	SBR	FA	FR	G/POS	TPR
1965	NY-A	51	108	13	28	1	0	1	9	6	6	.259	.298	.296	70	-4	2	1	0	.923	3	3-17/2-7,S-1	-0.3
1966	NY-A	96	312	37	83	10	4	6	28	27	24	.266	.326	.381	107	2	5	3	-0	.970	-19	S-63,2-16/3-4	-1.1
1967	NY-A	143	588	74	160	17	0	3	29	42	64	.272	.321	.316	92	-6	21	4	4	**.990**	15	*2-140	2.5
1968	NY-A	148	579	52	133	6	2	2	26	23	46	.230	.259	.254	58	-30	20	7	2	.984	**30**	*2-139	1.1
1969	NY-A	156	641	82	183	26	7	4	48	53	41	.285	.340	.367	101	1	33	13	2	.982	-4	*2-156	1.2
1970	NY-A	158	686	81	172	24	4	4	46	35	35	.251	.289	.309	68	-31	23	7	3	.979	-7	*2-157	-2.2
1971	NY-A	159	625	76	156	23	7	2	41	64	43	.250	.321	.318	87	-11	17	7	1	.981	-3	*2-156	0.1
1972	NY-A	147	547	65	132	20	2	3	37	56	44	.241	.316	.302	87	-8	18	6	2	.985	6	*2-143	1.0
1973	NY-A	148	590	60	155	21	4	2	35	47	48	.263	.319	.308	80	-15	11	10	-3	.979	8	*2-147	-0.1
1974	NY-A	24	47	3	11	1	0	0	4	4	5	.234	.294	.255	60	-2	1	0	0	1.000	-6	2-20/D-1	-0.7
	SD-N	42	90	5	17	1	0	0	4	8	6	.189	.255	.200	30	-8	0	0	0	.978	-4	2-21	-1.3
Total	10	1272	4813	548	1230	150	23	27	304	365	362	.256	.310	.313	82	-112	151	58	11	.983	19	*2-1102/S-64,3-21,D	0.3

■ NIG CLARKE
Clarke, Jay Justin b: 12/15/1882, Amherstburg, Ont., Canada d: 6/15/49, River Rouge, Mich BL/TR, 5'8", 165 lbs. Deb: 4/26/05

YEAR	TM/L	G	AB	R	H	2B	3B	HR	RBI	BB	SO	AVG	OBP	SLG	PRO+	BR/A	SB	CS	SBR	FA	FR	G/POS	TPR
1905	Cle-A	5	9	2	1	1	0	0	1	1		.111	.200	.222	33	-1	0			1.000	-2	/C-5	-0.2
	Det-A	3	7	1	3	0	0	1	0	0		.429	.500	.857	326	2	0			1.000	1	/C-2	0.2
	Cle-A	37	114	9	23	5	1	0	8	10		.202	.266	.263	67	-4	0			.961	-1	C-37	-0.3
	Yr	45	130	12	27	6	1	1	10	11		.208	.275	.292	79	-3	0			.965	-2	C-44	-0.1
1906	Cle-A	57	179	22	64	12	4	1	21	13		.358	.404	.486	181	16	3			.982	-1	C-54	2.2
1907	Cle-A	120	390	44	105	19	6	3	33	35		.269	.333	.372	123	10	3			.961	-11	*C-115	1.0
1908	Cle-A	97	290	34	70	8	6	1	27	30		.241	.315	.321	106	2	6			.969	-8	C-90	0.3
1909	Cle-A	55	164	15	45	4	2	0	14	9		.274	.316	.323	98	-1	1			.952	-3	C-44	0.1
1910	Cle-A	21	58	4	9	2	0	0	2	9		.155	.258	.190	40	-4	0			.974	3	C-17	0.0
1911	StL-A	82	256	25	55	10	1	0	18	26		.215	.287	.262	56	-15	2			.926	-5	C-73/1-4	-1.3
1919	Phi-A	26	62	4	15	3	0	0	2	4	5	.242	.299	.290	72	-2	1			.969	0	C-22	0.0
1920	Pit-N	3	7	0	0	0	0	0	0	2	4	.000	.222	.000	-32	-1	0	0	0	1.000	1	/C-3	0.0
Total	9	506	1536	157	390	64	20	6	127	138	9	.254	.318	.333	102	3	16	0		.960	-25	C-462/1-4	2.2

■ JOSH CLARKE
Clarke, Joshua Baldwin "Pepper" b: 3/8/1879, Winfield, Kan. d: 7/2/62, Ventura, Cal. BL/TR, 5'10", 180 lbs. Deb: 6/15/1898 F

YEAR	TM/L	G	AB	R	H	2B	3B	HR	RBI	BB	SO	AVG	OBP	SLG	PRO+	BR/A	SB	CS	SBR	FA	FR	G/POS	TPR
1898	Lou-N	6	18	0	3	0	0	0	1		1	.167	.211	.167	9	-2	0			.917	-1	/O-5	-0.3
1905	StL-N	50	167	31	43	3	2	3	18	27		.257	.361	.353	117	4	8			.942	-8	O-26,2-16/S-4	-0.5
1908	Cle-A	131	492	70	119	8	4	1	21	76		.242	.348	.280	104	6	37			.963	-3	*O-131	-0.2
1909	Cle-A	4	12	1	0	0	0	0	0	2		.000	.143	.000	-52	-2	0			.600	-2	/O-4	-0.4
1911	Bos-N	32	120	16	28	7	3	1	4	29	22	.233	.387	.367	103	1	6			.938	4	O-30	0.3
Total	5	223	809	118	193	18	9	5	43	135	22	.239	.351	.302	102	8	51			.949	-9	O-196/2-16,S-4	-1.1

■ GREY CLARKE
Clarke, Richard Grey "Noisy" b: 9/26/12, Fulton, Ala. d: 11/25/93, Kannapolis, N.C. BR/TR, 5'9", 183 lbs. Deb: 4/19/44

YEAR	TM/L	G	AB	R	H	2B	3B	HR	RBI	BB	SO	AVG	OBP	SLG	PRO+	BR/A	SB	CS	SBR	FA	FR	G/POS	TPR
1944	Chi-A	63	169	14	44	10	1	0	27	22	6	.260	.352	.331	97	0	0	4	-2	.941	1	3-45	-0.1

■ SUMPTER CLARKE
Clarke, Sumpter Mills b: 10/18/1897, Savannah, Ga. d: 3/16/62, Knoxville, Tenn. BR/TR, 5'11", 170 lbs. Deb: 9/27/20 F

YEAR	TM/L	G	AB	R	H	2B	3B	HR	RBI	BB	SO	AVG	OBP	SLG	PRO+	BR/A	SB	CS	SBR	FA	FR	G/POS	TPR
1920	Chi-N	1	3	0	1	0	0	0	0	0	1	.333	.333	.333	90	-0	0	0	0	1.000	-0	/3-1	0.0
1923	Cle-A	1	3	0	0	0	0	0	0	0	1	.000	.000	.000	-99	-1	0	0	0	1.000	-0	/O-1	-0.1
1924	Cle-A	35	104	17	24	6	1	0	11	6	12	.231	.273	.308	49	-8	0	0	0	1.000	-5	O-33	-1.5
Total	3	37	110	17	25	6	1	0	11	6	13	.227	.267	.300	46	-9	0	0	0	1.000	-6	/O-34,3-1	-1.6

■ TOMMY CLARKE
Clarke, Thomas Aloysius b: 5/9/1888, New York, N.Y. d: 8/14/45, Corona, N.Y. BR/TR, 5'11", 175 lbs. Deb: 8/26/09

YEAR	TM/L	G	AB	R	H	2B	3B	HR	RBI	BB	SO	AVG	OBP	SLG	PRO+	BR/A	SB	CS	SBR	FA	FR	G/POS	TPR
1909	Cin-N	18	52	8	13	3	2	0	10	6		.250	.328	.385	122	1	3			.965	5	C-17	0.8
1910	Cin-N	64	151	19	42	6	5	1	20	19	17	.278	.370	.404	131	6	1			.971	-1	C-56	1.0
1911	Cin-N	86	203	20	49	6	1	1	25	25	22	.241	.328	.355	94	-2	4			.970	2	C-81/1-1	0.7
1912	Cin-N	72	146	19	41	7	2	0	22	28	14	.281	.400	.356	111	4	9			.983	5	C-63	1.3

YEAR	TM/L	G	AB	R	H	2B	3B	HR	RBI	BB	SO	AVG	OBP	SLG	PRO+	BR/A	SB	CS	SBR	FA	FR	G/POS	TPR
1913	Cin-N	114	330	29	87	11	8	1	38	39	40	.264	.345	.355	100	1	2			.979	-13	*C-100	-0.4
1914	Cin-N	113	313	30	82	13	7	2	25	31	30	.262	.332	.367	105	2	6			.973	-4	*C-106	0.7
1915	Cin-N	96	226	23	65	7	2	0	21	33	22	.288	.381	.336	116	6	7	3	0	.981	-4	C-72	0.8
1916	Cin-N	78	177	10	42	10	1	0	17	24	20	.237	.328	.305	97	0	8			.965	-10	C-51	-0.7
1917	Cin-N	58	110	11	32	3	3	1	13	11	12	.291	.361	.400	139	5	2			.991	-5	C-29	0.2
1918	Chi-N	1	0	0	0	0	0	0	0	0	0	—	—	—	—		0			.000	0	/C-1	0.0
Total	10	700	1708	169	453	66	37	6	191	216	177	.265	.351	.358	109	24	42	3		.975	-26	C-576/1-1	4.4

■ BOILERYARD CLARKE
Clarke, William Jones   b: 10/18/1868, New York, N.Y.   d: 7/29/59, Princeton, N.J.   BR/TR, 5'11.5", 170 lbs.   Deb: 5/1/1893

YEAR	TM/L	G	AB	R	H	2B	3B	HR	RBI	BB	SO	AVG	OBP	SLG	PRO+	BR/A	SB	CS	SBR	FA	FR	G/POS	TPR
1893	Bal-N	49	183	23	32	1	3	1	24	19	14	.175	.274	.230	34	-18	2			.909	-3	C-38,1-11	-1.4
1894	Bal-N	28	100	18	24	8	0	1	19	16	14	.240	.361	.350	69	-5	2			.903	-3	C-23/1-5	-0.4
1895	*Bal-N	67	241	38	70	15	3	0	35	13	18	.290	.350	.378	85	-6	8			.938	6	C-60/1-6	0.5
1896	Bal-N	80	300	48	89	14	7	2	71	14	12	.297	.345	.410	97	-2	7			.948	-11	C-67,1-14	-0.5
1897	*Bal-N	64	241	32	65	7	1	1	38	9		.270	.320	.320	69	-11	5			.939	-15	C-59/1-4	-1.6
1898	Bal-N	82	285	26	69	5	2	0	27	4		.242	.289	.274	60	-15	3			.962	3	C-70,1-10	-0.4
1899	Bos-N	60	223	25	50	3	2	2	32	10		.224	.270	.283	47	-17	2			.940	-1	C-60	-1.2
1900	Bos-N	81	270	35	85	5	2	1	30	9		.315	.344	.359	84	-7	0			.928	7	C-67/1-8	0.6
1901	Was-A	110	422	58	118	15	5	3	54	23		.280	.335	.360	94	-3	7			.952	-9	*C-107/1-3	-0.1
1902	Was-A	87	291	31	78	15	0	6	40	23		.268	.330	.381	96	-2	1			**.972**	-3	C-87	0.4
1903	Was-A	126	465	35	111	14	6	2	38	15		.239	.273	.308	72	-16	12			.981	-11	1-88,C-37	-2.5
1904	Was-A	85	275	23	58	8	1	0	17	17		.211	.269	.247	65	-10	5			.977	0	C-52,1-29	-0.6
1905	NY-N	31	50	2	9	0	1	0	4	4		.180	.241	.240	42	-4	1			.973	-1	1-15,C-12	-0.4
Total	13	950	3346	394	858	110	32	20	429	176	58	.256	.310	.326	75	-115	54			.947	-39	C-739,1-193	-7.6

■ STU CLARKE
Clarke, William Stuart   b: 1/24/06, San Francisco, Cal   d: 8/26/85, Hayward, Cal.   BR/TR, 5'8.5", 160 lbs.   Deb: 7/17/29

YEAR	TM/L	G	AB	R	H	2B	3B	HR	RBI	BB	SO	AVG	OBP	SLG	PRO+	BR/A	SB	CS	SBR	FA	FR	G/POS	TPR
1929	Pit-N	57	178	20	47	5	7	2	21	19	21	.264	.338	.404	81	-5	3			.919	-8	S-41,3-15/2-1	-0.8
1930	Pit-N	4	9	2	4	0	1	0	2	1	0	.444	.500	.667	178	1	0			1.000	-1	/2-2	0.0
Total	2	61	187	22	51	5	8	2	23	20	21	.273	.346	.417	86	-4	3			1.000	-9	/S-41,3-15,2-3	-0.8

■ BUZZ CLARKSON
Clarkson, James Buster   b: 3/13/15, Hopkins, S.C.   d: 1/18/89, Jeannette, Pa.   BR/TR, 5'11", 210 lbs.   Deb: 4/30/52

YEAR	TM/L	G	AB	R	H	2B	3B	HR	RBI	BB	SO	AVG	OBP	SLG	PRO+	BR/A	SB	CS	SBR	FA	FR	G/POS	TPR
1952	Bos-N	14	25	3	5	0	0	1	3	3	3	.200	.286	.200	38	-2	0	0	0	.938	-2	/S-6,3-2	-0.4

■ ELLIS CLARY
Clary, Ellis "Cat"   b: 9/11/16, Valdosta, Ga.   BR/TR, 5'8", 160 lbs.   Deb: 6/7/42   C

YEAR	TM/L	G	AB	R	H	2B	3B	HR	RBI	BB	SO	AVG	OBP	SLG	PRO+	BR/A	SB	CS	SBR	FA	FR	G/POS	TPR
1942	Was-A	76	240	34	66	9	0	0	16	45	25	.275	.394	.313	101	3	2	0	1	.969	-17	2-69/3-2	-0.9
1943	Was-A	73	254	36	65	19	1	0	19	44	31	.256	.370	.339	112	6	8	4	0	.945	-8	3-68/S-1	-0.1
	StL-A	23	69	15	19	2	0	0	5	11	6	.275	.373	.304	98	0	1	2	-1	.972	-1	3-14/2-3	-0.1
	Yr	96	323	51	84	21	1	0	24	55	37	.260	.371	.331	109	6	9	6	-1	.949	-9	3-82/2-3,S-1	-0.2
1944	*StL-A	25	49	6	13	1	1	0	4	12	9	.265	.410	.327	106	1	1			1.000	-1	3-11/2-6	0.0
1945	StL-A	26	38	6	8	1	0	1	2	2	3	.211	.250	.316	61	-2	0	2	-1	.947	3	3-16/2-3	0.0
Total	4	223	650	97	171	32	2	1	46	114	74	.263	.376	.323	103	8	12	8	-1	.953	-25	3-111/2-81,S-1	-1.1

■ DAIN CLAY
Clay, Dain Elmer "Sniffy" or "Ding-A-Ling"   b: 7/10/19, Hicksville, Ohio   d: 8/28/94, Chula Vista, Cal.   BR/TR, 5'10.5", 160 lbs.   Deb: 6/12/43

YEAR	TM/L	G	AB	R	H	2B	3B	HR	RBI	BB	SO	AVG	OBP	SLG	PRO+	BR/A	SB	CS	SBR	FA	FR	G/POS	TPR
1943	Cin-N	49	93	19	25	2	0	0	9	8	14	.269	.333	.376	106	1	1			.936	-9	O-33	-1.0
1944	Cin-N	110	356	51	89	15	0	0	17	17	18	.250	.290	.292	67	-16	8			.993	-2	O-98	-2.3
1945	Cin-N	153	656	81	184	29	2	1	50	37	58	.280	.321	.335	84	-15	19			.989	6	*O-152	-1.7
1946	Cin-N	121	435	52	99	17	0	2	22	53	40	.228	.318	.280	73	-14	11			**.988**	7	*O-120	-1.3
Total	4	433	1540	203	397	63	6	3	98	115	130	.258	.314	.312	79	-44	39			.987	3	O-403	-6.3

■ BILL CLAY
Clay, Frederick C.   b: 11/23/1874, Baltimore, Md.   d: 10/12/17, York, Pa.   TR,   Deb: 8/8/02

YEAR	TM/L	G	AB	R	H	2B	3B	HR	RBI	BB	SO	AVG	OBP	SLG	PRO+	BR/A	SB	CS	SBR	FA	FR	G/POS	TPR
1902	Phi-N	3	8	1	2	0	0	0	1	0		.250	.250	.250	54	-0	0			.750	-1	/O-3	-0.2

■ ROYCE CLAYTON
Clayton, Royce Spencer   b: 1/2/70, Burbank, Cal.   BR/TR, 6', 175 lbs.   Deb: 9/20/91

YEAR	TM/L	G	AB	R	H	2B	3B	HR	RBI	BB	SO	AVG	OBP	SLG	PRO+	BR/A	SB	CS	SBR	FA	FR	G/POS	TPR
1991	SF-N	9	26	0	3	1	0	0	2	1	6	.115	.148	.154	-15	-4	0	0	0	.880	-6	/S-8	-1.0
1992	SF-N	98	321	31	72	7	4	4	24	26	63	.224	.282	.308	71	-13	8	4	0	.973	-9	S-94/3-1	-1.6
1993	SF-N	153	549	54	155	21	5	6	70	38	91	.282	.334	.372	91	-7	11	10	-3	.963	1	*S-153	0.3
1994	SF-N	108	385	38	91	14	6	3	30	30	74	.236	.297	.327	66	-20	23	3	5	.973	7	*S-108	0.2
1995	SF-N	138	509	56	124	29	3	5	58	38	109	.244	.300	.342	71	-22	24	9	2	.969	4	*S-136	-0.4
1996	*StL-N	129	491	64	136	20	4	6	35	33	89	.277	.324	.371	82	-13	33	15	1	.972	1	*S-113	0.0
Total	6	635	2281	243	581	92	22	24	219	166	432	.255	.309	.346	77	-77	99	41	5	.969	-3	S-612/3-1	-2.5

■ CHET CLEMENS
Clemens, Chester Spurgeon   b: 5/10/17, San Fernando, Cal.   BR/TR, 6', 175 lbs.   Deb: 9/13/39

YEAR	TM/L	G	AB	R	H	2B	3B	HR	RBI	BB	SO	AVG	OBP	SLG	PRO+	BR/A	SB	CS	SBR	FA	FR	G/POS	TPR
1939	Bos-N	9	23	2	5	0	0	0	1	1	3	.217	.250	.217	29	-2	1			.867	-1	/O-7	-0.4
1944	Bos-N	19	17	7	3	1	1	0	2	2	2	.176	.263	.353	69	-1	0			1.000	-2	/O-7	-0.3
Total	2	28	40	9	8	1	1	0	3	3	5	.200	.256	.275	46	-3	1			.905	-3	/O-14	-0.7

■ CLEM CLEMENS
Clemens, Clement Lambert "Count" (b: Clement Lambert Ulatowski)   b: 11/21/1886, Chicago, Ill.   d: 11/2/67, St.Petersburg, Fla.   BR/TR, 5'11", 176 lbs.   Deb: 5/15/14

YEAR	TM/L	G	AB	R	H	2B	3B	HR	RBI	BB	SO	AVG	OBP	SLG	PRO+	BR/A	SB	CS	SBR	FA	FR	G/POS	TPR
1914	Chi-F	13	27	4	4	0	0	0	3	1	0	.148	.233	.148	6	-4	0			.950	-1	/C-8	-0.5
1915	Chi-F	11	22	3	3	1	0	0	3	1	0	.136	.174	.182	-3	-3	0			1.000	-1	/C-9,2-2	-0.2
1916	Chi-N	10	15	0	0	0	0	0	0	3	6	.000	.063	.000	-72	-3	0			.941	1	/C-9	-0.3
Total	3	34	64	7	7	1	0	0	5	5	6	.109	.174	.125	-15	-10	0			.962	-1	/C-26,2-2	-1.1

■ DOUG CLEMENS
Clemens, Douglas Horace   b: 6/9/39, Leesport, Pa.   BL/TR, 6', 180 lbs.   Deb: 10/2/60

YEAR	TM/L	G	AB	R	H	2B	3B	HR	RBI	BB	SO	AVG	OBP	SLG	PRO+	BR/A	SB	CS	SBR	FA	FR	G/POS	TPR
1960	StL-N	1	0	0	0	0	0	0	0	0	0						0	0	0	1.000	0	/O-1	0.0
1961	StL-N	6	12	1	2	0	0	0	3	1		.167	.333	.250	53	-1	0	0	0	.667	-1	/O-3	-0.2
1962	StL-N	48	93	12	22	1	1	0	12	19	17	.237	.355	.301	71	-3	0	0	0	.974	-6	O-34	-1.1
1963	StL-N	5	6	1	1	0	0	0	2	1	2	.167	.286	.667	151	0	0	0	0	1.000	0	/O-3	0.1
1964	StL-N	33	78	8	16	4	3	1	9	6	16	.205	.271	.372	73	-3	0	0	0	.970	0	O-22	-0.4
	Chi-N	54	140	23	39	10	2	2	12	18	22	.279	.365	.421	116	3	0	0	0	.923	0	O-40	0.2
	Yr	87	218	31	55	14	5	3	21	24	38	.252	.332	.404	100	0	0	0	0	.937	1	O-62	-0.2
1965	Chi-N	128	340	36	75	11	0	4	26	38	53	.221	.300	.288	66	-15	5	8	-3	.981	-6	*O-105	-2.9
1966	Phi-N	79	121	10	31	1	0	1	15	16	25	.256	.353	.289	81	-2	1			1.000	0	O-28/1-1	-0.4
1967	Phi-N	69	73	2	13	5	0	0	4	8	15	.178	.268	.247	48	-5	0			1.000	0	O-10	-0.8
1968	Phi-N	29	57	6	12	1	1	0	7	3	13	.211	.297	.368	99	0	0			1.000	0	O-17	-0.2
Total	9	452	920	99	211	34	7	12	88	114	166	.229	.319	.321	78	-25	6	8	-3	.969	-16	O-263/1-1	-5.7

■ BOB CLEMENS
Clemens, Robert Baxter   b: 8/9/1886, Mt.Hebron, Mo.   d: 4/5/64, Marshall, Mo.   BR/TR, 5'9", 163 lbs.   Deb: 9/17/14

YEAR	TM/L	G	AB	R	H	2B	3B	HR	RBI	BB	SO	AVG	OBP	SLG	PRO+	BR/A	SB	CS	SBR	FA	FR	G/POS	TPR
1914	StL-A	7	13	1	3	0	1	0	3	2	1	.231	.375	.385	134	1	0	2	-1	.750	-1	/O-5	-0.2

■ WALLY CLEMENT
Clement, Wallace Oakes   b: 7/21/1881, Auburn, Me.   d: 11/1/53, Coral Gables, Fla.   BL/TR, 5'11", 175 lbs.   Deb: 8/17/08

YEAR	TM/L	G	AB	R	H	2B	3B	HR	RBI	BB	SO	AVG	OBP	SLG	PRO+	BR/A	SB	CS	SBR	FA	FR	G/POS	TPR
1908	Phi-N	16	36	0	8	3	0	0	0	1		.222	.222	.306	66	-1	4			1.000	4	/O-8	0.2
1909	Phi-N	3	3	0	0	0	0	0	0	0		.000	.000	.000	-99	-1	0			.000	0	H	-0.1
	Bro-N	92	340	35	88	8	4	0	17	18		.259	.296	.306	90	-5	11			.965	0	O-88	-0.5
	Yr	95	343	35	88	8	4	0	17	18		.257	.294	.303	88	-6	11			.965	4	O-88	-0.6
Total	2	111	379	35	96	11	4	0	18	18		.253	.287	.303	86	-7	13			.970	7	/O-96	-0.4

■ ROBERTO CLEMENTE
Clemente, Roberto (Walker) "Bob"   b: 8/18/34, Carolina, P.R.   d: 12/31/72, San Juan, P.R.   BR/TR, 5'11", 175 lbs.   Deb: 4/17/55   H

YEAR	TM/L	G	AB	R	H	2B	3B	HR	RBI	BB	SO	AVG	OBP	SLG	PRO+	BR/A	SB	CS	SBR	FA	FR	G/POS	TPR
1955	Pit-N	124	474	48	121	23	11	5	47	18	60	.255	.285	.382	76	-17	2	4	-1	.978	12	*O-118	-1.4
1956	Pit-N	147	543	66	169	30	7	7	60	13	58	.311	.332	.431	105	3	6	6	-2	.957	7	*O-139/2-2,3-1	-0.4
1957	Pit-N	111	451	42	114	17	7	4	30	23	45	.253	.289	.348	72	-18	0	4	-2	.979	13	*O-109	-1.4
1958	Pit-N	140	519	69	150	24	10	6	50	31	41	.289	.324	.408	96	-4	8	2	1	.982	25	*O-135	1.6
1959	Pit-N	105	432	60	128	17	7	4	50	15	51	.296	.324	.396	91	-6	2	3	0	.948	9	*O-104	-0.3

YEAR	TM/L	G	AB	R	H	2B	3B	HR	RBI	BB	SO	AVG	OBP	SLG	PRO+	BR/A	SB	CS	SBR	FA	FR	G/POS	TPR
1960	*Pit-N★	144	570	89	179	22	6	16	94	39	72	.314	.360	.458	121	16	4	5	-2	.971	3	*O-142	1.1
1961	Pit-N★	146	572	100	201	30	10	23	89	35	59	**.351**	.392	.559	148	38	4	1	1	.969	14	*O-144	4.4
1962	Pit-N★	144	538	95	168	28	9	10	74	35	73	.312	.355	.454	115	11	6	4	-1	.973	13	*O-142	1.5
1963	Pit-N★	152	600	77	192	23	8	17	76	31	64	.320	.357	.470	135	26	12	2	2	.958	-3	*O-151	1.9
1964	Pit-N★	155	622	95	**211**	40	7	12	87	51	87	**.339**	.391	.484	145	37	5	2	0	.968	11	*O-154	4.2
1965	Pit-N★	152	589	91	194	21	14	10	65	43	78	**.329**	.380	.463	136	28	8	0	2	.968	9	*O-145	3.4
1966	Pit-N★	154	638	105	202	31	11	29	119	46	109	.317	.363	.536	146	38	7	5	-1	.965	15	*O-154	4.6
1967	Pit-N★	147	585	103	**209**	26	10	23	110	41	103	**.357**	.402	.554	170	52	9	1	2	.970	9	*O-145	5.8
1968	Pit-N	132	502	74	146	18	12	18	57	51	77	.291	.357	.482	152	31	2	3	-1	.984	12	*O-131	3.9
1969	Pit-N★	138	507	87	175	20	**12**	19	91	56	73	.345	.413	.544	170	47	4	1	1	.980	7	*O-135	4.9
1970	Pit-N★	108	412	65	145	22	10	14	60	38	66	.352	.409	.556	159	34	3	0	1	.966	7	*O-104	3.5
1971	*Pit-N★	132	522	82	178	29	8	13	86	26	65	.341	.372	.502	146	29	1	2	-1	.993	10	*O-124	3.5
1972	*Pit-N†	102	378	68	118	19	7	10	60	29	49	.312	.361	.479	140	18	0	0	0	1.000	6	O-94	2.1
Total	18	2433	9454	1416	3000	440	166	240	1305	621	1230	.317	.362	.475	130	363	83	46	-3	.973	175	*O-2370/2-2,3-1	42.9

■ ED CLEMENTS
Clements, Edward b: Philadelphia, Pa. Deb: 6/24/1890

YEAR	TM/L	G	AB	R	H	2B	3B	HR	RBI	BB	SO	AVG	OBP	SLG	PRO+	BR/A	SB	CS	SBR	FA	FR	G/POS	TPR
1890	Pit-N	1	1	0	0	0	0	0	0	0	0	.000	.000	.000	-99	-0	0			.400	-0	/S-1	-0.1

■ JACK CLEMENTS
Clements, John J. b: 7/24/1864, Philadelphia, Pa. d: 5/23/41, Norristown, Pa. BL/TL, 5'8.5", 204 lbs. Deb: 4/22/1884 M

YEAR	TM/L	G	AB	R	H	2B	3B	HR	RBI	BB	SO	AVG	OBP	SLG	PRO+	BR/A	SB	CS	SBR	FA	FR	G/POS	TPR
1884	Phi-U	41	177	37	50	13	2	3		9		.282	.317	.429	134	2				.764	1	O-22,C-20/S-1	0.3
	Phi-N	9	30	3	7	0	0	0	0	4	8	.233	.324	.233	82	-0				.827	1	/C-9	0.1
1885	Phi-N	52	188	14	36	11	3	1	14	2	30	.191	.200	.298	61	-8				.891	-8	C-41,O-11	-1.2
1886	Phi-N	54	185	15	38	5	1	0	11	7	34	.205	.234	.243	45	-12	4			.930	12	C-47/O-7	0.4
1887	Phi-N	66	246	48	69	13	7	1	47	9	24	.280	.317	.402	93	-3	7			.940	9	C-59/3-4,S-3	0.9
1888	Phi-N	86	326	26	80	8	4	1	32	10	36	.245	.276	.304	81	-8	3			.927	-1	C-85/O-1	0.0
1889	Phi-N	78	310	51	88	17	1	4	35	29	21	.284	.347	.384	96	-3	3			.916	-7	C-78	-0.2
1890	Phi-N	97	381	64	120	23	8	7	74	45	30	.315	.392	.472	148	22	10			.944	3	C-91/1-5,M	2.9
1891	Phi-N	107	423	58	131	29	4	4	75	43	19	.310	.380	.426	131	16	3			.927	-5	*C-107/1-2	1.9
1892	Phi-N	109	402	50	106	25	6	3	76	43	40	.264	.339	.415	128	13	7			.950	6	*C-109	2.4
1893	Phi-N	94	376	64	107	20	3	17	80	39	29	.285	.360	.489	125	11	3			.942	-12	*C-92/1-1	0.6
1894	Phi-N	45	159	26	55	6	5	3	36	24	7	.346	.455	.563	134	11	6			.946	-2	C-45	1.0
1895	Phi-N	88	322	64	127	27	2	13	75	22	7	.394	.446	.612	170	32	3			.969	-10	*C-88	2.4
1896	Phi-N	57	184	35	66	5	7	5	45	17	14	.359	.427	.543	157	15	2			.966	-4	C-53	1.4
1897	Phi-N	55	185	18	44	4	2	6	36	12		.238	.305	.378	82	-6	3			.962	-2	C-49	-0.2
1898	StL-N	99	335	39	86	19	5	3	41	21		.257	.314	.370	94	-4	1			**.971**	-6	C-86	-0.2
1899	Cle-N	4	12	1	3	0	0	0				.250	.308	.250	58	-1				.938	0	/C-4	0.0
1900	Bos-N	42	42	6	13	1	0	1	10	3		.310	.370	.405	101	-0				.948	1	C-10	0.2
Total	17	1157	4283	619	1226	226	60	77	687	339	299	.286	.347	.421	116	78	55			.937	-26	*C-1073/O-41,13S	12.7

■ VERNE CLEMONS
Clemons, Verne James "Stinger" or "Tubby" b: 9/8/1891, Clemons, Iowa d: 5/5/59, Bay Pines, Fla. BR/TR, 5'9.5", 190 lbs. Deb: 4/22/16

YEAR	TM/L	G	AB	R	H	2B	3B	HR	RBI	BB	SO	AVG	OBP	SLG	PRO+	BR/A	SB	CS	SBR	FA	FR	G/POS	TPR
1916	StL-A	4	7	0	1	1	0	0	0	0	1	.143	.143	.286	30	-1	0			.889	0	/C-2	0.0
1919	StL-N	88	239	14	63	13	2	2	22	26	13	.264	.336	.360	116	5	4			.982	2	C-75	1.5
1920	StL-N	112	338	17	95	10	6	1	36	30	12	.281	.340	.355	103	2	1	1	-0	.977	-6	*C-103	0.2
1921	StL-N	117	341	29	109	16	2	2	48	33	17	.320	.380	.396	108	5	0	0	0	.985	-4	*C-107	0.6
1922	StL-N	71	160	9	41	4	0	0	15	18	5	.256	.331	.281	62	-8	1	0	0	.996	3	C-63	-0.3
1923	StL-N	57	130	6	37	9	1	0	13	10	11	.285	.345	.369	90	-2	0	0	0	.981	5	C-41	0.5
1924	StL-N	25	56	3	18	3	0	0	6	2	3	.321	.345	.375	94	-0	0	0	0	.983	-2	C-17	-0.1
Total	7	474	1271	78	364	56	11	5	140	119	62	.286	.348	.360	99	0	6	1		.983	-2	C-408	2.4

■ DONN CLENDENON
Clendenon, Donn Alvin b: 7/15/35, Neosho, Mo. BR/TR, 6'3.5", 210 lbs. Deb: 9/22/61

YEAR	TM/L	G	AB	R	H	2B	3B	HR	RBI	BB	SO	AVG	OBP	SLG	PRO+	BR/A	SB	CS	SBR	FA	FR	G/POS	TPR
1961	Pit-N	9	35	7	11	1	1	0	2	5	10	.314	.400	.400	113	1	0	0	0	1.000	1	/O-8	0.1
1962	Pit-N	80	222	39	67	8	5	7	28	26	58	.302	.378	.477	128	9	16	4	2	.990	-1	1-52,O-19	0.6
1963	Pit-N	154	563	65	155	28	7	15	57	39	136	.275	.328	.430	116	10	22	13	-1	.991	7	*1-151	1.0
1964	Pit-N	133	457	53	129	23	8	12	64	26	96	.282	.324	.446	115	8	12	8	-1	.989	-1	*1-119	0.1
1965	Pit-N	162	612	89	184	32	14	14	96	48	128	.301	.356	.467	129	23	9	9	-3	.984	5	*1-158/3-1	1.5
1966	Pit-N	155	571	80	171	22	10	28	98	52	142	.299	.360	.520	141	31	8	7	-2	.985	-1	*1-152	1.8
1967	Pit-N	131	478	46	119	15	2	13	56	34	107	.249	.300	.370	90	-7	4	4	-1	.988	1	*1-123	-1.2
1968	Pit-N	158	584	63	150	20	6	17	87	47	163	.257	.313	.399	114	9	10	3	1	.990	10	*1-155	0.5
1969	Mon-N	38	129	14	31	6	1	4	14	9	32	.240	.274	.395	85	-3	0	2	-1	.987	4	1-24,O-11	-0.3
	*NY-N	72	202	31	51	5	0	12	37	19	62	.252	.323	.455	113	3	3	2	-0	.984	-4	1-58/O-1	-0.5
	Yr	110	331	45	82	11	1	16	51	25	94	.248	.304	.432	103	-0	3	4	-2	.985	0	1-82,O-12	-0.8
1970	NY-N	121	396	65	114	18	3	22	97	39	91	.288	.353	.515	129	15	4	1	1	.991	-2	*1-100	0.5
1971	NY-N	88	263	29	65	10	0	11	37	21	78	.247	.305	.411	103	-0	1	2	-1	.985	-2	1-72	-0.9
1972	StL-N	61	136	13	26	4	0	4	9	17	37	.191	.281	.309	68	-6	1	2	-1	.986	3	1-36	-0.6
Total	12	1362	4648	594	1273	192	57	159	682	379	1140	.274	.331	.442	117	94	90	57	-7	.988	20	*1-1200/O-39,3-1	3.0

■ ELMER CLEVELAND
Cleveland, Elmer Ellsworth b: 9/15/1862, Washington, D.C. d: 10/8/13, Zimmerman, Pa. BR/TR, Deb: 8/29/1884

YEAR	TM/L	G	AB	R	H	2B	3B	HR	RBI	BB	SO	AVG	OBP	SLG	PRO+	BR/A	SB	CS	SBR	FA	FR	G/POS	TPR
1884	Cin-U	29	115	24	37	9	2	0		4		.322	.345	.435	125	-0				.843	2	3-29	0.2
1888	NY-N	9	34	6	8	0	2	2	5	3	1	.235	.297	.529	161	2	1			.667	-7	/3-9	-0.4
	Pit-N	30	108	10	24	2	1	2	11	5	23	.222	.270	.315	93	-1	3			.831	-9	3-30	-0.9
	Yr	39	142	16	32	2	3	4	16	8	24	.225	.276	.366	110	2	4			.806	-15	3-39	-1.3
1891	Col-a	12	41	12	7	0	0	0	4	12	9	.171	.370	.171	59	-1	4			.843	3	3-12	-0.2
Total	3	80	298	52	76	11	5	4	20	24	33	.255	.317	.366	110	0	8			.830	-10	/3-80	-0.9

■ STAN CLIBURN
Cliburn, Stanley Gene b: 12/19/56, Jackson, Miss. BR/TR, 6', 195 lbs. Deb: 5/6/80 F

YEAR	TM/L	G	AB	R	H	2B	3B	HR	RBI	BB	SO	AVG	OBP	SLG	PRO+	BR/A	SB	CS	SBR	FA	FR	G/POS	TPR
1980	Cal-A	54	56	7	10	2	0	2	6	3	9	.179	.220	.321	48	-4	0	0	0	.971	5	C-54	0.2

■ HARLOND CLIFT
Clift, Harlond Benton "Darkie" b: 8/12/12, ElReno, Okla. d: 4/27/92, Yakima, Wash. BR/TR, 5'11", 180 lbs. Deb: 4/17/34

YEAR	TM/L	G	AB	R	H	2B	3B	HR	RBI	BB	SO	AVG	OBP	SLG	PRO+	BR/A	SB	CS	SBR	FA	FR	G/POS	TPR
1934	StL-A	147	572	104	149	30	10	14	56	84	100	.260	.357	.421	92	-7	7	2	1	.929	-16	*3-141	-1.6
1935	StL-A	137	475	101	140	26	4	11	69	83	39	.295	.406	.436	113	11	0	3	-2	.934	-6	*3-127/2-6	0.8
1936	StL-A	152	576	145	174	40	11	20	73	115	68	.302	.424	.514	127	27	12	4	1	.951	3	*3-152	3.2
1937	StL-A☆	155	571	103	175	36	7	29	118	98	80	.306	.413	.546	139	35	8	5	-1	.947	**41**	*3-155	**7.2**
1938	StL-A	149	534	119	155	25	7	34	118	118	67	.290	.423	.554	143	38	10	5	0	**.962**	14	*3-149	4.8
1939	StL-A	151	526	90	142	25	2	15	84	**111**	55	.270	.402	.411	106	9	4	3	-1	.953	12	*3-149	2.0
1940	StL-A	150	523	92	143	29	5	20	87	104	62	.273	.396	.463	119	18	9	8	-2	**.959**	4	*3-147	2.1
1941	StL-A	154	584	108	149	38	9	17	84	113	93	.255	.376	.430	109	9	6	4	-1	.959	1	*3-154	1.3
1942	StL-A	143	541	108	148	39	4	7	55	106	48	.274	.394	.399	122	20	6	4	-1	.941	-1	*3-141/S-1	2.0
1943	StL-A	105	379	43	88	11	3	3	25	54	37	.232	.329	.301	83	-7	5	4	-1	.950	19	*3-104	1.3
	Was-A	8	30	4	9	0	0	0	4	5	3	.300	.417	.300	115	1	0	0	0	.968	-1	/3-8	0.1
	Yr	113	409	47	97	11	3	3	29	59	40	.237	.336	.301	85	-6	5	4	-1	.951	18	*3-112	1.4
1944	Was-A	12	44	4	7	1	0	0	3	3	3	.159	.213	.227	27	-4	0	0	0	.842	-3	3-12	-0.7
1945	Was-A	119	375	49	79	12	0	8	53	76	58	.211	.349	.307	99	-3	2	1	-0	.934	-4	*3-111	0.5
Total	12	1582	5730	1070	1558	309	62	178	829	1070	713	.272	.390	.441	115	152	69	43	-5	.948	63	*3-1550/2-6,S-1	22.7

■ FLEA CLIFTON
Clifton, Herman Earl b: 12/12/09, Cincinnati, Ohio BR/TR, 5'10", 160 lbs. Deb: 4/29/34

YEAR	TM/L	G	AB	R	H	2B	3B	HR	RBI	BB	SO	AVG	OBP	SLG	PRO+	BR/A	SB	CS	SBR	FA	FR	G/POS	TPR
1934	Det-A	16	16	3	1	0	0	0	1	1	2	.063	.118	.063	-52	-4	0	0	0	1.000	2	/3-4,2-1	-0.2
1935	*Det-A	43	110	15	28	5	0	0	9	5	13	.255	.293	.300	56	-7	2	1	0	.934	-1	3-21/2-5,S-4	-0.7
1936	Det-A	13	26	5	5	1	0	0	1	4	3	.192	.300	.231	33	-3	0	1	-1	.926	0	/S-6,3-2,2-1	-0.3
1937	Det-A	15	43	4	5	1	0	0	2	7	10	.116	.240	.140	-2	-7	0	0	0	.958	-0	/3-7,S-4,2-3	-0.5
Total	4	87	195	27	39	7	0	0	13	17	28	.200	.268	.236	30	-20	2	2	0	.937	-0	/3-34,S-14,2-10	-1.7

YEAR	TM/L	G	AB	R	H	2B	3B	HR	RBI	BB	SO	AVG	OBP	SLG	PRO+	BR/A	SB	CS	SBR	FA	FR	G/POS	TPR

■ MONK CLINE   Cline, John P.   b: 3/3/1858, Louisville, Ky.   d: 9/23/16, Louisville, Ky.   BL/TL, 5'4", 150 lbs.   Deb: 7/4/1882

YEAR	TM/L	G	AB	R	H	2B	3B	HR	RBI	BB	SO	AVG	OBP	SLG	PRO+	BR/A	SB	CS	SBR	FA	FR	G/POS	TPR
1882	Bal-a	44	172	18	38	6	2	0		3		.221	.234	.279	79	-3				.825	6	O-39/S-8,2-2,3-1	0.3
1884	Lou-a	94	396	91	115	16	7	2	39	27		.290	.342	.381	142	19				.875	6	*O-90/S-6	2.1
1885	Lou-a	2	9	0	2	1	0	0		2		.222	.222	.333	74	-0				1.000	-1	/O-1,3-1	-0.1
1888	KC-a	73	293	45	69	13	2	0	19	20		.235	.289	.294	82	-7	29			.883	5	O-70/2-3,3-1	-0.3
1891	Lou-a	21	76	13	23	3	1	0	12	19	3	.303	.442	.368	134	5	2			.906	-3	O-21	0.1
Total	5	234	946	167	247	39	12	2	72	69	3	.261	.315	.334	111	14	31			.867	14	O-221/S-14,2-5,3-3	2.1

■ TY CLINE   Cline, Tyrone Alexander   b: 6/15/39, Hampton, S.C.   BL/TL, 6'0.5", 170 lbs.   Deb: 9/14/60

YEAR	TM/L	G	AB	R	H	2B	3B	HR	RBI	BB	SO	AVG	OBP	SLG	PRO+	BR/A	SB	CS	SBR	FA	FR	G/POS	TPR
1960	Cle-A	7	26	2	8	1	0	0		4		.308	.308	.423	99	-0	0	0	0	1.000	2	/O-6	0.1
1961	Cle-A	12	43	9	9	2	1	0	1	6	1	.209	.333	.302	73	-1	1	0	0	1.000	-2	O-12	-0.4
1962	Cle-A	118	375	53	93	15	5	2	28	28	50	.248	.309	.331	74	-14	5	4	-1	.992	3	*O-107	-1.8
1963	Mil-N	72	174	17	41	2	1	0	10	10	31	.236	.285	.259	58	-9	2	1	0	.992	-0	O-62	-1.3
1964	Mil-N	101	116	22	35	4	2	1	13	8	22	.302	.362	.397	113	2	0	1	-1	.982	-10	O-54/1-6	-1.0
1965	Mil-N	123	220	27	42	5	3	0	10	16	50	.191	.246	.241	37	-18	2	2	-1	.969	-6	O-86/1-5	-2.9
1966	Chi-N	7	17	3	6	0	0	0	2	0	2	.353	.353	.353	96	-0	1	0	0	1.000	-1	/O-5	-0.1
	Atl-N	42	71	12	18	0	0	0	6	3	11	.254	.303	.254	56	-4	2	1	0	1.000	-6	O-19/1-6	-1.1
	Yr	49	88	15	24	0	0	0	8	3	13	.273	.312	.273	63	-4	3	1	0	1.000	-6	O-24/1-6	-1.1
1967	Atl-N	10	8	0	0	0	0	0	0	0	3	.000	.111	.000	-66	-2	0	1	0	1.000	-0	/O-1	-0.2
	SF-N	64	122	18	33	5	5	0	4	9	13	.270	.326	.393	106	1	2	1	0	1.000	-6	O-37	-0.7
	Yr	74	130	18	33	5	5	0	4	9	16	.254	.312	.369	96	-1	2	1	0	1.000	-6	O-38	-0.9
1968	SF-N	116	291	37	65	6	3	1	28	11	26	.223	.254	.275	59	-15	0	2	-1	.971	-4	O-70,1-24	-2.8
1969	Mon-N	101	209	26	50	5	3	2	12	32	22	.239	.346	.321	87	-2	4	3	-1	.988	-0	O-41,1-17	-0.7
1970	Mon-N	2	2	0	1	0	0	0	0	0	0	.500	.500	.500	169	0	0	0	0	.000	0	H	0.0
	*Cin-N	48	63	13	17	7	1	0	8	12	11	.270	.387	.413	114	2	1	2	-1	.966	-2	O-20/1-2	-0.2
	Yr	50	65	13	18	7	1	0	8	12	11	.277	.390	.415	115	2	1	2	-1	.966	-2	O-20/1-2	-0.2
1971	Cin-N	69	97	12	19	1	0	0	1	18	16	.196	.333	.206	57	-5	2	2	-1	1.000	-5	O-28/1-2	-1.2
Total	12	892	1834	251	437	53	25	6	125	153	262	.238	.304	.304	72	-65	22	19	-5	.986	-38	O-548/1-62	-14.2

■ GENE CLINES   Clines, Eugene Anthony   b: 10/6/46, San Pablo, Cal.   BR/TR, 5'9", 170 lbs.   Deb: 6/28/70   C

YEAR	TM/L	G	AB	R	H	2B	3B	HR	RBI	BB	SO	AVG	OBP	SLG	PRO+	BR/A	SB	CS	SBR	FA	FR	G/POS	TPR
1970	Pit-N	31	37	4	15	2	0	0	3	2	5	.405	.436	.459	143	2	2	1	0	1.000	-2	/O-7	0.0
1971	*Pit-N	97	273	52	84	12	4	1	24	22	36	.308	.366	.392	115	6	15	6	1	.981	2	O-74	0.6
1972	*Pit-N	107	311	52	104	15	6	0	17	16	47	.334	.371	.421	127	11	12	6	0	.958	-9	O-83	-0.1
1973	Pit-N	110	304	42	80	11	3	1	23	26	36	.263	.327	.329	84	-6	8	7	-2	.968	-2	O-77	-1.3
1974	*Pit-N	107	276	29	62	5	1	0	14	30	40	.225	.310	.250	60	-14	14	2	3	.989	2	O-78	-1.2
1975	NY-N	82	203	25	46	6	3	0	10	11	21	.227	.270	.286	57	-12	4	4	-1	.982	-4	O-60	-2.0
1976	Tex-A	116	446	52	123	6	3	0	38	16	52	.276	.307	.316	81	-11	11	9	-2	.987	3	*O-103,D-10	-1.6
1977	Chi-N	101	239	27	70	12	2	3	41	25	25	.293	.362	.397	93	-2	1	2	-1	.986	-8	O-63	-1.3
1978	Chi-N	109	229	31	59	10	2	0	17	21	28	.258	.323	.319	71	-8	4	3	-1	.978	-7	O-66	-2.0
1979	Chi-N	10	10	0	2	0	0	0	0	1	1	.200	.200	.200	9	-1	0	0	0	.000	0	/H	-0.2
Total	10	870	2328	314	645	85	24	5	187	169	291	.277	.331	.341	88	-36	71	40	-3	.979	-24	O-611/D-10	-9.1

■ BILLY CLINGMAN   Clingman, William Frederick   b: 11/21/1869, Cincinnati, Ohio   d: 5/14/58, Cincinnati, Ohio   BB/TR, 5'11", 150 lbs.   Deb: 9/9/1890

YEAR	TM/L	G	AB	R	H	2B	3B	HR	RBI	BB	SO	AVG	OBP	SLG	PRO+	BR/A	SB	CS	SBR	FA	FR	G/POS	TPR
1890	Cin-N	7	27	2	7	1	0	0	5	1	0	.259	.286	.296	70	-1	0			.892	-1	/S-6,2-1	-0.1
1891	Cin-a	1	5	0	1	1	0	0	0	0	0	.200	.200	.400	65	-0	0			.667	-1	/2-1	-0.1
1895	Pit-N	106	382	69	99	16	4	0	45	41	43	.259	.334	.322	74	-14	19			.887	14	*3-106	0.1
1896	Lou-N	121	423	57	99	10	2	2	37	57	51	.234	.329	.281	64	-20	19			.925	24	*3-121	0.5
1897	Lou-N	113	395	59	90	14	7	2	47	37		.228	.302	.314	65	-20	14			**.947**	29	*3-113	1.0
1898	Lou-N	154	538	65	138	12	6	0	50	51		.257	.327	.301	81	-12	15			.914	15	3-79,S-74/O-1,2-1	0.7
1899	Lou-N	109	366	67	96	15	4	2	44	46		.262	.349	.342	90	-4	13			.916	-4	*S-109	0.0
1900	Chi-N	47	159	15	33	6	0	0	11	17		.208	.292	.245	51	-10	6			.872	-12	S-47	-1.7
1901	Was-A	137	480	66	116	10	7	2	55	42		.242	.308	.304	71	-18	10			**.932**	18	*S-137	1.0
1903	Cle-A	21	64	10	18	1	0	0	7	11		.281	.387	.328	118	2	2			.932	-0	2-11/S-7,3-3	0.3
Total	10	816	2839	410	697	86	31	8	301	303	94	.246	.323	.306	74	-97	98			.919	80	3-422,S-380/2-14,O	1.7

■ JIM CLINTON   Clinton, James Lawrence "Big Jim"   b: 8/10/1850, New York, N.Y.   d: 9/3/21, Brooklyn, N.Y.   BR/TR, 5'8.5", 174 lbs.   Deb: 5/18/1872   MU

YEAR	TM/L	G	AB	R	H	2B	3B	HR	RBI	BB	SO	AVG	OBP	SLG	PRO+	BR/A	SB	CS	SBR	FA	FR	G/POS	TPR
1872	Eck-n	25	97	12	25	3	1	0	6	0	2	.258	.258	.309	87	-0	0	1	-1	.792	-6	O-11,3-10/2-3,CS	-0.6
1873	Res-n	9	38	5	9	1	0	0	4	0	0	.237	.237	.263	52	-2	0	0	0	.697	-1	/3-9	-0.2
1874	Atl-n	2	11	3	2	1	0	0	2	0	2	.182	.182	.273	49	-1	0	1	0	.444	-2	/2-1,O-1	-0.2
1875	Atl-n	22	81	3	10	1	0	0	0	0	0	.123	.123	.123	-16	-8	0	0	0	.830	3	P-17/O-7,1-5,2-1	-0.1
1876	Lou-N	16	65	8	22	2	0	0	6	3	0	.338	.338	.369	115	0				.783	1	O-14/1-1,P-1	0.1
1882	Wor-N	26	98	9	16	2	0	0	3	7	13	.163	.219	.184	30	-7				.734	-4	O-26	-1.0
1883	Bal-a	94	399	69	125	16	8	0		27		.313	.357	.393	137	16				.842	5	*O-92/2-2	1.8
1884	Bal-a	104	437	82	118	12	6	4		29		.270	.324	.352	119	10				.807	-1	*O-104/2-1	0.6
1885	Cin-a	105	408	48	97	5	5	0	34	15		.238	.277	.275	73	-12				.877	-0	*O-105	-1.4
1886	Bal-a	23	83	8	15	1	0	0	6	4		.181	.227	.193	33	-6	3			.894	-0	O-23	-0.6
Total	4 n	58	227	23	46	5	1	0	12	0	4	.203	.203	.233	45	-11	0	1	-1	.699	-4	/3-19,O-19,P12SC	-1.1
Total	6	368	1490	224	393	38	19	4	43	82	13	.264	.311	.323	101	-0	3			.838	0	O-364/2-3,P-1,1-1	-0.6

■ LOU CLINTON   Clinton, Lucien Louis   b: 10/13/37, Ponca City, Okla.   BR/TR, 6'1", 185 lbs.   Deb: 4/22/60

YEAR	TM/L	G	AB	R	H	2B	3B	HR	RBI	BB	SO	AVG	OBP	SLG	PRO+	BR/A	SB	CS	SBR	FA	FR	G/POS	TPR
1960	Bos-A	96	298	37	68	17	5	6	37	20	66	.228	.283	.379	75	-11	4	3	-1	.966	2	O-89	-1.4
1961	Bos-A	17	51	4	13	2	1	0	3	2	10	.255	.283	.333	63	-3	0	0	0	1.000	1	O-13	0.0
1962	Bos-A	114	398	63	117	24	10	18	75	34	79	.294	.351	.540	132	16	2	1	0	.979	1	*O-103	1.2
1963	Bos-A	148	560	71	130	23	7	22	77	49	118	.232	.295	.416	94	-6	0	0	0	.982	11	*O-146	-0.3
1964	Bos-A	37	120	15	31	4	3	6	9	9	33	.258	.310	.417	95	-1	1	0	0	1.000	5	O-35	0.3
	LA-A	91	306	30	76	18	0	9	38	31	40	.248	.320	.395	108	2	3	0	1	.985	3	O-86	0.2
	Yr	128	426	45	107	22	3	12	44	40	73	.251	.317	.401	104	1	4	0	1	.990	7	*O-121	0.5
1965	Cal-A	89	222	29	54	12	3	1	8	23	37	.243	.317	.338	88	-3	2	4	-1	.983	-0	O-73	-0.9
	KC-A	1	1	0	0	0	0	0	0	0	0	.000	.000	.000	-99	-0	0	0	0	.000	-0	/O-1	-0.1
	Cle-A	12	34	2	6	1	0	1	2	3	7	.176	.243	.294	51	-2	0	0	0	.941	-0	/O-9	-0.3
	Yr	102	257	31	60	13	3	2	10	26	44	.233	.306	.331	83	-6	2	4	-1	.977	-2	O-83	-1.3
1966	NY-A	80	159	18	35	10	2	5	21	16	27	.220	.291	.403	101	-0	0	1	0	.976	-6	O-63	-0.9
1967	NY-A	6	4	1	2	1	0	0	2	1	1	.500	.600	.750	308	1	0	0	0	.000	-0	/O-1	0.1
Total	8	691	2153	270	532	112	31	65	269	188	418	.247	.310	.418	99	-7	12	7	-1	.980	15	O-619	-2.1

■ ED CLOUGH   Clough, Edgar George "Big Ed" or "Spec"   b: 10/28/06, Wiconisco, Pa.   d: 1/30/44, Harrisburg, Pa.   BL/TL, 6', 188 lbs.   Deb: 8/28/24

YEAR	TM/L	G	AB	R	H	2B	3B	HR	RBI	BB	SO	AVG	OBP	SLG	PRO+	BR/A	SB	CS	SBR	FA	FR	G/POS	TPR
1924	StL-N	7	14	0	1	0	0	0	1	0	3	.071	.071	.071	-63	-3	0	0	0	1.000	-0	O-6	-0.3
1925	StL-N	3	4	0	1	0	0	0	0	1	0	.250	.250	.250	28	-0	0	0	0	1.000	-0	/P-3	0.0
1926	StL-N	1	1	0	0	0	0	0	0	0	0	.000	.000	.000	-96	-0	0	0	0	.000	-0	/P-1	0.0
Total	3	11	19	0	2	0	0	0	1	1	3	.105	.105	.105	-44	-4	0	0	0	1.000	-0	/O-6,P-4	-0.3

■ OTIS CLYMER   Clymer, Otis Edgar   b: 1/27/1876, Pine Grove, Pa.   d: 2/27/26, St.Paul, Minn.   BB/TR, 5'11", 180 lbs.   Deb: 4/14/05

YEAR	TM/L	G	AB	R	H	2B	3B	HR	RBI	BB	SO	AVG	OBP	SLG	PRO+	BR/A	SB	CS	SBR	FA	FR	G/POS	TPR
1905	Pit-N	96	365	74	108	11	5	2	23	19		.296	.332	.353	102	-2	23			.986	-2	O-89/1-1	-0.6
1906	Pit-N	11	45	7	11	0	1	0	1	3		.244	.292	.289	78	-1	1			.900	-1	O-11	-0.3
1907	Pit-N	22	66	8	15	2	0		4	5		.227	.311	.258	77	-1	4			.923	-3	O-15/1-1	-0.3
	Was-A	57	206	30	65	5	5	1	16	18		.316	.382	.403	163	15	18			.912	-4	O-51/1-1	1.0
1908	Was-A	110	368	32	93	11	4	0	35	20		.253	.291	.313	105	1	19			.933	-8	O-82,2-13/3-2	-1.2
1909	Was-A	45	138	11	27	5	0	0	4	7		.196	.284	.261	76	-4	7			.922	-4	O-41	-1.1
1913	Chi-N	30	105	16	24	5	1	0	7	14	18	.229	.319	.295	76	-3	9			.933	-2	O-26	-0.6
	Bos-N	14	37	4	12	3	0	0	6	3	3	.324	.375	.459	135	2	2			.880	-2	O-11	-0.1

YEAR	TM/L	G	AB	R	H	2B	3B	HR	RBI	BB	SO	AVG	OBP	SLG	PRO+	BR/A	SB	CS	SBR	FA	FR	G/POS	TPR
	Yr	44	142	20	36	8	2	0	13	17	21	.254	.333	.338	91	-1	11			.918	-4	O-37	-0.7
Total	6	385	1330	182	355	42	19	2	98	99	21	.267	.322	.332	106	8	83			.939	-25	O-326/2-13,1-3,3-2	-3.4

■ BILL CLYMER
Clymer, William Johnston "Derby Day Bill" b: 12/18/1873, Philadelphia, Pa. d: 12/26/36, Philadelphia, Pa.   Deb: 6/26/1891 C

YEAR	TM/L	G	AB	R	H	2B	3B	HR	RBI	BB	SO	AVG	OBP	SLG	PRO+	BR/A	SB	CS	SBR	FA	FR	G/POS	TPR
1891	Phi-a	3	11	0	0	0	0	0	0	1	2	.000	.154	.000	-54	-2	1			.867	-2	/S-3	-0.3

■ PETE COACHMAN
Coachman, Bobby Dean b: 11/11/61, Cottonwood, Ala. BR/TR, 5'9", 175 lbs. Deb: 8/18/90

YEAR	TM/L	G	AB	R	H	2B	3B	HR	RBI	BB	SO	AVG	OBP	SLG	PRO+	BR/A	SB	CS	SBR	FA	FR	G/POS	TPR
1990	Cal-A	16	45	3	14	3	0	0	5	1	7	.311	.354	.378	107	0	0	1	-1	.958	1	/3-9,2-2,D-2	0.1

■ GIL COAN
Coan, Gilbert Fitzgerald b: 5/18/22, Monroe, N.C. BL/TR, 6', 180 lbs. Deb: 4/27/46

YEAR	TM/L	G	AB	R	H	2B	3B	HR	RBI	BB	SO	AVG	OBP	SLG	PRO+	BR/A	SB	CS	SBR	FA	FR	G/POS	TPR
1946	Was-A	59	134	17	28	3	2	3	9	7	37	.209	.269	.328	70	-6	2	2	-1	.969	-2	O-29	-1.0
1947	Was-A	11	42	5	21	3	2	0	3	5	6	.500	.553	.667	245	8	2	1	0	1.000	5	O-11	0.8
1948	Was-A	138	513	56	119	13	9	7	60	41	78	.232	.298	.333	70	-24	23	9	2	.970	12	*O-131	-1.7
1949	Was-A	111	358	36	78	7	8	3	25	29	53	.218	.278	.330	56	-24	9	6	-1	.975	2	O-97	-2.8
1950	Was-A	104	366	58	111	17	4	7	50	28	46	.303	.359	.429	106	2	10	5	0	.970	-3	O-98	-0.4
1951	Was-A	135	538	85	163	25	7	9	62	39	62	.303	.357	.426	113	9	8	5	-1	.965	22	*O-132	2.4
1952	Was-A	107	332	50	68	11	6	5	20	32	35	.205	.277	.319	68	-15	9	4	0	.984	0	O-86	-1.9
1953	Was-A	68	168	28	33	1	4	2	17	22	23	.196	.301	.286	60	-9	7	0	2	1.000	4	O-46	-0.5
1954	Bal-A	94	265	29	74	11	1	2	20	16	17	.279	.323	.351	91	-4	9	4	0	.968	-1	O-67	-1.0
1955	Bal-A	61	130	18	31	7	1	1	11	13	15	.238	.313	.331	79	-4	4	0	0	.983	-4	O-43	-1.0
	Chi-A	17	17	0	3	0	0	0	1	0	5	.176	.176	.176	-5	-2	0	0	0	1.000	-1	/O-3	-0.3
	Yr	78	147	18	34	7	1	1	12	13	20	.231	.298	.313	68	-7	4	0	0	.984	-5	O-46	-1.3
	NY-N	9	13	0	2	0	0	0	0	0	1	.154	.154	.154	-18	-2	0	0	0	1.000	-2	/O-6	-0.5
1956	NY-N	4	1	2	0	0	0	0	0	0	1	.000	.000	.000	-99	-0	0	0	0	.000	0	H	0.0
Total	11	918	2877	384	731	98	44	39	278	232	384	.254	.316	.359	84	-73	83	38	2	.973	24	O-749	-7.9

■ JOE COBB
Cobb, Joseph Stanley (b: Joseph Stanley Serafin) b: 1/24/1895, Hudson, Pa. d: 12/24/47, Allentown, Pa. BR/TR, 5'9", 170 lbs. Deb: 4/25/18

YEAR	TM/L	G	AB	R	H	2B	3B	HR	RBI	BB	SO	AVG	OBP	SLG	PRO+	BR/A	SB	CS	SBR	FA	FR	G/POS	TPR
1918	Det-A	1	0	0	0	0	0	0	0	1	0	—	1.000	—	210	0	0			.000	0	H	0.0

■ TY COBB
Cobb, Tyrus Raymond "The Georgia Peach" b: 12/18/1886, Narrows, Ga. d: 7/17/61, Atlanta, Ga. BL/TR, 6'1", 175 lbs. Deb: 8/30/05 MH

YEAR	TM/L	G	AB	R	H	2B	3B	HR	RBI	BB	SO	AVG	OBP	SLG	PRO+	BR/A	SB	CS	SBR	FA	FR	G/POS	TPR
1905	Det-A	41	150	19	36	6	0	1	15	10		.240	.287	.300	86	-3	2			.958	2	O-41	-0.3
1906	Det-A	98	358	45	113	15	5	1	34	19		.316	.355	.394	131	12	23			.961	6	O-96	1.5
1907	*Det-A	150	605	97	212	28	14	5	119	24		.350	.380	.468	164	40	49			.961	11	*O-150	5.0
1908	*Det-A	150	581	88	188	36	20	4	108	34		.324	.367	.475	166	40	39			.944	4	*O-150	4.2
1909	*Det-A	156	573	116	216	33	10	9	107	48		.377	.431	.517	190	58	76			.946	3	*O-156	6.1
1910	Det-A	140	506	106	194	35	13	8	91	64		.383	.456	.551	202	60	65			.958	9	*O-137	6.7
1911	Det-A	146	591	147	248	47	24	8	127	44		.420	.467	.621	193	71	83			.957	11	*O-146	7.1
1912	Det-A	140	553	120	226	30	23	7	83	43		.409	.456	.584	203	72	61			.940	1	*O-140	6.4
1913	Det-A	122	428	70	167	18	16	4	67	58	31	.390	.467	.535	196	53	51			.947	3	*O-119	5.3
1914	Det-A	98	345	69	127	22	11	2	57	57	22	.368	.466	.513	188	40	35	17	0	.949	-10	O-96	2.8
1915	Det-A	156	563	144	208	31	13	3	99	118	43	.369	.486	.487	182	64	96	38	6	.951	-3	*O-156	6.2
1916	Det-A	145	542	113	201	31	10	5	68	78	39	.371	.452	.493	177	53	68	24	6	.953	-2	*O-143/1-1	5.4
1917	Det-A	152	588	107	225	44	24	6	102	61	34	.383	.444	.570	210	75	55			.973	13	*O-152	8.5
1918	Det-A	111	421	83	161	19	14	3	64	41	21	.382	.440	.515	196	48	34			.975	2	O-95,1-13/P-2,23	4.8
1919	Det-A	124	497	92	191	36	13	1	70	38	22	.384	.429	.515	168	44	28			.973	-2	*O-123	3.5
1920	Det-A	112	428	86	143	28	8	2	63	58	28	.334	.416	.451	133	22	15	10	-2	.966	-7	*O-112	0.5
1921	Det-A	128	507	124	197	37	16	12	101	56	19	.389	.452	.596	167	52	22	15	-2	.970	13	*O-121,M	4.9
1922	Det-A	137	526	99	211	42	16	4	99	55	24	.401	.462	.565	172	57	9	13	-5	.980	4	*O-134,M	4.3
1923	Det-A	145	556	103	189	40	7	6	88	66	14	.340	.413	.469	135	29	9	10	-3	.969	4	*O-141,M	2.0
1924	Det-A	155	625	115	211	38	10	4	78	85	18	.338	.418	.450	126	26	23	14	-2	.986	6	*O-155,M	1.8
1925	Det-A	121	415	97	157	31	12	12	102	65	12	.378	.468	.598	171	47	13	9	-2	.948	-2	*O-105/P-1,M	3.3
1926	Det-A	79	233	48	79	18	5	4	62	26	2	.339	.408	.511	137	12	9	4	0	.950	-5	O-55,M	0.4
1927	Phi-A	134	490	104	175	32	7	5	93	67	12	.357	.440	.482	131	25	22	16	-3	.969	-5	*O-127	0.9
1928	Phi-A	95	353	54	114	27	4	1	40	34	16	.323	.389	.431	112	7	5	8	-3	.964	-1	O-85	-0.3
Total	24	3035	11434	2246	4189	724	295	117	1937	1249	357	.366	.433	.512	167	1004	892	178		.961	56	*O-2935/1-14,P32	91.0

■ DAVE COBLE
Coble, David Lamar b: 12/24/12, Monroe, N.C. d: 10/15/71, Orlando, Fla. BR/TR, 6'1", 183 lbs. Deb: 5/1/39

YEAR	TM/L	G	AB	R	H	2B	3B	HR	RBI	BB	SO	AVG	OBP	SLG	PRO+	BR/A	SB	CS	SBR	FA	FR	G/POS	TPR
1939	Phi-N	15	25	2	7	1	0	0	0	3	3	.280	.280	.320	63	-1	0			.938	-1	C-13	-0.2

■ GEORGE COCHRAN
Cochran, George Leslie b: 2/12/1889, Rusk, Tex. d: 5/21/60, Harbor City, Cal. TR , Deb: 7/29/18

YEAR	TM/L	G	AB	R	H	2B	3B	HR	RBI	BB	SO	AVG	OBP	SLG	PRO+	BR/A	SB	CS	SBR	FA	FR	G/POS	TPR
1918	Bos-A	24	60	7	7	0	0	0	3	10	6	.117	.264	.117	15	-6	3			.960	-4	3-22/S-1	-1.0

■ DAVE COCHRANE
Cochrane, David Carter b: 1/31/63, Riverside, Cal. BB/TR, 6'2", 180 lbs. Deb: 9/2/86

YEAR	TM/L	G	AB	R	H	2B	3B	HR	RBI	BB	SO	AVG	OBP	SLG	PRO+	BR/A	SB	CS	SBR	FA	FR	G/POS	TPR
1986	Chi-A	19	62	4	12	2	0	1	2	5	22	.194	.254	.274	42	-5	0	0	0	.872	-3	3-18/S-1	-0.8
1989	Sea-A	54	102	13	24	4	1	3	7	14	27	.235	.333	.382	98	-0	0	2	-1	.905	-13	S-30/1-9,3-9,2OC	-1.5
1990	Sea-A	15	20	0	3	0	0	0	0	8	6	.150	.150	.150	-16	-3	0	0	0	1.000	0	/S-5,1-3,3-3,C-1	-0.3
1991	Sea-A	65	178	16	44	13	0	2	9	9	38	.247	.287	.354	76	-6	0	1	-1	.969	-14	O-26,C-19,3-13,/1D	-2.1
1992	Sea-A	65	152	10	38	5	0	2	12	12	34	.250	.309	.322	77	-5	1	0	0	.879	-8	O-25,C-21,3/1SD2	-1.2
Total	5	218	514	43	121	24	1	8	43	40	129	.235	.294	.333	73	-19	1	3	-2	.925	-38	/O-54,3-53,CS12D	-5.9

■ MICKEY COCHRANE
Cochrane, Gordon Stanley b: 4/6/03, Bridgewater, Mass. d: 6/28/62, Lake Forest, Ill. BL/TR, 5'10.5", 180 lbs. Deb: 4/14/25 MCH

YEAR	TM/L	G	AB	R	H	2B	3B	HR	RBI	BB	SO	AVG	OBP	SLG	PRO+	BR/A	SB	CS	SBR	FA	FR	G/POS	TPR
1925	Phi-A	134	420	69	139	21	5	6	55	44	19	.331	.397	.448	107	5	7	4	-0	.984	-10	*C-133	0.1
1926	Phi-A	120	370	50	101	8	9	8	47	56	15	.273	.369	.408	97	-1	5	2	0	.975	12	*C-115	1.7
1927	Phi-A	126	432	80	146	20	6	12	80	50	7	.338	.409	.495	127	17	9	6	-1	.986	3	*C-123	2.6
1928	Phi-A	131	468	92	137	26	12	10	57	76	25	.293	.395	.464	122	16	7	2	-2	.966	2	*C-130	2.6
1929	*Phi-A	135	514	113	170	37	8	7	95	69	8	.331	.412	.475	123	19	7	6	-2	.983	8	*C-135	3.6
1930	*Phi-A	130	487	110	174	42	5	10	85	55	18	.357	.424	.526	133	25	5	0	2	.993	6	*C-130	4.0
1931	*Phi-A	122	459	87	160	31	6	17	89	56	21	.349	.423	.553	146	30	2	3	-1	.986	10	*C-117	4.3
1932	Phi-A	139	518	118	152	35	4	23	112	100	22	.293	.412	.510	132	27	0	1	-1	.993	10	*C-137/O-1	4.1
1933	Phi-A	130	429	104	138	30	4	15	60	106	22	.322	.459	.515	156	41	8	5	-1	.989	-7	*C-128	3.7
1934	*Det-A★	129	437	74	140	32	1	2	76	78	26	.320	.428	.412	117	16	8	4	-0	.988	-4	*C-124,M	1.6
1935	*Det-A☆	115	411	93	131	33	3	5	47	96	15	.319	.452	.450	139	30	5	5	-2	.989	-5	*C-110,M	2.7
1936	Det-A	44	126	24	34	8	0	2	17	46	15	.270	.465	.381	111	5	1	1	-0	.983	-9	C-42,M	-0.1
1937	Det-A	27	98	27	30	10	1	2	12	25	4	.306	.452	.490	134	6	1	0	0	1.000	-2	C-27,M	0.5
Total	13	1482	5169	1041	1652	333	64	119	832	857	217	.320	.419	.478	127	237	64	46	-8	.985	14	*C-1451/O-1	31.4

■ JIM COCKMAN
Cockman, James b: 4/26/1873, Guelph, Ont., Can. d: 9/28/47, Guelph, Ont., Can. BR/TR, 5'6", 145 lbs. Deb: 9/28/05

YEAR	TM/L	G	AB	R	H	2B	3B	HR	RBI	BB	SO	AVG	OBP	SLG	PRO+	BR/A	SB	CS	SBR	FA	FR	G/POS	TPR
1905	NY-A	13	38	5	4	0	0	0	2	4		.105	.190	.105	-5	-4	2			.875	-2	3-13	-0.7

■ ALAN COCKRELL
Cockrell, Atlee Alan b: 12/5/62, Kansas City, Kan. BR/TR, 6'2", 210 lbs. Deb: 9/7/96

YEAR	TM/L	G	AB	R	H	2B	3B	HR	RBI	BB	SO	AVG	OBP	SLG	PRO+	BR/A	SB	CS	SBR	FA	FR	G/POS	TPR
1996	Col-N	9	8	0	2	1	0	0	2	0	4	.250	.250	.375	48	-1	0	0	0	.000	-0	/O-1	-0.1

■ JACK COFFEY
Coffey, John Francis b: 1/28/1887, New York, N.Y. d: 2/14/66, Bronx, N.Y. BR/TR, 5'11", 178 lbs. Deb: 6/23/09

YEAR	TM/L	G	AB	R	H	2B	3B	HR	RBI	BB	SO	AVG	OBP	SLG	PRO+	BR/A	SB	CS	SBR	FA	FR	G/POS	TPR
1909	Bos-N	73	257	21	48	4	4	0	20	11		.187	.229	.233	41	-18	2			.896	-12	S-73	-3.2
1918	Det-A	22	67	7	14	0	2	0	4	8	6	.209	.303	.269	75	-2	2			.957	0	2-22	-0.1
	Bos-A	15	44	5	7	1	0	1	2	3	2	.159	.213	.250	40	-3	0			.955	0	3-14/2-1	-0.1
	Yr	37	111	12	21	1	2	1	6	11	8	.189	.268	.261	62	-5	2			.959	2	2-23,3-14	-0.2
Total	2	110	368	33	69	5	6	1	26	22	8	.188	.241	.242	48	-23	4			.896	-9	/S-73,2-23,3-14	-3.4

■ FRANK COGGINS
Coggins, Franklin b: 5/22/44, Griffin, Ga. BB/TR, 6'2", 187 lbs. Deb: 9/10/67

YEAR	TM/L	G	AB	R	H	2B	3B	HR	RBI	BB	SO	AVG	OBP	SLG	PRO+	BR/A	SB	CS	SBR	FA	FR	G/POS	TPR
1967	Was-A	19	75	9	23	3	0	1	8	2	17	.307	.325	.387	114	1	1	0	0	.964	3	2-19	0.6
1968	Was-A	62	171	15	30	6	1	0	7	9	33	.175	.217	.222	34	-14	1	1	-0	.953	4	2-52	-0.9

YEAR	TM/L	G	AB	R	H	2B	3B	HR	RBI	BB	SO	AVG	OBP	SLG	PRO+	BR/A	SB	CS	SBR	FA	FR	G/POS	TPR
1972	Chi-N	6	1	1	0	0	0	0	0	1	0	.000	.500	.000	48	0	0	0	0	.000	0	H	0.0
Total	3	87	247	25	53	9	1	1	15	12	50	.215	.251	.271	59	-13	2	1	0	.957	7	/2-71	-0.3

■ RICH COGGINS
Coggins, Richard Allen b: 12/7/50, Indianapolis, Ind. BL/TL, 5'8", 170 lbs. Deb: 8/29/72

YEAR	TM/L	G	AB	R	H	2B	3B	HR	RBI	BB	SO	AVG	OBP	SLG	PRO+	BR/A	SB	CS	SBR	FA	FR	G/POS	TPR
1972	Bal-A	16	39	5	13	4	0	0	1	1	6	.333	.350	.436	129	1	0	2	-1	1.000	2	O-13	0.2
1973	*Bal-A	110	389	54	124	19	9	7	41	28	24	.319	.365	.468	134	16	17	9	-0	.987	-3	*O-101/D-1	0.9
1974	*Bal-A	113	411	53	100	13	3	4	32	29	31	.243	.301	.319	81	-10	26	6	4	.984	-7	*O-105	-1.9
1975	Mon-N	13	37	1	10	3	1	0	4	1	7	.270	.289	.405	87	-1	0	0	0	1.000	-1	O-10	-0.3
	NY-A	51	107	7	24	1	0	1	6	7	16	.224	.272	.262	52	-7	3	3	-1	.970	-3	O-36/D-9	-1.2
1976	NY-A	7	4	1	1	0	0	0	1	0	1	.250	.250	.250	47	-0	1	0	0	1.000	-0	/O-2	0.0
	Chi-A	32	96	4	15	2	0	0	5	6	15	.156	.206	.177	13	-10	3	1	0	1.000	-4	O-26/D-1	-1.6
	Yr	39	100	5	16	2	0	0	6	6	16	.160	.208	.180	14	-11	4	1	1	1.000	-4	O-28/D-1	-1.6
Total	5	342	1083	125	287	42	13	12	90	72	100	.265	.314	.361	93	-11	50	21	2	.986	-17	O-293/D-11	-3.9

■ ED COGSWELL
Cogswell, Edward b: 2/25/1854, England d: 7/27/1888, Fitchburg, Mass. BR/TR, 5'8", 150 lbs. Deb: 7/11/1879

YEAR	TM/L	G	AB	R	H	2B	3B	HR	RBI	BB	SO	AVG	OBP	SLG	PRO+	BR/A	SB	CS	SBR	FA	FR	G/POS	TPR
1879	Bos-N	49	236	51	76	8	1	1	18	8	5	.322	.344	.377	135	8				.967	1	1-49	0.7
1880	Tro-N	47	209	41	63	7	3	0	13	11	10	.301	.336	.364	130	6				.961	1	1-47	0.3
1882	Wor-N	13	51	10	7	1	0	0	1	6	6	.137	.228	.157	26	-4				.937	-1	1-13	-0.6
Total	3	109	496	102	146	16	4	1	32	25	21	.294	.328	.349	121	11				.960	1	1-109	0.4

■ ALTA COHEN
Cohen, Alta Albert "Schoolboy" b: 12/25/08, New York, N.Y. BL/TL, 5'10.5", 170 lbs. Deb: 4/15/31

YEAR	TM/L	G	AB	R	H	2B	3B	HR	RBI	BB	SO	AVG	OBP	SLG	PRO+	BR/A	SB	CS	SBR	FA	FR	G/POS	TPR
1931	Bro-N	1	3	1	2	0	0	0	0	0	0	.667	.667	.667	261	1	0			1.000	1	/O-1	0.2
1932	Bro-N	9	32	1	5	1	0	0	1	3	7	.156	.229	.188	14	-4	0			.850	1	/O-8	-0.4
1933	Phi-N	19	32	6	6	1	0	0	1	6	4	.188	.316	.219	49	-2	0			1.000	-0	/O-7	-0.2
Total	3	29	67	8	13	2	0	0	2	9	11	.194	.289	.224	42	-5	0			.925	2	/O-16	-0.4

■ ANDY COHEN
Cohen, Andrew Howard b: 10/25/04, Baltimore, Md. d: 10/29/88, ElPaso, Tex. BR/TR, 5'8", 155 lbs. Deb: 6/6/26 FMC

YEAR	TM/L	G	AB	R	H	2B	3B	HR	RBI	BB	SO	AVG	OBP	SLG	PRO+	BR/A	SB	CS	SBR	FA	FR	G/POS	TPR
1926	NY-N	32	35	4	9	0	0	0	8	1	2	.257	.278	.314	60	-2	0			.792	2	2-10,S-10/3-2	0.0
1928	NY-N	129	504	64	138	24	7	9	59	31	17	.274	.318	.403	87	-11	3			.969	3	*2-126/S-3,3-1	-0.4
1929	NY-N	101	347	40	102	12	2	5	47	11	15	.294	.319	.383	73	-15	3			.964	12	2-94/S-1,3-1	0.1
Total	3	262	886	108	249	36	10	14	114	43	34	.281	.317	.392	81	-28	6			.964	16	2-230/S-14,3-4	-0.3

■ JIMMIE COKER
Coker, Jimmie Goodwin b: 3/28/36, Holly Hill, S.C. d: 10/29/91, Throckmorton, Tex. BR/TR, 5'11", 195 lbs. Deb: 9/11/58

YEAR	TM/L	G	AB	R	H	2B	3B	HR	RBI	BB	SO	AVG	OBP	SLG	PRO+	BR/A	SB	CS	SBR	FA	FR	G/POS	TPR
1958	Phi-N	2	6	0	1	0	0	0	0	0	0	.167	.167	.167	-12	-1	0	0	0	1.000	0	/C-2	-0.1
1960	Phi-N	81	252	18	54	5	3	6	34	23	45	.214	.290	.329	69	-11	0	3	-2	.982	2	C-76	-0.6
1961	Phi-N	11	25	3	10	1	0	1	4	7	4	.400	.531	.560	193	4	1	0	0	.984	1	C-11	0.5
1962	Phi-N	5	3	0	0	0	0	0	1	1	2	.000	.250	.000	-27	-1	0	0	0	.000	0	H	-0.1
1963	SF-N	4	5	0	1	0	0	0	0	1	2	.200	.333	.200	58	-0	0	0	0	1.000	-1	/C-2	-0.1
1964	Cin-N	11	32	3	10	2	0	1	4	3	5	.313	.371	.469	130	1	0	0	0	1.000	1	C-11	0.4
1965	Cin-N	24	61	3	15	2	0	2	9	8	16	.246	.333	.377	93	-0	0	0	0	.993	5	C-19	0.6
1966	Cin-N	50	111	9	28	3	0	4	14	8	5	.252	.303	.387	83	-3	0	1	-1	.979	-2	C-39/O-2	0.3
1967	Cin-N	45	97	8	18	2	1	2	4	4	20	.186	.218	.289	39	-8	0	1	-1	.976	-0	C-34	-0.8
Total	9	233	592	44	137	15	4	16	70	55	99	.231	.301	.351	77	-18	1	5	-3	.983	13	C-194/O-2	0.1

■ ROCKY COLAVITO
Colavito, Rocco Domenico b: 8/10/33, New York, N.Y. BR/TR, 6'3", 190 lbs. Deb: 9/10/55 C

YEAR	TM/L	G	AB	R	H	2B	3B	HR	RBI	BB	SO	AVG	OBP	SLG	PRO+	BR/A	SB	CS	SBR	FA	FR	G/POS	TPR
1955	Cle-A	5	9	3	4	2	0	0	0	0	2	.444	.444	.667	189	1	0	0	0	1.000	0	/O-2	0.3
1956	Cle-A	101	322	55	89	11	4	21	65	49	46	.276	.375	.531	134	15	0	1	-1	.968	-1	O-98	0.9
1957	Cle-A	134	461	66	116	26	0	25	84	71	80	.252	.353	.471	124	15	1	6	-3	.962	12	*O-130	1.7
1958	Cle-A	143	489	80	148	26	3	41	113	84	89	.303	.407	**.620**	183	56	0	2	-1	.981	2	*O-129,1-11/P-1	5.0
1959	Cle-A★	154	588	90	151	24	0	**42**	111	71	86	.257	.339	.512	135	35	3	3	-0	.985	12	*O-154	2.9
1960	Det-A	145	555	67	138	18	1	35	87	53	80	.249	.319	.474	108	4	3	6	-3	.976	7	*O-144	0.1
1961	Det-A★	163	583	129	169	30	2	45	140	113	75	.290	.407	.580	156	48	1	2	-1	.975	10	*O-161	4.7
1962	Det-A★	161	601	90	164	30	2	37	112	96	68	.273	.375	.514	132	27	2	0	1	.992	18	*O-161	3.6
1963	Det-A	160	597	91	162	29	2	22	91	84	78	.271	.362	.437	119	16	0	0	0	.988	7	*O-159	1.6
1964	KC-A★	160	588	89	161	31	2	34	102	83	56	.274	.366	.507	136	30	3	1	0	.973	3	*O-159	2.6
1965	Cle-A★	162	592	92	170	25	2	26	**108**	**93**	63	.287	.387	.468	140	34	1	1	-0	**1.000**	4	*O-162	3.1
1966	Cle-A★	151	533	68	127	13	0	30	72	76	81	.238	.337	.432	119	14	2	1	0	.982	7	*O-146	1.5
1967	Cle-A	63	191	10	46	9	0	5	21	24	31	.241	.336	.366	104	1	2	2	-1	.962	-4	O-50	-0.6
	Chi-A	60	190	20	42	4	1	3	29	25	10	.221	.312	.300	85	-3	1	-1	0	.977	-7	O-58	-1.4
	Yr	123	381	30	88	13	1	8	50	49	41	.231	.320	.333	95	-2	3	3	-1	.970	-11	*O-108	-2.0
1968	LA-N	40	113	8	23	3	0	3	11	15	18	.204	.297	.310	89	-1	0	1	-1	1.000	-1	O-33	-0.6
	NY-A	39	91	13	20	2	2	5	13	14	17	.220	.330	.451	139	4	0	0	0	.933	-4	O-28/P-1	-0.2
Total	14	1841	6503	971	1730	283	21	374	1159	951	880	.266	.362	.489	132	287	19	27	-11	.980	66	*O-1774/1-11,P-2	25.2

■ MIKE COLBERN
Colbern, Michael Malloy b: 4/19/55, Santa Monica, Cal. BR/TR, 6'3", 205 lbs. Deb: 7/18/78

YEAR	TM/L	G	AB	R	H	2B	3B	HR	RBI	BB	SO	AVG	OBP	SLG	PRO+	BR/A	SB	CS	SBR	FA	FR	G/POS	TPR
1978	Chi-A	48	141	11	38	5	1	2	20	1	36	.270	.285	.362	80	-4	0	1	-1	.969	0	C-47/D-1	-0.4
1979	Chi-A	32	83	5	20	5	1	0	8	4	25	.241	.276	.325	61	-5	0	0	0	.971	3	C-32	-0.1
Total	2	80	224	16	58	10	2	2	28	5	61	.259	.281	.348	73	-9	0	1	-1	.970	3	/C-79,D-1	-0.5

■ CRAIG COLBERT
Colbert, Craig Charles b: 2/13/65, Iowa City, Iowa BR/TR, 6', 190 lbs. Deb: 4/6/92

YEAR	TM/L	G	AB	R	H	2B	3B	HR	RBI	BB	SO	AVG	OBP	SLG	PRO+	BR/A	SB	CS	SBR	FA	FR	G/POS	TPR
1992	SF-N	49	126	10	29	5	2	1	16	9	22	.230	.281	.325	76	-4	1	0	0	.994	-7	C-35/3-9,2-2	-1.0
1993	SF-N	23	37	2	6	2	0	1	5	3	13	.162	.225	.297	40	-3	0	0	0	.982	2	C-10/2-2,3-1	-0.1
Total	2	72	163	12	35	7	2	2	21	12	35	.215	.269	.319	67	-7	1	0	0	.990	-5	/C-45,3-10,2-4	-1.1

■ NATE COLBERT
Colbert, Nathan b: 4/9/46, St.Louis, Mo. BR/TR, 6'2", 209 lbs. Deb: 4/14/66

YEAR	TM/L	G	AB	R	H	2B	3B	HR	RBI	BB	SO	AVG	OBP	SLG	PRO+	BR/A	SB	CS	SBR	FA	FR	G/POS	TPR
1966	Hou-N	19	7	3	0	0	0	0	0	0	4	.000	.000	.000	-99	-2	0	0	0	.000	0	H	-0.2
1968	Hou-N	20	53	5	8	1	0	0	4	1	23	.151	.167	.170	1	-6	1	1	-0	.952	-1	O-11/1-5	-1.0
1969	SD-N	139	483	64	123	20	9	24	66	45	123	.255	.322	.482	128	15	6	4	-1	.990	1	*1-134	0.5
1970	SD-N	156	572	84	148	17	6	38	86	56	150	.259	.329	.509	126	18	3	5	-2	.991	-8	*1-153/3-1	-0.6
1971	SD-N★	156	565	81	149	25	3	27	84	63	119	.264	.342	.462	135	24	5	2	0	.993	1	*1-153	1.1
1972	SD-N★	151	563	87	141	27	2	38	111	70	127	.250	.335	.508	147	32	15	6	1	.996	7	*1-150	2.8
1973	SD-N★	145	529	73	143	25	2	22	80	54	146	.270	.347	.450	130	20	9	8	-2	.992	3	*1-144	0.9
1974	SD-N	119	368	53	76	16	0	14	54	62	108	.207	.323	.364	96	-2	10	2	2	.988	8	1-79,O-48	0.2
1975	Det-A	45	156	16	23	4	2	4	18	17	52	.147	.231	.276	41	-13	0	2	-1	.982	-4	1-44/D-1	-2.1
	Mon-N	38	81	10	14	4	1	4	11	5	31	.173	.230	.395	68	-4	0	1	-1	.988	-1	1-22	-0.6
1976	Mon-N	14	40	5	8	2	0	2	6	9	16	.200	.347	.400	107	1	3	1	0	1.000	1	/O-7,1-6	0.1
	Oak-A	2	5	0	0	0	0	0	1	1	1	.000	.167	.000	-50	-0	0	0	0	.000	0	/D-2	-0.1
Total	10	1004	3422	481	833	141	25	173	520	383	902	.243	.324	.451	120	81	52	31	-3	.991	5	1-890/O-66,D-3,3-1	1.0

■ GREG COLBRUNN
Colbrunn, Gregory Joseph b: 7/26/69, Fontana, Cal. BR/TR, 6', 190 lbs. Deb: 7/9/92

YEAR	TM/L	G	AB	R	H	2B	3B	HR	RBI	BB	SO	AVG	OBP	SLG	PRO+	BR/A	SB	CS	SBR	FA	FR	G/POS	TPR
1992	Mon-N	52	168	12	45	8	0	2	18	6	34	.268	.301	.351	85	-4	3	2	-0	.992	-1	1-47	-0.9
1993	Mon-N	70	153	15	39	9	0	4	23	6	33	.255	.287	.392	76	-5	4	2	0	.995	1	1-61	-0.8
1994	Fla-N	47	155	17	47	10	0	6	31	9	27	.303	.349	.484	111	2	1	1	0	.988	-1	1-41	-0.2
1995	Fla-N	138	528	70	146	22	1	23	89	22	69	.277	.313	.453	99	-3	11	3	2	.996	-1	*1-134	-1.4
1996	Fla-N	141	511	60	146	26	2	16	69	25	76	.286	.336	.438	107	4	4	5	-2	.995	5	*1-134	-0.6
Total	5	448	1515	174	423	75	3	51	230	68	239	.279	.321	.434	99	-6	23	13	1	.994	3	1-417	-3.9

■ ALEX COLE
Cole, Alexander b: 8/17/65, Fayetteville, N.C. BL/TL, 6'2", 170 lbs. Deb: 7/27/90

YEAR	TM/L	G	AB	R	H	2B	3B	HR	RBI	BB	SO	AVG	OBP	SLG	PRO+	BR/A	SB	CS	SBR	FA	FR	G/POS	TPR
1990	Cle-A	63	227	43	68	5	4	0	13	28	38	.300	.379	.357	107	3	40	6	7	.961	2	O-59/D-1	1.0
1991	Cle-A	122	387	58	114	17	3	0	21	58	47	.295	.388	.354	106	6	27	17	-2	.970	1	*O-107/D-6	0.2
1992	Cle-A	41	97	11	20	1	0	0	5	10	21	.206	.287	.216	44	-7	9	2	1	.971	-4	O-24/D-4	-1.0
	*Pit-N	64	205	33	57	3	7	0	10	18	46	.278	.336	.361	99	-0	7	4	0	.989	1	O-53	-0.2

YEAR	TM/L	G	AB	R	H	2B	3B	HR	RBI	BB	SO	AVG	OBP	SLG	PRO+	BR/A	SB	CS	SBR	FA	FR	G/POS	TPR
1993	Col-N	126	348	60	89	9	4	0	24	43	58	.256	.341	.305	64	-17	30	13	1	.982	2	O-93	-1.6
1994	Min-A	105	345	68	102	15	5	4	23	44	60	.296	.377	.403	101	2	29	8	4	.969	-0	*O-100/D-1	0.3
1995	Min-A	28	79	10	27	3	2	1	14	8	15	.342	.409	.468	127	3	1	3	-2	.938	-3	O-23/D-2	-0.1
1996	Bos-A	24	72	13	16	5	1	0	7	8	11	.222	.300	.319	55	-5	5	3	-0	.974	-3	O-24	-0.8
Total	7	573	1760	286	493	58	26	5	117	217	296	.280	.361	.351	91	-15	148	59	9	.971	-7	O-483/D-14	-2.2

■ DICK COLE
Cole, Richard Roy   b: 5/6/26, Long Beach, Cal.   BR/TR, 6'2", 175 lbs.   Deb: 4/27/51   C

YEAR	TM/L	G	AB	R	H	2B	3B	HR	RBI	BB	SO	AVG	OBP	SLG	PRO+	BR/A	SB	CS	SBR	FA	FR	G/POS	TPR
1951	StL-N	15	36	4	7	1	0	0	3	6	5	.194	.310	.222	45	-3	0	0	0	.969	5	2-14	0.2
	Pit-N	42	106	9	25	4	0	1	11	19	9	.236	.331	.302	69	-4	0	1	-1	.981	-2	2-34/S-8	-0.5
	Yr	57	142	13	32	5	0	1	14	21	14	.225	.325	.282	63	-7	0	1	-1	.978	2	2-48/S-8	-0.3
1953	Pit-N	97	235	29	64	13	1	0	23	38	26	.272	.374	.336	87	-3	2	2	-1	.965	-3	S-77/2-7,1-1	-0.2
1954	Pit-N	138	486	40	131	22	5	1	40	41	48	.270	.326	.342	75	-17	0	0	0	.949	-11	S-66,3-55,2-17	-2.3
1955	Pit-N	77	239	16	54	8	3	0	21	18	22	.226	.286	.285	53	-16	0	0	0	.935	1	3-33,2-24,S-12	-1.3
1956	Pit-N	72	99	7	21	2	1	0	9	11	9	.212	.291	.253	49	-7	0	0	0	.947	-5	3-18,2-12/S-6	-1.4
1957	Mil-N	15	14	1	1	0	0	0	0	3	5	.071	.235	.071	-13	-2	0	0	0	.952	0	2-10/1-1,3-1	-0.2
Total	6	456	1215	106	303	50	10	2	107	132	124	.249	.324	.312	69	-52	2	3	-1	.961	-19	S-169,2-118,3/1	-5.7

■ STU COLE
Cole, Stewart Bryan   b: 2/7/66, Charlotte, N.C.   BR/TR, 6'1", 175 lbs.   Deb: 9/5/91

YEAR	TM/L	G	AB	R	H	2B	3B	HR	RBI	BB	SO	AVG	OBP	SLG	PRO+	BR/A	SB	CS	SBR	FA	FR	G/POS	TPR
1991	KC-A	9	7	1	1	0	0	0	2	2	1	.143	.333	.143	37	-1	0	0	0	1.000	0	/2-5,S-1,D-2	0.0

■ WILLIS COLE
Cole, Willis Russell   b: 1/6/1882, Milton Junction, Wis.   d: 10/11/65, Madison, Wis.   BR/TR, 5'8", 170 lbs.   Deb: 8/22/09

YEAR	TM/L	G	AB	R	H	2B	3B	HR	RBI	BB	SO	AVG	OBP	SLG	PRO+	BR/A	SB	CS	SBR	FA	FR	G/POS	TPR
1909	Chi-A	46	165	17	39	7	3	0	16	16		.236	.308	.315	101	0	3			.889	-3	O-46	-0.6
1910	Chi-A	22	80	6	14	2	1	0	2	4		.175	.224	.225	42	-5	0			.974	1	O-22	-0.7
Total	2	68	245	23	53	9	4	0	18	20		.216	.281	.286	82	-5	3			.912	-3	/O-68	-1.3

■ CHOO CHOO COLEMAN
Coleman, Clarence   b: 8/25/37, Orlando, Fla.   BL/TR, 5'9", 165 lbs.   Deb: 4/16/61

YEAR	TM/L	G	AB	R	H	2B	3B	HR	RBI	BB	SO	AVG	OBP	SLG	PRO+	BR/A	SB	CS	SBR	FA	FR	G/POS	TPR
1961	Phi-N	34	47	3	6	1	0	0	4	2	8	.128	.180	.149	-12	-8	0	0	0	.977	-1	C-14	-0.8
1962	NY-N	55	152	24	38	2	2	6	17	11	24	.250	.305	.441	96	-1	2	4	-2	.995	-9	C-44	-1.0
1963	NY-N	106	247	22	44	0	0	3	9	24	49	.178	.264	.215	39	-19	5	5	-2	.969	3	C-91/O-1	-1.6
1966	NY-N	6	16	2	3	0	0	0	0	0	4	.188	.188	.188	5	-2	0	0	0	.963	0	/C-5	-0.2
Total	4	201	462	51	91	8	2	9	30	37	85	.197	.267	.281	52	-30	7	9	-3	.977	-6	C-154/O-1	-3.6

■ CURT COLEMAN
Coleman, Curtis Hancock   b: 2/18/1887, Salem, Ore.   d: 7/1/80, Newport, Ore.   BL/TR, 5'11", 180 lbs.   Deb: 4/13/12

YEAR	TM/L	G	AB	R	H	2B	3B	HR	RBI	BB	SO	AVG	OBP	SLG	PRO+	BR/A	SB	CS	SBR	FA	FR	G/POS	TPR
1912	NY-A	12	37	8	9	4	0	0	4	7		.243	.364	.351	99	0				.865	0	3-10	0.0

■ DAVE COLEMAN
Coleman, David Lee   b: 10/26/50, Dayton, Ohio   BR/TR, 6'3", 195 lbs.   Deb: 4/13/77

YEAR	TM/L	G	AB	R	H	2B	3B	HR	RBI	BB	SO	AVG	OBP	SLG	PRO+	BR/A	SB	CS	SBR	FA	FR	G/POS	TPR
1977	Bos-A	11	12	1	0	0	0	0	0	1	3	.000	.077	.000	-69	-3	0	0	0	1.000	-3	/O-9	-0.6

■ JERRY COLEMAN
Coleman, Gerald Francis   b: 9/14/24, San Jose, Cal.   BR/TR, 6', 170 lbs.   Deb: 4/20/49   M

YEAR	TM/L	G	AB	R	H	2B	3B	HR	RBI	BB	SO	AVG	OBP	SLG	PRO+	BR/A	SB	CS	SBR	FA	FR	G/POS	TPR
1949	*NY-A	128	447	54	123	21	5	2	42	63	44	.275	.367	.354	92	-4	3	6	-1	**.981**	1	*2-122/S-4	0.2
1950	*NY-A★	153	522	69	150	19	6	6	69	67	38	.287	.372	.381	96	-2	3	2	-0	.977	-15	*2-152/S-6	-1.1
1951	*NY-A	121	362	48	90	11	2	3	43	31	36	.249	.315	.315	73	-14	6	1	1	.968	3	*2-102,S-18	-0.4
1952	NY-A	11	42	6	17	2	1	0	4	5	4	.405	.468	.500	180	5	0	1	-1	.971	3	2-11	0.7
1953	NY-A	8	10	1	2	0	0	0	0	2	2	.200	.200	.200	9	-1	0	0	0	1.000	1	/2-7,S-1	0.1
1954	NY-A	107	300	39	65	7	1	3	21	26	29	.217	.279	.277	54	-19	3	0	1	.977	18	2-79,S-30/3-1	0.5
1955	*NY-A	43	96	12	22	5	0	0	8	11	11	.229	.321	.281	64	-5	0	2	-1	.966	-2	S-29,2-13/3-1	-0.5
1956	*NY-A	80	183	15	47	5	1	0	18	18	12	.257	.306	.295	61	-10	1	2	-1	.979	17	2-41,S-24,3-18	0.9
1957	*NY-A	72	157	23	42	7	2	2	12	20	21	.268	.354	.376	101	1	1	1	-0	.969	5	2-45,3-21/S-4	0.8
Total	9	723	2119	267	558	77	18	16	217	235	218	.263	.341	.339	83	-49	22	15	-2	.976	31	2-572,S-116/3-41	1.2

■ GORDY COLEMAN
Coleman, Gordon Calvin   b: 7/5/34, Rockville, Md.   d: 3/12/94, Cincinnati, Ohio   BL/TR, 6'2", 218 lbs.   Deb: 9/19/59

YEAR	TM/L	G	AB	R	H	2B	3B	HR	RBI	BB	SO	AVG	OBP	SLG	PRO+	BR/A	SB	CS	SBR	FA	FR	G/POS	TPR
1959	Cle-A	6	15	5	8	0	1	0	2	1	2	.533	.563	.667	245	3	0	0	0	.955	0	/1-3	0.3
1960	Cin-N	66	251	26	68	10	1	6	23	12	32	.271	.309	.390	89	-4	1	1	-0	.998	1	1-66	-0.3
1961	*Cin-N	150	520	63	149	27	4	26	87	45	67	.287	.346	.504	120	14	1	3	-2	.991	7	*1-150	0.7
1962	Cin-N	136	476	73	132	13	1	28	86	36	68	.277	.332	.485	113	7	2	3	-1	.989	-1	*1-128	-0.4
1963	Cin-N	123	365	38	90	20	2	14	59	29	51	.247	.306	.427	105	2	1	0	0	.987	-1	*1-107	-0.1
1964	Cin-N	89	198	18	48	6	2	5	27	13	30	.242	.292	.369	82	-5	2	0	1	.990	4	1-49	-0.3
1965	Cin-N	108	325	39	98	19	0	14	57	24	38	.302	.351	.489	125	10	0	0	0	.991	-1	1-89	0.5
1966	Cin-N	91	227	20	57	7	0	5	37	16	45	.251	.300	.348	73	-8	2	1	0	.986	-1	1-65	-1.3
1967	Cin-N	4	7	0	0	0	0	0	0	1	0	.000	.125	.000	-55	-1	0	0	0	1.000	0	/1-2	-0.2
Total	9	773	2384	282	650	102	11	98	387	177	333	.273	.326	.448	100	8	9	8	-2	.990	16	1-659	-1.1

■ JOHN COLEMAN
Coleman, John Francis   b: 3/6/1863, Saratoga Springs, N.Y   d: 5/31/22, Detroit, Mich.   BL/TR, 5'9.5", 170 lbs.   Deb: 5/1/1883

YEAR	TM/L	G	AB	R	H	2B	3B	HR	RBI	BB	SO	AVG	OBP	SLG	PRO+	BR/A	SB	CS	SBR	FA	FR	G/POS	TPR
1883	Phi-N	90	354	33	83	12	8	0	32	15	39	.234	.266	.314	83	-6				.886	10	P-65,O-31/2-1	0.5
1884	Phi-N	43	171	16	42	7	2	0	22	8	20	.246	.279	.310	89	-2				.844	2	O-27,P-21/1-2	-0.1
	Phi-a	28	107	16	22	2	3	2	2	5		.206	.241	.336	81	-3				.743	-1	O-24/P-3,1-2	-0.4
1885	Phi-a	96	398	71	119	15	11	3	70	25		.299	.345	.415	131	13				.844	-1	O-93/P-8	0.8
1886	Phi-a	121	492	67	121	18	16	0	65	33		.246	.296	.348	100	-1	28			.862	2	*O-115/1-6,P-3,2-1	-0.2
	Pit-a	11	43	3	15	2	1	0	9	2		.349	.378	.442	157	3	1			.786	-2	O-11	0.0
	Yr	132	535	70	136	20	17	0	74	35		.254	.302	.355	105	2	29			.858	0	*O-126/1-6,P-3,2-1	-0.2
1887	Pit-N	115	475	75	139	21	11	2	54	31	40	.293	.337	.396	110	7	25			.899	1	*O-115/1-2	0.4
1888	Pit-N	116	438	49	101	11	4	0	26	29	52	.231	.285	.274	85	-6	15			.928	0	O-91,1-25	-0.9
1889	Phi-a	6	19	1	1	0	0	0	1	1	3	.053	.100	.053	-57	-4	1			.929	0	/P-5,O-1	-0.1
1890	Pit-N	3	11	1	2	0	0	0	0	3	0	.182	.357	.182	66	-0	1			1.000	-1	/O-2,P-2	-0.1
Total	8	629	2508	332	645	88	56	7	279	152	154	.257	.302	.345	100	2	71			.873	11	O-510,P-107/1-37,2	-0.1

■ ED COLEMAN
Coleman, Parke Edward   b: 12/1/01, Canby, Ore.   d: 8/5/64, Oregon City, Ore.   BL/TR, 6'2", 200 lbs.   Deb: 4/15/32

YEAR	TM/L	G	AB	R	H	2B	3B	HR	RBI	BB	SO	AVG	OBP	SLG	PRO+	BR/A	SB	CS	SBR	FA	FR	G/POS	TPR
1932	Phi-A	26	73	13	25	7	1	1	13	1	6	.342	.351	.507	115	1	1	0	0	1.000	1	O-16	0.1
1933	Phi-A	102	388	48	109	26	3	6	68	19	51	.281	.318	.410	91	-7	0	0	0	.948	-1	O-89	-1.2
1934	Phi-A	101	329	53	92	14	6	14	60	29	34	.280	.342	.486	116	6	0	1	-1	.980	-2	O-86	0.0
1935	Phi-A	10	13	0	1	0	0	0	0	3		.077	.077	.077	-61	-3	0	0	0	.000	-0	/O-1	-0.3
	StL-A	108	397	66	114	15	9	17	71	53	41	.287	.373	.499	118	10	0	2	-1	.974	-3	*O-102	0.2
	Yr	118	410	66	115	15	9	17	71	56	44	.280	.364	.485	113	7	0	2	-1	.974	-3	*O-103	-0.1
1936	StL-A	92	137	13	40	5	4	2	34	15	17	.292	.366	.431	93	-2	0	0	0	.939	-3	O-18	-0.4
Total	5	439	1337	193	381	67	23	40	246	117	152	.285	.345	.459	105	6	1	3	-2	.966	-8	O-312	-1.6

■ RAY COLEMAN
Coleman, Raymond Leroy   b: 6/4/22, Dunsmuir, Cal.   BL/TR, 5'11", 170 lbs.   Deb: 4/22/47

YEAR	TM/L	G	AB	R	H	2B	3B	HR	RBI	BB	SO	AVG	OBP	SLG	PRO+	BR/A	SB	CS	SBR	FA	FR	G/POS	TPR
1947	StL-A	110	343	34	89	9	7	2	30	26	32	.259	.314	.344	81	-9	2	5	-2	.984	-2	O-93	-1.9
1948	StL-A	17	29	2	5	0	1	0	2	2	5	.172	.226	.241	24	-3	1	0	0	.889	1	/O-5	-0.4
	Phi-A	68	210	32	51	6	6	0	21	31	17	.243	.340	.329	78	-6	4	3	-1	.978	-2	O-53	-0.5
	Yr	85	239	34	56	6	7	0	23	33	22	.234	.327	.318	72	-10	5	3	-0	.972	-1	O-58	-1.2
1950	StL-A	117	384	54	104	25	6	8	55	32	35	.271	.330	.430	90	-8	7	5	-1	.985	3	O-98	-0.9
1951	StL-A	91	341	41	96	16	5	3	55	24	32	.282	.329	.402	94	-4	3	4	-1	.975	-1	O-87	-0.7
	Chi-A	51	181	21	50	8	5	3	21	15	14	.276	.332	.448	112	2	2	3	-1	.980	-3	O-51	-0.4
	Yr	142	522	62	146	24	12	8	76	39	46	.280	.330	.418	100	-2	5	7	-3	.977	-4	*O-138	-1.1
1952	Chi-A	85	195	19	42	7	2	1	14	13	17	.215	.264	.292	54	-12	1	5	-3	.978	-7	O-73	-2.2
	StL-A	20	46	5	9	3	0	1	5	5	4	.196	.288	.261	52	-3	1	0	0	1.000	-2	O-16	-0.6
	Yr	105	241	24	51	10	2	2	19	18	21	.212	.269	.286	54	-15	2	5	-3	.980	-9	O-89	-2.8
Total	5	559	1729	208	446	74	33	20	199	148	158	.258	.318	.374	84	-43	19	20	-6	.980	-9	O-476	-7.9

■ BOB COLEMAN
Coleman, Robert Hunter   b: 9/26/1890, Huntingburg, Ind.   d: 7/16/59, Boston, Mass.   BR/TR, 6'2", 190 lbs.   Deb: 6/13/13   MC

YEAR	TM/L	G	AB	R	H	2B	3B	HR	RBI	BB	SO	AVG	OBP	SLG	PRO+	BR/A	SB	CS	SBR	FA	FR	G/POS	TPR
1913	Pit-N	24	50	5	9	2	0	0	9	7	8	.180	.281	.220	46	-3	0			.978	-4	C-24	-0.6

YEAR	TM/L	G	AB	R	H	2B	3B	HR	RBI	BB	SO	AVG	OBP	SLG	PRO+	BR/A	SB	CS	SBR	FA	FR	G/POS	TPR
1914	Pit-N	73	150	11	40	4	1	1	14	15	32	.267	.333	.327	101	0	3			.977	2	C-72	0.7
1916	Cle-A	19	28	3	6	2	0	0	4	7	6	.214	.371	.286	92	0	0			.972	-3	C-12	-0.2
Total	3	116	228	19	55	8	1	1	27	29	46	.241	.327	.298	87	-3	3			.976	-5	C-108	-0.1

■ VINCE COLEMAN
Coleman, Vincent Maurice b: 9/22/61, Jacksonville, Fla. BB/TR, 6′, 170 lbs. Deb: 4/18/85

YEAR	TM/L	G	AB	R	H	2B	3B	HR	RBI	BB	SO	AVG	OBP	SLG	PRO+	BR/A	SB	CS	SBR	FA	FR	G/POS	TPR
1985	*StL-N	151	636	107	170	20	10	1	40	50	115	.267	.321	.335	84	-13	**110**	25	**18**	.979	9	*O-150	0.9
1986	StL-N	154	600	94	139	13	8	0	29	60	98	.232	.304	.280	63	-30	**107**	14	**24**	.972	9	*O-149	-0.2
1987	*StL-N	151	623	121	180	14	10	3	43	70	126	.289	.364	.358	90	-6	**109**	22	**20**	.970	9	*O-150	1.7
1988	StL-N★	153	616	77	160	20	10	3	38	49	111	.260	.315	.339	87	-10	**81**	27	8	.971	5	*O-150	-0.2
1989	StL-N★	145	563	94	143	21	9	2	28	50	90	.254	.317	.334	84	-11	**65**	10	**14**	.962	5	*O-142	-0.7
1990	StL-N	124	497	73	145	18	9	6	39	35	88	.292	.341	.400	103	2	**77**	17	**13**	.981	8	*O-120	2.0
1991	NY-N	72	278	45	71	7	5	1	17	39	47	.255	.347	.327	91	-2	37	14	3	.979	0	O-70	-0.1
1992	NY-N	71	229	37	63	11	1	2	21	27	41	.275	.357	.358	104	2	24	9	2	.991	-1	O-61	0.2
1993	NY-N	92	373	64	104	14	8	2	25	21	58	.279	.317	.375	86	-8	38	13	4	.982	0	O-90	-0.6
1994	KC-A	104	438	61	105	14	12	2	33	29	72	.240	.288	.340	59	-27	50	8	10	.962	0	O-99/D-5	-1.8
1995	KC-A	75	293	39	84	13	4	4	20	27	48	.287	.349	.399	93	-3	26	9	2	.975	-3	O-69/D-4	-0.5
	*Sea-A	40	162	27	47	10	2	1	9	10	32	.290	.335	.395	88	-3	16	7	1	.988	4	O-38	0.0
	Yr	115	455	66	131	23	6	5	29	37	80	.288	.344	.398	91	-6	42	16	3	.980	1	*O-107/D-4	-0.5
1996	Cin-N	33	84	10	13	1	1	1	4	9	31	.155	.237	.226	23	-9	12	2	2	.968	0	O-20	-0.7
Total	12	1365	5392	849	1424	176	89	28	346	476	957	.264	.326	.345	83	-119	752	177	119	.974	35	*O-1308/D-9	0.0

■ CAD COLES
Coles, Cadwallader b: 1/17/1886, Rock Hill, S.C. d: 6/30/42, Miami, Fla. BL/TR, 6′0.5″, 174 lbs. Deb: 4/16/14

YEAR	TM/L	G	AB	R	H	2B	3B	HR	RBI	BB	SO	AVG	OBP	SLG	PRO+	BR/A	SB	CS	SBR	FA	FR	G/POS	TPR
1914	KC-F	78	194	17	49	7	3	1	25	5	30	.253	.271	.335	67	-13	6			.889	-7	O-39/1-3	-2.3

■ CHUCK COLES
Coles, Charles Edward b: 6/27/31, Fredericktown, Pa d: 1/25/96, Myrtle Beach, S.C. BL/TL, 5′9″, 180 lbs. Deb: 9/19/58

YEAR	TM/L	G	AB	R	H	2B	3B	HR	RBI	BB	SO	AVG	OBP	SLG	PRO+	BR/A	SB	CS	SBR	FA	FR	G/POS	TPR
1958	Cin-N	5	11	0	2	1	0	0	2	2	6	.182	.308	.273	52	-1	0	0	0	1.000	1	/O-4	0.0

■ DARNELL COLES
Coles, Darnell b: 6/2/62, San Bernardino, Cal BR/TR, 6′1″, 185 lbs. Deb: 9/4/83

YEAR	TM/L	G	AB	R	H	2B	3B	HR	RBI	BB	SO	AVG	OBP	SLG	PRO+	BR/A	SB	CS	SBR	FA	FR	G/POS	TPR
1983	Sea-A	27	92	9	26	7	0	1	6	7	12	.283	.333	.391	95	-1	0	3	-2	.941	-3	3-26	-0.6
1984	Sea-A	48	143	15	23	3	1	0	6	17	26	.161	.259	.196	28	-14	2	1	0	.918	-3	3-42/O-3,D-3	-1.8
1985	Sea-A	27	59	8	14	4	0	1	5	9	17	.237	.348	.356	93	-0	0	1	-1	.918	1	S-15/3-7,O-2,D-2	0.1
1986	Det-A	142	521	67	142	30	2	20	86	45	84	.273	.337	.453	113	9	6	2	1	.938	-5	*3-133/S-2,O-2,D-7	0.1
1987	Det-A	53	149	14	27	5	1	4	15	15	23	.181	.265	.309	54	-10	0	1	-1	.847	-5	3-36/1-9,O-8,S-1,D	-1.6
	Pit-N	40	119	20	27	8	0	6	24	19	20	.227	.338	.445	105	1	1	3	-1	1.000	-5	O-26,3-10/1-1	-0.7
1988	Pit-N	68	211	20	49	13	1	5	36	20	41	.232	.308	.374	96	-1	1	1	-0	.990	-3	O-55/1-1,3-1	-0.7
	Sea-A	55	195	32	57	10	1	10	34	17	26	.292	.361	.508	134	9	3	2	-0	.986	-3	O-47/1-1,D-7	0.4
1989	Sea-A	146	535	54	135	21	3	10	59	27	61	.252	.296	.359	81	-14	5	4	-1	.975	7	O-89,3-26,1-18/D-12	-1.1
1990	Sea-A	37	107	9	23	5	1	2	16	4	17	.215	.250	.336	62	-6	0	0	-0	.970	1	O-20/3-6,1-4,D-1	-0.5
	Det-A	52	108	13	22	2	0	1	4	12	21	.204	.283	.250	50	-7	0	4	-2	1.000	-0	D-30,O-11/3-8	-1.2
	Yr	89	215	22	45	7	1	3	20	16	38	.209	.267	.293	56	-13	0	4	-2	.977	-0	O-31,D-31,3-14/1-4	-1.7
1991	SF-N	11	14	1	3	0	0	0	0	0	2	.214	.214	.214	22	-1	0	0	-0	.000	-1	/O-3,1-1	-0.3
1992	Cin-N	55	141	16	44	11	2	3	18	3	15	.312	.326	.482	123	4	1	0	-0	1.000	1	3-23,1-20/O-5	0.4
1993	Tor-A	64	194	26	49	9	1	4	26	16	29	.253	.322	.371	85	-4	1	1	-0	.957	-9	O-44,3-16/1-1,D-1	-1.4
1994	Tor-A	48	143	15	30	6	1	4	15	10	25	.210	.266	.350	57	-10	0	0	-0	.980	-3	O-29,1-10/3-7,D-1	-1.3
1995	StL-N	63	138	13	31	7	0	3	16	16	20	.225	.310	.341	74	-5	0	0	-0	.951	-6	3-22,1-18/O-1	-1.2
Total	13	936	2869	332	702	141	14	74	366	237	439	.245	.310	.381	88	-51	20	23	-8	.922	-40	3-363,O-345/1DS	-11.4

■ CHRIS COLETTA
Coletta, Christopher Michael b: 8/2/44, Brooklyn, N.Y. BL/TL, 5′11″, 190 lbs. Deb: 8/15/72

YEAR	TM/L	G	AB	R	H	2B	3B	HR	RBI	BB	SO	AVG	OBP	SLG	PRO+	BR/A	SB	CS	SBR	FA	FR	G/POS	TPR
1972	Cal-A	14	30	5	9	1	0	1	7	1	4	.300	.323	.433	131	1	0	0	0	1.000	-2	/O-7	-0.1

■ ED COLGAN
Colgan, William H. b: E.St.Louis, Ill. d: 8/8/1895, Great Falls, Mont. 180 lbs. Deb: 5/3/1884

YEAR	TM/L	G	AB	R	H	2B	3B	HR	RBI	BB	SO	AVG	OBP	SLG	PRO+	BR/A	SB	CS	SBR	FA	FR	G/POS	TPR
1884	Pit-a	48	161	10	25	4	1	0		3		.155	.171	.193	18	-14				.906	2	C-44/O-4	-0.8

■ COLLINS
Collins Deb: 9/12/1892

YEAR	TM/L	G	AB	R	H	2B	3B	HR	RBI	BB	SO	AVG	OBP	SLG	PRO+	BR/A	SB	CS	SBR	FA	FR	G/POS	TPR
1892	StL-N	1	2	0	0	0	0	0	0	0	0	.000	.000	.000	-99	-0	0			1.000	0	/O-1	0.0

■ CHUB COLLINS
Collins, Charles Augustine b: 10/12/1857, Dundas, Ont., Canada d: 5/20/14, Dundas, Ont., Can. BB, 5′11.5″, 165 lbs. Deb: 5/1/1884

YEAR	TM/L	G	AB	R	H	2B	3B	HR	RBI	BB	SO	AVG	OBP	SLG	PRO+	BR/A	SB	CS	SBR	FA	FR	G/POS	TPR
1884	Buf-N	45	169	24	30	6	0	0	20	14	36	.178	.240	.213	42	-11				.914	0	2-42/S-3	-0.9
	Ind-a	38	138	18	31	3	1	0		9		.225	.272	.261	77	-3				.886	-8	2-38	-1.0
1885	Det-N	14	55	8	10	0	2	0	6	0	11	.182	.182	.255	40	-4				.792	-8	S-14	-1.1
Total	2	97	362	50	71	9	3	0	26	23	47	.196	.244	.238	55	-18				.901	-16	/2-80,S-17	-3.0

■ WILSON COLLINS
Collins, Cyril Wilson b: 5/7/1889, Pulaski, Tenn. d: 2/28/41, Knoxville, Tenn. BR/TR, 5′9.5″, 165 lbs. Deb: 5/12/13

YEAR	TM/L	G	AB	R	H	2B	3B	HR	RBI	BB	SO	AVG	OBP	SLG	PRO+	BR/A	SB	CS	SBR	FA	FR	G/POS	TPR
1913	Bos-N	16	3	3	1	0	0	0	0	0	1	.333	.333	.333	89	-0	0			1.000	-4	/O-9	-0.4
1914	Bos-N	27	35	5	9	0	0	0	1	2	8	.257	.297	.257	66	-1	0			.917	-4	O-19	-0.7
Total	2	43	38	8	10	0	0	0	1	2	9	.263	.300	.263	68	-1	0			.926	-8	/O-28	-1.1

■ DAN COLLINS
Collins, Daniel Thomas b: 7/12/1854, St.Louis, Mo. d: 9/21/1883, New Orleans, La. Deb: 6/8/1874

YEAR	TM/L	G	AB	R	H	2B	3B	HR	RBI	BB	SO	AVG	OBP	SLG	PRO+	BR/A	SB	CS	SBR	FA	FR	G/POS	TPR
1874	Chi-n	3	12	1	1	0	0	0	0	2		.083	.083	.167	-22	-2	1	0		1.000	0	/P-2,O-2,S-1	-0.1
1876	Lou-N	7	28	3	4	1	0	0	9	0	2	.143	.143	.179	5	-3				.909	1	/O-7	-0.2

■ DAVE COLLINS
Collins, David S b: 10/20/52, Rapid City, S.D. BB/TL, 5′11″, 175 lbs. Deb: 6/7/75 C

YEAR	TM/L	G	AB	R	H	2B	3B	HR	RBI	BB	SO	AVG	OBP	SLG	PRO+	BR/A	SB	CS	SBR	FA	FR	G/POS	TPR
1975	Cal-A	93	319	41	85	13	4	3	29	36	55	.266	.343	.361	106	3	24	10	1	.988	4	O-75,D-12	0.5
1976	Cal-A	99	365	45	96	12	1	4	28	40	55	.263	.336	.334	103	2	32	19	-2	.994	3	O-71,D-22	-0.1
1977	Sea-A	120	402	46	96	9	3	5	28	33	66	.239	.301	.313	69	-17	25	10	2	.985	0	O-73,D-40	-1.9
1978	Cin-N	102	102	13	22	1	0	0	7	15	18	.216	.316	.225	54	-6	7	7	-2	.969	-4	O-24	-1.3
1979	*Cin-N	122	396	59	126	16	4	3	35	27	48	.318	.365	.402	108	5	16	9	-1	.976	-9	O-91,1-10	-0.9
1980	Cin-N	144	551	94	167	20	4	3	35	53	68	.303	.367	.370	106	6	79	21	11	.986	3	*O-141	1.6
1981	Cin-N	95	360	63	98	18	6	3	23	41	41	.272	.356	.381	107	4	26	10	2	.977	1	O-94	0.5
1982	NY-A	111	348	41	88	12	3	3	25	28	49	.253	.318	.330	80	-9	13	8	-1	.992	-5	O-60,1-52/D-1	-1.9
1983	Tor-A	118	402	55	109	12	4	1	34	43	67	.271	.345	.328	81	-9	31	7	5	.989	6	*O-112/1-5,D-1	-0.9
1984	Tor-A	128	441	59	136	24	**15**	2	44	32	41	.308	.369	.444	119	12	60	14	10	.991	4	*O-108/1-6,D-4	1.9
1985	Oak-A	112	379	52	95	16	4	4	29	29	37	.251	.306	.346	84	-9	29	8	4	.978	6	O-91	-0.1
1986	Det-A	124	419	44	113	18	2	1	27	44	49	.270	.342	.329	84	-8	27	12	1	.995	3	O-94,D-24	-0.7
1987	Cin-N	57	85	19	25	5	0	0	5	11	12	.294	.388	.353	94	1	9	0	3	1.000	-1	O-21	0.1
1988	Cin-N	99	174	12	41	6	2	0	14	11	27	.236	.289	.293	65	-8	7	2	1	.965	-4	O-35/1-3	-1.2
1989	Cin-N	78	106	12	25	4	0	0	7	10	17	.236	.302	.274	63	-5	3	1	0	1.000	0	O-16	-0.3
1990	StL-N	99	58	12	13	1	0	0	3	13	10	.224	.366	.241	70	-2	7	1	2	1.000	-6	1-49,O-12	-0.6
Total	16	1701	4907	667	1335	187	52	32	373	467	660	.272	.340	.351	93	-40	395	139	35	.986	3	*O-1118,1-125,D-104	-4.6

■ EDDIE COLLINS
Collins, Edward Trowbridge Jr. b: 11/23/16, Lansdowne, Pa. BL/TR, 5′10″, 175 lbs. Deb: 7/4/39 F

YEAR	TM/L	G	AB	R	H	2B	3B	HR	RBI	BB	SO	AVG	OBP	SLG	PRO+	BR/A	SB	CS	SBR	FA	FR	G/POS	TPR
1939	Phi-A	32	21	6	5	1	0	0	0	3		.238	.238	.286	34	-2	1	0	0	1.000	-0	/O-6,2-1	-0.2
1941	Phi-A	80	219	29	53	6	3	0	12	20	24	.242	.305	.297	61	-12	2	1	0	.968	-0	O-50	-1.5
1942	Phi-A	20	34	6	8	2	0	0	4	4	2	.235	.316	.294	72	-1	1	0	0	.800	-4	/O-9	-0.5
Total	3	132	274	41	66	9	3	0	16	24	29	.241	.302	.296	61	-15	4	1	0	.959	-4	/O-65,2-1	-2.2

■ EDDIE COLLINS
Collins, Edward Trowbridge Sr. "Cocky" (a.k.a. Edward T. Sullivan In 1906)
b: 5/2/1887, Millerton, N.Y. d: 3/25/51, Boston, Mass. BL/TR, 5′9″, 175 lbs. Deb: 9/17/06 FMCH

YEAR	TM/L	G	AB	R	H	2B	3B	HR	RBI	BB	SO	AVG	OBP	SLG	PRO+	BR/A	SB	CS	SBR	FA	FR	G/POS	TPR
1906	Phi-A	6	15	2	3	0	0	0	0	0		.200	.200	.200	25	-1	1			.900	-0	/S-3,2-1,3-1	-0.2
1907	Phi-A	14	23	0	8	0	1	0	2	0		.348	.348	.435	146	1	0			.833	1	/S-6	0.2
1908	Phi-A	102	330	39	90	18	7	1	40	16		.273	.312	.379	116	5	8			.944	-12	2-47,S-28,O-10	-0.8
1909	Phi-A	153	571	104	198	30	10	3	56	62		.347	.416	.450	170	47	67			**.967**	8	*2-152/S-1	5.7

YEAR	TM/L	G	AB	R	H	2B	3B	HR	RBI	BB	SO	AVG	OBP	SLG	PRO+	BR/A	SB	CS	SBR	FA	FR	G/POS	TPR
1910	*Phi-A	153	581	81	188	16	15	3	81	49		.324	.382	.418	152	34	**81**			**.972**	**34**	*2-153	7.0
1911	*Phi-A	132	493	92	180	22	13	3	73	62		.365	.451	.481	163	45	38			.967	3	*2-132	4.4
1912	Phi-A	153	543	**137**	189	25	11	0	64	101		.348	.450	.435	159	48	63			.955	15	*2-153	5.8
1913	*Phi-A	148	534	**125**	184	23	13	3	73	85	37	.345	**.441**	.453	165	48	55			.965	16	*2-148	6.4
1914	*Phi-A	152	526	**122**	181	23	14	2	85	97	31	.344	**.452**	.452	**179**	**56**	58	30	-1	**.970**	0	*2-152	5.9
1915	Chi-A	155	521	118	173	22	10	4	77	**119**	27	.332	.460	.436	163	48	46	30	-4	**.974**	13	*2-155	6.1
1916	Chi-A	155	545	87	168	14	17	0	52	86	36	.308	.405	.396	139	29	40	21	-1	**.976**	-6	*2-155	3.0
1917	*Chi-A	156	564	91	163	18	12	0	67	89	16	.289	.389	.363	127	22	53			.969	-26	*2-156	0.5
1918	Chi-A	97	330	51	91	8	2	2	30	73	13	.276	.407	.330	121	13	22			.974	-1	2-96	2.0
1919	*Chi-A	140	518	87	165	19	7	4	80	68	27	.319	.400	.405	126	20	**33**			.974	3	*2-140	3.1
1920	Chi-A	153	602	117	224	38	13	3	76	69	19	.372	.438	.493	146	42	20	8	1	**.976**	-4	*2-153	5.6
1921	Chi-A	139	526	79	177	20	10	2	58	66	11	.337	.412	.424	115	15	12	10	-2	.968	27	*2-136	4.0
1922	Chi-A	154	598	92	194	20	12	1	69	73	16	.324	.401	.403	110	12	20	12	-1	**.976**	-10	*2-154	0.5
1923	Chi-A	145	505	89	182	22	5	5	67	84	8	.360	.455	.453	141	36	**48**	29	-3	.975	-4	*2-142	2.9
1924	Chi-A	152	556	108	194	27	7	6	86	89	16	.349	.441	.455	136	34	**42**	17	2	**.977**	-7	*2-150,M	2.9
1925	Chi-A	118	425	80	147	26	3	3	80	87	8	.346	.461	.442	137	31	19	6	2	.970	-9	*2-116,M	2.4
1926	Chi-A	106	375	66	129	32	4	1	62	62	8	.344	.441	.459	140	25	13	8	-1	.973	-6	*2-101,M	2.0
1927	Phi-A	95	226	50	76	12	1	1	15	56	9	.336	.468	.412	123	12	6	2	1	.965	-7	2-56/S-1	0.6
1928	Phi-A	36	33	3	10	3	0	0	7	4	4	.303	.378	.394	100	0	0	0	0	.000	-2	/2-2,S-1	-0.1
1929	Phi-A	9	7	0	0	0	0	0	0	2	0	.000	.222	.000	-37	-1	0	0	0	.000	0	H	-0.1
1930	Phi-A	3	2	1	1	0	0	0	0	0	0	.500	.500	.500	148	0	0	0	0	.000	0	H	0.0
Total	25	2826	9949	1821	3315	438	187	47	1300	1499	286	.333	.424	.429	142	622	744	173		.970	41	*2-2650/S-40,O-10,3	69.8

■ HUB COLLINS
Collins, Hubert B.   b: 4/15/1864, Louisville, Ky.   d: 5/21/1892, Brooklyn, N.Y.   BR/TR, 5'8", 160 lbs.   Deb: 9/4/1886

YEAR	TM/L	G	AB	R	H	2B	3B	HR	RBI	BB	SO	AVG	OBP	SLG	PRO+	BR/A	SB	CS	SBR	FA	FR	G/POS	TPR
1886	Lou-a	27	101	12	29	3	2	0		10	5	.287	.321	.356	106	-2	7			.885	-2	O-24/3-2,S-1,2-1,1	-0.2
1887	Lou-a	130	559	122	162	22	8	1	66	39		.290	.338	.363	94	-6	71			.887	-8	*O-109,2-10/1-8,S3	-1.3
1888	Lou-a	116	485	117	149	26	11	2	50	41		.307	.366	.419	154	30	62			.890	13	O-82,2-19,S-15	3.7
	Bro-a	12	42	16	13	5	1	0	3	9		.310	.442	.476	195	5	9			.897	-3	2-12	0.3
	Yr	128	527	133	162	**31**	12	2	53	50		.307	.373	.423	158	35	71			.890	10	O-82,2-31,S-15	**4.0**
1889	*Bro-a	138	560	139	149	18	3	2	73	80	41	.266	.365	.320	95	-0	65			.929	-2	*2-138	0.4
1890	*Bro-N	129	510	**148**	142	32	7	3	69	85	47	.278	.385	.386	124	18	85			.945	5	*2-129	2.7
1891	Bro-N	107	435	82	120	16	5	3	31	59	63	.276	.365	.356	111	8	32			.910	-22	2-72,O-35	-1.1
1892	Bro-N	21	87	17	26	5	1	0	17	14	13	.299	.396	.379	140	5	4			.925	-2	O-21	0.2
Total	7	680	2779	653	790	127	38	11	319	332	164	.284	.365	.369	115	60	335			.928	-21	2-381,O-271/S13	4.7

■ HUGH COLLINS
Collins, Hugh   150 lbs.   Deb: 8/1/1887

YEAR	TM/L	G	AB	R	H	2B	3B	HR	RBI	BB	SO	AVG	OBP	SLG	PRO+	BR/A	SB	CS	SBR	FA	FR	G/POS	TPR
1887	NY-a	1	4	0	1	0	0	0	0	0	0	.250	.250	.250	41	-0	0			.250	-1	/C-1	-0.1

■ RIPPER COLLINS
Collins, James Anthony   b: 3/30/04, Altoona, Pa.   d: 4/15/70, New Haven, Conn.   BB/TL, 5'9", 165 lbs.   Deb: 4/18/31   C

YEAR	TM/L	G	AB	R	H	2B	3B	HR	RBI	BB	SO	AVG	OBP	SLG	PRO+	BR/A	SB	CS	SBR	FA	FR	G/POS	TPR
1931	*StL-N	89	279	34	84	20	10	4	59	18	24	.301	.350	.487	118	6	1			.995	5	1-68/O-3	0.5
1932	StL-N	149	549	82	153	28	8	21	91	38	67	.279	.329	.474	110	6	4			.999	-5	1-81,O-60	-0.9
1933	StL-N	132	493	66	153	26	7	10	68	38	49	.310	.363	.452	125	16	7			.994	3	*1-123	0.7
1934	*StL-N	154	600	116	200	40	12	**35**	128	57	50	.333	.393	**.615**	155	45	2			.991	6	*1-154	3.8
1935	StL-N★	150	578	109	181	36	10	23	122	65	45	.313	.385	.529	138	30	0			.987	1	*1-150	1.4
1936	StL-N★	103	277	48	81	15	3	13	48	48	30	.292	.399	.509	143	18	1			.990	-7	1-61/O-9	0.9
1937	Chi-N★	115	456	77	125	16	5	16	71	32	46	.274	.329	.436	102	0	2			.991	1	*1-111	-1.2
1938	*Chi-N	143	490	78	131	22	8	13	61	54	48	.267	.344	.424	107	5	1			**.996**	10	*1-135	-0.1
1941	Pit-N	49	62	5	13	2	2	0	11	6	14	.210	.279	.306	65	-3	0			.947	-0	1-11/O-3	-0.4
Total	9	1084	3784	615	1121	205	65	135	659	356	373	.296	.360	.492	125	123	18			.992	19	1-894/O-75	4.7

■ JIMMY COLLINS
Collins, James Joseph   b: 1/16/1870, Buffalo, N.Y.   d: 3/6/43, Buffalo, N.Y.   BR/TR, 5'9", 178 lbs.   Deb: 4/19/1895   MH

YEAR	TM/L	G	AB	R	H	2B	3B	HR	RBI	BB	SO	AVG	OBP	SLG	PRO+	BR/A	SB	CS	SBR	FA	FR	G/POS	TPR
1895	Bos-N	11	38	10	8	3	0	1	8	4	4	.211	.302	.368	67	-2	0			.714	-2	O-10	-0.4
	Lou-N	96	373	65	104	17	5	6	49	33	16	.279	.352	.393	100	0	12			.926	21	3-77,O-18/2-2,S-1	1.7
	Yr	107	411	75	112	20	5	7	57	37	20	.273	.347	.397	96	-2	12			.926	19	3-77,O-28/2-2,S-1	1.3
1896	Bos-N	84	304	48	90	10	9	1	46	30	12	.296	.374	.398	98	-1	10			.909	20	3-80/S-4	1.7
1897	*Bos-N	134	529	103	183	28	13	6	132	41		.346	.400	.482	125	17	14			.917	21	*3-134	3.5
1898	Bos-N	152	597	107	196	35	5	**15**	111	40		.328	.377	.479	138	26	12			.932	15	*3-152	3.8
1899	Bos-N	151	599	98	166	28	11	5	92	40		.277	.335	.386	89	-12	12			.943	21	*3-151	0.9
1900	Bos-N	142	586	104	178	25	5	6	95	34		.304	.352	.394	94	-7	23			.935	10	*3-141/S-1	0.4
1901	Bos-A	138	564	108	187	42	16	6	94	34		.332	.375	.495	142	30	19			.914	14	*3-138,M	4.0
1902	Bos-A	108	429	71	138	21	6	6	61	24		.322	.360	.459	123	12	18			**.954**	9	*3-107,M	2.0
1903	*Bos-A	130	540	88	160	33	17	5	72	24		.296	.329	.448	125	14	23			**.952**	12	*3-130,M	2.9
1904	Bos-A	156	631	85	171	33	13	3	67	27		.271	.306	.379	110	6	17			.945	7	*3-156,M	1.9
1905	Bos-A	131	508	66	140	26	5	4	65	37		.276	.330	.370	120	11	18			.923	4	*3-131,M	2.2
1906	Bos-A	37	142	17	39	8	4	1	16	4		.275	.295	.408	112	2	4			.911	2	3-32,M	0.6
1907	Bos-A	41	158	13	46	8	0	0	10	10		.291	.333	.342	116	3	4			.874	-8	3-41	-0.4
	Phi-A	99	364	38	99	21	0	0	35	24		.272	.331	.330	108	4	4			.904	-2	3-98	0.5
	Yr	140	522	51	145	29	0	0	45	34		.278	.332	.333	110	6	8			.895	-10	*3-139	0.1
1908	Phi-A	115	433	34	94	14	3	0	30	20		.217	.258	.263	65	-17	5			.928	-7	*3-115	-2.2
Total	14	1725	6795	1055	1999	352	116	65	983	426	32	.294	.343	.409	112	85	194			.929	137	*3-1683/O-28,S-6,2	23.1

■ ZIP COLLINS
Collins, John Edgar   b: 5/2/1892, Brooklyn, N.Y.   d: 12/19/83, Manassas, Va.   BL/TL, 5'11", 152 lbs.   Deb: 7/31/14

YEAR	TM/L	G	AB	R	H	2B	3B	HR	RBI	BB	SO	AVG	OBP	SLG	PRO+	BR/A	SB	CS	SBR	FA	FR	G/POS	TPR
1914	Pit-N	49	182	14	44	2	0	0	15	8	10	.242	.277	.253	61	-9	3			.962	1	O-49	-1.2
1915	Pit-N	101	354	51	104	8	5	1	23	24	38	.294	.340	.353	112	5	6	7	-2	.942	5	O-89	0.3
	Bos-N	5	14	3	4	1	1	0	0	2	1	.286	.375	.500	171	1	1			1.000	0	/O-4	0.2
	Yr	106	368	54	108	9	6	1	23	26	39	.293	.342	.359	114	6	7	7	-2	.944	5	O-93	0.5
1916	Bos-N	93	268	39	56	6	1	1	18	18	42	.209	.261	.246	66	-11	4			.947	-6	O-78	-2.4
1917	Bos-N	9	27	3	4	0	1	0	2	0	1	.148	.148	.222	14	-3	0			1.000	1	/O-5	-0.3
1921	Phi-A	24	71	14	20	5	1	0	5	6	5	.282	.354	.380	87	-1	1	2	-1	.915	0	O-20	-0.3
Total	5	281	916	124	232	17	14	2	63	58	100	.253	.301	.309	89	-18	15	9		.946	1	O-245	-3.7

■ SHANO COLLINS
Collins, John Francis   b: 12/4/1885, Charlestown, Mass.   d: 9/10/55, Newton, Mass.   BR/TR, 6', 185 lbs.   Deb: 4/21/10   FM

YEAR	TM/L	G	AB	R	H	2B	3B	HR	RBI	BB	SO	AVG	OBP	SLG	PRO+	BR/A	SB	CS	SBR	FA	FR	G/POS	TPR
1910	Chi-A	97	315	29	62	10	6	1	24	25		.197	.258	.289	74	-10	10			.949	4	O-66,1-28	-1.0
1911	Chi-A	106	370	48	97	16	12	4	48	20		.262	.309	.403	101	-2	14			.978	4	1-98/2-3,O-3	0.2
1912	Chi-A	153	599	75	168	34	10	2	81	29		.290	.330	.394	110	5	26			.969	3	*O-105,1-46	0.2
1913	Chi-A	148	535	53	128	26	9	1	47	32	60	.239	.286	.327	80	-15	22			.949	1	*O-147	-2.2
1914	Chi-A	154	598	61	164	34	6	3	65	27	49	.274	.312	.376	108	3	30	24	-5	.970	6	*O-154	-0.5
1915	Chi-A	153	576	73	148	24	17	2	85	28	50	.257	.298	.366	96	-6	38	19	0	.963	3	*O-104,1-47	-1.1
1916	Chi-A	143	527	74	128	28	12	0	42	59	51	.243	.323	.342	98	-1	16			.959	8	*O-137/1-4	-0.1
1917	*Chi-A	82	252	38	59	13	3	1	14	10	27	.234	.269	.321	78	-8	14			.992	-2	O-73	-1.4
1918	Chi-A	103	365	30	100	18	11	1	56	17	19	.274	.310	.392	111	2	7			.973	14	O-93/1-5	1.2
1919	*Chi-A	63	179	21	50	6	3	1	16	7	11	.279	.317	.363	90	-3	3			.957	1	O-46/1-8	-0.5
1920	Chi-A	133	495	70	150	21	10	1	63	23	24	.303	.339	.392	93	-6	12	9	-2	.988	-9	*1-116,O-13	-1.9
1921	Bos-A	141	542	63	155	29	12	4	69	18	38	.286	.314	.406	85	-15	15	8	-0	.966	-3	*O-139/1-3	-2.0
1922	Bos-A	135	472	33	128	24	7	1	52	7	30	.271	.289	.358	68	-23	7	9	-3	.951	-7	*O-117/1-1	-4.2
1923	Bos-A	97	342	41	79	10	5	0	18	11	29	.231	.265	.289	46	-28	7	8	-3	.953	-2	O-89	-3.7
1924	Bos-A	89	240	37	70	17	5	0	28	18	17	.292	.349	.400	94	-3	4	6	-2	.945	-10	O-56,1-12	-1.8
1925	Bos-A	2	3	1	1	0	0	0	0	0	0	.333	.333	.333	70	-0	0			.000	0	/O-1	-0.1
Total	16	1799	6390	747	1687	310	133	22	709	331	405	.264	.306	.364	90	-109	225	83		.962	16	*O-1343,1-368/2-3	-18.9

YEAR	TM/L	G	AB	R	H	2B	3B	HR	RBI	BB	SO	AVG	OBP	SLG	PRO+	BR/A	SB	CS	SBR	FA	FR	G/POS	TPR

■ JOE COLLINS
Collins, Joseph Edward (b: Joseph Edward Kollonige) b: 12/3/22, Scranton, Pa. d: 8/30/89, Union, N.J. BL/TL, 6', 185 lbs. Deb: 9/25/48

YEAR	TM/L	G	AB	R	H	2B	3B	HR	RBI	BB	SO	AVG	OBP	SLG	PRO+	BR/A	SB	CS	SBR	FA	FR	G/POS	TPR
1948	NY-A	5	5	0	1	1	0	0	2	0	1	.200	.200	.400	58	-0	0	0	0	.000	0	H	0.0
1949	NY-A	7	10	2	1	0	0	0	4	6	2	.100	.438	.100	46	-0	0	0	0	.920	-1	/1-5	-0.2
1950	*NY-A	108	205	47	48	8	3	8	28	31	34	.234	.335	.420	95	-2	5	0	2	.987	0	1-99/O-2	-0.2
1951	*NY-A	125	262	52	75	8	5	9	48	34	23	.286	.368	.458	127	10	9	7	-2	.987	4	*1-114,O-15	0.8
1952	*NY-A	122	428	69	120	16	8	18	59	55	47	.280	.364	.481	142	23	4	2	0	.990	-3	*1-119	1.7
1953	*NY-A	127	387	72	104	11	2	17	44	59	36	.269	.365	.439	121	11	2	6	-3	.989	1	*1-113/O-4	0.5
1954	NY-A	130	343	67	93	20	2	12	46	51	37	.271	.365	.446	126	12	2	2	-1	.992	1	*1-117	0.9
1955	*NY-A	105	278	40	65	9	1	13	46	45	44	.234	.343	.414	104	2	0	2	-1	.998	5	1-73,O-27	0.2
1956	*NY-A	100	262	38	59	5	3	7	43	34	33	.225	.316	.347	78	-9	3	1	0	.990	2	O-51,1-43	-1.0
1957	*NY-A	79	149	17	30	1	0	2	10	24	18	.201	.312	.248	56	-8	2	1	0	.987	-3	1-32,O-15	-1.4
Total	10	908	2329	404	596	79	24	86	329	338	263	.256	.351	.421	112	37	27	21	-5	.990	7	1-715,O-114	1.3

■ KEVIN COLLINS
Collins, Kevin Michael "Casey" b: 8/4/46, Springfield, Mass. BL/TR, 6'2", 190 lbs. Deb: 9/1/65

YEAR	TM/L	G	AB	R	H	2B	3B	HR	RBI	BB	SO	AVG	OBP	SLG	PRO+	BR/A	SB	CS	SBR	FA	FR	G/POS	TPR
1965	NY-N	11	23	3	4	1	0	0	1	0	9	.174	.208	.217	21	-2	0	1	-1	1.000	-1	/3-7,S-3	-0.5
1967	NY-N	4	10	1	1	0	0	0	0	0	3	.100	.100	.100	-43	-2	1	0	0	1.000	-0	/2-2	-0.2
1968	NY-N	58	154	12	31	5	2	1	13	7	37	.201	.236	.279	54	-9	0	1	-1	.955	-7	3-40/2-6,S-1	-1.8
1969	NY-N	16	40	1	6	3	0	1	2	3	10	.150	.209	.300	40	-3	0	0	0	.925	3	3-14	-0.1
	Mon-N	52	96	5	23	5	1	2	12	8	16	.240	.298	.375	87	-2	0	0	0	1.000	-7	2-20,3-16	-0.9
	Yr	68	136	6	29	8	1	3	14	11	26	.213	.272	.353	73	-5	0	0	0	.917	-4	3-30,2-20	-1.0
1970	Det-A	25	24	2	5	1	0	0	3	1	10	.208	.240	.375	67	-1	0	0	0	1.000	-0	/1-1	-0.1
1971	Det-A	35	41	6	11	2	1	1	4	0	12	.268	.268	.439	94	-1	0	0	0	1.000	1	/3-4,O-2,2-1	0.0
Total	6	201	388	30	81	17	4	6	34	20	97	.209	.248	.320	62	-20	1	2	-1	.944	-11	/3-81,2-29,S-4,O1	-3.6

■ ORTH COLLINS
Collins, Orth Stein "Buck" b: 4/27/1880, Lafayette, Ind. d: 12/13/49, Ft.Lauderdale, Fla BL/TR, 6', 150 lbs. Deb: 6/1/04

YEAR	TM/L	G	AB	R	H	2B	3B	HR	RBI	BB	SO	AVG	OBP	SLG	PRO+	BR/A	SB	CS	SBR	FA	FR	G/POS	TPR
1904	NY-A	5	17	3	6	1	1	0	1	1	1	.353	.389	.529	180	1	0			1.000	2	/O-5	0.4
1909	Was-A	8	7	0	0	0	0	0	0	0	0	.000	.000	.000	-99	-2	0			1.000	-1	/O-2,P-1	-0.2
Total	2	13	24	3	6	1	1	0	1	1	1	.250	.280	.375	104	-0	0			1.000	1	/O-7,P-1	0.2

■ RIP COLLINS
Collins, Robert Joseph b: 9/18/09, Pittsburgh, Pa. d: 4/19/69, Pittsburgh, Pa. BR/TR, 5'11", 176 lbs. Deb: 4/28/40

YEAR	TM/L	G	AB	R	H	2B	3B	HR	RBI	BB	SO	AVG	OBP	SLG	PRO+	BR/A	SB	CS	SBR	FA	FR	G/POS	TPR
1940	Chi-N	47	120	11	25	3	0	1	14	14	18	.208	.296	.258	55	-7	4			.951	-3	C-42	-0.7
1944	NY-A	3	3	0	1	0	0	0	0	1	0	.333	.500	.333	136	-0	0	0	0	1.000	-0	/C-3	0.1
Total	2	50	123	11	26	3	0	1	14	15	18	.211	.302	.260	58	-7	4	0		.953	-2	/C-45	-0.6

■ PAT COLLINS
Collins, Tharon Leslie b: 9/13/1896, Sweet Sprgs., Mo. d: 5/20/60, Kansas City, Kan. BR/TR, 5'9", 178 lbs. Deb: 9/5/19

YEAR	TM/L	G	AB	R	H	2B	3B	HR	RBI	BB	SO	AVG	OBP	SLG	PRO+	BR/A	SB	CS	SBR	FA	FR	G/POS	TPR
1919	StL-A	11	21	2	3	1	0	0	1	4	2	.143	.280	.190	32	-2				.929	-1	/C-5	-0.2
1920	StL-A	23	28	5	6	1	0	0	6	3	5	.214	.290	.250	43	-2	0	0	0	1.000	-2	/C-7	-0.4
1921	StL-A	58	111	9	27	3	0	1	10	16	17	.243	.339	.297	60	-6	1	0	0	.961	-1	C-31	-0.5
1922	StL-A	63	127	14	39	6	0	8	23	21	21	.307	.405	.543	140	8	0	1	-1	.980	6	C-28/1-5	1.4
1923	StL-A	85	181	9	32	8	0	3	30	15	45	.177	.240	.271	32	-18	0	0	0	.980	-1	C-47	-1.7
1924	StL-A	32	54	9	17	2	0	1	11	11	14	.315	.431	.407	110	1	0	1	-1	.969	-1	C-20	0.1
1926	*NY-A	102	290	41	83	11	3	7	35	73	57	.286	.433	.417	124	15	3	2	-0	.971	2	*C-100	2.2
1927	*NY-A	92	251	38	69	9	3	7	36	54	24	.275	.407	.418	118	9	0	1	-1	.976	-7	C-89	0.7
1928	*NY-A	70	136	18	30	5	0	6	14	35	16	.221	.380	.390	106	2	0	0	0	.977	-5	C-70	0.2
1929	Bos-N	7	5	1	0	0	0	0	0	2	3	.000	.375	.000	2	-1	0	0	0	1.000	1	/C-6	0.1
Total	10	543	1204	146	306	46	6	33	168	235	202	.254	.378	.385	98	5	4	5		.974	-7	C-403/1-5	1.9

■ BILL COLLINS
Collins, William J. b: 1863, Dublin, Ireland d: 6/8/1893, New York, N.Y. BR , Deb: 10/5/1889

YEAR	TM/L	G	AB	R	H	2B	3B	HR	RBI	BB	SO	AVG	OBP	SLG	PRO+	BR/A	SB	CS	SBR	FA	FR	G/POS	TPR
1889	Phi-a	1	4	0	1	0	0	0	1	1	0	.250	.400	.250	88	0	0			.800	-1	/C-1	0.0
1890	Phi-a	1	1	0	0	0	0	0	0	0	0	.000	.000	.000	-99	-0	0			.500	-0	/S-1	0.0
1891	Cle-N	2	3	0	0	0	0	0	0	0	0	.000	.000	.000	-96	-1	0			.000	1	/O-1,C-1	0.0
Total	3	4	8	0	1	0	0	0	1	1	0	.125	.222	.125	1	-1	1			.867	0	/C-2,O-1,S-1	0.0

■ BILL COLLINS
Collins, William Shirley b: 3/27/1882, Chesterton, Ind. d: 6/26/61, San Bernardino, Cal. BB/TR, 6', 170 lbs. Deb: 4/14/10

YEAR	TM/L	G	AB	R	H	2B	3B	HR	RBI	BB	SO	AVG	OBP	SLG	PRO+	BR/A	SB	CS	SBR	FA	FR	G/POS	TPR
1910	Bos-N	151	584	67	141	6	7	3	40	43	48	.241	.308	.291	72	-21	36			**.977**	13	*O-151	-1.7
1911	Bos-N	17	44	8	6	1	1	0	8	1	8	.136	.156	.205	0	-6	4			1.000	0	O-13/3-1	-0.6
	Chi-N	7	3	2	1	1	0	0	0	1	0	.333	.500	.667	225	1	0			1.000	-2	/O-4	-0.1
	Yr	24	47	10	7	2	1	0	8	2	8	.149	.184	.234	16	-6	4			1.000	-2	O-17/3-1	-0.7
1913	Bro-N	32	95	8	18	1	0	0	4	8	11	.189	.267	.200	33	-8	2			.921	-3	O-27	-1.3
1914	Buf-F	21	47	6	7	2	2	0	2	1	8	.149	.167	.277	19	-6	0			.864	-1	O-15	-0.8
Total	4	228	773	91	173	11	10	3	54	54	75	.224	.287	.276	60	-41	42			.966	7	O-210/3-1	-4.5

■ BILL COLLVER
Collver, William J. b: 3/21/1867, Clyde, Ohio d: 3/24/1888, Detroit, Mich. Deb: 7/4/1885

YEAR	TM/L	G	AB	R	H	2B	3B	HR	RBI	BB	SO	AVG	OBP	SLG	PRO+	BR/A	SB	CS	SBR	FA	FR	G/POS	TPR
1885	Bos-N	1	4	0	0	0	0	0	0	0	1	.000	.000	.000	-99	-1				.000	-0	/O-1	-0.1

■ FRANK COLMAN
Colman, Frank Lloyd b: 3/2/18, London, Ont., Canada d: 2/19/83, London, Ont., Can. BL/TL, 5'11", 188 lbs. Deb: 9/12/42

YEAR	TM/L	G	AB	R	H	2B	3B	HR	RBI	BB	SO	AVG	OBP	SLG	PRO+	BR/A	SB	CS	SBR	FA	FR	G/POS	TPR
1942	Pit-N	10	37	2	5	0	0	0	2	2	2	.135	.179	.216	15	-4	0			1.000	1	/O-8	-0.4
1943	Pit-N	32	59	9	16	2	2	0	4	8	7	.271	.358	.373	108	1	0			1.000	0	O-11	-0.2
1944	Pit-N	99	226	30	61	9	5	6	53	25	27	.270	.345	.434	113	4	0			.964	-3	O-53/1-6	-0.2
1945	Pit-N	77	153	18	32	11	1	4	30	9	16	.209	.253	.373	70	-7	0			.993	-1	1-22,O-12	-1.0
1946	Pit-N	26	53	3	9	0	0	1	6	2	7	.170	.214	.283	39	-4	0			1.000	-0	/O-8,1-2	-0.5
	NY-A	5	15	2	4	0	0	1	5	1	1	.267	.313	.467	114	0	0			1.000	-0	/O-5	0.0
1947	NY-A	22	28	2	3	0	0	0	5	2	6	.107	.167	.321	34	-3	0			1.000	-1	/O-6	-0.4
Total	6	271	571	66	130	22	8	12	105	49	66	.228	.291	.358	85	-14	0			.980	-4	O-103/1-30	-2.5

■ CRIS COLON
Colon, Cristobal b: 1/3/69, LaGuaira, Venez. BB/TR, 6'2", 180 lbs. Deb: 9/18/92

YEAR	TM/L	G	AB	R	H	2B	3B	HR	RBI	BB	SO	AVG	OBP	SLG	PRO+	BR/A	SB	CS	SBR	FA	FR	G/POS	TPR
1992	Tex-A	14	36	5	6	0	0	0	1	1	8	.167	.189	.167	0	-5	0	0	0	.946	3	S-14	-0.1

■ BOB COLUCCIO
Coluccio, Robert Pasquali b: 10/2/51, Centralia, Wash. BR/TR, 5'11", 183 lbs. Deb: 4/15/73

YEAR	TM/L	G	AB	R	H	2B	3B	HR	RBI	BB	SO	AVG	OBP	SLG	PRO+	BR/A	SB	CS	SBR	FA	FR	G/POS	TPR
1973	Mil-A	124	438	65	98	21	8	15	58	54	92	.224	.313	.411	105	2	13	6	0	.992	10	*O-108,D-11	0.7
1974	Mil-A	138	394	42	88	13	4	6	31	43	61	.223	.305	.322	81	-9	15	9	-1	.989	9	*O-131/D-2	-1.5
1975	Mil-A	22	62	8	12	0	1	1	5	11	11	.194	.324	.274	70	-2	1	4	-2	1.000	1	O-22	-0.5
	Chi-A	61	161	22	33	4	2	4	13	13	34	.205	.269	.329	67	-7	4	0	1	.980	-5	O-59/D-1	-1.4
	Yr	83	223	30	45	4	3	5	18	24	45	.202	.285	.314	68	-9	5	4	-1	.987	-5	O-81/D-1	-1.9
1977	Chi-A	20	37	4	10	0	0	0	7	6	2	.270	.372	.270	79	-1	0	2	-1	1.000	-2	/O-19	-0.5
1978	StL-N	5	3	0	0	0	0	0	0	2	2	.000	.250	.000	-25	-0	0	0	0	1.000	-1	/O-2	-0.1
Total	5	370	1095	141	241	38	15	26	114	128	202	.220	.306	.353	87	-18	33	21	-3	.990	2	O-341/D-14	-3.3

■ EARLE COMBS
Combs, Earle Bryan "The Kentucky Colonel" b: 5/14/1899, Pebworth, Ky. d: 7/21/76, Richmond, Ky. BL/TR, 6', 185 lbs. Deb: 4/16/24 CH

YEAR	TM/L	G	AB	R	H	2B	3B	HR	RBI	BB	SO	AVG	OBP	SLG	PRO+	BR/A	SB	CS	SBR	FA	FR	G/POS	TPR
1924	NY-A	24	35	10	14	5	0	0	2	4	2	.400	.462	.543	159	3	0	1	-1	1.000	-3	O-11	-0.1
1925	NY-A	150	593	117	203	36	13	3	61	65	43	.342	.411	.462	123	22	12	13	-4	.979	4	*O-150	1.1
1926	*NY-A	145	606	113	181	31	12	8	55	47	23	.299	.352	.429	105	2	8	6	-1	.970	1	*O-145	-0.8
1927	*NY-A	152	648	137	**231**	36	**23**	6	64	62	31	.356	.414	.511	143	41	15	6	1	.968	2	*O-152	3.2
1928	*NY-A	149	626	118	194	33	**21**	7	56	77	33	.310	.387	.463	127	25	10	8	-2	.980	8	*O-149	2.0
1929	NY-A	142	586	119	202	33	15	3	65	69	32	.345	.414	.468	135	32	11	7	-1	.966	-4	*O-141	1.7
1930	NY-A	137	532	129	183	30	**22**	7	82	74	26	.344	.424	.523	145	38	16	10	-1	.969	-4	*O-135	2.1
1931	NY-A	138	563	120	179	31	13	5	58	68	34	.318	.394	.446	128	24	11	3	2	.974	-0	*O-129	1.5
1932	*NY-A	144	591	143	190	32	10	9	65	81	16	.321	.405	.455	129	28	3	9	-5	.967	-7	*O-139	0.6
1933	NY-A	122	417	86	125	22	16	5	64	47	19	.300	.372	.465	128	16	6	4	-1	.975	-4	*O-104	0.6
1934	NY-A	63	251	47	80	13	5	2	25	40	9	.319	.412	.434	129	11	6			.993	-2	O-62	0.6

YEAR	TM/L	G	AB	R	H	2B	3B	HR	RBI	BB	SO	AVG	OBP	SLG	PRO+	BR/A	SB	CS	SBR	FA	FR	G/POS	TPR
1935	NY-A	89	298	47	84	7	4	3	35	36	10	.282	.359	.362	92	-3	1	3	-2	.993	-4	O-70	-1.0
Total	12	1455	5746	1186	1866	309	154	58	632	670	278	.325	.397	.462	127	241	96	71	-14	.974	-14	*O-1387	11.6

■ MERL COMBS

Combs, Merrill Russell   b: 12/11/19, Los Angeles, Cal.   d: 7/8/81, Riverside, Cal.   BL/TR, 6', 172 lbs.   Deb: 9/12/47   C

YEAR	TM/L	G	AB	R	H	2B	3B	HR	RBI	BB	SO	AVG	OBP	SLG	PRO+	BR/A	SB	CS	SBR	FA	FR	G/POS	TPR
1947	Bos-A	17	68	8	15	1	0	1	6	9	9	.221	.329	.279	65	-3	0	0	0	1.000	4	3-17	0.1
1949	Bos-A	14	24	5	5	1	0	0	1	9	0	.208	.424	.250	75	-0	0	0	0	.923	-0	/3-9,S-1	-0.1
1950	Bos-A	1	0	0	0	0	0	0	0	1	0	—	1.000	—	158	-0	0	0	0	.000	0	H	0.0
	Was-A	37	102	19	25	1	0	0	6	22	16	.245	.379	.255	68	-4	0	0	0	.966	-1	S-30	-0.2
	Yr	38	102	19	25	1	0	0	6	23	16	.245	.384	.255	69	-3	0	0	0	.966	-1	S-30	-0.2
1951	Cle-A	19	28	2	5	2	0	0	2	2	3	.179	.233	.250	32	-3	0	0	0	.960	5	S-16	0.2
1952	Cle-A	52	139	11	23	1	1	1	10	14	15	.165	.242	.209	28	-14	0	1	-1	.972	9	S-49/2-3	-0.3
Total	5	140	361	45	73	6	1	2	25	57	43	.202	.314	.241	52	-23	0	1	-1	.968	17	/S-96,3-26,2-3	-0.3

■ WAYNE COMER

Comer, Harry Wayne   b: 2/3/44, Shenandoah, Va.   BR/TR, 5'10", 175 lbs.   Deb: 9/17/67

YEAR	TM/L	G	AB	R	H	2B	3B	HR	RBI	BB	SO	AVG	OBP	SLG	PRO+	BR/A	SB	CS	SBR	FA	FR	G/POS	TPR
1967	Det-A	4	3	0	1	0	0	0	0	0	0	.333	.333	.333	95	-0	0	0	0	.000	-0	/O-1	0.0
1968	*Det-A	48	48	8	6	0	1	1	3	2	7	.125	.160	.229	16	-5	0	0	0	1.000	-5	O-27/C-1	-1.2
1969	Sea-A	147	481	88	118	18	1	15	54	82	79	.245	.356	.380	108	7	18	7	1	.980	3	*O-139/C-1,3-1	0.4
1970	Mil-A	13	17	1	1	0	0	0	1	0	3	.059	.059	.059	-67	-4	0	0	0	1.000	-1	/O-5	-0.5
	Was-A	77	129	21	30	4	0	0	8	22	16	.233	.349	.264	75	-3	4	1	1	.960	-10	O-58/3-1	-1.5
	Yr	90	146	22	31	4	0	0	9	22	19	.212	.320	.240	59	-7	4	1	1	.962	-11	O-63/3-1	-2.0
1972	Det-A	27	9	1	1	0	0	0	1	0	1	.111	.111	.111	-33	-1	0	1	-1	1.000	-5	O-17	-0.9
Total	5	316	687	119	157	22	2	16	67	106	106	.229	.333	.336	90	-7	22	9	1	.978	-18	O-247/3-2,C-2	-3.7

■ CHARLIE COMISKEY

Comiskey, Charles Albert "Commy" or "The Old Roman"   b: 8/15/1859, Chicago, Ill.   d: 10/26/31, Eagle River, Wis.   BR/TR, 6', 180 lbs.   Deb: 5/2/1882   MH

YEAR	TM/L	G	AB	R	H	2B	3B	HR	RBI	BB	SO	AVG	OBP	SLG	PRO+	BR/A	SB	CS	SBR	FA	FR	G/POS	TPR
1882	StL-a	78	329	58	80	9	5	1	45	4		.243	.252	.310	85	-6				.967	-1	*1-77/P-2	-1.4
1883	StL-a	96	401	87	118	17	9	2	64	11		.294	.313	.397	120	7				.963	-2	*1-96/O-1,M	-0.4
1884	StL-a	108	460	76	109	17	6	2	84	5		.237	.253	.313	81	-11				.969	-2	*1-108/2-1,P-1,M	-1.9
1885	*StL-a	83	340	68	87	15	7	2	44	14		.256	.293	.359	101	-1				.969	1	*1-83,M	-0.9
1886	*StL-a	131	578	95	147	15	9	3	76	10		.254	.267	.327	82	-15	41			.975	4	*1-122/2-9,O-2,M	-2.3
1887	*StL-a	125	538	139	180	22	5	4	103	27		.335	.374	.416	109	2	117			.976	3	*1-116/2-9,O-3,M	-0.5
1888	*StL-a	137	576	102	157	22	5	6	83	12		.273	.292	.359	98	-6	72			.970	-6	*1-133/O-5,2-3,M	-2.3
1889	StL-a	137	587	105	168	28	10	3	102	19	19	.286	.312	.383	86	-17	65			.970	-1	*1-134/O-3,2-3,PM	-2.3
1890	Chi-P	88	377	53	92	11	3	0	59	14	17	.244	.277	.289	49	-29	34			.965	-4	1-88,M	-2.9
1891	StL-a	141	580	86	152	16	2	3	93	33	25	.262	.310	.312	68	-30	41			.980	3	*1-141/O-2,M	-2.9
1892	Cin-N	141	551	61	125	14	6	3	71	32	16	.227	.274	.290	72	-20	30			.984	1	*1-141,M	-2.4
1893	Cin-N	64	259	38	57	12	1	0	26	11	2	.220	.257	.274	40	-23	9			.979	-6	1-64,M	-2.6
1894	Cin-N	61	220	26	58	8	0	0	33	5	5	.264	.289	.300	41	-22	10			.972	-4	1-60/O-1,M	-2.0
Total	13	1390	5796	994	1530	206	68	29	883	197	84	.264	.293	.338	82	-169	419			.973	-8	*1-1363/2-25,O-17,P	-24.8

■ JIM COMMAND

Command, James Dalton "Igor"   b: 10/15/28, Grand Rapids, Mich   BL/TR, 6'2", 200 lbs.   Deb: 6/20/54

YEAR	TM/L	G	AB	R	H	2B	3B	HR	RBI	BB	SO	AVG	OBP	SLG	PRO+	BR/A	SB	CS	SBR	FA	FR	G/POS	TPR
1954	Phi-N	9	18	1	4	1	0	1	6	2	4	.222	.300	.444	91	-0	0	0	0	.929	-0	/3-6	-0.1
1955	Phi-N	5	5	0	0	0	0	0	0	0	0	.000	.000	.000	-99	-1	0	0	0	.000	0	H	-0.1
Total	2	14	23	1	4	1	0	1	6	2	4	.174	.240	.348	52	-2	0	0	0	.929	-0	/3-6	-0.2

■ ADAM COMOROSKY

Comorosky, Adam Anthony   b: 12/9/05, Swoyersville, Pa.   d: 3/2/51, Swoyersville, Pa.   BR/TR, 5'10", 167 lbs.   Deb: 9/13/26

YEAR	TM/L	G	AB	R	H	2B	3B	HR	RBI	BB	SO	AVG	OBP	SLG	PRO+	BR/A	SB	CS	SBR	FA	FR	G/POS	TPR
1926	Pit-N	8	15	2	4	1	1	0	0	1	2	.267	.313	.467	102	-0	1			1.000	-1	/O-6	-0.2
1927	Pit-N	18	61	5	14	1	0	0	4	3	1	.230	.266	.246	35	-6	0			.978	-1	O-16	-0.5
1928	Pit-N	51	176	22	52	6	3	2	34	15	6	.295	.354	.398	92	-2	1			.968	-1	O-49	-0.5
1929	Pit-N	127	473	86	152	26	11	6	97	40	22	.321	.377	.461	104	3	19			.963	0	*O-121	-0.5
1930	Pit-N	152	597	112	187	47	**23**	12	119	51	33	.313	.371	.529	114	12	14			.969	1	*O-152	0.2
1931	Pit-N	99	350	37	85	12	1	1	48	34	28	.243	.310	.291	63	-17	11			.978	3	O-90	-2.1
1932	Pit-N	108	370	54	106	18	4	4	46	25	20	.286	.337	.389	96	-2	7			.981	7	O-92	0.0
1933	Pit-N	64	162	18	46	8	1	1	15	4	9	.284	.301	.364	89	-3	2			1.000	5	O-30	-0.5
1934	Cin-N	127	446	46	115	12	6	0	40	34	23	.258	.315	.312	70	-18	1			.970	1	*O-122	-2.2
1935	Cin-N	59	137	22	34	3	1	2	14	7	14	.248	.290	.328	68	-6	1			.953	-2	O-40	-0.9
Total	10	813	2787	404	795	134	51	28	417	214	158	.285	.339	.400	91	-39	57			.972	9	O-718	-7.2

■ PETE COMPTON

Compton, Anna Sebastian "Bash"   b: 9/28/1889, San Marcos, Tex.   d: 2/3/78, Kansas City, Mo.   BL/TL, 5'11", 170 lbs.   Deb: 9/6/11

YEAR	TM/L	G	AB	R	H	2B	3B	HR	RBI	BB	SO	AVG	OBP	SLG	PRO+	BR/A	SB	CS	SBR	FA	FR	G/POS	TPR
1911	StL-A	28	107	9	29	4	0	0	5	8		.271	.322	.308	79	-3	2			.917	1	O-28	-0.3
1912	StL-A	103	268	26	75	6	4	2	30	22		.280	.339	.354	102	1	11			.925	1	O-72	-0.2
1913	StL-A	63	100	14	18	5	2	0	17	13	13	.180	.274	.330	79	-3	2			.862	-4	O-21	-0.9
1915	StL-F	2	8	0	2	0	0	0	0	0	0	.250	.250	.250	39	-1	0			1.000	-1	/O-2	-0.2
	Bos-N	35	116	10	28	7	1	1	12	8	11	.241	.290	.345	96	-1	4	1	1	.971	0	O-31	-0.2
1916	Bos-N	34	98	13	20	2	0	0	8	7	7	.204	.264	.224	53	-5	5			.939	-2	O-30	-1.0
	Pit-N	5	16	1	1	0	0	0	0	2	5	.063	.211	.063	-14	-2	0			.917	0	/O-5	-0.3
	Yr	39	114	14	21	2	0	0	8	9	12	.184	.256	.202	43	-7	5			.936	-2	O-35	-1.3
1918	NY-N	21	60	5	13	0	1	0	5	5	4	.217	.277	.250	62	-3	2			.971	-1	O-19	-0.5
Total	6	291	773	78	186	24	8	5	80	65	40	.241	.303	.312	83	-17	26	1		.933	-6	O-208	-3.6

■ MIKE COMPTON

Compton, Michael Lynn   b: 8/15/44, Stamford, Tex.   BR/TR, 5'10", 180 lbs.   Deb: 4/17/70

YEAR	TM/L	G	AB	R	H	2B	3B	HR	RBI	BB	SO	AVG	OBP	SLG	PRO+	BR/A	SB	CS	SBR	FA	FR	G/POS	TPR
1970	Phi-N	47	110	8	18	0	1	1	7	9	22	.164	.240	.209	22	-12	0	0	0	.986	8	C-40	-0.3

■ CLINT CONATSER

Conatser, Clinton Astor "Connie"   b: 7/24/21, Los Angeles, Cal.   BR/TR, 5'11", 182 lbs.   Deb: 4/21/48

YEAR	TM/L	G	AB	R	H	2B	3B	HR	RBI	BB	SO	AVG	OBP	SLG	PRO+	BR/A	SB	CS	SBR	FA	FR	G/POS	TPR
1948	*Bos-N	90	224	30	62	9	3	3	23	32	27	.277	.370	.384	106	3	0			.974	-9	O-76	-0.9
1949	Bos-N	53	152	10	40	6	0	3	16	14	19	.263	.325	.362	89	0	0			.951	0	O-44	-0.4
Total	2	143	376	40	102	15	3	6	39	46	46	.271	.352	.375	99	0	0			.965	-8	O-120	-1.3

■ DAVE CONCEPCION

Concepcion, David Ismael (Benitez)   b: 6/17/48, Aragua, Venez.   BR/TR, 6'1", 180 lbs.   Deb: 4/6/70

YEAR	TM/L	G	AB	R	H	2B	3B	HR	RBI	BB	SO	AVG	OBP	SLG	PRO+	BR/A	SB	CS	SBR	FA	FR	G/POS	TPR
1970	*Cin-N	101	265	38	69	6	3	1	19	23	45	.260	.326	.317	73	-10	10	2	2	.945	-8	S-93/2-3	-0.6
1971	Cin-N	130	327	24	67	4	4	1	20	18	51	.205	.246	.251	42	-25	9	3	1	.974	-4	*S-112,2-10/3-7,O-5	-1.7
1972	Cin-N	119	378	40	79	13	2	2	29	32	65	.209	.274	.270	58	-21	13	6	0	.969	3	*S-114/3-9,2-1	-0.3
1973	Cin-N†	89	328	39	94	18	3	8	46	21	55	.287	.331	.433	116	6	22	5	4	.974	2	S-88/O-2	2.3
1974	Cin-N	160	594	70	167	25	1	14	82	44	79	.281	.337	.397	106	4	41	6	9	.963	9	*S-160/O-1	4.3
1975	*Cin-N★	140	507	62	139	23	1	5	49	39	51	.274	.328	.353	88	-9	33	6	6	.977	8	*S-130/3-6	2.1
1976	*Cin-N★	152	576	74	162	28	7	9	69	49	68	.281	.339	.401	107	5	21	10	0	.968	17	*S-150	4.1
1977	Cin-N★	156	572	59	155	26	3	8	64	46	77	.271	.325	.369	84	-13	29	7	5	**.986**	8	*S-156	1.7
1978	Cin-N★	153	565	75	170	33	4	6	67	51	83	.301	.360	.405	113	10	23	10	1	.969	-5	*S-152	2.7
1979	*Cin-N†	149	590	91	166	25	3	16	84	64	73	.281	.352	.415	108	7	19	7	2	.967	13	*S-148	3.8
1980	Cin-N	156	622	72	162	31	8	5	77	37	107	.260	.303	.360	84	-14	12	2	2	.978	-13	*S-155/2-1	-0.7
1981	Cin-N★	106	421	57	129	28	0	5	67	37	61	.306	.364	.409	117	10	4	5	-2	.960	4	*S-106	2.4
1982	Cin-N★	147	572	48	164	25	4	5	53	45	61	.287	.339	.371	96	-2	13	6	0	.977	13	*S-145/1-3,3-1	2.5
1983	Cin-N	143	528	54	123	22	4	1	47	56	81	.233	.307	.280	61	-26	14	9	-1	.979	-22	*S-139/3-6,1-1	-3.8
1984	Cin-N	154	531	46	130	26	4	4	58	52	72	.245	.312	.320	75	-17	22	6	3	.978	-35	*S-104,3-54/1-6	-4.3
1985	Cin-N	155	560	59	141	19	2	7	48	50	67	.252	.316	.330	77	-16	16	12	-2	.962	-32	*S-151/3-5	-3.9
1986	Cin-N	90	311	42	81	13	2	3	30	26	43	.260	.318	.344	79	-9	13	2	3	.965	-2	S-60,1-12,2-10,3-10	-0.3
1987	Cin-N	104	279	32	89	15	0	1	33	28	24	.319	.381	.384	99	1	4	3	-1	.992	9	2-59,1-26,3-13,S-2	0.2
1988	Cin-N	84	197	11	39	7	0	0	8	14	23	.198	.265	.244	45	-14	2	5	-0	.994	9	2-46,1-16,S-13/3P	-1.3
Total	19	2488	8723	993	2326	389	48	101	950	736	1186	.267	.325	.357	88	-133	321	109	31	.971	-44	*S-2178,2-130,3/1OP	9.2

■ ONIX CONCEPCION

Concepcion, Onix Cardona (Cardona)   b: 10/5/57, Dorado, P.R.   BR/TR, 5'6", 180 lbs.   Deb: 8/30/80

YEAR	TM/L	G	AB	R	H	2B	3B	HR	RBI	BB	SO	AVG	OBP	SLG	PRO+	BR/A	SB	CS	SBR	FA	FR	G/POS	TPR
1980	*KC-A	12	15	1	2	0	0	0	2	0	1	.133	.133	.133	-26	-3	0	0	0	.833	1	/S-6	-0.2

YEAR	TM/L	G	AB	R	H	2B	3B	HR	RBI	BB	SO	AVG	OBP	SLG	PRO+	BR/A	SB	CS	SBR	FA	FR	G/POS	TPR
1981	KC-A	2	0	0	0	0	0	0	0	0	0	—	—	—	—	0	0	0	0	.000	0	/S-1	0.0
1982	KC-A	74	205	17	48	9	1	0	15	5	18	.234	.256	.288	49	-14	2	1	0	.948	-2	S-46,2-24/D-1	-1.1
1983	KC-A	80	219	22	53	11	3	0	20	12	12	.242	.284	.320	66	-10	10	3	1	.913	1	3-31,2-28,S-21/D-1	-0.6
1984	*KC-A	90	287	36	81	9	2	1	23	14	33	.282	.322	.338	82	-7	9	6	-1	.972	3	S-85/2-6,3-1	0.4
1985	*KC-A	131	314	32	64	5	1	2	20	16	29	.204	.256	.245	38	-27	4	4	-1	.959	5	*S-128/2-2	-1.2
1987	Pit-N	1	1	0	1	0	0	0	0	0	0	1.000	1.000	1.000	429	0	0	0	0	.000	0	/H	0.0
Total	7	390	1041	108	249	34	7	3	80	47	93	.239	.279	.294	58	-60	25	14	-1	.960	8	S-287/2-60,3-32,D-2	-2.7

■ RAMON CONDE
Conde, Ramon Luis (Roman) "Wito"   b: 12/29/34, Juana Diaz, P.R.   BR/TR, 5'8", 172 lbs.   Deb: 7/17/62

YEAR	TM/L	G	AB	R	H	2B	3B	HR	RBI	BB	SO	AVG	OBP	SLG	PRO+	BR/A	SB	CS	SBR	FA	FR	G/POS	TPR
1962	Chi-A	14	16	0	0	0	0	0	1	3	3	.000	.158	.000	-54	-4	0	0	0	.889	-1	/3-7	-0.4

■ FRED CONE
Cone, Joseph Frederick   b: 5/1848, Rockford, Ill.   d: 4/13/09, Chicago, Ill.   5'9.5", 171 lbs.   Deb: 5/5/1871

YEAR	TM/L	G	AB	R	H	2B	3B	HR	RBI	BB	SO	AVG	OBP	SLG	PRO+	BR/A	SB	CS	SBR	FA	FR	G/POS	TPR
1871	Bos-n	19	77	17	20	3	1	0	16	8	2	.260	.329	.325	86	-1	12	1	3	.854	-0	O-18	0.1

■ BUNK CONGALTON
Congalton, William Millar   b: 1/24/1875, Guelph, Ont., Can.   d: 8/16/37, Cleveland, Ohio   BL/TL, 5'11", 190 lbs.   Deb: 4/18/02

YEAR	TM/L	G	AB	R	H	2B	3B	HR	RBI	BB	SO	AVG	OBP	SLG	PRO+	BR/A	SB	CS	SBR	FA	FR	G/POS	TPR
1902	Chi-N	45	179	14	40	3	0	1	24	7		.223	.253	.257	59	-9	3			.987	0	O-45	-1.3
1905	Cle-A	12	47	4	17	0	0	0	5	2		.362	.388	.362	136	2	3			.923	-1	O-12	0.0
1906	Cle-A	117	419	51	134	13	5	3	50	24		.320	.361	.396	139	18	12			.957	-9	*O-114	0.4
1907	Cle-A	9	22	2	4	0	0	0	2	4		.182	.308	.182	56	-1	0			1.000	0	/O-6	-0.1
	Bos-A	124	496	44	142	11	8	2	47	20		.286	.318	.353	115	7	13			.969	-3	*O-123	-0.1
	Yr	133	518	46	146	11	8	2	49	24		.282	.317	.346	112	6	13			.971	-2	*O-129	-0.2
Total	4	307	1163	115	337	27	13	6	128	57		.290	.326	.351	115	17	31			.967	-13	O-300	-1.1

■ TONY CONIGLIARO
Conigliaro, Anthony Richard   b: 1/7/45, Revere, Mass.   d: 2/24/90, Salem, Mass.   BR/TR, 6'3", 185 lbs.   Deb: 4/16/64   F

YEAR	TM/L	G	AB	R	H	2B	3B	HR	RBI	BB	SO	AVG	OBP	SLG	PRO+	BR/A	SB	CS	SBR	FA	FR	G/POS	TPR
1964	Bos-A	111	404	69	117	21	2	24	52	35	78	.290	.354	.530	135	18	2	4	-2	.973	6	*O-106	1.5
1965	Bos-A	138	521	82	140	21	5	**32**	82	51	116	.269	.340	.512	131	20	4	2	0	.976	14	*O-137	2.8
1966	Bos-A	150	558	77	148	26	7	28	93	52	112	.265	.333	.487	120	13	0	2	-1	.973	-0	*O-146	0.6
1967	Bos-A★	95	349	59	100	11	5	20	67	27	58	.287	.346	.519	141	17	4	6	-2	.983	9	O-95	1.4
1969	Bos-A	141	506	57	129	21	3	20	82	48	111	.255	.324	.427	103	1	2	4	-2	.981	-8	*O-137	-1.7
1970	Bos-A	146	560	89	149	20	1	36	116	43	93	.266	.327	.498	116	10	4	2	0	.977	3	*O-146	0.6
1971	Cal-A	74	266	23	59	18	0	4	15	23	52	.222	.286	.335	81	-8	3	3	-1	.994	6	O-72	-0.6
1975	Bos-A	21	57	8	7	1	0	2	9	8	9	.123	.231	.246	32	-5	1	0	0	.000	0	D-15	-0.6
Total	8	876	3221	464	849	139	23	166	516	287	629	.264	.330	.476	118	62	20	23	-8	.979	21	O-839/D-15	4.0

■ BILLY CONIGLIARO
Conigliaro, William Michael   b: 8/15/47, Revere, Mass.   BR/TR, 6', 190 lbs.   Deb: 4/11/69   F

YEAR	TM/L	G	AB	R	H	2B	3B	HR	RBI	BB	SO	AVG	OBP	SLG	PRO+	BR/A	SB	CS	SBR	FA	FR	G/POS	TPR
1969	Bos-A	32	80	14	23	6	2	4	7	9	23	.287	.367	.563	149	5	1	1	-0	.926	-7	O-24	-0.3
1970	Bos-A	114	398	59	108	16	3	18	58	35	73	.271	.341	.462	112	6	3	7	-3	.968	0	*O-108	-0.3
1971	Bos-A	101	351	42	92	26	1	11	33	25	68	.262	.311	.436	102	0	3	2	-0	.983	4	*O-100	-0.1
1972	Mil-A	52	191	22	44	6	2	7	16	8	54	.230	.261	.393	95	-2	1	0	0	.992	6	O-50	0.2
1973	*Oak-A	48	110	5	22	2	2	0	14	9	26	.200	.261	.255	48	-8	1	0	0	1.000	-2	O-40/2-1	-1.1
Total	5	347	1130	142	289	56	10	40	128	86	244	.256	.313	.429	103	1	9	10	-3	.980	2	O-322/2-1	-1.6

■ JEFF CONINE
Conine, Jeffrey Guy   b: 6/27/66, Tacoma, Wash.   BR/TR, 6'1", 205 lbs.   Deb: 9/16/90

YEAR	TM/L	G	AB	R	H	2B	3B	HR	RBI	BB	SO	AVG	OBP	SLG	PRO+	BR/A	SB	CS	SBR	FA	FR	G/POS	TPR
1990	KC-A	9	20	3	5	2	0	0	2	2	5	.250	.318	.350	88	-0	0	0	0	.977	0	/1-9	-0.1
1992	KC-A	28	91	10	23	5	2	0	9	8	23	.253	.313	.352	84	-2	0	0	0	1.000	-2	O-23/1-4	-0.5
1993	Fla-N	162	595	75	174	24	3	12	79	52	135	.292	.354	.403	97	-2	2	2	-1	.992	5	*O-147,1-43	-0.5
1994	Fla-N☆	115	451	60	144	27	6	18	82	40	92	.319	.376	.525	128	18	1	2	-0	.974	5	O-97,1-46	1.7
1995	Fla-N★	133	483	72	146	26	2	25	105	66	94	.302	.387	.520	136	26	2	0	1	.976	5	*O-118/1-14	2.7
1996	Fla-N	157	597	84	175	32	2	26	95	62	121	.293	.363	.484	126	22	1	4	-2	.975	5	*O-128/1-48	1.7
Total	6	604	2237	304	667	116	15	81	372	230	470	.298	.366	.472	119	62	6	8	-3	.981	16	O-513,1-164	5.0

■ JOCKO CONLAN
Conlan, John Bertrand   b: 12/6/1899, Chicago, Ill.   d: 4/16/89, Scottsdale, Ariz.   BL/TL, 5'7.5", 165 lbs.   Deb: 7/6/34   UH

YEAR	TM/L	G	AB	R	H	2B	3B	HR	RBI	BB	SO	AVG	OBP	SLG	PRO+	BR/A	SB	CS	SBR	FA	FR	G/POS	TPR
1934	Chi-A	63	225	35	56	11	3	0	16	19	7	.249	.310	.324	62	-13	2	2	-1	.955	-3	O-54	-1.8
1935	Chi-A	65	140	20	40	7	1	0	15	14	6	.286	.355	.350	81	-4	3	3	-1	.961	-3	O-37	-0.8
Total	2	128	365	55	96	18	4	0	31	33	13	.263	.327	.334	69	-17	5	5	-2	.957	-6	/O-91	-2.6

■ JOCKO CONLON
Conlon, Arthur Joseph   b: 12/10/1897, Woburn, Mass.   d: 8/5/87, Falmouth, Mass.   BR/TR, 5'7", 145 lbs.   Deb: 4/17/23

YEAR	TM/L	G	AB	R	H	2B	3B	HR	RBI	BB	SO	AVG	OBP	SLG	PRO+	BR/A	SB	CS	SBR	FA	FR	G/POS	TPR
1923	Bos-N	59	147	23	32	3	0	0	17	11	11	.218	.299	.238	45	-11	0	3	-2	.955	1	2-36/S-6,3-4	-1.0

■ BERT CONN
Conn, Albert Thomas   b: 9/22/1879, Philadelphia, Pa.   d: 11/2/44, Philadelphia, Pa.   TR   Deb: 9/16/1898

YEAR	TM/L	G	AB	R	H	2B	3B	HR	RBI	BB	SO	AVG	OBP	SLG	PRO+	BR/A	SB	CS	SBR	FA	FR	G/POS	TPR
1898	Phi-N	1	3	1	1	0	1	0	1	0		.333	.333	.667	291	1	0			1.000	-0	/P-1	0.0
1900	Phi-N	6	9	4	3	1	0	0	1	0		.333	.333	.444	115	0	0			.667	-1	P-4	0.0
1901	Phi-N	5	18	2	4	1	0	0	0	0		.222	.263	.278	56	-1	0			.880	-1	/2-5	-0.2
Total	3	12	30	7	8	2	1	0	2	0		.267	.290	.400	95	-0	0			.714	-2	/2-5,P-5	-0.2

■ FRITZIE CONNALLY
Connally, Fritzie Lee   b: 5/19/58, Bryan, Tex.   BR/TR, 6'3", 210 lbs.   Deb: 9/9/83

YEAR	TM/L	G	AB	R	H	2B	3B	HR	RBI	BB	SO	AVG	OBP	SLG	PRO+	BR/A	SB	CS	SBR	FA	FR	G/POS	TPR
1983	Chi-N	8	10	0	1	0	0	0	0	0	5	.100	.100	.100	-42	-2	0	0	0	1.000	0	/3-3	-0.2
1985	Bal-A	50	112	16	26	4	0	3	15	19	21	.232	.348	.348	94	-0	0	0	0	.976	-3	3-46/1-2,D-1	-0.4
Total	2	58	122	16	27	4	0	3	15	19	26	.221	.331	.328	83	-2	0	0	0	.977	-3	/3-49,1-2,D-1	-0.6

■ BRUCE CONNATSER
Connatser, Broadus Milburn   b: 9/19/02, Sevierville, Tenn   d: 1/27/71, Terre Haute, Ind.   BR/TR, 5'11.5", 170 lbs.   Deb: 9/15/31

YEAR	TM/L	G	AB	R	H	2B	3B	HR	RBI	BB	SO	AVG	OBP	SLG	PRO+	BR/A	SB	CS	SBR	FA	FR	G/POS	TPR
1931	Cle-A	12	49	5	14	3	0	0	4	2	3	.286	.327	.347	73	-2	0	0	0	1.000	1	1-12	-0.2
1932	Cle-A	23	60	8	14	3	1	0	4	4	8	.233	.281	.317	51	-4	1	0	0	1.000	0	1-14	-0.4
Total	2	35	109	13	28	6	1	0	8	6	11	.257	.302	.330	61	-6	1	0	0	1.000	0	/1-26	-0.6

■ FRANK CONNAUGHTON
Connaughton, Frank Henry   b: 1/1/1869, Clinton, Mass.   d: 12/1/42, Boston, Mass.   BR/TR, 5'9", 165 lbs.   Deb: 5/28/1894

YEAR	TM/L	G	AB	R	H	2B	3B	HR	RBI	BB	SO	AVG	OBP	SLG	PRO+	BR/A	SB	CS	SBR	FA	FR	G/POS	TPR
1894	Bos-N	46	171	42	59	9	2	2	33	16	8	.345	.407	.456	100	-0	3			.892	-3	S-33/C-7,O-4	-0.1
1896	NY-N	88	315	53	82	3	2	2	43	25	7	.260	.319	.302	66	-15	22			.892	-3	S-54,O-30	-1.1
1906	Bos-N	12	44	3	9	0	0	0	1	3		.205	.271	.205	50	-2	1			.918	-3	S-11/2-1	-0.5
Total	3	146	530	98	150	12	4	4	77	44	15	.283	.344	.343	78	-18	26			.894	-9	/S-98,O-34,C-7,2-1	-1.7

■ GENE CONNELL
Connell, Eugene Joseph   b: 5/10/06, Hazleton, Pa.   d: 8/31/37, Waverly, N.Y.   BR/TR, 6'0.5", 180 lbs.   Deb: 7/4/31   F

YEAR	TM/L	G	AB	R	H	2B	3B	HR	RBI	BB	SO	AVG	OBP	SLG	PRO+	BR/A	SB	CS	SBR	FA	FR	G/POS	TPR
1931	Phi-N	6	12	1	3	0	0	0	0	0	3	.250	.250	.250	32	-1	0			1.000	-1	/C-6	-0.1

■ JOE CONNELL
Connell, Joseph Bernard   b: 1/16/02, Bethlehem, Pa.   d: 9/21/77, Trexlertown, Pa.   BL/TL, 5'8", 165 lbs.   Deb: 6/15/26   F

YEAR	TM/L	G	AB	R	H	2B	3B	HR	RBI	BB	SO	AVG	OBP	SLG	PRO+	BR/A	SB	CS	SBR	FA	FR	G/POS	TPR
1926	NY-N	2	1	1	0	0	0	0	0	0	0	.000	.000	.000	-99	-1	0			.000	0	H	0.0

■ PETE CONNELL
Connell, Peter J.   b: Brooklyn, N.Y.   Deb: 9/3/1886

YEAR	TM/L	G	AB	R	H	2B	3B	HR	RBI	BB	SO	AVG	OBP	SLG	PRO+	BR/A	SB	CS	SBR	FA	FR	G/POS	TPR
1886	NY-a	1	5	0	0	0	0	0	0	0		.000	.000	.000	-99	-1	0			.667	-1	/3-1	-0.2

■ TERRY CONNELL
Connell, Terence G.   b: 6/17/1855, Philadelphia, Pa.   d: 3/25/24, Philadelphia, Pa.   Deb: 6/20/1874

YEAR	TM/L	G	AB	R	H	2B	3B	HR	RBI	BB	SO	AVG	OBP	SLG	PRO+	BR/A	SB	CS	SBR	FA	FR	G/POS	TPR
1874	Chi-n	1	4	0	0	0	0	0	0	0	0	.000	.000	.000	-99	-1	0	0	0	.429	-1	/C-1	-0.1

■ TOM CONNELLY
Connelly, Thomas Martin   b: 10/20/1897, Chicago, Ill.   d: 2/18/41, Hines, Ill.   BL/TR, 5'11.5", 165 lbs.   Deb: 9/24/20

YEAR	TM/L	G	AB	R	H	2B	3B	HR	RBI	BB	SO	AVG	OBP	SLG	PRO+	BR/A	SB	CS	SBR	FA	FR	G/POS	TPR
1920	NY-A	1	1	0	0	0	0	0	0	0	0	.000	.000	.000	-97	-0	0			.000	0	H	0.0
1921	NY-A	4	5	0	1	0	0	0	0	1	1	.200	.333	.200	38	-0	0			1.000	0	/O-3	-0.1
Total	2	5	6	0	1	0	0	0	0	1	1	.167	.286	.167	18	-1	0			1.000	0	/O-3	-0.1

■ ED CONNOLLY
Connolly, Edward Joseph Sr.   b: 7/17/08, Brooklyn, N.Y.   d: 11/12/63, Pittsfield, Mass.   BR/TR, 5'8.5", 180 lbs.   Deb: 9/20/29   F

YEAR	TM/L	G	AB	R	H	2B	3B	HR	RBI	BB	SO	AVG	OBP	SLG	PRO+	BR/A	SB	CS	SBR	FA	FR	G/POS	TPR
1929	Bos-A	5	8	0	0	0	0	0	0	0	2	.000	.000	.000	-99	-2	0			.889	-1	/C-5	-0.3
1930	Bos-A	27	48	1	9	2	0	0	7	4	3	.188	.250	.229	23	-6	0			1.000	-1	C-26	-0.5
1931	Bos-A	42	93	3	7	1	0	0	3	5	18	.075	.131	.086	-44	-20	0			.981	-1	C-41	-1.8

YEAR	TM/L	G	AB	R	H	2B	3B	HR	RBI	BB	SO	AVG	OBP	SLG	PRO+	BR/A	SB	CS	SBR	FA	FR	G/POS	TPR
1932	Bos-A	75	222	9	50	8	4	0	21	20	27	.225	.289	.297	54	-15	0	1	-1	.957	4	C-75	-0.8
Total	4	149	371	13	66	11	4	0	31	29	50	.178	.239	.229	23	-43	0	1	-1	.966	1	C-147	-3.4

■ RED CONNOLLY
Connolly, John M. b: 1863, New York, N.Y. d: 3/2/1896, New York, N.Y. Deb: 7/1/1886

YEAR	TM/L	G	AB	R	H	2B	3B	HR	RBI	BB	SO	AVG	OBP	SLG	PRO+	BR/A	SB	CS	SBR	FA	FR	G/POS	TPR
1886	StL-N	2	7	0	0	0	0	0	0	0	3	.000	.000	.000	-99	-2	0			.000	-1	/O-2	-0.2

■ JOE CONNOLLY
Connolly, Joseph Aloysius b: 2/12/1888, N.Smithfield, R.I. d: 9/1/43, Springfield, R.I. BL/TR, 5'7.5", 165 lbs. Deb: 4/10/13

YEAR	TM/L	G	AB	R	H	2B	3B	HR	RBI	BB	SO	AVG	OBP	SLG	PRO+	BR/A	SB	CS	SBR	FA	FR	G/POS	TPR
1913	Bos-N	126	427	79	120	18	11	5	57	66	47	.281	.379	.410	123	14	18			.954	-8	*O-124	0.1
1914	*Bos-N	120	399	64	122	28	10	9	65	49	36	.306	.393	.494	164	32	12			.974	-5	*O-118	2.2
1915	Bos-N	104	305	48	91	14	8	0	23	39	35	.298	.387	.397	144	18	13	12	-3	.971	-4	O-93	0.7
1916	Bos-N	62	110	11	25	5	2	0	12	14	13	.227	.320	.309	98	0	5			.980	-1	O-31	-0.2
Total	4	412	1241	202	358	65	31	14	157	168	131	.288	.380	.425	139	63	48	12		.967	-17	O-366	2.8

■ JOE CONNOLLY
Connolly, Joseph George "Coaster Joe" b: 6/4/1896, San Francisco, Cal d: 3/30/60, San Francisco, Cal BR/TR, 6', 170 lbs. Deb: 10/1/21

YEAR	TM/L	G	AB	R	H	2B	3B	HR	RBI	BB	SO	AVG	OBP	SLG	PRO+	BR/A	SB	CS	SBR	FA	FR	G/POS	TPR
1921	NY-N	2	4	0	0	0	0	0	0	0	1	.000	.200	.000	-42	-1	0	0	0	1.000	-0	/O-1	-0.1
1922	Cle-A	12	45	6	11	2	1	0	6	5	8	.244	.320	.333	70	-2	1	0	0	.972	2	O-12	-0.1
1923	Cle-A	52	109	25	33	10	1	3	25	13	7	.303	.377	.495	129	4	1	2	-1	.957	-10	O-39	-0.8
1924	Bos-A	14	10	1	1	0	0	0	1	2	2	.100	.250	.100	-8	-2	0	0	0	1.000	-1	/O-3	-0.2
Total	4	80	168	32	45	12	2	3	32	21	18	.268	.349	.417	100	-2	2	2	-1	.966	-9	O-55	-1.2

■ BUD CONNOLLY
Connolly, Mervin Thomas "Mike" b: 5/25/01, San Francisco, Cal d: 6/12/64, Berkeley, Cal. BR/TR, 5'8", 154 lbs. Deb: 5/3/25

YEAR	TM/L	G	AB	R	H	2B	3B	HR	RBI	BB	SO	AVG	OBP	SLG	PRO+	BR/A	SB	CS	SBR	FA	FR	G/POS	TPR
1925	Bos-A	43	107	12	28	7	1	0	21	23	9	.262	.392	.346	88	-1	0	3	-2	.950	-11	S-34/3-2	-0.9

■ TOM CONNOLLY
Connolly, Thomas Francis "Blackie" or "Ham" b: 12/30/1892, Boston, Mass. d: 5/14/66, Boston, Mass. BL/TR, 5'11", 175 lbs. Deb: 5/12/15

YEAR	TM/L	G	AB	R	H	2B	3B	HR	RBI	BB	SO	AVG	OBP	SLG	PRO+	BR/A	SB	CS	SBR	FA	FR	G/POS	TPR
1915	Was-A	50	141	14	26	3	2	0	7	14	19	.184	.268	.234	49	-9	5	4	-1	.970	-7	3-24,O-19/S-4	-1.7

■ NED CONNOR
Connor, Edward b: 1850, New York 5'9", 156 lbs. Deb: 5/18/1871

YEAR	TM/L	G	AB	R	H	2B	3B	HR	RBI	BB	SO	AVG	OBP	SLG	PRO+	BR/A	SB	CS	SBR	FA	FR	G/POS	TPR
1871	Tro-n	7	33	6	7	0	0	0	2	0	0	.212	.212	.212	22	-3	0	0	0	.878	-0	/1-4,O-3	-0.2

■ JIM CONNOR
Connor, James Matthew (b: James Matthew O'Connor) b: 5/11/1863, Port Jervis, N.Y. d: 9/3/50, Providence, R.I. BR/TR, Deb: 7/11/1892

YEAR	TM/L	G	AB	R	H	2B	3B	HR	RBI	BB	SO	AVG	OBP	SLG	PRO+	BR/A	SB	CS	SBR	FA	FR	G/POS	TPR
1892	Chi-N	9	34	0	2	0	0	0	0	1	7	.059	.111	.059	-48	-6	0			.917	-6	/2-9	-1.1
1897	Chi-N	77	285	40	83	10	5	3	38	24		.291	.355	.393	94	-3	10			.936	22	2-76	2.0
1898	Chi-N	138	505	51	114	9	9	0	67	42		.226	.289	.279	63	-24	11			.946	-3	*2-138	-1.7
1899	Chi-N	69	234	26	48	7	1	0	24	18		.205	.265	.244	41	-19	6			.942	4	2-44,3-25	-1.1
Total	4	293	1058	117	247	26	15	3	129	85	7	.233	.296	.295	64	-52	27			.942	18	2-267/3-25	-1.9

■ JOE CONNOR
Connor, Joseph Francis b: 12/8/1874, Waterbury, Conn. d: 11/8/57, Waterbury, Conn. BR/TR, 6'2", 185 lbs. Deb: 9/9/1895 F

YEAR	TM/L	G	AB	R	H	2B	3B	HR	RBI	BB	SO	AVG	OBP	SLG	PRO+	BR/A	SB	CS	SBR	FA	FR	G/POS	TPR
1895	StL-N	2	7	0	0	0	0	0	1	0	2	.000	.000	.000	-99	-2	0			1.000	1	/3-2	-0.1
1900	Bos-N	7	19	2	4	0	0	0	0	4	2	.211	.286	.211	34	-2	1			.971	2	/C-7	0.1
1901	Mil-A	38	102	10	28	3	1	1	9	6		.275	.321	.353	91	-1	4			.949	0	C-30/2-1,3-1,O-1	0.1
	Cle-A	37	121	13	17	3	1	0	6	7		.140	.200	.182	7	-15	2			.942	-0	C-32/O-4,S-1	-1.2
	Yr	75	223	23	45	6	2	1	15	13		.202	.255	.260	45	-16	6			.946	-0	C-62/O-5,2-1,3-1,S	-1.1
1905	NY-A	8	22	4	5	1	0	0	2	3		.227	.320	.217	79	-0	1			.978	5	/C-6,1-2	0.2
Total	4	92	271	29	54	7	2	1	22	18	2	.199	.257	.251	43	-21	8			.952	5	/C-75,O-5,3-3,1S2	-0.9

■ ROGER CONNOR
Connor, Roger b: 7/1/1857, Waterbury, Conn. d: 1/4/31, Waterbury, Conn. BL/TL, 6'3", 220 lbs. Deb: 5/1/1880 FMH

YEAR	TM/L	G	AB	R	H	2B	3B	HR	RBI	BB	SO	AVG	OBP	SLG	PRO+	BR/A	SB	CS	SBR	FA	FR	G/POS	TPR
1880	Tro-N	83	340	53	113	18	8	3	47	13	21	.332	.357	.459	166	22				.821	-10	*3-83	1.4
1881	Tro-N	85	367	55	107	17	6	2	31	15	20	.292	.319	.387	115	5				.950	2	*1-85	-0.1
1882	Tro-N	81	349	65	115	22	18	4	42	13	20	.330	.354	.530	188	34				.951	3	1-43,O-24,3-14	2.9
1883	NY-N	98	409	80	146	28	15	1	50	25	16	.357	.394	.506	173	36				.958	3	*1-98	2.4
1884	NY-N	116	477	98	151	28	4	4	82	38	32	.317	.367	.417	143	23				.860	3	2-67,O-37,3-12	2.4
1885	NY-N	110	455	102	169	23	15	1	65	51	8	.371	.435	.495	203	53				.975	3	*1-110	4.0
1886	NY-N	118	485	105	172	29	20	7	71	41	15	.355	.405	.540	183	48	17			.973	10	*1-118	3.9
1887	NY-N	127	471	113	134	26	22	17	104	75	50	.285	.392	.541	164	43	43			.993	5	*1-127	2.9
1888	*NY-N	134	481	98	140	15	17	14	71	73	44	.291	.389	.480	178	45	27			.982	1	*1-133/2-1	3.3
1889	*NY-N	131	496	117	157	32	17	13	130	93	46	.317	.426	.528	166	46	21			.977	-8	*1-131/3-1	2.5
1890	NY-P	123	484	133	169	24	15	14	103	88	32	.349	.450	.548	152	35	22			.985	11	*1-123	3.1
1891	NY-N	129	479	112	139	29	13	7	94	83	39	.290	.399	.449	153	35	27			.983	1	*1-129	2.7
1892	Phi-N	155	564	123	166	37	11	12	73	116	39	.294	.420	.463	167	51	22			.985	-6	*1-155	3.4
1893	NY-N	135	511	111	156	25	8	11	105	91	26	.305	.413	.450	129	23	24			.974	2	*1-135/3-1	1.7
1894	NY-N	22	82	10	24	7	0	1	14	8	0	.293	.356	.415	86	-2	2			.976	2	1-21/O-1	-0.1
	StL-N	99	380	83	122	28	25	7	79	51	17	.321	.410	.582	137	21	17			.974	5	1-99	2.0
	Yr	121	462	93	146	35	25	8	93	59	17	.316	.400	.552	128	19	19			.974	7	*1-120/O-1	2.0
1895	StL-N	103	398	78	131	29	9	8	77	63	10	.329	.423	.508	141	26	9			.986	4	*1-103	2.6
1896	StL-N	126	483	71	137	21	9	11	72	52	14	.284	.356	.433	112	7	10			.988	13	*1-126,M	1.8
1897	StL-N	22	83	13	19	3	1	1	12	13		.229	.333	.325	76	-3	3			.984	-0	1-22	-0.2
Total	18	1997	7794	1620	2467	441	233	138	1322	1002	449	.317	.397	.486	154	549	244			.978	42	*1-1758,3-111/2O	42.7

■ JERRY CONNORS
Connors, Jeremiah b: Cleveland, Ohio Deb: 7/11/1882

YEAR	TM/L	G	AB	R	H	2B	3B	HR	RBI	BB	SO	AVG	OBP	SLG	PRO+	BR/A	SB	CS	SBR	FA	FR	G/POS	TPR
1892	Phi-N	1	3	0	0	0	0	0	0	0	0	.000	.000	.000	-99	-1	0			.000	-0	/O-1	-0.1

■ JOE CONNORS
Connors, Joseph P. b: Paterson, N.J. Deb: 5/3/1884

YEAR	TM/L	G	AB	R	H	2B	3B	HR	RBI	BB	SO	AVG	OBP	SLG	PRO+	BR/A	SB	CS	SBR	FA	FR	G/POS	TPR
1884	Alt-U	3	11	0	1	0	0	0		0		.091	.091	.091	-44	-2				1.000	-0	/P-1,3-1,O-1	-0.2
	KC-U	3	11	2	1	0	0	0		1		.091	.167	.091	-23	-2				1.000	0	/O-2,P-2	0.0
	Yr	6	22	2	2	0	0	0		1		.091	.130	.091	-34	-4				.750	0	/P-3,O-3,3-1	-0.2

■ CHUCK CONNORS
Connors, Kevin Joseph Aloysius b: 4/10/21, Brooklyn, N.Y. d: 11/10/92, Los Angeles, Cal. BL/TL, 6'5", 190 lbs. Deb: 5/1/49

YEAR	TM/L	G	AB	R	H	2B	3B	HR	RBI	BB	SO	AVG	OBP	SLG	PRO+	BR/A	SB	CS	SBR	FA	FR	G/POS	TPR
1949	Bro-N	1	1	0	0	0	0	0	0	0	0	.000	.000	.000	-96	-0	0			.000	-0	H	0.0
1951	Chi-N	66	201	16	48	5	1	2	18	12	25	.239	.282	.303	56	-12	4	0	1	.984	-1	1-57	-1.5
Total	2	67	202	16	48	5	1	2	18	12	25	.238	.280	.302	56	-13	4	0		.984	-1	/1-57	-1.5

■ MERV CONNORS
Connors, Mervyn James b: 1/23/14, Berkeley, Cal. BR/TR, 6'2", 192 lbs. Deb: 9/4/37

YEAR	TM/L	G	AB	R	H	2B	3B	HR	RBI	BB	SO	AVG	OBP	SLG	PRO+	BR/A	SB	CS	SBR	FA	FR	G/POS	TPR
1937	Chi-A	28	103	12	24	4	1	2	12	14	19	.233	.325	.350	70	-5	2	1	0	.926	-3	3-28	-0.7
1938	Chi-A	24	62	14	22	4	0	6	13	9	17	.355	.437	.710	178	7	0	0	0	.979	0	1-16	0.5
Total	2	52	165	26	46	8	1	8	25	23	36	.279	.367	.485	111	2	2	1	0	.926	-3	/3-28,1-16	-0.2

■ BEN CONROY
Conroy, Bernard Patrick b: 3/14/1871, Philadelphia, Pa. d: 11/25/37, Philadelphia, Pa. 160 lbs. Deb: 4/21/1890

YEAR	TM/L	G	AB	R	H	2B	3B	HR	RBI	BB	SO	AVG	OBP	SLG	PRO+	BR/A	SB	CS	SBR	FA	FR	G/POS	TPR
1890	Phi-a	117	404	45	69	13	1	0	21	45		.171	.262	.208	40	-30	17			.893	-6	S-74,2-42/O-1	-2.6

■ WID CONROY
Conroy, William Edward b: 4/5/1877, Camden, N.J. d: 12/6/59, Mt.Holly, N.J. BR/TR, 5'9", 158 lbs. Deb: 4/25/01 C

YEAR	TM/L	G	AB	R	H	2B	3B	HR	RBI	BB	SO	AVG	OBP	SLG	PRO+	BR/A	SB	CS	SBR	FA	FR	G/POS	TPR
1901	Mil-A	131	503	74	129	20	6	5	64	36		.256	.316	.350	89	-7	21			.922	19	*S-118,3-12	1.9
1902	Pit-N	99	365	55	89	10	6	1	47	24		.244	.299	.312	86	-6	10			.925	8	S-95/O-3	0.8
1903	NY-A	126	503	74	137	23	12	1	45	32		.272	.322	.372	101	1	33			.919	3	*3-123/S-4	0.6
1904	NY-A	140	489	58	119	18	12	1	52	43		.243	.314	.335	100	1	30			.944	4	*3-110,S-27/O-3	1.0
1905	NY-A	101	385	55	105	19	11	2	25	32		.273	.329	.395	116	6	25			.928	7	3-48,O-25,S-17,1/2	1.5
1906	NY-A	148	567	67	139	17	10	4	54	47		.245	.303	.332	89	-8	32			.968	-1	O-97,S-49/3-2	-1.4
1907	NY-A	140	530	58	124	12	11	3	51	30		.234	.279	.315	83	-11	41			.955	0	*O-100,S-38	-0.5
1908	NY-A	141	531	44	126	22	3	1	39	14		.237	.258	.296	79	-14	23			.939	13	*3-119,2-12,O-10	0.3
1909	Was-A	139	488	44	119	13	4	1	20	37		.244	.298	.293	91	-5	24			.938	-0	3-120,2-13/O-5,S-1	-0.2
1910	Was-A	103	351	36	89	13	3	1	27	30		.254	.314	.311	100	0	11			.961	2	3-46,O-46/2-5	0.1
1911	Was-A	106	349	40	81	11	4	2	28	20		.232	.282	.304	64	-17	12			.930	6	3-85,O-15/2-1	-1.1
Total	11	1374	5061	605	1257	176	82	22	452	345		.248	.301	.329	91	-62	262			.934	71	3-665,S-349,O/21	3.0

YEAR	TM/L	G	AB	R	H	2B	3B	HR	RBI	BB	SO	AVG	OBP	SLG	PRO+	BR/A	SB	CS	SBR	FA	FR	G/POS	TPR

■ BILL CONROY Conroy, William Frederick "Pep" b: 1/9/1899, Chicago, Ill. d: 1/23/70, Chicago, Ill. BR/TR, 5'8.5", 160 lbs. Deb: 4/18/23

1923	Was-A	18	60	6	8	2	2	0	2	4	9	.133	.188	.233	11	-8	0	0	0	.926	-2	3-10/1-6,O-1	-0.9

■ BILL CONROY Conroy, William Gordon b: 2/26/15, Bloomington, Ill. BR/TR, 6', 185 lbs. Deb: 9/21/35

1935	Phi-A	1	4	0	1	1	0	0	0	1	0	.250	.400	.500	133	0	0	0	0	1.000	1	/C-1	0.1
1936	Phi-A	1	2	0	1	0	0	0	0	0	0	.500	.500	.500	151	0	0	0	0	1.000	-0	/C-1	0.0
1937	Phi-A	26	60	4	12	1	1	0	3	7	9	.200	.284	.250	36	-6	1	0	0	1.000	-1	C-18/1-1	-0.6
1942	Bos-A	83	250	22	50	4	2	4	20	40	47	.200	.315	.280	66	-11	2	0	1	.971	-1	C-83	-0.3
1943	Bos-A	39	89	13	16	5	0	1	6	18	19	.180	.336	.270	77	-2	0	0	0	.969	2	C-38	0.2
1944	Bos-A	19	47	6	10	2	0	0	4	11	9	.213	.362	.255	79	-1	0	0	0	.972	-0	C-19	0.2
Total	6	169	452	45	90	13	3	5	33	77	85	.199	.322	.274	66	-19	3	0	1	.974	1	C-160/1-1	-0.6

■ BILLY CONSOLO Consolo, William Angelo b: 8/18/34, Cleveland, Ohio BR/TR, 5'11", 180 lbs. Deb: 4/20/53 C

1953	Bos-A	47	65	9	14	2	1	1	6	2	23	.215	.239	.323	48	-5	1	2	-1	.808	10	3-16,2-11	0.4
1954	Bos-A	91	242	23	55	7	1	1	11	33	69	.227	.325	.277	59	-13	2	1	0	.953	-3	S-50,3-18,2-12	-1.2
1955	Bos-A	8	18	4	4	0	0	0	0	5	4	.222	.391	.222	63	-1	0	0	0	.889	-3	/2-4	-0.3
1956	Bos-A	48	11	13	2	0	0	0	1	3	5	.182	.357	.182	41	-1	0	0	0	.920	8	2-25	0.7
1957	Bos-A	68	196	26	53	6	1	4	19	23	48	.270	.347	.372	91	-2	1	3	-2	.933	12	S-42,2-16/3-2	1.3
1958	Bos-A	46	72	13	9	2	1	0	5	6	14	.125	.192	.181	3	-10	0	0	0	.925	7	2-13,S-11/3-1	-0.1
1959	Bos-A	10	14	3	3	1	0	0	0	2	5	.214	.313	.286	63	-1	0	0	0	.818	-2	/S-2	-0.2
	Was-A	79	202	25	43	5	3	0	10	36	54	.213	.332	.267	67	-8	1	0	0	.952	10	S-75/2-4	0.8
	Yr	89	216	28	46	6	3	0	10	38	59	.213	.331	.269	66	-9	1	0	0	.948	9	S-77/2-4	0.6
1960	Was-A	100	174	23	36	4	2	3	15	25	29	.207	.330	.305	68	-8	1	1	-0	.938	-1	S-82,2-12/3-2	-0.5
1961	Min-A	11	5	1	0	0	0	0	0	0	1	.000	.000	.000	-95	-1	0	0	0	1.000	0	/2-3,S-3,3-1	-0.1
1962	Phi-N	13	5	3	2	0	0	0	0	0	1	.400	.400	.400	119	0	0	0	0	.000	0	/3-1	0.0
	LA-A	28	20	4	2	0	0	0	0	3	11	.100	.217	.100	-12	-3	2	0	1	.917	3	3-20/S-4,2-1	-0.4
	KC-A	54	154	11	37	4	2	0	16	23	33	.240	.339	.292	68	-6	1	3	-2	.950	-1	S-48	-0.5
	Yr	82	174	15	39	4	2	0	16	26	44	.224	.325	.270	61	-9	3	3	-1	.944	2	S-52,3-20/2-1	-0.5
Total	10	603	1178	158	260	31	11	9	83	161	297	.221	.316	.289	63	-57	9	10	-3	.945	41	S-317,2-101/3-61	0.3

■ CHARLIE CONWAY Conway, Charles Connell b: 4/28/1886, Youngstown, Ohio d: 9/12/68, Youngstown, Ohio BR/TR, Deb: 4/15/11

1911	Was-A	2	3	0	1	0	0	0				.333	.333	1.000	272	1	0			.000	-1	/O-2	0.0

■ JACK CONWAY Conway, Jack Clements b: 7/30/19, Bryan, Tex. d: 6/11/93, Waco, Tex. BR/TR, 5'11.5", 175 lbs. Deb: 9/9/41

1941	Cle-A	2	2	0	1	0	0	0	1	0	0	.500	.500	.500	174	0	0	0	0	1.000	1	/S-2	0.1
1946	Cle-A	68	258	24	58	6	2	0	18	20	34	.225	.281	.264	56	-15	2	2	-1	.955	-7	2-50,S-14/3-3	-2.0
1947	Cle-A	34	50	3	9	2	0	0	5	3	8	.180	.226	.220	25	-5	0	0	0	.877	0	S-24/2-5,3-1	-0.5
1948	NY-N	24	49	8	12	2	1	1	3	5	10	.245	.315	.388	89	-1	0	0	0	.985	6	2-13/S-6,3-3	0.6
Total	4	128	359	35	80	10	3	1	27	28	54	.223	.279	.276	57	-21	2	2		.962	0	/2-68,S-46,3-7	-1.8

■ OWEN CONWAY Conway, Owen Sylvester b: 10/23/1890, New York, N.Y. d: 3/12/42, Philadelphia, Pa. TR, Deb: 6/21/15

1915	Phi-A	4	15	2	1	0	0	0	0	0	3	.067	.067	.067	-62	-3	0			.750	1	/3-4	-0.2

■ PETE CONWAY Conway, Peter J. b: 10/30/1866, Burmont, Pa. d: 1/13/03, Clifton Heights, Pa. BR/TR, 5'10.5", 162 lbs. Deb: 8/10/1885 F

1885	Buf-N	29	90	7	10	5	0	1	7	5	28	.111	.158	.200	15	-8				.889	-1	P-27/O-2,S-1,1-1	-0.2
1886	KC-N	51	194	22	47	8	2	1	18	5	34	.242	.261	.320	71	-7	3			.857	-1	O-31,P-23	-0.4
	Det-N	12	43	10	8	1	0	2	3	1	8	.186	.205	.349	64	-2	0			.846	-1	P-11/O-1	0.0
	Yr	63	237	32	55	9	2	3	21	6	42	.232	.251	.325	70	-9	3			.826	-2	P-34,O-32	-0.4
1887	*Det-N	24	95	16	22	5	1	1	7	2	9	.232	.247	.337	59	-6	0			.979	2	P-17/O-8	-0.2
1888	Det-N	45	167	28	46	4	2	3	23	8	25	.275	.320	.377	122	4	1			.938	2	P-45/O-1	0.0
1889	Pit-N	3	10	2	1	0	0	1	2	1	3	.100	.182	.400	67	-1	0			.875	-0	/P-3,O-1	0.0
Total	5	164	599	85	134	23	5	9	60	22	107	.224	.255	.324	74	-20	5			.907	2	P-126/O-44,1-1,S-1	-0.8

■ RIP CONWAY Conway, Richard Daniel b: 4/18/1896, White Bear Lake, Minn. d: 12/3/71, St.Paul, Minn. BL/TR, 5'6", 160 lbs. Deb: 4/16/18

1918	Bos-N	14	24	4	4	0	0	0	4	3	1	.167	.231	.167	23	-1	1			.810	-4	/2-5,3-1	-0.7

■ BILL CONWAY Conway, William F. b: 11/28/1861, Lowell, Mass. d: 12/28/43, Somerville, Mass. BR/TR, 5'8", 170 lbs. Deb: 7/28/1884 F

1884	Phi-N	1	4	0	0	0	0	0	0	0	1	.000	.000	.000	-99	-1				1.000	0	/C-1	-0.1
1886	Bal-a	7	14	4	2	0	0	0	3	7		.143	.429	.143	84	0	0			.925	-3	/C-7	-0.2
Total	2	8	18	4	2	0	0	0	3	7	1	.111	.360	.111	52	-0	0			.936	-3	/C-8	-0.3

■ ED CONWELL Conwell, Edward James "Irish" b: 1/29/1890, Chicago, Ill. d: 5/1/26, Chicago, Ill. BR/TR, 5'11", 155 lbs. Deb: 9/22/11

1911	StL-N	1	1	0	0	0	0	0	0	0	0	.000	.000	.000	-99	-0				.000	-0	/3-1	-0.1

■ HERB CONYERS Conyers, Herbert Leroy b: 1/8/21, Cowgill, Mo. d: 9/16/64, Cleveland, Ohio BL/TR, 6'5", 210 lbs. Deb: 4/18/50

1950	Cle-A	7	9	2	3	0	0	1	4	1	2	.333	.400	.667	175	1	1	0	0	1.000	-0	/1-1	0.1

■ DALE COOGAN Coogan, Dale Roger b: 8/14/30, Los Angeles, Cal. d: 3/8/89, Mission Viejo, Cal. BL/TL, 6'1", 190 lbs. Deb: 4/22/50

1950	Pit-N	53	129	19	31	6	1	1	13	17	24	.240	.338	.326	73	-5	0			.980	2	1-32	-0.3

■ DAN COOGAN Coogan, Daniel George b: 2/16/1875, Philadelphia, Pa. d: 10/28/42, Philadelphia, Pa. 128 lbs. Deb: 4/25/1895

1895	Was-N	26	77	9	17	2	1	0	7	13	6	.221	.333	.273	58	-4	1			.746	-11	S-18/C-5,O-2,3-1	-1.2

■ JIM COOK Cook, James Fitchie b: 11/10/1879, Dundee, Ill. d: 6/17/49, St.Louis, Mo. BR/TR, 5'9", 163 lbs. Deb: 7/2/03

1903	Chi-N	8	26	3	4	1	0	0	2	2		.154	.241	.192	25	-3	1			1.000	-2	/O-5,2-2,1-1	-0.4

■ DOC COOK Cook, Luther Almus b: 6/24/1886, Whitt, Tex. d: 6/30/73, Lawrenceburg, Tenn. BL/TR, 6', 170 lbs. Deb: 8/7/13

1913	NY-A	20	72	9	19	2	0	1	10	4		.264	.369	.319	101	1	1			.939	1	O-20	0.0
1914	NY-A	132	470	59	133	11	3	1	40	44	60	.283	.356	.326	105	4	26	32	-11	.949	-5	*O-127	-2.0
1915	NY-A	132	476	70	129	16	5	2	33	62	43	.271	.364	.338	111	8	29	18	-2	.959	1	*O-131	0.0
1916	NY-A	4	10	0	1	0	0	0	1	0	2	.100	.100	.100	-39	-2	0			1.000	-1	/O-3	-0.3
Total	4	288	1028	138	282	29	9	3	75	116	109	.274	.359	.329	106	11	56	50		.953	-4	O-281	-2.3

■ PAUL COOK Cook, Paul b: 5/5/1863, Caledonia, N.Y. d: 5/25/05, Rochester, N.Y. BR/TR, Deb: 9/13/1884

1884	Phi-N	3	12	0	1	0	0	0	0	0	2	.083	.083	.083	-50	-2				.818	-2	/C-3	-0.3
1886	Lou-a	66	262	28	54	5	2	0	14	10		.206	.235	.240	46	-17	6			.945	-9	1-43,C-21/O-2	-2.6
1887	Lou-a	61	223	34	55	4	2	0	17	11		.247	.294	.283	60	-12	15			.916	-10	C-55/1-6	-1.4
1888	Lou-a	57	185	20	34	2	0	0	13	5		.184	.222	.195	35	-13	9			.901	-14	C-53/O-4,S-1	-2.1
1889	Lou-a	81	286	34	65	10	1	0	15	15	48	.227	.287	.269	60	-15	11			.925	5	C-74/O-7,S-1,1-1	-0.3
1890	Bro-P	58	218	32	55	3	3	0	31	14	18	.252	.303	.294	56	-14	7			.890	-8	C-36,1-21/O-1	-1.0
1891	Lou-a	45	153	21	35	3	1	0	23	11		.229	.285	.261	57	-9	4			.909	-9	C-35,1-10	-1.4
	StL-a	7	25	3	5	0	0	1	1	2		.200	.259	.200	28	-3	0			.921	3	/C-7	0.1
	Yr	52	178	24	40	3	1	0	24	12	19	.225	.281	.253	52	-11	4			.912	-6	C-42,1-10	-1.3
Total	7	378	1364	172	304	27	9	0	114	67	87	.223	.270	.256	52	-84	52			.906	-35	C-284/1-81,O-14,S-2	-9.0

■ CLIFF COOK Cook, Raymond Clifford b: 8/20/36, Dallas, Tex. BR/TR, 6', 188 lbs. Deb: 9/9/59

1959	Cin-N	9	21	3	8	2	1	2	5	2	8	.381	.435	.571	161	2	1	0	0	.909	1	/3-9	0.3
1960	Cin-N	54	149	9	31	7	0	3	13	8	51	.208	.248	.315	52	-10	0	0	0	.954	4	3-47/O-4	-0.7
1961	Cin-N	4	5	0	0	0	0	0	0	0	1	.000	.000	.000	-99	-1	0	0	0	1.000	0	/3-1	-0.1
1962	Cin-N	6	5	0	0	0	0	0	0	0	0	.000	.000	.000	-97	-1	0	0	0	1.000	-0	/3-4	-0.2
	NY-N	40	112	12	26	6	1	2	9	4	34	.232	.277	.357	68	-5	0	0	0	.875	-8	3-16,O-10	-1.4
	Yr	46	117	12	26	6	1	2	9	4	36	.222	.266	.342	61	-7	0	0	0	.878	-8	3-20,O-10	-1.6

YEAR	TM/L	G	AB	R	H	2B	3B	HR	RBI	BB	SO	AVG	OBP	SLG	PRO+	BR/A	SB	CS	SBR	FA	FR	G/POS	TPR
1963	NY-N	50	106	9	15	2	1	2	8	12	37	.142	.229	.236	34	-9	0	1	-1	1.000	4	O-21/3-9,1-5	-0.7
Total	5	163	398	33	80	17	3	5	35	26	136	.201	.255	.312	54	-25	2	1		.937	0	/3-86,O-35,1-5	-2.8

■ DUSTY COOKE   Cooke, Allen Lindsey b: 6/23/07, Swepsonville, N.C. d: 11/21/87, Raleigh, N.C. BL/TR, 6'1", 205 lbs. Deb: 4/15/30 MC

YEAR	TM/L	G	AB	R	H	2B	3B	HR	RBI	BB	SO	AVG	OBP	SLG	PRO+	BR/A	SB	CS	SBR	FA	FR	G/POS	TPR
1930	NY-A	92	216	43	55	12	3	6	29	32	61	.255	.353	.421	100	0	4	6	-2	.978	-6	O-73	-1.1
1931	NY-A	27	39	10	13	1	0	1	6	8	11	.333	.447	.436	141	3	4	1	0	1.000	-1	O-11	0.2
1932	NY-A	3	0	1	0	0	0	0	0	1	0	—	1.000	—	191	0	0	0	0	.000	0	H	0.0
1933	Bos-A	119	454	86	133	35	10	5	54	67	71	.293	.386	.447	121	15	7	5	-1	.956	-6	*O-118	-0.9
1934	Bos-A	74	168	34	41	8	5	1	26	36	25	.244	.377	.369	87	-2	7	2	1	.976	-4	O-44	-0.7
1935	Bos-A	100	294	51	90	18	6	3	34	46	24	.306	.400	.439	109	5	6	8	-3	.972	-6	O-82	-0.6
1936	Bos-A	111	341	58	93	20	3	6	47	72	48	.273	.401	.402	93	-2	4	3	-1	.972	2	O-91	-0.4
1938	Cin-N	82	233	41	64	15	1	2	33	28	36	.275	.355	.373	103	2	0	0		.963	3	O-51	0.3
Total	8	608	1745	324	489	109	28	24	229	290	276	.280	.384	.416	106	21	32	25		.969	-30	O-470	-3.2

■ FRED COOKE   Cooke, Frederick B. b: Paulding, Ohio Deb: 7/30/1897

| 1897 | Cle-N | 5 | 17 | 2 | 5 | 2 | 0 | 0 | 3 | 3 | | .294 | .400 | .412 | 109 | 0 | 0 | | | .857 | 1 | /O-5 | 0.1 |

■ BRENT COOKSON   Cookson, Brent Adam b: 9/7/69, Van Nuys, Cal. BR/TR, 5'11", 200 lbs. Deb: 8/12/95

| 1995 | KC-A | 22 | 35 | 2 | 5 | 1 | 0 | 0 | 5 | 2 | 7 | .143 | .189 | .171 | -5 | -5 | 1 | 0 | 0 | 1.000 | -2 | O-12/D-2 | -0.7 |

■ SCOTT COOLBAUGH   Coolbaugh, Scott Robert b: 6/13/66, Binghamton, N.Y. BR/TR, 5'11", 185 lbs. Deb: 9/2/89

YEAR	TM/L	G	AB	R	H	2B	3B	HR	RBI	BB	SO	AVG	OBP	SLG	PRO+	BR/A	SB	CS	SBR	FA	FR	G/POS	TPR
1989	Tex-A	25	51	7	14	1	0	2	7	4	12	.275	.327	.412	105	0	0	0	0	.958	5	3-23/D-2	0.5
1990	Tex-A	67	180	21	36	6	0	2	13	15	47	.200	.265	.267	49	-12	1	0	0	.941	7	3-66	-0.5
1991	SD-N	60	180	12	39	8	1	2	15	19	45	.217	.295	.306	67	-8	0	3	-2	.952	4	3-54	-0.6
1994	StL-N	15	21	4	4	0	0	2	6	1	4	.190	.227	.476	79	-1	0	0	0	1.000	0	/1-4,3-4	-0.1
Total	4	167	432	44	93	15	1	8	41	39	108	.215	.283	.310	65	-20	1	3	-2	.949	16	3-147/1-4,D-2	-0.7

■ DUFF COOLEY   Cooley, Duff Gordon "Dick" b: 3/29/1873, Leavenworth, Kan. d: 8/9/37, Dallas, Tex. BL/TR, 5'11", 158 lbs. Deb: 7/27/1893

YEAR	TM/L	G	AB	R	H	2B	3B	HR	RBI	BB	SO	AVG	OBP	SLG	PRO+	BR/A	SB	CS	SBR	FA	FR	G/POS	TPR
1893	StL-N	29	107	20	37	2	3	0	21	8	9	.346	.391	.421	115	2	8			.947	-9	O-15,C-10/S-5	-0.5
1894	StL-N	54	206	35	61	3	1	1	21	12	16	.296	.335	.335	62	-13	7			.833	-11	O-39,3-13/S-1,1-1	-2.0
1895	StL-N	132	563	106	191	9	20	7	75	36	29	.339	.382	.464	119	15	27			.936	11	*O-124/3-5,S-3,C-1	1.3
1896	StL-N	40	166	29	51	5	3	0	13	7	3	.307	.335	.373	90	-3	12			.959	-1	O-40	-0.6
	Phi-N	64	287	63	88	6	4	2	22	18	16	.307	.348	.376	92	-4	18			.901	-5	O-64	-1.1
	Yr	104	453	92	139	11	7	2	35	25	19	.307	.343	.375	91	-6	30			.923	-5	*O-104	-1.7
1897	Phi-N	133	566	124	186	14	13	4	40	51		.329	.386	.420	116	14	31			.960	-5	*O-131/1-2	0.9
1898	Phi-N	149	629	123	196	24	12	4	55	48		.312	.364	.407	126	21	17			.943	4	*O-149	1.2
1899	Phi-N	94	406	75	112	15	8	1	31	29		.276	.330	.360	92	-5	15			.971	-5	1-79,O-14/2-1	-1.0
1900	Pit-N	66	249	30	50	8	1	0	22	14		.201	.243	.241	34	-23	9			.989	-5	1-66	-2.6
1901	Bos-N	63	240	27	62	13	3	0	27	14		.258	.302	.338	78	-7	5			.943	2	O-53,1-10	-0.9
1902	Bos-N	135	548	73	162	26	8	0	58	34		.296	.339	.372	118	11	27			.952	-6	*O-127/1-7	-0.4
1903	Bos-N	138	553	76	160	26	10	1	70	44		.289	.342	.378	109	6	27			.952	-5	*O-126,1-13	-0.7
1904	Bos-N	122	467	41	127	18	7	5	70	24		.272	.312	.373	115	2	14			.976	-7	*O-116/1-6	-0.8
1905	Det-A	97	377	25	93	11	9	1	32	26		.247	.297	.332	99	-1	7			.959	7	O-96	0.2
Total	13	1316	5364	847	1576	180	102	26	557	365	73	.294	.341	.380	104	20	224			.945	-22	*O-1094,1-184/3CS2	-7.0

■ CECIL COOMBS   Coombs, Cecil Lysander b: 3/18/1888, Moweaqua, Ill. d: 11/25/75, Fort Worth, Tex. BR/TR, 5'9", 160 lbs. Deb: 8/7/14

| 1914 | Chi-A | 7 | 23 | 1 | 4 | 1 | 0 | 0 | 1 | 1 | 7 | .174 | .208 | .217 | 28 | -2 | 0 | 1 | -1 | 1.000 | 1 | /O-7 | -0.3 |

■ JACK COOMBS   Coombs, John Wesley "Colby Jack" b: 11/18/1882, LeGrand, Iowa d: 4/15/57, Palestine, Tex. BB/TR, 6', 185 lbs. Deb: 7/5/06 MC

YEAR	TM/L	G	AB	R	H	2B	3B	HR	RBI	BB	SO	AVG	OBP	SLG	PRO+	BR/A	SB	CS	SBR	FA	FR	G/POS	TPR
1906	Phi-A	24	67	9	16	2	0	0	3	1		.239	.261	.269	64	-3	2			.967	-0	P-23	0.0
1907	Phi-A	24	48	4	8	0	0	1	4	0		.167	.167	.229	25	-4	1			.979	4	P-23	0.0
1908	Phi-A	78	220	24	56	9	5	1	23	9		.255	.287	.355	101	-1	6			.990	6	O-47,P-26/1-1	0.4
1909	Phi-A	37	83	4	14	0	0	0	10	4		.169	.216	.217	36	-6	1			.973	-0	P-30	0.0
1910	*Phi-A	46	132	20	29	3	0	0	9	7		.220	.270	.242	61	-6	3			.990	-5	P-45	0.0
1911	*Phi-A	52	141	31	45	6	1	2	23	8		.319	.356	.418	118	3	5			.913	-3	P-47	0.0
1912	Phi-A	56	110	10	28	3	0	0	13	14		.255	.344	.273	80	-2	1			1.000	-1	P-40	0.0
1913	Phi-A	2	3	1	1	1	0	0	0	0	2	.333	.333	.667	195	-0				.500	-1	/P-2	0.0
1914	Phi-A	5	11	0	3	1	0	0	2	1	1	.273	.333	.364	114	-0	1		-1	1.000	-1	/P-2,O-2	-0.1
1915	Bro-N	29	75	8	21	1	1	0	5	2	17	.280	.299	.320	86	-1	0			.980	-4	P-29	0.0
1916	*Bro-N	27	61	2	11	2	0	0	3	2	10	.180	.206	.213	28	-5	0			1.000	-6	P-27	0.0
1917	Bro-N	32	44	4	10	0	1	0	2	4	9	.227	.292	.273	72	-1	1			.971	-3	P-31	0.0
1918	Bro-N	46	113	6	19	3	2	0	3	7	5	.168	.223	.230	38	-8	1			.962	-7	P-27,O-13	-0.8
1920	Det-A	2	2	0	0	0	0	0	0	0	0	.000	.000	.000	-99	-1	0	0	0	1.000	-0	/P-2	0.0
Total	14	460	1110	123	261	34	10	4	100	59	44	.235	.278	.295	74	-35	21	2		.966	-24	P-354/O-62,1-1	-0.5

■ RON COOMER   Coomer, Ronald Bryan b: 11/18/66, Crest Hill, Ill. BR/TR, 5'11", 195 lbs. Deb: 8/1/95

1995	Min-A	37	101	15	26	3	1	5	19	9	15	.257	.324	.455	100	-0	0	1	-1	.993	1	1-22,3-13/O-1,D-4	-0.1
1996	Min-A	95	233	34	69	12	1	12	41	17	24	.296	.344	.511	110	3	3	0	1	.993	1	1-57,O-23/3-9,D-3	0.0
Total	2	132	334	49	95	15	2	17	60	26	35	.284	.338	.494	107	3	3	1	0	.993	2	/1-79,O-24,3-22,D-7	-0.1

■ WILLIAM COON   Coon, William K. b: 3/21/1855, Pennsylvania d: 8/30/15, Burlington, N.J. Deb: 9/4/1875

| 1875 | Ath-n | 4 | 12 | 1 | 2 | 0 | 0 | 0 | 1 | 0 | | .167 | .167 | .167 | 15 | -1 | 1 | 0 | 0 | .810 | -0 | /C-4,O-1 | -0.1 |
| 1876 | Phi-N | 54 | 220 | 30 | 50 | 5 | 1 | 0 | 22 | 2 | 4 | .227 | .234 | .259 | 65 | -8 | | | | .761 | -15 | O-29,C-18/3-4,2P | -2.0 |

■ JIMMY COONEY   Cooney, James Edward "Scoops" b: 8/24/1894, Cranston, R.I. d: 8/7/91, Warwick, R.I. BR/TR, 5'11", 160 lbs. Deb: 9/22/17 F

YEAR	TM/L	G	AB	R	H	2B	3B	HR	RBI	BB	SO	AVG	OBP	SLG	PRO+	BR/A	SB	CS	SBR	FA	FR	G/POS	TPR
1917	Bos-A	11	36	4	8	1	0	0	3	6	2	.222	.333	.250	79	-1	0			1.000	5	2-10/S-1	0.5
1919	NY-N	5	14	3	3	0	0	0	1	0	0	.214	.214	.214	29	-1	0			1.000	-1	/S-4,2-1	-0.2
1924	StL-N	110	383	44	113	20	8	1	57	20	20	.295	.330	.397	96	-3	12	10	-2	.969	1	S-99/3-7,2-1	0.6
1925	StL-N	54	187	27	51	11	2	0	18	4	5	.273	.292	.353	62	-11	1	3	-2	.976	-11	S-37,2-15/O-1	-1.8
1926	Chi-N	141	513	52	129	18	5	1	47	23	10	.251	.288	.312	61	-29	11			.972	19	*S-141	0.6
1927	Chi-N	33	132	16	32	2	0	0	6	8	7	.242	.286	.258	46	-10	1			.973	-2	S-33	-0.9
	Phi-N	76	259	33	70	12	1	0	15	13	9	.270	.305	.324	68	-12	4			.980	17	S-74	1.2
	Yr	109	391	49	102	14	1	0	21	21	16	.261	.299	.302	61	-22	5			.978	15	*S-107	0.3
1928	Bos-N	58	51	2	7	0	0	0	2	2	5	.137	.170	.137	-20	-9	1			.982	3	S-11/2-4	-0.6
Total	7	448	1575	181	413	64	16	2	150	76	58	.262	.298	.327	67	-75	30	13		.974	30	S-400/2-31,3-7,O-1	-0.6

■ JIMMY COONEY   Cooney, James Joseph b: 7/9/1865, Cranston, R.I. d: 7/1/03, Cranston, R.I. BB/TR, 5'9", 155 lbs. Deb: 4/19/1890 F

1890	Chi-N	135	574	114	156	19	10	4	52	73	23	.272	.360	.361	106	5	45			.936	1	*S-135/C-1	1.2
1891	Chi-N	118	465	84	114	15	3	0	42	48	17	.245	.318	.290	78	-12	21			.917	8	*S-118	0.3
1892	Chi-N	65	238	18	41	1	0	0	20	23	5	.172	.248	.176	29	-20	10			.912	-8	S-65	-2.3
	Was-N	6	25	5	4	0	1	0	4	4	3	.160	.276	.240	58	-1	1			.862	-3	/S-6	-0.4
	Yr	71	263	23	45	1	1	0	24	27	8	.171	.251	.183	31	-21	11			.908	-11	S-71	-2.7
Total	3	324	1302	221	315	35	14	4	118	148	48	.242	.324	.300	82	-29	77			.923	-2	S-324/C-1	-1.2

■ JOHNNY COONEY   Cooney, John Walter b: 3/18/01, Cranston, R.I. d: 7/8/86, Sarasota, Fla. BR/TL, 5'10", 165 lbs. Deb: 4/19/21 FMC

YEAR	TM/L	G	AB	R	H	2B	3B	HR	RBI	BB	SO	AVG	OBP	SLG	PRO+	BR/A	SB	CS	SBR	FA	FR	G/POS	TPR
1921	Bos-N	8	5	0	1	0	0	0	0	0	0	.200	.200	.200	7	-1	0			1.000	0	/P-8	0.0
1922	Bos-N	4	8	0	0	0	0	0	0	0	1	.000	.000	.000	-99	-2	0			1.000	0	/P-4	0.0
1923	Bos-N	42	66	7	25	1	0	0	3	4	2	.379	.414	.394	119	2	0	1	-1	1.000	0	P-23,O-11/1-1	0.0
1924	Bos-N	55	130	10	33	4	0	0	4	9	5	.254	.302	.285	61	-7	0	4	-2	.962	0	P-34,O-16/1-1	-0.4
1925	Bos-N	54	103	17	33	7	0	0	13	6	4	.320	.346	.388	96	-1	1	0	0	.949	1	P-31/1-3,O-1	-0.1
1926	Bos-N	64	126	17	38	3	2	0	18	13	7	.302	.367	.357	105	1	6			.996	5	1-31,P-19/O-1	0.3
1927	Bos-N	10	3	0	0	0	0	0	0	0	0	.000	.000	.000	-99	-0	0			1.000	0	H	0.0

YEAR	TM/L	G	AB	R	H	2B	3B	HR	RBI	BB	SO	AVG	OBP	SLG	PRO+	BR/A	SB	CS	SBR	FA	FR	G/POS	TPR
1928	Bos-N	33	41	2	7	0	0	0	2	4	3	.171	.244	.171	11	-5	0			1.000	2	P-24/1-3,O-2	-0.2
1929	Bos-N	41	72	10	23	4	1	0	6	3	3	.319	.355	.403	91	-1	1			1.000	2	O-16,P-14	-0.1
1930	Bos-N	4	3	0	0	0	0	0	0	0	0	.000	.000	.000	-99	-1	0			1.000	1	/P-2	0.0
1935	Bro-N	10	29	3	9	0	1	0	1	3	2	.310	.375	.379	106	0	0			1.000	-1	O-10	-0.1
1936	Bro-N	130	507	71	143	17	5	0	30	24	15	.282	.315	.335	74	-18	3			.994	8	*O-130	-1.6
1937	Bro-N	120	430	61	126	18	5	0	37	22	10	.293	.327	.358	85	-9	5			.976	6	*O-111/1-2	-0.7
1938	Bos-N	120	432	45	117	25	5	0	17	22	12	.271	.308	.352	90	-8	2			.982	-10	*O-110,1-13	-2.2
1939	Bos-N	118	368	39	101	8	1	2	27	21	8	.274	.317	.318	77	-12	2			.992	-6	*O-116/1-2	-2.2
1940	Bos-N	108	365	40	116	14	3	0	21	25	9	.318	.363	.373	109	5	4			.992	-1	O-99/1-7	-0.1
1941	Bos-N	123	442	52	141	25	2	0	29	27	15	.319	.358	.385	114	8	3			.996	4	*O-111/1-4	0.5
1942	Bos-N	74	198	23	41	6	0	0	7	23	5	.207	.290	.237	56	-10	2			.984	-14	O-54,1-23	-3.1
1943	Bro-N	37	34	7	7	0	0	0	2	4	3	.206	.289	.206	44	-2	1			1.000	-0	/1-3,O-2	-0.3
1944	Bro-N	7	4	0	3	0	0	0	1	0	0	.750	.750	.750	329	1	0			1.000	-0	/O-2	0.1
	NY-A	10	8	1	1	0	0	0	1	1	0	.125	.222	.125	1	-1	0	0	0	1.000	-0	/O-1	-0.1
Total	20	1172	3372	408	965	130	26	2	219	208	107	.286	.329	.342	87	-63	30	5		.988	-6	O-794,P-159/1-93	-10.1

■ PHIL COONEY
Cooney, Philip Clarence (b: Philip Clarence Cohen) b: 9/14/1882, New York, N.Y. d: 10/6/57, New York, N.Y. BL/TR, 5'8", 155 lbs. Deb: 9/27/05

YEAR	TM/L	G	AB	R	H	2B	3B	HR	RBI	BB	SO	AVG	OBP	SLG	PRO+	BR/A	SB	CS	SBR	FA	FR	G/POS	TPR
1905	NY-A	1	3	0	0	0	0	0	0	0	0	.000	.000	.000	-90	-1	0			1.000	-0	/3-1	-0.1

■ BILL COONEY
Cooney, William A. "Cush" b: 4/7/1883, Boston, Mass. d: 11/6/28, Roxbury, Mass. TR , Deb: 9/22/09

YEAR	TM/L	G	AB	R	H	2B	3B	HR	RBI	BB	SO	AVG	OBP	SLG	PRO+	BR/A	SB	CS	SBR	FA	FR	G/POS	TPR
1909	Bos-N	5	10	0	3	0	0	0	1	0	0	.300	.300	.300	82	-0	0			.500	-0	/P-3,2-1,S-1	0.0
1910	Bos-N	8	12	2	3	0	0	0	1	2	0	.250	.357	.250	74	-0	0			.000	-1	/O-2	-0.1
Total	2	13	22	2	6	0	0	0	1	2	0	.273	.333	.273	78	-1	0			.500	-1	/P-3,O-2,S-1,2-1	-0.1

■ CECIL COOPER
Cooper, Cecil Celester b: 12/20/49, Brenham, Tex. BL/TL, 6'2", 190 lbs. Deb: 9/8/71

YEAR	TM/L	G	AB	R	H	2B	3B	HR	RBI	BB	SO	AVG	OBP	SLG	PRO+	BR/A	SB	CS	SBR	FA	FR	G/POS	TPR
1971	Bos-A	14	42	9	13	4	1	0	3	5	4	.310	.396	.452	130	2	1	0	0	.988	-2	1-11	-0.1
1972	Bos-A	12	17	0	4	1	0	0	2	2	5	.235	.316	.294	78	-0	0	0	0	1.000	-1	/1-3	-0.1
1973	Bos-A	30	101	12	24	2	0	3	11	7	12	.238	.287	.347	73	-4	1	2	-1	.984	-0	1-29	-0.7
1974	Bos-A	121	414	55	114	24	1	8	43	32	74	.275	.329	.396	101	-0	2	5	-2	.983	-1	1-74,D-41	-1.0
1975	*Bos-A	106	305	49	95	17	6	14	44	19	33	.311	.358	.544	140	14	1	4	-2	.995	2	D-54,1-35	1.2
1976	Bos-A	123	451	66	127	22	6	15	78	16	62	.282	.308	.457	109	2	7	1	2	.994	-1	1-66,D-53	-0.3
1977	Mil-A	160	643	86	193	31	7	20	78	28	110	.300	.329	.463	113	10	13	8	-1	.992	5	*1-148,D-10	0.5
1978	Mil-A	107	407	60	127	23	4	13	54	32	72	.312	.362	.474	133	17	3	4	-2	.988	1	1-84,D-19	1.2
1979	Mil-A★	150	590	83	182	44	1	24	106	56	77	.308	.368	.508	134	27	15	3	3	.993	-8	*1-135,D-15	1.2
1980	Mil-A★	153	622	96	219	33	4	25	122	39	42	.352	.392	.539	157	47	17	6	2	.997	4	*1-142,D-11	4.3
1981	*Mil-A	106	416	70	133	35	1	12	60	28	30	.320	.367	.495	154	27	5	4	-1	.992	-0	*1-101/D-5	2.1
1982	*Mil-A★	155	654	104	205	38	3	32	121	32	53	.313	.345	.528	145	36	2	3	-1	.997	-1	*1-154/D-1	2.5
1983	Mil-A★	160	661	106	203	37	3	30	126	37	63	.307	.345	.508	142	34	2	1	0	.993	-10	*1-158/D-2	1.5
1984	Mil-A	148	603	63	166	28	3	11	67	27	59	.275	.309	.386	95	-6	8	2	1	.991	3	*1-122,D-26	-1.0
1985	Mil-A	154	631	82	185	39	8	16	99	30	77	.293	.327	.456	112	9	10	3	1	.986	-2	*1-123,D-30	0.0
1986	Mil-A	134	542	46	140	24	1	12	75	41	87	.258	.312	.373	83	-13	1	2	-1	.988	-4	1-90,D-44	-2.6
1987	Mil-A	63	250	25	62	13	0	6	36	17	51	.248	.296	.372	74	-10	0	0	0	.000	0	D-62	-1.1
Total	17	1896	7349	1012	2192	415	47	241	1125	448	911	.298	.340	.466	121	193	89	49	-3	.992	-13	*1-1475,D-373	7.6

■ CLAUDE COOPER
Cooper, Claude William b: 4/1/1892, Troup, Tex. d: 1/21/74, Plainview, Tex. BL/TL, 5'9", 158 lbs. Deb: 4/14/13

YEAR	TM/L	G	AB	R	H	2B	3B	HR	RBI	BB	SO	AVG	OBP	SLG	PRO+	BR/A	SB	CS	SBR	FA	FR	G/POS	TPR
1913	*NY-N	27	30	11	9	4	0	0	4	4	6	.300	.382	.433	132	1	3			.895	-5	O-15	-0.4
1914	Bro-F	113	399	56	96	14	11	0	25	26	60	.241	.294	.346	74	-22	25			.926	-1	*O-101	-2.9
1915	Bro-F	153	527	75	155	26	12	2	63	77	78	.294	.388	.400	123	11	31			.958	18	*O-121,1-32	2.4
1916	Phi-N	56	104	9	20	2	0	0	11	7	15	.192	.250	.212	41	-7	1			.945	-3	O-29/1-1	-1.3
1917	Phi-N	24	29	5	3	1	0	0	1	5	4	.103	.235	.138	15	-3	0			.923	-4	O-12	-0.9
Total	5	373	1089	156	283	47	23	4	104	119	163	.260	.338	.356	95	-19	60			.943	5	O-278/1-33	-3.1

■ GARY COOPER
Cooper, Gary Clifton b: 8/13/64, Lynwood, Cal. BR/TR, 6'1", 200 lbs. Deb: 9/15/91

YEAR	TM/L	G	AB	R	H	2B	3B	HR	RBI	BB	SO	AVG	OBP	SLG	PRO+	BR/A	SB	CS	SBR	FA	FR	G/POS	TPR
1991	Hou-N	9	16	1	4	1	0	0	2	3	6	.250	.368	.313	99	0	0	0	0	.833	-2	/3-4	-0.2

■ GARY COOPER
Cooper, Gary Nathaniel b: 12/22/56, Savannah, Ga. BB/TR, 6'3", 175 lbs. Deb: 8/25/80

YEAR	TM/L	G	AB	R	H	2B	3B	HR	RBI	BB	SO	AVG	OBP	SLG	PRO+	BR/A	SB	CS	SBR	FA	FR	G/POS	TPR
1980	Atl-N	21	2	3	0	0	0	0	0	0	1	.000	.000	.000	-97	-1	2	1	0	1.000	-4	O-13	-0.4

■ PAT COOPER
Cooper, Orge Patterson b: 11/26/17, Albemarle, N.C. d: 3/15/93, Charlotte, N.C. BR/TR, 6'3", 180 lbs. Deb: 5/11/46

YEAR	TM/L	G	AB	R	H	2B	3B	HR	RBI	BB	SO	AVG	OBP	SLG	PRO+	BR/A	SB	CS	SBR	FA	FR	G/POS	TPR
1946	Phi-A	1	0	0	0	0	0	0	0	0	0	—	—	—	—	—	0	0	0	.000	-0	/P-1	0.0
1947	Phi-A	13	16	0	4	2	0	0	3	0	5	.250	.250	.375	71	-1	0	0	0	1.000	-0	/1-1	-0.1
Total	2	14	16	0	4	2	0	0	3	0	5	.250	.250	.375	71	-1	0	0	0	1.000	-0	/1-1,P-1	-0.1

■ SCOTT COOPER
Cooper, Scott Kendrick b: 10/13/67, St.Louis, Mo. BL/TR, 6'3", 200 lbs. Deb: 9/5/90

YEAR	TM/L	G	AB	R	H	2B	3B	HR	RBI	BB	SO	AVG	OBP	SLG	PRO+	BR/A	SB	CS	SBR	FA	FR	G/POS	TPR
1990	Bos-A	2	1	0	0	0	0	0	0	0	1	.000	.000	.000	-96	-0	0	0	0	.000	0	/H	0.0
1991	Bos-A	14	35	6	16	4	2	0	7	2	2	.457	.486	.686	210	5	0	0	0	.933	2	3-13	0.7
1992	Bos-A	123	337	34	93	21	0	5	33	37	33	.276	.348	.383	98	-1	1	1	-0	.990	8	1-62,3-47/2-1,SD	0.4
1993	Bos-A★	156	526	67	147	29	3	9	63	58	81	.279	.357	.397	96	-2	5	2	0	.937	-17	*3-154/1-2,S-1	-1.8
1994	Bos-A★	104	369	49	104	16	4	13	53	30	65	.282	.338	.453	97	-2	0	3	-2	.944	8	*3-104	0.3
1995	StL-N	118	374	29	86	18	2	3	40	49	85	.230	.320	.313	69	-16	0	3	-2	.945	9	3-110	-0.8
Total	6	517	1642	185	446	88	11	30	196	176	267	.272	.345	.393	93	-16	6	9	-4	.945	10	3-428/1-64,D-2,S2	-1.2

■ WALKER COOPER
Cooper, William Walker "Walk" b: 1/8/15, Atherton, Mo. d: 4/11/91, Scottsdale, Ariz. BR/TR, 6'3", 210 lbs. Deb: 9/25/40 FC

YEAR	TM/L	G	AB	R	H	2B	3B	HR	RBI	BB	SO	AVG	OBP	SLG	PRO+	BR/A	SB	CS	SBR	FA	FR	G/POS	TPR
1940	StL-N	6	19	3	6	1	0	0	2	2	2	.316	.381	.368	102	0	1			1.000	-0	/C-6	0.0
1941	StL-N	68	200	19	49	9	1	1	20	13	14	.245	.291	.315	66	-9	1			.966	4	C-63	-0.1
1942	*StL-N★	125	438	58	123	32	7	7	65	29	29	.281	.327	.434	113	5	4			.972	3	*C-115	1.8
1943	*StL-N★	122	449	52	143	30	4	9	81	19	19	.318	.349	.463	128	14	1			.975	-3	*C-112	2.0
1944	*StL-N★	112	397	56	126	25	5	13	72	20	19	.317	.352	.504	136	17	4			.980	4	C-97	2.7
1945	StL-N	4	18	3	7	0	0	0	1	0	1	.389	.389	.389	114	0	0			.966	1	/C-4	0.2
1946	NY-N★	87	280	29	75	10	1	8	46	17	12	.268	.310	.396	99	-2	0			.972	-12	C-73	-1.0
1947	NY-N★	140	515	79	157	24	8	35	122	24	43	.305	.339	.586	141	25	2			.979	-9	*C-132	2.4
1948	NY-N★	91	290	40	77	12	0	16	54	28	29	.266	.332	.472	115	5	1			.979	-13	C-79	-0.2
1949	NY-N	42	147	14	31	4	2	4	21	7	8	.211	.261	.347	62	-8	0			.982	-0	C-40	-0.8
	Cin-N☆	82	307	34	86	9	2	16	62	21	24	.280	.330	.479	113	4	0			.978	-3	C-77	0.6
	Yr	124	454	48	117	13	4	20	83	28	32	.258	.308	.436	97	-4	0			.979	-5	*C-117	-0.2
1950	Cin-N	15	47	3	9	3	0	0	4	0	5	.191	.191	.255	16	-6	0			.972	1	C-13	-0.4
	Bos-N☆	102	337	52	111	19	3	14	60	30	26	.329	.389	.528	148	23	1			.973	-5	C-88	2.1
	Yr	117	384	55	120	22	3	14	64	30	31	.313	.367	.495	132	16	1			.973	-4	*C-101	1.7
1951	Bos-N	109	342	42	107	14	1	18	59	28	18	.313	.367	.518	145	20	1	1	-0	.981	-2	C-90	2.2
1952	Bos-N	102	349	33	82	12	1	10	55	22	32	.235	.282	.361	80	-11	1	0	0	.983	-4	C-89	-1.0
1953	Mil-N	53	137	12	30	6	0	3	16	12	15	.219	.287	.328	64	-8	1	0	0	.983	-5	C-35	-1.0
1954	Pit-N	14	15	0	3	2	0	0	1	2	1	.200	.294	.333	64	-1	0	0	0	1.000	-0	/C-2	-0.1
	Chi-N	57	158	21	49	10	2	7	32	21	23	.310	.398	.532	138	9	0	0	0	.978	-2	C-48	0.9
	Yr	71	173	21	52	12	2	7	33	23	24	.301	.389	.514	132	8	0	0	0	.978	-2	C-50	0.8
1955	Chi-N	54	111	11	31	8	1	7	15	6	19	.279	.322	.559	128	4	0	0	0	.961	-11	C-31	-0.6
1956	StL-N	40	68	5	18	5	1	2	14	3	8	.265	.296	.456	98	-0	0			.984	-3	C-16	-0.3
1957	StL-N	48	78	3	24	5	1	3	12	6	13	.308	.357	.513	126	2	0			.957	-2	C-13	-0.1
Total	18	1473	4702	573	1341	240	40	173	812	309	357	.285	.332	.464	116	82	18	1		.977	-63	*C-1223	9.3

■ JOEY CORA
Cora, Jose Manuel (Amaro) b: 5/14/65, Caguas, P.R. BB/TR, 5'8", 150 lbs. Deb: 4/6/87

YEAR	TM/L	G	AB	R	H	2B	3B	HR	RBI	BB	SO	AVG	OBP	SLG	PRO+	BR/A	SB	CS	SBR	FA	FR	G/POS	TPR
1987	SD-N	77	241	23	57	7	2	0	13	28	26	.237	.319	.282	63	-12	15	11	-2	.975	-2	2-66/S-6	-1.3
1989	SD-N	12	19	5	6	1	0	0	1	1	0	.316	.350	.368	105	0	1	0	0	.960	2	/S-7,3-2,2-1	0.3

YEAR	TM/L	G	AB	R	H	2B	3B	HR	RBI	BB	SO	AVG	OBP	SLG	PRO+	BR/A	SB	CS	SBR	FA	FR	G/POS	TPR
1990	SD-N	51	100	12	27	3	0	0	2	6	9	.270	.311	.300	68	-4	8	3	1	.833	-3	S-21,2-15/C-1	-0.6
1991	Chi-A	100	228	37	55	2	3	0	18	20	21	.241	.316	.276	67	-10	11	6	0	.970	-9	2-80/S-5,D-2	-1.8
1992	Chi-A	68	122	27	30	7	1	0	9	22	13	.246	.378	.320	99	1	10	3	1	.984	5	2-28,D-18/S-6,3-5	0.7
1993	*Chi-A	153	579	95	155	15	13	2	51	67	63	.268	.353	.349	91	-5	20	8	1	.974	-16	*2-151/3-3	-1.5
1994	Chi-A	90	312	55	86	13	4	2	30	38	32	.276	.358	.362	88	-4	8	4	0	.978	-13	2-84/D-1	-1.3
1995	*Sea-A	120	427	64	127	19	2	3	39	37	31	.297	.362	.372	91	-5	18	7	1	.955	-27	*2-112/S-1,D-1	-2.2
1996	Sea-A	144	530	90	154	37	6	6	45	35	32	.291	.340	.417	91	-7	5	5	-2	.979	-20	2-140/3-1	-1.9
Total	9	815	2558	408	697	104	31	13	208	254	227	.272	.346	.353	86	-46	96	47	1	.972	-84	2-677/S-46,D-22,3C	-9.6

■ GENE CORBETT
Corbett, Eugene Louis b: 10/25/13, Winona, Minn. BL/TR, 6'1.5", 190 lbs. Deb: 9/19/36

YEAR	TM/L	G	AB	R	H	2B	3B	HR	RBI	BB	SO	AVG	OBP	SLG	PRO+	BR/A	SB	CS	SBR	FA	FR	G/POS	TPR
1936	Phi-N	6	21	1	3	0	0	0	2	2	3	.143	.217	.143	-1	-3	0			1.000	-1	/1-6	-0.4
1937	Phi-N	7	12	4	4	2	0	0	1	0	0	.333	.333	.500	114	0	0			.800	-1	/3-3,2-1	-0.1
1938	Phi-N	24	75	7	6	1	0	2	7	6	11	.080	.148	.173	-12	-12	0			.995	-1	1-22	-1.5
Total	3	37	108	12	13	3	0	2	10	8	14	.120	.181	.204	5	-15	0			.996	-2	/1-28,3-3,2-1	-2.0

■ CLAUDE CORBITT
Corbitt, Claude Elliott b: 7/21/15, Sunbury, N.C. d: 5/1/78, Cincinnati, Ohio BR/TR, 5'10", 170 lbs. Deb: 9/23/45

YEAR	TM/L	G	AB	R	H	2B	3B	HR	RBI	BB	SO	AVG	OBP	SLG	PRO+	BR/A	SB	CS	SBR	FA	FR	G/POS	TPR
1945	Bro-N	2	4	1	2	0	0	0	0	1	0	.500	.600	.500	209	1				1.000	0	/3-2	0.1
1946	Cin-N	82	274	25	68	10	1	1	16	23	13	.248	.309	.303	77	-9	3			.947	-13	S-77	-1.9
1948	Cin-N	87	258	24	66	11	0	0	18	14	16	.256	.297	.298	64	-13	4			.973	-8	2-52,3-16,S-11	-1.8
1949	Cin-N	44	94	10	17	1	0	0	3	9	1	.181	.252	.191	20	-10	1			.984	-6	S-18,2-17/3-1	-1.5
Total	4	215	630	60	153	22	1	1	37	47	30	.243	.297	.286	63	-31	8			.956	-26	S-106/2-69,3-19	-5.1

■ ART CORCORAN
Corcoran, Arthur Andrew "Bunny" b: 11/23/1894, Roxbury, Mass. d: 7/27/58, Chelsea, Mass. TR, Deb: 9/9/15

YEAR	TM/L	G	AB	R	H	2B	3B	HR	RBI	BB	SO	AVG	OBP	SLG	PRO+	BR/A	SB	CS	SBR	FA	FR	G/POS	TPR
1915	Phi-A	1	4	0	0	0	0	0	0	0	2	.000	.000	.000	-99	-1	0			1.000	-1	/3-1	-0.1

■ JOHN CORCORAN
Corcoran, John A. b: 1873, Cincinnati, Ohio d: 11/2/01, Cincinnati, Ohio TL, Deb: 9/17/1895

YEAR	TM/L	G	AB	R	H	2B	3B	HR	RBI	BB	SO	AVG	OBP	SLG	PRO+	BR/A	SB	CS	SBR	FA	FR	G/POS	TPR
1895	Pit-N	6	20	0	3	0	0	0	1	0	2	.150	.150	.150	-24	-4	0			.895	-1	/S-4,3-2	-0.4

■ JACK CORCORAN
Corcoran, John H. b: 1860, Lowell, Mass. Deb: 5/1/1884

YEAR	TM/L	G	AB	R	H	2B	3B	HR	RBI	BB	SO	AVG	OBP	SLG	PRO+	BR/A	SB	CS	SBR	FA	FR	G/POS	TPR
1884	Bro-a	52	185	17	39	4	3	0		8		.211	.251	.265	68	-6				.873	-9	C-38/O-9,2-4,S-2,P	-1.1

■ LARRY CORCORAN
Corcoran, Lawrence J. b: 8/10/1859, Brooklyn, N.Y. d: 10/14/1891, Newark, N.J. BL/TR, 120 lbs. Deb: 5/1/1880 F

YEAR	TM/L	G	AB	R	H	2B	3B	HR	RBI	BB	SO	AVG	OBP	SLG	PRO+	BR/A	SB	CS	SBR	FA	FR	G/POS	TPR
1880	Chi-N	72	286	41	66	11	1	0	25	10	33	.231	.257	.276	76	-7				.957	3	*P-63/O-8,S-8	-0.3
1881	Chi-N	47	189	25	42	8	0	0	9	5	22	.222	.242	.265	57	-9				.893	-1	P-45/S-2,O-1	0.0
1882	Chi-N	40	169	23	35	10	2	1	24	6	18	.207	.234	.308	69	-6				.919	1	P-39/3-1	0.0
1883	Chi-N	68	263	40	55	12	7	0	25	6	62	.209	.227	.308	57	-14				.906	-3	P-56,O-13/S-3,2-1	-0.6
1884	Chi-N	64	251	43	61	3	4	1	19	10	33	.243	.272	.299	73	-9				.882	7	P-60/O-4,S-2	-0.1
1885	Chi-N	7	22	6	6	1	0	0	4	6	1	.273	.429	.318	126	1				.905	0	/P-7,S-1	0.0
	NY-N	3	14	3	5	0	0	0	2	0	1	.357	.357	.357	133	0				1.000	1	/P-3	0.0
	Yr	10	36	9	11	1	0	0	6	6	2	.306	.405	.333	128	1				.935	1	P-10/S-1	0.0
1886	NY-N	1	4	0	0	0	0	0	0	0	0	.000	.000	.000	-99	-1	0			.000	-1	/O-1	-0.2
	Was-N	21	81	9	15	2	1	0	3	7	14	.185	.250	.235	51	-4	3			.619	-3	O-11/S-9,P-2	-0.6
	Yr	22	85	9	15	2	1	0	3	7	16	.176	.239	.224	44	-5	3			.591	-3	O-12/S-9,P-2	-0.8
1887	Ind-N	3	10	2	2	0	0	0	0	2	1	.200	.333	.200	53	-1	2			1.000	1	/O-2,P-2	0.0
Total	8	326	1289	192	287	47	15	2	111	52	187	.223	.253	.287	67	-50	5			.910	3	P-277/O-40,S-25,23	-1.8

■ MICKEY CORCORAN
Corcoran, Michael Joseph b: 8/26/1882, Buffalo, N.Y. d: 12/9/50, Buffalo, N.Y. BR/TR, 5'8", 165 lbs. Deb: 9/15/10

YEAR	TM/L	G	AB	R	H	2B	3B	HR	RBI	BB	SO	AVG	OBP	SLG	PRO+	BR/A	SB	CS	SBR	FA	FR	G/POS	TPR
1910	Cin-N	14	46	3	10	3	0	0	7	5	9	.217	.308	.283	76	-1	0			.911	-1	2-14	-0.2

■ TOMMY CORCORAN
Corcoran, Thomas William "Corky" b: 1/4/1869, New Haven, Conn. d: 6/25/60, Plainfield, Conn. BR/TR, 5'9", 164 lbs. Deb: 4/19/1890 U

YEAR	TM/L	G	AB	R	H	2B	3B	HR	RBI	BB	SO	AVG	OBP	SLG	PRO+	BR/A	SB	CS	SBR	FA	FR	G/POS	TPR
1890	Pit-P	123	503	80	117	14	13	1	61	36	45	.233	.289	.318	68	-24	43			.884	4	*S-123	-1.0
1891	Phi-a	133	511	84	130	11	15	7	71	29	56	.254	.307	.376	93	-8	30			**.911**	12	*S-133	1.0
1892	Bro-N	151	613	77	145	11	6	1	74	34	51	.237	.281	.279	72	-21	39			**.925**	-2	*S-151	-1.5
1893	Bro-N	115	459	61	126	11	10	2	58	27	12	.275	.318	.355	82	-13	14			.907	14	*S-115	0.5
1894	Bro-N	129	576	123	173	21	20	5	92	25	17	.300	.329	.432	89	-13	33			.904	-4	*S-129	-0.8
1895	Bro-N	127	535	81	142	17	10	2	69	23	11	.265	.299	.346	72	-23	17			.924	18	*S-127	-0.8
1896	Bro-N	132	532	63	154	15	7	3	73	15	13	.289	.310	.361	81	-16	16			.926	24	*S-132	1.0
1897	Cin-N	109	445	76	128	30	5	3	57	13		.288	.311	.398	81	-15	15			.913	6	S-63,2-47	-0.4
1898	Cin-N	153	619	80	155	28	15	2	87	26		.250	.283	.354	77	-22	19			.932	14	*S-153	-0.1
1899	Cin-N	137	537	91	149	11	8	0	81	28		.278	.316	.328	75	-19	32			.931	4	*S-123,2-14	-0.4
1900	Cin-N	127	523	64	128	21	9	1	54	22		.245	.278	.325	68	-24	27			.921	5	*S-124/2-5	-1.8
1901	Cin-N	31	115	14	24	3	0	0	15	11		.209	.278	.287	68	-5	6			.919	4	S-30	0.2
1902	Cin-N	138	538	54	136	18	4	0	54	11		.253	.268	.301	69	-21	20			.926	-13	*S-137/2-1	-2.8
1903	Cin-N	115	459	61	113	18	7	2	73	12		.246	.267	.329	63	-25	12			.943	6	*S-115	-1.3
1904	Cin-N	150	578	55	133	17	9	2	74	19		.230	.257	.301	66	-25	19			**.936**	2	*S-150	-2.0
1905	Cin-N	151	605	70	150	21	11	2	85	23		.248	.277	.329	72	-23	28			**.952**	20	*S-151	0.0
1906	Cin-N	117	430	29	89	13	1	1	33	19		.207	.242	.249	51	-25	9			.941	-9	*S-117	-1.6
1907	NY-N	62	226	21	60	9	2	0	24	7		.265	.288	.323	88	-4	9			.939	-5	2-62	-1.1
Total	18	2200	8804	1184	2252	289	155	34	1135	382	205	.256	.289	.335	74	-327	387			.924	106	*S-2073,2-129	-12.1

■ TIM CORCORAN
Corcoran, Timothy Michael b: 3/19/53, Glendale, Cal. BL/TL, 5'11", 175 lbs. Deb: 5/18/77

YEAR	TM/L	G	AB	R	H	2B	3B	HR	RBI	BB	SO	AVG	OBP	SLG	PRO+	BR/A	SB	CS	SBR	FA	FR	G/POS	TPR
1977	Det-A	55	103	13	29	3	0	3	15	6	9	.282	.321	.398	90	-2	0	1	-1	1.000	-0	O-18/D-3	-0.3
1978	Det-A	116	324	37	86	13	1	1	27	24	27	.265	.326	.321	80	-8	3	2	-0	.985	-6	*O-109/D-1	-1.9
1979	Det-A	18	22	4	5	1	0	0	6	4	2	.227	.346	.273	67	-1	1	1	-0	1.000	-1	/O-9,1-5,D-2	-0.2
1980	Det-A	84	153	20	44	7	1	3	18	22	10	.288	.381	.405	113	3	0	2	-1	.985	-2	1-48,O-18/D-5	-0.4
1981	Min-A	22	51	4	9	3	0	0	4	6	7	.176	.263	.235	42	-4	0	0	0	1.000	-1	1-16/D-3	-0.4
1983	Phi-N	3	0	0	0	0	0	0	0	0	0	—	—	—	—	0	0	0		1.000	0	/1-3	0.0
1984	Phi-N	102	208	30	71	13	1	5	36	37	27	.341	.443	.486	158	18	0	1	-1	.997	-4	1-51,O-17	1.1
1985	Phi-N	103	182	11	39	6	1	0	22	29	20	.214	.322	.258	63	-8	0	0	0	.993	-3	1-59/O-3	-1.3
1986	NY-N	6	7	1	0	0	0	0	0	2	0	.000	.222	.000	-34	-1	0	0	0	1.000	0	/1-1	-0.1
Total	9	509	1050	120	283	46	4	12	128	130	102	.270	.354	.355	96	-2	4	7	-3	.993	-15	1-183,O-174/D-14	-3.3

■ WIL CORDERO
Cordero, Wilfredo (Nieva) b: 10/3/71, Mayaguez, P.R. BR/TR, 6'2", 185 lbs. Deb: 7/24/92

YEAR	TM/L	G	AB	R	H	2B	3B	HR	RBI	BB	SO	AVG	OBP	SLG	PRO+	BR/A	SB	CS	SBR	FA	FR	G/POS	TPR
1992	Mon-N	45	126	17	38	4	1	2	8	9	31	.302	.353	.397	113	2	0	0	0	.949	-2	S-35/2-9	-0.2
1993	Mon-N	138	475	56	118	32	2	10	58	34	60	.248	.308	.387	81	-13	12	3	2	.941	-16	*S-134/3-2	-1.7
1994	Mon-N★	110	415	65	122	30	3	15	63	41	62	.294	.366	.489	119	12	16	3	3	.952	-9	*S-109	1.5
1995	Mon-N	131	514	64	147	35	2	10	49	36	88	.286	.343	.420	97	-2	9	5	-0	.960	-22	*S-105,O-26	-1.5
1996	Bos-A	59	198	29	57	14	0	3	37	11	31	.288	.332	.404	82	-6	2	1	0	.949	-5	2-37,D-13/1-1	-0.1
Total	5	483	1728	231	482	115	8	40	215	131	272	.279	.339	.424	97	-7	39	12	5	.950	-49	S-383/2-46,O,D31	-2.0

■ MARTY CORDOVA
Cordova, Martin Keevin b: 7/10/69, Las Vegas, Nev. BR/TR, 6', 200 lbs. Deb: 4/26/95

YEAR	TM/L	G	AB	R	H	2B	3B	HR	RBI	BB	SO	AVG	OBP	SLG	PRO+	BR/A	SB	CS	SBR	FA	FR	G/POS	TPR
1995	Min-A	137	512	81	142	27	4	24	84	52	111	.277	.355	.486	116	11	20	7	2	.986	9	*O-137	2.6
1996	Min-A	145	569	97	176	46	1	16	111	53	96	.309	.376	.478	112	11	11	5	0	.991	13	*O-145	1.8
Total	2	282	1081	178	318	73	5	40	195	105	207	.294	.366	.482	114	22	31	12	2	.989	32	O-282	4.4

■ FRED COREY
Corey, Frederick Harrison b: 1857, S.Kingston, R.I. d: 11/27/12, Providence, R.I. BR/TR, Deb: 5/1/1878

YEAR	TM/L	G	AB	R	H	2B	3B	HR	RBI	BB	SO	AVG	OBP	SLG	PRO+	BR/A	SB	CS	SBR	FA	FR	G/POS	TPR
1878	Pro-N	7	21	3	3	0	0	0	1	0		.143	.143	.143	-6	-2				1.000	-0	/P-5,2-2,1-1	-0.1
1880	Wor-N	41	138	11	24	8	1	0	6	4	27	.174	.197	.246	45	-8				.759	-11	O-29,P-25/S-3,31	-0.6
1881	Wor-N	51	203	22	45	8	4	0	10	5	10	.222	.240	.300	65	-8				.827	2	O-25,P-23/S-7	-0.2
1882	Wor-N	64	255	33	63	7	12	0	29	5	31	.247	.262	.369	47	-9				.847	-13	S-26,P-21,O-15/31	-1.2
1883	Phi-a	71	298	45	77	11	8	1	40	12		.258	.287	.336	92	-4						3-34,P-18,O/2SC	-0.6
1884	Phi-a	104	439	64	121	17	16	5			17	.276	.306	.421	127	11				**.887**	13	*3-104	2.2

YEAR	TM/L	G	AB	R	H	2B	3B	HR	RBI	BB	SO	AVG	OBP	SLG	PRO+	BR/A	SB	CS	SBR	FA	FR	G/POS	TPR
1885	Phi-a	94	384	61	94	14	8	1	38	17		.245	.282	.331	88	-7				.872	8	*3-92/S-1,P-1	0.2
Total	7	432	1738	239	427	70	43	7	124	60	70	.246	.273	.348	93	-20				.863	-4	3-237/P-93,OS21C	-1.0

■ MARK COREY
Corey, Mark Mundell   b: 11/3/55, Tucumcari, N.Mex.   BR/TR, 6'2", 200 lbs.   Deb: 9/1/79

YEAR	TM/L	G	AB	R	H	2B	3B	HR	RBI	BB	SO	AVG	OBP	SLG	PRO+	BR/A	SB	CS	SBR	FA	FR	G/POS	TPR
1979	Bal-A	13	13	1	2	0	0	0	0	1	4	.154	.154	.154	-17	-2	1	0	0	1.000	-3	O-11/D-1	-0.5
1980	Bal-A	36	36	7	10	2	0	1	2	5	7	.278	.366	.417	115	1	0	1	-1	1.000	-10	O-34	-1.0
1981	Bal-A	10	8	2	0	0	0	0	0	2	2	.000	.000	.000	-38	-1	0	0	0	1.000	-2	/O-9	-0.4
Total	3	59	57	10	12	2	0	1	3	7	13	.211	.297	.298	65	-3	1	1	0	1.000	-15	/O-54,D-1	-1.9

■ CHUCK CORGAN
Corgan, Charles Howard   b: 12/4/02, Wagoner, Okla.   d: 6/13/28, Wagoner, Okla.   BB/TR, 5'11", 180 lbs.   Deb: 9/19/25

YEAR	TM/L	G	AB	R	H	2B	3B	HR	RBI	BB	SO	AVG	OBP	SLG	PRO+	BR/A	SB	CS	SBR	FA	FR	G/POS	TPR
1925	Bro-N	14	47	4	8	1	0	0	3		9	.170	.220	.234	16	-6	0	0	0	.908	4	S-14	-0.1
1927	Bro-N	19	57	3	15	1	0	0	1	4	4	.263	.311	.281	59	-3	0			.969	-1	2-13/S-3	-0.3
Total	2	33	104	7	23	2	1	0	1	7	13	.221	.270	.260	40	-9	0			.900	3	/S-17,2-13	-0.4

■ ROY CORHAN
Corhan, Roy George "Irish"   b: 10/21/1887, Indianapolis, Ind.   d: 11/24/58, San Francisco, Cal   BR/TR, 5'9.5", 165 lbs.   Deb: 4/20/11

YEAR	TM/L	G	AB	R	H	2B	3B	HR	RBI	BB	SO	AVG	OBP	SLG	PRO+	BR/A	SB	CS	SBR	FA	FR	G/POS	TPR
1911	Chi-A	43	131	14	28	6	2	0	8	15		.214	.304	.290	68	-5	2			.924	11	S-43	0.8
1916	StL-N	92	295	30	62	6	3	0	18	20	31	.210	.265	.251	59	-14	15			.917	1	S-84	-0.9
Total	2	135	426	44	90	12	5	0	26	35	31	.211	.277	.263	62	-19	17			.920	12	S-127	-0.1

■ POP CORKHILL
Corkhill, John Stewart   b: 4/11/1858, Parkesburg, Pa.   d: 4/4/21, Pennsauken, N.J.   BL/TR, 5'10", 180 lbs.   Deb: 5/1/1883

YEAR	TM/L	G	AB	R	H	2B	3B	HR	RBI	BB	SO	AVG	OBP	SLG	PRO+	BR/A	SB	CS	SBR	FA	FR	G/POS	TPR
1883	Cin-a	88	375	53	81	10	8	2	46	3		.216	.222	.301	63	-16				.930	1	*O-85/S-2,2-2,1-2	-1.4
1884	Cin-a	110	452	85	124	13	11	4	70	4		.274	.290	.378	111	4				.934	10	*O-92,S-11/1-6,3P	1.0
1885	Cin-a	112	440	64	111	10	8	1	53	7		.252	.275	.318	85	-8				.938	17	*O-110/P-8,1-3	0.5
1886	Cin-a	129	540	81	143	9	7	5	97	23		.265	.302	.335	96	-4	24			.919	-0	*O-112,3-12/1-7,SP	0.2
1887	Cin-a	128	541	79	168	19	11	5	97	14		.311	.333	.414	105	1	30			.952	15	*O-128/P-5	1.1
1888	Cin-a	118	490	68	133	11	9	1	74	15		.271	.299	.337	98	-3	27			.958	7	*O-116/P-2,1-1,2-1	0.0
	Bro-a	19	71	17	27	4	3	1	19	4		.380	.429	.563	217	9	3			.980	2	O-19	0.9
	Yr	137	561	85	160	15	12	2	93	19		.285	.316	.365	113	5	30			.961	8	*O-135/P-2,1-1,2-1	0.9
1889	*Bro-a	138	537	91	134	21	9	8	78	42	24	.250	.308	.367	91	-8	22			.949	12	*O-138/S-1,1-1	0.1
1890	Bro-N	51	204	23	46	4	2	1	21	15	11	.225	.279	.279	62	-10	6			.977	4	O-48/1-6	-0.7
1891	Phi-a	83	349	50	73	7	7	0	31	26	15	.209	.268	.269	52	-23	12			.956	7	O-83	-1.7
	Cin-N	1	4	0	0	0	0	0	0	0	1	.000	.000	.000	-99	-1	0			1.000	1	/O-1	0.0
	Pit-N	41	145	16	33	1	1	3	20	7	10	.228	.268	.310	70	-6	7			.935	2	O-41	-0.5
	Yr	42	149	16	33	1	1	3	20	7	11	.221	.261	.302	65	-7	7			.939	3	O-42	-0.5
1892	Pit-N	68	256	23	47	1	4	0	25	12	19	.184	.229	.219	35	-20	6			.953	7	O-68	-1.5
Total	10	1086	4404	650	1120	110	80	31	631	174	80	.254	.288	.337	87	-86	137			.947	83	*O-1041/1-26,PS32	-2.8

■ PAT CORRALES
Corrales, Patrick   b: 3/20/41, Los Angeles, Cal.   BR/TR, 6', 195 lbs.   Deb: 8/2/64   MC

YEAR	TM/L	G	AB	R	H	2B	3B	HR	RBI	BB	SO	AVG	OBP	SLG	PRO+	BR/A	SB	CS	SBR	FA	FR	G/POS	TPR
1964	Phi-N	2	1	1	0	0	0	0	0	0	0	.000	.500	.000	55	0	0	0	0	.000	0	H	0.0
1965	Phi-N	63	174	16	39	8	1	2	15	25	42	.224	.325	.316	83	-3	0	0	0	.982	-3	C-62	-0.4
1966	StL-N	28	72	5	13	2	0	0	3	2	17	.181	.224	.208	21	-8	1	0	0	.975	9	C-27	0.3
1968	Cin-N	20	56	3	15	4	0	0	6	6	16	.268	.349	.339	101	0	0	0	0	.991	0	C-20	0.2
1969	Cin-N	29	72	10	19	5	0	1	5	8	17	.264	.346	.375	97	-0	0	1	-1	.986	3	C-29	0.4
1970	*Cin-N	43	106	9	25	5	1	1	10	8	22	.236	.289	.330	65	-5	0	0	0	.983	4	C-42	0.0
1971	Cin-N	40	94	6	17	2	0	0	6	6	17	.181	.230	.202	24	-9	0	0	0	.980	-1	C-39	-0.8
1972	Cin-N	2	1	0	0	0	0	0	0	2	0	.000	.667	.000	110	0	0	0	0	1.000	0	/C-2	0.2
	SD-N	44	119	6	23	0	0	0	6	11	26	.193	.267	.193	35	-10	0	0	0	.993	4	C-43	-0.5
	Yr	46	120	6	23	0	0	0	6	13	26	.192	.276	.192	38	-10	0	0	0	.993	5	C-45	-0.3
1973	SD-N	29	72	7	15	2	1	0	3	6	10	.208	.278	.264	55	-4	0	0	0	.986	-1	C-28	-0.5
Total	9	300	767	63	166	28	4	4	54	75	167	.216	.292	.276	61	-39	1	1	-0	.984	18	C-292	-1.1

■ ROD CORREIA
Correia, Ronald Douglas   b: 9/13/67, Providence, R.I.   BR/TR, 5'11", 180 lbs.   Deb: 6/20/93

YEAR	TM/L	G	AB	R	H	2B	3B	HR	RBI	BB	SO	AVG	OBP	SLG	PRO+	BR/A	SB	CS	SBR	FA	FR	G/POS	TPR
1993	Cal-A	64	128	12	34	5	0	0	9	6	20	.266	.319	.305	66	-6	2	4	-2	.981	18	S-40,2-11/3-3,D-6	1.2
1994	Cal-A	6	17	4	4	1	0	0	0	0	3	.235	.316	.294	58	-1	0	0	0	1.000	-2	/2-5,S-1	-0.2
1995	Cal-A	14	21	3	5	1	1	0	3	0	5	.238	.238	.381	58	-1	0	0	0	.850	3	/S-7,2-3,3-2,D-1	0.2
Total	3	84	166	19	43	7	1	0	12	6	25	.259	.309	.313	65	-8	2	4	-2	.968	19	/S-48,2-19,D-7,3-5	1.2

■ VIC CORRELL
Correll, Victor Crosby   b: 2/5/46, Washington, D.C.   BR/TR, 5'10", 185 lbs.   Deb: 10/4/72

YEAR	TM/L	G	AB	R	H	2B	3B	HR	RBI	BB	SO	AVG	OBP	SLG	PRO+	BR/A	SB	CS	SBR	FA	FR	G/POS	TPR
1972	Bos-A	1	4	1	2	0	0	0	1	0	1	.500	.500	.500	188	0	0	0	0	1.000	1	/C-1	0.1
1974	Atl-N	73	202	20	48	15	1	4	29	21	38	.238	.322	.381	92	-2	0	0	0	.988	6	C-59	0.6
1975	Atl-N	103	325	37	70	12	1	11	39	42	66	.215	.307	.360	82	-8	0	2	-1	.973	-2	C-97	-0.8
1976	Atl-N	69	200	26	45	6	2	5	16	21	37	.225	.302	.350	80	-5	0	1	-1	.981	3	C-65	-0.1
1977	Atl-N	54	144	16	30	7	0	7	16	22	33	.208	.317	.403	82	-4	2	3	-1	.973	4	C-49	-0.2
1978	Cin-N	52	105	9	25	7	0	1	6	8	17	.238	.292	.333	74	-4	0	0	0	.980	1	C-52	-0.3
1979	Cin-N	48	133	14	31	12	0	1	15	14	26	.233	.311	.346	78	-4	0	0	0	.992	7	C-47	0.4
1980	Cin-N	10	19	1	8	1	0	0	3	0	1	.421	.421	.474	149	1	0	0	0	.919	-0	C-10	0.1
Total	8	410	1132	124	259	60	4	29	125	128	220	.229	.312	.366	83	-26	2	8	-4	.979	18	C-380	-0.2

■ PHIL CORRIDAN
Corridan, Philip   Deb: 7/16/1884

YEAR	TM/L	G	AB	R	H	2B	3B	HR	RBI	BB	SO	AVG	OBP	SLG	PRO+	BR/A	SB	CS	SBR	FA	FR	G/POS	TPR
1884	CP-U	2	7	1	1	0	0	0	0	0		.143	.143	.143	-13	-1				.800	-1	/2-2,O-1	-0.2

■ JOHN CORRIDEN
Corriden, John Michael Jr.   b: 10/6/18, Logansport, Ind.   BB/TR, 5'6", 160 lbs.   Deb: 4/20/46   F

YEAR	TM/L	G	AB	R	H	2B	3B	HR	RBI	BB	SO	AVG	OBP	SLG	PRO+	BR/A	SB	CS	SBR	FA	FR	G/POS	TPR
1946	Bro-N	1	0	1	0	0	0	0	0	0		—	—	—	—	—				.000	0	R	0.0

■ RED CORRIDEN
Corriden, John Michael Sr.   b: 9/4/1887, Logansport, Ind.   d: 9/28/59, Indianapolis, Ind   BR/TR, 5'9", 165 lbs.   Deb: 9/8/10   FMC

YEAR	TM/L	G	AB	R	H	2B	3B	HR	RBI	BB	SO	AVG	OBP	SLG	PRO+	BR/A	SB	CS	SBR	FA	FR	G/POS	TPR
1910	StL-A	26	84	19	13	3	0	1	4	13		.155	.297	.226	68	-2	5			.902	4	S-14,3-12	0.3
1912	Det-A	38	138	22	28	6	0	0	5	15		.203	.286	.246	54	-8	4			.929	-4	3-25/2-7,S-3	-1.2
1913	Chi-N	46	97	13	17	3	0	2	9	10	14	.175	.252	.268	48	-7	4			.907	-1	S-37/2-2,3-1	-0.6
1914	Chi-N	107	318	42	73	9	5	3	29	35	33	.230	.323	.318	91	-3	13			.894	-33	S-91/3-8,2-3	-3.1
1915	Chi-N	6	3	1	0	0	0	0	0	2	0	.000	.571	.000	79	1	0			.667	-1	/3-1,O-1	0.0
Total	5	223	640	97	131	21	5	6	47	75	48	.205	.304	.281	74	-19	26			.896	-35	S-145/3-47,2-12,O-1	-4.6

■ JESS CORTAZZO
Cortazzo, John Francis   b: 9/26/04, Wilmerding, Pa.   d: 3/4/63, Pittsburgh, Pa.   BR/TR, 5'3.5", 142 lbs.   Deb: 9/1/23

YEAR	TM/L	G	AB	R	H	2B	3B	HR	RBI	BB	SO	AVG	OBP	SLG	PRO+	BR/A	SB	CS	SBR	FA	FR	G/POS	TPR
1923	Chi-A	1	1	0	0	0	0	0	0	0	0	.000	.000	.000	-99	-0	0			.000	0	H	0.0

■ JOE COSCARART
Coscarart, Joseph Marvin   b: 11/18/09, Escondido, Cal.   d: 4/5/93, Sequim, Wash.   BR/TR, 6', 185 lbs.   Deb: 4/26/35   F

YEAR	TM/L	G	AB	R	H	2B	3B	HR	RBI	BB	SO	AVG	OBP	SLG	PRO+	BR/A	SB	CS	SBR	FA	FR	G/POS	TPR
1935	Bos-N	86	284	30	67	11	2	1	29	16	28	.236	.277	.299	59	-17	2			.962	-4	3-41,S-27,2-15	-1.7
1936	Bos-N	104	367	28	90	11	2	2	44	19	37	.245	.292	.302	64	-19	0			.935	2	3-97/S-6,2-1	-1.3
Total	2	190	651	58	157	22	4	3	73	35	65	.241	.285	.301	62	-35	2			.943	-3	3-138/S-33,2-16	-3.0

■ PETE COSCARART
Coscarart, Peter Joseph   b: 6/16/13, Escondido, Cal.   BR/TR, 5'11.5", 175 lbs.   Deb: 4/26/38   F

YEAR	TM/L	G	AB	R	H	2B	3B	HR	RBI	BB	SO	AVG	OBP	SLG	PRO+	BR/A	SB	CS	SBR	FA	FR	G/POS	TPR
1938	Bro-N	32	79	10	12	3	0	0	6	9	18	.152	.256	.190	24	-8	0			.955	1	2-27	-0.6
1939	Bro-N	115	419	59	116	22	2	4	43	46	43	.277	.354	.368	91	-4	10			.960	-8	*2-107/3-4,S-2	-0.6
1940	Bro-N★	143	506	55	120	24	4	9	58	53	59	.237	.311	.354	78	-15	5			.958	-32	*2-140	-3.8
1941	*Bro-N	43	62	13	8	0	0	0	5	7	12	.129	.217	.145	3	-8	1			.948	5	2-19/S-1	-0.2
1942	Pit-N	133	487	57	111	12	4	3	29	38	56	.228	.288	.287	67	-20	2			.952	-18	*S-108,2-25	-3.3
1943	Pit-N	133	491	57	119	19	6	0	48	46	48	.242	.307	.305	75	-16	4			.961	-6	2-85/S-47,3-1	-1.4
1944	Pit-N	139	554	89	146	30	4	4	42	41	57	.264	.315	.354	85	-12	10			.967	-7	*2-136/S-4,O-1	-1.4
1945	Pit-N	123	392	59	95	17	2	8	38	55	55	.242	.341	.357	91	-4	2			.978	21	*2-122/S-1	2.4
1946	Pit-N	3	2	0	1	1	0	0	0	0	0	.500	.500	1.000	312	1	0			.000	0	/S-1	0.1
Total	9	864	2992	399	728	129	22	28	269	295	361	.243	.314	.329	78	-87	34			.963	-43	2-661,S-164/3-5,O-1	-8.6

YEAR	TM/L	G	AB	R	H	2B	3B	HR	RBI	BB	SO	AVG	OBP	SLG	PRO+	BR/A	SB	CS	SBR	FA	FR	G/POS	TPR

■ RAY COSEY   Cosey, Donald Ray b: 2/15/56, San Rafael, Cal. BL/TL, 5'10", 185 lbs. Deb: 4/14/80

1980	Oak-A	9	9	0	1	0	0	0	0	0	0	.111	.111	.111	-42	-2	0	0	0	.000	0	/H	-0.2

■ DAN COSTELLO   Costello, Daniel Francis "Dashing Dan" b: 9/9/1891, Jessup, Pa. d: 3/26/36, Pittsburgh, Pa. BL/TR, 6'0.5", 185 lbs. Deb: 7/2/13

1913	NY-A	2	2	1	1	0	0	0	0	0	0	.500	.500	.500	192	0	0			.000	0	H	0.0
1914	Pit-N	21	64	7	19	1	0	0	5	8	16	.297	.375	.313	110	1	2			.970	-1	O-20	-0.1
1915	Pit-N	71	125	16	27	4	1	0	11	7	23	.216	.258	.264	59	-6	7	1	2	.893	-5	O-22/1-1	-1.3
1916	Pit-N	60	159	11	38	1	3	0	8	6	23	.239	.267	.283	68	-6	3			.976	-2	O-41	-1.2
Total	4	154	350	35	85	6	4	0	24	21	62	.243	.286	.283	73	-11	12	1		.959	-9	/O-83,1-1	-2.6

■ TIM COSTO   Costo, Timothy Roger b: 2/16/69, Melrose Park, Ill. BR/TR, 6'5", 220 lbs. Deb: 9/18/92

1992	Cin-N	12	36	3	8	2	0	0	2	5	6	.222	.317	.278	68	-1	0	0	0	1.000	0	1-12	-0.2
1993	Cin-N	31	98	13	22	5	0	3	12	4	17	.224	.255	.367	64	-5	0	0	0	.980	0	O-26/1-2,3-2	-0.6
Total	2	43	134	16	30	7	0	3	14	9	23	.224	.273	.343	66	-7	0	0	0	1.000	1	/O-26,1-14,3-2	-0.8

■ HENRY COTE   Cote, Henry Joseph b: 2/19/1864, Troy, N.Y. d: 4/28/40, Troy, N.Y. 5'9.5", 165 lbs. Deb: 9/16/1894

1894	Lou-N	10	31	7	9	2	0	0	3	6		.290	.389	.484	117	-1	2			.918	5	C-10	0.5
1895	Lou-N	10	33	10	10	0	0	0	5	3	3	.303	.361	.303	77	-1	2			.872	-3	C-10	-0.3
Total	2	20	64	17	19	2	2	0	8	8	9	.297	.375	.391	98	-1	0		4	.900	2	/C-20	0.2

■ PETE COTE   Cote, Warren Peter b: 8/30/02, Cambridge, Mass. d: 10/17/87, Middleton, Mass. BR/TR, 5'6", 148 lbs. Deb: 6/18/26

| 1926 | NY-N | 2 | 1 | 0 | 0 | 0 | 0 | 0 | 0 | 0 | 0 | .000 | .000 | .000 | -99 | -0 | 0 | | | .000 | 0 | H | 0.0 |

■ ED COTTER   Cotter, Edward Christopher b: 7/4/04, Hartford, Conn. d: 6/14/59, Hartford, Conn. BR/TR, 6', 185 lbs. Deb: 6/12/26

| 1926 | Phi-N | 17 | 26 | 3 | 8 | 0 | 1 | 0 | 1 | 1 | 4 | .308 | .333 | .385 | 88 | -0 | 1 | | | .833 | 0 | /3-8,S-5 | 0.0 |

■ HOOKS COTTER   Cotter, Harvey Louis b: 5/22/1900, Holden, Mo. d: 8/6/55, Los Angeles, Cal. BL/TL, 5'10", 160 lbs. Deb: 4/15/22

1922	Chi-N	1	1	0	1	1	0	0	0	0	0	1.000	1.000	2.000	644	1	0	0	0	.000	0	H	0.1
1924	Chi-N	98	310	39	81	16	4	4	33	36	31	.261	.338	.377	91	-4	3	5	-2	.989	4	1-90	-0.7
Total	2	99	311	39	82	17	4	4	33	36	31	.264	.340	.383	92	-3	3	5	-2	.989	4	/1-90	-0.6

■ DICK COTTER   Cotter, Richard Raphael b: 10/12/1889, Manchester, N.H. d: 4/4/45, Brooklyn, N.Y. BR/TR, 5'11", 172 lbs. Deb: 8/17/11

1911	Phi-N	20	46	2	13	0	0	0	5	5	7	.283	.353	.283	78	-1	1			.975	-2	C-17	-0.1
1912	Chi-N	26	54	6	15	0	2	0	10	6	13	.278	.361	.352	96	-0	1			.954	-3	C-24	-0.2
Total	2	46	100	8	28	0	2	0	15	11	20	.280	.357	.320	87	-1	1			.964	-5	/C-41	-0.3

■ TOM COTTER   Cotter, Thomas B. b: 9/30/1866, Waltham, Mass. d: 11/22/06, Brookline, Mass. BR/TR, 5'10.5", 149 lbs. Deb: 9/3/1891

| 1891 | Bos-a | 6 | 12 | 1 | 3 | 0 | 0 | 0 | 4 | 1 | 2 | .250 | .308 | .250 | 61 | -1 | 0 | | | .938 | -1 | /C-5,O-1 | -0.1 |

■ CHUCK COTTIER   Cottier, Charles Keith b: 1/8/36, Delta, Colo. BR/TR, 5'10.5", 175 lbs. Deb: 4/17/59 MC

1959	Mil-N	10	24	1	3	1	0	0	1	3	7	.125	.222	.167	6	-3	0	0	0	.976	1	2-10	-0.2
1960	Mil-N	95	229	29	52	9	0	3	19	14	21	.227	.278	.301	63	-12	1	0	0	.968	17	2-92	1.2
1961	Det-A	10	7	2	2	0	0	0	1	1	1	.286	.375	.286	77	-0	0	0	0	.889	1	/S-8,2-2	0.1
	Was-A	101	337	37	79	14	4	2	34	30	51	.234	.299	.318	66	-16	9	1	2	.982	15	*2-100	1.2
	Yr	111	344	39	81	14	4	2	35	31	52	.235	.301	.317	66	-17	9	1	2	.982	17	*2-102/S-8	1.3
1962	Was-A	136	443	50	107	14	6	6	40	44	57	.242	.313	.341	76	-15	14	8	-1	.981	21	*2-134	1.8
1963	Was-A	113	337	30	69	16	4	5	21	24	63	.205	.258	.320	61	-18	2	1	0	.963	13	2-85,S-24/3-1	0.1
1964	Was-A	73	137	16	23	6	2	3	10	19	33	.168	.269	.307	60	-7	2	0	1	.982	14	2-53/3-3,S-2	1.0
1965	Was-A	7	1	1	0	0	0	0	0	0	0	.000	.000	.000	-99	-1	0	0	0	.000	0	H	0.0
1968	Cal-A	33	67	2	13	4	1	0	1	2	15	.194	.217	.284	53	-4	0	0	0	.963	2	3-27/2-4	-0.3
1969	Cal-A	2	2	0	0	0	0	0	0	0	0	.000	.000	.000	-99	-1	0	0	0	1.000	-0	/2-2	-0.1
Total	9	580	1584	168	348	63	17	19	127	137	248	.220	.284	.317	65	-77	28	10	2	.976	81	2-482/S-34,3-31	4.8

■ HENRY COTTO   Cotto, Henry b: 1/5/61, New York, N.Y. BR/TR, 6'2", 178 lbs. Deb: 4/5/84

1984	*Chi-N	105	146	24	40	5	0	6	8	10	23	.274	.325	.308	72	-5	9	3	1	.984	-12	O-88	-1.8
1985	NY-A	34	56	4	17	3	0	1	6	3	12	.304	.339	.375	98	-0	1	1	-0	.977	-7	O-30	-0.8
1986	NY-A	35	80	11	17	3	0	1	6	2	17	.213	.232	.287	41	-7	3	0	1	1.000	-2	O-57	-0.8
1987	NY-A	68	149	21	35	10	0	5	20	6	35	.235	.269	.403	76	-6	4	2	0	.989	-8	O-57	-1.4
1988	Sea-A	133	386	50	100	18	1	8	33	23	53	.259	.304	.373	85	-8	27	3	6	.992	-5	*O-120/D-2	-1.0
1989	Sea-A	100	295	44	78	11	2	9	33	12	44	.264	.300	.407	94	-3	10	4	1	.988	-7	O-90/D-2	-1.1
1990	Sea-A	127	355	40	92	14	3	4	33	22	52	.259	.310	.349	83	-8	21	3	5	.990	-9	*O-118/D-3	-1.5
1991	Sea-A	66	177	35	54	6	2	6	23	10	27	.305	.349	.463	123	5	16	3	3	.981	-5	O-56/D-6	0.2
1992	Sea-A	108	294	42	76	11	1	5	27	14	49	.259	.294	.354	80	-8	23	2	6	1.000	-10	O-92/D-3	-1.4
1993	Sea-A	54	105	10	20	1	0	2	7	2	22	.190	.213	.257	25	-11	5	4	-1	.983	-3	O-34,D-15	-1.6
	Fla-N	54	135	15	40	7	0	3	14	3	18	.296	.317	.415	89	-2	11	1	3	.977	-4	O-46	-0.4
Total	10	884	2178	296	569	87	9	44	210	107	352	.261	.301	.370	83	-54	130	26	23	.989	-70	O-760/D-32	-11.6

■ DENNIS COUGHLIN   Coughlin, Dennis F. Deb: 4/27/1872

| 1872 | Nat-n | 8 | 37 | 5 | 12 | 1 | 0 | 0 | 7 | 0 | 0 | .324 | .324 | .351 | 92 | -1 | 0 | 0 | 0 | .941 | 1 | /O-5,1-1,2-1,S-1 | 0.0 |

■ ED COUGHLIN   Coughlin, Edward E. b: 8/5/1861, Hartford, Conn. d: 12/25/52, Hartford, Conn. Deb: 5/15/1884

| 1884 | Buf-N | 1 | 4 | 0 | 1 | 0 | 0 | 0 | 1 | 0 | 2 | .250 | .250 | .250 | 56 | -0 | | | | .750 | 0 | /O-1,P-1 | 0.0 |

■ BILL COUGHLIN   Coughlin, William Paul "Scranton Bill" b: 7/12/1878, Scranton, Pa. d: 5/7/43, Scranton, Pa. BR/TR, 5'9", 140 lbs. Deb: 8/9/1899

1899	Was-N	6	24	2	3	0	1	0	3	1		.125	.160	.208	1	-3	1			.818	-1	/3-6	-0.4
1901	Was-A	137	506	75	139	17	13	6	68	25		.275	.317	.395	98	-3	16			.922	-1	*3-137	-0.1
1902	Was-A	123	469	84	141	27	4	6	71	26		.301	.348	.414	110	-3	29			.926	12	3-66,S-31,2-26	1.9
1903	Was-A	125	473	56	116	18	3	1	31	9		.245	.267	.302	69	-18	30			.952	4	*3-119/S-4,2-2	-1.3
1904	Was-A	65	265	28	73	15	4	0	17	9		.275	.307	.362	113	3	10			.939	-3	3-64	0.8
	Det-A	56	206	22	47	6	0	0	17	5		.228	.257	.257	65	-8	1			.929	-3	3-56	-1.1
	Yr	121	471	50	120	21	4	0	34	14		.255	.285	.316	92	-5	11			.935	-1	*3-120	-0.3
1905	Det-A	137	489	48	123	20	6	0	44	34		.252	.309	.317	98	-1	16			.914	-9	*3-136	-0.6
1906	Det-A	147	498	54	117	15	5	2	60	36		.235	.293	.297	83	-10	31			.940	-11	*3-147	-1.7
1907	*Det-A	134	519	80	126	10	2	0	46	35		.243	.301	.270	79	-11	15			.930	-3	*3-133	-3.3
1908	*Det-A	119	405	32	87	5	1	0	23	23		.215	.269	.232	61	-17	10			.941	-16	*3-119	-3.3
Total	9	1049	3854	481	972	133	39	15	380	203		.252	.299	.319	86	-63	159			.931	-32	3-983/S-35,2-28	-7.6

■ MARLAN COUGHTRY   Coughtry, James Marlan b: 9/11/34, Hollywood, Cal. BL/TR, 6'1", 170 lbs. Deb: 9/2/60

1960	Bos-A	15	19	3	3	0	0	0	0	5	8	.158	.333	.158	36	-1	0	0	0	.909	1	2-13/3-1	0.0
1962	LA-A	11	22	0	4	0	0	0	2	0	6	.182	.182	.182	-2	-3	0	0	0	.867	3	/3-5,2-2	0.0
	KC-A	6	11	1	2	0	0	0	1	4		.182	.400	.182	60	-0	0	0	0	.917	1	/3-3	0.1
	Cle-A	3	2	1	1	0	0	0	1	1		.500	.667	.500	226	-0	0	0	0	.000	0	H	0.1
	Yr	20	35	2	7	0	0	0	4	5	10	.200	.300	.200	38	-3	0	0	0	.889	4	/3-8,2-2	0.2
Total	2	35	54	5	10	0	0	0	4	10	18	.185	.313	.185	37	-4	0	0	0	.915	6	/2-15,3-9	0.2

■ BOB COULSON   Coulson, Robert Jackson b: 6/17/1887, Courtney, Pa. d: 9/11/53, Washington, Pa. BR/TR, 5'10.5", 175 lbs. Deb: 8/4/08

1908	Cin-N	8	18	3	6	1	1	0	1	3		.333	.429	.500	202	2	0			1.000	1	/O-6	0.3
1910	Bro-N	25	89	14	22	4	1	1	13	6	14	.247	.302	.404	109	-0	9			.922	1	O-25	0.0
1911	Bro-N	146	521	52	122	23	7	0	50	42	78	.234	.301	.305	73	-19	32			.968	1	*O-145	-2.6
1914	Pit-F	18	64	7	13	1	0	0	3	7	10	.203	.282	.219	38	-6	2			.931	-2	O-18	-1.0
Total	4	197	692	76	163	28	12	1	67	58	102	.236	.303	.315	77	-23	43			.960	0	O-194	-3.3

YEAR	TM/L	G	AB	R	H	2B	3B	HR	RBI	BB	SO	AVG	OBP	SLG	PRO+	BR/A	SB	CS	SBR	FA	FR	G/POS	TPR

■ CHIP COULTER
Coulter, Thomas Lee b: 6/5/45, Steubenville, O. BB/TR, 5'10", 172 lbs. Deb: 9/18/69

YEAR	TM/L	G	AB	R	H	2B	3B	HR	RBI	BB	SO	AVG	OBP	SLG	PRO+	BR/A	SB	CS	SBR	FA	FR	G/POS	TPR
1969	StL-N	6	19	3	6	1	1	0	4	2	6	.316	.381	.474	138	1	0	1	-1	.960	-0	/2-6	0.1

■ CRAIG COUNSELL
Counsell, Craig John b: 8/21/70, South Bend, Ind. BL/TR, 6', 180 lbs. Deb: 9/17/95

YEAR	TM/L	G	AB	R	H	2B	3B	HR	RBI	BB	SO	AVG	OBP	SLG	PRO+	BR/A	SB	CS	SBR	FA	FR	G/POS	TPR
1995	Col-N	3	1	0	0	0	0	0	0	0	0	.000	.500	.000	36	-0	0	0	0	1.000	0	/S-3	0.0

■ CLINT COURTNEY
Courtney, Clinton Dawson "Scrap Iron" b: 3/16/27, Hall Summit, La. d: 6/16/75, Rochester, N.Y. BL/TR, 5'8", 180 lbs. Deb: 9/29/51 C

YEAR	TM/L	G	AB	R	H	2B	3B	HR	RBI	BB	SO	AVG	OBP	SLG	PRO+	BR/A	SB	CS	SBR	FA	FR	G/POS	TPR
1951	NY-A	1	2	0	0	0	0	0	0	0	1	.000	.333	.000	-5	-0	0	0	0	.800	0	/C-1	0.0
1952	StL-A	119	413	38	118	24	3	5	50	39	26	.286	.349	.395	104	2	0	2	-1	**.996**	3	*C-113	0.9
1953	StL-A	106	355	28	89	12	2	4	19	25	20	.251	.302	.330	69	-16	0	1	-1	.980	-5	*C-103	-1.7
1954	Bal-A	122	397	25	107	18	3	4	37	30	7	.270	.326	.360	95	-4	2	1	0	.990	-3	*C-111	-0.2
1955	Chi-A	19	37	7	14	3	0	1	10	7	0	.378	.477	.541	168	4	0	0	0	1.000	-1	C-17	0.3
	Was-A	75	238	26	71	8	4	2	30	19	9	.298	.353	.391	105	1	0	0	0	.983	-14	C-67	-1.0
	Yr	94	275	33	85	11	4	3	40	26	9	.309	.371	.411	114	5	0	0	0	.985	-15	C-84	-0.7
1956	Was-A	101	283	31	85	20	3	5	44	20	10	.300	.365	.445	113	5	0	5	-3	.979	-15	C-76	-1.0
1957	Was-A	91	232	23	62	14	1	6	27	16	11	.267	.346	.414	108	3	0	0	0	.994	-1	C-59	0.4
1958	Was-A	134	450	46	113	18	0	8	62	48	23	.251	.335	.344	89	-6	1	5	-3	.991	-3	*C-128	-0.4
1959	Was-A	72	189	19	44	4	1	2	18	20	19	.233	.310	.296	68	-8	0	1	-1	.987	-13	C-53	-1.9
1960	Bal-A	83	154	14	35	3	0	1	12	30	14	.227	.380	.266	79	-2	0	1	-1	.975	4	C-58	0.4
1961	KC-A	1	1	0	0	0	0	0	0	0	0	.000	.000	.000	-98	-0	0	0	0	.000	0	H	0.0
	Bal-A	22	45	3	12	2	0	0	4	10	3	.267	.400	.311	96	0	0	0	0	1.000	1	C-16	0.2
	Yr	23	46	3	12	2	0	0	4	10	3	.261	.393	.304	92	0	0	0	0	1.000	1	C-16	0.2
Total	11	946	2796	260	750	126	17	38	313	264	143	.268	.341	.366	94	-21	3	16	-9	.987	-45	C-802	-4.0

■ ERNIE COURTNEY
Courtney, Edward Ernest b: 1/20/1875, Des Moines, Iowa d: 2/29/20, Buffalo, N.Y. BL/TR, 5'10", Deb: 4/17/02

YEAR	TM/L	G	AB	R	H	2B	3B	HR	RBI	BB	SO	AVG	OBP	SLG	PRO+	BR/A	SB	CS	SBR	FA	FR	G/POS	TPR
1902	Bos-N	48	165	23	36	3	0	0	17	13		.218	.291	.236	62	-7	3			.974	-1	O-39/S-3	-1.1
	Bal-A	1	4	3	2	0	1	0	1	1		.500	.600	1.000	324	1	0			1.000	0	/3-1	0.1
1903	NY-A	25	79	7	21	3	3	1	8	7		.266	.341	.418	119	2	1			.916	-3	S-19/2-4,1-1	0.1
	Det-A	23	74	7	17	0	0	0	6	5		.230	.305	.230	64	-3	1			.938	-4	3-13/S-9	-0.7
	Yr	48	153	14	38	3	3	1	14	12		.248	.324	.327	94	-1	2			.921	-6	S-28,3-13/2-4,1-1	-0.6
1905	Phi-N	155	601	77	165	14	7	2	77	47		.275	.334	.331	102	2	17			.923	-17	*3-155	-1.0
1906	Phi-N	116	398	53	94	12	2	0	42	45		.236	.315	.276	84	-6	6			.923	-11	3-96,1-13/O-3,S-1	-1.6
1907	Phi-N	130	440	42	107	17	4	2	43	55		.243	.335	.314	105	4	6			.907	-8	3-75,1-48/O-4,2S	-0.3
1908	Phi-N	60	160	14	29	3	0	0	6	15		.181	.260	.200	46	-9	1			.915	-7	3-22,1-13/2-5,S-2	-1.8
Total	6	558	1921	226	471	52	17	5	200	188		.245	.321	.298	91	-15	35			.920	-49	3-362/1-75,O-46,S2	-6.3

■ DEE COUSINEAU
Cousineau, Edward Thomas b: 12/16/1898, Watertown, Mass. d: 7/14/51, Watertown, Mass. BR/TR, 6', 170 lbs. Deb: 10/6/23

YEAR	TM/L	G	AB	R	H	2B	3B	HR	RBI	BB	SO	AVG	OBP	SLG	PRO+	BR/A	SB	CS	SBR	FA	FR	G/POS	TPR
1923	Bos-N	1	2	1	2	0	0	0	0	0	0	1.000	1.000	1.000	447	1	0	0	0	.000	0	/C-1	0.1
1924	Bos-N	3	2	0	0	0	0	0	2	0	0	.000	.000	.000	-99	-1	0	0	0	.500	-1	/C-3	-0.1
1925	Bos-N	1	0	0	0	0	0	0	0	0	0	—	—	—		0	0	0	0	.500	0	/C-1	0.0
Total	3	5	4	1	2	0	0	0	2	0	0	.500	.500	.500	174	0	0	0	0	.500	-1	/C-5	0.0

■ JACK COVENEY
Coveney, John Patrick b: 6/10/1880, S.Natick, Mass. d: 3/28/61, Wayland, Mass. BR/TR, 5'9", 175 lbs. Deb: 9/19/03

YEAR	TM/L	G	AB	R	H	2B	3B	HR	RBI	BB	SO	AVG	OBP	SLG	PRO+	BR/A	SB	CS	SBR	FA	FR	G/POS	TPR
1903	StL-N	4	14	0	2	0	0	0	0	0	0	.143	.143	.143	-19	-2	0			.923	1	/C-4	-0.1

■ SAM COVINGTON
Covington, Clarence Otto b: 12/17/1892, Henryville, Tenn. d: 1/4/63, Denison, Tex. BL/TR, 6'1", 190 lbs. Deb: 8/25/13 F

YEAR	TM/L	G	AB	R	H	2B	3B	HR	RBI	BB	SO	AVG	OBP	SLG	PRO+	BR/A	SB	CS	SBR	FA	FR	G/POS	TPR
1913	StL-A	20	60	3	9	0	1	0	4	4	6	.150	.203	.183	14	-7	3			.994	3	1-16	-0.4
1917	Bos-N	17	66	8	13	2	0	1	10	5	5	.197	.264	.273	69	-2	1			.994	0	1-17	-0.3
1918	Bos-N	3	3	0	1	0	0	0	0	0	0	.333	.333	.333	108	0	0			.000	0	H	0.0
Total	3	40	129	11	23	2	1	1	14	9	11	.178	.237	.233	43	-9	4			.994	3	/1-33	-0.7

■ WES COVINGTON
Covington, John Wesley b: 3/27/32, Laurinburg, N.C. BL/TR, 6'1", 205 lbs. Deb: 4/19/56

YEAR	TM/L	G	AB	R	H	2B	3B	HR	RBI	BB	SO	AVG	OBP	SLG	PRO+	BR/A	SB	CS	SBR	FA	FR	G/POS	TPR
1956	Mil-N	75	138	17	39	4	0	2	16	16	20	.283	.361	.355	100	0	1	0	0	.979	-3	O-35	-0.4
1957	*Mil-N	96	328	51	93	4	8	21	65	29	46	.284	.345	.537	143	18	4	1	1	.981	-8	O-89	1.4
1958	*Mil-N	90	294	43	97	12	1	24	74	20	35	.330	.382	.622	175	30	0	0	0	.953	-4	O-82	2.1
1959	Mil-N	103	373	38	104	17	3	7	45	26	41	.279	.331	.397	101	-0	0	1	-1	.962	-3	O-94	-0.8
1960	Mil-N	95	281	25	70	16	1	10	35	15	37	.249	.290	.420	99	-2	1	2	-1	.964	-5	O-72	-1.1
1961	Mil-N	9	21	3	4	1	0	0	0	2	4	.190	.261	.238	36	-2	0	0	0	1.000	-1	/O-5	-0.4
	Chi-A	22	59	5	17	1	0	4	15	4	5	.288	.333	.508	123	2	0	0	0	.900	-1	O-14	0.0
	KC-A	17	44	3	7	0	0	1	6	4	7	.159	.260	.227	31	-4	0	0	0	1.000	-2	O-12	-0.7
	Yr	39	103	8	24	1	0	5	21	8	12	.233	.301	.388	83	-3	0	0	0	.941	-3	O-26	-0.7
	Phi-N	57	165	23	50	9	0	7	26	15	17	.303	.361	.485	124	5	0	0	0	.950	-5	O-45	-0.2
1962	Phi-N	116	304	36	86	12	1	9	44	19	44	.283	.329	.418	102	0	0	0	0	.944	-7	O-88	-1.1
1963	Phi-N	119	353	46	107	24	1	17	64	26	56	.303	.354	.521	150	22	1	0	0	.937	-8	*O-101	1.1
1964	Phi-N	129	339	37	95	18	0	13	58	38	50	.280	.358	.448	127	13	0	0	0	.972	-9	*O-99	0.0
1965	Phi-N	101	235	27	58	10	1	15	45	26	47	.247	.324	.489	128	8	0	0	0	.968	-6	O-64	0.4
1966	Chi-N	9	11	0	1	0	0	0	0	1	2	.091	.167	.091	-26	-2	0	0	0	1.000	-0	/O-1	-0.2
	*LA-N	37	33	1	4	0	1	1	6	6	5	.121	.264	.227	63	-2	0	0	0	1.000	-0	/O-2	-0.2
	Yr	46	44	1	5	0	1	1	6	7	7	.114	.264	.227	41	-3	0	0	0	1.000	-0	/O-3	-0.4
Total	11	1075	2978	355	832	128	17	131	499	247	414	.279	.339	.466	123	86	7	4	-0	.961	-49	O-803	-0.1

■ BILLY COWAN
Cowan, Billy Rolland b: 8/28/38, Calhoun City, Miss. BR/TR, 6', 170 lbs. Deb: 9/9/63

YEAR	TM/L	G	AB	R	H	2B	3B	HR	RBI	BB	SO	AVG	OBP	SLG	PRO+	BR/A	SB	CS	SBR	FA	FR	G/POS	TPR
1963	Chi-N	14	36	1	9	1	1	1	2	0	11	.250	.250	.417	84	-1	0	1	-1	.917	-2	O-10	-0.4
1964	Chi-N	139	497	52	120	16	4	19	50	18	128	.241	.269	.404	83	-12	12	3	2	.968	-3	*O-134	-2.1
1965	NY-N	82	156	16	28	8	2	3	9	4	45	.179	.205	.314	45	-12	3	2	-0	1.000	-8	O-61/2-2,S-1	-2.3
	Mil-N	19	27	4	5	1	0	0	0	0	9	.185	.185	.222	14	-3	0	0	0	1.000	-2	O-10	-0.5
	Yr	101	183	20	33	9	2	3	9	4	54	.180	.202	.301	41	-15	3	2	-0	1.000	-10	O-71/2-2,S-1	-2.8
1967	Phi-N	34	59	11	9	0	0	3	6	4	14	.153	.206	.305	44	-4	1	0	0	1.000	-4	O-20/2-1,3-1	-0.9
1969	NY-A	32	48	5	8	0	0	1	3	3	9	.167	.216	.229	25	-5	0	0	0	1.000	-0	O-14	-0.7
	Cal-A	28	56	10	17	1	0	4	10	3	9	.304	.350	.536	152	3	0	0	0	1.000	-0	O-13/1-6	0.3
	Yr	60	104	15	25	1	0	5	13	6	18	.240	.288	.394	93	-1	0	0	0	1.000	-0	O-27/1-6	-0.4
1970	Cal-A	68	134	20	37	9	1	5	25	11	29	.276	.330	.470	124	4	0	1	-1	.929	-6	O-27,1-14/3-2	-0.5
1971	Cal-A	74	174	12	48	9	0	4	20	7	41	.276	.304	.391	103	-0	1	1	-0	1.000	-0	O-40/1-5	-0.5
1972	Cal-A	3	3	0	0	0	0	0	0	0	0	.000	.000	.000	-99	-0	0	0	0	.000	0	H	-0.1
Total	8	493	1190	131	281	44	8	40	125	50	297	.236	.269	.387	83	-31	17	8	-0	.977	-28	O-329/1-25,3-3,2S	-7.7

■ AL COWENS
Cowens, Alfred Edward b: 10/25/51, Los Angeles, Cal. BR/TR, 6'2", 200 lbs. Deb: 4/6/74

YEAR	TM/L	G	AB	R	H	2B	3B	HR	RBI	BB	SO	AVG	OBP	SLG	PRO+	BR/A	SB	CS	SBR	FA	FR	G/POS	TPR
1974	KC-A	110	269	28	65	7	1	4	25	23	38	.242	.304	.286	67	-11	5	0	2	.988	-9	*O-102/3-2,D-4	-2.3
1975	KC-A	120	328	44	91	13	8	4	42	23	36	.277	.342	.402	107	3	12	7	-1	.978	-10	*O-113/D-2	-1.1
1976	*KC-A	152	581	71	154	23	6	3	59	26	50	.265	.300	.341	87	-11	23	16	-3	.986	5	*O-148/D-1	-1.5
1977	*KC-A	162	606	98	189	32	14	23	112	41	64	.312	.363	.525	138	30	16	12	-2	.982	3	*O-159/D-1	2.4
1978	*KC-A	132	485	63	133	24	8	5	63	31	54	.274	.326	.388	97	-2	14	6	1	.990	-2	*O-127/3-5,D-2	-0.5
1979	KC-A	136	516	69	152	18	7	9	73	40	44	.295	.349	.409	102	1	10	8	-2	.986	-0	*O-134/D-1	-0.6
1980	Cal-A	34	119	11	27	7	0	1	17	12	21	.227	.303	.294	66	-5	1	2	-1	1.000	0	O-30/D-1	-0.7
	Det-A	108	403	58	113	15	3	6	42	37	40	.280	.342	.370	93	-3	5	6	-2	.986	2	*O-107/D-1	-0.8
	Yr	142	522	69	140	20	3	6	59	49	61	.268	.333	.352	87	-8	6	8	-3	.989	3	*O-137/D-2	-1.5
1981	Det-A	85	253	27	66	11	4	1	18	22	36	.261	.322	.348	93	-3	3	3	-1	.994	-6	O-83	-1.3
1982	Sea-A	146	560	72	151	39	8	20	78	46	81	.270	.326	.475	114	9	11	7	-1	.987	5	*O-145/D-1	1.1
1983	Sea-A	110	356	39	73	19	2	7	35	23	68	.205	.257	.329	58	-21	10	2	2	.985	2	O-70,D-34	-2.1
1984	Sea-A	139	524	60	145	34	2	15	78	27	83	.277	.315	.435	106	3	9	5	-0	.987	-2	*O-130/D-7	-0.4
1985	Sea-A	122	452	59	120	32	5	14	69	30	56	.265	.313	.451	105	2	0	0	0	.967	-5	*O-110/D-5	

YEAR	TM/L	G	AB	R	H	2B	3B	HR	RBI	BB	SO	AVG	OBP	SLG	PRO+	BR/A	SB	CS	SBR	FA	FR	G/POS	TPR
1986	Sea-A	28	82	5	15	4	0	0	6	3	18	.183	.212	.232	20	-9	1	0	0	.971	-0	O-19/D-1	-0.9
Total	13	1584	5534	704	1494	276	68	108	717	389	659	.270	.322	.403	98	-18	120	74	-8	.985	-5	*O-1477/D-61,3-7	-8.7

■ DICK COX
Cox, Elmer Joseph   b: 9/30/1897, Pasadena, Cal.   d: 6/1/66, Morro Bay, Cal.   BR/TR, 5'7.5", 158 lbs.   Deb: 4/16/25

YEAR	TM/L	G	AB	R	H	2B	3B	HR	RBI	BB	SO	AVG	OBP	SLG	PRO+	BR/A	SB	CS	SBR	FA	FR	G/POS	TPR
1925	Bro-N	122	434	68	143	23	10	7	64	37	29	.329	.382	.477	121	14	4	3	-1	.968	-4	*O-111	0.2
1926	Bro-N	124	398	53	118	17	4	1	45	46	20	.296	.375	.367	102	3	6			.964	-8	*O-117	-1.2
Total	2	246	832	121	261	40	14	8	109	83	49	.314	.379	.424	112	17	10	3		.966	-12	O-228	-1.0

■ FRANK COX
Cox, Francis Bernard "Runt"   b: 8/29/1857, Waltham, Mass.   d: 6/24/28, Hartford, Conn.   5'6",   Deb: 8/13/1884

YEAR	TM/L	G	AB	R	H	2B	3B	HR	RBI	BB	SO	AVG	OBP	SLG	PRO+	BR/A	SB	CS	SBR	FA	FR	G/POS	TPR
1884	Det-N	27	102	6	13	3	1	0	2	2	36	.127	.144	.176	0	-11				.812	-4	S-27	-1.3

■ JIM COX
Cox, James Charles   b: 5/28/50, Bloomington, Ill.   BR/TR, 5'11", 175 lbs.   Deb: 7/19/73

YEAR	TM/L	G	AB	R	H	2B	3B	HR	RBI	BB	SO	AVG	OBP	SLG	PRO+	BR/A	SB	CS	SBR	FA	FR	G/POS	TPR
1973	Mon-N	9	15	1	2	1	0	0	1	4	1	.133	.188	.200	7	-2	0	0	0	.950	-1	/2-7	-0.2
1974	Mon-N	77	236	29	52	9	1	2	26	23	36	.220	.292	.292	61	-12	2	3	-1	.968	15	2-72	0.4
1975	Mon-N	11	27	1	7	1	0	1	5	1	2	.259	.286	.407	87	-1	1	0	0	1.000	1	/2-8	0.0
1976	Mon-N	13	29	2	5	0	1	0	2	2	2	.172	.226	.241	31	-3	0	0	0	.958	1	2-11	-0.1
Total	4	110	307	33	66	11	2	3	33	27	44	.215	.281	.293	58	-17	3	3	-1	.969	16	/2-98	0.1

■ JEFF COX
Cox, Jeffrey Lindon   b: 11/9/55, Los Angeles, Cal.   BR/TR, 5'11", 170 lbs.   Deb: 7/1/80

YEAR	TM/L	G	AB	R	H	2B	3B	HR	RBI	BB	SO	AVG	OBP	SLG	PRO+	BR/A	SB	CS	SBR	FA	FR	G/POS	TPR
1980	Oak-A	59	169	20	36	3	0	0	9	14	23	.213	.273	.231	43	-13	8	5	-1	.979	-16	2-58	-2.6
1981	Oak-A	2	0	0	0	0	0	0	0	0	0	—	—	—	—	—	0	0	0	1.000	0	/2-1	0.0
Total	2	61	169	20	36	3	0	0	9	14	23	.213	.273	.231	43	-13	8	5	-1	.979	-16	/2-59	-2.6

■ LARRY COX
Cox, Larry Eugene   b: 9/11/47, Bluffton, Ohio   d: 2/17/90, Bellefontaine, Ohio   BR/TR, 5'11", 190 lbs.   Deb: 4/18/73   C

YEAR	TM/L	G	AB	R	H	2B	3B	HR	RBI	BB	SO	AVG	OBP	SLG	PRO+	BR/A	SB	CS	SBR	FA	FR	G/POS	TPR
1973	Phi-N	1	0	0	0	0	0	0	0	0	0				0	-0	0	0	0	1.000	-0	/C-1	0.0
1974	Phi-N	30	53	5	9	2	0	0	4	4	9	.170	.241	.208	25	-5	0	0	0	.990	0	C-29	-0.4
1975	Phi-N	11	5	0	1	0	0	0	1	1	0	.200	.333	.200	49	-0	1	0	0	1.000	0	C-10	0.0
1977	Sea-A	35	93	6	23	6	0	2	6	10	12	.247	.320	.376	90	-1	1	1	-0	.970	-1	C-35	-0.2
1978	Chi-N	59	121	10	34	5	0	2	18	12	16	.281	.346	.372	90	-2	0	0	0	.967	2	C-58	0.1
1979	Sea-A	100	293	32	63	11	3	4	36	22	39	.215	.270	.314	56	-18	2	1	0	.981	-2	C-99	-1.7
1980	Sea-A	105	243	18	49	6	2	4	20	19	36	.202	.260	.292	50	-17	1	2	-1	**.993**	12	*C-104	-0.3
1981	Tex-A	5	13	0	3	1	0	0	0	4	4	.231	.231	.308	57	-1	0	0	0	1.000	3	/C-5	0.3
1982	Chi-N	2	4	1	0	0	0	0	0	2	1	.000	.333	.000	1	-0	0	0	0	1.000	1	/C-2	0.1
Total	9	348	825	72	182	31	5	12	85	70	117	.221	.282	.314	61	-45	5	4	-1	.983	15	C-343	-2.1

■ BOBBY COX
Cox, Robert Joseph   b: 5/21/41, Tulsa, Okla.   BR/TR, 5'11", 180 lbs.   Deb: 4/14/68   MC

YEAR	TM/L	G	AB	R	H	2B	3B	HR	RBI	BB	SO	AVG	OBP	SLG	PRO+	BR/A	SB	CS	SBR	FA	FR	G/POS	TPR
1968	NY-A	135	437	33	100	15	1	7	41	41	85	.229	.302	.316	90	-5	3	2	-0	.957	-5	*3-132	-1.2
1969	NY-A	85	191	17	41	7	1	2	17	34	41	.215	.336	.293	80	-4	0	1	-1	.935	11	3-56/2-6	0.7
Total	2	220	628	50	141	22	2	9	58	75	126	.225	.313	.309	87	-9	3	3	-1	.950	6	3-188/2-6	-0.5

■ BILLY COX
Cox, William Richard   b: 8/29/19, Newport, Pa.   d: 3/30/78, Harrisburg, Pa.   BR/TR, 5'10", 150 lbs.   Deb: 9/20/41

YEAR	TM/L	G	AB	R	H	2B	3B	HR	RBI	BB	SO	AVG	OBP	SLG	PRO+	BR/A	SB	CS	SBR	FA	FR	G/POS	TPR
1941	Pit-N	10	37	4	10	3	1	0	2	3	2	.270	.325	.405	105	0				.943	2	S-10	0.3
1946	Pit-N	121	411	32	119	22	6	2	36	26	15	.290	.333	.387	101	-0	4			.935	-16	*S-114	-1.0
1947	Pit-N	132	529	75	145	30	7	15	54	29	28	.274	.313	.442	96	-5	5			.968	-13	*S-129	-1.1
1948	Bro-N	88	237	36	59	13	2	3	15	38	19	.249	.353	.359	90	-3	3			.958	-4	3-70/S-6,2-1	-0.7
1949	*Bro-N	100	390	48	91	18	2	8	40	30	18	.233	.290	.351	68	-18	5			.964	9	*3-100	-1.1
1950	Bro-N	119	451	62	116	17	2	8	44	35	24	.257	.311	.357	74	-17	6			**.957**	12	*3-107,2-13/S-9	-0.6
1951	Bro-N	142	455	62	127	25	4	9	51	37	30	.279	.336	.411	98	-2	5	5	-2	.967	-8	*3-139/S-1	-1.3
1952	*Bro-N	116	455	56	118	12	3	6	34	25	32	.259	.301	.358	76	-15	10	12	-4	.970	-9	*3-100,S-10/2-9	-3.0
1953	*Bro-N	100	327	44	95	18	1	10	44	37	21	.291	.363	.443	106	3	2	2	-1	.974	-2	3-89/S-6,2-1	-0.1
1954	Bro-N	77	226	26	53	9	2	2	17	21	13	.235	.300	.319	59	-13	0	0	0	.961	-2	3-58,2-11/S-8	-1.1
1955	Bal-A	53	194	25	41	7	2	3	14	17	16	.211	.275	.314	63	-11	1	2	-1	.969	-9	3-37,2-18/S-6	-2.1
Total	11	1058	3712	470	974	174	32	66	351	298	218	.262	.318	.380	85	-82	42	21		.965	-36	3-700,S-299/2-53	-11.8

■ TED COX
Cox, William Ted   b: 1/24/55, Oklahoma City, Okla   BR/TR, 6'3", 195 lbs.   Deb: 9/18/77

YEAR	TM/L	G	AB	R	H	2B	3B	HR	RBI	BB	SO	AVG	OBP	SLG	PRO+	BR/A	SB	CS	SBR	FA	FR	G/POS	TPR
1977	Bos-A	13	58	11	21	3	1	6	6	3	6	.362	.393	.500	127	2	0	0	0	.000	0	D-13	0.2
1978	Cle-A	82	227	14	53	7	0	1	19	16	30	.233	.287	.278	60	-12	0	1	-1	.980	-5	O-38,3-20,D-12/1S	-2.0
1979	Cle-A	78	189	17	40	6	0	4	22	14	27	.212	.273	.307	56	-12	3	4	-2	.964	1	3-52,O-16/2-4,D-1	-1.3
1980	Sea-A	83	247	17	60	9	0	2	23	19	25	.243	.297	.304	64	-12	0	0	0	.945	-2	3-80	-1.5
1981	Tor-A	16	50	6	15	4	0	2	9	5	10	.300	.364	.500	138	2	0	0	-1	.897	-4	3-14/1-1,D-1	-0.3
Total	5	272	771	65	189	29	1	10	79	57	98	.245	.300	.324	71	-31	3	6	-3	.947	-10	3-166/O-54,D12S	-4.9

■ TOOTS COYNE
Coyne, Martin Albert   b: 10/20/1894, St.Louis, Mo.   d: 9/18/39, St.Louis, Mo.   TR,   Deb: 9/28/14

YEAR	TM/L	G	AB	R	H	2B	3B	HR	RBI	BB	SO	AVG	OBP	SLG	PRO+	BR/A	SB	CS	SBR	FA	FR	G/POS	TPR
1914	Phi-A	1	2	0	0	0	0	0	0	0	0	.000	.000	.000	-99	-0	0	0	0	1.000	-0	/3-1	-0.1

■ ESTEL CRABTREE
Crabtree, Estel Crayton "Crabby"   b: 8/19/03, Crabtree, Ohio   d: 1/4/67, Logan, Ohio   BL/TR, 6', 168 lbs.   Deb: 4/18/29   C

YEAR	TM/L	G	AB	R	H	2B	3B	HR	RBI	BB	SO	AVG	OBP	SLG	PRO+	BR/A	SB	CS	SBR	FA	FR	G/POS	TPR
1929	Cin-N	1	1	0	0	0	0	0	0	0	0	.000	.000	.000	-99	-0	0			.000	0	H	0.0
1931	Cin-N	117	443	70	119	12	12	4	37	23	33	.269	.309	.377	89	-8	3			.974	10	*O-101/3-4,1-2	-0.5
1932	Cin-N	108	402	38	110	14	9	2	35	23	26	.274	.316	.368	86	-8	2			.990	9	O-95	-0.5
1933	StL-N	23	34	6	9	3	0	0	3	2	3	.265	.306	.353	83	-1	1			.947	-2	/O-7	-0.1
1941	StL-N	77	167	27	57	6	3	5	28	26	24	.341	.439	.503	154	13	1			1.000	-8	O-50/3-1	0.3
1942	StL-N	10	9	1	3	2	0	0	2	1	3	.333	.400	.556	166	1	0			.000	0	H	0.1
1943	Cin-N	95	254	25	70	12	0	2	26	25	17	.276	.345	.346	101	1	1			.939	-5	O-65	-0.8
1944	Cin-N	58	98	7	28	4	1	0	11	13	3	.286	.369	.347	106	1	0			1.000	-4	O-19/1-2	-0.4
Total	8	489	1408	174	396	53	25	13	142	113	109	.281	.339	.382	100	-2	8			.976	-0	O-337/3-5,1-4	-1.9

■ HARRY CRAFT
Craft, Harry Francis "Wildfire"   b: 4/19/15, Ellisville, Miss.   d: 8/3/95, Conroe, Tex.   BR/TR, 6'1", 185 lbs.   Deb: 9/19/37   MC

YEAR	TM/L	G	AB	R	H	2B	3B	HR	RBI	BB	SO	AVG	OBP	SLG	PRO+	BR/A	SB	CS	SBR	FA	FR	G/POS	TPR
1937	Cin-N	10	42	7	13	2	1	0	4	1	3	.310	.326	.405	102	-0	0			1.000	0	O-10	0.0
1938	Cin-N	151	612	70	165	28	9	15	83	29	46	.270	.305	.418	100	-3	3			.983	16	*O-151	0.9
1939	*Cin-N	134	502	58	129	20	7	13	67	27	54	.257	.299	.402	86	-11	5			.981	3	*O-134	-1.3
1940	*Cin-N	115	422	47	103	18	5	6	48	17	46	.244	.277	.353	72	-17	2			**.997**	6	*O-109/1-2	-1.7
1941	Cin-N	119	413	48	103	15	2	10	59	33	43	.249	.308	.368	90	-7	4			.983	-1	*O-115	-1.2
1942	Cin-N	37	113	7	20	2	1	0	6	3	11	.177	.205	.212	22	-11	0			.987	1	O-33	-1.3
Total	6	566	2104	237	533	85	25	44	267	110	203	.253	.294	.380	85	-49	14			.986	28	O-552/1-2	-4.6

■ ROD CRAIG
Craig, Rodney Paul   b: 1/12/58, Los Angeles, Cal.   BB/TR, 6'1", 195 lbs.   Deb: 9/11/79

YEAR	TM/L	G	AB	R	H	2B	3B	HR	RBI	BB	SO	AVG	OBP	SLG	PRO+	BR/A	SB	CS	SBR	FA	FR	G/POS	TPR
1979	Sea-A	16	52	9	20	1	0	6	1	5	.385	.396	.577	156	4	1	1	-0	.923	-2	O-15	0.1
1980	Sea-A	70	240	30	57	15	1	3	20	17	35	.237	.293	.346	74	-9	3	6	-3	.987	-2	O-63	-1.6
1982	Cle-A	49	65	7	15	2	0	0	1	4	6	.231	.275	.262	49	-5	3	1	0	.966	-4	O-22/D-4	-0.9
1986	Chi-A	10	10	3	2	0	0	0	0	2	2	.200	.333	.200	48	-1	0	0	0	.000	-1	/O-2	-0.1
Total	4	145	367	49	94	25	2	3	27	24	48	.256	.305	.360	80	-10	7	8	-3	.977	-9	O-102/D-4	-2.5

■ DOC CRAMER
Cramer, Roger Maxwell "Flit"   b: 7/22/05, Beach Haven, N.J.   d: 9/9/90, Manahawkin, N.J.   BL/TR, 6'2", 185 lbs.   Deb: 9/18/29   C

YEAR	TM/L	G	AB	R	H	2B	3B	HR	RBI	BB	SO	AVG	OBP	SLG	PRO+	BR/A	SB	CS	SBR	FA	FR	G/POS	TPR
1929	Phi-A	2	6	0	0	0	0	0	0	0	2	.000	.000	.000	-97	-2	0	0	0	1.000	1	/O-1	-0.1
1930	Phi-A	30	82	12	19	1	0	0	8	2	6	.232	.250	.268	30	-9	0	0	0	.927	-2	O-21/S-1	-1.1
1931	*Phi-A	65	223	37	58	8	2	2	20	11	15	.260	.301	.341	64	-12	3	1	0	.979	1	O-55	-1.4
1932	Phi-A	92	384	73	129	27	8	3	46	17	27	.336	.367	.461	109	4	3	1	0	.976	8	O-86	0.7
1933	Phi-A	152	661	109	195	27	11	8	75	36	24	.295	.331	.396	91	-10	5	4	0	.985	-5	*O-152	-1.4
1934	Phi-A	153	649	99	202	29	9	6	46	40	35	.311	.353	.411	100	-1	5	5	-3	.985	5	*O-152	-0.4
1935	Phi-A★	149	644	96	214	37	4	5	70	37	21	.332	.373	.416	105	4	6	7	-2	.975	4	*O-149	0.0
1936	Bos-A	154	643	99	188	31	7	6	41	49	20	.292	.347	.362	71	-29	4	8	-2	.975	16	*O-154	-1.9
1937	Bos-A☆	133	560	90	171	22	11	0	51	35	14	.305	.351	.384	82	-15	1	6	-3	.969	6	*O-133	-1.4

YEAR	TM/L	G	AB	R	H	2B	3B	HR	RBI	BB	SO	AVG	OBP	SLG	PRO+	BR/A	SB	CS	SBR	FA	FR	G/POS	TPR
1938	Bos-A★	148	658	116	198	36	8	0	71	51	19	.301	.354	.380	80	-20	4	9	-4	.986	9	*O-148/P-1	-1.8
1939	Bos-A★	137	589	110	183	30	6	0	56	36	17	.311	.352	.382	85	-13	3	3	-1	.984	2	*O-135	-1.6
1940	Bos-A☆	150	661	94	**200**	27	12	1	51	36	29	.303	.340	.384	84	-16	3	5	-2	.969	-5	*O-149	-3.0
1941	Was-A	154	660	93	180	25	6	2	66	37	15	.273	.317	.338	77	-23	4	1	1	.984	-7	*O-152	-3.8
1942	Det-A	151	630	71	166	26	4	0	43	43	18	.263	.314	.317	72	-24	4	4	-1	.981	-0	*O-150	-3.4
1943	Det-A	140	606	79	182	18	4	1	43	31	13	.300	.335	.348	93	-6	4	3	-1	.989	1	*O-138	-1.4
1944	Det-A	143	578	69	169	20	9	2	42	37	21	.292	.337	.369	96	-3	6	5	-1	.980	-8	*O-141	-2.1
1945	*Det-A	141	541	62	149	22	8	6	58	36	21	.275	.324	.379	97	-3	2	9	-5	**.991**	-8	*O-140	-2.5
1946	Det-A	68	204	26	60	8	2	1	26	15	8	.294	.342	.368	93	-2	3	0	1	1.000	-6	O-50	-1.0
1947	Det-A	73	157	21	42	2	2	2	30	20	5	.268	.350	.344	91	-2	0	4	-2	.965	-2	O-35	-0.8
1948	Det-A	4	4	1	0	0	0	0	1	3	0	.000	.429	.000	19	-0	0	0	0	1.000	-0	/O-1	-0.2
Total	20	2239	9140	1357	2705	396	109	37	842	572	345	.296	.340	.375	87	-180	62	73	-25	.979	19	*O-2142/P-1,S-1	-28.4

■ DICK CRAMER   Cramer, William B. b: Brooklyn, N.Y. d: 8/12/1885, Camden, N.J.   Deb: 5/12/1883

YEAR	TM/L	G	AB	R	H	2B	3B	HR	RBI	BB	SO	AVG	OBP	SLG	PRO+	BR/A	SB	CS	SBR	FA	FR	G/POS	TPR
1883	NY-N	2	6	0	0	0	0	0	0	1	5	.000	.143	.000	-52	-1				.000	-1	/O-2	-0.2

■ DEL CRANDALL   Crandall, Delmar Wesley b: 3/5/30, Ontario, Cal. BR/TR, 6'1", 195 lbs.   Deb: 6/17/49   MC

YEAR	TM/L	G	AB	R	H	2B	3B	HR	RBI	BB	SO	AVG	OBP	SLG	PRO+	BR/A	SB	CS	SBR	FA	FR	G/POS	TPR
1949	Bos-N	67	228	21	60	10	1	4	34	9	18	.263	.291	.368	80	-7	2			.982	7	C-63	0.3
1950	Bos-N	79	255	21	56	11	0	4	37	13	24	.220	.257	.310	52	-19	0			.967	3	C-75/1-1	-1.3
1953	Mil-N†	116	382	55	104	13	1	15	51	33	47	.272	.330	.429	102	0	2	1	0	.986	15	*C-108	1.9
1954	Mil-N☆	138	463	60	112	18	2	21	64	40	56	.242	.306	.425	94	-6	0	3	-2	.989	14	*C-136	1.2
1955	Mil-N★	133	440	61	104	15	2	26	62	40	56	.236	.303	.457	103	-0	2	1	0	**.996**	3	*C-131	0.3
1956	Mil-N†	112	311	37	74	14	2	16	48	35	30	.238	.317	.450	110	3	1	2	-1	**.996**	3	*C-109	1.0
1957	*Mil-N	118	383	45	97	11	2	15	46	30	38	.253	.309	.410	98	-2	1	2	-1	.987	-8	*C-102/O-9,1-1	-0.8
1958	*Mil-N★	131	427	50	116	23	1	18	63	48	38	.272	.344	.457	122	12	4	1	1	**.990**	6	*C-124	2.6
1959	Mil-N★	150	518	65	133	19	2	21	72	46	48	.257	.321	.423	105	2	5	1	1	**.994**	6	*C-146	1.7
1960	Mil-N★	142	537	81	158	14	1	19	77	34	36	.294	.341	.430	118	12	4	6	-2	.988	-15	*C-141	0.3
1961	Mil-N	15	30	3	6	3	0	0	1	1	0	.200	.226	.300	40	-3	0	0	0	1.000	-2	/C-5	-0.4
1962	Mil-N	107	350	35	104	12	3	8	45	27	24	.297	.351	.417	108	4	3	4	-2	**.994**	-4	C-90/1-5	0.2
1963	Mil-N	86	259	18	52	4	0	3	28	18	22	.201	.253	.251	46	-18	1	4	-2	.991	5	C-75/1-7	-1.4
1964	SF-N	69	195	12	45	8	1	3	11	22	21	.231	.309	.328	78	-5	0	3	-2	.993	13	C-65	0.8
1965	Pit-N	60	140	11	30	2	0	2	10	14	10	.214	.290	.271	59	-7	1	0	0	.996	5	C-60	0.0
1966	Cle-A	50	108	10	25	2	0	4	8	14	9	.231	.320	.361	95	-1	0	0	0	.991	15	C-49	1.8
Total	16	1573	5026	585	1276	179	18	179	657	424	477	.254	.315	.404	87	-35	26	**28**		.989	61	*C-1479/1-14,0-9	8.2

■ DOC CRANDALL   Crandall, James Otis b: 10/8/1887, Wadena, Ind. d: 8/17/51, Bell, Cal. BR/TR, 5'10.5", 180 lbs.   Deb: 4/24/08

YEAR	TM/L	G	AB	R	H	2B	3B	HR	RBI	BB	SO	AVG	OBP	SLG	PRO+	BR/A	SB	CS	SBR	FA	FR	G/POS	TPR
1908	NY-N	34	72	8	16	4	0	2	6	4		.222	.273	.361	97	-1	0			.985	-2	P-32/2-1	0.0
1909	NY-N	30	41	4	10	0	1	1	1	1		.244	.262	.366	93	-1	0			.941	2	P-30	0.0
1910	NY-N	45	73	10	25	2	4	1	13	5	7	.342	.385	.521	163	5	0			.984	-2	P-42/S-1	0.0
1911	*NY-N	61	113	12	27	1	4	2	21	8	16	.239	.295	.372	83	-3	2			.958	-0	P-41/S-6,2-3	-0.2
1912	*NY-N	50	80	9	25	6	2	0	19	6	7	.313	.360	.438	114	1	0			.957	0	P-37/2-1,1-1	0.0
1913	*NY-N	31	25	4	7	2	1	0	2	1	5	.280	.308	.440	111	0	0			1.000	1	P-24/2-2	0.0
	StL-N	2	2	0	0	0	0	0	0	0	2	.000	.000	.000	-99	-1	0			.000	0	H	-0.1
	*NY-N	15	22	3	8	2	0	0	2	0	3	.364	.417	.455	148	1	0			1.000	1	P-11	0.0
	Yr	48	49	7	15	4	1	0	4	3	10	.306	.346	.429	120	1	0			1.000	2	P-35/2-2	0.0
1914	StL-F	118	278	40	86	16	5	2	41	58	32	.309	.429	.424	126	9	3			.926	-18	2-63,P-27/S-1,0-1	-1.1
1915	StL-F	84	141	18	40	2	2	1	19	27	15	.284	.406	.348	107	1	4			.958	1	P-51	0.0
1916	StL-A	16	12	0	1	0	0	0	0	2	4	.083	.214	.083	-11	-0	0			.000	-0	/P-2	0.0
1918	Bos-N	14	28	1	8	0	0	0	2	4	3	.286	.375	.286	107	0	0			1.000	0	/P-5,O-3	0.0
Total	10	500	887	109	253	35	19	9	126	118	**94**	.285	.372	.398	114	13	9			.962	-18	P-302/2-71,S-8,01	-1.4

■ ED CRANE   Crane, Edward Nicholas "Cannon-Ball" b: 5/27/1862, Boston, Mass. d: 9/19/1896, Rochester, N.Y. BR/TR, 5'10.5", 204 lbs.   Deb: 4/17/1884

YEAR	TM/L	G	AB	R	H	2B	3B	HR	RBI	BB	SO	AVG	OBP	SLG	PRO+	BR/A	SB	CS	SBR	FA	FR	G/POS	TPR
1884	Bos-U	101	428	83	122	23	6	12	14			.285	.308	.451	129	2				.826	-5	0-57,C-42/1-5,P-4	-0.2
1885	Pro-N	1	2	0	0	0	0	0	0	1	1	.000	.333	.000	16	-0				.500	0	/O-1	0.0
	Buf-N	13	51	5	14	0	1	2	9	3	8	.275	.315	.431	135	2				.769	-3	O-13	-0.1
	Yr	14	53	5	14	0	1	2	9	4	9	.264	.316	.415	131	2				.750	-2	O-14	-0.1
1886	Was-N	80	292	20	50	11	3	0	20	13	54	.171	.207	.229	34	-22	8			.866	3	0-68,P-10/C-4	-1.7
1888	*NY-N	12	37	3	6	2	0	1	2	3	11	.162	.225	.297	66	-1	1			.867	1	P-12	0.0
1889	*NY-N	29	103	16	21	1	0	2	11	13	21	.204	.293	.272	58	-6	6			.762	-4	P-29/1-1	0.0
1890	NY-P	43	146	27	46	5	4	0	16	10	26	.315	.363	.404	96	-2	5			.846	-3	P-43	0.0
1891	Cin-a	34	110	13	17	0	0	1	7	8	28	.155	.212	.182	12	-13	4			.822	-1	P-32/O-3	-0.1
	Cin-N	15	46	3	5	0	0	0	2	3	12	.109	.163	.109	-20	-7	3			.906	0	P-15	0.0
1892	NY-N	48	163	20	40	1	1	0	14	11	30	.245	.297	.264	71	-6	2			.821	-1	P-47/O-1	-0.1
1893	NY-N	12	26	8	12	1	0	0	3	7	0	.462	.576	.500	186	4	0			.889	-1	P-10/1-1,O-1	0.0
	Bro-N	3	5	1	2	1	0	0	0	0	0	.400	.400	.600	172	0	0			.500	-1	/P-2,O-1	0.0
	Yr	15	31	9	14	2	0	0	3	7	0	.452	.553	.516	186	5	0			.850	-2	P-12/O-2,1-1	0.0
Total	9	391	1409	199	335	45	15	18	**84**	86	**191**	.238	.283	.329	80	-49	29			.842	-15	P-204,0-145/C-46,1	-2.2

■ FRED CRANE   Crane, Frederic William Hotchkiss b: 11/4/1840, Old Saybrook, Conn. d: 4/27/25, Brooklyn, N.Y.   Deb: 5/26/1873

YEAR	TM/L	G	AB	R	H	2B	3B	HR	RBI	BB	SO	AVG	OBP	SLG	PRO+	BR/A	SB	CS	SBR	FA	FR	G/POS	TPR
1873	Res-n	1	4	0	1	0	0	0	0	0	0	.250	.250	.250	53	-0	0	0	0	.667	-1	/2-1	-0.1
1875	Atl-n	21	81	7	17	1	0	0	4	0	4	.210	.210	.222	58	-3	0	0	0	.953	1	1-20/S-1,O-1	-0.1
Total	2 n	22	85	7	18	1	0	0	5	0	4	.212	.212	.224	57	-3	0	0	0	.953	1	/1-20,O-1,S-1,2-1	-0.2

■ SAM CRANE   Crane, Samuel Byren "Lucky" or "Red" b: 9/13/1894, Harrisburg, Pa. d: 11/12/55, Philadelphia, Pa. BR/TR, 5'11.5", 154 lbs.   Deb: 10/2/14

YEAR	TM/L	G	AB	R	H	2B	3B	HR	RBI	BB	SO	AVG	OBP	SLG	PRO+	BR/A	SB	CS	SBR	FA	FR	G/POS	TPR
1914	Phi-A	2	6	0	0	0	0	0	0	2	3	.000	.250	.000	-25	-1	0			.929	1	/S-2	0.0
1915	Phi-A	8	23	3	2	2	0	0	1	0	4	.087	.087	.174	-23	-4	0			.900	2	/S-6,2-1	-0.1
1916	Phi-A	2	4	1	1	0	0	0	0	2	1	.250	.500	.250	132	0	0			1.000	-0	/S-2	0.0
1917	Was-A	32	95	6	17	2	0	0	4	4	14	.179	.212	.200	26	-9	0			.889	-4	S-32	-1.3
1920	Cin-N	54	144	20	31	4	0	0	9	7	9	.215	.261	.243	46	-10	5	4	-1	.945	-9	S-25,3-10/2-4,0-3	-1.9
1921	Cin-N	73	215	20	50	10	2	0	16	14	14	.233	.292	.298	59	-13	2	5	-2	.953	-17	S-63/3-2,O-1	-2.6
1922	Bro-N	3	8	1	2	1	0	0	0	0	1	.250	.333	.375	83	-0	0	0	0	.875	-1	/S-3	0.2
Total	7	174	495	51	103	19	2	0	30	29	46	.208	.262	.255	46	-35	7	**9**		.931	-25	S-133/3-12,2-5,0-4	-5.7

■ SAM CRANE   Crane, Samuel Newhall b: 1/2/1854, Springfield, Mass. d: 6/26/25, New York, N.Y. BR/TR,   Deb: 5/1/1880   M

YEAR	TM/L	G	AB	R	H	2B	3B	HR	RBI	BB	SO	AVG	OBP	SLG	PRO+	BR/A	SB	CS	SBR	FA	FR	G/POS	TPR
1880	Buf-N	10	31	4	4	0	0	0	2	1	8	.129	.156	.129	-2	-3				.866	-2	2-10/O-1,M	-0.5
1883	NY-a	96	349	57	82	8	5	0	13			.235	.262	.287	73	-11				.859	-10	*2-96/O-1	-1.7
1884	Cin-U	80	309	56	72	9	3	1	11			.233	.259	.291	62	-24				.858	-9	*2-80,M	-2.8
1885	Det-N	68	245	23	47	4	6	1	20	13	45	.192	.233	.269	62	-10				.908	-5	2-68	-1.2
1886	Det-N	47	185	24	26	2	2	1	12	8	34	.141	.176	.189	11	-20	8			.903	1	2-38/S-8,O-4	-1.6
	StL-N	39	116	10	20	3	1	0	7	13	27	.172	.256	.216	48	-7	6			.897	-11	2-39	-1.4
	Yr	86	301	34	46	5	3	1	19	21	61	.153	.208	.199	25	-27	14			.900	-10	2-77/S-8,O-4	-3.0
1887	Was-N	7	30	6	9	1	0	0	3			.300	.323	.400	105	0				.865	-1	/S-7	0.0
1890	NY-N	2	6	0	0	0	0	0	0		1	.000	.000	.000	-99	-2	1			.778	-1	/1-1,O-1	-0.2
	Pit-N	22	82	3	16	3	0	0	3		5	.195	.205	.232	31	-7	5			.880	3	2-15/S-7,O-1	-0.2
	NY-N	2	6	0	0	0	0	0	0		2	.000	.000	.000	-99	-2	0			1.000	1	/2-2	0.0
	Yr	26	94	3	16	3	0	0	3	0	7	.170	.179	.202	12	-11	6			.883	3	2-17/S-7,O-2,1-1	-0.5
Total	7	373	1359	183	276	30	18	3	**45**	60	**127**	.203	.237	.258	53	-85	25			.878	-33	2-348/S-22,O-8,1-1	-9.7

■ GAVVY CRAVATH   Cravath, Clifford Carlton "Cactus" b: 3/23/1881, Escondido, Cal. d: 5/23/63, Laguna Beach, Cal. BR/TR, 5'10.5", 186 lbs.   Deb: 4/18/08   MC

YEAR	TM/L	G	AB	R	H	2B	3B	HR	RBI	BB	SO	AVG	OBP	SLG	PRO+	BR/A	SB	CS	SBR	FA	FR	G/POS	TPR
1908	Bos-A	94	277	43	71	10	11	1	34	38		.256	.354	.383	136	12	6			.925	-2	O-77/1-5	0.8
1909	Chi-A	19	50	7	9	0	0	1	8	19		.180	.406	.240	109	2	3			.944	-2	O-18	-0.1

YEAR	TM/L	G	AB	R	H	2B	3B	HR	RBI	BB	SO	AVG	OBP	SLG	PRO+	BR/A	SB	CS	SBR	FA	FR	G/POS	TPR
	Was-A	4	6	0	0	0	0	0	1	1		.000	.143	.000	-57	-1	0			1.000	1	/O-1	-0.1
	Yr	23	56	7	9	0	0	1	9	20		.161	.382	.214	93	1	3			.947	-2	O-19	-0.2
1912	Phi-N	130	436	63	124	30	9	11	70	47	77	.284	.358	.470	118	9	15			.966	5	*O-113	0.8
1913	Phi-N	147	525	78	**179**	34	14	**19**	**128**	55	63	.341	.407	**.568**	**169**	**46**	10			.958	-4	*O-141	3.7
1914	Phi-N	149	499	76	149	27	8	**19**	100	83	72	.299	.402	.499	**157**	36	14			.930	3	*O-143	3.5
1915	*Phi-N	150	522	**89**	149	31	7	**24**	115	86	77	.285	**.393**	.510	170	46	11	9	-2	.946	9	*O-149	**4.9**
1916	Phi-N	137	448	70	127	21	8	11	70	64	89	.283	**.379**	.440	146	26	9			.966	-3	*O-130	1.8
1917	Phi-N	140	503	70	141	29	16	**12**	83	70	83	.280	.369	.473	151	31	6			.946	-3	*O-139	2.2
1918	Phi-N	121	426	43	99	27	5	**8**	54	54	46	.232	.320	.376	105	3	7			.931	-4	*O-118	-0.9
1919	Phi-N	83	214	34	73	18	5	**12**	45	35	21	.341	.438	.640	207	28	8			.914	-5	O-56,M	2.2
1920	Phi-N	46	45	2	13	5	0	1	11	9	12	.289	.407	.667	144	3	0	0	0	.667	-2	/O-5,M	0.1
Total	11	1220	3951	575	1134	232	83	119	719	561	514	.287	.380	.478	149	240	89	9		.944	-6	*O-1090/1-5	18.9

■ BILL CRAVER   Craver, William H. b: 6/1844, Troy, N.Y. d: 6/17/01, Troy, N.Y. BR/TR, 5'9", 160 lbs. Deb: 5/9/1871 M

YEAR	TM/L	G	AB	R	H	2B	3B	HR	RBI	BB	SO	AVG	OBP	SLG	PRO+	BR/A	SB	CS	SBR	FA	FR	G/POS	TPR
1871	Tro-n	27	118	26	38	8	1	0	26	3	0	.322	.339	.407	112		2	6	3	.870	7	2-18/S-4,C-3,1OM	0.5
1872	Bal-n	35	179	55	50	3	2	0	23	5	2	.279	.299	.318	86	-4	7	1	2	.873	7	C-27/O-4,2-2,3-2,M	0.3
1873	Bal-n	41	196	45	57	9	2	0	28	2	3	.291	.298	.357	94	-1	2	3	-1	.917	5	C-22,S-15/O-7,1-3	0.1
1874	Phi-n	55	265	68	91	19	11	0	56	4	2	.343	.353	.498	164	17	**11**	3	2	.807	6	*2-54/C-5,1-1	1.7
1875	Cen-n	14	65	8	18	4	2	0	5	2	4	.277	.299	.400	153	4	1	0	0	.773	4	/S-9,3-4,1-1,M	0.6
	Ath-n	54	260	71	83	11	11	2	40	4	5	.319	.330	.469	157	12	8	4	0	.856	-6	2-54/C-2,3-1	0.4
	Yr	68	325	79	101	15	**13**	2	45	6	9	.311	.323	.455	156	16	9	4	0	.856	-2	2-54/S-9,3-5,C-2,1	1.0
1876	NY-N	56	246	54	55	4	0	0	22	2	7	.224	.230	.240	65	-8				.814	-21	2-42,C-11/S-6,M	-2.6
1877	Lou-N	57	238	33	63	5	2	0	29	5	11	.265	.280	.303	71	-10				.904	-1	*S-57	-0.8
Total	5 n	226	1083	273	337	54	29	2	178	20	16	.311	.324	.420	129	30	35	14	2	.834	22	2-128/C-59,SO31	3.6
Total	2	113	484	57	118	9	2	0	51	7	18	.244	.255	.271	69	-18				.897	-22	/S-63,2-42,C-11	-3.4

■ PAT CRAWFORD   Crawford, Clifford Rankin b: 1/28/02, Society Hill, S.C. d: 1/25/94, Morehead City, N.C BL/TR, 5'11", 170 lbs. Deb: 4/18/29

YEAR	TM/L	G	AB	R	H	2B	3B	HR	RBI	BB	SO	AVG	OBP	SLG	PRO+	BR/A	SB	CS	SBR	FA	FR	G/POS	TPR
1929	NY-N	65	57	13	17	3	0	3	24	11	5	.298	.412	.509	127	3	1			1.000	-0	/1-7,3-1	0.2
1930	NY-N	25	76	11	21	3	2	3	17	7	2	.276	.345	.487	100	-0	0			.966	-0	2-18/1-1	-0.3
	Cin-N	76	224	24	65	7	1	3	26	23	10	.290	.359	.371	81	-6	2			.969	-8	2-54,1-13	-1.2
	Yr	101	300	35	86	10	3	6	43	30	12	.287	.355	.400	86	-7	2			.968	-12	2-72,1-14	-1.5
1933	StL-N	91	224	24	60	8	2	0	21	14	9	.268	.317	.321	78	-6	1			.986	3	1-29,2-15/3-7	-0.6
1934	*StL-N	61	70	3	19	2	0	0	16	5	3	.271	.320	.300	63	-4	0			.900	2	/3-9,2-4	-0.1
Total	4	318	651	75	182	23	5	9	104	60	29	.280	.344	.372	85	-13	4			.969	-8	/2-91,1-50,3-17	-2.0

■ FORREST CRAWFORD   Crawford, Forrest A. b: 5/10/1881, Rockdale, Tex. d: 3/29/08, Austin, Tex. BL/TR, Deb: 7/30/06

YEAR	TM/L	G	AB	R	H	2B	3B	HR	RBI	BB	SO	AVG	OBP	SLG	PRO+	BR/A	SB	CS	SBR	FA	FR	G/POS	TPR
1906	StL-N	45	145	8	30	3	1	0	11	7		.207	.248	.241	55	-8	1			.927	-10	S-39/3-6	-1.8
1907	StL-N	7	22	0	5	0	0	0	3	2		.227	.292	.227	65	-1	0			.912	-1	/S-7	-0.2
Total	2	52	167	8	35	3	1	0	14	9		.210	.254	.240	56	-9	1			.924	-11	/S-46,3-6	-2.0

■ GEORGE CRAWFORD   Crawford, George Deb: 10/8/1890

YEAR	TM/L	G	AB	R	H	2B	3B	HR	RBI	BB	SO	AVG	OBP	SLG	PRO+	BR/A	SB	CS	SBR	FA	FR	G/POS	TPR
1890	Phi-a	5	17	1	2	0	0	0	3	0		.118	.118	.118	-31	-3	1			1.000	1	/O-4,S-1	-0.2

■ GLENN CRAWFORD   Crawford, Glenn Martin "Shorty" b: 12/2/13, North Branch, Mich. d: 1/2/72, Saginaw, Mich. BL/TR, 5'9", 165 lbs. Deb: 4/22/45

YEAR	TM/L	G	AB	R	H	2B	3B	HR	RBI	BB	SO	AVG	OBP	SLG	PRO+	BR/A	SB	CS	SBR	FA	FR	G/POS	TPR
1945	StL-N	4	3	0	0	0	0	0	0	1	0	.000	.250	.000	-26	-0	0			.000	-1	/O-1	-0.1
	Phi-N	82	302	41	89	13	2	2	24	36	15	.295	.372	.371	110	5	5			.976	-1	O-38,S-34,2-14	0.5
	Yr	86	305	41	89	13	2	2	24	37	15	.292	.370	.367	108	4	5			.976	-2	O-39,S-34,2-14	0.4
1946	Phi-N	1	1	0	0	0	0	0	0	0	0	.000	.000	.000	-99	-0	0			.000	0	H	0.0
Total	2	87	306	41	89	13	2	2	24	37	15	.291	.369	.366	108	4	5			—	0	/O-39,S-34,2-14	0.4

■ KEN CRAWFORD   Crawford, Kenneth Daniel b: 10/31/1894, South Bend, Ind. d: 11/11/76, Pittsburgh, Pa. BL/TR, 5'9", 145 lbs. Deb: 9/6/15

YEAR	TM/L	G	AB	R	H	2B	3B	HR	RBI	BB	SO	AVG	OBP	SLG	PRO+	BR/A	SB	CS	SBR	FA	FR	G/POS	TPR
1915	Bal-F	23	82	4	20	2	1	0	7	1	18	.244	.253	.293	52	-7	0			.978	-2	1-14/O-4	-1.0

■ JAKE CRAWFORD   Crawford, Rufus b: 3/20/28, Campbell, Mo. BR/TR, 6'1.5", 185 lbs. Deb: 9/7/52

YEAR	TM/L	G	AB	R	H	2B	3B	HR	RBI	BB	SO	AVG	OBP	SLG	PRO+	BR/A	SB	CS	SBR	FA	FR	G/POS	TPR
1952	StL-A	7	11	1	2	1	0	0	1	1	5	.182	.250	.273	44	-1	1	0	0	1.000	-0	/O-3	-0.1

■ SAM CRAWFORD   Crawford, Samuel Earl "Wahoo Sam" b: 4/18/1880, Wahoo, Neb. d: 6/15/68, Hollywood, Cal. BL/TL, 6', 190 lbs. Deb: 9/10/1899 H

YEAR	TM/L	G	AB	R	H	2B	3B	HR	RBI	BB	SO	AVG	OBP	SLG	PRO+	BR/A	SB	CS	SBR	FA	FR	G/POS	TPR
1899	Cin-N	31	127	25	39	3	7	1	20	2		.307	.318	.465	111	1	6			.970	2	O-31	0.1
1900	Cin-N	101	389	68	101	15	15	7	59	28		.260	.314	.429	107	1	14			.948	12	*O-95	0.5
1901	Cin-N	131	515	91	170	20	16	**16**	104	37		.330	.378	.524	172	44	13			.923	3	*O-127	3.6
1902	Cin-N	140	555	92	185	18	**22**	3	78	47		.333	.386	.461	147	29	16			.932	4	*O-140	2.5
1903	Det-A	137	550	88	184	23	**25**	4	89	25		.335	.366	.489	159	37	18			.960	4	*O-137	3.3
1904	Det-A	150	562	49	143	22	16	2	73	44		.254	.309	.361	115	9	20			.973	4	*O-150	0.5
1905	Det-A	154	575	73	171	38	10	6	75	50		.297	.357	.430	148	30	22			**.988**	12	*O-103,1-51	3.9
1906	Det-A	145	563	65	166	25	16	2	72	38		.295	.341	.407	130	18	24			.984	1	*O-116,1-32	1.4
1907	*Det-A	144	582	**102**	188	34	17	4	81	37		.323	.366	.460	157	35	18			.965	9	*O-144/1-2	4.1
1908	*Det-A	152	591	102	184	33	16	**7**	80	37		.311	.355	.457	157	34	15			.970	-4	*O-134,1-17	2.3
1909	*Det-A	156	589	83	185	**35**	14	6	97	47		.314	.366	.452	151	32	30			.965	-7	*O-139,1-18	2.3
1910	Det-A	154	588	83	170	26	**19**	5	**120**	37		.289	.332	.423	128	16	20			.963	-11	*O-153/1-1	-0.2
1911	Det-A	146	574	109	217	36	14	7	115	61		.378	.438	.526	160	46	37			.975	-12	*O-146	2.6
1912	Det-A	149	581	81	189	30	21	4	109	42		.325	.373	.470	145	31	41			.984	-17	*O-149	0.7
1913	Det-A	153	609	78	193	32	**23**	9	83	52	28	.317	.371	.489	154	37	13			.964	-10	*O-140,1-13	2.2
1914	Det-A	157	582	74	183	22	**26**	8	104	69	31	.314	.388	.483	157	39	25	16	-2	.977	-8	*O-157	2.4
1915	Det-A	156	612	81	183	31	**19**	4	**112**	66	29	.299	.367	.431	132	22	24	14	-1	.974	-14	*O-156	0.6
1916	Det-A	100	322	41	92	11	13	0	42	37	10	.286	.359	.401	124	9	10			.978	-10	O-79/1-2	-0.6
1917	Det-A	61	104	6	18	4	0	2	12	4	6	.173	.204	.269	44	-7	0			.988	-3	1-15/O-3	-1.2
Total	19	2517	9570	1391	2961	458	309	97	1525	760	104	.309	.362	.452	143	464	366	30		.965	-48	*O-2299,1-151	30.4

■ WILLIE CRAWFORD   Crawford, Willie Murphy b: 9/7/46, Los Angeles, Cal. BL/TL, 6'1", 205 lbs. Deb: 9/16/64

YEAR	TM/L	G	AB	R	H	2B	3B	HR	RBI	BB	SO	AVG	OBP	SLG	PRO+	BR/A	SB	CS	SBR	FA	FR	G/POS	TPR
1964	LA-N	10	16	3	5	1	0	0	1	1	7	.313	.353	.375	113	0	1	1	-0	1.000	0	/O-4	0.0
1965	*LA-N	52	27	10	4	0	0	0	0	2	8	.148	.207	.148	2	-4	2	0	1	1.000	-2	/O-8	-0.5
1966	LA-N	6	0	1	0	0	0	0	0	0	0	—	—	—	—	0	0	0	0	.000	0	R	0.0
1967	LA-N	4	4	0	1	0	0	0	0	1	3	.250	.400	.250	98	0	0	0	0	.000	-1	/O-1	-0.1
1968	LA-N	61	175	25	44	12	1	4	14	20	64	.251	.335	.400	130	6	3	3	-2	.966	3	O-48	0.6
1969	LA-N	129	389	64	96	17	5	11	40	49	85	.247	.331	.411	112	4	4	4	-0	.973	-4	*O-113	-0.6
1970	LA-N	109	299	48	70	8	6	4	40	33	88	.234	.314	.381	89	-5	4	4	-1	.960	-1	O-94	-1.1
1971	LA-N	114	342	64	96	16	6	9	40	28	49	.281	.337	.442	126	11	5	2	0	.981	-7	O-97	0.0
1972	LA-N	96	243	28	61	7	3	8	27	35	55	.251	.350	.403	116	6	4	2	0	.983	-8	O-74	-0.5
1973	LA-N	145	457	75	135	26	2	14	66	78	91	.295	.399	.453	142	28	12	5	1	.978	1	O-138	2.5
1974	*LA-N	139	466	73	138	23	4	11	61	64	88	.295	.380	.432	132	21	5	8	-3	.966	-7	*O-133	0.6
1975	LA-N	124	373	46	98	15	2	6	46	49	43	.263	.348	.386	108	4	5	5	-2	.990	-5	*O-113	-0.6
1976	StL-N	120	392	49	119	17	5	9	50	37	53	.304	.365	.441	127	14	2	1	0	.982	-1	*O-107	0.9
1977	Hou-N	42	114	14	29	3	0	2	18	16	19	.254	.346	.333	91	-1	0	0	0	.959	-2	O-30	-0.4
	Oak-A	59	136	7	25	7	1	1	16	18	20	.184	.279	.272	52	-9	0	0	0	.978	2	O-22,D-18	-0.8
Total	14	1210	3435	507	921	152	35	86	419	431	664	.268	.351	.408	117	77	47	36	-8	.975	-30	O-982/D-18	-0.0

■ GEORGE CREAMER   Creamer, George W. (b: George W. Triebel) b: 1855, Philadelphia, Pa. d: 6/27/1886, Philadelphia, Pa. BR/TR, 6'2", Deb: 5/1/1878 M

YEAR	TM/L	G	AB	R	H	2B	3B	HR	RBI	BB	SO	AVG	OBP	SLG	PRO+	BR/A	SB	CS	SBR	FA	FR	G/POS	TPR
1878	Mil-N	50	193	30	41	7	3	0	15	5	15	.212	.232	.280	63	-8				.839	-5	2-28,O-17/3-6	-1.1
1879	Syr-N	15	60	3	13	2	0	0	3	1	2	.217	.230	.250	65	-2				.825	-10	2-10/S-3,O-2	-1.0
1880	Wor-N	85	306	40	61	6	3	0	27	4	21	.199	.210	.239	47	-17				.883	-7	*2-85	-1.9
1881	Wor-N	80	309	42	64	9	2	0	25	11	27	.207	.234	.249	49	-18				.904	-9	*2-80	-2.2
1882	Wor-N	81	286	27	65	16	4	0	29	14	24	.227	.263	.336	88	-4				.907	11	*2-81	0.8

YEAR	TM/L	G	AB	R	H	2B	3B	HR	RBI	BB	SO	AVG	OBP	SLG	PRO+	BR/A	SB	CS	SBR	FA	FR	G/POS	TPR
1883	Pit-a	91	369	54	94	7	9	0		20		.255	.293	.322	103	2				.897	8	*2-91	1.0
1884	Pit-a	98	339	38	62	8	5	0		16		.183	.224	.236	49	-18				.937	16	*2-98,M	0.0
Total	7	500	1862	234	400	55	28	1	99	71	89	.215	.244	.276	67	-65				.901	6	2-473/O-19,3-6,S-3	-4.4

■ BIRDIE CREE   Cree, William Franklin   b: 10/23/1882, Khedive, Pa.   d: 11/8/42, Sunbury, Pa.   BR/TR, 5'6", 150 lbs.   Deb: 9/17/08

YEAR	TM/L	G	AB	R	H	2B	3B	HR	RBI	BB	SO	AVG	OBP	SLG	PRO+	BR/A	SB	CS	SBR	FA	FR	G/POS	TPR
1908	NY-A	21	78	5	21	0	2	0	4	7		.269	.345	.321	115	2	1			1.000	1	O-21	0.2
1909	NY-A	104	343	48	90	6	3	2	27	30		.262	.338	.315	105	3	10			.949	-7	O-79/S-6,2-4,3-1	-0.7
1910	NY-A	134	467	58	134	19	16	4	73	40		.287	.353	.422	135	18	28			.955	-12	*O-134	-0.1
1911	NY-A	137	520	90	181	30	22	4	88	56		.348	.415	.513	149	33	48			.964	0	*O-132/S-4,2-2	2.6
1912	NY-A	50	190	25	63	11	6	0	22	20		.332	.409	.453	138	10	12			.948	5	O-50	1.2
1913	NY-A	145	534	51	145	25	6	1	63	50	51	.272	.338	.346	100	0	22			.976	-4	*O-144	-1.1
1914	NY-A	77	275	45	85	18	5	0	40	30	24	.309	.389	.411	141	14	4	9	-4	.976	7	O-76	1.5
1915	NY-A	74	196	23	42	5	0	0	15	36	22	.214	.353	.276	88	-1	7	8	-3	.945	-3	O-53	-1.0
Total	8	742	2603	345	761	117	62	11	332	269	97	.292	.368	.398	124	78	132	17		.965	-13	O-689/S-10,2-6,3-1	2.6

■ CONNIE CREEDEN   Creeden, Cornelius Stephen   b: 7/21/15, Danvers, Mass.   d: 11/30/69, Santa Ana, Cal.   BL/TL, 6'1", 200 lbs.   Deb: 4/28/43

| 1943 | Bos-N | 5 | 4 | 0 | 1 | 0 | 0 | 0 | 1 | 0 | | .250 | .400 | .250 | 91 | 0 | 0 | | | .000 | 0 | H | 0.0 |

■ PAT CREEDEN   Creeden, Patrick Francis "Whoops"   b: 5/23/06, Newburyport, Mass.   d: 4/20/92, Brockton, Mass.   BL/TR, 5'8", 175 lbs.   Deb: 4/14/31

| 1931 | Bos-A | 5 | 8 | 0 | 0 | 0 | 0 | 0 | 0 | 0 | 3 | .000 | .111 | .000 | -73 | -2 | 0 | 0 | 0 | .846 | 1 | /2-2 | -0.2 |

■ MARTY CREEGAN   Creegan, Martin   b: San Francisco, Cal.   161 lbs.   Deb: 4/17/1884

| 1884 | Was-U | 9 | 33 | 4 | 5 | 0 | 0 | 0 | | 1 | | .152 | .176 | .152 | 0 | -5 | | | | .667 | -1 | /O-6,C-3,3-2,1-1 | -0.5 |

■ GUS CREELY   Creely, August L.   b: 6/6/1870, Florissant, Mo.   d: 4/22/34, St.Louis, Mo.   5'6", 150 lbs.   Deb: 10/9/1890

| 1890 | StL-a | 4 | 15 | 0 | 0 | 0 | 0 | 0 | 0 | 0 | | .000 | .000 | .000 | -88 | -4 | 1 | | | .769 | -3 | /S-4 | -0.6 |

■ PETE CREGAN   Cregan, Peter James "Peekskill Pete"   b: 4/13/1875, Kingston, N.Y.   d: 5/18/45, New York, N.Y.   BR/TR, 5'7.5", 150 lbs.   Deb: 9/8/1899

1899	NY-N	1	2	0	0	0	0	0	0	0		.000	.000	.000	-99	-1	0			1.000	-0	/O-1	-0.1
1903	Cin-N	6	19	0	2	0	0	0	0	1		.105	.190	.105	-13	-3	0			.769	-1	/O-6	-0.4
Total	2	7	21	0	2	0	0	0	0	1		.095	.174	.095	-21	-3	0			.786	-2	/O-7	-0.5

■ BERNIE CREGER   Creger, Bernard Odell   b: 3/21/27, Wytheville, Va.   BR/TR, 6', 175 lbs.   Deb: 4/29/47

| 1947 | StL-N | 15 | 16 | 3 | 3 | 1 | 0 | 0 | 1 | 3 | | .188 | .235 | .250 | 28 | -2 | 1 | | | .828 | -3 | S-13 | -0.5 |

■ CREEPY CRESPI   Crespi, Frank Angelo Joseph   b: 2/16/18, St.Louis, Mo.   d: 3/1/90, Florissant, Mo.   BR/TR, 5'8.5", 175 lbs.   Deb: 9/14/38

1938	StL-N	7	19	2	5	2	0	0	1	2	7	.263	.333	.368	88	-0	0			.813	-2	/S-7	-0.2
1939	StL-N	15	29	3	5	1	0	0	6	3	6	.172	.250	.207	23	-3	0			.962	-0	/2-6,S-4	-0.3
1940	StL-N	3	11	2	3	1	0	0	0	1	2	.273	.333	.364	87	-0	1			1.000	-1	/3-2,S-1	-0.1
1941	StL-N	146	560	85	156	24	2	4	46	57	58	.279	.355	.350	90	-3	4			.962	0	*2-145	0.7
1942	*StL-N	93	292	35	71	4	2	0	35	27	29	.243	.309	.271	65	-12	4			.967	-5	2-83/S-5	-1.3
Total	5	264	911	125	240	32	4	4	88	90	102	.263	.336	.321	82	-20	8			.963	-7	2-234/S-17,3-2	-1.2

■ FELIPE CRESPO   Crespo, Felipe Javier (Clausio)   b: 3/5/73, Rio Piedras, P.R.   BB/TR, 5'11", 195 lbs.   Deb: 4/28/96

| 1996 | Tor-A | 22 | 49 | 6 | 9 | 4 | 1 | 2 | 4 | 12 | 13 | .184 | .375 | .265 | 65 | -2 | 1 | 0 | 0 | .982 | 3 | 2-10/3-6,1-2 | 0.2 |

■ LOU CRIGER   Criger, Louis   b: 2/3/1872, Elkhart, Ind.   d: 5/14/34, Tucson, Ariz.   BR/TR, 5'10", 165 lbs.   Deb: 9/21/1896

1896	Cle-N	2	5	0	0	0	0	0	0	1	0	.000	.167	.000	-51	-1	1			1.000	1	/C-1	0.0
1897	Cle-N	39	138	15	31	4	1	0	22	23		.225	.340	.268	58	-8	5			.937	-1	C-37/1-2	-0.4
1898	Cle-N	84	287	43	80	13	4	1	32	40		.279	.377	.362	113	7	2			.957	15	C-82	2.8
1899	StL-N	77	258	39	66	4	5	2	44	28		.256	.286	.333	81	-6	14			.953	6	C-75/3-1	0.3
1900	StL-N	80	288	31	78	8	6	2	38	4		.271	.286	.361	78	-10	5			.953	6	C-75/3-1	0.3
1901	Bos-A	76	268	26	62	6	3	0	24	11		.231	.270	.276	52	-17	7			.967	22	C-68/1-8	1.0
1902	Bos-A	83	266	32	68	16	6	0	28	27		.256	.324	.361	87	-5	7			.965	14	C-80/O-1	1.7
1903	*Bos-A	96	317	41	61	7	10	3	31	26		.192	.256	.306	65	-14	5			.979	23	C-96	2.0
1904	Bos-A	98	299	34	63	10	5	2	34	27		.211	.283	.298	79	-7	1			.981	19	C-95	2.5
1905	Bos-A	109	313	33	62	6	7	1	36	54		.198	.322	.272	88	-2	5			.972	5	*C-109	1.5
1906	Bos-A	7	17	0	3	1	0	0	1	0		.176	.222	.235	43	-1	1			.981	0	/C-6	0.4
1907	Bos-A	75	226	12	41	4	0	0	14	19		.181	.251	.199	44	-14	2			.978	-0	C-75	-0.8
1908	Bos-A	84	237	12	45	4	2	0	25	13		.190	.232	.224	47	-14	1			.980	13	C-84	0.7
1909	StL-A	74	212	15	36	1	1	0	9	36		.170	.261	.184	44	-13	2			.986	8	C-73	0.2
1910	NY-A	27	69	3	13	2	0	0	4	10		.188	.291	.217	56	-3	0			.993	-1	C-27	-0.3
1912	StL-A	3	2	1	0	0	0	0	0	0		.000	.000	.000	-99	-1	0			1.000	1	/C-1	0.0
Total	16	1012	3202	337	709	86	50	11	342	309	0	.221	.295	.290	72	-108	58			.971	130	C-984/1-10,0-1,3-1	11.7

■ DAVE CRIPE   Cripe, David Gordon   b: 4/7/51, Ramona, Cal.   BR/TR, 6', 180 lbs.   Deb: 9/10/78

| 1978 | KC-A | 7 | 13 | 1 | 2 | 0 | 0 | 0 | 1 | 0 | 2 | .154 | .154 | .154 | -13 | -2 | 0 | 0 | 0 | 1.000 | -2 | /3-5 | -0.4 |

■ DAVE CRISCIONE   Criscione, David Gerald   b: 9/2/51, Dunkirk, N.Y.   BR/TR, 5'8", 185 lbs.   Deb: 7/17/77

| 1977 | Bal-A | 7 | 9 | 1 | 3 | 0 | 0 | 1 | 1 | 0 | 1 | .333 | .333 | .667 | 176 | 1 | 0 | 0 | 0 | 1.000 | -1 | /C-7 | 0.0 |

■ TONY CRISCOLA   Criscola, Anthony Paul   b: 7/9/15, Walla Walla, Wash.   BL/TR, 5'11.5", 180 lbs.   Deb: 4/15/42

1942	StL-A	91	158	17	47	9	2	1	13	8	13	.297	.331	.399	103	0	2	2	-1	.955	-14	O-52	-1.7
1943	StL-A	29	52	4	8	0	0	0	1	8	7	.154	.267	.154	24	-5	0	0	0	.960	-2	O-13	-0.8
1944	Cin-N	64	157	14	36	3	2	0	14	14	12	.229	.297	.274	64	-7	0			.977	1	O-35	-0.8
Total	3	184	367	35	91	12	4	1	28	30	32	.248	.307	.311	75	-12	2	2	2	.966	-15	O-100	-3.3

■ PAT CRISHAM   Crisham, Patrick J.   b: 6/4/1877, Amesbury, Mass.   d: 6/12/15, Syracuse, N.Y.   6', 168 lbs.   Deb: 5/5/1899

| 1899 | Bal-N | 53 | 172 | 23 | 50 | 5 | 3 | 0 | 20 | 4 | | .291 | .311 | .355 | 78 | -6 | 4 | | | .979 | -5 | 1-26,C-22 | -0.8 |

■ JOE CRISP   Crisp, Joseph Shelby   b: 7/8/1889, Higginsville, Mo.   d: 2/5/39, Kansas City, Mo.   BR/TR, 6'4", 200 lbs.   Deb: 9/2/10

1910	StL-A	1	1	0	0	0	0	0	0	0		.000	.000	.000	-99	-0	0			1.000	0	/C-1	0.0
1911	StL-A	1	1	0	1	0	0	0	0	0		1.000	1.000	1.000	477	0	0			.000	0	/H	0.0
Total	2	2	2	0	1	0	0	0	0	0		.500	.500	.500	206	0	0			1.000	0	/C-1	0.0

■ DODE CRISS   Criss, Dode   b: 3/12/1885, Sherman, Miss.   d: 9/8/55, Sherman, Miss.   BL/TR, 6'2", 200 lbs.   Deb: 4/20/08

1908	StL-A	64	82	15	28	6	0	0	14	9		.341	.407	.415	166	6	1			.933	-1	O-11/P-9,1-1	0.0
1909	StL-A	35	48	2	14	6	1	0	7	0		.292	.306	.458	152	2	0			1.000	-1	P-11	0.0
1910	StL-A	70	91	11	21	4	2	1	11	11		.231	.320	.352	118	0	2			.983	-1	1-11/P-6	0.1
1911	StL-A	58	83	10	21	3	1	2	15	11		.253	.347	.386	109	1	0			.956	-2	1-14/P-4	-0.1
Total	4	227	304	38	84	19	4	3	47	31		.276	.348	.395	133	11	3			.964	-5	/P-30,1-26,O-11	0.5

■ CHES CRIST   Crist, Chester Arthur "Squak"   b: 2/10/1882, Cozaddale, Ohio   d: 1/7/57, Cincinnati, Ohio   BR/TR, 5'11", 165 lbs.   Deb: 5/18/06

| 1906 | Phi-N | 6 | 11 | 1 | 0 | 0 | 0 | 0 | | | | .000 | .083 | .000 | -74 | -2 | 0 | | | .800 | -3 | /C-6 | -0.6 |

■ HUGHIE CRITZ   Critz, Hugh Melville   b: 9/17/1900, Starkville, Miss.   d: 1/10/80, Greenwood, Miss.   BR/TR, 5'8", 147 lbs.   Deb: 5/31/24

1924	Cin-N	102	413	67	133	15	14	3	35	19	18	.322	.352	.448	115	7	19	11	-1	.956	2	2-96/S-1	1.0
1925	Cin-N	144	541	74	150	14	8	2	51	34	17	.277	.321	.344	72	-23	13	13	-4	.970	22	*2-144	-0.3
1926	Cin-N	155	607	96	164	24	14	3	79	39	25	.270	.314	.371	87	-12	7			.981	24	*2-155	1.6
1927	Cin-N	113	396	50	110	10	8	4	49	16	18	.278	.306	.374	84	-10	7			.969	-2	2-113	-0.8
1928	Cin-N	153	641	69	190	21	11	5	52	37	24	.296	.335	.387	90	-11	18			.971	-17	2-153	-2.3
1929	Cin-N	107	425	55	105	17	9	1	50	27	21	.247	.292	.336	58	-29	9			.974	4	2-106/S-1	-1.9
1930	Cin-N	28	104	15	24	3	2	0	11	6	6	.231	.273	.298	40	-10	1			.987	-3	2-28	-1.1

YEAR	TM/L	G	AB	R	H	2B	3B	HR	RBI	BB	SO	AVG	OBP	SLG	PRO+	BR/A	SB	CS	SBR	FA	FR	G/POS	TPR
	NY-N	124	558	93	148	17	11	4	50	24	26	.265	.296	.357	58	-39	7			.972	5	*2-124	-2.4
	Yr	152	662	108	172	20	13	4	61	30	32	.260	.292	.347	55	-49	8			**.974**	2	*2-152	-3.5
1931	NY-N	66	238	33	69	7	2	4	17	8	17	.290	.313	.387	89	-4	4			.984	0	2-54	0.0
1932	NY-N	151	659	90	182	32	7	2	50	34	27	.276	.313	.355	81	-18	3			.974	1	*2-151	-0.9
1933	*NY-N	133	558	68	137	18	5	2	33	23	24	.246	.279	.306	68	-23	4			**.982**	**47**	*2-133	3.2
1934	NY-N	137	571	77	138	17	1	6	40	19	24	.242	.269	.306	55	-37	3			**.978**	**25**	*2-137	-0.3
1935	NY-N	65	219	19	41	0	3	2	14	3	10	.187	.198	.242	18	-25	2			.966	3	2-59	-1.8
Total	12	1478	5930	832	1591	195	95	38	531	289	257	.268	.303	.352	74	-235	97	24		.974	111	*2-1453/S-2	-6.0

■ **DAVEY CROCKETT** Crockett, Daniel Solomon b: 10/5/1875, Roanoke, Va. d: 2/23/61, Charlottesville, Va. BL/TR, 6'1", 175 lbs. Deb: 7/11/01

YEAR	TM/L	G	AB	R	H	2B	3B	HR	RBI	BB	SO	AVG	OBP	SLG	PRO+	BR/A	SB	CS	SBR	FA	FR	G/POS	TPR
1901	Det-A	28	102	10	29	2	0	0	14	6		.284	.336	.343	85	-2	1			.968	-0	1-27	-0.3

■ **ART CROFT** Croft, Arthur F. b: 1/23/1855, St.Louis, Mo. d: 3/16/1884, St.Louis, Mo. Deb: 5/4/1875

YEAR	TM/L	G	AB	R	H	2B	3B	HR	RBI	BB	SO	AVG	OBP	SLG	PRO+	BR/A	SB	CS	SBR	FA	FR	G/POS	TPR
1875	RS-n	19	75	5	15	3	0	0	2	0	2	.200	.200	.240	58	-3	5	1	1	.800	-4	O-19	-0.5
1877	StL-N	54	220	23	51	5	2	0	27	1	15	.232	.235	.273	63	-9				.971	-3	1-28,O-25/2-1	-1.1
1878	Ind-N	60	222	22	35	6	0	0	16	5	23	.158	.176	.185	22	-18				.963	-1	*1-51/O-9	-2.0
Total	2	114	442	45	86	11	2	0	43	6	38	.195	.205	.229	43	-26				.965	-4	/1-79,O-34,2-1	-3.1

■ **HARRY CROFT** Croft, Henry T. b: 8/1/1875, Chicago, Ill. d: 12/11/33, Oak Park, Ill. Deb: 5/19/1899

YEAR	TM/L	G	AB	R	H	2B	3B	HR	RBI	BB	SO	AVG	OBP	SLG	PRO+	BR/A	SB	CS	SBR	FA	FR	G/POS	TPR
1899	Lou-N	2	2	0	0	0	0	0	0	0		.000	.000	.000	-99	-1	0			.000	0	/H	0.0
	Phi-N	2	7	0	1	0	0	0	0	1		.143	.250	.143	9	-1	0			1.000	-1	/2-2	-0.1
	Yr	4	9	0	1	0	0	0	0	1		.111	.200	.111	-14	-1	0			1.000	-1	/2-2	-0.1
1901	Chi-N	3	12	1	4	0	0	0	4	0		.333	.333	.333	97	-0	0			1.000	1	/O-3	0.2
Total	2	7	21	1	5	0	0	0	4	1		.238	.273	.238	47	-1	0			1.000	2	/O-3,2-2	0.1

■ **FRED CROLIUS** Crolius, Fred Joseph b: 12/16/1876, Jersey City, N.J. d: 8/25/60, Ormond Beach, Fla. Deb: 4/19/01

YEAR	TM/L	G	AB	R	H	2B	3B	HR	RBI	BB	SO	AVG	OBP	SLG	PRO+	BR/A	SB	CS	SBR	FA	FR	G/POS	TPR
1901	Bos-N	49	200	22	48	4	1	1	13	9		.240	.306	.285	66	-9	6			.850	-8	O-49	-2.0
1902	Pit-N	9	38	4	10	2	1	0	7	0		.263	.263	.368	91	-1	0			1.000	-1	/O-9	-0.2
Total	2	58	238	26	58	6	2	1	20	9		.244	.300	.298	69	-9	6			.868	-8	/O-58	-2.2

■ **WARREN CROMARTIE** Cromartie, Warren Livingston b: 9/29/53, Miami Beach, Fla. BL/TL, 6', 192 lbs. Deb: 9/6/74

YEAR	TM/L	G	AB	R	H	2B	3B	HR	RBI	BB	SO	AVG	OBP	SLG	PRO+	BR/A	SB	CS	SBR	FA	FR	G/POS	TPR
1974	Mon-N	8	17	2	3	0	0	0	0	3	3	.176	.300	.176	34	-1	1	0	0	1.000	-1	/O-6	-0.2
1976	Mon-N	33	81	8	17	1	0	0	2	1	5	.210	.220	.222	25	-8	1	2	-1	.943	-2	O-20	-1.2
1977	Mon-N	155	620	64	175	41	7	5	50	33	40	.282	.323	.395	94	-6	10	3	-1	.976	12	*O-155	0.1
1978	Mon-N	159	607	77	180	32	6	10	56	33	60	.297	.340	.418	112	9	8	8	-2	.978	25	*O-158/1-4	2.5
1979	Mon-N	158	659	84	181	46	5	8	46	38	78	.275	.315	.396	94	-7	8	7	-2	.976	20	*O-158	0.5
1980	Mon-N	162	597	74	172	33	5	14	70	51	64	.288	.346	.430	115	12	8	8	-2	.991	-6	*1-158/O-2	-0.5
1981	*Mon-N	99	358	41	109	19	2	6	42	39	27	.304	.373	.419	123	11	2	3	-1	.992	-1	1-62,O-38	0.5
1982	Mon-N	144	497	59	126	24	3	14	62	69	60	.254	.348	.398	106	5	3	0	1	.979	11	O-136/1-9	1.4
1983	Mon-N	120	360	37	100	26	2	6	43	43	48	.278	.356	.386	106	4	8	3	1	.973	12	*O-101/1-1	1.5
1991	KC-A	69	131	13	41	7	1	2	20	15	18	.313	.384	.420	122	4	1	3	-2	.996	-4	1-29/O-6,D-1	-0.3
Total	10	1107	3927	459	1104	229	32	61	391	325	403	.281	.339	.402	105	22	50	37	-7	.977	68	O-780,1-263/D-1	4.3

■ **TRIPP CROMER** Cromer, Roy Bunyan b: 11/21/67, Lake City, S.C. BR/TR, 6'2", 165 lbs. Deb: 9/7/93

YEAR	TM/L	G	AB	R	H	2B	3B	HR	RBI	BB	SO	AVG	OBP	SLG	PRO+	BR/A	SB	CS	SBR	FA	FR	G/POS	TPR
1993	StL-N	10	23	1	2	0	0	0	0	1	6	.087	.125	.087	-43	-5	0	0	0	.912	1	/S-9	-0.3
1994	StL-N	2	0	1	0	0	0	0	0	0	0					0	0	0	0	.000	-1	/S-2	-0.1
1995	StL-N	105	345	36	78	19	0	5	18	14	66	.226	.264	.325	54	-23	0	0	0	.960	2	S-95,2-11	-1.3
Total	3	117	368	38	80	19	0	5	18	15	72	.217	.256	.310	49	-28	0	0	0	.954	2	S-106/2-11	-1.7

■ **NED CROMPTON** Crompton, Edward b: 2/12/1889, Liverpool, England d: 9/28/50, Aspinwall, Pa. BL/TL, 5'10.5", 175 lbs. Deb: 9/13/09

YEAR	TM/L	G	AB	R	H	2B	3B	HR	RBI	BB	SO	AVG	OBP	SLG	PRO+	BR/A	SB	CS	SBR	FA	FR	G/POS	TPR
1909	StL-A	17	63	7	10	2	1	0	2	7		.159	.254	.222	54	-3	1			.909	-1	O-17	-0.3
1910	Cin-N	1	2	0	0	0	0	0	0	0	2	.000	.000	.000	-99	-1	0			.000	-1	/O-1	-0.1
Total	2	18	65	7	10	2	1	0	2	7	2	.154	.247	.215	49	-4	1			.909	-1	/O-18	-0.4

■ **HERB CROMPTON** Crompton, Herbert Bryan "Workhorse" b: 11/7/11, Taylor Ridge, Ill. d: 8/5/63, Moline, Ill. BR/TR, 6', 185 lbs. Deb: 4/26/37

YEAR	TM/L	G	AB	R	H	2B	3B	HR	RBI	BB	SO	AVG	OBP	SLG	PRO+	BR/A	SB	CS	SBR	FA	FR	G/POS	TPR
1937	Was-A	2	3	0	1	0	0	0	0	0	0	.333	.333	.333	72	-0	0	0	0	1.000	0	/C-2	0.0
1945	NY-A	36	99	6	19	3	0	0	12	2	7	.192	.208	.222	24	-10	0	0	0	.984	1	C-33	-0.8
Total	2	38	102	6	20	3	0	0	12	2	7	.196	.212	.225	25	-10	0	0	0	.984	1	/C-35	-0.8

■ **CHRIS CRON** Cron, Christopher John b: 3/31/64, Albuquerque, N.Mex. BR/TR, 6'2", 200 lbs. Deb: 8/15/91

YEAR	TM/L	G	AB	R	H	2B	3B	HR	RBI	BB	SO	AVG	OBP	SLG	PRO+	BR/A	SB	CS	SBR	FA	FR	G/POS	TPR
1991	Cal-A	6	15	0	2	0	0	0	0	2	5	.133	.235	.133	5	-2	0	0	0	1.000	1	/1-5,D-1	-0.1
1992	Chi-A	6	10	0	0	0	0	0	0	0	4	.000	.000	.000	-99	-3	0	0	0	.923	-1	/1-5,O-1	-0.3
Total	2	12	25	0	2	0	0	0	0	2	9	.080	.148	.080	-35	-5	0	0	0	.980	1	/1-10,O-1,D-1	-0.4

■ **DAN CRONIN** Cronin, Daniel T. b: 4/1/1857, S.Boston, Mass. d: 11/30/1885, Boston, Mass. 5'8", 170 lbs. Deb: 7/9/1884

YEAR	TM/L	G	AB	R	H	2B	3B	HR	RBI	BB	SO	AVG	OBP	SLG	PRO+	BR/A	SB	CS	SBR	FA	FR	G/POS	TPR
1884	CP-U	1	4	1	1	0	0	0		0		.250	.250	.250	52	-0				.200	-2	/2-1	-0.2
	StL-U	1	5	0	0	0	0	0		0		.000	.000	.000	-97	-1				.000	-1	/O-1	-0.2
	Yr	2	9	1	1	0	0	0		0		.111	.111	.111	-32	-2				.000	-3	/2-1,O-1	-0.4

■ **JIM CRONIN** Cronin, James John b: 8/7/05, Richmond, Cal. d: 6/10/83, Concord, Cal. BB/TR, 5'10.5", 150 lbs. Deb: 7/4/29

YEAR	TM/L	G	AB	R	H	2B	3B	HR	RBI	BB	SO	AVG	OBP	SLG	PRO+	BR/A	SB	CS	SBR	FA	FR	G/POS	TPR
1929	Phi-A	25	56	7	13	2	1	0	4	5	7	.232	.295	.304	52	-4	0	0	0	.966	5	2-10/S-9,3-4	0.2

■ **JOE CRONIN** Cronin, Joseph Edward b: 10/12/06, San Francisco, Cal d: 9/7/84, Osterville, Mass. BR/TR, 5'11.5", 180 lbs. Deb: 4/29/26 MH

YEAR	TM/L	G	AB	R	H	2B	3B	HR	RBI	BB	SO	AVG	OBP	SLG	PRO+	BR/A	SB	CS	SBR	FA	FR	G/POS	TPR
1926	Pit-N	38	83	9	22	2	2	0	11	6	15	.265	.315	.337	72	-3	0			.977	6	2-27/S-7	0.3
1927	Pit-N	12	22	2	5	1	0	0	3	2	3	.227	.292	.273	48	-2	0			1.000	-4	/2-7,S-4,1-1	-0.5
1928	Was-A	63	227	23	55	10	4	0	25	22	27	.242	.309	.322	66	-11	4	0	1	.953	8	S-63	0.5
1929	Was-A	145	494	72	139	29	8	8	61	85	37	.281	.388	.421	107	8	5	9	-4	.923	6	*S-143/2-1	2.6
1930	Was-A	154	587	127	203	41	9	13	126	72	36	.346	.422	.513	135	33	17	10	-1	.960	26	*S-154	6.7
1931	Was-A	156	611	103	187	44	13	12	126	81	52	.306	.391	.480	127	25	10	9	-2	.950	13	*S-155	4.6
1932	Was-A	143	557	95	177	43	**18**	6	116	66	45	.318	.393	.492	129	25	7	5	-2	**.959**	6	*S-141	3.9
1933	*Was-A★	152	602	89	186	**45**	11	5	118	87	49	.309	.398	.445	124	23	5	4	-1	**.960**	10	*S-152,M	4.0
1934	Was-A★	127	504	68	143	30	9	7	101	53	28	.284	.353	.421	103	1	8	0	2	.951	18	*S-127,M	2.7
1935	Bos-A★	144	556	70	164	37	14	9	95	63	40	.295	.370	.460	106	5	3	3	-1	.949	-13	*S-139/1-2,M	-0.2
1936	Bos-A	81	295	36	83	22	4	2	43	32	21	.281	.354	.403	82	-9	1	3	-2	.930	2	S-60,3-21,M	-0.7
1937	Bos-A★	148	570	102	175	40	4	18	110	84	73	.307	.402	.486	118	17	5	3	-0	.958	-13	*S-148,M	1.3
1938	Bos-A★	143	530	98	172	**51**	5	17	94	91	60	.325	.428	.536	134	29	7	5	-1	.954	7	*S-142,M	4.2
1939	Bos-A★	143	520	97	160	33	3	19	107	87	48	.308	.407	.492	124	20	6	6	-2	.959	6	*S-142,M	3.4
1940	Bos-A	149	548	104	156	35	6	24	111	83	65	.285	.380	.502	122	17	7	5	-1	.948	-8	*S-146/3-2,M	2.9
1941	Bos-A★	143	518	98	161	38	8	16	95	82	55	.311	.406	.508	137	29	1	4	-2	.958	-8	*S-119,3-22/O-1,M	2.7
1942	Bos-A	45	79	7	24	8	0	4	24	15	21	.304	.415	.494	150	6	0	1	-1	.865	-1	3-11/1-5,S-1,M	0.4
1943	Bos-A	59	77	8	24	4	0	5	29	11	4	.312	.398	.558	176	7	0	0	0	.968	0	3-10,M	0.8
1944	Bos-A	76	191	24	46	7	0	5	28	34	19	.241	.358	.356	106	3	1	0	0	.981	-2	1-49,M	-0.4
1945	Bos-A	3	8	1	3	1	0	0	1	1	0	.375	.545	.375	165	1	0	0	0	1.000	1	/3-3,M	0.0
Total	20	2124	7579	1233	2285	515	118	170	1424	1059	700	.301	.390	.468	119	223	87	71		.951	68	*S-1843/3-69,12O	39.4

■ **BILL CRONIN** Cronin, William Patrick "Crungy" b: 12/26/02, W.Newton, Mass. d: 10/26/66, Newton, Mass. BR/TR, 5'9", 167 lbs. Deb: 7/4/28

YEAR	TM/L	G	AB	R	H	2B	3B	HR	RBI	BB	SO	AVG	OBP	SLG	PRO+	BR/A	SB	CS	SBR	FA	FR	G/POS	TPR
1928	Bos-N	3	2	1	0	0	0	0	0	1	0	.000	.333	.000	-6	-0				1.000	-0	/C-3	0.0
1929	Bos-N	6	9	0	1	0	0	0	0	0	0	.111	.111	.111	-47	-2				1.000	1	/C-6	-0.1
1930	Bos-N	66	178	19	45	9	1	0	17	4	8	.253	.277	.315	44	-16				.983	7	C-64	-0.5
1931	Bos-N	51	107	8	22	6	1	0	10	7	5	.206	.267	.280	49	-8				.941	1	C-50	-0.5
Total	4	126	296	28	68	15	3	0	27	12	13	.230	.269	.294	43	-26	0			.968	9	C-123	-1.0

YEAR	TM/L	G	AB	R	H	2B	3B	HR	RBI	BB	SO	AVG	OBP	SLG	PRO+	BR/A	SB	CS	SBR	FA	FR	G/POS	TPR

■ TOM CROOKE Crooke, Thomas Aloysius b: 7/26/1884, Washington, D.C. d: 4/5/29, Quantico, Va. BR/TR, 6', 180 lbs. Deb: 9/29/09

1909	Was-A	3	7	2	2	1	0	0	2	2		.286	.444	.429	184	1			1	.969	-1	/1-3	0.0
1910	Was-A	8	21	1	4	1	0	0	1	1		.190	.227	.238	48	-1			0	1.000	-0	/1-5	-0.2
Total	2	11	28	3	6	2	0	0	3	3		.214	.290	.286	85	-0			1	.988	-1	/1-8	-0.2

■ JACK CROOKS Crooks, John Charles b: 11/9/1865, St.Paul, Minn. d: 2/2/18, St.Louis, Mo. BR/TR, 5'10", 170 lbs. Deb: 9/26/1889 M

1889	Col-a	12	43	13	14	2	3	0	7	10	4	.326	.463	.512	187	6	10			.987	5	2-12	0.9
1890	Col-a	135	485	86	107	5	4	1	62	96		.221	.357	.254	86	-1	57			.937	-4	*2-134/3-1,O-1	0.3
1891	Col-a	138	519	110	127	19	13	0	46	103	47	.245	.379	.331	110	13	50			.957	20	*2-138	3.3
1892	StL-N	128	445	82	95	7	4	7	38	**136**	52	.213	.400	.294	116	20	23			.929	-7	*2-101,3-25/O-2,M	1.5
1893	StL-N	128	448	93	106	10	9	1	48	**121**	37	.237	.408	.306	91	2	31			.908	4	*3-123/S-4,C-1	0.7
1895	Was-N	117	409	80	114	19	8	6	57	68	39	.279	.392	.408	108	7	36			.956	12	*2-117	2.1
1896	Was-N	25	84	20	24	3	0	3	20	16	8	.286	.406	.429	120	3	2			.916	-3	2-20/3-4	0.1
	Lou-N	39	122	19	29	5	1	2	15	20	8	.238	.354	.344	88	-2	8			.925	5	2-39	0.5
	Yr	64	206	39	53	8	1	5	35	36	16	.257	.376	.379	101	2	10			.922	2	2-59/3-4	0.6
1898	StL-N	72	225	33	52	4	2	1	20	40		.231	.359	.280	82	-3	3			.959	7	2-66/3-3,S-2,O-1	0.7
Total	8	794	2780	536	668	74	44	21	313	610	195	.240	.385	.321	102	44	220			.946	39	2-627,3-156/S-6,OC	10.1

■ ED CROSBY Crosby, Edward Carlton b: 5/26/49, Long Beach, Cal. BL/TR, 6'2", 180 lbs. Deb: 7/12/70

1970	StL-N	38	95	9	24	4	1	0	6	7	5	.253	.311	.316	67	-4	0	0	0	.954	-1	S-35/3-3,2-2	-0.2
1972	StL-N	101	276	27	60	9	1	0	19	18	27	.217	.270	.257	51	-18	1	1	-0	.979	-6	S-43,2-38,3-14	-1.9
1973	StL-N	22	39	4	5	2	1	0	1	4	4	.128	.209	.231	22	-4	0	0	0	.938	-3	/S-7,2-5,3-4	-0.7
	*Cin-N	36	51	4	11	1	0	0	5	7	12	.216	.333	.275	74	-2	0	1	-1	.953	5	S-29/2-5	0.5
	Yr	58	90	8	16	3	2	0	6	11	16	.178	.282	.256	52	-6	0	1	-1	.950	2	S-36,2-10/3-4	-0.2
1974	Cle-A	37	86	11	18	3	0	0	6	6	12	.209	.261	.244	46	-6	0	1	-1	.926	-10	3-18,S-13/2-3	-1.6
1975	Cle-A	61	128	12	30	3	0	0	7	13	14	.234	.305	.258	60	-6	0	4	-2	.974	4	S-30,2-19,3-13	-0.2
1976	Cle-A	2	2	0	1	0	0	0	0	0	0	.500	.500	.500	195	0	0	0	0	1.000	1	/3-1,D-1	0.1
Total	6	297	677	67	149	22	4	0	44	55	74	.220	.284	.264	55	-40	1	7	-4	.964	-11	S-157/2-72,3-53,D-1	-4.0

■ FRANKIE CROSETTI Crosetti, Frank Peter Joseph "Crow" b: 10/4/10, San Francisco, Cal. BR/TR, 5'10", 165 lbs. Deb: 4/12/32 C

1932	*NY-A	116	398	47	96	20	9	5	57	51	51	.241	.335	.374	88	-7	3	2	-0	.937	-5	S-84,3-33/2-1	-0.4
1933	NY-A	136	451	71	114	20	5	9	60	55	40	.253	.337	.379	95	-3	4	1	1	.936	-8	*S-133	-0.2
1934	NY-A	138	554	85	147	22	10	11	67	61	58	.265	.344	.401	98	-3	5	6	-2	.945	-10	*S-119,3-23/2-1	-0.6
1935	NY-A	87	305	49	78	17	6	8	50	41	27	.256	.351	.430	107	3	3	1	0	.963	-7	S-87	0.1
1936	*NY-A★	151	632	137	182	35	7	15	78	90	83	.288	.387	.437	107	8	18	7	1	.948	-8	*S-151	1.0
1937	*NY-A	149	611	127	143	29	5	11	49	86	105	.234	.340	.352	74	-24	13	7	-0	.948	2	*S-147	-1.1
1938	*NY-A	157	631	113	166	35	3	9	55	106	97	.263	.382	.371	90	-7	27	12	1	.948	18	*S-157	2.2
1939	*NY-A☆	152	656	109	153	25	5	10	56	65	81	.233	.315	.332	67	-33	11	7	-1	.968	8	*S-152	-1.2
1940	NY-A	145	546	84	106	23	4	4	31	72	77	.194	.299	.273	52	-39	14	8	-1	.954	-14	*S-145	-4.0
1941	NY-A	50	148	13	33	2	2	1	22	18	14	.223	.320	.284	62	-8	0	2	-1	.944	10	S-32,3-13	0.3
1942	*NY-A	74	285	50	69	5	5	4	23	31	31	.242	.335	.337	91	-3	1	1	-0	.951	-3	3-62/S-8,2-2	-0.4
1943	*NY-A	95	348	36	81	8	1	2	20	36	47	.233	.317	.279	74	-10	4	4	-1	.946	3	S-90	-0.2
1944	NY-A	55	197	20	47	4	2	5	30	11	21	.239	.299	.355	84	-5	3	0	1	.960	-9	*S-126	-0.9
1945	NY-A	130	441	57	105	12	0	4	48	59	65	.238	.341	.293	81	-8	7	1	2	.946	-8	*S-126	-0.5
1946	NY-A	28	59	4	17	3	0	0	3	8	2	.288	.382	.339	101	1	0	3	-2	.940	7	S-24	0.7
1947	NY-A	3	1	0	0	0	0	0	0	0	0	.000	.000	.000	-99	-0	0	0	0	.000	0	/2-1,S-1	0.0
1948	NY-A	17	14	4	4	0	1	0	2	2	0	.286	.375	.429	115	0	0	0	0	1.000	0	/2-6,S-5	0.1
Total	17	1683	6277	1006	1541	260	65	98	649	792	799	.245	.341	.354	84	-137	113	62	-3	.949	-24	*S-1516,3-131/2-11	-5.1

■ AMOS CROSS Cross, Amos C. b: 1861, Czechoslovakia d: 7/16/1888, Cleveland, Ohio Deb: 4/22/1885 F

1885	Lou-a	35	130	11	37	2	1	0	14	0		.285	.290	.315	91	-2				.936	-1	C-35	0.0
1886	Lou-a	74	283	51	78	14	6	1	42	44		.276	.375	.378	129	10	13			.910	-16	C-51,1-20/S-2,O-1	-0.3
1887	Lou-a	8	28	0	3	0	0	0	0	1		.107	.138	.107	-31	-5	0			.808	-4	/C-5,1-2,O-1	-0.8
Total	3	117	441	62	118	16	7	1	56	45		.268	.338	.342	108	4	13			.916	-22	/C-91,1-22,O-2,S-2	-1.1

■ CLARENCE CROSS Cross, Clarence (b: Clarence Crause) b: 3/4/1856, St.Louis, Mo. d: 6/23/31, Seattle, Wash. Deb: 5/5/1884

1884	Alt-U	2	7	1	4	1	0	0		2		.571	.667	.714	314	2				.500	-2	/3-2	0.0
	Phi-U	2	9	0	2	0	0	0		0		.222	.222	.222	38	-1				.545	-2	/S-2	-0.2
	KC-U	25	93	13	20	1	0	0		6		.215	.263	.226	57	-8				.836	3	S-24/3-1	-0.4
	Yr	29	109	14	26	2	0	0		8		.239	.291	.257	76	-6				.813	-1	S-26/3-3	-0.6
1887	NY-a	16	55	9	11	2	1	0	5	2		.200	.267	.273	53	-3	0			.833	-3	S-13/3-4	-0.5
Total	2	45	164	23	37	4	1	0	5	10		.226	.282	.262	67	-10	0			.818	-4	/S-39,3-7	-1.1

■ FRANK CROSS Cross, Frank Atwell "Mickey" b: 1/20/1873, Cleveland, Ohio d: 11/2/32, Geauga Lake, Ohio TR, Deb: 5/20/01 F

1901	Cle-A	1	5	0	3	0	0	0	0	0	0	.600	.600	.600	243	1	0			.000	-0	/O-1	0.0

■ JEFF CROSS Cross, Joffre James b: 8/28/18, Tulsa, Okla. BR/TR, 5'11", 160 lbs. Deb: 9/27/42

1942	StL-N	1	4	0	1	0	0	0	1	0	0	.250	.250	.250	43	-0	0			1.000	-1	/S-1	-0.1
1946	StL-N	49	69	17	15	3	0	0	6	10	6	.217	.316	.261	62	-3	4			.970	6	S-17/2-8,3-1	0.3
1947	StL-N	51	49	4	5	1	0	0	3	10	6	.102	.254	.122	3	-7	0			.947	5	3-15,S-14/2-2	-0.1
1948	StL-N	2	0	0	0	0	0	0	0	0	0	—	—	—			0			.000	0	R	0.0
	Chi-N	16	20	1	2	0	0	0	0	0	4	.100	.100	.100	-48	-4	0			.786	-4	/S-9,2-1	-0.8
	Yr	18	20	1	2	0	0	0	0	0	4	.100	.100	.100	-47	-4	0			.786	-4	/S-9,2-1	-0.8
Total	4	119	142	22	23	4	0	0	10	20	18	.162	.265	.190	26	-14	4			.932	7	/S-41,3-16,2-11	-0.7

■ LAVE CROSS Cross, Lafayette Napoleon b: 5/12/1866, Milwaukee, Wis. d: 9/6/27, Toledo, Ohio BR/TR, 5'8.5", 155 lbs. Deb: 4/23/1887 FM

1887	Lou-a	54	203	32	54	8	3	0	26	15		.266	.320	.335	81	-5	15			.916	-3	C-44,O-10	-0.3
1888	Lou-a	47	181	20	41	3	0	0	15	2		.227	.239	.243	56	-9	10			.929	1	C-37,O-12/S-2	-0.5
1889	Phi-a	55	199	22	44	8	2	0	23	14	9	.221	.272	.281	58	-11	11			.934	19	C-55	1.1
1890	Phi-P	63	245	42	73	7	8	3	47	12	6	.298	.331	.429	100	-2	5			.885	2	C-49,O-15	0.3
1891	Phi-a	110	402	66	121	20	14	5	52	38	23	.301	.366	.458	131	14	14			.971	-4	O-43,C-43,3-24/S2	1.2
1892	Phi-N	140	541	84	149	15	10	4	69	39	16	.275	.328	.362	109	-2	18			.921	-2	3-65,C-39,O-25,2/S	0.6
1893	Phi-N	96	415	81	124	17	6	4	78	26	7	.299	.342	.398	96	-4	18			.974	15	C-40,3-30,O-10,S/1	1.3
1894	Phi-N	119	529	123	204	34	9	7	125	29	7	.386	.421	.524	130	25	21			.919	20	*3-100,C-16/S-7,2-1	3.6
1895	Phi-N	125	535	95	145	26	9	2	101	35	8	.271	.319	.364	76	-21	21			**.940**	34	*3-125	1.2
1896	Phi-N	106	406	63	104	23	5	1	73	32	14	.256	.312	.345	74	-16	8			.937	13	3-61,S-37/2-6,OC	0.0
1897	Phi-N	88	344	37	89	17	5	3	51	10		.259	.282	.363	71	-16	10			.912	2	3-47,2-38/O-2,S-1	-0.9
1898	StL-N	151	602	71	191	28	3	0	79	28		.317	.348	.405	113	7	14			**.945**	18	*3-149/S-2	2.5
1899	Cle-N	38	154	15	44	5	0	1	20	8		.286	.325	.338	88	-3	2			.955	4	3-38,M	0.1
	StL-N	103	403	61	122	14	5	4	64	17		.303	.333	.392	96	-4	11			.960	29	*3-103	2.4
	Yr	141	557	76	166	19	5	5	84	25		.298	.330	.377	94	-6	13			**.959**	33	*3-141	2.5
1900	StL-N	16	61	6	18	1	0	0	6	1		.295	.306	.311	71	-2	1			.962	1	*3-16	-0.1
	*Bro-N	117	461	73	135	14	6	4	67	25		.293	.332	.375	90	-8	20			.943	3	*3-117	-0.4
	Yr	133	522	79	153	15	6	4	73	26		.293	.329	.368	88	-10	21			**.945**	4	*3-133	-0.5
1901	Phi-A	100	424	82	139	28	12	2	73	19		.328	.358	.465	121	10	23			.919	5	*3-100	1.5
1902	Phi-A	137	559	90	191	39	4	0	108	27		.342	.374	.440	120	14	25			.942	7	*3-137	2.1
1903	Phi-A	137	559	60	163	22	4	2	90	10		.292	.304	.356	93	-6	14			.950	-3	*3-136/1-1	-0.7
1904	Phi-A	155	607	73	176	31	10	1	71	13		.290	.310	.379	112	6	10			.936	-10	*3-155	-0.6
1905	*Phi-A	147	587	69	156	29	5	0	77	26		.266	.299	.332	98	-2	8			.928	-9	*3-147	-0.6
1906	Was-A	130	494	55	130	14	6	1	46	28		.263	.303	.322	100	-1	19			**.952**	-3	*3-130	0.0

YEAR	TM/L	G	AB	R	H	2B	3B	HR	RBI	BB	SO	AVG	OBP	SLG	PRO+	BR/A	SB	CS	SBR	FA	FR	G/POS	TPR
1907	Was-A	41	161	13	32	8	0	0	10	10		.199	.246	.248	62	-7	3			.978	7	3-41	0.1
Total	21	2275	9072	1333	2645	411	135	47	1371	464	90	.292	.328	.382	99	-34	301			.938	146	*3-1721,C-324,O/S21	14.6

■ MONTE CROSS

Cross, Montford Montgomery   b: 8/31/1869, Philadelphia, Pa.   d: 6/21/34, Philadelphia, Pa.   BR/TR, 5'8.5", 148 lbs.   Deb: 9/27/1892 U

YEAR	TM/L	G	AB	R	H	2B	3B	HR	RBI	BB	SO	AVG	OBP	SLG	PRO+	BR/A	SB	CS	SBR	FA	FR	G/POS	TPR
1892	Bal-N	15	50	5	8	0	0	0	2	4	10	.160	.222	.160	16	-5	2			.864	-3	S-15	-0.7
1894	Pit-N	13	43	14	19	1	5	2	13	5	4	.442	.520	.837	225	9	6			.924	2	S-13	0.8
1895	Pit-N	108	393	67	101	14	13	3	54	38	38	.257	.327	.382	87	-8	39			.883	-13	*S-107/2-1	-1.3
1896	StL-N	125	427	66	104	10	6	6	52	58	48	.244	.342	.337	83	-9	40			.892	-12	*S-125	-1.4
1897	StL-N	131	462	59	132	17	11	4	55	62		.286	.379	.396	107	6	38			.920	28	*S-131	3.1
1898	Phi-N	149	525	68	135	25	5	1	50	55		.257	.337	.330	95	-2	20			.907	15	*S-149	1.8
1899	Phi-N	154	557	85	143	25	6	3	65	56		.257	.335	.339	88	-8	26			.909	2	*S-154	0.5
1900	Phi-N	131	466	59	94	11	3	3	62	51		.202	.289	.258	52	-30	19			.928	-3	*S-131	-2.0
1901	Phi-N	139	483	49	95	14	1	1	44	52		.197	.281	.236	50	-30	24			.924	-16	*S-139	-3.4
1902	Phi-A	137	497	72	115	22	2	3	59	32		.231	.289	.302	61	-26	17			.927	11	*S-137	-0.7
1903	Phi-A	137	470	44	116	21	2	3	45	49		.247	.326	.319	90	-4	31			.940	5	*S-137/2-1	1.0
1904	Phi-A	153	503	33	95	23	4	1	38	46		.189	.266	.256	62	-20	19			.937	-16	*S-153	-3.6
1905	*Phi-A	79	252	28	67	17	2	0	24	19		.266	.332	.349	114	4	8			.929	-4	S-77/2-2	0.2
1906	Phi-A	134	445	32	89	23	3	1	40	50		.200	.291	.272	74	-12	22			.938	4	*S-134	-0.4
1907	Phi-A	77	248	37	51	9	5	0	18	39		.206	.316	.282	89	-2	17			.954	12	S-74	1.3
Total	15	1682	5821	718	1364	232	68	31	621	616	100	.234	.316	.314	80	-138	328			.920	15	*S-1676/2-4	-4.8

■ FRANK CROSSIN

Crossin, Frank Patrick   b: 6/15/1891, Avondale, Pa.   d: 12/6/65, Kingston, Pa.   BR/TR, 5'10", 160 lbs.   Deb: 9/24/12

YEAR	TM/L	G	AB	R	H	2B	3B	HR	RBI	BB	SO	AVG	OBP	SLG	PRO+	BR/A	SB	CS	SBR	FA	FR	G/POS	TPR
1912	StL-A	8	22	2	5	0	0	0	2	1		.227	.261	.227	41	-2	1			.920	-5	/C-8	-0.6
1913	StL-A	4	4	1	1	0	0	0	0	1	1	.250	.500	.250	124	0	0			.857	-1	/C-2	0.0
1914	StL-A	43	90	5	11	1	1	0	5	10	10	.122	.225	.156	15	-9	3			.934	-1	C-41	-0.7
Total	3	55	116	8	17	1	1	0	7	12	11	.147	.244	.172	25	-10	4			.930	-6	/C-51	-1.3

■ JOE CROTTY

Crotty, Joseph P.   b: 12/24/1860, Cincinnati, O.   d: 6/22/26, Minneapolis, Minn   BR/TR,   Deb: 5/4/1882

YEAR	TM/L	G	AB	R	H	2B	3B	HR	RBI	BB	SO	AVG	OBP	SLG	PRO+	BR/A	SB	CS	SBR	FA	FR	G/POS	TPR
1882	Lou-a	5	20	1	2	0	0	0		0		.100	.100	.100	-34	-3				.882	-0	/C-5	-0.3
	StL-a	8	28	2	4	1	0	0		3		.143	.226	.179	37	-2				.882	-1	/C-7,O-1	-0.3
	Yr	13	48	3	6	1	0	0		3		.125	.176	.146	10	-4				.882	-2	C-12/O-1	-0.6
1884	Cin-U	21	84	11	22	4	2	1		1		.262	.271	.393	92	-4				.896	-7	C-21	-0.8
1885	Lou-a	39	129	14	20	2	0	0	7	3		.155	.193	.171	15	-12				.931	1	C-38/1-1	-0.7
1886	NY-a	14	47	6	8	0	1	0	2	4		.170	.250	.213	48	-3	3			.933	-3	C-14	-0.0
Total	4	87	308	34	56	7	3	1	9	11		.182	.220	.234	42	-23	3			.915	-10	/C-85,1-1,O-1	-2.4

■ JACK CROUCH

Crouch, Jack Albert "Roxy"   b: 6/12/03, Salisbury, N.C.   d: 8/25/72, Leesburg, Fla.   BR/TR, 5'9", 165 lbs.   Deb: 9/18/30

YEAR	TM/L	G	AB	R	H	2B	3B	HR	RBI	BB	SO	AVG	OBP	SLG	PRO+	BR/A	SB	CS	SBR	FA	FR	G/POS	TPR
1930	StL-A	6	14	1	2	1	0	0	1	1	3	.143	.200	.214	5	-2	0	0	0	1.000	1	/C-5	-0.1
1931	StL-A	8	12	0	0	0	0	0	1	0	4	.000	.000	.000	-97	-3	0	0	0	.895	1	/C-7	-0.3
1933	StL-A	19	30	1	5	0	0	1	5	2	6	.167	.219	.267	26	-3	0	0	0	1.000	-1	/C-9	-0.3
	Cin-N	10	16	5	2	0	0	0	1	3	4	.125	.222	.125	1	-2	1			1.000	2	/C-6	0.0
Total	3	43	72	7	9	1	0	1	8	3	13	.125	.182	.181	-3	-11	1	0		.976	3	/C-27	-0.7

■ FRANK CROUCHER

Croucher, Frank Donald "Dingle"   b: 7/23/14, San Antonio, Tex.   d: 5/21/80, Houston, Tex.   BR/TR, 5'11", 165 lbs.   Deb: 4/18/39

YEAR	TM/L	G	AB	R	H	2B	3B	HR	RBI	BB	SO	AVG	OBP	SLG	PRO+	BR/A	SB	CS	SBR	FA	FR	G/POS	TPR
1939	Det-A	97	324	38	87	15	6	5	40	16	42	.269	.303	.361	64	-18	2	2	-1	.934	-8	S-93/2-3	-1.8
1940	*Det-A	37	57	3	6	0	0	0	2	4	5	.105	.164	.105	-26	-11	0	0	0	.936	-2	S-26/2-7,3-1	-1.1
1941	Det-A	136	489	51	124	21	4	2	39	33	72	.254	.305	.325	61	-28	2	0	1	.935	-3	*S-136	-2.0
1942	Was-A	26	65	2	18	1	1	0	5	3	9	.277	.309	.323	79	-2	0	0	0	.950	5	2-18	0.4
Total	4	296	935	94	235	37	5	7	86	56	128	.251	.296	.324	58	-59	4	2	0	.934	-8	S-255/2-28,3-1	-4.5

■ BUCK CROUSE

Crouse, Clyde Elsworth   b: 1/6/1897, Anderson, Ind.   d: 10/23/83, Muncie, Ind.   BL/TR, 5'8", 158 lbs.   Deb: 8/1/23

YEAR	TM/L	G	AB	R	H	2B	3B	HR	RBI	BB	SO	AVG	OBP	SLG	PRO+	BR/A	SB	CS	SBR	FA	FR	G/POS	TPR
1923	Chi-A	23	70	6	18	2	1	0	7	3	4	.257	.297	.357	73	-3	0	0	0	.955	-2	C-22	-0.4
1924	Chi-A	94	305	30	79	10	1	1	44	23	12	.259	.319	.308	64	-16	3	2	-0	.945	1	C-90	-0.9
1925	Chi-A	54	131	18	46	7	0	2	25	12	4	.351	.410	.450	125	5	1	2	-1	.952	2	C-48	0.3
1926	Chi-A	49	135	10	32	4	1	0	17	14	7	.237	.309	.281	57	-8	0	0	0	.985	3	C-45	-0.3
1927	Chi-A	85	222	22	53	11	0	0	20	21	10	.239	.307	.288	57	-14	4	1	1	.972	7	C-81	-0.2
1928	Chi-A	78	218	17	55	8	2	2	20	19	14	.252	.315	.321	68	-10	3	4	-2	.959	4	C-76	-0.7
1929	Chi-A	45	107	11	29	7	0	2	12	5	7	.271	.316	.393	82	-3	2	0	1	.979	6	C-40	0.6
1930	Chi-A	42	118	14	30	8	1	1	15	17	10	.254	.348	.339	78	-4	1	1	-0	.979	7	C-38	0.6
Total	8	470	1306	128	342	54	6	8	160	114	68	.262	.326	.331	72	-53	14	10	-2	.964	18	C-440	-0.9

■ DON CROW

Crow, Donald Le Roy   b: 8/18/58, Yakima, Wash.   BR/TR, 6'4", 200 lbs.   Deb: 7/25/82

YEAR	TM/L	G	AB	R	H	2B	3B	HR	RBI	BB	SO	AVG	OBP	SLG	PRO+	BR/A	SB	CS	SBR	FA	FR	G/POS	TPR
1982	LA-N	4	4	0	0	0	0	0	0	0	3	.000	.000	.000	-99	-1	0	0	0	1.000	1	/C-4	0.0

■ GEORGE CROWE

Crowe, George Daniel "Big George"   b: 3/22/21, Whiteland, Ind.   BL/TL, 6'2", 212 lbs.   Deb: 4/16/52

YEAR	TM/L	G	AB	R	H	2B	3B	HR	RBI	BB	SO	AVG	OBP	SLG	PRO+	BR/A	SB	CS	SBR	FA	FR	G/POS	TPR
1952	Bos-N	73	217	25	56	13	1	4	20	18	25	.258	.329	.382	100	-0	6	0		.985	2	1-55	-0.1
1953	Mil-N	47	42	6	12	2	0	2	6	2	7	.286	.333	.476	115	1	0	0	0	1.000	0	/1-9	0.1
1955	Mil-N	104	303	41	85	12	4	15	55	45	44	.281	.375	.495	135	16	0	0	0	.989	5	1-79	1.3
1956	Cin-N	77	144	22	36	2	1	10	23	11	28	.250	.312	.486	104	0	0	0	0	.988	2	1-32	0.1
1957	Cin-N	133	494	71	134	31	1	31	92	32	62	.271	.317	.504	108	4	1	1	-0	.989	-2	*1-120	-0.5
1958	Cin-N☆	111	345	31	95	12	5	7	61	41	51	.275	.352	.400	94	-2	0	0	0	.992	-3	1-93/2-1	-1.0
1959	StL-N	77	103	14	31	6	0	8	29	5	12	.301	.333	.592	132	4	0	0	0	1.000	4	1-14	0.6
1960	StL-N	73	72	5	17	3	0	4	13	5	16	.236	.286	.444	89	-1	0	0	0	1.000	0	/1-5	-0.1
1961	StL-N	7	7	0	1	0	0	0	0	0	0	.143	.143	.143	-22	-1	0	0	0	.000	0	H	-0.1
Total	9	702	1727	215	467	70	12	81	299	159	246	.270	.335	.466	109	20	3	2	-0	.990	1-407/2-1	0.3

■ ED CROWLEY

Crowley, Edgar Jewel   b: 8/20/06, Watkinsville, Ga.   d: 4/14/70, Birmingham, Ala.   BR/TR, 6'1", 180 lbs.   Deb: 6/21/28

YEAR	TM/L	G	AB	R	H	2B	3B	HR	RBI	BB	SO	AVG	OBP	SLG	PRO+	BR/A	SB	CS	SBR	FA	FR	G/POS	TPR
1928	Was-A	2	1	0	0	0	0	0	0	0	0	.000	.000	.000	-99	-0	0	0	0	.000	-0	/3-2	-0.1

■ JOHN CROWLEY

Crowley, John A.   b: 1/12/1862, Lawrence, Mass.   d: 9/23/1896, Lawrence, Mass.   5'10", 164 lbs.   Deb: 5/1/1884

YEAR	TM/L	G	AB	R	H	2B	3B	HR	RBI	BB	SO	AVG	OBP	SLG	PRO+	BR/A	SB	CS	SBR	FA	FR	G/POS	TPR
1884	Phi-N	48	168	26	41	7	3	0	19	15	21	.244	.306	.321	102	1				.832	-23	C-48	-1.6

■ TERRY CROWLEY

Crowley, Terrence Michael   b: 2/16/47, Staten Island, N.Y.   BL/TL, 6', 180 lbs.   Deb: 9/4/69 C

YEAR	TM/L	G	AB	R	H	2B	3B	HR	RBI	BB	SO	AVG	OBP	SLG	PRO+	BR/A	SB	CS	SBR	FA	FR	G/POS	TPR
1969	Bal-A	7	18	0	6	0	0	3	1	4	.333	.368	.333	97	-0	0	0	1.000	0	/1-3,O-2	0.0
1970	*Bal-A	83	152	25	39	5	0	5	20	35	26	.257	.396	.388	116	5	2	0	1	.973	-5	O-27,1-23	-0.2
1971	Bal-A	18	23	2	4	0	0	0	1	3	4	.174	.269	.174	28	-2	0	0	0	1.000	-2	/O-6,1-2	-0.5
1972	Bal-A	97	247	30	57	10	0	11	29	32	26	.231	.321	.405	112	4	0	0	0	.990	-7	O-68,1-15	-0.7
1973	*Bal-A	54	131	16	27	4	0	3	15	16	14	.206	.297	.305	71	-5	0	0	0	.867	-1	D-23,O-10/1-7	-0.7
1974	Cin-N	84	125	11	30	12	0	1	20	10	16	.240	.301	.360	86	-3	0	0	0	1.000	-2	O-22/1-7	-0.6
1975	*Cin-N	66	71	8	19	6	0	1	11	7	6	.268	.333	.394	100	-0	0	0	0	1.000	1	1-4,O-4	-0.0
1976	Atl-N	7	6	0	0	0	0	0	1	0	0	.000	.000	.000	-94	-2	0	0	0	.000	0	H	-0.2
	Bal-A	33	61	5	15	1	0	0	5	7	11	.246	.333	.262	81	-1	0	0	0	1.000	1	D-17/1-1	-0.1
1977	Bal-A	18	22	3	8	1	0	1	6	2	4	.364	.391	.545	162	2	0	0	0	1.000	-1	/1-1,D-2	0.2
1978	Bal-A	62	95	8	24	2	0	0	12	8	12	.253	.317	.274	72	-3	0	0	0	1.000	0	D-17/O-2,1-1	-0.4
1979	*Bal-A	61	63	8	20	5	1	1	8	14	13	.317	.449	.476	155	6	0	0	0	1.000	-0	D-15/1-2	0.5
1980	Bal-A	92	233	33	67	8	0	12	50	29	21	.288	.366	.476	130	10	0	0	0	1.000	1	D-65/1-3	0.9
1981	Bal-A	68	134	12	33	6	0	4	25	29	12	.246	.380	.381	120	5	0	0	0	1.000	4	D-42/1-4	0.3
1982	Bal-A	65	93	8	22	2	0	3	17	21	9	.237	.377	.355	103	1	0	0	0	.988	0	D-14,1-10	0.1
1983	Mon-N	50	44	2	8	0	0	0	5	6	8	.182	.333	.182	47	-3	0	0	0	1.000	0	1-4	-0.4
Total	15	865	1518	174	379	62	1	42	229	222	181	.250	.348	.375	104	13	3	0	1	.980	-13	D-195,O-141/1-87	-1.7

YEAR	TM/L	G	AB	R	H	2B	3B	HR	RBI	BB	SO	AVG	OBP	SLG	PRO+	BR/A	SB	CS	SBR	FA	FR	G/POS	TPR

■ BILL CROWLEY   Crowley, William Michael   b: 4/8/1857, Philadelphia, Pa.   d: 7/14/1891, Gloucester, N.J.   BR/TR, 5'7.5", 159 lbs.   Deb: 4/26/1875

1875	Phi-n	9	37	4	3	0	0	0	3	1	0	.081	.105	.081	-33	-5	0	0	0	.800	-0	/3-4,O-4,1-1	-0.5
1877	Lou-N	61	238	30	67	9	3	1	23	4	13	.282	.293	.357	88	-6				.849	9	*O-58/S-2,C-2,32	0.1
1879	Buf-N	60	261	41	75	9	5	0	30	6	14	.287	.303	.360	115	4				.809	-0	O-43,C-10/1-7,2-3	0.1
1880	Buf-N	85	354	57	95	16	4	0	20	19	23	.268	.306	.336	115	6				.824	1	*O-74,C-22	0.5
1881	Bos-N	72	279	33	71	12	0	0	31	14	15	.254	.290	.297	89	-3				.880	-1	*O-72	-0.5
1883	Phi-a	23	96	16	24	4	3	0	16	3		.250	.273	.354	93	-1				.810	-2	O-22/1-1	-0.3
	Cle-N	11	41	3	12	5	0	0	5	1	7	.293	.310	.415	119	1				.923	-3	O-11	-0.2
1884	Bos-N	108	407	50	110	14	6	6	61	33	74	.270	.325	.378	121	10				.870	-5	*O-108	0.3
1885	Buf-N	92	344	29	83	14	1	1	36	21	32	.241	.285	.297	85	-6				.874	-5	*O-92	-1.2
Total	7	512	2020	259	537	83	22	8	222	101	178	.266	.301	.341	103	5				.853	-6	O-480/C-34,1-8,2S3	-1.2

■ WALTON CRUISE   Cruise, Walton Edwin   b: 5/6/1890, Childersburg, Ala.   d: 1/9/75, Sylacauga, Ala.   BL/TR, 6', 175 lbs.   Deb: 4/14/14

1914	StL-N	95	256	20	58	9	3	4	28	25	42	.227	.303	.332	90	-3	3			.976	-3	O-81	-1.0
1916	StL-N	3	3	0	2	0	0	0	0	1	0	.667	.750	.667	339	1	0			1.000	-1	/O-2	0.0
1917	StL-N	153	529	70	156	20	10	5	59	38	73	.295	.343	.399	131	18	16			.965	-14	*O-152	-0.4
1918	StL-N	70	240	34	65	5	4	6	39	30	26	.271	.359	.400	136	11	2			.964	-7	O-65	0.0
1919	StL-N	9	21	0	2	1	0	0	0	1	6	.095	.136	.143	-17	-3	0			.833	-2	/O-5,1-2	-0.6
	Bos-N	73	241	23	52	7	0	1	21	17	29	.216	.267	.257	61	-11	8			.978	-5	O-66	-2.4
	Yr	82	262	23	54	8	0	1	21	18	35	.206	.257	.248	55	-14	8			.971	-7	O-71/1-2	-3.0
1920	Bos-N	91	288	40	80	7	5	1	21	31	21	.278	.352	.347	106	3	5	3	-0	.950	-7	O-82	-1.1
1921	Bos-N	108	344	47	119	16	7	8	55	48	24	.346	.429	.503	154	29	10	8	-2	.963	-6	*O-102/1-2	1.4
1922	Bos-N	104	352	51	98	15	10	4	46	44	20	.278	.360	.412	103	2	4	4	-1	.948	-0	*O-100/1-2	-0.6
1923	Bos-N	21	38	4	8	2	0	0	0	3	2	.211	.268	.263	42	-3	1	0		.952	-3	/O-9	-0.4
1924	Bos-N	9	9	4	4	1	0	1	3	0	2	.444	.444	.889	260	1	0	0		.000	0	H	0.2
Total	10	736	2321	293	644	83	39	30	272	238	250	.277	.348	.386	114	44	49	15		.962	-45	O-664/1-6	-4.9

■ GENE CRUMLING   Crumling, Eugene Leon   b: 4/5/22, Wrightsville, Pa.   BR/TR, 6', 180 lbs.   Deb: 9/11/45

| 1945 | StL-N | 6 | 12 | 0 | 1 | 0 | 0 | 0 | 0 | 1 | 1 | .083 | .083 | .083 | -52 | -2 | 0 | | | 1.000 | 2 | /C-6 | -0.1 |

■ BUDDY CRUMP   Crump, Arthur Elliott   b: 11/29/01, Norfolk, Va.   d: 9/7/76, Raleigh, N.C.   BL/TL, 5'10", 156 lbs.   Deb: 9/28/24

| 1924 | NY-N | 1 | 4 | 0 | 0 | 0 | 0 | 0 | 0 | 0 | 0 | .000 | .000 | .000 | -99 | -1 | 0 | 0 | 0 | .500 | -1 | /O-1 | -0.2 |

■ PRESS CRUTHERS   Cruthers, Charles Preston   b: 9/8/1890, Marshallton, Del.   d: 12/27/76, Kenosha, Wis.   BR/TR, 5'9", 152 lbs.   Deb: 9/29/13

1913	Phi-A	3	12	0	3	1	0	0	0	0	0	.250	.250	.333	72	-1				.923	-3	/2-3	-0.4
1914	Phi-A	4	15	1	3	0	1	0	0	0	4	.200	.200	.333	63	-1	0	1	-1	1.000	1	/2-4	0.0
Total	2	7	27	1	6	1	1	0	0	0	4	.222	.222	.333	67	-1	0	1		.973	-1	/2-7	-0.4

■ TOMMY CRUZ   Cruz, Cirilo (Dilan)   b: 2/15/51, Arroyo, P.R.   BL/TL, 5'9", 165 lbs.   Deb: 9/4/73   F

1973	StL-N	3	0	1	0	0	0	0	0	0	0	—	—	—	—	0	0	0	0	.000	-0	/O-1	0.0
1977	Chi-A	4	2	1	0	0	0	0	0	0	0	.000	.000	.000	-99	-1	0	0	0	1.000	-1	/O-2	-0.1
Total	2	7	2	2	0	0	0	0	0	0	0	.000	.000	.000	-99	-1	0	0	0	1.000	-1	/O-3	-0.1

■ FAUSTO CRUZ   Cruz, Fausto (Santiago)   b: 5/1/72, Monte Cristi, D.R.   BR/TR, 5'10", 165 lbs.   Deb: 4/10/94

1994	Oak-A	17	28	2	3	0	0	0	4	6	6	.107	.219	.107	-14	-5	0	0	0	.960	3	S-10/3-4,2-1	-0.1
1995	Oak-A	8	23	0	5	0	0	0	5	3	5	.217	.308	.217	42	-2	1	1	-0	.971	-1	/S-8	-0.2
1996	Det-A	14	38	5	9	2	0	0	0	1	11	.237	.256	.289	38	-4	0	0	0	.906	-0	/2-8,S-4,D-1	-0.3
Total	3	39	89	7	17	2	0	0	9	8	22	.191	.258	.213	24	-10	1	1	0	.934	2	/S-22,2-9,3-4,D-1	-0.6

■ HECTOR CRUZ   Cruz, Hector Louis (Dilan) "Heity"   b: 4/2/53, Arroyo, P.R.   BR/TR, 5'11", 170 lbs.   Deb: 8/11/73   F

1973	StL-N	11	11	1	0	0	0	0	0	1	3	.000	.083	.000	-75	-3	0	0	0	1.000	-1	/O-5	-0.4
1975	StL-N	23	48	7	7	2	2	0	6	2	4	.146	.180	.271	23	-5	0	0	0	.800	-1	3-12/O-6	-0.7
1976	StL-N	151	526	54	120	17	1	13	71	42	119	.228	.288	.338	77	-17	1	0	0	.964	-9	*O-106/3-2	-4.2
1977	StL-N	118	339	50	80	19	2	6	42	46	56	.236	.329	.357	85	-6	4	3	-1	.964	-9	*O-106/3-2	-2.0
1978	Chi-N	30	76	8	18	5	0	2	9	3	6	.237	.266	.382	70	-3	0	0	0	1.000	-1	O-14/3-7	-0.4
	SF-N	79	197	19	44	8	1	6	24	21	39	.223	.301	.365	89	-3	0	2	-1	.978	-5	O-53,3-14	-1.2
	Yr	109	273	27	62	13	1	8	33	24	45	.227	.292	.370	83	-7	0	2	-1	.983	-5	O-67,3-21	-1.6
1979	SF-N	16	25	2	3	0	0	0	1	3	7	.120	.214	.120	-7	-4	0	0	0	1.000	-2	/O-6,3-2	-0.6
	*Cin-N	74	182	24	44	10	2	4	27	31	39	.242	.352	.385	100	1	0	1	-1	.984	-7	/O-69	-1.0
	Yr	90	207	26	47	10	2	4	28	34	46	.227	.336	.353	89	-3	0	1	-1	.985	-9	O-75/3-2	-1.6
1980	Cin-N	52	75	5	16	4	1	5	8	5	16	.213	.289	.333	73	-3	0	0	0	.955	-4	O-29	-0.8
1981	Chi-N	53	109	15	25	5	0	7	15	17	24	.229	.333	.468	120	3	2	2	-1	.925	-6	3-18,O-16	-0.4
1982	Chi-N	17	19	1	4	1	0	0	2	4	4	.211	.286	.263	53	-1	0	0	0	1.000	-2	/O-4	-0.3
Total	9	624	1607	186	361	71	9	39	200	176	317	.225	.303	.353	81	-42	7	8	-3	.975	-57	O-308,3-203	-12.0

■ HENRY CRUZ   Cruz, Henry (Acosta)   b: 2/27/52, Christiansted, V.I.   BL/TL, 6', 175 lbs.   Deb: 4/18/75

1975	LA-N	53	94	8	25	3	1	5	7	6	6	.266	.317	.319	80	-3	1	1	-0	.960	-1	O-41	-1.5
1976	LA-N	49	88	8	16	2	1	4	14	9	11	.182	.258	.364	76	-3	0	2	-1	.976	-3	O-23	-0.9
1977	Chi-A	16	21	3	6	0	0	2	5	1	3	.286	.318	.571	137	1	0	0	0	.833	-3	/O-9	-0.2
1978	Chi-A	53	77	13	17	2	1	2	10	8	11	.221	.302	.351	82	-2	0	1	-1	1.000	-5	O-40/D-1	-0.8
Total	4	171	280	32	64	7	3	8	34	25	31	.229	.294	.361	84	-1	1	4	-2	.974	-22	O-113/D-1	-3.4

■ JACOB CRUZ   Cruz, Jacob   b: 1/28/73, Oxnard, Cal.   BL/TL, 6', 175 lbs.   Deb: 7/18/96

| 1996 | SF-N | 33 | 77 | 10 | 18 | 3 | 0 | 2 | 10 | 12 | 14 | .234 | .352 | .390 | 99 | 0 | 0 | 1 | -1 | .977 | 0 | O-23 | -0.1 |

■ JOSE CRUZ   Cruz, Jose (Dilan)   b: 8/8/47, Arroyo, P.R.   BL/TL, 6', 175 lbs.   Deb: 9/19/70   F

1970	StL-N	6	17	2	6	1	0	0	1	4	0	.353	.500	.412	144	2	0	0	0	1.000	2	/O-4	0.3
1971	StL-N	83	292	46	80	13	2	9	27	49	35	.274	.380	.425	123	10	6	3	0	.975	2	O-83	0.9
1972	StL-N	117	332	33	78	14	4	2	23	36	54	.235	.312	.319	81	-8	9	7	1	.979	4	*O-102	-0.8
1973	StL-N	132	406	51	92	22	5	10	57	51	66	.227	.314	.379	92	-5	10	4	1	.979	0	*O-118	-1.0
1974	StL-N	107	161	24	42	4	3	5	20	20	27	.261	.343	.416	112	3	4	2	0	.975	-6	O-53/1-1	-0.5
1975	Hou-N	120	315	44	81	15	2	9	49	52	44	.257	.364	.403	121	10	6	3	0	.980	4	O-94	1.1
1976	Hou-N	133	439	49	133	21	5	4	61	53	46	.303	.378	.401	133	19	28	11	2	.972	10	O-125	2.7
1977	Hou-N	157	579	87	173	31	10	17	87	69	67	.299	.373	.475	138	30	44	23	-1	.973	4	*O-155	2.7
1978	Hou-N	153	565	79	178	34	9	10	83	57	57	.315	.380	.460	144	32	37	9	6	.975	3	*O-152/1-2	3.6
1979	Hou-N	157	558	73	161	33	9	9	72	72	66	.289	.370	.421	122	18	36	14	2	.959	9	*O-156	2.3
1980	*Hou-N☆	160	612	79	185	29	7	11	91	60	66	.302	.365	.426	130	24	36	11	4	.969	15	*O-158	3.9
1981	Hou-N	107	409	53	109	15	6	13	55	35	49	.267	.324	.425	117	7	5	7	-3	.984	-0	*O-105	1.1
1982	Hou-N	155	570	62	157	27	2	9	68	60	67	.275	.345	.377	110	8	21	11	-0	.964	14	*O-155	1.8
1983	Hou-N	160	594	85	**189**	28	8	14	92	65	86	.318	.386	.463	143	34	30	16	-1	.979	8	*O-160	3.9
1984	Hou-N	160	600	96	187	28	13	12	95	73	68	.312	.386	.462	148	38	22	9	2	.976	13	*O-160	4.9
1985	Hou-N★	141	544	69	163	34	4	9	79	43	74	.300	.351	.426	111	14	16	5	2	.971	10	*O-137	2.2
1986	*Hou-N	141	479	48	133	22	4	10	72	55	86	.278	.352	.403	111	7	3	4	-2	.984	6	O-97	0.8
1987	Hou-N	126	365	47	88	17	4	11	38	36	65	.241	.309	.400	90	-6	4	3	0	.984	6	O-134	-0.3
1988	NY-A	38	80	9	16	2	0	1	7	8	1	.200	.273	.262	51	-5	0	1	-1	.889	-2	D-12/O-8	-0.8
Total	19	2353	7917	1036	2251	391	94	165	1077	898	1031	.284	.358	.420	122	232	317	136	14	.974	111	*O-2156/D-12,1-3	28.8

■ JULIO CRUZ   Cruz, Julio Luis   b: 12/2/54, Brooklyn, N.Y.   BB/TR, 5'9", 165 lbs.   Deb: 7/4/77

1977	Sea-A	60	199	25	51	3	1	1	7	24	29	.256	.336	.296	75	-6	15	6	1	.983	2	2-54/D-1	0.1
1978	Sea-A	147	550	77	129	13	7	1	25	69	66	.235	.321	.269	68	-21	59	10	**12**	**.987**	8	*2-141/S-5,D-1	0.9
1979	Sea-A	107	414	70	112	16	2	1	29	62	61	.271	.366	.326	87	-5	49	9	9	.979	17	*2-107	2.7

YEAR	TM/L	G	AB	R	H	2B	3B	HR	RBI	BB	SO	AVG	OBP	SLG	PRO+	BR/A	SB	CS	SBR	FA	FR	G/POS	TPR
1980	Sea-A	119	422	66	88	9	3	2	16	59	49	.209	.307	.258	56	-24	45	7	9	.983	1	*2-115/D-3	-0.7
1981	Sea-A	94	352	57	90	12	3	2	24	39	40	.256	.335	.324	87	-5	43	8	**8**	.982	8	2-92/S-1	1.8
1982	Sea-A	154	549	83	133	22	5	8	49	57	71	.242	.317	.344	79	-15	46	13	6	.987	4	*2-151/S-2,3-1,D-2	0.3
1983	Sea-A	61	181	24	46	10	1	2	12	20	22	.254	.335	.354	86	-3	33	6	6	.984	7	2-60/D-1	1.3
	*Chi-A	99	334	47	84	9	4	1	40	29	44	.251	.315	.311	71	-13	24	6	4	.983	10	2-97	0.5
	Yr	160	515	71	130	19	5	3	52	49	66	.252	.322	.326	76	-16	57	12	10	.983	17	*2-157/D-1	1.8
1984	Chi-A	143	415	42	92	14	4	5	43	45	58	.222	.298	.311	66	-19	14	6	1	.976	22	*2-141	0.9
1985	Chi-A	91	234	28	46	2	3	0	15	32	40	.197	.299	.231	46	-17	8	5	-1	.982	13	2-87/D-2	-0.2
1986	Chi-A	81	209	38	45	2	0	0	19	42	28	.215	.347	.225	58	-11	7	2	1	.985	2	2-78/D-3	-0.5
Total	10	1156	3859	557	916	113	27	23	279	478	508	.237	.324	.299	71	-138	343	78	56	.983	93	*2-1123/D-13,S-8,3	7.1

■ TODD CRUZ   Cruz, Todd Ruben   b: 11/23/55, Highland Park, Mich   BR/TR, 6', 175 lbs.   Deb: 9/4/78

YEAR	TM/L	G	AB	R	H	2B	3B	HR	RBI	BB	SO	AVG	OBP	SLG	PRO+	BR/A	SB	CS	SBR	FA	FR	G/POS	TPR
1978	Phi-N	3	4	0	2	0	0	0	2	0	0	.500	.500	.500	178	0	0	1	-1	1.000	2	/S-2	0.1
1979	KC-A	55	118	9	24	7	0	2	15	3	19	.203	.230	.314	44	-9	0	1	-1	.974	4	S-48/3-9	-0.3
1980	Cal-A	18	40	5	11	3	0	1	5	5	8	.275	.356	.425	116	1	0	0	0	.860	-6	S-12/3-4,2-1,0-1	-0.4
	Chi-A	90	293	23	68	11	1	2	18	9	54	.232	.260	.297	52	-19	2	1	0	.956	5	S-90	-0.4
	Yr	108	333	28	79	14	1	3	23	14	62	.237	.272	.312	60	-18	2	1	0	.948	-1	*S-102/3-4,2-1,0-1	-0.8
1982	Sea-A	136	492	44	113	20	2	16	57	12	95	.230	.248	.376	67	-24	2	10	-5	.963	19	*S-136	0.3
1983	Sea-A	65	216	21	41	4	2	7	21	7	56	.190	.222	.324	46	-16	1	3	-2	.964	21	S-63	0.9
	*Bal-A	81	221	16	46	9	1	3	27	15	52	.208	.262	.299	55	-14	3	4	-2	.942	3	3-79/2-2	-1.2
	Yr	146	437	37	87	13	3	10	48	22	108	.199	.242	.311	51	-30	4	7	-3	.942	25	3-79,S-63/2-2	-0.3
1984	Bal-A	96	142	15	31	4	0	3	19	8	33	.218	.265	.310	60	-8	1	4	-2	.955	11	3-89/P-1,D-1	0.1
Total	6	544	1526	133	336	58	6	34	154	59	317	.220	.253	.333	59	-89	9	24	-12	.960	60	S-351,3-181/2DPO	-0.9

■ MIKE CUBBAGE   Cubbage, Michael Lee   b: 7/21/50, Charlottesville, Va.   BL/TR, 6', 180 lbs.   Deb: 4/7/74   MC

YEAR	TM/L	G	AB	R	H	2B	3B	HR	RBI	BB	SO	AVG	OBP	SLG	PRO+	BR/A	SB	CS	SBR	FA	FR	G/POS	TPR
1974	Tex-A	9	15	0	0	0	0	0	0	0	4	.000	.000	.000	-99	-4	0	0	0	1.000	2	/3-3,2-2	-0.2
1975	Tex-A	58	143	12	32	6	0	4	21	18	14	.224	.311	.350	87	-2	0	0	0	.962	2	2-37/3-3,D-2	0.1
1976	Tex-A	14	32	2	7	0	0	0	0	7	7	.219	.359	.219	70	-1	0	0	0	1.000	-0	/2-5,3-1,D-6	-0.1
	Min-A	104	342	40	89	19	5	3	49	42	37	.260	.346	.371	108	4	1	1	-0	.940	3	3-99/2-2,D-2	0.6
	Yr	118	374	42	96	19	5	3	49	49	44	.257	.347	.358	105	3	1	1	-0	.940	2	*3-100/D-8,2-7	0.5
1977	Min-A	129	417	60	110	16	5	9	55	37	49	.264	.324	.391	95	-3	1	4	-2	.952	9	*3-126/D-1	0.2
1978	Min-A	125	394	40	111	12	7	7	57	40	44	.282	.349	.401	108	5	3	1	0	.971	2	*3-115/2-5	0.5
1979	Min-A	94	243	26	67	10	1	2	23	39	26	.276	.376	.350	94	-1	1	8	-5	.928	-12	3-63/D-21/1-1,2-1	-1.8
1980	Min-A	103	285	29	70	9	0	8	42	23	37	.246	.304	.361	76	-4	1	0	-1	.996	1	1-72,3-32/2-1,D-1	-0.7
1981	NY-N	67	80	9	17	2	2	1	4	9	15	.213	.292	.325	76	-3	0	0	0	.963	1	3-12	-0.2
Total	8	703	1951	218	503	74	20	34	251	215	233	.258	.333	.369	94	-14	6	15	-7	.952	12	3-454/1-73,2-53,D	-1.6

■ AL CUCCINELLO   Cuccinello, Alfred Edward   b: 11/26/14, Long Island City, N.Y.   BR/TR, 5'10", 165 lbs.   Deb: 5/17/35   F

YEAR	TM/L	G	AB	R	H	2B	3B	HR	RBI	BB	SO	AVG	OBP	SLG	PRO+	BR/A	SB	CS	SBR	FA	FR	G/POS	TPR
1935	NY-N	54	165	27	41	7	1	4	20	1	20	.248	.262	.376	70	-7	0			.951	6	2-48/3-2	0.1

■ TONY CUCCINELLO   Cuccinello, Anthony Francis "Cooch" or "Chick"
b: 11/8/07, Long Island City, N.Y.   d: 9/21/95, Tampa, Fla.   BR/TR, 5'7", 160 lbs.   Deb: 4/15/30   FC

YEAR	TM/L	G	AB	R	H	2B	3B	HR	RBI	BB	SO	AVG	OBP	SLG	PRO+	BR/A	SB	CS	SBR	FA	FR	G/POS	TPR
1930	Cin-N	125	443	64	138	22	5	10	78	47	44	.312	.380	.451	105	4	5			.920	-19	*3-109,2-15/S-4	-0.7
1931	Cin-N	154	575	67	181	39	11	2	93	54	28	.315	.374	.431	123	19	1			.969	5	*2-154	3.3
1932	Bro-N	154	597	76	168	32	6	12	77	46	47	.281	.337	.415	103	2	5			.973	19	*2-154	2.9
1933	Bro-N★	134	485	58	122	31	4	9	65	44	40	.252	.316	.388	105	2	4			.977	-19	*2-120,3-14	-0.9
1934	Bro-N	140	528	59	138	32	2	14	94	49	45	.261	.325	.409	100	-1	0			.974	12	*2-101,3-43	1.8
1935	Bro-N	102	360	49	105	20	3	8	53	40	35	.292	.366	.431	116	9	3			.977	8	2-64,3-36	1.9
1936	Bos-N	150	565	68	174	26	3	7	86	58	49	.308	.374	.402	116	14	5			.971	22	*2-150	4.5
1937	Bos-N	152	575	77	156	36	4	11	80	61	40	.271	.341	.405	112	9	2			.967	-10	*2-151	1.0
1938	Bos-N☆	147	555	62	147	25	2	9	76	52	32	.265	.331	.366	102	0	4			.974	-26	*2-147	-1.7
1939	Bos-N	81	310	42	95	17	1	2	40	26	26	.306	.360	.387	109	4	5			.970	4	2-80	0.5
1940	Bos-N	34	126	14	34	9	0	0	19	8	9	.270	.319	.341	87	-2	1			.978	1	3-33	0.0
	NY-N	88	307	26	64	9	3	6	36	16	42	.208	.248	.300	50	-21	1			.987	2	2-47,3-37	-1.3
	Yr	122	433	40	98	18	2	5	55	24	51	.226	.269	.312	60	-24	2			.971	6	3-70,2-47	-1.3
1942	Bos-N	40	104	8	21	3	0	1	8	9	11	.202	.265	.260	55	-6	1			.907	-4	3-20,2-14	-1.0
1943	Bos-N	13	19	0	0	0	0	0	2	3	1	.000	.136	.000	-60	-4	0			.929	0	/3-4,2-2,S-1	-0.4
	Chi-A	34	103	5	28	5	0	2	11	13	13	.272	.353	.379	114	2	3	1	0	.965	-2	3-30	0.1
1944	Chi-A	38	130	5	34	3	0	0	17	6	16	.262	.304	.285	70	-5	0	0	0	.959	-2	3-30/2-6	-0.7
1945	Chi-A†	118	402	50	124	25	3	2	49	45	19	.308	.379	.400	130	16	6	2	1	.936	-5	*3-112	1.5
Total	15	1704	6184	730	1729	334	46	94	884	579	497	.280	.343	.394	105	41	42	3		.973	-18	*2-1205,3-468/S-5	10.8

■ JIM CUDWORTH   Cudworth, James Alaric "Cuddy"   b: 8/22/1858, Fairhaven, Mass.   d: 12/21/43, Middleboro, Mass.   BR/TR, 6', 165 lbs.   Deb: 7/27/1884

YEAR	TM/L	G	AB	R	H	2B	3B	HR	RBI	BB	SO	AVG	OBP	SLG	PRO+	BR/A	SB	CS	SBR	FA	FR	G/POS	TPR
1884	KC-U	32	116	7	17	3	1	0		2		.147	.161	.190	7	-17				.963	2	1-19,O-12/P-2	-1.4

■ MANUEL CUETO   Cueto, Manuel "Potato"   b: 2/8/1892, Guanajay, Cuba   d: 6/29/42, Regla, Cuba   BR/TR, 5'5", 157 lbs.   Deb: 6/25/14

YEAR	TM/L	G	AB	R	H	2B	3B	HR	RBI	BB	SO	AVG	OBP	SLG	PRO+	BR/A	SB	CS	SBR	FA	FR	G/POS	TPR
1914	StL-F	19	43	2	4	0	0	0	2	5	0	.093	.188	.093	-21	-8	0			.941	-1	3-10/S-5,2-2	-0.9
1917	Cin-N	56	140	10	28	3	0	1	11	16	17	.200	.287	.243	66	-5	4			.963	-1	O-38/2-6,C-5	-0.9
1918	Cin-N	47	108	14	32	5	1	0	14	19	5	.296	.406	.361	137	6	4			.929	-14	O-19,2-10/S-9,C-6	-0.8
1919	Cin-N	29	88	10	22	2	0	0	4	10	4	.250	.340	.273	88	-1	5			.982	4	O-25/3-1	0.1
Total	4	151	379	36	86	10	1	1	31	50	26	.227	.323	.266	80	-8	13			.964	-13	/O-82,2-18,S-14,C3	-2.5

■ JOHN CUFF   Cuff, John J.   b: 6/1864, Jersey City, N.J.   Deb: 9/11/1884

YEAR	TM/L	G	AB	R	H	2B	3B	HR	RBI	BB	SO	AVG	OBP	SLG	PRO+	BR/A	SB	CS	SBR	FA	FR	G/POS	TPR
1884	Bal-U	3	11	1	1	0	0	0		1		.091	.167	.182	5	-2				.920	0	/C-3	-0.1

■ LEON CULBERSON   Culberson, Delbert Leon "Lee"   b: 8/6/19, Halls, Ga.   d: 9/17/89, Rome, Ga.   BR/TR, 5'11", 180 lbs.   Deb: 5/16/43

YEAR	TM/L	G	AB	R	H	2B	3B	HR	RBI	BB	SO	AVG	OBP	SLG	PRO+	BR/A	SB	CS	SBR	FA	FR	G/POS	TPR
1943	Bos-A	81	312	36	85	16	6	3	34	31	35	.272	.338	.391	111	4	14	0	4	.978	6	O-79	1.0
1944	Bos-A	75	282	41	67	11	5	2	21	20	20	.238	.288	.333	78	-9	6	4	-1	.979	-3	O-72	-1.7
1945	Bos-A	97	331	26	91	21	6	6	45	20	37	.275	.316	.429	113	4	4	3	-1	.967	5	O-91	0.3
1946	*Bos-A	59	179	34	56	10	1	3	18	16	19	.313	.369	.430	116	4	3	2	-0	.967	-7	O-49/3-4	-0.5
1947	Bos-A	47	84	10	20	1	0	0	11	12	10	.238	.354	.250	65	-3	1	1	-0	.974	-4	O-25/3-4	-0.9
1948	Was-A	12	29	1	5	0	0	0	2	8	5	.172	.351	.172	43	-2	0	0	0	1.000	-3	O-11	-0.5
Total	6	371	1217	148	324	59	18	14	131	107	126	.266	.327	.379	100	-3	28	10	2	.974	-0	O-327/3-8	-2.3

■ JOHN CULLEN   Cullen, John J.   b: Marysville, Cal.   Deb: 8/18/1884

YEAR	TM/L	G	AB	R	H	2B	3B	HR	RBI	BB	SO	AVG	OBP	SLG	PRO+	BR/A	SB	CS	SBR	FA	FR	G/POS	TPR
1884	Wil-U	9	31	2	6	0	0	0		1		.194	.219	.194	25	-4				.750	-1	/O-6,S-3	-0.5

■ TIM CULLEN   Cullen, Timothy Leo   b: 2/16/42, San Francisco, Cal.   BR/TR, 6'1", 185 lbs.   Deb: 8/8/66

YEAR	TM/L	G	AB	R	H	2B	3B	HR	RBI	BB	SO	AVG	OBP	SLG	PRO+	BR/A	SB	CS	SBR	FA	FR	G/POS	TPR
1966	Was-A	18	34	8	8	0	0	0		2	8	.235	.278	.265	57	-2	0	0	0	.889	1	/3-8,2-5	0.0
1967	Was-A	124	402	35	95	7	0	2	31	40	47	.236	.307	.269	74	-12	4	5	-2	.951	15	S-69,2-46,3-15/O-1	1.1
1968	Chi-A	72	155	16	31	3	0	0	13	15	23	.200	.275	.284	69	-6	0	0	0	.966	6	2-71	0.3
	Was-A	47	114	8	31	4	2	1	16	7	12	.272	.325	.368	113	2	0	0	0	.968	-1	S-33,2-16/3-3	0.4
	Yr	119	269	24	62	11	2	3	29	22	35	.230	.296	.320	87	-4	0	0	0	.965	5	2-87,S-33/3-3	0.7
1969	Was-A	119	249	22	52	10	2	1	15	14	27	.209	.257	.249	44	-19	1	1	-0	.981	12	*2-105/S-9,3-1	-0.1
1970	Was-A	123	262	22	56	10	2	1	18	31	38	.214	.304	.279	65	-12	3	2	-1	**.994**	27	*2-112/S-6	2.1
1971	Was-A	125	403	34	77	13	4	2	26	33	47	.191	.252	.258	47	-29	2	0	1	.997	21	2-78,S-62	0.5
1972	*Oak-A	72	142	10	37	3	0	0	11	5	17	.261	.286	.331	88	-3	0	1	-1	.952	-2	2-65/3-4,S-1	-0.2
Total	7	700	1761	155	387	57	9	9	134	147	219	.220	.283	.278	65	-80	10	9	-2	.979	80	2-498,S-180/3-31,O	4.1

■ ROY CULLENBINE   Cullenbine, Roy Joseph   b: 10/18/13, Nashville, Tenn.   d: 5/28/91, Mt.Clemens, Mich.   BB/TR, 6'1", 190 lbs.   Deb: 4/19/38

YEAR	TM/L	G	AB	R	H	2B	3B	HR	RBI	BB	SO	AVG	OBP	SLG	PRO+	BR/A	SB	CS	SBR	FA	FR	G/POS	TPR
1938	Det-A	25	67	12	19	9	1	0	9	12	9	.284	.392	.388	91	-1	2	0	1	1.000	-0	O-17	-0.1
1939	Det-A	75	179	31	43	9	2	6	23	34	29	.240	.362	.413	91	-2	0	1	-1	.902	-5	O-46/1-2	-0.9

YEAR	TM/L	G	AB	R	H	2B	3B	HR	RBI	BB	SO	AVG	OBP	SLG	PRO+	BR/A	SB	CS	SBR	FA	FR	G/POS	TPR
1940	Bro-N	22	61	8	11	1	0	1	9	23	11	.180	.405	.246	78	-0	2			1.000	1	O-19	-0.1
	StL-A	86	257	41	59	11	2	7	31	50	34	.230	.359	.370	87	-4	0	1	-1	.975	-2	O-57/1-6	-1.0
1941	StL-A★	149	501	82	159	29	9	9	98	121	43	.317	.452	.465	138	35	6	4	-1	.964	1	*O-120,1-22	2.5
1942	StL-A	38	109	15	21	7	1	2	14	30	20	.193	.367	.330	95	0	0	1	-1	.930	1	O-27/1-5	-0.1
	Was-A	64	241	30	69	19	0	2	35	44	18	.286	.396	.390	123	9	1	2	-1	.966	8	O-35,3-28	1.5
	*NY-A	21	77	16	28	7	0	2	17	18	2	.364	.484	.532	190	10	0	1	-1	.980	2	O-19/1-1	1.1
	Yr	123	427	61	118	33	1	6	66	92	40	.276	.405	.400	127	20	1	4	-2	.959	11	O-81,3-28/1-6	2.5
1943	Cle-A	138	488	66	141	24	4	8	56	96	58	.289	.407	.404	146	33	3	4	-2	.981	3	*O-121,1-13	2.9
1944	Cle-A☆	154	571	98	162	34	5	16	80	87	49	.284	.380	.445	141	31	4	4	-1	.967	-2	*O-151	2.1
1945	Cle-A	8	13	3	1	1	0	0	0	11	0	.077	.500	.154	97	1	0	0	0	1.000	-2	/O-4,3-3	-0.1
	*Det-A	146	523	80	145	27	5	18	93	102	36	.277	.398	.451	137	28	2	0	1	.980	13	*O-146	3.5
	Yr	154	536	83	146	28	5	18	93	**113**	36	.272	.402	.444	137	29	2	0	1	.980	11	O-150/3-3	3.4
1946	Det-A	113	328	63	110	21	0	15	56	88	39	.335	.477	.537	172	37	3	0	1	.965	2	O-81,1-21	3.5
1947	Det-A	142	464	82	104	18	1	24	78	137	51	.224	.401	.422	125	21	3	2	-0	.989	16	*1-138	3.3
Total	10	1181	3879	627	1072	209	32	110	599	853	399	.276	.408	.432	132	199	26	**20**		.969	34	O-843,1-208/3-31	18.1

■ DICK CULLER   Culler, Richard Broadus b: 1/15/15, High Point, N.C. d: 6/16/64, Chapel Hill, N.C. BR/TR, 5'9.5", 155 lbs. Deb: 9/19/36

YEAR	TM/L	G	AB	R	H	2B	3B	HR	RBI	BB	SO	AVG	OBP	SLG	PRO+	BR/A	SB	CS	SBR	FA	FR	G/POS	TPR
1936	Phi-A	9	38	3	9	0	0	0	1	1	3	.237	.256	.237	23	-5	0	0	0	.946	-3	/2-7,S-2	-0.7
1943	Chi-A	53	148	9	32	5	1	0	11	16	11	.216	.297	.264	65	-6	4	5	-2	.950	11	3-26,2-19/S-3	0.4
1944	Bos-N	8	28	2	2	0	0	0	4	2		.071	.188	.071	-24	-5	0			.904	2	/S-8	-0.2
1945	Bos-N	136	527	87	138	12	1	2	30	50	35	.262	.328	.300	75	-17	7			.954	-8	*S-126/3-6	-1.5
1946	Bos-N	134	482	70	123	15	3	0	33	62	18	.255	.342	.299	82	-9	7			.948	-8	*S-132	-1.1
1947	Bos-N	77	214	20	53	5	1	0	19	19	15	.248	.309	.280	59	-12	1			.967	3	S-77	-0.6
1948	Chi-N	48	89	4	15	2	0	0	5	13	3	.169	.275	.191	29	-9	0			.968	16	S-43/2-2	0.9
1949	NY-N	7	1	0	0	0	0	0	0	0	1	.000	.500	.000	45	0	0			.889	2	/S-7	0.2
Total	8	472	1527	195	372	39	6	2	99	166	87	.244	.320	.281	68	-62	19	**5**		.954	14	S-398/3-32,2-28	-2.6

■ NICK CULLOP   Cullop, Henry Nicholas "Tomato Face" (b: Heinrich Nicholas Kolop) b: 10/16/1900, St.Louis, Mo. d: 12/8/78, Westerville, Ohio BR/TR, 6', 200 lbs. Deb: 4/14/26

YEAR	TM/L	G	AB	R	H	2B	3B	HR	RBI	BB	SO	AVG	OBP	SLG	PRO+	BR/A	SB	CS	SBR	FA	FR	G/POS	TPR
1926	NY-A	2	2	0	1	0	0	0	0	0	1	.500	.500	.500	164	0	0	0	0	.000	0	H	0.0
1927	Was-A	15	23	2	5	2	0	0	1	1	6	.217	.250	.304	44	-2	0	0	0	1.000	-1	/O-5,1-1	-0.3
	Cle-A	32	68	9	16	2	3	1	8	9	19	.235	.333	.397	88	-1	0	4	-2	.982	3	O-20/P-1	-0.2
	Yr	47	91	11	21	4	3	1	9	10	25	.231	.314	.374	78	-3	0	4	-2	.984	2	O-25/1-1,P-1	-0.5
1929	Bro-N	13	41	7	8	2	2	1	5	8	7	.195	.327	.415	84	-1	0			1.000	1	O-11/1-1	-0.2
1930	Cin-N	7	22	2	4	0	0	1	5	1	9	.182	.217	.318	29	-3	0			1.000	0	/O-5	-0.2
1931	Cin-N	104	334	29	88	23	7	8	48	21	86	.263	.309	.446	107	1	0			.968	2	O-83	-0.4
Total	5	173	490	49	122	29	12	11	67	40	128	.249	.308	.424	96	-6	0	**4**		.975	2	O-124/1-2,P-1	-1.3

■ WIL CULMER   Culmer, Wilfred Hillard b: 11/11/58, Nassau, Bahamas BR/TR, 6'4", 210 lbs. Deb: 4/12/83

YEAR	TM/L	G	AB	R	H	2B	3B	HR	RBI	BB	SO	AVG	OBP	SLG	PRO+	BR/A	SB	CS	SBR	FA	FR	G/POS	TPR
1983	Cle-A	7	19	0	2	0	0	0	1	0	4	.105	.105	.105	-40	-4	0	1	-1	1.000	-1	/O-4,D-2	-0.6

■ BENNY CULP   Culp, Benjamin Baldy b: 1/19/14, Philadelphia, Pa. BR/TR, 5'9", 175 lbs. Deb: 9/17/42 C

YEAR	TM/L	G	AB	R	H	2B	3B	HR	RBI	BB	SO	AVG	OBP	SLG	PRO+	BR/A	SB	CS	SBR	FA	FR	G/POS	TPR
1942	Phi-N	1	0	0	0	0	0	0	0	0						0	0			.500	-0	C-1	0.0
1943	Phi-N	10	24	4	5	1	0	0	2	3	3	.208	.296	.250	61	-1	0			.958	-3	C-10	-0.3
1944	Phi-N	4	2	1	0	0	0	0	0	0	0	.000	.000	.000	-99	-1	0			1.000	0	C-1	0.0
Total	3	15	26	5	5	1	0	0	2	3	3	.192	.276	.231	49	-2	0			.926	-3	C-12	-0.3

■ JACK CUMMINGS   Cummings, John William b: 4/1/04, Pittsburgh, Pa. d: 10/5/62, W.Mifflin, Pa. BR/TR, 6', 195 lbs. Deb: 9/11/26

YEAR	TM/L	G	AB	R	H	2B	3B	HR	RBI	BB	SO	AVG	OBP	SLG	PRO+	BR/A	SB	CS	SBR	FA	FR	G/POS	TPR
1926	NY-N	7	16	3	5	3	0	0	4	2	2	.313	.450	.500	157	0	0			.958	0	/C-6	0.2
1927	NY-N	43	80	8	29	6	1	2	14	5	10	.363	.407	.538	151	6	0			.974	-5	C-34	0.2
1928	NY-N	33	27	4	9	2	0	2	9	3	4	.333	.400	.630	165	2	0			.833	-2	/C-4	0.2
1929	NY-N	3	3	0	1	0	0	0	0	0	1	.333	.333	.333	66	-0	0			1.000	-0	/C-1	0.0
	Bos-N	3	6	0	1	0	0	0	1	0	2	.167	.167	.167	-18	-1	0			.667	-1	/C-3	-0.2
	Yr	6	9	0	2	0	0	0	1	0	2	.222	.222	.222	11	-1	0			.714	-1	/C-4	-0.2
Total	4	89	132	15	45	11	1	4	28	12	18	.341	.400	.530	145	8	0			.947	-6	/C-48	0.4

■ MIDRE CUMMINGS   Cummings, Midre Almeric b: 10/14/71, St.Croix, V.I. BB/TR, 6'1", 190 lbs. Deb: 9/10/93

YEAR	TM/L	G	AB	R	H	2B	3B	HR	RBI	BB	SO	AVG	OBP	SLG	PRO+	BR/A	SB	CS	SBR	FA	FR	G/POS	TPR
1993	Pit-N	13	36	5	4	1	0	0	3	4	9	.111	.200	.139	-7	-5	0	0	0	1.000	-1	O-11	-0.7
1994	Pit-N	24	86	11	21	4	0	1	12	4	18	.244	.286	.326	58	-5	0	0	0	.962	0	O-24	-0.6
1995	Pit-N	59	152	13	37	7	1	2	15	13	30	.243	.303	.342	68	-7	1	0	0	.988	1	O-41	-0.8
1996	Pit-N	24	85	11	19	3	1	3	7	0	16	.224	.224	.388	56	-6	0	0	0	.980	0	/O-97	-0.5
Total	4	120	359	40	81	15	2	6	37	21	73	.226	.270	.329	56	-23	1	0	0	.980	0	/O-97	-2.6

■ GEORGE CUNNINGHAM   Cunningham, George Harold b: 7/13/1894, Sturgeon Lake, Minn. d: 3/10/72, Chattanooga, Tenn. BR/TR, 5'11", 185 lbs. Deb: 4/14/16

YEAR	TM/L	G	AB	R	H	2B	3B	HR	RBI	BB	SO	AVG	OBP	SLG	PRO+	BR/A	SB	CS	SBR	FA	FR	G/POS	TPR
1916	Det-A	35	41	7	11	2	2	0	3	8	12	.268	.388	.415	136	2	0			.948	1	P-35	0.0
1917	Det-A	44	34	5	6	0	0	0	3	3	13	.176	.243	.265	55	-2	0			.922	1	P-44	0.0
1918	Det-A	56	112	11	25	4	1	0	16	16	34	.223	.320	.277	84	-2	2			.923	-6	P-27,O-20	-0.8
1919	Det-A	26	23	4	5	0	0	0	5	9	8	.217	.438	.217	89	1	0			.857	-0	P-17	0.0
1921	Det-A	1	0	0	0	0	0	0	0	0	0	—	—	—		0	0	0	0	1.000	-0	/O-1	0.0
Total	5	162	210	27	47	6	3	0	13	36	67	.224	.337	.295	91	-1	2	**0**		.923	-4	P-123/O-21	-0.8

■ JOE CUNNINGHAM   Cunningham, Joseph Robert b: 8/27/31, Paterson, N.J. BL/TL, 6'1", 190 lbs. Deb: 6/30/54 C

YEAR	TM/L	G	AB	R	H	2B	3B	HR	RBI	BB	SO	AVG	OBP	SLG	PRO+	BR/A	SB	CS	SBR	FA	FR	G/POS	TPR
1954	StL-N	85	310	40	88	11	3	11	50	43	40	.284	.375	.445	112	6	1	1	-0	.989	2	1-85	0.3
1956	StL-N	4	3	1	0	0	0	0	0	1	0	.000	.250	.000	-25	-1	0	0	0	1.000	-0	/1-1	-0.1
1957	StL-N	122	261	50	83	15	0	9	52	56	29	.318	.447	.479	146	20	3	3	-1	1.000	-3	1-57,O-46	1.2
1958	StL-N	131	337	61	105	20	3	12	57	82	23	.312	.450	.496	144	26	4	4	-1	.997	-6	1-67,O-66	1.3
1959	StL-N★	144	458	65	158	28	6	7	60	88	47	.345	**.456**	.478	140	31	2	6	-3	.972	-7	*O-121,1-35	1.4
1960	StL-N	139	492	68	138	28	3	6	39	59	59	.280	.364	.386	97	-0	1	7	-4	.950	-7	*O-116,1-15	-1.9
1961	StL-N	113	322	60	92	11	2	7	40	53	32	.286	.404	.398	104	4	1	0	0	.964	-9	O-86,1-10	-1.0
1962	Chi-A	149	526	91	155	32	7	8	70	101	33	.295	.415	.428	128	26	3	3	-1	**.994**	-6	*1-143/O-5	0.9
1963	Chi-A	67	210	32	60	12	1	1	31	33	23	.286	.393	.367	116	6	1	0	0	.989	-7	1-58	-0.3
1964	Chi-A	40	108	13	27	7	0	0	10	14	15	.250	.352	.315	90	-1	0	1	-1	.996	-1	1-41	-0.3
	Was-A	49	126	15	27	4	0	0	7	23	12	.214	.344	.246	68	-4	0	1	-1	.997	-4	1-41	-1.1
	Yr	89	234	28	54	11	0	0	17	37	27	.231	.348	.278	78	-5	0	2	-1	.997	-5	1-74	-1.4
1965	Was-A	95	201	29	46	9	1	3	20	46	27	.229	.375	.328	103	3	0	1	-1	.986	-4	1-59	-0.5
1966	Was-A	3	8	0	1	0	0	0	0	1	1	.125	.125	.125	-28	-1	0	0	0	1.000	1	/1-3	0.0
Total	12	1141	3362	525	980	177	26	64	436	599	369	.291	.406	.417	119	116	16	27	-11	.993	-51	1-607,O-440	-0.1

■ RAY CUNNINGHAM   Cunningham, Raymond Lee b: 1/17/05, Mesquite, Tex. BR/TR, 5'7.5", 150 lbs. Deb: 9/16/31

YEAR	TM/L	G	AB	R	H	2B	3B	HR	RBI	BB	SO	AVG	OBP	SLG	PRO+	BR/A	SB	CS	SBR	FA	FR	G/POS	TPR
1931	StL-N	3	4	0	0	0	0	0	1	0	0	.000	.000	.000	-96	-1	0			1.000	1	/3-3	0.0
1932	StL-N	11	22	4	4	1	0	0	0	3	4	.182	.280	.227	37	-2	0			1.000	3	/3-8,2-2	0.1
Total	2	14	26	4	4	1	0	0	1	3	4	.154	.241	.192	18	-3	0			1.000	4	/3-11,2-2	0.1

■ BILL CUNNINGHAM   Cunningham, William Aloysius b: 7/30/1895, San Francisco, Cal. d: 9/26/53, Colusa, Cal. BR/TR, 5'8", 155 lbs. Deb: 7/14/21 C

YEAR	TM/L	G	AB	R	H	2B	3B	HR	RBI	BB	SO	AVG	OBP	SLG	PRO+	BR/A	SB	CS	SBR	FA	FR	G/POS	TPR
1921	NY-N	40	76	10	21	2	1	2	12	3	8	.276	.313	.368	79	-2	0	1	-1	1.000	-4	O-20	-0.8
1922	*NY-N	85	229	37	75	15	2	2	33	7	9	.328	.350	.437	101	-0	4	5	-2	.988	-4	O-71/3-1	-0.9
1923	*NY-N	79	203	22	55	7	1	5	27	10	9	.271	.305	.389	83	-6	1	2	-1	.992	-7	O-68/2-4	-1.5
1924	Bos-N	114	437	44	119	15	8	0	40	32	27	.272	.326	.350	85	-9	8	5	-1	.970	6	*O-109	-1.1
Total	4	318	945	113	270	39	12	9	112	52	48	.286	.326	.381	88	-17	13	13	-3	.982	-8	O-268/2-4,3-1	-4.3

■ BILL CUNNINGHAM   Cunningham, William John b: 6/9/1888, Schenectady, N.Y. d: 2/21/46, Schenectady, N.Y. BR/TR, 5'9", 170 lbs. Deb: 9/12/10

YEAR	TM/L	G	AB	R	H	2B	3B	HR	RBI	BB	SO	AVG	OBP	SLG	PRO+	BR/A	SB	CS	SBR	FA	FR	G/POS	TPR
1910	Was-A	21	74	3	22	5	1	0	14	12		.297	.402	.392	156	5	4			.957	-5	2-21	0.0

YEAR	TM/L	G	AB	R	H	2B	3B	HR	RBI	BB	SO	AVG	OBP	SLG	PRO+	BR/A	SB	CS	SBR	FA	FR	G/POS	TPR
1911	Was-A	94	331	34	63	10	5	3	37	19		.190	.239	.278	45	-26	10			.932	-13	2-93	-4.1
1912	Was-A	8	27	5	5	1	0	1	8	3		.185	.267	.333	71	-1	2			.962	-3	/2-7,S-1	-0.4
Total	3	123	432	42	90	16	6	4	59	34		.208	.271	.301	64	-21	16			.938	-21	2-121/S-1	-4.5

■ DOC CURLEY
Curley, Walter James   b: 3/12/1874, Upton, Mass.   d: 9/23/20, Framingham, Mass.   BR/TR,   Deb: 9/12/1899

YEAR	TM/L	G	AB	R	H	2B	3B	HR	RBI	BB	SO	AVG	OBP	SLG	PRO+	BR/A	SB	CS	SBR	FA	FR	G/POS	TPR
1899	Chi-N	10	37	7	4	0	1	0	2	3		.108	.233	.162	9	-5	0			.907	-6	2-10	-0.9

■ PETE CURREN
Curren, Peter   b: Baltimore, Md.   175 lbs.   Deb: 9/12/1876

YEAR	TM/L	G	AB	R	H	2B	3B	HR	RBI	BB	SO	AVG	OBP	SLG	PRO+	BR/A	SB	CS	SBR	FA	FR	G/POS	TPR
1876	Phi-N	3	12	5	4	1	0	0	2	0	0	.333	.333	.417	150	1				.588	-1	/C-2,O-1	0.0

■ PERRY CURRIN
Currin, Perry Gilmore   b: 9/27/28, Washington, D.C.   BL/TR, 6', 175 lbs.   Deb: 6/29/47

YEAR	TM/L	G	AB	R	H	2B	3B	HR	RBI	BB	SO	AVG	OBP	SLG	PRO+	BR/A	SB	CS	SBR	FA	FR	G/POS	TPR
1947	StL-A	3	2	0	0	0	0	0	0	1	0	.000	.333	.000	-3	-0	0	0	0	1.000	1	/S-1	0.1

■ TONY CURRY
Curry, George Anthony   b: 12/22/38, Nassau, Bahamas   BL/TL, 5'11", 185 lbs.   Deb: 4/12/60

YEAR	TM/L	G	AB	R	H	2B	3B	HR	RBI	BB	SO	AVG	OBP	SLG	PRO+	BR/A	SB	CS	SBR	FA	FR	G/POS	TPR
1960	Phi-N	95	245	26	64	14	2	6	34	16	53	.261	.309	.408	94	-2	0	2	-1	.925	-8	O-64	-1.4
1961	Phi-N	15	36	3	7	2	0	0	3	1	8	.194	.216	.250	24	-4	0	0	0	.833	-0	/O-8	-0.5
1966	Cle-A	19	16	4	2	0	0	0	3	3	8	.125	.263	.125	16	-2	0	0	0	.000	0	H	-0.2
Total	3	129	297	33	73	16	2	6	40	20	69	.246	.296	.374	82	-8	0	2	-1	.915	-8	/O-72	-2.1

■ JIM CURRY
Curry, James L.   b: 3/10/1893, Camden, N.J.   d: 8/2/38, Grenloch, N.J.   BR/TR, 5'11", 160 lbs.   Deb: 10/2/09

YEAR	TM/L	G	AB	R	H	2B	3B	HR	RBI	BB	SO	AVG	OBP	SLG	PRO+	BR/A	SB	CS	SBR	FA	FR	G/POS	TPR
1909	Phi-A	1	4	1	1	0	0	0	0	0		.250	.250	.250	57	-0	0			1.000	-1	/2-1	-0.1
1911	NY-A	4	11	3	2	0	0	0	0	0	1	.182	.250	.182	20	-1	0			.773	-1	/2-4	-0.3
1918	Det-A	5	20	1	5	1	0	0	0	0	0	.250	.286	.300	80	-1	0			.952	-3	/2-5	-0.3
Total	3	10	35	5	8	1	0	0	0	0		.229	.270	.257	56	-1	0			.867	-5	/2-10	-0.7

■ CHAD CURTIS
Curtis, Chad David   b: 11/6/68, Marion, Ind.   BR/TR, 5'10", 175 lbs.   Deb: 4/8/92

YEAR	TM/L	G	AB	R	H	2B	3B	HR	RBI	BB	SO	AVG	OBP	SLG	PRO+	BR/A	SB	CS	SBR	FA	FR	G/POS	TPR
1992	Cal-A	139	441	59	114	16	2	10	46	51	71	.259	.343	.372	100	1	43	18	2	.978	-3	*O-135/D-1	-0.2
1993	Cal-A	152	583	94	166	25	3	6	59	70	89	.285	.365	.369	95	-2	48	24	0	.980	17	*O-151/2-3	1.1
1994	Cal-A	114	453	67	116	23	4	11	50	37	69	.256	.319	.397	82	-13	25	11	1	.988	15	*O-114	0.0
1995	Det-A	144	586	96	157	29	3	21	67	70	93	.268	.353	.435	104	4	27	15	-1	.992	2	*O-144	0.1
1996	Det-A	104	400	65	105	20	1	10	37	53	73	.262	.350	.393	88	-7	16	10	-1	.965	-7	*O-104	-1.6
	*LA-N	43	104	20	22	5	0	2	9	17	22	.212	.322	.317	76	-3	2	1	0	.985	-3	O-40	-0.7
Total	5	696	2567	401	680	118	13	60	268	298	410	.265	.347	.391	94	-20	161	79	1	.982	21	O-688/2-3,D-1	-1.3

■ ERVIN CURTIS
Curtis, Ervin Duane   b: 12/27/1861, Coldwater, Mich.   d: 2/14/45, N.Adams, Mass.   BL/TL, 5'8.5", 157 lbs.   Deb: 7/15/1891

YEAR	TM/L	G	AB	R	H	2B	3B	HR	RBI	BB	SO	AVG	OBP	SLG	PRO+	BR/A	SB	CS	SBR	FA	FR	G/POS	TPR
1891	Cin-N	27	108	11	29	3	3	1	13	9	19	.269	.331	.380	106	1	3			.862	-0	O-27	-0.1
	Was-a	29	103	17	26	3	2	0	12	13	16	.252	.347	.320	96	-0	2			.797	-1	O-29	-0.2
Total	1	56	211	28	55	6	5	1	25	22	35	.261	.339	.351	101	0	5			.829	-2	/O-56	-0.3

■ GENE CURTIS
Curtis, Eugene Holmes "Eude"   b: 5/5/1883, Bethany, W.Va.   d: 1/1/19, Steubenville, Ohio   BR/TR, 6'3", 220 lbs.   Deb: 9/21/03

YEAR	TM/L	G	AB	R	H	2B	3B	HR	RBI	BB	SO	AVG	OBP	SLG	PRO+	BR/A	SB	CS	SBR	FA	FR	G/POS	TPR
1903	Pit-N	5	19	2	8	1	0	0	3			.421	.450	.474	158	1	0			.833	-0	/O-5	0.1

■ FRED CURTIS
Curtis, Frederick Marion   b: 10/30/1880, Beaver Lake, Mich.   d: 4/5/39, Minneapolis, Minn.   BR/TR, 6'1",   Deb: 7/24/05

YEAR	TM/L	G	AB	R	H	2B	3B	HR	RBI	BB	SO	AVG	OBP	SLG	PRO+	BR/A	SB	CS	SBR	FA	FR	G/POS	TPR
1905	NY-A	2	9	0	2	1	0	0	2	1		.222	.300	.333	90	-0	1			1.000	-0	/1-2	0.0

■ HARRY CURTIS
Curtis, Harry Albert   b: 2/19/1883, Portland, Maine   d: 8/1/51, Evanston, Ill.   TR , 5'10.5", 170 lbs.   Deb: 8/28/07

YEAR	TM/L	G	AB	R	H	2B	3B	HR	RBI	BB	SO	AVG	OBP	SLG	PRO+	BR/A	SB	CS	SBR	FA	FR	G/POS	TPR
1907	NY-N	6	9	2	2	0	0	0	1	2		.222	.364	.222	81	-0	2			.909	0	/C-6	0.0

■ GUY CURTRIGHT
Curtright, Guy Paxton   b: 10/18/12, Holliday, Mo.   BR/TR, 5'11", 200 lbs.   Deb: 4/21/43

YEAR	TM/L	G	AB	R	H	2B	3B	HR	RBI	BB	SO	AVG	OBP	SLG	PRO+	BR/A	SB	CS	SBR	FA	FR	G/POS	TPR
1943	Chi-A	138	488	67	142	20	7	3	48	69	60	.291	.382	.379	123	16	13	12	-3	.972	-2	*O-128	0.5
1944	Chi-A	72	198	22	50	8	2	2	23	23	21	.253	.330	.343	94	-1	4	3	-1	.948	1	O-51	-0.3
1945	Chi-A	98	324	51	91	15	7	4	32	39	29	.281	.358	.407	125	10	3	4	-0	.986	1	O-84	0.6
1946	Chi-A	23	55	7	11	2	0	0	5	11	14	.200	.333	.236	63	-2	0	1	-1	1.000	1	O-15	-0.3
Total	4	331	1065	147	294	45	16	9	108	142	124	.276	.363	.374	115	23	20	20	-6	.973	2	O-278	0.5

■ TONY CUSICK
Cusick, Andrew Daniel "Andy"   b: 12/1857, Fall River, Mass.   d: 8/6/29, Chicago, Ill.   BR/TR, 5'9.5", 190 lbs.   Deb: 8/21/1884

YEAR	TM/L	G	AB	R	H	2B	3B	HR	RBI	BB	SO	AVG	OBP	SLG	PRO+	BR/A	SB	CS	SBR	FA	FR	G/POS	TPR
1884	Wil-U	11	34	0	5	0	0	0			1	.147	.171	.147	-3	-5				.871	-0	/C-6,S-3,O-3,2-1,3	-0.4
	Phi-N	9	29	2	4	0	0	0	1	0	3	.138	.138	.138	-14	-4				.930	4	/C-9	0.1
1885	Phi-N	39	141	12	25	1	0	0	5	1	24	.177	.183	.184	19	-12				.808	-3	C-38/O-1	-1.2
1886	Phi-N	29	104	10	23	5	1	0	4	3	14	.221	.243	.288	61	-5	1			.891	-6	C-25/O-3,1-1	-0.7
1887	Phi-N	7	24	3	7	1	0	0	5	3	1	.292	.393	.333	98	-0	0			.643	-3	/C-4,1-3,2-1	-0.3
Total	4	95	332	27	64	7	1	0	15	8	42	.193	.214	.220	35	-26	1			.844	-8	/C-82,O-7,1-4,S23	-2.5

■ JACK CUSICK
Cusick, John Peter   b: 6/12/28, Weehawken, N.J.   d: 11/17/89, Edgewood, N.J.   BR/TR, 6', 170 lbs.   Deb: 4/24/51

YEAR	TM/L	G	AB	R	H	2B	3B	HR	RBI	BB	SO	AVG	OBP	SLG	PRO+	BR/A	SB	CS	SBR	FA	FR	G/POS	TPR
1951	Chi-N	65	164	16	29	3	2	2	16	17	29	.177	.254	.256	37	-15	2	1	0	.953	-2	S-56	-1.3
1952	Bos-N	49	78	5	13	1	0	0	6	6	9	.167	.226	.179	14	-9	0	1	-1	.969	-2	S-28/3-3	-1.1
Total	2	114	242	21	42	4	2	2	22	23	38	.174	.245	.231	30	-24	2	2	-1	.958	-4	/S-84,3-3	-2.4

■ NED CUTHBERT
Cuthbert, Edgar Edward   b: 6/20/1845, Philadelphia, Pa.   d: 2/6/05, St.Louis, Mo.   BR/TR, 5'6", 140 lbs.   Deb: 5/20/1871   MU

YEAR	TM/L	G	AB	R	H	2B	3B	HR	RBI	BB	SO	AVG	OBP	SLG	PRO+	BR/A	SB	CS	SBR	FA	FR	G/POS	TPR
1871	Ath-n	28	150	47	37	7	5	3	30	10	2	.247	.294	.420	103	1	16	2	4	.890	4	*O-27/C-1	0.6
1872	Ath-n	47	260	83	88	10	1	1	47	6	10	.338	.353	.388	127	8	14	2	6	.858	-3	*O-47	0.6
1873	Phi-n	51	278	78	77	5	3	2	33	2	4	.277	.282	.338	80	-8	**13**	2	**3**	.848	-6	*O-51	-0.6
1874	Chi-n	58	295	65	79	6	1	2	22	5	5	.268	.280	.315	90	-3	8	0	2	.806	-0	*O-55/C-4	0.0
1875	StL-n	68	319	68	78	9	2	0	17	3	8	.245	.252	.285	95	-0	18	1	5	.860	-13	*O-67/C-3,2-1	-0.6
1876	StL-N	63	283	46	70	10	1	0	25	7	4	.247	.266	.290	90	-2				.843	-8	*O-63	-1.0
1877	Cin-N	12	56	6	10	5	0	0	2	1	2	.179	.193	.268	49	-3				.830	4	O-12	0.1
1882	StL-a	60	233	28	52	16	5	0		17		.223	.276	.335	101	0				.896	-4	*O-60,M	-0.4
1883	StL-a	21	71	3	12	1	0	0	3	4		.169	.213	.183	27	-6				.794	-1	O-20/1-1	-0.6
1884	Bal-U	44	168	29	34	5	0	0		10		.202	.247	.232	42	-17				.750	-5	O-44	-2.1
Total	5 n	252	1302	341	359	37	11	8	149	26	29	.276	.290	.339	98	-2	69	9	15	.846	-17	O-247/C-8,2-1	0.0
Total	5	200	811	112	178	37	6	0	30	39	6	.219	.255	.280	73	-28				.833	-14	O-199/1-1	-4.0

■ GEORGE CUTSHAW
Cutshaw, George William "Clancy"   b: 7/27/1887, Wilmington, Ill.   d: 8/22/73, San Diego, Cal.   BR/TR, 5'9", 160 lbs.   Deb: 4/25/12

YEAR	TM/L	G	AB	R	H	2B	3B	HR	RBI	BB	SO	AVG	OBP	SLG	PRO+	BR/A	SB	CS	SBR	FA	FR	G/POS	TPR
1912	Bro-N	102	357	41	100	14	4	0	28	31	16	.280	.341	.342	91	-4	16			.958	8	2-91/3-5,S-1	0.2
1913	Bro-N	147	592	72	158	23	13	7	80	39	22	.267	.315	.385	97	-4	39			.957	18	*2-147	1.2
1914	Bro-N	153	583	69	150	22	12	2	78	30	32	.257	.297	.346	89	-10	34			.959	28	*2-153	1.8
1915	Bro-N	154	566	68	139	18	9	0	62	34	35	.246	.293	.309	81	-13	28	23	-5	**.971**	17	*2-154	0.0
1916	*Bro-N	154	581	58	151	21	4	2	63	25	32	.260	.292	.320	85	-11	27	20	-4	.958	7	*2-154	-0.2
1917	Bro-N	135	487	42	132	17	7	4	49	21	26	.271	.292	.347	93	-5	22			.963	-9	*2-134	-0.9
1918	Pit-N	126	463	56	132	16	10	5	68	27	18	.285	.326	.395	115	7	25			.964	-3	*2-126	1.4
1919	Pit-N	139	512	49	124	15	9	3	51	30	22	.242	.287	.320	79	-13	36			**.980**	-11	*2-139	-2.0
1920	Pit-N	131	488	56	123	16	8	0	47	23	10	.252	.287	.318	71	-18	17	14	-3	.968	1	*2-129	-1.0
1921	Pit-N	98	350	46	119	18	4	0	53	11	11	.340	.362	.414	102	1	14	5	1	.951	-15	2-84	-1.1
1922	Det-A	132	499	57	133	14	8	2	61	20	13	.267	.300	.339	68	-24	11	5	0	.972	9	*2-132	-1.1
1923	Det-A	45	143	15	32	7	1	0	13	9	5	.224	.279	.259	43	-12	2	1	0	.988	12	2-43/3-2	-0.1
Total	12	1516	5621	629	1487	195	89	25	653	300	242	.265	.305	.344	86	-106	271	68		.965	61	*2-1486/3-7,S-1	-2.5

■ KIKI CUYLER
Cuyler, Hazen Shirley   b: 8/30/1898, Harrisville, Mich.   d: 2/11/50, Ann Arbor, Mich.   BR/TR, 5'10.5", 180 lbs.   Deb: 9/29/21   CH

YEAR	TM/L	G	AB	R	H	2B	3B	HR	RBI	BB	SO	AVG	OBP	SLG	PRO+	BR/A	SB	CS	SBR	FA	FR	G/POS	TPR
1921	Pit-N	1	3	0	0	0	0	0	0	0	0	.000	.000	.000	-97	-1	0	0	0	1.000	-0	/O-1	-0.1
1922	Pit-N	1	0	0	0	0	0	0	0	0	0				0	0	0	0	0	.000	0	R	0.0
1923	Pit-N	11	40	4	10	1	1	0	2	5	3	.250	.348	.325	77	-1	2	1	-1	.931	-1	O-11	-0.4
1924	Pit-N	117	466	94	165	27	16	9	85	30	62	.354	.402	.539	147	30	32	11	3	.943	5	*O-114	3.0
1925	*Pit-N	153	617	**144**	220	43	**26**	18	102	58	56	.357	.423	.598	148	44	41	13	5	.967	7	*O-153	4.1

YEAR	TM/L	G	AB	R	H	2B	3B	HR	RBI	BB	SO	AVG	OBP	SLG	PRO+	BR/A	SB	CS	SBR	FA	FR	G/POS	TPR
1926	Pit-N	157	614	**113**	197	31	15	8	92	50	66	.321	.380	.459	119	16	**35**			.968	13	*O-157	1.8
1927	Pit-N	85	285	60	88	13	7	3	31	37	36	.309	.394	.435	114	7	20			.980	1	O-73	0.3
1928	Chi-N	133	499	92	142	25	9	17	79	51	61	.285	.359	.473	117	12	37			.982	6	*O-127	0.9
1929	*Chi-N	139	509	111	183	29	7	15	102	66	56	.360	.438	.532	139	33	43			.974	-0	*O-129	2.2
1930	Chi-N	156	642	155	228	50	17	13	134	72	49	.355	.428	.547	133	36	37			.980	12	*O-156	3.2
1931	Chi-N	154	613	110	202	37	12	9	88	72	54	.330	.404	.473	133	30	13			.970	-4	*O-153	1.6
1932	*Chi-N	110	446	58	130	19	9	10	77	29	43	.291	.340	.442	109	5	9			.969	-7	*O-109	-0.8
1933	Chi-N	70	262	37	83	13	3	5	35	21	29	.317	.376	.447	135	12	4			.978	-7	O-69	0.1
1934	Chi-N★	142	559	80	189	**42**	8	6	69	31	62	.338	.377	.474	129	22	15			.971	0	*O-142	1.6
1935	Chi-N	45	157	22	42	5	1	4	18	10	16	.268	.331	.389	92	-2	3			.981	-1	O-42	-0.4
	Cin-N	62	223	36	56	8	3	2	22	27	18	.251	.337	.341	85	-4	5			.985	-3	O-57	-0.8
	Yr	107	380	58	98	13	4	6	40	37	34	.258	.335	.361	88	-6	8			.983	-3	O-99	-1.2
1936	Cin-N	144	567	96	185	29	11	7	74	47	67	.326	.380	.453	132	25	16			.974	-4	*O-140	1.5
1937	Cin-N	117	406	48	110	12	4	0	32	36	50	.271	.333	.320	82	-9	10			.973	-8	O-106	-2.1
1938	Bro-N	82	253	45	69	10	8	2	23	34	23	.273	.363	.399	107	3	6			.993	0	O-68	0.1
Total	18	1879	7161	1305	2299	394	157	128	1065	676	752	.321	.386	.474	125	258	328	27		.972	12	*O-1807	15.8

■ MILT CUYLER

Cuyler, Milton b: 10/7/68, Macon, Ga. BB/TR, 5'10", 175 lbs. Deb: 9/6/90

YEAR	TM/L	G	AB	R	H	2B	3B	HR	RBI	BB	SO	AVG	OBP	SLG	PRO+	BR/A	SB	CS	SBR	FA	FR	G/POS	TPR
1990	Det-A	19	51	8	13	3	1	0	8	5	10	.255	.321	.353	88	-1	1	2	-1	.976	0	O-17	-0.2
1991	Det-A	154	475	77	122	15	7	3	33	52	92	.257	.336	.337	86	-8	41	10	6	.986	8	*O-151	0.3
1992	Det-A	89	291	39	70	11	1	3	28	10	62	.241	.275	.316	65	-14	13	9	1	.983	-0	O-89	-1.7
1993	Det-A	82	249	46	53	11	4	0	19	19	53	.213	.277	.313	59	-15	13	2	3	.968	1	O-80	-1.2
1994	Det-A	48	116	20	28	3	1	1	11	13	21	.241	.323	.310	64	-6	5	3	-0	.975	-9	O-36/D-2	-1.5
1995	Det-A	41	88	15	18	1	4	0	5	8	16	.205	.271	.307	50	-7	2	1	0	.929	-4	O-36/D-2	-1.1
1996	Bos-A	50	110	19	22	1	2	2	12	13	19	.200	.302	.300	51	-7	3	0	0	.972	-3	O-45/D-2	-1.0
Total	7	483	1380	224	326	45	23	9	116	120	273	.236	.305	.322	69	-58	77	26	8	.977	-7	O-463/D-4	-6.4

■ AL CYPERT

Cypert, Alfred Boyd "Cy" b: 8/8/1889, Little Rock, Ark. d: 1/9/73, Washington, D.C. BR/TR, 5'10.5", 150 lbs. Deb: 6/27/14

YEAR	TM/L	G	AB	R	H	2B	3B	HR	RBI	BB	SO	AVG	OBP	SLG	PRO+	BR/A	SB	CS	SBR	FA	FR	G/POS	TPR
1914	Cle-A	1	1	0	0	0	0	0	0	0		.000	.000	.000	-96	-0	0			.000	0	/3-1	0.0

■ PAUL DADE

Dade, Lonnie Paul b: 12/7/51, Seattle, Wash. BR/TR, 6', 195 lbs. Deb: 9/12/75

YEAR	TM/L	G	AB	R	H	2B	3B	HR	RBI	BB	SO	AVG	OBP	SLG	PRO+	BR/A	SB	CS	SBR	FA	FR	G/POS	TPR
1975	Cal-A	11	30	5	6	4	0	0	1	6	7	.200	.333	.333	96	-0	0	0	0	1.000	1	/O-3,3-1,D-7	0.0
1976	Cal-A	13	9	2	1	0	0	0	1	3	3	.111	.333	.111	36	-1	0	0	0	.750	0	/O-4,2-2,3-1,D-1	-0.0
1977	Cle-A	134	461	65	134	15	3	3	45	32	58	.291	.339	.356	93	-4	16	8	0	.989	-7	O-99,3-26/2-1,D-7	-1.6
1978	Cle-A	93	307	37	78	12	1	3	20	34	45	.254	.332	.329	88	-4	12	9	-2	.962	4	O-81/D-9	-0.8
1979	Cle-A	44	170	22	48	4	1	3	18	12	22	.282	.330	.371	88	-3	12	6	0	.962	4	O-37/3-2,D-4	-0.2
	SD-N	76	283	38	78	19	2	1	19	14	48	.276	.314	.367	91	-4	13	5	1	.949	6	3-70/O-4	0.1
1980	SD-N	68	53	17	10	0	0	0	3	12	10	.189	.338	.189	54	-3	4	5	-2	.846	1	3-21/O-8,2-1	-0.3
Total	6	439	1313	186	355	54	7	10	107	113	193	.270	.331	.345	89	-19	57	33	-3	.970	4	O-236,3-121/D-28,2	-2.8

■ ANGELO DAGRES

Dagres, Angelo George "Junior" b: 8/22/34, Newburyport, Mass. BL/TL, 5'11", 175 lbs. Deb: 9/11/55

YEAR	TM/L	G	AB	R	H	2B	3B	HR	RBI	BB	SO	AVG	OBP	SLG	PRO+	BR/A	SB	CS	SBR	FA	FR	G/POS	TPR
1955	Bal-A	8	15	5	4	0	0	0	3	1	2	.267	.313	.267	61	-1	0	0	0	.818	-1	/O-5	-0.2

■ BILL DAHLEN

Dahlen, William Frederick "Bad Bill" b: 1/5/1870, Nelliston, N.Y. d: 12/5/50, Brooklyn, N.Y. BR/TR, 5'9", 180 lbs. Deb: 4/22/1891 M

YEAR	TM/L	G	AB	R	H	2B	3B	HR	RBI	BB	SO	AVG	OBP	SLG	PRO+	BR/A	SB	CS	SBR	FA	FR	G/POS	TPR
1891	Chi-N	135	549	114	143	18	13	9	76	67	60	.260	.348	.390	115	9	21			.887	9	3-84,O-37,S-15	2.0
1892	Chi-N	143	581	114	169	23	19	5	58	45	56	.291	.347	.422	131	19	60			.909	25	S-72,3-68/O-2,2-1	4.6
1893	Chi-N	116	485	113	146	28	15	5	64	58	30	.301	.381	.452	123	15	31			.892	4	*S-88,O-17,2-10,/3	1.8
1894	Chi-N	121	502	149	179	32	14	15	107	76	33	.357	.444	.566	135	28	42			.898	32	S-66,3-55	**4.8**
1895	Chi-N	129	516	106	131	19	10	7	62	61	38	.254	.344	.370	79	-18	38			.904	36	*S-129/O-1	1.9
1896	Chi-N	125	474	137	167	30	19	9	74	64	36	.352	.438	.553	154	37	51			.915	25	*S-125	5.5
1897	Chi-N	75	276	67	80	18	8	6	40	43		.290	.399	.478	126	11	15			.930	28	S-75	3.4
1898	Chi-N	142	521	96	151	35	8	1	79	58		.290	.385	.393	123	18	27			.921	26	*S-142	**4.6**
1899	Bro-N	121	428	87	121	20	7	4	76	67		.283	.398	.395	115	12	29			.941	17	*S-110,3-11	3.4
1900	*Bro-N	133	483	87	125	16	11	1	69	73		.259	.364	.344	90	-5	31			.938	20	*S-133	2.3
1901	Bro-N	131	511	69	136	17	9	4	82	30		.266	.313	.358	92	-6	23			.929	14	*S-129/2-2	1.8
1902	Bro-N	138	527	67	139	25	8	2	74	43		.264	.329	.353	109	6	20			.916	-6	*S-138	0.8
1903	Bro-N	138	474	71	124	17	9	1	64	82		.262	.373	.342	107	8	34			**.948**	18	*S-138	3.0
1904	NY-N	145	523	70	140	26	2	2	**80**	44		.268	.326	.337	100	0	47			.930	28	*S-145	3.3
1905	*NY-N	148	520	67	126	20	4	7	81	62		.242	.337	.337	99	1	37			.948	20	*S-147/O-1	2.4
1906	NY-N	143	471	63	113	18	3	1	49	76		.240	.357	.297	102	5	16			.938	0	*S-143	1.1
1907	NY-N	143	464	40	96	20	1	0	34	51		.207	.291	.254	69	-16	11			.941	7	*S-143	-0.5
1908	Bos-N	144	524	50	125	23	2	3	48	35		.239	.296	.307	94	-4	10			.952	**38**	*S-144	4.2
1909	Bos-N	69	197	22	46	6	1	2	16	29		.234	.332	.305	93	-1	4			.908	9	S-49/2-6,3-2	1.0
1910	Bro-N	3	2	0	0	0	0	0	0	0	0	.000	.000	.000	-99	-1	0			.000	0	HM	-0.1
1911	Bro-N	3	3	0	0	0	0	0	0	0	3	.000	.000	.000	-99	-1	0			1.000	2	/S-1,M	0.1
Total	21	2443	9031	1589	2457	413	163	84	1233	1064	269	.272	.358	.382	109	121	547			.927	348	*S-2132,3-223/O2	51.4

■ BABE DAHLGREN

Dahlgren, Ellsworth Tenney b: 6/15/12, San Francisco, Cal. d: 9/4/96, Arcadia, Cal. BR/TR, 6', 190 lbs. Deb: 4/16/35 C

YEAR	TM/L	G	AB	R	H	2B	3B	HR	RBI	BB	SO	AVG	OBP	SLG	PRO+	BR/A	SB	CS	SBR	FA	FR	G/POS	TPR
1935	Bos-A	149	525	77	138	27	7	9	63	56	67	.263	.337	.392	83	-14	6	5	-0	.988	-7	*1-149	-3.7
1936	Bos-A	16	57	6	16	3	1	1	7	7	1	.281	.359	.421	87	-1	2	1	0	.980	-1	1-16	-0.3
1937	NY-A	1	1	0	0	0	0	0	0	0	0	.000	.000	.000	-99	-0	0	0	0	.000	0	H	0.0
1938	NY-A	27	43	8	8	1	0	0	1	1	7	.186	.205	.209	4	-6	0	0	0	.826	-1	/3-8,1-6	-0.7
1939	*NY-A	144	531	71	125	18	6	15	89	57	54	.235	.312	.377	76	-20	2	3	-1	.991	-7	*1-144	-4.1
1940	NY-A	155	568	51	150	24	4	12	73	46	54	.264	.325	.384	86	-12	1	1	-0	.990	-10	*1-155	-3.6
1941	Bos-N	44	166	20	39	8	1	7	30	16	13	.235	.306	.422	108	1	0			.993	-2	1-39/3-5	0.1
	Chi-N	99	359	50	101	20	1	16	59	43	39	.281	.360	.476	139	18	2			.991	-8	1-98	0.2
	Yr	143	525	70	140	28	2	23	89	59	52	.267	.343	.459	129	19	2			.992	-6	*1-137/3-5	0.3
1942	Chi-N	17	56	4	12	1	0	0	6	4	2	.214	.267	.232	48	-4	0			.986	1	1-14	-0.4
	StL-A	2	2	0	0	0	0	0	0	0	0	.000	.000	.000	-99	-1	0	0	0	.000	0	H	-0.1
	Bro-N	17	19	2	1	0	0	0	0	0	6	.053	.217	.053	-19	-3	0			1.000	1	1-10	-0.2
1943	Phi-N★	136	508	55	146	19	2	5	56	50	39	.287	.354	.362	111	8	2			.988	-23	1-73,3-35,S-25/C-1	-1.8
1944	Pit-N	158	599	67	173	28	7	12	101	47	56	.289	.347	.419	110	7	2			.987	8	*1-158	0.7
1945	Pit-N	144	531	57	133	24	8	6	75	51	51	.250	.318	.354	84	-12	1			**.996**	1	*1-144	-2.1
1946	StL-A	28	80	2	14	1	0	0	9	8	13	.175	.250	.188	22	-8	0	1	-1	.981	1	1-24	-0.9
Total	12	1137	4045	470	1056	174	37	82	569	390	401	.261	.329	.383	92	-49	18	11		.990	-44	*1-1030/3-48,S-25,C	-16.9

■ JOHN DAILEY

Dailey, John G. b: Brooklyn, N.Y. Deb: 7/12/1875

YEAR	TM/L	G	AB	R	H	2B	3B	HR	RBI	BB	SO	AVG	OBP	SLG	PRO+	BR/A	SB	CS	SBR	FA	FR	G/POS	TPR
1875	Was-n	27	110	16	20	5	4	0		1		.182	.182	.300	67	-3	3	2	-0	.810	-3	S-20/3-5,2-2	-0.7
	Atl-n	2	8	3	1	0	0	0		0	1	.125	.125	.125	-15	-1	0	0	0	1.000	0	/O-2,1-1,S-1	-0.4
	Yr	29	118	19	21	5	4	0	13	0	2	.178	.178	.288	62	-4	3	2	-0	.797	-3	S-21/3-5,2-2,O-2,1	-1.1

■ VINCE DAILEY

Dailey, Vincent Perry b: 12/25/1864, Osceola, Pa. d: 11/14/19, Hornell, N.Y. 6', 200 lbs. Deb: 4/21/1890

YEAR	TM/L	G	AB	R	H	2B	3B	HR	RBI	BB	SO	AVG	OBP	SLG	PRO+	BR/A	SB	CS	SBR	FA	FR	G/POS	TPR
1890	Cle-N	64	246	41	71	5	7	0	32	33	23	.289	.373	.366	118	6	17			.859	0	O-64/P-2	0.4

■ CON DAILY

Daily, Cornelius F. b: 9/11/1864, Blackstone, Mass. d: 6/14/28, Brooklyn, N.Y. BL, 6', 192 lbs. Deb: 6/9/1884 F

YEAR	TM/L	G	AB	R	H	2B	3B	HR	RBI	BB	SO	AVG	OBP	SLG	PRO+	BR/A	SB	CS	SBR	FA	FR	G/POS	TPR
1884	Phi-U	2	8	0	0	0	0	0		0		.000	.000	.000	-99	-2				.857	-1	/C-2	-0.3
1885	Pro-N	60	223	20	58	6	1	0	19	12	20	.260	.298	.296	96	-1				.876	-1	C-48/1-7,O-6	0.2
1886	Bos-N	50	180	25	43	4	2	0	21	19	29	.239	.312	.283	85	-2	2			.911	-11	C-49/O-1	-0.7
1887	Bos-N	36	120	12	19	5	0	0	13	9	8	.158	.229	.200	20	-13	7			.889	-2	C-36	-1.0
1888	Ind-N	57	202	14	44	6	1	0	14	10	28	.218	.255	.257	62	-8	5			.893	-1	C-42/O-5,3-5,1-5,2	-0.6
1889	Ind-N	62	219	35	55	6	2	0	26	28	21	.251	.347	.297	79	-5	14			.887	-12	C-51/O-6,1-6,3-1	-1.1

YEAR	TM/L	G	AB	R	H	2B	3B	HR	RBI	BB	SO	AVG	OBP	SLG	PRO+	BR/A	SB	CS	SBR	FA	FR	G/POS	TPR
1890	Bro-P	46	168	20	42	6	3	0	35	15	14	.250	.315	.321	66	-9	6			.879	-7	C-40/1-6,O-1	-1.0
1891	Bro-N	60	206	25	66	10	1	0	30	15	13	.320	.378	.379	121	6	7			.925	-0	C-55/O-3,S-2,1-1	0.9
1892	Bro-N	80	278	38	65	10	1	0	28	38	21	.234	.234	.277	87	-3	18			.943	-2	C-68,O-13	0.0
1893	Bro-N	61	215	33	57	4	2	1	32	20	12	.265	.342	.316	79	-6	13			.935	-1	C-51/O-9	-0.2
1894	Bro-N	67	234	40	60	14	7	0	32	31	22	.256	.351	.376	81	-7	8			.930	-2	C-60/1-7	-0.3
1895	Bro-N	40	142	17	30	3	2	1	11	10	18	.211	.268	.282	46	-12	3			.956	-3	C-39/O-1	-0.9
1896	Chi-N	9	27	1	2	0	0	0	1	1	2	.074	.107	.074	-50	-6	1			.969	-2	/C-9	-0.6
Total	13	630	2222	280	541	74	22	2	262	208	208	.243	.314	.299	76	-68	94			.912	-43	C-550/O-45,13S2	-5.6

■ ED DAILY
Daily, Edward M.   b: 9/7/1862, Providence, R.I.   d: 10/21/1891, Washington, D.C.   BR/TR, 5'10.5", 174 lbs.   Deb: 5/4/1885   F

YEAR	TM/L	G	AB	R	H	2B	3B	HR	RBI	BB	SO	AVG	OBP	SLG	PRO+	BR/A	SB	CS	SBR	FA	FR	G/POS	TPR
1885	Phi-N	50	184	22	38	8	2	1	13	0	25	.207	.207	.288	60	-8				.891	-4	P-50	0.0
1886	Phi-N	79	309	40	70	17	1	4	50	7	34	.227	.244	.327	72	-11	23			.827	5	O-56,P-27	-0.5
1887	Phi-N	26	106	18	30	11	1	1	17	3	9	.283	.303	.434	97	-1	8			.659	-6	O-22/P-6	-0.7
	Was-N	78	311	39	78	6	10	2	36	14	27	.251	.285	.354	81	-8	26			.855	-5	O-77/P-1	-1.3
	Yr	104	417	57	108	17	11	3	53	17	36	.259	.290	.374	85	-9	34			.812	-11	O-99/P-7	-2.0
1888	Was-N	110	453	56	102	8	4	7	39	7	42	.225	.239	.307	77	-12	44			.912	4	*O-100/P-9,1-1	-1.1
1889	Col-a	136	578	105	148	22	8	3	70	38	65	.256	.303	.337	87	-11	60			.854	-3	*O-136/P-2	-1.5
1890	Bro-a	91	394	68	94	15	7	1	39	24		.239	.284	.320	81	-11	49			.892	6	O-64/P-27	-0.5
	NY-N	4	15	1	2	1	0	0	1	0	4	.133	.133	.200	-3	-2	0			.500	0	/O-3,P-2	-0.1
	*Lou-a	23	80	24	20	0	2	0	9	13		.250	.355	.300	95	0	13			.925	1	P-12,O-11	-0.1
1891	Lou-a	22	64	10	16	2	0	0	8	6		.250	.342	.281	80	-1	4			.884	5	P-15/O-7	-0.1
	Was-a	21	79	13	18	2	0	0	6	11	10	.228	.322	.253	68	-3	8			.719	-4	O-21	-0.6
	Yr	43	143	23	34	4	0	0	14	19	16	.238	.331	.266	73	-4	12			.750	-3	O-28,P-15	-0.7
Total	7	640	2573	396	616	92	35	19	288	125	222	.239	.276	.325	80	-69	235			.857	-6	O-497,P-151/1-1	-6.5

■ GEORGE DAISEY
Daisey, George K.   b: Altoona, Pa.   5'11", 190 lbs.   Deb: 5/31/1884

YEAR	TM/L	G	AB	R	H	2B	3B	HR	RBI	BB	SO	AVG	OBP	SLG	PRO+	BR/A	SB	CS	SBR	FA	FR	G/POS	TPR
1884	Alt-U	1	4	0	0	0	0	0		0		.000	.000	.000	-99	-1				.000	-1	/O-1	-0.2

■ PETE DALENA
Dalena, Peter Martin   b: 6/26/60, Fresno, Cal.   BL/TR, 5'11", 200 lbs.   Deb: 7/7/89

YEAR	TM/L	G	AB	R	H	2B	3B	HR	RBI	BB	SO	AVG	OBP	SLG	PRO+	BR/A	SB	CS	SBR	FA	FR	G/POS	TPR
1989	Cle-A	5	7	0	1	1	0	0	0	0	3	.143	.143	.286	18	-1	0	0	0	.000	0	/D-1	-0.1

■ MARK DALESANDRO
Dalesandro, Mark Anthony   b: 5/14/68, Chicago, Ill.   BR/TR, 6', 185 lbs.   Deb: 6/6/94

YEAR	TM/L	G	AB	R	H	2B	3B	HR	RBI	BB	SO	AVG	OBP	SLG	PRO+	BR/A	SB	CS	SBR	FA	FR	G/POS	TPR
1994	Cal-A	19	25	5	5	1	0	1	2	2	4	.200	.259	.360	57	-2	0	0	0	1.000	-3	C-11/3-5,O-2	-0.4
1995	Cal-A	11	10	1	1	1	0	0	0	0	2	.100	.100	.200	-25	-2	0	0	0	1.000	0	/C-8,O-1,D-1	-0.2
Total	2	30	35	6	6	2	0	1	2	2	6	.171	.216	.314	35	-4	0	0	0	1.000	0	/C-19,3-5,O-3,D-1	-0.6

■ JOHN DALEY
Daley, John Francis   b: 5/25/1887, Pittsburgh, Pa.   d: 8/31/88, Mansfield, Ohio   BR/TR, 5'7.5", 155 lbs.   Deb: 7/19/12

YEAR	TM/L	G	AB	R	H	2B	3B	HR	RBI	BB	SO	AVG	OBP	SLG	PRO+	BR/A	SB	CS	SBR	FA	FR	G/POS	TPR
1912	StL-A	18	52	7	9	0	0	1		3	9	.173	.317	.231	60	-2	4			.833	-4	S-17	-0.5

■ JUD DALEY
Daley, Judson Lawrence   b: 3/14/1884, S.Coventry, Conn.   d: 1/26/67, Gadsden, Ala.   BL/TR, 5'8", 172 lbs.   Deb: 9/19/11

YEAR	TM/L	G	AB	R	H	2B	3B	HR	RBI	BB	SO	AVG	OBP	SLG	PRO+	BR/A	SB	CS	SBR	FA	FR	G/POS	TPR
1911	Bro-N	19	65	8	15	2	1	0	7	2	8	.231	.286	.292	65	-3	2			.952	2	O-16	-0.3
1912	Bro-N	61	199	22	51	9	1	1	13	24	17	.256	.342	.327	87	-3	2			.947	2	O-55	-0.4
Total	2	80	264	30	66	11	2	1	20	26	25	.250	.329	.318	82	-6	4			.949	3	/O-71	-0.7

■ PETE DALEY
Daley, Peter Harvey   b: 1/14/30, Grass Valley, Cal.   BR/TR, 6', 195 lbs.   Deb: 5/3/55

YEAR	TM/L	G	AB	R	H	2B	3B	HR	RBI	BB	SO	AVG	OBP	SLG	PRO+	BR/A	SB	CS	SBR	FA	FR	G/POS	TPR
1955	Bos-A	17	50	4	11	2	1	0	5	3	6	.220	.264	.300	47	-4	0	0	0	1.000	3	C-14	0.0
1956	Bos-A	59	187	22	50	11	3	5	29	18	30	.267	.338	.439	92	-3	0	0	0	.992	-10	C-57	-1.0
1957	Bos-A	78	191	17	43	10	0	3	25	16	31	.225	.288	.325	64	-10	0	0	0	**1.000**	-2	C-77	-1.0
1958	Bos-A	27	56	10	18	2	1	2	8	7	11	.321	.397	.500	136	3	0	0	0	.990	2	C-27	0.6
1959	Bos-A	65	169	9	38	7	0	1	11	13	31	.225	.280	.284	53	-11	1	1	-0	.996	2	C-58	-0.6
1960	KC-A	73	228	19	60	10	2	5	25	16	41	.263	.311	.390	88	-4	0	0	0	.990	-5	C-61/O-1	-0.5
1961	Was-A	72	203	12	39	7	1	2	17	14	37	.192	.244	.266	37	-18	0	1	-1	.988	7	C-72	-1.0
Total	7	391	1084	93	259	49	8	18	120	87	187	.239	.297	.349	71	-47	2	2	-1	.993	-2	C-366/O-1	-3.5

■ TOM DALEY
Daley, Thomas Francis "Pete"   b: 11/13/1884, DuBois, Pa.   d: 12/2/34, Los Angeles, Cal.   BL/TR, 5'5", 168 lbs.   Deb: 8/29/08

YEAR	TM/L	G	AB	R	H	2B	3B	HR	RBI	BB	SO	AVG	OBP	SLG	PRO+	BR/A	SB	CS	SBR	FA	FR	G/POS	TPR
1908	Cin-N	14	46	5	5	0	0	0		1	3	.109	.196	.109	-2	-5	1			1.000	-0	O-13	-0.7
1913	Phi-A	62	141	13	36	2	1	0	11	13	28	.255	.327	.284	81	-3	4			.963	-1	O-39	-0.6
1914	Phi-A	28	86	17	22	1	3	0	7	12	14	.256	.347	.337	110	1	4	7	-3	1.000	2	O-24	-0.1
	NY-A	69	191	36	48	6	4	0	9	38	13	.251	.378	.325	112	5	8	8	-2	.958	9	O-58	0.6
	Yr	97	277	53	70	7	7	0	16	50	27	.253	.369	.329	111	6	12	15	-5	.969	7	O-82	0.5
1915	NY-A	10	8	2	2	0	0	0	1	2	2	.250	.400	.250	95	0	1			1.000	-0	/O-2	-0.8
Total	4	183	472	73	113	9	8	0	29	68	57	.239	.341	.292	92	-2	18	15		.970	6	O-136	-0.8

■ DOM DALLESSANDRO
Dallessandro, Nicholas Dominic "Dim Dom"   b: 10/3/13, Reading, Pa.   d: 4/29/88, Indianapolis, Ind.   BL/TL, 5'6", 168 lbs.   Deb: 4/24/37

YEAR	TM/L	G	AB	R	H	2B	3B	HR	RBI	BB	SO	AVG	OBP	SLG	PRO+	BR/A	SB	CS	SBR	FA	FR	G/POS	TPR
1937	Bos-A	68	147	18	34	4	0	1	11	27	16	.231	.351	.293	61	-8	2	1	0	.965	-5	O-35	-1.3
1940	Chi-N	107	287	33	77	19	6	1	36	34	13	.268	.348	.387	104	2	4			.969	-3	O-74	-0.4
1941	Chi-N	140	486	73	132	36	2	6	85	68	37	.272	.362	.391	116	12	3			.987	-2	*O-131	0.2
1942	Chi-N	96	264	30	69	12	4	4	43	36	18	.261	.350	.383	119	7	4			.986	-2	O-66	0.2
1943	Chi-N	87	176	13	39	7	1	3	31	40	14	.222	.369	.318	101	2	1			.967	-4	O-45	-0.4
1944	Chi-N	117	381	53	116	19	4	8	74	61	29	.304	.400	.438	137	21	4			.982	-2	*O-106	1.3
1946	Chi-N	65	89	4	20	2	2	1	9	23	12	.225	.384	.326	104	2	1			.971	-3	O-20	-0.2
1947	Chi-N	66	115	18	33	11	4	1	14	21	11	.287	.397	.391	115	3	0			1.000	-2	O-28	-0.0
Total	8	746	1945	242	520	110	23	22	303	310	150	.267	.369	.381	112	40	16	1		.980	-22	O-505	-0.6

■ ABNER DALRYMPLE
Dalrymple, Abner Frank   b: 9/9/1857, Warren, Ill.   d: 1/25/39, Warren, Ill.   BL/TR, 5'10.5", 175 lbs.   Deb: 5/1/1878

YEAR	TM/L	G	AB	R	H	2B	3B	HR	RBI	BB	SO	AVG	OBP	SLG	PRO+	BR/A	SB	CS	SBR	FA	FR	G/POS	TPR
1878	Mil-N	61	271	52	96	10	4	0	15	6	29	**.354**	.368	.421	149	13				.832	7	*O-61	1.5
1879	Chi-N	71	333	47	97	25	1	0	23	4	29	.291	.300	.372	113	4				.728	-13	*O-71	-1.2
1880	Chi-N	86	382	**91**	**126**	25	12	0	36	3	18	.330	.335	.458	157	20				.859	4	*O-86	2.1
1881	Chi-N	82	362	72	117	22	4	1	37	15	22	.323	.350	.414	133	13				.835	-7	*O-82	0.4
1882	Chi-N	84	397	96	117	25	11	1	36	14	18	.295	.319	.421	129	12				.877	3	*O-84	1.0
1883	Chi-N	80	363	78	108	24	4	2	37	11	29	.298	.318	.402	111	3				.826	-1	*O-80	0.2
1884	Chi-N	111	521	111	161	18	9	22	69	14	39	.309	.327	.505	146	23				.882	1	*O-111	2.0
1885	*Chi-N	113	492	109	135	27	12	11	61	46	42	.274	.336	.445	131	13				.879	-1	*O-113	0.9
1886	*Chi-N	82	331	62	77	7	12	3	26	33	44	.233	.302	.353	86	-8	16			.952	-0	*O-82	-0.6
1887	Pit-N	92	358	45	76	18	5	2	31	45	43	.212	.311	.307	77	-9	29			.900	-2	*O-92	-1.1
1888	Pit-N	57	227	19	50	9	2	0	14	6	28	.220	.247	.278	72	-7	7			.909	-2	*O-57	-1.1
1891	Mil-a	32	135	31	42	7	5	1	22	7	18	.311	.345	.459	108	-1	6			.909	-1	O-32	-0.2
Total	12	951	4172	813	1202	217	81	43	407	204	359	.288	.323	.410	120	76	58			.863	-4	O-951	4.4

■ CLAY DALRYMPLE
Dalrymple, Clayton Errol   b: 12/3/36, Chico, Cal.   BL/TR, 6', 199 lbs.   Deb: 4/24/60

YEAR	TM/L	G	AB	R	H	2B	3B	HR	RBI	BB	SO	AVG	OBP	SLG	PRO+	BR/A	SB	CS	SBR	FA	FR	G/POS	TPR
1960	Phi-N	82	158	11	43	6	2	4	21	15	21	.272	.347	.411	106	2	0	0	0	.966	-5	C-48	-0.1
1961	Phi-N	129	378	23	83	11	1	5	42	30	30	.220	.284	.294	54	-25	0	2	-1	.978	0	*C-122	-2.0
1962	Phi-N	123	370	40	102	13	3	11	54	70	32	.276	.396	.416	122	15	1	3	-2	.987	-12	*C-119	0.6
1963	Phi-N	142	452	40	114	15	3	10	49	45	55	.252	.327	.365	100	1	0	2	-1	.981	-1	*C-142	0.6
1964	Phi-N	127	382	36	91	16	3	6	46	39	40	.238	.309	.343	84	-8	0	1	-1	.991	3	*C-124	0.0
1965	Phi-N	103	301	14	64	5	4	9	34	34	37	.213	.293	.302	69	-12	0	1	-1	.993	18	*C-102	1.0
1966	Phi-N	114	331	30	81	13	3	4	39	60	57	.245	.365	.338	97	1	0	4	-0	.993	-4	*C-110	0.4
1967	Phi-N	101	268	12	46	7	1	3	21	36	49	.172	.272	.239	47	-18	1	2	-1	.994	20	C-97	0.7
1968	Phi-N	85	241	19	50	9	3	2	26	22	52	.207	.277	.290	70	-9	1	2	-1	.990	-3	C-80	-0.9
1969	*Bal-A	37	80	8	19	1	1	3	6	13	8	.237	.344	.387	103	1	0	0	0	1.000	6	C-30	0.3
1970	Bal-A	13	32	4	7	1	0	1	3	6	4	.219	.359	.344	94	-0	1			1.000	6	C-11	0.6

YEAR	TM/L	G	AB	R	H	2B	3B	HR	RBI	BB	SO	AVG	OBP	SLG	PRO+	BR/A	SB	CS	SBR	FA	FR	G/POS	TPR
1971	Bal-A	23	49	6	10	1	0	1	6	16	13	.204	.409	.286	101	1	0	0	0	.971	2	C-18	0.4
Total	12	1079	3042	243	710	98	23	55	327	387	403	.233	.324	.335	85	-51	3	13	-7	.987	27	*C-1003	1.6

■ BILL DALRYMPLE   Dalrymple, William Dunn b: 2/7/1891, Baltimore, Md. d: 7/14/67, San Diego, Cal. TR , Deb: 7/6/15

1915	StL-A	3	2	0	0	0	0	0	0	0	0	.000	.000	.000	-99	-0	0			1.000	0	/3-1	0.0

■ JACK DALTON   Dalton, Talbot Percy b: 7/3/1885, Henderson, Tenn. BR/TR, 5'10.5", 187 lbs. Deb: 6/20/10

1910	Bro-N	77	273	33	62	9	4	1	21	26	30	.227	.304	.300	79	-7	5			.966	3	O-72	-0.9
1914	Bro-N	128	442	65	141	13	8	1	45	53	39	.319	.396	.391	131	19	19			.965	-3	*O-116	1.1
1915	Buf-F	132	437	68	128	17	3	2	46	50	38	.293	.368	.359	103	-3	28			.966	-5	*O-119	-1.5
1916	Det-A	8	11	1	2	0	0	0	0	0	5	.182	.182	.182	9	-1	0			1.000	-1	/O-4	-0.3
Total	4	345	1163	167	333	39	15	4	112	129	112	.286	.362	.356	107	7	52			.966	-7	O-311	-1.6

■ BERT DALY   Daly, Albert Joseph b: 4/8/1881, Bayonne, N.J. d: 9/3/52, Bayonne, N.J. BR/TR, 5'9", 170 lbs. Deb: 8/7/03

1903	Phi-A	10	21	2	4	0	2	0	4	1		.190	.227	.381	76	-1	0			.700	-4	/2-4,3-3,S-1	-0.5

■ SUN DALY   Daly, James J. b: 1/6/1865, Rutland, Vt. d: 4/30/38, Albany, N.Y. Deb: 9/30/1892

1892	Bal-N	13	48	5	12	0	2	0	7	1	4	.250	.265	.333	79	-2	0			.923	0	O-13	-0.2

■ JOE DALY   Daly, Joseph John b: 9/21/1868, Conshohocken, Pa. d: 3/21/43, Philadelphia, Pa. TR, 5'8", 157 lbs. Deb: 9/19/1890 F

1890	Phi-a	21	75	8	21	4	1	0	7	3		.280	.308	.360	99	-1	1			.900	-6	O-14/C-9	-0.5
1891	Cle-N	1	3	0	0	0	0	0	0	0	2	.000	.000	.000	-96	-1	0			1.000	0	/O-1	-0.1
1892	Bos-N	1	0	0	0	0	0	0	0	0	0	—	—	—	—	-0	0			1.000	0	/C-1	0.0
Total	3	23	78	8	21	4	1	0	7	3	2	.269	.296	.346	91	-1	1			.909	-6	O-15,C-10	-0.6

■ TOM DALY   Daly, Thomas Daniel b: 12/12/1891, St.John, N.B., Can. d: 11/7/46, Medford, Mass. BR/TR, 5'11.5", 171 lbs. Deb: 9/23/13 C

1913	Chi-A	1	3	0	0	0	0	0	0	0	0	.000	.000	.000	-99	-1	0			1.000	1	/C-1	0.0
1914	Chi-A	62	133	13	31	2	0	0	8	7	13	.233	.271	.248	57	-7	3	4	-2	.909	-10	O-23/3-5,C-4,1-2	-2.2
1915	Chi-A	29	47	5	9	1	0	0	3	5	9	.191	.269	.213	43	-3	0			.958	-3	C-19/1-1	-0.5
1916	Cle-A	31	73	3	16	1	1	0	8	1	2	.219	.230	.260	45	-5	0			.982	-2	C-25/O-1	-0.6
1918	Chi-N	1	1	0	0	0	0	0	0	0	0	.000	.000	.000	-98	-0	0			.667	-0	/C-1	0.0
1919	Chi-N	25	50	4	11	0	1	0	1	2	5	.220	.250	.260	53	-3	0			.956	-2	C-18	-0.5
1920	Chi-N	44	90	12	28	6	0	0	13	2	6	.311	.333	.378	102	0	1	1	-0	.981	-3	C-29	-0.2
1921	Chi-N	51	143	12	34	7	1	0	22	8	8	.238	.278	.301	53	-10	1	2	-1	.973	4	C-47	-0.4
Total	8	244	540	49	129	17	3	0	55	25	43	.239	.274	.281	59	-29	5	7		.972	-15	C-144/O-24,3-5,1-3	-4.4

■ TOM DALY   Daly, Thomas Peter "Tido" b: 2/7/1866, Philadelphia, Pa. d: 10/29/38, Brooklyn, N.Y. BB/TR, 5'7", 170 lbs. Deb: 4/30/1887 F

1887	Chi-N	74	256	45	53	10	4	2	17	22	25	.207	.270	.301	52	-19	29			.935	33	C-64/O-8,S-2,2-2,1	1.7
1888	Chi-N	65	219	34	42	2	6	0	29	10	26	.192	.230	.256	51	-12	10			.939	20	C-62/O-4	1.3
1889	Was-N	71	250	39	75	13	5	1	40	38	28	.300	.394	.404	131	12	18			.917	3	C-57/1-8,2-4,O-3,S	1.7
1890	*Bro-N	82	292	55	71	9	4	5	43	32	43	.243	.326	.353	97	-1	20			.953	7	C-69,1-12/O-1	1.0
1891	Bro-N	58	200	29	50	11	5	2	27	21	34	.250	.327	.385	108	2	7			.881	-6	C-26,1-15,S-11,O-7	-0.2
1892	Bro-N	124	446	76	114	15	6	4	51	64	61	.256	.355	.343	116	11	34			.897	-11	3-57,O-30,C-27,2-10	0.3
1893	Bro-N	126	470	94	136	21	14	8	70	76	65	.289	.388	.445	127	19	32			.915	-18	2-82,3-45	0.3
1894	Bro-N	123	492	135	168	22	10	8	82	77	42	.341	.436	.476	129	27	51			.908	-19	*2-123	1.1
1895	Bro-N	120	455	89	128	17	8	2	68	52	52	.281	.359	.367	95	-2	28			.930	-19	*2-120	-1.1
1896	Bro-N	67	224	43	63	13	6	3	29	33	25	.281	.385	.433	122	8	19			.909	-2	2-66/C-1	0.9
1898	Bro-N	23	73	11	24	3	1	0	11	14		.329	.443	.397	142	5	6			.993	3	2-23	0.9
1899	Bro-N	141	498	95	156	24	9	5	88	69		.313	.409	.428	127	21	43			.929	16	*2-141	4.0
1900	*Bro-N	97	343	72	107	17	3	4	55	46		.312	.403	.414	118	10	27			.921	-8	2-93/1-3,O-2	0.6
1901	Bro-N	133	520	88	164	38	10	3	90	42		.315	.371	.444	132	21	31			.944	11	*2-133	3.6
1902	Chi-A	137	489	57	110	22	3	1	54	55		.225	.303	.288	68	-20	19			.957	-15	*2-137	-2.9
1903	Chi-A	43	150	20	31	11	0	0	19	20		.207	.304	.280	80	-3	6			.948	-13	2-43	-0.9
	Cin-N	80	307	42	90	14	9	1	38	16		.293	.332	.407	99	-2	5			.937	-10	2-79	-0.9
Total	16	1564	5684	1024	1582	262	103	49	811	687	401	.278	.361	.387	108	77	385			.931	-28	*2-1056,C-306,3/O1S	10.7

■ BILL DAM   Dam, Elbridge Rust b: 4/4/1885, Cambridge, Mass. d: 6/22/30, Quincy, Mass. Deb: 8/23/09

1909	Bos-N	1	2	1	1	1	0	0	1		1	.500	.667	1.000	398	1	0			1.000	-0	/O-1	0.1

■ JACK DAMASKA   Damaska, Jack Lloyd b: 8/21/37, Beaver Falls, Pa. BR/TR, 5'11", 168 lbs. Deb: 7/3/63

1963	StL-N	5	5	1	1	0	0	0	1	0	4	.200	.200	.200	14	-1	0			.000	-0	/2-1,O-1	-0.1

■ JOHNNY DAMON   Damon, Johnny David b: 11/5/73, Fort Riley, Kan. BL/TL, 6', 175 lbs. Deb: 8/12/95

1995	KC-A	47	188	32	53	11	5	3	23	12	22	.282	.328	.441	97	-1	7	0	2	.991	-2	O-47	-0.3
1996	KC-A	145	517	61	140	22	5	6	50	31	64	.271	.316	.368	74	-21	25	5	5	.983	2	*O-144/D-1	-1.7
Total	2	192	705	93	193	33	10	9	73	43	86	.274	.319	.387	80	-22	32	5	7	.985	0	O-191/D-1	-2.0

■ HARRY DAMRAU   Damrau, Harry Robert (Also Known As Arthur Lee Whitehorn)
b: 9/11/1890, Newburgh, N.Y. d: 8/21/57, Staten Island, N.Y BR/TR, 5'10", 178 lbs. Deb: 9/17/15

1915	Phi-A	16	56	4	11	1	0	0	5	3		.196	.262	.214	44	-4	1	1	-0	.870	-4	3-16	-0.8

■ JAKE DANIEL   Daniel, Handley Jacob b: 4/22/11, Roanoke, Ala. BL/TL, 5'11", 175 lbs. Deb: 7/24/37

1937	Bro-N	12	27	3	5	1	0	0	3	3	4	.185	.267	.222	34	-2	0			1.000	-0	/1-7	-0.3

■ BERT DANIELS   Daniels, Bernard Elmer b: 10/13/1882, Danville, Ill. d: 6/6/58, Cedar Grove, N.J. BR/TR, 5'9.5", 180 lbs. Deb: 6/25/10

1910	NY-A	95	356	68	90	13	8	1	17	41		.253	.356	.343	112	7	41			.957	3	O-85/3-6,1-4	0.6
1911	NY-A	131	462	74	132	16	9	2	31	48		.286	.375	.372	102	2	40			.941	1	*O-120	-0.3
1912	NY-A	135	496	72	136	25	11	2	41	51		.274	.363	.381	106	4	37			.945	5	*O-131	0.3
1913	NY-A	94	320	52	69	13	5	0	22	44	36	.216	.343	.287	85	-4	27			.966	1	O-71	-0.7
1914	Cin-N	71	269	29	59	9	7	0	19	19	40	.219	.276	.305	70	-10	14			.974	0	O-71	-1.5
Total	5	526	1903	295	486	76	40	6	130	203	76	.255	.349	.345	98	-1	159			.953	10	O-494/3-6,1-4	-1.6

■ TONY DANIELS   Daniels, Frederick Clinton b: 12/28/24, Gastonia, N.C. BR/TR, 5'9.5", 185 lbs. Deb: 6/12/45

1945	Phi-N	76	230	15	46	3	0	2	10	12	22	.200	.249	.230	35	-20	1			.955	7	2-75/3-1	-0.9

■ JACK DANIELS   Daniels, Harold Jack "Sour Mash Jack" b: 12/21/27, Chester, Pa. BL/TL, 5'10", 165 lbs. Deb: 4/18/52

1952	Bos-N	106	219	31	41	5	1	2	14	28	30	.187	.288	.247	51	-14	3	3	-1	.977	-9	O-87	-2.8

■ KAL DANIELS   Daniels, Kalvoski b: 8/20/63, Vienna, Ga. BL/TR, 5'11", 195 lbs. Deb: 4/9/86

1986	Cin-N	74	181	34	58	10	4	6	23	22	30	.320	.400	.519	145	11	15	2	3	.967	-0	O-47	1.4
1987	Cin-N	108	368	73	123	24	1	26	64	60	62	.334	.429	.617	166	36	26	3	8	.968	3	O-94	3.8
1988	Cin-N	140	495	95	144	29	1	18	64	87	94	.291	.400	.463	141	30	27	6	5	.982	3	*O-137	3.6
1989	Cin-N	44	133	26	29	11	0	2	9	36	28	.218	.392	.346	109	3	6	4	-1	1.000	2	O-38	0.4
	LA-N	11	38	7	13	2	0	2	8	7	5	.342	.444	.553	187	5	3	0	1	1.000	0	O-11	0.5
	Yr	55	171	33	42	13	0	4	17	43	33	.246	.403	.392	125	8	9	4	0	1.000	2	O-49	0.9
1990	LA-N	130	450	81	133	23	1	27	94	68	104	.296	.389	.531	156	35	4	3	-1	.987	2	*O-127	3.4
1991	LA-N	137	461	54	115	15	1	17	73	63	116	.249	.341	.397	109	6	6	1	0	.979	1	*O-132	0.5
1992	LA-N	35	104	9	24	5	0	2	8	10	30	.231	.304	.337	83	-2	0	0	0	.964	-2	O-21/1-8	-0.6
	Chi-N	48	108	12	27	6	0	4	17	12	24	.250	.331	.417	108	1	0	0	0	1.000	0	O-28	-0.2
	Yr	83	212	21	51	11	0	6	25	22	54	.241	.318	.377	95	-1	0	0	0	.984	-4	O-49/1-8	-0.8
Total	7	727	2338	391	666	125	8	104	360	365	493	.285	.385	.479	137	125	87	26	11	.980	8	O-635/1-8	12.8

YEAR	TM/L	G	AB	R	H	2B	3B	HR	RBI	BB	SO	AVG	OBP	SLG	PRO+	BR/A	SB	CS	SBR	FA	FR	G/POS	TPR

■ LAW DANIELS Daniels, Lawrence Long b: 7/14/1862, Newton, Mass. d: 1/7/29, Waltham, Mass. BR/TR, 5'10", 170 lbs. Deb: 4/25/1887

1887	Bal-a	48	165	23	41	5	1	0	32	8		.248	.287	.291	65	-7	7			.845	-8	C-26,O-15/1-4,2S3	-1.1
1888	KC-a	61	218	32	45	2	0	2	28	14		.206	.264	.243	59	-10	20			.855	-2	O-30,C-29/3-2,S-1	-1.0
Total	2	109	383	55	86	7	1	2	60	22		.225	.274	.264	62	-18	27			.859	-10	/C-55,O-45,1-4,3S2	-2.1

■ BUCK DANNER Danner, Henry Frederick b: 6/8/1891, Dedham, Mass. d: 9/21/49, Boston, Mass. BR/TR, 5'6", 135 lbs. Deb: 9/17/15

1915	Phi-A	3	12	1	3	0	0	0	0	0	1	.250	.250	.250	51	-1	1			.750	-3	/S-3	-0.3

■ HARRY DANNING Danning, Harry "Harry The Horse" b: 9/6/11, Los Angeles, Cal. BR/TR, 6'1", 190 lbs. Deb: 7/30/33 F

1933	NY-N	3	2	0	0	0	0	0	0	0	0	.000	.333	.000	2	-0	0			1.000	0	/C-1	0.0
1934	NY-N	53	97	8	32	7	0	1	7	1	9	.330	.337	.433	107	1	1			.989	-0	C-37	0.1
1935	NY-N	65	152	16	37	11	1	2	20	9	16	.243	.286	.368	76	-6	0			.978	3	C-44	-0.1
1936	*NY-N	32	69	3	11	2	2	0	4	1	5	.159	.183	.246	15	-8	0			.988	2	C-24	-0.6
1937	*NY-N	93	292	30	84	12	4	8	51	18	20	.288	.331	.438	106	2	0			.982	-5	C-86	0.1
1938	NY-N☆	120	448	59	137	26	3	9	60	23	40	.306	.345	.438	113	7	1			.984	-8	*C-114	0.5
1939	NY-N☆	135	520	79	163	28	5	16	74	35	42	.313	.359	.479	122	15	4			.991	7	*C-132	2.9
1940	NY-N★	140	524	65	157	34	4	13	91	35	31	.300	.349	.454	119	12	3			.980	7	*C-131	2.9
1941	NY-N★	130	459	58	112	22	4	7	56	30	25	.244	.292	.355	80	-13	1			.993	7	*C-116/1-1	0.4
1942	NY-N	119	408	45	114	20	3	1	34	34	29	.279	.335	.350	100	-0	3			.979	-5	*C-116	0.5
Total	10	890	2971	363	847	162	26	57	397	187	217	.285	.330	.415	104	9	13			.985	8	C-801/1-1	6.7

■ IKE DANNING Danning, Ike b: 1/20/05, Los Angeles, Cal. d: 3/30/83, Santa Monica, Cal BR/TR, 5'10", 160 lbs. Deb: 9/21/28 F

1928	StL-A	2	6	0	3	0	0	0	1	1	2	.500	.571	.500	178	1	0	0	0	.917	1	/C-2	0.1

■ FATS DANTONIO Dantonio, John James b: 12/31/18, New Orleans, La. d: 5/28/93, New Orleans, La. BR/TR, 5'8", 165 lbs. Deb: 9/18/44

1944	Bro-N	3	7	0	1	0	0	0	0	0	1	.143	.143	.143	-20	-1	0			.846	0	/C-3	-0.1
1945	Bro-N	47	128	12	32	6	1	0	12	11	6	.250	.309	.313	74	-5	3			.929	-5	C-45	-0.8
Total	2	50	135	12	33	6	1	0	12	11	7	.244	.301	.304	69	-6	3			.923	-5	/C-48	-0.9

■ BABE DANZIG Danzig, Harold P. b: 4/30/1887, Binghamton, N.Y. d: 7/14/31, San Francisco, Cal. BR/TR, 6'2", 205 lbs. Deb: 4/12/09

1909	Bos-A	6	13	0	2	0	0	0	0	0	2	.154	.313	.154	47	-1	0			.960	-1	/1-3	-0.2

■ CLIFF DAPPER Dapper, Clifford Roland b: 1/2/20, Los Angeles, Cal. BR/TR, 6'2", 190 lbs. Deb: 4/19/42

1942	Bro-N	8	17	2	8	1	0	1	9	2	2	.471	.526	.706	255	3	0			1.000	-0	/C-8	0.4

■ CLIFF DARINGER Daringer, Clifford Clarence "Shanty" b: 4/10/1885, Hayden, Ind. d: 12/26/71, Sacramento, Cal. BL/TR, 5'7.5", 155 lbs. Deb: 4/20/14 F

1914	KC-F	64	160	12	42	2	1	0	16	11	7	.262	.322	.287	70	-9	9			.944	6	S-24,3-19,2-14	-0.1

■ ROLLA DARINGER Daringer, Rolla Harrison b: 11/15/1888, N.Vernon, Ind. d: 5/23/74, Seymour, Ind. BL/TR, 5'10", 155 lbs. Deb: 9/19/14 F

1914	StL-N	2	4	1	2	1	0	0	0	1	2	.500	.600	.750	304	1	0			.667	-1	/S-1	0.0
1915	StL-N	10	23	3	2	0	0	0	0	9	5	.087	.344	.087	33	-1	0	1	-1	.947	-3	S-10	-0.5
Total	2	12	27	4	4	1	0	0	0	10	7	.148	.378	.185	72	-0	0	1		.927	-4	/S-11	-0.5

■ ALVIN DARK Dark, Alvin Ralph "Blackie" b: 1/7/22, Comanche, Okla. BR/TR, 5'11", 185 lbs. Deb: 7/14/46 MC

1946	Bos-N	15	13	0	3	3	0	0	1	0	3	.231	.231	.462	93	-0	0			.905	2	S-12/O-1	0.2
1948	*Bos-N	137	543	85	175	39	6	3	48	24	36	.322	.353	.433	114	9	4			.963	-12	*S-133	0.4
1949	Bos-N	130	529	74	146	23	5	3	53	31	43	.276	.317	.355	85	-13	5			.961	-4	*S-125/3-4	-0.7
1950	NY-N	154	587	79	164	36	5	16	67	39	60	.279	.331	.440	100	-1	9			.962	-15	*S-154	-0.4
1951	*NY-N★	156	646	114	196	41	7	14	69	42	39	.303	.352	.454	114	11	12	7	-1	.944	1	*S-156	2.3
1952	NY-N☆	151	589	92	177	39	3	14	73	47	39	.301	.357	.431	117	13	6	6	-2	.965	3	*S-150	2.6
1953	NY-N	155	647	126	194	41	6	23	88	28	34	.300	.335	.488	109	7	7	2	1	.967	8	*S-110,2-26,O/3P	2.4
1954	*NY-N★	154	644	98	189	26	6	20	70	27	40	.293	.327	.446	98	-3	5	3	-0	.956	4	*S-154	1.3
1955	NY-N	115	475	77	134	20	3	9	45	22	32	.282	.321	.394	88	-9	2	1	0	.962	-14	*S-115	-1.2
1956	NY-N	48	206	19	52	12	0	2	17	8	13	.252	.284	.340	67	-10	0	0	-0	.961	-5	S-48	-1.1
	StL-N	100	413	54	118	14	7	4	37	21	33	.286	.323	.383	77	-7	3	1	0	.959	2	S-99	0.0
	Yr	148	619	73	170	26	7	6	54	29	46	.275	.310	.368	82	-16	3	1	0	.960	-2	*S-147	-1.1
1957	StL-N	140	583	80	169	25	8	4	64	29	56	.290	.328	.381	88	-10	3	4	-2	.965	6	*S-139/3-1	0.8
1958	StL-N	18	64	7	19	0	0	1	5	2	6	.297	.318	.344	72	-2	0	0	-0	.943	-3	/S-8,3-8	-0.5
	Chi-N	114	464	54	137	16	4	3	43	29	23	.295	.343	.366	89	-7	1	1	-0	.949	-3	*3-111	-0.9
	Yr	132	528	61	156	16	4	4	48	31	29	.295	.340	.364	87	-9	1	1	-0	.948	-6	*3-119/S-8	-1.4
1959	Chi-N	136	477	60	126	22	9	6	45	55	50	.264	.344	.386	95	-3	1	1	-0	.948	-3	*3-131/1-4,S-1	-0.5
1960	Phi-N	55	198	29	48	5	1	3	14	19	14	.242	.315	.323	75	-6	1	1	-0	.953	-8	3-53/1-1	-1.5
	Mil-N	50	141	16	42	6	2	1	18	7	13	.298	.336	.390	106	1	0	0	-0	.960	-1	O-25,1-10/3-4,2-3	-0.2
	Yr	105	339	45	90	11	3	4	32	26	27	.265	.323	.351	88	-6	1	1	-0	.954	-8	3-57,O-25,1-11,/2-3	-1.7
Total	14	1828	7219	1064	2089	358	72	126	757	430	534	.289	.334	.411	98	-30	59	27		.960	-43	*S-1404,3-320/O21P	3.0

■ DELL DARLING Darling, Conrad b: 12/21/1861, Erie, Pa. d: 11/20/04, Erie, Pa. BR/TR, 5'8", 170 lbs. Deb: 7/3/1883

1883	Buf-N	6	18	1	3	0	1	0	2	5	.167	.250	.167	29	-1				.875	-2	/C-6	-0.3
1887	Chi-N	38	141	28	45	7	4	3	20	22	18	.319	.411	.489	132	6	19			.786	2	O-20,C-20	0.8
1888	Chi-N	20	75	12	16	3	1	2	7	3	12	.213	.253	.360	87	-1	0			.932	5	C-20	0.3
1889	Chi-N	36	120	14	23	1	1	0	7	25	22	.192	.331	.217	52	-7	5			.960	4	C-36	0.0
1890	Chi-P	58	221	45	57	12	4	2	39	29	28	.258	.352	.376	91	-3	5			.957	-9	1-29,S-15/C-9,O23	-1.0
1891	StL-a	17	53	9	7	1	3	0	9	10	11	.132	.270	.264	46	-4	0			.894	2	C-17/2-2,S-1	-0.1
Total	6	175	628	109	151	24	13	7	83	91	96	.240	.340	.354	87	-12	29			.923	-1	C-108/1-29,OS23	-0.3

■ JACK DARRAGH Darragh, James S. b: 7/17/1866, Ebensburg, Pa. d: 8/12/39, Rochester, Pa. Deb: 5/13/1891

1891	Lou-a	1	2	0	1	0	0	0	0	0	0	.500	.500	.500	189	0	0			1.000	0	/1-1	0.0

■ BOBBY DARWIN Darwin, Arthur Bobby Lee b: 2/16/43, Los Angeles, Cal. BR/TR, 6'2", 200 lbs. Deb: 9/30/62

1962	LA-A	1	1	0	0	0	0	0	0	0	1	.000	.000	.000	-99	-0	0	0	0	.000	-0	/P-1	0.0
1969	LA-N	6	0	1	0	0	0	0	0	0	0	—	—	—	—	-0	0	0	0	.000	-0	/P-3	0.0
1971	LA-N	11	20	2	5	1	0	1	4	2	9	.250	.318	.450	123	0	0	0	0	1.000	-0	/O-4	0.0
1972	Min-A	145	513	48	137	20	2	22	80	38	145	.267	.327	.442	122	13	2	3	-1	.980	-1	*O-142	0.5
1973	Min-A	145	560	69	141	20	2	18	90	46	137	.252	.312	.391	93	-6	5	2	0	.980	-2	*O-140/D-1	-1.0
1974	Min-A	152	575	67	152	13	7	25	94	37	127	.264	.324	.442	115	10	1	3	-2	.970	-2	*O-142	-0.8
1975	Min-A	48	169	26	37	6	0	5	18	18	44	.219	.309	.343	83	-4	0	2	0	.969	-4	O-27,D-19	-0.8
	Mil-A	55	186	19	46	6	2	8	23	11	54	.247	.300	.430	104	0	4	1	1	.978	1	O-43/D-9	0.0
	Yr	103	355	45	83	12	2	13	41	29	98	.234	.304	.389	94	-4	4	3	1	.975	-3	O-70,D-28	-0.8
1976	Mil-A	25	73	6	18	3	1	5	6	16	.247	.321	.356	100	0	0	0	0	.977	-1	O-21/D-1	-0.2
	Bos-A	43	106	9	19	5	2	3	13	2	35	.179	.216	.349	57	-6	1	0	0	.964	-2	O-17,D-16	-0.9
	Yr	68	179	15	37	8	3	4	18	8	51	.207	.260	.352	73	-7	1	0	0	.972	-3	O-38,D-17	-1.1
1977	Bos-A	4	9	1	2	1	0	0	1	0	4	.222	.222	.333	44	-1	0	0	0	.500	-0	/O-1,D-2	-0.1
	Chi-N	11	12	2	2	1	0	0	0	0	5	.167	.167	.250	9	-2	0	0	0	.000	-0	/O-1	-0.2
Total	9	646	2224	250	559	76	16	83	328	160	577	.251	.312	.412	103	4	15	9	-1	.976	-8	O-538/D-48,P-4	-2.7

■ DOUG DASCENZO Dascenzo, Douglas Craig b: 6/30/64, Cleveland, Ohio BB/TL, 5'7", 150 lbs. Deb: 9/2/88

1988	Chi-N	26	75	9	16	3	0	0	4	9	4	.213	.298	.253	57	-4	6	1	1	1.000	2	O-20	-0.1
1989	Chi-N	47	139	20	23	1	0	1	12	13	13	.165	.237	.194	23	-14	6	3	0	1.000	0	O-45	-1.8
1990	Chi-N	113	241	27	61	9	5	1	26	21	18	.253	.316	.344	76	-8	15	6	1	1.000	-18	*O-107/P-1	-2.7
1991	Chi-N	118	239	40	61	11	0	1	18	24	26	.255	.328	.314	78	-6	14	7	0	.985	-19	O-86/P-3	-2.8
1992	Chi-N	139	376	37	96	13	4	0	20	27	32	.255	.305	.311	73	-13	6	8	-3	.978	-17	*O-122	-3.8
1993	Tex-A	76	146	20	29	5	2	1	10	8	22	.199	.240	.288	43	-12	1	4	0	.990	-12	O-68/D-2	-2.4

YEAR	TM/L	G	AB	R	H	2B	3B	HR	RBI	BB	SO	AVG	OBP	SLG	PRO+	BR/A	SB	CS	SBR	FA	FR	G/POS	TPR
1996	SD-N	21	9	3	1	0	0	0	0	1	2	.111	.200	.111	-16	-2	0	1	-1	1.000	-3	O-10	-0.5
Total	7	540	1225	156	287	42	10	5	90	103	117	.234	.295	.297	64	-58	49	26	-1	.990	-69	O-458/P-4,D-2	-14.1

■ WALLY DASHIELL
Dashiell, John Wallace b: 5/9/02, Jewett, Tex. d: 5/20/72, Pensacola, Fla. BR/TR, 5'9.5", 170 lbs. Deb: 4/20/24

YEAR	TM/L	G	AB	R	H	2B	3B	HR	RBI	BB	SO	AVG	OBP	SLG	PRO+	BR/A	SB	CS	SBR	FA	FR	G/POS	TPR
1924	Chi-A	1	2	0	0	0	0	0	0	0	0	.000	.000	.000	-99	-1	0	0	0	.667	-1	/S-1	-0.1

■ JEFF DATZ
Datz, Jeffrey William b: 11/28/59, Camden, N.J. BR/TR, 6'4", 220 lbs. Deb: 9/5/89

YEAR	TM/L	G	AB	R	H	2B	3B	HR	RBI	BB	SO	AVG	OBP	SLG	PRO+	BR/A	SB	CS	SBR	FA	FR	G/POS	TPR
1989	Det-A	7	10	0	2	0	0	0	0	1	1	.200	.333	.200	55	-0	0	0	0	1.000	0	/C-6,D-1	0.0

■ HARRY DAUBERT
Daubert, Harry "Jake" b: 6/19/1892, Columbus, Ohio d: 1/8/44, Detroit, Mich. BR/TR, 6', 160 lbs. Deb: 9/4/15

YEAR	TM/L	G	AB	R	H	2B	3B	HR	RBI	BB	SO	AVG	OBP	SLG	PRO+	BR/A	SB	CS	SBR	FA	FR	G/POS	TPR
1915	Pit-N	1	1	0	0	0	0	0	0	0	1	.000	.000	.000	-99	0	0			.000	0	H	0.0

■ JAKE DAUBERT
Daubert, Jacob Ellsworth b: 4/7/1884, Shamokin, Pa. d: 10/9/24, Cincinnati, Ohio BL/TL, 5'10.5", 160 lbs. Deb: 4/14/10

YEAR	TM/L	G	AB	R	H	2B	3B	HR	RBI	BB	SO	AVG	OBP	SLG	PRO+	BR/A	SB	CS	SBR	FA	FR	G/POS	TPR
1910	Bro-N	144	552	67	146	15	15	8	50	47	53	.264	.328	.389	112	7	23			.989	-3	*1-144	0.4
1911	Bro-N	149	573	89	176	17	8	5	45	51	56	.307	.366	.391	117	12	32			.989	2	*1-149	1.4
1912	Bro-N	145	559	81	172	19	16	3	66	48	45	.308	.369	.415	119	14	29			.993	0	*1-143	1.2
1913	Bro-N	139	508	76	178	17	7	2	52	44	40	.350	.405	.423	133	23	25			.991	3	*1-139	2.5
1914	Bro-N	126	474	89	156	17	7	6	45	30	34	.329	.375	.432	137	20	25			.993	-6	*1-126	1.2
1915	Bro-N	150	544	62	164	21	8	2	47	57	48	.301	.369	.381	125	17	11	13	-5	.993	9	*1-150	1.9
1916	*Bro-N	127	478	75	151	16	7	3	33	38	39	.316	.371	.397	132	19	21	7	2	.993	4	*1-126	2.2
1917	Bro-N	125	468	59	122	4	4	2	30	51	30	.261	.341	.299	94	-1	11			.991	6	*1-125	0.1
1918	Bro-N	108	396	50	122	12	15	2	47	27	18	.308	.360	.429	141	18	10			.991	0	*1-105	1.6
1919	*Cin-N	140	537	79	148	10	12	2	44	35	23	.276	.322	.350	105	3	11			.989	-2	*1-140	-0.4
1920	Cin-N	142	553	97	168	28	13	4	48	47	29	.304	.362	.423	127	19	11	13	-5	.990	-9	*1-140	0.2
1921	Cin-N	136	516	69	158	18	12	2	64	24	16	.306	.341	.399	100	-1	12	6	0	.993	-1	*1-136	-0.2
1922	Cin-N	156	610	114	205	15	22	12	66	56	21	.336	.395	.492	130	27	14	17	-6	.994	-0	*1-156	1.3
1923	Cin-N	125	500	63	146	27	10	2	54	40	20	.292	.349	.398	99	-1	11	12	-4	.993	6	*1-121	-0.5
1924	Cin-N	102	405	47	114	14	9	1	31	28	17	.281	.331	.368	88	-7	5	10	-5	.990	7	*1-102	-1.1
Total	15	2014	7673	1117	2326	250	165	56	722	623	489	.303	.360	.401	117	170	251	78		.991	19	*1-2002	11.8

■ RICH DAUER
Dauer, Richard Fremont b: 7/27/52, San Bernardino, Cal. BR/TR, 6', 180 lbs. Deb: 9/11/76 C

YEAR	TM/L	G	AB	R	H	2B	3B	HR	RBI	BB	SO	AVG	OBP	SLG	PRO+	BR/A	SB	CS	SBR	FA	FR	G/POS	TPR
1976	Bal-A	11	39	0	4	0	0	0	3	1	3	.103	.146	.103	-28	-6	0	0	0	1.000	-3	2-10	-0.9
1977	Bal-A	96	304	38	74	15	1	5	25	20	28	.243	.294	.349	79	-9	1	0	0	.982	6	2-83/3-9,D-2	-0.2
1978	Bal-A	133	459	57	121	23	0	6	46	26	22	.264	.303	.353	89	-8	0	4	-2	.998	3	2-87,3-52/D-1	-0.2
1979	*Bal-A	142	479	63	123	20	0	9	61	36	36	.257	.310	.355	82	-13	0	1	-1	.979	-5	*2-103,3-44	-1.2
1980	Bal-A	152	557	71	158	32	0	6	63	46	19	.284	.342	.352	91	-6	3	2	-0	.991	-4	2-137,3-35	-0.2
1981	Bal-A	96	369	41	97	27	0	4	38	27	18	.263	.318	.369	98	-1	0	0	0	.989	-14	2-94/3-4	-1.0
1982	Bal-A	158	558	75	156	24	2	8	57	50	34	.280	.340	.373	96	-2	0	1	-1	.987	-36	*2-123,3-61	-3.5
1983	*Bal-A	140	459	49	108	19	0	5	41	47	29	.235	.309	.309	72	-17	1	1	-0	.988	-29	*2-131,3-17	-4.1
1984	Bal-A	127	397	29	101	26	0	2	24	24	23	.254	.297	.335	76	-13	1	3	-2	.980	-19	2-123/3-3	-2.9
1985	Bal-A	85	208	25	42	7	0	2	14	20	7	.202	.275	.264	50	-14	0	1	-1	.990	-5	2-73,3-17/1-1	-0.8
Total	10	1140	3829	448	984	193	3	43	372	297	219	.257	.313	.343	83	-89	6	13	-6	.987	-96	2-964,3-242/D-3,1-1	-14.6

■ DOC DAUGHERTY
Daugherty, Harold Ray b: 10/12/27, Paris, Pa. BR/TR, 6', 180 lbs. Deb: 4/22/51

YEAR	TM/L	G	AB	R	H	2B	3B	HR	RBI	BB	SO	AVG	OBP	SLG	PRO+	BR/A	SB	CS	SBR	FA	FR	G/POS	TPR
1951	Det-A	1	1	0	0	0	0	0	0	0	1	.000	.000	.000	-99	-0	0	0	0	.000	0	H	0.0

■ JACK DAUGHERTY
Daugherty, John Michael b: 7/3/60, Hialeah, Fla. BB/TL, 6' ", 188 lbs. Deb: 9/1/87

YEAR	TM/L	G	AB	R	H	2B	3B	HR	RBI	BB	SO	AVG	OBP	SLG	PRO+	BR/A	SB	CS	SBR	FA	FR	G/POS	TPR
1987	Mon-N	11	10	1	1	1	0	0	1	0	3	.100	.100	.200	-22	-2	0	0	0	1.000	0	/1-1	-0.2
1989	Tex-A	52	106	15	32	4	2	1	10	11	21	.302	.373	.406	117	3	2	1	0	1.000	1	1-23/O-5,D-8	0.1
1990	Tex-A	125	310	36	93	20	2	6	47	22	49	.300	.350	.435	118	7	0	0	0	.982	-3	O-42,1-30,D-21	0.1
1991	Tex-A	58	144	8	28	3	2	1	11	16	23	.194	.275	.264	51	-10	1	0	0	.981	-4	O-37,1-11/D-1	-1.5
1992	Tex-A	59	127	13	26	9	0	0	9	16	21	.205	.299	.276	64	-6	2	1	0	.939	-4	O-26,D-13/1-8	-1.1
1993	Hou-N	4	3	0	1	0	0	0	0	0	0	.333	.333	.333	82	-0	0	0	0	.000	0	/1-1,O-1	0.0
	Cin-N	46	59	7	13	2	0	2	9	11	15	.220	.343	.356	87	-1	0	0	0	.917	-4	O-16/1-2	-0.5
	Yr	50	62	7	14	2	0	2	9	11	15	.226	.342	.355	87	-1	0	0	0	.923	-4	O-17/1-3	-0.5
Total	6	355	759	80	194	39	6	10	87	76	132	.256	.327	.362	92	-8	5	2	0	.969	-15	O-127/1-76,D-43	-3.0

■ BOB DAUGHTERS
Daughters, Robert Francis "Red" b: 8/5/14, Cincinnati, Ohio d: 8/22/88, Southbury, Conn. BR/TR, 6'2", 185 lbs. Deb: 4/24/37

YEAR	TM/L	G	AB	R	H	2B	3B	HR	RBI	BB	SO	AVG	OBP	SLG	PRO+	BR/A	SB	CS	SBR	FA	FR	G/POS	TPR
1937	Bos-A	1	0	1	0	0	0	0	0	0	0	—	—	—	—	0	0	0	0	.000	0	R	0.0

■ DARREN DAULTON
Daulton, Darren Arthur b: 1/3/62, Arkansas City, Kan. BL/TR, 6'2", 195 lbs. Deb: 9/25/83

YEAR	TM/L	G	AB	R	H	2B	3B	HR	RBI	BB	SO	AVG	OBP	SLG	PRO+	BR/A	SB	CS	SBR	FA	FR	G/POS	TPR
1983	Phi-N	2	3	1	1	0	0	0	0	0	0	.333	.500	.333	137	0	0	0	0	1.000	-0	/C-2	0.0
1985	Phi-N	36	103	14	21	3	1	4	11	16	37	.204	.311	.369	87	-2	3	0	1	.994	-4	C-28	0.1
1986	Phi-N	49	138	18	31	4	0	8	21	38	41	.225	.395	.428	123	6	2	3	-1	.985	-4	C-48	0.3
1987	Phi-N	53	129	10	25	6	0	3	13	16	37	.194	.283	.310	55	-8	2	1	0	.991	1	C-40/1-1	-0.5
1988	Phi-N	58	144	13	30	6	0	1	12	17	26	.208	.292	.271	61	-7	2	1	0	.977	-6	C-44/1-1	-1.1
1989	Phi-N	131	368	29	74	12	2	8	44	52	58	.201	.303	.310	76	-11	2	1	0	.984	-11	*C-126	-1.7
1990	Phi-N	143	459	62	123	30	1	12	57	72	72	.268	.370	.416	116	12	7	1	2	.989	-9	*C-139	1.4
1991	Phi-N	89	285	36	56	12	0	12	42	41	66	.196	.302	.365	88	-5	5	0	2	.985	-17	C-88	-1.6
1992	Phi-N★	145	485	80	131	32	5	27	109	88	103	.270	.389	.524	157	38	11	2	2	.987	-14	*C-141	3.6
1993	*Phi-N★	147	510	90	131	35	4	24	105	117	111	.257	.397	.482	136	30	5	2	0	.991	-9	*C-146	3.1
1994	Phi-N	69	257	43	77	17	1	15	56	33	43	.300	.380	.549	136	13	4	1	1	.994	7	C-68	2.4
1995	Phi-N★	98	342	44	85	19	3	9	55	55	52	.249	.359	.401	100	1	3	0	1	.994	-7	C-95	0.2
1996	Phi-N	5	12	3	2	0	0	0	0	7	5	.167	.500	.167	84	0	0	0	0	1.000	-1	/O-5	0.0
Total	13	1025	3235	443	787	176	17	123	525	553	652	.243	.357	.422	113	68	44	9	8	.989	-69	C-965/O-5,1-2	6.2

■ YO-YO DAVALILLO
Davalillo, Pompeyo Antonio (Romero) b: 6/30/31, Caracas, Venez. BR/TR, 5'3", 140 lbs. Deb: 8/1/53 F

YEAR	TM/L	G	AB	R	H	2B	3B	HR	RBI	BB	SO	AVG	OBP	SLG	PRO+	BR/A	SB	CS	SBR	FA	FR	G/POS	TPR
1953	Was-A	19	58	10	17	1	0	0	2	1	7	.293	.305	.310	68	-3	1	0	0	.935	2	S-17	0.0

■ VIC DAVALILLO
Davalillo, Victor Jose (Romero) b: 7/31/36, Cabimas, Venez. BL/TL, 5'7", 155 lbs. Deb: 4/9/63 F

YEAR	TM/L	G	AB	R	H	2B	3B	HR	RBI	BB	SO	AVG	OBP	SLG	PRO+	BR/A	SB	CS	SBR	FA	FR	G/POS	TPR
1963	Cle-A	90	370	44	108	18	5	7	36	16	41	.292	.323	.424	108	3	3	3	-1	.988	17	O-89	1.5
1964	Cle-A	150	577	64	156	26	2	6	51	34	77	.270	.312	.354	89	-12	21	11	-0	.986	16	*O-143	-0.3
1965	Cle-A★	142	505	67	152	19	1	5	40	35	50	.301	.346	.372	103	2	26	7	4	.988	15	*O-134	1.6
1966	Cle-A	121	344	42	86	6	4	3	19	24	37	.250	.299	.317	77	-10	8	6	-1	.986	0	*O-108	-1.6
1967	Cle-A	139	359	47	103	17	5	2	22	10	30	.287	.308	.379	101	-1	6	7	-2	.986	-8	*O-125	-1.7
1968	Cle-A	51	180	15	43	2	2	2	13	3	19	.239	.255	.317	74	-6	8	6	-1	.967	2	O-49	-0.9
	Cal-A	93	339	34	101	15	4	1	18	15	34	.298	.328	.375	117	6	17	10	-1	.995	6	O-86	0.7
	Yr	144	519	49	144	17	7	3	31	18	53	.277	.303	.355	102	-1	25	16	-2	.987	8	*O-135	-0.2
1969	Cal-A	33	71	10	11	1	1	0	1	6	5	.155	.231	.197	22	-7	1	0	0	1.000	-2	O-22/1-3	-1.0
	StL-N	63	98	15	26	3	0	2	10	7	8	.265	.314	.357	87	-2	1	1	0	1.000	-2	O-23/P-2	-0.5
1970	StL-N	111	183	29	57	14	3	1	33	13	19	.311	.357	.437	109	2	4	1	1	.972	-8	O-54	-0.7
1971	*Pit-N	99	295	48	84	14	6	1	33	11	31	.285	.318	.383	97	-2	10	2	2	.983	-2	O-61,1-16	-0.6
1972	*Pit-N	117	368	59	117	19	2	4	28	26	44	.318	.368	.413	124	11	14	1	4	.979	-1	O-97/1-8	1.1
1973	Pit-N	59	83	9	15	1	0	1	3	2	7	.181	.200	.229	19	-9	2	2	-0	.977	-0	1-10,O-10	-1.2
	*Oak-A	38	64	5	12	1	0	0	4	3	4	.188	.224	.203	22	-7	1	0	0	.967	-2	O-19/1-8,D-2	-0.9
1974	Oak-A	17	23	0	4	0	0	0	3	1	6	.174	.240	.174	22	-2	0	0	0	1.000	-2	/O-6,D-4	-0.5
1977	*LA-N	24	48	3	15	2	0	0	4	0	6	.313	.313	.354	79	-1	0	0	0	1.000	-3	O-12	-0.1
1978	LA-N	75	77	15	24	1	1	1	11	3	7	.312	.338	.390	103	0	2	0	0	1.000	-0	/O-25/1-1	-0.1
1979	LA-N	29	27	2	7	2	0	0	6	1	5	.259	.310	.296	67	-1	0	0	0	1.000	-1	/O-3	-0.1
1980	LA-N	7	6	1	1	0	0	0	0	0	1	.167	.167	.167	-7	-1	0	0	0	1.000	-0	/1-1	-0.1
Total	16	1458	4017	509	1122	160	37	36	329	212	422	.279	.317	.364	94	-36	125	58	3	.986	19	*O-1066/1-47,D-6,P	-6.4

YEAR	TM/L	G	AB	R	H	2B	3B	HR	RBI	BB	SO	AVG	OBP	SLG	PRO+	BR/A	SB	CS	SBR	FA	FR	G/POS	TPR
■ JERRY DaVANON					DaVanon, Frank Gerald b: 8/21/45, Oceanside, Cal. BR/TR, 5'11", 175 lbs. Deb: 4/11/69																		
1969	SD-N	24	59	4	8	1	0	0	3	3	12	.136	.177	.153	-7	-8	0	3	-2	.932	0	2-15/S-7	-0.9
	StL-N	16	40	7	12	3	0	1	7	6	8	.300	.391	.450	135	2	0	0	0	.958	1	S-16	0.4
	Yr	40	99	11	20	4	0	1	10	9	20	.202	.269	.273	53	-6	0	3	-2	.959	1	S-23,2-15	-0.5
1970	StL-N	11	18	2	2	1	0	0	0	2	5	.111	.200	.167	-1	-3	0	0	0	1.000	0	/3-5,2-3	0.0
1971	Bal-A	38	81	14	19	5	0	0	4	12	20	.235	.340	.296	82	-1	0	0	0	.970	-3	2-20,S-11/3-3,1-1	-0.3
1973	Cal-A	41	49	6	12	3	0	0	2	3	9	.245	.288	.306	73	-2	1	2	-1	.927	5	S-14,2-12/3-7	0.4
1974	StL-N	30	40	4	6	1	0	0	4	4	5	.150	.261	.175	24	-4	0	1	-1	.840	-2	S-14/3-8,2-7,O-1	-0.6
1975	Hou-N	32	97	15	27	4	2	1	10	16	7	.278	.386	.392	125	4	2	0	1	.944	2	S-21/2-9,3-3	1.0
1976	Hou-N	61	107	19	31	3	3	1	20	21	12	.290	.411	.402	144	7	0	2	-1	.980	5	2-17,S-17/3-9	1.2
1977	StL-N	9	8	2	0	0	0	0	0	1	2	.000	.111	.000	-68	-2	0	0	0	.923	1	/2-5	0.0
Total	8	262	499	73	117	21	5	3	50	68	80	.234	.332	.315	86	-7	3	8	-4	.936	11	S-100/2-88,3-35,O1	1.2
■ JIM DAVENPORT					Davenport, James Houston b: 8/17/33, Siluria, Ala. BR/TR, 5'11", 175 lbs. Deb: 4/15/58 MC																		
1958	SF-N	134	434	70	111	22	3	12	41	33	64	.256	.319	.403	92	-6	1	3	-2	.960	-4	*3-130/S-5	-1.0
1959	SF-N	123	469	65	121	16	3	6	38	28	65	.258	.303	.343	73	-18	0	1	-1	**.978**	-3	*3-121/S-1	-2.2
1960	SF-N	112	363	43	91	15	3	6	38	26	58	.251	.308	.358	87	-7	0	2	-1	**.961**	-1	*3-103/S-7	-0.9
1961	SF-N	137	436	64	121	28	4	12	65	45	65	.278	.348	.443	112	7	4	3	-1	.965	8	*3-132	1.6
1962	*SF-N★	144	485	83	144	25	5	14	58	45	76	.297	.359	.456	119	13	2	5	-2	.952	4	*3-141	1.6
1963	SF-N	147	460	40	116	19	3	4	36	32	87	.252	.301	.333	83	-10	5	2	0	.962	1	*3-127,2-22/S-1	-0.8
1964	SF-N	116	297	24	70	10	6	2	26	29	46	.236	.304	.330	77	-2	5	0	1	.979	-4	S-64,3-41,2-30	-0.7
1965	SF-N	106	271	29	68	14	3	4	31	21	47	.251	.307	.369	87	-5	7	4	-2	.949	-21	3-39,S-37,2-26	-2.4
1966	SF-N	111	305	42	76	8	4	9	30	22	40	.249	.302	.370	83	-7	1	5	-1	.961	-18	S-58,3-36,2-21,/1-2	-2.2
1967	SF-N	124	295	42	81	10	3	5	30	39	50	.275	.367	.380	116	7	1	4	-2	1.000	1	3-64,S-28,2-12	0.9
1968	SF-N	113	272	27	61	1	1	1	17	26	32	.224	.292	.246	63	-12	0	3	-2	.960	-7	3-82,S-17/2-1	-2.2
1969	SF-N	112	303	20	73	10	1	2	42	29	37	.241	.307	.300	72	-11	0	1	-1	.967	1	*3-104/1-1,S-1,O-1	-1.1
1970	SF-N	22	37	3	9	1	0	0	4	7	6	.243	.364	.270	73	-1	0	0	0	1.000	1	3-10	-0.4
Total	13	1501	4427	552	1142	177	37	77	456	382	673	.258	.320	.367	90	-58	16	25	-10	.964	-43	*3-1130,S-219,2/10	-9.8
■ ANDRE DAVID					David, Andre Anter b: 5/18/58, Hollywood, Cal. BL/TL, 6', 170 lbs. Deb: 6/29/84																		
1984	Min-A	33	48	5	12	2	0	1	5	7	11	.250	.357	.354	93	-0	0	0	0	1.000	-3	O-14/D-2	-0.4
1986	Min-A	5	5	0	1	0	0	0	0	0	2	.200	.333	.200	48	-0	0	0	0	.000	0	/D-1	0.0
Total	2	38	53	5	13	2	0	1	5	7	13	.245	.355	.340	89	-1	0	0	0	1.000	-3	/O-14,D-3	-0.4
■ CLAUDE DAVIDSON					Davidson, Claude Boucher "Davey" b: 10/13/1896, Boston, Mass. d: 4/18/56, Weymouth, Mass. BL/TR, 5'11", 155 lbs. Deb: 4/25/18																		
1918	Phi-A	31	81	4	15	1	0	0	4	5	9	.185	.233	.198	29	-7	0			.943	-7	2-15/O-8,3-1	-1.5
1919	Was-A	2	7	1	3	0	0	0	0	1	1	.429	.500	.429	163	1	0			1.000	-0	/3-2	0.1
Total	2	33	88	5	18	1	0	0	4	6	10	.205	.255	.216	41	-6	0			1.000	-7	/2-15,O-8,3-3	-1.4
■ HOMER DAVIDSON					Davidson, Homer Hurd "Divvy" b: 10/14/1884, Cleveland, Ohio d: 7/26/48, Detroit, Mich. BR/TR, 5'10.5", 155 lbs. Deb: 4/25/08																		
1908	Cle-A	9	4	2	0	0	0	0	0	0		.000	.000	.000	-99	-1	1			1.000	2	/C-5,O-1	0.1
■ MARK DAVIDSON					Davidson, John Mark b: 2/15/61, Knoxville, Tenn. BR/TR, 6'2", 190 lbs. Deb: 6/20/86																		
1986	Min-A	36	68	5	8	3	0	0	2	6	22	.118	.189	.162	-3	-10	2	3	-1	.980	-4	O-31/D-3	-1.5
1987	*Min-A	102	150	32	40	4	1	1	14	13	26	.267	.325	.327	71	-6	9	2	2	1.000	-14	O-86/D-9	-1.8
1988	Min-A	100	106	22	23	7	0	1	10	10	20	.217	.291	.311	67	-5	3	3	-1	.955	-8	O-91/3-1,D-3	-2.3
1989	Hou-N	33	65	7	13	2	1	1	5	7	14	.200	.278	.308	70	-3	1	0	0	1.000	-3	O-23	-0.6
1990	Hou-N	57	130	12	38	5	1	1	11	10	18	.292	.343	.369	99	-0	3	3	-2	.981	-2	O-51	-0.5
1991	Hou-N	85	142	10	27	6	0	2	15	12	28	.190	.263	.275	54	-9	0	0	0	1.000	-11	O-63	-2.2
Total	6	413	661	88	149	27	3	6	57	58	128	.225	.291	.303	64	-32	15	11	-2	.983	-49	O-345/D-15,3-1	-8.9
■ BILL DAVIDSON					Davidson, William Simpson b: 5/10/1884, Lafayette, Ind. d: 5/23/54, Lincoln, Neb. BR/TR, 5'10", 170 lbs. Deb: 9/29/09																		
1909	Chi-N	2	7	2	1	0	0	0	0	1		.143	.250	.143	22	-1	1			1.000	-0	/O-2	-0.1
1910	Bro-N	136	509	48	121	13	7	0	34	24	54	.238	.277	.291	68	-22	27			.961	-7	*O-131	-3.8
1911	Bro-N	87	292	33	68	3	4	1	26	16	21	.233	.275	.281	58	-17	18			.956	-5	O-74	-2.6
Total	3	225	808	83	190	16	11	1	60	41	75	.235	.276	.286	64	-40	46			.959	-12	O-207	-6.5
■ CHICK DAVIES					Davies, Lloyd Garrison b: 3/6/1892, Peabody, Mass. d: 9/5/73, Middletown, Conn. BL/TL, 5'8", 145 lbs. Deb: 7/11/14																		
1914	Phi-A	19	46	6	11	3	1	0	5	5	13	.239	.314	.348	103	-0	1			.926	0	O-10/P-1	0.0
1915	Phi-A	56	132	13	24	5	3	0	11	14	31	.182	.270	.265	62	-6	2	4	-2	.973	4	O-32/P-4	-0.6
1925	NY-N	4	6	1	0	0	0	0	0	0	1	.000	.000	.000	-99	-2	0	0	0	1.000	0	/P-2,O-1	-0.1
1926	NY-N	38	18	4	4	0	0	0	1	3	5	.222	.333	.222	53	-1	0			.938	1	P-38	0.0
Total	4	117	202	24	39	8	4	0	17	22	50	.193	.279	.272	65	-9	3	4		.938	6	/P-45,O-43	-0.7
■ LEFTY DAVIS					Davis, Alphonzo De Ford b: 2/4/1875, Nashville, Tenn. d: 2/4/19, Collins, N.Y. BL/TL, 5'10", 170 lbs. Deb: 4/18/01																		
1901	Bro-N	25	91	11	19	2	0	1	9	10		.209	.287	.231	50	-6	4			.822	-5	O-24/2-1	-1.2
	Pit-N	87	335	87	105	8	11	2	33	56		.313	.415	.421	138	19	22			.975	7	O-86	1.9
	Yr	112	426	98	124	10	11	3	42	66		.291	.389	.380	120	13	26			.942	-2	*O-110/2-1	0.7
1902	Pit-N	59	232	52	65	7	3	0	20	35		.280	.377	.336	116	6	19			.945	-2	O-59	0.0
1903	NY-A	104	372	54	88	10	0	0	25	43		.237	.319	.263	72	-11	11			.906	-7	*O-102/S-1	-2.6
1907	Cin-N	73	266	28	61	5	5	1	25	23		.229	.293	.297	82	-6	9			.972	5	O-70	-0.4
Total	4	348	1296	232	338	32	19	3	110	167		.261	.348	.322	98	2	65			.939	-2	O-341/S-1,2-1	-2.3
■ ALVIN DAVIS					Davis, Alvin Glenn b: 9/9/60, Riverside, Cal. BL/TR, 6'1", 195 lbs. Deb: 4/11/84																		
1984	Sea-A★	152	567	80	161	34	3	27	116	97	78	.284	.395	.497	147	39	5	4	-1	.992	-4	*1-147/D-7	2.5
1985	Sea-A	155	578	78	166	33	1	18	78	90	71	.287	.385	.441	125	22	1	2	-1	.992	-5	*1-154	0.7
1986	Sea-A	135	479	66	130	18	1	18	72	76	68	.271	.375	.426	116	13	0	3	-2	.986	1	*1-101,D-32	0.4
1987	Sea-A	157	580	86	171	37	2	29	100	72	84	.295	.375	.516	126	22	0	0	0	.994	-7	*1-157	0.3
1988	Sea-A	140	478	67	141	24	1	18	69	95	53	.295	.416	.462	139	29	1	1	-0	.994	-6	*1-115,D-25	1.3
1989	Sea-A	142	498	84	152	30	1	21	95	101	49	.305	.428	.496	155	41	0	1	-1	.992	-3	*1-125,D-14	2.7
1990	Sea-A	140	494	63	140	21	0	17	68	85	68	.283	.393	.429	128	22	0	2	-1	.994	-1	D-87,1-52	1.3
1991	Sea-A	145	462	39	102	15	1	12	69	56	78	.221	.305	.351	77	-14	0	3	-2	1.000	-1	*D-126,1-14	-2.3
1992	Cal-A	40	104	5	26	8	0	0	16	13	19	.250	.333	.327	85	-2	0	0	0	.995	-1	1-22/D-9	-0.4
Total	9	1206	4240	568	1189	220	10	160	683	685	558	.280	.384	.450	127	172	7	16	-8	.992	-26	1-887,D-300	6.5
■ BILL DAVIS					Davis, Arthur Willard b: 6/6/42, Graceville, Minn. BL/TL, 6'7", 215 lbs. Deb: 9/16/65																		
1965	Cle-A	10	10	0	3	1	0	0	0	0	1	.300	.300	.400	96	-0	0	0	0	.000	0	H	0.0
1966	Cle-A	23	38	2	6	1	0	1	4	6	9	.158	.273	.263	55	-2	0	0	0	.981	-0	/1-9	-0.3
1969	SD-N	31	57	1	10	1	0	0	1	8	18	.175	.288	.193	39	-4	0	0	0	.992	-1	1-14	-0.7
Total	3	64	105	3	19	3	0	1	5	14	28	.181	.283	.238	50	-7	0	0	0	.988	-1	/1-23	-1.0
■ BROCK DAVIS					Davis, Bryshear Barnett b: 10/19/43, Oakland, Cal. BL/TL, 5'10", 168 lbs. Deb: 4/9/63																		
1963	Hou-N	34	55	7	11	2	0	1	2	4	10	.200	.254	.291	60	-3	0	2	-1	.864	-2	O-14	-0.6
1964	Hou-N	1	3	0	0	0	0	0	0	1	1	.000	.250	.000	-24	-0	0	0	0	1.000	0	/O-1	0.0
1966	Hou-N	10	27	2	4	1	0	0	1	5	4	.148	.281	.185	35	-2	1	0	0	1.000	-0	/O-7	-0.3
1970	Chi-N	6	3	0	0	0	0	0	0	0		.000	.000	.000	-89	-1	0	0	0	.000	0	/O-1	-0.1
1971	Chi-N	106	301	22	77	7	5	0	28	35	34	.256	.337	.312	74	-9	0	6	-4	.982	4	O-93	-1.4
1972	Mil-A	85	154	17	49	2	0	0	12	12	23	.318	.367	.331	111	2	6	4	-1	.970	-5	O-43	-0.5
Total	6	242	543	48	141	12	5	1	43	57	73	.260	.332	.306	79	-13	7	10	-4	.973	-3	O-159	-2.9
■ CHILI DAVIS					Davis, Charles Theodore b: 1/17/60, Kingston, Jamaica BB/TR, 6'3", 195 lbs. Deb: 4/10/81																		
1981	SF-N	8	15	1	2	1	0	0	0	0	2	.133	.188	.133	-8	-2	2	0	1	1.000	-1	/O-6	-0.3

YEAR	TM/L	G	AB	R	H	2B	3B	HR	RBI	BB	SO	AVG	OBP	SLG	PRO+	BR/A	SB	CS	SBR	FA	FR	G/POS	TPR
1982	SF-N	154	641	86	167	27	6	19	76	45	115	.261	.311	.410	100	-1	24	13	-1	.972	18	*O-153	1.2
1983	SF-N	137	486	54	113	21	2	11	59	55	108	.233	.311	.352	86	-10	10	12	-4	.976	13	*O-133	-0.5
1984	SF-N★	137	499	87	157	21	6	21	81	42	74	.315	.369	.507	149	31	12	8	-1	.971	8	*O-123	3.4
1985	SF-N	136	481	53	130	25	2	13	56	62	74	.270	.354	.412	119	13	15	7	0	.980	13	*O-126	2.2
1986	SF-N★	153	526	71	146	28	3	13	70	84	96	.278	.378	.416	125	20	16	13	-3	.972	-2	*O-148	1.1
1987	*SF-N	149	500	80	125	22	1	24	76	72	109	.250	.347	.442	113	9	16	9	-1	.975	-13	*O-135	-0.9
1988	Cal-A	158	600	81	161	29	3	21	93	56	118	.268	.331	.432	115	11	9	10	-3	.942	-4	*O-153/D-3	-0.1
1989	Cal-A	154	560	81	152	24	1	22	90	61	109	.271	.343	.436	120	14	3	0	1	.979	-4	*O-147/D-6	0.7
1990	Cal-A	113	412	58	109	17	1	12	58	61	89	.265	.359	.398	114	9	1	2	-1	.965	-3	D-60,O-52	0.3
1991	*Min-A	153	534	84	148	34	1	29	93	95	117	.277	.387	.507	139	30	5	6	-2	1.000	-0	*D-150/O-2	2.1
1992	Min-A	138	444	63	128	27	2	12	66	73	76	.288	.392	.439	128	19	4	5	-2	1.000	-1	*D-125/O-4,1-1	1.2
1993	Cal-A	153	573	74	139	32	0	27	112	71	135	.243	.327	.440	101	-0	4	1	1	1.000	-0	*D-150/P-1	-0.6
1994	Cal-A★	108	392	72	122	18	1	26	84	69	84	.311	.416	.561	147	29	3	2	-1	1.000	0	*D-106/O-2	2.1
1995	Cal-A	119	424	81	135	23	0	20	86	89	79	.318	.437	.514	148	34	3	3	-1	1.000	0	*D-119	1.3
1996	Cal-A	145	530	73	155	24	0	28	95	86	99	.292	.391	.496	125	22	5	2	0	1.000	0	*D-143	1.1
Total	16	2115	7617	1099	2089	372	29	298	1195	1022	1484	.274	.361	.448	121	226	132	93	-16	.971	24	*O-1184,D-862/P-1,1	15.3

■ DOUG DAVIS

Davis, Douglas Raymond b: 9/24/62, Bloomsburg, Pa. BR/TR, 6', 180 lbs. Deb: 7/8/88

YEAR	TM/L	G	AB	R	H	2B	3B	HR	RBI	BB	SO	AVG	OBP	SLG	PRO+	BR/A	SB	CS	SBR	FA	FR	G/POS	TPR
1988	Cal-A	6	12	1	0	0	0	0	0	0	3	.000	.077	.000	-79	-3	0	0	0	1.000	-3	/C-3,3-3	-0.6
1992	Tex-A	1	1	0	1	0	0	0	0	0	0	1.000	1.000	1.000	479	0	0	0	0	1.000		/C-1	0.0
Total	2	7	13	1	1	0	0	0	0	0	3	.077	.143	.077	-38	-2	0	0	0	1.000	-3	/C-4,3-3	-0.6

■ ERIC DAVIS

Davis, Eric Keith b: 5/29/62, Los Angeles, Cal. BR/TR, 6'3", 175 lbs. Deb: 5/19/84

YEAR	TM/L	G	AB	R	H	2B	3B	HR	RBI	BB	SO	AVG	OBP	SLG	PRO+	BR/A	SB	CS	SBR	FA	FR	G/POS	TPR
1984	Cin-N	57	174	33	39	10	1	10	30	24	48	.224	.322	.466	114	3	10	2	2	.992	1	O-51	0.5
1985	Cin-N	56	122	26	30	3	3	8	18	7	39	.246	.287	.516	114	2	16	3	3	.987	-6	O-47	-0.3
1986	Cin-N	132	415	97	115	15	3	27	71	68	100	.277	.380	.523	140	23	80	11	11	.975	-9	*O-121	2.9
1987	Cin-N★	129	474	120	139	23	4	37	100	84	134	.293	.401	.593	152	36	50	6	11	.990	28	*O-128	**6.9**
1988	Cin-N	135	472	81	129	18	3	26	93	65	124	.273	.365	.489	138	23	35	3	9	.981	-0	*O-130	3.0
1989	Cin-N	131	462	74	130	14	2	34	101	68	116	.281	.375	.541	154	32	21	7	2	.984	-2	*O-125	3.4
1990	*Cin-N	127	453	84	118	26	2	24	86	60	100	.260	.350	.486	122	13	21	3	5	.993	7	*O-122	2.2
1991	Cin-N	89	285	39	67	10	0	11	33	48	92	.235	.355	.386	104	3	14	2	3	.985	6	O-81	1.1
1992	LA-N	76	267	21	61	8	1	5	32	36	71	.228	.327	.322	86	-4	19	1	5	.961	-5	O-74	-0.6
1993	LA-N	108	376	57	88	17	0	14	53	41	88	.234	.311	.391	92	-5	33	5	7	.991	6	*O-103	0.9
	Det-A	23	75	14	19	1	1	6	15	14	18	.253	.371	.533	141	4	2	2	-1	.981	1	O-18/D-5	0.4
1994	Det-A	37	120	19	22	4	0	3	13	18	45	.183	.290	.292	50	-9	5	0	2	.989	-1	O-35	-0.9
1996	Cin-N	129	415	81	119	20	0	26	83	70	121	.287	.397	.523	141	26	23	9	2	.989	2	*O-126/1-1	2.5
Total	12	1229	4110	746	1076	169	20	231	728	603	1096	.262	.360	.481	129	148	329	54	66	.985	35	*O-1161/D-5,1-1	22.0

■ GEORGE DAVIS

Davis, George Stacey b: 8/23/1870, Cohoes, N.Y. d: 10/17/40, Philadelphia, Pa. BB/TR, 5'9", 180 lbs. Deb: 4/19/1890

YEAR	TM/L	G	AB	R	H	2B	3B	HR	RBI	BB	SO	AVG	OBP	SLG	PRO+	BR/A	SB	CS	SBR	FA	FR	G/POS	TPR
1890	Cle-N	136	526	98	139	22	9	6	73	53	34	.264	.336	.375	109	6	22			.946	M	*O-133/2-2,S-1	1.2
1891	Cle-N	136	570	115	165	35	12	3	89	53	29	.289	.354	.409	117	11	42			.931	14	*O-116,3-22/P-3	1.9
1892	*Cle-N	144	597	95	144	27	12	5	82	58	51	.241	.312	.352	97	-4	36			.914	-10	3-79,O-44,S-20,2/3	-1.1
1893	NY-N	133	549	112	195	22	27	11	119	42	20	.355	.410	.554	155	40	37			.884	0	*3-133/S-1	3.4
1894	*NY-N	122	477	120	168	26	19	8	91	66	10	.352	.435	.537	134	28	40			.908	-1	*3-122	2.0
1895	NY-N	110	430	108	146	36	9	5	101	55	12	.340	.417	.500	139	26	48			.881	15	3-80,1-14,2-10/OM	3.4
1896	NY-N	124	494	98	158	25	12	6	99	50	24	.320	.387	.455	125	18	48			.917	11	3-74,S-45/O-3,1-3	2.7
1897	NY-N	130	519	112	183	31	10	10	**136**	41		.353	.407	.509	145	33	65			.926	22	*S-129	4.8
1898	NY-N	121	486	80	149	20	5	2	86	32		.307	.351	.381	113	7	26			.933	**35**	*S-121	4.4
1899	NY-N	108	416	68	140	21	5	1	57	37		.337	.393	.418	127	16	34			**.945**	**46**	*S-108	**6.2**
1900	NY-N	114	426	69	136	20	4	3	61	35		.319	.376	.406	121	13	29			**.944**	29	*S-114,M	4.6
1901	NY-N	130	491	69	148	26	7	7	65	40		.301	.356	.426	131	19	27			.939	23	*S-113,3-17,M	4.9
1902	Chi-A	132	485	76	145	27	7	3	93	65		.299	.386	.402	124	19	31			**.951**	-2	*S-129/1-3	2.3
1903	NY-N	4	15	2	4	0	0	0	1	1		.267	.313	.267	63	-1	0			.870	-2	/S-4	-0.2
1904	Chi-A	152	563	75	142	27	15	1	69	43		.252	.311	.359	116	10	32			.937	17	*S-152	3.4
1905	Chi-A	151	550	74	153	29	1	1	55	60		.278	.353	.340	125	18	31			**.948**	17	*S-151	**4.1**
1906	*Chi-A	133	484	63	134	26	6	0	80	41		.277	.338	.355	120	12	27			.946	10	*S-129/2-1	2.8
1907	Chi-A	132	466	59	111	16	2	1	52	47		.238	.313	.288	95	-1	15			.949	8	*S-132	1.1
1908	Chi-A	128	419	41	91	14	1	0	26	41		.217	.298	.255	81	-7	22			.960	4	2-95,S-23/1-4	-0.4
1909	Chi-A	28	68	5	9	1	0	0	2	10		.132	.253	.147	28	-5	4			.986	1	1-17/2-2	-0.5
Total	20	2368	9031	1539	2660	451	163	73	1437	870	<u>180</u>	.295	.361	.405	121	255	616			.940	249	*S-1372,3-527,O2/1P	51.0

■ KIDDO DAVIS

Davis, George Willis b: 2/12/02, Bridgeport, Conn. d: 3/4/83, Bridgeport, Conn. BR/TR, 5'11", 178 lbs. Deb: 6/15/26

YEAR	TM/L	G	AB	R	H	2B	3B	HR	RBI	BB	SO	AVG	OBP	SLG	PRO+	BR/A	SB	CS	SBR	FA	FR	G/POS	TPR
1926	NY-A	1	0	0	0	0	0	0	0	0	0	—	—	—	—	0	0	0	0	.000	-0	/O-1	0.0
1932	Phi-N	137	576	100	178	39	6	5	57	44	56	.309	.359	.424	98	-2	16			.975	14	*O-133	0.4
1933	*NY-N	126	434	61	112	20	4	7	37	25	30	.258	.298	.371	92	-6	10			.988	-10	*O-120	-2.3
1934	StL-N	16	33	6	10	3	0	1	4	3	1	.303	.361	.485	117	1	1			.960	1	/O-9	0.1
	Phi-N	100	393	50	115	25	5	3	48	27	28	.293	.338	.405	86	-8	1			.991	17	*O-100	0.5
	Yr	116	426	56	125	28	5	4	52	30	29	.293	.340	.411	89	-7	2			.988	18	*O-109	0.6
1935	NY-N	47	91	16	24	7	1	2	6	10	4	.264	.343	.429	108	1	2			.977	-1	O-21	-0.1
1936	*NY-N	47	67	6	16	1	0	0	5	6	5	.239	.301	.254	51	-4	0			1.000	-1	O-22	-0.6
1937	NY-N	56	76	20	20	10	0	0	9	10	7	.263	.356	.395	103	0	1			.932	-10	O-37	-1.0
	Cin-N	40	136	19	35	6	0	1	5	16	6	.257	.340	.324	85	-2	1			.959	2	O-35	-1.2
	Yr	96	212	39	55	16	0	1	14	26	13	.259	.346	.349	90	-2	2			.951	-8	O-72	-1.2
1938	Cin-N	5	18	3	5	1	0	0	3	1	0	.278	.316	.333	81	-0	0			1.000	-1	/O-5	-0.1
Total	8	575	1824	281	515	112	16	19	171	142	141	.282	.336	.393	92	-20	32	0		.980	10	O-483	-3.3

■ GERRY DAVIS

Davis, Gerald Edward b: 12/25/58, Trenton, N.J. BR/TR, 6', 185 lbs. Deb: 9/20/83

YEAR	TM/L	G	AB	R	H	2B	3B	HR	RBI	BB	SO	AVG	OBP	SLG	PRO+	BR/A	SB	CS	SBR	FA	FR	G/POS	TPR
1983	SD-N	5	15	3	5	2	0	0	1	3	4	.333	.444	.467	158	1	1	0	0	1.000	1	/O-5	0.2
1985	SD-N	44	58	10	17	3	1	0	2	5	7	.293	.349	.379	105	0	0	0	0	.952	-4	O-23	-0.4
Total	2	49	73	13	22	5	1	0	3	8	11	.301	.370	.397	117	2	1	0	0	.967	-3	/O-28	-0.2

■ GLENN DAVIS

Davis, Glenn Earle b: 3/28/61, Jacksonville, Fla. BR/TR, 6'3", 210 lbs. Deb: 9/2/84

YEAR	TM/L	G	AB	R	H	2B	3B	HR	RBI	BB	SO	AVG	OBP	SLG	PRO+	BR/A	SB	CS	SBR	FA	FR	G/POS	TPR
1984	Hou-N	18	61	6	13	5	0	2	8	4	12	.213	.262	.393	88	-1	0	0	0	.988	2	1-16	0.0
1985	Hou-N	100	350	51	95	11	0	20	64	27	68	.271	.336	.474	128	12	0	0	0	.985	-2	1-89/O-9	0.4
1986	*Hou-N★	158	574	91	152	32	3	31	101	64	72	.265	.348	.493	133	24	3	1	0	.992	2	*1-156	1.6
1987	Hou-N	151	578	70	145	35	2	27	93	47	84	.251	.313	.458	105	2	4	1	1	.991	7	*1-151	-0.6
1988	Hou-N	152	561	78	152	26	0	30	99	53	77	.271	.346	.478	140	27	4	3	-1	**.996**	0	*1-151	1.5
1989	Hou-N★	158	581	87	156	26	1	34	89	69	123	.269	.353	.492	144	32	4	2	0	.992	3	*1-156	2.4
1990	Hou-N	93	327	44	82	15	4	22	64	46	54	.251	.357	.523	143	19	8	3	1	.995	-3	1-91	1.0
1991	Bal-A	49	176	29	40	9	1	10	28	16	29	.227	.310	.460	115	3	4	0	1	.976	2	1-36,D-12	0.5
1992	Bal-A	106	398	46	110	15	2	13	48	37	65	.276	.341	.422	110	5	1	0	0	1.000	-0	*D-103/1-2	0.1
1993	Bal-A	30	113	8	20	1	0	1	9	7	29	.177	.231	.230	24	-12	0	1	-1	.990	-2	1-22/D-7	-1.6
Total	10	1015	3719	510	965	177	13	190	603	370	613	.259	.335	.467	124	111	28	11	2	.991	6	1-870,D-122/O-9	5.3

■ HARRY DAVIS

Davis, Harry Albert "Stinky" b: 5/7/08, Shreveport, La. BL/TL, 5'10.5", 160 lbs. Deb: 4/13/32

YEAR	TM/L	G	AB	R	H	2B	3B	HR	RBI	BB	SO	AVG	OBP	SLG	PRO+	BR/A	SB	CS	SBR	FA	FR	G/POS	TPR
1932	Det-A	141	590	92	159	32	13	4	74	60	53	.269	.339	.388	84	-14	12	7	-1	.989	-5	*1-141	-2.9
1933	Det-A	66	173	24	37	8	2	0	14	22	8	.214	.303	.283	55	-11	7	2	-1	.978	-5	1-44	-2.0
1937	StL-A	120	450	89	124	25	3	3	35	71	26	.276	.374	.364	86	-7	2	7	-2	.991	-4	1-112/O-1	-2.4
Total	3	327	1213	205	320	65	18	7	123	153	87	.264	.347	.364	81	-32	21	16	-3	.988	-14	1-297/O-1	-7.3

YEAR	TM/L	G	AB	R	H	2B	3B	HR	RBI	BB	SO	AVG	OBP	SLG	PRO+	BR/A	SB	CS	SBR	FA	FR	G/POS	TPR

■ HARRY DAVIS   Davis, Harry H (b: Harry Davis) "Jasper"   b: 7/19/1873, Philadelphia, Pa.   d: 8/11/47, Philadelphia, Pa.   BR/TR, 5'10", 180 lbs.   Deb: 9/21/1895   M

YEAR	TM/L	G	AB	R	H	2B	3B	HR	RBI	BB	SO	AVG	OBP	SLG	PRO+	BR/A	SB	CS	SBR	FA	FR	G/POS	TPR
1895	NY-N	7	24	1	7	0	1	0	6	2	0	.292	.346	.375	88	-0	1			.957	0	/1-7	0.0
1896	NY-N	64	233	43	64	11	10	2	50	31	20	.275	.372	.433	115	5	16			.883	-4	O-40,1-23	-0.1
	Pit-N	44	168	24	32	5	6	0	23	13	21	.190	.257	.292	46	-14	9			.966	0	1-35,O-10/S-1	-1.2
	Yr	108	401	67	96	16	16	2	73	44	41	.239	.325	.374	87	-8	25			.973	-4	1-58,O-50/S-1	-1.3
1897	Pit-N	111	429	70	131	10	28	2	63	26		.305	.359	.473	123	13	21			.965	-12	1-64,3-32,O-14,/S-1	0.1
1898	Pit-N	58	222	31	65	9	13	1	24	12		.293	.332	.464	130	7	7			.980	0	1-53/O-6	0.4
	Lou-N	37	138	18	30	5	2	1	16	7		.217	.255	.304	61	-7	6			.967	0	1-34/2-2,O-1	-0.7
	Was-N	1	3	0	0	0	0	0	0	0		.000	.000	.000	-99	-1	0			.875	-1	/1-1	-0.1
	Yr	96	363	49	95	14	15	2	40	19		.262	.300	.399	102	-1	13			.974	-2	1-88/O-7,2-2	-0.4
1899	Was-N	18	64	3	12	2	3	0	8	8		.188	.288	.313	65	-3	2			.988	1	1-18	-0.4
1901	Phi-A	117	496	92	152	28	10	8	76	23		.306	.340	.452	113	6	21			.976	8	*1-117	1.2
1902	Phi-A	133	561	89	172	**43**	8	6	92	30		.307	.343	.444	112	7	28			.984	7	*1-128/O-5	1.1
1903	Phi-A	106	420	77	125	28	7	6	55	24		.298	.343	.440	128	13	24			.972	-1	*1-104/O-2	1.1
1904	Phi-A	102	404	54	125	21	11	**10**	62	23		.309	.350	.490	156	24	12			.983	-1	*1-102	2.3
1905	*Phi-A	150	607	**93**	173	**47**	6	**8**	**83**	43		.285	.334	.422	137	23	36			.985	1	*1-150	2.1
1906	Phi-A	145	551	94	161	42	7	**12**	**96**	49		.292	.355	.459	150	30	23			.975	-0	*1-145	2.8
1907	Phi-A	149	582	84	155	**35**	8	8	87	42		.266	.318	.395	124	14	20			.977	4	*1-149	1.5
1908	Phi-A	147	513	65	127	23	9	5	62	61		.248	.332	.357	116	10	20			.986	1	*1-147	0.9
1909	Phi-A	149	530	73	142	22	11	4	75	51		.268	.338	.374	122	13	20			.988	-5	*1-149	0.8
1910	*Phi-A	139	492	61	122	19	4	1	41	53		.248	.332	.309	102	3	17			.986	-4	*1-139	-0.2
1911	*Phi-A	57	183	27	36	9	1	1	22	24		.197	.297	.273	60	-9	2			.977	2	1-53	-0.8
1912	Cle-A	2	5	0	0	0	0	0	0	0		.000	.000	.000	-97	-0	0			.941	0	/1-2,M	-0.1
1913	Phi-A	7	17	2	6	2	0	0	4	1	4	.353	.389	.471	155	1	0			1.000	1	/1-6	0.2
1914	Phi-A	5	7	0	3	1	0	0	2	1	0	.429	.556	.429	204	1	0	2	-1	1.000	-0	/1-1	0.0
1915	Phi-A	5	3	0	1	0	0	0	4	0	0	.333	.333	.333	103	-0	0			.000	0	/1-1	0.0
1916	Phi-A	1	0	0	0	0	0	0	0	1	0	—	1.000	—	213	-0	0			.000	0	H	0.0
1917	Phi-A	1	1	0	0	0	0	0	0	0		.000	.000	.000	-99	-0	0			.000	0	H	0.0
Total	22	1755	6653	1001	1841	361	145	75	951	525	45	.277	.335	.408	119	135	285	2		.980	-7	*1-1628/O-78,32S	10.9

■ TOMMY DAVIS   Davis, Herman Thomas   b: 3/21/39, Brooklyn, N.Y.   BR/TR, 6'2", 205 lbs.   Deb: 9/22/59   C

YEAR	TM/L	G	AB	R	H	2B	3B	HR	RBI	BB	SO	AVG	OBP	SLG	PRO+	BR/A	SB	CS	SBR	FA	FR	G/POS	TPR
1959	LA-N	1	1	0	0	0	0	0	0	0	0	.000	.000	.000	-93	-0	0	0	0	.000	0	H	0.0
1960	LA-N	110	352	43	97	18	1	11	44	13	35	.276	.305	.426	92	-5	6	2	1	.975	-0	O-87/3-5	-0.9
1961	LA-N	132	460	60	128	13	2	15	58	32	53	.278	.328	.413	87	-9	10	4	1	.973	-12	O-86,3-59	-2.4
1962	LA-N★	163	665	120	**230**	27	9	27	**153**	33	65	**.346**	.379	.535	151	45	18	6	2	.961	1	*O-146,3-39	3.9
1963	*LA-N★	146	556	69	181	19	3	16	88	29	59	**.326**	.363	.457	144	30	15	10	-2	.969	-7	*O-129,3-40	1.6
1964	LA-N	152	592	70	163	20	5	14	86	29	68	.275	.314	.397	106	3	11	8	-2	.982	14	*O-148	0.8
1965	LA-N	17	60	3	15	1	1	0	9	2	4	.250	.274	.300	66	-3	2	1	0	1.000	0	O-16	-0.4
1966	*LA-N	100	313	27	98	11	1	3	27	16	36	.313	.347	.383	111	4	3	3	-1	.972	-2	O-79/3-2	-0.3
1967	NY-N	154	577	72	174	32	0	16	73	31	71	.302	.345	.440	125	17	9	3	0	.975	-2	*O-149/1-1	0.9
1968	Chi-A	132	456	30	122	5	3	8	50	16	48	.268	.292	.344	91	-6	4	2	0	.962	-4	O-116/1-6	-1.9
1969	Sea-A	123	454	52	123	29	1	6	80	30	46	.271	.322	.379	97	-3	19	4	3	.967	-7	*O-112/1-1	-1.3
	Hou-N	24	79	2	19	3	0	1	9	8	9	.241	.318	.316	80	-2	1	1	-0	1.000	0	O-21	-0.4
1970	Hou-N	57	213	24	60	12	2	3	30	7	25	.282	.305	.399	91	-4	3	1	0	.949	-4	O-53	-0.7
	Chi-N	11	42	4	11	2	0	2	8	1	1	.262	.279	.452	83	-1	0	0	0	.938	-1	O-10	-0.2
	Yr	68	255	28	71	14	2	5	38	8	26	.278	.300	.408	89	-5	3	1	0	.947	-2	O-63	-0.9
	Oak-A	66	200	17	58	9	1	1	27	8	18	.290	.321	.360	91	-3	2	4	-2	.963	-7	O-45/1-8	-1.5
1971	*Oak-A	79	219	26	71	8	1	3	42	15	19	.324	.368	.411	123	6	7	1	2	.989	2	1-35,O-16/2-3,3-2	0.7
1972	Chi-N	15	26	3	7	1	0	0	6	2	3	.269	.321	.308	72	-1	0	1	-1	1.000	0	/1-3,O-2	-0.2
	Bal-A	26	82	9	21	3	0	2	6	6	18	.256	.307	.293	77	-2	0	0	1	1.000	0	O-18/1-3	-0.3
1973	*Bal-A	137	552	53	169	20	3	7	89	30	56	.306	.343	.391	107	5	11	3	2	.971	-0	*D-127/1-4	0.2
1974	*Bal-A	158	626	67	181	20	1	11	84	34	49	.289	.329	.377	106	4	6	2	1	.000	0	*D-155	0.0
1975	Bal-A	116	460	43	130	14	1	6	57	23	52	.283	.317	.357	96	-2	2	0	1	.000	0	*D-111	-0.6
1976	Cal-A	72	219	16	58	5	0	3	26	15	18	.265	.315	.329	95	-2	0	1	-1	1.000	-0	D-54/1-1	-0.4
	KC-A	8	19	1	5	0	0	0	0	1	0	.263	.300	.263	65	-1	0	0	0	.000	0	/D-3	-0.1
	Yr	80	238	17	63	5	0	3	26	16	18	.265	.314	.324	92	-3	0	1	-1	1.000	-0	D-54/H-3,1-1	-0.4
Total	18	1999	7223	811	2121	272	35	153	1052	381	754	.294	.332	.405	109	68	136	59	5	.970	-27	*O-1233,D-450,3/12	-3.5

■ IKE DAVIS   Davis, Isaac Marion   b: 6/14/1895, Pueblo, Col.   d: 4/2/84, Tucson, Ariz.   BR/TR, 5'7", 140 lbs.   Deb: 4/23/19

YEAR	TM/L	G	AB	R	H	2B	3B	HR	RBI	BB	SO	AVG	OBP	SLG	PRO+	BR/A	SB	CS	SBR	FA	FR	G/POS	TPR
1919	Was-A	8	14	0	0	0	0	0	0	0	6	.000	.000	.000	-99	-4				.857	-2	/S-4	-0.6
1924	Chi-A	10	33	5	8	1	1	0	4	2	5	.242	.286	.333	61	-2	0	0	0	.940	1	S-10	0.0
1925	Chi-A	146	562	105	135	31	9	0	61	71	58	.240	.333	.327	72	-24	19	14	-3	.937	8	S-144	-0.3
Total	3	164	609	110	143	32	10	0	65	73	69	.235	.324	.320	68	-29	19	14		.936	8	S-158	-0.9

■ IRA DAVIS   Davis, J. Ira "Slats"   b: 7/8/1870, Philadelphia, Pa.   d: 12/21/42, Brooklyn, N.Y.   162 lbs.   Deb: 4/22/1899

YEAR	TM/L	G	AB	R	H	2B	3B	HR	RBI	BB	SO	AVG	OBP	SLG	PRO+	BR/A	SB	CS	SBR	FA	FR	G/POS	TPR
1899	NY-N	6	17	3	4	1	1	0	2	0		.235	.235	.412	79	-1	1			.750	-0	/S-3,1-2	-0.1

■ JACKE DAVIS   Davis, Jacke Sylvesta   b: 3/5/36, Carthage, Tex.   BR/TR, 5'11", 160 lbs.   Deb: 4/19/62

YEAR	TM/L	G	AB	R	H	2B	3B	HR	RBI	BB	SO	AVG	OBP	SLG	PRO+	BR/A	SB	CS	SBR	FA	FR	G/POS	TPR
1962	Phi-N	48	75	9	16	0	1	1	6	4	20	.213	.253	.280	44	-6	1	0	0	.926	-6	O-26	-1.2

■ JUMBO DAVIS   Davis, James J.   b: 9/5/1861, New York, N.Y.   d: 2/14/21, St.Louis, Mo.   BL/TR, 5'11", 195 lbs.   Deb: 7/27/1884   U

YEAR	TM/L	G	AB	R	H	2B	3B	HR	RBI	BB	SO	AVG	OBP	SLG	PRO+	BR/A	SB	CS	SBR	FA	FR	G/POS	TPR
1884	KC-U	7	29	3	6	0	0	0		.207	.207	.207	30	-3					.633	-2	/3-7	-0.5
1886	Bal-a	60	216	23	42	5	2	1	20	11		.194	.240	.250	55	-11	12			.848	5	3-60	-0.4
1887	Bal-a	130	485	81	150	23	**19**	8	109	28		.309	.353	.485	141	25	49			.826	4	3-87,S-43	2.4
1888	KC-a	121	491	70	131	22	8	3	61	20		.267	.304	.363	106	1	42			.843	30	*3-113/S-8	3.0
1889	KC-a	62	241	40	64	4	3	0	30	17	35	.266	.319	.307	74	-9	25			.803	-1	3-62	-0.6
	StL-a	2	4	1	0	0	0	0	0	1	1	.000	.200	.000	-36	-1	0			1.000	-0	/S-1,O-1	-0.1
	Yr	64	245	41	64	4	3	0	30	18	36	.261	.317	.302	72	-9	25			.803	-1	3-62/S-1,O-1	-0.7
1890	StL-a	21	71	8	18	3	1	0	13	9		.254	.338	.324	83	-2	5			.731	-1	3-21	-0.2
	Bro-a	38	142	33	43	9	2	2	28	15		.303	.385	.437	147	8	10			.845	-5	3-38	0.4
	Yr	59	213	41	61	12	3	2	41	24		.286	.369	.399	123	6	15			.800	-5	3-59	0.2
1891	Was-a	12	44	7	14	3	0	0	9	7	5	.318	.412	.477	162	4	8			.820	-2	3-12	0.2
Total	7	453	1723	266	468	69	37	14	**270**	108	**41**	.272	.322	.379	107	12	151			.824	28	3-400/S-52,O-1	4.2

■ JODY DAVIS   Davis, Jody Richard   b: 11/12/56, Gainesville, Ga.   BR/TR, 6'3", 210 lbs.   Deb: 4/21/81

YEAR	TM/L	G	AB	R	H	2B	3B	HR	RBI	BB	SO	AVG	OBP	SLG	PRO+	BR/A	SB	CS	SBR	FA	FR	G/POS	TPR
1981	Chi-N	56	180	14	46	5	1	4	21	21	28	.256	.337	.361	94	-1	0	1	-1	.972	-1	C-56	-0.1
1982	Chi-N	130	418	41	109	20	2	12	52	36	92	.261	.321	.404	99	-1	0	1	-1	.984	8	*C-129	1.1
1983	Chi-N	151	510	56	138	31	2	24	84	59	93	.271	.317	.480	113	7	0	2	-1	.984	-14	*C-150	-0.2
1984	*Chi-N★	150	523	55	134	25	2	19	94	47	99	.256	.319	.421	97	-3	5	6	-2	.984	4	*C-146	0.7
1985	Chi-N	142	482	47	112	30	0	17	58	48	83	.232	.302	.400	85	-10	1	0	0	.990	-1	*C-138	-0.4
1986	Chi-N★	148	528	61	132	27	2	21	74	41	110	.250	.304	.428	92	-7	0	1	-1	.992	0	*C-145/1-1	0.6
1987	Chi-N	125	428	57	106	12	2	19	51	52	91	.248	.332	.418	93	-4	1	0	0	.989	-3	*C-123	0.1
1988	Chi-N	88	249	19	57	9	0	6	33	29	51	.229	.312	.337	83	-5	0	3	-2	.995	-4	C-74	-0.7
	Atl-N	2	8	2	2	0	0	1	3	0	1	.250	.250	.625	137	0	0	0	0	1.000	1	/C-2	0.1
	Yr	90	257	21	59	9	0	7	36	29	52	.230	.310	.346	84	-5	0	3	-2	.995	-4	C-76	-0.6
1989	Atl-N	78	231	12	39	5	1	4	19	23	61	.169	.247	.242	39	-18	0	0	0	.985	-9	C-72/1-2	-2.6
1990	Atl-N	12	28	0	2	0	0	0	3	0	8	.071	.161	.071	-32	-5	0	0	0	1.000	0	/1-6,C-4	-0.4
Total	10	1082	3585	364	877	164	11	127	490	333	712	.245	.310	.403	91	-48	7	16	-8	.987	-15	*C-1039/1-9	-1.8

■ JOHN DAVIS   Davis, John Humphrey "Red"   b: 7/15/15, Laurel Run, Pa.   BR/TR, 5'11", 172 lbs.   Deb: 9/9/41

YEAR	TM/L	G	AB	R	H	2B	3B	HR	RBI	BB	SO	AVG	OBP	SLG	PRO+	BR/A	SB	CS	SBR	FA	FR	G/POS	TPR
1941	NY-N	21	70	8	15	3	0	0	5	8	12	.214	.295	.257	55	-4	0			.970	1	3-21	-0.2

YEAR	TM/L	G	AB	R	H	2B	3B	HR	RBI	BB	SO	AVG	OBP	SLG	PRO+	BR/A	SB	CS	SBR	FA	FR	G/POS	TPR

■ CRASH DAVIS   Davis, Lawrence Columbus b: 7/14/19, Canon, Ga. BR/TR, 6′, 173 lbs. Deb: 6/15/40

1940	Phi-A	23	67	4	18	1	1	0	9	3	10	.269	.310	.313	63	-4	1	0	0	.963	4	2-19/S-1	0.1
1941	Phi-A	39	105	8	23	3	0	0	8	11	16	.219	.293	.248	45	-8	0	0	0	.952	2	2-20,1-12	-0.5
1942	Phi-A	86	272	31	61	8	1	2	26	21	30	.224	.282	.283	60	-15	1	0	0	.965	-6	2-57,S-26/1-3	-1.6
Total	3	148	444	43	102	12	2	2	43	35	56	.230	.289	.279	57	-26	2	0	1	.961	0	/2-96,S-27,1-15	-2.0

■ MARK DAVIS   Davis, Mark Anthony b: 11/25/64, San Diego, Cal. BR/TR, 6′, 180 lbs. Deb: 7/2/91 F

1991	Cal-A	3	2	0	0	0	0	0	0	0	0	.000	.000	.000	-99	-1	0	0	0	.500	-1	/O-3	-0.2

■ MIKE DAVIS   Davis, Michael Dwayne b: 6/11/59, San Diego, Cal. BL/TL, 6′3″, 185 lbs. Deb: 4/10/80 F

1980	Oak-A	51	95	11	20	2	1	1	8	7	14	.211	.265	.284	54	-6	2	1	0	1.000	1	O-18/1-7,D-6	-0.6
1981	*Oak-A	17	20	0	1	1	0	0	0	2	4	.050	.136	.100	-33	-3	0	0	0	1.000	-0	/O-2,1-1,D-3	-0.4
1982	Oak-A	23	75	12	30	4	0	1	10	2	8	.400	.416	.493	155	5	3	2	-0	.946	-1	O-13/1-7	0.4
1983	Oak-A	128	443	61	122	24	4	8	62	27	74	.275	.324	.402	105	2	32	15	1	.974	9	*O-121/D-3	0.8
1984	Oak-A	134	382	47	88	18	3	9	46	31	66	.230	.290	.364	85	-9	14	9	-1	.961	-1	*O-127/D-4	-1.4
1985	Oak-A	154	547	92	157	34	1	24	82	50	99	.287	.349	.484	135	25	24	10	1	.979	2	*O-151	2.3
1986	Oak-A	142	489	77	131	28	3	19	55	34	91	.268	.317	.454	115	8	27	4	6	.973	2	*O-139	1.1
1987	Oak-A	139	494	69	131	32	1	22	72	42	94	.265	.324	.468	114	8	19	7	2	.942	-7	*O-124,D-14	-0.1
1988	*LA-N	108	281	29	55	11	2	2	17	25	59	.196	.261	.270	55	-17	7	3	0	.961	-9	O-76	-3.0
1989	LA-N	67	173	21	43	7	1	5	19	16	28	.249	.312	.387	101	-0	6	5	-1	.987	-3	O-48	-0.6
Total	10	963	2999	419	778	161	16	91	371	236	537	.259	.316	.415	105	14	134	56	7	.968	-8	O-819/D-30,1-15	-1.5

■ ODIE DAVIS   Davis, Odie Ernest b: 8/13/55, San Antonio, Tex. BR/TR, 6′1″, 178 lbs. Deb: 9/3/80

1980	Tex-A	17	8	0	1	0	0	0	0	0	2	.125	.125	.125	-32	-1	0	0	0	.880	5	S-13/3-1	0.3

■ OTIS DAVIS   Davis, Otis Allen "Scat" b: 9/24/20, Charleston, Ark. BL/TL, 6′, 160 lbs. Deb: 4/22/46

1946	Bro-N	1	0	1	0	0	0	0	0	0	0	—	—	—	—	0	0			1.000	0	R	0.0

■ DICK DAVIS   Davis, Richard Earl b: 9/25/53, Long Beach, Cal. BR/TR, 6′3″, 195 lbs. Deb: 7/12/77

1977	Mil-A	22	51	7	14	2	0	0	6	1	8	.275	.288	.314	64	-3	0	0	0	1.000	-2	O-12/D-6	-0.5
1978	Mil-A	69	218	28	54	10	1	5	26	7	23	.248	.278	.372	81	-6	2	5	-2	1.000	-1	D-34,O-28	-1.2
1979	Mil-A	91	335	51	89	13	1	12	41	16	46	.266	.299	.418	91	-5	3	3	-1	.973	-0	D-53,O-35	-0.9
1980	Mil-A	106	365	50	99	26	2	4	30	11	43	.271	.298	.386	89	-7	5	3	-0	.971	-2	D-63,O-38	-1.3
1981	*Phi-N	45	96	12	32	6	1	2	19	8	13	.333	.390	.479	139	5	3	2	-1	.974	-4	O-32	-0.1
1982	Phi-N	28	68	5	19	3	1	2	7	2	9	.279	.300	.441	103	-0	1	0	0	1.000	-0	O-16	0.0
	Tor-A	3	7	0	2	0	0	0	2	0	1	.286	.286	.286	53	-0	0	0	0	1.000	-0	/O-1,D-1	-0.1
	Pit-N	39	77	7	14	2	1	2	10	5	9	.182	.232	.312	49	-5	0	0	0	.971	-4	O-28	-1.0
Total	6	403	1217	160	323	62	7	27	141	50	152	.265	.298	.394	89	-22	13	13	-4	.981	-14	O-190,D-157	-5.1

■ BRANDY DAVIS   Davis, Robert Brandon b: 9/10/28, Newark, Del. BR/TR, 6′, 170 lbs. Deb: 4/15/52 C

1952	Pit-N	55	95	14	17	1	1	0	1	11	28	.179	.264	.211	32	-9	9	2	2	.932	-3	O-29	-1.1
1953	Pit-N	12	39	5	8	2	0	0	2	0	3	.205	.205	.256	20	-5	2	2	-1	.955	0	/O-9	-0.6
Total	2	67	134	19	25	3	1	0	3	11	31	.187	.248	.224	29	-13	9	4	0	.938	-3	/O-38	-1.7

■ BOB DAVIS   Davis, Robert John Eugene b: 3/1/52, Pryor, Okla. BR/TR, 6′, 180 lbs. Deb: 4/6/73

1973	SD-N	5	11	1	1	0	0	0	0	0	5	.091	.091	.091	-54	-2	0	0	0	.941	2	/C-5	-0.1
1975	SD-N	43	128	6	30	3	2	0	7	11	31	.234	.310	.289	71	-5	0	0	0	.986	3	C-43	0.0
1976	SD-N	51	83	7	17	0	1	0	5	5	13	.205	.250	.229	40	-7	0	0	0	.965	4	C-47	-0.2
1977	SD-N	48	94	9	17	2	0	1	10	5	24	.181	.238	.234	30	-10	0	0	0	.975	-1	C-46	-1.0
1978	SD-N	19	40	3	8	1	0	0	2	1	5	.200	.220	.225	26	-4	0	1	-1	.960	-2	C-16	-0.7
1979	Tor-A	32	89	6	11	2	0	1	8	6	11	.124	.188	.180	-0	-13	0	0	0	.984	-2	C-32	-1.3
1980	Tor-A	91	218	18	47	11	0	4	19	12	48	.216	.260	.321	56	-14	0	0	0	.983	-2	C-89	-1.3
1981	Cal-A	1	2	0	0	0	0	0	0	0	1	.000	.000	.000	-99	-1	0	0	0	1.000	-0	/C-1	-0.1
Total	8	290	665	50	131	19	3	6	51	40	118	.197	.250	.262	42	-54	0	1	-1	.978	0	C-279	-4.7

■ RON DAVIS   Davis, Ronald Everette b: 10/21/41, Roanoke Rapids, N.C d: 9/5/92, Houston, Tex. BR/TR, 6′, 180 lbs. Deb: 8/1/62

1962	Hou-N	6	14	1	3	1	0	0	1	1	7	.214	.267	.214	33	-1	1	0	0	1.000	-1	/O-5	-0.2
1966	Hou-N	48	194	21	48	10	1	2	19	13	26	.247	.308	.340	86	-4	2	2	-1	.982	6	O-48	-0.1
1967	Hou-N	94	285	31	73	19	1	7	38	17	48	.256	.303	.404	104	0	5	3	-0	.976	-0	O-80	-0.4
1968	Hou-N	52	217	22	46	10	1	2	12	13	48	.212	.269	.281	67	-9	0	4	-2	.971	6	O-52	-0.9
	*StL-N	33	79	11	14	4	2	0	5	5	17	.177	.226	.278	51	-5	1	0	0	.979	0	O-25	-0.6
	Yr	85	296	33	60	14	3	2	17	18	65	.203	.258	.280	63	-14	1	4	-2	.973	6	O-77	-1.5
1969	Pit-N	62	64	10	15	0	0	0	4	7	14	.234	.310	.281	68	-3	0	0	0	.933	-13	O-51	-1.8
Total	5	295	853	96	199	44	6	10	79	56	160	.233	.288	.334	82	-21	9	9	-3	.974	-2	O-261	-4.0

■ RUSS DAVIS   Davis, Russell Stuart b: 9/13/69, Birmingham, Ala. BR/TR, 6′, 170 lbs. Deb: 7/6/94

1994	NY-A	4	14	0	2	0	0	0	1	0	4	.143	.143	.143	-27	-3	0	0	0	1.000	0	/3-4	-0.3
1995	*NY-A	40	98	14	27	5	2	2	12	10	26	.276	.349	.429	102	0	0	0	0	.968	3	3-34/1-2,D-4	0.3
1996	Sea-A	51	167	24	39	9	0	5	18	17	50	.234	.312	.377	73	-7	2	0	1	.933	-8	3-51	-1.3
Total	3	95	279	38	68	14	2	7	31	27	80	.244	.317	.384	79	-9	2	0	1	.949	-5	/3-89,D-4,1-2	-1.3

■ STEVE DAVIS   Davis, Steven Michael b: 12/30/53, Oakland, Cal. BR/TR, 6′1″, 200 lbs. Deb: 9/23/79

1979	Chi-N	3	4	0	0	0	0	0	0	0	0	.000	.000	.000	-99	-1	0	0	0	1.000	0	/2-3,3-1	-0.1

■ TOD DAVIS   Davis, Thomas Oscar b: 7/24/24, Los Angeles, Cal. d: 12/31/78, W.Covina, Cal. BR/TR, 6′2″, 190 lbs. Deb: 4/27/49

1949	Phi-A	31	75	7	20	1	1	0	6	9	16	.267	.345	.333	83	-2	1			.912	-1	S-14,3-12/2-1	-0.2
1951	Phi-A	11	15	0	1	0	0	0	0	1	3	.067	.125	.067	-46	-3	0	0	0	1.000	-0	/2-2,3-1	-0.3
Total	2	42	90	7	21	1	1	0	6	10	19	.233	.310	.289	61	-5	1			.966	-1	/S-14,3-13,2-3	-0.5

■ TRENCH DAVIS   Davis, Trench Neal b: 9/12/60, Baltimore, Md. BL/TL, 6′3″, 171 lbs. Deb: 6/4/85

1985	Pit-N	2	7	1	1	0	0	0	0	0	0	.143	.143	.143	-20	-1	1	0	0	.667	-1	/O-2	-0.2
1986	Pit-N	15	23	2	3	0	0	0	1	0	4	.130	.130	.130	-27	-4	0	0	0	.917	-0	/O-7	-0.5
1987	Atl-N	6	3	0	0	0	0	0	0	0	0	.000	.000	.000	-95	-2	0	0	0	.000	0	/H	-0.1
Total	3	23	33	3	4	0	0	0	1	0	5	.121	.121	.121	-32	-6	1	0	0	.867	-1	/O-9	-0.8

■ SPUD DAVIS   Davis, Virgil Lawrence b: 12/20/04, Birmingham, Ala. d: 8/14/84, Birmingham, Ala. BR/TR, 6′1″, 197 lbs. Deb: 4/30/28 MC

1928	StL-N	2	5	1	1	0	0	0	1	1	0	.200	.333	.200	42	-0	0			.750	-1	/C-2	-0.1
	Phi-N	67	163	16	46	2	0	3	18	15	11	.282	.343	.350	79	-5	0			.980	3	C-49	0.2
	Yr	69	168	17	47	2	0	3	19	16	11	.280	.342	.345	78	-5	0			.971	2	C-51	0.1
1929	Phi-N	98	263	31	90	18	0	7	48	19	17	.342	.391	.490	110	4	1			.961	-12	C-89	-0.1
1930	Phi-N	106	329	41	103	16	1	14	65	17	20	.313	.349	.495	94	-4	1			.986	-2	C-96	0.1
1931	Phi-N	120	393	30	128	32	1	4	51	36	28	.326	.382	.443	112	7	0			.994	1	*C-114	1.6
1932	Phi-N	125	402	44	135	23	5	14	70	40	39	.336	.399	.522	130	17	1			.987	-3	*C-120	2.0
1933	Phi-N	141	495	51	173	28	9	9	65	39	24	.349	.395	.473	130	19	2			.983	-11	*C-132	1.7
1934	*StL-N	107	347	45	104	24	4	9	65	34	27	.300	.366	.464	113	6	0			.988	1	C-94	1.2
1935	StL-N	102	315	28	100	24	2	6	60	30	30	.317	.386	.416	111	6	0			**.992**	-5	C-81/1-5	0.4
1936	StL-N	112	363	24	99	26	2	4	59	35	34	.273	.342	.388	97	-2	0			.985	-13	*C-103/3-2	-1.0
1937	Cin-N	76	209	19	56	10	1	3	33	23	15	.268	.341	.368	97	-1	0			.980	12	C-59	1.4
1938	Cin-N	12	36	3	6	1	0	0	1	5	6	.167	.286	.194	35	-3	0			.962	-0	C-11	-0.2
	Phi-N	70	215	11	53	7	0	2	23	14	14	.247	.293	.307	67	-10	1			.980	-12	C-63	-1.9
	Yr	82	251	14	59	8	0	2	24	19	20	.235	.292	.291	62	-13	1			.977	-12	C-74	-2.1
1939	Phi-N	87	202	10	62	8	1	0	24	14	20	.307	.383	.356	103	2	0			**1.000**	-2	C-85	0.3

YEAR	TM/L	G	AB	R	H	2B	3B	HR	RBI	BB	SO	AVG	OBP	SLG	PRO+	BR/A	SB	CS	SBR	FA	FR	G/POS	TPR
1940	Pit-N	99	285	23	93	14	1	5	39	35	20	.326	.404	.435	132	14	0			.967	-6	C-87	1.4
1941	Pit-N	57	107	3	27	4	1	0	6	11	11	.252	.322	.308	78	-3	0			1.000	-2	C-49	-0.2
1944	Pit-N	54	93	6	28	7	0	2	14	10	8	.301	.369	.441	122	3	0			.966	-1	C-35	0.3
1945	Pit-N	23	33	2	8	2	0	0	6	2	2	.242	.306	.303	67	-1	0			.968	-0	C-13	-0.1
Total	16	1458	4255	388	1312	244	22	77	647	386	326	.308	.369	.430	108	49	6			.984	-55	*C-1282/1-5,3-2	7.0

■ BUTCH DAVIS   Davis, Wallace McArthur b: 6/19/58, Martin Co., N.C.   BR/TR, 6′, 190 lbs.   Deb: 8/23/83

YEAR	TM/L	G	AB	R	H	2B	3B	HR	RBI	BB	SO	AVG	OBP	SLG	PRO+	BR/A	SB	CS	SBR	FA	FR	G/POS	TPR
1983	KC-A	33	122	13	42	2	6	2	18	4	19	.344	.365	.508	137	6	4	3	-1	.977	2	O-33	0.6
1984	KC-A	41	116	11	17	3	0	2	12	10	19	.147	.214	.224	21	-12	4	3	-1	.959	-1	O-35/D-2	-1.5
1987	Pit-N	7	7	3	1	1	0	0	0	1	3	.143	.250	.286	41	-1	0	0	0	1.000	0	/O-1	0.0
1988	Bal-A	13	25	2	6	1	0	0	0	0	6	.240	.240	.280	46	-2	1	0	0	1.000	-0	O-10/D-1	-0.2
1989	Bal-A	5	6	1	1	1	0	0	0	0	3	.167	.167	.333	39	-1	0	0	0	1.000	-0	/O-3,D-1	-0.1
1991	LA-N	1	1	0	0	0	0	0	0	0	0	.000	.000	.000	-99	-0	0	0	0	.000	0	/H	0.0
1993	Tex-A	62	159	24	39	10	4	3	20	5	28	.245	.273	.415	85	-4	3	1	0	.960	-2	O-44,D-11	-0.6
1994	Tex-A	4	17	2	4	3	0	0	0	0	3	.235	.235	.412	63	-1	1	0	0	1.000	1	/O-4	0.0
Total	8	166	453	56	110	21	10	7	50	20	83	.243	.276	.380	78	-15	13	7	-0	.969	-1	O-130/D-15	-1.8

■ WILLIE DAVIS   Davis, William Henry b: 4/15/40, Mineral Springs, Ark.   BL/TL, 6′2.5″, 181 lbs.   Deb: 9/8/60

YEAR	TM/L	G	AB	R	H	2B	3B	HR	RBI	BB	SO	AVG	OBP	SLG	PRO+	BR/A	SB	CS	SBR	FA	FR	G/POS	TPR
1960	LA-N	22	88	12	28	6	1	2	10	4	12	.318	.348	.477	116	2	3	5	-2	.981	1	O-22	-0.1
1961	LA-N	128	339	56	86	19	6	12	45	27	46	.254	.318	.451	93	-4	12	5	1	.983	-3	*O-114	-1.1
1962	LA-N	157	600	103	171	18	**10**	21	85	42	72	.285	.338	.453	117	13	32	7	5	.963	13	*O-156	2.1
1963	*LA-N	156	515	60	126	19	8	9	60	25	61	.245	.284	.365	92	-8	25	11	1	.978	14	*O-153	0.0
1964	LA-N	157	613	91	180	23	7	12	77	22	59	.294	.319	.413	112	7	42	13	5	.983	25	*O-155	3.1
1965	*LA-N	142	558	52	133	24	3	10	57	14	81	.238	.266	.346	76	-20	25	9	2	.967	9	*O-141	-1.6
1966	*LA-N	153	624	74	177	31	6	11	61	15	68	.284	.305	.405	104	-0	21	10	0	.970	9	*O-152	0.3
1967	LA-N	143	569	65	146	27	9	6	41	29	65	.257	.296	.367	97	-5	20	6	2	.971	3	*O-138	-0.7
1968	LA-N	160	643	86	161	24	10	7	31	31	88	.250	.286	.351	98	-5	36	10	5	.973	5	*O-158	-0.4
1969	LA-N	129	498	66	155	23	8	11	59	33	39	.311	.359	.456	136	22	24	10	1	.979	5	*O-125	2.2
1970	LA-N	146	593	92	181	23	**16**	8	93	29	54	.305	.339	.438	111	7	38	14	3	.992	15	*O-143	1.7
1971	LA-N★	158	641	84	198	33	10	10	74	23	47	.309	.333	.438	124	17	20	8	1	.981	12	*O-157	2.3
1972	LA-N	149	615	81	178	22	7	19	79	27	61	.289	.320	.441	117	11	20	3	4	.987	11	*O-146	2.0
1973	LA-N★	152	599	82	171	29	9	16	77	29	62	.285	.324	.444	116	10	17	5	2	.980	4	*O-146	0.9
1974	Mon-N	153	611	86	180	27	9	12	89	27	69	.295	.328	.427	104	1	25	7	3	.969	6	*O-151	0.4
1975	Tex-A	42	169	16	42	8	2	5	17	4	25	.249	.270	.408	90	-1	13	5	1	.990	-1	O-42	-0.5
	StL-N	98	350	41	102	19	6	6	50	14	27	.291	.326	.431	105	1	10	1	2	.970	2	O-89	0.3
1976	SD-N	141	493	61	132	18	10	5	46	19	34	.268	.298	.375	98	-4	14	2	3	.992	5	*O-128	0.2
1979	*Cal-A	43	56	9	14	2	1	0	2	4	6	.250	.300	.321	70	-2	1	0	0	1.000	-1	/O-7,D-6	-0.3
Total	18	2429	9174	1217	2561	395	138	182	1053	418	977	.279	.314	.412	106	40	398	131	41	.978	137	*O-2323/D-6	10.8

■ ANDRE DAWSON   Dawson, Andre Nolan b: 7/10/54, Miami, Fla.   BR/TR, 6′3″, 195 lbs.   Deb: 9/11/76

YEAR	TM/L	G	AB	R	H	2B	3B	HR	RBI	BB	SO	AVG	OBP	SLG	PRO+	BR/A	SB	CS	SBR	FA	FR	G/POS	TPR
1976	Mon-N	24	85	9	20	4	1	0	7	5	13	.235	.278	.306	63	-4	1	2	-1	.969	0	O-24	-0.4
1977	Mon-N	139	525	64	148	26	9	19	65	34	93	.282	.328	.474	116	9	21	7	2	.989	7	*O-136	1.3
1978	Mon-N	157	609	84	154	24	8	25	72	30	128	.253	.301	.442	106	2	28	11	2	.988	21	*O-153	1.9
1979	Mon-N	155	639	90	176	24	12	25	92	27	115	.275	.311	.468	111	6	35	10	5	.988	6	*O-153	1.0
1980	Mon-N	151	577	96	178	41	7	17	87	44	69	.308	.364	.492	137	27	34	9	5	.986	20	*O-147	4.8
1981	*Mon-N★	103	394	71	119	21	3	24	64	35	50	.302	.369	.553	157	28	26	4	5	.980	18	*O-103	5.0
1982	Mon-N★	148	608	107	183	37	7	23	83	34	96	.301	.346	.498	131	23	39	10	6	.982	21	*O-147	4.7
1983	Mon-N★	159	633	104	**189**	36	10	32	113	38	81	.299	.347	.539	143	33	25	11	1	.980	14	*O-157	4.5
1984	Mon-N	138	533	73	132	23	6	17	86	41	80	.248	.304	.409	103	0	13	5	1	.975	16	*O-134	1.3
1985	Mon-N	139	529	65	135	27	2	23	91	29	92	.255	.299	.444	112	5	13	4	2	.973	-4	*O-131	-0.2
1986	Mon-N	130	496	65	141	32	2	20	78	37	79	.284	.341	.478	125	15	18	12	-2	.986	-0	*O-127	0.9
1987	Chi-N★	153	621	90	178	24	2	**49**	**137**	32	103	.287	.329	.568	127	21	11	3	2	.986	6	*O-152	2.3
1988	Chi-N★	157	591	78	179	31	8	24	79	37	73	.303	.348	.504	136	25	12	4	1	.989	-1	*O-147	2.5
1989	*Chi-N★	118	416	62	105	18	6	21	77	35	62	.252	.312	.476	114	6	8	5	-1	.987	5	*O-112	0.8
1990	Chi-N★	147	529	72	164	28	5	27	100	42	65	.310	.363	.535	134	23	16	2	4	.981	-0	*O-139	2.4
1991	Chi-N★	149	563	69	153	21	4	31	104	22	80	.272	.305	.488	114	8	4	5	-2	.988	-1	*O-137	0.1
1992	Chi-N	143	542	60	150	27	2	22	90	30	70	.277	.319	.456	114	8	6	2	1	.992	-1	*O-139	0.5
1993	Bos-A	121	461	44	126	29	1	13	67	17	49	.273	.318	.425	92	-6	2	1	0	1.000	0	D-97,O-20	-1.0
1994	Bos-A	75	292	34	70	18	0	16	48	9	53	.240	.272	.466	82	-9	2	2	-1	.000	0	D-74	-1.3
1995	Fla-N	79	226	30	58	10	3	8	37	9	45	.257	.309	.434	93	-3	0	1	0	.908	-6	O-59	-1.0
1996	Fla-N	42	58	6	16	2	0	2	14	2	13	.276	.311	.414	93	-1	0	0	0	.833	-1	/O-6	-0.5
Total	21	2627	9927	1373	2774	503	98	438	1591	589	1509	.279	.327	.482	119	216	314	109	29	.983	123	*O-2323,D-171	29.9

■ BOOTS DAY   Day, Charles Frederick b: 8/31/47, Ilion, N.Y.   BL/TL, 5′9″, 160 lbs.   Deb: 6/15/69

YEAR	TM/L	G	AB	R	H	2B	3B	HR	RBI	BB	SO	AVG	OBP	SLG	PRO+	BR/A	SB	CS	SBR	FA	FR	G/POS	TPR
1969	StL-N	11	6	1	0	0	0	0	0	1	1	.000	.143	.000	-57	-1	0	0	0	.000	-0	/O-1	-0.2
1970	Chi-N	11	8	2	2	0	0	0	0	0	3	.250	.250	.250	31	-1	0	0	0	.875	1	/O-7	-0.2
	Mon-N	41	108	14	29	4	0	0	5	6	18	.269	.307	.306	65	-5	3	2	-0	.987	1	O-35	-0.6
	Yr	52	116	16	31	4	0	0	5	6	21	.267	.303	.302	61	-6	3	2	-0	.976	-0	O-42	-0.8
1971	Mon-N	127	371	53	105	10	2	4	33	33	39	.283	.343	.353	97	-1	9	4	0	.982	4	*O-120	-0.2
1972	Mon-N	128	386	32	90	7	4	0	30	29	44	.233	.288	.272	59	-20	3	6	-3	.979	3	*O-117	-3.5
1973	Mon-N	101	207	36	57	7	0	4	28	21	28	.275	.342	.367	93	-2	0	3	-2	1.000	-9	O-51	-1.5
1974	Mon-N	52	65	8	12	0	0	0	2	5	8	.185	.243	.185	20	-7	0	0	0	1.000	-2	O-16	-1.0
Total	6	471	1151	146	295	28	6	8	98	95	141	.256	.314	.312	75	-37	15	15	-5	.983	-13	O-347	-7.2

■ BRIAN DAYETT   Dayett, Brian Kelly b: 1/22/57, New London, Conn.   BR/TR, 5′10″, 180 lbs.   Deb: 9/11/83

YEAR	TM/L	G	AB	R	H	2B	3B	HR	RBI	BB	SO	AVG	OBP	SLG	PRO+	BR/A	SB	CS	SBR	FA	FR	G/POS	TPR
1983	NY-A	11	29	3	6	1	0	0	5	2	4	.207	.258	.276	49	-2	0	0	0	1.000	1	/O-9	-0.1
1984	NY-A	64	127	14	31	8	0	4	23	9	14	.244	.299	.402	96	-1	0	0	0	.988	-9	O-62/D-1	-1.1
1985	Chi-N	22	26	1	6	0	0	1	6	0	5	.231	.259	.346	61	-1	0	0	0	1.000	-0	O-10	-0.4
1986	Chi-N	24	67	7	18	4	0	4	11	6	10	.269	.329	.507	118	1	0	1	-1	1.000	-4	O-24	-0.3
1987	Chi-N	97	177	20	49	14	1	5	25	20	37	.277	.350	.452	106	2	0	0	0	1.000	-13	O-78	-1.3
Total	5	218	426	45	110	26	2	14	68	37	71	.258	.320	.427	99	-2	0	1	-1	.995	-26	O-183/D-1	-3.2

■ CHARLIE DEAL   Deal, Charles Albert b: 10/30/1891, Wilkinsburg, Pa.   d: 9/16/79, Covina, Cal.   BR/TR, 6′, 160 lbs.   Deb: 7/19/12

YEAR	TM/L	G	AB	R	H	2B	3B	HR	RBI	BB	SO	AVG	OBP	SLG	PRO+	BR/A	SB	CS	SBR	FA	FR	G/POS	TPR
1912	Det-A	42	142	13	32	4	2	0	11	9		.225	.272	.282	60	-8	4			.942	10	3-41	0.3
1913	Det-A	16	50	3	11	0	2	0	3	1	7	.220	.235	.300	57	-3	2			.862	2	3-15	-0.1
	Bos-N	10	36	6	11	1	0	0	3	2	1	.306	.359	.333	96	-0	1			.935	-6	2-10	-0.7
1914	*Bos-N	79	257	17	54	13	2	0	23	20	23	.210	.270	.276	63	-12	4			.948	-3	3-74/S-1	-1.6
1915	StL-F	65	223	21	72	12	4	1	27	12	16	.323	.357	.426	114	1	10			.951	5	3-65	0.8
1916	StL-A	23	74	7	10	1	0	0	10	6	3	.135	.200	.149	5	-9	4			.970	-2	3-22/2-1	-1.1
	Chi-N	2	8	2	2	1	0	0	3	0	0	.250	.250	.375	82	-0	0			1.000	-0	/3-2	0.2
1917	Chi-N	135	449	46	114	11	3	0	47	19	18	.254	.284	.292	71	-16	6			.957	7	*3-130	-0.7
1918	*Chi-N	119	414	43	99	9	3	2	34	21	13	.239	.279	.290	72	-14	11			.964	-2	*3-118	-1.6
1919	Chi-N	116	405	37	117	23	5	2	52	12	12	.289	.316	.385	110	3	11			**.973**	7	*3-116	1.7
1920	Chi-N	129	450	48	108	10	5	3	39	20	14	.240	.280	.304	68	-19	5	8	-3	**.973**	10	*3-128	-0.7
1921	Chi-N	115	422	52	122	19	8	3	66	13	9	.289	.310	.393	85	-10	3	5	-2	**.973**	4	*3-112	0.9
Total	10	851	2930	295	752	104	34	11	318	135	_121_	.257	.293	.327	79	-86	65	_13_		.958	41	3-823/2-11,S-1	-2.6

■ LINDSAY DEAL   Deal, Fred Lindsay b: 9/3/11, Lenoir, N.C.   d: 4/18/79, Little Rock, Ark.   BL/TR, 6′, 175 lbs.   Deb: 9/13/39

YEAR	TM/L	G	AB	R	H	2B	3B	HR	RBI	BB	SO	AVG	OBP	SLG	PRO+	BR/A	SB	CS	SBR	FA	FR	G/POS	TPR
1939	Bro-N	4	7	0	0	0	0	0	0	0	2	.000	.000	.000	-97	-2	0			1.000	0	/O-1	-0.2

YEAR	TM/L	G	AB	R	H	2B	3B	HR	RBI	BB	SO	AVG	OBP	SLG	PRO+	BR/A	SB	CS	SBR	FA	FR	G/POS	TPR

■ SNAKE DEAL
Deal, John Wesley b: 1/21/1879, Lancaster, Pa. d: 5/9/44, Harrisburg, Pa. BR/TR, 6′, 164 lbs. Deb: 7/9/06

YEAR	TM/L	G	AB	R	H	2B	3B	HR	RBI	BB	SO	AVG	OBP	SLG	PRO+	BR/A	SB	CS	SBR	FA	FR	G/POS	TPR
1906	Cin-N	65	231	13	48	4	3	0	21	6		.208	.228	.251	47	-15	15			.985	2	1-65	-1.6

■ PAT DEALY
Dealy, Patrick E. b: Burlington, Vt. d: 12/16/24, Buffalo, N.Y. BR/TR, 5′8″, 145 lbs. Deb: 9/30/1884

YEAR	TM/L	G	AB	R	H	2B	3B	HR	RBI	BB	SO	AVG	OBP	SLG	PRO+	BR/A	SB	CS	SBR	FA	FR	G/POS	TPR
1884	StP-U	5	15	2	2	0	0	0		0		.133	.133	.133	-35	-4				.871	3	/C-4,O-1	-0.1
1885	Bos-N	35	130	18	29	4	1	1	9	2	14	.223	.235	.292	72	-4				.903	0	C-29/3,3,O-2,S-2,1	-0.1
1886	Bos-N	15	46	9	15	1	1	0	3	4	4	.326	.380	.391	140	2	5			.929	-2	C-14/O-1	0.2
1887	Was-N	58	212	33	55	8	2	1	18	8	8	.259	.293	.330	77	-7	36			.931	-7	C-28,S-23/O-5,3-5	-0.9
1890	Syr-a	18	66	9	12	1	0	0	4	5		.182	.250	.197	36	-5	4			.900	-6	C-10/3-6,O-2	-0.9
Total 5		131	469	71	113	14	4	2	34	19	26	.241	.275	.301	74	-17	45			.914	-12	/C-85,S-25,3-14,O1	-1.8

■ CHUBBY DEAN
Dean, Alfred Lovill b: 8/24/16, Mt.Airy, N.C. d: 12/21/70, Riverside, Cal. BL/TL, 5′11″, 181 lbs. Deb: 4/14/36

YEAR	TM/L	G	AB	R	H	2B	3B	HR	RBI	BB	SO	AVG	OBP	SLG	PRO+	BR/A	SB	CS	SBR	FA	FR	G/POS	TPR
1936	Phi-A	111	342	41	98	21	3	1	48	24	24	.287	.337	.374	77	-13	3	2	-0	.989	-1	1-77	-1.9
1937	Phi-A	104	309	36	81	14	4	2	31	42	10	.262	.350	.353	79	-9	2	1	0	.991	-2	1-78/P-2	-1.9
1938	Phi-A	16	20	3	6	2	0	0	1	4	1	.300	.333	.400	85	-1	0	0	0	1.000	1	/P-6	0.0
1939	Phi-A	80	77	12	27	4	0	0	19	8	4	.351	.412	.403	111	2	0	0	0	.935	1	P-54	0.0
1940	Phi-A	67	90	6	26	2	0	0	6	16	9	.289	.396	.311	88	-1	0	0	0	.976	1	P-30/1-1	0.0
1941	Phi-A	27	37	0	9	2	0	0	9	4	3	.243	.317	.297	65	-2	0	0	0	1.000	1	P-18/1-1	0.0
	Cle-A	17	25	2	4	1	0	0	2	3	2	.160	.250	.200	21	-3	0	0	0	1.000	1	/P-8	0.0
	Yr	44	62	2	13	3	0	0	11	7	5	.210	.290	.258	48	-5	0	0	0	1.000	1	P-26/1-1	0.0
1942	Cle-A	70	101	4	27	1	0	0	7	11	7	.267	.339	.277	79	-2	0	0	0	.939	-3	P-27	0.0
1943	Cle-A	41	46	2	9	0	0	0	5	6	2	.196	.288	.196	45	-3	0	0	0	.929	-1	P-17	0.0
Total 8		533	1047	106	287	47	7	3	128	115	65	.274	.347	.341	79	-32	5	3	-0	.964	-5	P-162,1-157	-3.8

■ TOMMY DEAN
Dean, Tommy Douglas b: 8/30/45, Iuka, Miss. BR/TR, 6′, 165 lbs. Deb: 9/17/67

YEAR	TM/L	G	AB	R	H	2B	3B	HR	RBI	BB	SO	AVG	OBP	SLG	PRO+	BR/A	SB	CS	SBR	FA	FR	G/POS	TPR
1967	LA-N	12	28	1	4	1	0	0	2	0	9	.143	.143	.179	-9	-4	0	0	0	.981	6	S-12	0.3
1969	SD-N	101	273	14	48	9	2	2	9	27	54	.176	.252	.245	42	-21	0	3	-2	.978	4	S-97/2-2	-1.1
1970	SD-N	61	158	18	35	5	1	2	13	11	29	.222	.272	.304	56	-10	2	0	1	.974	6	S-55	0.2
1971	SD-N	41	70	2	8	0	0	0	1	4	13	.114	.162	.114	-22	-11	1	0	0	.969	6	S-28,3-11/2-1	-0.3
Total 4		215	529	35	95	15	3	4	25	42	105	.180	.241	.242	36	-47	3	3	-1	.976	23	S-192/3-11,2-3	-0.9

■ HARRY DEANE
Deane, John Henry b: 5/6/1846, Trenton, N.J. d: 5/31/25, Indianapolis, Ind. 5′7″, 150 lbs. Deb: 7/20/1871 M

YEAR	TM/L	G	AB	R	H	2B	3B	HR	RBI	BB	SO	AVG	OBP	SLG	PRO+	BR/A	SB	CS	SBR	FA	FR	G/POS	TPR
1871	Kek-n	6	22	3	4	1	0	0	2	0		.182	.250	.273	49	-1				1.000	2	/O-6,M	0.0
1874	Bal-n	47	203	29	50	8	1	0	13	5	3	.246	.264	.296	80	-4	2	1	0	.818	-4	*O-46/2-2,S-1	-0.6
Total 2 n		53	225	32	54	8	2	0	15	7	3	.240	.263	.293	76	-6	2	1	0	.850	-2	/O-52,2-2,S-1	-0.6

■ BUDDY DEAR
Dear, Paul Stanford b: 12/1/05, Norfolk, Va. d: 8/29/89, Radford, Va. BR/TR, 5′8″, 143 lbs. Deb: 9/9/27

YEAR	TM/L	G	AB	R	H	2B	3B	HR	RBI	BB	SO	AVG	OBP	SLG	PRO+	BR/A	SB	CS	SBR	FA	FR	G/POS	TPR
1927	Was-A	2	1	1	0	0	0	0	0	0	0	.000	.000	.000	-99	-0				.000	0	/2-1	0.0

■ CHARLIE DeARMOND
DeArmond, Charles Hommer "Hummer" b: 2/13/1877, Okeana, Ohio d: 12/17/33, Morning Sun, Ohio BR/TR, 5′10″, 165 lbs. Deb: 9/19/03

YEAR	TM/L	G	AB	R	H	2B	3B	HR	RBI	BB	SO	AVG	OBP	SLG	PRO+	BR/A	SB	CS	SBR	FA	FR	G/POS	TPR
1903	Cin-N	11	39	10	11	2	1	0	7	3		.282	.349	.385	98	-0	1			.878	-1	3-11	-0.1

■ JOHN DEASLEY
Deasley, John b: 1/1861, Philadelphia, Pa. d: 12/25/10, Philadelphia, Pa. Deb: 6/17/1884 F

YEAR	TM/L	G	AB	R	H	2B	3B	HR	RBI	BB	SO	AVG	OBP	SLG	PRO+	BR/A	SB	CS	SBR	FA	FR	G/POS	TPR
1884	Was-U	31	134	20	29	1	1	0		3		.216	.234	.239	45	-13				.836	0	S-31	-1.1
	KC-U	13	40	3	7	2	0	0		2		.175	.214	.225	38	-4				.833	-0	S-13	-0.4
	Yr	44	174	23	36	3	1	0		5		.207	.229	.236	44	-17				.835	0	S-44	-1.5

■ PAT DEASLEY
Deasley, Thomas H. b: 11/17/1857, Ireland d: 4/1/43, Philadelphia, Pa. BR/TR, 5′8.5″, 154 lbs. Deb: 5/18/1881 F

YEAR	TM/L	G	AB	R	H	2B	3B	HR	RBI	BB	SO	AVG	OBP	SLG	PRO+	BR/A	SB	CS	SBR	FA	FR	G/POS	TPR
1881	Bos-N	43	147	13	35	5	2	0	8	5	10	.238	.263	.299	80	-3				.914	-4	C-28/O-7,S-7,1-2	-0.6
1882	Bos-N	67	264	36	70	8	0	0	29	7	22	.265	.284	.295	86	-4				**.958**	2	*C-56,O-14/S-1	-0.1
1883	StL-a	58	206	27	53	2	1	0	15	6		.257	.278	.277	75	-6				**.930**	8	C-56/O-2	0.5
1884	StL-a	75	254	27	52	5	4	0		7		.205	.235	.256	58	-12				.919	14	*C-75/O-2,1-1	0.7
1885	NY-N	54	207	22	53	5	1	0	24	9	20	.256	.287	.290	88	-3				.935	8	C-54/O-2,S-1	0.9
1886	NY-N	41	143	18	38	6	1	0	17	4	12	.266	.286	.322	84	-3	2			.925	7	C-30,O-15	0.5
1887	NY-N	30	118	12	37	5	0	0	23	7	7	.314	.367	.356	107	2	3			.867	-13	C-24/3-7,S-1	-0.8
1888	Was-N	34	127	6	20	1	0	0	4	2	18	.157	.171	.165	8	-13	2			.922	8	C-31/O-1,S-1,2-1	-0.2
Total 8		402	1466	161	358	37	9	0	120	49	89	.244	.271	.282	75	-42	7			.927	28	C-354/O-43,S312	0.9

■ HANK DeBERRY
DeBerry, John Herman b: 12/29/1894, Savannah, Tenn. d: 9/10/51, Savannah, Tenn. BR/TR, 5′11″, 195 lbs. Deb: 9/12/16

YEAR	TM/L	G	AB	R	H	2B	3B	HR	RBI	BB	SO	AVG	OBP	SLG	PRO+	BR/A	SB	CS	SBR	FA	FR	G/POS	TPR
1916	Cle-A	15	33	7	9	4	0	0	4	6	9	.273	.385	.394	126	-3	0			1.000	-3	C-14	-0.1
1917	Cle-A	25	33	3	9	2	0	0	1	2	7	.273	.333	.333	96	-0	0			.968	1	/C-9	0.1
1922	Bro-N	85	259	29	78	10	1	3	35	20	9	.301	.354	.382	91	-3	4	1	1	.971	-2	C-81	-0.1
1923	Bro-N	78	235	21	67	11	6	0	48	20	12	.285	.346	.396	98	-1	2	1	0	.971	6	C-60	1.0
1924	Bro-N	77	218	20	53	10	3	3	26	20	21	.243	.307	.358	80	-6	0	1	-1	.993	23	C-63	1.9
1925	Bro-N	67	193	26	50	8	1	2	24	16	8	.259	.322	.342	72	-8	2	2	-1	.981	19	C-55	1.3
1926	Bro-N	48	115	6	33	11	0	0	13	8	5	.287	.333	.383	94	-1	0			.976	8	C-37	0.9
1927	Bro-N	68	201	15	47	3	2	1	29	17	8	.234	.294	.284	55	-13	1			.988	23	C-67	1.5
1928	Bro-N	82	258	19	65	8	2	0	23	18	15	.252	.301	.298	58	-16	3			.977	18	C-80	0.9
1929	Bro-N	68	210	13	55	11	1	1	25	17	15	.262	.317	.338	64	-12	1			.991	6	C-68	0.7
1930	Bro-N	35	95	11	28	3	0	0	14	4	10	.295	.323	.326	58	-6	0			.978	12	C-35	0.7
Total 11		648	1850	170	494	81	16	11	234	148	119	.267	.323	.346	76	-65	13	5		.982	113	C-569	8.1

■ ADAM DEBUS
Debus, Adam Joseph b: 10/7/1892, Chicago, Ill. d: 5/13/77, Chicago, Ill. BR/TR, 5′10.5″, 150 lbs. Deb: 7/14/17

YEAR	TM/L	G	AB	R	H	2B	3B	HR	RBI	BB	SO	AVG	OBP	SLG	PRO+	BR/A	SB	CS	SBR	FA	FR	G/POS	TPR
1917	Pit-N	38	131	9	30	4	1	0	11	11	13	.229	.279	.328	83	-3	2			.898	-6	S-21,3-18	-0.9

■ DOUG DeCINCES
DeCinces, Douglas Vernon b: 8/29/50, Burbank, Cal. BR/TR, 6′2″, 194 lbs. Deb: 9/9/73

YEAR	TM/L	G	AB	R	H	2B	3B	HR	RBI	BB	SO	AVG	OBP	SLG	PRO+	BR/A	SB	CS	SBR	FA	FR	G/POS	TPR
1973	Bal-A	10	18	2	2	0	0	0	0	1	5	.111	.158	.111	-23	-3	0	0	0	.895	3	/3-8,2-2,S-1	0.0
1974	Bal-A	1	1	0	0	0	0	0	0	1	0	.000	.500	.000	55	0	0	0	0	1.000	0	/3-1	0.0
1975	Bal-A	61	167	20	42	6	3	4	23	13	32	.251	.309	.395	105	0	0	1	-1	.947	3	3-34,S-13,2-11,/1-2	0.4
1976	Bal-A	129	440	36	103	17	2	11	42	29	68	.234	.285	.357	93	-6	8	4	0	.941	-1	*3-109,2-17,1/SD	-0.8
1977	Bal-A	150	522	63	135	28	3	19	69	64	86	.259	.342	.433	117	12	8	8	-2	.958	10	*3-148/1-1,2-1,D-1	1.8
1978	Bal-A	142	511	72	146	37	1	28	80	46	81	.286	.347	.526	152	32	7	7	-2	.975	10	*3-130,2-12	4.0
1979	*Bal-A	120	422	67	97	27	1	16	61	54	68	.230	.322	.412	100	-0	5	3	-0	.964	-3	*3-120	-0.4
1980	Bal-A	145	489	64	122	23	2	16	64	49	83	.249	.322	.403	98	-2	11	6	-0	.960	25	*3-142/1-1	2.0
1981	Bal-A	100	346	49	91	23	2	13	55	41	32	.263	.343	.454	128	12	0	3	-2	.942	-2	*3-100/1-1,O-1	0.7
1982	*Cal-A	153	575	94	173	42	5	30	97	66	80	.301	.374	.548	149	38	7	5	-1	.961	21	*3-153/S-2	5.3
1983	Cal-A★	95	370	49	104	19	3	18	65	32	56	.281	.338	.495	127	13	2	0	1	.955	9	3-84,D-10	2.0
1984	Cal-A	146	547	77	147	23	3	20	82	53	79	.269	.333	.431	111	7	4	1	1	.964	-5	*3-140/D-5	-1.0
1985	Cal-A	120	427	50	104	22	1	20	78	47	71	.244	.321	.440	107	3	1	4	-2	.958	-10	*3-111/D-3	-1.0
1986	*Cal-A	140	512	69	131	20	3	26	96	52	91	.256	.327	.459	112	8	2	2	-0	.965	-8	*3-132/S-1,D-3	-0.3
1987	Cal-A	133	453	65	106	23	0	16	63	70	87	.234	.339	.391	96	-2	3	4	-2	.948	-3	*3-128/1-4,S-1,D-1	-0.7
	StL-A	4	9	1	2	2	0	0	1	0	2	.222	.222	.444	70	-0	0	0	0	.833	1	/3-3	0.0
Total 15		1649	5809	778	1505	312	29	237	879	618	904	.259	.333	.445	116	113	58	48	-11	.958	49	*3-1543/2-43,D1SO	13.1

■ HARRY DECKER
Decker, Earle Harry b: 9/3/1854, Lockport, Ill. BR/TR, 5′11″, 180 lbs. Deb: 8/23/1884

YEAR	TM/L	G	AB	R	H	2B	3B	HR	RBI	BB	SO	AVG	OBP	SLG	PRO+	BR/A	SB	CS	SBR	FA	FR	G/POS	TPR
1884	Ind-a	4	15	1	4	1	0	0		1		.267	.313	.333	114	0				.870	-3	/C-4	-0.3
	KC-U	23	75	8	10	2	0	0		5		.133	.188	.160	7	-11				.813	-4	O-16,C-11	-0.8
1886	Det-N	14	54	2	12	1	0	0	5	2	9	.222	.250	.241	48	-3	0			.871	4	C-14/O-1	0.2
	Was-N	7	23	0	5	1	0	0	2	0	5	.217	.250	.348	85	-0	0			.946	1	/C-4,3-2,S-1	0.1
	Yr	21	77	2	17	2	1	0	7	3	14	.221	.250	.273	59	-4	0			.886	2	C-18/3-2,O-1,S-1	0.2
1889	Phi-N	11	30	4	3	0	0	0	2	1	5	.100	.156	.100	-25	-5	1			.857	-1	/2-7,C-3,O-1	-0.5
1890	Phi-N	5	19	5	7	1	0	0	2	4	1	.368	.478	.421	159	2	4			.938	-1	/1-2,O-2,C-1	0.0

YEAR	TM/L	G	AB	R	H	2B	3B	HR	RBI	BB	SO	AVG	OBP	SLG	PRO+	BR/A	SB	CS	SBR	FA	FR	G/POS	TPR
	Pit-N	92	354	52	97	14	3	5	38	26	36	.274	.324	.373	116	6	8			.909	-26	C-70,1-16/O-4,2S	-1.3
	Yr	97	373	57	104	15	3	5	40	30	37	.279	.333	.375	119	8	12			.909	-27	C-71,1-18/O-6,2S	-1.3
Total	4	156	570	72	138	20	4	5	49	41	56	.242	.293	.318	87	-11	13			.903	-25	C-107/O-24,12S3	-2.6

■ FRANK DECKER
Decker, Frank b: 2/26/1856, St.Louis, Mo. d: 2/5/40, St.Louis, Mo. BR/TR Deb: 6/25/1879

YEAR	TM/L	G	AB	R	H	2B	3B	HR	RBI	BB	SO	AVG	OBP	SLG	PRO+	BR/A	SB	CS	SBR	FA	FR	G/POS	TPR
1879	Syr-N	3	10	0	1	0	0	0	0	0	3	.100	.100	.100	-38	-1				.714	-2	/C-2,O-1,1-1	-0.3
1882	StL-a	2	8	0	2	0	0	0	1	0		.250	.250	.250	66	-0				.813	-0	/2-2	0.0
Total	2	5	18	0	3	0	0	0	1	0	3	.167	.167	.167	12	-2				.813	-2	/2-2,C-2,1-1,0-1	-0.3

■ GEORGE DECKER
Decker, George A "Gentleman George" b: 6/1/1869, York, Pa. d: 6/7/09, Patton, Cal. BL/TL, 6'1", 180 lbs. Deb: 7/11/1892

YEAR	TM/L	G	AB	R	H	2B	3B	HR	RBI	BB	SO	AVG	OBP	SLG	PRO+	BR/A	SB	CS	SBR	FA	FR	G/POS	TPR
1892	Chi-N	78	291	32	66	6	7	1	28	20	49	.227	.277	.306	75	-10	9			.876	-12	O-62,2-16	-2.2
1893	Chi-N	81	328	57	89	9	8	2	48	24	22	.271	.325	.366	85	-8	22			.878	-9	O-33,1-27,2-20,/S-2	-1.6
1894	Chi-N	91	384	74	120	17	6	8	92	24	17	.313	.361	.451	90	-8	23			.974	-8	1-48,O-29/3-7,2S	-1.4
1895	Chi-N	73	297	51	82	9	7	2	41	17	22	.276	.324	.374	75	-13	11			.910	-8	O-57,1-11/3-3,S2	-2.0
1896	Chi-N	107	421	68	118	23	11	5	61	23	14	.280	.318	.423	91	-8	20			.928	-3	O-71,1-36	-1.4
1897	Chi-N	111	428	72	124	12	7	5	63	24		.290	.333	.386	86	-10	11			.925	-3	O-75,1-38/2-1	-1.5
1898	StL-N	76	286	26	74	10	0	1	45	20		.259	.314	.304	76	-9	4			.980	-7	1-75	-1.6
	Lou-N	42	148	27	44	4	3	0	19	9		.297	.342	.365	104	1	9			.993	-1	1-32/O-6	-0.1
	Yr	118	434	53	118	14	3	1	64	29		.272	.323	.325	85	-9	13			**.984**	-9	*1-107/O-6	-1.7
1899	Lou-N	38	135	13	36	8	0	1	18	12		.267	.336	.348	88	-2	3			.968	-3	1-38	-0.4
	Was-N	4	9	0	0	0	0	0	0	0		.000	.000	.000	-99	-2	0			.955	-1	/1-2,O-1	-0.3
	Yr	42	144	13	36	8	0	1	18	12		.250	.316	.326	77	-5	3			.967	-3	1-40/O-1	-0.7
Total	8	701	2727	420	753	98	49	25	415	173	124	.276	.324	.376	84	-70	112			.900	-54	O-334,1-307/23S	-12.5

■ STEVE DECKER
Decker, Steven Michael b: 10/25/65, Rock Island, Ill. BR/TR, 6'3", 205 lbs. Deb: 9/18/90

YEAR	TM/L	G	AB	R	H	2B	3B	HR	RBI	BB	SO	AVG	OBP	SLG	PRO+	BR/A	SB	CS	SBR	FA	FR	G/POS	TPR
1990	SF-N	15	54	5	16	2	0	3	8	1	10	.296	.309	.500	123	1	0	0	0	.989	2	C-15	0.4
1991	SF-N	79	233	11	48	7	1	5	24	16	44	.206	.266	.309	63	-12	0	1	-1	.984	-3	C-78	-1.2
1992	SF-N	15	43	3	7	1	0	0	1	3	6	.163	.280	.186	36	-3	0	0	0	1.000	2	C-15	0.0
1993	Fla-N	8	15	0	0	0	0	0	1	3	3	.000	.167	.000	-48	-3	0	0	0	.968	1	/C-5	-0.2
1995	Fla-N	51	133	12	30	2	1	3	13	19	22	.226	.322	.323	71	-5	1	0	0	.985	6	C-46/1-2	0.4
1996	SF-N	57	122	16	28	1	0	1	12	15	26	.230	.314	.262	56	-7	0	0	0	1.000	3	C-30/1-3,3-2	-0.3
	Col-N	10	25	8	8	2	0	1	8	3	3	.320	.393	.520	107	0	1	0	0	1.000	2	C-10	0.3
	Yr	67	147	24	36	3	0	2	20	18	29	.245	.327	.306	68	-6	1	0	0	1.000	5	C-40/1-3,3-2	0.0
Total	6	235	625	55	137	15	2	13	67	63	115	.219	.295	.312	66	-30	1	1	0	.989	13	C-199/1-5,3-2	-0.6

■ ARTIE DEDE
Dede, Arthur Richard b: 7/12/1895, Brooklyn, N.Y. d: 9/6/71, Keene, N.H. BR/TR, 5'9", 155 lbs. Deb: 10/4/16

YEAR	TM/L	G	AB	R	H	2B	3B	HR	RBI	BB	SO	AVG	OBP	SLG	PRO+	BR/A	SB	CS	SBR	FA	FR	G/POS	TPR
1916	Bro-N	1	1	0	0	0	0	0	0	0	0	.000	.000	.000	-97	-0				1.000	-0	/C-1	-0.1

■ ROD DEDEAUX
Dedeaux, Raoul Martial b: 2/17/15, New Orleans, La. BR/TR, 5'11", 160 lbs. Deb: 9/28/35

YEAR	TM/L	G	AB	R	H	2B	3B	HR	RBI	BB	SO	AVG	OBP	SLG	PRO+	BR/A	SB	CS	SBR	FA	FR	G/POS	TPR
1935	Bro-N	2	4	0	1	0	0	0	1	0	0	.250	.250	.250	36	-0	0			.857	0	/S-2	-0.1

■ JIM DEE
Dee, James D. b: Buffalo, N.Y. Deb: 7/30/1884

YEAR	TM/L	G	AB	R	H	2B	3B	HR	RBI	BB	SO	AVG	OBP	SLG	PRO+	BR/A	SB	CS	SBR	FA	FR	G/POS	TPR
1884	Pit-a	12	40	0	5	0	0	0		1		.125	.146	.125	-10	-5				.860	1	S-12	-0.3

■ SHORTY DEE
Dee, Maurice Leo b: 10/4/1889, Halifax, N.S., Can. d: 8/12/71, Jamaica Plain, Mass. BR/TR, 5'6", 155 lbs. Deb: 9/14/15

YEAR	TM/L	G	AB	R	H	2B	3B	HR	RBI	BB	SO	AVG	OBP	SLG	PRO+	BR/A	SB	CS	SBR	FA	FR	G/POS	TPR
1915	StL-A	1	3	1	0	0	0	0	0	1	0	.000	.250	.000	-26	-0	0	1	-1	.500	-1	/S-1	-0.3

■ ROB DEER
Deer, Robert George b: 9/29/60, Orange, Cal. BR/TR, 6'3", 210 lbs. Deb: 9/4/84

YEAR	TM/L	G	AB	R	H	2B	3B	HR	RBI	BB	SO	AVG	OBP	SLG	PRO+	BR/A	SB	CS	SBR	FA	FR	G/POS	TPR
1984	SF-N	13	24	5	4	0	0	3	3	7	10	.167	.375	.542	160	2	1	1	-0	.905	0	/O-9	0.2
1985	SF-N	78	162	22	30	5	1	8	20	23	71	.185	.286	.377	88	-3	0	1	-1	.982	-4	O-37,1-10	-1.0
1986	Mil-A	134	466	75	108	17	3	33	86	72	179	.232	.338	.494	119	12	5	2	0	.974	5	*O-131/1-4	1.5
1987	Mil-A	134	474	71	113	15	2	28	80	86	186	.238	.361	.456	112	9	12	4	1	.974	8	*O-123,1-12/D-4	1.3
1988	Mil-A	135	492	71	124	24	0	23	85	51	153	.252	.331	.441	113	8	9	5	0	.990	7	*O-133/D-1	1.1
1989	Mil-A	130	466	72	98	18	2	26	65	60	158	.210	.306	.425	105	2	4	8	-4	.972	5	*O-125/D-5	0.0
1990	Mil-A	134	440	57	92	15	1	27	69	64	147	.209	.315	.432	108	4	2	3	-1	.970	9	*O-117,1-21/D-1	0.8
1991	Det-A	134	448	64	80	14	2	25	64	89	175	.179	.315	.386	91	-5	1	3	-2	.978	11	*O-132/D-2	0.2
1992	Det-A	110	393	66	97	20	1	32	64	51	131	.247	.338	.547	143	21	4	2	0	.983	5	*O-106/D-2	2.4
1993	Det-A	90	323	48	70	11	0	14	39	38	120	.217	.305	.381	84	-8	3	2	0	.975	5	O-86/D-4	-0.5
	Bos-A	38	143	18	28	6	1	7	16	20	49	.196	.303	.399	82	-4	2	0	1	.970	5	O-36/D-2	0.1
	Yr	128	466	66	98	17	1	21	55	58	169	.210	.304	.386	83	-12	5	2	0	.973	9	O-122/D-6	-0.4
1996	SD-N	25	50	9	9	0	0	3	9	14	30	.180	.359	.480	125	2	0	0	0	1.000	-2	O-18	0.0
Total	11	1155	3881	578	853	148	13	230	600	575	1409	.220	.325	.442	108	40	43	31	-6	.977	56	*O-1053/1-47,D-21	6.1

■ CHARLIE DEES
Dees, Charles Henry b: 6/24/35, Birmingham, Ala. BL/TL, 6'1", 173 lbs. Deb: 5/26/63

YEAR	TM/L	G	AB	R	H	2B	3B	HR	RBI	BB	SO	AVG	OBP	SLG	PRO+	BR/A	SB	CS	SBR	FA	FR	G/POS	TPR
1963	LA-A	60	202	23	62	11	1	3	27	11	31	.307	.367	.416	126	7	3	3	-1	.986	-2	1-56	0.2
1964	LA-A	26	26	3	2	1	0	0	1	1	4	.077	.143	.115	-30	-5	1	3	-1	.981	0	1-12	-0.6
1965	Cal-A	12	32	1	5	0	0	0	1	1	8	.156	.182	.156	-3	-4	1	2	-1	.986	-1	/1-8	-0.7
Total	3	98	260	27	69	12	1	3	29	13	43	.265	.323	.354	95	-2	5	7	-3	.986	-3	/1-76	-1.1

■ TONY DeFATE
DeFate, Clyde Herbert b: 2/22/1895, Kansas City, Mo. d: 9/3/63, New Orleans, La. BR/TR, 5'8.5", 158 lbs. Deb: 4/18/17

YEAR	TM/L	G	AB	R	H	2B	3B	HR	RBI	BB	SO	AVG	OBP	SLG	PRO+	BR/A	SB	CS	SBR	FA	FR	G/POS	TPR
1917	StL-N	14	14	0	2	0	0	0	1	4	5	.143	.333	.143	50	-1	0			1.000	-1	/3-5,2-1	-0.1
	Det-A	3	2	1	0	0	0	0	0	0	1	.000	.000	.000	-99	-0	0			1.000	-0	/2-1	-0.1
Total	1	17	16	1	2	0	0	0	1	4	6	.125	.300	.125	33	-1	0			1.000	-1	/3-5,2-2	-0.2

■ ARTURO DeFREITAS
DeFreitas, Arturo Marcelino (Simon) b: 4/26/53, San Pedro De Macoris, D.R. BR/TR, 6'2", 195 lbs. Deb: 9/7/78

YEAR	TM/L	G	AB	R	H	2B	3B	HR	RBI	BB	SO	AVG	OBP	SLG	PRO+	BR/A	SB	CS	SBR	FA	FR	G/POS	TPR
1978	Cin-N	9	19	1	4	1	0	1	2	1	4	.211	.250	.421	84	-1	0	0	0	1.000	0	/1-6	-0.1
1979	Cin-N	23	34	2	7	2	0	0	4	0	16	.206	.206	.265	27	-3	0	0	0	.974	-1	/1-6,O-1	-0.5
Total	2	32	53	3	11	3	0	1	6	1	20	.208	.222	.321	47	-4	0	0	0	.988	-1	/1-12,O-1	-0.6

■ RUBE DeGROFF
DeGroff, Edward Arthur b: 9/2/1879, Hyde Park, N.Y. d: 12/17/55, Poughkeepsie, N.Y. BL, 5'11", Deb: 9/22/05

YEAR	TM/L	G	AB	R	H	2B	3B	HR	RBI	BB	SO	AVG	OBP	SLG	PRO+	BR/A	SB	CS	SBR	FA	FR	G/POS	TPR
1905	StL-N	15	56	3	14	2	1	0	5	5		.250	.311	.321	91	-1	1			.909	-0	O-15	-0.1
1906	StL-N	1	4	1	0	0	0	0	0	0		.000	.000	.000	-99	-1	0			.000	-0	/O-1	-0.2
Total	2	16	60	4	14	2	1	0	5	5		.233	.292	.300	80	-2	1			.909	-0	/O-16	-0.3

■ HERMAN DEHLMAN
Dehlman, Herman J. "Dutch" b: 1850, Catasauqua, Pa. d: 3/13/1885, Wilkes-Barre, Pa. Deb: 5/2/1872

YEAR	TM/L	G	AB	R	H	2B	3B	HR	RBI	BB	SO	AVG	OBP	SLG	PRO+	BR/A	SB	CS	SBR	FA	FR	G/POS	TPR
1872	Atl-n	37	165	30	36	3	1	0	14	3	1	.218	.232	.248	41	-14	4	2	0	.928	-3	*1-37	-1.0
1873	Atl-n	54	221	50	52	4	1	0	17	9	7	.235	.265	.262	64	-7	5	0	2	.929	-4	*1-54/S-1	-0.5
1874	Atl-n	53	218	40	49	3	1	0	18	7	5	.225	.249	.248	68	-6	2	0	1	.944	0	*1-53	-0.5
1875	StL-n	67	254	42	57	12	2	0	14	11	21	.224	.257	.287	98	-1	23	9	2	**.955**	1	*1-67/O-2	0.3
1876	StL-N	64	245	40	45	8	0	0	18	5	10	.184	.213	.208	43	-13				.958	0	*1-64	-1.3
1877	StL-N	32	119	24	22	4	0	0	11	7	21	.185	.230	.218	44	-7				.931	-3	*1-31/O-1	-0.9
Total	4 n	211	858	162	194	22	5	0	63	30	34	.226	.252	.263	65	-26	34	11	4	.941	-5	1-211/O-2,S-1	-1.7
Total	2	96	364	64	67	12	0	0	20	16	31	.184	.218	.212	43	-20				.950	-3	1-95,O-1	-2.2

■ JIM DEIDEL
Deidel, James Lawrence b: 6/6/49, Denver, Col. BR/TR, 6'2", 195 lbs. Deb: 5/31/74

YEAR	TM/L	G	AB	R	H	2B	3B	HR	RBI	BB	SO	AVG	OBP	SLG	PRO+	BR/A	SB	CS	SBR	FA	FR	G/POS	TPR
1974	NY-A	2	2	0	0	0	0	0	0	0	0	.000	.000	.000	-99	-1	0	0	0	1.000	1	/C-2	0.1

■ PEP DEININGER
Deininger, Otto Charles b: 10/10/1877, Wasseralfingen, Germany d: 9/25/50, Boston, Mass. BL/TL, 5'8.5", 180 lbs. Deb: 4/26/02

YEAR	TM/L	G	AB	R	H	2B	3B	HR	RBI	BB	SO	AVG	OBP	SLG	PRO+	BR/A	SB	CS	SBR	FA	FR	G/POS	TPR
1902	Bos-A	2	6	0	2	1	0	0	0	0		.333	.333	.833	210	1				1.000	-1	/P-2	0.0
1908	Phi-N	1	0	0	0	—	—	—	—	—	—	—	—	—	—	0				.000	-0	/O-1	-0.1
1909	Phi-N	55	169	22	44	9	0	0	16	11		.260	.309	.314	93	-2	5			.989	-0	O-45/2-1	-0.6
Total	3	58	175	22	46	10	1	0	16	11		.263	.310	.331	97	-1	5			.989	-3	O-46,P-2,2-1	-0.7

YEAR	TM/L	G	AB	R	H	2B	3B	HR	RBI	BB	SO	AVG	OBP	SLG	PRO+	BR/A	SB	CS	SBR	FA	FR	G/POS	TPR

■ PAT DEISEL   Deisel, Edward b: 4/29/1876, Ripley, Ohio   d: 4/17/48, Cincinnati, Ohio   BR/TR, 5'5", 145 lbs.   Deb: 8/21/02

YEAR	TM/L	G	AB	R	H	2B	3B	HR	RBI	BB	SO	AVG	OBP	SLG	PRO+	BR/A	SB	CS	SBR	FA	FR	G/POS	TPR
1902	Bro-N	1	3	0	2	0	0	0	1	1		.667	.800	.667	350	1				1.000	0	/C-1	0.1
1903	Cin-N	2	0	0	0	0	0	0	0	0	1	—	1.000	—	174	0				.000	0	/C-1	0.0
Total	2	3	3	0	2	0	0	0	1	2		.667	.833	.667	352	2				1.000	0	/C-2	0.1

■ BILL DEITRICK   Deitrick, William Alexander b: 4/20/02, Hanover Co., Va.   d: 5/6/46, Bethesda, Md.   BR/TR, 5'10", 160 lbs.   Deb: 9/19/27

YEAR	TM/L	G	AB	R	H	2B	3B	HR	RBI	BB	SO	AVG	OBP	SLG	PRO+	BR/A	SB	CS	SBR	FA	FR	G/POS	TPR
1927	Phi-N	5	6	1	1	0	0	0	0	0	0	.167	.167	.167	-10	-1	0			.750	-1	/S-5	-0.2
1928	Phi-N	52	100	13	20	6	0	0	7	17	10	.200	.322	.260	52	-7	1			1.000	-2	O-21/S-8	-0.9
Total	2	57	106	14	21	6	0	0	7	17	10	.198	.315	.255	49	-8	1			.895	-3	/O-21,S-13	-1.1

■ MIKE DEJAN   Dejan, Michael Dan b: 1/13/15, Cleveland, Ohio   d: 2/2/53, W.Los Angeles, Cal.   BL/TL, 6'1", 185 lbs.   Deb: 7/13/40

YEAR	TM/L	G	AB	R	H	2B	3B	HR	RBI	BB	SO	AVG	OBP	SLG	PRO+	BR/A	SB	CS	SBR	FA	FR	G/POS	TPR
1940	Cin-N	12	16	1	3	0	0	0	2	3	3	.188	.316	.313	73	-1	0			1.000	-0	/O-2	-0.1

■ IVAN DeJESUS   DeJesus, Ivan (Alvarez) b: 1/9/53, Santurce, P.R.   BR/TR, 5'11", 175 lbs.   Deb: 9/13/74

YEAR	TM/L	G	AB	R	H	2B	3B	HR	RBI	BB	SO	AVG	OBP	SLG	PRO+	BR/A	SB	CS	SBR	FA	FR	G/POS	TPR
1974	LA-N	3	3	1	1	0	0	0	0	0	2	.333	.333	.333	91	-0	0	0	0	1.000	-1	/S-2	-0.1
1975	LA-N	63	87	10	16	2	1	0	2	11	15	.184	.276	.230	43	-7	1	2	-1	.974	7	S-63	0.3
1976	LA-N	22	41	4	7	2	1	0	2	4	9	.171	.244	.268	46	-3	0	1	-1	.950	5	S-13/3-7	0.3
1977	Chi-N	155	624	91	166	31	7	3	40	56	90	.266	.330	.353	75	-21	24	12	0	.962	36	*S-154	3.2
1978	Chi-N	160	619	104	172	24	7	3	35	74	78	.278	.357	.354	88	-8	41	12	5	.967	13	*S-160	3.1
1979	Chi-N	160	636	92	180	26	10	5	52	59	82	.283	.346	.379	89	-9	24	20	-5	.959	1	*S-160	0.5
1980	Chi-N	157	618	78	160	26	3	3	33	60	81	.259	.328	.325	77	-17	44	16	4	.969	8	*S-156	1.3
1981	Chi-N	106	403	49	78	8	4	0	13	46	61	.194	.276	.233	44	-29	21	9	1	.959	10	*S-106	-0.8
1982	Phi-N	161	536	53	128	21	5	3	59	54	70	.239	.311	.313	73	-18	14	4	2	.973	-8	*S-154/3-7	-1.0
1983	*Phi-N	158	497	60	126	15	7	4	45	53	77	.254	.325	.336	85	-10	11	4	1	.966	-14	*S-158	-0.8
1984	Phi-N	144	435	40	112	15	3	0	35	43	76	.257	.327	.306	77	-12	12	5	1	.951	-21	*S-141	-2.1
1985	*StL-N	59	72	11	16	5	0	0	7	4	16	.222	.263	.292	55	-4	2	2	-1	1.000	1	3-20,S-13	-0.2
1986	NY-A	7	4	1	0	0	0	0	0	0	1	.000	.200	.000	-40	-1	0	0	0	.900	1	/S-7	-0.1
1987	SF-N	9	10	0	2	0	0	0	1	0	2	.200	.200	.200	7	-1	0	1	-1	.840	2	/S-9	0.1
1988	Det-A	7	17	1	3	0	0	0	0	3	6	.176	.222	.176	14	-2	0	0	0	.893	1	/S-7	-0.1
Total	15	1371	4602	595	1167	175	48	21	324	466	664	.254	.324	.326	76	-142	194	88	5	.963	41	*S-1303/3-34	3.6

■ MARK DeJOHN   DeJohn, Mark Stephen b: 9/18/53, Middletown, Conn.   BB/TR, 5'11", 170 lbs.   Deb: 4/28/82   C

YEAR	TM/L	G	AB	R	H	2B	3B	HR	RBI	BB	SO	AVG	OBP	SLG	PRO+	BR/A	SB	CS	SBR	FA	FR	G/POS	TPR
1982	Det-A	24	21	1	4	2	0	0	1	4	4	.190	.320	.286	68	-1	1	0	0	.978	6	S-20/3-4,2-1	0.6

■ BILL DeKONING   DeKoning, William Callahan b: 12/19/18, Brooklyn, N.Y.   d: 7/26/79, Palm Harbor, Fla.   BR/TR, 5'11", 185 lbs.   Deb: 5/27/45

YEAR	TM/L	G	AB	R	H	2B	3B	HR	RBI	BB	SO	AVG	OBP	SLG	PRO+	BR/A	SB	CS	SBR	FA	FR	G/POS	TPR
1945	NY-N	3	1	0	0	0	0	0	0	0	1	.000	.000	.000	-99	-0	0			1.000	-0	/C-2	0.0

■ ED DELAHANTY   Delahanty, Edward James "Big Ed" b: 10/30/1867, Cleveland, Ohio   d: 7/2/03, Niagara Falls, Ont., Canada   BR/TR, 6'1", 170 lbs.   Deb: 5/22/1888   FH

YEAR	TM/L	G	AB	R	H	2B	3B	HR	RBI	BB	SO	AVG	OBP	SLG	PRO+	BR/A	SB	CS	SBR	FA	FR	G/POS	TPR
1888	Phi-N	74	290	40	66	12	2	1	31	12	26	.228	.261	.293	73	-9	38			.872	-10	2-56,O-17	-1.7
1889	Phi-N	56	246	37	72	13	3	0	27	14	17	.293	.333	.370	89	-5	19			.956	-13	O-31,2-24/S-1	-1.5
1890	Cle-P	115	517	107	153	26	13	3	64	24	30	.296	.337	.414	109	5	25			.830	-7	S-76,2-20,O-18/3,1	0.2
1891	Phi-N	128	543	92	132	19	9	5	86	33	50	.243	.296	.339	83	-14	25			.909	1	*O-99,1-27/2-3	-1.5
1892	Phi-N	123	477	79	146	30	21	6	91	31	32	.306	.360	.495	158	30	29			.944	10	*O-121/3-4	4.3
1893	Phi-N	132	595	145	219	35	18	19	146	47	20	.368	.423	.583	167	53	37			.948	31	*O-117,2-15/1-6	6.3
1894	Phi-N	114	489	147	199	39	18	4	131	60	16	.407	.478	.585	159	50	21			.925	17	*O-88,1-12/3-9,S2	4.7
1895	Phi-N	116	480	149	194	49	10	11	106	86	31	.404	.500	.617	186	66	46			.944	-0	*O-103/S-9,2-6,3-1	4.7
1896	Phi-N	123	499	131	198	44	17	13	126	62	22	.397	.472	.631	192	67	37			.952	14	*O-99,1-22/2-1	6.0
1897	Phi-N	129	530	109	200	40	15	5	96	60		.377	.444	.538	162	49	26			.970	9	*O-129/1-1	4.0
1898	Phi-N	144	548	115	183	36	9	4	92	77		.334	.426	.454	159	46	58			.964	6	*O-144	3.7
1899	Phi-N	146	581	135	238	55	9	9	137	55		.410	.464	.582	193	73	30			.969	0	*O-143	5.6
1900	Phi-N	131	539	82	174	32	10	2	109	41		.323	.378	.430	124	17	16			.981	-3	*1-130	1.2
1901	Phi-N	139	542	106	192	38	16	8	108	65		.354	.427	.528	173	51	29			.949	-4	O-84,1-58	3.8
1902	Was-A	123	473	103	178	43	14	10	93	62		.376	.453	.590	186	56	16			.961	2	*O-111,1-13	4.7
1903	Was-A	42	156	22	52	11	1	1	21	12		.333	.388	.436	144	9	3			.962	2	O-40/1-1	0.8
Total	16	1835	7505	1599	2596	522	185	101	1464	741	244	.346	.411	.505	152	543	455			.951	56	*O-1344,1-271,2/S3	44.3

■ FRANK DELAHANTY   Delahanty, Frank George "Pudgie" b: 1/29/1883, Cleveland, Ohio   d: 7/22/66, Cleveland, Ohio   BR/TR, 5'9", 160 lbs.   Deb: 8/23/05   F

YEAR	TM/L	G	AB	R	H	2B	3B	HR	RBI	BB	SO	AVG	OBP	SLG	PRO+	BR/A	SB	CS	SBR	FA	FR	G/POS	TPR
1905	NY-A	9	27	0	6	1	0	0	2	1		.222	.250	.259	55	-1	0			.932	-1	/1-5,O-3	-0.3
1906	NY-A	92	307	37	73	11	8	2	41	16		.238	.282	.345	87	-6	11			.954	3	O-86	-0.7
1907	Cle-A	15	52	3	9	0	1	0	4	4		.173	.232	.212	41	-3	2			.917	-0	O-15	-0.5
1908	NY-A	37	125	12	32	1	2	0	10	10		.256	.316	.296	98	-0	9			.957	-0	O-36	-0.3
1914	Buf-F	79	274	29	55	4	7	2	27	23	19	.201	.265	.288	50	-24	21			.976	-6	O-78	-3.5
	Pit-F	41	159	25	38	4	4	1	7	11	11	.239	.297	.333	72	-9	7			.984	-3	O-36/2-4	-1.4
	Yr	120	433	54	93	8	11	3	34	34	30	.215	.277	.305	58	-33	28			.979	-8	*O-114/2-4	-4.9
1915	Pit-F	14	42	3	10	1	0	0	3	1	0	.238	.256	.262	46	-4	0			1.000	1	O-11	-0.4
Total	6	287	986	109	223	22	22	5	94	66	30	.226	.280	.308	70	-47	50			.964	-7	O-265/1-5,2-4	-7.1

■ JIM DELAHANTY   Delahanty, James Christopher b: 6/20/1879, Cleveland, Ohio   d: 10/17/53, Cleveland, Ohio   BR/TR, 5'10.5", 170 lbs.   Deb: 4/19/01   F

YEAR	TM/L	G	AB	R	H	2B	3B	HR	RBI	BB	SO	AVG	OBP	SLG	PRO+	BR/A	SB	CS	SBR	FA	FR	G/POS	TPR
1901	Chi-N	17	63	4	12	2	0	0	4	3		.190	.239	.222	35	-5	5			.877	-1	3-17/2-1	-0.6
1902	NY-N	7	26	3	6	1	0	0	3	1		.231	.259	.269	64	-1	0			.917	-1	/O-7	-0.2
1904	Bos-N	142	499	56	142	27	8	3	60	27		.285	.333	.389	127	15	16			.888	1	*3-113,2-18/O-9,P-1	1.9
1905	Bos-N	125	461	50	119	11	8	5	55	28		.258	.315	.349	100	-1	12			.962	-7	*O-124/P-1	-1.5
1906	Cin-N	115	379	63	106	21	4	1	39	45		.280	.371	.364	124	12	21			.903	-19	*3-105/S-5,O-2	-0.4
1907	StL-A	33	95	8	21	3	0	0	6	5		.221	.275	.253	68	-3	6			.889	-1	3-21/O-4,2-2	-0.4
	Was-A	108	404	44	118	18	7	2	54	36		.292	.367	.386	152	24	18			.941	-12	2-68,3-27/O-9,1-4	1.3
	Yr	141	499	52	139	21	7	2	60	41		.279	.350	.361	135	20	24			.942	-13	2-70,3-48,O-13/1-4	0.9
1908	Was-A	83	287	33	91	11	4	1	30	24		.317	.376	.394	164	20	16			.963	-3	2-80	2.5
1909	Was-A	90	302	18	67	13	5	1	21	23		.222	.290	.308	93	-3	4			.956	-3	2-85	-0.5
	*Det-A	46	150	29	38	10	1	0	20	17		.253	.364	.333	115	4	9			.943	-7	2-46	-0.5
	Yr	136	452	47	105	23	6	1	41	40		.232	.316	.316	101	2	13			.951	-10	*2-131	-1.3
1910	Det-A	106	378	67	111	16	2	3	45	43		.294	.379	.370	126	13	15			.940	-15	*2-106	-0.5
1911	Det-A	144	542	83	184	30	14	3	94	56		.339	.411	.463	137	27	15			.978	-10	1-71,2-59,3-13	1.6
1912	Det-A	79	266	34	76	14	1	0	41	42		.286	.387	.346	117	9	9			.930	-2	2-44,O-33	0.1
1914	Bro-F	74	214	28	62	13	5	0	15	25	21	.290	.372	.397	110	6	2			.957	-19	2-55/1-5	-2.0
1915	Bro-F	17	25	0	6	1	0	0	2	3	3	.240	.345	.280	77	-1	1			.857	-1	/2-4	-0.2
Total	13	1186	4091	520	1159	191	59	19	489	378	24	.283	.357	.373	122	110	151			.946	-97	2-568,3-296,O/1SP	0.3

■ JOE DELAHANTY   Delahanty, Joseph Nicholas b: 10/18/1875, Cleveland, Ohio   d: 1/9/36, Cleveland, Ohio   BR/TR, 5'9", 168 lbs.   Deb: 9/30/07   F

YEAR	TM/L	G	AB	R	H	2B	3B	HR	RBI	BB	SO	AVG	OBP	SLG	PRO+	BR/A	SB	CS	SBR	FA	FR	G/POS	TPR
1907	StL-N	7	22	3	7	0	0	1	2	0		.318	.318	.455	147	1	3			.933	-1	/O-7	0.0
1908	StL-N	140	499	37	127	14	11	6	44	32		.255	.309	.333	110	5	11			.977	-5	*O-138	-0.6
1909	StL-N	123	411	28	88	16	4	2	54	42		.214	.292	.287	85	-7	10			.985	-16	O-63,2-48	-3.0
Total	3	270	932	68	222	30	15	4	100	74		.238	.301	.315	100	-1	24			.978	-21	O-208/2-48	-3.6

■ TOM DELAHANTY   Delahanty, Thomas James b: 3/9/1872, Cleveland, Ohio   d: 1/10/51, Sanford, Fla.   BL/TR, 5'8", 175 lbs.   Deb: 9/29/1894   F

YEAR	TM/L	G	AB	R	H	2B	3B	HR	RBI	BB	SO	AVG	OBP	SLG	PRO+	BR/A	SB	CS	SBR	FA	FR	G/POS	TPR
1894	Phi-N	1	4	0	1	0	0	0	0	0		.250	.250	.250	21	-1	0			.875	-2	/2-1	0.0
1896	Cle-N	16	56	11	13	4	0	0	4	8	1	.232	.338	.304	66	-3	4			.823	-1	3-16	-0.3
	Pit-N	1	3	1	1	0	0	0	0	0		.333	.333	.333	79	-0	0			.750	-1	/S-1	-0.0
	Yr	17	59	12	14	4	0	0	4	8		.237	.338	.305	67	-3	4			.823	-2	3-16/S-1	-0.3
1897	Lou-N	1	4	1	1	0	0	0	2	0		.250	.250	.500	99	-0	0			.333	-2	/2-1	-0.2
Total	3	19	67	13	16	4	0	0	6	8	5	.239	.329	.313	66	-4	4			.727	-4	/3-16,2-2,S-1	-0.5

YEAR	TM/L	G	AB	R	H	2B	3B	HR	RBI	BB	SO	AVG	OBP	SLG	PRO+	BR/A	SB	CS	SBR	FA	FR	G/POS	TPR

■ MIKE de la HOZ
de la Hoz, Miguel Angel (Piloto)   b: 10/2/38, Havana, Cuba   BR/TR, 5'11", 175 lbs.   Deb: 7/22/60

	1960	Cle-A	49	160	20	41	6	2	6	23	9	12	.256	.300	.431	98	-1	0	0	0	.950	-15	S-38/3-8	-1.3
	1961	Cle-A	61	173	20	45	10	0	3	23	7	10	.260	.297	.370	79	-6	0	0	0	.969	3	2-17,S-17,3-16	0.0
	1962	Cle-A	12	12	0	1	0	0	0	0	0	3	.083	.083	.083	-57	-3	0	0	0	1.000	-0	/2-2	-0.3
	1963	Cle-A	67	150	15	40	10	0	5	25	9	29	.267	.313	.433	107	1	0	0	0	.962	4	2-34/3-6,S-2,O-2	0.9
	1964	Mil-N	78	189	25	55	7	1	4	12	14	22	.291	.346	.402	109	2	1	1	-0	.968	-4	2-25,3-25/S-8	0.0
	1965	Mil-N	81	176	15	45	3	2	2	11	8	21	.256	.296	.330	75	-6	0	1	-1	.963	-10	S-41,3-22,2-10/1-1	-1.6
	1966	Atl-N	71	110	11	24	3	0	2	7	5	18	.218	.252	.300	52	-7	0	1	-1	.950	-2	3-30/2-8,S-1	-1.1
	1967	Atl-N	74	143	10	29	3	0	3	14	4	14	.203	.224	.287	46	-10	1	0	0	1.000	-4	2-23,3-22/S-1	-1.5
	1969	Cin-N	1	1	0	0	0	0	0	0	0	1	.000	.000	.000	-95	-0	0	0	0	.000	0	H	0.0
Total	9		494	1114	116	280	42	5	25	115	56	130	.251	.292	.365	82	-29	2	3	-1	.936	-28	3-129,2-119,S/O1	-4.9

■ BILL DeLANCEY
DeLancey, William Pinkney   b: 11/28/11, Greensboro, N.C.   d: 11/28/46, Phoenix, Ariz.   BL/TR, 5'11.5", 185 lbs.   Deb: 9/11/32

	1932	StL-N	8	26	1	5	0	2	0	2	2	1	.192	.250	.346	57	-2	0			.930	1	/C-8	-0.1
	1934	*StL-N	93	253	41	80	18	3	13	40	41	37	.316	.414	.565	150	18	1			.980	5	C-77	2.5
	1935	StL-N	103	301	37	84	14	5	6	41	42	34	.279	.369	.419	107	4	0			.971	-2	C-83	0.6
	1940	StL-N	15	18	0	4	0	0	0	2	0	2	.222	.222	.222	22	-2	0			.929	1	C-12	0.0
Total	4		219	598	79	173	32	10	19	85	85	74	.289	.380	.472	121	19	1			.972	4	C-180	3.0

■ BILL DELANEY
Delaney, William L.   b: 3/4/1863, Cincinnati, O.   d: 3/1/42, Canton, Ohio   BR/TR,   Deb: 8/21/1890

| | 1890 | Cle-N | 36 | 116 | 16 | 22 | 1 | 1 | 1 | 7 | 21 | 19 | .190 | .314 | .241 | 64 | -5 | 5 | | | .926 | -10 | 2-36 | -1.1 |

■ JESUS de la ROSA
de la Rosa, Jesus (b: Jesus De Los Santos (De La Rosa))   b: 8/5/53, Santo Domingo, D.R.   BR/TR, 6'1", 153 lbs.   Deb: 8/2/75

| | 1975 | Hou-N | 3 | 3 | 1 | 1 | 1 | 0 | 0 | 0 | 0 | 0 | .333 | .333 | .667 | 186 | 0 | 0 | 0 | 0 | .000 | 0 | H | 0.0 |

■ ALEX DELGADO
Delgado, Alexander   b: 1/11/71, Palmerejo, Venez.   BR/TR, 6', 160 lbs.   Deb: 4/4/96

| | 1996 | Bos-A | 26 | 20 | 5 | 5 | 0 | 0 | 0 | 1 | 3 | 3 | .250 | .348 | .250 | 53 | -1 | 0 | 0 | 0 | .889 | -2 | C-14/O-6,3-4,1-1,2 | -0.3 |

■ CARLOS DELGADO
Delgado, Carlos Juan (Hernandez)   b: 6/25/72, Mayaguez, P.R.   BL/TR, 6'3", 215 lbs.   Deb: 10/1/93

	1993	Tor-A	2	1	0	0	0	0	0	0	1	0	.000	.500	.000	47	0	0	0	0	1.000	0	/C-1,D-1	0.0
	1994	Tor-A	43	130	17	28	2	0	9	24	25	46	.215	.354	.438	103	1	1	1	-0	.966	-4	O-41/C-1	-0.4
	1995	Tor-A	37	91	7	15	3	0	3	11	6	26	.165	.216	.297	32	-9	0	0	0	1.000	1	O-17/1-4,D-7	-0.9
	1996	Tor-A	138	488	68	132	28	2	25	92	58	139	.270	.359	.490	111	8	0	0	0	.983	-2	*D-108,1-27	-0.4
Total	4		220	710	92	175	33	2	37	127	90	211	.246	.341	.455	100	-1	1	1	-0	.979	-6	D-116/O-58,1-31,C-2	-1.7

■ PUCHY DELGADO
Delgado, Luis Felipe (Robles)   b: 2/2/54, Hatillo, P.R.   BB/TL, 5'11", 170 lbs.   Deb: 9/6/77

| | 1977 | Sea-A | 13 | 22 | 4 | 4 | 0 | 0 | 0 | 2 | 1 | 8 | .182 | .217 | .182 | 10 | -3 | 0 | 0 | 0 | 1.000 | 0 | O-13 | -0.5 |

■ WILSON DELGADO
Delgado, Wilson (Duran)   b: 7/15/75, San Cristobal, D.R.   BB/TR, 5'11", 165 lbs.   Deb: 9/24/96

| | 1996 | SF-N | 6 | 22 | 3 | 8 | 0 | 0 | 0 | 2 | 1 | 5 | .364 | .440 | .364 | 120 | 1 | 0 | 0 | 0 | .960 | -2 | /S-6 | 0.0 |

■ BOBBY Del GRECO
Del Greco, Robert George   b: 4/7/33, Pittsburgh, Pa.   BR/TR, 5'11", 190 lbs.   Deb: 4/16/52

	1952	Pit-N	99	341	34	74	14	2	1	20	38	70	.217	.301	.279	60	-18	6	5	-1	.977	6	O-93	-1.8
	1956	Pit-N	14	20	4	4	0	0	2	3	3	3	.200	.304	.500	114	0	0	0	0	1.000	0	/O-7,3-3	-0.2
		StL-N	102	270	29	58	16	2	5	18	32	50	.215	.312	.344	76	-9	1	1	-0	.987	-9	O-99	-2.3
		Yr	116	290	33	62	16	2	7	21	35	53	.214	.311	.355	79	-8	1	1	-0	.987	-10	*O-106/3-3	-2.5
	1957	Chi-N	20	40	2	8	2	0	0	3	10	17	.200	.360	.250	69	-1	1	0	0	.967	-2	O-16	-0.3
		NY-A	8	7	3	3	0	0	0	0	2	2	.429	.556	.429	175	1	0	0	0	1.000	1	/O-6	-0.1
	1958	NY-A	12	5	1	1	0	0	0	0	1	1	.200	.333	.200	52	-0	0	0	-1	1.000	-4	/O-12	-0.5
	1960	Phi-N	100	300	48	71	16	4	10	26	54	64	.237	.355	.417	110	5	1	5	-3	.970	12	O-89	1.0
	1961	Phi-N	41	112	14	29	5	0	2	11	12	17	.259	.346	.357	88	-2	0	0	0	1.000	1	O-32/2-1,3-1	-0.2
		KC-A	74	239	34	55	14	1	5	21	30	31	.230	.319	.360	79	-7	0	0	0	.983	5	O-73	-0.5
	1962	KC-A	132	338	61	86	21	1	9	38	49	62	.254	.370	.402	103	3	4	1	1	.984	0	*O-124	-0.2
	1963	KC-A	121	306	40	65	7	1	8	29	40	52	.212	.313	.320	74	-10	1	2	-1	.981	-6	*O-110/3-2	-2.3
	1965	Phi-N	8	4	1	0	0	0	0	0	0	3	.000	.000	.000	-99	-1	0	0	0	.000	-1	/O-4	-0.2
Total	9		731	1982	271	454	95	11	42	169	271	372	.229	.331	.352	84	-38	16	15	-4	.981	-2	O-665/3-6,2-1	-7.6

■ JUAN DELIS
Delis, Juan Francisco   b: 2/27/28, Santiago De Cuba, Cuba   BR/TR, 5'11", 170 lbs.   Deb: 4/16/55

| | 1955 | Was-A | 54 | 132 | 12 | 25 | 3 | 1 | 0 | 11 | 3 | 15 | .189 | .219 | .227 | 21 | -15 | 1 | 2 | -1 | .918 | -2 | 3-24/O-8,2-1 | -1.8 |

■ EDDIE DELKER
Delker, Edward Alberts   b: 4/17/06, Palo Alto, Pa.   BR/TR, 5'10.5", 170 lbs.   Deb: 4/28/29

	1929	StL-N	22	40	5	6	0	1	0	3	2	12	.150	.227	.200	7	-6	0			.750	-2	/S-9,2-7,3-3	-0.7
	1931	StL-N	1	2	0	1	1	0	0	2	0	0	.500	.500	1.000	283	0	0			1.000	-0	/3-1	0.0
	1932	StL-N	20	42	1	5	4	0	0	2	8	7	.119	.260	.214	28	-4	0			1.000	4	2-10/3-5,S-4	0.1
		Phi-N	30	62	7	10	1	1	1	7	6	14	.161	.235	.258	29	-6	0			.925	-1	2-27	-0.7
		Yr	50	104	8	15	5	1	1	9	14	21	.144	.246	.240	29	-11	0			.946	3	2-37/3-5,S-4	-0.6
	1933	Phi-N	25	41	6	7	3	1	0	1	0	12	.171	.171	.293	27	-4	0			.968	5	2-17/3-4	0.3
Total	4		98	187	19	29	9	3	1	15	16	45	.155	.229	.251	26	-20	0			.952	6	2-61,3-13,S-13	-1.0

■ BERT DELMAS
Delmas, Albert Charles   b: 5/20/11, San Francisco, Cal   d: 12/4/79, Huntington Beach, Cal.   BL/TR, 5'11", 165 lbs.   Deb: 9/10/33

| | 1933 | Bro-N | 12 | 28 | 4 | 7 | 0 | 0 | 0 | 0 | 1 | 7 | .250 | .276 | .250 | 53 | -2 | 0 | | | .912 | -3 | 2-10 | -0.5 |

■ LUIS de los SANTOS
de los Santos, Luis Manuel (Martinez)   b: 12/29/66, San Cristobal, D.R.   BR/TR, 6'5", 205 lbs.   Deb: 9/7/88

	1988	KC-A	11	22	1	2	1	1	0	1	4	4	.091	.231	.227	29	-2	0	0	0	1.000	-0	/1-5,D-3	-0.3
	1989	KC-A	28	87	6	22	3	1	0	6	5	14	.253	.293	.310	71	-3	0	0	0	.986	3	1-27	-0.5
	1991	Det-A	16	30	1	5	2	0	0	0	2	4	.167	.219	.233	25	-3	0	0	0	1.000	-0	/O-3,1-2,3-2,D-9	-0.4
Total	3		55	139	8	29	6	2	0	7	11	22	.209	.267	.281	53	-9	0	0	0	.988	-1	/1-34,D-12,O-3,3-2	-1.2

■ GARTON Del SAVIO
Del Savio, Garton Orville   b: 11/26/13, New York, N.Y.   BR/TR, 5'9.5", 165 lbs.   Deb: 4/24/43

| | 1943 | Phi-N | 4 | 11 | 0 | 1 | 0 | 0 | 0 | 0 | 1 | 0 | .091 | .167 | .091 | -26 | -2 | 0 | | | .857 | 0 | /S-4 | -0.1 |

■ JIM DELSING
Delsing, James Henry   b: 11/13/25, Rudolph, Wis.   BL/TR, 5'10", 175 lbs.   Deb: 4/21/48

	1948	Chi-A	20	63	6	12	0	0	0	5	5	12	.190	.261	.190	22	-7	0	0	0	1.000	-1	O-15	-0.9
	1949	NY-A	9	20	5	7	1	0	1	3	1	2	.350	.381	.550	145	1	0	0	0	1.000	-0	/O-5	-0.1
	1950	NY-A	12	10	2	4	0	0	0	2	2	0	.400	.500	.400	137	1	0	0	0	.000	0	H	0.1
		StL-A	69	209	25	55	5	2	6	15	20	23	.263	.328	.306	85	-12	1	4	-2	.994	2	O-53	-1.4
		Yr	81	219	27	59	5	2	6	17	22	23	.269	.336	.311	65	-11	1	4	-2	.994	2	O-53	-1.3
	1951	StL-A	131	449	59	112	20	2	8	45	56	39	.249	.338	.356	85	-9	2	9	-5	.983	9	*O-124	-0.9
	1952	StL-A	93	298	34	76	13	6	1	34	25	29	.255	.323	.349	85	-6	3	3	-1	.986	1	O-85	-1.1
		Det-A	33	113	14	31	2	1	3	15	11	8	.274	.344	.389	103	1	0	1	0	.958	-0	O-32	-0.1
		Yr	126	411	48	107	15	7	4	49	36	37	.260	.329	.360	90	-6	3	4	-1	.979	-1	O-117	-1.2
	1953	Det-A	138	479	77	138	26	11	11	62	66	39	.288	.380	.436	121	15	1	3	-2	.992	-2	*O-133	0.7
	1954	Det-A	122	371	39	92	24	2	6	38	49	38	.248	.337	.372	96	-2	4	4	-1	**.996**	-1	*O-108	-1.3
	1955	Det-A	114	356	49	85	15	2	10	60	48	40	.239	.331	.376	92	-4	0	0	1	.995	-5	*O-101	-1.3
	1956	Det-A	10	12	0	0	0	0	0	0	2	2	.000	.250	.000	-29	-2	0	0	0	1.000	1	/O-3	-0.3
		Chi-A	55	41	11	5	1	0	0	2	10	13	.122	.294	.195	31	-4	1	0	0	.957	-8	O-29	-0.8
		Yr	65	53	11	5	1	0	0	2	13	16	.094	.284	.151	17	-6	1	0	0	.962	-8	O-32	-1.5
	1960	KC-A	16	40	2	5	2	0	0	1	8	5	.125	.302	.325	69	-2	0	0	0	1.000	-8	/O-5	-0.1
Total	10		822	2461	322	627	112	21	40	286	299	251	.255	.340	.366	91	-31	15	23	-9	.989	-8	O-698	-7.4

■ JOE DeMAESTRI
DeMaestri, Joseph Paul "Oats"   b: 12/9/28, San Francisco, Cal.   BR/TR, 6', 174 lbs.   Deb: 4/19/51

| | 1951 | Chi-A | 56 | 74 | 8 | 15 | 0 | 2 | 1 | 3 | 5 | 11 | .203 | .253 | .297 | 49 | -6 | 0 | 4 | -2 | .959 | 6 | S-27,2-11/3-8 | -0.1 |

YEAR	TM/L	G	AB	R	H	2B	3B	HR	RBI	BB	SO	AVG	OBP	SLG	PRO+	BR/A	SB	CS	SBR	FA	FR	G/POS	TPR
1952	StL-A	81	186	13	42	9	1	1	18	8	25	.226	.258	.301	54	-12	0	1	-1	.939	2	S-77/2-1,3-1	-0.7
1953	Phi-A	111	420	53	107	17	3	6	35	24	39	.255	.297	.352	72	-17	0	1	-1	.964	-16	*S-108	-2.7
1954	Phi-A	146	539	49	124	16	3	8	40	20	63	.230	.262	.315	57	-33	1	4	-2	.965	-6	*S-142/2-1,3-1	-3.0
1955	KC-A	123	457	42	114	14	1	6	37	20	47	.249	.285	.324	63	-25	3	5	-2	.964	-12	*S-122	-2.9
1956	KC-A	133	434	41	101	16	1	6	39	25	73	.233	.279	.316	57	-28	3	3	-1	.964	6	*S-132/2-2	-1.3
1957	KC-A☆	135	461	44	113	14	6	9	33	22	82	.245	.282	.360	73	-18	6	1	1	**.980**	-7	*S-134	-1.2
1958	KC-A	139	442	32	97	11	1	6	38	16	84	.219	.248	.290	47	-32	1	0	0	**.980**	11	*S-137	-1.0
1959	KC-A	118	352	31	86	16	5	6	34	28	65	.244	.307	.369	83	-8	1	0	0	.957	5	*S-115	0.6
1960	*NY-A	49	35	8	8	1	0	0	2	0	9	.229	.229	.257	33	-3	0	0	0	.952	7	2-19,S-17	0.4
1961	NY-A	30	41	1	6	0	0	0	2	0	13	.146	.146	.146	-23	-7	0	0	0	.981	7	S-18/2-5,3-4	0.1
Total	11	1121	3441	322	813	114	23	49	281	168	511	.236	.275	.325	62	-190	15	19	-7	.967	4	*S-1029/2-39,3-14	-11.8

■ FRANK DEMAREE

Demaree, Joseph Franklin (b: Joseph Franklin Dimaria) b: 6/10/10, Winters, Cal. d: 8/30/58, Los Angeles, Cal. BR/TR, 5'11.5", 185 lbs. Deb: 7/22/32

YEAR	TM/L	G	AB	R	H	2B	3B	HR	RBI	BB	SO	AVG	OBP	SLG	PRO+	BR/A	SB	CS	SBR	FA	FR	G/POS	TPR
1932	*Chi-N	23	56	4	14	3	0	0	6	2	7	.250	.288	.304	60	-3	1			1.000	-1	O-17	-0.5
1933	Chi-N	134	515	68	140	24	6	6	51	22	42	.272	.304	.377	94	-5	4			.965	0	*O-133	-1.2
1935	*Chi-N	107	385	60	125	19	4	2	66	26	23	.325	.369	.410	108	5	6			.973	-2	O-98	0.0
1936	Chi-N★	154	605	93	212	34	3	16	96	49	30	.350	.400	.496	137	31	4			.968	-2	*O-154	2.2
1937	Chi-N★	154	615	104	199	36	6	17	115	57	31	.324	.382	.485	129	24	6			.980	2	*O-154	2.0
1938	*Chi-N	129	476	63	130	15	7	8	62	45	34	.273	.341	.384	96	-2	1			.972	-8	*O-125	-1.4
1939	NY-N	150	560	68	170	27	2	11	79	66	40	.304	.381	.418	114	12	2			.986	-1	*O-150	0.6
1940	NY-N	121	460	68	139	18	6	7	61	45	39	.302	.364	.413	113	9	5			.980	-6	O-119	-0.3
1941	NY-N	16	35	3	6	0	0	0	1	4	1	.171	.256	.171	22	-4	0			1.000	-0	O-10	-0.5
	Bos-N	48	113	20	26	5	2	2	15	12	5	.230	.304	.363	91	-2	2			1.000	-4	O-28	-0.7
	Yr	64	148	23	32	5	2	2	16	16	6	.216	.293	.318	74	-5	2			1.000	-5	O-38	-1.2
1942	Bos-N	64	187	18	42	5	0	3	24	17	10	.225	.289	.299	74	-6	2			1.000	-4	O-49	-0.6
1943	*StL-N	39	86	5	25	2	0	0	9	8	4	.291	.351	.314	89	-1	1			1.000	-3	O-23	-0.6
1944	StL-A	16	51	4	13	2	0	0	3	6	3	.255	.332	.294	76	-1	0	0	0	.969	-1	O-16	-0.3
Total	12	1155	4144	578	1241	190	36	72	591	359	269	.299	.357	.415	110	57	33	0	0	.978	-22	*O-1076	-1.3

■ BILLY DeMARS

DeMars, William Lester "Kid" b: 8/26/25, Brooklyn, N.Y. BR/TR, 5'10", 160 lbs. Deb: 5/18/48 C

YEAR	TM/L	G	AB	R	H	2B	3B	HR	RBI	BB	SO	AVG	OBP	SLG	PRO+	BR/A	SB	CS	SBR	FA	FR	G/POS	TPR
1948	Phi-A	18	29	3	5	0	0	0	1	5	3	.172	.294	.172	26	-3	0	0	0	.927	4	/S-9,2-1,3-1	0.1
1950	StL-A	61	178	25	44	5	1	0	13	22	13	.247	.330	.287	57	-11	0	1	-1	.933	-7	S-54/3-5	-1.4
1951	StL-A	1	4	1	1	0	0	0	0	1	0	.250	.400	.250	76	-0	0	0	0	1.000	-0	/S-1	-0.0
Total	3	80	211	29	50	5	1	0	14	28	16	.237	.326	.270	53	-14	0	1	-1	.933	-4	/S-64,3-6,2-1	-1.3

■ JOHN DeMERIT

DeMerit, John Stephen "Thumper" b: 1/8/36, West Bend, Wis. BR/TR, 6'1.5", 195 lbs. Deb: 6/18/57

YEAR	TM/L	G	AB	R	H	2B	3B	HR	RBI	BB	SO	AVG	OBP	SLG	PRO+	BR/A	SB	CS	SBR	FA	FR	G/POS	TPR
1957	*Mil-N	33	34	8	5	0	0	0	1	0	8	.147	.147	.147	-22	-6	1	0	0	1.000	-3	O-13	-0.9
1958	Mil-N	3	3	1	2	0	0	0	0	0	0	.667	.667	.667	278	1	0	0	0	1.000	-1	/O-2	-0.1
1959	Mil-N	11	5	4	1	0	0	0	0	1	2	.200	.333	.200	51	-0	0	0	0	1.000	-0	/O-4	-0.1
1961	Mil-N	32	74	5	12	3	0	2	5	5	19	.162	.225	.284	36	-7	0	0	0	1.000	0	O-21	-0.8
1962	NY-N	14	16	3	3	0	0	1	2	2	4	.188	.278	.375	72	-1	0	0	0	1.000	-3	/O-9	-0.4
Total	5	93	132	21	23	3	0	3	7	8	33	.174	.227	.265	32	-13	1	0	0	1.000	-6	/O-49	-2.2

■ DON DEMETER

Demeter, Donald Lee b: 6/25/35, Oklahoma City, Okla BR/TR, 6'4", 190 lbs. Deb: 9/18/56

YEAR	TM/L	G	AB	R	H	2B	3B	HR	RBI	BB	SO	AVG	OBP	SLG	PRO+	BR/A	SB	CS	SBR	FA	FR	G/POS	TPR
1956	Bro-N	3	3	1	1	0	0	0	1	0	1	.333	.333	1.333	297	1	0	0	0	1.000	-0	/O-1	0.0
1958	LA-N	43	106	11	20	2	0	5	8	5	32	.189	.225	.349	48	-8	2	3	-1	1.000	-4	O-39	-1.6
1959	*LA-N	139	371	55	95	11	1	18	70	16	87	.256	.298	.437	86	-8	5	6	-2	.983	-6	*O-124	-2.1
1960	LA-N	64	168	23	46	7	1	9	29	8	34	.274	.311	.488	108	1	0	1	-1	.989	-8	O-62	-1.0
1961	LA-N	15	29	3	5	0	0	1	2	3	6	.172	.250	.276	36	-3	0	0	0	.950	1	O-14	-0.4
	Phi-N	106	382	54	98	18	4	20	68	19	74	.257	.300	.482	105	1	2	1	0	.995	6	O-79,1-22	0.1
	Yr	121	411	57	103	18	4	21	70	22	80	.251	.297	.467	99	-2	2	1	0	.990	5	O-93,1-22	-0.3
1962	Phi-N	153	550	85	169	24	3	29	107	41	93	.307	.366	.520	139	29	2	7	-4	.937	-13	*3-105,O-63/1-1	1.0
1963	Phi-N	154	515	63	133	20	2	22	83	31	93	.258	.308	.433	112	7	1	4	-2	**1.000**	-7	*O-119,3-43,1-26	-0.8
1964	Det-A	134	441	57	113	22	1	22	80	17	85	.256	.292	.460	104	0	4	1	1	1.000	-0	O-88,1-23	-0.6
1965	Det-A	122	389	50	108	16	4	16	58	23	65	.278	.328	.463	121	9	4	2	0	.988	-2	O-82,1-34	0.3
1966	Det-A	32	99	12	21	5	0	5	12	5	19	.212	.235	.414	81	-3	1	0	0	.985	5	O-27/1-4	-0.1
	Bos-A	73	226	31	66	13	1	9	29	5	42	.292	.310	.478	111	2	1	0	0	.982	-2	O-57/1-2	-0.1
	Yr	105	325	43	87	18	1	14	41	8	61	.268	.287	.458	102	-0	2	0	1	.984	3	O-84/1-6	0.0
1967	Bos-A	20	43	7	12	6	0	2	4	3	11	.279	.326	.465	122	1	0	0	0	1.000	-1	O-12/3-1	0.0
	Cle-A	51	121	15	25	4	0	5	12	6	16	.207	.256	.364	80	-3	0	0	0	.985	-0	O-35/3-1	-0.7
	Yr	71	164	22	37	10	0	6	16	9	27	.226	.274	.390	92	-2	0	0	0	.988	-3	O-47/3-2	-0.7
Total	11	1109	3443	467	912	147	17	163	563	180	658	.265	.309	.459	108	26	22	25	-8	.990	-37	O-802,3-150,1-112	-5.8

■ STEVE DEMETER

Demeter, Stephen b: 1/27/35, Homer City, Pa. BR/TR, 5'9.5", 185 lbs. Deb: 7/29/59 C

YEAR	TM/L	G	AB	R	H	2B	3B	HR	RBI	BB	SO	AVG	OBP	SLG	PRO+	BR/A	SB	CS	SBR	FA	FR	G/POS	TPR
1959	Det-A	11	18	1	2	1	0	0	1	0	1	.111	.111	.167	-24	-3	0	0	0	.909	1	/3-4	-0.2
1960	Cle-A	4	5	0	0	0	0	0	0	0	0	.000	.000	.000	-99	-1	0	0	0	1.000	0	/3-3	-0.1
Total	2	15	23	1	2	1	0	0	1	0	2	.087	.087	.130	-40	-4	0	0	0	.933	1	/3-7	-0.3

■ RAY DEMMITT

Demmitt, Charles Raymond b: 2/2/1884, Illiopolis, Ill. d: 2/19/56, Glen Ellyn, Ill. BL/TR, 5'8", 170 lbs. Deb: 4/12/09

YEAR	TM/L	G	AB	R	H	2B	3B	HR	RBI	BB	SO	AVG	OBP	SLG	PRO+	BR/A	SB	CS	SBR	FA	FR	G/POS	TPR
1909	NY-A	123	427	68	105	12	12	4	30	55		.246	.340	.358	120	11	16			.908	5	*O-109	1.3
1910	StL-A	10	23	4	4	1	0	0	2	3		.174	.296	.217	65	-1	0			1.000	-1	/O-8	0.0
1914	Det-A	1	0	0	0	0	0	0	0	0		—	—	—	—	0	0			.000	0	R	0.0
	Chi-A	146	515	63	133	13	12	2	46	61	48	.258	.344	.342	108	6	12	20	-8	.953	-5	*O-142	-1.6
	Yr	147	515	63	133	13	12	2	46	61	48	.258	.344	.342	108	6	12	20	-8	.953	-5	*O-142	-1.6
1915	Chi-A	9	6	0	0	0	0	0	0	1	2	.000	.143	.000	-55	-1	0			1.000	-1	/O-3	-0.2
1917	StL-A	14	53	6	15	2	1	0	7	0	8	.283	.296	.377	109	0	1			1.000	-3	O-14	-0.0
1918	StL-A	116	405	45	114	23	5	1	61	38	35	.281	.346	.370	120	9	10			.951	-3	*O-114	1.1
1919	StL-A	79	202	19	48	11	2	1	19	14	27	.238	.290	.327	71	-8	3			.868	-7	O-49	-2.0
Total	7	498	1631	205	419	61	33	8	165	172	120	.257	.334	.349	108	16	42	20		.934	-3	O-439	-1.8

■ GENE DeMONTREVILLE

DeMontreville, Eugene Napoleon b: 3/26/1874, St.Paul, Minn. d: 2/18/35, Memphis, Tenn. BR/TR, 5'8", 165 lbs. Deb: 8/20/1894 F

YEAR	TM/L	G	AB	R	H	2B	3B	HR	RBI	BB	SO	AVG	OBP	SLG	PRO+	BR/A	SB	CS	SBR	FA	FR	G/POS	TPR
1894	Pit-N	2	8	0	2	0	0	0	0	1	4	.250	.333	.250	43	-1	0			.889	1	/S-2	-0.1
1895	Was-N	12	46	7	10	1	3	0	9	3	4	.217	.265	.370	63	-3	5			.929	4	S-12	0.1
1896	Was-N	133	533	94	183	24	5	8	77	29	27	.343	.381	.452	119	13	28			.890	16	*S-133	2.8
1897	Was-N	133	566	92	193	27	8	3	93	21		.341	.366	.433	111	7	30			.886	10	*S-99,2-33	1.8
1898	Bal-N	151	567	93	186	19	2	0	86	52		.328	.394	.369	117	14	49			.944	0	*2-123,S-28	2.2
1899	Chi-N	82	310	43	87	6	3	0	40	17		.281	.328	.319	80	-8	26			.902	9	S-82	0.7
	Bal-N	60	240	40	67	13	1	0	36	10		.279	.313	.379	85	-6	21			.961	9	2-60	0.5
	Yr	142	550	83	154	19	4	0	76	27		.280	.322	.345	82	-14	47			.902	18	S-82,2-60	1.2
1900	Bro-N	69	234	34	57	7	0	0	28	10		.244	.289	.286	54	-15	21			.952	0	2-48,S-12/3-7,O1	-1.1
1901	Bos-N	140	577	83	173	14	4	5	72	17		.300	.321	.364	90	-9	25			**.954**	5	*2-120,3-20	0.1
1902	Bos-N	124	481	51	125	16	5	0	53	12		.260	.278	.314	82	-12	23			.940	-17	*2-112,S-10	-2.5
1903	Was-A	12	44	0	12	0	0	0	0	2		.273	.273	.318	75	-1	0			.931	-1	/2-11,S-1	-0.6
1904	StL-N	8	9	2	1	0	0	0	0	2		.111	.273	.111	25	-1	0			1.000	-1	/2-3	-0.1
Total	11	922	3615	537	1096	130	35	17	497	174	35	.303	.340	.373	97	-21	228			.948	31	2-510,S-379/310	3.8

■ LEE DeMONTREVILLE

DeMontreville, Leon b: 9/23/1875, Washington Co., Minn. d: 3/22/62, Pelham Manor, N.Y. BR/TR, 5'7", 140 lbs. Deb: 7/10/03 F

YEAR	TM/L	G	AB	R	H	2B	3B	HR	RBI	BB	SO	AVG	OBP	SLG	PRO+	BR/A	SB	CS	SBR	FA	FR	G/POS	TPR
1903	StL-N	26	70	8	17	3	1	0	7	8		.243	.338	.314	89	-1	3			.901	-3	S-15/2-4,O-1	-0.3

YEAR	TM/L	G	AB	R	H	2B	3B	HR	RBI	BB	SO	AVG	OBP	SLG	PRO+	BR/A	SB	CS	SBR	FA	FR	G/POS	TPR

■ **RICK DEMPSEY**   Dempsey, John Rikard   b: 9/13/49, Fayetteville, Tenn.   BR/TR, 6', 190 lbs.   Deb: 9/23/69

YEAR	TM/L	G	AB	R	H	2B	3B	HR	RBI	BB	SO	AVG	OBP	SLG	PRO+	BR/A	SB	CS	SBR	FA	FR	G/POS	TPR
1969	Min-A	5	6	1	3	1	0	0	0	1	0	.500	.571	.667	240	1	0	0	0	.833	-1	/C-3	0.0
1970	Min-A	5	7	1	0	0	0	0	0	1	1	.000	.125	.000	-62	-2	0	0	0	.923	0	/C-3	-0.2
1971	Min-A	6	13	2	4	1	0	0	0	1	1	.308	.357	.385	107	0	0	0	0	.944	0	/C-6	0.2
1972	Min-A	25	40	0	8	1	0	0	0	6	8	.200	.304	.225	56	-2	0	0	0	.986	-1	/C-23	-0.3
1973	NY-A	6	11	0	2	0	0	0	0	1	3	.182	.250	.182	24	-1	0	0	0	.818	-2	/C-5	-0.3
1974	NY-A	43	109	12	26	3	0	2	12	8	7	.239	.291	.321	77	-3	1	0	0	.978	4	C-31/O-2,D-1	0.2
1975	NY-A	71	145	18	38	8	0	1	11	21	15	.262	.355	.338	98	0	0	0	0	.977	3	C-19,D-18/O-8,3-1	0.3
1976	NY-A	21	42	1	5	0	0	0	2	5	4	.119	.213	.119	-1	-5	0	0	0	1.000	2	/C-9,O-4	-0.3
	Bal-A	59	174	11	37	2	0	0	10	13	17	.213	.275	.224	50	-11	1	1	-0	.987	5	C-58/O-3	-0.5
	Yr	80	216	12	42	2	0	0	12	18	21	.194	.263	.204	40	-16	1	1	-0	.988	7	C-67/O-7	-0.8
1977	Bal-A	91	270	27	61	7	4	3	34	34	34	.226	.317	.315	78	-8	2	3	-1	.977	-2	C-91	-0.9
1978	Bal-A	136	441	41	114	25	0	6	32	48	54	.259	.331	.356	99	-0	7	3	0	.985	-5	*C-135	-0.1
1979	*Bal-A	124	368	48	88	23	0	6	41	38	37	.239	.310	.351	81	-10	0	1	-1	.990	19	*C-124	1.0
1980	Bal-A	119	362	51	95	26	3	9	40	36	45	.262	.334	.425	108	4	3	1	0	.987	8	*C-112/O-6,1-2,D-1	1.7
1981	Bal-A	92	251	24	54	10	1	6	15	32	36	.215	.306	.335	85	-5	0	1	-1	**.998**	3	C-90/D-1	0.1
1982	Bal-A	125	344	35	88	15	1	5	36	46	37	.256	.344	.349	91	-3	0	3	-2	.991	0	*C-124/D-1	0.0
1983	*Bal-A	128	347	33	80	16	2	4	32	40	54	.231	.315	.323	78	-10	1	1	-0	**.997**	21	*C-128	1.5
1984	Bal-A	109	330	37	76	11	0	11	34	40	58	.230	.315	.364	89	-5	1	2	-1	.992	-4	*C-108	-0.5
1985	Bal-A	132	362	54	92	19	0	12	52	50	87	.254	.346	.406	108	5	0	1	-1	.987	-11	*C-131	0.0
1986	Bal-A	122	327	42	68	15	1	13	29	45	78	.208	.309	.379	87	-6	1	0	0	.990	5	*C-121	0.6
1987	Cle-A	60	141	16	25	10	0	1	9	23	29	.177	.297	.270	51	-10	0	0	0	.984	1	C-59	-0.5
1988	*LA-N	77	167	25	42	13	0	7	30	25	44	.251	.349	.455	133	7	1	0	0	.989	5	C-74	1.7
1989	LA-N	79	151	16	27	7	0	4	16	30	37	.179	.319	.305	80	-3	1	0	0	.984	3	C-62	0.3
1990	LA-N	62	128	13	25	5	0	2	15	23	29	.195	.318	.281	68	-5	0	0	0	.992	0	C-53	-0.2
1991	Mil-A	61	147	15	34	5	0	4	21	23	20	.231	.335	.347	91	-1	0	2	-1	.993	4	C-56/P-2,1-1	0.4
1992	Bal-A	8	9	2	1	0	0	0	0	2	1	.111	.273	.111	11	-1	0	0	0	1.000	-1	/C-8	-0.2
Total	24	1766	4692	525	1093	223	12	96	471	592	736	.233	.321	.347	88	-72	20	19	-5	.988	59	*C-1633/O-23,D1P3	4.2

■ **TOD DENNEHEY**   Dennehey, Thomas Francis   b: 5/12/1899, Philadelphia, Pa.   d: 8/8/77, Philadelphia, Pa.   BL/TL, 5'10", 180 lbs.   Deb: 4/21/23

YEAR	TM/L	G	AB	R	H	2B	3B	HR	RBI	BB	SO	AVG	OBP	SLG	PRO+	BR/A	SB	CS	SBR	FA	FR	G/POS	TPR
1923	Phi-N	9	24	4	7	2	0	0	2	1	3	.292	.320	.375	74	-1	0	0	0	1.000	-1	/O-9	-0.2

■ **OTTO DENNING**   Denning, Otto George "Dutch"   b: 12/28/12, Hays, Kan.   d: 5/25/92, Chicago, Ill.   BR/TR, 6', 180 lbs.   Deb: 4/15/42

YEAR	TM/L	G	AB	R	H	2B	3B	HR	RBI	BB	SO	AVG	OBP	SLG	PRO+	BR/A	SB	CS	SBR	FA	FR	G/POS	TPR
1942	Cle-A	92	214	15	45	14	0	1	19	18	14	.210	.275	.290	62	-11	0	0	0	**.992**	-2	C-78/O-2	-0.9
1943	Cle-A	37	129	8	31	6	0	0	13	5	1	.240	.269	.287	67	-6	3	1	0	.966	-3	1-34	-1.2
Total	2	129	343	23	76	20	0	1	32	23	15	.222	.272	.289	64	-17	3	1	0	**.99**	-6	/C-78,1-34,O-2	-2.1

■ **JERRY DENNY**   Denny, Jeremiah Dennis (b: Jeremiah Dennis Eldridge)   b: 3/16/1859, New York, N.Y.   d: 8/16/27, Houston, Tex.   BR/TR, 5'11.5", 180 lbs.   Deb: 5/2/1881

YEAR	TM/L	G	AB	R	H	2B	3B	HR	RBI	BB	SO	AVG	OBP	SLG	PRO+	BR/A	SB	CS	SBR	FA	FR	G/POS	TPR
1881	Pro-N	85	320	38	77	16	2	1	24	5	44	.241	.252	.313	78	-8				.840	6	*3-85	-0.1
1882	Pro-N	84	329	54	81	10	9	2	42	4	46	.246	.255	.350	92	-3				.861	13	*3-84	1.0
1883	Pro-N	98	393	73	108	26	8	8	55	9	48	.275	.291	.443	116	6				**.876**	10	*3-98	1.4
1884	*Pro-N	110	439	57	109	22	9	6	59	14	58	.248	.272	.380	105	2				.874	-2	*3-99/1-9,2-3,C-1	0.0
1885	Pro-N	83	318	40	71	14	4	3	24	12	53	.223	.252	.321	88	-4				.869	-0	*3-83	-0.3
1886	StL-N	119	475	58	122	24	6	9	62	14	68	.257	.278	.389	108	4	16			.895	23	*3-117/S-3	2.6
1887	Ind-N	122	510	86	165	34	12	11	97	15	22	.324	.344	.502	137	23	29			.889	23	*3-116/S-4,O-1,2-1	4.0
1888	Ind-N	126	524	92	137	27	7	12	63	9	79	.261	.277	.408	114	6	32			.894	25	*3-96,S-25/2-5,OP	3.2
1889	Ind-N	133	578	96	163	24	0	18	112	27	63	.282	.314	.417	101	-2	22			**.913**	12	*3-123/2-7,S-5	1.3
1890	NY-N	114	437	50	93	18	7	3	42	28	62	.213	.270	.307	66	-19	11			.889	5	*3-106/S-7,2-1	-0.9
1891	NY-N	4	16	1	4	1	0	0	1	0	3	.250	.250	.313	66	-1	2			.700	-3	/3-4	-0.3
	Cle-N	36	138	17	31	5	0	0	21	12	23	.225	.291	.261	59	-7	3			.884	-3	3-29/O-7	-0.8
	Phi-N	19	73	5	21	1	1	0	11	4	6	.288	.325	.329	88	-1	1			.977	-1	1-12/3-7	-0.2
	Yr	59	227	22	56	7	1	0	33	16	32	.247	.299	.286	69	-9	6			.876	-8	3-40,1-12/O-7	-1.3
1893	Lou-N	44	175	22	43	5	4	1	22	9	15	.246	.283	.337	70	-8	4			.920	1	S-42/3-2	-0.5
1894	Lou-N	60	221	26	61	11	7	0	32	13	12	.276	.325	.389	71	-9	10			.874	3	3-60	-0.3
Total	13	1237	4946	714	1286	238	76	74	667	173	602	.260	.287	.384	99	-22	130			.882	109	*3-1109/S-86,120PC	9.9

■ **DREW DENSON**   Denson, Andrew   b: 11/16/65, Cincinnati, Ohio   BB/TR, 6'5", 210 lbs.   Deb: 9/13/89

YEAR	TM/L	G	AB	R	H	2B	3B	HR	RBI	BB	SO	AVG	OBP	SLG	PRO+	BR/A	SB	CS	SBR	FA	FR	G/POS	TPR
1989	Atl-N	12	36	1	9	1	0	0	5	0	9	.250	.308	.278	67	-1	1	0	0	.988	2	1-12	0.0
1993	Chi-A	4	5	0	1	0	0	0	0	2	2	.200	.200	.200	8	-1	0	0	0	.800	-0	/1-3	-0.1
Total	2	16	41	1	10	1	0	0	5	3	11	.244	.295	.268	60	-2	1	0	0	.977	2	/1-15	-0.1

■ **BUCKY DENT**   Dent, Russell Earl (b: Russell Earl O'Dey)   b: 11/25/51, Savannah, Ga.   BR/TR, 5'11", 181 lbs.   Deb: 6/1/73   MC

YEAR	TM/L	G	AB	R	H	2B	3B	HR	RBI	BB	SO	AVG	OBP	SLG	PRO+	BR/A	SB	CS	SBR	FA	FR	G/POS	TPR
1973	Chi-A	40	117	17	29	2	0	0	10	10	18	.248	.313	.265	62	-6	2	3	-1	.963	5	S-36/2-3,3-1	0.3
1974	Chi-A	154	496	55	136	15	3	5	45	28	48	.274	.317	.347	89	-7	3	4	-2	.972	9	*S-154	2.0
1975	Chi-A★	157	602	52	159	29	4	3	58	36	48	.264	.306	.341	81	-15	2	4	-2	**.981**	27	*S-157	2.7
1976	Chi-A	158	562	44	138	18	4	2	52	43	45	.246	.301	.302	77	-16	3	5	-2	.976	-6	*S-158	-0.5
1977	*NY-A	158	477	54	118	18	4	8	49	39	28	.247	.306	.352	80	-14	1	1	-0	.974	-11	*S-158	-0.8
1978	*NY-A	123	379	40	92	11	1	5	40	23	24	.243	.290	.317	72	-14	3	1	0	.981	-8	*S-123	-0.7
1979	NY-A	141	431	47	99	14	2	2	32	37	30	.230	.292	.285	58	-25	0	0	0	.977	32	*S-141	2.2
1980	*NY-A★	141	489	57	128	26	2	5	52	48	37	.262	.330	.354	89	-7	3	3	-2	**.982**	13	*S-141	2.1
1981	NY-A★	73	227	22	54	11	0	7	27	19	17	.238	.302	.379	97	-1	0	1	-1	.970	-2	S-73	0.4
1982	NY-A	59	160	11	27	1	1	0	9	8	11	.169	.208	.188	10	-20	0	0	0	.962	17	S-58	0.2
	Tex-A	46	146	16	32	9	0	1	14	13	10	.219	.283	.301	64	-7	0	0	0	.980	-1	S-45	-0.5
	Yr	105	306	27	59	10	1	1	23	21	21	.193	.245	.242	35	-27	0	0	0	.970	15	*S-103	-0.3
1983	Tex-A	131	417	36	99	15	2	2	34	23	31	.237	.279	.297	60	-23	3	7	-3	.979	-8	*S-129/D-1	-2.2
1984	KC-A	11	9	2	3	0	0	0	1	1	2	.333	.400	.333	105	0	0	0	0	1.000	-1	/S-9,3-2	0.0
Total	12	1392	4512	451	1114	169	23	40	423	328	343	.247	.300	.321	74	-155	17	29	-12	.976	66	*S-1382/3-3,2-3,D-1	5.2

■ **SAM DENTE**   Dente, Samuel Joseph "Blackie"   b: 4/26/22, Harrison, N.J.   BR/TR, 5'11", 175 lbs.   Deb: 7/10/47

YEAR	TM/L	G	AB	R	H	2B	3B	HR	RBI	BB	SO	AVG	OBP	SLG	PRO+	BR/A	SB	CS	SBR	FA	FR	G/POS	TPR
1947	Bos-A	46	168	14	39	4	2	0	11	19	15	.232	.310	.280	60	-9	0	1	-1	.939	-3	3-46	-1.3
1948	StL-A	98	267	26	72	11	2	0	22	22	8	.270	.328	.326	72	-11	1	3	-2	.958	-2	S-76/3-6	-1.0
1949	Was-A	153	590	48	161	24	4	1	53	31	24	.273	.309	.332	71	-26	4	1	0	.957	-9	*S-153	-2.6
1950	Was-A	155	603	56	144	20	5	2	59	39	19	.239	.286	.299	52	-45	1	1	0	.952	1	*S-128,2-29	-3.1
1951	Was-A	88	273	21	65	8	1	0	29	25	10	.238	.302	.275	58	-16	3	0	1	.962	3	S-65,2-10/3-5	-0.7
1952	Chi-A	62	145	12	32	7	0	0	11	5	8	.221	.257	.234	37	-12	0	0	0	.942	2	S-27,3-18/2-6,01	-0.9
1953	Chi-A	2	0	0	0	0	0	0	0	0	0	—	—	—		0	0	0	0	.000	0	/S-1	0.0
1954	*Cle-A	68	169	18	45	7	1	1	19	14	4	.266	.322	.337	79	-5	0	0	0	.971	-3	S-60/2-7	-0.4
1955	Cle-A	73	105	10	27	4	0	0	10	12	8	.257	.333	.295	68	-4	0	0	0	.958	7	S-53,3-13/2-4	0.5
Total	9	745	2320	205	585	78	16	4	214	167	96	.252	.303	.305	62	-128	9	9	-3	.958	-5	*S-563/3-88,2-56,01	-9.5

■ **MIKE DePANGHER**   DePangher, Michael Anthony   b: 9/11/1858, Marysville, Cal.   d: 7/7/15, San Francisco, Cal   BL, 5'8", 190 lbs.   Deb: 8/8/1884

YEAR	TM/L	G	AB	R	H	2B	3B	HR	RBI	BB	SO	AVG	OBP	SLG	PRO+	BR/A	SB	CS	SBR	FA	FR	G/POS	TPR
1884	Phi-N	4	10	0	2	0	0	0	0	1		.200	.273	.200	54	-0				.920	1	/C-4	0.0

■ **TONY DePHILLIPS**   DePhillips, Anthony Andrew   b: 9/20/12, New York, N.Y.   d: 5/5/94, Port Jefferson, N.Y.   BR/TR, 6'2", 185 lbs.   Deb: 4/25/43

YEAR	TM/L	G	AB	R	H	2B	3B	HR	RBI	BB	SO	AVG	OBP	SLG	PRO+	BR/A	SB	CS	SBR	FA	FR	G/POS	TPR
1943	Cin-N	35	20	0	2	1	0	0	2	1	5	.100	.143	.150	-16	-3	0	0	0	.981	5	C-35	0.3

■ **GENE DERBY**   Derby, Eugene A.   b: 2/3/1860, Fitchburg, Mass.   5'7", 160 lbs.   Deb: 9/3/1885

YEAR	TM/L	G	AB	R	H	2B	3B	HR	RBI	BB	SO	AVG	OBP	SLG	PRO+	BR/A	SB	CS	SBR	FA	FR	G/POS	TPR
1885	Bal-a	10	31	4	4	0	0	0	2	1		.129	.182	.129	-1	-3				.952	1	/C-9,O-1	-0.2

YEAR	TM/L	G	AB	R	H	2B	3B	HR	RBI	BB	SO	AVG	OBP	SLG	PRO+	BR/A	SB	CS	SBR	FA	FR	G/POS	TPR

■ BOB DERNIER Dernier, Robert Eugene b: 1/5/57, Kansas City, Mo. BR/TR, 6', 165 lbs. Deb: 9/7/80

1980	Phi-N	10	7	5	4	0	0	0	1	1	0	.571	.625	.571	224	1	3	0	1	1.000	0	/O-3	0.3
1981	Phi-N	10	4	0	3	0	0	0	0	0	0	.750	.750	.750	313	1	2	1	0	1.000	-2	/O-5	-0.1
1982	Phi-N	122	370	56	92	10	2	4	21	36	69	.249	.317	.319	77	-11	42	12	5	.981	-0	*O-119	-0.9
1983	*Phi-N	122	221	41	51	10	0	1	15	18	21	.231	.289	.290	61	-11	35	7	6	.988	-1	*O-107	-1.9
1984	*Chi-N	143	536	94	149	26	5	3	32	63	60	.278	.356	.362	94	-3	45	17	3	.986	5	*O-140	0.1
1985	Chi-N	121	469	63	119	20	3	1	21	40	44	.254	.316	.316	70	-18	31	8	5	.972	9	*O-116	-0.9
1986	Chi-N	108	324	32	73	14	1	4	18	22	41	.225	.275	.312	57	-19	27	2	7	.987	1	*O-105	-1.4
1987	Chi-N	93	199	38	63	4	4	8	21	19	19	.317	.379	.497	125	7	16	7	1	.989	-12	O-71	-0.5
1988	Phi-N	68	166	19	48	3	1	1	10	9	19	.289	.330	.337	90	-2	13	6	0	.980	-4	O-54	-0.8
1989	Phi-N	107	187	26	32	5	0	1	13	14	28	.171	.229	.214	27	-18	4	3	-1	.970	-13	O-74	-3.5
Total	10	904	2483	374	634	92	16	23	152	222	301	.255	.318	.333	77	-73	218	63	28	.982	-26	O-794	-9.6

■ CLAUD DERRICK Derrick, Claud Lester "Deek" b: 6/11/1886, Burton, Ga. d: 7/15/74, Clayton, Ga. BR/TR, 6', 175 lbs. Deb: 9/8/10

1910	Phi-A	2	1	0	0	0	0	0	0	0	0	.000	.000	.000	-99	-0	0			.500	-0	/S-1	-0.1
1911	Phi-A	36	100	14	23	1	2	0	5	7		.230	.294	.280	61	-5	7			.960	1	2-21/S-6,1-3,3-2	-0.5
1912	Phi-A	21	58	7	14	0	1	0	7	5		.241	.313	.276	71	-2	1			.884	1	S-18	0.0
1913	NY-A	23	65	7	19	1	0	1	7	5	8	.292	.352	.354	106	1	2			.874	3	S-17/3-4,2-1	0.2
1914	Cin-N	3	6	2	2	1	0	0	1	0		.333	.333	.500	142	0	1			.889	0	/S-2	0.1
	Chi-N	28	96	5	21	3	1	0	13	5	13	.219	.257	.271	57	-5	2			.895	3	/S-28	-0.1
	Yr	31	102	7	23	4	1	0	14	5	13	.225	.262	.284	62	-5	3			.894	3	S-30	0.0
Total	5	113	326	35	79	6	4	1	33	22	21	.242	.298	.294	72	-12	13			.892	4	/S-72,2-22,3-6,1-3	-0.4

■ MIKE DERRICK Derrick, James Michael b: 9/19/43, Columbia, S.C. BL/TR, 6', 190 lbs. Deb: 4/9/70

| 1970 | Bos-A | 24 | 33 | 3 | 7 | 1 | 0 | 0 | 5 | 0 | 11 | .212 | .212 | .242 | 23 | -3 | 0 | 1 | -1 | 1.000 | 0 | /O-2,1-1 | -0.4 |

■ RUSS DERRY Derry, Alva Russell b: 10/7/16, Princeton, Mo. BL/TR, 6'1", 180 lbs. Deb: 7/4/44

1944	NY-A	38	114	14	29	3	0	4	14	20	19	.254	.366	.386	111	2	1	0	0	.949	-1	O-28	0.0
1945	NY-A	78	253	37	57	6	2	13	45	31	49	.225	.312	.419	107	1	1	0	0	.978	0	O-68	-0.2
1946	Phi-A	69	184	17	38	8	5	0	14	27	54	.207	.311	.304	73	-6	0	0	0	.985	4	O-50	-0.5
1949	StL-N	2	2	0	0	0	0	0	0	0	2	.000	.000	.000	-96	-1	0			.000	0	H	-0.1
Total	4	187	553	68	124	17	7	17	73	78	124	.224	.322	.373	95	-4	2	0		.976	3	O-146	-0.8

■ JOE DeSA DeSa, Joseph b: 7/27/59, Honolulu, Hawaii d: 12/20/86, San Juan, P.R. BL/TL, 5'11", 170 lbs. Deb: 9/6/80

1980	StL-N	7	11	0	3	0	0	0	0	0	0	.273	.273	.273	51	-1	0	0	0	1.000	-0	/1-1,O-1	-0.1
1985	Chi-A	28	44	5	8	2	0	2	7	3	6	.182	.234	.364	58	-3	0	0	0	1.000	1	/1-9,O-1,D-4	-0.2
Total	2	35	55	5	11	2	0	2	7	3	8	.200	.241	.345	57	-3	0	0	0	1.000	1	/1-10,D-4,O-2	-0.3

■ GENE DESAUTELS Desautels, Eugene Abraham "Red" b: 6/13/07, Worcester, Mass. d: 11/5/94, Flint, Mich. BR/TR, 5'11", 170 lbs. Deb: 6/22/30

1930	Det-A	42	126	13	24	4	2	0	9	7	9	.190	.239	.254	25	-15	2	0	1	.996	9	C-42	-0.2
1931	Det-A	3	11	1	1	0	0	0	1	0	1	.091	.091	.091	-50	-2	0	0	0	1.000	-1	/C-3	-0.3
1932	Det-A	28	72	8	17	2	0	0	2	13	11	.236	.360	.264	62	-4	0	0	0	.984	4	C-24	0.2
1933	Det-A	30	42	5	6	1	0	0	4	4	6	.143	.234	.167	8	-6	0	0	0	.976	2	C-30	-0.2
1937	Bos-A	96	305	33	74	10	3	0	27	36	26	.243	.325	.295	55	-20	1	2	-1	**.993**	4	C-94	-1.2
1938	Bos-A	108	333	47	97	16	2	2	48	57	31	.291	.396	.369	89	-4	1	1	-0	.985	6	*C-108	0.6
1939	Bos-A	76	226	26	55	14	0	0	21	33	13	.243	.340	.305	64	-12	3	1	0	.994	10	C-73	0.2
1940	Bos-A	71	222	19	50	7	0	0	17	32	13	.225	.328	.266	54	-14	0	1	-1	.992	-3	C-70	-1.2
1941	Cle-A	66	189	20	38	5	1	1	17	14	12	.201	.260	.254	38	-17	1	0	0	.997	6	C-66	-0.6
1942	Cle-A	62	162	14	40	5	0	0	9	12	13	.247	.303	.278	68	-7	1	0	0	.975	-8	C-61	-1.1
1943	Cle-A	68	185	14	38	6	1	0	19	11	16	.205	.250	.249	49	-12	2	0	1	.982	2	C-66	-0.7
1945	Cle-A	10	9	1	1	0	0	0	0	1	1	.111	.200	.111	-9	-1	0	0	0	1.000	0	C-10	-0.1
1946	Phi-A	52	130	10	28	3	1	0	13	12	16	.215	.282	.254	51	-8	1	1	-0	.989	2	C-52	-0.5
Total	13	712	2012	211	469	73	11	3	187	232	168	.233	.315	.285	57	-122	12	6	0	.989	31	C-699	-5.1

■ DELINO DeSHIELDS DeShields, Delino Lamont b: 1/15/69, Seaford, Del. BL/TR, 6'1", 170 lbs. Deb: 4/9/90

1990	Mon-N	129	499	69	144	28	6	4	45	66	96	.289	.376	.393	116	13	42	22	-1	.981	-8	*2-128	0.7
1991	Mon-N	151	563	83	134	15	4	10	51	95	151	.238	.350	.332	94	-1	56	23	3	.962	-22	*2-148	-1.7
1992	Mon-N	135	530	82	155	19	8	7	56	54	108	.292	.361	.398	116	12	46	15	5	.976	-22	*2-134	-0.3
1993	Mon-N	123	481	75	142	17	7	2	29	72	64	.295	.389	.372	101	4	43	10	7	.983	-1	*2-123	1.4
1994	LA-N	89	320	51	80	11	3	2	33	54	53	.250	.358	.322	85	-6	27	7	4	.986	6	2-88,S-10	0.8
1995	*LA-N	127	425	66	109	18	3	8	37	63	83	.256	.354	.369	100	1	39	14	3	.980	1	*2-113	1.1
1996	*LA-N	154	581	75	130	12	8	5	41	53	124	.224	.290	.298	60	-34	48	11	**8**	.975	-18	*2-154	-3.4
Total	7	908	3399	501	894	120	39	38	292	457	679	.263	.353	.355	96	-11	301	102	29	.977	-64	2-888/S-10	-1.4

■ ORESTES DESTRADE Destrade, Orestes (Cucuas) b: 5/8/62, Santiago De Cuba, Cuba BB/TR, 6'4", 210 lbs. Deb: 9/11/87

1987	NY-A	9	19	5	5	0	0	1	5	5	.263	.417	.263	87	-0	0	0	0	1.000	-0	/1-3,D-2	0.0
1988	Pit-N	36	47	2	7	1	0	1	3	5	17	.149	.231	.234	34	-4	0	0	0	1.000	-1	/1-8	-0.6
1993	Fla-N	153	569	61	145	20	3	20	87	58	130	.255	.327	.406	90	-8	0	2	-1	.987	-7	*1-152	-2.9
1994	Fla-N	39	130	12	27	4	0	5	15	19	32	.208	.318	.354	73	-5	1	0	0	.983	-3	1-37	-1.1
Total	4	237	765	80	184	25	3	26	106	87	184	.241	.322	.383	84	-17	1	2	-1	.987	-11	1-200/D-2	-4.6

■ BOB DETHERAGE Detherage, Robert Wayne b: 9/20/54, Springfield, Mo. BR/TR, 6', 180 lbs. Deb: 4/11/80

| 1980 | KC-A | 20 | 26 | 2 | 8 | 2 | 0 | 1 | 7 | 1 | 4 | .308 | .333 | .500 | 124 | 1 | 1 | 1 | -0 | 1.000 | -7 | O-20 | -0.7 |

■ GEORGE DeTORE DeTore, George Francis b: 11/11/06, Utica, N.Y. d: 2/7/91, Utica, N.Y. BR/TR, 5'8", 170 lbs. Deb: 9/14/30 C

1930	Cle-A	3	12	0	2	1	0	0	2	0	2	.167	.167	.250	4	-2	0	0	0	.750	-2	/3-3	-0.3
1931	Cle-A	30	56	3	15	6	0	0	7	8	2	.268	.359	.375	88	-1	0	2	-1	.958	4	3-13,S-10/2-3	0.3
Total	2	33	68	3	17	7	0	0	9	8	4	.250	.329	.353	74	-3	0	2	-1	.929	2	/3-16,S-10,2-3	0.0

■ DUCKY DETWEILER Detweiler, Robert Sterling b: 2/15/19, Trumbauersville, Pa. BR/TR, 5'11", 178 lbs. Deb: 9/12/42

1942	Bos-N	12	44	3	14	2	1	0	5	5	7	.318	.348	.409	123	1	0			.929	-4	3-12	-0.3
1946	Bos-N	1	1	0	0	0	0	0	0	0	0	.000	.000	.000	-99	-0	0			.000	0	H	0.0
Total	2	13	45	3	14	2	1	0	5	5	7	.311	.340	.400	118	1	0			.929	-4	3-12	-0.3

■ CESAR DEVAREZ Devarez, Cesar Salvatore (Santana) b: 9/22/69, San Francisco De Macoris, D.R. BR/TR, 5'10", 175 lbs. Deb: 6/2/95

1995	Bal-A	6	4	0	0	0	0	0	0	0	0	.000	.000	.000	-99	-1	0	0	0	1.000	1	/C-6	0.0
1996	Bal-A	10	18	3	2	0	1	0	1	0	3	.111	.158	.222	-5	-3	0	0	0	1.000	1	C-10	-0.2
Total	2	16	22	3	2	0	1	0	1	0	3	.091	.130	.182	-22	-4	0	0	0	1.000	2	C-16	-0.2

■ MIKE DEVEREAUX Devereaux, Michael b: 4/10/63, Casper, Wyo. BR/TR, 6' ", 195 lbs. Deb: 9/2/87

1987	LA-N	19	54	7	12	3	0	0	4	3	10	.222	.263	.278	45	-4	3	1	0	1.000	-2	O-18	-0.6
1988	LA-N	30	43	4	5	1	0	0	2	2	10	.116	.156	.140	-15	-6	0	1	-1	1.000	-5	O-26	-1.4
1989	Bal-A	122	391	55	104	14	3	8	46	36	60	.266	.331	.379	103	3	22	11	0	.983	-4	*O-112/D-5	-0.5
1990	Bal-A	108	367	48	88	18	1	12	49	28	48	.240	.294	.392	93	-5	13	12	-3	.983	6	*O-104/D-3	-0.5
1991	Bal-A	149	608	82	158	27	10	19	59	47	115	.260	.315	.431	109	5	16	9	-1	.993	12	*O-149	1.2
1992	Bal-A	156	653	76	180	29	11	24	107	44	94	.276	.325	.464	116	11	10	8	0	.988	2	*O-155	1.2
1993	Bal-A	131	527	72	132	31	3	14	75	43	99	.250	.308	.400	85	-12	3	4	-1	.988	2	*O-130	-1.3
1994	Bal-A	85	301	35	61	8	2	9	33	22	72	.203	.259	.332	49	-24	1	2	-1	.995	0	O-84/D-1	-2.5
1995	Chi-A	92	333	48	92	21	1	10	55	25	51	.306	.355	.465	117	7	6	6	-2	.985	3	O-90	0.6
	*Atl-N	29	55	7	14	3	0	1	8	2	11	.255	.281	.364	66	-3	0	1	0	1.000	-2	O-27	-0.4
1996	*Bal-A	127	323	49	74	11	3	8	34	34	53	.229	.306	.350	66	-17	8	2	1	.983	-19	*O-112/D-10	-3.4
Total	10	1048	3655	483	930	166	33	105	472	286	623	.254	.311	.404	96	-46	84	55	-8	.988	-3	*O-1007/D-19	-7.6

YEAR	TM/L	G	AB	R	H	2B	3B	HR	RBI	BB	SO	AVG	OBP	SLG	PRO+	BR/A	SB	CS	SBR	FA	FR	G/POS	TPR

■ JIM DEVINE — Devine, Walter James b: 10/5/1858, Brooklyn, N.Y. d: 1/11/05, Syracuse, N.Y. TL , Deb: 5/9/1883

1883	Bal-a	2	9	4	2	0	0	0		0		.222	.222	.222	42	-1				.500	-1	/P-2,O-1	0.0
1886	NY-N	1	3	0	0	0	0	0	0	0	1	.000	.000	.000	-99	-1	0			.000	-0	/O-1	-0.1
Total	2	3	12	4	2	0	0	0	0	0	1	.167	.167	.167	6	-1	0			—	-1	/O-2,P-2	-0.1

■ MICKEY DEVINE — Devine, William Patrick b: 5/9/1892, Albany, N.Y. d: 10/1/37, Albany, N.Y. BR/TR, 5'10", 165 lbs. Deb: 8/2/18

1918	Phi-N	4	8	0	1	1	0	0	0	0	1	.125	.125	.250	13	-1				.909	0	/C-3	-0.1
1920	Bos-A	8	12	1	2	0	0	0	0	1	2	.167	.231	.167	7	-2	1	0	0	.955	1	/C-5	0.0
1925	NY-N	21	33	6	9	3	0	0	4	2	3	.273	.314	.364	76	-1	0	0	0	.933	2	C-11/3-1	0.1
Total	3	33	53	7	12	4	0	0	4	3	6	.226	.268	.302	51	-4	1	0		.936	2	/C-19,3-1	0.0

■ BERNIE DeVIVEIROS — DeViveiros, Bernard John b: 4/19/01, Oakland, Cal. d: 7/5/94, Oakland, Cal. BR/TR, 5'7", 160 lbs. Deb: 9/13/24

1924	Chi-A	1	1	0	0	0	0	0	0	0	0	.000	.000	.000	-99	-0	0	0	0	.333	-1	/S-1	-0.1
1927	Det-A	24	22	4	5	1	0	0	2	2	8	.227	.292	.273	46	-2	1	0	0	.913	0	S-14/3-1	-0.1
Total	2	25	23	4	5	1	0	0	2	2	8	.217	.280	.261	40	-2	1	0	0	.846	-1	/S-15,3-1	-0.2

■ ART DEVLIN — Devlin, Arthur McArthur b: 10/16/1879, Washington, D.C. d: 9/18/48, Jersey City, N.J. BR/TR, 6', 175 lbs. Deb: 4/14/04 C

1904	NY-N	130	474	81	133	16	8	1	66	62		.281	.371	.354	119	13	33			.907	7	*3-130	2.5
1905	*NY-N	153	525	74	129	14	7	2	61	66		.246	.344	.310	94	-1	59			.932	5	*3-153	1.0
1906	NY-N	148	498	76	149	23	8	2	65	74		.299	.396	.390	142	27	54			.944	28	*3-148	6.5
1907	NY-N	143	491	61	136	16	2	1	54	63		.277	.376	.324	116	12	38			.940	0	*3-140/S-3	1.9
1908	NY-N	157	534	59	135	18	4	2	45	62		.253	.346	.313	106	6	19			.947	13	*3-157	2.8
1909	NY-N	143	491	61	130	19	8	0	56	65		.265	.362	.336	115	11	26			.934	18	*3-143	3.7
1910	NY-N	147	493	71	128	17	5	0	67	62	32	.260	.353	.327	98	1	28			.933	5	*3-147	1.0
1911	NY-N	95	260	42	71	16	2	0	25	42	19	.273	.386	.350	103	3	9			.944	2	3-79/1-6,2-6,S-6	0.6
1912	Bos-N	124	436	59	126	18	8	0	54	51	37	.289	.367	.367	99	1	11			.992	-1	1-69,S-26,3-26,/O-1	0.1
1913	Bos-N	73	210	19	48	7	5	0	12	29	17	.229	.328	.310	81	-4	8			.973	9	3-69	0.5
Total	10	1313	4412	603	1185	164	57	10	505	576	105	.269	.364	.338	109	68	285			.938	86	*3-1192/1-75,S2O	20.6

■ JIM DEVLIN — Devlin, James Alexander b: 1849, Philadelphia, Pa. d: 10/10/1883, Philadelphia, Pa. BR/TR, 5'11", 175 lbs. Deb: 4/21/1873

1873	Phi-n	23	99	18	24	4	4	0	10	2	4	.242	.257	.364	79	-3	0	0	0	.938	-3	1-12/3-6,S-5,O-1	-0.4
1874	Chi-n	45	203	26	58	5	0	0	27	2	9	.286	.293	.310	93	-2	2	1	0	.930	-3	1-24,O-17/3-5	-0.3
1875	Chi-n	69	318	60	92	17	6	0	40	4	4	.289	.298	.381	133	10	6	1	1	.934	-0	1-42,P-28/O-4	0.5
1876	Lou-N	68	298	38	94	14	1	0	28	1	11	.315	.318	.369	109	-1				.941	2	*P-68/1-1	0.0
1877	Lou-N	61	268	38	72	6	3	1	27	7	27	.269	.287	.325	78	-9				.933	2	*P-61	0.0
Total	3 n	137	620	104	174	26	10	0	77	8	17	.281	.290	.355	110	5	8	2	1	.933	-6	/1-78,P-28,O-22,3S	-0.2
Total	2	129	566	76	166	20	4	1	55	8	38	.293	.303	.348	94	-10				.937	4	P-129/1-1	0.0

■ JIM DEVLIN — Devlin, James Raymond b: 8/25/22, Plains, Pa. BL/TR, 5'11.5", 165 lbs. Deb: 4/27/44

| 1944 | Cle-A | 1 | 1 | 0 | 0 | 0 | 0 | 0 | 0 | 0 | 0 | .000 | .000 | .000 | -99 | -0 | 0 | 0 | 0 | 1.000 | 0 | /C-1 | 0.0 |

■ REX DeVOGT — DeVogt, Rex Eugene b: 1/4/1888, Clare, Mich. d: 11/9/35, Alma, Mich. BR/TR, 5'9", 170 lbs. Deb: 4/17/13

| 1913 | Bos-N | 3 | 6 | 0 | 0 | 0 | 0 | 0 | 0 | 0 | 3 | .000 | .000 | .000 | -98 | -2 | 0 | | | .941 | 1 | /C-3 | 0.0 |

■ JOSH DEVORE — Devore, Joshua D. b: 11/13/1887, Murray City, Ohio d: 10/6/54, Chillicothe, Ohio BL/TL, 5'6", 160 lbs. Deb: 9/25/08

1908	NY-N	5	6	1	1	0	0	0	0	0		.167	.286	.167	43	-0	1			1.000	-1	/O-2	-0.1
1909	NY-N	22	28	6	4	1	0	0	1	2		.143	.250	.179	33	-2	3			.824	-4	O-12	-0.7
1910	NY-N	133	490	92	149	11	10	2	27	46	67	.304	.371	.380	119	12	43			.929	-12	*O-130	-0.6
1911	*NY-N	149	565	96	158	19	10	3	50	81	69	.280	.376	.365	104	6	61			.934	1	*O-149	-0.1
1912	*NY-N	106	327	66	90	14	6	2	37	51	43	.275	.381	.373	104	3	27			.918	-8	O-96	-0.9
1913	NY-N	16	21	4	4	0	1	0	1	3	4	.190	.320	.286	73	-1	6			1.000	-0	/O-8	-0.3
	Cin-N	66	217	30	58	6	4	3	14	12	21	.267	.309	.373	95	-2	17			.920	-3	O-57	-0.8
	Phi-N	23	39	9	11	1	0	0	5	4	7	.282	.364	.308	89	-0	0			.889	-3	O-14	-0.4
	Yr	105	277	43	73	7	5	3	20	19	32	.264	.318	.357	92	-3	23			.919	-9	O-79	-1.5
1914	Phi-N	30	53	5	16	2	0	0	7	4	5	.302	.351	.340	99	-0	2			.947	2	/O-9	0.2
	*Bos-N	51	128	22	29	4	0	1	5	18	14	.227	.327	.281	82	-2	2			.915	-8	O-42	-1.3
	Yr	81	181	27	45	6	0	1	12	22	19	.249	.333	.298	87	-2	2			.923	-6	O-51	-1.1
Total	7	601	1874	331	520	58	31	11	149	222	230	.277	.361	.359	103	13	160			.925	-38	O-519	-5.0

■ AL DeVORMER — DeVormer, Albert E. b: 8/19/1891, Grand Rapids, Mich d: 8/29/66, Grand Rapids, Mich BR/TR, 6'0.5", 175 lbs. Deb: 8/4/18

1918	Chi-A	8	19	2	5	2	0	0	0	0	4	.263	.263	.368	90	-0	1			1.000	-2	/C-6,O-1	-0.2
1921	*NY-A	22	49	6	17	4	0	0	7	2	4	.347	.373	.429	102	0	2	0	1	.950	-1	C-17	0.1
1922	NY-A	24	59	8	12	4	1	0	11	1	6	.203	.217	.305	34	-6	0	0	0	.968	-1	C-17/1-1	-0.6
1923	Bos-A	74	209	20	54	7	3	0	18	6	21	.258	.282	.321	58	-13	0	0	1	.979	-4	C-55/1-2	-0.9
1927	NY-N	68	141	14	35	3	1	2	21	11	11	.248	.312	.326	71	-6	1			.953	-4	C-54/1-3	-0.8
Total	5	196	477	50	123	20	5	2	57	20	46	.258	.292	.333	65	-25	7	0		.967	-7	C-149/1-6,O-1	-2.4

■ WALT DEVOY — Devoy, Walter Joseph b: 3/14/1886, St.Louis, Mo. d: 12/17/53, St.Louis, Mo. 5'11", 165 lbs. Deb: 9/13/09

| 1909 | StL-A | 19 | 69 | 7 | 17 | 3 | 1 | 0 | 8 | 3 | | .246 | .278 | .319 | 95 | -1 | 4 | | | .944 | -2 | O-16/1-3 | -0.3 |

■ JEFF DeWILLIS — DeWillis, Jeffrey Allen b: 4/13/65, Houston, Tex. BR/TR, 6'2", 170 lbs. Deb: 4/19/87

| 1987 | Tor-A | 13 | 25 | 2 | 3 | 1 | 0 | 1 | 2 | 2 | 12 | .120 | .185 | .280 | 21 | -3 | 0 | 0 | 0 | .964 | 2 | C-13 | -0.1 |

■ CHARLIE DEXTER — Dexter, Charles Dana b: 6/15/1876, Evansville, Ind. d: 6/9/34, Cedar Rapids, Iowa BR/TR, 5'7", 155 lbs. Deb: 4/17/1896

1896	Lou-N	107	402	65	112	18	7	3	37	17	34	.279	.318	.381	87	-9	21			.903	-3	C-55,O-47	-0.8
1897	Lou-N	76	257	43	72	12	5	2	46	21		.280	.342	.389	96	-2	12			.907	-5	O-32,C-23,3-14,/S-2	-0.5
1898	Lou-N	112	421	76	132	13	5	1	66	26		.314	.363	.375	114	7	44			.958	-1	O-95/2-8,C-7	0.1
1899	Lou-N	80	295	47	76	7	1	1	33	21		.258	.318	.298	69	-12	21			.942	0	O-71/S-6	-1.3
1900	Chi-N	40	125	7	25	5	0	2	20	1		.200	.213	.288	39	-11	2			.943	8	C-22,O-13/2-1	-0.9
1901	Chi-N	116	460	46	123	9	5	1	66	16		.267	.302	.315	82	-11	22			.982	3	1-54,3-25,O-21,2/C	-0.9
1902	Chi-N	69	266	30	60	12	0	2	26	19		.226	.290	.293	82	-5	13			.853	-13	3-39,1-22,O-10	-2.0
	Bos-N	48	183	33	47	3	1	0	18	16		.257	.323	.290	88	-2	16			.901	-4	S-22,2-19/O-7,3-1	-0.4
	Yr	117	449	63	107	15	1	2	44	35		.238	.303	.292	85	-7	29			.854	-16	3-40,1-22,S-22,2O	-2.4
1903	Bos-N	85	457	82	102	15	1	3	34	61		.223	.323	.280	75	-12	32			.941	-10	*O-106/S-9,C-6	-2.7
Total	8	771	2866	429	749	94	24	16	346	198	34	.261	.318	.328	85	-57	183			.942	-22	O-402,C-116/312S	-8.7

■ ALEX DIAZ — Diaz, Alexis b: 10/5/68, Brooklyn, N.Y. BB/TR, 5'11", 175 lbs. Deb: 7/25/92

1992	Mil-A	22	9	5	1	0	0	0	1	0	0	.111	.111	.111	-38	-2	3	2	-0	1.000	-4	O-11/D-2	-0.7
1993	Mil-A	32	69	9	22	2	0	0	1	0	12	.319	.319	.348	80	-2	5	3	-0	.979	-4	O-28/D-1	-0.6
1994	Mil-A	79	187	17	47	5	7	1	17	10	19	.251	.289	.369	65	-10	5	5	-2	.993	-9	O-73/2-2,D-1	-2.0
1995	*Sea-A	103	270	44	67	14	3	0	27	13	27	.248	.288	.333	60	-16	18	8	1	.987	-7	O-88	-2.3
1996	Sea-A	38	79	11	19	2	0	1	5	2	8	.241	.277	.304	47	-6	6	3	-1	.982	-1	O-28/D-1	-0.7
Total	5	274	614	86	156	23	7	5	51	25	66	.254	.288	.339	61	-36	37	21	-2	.988	-25	O-228/D-5,2-2	-6.3

■ BO DIAZ — Diaz, Baudilio Jose (Seijas) b: 3/23/53, Cua, Venezuela d: 11/23/90, Caracas, Venez. BR/TR, 5'11", 190 lbs. Deb: 9/6/77

1977	Bos-A	2	1	0	0	0	0	0	0	0	0	.000	.000	.000	-90	-0	0	0		1.000	1	/C-2	0.0
1978	Cle-A	44	127	12	30	4	0	2	11	4	17	.236	.260	.315	61	-7	0	0	0	.971	-1	C-44	-0.7
1979	Cle-A	15	32	0	5	2	0	0	5	1	6	.156	.206	.219	15	-4	0	0	0	.958	4	C-15	-0.6
1980	Cle-A	76	207	15	47	11	2	3	32	7	27	.227	.252	.343	61	-12	1	0	0	.989	3	C-75	-0.6
1981	Cle-A★	63	182	25	57	19	0	7	38	13	23	.313	.362	.533	157	13	2	2	-1	.975	3	C-51/D-3	1.1
1982	Phi-N	144	525	69	151	29	1	18	85	36	87	.288	.337	.450	116	10	3	6	-3	.989	-9	*C-144	0.4
1983	*Phi-N	136	471	49	111	17	0	15	64	38	57	.236	.295	.367	84	-11	1	4	-2	.986	14	*C-134	0.7

Year	Tm/L	G	AB	R	H	2B	3B	HR	RBI	BB	SO	AVG	OBP	SLG	PRO+	BR/A	SB	CS	SBR	FA	FR	G/POS	TPR
1984	Phi-N	27	75	5	16	4	0	1	9	5	13	.213	.262	.307	58	-4	0	0	0	.992	-0	C-23	-0.4
1985	Phi-N	26	76	9	16	5	1	2	16	6	7	.211	.268	.382	78	-3	0	0	0	.972	2	C-24	0.1
	Cin-N	51	161	12	42	8	0	3	15	15	18	.261	.328	.366	89	-2	0	0	0	.988	9	C-51	0.9
	Yr	77	237	21	58	13	1	5	31	21	25	.245	.309	.371	86	-5	0	0	0	.983	11	C-75	1.0
1986	Cin-N	134	474	50	129	21	0	10	56	40	52	.272	.328	.380	91	-6	1	1	-0	.984	-6	*C-134	-0.4
1987	Cin-N★	140	496	49	134	28	1	15	82	19	73	.270	.304	.421	86	-11	1	0	0	.992	-6	*C-137	-0.7
1988	Cin-N	92	315	26	69	9	0	10	35	7	41	.219	.238	.343	63	-16	0	2	-1	.990	-3	C-88	-1.5
1989	Cin-N	43	132	6	27	5	0	1	8	6	7	.205	.239	.265	43	-10	0	2	-1	.984	-0	C-43	-1.0
Total	13	993	3274	327	834	162	5	87	452	198	429	.255	.300	.387	87	-63	9	17	-8	.986	3	C-965/D-3	-2.1

■ CARLOS DIAZ
Diaz, Carlos Francisco b: 12/24/64, Elizabeth, N.J. BR/TR, 6'3", 195 lbs. Deb: 5/8/90

Year	Tm/L	G	AB	R	H	2B	3B	HR	RBI	BB	SO	AVG	OBP	SLG	PRO+	BR/A	SB	CS	SBR	FA	FR	G/POS	TPR
1990	Tor-A	9	3	1	1	0	0	0	0	0	2	.333	.333	.333	85	-0	0	0	0	1.000	2	/C-9	0.2

■ EDGAR DIAZ
Diaz, Edgar (Serrano) b: 2/8/64, Santurce, P.R. BR/TR, 6', 155 lbs. Deb: 9/16/86

Year	Tm/L	G	AB	R	H	2B	3B	HR	RBI	BB	SO	AVG	OBP	SLG	PRO+	BR/A	SB	CS	SBR	FA	FR	G/POS	TPR
1986	Mil-A	5	13	0	3	0	0	0	0	0	3	.231	.286	.231	41	-1	0	0	0	.875	-1	/S-5	-0.1
1990	Mil-A	86	218	27	59	2	2	0	14	21	32	.271	.338	.298	80	-5	3	2	-0	.950	-1	S-65,2-15/3-7,D-1	-0.1
Total	2	91	231	27	62	2	2	0	14	22	35	.268	.335	.294	78	-6	3	2	-0	.946	-1	/S-70,2-15,3-7,D-1	-0.2

■ EINAR DIAZ
Diaz, Einar Antonio b: 12/28/72, Chiriqui, Panama BR/TR, 5'10", 165 lbs. Deb: 9/9/96

Year	Tm/L	G	AB	R	H	2B	3B	HR	RBI	BB	SO	AVG	OBP	SLG	PRO+	BR/A	SB	CS	SBR	FA	FR	G/POS	TPR
1996	Cle-A	4	1	0	0	0	0	0	0	0	0	.000	.000	.000	-99	-0	0	0	0	1.000	1	/C-4	0.0

■ MARIO DIAZ
Diaz, Mario Rafael (Torres) b: 1/10/62, Humacao, P.R. BR/TR, 5'10", 160 lbs. Deb: 9/12/87

Year	Tm/L	G	AB	R	H	2B	3B	HR	RBI	BB	SO	AVG	OBP	SLG	PRO+	BR/A	SB	CS	SBR	FA	FR	G/POS	TPR
1987	Sea-A	11	23	4	7	0	1	0	3	0	4	.304	.304	.391	79	-1	0	0	0	.972	4	S-10	0.3
1988	Sea-A	28	72	6	22	5	0	0	9	3	5	.306	.333	.375	94	-1	0	0	0	.985	-4	S-21/2-4,1-1,3-1	-0.3
1989	Sea-A	52	74	9	10	0	0	0	7	7	7	.135	.210	.176	9	-9	0	0	0	.930	-9	S-37,2-14/3-3	-1.7
1990	NY-N	16	22	0	3	1	0	0	1	0	3	.136	.136	.182	-13	-3	0	0	0	.958	2	S-10/2-1	-0.2
1991	Tex-A	96	182	24	48	7	0	1	22	15	18	.264	.320	.319	79	-5	0	1	-1	.962	-2	S-65,2-20/3-8,D-1	-0.5
1992	Tex-A	19	31	2	7	1	0	0	1	1	2	.226	.250	.258	44	-2	0	1	-1	.975	1	S-16/2-3,3-1	-0.1
1993	Tex-A	71	205	24	56	10	1	2	24	8	13	.273	.304	.361	81	-6	1	0	0	.986	-4	S-57,3-12/1-1	-0.6
1994	Fla-N	32	77	10	25	4	2	0	11	6	6	.325	.381	.429	107	1	0	0	0	.964	-0	3-11/2-7,S-7	0.1
1995	Fla-N	49	87	5	20	3	0	1	6	1	12	.230	.239	.299	41	-8	0	0	0	.944	-2	/2-9,S-5,3-3	-0.8
Total	9	374	773	84	198	31	4	5	84	41	70	.256	.295	.326	69	-33	1	2	-1	.972	-15	S-228/2-58,3-39,1D	-3.8

■ MIKE DIAZ
Diaz, Michael Anthony b: 4/15/60, San Francisco, Cal. BR/TR, 6'2", 195 lbs. Deb: 9/15/83

Year	Tm/L	G	AB	R	H	2B	3B	HR	RBI	BB	SO	AVG	OBP	SLG	PRO+	BR/A	SB	CS	SBR	FA	FR	G/POS	TPR
1983	Chi-N	6	7	2	2	1	0	0	1	0	0	.286	.286	.429	91	-0	0	0	0	1.000	-0	/C-3	-0.1
1986	Pit-N	97	209	22	56	9	0	12	36	19	43	.268	.335	.483	120	5	0	1	-1	.966	-5	O-38,1-20/3-5,C-1	-0.3
1987	Pit-N	103	241	28	58	8	2	16	48	31	42	.241	.335	.490	114	4	1	0	0	.960	-6	O-37,1-32/C-8	-0.4
1988	Pit-N	47	74	6	17	0	0		5	16	13	.230	.367	.270	87	-0	0	0	0	1.000	-5	O-19/1-6,C-1	-0.6
	Chi-A	40	152	12	36	6	0	3	12	5	30	.237	.266	.336	67	-7	0	1	-1	.987	2	1-39/D-1	-1.3
Total	4	293	683	70	169	27	2	31	102	71	128	.247	.324	.429	103	2	1	2	-1	.988	-18	/1-97,O-94,C-13,3D	-2.7

■ PAUL DICKEN
Dicken, Paul Franklin b: 10/2/43, DeLand, Fla. BR/TR, 6'5", 195 lbs. Deb: 6/7/64

Year	Tm/L	G	AB	R	H	2B	3B	HR	RBI	BB	SO	AVG	OBP	SLG	PRO+	BR/A	SB	CS	SBR	FA	FR	G/POS	TPR
1964	Cle-A	11	11	0	0	0	0	0	0	0	5	.000	.000	.000	-99	-3	0	0	0	.000	0	H	-0.3
1966	Cle-A	2	2	0	0	0	0	0	0	0	1	.000	.000	.000	-99	-1	0	0	0	.000	0	H	-0.1
Total	2	13	13	0	0	0	0	0	0	0	6	.000	.000	.000	-99	-3	0	0	0		0	-0,-0	-0.4

■ BUTTERCUP DICKERSON
Dickerson, Lewis Pessano b: 10/11/1858, Tyaskin, Md. d: 7/23/20, Baltimore, Md. BL/TR, 5'6", 140 lbs. Deb: 7/15/1878

Year	Tm/L	G	AB	R	H	2B	3B	HR	RBI	BB	SO	AVG	OBP	SLG	PRO+	BR/A	SB	CS	SBR	FA	FR	G/POS	TPR
1878	Cin-N	29	123	17	38	5	1	0	9	0	7	.309	.309	.366	134	4				.877	-1	O-29	0.1
1879	Cin-N	81	350	73	102	18	**14**	2	57	3	27	.291	.297	.440	147	17				.801	-4	*O-81	0.8
1880	Tro-N	30	119	15	23	2	2	0	10	2	3	.193	.207	.244	49	-6				.903	6	O-30/S-1	-0.1
	Wor-N	31	133	22	39	8	6	0	20	1	2	.293	.299	.444	136	4				.852	-2	O-31	0.1
	Yr	61	252	37	62	10	8	0	30	3	5	.246	.255	.349	96	-2				.883	4	O-61/S-1	0.0
1881	Wor-N	80	367	48	116	18	6	1	31	8	8	.316	.331	.406	123	8				.892	10	*O-80	1.5
1883	Pit-a	85	354	62	88	15	1	0			18	.249	.285	.297	92	-2				.798		*O-78/S-8,2-2	-0.2
1884	StL-U	46	211	49	77	15	1	0			8	.365	.388	.445	147	6				.895	5	O-42/3-4	0.9
	Bal-a	13	56	9	12	2	1	0			4	.214	.290	.286	85	-1				.941	-2	O-12/3-1	-0.3
	Lou-a	8	28	6	4	0	2	1			3	.143	.226	.393	103	0				.813	-1	/O-8	0.0
	Yr	21	84	15	16	2	3	1			7	.190	.269	.321	91	-1				.879	-3	O-20/3-1	-0.3
1885	Buf-N	5	21	1	1	0	0	0		1	4	.048	.136	.095	-38	-3				1.000	1	/O-5	-0.3
Total	7	408	1762	302	500	84	34	4	127	48	51	.284	.304	.377	118	28				.854	12	O-396/S-9,3-5,2-2	2.5

■ GEORGE DICKEY
Dickey, George Willard "Skeets" b: 7/10/15, Kensett, Ark. d: 6/16/76, DeWitt, Ark. BB/TR, 6'2", 180 lbs. Deb: 9/21/35 F

Year	Tm/L	G	AB	R	H	2B	3B	HR	RBI	BB	SO	AVG	OBP	SLG	PRO+	BR/A	SB	CS	SBR	FA	FR	G/POS	TPR
1935	Bos-A	5	11	1	0	0	0	0	0	1	3	.000	.083	.000	-72	-4	0	0	0	1.000	-1	/C-4	-0.4
1936	Bos-A	10	23	0	1	0	0	0	0	2	3	.043	.120	.087	-46	-5	0	0	0	.912	0	/C-10	-0.4
1941	Chi-A	32	55	6	11	1	0	2	8	5	7	.200	.267	.327	57	-4	0	0	0	1.000	1	C-17	-0.2
1942	Chi-A	59	116	6	27	3	0	1	17	9	11	.233	.288	.284	63	-6	0	0	0	.918	-4	C-29	-0.8
1946	Chi-A	37	78	8	15	1	0		1	12	13	.192	.300	.205	45	-5	0	2	-1	1.000	-2	C-30	-0.4
1947	Chi-A	83	211	15	47	6	0	1	27	34	25	.223	.331	.265	69	-8	4	2	-1	.985	2	C-80	-0.1
Total	6	226	494	36	101	12	0	4	54	63	62	.204	.294	.253	53	-31	4	4	-1	.974	-0	C-170	-2.3

■ BILL DICKEY
Dickey, William Malcolm b: 6/6/07, Bastrop, La. d: 11/12/93, Little Rock, Ark. BL/TR, 6'1.5", 185 lbs. Deb: 8/15/28 FMCH

Year	Tm/L	G	AB	R	H	2B	3B	HR	RBI	BB	SO	AVG	OBP	SLG	PRO+	BR/A	SB	CS	SBR	FA	FR	G/POS	TPR
1928	NY-A	10	15	1	3	1	1	0	2	0	2	.200	.200	.400	56	-1	0	0	0	1.000	-1	/C-6	-0.2
1929	NY-A	130	447	60	145	30	6	10	65	14	16	.324	.346	.485	120	10	4	3	-1	.979	1	*C-127	2.1
1930	NY-A	109	366	55	124	25	7	5	65	21	14	.339	.375	.486	122	11	7	1	2	.977	-12	*C-101	0.9
1931	NY-A	130	477	65	156	17	10	6	78	39	20	.327	.378	.442	122	15	2	1	0	**.996**	4	*C-125	2.5
1932	*NY-A	108	423	66	131	20	4	15	84	34	13	.310	.361	.482	123	13	2	4	-2	.987	-2	*C-108	1.4
1933	NY-A☆	130	478	58	152	24	8	14	97	47	14	.318	.381	.490	138	25	3	4	-2	.993	0	*C-127	2.9
1934	NY-A★	104	395	56	127	24	4	12	72	38	18	.322	.384	.494	134	19	0	3	-2	.986	-2	*C-104	1.9
1935	NY-A	120	448	54	125	26	6	14	81	35	11	.279	.339	.458	111	5	1	1	-0	**.995**	-2	*C-118	0.9
1936	*NY-A★	112	423	99	153	26	8	22	107	46	16	.362	.428	.617	161	39	0	2	-2	.976	0	*C-107	3.8
1937	*NY-A★	140	530	87	176	35	2	29	133	73	22	.332	.417	.570	145	37	3	2	-0	.991	12	*C-137	5.1
1938	*NY-A★	132	454	84	142	27	4	27	115	75	22	.313	.412	.568	144	31	3	0	1	.987	-4	*C-126	3.7
1939	*NY-A★	128	480	98	145	23	3	24	105	77	37	.302	.403	.512	135	26	5	0	2	**.989**	8	*C-126	3.9
1940	NY-A★	106	372	45	92	11	1	9	54	48	32	.247	.336	.355	83	-9	3	2	-1	.994	-1	*C-102	-0.3
1941	*NY-A★	109	348	35	99	15	5	7	71	45	17	.284	.371	.417	110	5	2	2	1	**.994**	1	*C-104	1.4
1942	*NY-A†	82	268	28	79	13	1	2	37	26	11	.295	.359	.373	108	2	1	1	-1	.976	3	C-80	1.2
1943	*NY-A☆	85	242	29	85	18	2	4	33	41	12	.351	.445	.492	173	24	2	1	0	.994	0	C-71	2.9
1946	NY-A★	54	134	10	35	8	0	2	10	25	12	.261	.357	.366	101	1	0	1	-1	.987	10	C-39,M	1.3
Total	17	1789	6300	930	1969	343	72	202	1209	678	289	.313	.382	.486	128	252	36	29	-7	.988	24	*C-1708	35.4

■ JOHNNY DICKSHOT
Dickshot, John Oscar "Ugly" (b: John Oscar Dicksus) b: 1/24/10, Waukegan, Ill. BR/TR, 6', 195 lbs. Deb: 4/16/36

Year	Tm/L	G	AB	R	H	2B	3B	HR	RBI	BB	SO	AVG	OBP	SLG	PRO+	BR/A	SB	CS	SBR	FA	FR	G/POS	TPR
1936	Pit-N	9	9	2	2	0	0	0	0	1		.222	.300	.222	42	-1				.000	-1	/O-1	-0.1
1937	Pit-N	82	264	42	67	8	4	3	33	26	36	.254	.348	.348	82	-6	0			.950	-2	O-64	-1.1
1938	Pit-N	29	35	3	8	0	0	0	4	8	5	.229	.372	.229	68	-1	3			1.000	-1	O-10	-0.3
1939	NY-N	10	34	3	8	0	0	0	5	5	9	.235	.333	.235	55	-2	0			1.000	-1	O-10	-0.3
1944	Chi-A	62	162	18	41	8	5	0	15	10	10	.253	.313	.364	94	-2	7			.974	-3	O-40	-0.6
1945	Chi-A	130	486	74	147	19	6	4	58	48	41	.302	.366	.407	128	17	18	3	**4**	.971	1	*O-124	1.5
Total	6	322	990	142	273	35	19	7	116	101	97	.276	.345	.371	104	5	23	3		.968	-7	O-249	-0.9

■ BOB DIDIER
Didier, Robert Daniel b: 2/16/49, Hattiesburg, Miss. BB/TR, 6', 190 lbs. Deb: 4/7/69 C

Year	Tm/L	G	AB	R	H	2B	3B	HR	RBI	BB	SO	AVG	OBP	SLG	PRO+	BR/A	SB	CS	SBR	FA	FR	G/POS	TPR
1969	*Atl-N	114	352	30	90	16	1	0	32	34	39	.256	.321	.307	76	-10	1	3	-2	.994	-2	*C-114	-0.9
1970	Atl-N	57	168	9	25	2	1	0	7	12	11	.149	.210	.173	3	-23	1	0	0	.988	1	C-57	-1.9

YEAR	TM/L	G	AB	R	H	2B	3B	HR	RBI	BB	SO	AVG	OBP	SLG	PRO+	BR/A	SB	CS	SBR	FA	FR	G/POS	TPR
1971	Atl-N	51	155	9	34	4	1	0	5	6	17	.219	.248	.258	41	-12	0	0	0	1.000	3	C-50	-0.8
1972	Atl-N	13	40	5	12	2	1	0	5	2	4	.300	.349	.400	103	0	0	0	0	1.000	3	C-11	0.2
1973	Det-A	7	22	3	10	1	0	0	1	3	0	.455	.520	.500	177	2	0	0	0	1.000	2	/C-7	0.5
1974	Bos-A	5	14	0	1	0	0	0	1	2	1	.071	.188	.071	-22	-2	0	0	0	.968	1	/C-5	-0.1
Total	6	247	751	56	172	25	4	0	51	59	72	.229	.287	.273	55	-45	2	3	-1	.994	6	C-244	-3.0

■ ERNIE DIEHL
Diehl, Ernest Guy   b: 10/2/1877, Cincinnati, Ohio   d: 11/6/58, Miami, Fla.   BR/TR, 6'1", 190 lbs.   Deb: 5/31/03

YEAR	TM/L	G	AB	R	H	2B	3B	HR	RBI	BB	SO	AVG	OBP	SLG	PRO+	BR/A	SB	CS	SBR	FA	FR	G/POS	TPR
1903	Pit-N	1	3	0	1	0	0	0	0	0	0	.333	.333	.333	87	-0				.000	-1	/O-1	-0.1
1904	Pit-N	12	37	6	6	0	0	0		4	6	.162	.311	.162	46	-2	3			1.000	1	/O-7,S-4	-0.1
1906	Bos-N	3	11	1	5	0	1	0		0	0	.455	.455	.636	247	2	0			1.000	0	/O-2,S-1	0.2
1909	Bos-N	1	4	1	2	1	0	0		0	0	.500	.500	.750	275	1	0			.800	1	/O-1	0.1
Total	4	17	55	8	14	1	1	0		4	6	.255	.349	.309	101	0	3			.944	2	/O-11,S-5	0.1

■ CHUCK DIERING
Diering, Charles Edward Allen   b: 2/5/23, St.Louis, Mo.   BR/TR, 5'10", 165 lbs.   Deb: 4/15/47

YEAR	TM/L	G	AB	R	H	2B	3B	HR	RBI	BB	SO	AVG	OBP	SLG	PRO+	BR/A	SB	CS	SBR	FA	FR	G/POS	TPR
1947	StL-N	105	74	22	16	3	1	2	11	19	22	.216	.383	.365	95	-0	3			1.000	-22	O-75	-2.3
1948	StL-N	7	7	2	0	0	0	0	0	2	2	.000	.222	.000	-33	-1	1			1.000	-1	/O-5	-0.2
1949	StL-N	131	369	60	97	21	8	3	38	35	49	.263	.328	.388	87	-7	1			.987	-2	*O-124	-1.4
1950	StL-N	89	204	34	51	12	0	3	18	35	38	.250	.360	.353	84	-4	1			.989	-1	O-81	-0.7
1951	StL-N	64	85	9	22	5	1	0	8	6	15	.259	.308	.341	74	-3	0	1	-1	1.000	-8	O-44	-1.3
1952	NY-N	41	23	2	4	1	1	0	2	4	3	.174	.296	.304	66	-1	0	2	-1	1.000	-10	O-36	-1.3
1954	Bal-A	128	418	35	108	14	1	2	29	56	57	.258	.351	.311	89	-3	3	7	-3	.983	13	*O-119	0.0
1955	Bal-A	137	371	38	95	16	2	3	31	57	45	.256	.355	.334	93	-3	5	8	-3	.976	5	*O-107,3-34,S-12	-0.6
1956	Bal-A	50	97	15	18	4	0	1	4	23	19	.186	.342	.258	65	-4	2	5	-2	1.000	-4	O-40/3-2	-1.2
Total	9	752	1648	217	411	76	14	14	141	237	250	.249	.346	.338	86	-27	16	23		.987	-31	O-631/3-36,S-12	-9.0

■ DICK DIETZ
Dietz, Richard Allen   b: 9/18/41, Crawfordsville, Ind.   BR/TR, 6'1", 195 lbs.   Deb: 6/18/66

YEAR	TM/L	G	AB	R	H	2B	3B	HR	RBI	BB	SO	AVG	OBP	SLG	PRO+	BR/A	SB	CS	SBR	FA	FR	G/POS	TPR
1966	SF-N	13	23	1	1	0	0	0	0	0	0	.043	.083	.043	-62	-5	0	0	0	1.000	-1	/C-6	-0.6
1967	SF-N	56	120	10	27	3	0	4	19	25	44	.225	.363	.350	106	2	0	1	-1	.983	0	C-43	0.4
1968	SF-N	98	301	21	82	14	2	6	38	34	68	.272	.348	.392	122	9	1	1	-0	.976	-8	C-90	0.7
1969	SF-N	79	244	28	56	8	1	11	35	53	53	.230	.373	.406	120	8	0	0	0	.973	-5	C-73	0.7
1970	SF-N★	148	493	82	148	36	2	22	107	109	106	.300	.430	.515	154	42	0	1	-1	.984	-18	*C-139	3.0
1971	*SF-N	142	453	58	114	19	0	19	72	97	86	.252	.388	.419	131	22	1	3	-2	.982	-12	*C-135	1.5
1972	LA-N	27	56	4	9	1	0	1	6	14	11	.161	.329	.232	63	-2	0	0	1	1.000	3	C-22	0.3
1973	Atl-N	83	139	22	41	8	1	3	24	49	25	.295	.479	.432	143	12	0	0	0	.989	1	1-36,C-20	1.1
Total	8	646	1829	226	478	89	6	66	301	381	402	.261	.392	.425	130	88	4	6	-2	.980	-39	C-528/1-36	7.1

■ ROY DIETZEL
Dietzel, Leroy Louis   b: 1/9/31, Baltimore, Md.   BR/TR, 6', 190 lbs.   Deb: 9/2/54

YEAR	TM/L	G	AB	R	H	2B	3B	HR	RBI	BB	SO	AVG	OBP	SLG	PRO+	BR/A	SB	CS	SBR	FA	FR	G/POS	TPR
1954	Was-A	9	21	1	5	0	0	0	1	5	4	.238	.385	.238	78	-0	0	0	0	.960	-2	/2-7,3-2	-0.2

■ JAY DIFANI
Difani, Clarence Joseph   b: 12/21/23, Crystal City, Mo.   BR/TR, 6', 170 lbs.   Deb: 4/23/48

YEAR	TM/L	G	AB	R	H	2B	3B	HR	RBI	BB	SO	AVG	OBP	SLG	PRO+	BR/A	SB	CS	SBR	FA	FR	G/POS	TPR
1948	Was-A	2	2	0	0	0	0	0	0	0	2	.000	.000	.000	-99	-1	0	0	0	.000	0	H	-0.1
1949	Was-A	2	2	0	1	1	0	0	0	0	0	1.000	1.000	2.000	699	1	0	0	0	1.000	0	/2-1	0.1
Total	2	4	3	0	1	1	0	0	0	0	2	.333	.333	.667	166	0	0	0	0	1.000	0	/2-1	0.0

■ MIKE DIFELICE
Difelice, Michael William   b: 5/28/69, Philadelphia, Pa.   BR/TR, 6'2", 205 lbs.   Deb: 9/1/96

YEAR	TM/L	G	AB	R	H	2B	3B	HR	RBI	BB	SO	AVG	OBP	SLG	PRO+	BR/A	SB	CS	SBR	FA	FR	G/POS	TPR
1996	StL-N	4	7	0	2	1	0	0	2	0	1	.286	.286	.429	85	-0	0	0	0	1.000	1	/C-4	0.1

■ STEVE DIGNAN
Dignan, Stephen E.   b: 5/16/1859, Boston, Mass.   d: 7/11/1881, Boston, Mass.   Deb: 6/1/1880

YEAR	TM/L	G	AB	R	H	2B	3B	HR	RBI	BB	SO	AVG	OBP	SLG	PRO+	BR/A	SB	CS	SBR	FA	FR	G/POS	TPR
1880	Bos-N	8	34	4	11	1	0	0	4	0	3	.324	.324	.353	133	1				.684	0	/O-8	0.1
	Wor-N	3	10	1	3	0	1	0	2	0	1	.300	.300	.500	153	0				.750	-1	/O-3	0.0
	Yr	11	44	5	14	1	1	0	6	0	4	.318	.318	.386	137	2				.696	-1	O-11	0.1

■ DON DILLARD
Dillard, David Donald   b: 1/8/37, Greenville, S.C.   BL/TR, 6'1", 200 lbs.   Deb: 4/24/59

YEAR	TM/L	G	AB	R	H	2B	3B	HR	RBI	BB	SO	AVG	OBP	SLG	PRO+	BR/A	SB	CS	SBR	FA	FR	G/POS	TPR
1959	Cle-A	10	10	0	4	0	0	0	1	0	2	.400	.400	.400	125	0	0	0	0	.000	0	H	0.0
1960	Cle-A	6	7	0	1	0	0	0	0	1	3	.143	.250	.143	9	-0	0	0	0	.000	0	/O-1	-0.1
1961	Cle-A	74	147	27	40	5	0	7	17	15	28	.272	.340	.449	112	2	0	0	0	1.000	-4	O-39	-0.3
1962	Cle-A	95	174	22	40	5	1	5	14	11	25	.230	.276	.356	71	-8	0	1	-1	.965	-10	O-50	-2.1
1963	Mil-N	67	119	9	28	6	4	1	12	5	21	.235	.272	.378	86	-2	0	2	-1	.951	-0	O-30	-0.5
1965	Mil-N	20	19	1	3	0	0	1	3	0	6	.158	.158	.316	30	-2	0	0	0	.000	-0	/O-1	-0.2
Total	6	272	476	59	116	16	5	14	47	32	85	.244	.293	.387	86	-10	0	3	-2	.976	-15	O-121	-3.2

■ PAT DILLARD
Dillard, Robert Lee   b: 6/12/1873, Chattanooga, Tenn   d: 7/22/07, Denver, Colo.   BL/TR, 6', 180 lbs.   Deb: 4/21/00

YEAR	TM/L	G	AB	R	H	2B	3B	HR	RBI	BB	SO	AVG	OBP	SLG	PRO+	BR/A	SB	CS	SBR	FA	FR	G/POS	TPR
1900	StL-N	57	183	24	42	5	2	0	12	13		.230	.284	.279	56	-11	7			.942	-4	O-26,3-21/S-3	-1.5

■ STEVE DILLARD
Dillard, Stephen Bradley   b: 2/8/51, Memphis, Tenn.   BR/TR, 6'1", 180 lbs.   Deb: 9/28/75

YEAR	TM/L	G	AB	R	H	2B	3B	HR	RBI	BB	SO	AVG	OBP	SLG	PRO+	BR/A	SB	CS	SBR	FA	FR	G/POS	TPR
1975	Bos-A	1	5	2	2	0	0	0	0	0	0	.400	.400	.400	117	0	1	0	0	1.000	1	/2-1	0.1
1976	Bos-A	57	167	22	46	14	0	1	15	17	20	.275	.342	.377	99	-0	6	4	-1	.918	-4	3-18,2-17,S-12,D-7	-0.3
1977	Bos-A	66	141	22	34	7	0	1	13	7	13	.241	.277	.312	54	-9	4	3	-1	.967	8	2-45/S-9,D-6	0.1
1978	Det-A	56	130	21	29	5	2	0	6	6	11	.223	.257	*.292	53	-8	1	2	-1	.958	17	2-41/D-4	1.0
1979	Chi-N	89	166	31	47	6	1	3	24	17	24	.283	.353	.422	101	0	1	0	0	.988	9	2-60/3-9	1.3
1980	Chi-N	100	244	31	55	8	1	4	27	20	54	.225	.287	.316	63	-12	2	2	-1	.908	2	3-51,2-38/S-2	-1.0
1981	Chi-N	53	119	18	26	7	1	2	11	8	20	.218	.268	.345	70	-5	0	0	0	.974	3	2-32/3-7,S-2	-0.1
1982	Chi-A	16	41	1	7	3	1	0	5	1	5	.171	.190	.293	30	-4	0	1	-1	.959	3	2-16	-0.1
Total	8	438	1013	148	246	50	6	13	102	76	147	.243	.297	.343	73	-38	15	12	-3	.973	37	2-250/3-85,S-25,D	1.0

■ PICKLES DILLHOEFER
Dillhoefer, William Martin   b: 10/13/1894, Cleveland, Ohio   d: 2/23/22, St.Louis, Mo.   BR/TR, 5'7", 154 lbs.   Deb: 4/16/17

YEAR	TM/L	G	AB	R	H	2B	3B	HR	RBI	BB	SO	AVG	OBP	SLG	PRO+	BR/A	SB	CS	SBR	FA	FR	G/POS	TPR
1917	Chi-N	42	95	3	12	1	1	0	8	2	9	.126	.144	.158	-7	-12	1			.985	8	C-37	-0.2
1918	Phi-N	8	11	0	1	0	0	0	0	1	1	.091	.167	.091	-19	-2	2			.923	-1	/C-6	-0.2
1919	StL-N	45	108	11	23	3	2	0	12	8	6	.213	.267	.278	68	-4	5			.967	-5	C-39	-0.7
1920	StL-N	76	224	26	59	8	3	0	13	13	7	.263	.304	.326	84	-5	2	1	0	.953	-0	C-74	-0.1
1921	StL-N	76	162	19	39	4	4	0	15	11	7	.241	.289	.315	61	-9	2	1	0	.953	2	C-69	-0.5
Total	5	247	600	59	134	16	10	0	48	35	30	.223	.266	.283	58	-32	12	2		.961	4	C-225	-1.7

■ BOB DILLINGER
Dillinger, Robert Bernard "Duke"   b: 9/17/18, Glendale, Cal.   BR/TR, 5'11.5", 170 lbs.   Deb: 4/16/46

YEAR	TM/L	G	AB	R	H	2B	3B	HR	RBI	BB	SO	AVG	OBP	SLG	PRO+	BR/A	SB	CS	SBR	FA	FR	G/POS	TPR
1946	StL-A	83	225	33	63	6	3	0	11	19	30	.280	.341	.333	85	-4	8	1	2	.922	-3	3-54/S-1	-0.5
1947	StL-A	137	571	70	168	23	6	3	37	56	38	.294	.361	.371	102	2	34	11	2	.958	2	*3-137	0.8
1948	StL-A	153	644	110	207	34	10	2	44	65	34	.321	.385	.415	110	9	28	11	2	.955	-16	*3-153	-0.6
1949	StL-A★	137	544	68	176	22	13	1	51	51	40	.324	.385	.417	108	6	20	14	-2	.938	-25	*3-133	-2.4
1950	Phi-A	84	356	55	110	21	9	3	41	31	20	.309	.366	.444	109	4	5	3	-0	.957	-2	3-84	0.0
	Pit-N	58	222	23	64	8	2	1	9	13	22	.288	.328	.356	77	-7	4			.957	-2	3-51	-0.6
1951	Pit-N	12	43	3	10	3	0	0	1		0	.233	.250	.302	47	-3	2	0	1	.963	-2	3-10	-0.5
	Chi-A	89	299	39	90	6	4	0	20	15	17	.301	.337	.348	87	-6	5	5	-2	.930	-6	3-70	-1.4
Total	6	753	2904	401	888	123	47	10	213	251	201	.306	.363	.391	100	1	106	47		.948	-50	3-692/S-1	-5.2

■ POP DILLON
Dillon, Frank Edward   b: 10/17/1873, Normal, Ill.   d: 9/12/31, Pasadena, Cal.   BL/TR, 6'1", 185 lbs.   Deb: 9/8/1899

YEAR	TM/L	G	AB	R	H	2B	3B	HR	RBI	BB	SO	AVG	OBP	SLG	PRO+	BR/A	SB	CS	SBR	FA	FR	G/POS	TPR
1899	Pit-N	30	121	21	31	5	0	0	20	5		.256	.286	.298	60	-7	5			.988	1	1-30	-0.5
1900	Pit-N	5	18	3	2	0	0	0	0	0		.111	.111	.167	-24	-3	0			.981	1	/1-5	-0.2
1901	Det-A	74	281	40	81	14	6	1	42	15		.288	.324	.391	94	-3	14			.979	3	1-74	-0.2
1902	Det-A	66	243	21	50	6	3	0	22	16		.206	.255	.255	41	-19	2			.976	5	1-66	-1.5
	Bal-A	2	7	1	2	0	0	0	0	2		.286	.444	.571	173	1	0			.960	0	/1-2	0.1
	Yr	68	250	22	52	6	3	0	22	18		.208	.261	.264	45	-19	2			.975	6	1-68	-1.4

YEAR	TM/L	G	AB	R	H	2B	3B	HR	RBI	BB	SO	AVG	OBP	SLG	PRO+	BR/A	SB	CS	SBR	FA	FR	G/POS	TPR
1904	Bro-N	135	511	60	132	18	6	0	31	40		.258	.313	.317	97	-2	13			.982	3	*1-134	-0.1
Total	5	312	1181	146	298	44	16	1	116	78		.252	.299	.319	79	-33	34			.980	14	1-311	-2.4

■ JOHN DILLON　Dillon, John　Deb: 5/8/1875　F

YEAR	TM/L	G	AB	R	H	2B	3B	HR	RBI	BB	SO	AVG	OBP	SLG	PRO+	BR/A	SB	CS	SBR	FA	FR	G/POS	TPR
1875	RS-n	1	1	0	0	0	0	0	0	0	0	.000	.000	.000	-99	-0	0	0	0	.000	0	/S-1	0.0

■ PACKY DILLON　Dillon, Packard Andrew　b: St.Louis, Mo.　d: 1/8/1890, Guelph, Ont., Canada　Deb: 5/4/1875　F

YEAR	TM/L	G	AB	R	H	2B	3B	HR	RBI	BB	SO	AVG	OBP	SLG	PRO+	BR/A	SB	CS	SBR	FA	FR	G/POS	TPR
1875	RS-n	3	13	1	3	1	0	0	1	0	0	.231	.231	.308	94	-0	0	0	0	.923	-2	/C-3	-0.2

■ MIGUEL DILONE　Dilone, Miguel Angel (Reyes)　b: 11/1/54, Santiago, D.R.　BB/TR, 6', 160 lbs.　Deb: 9/2/74

YEAR	TM/L	G	AB	R	H	2B	3B	HR	RBI	BB	SO	AVG	OBP	SLG	PRO+	BR/A	SB	CS	SBR	FA	FR	G/POS	TPR
1974	Pit-N	12	2	3	0	0	0	0	0	0	1	.000	.333	.000	-1	-0	2	0	1	1.000	-1	/O-2	0.0
1975	Pit-N	18	6	8	0	0	0	0	0	0	1	.000	.000	.000	-99	-2	2	2	-1	1.000	-0	/O-2	-0.3
1976	Pit-N	16	17	7	4	0	0	0	0	0	0	.235	.235	.235	34	-1	5	1	1	1.000	1	/O-3	-0.3
1977	Pit-N	29	44	5	6	0	0	0	0	2	3	.136	.174	.136	-15	-7	12	0	4	1.000	-3	O-17	-0.7
1978	Oak-A	135	258	34	59	8	0	1	14	23	30	.229	.294	.271	63	-12	50	23	1	.985	-7	O-99,D-11/3-3	-2.2
1979	Oak-A	30	91	15	17	1	2	1	6	6	7	.187	.237	.275	40	-8	15	6	1	.959	-2	O-25	-1.2
	Chi-N	43	36	14	11	0	0	0	1	2	5	.306	.342	.306	71	-1	15	5	2	1.000	-5	O-22	-0.5
1980	Cle-A	132	528	82	180	30	9	0	40	28	45	.341	.376	.432	120	15	61	18	8	.973	-0	*O-118,D-11	1.6
1981	Cle-A	72	269	33	78	5	5	0	19	18	28	.290	.334	.346	98	-1	29	10	3	.971	6	O-56,D-11	0.6
1982	Cle-A	104	379	50	89	12	3	3	25	25	36	.235	.286	.306	63	-19	33	5	7	.964	-3	O-97/D-1	-1.8
1983	Cle-A	32	68	15	13	3	1	0	7	10	5	.191	.295	.265	53	-4	5	1	1	1.000	1	O-19	-0.3
	Chi-A	4	3	1	0	0	0	0	0	0	0	.000	.000	.000	-96	-1	1	0	0	1.000	-1	/O-2,D-2	-0.1
	Yr	36	71	16	13	3	1	0	7	10	5	.183	.284	.254	47	-5	6	1	1	1.000	0	O-21/D-2	-0.4
	Pit-N	7	0	1	0	0	0	0	0	0	0					0	2	0	1	.000	0	/R	0.0
1984	Mon-N	88	169	28	47	8	2	1	10	17	18	.278	.348	.367	106	1	27	2	7	.987	1	O-41	0.9
1985	Mon-N	51	84	10	16	0	2	0	6	6	11	.190	.244	.238	38	-7	7	3	0	.974	-2	O-22	-1.0
	SD-N	27	46	8	10	0	1	0	1	4	8	.217	.280	.261	53	-3	10	3	1	.917	-2	O-14	-0.4
	Yr	78	130	18	26	0	3	0	7	10	19	.200	.257	.246	43	-10	17	6	2	.952	-4	O-36	-1.4
Total	12	800	2000	314	530	67	25	6	129	142	197	.265	.316	.333	81	-51	267	78	33	.975	-16	O-539/D-36,3-3	-5.4

■ DOM DiMAGGIO　DiMaggio, Dominic Paul "The Little Professor"　b: 2/12/17, San Francisco, Cal.　BR/TR, 5'9", 168 lbs.　Deb: 4/16/40　F

YEAR	TM/L	G	AB	R	H	2B	3B	HR	RBI	BB	SO	AVG	OBP	SLG	PRO+	BR/A	SB	CS	SBR	FA	FR	G/POS	TPR
1940	Bos-A	108	418	81	126	32	6	8	46	41	46	.301	.367	.464	109	9	7	6	-2	.977	10	O-94	0.8
1941	Bos-A★	144	584	117	165	37	6	8	58	90	57	.283	.385	.408	107	8	13	6	0	.964	9	*O-144	0.6
1942	Bos-A☆	151	622	110	178	36	8	14	48	70	52	.286	.364	.437	121	17	16	10	-1	.987	17	*O-151	2.5
1946	*Bos-A★	142	534	85	169	24	7	7	73	66	58	.316	.393	.427	122	17	10	6	-1	.985	7	*O-142	1.8
1947	Bos-A	136	513	75	145	21	5	8	71	74	62	.283	.376	.390	105	5	10	6	-1	.977	19	*O-134	1.7
1948	Bos-A	155	648	127	185	40	4	9	87	101	58	.285	.383	.401	104	5	10	2	2	.981	16	*O-155	1.4
1949	Bos-A	145	605	126	186	34	5	8	60	96	55	.307	.404	.420	110	11	9	7	-2	.977	14	*O-145	1.6
1950	Bos-A★	141	588	131	193	30	11	7	70	82	68	.328	.414	.452	111	11	15	4	2	.983	9	*O-140	1.5
1951	Bos-A★	146	639	113	189	34	4	12	72	73	53	.296	.370	.418	103	2	4	7	-3	.973	3	*O-146	-0.4
1952	Bos-A★	128	486	81	143	20	1	6	33	57	61	.294	.371	.377	100	2	6	8	-3	.975	-0	*O-123	-0.7
1953	Bos-A	3	3	0	1	0	0	0	0	0	0	.333	.333	.333	76	-0	0	0	0	.000	0	H	0.0
Total	11	1399	5640	1046	1680	308	57	87	618	750	571	.298	.383	.419	109	84	100	62	-7	.978	101	*O-1373	10.8

■ JOE DiMAGGIO　DiMaggio, Joseph Paul "Joltin' Joe" or "The Yankee Clipper"　b: 11/25/14, Martinez, Cal.　BR/TR, 6'2", 193 lbs.　Deb: 5/3/36　FCH

YEAR	TM/L	G	AB	R	H	2B	3B	HR	RBI	BB	SO	AVG	OBP	SLG	PRO+	BR/A	SB	CS	SBR	FA	FR	G/POS	TPR
1936	*NY-A★	138	637	132	206	44	15	29	125	24	39	.323	.352	.576	130	23	4	0	1	.978	15	*O-138	3.0
1937	*NY-A★	151	621	151	215	35	15	46	167	64	37	.346	.412	.673	168	60	3	0	1	.962	11	*O-150	6.0
1938	*NY-A★	145	599	129	194	32	13	32	140	59	21	.324	.386	.581	140	33	6	1	1	.963	4	*O-145	3.0
1939	*NY-A★	120	462	108	176	32	6	30	126	52	20	.381	.448	.671	185	58	3	0	1	.986	8	*O-117	5.7
1940	*NY-A★	132	508	93	179	28	9	31	133	61	30	.352	.425	.626	176	56	1	2	0	.978	1	*O-130	4.5
1941	*NY-A★	139	541	122	193	43	11	30	125	76	13	.357	.440	.643	186	66	4	2	0	.978	10	*O-139	6.4
1942	NY-A☆	154	610	123	186	29	13	21	114	68	36	.305	.376	.498	148	37	4	2	0	.981	2	*O-154	3.1
1946	NY-A☆	132	503	81	146	20	8	25	95	59	24	.290	.367	.511	142	27	1	0	0	.982	4	*O-131	2.5
1947	*NY-A★	141	534	97	168	31	10	20	97	64	32	.315	.391	.522	154	38	3	0	1	.997	-13	*O-139	1.8
1948	NY-A★	153	594	110	190	26	11	39	155	67	30	.320	.396	.598	164	50	1	1	-0	.972	4	*O-152	4.3
1949	NY-A★	76	272	58	94	14	6	14	67	55	18	.346	.459	.596	178	32	0	1	-1	.985	-1	O-76	2.5
1950	*NY-A★	139	525	114	158	33	10	32	122	80	33	.301	.394	.585	152	39	0	0	0	.976	5	*O-137/1-1	3.1
1951	*NY-A☆	116	415	72	109	22	4	12	71	61	36	.263	.365	.422	117	10	0	0	0	.990	4	*O-113	1.0
Total	13	1736	6821	1390	2214	389	131	361	1537	790	369	.325	.398	.579	156	529	30	9	4	.978	51	*O-1721/1-1	46.9

■ VINCE DiMAGGIO　DiMaggio, Vincent Paul　b: 9/6/12, Martinez, Cal.　d: 10/3/86, N.Hollywood, Cal.　BR/TR, 5'11", 183 lbs.　Deb: 4/19/37　F

YEAR	TM/L	G	AB	R	H	2B	3B	HR	RBI	BB	SO	AVG	OBP	SLG	PRO+	BR/A	SB	CS	SBR	FA	FR	G/POS	TPR
1937	Bos-N	132	493	56	126	18	4	13	69	44	111	.256	.311	.387	98	-4	8			.982	16	*O-130	0.7
1938	Bos-N	150	540	71	123	28	3	14	61	65	134	.228	.313	.369	96	-4	11			.973	13	*O-149/2-1	0.5
1939	Cin-N	8	14	1	1	1	0	0	2	2	10	.071	.188	.143	-10	-2	0			1.000	-0	/O-7	-0.2
1940	Cin-N	2	4	2	1	0	0	0	0	1	0	.250	.400	.250	82	-0	0			1.000	-0	/O-1	0.0
	Pit-N	110	356	59	103	26	6	19	54	37	83	.289	.364	.522	143	20	11			.979	-2	*O-108	1.3
	Yr	112	360	61	104	26	6	19	54	38	83	.289	.365	.519	142	20	11			.979	-2	*O-109	1.3
1941	Pit-N	151	528	73	141	27	5	21	100	68	100	.267	.354	.456	128	19	10			.976	7	*O-151	1.7
1942	Pit-N	143	496	57	118	22	3	15	75	52	87	.238	.311	.385	101	-1	10			.978	20	*O-138	1.3
1943	Pit-N★	157	580	64	144	41	2	15	88	70	126	.248	.329	.403	107	5	11			.985	15	*O-156/S-1	1.2
1944	Pit-N★	109	342	41	82	22	4	9	50	33	83	.240	.307	.401	94	-4	6			.984	-6	*O-101/3-1	-1.5
1945	Phi-N	127	452	64	116	25	3	19	84	43	91	.257	.321	.451	117	7	12			.994	10	*O-121	1.1
1946	Phi-N	6	19	1	4	1	0	0	1	0	7	.211	.211	.263	35	-2	0			1.000	-1	/O-6	-0.3
	NY-N	15	25	2	0	0	0	0	0	2	12	.000	.074	.000	-78	-6	0			.967	-1	O-13	-0.8
	Yr	21	44	3	4	1	0	0	1	2	19	.091	.130	.114	-31	-8	0			.975	-2	O-19	-1.1
Total	10	1110	3849	491	959	209	24	125	584	412	837	.249	.324	.413	108	29	79			.981	70	*O-1081/3-1,S-1,2-1	5.0

■ MIKE DIMMEL　Dimmel, Michael Wayne　b: 10/16/54, Albert Lea, Minn.　BR/TR, 6', 180 lbs.　Deb: 9/2/77

YEAR	TM/L	G	AB	R	H	2B	3B	HR	RBI	BB	SO	AVG	OBP	SLG	PRO+	BR/A	SB	CS	SBR	FA	FR	G/POS	TPR
1977	Bal-A	25	5	8	0	0	0	0	0	0	1	.000	.000	.000	-99	-1	0	0	0	1.000	-6	O-23	-0.7
1978	Bal-A	8	0	2	0	0	0	0	0	0	0	—	—	—		0	0	1	-1	.667	-3	/O-7	-0.4
1979	StL-N	6	3	1	1	0	0	0	0	0	0	.333	.333	.333	82	-0	0	1	-1	1.000	-2	/O-5	-0.3
Total	3	39	8	11	1	0	0	0	0	0	1	.125	.125	.125	-42	-1	0	2	-1	.952	-11	/O-35	-1.4

■ KERRY DINEEN　Dineen, Kerry Michael　b: 7/1/52, Englewood, N.J.　BL/TL, 5'11", 165 lbs.　Deb: 6/14/75

YEAR	TM/L	G	AB	R	H	2B	3B	HR	RBI	BB	SO	AVG	OBP	SLG	PRO+	BR/A	SB	CS	SBR	FA	FR	G/POS	TPR
1975	NY-A	7	22	3	8	1	0	0	1	2	1	.364	.417	.409	136	1	0	0	0	1.000	0	/O-7	0.1
1976	NY-A	4	7	0	2	0	0	0	1	2	2	.286	.375	.286	96	0	0	1	-0	.900	-0	/O-4	-0.1
1978	Phi-N	5	8	0	2	1	0	0	0	0	0	.250	.333	.375	97	-0	0	0	0	1.000	-0	/O-1	0.0
Total	3	16	37	3	12	2	0	0	2	4	3	.324	.390	.378	120	1	0	1	-0	.967	-0	/O-12	0.0

■ VANCE DINGES　Dinges, Vance George　b: 5/29/15, Elizabeth, N.J.　d: 10/4/90, Harrisonburg, Va.　BL/TL, 6'2", 175 lbs.　Deb: 4/17/45

YEAR	TM/L	G	AB	R	H	2B	3B	HR	RBI	BB	SO	AVG	OBP	SLG	PRO+	BR/A	SB	CS	SBR	FA	FR	G/POS	TPR
1945	Phi-N	109	397	46	114	15	4	1	36	35	17	.287	.346	.353	97	-1	5			.986	-1	O-65,1-42	-0.8
1946	Phi-N	50	104	7	32	5	1	0	10	9	12	.308	.363	.404	121	3	2			.985	0	1-26/O-1	0.1
Total	2	159	501	53	146	20	5	2	46	44	29	.291	.350	.363	102	1	7			.986	-1	/1-68,O-66	-0.7

■ BOB DiPIETRO　DiPietro, Robert Louis Paul　b: 9/1/27, San Francisco, Cal　BR/TR, 5'11", 185 lbs.　Deb: 9/23/51

YEAR	TM/L	G	AB	R	H	2B	3B	HR	RBI	BB	SO	AVG	OBP	SLG	PRO+	BR/A	SB	CS	SBR	FA	FR	G/POS	TPR
1951	Bos-A	4	11	0	1	0	0	0	0	1	0	.091	.167	.091	-26	-0	0	0	0	.833	0	/O-3	-0.2

■ GARY DiSARCINA　DiSarcina, Gary Thomas　b: 11/19/67, Malden, Mass.　BR/TR, 6'1", 170 lbs.　Deb: 9/23/89

YEAR	TM/L	G	AB	R	H	2B	3B	HR	RBI	BB	SO	AVG	OBP	SLG	PRO+	BR/A	SB	CS	SBR	FA	FR	G/POS	TPR
1989	Cal-A	2	0	0	0	0	0	0	0	0	0					0	0	0	0	.000	0	/S-1	0.0
1990	Cal-A	18	57	8	8	1	0	0	0	3	10	.140	.183	.193	5	-7	1	0	0	.940	2	S-14/2-3	-0.4
1991	Cal-A	18	57	5	12	2	0	0	3	3	4	.211	.274	.246	45	-4	0	0	0	.915	-1	S-10/2-7,3-2	-0.4
1992	Cal-A	157	518	48	128	19	0	3	42	20	50	.247	.284	.301	64	-25	9	7	-2	.967	12	*S-157	-0.4

YEAR	TM/L	G	AB	R	H	2B	3B	HR	RBI	BB	SO	AVG	OBP	SLG	PRO+	BR/A	SB	CS	SBR	FA	FR	G/POS	TPR
1993	Cal-A	126	416	44	99	20	1	3	45	15	38	.238	.275	.313	56	-26	5	7	-3	.975	-13	*S-126	-3.1
1994	Cal-A	112	389	53	101	14	2	3	33	18	28	.260	.296	.329	60	-23	3	7	-3	.983	8	*S-110	-0.8
1995	Cal-A★	99	362	61	111	28	6	5	41	20	25	.307	.346	.459	108	4	7	4	-0	.986	-4	S-98	0.7
1996	Cal-A	150	536	62	137	26	4	5	48	21	36	.256	.286	.347	60	-33	2	1	0	.971	5	*S-150	-1.3
Total	8	682	2335	281	596	110	14	19	212	100	191	.255	.292	.339	66	-116	27	26	-8	.973	8	S-666/2-10,3-2	-5.7

■ BENNY DISTEFANO
Distefano, Benito James   b: 1/23/62, Brooklyn, N.Y.   BL/TL, 6'1", 195 lbs.   Deb: 5/18/84

YEAR	TM/L	G	AB	R	H	2B	3B	HR	RBI	BB	SO	AVG	OBP	SLG	PRO+	BR/A	SB	CS	SBR	FA	FR	G/POS	TPR
1984	Pit-N	45	78	10	13	1	2	3	9	5	13	.167	.226	.346	59	-5	0	1	-1	.946	1	O-20,1-17	-0.5
1986	Pit-N	31	39	3	7	1	0	1	5	1	5	.179	.200	.282	31	-4	0	0	0	1.000	-1	/O-9,1-1	-0.5
1988	Pit-N	16	29	6	10	3	1	1	6	3	4	.345	.406	.621	194	3	0	0	0	1.000	-0	/1-5,O-2	0.3
1989	Pit-N	96	154	12	38	8	0	2	15	17	30	.247	.333	.338	96	-1	1	0	0	.981	-3	1-48/C-3,O-1	-0.6
1992	Hou-N	52	60	4	14	0	2	0	7	5	14	.233	.303	.300	75	-2	0	0	0	1.000	-0	O-12/1-6	-0.3
Total	5	240	360	35	82	13	5	7	42	31	66	.228	.298	.350	85	-7	1	1	-0	.985	-3	/1-77,O-44,C-3	-1.6

■ DUTCH DISTEL
Distel, George Adam   b: 4/15/1896, Madison, Ind.   d: 2/12/67, Madison, Ind.   BR/TR, 5'9", 165 lbs.   Deb: 6/21/18

YEAR	TM/L	G	AB	R	H	2B	3B	HR	RBI	BB	SO	AVG	OBP	SLG	PRO+	BR/A	SB	CS	SBR	FA	FR	G/POS	TPR
1918	StL-N	8	17	3	3	1	1	0	2	3	6	.176	.263	.353	90	-0	0			.900	-2	/2-5,S-2,O-1	-0.2

■ JACK DITTMER
Dittmer, John Douglas   b: 1/10/28, Elkader, Iowa   BL/TR, 6'1", 175 lbs.   Deb: 6/17/52

YEAR	TM/L	G	AB	R	H	2B	3B	HR	RBI	BB	SO	AVG	OBP	SLG	PRO+	BR/A	SB	CS	SBR	FA	FR	G/POS	TPR
1952	Bos-N	93	326	26	63	7	2	7	41	26	26	.193	.255	.291	53	-21	1	0	0	.982	6	2-90	-1.1
1953	Mil-N	138	504	54	134	22	1	9	63	18	35	.266	.293	.367	75	-20	1	0	0	.965	-29	*2-138	-4.0
1954	Mil-N	66	192	22	47	8	0	6	20	19	17	.245	.322	.380	88	-4	0	1	-1	.977	-3	2-55	-0.4
1955	Mil-N	38	72	4	9	1	1	1	4	5	15	.125	.171	.208	0	-11	0	0	0	.977	-2	2-28	-1.1
1956	Mil-N	44	102	8	25	4	0	1	6	8	8	.245	.300	.314	69	-4	0	0	0	.979	3	2-42	0.0
1957	Det-A	16	22	3	5	1	0	0	2	2	1	.227	.292	.273	54	-1	0	0	0	1.000	-1	/3-3,2-1	-0.2
Total	6	395	1218	117	283	43	4	24	136	77	102	.232	.281	.333	66	-61	2	1	0	.974	-26	2-354/3-3	-6.8

■ MOXIE DIVIS
Divis, Edward George   b: 1/16/1894, Cleveland, Ohio   d: 12/19/55, Lakewood, Ohio   Deb: 8/4/16

YEAR	TM/L	G	AB	R	H	2B	3B	HR	RBI	BB	SO	AVG	OBP	SLG	PRO+	BR/A	SB	CS	SBR	FA	FR	G/POS	TPR
1916	Phi-A	3	6	0	1	0	0	0	1	0	2	.167	.167	.167	-4	-1	0			1.000	1	/O-1	0.0

■ LEO DIXON
Dixon, Leo Moses   b: 9/4/1894, Chicago, Ill.   d: 4/11/84, Chicago, Ill.   BR/TR, 5'11", 170 lbs.   Deb: 4/14/25

YEAR	TM/L	G	AB	R	H	2B	3B	HR	RBI	BB	SO	AVG	OBP	SLG	PRO+	BR/A	SB	CS	SBR	FA	FR	G/POS	TPR
1925	StL-A	76	205	27	46	11	1	1	19	24	42	.224	.318	.302	55	-14	3	2	-0	.981	9	C-75	-0.2
1926	StL-A	33	89	7	17	3	1	0	8	11	14	.191	.294	.247	40	-8	1	4	-2	.977	4	C-33	-0.4
1927	StL-A	36	103	6	20	3	1	0	12	7	6	.194	.245	.243	26	-11	0	1	-1	.937	3	C-35	-0.6
1929	Cin-N	14	30	0	5	2	0	0	2	3	7	.167	.242	.233	19	-4	0			1.000	4	C-14	0.1
Total	4	159	427	40	88	19	3	1	41	45	69	.206	.291	.272	43	-37	4	7		.971	21	C-157	-1.1

■ WALT DOANE
Doane, Walter Rudolph   b: 3/12/1887, Bellevue, Idaho   d: 10/19/35, W.Brandywine, Pa.   BL/TR, 6', 165 lbs.   Deb: 9/20/09

YEAR	TM/L	G	AB	R	H	2B	3B	HR	RBI	BB	SO	AVG	OBP	SLG	PRO+	BR/A	SB	CS	SBR	FA	FR	G/POS	TPR
1909	Cle-A	4	9	1	1	0	0	0	0	1		.111	.200	.111	-1	-1	0			.778	1	/O-2,P-1	0.0
1910	Cle-A	6	7	0	2	1	0	0	2	1		.286	.375	.429	150	0	0			.750	-1	/P-6	0.0
Total	2	10	16	1	3	1	0	0	2	2		.188	.278	.250	64	-1	0			.800	-0	/P-7,O-2	0.0

■ DAN DOBBEK
Dobbek, Daniel John   b: 12/6/34, Ontonagon, Mich.   BL/TR, 6', 195 lbs.   Deb: 9/9/59

YEAR	TM/L	G	AB	R	H	2B	3B	HR	RBI	BB	SO	AVG	OBP	SLG	PRO+	BR/A	SB	CS	SBR	FA	FR	G/POS	TPR
1959	Was-A	16	60	8	15	1	2	1	5	5	13	.250	.308	.383	89	-1	0	0	0	1.000	1	O-16	-0.1
1960	Was-A	110	248	32	54	8	2	10	30	35	41	.218	.317	.387	90	-4	4	3	-1	.973	-8	O-78	-1.5
1961	Min-A	72	125	12	21	3	1	4	14	13	18	.168	.257	.304	47	-10	1	2	-1	.985	-9	O-48	-2.1
Total	3	198	433	52	90	12	5	15	49	53	72	.208	.299	.363	77	-14	5	5	-2	.980	-16	O-142	-3.7

■ JOHN DOBBS
Dobbs, John Gordon   b: 6/3/1875, Chattanooga, Tenn.   d: 9/9/34, Charlotte, N.C.   BL/TR, 5'9.5", 170 lbs.   Deb: 4/20/01

YEAR	TM/L	G	AB	R	H	2B	3B	HR	RBI	BB	SO	AVG	OBP	SLG	PRO+	BR/A	SB	CS	SBR	FA	FR	G/POS	TPR
1901	Cin-N	109	435	71	119	17	4	2	27	36		.274	.338	.345	105	3	19			.948	-7	*O-100/3-8	-1.0
1902	Cin-N	63	256	39	76	7	3	1	16	19		.297	.348	.359	108	4	7			.963	8	O-63	0.6
	Chi-N	59	235	31	71	8	2	0	35	18		.302	.352	.353	121	6	3			.977	1	O-59	0.3
	Yr	122	491	70	147	15	5	1	51	37		.299	.350	.356	114	8	10			.970	9	*O-122	0.9
1903	Chi-N	16	61	8	14	1	1	0	4	7		.230	.329	.279	76	-2	0			1.000	1	O-16	-0.2
	Bro-N	111	414	61	98	15	7	2	59	48		.237	.323	.321	86	-6	23			.966	4	*O-110	-0.9
	Yr	127	475	69	112	16	8	2	63	55		.236	.324	.316	85	-8	23			.970	4	*O-126	-1.1
1904	Bro-N	101	363	36	90	16	2	0	30	28		.248	.304	.303	90	-4	11			.936	0	O-92/2-2,S-2	-1.0
1905	Bro-N	123	460	59	117	21	4	2	36	31		.254	.304	.330	96	-3	15			.938	-6	*O-123	-1.6
Total	5	582	2224	305	585	85	23	7	207	187		.263	.325	.331	98	-4	78			.954	-0	O-563/3-8,S-2,2-2	-3.8

■ LARRY DOBY
Doby, Lawrence Eugene   b: 12/13/24, Camden, S.C.   BL/TR, 6'1", 182 lbs.   Deb: 7/5/47   MC

YEAR	TM/L	G	AB	R	H	2B	3B	HR	RBI	BB	SO	AVG	OBP	SLG	PRO+	BR/A	SB	CS	SBR	FA	FR	G/POS	TPR
1947	Cle-A	29	32	3	5	1	0	2	1	1	11	.156	.182	.188	3	-4	0	0	0	1.000	-1	/2-4,1-1,S-1	-0.5
1948	*Cle-A	121	439	83	132	23	9	14	66	54	77	.301	.384	.490	135	21	9	9	-3	.955	3	*O-114	1.5
1949	Cle-A★	147	547	106	153	25	3	24	85	91	90	.280	.389	.468	129	23	10	9	-2	.976	-7	*O-147	0.6
1950	Cle-A★	142	503	110	164	25	5	25	102	98	71	.326	**.442**	.545	156	46	8	6	-1	.987	-6	*O-140	3.1
1951	Cle-A★	134	447	84	132	27	5	20	69	101	81	.295	.428	.512	163	43	4	1	1	.977	-1	*O-132	3.6
1952	Cle-A★	140	519	**104**	143	26	8	**32**	104	90	111	.276	.383	**.541**	166	45	5	2	0	.986	11	*O-136	**5.1**
1953	Cle-A★	149	513	92	135	18	5	29	102	96	121	.263	.385	.487	138	29	3	2	-0	.984	-7	*O-146	1.6
1954	*Cle-A★	153	577	94	157	18	4	**32**	**126**	85	94	.272	.368	.484	130	23	3	1	0	.995	6	*O-153	2.4
1955	Cle-A☆	131	491	91	143	17	5	26	75	61	100	.291	.372	.505	129	19	2	0	1	.994	3	*O-129	1.7
1956	Chi-A	140	504	89	135	22	3	24	102	102	105	.268	.395	.466	125	20	0	1	-1	.987	-6	*O-137	1.8
1957	Chi-A	119	416	57	120	27	2	14	79	56	79	.288	.376	.464	127	16	2	3	-1	.985	-4	*O-110	0.5
1958	Chi-A	89	247	41	70	10	1	13	45	26	49	.283	.352	.490	132	10	0	2	-1	1.000	1	O-68	0.7
1959	Det-A	18	55	5	12	3	1	0	4	8	6	.218	.317	.309	69	-2	0	0	0	.960	-1	O-16	-0.4
	Chi-A	21	58	1	14	1	0	9	2	13	.241	.267	.293	54	-4	0	0	-1	.955	-1	O-12/1-2	-0.5
	Yr	39	113	6	26	4	1	0	13	10	22	.230	.293	.301	61	-6	1	0	0	.957	-1	O-28/1-2	-0.9
Total	13	1533	5348	960	1515	243	52	253	970	871	1011	.283	.387	.490	137	285	47	36	-8	.983	-1	*O-1440/2-4,1-3,S-1	21.2

■ ORAN DODD
Dodd, Oran A.   b: 9/14/1889, Bagwell, Tex.   d: 3/31/29, Newport, Ark.   BR/TR, 5'8", 150 lbs.   Deb: 7/26/12

YEAR	TM/L	G	AB	R	H	2B	3B	HR	RBI	BB	SO	AVG	OBP	SLG	PRO+	BR/A	SB	CS	SBR	FA	FR	G/POS	TPR
1912	Pit-N	5	9	0	0	0	0	0	1	1	3	.000	.100	.000	-73	-2	0			1.000	0	/3-4,2-1	-0.2

■ TOM DODD
Dodd, Thomas Marion   b: 8/15/58, Portland, Ore.   BR/TR, 6', 190 lbs.   Deb: 7/25/86

YEAR	TM/L	G	AB	R	H	2B	3B	HR	RBI	BB	SO	AVG	OBP	SLG	PRO+	BR/A	SB	CS	SBR	FA	FR	G/POS	TPR
1986	Bal-A	8	13	1	3	0	0	1	2	2	2	.231	.375	.462	128	1	0	0	0	.000	-0	/3-1,D-6	0.0

■ JOHN DODGE
Dodge, John Lewis   b: 4/27/1889, Bolivar, Tenn.   d: 6/19/16, Mobile, Ala.   BR/TR, 5'11.5", 165 lbs.   Deb: 8/29/12

YEAR	TM/L	G	AB	R	H	2B	3B	HR	RBI	BB	SO	AVG	OBP	SLG	PRO+	BR/A	SB	CS	SBR	FA	FR	G/POS	TPR
1912	Phi-N	30	92	3	11	1	0	0	3	4	11	.120	.156	.130	-20	-15	2			1.000	8	3-23/2-5,S-1	-0.8
1913	Phi-N	3	3	0	1	0	0	0	0	0	0	.333	.600	.333	164	1	0			1.000	-1	/S-3	0.0
	Cin-N	94	323	35	78	8	8	4	45	10	34	.241	.269	.353	77	-11	11			.908	2	3-91	-0.9
	Yr	97	326	35	79	8	8	4	45	10	34	.242	.274	.353	78	-10	11			.908	1	3-91/S-3	-0.9
Total	2	127	418	38	90	9	8	4	48	14	45	.215	.248	.304	55	-26	13			.926	8	3-114/2-5,S-4	-1.7

■ PAT DODSON
Dodson, Patrick Neal   b: 10/11/59, Santa Monica, Cal.   BL/TL, 6'4", 210 lbs.   Deb: 9/5/86

YEAR	TM/L	G	AB	R	H	2B	3B	HR	RBI	BB	SO	AVG	OBP	SLG	PRO+	BR/A	SB	CS	SBR	FA	FR	G/POS	TPR
1986	Bos-A	9	12	3	5	2	0	1	3	3	3	.417	.533	.833	264	3	0	0	0	1.000	-1	/1-7	0.2
1987	Bos-A	26	42	4	7	3	0	2	6	8	13	.167	.300	.381	77	-1	0	0	0	1.000	-1	1-21/D-1	-0.3
1988	Bos-A	17	45	5	8	3	1	1	4	6	17	.178	.275	.356	72	-2	0	0	0	1.000	2	1-17	-0.1
Total	3	52	99	12	20	8	1	4	10	17	33	.202	.319	.424	97	-0	0	0	0	1.000	0	/1-45,D-1	-0.2

■ BOBBY DOERR
Doerr, Robert Pershing   b: 4/7/18, Los Angeles, Cal.   BR/TR, 5'11", 175 lbs.   Deb: 4/20/37   CH

YEAR	TM/L	G	AB	R	H	2B	3B	HR	RBI	BB	SO	AVG	OBP	SLG	PRO+	BR/A	SB	CS	SBR	FA	FR	G/POS	TPR
1937	Bos-A	55	147	22	33	5	1	2	14	18	25	.224	.313	.313	56	-10	2	4	-2	.973	4	2-47	-0.5
1938	Bos-A	145	509	70	147	26	7	5	80	59	39	.289	.363	.397	86	-11	5	10	-5	.968	**27**	*2-145	-0.1
1939	Bos-A	127	525	75	167	28	2	12	73	38	32	.318	.365	.448	103	1	5	10	-6	.976	27	*2-126	2.7
1940	Bos-A	151	595	87	173	37	10	22	105	57	53	.291	.353	.497	113	10	10	5	0	.977	18	*2-151	3.6
1941	Bos-A★	132	500	74	141	28	4	16	93	43	43	.282	.339	.450	105	2	1	3	-2	.971	-6	*2-132	0.3

YEAR	TM/L	G	AB	R	H	2B	3B	HR	RBI	BB	SO	AVG	OBP	SLG	PRO+	BR/A	SB	CS	SBR	FA	FR	G/POS	TPR
1942	Bos-A☆	144	545	71	158	35	5	15	102	67	55	.290	.369	.455	127	19	4	4	-1	**.975**	11	*2-142	3.8
1943	Bos-A★	155	604	78	163	32	3	16	75	62	59	.270	.339	.412	117	12	8	8	-2	**.990**	15	*2-155	3.5
1944	Bos-A★	125	468	95	152	30	10	15	81	58	31	.325	.399	**.528**	166	39	5	2	0	.976	4	*2-125	5.2
1946	*Bos-A★	151	583	95	158	34	9	18	116	66	67	.271	.346	.453	115	11	5	6	-2	**.986**	27	*2-151	4.8
1947	Bos-A★	146	561	79	145	23	10	17	95	59	47	.258	.329	.426	101	-1	3	3	-1	.981	24	*2-146	3.3
1948	Bos-A★	140	527	94	150	23	6	27	111	83	49	.285	.386	.505	129	21	3	2	-0	.993	8	*2-138	3.6
1949	Bos-A	139	541	91	167	30	9	18	109	75	33	.309	.393	.497	126	19	2	2	-1	.980	28	*2-139	5.0
1950	Bos-A★	149	586	103	172	29	11	27	120	67	42	.294	.367	.519	114	9	3	4	-2	**.988**	9	*2-149	2.1
1951	Bos-A★	106	402	60	116	21	2	13	73	57	33	.289	.378	.448	112	7	2	1	-0	.981	6	*2-106	1.7
Total	14	1865	7093	1094	2042	381	89	223	1247	809	608	.288	.362	.461	114	127	54	64	-22	.980	181	*2-1852	39.0

■ JOHN DOHERTY   Doherty, John Michael b: 8/22/51, Woburn, Mass. BL/TL, 5'11", 185 lbs. Deb: 6/1/74

YEAR	TM/L	G	AB	R	H	2B	3B	HR	RBI	BB	SO	AVG	OBP	SLG	PRO+	BR/A	SB	CS	SBR	FA	FR	G/POS	TPR
1974	Cal-A	74	223	20	57	14	1	3	15	8	13	.256	.281	.368	91	-4	2	1	0	.991	-1	1-70/D-2	-0.9
1975	Cal-A	30	94	7	19	3	0	1	12	8	12	.202	.265	.266	54	-6	1	1	-0	.983	-1	1-26/D-1	-0.9
Total	2	104	317	27	76	17	1	4	27	16	25	.240	.276	.338	80	-10	3	2	-0	.989	-2	/1-96,D-3	-1.8

■ COZY DOLAN   Dolan, Albert J. (b: James Alberts) b: 12/23/1889, Chicago, Ill. d: 12/10/58, Chicago, Ill. BR/TR, 5'10", 160 lbs. Deb: 8/15/09 C

YEAR	TM/L	G	AB	R	H	2B	3B	HR	RBI	BB	SO	AVG	OBP	SLG	PRO+	BR/A	SB	CS	SBR	FA	FR	G/POS	TPR
1909	Cin-N	3	6	2	1	0	0	0	0	2		.167	.375	.167	69	-1	0			.750	-1	/3-3	-0.1
1911	NY-A	19	69	19	21	1	2	0	6	8		.304	.385	.377	106	1	12			.947	-1	3-19	0.0
1912	NY-A	18	60	15	12	1	3	0	11	5		.200	.273	.317	64	-3	5			.768	-5	3-17	-0.8
	Phi-N	11	50	8	14	2	2	0	7	1	10	.280	.294	.400	83	-1	3			.872	-1	3-11	-0.2
1913	Phi-N	55	126	15	33	4	0	0	8	1	21	.262	.273	.294	59	-7	9			.905	-7	O-12,S-10/2-9,31	-1.4
	Pit-N	35	133	22	27	5	2	0	9	15	14	.203	.289	.271	63	-6	14			.937	-1	3-35	-0.7
	Yr	90	259	37	60	9	2	0	17	16	35	.232	.282	.282	61	-13	23			.932	-9	3-39,O-12,S-10/21	-2.1
1914	StL-N	126	421	76	101	16	3	4	32	55	74	.240	.335	.321	96	-0	42			.955	-8	O-96,3-27	-1.3
1915	StL-N	111	322	53	90	14	9	2	38	34	37	.280	.356	.398	127	11	17	11	-2	.929	-11	O-98	-0.6
1922	NY-N	1	0	0	0	0	0	0	0	0		—	—	—	—	0	0	0	0	.000	0	R	0.0
Total	7	379	1187	210	299	43	21	6	111	121	156	.252	.328	.339	95	-6	102	11		.940	-34	O-206,3-116/S21	-5.1

■ JOE DOLAN   Dolan, Joseph b: 2/24/1873, Baltimore, Md. d: 3/24/38, Omaha, Neb. TR, 5'10", 155 lbs. Deb: 8/11/1896

YEAR	TM/L	G	AB	R	H	2B	3B	HR	RBI	BB	SO	AVG	OBP	SLG	PRO+	BR/A	SB	CS	SBR	FA	FR	G/POS	TPR
1896	Lou-N	44	165	14	35	2	1	3	18	9	12	.212	.253	.291	45	-14	6			.940	10	S-44	-0.2
1897	Lou-N	36	133	10	28	2	2	0	7	8		.211	.271	.256	41	-11	6			.849	-3	S-18,2-18	-1.2
1899	Phi-N	61	222	27	57	6	3	1	30	11		.257	.298	.324	73	-9	3			.915	-11	2-61	-1.5
1900	Phi-N	74	257	39	51	7	3	1	27	16		.198	.259	.261	44	-20	10			.931	3	3-31,2-29,S-12	-1.4
1901	Phi-N	10	37	0	3	0	0	0	2	2		.081	.128	.081	-38	-6	2			.973	-3	2-10	-0.9
	Phi-A	98	338	50	73	21	2	1	38	26		.216	.282	.299	58	-19	3			.881	16	S-61,3-35/2-1,O-1	0.1
Total	5	323	1152	140	247	38	11	7	122	72	12	.214	.270	.282	51	-79	28			.902	1	S-135,2-119/3-66,O	-5.1

■ BIDDY DOLAN   Dolan, Leon Mark b: 7/9/1881, Onalaska, Wis. d: 7/15/50, Indianapolis, Ind BR/TR, 6', Deb: 4/16/14

YEAR	TM/L	G	AB	R	H	2B	3B	HR	RBI	BB	SO	AVG	OBP	SLG	PRO+	BR/A	SB	CS	SBR	FA	FR	G/POS	TPR
1914	Ind-F	32	103	13	23	4	2	1	15	12	13	.223	.316	.330	69	-6	5			.979	1	1-31	-0.6

■ COZY DOLAN   Dolan, Patrick Henry b: 12/3/1872, Cambridge, Mass. d: 3/29/07, Louisville, Ky. BL/TL, 5'10", 160 lbs. Deb: 4/26/1895

YEAR	TM/L	G	AB	R	H	2B	3B	HR	RBI	BB	SO	AVG	OBP	SLG	PRO+	BR/A	SB	CS	SBR	FA	FR	G/POS	TPR
1895	Bos-N	26	83	12	20	4	1	0	7	6	7	.241	.300	.313	54	-6	3			.949	3	P-25/O-1	-0.1
1896	Bos-N	6	14	4	2	0	0	0	0	0	1	.143	.143	.143	-23	-3	0			.765	-0	/P-6	0.0
1900	Chi-N	13	48	5	13	1	0	0	2	2		.271	.300	.292	66	-2	2			.826	-2	O-13	-0.4
1901	Chi-N	43	171	29	45	1	2	0	16	7		.263	.296	.292	74	-6	3			.878	2	O-41	-0.7
	Bro-N	66	253	33	66	11	1	0	29	17		.261	.313	.312	79	-7	7			.967	-2	O-64	-1.3
	Yr	109	424	62	111	12	3	0	45	24		.262	.306	.304	77	-12	10			.931	0	*O-105	-2.0
1902	Bro-N	141	592	72	166	16	7	1	54	33		.280	.324	.336	103	1	24			.936	-9	*O-141	-1.8
1903	Chi-A	27	104	16	27	5	1	0	7	6		.260	.313	.327	96	-0	5			.971	2	1-19/O-4	0.1
	Cin-N	93	385	64	111	20	3	0	58	28		.288	.340	.356	88	-7	11			.937	-7	O-93	-1.9
1904	Cin-N	129	465	88	132	8	10	6	51	39		.284	.342	.383	113	6	19			.939	-4	*O-102,1-24	-0.4
1905	Cin-N	22	77	7	18	2	1	0	4	7		.234	.306	.286	69	-3	2			.965	-4	1-13/O-9	-0.8
	Bos-N	112	433	44	119	11	7	3	48	27		.275	.322	.353	103	1	21			.946	4	*O-111/P-2,1-2	-0.8
	Yr	134	510	51	137	13	8	3	52	34		.269	.319	.343	97	-2	23			.931	0	*O-120,1-15/P-2	-0.8
1906	Bos-N	152	549	54	136	20	4	0	39	55		.248	.318	.299	95	-2	17			.928	-2	*O-144/2-7,P-2,1-1	-1.2
Total	9	830	3174	428	855	99	37	10	315	227	8	.269	.322	.333	94	-27	114			.931	-18	*O-723/1-59,P-35,2-7	-8.5

■ TOM DOLAN   Dolan, Thomas J. b: 1/10/1859, New York, N.Y. d: 1/16/13, St.Louis, Mo. BR/TR, Deb: 9/30/1879

YEAR	TM/L	G	AB	R	H	2B	3B	HR	RBI	BB	SO	AVG	OBP	SLG	PRO+	BR/A	SB	CS	SBR	FA	FR	G/POS	TPR
1879	Chi-N	1	4	0	0	0	0	0	0	0	0	.000	.000	.000	-94	-1				1.000	1	/C-1	0.0
1882	Buf-N	22	89	12	14	0	1	0	8	2	11	.157	.176	.180	14	-8				.941	-8	C-18/O-4,3-2	-1.5
1883	StL-a	81	295	32	63	9	2	1	18	9		.214	.237	.268	59	-14				.957	13	C-42,O-40/P-1	-0.3
1884	StL-a	35	137	19	36	6	2	0				.263	.299	.336	103	0				.873	-6	C-34/O-2	-0.3
	StL-U	19	69	9	13	3	0	0		4		.188	.233	.232	40	-7				.897	11	C-14/3-3,O-2	0.4
1885	StL-N	3	9	1	2	0	0	0		2	1	.222	.364	.222	99	0				.810	-1	/C-3	0.0
1886	StL-N	15	44	8	11	3	0	0	1	7	9	.250	.353	.318	113	1	2			.928	5	C-15	0.8
	Bal-a	38	125	13	19	3	2	0	12	8		.152	.203	.208	30	-10	8			.918	-6	C-35/O-3	-1.1
1888	StL-a	11	36	1	7	1	0	0	1	1		.194	.216	.222	37	-3	1			.914	-0	C-11	-0.2
Total	7	225	808	95	165	25	7	1	40	39	23	.204	.242	.256	57	-42	11			.916	9	C-173/O-51,3-5,P-1	-1.9

■ LESTER DOLE   Dole, Lester Carrington b: 7/8/1855, Meriden, Conn. d: 12/10/18, Concord, N.H. 5'11", Deb: 5/27/1875

YEAR	TM/L	G	AB	R	H	2B	3B	HR	RBI	BB	SO	AVG	OBP	SLG	PRO+	BR/A	SB	CS	SBR	FA	FR	G/POS	TPR
1875	NH-n	1	4	1	2	0	0	0	0	0	0	.500	.500	.500	285	1	0	0	0	.750	0	/O-1	0.1

■ FRANK DOLJACK   Doljack, Frank Joseph "Dolie" b: 10/5/07, Cleveland, Ohio d: 1/23/48, Cleveland, Ohio BR/TR, 5'11", 175 lbs. Deb: 9/4/30

YEAR	TM/L	G	AB	R	H	2B	3B	HR	RBI	BB	SO	AVG	OBP	SLG	PRO+	BR/A	SB	CS	SBR	FA	FR	G/POS	TPR
1930	Det-A	20	74	10	19	5	1	2	11	2	11	.257	.286	.473	87	-2	0	1	-1	.930	-2	O-20	-0.3
1931	Det-A	63	187	20	52	13	3	4	20	15	17	.278	.335	.444	100	-1	3	2	-0	.925	3	O-54	-0.1
1932	Det-A	8	26	5	10	1	0	1	7	2	2	.385	.429	.538	143	2	1	0	0	1.000	-2	/O-6	0.0
1933	Det-A	42	147	18	42	5	2	0	22	14	13	.286	.348	.347	83	-3	2	6	-3	.941	-7	O-37	-0.6
1934	*Det-A	56	120	15	28	7	1	1	19	13	15	.233	.313	.333	67	-6	2	1	0	.943	-3	O-30/1-3	-0.9
1943	Cle-A	3	7	0	0	0	0	0	1	1	2	.000	.125	.000	-66	-1	0	0	0	1.000	-1	/O-2	-0.2
Total	6	192	561	68	151	31	7	9	85	47	60	.269	.329	.398	87	-12	8	10	-4	.934	-0	O-149/1-3	-2.1

■ ART DOLL   Doll, Arthur James "Moose" b: 5/7/13, Chicago, Ill. d: 4/28/78, Calumet City, Ill. BR/TR, 6'1", 190 lbs. Deb: 9/21/35

YEAR	TM/L	G	AB	R	H	2B	3B	HR	RBI	BB	SO	AVG	OBP	SLG	PRO+	BR/A	SB	CS	SBR	FA	FR	G/POS	TPR
1935	Bos-N	3	10	0	1	0	0	0	0	0	1	.100	.100	.100	-50	-2	0			.867	0	/C-3	-0.2
1936	Bos-N	1	2	0	0	0	0	0	0	0	2	.000	.000	.000	-99	-1	0			1.000	-0	/P-1	0.0
1938	Bos-N	3	1	0	1	0	0	0	0	0	0	1.000	1.000	1.000	501	1	0			1.000	-0	/P-3	0.0
Total	3	7	13	0	2	0	0	0	0	0	3	.154	.154	.154	-18	-2	0			1.000	-0	/P-4,C-3	-0.2

■ SHE DONAHUE   Donahue, Charles Michael b: 6/29/1877, Oswego, N.Y. d: 8/28/47, New York, N.Y. BR/TR, 5'9", Deb: 4/29/04

YEAR	TM/L	G	AB	R	H	2B	3B	HR	RBI	BB	SO	AVG	OBP	SLG	PRO+	BR/A	SB	CS	SBR	FA	FR	G/POS	TPR
1904	StL-N	4	15	1	4	0	0	0	2	0		.267	.267	.267	68	-1	3			.846	-3	/2-3,S-1	-0.4
	Phi-N	58	200	21	43	4	0	0	14	3		.215	.227	.235	44	-13	7			.857	-17	S-29,3-24/1-3,2-2	-3.1
	Yr	62	215	22	47	4	0	0	16	3		.219	.229	.237	46	-14	10			.852	-20	S-30,3-24/2-5,1-3	-3.5

■ JIM DONAHUE   Donahue, James Augustus b: 1/8/1862, Lockport, Ill. d: 4/19/35, Lockport, Ill. BR/TR, 6', 175 lbs. Deb: 4/19/1886

YEAR	TM/L	G	AB	R	H	2B	3B	HR	RBI	BB	SO	AVG	OBP	SLG	PRO+	BR/A	SB	CS	SBR	FA	FR	G/POS	TPR
1886	NY-a	49	186	14	37	0	0	0	9	10		.199	.251	.199	44	-11	1			.803	-2	O-32,C-19	-1.1
1887	NY-a	60	220	33	62	4	1	1	29	21		.282	.350	.323	92	-1	6			.890	-8	C-51/O-5,1-4,3-1,2	-0.3
1888	KC-a	88	337	29	79	11	3	1	28	21		.234	.281	.294	79	-9	12			.902	-11	C-67,O-18/3-5,2-1	-1.3
1889	KC-a	67	252	30	59	5	4	0	32	21	20	.234	.293	.286	61	-13	12			.887	-8	C-46,O-14,3-10	-1.5
1891	Col-a	77	280	27	61	4	3	0	35	31	18	.218	.296	.254	62	-13	2			.942	5	C-75/O-1,1-1	-0.3
Total	5	341	1275	133	298	24	11	2	133	104	38	.234	.295	.275	69	-48	33			.911	-25	C-258/O-70,3-16,12	-4.5

YEAR	TM/L	G	AB	R	H	2B	3B	HR	RBI	BB	SO	AVG	OBP	SLG	PRO+	BR/A	SB	CS	SBR	FA	FR	G/POS	TPR

■ JIGGS DONAHUE
Donahue, John Augustus b: 7/13/1879, Springfield, Ohio d: 7/19/13, Columbus, Ohio BL/TL, 6'1", 178 lbs. Deb: 9/10/00 F

1900	Pit-N	3	10	1	2	0	1	0	3	0		.200	.200	.400	63	-1	1			.889	-1	/C-2,O-1	-0.2
1901	Pit-N	2	0	0	0	0	0	0	0	0		—	—	—	—	0	0			.000	-1	/C-1,O-1	-0.1
	Mil-A	37	107	10	34	5	4	0	16	10		.318	.387	.439	135	5	4			.933	-2	C-19,1-13	0.5
1902	StL-A	30	89	11	21	1	1	1	7	12		.236	.327	.303	76	-2	2			.956	-1	C-23/1-5	-0.1
1904	Chi-A	102	367	46	91	9	7	1	48	25		.248	.298	.319	99	-1	18			.979	7	*1-101	0.4
1905	Chi-A	149	533	71	153	22	4	1	76	44		.287	.346	.349	126	16	32			**.988**	8	*1-149	2.1
1906	*Chi-A	154	556	70	143	17	7	1	57	48		.257	.320	.318	103	2	36			**.988**	9	*1-154	0.7
1907	Chi-A	157	609	75	158	16	4	0	68	28		.259	.295	.299	93	-6	27			**.994**	21	*1-157	1.1
1908	Chi-A	93	304	22	62	8	2	0	22	25		.204	.271	.243	69	-10	14			.994	5	1-83	-0.8
1909	Chi-A	2	4	0	0	0	0	0	2	1		.000	.200	.000	-38	-1	0			1.000	-0	/1-2	-0.1
	Was-A	84	283	13	67	12	1	0	28	22		.237	.294	.286	87	-4	9			.984	-4	1-81	-1.0
	Yr	86	287	13	67	12	1	0	30	23		.233	.293	.282	86	-5	9			.984	-4	1-83	-1.1
Total	9	813	2862	319	731	90	31	4	327	215		.255	.311	.313	99	-1	143			.987	40	1-745/C-45,O-2	2.5

■ JOHN DONAHUE
Donahue, John Frederick "Jiggs" b: 4/19/1894, Roxbury, Mass. d: 10/3/49, Boston, Mass. BB/TR, 5'8", 170 lbs. Deb: 9/25/23

1923	Bos-A	10	36	5	10	4	0	0	1	4	5	.278	.350	.389	94	-0	0	1	-1	1.000	3	/O-9	0.2

■ PAT DONAHUE
Donahue, Patrick William b: 11/8/1884, Springfield, Ohio d: 1/31/66, Springfield, Ohio BR/TR, 6', 175 lbs. Deb: 5/29/08 F

1908	Bos-A	35	86	8	17	2	0	1	6	9		.198	.289	.256	75	-2	0			.959	0	C-32/1-3	0.1
1909	Bos-A	64	176	14	42	4	1	2	25	17		.239	.309	.307	93	-1	2			.982	-3	C-58	0.1
1910	Bos-A	2	4	0	0	0	0	0	0	0		.000	.000	.000	-98	-1	0			1.000	0	/C-1	-0.1
	Phi-A	14	34	2	5	0	0	0	4	3		.147	.237	.147	21	-3	1			1.000	1	C-13	0.2
	Cle-A	2	6	0	1	0	0	0	0	0		.167	.167	.167	4	-1	0			1.000	-1	/C-2,1-1	-0.1
	Phi-A	1	1	0	0	0	0	0	0	0		.000	.000	.000	-99	-0	0			1.000	1	/C-1	0.0
	Yr	19	45	2	6	0	0	0	4	3		.133	.204	.133	6	-5	1			1.000	3	C-17/1-1	0.0
Total	3	118	307	24	65	6	1	3	35	29		.212	.288	.267	75	-8	3			.978	1	C-107/1-4	0.2

■ TIM DONAHUE
Donahue, Timothy Cornelius "Bridget" b: 6/8/1870, Raynham, Mass. d: 6/12/02, Taunton, Mass. BL/TR, 5'11", 180 lbs. Deb: 7/28/1891

1891	Bos-a	4	7	0	0	0	0	0	0	5		.000	.000	.000	-99	-2	0			.833	-1	/C-4	-0.3
1895	Chi-N	63	219	29	59	9	1	2	36	20	25	.269	.339	.347	73	-9	5			.915	-2	C-63	-0.4
1896	Chi-N	57	188	27	41	10	1	0	20	11	15	.218	.276	.282	45	-15	11			.937	5	C-57	-0.3
1897	Chi-N	58	188	28	45	7	3	0	21	9		.239	.281	.309	54	-13	3			.947	7	C-55/S-2,1-1	0.0
1898	Chi-N	122	396	52	87	12	3	0	39	49		.220	.318	.265	68	-15	17			.962	6	*C-122	0.3
1899	Chi-N	92	278	39	69	10	3	0	29	34		.248	.345	.302	80	-6	10			.951	4	C-91/1-1	0.4
1900	Chi-N	67	216	21	51	10	1	0	17	19		.236	.313	.292	70	-8	8			.928	-7	C-66/2-1	-0.9
1902	Was-A	3	8	0	2	0	0	0	1	0		.250	.250	.250	39	-1	0			1.000	0	/C-3	0.0
Total	8	466	1500	196	354	57	12	2	163	142	45	.236	.314	.294	66	-70	54			.943	11	C-461/1-2,S-2,2-1	-1.2

■ JOHN DONALDSON
Donaldson, John David b: 5/5/43, Charlotte, N.C. BL/TR, 5'11", 165 lbs. Deb: 8/26/66

1966	KC-A	15	30	4	4	0	0	1	3	4		.133	.212	.133	2	-4	1	0	0	1.000	-2	/2-9	-0.6
1967	KC-A	105	377	40	104	16	5	0	28	37	39	.276	.344	.345	107	4	6	3	0	.982	-18	*2-101/S-1	-0.8
1968	Oak-A	127	363	37	80	9	2	2	27	45	44	.220	.310	.273	82	-7	5	5	-2	.971	-4	2-98/3-5,S-1	-0.8
1969	Oak-A	12	13	1	1	0	0	0	0	2	4	.077	.200	.077	-21	-2	0	0	0	.857	0	2-1	-0.2
	Sea-A	95	338	22	79	8	3	1	19	36	36	.234	.307	.284	67	-14	6	1	1	.974	-1	2-90/3-2,S-1	-0.6
	Yr	107	351	23	80	8	3	1	19	38	40	.228	.303	.276	64	-16	6	1	1	.972	0	2-91/3-2,S-1	-0.8
1970	Oak-A	41	89	4	22	2	1	1	11	9	6	.247	.316	.326	80	-2	1	0	0	.986	-3	2-21/S-6,3-1	-0.3
1974	Oak-A	10	15	1	2	0	0	0	0	0	0	.133	.133	.133	-25	-2	0	0	0	.962	1	/2-7,3-3	-0.2
Total	6	405	1225	96	292	35	11	4	86	132	133	.238	.314	.295	81	-28	19	9	0	.976	-26	2-327/3-11,S-9	-3.5

■ LEN DONDERO
Dondero, Leonard Peter "Mike" b: 9/12/03, Newark, Cal. BR/TR, 5'11", 178 lbs. Deb: 4/21/29

1929	StL-A	19	31	2	6	0	0	1	8	0	4	.194	.194	.290	22	-4	0	0	0	.857	-3	3-10/2-5	-0.6

■ MIKE DONLIN
Donlin, Michael Joseph "Turkey Mike" b: 5/30/1878, Peoria, Ill. d: 9/24/33, Hollywood, Cal. BL/TL, 5'9", 170 lbs. Deb: 7/19/1899

1899	StL-N	66	266	49	86	9	6	0	27	17		.323	.366	.470	126	8	20			.873	-7	O-51,1-13/S-3,P-3	-0.4
1900	StL-N	78	276	40	90	8	6	10	48	14		.326	.361	.507	139	13	14			.922	-4	O-47,1-21	0.5
1901	Bal-A	121	476	107	162	23	13	5	67	53		.340	.409	.475	138	25	33			.918	-9	O-74,1-47	2.5
1902	Cin-N	34	143	30	41	5	4	0	9	9		.287	.333	.378	109	1	9			.877	-1	O-32/P-1,S-1	-0.2
1903	Cin-N	126	496	110	174	25	18	7	67	56		.351	.420	.556	150	30	26			.900	-3	*O-118/1-7	2.0
1904	Cin-N	60	236	42	84	11	7	1	38	18		.356	.406	.475	158	15	21			.872	-3	O-53/1-6	1.0
	NY-N	42	132	17	37	7	3	2	14	10		.280	.340	.424	130	4	1			.918	-7	O-37	-0.4
	Yr	102	368	59	121	18	10	3	52	28		.329	.382	.457	148	20	22			.886	-9	O-90/1-6	0.6
1905	*NY-N	150	606	**124**	216	31	16	7	80	56		.356	.413	.495	166	49	33			.934	-12	*O-150	3.1
1906	NY-N	37	121	15	38	5	1	1	14	11		.314	.371	.397	136	5	9			.929	-6	O-29/1-1	-0.3
1908	NY-N	155	593	71	198	26	13	6	106	23		.334	.364	.452	153	32	30			.977	0	*O-155	3.0
1911	NY-N	12	12	3	4	0	0	1	0	1	1	.333	.333	.583	150	1	2			1.000	1	/O-3	-0.1
	Bos-N	56	222	33	70	16	1	2	34	22	17	.315	.377	.423	115	4	7			.912	-3	O-56	-0.2
	Yr	68	234	36	74	16	1	3	35	22	18	.316	.375	.432	117	5	9			.913	-4	O-59	-0.3
1912	Pit-N	77	244	27	77	9	8	2	35	20	16	.316	.370	.443	124	7	8			.982	-2	O-62	0.2
1914	NY-N	35	31	1	5	1	1	1	3	3	5	.161	.235	.355	77	-1	0			.000	0	H	-0.1
Total	12	1049	3854	669	1282	176	97	51	543	312	39	.333	.386	.468	142	193	213			.924	-37	O-867/1-95,P-4,S-4	10.6

■ JIM DONNELLY
Donnelly, James B. b: 7/19/1865, New Haven, Conn. d: 3/5/15, New Haven, Conn. BR/TR, 5'10.5", 155 lbs. Deb: 7/11/1884

1884	KC-U	6	23	2	3	1	0	0	1			.130	.167	.174	4	-3				.536	-4	/3-5,C-1	-0.6
	Ind-a	40	134	22	34	2	2	0		5		.254	.301	.299	99	0				.850	-5	3-24/S-8,O-6,2-2	-0.4
1885	Det-N	56	211	24	49	4	3	1	22	10	29	.232	.267	.294	81	-4				.850	-3	3-55/1-1	-0.6
1886	KC-N	113	438	51	88	11	3	0	38	36	57	.201	.262	.240	50	-26	16			.845	9	*3-113	-2.2
1887	Was-N	117	425	51	85	9	6	1	46	16	26	.200	.234	.256	38	-35	42			.867	16	*3-115/S-2	-1.4
1888	Was-N	122	428	43	86	9	4	0	23	20	16	.201	.242	.241	57	-20	44			.875	-5	*3-117/S-5	-2.2
1889	Was-N	4	13	3	2	0	0	0	2	0		.154	.267	.154	20	-1	1			.667	-4	/3-4	-0.2
1890	StL-a	11	42	11	14	0	0	0	3	8		.333	.451	.333	115	1	5			.795	-3	3-11	-0.1
1891	Col-a	17	54	6	13	0	0	0	9	13	5	.241	.388	.241	85	0	7			.855	3	3-17	0.3
1896	Bal-N	106	396	70	130	14	10	0	71	34	11	.328	.387	.414	110	6	38			.884	-3	*3-106	0.5
1897	Pit-N	44	161	22	31	4	1	0	14	16		.193	.270	.217	31	-16	14			.920	1	3-44	-1.2
	NY-N	23	85	19	16	3	0	0	11	9		.188	.266	.224	31	-8	6			.869	-6	3-23	-1.2
	Yr	67	246	41	47	7	1	0	25	25		.191	.268	.220	31	-24	20			.905	-5	3-67	-2.4
1898	StL-N	1	1	0	1	0	0	0	0	0		1.000	1.000	1.000	463	0	0			.500	0	/3-1	0.0
Total	11	660	2411	324	552	57	28	2	237	170	144	.229	.284	.278	65	-107	173			.862	-8	3-635/S-15,O-6,21C	-9.3

■ JOHN DONNELLY
Donnelly, John b: Elizabeth, N.J. Deb: 4/14/1873 F

1873	Was-n	30	137	15	35	1	0	0	20	1	0	.255	.261	.263	58	-6	0	0	0	.783	1	S-13,2-12/O-6,3-1	-0.5
1874	Phi-n	6	22	2	5	0	0	0	2	0	0	.227	.227	.227	45	-1	0	0	0	.667	-3	/O-3,S-2,2-1	-0.3
Total	2 n	36	159	17	40	1	0	0	22	1	0	.252	.256	.258	56	-8	0	0	0	.763	-2	/S-15,2-13,O-9,3-1	-0.8

■ PETE DONNELLY
Donnelly, Peter J. b: 10/8/1849, Philadelphia, Pa. d: 10/1/1890, Jersey City, N.J. Deb: 5/13/1871 F

1871	Kek-n	9	34	7	7	1	1	0	3	1	2	.206	.229	.294	48	-2	0	0	0	.714	-5	/O-9,3-2	-0.5

■ CHRIS DONNELS
Donnels, Chris Barton b: 4/21/66, Los Angeles, Cal. BL/TR, 6', 185 lbs. Deb: 5/7/91

1991	NY-N	37	89	7	20	2	0	0	5	14	19	.225	.330	.247	65	-4	1	1	-0	1.000	3	1-15,3-11	-0.2
1992	NY-N	45	121	8	21	4	0	0	6	17	25	.174	.275	.207	39	-9	1	0	0	.941	4	3-29,2-12	-0.6
1993	Hou-N	88	179	18	46	14	2	2	24	19	33	.257	.328	.391	95	-1	2	0	1	.898	-2	3-31,1-23/2-1	-0.2

YEAR	TM/L	G	AB	R	H	2B	3B	HR	RBI	BB	SO	AVG	OBP	SLG	PRO+	BR/A	SB	CS	SBR	FA	FR	G/POS	TPR
1994	Hou-N	54	86	12	23	5	0	3	5	13	18	.267	.364	.430	112	2	1	0	0	1.000	1	3-14/1-4,2-4	0.2
1995	Hou-N	19	30	4	9	0	0	0	2	3	6	.300	.364	.300	83	-1	0	0	0	.818	-2	/3-9,2-1	-0.2
	Bos-A	40	91	13	23	2	2	2	11	9	18	.253	.320	.385	80	-3	0	0	0	.927	1	3-27/1-8,2-3	-0.2
Total	5	283	596	62	142	27	4	7	53	75	119	.238	.323	.332	79	-16	5	1	1	.929	6	3-121/1-50,2-21	-1.2

■ JOE DONOHUE   Donohue, Joseph F.   b: 1869, Syracuse, N.Y.   Deb: 8/24/1891

YEAR	TM/L	G	AB	R	H	2B	3B	HR	RBI	BB	SO	AVG	OBP	SLG	PRO+	BR/A	SB	CS	SBR	FA	FR	G/POS	TPR
1891	Phi-N	6	22	2	7	1	0	0	2	1	3	.318	.375	.364	113	0	0			1.000	-0	/O-4,S-2	0.0

■ TOM DONOHUE   Donohue, Thomas James   b: 11/15/52, Mineola, N.Y.   BR/TR, 6', 185 lbs.   Deb: 4/6/79

YEAR	TM/L	G	AB	R	H	2B	3B	HR	RBI	BB	SO	AVG	OBP	SLG	PRO+	BR/A	SB	CS	SBR	FA	FR	G/POS	TPR
1979	Cal-A	38	107	13	24	3	1	3	14	3	29	.224	.259	.355	66	-5	2	0	1	.981	-3	C-38	-0.6
1980	Cal-A	84	218	18	41	4	1	2	14	7	63	.188	.217	.243	26	-22	5	1	1	.986	-10	C-84	-2.9
Total	2	122	325	31	65	7	2	5	28	10	92	.200	.231	.280	40	-28	7	1	2	.985	-12	C-122	-3.5

■ FRED DONOVAN   Donovan, Frederick Maurice   b: 7/4/1864, New Hampshire   d: 3/7/16, Bloomington, Ill.   BR/TR,   Deb: 6/23/1895

YEAR	TM/L	G	AB	R	H	2B	3B	HR	RBI	BB	SO	AVG	OBP	SLG	PRO+	BR/A	SB	CS	SBR	FA	FR	G/POS	TPR
1895	Cle-N	3	12	1	1	0	0	0	1	1	2	.083	.154	.083	-36	-2	0			.938	-0	/C-3	-0.2

■ JERRY DONOVAN   Donovan, Jeremiah Francis   b: 9/3/1876, Lock Haven, Pa.   d: 6/27/38, St.Petersburg, Fla.   BR/TR,   Deb: 4/12/06   F

YEAR	TM/L	G	AB	R	H	2B	3B	HR	RBI	BB	SO	AVG	OBP	SLG	PRO+	BR/A	SB	CS	SBR	FA	FR	G/POS	TPR
1906	Phi-N	61	166	11	33	4	0	0	15	6		.199	.236	.223	43	-11	2			.955	-4	C-53/S-1,O-1	-1.2

■ MIKE DONOVAN   Donovan, Michael Berchman   b: 10/18/1881, Brooklyn, N.Y.   d: 2/3/38, New York, N.Y.   BR/TR, 5'8", 155 lbs.   Deb: 5/29/04

YEAR	TM/L	G	AB	R	H	2B	3B	HR	RBI	BB	SO	AVG	OBP	SLG	PRO+	BR/A	SB	CS	SBR	FA	FR	G/POS	TPR
1904	Cle-A	2	2	0	0	0	0	0	0	0	0	.000	.000	.000	-99	-0	0			.000	0	/S-1	-0.1
1908	NY-A	5	19	2	5	1	0	0	2	0		.263	.263	.316	87	-0	0			1.000	1	/3-5	0.1
Total	2	7	21	2	5	1	0	0	2	0		.238	.238	.286	69	-1	0			1.000	0	/3-5,S-1	0.0

■ PATSY DONOVAN   Donovan, Patrick Joseph   b: 3/16/1865, County Cork, Ireland   d: 12/25/53, Lawrence, Mass.   BL/TL, 5'11.5", 175 lbs.   Deb: 4/19/1890   M

YEAR	TM/L	G	AB	R	H	2B	3B	HR	RBI	BB	SO	AVG	OBP	SLG	PRO+	BR/A	SB	CS	SBR	FA	FR	G/POS	TPR
1890	Bos-N	32	140	17	36	0	0	0	9	8	17	.257	.307	.257	60	-7	10			.891	-5	O-32	-1.2
	*Bro-N	28	105	17	23	5	1	0	8	5	5	.219	.268	.286	61	-5	3			1.000	2	O-28	-0.4
	Yr	60	245	34	59	5	1	0	17	13	22	.241	.290	.269	61	-13	13			.952	-3	O-60	-1.6
1891	Lou-a	105	439	73	141	10	3	2	53	30	18	.321	.375	.371	115	9	27			.912	5	*O-105	0.9
	Was-a	17	70	9	14	1	0	0	3	4	5	.200	.243	.214	33	-6	1			.857	-2	O-17	-0.8
	Yr	122	509	82	155	11	3	2	56	34	23	.305	.358	.350	104	3	28			.907	2	*O-122	0.1
1892	Was-N	40	163	29	39	3	3	0	12	11	13	.239	.295	.294	81	-4	16			.844	1	O-40	-0.4
	Pit-N	90	388	77	114	15	3	2	26	20	16	.294	.333	.363	110	4	40			.872	-3	O-90	-0.3
	Yr	130	551	106	153	18	6	2	38	31	29	.278	.322	.343	102	0	56			.862	-2	*O-130	-0.7
1893	Pit-N	113	499	114	158	5	8	2	56	42	8	.317	.373	.371	100	1	46			.937	-1	*O-112	-0.5
1894	Pit-N	132	576	145	174	21	10	4	76	33	12	.302	.345	.394	79	-21	41			.932	8	*O-132	-1.7
1895	Pit-N	125	519	114	160	17	6	1	58	47	19	.308	.375	.370	98	1	36			.961	-5	*O-125	-1.2
1896	Pit-N	131	573	113	183	20	5	3	59	35	18	.319	.360	.387	104	4	48			.954	7	*O-131	0.0
1897	Pit-N	120	479	82	154	16	7	0	57	25		.322	.360	.384	104	3	34			.949	1	*O-120,M	-0.7
1898	Pit-N	147	610	112	184	16	9	0	37	34		.302	.346	.357	104	2	41			.928	0	*O-147	-0.7
1899	Pit-N	121	531	82	156	11	7	1	55	17		.294	.322	.347	84	-13	26			.941	-12	*O-121,M	-3.1
1900	StL-N	126	503	78	159	11	1	0	61	38		.316	.368	.342	97	-1	**45**			.951	-5	*O-124	-1.3
1901	StL-N	130	531	92	161	23	5	1	73	27		.303	.344	.371	113	9	28			.979	4	*O-129,M	0.2
1902	StL-N	126	502	70	158	12	4	0	35	28		.315	.363	.355	126	16	34			.959	10	*O-126,M	1.9
1903	StL-N	105	410	63	134	15	3	0	39	25		.327	.370	.378	117	9	25			.952	-1	*O-105,M	0.2
1904	Was-A	125	436	30	100	6	0	0	19	24		.229	.271	.243	64	-17	17			.963	9	*O-122,M	-1.7
1906	Bro-N	7	21	1	5	0	0	0	0	0		.238	.238	.238	53	-1	0			1.000	-1	/O-6,M	-0.2
1907	Bro-N	1	1	0	0	0	0	0	0	0		.000	.000	.000	-99	-0	0			1.000	0	/O-1,M	0.0
Total	17	1821	7496	1318	2253	207	75	16	736	453	131	.301	.347	.355	98	-22	518			.941	13	*O-1813	-11.0

■ TOM DONOVAN   Donovan, Thomas Joseph   b: 1/1/1873, West Troy, N.Y.   d: 3/25/33, Watervliet, N.Y.   BR/TR, 6'2", 168 lbs.   Deb: 9/10/01   F

YEAR	TM/L	G	AB	R	H	2B	3B	HR	RBI	BB	SO	AVG	OBP	SLG	PRO+	BR/A	SB	CS	SBR	FA	FR	G/POS	TPR
1901	Cle-A	18	71	9	18	3	1	0	5	0		.254	.254	.324	62	-4	1			.862	-1	O-18/P-1	-0.5

■ BILL DONOVAN   Donovan, William Edward "Wild Bill"   b: 10/13/1876, Lawrence, Mass.   d: 12/9/23, Forsyth, N.Y.   BR/TR, 5'11", 190 lbs.   Deb: 4/22/1898   MC

YEAR	TM/L	G	AB	R	H	2B	3B	HR	RBI	BB	SO	AVG	OBP	SLG	PRO+	BR/A	SB	CS	SBR	FA	FR	G/POS	TPR
1898	Was-N	39	103	11	17	2	2	2	8	4		.165	.211	.282	41	-8	2			.933	1	O-20,P-17/S-1,2-1	-0.5
1899	Bro-N	5	13	2	3	1	0	0	0	0		.231	.231	.308	46	-1	0			.857	-0	/P-5	0.0
1900	Bro-N	5	13	0	0	0	0	0	2	0		.000	.000	.000	-94	-3	0			1.000	1	/P-5	0.0
1901	Bro-N	46	135	16	23	3	0	2	13	8		.170	.217	.237	31	-12	1			.927	-1	P-45	0.0
1902	Bro-N	48	161	16	28	3	2	1	16	9		.174	.227	.236	42	-11	7			.948	2	P-35/1-8,O-4,2-1	-0.3
1903	Det-A	40	124	11	30	3	2	0	12	4		.242	.266	.298	71	-4	3			.938	-2	P-35/S-2,2-1,O-1	0.1
1904	Det-A	46	140	12	38	2	1	1	6	3		.271	.287	.321	95	-1	2			.967	-3	P-34/1-8,O-1	-0.4
1905	Det-A	44	130	16	25	4	0	0	5	12		.192	.266	.223	55	-6	8			.933	-0	P-34/O-8,2-2	0.1
1906	Det-A	28	91	5	11	0	1	0	0	1		.121	.130	.143	-14	-12	6			.961	-1	P-25/2-3,O-1	-0.2
1907	*Det-A	37	109	20	29	7	2	0	19	6		.266	.304	.367	110	1	4			.945	-6	P-32	0.0
1908	*Det-A	30	82	5	13	1	0	0	2	10		.159	.250	.171	36	-5	2			.917	-6	P-29	0.0
1909	*Det-A	22	45	6	9	0	0	0	1	2		.200	.250	.200	41	-3	0			.974	-2	P-21	0.0
1910	Det-A	26	69	6	10	1	0	0	2	5		.145	.203	.159	13	-7	0			.955	-6	P-26	0.0
1911	Det-A	24	60	11	12	3	1	0	6	11		.200	.324	.333	79	-2	1			.935	-5	P-20	0.0
1912	Det-A	6	13	3	1	0	0	0	0	1		.077	.143	.077	-38	-2	0			1.000	-2	/P-3,1-2,O-2	-0.3
1915	NY-A	10	12	1	1	0	0	0	0	1	6	.083	.154	.083	-29	-2	0			1.000	-1	/P-9,M	0.0
1916	NY-A	1	0	0	0	0	0	0	0	0		—	—	—	—		0			1.000	0	/P-1,M	0.0
1918	Det-A	2	2	1	1	0	0	0	1	0		.500	.500	.500	210		0			1.000	-0	/P-2	0.0
Total	18	459	1302	142	251	30	11	7	93	77	6	.193	.241	.249	49	-80	36			.944	-30	P-378/O-37,1-18,2S	-1.5

■ RED DOOIN   Dooin, Charles Sebastian   b: 6/12/1879, Cincinnati, Ohio   d: 5/14/52, Rochester, N.Y.   BR/TR, 5'9.5", 165 lbs.   Deb: 4/18/02   M

YEAR	TM/L	G	AB	R	H	2B	3B	HR	RBI	BB	SO	AVG	OBP	SLG	PRO+	BR/A	SB	CS	SBR	FA	FR	G/POS	TPR
1902	Phi-N	94	333	20	77	7	3	0	35	10		.231	.262	.270	64	-14	8			.950	5	C-84/O-6	-0.1
1903	Phi-N	62	188	18	41	5	1	0	14	8		.218	.254	.255	47	-13	9			.940	-4	C-51/1-1,O-1	-1.2
1904	Phi-N	108	355	41	86	11	4	6	36	8		.242	.261	.346	90	-6	15			.938	7	C-96/1-4,O-3,3-1	1.2
1905	Phi-N	113	380	45	95	13	5	0	36	10		.250	.269	.311	75	-13	12			.965	8	*C-107/3-1	0.6
1906	Phi-N	113	351	25	86	19	1	0	32	13		.245	.274	.305	80	-9	15			.948	-10	*C-107	-1.0
1907	Phi-N	101	313	18	66	8	4	0	14	15		.211	.252	.262	62	-14	10			.959	2	C-94/2-1,O-1	-0.4
1908	Phi-N	133	435	28	108	17	4	0	41	17		.248	.283	.306	85	-8	20			.966	12	*C-132	1.8
1909	Phi-N	141	468	42	105	14	1	0	38	21		.224	.264	.271	66	-20	14			.958	4	*C-140	-0.3
1910	Phi-N	103	331	30	80	13	4	0	30	22	17	.242	.289	.305	71	-13	10			.956	-4	C-91/O-3,M	-0.8
1911	Phi-N	74	247	18	81	15	1	1	16	14	12	.328	.366	.409	115	4	6			.967	5	C-74,M	1.6
1912	Phi-N	69	184	20	43	9	0	0	22	5	12	.234	.262	.283	46	-14	8			.958	-9	C-58,M	-0.9
1913	Phi-N	55	129	6	33	4	1	0	13	3	9	.256	.273	.302	62	-7	1			.962	3	C-50,M	-0.1
1914	Phi-N	53	118	10	21	2	0	0	8	4	14	.178	.205	.220	25	-11	4			.967	-0	C-40/O-2,M	-1.0
1915	Cin-N	10	31	2	10	0	0	0	2	5		.323	.364	.323	106	0	1			.915	-4	C-10	-0.3
	NY-N	46	124	9	27	2	2	0	5	15		.218	.236	.266	55	-7	0	2	-1	.964	1	C-46	-0.5
	Yr	56	155	11	37	2	2	0	7	20		.239	.262	.277	66	-7	1	2	-1	.956	-3	C-56	-0.8
1916	NY-N	15	17	1	2	0	0	0	0	0	3	.118	.118	.118	-29	-3	0			.972	5	C-15	-0.2
Total	15	1290	4004	333	961	139	31	10	344	155	87	.240	.272	.298	72	-148	133	2		.957	25	*C-1195/O-16,132	-1.6

■ MICKEY DOOLAN   Doolan, Michael Joseph "Doc" (b: Michael Joseph Doolittle)   b: 5/7/1880, Ashland, Pa.   d: 11/1/51, Orlando, Fla.   BR/TR, 5'10.5", 170 lbs.   Deb: 4/14/05   C

YEAR	TM/L	G	AB	R	H	2B	3B	HR	RBI	BB	SO	AVG	OBP	SLG	PRO+	BR/A	SB	CS	SBR	FA	FR	G/POS	TPR
1905	Phi-N	136	492	53	125	27	11	6	48	24		.254	.292	.360	97	-4	17			.935	-9	*S-135	-1.1
1906	Phi-N	154	535	41	123	19	7	1	55	27		.230	.270	.297	77	-16	16			.930	6	*S-154	-0.6
1907	Phi-N	145	509	33	104	19	7	1	47	25		.204	.243	.275	63	-23	14			.929	14	*S-145	-0.6
1908	Phi-N	129	445	29	104	25	4	2	49	17		.234	.267	.321	85	-9	5			.939	-8	*S-129	-0.7
1909	Phi-N	147	493	39	108	12	10	0	35	37		.219	.276	.290	75	-15	10			.939	**25**	*S-147	1.3
1910	Phi-N	148	536	58	141	31	6	2	57	35	56	.263	.315	.354	92	-7	16			**.948**	21	*S-148	2.1

YEAR	TM/L	G	AB	R	H	2B	3B	HR	RBI	BB	SO	AVG	OBP	SLG	PRO+	BR/A	SB	CS	SBR	FA	FR	G/POS	TPR
1911	Phi-N	146	512	51	122	23	6	1	49	44	65	.238	.301	.313	71	-21	14			.936	20	*S-145	0.9
1912	Phi-N	146	532	47	137	26	6	1	62	34	59	.258	.305	.335	70	-23	6			.950	8	*S-146	-0.2
1913	Phi-N	151	518	32	113	12	6	1	43	29	68	.218	.262	.270	50	-34	17			.941	17	*S-148/2-3	-0.3
1914	Bal-F	145	486	58	119	23	6	1	53	40	47	.245	.311	.323	71	-27	30			**.949**	**29**	*S-145	1.5
1915	Bal-F	119	404	41	75	13	7	2	21	24	39	.186	.238	.267	41	-39	10			.946	32	*S-119	0.3
	Chi-F	24	86	9	23	1	1	0	9	2	7	.267	.292	.302	72	-5	5			.914	1	S-24	-0.2
	Yr	143	490	50	98	14	8	2	30	26	46	.200	.248	.273	46	-44	15			.941	**33**	*S-143	0.1
1916	Chi-N	28	70	4	15	2	1	0	5	8	7	.214	.295	.271	67	-3	0			.918	3	S-24	0.2
	NY-N	18	51	4	12	3	1	1	3	2	4	.235	.264	.392	106	0	1			.975	2	S-16/2-2	0.3
	Yr	46	121	8	27	5	2	1	8	10	11	.223	.282	.322	82	-3	1			.939	4	S-40/2-2	0.5
1918	Bro-N	92	308	14	55	8	2	0	18	22	24	.179	.233	.218	38	-23	8			**.968**	10	2-91	-0.8
Total	13	1728	5977	513	1376	244	81	15	554	370	<u>376</u>	.230	.279	.306	71	-248	173			.940	178	*S-1625/2-96	2.1

■ HARRY DOOMS
Dooms, Henry E. "Jack" b: 1/30/1867, St.Louis, Mo. d: 12/14/1899, St.Louis, Mo. Deb: 8/7/1892

YEAR	TM/L	G	AB	R	H	2B	3B	HR	RBI	BB	SO	AVG	OBP	SLG	PRO+	BR/A	SB	CS	SBR	FA	FR	G/POS	TPR
1892	Lou-N	1	4	0	0	0	0	0	1	3		.000	.200	.000	-42	-1	0			.000	-1	/O-1	-0.1

■ TOM DORAN
Doran, Thomas J. "Long Tom" b: 12/2/1880, Westchester Co., N.Y. d: 6/22/10, New York, N.Y. BL/TR, 5'11", 152 lbs. Deb: 4/19/04

YEAR	TM/L	G	AB	R	H	2B	3B	HR	RBI	BB	SO	AVG	OBP	SLG	PRO+	BR/A	SB	CS	SBR	FA	FR	G/POS	TPR
1904	Bos-A	12	32	1	4	0	1	0	0	4		.125	.243	.188	35	-2	1			.898	-5	C-11	-0.7
1905	Bos-A	3	3	0	0	0	0	0	0	0		.000	.000	.000	-99	-1	0			1.000	0	/C-1	0.0
	Det-A	34	94	8	15	3	0	0	4	8		.160	.248	.191	40	-6	2			.963	-5	/C-32	-0.9
	Yr	37	97	8	15	3	0	0	4	8		.155	.241	.186	35	-7	2			.964	-5	/C-33	-0.9
1906	Bos-A	2	3	1	0	0	0	0	0	0		.000	.000	.000	-99	-1	0			1.000	0	/C-2	-0.1
Total	3	51	132	10	19	3	1	0	4	12		.144	.236	.182	33	-10	3			.950	-10	/C-46	-1.7

■ BILL DORAN
Doran, William Donald b: 5/28/58, Cincinnati, Ohio BB/TR, 5'11", 175 lbs. Deb: 9/6/82

YEAR	TM/L	G	AB	R	H	2B	3B	HR	RBI	BB	SO	AVG	OBP	SLG	PRO+	BR/A	SB	CS	SBR	FA	FR	G/POS	TPR
1982	Hou-N	26	97	11	27	3	0	0	6	4	11	.278	.307	.309	79	-3	5	0	2	.975	-3	2-26	-0.3
1983	Hou-N	154	535	70	145	12	7	8	39	86	67	.271	.372	.364	112	11	12	12	-4	.979	5	*2-153	2.0
1984	Hou-N	147	548	92	143	18	11	4	41	66	69	.261	.343	.356	104	4	21	12	-1	.986	6	*2-139,S-13	1.5
1985	Hou-N	148	578	84	166	31	6	14	59	71	69	.287	.365	.434	126	21	23	15	-2	.980	7	*2-147	3.2
1986	*Hou-N	145	550	92	152	29	3	6	37	81	57	.276	.371	.373	109	9	42	19	1	.974	-42	*2-144	-2.7
1987	Hou-N	162	625	82	177	23	3	16	79	82	64	.283	.369	.406	109	10	31	11	3	**.992**	-16	*2-162/S-3	0.4
1988	Hou-N	132	480	66	119	18	1	7	53	65	60	.248	.339	.333	97	-0	17	4	3	**.987**	-3	*2-130	0.5
1989	Hou-N	142	507	65	111	25	2	8	58	59	63	.219	.303	.323	82	-12	22	3	5	.980	-27	*2-138	-3.2
1990	Hou-N	109	344	49	99	21	2	6	32	71	53	.288	.410	.413	131	18	18	9	0	.989	-11	2-99	0.9
	Cin-N	17	59	10	22	8	0	1	5	8	5	.373	.448	.559	168	6	5	0	2	.985	1	2-12/3-4	0.9
	Yr	126	403	59	121	29	2	7	37	79	58	.300	.415	.434	137	24	23	9	2	.988	-10	*2-111/3-4	1.8
1991	Cin-N	111	361	51	101	12	6	6	35	46	39	.280	.361	.374	103	3	5	4	-0	.981	-14	2-88/O-6,1-4	-1.1
1992	Cin-N	132	387	48	91	16	2	8	47	64	40	.235	.344	.349	94	-1	7	4	-0	.988	-9	*2-104,1-25	-1.0
1993	Mil-A	28	60	7	13	4	0	0	6	6	3	.217	.288	.283	55	-4	1	0	0	.964	-5	2-17/1-4	-0.9
Total	12	1453	5131	727	1366	220	39	84	497	709	600	.266	.356	.373	107	62	209	93	7	.983	-112	*2-1359/1-33,SO3	0.2

■ BILL DORAN
Doran, William James b: 6/14/1898, San Francisco, Cal. d: 3/9/78, Santa Monica, Cal. BL/TR, 5'11.5", 175 lbs. Deb: 6/23/22

YEAR	TM/L	G	AB	R	H	2B	3B	HR	RBI	BB	SO	AVG	OBP	SLG	PRO+	BR/A	SB	CS	SBR	FA	FR	G/POS	TPR
1922	Cle-A	3	2	0	1	0	0	0	0	1	0	.500	.667	.500	206	0	0	0	0	.000	0	/3-2	0.0

■ JERRY DORGAN
Dorgan, Jeremiah F. b: 1856, Meriden, Conn. d: 6/10/1891, New Haven, Conn. BL/TR, 165 lbs. Deb: 7/8/1880 F

YEAR	TM/L	G	AB	R	H	2B	3B	HR	RBI	BB	SO	AVG	OBP	SLG	PRO+	BR/A	SB	CS	SBR	FA	FR	G/POS	TPR
1880	Wor-N	10	35	2	7	1	0	0	1	0	1	.200	.200	.229	41	-2				.750	-3	/O-9,C-1	-0.5
1882	Phi-a	44	181	25	51	9	1	0	24	4		.282	.297	.343	103	-1				.880	-1	C-25,O-22/3-1	-0.1
1884	Ind-a	34	141	22	42	6	1	0		2		.298	.317	.355	122	3				.793	-2	O-29/C-5	0.1
	Bro-a	4	13	2	4	0	0	0		0		.308	.308	.308	101	-0				.921	2	/C-4	0.2
	Yr	38	154	24	46	6	1	0		2		.299	.316	.351	120	3				.793	0	O-29/C-9	0.3
1885	Det-N	39	161	23	46	6	2	0	24	8	10	.286	.320	.348	115	3				.857	-3	O-39	-0.2
Total	4	131	531	74	150	22	4	0	<u>49</u>	14	<u>11</u>	.282	.303	.339	107	3				.817	-7	/O-99,C-35,3-1	-0.5

■ MIKE DORGAN
Dorgan, Michael Cornelius b: 10/2/1853, Middletown, Conn. d: 4/26/09, Hartford, Conn. BR/TR, 5'9", 180 lbs. Deb: 5/8/1877 FM

YEAR	TM/L	G	AB	R	H	2B	3B	HR	RBI	BB	SO	AVG	OBP	SLG	PRO+	BR/A	SB	CS	SBR	FA	FR	G/POS	TPR
1877	StL-N	60	266	45	82	9	7	0	23	9	13	.308	.331	.395	135	11				.824	-8	*O-50,C-12/3-2,S2	0.1
1879	Syr-N	59	270	38	72	11	5	1	17	4	13	.267	.277	.356	120	6				.954	-5	1-21,O-16,3/SCP2	0.0
1880	Pro-N	79	321	45	79	10	1	0	31	10	18	.246	.269	.283	90	-3				.858	2	*O-77/3-2,P-1,M	-0.3
1881	Wor-N	51	220	36	61	5	0	0	18	8	4	.277	.303	.300	85	-4				.953	1	1-26,O-23/S-2,M	-0.6
	Det-N	8	34	5	8	1	0	0	5	1	0	.235	.257	.265	62	-1				1.000	-0	/O-5,3-2,1-1	-0.2
	Yr	59	254	41	69	6	0	0	23	9	4	.272	.297	.295	82	-5				.897	0	O-28,1-27/S-2,3-2	-0.8
1883	NY-N	64	261	32	61	11	3	0	27	2	23	.234	.240	.299	63	-11				.847	-5	O-59/C-6,P-1	-1.5
1884	NY-N	83	341	61	94	11	6	1	48	13	27	.276	.302	.352	103	0				.851	1	O-64/P-14/C-6,2-3	0.0
1885	NY-N	89	347	60	113	17	8	0	46	11	24	.326	.346	.421	149	18				.905	-7	*O-88/1-1	1.2
1886	NY-N	118	442	61	129	19	4	2	79	29	37	.292	.335	.367	112	6	9			.888	-8	*O-116/1-3	-0.4
1887	NY-N	71	283	41	73	9	0	0	34	15	20	.258	.302	.293	69	-11	22			.870	-1	O-69/1-2	-1.2
1890	Syr-a	33	139	19	30	8	0	0	18	16		.216	.301	.273	77	-3	6			.900	-2	O-33	-0.6
Total	10	715	2924	443	802	112	34	4	346	118	<u>179</u>	.274	.303	.340	102	8	39			.867	-30	O-600/1-54,CP3S2	-3.5

■ CHARLIE DORMAN
Dorman, Charles William "Slats" b: 4/23/1898, San Francisco, Cal d: 11/15/28, San Francisco, Cal BR/TR, 6'2", 185 lbs. Deb: 5/14/23

YEAR	TM/L	G	AB	R	H	2B	3B	HR	RBI	BB	SO	AVG	OBP	SLG	PRO+	BR/A	SB	CS	SBR	FA	FR	G/POS	TPR
1923	Chi-A	1	2	0	1	0	0	0	0	0	0	.500	.500	.500	166	0	0	0	0	1.000	-0	/C-1	0.0

■ RED DORMAN
Dorman, Dwight Dexter "Curlie" b: 10/3/05, Jacksonville, Ill. d: 12/7/74, Anaheim, Cal. BR/TR, 5'10.5", 180 lbs. Deb: 8/21/28

YEAR	TM/L	G	AB	R	H	2B	3B	HR	RBI	BB	SO	AVG	OBP	SLG	PRO+	BR/A	SB	CS	SBR	FA	FR	G/POS	TPR
1928	Cle-A	25	77	12	28	6	0	1	19	6	6	.364	.430	.442	128	4	1	0	0	.915	-3	O-24	0.0

■ BRIAN DORSETT
Dorsett, Brian Richard b: 4/9/61, Terre Haute, Ind. BR/TR, 6'3", 215 lbs. Deb: 9/8/87

YEAR	TM/L	G	AB	R	H	2B	3B	HR	RBI	BB	SO	AVG	OBP	SLG	PRO+	BR/A	SB	CS	SBR	FA	FR	G/POS	TPR
1987	Cle-A	5	11	2	3	0	0	1	3	0	3	.273	.333	.545	127	0	0	0	0	1.000	-2	/C-4	-0.1
1988	Cal-A	7	11	0	1	0	0	0	2	1	5	.091	.167	.091	-26	-2	0	0	0	1.000	1	/C-7	-0.1
1989	NY-A	8	22	3	8	1	0	0	4	1	3	.364	.391	.409	127	1	0	0	0	1.000	-0	/C-8	0.1
1990	NY-A	14	35	2	5	2	0	0	0	2	4	.143	.189	.200	9	-4	0	0	0	1.000	-1	/C-9,D-5	-0.5
1991	SD-N	11	12	0	1	0	0	0	1	0	3	.083	.083	.083	-51	-2	0	0	0	1.000	0	/1-2	-0.2
1993	Cin-N	25	63	7	16	4	0	2	12	3	14	.254	.288	.413	85	-2	0	0	0	1.000	0	C-18/1-3	0.1
1994	Cin-N	76	216	21	53	8	0	5	26	21	33	.245	.315	.352	74	-8	0	0	0	.991	-1	C-73/1-1	-0.5
1996	Chi-N	17	41	3	5	0	0	1	3	4	8	.122	.200	.195	5	-6	0	0	0	1.000	1	C-15	-0.4
Total	8	163	411	38	92	15	0	9	51	32	73	.224	.283	.326	62	-23	0	0	0	.995	-0	C-134/1-6,D-5	-1.6

■ JERRY DORSEY
Dorsey, Jeremiah b: 1885, Oakland, Cal. BL/TL, 5'11", 175 lbs. Deb: 9/23/11

YEAR	TM/L	G	AB	R	H	2B	3B	HR	RBI	BB	SO	AVG	OBP	SLG	PRO+	BR/A	SB	CS	SBR	FA	FR	G/POS	TPR
1911	Pit-N	2	6	0	0	0	0	0	0	0	1	.000	.000	.000	-96	-2	0			1.000	0	/O-1	-0.1

■ JERRY DORSEY
Dorsey, Michael Jeremiah b: 1854, Canada d: 11/3/38, Auburn, N.Y. Deb: 7/9/1884

YEAR	TM/L	G	AB	R	H	2B	3B	HR	RBI	BB	SO	AVG	OBP	SLG	PRO+	BR/A	SB	CS	SBR	FA	FR	G/POS	TPR
1884	Bal-U	1	3	0	0	0	0	0	0	0		.000	.000	.000	-91	-1				.000	-0	/O-1,P-1	-0.1

■ HERM DOSCHER
Doscher, John Henry Sr. b: 12/20/1852, New York, N.Y. d: 3/20/34, Buffalo, N.Y. BR/TR, 5'10", 182 lbs. Deb: 9/4/1872 FU

YEAR	TM/L	G	AB	R	H	2B	3B	HR	RBI	BB	SO	AVG	OBP	SLG	PRO+	BR/A	SB	CS	SBR	FA	FR	G/POS	TPR
1872	Atl-n	6	25	4	9	0	0	0		0	1	.360	.360	.360	104	-0	0	0	0	.769	1	/O-6	0.0
1873	Atl-n	1	6	1	1	0	0	0	1	0	0	.167	.167	.167	-1	-1	0	0	0	.500	-0	/O-1	-0.1
1875	Was-n	22	81	5	15	0	0	0	5	0	0	.185	.185	.235	46	-4	1	0	0	.752	1	3-22	-0.2
1879	Tro-N	47	191	16	42	8	0	0	18	2	10	.220	.228	.262	65	-7				.806	-4	3-47	-0.9
	Chi-N	3	11	1	2	0	0	0	1	0	3	.182	.182	.182	19	-1				.700	1	/3-3	-0.2
	Yr	50	202	17	44	8	0	0	19	2	13	.218	.225	.257	62	-8				.800	-3	3-50	-1.1
1881	Cle-N	5	19	2	4	0	0	0	0	0	0	.211	.211	.211	35	-1				.895	-0	/3-5	-0.2
1882	Cle-N	25	104	7	25	2	0	0	10	0	6	.240	.240	.260	62	-4				.857	-3	3-22/O-2,S-1	-0.5
Total	3 n	29	112	10	25	0	0	0	11	0	7	.223	.223	.259	60	-5				.733	1	/3-3,O-7	-0.3
Total	3	80	325	26	73	10	0	0	29	2	26	.225	.229	.255	61	-13				.823	-7	/3-77,O-2,S-1	-1.8

YEAR	TM/L	G	AB	R	H	2B	3B	HR	RBI	BB	SO	AVG	OBP	SLG	PRO+	BR/A	SB	CS	SBR	FA	FR	G/POS	TPR

■ **DAVID DOSTER**   Doster, David Eric b: 10/8/70, Ft.Wayne, Ind.   BR/TR, 5'10", 185 lbs.   Deb: 6/16/96

| 1996 | Phi-N | 39 | 105 | 14 | 28 | 8 | 0 | 1 | 8 | 7 | 21 | .267 | .313 | .371 | 77 | -3 | 0 | 0 | 0 | .973 | -1 | 2-24/3-1 | -0.3 |

■ **DUTCH DOTTERER**   Dotterer, Henry John b: 11/11/31, Syracuse, N.Y.   BR/TR, 6', 209 lbs.   Deb: 9/25/57

1957	Cin-N	4	12	0	1	0	0	0	2	1	2	.083	.154	.083	-32	-2	0	0	0	1.000	-1	/C-4	-0.3
1958	Cin-N	11	28	1	7	1	0	1	2	2	4	.250	.300	.393	77	-1	0	0	0	.981	4	/C-8	0.3
1959	Cin-N	52	161	21	43	7	0	2	17	16	23	.267	.333	.348	79	-4	0	0	0	.992	-0	C-51	-0.2
1960	Cin-N	33	79	4	18	5	0	2	11	13	10	.228	.337	.367	91	-1	0	1	-1	.979	1	C-31	0.1
1961	Was-A	7	19	1	5	2	0	0	1	3	5	.263	.364	.368	98	0	0	0	0	1.000	2	/C-7	0.2
Total	5	107	299	27	74	15	0	5	33	35	44	.247	.326	.348	79	-8	0	1	-1	.988	7	C-101	0.1

■ **CHARLIE DOUGHERTY**   Dougherty, Charles William b: 2/7/1862, Darlington, Wis. d: 2/18/25, Milwaukee, Wis.   Deb: 4/17/1884

| 1884 | Alt-U | 23 | 85 | 6 | 22 | 5 | 0 | 0 | | 2 | | .259 | .276 | .318 | 78 | -5 | | | | .854 | 0 | 2-16/O-8,S-1 | -0.4 |

■ **PATSY DOUGHERTY**   Dougherty, Patrick Henry b: 10/27/1876, Andover, N.Y. d: 4/30/40, Bolivar, N.Y.   BL/TR, 6'2", 190 lbs.   Deb: 4/19/02

1902	Bos-A	108	438	77	150	12	6	0	34	42		.342	.407	.397	120	14	20			.899	-9	*O-102/3-1	-0.2
1903	*Bos-A	139	590	**107**	**195**	19	12	4	59	33		.331	.372	.424	131	22	35			.952	6	*O-139	1.8
1904	Bos-A	49	195	33	53	5	4	0	4	25		.272	.355	.338	113	4	10			.925	0	O-49	0.1
	NY-A	106	452	80	128	13	10	6	22	19		.283	.316	.396	119	9	11			.925	-8	*O-106	-0.7
	Yr	155	647	**113**	181	18	14	6	26	44		.280	.329	.379	117	12	21			.925	-8	*O-155	-0.6
1905	NY-A	116	418	56	110	9	6	3	29	28		.263	.319	.335	96	-2	17			.898	-6	*O-108/3-1	-1.4
1906	NY-A	12	52	3	10	2	0	0	4	0		.192	.192	.231	29	-4	0			1.000	2	O-12	-0.3
	*Chi-A	75	253	30	59	9	4	0	27	19		.233	.295	.312	92	-2	11			.985	-1	O-74	-0.8
	Yr	87	305	33	69	11	4	0	31	19		.226	.278	.298	81	-7	11			.987	1	O-86	-1.1
1907	Chi-A	148	533	69	144	17	2	1	59	36		.270	.322	.315	107	4	33			.946	-7	*O-148	-0.9
1908	Chi-A	138	482	68	134	11	6	0	45	58		.278	.367	.326	128	18	**47**			.947	-15	*O-128	-0.2
1909	Chi-A	139	491	71	140	23	13	1	55	51		.285	.359	.391	143	24	36			.942	-16	*O-138	0.4
1910	Chi-A	127	443	45	110	8	6	1	43	41		.248	.318	.300	98	-1	22			.923	-13	*O-121	-2.2
1911	Chi-A	76	211	39	61	10	9	0	32	26		.289	.380	.422	128	8	19			.933	-6	O-56	0.0
Total	10	1233	4558	678	1294	138	78	17	413	378		.284	.346	.360	117	94	261			.935	-75	*O-1181/3-2	-4.4

■ **JOHN DOUGLAS**   Douglas, John Franklin b: 9/14/17, Thayer, W.Va. d: 2/11/84, Miami, Fla.   BL/TL, 6'2.5", 195 lbs.   Deb: 4/21/45

| 1945 | Bro-N | 5 | 9 | 0 | 0 | 0 | 0 | 0 | 0 | 2 | 4 | .000 | .182 | .000 | -47 | -2 | 0 | | | .971 | -1 | /1-4 | -0.3 |

■ **ASTYANAX DOUGLASS**   Douglass, Astyanax Saunders b: 9/19/1899, Covington, Tex. d: 1/26/75, ElPaso, Tex.   BL/TR, 6'1", 190 lbs.   Deb: 7/30/21

1921	Cin-N	4	7	1	1	0	0	0	0	0	1	.143	.143	.143	-25	-1	0	0	0	1.000	-0	/C-4	-0.1
1925	Cin-N	7	17	1	3	0	0	0	1	1	3	.176	.222	.176	3	-2	0	0	0	.889	-1	/C-7	-0.3
Total	2	11	24	2	4	0	0	0	1	1	4	.167	.200	.167	-4	-4	0	0	0	.926	-0	/C-11	-0.4

■ **KLONDIKE DOUGLASS**   Douglass, William Bingham b: 5/10/1872, Boston, Pa. d: 12/13/53, Bend, Ore.   BL/TR, 6', 200 lbs.   Deb: 4/23/1896

1896	StL-N	81	296	42	78	6	4	1	28	35	15	.264	.351	.321	81	-7	18			.894	-7	O-74/C-6,S-2	-1.6
1897	StL-N	125	516	77	170	15	3	6	50	52		.329	.403	.405	116	14	12			.948	-11	C-61,O-43,1-17,/3S	0.6
1898	Phi-N	146	582	105	150	26	4	2	48	55		.258	.333	.326	93	-4	18			.976	2	*1-146	-0.2
1899	Phi-N	77	275	26	70	6	6	0	27	10		.255	.296	.320	71	-11	7			.970	-5	C-66/3-4,1-4,O-1	-1.0
1900	Phi-N	50	160	23	48	9	4	0	25	13		.300	.360	.406	112	3	6			.934	-3	C-47/3-2	0.3
1901	Phi-N	51	173	14	56	6	1	0	23	11		.324	.371	.370	113	3	10			.979	0	C-41/1-6,O-2	0.8
1902	Phi-N	109	408	37	95	12	3	0	37	23		.233	.274	.277	70	-15	6			.986	-7	1-69,C-29,O-10	-2.2
1903	Phi-N	105	377	43	96	5	4	1	36	28		.255	.308	.297	75	-12	6			.985	-1	1-97	-1.4
1904	Phi-N	3	10	1	3	0	0	0	1	0		.300	.364	.300	109	0	0			.970	-0	/1-3	0.0
Total	9	747	2797	368	766	85	29	10	275	227	15	.274	.337	.336	91	-28	84			.981	-31	1-342,C-250,O/3S	-4.7

■ **TAYLOR DOUTHIT**   Douthit, Taylor Lee b: 4/22/01, Little Rock, Ark. d: 5/28/86, Fremont, Cal.   BR/TR, 5'11.5", 175 lbs.   Deb: 9/14/23

1923	StL-N	9	27	3	5	0	2	0	4		.185	.185	.333	35	-3	1	0	0	1.000	-0	/O-7	-0.3
1924	StL-N	53	173	24	48	13	4	0	13	16	19	.277	.349	.364	93	-1	4	3	-1	.976	2	O-50	-0.3
1925	StL-N	30	73	13	20	3	1	1	8	2	6	.274	.312	.384	75	-3	0	0	0	.981	-1	O-21	-0.4
1926	*StL-N	139	530	96	163	20	4	3	52	55	46	.308	.375	.377	99	1	23			.958	18	*O-138	0.9
1927	StL-N	130	488	81	128	29	6	5	50	52	45	.262	.336	.377	88	-8	6			.964	8	*O-125	-0.8
1928	*StL-N	154	648	111	191	35	3	3	43	84	36	.295	.384	.372	97	0	11			.984	24	*O-154	1.4
1929	StL-N	150	613	128	206	42	7	9	62	79	49	.336	.416	.471	118	20	8			.974	4	*O-150	1.3
1930	*StL-N	154	664	109	201	41	10	7	93	60	42	.303	.364	.426	87	-13	4			.964	8	*O-154	-1.4
1931	StL-N	36	133	21	44	11	2	1	21	11	9	.331	.386	.466	123	4	1			.972	5	O-36	0.2
	Cin-N	95	374	42	98	9	1	0	24	42	24	.262	.340	.291	76	-11	4			.983	5	O-95	-1.3
	Yr	131	507	63	142	20	3	1	45	53	33	.280	.352	.337	89	-6	5			.980	5	*O-131	-1.1
1932	Cin-N	96	333	28	81	12	1	0	25	31	29	.243	.311	.285	64	-16	3			.985	-0	O-88	-2.0
1933	Cin-N	1	0	1	0	0	0	0	0	0	0	—	—	—	—		0			.000	0	R	0.0
	Chi-N	27	71	8	16	5	0	0	5	11	7	.225	.329	.296	80	-1	2			.930	-0	O-18	-0.3
	Yr	28	71	9	16	5	0	0	5	11	7	.225	.329	.296	80	-1	2			.930	-0	O-18	-0.3
Total	11	1074	4127	665	1201	220	38	29	396	443	312	.291	.364	.384	93	-31	67	3		.972	69	*O-1036	-3.0

■ **CLARENCE DOW**   Dow, Clarence G. b: 10/11/1854, Charlestown, Mass. d: 3/11/1893, West Somerville, Mass.   Deb: 9/22/1884

| 1884 | Bos-U | 1 | 6 | 1 | 2 | 0 | 0 | 0 | | 0 | | .333 | .333 | .333 | 104 | -0 | | | | .333 | -1 | /O-1 | -0.1 |

■ **JOHN DOWD**   Dowd, John Leo (b: John Leo O'Dowd) b: 1/3/1891, Weymouth, Mass. d: 1/31/81, Ft.Lauderdale, Fla   BR/TR, 5'8", 170 lbs.   Deb: 7/3/12

| 1912 | NY-A | 10 | 31 | 1 | 6 | 1 | 0 | 0 | | 6 | | .194 | .342 | .226 | 60 | -1 | | | | .840 | -3 | S-10 | -0.4 |

■ **SNOOKS DOWD**   Dowd, Raymond Bernard b: 12/20/1897, Springfield, Mass. d: 4/4/62, Northampton, Mass.   BR/TR, 5'8", 163 lbs.   Deb: 4/27/19

1919	Det-A	1	0	0	0	0	0	0	0	0	0	—	—	—			0	0		.000	0	R	0.0
	Phi-A	13	18	4	3	0	0	0	0	6	5	.167	.167	.167	-6	-3	2			.800	1	/2-3,S-2,3-1,0-1	-0.2
	Yr	14	18	4	3	0	0	0	0	6	5	.167	.167	.167	-6	-3	2			.800	1	/2-3,S-2,3-1,0-1	-0.2
1926	Bro-N	2	8	0	0	0	0	0	0	0	0	.000	.000	.000	-99	-2	0			1.000	-2	/2-2	-0.5
Total	2	16	26	4	3	0	0	0	0	6	5	.115	.115	.115	-36	-5	2			.875	-1	/2-5,S-2,0-1,3-1	-0.7

■ **TOMMY DOWD**   Dowd, Thomas Jefferson "Buttermilk Tommy" b: 4/20/1869, Holyoke, Mass. d: 7/2/33, Holyoke, Mass.   BR/TR, 5'8", 173 lbs.   Deb: 4/8/1891 M

1891	Bos-a	4	11	1	1	0	0	0	0	0	1	.091	.091	.091	-49	-7	0			.000	-2	/O-4	-0.3
	Was-a	112	464	66	120	9	10	1	44	19	44	.259	.291	.328	80	-14	39			.885	-17	*2-107/O-5	-2.3
	Yr	116	475	67	121	9	10	1	44	19	45	.255	.286	.322	77	-16	39			.885	-19	*2-107/O-9	-2.6
1892	Was-N	144	584	94	142	9	12	1	50	34	49	.243	.286	.298	79	-16	49			.891	-33	2-98,O-23,3-18,/S-6	-4.4
1893	StL-N	132	581	114	164	18	7	1	54	49	23	.282	.340	.343	81	-16	59			.944	-3	*O-132/2-1	-1.6
1894	StL-N	123	524	92	142	16	8	4	62	54	33	.271	.341	.355	68	-27	31			.930	-7	*O-117/2-7,3-1	-3.3
1895	StL-N	129	505	95	163	19	17	7	74	30	31	.323	.364	.469	116	10	30			.927	-7	*O-115,3-17/2-2	-1.6
1896	StL-N	126	521	93	138	17	11	5	46	42	19	.265	.322	.369	85	-12	40			.920	-13	2-78,O-48,M	-2.1
1897	StL-N	35	145	25	38	9	1	0	9	6		.262	.291	.338	67	-7	11			.915	-7	O-30/2-5,M	-1.4
	Phi-N	91	391	68	114	14	4	0	43	19		.292	.324	.348	79	-12	30			.919	-6	O-73,2-19	-1.9
	Yr	126	536	93	152	23	5	0	52	25		.284	.316	.345	76	-19	41			.918	-13	*O-103,2-24	-3.3
1898	StL-N	139	586	70	143	17	7	0	32	30		.244	.287	.297	66	-27	16			.920	-17	*O-129,2-11	-5.0
1899	Cle-N	147	605	81	168	17	7	2	35	48		.278	.333	.336	90	-8	28			.954	-2	*O-147	-1.9
1901	Bos-N	138	594	104	159	18	7	3	52	38		.268	.315	.337	82	-14	33			.937	1	*O-137/1-2,3-1	-2.1
Total	10	1320	5511	903	1492	163	88	24	501	369	200	.271	.319	.345	82	-146	366			.933	-106	O-960,2-328/3S1	-26.9

■ **KEN DOWELL**   Dowell, Kenneth Allen b: 1/19/61, Sacramento, Cal.   BR/TR, 5'9", 160 lbs.   Deb: 6/24/87

| 1987 | Phi-N | 15 | 39 | 4 | 5 | 0 | 0 | 0 | 1 | 2 | 5 | .128 | .171 | .128 | -19 | -7 | 0 | 0 | 0 | 1.000 | 0 | S-15 | -0.5 |

YEAR	TM/L	G	AB	R	H	2B	3B	HR	RBI	BB	SO	AVG	OBP	SLG	PRO+	BR/A	SB	CS	SBR	FA	FR	G/POS	TPR

■ JOE DOWIE   Dowie, Joseph E.   b: 7/15/1865, New Orleans, La.   d: 3/4/17, New Orleans, La.   5'8", 150 lbs.   Deb: 7/10/1889

| 1889 | Bal-a | 20 | 75 | 12 | 17 | 5 | 0 | 0 | 8 | 2 | 10 | .227 | .266 | .293 | 58 | -4 | 5 | | | .947 | 0 | O-20 | -0.4 |

■ RED DOWNEY   Downey, Alexander Cummings   b: 2/6/1889, Aurora, Ind.   d: 7/10/49, Detroit, Mich.   BL/TL, 5'11", 174 lbs.   Deb: 9/14/09

| 1909 | Bro-N | 19 | 78 | 7 | 20 | 1 | 0 | 0 | 8 | 2 | | .256 | .275 | .269 | 71 | -3 | 4 | | | 1.000 | -1 | O-19 | -0.6 |

■ TOM DOWNEY   Downey, Thomas Edward   b: 1/1/1884, Lewiston, Me.   d: 8/3/61, Passaic, N.J.   BR/TR, 5'10", 178 lbs.   Deb: 5/7/09

1909	Cin-N	119	416	39	96	9	6	1	32	32		.231	.287	.288	79	-10	16			.909	-6	*S-119/C-1	-1.6
1910	Cin-N	111	378	43	102	9	3	2	32	34	28	.270	.335	.325	97	-1	12			.879	-7	S-68,3-41	-0.5
1911	Cin-N	111	360	50	94	16	7	0	36	44	38	.261	.345	.344	97	-1	10			.906	-12	S-93/2-6,3-5,1-2,O	-0.7
1912	Phi-N	54	171	27	50	6	3	1	23	21	20	.292	.370	.380	99	-0	3			.893	-3	3-46/S-3	-0.2
	Chi-N	13	22	4	4	0	0	0	4	1	5	.182	.217	.364	58	-1	0			.792	1	/S-5,3-3,2-1	0.0
	Yr	67	193	31	54	6	5	1	27	22	25	.280	.353	.378	95	-1	3			.892	-2	3-49/S-8,2-1	-0.3
1914	Buf-F	151	541	69	118	20	3	2	42	40	55	.218	.273	.277	49	-47	35			**.962**	13	*2-129,S-16/3-5	-3.6
1915	Buf-F	92	282	24	56	9	1	1	19	26	26	.199	.269	.248	45	-25	11			.930	2	2-48,3-35/S-2,1-1	-2.3
Total	6	651	2170	256	520	69	25	7	188	198	<u>172</u>	.240	.306	.304	74	-86	87			.901	-12	S-306,2-184,3/10C	-8.9

■ BRIAN DOWNING   Downing, Brian Jay   b: 10/9/50, Los Angeles, Cal.   BR/TR, 5'10", 194 lbs.   Deb: 5/31/73

1973	Chi-A	34	73	5	13	1	0	2	4	10	17	.178	.277	.274	54	-4	0	0	0	1.000	0	O-13,C-11/3-8,D-1	-0.4
1974	Chi-A	108	293	41	66	12	1	10	39	51	72	.225	.344	.375	104	3	0	1	-1	.994	-7	C-63,O-39/D-9	-0.3
1975	Chi-A	138	420	58	101	12	1	7	41	76	75	.240	.361	.324	93	-1	13	4	2	.990	2	*C-137/D-1	0.9
1976	Chi-A	104	317	38	81	14	0	3	30	40	55	.256	.341	.328	96	-1	7	3	0	.988	-12	C-93,D-11	-1.0
1977	Chi-A	69	169	28	48	4	2	4	25	34	21	.284	.410	.402	123	7	1	2	-1	.983	5	C-61/O-3,D-2	1.0
1978	Cal-A	133	412	42	105	15	0	7	46	52	47	.255	.347	.342	98	0	3	2	-0	.993	-7	*C-128/D-2	-0.3
1979	*Cal-A★	148	509	87	166	27	3	12	75	77	57	.326	.420	.462	142	34	3	3	-1	.985	-2	*C-129,D-18	1.5
1980	Cal-A	30	93	5	27	6	0	2	25	12	12	.290	.371	.419	119	3	0	2	-1	1.000	-4	C-16,D-13	-0.2
1981	Cal-A	93	317	47	79	14	0	9	41	46	35	.249	.351	.379	110	5	1	1	-0	.990	-9	O-56,C-37/D-5	-0.4
1982	*Cal-A	158	623	109	175	37	2	28	84	86	58	.281	.373	.482	132	29	2	1	0	**1.000**	2	*O-158	2.6
1983	Cal-A	113	403	68	99	15	1	19	53	62	59	.246	.353	.429	115	9	1	2	-0	.994	-0	O-84,D-26	0.5
1984	Cal-A	156	539	65	148	28	2	23	91	70	66	.275	.365	.462	128	21	0	4	-2	**1.000**	1	*O-131,D-21	1.6
1985	Cal-A	150	520	80	137	23	1	20	85	78	61	.263	.373	.427	119	16	5	3	-0	.992	2	*O-121,D-25	1.3
1986	*Cal-A	152	513	90	137	27	4	20	95	90	84	.267	.394	.452	131	26	4	4	-0	.989	1	*O-138,D-10	2.1
1987	Cal-A	155	567	110	154	29	3	29	77	**106**	85	.272	.401	.487	139	36	5	5	-2	1.000	-3	*D-118,O-34	2.6
1988	Cal-A	135	484	80	117	18	2	25	64	81	63	.242	.366	.442	129	21	3	4	-0	.000		*D-132	1.6
1989	Cal-A	142	544	59	154	25	2	14	59	56	87	.283	.356	.414	118	14	0	2	-1	.000		*D-141	0.9
1990	Cal-A	96	330	47	90	18	2	14	51	50	45	.273	.378	.467	138	18	0	0	0	.000		D-87	1.5
1991	Tex-A	123	407	76	113	17	2	17	49	58	70	.278	.378	.455	132	19	1	1	-0	.000		*D-109	1.4
1992	Tex-A	107	320	53	89	18	0	10	39	62	58	.278	.408	.428	139	20	1	0	0	.000		D-93	1.7
Total	20	2344	7853	1188	2099	360	28	275	1073	1197	1127	.267	.373	.425	122	276	50	44	-11	.995	-51	D-824,O-777,C/3	18.6

■ RED DOWNS   Downs, Jerome Willis   b: 8/22/1883, Neola, Iowa   d: 10/19/39, Council Bluffs, Ia   BR/TR, 5'11", 155 lbs.   Deb: 5/2/07

1907	Det-A	105	374	28	82	13	5	1	42	13		.219	.249	.289	69	-14	3			.930	-24	2-80,O-20-S-1,3-1	-4.5
1908	*Det-A	84	289	29	64	10	3	1	35	5		.221	.237	.287	67	-11	2			.925	1	2-82/3-1	-1.3
1912	Bro-N	9	32	2	8	3	0	0	3	1	5	.250	.273	.344	71	-1	3			.881	-1	/2-9	-0.3
	Chi-N	43	95	9	25	4	3	1	14	9	17	.263	.327	.400	99	-0	5			.907	0	2-16/S-9,3-5	0.2
	Yr	52	127	11	33	7	3	1	17	10	22	.260	.314	.386	92	-2	8			.896	-1	2-25/S-9,3-5	-0.1
Total	3	241	790	68	179	30	11	3	94	28	<u>22</u>	.227	.256	.304	72	-27	13			.924	-23	2-187/O-20,S-10,3-7	-5.9

■ TOM DOWSE   Dowse, Thomas Joseph   b: 8/12/1866, Ireland   d: 12/14/46, Riverside, Cal.   BR/TR, 5'11", 175 lbs.   Deb: 4/21/1890

1890	Cle-N	40	159	20	33	2	1	0	9	12	22	.208	.267	.233	47	-11	3			.870	-3	O-26,1-10/C-3,P-1	-1.3
1891	Col-a	55	201	24	45	7	0	0	22	13	22	.224	.278	.259	57	-11	2			.919	-6	C-51/O-5	-1.2
1892	Lou-N	41	145	10	21	2	0	0	7	2	15	.145	.173	.159	1	-17	1			.918	-2	C-29,1-11/O-3,2-1	-1.3
	Cin-N	1	4	0	0	0	0	0	0	0	0	.000	.000	.000	-99	-0	0			1.000	-1	/C-1	-0.2
	Phi-N	16	54	3	10	2	0	0	6	2	4	.185	.228	.185	25	-5	1			.973	-1	C-15	-0.4
	Was-N	7	27	5	7	0	0	0	2	0	3	.259	.259	.296	70	-1	0			.800	0	/O-4,C-3	-0.1
	Yr	65	230	18	38	3	0	0	15	4	22	.165	.193	.178	13	-24	2			.931	1	C-48,1-11/O-7,2-1	-2.0
Total	3	160	590	62	116	12	1	0	46	29	66	.197	.243	.220	38	-46	6			.921	-9	C-102/O-38,1-21,2P	-4.5

■ BRIAN DOYLE   Doyle, Brian Reed   b: 1/26/55, Glasgow, Ky.   BL/TR, 5'10", 160 lbs.   Deb: 4/30/78   F

1978	*NY-A	39	52	6	10	3	0	0	3	0	3	.192	.192	.192	9	-6	0	3	-2	.989	13	2-29/S-7,3-5	0.6
1979	NY-A	20	32	2	4	2	0	0	5	3	1	.125	.200	.188	5	-4	0	0	0	.944	1	2-13/3-6	-0.3
1980	NY-A	34	75	8	13	1	0	1	5	6	7	.173	.235	.227	27	-7	1	1	-0	.953	5	2-20,S-12/3-2	-0.1
1981	Oak-A	17	40	2	5	0	0	0	3	1	2	.125	.146	.125	-22	-6	0	1	-1	1.000	1	2-17	-0.5
Total	4	110	199	18	32	3	0	1	13	10	13	.161	.201	.191	10	-24	1	5	-3	.977	20	/2-79,S-19,3-13	-0.3

■ CONNY DOYLE   Doyle, Cornelius J.   b: 1862, Ireland   d: 7/29/21, ElPaso, Tex.   5'10", 185 lbs.   Deb: 6/23/1883

1883	Phi-N	16	68	3	15	3	2	0	3	0	15	.221	.221	.338	69	-2				.788	-1	O-16	-0.3
1884	Pit-a	15	58	8	17	3	2	0		2		.293	.317	.414	134	2				.818	-1	O-14/S-1	0.0
Total	2	31	126	11	32	6	4	0	<u>3</u>	2	15	.254	.266	.365	100	-0				.800	-3	/O-30,S-1	-0.3

■ DANNY DOYLE   Doyle, Howard James   b: 1/24/17, McLoud, Okla.   BB/TR, 6'1", 195 lbs.   Deb: 9/14/43

| 1943 | Bos-A | 13 | 43 | 2 | 9 | 1 | 0 | 0 | 6 | 7 | 9 | .209 | .320 | .233 | 62 | -2 | 0 | 1 | -1 | .964 | -2 | C-13 | -0.4 |

■ JIM DOYLE   Doyle, James Francis   b: 12/25/1881, Detroit, Mich.   d: 2/1/12, Syracuse, N.Y.   BR/TR, 5'10", 168 lbs.   Deb: 5/4/10

1910	Cin-N	7	13	1	2	2	0	0	1	0	2	.154	.154	.308	36	-1	0			.875	-1	/3-3,O-1	-0.3
1911	Chi-N	130	472	69	133	23	12	5	62	40	54	.282	.340	.413	110	5	19			.922	10	*3-127	1.6
Total	2	137	485	70	135	25	12	5	63	40	56	.278	.336	.410	108	4	19			.921	8	3-130/O-1	1.3

■ JEFF DOYLE   Doyle, Jeffrey Donald   b: 10/2/56, Havre, Mont.   BB/TR, 5'9", 160 lbs.   Deb: 9/13/83

| 1983 | StL-N | 13 | 37 | 4 | 11 | 1 | 2 | 0 | 2 | 1 | 3 | .297 | .316 | .432 | 105 | 0 | 0 | 0 | 0 | .966 | 1 | 2-12 | 0.2 |

■ JACK DOYLE   Doyle, John Joseph "Dirty Jack"   b: 10/25/1869, Killorglin, Ireland   d: 12/31/58, Holyoke, Mass.   BR/TR, 5'9", 155 lbs.   Deb: 8/27/1889   MU

1889	Col-a	11	36	6	10	1	1	0	3	6	6	.278	.381	.361	118	1	9			.897	-3	/C-7,O-3,2-2	-0.1
1890	Col-a	77	298	47	80	17	7	2	44	13		.268	.299	.393	111	2	27			.887	-6	C-38,S-25/O-9,23	0.1
1891	Cle-N	69	250	43	69	14	4	0	43	26	44	.276	.351	.364	104	1	24			.897	-3	C-29,O-21,3-20,S-1	0.1
1892	Cle-N	24	88	17	26	4	1	1	14	6	10	.295	.340	.398	118	2	5			.875	-1	O-12/C-9,1-1,S-1	-0.1
	NY-N	90	366	61	109	22	1	5	55	18	30	.298	.336	.404	126	10	42			.864	-18	2-31,C-26,O-17,3/S	-0.5
	Yr	114	454	78	135	26	2	6	69	24	40	.297	.337	.403	124	11	47			.890	-18	C-35,2-31,O3/S1	-0.4
1893	NY-N	82	358	56	102	17	5	1	51	20	12	.285	.383	.415	112	5	40			.919	0	C-48,O-29/S-4,31	0.9
1894	*NY-N	105	422	90	155	30	8	3	100	35	3	.367	.420	.498	121	15	42			.965	-7	*1-99/C-6	1.2
1895	NY-N	82	319	52	100	21	5	1	66	24	12	.313	.365	.408	102	1	35			.968	-2	1-58,2-13/3-6,CM	0.1
1896	*Bal-N	118	487	116	165	29	4	2	101	42	15	.339	.400	.421	115	11	73			.974	-11	*1-118/2-1	0.2
1897	*Bal-N	114	460	91	163	29	4	2	87	29		.354	.394	.448	122	14	62			.979	5	*1-114	1.6
1898	Was-N	43	177	26	54	2	2	0	26	7		.305	.335	.373	103	0	9			.963	-2	1-38/2-5,M	-0.2
	NY-N	82	297	42	84	15	3	1	43	12		.283	.317	.364	98	-2	14			.860	0	O-38,1-24,S-15,/3C	-0.3
	Yr	125	474	68	138	17	5	1	69	19		.291	.324	.367	100	-2	23			.970	-2	1-62,O-38,S/23C	-0.5
1899	NY-N	118	448	55	134	15	5	3	76	33		.299	.353	.384	106	3	35			.976	6	*1-113/C-5	0.9
1900	NY-N	133	505	69	135	24	1	1	66	34		.267	.317	.325	81	-13	34			.971	6	*1-133	-0.6
1901	Chi-N	75	285	21	66	9	0	0	39	7		.232	.259	.277	59	-15	8			.973	7	1-75	-0.9
1902	NY-N	49	186	21	56	13	0	1	19	10		.301	.340	.387	125	5	12			.991	4	1-49	0.8
	Was-A	78	312	52	77	15	2	1	20	29		.247	.311	.317	74	-11	6			.929	-11	2-68/1-7,O-4,C-2	-1.9

YEAR	TM/L	G	AB	R	H	2B	3B	HR	RBI	BB	SO	AVG	OBP	SLG	PRO+	BR/A	SB	CS	SBR	FA	FR	G/POS	TPR
1903	Bro-N	139	524	84	164	27	6	0	91	54		.313	.383	.387	123	17	34			.981	2	*1-139	1.6
1904	Bro-N	8	22	2	5	1	0	0	2	6		.227	.414	.273	116	1	1			1.000	1	/1-8	0.2
	Phi-N	66	236	20	52	10	3	1	22	19		.220	.281	.301	83	-5	4			.977	4	1-65/2-1	-0.3
	Yr	74	258	22	57	11	3	1	24	25		.221	.295	.298	86	-4	5			.980	5	1-73/2-1	-0.1
1905	NY-A	1	3	0	0	0	0	0	0	0		.000	.000	.000	-90	-1	0			.833	-1	/1-1	-0.1
Total	17	1564	6039	971	1806	315	64	26	968	437	132	.299	.351	.385	106	42	516			.975	-20	*1-1043,C-176,O2/S3	2.9

■ JOE DOYLE Doyle, Joseph K. b: Cincinnati, Ohio Deb: 4/20/1872

YEAR	TM/L	G	AB	R	H	2B	3B	HR	RBI	BB	SO	AVG	OBP	SLG	PRO+	BR/A	SB	CS	SBR	FA	FR	G/POS	TPR
1872	Nat-n	9	41	6	12	1	0	0	9	0	0	.293	.293	.317	75	-2	0	0	0	.667	-4	/S-8,2-1	-0.4

■ LARRY DOYLE Doyle, Lawrence Joseph "Laughing Larry" b: 7/31/1886, Caseyville, Ill. d: 3/1/74, Saranac Lake, N.Y. BL/TR, 5'10", 165 lbs. Deb: 7/22/07

YEAR	TM/L	G	AB	R	H	2B	3B	HR	RBI	BB	SO	AVG	OBP	SLG	PRO+	BR/A	SB	CS	SBR	FA	FR	G/POS	TPR
1907	NY-N	69	227	16	59	3	0	0	16	20		.260	.320	.273	83	-4	3			.917	-22	2-69	-3.1
1908	NY-N	104	377	65	116	16	9	0	33	22		.308	.354	.398	134	13	17			.935	-10	*2-102	0.3
1909	NY-N	147	570	86	172	27	11	6	49	45		.302	.360	.419	140	25	31			.940	-18	*2-144	0.5
1910	NY-N	151	575	97	164	21	14	8	69	71	26	.285	.369	.412	128	20	39			.930	-17	*2-151	0.0
1911	*NY-N	143	526	102	163	25	25	13	77	71	39	.310	.397	.527	153	36	38			.944	-24	*2-141	0.8
1912	*NY-N	143	558	98	184	33	8	10	90	56	20	.330	.393	.471	132	24	36			.948	-8	*2-143	1.2
1913	*NY-N	132	482	67	135	25	6	5	73	59	29	.280	.364	.388	114	10	38			.955	-13	*2-130	-0.5
1914	NY-N	145	539	87	140	19	8	5	63	58	25	.260	.343	.353	111	8	17			.959	-19	*2-145	-1.3
1915	NY-N	150	591	86	189	40	10	4	70	32	28	.320	.358	.442	150	32	22	18	-4	.947	-7	*2-147	2.5
1916	NY-N	113	441	55	118	24	10	2	47	27	23	.268	.316	.381	120	9	17			.960	16	2-113	3.1
	Chi-N	9	38	6	15	5	1	2	7	1	1	.395	.410	.658	203	4	2			.982	5	/2-9	1.0
	Yr	122	479	61	133	29	11	3	54	28	24	.278	.323	.403	127	14	19			.962	20	*2-122	4.1
1917	Chi-N	135	476	48	121	19	5	6	61	48	28	.254	.323	.353	99	-0	5			.952	-2	*2-128	0.4
1918	NY-N	75	257	38	67	7	4	3	36	37	10	.261	.354	.354	118	7	10			.969	-12	2-73	-0.1
1919	NY-N	113	381	61	110	14	10	7	52	31	17	.289	.350	.433	136	16	12			.956	2	*2-100	2.5
1920	NY-N	137	471	48	134	21	2	4	50	47	28	.285	.352	.363	107	5	11	9	-2	.967	-26	*2-133	-2.0
Total	14	1766	6509	960	1887	299	123	74	793	625	274	.290	.357	.408	126	206	298	27		.949	-155	*2-1728	5.3

■ DENNY DOYLE Doyle, Robert Dennis b: 1/17/44, Glasgow, Ky. BL/TR, 5'9", 175 lbs. Deb: 4/7/70 F

YEAR	TM/L	G	AB	R	H	2B	3B	HR	RBI	BB	SO	AVG	OBP	SLG	PRO+	BR/A	SB	CS	SBR	FA	FR	G/POS	TPR
1970	Phi-N	112	413	43	86	10	7	2	16	33	64	.208	.267	.281	48	-31	6	5	-1	.978	-16	*2-103	-4.1
1971	Phi-N	95	342	34	79	12	1	3	24	19	31	.231	.281	.298	64	-16	4	2	0	.967	4	2-91	-0.5
1972	Phi-N	123	442	33	110	14	2	1	26	31	33	.249	.298	.296	68	-18	6	7	-2	.982	-9	*2-119	-2.6
1973	Phi-N	116	370	45	101	9	3	3	26	31	32	.273	.329	.338	83	-8	1	3	-2	.974	9	*2-114	0.6
1974	Cal-A	147	511	47	133	19	2	1	34	25	24	.260	.296	.311	79	-14	6	7	-2	.983	16	2-146/S-2	0.7
1975	Cal-A	4	15	0	1	0	0	0	0	1	1	.067	.125	.067	-48	-3	0	0	0	.926	2	/2-6,3-1	-0.1
	*Bos-A	89	310	50	96	21	4	3	36	14	11	.310	.342	.429	107	2	5	7	-3	.974	-31	2-84/3-6,S-2	-2.8
	Yr	97	325	50	97	21	4	3	36	15	12	.298	.331	.412	102	-0	5	7	-3	.970	-29	2-90/3-7,S-2	-2.9
1976	Bos-A	117	432	51	108	15	5	0	26	22	39	.250	.286	.308	66	-19	8	5	-1	.977	-25	*2-112	-4.0
1977	Bos-A	137	455	54	109	13	6	2	49	29	50	.240	.291	.308	57	-27	2	4	-2	.979	-10	2-137	-3.0
Total	8	944	3290	357	823	113	28	16	237	205	310	.250	.296	.316	70	-135	38	40	-13	.977	-61	2-912/3-7,S-4	-15.8

■ D. J. DOZIER Dozier, William Henry b: 9/21/65, Norfolk, Va. BR/TR, 6', 202 lbs. Deb: 5/6/92

YEAR	TM/L	G	AB	R	H	2B	3B	HR	RBI	BB	SO	AVG	OBP	SLG	PRO+	BR/A	SB	CS	SBR	FA	FR	G/POS	TPR
1992	NY-N	25	47	4	9	2	0	0	2	4	19	.191	.269	.234	44	-3	4	0	1	.971	0	O-17	-0.2

■ DELOS DRAKE Drake, Delos Daniel b: 12/3/1886, Girard, Ohio d: 10/3/65, Findlay, Ohio BR/TL, 5'11.5", 170 lbs. Deb: 4/30/11

YEAR	TM/L	G	AB	R	H	2B	3B	HR	RBI	BB	SO	AVG	OBP	SLG	PRO+	BR/A	SB	CS	SBR	FA	FR	G/POS	TPR
1911	Det-A	95	315	37	88	9	9	1	36	17		.279	.324	.375	90	-5	20			.942	-10	O-83/1-2	-1.9
1914	StL-F	138	514	51	129	18	8	3	42	31	57	.251	.295	.335	68	-31	17			.957	-1	*O-116,1-18	-4.0
1915	StL-F	102	343	32	91	23	4	1	41	23	27	.265	.313	.364	86	-12	6			.974	-5	O-97/1-1	-2.3
Total	3	335	1172	120	308	50	21	5	119	71	84	.263	.308	.354	79	-48	43			.959	-16	O-296/1-21	-8.2

■ LARRY DRAKE Drake, Larry Francis b: 5/4/21, McKinney, Tex. d: 7/14/85, Houston, Tex. BL/TR, 6'1.5", 195 lbs. Deb: 7/20/45

YEAR	TM/L	G	AB	R	H	2B	3B	HR	RBI	BB	SO	AVG	OBP	SLG	PRO+	BR/A	SB	CS	SBR	FA	FR	G/POS	TPR
1945	Phi-A	1	2	0	0	0	0	0	0	0	2	.000	.000	.000	-99	-1	0	0	0	1.000	-0	/O-1	-0.1
1948	Was-A	4	7	0	2	0	0	0	1	1	3	.286	.375	.286	79	-0	0	0	0	1.000	-0	/O-2	-0.1
Total	2	5	9	0	2	0	0	0	1	1	5	.222	.300	.222	44	-0	0	0	0	1.000	-0	/O-3	-0.2

■ LYMAN DRAKE Drake, Lyman Daniel b: 2/9/1852, Berea, Ohio d: 2/6/32, Muskegon, Mich. 6', Deb: 6/29/1884

YEAR	TM/L	G	AB	R	H	2B	3B	HR	RBI	BB	SO	AVG	OBP	SLG	PRO+	BR/A	SB	CS	SBR	FA	FR	G/POS	TPR
1884	Was-a	2	7	0	2	1	0	0	2	0	0	.286	.286	.429	147	0				.000	-1	/O-2	-0.1

■ SAMMY DRAKE Drake, Samuel Harrison b: 10/7/34, Little Rock, Ark. BB/TR, 5'11", 175 lbs. Deb: 4/17/60 F

YEAR	TM/L	G	AB	R	H	2B	3B	HR	RBI	BB	SO	AVG	OBP	SLG	PRO+	BR/A	SB	CS	SBR	FA	FR	G/POS	TPR
1960	Chi-N	15	15	5	1	0	0	0	0	1	4	.067	.125	.067	-46	-3	0	0	0	1.000	-1	/3-6,2-2	-0.4
1961	Chi-N	13	5	1	0	0	0	0	0	1	1	.000	.167	.000	-50	-1	0	0	0	1.000	-0	/O-1	-0.1
1962	NY-N	25	52	2	10	0	0	0	7	6	12	.192	.276	.192	28	-5	0	0	0	.977	-2	2-10/3-6	-0.6
Total	3	53	72	8	11	0	0	0	7	8	17	.153	.237	.153	8	-9	0	0	0	.978	-3	/2-12,3-12,O-1	-1.1

■ SOLLY DRAKE Drake, Solomon Louis b: 10/23/30, Little Rock, Ark. BB/TR, 6', 170 lbs. Deb: 4/17/56 F

YEAR	TM/L	G	AB	R	H	2B	3B	HR	RBI	BB	SO	AVG	OBP	SLG	PRO+	BR/A	SB	CS	SBR	FA	FR	G/POS	TPR
1956	Chi-N	65	215	29	55	9	1	2	15	23	35	.256	.331	.335	81	-5	9	5	-0	.993	2	O-53	-0.6
1959	LA-N	9	8	2	2	0	0	0	0	1	3	.250	.333	.250	54	-0	1	0	0	.667	-1	/O-4	-0.2
	Phi-N	67	62	10	9	1	0	0	3	8	15	.145	.243	.161	10	-8	5	5	-2	1.000	-10	O-37	-2.0
	Yr	76	70	12	11	1	0	0	3	9	18	.157	.253	.171	15	-8	6	5	-1	.974	-11	O-41	-2.2
Total	2	141	285	41	66	10	1	2	18	32	53	.232	.311	.295	64	-14	15	10	-2	.989	-9	/O-94	-2.8

■ JAKE DRAUBY Drauby, Jacob C. b: 1865, Harrisburg, Pa. 5'10", 163 lbs. Deb: 10/3/1892

YEAR	TM/L	G	AB	R	H	2B	3B	HR	RBI	BB	SO	AVG	OBP	SLG	PRO+	BR/A	SB	CS	SBR	FA	FR	G/POS	TPR
1892	Was-N	10	34	3	7	0	1	0	3	2	12	.206	.250	.265	57	-2	0			.763	-2	3-10	-0.3

■ BILL DREESEN Dreesen, William Richard b: 7/26/04, New York, N.Y. d: 11/9/71, Mt.Vernon, N.Y. BL/TR, 5'7.5", 160 lbs. Deb: 5/1/31

YEAR	TM/L	G	AB	R	H	2B	3B	HR	RBI	BB	SO	AVG	OBP	SLG	PRO+	BR/A	SB	CS	SBR	FA	FR	G/POS	TPR
1931	Bos-N	48	180	38	40	10	4	1	10	23	23	.222	.310	.339	77	-6	1			.910	-8	3-47	-1.1

■ BILL DRESCHER Drescher, William Clayton "Dutch" b: 5/23/21, Congers, N.Y. d: 5/15/68, Haverstraw, N.Y. BL/TR, 6'2", 190 lbs. Deb: 4/19/44

YEAR	TM/L	G	AB	R	H	2B	3B	HR	RBI	BB	SO	AVG	OBP	SLG	PRO+	BR/A	SB	CS	SBR	FA	FR	G/POS	TPR
1944	NY-A	4	7	0	1	0	0	0	0	0	0	.143	.143	.143	-18	-1	0	0	0	.875	0	/C-1	-0.1
1945	NY-A	48	126	10	34	3	1	0	15	8	5	.270	.313	.310	77	-4	0	2	-1	.991	-8	C-33	-1.2
1946	NY-A	5	6	0	2	1	0	0	1	0	0	.333	.333	.500	129	0	0	0	0	1.000	1	/C-3	0.1
Total	3	57	139	10	37	4	1	0	16	8	5	.266	.306	.309	75	-5	0	2	-1	.985	-7	/C-37	-1.2

■ CHUCK DRESSEN Dressen, Charles Walter b: 9/20/1898, Decatur, Ill. d: 8/10/66, Detroit, Mich. BR/TR, 5'5.5", 146 lbs. Deb: 4/17/25 MC

YEAR	TM/L	G	AB	R	H	2B	3B	HR	RBI	BB	SO	AVG	OBP	SLG	PRO+	BR/A	SB	CS	SBR	FA	FR	G/POS	TPR
1925	Cin-N	76	215	35	59	8	2	3	19	12	4	.274	.319	.372	78	-7	5	3	-0	.951	-5	3-47/2-5,O-4	-0.3
1926	Cin-N	127	474	76	126	27	11	4	48	49	31	.266	.338	.395	99	-1	0			.966	17	*3-123/S-1,O-1	2.3
1927	Cin-N	144	548	78	160	36	10	2	55	71	32	.292	.374	.405	113	12	7			.967	12	*3-142/S-2	3.0
1928	Cin-N	135	498	72	145	26	3	1	59	43	22	.291	.355	.361	89	-7	10			.938	-2	*3-135	-0.2
1929	Cin-N	110	401	49	98	22	3	1	36	41	21	.244	.321	.322	63	-23	8			.932	-20	3-98/2-8	-3.6
1930	Cin-N	33	19	0	4	0	0	0	1	3		.211	.250	.211	14	-3	0			1.000	3	3-10/2-3	0.0
1931	Cin-N	5	15	0	1	0	0	0	0	0	3	.067	.125	.067	-50	-3	0			.846	-0	/3-4	-0.3
1933	NY-N	16	45	3	10	4	0	0	3	1	4	.222	.239	.311	57	-3	0			.972	6	3-16	-0.2
Total	8	646	2215	313	603	123	29	11	221	219	118	.272	.343	.369	89	-35	30			.953	12	3-575/2-16,O-5,S-3	0.7

■ LEE DRESSEN Dressen, Lee August b: 7/23/1889, Ellinwood, Kan. d: 6/30/31, Diller, Neb. BL/TL, 6', 165 lbs. Deb: 4/21/14

YEAR	TM/L	G	AB	R	H	2B	3B	HR	RBI	BB	SO	AVG	OBP	SLG	PRO+	BR/A	SB	CS	SBR	FA	FR	G/POS	TPR
1914	StL-N	46	103	16	24	2	1	0	7	11	20	.233	.307	.272	73	-3	2			.982	-1	1-38	-0.6
1918	Det-A	31	107	10	19	1	2	0	3	21	10	.178	.323	.224	68	-3	2			.988	-3	1-30	-0.9
Total	2	77	210	26	43	3	3	0	10	32	30	.205	.316	.248	71	-6	4			.985	-5	/1-68	-1.5

■ CAMERON DREW Drew, Cameron Steward b: 2/12/64, Boston, Mass. BL/TR, 6'5", 230 lbs. Deb: 9/9/88

YEAR	TM/L	G	AB	R	H	2B	3B	HR	RBI	BB	SO	AVG	OBP	SLG	PRO+	BR/A	SB	CS	SBR	FA	FR	G/POS	TPR
1988	Hou-N	7	16	1	3	0	1	0	1	0	1	.188	.188	.313	43	-1	0	0	0	1.000	0	/O-5	-0.1

YEAR	TM/L	G	AB	R	H	2B	3B	HR	RBI	BB	SO	AVG	OBP	SLG	PRO+	BR/A	SB	CS	SBR	FA	FR	G/POS	TPR

■ DAVE DREW   Drew, David   Deb: 5/14/1884

1884	Phi-U	2	9	1	4	0	0	0		0		.444	.444	.444	184	1				.000	-0	/P-1,2-1,S-1	0.1
	Was-U	13	53	8	16	1	2	0		1		.302	.315	.396	118	-0				.806	1	/S-8,1-5,O-1	0.0
	Yr	15	62	9	20	1	2	0		1		.323	.333	.403	127	0				.813	1	/S-9,1-5,P-1,2-1,O	0.1

■ FRANK DREWS   Drews, Frank John   b: 5/25/16, Buffalo, N.Y.   d: 4/22/72, Buffalo, N.Y.   BR/TR, 5′10″, 175 lbs.   Deb: 8/13/44

1944	Bos-N	46	141	14	29	9	1	0	10	25	14	.206	.329	.284	71	-5	0			.959	1	2-46	-0.2
1945	Bos-N	49	147	13	30	4	1	0	19	16	18	.204	.282	.245	47	-10	0			.976	5	2-48	-0.3
Total	2	95	288	27	59	13	2	0	29	41	32	.205	.306	.264	59	-15	0			.967	5	/2-94	-0.5

■ DAN DRIESSEN   Driessen, Daniel   b: 7/29/51, Hilton Head Island, S.C.   BL/TR, 5′11″, 190 lbs.   Deb: 6/9/73

1973	*Cin-N	102	366	49	110	15	2	4	47	24	37	.301	.347	.385	108	4	8	3	1	.946	-10	3-87,1-35/O-1	-0.7
1974	Cin-N	150	470	63	132	23	6	7	56	48	62	.281	.349	.400	111	6	10	5	0	.915	-21	*3-126,1-47/O-3	-1.7
1975	*Cin-N	88	210	38	59	8	1	7	38	35	30	.281	.389	.429	124	8	10	3	1	.986	-5	1-41,O-29	0.1
1976	*Cin-N	98	219	32	54	11	1	7	44	43	32	.247	.370	.402	116	6	14	1	4	.997	-3	1-40,O-20	0.3
1977	Cin-N	151	536	75	161	31	4	17	91	64	85	.300	.378	.468	123	18	31	13	2	.994	-3	*1-148	0.8
1978	Cin-N	153	524	68	131	23	3	16	75	70	79	.250	.348	.397	108	7	28	9	3	.996	3	*1-151	0.4
1979	*Cin-N	150	515	72	129	24	3	18	75	62	77	.250	.334	.414	102	2	11	5	0	.993	-3	*1-143	-1.0
1980	Cin-N	154	524	81	139	36	1	14	93	60	68	.265	.382	.418	123	20	19	6	2	.995	-4	*1-151	0.9
1981	Cin-N	82	233	35	55	14	0	7	33	40	31	.236	.353	.386	108	3	2	4	-2	.995	-5	1-74	-0.8
1982	Cin-N	149	516	64	139	25	1	17	57	82	62	.269	.372	.421	119	15	11	6	-0	.998	-7	*1-144	0.3
1983	Cin-N	122	386	57	107	17	1	12	57	75	51	.277	.395	.420	121	14	6	4	-1	.996	-2	*1-112	0.5
1984	Cin-N	81	218	27	61	13	0	7	28	37	25	.280	.384	.436	124	8	2	1	0	.991	-4	1-70	0.1
	Mon-N	51	169	20	43	11	0	9	32	17	15	.254	.323	.479	128	6	0	1	-1	.995	-4	1-45	0.1
	Yr	132	387	47	104	24	0	16	60	54	40	.269	.358	.455	126	14	2	2	-1	.992	-5	*1-115	0.2
1985	Mon-N	91	312	31	78	18	0	6	25	33	29	.250	.326	.365	99	-1	2	1	-1	.997	1	1-88	-0.4
	SF-N	54	181	22	42	8	0	3	22	17	22	.232	.302	.326	79	-5	0	0	-1	.998	-2	1-49	-1.0
	Yr	145	493	53	120	26	0	9	47	50	51	.243	.317	.351	92	-6	2	2	-1	.997	1	*1-137	-1.4
1986	SF-N	15	16	2	3	2	0	0	0	4	4	.188	.350	.313	89	-0	0	0	0	1.000	1	/1-4	0.0
	Hou-N	17	24	5	7	1	0	1	3	5	2	.292	.414	.458	144	2	0	0	0	1.000	-0	1-12	0.1
	Yr	32	40	7	10	3	0	1	3	9	6	.250	.388	.400	122	2	0	0	0	1.000	0	1-16	0.1
1987	*StL-N	24	60	5	14	2	0	1	11	7	8	.233	.313	.317	66	-3	0	0	0	.993	-0	1-21	-0.4
Total	15	1732	5479	746	1464	282	23	153	763	761	719	.267	.359	.411	113	109	154	63	8	.995	-64	*1-1375,3-213/O-53	-2.7

■ LEW DRILL   Drill, Lewis L   b: 5/9/1877, Browerville, Minn.   d: 7/4/69, St.Paul, Minn.   BR/TR, 5′6″, 186 lbs.   Deb: 4/23/02

1902	Was-A	38	123	21	34	7	2	1	16	16		.276	.369	.390	110	2				.919	-11	C-28/2-4,O-4,3-1	-0.6
	Bal-A	2	8	2	2	0	0	0	0	0		.250	.250	.250	37	-1				1.000	1	/C-1,1-1	0.0
	Was-A	33	98	12	24	3	2	0	13	10		.245	.327	.316	78	-3				.926	-4	C-25/O-4,2-1	-0.4
	Yr	73	229	35	60	10	4	1	29	26		.262	.347	.354	94	-1				.924	-15	C-54/O-8,2-5,3-1,1	-1.0
1903	Was-A	51	154	11	39	9	3	0	23	15		.253	.331	.351	103	1				.966	-4	C-47/1-3	0.2
1904	Was-A	46	142	17	38	7	1	1	11	21		.268	.385	.366	140	8				.934	-7	C-29,O-14	0.4
	Det-A	51	160	7	39	6	1	0	13	20		.244	.335	.294	103	1				.950	-7	C-49/1-2	0.0
	Yr	97	302	24	77	13	3	1	24	41		.255	.359	.328	121	10				.944	-14	C-78,O-14/1-2	0.4
1905	Det-A	72	211	17	55	9	0	0	24	32		.261	.366	.303	112	5				.970	-2	C-71	1.1
Total	4	293	896	87	231	41	10	2	100	114		.258	.353	.333	108	14		21		.953	-34	C-250/O-22,1-6,23	0.7

■ JIM DRISCOLL   Driscoll, James Bernard   b: 5/14/44, Medford, Mass.   BL/TR, 5′11″, 175 lbs.   Deb: 6/17/70

1970	Oak-A	21	52	2	10	0	0	1	2	2	15	.192	.236	.252	35	-5	0	0	0	.967	-3	/2-7,S-7	-0.6
1972	Tex-A	15	18	0	0	0	0	0	0	2	3	.000	.100	.000	-72	-4	0	0	0	.900	1	/2-4,3-2	-0.3
Total	2	36	70	2	10	0	0	1	2	4	18	.143	.200	.186	9	-8	0	0	0	.950	-1	/2-11,S-7,3-2	-0.9

■ DENNY DRISCOLL   Driscoll, John F.   b: 11/19/1855, Lowell, Mass.   d: 7/11/1886, Lowell, Mass.   BL/TL, 5′10.5″, 160 lbs.   Deb: 7/1/1880

1880	Buf-N	18	65	1	10	1	0	0	4	1	7	.154	.167	.169	14	-6				.895	-2	O-14/P-6	-0.6
1882	Pit-a	23	80	12	11	2	0	1		3		.138	.169	.200	25	-6				.885	-4	P-23	0.0
1883	Pit-a	41	148	19	27	2	1	0		4		.182	.204	.209	35	-10				.890	4	P-41/O-4,3-1	-0.2
1884	Lou-a	13	48	5	9	1	0	0	1	2		.188	.220	.208	42	-3				.816	2	P-13/O-2	-0.1
1885	Buf-N	7	19	2	3	0	0	0	0	2	5	.158	.238	.158	29	-1				.719	-5	/2-7	-0.6
Total	5	102	360	39	60	6	1	1	5	12	12	.167	.194	.197	30	-26				.872	-5	/P-83,O-20,2-7,3-1	-1.5

■ PADDY DRISCOLL   Driscoll, John Leo   b: 1/11/1895, Evanston, Ill.   d: 6/28/68, Chicago, Ill.   BR/TR, 5′8.5″, 155 lbs.   Deb: 6/12/17

1917	Chi-N	13	28	2	3	1	0	0	3	2	6	.107	.167	.143	-4	-3	2			.882	2	/2-8,3-2,S-1	-0.1

■ MIKE DRISSEL   Drissel, Michael F.   b: 12/19/1864, St.Louis, Mo.   d: 2/26/13, St.Louis, Mo.   BR/TR, 5′11″,   Deb: 9/5/1885

1885	StL-a	6	20	0	1	0	0	0	0	0		.050	.050	.050	-65	-4				.971	-0	/C-6	-0.3

■ WALT DROPO   Dropo, Walter "Moose"   b: 1/30/23, Moosup, Conn.   BR/TR, 6′5″, 220 lbs.   Deb: 4/19/49

1949	Bos-A	11	41	3	6	2	0	1	4	3	9	.146	.205	.195	6	-6	0	0	0	1.000	-1	1-11	-0.7
1950	Bos-A★	136	559	101	180	28	8	34	144	45	75	.322	.378	.583	130	21	0	0	0	.988	-4	*1-134	1.3
1951	Bos-A	99	360	37	86	14	0	11	57	38	52	.239	.312	.369	76	-13	0	0	0	.987	-1	1-93	-1.8
1952	Bos-A	37	132	13	35	7	1	6	27	11	22	.265	.331	.470	112	2	0	0	0	.994	-1	1-35	-0.1
	Det-A	115	459	56	128	17	3	23	70	26	63	.279	.320	.479	120	9	2	2	-1	.989	-1	*1-115	0.3
	Yr	152	591	69	163	24	4	29	97	37	85	.276	.323	.477	118	10	2	2	-1	.990	-2	*1-150	0.2
1953	Det-A	152	606	61	150	30	3	13	96	29	69	.248	.289	.371	78	-21	0	1	-1	.990	12	*1-150	-1.5
1954	Det-A	107	320	27	90	14	2	4	44	24	41	.281	.331	.375	95	-3	0	1	-1	.996	1	1-95	-0.7
1955	Chi-A	141	453	55	127	15	2	19	79	34	71	.280	.344	.448	109	4	0	1	-1	.995	-5	*1-140	-0.9
1956	Chi-A	125	361	42	96	13	1	8	52	37	51	.266	.339	.374	87	-7	1	0	0	.993	-3	*1-117	-1.6
1957	Chi-A	93	223	24	57	9	0	13	49	16	40	.256	.305	.439	101	-1	0	1	-1	.987	2	1-69	-0.3
1958	Chi-A	28	52	3	10	1	0	2	8	5	11	.192	.276	.327	67	-2	0	0	0	1.000	1	1-16	-0.3
	Cin-N	63	162	18	47	7	2	7	31	12	31	.290	.343	.488	111	2	0	0	0	1.000	1	1-43	0.1
1959	Cin-N	26	39	4	4	1	0	1	2	4	7	.103	.205	.205	9	-5	0	0	0	1.000	2	1-23	-0.4
	Bal-A	62	151	17	42	9	0	6	21	12	20	.278	.331	.457	117	3	0	0	0	.990	-2	1-54/3-2	-0.1
1960	Bal-A	79	179	16	48	8	0	4	21	20	19	.268	.345	.380	97	-0	1	-1	-1	.993	-1	1-67/3-1	-0.6
1961	Bal-A	14	27	1	7	0	0	0	4	2	4	.259	.355	.370	97	-0	0	0	0	1.000	1	1-12	0.0
Total	13	1288	4124	478	1113	168	22	152	704	328	582	.270	.327	.432	100	-17	5	6	-2	.992	-1	*1-1174/3-3	-7.3

■ KEITH DRUMRIGHT   Drumright, Keith Alan   b: 10/21/54, Springfield, Mo.   BL/TR, 5′10″, 170 lbs.   Deb: 9/1/78

1978	Hou-N	17	55	5	9	0	0	0	2	3	4	.164	.207	.164	5	-7	0	1	-1	.944	-1	2-17	-0.8
1981	*Oak-A	31	86	8	25	1	1	0	11	4	4	.291	.322	.326	91	-1	0	0	0	.989	-5	2-19/D-5	-0.6
Total	2	48	141	13	34	1	1	0	13	7	8	.241	.277	.262	58	-8	0	1	-1	.969	-6	/2-36,D-5	-1.4

■ JEAN DUBUC   Dubuc, Jean Joseph Octave Arthur "Chauncey"   b: 9/15/1888, St.Johnsbury, Vt.   d: 8/28/58, Fort Myers, Fla.   BR/TR, 5′10.5″, 185 lbs.   Deb: 6/25/08   C

1908	Cin-N	15	29	2	4	1	0	0	2	0		.138	.138	.172	-3	-3	0			.943	1	P-15	0.0
1909	Cin-N	19	18	1	3	0	0	0	0	2		.167	.250	.167	30	-1	0			.844	0	P-19	0.0
1912	Det-A	40	108	16	29	6	2	1	9	3		.269	.295	.389	98	-1	0			.972	5	P-37/O-2	0.0
1913	Det-A	68	135	17	36	5	3	2	11	2	17	.267	.277	.393	97	-2	1			.953	6	P-36/O-3	-0.2
1914	Det-A	71	124	9	28	8	1	1	7	11	11	.226	.273	.331	79	-4	1			.942	3	P-36	0.0
1915	Det-A	60	112	7	23	0	1	0	14	8	15	.205	.258	.241	47	-7	0			.969	1	P-39	0.0
1916	Det-A	52	78	3	20	0	0	0	7	7	12	.256	.318	.308	85	-1	0			.952	3	P-36	0.0
1918	*Bos-A	5	6	0	1	0	0	0	0	0	2	.167	.286	.167	37	-0	0			1.000	-0	/P-2	0.0
1919	NY-N	37	42	2	6	3	0	0	6	0	6	.143	.143	.214	7	-5	0			.964	2	P-36	0.0
Total	9	367	652	57	150	23	10	4	56	30	63	.230	.266	.314	72	-25	2			.952	22	P-256/O-5	-0.2

YEAR	TM/L	G	AB	R	H	2B	3B	HR	RBI	BB	SO	AVG	OBP	SLG	PRO+	BR/A	SB	CS	SBR	FA	FR	G/POS	TPR

■ ROB DUCEY   Ducey, Robert Thomas   b: 5/24/65, Toronto, Ont., Can.   BL/TR, 6'2", 175 lbs.   Deb: 5/1/87

YEAR	TM/L	G	AB	R	H	2B	3B	HR	RBI	BB	SO	AVG	OBP	SLG	PRO+	BR/A	SB	CS	SBR	FA	FR	G/POS	TPR
1987	Tor-A	34	48	12	9	1	0	1	6	8	10	.188	.304	.271	53	-3	2	0	1	1.000	-7	O-28/D-1	-0.9
1988	Tor-A	27	54	15	17	4	1	0	6	5	7	.315	.373	.426	123	2	1	0	0	1.000	-6	O-26/D-1	-0.4
1989	Tor-A	41	76	5	16	4	0	0	7	9	25	.211	.294	.263	59	-4	2	1	0	1.000	-2	O-35/D-1	-0.6
1990	Tor-A	19	53	7	16	5	0	0	7	7	15	.302	.393	.396	119	2	1	1	-0	1.000	-0	O-19	0.1
1991	*Tor-A	39	68	8	16	2	2	1	4	6	26	.235	.297	.368	80	-2	2	0	1	.892	-4	O-24/D-2	-0.5
1992	Tor-A	23	21	3	1	1	0	0	0	0	10	.048	.048	.095	-58	-4	0	1	-1	1.000	-3	O-13/D-4	-0.9
	Cal-A	31	59	4	14	3	0	0	2	5	12	.237	.297	.288	64	-3	2	3	-1	.944	-1	O-20/D-1	-0.5
	Yr	54	80	7	15	4	0	0	2	5	22	.188	.235	.237	32	-7	2	4	-2	.957	-4	O-33/D-5	-1.4
1993	Tex-A	27	85	15	24	6	3	2	9	10	17	.282	.358	.494	132	4	2	3	-1	1.000	-2	O-26	0.0
1994	Tex-A	11	29	1	5	1	0	0	1	2	1	.172	.226	.207	13	-4	0	0	0	.882	-2	O-10	-0.5
Total	8	252	493	70	118	27	6	4	42	52	123	.239	.313	.343	80	-13	12	9	-2	.975	-26	O-201/D-10	-4.2

■ JOHN DUDRA   Dudra, John Joseph   b: 5/27/16, Assumption, Ill.   d: 10/24/65, Pana, Ill.   BR/TR, 5'11.5", 175 lbs.   Deb: 9/7/41

YEAR	TM/L	G	AB	R	H	2B	3B	HR	RBI	BB	SO	AVG	OBP	SLG	PRO+	BR/A	SB	CS	SBR	FA	FR	G/POS	TPR
1941	Bos-N	14	25	3	9	3	1	0	3	3	4	.360	.429	.560	185	3	0				.933	0	/2-5,3-5,1-1,S-1	0.3

■ PAT DUFF   Duff, Patrick Henry   b: 5/6/1875, Providence, R.I.   d: 9/11/25, Providence, R.I.   TR ,   Deb: 4/16/06

YEAR	TM/L	G	AB	R	H	2B	3B	HR	RBI	BB	SO	AVG	OBP	SLG	PRO+	BR/A	SB	CS	SBR	FA	FR	G/POS	TPR
1906	Was-A	1	1	0	0	0	0	0	0	0		.000	.000	.000	-99	-0	0				.000	0	H	0.0

■ CHARLIE DUFFEE   Duffee, Charles Edward "Home Run"   b: 1/27/1866, Mobile, Ala.   d: 12/24/1894, Mobile, Ala.   BR/TR,   Deb: 4/17/1889

YEAR	TM/L	G	AB	R	H	2B	3B	HR	RBI	BB	SO	AVG	OBP	SLG	PRO+	BR/A	SB	CS	SBR	FA	FR	G/POS	TPR
1889	StL-a	137	509	93	124	15	11	16	86	60	81	.244	.327	.411	97	-7	21				.936	18	*O-132/3-5,2-2	0.6
1890	StL-a	98	378	68	104	11	7	3	54	37		.275	.344	.365	96	-5	20				.951	10	O-66,3-33/S-1	0.3
1891	Col-a	137	552	86	166	28	4	10	90	42	36	.301	.353	.420	129	18	41				.927	11	*O-128/3-7,S-2	2.2
1892	Was-N	132	492	64	122	12	11	6	51	36	33	.248	.302	.354	101	-1	28				.913	19	*O-125/3-6,1-4	1.2
1893	Cin-N	4	12	3	2	1	0	0	0	5	0	.167	.412	.250	76	-0	0				.400	-2	/O-4	-0.2
Total	5	508	1943	314	518	67	33	35	281	180	150	.267	.332	.389	106	5	110				.927	56	O-455/3-51,1-4,S2	4.1

■ ED DUFFY   Duffy, Edward Charles   b: 1844, Ireland   d: 6/21/1889, Brooklyn, N.Y.   TR , 5'7.5", 152 lbs.   Deb: 5/8/1871

YEAR	TM/L	G	AB	R	H	2B	3B	HR	RBI	BB	SO	AVG	OBP	SLG	PRO+	BR/A	SB	CS	SBR	FA	FR	G/POS	TPR
1871	Chi-n	26	121	30	28	5	0	0	15	3	2	.231	.250	.273	45	-10	11	4	1	.750	-3	*S-26/3-1	-0.8

■ FRANK DUFFY   Duffy, Frank Thomas   b: 10/14/46, Oakland, Cal.   BR/TR, 6'1", 180 lbs.   Deb: 9/4/70

YEAR	TM/L	G	AB	R	H	2B	3B	HR	RBI	BB	SO	AVG	OBP	SLG	PRO+	BR/A	SB	CS	SBR	FA	FR	G/POS	TPR
1970	Cin-N	6	11	1	2	2	0	0	1	1	2	.182	.250	.364	62	-1	1	0	0	1.000	1	/S-5	0.1
1971	Cin-N	13	16	0	3	1	0	0	1	1	2	.188	.235	.250	38	-1	0	0	0	.944	5	S-10	0.4
	*SF-N	21	28	4	5	0	0	0	2	0	10	.179	.179	.179	1	-4	0	0	0	.968	5	/S-6,2-1,3-1	0.2
	Yr	34	44	4	8	1	0	0	3	1	12	.182	.200	.205	15	-5	0	0	0	.955	10	S-16/2-1,3-1	0.6
1972	Cle-A	130	385	23	92	16	4	3	27	31	54	.239	.297	.325	82	-8	6	2	1	.977	3	*S-126	1.2
1973	Cle-A	116	361	34	95	16	4	8	50	25	41	.263	.314	.396	97	-2	6	6	-2	.986	12	*S-115	2.3
1974	Cle-A	158	549	62	128	18	0	8	48	30	64	.233	.273	.310	68	-23	7	8	-3	.980	14	*S-158	-1.5
1975	Cle-A	146	482	44	117	22	2	1	47	27	60	.243	.286	.303	66	-22	10	10	-3	.977	14	*S-145	0.4
1976	Cle-A	133	392	38	83	11	2	2	30	29	50	.212	.270	.265	58	-21	10	0	0	.983	11	*S-132	0.7
1977	Cle-A	122	334	30	67	13	2	4	31	21	47	.201	.248	.287	47	-25	8	3	1	.967	3	*S-121	-1.1
1978	Bos-A	64	104	12	27	5	0	0	4	6	11	.260	.306	.308	66	-5	1	1	-0	.960	6	3-22,S-21,2-12/D-6	0.4
1979	Bos-A	6	3	0	0	0	0	0	0	1	1	.000	.000	.000	-95	-1	0	0	0	1.000	1	/2-3,1-1	0.0
Total	10	915	2665	248	619	104	14	26	240	171	342	.232	.281	.311	69	-112	49	30	-3	.977	53	S-839/3-23,2-16,D1	3.1

■ HUGH DUFFY   Duffy, Hugh   b: 11/26/1866, Cranston, R.I.   d: 10/19/54, Boston, Mass.   BR/TR, 5'7", 168 lbs.   Deb: 6/23/1888   MCH

YEAR	TM/L	G	AB	R	H	2B	3B	HR	RBI	BB	SO	AVG	OBP	SLG	PRO+	BR/A	SB	CS	SBR	FA	FR	G/POS	TPR
1888	Chi-N	71	298	60	84	10	4	7	41	9	32	.282	.305	.413	119	5	13				.910	5	O-67/S-3,3-1	0.8
1889	Chi-N	136	584	144	172	21	7	12	89	46	30	.295	.348	.416	108	4	52				.894	-15	*O-126,S-10	-1.3
1890	Chi-P	138	596	161	191	36	16	7	82	59	20	.320	.384	.470	122	16	78				.917	13	*O-137	2.0
1891	Bos-a	127	536	134	180	20	8	9	110	61	29	.336	.408	.453	149	34	85				.917	0	*O-124/3-3,S-1	2.6
1892	*Bos-N	147	612	125	184	28	12	5	81	60	37	.301	.364	.410	123	14	51				.942	-9	*O-146/3-2	-0.1
1893	Bos-N	131	560	147	203	23	7	6	118	50	13	.363	.416	.461	123	16	44				.953	-2	*O-131	0.6
1894	Bos-N	125	539	160	237	51	16	18	145	66	15	.440	.502	.694	172	61	48				.927	4	*O-124/S-2	4.3
1895	Bos-N	130	531	110	187	30	6	9	100	63	16	.352	.425	.482	124	18	42				.945	6	*O-130	1.1
1896	Bos-N	131	527	97	158	16	8	5	113	52	19	.300	.365	.389	93	-6	39				.957	0	*O-120/2-9,S-2	-1.3
1897	*Bos-N	134	550	130	187	25	10	11	129	52		.340	.403	.482	125	18	41				.975	-1	*O-129/2-6,S-2	0.7
1898	Bos-N	152	568	97	169	13	3	8	108	59		.298	.365	.373	106	4	29				.956	2	*O-152/3-1,1-1,C-1	-0.4
1899	Bos-N	147	588	103	164	29	7	5	102	39		.279	.327	.378	85	-15	26				.970	-4	*O-147	-2.7
1900	Bos-N	55	181	27	55	5	4	2	31	16		.304	.360	.409	100	-1	11				.957	-1	O-49/2-1	-0.5
1901	Mil-A	79	285	40	86	15	9	2	45	16		.302	.341	.439	121	7	12				.967	-6	O-77,M	-0.4
1904	Phi-N	18	46	10	13	1	1	0	5	13		.283	.441	.348	150	4	3				.850	-3	O-14,M	0.0
1905	Phi-N	15	40	7	12	2	1	0	3	1		.300	.317	.400	117	1	0				.909	1	/O-8,M	0.1
1906	Phi-N	1	1	0	0	0	0	0	0	0		.000	.000	.000	-99	-0	0				.000	0	HM	0.0
Total	17	1737	7042	1552	2282	325	119	106	1302	662	211	.324	.384	.449	121	181	574				.943	-10	*O-1681/S-20,23C1	5.5

■ JOE DUGAN   Dugan, Joseph Anthony "Jumping Joe"   b: 5/12/1897, Mahanoy City, Pa.   d: 7/7/82, Norwood, Mass.   BR/TR, 5'11", 160 lbs.   Deb: 7/5/17

YEAR	TM/L	G	AB	R	H	2B	3B	HR	RBI	BB	SO	AVG	OBP	SLG	PRO+	BR/A	SB	CS	SBR	FA	FR	G/POS	TPR
1917	Phi-A	43	134	9	26	8	0	0	16	3	16	.194	.229	.254	48	-9	0				.917	1	S-39/2-2	-0.7
1918	Phi-A	121	411	26	80	11	3	3	34	16	55	.195	.230	.258	47	-28	4				.930	17	S-86,2-34	-0.6
1919	Phi-A	104	387	25	105	17	2	1	30	11	30	.271	.300	.333	77	-13	9				.929	1	S-98/2-4,3-2	-0.6
1920	Phi-A	123	491	65	158	40	5	3	60	19	51	.322	.351	.442	108	4	5	8	-3	.948	-1	3-60,S-32,2-31	0.6
1921	Phi-A	119	461	54	136	22	6	10	58	28	45	.295	.342	.434	96	-4	5	1	1	.953	-25	*3-119	-1.9
1922	Bos-A	84	341	45	98	22	3	3	38	9	28	.287	.308	.396	83	-10	2	3	-1	.943	-9	3-64,S-21	-1.3
	*NY-A	60	252	44	72	9	1	3	25	13	21	.286	.331	.365	79	-8	1	0	0	.967	-10	3-60	-1.2
	Yr	144	593	89	170	31	4	6	63	22	49	.287	.318	.383	81	-17	3	3	-1	.954	-19	*3-124,S-21	-2.5
1923	*NY-A	146	644	111	182	30	7	7	67	25	41	.283	.311	.384	81	-20	4	2	0	.974	-11	*3-146	-1.8
1924	NY-A	148	610	105	184	31	7	3	56	31	33	.302	.341	.390	88	-12	1	2	-1	.962	-15	*3-148/2-2	-1.5
1925	NY-A	102	404	50	118	19	4	0	31	19	20	.292	.330	.359	76	-15	2	4	-2	.970	7	3-96	-0.3
1926	*NY-A	123	434	39	125	19	5	1	64	26	16	.288	.328	.362	81	-13	2	4	-2	.955	-16	*3-122	-2.2
1927	*NY-A	112	387	44	104	24	3	2	43	27	37	.269	.321	.362	79	-12	1	4	-2	.938	-19	*3-111	-2.8
1928	*NY-A	94	312	33	86	15	0	6	34	16	15	.276	.317	.381	85	-7	0	0	0	.952	-18	3-91/2-1	-2.0
1929	Bos-A	60	125	14	38	10	0	0	15	8	8	.304	.346	.384	84	-3	0				.918	-9	3-24/S-5,2-2,O-2	-1.0
1931	Det-A	8	17	1	4	0	0	0	0	0	0	.235	.235	.235	23	-2	0	0	0	.900	-1	/3-5	-0.2
Total	14	1447	5410	665	1516	277	46	42	571	250	419	.280	.317	.372	82	-152	37	28		.957	-107	*3-1048,S-281/2O	-17.5

■ BILL DUGAN   Dugan, William H.   b: 1864, New York, N.Y.   d: 7/24/21, New York, N.Y.   Deb: 8/5/1884   F

YEAR	TM/L	G	AB	R	H	2B	3B	HR	RBI	BB	SO	AVG	OBP	SLG	PRO+	BR/A	SB	CS	SBR	FA	FR	G/POS	TPR
1884	Ric-a	9	28	4	3	1	0	0	0			.107	.138	.143	-8	-3				.889	-3	/C-9	-0.5
	KC-U	3	6	0	0	0	0	0	0			.000	.000	.000	-99	-2				.400	-1	/O-3	-0.3
Total	1	12	34	4	3	1	0	0	0			.088	.114	.118	-26	-5				.889	-4	/C-9,O-3	-0.8

■ GUS DUGAS   Dugas, Augustin Joseph   b: 3/24/07, St.Jean Dematha, Que., Canada   BL/TL, 5'9", 165 lbs.   Deb: 9/17/30

YEAR	TM/L	G	AB	R	H	2B	3B	HR	RBI	BB	SO	AVG	OBP	SLG	PRO+	BR/A	SB	CS	SBR	FA	FR	G/POS	TPR
1930	Pit-N	9	31	8	9	2	0	1	7	4		.290	.421	.355	90	-0	0				.864	-1	/O-9	-0.2
1932	Pit-N	55	97	13	23	3	3	3	12	7	11	.237	.288	.423	90	-2	0				.952	-3	O-20	-0.5
1933	Phi-N	37	71	4	12	3	0	0	9	1	9	.169	.181	.211	10	-7	0				.984	-0	1-11/O-1	-1.0
1934	Was-A	24	19	2	1	1	0	0	2	6	7	.053	.192	.105	-25	-4	0	0	0	1.000	-0	/O-2	-0.4
Total	4	125	218	27	45	9	3	4	23	18	27	.206	.267	.317	54	-14	0	0	0	.926	-4	/O-32,1-11	-2.1

■ DAN DUGDALE   Dugdale, Daniel Edward   b: 10/28/1864, Peoria, Ill.   d: 3/9/34, Seattle, Wash.   5'8", 180 lbs.   Deb: 5/20/1886

YEAR	TM/L	G	AB	R	H	2B	3B	HR	RBI	BB	SO	AVG	OBP	SLG	PRO+	BR/A	SB	CS	SBR	FA	FR	G/POS	TPR
1886	KC-N	12	40	4	7	0	0	0	2	1	9	.175	.214	.175	18	-4	1				.884	-2	/C-7,O-6	-0.5
1894	Was-N	38	134	19	32	4	2	0	16	13	14	.239	.306	.299	48	-11	7				.874	-5	C-33/3-3,O-2	-1.1
Total	2	50	174	23	39	4	2	0	18	15	27	.224	.286	.270	42	-15	8				.877	-7	/C-40,O-8,3-3	-1.6

YEAR	TM/L	G	AB	R	H	2B	3B	HR	RBI	BB	SO	AVG	OBP	SLG	PRO+	BR/A	SB	CS	SBR	FA	FR	G/POS	TPR

■ OSCAR DUGEY   Dugey, Oscar Joseph "Jake"   b: 10/25/1887, Palestine, Tex.   d: 1/1/66, Dallas, Tex.   BR/TR, 5'8", 160 lbs.   Deb: 9/13/13   C

1913	Bos-N	5	8	1	2	0	0	0	0	1	1	.250	.333	.250	67	-0	0			.500	-1	/3-2,2-1,S-1	-0.1
1914	Bos-N	58	109	17	21	2	0	1	10	10	15	.193	.267	.239	51	-6	10			.933	-2	O-16,2-16/3-1	-1.0
1915	*Phi-N	42	39	4	6	1	0	0	0	7	5	.154	.283	.179	41	-3	2	1	0	.941	3	2-14	0.0
1916	Phi-N	41	50	9	11	3	0	1	9	8		.220	.339	.280	88	-0	3			.967	3	2-12	0.3
1917	Phi-N	44	72	12	14	4	1	0	9	4	9	.194	.237	.278	55	-4	2			.871	0	2-15/O-4	-0.4
1920	Bos-N	5	0	2	0	0	0	0	0	0	0	—	—	—	—	0	0	0	0	.000	0	R	0.0
Total	6	195	278	45	54	10	1	1	20	31	38	.194	.277	.248	58	-14	17	1		.915	3	/2-58,O-20,3-3,S-1	-1.2

■ JIM DUGGAN   Duggan, James Elmer "Mer"   b: 6/1/1885, Whiteland, Ind.   d: 12/5/51, Indianapolis, Ind.   BL/TL, 5'10", 165 lbs.   Deb: 6/29/11

| 1911 | StL-A | 1 | 4 | 1 | 0 | 0 | 0 | 0 | 0 | 0 | | .000 | .200 | .000 | -44 | -1 | 0 | | | 1.000 | 0 | /1-1 | -0.1 |

■ TOM DUNBAR   Dunbar, Thomas Jerome   b: 11/24/59, Graniteville, S.C.   BL/TL, 6'2", 192 lbs.   Deb: 9/7/83

1983	Tex-A	12	24	3	6	0	0	0	3	5	7	.250	.379	.250	79	-0	3	1	0	.875	-3	/O-9,D-1	-0.3
1984	Tex-A	34	97	9	25	2	0	2	10	6	16	.258	.301	.340	75	-3	1	0	0	.939	-3	O-20/D-6	-0.6
1985	Tex-A	45	104	7	21	4	0	1	5	12	9	.202	.291	.269	54	-6	0	3	-2	.933	-3	D-18,O-14	-1.2
Total	3	91	225	19	52	6	0	3	18	23	32	.231	.305	.298	66	-10	4	4	-1	.929	-9	/O-43,D-25	-2.1

■ DAVE DUNCAN   Duncan, David Edwin   b: 9/26/45, Dallas, Tex.   BR/TR, 6'2", 200 lbs.   Deb: 5/6/64   C

1964	KC-A	25	53	2	9	0	1	1	5	2	20	.170	.200	.264	27	-5	0	0	0	.981	3	C-22	-0.1
1967	KC-A	34	101	9	19	4	0	5	11	4	50	.188	.219	.376	75	-4	0	1	-1	.979	-6	C-32	-1.0
1968	Oak-A	82	246	15	47	4	0	7	28	25	68	.191	.268	.293	73	-8	1	2	-1	.987	0	C-79	-0.4
1969	Oak-A	58	127	11	16	3	0	3	22	19	41	.126	.240	.220	31	-12	0	0	0	.982	-12	C-56	-2.3
1970	Oak-A	86	232	21	60	7	0	10	29	22	38	.259	.323	.418	107	1	0	0	0	.978	3	C-73	0.8
1971	*Oak-A☆	103	363	39	92	13	1	15	40	28	77	.253	.309	.419	106	2	1	1	-0	.984	3	*C-102	0.9
1972	*Oak-A	121	403	39	88	13	0	19	59	34	68	.218	.287	.392	106	1	0	2	-1	.993	2	*C-113	0.7
1973	Cle-A	95	344	43	80	11	1	17	43	35	86	.233	.309	.419	101	-0	3	3	-1	.988	-1	C-86/D-9	0.2
1974	Cle-A	136	425	45	85	10	1	16	46	42	91	.200	.275	.341	77	-13	0	4	-2	.976	-8	C-134/1-3,D-1	-1.9
1975	Bal-A	96	307	30	63	7	0	12	41	16	82	.205	.247	.345	70	-14	0	0	0	.982	-7	C-95	-1.7
1976	Bal-A	93	284	20	58	7	0	4	17	25	56	.204	.271	.271	63	-13	0	0	0	.985	-11	C-93	-2.3
Total	11	929	2885	274	617	79	4	109	341	252	677	.214	.280	.357	85	-65	5	13	-6	.984	-32	C-885/D-10,1-3	-7.1

■ JIM DUNCAN   Duncan, James William   b: 7/1/1871, Saltsburg, Pa.   d: 10/16/01, Foxburg, Pa.   BR/TR, 5'8", 140 lbs.   Deb: 7/18/1899

1899	Was-N	15	47	5	11	2	0	0	5	4		.234	.294	.277	57	-3	1			.940	-1	C-14	-0.2
	Cle-N	31	105	9	24	2	3	2	9	4		.229	.257	.362	74	-4	0			.971	-4	1-17,C-14	-0.7
	Yr	46	152	14	35	4	3	2	14	8		.230	.269	.336	69	-7	1			.904	-5	C-28,1-17	-0.9

■ PAT DUNCAN   Duncan, Louis Baird   b: 10/6/1893, Coalton, Ohio   d: 7/17/60, Columbus, Ohio   BR/TR, 5'9", 170 lbs.   Deb: 7/16/15

1915	Pit-N	3	5	0	1	0	0	0	0	0	1	.200	.200	.200	22	-0	0			1.000	-0	/O-1	-0.1
1919	*Cin-N	31	90	9	22	3	3	2	17	8	7	.244	.306	.411	118	2	2			.982	-1	O-27	-0.1
1920	Cin-N	154	576	75	170	16	11	2	83	42	42	.295	.350	.372	109	7	18	18	-5	.964	5	*O-154	-0.5
1921	Cin-N	145	532	57	164	27	10	2	60	44	33	.308	.367	.408	110	8	7	18	-9	.971	9	*O-145	-0.3
1922	Cin-N	151	607	94	199	44	12	8	94	40	31	.328	.370	.479	120	16	12	28	-13	.971	4	*O-151	-0.4
1923	Cin-N	147	566	92	185	26	8	7	83	30	27	.327	.363	.438	113	9	15	13	-3	.993	-1	*O-146	-0.4
1924	Cin-N	96	319	34	86	21	6	2	37	20	23	.270	.313	.392	89	-6	1	7	-4	.927	-14	O-83	-2.9
Total	7	727	2695	361	827	137	50	23	374	184	164	.307	.355	.420	110	36	55	84		.970	2	O-707	-4.7

■ MARIANO DUNCAN   Duncan, Mariano (Nalasco)   b: 3/13/63, San Pedro De Macoris, D.R.   BR/TR, 6', 185 lbs.   Deb: 4/9/85

1985	*LA-N	142	562	74	137	24	6	6	39	38	113	.244	.295	.340	79	-16	38	8	7	.954	-8	*S-123,2-19	-0.6
1986	LA-N	109	407	47	93	7	0	8	30	30	78	.229	.285	.355	67	-19	48	13	7	.951	-2	*S-106	-0.4
1987	LA-N	76	261	31	56	8	1	6	18	17	62	.215	.268	.322	57	-17	11	1	3	.930	-1	S-67/2-7,O-2	-0.9
1989	LA-N	49	84	9	21	5	1	0	8	0	15	.250	.267	.333	72	-3	3	3	-1	.943	-0	S-16/2-8,O-7	-0.4
	Cin-N	45	174	23	43	10	1	3	13	8	36	.247	.292	.368	85	-4	6	2	1	.955	-7	S-44/2-5	-0.8
	Yr	94	258	32	64	15	2	3	21	8	51	.248	.284	.357	81	-7	9	5	-0	.952	-8	S-60,2-13/O-7	-1.2
1990	*Cin-N	125	435	67	133	22	**11**	10	55	24	67	.306	.348	.476	119	10	13	7	-0	.973	1	*2-115,S-12/O-1	1.4
1991	Cin-N	100	333	46	86	7	4	12	40	12	57	.258	.290	.441	92	-5	5	4	-1	.974	-6	2-62,S-32/O-7	-0.9
1992	Phi-N	142	574	71	153	40	3	8	50	17	108	.267	.294	.389	92	-8	23	3	5	.976	-23	O-65,2-52,S-42,/3-4	-2.5
1993	*Phi-N	124	496	68	140	26	4	11	73	12	88	.282	.305	.417	92	-7	6	5	-1	.969	-28	2-65,S-59	-3.0
1994	Phi-N★	88	347	49	93	22	1	8	48	17	72	.268	.310	.406	83	-9	10	2	2	.972	-17	2-37,3-28,S-19,/1-6	-2.1
1995	Phi-N	52	196	20	56	12	1	3	23	0	43	.286	.289	.403	80	-6	1	2	-1	.957	5	2-24,S-14,1-12,/3-1	0.0
	*Cin-N	29	69	16	20	2	1	3	13	5	19	.290	.338	.478	113	1	0	1	-0	.963	-3	/2-7,1-6,S-6,0-3	-0.2
	Yr	81	265	36	76	14	2	6	36	5	62	.287	.303	.423	88	-5	1	3	-2	.958	2	2-31,S-20,1-18,/O3	-0.2
1996	*NY-A	109	400	62	136	34	3	8	56	9	77	.340	.356	.500	111	6	4	3	-1	.975	-25	*2-104/3-3,O-3,D-2	-1.2
Total	11	1190	4338	583	1167	219	37	86	466	189	835	.269	.305	.396	89	-77	168	54	18	.951	-114	S-540,2-505/O31D	-11.6

■ TAYLOR DUNCAN   Duncan, Taylor McDowell   b: 5/12/53, Memphis, Tenn.   BR/TR, 6', 170 lbs.   Deb: 9/15/77

1977	StL-N	8	12	2	4	0	0	1	2	2	1	.333	.429	.583	172	1	0	0	0	1.000	-2	/3-5	-0.1
1978	Oak-A	104	319	25	82	15	2	2	37	19	38	.257	.299	.335	82	-8	1	2	-1	.953	-21	3-84,2-11/S-1,D-7	-3.2
Total	2	112	331	27	86	15	2	3	39	21	39	.260	.304	.344	86	-7	1	2	-1	.953	-23	/3-89,2-11,D-7,S-1	-3.3

■ VERN DUNCAN   Duncan, Vernon Van Duke   b: 1/6/1890, Clayton, N.C.   d: 6/1/54, Daytona Beach, Fla   BL/TR, 5'9", 155 lbs.   Deb: 9/11/13

1913	Phi-N	8	12	3	5	1	0	0	1	0	3	.417	.417	.500	155	1	0			1.000	-0	/O-3	0.1
1914	Bal-F	157	557	99	160	20	8	2	53	67	55	.287	.375	.363	98	-7	13			.914	-3	*O-148/3-8,2-1	-1.7
1915	Bal-F	146	531	68	142	18	4	2	43	54	40	.267	.337	.328	85	-17	19			.965	-0	*O-124,3-21/2-1	-2.4
Total	3	311	1100	170	307	39	12	4	97	121	98	.279	.357	.347	93	-23	32			.939	-3	O-275/3-29,2-2	-4.0

■ GUS DUNDON   Dundon, Augustus Joseph   b: 7/10/1874, Columbus, Ohio   d: 9/1/40, Pittsburg, Pa.   BR/TR, 5'10", 165 lbs.   Deb: 4/14/04

1904	Chi-A	108	373	40	85	9	3	0	36	30		.228	.292	.268	81	-7	19			**.973**	-15	*2-103/3-3,S-2	-2.2
1905	Chi-A	106	364	30	70	7	0	0	22	23		.192	.248	.228	53	-19	14			.983	13	*2-100/S-6	-0.5
1906	Chi-A	33	96	7	13	1	0	0	4	11		.135	.224	.146	17	-9	4			.921	7	2-18,S-14	-0.1
Total	3	247	833	77	168	17	6	0	62	64		.202	.265	.236	61	-35	37			.972	6	2-221/S-22,3-3	-2.8

■ ED DUNDON   Dundon, Edward Joseph "Dummy"   b: 7/10/1859, Columbus, Ohio   d: 8/18/1893, Columbus, Ohio   TR ,   Deb: 6/2/1883

1883	Col-a	26	93	8	15	1	0	0		3		.161	.188	.172	18	-8				.804	0	P-20/O-9,2-1	-0.2
1884	Col-a	26	86	6	12	2	2	0		5		.140	.196	.209	35	-6				.966	3	O-16,P-11/1-3	-0.2
Total	2	52	179	14	27	3	2	0		8		.151	.191	.190	26	-14				.866	4	/P-31,O-25,1-3,2-1	-0.4

■ SAM DUNGAN   Dungan, Samuel Morrison   b: 7/29/1866, Ferndale, Cal.   d: 3/16/39, Santa Ana, Cal.   BR , 5'11", 180 lbs.   Deb: 4/12/1892

1892	Chi-N	113	433	46	123	19	7	0	53	35	19	.284	.346	.360	112	6	15			.905	-6	*O-113	-0.5
1893	Chi-N	107	465	86	138	23	7	2	64	29	8	.297	.350	.389	98	-2	11			.920	4	*O-107	-0.3
1894	Chi-N	10	39	5	9	3	0	1	3	7	1	.231	.348	.282	51	-3	1			1.000	0	/O-10	-0.3
	Lou-N	8	32	6	11	1	0	0	3	4	1	.344	.417	.375	99	0	2			.941	0	/O-8	0.0
	Yr	18	71	11	20	4	0	1	6	11	2	.282	.378	.324	71	-3	3			.971	1	/O-18	-0.2
1900	Chi-N	6	15	1	4	0	0	0	1	1		.267	.313	.267	63	-1	0			.800	-1	/O-3	-0.2
1901	Was-A	138	559	70	179	26	12	1	73	40		.320	.368	.415	118	14	9			.947	-5	*O-104,1-35	0.1
Total	5	382	1543	214	464	71	26	3	197	116	29	.301	.356	.386	107	14	38			.924	-8	O-345/1-35	1.2

■ LEE DUNHAM   Dunham, Leland Huffield   b: 6/9/02, Atlanta, Ill.   d: 5/11/61, Atlanta, Ill.   BL/TL, 5'11", 185 lbs.   Deb: 4/17/26

| 1926 | Phi-N | 5 | 4 | 0 | 1 | 0 | 0 | 0 | 1 | 0 | | .250 | .250 | .250 | 33 | -0 | 0 | | | 1.000 | -0 | /1-2 | 0.0 |

■ FRED DUNLAP   Dunlap, Frederick C. "Sure Shot"   b: 5/21/1859, Philadelphia, Pa.   d: 12/1/02, Philadelphia, Pa.   BR/TR, 5'8", 165 lbs.   Deb: 5/1/1880   M

| 1880 | Cle-N | 85 | 373 | 61 | 103 | **27** | 9 | 4 | 30 | 7 | 32 | .276 | .289 | .429 | 143 | 16 | | | | .911 | 8 | *2-85 | 2.7 |

YEAR	TM/L	G	AB	R	H	2B	3B	HR	RBI	BB	SO	AVG	OBP	SLG	PRO+	BR/A	SB	CS	SBR	FA	FR	G/POS	TPR
1881	Cle-N	80	351	60	114	25	4	3	24	18	24	.325	.358	.444	159	24				.909	6	*2-79/3-1	3.0
1882	Cle-N	84	364	68	102	19	4	0	28	23	26	.280	.323	.354	121	9				.900	18	*2-84,M	2.6
1883	Cle-N	93	396	81	129	34	2	4	37	22	21	.326	.361	.452	147	22				.911	8	*2-93/O-1	2.7
1884	StL-U	101	449	160	185	39	8	13		29		.412	.448	.621	213	49				.926	31	*2-100/O-1,P-1,M	6.9
1885	StL-N	106	423	70	114	11	5	2	25	41	24	.270	.334	.333	124	13				.934	26	*2-106,M	4.0
1886	StL-N	71	285	53	76	15	2	3	32	28	30	.267	.332	.365	119	8	7			.931	16	2-71/O-1	2.4
	Det-N	51	196	32	56	8	3	4	37	16	21	.286	.340	.418	126	6	13			.918	3	2-51	1.0
	Yr	122	481	85	132	23	5	7	69	44	51	.274	.335	.387	122	14	20			.926	19	*2-122/O-1	3.4
1887	*Det-N	65	272	60	72	13	10	5	45	25	12	.265	.327	.441	108	2	15			.948	24	2-65/P-1	2.3
1888	Pit-N	82	321	41	84	12	4	1	36	16	30	.262	.303	.333	111	4	24			.940	12	2-82	1.9
1889	Pit-N	121	451	59	106	19	0	2	65	46	33	.235	.309	.290	75	-14	21			.950	-6	*2-121,M	-1.2
1890	Pit-N	17	64	9	11	1	1	0	3	7	6	.172	.264	.219	46	-4	2			.874	-3	2-17	-0.5
	NY-P	1	4	1	2	0	0	0	0	0	0	.500	.500	.500	154	0	0			1.000	-1	/2-1	-0.1
1891	Was-a	8	25	4	5	1	1	0	4	5	4	.200	.355	.320	98	0	3			.818	-3	/2-8	-0.3
Total	12	965	3974	759	1159	224	53	41	366	283	263	.292	.340	.406	132	136	85			.924	137	2-963/O-3,P-2,3-1	27.4

■ GRANT DUNLAP
Dunlap, Grant Lester "Snap" b: 12/20/23, Stockton, Cal. BR/TR, 6'2", 180 lbs. Deb: 4/21/53

YEAR	TM/L	G	AB	R	H	2B	3B	HR	RBI	BB	SO	AVG	OBP	SLG	PRO+	BR/A	SB	CS	SBR	FA	FR	G/POS	TPR
1953	StL-N	16	17	2	6	0	1	1	3	0	2	.353	.353	.647	154	1	0	0	0	.000	-0	/O-1	0.1

■ BILL DUNLAP
Dunlap, William James b: 5/1/09, Palmer, Mass. d: 11/29/80, Reading, Pa. BR/TR, 5'11", 170 lbs. Deb: 9/2/29

YEAR	TM/L	G	AB	R	H	2B	3B	HR	RBI	BB	SO	AVG	OBP	SLG	PRO+	BR/A	SB	CS	SBR	FA	FR	G/POS	TPR
1929	Bos-N	10	29	6	12	0	1	1	4	4	4	.414	.485	.586	171	3	0			.889	-1	/O-9	0.1
1930	Bos-N	16	29	3	2	1	0	0	0	0	6	.069	.069	.103	-61	-8	0			1.000	-1	/O-7	-0.8
Total	2	26	58	9	14	1	1	1	4	4	10	.241	.290	.345	57	-4	0			.939	-2	/O-16	-0.7

■ JACK DUNLEAVY
Dunleavy, John Francis b: 9/14/1879, Harrison, N.J. d: 4/11/44, S.Norwalk, Conn. TL, 5'6", 167 lbs. Deb: 5/30/03

YEAR	TM/L	G	AB	R	H	2B	3B	HR	RBI	BB	SO	AVG	OBP	SLG	PRO+	BR/A	SB	CS	SBR	FA	FR	G/POS	TPR
1903	StL-N	61	193	23	48	3	3	0	10	13		.249	.306	.295	74	-6	10			.972	6	O-38,P-14	-0.2
1904	StL-N	51	172	23	40	7	3	1	14	16		.233	.305	.326	99	-0	8			.987	1	O-44/P-7	-0.3
1905	StL-N	119	435	52	105	8	8	1	25	55		.241	.328	.303	91	-3	15			.962	2	*O-118/2-1	-0.7
Total	3	231	800	98	193	18	14	2	49	84		.241	.318	.306	89	-9	33			.969	9	O-200/P-21,2-1	-1.2

■ GEORGE DUNLOP
Dunlop, George Henry b: 7/19/1888, Meriden, Conn. d: 12/12/72, Meriden, Conn. BR/TR, 5'10", 170 lbs. Deb: 9/9/13

YEAR	TM/L	G	AB	R	H	2B	3B	HR	RBI	BB	SO	AVG	OBP	SLG	PRO+	BR/A	SB	CS	SBR	FA	FR	G/POS	TPR
1913	Cle-A	7	17	3	4	1	0	0	0	0	5	.235	.235	.294	53	-1	0			.923	1	/S-4,3-3	0.0
1914	Cle-A	1	3	0	0	0	0	0	0	0	1	.000	.250	.000	-23	-0	0			1.000	-1	/S-1	-0.2
Total	2	8	20	3	4	1	0	0	0	1	6	.200	.238	.250	42	-1	0			.929	0	/S-5,3-3	-0.2

■ JACK DUNN
Dunn, John Joseph b: 10/6/1872, Meadville, Pa. d: 10/22/28, Towson, Md. BR/TR, 5'9", Deb: 5/6/1897

YEAR	TM/L	G	AB	R	H	2B	3B	HR	RBI	BB	SO	AVG	OBP	SLG	PRO+	BR/A	SB	CS	SBR	FA	FR	G/POS	TPR
1897	Bro-N	36	131	20	29	4	0	0	17	4		.221	.244	.252	33	-13	2			.911	-1	P-25/2-4,O-3,3-3,S	-0.5
1898	Bro-N	51	167	21	41	0	1	0	19	7		.246	.280	.257	54	-10	3			.939	-1	P-41/O-4,S-4,3-2	-0.2
1899	Bro-N	43	122	21	30	2	1	0	16	3		.246	.270	.279	49	-9	3			.963	3	P-41/S-1	0.0
1900	Bro-N	10	26	2	6	0	0	0	0	1		.231	.259	.231	34	-2	0			.960	1	P-10	0.0
	Phi-N	10	33	3	10	1	0	0	5	0		.303	.303	.333	76	-1	1			.920	-1	P-10	0.0
	Yr	20	59	5	16	1	0	0	6	1		.271	.283	.288	56	-4	1			.940	1	P-20	0.0
1901	Phi-N	2	1	1	1	0	0	0	0	0		1.000	1.000	1.000	471	1	0			1.000	-0	/P-2	0.0
	Bal-A	96	362	41	90	9	4	0	36	21		.249	.301	.296	63	-18	10			.872	-7	3-67,S-19/P-9,2O	-2.0
1902	NY-N	100	342	26	72	11	1	0	14	20		.211	.256	.249	56	-18	13			.962	-10	O-43,S-36,3-18/P2	-2.9
1903	NY-N	78	257	35	62	15	1	0	37	15		.241	.291	.307	68	-11	12			.907	-7	S-27,3-25,2-19/O-1	-1.5
1904	NY-N	64	181	27	56	12	2	1	19	11		.309	.356	.414	132	6	11			.914	-8	3-28,S-10/2-9,OP	-0.1
Total	8	490	1622	197	397	54	10	1	164	83		.245	.287	.292	66	-75	55			.890	-31	3-143,P-142/SO2	-7.2

■ JOE DUNN
Dunn, Joseph Edward b: 3/11/1885, Springfield, Ohio d: 3/19/44, Springfield, Ohio BR/TR, 5'9", 160 lbs. Deb: 9/12/08

YEAR	TM/L	G	AB	R	H	2B	3B	HR	RBI	BB	SO	AVG	OBP	SLG	PRO+	BR/A	SB	CS	SBR	FA	FR	G/POS	TPR
1908	Bro-N	20	64	3	11	3	0	0	5	0		.172	.172	.219	26	-6	0			.957	7	C-20	0.4
1909	Bro-N	10	25	1	4	1	0	0	2	0		.160	.192	.200	23	-2	0			.952	-2	/C-7	-0.4
Total	2	30	89	4	15	4	0	0	7	0		.169	.178	.213	25	-8	0			.956	6	/C-27	0.0

■ RON DUNN
Dunn, Ronald Ray b: 1/24/50, Oklahoma City, Okla BR/TR, 5'11", 180 lbs. Deb: 9/3/74

YEAR	TM/L	G	AB	R	H	2B	3B	HR	RBI	BB	SO	AVG	OBP	SLG	PRO+	BR/A	SB	CS	SBR	FA	FR	G/POS	TPR
1974	Chi-N	23	68	6	20	7	0	2	15	12	8	.294	.400	.485	141	4	0	0	0	.917	-7	2-21/3-6	-0.2
1975	Chi-N	32	44	2	7	3	0	1	6	6	17	.159	.260	.295	52	-3	0	0	0	.957	-1	3-11/O-2,2-1	-0.4
Total	2	55	112	8	27	10	0	3	21	18	25	.241	.346	.411	106	1	0	0	0	.918	-7	/2-22,3-17,O-2	-0.6

■ STEVE DUNN
Dunn, Stephen B. b: 12/21/1858, London, Ont., Can. d: 5/5/33, London, Ont., Can. 5'9.5", 173 lbs. Deb: 9/27/1884

YEAR	TM/L	G	AB	R	H	2B	3B	HR	RBI	BB	SO	AVG	OBP	SLG	PRO+	BR/A	SB	CS	SBR	FA	FR	G/POS	TPR
1884	StP-U	9	32	2	8	0	0	0		2	0	.250	.250	.313	128	-2				.972	1	/1-9,3-1	-0.1

■ STEVE DUNN
Dunn, Steven Robert b: 4/18/70, Champaign, Ill. BL/TL, 6'4", 225 lbs. Deb: 5/3/94

YEAR	TM/L	G	AB	R	H	2B	3B	HR	RBI	BB	SO	AVG	OBP	SLG	PRO+	BR/A	SB	CS	SBR	FA	FR	G/POS	TPR
1994	Min-A	14	35	4	8	5	0	0	4	1	12	.229	.250	.371	57	-2	0	0	0	.990	1	1-12	-0.2
1995	Min-A	5	6	0	0	0	0	0	0	1	3	.000	.143	.000	-59	-1	0	0	0	1.000	-0	/1-3	-0.2
Total	2	19	41	4	8	5	0	0	4	2	15	.195	.233	.317	40	-4	0	0	0	.990	1	/1-15	-0.4

■ TODD DUNN
Dunn, Todd Kent b: 7/29/70, Tulsa, Okla. BR/TR, 6'5", 220 lbs. Deb: 9/8/96

YEAR	TM/L	G	AB	R	H	2B	3B	HR	RBI	BB	SO	AVG	OBP	SLG	PRO+	BR/A	SB	CS	SBR	FA	FR	G/POS	TPR
1996	Mil-A	6	10	2	3	1	0	0	1	0		.300	.300	.400	71	-0	0	0	0	1.000	-1	/O-6	-0.2

■ SHAWON DUNSTON
Dunston, Shawon Donnell b: 3/21/63, Brooklyn, N.Y. BR/TR, 6'1", 175 lbs. Deb: 4/9/85

YEAR	TM/L	G	AB	R	H	2B	3B	HR	RBI	BB	SO	AVG	OBP	SLG	PRO+	BR/A	SB	CS	SBR	FA	FR	G/POS	TPR
1985	Chi-N	74	250	40	65	12	4	4	18	19	42	.260	.312	.388	85	-5	11	3	2	.958	13	S-73	1.7
1986	Chi-N	150	581	66	145	37	3	17	68	21	114	.250	.279	.411	82	-16	13	11	-3	.961	20	*S-149	1.6
1987	Chi-N	95	346	40	85	18	3	5	22	10	68	.246	.269	.358	62	-19	12	3	2	.969	5	S-94	-0.5
1988	Chi-N☆	155	575	69	143	23	6	9	56	16	108	.249	.272	.357	76	-19	30	9	4	.973	6	*S-151	0.3
1989	*Chi-N	138	471	52	131	20	6	9	60	30	86	.278	.323	.403	99	-1	19	11	-1	.972	7	*S-138	1.6
1990	Chi-N★	146	545	73	143	22	8	17	66	15	87	.262	.286	.426	87	-12	25	5	5	.970	6	*S-144	1.0
1991	Chi-N	142	492	59	128	22	7	12	50	23	64	.260	.299	.407	92	-6	21	6	3	.968	-6	*S-142	0.1
1992	Chi-N	18	73	8	23	3	1	0	2	3	13	.315	.342	.384	103	0	2	3	-1	.986	-5	S-18	-0.5
1993	Chi-N	7	10	3	4	2	0	0	2	0	1	.400	.400	.600	166	1	0	0	0	1.000	-1	/S-2	0.0
1994	Chi-N	88	331	38	92	19	0	11	35	16	48	.278	.315	.435	94	-4	3	8	-4	.966	-7	S-84	-0.7
1995	Chi-N	127	477	58	141	30	6	14	69	10	75	.296	.318	.472	107	3	10	5	0	.969	-12	*S-125	0.2
1996	SF-N	82	287	27	86	12	2	5	25	13	40	.300	.332	.408	98	-1	8	0	2	.957	-2	S-78	0.5
Total	12	1222	4438	533	1186	220	46	103	473	176	746	.267	.299	.407	88	-81	154	64	8	.967	25	*S-1198	5.3

■ DAN DURAN
Duran, Daniel James b: 3/16/54, Palo Alto, Cal. BL/TL, 5'11", 190 lbs. Deb: 4/17/81

YEAR	TM/L	G	AB	R	H	2B	3B	HR	RBI	BB	SO	AVG	OBP	SLG	PRO+	BR/A	SB	CS	SBR	FA	FR	G/POS	TPR
1981	Tex-A	13	16	1	4	0	0	0	1	1		.250	.294	.250	61	-1	0	0	0	1.000	-1	/O-7,1-1	-0.2

■ MIKE DURANT
Durant, Michael Joseph b: 9/14/69, Columbus, Ohio BR/TR, 6'2", 200 lbs. Deb: 4/3/96

YEAR	TM/L	G	AB	R	H	2B	3B	HR	RBI	BB	SO	AVG	OBP	SLG	PRO+	BR/A	SB	CS	SBR	FA	FR	G/POS	TPR
1996	Min-A	40	81	15	17	3	0	0	5	10	15	.210	.297	.247	39	-7	3	0	1	.975	9	C-37	0.4

■ KID DURBIN
Durbin, Blaine Alphonsus b: 9/10/1886, Lamar, Mo. d: 9/11/43, Kirkwood, Mo. BL/TL, 5'8", 155 lbs. Deb: 4/24/07

YEAR	TM/L	G	AB	R	H	2B	3B	HR	RBI	BB	SO	AVG	OBP	SLG	PRO+	BR/A	SB	CS	SBR	FA	FR	G/POS	TPR
1907	Chi-N	11	18	2	6	0	0	0	0	1		.333	.368	.333	113	0				1.000	0	P-5,O-5	0.0
1908	Chi-N	14	28	3	7	1	0	0	2	0		.250	.323	.286	91	-0				1.000	-3	O-14	-0.4
1909	Cin-N	6	5	1	1	0	0	0	0	0		.200	.333	.200	66	-0				.000	0	H	0.0
	Pit-N	1	0	0	0	0	0	0	0	0		—	—	—		0				.000	0	R	0.0
	Yr	7	5	1	1	0	0	0	0	0		.200	.333	.200	65	-0				.000	0	-0,-0	0.0
Total	3	32	51	6	14	1	0	0	2	1		.275	.339	.294	96	-0				1.000	-2	/O-19,P-5	-0.4

■ JOE DURHAM
Durham, Joseph Vann "Pop" b: 7/31/31, Newport News, Va. BR/TR, 6'1", 186 lbs. Deb: 9/10/54

YEAR	TM/L	G	AB	R	H	2B	3B	HR	RBI	BB	SO	AVG	OBP	SLG	PRO+	BR/A	SB	CS	SBR	FA	FR	G/POS	TPR
1954	Bal-A	10	40	4	9	0	0	1	3	4	7	.225	.295	.300	68	-2	0	0	0	.917	-1	O-10	-0.3
1957	Bal-A	77	157	19	29	2	0	4	17	16	42	.185	.260	.274	49	-11	1	1	-0	1.000	-11	O-59	-2.7

YEAR	TM/L	G	AB	R	H	2B	3B	HR	RBI	BB	SO	AVG	OBP	SLG	PRO+	BR/A	SB	CS	SBR	FA	FR	G/POS	TPR
1959	StL-N	6	5	2	0	0	0	0	0	0	1	.000	.000	.000	-94	-1	0	0	0	1.000	0	/O-1	-0.1
Total	3	93	202	25	38	2	0	5	20	20	50	.188	.261	.272	49	-15	1	1	-0	.979	-12	/O-70	-3.1

■ **LEON DURHAM**   Durham, Leon   b: 7/31/57, Cincinnati, Ohio   BL/TL, 6′2″, 210 lbs.   Deb: 5/27/80

YEAR	TM/L	G	AB	R	H	2B	3B	HR	RBI	BB	SO	AVG	OBP	SLG	PRO+	BR/A	SB	CS	SBR	FA	FR	G/POS	TPR
1980	StL-N	96	303	42	82	15	4	8	42	18	55	.271	.314	.426	101	-0	8	5	-1	.987	7	O-78/1-8	0.3
1981	Chi-N	87	328	42	95	14	6	10	35	27	53	.290	.344	.460	121	8	25	11	1	.970	2	O-83/1-3	0.9
1982	Chi-N☆	148	539	84	168	33	7	22	90	66	77	.312	.389	.521	148	35	28	14	0	.963	-3	*O-143/1-1	2.9
1983	Chi-N★	100	337	58	87	18	8	12	55	66	83	.258	.384	.466	128	15	12	6	0	.966	-7	O-95/1-6	0.5
1984	*Chi-N	137	473	86	132	30	4	23	96	69	86	.279	.372	.505	132	20	16	8	0	.994	6	*1-130	2.0
1985	Chi-N	153	542	58	153	32	2	21	75	64	99	.282	.358	.465	116	11	7	6	-2	.995	3	*1-151	0.3
1986	Chi-N	141	484	66	127	18	7	20	65	67	98	.262	.353	.452	112	8	8	7	-2	.995	-7	*1-141	-1.0
1987	Chi-N	131	439	70	120	22	1	27	63	51	92	.273	.349	.513	120	12	2	2	-1	.990	-9	*1-123	-0.6
1988	Chi-N	24	73	10	16	6	1	3	6	9	20	.219	.305	.452	110	1	0	1	-1	.995	1	1-20	-0.1
	Cin-N	21	51	4	11	3	0	1	2	5	12	.216	.286	.333	74	-2	0	0	0	.993	-1	1-17	-0.4
	Yr	45	124	14	27	9	1	4	8	14	32	.218	.297	.403	95	-1	0	1	-1	.994	-0	1-37	-0.5
1989	StL-N	29	18	2	1	0	0	1	2	4	5	.056	.190	.111	-11	-3	0	1	-1	.961	1	1-18	-0.3
Total	10	1067	3587	522	992	192	40	147	530	444	679	.277	.358	.475	122	105	106	61	-5	.994	-8	1-618,O-399	4.5

■ **RAY DURHAM**   Durham, Ray   b: 11/30/71, Charlotte, N.C.   BB/TR, 5′8″, 170 lbs.   Deb: 4/26/95

YEAR	TM/L	G	AB	R	H	2B	3B	HR	RBI	BB	SO	AVG	OBP	SLG	PRO+	BR/A	SB	CS	SBR	FA	FR	G/POS	TPR
1995	Chi-A	125	471	68	121	27	6	7	51	31	83	.257	.311	.384	83	-12	18	5	2	.973	-29	*2-122/D-1	-3.0
1996	Chi-A	156	557	79	153	33	5	10	65	58	95	.275	.354	.406	97	-2	30	4	7	.984	-21	*2-150/D-3	-0.6
Total	2	281	1028	147	274	60	11	17	116	89	178	.267	.335	.396	91	-15	48	9	9	.979	-50	2-272/D-4	-3.6

■ **BOBBY DURNBAUGH**   Durnbaugh, Robert Eugene "Scroggy"   b: 1/15/33, Dayton, Ohio   BR/TR, 5′8″, 170 lbs.   Deb: 9/22/57

YEAR	TM/L	G	AB	R	H	2B	3B	HR	RBI	BB	SO	AVG	OBP	SLG	PRO+	BR/A	SB	CS	SBR	FA	FR	G/POS	TPR
1957	Cin-N	2	1	0	0	0	0	0	0	0	0	.000	.000	.000	-93	-0	0	0	0	.500	-0	/S-2	0.0

■ **GEORGE DURNING**   Durning, George Dewey   b: 5/9/1898, Philadelphia, Pa.   d: 4/18/86, Tampa, Fla.   BR/TR, 5′11″, 175 lbs.   Deb: 9/12/25

YEAR	TM/L	G	AB	R	H	2B	3B	HR	RBI	BB	SO	AVG	OBP	SLG	PRO+	BR/A	SB	CS	SBR	FA	FR	G/POS	TPR
1925	Phi-N	5	14	3	5	0	0	0	1	2	1	.357	.438	.357	97	0	0	0	0	1.000	2	/O-4	0.2

■ **LEO DUROCHER**   Durocher, Leo Ernest "Lippy"   b: 7/27/05, W.Springfield, Mass.   d: 10/7/91, Palm Springs, Cal.   BR/TR, 5′10″, 160 lbs.   Deb: 10/2/25   MCH

YEAR	TM/L	G	AB	R	H	2B	3B	HR	RBI	BB	SO	AVG	OBP	SLG	PRO+	BR/A	SB	CS	SBR	FA	FR	G/POS	TPR
1925	NY-A	2	1	1	0	0	0	0	0	0	0	.000	.000	.000	-99	-0	0			.000	0	H	0.0
1928	*NY-A	102	296	46	80	8	6	0	31	22	52	.270	.327	.338	77	-10	1	4	-2	.948	12	2-66,S-29	0.5
1929	NY-A	106	341	53	84	4	5	0	32	34	33	.246	.320	.287	62	-19	3	1	0	.958	**26**	S-93,2-12	1.7
1930	Cin-N	119	354	31	86	15	3	3	32	20	45	.243	.287	.328	51	-29	0			.959	10	*S-103,2-13	-0.7
1931	Cin-N	121	361	26	82	11	5	1	29	18	32	.227	.264	.294	53	-25	0			.965	-4	*S-120	-1.9
1932	Cin-N	143	457	43	99	22	5	1	33	36	40	.217	.275	.293	55	-29	3			.960	-14	*S-142	-3.1
1933	Cin-N	16	51	6	11	1	0	1	3	4	5	.216	.273	.294	63	-2	0			.953	6	S-16	0.4
	StL-N	123	395	45	102	18	4	2	41	26	32	.258	.306	.339	80	-10	3			.961	-1	*S-123	-0.3
	Yr	139	446	51	113	19	4	3	44	30	37	.253	.302	.334	78	-13	3			**.960**	5	*S-139	0.1
1934	*StL-N	146	500	62	130	26	5	3	70	33	40	.260	.308	.350	71	-20	2			.957	1	*S-146	-1.1
1935	StL-N	143	513	62	136	23	5	8	78	29	46	.265	.304	.371	79	-16	4			.963	9	*S-142	0.1
1936	StL-N★	136	510	57	146	22	3	1	58	29	47	.286	.327	.347	82	-13	3			**.971**	-11	*S-136	-1.5
1937	StL-N	135	477	46	97	11	3	1	47	38	36	.203	.262	.245	38	-41	6			.959	-11	*S-134	-4.3
1938	Bro-N★	141	479	41	105	18	5	1	56	47	30	.219	.293	.284	58	-27	3			**.966**	-5	*S-141	-2.1
1939	Bro-N	116	390	42	108	21	6	1	34	27	24	.277	.325	.369	83	-9	2			.957	-7	S-113/3-1,M	-0.7
1940	Bro-N☆	62	160	10	37	9	1	1	14	12	13	.231	.285	.319	62	-8	1			.959	1	S-53/2-4,M	-0.4
1941	Bro-N	18	42	2	12	1	0	0	6	1	3	.286	.302	.310	70	-2	0			.917	-0	S-12/2-1,M	-0.1
1943	Bro-N	6	18	1	4	0	0	0	1	1	2	.222	.263	.222	41	-1	0			1.000	2	/S-6,M	0.1
1945	Bro-N	2	5	1	1	0	0	0	0	0	0	.200	.200	.200	11	-1	0			1.000	1	/2-2,M	0.0
Total	17	1637	5350	575	1320	210	56	24	567	377	480	.247	.299	.320	66	-262	31	5		.961	16	*S-1509/2-98,3-1	-13.4

■ **RED DURRETT**   Durrett, Elmer Cable   b: 2/3/21, Sherman, Tex.   d: 1/17/92, Waxahachie, Tex.   BL/TL, 5′10″, 170 lbs.   Deb: 9/14/44

YEAR	TM/L	G	AB	R	H	2B	3B	HR	RBI	BB	SO	AVG	OBP	SLG	PRO+	BR/A	SB	CS	SBR	FA	FR	G/POS	TPR
1944	Bro-N	11	32	3	5	1	0	1	1	7	10	.156	.308	.281	68	-1	0			.933	1	/O-9	0.0
1945	Bro-N	8	16	2	2	0	0	0	0	3	3	.125	.263	.125	10	-2	0			1.000	-1	/O-4	-0.3
Total	2	19	48	5	7	1	0	1	1	10	13	.146	.293	.229	48	-3	0			.947	1	/O-13	-0.3

■ **CEDRIC DURST**   Durst, Cedric Montgomery   b: 8/23/1896, Austin, Tex.   d: 2/16/71, San Diego, Cal.   BL/TL, 5′11″, 160 lbs.   Deb: 5/30/22

YEAR	TM/L	G	AB	R	H	2B	3B	HR	RBI	BB	SO	AVG	OBP	SLG	PRO+	BR/A	SB	CS	SBR	FA	FR	G/POS	TPR
1922	StL-A	15	12	5	4	1	0	0	0	0	1	.333	.333	.417	91	-0	0	0	0	.857	-2	/O-6	-0.2
1923	StL-A	45	85	12	18	0	5	0	11	8	14	.212	.280	.412	76	-4	0	0	0	.980	-2	O-10/1-8	-0.7
1926	StL-A	80	219	32	52	7	5	3	16	22	19	.237	.310	.356	70	-10	0	5	-3	.980	2	O-57/1-4	-1.5
1927	*NY-A	65	129	18	32	4	3	0	25	6	7	.248	.281	.326	59	-8	0	3	-2	.980	-7	O-36/1-2	-1.8
1928	*NY-A	74	135	18	34	2	1	2	10	7	9	.252	.289	.326	63	-7	1	0	0	.983	-3	O-33/1-3	-1.1
1929	NY-A	92	202	32	52	3	5	4	31	16	25	.257	.309	.361	77	-8	3	2	-0	.987	-0	O-72/1-1	-1.1
1930	NY-A	8	19	0	3	1	0	0	5	0	1	.158	.158	.211	-8	-3	0	0	0	1.000	-0	/O-6	-0.2
	Bos-A	102	302	29	74	19	5	1	24	17	24	.245	.290	.351	64	-17	3	1	0	.968	-2	O-75	-2.2
	Yr	110	321	29	77	20	5	1	29	17	25	.240	.282	.343	60	-20	3	1	0	.970	-2	O-81	-2.5
Total	7	481	1103	164	269	37	24	10	122	75	100	.244	.294	.351	67	-57	7	11	-5	.979	-15	O-295/1-18	-8.9

■ **ERV DUSAK**   Dusak, Ervin Frank "Four Sack"   b: 7/29/20, Chicago, Ill.   d: 11/6/94, Glendale Heights, Ill.   BR/TR, 6′2″, 185 lbs.   Deb: 9/18/41

YEAR	TM/L	G	AB	R	H	2B	3B	HR	RBI	BB	SO	AVG	OBP	SLG	PRO+	BR/A	SB	CS	SBR	FA	FR	G/POS	TPR
1941	StL-N	6	14	1	2	0	0	0	3	2	6	.143	.250	.143	12	-2	1			1.000	1	/O-4	0.0
1942	StL-N	12	27	4	5	3	0	0	3	3	7	.185	.267	.296	60	-1	0			1.000	0	/O-8,3-1	-0.1
1946	*StL-N	100	275	38	66	9	1	9	42	33	63	.240	.321	.378	94	-2	7			.993	3	O-77,3-11/2-2	-0.2
1947	StL-N	111	328	56	93	7	3	6	28	50	34	.284	.378	.378	97	0	1			.970	1	O-89/3-7	0.3
1948	StL-N	114	311	60	65	9	2	6	19	49	55	.209	.317	.309	66	-14				.992	-5	O-68,2-29/3-9,PS	-2.1
1949	StL-N	1	0	1	0	0						.000	—	—	—	-0	0			.000	0	R	0.0
1950	StL-N	23	12	1	1	0	0	0	0	0	3	.083	.083	.167	-34	-2	0			1.000	0	P-14/O-2	-0.1
1951	StL-N	5	2	1	1	0	0	1	1	0	1	.500	.500	2.000	537	1	0			1.000	0	/P-5	0.0
	Pit-N	21	39	6	12	3	0	1	7	3	11	.308	.357	.462	115	1	0			1.000	-6	O-12/P-3,2-2,3-2	-0.5
	Yr	26	41	7	13	3	0	2	8	3	12	.317	.364	.537	136	2	0			1.000	-6	O-12/P-8,2-2,3-2	-0.5
1952	Pit-N	20	27	1	6	0	0	0	3	2	8	.222	.276	.333	66	-1	0			.818	-2	O-11	-0.3
Total	9	413	1035	168	251	32	6	24	106	142	188	.243	.334	.355	84	-21	12	0		.981	-6	O-271/2-33,3-30,PS	-3.6

■ **AL DWIGHT**   Dwight, Albert Ward   b: 1/4/1856, New York, N.Y.   d: 2/20/03, San Francisco, Cal   Deb: 6/19/1884

YEAR	TM/L	G	AB	R	H	2B	3B	HR	RBI	BB	SO	AVG	OBP	SLG	PRO+	BR/A	SB	CS	SBR	FA	FR	G/POS	TPR
1884	KC-U	12	43	8	10	2	0	0				.233	.267	.279	75	-3				.953	-1	C-10/O-1,2-1	-0.2

■ **JIM DWYER**   Dwyer, James Edward "Pig Pen"   b: 1/3/50, Evergreen Park, Ill.   BL/TL, 5′10″, 175 lbs.   Deb: 6/10/73

YEAR	TM/L	G	AB	R	H	2B	3B	HR	RBI	BB	SO	AVG	OBP	SLG	PRO+	BR/A	SB	CS	SBR	FA	FR	G/POS	TPR
1973	StL-N	28	57	17	11	1	1	0	1	5	7	.193	.207	.246	25	-6	0	0	0	1.000	-2	O-20	-0.9
1974	StL-N	74	86	13	24	1	0	2	11	11	16	.279	.367	.360	105	1	0	0	0	1.000	-3	O-25/1-3	-0.3
1975	StL-N	21	31	4	6	1	0	0	4	5	8	.194	.286	.226	42	-2	0	0	0	1.000	-1	/O-9	-0.3
	Mon-N	60	175	22	50	7	1	3	20	23	30	.286	.389	.389	106	2	4	1	1	.959	1	O-52	0.2
	Yr	81	206	26	56	8	1	3	21	27	36	.272	.356	.364	96	-0	4	1	1	.966	1	O-61	-0.1
1976	Mon-N	50	92	7	17	3	1	0	5	11	10	.185	.272	.239	44	-7	0	0	0	.970	-2	O-19	-1.0
	NY-N	11	13	2	2	0	0	0	0	2	1	.154	.267	.154	23	-1	0	0	0	1.000	-0	/O-2	-0.2
	Yr	61	105	9	19	3	1	0	5	13	11	.181	.271	.229	42	-8	0	0	0	.972	-2	O-21	-1.2
1977	StL-N	13	31	3	7	1	0	0	2	4	5	.226	.351	.258	68	-1	0	0	0	1.000	26	O-12	-0.4
1978	StL-N	34	65	8	14	3	0	1	4	9	3	.215	.320	.308	77	-1	2	1	0	.952	-4	O-22	-0.7
	SF-N	73	173	22	39	9	0	5	22	28	29	.225	.333	.387	105	1	6	0	2	.987	1	O-36,1-29	0.2
	Yr	107	238	30	53	12	2	6	26	37	32	.223	.329	.366	97	-1	8	1	2	.979	-3	O-58,1-29	-0.5
1979	Bos-A	76	113	19	30	7	0	2	14	17	9	.265	.366	.381	96	-0	3	1	0	.981	-0	1-25,O-19/D-4	-0.1
1980	Bos-A	93	260	41	74	11	4	9	38	28	23	.285	.359	.438	111	4	3	2	-0	.975	-3	O-65,D-12/1-9	-0.1
1981	Bal-A	68	134	16	30	0	1	3	10	20	19	.224	.325	.306	83	-2	0	0	-1	.977	-11	O-59/1-3,D-1	-1.6
1982	Bal-A	71	148	28	45	4	3	6	15	27	24	.304	.411	.493	148	11	2	0	-1	.976	-8	O-49/1-1,D-1	0.3

YEAR	TM/L	G	AB	R	H	2B	3B	HR	RBI	BB	SO	AVG	OBP	SLG	PRO+	BR/A	SB	CS	SBR	FA	FR	G/POS	TPR
1983	*Bal-A	100	196	37	56	17	1	8	38	31	29	.286	.383	.505	145	13	1	1	-0	.966	-7	O-56,D-10/1-4	0.3
1984	Bal-A	76	161	22	41	9	1	2	21	23	24	.255	.348	.360	98	0	0	2	-1	.966	-4	O-52/D-3	-0.6
1985	Bal-A	101	233	35	58	8	3	7	36	37	31	.249	.354	.399	109	4	0	3	-2	.993	-3	O-78/D-3	-0.3
1986	Bal-A	94	160	18	39	13	1	8	31	23	31	.244	.346	.488	126	6	0	2	-1	1.000	-0	O-24,D-24/1-1	0.3
1987	Bal-A	92	241	54	66	7	1	15	33	37	57	.274	.387	.498	132	11	4	1	1	1.000	-1	D-41,O-30	0.9
1988	Bal-A	35	53	3	12	0	0	0	3	12	11	.226	.369	.226	73	-1	0	0	0	1.000	-0	D-17/O-2	-0.2
	Min-A	20	41	6	12	1	0	2	15	13	8	.293	.473	.463	159	4	0	0	0	.000	0	D-13	0.4
	Yr	55	94	9	24	1	0	2	18	25	19	.255	.417	.330	113	3	0	0	0	1.000	-0	D-30/O-2	0.2
1989	Min-A	88	225	34	71	11	0	3	23	28	23	.316	.391	.404	117	6	2	0	1	.000	-0	D-74/O-1	0.4
	Mon-N	13	10	1	3	1	0	0	2	1	1	.300	.364	.400	116	0	0	0	0	.000	0	H	0.0
1990	Min-A	37	63	7	12	0	0	1	5	12	7	.190	.320	.238	55	-3	0	0	0	1.000	-0	D-23/O-2	-0.5
Total	18	1328	2761	409	719	115	17	77	349	402	402	.260	.357	.398	107	37	26	15	-1	.979	-50	O-634,D-226/1-75	-4.2

■ JOHN DWYER
Dwyer, John E.   Deb: 5/16/1882

YEAR	TM/L	G	AB	R	H	2B	3B	HR	RBI	BB	SO	AVG	OBP	SLG	PRO+	BR/A	SB	CS	SBR	FA	FR	G/POS	TPR
1882	Cle-N	1	3	0	0	0	0	0	1	0	0	.000	.000	.000	-99	-1				.000	-1	/O-1,C-1	-0.2

■ DOUBLE JOE DWYER
Dwyer, Joseph Michael   b: 3/27/03, Orange, N.J.   d: 10/21/92, Glen Ridge, N.J.   BL/TL, 5'9", 186 lbs.   Deb: 4/20/37

YEAR	TM/L	G	AB	R	H	2B	3B	HR	RBI	BB	SO	AVG	OBP	SLG	PRO+	BR/A	SB	CS	SBR	FA	FR	G/POS	TPR
1937	Cin-N	12	11	2	3	0	0	0	3	1	0	.273	.333	.273	70	-0				.000	0	H	0.0

■ JERRY DYBZINSKI
Dybzinski, Jerome Matthew   b: 7/7/55, Cleveland, Ohio   BR/TR, 6'2", 180 lbs.   Deb: 4/11/80

YEAR	TM/L	G	AB	R	H	2B	3B	HR	RBI	BB	SO	AVG	OBP	SLG	PRO+	BR/A	SB	CS	SBR	FA	FR	G/POS	TPR
1980	Cle-A	114	248	32	57	11	1	1	23	13	35	.230	.274	.294	55	-15	4	1	1	.971	21	S-73,2-29/3-4,D-2	1.3
1981	Cle-A	48	57	10	17	0	0	0	6	5	8	.298	.355	.298	91	-0	7	1	2	.970	8	S-34/2-3,3-3,D-1	1.1
1982	Cle-A	80	212	19	49	6	2	0	22	21	25	.231	.309	.278	63	-10	3	5	-2	.957	17	S-77/3-3	1.1
1983	*Chi-A	127	256	30	59	10	1	1	32	18	29	.230	.286	.289	57	-15	11	4	1	.966	-1	*S-118/3-9	-0.5
1984	Chi-A	94	132	17	31	5	1	1	10	13	12	.235	.313	.311	70	-5	7	2	1	.974	18	S-76,3-14/2-1,D-1	1.8
1985	Pit-N	5	4	0	0	0	0	0	0	0	0	.000	.000	.000	-99	-1	0	0	0	.900	1	/S-5	0.0
Total	6	468	909	108	213	32	5	3	93	70	109	.234	.296	.290	61	-47	32	13	2	.966	67	S-383/3-33,2-33,D-4	4.8

■ JIM DYCK
Dyck, James Robert   b: 2/3/22, Omaha, Neb.   BR/TR, 6'2", 205 lbs.   Deb: 9/27/51

YEAR	TM/L	G	AB	R	H	2B	3B	HR	RBI	BB	SO	AVG	OBP	SLG	PRO+	BR/A	SB	CS	SBR	FA	FR	G/POS	TPR
1951	StL-A	4	15	1	1	0	0	0	0	0	1	.067	.125	.067	-46	-3	0	0	0	1.000	0	/3-4	-0.3
1952	StL-A	122	402	60	108	22	3	15	64	50	68	.269	.354	.450	119	10	0	4	-2	.962	9	3-74,O-48	1.4
1953	StL-A	112	334	38	71	15	1	9	27	38	40	.213	.299	.344	72	-14	3	2	-0	.981	-6	O-55,3-51	-2.3
1954	Cle-A	2	1	0	1	0	0	0	0	1	0	1.000	1.000	1.000	441	1	0	0	0	.000	0	H	0.1
1955	Bal-A	61	197	32	55	13	1	2	22	22	21	.279	.372	.386	112	4	0	0	0	.989	0	O-45,3-17	0.2
1956	Bal-A	11	23	3	5	2	0	0	0	10	5	.217	.455	.304	112	1	0	0	0	.923	-0	/O-9	0.1
	Cin-N	18	11	5	1	0	0	0	0	3	5	.091	.286	.091	7	-1	0	0	0	1.000	0	/1-1,3-1	-0.1
Total	6	330	983	139	242	52	5	26	114	131	140	.246	.339	.389	98	-2	4	6	-2	.982	3	O-157,3-147/1-1	-0.9

■ JERMAINE DYE
Dye, Jermaine Terrell   b: 1/28/74, Oakland, Cal.   BR/TR, 6'4", 210 lbs.   Deb: 5/17/96

YEAR	TM/L	G	AB	R	H	2B	3B	HR	RBI	BB	SO	AVG	OBP	SLG	PRO+	BR/A	SB	CS	SBR	FA	FR	G/POS	TPR
1996	*Atl-N	98	292	32	82	16	0	12	37	8	67	.281	.307	.459	93	-4	1	4	-2	.950	-6	O-92	-1.4

■ BEN DYER
Dyer, Benjamin Franklin   b: 2/13/1893, Chicago, Ill.   d: 8/7/59, Kenosha, Wis.   BR/TR, 5'10", 170 lbs.   Deb: 5/23/14

YEAR	TM/L	G	AB	R	H	2B	3B	HR	RBI	BB	SO	AVG	OBP	SLG	PRO+	BR/A	SB	CS	SBR	FA	FR	G/POS	TPR
1914	NY-N	7	4	1	1	0	0	0	0	0	1	.250	.250	.250	50	-0	1			1.000	1	/S-6,2-1	0.1
1915	NY-N	7	19	4	4	0	1	0	0	4	3	.211	.375	.316	117	1	0			.889	-1	/3-6,S-1	-0.1
1916	Det-A	4	14	4	4	1	0	0	1	1	1	.286	.333	.357	104	0	0			1.000	-2	/S-4	-0.2
1917	Det-A	30	67	6	14	5	0	0	0	2	17	.209	.232	.284	57	-4	3			.846	2	S-14/3-8	-0.1
1918	Det-A	13	18	1	5	0	0	0	2	0	6	.278	.278	.278	71	-1	0			1.000	0	/P-2,1-2,O-2,2-1	-0.1
1919	Det-A	44	85	11	21	4	0	0	15	8	19	.247	.312	.294	72	-3	0			.953	6	3-23,S-11/O-1	0.4
Total	6	105	207	27	49	10	1	0	18	15	47	.237	.291	.295	74	-7	4			.937	7	/3-37,S-36,O-3,1P2	0.2

■ DUFFY DYER
Dyer, Don Robert   b: 8/15/45, Dayton, Ohio   BR/TR, 6', 195 lbs.   Deb: 9/21/68   C

YEAR	TM/L	G	AB	R	H	2B	3B	HR	RBI	BB	SO	AVG	OBP	SLG	PRO+	BR/A	SB	CS	SBR	FA	FR	G/POS	TPR
1968	NY-N	1	3	0	1	0	0	0	0	0	1	.333	.500	.333	153	0	0	0	0	1.000	0	/C-1	0.1
1969	*NY-N	29	74	5	19	3	1	3	12	4	22	.257	.295	.446	103	-0	0	0	0	.991	-1	C-19	0.0
1970	NY-N	59	148	8	31	1	0	2	12	21	32	.209	.308	.257	53	-9	1	1	-0	.991	2	C-57	-0.6
1971	NY-N	59	169	13	39	7	1	2	18	14	45	.231	.293	.320	75	-6	0	1	-0	.992	0	C-53	-0.4
1972	NY-N	94	325	33	75	17	3	8	36	28	71	.231	.302	.375	94	-3	0	1	-1	.993	18	C-91/O-1	1.9
1973	NY-N	70	189	9	35	6	1	1	9	13	40	.185	.245	.243	36	-16	0	1	-1	.994	-1	C-60	-1.7
1974	NY-N	63	142	14	30	1	1	0	10	18	15	.211	.304	.232	53	-8	0	0	0	.982	-4	C-45	-1.2
1975	*Pit-N	48	132	8	30	5	3	2	16	6	22	.227	.266	.364	74	-5	0	0	0	.990	6	C-36	0.2
1976	Pit-N	69	184	12	41	8	0	3	9	29	35	.223	.338	.315	85	-3	0	0	0	.994	7	C-58	0.6
1977	Pit-N	94	270	27	65	11	1	3	19	54	49	.241	.373	.322	86	-3	6	0	2	**.996**	3	C-93	0.6
1978	Pit-N	58	175	7	37	8	0	0	13	18	32	.211	.296	.269	56	-10	2	1	0	.991	6	C-55	0.6
1979	Mon-N	28	74	4	18	6	0	1	8	9	17	.243	.325	.365	89	-1	0	0	0	.993	7	C-27	0.6
1980	Det-A	48	108	11	20	1	0	4	11	13	34	.185	.273	.306	57	-0	0	0	0	.986	3	C-37,D-10	-0.3
1981	Det-A	2	0	0	0	0	0	0	0	0	0	—	—	—	—	0	0	0	0	.000	0	/C-2	0.0
Total	14	722	1993	151	441	74	11	30	173	228	415	.221	.307	.315	73	-71	10	4	1	.992	46	C-634/D-10,O-1	-0.5

■ EDDIE DYER
Dyer, Edwin Hawley   b: 10/11/1900, Morgan City, La.   d: 4/20/64, Houston, Tex.   BL/TL, 5'11.5", 168 lbs.   Deb: 7/8/22   M

YEAR	TM/L	G	AB	R	H	2B	3B	HR	RBI	BB	SO	AVG	OBP	SLG	PRO+	BR/A	SB	CS	SBR	FA	FR	G/POS	TPR
1922	StL-N	6	3	1	1	1	0	0	0	0	0	.333	.333	.667	159	0	0	0	0	1.000	0	/P-2	0.0
1923	StL-N	35	45	17	12	3	0	2	5	3	5	.267	.313	.467	105	0	1	0	0	1.000	-1	/O-8,P-4	-0.1
1924	StL-N	50	76	8	18	2	3	0	8	3	8	.237	.266	.342	63	-4	0	0	0	.909	0	P-29/O-1	-0.1
1925	StL-N	31	31	4	3	1	0	0	0	3	1	.097	.176	.129	-20	-6	1	1	-0	.917	0	P-27	0.0
1926	StL-N	6	2	1	1	0	0	0	0	0	0	.500	.500	.500	164	0	0	0	0	1.000	0	/P-6	0.0
1927	StL-N	1	0	0	0	0	0	0	0	0	1	—	1.000	—	181	0	0	0	0	.000	-0	/P-1	0.0
Total	6	129	157	31	35	7	3	2	13	10	14	.223	.269	.344	61	-9	3		<u>1</u>	.921	-0	/P-69,O-9	-0.2

■ JIMMY DYKES
Dykes, James Joseph   b: 11/10/1896, Philadelphia, Pa.   d: 6/15/76, Philadelphia, Pa.   BR/TR, 5'9", 185 lbs.   Deb: 5/6/18   MC

YEAR	TM/L	G	AB	R	H	2B	3B	HR	RBI	BB	SO	AVG	OBP	SLG	PRO+	BR/A	SB	CS	SBR	FA	FR	G/POS	TPR
1918	Phi-A	59	186	13	35	3	3	0	13	19	32	.188	.267	.237	51	-11	3			.940	10	2-56/3-1	0.3
1919	Phi-A	17	49	4	9	1	0	0	1	7	11	.184	.286	.204	38	-4	0			.945	6	2-16	0.1
1920	Phi-A	142	546	81	140	25	4	6	35	55	73	.256	.334	.361	83	-13	6	9	-4	.957	17	*2-108,3-34	0.6
1921	Phi-A	155	613	88	168	32	13	16	77	60	75	.274	.343	.447	102	1	6	5	-1	.954	25	*2-155	2.7
1922	Phi-A	145	501	66	138	23	7	12	68	50	98	.275	.359	.421	100	0	6	4	-1	.945	-8	*3-141/2-5	-0.4
1923	Phi-A	124	416	50	105	28	1	4	43	35	40	.252	.318	.353	76	-15	6	4	-1	.964	4	*2-102,S-20/3-2	-0.9
1924	Phi-A	110	410	68	128	26	6	3	58	38	60	.312	.372	.427	105	3	1	3	-2	.961	16	2-77,3-27/S-4	1.9
1925	Phi-A	122	465	93	150	32	11	5	55	49	34	.323	.393	.471	111	8	3	2	0	.944	10	3-64,2-58/S-2	2.1
1926	Phi-A	124	429	54	123	32	5	1	44	49	34	.287	.370	.392	93	-3	6	2	1	.950	**26**	3-82,2-44/S-1	2.8
1927	Phi-A	121	417	61	135	33	6	3	60	44	23	.324	.394	.453	113	8	2	3	-1	.989	-3	1-82,3-25/S-5,O2P	0.0
1928	Phi-A	85	242	39	67	11	0	5	30	27	21	.277	.361	.384	93	-2	2	2	-1	.982	-2	2-32,S-22,3-20,/1O	0.0
1929	*Phi-A	119	401	76	131	34	6	13	79	51	25	.327	.412	.539	138	23	8	3	1	.928	-11	S-60,3-48,2-12	2.1
1930	*Phi-A	125	435	69	131	28	4	6	73	74	53	.301	.414	.425	109	-3	3	3	-1	.960	-13	*3-123/O-1	0.2
1931	*Phi-A	101	355	48	97	28	3	2	46	49	47	.273	.371	.389	94	-2	1	2	-1	.974	-2	3-87,S-15	0.2
1932	Phi-A	153	558	71	148	29	5	7	90	77	65	.265	.358	.373	87	-10	8	2	1	**.980**	-5	*3-141,S-10/2-1	-0.2
1933	Chi-A★	151	554	49	144	22	6	1	68	69	37	.260	.354	.327	85	-9	3	7	0	.953	-1	*3-151	-0.4
1934	Chi-A☆	127	456	52	122	17	4	7	82	64	28	.268	.363	.368	86	-8	1	4	0	.944	-5	3-74,1-27,2-27,M	-1.0
1935	Chi-A	117	403	45	116	24	2	4	61	59	28	.288	.381	.387	97	-0	4	3	-1	.953	-5	3-98,1-16/2-3,M	-0.4
1936	Chi-A	127	435	62	116	36	1	3	60	61	36	.267	.362	.366	77	-15	1	3	-1	.951	-6	3-125,M	-1.7
1937	Chi-A	30	85	10	26	5	0	1	23	9	7	.306	.372	.400	95	-1	0	0	0	.993	0	1-15,3-11,M	0.1
1938	Chi-A	26	89	9	27	4	2	0	13	10	8	.303	.374	.461	105	1	0	0	0	.941	1	2-23/S-1,3-1,M	0.1
1939	Chi-A	2	1	0	0	0	0	0	0	0	0	.000	.000	.000	-97	-0	0	0	0	.667	0	/3-2,M	0.0
Total	22	2282	8046	1108	2256	453	90	108	1071	958	850	.280	.365	.399	96	-42	70	<u>55</u>		.952	56	*3-1257,2-722,1S/OP	9.2

YEAR	TM/L	G	AB	R	H	2B	3B	HR	RBI	BB	SO	AVG	OBP	SLG	PRO+	BR/A	SB	CS	SBR	FA	FR	G/POS	TPR

■ LENNY DYKSTRA　　Dykstra, Leonard Kyle　b: 2/10/63, Santa Ana, Cal.　　BL/TL, 5'10", 167 lbs.　Deb: 5/3/85

1985	NY-N	83	236	40	60	9	3	1	19	30	24	.254	.341	.331	91	-2	15	2	3	.994	4	O-74	0.3
1986	*NY-N	147	431	77	127	27	7	8	45	58	55	.295	.378	.445	130	18	31	7	5	.990	4	*O-139	2.4
1987	NY-N	132	431	86	123	37	3	10	43	40	67	.285	.352	.455	118	10	27	7	4	.988	1	*O-118	1.1
1988	*NY-N	126	429	57	116	19	3	8	33	30	43	.270	.323	.385	107	3	30	8	4	.996	7	*O-112	1.2
1989	NY-N	56	159	27	43	12	1	3	13	23	15	.270	.370	.415	130	7	13	1	3	.984	2	O-51	1.2
	Phi-N	90	352	39	78	20	3	4	19	37	38	.222	.297	.330	79	-10	17	11	-2	.991	7	O-88	-0.7
	Yr	146	511	66	121	32	4	7	32	60	53	.237	.321	.356	95	-3	30	12	2	.988	9	*O-139	0.5
1990	Phi-N★	149	590	106	**192**	35	3	9	60	89	48	.325	.420	.441	137	35	33	5	7	.987	20	O-149	5.8
1991	Phi-N	63	246	48	73	13	5	3	12	37	20	.297	.391	.427	131	11	24	4	5	.977	8	O-63	2.3
1992	Phi-N	85	345	53	104	18	0	6	39	40	32	.301	.379	.406	123	11	30	5	6	.989	13	O-85	3.0
1993	*Phi-N	161	637	**143**	**194**	44	6	19	66	**129**	64	.305	.423	.482	144	45	37	12	4	.979	17	O-160	6.1
1994	Phi-N†	84	315	68	86	26	5	5	24	68	44	.273	.405	.435	116	10	15	4	2	.984	9	O-82	1.9
1995	Phi-N★	62	254	37	67	15	1	2	18	33	28	.264	.355	.354	87	-4	10	5	0	.987	6	O-61	0.1
1996	Phi-N	40	134	21	35	6	3	3	13	26	25	.261	.389	.418	110	3	3	1	0	1.000	7	O-39	0.8
Total	12	1278	4559	802	1298	281	43	81	404	640	503	.285	.376	.419	120	139	285	72	42	.987	103	*O-1221	25.5

■ JOHN DYLER　　Dyler, John F.　b: 6/1852, Louisville, Ky.　　Deb: 7/22/1882　U

1882	Lou-a	1	4	0	0	0	0	0	0		0	.000	.000	.000	-99	-1				.000	-0	/O-1	-0.1

■ DON EADDY　　Eaddy, Donald Johnson　b: 2/16/34, Grand Rapids, Mich　BR/TR, 5'11", 165 lbs.　Deb: 4/24/59

1959	Chi-N	15	1	3	0	0	0	0	0	0	1	.000	.000	.000	-99	-0				.500	1	/3-1	0.0

■ TRUCK EAGAN　　Eagan, Charles Eugene　b: 8/10/1877, San Francisco, Cal　d: 3/19/49, San Francisco, Cal　BR/TR, 5'11", 190 lbs.　Deb: 5/1/01

1901	Pit-N	4	12	0	1	0	0	0	2	0		.083	.083	.083	-50	-2	1			.923	-1	/S-3	-0.3
	Cle-A	5	18	2	3	0	1	0	2	1		.167	.211	.278	36	-2	0			1.000	1	/2-5,3-1	-0.1
Total	1	9	30	2	4	0	1	0	4	1		.133	.161	.200	2	-4	1			1.000	-1	/2-5,S-3,3-1	-0.4

■ BILL EAGAN　　Eagan, William "Bad Bill"　b: 6/1/1869, Camden, N.J.　d: 2/13/05, Denver, Colo.　Deb: 4/8/1891

1891	StL-a	83	302	49	65	11	4	4	43	44	54	.215	.321	.318	72	-14	21			.929	20	2-83	0.8
1893	Chi-N	6	19	3	5	0	0	0	2	5	5	.263	.417	.263	83	-0	4			.912	0	/2-6	0.0
1898	Pit-N	19	61	14	20	2	3	0	5	8		.328	.453	.459	165	6	1			.914	3	2-17	0.9
Total	3	108	382	66	90	13	7	4	50	57	59	.236	.348	.338	86	-8	26			.925	23	2-106	1.7

■ BILL EAGLE　　Eagle, William Lycurgus　b: 7/25/1877, Rockville, Md.　d: 4/27/51, Churchton, Md.　Deb: 8/20/1898

1898	Was-N	4	13	0	4	1	0	0	2	0		.308	.308	.385	98	-0	1			.750	0	/O-4	0.0

■ CHARLIE EAKLE　　Eakle, Charles Emory　b: 9/27/1887, Maryland　d: 6/15/59, Baltimore, Md.　Deb: 8/20/15

1915	Bal-F	2	7	0	2	0	0	0	0	0		.286	.286	.429	97	-0	1			.600	-2	/2-2	-0.3

■ HOWARD EARL　　Earl, Howard J. "Slim Jim"　b: 2/27/1869, Massachusetts　d: 12/22/16, North Bay, N.Y.　6'2", 180 lbs.　Deb: 4/19/1890

1890	Chi-N	92	384	57	95	10	3	7	51	18	47	.247	.285	.344	80	-12	17			.861	-4	O-49,2-39/S-4,1-3	-1.3
1891	Mil-a	31	129	21	32	5	2	1	17	5	13	.248	.281	.341	65	-8	3			.978	-1	O-30/1-2	-0.9
Total	2	123	513	78	127	15	5	8	68	23	60	.248	.284	.343	76	-20	20			.904	-5	/O-79,2-39,1-5,S-4	-2.2

■ SCOTT EARL　　Earl, William Scott　b: 9/18/60, Seymour, Ind.　BR/TR, 5'11", 165 lbs.　Deb: 9/10/84

1984	Det-A	14	35	3	4	0	1	0	1	0	9	.114	.114	.171	-22	-6	1	0	0	.959	1	2-14	-0.4

■ BILLY EARLE　　Earle, William Moffat "The Little Globetrotter"　b: 11/10/1867, Philadelphia, Pa.　d: 5/30/46, Omaha, Neb.　BR/TR, 5'10.5", 170 lbs.　Deb: 4/27/1889

1889	Cin-a	53	169	37	45	4	7	4	31	30	24	.266	.386	.444	132	7	26			.776	-2	O-26,C-23/1-5	0.5
1890	StL-a	22	73	16	17	3	1	0	12	7		.233	.317	.301	72	-3	6			.955	5	C-18/O-3,S-1,3-1,2	0.3
1892	Pit-N	5	13	5	7	2	0	0	3	4	1	.538	.647	.692	304	4	2			.909	-1	/C-5	0.3
1893	Pit-N	27	95	21	24	4	4	2	15	7	6	.253	.304	.442	99	-1	1			.959	1	C-27	0.1
1894	Lou-N	21	65	10	23	1	0	0	7	9	3	.354	.432	.369	102	1	2			.954	3	C-18/1-1,2-1,3-1,0	0.4
	Bro-N	14	50	13	17	6	0	0	6	6	2	.340	.421	.460	121	2	4			.930	-2	C-12/2-1	0.1
	Yr	35	115	23	40	7	0	0	13	15	5	.348	.427	.409	110	3	6			.944	2	C-30/2-2,1-1,3-1,0	0.5
Total	5	142	465	102	133	20	12	6	74	63	36	.286	.378	.419	114	10	41			.929	5	C-103/O-30,1-6,23S	1.7

■ JAKE EARLY　　Early, Jacob Willard　b: 5/19/15, Kings Mountain, N.C.　d: 5/31/85, Melbourne, Fla.　BL/TR, 5'11", 168 lbs.　Deb: 5/4/39

1939	Was-A	32	84	8	22	7	2	0	14	5	14	.262	.303	.393	83	-3	0	0	-0	.963	-1	C-24	-0.2
1940	Was-A	80	206	26	53	8	4	5	14	23	22	.257	.335	.408	98	-1	0	1	-1	.969	5	C-56	0.7
1941	Was-A	104	355	42	102	20	7	10	54	24	38	.287	.338	.448	117	6	6	0	-1	.965	-11	*C-100	0.3
1942	Was-A	104	353	31	72	14	2	3	46	37	37	.204	.281	.280	59	-19	0	0	-0	.981	-2	C-98	-1.5
1943	Was-A★	126	423	37	109	23	2	5	60	53	43	.258	.346	.362	111	6	5	3	-0	.980	-8	*C-122	0.7
1946	Was-A	64	189	13	38	6	0	4	18	23	27	.201	.288	.296	67	-9	0	0	-0	.960	2	C-64	-0.3
1947	StL-A	87	214	25	48	9	3	3	19	54	34	.224	.381	.336	98	2	0	1	-1	.989	3	C-85	0.3
1948	Was-A	97	246	22	54	7	2	1	28	36	33	.220	.322	.276	62	-13	2	1	-0	.991	4	C-92	-0.5
1949	Was-A	53	138	12	34	4	0	1	11	26	11	.246	.370	.297	79	-3	0	1	-1	.973	-4	C-53	-0.4
Total	9	747	2208	216	532	98	23	32	264	281	259	.241	.330	.350	89	-33	7	8	-3	.976	-19	C-694	-0.9

■ MIKE EASLER　　Easler, Michael Anthony　b: 11/29/50, Cleveland, Ohio　BL/TR, 6'1", 196 lbs.　Deb: 9/5/73　C

1973	Hou-N	6	7	1	0	0	0	0	0	2	4	.000	.222	.000	-34	-1	0	0	0	.500	-1	/O-2	-0.2
1974	Hou-N	15	15	0	1	0	0	0	0	0	5	.067	.067	.067	-65	-3	0	0	0	.000	0	H	-0.4
1975	Hou-N	5	5	0	0	0	0	0	0	0	1	.000	.000	.000	-99	-1	0	0	0	.000	0	H	-0.2
1976	Cal-A	21	54	6	13	1	1	0	4	2	11	.241	.268	.296	69	-2	1	1	-0	.000	0	D-16	-0.3
1977	Pit-N	10	18	3	8	0	1	0	5	0	1	.444	.444	.722	202	3	0	0	0	1.000	-0	/O-4	0.2
1979	*Pit-N	55	54	8	15	1	1	2	11	8	13	.278	.371	.444	116	1	0	1	-1	.000	-2	/O-4	-0.1
1980	Pit-N	132	393	66	133	27	3	21	74	43	65	.338	.404	.583	170	36	5	5	-4	.986	-8	*O-119	2.1
1981	Pit-N★	95	339	43	97	18	5	7	42	24	45	.286	.333	.431	112	5	4	7	-3	.980	7	O-90	0.6
1982	Pit-N	142	475	52	131	27	2	15	58	40	85	.276	.340	.454	112	7	1	1	-0	.973	1	*O-138	0.4
1983	Pit-N	115	381	44	117	17	2	10	54	22	64	.307	.350	.441	115	7	4	2	0	.965	-3	*O-105	0.1
1984	Bos-A	156	601	87	188	31	5	27	91	58	134	.313	.377	.516	138	31	1	1	-0	.976	2	*D-126,1-29	2.7
1985	Bos-A	155	568	71	149	29	4	16	74	53	102	.262	.329	.412	97	-2	0	1	-1	.914	-2	*D-130,O-20	-0.8
1986	NY-A	146	490	64	148	26	2	14	78	49	87	.302	.365	.449	122	15	2	1	0	.958	-1	*D-129,O-11	1.2
1987	Phi-N	33	110	7	31	4	0	1	10	6	20	.282	.319	.345	74	-4	0	1	-0	.981	0	O-30	-0.4
	NY-A	65	167	13	47	6	0	4	21	14	32	.281	.341	.394	94	-1	1	0	0	1.000	-0	D-32,O-15	-0.3
Total	14	1151	3677	465	1078	189	25	118	522	321	696	.293	.353	.454	118	88	20	26	-10	.974	-5	O-538,D-433/1-29	4.6

■ DAMION EASLEY　　Easley, Jacinto Damion　b: 11/11/69, New York, N.Y.　BR/TR, 5'11", 155 lbs.　Deb: 8/13/92

1992	Cal-A	47	151	14	39	5	0	1	12	8	26	.258	.309	.311	74	-5	9	5	-0	.970	8	3-45/S-3	0.3
1993	Cal-A	73	230	33	72	13	2	2	22	28	35	.313	.395	.413	114	5	6	6	-2	.978	-11	2-54,3-14/D-1	-0.5
1994	Cal-A	88	316	41	68	16	1	6	30	29	48	.215	.289	.329	58	-20	4	5	-2	.953	-7	3-47,2-40	-2.5
1995	Cal-A	114	357	35	77	14	2	4	35	32	47	.216	.291	.300	55	-24	5	2	-0	.981	-8	2-88,S-25	-2.3
1996	Cal-A	28	45	4	7	1	0	2	7	6	12	.156	.255	.311	43	-4	0	0	0	.943	3	S-13/2-9,3-3,O-2,D	0.0
	Det-A	21	67	10	23	1	0	2	10	4	13	.343	.389	.448	112	1	3	1	0	.974	-1	2-8,S-8,3-2,D-1	0.1
	Yr	49	112	14	30	2	0	4	17	10	25	.268	.333	.393	84	-3	3	1	0	.951	2	S-21,2-17/3-5,DO	0.1
Total	5	371	1166	137	286	50	5	17	116	107	181	.245	.318	.340	73	-46	27	19	-3	.982	-15	2-199,3-111/SDO	-4.9

■ CARL EAST　　East, Carlton William　b: 8/27/1894, Marietta, Ga.　d: 1/15/53, Whitesburg, Ga.　BL/TR, 6'2", 178 lbs.　Deb: 8/24/15

1915	StL-A	1	1	0	0	0	0	0	0	0	0	.000	.000	.000	-99	-0	1			.000	-0	/P-1	0.0

YEAR	TM/L	G	AB	R	H	2B	3B	HR	RBI	BB	SO	AVG	OBP	SLG	PRO+	BR/A	SB	CS	SBR	FA	FR	G/POS	TPR
1924	Was-A	2	6	1	2	1	0	0	2	2	1	.333	.500	.500	163	1	0	0	0	.800	-0	/O-2	0.0
Total	2	3	7	1	2	1	0	0	2	2	1	.286	.444	.429	134	0	0	0		.800	-1	/O-2,P-1	0.0

■ HARRY EAST   East, Henry H.   b: 4/1863, St.Louis, Mo.   Deb: 6/17/1882

YEAR	TM/L	G	AB	R	H	2B	3B	HR	RBI	BB	SO	AVG	OBP	SLG	PRO+	BR/A	SB	CS	SBR	FA	FR	G/POS	TPR
1882	Bal-a	1	4	0	0	0	0	0		0		.000	.000	.000	-99	-1				.600	-0	/3-1	-0.1

■ LUKE EASTER   Easter, Luscious Luke   b: 8/4/15, Jonestown, Miss.   d: 3/29/79, Euclid, Ohio   BL/TR, 6'4.5", 240 lbs.   Deb: 8/11/49 C

YEAR	TM/L	G	AB	R	H	2B	3B	HR	RBI	BB	SO	AVG	OBP	SLG	PRO+	BR/A	SB	CS	SBR	FA	FR	G/POS	TPR
1949	Cle-A	21	45	6	10	3	0	0	2	8	6	.222	.340	.289	68	-2	0	1	-1	1.000	-4	O-12	-0.7
1950	Cle-A	141	540	96	151	20	4	28	107	70	95	.280	.373	.487	123	17	0	3	-2	.991	-3	*1-128,O-13	0.8
1951	Cle-A	128	486	65	131	12	5	27	103	37	71	.270	.333	.481	125	13	0	1	-1	.988	-7	*1-125	0.0
1952	Cle-A	127	437	63	115	10	3	31	97	44	84	.263	.337	.513	144	22	1	1	-0	.983	4	*1-118	2.2
1953	Cle-A	68	211	26	64	9	0	7	31	15	35	.303	.361	.445	120	5	0	2	-1	.981	-2	1-56	0.0
1954	Cle-A	6	6	0	1	0	0	0	0	0	2	.167	.167	.167	-8	-1	0	0	0	.000	0	H	-0.1
Total	6	491	1725	256	472	54	12	93	340	174	293	.274	.350	.481	126	55	1	8	-5	.986	-12	1-427/O-25	2.2

■ HENRY EASTERDAY   Easterday, Henry P.   b: 9/16/1864, Philadelphia, Pa.   d: 3/30/1895, Philadelphia, Pa.   BR/TR, 5'6", 145 lbs.   Deb: 6/23/1884

YEAR	TM/L	G	AB	R	H	2B	3B	HR	RBI	BB	SO	AVG	OBP	SLG	PRO+	BR/A	SB	CS	SBR	FA	FR	G/POS	TPR
1884	Phi-U	28	115	12	28	5	0	0		5		.243	.275	.287	76	-7				.875	6	S-28	0.0
1888	KC-a	115	401	42	76	7	6	3	37	31		.190	.256	.259	61	-18	23			.888	26	*S-115	1.0
1889	Col-a	95	324	43	56	5	8	4	34	41	57	.173	.270	.275	58	-17	10			.890	12	S-89/2-5,3-1	-0.5
1890	Col-a	58	197	25	31	5	1	0	17	23		.157	.249	.208	37	-15	5			.879	8	S-58	-0.5
	Phi-a	19	68	17	10	1	0	1	3	10		.147	.256	.206	37	-5	4			.860	-2	S-19	-0.5
	Lou-a	7	24	2	2	0	0	0	1	2		.083	.154	.083	-21	-4	1			.886	1	/S-6,3-1	-0.2
	Yr	84	289	44	43	6	1	2	21	35		.149	.245	.197	32	-24	10			.875	8	S-83/3-1	-1.2
Total	4	322	1129	141	203	23	15	9	92	112	57	.180	.259	.251	54	-66	43			.884	50	S-315/2-5,3-2	-0.2

■ PAUL EASTERLING   Easterling, Paul   b: 9/28/05, Reidsville, Ga.   d: 3/15/93, Reidsville, Ga.   BR/TR, 5'11", 180 lbs.   Deb: 4/11/28

YEAR	TM/L	G	AB	R	H	2B	3B	HR	RBI	BB	SO	AVG	OBP	SLG	PRO+	BR/A	SB	CS	SBR	FA	FR	G/POS	TPR
1928	Det-A	43	114	17	37	7	1	3	12	8	24	.325	.374	.482	122	3	2	1	0	.921	-2	O-34	-0.1
1930	Det-A	29	79	7	16	6	0	1	14	6	18	.203	.259	.316	44	-7	0	1	-1	1.000	-2	O-25	-1.0
1938	Phi-A	4	7	1	2	0	0	0	0	1	2	.286	.375	.286	70	-0	0	0	0	.750	-0	/O-1	0.0
Total	3	76	200	25	55	13	1	4	26	15	44	.275	.329	.410	88	-4	2	2	-1	.938	-4	/O-60	-1.1

■ TED EASTERLY   Easterly, Theodore Harrison   b: 4/20/1885, Lincoln, Neb.   d: 7/6/51, Clearlake Highlands, Cal.   BL/TR, 5'8", 165 lbs.   Deb: 4/17/09

YEAR	TM/L	G	AB	R	H	2B	3B	HR	RBI	BB	SO	AVG	OBP	SLG	PRO+	BR/A	SB	CS	SBR	FA	FR	G/POS	TPR
1909	Cle-A	98	287	32	75	14	10	1	27	13		.261	.293	.390	111	2	8			.965	0	C-76	1.0
1910	Cle-A	110	363	34	111	16	6	0	55	21		.306	.344	.383	126	10	10			.964	-8	C-65,O-32	0.7
1911	Cle-A	99	287	34	93	19	5	1	37	8		.324	.345	.436	116	4	6			.910	-12	O-54,C-22	-0.8
1912	Cle-A	65	186	17	55	4	0	2	21	7		.296	.328	.349	91	-3	3			.958	-4	C-51	-0.2
	Chi-A	30	55	5	20	2	0	0	14	2		.364	.386	.400	129	2	1			.964	-4	C-10/O-1	-0.1
	Yr	95	241	22	75	6	0	2	35	9		.311	.341	.361	100	-1	4			.959	-8	C-61/O-1	-0.3
1913	Chi-A	60	97	3	23	1	0	0	8	4	9	.237	.267	.247	51	-6	2			.976	2	C-19	-0.2
1914	KC-F	134	436	58	146	20	12	1	67	31	25	.335	.384	.443	130	11	10			.969	-18	*C-128	0.4
1915	KC-F	110	309	32	84	12	5	3	32	21	15	.272	.320	.372	99	-2	6			.969	4	C-88	0.5
Total	7	706	2020	215	607	88	38	8	261	107	49	.300	.338	.394	112	14	42			.965	-41	C-459/O-87	1.3

■ ROY EASTERWOOD   Easterwood, Roy Charles "Shag"   b: 1/12/15, Waxahachie, Tex.   d: 8/24/84, Graham, Tex.   BR/TR, 6'0.5", 196 lbs.   Deb: 4/21/44

YEAR	TM/L	G	AB	R	H	2B	3B	HR	RBI	BB	SO	AVG	OBP	SLG	PRO+	BR/A	SB	CS	SBR	FA	FR	G/POS	TPR
1944	Chi-N	17	33	1	7	2	0	1	2	1	11	.212	.235	.364	67	-2	0			1.000	-1	C-12	-0.2

■ JOHN EASTON   Easton, John David "Goose"   b: 3/4/33, Trenton, N.J.   BR/TR, 6'2", 185 lbs.   Deb: 6/19/55

YEAR	TM/L	G	AB	R	H	2B	3B	HR	RBI	BB	SO	AVG	OBP	SLG	PRO+	BR/A	SB	CS	SBR	FA	FR	G/POS	TPR
1955	Phi-N	1	0	0	0	0	0	0	0	0		—	—	—		0	0	0	0	.000	0	R	0.0
1959	Phi-N	3	3	0	0	0	0	0	0	0	3	.000	.000	.000	-98	-1	0	0	0	.000	0	H	-0.1
Total	2	4	3	0	0	0	0	0	0	0	3	.000	.000	.000	-98	-1	0	0	0	.000	0	-0,-0	-0.1

■ EDDIE EAYRS   Eayrs, Edwin   b: 11/10/1890, Blackstone, Mass.   d: 11/30/69, Warwick, R.I.   BL/TL, 5'7", 160 lbs.   Deb: 6/30/13

YEAR	TM/L	G	AB	R	H	2B	3B	HR	RBI	BB	SO	AVG	OBP	SLG	PRO+	BR/A	SB	CS	SBR	FA	FR	G/POS	TPR
1913	Pit-N	4	6	0	1	0	0	0	0	1		.167	.167	.167	-5	-1	0			.667	-0	/P-2	0.0
1920	Bos-N	87	244	31	80	5	2	1	24	30	18	.328	.410	.377	133	12	4	3	-1	.950	-4	O-63/P-7	0.1
1921	Bos-N	15	15	0	1	0	0	0	0	4		.067	.263	.067	-68	-4	0	0	0	.000	-0	/P-2	-0.1
	Bro-N	8	6	1	1	0	0	0	2	0		.167	.375	.167	47	-0	0	0	0	.000	-1	/O-1	-0.1
	Yr	23	21	1	2	0	0	0	2	4		.095	.174	.095	-27	-4	0	0	0	.000	-1	/P-2,O-1	-0.1
Total	3	114	271	32	83	5	2	1	26	32	23	.306	.388	.351	116	7	4	3		.950	-5	O-64,P-11	0.0

■ HI EBRIGHT   Ebright, Hiram C. "Buck"   b: 6/12/1859, Lancaster Co., Pa   d: 10/24/16, Milwaukee, Wis.   BR/TR,   Deb: 4/24/1889

YEAR	TM/L	G	AB	R	H	2B	3B	HR	RBI	BB	SO	AVG	OBP	SLG	PRO+	BR/A	SB	CS	SBR	FA	FR	G/POS	TPR
1889	Was-N	16	59	9	15	2	2	1	6	3	8	.254	.302	.407	103	-0	1			.875	4	/C-9,O-4,S-3	0.4

■ ANGEL ECHEVARRIA   Echevarria, Angel Santos   b: 5/25/71, Bridgeport, Conn.   BR/TR, 6'4", 215 lbs.   Deb: 7/15/96

YEAR	TM/L	G	AB	R	H	2B	3B	HR	RBI	BB	SO	AVG	OBP	SLG	PRO+	BR/A	SB	CS	SBR	FA	FR	G/POS	TPR
1996	Col-N	26	21	2	6	0	0	0	2	6	5	.286	.375	.286	60	-1	0	0	0	1.000	-4	O-11	-0.5

■ JOHNNY ECHOLS   Echols, John Gresham   b: 1/9/17, Atlanta, Ga.   d: 11/13/72, Atlanta, Ga.   BR/TR, 5'10.5", 175 lbs.   Deb: 5/24/39

YEAR	TM/L	G	AB	R	H	2B	3B	HR	RBI	BB	SO	AVG	OBP	SLG	PRO+	BR/A	SB	CS	SBR	FA	FR	G/POS	TPR
1939	StL-N	2	0	0	0	0	0	0	0	0	0	—	—	—		0	0			.000	0	R	0.0

■ OX ECKHARDT   Eckhardt, Oscar George   b: 12/23/01, Yorktown, Tex.   d: 4/22/51, Yorktown, Tex.   BL/TR, 6'1", 185 lbs.   Deb: 4/16/32

YEAR	TM/L	G	AB	R	H	2B	3B	HR	RBI	BB	SO	AVG	OBP	SLG	PRO+	BR/A	SB	CS	SBR	FA	FR	G/POS	TPR
1932	Bos-N	8	8	1	2	0	0	0	1	0	1	.250	.250	.250	36	-1	0			.000	0	H	-0.1
1936	Bro-N	16	44	5	8	1	0	1	6	5	2	.182	.265	.273	45	-3	0			1.000	1	O-10	-0.3
Total	2	24	52	6	10	1	0	1	7	5	3	.192	.263	.269	43	-4	0			1.000	1	/O-10	-0.4

■ CHARLIE EDEN   Eden, Charles M.   b: 1/18/1855, Lexington, Ky.   d: 9/17/20, Cincinnati, Ohio   BL/TL, 168 lbs.   Deb: 8/17/1877

YEAR	TM/L	G	AB	R	H	2B	3B	HR	RBI	BB	SO	AVG	OBP	SLG	PRO+	BR/A	SB	CS	SBR	FA	FR	G/POS	TPR
1877	Chi-N	15	55	9	12	0	1	0	5	3	6	.218	.259	.255	56	-3				.679	-2	O-15	-0.5
1879	Cle-N	81	353	40	96	31	7	3	34	6	20	.272	.284	.425	131	12				.808	-4	*O-80/1-3,C-1	0.3
1884	Pit-a	32	122	12	33	7	4	1		7		.270	.341	.418	144	6				.759	-4	O-31/P-2	0.2
1885	Pit-a	98	405	57	103	18	6	0	38	17		.254	.298	.328	99	-0				.814	-16	*O-96/P-4,3-2	-1.6
Total	4	226	935	118	244	56	18	4	77	33	26	.261	.296	.372	114	14				.793	-25	O-222/P-6,1-3,3C	-1.7

■ MIKE EDEN   Eden, Edward Michael   b: 5/22/49, Fort Clayton, Canal Zone   BB/TR, 5'10", 170 lbs.   Deb: 8/2/76

YEAR	TM/L	G	AB	R	H	2B	3B	HR	RBI	BB	SO	AVG	OBP	SLG	PRO+	BR/A	SB	CS	SBR	FA	FR	G/POS	TPR
1976	Atl-N	5	8	0	0	0	0	0	1	0	0	.000	.000	.000	-94	-2	0	0	0	1.000	1	/2-2	-0.1
1978	Chi-A	10	17	1	2	0	0	0	0	4	0	.118	.286	.118	17	-2	0	0	0	.905	-0	/S-5,2-4	-0.1
Total	2	15	25	1	2	0	0	0	1	4	0	.080	.207	.080	-16	-4	0	0	0	1.000	0	/2-6,S-5	-0.2

■ STUMP EDINGTON   Edington, Jacob Frank   b: 7/4/1891, Koleen, Ind.   d: 11/11/69, Bastrop, La.   BL/TL, 5'8", 170 lbs.   Deb: 6/20/12

YEAR	TM/L	G	AB	R	H	2B	3B	HR	RBI	BB	SO	AVG	OBP	SLG	PRO+	BR/A	SB	CS	SBR	FA	FR	G/POS	TPR
1912	Pit-N	15	53	4	16	0	2	0	12	3	1	.302	.339	.377	97	-0	0			1.000	1	O-14	0.0

■ DAVE EDLER   Edler, David Delmar   b: 8/5/56, Sioux City, Iowa   BR/TR, 6', 185 lbs.   Deb: 9/4/80

YEAR	TM/L	G	AB	R	H	2B	3B	HR	RBI	BB	SO	AVG	OBP	SLG	PRO+	BR/A	SB	CS	SBR	FA	FR	G/POS	TPR
1980	Sea-A	28	89	11	20	1	0	3	9	6	16	.225	.289	.337	70	-4	2	3	-1	.965	-4	3-28	-0.2
1981	Sea-A	29	78	7	11	3	0	0	5	11	13	.141	.256	.179	26	-7	3	3	-1	.884	-3	3-26/S-1	-1.2
1982	Sea-A	40	104	14	29	2	2	2	18	11	13	.279	.348	.394	100	0	4	2	0	.922	3	3-31/O-2,D-2	0.2
1983	Sea-A	29	63	2	12	1	1	1	4	5	11	.190	.261	.286	49	-4	3	3	-1	.875	-2	3-13/1-5,O-1,D-6	-0.7
Total	4	126	334	34	72	7	3	6	36	35	53	.216	.294	.308	66	-15	12	11	-3	.922	-6	/3-98,D-8,1-5,OS	-1.9

■ JIM EDMONDS   Edmonds, James Patrick   b: 6/27/70, Fullerton, Cal.   BL/TL, 6'1", 190 lbs.   Deb: 9/9/93

YEAR	TM/L	G	AB	R	H	2B	3B	HR	RBI	BB	SO	AVG	OBP	SLG	PRO+	BR/A	SB	CS	SBR	FA	FR	G/POS	TPR
1993	Cal-A	18	61	5	15	4	1	0	4	2	16	.246	.270	.344	62	-3	0	2	-1	.981	5	O-17	0.0
1994	Cal-A	94	289	35	79	13	1	5	37	30	72	.273	.344	.377	85	-6	4	2	0	.981	0	O-77,1-22	-0.9
1995	Cal-A★	141	558	120	162	30	4	33	107	51	130	.290	.355	.536	129	22	1	4	-2	.998	19	*O-139	3.3
1996	Cal-A	114	431	73	131	28	3	27	66	46	101	.304	.376	.571	138	24	4	0	1	.997	7	*O-111/D-1	2.6
Total	4	367	1339	233	387	75	9	65	214	129	319	.289	.356	.504	119	36	9	8	-2	.993	32	O-344/1-22,D-1	5.0

■ BOB EDMONDSON   Edmondson, Robert E.   b: 4/30/1879, Paris, Ky.   d: 8/14/31, Lawrence, Kan.   BR/TR, 5'11", 185 lbs.   Deb: 9/15/06

YEAR	TM/L	G	AB	R	H	2B	3B	HR	RBI	BB	SO	AVG	OBP	SLG	PRO+	BR/A	SB	CS	SBR	FA	FR	G/POS	TPR
1906	Was-A	3	3	1	1	0	0	0	0	0	0	.333	.333	.333	114	0	0			1.000	-0	/P-2,O-1	0.0
1908	Was-A	26	80	5	15	4	1	0		2	7	.188	.261	.262	77	-2	0			.878	-2	O-24	-0.6
Total	2	29	83	6	16	4	1	0		2	7	.193	.264	.265	78	-2	0			.878	-2	/O-25,P-2	-0.6

■ EDDIE EDMONSON   Edmonson, Earl Edward   b: 11/20/1889, Hopewell, Pa.   d: 5/10/71, Leesburg, Fla.   BL/TR, 6', 175 lbs.   Deb: 10/4/13

YEAR	TM/L	G	AB	R	H	2B	3B	HR	RBI	BB	SO	AVG	OBP	SLG	PRO+	BR/A	SB	CS	SBR	FA	FR	G/POS	TPR
1913	Cle-A	2	5	0	0	0	0	0	0	0	0	.000	.000	.000	-97	-1	0			1.000	-1	/1-1,O-1	-0.2

■ BRUCE EDWARDS   Edwards, Charles Bruce "Bull"   b: 7/15/23, Quincy, Ill.   d: 4/25/75, Sacramento, Cal.   BR/TR, 5'7", 194 lbs.   Deb: 6/23/46

YEAR	TM/L	G	AB	R	H	2B	3B	HR	RBI	BB	SO	AVG	OBP	SLG	PRO+	BR/A	SB	CS	SBR	FA	FR	G/POS	TPR
1946	Bro-N	92	292	24	78	13	5	1	25	34	20	.267	.348	.356	99	0	1			.982	6	C-91	1.2
1947	*Bro-N★	130	471	53	139	15	8	9	80	49	55	.295	.364	.418	103	3	2			.983	5	*C-128	1.6
1948	Bro-N	96	286	36	79	17	2	8	54	26	28	.276	.341	.434	105	1	4			.984	-8	C-48,O-21,3-14,/1-1	-0.5
1949	*Bro-N	64	148	24	31	3	0	8	25	25	15	.209	.324	.392	87	-3	0			.990	-3	C-41/O-4,3-1	-0.4
1950	Bro-N	50	142	16	26	4	1	8	16	13	22	.183	.256	.394	67	-8	1			.980	-8	C-38/1-2	-0.9
1951	Bro-N	17	36	6	9	2	0	1	8	1	3	.250	.270	.389	74	-1	0	0	0	1.000	0	/C-9	-0.1
	Chi-N☆	51	141	19	33	9	2	3	17	16	14	.234	.316	.390	87	-3	1	2	-1	.962	-3	C-28/1-9	-0.6
	Yr	68	177	25	42	11	2	4	25	17	17	.237	.308	.390	85	-4	1	2	-1	.971	-3	C-37/1-9	-0.7
1952	Chi-N	50	94	7	23	2	2	1	12	8	12	.245	.304	.340	77	-3	0	0	0	.989	-3	C-22/2-1	-0.5
1954	Chi-N	4	3	1	0	0	0	0	1	2	2	.000	.400	.000			0			.000	0	H	0.0
1955	Was-A	30	57	5	10	2	0	0	3	16	6	.175	.356	.211	58	-3	0	0	1	.980	7	C-22/3-5	0.4
1956	Cin-N	7	5	0	1	0	0	0	0	0	2	.200	.200	.200	8	-1	0			.000	-1	/C-2,2-1,3-1	-0.1
Total	10	591	1675	191	429	67	20	39	241	190	179	.256	.335	.390	93	-17	9	3		.982	-3	C-429/O-25,3-21,12	0.1

■ DAVE EDWARDS   Edwards, David Leonard   b: 2/24/54, Los Angeles, Cal.   BR/TR, 6', 177 lbs.   Deb: 9/11/78   F

YEAR	TM/L	G	AB	R	H	2B	3B	HR	RBI	BB	SO	AVG	OBP	SLG	PRO+	BR/A	SB	CS	SBR	FA	FR	G/POS	TPR
1978	Min-A	15	44	7	11	3	0	1	3	7	13	.250	.377	.386	113	1	1	1	-0	.950	1	O-15	0.1
1979	Min-A	96	229	42	57	8	0	3	35	24	45	.249	.323	.389	88	-4	6	3	0	.983	-4	O-86/D-3	-1.0
1980	Min-A	81	200	26	50	9	1	2	20	12	51	.250	.296	.335	68	-9	3	3	0	.932	-6	O-72/D-3	-1.7
1981	SD-N	58	112	13	24	4	1	2	13	11	24	.214	.285	.321	77	-4	3	1	0	.970	-5	O-49	-1.0
1982	SD-N	71	55	7	10	2	0	1	2	1	14	.182	.196	.273	32	-5	0	0	0	.944	-14	O-45/1-1	-2.1
Total	5	321	640	95	152	26	2	14	73	55	147	.237	.302	.350	77	-21	12	6	0	.958	-28	O-267/D-6,1-1	-5.7

■ HANK EDWARDS   Edwards, Henry Albert   b: 1/29/19, Elmwood Place, O.   d: 6/22/88, Santa Ana, Cal.   BL/TL, 6', 190 lbs.   Deb: 9/10/41

YEAR	TM/L	G	AB	R	H	2B	3B	HR	RBI	BB	SO	AVG	OBP	SLG	PRO+	BR/A	SB	CS	SBR	FA	FR	G/POS	TPR
1941	Cle-A	16	68	10	15	1	1	1	6	2	4	.221	.243	.353	47	-5	0	0	0	.929	-1	O-16	-0.7
1942	Cle-A	13	48	6	12	2	0	0	7	5	8	.250	.321	.333	89	-1	2	1	0	.968	-1	O-12	-0.1
1943	Cle-A	92	297	38	82	18	6	3	28	30	34	.276	.343	.407	127	9	4	8	-4	.983	-5	O-74	-0.3
1946	Cle-A	124	458	62	138	33	**16**	10	54	43	48	.301	.361	.509	151	28	1	3	-2	.968	1	*O-123	2.3
1947	Cle-A	108	393	54	102	12	3	15	59	31	55	.260	.315	.420	106	1	1	3	-2	.990	-7	O-100	-1.3
1948	Cle-A	55	160	27	43	9	2	3	18	18	18	.269	.346	.406	102	0	1	1	-0	.987	-3	O-41	-0.5
1949	Cle-A	5	15	3	4	0	0	1	1	1	2	.267	.313	.467	107	0	0	0	0	1.000	-	/O-5	-0.1
	Chi-N	58	176	25	51	8	1	7	21	19	22	.290	.359	.500	131	7	0			.988	-4	O-51	0.1
1950	Chi-N	41	110	13	40	11	1	2	21	10	13	.364	.417	.536	150	8	0			.976	-3	O-29	0.4
1951	Bro-N	35	31	1	7	3	0	0	3	4	9	.226	.314	.323	70	-1	0	0	0	.000	0	H	-0.1
	Cin-N	41	127	14	40	9	1	3	20	13	17	.315	.379	.472	126	5	0	2	-1	.985	-1	O-34	-0.1
	Yr	76	158	15	47	12	1	3	23	17	26	.297	.366	.443	115	3	0	2	-1	.985	-3	O-34	-0.2
1952	Cin-N	74	184	24	52	7	6	6	28	19	22	.283	.350	.484	129	7	0	3	-2	.988	-4	O-51	-0.1
	Chi-A	8	18	2	6	0	0	0	1	0	2	.333	.333	.333	85	-0	0			1.000	-	/O-3	0.0
1953	StL-A	65	106	6	21	3	0	0	9	13	10	.198	.286	.226	39	-9	0	1	-1	1.000	-1	O-21	-1.1
Total	11	735	2191	285	613	116	41	51	276	208	264	.280	.343	.440	119	48	9	22		.981	-31	O-560	-1.8

■ DOC EDWARDS   Edwards, Howard Rodney   b: 12/10/36, Red Jacket, W.Va.   BR/TR, 6'2", 215 lbs.   Deb: 4/21/62   MC

YEAR	TM/L	G	AB	R	H	2B	3B	HR	RBI	BB	SO	AVG	OBP	SLG	PRO+	BR/A	SB	CS	SBR	FA	FR	G/POS	TPR
1962	Cle-A	53	143	13	39	6	0	3	9	9	14	.273	.325	.378	91	-2	0	0	0	.992	9	C-39	0.8
1963	Cle-A	10	31	6	8	2	0	0	0	2	6	.258	.303	.323	76	-1	0	0	0	.988	5	C-10	0.4
	KC-A	71	240	16	60	12	0	6	35	11	23	.250	.289	.375	80	-7	0	1	-1	.987	-5	C-63	-1.1
	Yr	81	271	22	68	14	0	6	35	13	29	.251	.290	.369	79	-8	0	1	-1	.987	-0	C-73	-0.7
1964	KC-A	97	294	25	66	10	0	5	28	13	40	.224	.265	.310	57	-17	0	1	-1	.986	1	C-79/1-7	-1.4
1965	KC-A	6	20	1	3	0	0	0	0	0	2	.150	.190	.150	-2	-3	0	0	0	1.000	-0	/C-6	-0.3
	NY-A	45	100	3	19	3	0	1	9	13	14	.190	.289	.250	55	-6	1	2	-1	.986	2	C-43	-0.3
	Yr	51	120	4	22	3	0	1	9	14	16	.183	.274	.233	46	-8	1	2	-1	.988	2	C-49	-0.6
1970	Phi-N	35	78	5	21	3	0	0	6	4	10	.269	.313	.269	59	-4	0	0	0	.970	6	C-34	0.3
Total	5	317	906	69	216	33	0	15	87	53	109	.238	.287	.325	68	-39	1	4	-2	.986	18	C-274/1-7	-1.6

■ JOHNNY EDWARDS   Edwards, John Alban   b: 6/10/38, Columbus, Ohio   BL/TR, 6'4", 220 lbs.   Deb: 6/27/61

YEAR	TM/L	G	AB	R	H	2B	3B	HR	RBI	BB	SO	AVG	OBP	SLG	PRO+	BR/A	SB	CS	SBR	FA	FR	G/POS	TPR
1961	*Cin-N	52	145	14	27	5	0	2	14	18	28	.186	.280	.262	45	-11	0	1	0	.982	-4	C-52	-1.2
1962	Cin-N	133	452	47	115	28	5	8	50	45	70	.254	.323	.392	88	-8	1	1	-0	.987	12	*C-130	0.9
1963	Cin-N★	148	495	46	128	19	4	11	67	45	93	.259	.325	.380	99	-0	1	5	-3	**.995**	13	*C-148	1.7
1964	Cin-N★	126	423	47	119	23	1	7	55	34	65	.281	.336	.390	100	0	1	2	-1	.992	23	*C-120	2.9
1965	Cin-N☆	114	371	47	99	22	2	17	51	50	45	.267	.355	.474	123	12	0	0	0	.990	5	*C-110	2.3
1966	Cin-N	98	282	24	54	6	0	6	39	31	42	.191	.272	.284	50	-19	1	3	-2	.992	9	C-98	-0.6
1967	Cin-N	80	209	10	43	6	0	2	20	16	28	.206	.262	.263	46	-15	1	4	-2	.990	15	C-73	0.2
1968	*StL-N	85	230	14	55	9	1	3	29	16	20	.239	.291	.326	86	-4	1	1	-0	.992	2	C-54	0.1
1969	Hou-N	151	496	52	115	20	6	6	50	53	69	.232	.309	.333	81	-12	2	1	0	**.994**	11	*C-151	0.1
1970	Hou-N	140	458	46	101	16	4	7	49	51	63	.221	.300	.319	69	-21	1	2	-1	**.995**	13	*C-139	-0.1
1971	Hou-N	106	317	18	74	13	4	1	23	26	38	.233	.292	.309	72	-12	1	1	-0	**.995**	8	*C-104	-0.1
1972	Hou-N	108	333	39	89	16	2	5	40	50	39	.267	.366	.373	113	7	2	4	-2	.988	-8	*C-105	0.1
1973	Hou-N	79	250	24	61	10	2	5	27	19	23	.244	.303	.360	83	-6	0	1	-0	.989	-1	C-76	-0.4
1974	Hou-N	50	117	8	26	4	1	0	10	11	12	.222	.295	.325	76	-5	1	0	0	.989	5	C-32	0.2
Total	14	1470	4577	430	1106	202	32	81	524	465	635	.242	.314	.353	85	-92	15	23	-9	.992	97	*C-1392	6.1

■ MARSHALL EDWARDS   Edwards, Marshall Lynn   b: 8/27/52, Fort Lewis, Wash.   BL/TL, 5'9", 157 lbs.   Deb: 4/11/81   F

YEAR	TM/L	G	AB	R	H	2B	3B	HR	RBI	BB	SO	AVG	OBP	SLG	PRO+	BR/A	SB	CS	SBR	FA	FR	G/POS	TPR
1981	*Mil-A	40	58	10	14	1	1	0	4	0	2	.241	.241	.293	56	-3	6	2	1	.979	-9	O-36/D-1	-1.3
1982	*Mil-A	69	178	24	44	4	1	2	14	9	14	.247	.264	.315	62	-10	10	4	1	.984	-2	O-54/D-6	-1.2
1983	Mil-A	51	74	14	22	1	1	0	5	5	9	.297	.307	.338	84	-2	5	5	-2	1.000	-3	O-35/D-4	-0.7
Total	3	160	310	48	80	6	3	2	23	15	25	.258	.270	.316	66	-15	21	11	-0	.987	-13	O-125/D-11	-3.2

■ MIKE EDWARDS   Edwards, Michael Lewis   b: 8/27/52, Fort Lewis, Wash.   BR/TR, 5'10", 154 lbs.   Deb: 9/10/77   F

YEAR	TM/L	G	AB	R	H	2B	3B	HR	RBI	BB	SO	AVG	OBP	SLG	PRO+	BR/A	SB	CS	SBR	FA	FR	G/POS	TPR
1977	Pit-N	7	6	1	0	0	0	0	0	0	1	.000	.143	.000	-56	-2	0	2	-1	1.000	3	/2-4	0.1
1978	Oak-A	142	414	48	113	16	2	1	23	16	32	.273	.303	.329	82	-11	27	21	-5	.964	-28	*2-133/S-9,D-4	-3.5
1979	Oak-A	122	400	35	93	12	2	1	23	15	37	.233	.264	.280	49	-29	10	6	-1	.962	-14	*2-113/S-3,D-2	-3.5
1980	Oak-A	46	59	10	14	0	0	0	3	1	5	.237	.250	.237	37	-5	1	1	-0	.971	-4	2-23/O-1,D-5	-0.1
Total	4	317	879	94	220	28	4	2	49	32	77	.250	.281	.298	63	-46	38	30	-7	.964	-34	2-273/S-12,D-11,O-1	-7.0

■ RALPH EDWARDS   Edwards, Ralph Strunk   b: 12/14/1882, Brewster, N.Y.   d: 1/5/49, White Plains, N.Y.   BR/TR, 5'9", 165 lbs.   Deb: 9/17/15

YEAR	TM/L	G	AB	R	H	2B	3B	HR	RBI	BB	SO	AVG	OBP	SLG	PRO+	BR/A	SB	CS	SBR	FA	FR	G/POS	TPR
1915	Phi-A	2	5	0	0	0	0	0	0	0	3	.000	.000	.000	-99	-1	0			1.000	-1	/2-1	-0.3

■ ROBERT EENHOORN   Eenhoorn, Robert Franciscus   b: 2/9/68, Rotterdam, Holland   BR/TR, 6'3", 170 lbs.   Deb: 4/27/94

YEAR	TM/L	G	AB	R	H	2B	3B	HR	RBI	BB	SO	AVG	OBP	SLG	PRO+	BR/A	SB	CS	SBR	FA	FR	G/POS	TPR
1994	NY-A	3	4	1	2	1	0	0	0	0	0	.500	.500	.750	225	0	0	0	0	1.000	0	/S-3	0.0
1995	NY-A	5	14	1	2	0	0	0	2	1	3	.143	.200	.214	8	-2	0	0	0	1.000	-1	/2-3,S-2	-0.3
1996	NY-A	12	14	2	1	0	0	0	0	2	3	.071	.188	.071	-30	-3	0	0	0	1.000	-1	2-10/3-2	0.0
	Cal-A	6	15	1	4	0	0	0	0	0	2	.267	.267	.267	36	-1	0	0	0	.875	-3	/S-4,2-2	-0.2
	Yr	18	29	3	5	0	0	0	0	2	5	.172	.226	.172	3	-4	0	0	0	.971	-4	2-12/S-4,3-2	-0.2
Total	3	26	47	5	9	2	0	0	4	3	8	.191	.240	.234	22	-5	0	0	0	.980	-1	/2-15,S-9,3-2	-0.5

YEAR	TM/L	G	AB	R	H	2B	3B	HR	RBI	BB	SO	AVG	OBP	SLG	PRO+	BR/A	SB	CS	SBR	FA	FR	G/POS	TPR

■ BEN EGAN   Egan, Arthur Augustus b: 11/20/1883, Augusta, N.Y. d: 2/18/68, Sherrill, N.Y. BR/TR, 6′, 195 lbs. Deb: 9/29/08 C

1908	Phi-A	2	6	1	1	1	0	0	0	1		.167	.286	.333	95	-0	0			.933	0	/C-2	0.0
1912	Phi-A	49	138	9	24	3	4	0	13	6		.174	.208	.254	33	-13	3			.958	4	C-46	-0.5
1914	Cle-A	29	88	7	20	2	1	0	11	3	20	.227	.277	.273	63	-4	0	1	-1	.975	4	C-27	0.2
1915	Cle-A	42	120	4	13	3	0	0	6	8	14	.108	.164	.133	-11	-16	0			.970	8	C-40	-0.6
Total	4	122	352	21	58	9	5	0	30	18	34	.165	.212	.219	27	-33	3	1		.966	16	C-115	-0.9

■ JIM EGAN   Egan, James K. "Troy Terrier" b: 1858, Derby, Conn. d: 9/26/1884, New Haven, Conn. TL Deb: 5/15/1882

1882	Tro-N	30	115	15	23	3	2	0	10	1	21	.200	.207	.261	51	-6				.625	-8	O-18,P-12/C-2	-0.8

■ DICK EGAN   Egan, Richard Joseph b: 6/23/1884, Portland, Ore. d: 7/7/47, Oakland, Cal. BR/TR, 5′11″, 162 lbs. Deb: 9/15/08

1908	Cin-N	18	68	8	14	3	1	0	5	2		.206	.229	.279	64	-3	7			.891	-3	2-18	-0.7
1909	Cin-N	127	480	59	132	14	3	2	53	37		.275	.329	.329	105	3	39			.950	24	*2-116,S-10	2.7
1910	Cin-N	135	474	70	116	11	5	0	46	53	38	.245	.322	.289	82	-10	41			.961	-11	*2-131/S-3	-2.5
1911	Cin-N	153	558	80	139	11	5	1	56	59	50	.249	.322	.292	75	-18	37			.949	10	*2-152	-1.1
1912	Cin-N	149	507	69	125	14	5	0	52	56	26	.247	.324	.294	72	-19	24			**.973**	3	*2-149	-1.9
1913	Cin-N	60	195	15	55	7	3	0	22	15	13	.282	.333	.349	95	-1	6			.972	-5	2-37,S-17/3-2	-0.5
1914	Bro-N	106	337	30	76	10	3	1	21	22	25	.226	.273	.282	64	-15	8			.914	-9	S-83,3-10/O-3,21	-1.9
1915	Bro-N	3	3	0	0	0	0	0	0	0	0	.000	.000	.000	-98	-1	0			.000	0	H	-0.1
	Bos-N	83	220	20	57	9	1	0	21	28	18	.259	.343	.309	102	2	3	4	-2	.974	-2	O-24,2-22,S-10/13	-0.2
	Yr	86	223	20	57	9	1	0	21	28	18	.256	.339	.305	100	1	3	4	-2	.974	-2	O-24,2-22,S-10/13	-0.3
1916	Bos-N	83	238	23	53	8	3	0	16	19	21	.223	.280	.282	76	-7	2			.949	-21	2-59,S-12/3-8	-3.0
Total	9	917	3080	374	767	87	29	4	292	291	191	.249	.315	.300	82	-69	167	4		.956	-14	2-686,S-135/O31	-9.2

■ TOM EGAN   Egan, Thomas Patrick b: 6/9/46, Los Angeles, Cal. BR/TR, 6′4″, 218 lbs. Deb: 5/27/65

1965	Cal-A	18	38	3	10	0	1	0	1	3	12	.263	.317	.316	82	-1	0	0	0	1.000	-0	C-16	0.0
1966	Cal-A	7	11	0	0	0	0	0	0	1	5	.000	.083	.000	-76	-2	0	0	0	1.000	2	/C-6	-0.1
1967	Cal-A	1	1	0	0	0	0	0	0	0	0	.000	.000	.000	-99	-0	0	0	0	1.000	0	/C-1	0.0
1968	Cal-A	16	43	2	5	1	0	1	4	2	15	.116	.156	.209	10	-5	0	0	0	1.000	14	C-14	-0.3
1969	Cal-A	46	120	7	17	1	0	5	16	17	41	.142	.254	.275	50	-8	0	1	-1	.985	6	C-46	0.0
1970	Cal-A	79	210	14	50	6	0	4	20	14	67	.238	.289	.324	71	-9	0	0	0	.988	-1	C-79	-0.7
1971	Chi-A	85	251	29	60	11	1	10	34	26	94	.239	.320	.410	102	1	1	0	0	.986	3	C-77/1-1	0.7
1972	Chi-A	50	141	8	27	3	0	2	9	4	48	.191	.224	.255	42	-10	0	0	0	.986	3	C-46	-0.6
1974	Cal-A	43	94	4	11	0	0	0	4	8	40	.117	.194	.117	-9	-13	0	0	0	.996	16	C-41	0.4
1975	Cal-A	28	70	7	16	3	1	0	3	5	14	.229	.280	.300	69	-3	0	0	0	.965	4	C-28	0.2
Total	10	373	979	74	196	25	3	22	91	80	336	.200	.267	.299	62	-51	2	1	0	.987	35	C-354/1-1	-0.4

■ ELMER EGGERT   Eggert, Elmer Albert "Mose" b: 1/29/02, Rochester, N.Y. d: 4/9/71, Rochester, N.Y. BR/TR, 5′9″, 160 lbs. Deb: 4/27/27

1927	Bos-A	5	3	0	0	0	0	0	0	1	1	.000	.250	.000	-31	-1	0	0	0	.000	0	/2-1	-0.1

■ DAVE EGGLER   Eggler, David Daniel b: 4/30/1851, Brooklyn, N.Y. d: 4/5/02, Buffalo, N.Y. BR/TR, 5′9″, 165 lbs. Deb: 5/18/1871

1871	Mut-n	33	147	37	47	7	3	0	18	4	3	.320	.348	.408	124	6	14	3	2	.910	6	*O-33	1.0
1872	Mut-n	56	290	94	98	20	6	0	20	8	9	.338	.356	.407	143	16	**18**	5	2	.922	15	*O-56	2.5
1873	Mut-n	53	268	82	90	13	4	0	34	5	2	.336	.348	.414	126	9	4	1	1	.862	5	*O-53/3-1	1.1
1874	Phi-n	58	299	70	95	13	8	0	31	5	1	.318	.329	.415	132	9	5	6	-2	**.906**	4	*O-57/2-2	1.4
1875	Ath-n	66	295	66	89	13	7	0	33	1	10	.302	.304	.393	126	5	6	5	-1	**.921**	9	*O-66	0.7
1876	Phi-N	39	174	28	52	4	0	0	19	2	4	.299	.307	.322	111	2				.913	5	O-39	0.6
1877	Chi-N	33	136	20	36	3	0	0	20	1	5	.265	.270	.287	67	-6				.861	3	O-33	-0.4
1879	Buf-N	78	317	41	66	5	7	0	27	11	41	.208	.235	.268	64	-12				.919	-6	O-78	-2.0
1883	Bal-a	53	202	15	38	2	0	0	7	1		.188	.192	.198	25	-17				.916	1	O-53	-1.5
	Buf-N	38	153	13	38	2	1	0	13	2	29	.248	.258	.275	61	-7				.845	1	O-38	-0.8
1884	Buf-N	63	241	25	47	3	1	0	20	6	54	.195	.215	.216	35	-18				.887	1	O-63	-1.7
1885	Buf-N	6	24	0	2	0	0	0	0	2	4	.083	.154	.083	-21	-3				.938	1	/O-6	-0.3
Total	5 n	266	1299	349	419	66	22	0	136	23	25	.323	.334	.407	131	45	47	20	2	.905	39	O-265/2-2,3-1	6.7
Total	6	310	1247	142	279	19	9	0	106	25	137	.224	.239	.253	56	-61				.894	3	O-310	-6.1

■ RED EHRET   Ehret, Philip Sydney b: 8/31/1868, Louisville, Ky. d: 7/28/40, Cincinnati, Ohio BR/TR, 6′, 175 lbs. Deb: 7/7/1888

1888	KC-a	17	63	4	12	4	0	0	4	1		.190	.203	.254	43	-4	1			.750	-4	O-10/P-7,2-1,1-1	-0.7
1889	Lou-a	67	258	27	65	6	6	1	31	4	23	.252	.263	.333	71	-11	4			.891	-1	P-45,O-22/S-1,32	-0.7
1890	*Lou-a	43	146	11	31	2	1	0	10	1		.212	.218	.240	36	-12	1			.859	-3	P-43	0.0
1891	Lou-a	26	91	9	22	2	1	0	9	5	15	.242	.281	.286	63	-5	3			.871	-1	P-26	0.0
1892	Pit-N	40	132	12	34	2	0	0	19	7	22	.258	.295	.273	72	-5	1			.855	-4	P-39	0.0
1893	Pit-N	40	136	16	24	3	0	1	17	10	18	.176	.233	.221	21	-16	1			.893	1	P-39	0.0
1894	Pit-N	46	135	6	23	4	1	0	11	8	22	.170	.217	.215	4	-21	0			.859	-1	P-46	0.0
1895	StL-N	37	96	13	21	2	1	1	9	6	12	.219	.265	.292	44	-5	0			.848	0	P-37	0.0
1896	Cin-N	34	102	10	20	2	0	1	20	10	12	.196	.268	.245	33	-10	2			.923	-1	P-34/1-1	0.0
1897	Cin-N	34	66	6	13	2	0	0	6	4		.197	.254	.227	26	-7	2			.957	-1	P-34	0.0
1898	Lou-N	13	40	3	9	3	1	0	4	1		.225	.262	.350	76	-1	0			.800	-1	P-12	0.0
Total	11	397	1265	117	274	32	11	4	140	57	124	.217	.252	.269	44	-101	15			.882	-12	P-362/O-32,1-2,23S	-1.4

■ HACK EIBEL   Eibel, Henry Hack b: 12/6/1893, Brooklyn, N.Y. d: 10/16/45, Macon, Ga. BL/TL, 5′11″, 220 lbs. Deb: 6/13/12

1912	Cle-A	1	3	0	0	0	0	0	0	0	0	.000	.000	.000	-97	-1	0			.000	-0	/O-1	-0.1
1920	Bos-A	29	43	4	8	2	0	0	6	3	6	.186	.239	.233	26	-5	1	1	-0	.800	-2	/O-5,P-3,1-1	-0.6
Total	2	30	46	4	8	2	0	0	6	3	6	.174	.224	.217	19	-5	1	1		.800	-2	/O-6,P-3,1-1	-0.7

■ IKE EICHRODT   Eichrodt, Frederick George b: 1/6/03, Chicago, Ill. d: 7/14/65, Indianapolis, Ind BR/TR, 5′11.5″, 167 lbs. Deb: 9/7/25

1925	Cle-A	15	52	4	12	3	1	0	4	2	7	.231	.259	.327	48	-4	0	0	0	.938	-2	O-13	-0.7
1926	Cle-A	37	80	14	25	7	1	0	7	2	11	.313	.329	.425	95	-1	1	0	0	.976	-4	O-27	-0.5
1927	Cle-A	85	267	24	59	19	2	0	25	16	25	.221	.265	.307	48	-21	2	3	-1	.979	1	O-81	-2.5
1931	Chi-A	34	117	9	25	5	1	0	15	1	8	.214	.220	.274	31	-12	0	0	0	1.000	-5	O-32	-1.8
Total	4	171	516	51	121	34	5	0	51	21	51	.234	.264	.320	52	-39	3	3	-1	.979	-9	O-153	-5.5

■ JIM EISENREICH   Eisenreich, James Michael b: 4/18/59, St.Cloud, Minn. BL/TL, 5′11″, 195 lbs. Deb: 4/6/82

1982	Min-A	34	99	10	30	6	0	2	9	11	13	.303	.378	.424	117	3	0	0	0	.973	-1	O-30	0.1
1983	Min-A	2	7	1	2	1	0	0	0	1	1	.286	.375	.429	116	0	0	0	0	1.000	1	/O-2	0.1
1984	Min-A	12	32	1	7	1	0	0	3	2	4	.219	.265	.250	41	-3	0	0	0	1.000	-1	/O-3,D-6	-0.3
1987	KC-A	44	105	10	25	8	2	4	21	7	13	.238	.286	.467	93	-2	1	1	-0	.000	0	D-26	-0.2
1988	KC-A	82	202	26	44	8	1	1	19	6	31	.218	.240	.282	45	-15	9	3	1	.965	-8	O-64,D-13	-2.4
1989	KC-A	134	475	64	139	33	7	9	59	37	44	.293	.344	.448	122	13	27	8	3	.989	-11	*O-123,D-10	0.2
1990	KC-A	142	496	61	139	29	7	5	51	42	51	.280	.338	.397	106	4	12	14	-5	**.996**	-9	*O-138/D-2	-1.4
1991	KC-A	135	375	47	113	22	3	2	47	20	35	.301	.333	.392	101	1	5	3	-0	.973	-17	*O-105,1-15/D-1	-2.0
1992	KC-A	113	353	31	95	13	3	2	28	24	36	.269	.316	.340	81	-9	11	6	-0	.995	-4	O-88/D-8	-1.3
1993	*Phi-N	153	362	51	115	17	4	7	54	26	36	.318	.365	.445	117	9	5	2	0	.996	-6	*O-137/1-1	0.2
1994	Phi-N	104	290	42	87	15	4	4	43	33	31	.300	.373	.421	104	3	6	1	1	.996	-1	O-93	0.1
1995	Phi-N	129	377	46	119	22	2	10	55	38	44	.316	.380	.464	122	10	10	0	3	**1.000**	1	*O-111	1.2
1996	Phi-N	113	338	45	122	24	3	3	41	31	32	.361	.416	.476	131	16	11	1	3	.977	1	O-91	1.7
Total	13	1197	3511	435	1037	199	36	49	430	278	371	.295	.348	.414	106	31	99	38		.988	-53	O-985/D-66,1-16	-4.0

■ ELAND   Eland Deb: 4/14/1873

1873	Mar-n	1	3	0	0	0	0	0	0	0	0	.000	.000	.000	-99	-1	0	0	0	.667	-0	/O-1	-0.1

YEAR	TM/L	G	AB	R	H	2B	3B	HR	RBI	BB	SO	AVG	OBP	SLG	PRO+	BR/A	SB	CS	SBR	FA	FR	G/POS	TPR
■ KID ELBERFELD			Elberfeld, Norman Arthur "The Tabasco Kid"			b: 4/13/1875, Pomeroy, Ohio			d: 1/13/44, Chattanooga, Tenn.						BR/TR, 5'7", 158 lbs.		Deb: 5/30/1898	M				
1898	Phi-N	14	38	1	9	4	0	0	7	5		.237	.420	.342	124	2	0			.795	-5	3-14	-0.3
1899	Cin-N	41	138	23	36	4	2	0	22	15		.261	.378	.319	90	-1	5			.878	-4	S-24,3-18	-0.3
1901	Det-A	121	432	76	133	21	11	3	76	57		.308	.397	.428	123	15	23			.907	22	*S-121	4.2
1902	Det-A	130	488	70	127	17	6	1	64	55		.260	.348	.326	86	-7	19			.921	9	*S-130	0.9
1903	Det-A	35	132	29	45	5	3	0	19	11		.341	.412	.424	156	10	6			.932	6	S-34/3-1	1.7
	NY-A	90	349	49	100	18	5	0	45	22		.287	.346	.367	107	4	16			.914	7	S-90	1.5
	Yr	125	481	78	145	23	8	0	64	33		.301	.365	.383	120	13	22			.919	13	*S-124/3-1	3.2
1904	NY-A	122	445	55	117	13	5	2	46	37		.263	.337	.328	106	4	18			.933	15	*S-122	2.6
1905	NY-A	111	390	48	102	18	2	0	53	23		.262	.329	.318	95	-2	18			.908	-5	*S-108	-0.5
1906	NY-A	99	346	59	106	11	5	2	31	30		.306	.378	.384	126	11	19			.925	-4	S-98	1.2
1907	NY-A	120	447	61	121	17	6	0	51	36		.271	.343	.336	108	5	22			.930	8	*S-118	1.7
1908	NY-A	19	56	11	11	3	0	0	5	6		.196	.328	.250	87	-0	1			.916	-3	S-17,M	-0.3
1909	NY-A	106	379	47	90	9	5	0	26	28		.237	.314	.288	89	-4	23			.943	-5	S-61,3-44	-0.4
1910	Was-A	127	455	53	114	9	2	2	42	35		.251	.322	.292	97	-1	19			**.943**	-10	*3-113,2-10/S-3	-0.8
1911	Was-A	127	404	58	110	19	4	0	47	65		.272	.405	.339	110	11	24			.957	10	2-68,3-52	2.0
1914	Bro-N	30	62	7	14	1	0	0	1	2	4	.226	.304	.242	62	-3	0			.901	-4	S-18/2-1	-0.6
Total	14	1292	4561	647	1235	169	56	10	535	427	4	.271	.355	.339	105	44	213			.920	41	S-944,3-242/2-79	12.6
■ GEORGE ELDER			Elder, George Rezin			b: 3/10/21, Lebanon, Ky.				BL/TR, 5'11", 180 lbs.			Deb: 7/22/49								
1949	StL-A	41	44	9	11	3	0	0	2	4	11	.250	.313	.318	64	-2	0	0	0	1.000	-1	O-10	-0.4
■ LEE ELIA			Elia, Lee Constantine			b: 7/16/37, Philadelphia, Pa.				BR/TR, 5'11", 175 lbs.			Deb: 4/23/66	MC							
1966	Chi-A	80	195	16	40	5	2	3	22	15	39	.205	.269	.297	67	-9	0	1	-1	.954	4	S-75	0.0
1968	Chi-N	15	17	1	3	0	0	0	3	0	6	.176	.222	.176	20	-2	0	0	0	1.000	-1	/S-2,2-1,3-1	-0.3
Total	2	95	212	17	43	5	2	3	25	15	45	.203	.265	.288	63	-10	0	1	-1	.954	3	/S-77,3-1,2-1	-0.3
■ PETE ELKO			Elko, Peter "Piccolo Pete"			b: 6/17/18, Wilkes-Barre, Pa.			d: 9/17/93, Wilkes-Barre, Pa.		BR/TR, 5'11", 185 lbs.			Deb: 9/17/43								
1943	Chi-N	9	30	1	4	0	0	0	4	5		.133	.235	.133	8	-3	0			.852	-2	/3-9	-0.6
1944	Chi-N	7	22	2	5	1	0	0	0	0	0	.227	.227	.273	40	-2	0			1.000	-0	/3-6	-0.2
Total	2	16	52	3	9	1	0	0	4	5		.173	.232	.192	22	-5	0			.902	-2	/3-15	-0.8
■ ROY ELLAM			Ellam, Roy "Whitey" or "Slippery"			b: 2/8/1886, W.Conshohocken, Pa.			d: 10/28/48, Conshohocken, Pa.		BR/TR, 5'10.5", 203 lbs.			Deb: 9/18/09								
1909	Cin-N	10	21	4	4	0	1	1	4	7		.190	.393	.429	156	2	1			.895	-1	/S-9	0.1
1918	Pit-N	26	77	9	10	1	1	0	2	17	17	.130	.302	.169	43	-4	2			.924	-8	S-26	-1.3
Total	2	36	98	13	14	1	2	1	6	24	17	.143	.323	.224	67	-3	3			.917	-10	/S-35	-1.2
■ FRANK ELLERBE			Ellerbe, Francis Rogers "Governor"			b: 12/25/1895, Marion Co., S.C.			d: 7/8/88, Latta, S.C.		BR/TR, 5'10.5", 165 lbs.			Deb: 8/28/19								
1919	Was-A	28	105	13	29	4	1	0	16	2	15	.276	.290	.333	75	-4	5			.945	-4	S-28	-0.7
1920	Was-A	101	336	38	98	14	2	0	36	19	23	.292	.331	.345	82	-9	5	4	-1	.934	5	3-75,S-19/O-1	-0.7
1921	Was-A	10	10	1	2	0	1	0	1	0	2	.200	.200	.400	52	-1	0	0	0	.000	-5	H	-0.1
	StL-A	105	430	65	124	20	12	2	49	22	42	.288	.327	.405	81	-14	1	6	-3	.953	2	*3-105	-0.7
	Yr	115	440	66	126	20	13	2	50	22	44	.286	.325	.405	81	-14	1	6	-3	.953	2	*3-105	-0.8
1922	StL-A	91	342	42	84	16	3	1	33	25	36	.246	.303	.319	60	-20	1	1	-0	.955	16	3-91	0.2
1923	StL-A	18	49	6	9	0	0	0	1	1	5	.184	.200	.184	1	-7	0	0	0	.967	-3	3-14	-0.9
1924	StL-A	21	61	7	12	3	0	0	2	2	3	.197	.222	.246	19	-7	0	1	-1	.953	-3	3-21	-0.4
	Cle-A	46	120	7	31	1	3	1	14	1	10	.258	.270	.342	56	-8	0	0	0	.975	5	3-39/2-2	-0.1
	Yr	67	181	14	43	4	3	1	16	3	13	.238	.254	.309	44	-16	0	1	-1	.967	8	3-60/2-2	-0.5
Total	6	420	1453	179	389	58	22	4	152	72	136	.268	.306	.346	68	-70	12	13		.952	14	3-345/S-47,2-2,0-1	-3.7
■ JOE ELLICK			Ellick, Joseph J.			b: 4/3/1854, Cincinnati, Ohio			d: 4/21/23, Kansas City, Kan.		5'10", 162 lbs.			Deb: 5/13/1875	MU							
1875	RS-n	7	27	1	6	1	0	0		0	1	.222	.222	.259	74	-1	1	0	MU	.471	-3	/3-5,O-2	-0.3
1878	Mil-N	3	13	2	2	0	0	0	1	0	1	.154	.154	.154	1	-1				.769	-3	/C-2,3-1,P-1	-0.3
1880	Wor-N	5	18	1	1	0	0	0		0	2	.056	.105	.056	-40	-3				.882	0	/3-5	-0.2
1884	CP-U	92	394	71	93	11	0	0		16		.236	.266	.264	61	-29				.903	-2	O-57,S-33/2-4,M	-2.9
	KC-U	2	8	0	0	0	0	0		0		.000	.000	.000	-99	-2				.778	-1	/2-1,O-1	-0.3
	Bal-U	7	27	2	4	0	0	0		2		.148	.207	.148	8	-4				.714	-1	/S-6,O-1	-0.4
	Yr	101	429	73	97	11	0	0		18		.226	.257	.252	55	-35				.894	-3	O-59,S-39/2-5	-3.6
Total	3	109	460	76	100	11	0	0	1	19	3	.217	.248	.241	50	-40				.889	-6	/O-59,S-39,3-6,2CP	-4.1
■ LARRY ELLIOT			Elliot, Lawrence Lee			b: 3/5/38, San Diego, Cal.				BL/TL, 6'2", 200 lbs.			Deb: 4/19/62								
1962	Pit-N	8	10	2	3	0	0	1	2	0	1	.300	.300	.600	135	0	0	0	0	1.000	-1	/O-3	0.0
1963	Pit-N	4	4	0	0	0	0	0	0	0	1	.000	.000	.000	-99	-1	0	0	0	.000	0	H	-0.1
1964	NY-N	80	224	27	51	8	0	9	22	28	55	.228	.322	.384	100	0	1	2	-1	.985	-2	O-63	-0.5
1966	NY-N	65	199	24	49	14	2	5	32	17	46	.246	.306	.412	100	0	0	0	0	.912	0	O-54	-0.3
Total	4	157	437	53	103	22	2	15	56	45	105	.236	.311	.398	99	-1	1	3	-2	.956	-2	O-120	-0.9
■ ALLEN ELLIOTT			Elliott, Allen Clifford "Ace"			b: 12/25/1897, St.Louis, Mo.			d: 5/6/79, St.Louis, Mo.		BL/TR, 6', 170 lbs.			Deb: 6/14/23								
1923	Chi-N	53	168	21	42	8	2	2	29	2	12	.250	.267	.357	63	-9	3	3	-1	.992	-2	1-52	-1.4
1924	Chi-N	10	14	0	2	0	0	0	0	0	1	.143	.143	.143	-23	-2	0	0	0	1.000	0	1-10	-0.3
Total	2	63	182	21	44	8	2	2	29	2	13	.242	.258	.341	57	-12	3	3	-1	.992	-2	/1-62	-1.7
■ CARTER ELLIOTT			Elliott, Carter Ward			b: 11/29/1893, Atchison, Kan.			d: 5/21/59, Palm Springs, Cal.		BL/TR, 5'11", 165 lbs.			Deb: 9/10/21								
1921	Chi-N	12	28	5	7	2	0	0	5	3		.250	.364	.321	83	-0	0	0	0	.964	4	S-10	0.4
■ GENE ELLIOTT			Elliott, Eugene Birminghouse			b: 2/8/1889, Fayette Co., Pa.			d: 1/5/76, Huntingdon, Pa.		BL/TR, 5'7", 150 lbs.			Deb: 4/13/11								
1911	NY-A	5	13	1	1	1	0	0	1	2		.077	.200	.154	-1	-2	0			.000	-1	/O-2,3-1	-0.3
■ ROWDY ELLIOTT			Elliott, Harold B.			b: 7/8/1890, Kokomo, Ind.			d: 2/12/34, San Francisco, Cal.		BR/TR, 5'9", 160 lbs.			Deb: 9/24/10								
1910	Bos-N	3	2	0	0	0	0	0	0	0		.000	.000	.000	-96	-0	0			1.000	-0	/C-1	-0.1
1916	Chi-N	23	55	5	14	3	0	0	3	5		.255	.293	.309	77	-2	1			.969	-1	C-18	-0.1
1917	Chi-N	85	223	18	56	8	5	0	28	11	11	.251	.292	.332	84	1	4			.969	4	C-73	0.5
1918	Chi-N	5	10	0	0	0	0	0	0	2	1	.000	.167	.000	-47	-2	0			.952	0	/C-5	-0.1
1920	Bro-N	41	112	13	27	4	0	1	13	3	6	.241	.267	.304	62	-9	1			.964	5	C-39	0.1
Total	5	157	402	36	97	15	5	1	44	19	23	.241	.281	.311	73	-14	7	5	0	.967	8	C-136	0.3
■ HARRY ELLIOTT			Elliott, Harry Lewis			b: 12/30/23, San Francisco, Cal				BR/TR, 5'9", 175 lbs.			Deb: 8/1/53								
1953	StL-N	24	59	6	15	6	1	1	6	3	8	.254	.302	.441	91	-1	0	0	0	1.000	1	O-17	-0.1
1955	StL-N	68	117	9	30	4	0	1	12	11	9	.256	.326	.316	71	-5	0	2	-1	.978	-2	O-28	-0.9
Total	2	92	176	15	45	10	1	2	18	14	17	.256	.318	.358	78	-6	0	2	-1	.988	-2	/O-45	-1.0
■ RANDY ELLIOTT			Elliott, Randy Lee			b: 6/5/51, Oxnard, Cal.				BR/TR, 6'2", 190 lbs.			Deb: 9/10/72								
1972	SD-N	14	49	5	10	3	0	2	6	2	11	.204	.235	.306	57	-3	0	0	0	1.000	1	O-13	-0.3
1974	SD-N	13	33	5	7	1	0	1	2	7	9	.212	.350	.333	96	0	0	1	-1	1.000	-2	O-11/1-1	-0.4
1977	SF-N	73	167	17	40	5	1	7	26	8	24	.240	.278	.407	82	-5	0	0	0	.973	1	O-46	-0.7
1980	Oak-A	14	39	4	5	3	0	0	1	1	13	.128	.150	.205	-4	-6	0	0	0	.000	0	D-11	-0.3
Total	4	114	288	31	62	12	2	8	35	18	57	.215	.264	.354	69	-14	0	3	-2	.982	-1	/O-70,D-11,1-1	-2.0
■ BOB ELLIOTT			Elliott, Robert Irving "Mr. Team"			b: 11/26/16, San Francisco, Cal.			d: 5/4/66, San Diego, Cal.		BR/TR, 6', 185 lbs.			Deb: 9/2/39	MC							
1939	Pit-N	32	129	18	43	10	3	3	19	9	4	.333	.377	.527	143	7	0			.978	3	O-30	0.9
1940	Pit-N	148	551	88	161	34	11	5	64	45	28	.292	.348	.421	112	9	13			.978	2	*O-147	0.3
1941	Pit-N★	141	527	74	144	24	10	3	76	46	52	.273	.333	.374	105	5	6			.970	2	*O-139	-0.2

YEAR	TM/L	G	AB	R	H	2B	3B	HR	RBI	BB	SO	AVG	OBP	SLG	PRO+	BR/A	SB	CS	SBR	FA	FR	G/POS	TPR
1942	Pit-N★	143	560	75	166	26	7	9	89	52	35	.296	.358	.416	123	16	2			.927	-2	*3-142/O-1	1.7
1943	Pit-N	156	581	82	183	30	12	7	101	56	24	.315	.376	.444	132	23	4			.949	-8	*3-151/2-2,S-1	1.9
1944	Pit-N★	143	538	85	160	28	16	10	108	75	42	.297	.383	.465	132	24	9			.944	-1	*3-140/S-1	2.5
1945	Pit-N†	144	541	80	157	36	6	8	108	64	38	.290	.366	.423	115	11	5			.928	8	3-81,O-61	1.8
1946	Pit-N	140	486	50	128	25	3	5	68	64	44	.263	.351	.358	99	1	6			.995	3	O-92,3-43	0.0
1947	Bos-N†	150	555	93	176	35	5	22	113	87	60	.317	.410	.517	148	40	3			**.956**	-2	*3-148	3.7
1948	*Bos-N★	151	540	99	153	24	5	23	100	**131**	57	.283	.423	.467	145	40	6			.945	-10	*3-150	2.8
1949	Bos-N	139	482	77	135	29	5	17	76	90	38	.280	.395	.467	138	28	0			.963	11	*3-130	3.5
1950	Bos-N	142	531	94	162	28	5	24	107	68	67	.305	.386	.512	143	33	2			.952	-17	*3-137	1.3
1951	Bos-N★	136	480	73	137	29	2	15	70	65	56	.285	.371	.448	128	19	2	0	1	.941	-8	*3-127	1.1
1952	NY-N	98	272	33	62	6	2	10	35	36	20	.228	.323	.375	92	-3	1	0	0	.978	-6	O-65,3-13	-1.1
1953	StL-A	48	160	19	40	7	1	5	29	30	18	.250	.368	.400	105	2	0	1	-1	.954	-2	3-45	-0.1
	Chi-A	67	208	24	54	11	1	4	32	31	21	.260	.358	.380	96	-0	1	1	-0	.963	-11	3-58/O-2	-1.3
	Yr	115	368	43	94	18	2	9	61	61	39	.255	.363	.389	100	1	1	2	-1	.959	-12	*3-103/O-2	-1.4
Total	15	1978	7141	1064	2061	382	94	170	1195	967	604	.289	.375	.440	124	252	60	2		.947	-38	*3-1365,O-537/S-2,2	18.8

■ BEN ELLIS
Ellis, Benjamin Franklin b: 7/1870, New York, N.Y. 5'10", 165 lbs. Deb: 7/16/1896

YEAR	TM/L	G	AB	R	H	2B	3B	HR	RBI	BB	SO	AVG	OBP	SLG	PRO+	BR/A	SB	CS	SBR	FA	FR	G/POS	TPR
1896	Phi-N	4	16	0	1	0	0	0		3	6	.063	.211	.063	-26	-3	0			.800	-1	/S-2,3-2	-0.3

■ RUBE ELLIS
Ellis, George William b: 11/17/1885, Downey, Cal. d: 3/13/38, Rivera, Cal. BL/TL, 6', 170 lbs. Deb: 4/15/09

YEAR	TM/L	G	AB	R	H	2B	3B	HR	RBI	BB	SO	AVG	OBP	SLG	PRO+	BR/A	SB	CS	SBR	FA	FR	G/POS	TPR
1909	StL-N	149	575	76	154	10	9	3	46	54		.268	.334	.332	114	9	16			.955	13	*O-145	1.8
1910	StL-N	142	550	87	142	18	8	4	54	62	70	.258	.339	.342	102	2	25			.942	0	*O-141	-0.5
1911	StL-N	155	555	69	139	20	11	2	66	66	64	.250	.332	.337	90	-7	9			.938	1	*O-148	-1.5
1912	StL-N	109	305	47	82	18	2	4	33	34	36	.269	.342	.380	100	-0	6			.929	0	O-76	-0.4
Total	4	555	1985	279	517	66	30	13	199	216	170	.260	.336	.344	101	4	56			.943	14	O-510	-0.6

■ JOHN ELLIS
Ellis, John Charles b: 8/21/48, New London, Conn. BR/TR, 6'2.5", 225 lbs. Deb: 5/17/69

YEAR	TM/L	G	AB	R	H	2B	3B	HR	RBI	BB	SO	AVG	OBP	SLG	PRO+	BR/A	SB	CS	SBR	FA	FR	G/POS	TPR
1969	NY-A	22	62	2	18	4	0	1	8	1	11	.290	.313	.403	103	-0	0	2	-1	.978	1	C-15	0.0
1970	NY-A	78	226	24	56	12	1	7	29	18	47	.248	.309	.403	100	-1	0	1	-1	.992	1	1-53/3-5,C-2	-0.5
1971	NY-A	83	238	16	58	12	1	3	34	23	42	.244	.326	.340	95	-2	0	0	0	.990	-3	1-65/C-2	-1.1
1972	NY-A	52	136	13	40	5	1	5	25	8	22	.294	.333	.456	138	6	0	0	0	.965	1	C-25/1-8	0.8
1973	Cle-A	127	437	59	118	12	2	14	68	46	57	.270	.344	.403	108	5	0	0	0	.980	-18	C-72,D-38,1-12	-1.2
1974	Cle-A	128	477	58	136	23	6	10	64	32	53	.285	.331	.421	116	9	1	2	-1	.992	-8	1-69,C-42,D-21	-0.4
1975	Cle-A	92	296	22	68	11	1	7	32	14	33	.230	.269	.345	72	-12	0	1	-1	.976	-8	C-84/1-2,D-3	-1.7
1976	Tex-A	11	31	4	13	2	0	1	8	0	4	.419	.419	.581	187	3	0	0	0	1.000	-1	/C-7,D-3	0.2
1977	Tex-A	49	119	7	28	7	0	4	15	8	26	.235	.283	.395	82	-3	0	0	0	1.000	-2	C-16,D-15/1-8	-0.6
1978	Tex-A	34	94	7	23	4	0	3	17	6	20	.245	.290	.383	88	-2	0	1	-1	.958	-2	C-22/D-7	-0.4
1979	Tex-A	111	316	33	90	12	0	12	61	15	55	.285	.321	.437	103	1	2	2	-1	.978	-3	D-62,1-30/C-7	-0.7
1980	Tex-A	73	182	12	43	9	1	1	23	14	23	.236	.294	.313	69	-8	3	0	1	.992	-2	1-39,D-20/C-3	-1.2
1981	Tex-A	23	58	2	8	3	0	1	7	5	10	.138	.219	.241	34	-5	0	1	-1	.993	-1	1-18/D-1	-0.8
Total	13	883	2672	259	699	116	13	69	391	190	403	.262	.315	.392	99	-10	6	10	-4	.989	-46	1-304,C-297,D/3	-7.6

■ ROB ELLIS
Ellis, Robert Walter b: 7/3/50, Grand Rapids, Mich. BR/TR, 5'11", 180 lbs. Deb: 6/18/71

YEAR	TM/L	G	AB	R	H	2B	3B	HR	RBI	BB	SO	AVG	OBP	SLG	PRO+	BR/A	SB	CS	SBR	FA	FR	G/POS	TPR
1971	Mil-A	36	111	9	22	2	0	0	6	12	24	.198	.282	.216	43	-8	0	2	-1	.923	-7	3-19,O-15	-1.9
1974	Mil-A	22	48	4	14	2	0	0	4	1	11	.292	.346	.333	97	-0	0	0	0	1.000	-1	O-11/3-1,D-9	-0.1
1975	Mil-A	6	7	3	2	0	0	0	0	0	0	.286	.286	.286	62	-0	0	0	0	1.000	-2	/O-5,D-1	-0.2
Total	3	64	166	16	38	4	0	0	10	16	35	.229	.301	.253	59	-8	0	2	-1	.976	-10	/O-31,3-20,D-10	-2.2

■ BABE ELLISON
Ellison, Herbert Spencer "Bert" b: 11/15/1895, Rutland, Ark. d: 8/11/55, San Francisco, Cal BR/TR, 5'11", 170 lbs. Deb: 9/18/16

YEAR	TM/L	G	AB	R	H	2B	3B	HR	RBI	BB	SO	AVG	OBP	SLG	PRO+	BR/A	SB	CS	SBR	FA	FR	G/POS	TPR
1916	Det-A	2	7	0	1	0	0	0	0	0	0	.143	.143	.143	-14	-1	0			1.000	-1	/3-2	-0.3
1917	Det-A	9	29	2	5	1	2	0	4	6	3	.172	.333	.448	139	1	0			.980	-2	/1-9	-0.1
1918	Det-A	7	23	1	6	1	0	0	2	3	1	.261	.346	.304	100	0	1			1.000	-0	/O-4,2-3	0.0
1919	Det-A	56	134	18	29	4	0	0	11	13	24	.216	.291	.246	53	-8	4			.966	-7	2-25,O-10/S-1	-1.5
1920	Det-A	61	155	11	34	7	2	0	21	8	26	.219	.258	.290	46	-12	4	1	1	.997	-3	1-38/O-4,3-1	-1.1
Total	5	135	348	32	75	13	4	1	39	30	55	.216	.282	.284	58	-20	9	1		.994	-9	/1-47,2-28,O-18,3S	-3.0

■ VERDO ELMORE
Elmore, Verdo Wilson "Ellie" b: 12/10/1899, Gordo, Ala. d: 8/5/69, Birmingham, Ala. BL/TL, 5'11", 185 lbs. Deb: 9/11/24

YEAR	TM/L	G	AB	R	H	2B	3B	HR	RBI	BB	SO	AVG	OBP	SLG	PRO+	BR/A	SB	CS	SBR	FA	FR	G/POS	TPR
1924	StL-A	7	17	2	3	3	0	0	0	1	3	.176	.222	.353	44	-2	0	0	0	.000	-2	/O-3	-0.3

■ ROY ELSH
Elsh, Eugene Reybold b: 3/1/1892, Penns Grove, N.J. d: 11/12/78, Philadelphia, Pa. BR/TR, 5'9", 165 lbs. Deb: 4/19/23

YEAR	TM/L	G	AB	R	H	2B	3B	HR	RBI	BB	SO	AVG	OBP	SLG	PRO+	BR/A	SB	CS	SBR	FA	FR	G/POS	TPR
1923	Chi-A	81	209	28	52	7	2	0	24	16	23	.249	.305	.301	61	-12	16	8	0	.957	1	O-57	-1.4
1924	Chi-A	60	147	21	45	9	1	0	11	10	14	.306	.350	.381	91	-2	6	1	0	.953	-6	O-38/1-2	-0.8
1925	Chi-A	32	48	6	9	1	0	0	4	5	7	.188	.264	.208	22	-6	2	0	1	.964	0	O-16/1-3	-0.6
Total	3	173	404	55	106	17	3	0	39	31	44	.262	.317	.319	67	-20	24	9	2	.957	-6	O-111/1-5	-2.8

■ KEVIN ELSTER
Elster, Kevin Daniel b: 8/3/64, San Pedro, Cal. BR/TR, 6'2", 180 lbs. Deb: 9/2/86

YEAR	TM/L	G	AB	R	H	2B	3B	HR	RBI	BB	SO	AVG	OBP	SLG	PRO+	BR/A	SB	CS	SBR	FA	FR	G/POS	TPR
1986	*NY-N	19	30	3	5	1	0	0	0	3	8	.167	.242	.200	24	-3	0	0	0	.962	4	S-19	0.2
1987	NY-N	5	10	1	4	2	0	0	1	0	1	.400	.400	.600	169	1	0	0	0	.909	-0	/S-3	0.1
1988	*NY-N	149	406	41	87	11	1	9	37	35	47	.214	.282	.313	74	-14	2	0	1	.977	5	*S-148	0.2
1989	NY-N	151	458	52	106	25	2	10	55	34	77	.231	.287	.360	88	-8	4	3	-1	.976	7	*S-150	1.0
1990	NY-N	92	314	36	65	20	1	9	45	30	54	.207	.278	.363	75	-11	2	0	0	.960	15	S-92	1.1
1991	NY-N	115	348	33	84	16	2	6	36	40	53	.241	.321	.351	90	-4	2	3	-1	.970	11	*S-107	1.3
1992	NY-N	6	18	0	4	0	0	0	0	2	2	.222	.222	.222	27	-2	0	0	0	1.000	-1	/S-5	-0.1
1994	NY-A	7	20	0	0	0	0	0	0	1	6	.000	.048	.000	-90	-6	0	0	0	1.000	5	/S-7	-0.1
1995	NY-A	10	17	1	2	1	0	0	1	1	2	.118	.167	.176	-11	-3	0	0	0	1.000	5	S-10/2-1	-0.1
	Phi-N	26	53	10	11	4	1	1	9	7	14	.208	.311	.377	80	-2	0	0	0	.982	0	S-19/1-4,3-2	-0.1
1996	*Tex-A	157	515	79	130	32	2	24	99	52	138	.252	.323	.462	89	-10	4	1	1	.981	4	*S-157	0.7
Total	10	737	2189	256	498	112	9	59	282	203	405	.228	.296	.368	81	-63	14	7	0	.974	51	*S-717/1-4,3-2,2-1	4.1

■ BONES ELY
Ely, William Frederick b: 6/7/1863, N.Girard, Pa. d: 1/10/52, Berkeley, Cal. BR/TR, 6'1", 155 lbs. Deb: 6/19/1884

YEAR	TM/L	G	AB	R	H	2B	3B	HR	RBI	BB	SO	AVG	OBP	SLG	PRO+	BR/A	SB	CS	SBR	FA	FR	G/POS	TPR
1884	Buf-N	1	4	0	0	0	0	0	0	0	2	.000	.000	.000	-97	-1				.000	-1	/O-1,P-1	-0.1
1886	Lou-a	10	32	5	5	0	0	0		6	2	.156	.206	.156	13	-3	1			1.000	-0	/P-6,O-5	-0.2
1890	Syr-a	119	496	72	130	16	6	0	64	31		.262	.308	.319	95	-4	44			.915	19	O-78,S-36/1-4,23P	1.3
1891	Bro-N	31	111	9	17	1	0	1	11	7	9	.153	.203	.171	9	-13	4			.870	8	S-28/3-2,2-1	-0.3
1893	StL-N	44	178	25	45	1	6	0	16	17	13	.253	.318	.326	71	-8	2			.905	-3	S-44	-0.3
1894	StL-N	127	510	85	156	20	12	12	89	30	34	.306	.344	.463	93	-9	23			.901	1	*S-126/2-1,P-1	-0.1
1895	StL-N	117	467	68	121	16	2	1	46	19	17	.259	.288	.308	85	-32	28			.925	6	*S-117	-1.7
1896	Pit-N	128	537	85	153	15	9	3	77	33	33	.285	.326	.363	85	-12	18			.918	-2	*S-128	-0.8
1897	Pit-N	133	516	63	146	20	8	2	74	25		.283	.317	.364	83	-14	10			.927	3	*S-133	-0.7
1898	Pit-N	148	519	49	110	14	5	2	44	24		.212	.247	.270	49	-36	6			**.943**	8	*S-148	-2.0
1899	Pit-N	138	522	66	145	18	4	1	72	22		.278	.313	.352	83	-14	8			.928	3	*S-132/2-6	0.0
1900	*Pit-N	130	475	60	116	6	6	0	51	17		.244	.272	.282	53	-31	6			.935	13	*S-130	-0.8
1901	Pit-N	65	240	18	50	6	3	0	26	6		.208	.234	.258	41	-18	6			.916	-8	S-64/3-1	-2.1
	Phi-A	45	171	11	37	8	2	0	16	3		.216	.230	.275	38	-15	6			.913	1	S-45	-0.9
1902	Was-A	105	381	39	100	11	2	0	62	21		.262	.301	.310	69	-16	3			.923	-9	*S-105	-1.8
Total	14	1341	5159	655	1331	149	68	24	656	257	108	.258	.295	.327	69	-225	164			.923	39	*S-1236/O-84,2P31	-10.9

■ CHESTER EMERSON
Emerson, Chester Arthur "Chuck" b: 10/27/1889, Stow, Me. d: 7/2/71, Augusta, Me. BL/TR, 5'8", 165 lbs. Deb: 9/27/11

YEAR	TM/L	G	AB	R	H	2B	3B	HR	RBI	BB	SO	AVG	OBP	SLG	PRO+	BR/A	SB	CS	SBR	FA	FR	G/POS	TPR
1911	Phi-A	7	18	2	4	0	0	0	0		6	.222	.417	.222	82	0	1			1.000	0	/O-7	0.0
1912	Phi-A	1	1	0	0	0	0	0	0	0	0	.000	.000	.000	-99	-0	0			.000	0	H	0.0
Total	2	8	19	2	4	0	0	0	0		6	.211	.400	.211	74	-0	1			1.000	1	/O-7	0.0

■ CAL EMERY
Emery, Calvin Wayne   b: 6/28/37, Centre Hall, Pa.   BL/TL, 6'2", 205 lbs.   Deb: 7/15/63   C

YEAR	TM/L	G	AB	R	H	2B	3B	HR	RBI	BB	SO	AVG	OBP	SLG	PRO+	BR/A	SB	CS	SBR	FA	FR	G/POS	TPR
1963	Phi-N	16	19	0	3	1	0	0	0	0	2	.158	.158	.211	5	-2	0	0	0	1.000	-0	/1-2	-0.3

■ SPOKE EMERY
Emery, Herrick Smith   b: 12/10/1898, Bay City, Mich.   d: 6/2/75, Cape Canaveral, Fla.   BR/TR, 5'9", 165 lbs.   Deb: 7/18/24

YEAR	TM/L	G	AB	R	H	2B	3B	HR	RBI	BB	SO	AVG	OBP	SLG	PRO+	BR/A	SB	CS	SBR	FA	FR	G/POS	TPR
1924	Phi-N	5	3	3	2	0	0	0	0	0	0	.667	.667	.667	230	1	0	1		1.000	-0	/O-1	0.0

■ FRANK EMMER
Emmer, Frank William   b: 2/17/1896, Crestline, Ohio   d: 10/18/63, Homestead, Fla.   BR/TR, 5'8", 150 lbs.   Deb: 4/25/16

YEAR	TM/L	G	AB	R	H	2B	3B	HR	RBI	BB	SO	AVG	OBP	SLG	PRO+	BR/A	SB	CS	SBR	FA	FR	G/POS	TPR
1916	Cin-N	42	89	8	13	3	1	0	2	7	27	.146	.208	.202	27	-8	1			.899	5	S-29/O-2,2-1,3-1	-0.2
1926	Cin-N	80	224	22	44	7	6	0	18	13	30	.196	.244	.281	42	-19	1			.918	-7	S-79	-1.9
Total	2	122	313	30	57	10	7	0	20	20	57	.182	.234	.259	38	-26	2			.913	-3	S-108/O-2,3-1,2-1	-2.1

■ BOB EMMERICH
Emmerich, Robert George   b: 8/1/1897, New York, N.Y.   d: 11/22/48, Bridgeport, Conn.   BR/TR, 5'3", 155 lbs.   Deb: 9/22/23

YEAR	TM/L	G	AB	R	H	2B	3B	HR	RBI	BB	SO	AVG	OBP	SLG	PRO+	BR/A	SB	CS	SBR	FA	FR	G/POS	TPR
1923	Bos-N	13	24	3	2	0	0	0	0	2	3	.083	.154	.083	-37	-5	1	1	-0	1.000	-1	/O-8	-0.6

■ ANGELO ENCARNACION
Encarnacion, Angelo Benjamin   b: 4/18/73, Santo Domingo, D.R.   BR/TR, 5'8", 180 lbs.   Deb: 5/2/95

YEAR	TM/L	G	AB	R	H	2B	3B	HR	RBI	BB	SO	AVG	OBP	SLG	PRO+	BR/A	SB	CS	SBR	FA	FR	G/POS	TPR
1995	Pit-N	58	159	18	36	7	2	1	10	13	28	.226	.285	.333	61	-9	1	1	-0	.979	6	C-55	0.0
1996	Pit-N	7	22	3	7	2	0	0	1	0	5	.318	.318	.409	87	-0	0	0	0	.951	-1	/C-7	-0.1
Total	2	65	181	21	43	9	2	1	11	13	33	.238	.289	.343	64	-9	1	1	-0	.976	6	/C-62	-0.1

■ BILL ENDICOTT
Endicott, William Franklin   b: 9/4/18, Acorn, Mo.   BL/TL, 5'11.5", 175 lbs.   Deb: 4/21/46

YEAR	TM/L	G	AB	R	H	2B	3B	HR	RBI	BB	SO	AVG	OBP	SLG	PRO+	BR/A	SB	CS	SBR	FA	FR	G/POS	TPR
1946	StL-N	20	20	2	4	0	0	0	3	4		.200	.333	.350	90	-0	0			1.000	-0	/O-2	0.0

■ CLYDE ENGLE
Engle, Arthur Clyde "Hack"   b: 3/19/1884, Dayton, Ohio   d: 12/26/39, Boston, Mass.   BR/TR, 5'10", 190 lbs.   Deb: 4/12/09

YEAR	TM/L	G	AB	R	H	2B	3B	HR	RBI	BB	SO	AVG	OBP	SLG	PRO+	BR/A	SB	CS	SBR	FA	FR	G/POS	TPR
1909	NY-A	135	492	66	137	20	5	3	71	47		.278	.347	.358	122	13	18			.946	14	*O-134	2.4
1910	NY-A	5	13	0	3	0	0	0	0	2		.231	.333	.231	73	-0	1			.857	-0	/O-3	-0.1
	Bos-A	106	363	59	96	18	7	2	38	31		.264	.326	.369	115	5	12			.915	-8	3-51,2-27,O-15,/S-7	0.7
	Yr	111	376	59	99	18	7	2	38	33		.263	.326	.364	113	5	13			.915	-0	3-51,2-27,O-18,/S-7	0.6
1911	Bos-A	146	514	58	139	13	3	2	48	51		.270	.343	.319	86	-8	24			.975	-4	1-65,3-51,2-13,O-10	-1.2
1912	*Bos-A	58	171	32	40	5	3	0	18	28		.234	.348	.298	81	-3	12			.977	-8	1-25,2-15,3-11,/SO	-1.2
1913	Bos-A	143	498	75	144	17	12	6	50	53	41	.289	.363	.384	116	10	28			.987	-7	*1-133/O-2	0.1
1914	Bos-A	59	134	14	26	2	0	0	9	14	11	.194	.275	.209	46	-8	4	9	-4	.976	-1	1-29/2-5,3-3,O-1	-2.0
	Buf-F	32	110	12	28	4	1	0	12	11	18	.255	.328	.309	73	-6	5			.889	-7	3-23/O-9	-1.3
1915	Buf-F	141	501	56	131	22	8	3	71	34	43	.261	.312	.355	86	-17	24			.969	-3	*O-100,2-21,3-17,/1	-2.7
1916	Cle-A	11	26	1	4	0	0	0	1	0	6	.154	.154	.154	-7	-3	0			.810	-2	/3-7,1-2,O-1	-0.6
Total	8	836	2822	373	748	101	39	12	318	271	119	.265	.335	.341	97	-19	128	9		.959	-21	O-276,1-255,3/2S	-5.9

■ CHARLIE ENGLE
Engle, Charlie August "Cholly"   b: 8/27/03, New York, N.Y.   d: 10/12/83, San Antonio, Tex.   BR/TR, 5'8", 145 lbs.   Deb: 9/14/25

YEAR	TM/L	G	AB	R	H	2B	3B	HR	RBI	BB	SO	AVG	OBP	SLG	PRO+	BR/A	SB	CS	SBR	FA	FR	G/POS	TPR
1925	Phi-A	1	0	0	0	0	0	0	0	0	0	—	—	—		0	0	0	0	.000	0	/S-1	0.0
1926	Phi-A	19	19	7	2	0	0	0	0	10	6	.105	.433	.105	43	-1	0	0	0	.930	2	S-16	0.2
1930	Pit-N	67	216	34	57	10	1	0	15	22	20	.264	.335	.319	59	-14	1			.975	-1	3-24,S-23,2-10	-0.9
Total	3	87	235	41	59	10	1	0	15	32	26	.251	.346	.302	59	-15	1			.937	2	/S-40,3-24,2-10	-0.7

■ DAVE ENGLE
Engle, Ralph David   b: 11/30/56, San Diego, Cal.   BR/TR, 6'3", 216 lbs.   Deb: 4/14/81

YEAR	TM/L	G	AB	R	H	2B	3B	HR	RBI	BB	SO	AVG	OBP	SLG	PRO+	BR/A	SB	CS	SBR	FA	FR	G/POS	TPR
1981	Min-A	82	248	29	64	14	4	5	32	13	37	.258	.298	.407	95	-2	0	1	-1	.980	-0	O-76/3-1,D-1	-0.6
1982	Min-A	58	186	20	42	7	2	4	16	10	22	.226	.269	.349	67	-9	0	0	0	.985	0	O-34,D-20	-1.0
1983	Min-A	120	374	46	114	22	4	8	43	28	39	.305	.355	.449	115	-3	8	2	1	.973	-19	C-73,D-29/O-4	-0.9
1984	Min-A☆	109	391	56	104	20	1	4	38	26	22	.266	.312	.353	80	-11	0	1	0	.981	-7	C-86,D-22	-1.5
1985	Min-A	70	172	28	44	8	2	7	25	21	28	.256	.337	.448	106	1	2	2	-1	.984	0	D-38,C-17/O-3	-1.5
1986	Det-A	35	86	6	22	7	0	0	4	7	13	.256	.312	.337	77	-3	0	0	0	1.000	-1	1-23/O-4,C-3,D-5	-0.5
1987	Mon-N	59	84	7	19	4	0	1	14	6	11	.226	.278	.310	54	-6	1	0	0	1.000	0	O-11/C-6,1-2,3-1	-0.6
1988	Mon-N	34	37	4	8	3	0	0	1	5	5	.216	.310	.297	72	-1	1	0	0	1.000	-1	/C-9,O-4,3-1	-0.2
1989	Mil-A	27	65	5	14	3	0	2	4	3	11	.215	.261	.354	72	-3	0	0	0	.973	-3	1-18/C-3,D-3	-0.4
Total	9	594	1643	201	431	88	13	31	181	120	190	.262	.314	.388	90	-25	5	5	-2	.979	-29	C-197,O-136/D-13	-5.7

■ CHARLIE ENGLISH
English, Charles Dewie   b: 4/8/10, Darlington, S.C.   BR/TR, 5'9.5", 160 lbs.   Deb: 7/23/32

YEAR	TM/L	G	AB	R	H	2B	3B	HR	RBI	BB	SO	AVG	OBP	SLG	PRO+	BR/A	SB	CS	SBR	FA	FR	G/POS	TPR
1932	Chi-A	24	63	7	20	3	1	1	8	7	3	.317	.348	.444	111	1	0	0	0	.821	-2	3-13/S-1	-0.1
1933	Chi-A	3	9	2	4	2	0	0	1	1	1	.444	.500	.667	216	2	0	0	0	.923	-1	/2-3	0.1
1936	NY-N	6	1	0	0	0	0	0	0	0	0	.000	.000	.000	-99	-0	0			.000	0	/2-1	0.0
1937	Cin-N	17	63	1	15	3	1	0	4	0	2	.238	.238	.317	52	-4	0			.958	-4	3-15/2-2	-0.2
Total	4	50	136	10	39	8	2	1	13	4	10	.287	.307	.397	90	-2	0			.897	-6	/3-28,2-6,S-1	-0.2

■ WOODY ENGLISH
English, Elwood George   b: 3/2/07, Fredonia, Ohio   BR/TR, 5'10", 155 lbs.   Deb: 4/26/27

YEAR	TM/L	G	AB	R	H	2B	3B	HR	RBI	BB	SO	AVG	OBP	SLG	PRO+	BR/A	SB	CS	SBR	FA	FR	G/POS	TPR
1927	Chi-N	87	334	46	97	14	4	1	28	16	26	.290	.325	.365	94	-8	1			.940	7	S-84/3-1	0.7
1928	Chi-N	116	475	68	142	22	4	2	34	30	28	.299	.343	.375	89	-8	4			.946	6	*S-114/3-2	1.1
1929	*Chi-N	144	608	131	168	29	3	1	52	68	50	.276	.352	.339	72	-25	13			.955	15	*S-144	0.8
1930	Chi-N	156	638	152	214	36	17	14	59	100	72	.335	.430	.511	125	30	3			.973	-13	3-83,S-78	2.7
1931	Chi-N	156	634	117	202	38	8	2	53	68	80	.319	.391	.413	114	15	12			.965	1	*S-138,3-18	3.1
1932	*Chi-N	127	522	70	142	23	7	3	47	55	73	.272	.344	.360	90	-6	5			.957	-2	3-93,S-38	0.1
1933	Chi-N★	105	398	54	104	19	2	3	41	53	44	.261	.348	.342	98	1	5			**.973**	-15	*3-103/S-1	-0.8
1934	Chi-N	109	421	65	117	26	5	3	31	48	65	.278	.353	.385	99	1	6			.971	-10	S-56,3-46/2-7	-0.4
1935	Chi-N	34	84	11	17	2	0	2	8	20	4	.202	.368	.298	81	-1	1			.868	-3	3-16,S-12	-0.5
1936	Chi-N	64	182	33	45	9	0	0	20	40	28	.247	.394	.297	86	-1	1			.976	1	S-42,3-17/2-1	0.3
1937	Bro-N	129	378	45	90	16	2	1	42	65	55	.238	.350	.299	77	-10	4			.956	-17	*S-116,2-11	-1.9
1938	Bro-N	34	72	9	18	2	0	0	7	8	11	.250	.333	.278	68	-3	2			.958	1	3-21/2-3,S-3	-0.2
Total	12	1261	4746	801	1356	236	52	32	422	571	536	.286	.366	.378	95	-14	57			.957	-31	S-826,3-400/2-22	5.0

■ GIL ENGLISH
English, Gilbert Raymond   b: 7/2/09, Glenola, N.C.   d: 8/31/96, Trinity, N.C.   BR/TR, 5'11", 180 lbs.   Deb: 9/20/31

YEAR	TM/L	G	AB	R	H	2B	3B	HR	RBI	BB	SO	AVG	OBP	SLG	PRO+	BR/A	SB	CS	SBR	FA	FR	G/POS	TPR
1931	NY-N	3	8	0	0	0	0	0	0	1	3	.000	.111	.000	-69	-2	0			1.000	-1	/3-3	-0.3
1932	NY-N	59	204	22	46	7	5	2	19	5	20	.225	.244	.338	56	-13	0			.931	4	3-39,S-23	-0.5
1936	Det-A	1	1	0	0	0	0	0	0	0	1	.000	.000	.000	-99	-0	0	0	0	1.000	0	/3-1	0.0
1937	Det-A	18	65	6	17	1	1	0	6	6	4	.262	.333	.323	65	-3	1	1	-0	.962	-8	2-12/3-6	-1.0
	Bos-N	79	269	25	78	5	2	2	37	23	27	.290	.348	.346	98	-1	3			.958	-7	3-71	-0.6
1938	Bos-N	53	165	17	41	6	0	2	21	15	16	.248	.315	.321	84	-4	3			.956	-4	3-43/O-3,2-2,S-2	-0.7
1944	Bro-N	27	79	4	12	3	0	1	7	6	7	.152	.212	.228	24	-8	0			.918	-3	S-13,3-11/2-2	-1.1
Total	6	240	791	74	194	22	7	8	90	56	78	.245	.298	.321	72	-31	5	1		.950	-18	3-174/S-38,2-16,O-3	-4.2

■ DEL ENNIS
Ennis, Delmer   b: 6/8/25, Philadelphia, Pa.   d: 2/8/96, Huntingdon Valley, Pa.   BR/TR, 6', 195 lbs.   Deb: 4/28/46

YEAR	TM/L	G	AB	R	H	2B	3B	HR	RBI	BB	SO	AVG	OBP	SLG	PRO+	BR/A	SB	CS	SBR	FA	FR	G/POS	TPR
1946	Phi-N★	141	540	70	169	30	6	17	73	39	65	.313	.364	.485	144	28	5			.975	14	*O-138	3.7
1947	Phi-N	139	541	71	149	25	6	12	81	37	51	.275	.325	.410	98	4	9			.979	9	*O-135	-0.1
1948	Phi-N	152	589	86	171	40	4	30	95	47	58	.290	.345	.525	135	25	2			.957	5	*O-151	2.2
1949	Phi-N	154	610	92	184	39	11	25	110	59	61	.302	.367	.525	140	32	2			.966	6	*O-154	3.0
1950	*Phi-N	153	595	92	185	34	8	31	**126**	56	59	.311	.372	.551	142	34	2			.970	6	*O-149	2.5
1951	Phi-N★	144	532	76	142	20	5	15	73	66	42	.267	.352	.408	105	5	2			.969	-1	*O-135	-0.2
1952	Phi-N	151	592	90	171	30	10	20	107	47	65	.289	.341	.475	125	18	6	4	-1	.970	4	*O-149	1.0
1953	Phi-N	152	578	79	165	23	2	29	125	57	53	.285	.355	.484	117	13	1	3	-2	.980	4	*O-150	0.9
1954	Phi-N	145	556	73	145	23	2	25	119	50	60	.261	.324	.444	98	-1	3			.957	3	*O-142/1-1	-0.6
1955	Phi-N★	146	564	82	167	24	7	29	120	46	46	.296	.351	.518	129	22	4			.987	6	*O-145	2.0
1956	Phi-N	153	630	80	164	23	3	26	95	33	62	.260	.303	.449	95	-6	3			.962	0	*O-153	-1.5
1957	StL-N	136	490	61	140	24	3	24	105	37	50	.286	.341	.494	117	11	3	3	-2	.943	-5	*O-127	-1.7
1958	StL-N	106	329	22	86	18	1	3	47	15	35	.261	.296	.350	67	-15	0	1	-1	.993	3	O-84	-1.7
1959	Cin-N	5	12	1	4	0	0	1	2	2		.333	.429	.333	103	-0	0			1.000	-0	/O-3	0.0

YEAR	TM/L	G	AB	R	H	2B	3B	HR	RBI	BB	SO	AVG	OBP	SLG	PRO+	BR/A	SB	CS	SBR	FA	FR	G/POS	TPR
	Chi-A	26	96	10	21	6	0	2	7	4	10	.219	.250	.344	62	-5	0	0	0	.909	-3	O-25	-1.0
Total	14	1903	7254	985	2063	358	69	288	1284	597	719	.284	.341	.472	117	154	45	19		.969	28	*O-1840/1-1	8.9

■ **RUSS ENNIS**   Ennis, Russell Elwood "Hack" b: 3/10/1897, Superior, Wis. d: 1/21/49, Superior, Wis.   BR/TR, 5'11.5", 160 lbs.   Deb: 9/19/26

| 1926 | Was-A | 1 | 0 | 0 | 0 | 0 | 0 | 0 | 0 | 0 | 0 | — | — | — | — | -0 | 0 | 0 | 0 | .000 | 0 | /C-1 | 0.0 |

■ **GEORGE ENRIGHT**   Enright, George Albert b: 5/9/54, New Britain, Conn.   BR/TR, 5'11", 175 lbs.   Deb: 8/8/76

| 1976 | Chi-A | 2 | 1 | 0 | 0 | 0 | 0 | 0 | 0 | 0 | 0 | .000 | .000 | .000 | -99 | -0 | 0 | 0 | 0 | 1.000 | 1 | /C-2 | 0.0 |

■ **MUTZ ENS**   Ens, Anton b: 11/8/1884, St.Louis, Mo.   d: 6/28/50, St.Louis, Mo.   BL/TL, 6'1", 180 lbs.   Deb: 9/2/12 F

| 1912 | Chi-A | 3 | 6 | 0 | 0 | 0 | 0 | 0 | 0 | 0 | 0 | .000 | .000 | .000 | -99 | -2 | 0 | | | .857 | -1 | /1-3 | -0.2 |

■ **JEWEL ENS**   Ens, Jewel Winklemeyer b: 8/24/1889, St.Louis, Mo.   d: 1/17/50, Syracuse, N.Y.   BR/TR, 5'10.5", 165 lbs.   Deb: 4/29/22   FMC

1922	Pit-N	47	142	18	42	7	3	0	17	7	9	.296	.338	.387	85	-3	3	0	1	.951	-17	2-29/3-3,1-2,S-1	-1.7
1923	Pit-N	12	29	3	8	1	1	0	5	0	3	.276	.276	.379	70	-1	2	0	1	.975	-0	/1-4,3-3	-0.1
1924	Pit-N	5	10	2	3	0	0	0	0	0	3	.300	.300	.300	60	-1	0	0		1.000	-0	/1-5	-0.1
1925	Pit-N	3	5	2	1	0	0	1	2	0	1	.200	.200	.800	133	0	0	0		1.000	-0	/1-3	0.0
Total	4	67	186	25	54	8	4	1	24	7	16	.290	.323	.392	83	-5	5	0	2	.990	-17	/2-29,1-14,3-6,S-1	-1.9

■ **CHARLIE ENWRIGHT**   Enwright, Charles Massey b: 10/6/1887, Sacramento, Cal.   d: 1/19/17, Sacramento, Cal.   BL/TR, 5'10"   Deb: 4/19/09

| 1909 | StL-N | 3 | 7 | 1 | 1 | 0 | 0 | 0 | 0 | 1 | | .143 | .333 | .143 | 51 | -0 | 0 | | | .444 | -3 | /S-2 | -0.4 |

■ **JACK ENZENROTH**   Enzenroth, Clarence Herman b: 11/4/1885, Mineral Point, Wis.   d: 2/21/44, Detroit, Mich.   BR/TR, 5'10", 164 lbs.   Deb: 5/1/14

1914	StL-A	3	6	0	1	0	0	0	0	0	0	.167	.444	.167	88	0	0	1	-1	.923	-1	/C-3	-0.2
	KC-F	26	67	7	12	4	1	0	5	5	19	.179	.236	.269	39	-7	0			.965	-2	C-24	-0.8
1915	KC-F	14	19	3	3	0	0	0	3	6	0	.158	.360	.158	50	-1	0			.973	2	/C-8	0.1
Total	2	43	92	10	16	4	1	0	8	13	22	.174	.283	.239	47	-8	0	1		.963	-1	/C-35	-0.9

■ **JIM EPPARD**   Eppard, James Gerhard b: 4/27/60, South Bend, Ind.   BL/TL, 6'2", 180 lbs.   Deb: 9/8/87

1987	Cal-A	8	9	2	3	0	0	0	2	0	0	.333	.455	.333	118	0	0	0	0	1.000	-0	/O-1	0.0
1988	Cal-A	56	113	7	32	3	1	0	14	11	15	.283	.347	.327	92	-1	0	0	0	.971	-0	O-17,D-10/1-6	-0.1
1989	Cal-A	12	12	0	3	0	0	0	0	2	4	.250	.308	.250	60	-1	0	0	0	1.000	-0	/1-4	-0.1
1990	Tor-A	6	5	0	1	0	0	0	0	1	2	.200	.333	.200	52	-0	0	0	0	.000	-0	/H	0.0
Total	4	82	139	9	39	3	1	0	16	14	21	.281	.351	.317	90	-1	0	0	0	.972	-1	/O-18,1-10,D-10	-0.3

■ **AUBREY EPPS**   Epps, Aubrey Lee "Yo-Yo" b: 3/3/12, Memphis, Tenn.   d: 11/13/84, Ackerman, Miss.   BR/TR, 5'10", 170 lbs.   Deb: 9/29/35

| 1935 | Pit-N | 1 | 4 | 1 | 3 | 0 | 1 | 0 | 3 | 0 | 0 | .750 | .750 | 1.250 | 414 | 2 | 0 | | | .750 | -0 | /C-1 | 0.1 |

■ **HAL EPPS**   Epps, Harold Franklin b: 3/26/14, Athens, Ga.   BL/TL, 6', 175 lbs.   Deb: 9/9/38

1938	StL-N	17	50	8	15	0	0	1	3	2	4	.300	.327	.360	84	-1	2			.963	-0	O-10	-0.2
1940	StL-N	11	15	6	3	0	0	0	1	0	3	.200	.200	.200	10	-2	0			.800	-1	/O-3	-0.3
1943	StL-A	8	35	2	10	4	0	0	1	3	4	.286	.342	.400	114	1	1	1	-0	1.000	-1	/O-8	-0.3
1944	StL-A	22	62	15	11	1	1	0	3	14	11	.177	.338	.226	59	-3	0	1	-1	.962	-1	/O-18	-0.3
	Phi-A	67	229	27	60	8	8	0	13	18	18	.262	.316	.367	96	-2	2	1	0	.973	-3	O-60	-0.8
	Yr	89	291	42	71	9	9	0	16	32	32	.244	.321	.337	88	-4	2	2	-1	.970	-2	/O-78	-1.1
Total	4	125	391	58	99	13	9	1	21	37	43	.253	.319	.340	86	-7	5	3		.968	-4	/O-99	-1.7

■ **MIKE EPSTEIN**   Epstein, Michael Peter "Superjew" b: 4/4/43, Bronx, N.Y.   BL/TL, 6'3.5", 230 lbs.   Deb: 9/16/66

1966	Bal-A	6	11	1	2	0	1	0	3	1	3	.182	.250	.364	75	-0	0	0	0	1.000	0	/1-4	0.0
1967	Bal-A	9	13	0	2	0	0	0	0	3	5	.154	.313	.154	42	-1	0	0	0	1.000	0	/1-3	-0.1
	Was-A	96	284	32	65	7	4	9	29	39	74	.229	.332	.377	114	5	1	4	-2	.987	-2	1-80	-0.3
	Yr	105	297	32	67	7	4	9	29	41	79	.226	.331	.367	110	5	1	4	-2	.988	-2	1-83	-0.4
1968	Was-A	123	385	40	90	8	2	13	33	48	91	.234	.339	.366	117	9	1	1	-0	.987	-1	*1-110	0.3
1969	Was-A	131	403	73	112	18	1	30	85	85	99	.278	.416	.551	178	45	3	6		.990	-1	*1-118	3.4
1970	Was-A	140	430	55	110	15	3	20	56	73	117	.256	.375	.444	131	20	2	3	-1	.992	-3	*1-122	0.5
1971	Was-A	24	85	6	21	1	1	1	9	12	31	.247	.366	.318	101	1	1	0	0	.992	-1	1-24	-0.2
	*Oak-A	104	329	43	77	13	0	18	51	62	71	.234	.368	.438	130	15	0	3	-2	.995	-2	1-96	0.3
	Yr	128	414	49	98	14	1	19	60	74	102	.237	.368	.413	124	15	1	3	-2	.994	-2	*1-120	0.1
1972	*Oak-A	138	455	63	123	18	2	26	70	68	68	.270	.378	.490	166	38	0	1	-1	.990	-2	*1-137	2.6
1973	Tex-A	27	85	9	16	3	0	6	14	19	19	.188	.324	.259	69	-3	0	0	0	.991	-1	1-25	-0.6
	Cal-A	91	312	30	67	8	2	9	32	34	54	.215	.302	.330	84	-7	0	0	0	.993	-1	1-86	-1.4
	Yr	118	397	39	83	11	2	9	38	48	73	.209	.307	.315	81	-10	0	0	0	.993	-1	*1-111	-2.0
1974	Cal-A	18	62	10	10	2	0	4	6	10	13	.161	.288	.387	98	-0	0	0	0	.993	-1	1-18	-0.1
Total	9	907	2854	362	695	93	16	130	380	448	645	.244	.360	.424	130	121	7	17	-8	.991	-10	1-823	4.4

■ **JOE ERAUTT**   Erautt, Joseph Michael "Stubby" b: 9/1/21, Vibank, Sask., Can.   d: 10/6/76, Portland, Ore.   BR/TR, 5'9", 175 lbs.   Deb: 5/9/50 F

1950	Chi-A	16	18	0	4	0	0	0	1	3	1	.222	.263	.222	26	-2	0	0	0	1.000	1	/C-5	-0.1
1951	Chi-A	16	25	3	4	1	0	0	3	2	3	.160	.276	.200	31	-2	0	0	0	.977	3	C-12	0.1
Total	2	32	43	3	8	1	0	0	4	5	4	.186	.271	.209	29	-4	0	0	0	.983	4	/C-17	0.0

■ **HANK ERICKSON**   Erickson, Henry Nels "Popeye" b: 11/11/07, Chicago, Ill.   d: 12/13/64, Louisville, Ky.   BR/TR, 6'1", 185 lbs.   Deb: 4/17/35

| 1935 | Cin-N | 37 | 88 | 9 | 23 | 4 | 1 | 2 | 4 | 6 | 4 | .261 | .323 | .375 | 90 | -1 | 0 | | | .972 | 2 | C-25 | 0.2 |

■ **CAL ERMER**   Ermer, Calvin Coolidge b: 11/10/23, Baltimore, Md.   BR/TR, 6'0.5", 175 lbs.   Deb: 9/26/47   MC

| 1947 | Was-A | 1 | 3 | 0 | 0 | 0 | 0 | 0 | 0 | 0 | 0 | .000 | .000 | .000 | -99 | -1 | 0 | 0 | 0 | 1.000 | 1 | /2-1 | 0.0 |

■ **FRANK ERNAGA**   Ernaga, Frank John b: 8/22/30, Susanville, Cal.   BR/TR, 6'1", 195 lbs.   Deb: 5/24/57

1957	Chi-N	20	35	9	11	3	2	2	7	9	14	.314	.455	.686	204	6	0	0	0	.950	-0	O-10	0.5
1958	Chi-N	9	8	0	1	0	0	0	0	0	2	.125	.125	.125	-34	-2	0	0	0	.000	0	H	-0.2
Total	2	29	43	9	12	3	2	2	7	9	16	.279	.404	.581	163	4	0	0	0	.950	-0	/O-10	0.3

■ **DARIN ERSTAD**   Erstad, Darin Charles b: 6/4/74, Jamestown, N.D.   BL/TL, 6'2", 195 lbs.   Deb: 6/14/96

| 1996 | Cal-A | 57 | 208 | 34 | 59 | 5 | 1 | 4 | 20 | 17 | 29 | .284 | .338 | .375 | 82 | -6 | 3 | 3 | -1 | .976 | 3 | O-48 | -0.5 |

■ **TEX ERWIN**   Erwin, Ross Emil b: 12/22/1885, Forney, Tex.   d: 4/5/53, Rochester, N.Y.   BL/TR, 6', 185 lbs.   Deb: 8/26/07

1907	Det-A	4	5	0	1	0	0	0	1	1		.200	.333	.200	68	-0	0			.909	0	/C-4	0.0
1910	Bro-N	81	202	15	38	3	1	1	10	24	12	.188	.278	.228	49	-13	3			.949	-1	C-68	-0.8
1911	Bro-N	91	218	30	59	13	2	2	34	31	23	.271	.367	.445	132	9	5			.971	-5	C-74	1.1
1912	Bro-N	59	133	14	28	3	0	2	14	18	16	.211	.305	.278	62	-7	1			.949	-2	C-41	-0.5
1913	Bro-N	20	31	6	8	1	0	0	3	4	5	.258	.343	.290	80	-1	0			.950	-3	/C-13	-0.3
1914	Bro-N	9	11	0	5	1	0	0	2	1	1	.455	.538	.455	192	1	1			1.000	-1	/C-4	0.1
	Cin-N	12	35	5	11	3	0	1	2	7	5	.314	.351	.486	144	2	0			.962	1	C-12	0.3
	Yr	21	46	5	16	4	0	1	4	8	6	.348	.391	.478	157	3	1			.966	-0	C-16	0.4
Total	6	276	635	70	150	23	3	11	70	82	60	.236	.326	.334	90	-8	10			.957	-11	C-216	-0.1

■ **NICK ESASKY**   Esasky, Nicholas Andrew b: 2/24/60, Hialeah, Fla.   BR/TR, 6'3", 205 lbs.   Deb: 6/19/83

1983	Cin-N	85	302	41	80	10	5	12	46	27	99	.265	.331	.450	111	4	6	2	1	.935	-10	3-84	-0.7
1984	Cin-N	113	322	30	62	10	5	10	45	52	103	.193	.305	.348	79	-9	1	2	-1	.910	-8	3-82,1-25	-2.1
1985	Cin-N	125	413	61	108	21	0	21	66	41	102	.261	.333	.465	115	8	3	4	-2	.946	-6	3-62,O-54,1-12	-1.1
1986	Cin-N	102	330	35	76	17	2	12	41	47	95	.230	.328	.403	96	-2	0	1	-1	.991	2	1-70,O-42/3-1	-1.1
1987	Cin-N	100	346	48	94	19	2	22	59	29	94	.272	.328	.529	117	7	0	0	0	.994	-11	1-93/3-1,O-1	-1.1
1988	Cin-N	122	391	40	95	17	2	15	62	48	104	.243	.332	.412	108	2	7	2	1	.994	*-9	*1-116	-1.4
1989	Bos-A	154	564	79	156	26	5	30	108	66	117	.277	.355	.500	130	22	0	2	-1	.996	-3	*1-153/O-1	1.3

YEAR	TM/L	G	AB	R	H	2B	3B	HR	RBI	BB	SO	AVG	OBP	SLG	PRO+	BR/A	SB	CS	SBR	FA	FR	G/POS	TPR
1990	Atl-N	9	35	2	6	0	0	0	0	4	14	.171	.256	.171	19	-4	0	0	0	.944	-2	/1-9	-0.6
Total	8	810	2703	336	677	120	21	122	427	314	712	.250	.332	.446	109	31	18	14	-3	.993	-45	1-478,3-230/O-98	-6.0

■ **NINO ESCALERA**   Escalera, Saturnino Cuadrado b: 12/1/29, Santurce, P.R. BL/TR, 5'10", 165 lbs. Deb: 4/17/54

| 1954 | Cin-N | 73 | 69 | 15 | 11 | 1 | 1 | 0 | 3 | 7 | 11 | .159 | .237 | .203 | 15 | -9 | 1 | 0 | 0 | .962 | 0 | O-14/1-8,S-1 | -0.8 |

■ **JIM ESCHEN**   Eschen, James Godrich b: 8/21/1891, Brooklyn, N.Y. d: 9/27/60, Sloatsburg, N.Y. BR/TR, 5'10.5", 160 lbs. Deb: 7/10/15 F

| 1915 | Cle-A | 15 | 42 | 11 | 10 | 1 | 0 | 0 | 2 | 5 | 9 | .238 | .319 | .262 | 73 | -1 | 0 | 1 | -1 | .968 | 1 | O-10 | -0.1 |

■ **LARRY ESCHEN**   Eschen, Lawrence Edward b: 9/22/20, Suffern, N.Y. BR/TR, 6', 180 lbs. Deb: 6/16/42 F

| 1942 | Phi-A | 12 | 11 | 0 | 0 | 0 | 0 | 0 | 0 | 4 | 6 | .000 | .267 | .000 | -22 | -2 | 0 | 0 | 0 | .824 | -1 | /S-7,2-1 | -0.3 |

■ **ANGEL ESCOBAR**   Escobar, Angel Rubenque (Rivas) b: 5/12/65, LaSabana, Venez. BB/TR, 6', 160 lbs. Deb: 5/17/88

| 1988 | SF-N | 3 | 3 | 1 | 1 | 0 | 0 | 0 | 0 | 0 | 0 | .333 | .333 | .333 | 96 | -0 | 0 | 0 | 0 | 1.000 | 0 | /S-1,3-1 | 0.0 |

■ **JOSE ESCOBAR**   Escobar, Jose Elias (Sanchez) b: 10/30/60, Las Flores, Venez. BR/TR, 5'10", 140 lbs. Deb: 4/13/91

| 1991 | Cle-A | 10 | 15 | 0 | 3 | 0 | 0 | 0 | 1 | 1 | 4 | .200 | .250 | .200 | 26 | -1 | 0 | 0 | 0 | 1.000 | 2 | /S-5,2-4,3-1 | 0.0 |

■ **JIMMY ESMOND**   Esmond, James Joseph b: 10/8/1889, Albany, N.Y. d: 6/26/48, Troy, N.Y. BR/TR, 5'11", 167 lbs. Deb: 4/20/11

1911	Cin-N	73	198	27	54	4	6	1	11	17	30	.273	.330	.369	99	-1	7			.918	1	S-44,3-14/2-2	0.2
1912	Cin-N	82	231	24	45	5	3	1	40	20	31	.195	.259	.255	42	-19	11			.930	-7	S-74	-2.0
1914	Ind-F	151	542	74	160	23	**15**	2	49	40	48	.295	.344	.404	93	-13	25			.919	-7	*S-151	-0.9
1915	New-F	155	569	79	147	20	10	5	62	59	54	.258	.329	.355	98	-11	18			.939	6	*S-155	0.8
Total	4	461	1540	204	406	52	34	9	162	136	163	.264	.324	.359	88	-44	61			.929	-8	S-424/3-14,2-2	-1.9

■ **JUAN ESPINO**   Espino, Juan (Reyes) b: 3/16/56, Bonao, D.R. BR/TR, 6'1", 190 lbs. Deb: 6/25/82

1982	NY-A	3	2	0	0	0	0	0	0	0	1	.000	.000	.000	-99	-1	0	0	0	1.000	0	/C-3	0.0
1983	NY-A	10	23	1	6	0	0	1	3	1	5	.261	.292	.391	89	-0	0	0	0	1.000	-0	C-10	0.0
1985	NY-A	9	11	0	4	0	0	0	0	0	0	.364	.364	.364	102	0	0	0	0	1.000	1	/C-9	0.1
1986	NY-A	27	37	1	6	2	0	0	5	2	9	.162	.205	.216	15	-4	0	0	0	.987	3	C-27	-0.1
Total	4	49	73	2	16	2	0	1	8	3	15	.219	.250	.288	48	-5	0	0	0	.993	4	/C-49	0.0

■ **ALVARO ESPINOZA**   Espinoza, Alvaro Alberto b: 2/19/62, Valencia, Venez. BR/TR, 6', 170 lbs. Deb: 9/14/84

1984	Min-A	1	0	0	0	0	0	0	0	0	0					0	0	0	0	.000	0	/S-1	0.0
1985	Min-A	32	57	5	15	2	0	0	9	1	9	.263	.288	.298	58	-3	0	1	-1	.949	7	S-31	0.4
1986	Min-A	37	42	4	9	1	0	0	1	1	10	.214	.233	.238	28	-4	0	1	-1	.941	6	2-19,S-18	0.2
1988	NY-A	3	0	0	0	0	0	0	0	0	0	.000	.000	.000	-99	-1	0	0	0	1.000	1	/2-2,S-1	0.0
1989	NY-A	146	503	51	142	23	1	0	41	14	60	.282	.303	.332	80	-14	3	3	-1	.970	17	*S-146	1.3
1990	NY-A	150	438	31	98	12	2	2	20	16	54	.224	.259	.274	49	-30	1	2	-1	.977	**21**	*S-150	0.2
1991	NY-A	148	480	51	123	23	2	5	33	16	57	.256	.283	.344	72	-19	4	1	1	.969	20	*S-147/3-2,P-1	1.3
1993	Cle-A	129	263	34	73	15	0	4	27	8	36	.278	.301	.380	82	-7	2	2	-1	.937	1	3-99,S-35/2-2	-0.5
1994	Cle-A	90	231	27	55	13	0	1	19	6	33	.238	.261	.307	46	-19	1	3	-2	.915	24	3-37,S-36,2-20,1-3	0.7
1995	*Cle-A	66	143	15	36	4	0	2	17	2	16	.252	.267	.322	52	-10	0	2	-1	.966	9	2-22,3-22,S-19/1D	-0.1
1996	Cle-A	59	112	12	25	4	2	4	11	6	18	.223	.281	.402	70	-6	1	1	-0	.947	3	3-20,1-18,S-16/2D	-0.4
	NY-N	48	134	19	41	7	2	4	16	4	19	.306	.326	.478	117	2	0	2	-1	.900	-6	3-38/S-7,2-1,1-1	-0.4
Total	11	909	2406	249	617	104	9	22	194	74	312	.256	.283	.335	68	-110	12	18	-7	.971	104	S-607,3-218/21DP	2.9

■ **SAMMY ESPOSITO**   Esposito, Samuel b: 12/15/31, Chicago, Ill. BR/TR, 5'9", 165 lbs. Deb: 9/28/52

1952	Chi-A	1	4	0	1	0	0	0	0	0	2	.250	.250	.250	39	-0	0	1	-1	.500	-1	/S-1	-0.3
1955	Chi-A	3	4	3	0	0	0	0	0	1	0	.000	.200	.000	-41	-1	0	0	0	1.000	-1	/3-2	-0.2
1956	Chi-A	81	184	30	42	8	2	3	25	24	19	.228	.374	.342	89	-1	1	2	-1	.962	4	3-61,S-19/2-3	0.2
1957	Chi-A	94	176	26	36	1	0	2	15	38	27	.205	.346	.256	66	-7	5	1	1	.960	16	3-53,S-22/2-4,0-1	1.3
1958	Chi-A	98	81	16	20	3	0	0	3	12	6	.247	.358	.284	81	-2	1	1	0	.979	8	3-63,S-22/2-2,0-1	1.0
1959	*Chi-A	69	66	12	11	1	0	1	5	11	16	.167	.286	.227	43	-5	0	1	-1	.979	9	3-45,S-14/2-2	0.4
1960	Chi-A	57	77	14	14	5	0	1	11	10	20	.182	.276	.286	53	-5	0	0	0	.929	1	3-37,S-11/2-5	-0.4
1961	Chi-A	63	94	12	16	5	0	1	8	12	21	.170	.264	.255	40	-8	0	0	0	.976	12	3-28,S-20,2-11	0.5
1962	Chi-A	75	81	14	19	1	0	0	4	17	13	.235	.367	.247	69	-3	2	1	-1	.846	3	3-41,S-20/2-7	0.2
1963	Chi-A	1	0	0	0	0	0	0	0	0	0	—	—	—			0	0	0	.000	0	R	0.0
	KC-A	18	25	3	5	1	0	0	2	3	3	.200	.286	.240	47	-2	0	0	0	1.000	-1	/2-7,S-4,3-3	-0.3
	Yr	19	25	3	5	1	0	0	2	3	3	.200	.286	.240	47	-2	0	0	0	1.000	-1	/2-7,S-4,3-3	-0.3
Total	10	560	792	130	164	27	2	8	73	145	127	.207	.333	.277	66	-33	7	7	-2	.957	51	3-333,S-133/2-41,O	2.4

■ **CECIL ESPY**   Espy, Cecil Edward b: 1/20/63, San Diego, Cal. BB/TR, 6'3", 195 lbs. Deb: 9/2/83

1983	LA-N	20	11	4	3	1	0	0	1	1	2	.273	.333	.364	94	-0	1	0	0	1.000	-5	O-15	-0.5
1987	Tex-A	14	8	1	0	0	0	0	0	0	3	.000	.111	.000	-67	-2	2	0	1	1.000	-1	/O-8	-0.2
1988	Tex-A	123	347	46	86	17	6	2	39	20	83	.248	.291	.349	76	-11	33	10	4	.972	-4	O-98,D-12/S-3,C12	-1.4
1989	Tex-A	142	475	65	122	12	7	3	31	38	99	.257	.315	.331	81	-12	45	20	2	.990	-3	*O-133/D-3	-1.7
1990	Tex-A	52	71	10	9	0	0	0	1	10	20	.127	.235	.127	4	-9	11	5	0	1.000	-7	O-39/2-1,D-4	-1.7
1991	*Pit-N	43	82	7	20	4	0	1	11	5	17	.244	.287	.329	74	-3	4	0	1	.966	-3	O-35	-0.6
1992	*Pit-N	112	194	21	50	7	3	1	20	15	40	.258	.311	.340	85	-4	6	3	0	.955	-20	O-82	-2.7
1993	Cin-N	40	60	6	14	2	0	0	5	14	13	.233	.378	.267	76	-1	2	2	-1	.931	-1	O-18	-0.3
Total	8	546	1248	160	304	43	16	7	108	104	277	.244	.303	.321	74	-42	103	40	7	.977	-43	O-428/D-19,S-3,2C1	-9.1

■ **CHUCK ESSEGIAN**   Essegian, Charles Abraham b: 8/9/31, Boston, Mass. BR/TR, 5'11", 202 lbs. Deb: 4/15/58

1958	Phi-N	39	114	15	28	5	2	5	16	12	34	.246	.317	.456	103	0	0	0	0	.952	1	O-30	-0.1
1959	StL-N	17	39	2	7	2	1	0	5	1	13	.179	.200	.282	25	-4	0	0	0	1.000	-1	/O-9	-0.6
	*LA-N	24	46	6	14	6	0	1	5	4	11	.304	.360	.500	118	1	0	0	0	1.000	-1	O-10	-0.1
	Yr	41	85	8	21	8	1	1	10	5	24	.247	.289	.400	76	-3	0	0	0	1.000	-2	O-19	-0.7
1960	LA-N	52	79	8	17	3	0	3	11	8	24	.215	.287	.367	73	-3	0	0	0	.968	0	O-18	-0.4
1961	Bal-A	1	1	0	0	0	0	0	0	0	0	.000	.000	.000	-99	-0	0	0	0	.000	0	H	0.0
	KC-A	4	6	1	2	1	0	0	1	1	2	.333	.429	.500	145	0	0	0	0	1.000	0	/O-1	0.1
	Cle-A	60	166	25	48	7	1	12	35	10	33	.289	.333	.560	138	8	0	0	0	.968	-2	O-49	0.4
	Yr	65	173	26	50	8	1	12	36	11	35	.289	.335	.555	137	8	0	0	0	.969	-2	O-50	0.5
1962	Cle-A	106	336	59	92	12	0	21	50	42	68	.274	.366	.497	134	16	0	0	0	.994	-4	O-90	0.7
1963	KC-A	101	231	23	52	9	0	5	27	19	48	.225	.287	.329	68	-10	0	0	0	.990	-0	O-53	-1.3
Total	6	404	1018	139	260	45	4	47	150	97	233	.255	.326	.446	106	6	0	0	0	.981	-7	O-260	-1.3

■ **JIM ESSIAN**   Essian, James Sarkis b: 1/2/51, Detroit, Mich. BR/TR, 6'2", 195 lbs. Deb: 9/15/73 M

1973	Phi-N	2	3	0	0	0	0	0	0	0	1	.000	.000	.000	-97	-1	0	0	0	1.000	-0	/C-1	-0.1
1974	Phi-N	17	20	1	2	0	0	0	0	2	1	.100	.182	.100	-19	-3	0	0	0	.976	1	C-15/1-1,3-1	-0.2
1975	Phi-N	2	1	1	1	0	0	0	1	0	0	1.000	1.000	1.000	439	1	0	0	0	1.000	0	/C-2	0.1
1976	Chi-A	78	199	20	49	7	0	0	21	23	28	.246	.327	.281	79	-4	2	1	0	.974	3	*C-77/1-2,3-1	0.0
1977	Chi-A	114	322	50	88	18	2	10	44	52	35	.273	.376	.435	120	10	1	4	-2	.986	5	*C-111/3-2	1.6
1978	Oak-A	126	278	21	62	9	1	3	26	44	22	.223	.329	.295	81	-6	2	1	0	.981	14	*C-119/1-3,2-1,D-1	1.1
1979	Oak-A	98	313	34	76	16	0	8	40	25	29	.243	.303	.371	85	-7	0	1	-1	.981	9	C-70,3-10/1-4,OD	0.4
1980	Oak-A	87	285	19	66	11	0	5	29	30	18	.232	.305	.323	78	-9	1	3	-2	.987	6	C-68/D-11/1-1	-0.3
1981	Chi-N	27	52	6	16	3	0	1	5	4	5	.308	.357	.365	111	1	0	0	0	.990	5	C-25/3-2	0.6
1982	Sea-A	48	153	14	42	8	0	3	20	11	7	.275	.327	.386	92	-2	2	0	1	.990	2	C-48	0.7
1983	Cle-A	48	93	11	19	4	0	2	11	16	8	.204	.321	.312	72	-3	0	1	-1	.989	1	C-47/3-1	0.1
1984	Oak-A	63	136	17	32	9	0	2	10	23	17	.235	.350	.346	100	1	1	1	-0	.985	11	C-59/3-1,D-1	1.3
Total	12	710	1855	194	453	85	3	33	207	231	171	.244	.330	.347	90	-22	9	13	-5	.984	63	C-642/3-18,D102	5.3

YEAR	TM/L	G	AB	R	H	2B	3B	HR	RBI	BB	SO	AVG	OBP	SLG	PRO+	BR/A	SB	CS	SBR	FA	FR	G/POS	TPR

■ BOBBY ESTALELLA   Estalella, Robert M   b: 8/23/74, Hialeah, Fla.   BR/TR, 6'1", 200 lbs.   Deb: 9/17/96 F

YEAR	TM/L	G	AB	R	H	2B	3B	HR	RBI	BB	SO	AVG	OBP	SLG	PRO+	BR/A	SB	CS	SBR	FA	FR	G/POS	TPR
1996	Phi-N	7	17	5	6	0	0	2	4	1	6	.353	.389	.706	176	2	1	0	0	1.000	-0	/C-4	0.2

■ BOBBY ESTALELLA   Estalella, Roberto (Ventoza)   b: 4/25/11, Cardenas, Cuba   d: 1/6/91, Hialeah, Fla.   BR/TR, 5'8", 180 lbs.   Deb: 9/7/35 F

YEAR	TM/L	G	AB	R	H	2B	3B	HR	RBI	BB	SO	AVG	OBP	SLG	PRO+	BR/A	SB	CS	SBR	FA	FR	G/POS	TPR
1935	Was-A	15	51	7	16	2	0	2	10	17	7	.314	.485	.471	153	5	1	0	0	.895	2	3-15	0.8
1936	Was-A	13	9	2	2	0	0	0	0	4	5	.222	.462	.667	186	1	0	0	0	.000	0	H	0.1
1939	Was-A	82	280	51	77	18	6	8	41	40	27	.275	.368	.468	121	8	2	3	-1	.964	-3	O-74	0.2
1941	StL-A	46	83	7	20	6	1	0	14	18	13	.241	.376	.337	87	-1	0	0	0	1.000	-4	O-17	-0.6
1942	Was-A	133	429	68	119	24	5	8	65	85	42	.277	.400	.413	130	21	5	2	0	.941	-14	3-78,O-36	0.7
1943	Phi-A	117	367	43	95	14	4	11	63	52	44	.259	.352	.409	123	11	1	3	-2	.975	-1	O-97	0.3
1944	Phi-A	140	506	54	151	17	9	7	60	59	60	.298	.374	.409	125	17	3	3	-1	.988	1	*O-128/1-6	0.8
1945	Phi-A	126	451	45	135	25	6	8	52	74	46	.299	.399	.435	142	26	1	6	-3	.988	1	*O-124	1.8
1949	Phi-A	8	20	2	5	0	0	0	3	1	2	.250	.286	.250	44	-2	0	0	0	1.000	0	/O-6	-0.2
Total	9	680	2196	279	620	106	33	44	308	350	246	.282	.383	.421	127	88	13	17	-6	.982	-21	O-482/3-93,1-6	3.9

■ DUDE ESTERBROOK   Esterbrook, Thomas John   b: 6/20/1857, Staten Is., N.Y.   d: 4/30/01, Middletown, N.Y.   BR/TR, 5'11", 167 lbs.   Deb: 5/1/1880 M

YEAR	TM/L	G	AB	R	H	2B	3B	HR	RBI	BB	SO	AVG	OBP	SLG	PRO+	BR/A	SB	CS	SBR	FA	FR	G/POS	TPR
1880	Buf-N	64	253	20	61	12	1	0		35	0	15	.241	.241	.296	80	-6				.939	-3	1-47,O-15/2-6,SC	-1.2
1882	Cle-N	45	179	13	44	4	3	0	19	5	12	.246	.266	.302	85	-3				.893	10	O-45/1-1	0.6
1883	NY-a	97	407	55	103	9	7	0		15		.253	.280	.310	86	-7				.871	-4	*3-97	-1.1
1884	*NY-a	112	477	110	150	29	11	1		12		.314	.345	.428	154	28				.886	9	*3-112	3.4
1885	NY-N	88	359	48	92	14	5	2	44	4	28	.256	.264	.340	96	-2				.885	2	*3-84/O-4	0.0
1886	NY-N	123	473	62	125	20	6	3	43	8	43	.264	.277	.351	89	-8	13			.895	-3	*3-123	-0.7
1887	NY-a	26	101	11	17	1	0	0	7	6		.168	.222	.178	13	-11	8			.950	-7	/1-9,O-7,S-5,2-5	-1.6
1888	Ind-N	64	246	21	54	8	0	0	17	2	20	.220	.232	.252	53	-13	11			.976	-3	1-61/3-3	-2.2
	Lou-a	23	93	9	21	6	0	0	7	3		.226	.265	.290	80	-2	5			.962	0	1-23	-0.4
1889	Lou-a	11	44	8	14	3	0	0	9	5	2	.318	.400	.386	127	2	6			.931	-1	/1-8,O-2,S-1,M	0.1
1890	NY-N	45	197	29	57	14	1	0	29	10	8	.289	.333	.371	105	1	12			.984	0	1-45	-0.2
1891	Bro-N	3	8	1	3	0	0	0	0	1	0	.375	.444	.375	140	0	0			1.000	-1	/O-2,2-1	0.0
Total	11	701	2837	387	741	120	34	6	210	70	129	.261	.284	.334	94	-22	55			.884	-1	3-419,1-194/O2SC	-3.3

■ FRANK ESTRADA   Estrada, Francisco (Soto)   b: 2/12/48, Navojoa, Mexico   BR/TR, 5'8", 182 lbs.   Deb: 9/14/71

YEAR	TM/L	G	AB	R	H	2B	3B	HR	RBI	BB	SO	AVG	OBP	SLG	PRO+	BR/A	SB	CS	SBR	FA	FR	G/POS	TPR
1971	NY-N	1	2	0	1	0	0	0	0	0	0	.500	.500	.500	187	0	0	0	0	1.000	-1	/C-1	-0.1

■ ANDY ETCHEBARREN   Etchebarren, Andrew Auguste   b: 6/20/43, Whittier, Cal.   BR/TR, 6'1", 197 lbs.   Deb: 9/26/62 C

YEAR	TM/L	G	AB	R	H	2B	3B	HR	RBI	BB	SO	AVG	OBP	SLG	PRO+	BR/A	SB	CS	SBR	FA	FR	G/POS	TPR
1962	Bal-A	2	6	0	2	1	0	0	1	0	2	.333	.333	.333	85	-0	0	0	0	.875	-1	/C-2	-0.1
1965	Bal-A	5	6	1	1	0	0	1	4	0	2	.167	.167	.667	123	0	0	0	0	1.000	3	/C-5	0.3
1966	*Bal-A☆	121	412	49	91	14	6	11	50	38	106	.221	.295	.364	89	-6	0	1	-1	.989	-4	*C-121	-0.3
1967	Bal-A☆	112	330	29	71	13	0	7	35	38	80	.215	.300	.318	83	-6	1	0	0	.989	0	*C-110	0.0
1968	Bal-A	74	189	20	44	11	2	5	20	19	46	.233	.313	.392	112	-3	0	0	0	.998	9	C-70	1.7
1969	*Bal-A	73	217	29	54	9	2	3	26	28	42	.249	.353	.350	96	-0	1	2	-1	.990	4	C-72	0.5
1970	*Bal-A	78	230	19	56	10	1	4	28	21	41	.243	.315	.348	82	-6	4	1	1	.984	2	C-76	0.5
1971	*Bal-A	70	222	21	60	8	0	9	29	16	40	.270	.322	.428	112	3	0	2	-1	.986	2	C-70	0.0
1972	Bal-A	71	188	11	38	6	1	2	21	17	43	.202	.279	.277	64	-8	0	2	-1	.992	7	C-70	0.2
1973	*Bal-A	54	152	16	39	9	1	2	23	12	21	.257	.319	.368	94	-1	0	1	-0	.991	2	C-51	0.0
1974	*Bal-A	62	180	13	40	8	0	2	15	6	26	.222	.251	.300	60	-10	1	0	0	.976	6	C-60	-0.1
1975	Bal-A	8	20	0	4	1	0	0	3	0	3	.200	.200	.250	28	-2	0	0	0	1.000	0	/C-7	-0.1
	Cal-A	31	100	10	28	0	1	3	17	14	19	.280	.368	.390	123	3	1	0	0	.981	-4	C-31	0.1
	Yr	39	120	10	32	1	1	3	20	14	22	.267	.343	.367	108	1	1	0	0	.983	-3	C-38	0.0
1976	Cal-A	103	247	15	56	9	1	0	21	24	37	.227	.305	.271	74	-7	0	2	-1	.980	6	*C-102	-0.1
1977	Cal-A	80	114	11	29	2	2	0	14	12	19	.254	.325	.307	77	-3	0	1	0	.987	1	C-80	-0.1
1978	Mil-A	4	5	1	2	1	0	0	1	0	0	.400	.500	.600	207	1	0	0	0	1.000	2	/C-4	0.3
Total	15	948	2618	245	615	101	17	49	309	246	529	.235	.308	.343	88	-41	13	14	-5	.987	32	C-931	2.8

■ BUCK ETCHISON   Etchison, Clarence Hampton   b: 1/27/15, Baltimore, Md.   d: 1/24/80, E.New Market, Md.   BL/TL, 6'1", 190 lbs.   Deb: 9/22/43

YEAR	TM/L	G	AB	R	H	2B	3B	HR	RBI	BB	SO	AVG	OBP	SLG	PRO+	BR/A	SB	CS	SBR	FA	FR	G/POS	TPR
1943	Bos-N	10	19	2	6	3	0	0	2	2	2	.316	.381	.474	148	1				.956	-1	/1-6	0.0
1944	Bos-N	109	308	30	66	16	0	8	33	33	50	.214	.292	.344	76	-10	1			.993	-1	1-85	-1.6
Total	2	119	327	32	72	19	0	8	35	35	52	.220	.299	.352	79	-9	1			.991	-2	/1-91	-1.6

■ BOBBY ETHERIDGE   Etheridge, Bobby Lamar "Luke"   b: 11/25/42, Greenville, Miss.   BR/TR, 5'9", 170 lbs.   Deb: 7/16/67

YEAR	TM/L	G	AB	R	H	2B	3B	HR	RBI	BB	SO	AVG	OBP	SLG	PRO+	BR/A	SB	CS	SBR	FA	FR	G/POS	TPR
1967	SF-N	40	115	13	26	7	1	1	15	7	12	.226	.299	.348	86	-2	0	1	-1	.925	-1	3-37	-0.4
1969	SF-N	56	131	13	34	9	1	1	10	19	26	.260	.358	.351	101	1	0	0	0	.899	-2	3-39/S-1	-0.1
Total	2	96	246	26	60	16	2	2	25	26	38	.244	.331	.350	94	-1	0	1	-1	.911	-4	/3-76,S-1	-0.5

■ NICK ETTEN   Etten, Nicholas Raymond Thomas   b: 9/19/13, Spring Grove, Ill.   d: 10/18/90, Hinsdale, Ill.   BL/TL, 6'2", 198 lbs.   Deb: 9/8/38

YEAR	TM/L	G	AB	R	H	2B	3B	HR	RBI	BB	SO	AVG	OBP	SLG	PRO+	BR/A	SB	CS	SBR	FA	FR	G/POS	TPR
1938	Phi-A	22	81	6	21	6	2	0	11	9	7	.259	.333	.395	81	-3	1	0	0	.987	-2	1-22	-0.6
1939	Phi-A	43	155	20	39	11	2	3	29	16	11	.252	.322	.406	87	-4	0	0	0	.990	-3	1-41	-1.0
1941	Phi-N	151	540	78	168	27	4	14	79	82	33	.311	.405	.454	147	36	9			.984	-3	*1-150	2.3
1942	Phi-N	139	459	37	121	21	3	8	41	67	26	.264	.357	.375	120	13	3			.985	1	*1-135	0.6
1943	*NY-A	154	583	78	158	35	5	14	107	76	31	.271	.355	.420	126	19	3	7	-3	.989	-11	*1-154	-0.5
1944	NY-A	154	573	88	168	25	4	**22**	91	**97**	29	.293	.399	.466	142	34	4	2	0	.989	4	*1-154	3.0
1945	NY-A†	152	565	77	161	24	4	18	**111**	90	23	.285	.387	.437	133	25	2	3	-1	.989	-9	*1-152	0.5
1946	NY-A	108	323	37	75	14	1	9	49	38	35	.232	.315	.365	88	-5	0	1	-1	.991	-4	1-84	-1.2
1947	Phi-N	14	41	5	10	4	0	1	8	5	4	.244	.326	.415	99	-0	0	0	0	.990	1	1-11	0.1
Total	9	937	3320	426	921	167	25	89	526	480	199	.277	.371	.423	125	115	22	13		.988	-22	1-903	3.2

■ FRED EUNICK   Eunick, Fernandas Bowen   b: 4/22/1892, Baltimore, Md.   d: 12/9/59, Baltimore, Md.   BR/TR, 5'6", 148 lbs.   Deb: 8/29/17

YEAR	TM/L	G	AB	R	H	2B	3B	HR	RBI	BB	SO	AVG	OBP	SLG	PRO+	BR/A	SB	CS	SBR	FA	FR	G/POS	TPR
1917	Cle-A	1	2	0	0	0	0	0	0	0	0	.000	.000	.000	-93	-0	0			1.000	-0	/3-1	-0.1

■ TONY EUSEBIO   Eusebio, Raul Antonio Bare (b: Raul Antontio Bare (Eusebio))   b: 4/27/67, San Jose De Los Llamos, D.R.   BR/TR, 6'2", 180 lbs.   Deb: 8/8/91

YEAR	TM/L	G	AB	R	H	2B	3B	HR	RBI	BB	SO	AVG	OBP	SLG	PRO+	BR/A	SB	CS	SBR	FA	FR	G/POS	TPR
1991	Hou-N	10	19	4	2	0	0	0	6	8		.105	.320	.158	41	-1	0	1	0	.981	2	/C-9	0.1
1994	Hou-N	55	159	18	47	9	1	5	30	8	33	.296	.329	.459	108	1	0	1	-1	.993	-5	C-52	-0.1
1995	Hou-N	113	368	46	110	21	1	6	58	31	59	.299	.358	.410	110	5	0	2	-1	.993	-13	*C-103	-0.2
1996	Hou-N	58	152	15	41	7	1	1	19	18	20	.270	.347	.362	96	-1	0	1	-1	.996	-9	C-47	-0.7
Total	4	236	698	83	200	38	4	12	107	63	120	.287	.348	.404	105	4	0	4	-2	.993	-24	C-211	-0.9

■ FRANK EUSTACE   Eustace, Frank John   b: 11/7/1873, New York, N.Y.   d: 10/20/32, Pottsville, Pa.   5'9", 160 lbs.   Deb: 4/17/1896

YEAR	TM/L	G	AB	R	H	2B	3B	HR	RBI	BB	SO	AVG	OBP	SLG	PRO+	BR/A	SB	CS	SBR	FA	FR	G/POS	TPR
1896	Lou-N	25	100	18	17	2	2	1	11	6	14	.170	.217	.260	26	-11	4			.841	-5	S-22/2-3	-1.3

■ EVANS   Evans   Deb: 6/1/1875

YEAR	TM/L	G	AB	R	H	2B	3B	HR	RBI	BB	SO	AVG	OBP	SLG	PRO+	BR/A	SB	CS	SBR	FA	FR	G/POS	TPR
1875	NH-n	1	4	1	2	0	0	0	1	0	0	.500	.500	.500	285	1	0	0	0	.000	-0	/O-1	0.0

■ AL EVANS   Evans, Alfred Hubert   b: 9/28/16, Kenly, N.C.   d: 4/6/79, Wilson, N.C.   BR/TR, 5'11", 190 lbs.   Deb: 9/13/39

YEAR	TM/L	G	AB	R	H	2B	3B	HR	RBI	BB	SO	AVG	OBP	SLG	PRO+	BR/A	SB	CS	SBR	FA	FR	G/POS	TPR
1939	Was-A	7	21	2	7	0	0	0	1	5	2	.333	.462	.333	115	1	0	0	0	.964	-1	/C-6	0.1
1940	Was-A	14	25	1	8	2	0	0	7	6	7	.320	.452	.400	131	2	1	0	0	1.000	0	/C-9	0.2
1941	Was-A	53	159	16	44	8	4	1	19	9	18	.277	.315	.396	91	-3	0	3	-2	.969	2	C-51	0.1
1942	Was-A	74	223	22	51	4	1	0	10	25	36	.229	.309	.256	60	-11	3	0	0	.961	-3	C-67	-0.9
1944	Was-A	14	22	5	2	0	0	0	2	2	6	.091	.167	.091	-27	-4	0	0	0	.933	-1	/C-8	-0.5
1945	Was-A	51	150	19	39	11	2	2	19	17	22	.260	.339	.400	125	4	2	0	0	.973	-6	C-41	-1.1
1946	Was-A	88	272	30	69	10	4	2	30	30	28	.254	.332	.342	94	-2	1	2	-1	.966	-12	C-81	-1.1
1947	Was-A	99	319	17	77	8	3	2	23	28	25	.241	.303	.304	71	-13	2	1	0	.989	-2	C-94	-0.9
1948	Was-A	93	228	19	59	8	2	2	26	38	20	.259	.367	.338	91	-2	1	1	-0	.983	-3	C-85	0.0
1949	Was-A	109	321	32	87	13	2	42	50	19	.271	.369	.346	92	-3	4	1	1	**.992**	-16	*C-107	-1.1

YEAR	TM/L	G	AB	R	H	2B	3B	HR	RBI	BB	SO	AVG	OBP	SLG	PRO+	BR/A	SB	CS	SBR	FA	FR	G/POS	TPR
1950	Was-A	90	289	24	68	8	3	2	30	29	21	.235	.309	.304	61	-18	0	0	0	.987	-13	C-88	-2.6
1951	Bos-A	12	24	1	3	1	0	0	2	4	2	.125	.250	.167	13	-3	0	0	0	1.000	1	C-10	-0.2
Total	12	704	2053	188	514	70	23	13	211	243	206	.250	.332	.326	82	-50	14	9	-1	.979	-56	C-647	-6.9

■ BARRY EVANS

Evans, Barry Steven b: 11/30/56, Atlanta, Ga. BR/TR, 6'1", 180 lbs. Deb: 9/4/78

YEAR	TM/L	G	AB	R	H	2B	3B	HR	RBI	BB	SO	AVG	OBP	SLG	PRO+	BR/A	SB	CS	SBR	FA	FR	G/POS	TPR
1978	SD-N	24	90	7	24	1	1	0	4	4	10	.267	.298	.300	73	-3	0	0	0	.947	1	3-24	-0.3
1979	SD-N	56	162	9	35	5	0	1	14	5	16	.216	.240	.265	40	-14	0	2	-1	.952	11	3-53/S-2,2-1	-0.4
1980	SD-N	73	125	11	29	3	2	0	14	17	21	.232	.324	.312	83	-3	1	1	-0	.983	-3	3-43,2-19/S-4,1-1	-0.5
1981	SD-N	54	93	11	30	5	0	0	7	9	9	.323	.382	.376	125	3	2	2	-1	.969	-4	3-24,1-10/2-6,S-2	-0.2
1982	NY-A	17	31	2	8	3	0	0	2	6	6	.258	.392	.355	109	1	0	0	0	1.000	1	/2-8,3-6,S-4	0.2
Total	5	224	501	40	126	17	3	2	41	41	62	.251	.309	.309	77	-16	3	5	-2	.960	7	3-150/2-34,S-12,1	-1.2

■ DARRELL EVANS

Evans, Darrell Wayne b: 5/26/47, Pasadena, Cal. BL/TR, 6'2", 205 lbs. Deb: 4/20/69 C

YEAR	TM/L	G	AB	R	H	2B	3B	HR	RBI	BB	SO	AVG	OBP	SLG	PRO+	BR/A	SB	CS	SBR	FA	FR	G/POS	TPR
1969	Atl-N	12	26	3	6	0	0	0	1	1	8	.231	.259	.231	38	-2	0	0	0	.917	-2	/3-6	-0.4
1970	Atl-N	12	44	4	14	1	1	0	9	7	5	.318	.423	.386	112	1	0	0	0	.941	-1	3-12	0.0
1971	Atl-N	89	260	42	63	11	1	12	38	39	54	.242	.343	.431	111	4	2	3	-1	.937	-3	3-72/O-3	0.6
1972	Atl-N	125	418	67	106	12	0	19	71	90	58	.254	.391	.419	119	14	4	2	0	.941	9	*3-123	2.3
1973	Atl-N★	161	595	114	167	25	8	41	104	**124**	104	.281	.407	.556	153	45	6	3	0	.953	8	*3-146,1-20	5.2
1974	Atl-N	160	571	99	137	21	3	25	79	**126**	88	.240	.383	.419	119	18	4	2	0	.955	16	*3-160	3.4
1975	Atl-N	156	567	82	138	22	2	22	73	105	106	.243	.364	.406	109	9	12	3	2	.938	23	*3-156/1-3	3.5
1976	Atl-N	44	139	11	24	0	0	1	10	30	33	.173	.320	.194	45	-9	3	0	1	.994	0	1-36/3-7	-1.1
	SF-N	92	257	42	57	9	1	10	36	42	38	.222	.331	.381	99	0	6	1	1	.991	9	1-83/3-5	0.5
	Yr	136	396	53	81	9	1	11	46	72	71	.205	.327	.316	80	-9	9	1	2	.992	9	*1-119,3-12	-0.6
1977	SF-N	144	461	64	117	18	3	17	72	69	50	.254	.355	.416	106	5	9	6	-1	.937	-1	O-81,1-41,3-35	-0.2
1978	SF-N	159	547	82	133	24	2	20	78	105	64	.243	.365	.404	119	17	4	5	-2	.952	10	*3-155	2.4
1979	SF-N	160	562	68	142	23	2	17	70	91	80	.253	.359	.391	112	11	6	7	-2	.943	22	*3-159	3.0
1980	SF-N	154	556	69	147	23	0	20	78	83	65	.264	.362	.414	119	15	17	5	2	.946	17	*3-140,1-14	3.3
1981	SF-N	102	357	51	92	13	4	12	48	54	33	.258	.358	.417	122	11	2	3	-1	.953	7	3-87,1-12	1.5
1982	SF-N★	141	465	64	119	20	4	16	61	77	64	.256	.364	.419	119	13	2	4	-1	.933	-2	3-84,1-49,S-13	0.7
1983	SF-N★	142	523	94	145	29	3	30	82	84	81	.277	.370	.516	151	36	6	6	-0	.993	1	*1-113,3-32/S-9	3.0
1984	*Det-A	131	401	60	93	11	1	16	63	77	70	.232	.356	.384	105	5	2	2	-1	.997	2	D-62,1-47,3-19	0.2
1985	Det-A	151	505	81	125	17	0	**40**	94	85	85	.248	.357	.519	137	26	0	4	-2	.984	11	*1-113,D-33/3-7	2.7
1986	Det-A	151	507	78	122	15	0	29	85	91	105	.241	.357	.442	116	13	3	2	-0	.998	11	*1-105,D-42/3-2	1.5
1987	*Det-A	150	499	90	128	20	0	34	99	100	84	.257	.383	.501	138	29	6	5	-1	.997	12	*1-105,D-44/3-7	2.9
1988	Det-A	144	437	48	91	9	0	22	64	84	89	.208	.337	.380	104	4	1	4	-2	.993	5	D-72,1-65	-0.1
1989	Atl-N	107	276	31	57	6	1	11	39	41	46	.207	.309	.355	87	-4	0	1	-1	.985	-5	1-50,3-28	-0.3
Total	21	2687	8973	1344	2223	329	36	414	1354	1605	1410	.248	.364	.431	119	263	98	68	-11	.946	165	*3-1442,1-856,D/OS	34.6

■ DWIGHT EVANS

Evans, Dwight Michael "Dewey" b: 11/3/51, Santa Monica, Cal. BR/TR, 6'2", 205 lbs. Deb: 9/16/72 C

YEAR	TM/L	G	AB	R	H	2B	3B	HR	RBI	BB	SO	AVG	OBP	SLG	PRO+	BR/A	SB	CS	SBR	FA	FR	G/POS	TPR
1972	Bos-A	18	57	2	15	3	1	1	6	7	13	.263	.344	.404	115	1	0	0	0	1.000	1	O-17	0.2
1973	Bos-A	119	282	46	63	13	1	10	32	40	52	.223	.322	.383	92	-3	5	0	2	.995	-6	*O-113/D-2	-1.1
1974	Bos-A	133	463	60	130	19	8	10	70	38	77	.281	.338	.421	110	5	4	4	-1	.990	11	*O-122/D-7	1.0
1975	*Bos-A	128	412	61	113	24	6	13	56	47	60	.274	.354	.456	118	9	3	4	-2	.987	18	*O-115/D-7	2.2
1976	Bos-A	146	501	61	121	34	5	17	62	57	92	.242	.326	.431	107	3	6	7	-2	**.994**	9	*O-145/D-1	0.5
1977	Bos-A	73	230	39	66	9	2	14	36	28	58	.287	.364	.526	125	7	4	2	0	.992	-2	O-63/D-6	0.3
1978	Bos-A★	147	497	75	123	24	2	24	63	65	119	.247	.337	.449	108	4	8	5	-1	.982	8	*O-142/D-4	0.6
1979	Bos-A	152	489	69	134	24	1	21	58	69	76	.274	.365	.456	114	10	6	9	-4	.988	10	*O-149	1.0
1980	Bos-A	148	463	72	123	37	5	18	60	64	98	.266	.361	.484	123	15	3	1	0	.982	2	*O-144/D-2	1.2
1981	Bos-A★	108	412	84	122	19	4	**22**	71	**85**	85	.296	.418	.522	160	**34**	3	2	-0	.993	14	*O-108	4.5
1982	Bos-A	162	609	122	178	37	7	32	98	112	125	.292	**.403**	.534	146	41	3	2	-0	.973	6	*O-161/D-1	4.2
1983	Bos-A	126	470	74	112	19	4	22	58	70	97	.238	.338	.436	104	3	3	0	1	.987	7	O-99,D-21	0.7
1984	Bos-A	162	630	**121**	186	37	8	32	104	96	115	.295	.392	.532	146	41	3	1	0	.994	2	*O-161/D-1	3.7
1985	Bos-A	159	617	110	162	29	1	29	78	**114**	105	.263	.382	.454	123	22	7	2	1	.990	3	*O-152/D-7	2.0
1986	*Bos-A	152	529	86	137	33	2	26	97	97	117	.259	.380	.476	131	25	3	3	-1	.983	5	*O-149/D-1	2.3
1987	Bos-A★	154	541	109	165	37	2	34	123	**106**	98	.305	.422	.569	155	46	4	6	-2	.982	-7	1-79,O-77/D-4	2.7
1988	*Bos-A	149	559	96	164	31	7	21	111	76	99	.293	.379	.487	135	27	5	1	1	.987	-6	O-85,1-64/D-6	1.4
1989	Bos-A	146	520	82	148	27	3	20	100	99	84	.285	.402	.463	135	27	3	4	-1	.981	2	O-77,D-69	2.5
1990	*Bos-A	123	445	66	111	18	3	13	63	67	73	.249	.353	.391	103	3	3	4	-2	.000	0	*D-122	-0.2
1991	Bal-A	101	270	35	73	9	1	6	38	54	54	.270	.396	.378	120	5	3	3	0	.984	0	O-67,D-21	0.7
Total	20	2606	8996	1470	2446	483	73	385	1384	1391	1697	.272	.373	.470	126	331	78	59	-12	.987	76	*O-2146,D-282,1-143	30.4

■ JOE EVANS

Evans, Joseph Patton "Doc" b: 5/15/1895, Meridian, Miss. d: 8/9/53, Gulfport, Miss. BR/TR, 5'9", 160 lbs. Deb: 7/3/15

YEAR	TM/L	G	AB	R	H	2B	3B	HR	RBI	BB	SO	AVG	OBP	SLG	PRO+	BR/A	SB	CS	SBR	FA	FR	G/POS	TPR
1915	Cle-A	42	109	17	28	4	2	0	11	22	18	.257	.382	.330	111	2	6	1	1	.885	-0	3-30/2-2	0.5
1916	Cle-A	33	82	4	12	1	0	0	1	7	12	.146	.213	.159	11	-9	4			.915	4	3-28	-0.5
1917	Cle-A	132	385	36	73	4	5	2	33	42	44	.190	.271	.242	53	-22	12			.939	1	*3-127	-1.9
1918	Cle-A	79	243	38	64	6	7	1	22	30	29	.263	.344	.358	102	1	7			.932	4	3-74	0.7
1919	Cle-A	21	14	9	1	0	0	0	0	2	1	.071	.188	.071	-24	-2	1			.923	4	/S-6	0.1
1920	*Cle-A	56	172	32	60	9	0	0	23	15	3	.349	.404	.506	136	9	6	2	1	.966	-2	O-43/S-6	0.4
1921	Cle-A	57	153	36	51	11	0	0	21	19	5	.333	.410	.405	107	3	4	1	1	.933	-1	O-47	0.0
1922	Cle-A	75	145	35	39	6	2	0	22	8	4	.269	.307	.338	67	-7	11	2	2	.969	-7	O-49	-1.4
1923	Was-A	106	372	42	98	15	3	0	38	27	18	.263	.311	.320	70	-16	6	4	-1	.982	-4	O-72,3-21/1-5	-2.3
1924	StL-A	77	209	30	53	3	3	0	19	24	12	.254	.330	.297	59	-12	4	4	-1	.969	2	O-47	-1.5
1925	StL-A	55	159	27	50	12	0	0	20	16	6	.314	.377	.390	90	-2	6	2	1	1.000	-1	O-47	-0.5
Total	11	733	2043	306	529	71	22	3	210	212	152	.259	.329	.328	79	-57	67	16		.971	-5	O-307,3-280/S12	-6.4

■ STEVE EVANS

Evans, Louis Richard b: 2/17/1885, Cleveland, Ohio d: 12/28/43, Cleveland, Ohio BL/TL, 5'10", 175 lbs. Deb: 4/16/08

YEAR	TM/L	G	AB	R	H	2B	3B	HR	RBI	BB	SO	AVG	OBP	SLG	PRO+	BR/A	SB	CS	SBR	FA	FR	G/POS	TPR
1908	NY-N	2	2	0	1	0	0	0	0	0	0	.500	.500	.500	209	0				.000	-1	/O-1	0.0
1909	StL-N	143	498	67	129	17	6	2	56	66		.259	.362	.329	122	16	14			.947	-4	*O-141/1-2	0.7
1910	StL-N	151	506	73	122	21	8	2	73	78	63	.241	.376	.322	109	11	10			.968	-6	*O-141,1-10	-0.2
1911	StL-N	154	547	74	161	24	13	5	71	46	52	.294	.369	.413	122	16	13			.972	-2	*O-150	0.6
1912	StL-N	135	491	59	139	23	9	6	72	36	51	.283	.353	.403	109	6	11			.942	-0	*O-134	-0.1
1913	StL-N	97	245	18	61	15	6	1	31	20	28	.249	.321	.371	99	-1	5			.983	-6	O-74/1-1	-1.0
1914	Bro-F	145	514	93	179	41	**15**	12	96	50	49	.348	.416	**.556**	165	38	18			.941	-5	*O-112,1-27	2.9
1915	Bro-F	63	216	44	64	14	4	3	30	35	22	.296	.411	.440	140	10	7			.960	-2	O-61/1-1	0.6
	Bal-F	88	340	50	107	20	6	1	37	28	34	.315	.379	.418	120	5	8			.925	-6	O-88/1-4	-0.5
	Yr	151	556	94	171	**34**	10	4	67	63	56	.308	.392	.426	128	15	15			.940	-8	*O-149/1-5	0.1
Total	8	978	3359	478	963	175	67	32	466	359	299	.287	.374	.407	125	101	86			.955	-31	O-902/1-45	3.0

■ JAKE EVANS

Evans, Uriah L. P. "Bloody Jake" b: 9/1856, Baltimore, Md. d: 1/16/07, Baltimore, Md. TR, 5'8", 154 lbs. Deb: 5/1/1879

YEAR	TM/L	G	AB	R	H	2B	3B	HR	RBI	BB	SO	AVG	OBP	SLG	PRO+	BR/A	SB	CS	SBR	FA	FR	G/POS	TPR
1879	Tro-N	72	280	30	65	9	5	0	17	5	18	.232	.246	.300	84	-4				.884	18	*O-72	0.9
1880	Tro-N	47	180	31	46	8	1	0	22	7	15	.256	.288	.311	96	-1				.906	0	O-47/P-1	-0.2
1881	Tro-N	83	315	35	76	11	5	0	28	14	30	.241	.274	.308	78	-8				.926	14	*O-83	0.4
1882	Wor-N	80	334	33	71	10	4	0	25	7	22	.213	.229	.266	57	-16				.910	20	*O-68,S-11/3-1,2P	0.4
1883	Cle-N	90	332	36	79	13	2	0	31	8	38	.238	.256	.289	66	-13				.902	9	*O-86/S-3,3-3,2P	-0.7
1884	Cle-N	80	313	32	81	18	3	1	38	15	49	.259	.293	.345	97	-2				**.917**	8	*O-76/2-4,S-2	0.4
1885	Bal-a	20	77	18	17	1	1	0	7		7	.221	.318	.260	85	-1				.894	5	O-20	0.1
Total	7	472	1831	215	435	70	21	1	168	63	172	.238	.268	.300	78	-45				.907	67	O-452/S-16,2-6,3P	1.3

■ CARL EVERETT

Everett, Carl Edward b: 6/3/70, Tampa, Fla. BB/TR, 6', 190 lbs. Deb: 7/1/93

YEAR	TM/L	G	AB	R	H	2B	3B	HR	RBI	BB	SO	AVG	OBP	SLG	PRO+	BR/A	SB	CS	SBR	FA	FR	G/POS	TPR
1993	Fla-N	11	19	0	2	0	0	0	0	3	9	.105	.150	.105	-29	-3	1	0	0	.857	-3	/O-8	-0.6
1994	Fla-N	16	51	7	11	1	0	2	6	3	15	.216	.259	.353	56	-3	4	0	1	1.000	-0	O-16	-0.3

YEAR	TM/L	G	AB	R	H	2B	3B	HR	RBI	BB	SO	AVG	OBP	SLG	PRO+	BR/A	SB	CS	SBR	FA	FR	G/POS	TPR
1995	NY-N	79	289	48	75	13	1	12	54	39	67	.260	.352	.436	110	4	2	5	-2	.981	5	O-77	0.4
1996	NY-N	101	192	29	46	8	1	1	16	21	53	.240	.327	.307	74	-7	6	0	2	.935	-2	O-55	-0.9
Total	4	207	551	84	134	22	2	15	76	64	144	.243	.329	.372	87	-10	13	5	1	.964	-1	O-156	-1.4

■ BILL EVERITT
Everitt, William Lee "Wild Bill" b:12/13/1868, Ft.Wayne, Ind. d:1/19/38, Denver, Colo. BL/TR, 6'0.5", 185 lbs. Deb:4/18/1895

YEAR	TM/L	G	AB	R	H	2B	3B	HR	RBI	BB	SO	AVG	OBP	SLG	PRO+	BR/A	SB	CS	SBR	FA	FR	G/POS	TPR
1895	Chi-N	133	550	129	197	16	10	3	88	33	42	.358	.399	.440	109	6	47			.854	-8	*3-130/2-3	0.0
1896	Chi-N	132	575	130	184	16	13	2	46	41	43	.320	.367	.403	99	-2	46			.882	-10	*3-97,O-35	-1.1
1897	Chi-N	92	379	63	119	14	7	5	39	36		.314	.373	.427	107	3	26			.864	-5	3-83/O-8	-0.1
1898	Chi-N	149	596	102	190	15	6	0	69	53		.319	.377	.364	113	11	28			.974	-2	*1-149	0.8
1899	Chi-N	136	536	87	166	17	5	1	74	31		.310	.351	.366	99	-1	30			.971	8	*1-136	0.7
1900	Chi-N	23	91	10	24	4	0	0	17	3		.264	.287	.308	67	-4	2			.979	-1	1-23	-0.5
1901	Was-A	33	115	14	22	3	2	0	8	15		.191	.301	.252	55	-6	7			.967	-4	1-33	-1.0
Total	7	698	2842	535	902	85	43	11	341	212	85	.317	.368	.389	103	-7	186			.973	-23	1-341,3-310/O-43,2	-1.2

■ JOHNNY EVERS
Evers, John Joseph "Crab" or "Trojan" b:7/21/1881, Troy, N.Y. d:3/28/47, Albany, N.Y. BL/TR, 5'9", 125 lbs. Deb:9/1/02 FMCH

YEAR	TM/L	G	AB	R	H	2B	3B	HR	RBI	BB	SO	AVG	OBP	SLG	PRO+	BR/A	SB	CS	SBR	FA	FR	G/POS	TPR
1902	Chi-N	26	90	7	20	0	0	0	2	3		.222	.263	.222	51	-5	1			.990	-1	2-18/S-8	-0.5
1903	Chi-N	124	464	70	136	27	3	0	52	19		.293	.325	.381	104	1	25			.937	-14	*2-110,S-11/3-2	-0.9
1904	Chi-N	152	532	49	141	14	7	0	47	28		.265	.307	.318	93	-5	26			.943	31	*2-152	3.2
1905	Chi-N	99	340	44	94	11	2	1	37	27		.276	.333	.329	94	-2	19			.937	3	2-99	0.1
1906	*Chi-N	154	533	65	136	17	6	1	51	36		.255	.305	.315	88	-8	49			.947	6	*2-153/3-1	-0.2
1907	*Chi-N	151	508	66	127	18	4	2	51	38		.250	.309	.313	89	-7	46			.964	**28**	*2-151	2.2
1908	*Chi-N	126	416	83	125	19	6	0	37	66		.300	.402	.375	143	23	36			.960	-4	*2-122/O-1	2.5
1909	Chi-N	127	463	88	122	19	6	1	24	73		.263	.369	.337	116	12	28			.942	3	*2-126	1.3
1910	Chi-N	125	433	87	114	11	7	0	28	108	18	.263	.413	.322	115	16	28			.950	-4	*2-125	1.0
1911	Chi-N	46	155	29	35	4	3	0	7	34	10	.226	.372	.290	86	-1	6			.975	-6	2-33,3-11	-0.8
1912	Chi-N	143	478	73	163	23	11	1	63	74	18	.341	**.431**	.441	139	29	16			.959	6	*2-143	3.1
1913	Chi-N	136	446	81	127	20	5	3	49	50	14	.285	.361	.372	109	6	11			.960	**30**	*2-136,M	3.5
1914	*Bos-N	139	491	81	137	20	3	1	40	87	26	.279	.390	.338	118	16	12			**.976**	-1	*2-139	2.0
1915	Bos-N	83	278	38	73	4	1	1	22	50	16	.263	.375	.295	109	6	7	8	-3	.959	-1	2-82	0.3
1916	Bos-N	71	241	33	52	4	1	0	15	40	19	.216	.330	.241	80	-4	5			.951	-7	2-71	-2.2
1917	Bos-N	24	83	5	16	0	0	0	13	8		.193	.302	.193	56	-4	1			.950	-7	2-24	-1.1
	Phi-N	56	183	20	41	5	1	1	12	30	13	.224	.333	.279	85	-2	8			.983	-5	2-49/3-7	-0.5
	Yr	80	266	25	57	5	1	1	12	43	21	.214	.324	.252	77	-5	9			.973	-12	2-73/3-7	-1.6
1922	Chi-A	1	3	0	0	0	0	0	1	2	0	.000	.400	.000	12	-0	0	0	0	1.000	-1	/2-1	0.0
1929	Bos-N	1	0	0	0	0	0	0	0	0		—	—	—	—		0			.000	-1	/2-1	-0.1
Total	18	1784	6137	919	1659	216	70	12	538	778	142	.270	.356	.334	106	71	324	8		.955	54	*2-1735/3-21,S-19,O	12.9

■ JOE EVERS
Evers, Joseph Francis b:9/10/1891, Troy, N.Y. d:1/4/49, Albany, N.Y. BR/TR, 5'9", 135 lbs. Deb:4/24/13 F

YEAR	TM/L	G	AB	R	H	2B	3B	HR	RBI	BB	SO	AVG	OBP	SLG	PRO+	BR/A	SB	CS	SBR	FA	FR	G/POS	TPR
1913	NY-N	1	0	0	0	0	0	0	0	0	0	—	—	—	—		0	0		.000	0	R	0.0

■ TOM EVERS
Evers, Thomas Francis b:3/31/1852, Troy, N.Y. d:3/23/25, Washington, D.C. TL, Deb:5/25/1882

YEAR	TM/L	G	AB	R	H	2B	3B	HR	RBI	BB	SO	AVG	OBP	SLG	PRO+	BR/A	SB	CS	SBR	FA	FR	G/POS	TPR
1882	Bal-a	1	4	0	0	0	0	0	0			.000	.000	.000	-99	-1				.500	-2	/2-1	-0.3
1884	Was-U	109	427	54	99	6	1	0	7			.232	.244	.251	52	-37				.869	11	*2-109	-2.0
Total	2	110	431	54	99	6	1	0	7			.230	.242	.248	51	-38				.866	9	2-110	-2.3

■ HOOT EVERS
Evers, Walter Arthur b:2/8/21, St.Louis, Mo. d:1/25/91, Houston, Tex. BR/TR, 6'2", 185 lbs. Deb:9/16/41 C

YEAR	TM/L	G	AB	R	H	2B	3B	HR	RBI	BB	SO	AVG	OBP	SLG	PRO+	BR/A	SB	CS	SBR	FA	FR	G/POS	TPR
1941	Det-A	1	4	0	0	0	0	0	0	0	2	.000	.000	.000	-91	-1	0	0		.000	-0	/O-1	-0.2
1946	Det-A	81	304	42	81	8	4	4	33	34	43	.266	.344	.359	91	-3	7	1	2	.975	0	O-76	-0.5
1947	Det-A	126	460	67	136	24	5	10	67	45	49	.296	.366	.435	119	11	8	7	-2	.978	8	*O-123	1.1
1948	Det-A★	139	538	81	169	33	6	10	103	51	31	.314	.378	.454	117	12	3	4	-2	.973	2	*O-138	0.5
1949	Det-A	132	432	68	131	21	6	7	72	70	38	.303	.403	.428	120	14	6	7	-2	.994	11	*O-123	1.6
1950	Det-A★	143	526	100	170	35	**11**	21	103	71	40	.323	.408	.551	139	30	5	9	-4	**.997**	16	*O-139	2.6
1951	Det-A	116	393	47	88	15	2	11	46	40	47	.224	.297	.356	76	-14	5	3	-0	.976	-4	*O-108	-2.3
1952	Det-A	1	1	0	1	0	0	0	0	0	0	1.000	1.000	1.000	454	0	0	0	0	.000	0	H	0.0
	Bos-A	106	401	53	105	17	4	14	59	29	55	.262	.318	.429	99	-2	5	2	0	.974	-5	*O-105	-1.2
	Yr	107	402	53	106	17	4	14	59	29	55	.264	.320	.430	100	-2	5	2	0	.974	-5	*O-105	-1.2
1953	Bos-A	99	300	39	72	10	1	11	31	23	41	.240	.301	.390	81	-9	2	1	0	.988	-7	O-93	-1.9
1954	Bos-A	6	8	1	0	0	0	0	0	0	2	.000	.000	.000	-90	-2	0	0	0	1.000	-0	/O-1	-0.2
	NY-N	12	11	1	1	0	0	1	3	0	6	.091	.091	.364	12	-2	0	0	0	1.000	-1	/O-4	-0.3
	Det-A	30	60	5	11	0	0	0	5	5	8	.183	.258	.250	40	-5	0	0	0	1.000	-4	O-24	-0.9
1955	Bal-A	60	185	21	44	10	1	6	30	19	28	.238	.309	.400	96	-2	1	0	0	.991	-4	O-55	-0.8
	Cle-A	39	66	10	19	7	1	2	9	3	12	.288	.319	.515	117	1	0	1	-1	1.000	-4	O-25	-0.2
	Yr	99	251	31	63	17	2	8	39	22	40	.251	.311	.430	101	-1	2	2	-1	.993	-8	O-80	-1.2
1956	Cle-A	3	0	1	0	0	0	0	0	1	0	—	1.000	—	180	0	0	0	0	.000	0	H	0.0
	Bal-A	48	112	20	27	3	0	1	4	24	18	.241	.375	.295	85	-1	1	0	0	.985	-3	O-36	-0.5
	Yr	51	112	21	27	3	0	1	4	25	18	.241	.380	.295	86	-3	1	0	0	.985	-3	O-36	-0.5
Total	12	1142	3801	556	1055	187	41	98	565	415	420	.278	.353	.426	106	27	45	36	-8	.983	-4	*O-1051	-3.4

■ GEORGE EWELL
Ewell, George b:Philadelphia, Pa. Deb:6/26/1871

YEAR	TM/L	G	AB	R	H	2B	3B	HR	RBI	BB	SO	AVG	OBP	SLG	PRO+	BR/A	SB	CS	SBR	FA	FR	G/POS	TPR
1871	Cle-n	1	3	0	0	0	0	0	0	0	0	.000	.000	.000	-99	-1	0	0	0	1.000	-0	/O-1	-0.1

■ JOHN EWING
Ewing, John "Long John" b:6/1/1863, Cincinnati, Ohio d:4/23/1895, Denver, Colo. TR, Deb:6/18/1883 F

YEAR	TM/L	G	AB	R	H	2B	3B	HR	RBI	BB	SO	AVG	OBP	SLG	PRO+	BR/A	SB	CS	SBR	FA	FR	G/POS	TPR
1883	StL-a	1	5	0	0	0	0	0	0			.000	.000	.000	-95	-1				.333	-1	/O-1	-0.2
1884	Cin-U	1	4	0	0	0	0	0	0			.000	.000	.000	-93	-1				1.000	-0	/O-1	-0.1
	Was-U	1	5	1	1	0	0	0	0			.200	.200	.600	138	0				.500	0	/O-1	0.0
	Yr	2	9	1	1	0	1	0	0			.111	.111	.333	29	-1				.600	0	/O-2	-0.1
1888	Lou-a	21	79	6	16	1	0	0	5	1		.203	.213	.241	46	-5	7			.907	0	P-21	0.0
1889	Lou-a	41	134	12	23	2	0	0	6	9	30	.172	.234	.187	21	-14	5			.953	2	P-40/1-1	0.0
1890	NY-P	35	114	18	24	2	1	2	17	5	35	.211	.244	.298	41	-11	2			.949	0	P-35	0.0
1891	NY-N	33	113	10	23	1	0	0	8	5	14	.204	.224	.212	28	-10	4			.917	0	P-33	0.0
Total	6	133	454	47	87	6	3	2	36	18	79	.192	.226	.231	31	-41	18			.935	2	P-129/O-3,1-1	-0.3

■ REUBEN EWING
Ewing, Reuben (b:Reuben Cohen) b:11/30/1899, Odessa, Russia d:10/5/70, W.Hartford, Conn. BR/TR, 5'4.5", 150 lbs. Deb:6/21/21

YEAR	TM/L	G	AB	R	H	2B	3B	HR	RBI	BB	SO	AVG	OBP	SLG	PRO+	BR/A	SB	CS	SBR	FA	FR	G/POS	TPR
1921	StL-N	3	1	0	0	0	0	0	0	0	1	.000	.000	.000	-99	-0	0	0	0	1.000	0	/S-1	0.0

■ SAM EWING
Ewing, Samuel James b:4/9/49, Lewisburg, Tenn. BL/TL, 6'3", 200 lbs. Deb:9/11/73

YEAR	TM/L	G	AB	R	H	2B	3B	HR	RBI	BB	SO	AVG	OBP	SLG	PRO+	BR/A	SB	CS	SBR	FA	FR	G/POS	TPR
1973	Chi-A	11	20	1	3	1	0	0	2	2	6	.150	.227	.200	20	-2	0	0	0	1.000	0	/1-4	-0.2
1976	Chi-A	19	41	3	9	2	1	0	2	2	8	.220	.256	.317	67	-2	0	0	0	1.000	-0	D-12/1-1	-0.2
1977	Tor-A	97	244	24	70	8	2	4	34	19	42	.287	.338	.385	95	-1	1	1	-0	.957	-5	O-46,D-27/1-2	-0.9
1978	Tor-A	40	56	3	10	0	2	0	9	5	9	.179	.246	.286	48	-4	0	0	0	1.000	-0	/O-3,D-9	-0.5
Total	4	167	361	31	92	11	3	6	47	28	65	.255	.308	.352	81	-9	1	1	-0	.959	-5	/O-49,D-48,1-7	-1.8

■ BUCK EWING
Ewing, William b:10/17/1859, Hoagland, Ohio d:10/20/06, Cincinnati, Ohio BR/TR, 5'10", 188 lbs. Deb:9/9/1880 FMH

YEAR	TM/L	G	AB	R	H	2B	3B	HR	RBI	BB	SO	AVG	OBP	SLG	PRO+	BR/A	SB	CS	SBR	FA	FR	G/POS	TPR
1880	Tro-N	13	45	1	8	0	0	0	5	1	3	.178	.196	.200	33	-3				.864	-4	C-10/O-4	-0.7
1881	Tro-N	67	272	40	68	14	7	0	25	7	8	.250	.269	.353	89	-4	25			.915	**25**	C-44,S-22/O-2,3-1	2.3
1882	Tro-N	74	328	67	89	16	7	6	41	10	8	.271	.293	.405	127	10	14			.887	14	3-44,C-25/2-4,O1P	2.3
1883	NY-N	88	376	90	114	11	13	**10**	41	20	14	.303	.338	.481	147	21				.922	4	C-63,O-14,3-11/S3	2.3
1884	NY-N	94	382	90	106	15	**20**	3	41	28	22	.277	.327	.445	137	16				.933	4	*C-80,O-12/S-3,3P	3.2
1885	NY-N	81	404	81	104	15	12	6	63	13	17	.304	.330	.471	159	21				.918	3	C-63,O-14/3-8,S1P	3.2
1886	NY-N	73	275	59	85	11	7	4	31	16	17	.309	.347	.444	138	12	18			.921	3	C-50,O-23/1-2	1.7
1887	NY-N	77	318	83	97	17	13	6	44	30	33	.305	.370	.497	146	20	26			.863	-1	3-51,2-19/C-8	1.8
1888	*NY-N	103	415	83	127	18	15	6	58	24	28	.306	.348	.465	159	27	53			.947	5	C-78,3-21/S-4,P-2	3.9

YEAR	TM/L	G	AB	R	H	2B	3B	HR	RBI	BB	SO	AVG	OBP	SLG	PRO+	BR/A	SB	CS	SBR	FA	FR	G/POS	TPR
1889	*NY-N	99	407	91	133	23	13	4	87	37	32	.327	.383	.477	139	20	34			.937	16	*C-97/P-3,O-1	3.8
1890	NY-P	83	352	98	119	19	15	8	72	39	12	.338	.406	.545	141	17	36			**.949**	14	C-81/2-1,P-1,M	3.0
1891	NY-N	14	49	8	17	2	1	0	18	5	5	.347	.407	.429	150	3	5			.881	-3	/2-8,C-6	0.1
1892	NY-N	105	393	58	122	10	15	8	76	38	26	.310	.371	.473	158	26	42			.974	8	1-73,C-30/2-2	3.0
1893	Cle-N	116	500	117	172	28	15	6	122	41	18	.344	.394	.496	128	17	47			.927	-1	*O-112/2-5,1-1,C-1	3.0
1894	Cle-N	53	211	32	53	12	4	2	39	24	9	.251	.328	.374	66	-13	18			.912	-2	O-52/2-1	-1.4
1895	Cin-N	105	434	90	138	24	13	5	94	30	22	.318	.363	.468	109	3	34			.976	8	*1-105,M	1.1
1896	Cin-N	69	263	41	73	14	4	1	38	29	13	.278	.349	.373	85	-6	41			.980	4	1-69,M	-0.1
1897	Cin-N	1	1	0	0	0	0	0	0	0	0	.000	.500	.000	36	0	0			.800	-0	/1-1,M	0.0
Total	18	1315	5363	1129	1625	250	178	71	883	392	294	.303	.351	.456	130	186	354			.931	101	C-636,1-253,O3/2SP	29.5

■ ART EWOLDT   Ewoldt, Arthur Lee "Sheriff"   b: 1/8/1894, Paullina, Iowa   d: 12/8/77, Des Moines, Iowa   BR/TR, 5'10", 165 lbs.   Deb: 9/17/19

YEAR	TM/L	G	AB	R	H	2B	3B	HR	RBI	BB	SO	AVG	OBP	SLG	PRO+	BR/A	SB	CS	SBR	FA	FR	G/POS	TPR
1919	Phi-A	9	32	2	7	1	0	0	2	1	1	.219	.242	.250	38	-3	0			1.000	0	/3-9	-0.2

■ HOMER EZZELL   Ezzell, Homer Estell   b: 2/28/1896, Victoria, Tex.   d: 8/3/76, San Antonio, Tex.   BR/TR, 5'10", 158 lbs.   Deb: 4/22/23

YEAR	TM/L	G	AB	R	H	2B	3B	HR	RBI	BB	SO	AVG	OBP	SLG	PRO+	BR/A	SB	CS	SBR	FA	FR	G/POS	TPR
1923	StL-A	88	279	31	68	6	0	0	14	15	20	.244	.287	.265	44	-23	4	3	-1	.961	8	3-73/2-8	-0.9
1924	Bos-A	90	277	35	75	8	4	0	32	14	21	.271	.311	.329	65	-15	12	5	1	.984	9	3-64,S-21/C-1	0.1
1925	Bos-A	58	186	40	53	6	4	0	15	19	18	.285	.351	.360	81	-5	9	7	-2	.916	-7	3-47/2-9	-1.0
Total	3	236	742	106	196	20	8	0	61	48	59	.264	.312	.313	61	-43	25	15	-1	.957	10	3-184/S-21,2-17,C-1	-1.8

■ JAY FAATZ   Faatz, Jayson S.   b: 10/24/1860, Weedsport, N.Y.   d: 4/10/23, Syracuse, N.Y.   BR/TR, 6'4",   Deb: 8/22/1884   M

YEAR	TM/L	G	AB	R	H	2B	3B	HR	RBI	BB	SO	AVG	OBP	SLG	PRO+	BR/A	SB	CS	SBR	FA	FR	G/POS	TPR
1884	Pit-a	29	112	18	27	2	3	0			1	.241	.274	.313	89	-1				.963	-1	1-29	-0.5
1888	Cle-a	120	470	73	124	10	2	0	51	12		.264	.312	.294	97	-1	64			**.989**	2	*1-120	-0.9
1889	Cle-N	117	442	50	102	12	5	2	38	17	28	.231	.275	.294	60	-24	27			.981	6	*1-117	-2.3
1890	Buf-P	32	111	18	21	0	2	1	16	9	5	.189	.297	.252	52	-7	2			.982	-3	1-32,M	-0.9
Total	4	298	1135	159	274	24	12	3	105	39	33	.241	.293	.292	76	-33	93			.982	4	1-298	-4.6

■ JORGE FABREGAS   Fabregas, Jorge   b: 3/13/70, Miami, Fla.   BL/TR, 6'3", 205 lbs.   Deb: 4/24/94

YEAR	TM/L	G	AB	R	H	2B	3B	HR	RBI	BB	SO	AVG	OBP	SLG	PRO+	BR/A	SB	CS	SBR	FA	FR	G/POS	TPR
1994	Cal-A	43	127	12	36	3	0	0	16	7	18	.283	.321	.307	62	-7	2	1	0	.987	-2	C-41	-0.6
1995	Cal-A	73	227	24	56	10	0	1	22	17	28	.247	.299	.304	58	-14	0	2	-1	.986	2	C-73	-0.8
1996	Cal-A	90	254	18	73	6	0	2	26	17	27	.287	.332	.335	71	-11	0	1	-1	.989	9	C-89/D-1	0.2
Total	3	206	608	54	165	19	0	3	64	41	73	.271	.317	.317	64	-32	2	4	-2	.988	9	C-203/D-1	-1.2

■ BUNNY FABRIQUE   Fabrique, Albert La Verne   b: 12/23/1887, Clinton, Mich.   d: 1/10/60, Ann Arbor, Mich.   BB/TR, 5'8.5", 150 lbs.   Deb: 10/4/16

YEAR	TM/L	G	AB	R	H	2B	3B	HR	RBI	BB	SO	AVG	OBP	SLG	PRO+	BR/A	SB	CS	SBR	FA	FR	G/POS	TPR
1916	Bro-N	2	2	0	0	0	0	0	0	0	1	.000	.000	.000	-97	-0	0			1.000	0	/S-2	0.0
1917	Bro-N	25	88	8	18	3	0	1	3	8	9	.205	.271	.273	65	-4	0			.874	-2	/S-21	-0.5
Total	2	27	90	8	18	3	0	1	3	8	10	.200	.265	.267	62	-4	0			.878	-2	/S-23	-0.5

■ LENNY FAEDO   Faedo, Leonardo Lago   b: 5/13/60, Tampa, Fla.   BR/TR, 6', 170 lbs.   Deb: 9/6/80

YEAR	TM/L	G	AB	R	H	2B	3B	HR	RBI	BB	SO	AVG	OBP	SLG	PRO+	BR/A	SB	CS	SBR	FA	FR	G/POS	TPR
1980	Min-A	5	8	1	2	1	0	0	0	0	0	.250	.250	.375	64	-0	0	0	0	.818	-1	/S-5	-0.1
1981	Min-A	12	41	3	8	0	1	0	6	1	5	.195	.214	.244	30	-4	0	0	0	.971	2	S-12	-0.1
1982	Min-A	90	255	16	62	8	0	3	22	16	22	.243	.290	.310	63	-13	1	0	0	.967	3	S-88/D-1	-0.2
1983	Min-A	51	173	16	48	7	0	1	18	4	19	.277	.294	.335	70	-7	0	0	0	.954	-15	S-51	-1.8
1984	Min-A	16	52	6	13	1	0	1	6	4	3	.250	.304	.327	71	-2	0	0	0	.968	-5	S-15/D-1	-0.6
Total	5	174	529	42	133	17	1	5	52	25	49	.251	.286	.316	64	-26	1	0	0	.961	-16	S-171/D-2	-2.8

■ FRED FAGIN   Fagin, Frederick H.   b: Cincinnati, Ohio   Deb: 6/25/1895

YEAR	TM/L	G	AB	R	H	2B	3B	HR	RBI	BB	SO	AVG	OBP	SLG	PRO+	BR/A	SB	CS	SBR	FA	FR	G/POS	TPR
1895	StL-N	1	3	0	1	0	0	0	2	0	0	.333	.333	.333	73	-0	0			.636	0	/C-1	0.0

■ FRANK FAHEY   Fahey, Francis Raymond   b: 1/22/1896, Milford, Mass.   d: 3/19/54, Boston, Mass.   BB/TR, 6'1", 190 lbs.   Deb: 4/25/18

YEAR	TM/L	G	AB	R	H	2B	3B	HR	RBI	BB	SO	AVG	OBP	SLG	PRO+	BR/A	SB	CS	SBR	FA	FR	G/POS	TPR
1918	Phi-A	10	17	2	3	1	0	0	1	0	3	.176	.176	.235	24	-2	0			1.000	-2	/O-5,P-3	-0.4

■ HOWARD FAHEY   Fahey, Howard Simpson "Cap" or "Kid"   b: 6/24/1892, Medford, Mass.   d: 10/24/71, Clearwater, Fla.   BR/TR, 5'7.5", 145 lbs.   Deb: 7/23/12

YEAR	TM/L	G	AB	R	H	2B	3B	HR	RBI	BB	SO	AVG	OBP	SLG	PRO+	BR/A	SB	CS	SBR	FA	FR	G/POS	TPR
1912	Phi-A	5	8	0	0	0	0	0	0	0	0	.000	.000	.000	-99	-2	0			1.000	-1	/3-2,2-1,S-1	-0.3

■ BILL FAHEY   Fahey, William Roger   b: 6/14/50, Detroit, Mich.   BL/TR, 6', 200 lbs.   Deb: 9/26/71   C

YEAR	TM/L	G	AB	R	H	2B	3B	HR	RBI	BB	SO	AVG	OBP	SLG	PRO+	BR/A	SB	CS	SBR	FA	FR	G/POS	TPR
1971	Was-A	2	8	0	0	0	0	0	0	0	0	.000	.000	.000	-99	-2	0	0	0	.909	-0	/C-2	-0.3
1972	Tex-A	39	119	8	20	2	0	1	10	12	23	.168	.250	.210	40	-9	4	0	1	.992	11	C-39	0.5
1974	Tex-A	6	16	1	4	0	0	0	0	0	1	.250	.250	.250	45	-1	0	0	0	1.000	-1	/C-6	-0.2
1975	Tex-A	21	37	3	11	1	1	0	3	1	0	.297	.316	.378	96	-0	0	0	0	.983	-1	C-21	-0.1
1976	Tex-A	38	80	12	20	2	0	1	9	11	6	.250	.348	.313	92	-0	1	0	0	.993	-3	C-38	0.2
1977	Tex-A	37	68	3	15	4	0	0	5	1	8	.221	.232	.279	38	-6	0	0	0	1.000	-5	C-34	-0.6
1979	SD-N	73	209	14	60	3	1	3	19	21	17	.287	.352	.378	106	2	1	1	0	.994	-3	C-68	0.1
1980	SD-N	93	241	18	62	4	0	1	22	21	16	.257	.317	.286	74	-8	2	0	1	.977	-4	C-85	-1.0
1981	Det-A	27	67	5	17	2	0	2	7	3	5	.254	.275	.328	71	-3	0	1	-1	.981	3	C-27	0.1
1982	Det-A	28	67	7	10	2	0	0	4	0	5	.149	.149	.179	-10	-10	1	0	0	1.000	5	C-28	-0.4
1983	Det-A	19	22	4	6	1	0	0	2	5	3	.273	.407	.318	106	0	0	0	0	1.000	1	C-18	0.1
Total	11	383	934	75	225	26	2	7	83	74	93	.241	.298	.296	69	-37	9	2	2	.989	11	C-366	-1.6

■ FERRIS FAIN   Fain, Ferris Roy "Burrhead"   b: 5/29/21, San Antonio, Tex.   BL/TL, 5'11", 186 lbs.   Deb: 4/15/47

YEAR	TM/L	G	AB	R	H	2B	3B	HR	RBI	BB	SO	AVG	OBP	SLG	PRO+	BR/A	SB	CS	SBR	FA	FR	G/POS	TPR
1947	Phi-A	136	461	70	134	28	6	7	71	95	34	.291	.414	.423	130	23	4	5	-2	.985	1	*1-132	1.8
1948	Phi-A	145	520	81	146	27	6	6	88	113	37	.281	.412	.396	115	16	10	5	0	.989	7	*1-145	2.3
1949	Phi-A	150	525	81	138	21	5	3	78	136	51	.263	.415	.339	104	11	8	1	**2**	.984	4	*1-150	1.4
1950	Phi-A★	151	522	83	147	25	4	10	83	133	26	.282	.430	.402	116	20	8	5	-1	.987	8	*1-151	2.3
1951	Phi-A★	117	425	63	146	30	3	6	57	80	20	**.344**	.451	.471	146	32	3	5	-2	.990	13	*1-108,O-11	3.6
1952	Phi-A☆	145	538	82	176	**43**	3	2	59	105	26	**.327**	**.438**	.429	133	30	3	5	-2	.984	16	*1-144	3.9
1953	Chi-A★	128	446	73	114	18	2	6	52	108	28	.256	.405	.345	101	7	3	2	-0	.989	10	*1-127	1.0
1954	Chi-A†	65	235	30	71	10	1	5	51	40	14	.302	.406	.417	121	9	5	1	1	.987	-4	1-64	0.2
1955	Det-A	58	140	23	37	8	0	2	23	52	12	.264	.464	.364	128	10	2	1	0	.988	1	1-44	0.8
	Cle-A	56	118	9	30	3	0	0	8	42	13	.254	.453	.280	97	3	3	0	1	.992	3	1-51	0.5
	Yr	114	258	32	67	11	0	2	31	94	25	.260	.459	.326	113	13	5	1	1	.990	4	1-95	1.3
Total	9	1151	3930	595	1139	213	30	48	570	904	261	.290	.425	.396	120	160	46	28	-3	.987	59	*1-1116/O-11	17.8

■ GEORGE FAIR   Fair, George T.   b: 1/14/1856, Boston, Mass.   d: 2/12/39, Roslindale, Mass.   5'7.5", 140 lbs.   Deb: 7/29/1876

YEAR	TM/L	G	AB	R	H	2B	3B	HR	RBI	BB	SO	AVG	OBP	SLG	PRO+	BR/A	SB	CS	SBR	FA	FR	G/POS	TPR
1876	NY-N	1	4	0	0	0	0	0	0	0	0	.000	.000	.000	-99	-1				.750	0	/2-1	-0.1

■ JIM FAIREY   Fairey, James Burke   b: 9/22/44, Orangeburg, S.C.   BL/TL, 5'10", 190 lbs.   Deb: 4/14/68

YEAR	TM/L	G	AB	R	H	2B	3B	HR	RBI	BB	SO	AVG	OBP	SLG	PRO+	BR/A	SB	CS	SBR	FA	FR	G/POS	TPR
1968	LA-N	99	156	17	31	3	3	1	10	9	32	.199	.242	.276	60	-8	1	1	-0	.944	-8	O-63	-2.1
1969	Mon-N	20	49	6	14	1	0	1	6	1	7	.286	.300	.367	86	-1	0	2	-1	.913	-3	O-13	-0.4
1970	Mon-N	92	211	35	51	9	3	3	25	14	38	.242	.295	.355	74	-8	1	3	-2	.978	-8	O-59	-2.0
1971	Mon-N	92	200	19	49	8	1	7	19	12	23	.245	.288	.310	69	-8	3	3	-1	.968	1	O-58	-1.2
1972	Mon-N	86	141	9	33	7	0	1	15	10	21	.234	.285	.305	66	-6	1	3	-2	.932	-7	O-37	-1.7
1973	LA-N	10	9	0	2	0	0	0	0	1	1	.222	.300	.222	49	-1	0	0	0	.000		H	-0.1
Total	6	399	766	86	180	28	7	14	74	47	122	.235	.281	.317	69	-32	6	12	-5	.957	-23	O-230	-7.5

■ RON FAIRLY   Fairly, Ronald Ray   b: 7/12/38, Macon, Ga.   BL/TL, 5'10", 181 lbs.   Deb: 9/9/58

YEAR	TM/L	G	AB	R	H	2B	3B	HR	RBI	BB	SO	AVG	OBP	SLG	PRO+	BR/A	SB	CS	SBR	FA	FR	G/POS	TPR
1958	LA-N	15	53	6	15	1	0	4	8	6	7	.283	.356	.415	100	0	0	0	0	.971	-1	O-15	-0.2
1959	*LA-N	118	244	27	58	12	1	4	23	31	29	.238	.326	.344	73	-9	0	4	-2	.963	-10	O-88	-2.5
1960	LA-N	14	37	6	4	0	1	0	3	7	6	.108	.159	.351	59	-2	0	0	0	1.000	-1	O-13	-0.4
1961	LA-N	111	245	42	79	15	2	10	48	48	22	.322	.435	.522	140	16	0	0	0	.989	-6	O-71,1-23	-0.4
1962	LA-N	147	460	80	128	15	7	14	71	75	59	.278	.383	.433	126	19	1	1	-0	.989	-23	*1-120,O-48	-1.3
1963	*LA-N	152	490	62	133	21	0	12	77	58	69	.271	.350	.388	120	13	5	2		**.995**	-11	*1-119,O-45	-0.5

YEAR TM/L	G	AB	R	H	2B	3B	HR	RBI	BB	SO	AVG	OBP	SLG	PRO+	BR/A	SB	CS	SBR	FA	FR	G/POS	TPR
1964 LA-N	150	454	62	116	19	5	10	74	65	59	.256	.351	.385	116	11	4	0	1	.987	-1	*1-141	0.5
1965 *LA-N	158	555	73	152	28	1	9	70	76	72	.274	.364	.377	117	14	2	0	1	.982	-1	*O-148,1-13	0.8
1966 *LA-N	117	351	53	101	20	0	14	61	52	38	.288	.383	.464	146	23	3	2	-0	.974	-15	O-98,1-25	0.3
1967 LA-N	153	486	45	107	19	0	10	55	54	51	.220	.299	.321	85	-10	1	4	-2	.986	-4	O-97,1-68	-2.6
1968 LA-N	141	441	32	103	15	1	4	43	41	61	.234	.305	.299	89	-6	2	2	-1	.989	0	*O-105,1-36	-1.7
1969 LA-N	30	64	3	14	3	2	0	8	9	6	.219	.315	.328	86	-1	0	0	0	.981	-1	1-12,O-10	-0.4
Mon-N	70	253	35	73	13	4	12	39	28	22	.289	.359	.514	142	13	1	0	0	.991	-1	1-52,O-21	1.0
Yr	100	317	38	87	16	6	12	47	37	28	.274	.350	.476	132	13	1	0	0	.989	-0	1-64,O-31	0.6
1970 Mon-N	119	385	54	111	19	0	15	61	72	64	.288	.406	.455	130	19	10	2	2	.995	5	*1-118/O-4	1.6
1971 Mon-N	146	447	58	115	23	0	13	71	81	65	.257	.377	.396	119	14	1	3	-2	.992	5	*1-135,O-10	0.6
1972 Mon-N	140	446	51	124	15	1	17	68	46	45	.278	.349	.430	118	11	3	4	-2	.985	6	O-70,1-68	0.8
1973 Mon-N★	142	413	70	123	13	1	17	49	86	33	.298	.422	.458	139	26	2	2	-1	.974	-8	*O-121/1-5	1.2
1974 Mon-N	101	282	35	69	9	1	12	43	57	28	.245	.374	.411	113	6	2	1	0	.989	1	1-67,O-20	0.2
1975 StL-N	107	229	32	69	13	2	7	37	45	22	.301	.422	.467	142	15	0	1	-1	.980	-0	1-56,O-20	1.1
1976 StL-N	73	110	13	29	4	0	0	21	23	12	.264	.391	.300	97	1	0	0	0	.995	3	1-27	0.2
Oak-A	15	46	9	11	1	0	3	10	9	12	.239	.347	.457	145	3	0	0	0	1.000	1	1-15	0.3
1977 Tor-A★	132	458	60	128	24	2	19	64	58	58	.279	.363	.465	122	14	0	4	-2	.986	3	D-58,1-40,O-33	1.0
1978 Cal-A	91	235	23	51	5	0	10	40	25	31	.217	.295	.366	88	-4	0	1	-1	.998	-2	1-78/D-5	-1.1
Total 21	2442	7184	931	1913	307	33	215	1044	1052	877	.266	.363	.408	117	186	35	33	-9	.991	-60	*1-1218/O-1037/D-63	-0.6

■ ANTON FALCH
Falch, Anton C.   b: 12/4/1860, Milwaukee, Wis.   d: 3/31/36, Wauwatosa, Wis.   6'6", 220 lbs.   Deb: 9/30/1884

YEAR TM/L	G	AB	R	H	2B	3B	HR	RBI	BB	SO	AVG	OBP	SLG	PRO+	BR/A	SB	CS	SBR	FA	FR	G/POS	TPR
1884 Mil-U	5	18	0	2	0	0	0		0	0	.111	.111	.111	-60	-5				.600	-1	/O-3,C-2	-0.6

■ BIBB FALK
Falk, Bibb August "Jockey"   b: 1/27/1899, Austin, Tex.   d: 6/8/89, Austin, Tex.   BL/TR, 6', 175 lbs.   Deb: 9/17/20   FMC

YEAR TM/L	G	AB	R	H	2B	3B	HR	RBI	BB	SO	AVG	OBP	SLG	PRO+	BR/A	SB	CS	SBR	FA	FR	G/POS	TPR
1920 Chi-A	7	17	1	5	1	1	0	2	0	5	.294	.294	.471	100	-0				1.000	-1	/O-4	-0.1
1921 Chi-A	152	585	62	167	31	11	5	82	37	69	.285	.330	.402	87	-13	4	4	-1	.958	-14	*O-149	-3.7
1922 Chi-A	131	483	58	144	27	1	12	79	27	55	.298	.335	.433	99	-2	2	6	-3	.963	-9	*O-129	-2.3
1923 Chi-A	87	274	44	84	18	6	5	38	25	12	.307	.367	.471	121	7	5	5	-2	.951	-7	O-80	-0.6
1924 Chi-A	138	526	77	185	37	4	6	99	47	21	.352	.406	.487	134	26	6	6	-2	.970	10	*O-134	2.3
1925 Chi-A	154	602	80	181	35	9	4	99	51	25	.301	.357	.409	99	-2	4	5	-2	.959	-4	*O-153	-1.7
1926 Chi-A	155	566	86	195	43	4	8	108	66	22	.345	.415	.477	137	32	9	10	-3	.992	8	*O-155	2.4
1927 Chi-A	145	535	76	175	35	6	9	83	52	19	.327	.391	.465	125	19	5	7	-3	.978	18	*O-145	2.4
1928 Chi-A	98	286	42	83	18	4	1	37	25	16	.290	.347	.392	95	-2	5	1	1	.972	2	O-78	-0.4
1929 Cle-A	125	426	65	133	30	7	13	93	42	14	.312	.374	.507	120	12	4	4	-1	.943	-4	*O-120	-0.1
1930 Cle-A	82	191	34	62	12	1	4	36	23	8	.325	.397	.461	113	4	2	0	1	.967	1	O-42	0.3
1931 Cle-A	79	161	30	49	13	1	2	28	17	13	.304	.371	.435	105	1	1	1	-0	.949	-3	O-33	-0.4
Total 12	1353	4652	655	1463	300	59	69	784	412	279	.314	.372	.449	113	82	47	49	-15	.967	-4	*O-1222	-1.9

■ CHARLIE FALLON
Fallon, Charles Augustus   b: 3/7/1881, New York, N.Y.   d: 6/10/60, Kings Park, N.Y.   BR/TR, 5'6",   Deb: 6/30/05

YEAR TM/L	G	AB	R	H	2B	3B	HR	RBI	BB	SO	AVG	OBP	SLG	PRO+	BR/A	SB	CS	SBR	FA	FR	G/POS	TPR
1905 NY-A	1	0	0	0	0	0	0	0	0	0	—	—	—			0	0		.000	0	R	0.0

■ GEORGE FALLON
Fallon, George Decatur "Flash"   b: 7/8/14, Jersey City, N.J.   d: 10/25/94, Lake Worth, Fla.   BR/TR, 5'9", 155 lbs.   Deb: 9/27/37

YEAR TM/L	G	AB	R	H	2B	3B	HR	RBI	BB	SO	AVG	OBP	SLG	PRO+	BR/A	SB	CS	SBR	FA	FR	G/POS	TPR
1937 Bro-N	4	8	0	2	1	0	0	0	0	0	.250	.333	.375	91	-0				.895	1	/2-4	0.1
1943 StL-N	36	78	6	18	1	0	0	5	2	9	.231	.259	.244	44	-6	0			.968	15	2-36	1.1
1944 *StL-N	69	141	16	28	6	0	1	9	16	11	.199	.285	.262	54	-8	1			.973	4	2-38,S-24/3-6	-0.2
1945 StL-N	24	55	4	13	2	1	0	7	6	6	.236	.311	.309	71	-2	1			.948	-2	S-20/2-4	-0.3
Total 4	133	282	26	61	10	1	1	21	25	26	.216	.285	.270	56	-16	2			.966	18	/2-82,S-44,3-6	0.7

■ PETE FALSEY
Falsey, Peter James   b: 4/24/1891, New Haven, Conn.   d: 5/23/76, Los Angeles, Cal.   BL/TL, 5'6.5", 132 lbs.   Deb: 7/16/14

YEAR TM/L	G	AB	R	H	2B	3B	HR	RBI	BB	SO	AVG	OBP	SLG	PRO+	BR/A	SB	CS	SBR	FA	FR	G/POS	TPR
1914 Pit-N	3	1	0	0	0	0	0	0	0	1	.000	.000	.000	-99	-0				.000	0	H	0.0

■ RIKKERT FANEYTE
Faneyte, Rikkert   b: 5/31/69, Amsterdam, Holland   BR/TR, 6'1", 170 lbs.   Deb: 8/29/93

YEAR TM/L	G	AB	R	H	2B	3B	HR	RBI	BB	SO	AVG	OBP	SLG	PRO+	BR/A	SB	CS	SBR	FA	FR	G/POS	TPR
1993 SF-N	7	15	2	2	0	0	0	0	2	4	.133	.235	.133	2	-2	0	0	0	1.000	-1	/O-6	-0.3
1994 SF-N	19	26	1	3	0	0	0	3	1	11	.115	.207	.231	15	-3	0	0	0	.900	-1	/O-6	-0.5
1995 SF-N	46	86	7	17	4	1	0	4	11	27	.198	.289	.267	49	-6	1	0	0	.981	-4	O-34	-1.0
1996 Tex-A	8	5	0	1	0	0	0	1	0	0	.200	.200	.200	1	-1	0	0	0	1.000	-1	/O-6,D-2	-0.1
Total 4	80	132	10	23	7	1	0	9	16	42	.174	.264	.242	35	-12	1	0	0	.976	-6	/O-52,D-2	-1.9

■ JIM FANNING
Fanning, William James   b: 9/14/27, Chicago, Ill.   BR/TR, 5'11", 180 lbs.   Deb: 9/11/54   MC

YEAR TM/L	G	AB	R	H	2B	3B	HR	RBI	BB	SO	AVG	OBP	SLG	PRO+	BR/A	SB	CS	SBR	FA	FR	G/POS	TPR
1954 Chi-N	11	38	2	7	0	0	0	1	1	7	.184	.205	.184	2	-5	0	0	0	1.000	-1	C-11	-0.6
1955 Chi-N	5	10	0	0	0	0	0	0	1	2	.000	.091	.000	-73	-3	0	0	0	1.000	3	/C-5	0.1
1956 Chi-N	1	4	0	1	0	0	0	0	0	0	.250	.250	.250	36	-0				.800	0	/C-1	0.0
1957 Chi-N	47	89	3	16	2	0	0	4	4	17	.180	.223	.202	16	-11	0	0	0	.981	2	C-35	-0.7
Total 4	64	141	5	24	2	0	0	5	6	26	.170	.209	.184	5	-19	0	0	0	.979	5	/C-52	-1.2

■ CARMEN FANZONE
Fanzone, Carmen Ronald   b: 8/30/43, Detroit, Mich.   BR/TR, 6', 200 lbs.   Deb: 7/21/70

YEAR TM/L	G	AB	R	H	2B	3B	HR	RBI	BB	SO	AVG	OBP	SLG	PRO+	BR/A	SB	CS	SBR	FA	FR	G/POS	TPR
1970 Bos-A	10	15	0	3	1	0	0	3	2	2	.200	.333	.267	63	-1	0	0	0	.750	0	/3-5	-0.1
1971 Chi-N	12	43	5	8	0	2	0	5	2	7	.186	.222	.372	57	-3	0	0	0	1.000	0	/O-6,3-3,1-2	-0.3
1972 Chi-N	86	222	26	50	11	0	8	42	35	45	.225	.338	.383	95	-1	2	3	-1	.923	3	3-36,1-21,2-13/SO	0.0
1973 Chi-N	64	150	22	41	7	0	6	22	20	38	.273	.359	.440	112	3	1	2	-1	.922	-3	3-25,1-24/O-6	-0.3
1974 Chi-N	65	158	13	30	6	0	4	22	15	27	.190	.269	.304	57	-9	0	1	-1	.885	-1	3-35,2-10/1-7,O-1	-1.2
Total 5	237	588	66	132	27	0	20	94	74	119	.224	.317	.372	86	-11	3	6	-3	.896	-1	3-104/1-54,2-23,OS	-1.9

■ PAUL FARIES
Faries, Paul Tyrrell   b: 2/20/65, Berkeley, Cal.   BR/TR, 5'10", 165 lbs.   Deb: 9/6/90

YEAR TM/L	G	AB	R	H	2B	3B	HR	RBI	BB	SO	AVG	OBP	SLG	PRO+	BR/A	SB	CS	SBR	FA	FR	G/POS	TPR
1990 SD-N	14	37	4	7	1	0	0	2	4	7	.189	.286	.216	40	-3	0	1	-1	1.000	6	/2-7,S-4,3-1	0.3
1991 SD-N	57	130	13	23	3	1	0	7	14	21	.177	.262	.215	35	-11	3	1	0	.988	8	2-36,3-12/S-8	-0.2
1992 SD-N	10	11	3	5	1	0	0	1	1	2	.455	.500	.545	193	1	0	1	0	1.000	-2	/2-4,3-2,S-1	0.0
1993 SF-N	15	36	6	8	2	1	0	4	1	4	.222	.243	.333	54	-2	2	0	1	1.000	-1	/2-7,S-4,3-1	-0.3
Total 4	96	214	26	43	7	2	0	14	20	34	.201	.275	.252	47	-15	5	2	0	.992	11	/2-54,S-17,3-16	-0.2

■ MONTY FARISS
Fariss, Monty Ted   b: 10/13/67, Cordell, Okla.   BR/TR, 6'4", 180 lbs.   Deb: 9/6/91

YEAR TM/L	G	AB	R	H	2B	3B	HR	RBI	BB	SO	AVG	OBP	SLG	PRO+	BR/A	SB	CS	SBR	FA	FR	G/POS	TPR
1991 Tex-A	19	31	6	8	1	0	1	6	7	11	.258	.395	.387	119	1	0	0	0	1.000	4	/O-8,2-4,D-4	0.5
1992 Tex-A	67	166	13	36	7	1	3	21	19	51	.217	.297	.295	77	-5	0	2	-1	1.000	-15	O-49,2-17/1-1,D-4	-2.3
1993 Fla-N	18	29	3	5	2	1	0	2	5	13	.172	.294	.310	59	-2	0	0	0	1.000	-1	/O-8	-0.2
Total 3	104	226	22	49	10	2	4	29	29	75	.217	.311	.332	81	-6	0	2	-1	1.000	-12	/O-65,2-21,D-8,1-1	-2.0

■ BOB FARLEY
Farley, Robert Jacob   b: 11/15/37, Watsontown, Pa.   BL/TL, 6'2", 200 lbs.   Deb: 4/15/61

YEAR TM/L	G	AB	R	H	2B	3B	HR	RBI	BB	SO	AVG	OBP	SLG	PRO+	BR/A	SB	CS	SBR	FA	FR	G/POS	TPR
1961 SF-N	13	20	3	2	0	0	0	0	3	5	.100	.217	.100	-13	-3	0	0	0	1.000	-1	/O-3,1-1	-0.4
1962 Chi-A	35	53	7	10	1	1	1	4	13	13	.189	.348	.302	77	-1	0	0	-1	.989	-1	1-14	-0.4
Det-A	36	50	9	8	2	0	1	4	14	10	.160	.344	.260	63	-2	0	0	0	.857	-4	O-11/1-6	-0.7
Yr	71	103	16	18	3	1	2	8	27	23	.175	.346	.282	70	-3	0	0	-1	.974	-5	1-20,O-11	-1.1
Total 2	84	123	19	20	3	1	2	9	30	28	.163	.327	.252	58	-7	0	0	-1	.975	-6	/1-21,O-14	-1.5

■ TOM FARLEY
Farley, Thomas T.   b: Chicago, Ill.   Deb: 6/24/1884

YEAR TM/L	G	AB	R	H	2B	3B	HR	RBI	BB	SO	AVG	OBP	SLG	PRO+	BR/A	SB	CS	SBR	FA	FR	G/POS	TPR
1884 Was-a	14	52	5	11	4	0	0				.212	.241	.288	81	-1				.867	1	O-14	0.0

■ ALEX FARMER
Farmer, Alexander Johnson   b: 5/9/1880, New York, N.Y.   d: 3/5/20, New York, N.Y.   BR/TR, 6', 175 lbs.   Deb: 9/1/08

YEAR TM/L	G	AB	R	H	2B	3B	HR	RBI	BB	SO	AVG	OBP	SLG	PRO+	BR/A	SB	CS	SBR	FA	FR	G/POS	TPR
1908 Bro-N	12	30	1	5	1	0	0	2	1	0	.167	.194	.200	27	-3	0			.966	-0	C-11	-0.2

■ JACK FARMER
Farmer, Floyd Haskell   b: 7/14/1892, Granville, Tenn.   d: 5/21/70, Columbia, La.   BR/TR, 6', 180 lbs.   Deb: 7/8/16

YEAR TM/L	G	AB	R	H	2B	3B	HR	RBI	BB	SO	AVG	OBP	SLG	PRO+	BR/A	SB	CS	SBR	FA	FR	G/POS	TPR
1916 Pit-N	55	166	10	45	6	4	0	14	7	24	.271	.309	.355	103	0	1			.929	-9	2-31,O-15/S-4,3-1	-1.0

YEAR	TM/L	G	AB	R	H	2B	3B	HR	RBI	BB	SO	AVG	OBP	SLG	PRO+	BR/A	SB	CS	SBR	FA	FR	G/POS	TPR
1918	Cle-A	7	9	1	2	0	0	0	1	0	3	.222	.300	.222	53	-0	2			.429	-2	/O-3	-0.3
Total	2	62	175	11	47	6	4	0	15	7	27	.269	.308	.349	100	-0	3			.829	-11	/2-31,O-18,S-4,3-1	-1.3

■ **BILL FARMER**   Farmer, William   b: 12/27/1870,   BR/TR, 5'11.5", 187 lbs.   Deb: 5/1/1888

YEAR	TM/L	G	AB	R	H	2B	3B	HR	RBI	BB	SO	AVG	OBP	SLG	PRO+	BR/A	SB	CS	SBR	FA	FR	G/POS	TPR
1888	Pit-N	2	4	0	0	0	0	0	0	0	1	.000	.000	.000	-99	-1	0			.667	0	/C-1,O-1	-0.1
	Phi-a	3	12	0	2	0	0	0	1	0	0	.167	.167	.167	7	-1	0			.960	0	/C-3	-0.1
Total	1	5	16	0	2	0	0	0	1	0	1	.125	.125	.125	-20	-2	0			.903	1	/C-4,O-1	-0.2

■ **SID FARRAR**   Farrar, Sidney Douglas   b: 8/10/1859, Paris Hill, Me.   d: 5/7/35, New York, N.Y.   TR, 5'10", 185 lbs.   Deb: 5/1/1883

YEAR	TM/L	G	AB	R	H	2B	3B	HR	RBI	BB	SO	AVG	OBP	SLG	PRO+	BR/A	SB	CS	SBR	FA	FR	G/POS	TPR
1883	Phi-N	99	377	41	88	19	8	0	29	4	37	.233	.241	.326	77	-9				.965	-0	*1-99	-1.7
1884	Phi-N	111	428	62	105	16	6	1	45	9	25	.245	.261	.318	85	-7				.966	5	*1-111	-1.4
1885	Phi-N	111	420	49	103	20	3	3	36	28	34	.245	.292	.329	103	2				.975	2	*1-111	-0.9
1886	Phi-N	118	439	55	109	19	7	5	50	16	47	.248	.275	.358	90	-6	10			**.980**	3	*1-118	-1.6
1887	Phi-N	116	443	83	125	20	9	4	72	42	29	.282	.358	.395	103	1	24			.977	3	*1-116	-0.7
1888	Phi-N	131	508	53	124	24	7	1	53	31	38	.244	.304	.325	96	-3	21			.979	3	*1-131	-1.2
1889	Phi-N	130	477	70	128	22	3	2	58	52	36	.268	.348	.342	86	-10	28			.978	-5	*1-130	-2.1
1890	Phi-P	127	481	84	123	17	11	3	69	51	23	.256	.333	.343	79	-15	9			.973	-2	*1-127	-1.9
Total	8	943	3573	497	905	157	53	18	412	233	269	.253	.305	.342	90	-47	92			.974	8	1-943	-11.5

■ **DUKE FARRELL**   Farrell, Charles Andrew   b: 8/31/1866, Oakdale, Mass.   d: 2/15/25, Boston, Mass.   BB/TR, 6'1", 208 lbs.   Deb: 4/21/1888

YEAR	TM/L	G	AB	R	H	2B	3B	HR	RBI	BB	SO	AVG	OBP	SLG	PRO+	BR/A	SB	CS	SBR	FA	FR	G/POS	TPR
1888	Chi-N	64	241	34	56	6	3	3	19	4	41	.232	.245	.320	73	-8	8			.874	-12	C-33,O-31/1-1	-1.7
1889	Chi-N	101	407	66	101	19	7	11	75	29	21	.248	.318	.410	98	-3	13			.910	4	C-76,O-25	0.6
1890	Chi-P	117	451	79	131	21	12	2	84	42	28	.290	.352	.404	98	-3	8			.929	**27**	C-90,1-22,O-10	2.4
1891	Bos-a	122	473	108	143	19	13	**12**	**110**	59	48	.302	.384	.474	147	28	21			.918	19	3-66,C-37,O-23,1-4	**4.4**
1892	Pit-N	152	605	96	130	10	13	8	77	46	53	.215	.276	.314	78	-18	20			.879	-3	*3-133,O-20	-1.6
1893	Was-N	124	511	84	144	13	13	4	75	47	12	.282	.348	.382	96	-3	11			.923	14	C-81,3-41/1-3	1.5
1894	*NY-N	114	401	47	114	20	12	4	66	35	15	.284	.344	.424	86	-11	9			.926	29	*C-104/3-5,1-4	2.2
1895	NY-N	90	312	38	90	16	9	1	58	38	18	.288	.371	.407	103	2	11			.941	-4	C-62,3-24/1-2	1.0
1896	NY-N	58	191	23	54	7	3	1	37	19	7	.283	.351	.366	92	-2	2			.954	-7	C-34,S-13/3-7	-0.4
	Was-N	37	130	18	39	7	3	1	30	7	3	.300	.345	.423	102	-0	2			1.000	-1	C-18,3-14	0.1
	Yr	95	321	41	93	14	6	2	67	26	10	.290	.349	.389	96	-2	4			.970	-7	C-52,3-21,S-13	-0.3
1897	Was-N	78	261	41	84	9	6	0	53	17		.322	.366	.402	103	1	8			.945	9	C-63/1-1	1.5
1898	Was-N	99	338	47	106	12	6	1	53	34		.314	.383	.393	123	11	12			.929	-6	C-61,1-28	1.0
1899	Was-N	5	12	2	4	1	0	0	1	2		.333	.429	.417	134	1	1			1.000	-0	/C-4	0.1
	Bro-N	80	254	40	76	10	7	2	55	35		.299	.399	.417	121	9	6			.948	11	C-78	2.3
	Yr	85	266	42	80	11	7	2	56	37		.301	.400	.417	122	9	7			.949	10	C-82	2.4
1900	*Bro-N	76	273	33	75	11	5	0	39	11		.275	.310	.352	78	-9	3			.944	-4	C-74	-0.6
1901	Bro-N	80	284	38	84	10	6	1	31	7		.296	.320	.384	101	-1	7			.979	6	C-59,1-17	1.1
1902	Bro-N	74	264	14	64	5	2	0	24	12		.242	.281	.277	71	-9	6			.976	7	C-49,1-24	0.3
1903	*Bos-A	17	52	5	21	5	1	0	8	5		.404	.466	.538	190	6	1			.960	-0	C-17	0.8
1904	Bos-A	68	198	11	42	9	0	0	15	15		.212	.281	.278	73	-6	1			.958	-7	C-56	-0.7
1905	Bos-A	7	21	2	6	1	0	0	2	1		.286	.318	.333	105	0	1			1.000	-2	/C-7	0.3
Total	18	1563	5679	826	1564	211	123	51	912	477	246	.275	.337	.383	99	-16	150			.938	91	*C-1003,3-290,O1/S	14.6

■ **DOC FARRELL**   Farrell, Edward Stephen   b: 12/26/01, Johnson City, N.Y.   d: 12/20/66, Livingston, N.J.   BR/TR, 5'8", 160 lbs.   Deb: 6/15/25

YEAR	TM/L	G	AB	R	H	2B	3B	HR	RBI	BB	SO	AVG	OBP	SLG	PRO+	BR/A	SB	CS	SBR	FA	FR	G/POS	TPR
1925	NY-N	27	56	6	12	1	0	0	4	6		.214	.267	.232	30	-6	0	1	-1	.900	1	S-13/3-7,2-1	-0.4
1926	NY-N	67	171	19	49	10	1	2	23	12	17	.287	.341	.392	98	-1	4			.950	-11	S-53/2-3	-0.7
1927	NY-N	42	142	13	55	10	1	3	34	12	11	.387	.442	.535	161	12	0			.919	-1	S-36/3-2	0.5
	Bos-N	110	424	44	124	13	2	1	58	14	21	.292	.315	.340	82	-12	0			.931	-4	S-57,2-40,3-18	-0.8
	Yr	152	566	57	179	23	3	4	92	26	32	.316	.348	.389	103	1	4			.926	-4	S-93,2-40,3-20	0.7
1928	Bos-N	134	483	36	104	14	2	3	43	26		.215	.263	.271	42	-42	3			*.933	-17	*S-132/2-1	-4.3
1929	Bos-N	5	8	0	1	0	0	0	2	0	1	.125	.125	.125	-39	-2	0			.000	-1	/2-1,S-1	-0.2
	NY-N	63	178	18	38	6	0	0	16	9	17	.213	.251	.247	24	-21	2			.925	7	3-28,2-25/S-4	-1.1
	Yr	68	186	18	39	6	0	0	18	9	18	.210	.246	.242	22	-23	2			.925	7	3-28,2-26/S-5	-1.3
1930	StL-N	23	61	3	13	1	1	0	6	4	2	.213	.262	.262	26	-7	1			.944	-3	S-15/2-6,1-1	-0.4
	Chi-N	46	113	21	33	6	0	1	16	9	5	.292	.344	.372	73	-5	0			.937	3	S-38/2-1	0.2
	Yr	69	174	24	46	7	1	1	22	13	7	.264	.316	.333	56	-12	1			.938	5	S-53/2-7,1-1	-0.2
1932	NY-A	26	63	4	11	1	0	0	4	2	8	.175	.212	.222	13	-8	0	0	0	.963	-1	2-16/S-5,1-2,3-1	-0.7
1933	NY-A	44	93	16	25	0	0	0	16	6		.269	.376	.269	78	-2	0	0	0	.947	-4	S-22,3-20	-0.4
1935	Bos-A	4	7	1	2	1	0	0	1	0		.286	.375	.429	101	0	0			.917	-1	/2-4	0.0
Total	9	591	1799	181	467	63	6	10	213	109	120	.260	.306	.320	66	-93	14	1		.934	-24	S-376,2-118/3-56,1	-7.3

■ **JACK FARRELL**   Farrell, John "Hartford Jack"   b: 1/2/1856, Hartford, Conn.   d: 11/15/16, Hartford, Conn.   Deb: 10/27/1874

YEAR	TM/L	G	AB	R	H	2B	3B	HR	RBI	BB	SO	AVG	OBP	SLG	PRO+	BR/A	SB	CS	SBR	FA	FR	G/POS	TPR
1874	Har-n	3	13	3	5	0	0	0	1	0		.385	.429	.385	155	1	0	0	0	1.000	0	/O-3	0.1

■ **JACK FARRELL**   Farrell, John A. "Moose"   b: 7/5/1857, Newark, N.J.   d: 2/10/14, Overbrook, N.J.   BR/TR, 5'9", 165 lbs.   Deb: 5/1/1879   M

YEAR	TM/L	G	AB	R	H	2B	3B	HR	RBI	BB	SO	AVG	OBP	SLG	PRO+	BR/A	SB	CS	SBR	FA	FR	G/POS	TPR
1879	Syr-N	54	241	40	73	6	2	1	24	3	13	.303	.311	.357	135	9				.870	-15	2-54	-0.2
	Pro-N	12	51	5	13	2	0	0	5	0	0	.255	.255	.294	82	-1				.915	7	2-12	0.6
	Yr	66	292	45	86	8	2	1	26	3	13	.295	.302	.346	125	8				.879	-7	2-66	0.4
1880	Pro-N	80	339	46	92	12	5	3	36	10	6	.271	.292	.363	125	9				.887	-8	*2-80	0.4
1881	Pro-N	84	345	69	82	16	5	5	36	29	23	.238	.297	.357	106	3				.881	-5	*2-82/O-3,M	0.1
1882	Pro-N	84	366	67	93	21	6	2	31	16	21	.254	.285	.361	106	2				.875	-5	*2-84	-0.1
1883	Pro-N	95	420	92	128	24	11	3	61	15	21	.305	.329	.436	126	12				**.924**	**25**	*2-95	**3.3**
1884	*Pro-N	111	469	70	102	13	6	1	37	35	44	.217	.272	.277	75	-12				.922	-4	2-109/3-3	-1.2
1885	Pro-N	68	257	27	53	7	1	1	19	10	25	.206	.236	.253	61	-11				.900	-15	2-68	-2.3
1886	Phi-N	17	60	7	11	0	1	0	3	3	11	.183	.222	.217	34	-5	1			.825	-3	2-17	-0.6
	Was-N	47	171	24	41	11	4	2	18	15	12	.240	.301	.386	114	3	12			.913	-13	2-47	-0.7
	Yr	64	231	31	52	11	5	2	21	18	23	.225	.281	.342	92	-2	13			.888	-15	2-64	-1.3
1887	Was-N	87	339	40	75	14	9	0	41	20	12	.221	.267	.316	64	-16	31			.876	-3	S-48,2-40	-1.9
1888	Bal-a	103	398	72	81	19	5	4	36	26		.204	.256	.307	82	-8	29			.902	11	S-54,2-52	0.6
1889	Bal-a	42	157	25	33	3	0	1	26	15	15	.210	.287	.248	52	-10	14			.891	-6	S-42	-1.1
Total	11	884	3613	584	877	148	55	23	370	197	205	.243	.283	.333	94	-24	87			.899	-38	2-740,S-144/3-3,O-3	-3.1

■ **JACK FARRELL**   Farrell, John J.   b: 6/16/1892, Chicago, Ill.   d: 3/24/18, Chicago, Ill.   BB/TR, 5'8", 145 lbs.   Deb: 4/16/14

YEAR	TM/L	G	AB	R	H	2B	3B	HR	RBI	BB	SO	AVG	OBP	SLG	PRO+	BR/A	SB	CS	SBR	FA	FR	G/POS	TPR
1914	Chi-F	156	524	58	123	23	4	0	35	52	65	.235	.307	.294	68	-32	12			.954	0	*2-155/S-3	-3.5
1915	Chi-F	70	222	27	48	10	1	0	14	25	18	.216	.298	.270	64	-14	8			.941	-5	2-70/S-1	-1.9
Total	2	226	746	85	171	33	5	0	49	77	83	.229	.305	.287	67	-46	20			.950	-4	2-225/S-4	-5.4

■ **JOHN FARRELL**   Farrell, John Sebastian   b: 12/4/1876, Covington, Ky.   d: 5/13/21, Kansas City, Mo.   BR/TR, 5'10", 160 lbs.   Deb: 4/26/01

YEAR	TM/L	G	AB	R	H	2B	3B	HR	RBI	BB	SO	AVG	OBP	SLG	PRO+	BR/A	SB	CS	SBR	FA	FR	G/POS	TPR
1901	Was-A	135	555	100	151	32	11	3	63	52		.272	.336	.386	101	1	25			.915	17	2-72,O-62/3-1	1.4
1902	StL-N	138	565	69	141	13	5	0	25	43		.250	.308	.290	88	-7	9			.947	**34**	*2-118,S-21	3.3
1903	StL-N	130	519	83	141	25	8	1	32	48		.272	.336	.356	100	0	17			.927	**28**	*2-118,O-12	3.0
1904	StL-N	131	509	72	130	23	3	0	20	46		.255	.320	.312	100	1	16			.934	16	*2-130	2.1
1905	StL-N	7	24	6	4	0	1	0	1	4		.167	.286	.250	62	-1	1			.892	-3	/2-7	-0.4
Total	5	541	2172	329	567	93	28	4	141	193		.261	.324	.335	97	-6	68			.932	92	2-445/O-74,S-21,3-1	9.4

■ **JOE FARRELL**   Farrell, Joseph F.   b: 1857, Brooklyn, N.Y.   d: 4/18/1893, Brooklyn, N.Y.   BR, 5'6", 160 lbs.   Deb: 5/1/1882

YEAR	TM/L	G	AB	R	H	2B	3B	HR	RBI	BB	SO	AVG	OBP	SLG	PRO+	BR/A	SB	CS	SBR	FA	FR	G/POS	TPR
1882	Det-N	69	283	34	70	12	2	1	24	4	20	.247	.258	.314	83	-6				.816	-11	3-42,2-18/S-9	-1.4
1883	Det-N	101	444	58	108	13	5	0	36	5	29	.243	.245	.295	69	-16				.845	13	*3-101	-0.3
1884	Det-N	110	461	59	104	10	5	3	41	14	66	.226	.248	.289	73	-14				.842	-7	*3-110/O-1	-1.8

YEAR	TM/L	G	AB	R	H	2B	3B	HR	RBI	BB	SO	AVG	OBP	SLG	PRO+	BR/A	SB	CS	SBR	FA	FR	G/POS	TPR
1886	Bal-a	73	301	36	63	8	3	1	31	12		.209	.240	.266	60	-14	5			.870	-15	2-45,3-27/O-1	-2.4
Total	4	353	1489	187	345	43	15	5	132	35	115	.232	.249	.291	71	-49	5			.840	-21	3-280/2-63,S-9,O-2	-5.9

■ **KERBY FARRELL**   Farrell, Major Kerby   b: 9/3/13, Leapwood, Tenn.   d: 12/17/75, Nashville, Tenn.   BL/TL, 5'11", 172 lbs.   Deb: 4/24/43   MC

YEAR	TM/L	G	AB	R	H	2B	3B	HR	RBI	BB	SO	AVG	OBP	SLG	PRO+	BR/A	SB	CS	SBR	FA	FR	G/POS	TPR
1943	Bos-N	85	280	11	75	14	1	0	21	16	15	.268	.307	.325	84	-6	1			.996	-5	1-69/P-5	-0.9
1945	Chi-A	103	396	44	102	11	3	0	34	24	18	.258	.300	.301	76	-12	4	9	-4	.989	-0	1-97	-2.5
Total	2	188	676	55	177	25	4	0	55	40	33	.262	.303	.311	80	-19	5	9		.992	1	1-166/P-5	-3.4

■ **BILL FARRELL**   Farrell, William   Deb: 5/3/1882

YEAR	TM/L	G	AB	R	H	2B	3B	HR	RBI	BB	SO	AVG	OBP	SLG	PRO+	BR/A	SB	CS	SBR	FA	FR	G/POS	TPR
1882	Phi-a	2	7	2	2	1	0	0	1	1		.286	.375	.429	153	0				.000	-1	/O-2,C-1	-0.1
1883	Bal-a	2	7	0	0	0	0	0		1		.000	.125	.000	-55	-1				.750	-1	/S-2	-0.2
Total	2	4	14	2	2	1	0	0	1	2		.143	.250	.214	51	-1				.750	-2	/S-2,O-2,C-1	-0.3

■ **JOHN FARROW**   Farrow, John Jacob   b: 11/8/1853, Verplanck, N.Y   d: 12/31/14, Perth Amboy, N.J.   BL/TR,   Deb: 4/28/1873

YEAR	TM/L	G	AB	R	H	2B	3B	HR	RBI	BB	SO	AVG	OBP	SLG	PRO+	BR/A	SB	CS	SBR	FA	FR	G/POS	TPR
1873	Res-n	12	48	2	8	1	0	0	3	0	3	.167	.167	.188	5	-5	0	0	0	.673	-3	/C-9,O-3,1-1,S-1	-0.6
1874	Atl-n	27	122	16	26	3	0	0	10	1	1	.213	.220	.238	53	-5	0	0	0	.694	-2	C-16,2-12/O-3	-0.6
1884	Bro-a	16	58	7	11	2	0	0		3		.190	.230	.224	48	-3				.915	-1	C-16	-0.2
Total	2 n	39	170	18	34	4	0	0	13	1	4	.200	.205	.224	38	-10				.686	-5	/C-25,2-12,O-6,S1	-1.2

■ **SAL FASANO**   Fasano, Salvatore Frank   b: 8/10/71, Chicago, Ill.   BR/TR, 6'2", 220 lbs.   Deb: 4/3/96

YEAR	TM/L	G	AB	R	H	2B	3B	HR	RBI	BB	SO	AVG	OBP	SLG	PRO+	BR/A	SB	CS	SBR	FA	FR	G/POS	TPR
1996	KC-A	51	143	20	29	2	0	6	19	14	25	.203	.283	.343	59	-9	1	1	-0	.984	10	C-51	0.3

■ **BUCK FAUSETT**   Fausett, Robert Shaw "Leaky"   b: 4/8/08, Sheridan, Ark.   d: 5/2/94, College Station, Tex.   BL/TR, 5'10", 170 lbs.   Deb: 4/18/44

YEAR	TM/L	G	AB	R	H	2B	3B	HR	RBI	BB	SO	AVG	OBP	SLG	PRO+	BR/A	SB	CS	SBR	FA	FR	G/POS	TPR
1944	Cin-N	13	31	2	3	0	1	0	1	2	1	.097	.125	.161	-21	-5	0			1.000	3	/3-6,P-2	-0.1

■ **JOE FAUTSCH**   Fautsch, Joseph Roamon   b: 2/28/1887, Minneapolis, Minn.   d: 3/16/71, New Hope, Minn.   BR/TR, 5'10", 162 lbs.   Deb: 4/24/16

YEAR	TM/L	G	AB	R	H	2B	3B	HR	RBI	BB	SO	AVG	OBP	SLG	PRO+	BR/A	SB	CS	SBR	FA	FR	G/POS	TPR
1916	Chi-A	1	1	0	0	0	0	0				.000	.000	.000	-99	-0	0			.000	0	H	0.0

■ **ERNIE FAZIO**   Fazio, Ernest Joseph   b: 1/25/42, Oakland, Cal.   BR/TR, 5'7", 165 lbs.   Deb: 7/3/62

YEAR	TM/L	G	AB	R	H	2B	3B	HR	RBI	BB	SO	AVG	OBP	SLG	PRO+	BR/A	SB	CS	SBR	FA	FR	G/POS	TPR
1962	Hou-N	12	12	3	1	0	0	0	1	2	5	.083	.214	.083	-18	-2	0	0	0	.783	0	S-10	-0.1
1963	Hou-N	102	228	31	42	10	3	2	5	27	70	.184	.273	.281	64	-11	4	4	-1	.972	-11	2-84/S-1,3-1	-1.8
1966	KC-A	27	34	3	7	0	1	0	2	4	10	.206	.289	.265	62	-2	1	0	0	1.000	2	2-10/S-4	0.1
Total	3	141	274	37	50	10	4	2	8	33	85	.182	.273	.270	60	-14	5	4	-1	.974	-9	/2-94,S-15,3-1	-1.8

■ **AL FEDEROFF**   Federoff, Alfred "Whitey"   b: 7/11/24, Bairdford, Pa.   BR/TR, 5'10.5", 165 lbs.   Deb: 9/27/51

YEAR	TM/L	G	AB	R	H	2B	3B	HR	RBI	BB	SO	AVG	OBP	SLG	PRO+	BR/A	SB	CS	SBR	FA	FR	G/POS	TPR
1951	Det-A	2	4	0	0	0	0	0	0	0	0	.000	.000	.000	-99	-1	0	0	0	.889	1	/2-1	0.0
1952	Det-A	74	231	14	56	4	2	0	14	16	13	.242	.294	.273	59	-13	1	0	0	.976	0	2-70/S-7	-0.9
Total	2	76	235	14	56	4	2	0	14	16	13	.238	.290	.272	56	-14	1	0	0	.973	1	/2-71,S-7	-0.9

■ **BILL FEHRING**   Fehring, William Paul "Dutch"   b: 5/31/12, Columbus, Ind.   BB/TR, 6', 195 lbs.   Deb: 6/25/34

YEAR	TM/L	G	AB	R	H	2B	3B	HR	RBI	BB	SO	AVG	OBP	SLG	PRO+	BR/A	SB	CS	SBR	FA	FR	G/POS	TPR
1934	Chi-A	1	1	0	0	0	0	0			1	.000	.000	.000	-97	0	0	0	0	1.000	0	/C-1	0.0

■ **EDDIE FEINBERG**   Feinberg, Edward Isadore "Itzzy"   b: 9/29/17, Philadelphia, Pa.   d: 4/20/86, Hollywood, Fla.   BB/TR, 5'9", 165 lbs.   Deb: 9/11/38

YEAR	TM/L	G	AB	R	H	2B	3B	HR	RBI	BB	SO	AVG	OBP	SLG	PRO+	BR/A	SB	CS	SBR	FA	FR	G/POS	TPR
1938	Phi-N	10	20	0	3	0	0	0	0	0	2	.150	.150	.150	-18	-3				.957	3	/S-4,O-2	0.0
1939	Phi-N	6	18	2	4	1	0	0	0	0	0	.222	.300	.278	58	-1				.909	-4	/2-4,S-1	-0.5
Total	2	16	38	2	7	1	0	0	0	2	1	.184	.225	.211	20	-4				.957	-2	/S-5,2-4,O-2	-0.5

■ **MIKE FELDER**   Felder, Michael Otis   b: 11/18/61, Vallejo, Cal.   BB/TR, 5'8", 160 lbs.   Deb: 9/11/85

YEAR	TM/L	G	AB	R	H	2B	3B	HR	RBI	BB	SO	AVG	OBP	SLG	PRO+	BR/A	SB	CS	SBR	FA	FR	G/POS	TPR
1985	Mil-A	15	56	8	11	1	0	0	5	6		.196	.262	.214	33	-5	4	1	1	1.000	-0	O-14	-0.5
1986	Mil-A	44	155	24	37	2	4	1	13	13	16	.239	.298	.323	67	-7	16	2	4	1.000	2	O-42/D-1	-0.3
1987	Mil-A	108	289	48	77	5	7	2	31	28	23	.266	.331	.353	79	-8	34	8	5	.975	-5	O-99/2-1,D-3	-0.4
1988	Mil-A	50	81	14	14	1	0	0	5	0	11	.173	.183	.185	3	-10	8	2	1	.976	-5	O-28,D-16/2-1	-1.5
1989	Mil-A	117	315	50	76	11	3	3	23	23	38	.241	.293	.324	74	-11	26	5	5	.985	-1	O-93,D-11,2-10	-0.9
1990	Mil-A	121	237	38	65	7	2	3	27	22	17	.274	.336	.359	95	-1	20	9	1	.972	-12	*O-109/2-1,3-1,D-1	-1.5
1991	SF-N	132	348	51	92	10	6	0	18	30	31	.264	.325	.328	87	-6	21	6	3	.985	-11	*O-107/3-3,2-1	-1.6
1992	SF-N	145	322	44	92	13	3	4	23	21	29	.286	.333	.382	108	3	14	4	2	.994	-20	*O-105/2-3	-1.9
1993	Sea-A	109	342	31	72	7	5	1	20	22	34	.211	.262	.269	43	-28	15	9	-1	.987	-3	O-95/3-2,D-6	-3.2
1994	Hou-N	58	117	10	28	2	2	0	13	4	12	.239	.264	.291	47	-9	3	0	1	.974	-6	O-32	-1.4
Total	10	899	2262	318	564	59	32	14	173	168	217	.249	.303	.322	73	-83	161	46	21	.984	-55	O-724/D-38,2-17,3-6	-13.2

■ **MARV FELDERMAN**   Felderman, Marvin Wilfred "Coonie"   b: 12/20/15, Bellevue, Iowa   BR/TR, 6'1", 187 lbs.   Deb: 4/19/42

YEAR	TM/L	G	AB	R	H	2B	3B	HR	RBI	BB	SO	AVG	OBP	SLG	PRO+	BR/A	SB	CS	SBR	FA	FR	G/POS	TPR
1942	Chi-N	3	6	0	1	0	0	0	0	1	4	.167	.286	.167	35	-0	0			1.000	1	/C-2	0.0

■ **GUS FELIX**   Felix, August Guenther   b: 5/24/1895, Cincinnati, Ohio   d: 5/12/60, Montgomery, Ala.   BR/TR, 6', 180 lbs.   Deb: 4/19/23

YEAR	TM/L	G	AB	R	H	2B	3B	HR	RBI	BB	SO	AVG	OBP	SLG	PRO+	BR/A	SB	CS	SBR	FA	FR	G/POS	TPR
1923	Bos-N	139	506	64	138	17	2	6	44	51	65	.273	.348	.354	88	-8	8	13	-5	.950	0	*O-123/2-5,3-4	-2.0
1924	Bos-N	59	204	25	43	7	1	1	10	18	16	.211	.275	.270	48	-15	2	5		.950	5	O-51	-1.5
1925	Bos-N	121	459	60	141	25	7	2	66	30	34	.307	.356	.405	103	2	5	5	-2	.972	10	*O-114	0.3
1926	Bro-N	134	432	64	121	21	7	3	53	51	32	.280	.360	.382	101	2	9			.956	-3	*O-125	-0.8
1927	Bro-N	130	445	43	118	21	8	0	57	39	47	.265	.327	.348	81	-12	6			.947	-3	*O-119	-2.2
Total	5	583	2046	256	561	91	25	12	230	189	194	.274	.341	.361	89	-31	28	21		.957	11	O-532/2-5,3-4	-6.2

■ **JUNIOR FELIX**   Felix, Junior Francisco (Sanchez)   b: 10/3/67, Laguna Salada, D.R.   BR/TR, 6', 170 lbs.   Deb: 5/3/89

YEAR	TM/L	G	AB	R	H	2B	3B	HR	RBI	BB	SO	AVG	OBP	SLG	PRO+	BR/A	SB	CS	SBR	FA	FR	G/POS	TPR
1989	*Tor-A	110	415	62	107	14	8	9	46	33	101	.258	.317	.395	101	0	18	12	-2	.966	3	*O-107/D-2	-0.1
1990	Tor-A	127	463	73	122	23	7	15	65	45	99	.263	.331	.441	112	7	13	8	-1	.966	2	O-125/D-1	0.4
1991	Cal-A	66	230	32	65	10	2	2	26	11	55	.283	.324	.370	91	-3	7	5	-1	.977	-6	O-65	-1.1
1992	Cal-A	139	509	63	125	22	5	9	72	33	128	.246	.294	.361	82	-13	8	8	-2	.983	7	*O-128/D-8	-1.2
1993	Fla-N	57	214	25	51	11	1	7	22	10	50	.238	.276	.397	73	-9	2	1	0	.940	-2	O-52	-1.2
1994	Det-A	86	301	54	92	25	1	13	49	26	76	.306	.376	.525	129	13	1	6	-3	.980	5	O-81/D-2	1.1
Total	6	585	2132	309	562	105	24	55	280	158	509	.264	.320	.413	99	-5	49	40	-9	.972	8	O-558/D-13	-2.1

■ **JACK FELLER**   Feller, Jack Leland   b: 12/10/36, Adrian, Mich.   BR/TR, 5'10.5", 185 lbs.   Deb: 9/13/58

YEAR	TM/L	G	AB	R	H	2B	3B	HR	RBI	BB	SO	AVG	OBP	SLG	PRO+	BR/A	SB	CS	SBR	FA	FR	G/POS	TPR
1958	Det-A	1	0	0	0	0	0	0	0	0							0	0	0	1.000	-0	/C-1	0.0

■ **HAPPY FELSCH**   Felsch, Oscar Emil   b: 8/22/1891, Milwaukee, Wis.   d: 8/17/64, Milwaukee, Wis.   BR/TR, 5'11", 175 lbs.   Deb: 4/14/15

YEAR	TM/L	G	AB	R	H	2B	3B	HR	RBI	BB	SO	AVG	OBP	SLG	PRO+	BR/A	SB	CS	SBR	FA	FR	G/POS	TPR
1915	Chi-A	121	427	65	106	18	11	3	53	51	59	.248	.334	.363	105	2	16	18	-6	.959	-3	*O-118	-1.4
1916	Chi-A	146	546	73	164	24	12	7	70	31	67	.300	.341	.427	129	16	13			.981	7	*O-141	1.7
1917	*Chi-A	152	575	75	177	17	10	6	102	33	52	.308	.352	.403	128	17	26			.985	19	*O-152	3.0
1918	Chi-A	53	206	16	52	2	1	1	20	15	13	.252	.306	.325	90	-3	6			.957	-7	O-53	-0.1
1919	*Chi-A	135	502	68	138	34	11	7	86	40	35	.275	.336	.428	113	7	19			.968	21	*O-135	2.1
1920	Chi-A	142	556	88	188	40	15	14	115	37	25	.338	.384	.540	143	31	8	13	-5	.981	18	*O-142	3.2
Total	6	749	2812	385	825	135	64	38	446	207	251	.293	.347	.427	123	70	88	31		.975	67	O-741	8.5

■ **JOHN FELSKE**   Felske, John Frederick   b: 5/30/42, Chicago, Ill.   BR/TR, 6'3", 195 lbs.   Deb: 7/26/68   MC

YEAR	TM/L	G	AB	R	H	2B	3B	HR	RBI	BB	SO	AVG	OBP	SLG	PRO+	BR/A	SB	CS	SBR	FA	FR	G/POS	TPR
1968	Chi-N	4	2	0	0	0	0	0	0	0	1	.000	.000	.000	-94	-0	0	0	0	.833	1	/C-3	0.0
1972	Mil-A	37	80	6	11	3	0	1	5	8	23	.138	.216	.213	28	-7	0	0	0	.972	-2	C-23/1-8	-1.0
1973	Mil-A	13	22	1	3	0	1	0	1	4	11	.136	.174	.227	12	-3	0	0	0	1.000	0	/C-7,1-6	-0.3
Total	3	54	104	7	14	3	1	1	6	12	35	.135	.204	.212	23	-10	0	0	0	.969	-1	/C-33,1-14	-1.3

■ **FRANK FENNELLY**   Fennelly, Francis John   b: 2/18/1860, Fall River, Mass.   d: 8/4/20, Fall River, Mass.   BR/TR, 5'8", 168 lbs.   Deb: 5/1/1884

YEAR	TM/L	G	AB	R	H	2B	3B	HR	RBI	BB	SO	AVG	OBP	SLG	PRO+	BR/A	SB	CS	SBR	FA	FR	G/POS	TPR
1884	Was-a	62	257	52	75	17	7	2		20		.292	.343	.436	172	21				.863	13	S-60/2-4	3.1
	Cin-a	28	122	42	43	5	8	2		11		.352	.415	.574	209	14				.813	-6	S-28	0.8
	Yr	90	379	94	118	22	15	4		31		.311	.367	.480	186	37				.849	7	S-88/2-4	3.9
1885	Cin-a	112	454	82	124	14	17	10	89	38		.273	.333	.445	142	21				.873	-11	*S-112	1.0

YEAR	TM/L	G	AB	R	H	2B	3B	HR	RBI	BB	SO	AVG	OBP	SLG	PRO+	BR/A	SB	CS	SBR	FA	FR	G/POS	TPR
1886	Cin-a	132	497	113	124	13	17	6	72	60		.249	.351	.380	125	15	32			.848	14	*S-132	2.6
1887	Cin-a	134	526	133	140	15	16	8	97	82		.266	.369	.401	112	10	74			.855	-9	*S-134	0.2
1888	Cin-a	120	448	64	88	8	7	2	56	63		.196	.297	.259	75	-12	43			.858	17	*S-112/2-4,O-4	0.7
	Phi-a	15	47	13	11	2	2	1	12	9		.234	.357	.426	151	3	5			.912	-1	S-15	0.2
	Yr	135	495	77	99	10	9	3	68	72		.200	.303	.275	82	-9	48			.863	16	*S-127/2-4,O-4	0.9
1889	Phi-a	138	513	70	132	20	5	1	64	65	78	.257	.344	.322	91	-4	15			.872	-20	*S-138	-1.4
1890	Bro-a	45	178	40	44	8	3	2	18	30		.247	.356	.360	115	4	6			.858	0	S-38/3-7	0.6
Total	7	786	3042	609	781	102	82	34	408	378	78	.257	.345	.378	118	72	175			.860	-4	S-769/2-8,3-7,O-4	7.8

■ BOBBY FENWICK

Fenwick, Robert Richard b: 12/10/46, Naha, Okinawa BR/TR, 5'9", 165 lbs. Deb: 4/26/72

YEAR	TM/L	G	AB	R	H	2B	3B	HR	RBI	BB	SO	AVG	OBP	SLG	PRO+	BR/A	SB	CS	SBR	FA	FR	G/POS	TPR
1972	Hou-N	36	50	7	9	3	0	0	4	3	13	.180	.226	.240	33	-4	0	1	-1	.945	3	2-17/S-4,3-2	-0.1
1973	StL-N	5	6	0	1	0	0	0	1	0	2	.167	.167	.167	-7	-1	0	0	0	.750	-1	/2-3	-0.2
Total	2	41	56	7	10	3	0	0	5	3	15	.179	.220	.232	29	-5	0	1	-1	.932	3	/2-20,S-4,3-2	-0.3

■ JOE FERGUSON

Ferguson, Joseph Vance b: 9/19/46, San Francisco, Cal. BR/TR, 6'2", 200 lbs. Deb: 9/12/70 C

YEAR	TM/L	G	AB	R	H	2B	3B	HR	RBI	BB	SO	AVG	OBP	SLG	PRO+	BR/A	SB	CS	SBR	FA	FR	G/POS	TPR
1970	LA-N	5	4	0	1	0	0	0	1	2	2	.250	.500	.250	112	0	0	0	0	1.000	0	/C-3	0.0
1971	LA-N	36	102	13	22	3	0	2	7	12	15	.216	.304	.304	77	-3	1	0	0	.983	-2	C-35	-0.4
1972	LA-N	8	24	2	7	3	0	-1	5	2	4	.292	.346	.542	152	2	0	0	0	.975	7	/C-7,O-2	0.3
1973	LA-N	136	487	84	128	26	0	25	88	87	81	.263	.376	.470	139	27	1	1	-0	.996	-0	*C-122,O-20	3.2
1974	*LA-N	111	349	54	88	14	1	16	57	75	73	.252	.384	.436	134	18	2	2	0	.988	-10	C-82,O-32	1.0
1975	LA-N	66	202	15	42	2	1	5	23	35	47	.208	.328	.302	79	-5	2	1	0	.994	-1	C-35,O-34	-0.6
1976	LA-N	54	185	24	41	7	0	6	18	25	41	.222	.318	.357	93	-2	2	0	1	.966	-0	O-39,C-17	-0.3
	StL-N	71	189	22	38	8	4	4	21	32	40	.201	.320	.349	89	-2	4	2	0	.978	3	C-48,O-14	0.2
	Yr	125	374	46	79	15	4	10	39	57	81	.211	.319	.353	91	-4	6	2	1	.975	2	C-65,O-53	-0.1
1977	Hou-N	132	421	59	108	21	3	16	61	85	79	.257	.381	.435	130	20	6	2	1	.985	-10	*C-122/1-1	1.4
1978	Hou-N	51	150	20	31	5	0	7	22	37	30	.207	.367	.380	118	5	0	0	0	.994	-6	C-51	0.1
	*LA-N	67	198	20	47	11	0	7	28	34	41	.237	.352	.399	110	3	1	2	-1	.984	-10	C-62/O-3	-0.7
	Yr	118	348	40	78	16	0	14	50	71	71	.224	.359	.391	113	8	1	2	-1	.989	-16	C-113/O-3	-0.6
1979	LA-N	122	363	54	95	14	0	20	69	70	68	.262	.384	.466	133	18	1	0	0	.981	-12	C-67,O-52	0.7
1980	LA-N	77	172	20	41	3	2	9	29	38	46	.238	.376	.436	128	8	2	2	-1	.982	-3	C-66/O-1	0.6
1981	LA-N	17	14	2	2	1	0	0	1	2	5	.143	.250	.214	34	-1	0	0	0	.000	0	/O-1	-0.2
	Cal-A	12	30	5	7	1	0	1	5	9	8	.233	.410	.367	125	2	0	0	0	.976	0	/C-8,O-4	0.2
1982	Cal-A	36	84	10	19	2	0	3	8	12	19	.226	.323	.357	87	-1	0	0	0	.993	5	C-32/O-3	0.5
1983	Cal-A	12	27	3	2	0	0	0	2	5	8	.074	.219	.074	-15	-4	0	0	0	.968	-2	/C-9,O-3	-0.6
Total	14	1013	3001	407	719	121	11	122	445	562	607	.240	.361	.409	117	84	22	12	-1	.987	-47	C-766,O-207/1-1	5.4

■ BOB FERGUSON

Ferguson, Robert Vavasour b: 1/31/1845, Brooklyn, N.Y. d: 5/3/1894, Brooklyn, N.Y. BB/TR, 5'9.5", 149 lbs. Deb: 5/18/1871 MU

YEAR	TM/L	G	AB	R	H	2B	3B	HR	RBI	BB	SO	AVG	OBP	SLG	PRO+	BR/A	SB	CS	SBR	FA	FR	G/POS	TPR
1871	Mut-n	33	158	30	38	6	1	0	25	3	2	.241	.255	.291	62	-6	4	4	-1	.774	4	*3-20,2-11/C-5,PM	-0.4
1872	Atl-n	37	165	33	46	5	0	0	19	3	0	.279	.292	.309	72	-8	4	2	0	.809	36	*3-37/C-1,M	1.7
1873	Atl-n	51	228	36	59	3	5	0	25	4	9	.259	.272	.316	83	-3	1	2	-1	.755	32	*3-50/P-4,M	1.8
1874	Atl-n	56	245	34	64	4	0	0	18	2	7	.261	.267	.278	85	-2	4	3	-1	.760	3	*3-55/C-2,P-1,M	0.0
1875	Har-n	85	366	65	88	10	4	0	43	3	5	.240	.247	.290	82	-8	2	1	0	.827	8	*3-85/P-1,M	0.0
1876	Har-N	69	310	48	82	8	5	0	32	2	11	.265	.269	.323	89	-5				.826	2	*3-69,M	-0.1
1877	Har-N	58	254	40	65	7	0	0	35	3	10	.256	.265	.299	86	-3				.841	17	*3-56/P-3,M	1.4
1878	Chi-N	61	259	44	91	10	2	0	39	10	12	.351	.375	.405	147	12				.881	16	*S-57/2-4,C-1,M	2.8
1879	Tro-N	30	123	18	31	5	2	0	4	4	3	.252	.276	.325	104	1				.808	2	3-24/2-6,M	0.4
1880	Tro-N	82	332	55	87	9	0	0	22	24	24	.262	.312	.289	100	0				.904	-3	*2-82,M	0.1
1881	Tro-N	85	339	56	96	13	5	1	35	29	12	.283	.340	.360	114	6				.904	-10	*2-85,M	-0.3
1882	Tro-N	81	319	44	82	15	2	0	32	23	21	.257	.307	.317	106	3				.914	-13	*2-79/S-2,M	-0.7
1883	Phi-N	86	329	39	85	9	2	0	27	18	21	.258	.297	.298	89	-3				.862	-8	*2-86/P-1,M	-0.8
1884	Pit-a	10	41	2	6	0	0	0	0	0	0	.146	.146	.146	-4	-5				.714	-3	/O-6,1-3,3-1,M	-0.3
Total	5 n	262	1162	198	295	28	10	0	130	15	23	.254	.263	.295	78	-27	15	12	-3	.787	82	3-247/2-11,C-8,P-7	3.1
Total	9	562	2306	346	625	76	20	1	226	113	114	.271	.305	.323	102	6				.895	0	2-342,3-150/SOP1C	2.2

■ FELIX FERMIN

Fermin, Felix Jose (Minaya) b: 10/9/63, Mao Valverde, D.R. BR/TR, 5'11", 179 lbs. Deb: 7/8/87

YEAR	TM/L	G	AB	R	H	2B	3B	HR	RBI	BB	SO	AVG	OBP	SLG	PRO+	BR/A	SB	CS	SBR	FA	FR	G/POS	TPR
1987	Pit-N	23	68	6	17	0	0	0	4	4	9	.250	.301	.250	48	-5	0	0	0	.980	4	S-23	-0.2
1988	Pit-N	43	87	9	24	0	0	0	2	8	10	.276	.357	.322	98	0	3	1	0	.955	-5	S-43	-0.3
1989	Cle-A	156	484	50	115	9	1	0	21	41	27	.238	.302	.260	59	-25	6	4	-1	.967	18	*S-153/2-2	0.4
1990	Cle-A	148	414	47	106	13	2	1	40	26	22	.256	.300	.304	70	-17	3	3	-1	.975	4	*S-147/2-1	-0.2
1991	Cle-A	129	424	30	111	13	2	0	31	26	27	.262	.309	.302	69	-17	5	4	-1	.980	1	*S-129	-0.7
1992	Cle-A	79	215	27	58	7	2	0	13	10	13	.270	.329	.321	84	-4	0	0	0	.971	-5	S-55,3-17/2-7,1-2	-0.6
1993	Cle-A	140	480	48	126	16	2	2	45	24	14	.262	.303	.317	67	-22	4	5	-2	.960	-29	*S-140	-4.1
1994	Sea-A	101	379	52	120	21	0	1	35	11	22	.317	.343	.380	84	-9	4	4	-1	.974	-6	S-77,2-25	-0.8
1995	*Sea-A	73	200	21	39	6	0	0	15	6	6	.195	.233	.225	20	-24	2	0	1	.971	13	S-46,2-29	-0.5
1996	Chi-N	11	16	4	2	1	0	0	1	2	0	.125	.222	.188	9	-2	0	0	0	.875	-3	/2-6,S-2	-0.2
Total	10	903	2767	294	718	86	11	4	207	166	147	.259	.307	.303	67	-124	27	21	-5	.971	-11	S-815/2-70,3-17,1-2	-7.4

■ ED FERNANDES

Fernandes, Edward Paul b: 3/11/18, Oakland, Cal. d: 11/27/68, Hayward, Cal. BB/TR, 5'9", 185 lbs. Deb: 6/9/40

YEAR	TM/L	G	AB	R	H	2B	3B	HR	RBI	BB	SO	AVG	OBP	SLG	PRO+	BR/A	SB	CS	SBR	FA	FR	G/POS	TPR
1940	Pit-N	28	33	1	4	1	0	0	2	7	6	.121	.275	.152	21	-3	0			.981	0	C-27	-0.2
1946	Chi-A	14	32	4	8	2	0	0	4	8	7	.250	.400	.313	105	1	0	0	0	.922	-1	C-12	0.0
Total	2	42	65	5	12	3	0	0	6	15	13	.185	.338	.231	61	-3	0	0	0	.952	-0	/C-39	-0.2

■ FRANK FERNANDEZ

Fernandez, Frank b: 4/16/43, Staten Island, N.Y. BR/TR, 6'1", 192 lbs. Deb: 9/12/67

YEAR	TM/L	G	AB	R	H	2B	3B	HR	RBI	BB	SO	AVG	OBP	SLG	PRO+	BR/A	SB	CS	SBR	FA	FR	G/POS	TPR
1967	NY-A	9	28	1	6	2	0	1	2	4	7	.214	.290	.393	104	0	1	1	-0	1.000	0	/C-7,O-2	0.0
1968	NY-A	51	135	15	23	6	1	7	30	35	50	.170	.341	.385	124	5	1	0	0	.989	6	C-45/O-4	1.5
1969	NY-A	89	229	34	51	6	1	12	29	65	68	.223	.401	.415	133	13	1	3	-2	.994	-8	C-65/O-14	0.8
1970	Oak-A	94	252	30	54	5	0	15	44	40	76	.214	.327	.413	106	2	0	1	-0	.993	-1	C-76/O-1	0.5
1971	Oak-A	2	4	0	0	0	0	0	0	1	2	.000	.200	.000	-40	-1	0	0	0	1.000	2	/C-2	0.1
	Was-A	18	30	0	3	0	0	0	4	4	10	.100	.206	.100	-12	-4	0	0	0	1.000	1	/O-6,C-1	-0.6
	Oak-A	2	5	1	1	1	0	0	1	0	1	.200	.200	.400	68	-0	0	0	0	1.000	-0	/C-1	-0.1
	Yr	22	39	1	4	1	0	0	5	5	13	.103	.205	.128	-4	-5	0	0	0	1.000	0	/O-6,C-4	-0.6
	Chi-N	17	41	11	7	1	0	4	17	15	17	.171	.414	.488	135	2	0	0	0	.980	0	C-16	0.3
1972	Chi-N	3	3	0	0	0	0	0	0	0	0	.000	.000	.000	-90	-1	0	0	0	1.000	-0	/C-1	-0.1
Total	6	285	727	92	145	21	2	39	116	164	231	.199	.351	.395	114	17	4	4	-1	.992	-2	C-214/O-27	2.4

■ NANNY FERNANDEZ

Fernandez, Froilan b: 10/25/18, Wilmington, Cal. d: 9/19/96, Lomita, Cal. BR/TR, 5'9", 170 lbs. Deb: 4/14/42

YEAR	TM/L	G	AB	R	H	2B	3B	HR	RBI	BB	SO	AVG	OBP	SLG	PRO+	BR/A	SB	CS	SBR	FA	FR	G/POS	TPR
1942	Bos-N	145	577	63	147	29	3	6	55	38	61	.255	.303	.347	92	-8	15			.914	6	3-98,O-44	-0.3
1946	Bos-N	115	372	37	95	15	2	2	42	30	44	.255	.313	.323	79	-10	1			.940	-2	3-81,S-18,O-14	-1.2
1947	Bos-N	83	209	16	43	4	0	2	21	22	20	.206	.281	.254	44	-17	2			.933	-13	S-62/O-8,3-6	-2.7
1950	Pit-N	65	198	23	51	11	0	6	27	19	17	.258	.326	.404	88	-4	2			.925	-3	3-52	-0.7
Total	4	408	1356	139	336	59	5	16	145	109	142	.248	.306	.334	80	-38	20			.925	-13	3-237/S-80,O-66	-4.9

■ CHICO FERNANDEZ

Fernandez, Humberto (Perez) b: 3/2/32, Havana, Cuba BR/TR, 6', 170 lbs. Deb: 7/14/56

YEAR	TM/L	G	AB	R	H	2B	3B	HR	RBI	BB	SO	AVG	OBP	SLG	PRO+	BR/A	SB	CS	SBR	FA	FR	G/POS	TPR
1956	Bro-N	34	66	11	15	1	0	0	9	3	10	.227	.261	.303	47	-5	2	3	-1	.978	7	S-25	0.2
1957	Phi-N	149	500	42	131	14	4	5	51	31	64	.262	.306	.336	75	-18	18	5	2	.960	-25	*S-149	-2.7
1958	Phi-N	148	522	38	120	18	5	6	51	37	48	.230	.283	.318	60	-31	12	6	0	.975	-12	*S-148	-3.0
1959	Phi-N	45	123	15	26	5	1	0	9	10	11	.211	.271	.268	43	-10	2	1	1	.958	-3	S-40/2-2	-1.0
1960	Det-A	133	435	44	105	13	3	4	35	39	50	.241	.305	.313	66	-21	13	4	0	.947	-4	*S-130	-1.4
1961	Det-A	133	435	41	108	15	4	4	40	36	45	.248	.306	.322	66	-21	8	5	-1	.958	-8	*S-121/3-8	-1.9
1962	Det-A	141	503	64	125	17	3	20	59	42	69	.249	.306	.410	88	-10	10	8	-1	.960	-27	*S-138/3-2,1-1	-2.4
1963	Det-A	15	49	3	7	1	0	0	2	6	11	.143	.236	.163	14	-6	0	1	-1	.947	2	S-14	-0.3

YEAR	TM/L	G	AB	R	H	2B	3B	HR	RBI	BB	SO	AVG	OBP	SLG	PRO+	BR/A	SB	CS	SBR	FA	FR	G/POS	TPR
	NY-N	58	145	12	29	6	0	1	9	9	30	.200	.247	.262	46	-10	3	0	1	.944	-16	S-45/3-5,2-3	-2.5
Total	8	856	2778	270	666	91	19	40	259	213	338	.240	.295	.329	67	-130	68	28	4	.960	-86	S-810/3-15,2-5,1-1	-15.0

■ CHICO FERNANDEZ
Fernandez, Lorenzo Marto (Mosquera) b: 4/23/39, Havana, Cuba BR/TR, 5'10", 160 lbs. Deb: 4/20/68

YEAR	TM/L	G	AB	R	H	2B	3B	HR	RBI	BB	SO	AVG	OBP	SLG	PRO+	BR/A	SB	CS	SBR	FA	FR	G/POS	TPR
1968	Bal-A	24	18	0	2	2	0	0	0	1	2	.111	.158	.111	-17	-3	0	0	0	.923	3	/S-7,2-4	0.0

■ TONY FERNANDEZ
Fernandez, Octavio Antonio (Castro) (b: Octavio Antonio Fernando (Castro)) b: 6/30/62, San Pedro De Macoris, D.R. BB/TR, 6'2", 175 lbs. Deb: 9/2/83

YEAR	TM/L	G	AB	R	H	2B	3B	HR	RBI	BB	SO	AVG	OBP	SLG	PRO+	BR/A	SB	CS	SBR	FA	FR	G/POS	TPR
1983	Tor-A	15	34	5	9	1	1	0	2	2	2	.265	.324	.353	81	-1	0	1	-1	1.000	-3	S-13/D-1	-0.4
1984	Tor-A	88	233	29	63	5	3	3	19	17	15	.270	.320	.356	84	-5	5	7	-3	.974	3	S-73,3-10/D-1	0.1
1985	*Tor-A	161	564	71	163	31	10	2	51	43	41	.289	.342	.390	97	-2	13	6	0	.962	5	*S-160	1.9
1986	Tor-A★	163	687	91	213	33	9	10	65	27	52	.310	.340	.428	105	4	25	12	0	.983	-3	*S-163	2.2
1987	Tor-A★	146	578	90	186	29	8	5	67	51	48	.322	.382	.426	112	11	32	12	2	.979	6	*S-146	3.0
1988	Tor-A	154	648	76	186	41	4	5	70	45	65	.287	.337	.386	101	1	15	5	2	.981	10	*S-154	2.5
1989	*Tor-A	140	573	64	147	25	9	11	64	29	51	.257	.296	.389	93	-7	22	6	3	.992	18	*S-140	2.6
1990	*Tor-A	161	635	84	175	27	17	4	66	71	70	.276	.355	.391	106	7	26	13	0	.989	9	*S-161	2.8
1991	SD-N	145	558	81	152	27	5	4	38	55	74	.272	.338	.360	93	-4	23	9	2	.972	-3	*S-145	1.2
1992	SD-N★	155	622	84	171	32	4	4	37	56	62	.275	.339	.359	96	-2	20	20	-6	.983	-17	*S-154	-1.6
1993	NY-N	48	173	20	39	5	2	1	14	25	19	.225	.327	.295	69	-7	6	2	1	.975	7	S-48	0.4
	*Tor-A	94	353	45	108	18	9	4	50	31	26	.306	.362	.442	114	7	15	8	-0	.985	5	S-94	1.8
1994	Cin-N	104	366	50	102	18	6	8	50	44	40	.279	.364	.426	106	4	12	7	-1	.991	2	3-93/S-9,2-5	0.6
1995	*NY-A	108	384	57	94	20	2	5	45	40	40	.245	.326	.346	76	-13	6	6	-2	.976	-13	*S-103/2-4	-1.7
Total	13	1682	6408	847	1808	312	89	66	638	538	605	.282	.342	.390	99	-8	220	114	-2	.980	38	*S-1563,3-103/2-9,D	15.4

■ AL FERRARA
Ferrara, Alfred John "The Bull" b: 12/22/39, Brooklyn, N.Y. BR/TR, 6'1", 203 lbs. Deb: 7/30/63

YEAR	TM/L	G	AB	R	H	2B	3B	HR	RBI	BB	SO	AVG	OBP	SLG	PRO+	BR/A	SB	CS	SBR	FA	FR	G/POS	TPR
1963	LA-N	21	44	2	7	0	0	1	1	6	9	.159	.275	.227	50	-3	0	0	0	.950	-1	O-11	-0.3
1965	LA-N	41	81	5	17	2	1	1	10	9	20	.210	.297	.296	72	-3	0	0	0	.927	-3	O-27	-0.8
1966	*LA-N	63	115	15	31	4	0	5	23	9	35	.270	.339	.435	123	3	0	0	0	.956	-3	O-32	-0.1
1967	LA-N	122	347	41	96	16	1	16	50	33	73	.277	.345	.467	142	17	0	1	-1	.978	-10	O-94	0.3
1968	LA-N	2	7	0	1	0	0	0	0	0	2	.143	.143	.143	-15	-1	0	0	0	.500	-1	/O-2	-0.2
1969	SD-N	138	366	39	95	22	1	14	56	45	69	.260	.352	.440	125	12	0	0	0	.958	-2	O-96	0.5
1970	SD-N	138	372	44	103	15	4	13	51	46	63	.277	.344	.444	123	13	0	0	0	.968	-8	O-96	0.0
1971	SD-N	17	17	0	2	1	0	0	2	5	5	.118	.318	.176	47	-1	0	0	0	1.000	-1	/O-2	-0.2
	Cin-N	32	33	2	6	0	0	1	5	3	10	.182	.270	.273	55	-2	0	0	0	1.000	-1	/O-7	-0.3
	Yr	49	50	2	8	1	0	1	7	8	15	.160	.288	.240	53	-3	0	0	0	1.000	-1	/O-7	-0.5
Total	8	574	1382	148	358	60	7	51	198	156	286	.259	.346	.423	120	36	0	1	-1	.962	-28	O-365	-1.1

■ MIKE FERRARO
Ferraro, Michael Dennis b: 8/18/44, Kingston, N.Y. BR/TR, 5'11", 175 lbs. Deb: 9/6/66 MC

YEAR	TM/L	G	AB	R	H	2B	3B	HR	RBI	BB	SO	AVG	OBP	SLG	PRO+	BR/A	SB	CS	SBR	FA	FR	G/POS	TPR
1966	NY-A	10	28	4	5	0	0	0	0	3	3	.179	.281	.179	37	-2	0	0	0	.926	1	3-10	-0.1
1968	NY-A	23	87	5	14	0	1	0	1	2	17	.161	.180	.184	11	-9	0	0	0	.975	4	3-22	-0.6
1969	Sea-A	5	4	0	0	0	0	0	0	1	0	.000	.200	.000	-41	-1	0	0	0	.000	0	H	-0.1
1972	Mil-A	124	381	19	97	18	1	2	29	17	41	.255	.286	.323	83	-9	0	5	-3	.950	-16	*3-115/S-1	-3.3
Total	4	162	500	28	116	18	2	2	30	23	61	.232	.267	.288	67	-21	0	5	-3	.953	-10	3-147/S-1	-4.1

■ RICK FERRELL
Ferrell, Richard Benjamin b: 10/12/05, Durham, N.C. d: 7/27/95, Bloomfield Hills, Mich. BR/TR, 5'10", 160 lbs. Deb: 4/19/29 FCH

YEAR	TM/L	G	AB	R	H	2B	3B	HR	RBI	BB	SO	AVG	OBP	SLG	PRO+	BR/A	SB	CS	SBR	FA	FR	G/POS	TPR
1929	StL-A	64	144	21	33	6	1	0	20	32	10	.229	.373	.285	69	-5	1	2	-1	.962	0	C-45	-0.2
1930	StL-A	101	314	43	84	18	4	1	41	46	10	.268	.363	.360	81	-8	1	4	-2	.983	-9	*C-101	-1.0
1931	StL-A	117	386	47	118	30	4	3	57	56	12	.306	.394	.427	112	8	2	3	-1	.973	4	*C-108	1.7
1932	StL-A	126	438	67	138	30	5	2	65	66	18	.315	.406	.420	108	7	5	5	-2	.986	-2	*C-120	1.1
1933	StL-A	22	72	8	18	2	0	1	5	12	4	.250	.357	.319	76	-2	2	0	1	.991	3	C-21	0.2
	Bos-A★	118	421	50	125	19	4	3	72	58	19	.297	.385	.382	105	5	2	2	-1	.990	0	*C-116	1.6
	Yr	140	493	58	143	21	4	4	77	70	23	.290	.381	.373	100	3	4	2	0	.990	3	*C-137	1.8
1934	Bos-A☆	132	437	50	130	29	4	1	48	66	20	.297	.390	.389	95	-2	0	0	0	.990	3	*C-128	0.7
1935	Bos-A☆	133	458	54	138	34	4	3	61	65	15	.301	.388	.413	100	2	5	8	-3	.979	13	*C-131	1.7
1936	Bos-A★	121	410	59	128	27	5	8	55	65	17	.312	.406	.461	108	6	0	1	-1	.987	9	*C-121	1.7
1937	Bos-A	18	65	8	20	2	0	1	4	15	4	.308	.438	.385	105	1	0	0	0	.990	0	C-18	0.2
	Was-A☆	86	279	31	64	6	0	1	32	50	18	.229	.348	.262	59	-16	1	1	-0	.987	-6	C-84	-1.6
	Yr	104	344	39	84	8	0	2	36	65	22	.244	.366	.285	68	-14	1	1	-0	.988	-6	*C-102	-1.4
1938	Was-A☆	135	411	55	120	24	5	1	58	75	17	.292	.401	.382	104	6	1	0	0	.981	-5	*C-131	0.7
1939	Was-A	87	274	32	77	13	1	0	31	41	12	.281	.377	.336	90	-2	3	1	-1	.976	-6	C-83	-0.4
1940	Was-A	103	326	35	89	18	2	0	28	43	15	.273	.363	.340	90	-3	1	1	-0	.980	-6	C-99	-0.2
1941	Was-A	21	66	8	18	5	0	0	13	15	4	.273	.407	.348	107	1	0	0	0	.980	-1	C-21	0.0
	StL-A	100	321	30	81	14	3	0	23	52	22	.252	.357	.333	81	-8	2	1	0	.995	-5	C-98	-0.4
	Yr	121	387	38	99	19	3	2	36	67	26	.256	.366	.336	85	-6	3	1	0	.992	-6	*C-119	-0.2
1942	StL-A	99	273	20	61	6	1	0	26	33	13	.223	.307	.253	57	-15	0	1	-1	.986	9	C-95	1.4
1943	StL-A	74	209	12	50	7	0	0	24	34	14	.239	.348	.273	81	-3	0	0	0	.987	13	C-70	1.2
1944	Was-A☆	99	339	14	94	11	1	0	25	46	13	.277	.364	.316	99	2	2	1	0	.981	3	*C-96	1.2
1945	Was-A†	91	286	33	76	12	1	1	38	43	13	.266	.366	.325	110	5	2	4	-2	.990	-2	C-83	0.6
1947	Was-A	37	99	10	30	11	0	0	12	14	7	.303	.389	.414	127	4	0	0	0	.994	3	C-37	0.9
Total	18	1884	6028	687	1692	324	45	28	734	931	277	.281	.378	.363	95	-17	29	35	-12	.984	20	*C-1806	10.1

■ WES FERRELL
Ferrell, Wesley Cheek b: 2/2/08, Greensboro, N.C. d: 12/9/76, Sarasota, Fla. BR/TR, 6'2", 195 lbs. Deb: 9/9/27 F

YEAR	TM/L	G	AB	R	H	2B	3B	HR	RBI	BB	SO	AVG	OBP	SLG	PRO+	BR/A	SB	CS	SBR	FA	FR	G/POS	TPR
1927	Cle-A	1	0	0	0	0	0	0	0	0	0	—	—	—			0	0	0	.000	-0	/P-1	0.0
1928	Cle-A	2	4	0	1	0	1	0	0	0	0	.250	.250	.750	152	0	0	0	0	1.000	0	/P-2	0.0
1929	Cle-A	47	93	12	22	5	3	1	12	9	28	.237	.283	.387	68	-5	0	0	0	.973	3	P-43	0.0
1930	Cle-A	53	118	19	35	8	3	0	14	12	15	.297	.362	.415	93	-1	0	0	0	.967	-3	P-43	0.0
1931	Cle-A	48	116	24	37	6	1	9	30	10	21	.319	.373	.621	149	7	0	0	0	.969	5	P-40	0.0
1932	Cle-A	55	128	14	31	5	2	2	18	6	21	.242	.276	.359	59	-8	0	0	0	.986	1	P-38	0.0
1933	Cle-A☆	61	140	26	38	7	0	7	26	20	22	.271	.363	.471	114	3	0	0	0	1.000	2	P-28,O-13	0.1
1934	Bos-A	34	78	12	22	4	0	4	17	7	15	.282	.341	.487	104	0	1	0	0	.969	-2	P-26	0.0
1935	Bos-A	75	150	25	52	5	1	7	32	21	16	.347	.427	.533	138	9	0	0	0	.977	2	P-41	0.0
1936	Bos-A	61	135	20	36	6	1	5	24	14	10	.267	.330	.437	84	-4	0	0	0	.962	-3	P-39	0.0
1937	Bos-A	18	33	7	12	2	0	1	9	7	3	.364	.475	.515	144	3	0	0	0	.964	2	P-12	0.0
	Was-A☆	53	106	7	27	5	0	0	16	9	18	.255	.313	.302	58	-7	0	0	0	.975	-1	P-25	0.0
	Yr	71	139	14	39	7	0	1	25	16	21	.281	.355	.353	81	-4	0	0	0	.971	1	P-37	0.0
1938	Was-A	26	49	6	11	2	0	1	6	15	7	.224	.406	.327	92	0	0	0	0	.976	1	P-23	0.0
	NY-A	5	12	1	2	1	0	0	1	1	4	.167	.231	.250	20	0	0	0	0	.917	1	/P-5	0.0
	Yr	31	61	7	13	3	0	1	7	16	11	.213	.377	.311	79	-1	0	0	0	.962	2	P-28	0.0
1939	NY-A	3	8	0	1	1	0	0	1	0	2	.125	.125	.250	-6	-1	0	0	0	1.000	0	/P-3	0.0
1940	Bro-N	2	2	0	0	0	0	0	0	0	0	.000	.000	.000	-94	-1	0	0	0	1.000	-0	/P-1	0.0
1941	Bos-N	4	4	2	2	0	0	1	2	0	0	.500	.600	1.250	430	2	0	0	0	1.000	-0	/P-4	0.0
Total	15	548	1176	175	329	57	12	38	208	129	185	.280	.351	.446	99	-5	2	0		.975	7	P-374/O-13	0.1

■ SERGIO FERRER
Ferrer, Sergio (Marrero) b: 1/29/51, Santurce, P.R. BB/TR, 5'7", 145 lbs. Deb: 4/5/74

YEAR	TM/L	G	AB	R	H	2B	3B	HR	RBI	BB	SO	AVG	OBP	SLG	PRO+	BR/A	SB	CS	SBR	FA	FR	G/POS	TPR
1974	Min-A	24	57	12	16	3	0	2	0	9	8	.281	.379	.351	107	1	3	2	-0	.855	-12	S-20/2-1	-1.0
1975	Min-A	32	81	14	20	3	1	0	2	3	11	.247	.316	.309	66	-4	3	4	-2	.924	-3	S-18,2-10/D-2	-0.5
1978	NY-N	37	33	8	7	0	0	0	1	4	7	.212	.316	.273	68	-1	0	1	0	.971	10	S-29/2-3,3-2	0.1
1979	NY-N	32	7	7	0	0	0	0	0	3	0	.000	.222	.000	-35	-1	1	1	-1	.833	6	3-12/S-5,2-4	0.3
Total	4	125	178	41	43	3	4	0	3	17	12	.242	.318	.303	76	-5	7	8	-3	.922	2	/S-72,2-18,3-14,D-2	-0.2

YEAR	TM/L	G	AB	R	H	2B	3B	HR	RBI	BB	SO	AVG	OBP	SLG	PRO+	BR/A	SB	CS	SBR	FA	FR	G/POS	TPR

■ HOBE FERRIS
Ferris, Albert Sayles   b: 12/7/1877, Providence, R.I.   d: 3/18/38, Detroit, Mich.   BR/TR, 5'8", 162 lbs.   Deb: 4/26/01

YEAR	TM/L	G	AB	R	H	2B	3B	HR	RBI	BB	SO	AVG	OBP	SLG	PRO+	BR/A	SB	CS	SBR	FA	FR	G/POS	TPR
1901	Bos-A	138	523	68	131	16	15	2	63	23		.250	.290	.350	78	-17	13			.930	9	*2-138/S-1	-0.2
1902	Bos-A	134	499	57	122	16	14	8	63	21		.244	.276	.381	79	-17	11			.952	27	*2-134	1.4
1903	*Bos-A	141	525	69	132	19	7	9	66	25		.251	.287	.366	90	-8	11			.950	15	*2-139/S-2	1.3
1904	Bos-A	156	563	50	120	23	10	3	63	23		.213	.245	.306	70	-20	7			.962	2	*2-156	-1.6
1905	Bos-A	142	523	51	115	24	16	6	59	23		.220	.253	.361	93	-7	11			.960	14	*2-142	0.9
1906	Bos-A	130	495	47	121	25	13	2	44	10		.244	.262	.360	94	-6	8			.960	9	*2-126/3-4	0.4
1907	Bos-A	150	561	41	135	25	2	4	60	10		.241	.254	.314	82	-14	11			.967	13	*2-150	-0.2
1908	StL-A	148	555	54	150	26	7	2	74	14		.270	.291	.353	108	3	6			.952	16	*3-148	2.7
1909	StL-A	148	556	36	120	18	5	4	50	12		.216	.232	.288	69	-23	11			.937	7	*3-114,2-34	-1.4
Total	9	1287	4800	473	1146	192	89	40	550	161		.239	.265	.341	84	-108	89			.954	111	*2-1019,3-266/S-3	3.3

■ WILLY FETZER
Fetzer, William McKinnon   b: 6/24/1884, Concord, N.C.   d: 5/3/59, Butner, N.C.   BL/TR, 5'10.5", 180 lbs.   Deb: 9/4/06

YEAR	TM/L	G	AB	R	H	2B	3B	HR	RBI	BB	SO	AVG	OBP	SLG	PRO+	BR/A	SB	CS	SBR	FA	FR	G/POS	TPR
1906	Phi-A	1	1	0	0	0	0	0	0	0		.000	.000	.000	-97	-0	0			.000	0	H	0.0

■ CHICK FEWSTER
Fewster, Wilson Lloyd   b: 11/10/1895, Baltimore, Md.   d: 4/16/45, Baltimore, Md.   BR/TR, 5'11", 160 lbs.   Deb: 9/19/17

YEAR	TM/L	G	AB	R	H	2B	3B	HR	RBI	BB	SO	AVG	OBP	SLG	PRO+	BR/A	SB	CS	SBR	FA	FR	G/POS	TPR
1917	NY-A	11	36	2	8	0	0	0	1	5	5	.222	.317	.222	64	-1	1			.919	2	2-11	0.1
1918	NY-A	5	2	1	1	0	0	0	0	0	0	.500	.500	.500	197	0	0			.000	0	/2-2	0.0
1919	NY-A	81	244	38	69	9	3	1	15	34	36	.283	.384	.357	108	5	8			.946	8	O-41,S-24/2-4,3-2	1.1
1920	NY-A	21	21	8	6	1	0	0	1	7	2	.286	.464	.333	110	1	0	1	-1	.840	1	/S-6,2-3	0.1
1921	*NY-A	66	207	44	58	19	0	1	19	28	43	.280	.382	.386	94	-1	4	4	-1	.974	-3	O-43,2-15	-0.7
1922	NY-A	44	132	20	32	4	1	1	9	16	23	.242	.324	.311	65	-7	2	4	-2	.975	1	O-38/2-2	-0.9
	Bos-A	23	83	8	24	4	1	0	9	6	10	.289	.344	.361	85	-2	8	3	1	.959	4	3-23	0.4
	Yr	67	215	28	56	8	2	1	18	22	33	.260	.332	.330	72	-8	10	7	-1	.975	5	O-38,3-23/2-2	-0.5
1923	Bos-A	90	284	32	67	10	1	0	15	39	35	.236	.334	.278	62	-14	7	14	-6	.938	-10	2-49,S-37/3-3	-2.6
1924	Cle-A	101	322	36	86	12	2	0	36	24	36	.267	.324	.317	65	-17	12	12	-4	.961	-22	2-94/3-5	-4.0
1925	Cle-A	93	294	39	73	16	1	1	38	36	25	.248	.330	.320	65	-15	6	9	-4	.939	-9	2-83,3-10/O-1	-2.5
1926	Bro-N	105	337	53	82	16	3	2	24	45	49	.243	.341	.326	82	-7	9			.953	-15	*2-103	-1.9
1927	Bro-N	4	1	1	0	0	0	0	0	0	0	.000	.000	.000	-99	-0	0			.000	0	H	0.0
Total	11	644	1963	282	506	91	12	6	167	240	264	.258	.346	.326	77	-59	57	47		.945	-43	2-366,O-123/S-67,3	-10.9

■ NEIL FIALA
Fiala, Neil Stephen   b: 8/24/56, St.Louis, Mo.   BL/TR, 6'1", 185 lbs.   Deb: 9/3/81

YEAR	TM/L	G	AB	R	H	2B	3B	HR	RBI	BB	SO	AVG	OBP	SLG	PRO+	BR/A	SB	CS	SBR	FA	FR	G/POS	TPR
1981	StL-N	3	3	0	0	0	0	0	0	0	1	.000	.000	.000	-97	-1	0	0	0	.000	0	/H	-0.1
	Cin-N	2	2	1	1	0	0	0	1	0	1	.500	.500	.500	181	0	0	0	0	.000	0	/H	0.0
	Yr	5	5	1	1	0	0	0	1	0	2	.200	.200	.200	13	-1	0	0	0	.000	0	-0,-0	-0.1

■ JIM FIELD
Field, James C.   b: 4/24/1863, Philadelphia, Pa.   d: 5/13/53, Atlantic City, N.J   6'1", 170 lbs.   Deb: 6/2/1883

YEAR	TM/L	G	AB	R	H	2B	3B	HR	RBI	BB	SO	AVG	OBP	SLG	PRO+	BR/A	SB	CS	SBR	FA	FR	G/POS	TPR
1883	Col-a	76	295	31	75	10	6	1		7		.254	.272	.339	104	2				.938	-7	*1-76	-1.1
1884	Col-a	105	417	74	97	9	7	4		23		.233	.292	.317	107	5				.958	-4	*1-105	-1.0
1885	Pit-a	56	209	28	50	9	1	1	15	13		.239	.306	.306	95	-1				.965	0	1-56	-0.7
	Bal-a	38	144	16	30	3	2	0	10	13		.208	.278	.257	71	-4				.963	1	1-38	-0.7
	Yr	94	353	44	80	12	3	1	25	26		.227	.295	.286	85	-5				.964	1	1-94	-1.4
1890	Roc-a	52	188	30	38	7	5	4	25	21		.202	.309	.356	104	1	8			.964	-4	1-51/P-2	-0.5
1898	Was-N	5	21	1	2	0	0	0	0	0		.095	.095	.095	-46	-4	1			.979	-0	/1-5	-0.4
Total	5	332	1274	180	292	38	21	10	50	77		.229	.288	.316	96	1	9			.956	-15	1-331/P-2	-4.4

■ SAM FIELD
Field, Samuel Jay   b: 10/12/1848, Philadelphia, Pa.   d: 10/28/04, Sinking Spring, Pa   BR/TR, 5'9.5", 182 lbs.   Deb: 5/19/1875

YEAR	TM/L	G	AB	R	H	2B	3B	HR	RBI	BB	SO	AVG	OBP	SLG	PRO+	BR/A	SB	CS	SBR	FA	FR	G/POS	TPR
1875	Cen-n	3	11	2	1	0	0	0	0	0	0	.091	.091	.091	-40	-1	0	0	0	.714	-1	/C-2,O-1	-0.2
	Was-n	5	16	0	5	0	0	0	1	0	1	.313	.313	.313	122	0	1	0	0	.731	-2	/C-4,O-1	-0.1
	Yr	8	27	2	6	0	0	0	1	0	1	.222	.222	.222	58	-1	1	0	0	.723	-3	/C-6,O-2	-0.3
1876	Cin-N	4	14	2	0	0	0	0	0	0	3	.000	.067	.000	-89	-3				.667	-3	/C-3,2-2	-0.5

■ CECIL FIELDER
Fielder, Cecil Grant   b: 9/21/63, Los Angeles, Cal.   BR/TR, 6'3", 230 lbs.   Deb: 7/20/85

YEAR	TM/L	G	AB	R	H	2B	3B	HR	RBI	BB	SO	AVG	OBP	SLG	PRO+	BR/A	SB	CS	SBR	FA	FR	G/POS	TPR
1985	*Tor-A	30	74	6	23	4	0	4	16	6	16	.311	.363	.527	137	4	0	0	0	.979	1	1-25	0.3
1986	Tor-A	34	83	7	13	2	0	4	13	6	27	.157	.222	.325	46	-7	0	0	0	1.000	-1	D-22/1-7,3-2,O-1	-0.8
1987	Tor-A	82	175	30	47	7	1	14	32	20	48	.269	.347	.560	132	8	0	1	-1	1.000	-1	D-55,1-16/3-2	0.4
1988	Tor-A	74	174	24	40	6	1	9	23	14	53	.230	.291	.431	99	-1	0	1	-1	.991	0	D-50,1-17/3-3,2-2	-0.3
1990	Det-A★	159	573	104	159	25	1	**51**	**132**	90	182	.277	.380	**.592**	167	50	0	1	-1	.989	3	*1-143,D-15	4.2
1991	Det-A★	162	624	102	163	25	0	44	**133**	78	151	.261	.349	.513	133	27	0	0	0	.993	-3	*1-122,D-42	1.4
1992	Det-A	155	594	80	145	22	0	35	**124**	73	151	.244	.329	.458	118	13	0	0	0	.991	0	*1-114,D-43	0.5
1993	Det-A★	154	573	80	153	23	0	30	117	90	125	.267	.370	.464	124	20	0	1	-1	.991	-2	*1-119,D-36	0.7
1994	Det-A	109	425	67	110	16	2	28	90	50	110	.259	.340	.504	113	7	0	0	0	.993	16	*1-102/D-7	1.2
1995	Det-A	136	494	70	120	18	1	31	82	75	116	.243	.348	.472	112	8	0	1	-1	.993	6	1-77,D-58	0.1
1996	Det-A	107	391	55	97	12	0	26	80	63	91	.248	.357	.478	109	5	2	0	1	.989	4	1-71,D-36	0.0
	*NY-A	53	200	30	52	8	0	13	37	24	48	.260	.345	.495	107	2	0	0	0	1.000	-1	D-43/1-9	-0.3
	Yr	160	591	85	149	20	0	39	117	87	139	.252	.353	.484	109	7	2	0	1	.990	3	1-80,D-79	-0.3
Total	11	1255	4380	655	1122	168	6	289	879	589	1118	.256	.349	.495	123	136	2	5	-2	.991	25	1-822,D-407/3-7,2O	7.4

■ BRUCE FIELDS
Fields, Bruce Alan   b: 10/6/60, Cleveland, Ohio   BL/TR, 6', 185 lbs.   Deb: 9/3/86

YEAR	TM/L	G	AB	R	H	2B	3B	HR	RBI	BB	SO	AVG	OBP	SLG	PRO+	BR/A	SB	CS	SBR	FA	FR	G/POS	TPR
1986	Det-A	16	43	4	12	1	0	0	6	1	6	.279	.295	.302	75	-1	1	1	-0	.962	-1	O-14/D-1	-0.3
1988	Sea-A	39	67	8	18	5	0	1	5	4	11	.269	.310	.388	90	-1	0	1	-1	1.000	-5	O-23/D-6	-0.7
1989	Sea-A	3	3	2	1	1	0	0	0	0	1	.333	.333	.667	170	0	0	0	0	.000	-0	/O-1	0.0
Total	3	58	113	14	31	7	1	1	11	5	18	.274	.305	.381	86	-2	1	2	-1	.980	-6	/O-38,D-7	-1.0

■ GEORGE FIELDS
Fields, George W.   b: 7/1853, Waterbury, Conn.   d: 9/22/33, Waterbury, Conn.   Deb: 5/2/1872

YEAR	TM/L	G	AB	R	H	2B	3B	HR	RBI	BB	SO	AVG	OBP	SLG	PRO+	BR/A	SB	CS	SBR	FA	FR	G/POS	TPR
1872	Man-n	18	87	16	21	3	1	0	9	0	2	.241	.241	.299	64	-9				.563	-13	3-12/O-5,S-1	-1.2

■ JOCKO FIELDS
Fields, John Joseph   b: 10/20/1864, Cork, Ireland   d: 10/14/50, Jersey City, N.J.   BR/TR, 5'10", 160 lbs.   Deb: 5/31/1887

YEAR	TM/L	G	AB	R	H	2B	3B	HR	RBI	BB	SO	AVG	OBP	SLG	PRO+	BR/A	SB	CS	SBR	FA	FR	G/POS	TPR
1887	Pit-N	43	164	26	44	9	2	0	17	7	13	.268	.306	.348	86	-3	7			.933	1	O-27,C-14/1-3,3P	-0.1
1888	Pit-N	45	169	22	33	7	1	0	15	8	19	.195	.232	.278	67	-6	9			.887	-5	O-29,C-14/3-3	-1.0
1889	Pit-N	75	289	41	90	22	5	2	43	29	30	.311	.376	.443	142	16	7			.860	-6	O-60,C-16	0.9
1890	Pit-P	126	526	101	148	18	20	9	86	57	52	.281	.355	.443	123	16	24			.879	-13	O-80,2-30,C-15,/S-4	0.3
1891	Pit-N	23	75	10	18	3	0	0	5	10	13	.240	.337	.280	82	-1	1			.897	-3	C-15/S-8	-0.2
	Phi-N	8	30	4	7	2	1	0	5	4	2	.233	.324	.367	98	-0	0			.769	-1	/C-8	-0.3
	Yr	31	105	14	25	5	1	0	10	14	15	.238	.333	.305	87	-1	1			.857	-7	C-23/S-8	-0.5
1892	NY-N	21	66	8	18	4	2	1	5	9	10	.273	.368	.394	133	3	2			.917	-1	O-11,C-10	0.2
Total	6	341	1319	212	358	65	32	12	176	124	139	.271	.338	.397	114	25	50			.883	-31	O-207/C-92,2S31P	-0.2

■ BIEN FIGUEROA
Figueroa, Bienvenido   b: 2/7/64, Santo Domingo, D.R.   BR/TR, 5'10", 170 lbs.   Deb: 5/17/92

YEAR	TM/L	G	AB	R	H	2B	3B	HR	RBI	BB	SO	AVG	OBP	SLG	PRO+	BR/A	SB	CS	SBR	FA	FR	G/POS	TPR
1992	StL-N	12	11	1	2	1	0	0	4	1	2	.182	.250	.273	49	-1	0	0	0	.938	1	/S-9,2-3	0.0

■ JESUS FIGUEROA
Figueroa, Jesus Maria (Figueroa)   b: 2/20/57, Santo Domingo, D.R.   BL/TL, 5'10", 160 lbs.   Deb: 4/22/80

YEAR	TM/L	G	AB	R	H	2B	3B	HR	RBI	BB	SO	AVG	OBP	SLG	PRO+	BR/A	SB	CS	SBR	FA	FR	G/POS	TPR
1980	Chi-N	115	198	20	50	5	1	0	16	10	16	.253	.308	.293	64	-9	2	1	0	.979	-4	O-57	-1.5

■ SAM FILE
File, Lawrence Samuel   b: 5/18/22, Chester, Pa.   BR/TR, 5'11", 160 lbs.   Deb: 9/10/40

YEAR	TM/L	G	AB	R	H	2B	3B	HR	RBI	BB	SO	AVG	OBP	SLG	PRO+	BR/A	SB	CS	SBR	FA	FR	G/POS	TPR
1940	Phi-A	7	13	0	1	0	0	0	1	0	1	.077	.077	.077	-60	-3	0			.850	1	/S-6,3-1	-0.2

■ STEVE FILIPOWICZ
Filipowicz, Stephen Charles "Flip"   b: 6/28/21, Donora, Pa.   d: 2/21/75, Wilkes-Barre, Pa.   BR/TR, 5'8", 195 lbs.   Deb: 9/3/44

YEAR	TM/L	G	AB	R	H	2B	3B	HR	RBI	BB	SO	AVG	OBP	SLG	PRO+	BR/A	SB	CS	SBR	FA	FR	G/POS	TPR
1944	NY-N	15	41	10	8	2	1	0	3	7	7	.195	.250	.293	52	-3	0			1.000	-1	O-10/C-1	-0.5
1945	NY-N	35	112	14	23	5	0	2	16	4	13	.205	.239	.304	50	-8	0			.935	-6	O-31	-1.6
1948	Cin-N	7	26	0	9	0	1	0	3	2	1	.346	.393	.423	125	1	0			1.000	-0	/O-7	0.0
Total	3	57	179	24	40	7	2	2	26	9	21	.223	.265	.318	61	-10	0			.961	-8	/O-48,C-1	-2.1

YEAR	TM/L	G	AB	R	H	2B	3B	HR	RBI	BB	SO	AVG	OBP	SLG	PRO+	BR/A	SB	CS	SBR	FA	FR	G/POS	TPR

■ JACK FIMPLE
Fimple, John Joseph b: 2/10/59, Darby, Pa. BR/TR, 6'2", 185 lbs. Deb: 7/30/83

YEAR	TM/L	G	AB	R	H	2B	3B	HR	RBI	BB	SO	AVG	OBP	SLG	PRO+	BR/A	SB	CS	SBR	FA	FR	G/POS	TPR
1983	*LA-N	54	148	16	37	8	1	2	22	11	39	.250	.302	.358	83	-4	1	0	0	.989	12	C-54	1.1
1984	LA-N	12	26	2	5	1	0	0	3	1	6	.192	.222	.231	28	-3	0	0	0	.983	2	C-12	-0.1
1986	LA-N	13	13	2	1	0	0	0	2	6	6	.077	.368	.077	32	-1	0	0	0	1.000	1	/C-7,1-1,2-1	0.0
1987	Cal-A	13	10	1	2	0	0	0	1	1	2	.200	.273	.200	29	-1	0	0	0	.913	1	C-13	0.0
Total	4	92	197	21	45	9	1	2	28	19	53	.228	.296	.315	70	-8	1	0	0	.986	15	/C-86,2-1,1-1	1.0

■ JIM FINIGAN
Finigan, James Leroy b: 8/19/28, Quincy, Ill. d: 5/16/81, Quincy, Ill. BR/TR, 5'11", 175 lbs. Deb: 4/25/54

YEAR	TM/L	G	AB	R	H	2B	3B	HR	RBI	BB	SO	AVG	OBP	SLG	PRO+	BR/A	SB	CS	SBR	FA	FR	G/POS	TPR
1954	Phi-A☆	136	487	57	147	25	6	7	51	64	66	.302	.383	.421	120	14	2	8	-4	.948	2	*3-136	1.0
1955	KC-A★	150	545	72	139	30	7	9	68	61	49	.255	.335	.385	92	-7	1	3	-2	.975	-7	2-90,3-59	-0.9
1956	KC-A	91	250	29	54	7	2	2	21	30	28	.216	.302	.284	55	-16	3	1	-0	.969	-1	2-52,3-32	-1.2
1957	Det-A	64	174	20	47	4	2	0	17	23	18	.270	.359	.316	84	-3	1	1	-0	.954	4	3-59/2-3	0.2
1958	SF-N	23	25	3	5	2	0	0	1	3	5	.200	.310	.280	59	-1	0	0	0	.917	-2	/2-8,3-4	-0.3
1959	Bal-A	48	119	14	30	6	0	1	10	9	10	.252	.305	.328	75	-4	1	0	0	.959	0	3-42/2-6,S-2	-0.3
Total	6	512	1600	195	422	74	17	19	168	190	176	.264	.344	.367	92	-17	8	13	-5	.948	-3	3-332,2-159/S-2	-1.5

■ BOB FINLEY
Finley, Robert Edward b: 11/25/15, Ennis, Tex. d: 1/2/86, W.Covina, Cal. BR/TR, 6'1", 200 lbs. Deb: 7/4/43

YEAR	TM/L	G	AB	R	H	2B	3B	HR	RBI	BB	SO	AVG	OBP	SLG	PRO+	BR/A	SB	CS	SBR	FA	FR	G/POS	TPR
1943	Phi-N	28	81	9	21	2	0	1	7	4	10	.259	.294	.321	81	-2	0			.962	3	C-24	0.2
1944	Phi-N	94	281	18	70	11	1	1	21	12	25	.249	.292	.306	71	-11	1			.967	-2	C-74	-0.9
Total	2	122	362	27	91	13	1	2	28	16	35	.251	.292	.309	73	-13	1			.966	1	/C-98	-0.7

■ STEVE FINLEY
Finley, Steven Allen b: 3/12/65, Paducah, Ky. BL/TL, 6'2", 175 lbs. Deb: 4/3/89

YEAR	TM/L	G	AB	R	H	2B	3B	HR	RBI	BB	SO	AVG	OBP	SLG	PRO+	BR/A	SB	CS	SBR	FA	FR	G/POS	TPR
1989	Bal-A	81	217	35	54	5	2	2	25	15	30	.249	.300	.318	77	-7	17	3	3	.986	-8	O-76/D-3	-1.4
1990	Bal-A	142	464	46	119	16	4	3	37	32	53	.256	.307	.328	80	-12	22	9	1	.977	-1	*O-133/D-2	-1.5
1991	Hou-N	159	596	84	170	28	10	8	54	42	65	.285	.334	.406	114	9	34	18	-1	.985	-6	*O-153	0.0
1992	Hou-N	162	607	84	177	29	13	5	55	58	63	.292	.356	.407	121	17	44	9	8	.993	10	*O-160	3.3
1993	Hou-N	142	545	69	145	15	13	8	44	28	65	.266	.306	.385	87	-12	19	6	2	.988	9	*O-140	-0.3
1994	Hou-N	94	373	64	103	16	5	11	33	28	52	.276	.330	.434	102	0	13	7	-0	.982	5	O-92	0.2
1995	SD-N	139	562	104	167	23	8	10	44	59	62	.297	.367	.420	111	9	36	12	4	.977	5	*O-138	1.3
1996	*SD-N	161	655	126	195	45	9	30	95	56	88	.298	.352	.531	137	33	22	8	7	.982	12	*O-160	4.0
Total	8	1080	4019	612	1130	177	64	77	387	318	478	.281	.337	.415	108	38	207	72	19	.984	26	*O-1052/D-5	5.6

■ BILL FINLEY
Finley, William James b: 10/4/1863, New York, N.Y. d: 10/6/12, Asbury Park, N.J. 5'3", 170 lbs. Deb: 7/12/1886

YEAR	TM/L	G	AB	R	H	2B	3B	HR	RBI	BB	SO	AVG	OBP	SLG	PRO+	BR/A	SB	CS	SBR	FA	FR	G/POS	TPR
1886	NY-N	13	44	2	8	0	0	0	5	1	8	.182	.200	.182	17	-4	2			.800	-3	/O-8,C-8	-0.6

■ NEAL FINN
Finn, Cornelius Francis "Mickey" b: 1/24/04, Brooklyn, N.Y. d: 7/7/33, Allentown, Pa. BR/TR, 5'11", 168 lbs. Deb: 4/21/30

YEAR	TM/L	G	AB	R	H	2B	3B	HR	RBI	BB	SO	AVG	OBP	SLG	PRO+	BR/A	SB	CS	SBR	FA	FR	G/POS	TPR
1930	Bro-N	87	273	42	76	13	0	3	30	26	18	.278	.350	.359	73	-11	3			.948	-6	2-81	-1.2
1931	Bro-N	118	413	46	113	22	2	0	45	21	42	.274	.314	.337	75	-14	2			.975	9	*2-112	-0.7
1932	Bro-N	65	189	22	45	5	2	0	14	11	15	.238	.284	.286	55	-12	2			.933	4	3-50/2-2,S-1	-0.5
1933	Phi-N	51	169	15	40	4	1	0	13	10	14	.237	.287	.272	54	-10	2			.964	-1	2-51	-0.9
Total	4	321	1044	125	274	44	5	3	102	68	89	.262	.314	.323	67	-48	9			.964	-3	2-246/3-50,S-1	-3.3

■ HAL FINNEY
Finney, Harold Wilson b: 7/30/05, Lafayette, Ala. d: 12/20/91, Lafayette, Ala. BR/TR, 5'11", 170 lbs. Deb: 6/24/31 F

YEAR	TM/L	G	AB	R	H	2B	3B	HR	RBI	BB	SO	AVG	OBP	SLG	PRO+	BR/A	SB	CS	SBR	FA	FR	G/POS	TPR
1931	Pit-N	10	26	2	8	1	0	0	2	0	1	.308	.333	.308	84	-1	1			1.000	-0	/C-6	0.0
1932	Pit-N	31	33	14	7	3	0	0	4	3	4	.212	.297	.303	63	-2	0			.971	-3	C-11	0.1
1933	Pit-N	56	133	17	31	4	1	1	18	3	19	.233	.250	.301	57	-8	0			.993	-2	C-47	-0.8
1934	Pit-N	5	0	3	0	0	0	0	0	0	0	—	1.000	—	188	0	0			.000	0	/C-1	0.0
1936	Pit-N	21	35	3	0	0	0	0	3	0	8	.000	.000	.000	-98	-10	0			.956	1	C-14	-0.8
Total	5	123	227	39	46	8	1	1	27	6	32	.203	.233	.260	37	-19	1			.983	1	/C-79	-1.5

■ LOU FINNEY
Finney, Louis Klopsche b: 8/13/10, Buffalo, Ala. d: 4/22/66, Lafayette, Ala. BL/TR, 6', 180 lbs. Deb: 9/12/31 F

YEAR	TM/L	G	AB	R	H	2B	3B	HR	RBI	BB	SO	AVG	OBP	SLG	PRO+	BR/A	SB	CS	SBR	FA	FR	G/POS	TPR
1931	Phi-A	9	24	7	9	0	1	0	3	6	1	.375	.516	.458	149	2	0	0	0	1.000	1	/O-8	0.3
1933	Phi-A	74	240	26	64	12	3	2	32	13	17	.267	.307	.371	78	-8	1	3	-2	.947	2	O-63	-1.0
1934	Phi-A	92	272	32	76	11	4	1	28	14	17	.279	.315	.360	77	-10	4	3	-1	.943	0	O-54,1-15	-1.3
1935	Phi-A	109	410	45	112	11	6	0	31	18	18	.273	.307	.329	65	-22	7	2	1	.943	-2	O-76,1-18	-2.6
1936	Phi-A	151	653	100	197	26	10	1	41	47	22	.302	.351	.377	81	-19	7	9	-3	.990	-4	1-78,O-73	-3.3
1937	Phi-A	92	379	53	95	14	9	1	20	20	16	.251	.288	.343	59	-25	2	5	-2	.989	-4	1-50,O-39/2-1	-3.6
1938	Phi-A	122	454	61	125	21	12	10	48	39	25	.275	.333	.441	94	-6	5	8	-3	.990	-3	1-64,O-46	-1.9
1939	Phi-A	9	22	1	3	0	0	0	1	2	0	.136	.208	.136	-10	-4	0	0	0	1.000	0	O-4	-0.3
	Bos-A	95	249	43	81	18	3	1	46	24	11	.325	.385	.434	105	2	2	5	-2	.986	-6	1-32,O-24	-1.0
	Yr	104	271	44	84	18	3	1	47	26	11	.310	.374	.410	96	-1	2	5	-2	.986	-6	1-32,O-28	-1.3
1940	Bos-A★	130	534	73	171	31	15	5	73	33	13	.320	.360	.463	107	5	5	2	0	.975	2	O-69,1-51	-0.2
1941	Bos-A	127	497	83	143	24	10	4	53	38	17	.288	.340	.400	93	-6	2	3	-1	.945	-3	O-92,1-24	-1.8
1942	Bos-A	113	397	58	113	16	7	3	61	29	11	.285	.335	.383	98	-2	3	3	-1	.976	2	O-95/1-2	-0.6
1944	Bos-A	68	251	37	72	11	2	0	32	23	7	.287	.347	.347	100	-1	1	0	-0	.987	-5	1-59/O-2	-0.8
1945	Bos-A	2	2	0	0	0	0	0	0	0	0	.000	.000	.000	-98	-0	0	0	0	.000	0	H	-0.1
	StL-A	57	213	24	59	8	4	2	22	21	6	.277	.345	.380	105	1	0	0	0	.986	-2	O-36,1-22/3-1	-0.4
	Yr	59	215	24	59	8	4	2	22	21	7	.274	.342	.377	103	1	0	0	0	.986	-2	O-36,1-22/3-1	-0.5
1946	StL-A	16	30	2	9	0	0	0	3	2	4	.300	.344	.300	77	-1	0	0	0	.938	0	/O-7	-0.1
1947	Phi-N	4	4	0	0	0	0	0	0	0	0	.000	.000	.000	-99	-1	0	0	0	.000	0	H	-0.1
Total	15	1270	4631	643	1329	203	85	31	494	329	186	.287	.336	.388	88	-92	39	45		.961	-22	O-688,1-415/3-1,2-1	-18.8

■ MIKE FIORE
Fiore, Michael Gary Joseph b: 10/11/44, Brooklyn, N.Y. BL/TL, 6', 185 lbs. Deb: 9/21/68

YEAR	TM/L	G	AB	R	H	2B	3B	HR	RBI	BB	SO	AVG	OBP	SLG	PRO+	BR/A	SB	CS	SBR	FA	FR	G/POS	TPR
1968	Bal-A	6	17	2	1	0	0	0	4	4	4	.059	.273	.059	5	-2	0	0	0	.943	-0	/1-5,O-1	-0.3
1969	KC-A	107	339	53	93	14	1	12	35	84	63	.274	.421	.428	137	21	4	4	-1	.988	10	1-91,O-13	2.3
1970	KC-A	25	72	6	13	2	0	0	4	13	24	.181	.306	.208	44	-5	1	1	-0	.986	1	1-20	-0.7
	Bos-A	41	50	5	7	0	0	0	4	8	4	.140	.259	.140	12	-6	0	0	0	1.000	1	1-17/O-2	-0.7
	Yr	66	122	11	20	2	0	0	8	21	28	.164	.287	.180	30	-11	1	1	-0	.991	1	1-37/O-2	-1.4
1971	Bos-A	51	62	9	11	2	0	0	6	12	14	.177	.311	.258	58	-3	0	3	-2	1.000	-1	1-12	-0.6
1972	StL-N	17	10	0	1	0	0	0	0	2	3	.100	.250	.100	3	-1	0	0	0	1.000	-1	1-6,O-1	-0.2
	SD-N	7	6	0	0	0	0	0	0	1	3	.000	.143	.000	-61	-2	0	0	0	.000	0	H	-0.1
	Yr	24	16	0	1	0	0	0	0	3	6	.063	.211	.063	-20	-2	0	0	0	1.000	-1	/1-6,O-1	-0.3
Total	5	254	556	75	126	18	1	13	50	124	115	.227	.370	.333	97	3	5	8	-3	.988	9	1-151/O-17	-0.3

■ DAN FIROVA
Firova, Daniel Michael b: 10/16/56, Refugio, Tex. BR/TR, 6', 185 lbs. Deb: 9/1/81

YEAR	TM/L	G	AB	R	H	2B	3B	HR	RBI	BB	SO	AVG	OBP	SLG	PRO+	BR/A	SB	CS	SBR	FA	FR	G/POS	TPR
1981	Sea-A	13	2	0	0	0	0	0	0	0	0	.000	.000	.000	-96	-0	0	0	0	1.000	1	C-13	0.0
1982	Sea-A	3	5	0	0	0	0	0	0	0	0	.000	.000	.000	-97	-1	0	0	0	.900	-0	/C-3	-0.1
1988	Cle-A	1	0	0	0	0	0	0	0	0	0	—	—	—	—	-0	0	0	0	.000	0	/C-1	0.0
Total	3	17	7	0	0	0	0	0	0	0	0	.000	.000	.000	-97	-2	0	0	0	.944	1	/C-17	-0.1

■ WILLIAM FISCHER
Fischer, William Charles b: 3/2/1891, New York, N.Y. d: 9/4/45, Richmond, Va. BL/TR, 6', 174 lbs. Deb: 6/11/13

YEAR	TM/L	G	AB	R	H	2B	3B	HR	RBI	BB	SO	AVG	OBP	SLG	PRO+	BR/A	SB	CS	SBR	FA	FR	G/POS	TPR
1913	Bro-N	62	165	16	44	9	4	1	12	10	5	.267	.313	.388	97	-1	0			.974	-3	C-51	0.0
1914	Bro-N	43	105	12	27	1	2	0	8	8	12	.257	.310	.305	81	-2	1			.958	3	C-30	0.3
1915	Chi-F	105	292	30	96	15	4	4	50	24	19	.329	.384	.449	142	11	5			.972	-6	C-80	1.2
1916	Chi-N	65	179	15	35	9	2	1	14	11	8	.196	.246	.285	57	-9	2			.973	4	C-56	-0.2
	Pit-N	42	113	11	29	7	1	1	6	10	3	.257	.323	.363	109	1	1			.974	5	C-35	1.0
	Yr	107	292	26	64	16	3	2	20	21	11	.219	.276	.315	76	-8	3			.973	8	C-91	0.8
1917	Pit-N	95	245	25	70	9	5	2	25	27	19	.286	.359	.376	121	7	11			.961	-9	C-69/1-2	0.4
Total	5	412	1099	109	301	50	15	10	115	90	66	.274	.332	.374	107	7	20			.969	-8	C-321/1-2	2.7

YEAR	TM/L	G	AB	R	H	2B	3B	HR	RBI	BB	SO	AVG	OBP	SLG	PRO+	BR/A	SB	CS	SBR	FA	FR	G/POS	TPR

■ MIKE FISCHLIN
Fischlin, Michael Thomas b: 9/13/55, Sacramento, Cal. BR/TR, 6'1", 165 lbs. Deb: 9/3/77

YEAR	TM/L	G	AB	R	H	2B	3B	HR	RBI	BB	SO	AVG	OBP	SLG	PRO+	BR/A	SB	CS	SBR	FA	FR	G/POS	TPR
1977	Hou-N	13	15	0	3	0	0	0	0	0	2	.200	.200	.200	8	-2	0	0	0	1.000	1	S-12	0.0
1978	Hou-N	44	86	3	10	1	0	0	4	9	.116	.165	.128	-19	-14	1	0	0	.928	-4	S-41	-1.6
1980	Hou-N	1	1	0	0	0	0	0	0	0	1	.000	.000	.000	-99	-0	0	0	0	1.000	-0	/S-1	0.0
1981	Cle-A	22	43	3	10	1	0	0	5	3	6	.233	.283	.256	57	-2	3	2	-0	.955	-0	S-19/2-1	-0.2
1982	Cle-A	112	276	34	74	12	1	0	21	34	36	.268	.353	.319	86	-4	9	5	-0	.970	-7	*S-101/3-8,2-6,C-1	-0.3
1983	Cle-A	95	225	31	47	5	2	2	23	26	32	.209	.296	.276	56	-13	9	2	2	.965	21	2-71,S-15/3-4,D-1	1.3
1984	Cle-A	85	133	17	30	4	2	1	14	12	20	.226	.290	.308	64	-6	2	2	-1	.981	18	2-55,3-17,S-15	1.3
1985	Cle-A	73	60	12	12	4	1	0	2	5	7	.200	.262	.300	54	-4	0	1	-1	.990	27	2-31,S-22/1-6,3D	2.3
1986	NY-A	71	102	9	21	2	0	0	3	8	29	.206	.264	.225	35	-9	0	1	-1	.955	7	S-42,2-27	-0.1
1987	Atl-N	1	0	0	0	0	0	0	0	0	0	—	—	—	—	—	0	0	0	.000	0	/R	0.0
Total	10	517	941	109	207	29	6	3	68	92	142	.220	.293	.273	57	-54	24	13	-1	.959	63	S-268,2-191/31DC	2.7

■ SAM FISHBURN
Fishburn, Samuel E. b: 5/15/1893, Haverhill, Mass. d: 4/11/65, Bethlehem, Pa. BR/TR, 5'9", 157 lbs. Deb: 9/30/19

YEAR	TM/L	G	AB	R	H	2B	3B	HR	RBI	BB	SO	AVG	OBP	SLG	PRO+	BR/A	SB	CS	SBR	FA	FR	G/POS	TPR
1919	StL-N	9	6	0	2	1	0	0	2	0	0	.333	.333	.500	158	0	0			1.000	0	/1-1,2-1	0.1

■ JOHN FISHEL
Fishel, John Alan b: 11/8/62, Fullerton, Cal. BR/TR, 5'11", 185 lbs. Deb: 7/14/88

YEAR	TM/L	G	AB	R	H	2B	3B	HR	RBI	BB	SO	AVG	OBP	SLG	PRO+	BR/A	SB	CS	SBR	FA	FR	G/POS	TPR
1988	Hou-N	19	26	1	6	0	0	1	2	3	6	.231	.310	.346	92	-0	0	0	0	1.000	-2	/O-6	-0.3

■ GUS FISHER
Fisher, August Harris b: 10/21/1885, Pottsboro, Tex. d: 4/8/72, Portland, Ore. BL/TR, 5'10", 175 lbs. Deb: 4/18/11

YEAR	TM/L	G	AB	R	H	2B	3B	HR	RBI	BB	SO	AVG	OBP	SLG	PRO+	BR/A	SB	CS	SBR	FA	FR	G/POS	TPR
1911	Cle-A	70	203	20	53	6	3	0	12	7		.261	.302	.320	73	-8	6			.956	8	C-58/1-1	0.5
1912	NY-A	4	10	1	1	0	0	0	0	0		.100	.100	.100	-40	-2	0			1.000	1	/C-4	-0.1
Total	2	74	213	21	54	6	3	0	12	7		.254	.293	.310	68	-10	6			.958	8	/C-62,1-1	0.4

■ CHARLES FISHER
Fisher, Charles Deb: 6/15/1889

YEAR	TM/L	G	AB	R	H	2B	3B	HR	RBI	BB	SO	AVG	OBP	SLG	PRO+	BR/A	SB	CS	SBR	FA	FR	G/POS	TPR
1889	Lou-a	1	2	0	1	0	0	0	0	0	0	.500	.500	.500	189	0	0			.000	-1	/O-1	0.0

■ CHARLES FISHER
Fisher, Charles G. (b: Charles G. Fish) b: 3/10/1852, Boxford, Mass. d: 2/18/17, Eagle, Alaska BL/TR, 5'8", 143 lbs. Deb: 6/7/1884

YEAR	TM/L	G	AB	R	H	2B	3B	HR	RBI	BB	SO	AVG	OBP	SLG	PRO+	BR/A	SB	CS	SBR	FA	FR	G/POS	TPR
1884	KC-U	10	40	3	8	2	0	0		0		.200	.200	.250	41	-4				.711	-0	/3-9,S-1	-0.4
	CP-U	1	3	1	2	0	0	0		1		.667	.750	.667	335	1				.500	1	/3-1	0.0
Yr		11	43	4	10	2	0	0		1		.233	.250	.279	68	-3				.702	-1	3-10/S-1	-0.4

■ SHOWBOAT FISHER
Fisher, George Aloys b: 1/16/1899, Wesley, Iowa d: 5/15/94, St.Cloud, Minn. BL/TR, 5'10", 170 lbs. Deb: 4/24/23

YEAR	TM/L	G	AB	R	H	2B	3B	HR	RBI	BB	SO	AVG	OBP	SLG	PRO+	BR/A	SB	CS	SBR	FA	FR	G/POS	TPR
1923	Was-A	13	23	4	6	2	0	0	2	4	3	.261	.370	.348	95	-0	0	0	0	.750	0	/O-5	0.0
1924	Was-A	15	41	7	9	1	0	0	6	6	6	.220	.319	.244	48	-3	2	0	1	.933	-2	O-11	-0.5
1930	*StL-N	92	254	49	95	18	6	8	61	25	21	.374	.432	.587	139	16	4			.962	-3	O-67	0.8
1932	StL-A	18	22	2	4	0	0	0	2	2	5	.182	.250	.182	13	-3	0	0	0	1.000	-1	/O-5	-0.4
Total	4	138	340	62	114	21	6	8	71	37	35	.335	.402	.503	119	10	6	0	1	.946	-6	/O-88	0.0

■ GEORGE FISHER
Fisher, George C. b: Wilmington, Del. BL, Deb: 8/9/1884

YEAR	TM/L	G	AB	R	H	2B	3B	HR	RBI	BB	SO	AVG	OBP	SLG	PRO+	BR/A	SB	CS	SBR	FA	FR	G/POS	TPR
1884	Cle-N	6	24	2	3	0	0	0		0	3	.125	.125	.125	-20	-3				.897	-3	/2-6,C-1	-0.6
	Wil-U	8	29	0	2	0	0	0		0		.069	.069	.069	-56	-6				.818	-1	/O-6,S-2	-0.7
Total	1	14	53	2	5	0	0	0		0	3	.094	.094	.094	-40	-10				.818	-4	/O-6,2-6,S-2,C-1	-1.3

■ HARRY FISHER
Fisher, Harry Devereux b: 1/3/26, Newbury, Ont., Can. d: 9/20/81, Waterloo, Ont., Canada BL/TR, 6', 180 lbs. Deb: 9/16/51

YEAR	TM/L	G	AB	R	H	2B	3B	HR	RBI	BB	SO	AVG	OBP	SLG	PRO+	BR/A	SB	CS	SBR	FA	FR	G/POS	TPR
1951	Pit-N	3	3	0	0	0	0	0	0	0	0	.000	.000	.000	-97	-1	0	0	0	.000	0	H	-0.1
1952	Pit-N	15	15	0	5	1	0	0	1	0	3	.333	.333	.400	100	-1	0	0	0	1.000	-1	/P-8	0.0
Total	2	18	18	0	5	1	0	0	1	0	3	.278	.278	.333	66	-1	0	0	0	1.000	-1	/P-8	-0.1

■ RED FISHER
Fisher, John Gus b: 6/22/1887, Pittsburgh, Pa. d: 1/31/40, Louisville, Ky. BL/TR, Deb: 4/25/10

YEAR	TM/L	G	AB	R	H	2B	3B	HR	RBI	BB	SO	AVG	OBP	SLG	PRO+	BR/A	SB	CS	SBR	FA	FR	G/POS	TPR
1910	StL-A	23	72	5	9	2	1	0	3	8		.125	.222	.181	28	-6	5			.935	-1	O-19	-0.9

■ NEWT FISHER
Fisher, Newton "Ike" b: 6/28/1871, Nashville, Tenn. d: 2/28/47, Norwood Park, Ill. BR/TR, 5'9.5", 171 lbs. Deb: 5/17/1898 F

YEAR	TM/L	G	AB	R	H	2B	3B	HR	RBI	BB	SO	AVG	OBP	SLG	PRO+	BR/A	SB	CS	SBR	FA	FR	G/POS	TPR
1898	Phi-N	9	26	3	3	1	0	0	0	0		.115	.148	.154	-14	-4	1			.844	-1	/C-8,3-1	-0.4

■ BOB FISHER
Fisher, Robert Taylor b: 11/3/1886, Nashville, Tenn. d: 8/4/63, Jacksonville, Fla. BR/TR, 5'9.5", 170 lbs. Deb: 6/3/12 F

YEAR	TM/L	G	AB	R	H	2B	3B	HR	RBI	BB	SO	AVG	OBP	SLG	PRO+	BR/A	SB	CS	SBR	FA	FR	G/POS	TPR
1912	Bro-N	82	257	27	60	10	3	0	26	14	32	.233	.273	.296	58	-16	7			.917	-14	S-74/2-1,3-1	-2.4
1913	Bro-N	132	474	42	124	11	10	4	54	10	43	.262	.278	.352	77	-16	16			.923	-19	*S-131	-2.4
1914	Chi-N	15	50	5	15	2	2	0	5	3	4	.300	.340	.420	126	1	2			.943	-1	S-15	0.1
1915	Chi-N	147	568	70	163	22	5	5	53	30	51	.287	.326	.370	110	6	9	20	-9	.933	-20	*S-145	-1.4
1916	Cin-N	61	136	9	37	4	0	0	11	8	14	.272	.313	.346	104	0	7			.905	-12	S-29/2-6,O-1	-1.1
1918	StL-N	63	246	36	78	11	3	2	20	15	11	.317	.356	.411	138	10	7			.979	19	2-63	3.5
1919	StL-N	3	11	0	3	1	0	0	1	0	2	.273	.273	.364	96	-0	0			.900	-1	/2-3	0.1
Total	7	503	1742	189	480	61	26	11	170	80	157	.276	.309	.359	96	-13	48	20		.925	-48	S-394/2-73,O,1,3-1	-3.6

■ WILBUR FISHER
Fisher, Wilbur McCullough b: 7/18/1894, Green Bottom, W.Va. d: 10/24/60, Welch, W.Va. BL/TR, 6', 174 lbs. Deb: 6/13/16

YEAR	TM/L	G	AB	R	H	2B	3B	HR	RBI	BB	SO	AVG	OBP	SLG	PRO+	BR/A	SB	CS	SBR	FA	FR	G/POS	TPR
1916	Pit-N	1	1	0	0	0	0	0	0	0	0	.000	.000	.000	-99	-0	0			.000	0	H	0.0

■ CHEROKEE FISHER
Fisher, William Charles b: 12/1845, Philadelphia, Pa. d: 9/26/12, New York, N.Y. BR/TR, 5'9", 164 lbs. Deb: 5/6/1871

YEAR	TM/L	G	AB	R	H	2B	3B	HR	RBI	BB	SO	AVG	OBP	SLG	PRO+	BR/A	SB	CS	SBR	FA	FR	G/POS	TPR
1871	Rok-n	25	123	24	28	3	3	1	22	3	1	.228	.246	.325	65	-5	1	2	-1	**.927**	4	*P-24/1-2,2-1	0.0
1872	Bal-n	46	225	39	52	10	3	1	36	2	5	.231	.238	.316	66	-10	0	1	-1	.761	-8	P-19,O-19,3-18	-1.2
1873	Ath-n	51	253	50	66	4	3	1	35	4	5	.261	.272	.312	68	-11	1	2	-1	.743	5	*O-45,P-13/2,3-1,1	-0.2
1874	Har-n	52	241	28	54	7	0	0	28	2	6	.224	.230	.253	52	-13	0	2	-1	.789	-7	P-39,O-12/3-7,S-2	-0.7
1875	Phi-n	41	177	26	41	3	1	0	11	1	6	.232	.236	.260	69	-6	4	3	-1	.896	-5	P-41/O-5	-0.1
1876	Cin-N	35	129	12	32	1	0	0	4	0	8	.248	.248	.256	80	-2				.793	-5	P-28,O-11/S-1,1-1	-0.3
1877	Chi-N	1	4	0	0	0	0	0	0	0	0	.000	.000	.000	-89	-1				.667	-0	/3-1	-0.1
1878	Pro-N	1	3	0	0	0	0	0	0	0	0	.000	.000	.000	-99	-1				1.000	0	/P-1	0.0
Total	5 n	215	1019	167	241	27	10	3	132	12	23	.237	.245	.291	64	-45	6	10	-4	.850	-10	P-136/O-81,321S	-2.2
Total	3	37	136	12	32	1	0	0	4	0	10	.235	.235	.243	68	-4				.803	-5	/P-29,O-11,3-1,1S	-0.4

■ CARLTON FISK
Fisk, Carlton Ernest "Pudge" b: 12/26/47, Bellows Falls, Vt. BR/TR, 6'2", 220 lbs. Deb: 9/18/69

YEAR	TM/L	G	AB	R	H	2B	3B	HR	RBI	BB	SO	AVG	OBP	SLG	PRO+	BR/A	SB	CS	SBR	FA	FR	G/POS	TPR
1969	Bos-A	2	5	0	0	0	0	0	0	0	2	.000	.000	.000	-95	-1	0	0	0	1.000	-1	/C-1	-0.3
1971	Bos-A	14	48	7	15	2	1	2	6	1	10	.313	.327	.521	128	1	0	0	0	.975	-1	C-14	0.1
1972	Bos-A★	131	457	74	134	28	**9**	22	61	52	83	.293	.370	.538	159	33	5	2	0	.984	1	*C-131	4.4
1973	Bos-A★	135	508	65	125	21	0	26	71	37	99	.246	.310	.441	103	10	7	2	1	.983	6	*C-131/D-3	1.3
1974	Bos-A†	52	187	36	56	12	1	11	26	24	23	.299	.385	.551	156	13	5	1	1	.980	-2	C-50/D-2	1.9
1975	*Bos-A	79	263	47	87	14	4	10	52	27	32	.331	.397	.529	147	16	4	3	-1	.979	-4	C-71/D-6	1.4
1976	Bos-A★	134	487	76	124	17	5	17	58	56	71	.255	.339	.415	107	4	12	5	1	.984	10	*C-133/D-1	1.9
1977	Bos-A★	152	536	106	169	26	3	26	102	75	85	.315	.408	.521	135	27	7	6	-2	.987	-5	*C-151	3.0
1978	Bos-A★	157	571	94	162	39	5	20	88	71	83	.284	.370	.475	123	17	7	2	1	.980	11	*C-154/O-1,D-1	3.4
1979	Bos-A	91	320	49	87	23	2	10	42	10	38	.272	.307	.450	96	-3	3	0	1	.982	-12	D-42,C-39/O-1	-1.3
1980	Bos-A★	131	478	73	138	25	3	18	62	36	62	.289	.355	.467	117	11	11	5	0	.983	-7	C-115/O-5,1-3,3D	0.8
1981	Chi-A★	96	338	44	89	12	0	7	45	38	37	.263	.358	.361	110	6	3	2	-0	.990	-2	C-95/1-3,3-1,O-1	0.7
1982	Chi-A★	135	476	66	127	17	3	14	65	46	60	.267	.339	.403	103	2	17	2	4	.994	-1	*C-133/1-2	1.0
1983	*Chi-A	138	488	85	141	26	4	26	86	46	88	.289	.357	.518	133	21	9	6	-1	.991	-2	*C-133/D-2	2.4
1984	Chi-A	102	359	54	83	20	1	21	43	26	60	.231	.292	.468	102	-1	6	0	2	.987	-17	C-90/D-5	-1.1
1985	Chi-A★	153	543	85	129	23	1	37	107	52	81	.238	.324	.488	114	19	17	9	-0	.989	-4	*C-130/D-28	1.1
1986	Chi-A	125	457	42	101	11	0	14	63	22	92	.221	.266	.337	61	-25	2	4	-2	.991	-6	C-71,O-31/D-22	-2.1
1987	Chi-A	135	454	68	116	22	1	23	71	39	72	.256	.325	.460	103	1	1	4	-2	.990	-5	*C-122/1-9,O-2,D-7	0.9
1988	Chi-A	76	253	37	70	8	1	19	50	37	40	.277	.380	.542	137	14	0	0	0	.995	8	C-74	2.0
1989	Chi-A	103	375	47	110	25	2	13	68	36	60	.293	.360	.475	137	18	1	3	0	**.993**	-15	C-90,D-13	0.8
1990	Chi-A	137	452	65	129	21	0	18	65	61	73	.285	.379	.451	134	22	7	2	1	.994	5	*C-116,D-14	3.5

YEAR	TM/L	G	AB	R	H	2B	3B	HR	RBI	BB	SO	AVG	OBP	SLG	PRO+	BR/A	SB	CS	SBR	FA	FR	G/POS	TPR
1991	Chi-A★	134	460	42	111	25	0	18	74	32	86	.241	.301	.413	98	-3	1	2	-1	.993	-2	*C-106,D-13,1-12	-0.1
1992	Chi-A	62	188	12	43	4	1	3	21	23	38	.229	.316	.309	77	-5	3	0	1	.993	-6	C-54/D-2	-0.7
1993	Chi-A	25	53	2	10	0	0	1	4	2	11	.189	.232	.245	29	-5	0	1	-1	1.000	-4	C-25	-0.9
Total	24	2499	8756	1276	2356	421	47	376	1330	849	1386	.269	.343	.457	116	176	128	58	4	.988	-44	*C-2229,D-166/O13	24.0

■ WES FISLER
Fisler, Weston Dickson "Icicle" b: 7/5/1841, Camden, N.J. d: 12/25/22, Philadelphia, Pa. 5'6", 137 lbs. Deb: 5/20/1871

YEAR	TM/L	G	AB	R	H	2B	3B	HR	RBI	BB	SO	AVG	OBP	SLG	PRO+	BR/A	SB	CS	SBR	FA	FR	G/POS	TPR
1871	Ath-n	28	147	43	41	8	2	0	16	3	2	.279	.293	.361	88	-2	6	3	0	**.972**	1	*1-26/2-2	0.0
1872	Ath-n	47	243	49	85	13	3	0	48	4	4	.350	.360	.428	141	11	3	0	1	.889	8	*2-47	1.1
1873	Ath-n	44	218	44	75	11	4	1	42	2	2	.344	.350	.445	125	5	2	1	0	**.855**	3	*2-36,1-10	0.3
1874	Ath-n	37	180	26	59	12	1	0	22	0	1	.328	.328	.406	123	3	2	0	1	.953	4	1-28/2-9,O-1	0.5
1875	Ath-n	58	268	54	74	13	3	0	31	4	4	.276	.287	.347	107	-0	1	4	-2	.958	-0	1-46,O-10/2-5	-0.2
1876	Phi-N	59	278	42	80	15	1	1	30	2	4	.288	.293	.360	117	5				.911	1	O-24,2-21,1-14,/S-1	0.4
Total	5 n	214	1056	216	334	57	13	1	159	13	13	.316	.325	.398	118	17	14	8	-1	.951	15	1-110/2-99,O-11	1.7

■ CHARLIE FITZBERGER
Fitzberger, Charles Casper b: 2/13/04, Baltimore, Md. d: 1/25/65, Baltimore, Md. BL/TL, 6'1.5", 170 lbs. Deb: 9/11/28

YEAR	TM/L	G	AB	R	H	2B	3B	HR	RBI	BB	SO	AVG	OBP	SLG	PRO+	BR/A	SB	CS	SBR	FA	FR	G/POS	TPR
1928	Bos-N	7	7	0	2	0	0	0	0	0	3	.286	.286	.286	52	-0	0			.000	0	H	0.0

■ DENNIS FITZGERALD
Fitzgerald, Dennis S. b: 3/1865, England d: 10/16/36, New Haven, Conn. 5'10", 160 lbs. Deb: 4/17/1890

YEAR	TM/L	G	AB	R	H	2B	3B	HR	RBI	BB	SO	AVG	OBP	SLG	PRO+	BR/A	SB	CS	SBR	FA	FR	G/POS	TPR
1890	Phi-a	2	8	0	2	0	0	0	0	0	0	.250	.250	.250	48	-1	0			.667	-2	/S-2	-0.2

■ ED FITZ GERALD
Fitz Gerald, Edward Raymond b: 5/21/24, Santa Ynez, Cal. BR/TR, 6', 180 lbs. Deb: 4/19/48 C

YEAR	TM/L	G	AB	R	H	2B	3B	HR	RBI	BB	SO	AVG	OBP	SLG	PRO+	BR/A	SB	CS	SBR	FA	FR	G/POS	TPR
1948	Pit-N	102	262	31	70	9	3	1	35	32	37	.267	.349	.336	84	-5	3			.961	-2	C-96	-0.1
1949	Pit-N	75	160	16	42	7	0	2	18	8	27	.262	.302	.344	71	-7	1			.974	-5	C-56	-0.9
1950	Pit-N	6	15	1	1	1	0	0	0	0	3	.067	.067	.133	-47	-3	0			.950	-1	/C-5	-0.3
1951	Pit-N	55	97	8	22	6	0	0	13	7	10	.227	.286	.289	53	-6	1	1	-0	.965	-2	C-38	-0.8
1952	Pit-N	51	73	4	17	1	0	1	7	7	15	.233	.300	.288	62	-4	0	2	-1	1.000	-1	C-18/3-2	-0.6
1953	Pit-N	6	17	2	2	1	0	0	1	0	2	.118	.118	.176	-25	-3	0	0	0	1.000	-1	/C-5	-0.4
	Was-A	88	288	23	72	13	0	3	39	19	34	.250	.299	.326	70	-12	2	1	0	.989	-3	C-85	-1.1
1954	Was-A	115	360	33	104	13	5	4	40	33	22	.289	.352	.386	108	3	0	1	-1	.973	-17	*C-107	-0.9
1955	Was-A	74	236	28	56	3	1	4	19	25	23	.237	.318	.309	73	-9	0	1	-0	.982	-7	C-72	-1.4
1956	Was-A	64	148	15	45	8	0	2	12	20	16	.304	.387	.399	108	2	0	0	0	.974	2	C-50	0.6
1957	Was-A	45	125	14	34	8	0	1	13	10	9	.272	.331	.360	90	-2	2	0	1	.963	-8	C-37	-0.7
1958	Was-A	58	114	7	30	3	0	0	11	8	15	.263	.311	.289	68	-5	0	0	0	.970	-6	C-21/1-5	-1.1
1959	Was-A	19	62	5	12	3	0	0	5	4	8	.194	.242	.242	34	-6	0	0	0	1.000	-1	C-16	-0.6
	Cle-A	49	129	12	35	6	1	1	4	12	14	.271	.343	.357	96	-1	0	0	0	.978	0	C-45	0.2
	Yr	68	191	17	47	9	1	1	9	16	22	.246	.311	.319	76	-6	0	0	0	.984	-1	C-61	-0.4
Total	12	807	2086	199	542	82	10	19	217	185	235	.260	.324	.336	80	-56	9	6		.975	-49	C-651/1-5,3-2	-8.2

■ HOWIE FITZGERALD
Fitzgerald, Howard Chumney "Lefty" b: 5/16/02, Eagle Lake, Tex. d: 2/27/59, Mathews, Tex. BL/TL, 5'11.5", 163 lbs. Deb: 9/17/22

YEAR	TM/L	G	AB	R	H	2B	3B	HR	RBI	BB	SO	AVG	OBP	SLG	PRO+	BR/A	SB	CS	SBR	FA	FR	G/POS	TPR
1922	Chi-N	10	24	3	8	1	0	0	4	3	2	.333	.407	.375	101	0	1	0	0	.818	-2	/O-6	-0.1
1924	Chi-N	7	19	1	3	0	0	0	2	0	2	.158	.158	.158	-15	-3	0	0	0	1.000	-2	/O-5	-0.5
1926	Bos-A	31	97	11	25	2	0	0	8	5	7	.258	.294	.278	51	-7	1	4	-2	.882	-5	O-23	-1.5
Total	3	48	140	15	36	3	0	0	14	8	11	.257	.297	.279	52	-10	2	4	-2	.878	-8	O-34	-2.1

■ MIKE FITZGERALD
Fitzgerald, Justin Howard b: 6/22/1890, San Mateo, Cal. d: 1/17/45, San Mateo, Cal. BL/TR, 5'8", 160 lbs. Deb: 6/20/11

YEAR	TM/L	G	AB	R	H	2B	3B	HR	RBI	BB	SO	AVG	OBP	SLG	PRO+	BR/A	SB	CS	SBR	FA	FR	G/POS	TPR
1911	NY-A	16	37	6	10	1	0	0	6	4		.270	.341	.297	74	-1	4			1.000	-0	/O-9	-0.3
1918	Phi-N	66	133	21	39	8	0	0	6	13	6	.293	.361	.353	110	2	3			.966	-14	/O-59	-1.6
Total	2	82	170	27	49	9	0	0	12	17	6	.288	.356	.341	102	1	7			.971	-15	/O-68	-1.9

■ MATTY FITZGERALD
Fitzgerald, Matthew William b: 8/31/1880, Albany, N.Y. d: 9/22/49, Albany, N.Y. BR/TR, 6', 185 lbs. Deb: 9/15/06

YEAR	TM/L	G	AB	R	H	2B	3B	HR	RBI	BB	SO	AVG	OBP	SLG	PRO+	BR/A	SB	CS	SBR	FA	FR	G/POS	TPR
1906	NY-N	4	6	2	4	0	0	0	2	0		.667	.667	.667	309	1	1			1.000	-1	/C-3	0.1
1907	NY-N	7	15	1	2	1	0	0	1	0		.133	.133	.200	4	-2	0			.952	-1	/C-6	-0.3
Total	2	11	21	3	6	1	0	0	3	0		.286	.286	.333	91	-0	1			.967	-2	/C-9	-0.2

■ MIKE FITZGERALD
Fitzgerald, Michael Patrick b: 3/28/64, Savannah, Ga. BR/TR, 6'1", 196 lbs. Deb: 6/23/88

YEAR	TM/L	G	AB	R	H	2B	3B	HR	RBI	BB	SO	AVG	OBP	SLG	PRO+	BR/A	SB	CS	SBR	FA	FR	G/POS	TPR
1988	StL-N	13	46	4	9	1	0	0	1	0	9	.196	.213	.217	23	-5	0	0	0	.990	-2	1-12	-0.8

■ MIKE FITZGERALD
Fitzgerald, Michael Roy b: 7/13/60, Long Beach, Cal. BR/TR, 5'11", 190 lbs. Deb: 9/13/83

YEAR	TM/L	G	AB	R	H	2B	3B	HR	RBI	BB	SO	AVG	OBP	SLG	PRO+	BR/A	SB	CS	SBR	FA	FR	G/POS	TPR
1983	NY-N	8	20	1	2	0	0	1	2	3	6	.100	.217	.250	29	-2	0	0	0	.957	2	/C-8	0.1
1984	NY-N	112	360	20	87	15	1	2	33	24	71	.242	.291	.306	69	-15	1	0	0	**.995**	8	*C-107	-0.2
1985	Mon-N	108	295	25	61	7	1	5	34	28	55	.207	.301	.288	70	-12	5	3	-0	.987	-6	*C-108	-1.3
1986	Mon-N	73	209	20	59	13	1	6	37	27	34	.282	.367	.440	123	7	3		-0	.993	-7	C-71	0.4
1987	Mon-N	107	287	32	69	11	0	3	36	42	54	.240	.339	.310	71	-11	3	4	-2	.981	-1	*C-104/1-1,2-1	-0.7
1988	Mon-N	63	155	17	42	6	1	5	23	19	22	.271	.351	.419	115	3	2	2	-1	.979	4	C-47/O-4	1.0
1989	Mon-N	100	290	33	69	18	0	7	42	35	61	.238	.324	.386	101	-0	0	3	-2	.984	-6	C-77/3-8,O-6	-0.3
1990	Mon-N	111	313	36	76	18	1	9	41	60	60	.243	.368	.393	114	8	8	1	2	.990	-4	C-98/O-6	1.2
1991	Mon-N	71	198	17	40	5	2	4	28	22	35	.202	.282	.308	67	-9	2	2	-1	.994	5	C-54/1-3,O-3	-0.4
1992	Cal-A	95	189	19	40	2	0	6	17	22	34	.212	.294	.317	71	-7	2	2	-1	.990	-15	C-74,O-11/3-3,12D	-2.0
Total	10	848	2316	220	545	95	9	48	293	292	432	.235	.323	.346	87	-37	31	20	-3	.988	-21	C-748/O-30,312D	-2.2

■ RAY FITZGERALD
Fitzgerald, Raymond Francis b: 12/5/04, Chicopee, Mass. d: 9/6/77, Westfield, Mass. BR/TR, 5'9", 168 lbs. Deb: 4/18/31

YEAR	TM/L	G	AB	R	H	2B	3B	HR	RBI	BB	SO	AVG	OBP	SLG	PRO+	BR/A	SB	CS	SBR	FA	FR	G/POS	TPR
1931	Cin-N	1	1	0	0	0	0	0	0	0	0	.000	.000	.000	-99	-0				.000	0	H	0.0

■ SHAUN FITZMAURICE
Fitzmaurice, Shaun Earle b: 8/25/42, Worcester, Mass. BR/TR, 6', 180 lbs. Deb: 9/9/66

YEAR	TM/L	G	AB	R	H	2B	3B	HR	RBI	BB	SO	AVG	OBP	SLG	PRO+	BR/A	SB	CS	SBR	FA	FR	G/POS	TPR
1966	NY-N	9	13	2	2	0	0	0		2	6	.154	.267	.154	21	-1	1	0	0	1.000	1	/O-5	-0.1

■ ED FITZPATRICK
Fitzpatrick, Edward Henry b: 12/9/1889, Lewistown, Pa. d: 10/23/65, Bethlehem, Pa. BR/TR, 5'8", 165 lbs. Deb: 4/17/15

YEAR	TM/L	G	AB	R	H	2B	3B	HR	RBI	BB	SO	AVG	OBP	SLG	PRO+	BR/A	SB	CS	SBR	FA	FR	G/POS	TPR
1915	Bos-N	105	303	54	67	19	3	0	24	43	36	.221	.344	.304	101	3	13	8	-1	.967	-5	2-71,O-29	-0.4
1916	Bos-N	83	216	17	46	8	0	1	18	15	26	.213	.280	.264	70	-7	5			.950	-12	2-46,O-28	-2.2
1917	Bos-N	63	178	20	45	8	4	0	17	12	22	.253	.318	.343	109	2	4			.929	-13	2-22,O-19,3-15	-1.2
Total	3	251	697	91	158	35	7	1	59	70	84	.227	.319	.301	94	-3	22	8		.956	-30	2-139/O-76,3-15	-3.8

■ TOM FITZSIMMONS
Fitzsimmons, Thomas William b: 4/6/1890, Oakland, Cal. d: 12/20/71, Oakland, Cal. BR/TR, 6'1", 190 lbs. Deb: 6/12/19

YEAR	TM/L	G	AB	R	H	2B	3B	HR	RBI	BB	SO	AVG	OBP	SLG	PRO+	BR/A	SB	CS	SBR	FA	FR	G/POS	TPR
1919	Bro-N	4	4	1	0	0	0	0	0	1	2	.000	.200	.000	-36	-1	0			.500	-1	/3-4	-0.2

■ MAX FLACK
Flack, Max John b: 2/5/1890, Belleville, Ill. d: 7/31/75, Belleville, Ill. BL/TL, 5'7", 148 lbs. Deb: 4/16/14

YEAR	TM/L	G	AB	R	H	2B	3B	HR	RBI	BB	SO	AVG	OBP	SLG	PRO+	BR/A	SB	CS	SBR	FA	FR	G/POS	TPR
1914	Chi-F	134	502	66	124	15	3	2	39	51	48	.247	.324	.301	75	-25	37			.973	-1	*O-133	-3.3
1915	Chi-F	141	523	88	164	20	14	3	45	40	21	.314	.365	.423	129	11	37			.969	2	*O-138	0.6
1916	Chi-N	141	465	65	120	14	3	2	20	42	43	.258	.320	.320	87	-7	24	19	-4	**.991**	2	*O-136	-1.8
1917	Chi-N	131	447	65	111	18	7	0	21	51	30	.248	.325	.320	91	-4	17			.947	-3	*O-117	-1.5
1918	*Chi-N	123	478	74	123	17	10	4	41	56	19	.257	.343	.360	112	8	17			.978	3	*O-121	0.4
1919	Chi-N	116	469	71	138	20	6	6	35	34	13	.294	.346	.392	121	12	18			.986	-0	*O-116	0.4
1920	Chi-N	135	520	85	157	30	6	4	49	52	15	.302	.373	.406	121	16	13	19	-8	.967	-5	*O-132	-0.8
1921	Chi-N	133	572	80	172	31	4	6	37	32	15	.301	.342	.400	96	-4	17	11	-2	**.989**	4	*O-130	-1.1
1922	Chi-N	17	54	7	12	1	0	0	6	2	4	.222	.250	.241	27	-6	2			.933	-2	O-15	-0.9
	StL-N	66	267	46	78	12	1	2	21	31	11	.292	.368	.367	95	-1	3	5	-2	.968	-4	O-66	-1.2
	Yr	83	321	53	90	13	1	2	27	33	15	.280	.349	.346	83	-8	5	6	-2	.961	-6	O-81	-2.1
1923	StL-N	128	505	82	147	16	9	3	28	41	16	.291	.348	.376	93	-5	7	8	-3	.951	-6	*O-121	-2.0
1924	StL-N	67	209	31	55	11	3	2	21	21	5	.263	.330	.373	90	-3	5	3	-2	.971	1	O-52	-0.7
1925	StL-N	79	241	23	60	7	2	3	28	21	9	.249	.309	.344	65	-13	3	3	-0	.991	-2	O-59	-1.8
Total	12	1411	5252	783	1461	212	72	35	391	474	253	.278	.342	.366	99	-21	200	71		.972	-12	*O-1336	-13.7

YEAR	TM/L	G	AB	R	H	2B	3B	HR	RBI	BB	SO	AVG	OBP	SLG	PRO+	BR/A	SB	CS	SBR	FA	FR	G/POS	TPR

■ WALLY FLAGER
Flager, Walter Leonard b: 11/3/21, Chicago Heights, Ill. d: 12/16/90, Keizer, Ore. BL/TR, 5'11", 160 lbs. Deb: 4/17/45

1945	Cin-N	21	52	5	11	1	0	0	6	8	5	.212	.317	.231	55	-3	0			.933	-7	S-15	-0.9
	Phi-N	49	168	21	42	4	1	2	15	17	15	.250	.323	.321	82	-4	1			.946	1	S-48/2-1	0.1
	Yr	70	220	26	53	5	1	2	21	25	20	.241	.321	.300	75	-7	1			.943	-6	S-63/2-1	-0.8

■ IRA FLAGSTEAD
Flagstead, Ira James "Pete" b: 9/22/1893, Montague, Mich. d: 3/13/40, Olympia, Wash. BR/TR, 5'9", 165 lbs. Deb: 7/20/17

1917	Det-A	4	4	0	0	0	0	0	0	0	1	.000	.000	.000	-99	-1	0			.000	-1	/O-2	-0.2
1919	Det-A	97	287	43	95	22	3	5	41	35	39	.331	.416	.481	155	22	6			.951	2	O-83	1.9
1920	Det-A	110	311	40	73	13	5	3	35	37	27	.235	.318	.338	76	-11	3	4	-2	.967	7	O-82	-1.2
1921	Det-A	85	259	40	79	16	2	0	31	21	21	.305	.371	.382	93	-2	8	4	0	.903	-5	S-55,O-12/2-8,3-1	-0.3
1922	Det-A	44	91	21	28	5	3	3	8	14	16	.308	.411	.527	148	7	0	1	-1	.967	-2	O-32	0.3
1923	Det-A	1	1	0	0	0	0	0	0	0	0	.000	.000	.000	-99	-0	0			.000	-0	H	0.0
	Bos-A	109	382	55	119	23	4	8	53	37	26	.312	.380	.455	119	10	7	10	-4	.965	19	*O-102/S-1	1.7
	Yr	110	383	55	119	23	4	8	53	37	26	.311	.379	.454	118	10	7	10	-4	.965	19	*O-102/S-1	1.7
1924	Bos-A	149	560	106	172	35	7	5	43	77	41	.307	.401	.421	112	13	10	13	-5	.975	-2	*O-144	-0.3
1925	Bos-A	148	572	84	160	38	2	6	61	63	30	.280	.356	.385	88	-10	5	6	-2	.976	**20**	*O-144	-0.2
1926	Bos-A	98	415	65	124	31	7	3	31	36	22	.299	.363	.429	109	5	4	6	-2	.982	9	O-98	0.4
1927	Bos-A	131	466	63	133	26	8	4	69	57	25	.285	.374	.401	103	4	12	2	2	**.986**	11	*O-129	0.8
1928	Bos-A	140	510	84	148	41	4	1	39	60	23	.290	.366	.392	101	2	12	9	-2	.973	5	*O-135	-0.3
1929	Bos-A	14	36	9	11	2	0	0	3	5	1	.306	.390	.361	97	0	1	3	-2	.955	-3	O-13	-0.5
	Was-A	18	39	5	7	1	0	0	9	4	5	.179	.256	.205	20	-5	1	0	0	.971	4	O-11	-0.2
	Yr	32	75	14	18	3	0	0	12	9	6	.240	.321	.280	57	-5	2	3	-1	.965	0	O-24	-0.7
	Pit-N	26	50	8	14	2	1	0	6	4	2	.280	.333	.360	70	-2	1			1.000	0	/O-9	-0.2
1930	Pit-N	44	156	21	39	7	4	2	21	17	9	.250	.324	.385	70	-8	1			.961	-3	O-40	-1.2
Total	13	1218	4139	644	1202	262	50	40	450	467	288	.290	.370	.407	103	23	71	58		.974	59	*O-1036/S-56,2-8,3	0.5

■ JOHN FLAHERTY
Flaherty, John Timothy b: 10/21/67, New York, N.Y. BR/TR, 6'1", 195 lbs. Deb: 4/12/92

1992	Bos-A	35	66	3	13	2	0	0	2	3	7	.197	.232	.227	27	-6	0	0	0	.982	-3	C-34	-0.9
1993	Bos-A	13	25	3	3	0	0	0	2	2	6	.120	.214	.200	11	-3	0	0	0	1.000	1	C-13	-0.4
1994	Det-A	34	40	2	6	1	0	0	4	1	11	.150	.171	.175	-11	-7	0	1	-1	1.000	6	C-33/D-1	-0.1
1995	Det-A	112	354	39	86	22	1	11	40	18	47	.243	.285	.404	77	-13	0	0	0	.982	-10	*C-112	-1.5
1996	Det-A	47	152	18	38	12	0	4	23	8	25	.250	.292	.408	75	-6	1	0	0	.981	-13	C-46	-1.4
	*SD-N	72	264	22	80	12	0	9	41	9	36	.303	.331	.451	109	2	2	3	-1	.990	-7	C-72	-0.1
Total	5	313	901	87	226	51	1	24	112	41	132	.251	.289	.390	76	-33	3	4	-2	.986	-28	C-310/D-1	-4.4

■ MARTIN FLAHERTY
Flaherty, Martin J. b: 9/24/1853, Worcester, Mass. d: 6/10/20, Providence, R.I. BL/TL, Deb: 8/18/1881

| 1881 | Wor-N | 1 | 2 | 0 | 0 | 0 | 0 | 0 | 0 | 0 | 2 | .000 | .000 | .000 | -95 | -0 | | | | .000 | -1 | /O-1 | -0.2 |

■ PAT FLAHERTY
Flaherty, Patrick Henry b: 1/31/1866, St.Louis, Mo. d: 1/28/46, Chicago, Ill. 5'9", 166 lbs. Deb: 7/11/1894

| 1894 | Lou-N | 38 | 145 | 15 | 43 | 5 | 3 | 0 | 15 | 9 | 6 | .297 | .342 | .372 | 77 | -5 | 2 | | | .855 | -5 | 3-38 | -0.8 |

■ PATSY FLAHERTY
Flaherty, Patrick Joseph b: 6/29/1876, Mansfield, Pa. d: 1/23/68, Alexandria, La. BL/TL, 5'8", 165 lbs. Deb: 9/8/1899

1899	Lou-N	7	24	3	5	1	1	0	6	3		.208	.296	.333	73	-1	0			.692	-1	/P-5,O-2	0.0
1900	Pit-N	4	9	0	1	0	0	0	0	0	1	.111	.200	.111	-13	-1	0			1.000	1	/P-4	0.0
1903	Chi-A	40	102	7	14	4	0	0	5	5		.137	.178	.176	7	-11	4			.914	3	P-40	0.0
1904	Chi-A	5	12	1	4	1	0	0	0	4		.333	.500	.417	199	2	0			.880	1	/P-5	0.0
	Pit-N	36	104	9	22	3	4	2	19	8		.212	.268	.375	95	-1	0			.965	5	P-29/O-2	0.0
1905	Pit-N	30	76	7	15	4	0	0	4	3		.197	.228	.303	56	-4	0			.894	2	P-27/O-2	-0.1
1907	Bos-N	41	115	9	22	3	2	2	11	2		.191	.212	.304	62	-6	1			.907	3	P-27/O-8	-0.1
1908	Bos-N	32	86	8	12	0	5	0	5	6		.140	.196	.186	22	-8	0			.961	0	P-31	0.0
1910	Phi-N	2	2	0	1	0	0	0	0	0		.500	.500	.500	186	0	0			.000	0	/P-1,O-1	0.0
1911	Bos-N	38	94	9	27	3	2	2	20	8	11	.287	.343	.426	106	0	2			.933	-4	O-19/P-4	-0.4
Total	9	235	624	53	123	19	13	6	70	40	11	.197	.247	.298	63	-30	9			.921	11	P-173/O-34	-0.6

■ AL FLAIR
Flair, Albert Dell "Broadway" b: 7/24/16, New Orleans, La. d: 7/25/88, New Orleans, La. BL/TL, 6'4", 195 lbs. Deb: 9/6/41

| 1941 | Bos-A | 10 | 30 | 3 | 6 | 2 | 1 | 0 | 2 | 1 | 1 | .200 | .226 | .333 | 45 | -3 | 1 | 1 | -0 | 1.000 | -0 | /1-8 | -0.3 |

■ CHARLIE FLANAGAN
Flanagan, Charles James b: 12/31/1891, Oakland, Cal. d: 1/8/30, San Francisco, Cal. BR/TR, 6', 175 lbs. Deb: 7/9/13

| 1913 | StL-A | 4 | 3 | 0 | 0 | 0 | 0 | 0 | 1 | 0 | | .000 | .250 | .000 | -26 | -1 | 0 | | | 1.000 | -1 | /3-1,O-1 | 0.0 |

■ ED FLANAGAN
Flanagan, Edward J. "Sleepy" b: 9/15/1861, Lowell, Mass. d: 11/10/26, Lowell, Mass. 6'1", 190 lbs. Deb: 4/16/1887

1887	Phi-a	19	80	12	20	5	0	1	10	3		.250	.286	.350	77	-3	3			.948	-1	1-19	-0.5
1889	Lou-a	23	88	11	22	7	3	0	8	7	11	.250	.305	.398	101	-0	1			.953	-1	1-23	-0.2
Total	2	42	168	23	42	12	3	1	18	10	11	.250	.296	.375	89	-3	4			.951	-2	/1-42	-0.7

■ STEAMER FLANAGAN
Flanagan, James Paul b: 4/20/1881, Kingston, Pa. d: 4/21/47, Wilkes-Barre, Pa. BL/TL, 6'1", 185 lbs. Deb: 9/25/05

| 1905 | Pit-N | 7 | 25 | 7 | 7 | 1 | 0 | 3 | 1 | | .280 | .308 | .400 | 108 | 0 | 3 | | | 1.000 | 1 | /O-5 | 0.1 |

■ JOHN FLANNERY
Flannery, John Michael b: 1/25/57, Long Beach, Cal. BR/TR, 6'3", 173 lbs. Deb: 9/2/77

| 1977 | Chi-A | 7 | 2 | 1 | 0 | 0 | 0 | 0 | 0 | 1 | 0 | .000 | .333 | .000 | -0 | 0 | 0 | 0 | 0 | 1.000 | 1 | /S-4,3-1,D-1 | 0.1 |

■ TIM FLANNERY
Flannery, Timothy Earl b: 9/29/57, Tulsa, Okla. BL/TR, 5'11", 175 lbs. Deb: 9/3/79 C

1979	SD-N	22	65	2	10	0	1	0	4	4	5	.154	.225	.185	14	-8	0	0	0	.991	2	2-21	-0.4
1980	SD-N	95	292	15	70	12	6	0	25	18	30	.240	.284	.281	62	-15	2	2	-1	.988	-4	2-53,3-41	-1.9
1981	SD-N	37	67	4	17	4	1	0	6	2	4	.254	.275	.343	80	-2	1	0	0	.967	-1	3-15/2-7	-0.3
1982	SD-N	122	379	40	100	11	7	0	30	30	32	.264	.321	.330	87	-7	4	5	1	.974	-24	*2-104/3-5,S-2	-2.7
1983	SD-N	92	214	24	50	7	3	3	19	20	23	.234	.314	.336	83	-5	2	1	-2	.969	10	3-52,2-21/S-7	0.5
1984	*SD-N	86	128	24	35	3	3	2	10	12	17	.273	.350	.391	108	2	4	1	-2	.944	-6	2-22,3-14,S-14	-0.2
1985	SD-N	126	384	50	108	14	3	1	40	58	39	.281	.388	.341	107	7	2	5	-2	.977	-19	*2-121/3-1	-1.1
1986	SD-N	134	368	48	103	11	2	3	28	54	61	.280	.379	.345	103	4	3	6	-3	.993	-7	*2-108,3-23/S-8	-0.2
1987	SD-N	106	276	23	63	5	1	0	20	42	30	.228	.334	.254	61	-14	2	4	-2	.986	3	2-84/3-8,S-2	-0.9
1988	SD-N	79	170	16	45	5	4	0	19	24	32	.265	.369	.341	107	3	2	3	-0	.972	-4	3-51/2-2,S-1	-0.2
1989	SD-N	73	130	9	30	5	0	0	8	13	20	.231	.301	.269	64	-6	0	0	1	.920	2	3-33/2-1	-0.4
Total	11	972	2473	255	631	77	25	9	209	277	293	.255	.338	.317	86	-41	22	22	-7	.982	-47	2-544,3-243/S-34	-7.8

■ ROY FLASKAMPER
Flaskamper, Raymond Harold "Flash" b: 10/31/01, St.Louis, Mo. d: 2/3/78, San Antonio, Tex. BB/TR, 5'7", 140 lbs. Deb: 8/16/27

| 1927 | Chi-A | 26 | 95 | 12 | 21 | 5 | 0 | 0 | 8 | 13 | 8 | .221 | .260 | .274 | 40 | -9 | 0 | 0 | 0 | .962 | 0 | S-25 | -0.6 |

■ FRANK FLEET
Fleet, Frank H. b: 1848, New York, N.Y. d: 6/13/1900, New York, N.Y. Deb: 10/18/1871

1871	Mut-n	1	6	1	2	0	0	0		0	0	.333	.333	.333	101	0	0	0	0	1.000	1	/P-1	0.0
1872	Eck-n	13	53	10	13	1	0	0	5	0	1	.245	.245	.264	67	-1	1	0	0	.760	3	3-10/2-2,O-2	0.1
1873	Res-n	22	90	11	23	2	0	0	10	1	2	.256	.264	.278	66	-3	0	1	-1	.864	1	2-9,S-9,P-3,3-2,1	-0.3
1874	Atl-n	22	97	18	22	0	0	0	10	1	1	.227	.235	.227	55	-4	0	0	0	.759	-4	C-13,2-11/O-1	-0.6
1875	StL-n	4	16	1	1	0	0	0	0	0		.063	.063	.063	-62	-2	0			.900	-0	/P-3,3-1,O-1	-0.1
	Atl-n	26	111	13	25	2	0	0	9	1	1	.225	.232	.243	75	-2	1	0	0	.719	-8	C-11,2-10/S-9,P3	-0.9
	Yr	30	127	14	26	2	0	0	9	1	1	.205	.211	.220	57	-4	1	0	0	.719	-8	C-11,2-10/S-9,P3O	-1.0
Total	5 n	88	373	54	86	5	0	0	36	3	5	.231	.237	.244	61	-13	2	1	0	.782	-6	/2-32,C-24,S3PO1	-1.8

■ ANGEL FLEITAS
Fleitas, Angel Felix Husta b: 11/10/14, Los Abreus, Cuba BR/TR, 5'9", 160 lbs. Deb: 7/5/48

| 1948 | Was-A | 15 | 13 | 1 | 1 | 0 | 0 | 0 | 1 | 3 | 5 | .077 | .250 | .077 | -11 | -2 | 0 | 2 | -1 | .952 | 3 | /S-7 | 0.0 |

YEAR	TM/L	G	AB	R	H	2B	3B	HR	RBI	BB	SO	AVG	OBP	SLG	PRO+	BR/A	SB	CS	SBR	FA	FR	G/POS	TPR

■ LES FLEMING Fleming, Leslie Harvey "Moe" b: 8/7/15, Singleton, Tex. d: 3/5/80, Cleveland, Tex. BL/TL, 5'10", 185 lbs. Deb: 4/22/39

1939	Det-A	8	16	0	0	0	0	0	1	0	4	.000	.000	.000	-93	-5	0	0	0	1.000	-0	/O-3	-0.5
1941	Cle-A	2	8	0	2	1	0	0	2	0	0	.250	.250	.375	67	-0	0	0	0	1.000	-0	/1-2	-0.1
1942	Cle-A	156	548	71	160	27	4	14	82	106	57	.292	.412	.432	146	38	6	8	-3	**.993**	-9	*1-156	1.7
1945	Cle-A	42	140	18	46	10	2	3	22	11	5	.329	.382	.493	160	10	0	0	0	.938	-2	O-33/1-5	0.6
1946	Cle-A	99	306	40	85	17	5	5	42	50	42	.278	.383	.444	140	17	1	0	0	.984	3	1-80/O-1	1.6
1947	Cle-A	103	281	39	68	14	2	4	43	53	42	.242	.362	.349	101	2	0	0	0	.989	4	1-77	0.3
1949	Pit-N	24	31	0	8	0	2	0	7	6	2	.258	.395	.387	108	1	0			1.000	-1	/1-5	0.0
Total	7	434	1330	168	369	69	15	29	199	226	152	.277	.386	.417	131	63	7	8		.990	-6	1-325/O-37	3.6

■ TOM FLEMING Fleming, Thomas Vincent "Sleuth" b: 11/20/1873, Philadelphia, Pa. d: 12/26/57, Boston, Mass. BL/TL, 5'11", 155 lbs. Deb: 9/19/1899

1899	NY-N	22	77	9	16	1	1	0	4	1		.208	.218	.247	28	-8	1			.909	-1	O-22	-0.9
1902	Phi-N	5	16	2	6	0	0	0	2	1		.375	.412	.375	143	1	0			1.000	0	/O-5	0.1
1904	Phi-N	3	6	0	0	0	0	0	0	0		.000	.000	.000	-99	-1	0			1.000	-0	/O-1	-0.1
Total	3	30	99	11	22	1	1	0	6	2		.222	.238	.253	39	-8	1			.920	-0	/O-28	-0.9

■ ART FLETCHER Fletcher, Arthur b: 1/5/1885, Collinsville, Ill. d: 2/6/50, Los Angeles, Cal. BR/TR, 5'10.5", 170 lbs. Deb: 4/15/09 MC

1909	NY-N	33	98	7	21	0	0	0	6	1		.214	.238	.235	46	-6	0			.893	4	S-22/2-7,3-6	-0.2
1910	NY-N	51	125	12	28	2	1	0	13	4	9	.224	.248	.256	47	-9	9			.895	-5	S-22,2-11,3-11	-1.4
1911	*NY-N	112	326	73	104	17	8	3	37	30	27	.319	.400	.429	128	13	20			.926	4	S-74,3-21,2-13	2.2
1912	*NY-N	129	419	64	118	17	9	1	57	16	29	.282	.330	.372	89	-7	16			.927	16	*S-126/2-2,3-1	1.9
1913	*NY-N	136	538	76	160	20	9	4	71	24	35	.297	.345	.390	109	6	32			.932	-7	*S-136	1.1
1914	NY-N	135	514	62	147	26	8	3	79	22	37	.286	.332	.379	115	8	15			.922	6	*S-135	2.7
1915	NY-N	149	562	59	143	17	7	3	74	6	36	.254	.280	.326	88	-10	12	18	-7	.936	**34**	*S-149	3.0
1916	NY-N	133	500	53	143	23	8	3	66	13	36	.286	.323	.382	122	11	15			.940	20	*S-133	4.3
1917	*NY-N	151	557	70	145	24	5	4	56	23	28	.260	.312	.343	104	2	12			**.956**	27	*S-151	4.1
1918	NY-N	124	468	51	123	20	2	0	47	18	26	.263	.311	.314	93	-4	12			**.959**	22	*S-124	2.6
1919	NY-N	127	484	54	135	20	5	3	54	9	28	.279	.300	.357	98	-3	6			.944	24	*S-127	3.2
1920	NY-N	41	171	21	44	7	2	0	24	1	15	.257	.282	.322	74	-6	3	2	-0	.914	-2	S-41	-0.5
	Phi-N	102	379	36	112	25	7	4	38	15	28	.296	.329	.430	112	5	4	6	-2	.958	12	*S-102	2.4
	Yr	143	550	57	156	32	9	4	62	16	43	.284	.315	.396	100	-1	7	8	-3	.945	10	*S-143	1.9
1922	Phi-N	110	396	46	111	20	5	7	53	21	14	.280	.325	.409	80	-13	3	2	-0	.939	7	*S-106	0.4
Total	13	1533	5541	684	1534	238	77	32	675	203	348	.277	.319	.365	100	-14	159	28		.939	162	*S-1448/3-39,2-33	25.8

■ DARRIN FLETCHER Fletcher, Darrin Glen b: 10/3/66, Elmhurst, Ill. BL/TR, 6'2", 195 lbs. Deb: 9/10/89 F

1989	LA-N	5	8	1	4	0	0	1	2	1	0	.500	.556	.875	308	2	0	0	0	1.000	0	/C-5	0.2
1990	LA-N	2	1	0	0	0	0	0	0	0	1	.000	.000	.000	-99	-0	0	0	0			/C-1	0.0
	Phi-N	9	22	3	3	1	0	0	1	1	5	.136	.174	.182	-2	-3	0	0	0	1.000	1	/C-6	-0.2
	Yr	11	23	3	3	1	0	0	1	1	6	.130	.167	.174	-6	-3	0	0	0	1.000	1	/C-7	-0.2
1991	Phi-N	46	136	5	31	8	0	1	12	5	15	.228	.255	.309	59	-8	0	1	-1	.992	3	C-45	-0.3
1992	Mon-N	83	222	13	54	10	2	2	26	14	28	.243	.294	.333	78	-7	0	2	-1	.995	-0	C-69	-0.5
1993	Mon-N	133	396	33	101	20	1	9	60	34	40	.255	.320	.379	84	-9	0	0	0	.988	-10	*C-127	-1.3
1994	Mon-N★	94	285	28	74	18	1	10	57	25	23	.260	.326	.435	95	-2	0	0	0	**.996**	-8	C-81	-0.6
1995	Mon-N	110	350	42	100	21	1	11	45	32	23	.286	.352	.446	105	3	0	1	-1	.994	-3	C-98	0.6
1996	Mon-N	127	394	41	105	22	0	12	57	27	42	.266	.320	.414	90	-6	0	0	0	.992	-17	*C-112	-1.5
Total	8	609	1814	166	472	100	5	46	260	139	177	.260	.320	.397	89	-30	0	4	-2	.993	-35	C-544	-3.6

■ ELBIE FLETCHER Fletcher, Elburt Preston b: 3/18/16, Milton, Mass. d: 3/9/94, Milton, Mass. BL/TL, 6', 180 lbs. Deb: 9/16/34

1934	Bos-N	8	4	4	2	0	0	0	0	2		.500	.500	.500	182	0	1			.875	-0	/1-1	0.0
1935	Bos-N	39	148	12	35	7	1	1	9	7	13	.236	.271	.318	63	-8	1			.997	2	1-39	-1.0
1937	Bos-N	148	539	56	133	22	4	1	38	56	64	.247	.321	.308	79	-16	3			.993	1	*1-148	-3.2
1938	Bos-N	147	529	71	144	24	7	6	48	60	40	.272	.351	.378	112	8	5			.990	10	*1-146	0.3
1939	Bos-N	35	106	14	26	2	0	0	6	19	5	.245	.365	.264	77	-2	1			.986	-5	1-31	-1.1
	Pit-N	102	370	49	112	23	4	12	71	48	28	.303	.386	.484	134	18	3			.993	-4	*1-101	0.4
	Yr	137	476	63	138	25	4	12	77	67	33	.290	.381	.435	122	16	4			.991	-9	*1-132	-0.7
1940	Pit-N	147	510	94	139	22	7	16	104	**119**	54	.273	**.418**	.437	137	33	5			.993	4	*1-147	2.3
1941	Pit-N	151	521	95	150	29	13	11	74	**118**	54	.288	**.421**	.457	148	39	5			.991	9	*1-151	3.7
1942	Pit-N	145	506	86	146	22	5	7	57	105	60	.289	**.417**	.393	134	28	0			.992	12	*1-144	3.2
1943	Pit-N★	154	544	91	154	24	5	9	70	95	49	.283	.395	.395	124	21	1			**.996**	3	*1-154	1.6
1946	Pit-N	148	532	72	136	25	8	4	66	111	37	.256	.384	.355	108	10	4			.995	1	*1-147	0.3
1947	Pit-N	69	157	22	38	9	1	1	22	29	24	.242	.364	.331	83	-3	2			.986	-0	1-50	-0.4
1949	Bos-N	122	413	57	108	19	3	11	51	84	65	.262	.396	.402	121	16	1			.991	0	*1-121	1.5
Total	12	1415	4879	723	1323	228	58	79	616	851	495	.271	.384	.390	118	145	32			.993	33	*1-1380	7.6

■ GEORGE FLETCHER Fletcher, George Horace Ellis b: 4/21/1845, Deb: 6/21/1872

| 1872 | Eck-n | 2 | 8 | 1 | 3 | 0 | 0 | 0 | | | | .375 | .375 | .375 | 155 | 1 | 0 | 0 | 0 | .500 | -1 | /O-2 | 0.0 |

■ FRANK FLETCHER Fletcher, Oliver Frank b: 3/6/1891, Hildreth, Ill. d: 10/7/74, St.Petersburg, Fla. BR/TR, 5'10", 165 lbs. Deb: 7/14/14

| 1914 | Phi-N | 1 | 1 | 0 | 0 | 0 | 0 | 0 | 0 | 0 | | .000 | .000 | .000 | -94 | -0 | 0 | | | .000 | 0 | H | 0.0 |

■ SCOTT FLETCHER Fletcher, Scott Brian b: 7/30/58, Fort Walton Beach, Fla. BR/TR, 5'11", 173 lbs. Deb: 4/25/81

1981	Chi-N	19	46	6	10	4	0	0	1	2	4	.217	.250	.304	54	-3	0	0	0	.972	6	2-13/S-4,3-1	0.4
1982	Chi-N	11	24	4	4	0	0	1	4	5		.167	.286	.167	29	-2	1	0	0	1.000	-0	S-11	-0.2
1983	*Chi-A	114	262	42	62	16	5	3	31	29	22	.237	.317	.370	85	-5	5	1	1	.965	18	*S-100,2-12/3-7,D-1	2.2
1984	Chi-A	149	456	46	114	13	3	3	35	46	46	.250	.329	.311	75	-14	10	4	1	.973	-4	*S-134,2-28/3-3	-0.1
1985	Chi-A	119	301	38	77	8	1	2	31	35	47	.256	.333	.309	74	-10	5	5	-2	.934	-3	3-55,S-44,2-37/D-2	-1.1
1986	Tex-A	147	530	82	159	34	5	3	50	47	59	.300	.360	.400	104	4	12	11	-3	.973	-6	*S-136,3-12,2-11/D	0.7
1987	Tex-A	156	588	82	169	28	4	5	63	61	66	.287	.359	.374	95	-3	13	12	-3	.966	3	*S-155	1.2
1988	Tex-A	140	515	59	142	19	4	0	47	62	34	.276	.367	.328	94	-1	8	5	-1	.983	1	*S-139	1.1
1989	Tex-A	83	314	47	75	14	1	0	22	38	41	.239	.325	.290	73	-10	1	1	-0	.960	-18	S-81	-2.2
	Chi-A	59	232	30	63	11	1	1	21	26	19	.272	.347	.341	97	-0	1	1	-0	1.000	-3	2-53/S-8,D-1	-0.1
	Yr	142	546	77	138	25	2	1	43	64	60	.253	.334	.311	83	-10	2	2		.957	-21	S-89,2-53/D-1	-2.3
1990	Chi-A	151	509	54	123	18	3	4	56	45	63	.242	.307	.312	75	-16	1	2	-0	.988	-6	*2-151	-2.3
1991	Chi-A	90	248	14	51	10	1	1	28	17	26	.206	.265	.266	48	-17	0	2	-1	.992	-6	2-86/3-4	-2.3
1992	Mil-A	123	386	53	106	18	3	3	51	30	33	.275	.328	.360	98	-1	17	10	-1	.992	10	*2-106,S-22/3-1	1.1
1993	Bos-A	121	480	81	137	31	2	5	45	37	35	.285	.343	.402	94	-4	16	3	3	.982	5	*2-116/S-2,3-1,D-1	0.7
1994	Bos-A	63	185	31	42	9	1	1	11	16	14	.227	.296	.335	59	-11	8	1	2	.996	19	2-53/D-4	1.1
1995	Det-A	67	182	19	42	10	1	1	17	19	27	.231	.314	.313	64	-5	4	2	-0	1.000	-3	2-63/S-3,1-1,D-1	0.3
Total	15	1612	5258	688	1376	243	38	34	510	514	541	.262	.334	.342	84	-104	99	58	-5	.971	30	S-839,2-729/3D1	0.6

■ ELMER FLICK Flick, Elmer Harrison b: 1/11/1876, Bedford, Ohio d: 1/9/71, Bedford, Ohio BL/TR, 5'9", 168 lbs. Deb: 5/2/1898 H

1898	Phi-N	134	453	84	137	16	13	6	81	86		.302	.430	.448	158	40	23			.931	7	*O-133	3.5
1899	Phi-N	127	485	98	166	22	11	2	98	42		.342	.407	.445	139	27	31			.931	9	*O-125	2.4
1900	Phi-N	138	545	106	200	32	16	11	**110**	56		.367	.441	.545	173	**55**	35			.914	3	*O-138	4.3
1901	Phi-N	138	540	112	180	32	17	8	88	52		.333	.399	.500	157	39	30			.962	15	*O-138	4.2
1902	Phi-A	11	37	15	11	2	1	0	3	6		.297	.435	.405	128	2	4			.947	-0	O-11	0.1
	Cle-A	110	424	70	126	19	11	2	61	47		.297	.371	.408	121	13	20			.929	-4	*O-110	0.1
	Yr	121	461	85	137	21	12	2	64	53		.297	.377	.408	121	15	24			.930	-4	*O-121	0.2
1903	Cle-A	140	523	81	155	23	16	2	51	51		.296	.368	.413	136	24	24			.955	1	*O-140	1.7
1904	Cle-A	150	579	97	177	31	17	6	56	51		.306	.371	.449	160	40	**38**			.955	10	*O-145/2-6	4.5
1905	Cle-A	132	500	72	154	29	**18**	4	64	53		**.308**	.383	**.462**	165	37	35			.939	1	*O-131/2-1	3.4

YEAR	TM/L	G	AB	R	H	2B	3B	HR	RBI	BB	SO	AVG	OBP	SLG	PRO+	BR/A	SB	CS	SBR	FA	FR	G/POS	TPR
1906	Cle-A	157	624	**98**	194	34	**22**	1	62	54		.311	.372	.441	156	40	**39**			.981	-12	*O-150/2-8	2.3
1907	Cle-A	147	549	80	166	15	**18**	3	58	64		.302	.386	.412	153	35	41			.956	1	*O-147	3.3
1908	Cle-A	9	35	4	8	1	1	0	2	3		.229	.289	.314	96	-0	0			1.000	-0	/O-9	-0.1
1909	Cle-A	66	235	28	60	10	2	0	15	22		.255	.322	.315	97	-0	9			.958	-4	O-61	-0.7
1910	Cle-A	24	68	5	18	2	1	0	7	10		.265	.359	.368	126	2	1			.955	-3	O-18	-0.2
Total	13	1483	5597	950	1752	268	164	48	756	597		.313	.389	.445	149	353	330			.947	23	*O-1456/2-15	28.8

■ **LEW FLICK**   Flick, Lewis Miller "Noisy"   b: 2/18/15, Bristol, Tenn.   d: 12/7/90, Weber City, Va.   BL/TL, 5'9", 155 lbs.   Deb: 9/28/43

1943	Phi-A	1	5	2	3	0	0	0	0	0	0	.600	.600	.600	253	1	0	0	0	1.000	0	/O-1	0.1
1944	Phi-A	19	35	1	4	0	0	0	2	1	2	.114	.139	.114	-28	-6	1	0	0	1.000	-1	/O-6	-0.7
Total	2	20	40	3	7	0	0	0	2	1	2	.175	.195	.175	6	-5	1	0	0	1.000	-1	/O-7	-0.6

■ **DON FLINN**   Flinn, Don Raphael   b: 11/17/1892, Bluff Dale, Tex.   d: 3/9/59, Waco, Tex.   BR/TR, 6'1", 185 lbs.   Deb: 9/2/17

1917	Pit-N	14	37	1	11	1	1	0	1	1	6	.297	.316	.378	109	0	1			1.000	0	O-12	0.0

■ **SILVER FLINT**   Flint, Frank Sylvester   b: 8/3/1855, Philadelphia, Pa.   d: 1/14/1892, Chicago, Ill.   BR/TR, 6', 180 lbs.   Deb: 5/4/1875 M

1875	RS-n	17	61	4	5	0	0	0	1	1	10	.082	.097	.082	-41	-8	2	0	1	.820	-2	C-16/O-2,3-1	-0.7
1878	Ind-N	63	254	23	57	7	0	0	18	2	15	.224	.230	.252	67	-8				.908	-1	*C-59/O-9	-0.8
1879	Chi-N	79	324	46	92	22	6	1	41	6	44	.284	.297	.398	120	6				.915	3	*C-78/O-1,M	1.0
1880	Chi-N	74	284	30	46	10	4	0	17	5	32	.162	.176	.225	33	-20				**.934**	8	*C-67,O-13	-1.0
1881	Chi-N	80	306	46	95	18	0	1	34	6	39	.310	.324	.379	115	4				.938	-5	*C-80/O-8,1-1	-0.1
1882	Chi-N	81	331	48	83	18	8	4	44	2	50	.251	.255	.390	99	-1				.935	-4	*C-81,O-10	-0.1
1883	Chi-N	85	332	57	88	23	4	0	32	3	69	.265	.272	.358	85	-7				.877	-8	*C-83,O-23	-0.9
1884	Chi-N	73	279	35	57	5	2	9	45	7	57	.204	.224	.333	67	-12				.884	-2	C-73	-0.6
1885	*Chi-N	68	249	27	52	8	2	1	17	2	52	.209	.215	.269	49	-16				**.927**	14	*C-68/O-1	0.3
1886	*Chi-N	54	173	30	35	6	2	1	13	12	36	.202	.254	.277	53	-11	1			.893	15	C-54/1-3	0.8
1887	Chi-N	49	187	22	50	8	6	3	21	4	28	.267	.283	.422	83	-6	7			.909	3	C-47/1-2	0.1
1888	Chi-N	22	77	6	14	3	0	0	3	1	21	.182	.203	.221	33	-6	1			.926	-2	C-22	-0.6
1889	Chi-N	15	56	6	13	1	0	1	9	3	18	.232	.271	.304	58	-3	1			.903	-1	C-15	-0.3
Total	12	743	2852	376	682	129	34	21	294	53	461	.239	.253	.330	78	-80	10	0		.913	19	C-727/O-65,1-6	-2.2

■ **CURT FLOOD**   Flood, Curtis Charles   b: 1/18/38, Houston, Tex.   d: 1/20/97, Los Angeles, Cal.   BR/TR, 5'9", 165 lbs.   Deb: 9/9/56

1956	Cin-N	5	1	0	0	0	0	0	0	0	1	.000	.000	.000	-94	-0	0	0	0	.000	0	H	0.0
1957	Cin-N	3	3	2	1	0	0	1	1	0	0	.333	.333	1.333	299	1	0	0	0	.000	-1	/3-2,2-1	0.0
1958	StL-N	121	422	50	110	17	2	10	41	31	56	.261	.317	.382	81	-12	2	12	-7	.978	19	*O-120/3-1	-0.5
1959	StL-N	121	208	24	53	7	3	7	26	16	35	.255	.308	.418	86	-5	2	1	0	.967	-19	*O-106/2-1	-2.7
1960	StL-N	140	396	37	94	20	1	8	38	35	54	.237	.306	.354	73	-14	0	3	-2	**.993**	1	*O-134/3-1	-2.2
1961	StL-N	132	335	53	108	15	5	2	21	35	33	.322	.391	.415	104	3	6	2	1	.984	2	*O-119	0.1
1962	StL-N	151	635	99	188	30	5	12	70	42	57	.296	.349	.416	95	-4	8	6	-1	.990	16	*O-151	0.1
1963	StL-N	158	662	112	200	34	9	5	63	42	57	.302	.346	.403	105	5	17	12	-2	.988	20	*O-158	1.4
1964	*StL-N★	162	679	97	211	25	3	5	46	43	53	.311	.356	.378	98	-0	8	11	-4	.988	13	*O-162	0.1
1965	StL-N	156	617	90	191	30	3	11	83	51	50	.310	.368	.421	111	10	9	3	1	.986	11	*O-151	1.6
1966	StL-N★	160	626	64	167	21	5	10	78	26	50	.267	.300	.364	83	-15	14	7	0	**1.000**	10	*O-159	-1.2
1967	StL-N	134	514	68	172	24	1	5	50	37	46	.335	.382	.414	129	20	2	2	-1	.988	11	*O-126	2.5
1968	*StL-N★	150	618	71	186	17	4	5	60	33	58	.301	.341	.366	114	10	11	6	-0	.983	18	*O-149	2.1
1969	StL-N	153	606	80	173	31	3	4	57	48	57	.285	.345	.366	99	-0	9	7	-2	.989	17	*O-152	0.7
1971	Was-A	13	35	4	7	0	0	0	2	3	5	.200	.300	.200	47	-2	0	1	-1	.941	-2	O-10	-0.6
Total	15	1759	6357	851	1861	271	44	85	636	444	609	.293	.344	.389	99	-4	88	73	-17	.987	114	*O-1697/3-4,2-2	1.4

■ **TIM FLOOD**   Flood, Timothy A.   b: 3/13/1877, Montgomery City, Mo.   d: 6/15/29, St.Louis, Mo.   BR/TR, 5'9", 160 lbs.   Deb: 9/24/1899

1899	StL-N	10	31	0	9	0	0	0	3	0	4	.290	.371	.290	81	-1	1			.878	-2	2-10	-0.2
1902	Bro-N	132	476	43	104	11	4	3	51	23		.218	.268	.277	68	-18	8			.942	-16	*2-132/O-1	-3.1
1903	Bro-N	89	309	27	77	15	2	0	32	15		.249	.291	.311	73	-11	14			.924	-9	2-84/S-2,O-1	-1.6
Total	3	231	816	70	190	26	6	3	86	42		.233	.280	.290	70	-30	23			.933	-26	2-226/S-2,O-2	-4.9

■ **KEVIN FLORA**   Flora, Kevin Scot   b: 6/10/69, Fontana, Cal.   BR/TR, 6', 180 lbs.   Deb: 9/27/91

1991	Cal-A	3	8	1	1	0	0	0	0	1	5	.125	.222	.125	-1	-1	1	0	0	.846	-2	/2-3	-0.3
1995	Cal-A	2	1	0	0	0	0	0	0	0	1	.000	.000	.000	-99	-0	0	0	0	.000	0	/D-1	0.0
	Phi-N	24	75	12	16	3	0	2	7	4	22	.213	.253	.333	53	-5	1	0	0	1.000	0	O-20	-0.6
Total	2	29	84	14	17	3	0	2	7	5	28	.202	.247	.310	46	-7	2	0	1	1.000	-2	/O-20,2-3,D-1	-0.9

■ **PAUL FLORENCE**   Florence, Paul Robert "Pep"   b: 4/22/1900, Chicago, Ill.   d: 5/28/86, Gainesville, Fla.   BB/TR, 6'1", 185 lbs.   Deb: 5/22/26

1926	NY-N	76	188	19	43	4	3	2	14	23	12	.229	.322	.314	73	-7	2			.937	-9	C-76	-1.1

■ **GIL FLORES**   Flores, Gilberto (Garcia)   b: 10/27/52, Ponce, P.R.   BR/TR, 6', 185 lbs.   Deb: 5/8/77

1977	Cal-A	104	342	41	95	19	4	1	26	23	39	.278	.325	.365	92	-4	12	10	-2	.978	-2	O-85/D-8	-1.2
1978	NY-N	11	29	8	8	0	1	0	1	3	5	.276	.344	.345	96	-0	1	0	0	.944	-1	/O-8	-0.1
1979	NY-N	70	93	9	18	1	1	1	10	8	17	.194	.265	.258	45	-7	2	0	0	.976	-7	O-32	-1.5
Total	3	185	464	58	121	20	6	2	37	34	61	.261	.314	.343	82	-11	15	10	-2	.976	-10	O-125/D-8	-2.8

■ **DICKIE FLOWERS**   Flowers, Charles Richard   b: 1850, Philadelphia, Pa.   d: 10/5/1892, Philadelphia, Pa.   Deb: 6/3/1871

1871	Tro-n	21	105	39	33	5	4	0	18	4	0	.314	.339	.438	120	2	8	2	1	.769	-3	*S-20/P-1,2-1	0.1
1872	Ath-n	3	15	1	4	0	0	0	4	2	2	.267	.353	.267	93	0	0	0	0	.643	-2	/S-3	-0.1
Total	2 n	24	120	40	37	5	4	0	22	6	2	.308	.341	.417	117	2	8	2	1	.757	-5	/S-23,2-1,P-1	0.0

■ **JAKE FLOWERS**   Flowers, D'Arcy Raymond   b: 3/16/02, Cambridge, Md.   d: 12/27/62, Clearwater, Fla.   BR/TR, 5'11.5", 170 lbs.   Deb: 9/7/23 C

1923	StL-N	13	32	0	3	1	0	0	2	2	7	.094	.147	.125	-28	-6	1	2	-1	.971	-1	/S-7,2-1,2,3-2	-0.7
1926	*StL-N	40	74	13	20	1	0	3	9	5	9	.270	.325	.405	92	-1	1			.984	2	2-11/1-3,S-1	0.0
1927	Bro-N	67	231	26	54	5	5	2	20	21	25	.234	.300	.325	67	-11	3			.944	-8	S-65/2-1	-1.2
1928	Bro-N	103	339	51	93	11	6	4	44	47	30	.274	.366	.360	92	-3	10			.971	-6	2-94/S-6	-0.6
1929	Bro-N	46	130	16	26	6	0	1	16	22	6	.200	.316	.269	47	-10	9			.962	-5	2-39	-1.3
1930	Bro-N	89	253	37	81	18	3	2	50	21	18	.320	.372	.439	96	-1	5			.949	-8	2-65/O-1	-0.5
1931	Bro-N	22	31	3	7	0	0	0	1	7	4	.226	.368	.226	64	-1	1			1.000	1	/2-6,S-1	0.1
	*StL-N	45	137	19	34	11	2	1	19	9	6	.248	.295	.387	79	-4	7			.971	3	S-24,2-21/3-1	0.1
	Yr	67	168	22	41	11	2	1	20	16	10	.244	.310	.357	77	-5	8			.991	4	2-27,S-25/3-1	0.2
1932	StL-N	67	247	35	63	11	2	3	18	31	18	.255	.341	.332	79	-6	7			.980	-0	3-54/S-7,2-2	-0.2
1933	Bro-N	78	210	28	49	11	2	2	22	24	15	.233	.312	.333	88	-3	13			.955	-11	2-36,2-19/3-8,0-1	-1.1
1934	Cin-N	13	9	1	3	0	0	0	1	1	1	.333	.455	.333	117	0	1			.000	0	H	0.0
Total	10	583	1693	229	433	75	18	16	201	190	139	.256	.333	.350	80	-47	58	2		.967	-34	2-260,S-147/310	-5.4

■ **CLIFF FLOYD**   Floyd, Cornelius Clifford   b: 12/5/72, Chicago, Ill.   BL/TL, 6'4", 220 lbs.   Deb: 9/18/93

1993	Mon-N	10	31	3	7	0	0	1	2	0	9	.226	.226	.323	43	-3	0	0	0	1.000	0	1-10	-0.4
1994	Mon-N	100	334	43	94	19	4	4	41	24	63	.281	.335	.398	89	-5	10	3	1	.991	-3	1-77,O-26	-1.3
1995	Mon-N	29	69	6	9	1	0	1	8	7	22	.130	.221	.188	9	-9	3	0	1	.987	-1	1-18/O-4	-1.0
1996	Mon-N	117	227	29	55	15	4	6	26	30	52	.242	.344	.423	98	-0	7	1	2	.960	-13	O-85/1-2	-1.4
Total	4	256	661	81	165	35	8	12	77	61	146	.250	.321	.381	82	-17	20	4	4	.958	-17	O-115,1-107	-4.1

■ **BUBBA FLOYD**   Floyd, Leslie Roe   b: 6/23/17, Dallas, Tex.   BR/TR, 5'11", 160 lbs.   Deb: 6/16/44

1944	Det-A	3	9	1	4	0	0	0	1	0	1	.444	.500	.556	191	1	0	0	0	1.000	-1	/S-3	0.0

■ **BOBBY FLOYD**   Floyd, Robert Nathan   b: 10/20/43, Hawthorne, Cal.   BR/TR, 6', 181 lbs.   Deb: 9/18/68

1968	Bal-A	5	9	0	1	1	0	0	0	0	3	.111	.111	.222	-1	-1	0	0	0	1.000	2	/S-4	0.1

YEAR	TM/L	G	AB	R	H	2B	3B	HR	RBI	BB	SO	AVG	OBP	SLG	PRO+	BR/A	SB	CS	SBR	FA	FR	G/POS	TPR
1969	Bal-A	39	84	7	17	4	0	0	1	6	17	.202	.256	.250	41	-7	0	0	0	.984	11	2-15,S-15/3-9	0.7
1970	Bal-A	3	2	0	0	0	0	0	0	0	2	.000	.000	.000	-99	-1	0	0	0	1.000	-1	/S-2,2-1	-0.1
	KC-A	14	43	5	14	4	0	0	9	4	9	.326	.383	.419	121	1	0	1	-1	.880	1	/S-8,3-6	0.3
	Yr	17	45	5	14	4	0	0	9	4	11	.311	.367	.400	111	1	0	1	-1	.882	1	S-10/3-6,2-1	0.2
1971	KC-A	31	66	8	10	3	0	0	2	7	21	.152	.233	.197	23	-7	0	0	0	.970	5	S-15/2-8,3-1	0.0
1972	KC-A	61	134	9	24	3	0	0	5	5	29	.179	.209	.201	23	-13	1	0	0	.967	-2	3-30,S-29/2-2	-1.4
1973	KC-A	51	78	10	26	3	1	0	8	4	14	.333	.366	.397	107	1	1	1	-0	1.000	9	2-25,S-24	1.1
1974	KC-A	10	9	1	1	0	0	0	0	2	4	.111	.273	.111	13	-1	0	0	0	1.000	2	/2-5,3-2,S-1	0.2
Total 7		214	425	40	93	18	1	0	26	28	99	.219	.267	.266	52	-27	2	2	-1	.940	27	/S-98,2-56,3-48	0.9

■ JOHN FLUHRER
Fluhrer, John L. (a.k.a. Wm. G. Morris 1 Game In 1915) b: 1/3/1894, Adrian, Mich. d: 7/17/46, Columbus, Ohio BR/TR, 5'9", 165 lbs. Deb: 9/5/15

YEAR	TM/L	G	AB	R	H	2B	3B	HR	RBI	BB	SO	AVG	OBP	SLG	PRO+	BR/A	SB	CS	SBR	FA	FR	G/POS	TPR
1915	Chi-N	6	6	0	2	0	0	0	0	1	0	.333	.429	.333	132	0	1			.500	-1	/O-2	0.0

■ ED FLYNN
Flynn, Edward J. b: 1/25/1864, Chicago, Ill. BL, 5'9", 165 lbs. Deb: 5/5/1887

YEAR	TM/L	G	AB	R	H	2B	3B	HR	RBI	BB	SO	AVG	OBP	SLG	PRO+	BR/A	SB	CS	SBR	FA	FR	G/POS	TPR
1887	Cle-a	7	27	0	5	1	0	0	4	1		.185	.214	.222	22	-3	3			.786	-0	/3-6,O-1	-0.2

■ GEORGE FLYNN
Flynn, George A. "Dibby" b: 5/24/1871, Chicago, Ill. d: 12/28/01, Chicago, Ill. Deb: 4/17/1896

YEAR	TM/L	G	AB	R	H	2B	3B	HR	RBI	BB	SO	AVG	OBP	SLG	PRO+	BR/A	SB	CS	SBR	FA	FR	G/POS	TPR
1896	Chi-N	29	106	15	27	1	2	0	4	11	9	.255	.336	.302	66	-5	12			.878	2	O-29	-0.4

■ JOCKO FLYNN
Flynn, John A. b: 6/30/1864, Lawrence, Mass. d: 12/30/07, Lawrence, Mass. TR, 5'6.5", 143 lbs. Deb: 5/1/1886

YEAR	TM/L	G	AB	R	H	2B	3B	HR	RBI	BB	SO	AVG	OBP	SLG	PRO+	BR/A	SB	CS	SBR	FA	FR	G/POS	TPR
1886	Chi-N	57	205	40	41	6	2	4	19	18	45	.200	.265	.307	64	-10	9			.916	-5	P-32,O-28	-1.0
1887	Chi-N	1	0	0	0	0	0	0	0	0	0	.---	.---	.---	—	0	0			.000	-1	/O-1	-0.1
Total 2		58	205	40	41	6	2	4	19	18	45	.200	.265	.307	64	-10	9			.850	-6	/P-32,O-29	-1.1

■ JOHN FLYNN
Flynn, John Anthony b: 9/7/1883, Providence, R.I. d: 3/23/35, Providence, R.I. BR/TR, 6'0.5", 175 lbs. Deb: 4/22/10

YEAR	TM/L	G	AB	R	H	2B	3B	HR	RBI	BB	SO	AVG	OBP	SLG	PRO+	BR/A	SB	CS	SBR	FA	FR	G/POS	TPR
1910	Pit-N	96	332	32	91	10	2	6	52	30	47	.274	.336	.370	100	-1	6			.977	-3	1-93	-0.4
1911	Pit-N	33	59	5	12	0	1	0	3	9	8	.203	.309	.237	52	-4	0			1.000	0	1-13/O-1	-0.3
1912	Was-A	20	71	9	12	4	1	0	5	7		.169	.253	.254	45	-5	2			.974	1	1-20	-0.4
Total 3		149	462	46	115	14	4	6	60	46	55	.249	.320	.335	85	-9	8			.978	-1	1-126/O-1	-1.1

■ JOE FLYNN
Flynn, Joseph b: Philadelphia, Pa. Deb: 4/18/1884

YEAR	TM/L	G	AB	R	H	2B	3B	HR	RBI	BB	SO	AVG	OBP	SLG	PRO+	BR/A	SB	CS	SBR	FA	FR	G/POS	TPR
1884	Phi-U	52	209	38	52	9	4	4			11	.249	.286	.388	111	-4				.778	-15	O-43,C-10/1-1,S-1	-1.7
	Bos-U	9	31	4	7	2	0	0			2	.226	.273	.290	72	-2				.864	4	/C-7,O-4,1-1	0.2
	Yr	61	240	42	59	11	4	4			11	.246	.285	.375	105	-6				.764	-11	O-47,C-17/1-2,S-1	-1.5

■ MIKE FLYNN
Flynn, Michael J. b: 3/15/1872, County Kildare, Ireland d: 6/16/41, Los Angeles, Cal. Deb: 8/31/1891

YEAR	TM/L	G	AB	R	H	2B	3B	HR	RBI	BB	SO	AVG	OBP	SLG	PRO+	BR/A	SB	CS	SBR	FA	FR	G/POS	TPR
1891	Bos-a	1	2	0	0	0	0	0	0	0	1	.000	.000	.000	-99	-1				1.000	1	/C-1	0.0

■ DOUG FLYNN
Flynn, Robert Douglas b: 4/18/51, Lexington, Ky. BR/TR, 5'11", 165 lbs. Deb: 4/9/75

YEAR	TM/L	G	AB	R	H	2B	3B	HR	RBI	BB	SO	AVG	OBP	SLG	PRO+	BR/A	SB	CS	SBR	FA	FR	G/POS	TPR
1975	Cin-N	89	127	17	34	7	0	1	20	11	13	.268	.326	.346	85	-3	3	0	1	.962	10	3-40,2-30,S-17	1.0
1976	*Cin-N	93	219	20	62	5	2	1	20	10	24	.283	.314	.338	83	-5	2	0	1	.988	-4	2-55,3-23/S-20	-0.4
1977	Cin-N	36	32	0	8	1	1	0	5	0	6	.250	.250	.344	56	-2	0	0		1.000	7	3-25/2-9,S-4	0.3
	NY-N	90	282	14	54	6	1	0	14	11	23	.191	.222	.220	20	-32	1	3	-2	.954	-13	S-65,2-29/3-2	-4.0
	Yr	126	314	14	62	7	2	0	19	11	29	.197	.225	.232	24	-34	1	3	-2	.956	-6	S-69,2-38/3-27	-3.5
1978	NY-N	156	532	37	126	12	8	0	36	30	50	.237	.279	.289	61	-28	3	5	-2	.986	2	*2-128,S-60	-1.7
1979	NY-N	157	555	35	135	19	5	4	61	17	46	.243	.266	.317	61	-32	0	3	-2	.983	1	*2-148,S-20	-2.3
1980	NY-N	128	443	46	113	9	8	0	24	22	20	.255	.290	.312	70	-18	2	2	-1	**.991**	3	*2-128/S-3	-0.9
1981	NY-N	105	325	24	72	12	4	1	20	11	19	.222	.247	.292	53	-21	1	2	-1	.987	12	*2-100/S-5	-0.3
1982	Tex-A	88	270	13	57	6	2	0	19	4	14	.211	.223	.248	31	-26	6	2	1	.989	4	2-55,S-35	-1.6
	Mon-N	58	193	13	47	6	2	0	20	4	23	.244	.259	.295	54	-12	0	2	-1	.983	2	2-58	-0.6
1983	Mon-N	143	452	44	107	18	4	0	26	19	38	.237	.268	.294	56	-27	2	1	0	.986	7	*2-107,S-37	-1.4
1984	Mon-N	124	366	23	89	12	1	0	17	12	41	.243	.267	.281	57	-22	0	1	0	.979	-3	2-88,S-34	-2.6
1985	Mon-N	9	6	0	1	0	0	0	0	0	0	.167	.167	.167	-7	-1	0	0	0	1.000		/2-6,S-1	-0.2
	Det-A	32	51	2	13	2	1	0	5	2	9	.255	.255	.333	60	-3	0	0	0	.984	8	2-20/S-8,3-4	0.6
Total 11		1308	3853	288	918	115	39	7	284	151	320	.238	.267	.294	57	-231	20	20	-6	.986	33	2-961,S-309/3-94	-13.9

■ CLIPPER FLYNN
Flynn, William b: 4/29/1849, Lansingburg, N.Y. d: 11/11/1881, Lansingburg, N.Y. TR, 5'7", 140 lbs. Deb: 5/9/1871

YEAR	TM/L	G	AB	R	H	2B	3B	HR	RBI	BB	SO	AVG	OBP	SLG	PRO+	BR/A	SB	CS	SBR	FA	FR	G/POS	TPR
1871	Tro-n	29	142	43	48	6	1	0	27	4	2	.338	.356	.394	114	2	3	3	-1	.955	5	1-19/O-8,2-1,3-1	0.5
1872	Oly-n	9	40	4	9	1	0	0	2	0	0	.225	.225	.250	48	-2	0	0		.900	-1	/1-9	-0.2
Total 2 n		38	182	47	57	7	1	0	29	4	2	.313	.328	.363	101	0	3	3	-1	.934	4	/1-28,O-8,3-1,2-1	0.3

■ JIM FOGARTY
Fogarty, James G. b: 2/12/1864, San Francisco, Cal d: 5/20/1891, Philadelphia, Pa. BR/TR, 5'10.5", 180 lbs. Deb: 5/1/1884 FM

YEAR	TM/L	G	AB	R	H	2B	3B	HR	RBI	BB	SO	AVG	OBP	SLG	PRO+	BR/A	SB	CS	SBR	FA	FR	G/POS	TPR
1884	Phi-N	97	378	42	80	12	6	1	37	20	54	.212	.251	.283	71	-12				.915	3	*O-78,3-14/2-4,SP	-0.9
1885	Phi-N	111	427	49	99	13	3	0	39	30	37	.232	.282	.276	83	-7				.941	25	*O-88,2-10/S-8,3-5	1.5
1886	Phi-N	77	280	54	82	13	5	3	47	42	16	.293	.385	.407	140	15	30			.953	-3	O-60,2-13/S-3,3P	0.9
1887	Phi-N	126	495	113	129	26	12	8	50	**82**	44	.261	.376	.410	112	9	102			.920	32	*O-123/S-2,3-2,2P	3.3
1888	Phi-N	121	454	72	107	14	6	1	35	53	66	.236	.325	.300	95	-1	58			.930	14	*O-117/3-5,S-1	1.0
1889	Phi-N	128	499	107	129	15	17	3	54	65	60	.259	.352	.375	95	-5	**99**			**.961**	19	*O-128/P-4	1.0
1890	Phi-P	91	347	71	83	17	6	4	58	59	50	.239	.364	.357	91	-4	36			.963	8	O-91/3-1,M	0.1
Total 7		751	2880	508	709	110	55	20	320	351	327	.246	.335	.343	98	-4	325			.940	98	O-685/3-30,2-28,SP	6.9

■ JOE FOGARTY
Fogarty, Joseph J. b: San Francisco, Cal. Deb: 9/18/1885 F

YEAR	TM/L	G	AB	R	H	2B	3B	HR	RBI	BB	SO	AVG	OBP	SLG	PRO+	BR/A	SB	CS	SBR	FA	FR	G/POS	TPR
1885	StL-N	2	8	1	1	0	0	0	0	0	1	.125	.125	.125	-20	-1				1.000	-0	/O-2	-0.1

■ LEE FOHL
Fohl, Leo Alexander b: 11/28/1876, Lowell, Ohio d: 10/30/65, Cleveland, Ohio BL/TR, 5'10", 175 lbs. Deb: 8/29/02 MC

YEAR	TM/L	G	AB	R	H	2B	3B	HR	RBI	BB	SO	AVG	OBP	SLG	PRO+	BR/A	SB	CS	SBR	FA	FR	G/POS	TPR
1902	Pit-N	1	3	0	0	0	0	0	1	0		.000	.000	.000	-97	-1	0			.875	0	/C-1	0.0
1903	Cin-N	4	14	3	5	1	1	0	2	0		.357	.400	.571	158	1	0			.955	0	/C-4	0.1
Total 2		5	17	3	5	1	1	0	3	0		.294	.333	.471	120	0	0			.933	0	/C-5	0.1

■ HANK FOILES
Foiles, Henry Lee b: 6/10/29, Richmond, Va. BR/TR, 6', 195 lbs. Deb: 4/21/53

YEAR	TM/L	G	AB	R	H	2B	3B	HR	RBI	BB	SO	AVG	OBP	SLG	PRO+	BR/A	SB	CS	SBR	FA	FR	G/POS	TPR
1953	Cin-N	5	13	1	2	0	0	0	0	1	2	.154	.214	.154	-2	-2	0	0	0	.909	-1	/C-3	-0.2
	Cle-A	7	7	2	1	0	0	0	0	0	1	.143	.250	.143	9	-1	0	0	0	.933	1	/C-7	0.0
1955	Cle-A	62	111	13	29	9	0	1	7	17	18	.261	.359	.369	93	-1	0	0	0	.988	14	C-41	1.4
1956	Cle-A	1	0	0	0	0	0	0	0	0	0	.---	.---	.---	—	0	0	0	0	.000	0	/C-1	0.0
	Pit-N	79	222	24	47	10	2	7	25	17	56	.212	.268	.369	71	-10	0	0	0	.988	-2	C-73	-1.0
1957	Pit-N★	109	281	32	76	10	4	9	36	37	53	.270	.355	.431	113	6	1	3	-2	.981	-6	*C-109	0.2
1958	Pit-N	104	264	31	54	10	2	8	30	45	53	.205	.323	.348	80	-7	0	1	-1	.990	8	*C-103	0.6
1959	Pit-N	53	80	10	18	3	0	3	4	7	16	.225	.287	.375	75	-3	0	0	0	1.000	5	C-51	0.7
1960	KC-A	6	7	1	4	0	1	0	0	3	2	.571	.700	.571	246	2	0	0	0	.900	-0	/C-2	0.2
	Cle-A	24	68	9	19	1	0	1	6	7	5	.279	.347	.338	89	-1	0	0	0	.982	0	C-22	0.1
	Det-A	26	56	5	14	3	0	0	3	1	8	.250	.263	.304	51	-4	1	0	0	1.000	4	C-22	0.1
	Yr	56	131	15	37	4	1	1	9	11	15	.282	.338	.336	83	-3	1	0	0	.987	5	C-46	0.5
1961	Bal-A	43	124	18	34	6	0	6	19	12	27	.274	.338	.468	117	3	0	2	0	.995	3	C-38	0.6
1962	Cin-N	43	131	17	36	6	1	7	25	13	39	.275	.340	.496	118	3	0	1	0	.981	-5	C-41	0.5
1963	Cin-N	1	3	0	0	0	0	0	0	1	0	.000	.250	.000	-21	-0	1	0	0	1.000	-0	/C-1	0.0
	LA-N	41	84	8	18	1	1	4	10	8	13	.214	.290	.393	95	-1	0	0	0	.974	3	C-30	0.5
1964	LA-A	4	4	0	1	0	0	0	0	0	2	.250	.250	.250	44	-0	0	0	0	.000	0	H	0.0
Total 11		608	1455	171	353	59	10	46	166	170	295	.243	.323	.392	92	-17	3	7	-3	.986	35	C-544	3.6

■ CURRY FOLEY
Foley, Charles Joseph b: 1/14/1856, Milltown, Ireland d: 10/20/1898, Boston, Mass. TL, 5'10", 160 lbs. Deb: 5/13/1879

YEAR	TM/L	G	AB	R	H	2B	3B	HR	RBI	BB	SO	AVG	OBP	SLG	PRO+	BR/A	SB	CS	SBR	FA	FR	G/POS	TPR
1879	Bos-N	35	146	16	46	3	1	0	17	3	4	.315	.329	.349	121	3				.857	-7	P-21,O-17/1-2	-0.4
1880	Bos-N	80	332	44	97	13	2	2	31	8	14	.292	.309	.361	130	10				.953	-3	P-36,O-35,1-25	0.0

YEAR	TM/L	G	AB	R	H	2B	3B	HR	RBI	BB	SO	AVG	OBP	SLG	PRO+	BR/A	SB	CS	SBR	FA	FR	G/POS	TPR
1881	Buf-N	83	375	58	96	20	2	1	25	7	27	.256	.270	.328	88	-5				.795	-4	O-55,1-27,P-10	-1.2
1882	Buf-N	84	341	51	104	16	4	3	49	12	26	.305	.329	.402	131	11				.833	0	*O-84/P-1	1.0
1883	Buf-N	23	111	23	30	5	3	0	6	4	12	.270	.296	.369	98	-0				.885	-2	O-23/P-1	-0.2
Total	5	305	1305	192	373	57	12	6	128	34	83	.286	.304	.362	114	19				.819	-16	O-214/P-69,1-54	-0.8

■ MARV FOLEY
Foley, Marvis Edwin b: 8/29/53, Stanford, Ky. BL/TR, 6', 195 lbs. Deb: 9/11/78 C

YEAR	TM/L	G	AB	R	H	2B	3B	HR	RBI	BB	SO	AVG	OBP	SLG	PRO+	BR/A	SB	CS	SBR	FA	FR	G/POS	TPR
1978	Chi-A	11	34	3	12	0	0	0	6	4	6	.353	.421	.353	119	1	0	1	-1	.938	-3	C-10	-0.2
1979	Chi-A	34	97	6	24	3	0	2	10	7	5	.247	.298	.340	72	-4	0	0	0	.993	-1	C-33	-0.4
1980	Chi-A	68	137	14	29	5	0	4	15	9	22	.212	.270	.336	65	-7	0	0	0	.991	2	C-64/1-3	-0.3
1982	Chi-A	27	36	1	4	0	0	0	1	6	4	.111	.238	.111	-0	-5	0	0	0	.980	1	C-15/3-2,1-1,D-1	-0.3
1984	Tex-A	63	115	13	25	2	0	6	19	15	24	.217	.313	.391	91	-1	0	0	0	.988	1	C-36/1-1,3-1,D-4	0.1
Total	5	203	419	37	94	10	0	12	51	41	61	.224	.298	.334	73	-16	0	1	-1	.986	0	C-158/D-5,1-5,3-3	-1.1

■ RAY FOLEY
Foley, Raymond Kirwin b: 6/23/06, Naugatuck, Conn. d: 3/22/80, Vero Beach, Fla. BL/TR, 5'11", 173 lbs. Deb: 7/4/28

YEAR	TM/L	G	AB	R	H	2B	3B	HR	RBI	BB	SO	AVG	OBP	SLG	PRO+	BR/A	SB	CS	SBR	FA	FR	G/POS	TPR
1928	NY-N	2	1	1	0	0	0	0	0	1	1	.000	.500	.000	41	0	0			.000	0	H	0.0

■ TOM FOLEY
Foley, Thomas J. b: 1847, Chicago, Ill. d: 1/4/1896, LaGrange, Ill. 5'9.5", 157 lbs. Deb: 5/8/1871

YEAR	TM/L	G	AB	R	H	2B	3B	HR	RBI	BB	SO	AVG	OBP	SLG	PRO+	BR/A	SB	CS	SBR	FA	FR	G/POS	TPR
1871	Chi-n	18	84	18	22	3	1	0	13	3	2	.262	.287	.321	67	-5	1	4	-2	.633	-5	O-16/C-4,3-1	-0.7

■ TOM FOLEY
Foley, Thomas Michael b: 9/9/59, Columbus, Ga. BL/TR, 6'1", 175 lbs. Deb: 4/9/83

YEAR	TM/L	G	AB	R	H	2B	3B	HR	RBI	BB	SO	AVG	OBP	SLG	PRO+	BR/A	SB	CS	SBR	FA	FR	G/POS	TPR
1983	Cin-N	68	98	7	20	4	1	0	9	13	17	.204	.297	.265	55	-6	1	0	0	.983	9	S-37/2-5	0.6
1984	Cin-N	106	277	26	70	8	3	5	27	24	36	.253	.312	.357	84	-6	3	2	-0	.965	1	S-83,2-10/3-1	0.1
1985	Cin-N	43	92	7	18	5	1	0	6	6	16	.196	.245	.272	42	-7	1	0	0	.983	3	2-18,S-15/3-1	-0.3
	Phi-N	46	158	17	42	8	0	3	17	13	18	.266	.322	.373	91	-2	1	3	-2	.981	-5	S-45	-0.4
	Yr	89	250	24	60	13	1	3	23	19	34	.240	.294	.336	73	-9	2	3	-1	.978	-5	S-60,2-18/3-1	-0.7
1986	Phi-N	39	61	8	18	2	1	0	5	10	11	.295	.394	.361	106	1	2	0	1	.975	0	S-24/2-1,3-1	0.3
	Mon-N	64	202	18	52	13	2	1	18	20	26	.257	.324	.356	88	-3	8	3	1	.965	-5	S-29,2-25,3-15	-0.5
	Yr	103	263	26	70	15	3	1	23	30	37	.266	.341	.357	92	-2	10	3	1	.970	-5	S-53,2-26,3-16	-0.2
1987	Mon-N	106	280	35	82	18	3	5	28	11	40	.293	.322	.432	95	-3	6	10	-4	.963	1	S-49,2-39/3-9	-0.1
1988	Mon-N	127	377	33	100	21	3	5	43	30	49	.265	.321	.377	95	-2	2	8	-4	.972	3	2-89,S-32/3-9	0.3
1989	Mon-N	122	375	34	86	19	2	7	39	45	53	.229	.317	.347	88	-5	2	3	-1	.988	20	*2-108,3-16,S-14,/P	1.8
1990	Mon-N	73	164	11	35	2	1	0	12	12	22	.213	.267	.238	42	-13	0	1	-1	.987	3	S-45,2-20/3-7,1-1	-0.9
1991	Mon-N	86	168	12	35	11	1	0	15	14	30	.208	.273	.286	58	-9	2	0	1	.967	-2	S-43,1-31/3-6,2-2	-1.0
1992	Mon-N	72	115	7	20	3	1	0	5	8	21	.174	.234	.217	29	-11	3	0	1	.967	6	S-33,2-13,1-12/3O	-0.2
1993	Pit-N	86	194	18	49	11	1	3	22	11	26	.253	.293	.366	75	-7	0	0	0	.993	1	2-35,1-12/3-7,S-6	-0.5
1994	Pit-N	59	123	13	29	7	0	3	15	13	18	.236	.309	.366	74	-5	0	0	0	.986	11	2-17,3-14/S-8,1-3	0.7
1995	Mon-N	11	24	2	5	2	0	0	2	2	4	.208	.269	.292	46	-2	1	0	0	1.000	1	/1-4,2-3	-0.3
Total	13	1108	2708	248	661	134	20	32	263	232	387	.244	.305	.344	78	-80	32	29	-8	.972	45	S-463,2-385/310P	-0.4

■ WILL FOLEY
Foley, William Brown b: 11/15/1855, Chicago, Ill. d: 11/12/16, Chicago, Ill. BR/TR, 5'9.5", 150 lbs. Deb: 8/23/1875

YEAR	TM/L	G	AB	R	H	2B	3B	HR	RBI	BB	SO	AVG	OBP	SLG	PRO+	BR/A	SB	CS	SBR	FA	FR	G/POS	TPR
1875	Chi-n	3	12	0	3	1	0	0	1	0	2	.250	.250	.333	100	-0	0	0	0	.813	1	/3-3	0.1
1876	Cin-N	58	221	19	50	3	2	0	9	0	14	.226	.226	.258	71	-6				.804	2	3-46,C-20	-0.2
1877	Cin-N	56	216	23	41	5	1	0	18	4	13	.190	.205	.222	39	-14				.836	6	*3-56	-0.5
1878	Mil-N	56	229	33	62	8	5	0	22	7	14	.271	.292	.349	103	0				.812	-9	*3-53/C-7	-0.6
1879	Cin-N	56	218	22	46	5	1	0	25	2	16	.211	.218	.243	55	-10				.820	3	3-29,O-25/2-3	-0.7
1881	Det-N	5	15	0	2	0	0	0	1	2	3	.133	.235	.133	18	-1				.769	-1	/3-5	-0.3
1884	CP-U	19	71	15	20	1	1	0	5	0		.282	.329	.324	99	-2				.804	-3	3-19	-0.3
Total	6	250	970	112	221	22	10	0	75	20	60	.228	.243	.271	70	-33				.817	-2	3-208/C-27,O-25,2-3	-2.8

■ TIM FOLI
Foli, Timothy John b: 12/8/50, Culver City, Cal. BR/TR, 6', 179 lbs. Deb: 9/11/70 C

YEAR	TM/L	G	AB	R	H	2B	3B	HR	RBI	BB	SO	AVG	OBP	SLG	PRO+	BR/A	SB	CS	SBR	FA	FR	G/POS	TPR
1970	NY-N	5	11	0	4	0	0	0	0	0	1	.364	.364	.364	95	-0	0	0	0	1.000	2	/S-2,3-2	0.2
1971	NY-N	97	288	32	65	12	2	2	24	18	50	.226	.274	.281	58	-16	5	0	2	.964	14	2-58,3-36,S-12/O-1	0.4
1972	Mon-N	149	540	45	130	12	2	2	35	25	43	.241	.282	.281	59	-28	11	7	-1	.966	9	*S-148/2-1	0.1
1973	Mon-N	126	458	37	110	11	0	2	36	28	40	.240	.285	.277	55	-28	6	3	0	.960	-3	*S-123/2-2,O-1	-0.3
1974	Mon-N	121	441	41	112	10	3	0	39	26	27	.254	.303	.290	63	-21	8	2	1	.971	19	*S-120/3-1	1.6
1975	Mon-N	152	572	64	136	25	2	1	29	36	49	.238	.285	.294	58	-32	13	3	2	.973	7	*S-151/2-1	-0.9
1976	Mon-N	149	546	41	144	36	1	6	54	16	33	.264	.285	.366	80	-16	6	5	-1	.975	7	*S-146/3-1	0.8
1977	Mon-N	13	57	2	10	5	1	0	3	0	4	.175	.175	.298	25	-6	0	0	0	1.000	1	S-13	-0.4
	SF-N	104	368	30	84	17	3	4	27	11	16	.228	.251	.323	53	-25	2	4	-2	.974	2	*S-102/2-1,3-1,O-1	-1.4
	Yr	117	425	32	94	22	4	4	30	11	20	.221	.241	.320	49	-31	2	4	-2	.977	3	*S-115/2-1,3-1,O-1	-1.8
1978	NY-N	113	413	37	106	21	1	1	27	14	30	.257	.284	.320	71	-17	2	5	-2	.966	-15	*S-112	-2.1
1979	NY-N	3	7	0	0	0	0	0	0	0	0	.000	.000	.000	-99	-2	0	0	0	1.000	1	/S-3	-0.1
	*Pit-N	133	525	70	153	23	1	1	65	28	14	.291	.338	.345	83	-12	6	5	-1	.978	-1	*S-132	0.2
	Yr	136	532	70	153	23	1	1	65	28	14	.288	.334	.340	81	-13	6	5	-1	.978	0	*S-135	0.1
1980	Pit-N	127	495	61	131	22	0	3	38	19	23	.265	.300	.327	74	-17	11	7	-1	**.981**	-0	*S-125	0.2
1981	Pit-N	86	316	32	78	12	2	0	20	17	10	.247	.287	.297	64	-15	7	7	-2	.965	-9	S-81	-2.0
1982	*Cal-A	150	480	46	121	14	2	3	56	14	22	.252	.276	.308	60	-26	2	4	-2	**.985**	8	*S-139/2-8,3-2	-0.7
1983	Cal-A	88	330	29	83	10	2	2	29	5	18	.252	.265	.300	56	-20	2	3	-1	.975	10	S-74,3-13	0.1
1984	NY-A	61	163	8	41	11	0	0	16	2	16	.252	.265	.319	63	-8	0	0	0	.950	2	S-28,2-21,3-10,/1-2	0.1
1985	Pit-N	19	37	1	7	0	0	0	2	1	6	.189	.268	.189	30	-3	0	0	0	.980	1	S-13	0.1
Total	16	1696	6047	576	1515	241	20	25	501	265	399	.251	.286	.309	64	-293	81	55	-9	.973	73	*S-1524/2-92,3O1	-5.2

■ DEE FONDY
Fondy, Dee Virgil b: 10/31/24, Slaton, Tex. BL/TL, 6'3", 196 lbs. Deb: 4/17/51

YEAR	TM/L	G	AB	R	H	2B	3B	HR	RBI	BB	SO	AVG	OBP	SLG	PRO+	BR/A	SB	CS	SBR	FA	FR	G/POS	TPR
1951	Chi-N	49	170	23	46	7	3	2	20	11	20	.271	.319	.388	88	-3	5	6	-2	.976	-3	1-44	-1.0
1952	Chi-N	145	554	69	166	21	9	10	67	28	60	.300	.334	.424	108	4	13	11	-3	.990	2	*1-143	-0.2
1953	Chi-N	150	595	79	184	24	11	18	78	44	106	.309	.358	.477	113	10	10	7	-1	.987	4	*1-149	0.6
1954	Chi-N	141	568	77	162	30	4	9	49	35	84	.285	.328	.400	87	-11	20	5	**3**	.993	7	*1-138	-0.8
1955	Chi-N	150	574	69	152	23	8	17	65	35	87	.265	.309	.422	92	-8	8	9	-3	.991	1	*1-147	-1.9
1956	Chi-N	137	543	52	146	22	9	9	46	20	74	.269	.295	.392	84	-13	9	7	-2	.985	-3	*1-133	-2.8
1957	Chi-N	11	51	3	16	3	1	0	2	0	9	.314	.314	.412	94	-1	1	2	-1	.991	-1	1-11	-0.2
	Pit-N	95	323	42	101	13	2	2	35	25	59	.313	.364	.384	104	2	11	5	0	.982	-3	1-73	-0.5
	Yr	106	374	45	117	16	3	2	37	25	68	.313	.357	.388	103	2	12	7	-1	.983	-4	1-84	-0.7
1958	Cin-N	89	124	23	27	1	1	1	11	5	27	.218	.248	.266	34	-12	7	1	2	.987	3	1-36,O-22	-1.3
Total	8	967	3502	437	1000	144	47	69	373	203	526	.286	.326	.413	95	-30	84	53	-7	.988	3	1-874/O-22	-8.2

■ LEW FONSECA
Fonseca, Lewis Albert b: 1/21/1899, Oakland, Cal. d: 11/26/89, Ely, Iowa BR/TR, 5'10.5", 180 lbs. Deb: 4/13/21 M

YEAR	TM/L	G	AB	R	H	2B	3B	HR	RBI	BB	SO	AVG	OBP	SLG	PRO+	BR/A	SB	CS	SBR	FA	FR	G/POS	TPR
1921	Cin-N	82	297	38	82	10	3	1	41	8	13	.276	.304	.340	74	-12	2	3	-1	.961	-3	2-50,1-16,O-16	-1.6
1922	Cin-N	81	291	55	105	20	3	4	45	14	18	.361	.390	.491	128	12	7	8	-3	.970	2	2-71	1.8
1923	Cin-N	65	237	33	66	11	4	3	28	9	16	.278	.310	.397	87	-5	4	0	1	.957	8	2-45,1-14	0.4
1924	Cin-N	20	57	5	13	2	1	0	9	4	4	.228	.279	.298	55	-4	1	0	0	1.000	-2	2-10/1-6	-0.6
1925	Phi-N	126	467	78	149	30	5	7	60	21	42	.319	.352	.450	95	-4	6	3	1	.956	-8	2-69,1-55	-1.3
1927	Cle-A	112	428	60	133	20	7	2	40	12	17	.311	.333	.404	90	-8	12	4	1	.973	-6	2-96,1-13	-0.9
1928	Cle-A	75	263	38	86	19	4	3	36	13	17	.327	.361	.464	114	5	4	2	0	1.000	5	1-56,3-15/S-4,2-1	0.5
1929	Cle-A	148	566	97	209	44	15	6	103	50	23	**.369**	.427	.532	140	34	19	11	-1	.995	6	*1-147	2.3
1930	Cle-A	40	129	20	36	9	0	2	17	7	7	.279	.316	.380	73	-6	0	0	0	.980	2	1-28/3-6	-0.5
1931	Cle-A	26	108	21	40	9	1	1	14	8	7	.370	.419	.500	133	5	2	3	-0	.993	0	1-26	0.3
	Chi-A	121	465	65	139	26	5	2	71	32	22	.299	.348	.389	99	-1	5	4	-1	.974	-17	O-95,2-21/1-2,3-1	-2.2
	Yr	147	573	86	179	35	6	3	85	40	29	.312	.361	.410	106	4	7	7	-1	.974	-16	O-95,1-28,2-21,3-1	-1.9
1932	Chi-A	18	37	0	5	1	0	0	6	1	5	.135	.158	.162	-18	-7	0	0	0	1.000	1	/O-8,P-1,M	-0.6
1933	Chi-A	23	59	8	12	2	0	2	15	7	6	.203	.288	.339	68	-3	0	0	0	1.000	2	1-12,M	-0.1
Total	12	937	3404	518	1075	203	50	31	485	186	199	.316	.355	.432	103	8	64	36	-2	.994	-3	1-375,2-363,O/3SP	-2.5

YEAR	TM/L	G	AB	R	H	2B	3B	HR	RBI	BB	SO	AVG	OBP	SLG	PRO+	BR/A	SB	CS	SBR	FA	FR	G/POS	TPR

■ CHAD FONVILLE Fonville, Chad Everett b: 3/5/71, Jacksonville, N.C. BB/TR, 5'6", 155 lbs. Deb: 4/28/95

YEAR	TM/L	G	AB	R	H	2B	3B	HR	RBI	BB	SO	AVG	OBP	SLG	PRO+	BR/A	SB	CS	SBR	FA	FR	G/POS	TPR
1995	Mon-N	14	12	2	4	0	0	0	0	0	3	.333	.333	.333	74	-0	0	2	-1	.000	0	/2-2	-0.2
	*LA-N	88	308	41	85	6	1	0	16	23	39	.276	.328	.302	74	-11	20	5	3	.971	-3	S-38,2-36,O-11	-0.6
	Yr	102	320	43	89	6	1	0	16	23	42	.278	.328	.303	73	-12	20	7	2	.971	-3	2-38,S-38,O-11	-0.8
1996	LA-N	103	201	34	41	4	1	0	13	17	31	.204	.266	.234	36	-19	7	2	1	.964	-3	O-35,2-23,S-20,3-2	-1.9
Total	2	205	521	77	130	10	2	0	29	40	73	.250	.304	.276	59	-30	27	9	3	.970	-6	2-61,S-58,O-46,3-2	-2.7

■ BARRY FOOTE Foote, Barry Clifton b: 2/16/52, Smithfield, N.C. BR/TR, 6'3", 210 lbs. Deb: 9/14/73 C

YEAR	TM/L	G	AB	R	H	2B	3B	HR	RBI	BB	SO	AVG	OBP	SLG	PRO+	BR/A	SB	CS	SBR	FA	FR	G/POS	TPR
1973	Mon-N	6	6	0	4	0	1	0	1	0	0	.667	.667	1.000	343	2	0	0	0	.000	0	H	0.2
1974	Mon-N	125	420	44	110	23	4	11	60	35	74	.262	.323	.414	100	-1	2	1	0	.984	9	*C-122	1.3
1975	Mon-N	118	387	25	75	16	1	7	30	17	48	.194	.230	.295	43	-31	0	1	-1	.985	11	*C-115	-1.7
1976	Mon-N	105	350	32	82	12	2	7	27	17	32	.234	.272	.340	70	-15	0	0	0	.989	7	C-96/3-2,1-1	-0.5
1977	Mon-N	15	49	4	12	3	1	2	8	4	10	.245	.302	.469	106	0	0	0	0	.988	0	C-13	0.1
	Phi-N	18	32	3	7	1	0	1	3	3	6	.219	.286	.344	65	-2	0	0	0	.980	-1	C-17	-0.2
	Yr	33	81	7	19	4	1	3	11	7	16	.235	.295	.420	88	-2	0	0	0	.985	-0	C-30	-0.1
1978	*Phi-N	39	57	4	9	0	0	1	4	1	11	.158	.172	.211	6	-7	0	0	0	1.000	2	C-31	-0.5
1979	Chi-N	132	429	47	109	26	0	16	56	34	49	.254	.316	.427	92	-6	0	0	0	.979	-3	*C-129	-0.4
1980	Chi-N	63	202	16	48	13	1	6	28	13	18	.238	.284	.401	83	-5	1	1	-0	.992	1	C-55	-0.3
1981	Chi-N	9	22	0	0	0	0	0	1	3	7	.000	.120	.000	-61	-9	0	0	0	1.000	-1	/C-8	-0.6
	*NY-A	40	125	12	26	4	0	6	10	8	21	.208	.256	.384	83	-3	0	0	0	.996	9	C-34/1-1,D-4	0.7
1982	NY-A	17	48	4	7	5	0	0	2	1	11	.146	.163	.250	12	-6	0	0	0	.973	-4	C-17	-0.9
Total	10	687	2127	191	489	103	10	57	230	136	287	.230	.279	.368	75	-78	10	6	-1	.985	31	C-637/D-4,1-2,3-2	-2.8

■ JIM FORAN Foran, James H. b: 1848, New York 5'6.5", 159 lbs. Deb: 5/4/1871

YEAR	TM/L	G	AB	R	H	2B	3B	HR	RBI	BB	SO	AVG	OBP	SLG	PRO+	BR/A	SB	CS	SBR	FA	FR	G/POS	TPR
1871	Kek-n	19	89	21	31	1	3	1	18	2	1	.348	.363	.461	132	3	1	0	0	.878	1	1-16/O-4	0.3

■ DAVY FORCE Force, David W. "Wee Davy" or "Tom Thumb" b: 7/27/1849, New York, N.Y. d: 6/21/18, Englewood, N.J. BR/TR, 5'4", 130 lbs. Deb: 5/5/1871

YEAR	TM/L	G	AB	R	H	2B	3B	HR	RBI	BB	SO	AVG	OBP	SLG	PRO+	BR/A	SB	CS	SBR	FA	FR	G/POS	TPR
1871	Oly-n	32	162	45	45	9	4	0	29	4	0	.278	.295	.383	98	0	8	0	2	.844	18	*S-31/3-1	1.3
1872	Tro-n	25	130	40	53	11	0	0	16	1	0	.408	.412	.492	175	11	2	2	-1	.871	4	3-16/S-9	0.9
	Bal-n	19	95	29	41	2	2	0	13	1	0	.432	.438	.495	178	8	3	0	1	.846	5	3-19	0.8
	Yr	44	225	69	94	13	2	0	29	2	0	.418	.423	.493	176	19	5	2	0	.857	8	3-35/S-9	1.7
1873	Bal-n	49	234	77	86	8	1	0	31	9	0	.368	.391	.410	139	12	1	0	0	.820	6	3-34,S-17/P-3	1.1
1874	Chi-n	59	294	61	92	9	0	0	26	3	1	.313	.320	.344	112	3	4	0	1	.802	11	*3-42,S-18/P-1	1.2
1875	Ath-n	77	386	78	120	22	5	0	49	7	5	.311	.323	.394	133	9	6	3	0	.887	10	*S-77/3-2	1.4
1876	Phi-N	60	284	48	66	6	0	0	17	5	3	.232	.246	.254	67	-9				.898	21	*S-60/3-2	1.0
	NY-N	1	3	0	0	0	0	0	0	0	0	.000	.000	.000	-99	-1				.833	0	/S-1	0.0
	Yr	61	287	48	66	6	0	0	17	5	3	.230	.243	.251	66	-10				.897	21	S-61/3-2	1.0
1877	StL-N	58	225	24	59	5	3	0	22	11	15	.262	.297	.311	97	-0				.914	6	*S-50/3-8	0.6
1879	Buf-N	79	316	36	66	5	2	0	8	13	37	.209	.240	.237	57	-14				.929	2	*S-78/3-1	-0.8
1880	Buf-N	81	290	22	49	10	0	0	17	10	35	.169	.197	.203	35	-19				.939	31	2-53,S-30	1.6
1881	Buf-N	75	278	21	50	9	1	0	15	11	29	.180	.211	.219	36	-20				.937	24	2-51,S-21/O-3,3-1	0.7
1882	Buf-N	73	278	39	67	10	1	1	28	12	17	.241	.272	.295	81	-6				.908	7	*S-61,3-11/2-1	0.4
1883	Buf-N	96	378	40	82	11	3	0	35	12	39	.217	.241	.262	52	-22				.884	-6	*S-78,3-13/2-7	-2.3
1884	Buf-N	106	403	47	83	13	3	0	36	27	41	.206	.256	.253	59	-19				.898	-3	*S-105/2-1	-1.9
1885	Buf-N	71	253	20	57	6	1	0	15	13	19	.225	.263	.257	66	-9				.882	-4	2-42,S-24/3-6	-1.0
1886	Was-N	68	242	26	44	5	1	0	16	17	26	.182	.236	.211	39	-17	9			.909	17	S-56/2-8,3-4	0.1
Total	5 n	261	1301	330	437	61	12	0	164	25	6	.336	.348	.401	132	43	24	5	4	.861	53	S-152,3-114/P-4	6.7
Total	10	768	2950	323	623	80	15	1	209	131	261	.211	.245	.249	58	-136	9			.908	96	S-564,2-163/3-46,O	-1.6

■ CURT FORD Ford, Curtis Glenn b: 10/11/60, Jackson, Miss. BL/TR, 5'10", 150 lbs. Deb: 6/22/85

YEAR	TM/L	G	AB	R	H	2B	3B	HR	RBI	BB	SO	AVG	OBP	SLG	PRO+	BR/A	SB	CS	SBR	FA	FR	G/POS	TPR
1985	StL-N	11	12	2	6	2	0	0	3	4	1	.500	.625	.667	264	3	1	0	0	.750	-2	/O-4	0.2
1986	StL-N	85	214	30	53	15	2	2	29	23	29	.248	.321	.364	89	-3	13	5	1	.975	1	O-64	-0.3
1987	*StL-N	89	228	32	65	9	5	3	26	14	32	.285	.329	.408	92	-3	11	8	-2	.981	1	O-75	-0.5
1988	StL-N	91	128	11	25	6	0	1	18	8	26	.195	.243	.266	45	-9	6	1	1	.965	-4	O-40/1-7	-1.4
1989	Phi-N	108	142	13	31	5	1	1	13	16	33	.218	.302	.289	70	-5	5	3	-0	1.000	-8	O-52/1-1,2-1	-1.6
1990	Phi-N	22	18	0	2	0	0	0	0	1	5	.111	.158	.111	-25	-3	0	0	0	1.000	-1	/O-3	-0.4
Total	6	406	742	88	182	37	8	7	89	66	126	.245	.309	.345	80	-20	36	17	1	.977	-12	O-238/1-8,2-1	-4.0

■ DAN FORD Ford, Darnell Glenn b: 5/19/52, Los Angeles, Cal. BR/TR, 6'1", 185 lbs. Deb: 4/12/75

YEAR	TM/L	G	AB	R	H	2B	3B	HR	RBI	BB	SO	AVG	OBP	SLG	PRO+	BR/A	SB	CS	SBR	FA	FR	G/POS	TPR
1975	Min-A	130	440	72	123	21	1	15	59	30	79	.280	.333	.434	114	7	6	7	-2	.988	-9	*O-120/D-3	-0.9
1976	Min-A	145	514	87	137	24	7	20	86	36	118	.267	.327	.457	125	15	17	6	2	.968	-5	*O-139/D-3	0.6
1977	Min-A	144	453	66	121	25	7	11	60	41	79	.267	.341	.426	109	6	6	4	-1	.964	-10	*O-137/D-3	-0.9
1978	Min-A	151	592	78	162	36	10	11	82	48	88	.274	.333	.424	109	7	7	7	-2	.977	-2	*O-149/D-1	-0.4
1979	*Cal-A	142	569	100	165	26	5	21	101	40	86	.290	.340	.464	118	13	8	5	-1	.977	7	*O-141	1.3
1980	Cal-A	65	226	22	63	11	0	7	26	19	45	.279	.340	.420	110	3	0	1	-0	.940	-2	O-45,D-15	-0.2
1981	Cal-A	97	375	53	104	14	1	5	48	23	71	.277	.328	.440	119	8	2	2	0	.960	-2	O-97	0.2
1982	Bal-A	123	421	46	99	21	3	10	43	23	71	.235	.281	.371	78	-14	5	2	0	.975	4	*O-119/D-1	-1.2
1983	*Bal-A	103	407	63	114	30	4	9	55	29	55	.280	.333	.440	113	6	9	2	2	.987	1	*O-103	0.5
1984	Bal-A	25	91	7	21	4	0	1	5	7	13	.231	.286	.308	66	-4	1	0	0	1.000	2	O-15/D-8	-0.3
1985	Bal-A	28	75	4	14	2	0	1	1	7	17	.187	.256	.253	41	-6	0	1	0	.000	0	D-28	-0.7
Total	11	1153	4163	598	1123	214	38	121	566	303	722	.270	.326	.427	109	40	61	37	-4	.974	-17	*O-1065/D-62	-2.0

■ ED FORD Ford, Edward L. b: 1862, Richmond, Va. 5'9.5", 160 lbs. Deb: 10/9/1884

YEAR	TM/L	G	AB	R	H	2B	3B	HR	RBI	BB	SO	AVG	OBP	SLG	PRO+	BR/A	SB	CS	SBR	FA	FR	G/POS	TPR
1884	Ric-a	2	5	0	0	0	0	0	0	0	0	.000	.000	.000	-99	-1				.556	1	/S-1,1-1	0.0

■ HOD FORD Ford, Horace Hills b: 7/23/1897, New Haven, Conn. d: 1/29/77, Winchester, Mass. BR/TR, 5'10", 165 lbs. Deb: 9/8/19

YEAR	TM/L	G	AB	R	H	2B	3B	HR	RBI	BB	SO	AVG	OBP	SLG	PRO+	BR/A	SB	CS	SBR	FA	FR	G/POS	TPR
1919	Bos-N	10	28	4	6	1	0	1	3	2	6	.214	.290	.286	77	-1	0			.946	3	/S-8,3-2	0.3
1920	Bos-N	88	257	16	62	12	5	1	30	18	25	.241	.296	.339	86	-5	3	3	-1	.972	15	2-59,S-18/1-4	1.3
1921	Bos-N	152	555	50	155	29	5	2	61	36	49	.279	.328	.360	87	-11	2	11	-6	.973	16	*2-119,S-33	0.5
1922	Bos-N	143	515	58	140	23	9	2	60	30	36	.272	.317	.363	78	-17	2	1	0	.953	-4	*S-115,2-28	-0.8
1923	Bos-N	111	380	27	103	16	7	2	50	31	30	.271	.326	.366	86	-8	1	1	0	.970	-9	2-95,S-19	-1.4
1924	Phi-N	145	530	58	144	27	5	3	53	27	40	.272	.308	.358	70	-23	1	9	-5	.970	12	*2-145	-1.5
1925	Bro-N	66	216	32	59	11	0	1	15	26	15	.273	.357	.338	81	-5	0	3	-2	.966	-0	S-66	-0.1
1926	Cin-N	57	197	14	55	6	1	0	18	14	12	.279	.336	.320	79	-5	1			.963	5	S-57	0.5
1927	Cin-N	115	409	45	112	16	2	1	46	33	34	.274	.331	.330	80	-11	0			.952	-8	*S-104,2-12	-0.8
1928	Cin-N	149	506	49	122	17	4	0	54	47	31	.241	.308	.291	58	-30	1			.972	12	*S-149	-0.1
1929	Cin-N	148	529	68	146	14	6	3	50	41	25	.276	.329	.342	70	-25	8			.953	8	*S-108,2-42	-0.1
1930	Cin-N	132	424	36	98	16	7	1	34	24	28	.231	.272	.309	42	-40	2			.974	2	S-74,2-66	-2.6
1931	Cin-N	84	175	18	40	8	1	0	13	13	13	.229	.286	.286	57	-11	0			.954	1	S-73/2-3,3-1	-0.5
1932	StL-N	1	2	0	0	0	0	0	0	0	0	.000	.000	.000	-97	-1	0			.750	0	/S-1	0.0
	Bos-N	40	95	9	26	5	2	0	6	6	9	.274	.324	.368	89	-1	0			.984	-3	2-20,S-16/3-2	-0.2
	Yr	41	97	9	26	5	2	0	6	6	9	.268	.317	.361	85	-2	0			.984	-3	2-20,S-17/3-2	-0.2
1933	Bos-N	5	15	0	1	0	0	0	1	1	0	.067	.222	.067	-16	-2	0			1.000	5	/S-5	0.3
Total	15	1446	4833	484	1269	200	55	16	494	351	354	.263	.316	.337	72	-198	21	28		.960	54	S-846,2-589/3-5,1-4	-5.2

■ TED FORD Ford, Theodore Henry b: 2/7/47, Vineland, N.J. BR/TR, 5'10", 180 lbs. Deb: 4/7/70

YEAR	TM/L	G	AB	R	H	2B	3B	HR	RBI	BB	SO	AVG	OBP	SLG	PRO+	BR/A	SB	CS	SBR	FA	FR	G/POS	TPR
1970	Cle-A	26	46	5	8	1	0	1	3	1	13	.174	.224	.261	32	-4	0	0	0	1.000	1	O-12	-0.4
1971	Cle-A	74	196	15	38	6	0	2	14	9	34	.194	.229	.255	34	-17	2	2	-1	1.000	-1	O-55	-2.2
1972	Tex-A	129	429	43	101	19	1	14	50	37	80	.235	.301	.382	107	2	4	3	-1	.977	9	*O-119	0.6
1973	Cle-A	11	40	3	9	0	1	0	2	3	7	.225	.262	.275	50	-3	1	0	0	1.000	-4	O-10	-0.7
Total	4	240	711	66	156	26	2	17	68	51	134	.219	.275	.333	76	-22	7	5	-1	.985	6	O-196	-2.7

YEAR	TM/L	G	AB	R	H	2B	3B	HR	RBI	BB	SO	AVG	OBP	SLG	PRO+	BR/A	SB	CS	SBR	FA	FR	G/POS	TPR

■ BROOK FORDYCE
Fordyce, Brook Alexander b: 5/7/70, New London, Conn. BR/TR, 6'1", 185 lbs. Deb: 4/26/95

YEAR	TM/L	G	AB	R	H	2B	3B	HR	RBI	BB	SO	AVG	OBP	SLG	PRO+	BR/A	SB	CS	SBR	FA	FR	G/POS	TPR
1995	NY-N	4	2	1	1	1	0	0	0	1	0	.500	.667	1.000	343	1	0	0	0	.000	0	-0,-0	0.1
1996	Cin-N	4	7	0	2	1	0	0	1	3	1	.286	.500	.429	149	1	0	0	0	1.000	-0	/C-4	0.1
Total	2	8	9	1	3	2	0	0	1	4	1	.333	.538	.556	192	2	0	0	0	1.000	-0	/C-4	0.2

■ FRANK FOREMAN
Foreman, Francis Isaiah "Monkey" b: 5/1/1863, Baltimore, Md. d: 11/19/57, Baltimore, Md. BL/TL, 6', 160 lbs. Deb: 5/15/1884 F

YEAR	TM/L	G	AB	R	H	2B	3B	HR	RBI	BB	SO	AVG	OBP	SLG	PRO+	BR/A	SB	CS	SBR	FA	FR	G/POS	TPR
1884	CP-U	3	11	0	1	0	0	0		0		.091	.091	.091	-45	-2				.857	-1	/P-3,O-2	-0.1
	KC-U	1	3	0	0	0	0	0		0		.000	.000	.000	-99	-1				.900	1	/P-1	0.0
	Yr	4	14	0	1	0	0	0		0		.071	.071	.071	-59	-3				.882	0	/P-4,O-2	-0.1
1885	Bal-a	3	14	4	4	0	1	0	2	0		.286	.286	.429	125	0				.800	-1	/P-3,O-1	0.0
1889	Bal-a	54	181	18	26	2	1	1	11	12	35	.144	.201	.182	9	-22	7			.853	-3	P-51/O-3	-0.1
1890	Cin-N	25	75	13	10	1	3	1	7	10	13	.133	.253	.267	52	-5	0			.867	-3	P-25/O-1	0.0
1891	Cin-N	1	4	0	1	1	0	0	0	0	0	.250	.250	.500	116	0	0			.000	-0	/O-1	0.0
	Was-a	50	153	26	34	4	5	4	19	23	35	.222	.339	.392	114	3	6			.952	-1	P-43/O-8	0.0
1892	Was-N	11	28	5	13	2	1	1	4	3	3	.464	.516	.786	301	7	0			.632	-1	P-11	0.0
	Bal-N	7	23	2	4	1	1	0	1	3	3	.174	.269	.304	71	-1	1			.750	-0	/O-5,P-4	-0.1
	Yr	18	51	7	17	3	3	1	4	6	6	.333	.404	.569	195	6	1			.731	-1	P-15/O-5	-0.1
1893	NY-N	2	3	0	0	0	0	0		0		.000	.000	.000	-99	-1	0			1.000	-0	/P-2	0.0
1895	Cin-N	32	94	14	29	7	0	0	11	4	14	.309	.350	.447	100	-0	3			.882	-3	P-32	0.0
1896	Cin-N	27	74	9	18	2	0	0	8	4	6	.243	.282	.270	43	-6	2			.912	-1	P-27	0.0
1901	Bos-A	1	4	0	0	0	0	0		0		.000	.000	.000	-99	-1	0			1.000	-0	/P-1	0.0
	Bal-A	24	80	12	26	2	0	0	10	3		.325	.349	.400	103	0	1			.887	-3	P-24	0.0
	Yr	25	84	12	26	2	0	0	10	3		.310	.333	.381	94	-1	1			.891	-3	P-25	0.0
1902	Bal-A	2	7	1	3	1	0	0		1		.429	.429	.571	168	1	0			.818	1	/P-2	0.0
Total	11	243	754	104	169	23	15	9	73	62	109	.224	.291	.330	74	-29	18			.881	-16	P-229/O-21	-0.3

■ TOM FORSTER
Forster, Thomas W. b: 5/1/1859, New York, N.Y. d: 7/17/46, New York, N.Y. BR, 5'9", 153 lbs. Deb: 8/4/1882

YEAR	TM/L	G	AB	R	H	2B	3B	HR	RBI	BB	SO	AVG	OBP	SLG	PRO+	BR/A	SB	CS	SBR	FA	FR	G/POS	TPR
1882	Det-N	21	76	5	7	0	0	0	2	5	12	.092	.148	.092	-21	-10				.830	-7	2-21	-1.5
1884	Pit-a	35	126	10	28	5	0	0		7		.222	.263	.262	71	-4				.897	6	S-28/3-6,2-1	0.2
1885	NY-a	57	213	28	47	7	2	0	18	17		.221	.281	.272	82	-3				.903	-12	2-52/O-5	-1.2
1886	NY-a	67	251	33	49	3	2	1	20	20		.195	.263	.235	59	-11	9			.891	-7	2-62/O-4,S-1	-1.4
Total	4	180	666	76	131	15	4	1	40	49	12	.197	.256	.236	59	-28	9			.885	-19	2-136/S-29,O-9,3-6	-3.9

■ ED FORSYTHE
Forsythe, Edward James b: 4/30/1887, Kingston, N.Y. d: 6/22/56, Hoboken, N.J. BR/TR, 5'10", 155 lbs. Deb: 10/2/15

YEAR	TM/L	G	AB	R	H	2B	3B	HR	RBI	BB	SO	AVG	OBP	SLG	PRO+	BR/A	SB	CS	SBR	FA	FR	G/POS	TPR
1915	Bal-F	1	3	0	0	0	0	0		0	1	.000	.250	.000	-26	-1	0			.667	-0	/3-1	-0.1

■ GEORGE FOSS
Foss, George Dueward "Deeby" b: 6/13/1897, Register, Ga. d: 11/10/69, Brandon, Fla. BR/TR, 5'10.5", 170 lbs. Deb: 4/16/21

YEAR	TM/L	G	AB	R	H	2B	3B	HR	RBI	BB	SO	AVG	OBP	SLG	PRO+	BR/A	SB	CS	SBR	FA	FR	G/POS	TPR
1921	Was-A	4	7	0	0	0	0	0	0	0	1	.000	.000	.000	-99	-2	0	0	0	.750	0	/3-1	-0.2

■ RAY FOSSE
Fosse, Raymond Earl b: 4/4/47, Marion, Ill. BR/TR, 6'2", 215 lbs. Deb: 9/8/67

YEAR	TM/L	G	AB	R	H	2B	3B	HR	RBI	BB	SO	AVG	OBP	SLG	PRO+	BR/A	SB	CS	SBR	FA	FR	G/POS	TPR
1967	Cle-A	7	16	1	1	0	0	0	0	0	5	.063	.063	.063	-62	-3	0	0	0	1.000	5	/C-7	0.2
1968	Cle-A	1	0	0	0	0	0	0	0	0	0	—	—	—	—	0	0	0	0	1.000	0	/C-1	0.0
1969	Cle-A	37	116	11	20	3	0	2	9	8	29	.172	.232	.250	34	-10	1	0	0	.977	3	C-37	-0.5
1970	Cle-A★	120	450	62	138	17	1	18	61	39	55	.307	.363	.469	122	13	1	5	-3	.989	6	*C-120	2.3
1971	Cle-A†	133	486	53	134	21	1	12	62	36	62	.276	.331	.397	97	-2	4	1	1	.988	-3	*C-126/1-4	-0.1
1972	Cle-A	134	457	42	110	20	1	10	41	45	46	.241	.313	.354	95	-3	5	1	1	.985	6	*C-124/1-3	1.0
1973	*Oak-A	143	492	37	126	23	2	7	52	25	62	.256	.293	.354	86	-11	2	2	-1	.987	2	*C-141/D-2	-0.3
1974	*Oak-A	69	204	20	40	8	3	4	23	11	31	.196	.244	.324	66	-10	1	1	-0	.973	-1	C-68/D-1	-0.9
1975	*Oak-A	82	136	14	19	3	2	0	12	8	19	.140	.193	.191	9	-16	0	0	-1	.981	6	C-82/1-1,2-1	-1.0
1976	Cle-A	90	276	26	83	9	1	2	30	20	20	.301	.348	.362	109	3	1	2	-1	.987	1	C-85/1-3,D-1	0.6
1977	Cle-A	78	238	25	63	7	1	6	27	7	26	.265	.294	.378	84	-6	0	5	-1	.983	9	C-77/1-1,D-1	0.2
	Sea-A	11	34	3	12	3	0	0	5	2	2	.353	.389	.441	127	1	0	1	-1	.968	-3	/C-8,D-2	-0.2
	Yr	89	272	28	75	10	1	6	32	9	28	.276	.306	.386	90	-4	0	6	-4	.982	5	C-85/D-3,1-1	0.0
1979	Mil-A	19	52	6	12	3	1	0	2	2	6	.231	.286	.327	65	-3	0	0	-0	1.000	-3	/C-13/1-1,D-5	-0.3
Total	12	924	2957	299	758	117	13	61	324	203	363	.256	.308	.367	90	-46	15	19	-7	.985	28	C-889/1-13,D-12,2-1	1.0

■ POP FOSTER
Foster, Clarence Francis b: 4/8/1878, New Haven, Conn. d: 4/16/44, Princeton, N.J. BR/TR, 5'8.5",   Deb: 9/13/1898

YEAR	TM/L	G	AB	R	H	2B	3B	HR	RBI	BB	SO	AVG	OBP	SLG	PRO+	BR/A	SB	CS	SBR	FA	FR	G/POS	TPR
1898	NY-N	32	112	10	30	6	1	0	9	0		.268	.268	.339	76	-4	0			.967	-5	O-21,3-10/S-2	-1.0
1899	NY-N	84	301	48	89	9	7	3	57	20		.296	.348	.402	109	3	7			.949	-10	O-84/S-1,3-1	-1.2
1900	NY-N	31	84	19	22	3	1	0	11	11		.262	.347	.321	89	-1	0			.925	-1	O-12/S-7,2-5	-0.3
1901	Was-A	103	392	65	109	16	9	6	54	41		.278	.352	.411	113	7	10			.925	-1	*O-102/S-2	-0.1
	Chi-A	12	35	4	10	2	2	1	6	4		.286	.359	.543	152	2	0			.909	-1	/O-9	0.0
	Yr	115	427	69	119	18	11	7	60	45		.279	.353	.422	116	9	10			.924	-2	O-111/S-2	-0.1
Total	4	262	924	146	260	36	20	10	137	76		.281	.341	.396	107	8	17			.938	-19	O-228/S-12,3-11,2-5	-2.6

■ EDDIE FOSTER
Foster, Edward Cunningham "Kid" b: 2/13/1887, Chicago, Ill. d: 1/15/37, Washington, D.C. BR/TR, 5'6.5", 145 lbs. Deb: 4/14/10

YEAR	TM/L	G	AB	R	H	2B	3B	HR	RBI	BB	SO	AVG	OBP	SLG	PRO+	BR/A	SB	CS	SBR	FA	FR	G/POS	TPR
1910	NY-A	30	83	5	11	2	0	0	1	8		.133	.217	.157	16	-8	2			.909	-2	S-22	-1.1
1912	Was-A	154	618	98	176	34	9	2	70	53		.285	.345	.379	106	4	27			.920	12	*3-154	1.7
1913	Was-A	106	409	56	101	11	5	1	41	36	31	.247	.309	.306	78	-11	22			.901	4	*3-105	-0.6
1914	Was-A	157	616	82	174	16	10	2	50	60	47	.282	.348	.351	106	5	31	18	-2	.929	-18	*3-157	-1.0
1915	Was-A	154	618	75	170	25	10	0	52	48	30	.275	.329	.348	101	-1	20	6	2	.919	-1	3-79,2-75	0.0
1916	Was-A	158	606	75	153	19	5	1	44	68	26	.252	.332	.317	96	-2	23	16	-3	.929	-16	3-84,2-72	-1.7
1917	Was-A	143	554	66	130	16	4	0	43	46	23	.235	.293	.292	80	-14	11			.935	-6	3-86,2-57	-1.7
1918	Was-A	129	519	70	147	19	3	0	29	41	20	.283	.339	.320	101	0	12			.936	2	*3-127/2-2	0.6
1919	Was-A	120	478	57	126	12	5	0	26	33	21	.264	.314	.310	76	-15	20			.946	7	3-115	-0.3
1920	Bos-A	117	386	48	100	17	6	0	41	42	17	.259	.336	.334	82	-10	10	4	1	.957	15	3-88,2-21	1.0
1921	Bos-A	120	412	51	117	18	6	0	35	57	15	.284	.371	.357	89	-5	13	7	-0	.943	-14	3-94,2-22	-1.2
1922	Bos-A	48	109	11	23	3	0	0	3	9	10	.211	.277	.239	36	-10	1	1	-0	.886	-11	3-28/S-3	-1.9
	StL-A	37	144	29	44	4	0	0	12	20	8	.306	.394	.333	88	-1	3	1	0	.916	-2	3-37	0.0
	Yr	85	253	40	67	7	0	0	15	29	18	.265	.345	.292	67	-11	4	2	0	.905	-12	3-65/S-3	-1.9
1923	StL-A	27	100	9	18	2	0	0	4	7	7	.180	.241	.200	16	-12	0	0	0	.961	-8	2-20/3-7	-1.9
Total	13	1500	5652	732	1490	191	71	6	451	528	255	.264	.329	.326	89	-81	195	53		.930	-41	*3-1161,2-269/S-25	-8.1

■ ELMER FOSTER
Foster, Elmer Ellsworth b: 8/15/1861, Minneapolis, Minn. d: 7/22/46, Deephaven, Minn. BR/TL, 5'10", 178 lbs. Deb: 6/18/1884

YEAR	TM/L	G	AB	R	H	2B	3B	HR	RBI	BB	SO	AVG	OBP	SLG	PRO+	BR/A	SB	CS	SBR	FA	FR	G/POS	TPR
1884	Phi-a	4	11	4	2	0	0	0		3		.182	.357	.182	76	-0				.885	-2	/C-4,O-1	-0.2
	Phi-U	1	3	0	1	0	0	0		0		.333	.333	1.000	313	1				.625	-1	/O-1	0.0
1886	NY-a	35	125	16	23	0	1	0	7	6		.184	.239	.200	40	-8	3			.853	-5	2-21,O-14	-0.7
1888	NY-N	37	136	15	20	3	2	0	10	9	20	.147	.216	.199	33	-10	13			.852	-2	O-37/3-1	-1.3
1889	NY-N	2	4	0	0	0	0	0		3	1	.000	.429	.000	25	-0	2			1.000	-0	/O-2	0.0
1890	Chi-N	27	105	20	26	4	2	5	23	9	21	.248	.325	.467	125	2	18			.986	0	O-27	0.3
1891	Chi-N	4	16	3	3	0	1	0	1	1	2	.188	.235	.375	77	-1	1			.875	-2	/O-4	-0.1
Total	6	110	400	60	75	7	6	6	41	32	44	.188	.261	.280	67	-16	37			.883	-4	/O-85,2-21,C-5,3-1	-2.0

■ GEORGE FOSTER
Foster, George Arthur b: 12/1/48, Tuscaloosa, Ala. BR/TR, 6'1", 185 lbs. Deb: 9/10/69

YEAR	TM/L	G	AB	R	H	2B	3B	HR	RBI	BB	SO	AVG	OBP	SLG	PRO+	BR/A	SB	CS	SBR	FA	FR	G/POS	TPR
1969	SF-N	9	5	1	2	0	0	0	4	0	1	.400	.400	.400	127	0	0	0	0	1.000	-3	/O-8	-0.3
1970	SF-N	9	19	2	6	1	1	0	4	2	5	.316	.381	.632	168	2	0	0	0	1.000	-0	/O-7	0.1
1971	SF-N	36	105	11	28	5	0	3	8	6	27	.267	.303	.400	100	-0	0	1	-1			O-30	-0.4
	Cin-N	104	368	39	86	18	4	10	50	23	93	.234	.291	.386	92	-5	7	6	-2	.986	11	*O-102	-0.1
	Yr	140	473	50	114	23	4	13	58	29	120	.241	.295	.389	94	-5	7	7	-2	.985	9	*O-132	-0.5
1972	*Cin-N	59	145	15	29	4	1	2	12	5	44	.200	.232	.283	48	-10	2	1	0	.973	-5	O-47	-1.8
1973	Cin-N	17	39	6	11	3	0	2	4	7		.282	.349	.667	185	4	0	0	-0	1.000	-3	O-13	0.0

YEAR	TM/L	G	AB	R	H	2B	3B	HR	RBI	BB	SO	AVG	OBP	SLG	PRO+	BR/A	SB	CS	SBR	FA	FR	G/POS	TPR
1974	Cin-N	106	276	31	73	18	0	7	41	30	52	.264	.345	.406	111	4	3	2	-0	.989	-16	O-98	-1.6
1975	*Cin-N	134	463	71	139	24	4	23	78	40	73	.300	.360	.518	139	22	2	1	0	.990	5	*O-125/1-1	2.3
1976	*Cin-N★	144	562	86	172	21	9	29	121	52	89	.306	.369	.530	149	34	17	3	3	.994	-2	*O-142/1-1	3.1
1977	Cin-N★	158	615	124	197	31	2	52	149	61	107	.320	.386	.631	165	54	6	4	-1	.992	16	*O-158	6.1
1978	Cin-N★	158	604	97	170	26	7	40	120	70	138	.281	.363	.546	151	39	4	4	-1	.971	7	*O-157	4.0
1979	*Cin-N★	121	440	68	133	18	3	30	98	59	105	.302	.388	.561	155	33	0	2	-1	.982	4	*O-116	3.1
1980	Cin-N	144	528	79	144	21	5	25	93	75	99	.273	.364	.473	132	23	1	0	0	.997	10	*O-141	2.9
1981	Cin-N	108	414	64	122	23	2	22	90	51	75	.295	.376	.519	150	26	4	0	1	.991	8	*O-108	3.4
1982	NY-N	151	550	64	136	23	2	13	70	50	123	.247	.312	.367	90	-8	1	1	-0	.974	12	*O-138	0.0
1983	NY-N	157	601	74	145	19	2	28	90	38	111	.241	.291	.419	95	-6	1	1	-1	.988	10	*O-153	-0.1
1984	NY-N	146	553	67	149	22	1	24	86	30	122	.269	.314	.443	112	7	2	2	-1	.976	11	*O-141	1.3
1985	NY-N	129	452	57	119	24	1	21	77	46	87	.263	.334	.460	123	13	0	1	-1	.976	1	*O-123	0.9
1986	NY-N	72	233	28	53	6	1	13	38	21	53	.227	.291	.429	99	-1	1	1	-0	.962	-0	O-62	-0.4
	Chi-A	15	51	2	11	1	0	2	11	4	7	.216	.259	.353	63	-3	0	0	0	1.000	1	O-11/D-3	-0.2
Total	18	1977	7023	986	1925	307	47	348	1239	666	1419	.274	.341	.480	127	227	51	31	-3	.984	65	*O-1880/D-3,1-2	22.3

■ LEO FOSTER
Foster, Leonard Norris b: 2/2/51, Covington, Ky. BR/TR, 5'11", 165 lbs. Deb: 7/9/71

YEAR	TM/L	G	AB	R	H	2B	3B	HR	RBI	BB	SO	AVG	OBP	SLG	PRO+	BR/A	SB	CS	SBR	FA	FR	G/POS	TPR
1971	Atl-N	9	10	1	0	0	0	0	0	0	1	.000	.000	.000	-94	-2	0	0	0	.900	2	/S-3	-0.1
1973	Atl-N	3	6	1	1	1	0	0	0	0	2	.167	.167	.333	33	-1	0	0	0	1.000	-0	/S-1	-0.1
1974	Atl-N	72	112	16	22	2	0	1	5	9	22	.196	.256	.241	38	-9	1	2	-1	.977	-1	S-43,2-10/3-3,O-1	-0.8
1976	NY-N	24	59	11	12	2	0	1	8	8	5	.203	.299	.288	71	-2	3	0	1	.920	-3	/3-9,S-7,2-3	0.0
1977	NY-N	36	75	6	17	3	0	0	6	5	14	.227	.284	.267	51	-5	3	1	0	.968	-4	2-20/S-8,3-2	-0.8
Total	5	144	262	35	52	8	0	2	26	22	44	.198	.263	.252	44	-20	7	3	0	.964	-3	/S-62,2-33,3-14,O-1	-1.8

■ REDDY FOSTER
Foster, Oscar E. b: 8/1864, Richmond, Va. d: 12/19/08, Richmond, Va. Deb: 6/3/1896

YEAR	TM/L	G	AB	R	H	2B	3B	HR	RBI	BB	SO	AVG	OBP	SLG	PRO+	BR/A	SB	CS	SBR	FA	FR	G/POS	TPR
1896	NY-N	1	1	0	0	0	0	0	0	0	0	.000	.000	.000	-99	-0	0			.000	0	H	0.0

■ ROY FOSTER
Foster, Roy b: 7/29/45, Bixby, Okla. BR/TR, 6', 185 lbs. Deb: 4/7/70

YEAR	TM/L	G	AB	R	H	2B	3B	HR	RBI	BB	SO	AVG	OBP	SLG	PRO+	BR/A	SB	CS	SBR	FA	FR	G/POS	TPR
1970	Cle-A	139	477	66	128	26	6	23	60	54	75	.268	.357	.468	120	13	3	3	-1	.965	-3	*O-131	0.2
1971	Cle-A	125	396	51	97	21	1	18	45	35	48	.245	.316	.439	103	0	6	1	1	.968	-1	*O-107	-0.5
1972	Cle-A	73	143	19	32	4	0	4	13	21	23	.224	.331	.336	96	-0	0	2	-1	.966	-6	O-45	-1.1
Total	3	337	1016	136	257	51	1	45	118	110	146	.253	.338	.438	110	13	9	6	-1	.967	-11	O-283	-1.4

■ BOB FOTHERGILL
Fothergill, Robert Roy "Fats" b: 8/16/1897, Massillon, Ohio d: 3/20/38, Detroit, Mich. BR/TR, 5'10.5", 230 lbs. Deb: 4/18/22

YEAR	TM/L	G	AB	R	H	2B	3B	HR	RBI	BB	SO	AVG	OBP	SLG	PRO+	BR/A	SB	CS	SBR	FA	FR	G/POS	TPR
1922	Det-A	42	152	20	49	12	6	1	29	8	9	.322	.356	.454	113	2	1	5	-3	.945	-7	O-38	-0.9
1923	Det-A	101	241	34	76	18	7	1	49	12	19	.315	.358	.419	106	2	5	4	-1	.977	-8	O-68	-1.1
1924	Det-A	54	166	28	50	8	3	0	15	5	13	.301	.326	.386	84	-4	2	3	-1	.968	-4	O-45	-1.1
1925	Det-A	71	204	38	72	14	0	2	28	6	3	.353	.377	.451	111	3	3	2	-0	.977	-2	O-59	-0.2
1926	Det-A	110	387	63	142	31	7	3	73	33	23	.367	.421	.506	139	22	4	12	-6	.961	-1	*O-103	0.8
1927	Det-A	143	527	93	189	38	9	9	114	47	31	.359	.413	.516	138	29	9	15	-6	.961	-6	*O-137	0.8
1928	Det-A	111	347	49	110	28	10	3	63	24	19	.317	.366	.481	119	9	8	3	1	.959	-3	O-90	0.0
1929	Det-A	115	277	42	98	24	9	6	62	11	11	.354	.378	.570	140	15	3	1	0	.967	-4	O-59	0.8
1930	Det-A	55	143	14	37	9	3	2	14	6	10	.259	.289	.406	72	-7	1	1	-0	.947	-5	O-38	-1.3
	Chi-A	52	135	10	40	9	0	0	24	4	8	.296	.326	.363	77	-5	0	0	0	.879	-3	O-31	-0.9
	Yr	107	278	24	77	18	3	2	38	10	18	.277	.307	.385	75	-11	1	1	-0	.913	-8	O-69	-2.2
1931	Chi-A	108	312	25	88	9	4	3	56	17	17	.282	.323	.365	86	-7	2	2	-1	.972	-5	O-74	-1.1
1932	Chi-A	116	346	36	102	24	1	7	50	27	10	.295	.348	.431	107	3	4	4	-1	.952	-11	O-86	-1.4
1933	Bos-A	28	32	1	11	1	0	0	5	2	4	.344	.382	.375	102	0	0	0	0	1.000	-1	/O-4	-0.1
Total	12	1106	3269	453	1064	225	52	36	582	202	177	.325	.368	.459	115	62	42	52	-19	.961	-53	O-832	-5.7

■ JACK FOURNIER
Fournier, John Frank b: 9/28/1889, AuSable, Mich. d: 9/5/73, Tacoma, Wash. BL/TR, 6', 195 lbs. Deb: 4/13/12

YEAR	TM/L	G	AB	R	H	2B	3B	HR	RBI	BB	SO	AVG	OBP	SLG	PRO+	BR/A	SB	CS	SBR	FA	FR	G/POS	TPR
1912	Chi-A	35	73	6	14	5	2	0	2	4		.192	.262	.315	67	-3	1			.988	3	1-17	-0.1
1913	Chi-A	68	172	20	40	8	5	1	23	21	23	.233	.323	.355	99	-0	9			.990	4	1-29,O-23	0.3
1914	Chi-A	109	379	44	118	14	9	6	44	31	44	.311	.368	.443	146	20	10	13	-5	.978	5	1-97/O-6	1.8
1915	Chi-A	126	422	86	136	20	18	5	77	64	37	.322	.429	.491	170	38	21	16	-3	.986	3	1-65,O-57	3.5
1916	Chi-A	105	313	36	75	13	9	4	44	36	40	.240	.328	.367	108	-3	19			.976	-3	1-85/O-1	-0.4
1917	Chi-A	1	1	0	0	0	0	0	0	0	1	.000	.000	.000	-98	-0	0			.000	0	H	0.0
1918	NY-A	27	100	9	35	6	1	0	12	7	7	.350	.393	.430	145	5	7			.976	-2	1-27	0.2
1920	StL-N	141	530	77	162	33	14	3	61	42	44	.306	.370	.438	136	25	26	20	-4	.983	1	*1-138	2.0
1921	StL-N	149	574	103	197	27	9	16	86	56	48	.343	.409	.505	144	37	20	22	-7	.987	-4	*1-149	2.1
1922	StL-N	128	404	64	119	23	9	10	61	40	21	.295	.368	.470	120	12	6	8	-3	.982	-2	*1-109/P-1	0.6
1923	Bro-N	133	515	91	181	30	13	22	102	63	28	.351	.411	.588	165	47	11	4	1	.985	4	*1-133	4.3
1924	Bro-N	154	563	93	188	25	4	27	116	83	46	.334	.428	.536	162	52	7	5	-1	.985	7	*1-153	4.7
1925	Bro-N	145	545	99	191	21	16	22	130	86	39	.350	.446	.569	162	54	4	6	-2	.989	5	*1-145	4.2
1926	Bro-N	87	243	39	69	9	2	11	48	30	16	.284	.365	.473	126	9	0			.986	-2	1-64	0.3
1927	Bos-N	122	374	55	106	18	2	10	53	44	16	.283	.368	.422	121	11	4			.989	0	*1-102	0.4
Total	15	1530	5208	822	1631	252	113	136	859	587	408	.313	.392	.483	143	308	145	<u>94</u>		.984	20	*1-1313/O-87,P-1	23.9

■ BILL FOUSER
Fouser, William C. b: 10/1855, Philadelphia, Pa. d: 3/1/19, Philadelphia, Pa. Deb: 4/22/1876

YEAR	TM/L	G	AB	R	H	2B	3B	HR	RBI	BB	SO	AVG	OBP	SLG	PRO+	BR/A	SB	CS	SBR	FA	FR	G/POS	TPR
1876	Phi-N	21	89	11	12	0	1	0	2	0	0	.135	.135	.157	-3	-9				.827	3	2-14/O-7,1-1	-0.5

■ DAVE FOUTZ
Foutz, David Luther "Scissors" b: 9/7/1856, Carroll Co., Md. d: 3/5/1897, Waverly, Ind. BR/TR, 6'2", 161 lbs. Deb: 7/29/1884 FM

YEAR	TM/L	G	AB	R	H	2B	3B	HR	RBI	BB	SO	AVG	OBP	SLG	PRO+	BR/A	SB	CS	SBR	FA	FR	G/POS	TPR
1884	StL-a	33	119	17	27	4	0	0	8			.227	.276	.261	73	-3				.940	-3	P-25,O-14	-0.5
1885	*StL-a	65	238	42	59	6	4	0	34	11		.248	.281	.307	82	-5				.899	6	P-47,1-15/O-4	-0.4
1886	*StL-a	102	414	66	116	18	9	3	59	9		.280	.297	.389	109	1	17			.949	4	P-59,O-34,1-11	0.0
1887	*StL-a	102	423	79	151	26	13	4	108	23		.357	.393	.508	136	16	22			.899	-4	O-50,P-40,1-15	0.3
1888	Bro-a	140	563	91	156	20	13	3	99	28		.277	.314	.375	121	11	35			.895	3	O-78,1-42,P-23	0.3
1889	*Bro-a	138	553	118	152	19	8	6	113	64	23	.275	.353	.371	106	5	43			.979	-3	*1-134,P-12	-0.7
1890	*Bro-N	129	509	106	154	25	13	6	98	52	25	.303	.368	.432	133	20	42			.978	-1	*1-113,O-13/P-5	1.1
1891	Bro-N	130	521	87	134	26	8	2	73	40	25	.257	.313	.349	93	-6	48			.976	-3	*1-124/P-6,S-1	-1.3
1892	Bro-N	61	220	33	41	5	3	1	26	14	14	.186	.235	.250	48	-14	19			.850	-2	O-29,P-27/1-6	-1.3
1893	Bro-N	130	557	91	137	20	10	7	67	32	34	.246	.287	.355	74	-24	39			.913	-6	O-77,1-54/P-6,M	-2.9
1894	Bro-N	72	293	40	90	12	4	0	51	14	13	.307	.341	.410	86	-7	14			.976	-3	1-72/P-1,M	-0.7
1895	Bro-N	31	115	14	34	4	1	0	21	4	1	.296	.319	.348	78	-4	1			.879	-5	O-20/1-8,M	-0.8
1896	Bro-N	2	8	0	2	0	0	0	2			.250	.333	.375	92	0				1.000	0	/O-1,1-1,M	0.0
Total	13	1135	4533	784	1253	186	91	31	749	300	136	.276	.323	.370						.977	-14	1-595,O-320,P/S	-6.9

■ FRANK FOUTZ
Foutz, Frank Hayes b: 4/8/1877, Baltimore, Md. d: 12/25/61, Lima, Ohio BR/TR, 5'11", 165 lbs. Deb: 4/26/01 F

YEAR	TM/L	G	AB	R	H	2B	3B	HR	RBI	BB	SO	AVG	OBP	SLG	PRO+	BR/A	SB	CS	SBR	FA	FR	G/POS	TPR
1901	Bal-A	20	72	13	17	4	1	2	14	2		.236	.321	.403	90	-1	0			.959	-0	1-20	-0.1

■ BOOB FOWLER
Fowler, Joseph Chester "Gink" b: 11/11/1900, Waco, Tex. d: 10/8/88, Dallas, Tex. BL/TR, 5'11.5", 180 lbs. Deb: 5/6/23

YEAR	TM/L	G	AB	R	H	2B	3B	HR	RBI	BB	SO	AVG	OBP	SLG	PRO+	BR/A	SB	CS	SBR	FA	FR	G/POS	TPR
1923	Cin-N	11	33	9	11	0	1	1	6	1	3	.333	.353	.485	121	1	0	0	0	.847	-1	S-10	0.1
1924	Cin-N	59	129	20	43	6	1	0	9	5	15	.333	.358	.395	103	1	2	2	-1	.936	-7	S-32/2-4,3-2	-0.4
1925	Cin-N	6	5	0	2	1	0	0	1	0	0	.400	.400	.600	155	0	0			.000	0	H	0.0
1926	Bos-A	2	8	1	1	0	0	0	1	0	1	.125	.125	.125	-36	-2	0			.800	0	/3-2	-0.1
Total	4	78	175	30	57	7	2	1	18	6	19	.326	.348	.406	102	0	3	2	-0	.910	-7	/S-42,3-4,2-4	-0.4

■ ANDY FOX
Fox, Andrew Junipero b: 1/12/71, Sacramento, Cal. BL/TR, 6'4", 205 lbs. Deb: 4/7/96

YEAR	TM/L	G	AB	R	H	2B	3B	HR	RBI	BB	SO	AVG	OBP	SLG	PRO+	BR/A	SB	CS	SBR	FA	FR	G/POS	TPR
1996	*NY-A	113	189	26	37	4	0	3	13	20	28	.196	.276	.265	37	-18	11	3	2	.958	13	2-72,3-31/S-9,OD	-0.1

■ CHARLIE FOX
Fox, Charles Francis "Irish" b: 10/7/21, New York, N.Y. BR/TR, 5'11", 180 lbs. Deb: 9/24/42 MC

YEAR	TM/L	G	AB	R	H	2B	3B	HR	RBI	BB	SO	AVG	OBP	SLG	PRO+	BR/A	SB	CS	SBR	FA	FR	G/POS	TPR
1942	NY-N	3	7	1	3	0	0	0	1	1	2	.429	.500	.429	172	1	0			1.000	-1	/C-3	0.0

YEAR	TM/L	G	AB	R	H	2B	3B	HR	RBI	BB	SO	AVG	OBP	SLG	PRO+	BR/A	SB	CS	SBR	FA	FR	G/POS	TPR

■ ERIC FOX   Fox, Eric Hollis   b: 8/15/63, Lemoore, Cal.   BB/TL, 5'10", 180 lbs.   Deb: 7/7/92

1992	*Oak-A	51	143	24	34	5	2	3	13	13	29	.238	.301	.364	90	-2	3	4	-2	.990	-5	O-43/D-4	-1.0
1993	Oak-A	29	56	5	8	1	0	1	5	2	7	.143	.172	.214	3	-8	0	2	-1	1.000	-3	O-26/D-2	-1.2
1994	Oak-A	26	44	7	9	2	0	1	1	3	8	.205	.255	.318	51	-3	2	0	1	1.000	-4	O-24	-0.7
1995	Tex-A	10	15	2	0	0	0	0	0	3	4	.000	.167	.000	-51	-3	0	0	0	1.000	-1	/O-8,D-1	-0.4
Total	4	116	258	38	51	8	2	5	19	21	48	.198	.258	.302	55	-17	5	6	-2	.995	-13	O-101/D-7	-3.3

■ PETE FOX   Fox, Ervin   b: 3/8/09, Evansville, Ind.   d: 7/5/66, Detroit, Mich.   BR/TR, 5'11", 165 lbs.   Deb: 4/12/33

1933	Det-A	128	535	82	154	26	13	7	57	23	38	.288	.320	.424	94	-7	9	6	-1	.978	1	*O-124	-1.3
1934	*Det-A	128	516	101	147	31	4	2	45	49	53	.285	.351	.364	85	-11	25	10	2	.974	8	*O-121	-0.6
1935	*Det-A	131	517	116	166	38	8	15	73	45	52	.321	.382	.513	134	24	14	4	2	.988	0	*O-125	2.0
1936	Det-A	73	220	46	67	12	1	4	26	34	23	.305	.405	.423	104	3	1	3	-2	.968	1	O-55	-0.1
1937	Det-A	148	628	116	208	39	8	12	82	41	43	.331	.372	.476	110	8	12	8	-1	.976	-3	*O-143	-0.1
1938	Det-A	155	634	91	186	35	10	7	96	31	39	.293	.328	.413	80	-21	16	7	1	.994	-2	*O-155	-2.5
1939	Det-A	141	519	69	153	24	6	7	66	35	41	.295	.342	.405	84	-13	23	12	-0	.970	9	*O-126	-0.9
1940	*Det-A	93	350	49	101	17	4	5	48	21	30	.289	.329	.403	81	-10	7	7	-2	.967	0	O-85	-1.6
1941	Bos-A	73	268	38	81	12	7	0	31	21	32	.302	.357	.399	98	-1	9	2	2	.977	-1	O-62	-0.4
1942	Bos-A	77	256	42	67	15	5	3	42	20	28	.262	.323	.395	98	-1	8	7	-2	.966	-9	O-71	-1.6
1943	Bos-A	127	489	54	141	24	4	2	44	34	40	.288	.337	.366	104	2	22	8	2	.961	-3	*O-125	-0.6
1944	Bos-A☆	121	496	70	156	37	6	1	64	27	34	.315	.354	.419	122	13	10	5	0	.987	-1	*O-119	0.5
1945	Bos-A	66	208	21	51	4	1	0	20	11	18	.245	.296	.274	64	-9	2	2	-1	.989	-6	O-57	-2.1
Total	13	1461	5636	895	1678	314	75	65	694	392	471	.298	.347	.415	98	-25	158	81	-1	.977	-7	*O-1368	-9.3

■ PADDY FOX   Fox, George B.   b: 12/1/1868, Pottstown, Pa.   d: 5/8/14, Philadelphia, Pa.   Deb: 7/13/1891

1891	Lou-a	6	19	1	2	0	1	0	2	2	3	.105	.261	.211	36	-2	0			.929	-2	/3-6	-0.3
1899	Pit-N	13	41	4	10	0	1	1	3	3		.244	.311	.366	86	-1	2			.971	2	/1-9,C-3	0.1
Total	2	19	60	5	12	0	2	1	5	5	3	.200	.294	.317	70	-2	2			.971	-1	/1-9,3-6,C-3	-0.2

■ NELLIE FOX   Fox, Jacob Nelson   b: 12/25/27, St.Thomas, Pa.   d: 12/1/75, Baltimore, Md.   BL/TR, 5'9", 150 lbs.   Deb: 6/8/47   C

1947	Phi-A	7	3	2	0	0	0	0	0	1	0	.000	.250	.000	-26	-0	0	0	0	1.000	0	/2-1	0.0
1948	Phi-A	3	13	0	2	0	0	0	0	1	0	.154	.214	.154	-1	-2	1	0	0	.950	-2	/2-3	-0.3
1949	Phi-A	88	247	42	63	6	2	0	21	32	9	.255	.354	.296	75	-8	2	2	-1	.982	-1	2-77	-0.6
1950	Chi-A	130	457	45	113	12	7	0	30	35	17	.247	.304	.304	58	-30	4	3	-1	.974	-0	*2-121	-2.4
1951	Chi-A★	147	604	93	189	32	12	4	55	43	11	.313	.372	.425	118	15	9	12	-5	.981	-3	*2-147	1.4
1952	Chi-A☆	152	648	76	**192**	25	10	0	39	34	14	.296	.334	.366	94	-6	5	5	-2	.985	-2	*2-151	0.8
1953	Chi-A★	154	624	92	178	31	8	3	72	36	18	.285	.344	.375	91	-7	4	5	-2	.983	-2	*2-154	0.3
1954	Chi-A★	155	631	111	**201**	24	8	3	47	51	12	.319	.374	.391	106	6	16	9	-1	.989	-6	*2-155	1.1
1955	Chi-A★	154	636	100	198	28	7	6	59	38	15	.311	.366	.406	104	4	7	9	-3	.974	27	*2-154	3.9
1956	Chi-A★	154	649	109	192	20	10	4	52	44	14	.296	.350	.376	90	-9	8	4	0	**.986**	3	*2-154	0.7
1957	Chi-A★	155	619	110	**196**	27	8	6	61	75	13	.317	.404	.415	124	24	5	6	-2	.986	21	*2-155	5.6
1958	Chi-A★	155	623	82	**187**	21	6	0	49	47	11	.300	.360	.353	99	1	5	6	-2	.985	2	*2-155	1.2
1959	*Chi-A★	156	624	84	191	34	6	2	70	71	13	.306	.383	.389	114	15	5	9	-2	**.988**	-3	*2-156	2.2
1960	Chi-A★	150	605	85	175	24	**10**	2	59	50	13	.289	.353	.392	97	-1	2	4	-2	.985	12	*2-149	2.4
1961	Chi-A★	159	606	67	152	11	5	2	51	59	12	.251	.326	.295	69	-25	3	2	-1	.982	-6	*2-159	-1.5
1962	Chi-A	157	621	79	166	27	7	2	54	38	12	.267	.317	.343	78	-19	1	6	-2	**.990**	1	*2-154	-0.3
1963	Chi-A★	137	539	54	140	19	0	2	42	24	17	.260	.300	.306	72	-20	0	2	-1	**.988**	-6	*2-134	-1.8
1964	Hou-N	133	442	45	117	12	6	0	28	27	13	.265	.322	.319	86	-8	0	2	-1	.977	-5	*2-115	-0.6
1965	Hou-N	21	41	3	11	0	1	0	2	2	0	.268	.286	.317	75	-1	0	0	0	1.000	-0	/3-6,1-2,2-1	-0.2
Total	19	2367	9232	1279	2663	355	112	35	790	719	216	.288	.349	.363	94	-73	76	80	-25	.984	42	*2-2295/3-6,1-2	11.9

■ JACK FOX   Fox, John Paul   b: 5/21/1885, Reading, Pa.   d: 6/28/63, Reading, Pa.   BR/TR, 5'10", 185 lbs.   Deb: 6/2/08

1908	Phi-A	9	30	2	6	0	0	0	0	0		.200	.200	.200	28	-2	2			.923	-1	/O-8	-0.4

■ BILL FOX   Fox, William Henry   b: 1/15/1872, Sturbridge, Mass.   d: 5/7/46, Minneapolis, Minn.   BB/TR, 5'10", 160 lbs.   Deb: 8/20/1897

1897	Was-N	4	14	4	4	0	0	0	1			.286	.333	.286	64	-1	0			.700	0	/S-2,2-2	0.0
1901	Cin-N	43	159	9	28	2	1	0	7	4		.176	.201	.201	18	-17	9			.948	5	2-43	-0.9
Total	2	47	173	13	32	2	1	0	7	5		.185	.212	.208	22	-17	9			.944	6	/2-45,S-2	-0.9

■ JIMMIE FOXX   Foxx, James Emory "Beast" or "Double X"   b: 10/22/07, Sudlersville, Md.   d: 7/21/67, Miami, Fla.   BR/TR, 6', 195 lbs.   Deb: 5/1/25   CH

1925	Phi-A	10	9	2	6	0	0	0	0	1	1	.667	.667	.778	249	2	0	0	0	.000	0	/C-1	0.2
1926	Phi-A	26	32	8	10	2	1	0	5	1	6	.313	.333	.438	94	-0	1	0	0	1.000	2	C-12/O-3	0.2
1927	Phi-A	61	130	23	42	6	5	3	20	14	11	.323	.393	.515	127	5	2	1	0	.975	-2	1-32/C-5	0.1
1928	Phi-A	118	400	85	131	29	10	13	79	60	43	.327	.416	.548	147	28	3	8	-4	.940	-2	3-60,1-30,C-19	2.4
1929	*Phi-A	149	517	123	183	23	9	33	118	103	70	.354	**.463**	.625	171	58	9	7	-2	.995	-4	*1-142/3-8	3.6
1930	*Phi-A	153	562	127	188	33	13	37	156	93	66	.335	.429	.637	159	51	7	7	-2	.990	-7	*1-153	2.8
1931	*Phi-A	139	515	93	150	32	10	30	120	73	84	.291	.380	.567	138	26	4	3	-1	.993	-3	*1-112,3-26/O-1	1.3
1932	Phi-A	154	585	**151**	213	33	9	**58**	169	116	96	.364	.469	**.749**	203	**90**	3	7	-3	**.994**	-5	*1-141,3-13	**6.5**
1933	Phi-A☆	149	573	125	204	37	9	**48**	163	96	93	**.356**	.449	**.703**	**199**	81	2	2	-1	.990	4	*1-149/S-1	**6.7**
1934	Phi-A★	150	539	120	180	28	6	44	130	**111**	75	.334	.449	.653	188	72	11	2	2	.993	-4	*1-140/3-9	6.1
1935	Phi-A★	147	535	118	185	33	7	**36**	115	114	99	.346	.461	**.636**	182	68	6	4	-1	**.997**	6	*1-121,C-26/3-2	**5.7**
1936	Bos-A★	155	585	130	198	32	8	41	143	105	119	.338	.440	.631	153	48	13	4	2	.991	-1	*1-139,O-16/3-1	3.1
1937	Bos-A★	150	569	111	162	24	6	36	127	99	96	.285	.392	.538	127	23	10	8	-2	**.994**	10	*1-150/C-1	1.3
1938	Bos-A★	149	565	139	197	33	9	50	175	**119**	76	**.349**	.462	**.704**	180	70	5	4	-1	.987	6	*1-149	**5.2**
1939	Bos-A☆	124	467	130	168	31	10	**35**	105	89	72	.360	**.464**	**.694**	185	61	4	3	-1	.992	7	*1-123/P-1	4.9
1940	Bos-A★	144	515	106	153	30	4	36	119	101	87	.297	.412	.581	148	38	4	7	-3	.990	-5	1-95,C-42/3-1	2.6
1941	Bos-A★	135	487	87	146	27	8	19	105	93	103	.300	.412	.505	138	29	2	4	-2	.992	7	*1-124/3-5,O-1	2.3
1942	Bos-A	30	100	18	27	4	0	5	14	18	25	.270	.392	.460	134	5	0	0	0	.996	6	1-27	1.0
	Chi-N	70	205	25	42	8	0	3	19	32	55	.205	.282	.288	69	-8	1			.983	-4	1-52/C-1	-1.6
1944	Chi-N	15	20	0	1	1	0	0	2	5	5	.050	.136	.100	-33	-4	0			1.000	2	/3-2,C-1	-0.2
1945	Phi-N	89	224	30	60	11	1	7	38	23	39	.268	.336	.420	112	3	0			.988	-3	1-40,3-14/P-9	-0.2
Total	20	2317	8134	1751	2646	458	125	534	1922	1452	1311	.325	.428	.609	161	746	87	<u>72</u>		.992	30	*1-1919,3-141,C/OPS	54.0

■ JOE FOY   Foy, Joseph Anthony   b: 2/21/43, New York, N.Y.   d: 10/12/89, Bronx, N.Y.   BR/TR, 6', 215 lbs.   Deb: 4/13/66

1966	Bos-A	151	554	97	145	23	8	15	63	91	80	.262	.368	.413	112	11	2	5	-2	.953	-1	*3-139,S-13	0.7
1967	*Bos-A	130	446	70	112	22	4	16	49	46	87	.251	.325	.426	111	6	8	6	-1	.921	-10	*3-118/O-1	-0.7
1968	Bos-A	150	515	65	116	18	2	10	60	84	91	.225	.338	.326	96	0	26	8	3	.935	2	*3-147/O-3	0.6
1969	KC-A	145	519	72	136	19	2	11	71	74	75	.262	.360	.370	104	5	37	15	2	.964	5	*3-113,1-16,O/S2	-0.3
1970	NY-N	99	322	39	76	12	0	6	37	68	58	.236	.376	.329	90	-1	22	13	-1	.937	-4	3-97	-0.4
1971	Was-N	41	128	12	30	8	0	0	11	27	14	.234	.368	.297	96	1	4	1	1	.960	1	3-37/2-3,S-1	0.5
Total	6	716	2484	355	615	102	16	58	291	390	405	.248	.354	.372	103	21	99	48	1	.943	-14	3-651/O-20,S-19,12	0.3

■ JULIO FRANCO   Franco, Julio Cesar (b: Julio Cesar Robles (Franco))   b: 8/23/58, Hato Mayor, D.R.   BR/TR, 6', 175 lbs.   Deb: 4/23/82

1982	Phi-N	16	29	3	8	1	0	0	3	2	4	.276	.323	.310	76	-1	1.000	-0				S-11/3-2	-0.2
1983	Cle-A	149	560	68	153	24	8	8	80	27	50	.273	.309	.387	87	-11	32	12	2	.961	-7	*S-149	-0.1
1984	Cle-A	160	658	82	188	22	5	3	79	43	68	.286	.335	.348	88	-10	19	10	-0	.955	-1	*S-159/D-1	0.5
1985	Cle-A	160	636	97	183	33	4	6	90	54	74	.288	.347	.381	100	1	13	9	-2	.949	-22	*S-151/2-8,D-1	-0.7
1986	Cle-A	149	599	80	183	30	5	10	74	32	66	.306	.341	.422	108	6	10	7	-1	.971	-5	*S-134,2-13/D-3	1.2
1987	Cle-A	128	495	86	158	24	3	8	52	57	56	.319	.389	.428	117	14	32	9	4	.963	-24	*S-111/2-9,D-8	0.4
1988	Cle-A	152	613	88	186	23	6	10	54	56	72	.303	.364	.409	113	11	25	11	3	.982	-10	*2-151/D-1	0.9
1989	Tex-A★	150	548	80	173	31	5	13	92	66	69	.316	.390	.462	137	28	21	3	5	.980	-6	*2-140,D-10	3.1
1990	Tex-A★	157	582	96	172	27	1	11	69	82	83	.296	.384	.402	120	18	31	10	3	.975	-2	*2-152/D-3	2.3

YEAR	TM/L	G	AB	R	H	2B	3B	HR	RBI	BB	SO	AVG	OBP	SLG	PRO+	BR/A	SB	CS	SBR	FA	FR	G/POS	TPR
1991	Tex-A☆	146	589	108	201	27	3	15	78	65	78	**.341**	.409	.474	146	38	36	9	5	.979	-31	*2-146	1.6
1992	Tex-A	35	107	19	25	7	0	2	8	15	17	.234	.328	.355	95	-1	1	1	-0	.906	-6	D-15/2-9,O-4	-0.7
1993	Tex-A	144	532	85	154	31	3	14	84	62	95	.289	.365	.438	119	15	9	3	1	.000	0	*D-140	1.0
1994	Chi-A	112	433	72	138	19	2	20	98	62	75	.319	.410	.510	138	26	8	1	2	.969	-1	D-99,1-14	1.9
1996	*Cle-A	112	432	72	139	20	1	14	76	61	82	.322	.409	.470	122	16	8	8	-2	.990	4	1-97,D-13	0.7
Total	14	1770	6813	1036	2061	319	46	134	937	684	889	.303	.369	.422	115	152	245	95	16	.960	-111	S-715,2-628,D1/O3	11.9

■ MATT FRANCO
Franco, Matthew Neil   b: 8/19/69, Santa Monica, Cal.   BL/TR, 6'2", 200 lbs.   Deb: 9/6/95

YEAR	TM/L	G	AB	R	H	2B	3B	HR	RBI	BB	SO	AVG	OBP	SLG	PRO+	BR/A	SB	CS	SBR	FA	FR	G/POS	TPR
1995	Chi-N	16	17	3	5	1	0	0	1	0	4	.294	.294	.353	71	-1	0	0	0	1.000	-1	/2-3,1-1,3-1	-0.2
1996	NY-N	14	31	3	6	1	0	1	2	1	5	.194	.242	.323	51	-2	0	0	0	.824	-1	/3-8,1-2	-0.3
Total	2	30	48	6	11	2	0	1	3	1	9	.229	.260	.333	58	-3	0	0	0	.824	-2	/3-9,1-3,2-3	-0.5

■ TITO FRANCONA
Francona, John Patsy   b: 11/4/33, Aliquippa, Pa.   BL/TL, 5'11", 190 lbs.   Deb: 4/17/56   F

YEAR	TM/L	G	AB	R	H	2B	3B	HR	RBI	BB	SO	AVG	OBP	SLG	PRO+	BR/A	SB	CS	SBR	FA	FR	G/POS	TPR
1956	Bal-A	139	445	62	115	16	4	9	57	51	60	.258	.336	.373	94	-5	11	5	0	.977	-8	*O-122,1-21	-1.8
1957	Bal-A	97	279	35	65	8	3	7	38	29	48	.233	.312	.358	88	-5	7	3	0	.992	-10	O-73/1-4	-1.9
1958	Chi-A	41	128	10	33	3	2	1	10	14	24	.258	.331	.336	86	-2	2	3	-1	1.000	-4	O-35	-0.9
	Det-A	45	69	11	17	5	0	0	10	15	16	.246	.381	.319	88	-0	0	0	0	1.000	-3	O-18/1-1	-0.5
	Yr	86	197	21	50	8	2	1	20	29	40	.254	.350	.330	86	-3	2	3	-1	1.000	-7	O-53/1-1	-1.4
1959	Cle-A	122	399	68	145	17	2	20	79	35	42	.363	.419	.566	174	**40**	2	0	1	.972	-4	O-64,1-35	3.1
1960	Cle-A	147	544	84	159	**36**	2	17	79	67	67	.292	.375	.460	128	22	4	1	1	.989	5	O-138,1-13	2.0
1961	Cle-A☆	155	592	87	178	30	8	16	85	56	52	.301	.365	.459	122	18	2	1	0	.987	4	*O-138,1-14	1.3
1962	Cle-A	158	621	82	169	28	5	14	70	47	74	.272	.330	.401	99	-2	3	2	-0	.986	2	*1-158	-1.1
1963	Cle-A	142	500	57	114	29	0	10	41	47	77	.228	.297	.346	80	-13	9	1	2	.986	-0	O-122,1-11	-2.2
1964	Cle-A	111	270	35	67	13	2	8	24	44	46	.248	.362	.400	113	6	1	3	-2	.985	-12	O-69,1-17	-1.2
1965	StL-N	81	174	15	45	6	2	5	19	17	30	.259	.325	.402	95	-1	0	0	0	.972	-9	O-34,1-13	-1.3
1966	StL-N	83	156	14	33	4	1	4	17	7	27	.212	.250	.327	59	-9	0	0	0	.987	-1	1-30/O-9	-1.0
1967	Phi-N	27	73	7	15	1	0	0	3	7	10	.205	.275	.219	43	-5	0	1	-1	1.000	1	1-24/O-1	-0.6
	Atl-N	82	254	28	63	5	1	6	25	20	34	.248	.305	.346	87	-4	1	0	0	.991	-1	1-56/O-7	-0.9
	Yr	109	327	35	78	6	1	6	28	27	44	.239	.299	.318	77	-10	1	1	-0	.993	-1	1-80/O-7	-1.5
1968	Atl-N	122	346	32	99	13	1	2	47	51	45	.286	.378	.347	118	10	3	0	1	.978	-8	O-65,1-33	-0.3
1969	Atl-N	51	88	5	26	1	0	2	22	13	10	.295	.386	.375	114	2	0	1	-1	.957	-0	O-15/1-7	0.0
	Oak-A	32	85	12	29	6	1	3	20	12	11	.341	.423	.541	175	9	0	0	0	.988	-2	1-19/O-1	0.5
1970	Oak-A	32	33	2	8	0	0	0	6	6	6	.242	.375	.333	100	0	0	0	0	1.000	1	/1-6,O-1	0.1
	Mil-A	52	65	4	15	3	0	0	4	6	15	.231	.296	.277	58	-4	1	0	0	1.000	1	1-13	-0.3
	Yr	84	98	6	23	3	0	0	10	12	21	.235	.324	.296	73	-3	1	0	0	1.000	2	1-19/O-1	-0.2
Total	15	1719	5121	650	1395	224	34	125	656	544	694	.272	.346	.403	108	56	46	21	1	.984	-49	O-911,1-475	-7.0

■ TERRY FRANCONA
Francona, Terry Jon   b: 4/22/59, Aberdeen, S.D.   BL/TL, 6'1", 190 lbs.   Deb: 8/19/81   FC

YEAR	TM/L	G	AB	R	H	2B	3B	HR	RBI	BB	SO	AVG	OBP	SLG	PRO+	BR/A	SB	CS	SBR	FA	FR	G/POS	TPR
1981	*Mon-N	34	95	11	26	0	1	1	8	5	6	.274	.317	.326	82	-2	1	0	0	1.000	1	O-26/1-1	-0.2
1982	Mon-N	46	131	14	42	3	0	0	9	8	11	.321	.360	.344	96	-0	2	3	-1	.936	-6	O-33,1-16	-0.9
1983	Mon-N	120	230	21	59	11	1	3	22	6	20	.257	.275	.352	73	-9	0	2	-1	.978	-2	O-51,1-47	-1.5
1984	Mon-N	58	214	18	74	19	2	1	18	5	12	.346	.364	.467	138	10	0	0	0	.994	6	1-50/O-6	1.3
1985	Mon-N	107	281	19	75	15	1	2	31	12	12	.267	.299	.349	86	-6	5	5	-2	.988	1	1-57,O-28/3-1	-0.9
1986	Chi-N	86	124	13	31	3	0	2	8	6	8	.250	.290	.323	64	-6	0	1	-1	1.000	-7	O-30,1-23	-1.6
1987	Cin-N	102	207	16	47	5	0	3	12	10	12	.227	.266	.295	46	-16	2	0	1	.995	3	1-57/O-8	-1.6
1988	Cle-A	62	212	24	66	8	0	1	12	5	18	.311	.327	.363	91	-3	0	0	0	.977	-3	D-38/1-5,O-5	-0.4
1989	Mil-A	90	233	26	54	10	1	3	23	8	20	.232	.257	.322	63	-12	2	1	0	.989	-2	1-46,D-23,O-16,/P-1	-1.8
1990	Mil-A	3	4	1	0	0	0	0	0	0	0	.000	.000	.000	-99	-1	0	0	0	1.000	-0	/1-2,D-1	-0.1
Total	10	708	1731	163	474	74	6	16	143	65	119	.274	.302	.351	81	-46	12	12	-4	.992	-4	1-304,O-203/DP3	-7.7

■ CHARLIE FRANK
Frank, Charles   b: 5/30/1870, Mobile, Ala.   d: 5/24/22, Memphis, Tenn.   5'10", 170 lbs.   Deb: 8/18/1893

YEAR	TM/L	G	AB	R	H	2B	3B	HR	RBI	BB	SO	AVG	OBP	SLG	PRO+	BR/A	SB	CS	SBR	FA	FR	G/POS	TPR
1893	StL-N	40	164	29	55	6	3	1	17	18	8	.335	.408	.427	122	5	8			.930	3	O-40	0.5
1894	StL-N	80	319	52	89	12	7	4	42	44	13	.279	.372	.398	86	-7	14			.869	-2	O-77/1-3,P-2	-1.1
Total	2	120	483	81	144	18	10	5	59	62	21	.298	.384	.408	97	-2	22			.889	1	O-117/1-3,P-2	-0.6

■ FRED FRANK
Frank, Frederick   b: 3/11/1874, Louisa, Ky.   d: 3/27/50, Ashland, Ky.   Deb: 9/27/1898

YEAR	TM/L	G	AB	R	H	2B	3B	HR	RBI	BB	SO	AVG	OBP	SLG	PRO+	BR/A	SB	CS	SBR	FA	FR	G/POS	TPR
1898	Cle-N	17	53	3	11	1	0			3	4	.208	.276	.264	56	-3	1			.915	3	O-17	-0.1

■ FRANKLIN
Franklin   Deb: 9/27/1884

YEAR	TM/L	G	AB	R	H	2B	3B	HR	RBI	BB	SO	AVG	OBP	SLG	PRO+	BR/A	SB	CS	SBR	FA	FR	G/POS	TPR
1884	Was-U	1	3	0	0	0	0	0		0	0	.000	.000	.000	-99	-1				1.000	0	/O-1	-0.1

■ MOE FRANKLIN
Franklin, Murray Asher   b: 4/1/14, Chicago, Ill.   d: 3/16/78, Harbor City, Cal.   BR/TR, 6', 175 lbs.   Deb: 8/12/41

YEAR	TM/L	G	AB	R	H	2B	3B	HR	RBI	BB	SO	AVG	OBP	SLG	PRO+	BR/A	SB	CS	SBR	FA	FR	G/POS	TPR
1941	Det-A	13	10	1	3	1	0	0	0	3	2	.300	.417	.400	106	0				.750	-1	/S-4,3-1	-0.1
1942	Det-A	48	154	24	40	7	0	2	16	7	5	.260	.301	.344	75	-5	0	0	0	.967	-6	S-32/2-7	-0.9
Total	2	61	164	25	43	8	0	2	16	9	7	.262	.309	.348	77	-5	0	0	0	.961	-7	/S-36,2-7,3-1	-1.0

■ HERMAN FRANKS
Franks, Herman Louis   b: 1/4/14, Price, Utah   BL/TR, 5'10.5", 187 lbs.   Deb: 4/27/39   MC

YEAR	TM/L	G	AB	R	H	2B	3B	HR	RBI	BB	SO	AVG	OBP	SLG	PRO+	BR/A	SB	CS	SBR	FA	FR	G/POS	TPR
1939	StL-N	17	17	1	1	0	0	0	3	3	3	.059	.200	.059	-26	-3	0			.973	3	C-13	0.0
1940	Bro-N	65	131	11	24	4	0	1	14	20	6	.183	.296	.237	46	-9	2			.990	9	C-43	0.2
1941	*Bro-N	57	139	10	28	7	0	1	14	14	13	.201	.275	.273	52	-9	0			.986	2	C-54/O-1	-0.3
1947	Phi-A	8	15	2	3	0	1	0	1	4	4	.200	.368	.333	94	0	0	0	0	1.000	-1	/C-4	-0.1
1948	Phi-A	40	98	10	22	7	1	1	14	16	11	.224	.345	.347	84	-2	0	0	0	.977	3	C-27	0.2
1949	NY-N	1	3	1	2	0	0	0	0	0	0	.667	.667	.667	259	1	0			1.000	0	/C-1	0.1
Total	6	188	403	35	80	18	2	3	43	57	37	.199	.302	.275	57	-22	2	0		.985	16	C-142/O-1	0.1

■ LOU FRAZIER
Frazier, Arthur Louis   b: 1/26/65, St.Louis, Mo.   BB/TR, 6'2", 175 lbs.   Deb: 4/8/93

YEAR	TM/L	G	AB	R	H	2B	3B	HR	RBI	BB	SO	AVG	OBP	SLG	PRO+	BR/A	SB	CS	SBR	FA	FR	G/POS	TPR
1993	Mon-N	112	189	27	54	7	1	1	16	16	24	.286	.341	.349	82	-4	17	2	4	.986	-8	O-60/1-8,2-1	-0.9
1994	Mon-N	76	140	25	38	3	1	0	14	18	23	.271	.358	.307	75	-4	20	4	4	1.000	-2	O-36/2-6,1-1	-0.3
1995	Mon-N	35	63	6	12	2	0	0	3	8	12	.190	.301	.222	39	-5	4	0	1	.973	-3	O-25/2-1	-0.8
	Tex-A	49	99	19	21	2	0	0	8	7	20	.212	.278	.232	34	-10	9	1	2	.973	-6	O-47/D-2	-1.3
1996	Tex-A	30	50	5	13	2	1	0	8	10	13	.260	.373	.340	77	-2	4	2	0	.971	1	O-15,D-13/2-1	-0.1
Total	4	302	541	82	138	16	3	1	46	57	89	.255	.333	.301	66	-25	54	9	11	.982	-17	O-183/D-15,2-9,1-9	-3.4

■ JOE FRAZIER
Frazier, Joseph Filmore   b: 10/6/22, Liberty, N.C.   BL/TR, 6', 180 lbs.   Deb: 8/31/47   M

YEAR	TM/L	G	AB	R	H	2B	3B	HR	RBI	BB	SO	AVG	OBP	SLG	PRO+	BR/A	SB	CS	SBR	FA	FR	G/POS	TPR
1947	Cle-A	9	14	1	1	0	0	0	1	0	0	.071	.133	.143	-24	-2	0	0	0	.857	-1	/O-5	-0.4
1954	StL-N	81	88	8	26	5	2	3	18	13	17	.295	.392	.500	129	4	0	0	0	.938	-1	O-11/1-1	0.3
1955	StL-N	58	70	12	14	1	0	4	9	6	12	.200	.273	.386	72	-3	0	0	0	1.000	-3	O-14	-0.6
1956	StL-N	14	19	1	4	2	0	1	4	3	3	.211	.318	.474	109	0	0	1	-1	.800	-3	/O-3	-0.1
	Cin-N	10	17	2	4	0	0	1	2	1	7	.235	.278	.412	77	-1	0	0	0	.000	-2	/O-4	-0.2
	Yr	24	36	3	8	2	0	2	6	4	10	.222	.300	.444	94	-1	0	1	-1	.800	-5	/O-7	-0.3
	Bal-A	45	74	7	19	6	0	1	12	11	6	.257	.360	.378	103	0	0	0	0	1.000	-0	/O-19	-0.0
Total	4	217	282	31	68	15	2	10	45	35	46	.241	.331	.415	97	-1	0	1	-1	.961	-7	/O-56,1-1	-1.0

■ JOHNNY FREDERICK
Frederick, John Henry   b: 1/26/02, Denver, Colo.   d: 6/18/77, Tigard, Ore.   BL/TL, 5'11", 165 lbs.   Deb: 4/18/29

YEAR	TM/L	G	AB	R	H	2B	3B	HR	RBI	BB	SO	AVG	OBP	SLG	PRO+	BR/A	SB	CS	SBR	FA	FR	G/POS	TPR
1929	Bro-N	148	628	127	206	**52**	6	24	75	39	34	.328	.372	.545	126	23	6			.975	8	*O-143	1.9
1930	Bro-N	142	616	120	206	44	11	17	76	46	34	.334	.383	.524	118	17	1			.990	12	*O-142	1.7
1931	Bro-N	146	611	81	165	34	8	17	71	31	46	.270	.312	.435	99	-3	2			.965	3	*O-145	-1.0
1932	Bro-N	118	384	54	115	28	2	16	56	25	33	.299	.349	.508	130	15	1			.976	-3	O-88	0.6
1933	Bro-N	147	556	65	171	22	7	7	46	33	40	.308	.350	.410	123	16	9			.971	-7	*O-138	0.3
1934	Bro-N	104	307	51	91	20	4	4	35	33	13	.296	.370	.407	114	7	4			.957	-3	O-77/1-1	0.1
Total	6	805	3102	498	954	200	35	85	377	210	176	.308	.357	.477	118	75	23			.974	9	O-733/1-1	3.6

YEAR	TM/L	G	AB	R	H	2B	3B	HR	RBI	BB	SO	AVG	OBP	SLG	PRO+	BR/A	SB	CS	SBR	FA	FR	G/POS	TPR

■ ED FREED   Freed, Edwin Charles   b: 8/22/19, Centre Valley, Pa.   d: 1/9/96, Chino, Cal.   BR/TR, 5'6", 165 lbs.   Deb: 9/11/42

| 1942 | Phi-N | 13 | 33 | 3 | 10 | 3 | 1 | 0 | 1 | 4 | 3 | .303 | .378 | .455 | 151 | 2 | | 1 | | 1.000 | -1 | O-11 | 0.0 |

■ ROGER FREED   Freed, Roger Vernon   b: 6/2/46, Los Angeles, Cal.   BR/TR, 6', 190 lbs.   Deb: 9/18/70

1970	Bal-A	4	13	0	2	0	0	0	1	3	4	.154	.313	.154	32	-1	0	0	0	1.000	0	/1-3,O-1	-0.1
1971	Phi-N	118	348	23	77	12	1	6	37	44	86	.221	.314	.313	78	-9	0	3	-2	.989	-5	*O-106/C-1	-2.2
1972	Phi-N	73	129	10	29	4	0	6	18	23	39	.225	.346	.395	108	2	0	1	-1	.971	-2	O-46	-0.2
1974	Cin-N	6	6	1	2	0	0	1	3	1	1	.333	.429	.833	251	1	0	0	0	1.000	-0	/1-1	0.1
1976	Mon-N	8	15	0	3	1	0	0	1	0	3	.200	.200	.267	30	-1	0	0	0	1.000	-0	/1-3,O-1	-0.2
1977	StL-N	49	83	10	33	2	1	5	21	11	9	.398	.468	.627	194	11	0	0	0	1.000	-2	1-18/O-6	0.8
1978	StL-N	52	92	3	22	6	0	2	20	8	17	.239	.300	.370	87	-2	1	0	0	.992	-1	1-15/O-6	-0.4
1979	StL-N	34	31	2	8	2	0	2	8	5	7	.258	.361	.516	135	1	0	0	0	.889	-1	/1-1	0.2
Total	8	344	717	49	176	27	2	22	109	95	166	.245	.337	.381	101	2	1	4	-2	.982	-10	O-166/1-41,C-1	-2.0

■ BILL FREEHAN   Freehan, William Ashley   b: 11/29/41, Detroit, Mich.   BR/TR, 6'2", 205 lbs.   Deb: 9/26/61

1961	Det-A	4	10	1	4	0	0	0	4	1	0	.400	.455	.400	127	0	0	0	0	1.000	1	/C-3	0.2
1963	Det-A	100	300	37	73	12	2	9	36	39	56	.243	.334	.387	98	-0	2	0	1	.995	-1	C-73,1-19	0.2
1964	Det-A☆	144	520	69	156	14	8	18	80	36	68	.300	.355	.462	123	16	5	1	1	.993	-2	*C-141/1-1	2.2
1965	Det-A★	130	431	45	101	15	0	10	43	39	63	.234	.308	.373	83	-9	4	2	0	.996	-1	*C-129	-0.4
1966	Det-A★	136	492	47	115	22	0	12	46	40	72	.234	.295	.352	83	-11	5	2	0	**.996**	0	*C-132/1-5	-0.2
1967	Det-A★	155	517	66	146	23	1	20	74	73	71	.282	.392	.447	143	31	1	2	-1	.992	-9	*C-147,1-11	3.2
1968	*Det-A★	155	540	73	142	24	2	25	84	65	64	.263	.367	.454	143	30	0	1	-1	.994	6	*C-138,1-21/O-1	4.8
1969	Det-A★	143	489	61	128	16	3	16	49	53	55	.262	.344	.405	104	3	1	2	-1	.992	4	*C-120,1-20	1.2
1970	Det-A★	117	395	44	95	17	3	16	52	52	48	.241	.335	.420	106	3	0	3	-2	**.997**	-16	*C-114	-0.8
1971	Det-A★	148	516	57	143	26	4	21	71	54	48	.277	.356	.465	126	17	2	7	-4	.996	-12	*C-144/O-1	0.8
1972	*Det-A★	111	374	51	98	18	2	10	56	48	51	.262	.355	.401	121	11	0	1	-1	.989	0	*C-105/1-1	1.6
1973	Det-A☆	110	380	33	89	10	1	6	29	40	30	.234	.325	.313	75	-11	0	0	0	**.995**	9	C-98/1-7,D-3	0.1
1974	Det-A	130	445	58	132	17	5	18	60	42	44	.297	.364	.479	136	20	2	0	1	.994	-8	1-65,C-63/D-1	1.1
1975	Det-A☆	120	427	42	105	17	3	14	47	32	56	.246	.308	.398	94	-4	2	0	0	.991	-8	*C-113/1-5	-0.7
1976	Det-A	71	237	22	64	10	1	5	27	12	27	.270	.308	.384	98	-1	0	0	0	.983	-2	C-61/1-2,D-3	-0.1
Total	15	1774	6073	706	1591	241	35	200	758	626	753	.262	.342	.412	111	94	24	21	-5	.993	-38	*C-1581,1-157/D-7,O	13.2

■ JERRY FREEMAN   Freeman, Frank Ellsworth "Buck"   b: 12/26/1879, Placerville, Cal.   d: 9/30/52, Los Angeles, Cal.   BL/TR, 6'2", 220 lbs.   Deb: 4/14/08

1908	Was-A	154	531	45	134	15	5	1	45	36		.252	.304	.305	107	3	6			.975	-13	*1-154	-1.4
1909	Was-A	19	48	2	8	0	1	0	3	4		.167	.245	.208	46	-3	3			.956	-2	1-14/O-1	-0.5
Total	2	173	579	47	142	15	6	1	48	40		.245	.299	.297	101	0	9			.974	-15	1-168/O-1	-1.9

■ JOHN FREEMAN   Freeman, John Edward   b: 1/24/01, Boston, Mass.   d: 4/14/58, Washington, D.C.   BR/TR, 5'8", 160 lbs.   Deb: 6/17/27

| 1927 | Bos-A | 4 | 2 | 0 | 0 | 0 | 0 | 0 | 0 | 0 | 0 | .000 | .000 | .000 | -99 | -1 | 0 | 0 | 0 | .000 | -2 | /O-3 | -0.2 |

■ BUCK FREEMAN   Freeman, John Frank   b: 10/30/1871, Catasauqua, Pa.   d: 6/25/49, Wilkes-Barre, Pa.   BL/TL, 5'9", 169 lbs.   Deb: 6/27/1891

1891	Was-a	5	18	1	4	1	0	0	1	2	2	.222	.300	.278	69	-1	0			.769	-1	/P-5	0.0
1898	Was-N	29	107	19	39	2	3	3	21	7		.364	.424	.523	171	10	2			.978	1	O-29	0.8
1899	Was-N	155	588	107	187	19	25	**25**	122	23		.318	.362	.563	154	38	21			.944	-12	*O-155/P-2	1.3
1900	Bos-N	117	418	58	126	19	13	6	65	25		.301	.355	.452	109	2	10			.950	-1	O-91,1-19	-1.4
1901	Bos-A	129	490	88	166	23	15	12	114	44		.339	.400	.520	157	37	17			.974	-5	*1-128/2-1,O-1	2.7
1902	Bos-A	138	564	75	174	38	19	11	**121**	32		.309	.352	.502	131	21	17			.944	-1	*O-138	1.1
1903	*Bos-A	141	567	74	163	39	20	**13**	**104**	30		.287	.328	.496	137	23	5			.933	-6	*O-141	0.9
1904	Bos-A	157	597	64	167	24	**19**	7	84	32		.280	.329	.412	126	17	7			.954	-6	*O-157	0.2
1905	Bos-A	130	455	59	109	20	8	3	49	46		.240	.316	.338	106	4	8			.973	-14	1-66,O-57/3-2	-1.6
1906	Bos-A	121	392	42	98	18	9	1	30	28		.250	.302	.349	104	1	5			.989	1	O-65,1-43/3-4	-0.2
1907	Bos-A	4	12	1	2	0	0	1	2	3		.167	.333	.417	140	1	0			1.000	0	/O-3	0.1
Total	11	1126	4208	588	1235	199	131	82	713	272	2	.293	.346	.462	131	152	92			.950	-53	O-837,1-256/P-7,32	3.9

■ LA VEL FREEMAN   Freeman, La Vel Maurice   b: 2/18/63, Oakland, Cal.   BL/TL, 5'9", 170 lbs.   Deb: 4/7/89

| 1989 | Mil-A | 2 | 3 | 1 | 0 | 0 | 0 | 0 | 0 | 0 | 2 | .000 | .000 | .000 | -99 | -1 | 0 | 0 | 0 | .000 | 0 | /D-2 | -0.1 |

■ GENE FREESE   Freese, Eugene Lewis "Augie"   b: 1/8/34, Wheeling, W.Va.   BR/TR, 5'11", 175 lbs.   Deb: 4/13/55   F

1955	Pit-N	134	455	69	115	21	8	14	44	34	57	.253	.310	.426	94	-5	5	1	1	.943	-2	3-65,2-57	-0.2
1956	Pit-N	65	207	17	43	9	0	3	14	16	45	.208	.274	.295	54	-13	2	1	0	.963	-7	3-47,2-26	-1.9
1957	Pit-N	114	346	44	98	18	2	6	31	17	42	.283	.321	.399	95	-3	9	4	0	.924	-3	3-74,2-10,O-10	-0.4
1958	Pit-N	17	18	1	3	0	0	1	2	1	2	.167	.211	.333	42	-2	0	0	0	.800	1	/3-1	-0.1
	StL-N	62	191	28	49	11	1	6	16	10	32	.257	.294	.419	83	-5	1	1	-0	.924	-25	S-28,2-14/3-3	-2.7
	Yr	79	209	29	52	11	1	7	18	11	34	.249	.286	.411	80	-7	1	1	-0	.924	-24	S-28,2-14/3-4	-2.8
1959	Phi-N	132	400	60	107	14	5	23	70	43	61	.268	.346	.500	120	11	8	4	0	.916	-24	*3-109/2-6	-1.2
1960	Chi-A	127	455	60	124	32	6	17	79	29	65	.273	.318	.481	114	7	10	6	-1	.946	-3	*3-122	0.5
1961	*Cin-N	152	575	78	159	27	2	26	87	27	78	.277	.309	.466	101	-1	8	2	1	.950	-17	*3-151/2-1	-1.6
1962	Cin-N	18	42	2	6	1	0	0	1	6	8	.143	.250	.167	14	-5	1	0	0	1.000	1	3-10	-0.7
1963	Cin-N	66	217	20	53	9	1	6	26	17	42	.244	.305	.378	93	-2	4	2	0	.930	-6	3-62/O-1	-0.9
1964	Pit-N	99	289	33	65	13	2	9	40	19	45	.225	.273	.377	81	-8	1	2	-1	.920	-6	3-72	-1.6
1965	Pit-N	43	80	6	21	4	0	0	8	6	18	.262	.330	.313	82	-2	0	0	0	.951	-1	3-19	-0.4
	Chi-A	17	32	2	9	0	1	1	4	5	9	.281	.378	.438	140	2	0	0	0	.824	-3	/3-8	-0.1
1966	Chi-A	48	106	8	22	2	0	3	10	8	20	.208	.270	.311	71	-4	2	1	0	.894	3	3-34	-0.2
	Hou-N	21	33	1	3	0	0	0	0	5	5	.091	.211	.091	-13	-5	1	0	0	.800	-2	/3-4,2-3,O-1	-0.2
Total	12	1115	3446	429	877	161	28	115	432	243	535	.254	.307	.418	94	-37	51	26	-0	.934	-90	3-781,2-117/S-28,O	-12.0

■ GEORGE FREESE   Freese, George Walter "Bud"   b: 9/12/26, Wheeling, W.Va.   BR/TR, 6', 190 lbs.   Deb: 4/29/53   FC

1953	Det-A	1	1	0	0	0	0	0	0	0	0	.000	.000	.000	-99	0	0	0	0	.000	0	H	0.0
1955	Pit-N	51	179	17	46	8	2	3	22	17	18	.257	.328	.374	87	-3	1	1	-0	.936	-8	3-50	-1.2
1961	Chi-N	9	7	0	2	0	0	0	1	1	4	.286	.375	.286	78	-0	0	0	0	.000	0	H	0.0
Total	3	61	187	17	48	8	2	3	23	18	22	.257	.329	.369	86	-4	1	1	-0	.936	-8	/3-50	-1.2

■ JIM FREGOSI   Fregosi, James Louis   b: 4/4/42, San Francisco, Cal.   BR/TR, 6'1", 190 lbs.   Deb: 9/14/61   M

1961	LA-A	11	27	7	6	0	0	0	3	1	4	.222	.250	.222	25	-3	0	0	0	.944	-0	S-11	-0.2
1962	LA-A	58	175	15	51	3	4	3	23	18	27	.291	.358	.406	108	2	2	1	0	.943	4	S-52	1.1
1963	LA-A	154	592	83	170	29	12	9	50	36	104	.287	.328	.422	115	10	2	4	-1	.964	5	*S-151	2.3
1964	LA-A★	147	505	86	140	22	9	18	72	72	87	.277	.372	.463	145	31	8	5	1	.966	1	*S-137	4.4
1965	Cal-A	161	602	66	167	19	7	15	64	54	107	.277	.341	.407	114	11	13	5	1	.968	5	*S-160	3.0
1966	Cal-A★	162	611	78	154	32	7	13	67	67	89	.252	.328	.391	109	7	17	8	0	.959	15	*S-162/1-1	3.9
1967	Cal-A★	151	590	75	171	23	6	9	56	49	77	.290	.349	.395	124	17	9	6	-1	.965	-7	*S-151	2.6
1968	Cal-A★	159	614	77	150	21	**13**	9	49	60	101	.244	.317	.365	110	-7	9	4	0	.962	-14	*S-159	1.1
1969	Cal-A★	161	580	78	151	26	6	12	47	93	86	.260	.364	.381	114	13	9	2	0	.972	-16	*S-160	1.7
1970	Cal-A★	158	601	95	167	33	5	22	82	69	92	.278	.355	.459	127	22	0	2	-1	.973	4	*S-150/1-6	4.2
1971	Cal-A	107	347	31	81	15	5	5	33	39	61	.233	.320	.336	90	-5	1	2	-0	.938	-10	S-74,1-18/O-7	-0.7
1972	NY-N	101	340	31	79	15	4	5	32	38	71	.232	.311	.344	88	-5	1	0	0	.935	-2	3-85/S-6,1-3	-1.4
1973	NY-N	45	124	7	29	4	1	0	11	20	25	.234	.340	.282	75	-3	1	0	0	.906	-6	S-17,3-17/1-3,O-1	-0.9
	Tex-A	45	157	25	42	6	2	6	16	12	31	.268	.319	.433	110	2	0	0	0	.918	-1	3-34,1-10/S-6	-0.7
1974	Tex-A	78	230	31	60	5	0	12	34	22	41	.261	.326	.439	121	6	0	1	-1	1.000	-1	1-47,3-32	0.1
1975	Tex-A	77	191	25	50	5	0	7	33	20	39	.262	.335	.398	107	2	0	1	-0	.985	2	1-54,D-13/3-4	0.1
1976	Tex-A	58	133	17	31	7	0	1	12	23	33	.233	.346	.331	97	0	0	1	-1	.995	-0	1-26,D-18/3-5	-0.1
1977	Tex-A	13	28	1	7	0	1	5	5	3		.250	.323	.393	93	-0	1			1.000	1	/1-5,D-3	0.0

YEAR	TM/L	G	AB	R	H	2B	3B	HR	RBI	BB	SO	AVG	OBP	SLG	PRO+	BR/A	SB	CS	SBR	FA	FR	G/POS	TPR
	Pit-N	36	56	10	16	1	1	3	16	13	10	.286	.420	.500	142	4	2	0	1	.981	-1	1-15/3-1	0.3
1978	Pit-N	20	20	3	4	1	0	0	1	6	8	.200	.385	.250	77	-0	0	0	0	.667	-1	/3-5,1-2,2-1	-0.2
Total	18	1902	6523	844	1726	264	78	151	706	715	1097	.265	.340	.398	114	118	76	40		.963	-40	*S-1396,1-190,3/DO2	20.6

■ VERN FREIBURGER
Freiburger, Vern Donald b: 12/19/23, Detroit, Mich. d: 2/27/90, Palm Springs, Cal. BR/TL, 6'1", 170 lbs. Deb: 9/6/41

YEAR	TM/L	G	AB	R	H	2B	3B	HR	RBI	BB	SO	AVG	OBP	SLG	PRO+	BR/A	SB	CS	SBR	FA	FR	G/POS	TPR
1941	Cle-A	2	8	0	1	0	0	0	1	0	2	.125	.125	.125	-35	-2	0	0	0	.947	1	/1-2	-0.1

■ HOWARD FREIGAU
Freigau, Howard Earl "Ty" b: 8/1/02, Dayton, Ohio d: 7/18/32, Chattanooga, Tenn BR/TR, 5'10.5", 160 lbs. Deb: 9/13/22

YEAR	TM/L	G	AB	R	H	2B	3B	HR	RBI	BB	SO	AVG	OBP	SLG	PRO+	BR/A	SB	CS	SBR	FA	FR	G/POS	TPR
1922	StL-N	3	1	0	0	0	0	0	0	0	0	.000	.000	.000	-99	-0	0	0	0	1.000	1	/S-2,3-1	0.1
1923	StL-N	113	358	30	94	18	1	1	35	25	36	.263	.314	.327	71	-15	5	4	-1	.929	2	S-87,2-16/1-9,30	-0.6
1924	StL-N	98	376	35	101	17	6	2	39	19	24	.269	.306	.362	80	-11	10	3	1	.958	8	3-98/S-2	0.0
1925	StL-N	9	26	2	4	0	0	0	0	2	1	.154	.214	.154	-4	-4	0	0	0	.936	3	/S-7,2-1	0.0
	Chi-N	117	476	77	146	22	10	8	71	30	31	.307	.349	.445	100	-1	10	6	-1	.913	-5	3-96,S-17/1-7	0.2
	Yr	126	502	79	150	22	10	8	71	32	32	.299	.342	.430	94	-5	10	6	-1	.913	-1	3-96,S-24/1-7,2-1	0.2
1926	Chi-N	140	508	51	137	27	7	3	51	43	42	.270	.327	.368	86	-10	6			.966	-3	*3-135/S-2,O-1	-0.4
1927	Chi-N	30	86	12	20	5	0	0	10	9	10	.233	.313	.291	62	-4	0			.883	1	3-30	-0.3
1928	Bro-N	17	34	6	7	2	0	0	3	1	3	.206	.229	.265	29	-4	0			.810	-4	3-10/S-1	-0.7
	Bos-N	52	109	11	28	8	1	1	17	9	14	.257	.319	.376	86	-3	1			.938	-10	S-14,2-11	-1.0
	Yr	69	143	17	35	10	1	1	20	10	17	.245	.299	.350	72	-6	1			.938	-13	S-15,2-11,3-10	-1.7
Total	7	579	1974	224	537	99	25	15	226	138	161	.272	.322	.370	82	-52	32	13		.940	-11	3-371,S-132/210	-2.7

■ CHARLIE FRENCH
French, Charles Calvin b: 10/12/1883, Indianapolis, Ind. d: 3/30/62, Indianapolis, Ind. BL/TR, 5'6", 140 lbs. Deb: 5/23/09

YEAR	TM/L	G	AB	R	H	2B	3B	HR	RBI	BB	SO	AVG	OBP	SLG	PRO+	BR/A	SB	CS	SBR	FA	FR	G/POS	TPR
1909	Bos-A	51	167	15	42	3	1	0		13	15	.251	.324	.281	90	-1	8			.921	-8	2-28,S-23	-1.1
1910	Bos-A	9	40	4	8	1	0	0		3	1	.200	.220	.225	38	-3	0			.889	1	/2-8	-0.3
	Chi-A	45	170	17	28	1	1	0		4	10	.165	.224	.182	29	-14	5			.930	-14	2-28,O-16	-3.4
	Yr	54	210	21	36	2	1	0		7	11	.171	.223	.190	31	-17	5			.919	-14	2-36,O-16	-3.7
Total	2	105	377	36	78	5	2	0		20	26	.207	.269	.231	58	-18	13			.920	-22	/2-64,S-23,O-16	-4.8

■ PAT FRENCH
French, Frank Alexander b: 9/22/1893, Dover, N.H. d: 7/13/69, Bath, Maine BR/TR, 6'1", 180 lbs. Deb: 7/2/17

YEAR	TM/L	G	AB	R	H	2B	3B	HR	RBI	BB	SO	AVG	OBP	SLG	PRO+	BR/A	SB	CS	SBR	FA	FR	G/POS	TPR
1917	Phi-A	3	2	0	0	0	0	0	0	0	0	.000	.000	.000	-99	-0	0	0	0	1.000	-0	/O-1	-0.1

■ RAY FRENCH
French, Raymond Edward b: 1/9/1895, Alameda, Cal. d: 4/3/78, Alameda, Cal. BR/TR, 5'9.5", 158 lbs. Deb: 9/17/20

YEAR	TM/L	G	AB	R	H	2B	3B	HR	RBI	BB	SO	AVG	OBP	SLG	PRO+	BR/A	SB	CS	SBR	FA	FR	G/POS	TPR
1920	NY-A	2	2	0	0	0	0	0	0	0	1	.000	.000	.000	-97	-1	0	0	0	.500	-0	/S-1	-0.1
1923	Bro-N	43	73	14	16	2	1	0	7	4	7	.219	.269	.274	45	-6	0	0	0	.874	4	S-30	0.0
1924	Chi-A	37	112	13	20	4	0	0	11	10	13	.179	.246	.214	20	-14	3	1	0	.927	-3	S-28/2-3	-1.2
Total	3	82	187	29	36	6	1	0	19	14	21	.193	.252	.235	28	-20	3	1	0	.897	2	/S-59,2-3	-1.3

■ JIM FRENCH
French, Richard James b: 8/13/41, Warren, Ohio BL/TR, 5'7", 182 lbs. Deb: 9/12/65

YEAR	TM/L	G	AB	R	H	2B	3B	HR	RBI	BB	SO	AVG	OBP	SLG	PRO+	BR/A	SB	CS	SBR	FA	FR	G/POS	TPR
1965	Was-A	13	37	4	11	0	0	1	7	9	5	.297	.435	.378	135	2	0	1	0	.974	-0	C-13	0.3
1966	Was-A	10	24	0	5	1	0	0	3	4	5	.208	.321	.250	67	-1	0	1	-1	.979	-1	C-10	-0.2
1967	Was-A	6	16	0	1	0	0	0	1	3	4	.063	.211	.063	-16	-2	0	0	0	.968	-1	/C-6	-0.3
1968	Was-A	59	165	9	32	5	0	1	10	19	19	.194	.281	.242	62	-7	1	0	0	.984	2	C-53	-0.3
1969	Was-A	63	158	14	29	6	3	2	13	41	15	.184	.352	.297	88	-1	0	0	0	.989	9	C-63	1.2
1970	Was-A	69	166	20	35	3	1	1	13	38	23	.211	.358	.259	76	-4	0	1	-1	.973	-6	C-62/O-1	-0.8
1971	Was-A	14	41	6	6	2	0	0	4	7	7	.146	.271	.195	36	-3	2	3	0	.985	-1	C-14	-0.5
Total	7	234	607	53	119	17	4	5	51	121	78	.196	.331	.262	74	-16	3	6	-3	.982	-0	C-221/O-1	-0.6

■ WALTER FRENCH
French, Walter Edward "Piggy" or "Fitz" b: 7/12/1899, Moorestown, N.J. d: 5/13/84, Mountain Home, Ark BL/TR, 5'7.5", 155 lbs. Deb: 9/15/23

YEAR	TM/L	G	AB	R	H	2B	3B	HR	RBI	BB	SO	AVG	OBP	SLG	PRO+	BR/A	SB	CS	SBR	FA	FR	G/POS	TPR
1923	Phi-A	16	39	7	9	3	0	0	2	5	7	.231	.318	.308	64	-2	0	1	-1	1.000	-1	O-10	-0.4
1925	Phi-A	67	100	20	37	9	0	0	14	1	9	.370	.376	.460	104	0	1	1	-0	.971	0	O-19	-0.1
1926	Phi-A	112	397	51	121	18	7	1	36	18	24	.305	.340	.393	86	-9	2	3	-1	.971	3	O-99	-1.4
1927	Phi-A	109	326	48	99	10	5	0	41	16	14	.304	.338	.365	78	-11	9	1	2	.956	0	O-94	-1.3
1928	Phi-A	48	74	9	19	4	0	0	7	2	5	.257	.286	.311	55	-5	1	0	-1	1.000	-1	O-19	-0.5
1929	*Phi-A	45	45	7	12	1	0	1	9	2	3	.267	.298	.356	65	-2	0	0	0	1.000	-3	O-10	-0.5
Total	6	397	981	142	297	45	12	2	109	44	62	.303	.336	.379	81	-29	13	7	-0	.968	-2	O-251	-4.4

■ BILL FRENCH
French, William b: Baltimore, Md. Deb: 4/14/1873

YEAR	TM/L	G	AB	R	H	2B	3B	HR	RBI	BB	SO	AVG	OBP	SLG	PRO+	BR/A	SB	CS	SBR	FA	FR	G/POS	TPR
1873	Mar-n	5	18	3	4	0	0	0	0	0	0	.222	.222	.222	42	-1	0	0	0	.905	-0	/1-2,O-2,P-1,3-1	0.0

■ LONNY FREY
Frey, Linus Reinhard "Junior" b: 8/23/10, St.Louis, Mo. BL/TR, 5'10", 160 lbs. Deb: 8/29/33

YEAR	TM/L	G	AB	R	H	2B	3B	HR	RBI	BB	SO	AVG	OBP	SLG	PRO+	BR/A	SB	CS	SBR	FA	FR	G/POS	TPR
1933	Bro-N	34	135	25	43	5	3	0	12	13	13	.319	.378	.400	128	5	4			.896	-14	S-34	-0.7
1934	Bro-N	125	490	77	139	24	5	8	57	52	54	.284	.358	.402	109	7	11			.945	13	*S-109,3-13	2.6
1935	Bro-N	131	515	88	135	35	11	11	77	66	68	.262	.352	.437	113	10	6			.937	-4	*S-127/2-4	1.3
1936	Bro-N	148	524	63	146	29	4	4	60	71	56	.279	.369	.372	99	2	7			.918	-32	*S-117,2-30/O-1	-2.1
1937	Chi-N	78	198	33	55	9	3	1	22	33	15	.278	.381	.369	100	1	6			.938	-19	S-30,2-13/3-9,O-5	-1.4
1938	Cin-N	124	501	76	133	26	6	4	36	49	50	.265	.331	.365	94	-4	4			.964	-8	*2-121/S-3	-0.4
1939	*Cin-N★	125	484	95	141	27	9	11	55	72	46	.291	.387	.452	124	18	5			.976	15	*2-124	4.0
1940	*Cin-N	150	563	102	150	23	6	8	54	80	48	.266	.361	.371	101	3	22			.977	18	*2-150	3.1
1941	Cin-N★	146	543	78	138	29	5	6	59	72	37	.254	.345	.359	98	-0	16			.970	-2	*2-145	0.8
1942	Cin-N	141	523	66	139	23	6	2	39	87	38	.266	.373	.344	111	11	9			.977	5	*2-140	2.6
1943	Cin-N★	144	586	78	154	20	7	2	43	76	56	.263	.347	.334	99	1	7			.985	12	*2-144	2.2
1946	Cin-N	111	333	46	82	10	3	3	24	63	31	.246	.358	.321	100	3	5			.963	-3	2-65,O-28	0.3
1947	Chi-N	24	43	4	9	0	0	0	3	10	1	.209	.277	.209	32	-4	0			1.000	-2	/2-9	-0.6
	*NY-A	24	28	10	5	2	0	0	2	10	1	.179	.410	.250	87	0	3	0	1	.923	3	/2-8	0.5
1948	NY-A	1	0	0	0	0	0	0	0	0	0	—	—	—	—	0	0	0	0	.000	-0	R	-0.0
	NY-N	29	51	6	13	1	0	1	6	4	6	.255	.309	.333	73	-2	0			.920	-2	2-13	-0.3
Total	14	1535	5517	848	1482	263	69	61	549	752	525	.269	.359	.374	104	50	105		0	.973	-18	2-966,S-420/O-34,3	11.9

■ PEPE FRIAS
Frias, Jesus Maria (Andujar) b: 7/14/48, San Pedro De Macoris, D.R. BR/TR, 5'10", 159 lbs. Deb: 4/6/73

YEAR	TM/L	G	AB	R	H	2B	3B	HR	RBI	BB	SO	AVG	OBP	SLG	PRO+	BR/A	SB	CS	SBR	FA	FR	G/POS	TPR
1973	Mon-N	100	225	19	52	10	1	0	22	10	24	.231	.267	.284	51	-15	1	3	-2	.950	17	S-46,2-44/3-6,O-1	0.6
1974	Mon-N	75	112	12	24	4	1	0	7	7	10	.214	.261	.268	45	-8	1	0	0	.962	17	S-30,3-27,2-15/O-3	1.1
1975	Mon-N	51	64	4	8	2	0	0	4	3	13	.125	.164	.156	-10	-10	0	1	-1	.938	14	S-29,3-11/2-7	0.5
1976	Mon-N	76	113	7	28	5	0	0	8	4	14	.248	.274	.292	58	-7	1	1	0	.957	14	2-35,S-35/3-4,O-1	1.1
1977	Mon-N	53	70	10	18	5	0	0	5	0	10	.257	.257	.271	43	-6	1	0	0	.978	8	2-16,S-14/3-1	0.3
1978	Mon-N	73	15	5	4	2	1	0	5	0	3	.267	.267	.533	120	1	0	0	0	1.000	13	2-61/S-3	1.4
1979	Atl-N	140	475	41	123	18	4	1	44	20	36	.259	.292	.320	62	-25	3	2	0	.954	-1	*S-137	-1.0
1980	Tex-A	116	227	27	55	7	1	0	10	4	23	.242	.259	.273	47	-16	5	1	1	.947	-16	*S-106/3-7,2-2	-2.4
	LA-N	14	9	1	2	1	0	0	0	0	0	.222	.222	.333	54	-1	0	0	0	.933	2	S-11	0.2
1981	LA-N	25	36	6	9	1	0	0	3	1	3	.250	.289	.278	64	-2	0	0	0	.906	-5	S-15/2-6,3-1	-0.6
Total	9	723	1346	132	323	49	8	1	108	49	136	.240	.269	.290	52	-88	12	8	-1	.951	63	S-426,2-186/3-57,O	1.2

■ BERNIE FRIBERG
Friberg, Bernard Albert (b: Gustaf Bernhard Friberg) b: 8/18/1899, Manchester, N.H. d: 12/8/58, Lynn, Mass. BR/TR, 5'11", 178 lbs. Deb: 8/20/19

YEAR	TM/L	G	AB	R	H	2B	3B	HR	RBI	BB	SO	AVG	OBP	SLG	PRO+	BR/A	SB	CS	SBR	FA	FR	G/POS	TPR
1919	Chi-N	8	20	3	4	1	0	0	2	1	1	.200	.200	.250	35	-2	0			1.000	-1	/O-7	-0.3
1920	Chi-N	50	114	11	24	5	1	0	7	6	20	.211	.250	.272	49	-8	2			.963	-1	2-24,O-24	-0.9
1922	Chi-N	97	296	51	92	8	2	0	23	37	37	.311	.391	.351	91	-2	8	10	-4	.972	-2	O-74/1-6,3-5,2-3	-1.2
1923	Chi-N	146	547	91	174	27	11	12	88	45	49	.318	.372	.473	122	16	13	19	-8	.955	4	*3-146	2.8
1924	Chi-N	142	495	67	138	19	3	5	82	66	53	.279	.369	.360	95	-1	19	27	-11	.954	4	*3-142	-0.2
1925	Chi-N	44	152	12	39	5	3	1	16	14	22	.257	.327	.349	72	-6	0			.889	-5	3-26,O-12/1-6,S-2	-1.1
	Phi-N	91	304	41	82	12	1	5	22	39	35	.270	.353	.365	77	-10	1			.965	2	2-77,3-14/P-1,C-1	-0.4
	Yr	135	456	53	121	17	4	6	38	53	57	.265	.344	.360	75	-16	1			.965	-2	2-77,3-40,O/1SPC	-1.5
1926	Phi-N	144	478	38	128	21	3	1	51	57	77	.268	.346	.331	79	-13	2			.976	22	*2-144	1.3

YEAR	TM/L	G	AB	R	H	2B	3B	HR	RBI	BB	SO	AVG	OBP	SLG	PRO+	BR/A	SB	CS	SBR	FA	FR	G/POS	TPR
1927	Phi-N	111	335	31	78	8	2	1	28	41	49	.233	.322	.278	61	-17	3			.959	25	*3-103/2-5	1.3
1928	Phi-N	52	94	11	19	3	0	1	7	12	16	.202	.292	.266	45	-7	0			.908	1	S-31/3-5,2-3,O-3,1	-0.4
1929	Phi-N	128	455	74	137	21	10	7	55	49	54	.301	.370	.437	93	-5	1			.923	-26	S-73,O-40/2-8,1-2	-2.2
1930	Phi-N	105	331	62	113	21	1	4	42	47	35	.341	.425	.447	104	4	1			.953	-4	2-44,O-35,S-12/3-8	0.1
1931	Phi-N	103	353	33	92	19	5	1	26	33	25	.261	.324	.351	75	-12	1			.955	6	2-64,3-25/1-5,S-3	-0.1
1932	Phi-N	61	154	17	37	8	2	0	14	19	23	.240	.324	.318	66	-7	0			.957	-1	2-56	-0.6
1933	Bos-A	17	41	5	13	3	0	0	9	6	1	.317	.404	.390	112	1	0	0	0	.950	1	/2-6,3-5,S-2	0.3
Total	14	1299	4169	544	1170	181	44	38	471	471	498	.281	.356	.373	87	-69	51	60		.953	32	3-479,2-434,OS/1CP	-1.0

■ JIM FRIDLEY Fridley, James Riley "Big Jim" b: 9/6/24, Philippi, W.Va. BR/TR, 6'2", 205 lbs. Deb: 4/15/52

YEAR	TM/L	G	AB	R	H	2B	3B	HR	RBI	BB	SO	AVG	OBP	SLG	PRO+	BR/A	SB	CS	SBR	FA	FR	G/POS	TPR
1952	Cle-A	62	175	23	44	2	0	4	16	14	40	.251	.311	.331	84	-4	3	3	-1	.978	-5	O-54	-1.3
1954	Bal-A	85	240	25	59	8	5	4	36	21	41	.246	.312	.371	93	-3	0	1	-1	.985	-1	O-67	-0.8
1958	Cin-N	5	9	2	2	2	0	0	1	0	2	.222	.222	.444	67	-0	0			1.000	0	/O-2	-0.1
Total	3	152	424	50	105	12	5	8	53	35	83	.248	.310	.356	89	-8	3	4	-2	.982	-7	O-123	-2.2

■ PAT FRIEL Friel, Patrick Henry b: 6/11/1860, Lewisburg, W.Va. d: 1/15/24, Providence, R.I. BB, 5'11", 170 lbs. Deb: 7/13/1890 F

YEAR	TM/L	G	AB	R	H	2B	3B	HR	RBI	BB	SO	AVG	OBP	SLG	PRO+	BR/A	SB	CS	SBR	FA	FR	G/POS	TPR
1890	Syr-a	62	261	51	65	8	2	3	21	17		.249	.302	.330	96	-2	34			.913	-6	O-62	-0.9
1891	Phi-a	2	8	2	2	1	0	0	0	0	0	.250	.250	.375	76	-0	0			1.000	-1	/O-2	-0.1
Total	2	64	269	53	67	9	2	3	21	17	0	.249	.301	.331	96	-2	34			.914	-7	/O-64	-1.0

■ BILL FRIEL Friel, William Edward b: 4/1/1876, Renovo, Pa. d: 12/24/59, St.Louis, Mo. BL/TR, 5'10", 165 lbs. Deb: 5/3/01 FUC

YEAR	TM/L	G	AB	R	H	2B	3B	HR	RBI	BB	SO	AVG	OBP	SLG	PRO+	BR/A	SB	CS	SBR	FA	FR	G/POS	TPR
1901	Mil-A	106	376	51	100	13	7	4	35	23		.266	.310	.370	92	-4	15			.866	-9	3-61,O-29/2-9,S-6	-1.2
1902	StL-A	80	267	26	64	9	2	2	20	14		.240	.283	.311	65	-13	4			.921	-14	O-33,2-25,1/3SPC	-2.5
1903	StL-A	97	351	46	80	11	8	0	25	23		.228	.279	.305	77	-10	4			.915	-11	2-63,3-24/O-9	-1.9
Total	3	283	994	123	244	33	17	6	80	60		.245	.293	.332	80	-27	23			.924	-33	/2-97,3-93,O1SCP	-5.6

■ FRANK FRIEND Friend, Frank B. (b: Frederick Freund) b: 7/5/1875, Jeffersonville, Ind. d: 11/5/33, Jeffersonville, Ind. TR, 5'10", 180 lbs. Deb: 8/2/1896

YEAR	TM/L	G	AB	R	H	2B	3B	HR	RBI	BB	SO	AVG	OBP	SLG	PRO+	BR/A	SB	CS	SBR	FA	FR	G/POS	TPR
1896	Lou-N	2	5	1	1	0	0	0	1	1		.200	.333	.200	44	-0	0			1.000	-0	/C-2	0.0

■ OWEN FRIEND Friend, Owen Lacey "Red" b: 3/21/27, Granite City, Ill. BR/TR, 6'1", 180 lbs. Deb: 10/2/49 C

YEAR	TM/L	G	AB	R	H	2B	3B	HR	RBI	BB	SO	AVG	OBP	SLG	PRO+	BR/A	SB	CS	SBR	FA	FR	G/POS	TPR
1949	StL-A	2	8	1	3	0	0	0	0	0	0	.375	.375	.375	95	-0	0	0	0	1.000	1	/2-2	0.1
1950	StL-A	119	372	48	88	15	2	8	50	40	68	.237	.312	.352	67	-19	2	1	0	.961	10	2-93,3-24/S-3	-0.5
1953	Det-A	31	96	10	17	4	0	3	10	6	9	.177	.233	.302	47	-8	0	1	-1	.947	4	2-26	-0.3
	Cle-A	34	68	7	16	2	0	2	13	5	16	.235	.288	.353	74	-3	0	0	0	1.000	6	2-19/S-8,3-1	0.4
	Yr	65	164	17	33	6	0	5	23	11	25	.201	.256	.329	58	-10	0	1	-1	.964	10	2-45/S-8,3-1	0.1
1955	Bos-A	14	42	3	11	3	0	0	2	4	11	.262	.326	.333	71	-2	0	0	0	.951	2	S-14/2-1	0.1
	Chi-N	6	10	0	1	0	0	0	0	0	3	.100	.100	.100	-47	-2	0	0	0	1.000	-1	/3-2,S-1	-0.3
1956	Chi-N	2	2	0	0	0	0	0	0	0	0	.000	.000	.000	-99	-1	0	0	0	.000	0	H	-0.1
Total	5	208	598	69	136	24	2	13	76	55	109	.227	.295	.339	63	-34	2	2	-1	.963	23	2-141/3-27,S-26	-0.6

■ BUCK FRIERSON Frierson, Robert Lawrence b: 7/29/17, Chicota, Tex. BR/TR, 6'3", 195 lbs. Deb: 9/9/41

YEAR	TM/L	G	AB	R	H	2B	3B	HR	RBI	BB	SO	AVG	OBP	SLG	PRO+	BR/A	SB	CS	SBR	FA	FR	G/POS	TPR
1941	Cle-A	5	11	2	3	1	0	0	2	1	1	.273	.333	.364	89	-0	0	0	0	1.000	-1	/O-3	-0.1

■ PETE FRIES Fries, Peter Martin b: 10/30/1857, Scranton, Pa. d: 7/30/37, Chicago, Ill. BL/TL, 5'8", 160 lbs. Deb: 8/10/1883

YEAR	TM/L	G	AB	R	H	2B	3B	HR	RBI	BB	SO	AVG	OBP	SLG	PRO+	BR/A	SB	CS	SBR	FA	FR	G/POS	TPR
1883	Col-a	3	10	1	3	0	0	0		0	1	.300	.364	.400	158	1				.857	0	/P-3	0.0
1884	Ind-a	1	3	0	1	1	0	0			1	.333	.500	.667	285	1				.333	0	/O-1	0.1
Total	2	4	13	1	4	2	0	0			2	.308	.400	.462	190	1				.857	0	/P-3,O-1	0.1

■ FRED FRINK Frink, Frederick Ferdinand b: 8/25/11, Macon, Ga. d: 5/19/95, Miami Springs, Fla. BR/TR, 6'1", 180 lbs. Deb: 7/1/34

YEAR	TM/L	G	AB	R	H	2B	3B	HR	RBI	BB	SO	AVG	OBP	SLG	PRO+	BR/A	SB	CS	SBR	FA	FR	G/POS	TPR
1934	Phi-N	2	0	0	0	0	0	0	0	0	0	—	—	—	—		0			.000	-1	/O-1	-0.1

■ CHARLIE FRISBEE Frisbee, Charles Augustus "Bunt" b: 2/2/1874, Dows, Iowa d: 11/7/54, Alden, Iowa BB/TR, 5'9", 175 lbs. Deb: 6/22/1899

YEAR	TM/L	G	AB	R	H	2B	3B	HR	RBI	BB	SO	AVG	OBP	SLG	PRO+	BR/A	SB	CS	SBR	FA	FR	G/POS	TPR
1899	Bos-N	42	152	22	50	4	2	0	20	9		.329	.374	.382	98	-1	10			.875	-2	O-40	-0.5
1900	NY-N	4	13	2	2	1	0	0	3	2		.154	.267	.231	40	-1	0			.400	-2	/O-4	-0.3
Total	2	46	165	24	52	5	2	0	23	11		.315	.365	.370	94	-2	10			.849	-4	O-44	-0.8

■ FRANKIE FRISCH Frisch, Frank Francis "The Fordham Flash" b: 9/9/1898, Bronx, N.Y. d: 3/12/73, Wilmington, Del. BB/TR, 5'11", 165 lbs. Deb: 6/14/19 MCH

YEAR	TM/L	G	AB	R	H	2B	3B	HR	RBI	BB	SO	AVG	OBP	SLG	PRO+	BR/A	SB	CS	SBR	FA	FR	G/POS	TPR
1919	NY-N	54	190	21	43	3	2	2	24	4	14	.226	.242	.295	62	-9	15			.972	4	2-29,3-20/S-1	-0.4
1920	NY-N	110	440	57	123	10	10	4	77	20	18	.280	.311	.375	97	-3	34	11	4	.967	9	*3-109/S-2	1.6
1921	*NY-N	153	618	121	211	31	17	8	100	42	28	.341	.384	.485	128	25	49	13	7	.936	4	3-93,2-61	4.3
1922	*NY-N	132	514	101	168	16	13	5	51	47	13	.327	.387	.438	111	9	31	17	-1	.975	13	2-85,3-53/S-1	2.5
1923	*NY-N	151	641	116	**223**	32	10	12	111	46	12	.348	.395	.485	133	30	29	12	2	**.973**	-8	*2-135,3-17	2.6
1924	*NY-N	145	603	**121**	198	33	15	7	69	56	24	.328	.387	.468	132	27	22	9	1	.972	25	*2-143,S-10/3-2	5.4
1925	NY-N	120	502	89	166	26	6	11	48	32	14	.331	.374	.472	119	14	21	12	-1	.931	3	3-46,2-42,S-39	2.3
1926	NY-N	135	545	75	171	29	4	5	44	33	16	.314	.353	.409	106	4	23			.975	11	2-127/3-7	1.9
1927	StL-N	153	617	112	208	31	11	10	78	43	10	.337	.387	.472	125	21	48			**.979**	49	*2-153/S-1	**7.3**
1928	*StL-N	141	547	107	164	29	9	10	86	64	17	.300	.374	.441	110	9	29			**.976**	3	*2-139	1.5
1929	StL-N	138	527	93	176	40	12	5	74	53	12	.334	.397	.484	116	14	24			.970	4	*2-121,3-13/S-1	1.4
1930	*StL-N	133	540	121	187	46	9	10	114	55	16	.346	.407	.520	118	18	15	28		.969	28	*2-123,3-10	4.4
1931	*StL-N	131	518	96	161	24	4	4	82	45	13	.311	.368	.396	101	2	28			.974	16	*2-129	2.6
1932	StL-N	115	486	59	142	26	2	3	60	25	13	.292	.327	.372	85	-10	18			.971	16	2-75,3-37/S-4	1.3
1933	StL-N★	147	585	74	177	32	6	4	66	48	16	.303	.358	.398	110	8	18			.982	-3	*2-132,S-15,M	1.5
1934	*StL-N★	140	550	74	168	30	6	3	75	45	10	.305	.359	.398	96	-2	11			.977	5	*2-115,3-25,M	1.0
1935	StL-N☆	103	354	52	104	16	2	1	55	33	16	.294	.356	.359	89	-5	2			.982	9	2-88/3-5,M	-0.5
1936	StL-N	93	303	40	83	10	0	1	26	36	10	.274	.353	.317	82	-6	2			.965	-13	2-60,3-22/S-1,M	-1.4
1937	StL-N	17	32	3	7	0	0	0	4	1	0	.219	.242	.281	41	-3	0			1.000	1	/2-5,M	-0.1
Total	19	2311	9112	1532	2880	466	138	105	1244	728	272	.316	.369	.432	110	142	419	74		.974	149	*2-1762,3-459/S-75	39.0

■ EMIL FRISK Frisk, John Emil b: 10/15/1874, Kalkaska, Mich. d: 1/27/22, Seattle, Wash. BL/TR, 6'1", 190 lbs. Deb: 9/2/1899

YEAR	TM/L	G	AB	R	H	2B	3B	HR	RBI	BB	SO	AVG	OBP	SLG	PRO+	BR/A	SB	CS	SBR	FA	FR	G/POS	TPR
1899	Cin-N	9	25	5	7	1	0	0	2	2		.280	.357	.320	85	-0	0			.950	-0	/P-9	0.0
1901	Det-A	20	48	10	15	3	0	1	7	3		.313	.365	.438	117	1	0			.851	2	P-11/O-2	0.0
1905	StL-A	124	429	58	112	11	6	3	36	42		.261	.342	.336	122	12	7			.923	-3	*O-115	0.0
1907	StL-A	5	4	0	1	0	0	0	4	0		.250	.400	.250	108	0	0			.000	0	H	0.0
Total	4	158	506	73	135	15	6	4	45	48		.267	.346	.344	119	13	7			.918	-5	O-117/P-20	0.0

■ HARRY FRITZ Fritz, Harry Koch "Dutchman" b: 9/30/1890, Philadelphia, Pa. d: 11/4/74, Columbus, Ohio BR/TR, 5'8", 170 lbs. Deb: 9/29/13

YEAR	TM/L	G	AB	R	H	2B	3B	HR	RBI	BB	SO	AVG	OBP	SLG	PRO+	BR/A	SB	CS	SBR	FA	FR	G/POS	TPR
1913	Phi-A	5	13	1	0	0	0	0	0	2		.000	.188	.000	-45	-2	0			.846	-1	/3-5	-0.4
1914	Chi-F	65	174	16	37	5	1	0	13	18	18	.213	.297	.253	54	-14	2			.912	-9	3-46/S-9,2-1	-2.2
1915	Chi-F	79	236	27	59	8	4	3	26	13	27	.250	.298	.356	89	-8	4			.964	-8	3-70/2-6,S-1	-1.5
Total	3	149	423	44	96	13	5	3	39	33	45	.227	.294	.303	70	-25	6			.941	-18	3-121/S-10,2-7	-4.1

■ LARRY FRITZ Fritz, Lawrence Joseph b: 2/14/49, E.Chicago, Ind. BL/TL, 6'2", 225 lbs. Deb: 5/30/75

YEAR	TM/L	G	AB	R	H	2B	3B	HR	RBI	BB	SO	AVG	OBP	SLG	PRO+	BR/A	SB	CS	SBR	FA	FR	G/POS	TPR
1975	Phi-N	1	1	0	0	0	0	0	0	0	0	.000	.000	.000	-96	-0	0	0	0	.000	0	H	0.0

■ DOUG FROBEL Frobel, Douglas Steven b: 6/6/59, Ottawa, Ont., Can. BL/TR, 6'4", 196 lbs. Deb: 9/5/82

YEAR	TM/L	G	AB	R	H	2B	3B	HR	RBI	BB	SO	AVG	OBP	SLG	PRO+	BR/A	SB	CS	SBR	FA	FR	G/POS	TPR
1982	Pit-N	16	34	5	7	2	0	2	3	1	11	.206	.229	.441	81	-1	1	1	-0	1.000	-1	O-12	-0.3
1983	Pit-N	32	60	10	17	4	1	3	11	4	17	.283	.328	.533	132	2	1	1	-0	.964	-4	O-24	-0.2
1984	Pit-N	126	276	33	56	9	3	12	28	24	84	.203	.272	.388	83	-7	5	4	-1	.977	6	*O-112	-1.0
1985	Pit-N	53	109	14	22	5	0	2	7	19	24	.202	.320	.248	62	-5	4	3	-1	.941	-3	O-36	-1.0
	Mon-N	12	23	3	3	1	0	1	4	2	6	.130	.200	.304	42	-2	0	0	-0	.923	-0	/O-6	-0.3
	Yr	65	132	17	25	6	0	3	11	21	30	.189	.301	.258	59	-7	4	3	-1	.938	-3	O-42	-1.3

YEAR	TM/L	G	AB	R	H	2B	3B	HR	RBI	BB	SO	AVG	OBP	SLG	PRO+	BR/A	SB	CS	SBR	FA	FR	G/POS	TPR
1987	Cle-A	29	40	5	4	0	0	2	5	5	13	.100	.200	.250	18	-5	0	0	0	1.000	-3	O-12/D-5	-0.8
Total	5	268	542	70	109	21	4	20	58	55	155	.201	.277	.365	78	-18	13	10	-2	.957	-10	O-202/D-5	-3.6

■ **BEN FROELICH** Froelich, William Palmer b: 11/12/1887, Pittsburgh, Pa. d: 9/1/16, Pittsburgh, Pa. BR/TR, Deb: 7/2/09

YEAR	TM/L	G	AB	R	H	2B	3B	HR	RBI	BB	SO	AVG	OBP	SLG	PRO+	BR/A	SB	CS	SBR	FA	FR	G/POS	TPR
1909	Phi-N	1	1	0	0	0	0	0	0	0	0	.000	.000	.000	-99	-0	0			.000	0	/C-1	0.0

■ **JERRY FRY** Fry, Jerry Ray b: 2/29/56, Salinas, Cal. BR/TR, 6', 185 lbs. Deb: 9/4/78

YEAR	TM/L	G	AB	R	H	2B	3B	HR	RBI	BB	SO	AVG	OBP	SLG	PRO+	BR/A	SB	CS	SBR	FA	FR	G/POS	TPR
1978	Mon-N	4	9	0	0	0	0	0	1	5	.000	.100	.000	-71	-2	0	0	0	1.000	1	/C-4	-0.1

■ **JEFF FRYE** Frye, Jeffrey Dustin b: 8/31/66, Oakland, Cal. BR/TR, 5'9", 180 lbs. Deb: 7/9/92

YEAR	TM/L	G	AB	R	H	2B	3B	HR	RBI	BB	SO	AVG	OBP	SLG	PRO+	BR/A	SB	CS	SBR	FA	FR	G/POS	TPR
1992	Tex-A	67	199	24	51	9	1	1	12	16	27	.256	.321	.327	85	-4	1	3	-2	.978	8	2-67	0.4
1994	Tex-A	57	205	37	67	20	3	0	18	29	23	.327	.413	.454	124	8	6	1	1	.983	-16	2-54/3-1,D-1	-0.4
1995	Tex-A	90	313	38	87	15	2	4	29	24	45	.278	.339	.377	84	-7	3	3	-1	.975	3	2-83	0.0
1996	Bos-A	105	419	74	120	27	2	4	41	54	57	.286	.374	.389	90	-5	18	4	3	.983	14	*2-100/O-5,S-3,D-1	1.7
Total	4	319	1136	173	325	71	8	9	100	123	152	.286	.363	.386	94	-7	28	11	2	.979	8	2-304/O-5,S-3,D3	1.7

■ **TRAVIS FRYMAN** Fryman, David Travis b: 3/25/69, Lexington, Ky. BR/TR, 6'1", 180 lbs. Deb: 7/7/90

YEAR	TM/L	G	AB	R	H	2B	3B	HR	RBI	BB	SO	AVG	OBP	SLG	PRO+	BR/A	SB	CS	SBR	FA	FR	G/POS	TPR
1990	Det-A	66	232	32	69	11	1	9	27	17	51	.297	.348	.470	126	7	3	3	-1	.915	5	3-48,S-17/D-1	1.3
1991	Det-A	149	557	65	144	36	3	21	91	40	149	.259	.312	.447	106	2	12	5	1	.946	-9	3-85,S-71	-0.1
1992	Det-A★	161	659	87	175	31	4	20	96	45	144	.266	.318	.416	104	1	8	4	0	.970	-4	*S-137,3-26	0.7
1993	Det-A★	151	607	98	182	37	5	22	97	77	128	.300	.382	.486	133	28	9	4	0	.953	-5	S-81,3-69/D-1	2.9
1994	Det-A★	114	464	66	122	34	5	18	85	45	128	.263	.335	.474	105	2	2	2	-1	.955	-5	*3-114	-0.3
1995	Det-A	144	567	79	156	21	5	15	81	63	100	.275	.351	.409	97	-2	4	2	0	.969	**27**	*3-144	2.3
1996	Det-A★	157	616	90	165	32	3	22	100	57	118	.268	.334	.437	93	-7	4	3	-1	**.979**	17	*3-128,S-29	1.0
Total	7	942	3702	517	1013	202	26	127	577	344	818	.274	.340	.445	107	33	42	23	-1	.963	24	3-614,S-335/D-2	7.8

■ **MIKE FUENTES** Fuentes, Michael Jay b: 7/11/58, Miami, Fla. BR/TR, 6'3", 190 lbs. Deb: 9/2/83

YEAR	TM/L	G	AB	R	H	2B	3B	HR	RBI	BB	SO	AVG	OBP	SLG	PRO+	BR/A	SB	CS	SBR	FA	FR	G/POS	TPR
1983	Mon-N	6	4	1	1	0	0	0	0	0	2	.250	.250	.250	39	-0	0	0	0	.000	0	/H	-0.1
1984	Mon-N	3	4	0	1	0	0	0	0	1	2	.250	.400	.250	90	-0	0	0	0	1.000	0	/O-1	0.0
Total	2	9	8	1	2	0	0	0	0	1	4	.250	.333	.250	67	-0	0	0	0	1.000	0	/O-1	-0.1

■ **TITO FUENTES** Fuentes, Rigoberto (Peat) b: 1/4/44, Havana, Cuba BB/TR, 5'11", 175 lbs. Deb: 8/18/65

YEAR	TM/L	G	AB	R	H	2B	3B	HR	RBI	BB	SO	AVG	OBP	SLG	PRO+	BR/A	SB	CS	SBR	FA	FR	G/POS	TPR
1965	SF-N	26	72	12	15	1	0	1	5	1	14	.208	.269	.222	39	-6	0	1	-1	.919	-7	S-18/2-7,3-1	-1.3
1966	SF-N	133	541	63	141	21	3	9	40	9	57	.261	.277	.360	73	-20	6	3	0	.957	-14	S-76,2-60	-2.3
1967	SF-N	133	344	27	72	12	1	5	29	27	61	.209	.267	.294	61	-17	4	3	-1	.980	25	*2-130/S-5	1.4
1969	SF-N	67	183	28	54	4	3	1	14	15	25	.295	.352	.366	103	1	2	4	-2	.925	-6	3-36,S-30	-0.5
1970	SF-N	123	435	49	116	13	7	2	32	36	52	.267	.327	.343	81	-12	4	5	-2	.966	-2	2-78,S-36,3-24	-0.7
1971	*SF-N	152	630	63	172	28	6	4	52	18	46	.273	.300	.356	86	-13	12	2	2	.973	1	*2-152	0.3
1972	SF-N	152	572	64	151	23	6	7	53	39	56	.264	.314	.379	95	-5	16	5	2	.964	-21	*2-152	-1.6
1973	SF-N	160	656	78	182	25	5	6	63	45	62	.277	.331	.358	87	-11	12	6	0	**.993**	-5	*2-160/3-1	-0.7
1974	SF-N	108	390	33	97	15	2	0	22	22	32	.249	.294	.297	63	-19	7	3	0	.979	-4	*2-103	-1.9
1975	SD-N	146	565	57	158	21	3	4	43	25	51	.280	.314	.349	89	-10	8	8	-2	.970	4	*2-142	-0.1
1976	SD-N	135	520	48	137	18	0	2	36	18	38	.263	.289	.310	76	-18	5	3	-0	.971	2	*2-127	-0.9
1977	Det-A	151	615	83	190	19	10	5	51	38	61	.309	.351	.397	98	-1	4	4	-1	.970	3	*2-151/D-1	1.1
1978	Oak-A	13	43	5	6	1	0	0	2	1	6	.140	.159	.163	-10	-6	0	0	0	.944	-12	2-13	-1.9
Total	13	1499	5566	610	1491	211	46	45	438	298	561	.268	.309	.347	82	-137	80	47	-4	.974	-37	*2-1275,S-165/3D	-9.1

■ **OLLIE FUHRMAN** Fuhrman, Alfred George b: 7/20/1896, Jordan, Minn. d: 1/11/69, Peoria, Ill. BB/TR, 5'11", 185 lbs. Deb: 4/13/22

YEAR	TM/L	G	AB	R	H	2B	3B	HR	RBI	BB	SO	AVG	OBP	SLG	PRO+	BR/A	SB	CS	SBR	FA	FR	G/POS	TPR
1922	Phi-A	6	6	1	2	1	0	0	0	0	0	.333	.333	.500	112	0	0	0	0	1.000	0	/C-4	0.0

■ **DOT FULGHUM** Fulghum, James Lavoisier b: 7/4/1900, Valdosta, Ga. d: 11/11/67, Miami, Fla. BR/TR, 5'8.5", 165 lbs. Deb: 9/15/21

YEAR	TM/L	G	AB	R	H	2B	3B	HR	RBI	BB	SO	AVG	OBP	SLG	PRO+	BR/A	SB	CS	SBR	FA	FR	G/POS	TPR
1921	Phi-A	2	2	0	0	0	0	0	0	1	1	.000	.333	.000	-9	-0	0	0	0	.000	0	/S-1	0.0

■ **NIG FULLER** Fuller, Charles F. b: 3/30/1879, Toledo, Ohio d: 11/12/47, Toledo, Ohio BR/TR, 5'11", 165 lbs. Deb: 7/1/02

YEAR	TM/L	G	AB	R	H	2B	3B	HR	RBI	BB	SO	AVG	OBP	SLG	PRO+	BR/A	SB	CS	SBR	FA	FR	G/POS	TPR
1902	Bro-N	3	9	0	0	0	0	0	0	0		.000	.000	.000	-99	-2	0			1.000	-1	/C-3	-0.3

■ **FRANK FULLER** Fuller, Frank Edward "Rabbit" b: 1/1/1893, Detroit, Mich. d: 10/29/65, Warren, Mich. BB/TR, 5'7", 150 lbs. Deb: 4/14/15

YEAR	TM/L	G	AB	R	H	2B	3B	HR	RBI	BB	SO	AVG	OBP	SLG	PRO+	BR/A	SB	CS	SBR	FA	FR	G/POS	TPR
1915	Det-A	14	32	6	5	0	0	0	2	9	7	.156	.341	.156	47	-2	2	3	-1	.962	-6	/2-9,S-1	-0.9
1916	Det-A	20	10	2	1	0	0	0	1	1	4	.100	.182	.100	-15	-1	3			.846	3	/2-8,S-1	0.1
1923	Bos-A	6	21	3	5	0	0	0	0	1	1	.238	.273	.238	35	-2	1	1	-0	.952	2	/2-6	0.0
Total	3	40	63	11	11	0	0	0	3	11	12	.175	.297	.175	35	-5	6	4		.938	-1	/2-23,S-2	-0.8

■ **HARRY FULLER** Fuller, Henry W. b: 12/5/1862, Cincinnati, Ohio d: 12/12/1895, Cincinnati, Ohio Deb: 4/8/1891 F

YEAR	TM/L	G	AB	R	H	2B	3B	HR	RBI	BB	SO	AVG	OBP	SLG	PRO+	BR/A	SB	CS	SBR	FA	FR	G/POS	TPR
1891	StL-a	1	2	0	0	0	0	0	0	0	1	.000	.000	.000	-87	-0	0			.000	-1	/3-1	-0.1

■ **JIM FULLER** Fuller, James Hardy b: 11/28/50, Bethesda, Md. BR/TR, 6'3", 215 lbs. Deb: 9/10/73

YEAR	TM/L	G	AB	R	H	2B	3B	HR	RBI	BB	SO	AVG	OBP	SLG	PRO+	BR/A	SB	CS	SBR	FA	FR	G/POS	TPR
1973	Bal-A	9	26	2	3	0	0	2	4	1	17	.115	.148	.346	36	-2	0	0	0	1.000	1	/O-5,1-2,D-1	-0.1
1974	Bal-A	64	189	17	42	11	0	7	28	8	68	.222	.265	.392	90	-4	1	0	0	.960	-2	O-59/1-4,D-2	-0.8
1977	Hou-N	34	100	5	16	6	0	2	9	10	45	.160	.243	.280	44	-8	0	1	-1	.983	5	O-27/1-1	-0.5
Total	3	107	315	24	61	17	0	11	41	19	130	.194	.249	.352	70	-14	1	1	-0	.969	4	/O-91,1-7,D-3	-1.4

■ **JOHN FULLER** Fuller, John Edward b: 1/29/50, Lynwood, Cal. BL/TL, 6'2", 180 lbs. Deb: 5/9/74

YEAR	TM/L	G	AB	R	H	2B	3B	HR	RBI	BB	SO	AVG	OBP	SLG	PRO+	BR/A	SB	CS	SBR	FA	FR	G/POS	TPR
1974	Atl-N	3	3	1	1	0	0	0	0	0	0	.333	.333	.333	83	-0	0	0	0	1.000	-0	/O-1	0.0

■ **VERN FULLER** Fuller, Vernon Gordon b: 3/1/44, Menomonie, Wis. BR/TR, 6'1", 170 lbs. Deb: 9/5/64

YEAR	TM/L	G	AB	R	H	2B	3B	HR	RBI	BB	SO	AVG	OBP	SLG	PRO+	BR/A	SB	CS	SBR	FA	FR	G/POS	TPR
1964	Cle-A	2	1	0	0	0	0	0	0	0	0	.000	.000	.000	-99	-0	0	0	0	.000	0	H	0.0
1966	Cle-A	16	47	7	11	2	1	2	2	7	6	.234	.357	.447	129	2	0	0	0	1.000	-4	2-16	-0.1
1967	Cle-A	73	206	18	46	10	4	0	21	19	55	.223	.301	.374	98	-1	2	3	-1	.986	0	2-64/S-2	0.2
1968	Cle-A	97	244	14	59	9	0	18	24	49	.242	.320	.291	87	-3	2	2	-1	.988	-12	2-73,3-23/S-4	-1.4
1969	Cle-A	108	254	25	60	11	3	4	22	20	53	.236	.297	.335	74	-9	2	1	0	.978	9	*2-102/3-7	0.6
1970	Cle-A	29	33	3	6	2	0	1	2	3	9	.182	.250	.333	57	-2	0	0	0	.919	-3	2-16/3-4,1-1	0.1
Total	6	325	785	67	182	33	4	14	65	73	172	.232	.307	.338	87	-13	6	6	-2	.982	-5	2-271/3-34,S-6,1-1	-0.6

■ **SHORTY FULLER** Fuller, William Benjamin b: 10/10/1867, Cincinnati, Ohio d: 4/11/04, Cincinnati, Ohio BR/TR, 5'6", 157 lbs. Deb: 7/19/1888 F

YEAR	TM/L	G	AB	R	H	2B	3B	HR	RBI	BB	SO	AVG	OBP	SLG	PRO+	BR/A	SB	CS	SBR	FA	FR	G/POS	TPR
1888	Was-N	49	170	11	31	5	2	0	12	10	14	.182	.232	.235	52	-9	6			.845	-6	S-47/2-2	-1.3
1889	StL-a	140	517	91	117	18	6	0	51	52	56	.226	.303	.284	60	-31	38			**.913**	0	*S-140	-1.9
1890	StL-a	130	526	118	146	9	9	1	40	73		.278	.377	.335	96	-4	60			.870	-1	*S-130	0.3
1891	StL-a	137	586	107	127	15	7	2	63	67	28	.217	.301	.276	57	-38	42			.856	-10	*S-103,2-39	-3.5
1892	NY-N	141	508	74	115	11	4	1	48	52	24	.226	.298	.270	73	-16	37			.888	1	*S-141	-0.8
1893	NY-N	130	474	78	112	14	8	0	51	60	21	.236	.325	.300	66	-23	26			.911	11	*S-130	-0.5
1894	*NY-N	93	368	81	104	14	4	2	46	52	16	.283	.374	.359	78	-12	32			.884	-4	*S-89/O-2,3-2,2-1	-0.9
1895	NY-N	126	458	82	103	11	3	0	32	64	34	.225	.323	.262	53	-30	15			.913	34	*S-126	0.8
1896	NY-N	18	72	10	12	0	0	0	7	14	5	.167	.310	.167	28	-7	4			.874	1	S-18	-0.5
Total	9	964	3679	652	867	97	43	6	350	444	**198**	.236	.323	.290	63	-168	260			.891	26	S-924/2-42,3-2,O-2	-8.3

■ **CHICK FULLIS** Fullis, Charles Philip b: 2/27/04, Girardville, Pa. d: 3/28/46, Ashland, Pa. BR/TR, 5'9", 170 lbs. Deb: 4/13/28

YEAR	TM/L	G	AB	R	H	2B	3B	HR	RBI	BB	SO	AVG	OBP	SLG	PRO+	BR/A	SB	CS	SBR	FA	FR	G/POS	TPR
1928	NY-N	11	5	1	5	0	0	0	1	1	0	.500	.500	.500	41	-0	0			.000	0	H	0.0
1929	NY-N	86	274	67	79	11	1	2	29	30	26	.288	.365	.412	92	-3	7			.962	-12	O-78	-1.8
1930	NY-N	13	6	2	0	0	0	0	0	0	1	.000	.000	.000	-99	-2	1			.000	-1	/O-2	-0.3
1931	NY-N	89	302	61	99	15	2	3	28	23	13	.328	.383	.421	119	8	13			.988	-4	O-68/2-9	0.1
1932	NY-N	96	235	35	70	14	3	1	21	11	12	.298	.332	.396	97	-1	1			.990	-8	O-55/2-1	-1.2
1933	Phi-N	151	647	91	200	31	7	1	45	36	34	.309	.350	.380	96	-3	18			.977	8	*O-151/3-1	-0.3
1934	Phi-N	28	102	8	23	6	0	0	12	10	4	.225	.301	.284	51	-7	0			.956	-3	O-27	-1.2

YEAR	TM/L	G	AB	R	H	2B	3B	HR	RBI	BB	SO	AVG	OBP	SLG	PRO+	BR/A	SB	CS	SBR	FA	FR	G/POS	TPR
	*StL-N	69	199	21	52	9	1	0	26	14	11	.261	.310	.317	64	-10	4			.969	-3	O-56	-1.4
	Yr	97	301	29	75	15	1	0	38	24	15	.249	.307	.306	59	-17	6			.966	-6	O-83	-2.6
1936	StL-N	47	89	15	25	6	1	0	6	7	11	.281	.331	.371	90	-1	0			1.000	-1	O-26	-0.3
Total	8	590	1855	305	548	92	14	12	167	132	113	.295	.347	.380	92	-19	46			.977	-23	O-463/2-10,3-1	-6.4

■ CHICK FULMER　Fulmer, Charles John　b: 2/12/1851, Philadelphia, Pa.　d: 2/15/40, Philadelphia, Pa.　BR/TR, 6′, 158 lbs.　Deb: 8/23/1871　FU

YEAR	TM/L	G	AB	R	H	2B	3B	HR	RBI	BB	SO	AVG	OBP	SLG	PRO+	BR/A	SB	CS	SBR	FA	FR	G/POS	TPR
1871	Rok-n	16	63	11	17	1	3	0	3	5	1	.270	.324	.381	106	1	0	0	0	.770	2	S-16/1-1	0.2
1872	Mut-n	36	166	28	51	1	1	1	14	2	3	.307	.315	.343	109	3	1	1	-0	.752	-1	3-22,S-14	0.0
1873	Phi-n	49	236	42	66	11	3	1	38	2	3	.280	.286	.364	88	-4	3	1	-0	.801	19	*S-49/P-2,C-1,1-1	0.9
1874	Phi-n	57	258	49	72	3	2	0	37	2	5	.279	.285	.306	86	-4	0	2	-1	.793	8	S-32,3-25	0.1
1875	Phi-n	69	295	50	65	6	1	0	24	0	6	.220	.220	.247	60	-12	10	4	1	.835	-1	*S-53,3-17	-1.3
1876	Lou-N	66	267	28	73	9	5	1	29	1	10	.273	.276	.356	93	-5				.861	-3	*S-66	-0.8
1879	Buf-N	76	306	30	82	11	5	0	28	5	34	.268	.280	.337	100	-0				.905	17	*2-76	2.0
1880	Buf-N	11	44	3	7	0	0	0	1	2	4	.159	.196	.159	21	-3				.882	-2	2-11	-0.5
1882	Cin-a	79	324	54	91	13	4	0	27	10		.281	.302	.346	112	3				.897	-13	*S-79	-0.6
1883	Cin-a	92	362	52	92	13	5	5	52	12		.254	.278	.359	98	-2				.863	-2	*S-92	-0.1
1884	Cin-a	31	114	13	20	2	1	0	8	1		.175	.183	.211	27	-9				.786	-5	S-29/O-2,3-1	-1.8
	StL-a	1	5	0	0	0	0	0		0		.000	.000	.000	-97	-1				.778	-1	2-1	-0.2
	Yr	32	119	13	20	2	1	0	8	1		.168	.175	.202	22	-10				.786	-5	S-29/O-2,3-1,2-1	-2.0
Total	5 n	227	1018	180	271	22	10	2	116	11	18	.266	.274	.313	85	-17	14	8	-1	.807	26	S-164/3-64,P-2,1C	-0.1
Total	6	356	1422	180	365	48	20	6	145	31	48	.257	.273	.331	92	-18				.867	-13	S-266/2-88,O-2,3-1	-2.0

■ CHRIS FULMER　Fulmer, Christopher　b: 7/4/1858, Tamaqua, Pa.　d: 11/9/31, Tamaqua, Pa.　BR/TR, 5′8″, 165 lbs.　Deb: 8/4/1884

YEAR	TM/L	G	AB	R	H	2B	3B	HR	RBI	BB	SO	AVG	OBP	SLG	PRO+	BR/A	SB	CS	SBR	FA	FR	G/POS	TPR
1884	Was-U	48	181	39	50	9	0	0		11		.276	.318	.326	99	-5				.937	0	C-34,O-16/1-5	-0.2
1886	Bal-a	80	270	54	66	9	3	1	30	48		.244	.363	.311	115	8	29			.949	-4	C-68,O-12/P-1	0.9
1887	Bal-a	56	201	52	54	11	4	0	32	36		.269	.382	.363	115	6	35			.913	-11	C-48/O-8	0.0
1888	Bal-a	52	166	20	31	5	1	0	10	21		.187	.286	.229	67	-5	10			.903	-16	C-45/O-7	-1.6
1889	Bal-a	16	58	11	15	3	1	0	13	6	12	.259	.338	.345	93	-1	2			.938	-5	O-14/C-2	-0.5
Total	5	252	876	176	216	37	9	1	85	122	12	.247	.343	.313	102	3	76			.929	-36	C-197/O-57,1-5,P-1	-1.4

■ WASHINGTON FULMER　Fulmer, Washington Fayette　b: 6/15/1840, Philadelphia, Pa.　d: 12/8/07, Philadelphia, Pa.　Deb: 7/19/1875　F

YEAR	TM/L	G	AB	R	H	2B	3B	HR	RBI	BB	SO	AVG	OBP	SLG	PRO+	BR/A	SB	CS	SBR	FA	FR	G/POS	TPR
1875	Atl-n	1	4	1	2	0	0	0	1	0	0	.500	.500	.500	285	1	0	0	0	.750	0	/O-1	0.1

■ DAVE FULTZ　Fultz, David Lewis　b: 5/29/1875, Staunton, Va.　d: 10/29/59, DeLand, Fla.　BR/TR, 5′11″, 170 lbs.　Deb: 7/1/1898

YEAR	TM/L	G	AB	R	H	2B	3B	HR	RBI	BB	SO	AVG	OBP	SLG	PRO+	BR/A	SB	CS	SBR	FA	FR	G/POS	TPR
1898	Phi-N	19	55	7	10	2	2	0	5	6		.182	.262	.291	61	-3	1			.871	-2	O-14/2-3,S-1	-0.5
1899	Phi-N	2	5	0	2	0	0	0	0	0		.400	.400	.400	124	0	1			.750	-7	/2-1,S-1	0.0
	Bal-N	57	210	31	62	3	2	0	18	13		.295	.342	.329	80	-6	17			.940	-1	O-31,3-20/2-2,1-1	-1.3
	Yr	59	215	31	64	3	2	0	18	13		.298	.343	.330	81	-6	18			.940	-7	O-31,3-20/2-3,S1	-1.3
1901	Phi-A	132	561	95	164	17	9	0	52	32		.292	.334	.355	87	-10	36			.935	-6	*O-106,2-18/S-9	-2.1
1902	Phi-A	129	506	109	153	20	5	1	49	62		.302	.381	.368	104	5	44			.961	-5	*O-114,2-16	-0.5
1903	NY-A	79	295	39	66	12	1	0	25	25		.224	.295	.271	67	-11	29			.933	-2	O-77/3-2	-1.9
1904	NY-A	97	339	39	93	17	4	2	32	24		.274	.324	.366	113	5	17			.976	3	O-90	0.3
1905	NY-A	129	422	49	98	13	3	0	42	39		.232	.308	.277	77	-10	44			.966	-6	*O-122	-2.4
Total	7	644	2393	369	648	84	26	3	223	201		.271	.332	.331	89	-31	189			.952	-22	O-554/2-40,3-22,S1	-8.4

■ MARK FUNDERBURK　Funderburk, Mark Clifford　b: 5/16/57, Charlotte, N.C.　BR/TR, 6′4″, 226 lbs.　Deb: 9/4/81

YEAR	TM/L	G	AB	R	H	2B	3B	HR	RBI	BB	SO	AVG	OBP	SLG	PRO+	BR/A	SB	CS	SBR	FA	FR	G/POS	TPR
1981	Min-A	8	15	2	3	1	0	0	2	1		.200	.294	.267	59	-1	0	0	0	1.000	-1	/O-6,D-1	-0.2
1985	Min-A	23	70	7	22	7	1	2	13	5	12	.314	.360	.529	132	3	0	1	-1	1.000	-1	D-15/O-5,1-1	0.1
Total	2	31	85	9	25	8	1	2	15	7	13	.294	.348	.482	120	2	0	1	-1	1.000	-2	/D-16,O-11,1-1	-0.1

■ LIZ FUNK　Funk, Elias Calvin　b: 10/28/04, LaCygne, Kan.　d: 1/16/68, Norman, Okla.　BL/TL, 5′8.5″, 160 lbs.　Deb: 4/26/29

YEAR	TM/L	G	AB	R	H	2B	3B	HR	RBI	BB	SO	AVG	OBP	SLG	PRO+	BR/A	SB	CS	SBR	FA	FR	G/POS	TPR
1929	NY-A	1	0	0	0	0	0	0	0	0	0	—	—	—		0	0	0	0	.000	0	R	0.0
1930	Det-A	140	527	74	145	26	11	4	65	29	39	.275	.319	.389	77	-19	12	6	0	.965	8	*O-129	-1.9
1932	Chi-A	122	440	59	114	21	5	2	40	43	19	.259	.325	.343	78	-14	17	15	-4	.979	4	*O-120	-1.7
1933	Chi-A	10	9	1	2	0	0	0	0	1	0	.222	.300	.222	42	-1	0	0	0	.000	-1	/O-2	-0.2
Total	4	273	976	134	261	47	16	6	105	73	58	.267	.322	.367	77	-34	29	21	-4	.972	14	O-251	-3.8

■ CARL FURILLO　Furillo, Carl Anthony "Skoonj" or "The Reading Rifle"
b: 3/8/22, Stony Creek Mills, Pa.　d: 1/21/89, Stony Creek Mills, Pa.　BR/TR, 6′, 190 lbs.　Deb: 4/16/46

YEAR	TM/L	G	AB	R	H	2B	3B	HR	RBI	BB	SO	AVG	OBP	SLG	PRO+	BR/A	SB	CS	SBR	FA	FR	G/POS	TPR
1946	Bro-N	117	335	29	95	18	6	3	35	31	20	.284	.346	.400	110	4	6			.984	9	*O-112	0.9
1947	*Bro-N	124	437	61	129	24	7	8	88	34	24	.295	.347	.431	103	1	5			.977	2	*O-121	-0.2
1948	Bro-N	108	364	55	108	20	4	4	44	43	32	.297	.374	.407	108	5	6			.983	9	*O-104	0.8
1949	*Bro-N	142	549	95	177	27	10	18	106	37	29	.322	.368	.506	127	19	4			.965	5	*O-142	1.7
1950	Bro-N	153	620	99	189	30	6	18	106	41	40	.305	.353	.460	110	8	8			.971	3	*O-153	0.4
1951	Bro-N	158	667	93	197	32	4	16	91	43	33	.295	.344	.427	104	3	8	7	-2	.986	16	*O-157	1.2
1952	*Bro-N☆	134	425	52	105	18	4	8	59	31	33	.247	.304	.351	80	-12	1	4	-2	.988	-1	*O-131	-2.0
1953	*Bro-N☆	132	479	82	165	38	6	21	92	34	32	.344	.393	.580	146	31	1	1	-0	.988	4	*O-131	2.9
1954	Bro-N	150	547	56	161	23	1	19	96	49	35	.294	.358	.444	104	3	2	4	-2	.972	4	*O-149	0.6
1955	*Bro-N	140	523	83	164	24	3	26	95	43	43	.314	.373	.520	130	22	4	5	-2	.981	-3	*O-140	1.1
1956	*Bro-N	149	523	66	151	30	0	21	83	57	41	.289	.360	.467	111	9	1	1	-0	.984	-9	*O-146	-0.9
1957	Bro-N	149	395	61	121	17	4	12	66	29	33	.306	.361	.461	108	5	0	2	-1	.988	-5	*O-107	-0.8
1958	LA-N	122	411	54	119	19	3	18	83	35	28	.290	.348	.482	113	7	0	2	-1	.975	-8	*O-119	-0.8
1959	*LA-N	50	93	8	27	4	0	0	13	7	11	.290	.340	.333	75	-3	0	0	0	.920	-5	O-25	-0.9
1960	LA-N	8	10	1	2	0	1	0	1	0	0	.200	.200	.400	56	-1	0	0	0	1.000	0	/O-2	-0.1
Total	15	1806	6378	895	1910	324	56	192	1058	514	436	.299	.356	.458	112	102	48	26		.979	22	*O-1739	3.3

■ EDDIE FUSSELBACK　Fusselback, Edward L.　b: 7/17/1856, Philadelphia, Pa.　d: 4/14/26, Philadelphia, Pa.　5′6″, 156 lbs.　Deb: 5/3/1882

YEAR	TM/L	G	AB	R	H	2B	3B	HR	RBI	BB	SO	AVG	OBP	SLG	PRO+	BR/A	SB	CS	SBR	FA	FR	G/POS	TPR
1882	StL-a	35	136	13	31	2	0	0		5		.228	.255	.243	66	-5				.853	2	C-19,O-15/P-4	-0.1
1884	Bal-U	68	303	60	86	16	3	1		3		.284	.291	.366	89	-14				.912	19	C-54/3-6,S-5,O-4	0.9
1885	Phi-a	5	19	2	6	1	0	0		2		.316	.316	.368	109	-1				.911	1	C-5	0.1
1888	Lou-a	1	4	0	1	0	0	0		0		.250	.250	.250	62	-0		0		1.000	0	/O-1	0.0
Total	4	109	462	75	124	19	3	2		10		.268	.281	.329	84	-19				.901	22	/C-78,O-20,3-6,SP	0.9

■ LES FUSSELMAN　Fusselman, Lester Leroy　b: 3/7/21, Pryor, Okla.　d: 5/21/70, Cleveland, Ohio　BR/TR, 6′1″, 195 lbs.　Deb: 4/16/52

YEAR	TM/L	G	AB	R	H	2B	3B	HR	RBI	BB	SO	AVG	OBP	SLG	PRO+	BR/A	SB	CS	SBR	FA	FR	G/POS	TPR
1952	StL-N	32	63	5	10	3	0	1	3	0	9	.159	.159	.254	13	-8	0	0	0	.991	3	C-32	-0.4
1953	StL-N	11	8	1	2	1	0	0	0	0	0	.250	.250	.375	60	-0	0	0	0	1.000	2	C-11	0.1
Total	2	43	71	6	12	4	0	1	3	0	9	.169	.169	.268	18	-8	0	0	0	.992	5	/C-43	-0.3

■ GABE GABLER　Gabler, William Louis　b: 8/4/30, St.Louis, Mo.　BL/TR, 6′1″, 190 lbs.　Deb: 9/16/58

YEAR	TM/L	G	AB	R	H	2B	3B	HR	RBI	BB	SO	AVG	OBP	SLG	PRO+	BR/A	SB	CS	SBR	FA	FR	G/POS	TPR
1958	Chi-N	3	3	0	0	0	0	0	0	0	0	.000	.000	.000	-99	-1	0	0	0	.000	0	H	-0.1

■ LEN GABRIELSON　Gabrielson, Leonard Gary　b: 2/14/40, Oakland, Cal.　BL/TR, 6′4″, 210 lbs.　Deb: 9/9/60　F

YEAR	TM/L	G	AB	R	H	2B	3B	HR	RBI	BB	SO	AVG	OBP	SLG	PRO+	BR/A	SB	CS	SBR	FA	FR	G/POS	TPR
1960	Mil-N	4	3	0	0	0	0	0	0	1	0	.000	.250	.000	-27	-1	0	0	0	.000	-0	/O-1	-0.1
1963	Mil-N	46	120	14	26	5	0	3	15	8	23	.217	.266	.333	72	-4	1	1	-0	1.000	-3	O-22,1-16/3-3	-1.0
1964	Mil-N	24	38	0	7	2	0	0	1	1	8	.184	.205	.237	24	-4	0	0	0	1.000	-1	1-12/O-2	-0.5
	Chi-N	89	272	22	67	11	2	5	23	19	37	.246	.298	.357	80	-7	0	4	-1	.984	-1	O-68/1-8	-1.2
	Yr	113	310	22	74	13	2	5	24	20	45	.239	.287	.342	74	-11	0	4	-1	.984	-2	O-70,1-20	-1.7
1965	Chi-N	28	48	4	12	0	3	5	7	16		.250	.431	.438	116	1	0	0	0	1.000	-0	O-14/1-1	-0.4
	SF-N	88	269	36	81	6	4	2	26	26	48	.301	.367	.405	114	6	1	0	0	.975	-3	O-77/1-5	0.4
	Yr	116	317	40	93	6	5	7	31	33	64	.293	.364	.410	114	7	1	0	0	.977	-3	O-91/1-6	0.0
1966	SF-N	94	240	27	52	9	0	4	16	21	51	.217	.280	.296	58	-13	0	1	-0	.948	-9	O-67/1-6	-2.8
1967	Cal-A	11	12	2	1	0	0	0	2	2	4	.083	.214	.083	-9	-2	0	0	0	.000	-0	/O-1	-0.2

YEAR	TM/L	G	AB	R	H	2B	3B	HR	RBI	BB	SO	AVG	OBP	SLG	PRO+	BR/A	SB	CS	SBR	FA	FR	G/POS	TPR
	LA-N	90	238	20	62	10	3	7	29	15	41	.261	.307	.416	114	3	3	1	0	.980	-4	O-68	-0.3
1968	LA-N	108	304	38	82	16	1	10	35	32	47	.270	.339	.428	140	14	1	1	-0	.976	-3	O-86	0.7
1969	LA-N	83	178	13	48	5	1	1	18	12	25	.270	.316	.326	86	-4	1	2	-1	.981	-7	O-47/1-2	-1.4
1970	LA-N	43	42	1	8	2	0	0	6	1	15	.190	.209	.238	20	-5	0	0	0	1.000	-0	/O-2,1-1	-0.5
Total	9	708	1764	178	446	64	12	37	176	145	315	.253	.311	.366	94	-15	20	12	-1	.977	-31	O-455/1-51,3-3	-7.3

■ LEN GABRIELSON
Gabrielson, Leonard Hilbourne   b: 9/8/15, Oakland, Cal.   BL/TL, 6'3", 210 lbs.   Deb: 4/21/39   F

YEAR	TM/L	G	AB	R	H	2B	3B	HR	RBI	BB	SO	AVG	OBP	SLG	PRO+	BR/A	SB	CS	SBR	FA	FR	G/POS	TPR
1939	Phi-N	5	18	3	4	0	0	0	1	2	3	.222	.300	.222	43	-1				.977	2	/1-5	0.0

■ EDDIE GAEDEL
Gaedel, Edward Carl   b: 6/8/25, Chicago, Ill.   d: 6/18/61, Chicago, Ill.   BR/TL, 3'7", 65 lbs.   Deb: 8/19/51

YEAR	TM/L	G	AB	R	H	2B	3B	HR	RBI	BB	SO	AVG	OBP	SLG	PRO+	BR/A	SB	CS	SBR	FA	FR	G/POS	TPR
1951	StL-A	1	0	0	0	0	0	0	0	1	0	—	1.000	—	182	0	0	0	0	.000	0	H	0.0

■ GARY GAETTI
Gaetti, Gary Joseph   b: 8/19/58, Centralia, Ill.   BR/TR, 6', 184 lbs.   Deb: 9/20/81

YEAR	TM/L	G	AB	R	H	2B	3B	HR	RBI	BB	SO	AVG	OBP	SLG	PRO+	BR/A	SB	CS	SBR	FA	FR	G/POS	TPR
1981	Min-A	9	26	4	5	0	0	2	3	0	6	.192	.192	.423	68	-1	0	0	0	1.000	1	/3-8,D-1	0.0
1982	Min-A	145	508	59	117	25	4	25	84	37	107	.230	.286	.443	94	-6	0	4	-2	.963	-3	*3-142/S-2,D-1	-1.5
1983	Min-A	157	584	81	143	30	3	21	78	54	121	.245	.313	.414	95	-5	7	1	2	.967	13	*3-154/S-3,D-1	0.7
1984	Min-A	162	588	55	154	29	4	5	65	44	81	.262	.318	.350	81	-15	11	5	0	.960	15	*3-154/O-8,S-2	-0.1
1985	Min-A	160	560	71	138	31	0	20	63	37	89	.246	.301	.409	87	-11	13	5	1	.962	17	*3-156/O-4,1-1,D-1	0.4
1986	Min-A	157	596	91	171	34	1	34	108	52	108	.287	.350	.518	129	23	14	15	-5	.956	19	*3-156/S-2,2-1,O-1	3.3
1987	*Min-A	154	584	95	150	36	2	31	109	37	92	.257	.304	.485	101	-1	10	7	-1	.973	-4	*3-150/D-2	-0.8
1988	Min-A★	133	468	66	141	29	2	28	88	36	85	.301	.358	.551	146	27	7	4	-0	.977	-6	*3-115/S-2,D-5	2.1
1989	Min-A★	130	498	63	125	11	4	19	75	25	87	.251	.291	.404	88	-10	6	2	1	.973	11	*3-125/1-2,D-3	-0.3
1990	Min-A	154	577	61	132	27	5	16	85	36	101	.229	.278	.376	76	-20	6	1	1	.959	14	*3-151/1-2,S-2	-0.4
1991	Cal-A	152	586	58	144	22	1	18	66	33	104	.246	.295	.379	85	-13	5	5	-2	.965	25	*3-152	1.1
1992	Cal-A	130	456	41	103	13	2	12	48	21	79	.226	.269	.342	70	-19	3	1	0	.927	13	3-67,1-44,D-17	-1.0
1993	Cal-A	20	50	3	9	2	0	0	4	5	12	.180	.255	.220	28	-5	1	0	0	.857	2	/3-7,1-6,D-5	-0.3
	KC-A	82	281	37	72	18	1	14	46	16	75	.256	.315	.477	103	0	0	3	-2	.974	5	3-72,1-18/D-1	0.3
	Yr	102	331	40	81	20	1	14	50	21	87	.245	.306	.438	92	-5	1	3	-2	.970	7	3-79,1-24/D-6	0.0
1994	KC-A	90	327	53	94	15	3	12	57	19	63	.287	.330	.462	97	-2	0	2	-1	.982	3	3-85/1-9	-0.1
1995	KC-A	137	514	76	134	27	0	35	96	47	91	.261	.332	.518	115	9	3	3	-1	.954	-5	*3-123,1-11/D-6	-1.3
1996	*StL-N	141	522	71	143	27	4	23	80	35	97	.274	.329	.473	108	5	2	2	-1	.970	-16	*3-133,1-14	-1.3
Total	16	2113	7725	985	1975	376	36	315	1155	534	1398	.256	.310	.436	98	-44	88	60	-10	.964	103	*3-1950,1-107/DOS2	2.9

■ FABIAN GAFFKE
Gaffke, Fabian Sebastian   b: 8/5/13, Milwaukee, Wis.   d: 2/8/92, Milwaukee, Wis.   BR/TR, 5'10", 185 lbs.   Deb: 9/9/36

YEAR	TM/L	G	AB	R	H	2B	3B	HR	RBI	BB	SO	AVG	OBP	SLG	PRO+	BR/A	SB	CS	SBR	FA	FR	G/POS	TPR
1936	Bos-A	15	55	5	7	2	0	1	3	4	5	.127	.200	.218	3	-9	0	0	0	1.000	-1	O-15	-1.0
1937	Bos-A	54	184	32	53	10	4	6	34	15	25	.288	.342	.484	102	-0	1	2	-1	.965	-4	O-50	-0.7
1938	Bos-A	15	10	2	1	0	0	0	1	3	2	.100	.308	.100	6	-1	0	0	0	.000	-0	/O-2,C-1	-0.2
1939	Bos-A	1	1	0	0	0	0	0	1	0	0	.000	.000	.000	-96	-0	0	0	0	.000	0	H	0.0
1941	Cle-A	4	4	0	1	0	0	0	0	2	2	.250	.500	.250	109	-0	0	0	0	1.000	-1	/O-2	0.0
1942	Cle-A	40	67	4	11	2	0	0	3	6	13	.164	.243	.194	25	-7	1	0	0	1.000	-2	O-16	-0.9
Total	6	129	321	43	73	14	4	7	42	30	47	.227	.297	.361	67	-17	2	2	-1	.979	-9	/O-85,C-1	-2.8

■ PHIL GAGLIANO
Gagliano, Philip Joseph   b: 12/27/41, Memphis, Tenn.   BR/TR, 6'1", 185 lbs.   Deb: 4/16/63   F

YEAR	TM/L	G	AB	R	H	2B	3B	HR	RBI	BB	SO	AVG	OBP	SLG	PRO+	BR/A	SB	CS	SBR	FA	FR	G/POS	TPR
1963	StL-N	10	5	1	2	0	0	0	1	1	1	.400	.500	.400	149	0	0	0	0	1.000	2	/2-3,3-1	0.2
1964	StL-N	40	58	5	15	4	0	1	9	3	10	.259	.295	.379	81	-1	0	1	-1	.918	1	2-12/O-2,1-1,3-1	-0.2
1965	StL-N	122	363	46	87	14	2	8	53	40	45	.240	.317	.355	81	-9	2	1	0	.960	-12	2-57,O-25,3-19	-1.8
1966	StL-N	90	213	23	54	8	2	2	15	24	29	.254	.332	.338	86	-3	2	1	0	.982	-4	3-41/1-8,O-5,2-1	-0.9
1967	*StL-N	73	217	20	48	7	0	2	21	19	26	.221	.287	.281	64	-10	0	0	0	.972	-13	2-27,3-25/1-4,S-2	-2.4
1968	*StL-N	53	105	13	24	4	2	0	13	7	12	.229	.283	.305	77	-3	0	0	0	.982	-3	2-17,3-10/O-5	-0.6
1969	StL-N	62	128	7	29	2	0	1	10	14	12	.227	.303	.266	60	-6	0	0	0	.989	-2	2-20/1-9,3-9,O-2	-0.7
1970	StL-N	18	32	0	6	0	0	0	2	1	3	.188	.212	.188	8	-4	0	1	-1	1.000	-1	/3-6,1-3,2-2	-0.6
	Chi-N	26	40	5	6	0	0	0	5	5	5	.150	.244	.150	7	-5	0	0	0	1.000	0	2-16/1-1,3-1	-0.4
	Yr	44	72	5	12	0	0	0	7	6	8	.167	.231	.167	8	-9	0	1	-1	.980	-0	2-18/3-7,1-4	-1.0
1971	Bos-A	47	68	11	22	5	0	0	13	11	5	.324	.418	.397	123	3	0	0	0	1.000	-5	O-11/2-7,3-4	-0.2
1972	Bos-A	52	82	9	21	4	1	0	10	10	13	.256	.337	.329	94	-0	1	0	0	.962	2	O-12/3-5,2-4,1-2	0.2
1973	*Cin-N	63	69	8	20	0	0	1	7	13	16	.290	.402	.319	108	2	0	0	0	.824	-1	/3-7,2-4,1-1,O-1	0.2
1974	Cin-N	46	31	2	2	0	0	0	0	15	7	.065	.370	.065	27	-2	0	0	0	1.000	0	/2-2,1-1,3-1	-0.2
Total	12	702	1411	150	336	50	7	14	159	163	184	.238	.319	.313	77	-40	5	4	-1	.969	-34	2-172,3-130/O1S	-7.5

■ RALPH GAGLIANO
Gagliano, Ralph Michael   b: 10/8/46, Memphis, Tenn.   BL/TR, 5'11", 170 lbs.   Deb: 9/21/65   F

YEAR	TM/L	G	AB	R	H	2B	3B	HR	RBI	BB	SO	AVG	OBP	SLG	PRO+	BR/A	SB	CS	SBR	FA	FR	G/POS	TPR
1965	Cle-A	1	0	0	0	0	0	0	0	0	0	—	—	—		0	0	0	0	.000	0	R	0.0

■ GREG GAGNE
Gagne, Gregory Carpenter   b: 11/12/61, Fall River, Mass.   BR/TR, 5'11", 185 lbs.   Deb: 6/5/83

YEAR	TM/L	G	AB	R	H	2B	3B	HR	RBI	BB	SO	AVG	OBP	SLG	PRO+	BR/A	SB	CS	SBR	FA	FR	G/POS	TPR
1983	Min-A	10	27	2	3	1	0	0	3	0	6	.111	.111	.148	-28	-5	0	0	0	.923	-5	S-10	-1.0
1984	Min-A	2	1	0	0	0	0	0	0	0	0	.000	.000	.000	-96	-0	0	0	0	.000	0	/H	0.0
1985	Min-A	114	293	37	66	15	3	2	23	20	57	.225	.282	.317	60	-16	10	4	1	.968	4	*S-106/D-5	-0.3
1986	Min-A	156	472	63	118	22	6	12	54	30	108	.250	.303	.398	87	-9	12	10	-2	.959	-16	*S-155/2-4	-1.3
1987	*Min-A	137	437	68	116	28	7	10	40	25	84	.265	.311	.430	91	-7	6	6	-2	.970	17	*S-136/O-4,2-1,D-1	1.8
1988	Min-A	149	461	70	109	20	6	14	48	27	110	.236	.289	.397	87	-9	15	7	0	.970	-15	*S-146/O-2,2-1,3-1	-1.3
1989	Min-A	149	460	69	125	29	7	9	48	17	80	.272	.301	.424	96	-4	11	4	1	.971	-4	*S-146/O-1	0.3
1990	Min-A	138	388	38	91	22	3	7	38	24	76	.235	.281	.361	73	-15	8	8	-2	.976	2	*S-135/O-1,D-2	-0.6
1991	*Min-A	139	408	52	108	23	3	8	42	26	72	.265	.314	.395	90	-6	11	9	-2	.984	4	*S-137/D-1	0.5
1992	Min-A	146	439	53	108	23	0	7	39	19	83	.246	.280	.346	72	-17	6	7	-2	.973	21	*S-141	1.1
1993	KC-A	159	540	66	151	32	3	10	57	33	93	.280	.321	.406	89	-10	10	12	-4	.986	5	*S-159	0.4
1994	KC-A	107	375	39	97	23	3	7	51	27	79	.259	.315	.392	78	-13	10	17	-7	.977	8	*S-106	-0.2
1995	KC-A	120	430	58	110	25	4	6	49	38	60	.256	.319	.374	79	-14	3	5	-2	.969	7	*S-118/D-2	0.2
1996	*LA-N	128	428	48	109	13	2	10	55	50	93	.255	.335	.364	92	-5	4	2	0	.965	12	*S-127	1.9
Total	14	1654	5159	663	1311	276	47	102	547	336	1001	.254	.304	.385	83	-129	106	91	-23	.972	40	*S-1622/D-11,O23	1.5

■ ED GAGNIER
Gagnier, Edward James   b: 4/16/1883, Paris, France   d: 9/13/46, Detroit, Mich.   BR/TR, 5'9", 170 lbs.   Deb: 4/14/14

YEAR	TM/L	G	AB	R	H	2B	3B	HR	RBI	BB	SO	AVG	OBP	SLG	PRO+	BR/A	SB	CS	SBR	FA	FR	G/POS	TPR
1914	Bro-F	94	337	22	63	12	2	0	25	13	24	.187	.219	.234	24	-42	8			.933	-1	S-88/3-6	-3.7
1915	Bro-F	20	50	8	13	1	0	0	4	10	5	.260	.393	.280	92	-1	2			.930	2	S-13/2-6	0.3
	Buf-F	1	2	0	0	0	0	0	0	0	0	.000	.000	.000	-98	-1	0			.800	-0	/2-1	-0.1
	Yr	21	52	8	13	1	0	0	4	10	5	.250	.381	.269	85	-1	2			.930	2	S-13/2-7	0.2
Total	2	115	389	30	76	13	2	0	29	23	29	.195	.244	.239	33	-43	10			.933	1	S-101/2-7,3-6	-3.5

■ CHICK GAGNON
Gagnon, Harold Dennis   b: 9/27/1897, Millbury, Mass.   d: 4/30/70, Wilmington, Del.   BR/TR, 5'7.5", 158 lbs.   Deb: 6/27/22

YEAR	TM/L	G	AB	R	H	2B	3B	HR	RBI	BB	SO	AVG	OBP	SLG	PRO+	BR/A	SB	CS	SBR	FA	FR	G/POS	TPR
1922	Det-A	10	4	2	1	0	0	0	0	0	2	.250	.250	.250	32	-0	0	0	0	.000	-1	/S-1,3-1	-0.1
1924	Was-A	4	5	1	1	0	0	0	1	0	0	.200	.200	.200	-3	-1	0	0	0	1.000	1	/S-2	0.0
Total	2	14	9	3	2	0	0	0	1	0	2	.222	.222	.222	16	-1	0	0	0	1.000	0	/S-3,3-1	-0.1

■ DEL GAINER
Gainer, Dellos Clinton "Sheriff"   b: 11/10/1886, Montrose, W.Va.   d: 1/29/47, Elkins, W.Va.   BR/TR, 6', 180 lbs.   Deb: 10/2/09

YEAR	TM/L	G	AB	R	H	2B	3B	HR	RBI	BB	SO	AVG	OBP	SLG	PRO+	BR/A	SB	CS	SBR	FA	FR	G/POS	TPR
1909	Det-A	2	5	0	1	0	0	0	0	0		.200	.200	.200	25	-0	0			.929	-0	/1-2	-0.1
1911	Det-A	70	248	32	75	11	4	2	25	20		.302	.366	.403	109	3	10			.975	-4	1-69	-0.1
1912	Det-A	52	179	28	43	5	6	0	20	18		.240	.320	.335	90	-2	14			.986	-3	1-50/O-1	-0.6
1913	Det-A	105	363	47	97	16	8	2	25	30	45	.267	.333	.372	108	3	10			.988	-5	*1-103	-0.3
1914	Det-A	1	0	0	0	0	0	0	0	0	0	—	—	—		0	0			1.000	0	/1-1	0.0
	Bos-A	38	84	11	20	9	2	2	13	8	14	.238	.312	.464	133	3	2	2	-1	.981	-3	1-18,2-11/O-1	-0.1
	Yr	39	84	11	20	9	2	2	13	8	14	.238	.312	.464	133	3	2	2	-1	.982	-3	1-19,2-11/O-1	-0.1
1915	*Bos-A	82	200	30	59	5	8	1	29	21	31	.295	.371	.415	139	9	7	2	1	.988	0	1-56/O-6	1.0
1916	*Bos-A	56	142	14	36	7	3	0	18	10	24	.254	.303	.359	98	-1	5			.997	1	1-48/2-2	-0.1
1917	Bos-A	52	172	28	53	10	2	2	19	15	21	.308	.374	.424	145	9	1			.989	-1	1-50	0.7

YEAR	TM/L	G	AB	R	H	2B	3B	HR	RBI	BB	SO	AVG	OBP	SLG	PRO+	BR/A	SB	CS	SBR	FA	FR	G/POS	TPR
1919	Bos-A	47	118	9	28	6	2	0	13	13	15	.237	.318	.322	85	-2	5			.978	-3	1-21,O-18	-0.7
1922	StL-N	43	97	19	26	7	4	2	23	14	6	.268	.360	.485	122	3	0	2	-1	.979	-1	1-26,O-10	-0.1
Total	10	548	1608	218	438	75	36	14	185	149	156	.272	.342	.390	113		24	54	6	.985	-19	1-444/O-36,2-13	-0.4

■ JAY GAINER
Gainer, Johnathan Keith   b: 10/8/66, Panama City, Fla.   BL/TL, 6', 190 lbs.   Deb: 5/14/93

YEAR	TM/L	G	AB	R	H	2B	3B	HR	RBI	BB	SO	AVG	OBP	SLG	PRO+	BR/A	SB	CS	SBR	FA	FR	G/POS	TPR
1993	Col-N	23	41	4	7	0	0	3	6	4	12	.171	.244	.390	57	-3	1	1	-0	.982	-1	/1-7	-0.5

■ JOE GAINES
Gaines, Arnesta Joe   b: 11/22/36, Bryan, Tex.   BR/TR, 6'1", 190 lbs.   Deb: 6/29/60

YEAR	TM/L	G	AB	R	H	2B	3B	HR	RBI	BB	SO	AVG	OBP	SLG	PRO+	BR/A	SB	CS	SBR	FA	FR	G/POS	TPR
1960	Cin-N	11	15	2	3	0	0	0	1	0	1	.200	.200	.200	10	-2	0	0	0	1.000	-1	/O-3	-0.3
1961	Cin-N	5	3	2	0	0	0	0	0	2	1	.000	.400	.000	18	-0	0	0	0	.500	-1	/O-3	-0.2
1962	Cin-N	64	52	12	12	3	0	1	7	8	16	.231	.333	.346	80	-1	0	0	0	1.000	-1	O-13	-0.4
1963	Bal-A	66	126	24	36	4	1	6	20	20	39	.286	.384	.476	145	8	2	1	0	.945	-6	O-39	0.1
1964	Bal-A	16	26	2	4	0	0	1	2	3	7	.154	.241	.269	42	-2	0	0	0	.846	0	/O-5	-0.2
	Hou-N	89	307	37	78	9	7	7	34	27	69	.254	.318	.397	106	2	8	2	1	.957	-2	O-81	-0.3
1965	Hou-N	100	229	21	52	8	1	6	31	18	59	.227	.292	.349	86	-5	4	1	1	.913	-8	O-65	-1.5
1966	Hou-N	11	13	4	1	1	0	0	0	3	5	.077	.250	.154	17	-1	0	0	0	.500	-1	/O-3	-0.3
Total	7	362	771	104	186	25	9	21	95	81	197	.241	.317	.379	99	-2	14	4	2	.934	-21	O-212	-3.1

■ TY GAINEY
Gainey, Telmanch   b: 12/25/60, Cheraw, S.C.   BL/TR, 6'1", 190 lbs.   Deb: 4/24/85

YEAR	TM/L	G	AB	R	H	2B	3B	HR	RBI	BB	SO	AVG	OBP	SLG	PRO+	BR/A	SB	CS	SBR	FA	FR	G/POS	TPR
1985	Hou-N	13	37	5	6	2	0	1	6	2	9	.162	.244	.162	16	-4	0	0	0	.913	-0	/O-9	-0.5
1986	Hou-N	26	50	6	15	3	1	1	6	6	19	.300	.375	.460	133	2	3	1	0	1.000	-3	O-19	-0.1
1987	Hou-N	18	24	1	3	0	0	0	1	2	9	.125	.192	.125	-14	-4	1	0	0	1.000	-0	/O-6	-0.4
Total	3	57	111	12	24	3	1	1	7	10	37	.216	.293	.288	62	-6	4	1	1	.968	-3	/O-34	-1.0

■ AUGIE GALAN
Galan, August John   b: 5/25/12, Berkeley, Cal.   d: 12/28/93, Fairfield, Cal.   BB/TR, 6', 175 lbs.   Deb: 4/29/34   C

YEAR	TM/L	G	AB	R	H	2B	3B	HR	RBI	BB	SO	AVG	OBP	SLG	PRO+	BR/A	SB	CS	SBR	FA	FR	G/POS	TPR
1934	Chi-N	66	192	31	50	6	2	2	22	16	15	.260	.317	.391	90	-3	4			.961	-9	2-43/3-3,S-1	-0.9
1935	*Chi-N	154	646	133	203	41	11	12	79	87	53	.314	.399	.467	131	31	22			.978	7	*O-154	3.1
1936	Chi-N★	145	575	74	152	26	4	8	81	67	50	.264	.344	.365	89	-8	16			.987	5	*O-145	-0.8
1937	Chi-N	147	611	104	154	24	10	18	78	79	48	.252	.339	.412	99	-1	23			.980	13	*O-140/2-8,S-2	0.7
1938	*Chi-N	110	395	52	113	16	9	6	69	49	17	.286	.368	.418	112	8	12			.987	2	*O-103	0.7
1939	Chi-N	148	549	104	167	36	8	6	71	75	26	.304	.392	.432	119	17	8			.970	-2	*O-145	0.9
1940	Chi-N	68	209	33	48	14	2	3	22	37	23	.230	.346	.359	96	-0	9			.984	0	O-54/2-2	-0.3
1941	Chi-N	65	120	18	25	3	0	1	13	22	10	.208	.331	.258	70	-4	0			.959	-5	O-31	-1.1
	*Bro-N	17	27	3	7	3	0	0	4	3	1	.259	.333	.370	94	-0	0			1.000	-0	/O-6	-0.1
	Yr	82	147	21	32	6	0	1	17	25	11	.218	.331	.279	74	-4	0			.967	-5	O-37	-1.2
1942	Bro-N	69	209	24	55	16	0	0	22	24	12	.263	.339	.340	97	-0	2			.990	-5	O-55/1-4,2-3	-0.8
1943	Bro-N★	139	495	83	142	26	3	9	67	103	39	.287	.412	.406	136	28	6			.981	16	*O-124,1-13	3.9
1944	Bro-N★	151	547	96	174	43	9	12	93	101	23	.318	.426	.495	162	49	4			.988	-2	*O-147/2-2	4.0
1945	Bro-N	152	576	114	177	36	7	9	92	114	27	.307	.423	.441	142	38	13			.988	-8	1-66,O-49,3-40	2.3
1946	Bro-N	99	274	53	85	22	5	3	38	68	21	.310	.451	.460	157	25	8			.935	-10	O-60,3-19,1-12	1.3
1947	Cin-N	124	392	60	123	18	2	6	61	94	19	.314	.449	.416	132	24	0			.988	-4	*O-118	1.4
1948	Cin-N	54	77	18	22	3	2	2	16	26	4	.286	.471	.455	157	8	0			.967	-2	O-18	0.5
1949	NY-N	22	17	0	1	1	0	0	2	5	3	.059	.273	.118	8	-2	0			1.000	-0	/1-3,O-1	-0.3
	Phi-A	12	26	4	8	2	0	0	0	9	2	.308	.486	.385	136	2	0	0	0	1.000	-1	/O-9	0.1
Total	16	1742	5937	1004	1706	336	74	100	830	979	393	.287	.390	.419	122	212	123	0		.981	-4	*O-1359/1-98,32S	14.6

■ ANDRES GALARRAGA
Galarraga, Andres Jose (b: Andres Jose Padovani (Galarraga))   b: 6/18/61, Caracas, Venez.   BR/TR, 6'3", 235 lbs.   Deb: 8/23/85

YEAR	TM/L	G	AB	R	H	2B	3B	HR	RBI	BB	SO	AVG	OBP	SLG	PRO+	BR/A	SB	CS	SBR	FA	FR	G/POS	TPR
1985	Mon-N	24	75	9	14	1	0	2	4	3	18	.187	.228	.280	44	-6	1	2	-1	.995	4	1-23	-0.5
1986	Mon-N	105	321	39	87	13	0	10	42	30	79	.271	.339	.405	105	-2	6	5	-1	.995	-1	*1-102	-1.4
1987	Mon-N	147	551	72	168	40	3	13	90	41	127	.305	.364	.459	113	10	7	10	-4	.993	0	*1-146	-0.4
1988	Mon-N★	157	609	99	184	42	8	29	92	39	153	.302	.354	.540	147	34	13	4	2	.991	-4	*1-156	2.0
1989	Mon-N	152	572	76	147	30	1	23	85	48	158	.257	.329	.434	115	10	12	5	1	.992	-4	*1-147	-0.4
1990	Mon-N	155	579	65	148	29	0	20	87	40	169	.256	.308	.409	99	-2	10	1	2	.993	-5	*1-154	-1.7
1991	Mon-N	107	375	34	82	13	2	9	33	23	86	.219	.268	.336	70	-16	5	6	-2	.991	2	*1-105	-2.4
1992	StL-N	95	325	38	79	14	2	10	39	11	69	.243	.285	.391	92	-5	5	4	-1	.991	4	1-90	-1.3
1993	Col-N★	120	470	71	174	35	4	22	98	24	73	.370	.408	.602	143	27	2	4	-2	.990	7	*1-119	2.2
1994	Col-N	103	417	77	133	21	0	31	85	19	93	.319	.360	.592	123	12	8	3	1	.992	-5	*1-103	-0.2
1995	*Col-N	143	554	89	155	29	3	31	106	32	146	.280	.334	.511	92	-11	12	2	2	.991	6	*1-142	-1.6
1996	Col-N	159	626	119	190	39	3	47	150	40	157	.304	.353	.601	115	7	18	8	1	.992	-2	*1-159/3-1	-0.9
Total	12	1467	5474	788	1561	306	26	247	911	350	1328	.285	.339	.486	112	63	99	54	-3	.992	-2	*1-1446/3-1	-6.6

■ MILT GALATZER
Galatzer, Milton   b: 5/4/07, Chicago, Ill.   d: 1/29/76, San Francisco, Cal   BL/TL, 5'10", 168 lbs.   Deb: 6/25/33

YEAR	TM/L	G	AB	R	H	2B	3B	HR	RBI	BB	SO	AVG	OBP	SLG	PRO+	BR/A	SB	CS	SBR	FA	FR	G/POS	TPR
1933	Cle-A	57	160	19	38	2	1	1	17	23	21	.237	.333	.281	61	-8	2	3	-1	.975	-0	O-40/1-5	-1.2
1934	Cle-A	49	196	29	53	10	2	0	15	21	8	.270	.344	.342	76	-7	3	2	-0	.980	3	O-49	-0.6
1935	Cle-A	93	259	45	78	9	3	0	19	35	8	.301	.389	.359	93	-1	4	5	-2	.934	-8	O-81	-1.3
1936	Cle-A	49	97	12	23	4	1	0	6	13	8	.237	.333	.299	57	-6	1	2	-1	.964	-8	O-42/P-1,1-1	-1.4
1939	Cin-N	3	5	0	0	0	0	0	0	0	1	.000	.000	.000	-99	-1	0			1.000	-0	/1-2	-0.2
Total	5	251	717	105	192	25	7	1	57	92	46	.268	.354	.326	75	-24	10	12		.959	-14	O-212/1-8,P-1	-4.7

■ AL GALLAGHER
Gallagher, Alan Mitchell Edward George Patrick Henry   b: 10/19/45, San Francisco, Cal.   BR/TR, 6', 180 lbs.   Deb: 4/7/70

YEAR	TM/L	G	AB	R	H	2B	3B	HR	RBI	BB	SO	AVG	OBP	SLG	PRO+	BR/A	SB	CS	SBR	FA	FR	G/POS	TPR
1970	SF-N	109	282	31	75	15	2	4	28	30	37	.266	.337	.376	92	-3	2	1	0	.971	-3	3-91	-0.3
1971	*SF-N	136	429	47	119	18	5	5	57	40	57	.277	.342	.378	105	-3	2	1	0	.951	-16	*3-128	-1.5
1972	SF-N	82	233	19	52	3	1	2	18	33	39	.223	.322	.270	69	-8	2	1	0	.974	-4	3-69	-1.4
1973	SF-N	5	9	1	2	0	0	0	1	0	0	.222	.300	.222	45	-1	0	0	0	.833	1	/3-5	-0.2
	Cal-A	110	311	16	85	9	1	0	26	35	31	.273	.349	.299	91	-3	1	3	-2	.961	4	3-98/2-1,S-1	0.0
Total	4	442	1264	114	333	42	9	11	130	138	164	.263	.338	.337	91	-12	7	6	-2	.961	-15	3-391/S-1,2-1	-3.4

■ SHORTY GALLAGHER
Gallagher, Charles William   b: 4/30/1872, Detroit, Mich.   d: 6/23/24, Detroit, Mich.   Deb: 8/13/01

YEAR	TM/L	G	AB	R	H	2B	3B	HR	RBI	BB	SO	AVG	OBP	SLG	PRO+	BR/A	SB	CS	SBR	FA	FR	G/POS	TPR
1901	Cle-A	2	4	0	0	0	0	0	0	0	0	.000	.000	.000	-99	-1	0			.667	-1	/O-2	-0.2

■ DAVE GALLAGHER
Gallagher, David Thomas   b: 9/20/60, Trenton, N.J.   BR/TR, 6', 180 lbs.   Deb: 4/12/87

YEAR	TM/L	G	AB	R	H	2B	3B	HR	RBI	BB	SO	AVG	OBP	SLG	PRO+	BR/A	SB	CS	SBR	FA	FR	G/POS	TPR
1987	Cle-A	15	36	2	4	1	1	0	1	2	5	.111	.158	.194	-7	-6	2	0	1	.972	0	O-14	-0.4
1988	Chi-A	101	347	59	105	15	3	5	31	29	40	.303	.356	.406	113	6	5	4	-1	1.000	-1	O-95/D-2	0.1
1989	Chi-A	161	601	74	160	22	6	1	46	46	79	.266	.320	.314	82	-14	5	6	-2	.993	1	*O-160/D-1	-2.0
1990	Chi-A	45	75	5	21	3	1	0	5	3	9	.280	.316	.347	87	-1	0	1	-1	.981	-6	O-37/D-4	-0.9
	Bal-A	23	51	7	11	1	0	2	4	3	7	.216	.273	.235	45	-1	1	1	-0	.980	2	O-20/D-2	-0.2
	Yr	68	126	12	32	4	1	0	7	7	12	.254	.299	.302	70	-5	1	2	-1	.980	-4	O-57/D-6	-1.1
1991	Cal-A	90	270	32	79	17	0	1	30	24	43	.293	.355	.367	100	1	2	4	-2	1.000	1	O-87/D-2	-0.2
1992	NY-N	98	175	20	42	11	1	1	21	19	16	.240	.318	.331	85	-3	4	5	-2	.982	-8	O-76	-1.5
1993	NY-N	99	201	34	55	12	2	6	28	20	18	.274	.339	.443	109	2	1	1	-0	1.000	-7	O-72/1-9	-0.6
1994	Atl-N	89	152	27	34	5	0	2	14	22	17	.224	.326	.296	62	-8	0	1	-1	.989	-9	O-77/1-1	-1.9
1995	Phi-N	62	157	12	50	12	0	1	12	16	20	.318	.382	.414	109	2	1	1	-0	1.000	-4	O-55	-0.3
	Cal-A	11	16	1	3	1	0	0	1	1	5	.188	.278	.250	39	-1	0	0	0	1.000	-1	/O-6,D-1	-0.1
Total	9	794	2081	273	564	100	10	17	190	187	251	.271	.333	.353	90	-25	20	24	-8	.993	-30	O-699/D-12,1-10	-8.0

■ JIM GALLAGHER
Gallagher, James E.   b: Findlay, Ohio   d: 3/29/1894, Scranton, Pa.   Deb: 9/4/1886

YEAR	TM/L	G	AB	R	H	2B	3B	HR	RBI	BB	SO	AVG	OBP	SLG	PRO+	BR/A	SB	CS	SBR	FA	FR	G/POS	TPR
1886	Was-N	1	5	1	1	0	0	0	0	0	0	.200	.200	.200	23	-0	0			.875	1	/S-1	0.0

■ JOHN GALLAGHER
Gallagher, John Carroll   b: 2/18/1892, Pittsburgh, Pa.   d: 3/30/52, Norfolk, Va.   BR/TR, 5'10.5", 156 lbs.   Deb: 8/20/15

YEAR	TM/L	G	AB	R	H	2B	3B	HR	RBI	BB	SO	AVG	OBP	SLG	PRO+	BR/A	SB	CS	SBR	FA	FR	G/POS	TPR
1915	Bal-F	40	126	11	25	4	0	0	4	5	22	.198	.229	.230	28	-14	1			.945	-2	2-37/S-5,3-1	-1.7

YEAR	TM/L	G	AB	R	H	2B	3B	HR	RBI	BB	SO	AVG	OBP	SLG	PRO+	BR/A	SB	CS	SBR	FA	FR	G/POS	TPR

■ JACKIE GALLAGHER
Gallagher, John Laurence b: 1/28/02, Providence, R.I. d: 9/10/84, Gladwyne, Pa. BL/TR, 5'10", 175 lbs. Deb: 8/24/23

1923	Cle-A	1	1	0	1	0	0	0	0	0	0	1.000	1.000	1.000	428	0	0	0	0	.000	-1	/O-1	0.0

■ JOE GALLAGHER
Gallagher, Joseph Emmett "Muscles" b: 3/7/14, Buffalo, N.Y. BR/TR, 6'2", 210 lbs. Deb: 4/20/39

1939	NY-A	14	41	8	10	0	1	2	9	3	8	.244	.311	.439	91	-1	1	0	0	1.000	-1	O-12	-0.2
	StL-A	71	266	41	75	17	2	9	40	17	42	.282	.327	.462	98	-2	0	1	-1	.944	2	O-67	-0.3
	Yr	85	307	49	85	17	3	11	49	20	50	.277	.325	.459	97	-3	1	1	-0	.950	1	O-79	-0.5
1940	StL-A	23	70	14	19	3	1	2	8	4	12	.271	.311	.429	88	-2	2	0	1	.966	-1	O-15	-0.3
	Bro-N	57	110	10	29	6	1	3	16	2	14	.264	.283	.418	86	-3	1			.941	-2	O-20	-0.6
Total	2	165	487	73	133	26	5	16	73	26	76	.273	.314	.446	93	-7	4	1		.950	-3	O-114	-1.4

■ GIL GALLAGHER
Gallagher, Lawrence Kirby b: 9/5/1896, Washington, D.C. d: 1/6/57, Washington, D.C. BB/TR, 5'8", 155 lbs. Deb: 9/13/22

| 1922 | Bos-N | 7 | 22 | 1 | 1 | 1 | 0 | 0 | 2 | 1 | 7 | .045 | .087 | .091 | -57 | -5 | 0 | 0 | 0 | .893 | -2 | /S-6 | -0.6 |

■ BOB GALLAGHER
Gallagher, Robert Collins b: 7/7/48, Newton, Mass. BL/TL, 6'3", 185 lbs. Deb: 5/17/72 F

1972	Bos-A	7	5	0	0	0	0	0	0	0	0	.000	.000	.000	-95	-1	0	0	0	.000	0	H	-0.1
1973	Hou-N	71	148	16	39	3	1	2	10	3	27	.264	.278	.338	70	-6	0	1	-1	1.000	-2	O-42/1-1	-1.1
1974	Hou-N	102	87	13	15	2	0	0	3	12	23	.172	.280	.195	36	-7	1	0	0	.978	-21	O-62/1-4	-3.0
1975	NY-N	33	15	5	2	1	0	0	0	1	6	.133	.188	.200	8	-2	0	0	0	.900	-5	O-16	-0.7
Total	4	213	255	34	56	6	1	2	13	16	56	.220	.268	.275	52	-17	1	1	-0	.985	-27	O-120/1-5	-4.9

■ WILLIAM GALLAGHER
Gallagher, William Howard b: 2/4/1874, Boston, Mass. d: 3/11/50, Worcester, Mass. Deb: 8/19/1896

| 1896 | Phi-N | 14 | 49 | 9 | 15 | 2 | 0 | 0 | 6 | 10 | 0 | .306 | .433 | .347 | 108 | 1 | 0 | | | .894 | -4 | S-14 | -0.2 |

■ BILL GALLAGHER
Gallagher, William John b: Philadelphia, Pa. TL , Deb: 5/2/1883

1883	Bal-a	16	61	9	10	3	1	0		3		.164	.203	.246	43	-4				.824	-2	/O-9,P-7,S-4	-0.3
	Phi-N	2	8	1	0	0	0	0		0	4	.000	.000	.000	-99	-2				1.000	-0	/O-2	-0.2
1884	Phi-U	3	11	1	1	0	0	0		0		.091	.091	.091	-48	-2				.800	1	/P-3	0.0
Total	2	21	80	11	11	3	1	0	0	3	4	.138	.169	.200	16	-8				.850	-2	/O-11,P-10,S-4	-0.5

■ STAN GALLE
Galle, Stanley Joseph (b: Stanley Joseph Galazewski) b: 2/7/19, Milwaukee, Wis. BR/TR, 5'7", 165 lbs. Deb: 4/14/42

| 1942 | Was-A | 13 | 18 | 3 | 2 | 0 | 0 | 0 | 1 | 1 | 0 | .111 | .158 | .111 | -24 | -3 | 0 | 0 | 0 | .857 | -1 | /3-3 | -0.4 |

■ MIKE GALLEGO
Gallego, Michael Anthony b: 10/31/60, Whittier, Cal. BR/TR, 5'8", 160 lbs. Deb: 4/11/85

1985	Oak-A	76	77	13	16	5	1	1	9	12	14	.208	.322	.338	87	-1	1	1	-0	.991	12	2-42,S-21,3-12	1.2
1986	Oak-A	20	37	2	10	2	0	0	4	1	6	.270	.289	.324	72	-1	0	2	-1	.986	9	2-19/3-2,S-1	0.6
1987	Oak-A	72	124	18	31	6	0	2	14	12	21	.250	.321	.347	83	-3	0	1	-1	.968	17	2-31,3-24,S-17	1.4
1988	*Oak-A	129	277	38	58	8	0	2	20	34	53	.209	.298	.260	60	-14	2	3	-1	.993	4	2-83,S-42,3-16	-0.8
1989	*Oak-A	133	357	45	90	14	2	3	30	35	43	.252	.329	.328	89	-4	7	5	-1	.967	18	S-94,2-41/3-3,D-1	2.0
1990	*Oak-A	140	389	36	80	13	2	3	34	35	50	.206	.278	.272	57	-22	5	5	-2	.990	14	2-83,S-38,3-27,OD	-0.6
1991	Oak-A	159	482	67	119	15	4	12	49	67	84	.247	.345	.358	103	4	6	9	-4	.989	-16	*2-135,S-55	-1.1
1992	NY-A	53	173	24	44	7	1	3	14	20	22	.254	.345	.358	98	0	0	1	-1	.990	1	2-40,S-14	0.3
1993	NY-A	119	403	63	114	20	1	10	54	50	65	.283	.368	.412	113	8	3	2	-0	.976	17	S-55,2-52,3-27,/D-1	2.9
1994	NY-A	89	306	39	73	17	1	6	41	38	46	.239	.330	.359	81	-8	0	1	-1	.970	20	S-72,2-26	1.6
1995	Oak-A	43	120	11	28	0	0	0	8	9	24	.233	.292	.233	41	-10	0	1	-1	.960	2	2-18,S-14,3-12	-0.8
1996	*StL-N	51	143	12	30	2	0	0	4	12	31	.210	.276	.224	34	-13	0	0	0	.985	7	2-43/3-7,S-1	-0.4
Total	12	1084	2888	368	693	109	12	42	281	325	459	.240	.324	.330	82	-66	24	31	-11	.986	102	2-613,S-424,3/DO	6.3

■ JIM GALLIGAN
Galligan, James M. b: 1862, Easton, Pa. d: 7/17/01, New York, N.Y. 5'10", 160 lbs. Deb: 9/2/1889

| 1889 | Lou-a | 31 | 120 | 6 | 20 | 0 | 2 | 0 | 7 | 6 | 17 | .167 | .213 | .200 | 18 | -13 | 1 | | | .915 | 2 | O-31 | -1.0 |

■ CHICK GALLOWAY
Galloway, Clarence Edward b: 8/4/1896, Clinton, S.C. d: 11/7/69, Clinton, S.C. BR/TR, 5'8", 160 lbs. Deb: 9/9/19

1919	Phi-A	17	63	2	9	0	0	0	4	1	8	.143	.156	.143	-16	-10	0			.969	1	S-17	-0.8
1920	Phi-A	98	298	28	60	9	3	0	18	22	22	.201	.259	.252	35	-28	2	2	-1	.928	4	S-84/2-4,3-3	-1.7
1921	Phi-A	131	465	42	123	28	5	3	47	29	43	.265	.310	.366	72	-21	12	7	-1	.922	-22	*S-110,3-20/2-1	-3.1
1922	Phi-A	155	571	83	185	26	9	6	69	39	39	.324	.368	.433	105	4	10	19	-8	.952	1	*S-155	1.3
1923	Phi-A	134	504	64	140	18	9	2	62	37	30	.278	.327	.361	80	-15	12	10	-2	.944	2	*S-134	-0.3
1924	Phi-A	129	464	41	128	16	4	3	48	23	23	.276	.311	.341	67	-23	11	12	-4	.952	2	*S-129	-1.0
1925	Phi-A	149	481	52	116	11	4	3	71	59	28	.241	.324	.299	55	-32	16	9	-1	.954	-3	*S-148	-1.9
1926	Phi-A	133	408	37	98	13	6	0	49	31	20	.240	.295	.301	53	-28	8	7	-2	.935	-13	*S-133	-3.0
1927	Phi-A	77	181	25	48	10	4	0	22	18	9	.265	.332	.365	76	-6	1	3	-2	.946	5	S-61/3-7	-0.4
1928	Det-A	53	148	17	39	5	2	1	17	15	3	.264	.331	.345	77	-5	7	2	1	.914	-3	S-22,3-21/1-1,O-1	-0.4
Total	10	1076	3583	391	946	136	46	17	407	274	225	.264	.317	.342	69	-165	79	71		.943	-28	S-993/3-51,2-5,O1	-10.7

■ JIM GALLOWAY
Galloway, James Cato "Bad News" b: 9/16/1887, Iredell, Tex. d: 5/3/50, Fort Worth, Tex. BB/TR, 6'3", 187 lbs. Deb: 8/24/12

| 1912 | StL-N | 21 | 54 | 4 | 10 | 0 | 0 | 0 | 4 | 5 | 8 | .185 | .254 | .222 | 32 | -5 | 2 | | | .971 | 1 | 2-16/S-1 | -0.4 |

■ JIM GALVIN
Galvin, James Joseph b: 8/11/07, Somerville, Mass. d: 9/30/69, Marietta, Ga. BR/TR, 5'11.5", 180 lbs. Deb: 9/27/30

| 1930 | Bos-A | 2 | 2 | 0 | 0 | 0 | 0 | 0 | 0 | 0 | 0 | .000 | .000 | .000 | -99 | -1 | 0 | 0 | 0 | .000 | 0 | H | -0.1 |

■ JOHN GALVIN
Galvin, John S. b: Brooklyn, N.Y. d: 4/20/04, Brooklyn, N.Y. Deb: 5/7/1872

| 1872 | Atl-n | 1 | 4 | 0 | 0 | 0 | 0 | 0 | 0 | 0 | 0 | .000 | .000 | .000 | -85 | -1 | 0 | 0 | 0 | .200 | -2 | /2-1 | -0.2 |

■ JOHN GAMBLE
Gamble, John Robert b: 2/10/48, Reno, Nev. BR/TR, 5'10", 165 lbs. Deb: 9/7/72

1972	Det-A	6	3	0	0	0	0	0	0	0	0	.000	.000	.000	-97	-1	0	0	0	1.000	1	/S-1	0.1
1973	Det-A	7	0	1	0	0	0	0	0	0	0	—	—	—		0	0	0	0	.000	0	R	0.0
Total	2	13	3	1	0	0	0	0	0	0	0	.000	.000	.000	-97	-1	0	0	0	1.000	1	/S-1	0.1

■ LEE GAMBLE
Gamble, Lee Jesse b: 6/28/10, Renovo, Pa. d: 10/5/94, Punxsutawney, Pa. BL/TR, 6'1", 170 lbs. Deb: 9/15/35

1935	Cin-N	2	4	2	2	1	0	0	2	1	0	.500	.600	.750	269	1	1			1.000	-0	/O-2	0.1
1938	Cin-N	53	75	13	24	3	1	0	5	6	6	.320	.320	.387	96	-1	0			1.000	-1	/O-9	-0.1
1939	*Cin-N	72	221	24	59	7	2	0	14	9	14	.267	.296	.317	64	-11	5			.989	-3	O-56	-1.6
1940	Cin-N	38	42	12	6	1	0	0	0	1	1	.143	.143	.167	-15	-4	0			1.000	0	/O-10	-0.7
Total	4	165	342	51	91	12	3	0	21	10	21	.266	.287	.319	64	-17	6			.993	-4	/O-77	-2.3

■ OSCAR GAMBLE
Gamble, Oscar Charles b: 12/20/49, Ramer, Ala. BL/TR, 5'11", 165 lbs. Deb: 8/27/69

1969	Chi-N	24	71	6	16	1	1	1	5	10	12	.225	.321	.310	69	-3	0	2	-1	.913	-2	O-24	-0.8
1970	Phi-N	88	275	31	72	12	4	1	19	27	37	.262	.330	.345	84	-6	5	4	-1	.956	-4	O-74	-1.0
1971	Phi-N	92	280	24	62	11	1	6	23	21	35	.221	.278	.332	72	-11	5	2	-0	.970	-4	O-80	-1.9
1972	Phi-N	74	135	17	32	5	2	1	13	19	16	.237	.335	.326	86	-2	0	1	-1	1.000	-0	O-35/1-1	-0.5
1973	Cle-A	113	390	56	104	11	3	20	44	34	37	.267	.330	.464	120	9	3	4	-2	.971	-4	D-70,O-37	0.3
1974	Cle-A	135	454	74	132	16	4	19	59	48	51	.291	.365	.469	140	23	4	5	-2	1.000	-1	*D-115,O-13	1.7
1975	Cle-A	121	348	60	91	16	3	15	45	53	45	.261	.362	.454	130	14	11	5	0	.987	-6	O-82,D-29	1.2
1976	*NY-A	110	340	43	79	13	1	17	57	38	38	.232	.317	.426	117	7	5	3	-0	.981	-0	*O-104/D-1	0.3
1977	Chi-A	137	408	75	121	22	2	31	83	54	54	.297	.387	.588	162	35	1	2	-1	.987	-5	D-79,O-49	2.4
1978	SD-N	126	375	46	103	15	3	7	47	51	45	.275	.370	.387	121	12	1	2	-0	.979	-5	*O-107	0.7
1979	Tex-A	64	161	27	54	6	0	8	32	37	15	.335	.462	.522	167	17	2	0	1	1.000	1	D-37,O-21	1.6
	NY-A	36	113	21	44	4	1	11	32	13	13	.389	.462	.735	219	19	0	0	0	.943	0	O-27/D-6	1.7
	Yr	100	274	48	98	10	1	19	64	50	28	.358	.458	.609	188	36	2	0	1	.969	1	O-48,D-43	3.3
1980	*NY-A	78	194	40	54	2	1	14	50	28	21	.278	.381	.567	159	16	0	1	-0	1.000	3	O-49,D-20	0.8
1981	NY-A	80	189	24	45	8	0	11	27	35	23	.238	.360	.439	131	6	0	0	0	1.000	0	O-43,D-33	0.3
1982	NY-A	108	316	49	86	21	2	18	57	58	47	.272	.392	.522	151	23	6	3	0	1.000	5	D-74,O-29	2.4

YEAR	TM/L	G	AB	R	H	2B	3B	HR	RBI	BB	SO	AVG	OBP	SLG	PRO+	BR/A	SB	CS	SBR	FA	FR	G/POS	TPR
1983	NY-A	74	180	26	47	10	2	7	26	25	23	.261	.361	.456	128	7	0	0	0	.942	-0	O-32,D-21	0.5
1984	NY-A	54	125	17	23	2	0	10	27	25	18	.184	.320	.440	112	2	1	0	0	1.000	-1	D-28,O-12	0.1
1985	Chi-A	70	148	20	30	5	0	4	20	34	22	.203	.355	.318	83	-2	0	0	0	.000	0	D-48	-0.3
Total	17	1584	4502	656	1195	188	31	200	666	610	546	.265	.358	.454	127	168	47	37	-8	.977	-15	O-818,D-561/1-1	9.5

■ DAFF GAMMONS   Gammons, John Ashley b: 3/17/1876, New Bedford, Mass. d: 9/24/63, E.Greenwich, R.I. BR/TR, 5'11", 170 lbs. Deb: 4/23/01

YEAR	TM/L	G	AB	R	H	2B	3B	HR	RBI	BB	SO	AVG	OBP	SLG	PRO+	BR/A	SB	CS	SBR	FA	FR	G/POS	TPR
1901	Bos-N	28	93	10	18	0	1	0		10	3	.194	.242	.215	30	-8	5			.880	-3	O-23/2-2,3-1	-1.2

■ CHICK GANDIL   Gandil, Arnold b: 1/19/1887, St.Paul, Minn. d: 12/13/70, Calistoga, Cal. BR/TR, 6'1.5", 190 lbs. Deb: 4/14/10

YEAR	TM/L	G	AB	R	H	2B	3B	HR	RBI	BB	SO	AVG	OBP	SLG	PRO+	BR/A	SB	CS	SBR	FA	FR	G/POS	TPR
1910	Chi-A	77	275	21	53	7	3	2	21	24		.193	.267	.262	69	-10	12			.989	7	1-74/O-2	-0.4
1912	Was-A	117	443	59	135	20	15	2	81	27		.305	.350	.431	122	11	21			.990	3	*1-117	1.1
1913	Was-A	148	550	61	175	25	8	1	72	36	33	.318	.363	.398	120	13	22			.990	8	*1-145	2.1
1914	Was-A	145	526	48	136	24	10	3	75	44	44	.259	.324	.359	101	-0	30	19	-2	.991	24	*1-145	1.9
1915	Was-A	136	485	53	141	20	15	2	64	29	33	.291	.340	.406	121	10	20	13	-2	.986	-1	*1-134	0.4
1916	Cle-A	146	533	51	138	26	9	0	72	36	48	.259	.312	.341	91	-7	13			.995	8	*1-145	-0.5
1917	*Chi-A	149	553	53	151	9	7	0	57	30	36	.273	.316	.315	91	-7	16			.995	-6	*1-149	-2.0
1918	Chi-A	114	439	49	119	18	4	0	55	27	19	.271	.319	.330	95	-4	9			.992	-3	*1-114	-1.2
1919	*Chi-A	115	441	54	128	24	7	1	60	20	20	.290	.325	.383	98	-2	10			.997	-4	*1-115	-1.1
Total	9	1147	4245	449	1176	173	78	11	557	273	233	.277	.327	.362	103	3	153	32		.992	36	*1-1138/O-2	0.3

■ BOB GANDY   Gandy, Robert Brinkley "String" b: 8/25/1893, Jacksonville, Fla. d: 6/19/45, Jacksonville, Fla BL/TR, 6'3", 180 lbs. Deb: 10/5/16

YEAR	TM/L	G	AB	R	H	2B	3B	HR	RBI	BB	SO	AVG	OBP	SLG	PRO+	BR/A	SB	CS	SBR	FA	FR	G/POS	TPR
1916	Phi-N	1	2	0	0	0	0	0	0	0	1	.000	.000	.000	-97	-0				1.000	0	/O-1	0.0

■ BOB GANLEY   Ganley, Robert Stephen b: 4/23/1875, Lowell, Mass. d: 10/9/45, Lowell, Mass. BL/TL, 5'7", 156 lbs. Deb: 9/1/05

YEAR	TM/L	G	AB	R	H	2B	3B	HR	RBI	BB	SO	AVG	OBP	SLG	PRO+	BR/A	SB	CS	SBR	FA	FR	G/POS	TPR
1905	Pit-N	32	127	12	40	1	2	0	7	8		.315	.356	.354	109	1	3			1.000	-2	O-32	-0.3
1906	Pit-N	137	511	63	132	7	6	0	31	41		.258	.316	.295	87	-8	19			.965	-2	*O-134	-1.8
1907	Was-A	154	605	73	167	10	5	1	35	54		.276	.337	.314	117	13	40			.940	9	*O-154	1.7
1908	Was-A	150	549	61	131	19	9	1	36	45		.239	.299	.311	107	4	30			.964	4	*O-150	0.2
1909	Was-A	19	63	5	16	3	0	0	5	1		.254	.266	.302	83	-2	4			1.000	-3	O-17	-0.6
	Phi-A	80	274	32	54	4	2	0	9	28		.197	.272	.226	56	-13	16			.980	8	O-77	-1.0
	Yr	99	337	37	70	7	2	0	14	29		.208	.270	.240	61	-15	20			.982	4	O-94	-1.6
Total	5	572	2129	246	540	44	24	2	123	177		.254	.313	.300	97	-4	112			.962	13	O-564	-1.8

■ BILL GANNON   Gannon, William G. b: 1876, New Haven, Conn. d: 4/26/27, Fort Worth, Tex. 5'9", 170 lbs. Deb: 9/9/01

YEAR	TM/L	G	AB	R	H	2B	3B	HR	RBI	BB	SO	AVG	OBP	SLG	PRO+	BR/A	SB	CS	SBR	FA	FR	G/POS	TPR
1901	Chi-N	15	61	2	9	0	0	0	0	1		.148	.161	.148	-11	-8	5			1.000	-1	O-15	-1.1

■ RON GANT   Gant, Ronald Edwin b: 3/2/65, Victoria, Tex. BR/TR, 6'", 192 lbs. Deb: 9/6/87

YEAR	TM/L	G	AB	R	H	2B	3B	HR	RBI	BB	SO	AVG	OBP	SLG	PRO+	BR/A	SB	CS	SBR	FA	FR	G/POS	TPR
1987	Atl-N	21	83	9	22	4	0	2	9	1	11	.265	.274	.386	69	-4	4	2	0	.972	-0	2-20	-0.3
1988	Atl-N	146	563	85	146	28	8	19	60	46	118	.259	.319	.439	110	6	19	10	-0	.963	-1	*2-122,3-22	1.0
1989	Atl-N	75	260	26	46	8	3	9	25	20	63	.177	.238	.335	61	-14	9	6	-1	.887	3	3-53,O-14	-1.3
1990	Atl-N	152	575	107	174	34	3	32	84	50	86	.303	.359	.539	136	26	33	16	0	.978	7	*O-146	3.0
1991	*Atl-N	154	561	101	141	35	3	32	105	71	104	.251	.341	.496	125	18	34	15	1	.983	8	*O-148	2.4
1992	*Atl-N★	153	544	74	141	22	6	17	80	45	101	.259	.324	.415	102	1	32	10	4	.986	-4	*O-147	-0.2
1993	Atl-N	157	606	113	166	27	4	36	117	67	117	.274	.348	.510	125	20	26	9	2	.962	-3	*O-155	1.6
1995	*Cin-N★	119	410	79	113	19	4	29	88	74	108	.276	.390	.554	146	28	23	8	2	.985	4	*O-117	3.0
1996	*StL-N	122	419	74	103	14	2	30	82	73	98	.246	.362	.504	125	15	13	4	2	.978	0	*O-116	1.9
Total	9	1099	4021	668	1052	191	33	206	650	447	806	.262	.339	.479	118	96	193	80	10	.979	19	O-843,2-142/3-75	11.1

■ JOE GANTENBEIN   Gantenbein, Joseph Steven "Sep" b: 8/25/16, San Francisco, Cal BL/TR, 5'9", 168 lbs. Deb: 4/20/39

YEAR	TM/L	G	AB	R	H	2B	3B	HR	RBI	BB	SO	AVG	OBP	SLG	PRO+	BR/A	SB	CS	SBR	FA	FR	G/POS	TPR
1939	Phi-A	111	348	47	101	14	4	4	36	32	22	.290	.353	.388	91	-4	1	5	-3	.948	-34	2-76,3-14/S-5	-3.4
1940	Phi-A	75	197	21	47	6	2	4	23	11	21	.239	.282	.350	64	-11	1	0	0	.930	-8	3-45/1-6,S-3,O-1	-1.7
Total	2	186	545	68	148	20	6	8	59	43	43	.272	.328	.374	82	-15	2	5	-2	.934	-42	/2-76,3-59,S-8,10	-5.1

■ JIM GANTNER   Gantner, James Elmer b: 1/5/53, Fond du Lac, Wis. BL/TR, 6', 180 lbs. Deb: 9/3/76 C

YEAR	TM/L	G	AB	R	H	2B	3B	HR	RBI	BB	SO	AVG	OBP	SLG	PRO+	BR/A	SB	CS	SBR	FA	FR	G/POS	TPR
1976	Mil-A	26	69	6	17	1	0	0	7	6	11	.246	.316	.261	71	-2	1	0	0	.982	-3	3-24/D-2	-0.6
1977	Mil-A	14	47	4	14	1	0	0	2	2	5	.298	.327	.383	93	-1	2	1	0	.902	1	3-14	0.1
1978	Mil-A	43	97	14	21	1	0	1	8	5	10	.216	.269	.258	49	-7	2	0	1	.980	5	2-21,3-15/1-1,S-1	0.0
1979	Mil-A	70	208	29	59	10	3	2	22	16	17	.284	.341	.389	96	-1	3	5	-2	.952	4	3-42,2-22/S-3,P-1	0.2
1980	Mil-A	132	415	47	117	21	3	4	40	30	29	.282	.332	.376	97	-2	11	10	-3	.938	-1	3-69,2-66/S-1	-0.2
1981	*Mil-A	107	352	35	94	14	1	2	33	29	29	.267	.328	.330	95	-2	3	6	-3	.984	16	*2-107	1.8
1982	*Mil-A	132	447	48	132	17	2	4	43	26	36	.295	.337	.369	100	-0	6	3	0	.985	9	*2-131	1.5
1983	Mil-A	161	603	85	170	23	8	11	74	38	46	.282	.331	.401	109	6	5	6	-2	.984	10	*2-158	2.1
1984	Mil-A	153	613	61	173	27	1	3	56	30	51	.282	.319	.344	87	-11	6	5	-1	.985	10	*2-153	0.3
1985	Mil-A	143	523	63	133	15	4	5	44	33	42	.254	.302	.327	73	-19	11	8	-2	.988	1	*2-124,3-24/S-1	-1.5
1986	Mil-A	139	497	58	136	25	1	7	38	26	50	.274	.318	.370	84	-11	13	7	-0	.985	-12	2-135/3-3,S-1,D-1	-1.8
1987	Mil-A	81	265	37	72	14	0	4	30	19	22	.272	.332	.370	84	-6	6	2	1	.984	5	2-57,3-38/D-1	-0.3
1988	Mil-A	155	539	67	149	28	2	0	47	34	50	.276	.323	.336	84	-11	20	8	1	.986	-8	*2-154/3-1	-1.2
1989	Mil-A	116	409	51	112	18	3	0	34	21	33	.274	.325	.333	86	-7	20	6	2	.987	9	*2-114/D-2	0.8
1990	Mil-A	88	323	36	85	8	5	0	25	19	19	.263	.328	.319	82	-7	18	3	4	.982	-7	2-80/3-9	-0.9
1991	Mil-A	140	526	63	149	27	4	2	47	27	34	.283	.322	.361	91	-7	4	6	-2	.976	3	3-90,2-59	-0.4
1992	Mil-A	101	256	22	63	12	1	1	18	12	17	.246	.280	.313	67	-12	6	2	1	.994	7	2-68,3-31/1-2,D-2	-0.3
Total	17	1801	6189	726	1696	262	38	47	568	383	501	.274	.322	.351	88	-100	137	78	-6	.985	50	*2-1449,3-360/DS1P	0.1

■ CHARLIE GANZEL   Ganzel, Charles William b: 6/18/1862, Waterford, Wis. d: 4/7/14, Quincy, Mass. BR/TR, 6', 161 lbs. Deb: 9/27/1884 F

YEAR	TM/L	G	AB	R	H	2B	3B	HR	RBI	BB	SO	AVG	OBP	SLG	PRO+	BR/A	SB	CS	SBR	FA	FR	G/POS	TPR
1884	StP-U	7	23	2	5	0	0	0		0		.217	.217	.217	59	-3				.956	-2	/C-6,O-1	-0.4
1885	Phi-N	34	125	15	21	3	1	0	6	4	13	.168	.194	.208	31	-9				.888	0	C-33/O-1	-0.6
1886	Phi-N	1	3	0	0	0	0	0	0	0	1	.000	.000	.000	-99	-1	0			.600	-1	/C-1	-0.1
	Det-N	57	158	28	58	7	2	1	31	7	22	.272	.295	.358	90	-3	5			.911	3	C-45/O-7,1-5	0.4
	Yr	58	216	28	58	7	2	1	31	7	23	.269	.291	.333	87	-4	5			.903	3	C-46/O-7,1-5	0.3
1887	*Det-N	57	227	40	59	6	5	0	20	8	2	.260	.288	.330	69	-10	3			.913	9	C-51/O-4,1-2,3-1	0.3
1888	Det-N	95	386	45	96	13	5	1	46	14	15	.249	.277	.316	89	-5	12			.900	-1	2-49,C-28/3-9,OS1	-0.1
1889	Bos-N	73	275	30	73	3	5	1	43	15	11	.265	.308	.324	72	-11	13			.927	5	C-39,O-26/1-7,S3	-0.3
1890	Bos-N	38	163	21	44	7	3	0	24	5	6	.270	.300	.350	83	-5	3			.958	5	C-22,O-15/S-3,2-1	0.1
1891	Bos-N	70	263	33	68	18	5	1	29	12	13	.259	.304	.376	87	-6	7			.956	4	C-59,O-13	0.2
1892	*Bos-N	54	198	25	53	9	3	0	25	18	12	.268	.332	.343	96	-2	7			.933	-6	C-51/O-2,1-1	-0.4
1893	Bos-N	73	281	50	75	10	2	1	48	22	9	.267	.325	.327	68	-14	11			.952	-2	C-40,O-23,1-10	-1.1
1894	Bos-N	70	266	51	74	7	4	3	56	19	6	.278	.326	.383	65	-17	1			.897	-3	C-59/1-7,O-3,S-2,2	-1.3
1895	Bos-N	80	277	38	73	2	1	5	52	24	6	.264	.325	.318	61	-17	1			.962	19	C-76/S-2,1-2	0.7
1896	Bos-N	47	179	28	47	2	1	0	18	9	5	.263	.305	.291	54	-12	1			.989	8	C-41/1-3,S-2	-0.1
1897	Bos-N	30	105	15	28	4	3	0	14	4		.267	.300	.362	70	-5	2			.942	2	C-27/1-2	0.0
Total	14	786	2984	421	774	91	45	10	412	161	121	.259	.301	.330	73	-120	60			.934	35	C-578,O-100/21S3	-2.7

■ BABE GANZEL   Ganzel, Foster Pirie b: 5/22/01, Malden, Mass. d: 2/6/78, Jacksonville, Fla. BR/TR, 5'10.5", 172 lbs. Deb: 9/19/27 F

YEAR	TM/L	G	AB	R	H	2B	3B	HR	RBI	BB	SO	AVG	OBP	SLG	PRO+	BR/A	SB	CS	SBR	FA	FR	G/POS	TPR
1927	Was-A	13	48	7	21	4	1	1	13	7	3	.438	.509	.667	206	7	0	0	0	.944	0	O-13	0.7
1928	Was-A	10	26	2	2	1	0	0	1	4	1	.077	.111	.115	-41	-5	0	0	0	1.000	-1	/O-7	-0.7
Total	2	23	74	9	23	5	1	1	14	11	4	.311	.378	.473	122	2	0	0	0	.957	-1	/O-20	0.0

■ JOHN GANZEL   Ganzel, John Henry b: 4/7/1874, Kalamazoo, Mich. d: 1/14/59, Orlando, Fla. BR/TR, 6'0.5", 195 lbs. Deb: 4/21/1898 FM

YEAR	TM/L	G	AB	R	H	2B	3B	HR	RBI	BB	SO	AVG	OBP	SLG	PRO+	BR/A	SB	CS	SBR	FA	FR	G/POS	TPR
1898	Pit-N	15	45	5	6	0	0	0	3	1		.133	.220	.133	-6	-0				.963	-1	1-12	-0.7
1900	Chi-N	78	284	29	78	14	4	4	32	10		.275	.316	.394	99	-2	5			.980	-4	1-78	-0.5
1901	NY-N	138	526	42	113	13	3	2	66	20		.215	.256	.262	52	-32	6			.986	2	*1-138	-3.2
1903	NY-A	129	476	62	132	25	7	3	71	30		.277	.336	.378	107	4	9			.988	7	*1-129	0.9

YEAR	TM/L	G	AB	R	H	2B	3B	HR	RBI	BB	SO	AVG	OBP	SLG	PRO+	BR/A	SB	CS	SBR	FA	FR	G/POS	TPR
1904	NY-A	130	465	50	121	16	10	6	48	24		.260	.309	.376	111	5	13			.988	-2	*1-118/2-9,S-1	0.1
1907	Cin-N	145	531	61	135	20	**16**	2	64	29		.254	.297	.363	102	-1	9			.990	1	*1-143	-0.5
1908	Cin-N	112	388	32	97	16	10	1	53	19		.250	.289	.351	107	1	6			**.990**	-2	*1-108,M	-0.3
Total	7	747	2715	281	682	104	50	18	336	136		.251	.298	.346	93	-29	48			.987	0	1-726/2-9,S-1	-4.2

■ JOE GARAGIOLA
Garagiola, Joseph Henry b: 2/12/26, St.Louis, Mo. BL/TR, 6′, 190 lbs. Deb: 5/26/46

YEAR	TM/L	G	AB	R	H	2B	3B	HR	RBI	BB	SO	AVG	OBP	SLG	PRO+	BR/A	SB	CS	SBR	FA	FR	G/POS	TPR
1946	*StL-N	74	211	21	50	4	1	3	22	23	25	.237	.312	.308	73	-7	0			.990	-5	C-70	-0.9
1947	StL-N	77	183	20	47	10	2	5	25	40	14	.257	.398	.415	111	4	0			.987	1	C-74	0.9
1948	StL-N	24	56	9	6	1	0	2	7	12	9	.107	.275	.232	36	-5	0			.990	2	C-23	-0.2
1949	StL-N	81	241	25	63	14	0	3	26	31	19	.261	.348	.357	85	-4	0			.984	7	C-80	0.7
1950	StL-N	34	88	8	28	6	1	2	20	10	7	.318	.388	.477	120	3	0			1.000	-3	C-30	0.1
1951	StL-N	27	72	9	14	3	2	1	9	9	7	.194	.284	.375	75	-3	0	0	0	1.000	-3	C-23	-0.4
	Pit-N	72	212	24	54	8	2	9	35	32	20	.255	.358	.439	110	3	4	1	1	.986	-9	C-61	-0.2
	Yr	99	284	33	68	11	4	11	44	41	27	.239	.339	.423	101	1	4	1	1	**.989**	-11	C-84	-0.6
1952	Pit-N	118	344	35	94	15	4	8	54	50	24	.273	.369	.410	113	7	0	1	-1	.978	-3	*C-105	0.9
1953	Pit-N	27	73	9	17	5	0	2	14	10	11	.233	.341	.384	89	-1	0	0		.989	-4	C-22	-0.3
	Chi-N	74	228	21	62	9	4	1	21	21	23	.272	.336	.360	80	-6	0	0		.988	0	C-68	-0.3
	Yr	101	301	30	79	14	4	3	35	31	34	.262	.337	.365	82	-7	0	0		.988	-4	C-90	-0.6
1954	Chi-N	63	153	16	43	5	0	5	21	28	12	.281	.405	.412	112	4	0	0	0	.982	-8	C-55	-0.1
	NY-N	5	11	1	3	2	0	1	1	1	2	.273	.333	.455	102	0	0	0	0	1.000	0	/C-3	0.0
	Yr	68	164	17	46	7	0	5	22	29	14	.280	.401	.415	112	4	0	0	0	.983	-8	C-58	-0.1
Total	9	676	1872	198	481	82	16	42	255	267	173	.257	.355	.385	96	-5	5	2		.986	-23	C-614	

■ MIKE GARBARK
Garbark, Nathaniel Michael (b: Nathaniel Michael Garbach)
b: 2/2/16, Houston, Tex. d: 8/31/94, Charlotte, N.C. BR/TR, 6′, 200 lbs. Deb: 4/18/44 F

YEAR	TM/L	G	AB	R	H	2B	3B	HR	RBI	BB	SO	AVG	OBP	SLG	PRO+	BR/A	SB	CS	SBR	FA	FR	G/POS	TPR
1944	NY-A	89	299	23	78	9	4	1	33	25	27	.261	.320	.328	82	-7	0	1	-1	.988	8	C-85	0.6
1945	NY-A	60	176	23	38	5	3	1	26	23	12	.216	.310	.295	73	-6	0	1	-1	.972	4	C-59	0.1
Total	2	149	475	46	116	14	7	2	59	48	39	.244	.316	.316	79	-12	0	2	-1	.982	12	C-144	0.7

■ BOB GARBARK
Garbark, Robert Michael (b: Robert Michael Garbach) b: 11/13/09, Houston, Tex. d: 8/15/90, Meadville, Pa. BR/TR, 5′11″, 178 lbs. Deb: 9/3/34 F

YEAR	TM/L	G	AB	R	H	2B	3B	HR	RBI	BB	SO	AVG	OBP	SLG	PRO+	BR/A	SB	CS	SBR	FA	FR	G/POS	TPR
1934	Cle-A	5	11	1	0	0	0	0	0	1	3	.000	.083	.000	-76	-3	0			1.000	-2	/C-5	-0.4
1935	Cle-A	6	18	4	6	1	0	0	4	5	1	.333	.478	.389	124	1	0	0	0	1.000	2	/C-6	0.3
1937	Chi-N	1	1	0	0	0	0	0	0	0	0	.000	.000	.000	-96	-0	0			.000	0	H	0.0
1938	Chi-N	23	54	2	14	0	0	0	5	1	0	.259	.273	.259	46	-4	0			1.000	1	C-20/1-1	-0.2
1939	Chi-N	24	21	1	3	0	0	0	0	0	3	.143	.143	.143	-23	-4	0			1.000	1	C-21	-0.3
1944	Phi-A	18	23	2	6	2	0	0	2	1	0	.261	.292	.348	83	-1	0			1.000	0	C-15	-0.1
1945	Bos-A	68	199	21	52	6	0	0	17	18	10	.261	.329	.291	79	-5	0	1	-1	.993	-3	C-67	-0.5
Total	7	145	327	31	81	9	0	0	28	26	17	.248	.307	.275	64	-15	0	1		.996	-2	C-134/1-1	-1.2

■ BARBARO GARBEY
Garbey, Barbaro (Garbey) b: 12/4/56, Santiago De Cuba, Cuba BR/TR, 5′10″, 170 lbs. Deb: 4/3/84

YEAR	TM/L	G	AB	R	H	2B	3B	HR	RBI	BB	SO	AVG	OBP	SLG	PRO+	BR/A	SB	CS	SBR	FA	FR	G/POS	TPR
1984	*Det-A	110	327	45	94	17	1	5	52	17	35	.287	.327	.391	98	-1	6	7	-2	.989	-5	1-65,3-20,D-17,O/2	-1.3
1985	Det-A	86	237	27	61	9	1	6	29	15	37	.257	.310	.380	88	-4	3	2	-0	.991	-2	1-37,O-24,D-21,/3-1	-0.9
1988	Tex-A	30	62	4	12	2	0	0	5	4	11	.194	.242	.226	31	-6	0	0	0	.900	-2	/O-8,1-7,3-3,D-7	-0.6
Total	3	226	626	76	167	28	2	11	86	36	83	.267	.312	.371	88	-11	9	9	-3	.990	-8	1-109/D-45,O-42,32	-2.8

■ ALEX GARBOWSKI
Garbowski, Alexander b: 6/25/25, Yonkers, N.Y BR/TR, 6′1″, 185 lbs. Deb: 4/16/52

YEAR	TM/L	G	AB	R	H	2B	3B	HR	RBI	BB	SO	AVG	OBP	SLG	PRO+	BR/A	SB	CS	SBR	FA	FR	G/POS	TPR
1952	Det-A	2	0	0	0	0	0	0	0	0	0	—	—	—	—	0	0	0	0	.000	0	R	0.0

■ KIKO GARCIA
Garcia, Alfonso Rafael b: 10/14/53, Martinez, Cal. BR/TR, 5′11″, 180 lbs. Deb: 9/11/76

YEAR	TM/L	G	AB	R	H	2B	3B	HR	RBI	BB	SO	AVG	OBP	SLG	PRO+	BR/A	SB	CS	SBR	FA	FR	G/POS	TPR
1976	Bal-A	11	32	2	7	1	1	1	4	0	4	.219	.219	.406	86	-1	2	1	0	1.000	1	S-11	0.1
1977	Bal-A	65	131	20	29	6	0	2	10	6	31	.221	.255	.313	58	-8	2	3	-1	.966	20	S-61/2-2	1.5
1978	Bal-A	79	186	17	49	6	4	0	13	7	43	.263	.290	.339	81	-5	7	1	2	.945	4	S-74/2-3	0.7
1979	*Bal-A	126	417	54	103	15	9	5	24	32	87	.247	.304	.362	82	-11	11	9	-2	.955	-18	*S-113,2-25/3-2,O-2	-1.9
1980	Bal-A	111	311	27	62	8	0	1	27	24	57	.199	.257	.235	36	-27	8	4	0	.974	2	S-96,2-27/O-1	-1.6
1981	*Hou-N	48	136	9	37	6	1	0	15	10	16	.272	.327	.331	91	-2	2	2	-1	.950	3	S-28,3-13/2-9	0.4
1982	Hou-N	34	76	5	16	5	0	1	5	3	15	.211	.241	.316	59	-5	1	0	0	.946	5	S-21/3-2,2-1	0.2
1983	Phi-N	84	118	22	34	7	1	2	9	9	20	.288	.344	.415	111	2	1	2	-1	.970	19	2-52,S-22,3-10	2.2
1984	Phi-N	57	60	6	14	2	0	0	5	4	11	.233	.281	.267	54	-4	0	0	0	.965	5	S-30,3-23/2-1	0.2
1985	Phi-N	4	3	0	0	0	0	0	0	0	1	.000	.000	.000	-97	-1	0	0	0	1.000	-1	/S-3,3-1	-0.2
Total	10	619	1470	162	351	56	16	12	112	95	285	.239	.287	.323	70	-61	34	22	-3	.961	39	S-459,2-120/3-51,O	1.6

■ CARLOS GARCIA
Garcia, Carlos Jesus (Guerrero) b: 10/15/67, Tachira, Venez. BR/TR, 6′1″, 185 lbs. Deb: 9/20/90

YEAR	TM/L	G	AB	R	H	2B	3B	HR	RBI	BB	SO	AVG	OBP	SLG	PRO+	BR/A	SB	CS	SBR	FA	FR	G/POS	TPR
1990	Pit-N	4	4	1	2	0	0	0	0	0	2	.500	.500	.500	183	0	0	0	0	1.000	1	/S-3	0.1
1991	Pit-N	12	24	2	6	0	1	1	8	1	8	.250	.280	.417	95	-0	0	0	0	.947	2	/S-9,3-2,2-1	0.2
1992	*Pit-N	22	39	4	8	1	0	0	4	0	9	.205	.205	.231	23	-4	0	0	0	.977	2	2-14/S-8	-0.1
1993	Pit-N	141	546	77	147	25	5	12	47	31	67	.269	.319	.399	91	-8	18	11	-1	.983	-26	*2-140/S-3	-3.1
1994	Pit-N★	98	412	49	114	15	2	6	28	16	67	.277	.310	.367	75	-15	18	9	0	.978	8	2-98	-0.2
1995	Pit-N	104	367	41	108	24	5	6	50	25	55	.294	.343	.420	98	-1	8	4	0	.982	14	2-92,S-15	1.9
1996	Pit-N	101	390	66	111	18	4	6	44	23	58	.285	.331	.397	88	-7	16	6	1	.985	5	2-77,S-19,3-14	0.3
Total	7	482	1782	240	496	83	15	30	174	96	266	.278	.322	.392	87	-35	60	30		.982	5	2-422/S-57,3-16	-0.9

■ DAMASO GARCIA
Garcia, Damaso Domingo (Sanchez) b: 2/7/55, Moca, D.R. BR/TR, 6′, 170 lbs. Deb: 6/24/78

YEAR	TM/L	G	AB	R	H	2B	3B	HR	RBI	BB	SO	AVG	OBP	SLG	PRO+	BR/A	SB	CS	SBR	FA	FR	G/POS	TPR
1978	NY-A	18	41	5	8	0	0	0	1	2	6	.195	.233	.195	22	-4	1	0	0	.959	2	2-16/S-3	-0.2
1979	NY-A	11	38	3	10	1	0	0	4	0	2	.263	.263	.289	50	-3	2	0	1	.902	-6	S-10/3-1	-0.6
1980	Tor-A	140	543	50	151	30	7	4	46	12	55	.278	.297	.381	81	-15	13	13	-4	.980	16	*2-138/D-1	0.5
1981	Tor-A	64	250	24	63	8	1	1	13	9	32	.252	.278	.304	64	-12	13	3	2	.972	-15	*2-62/D-1	-2.2
1982	Tor-A	147	597	89	185	32	3	5	42	21	44	.310	.339	.399	93	-6	54	20	4	.980	10	*2-141/D-4	1.6
1983	Tor-A	131	525	84	161	23	6	3	38	24	31	.307	.339	.390	94	-4	31	17	-1	.981	-16	*2-130	-1.5
1984	Tor-A★	152	633	79	180	32	5	5	46	16	46	.284	.312	.374	86	-13	46	12	7	.980	-14	*2-149/D-1	-1.5
1985	*Tor-A★	146	600	70	169	25	4	8	65	15	41	.282	.304	.377	83	-15	28	15	-1	.981	-34	*2-143	-4.5
1986	Tor-A	122	424	57	119	22	0	6	46	13	32	.281	.308	.375	83	-10	9	6	-1	.985	-7	*2-106,D-11/1-1	-1.4
1988	Atl-N	21	60	3	7	1	0	1	4	3	10	.117	.159	.183	-2	-8	1	0	0	.984	-4	2-13	-1.2
1989	Mon-N	80	203	26	55	9	1	3	18	15	20	.271	.321	.369	96	-1	5	4	0	.972	-2	2-62/3-1	0.6
Total	11	1032	3914	490	1108	183	27	36	323	130	322	.283	.311	.371	84	-91	203	90	7	.980	-62	2-960/D-18,S-13,31	-10.4

■ DANNY GARCIA
Garcia, Daniel Raphael b: 4/29/54, Brooklyn, N.Y. BL/TL, 6′1″, 182 lbs. Deb: 4/26/81

YEAR	TM/L	G	AB	R	H	2B	3B	HR	RBI	BB	SO	AVG	OBP	SLG	PRO+	BR/A	SB	CS	SBR	FA	FR	G/POS	TPR
1981	KC-A	12	14	4	2	0	0	0	0	0	2	.143	.143	.143	-18	-2	0	0	0	1.000	-2	/O-6,1-2	-0.4

■ FREDDY GARCIA
Garcia, Freddy Adrian (Felix) b: 8/1/72, LaRomana, D.R. BR/TR, 6′2″, 190 lbs. Deb: 5/3/95

YEAR	TM/L	G	AB	R	H	2B	3B	HR	RBI	BB	SO	AVG	OBP	SLG	PRO+	BR/A	SB	CS	SBR	FA	FR	G/POS	TPR
1995	Pit-N	42	57	5	8	1	0	1	8	1	17	.140	.246	.193	17	-7	0	1	-1	1.000	0	O-10/3-8	-0.6

■ KARIM GARCIA
Garcia, Gustavo Karim b: 10/29/75, Ciudad Obregon, Mexico BL/TL, 6′, 200 lbs. Deb: 9/2/95

YEAR	TM/L	G	AB	R	H	2B	3B	HR	RBI	BB	SO	AVG	OBP	SLG	PRO+	BR/A	SB	CS	SBR	FA	FR	G/POS	TPR
1995	LA-N	13	20	1	4	0	0	0	0	0	5	.200	.200	.200	6	-3	0	0	0	1.000	1	/O-5	-0.2
1996	LA-N	1	1	0	0	0	0	0	0	0	0	.000	.000	.000	-99	-3	0	0	0	.000	0	/H	0.0
Total	2	14	21	1	4	0	0	0	0	0	5	.190	.190	.190	1	-3	0	0	0	1.000	1	/O-5	-0.2

■ LEO GARCIA
Garcia, Leonardo Antonio (Peralta) b: 11/6/62, Santiago, D.R. BL/TL, 5′8″, 160 lbs. Deb: 4/6/87

YEAR	TM/L	G	AB	R	H	2B	3B	HR	RBI	BB	SO	AVG	OBP	SLG	PRO+	BR/A	SB	CS	SBR	FA	FR	G/POS	TPR
1987	Cin-N	31	30	8	6	1	0	2	5	4	9	.200	.294	.300	55	-2	3	1	0	1.000	-2	O-14	-0.4
1988	Cin-N	23	28	2	4	1	0	0	4	5	4	.143	.250	.179	24	-3	0	1	-1	1.000	-1	/O-9	-0.5
Total	2	54	58	10	10	2	0	2	9	8	13	.172	.273	.241	41	-5	3	2	-0	1.000	-4	/O-23	-0.9

YEAR	TM/L	G	AB	R	H	2B	3B	HR	RBI	BB	SO	AVG	OBP	SLG	PRO+	BR/A	SB	CS	SBR	FA	FR	G/POS	TPR

■ PEDRO GARCIA
Garcia, Pedro Modesto (Delfi) b: 4/17/50, Guayama, P.R. BR/TR, 5'10", 175 lbs. Deb: 4/6/73

1973	Mil-A	160	580	67	142	**32**	5	15	54	40	119	.245	.299	.395	96	-5	11	10	-3	.970	-12	*2-160	-1.0
1974	Mil-A	141	452	46	90	15	4	12	54	26	67	.199	.251	.330	66	-21	8	5	-1	.970	-11	*2-140	-2.7
1975	Mil-A	98	302	40	68	15	2	6	38	18	59	.225	.273	.348	74	-11	12	6	0	.985	19	2-94/D-1	1.3
1976	Mil-A	41	106	12	23	7	1	1	9	4	23	.217	.259	.340	73	-4	2	2	-1	.971	-3	2-39	-0.6
	Det-A	77	227	21	45	10	2	3	20	9	40	.198	.242	.300	56	-13	2	3	-1	.958	-0	2-77	-1.1
	Yr	118	333	33	68	17	3	4	29	13	63	.204	.247	.309	61	-17	4	5	-2	.962	-3	*2-116	-1.7
1977	Tor-A	41	130	10	27	10	1	0	9	5	21	.208	.254	.300	50	-9	0	0	0	.971	-2	2-34/D-4	-0.9
Total	5	558	1797	196	395	89	15	37	184	102	329	.220	.270	.348	75	-63	35	26	-5	.971	-8	2-544/D-5	-5.0

■ CHICO GARCIA
Garcia, Vinicio Uzcanga b: 12/24/24, Veracruz, Mexico BR/TR, 5'8", 170 lbs. Deb: 4/24/54

| 1954 | Bal-A | 39 | 62 | 6 | 7 | 0 | 2 | 0 | 5 | 8 | 3 | .113 | .214 | .177 | 9 | -8 | 0 | 0 | 0 | .962 | 8 | 2-24 | 0.0 |

■ NOMAR GARCIAPARRA
Garciaparra, Anthony Nomar b: 7/23/73, Whittier, Cal. BR/TR, 6', 165 lbs. Deb: 8/31/96

| 1996 | Bos-A | 24 | 87 | 11 | 21 | 2 | 3 | 4 | 16 | 4 | 14 | .241 | .275 | .471 | 81 | -3 | 5 | 0 | 2 | .988 | -5 | S-22/2-1,D-1 | -0.4 |

■ AL GARDELLA
Gardella, Alfred Stephan b: 1/11/18, New York, N.Y. BL/TL, 5'10", 172 lbs. Deb: 5/17/45 F

| 1945 | NY-N | 16 | 26 | 2 | 2 | 0 | 0 | 0 | 1 | 4 | 3 | .077 | .226 | .077 | -14 | -4 | 0 | | | .961 | -1 | /1-9,O-1 | -0.6 |

■ DANNY GARDELLA
Gardella, Daniel Lewis b: 2/26/20, New York, N.Y. BL/TL, 5'7.5", 160 lbs. Deb: 5/14/44 F

1944	NY-N	47	112	20	28	2	2	6	14	11	13	.250	.323	.464	120	2	0			.912	2	O-25	0.3
1945	NY-N	121	430	54	117	10	1	18	71	46	55	.272	.349	.426	113	7	2			.954	-2	O-94,1-15	-0.1
1950	StL-N	1	1	0	0	0	0	0	0	0	0	.000	.000	.000	-95	-0	0			.000	0	H	0.0
Total	3	169	543	74	145	12	3	24	85	57	68	.267	.343	.433	114	9	2			.943	-0	O-119/1-15	0.2

■ RON GARDENHIRE
Gardenhire, Ronald Clyde b: 10/24/57, Butzbach, Germany BR/TR, 6', 175 lbs. Deb: 9/1/81 C

1981	NY-N	27	48	2	13	1	0	0	3	5	9	.271	.340	.292	82	-1	2	2	-1	.969	4	S-18/2-6,3-1	0.4
1982	NY-N	141	384	29	92	17	1	3	33	23	55	.240	.283	.313	67	-17	5	6	-2	.956	15	*S-135/2-1,3-1	0.7
1983	NY-N	17	32	1	2	0	0	0	1	1	4	.063	.091	.063	-57	-7	0	0	0	1.000	0	S-15	-0.6
1984	NY-N	74	207	20	51	7	1	1	10	9	43	.246	.278	.304	64	-10	6	1	1	.947	-4	S-49,2-18/3-7	-0.9
1985	NY-N	26	39	5	7	2	1	0	2	8	11	.179	.319	.282	71	-1	0	0	0	.911	-1	S-13/2-5,3-2	-0.1
Total	5	285	710	57	165	27	3	4	49	46	122	.232	.279	.296	62	-36	13	9	-2	.955	15	S-230/2-30,3-11	-0.5

■ ALEX GARDNER
Gardner, Alexander b: 4/28/1861, Toronto, Ont., Can. d: 6/18/26, Danvers, Mass. Deb: 5/10/1884

| 1884 | Was-a | 1 | 3 | 0 | 0 | 0 | 0 | 0 | | 0 | 0 | .000 | .000 | .000 | -99 | -1 | | | | .600 | -1 | /C-1 | -0.1 |

■ ART GARDNER
Gardner, Arthur Junior b: 9/21/52, Madden, Miss. BL/TL, 5'11", 175 lbs. Deb: 9/2/75

1975	Hou-N	13	31	3	6	0	0	0	2	1	8	.194	.242	.194	24	-3	1	0	0	1.000	-1	/O-8	-0.4
1977	Hou-N	66	65	7	10	0	0	0	3	3	15	.154	.203	.154	-3	-10	0	0	0	1.000	-4	O-26	-1.4
1978	SF-N	7	3	2	0	0	0	0	0	0	2	.000	.000	.000	-99	-1	0	1	-1	1.000	0	H	-0.2
Total	3	86	99	12	16	0	0	0	5	4	25	.162	.210	.162	2	-14	1	1	-0	1.000	-4	/O-34	-2.0

■ EARLE GARDNER
Gardner, Earle McClurkin b: 1/24/1884, Sparta, Ill. d: 3/2/43, Sparta, Ill. BR/TR, 5'11", 160 lbs. Deb: 9/18/08

1908	NY-A	20	75	7	16	2	0	0	4	1		.213	.234	.240	53	-4	0			.947	4	2-20	0.0
1909	NY-A	22	85	12	28	4	0	0	15	3		.329	.352	.376	129	3	4			.945	-8	2-22	-0.6
1910	NY-A	86	271	36	66	4	2	1	24	21		.244	.303	.284	79	-6	9			.936	6	2-70	-0.2
1911	NY-A	102	357	36	94	13	2	0	39	20		.263	.312	.311	69	-15	14			.959	-3	*2-101	-2.0
1912	NY-A	43	160	14	45	3	1	0	26	5		.281	.303	.313	72	-6	11			.922	-5	2-43	-1.1
Total	5	273	948	105	249	26	5	1	108	50		.263	.305	.304	76	-29	38			.944	-5	2-256	-3.9

■ GID GARDNER
Gardner, Frank Washington b: 6/9/1859, Attleboro, Mass. d: 8/1/14, Cambridge, Mass. 165 lbs. Deb: 8/23/1879

1879	Tro-N	2	6	1	1	0	0	0	0	0	0	.167	.167	.167	11	-1				.429	-1	/P-2	0.0
1880	Cle-N	10	32	0	6	1	1	0	4	2	4	.188	.235	.281	76	-1				.850	-1	/P-9,O-1	0.0
1883	Bal-a	42	161	28	44	10	3	1		18		.273	.346	.391	133	6				.837	-1	O-35/2-4,3-3,P-2	0.5
1884	Bal-a	41	173	32	37	6	8	2		14		.214	.280	.376	108	1				.860	4	O-40/1-2	0.4
	CP-U	38	149	22	38	10	2	0		10		.255	.302	.349	97	-5				.872	6	O-29/3-8,P-1,2-1	-0.6
	Bal-U	1	4	0	1	0	0	0		0		.250	.250	.250	47	-0				.714	-0	/S-1	0.0
	Yr	39	153	22	39	10	2	0		10		.255	.301	.346	96	-5				.872	-0	O-29/3-8,P-1,2-1,S	-0.6
1885	Bal-a	44	170	22	37	5	4	0	17	12		.218	.269	.294	79	-4				.891	3	2-39/O-5,1-1,P-1	0.1
1887	Ind-N	18	63	8	11	1	0	1	8	12	11	.175	.307	.238	55	-3	7			1.000	-3	O-11/2-7	-0.6
1888	Was-N	1	3	0	1	0	0	0	0	1	1	.333	.500	.333	180	1				.750	-3	/S-1	0.1
	Phi-N	1	3	0	2	0	0	0	1	0		.667	.667	.667	310	1				1.000	-1	/2-1	0.0
	Was-N	1	1	0	0	0	0	0	0	0		.000	.000	.000	-99	-0				1.000	-0	/2-1	-0.1
	Yr	3	7	0	3	0	0	0	1	1	1	.429	.500	.429	202	1				1.000	-1	/2-2,S-1	0.0
Total	7	199	765	113	178	33	18	4	30	69	16	.233	.298	.339	99	-5	7			.855	0	O-121/2-53,P31S	-0.2

■ JEFF GARDNER
Gardner, Jeffrey Scott b: 2/4/64, Newport Beach, Cal. BL/TR, 5'11", 165 lbs. Deb: 9/10/91

1991	NY-N	13	37	3	6	1	0	0	1	4	6	.162	.244	.162	17	-4	0	0	0	.818	-2	/S-8,2-3	-0.6
1992	SD-N	15	19	0	2	0	0	0	0	1	8	.105	.150	.105	-26	-3	0	0	0	1.000	4	2-11	0.1
1993	SD-N	140	404	53	106	21	7	1	24	45	69	.262	.338	.356	85	-8	2	6	-3	.983	-8	*2-133/3-1,S-1	-1.6
1994	Mon-N	18	32	4	7	0	1	0	1	3	5	.219	.286	.281	48	-2	0	0	0	.714	-5	/3-9,2-4	-0.8
Total	4	186	492	60	121	21	8	1	26	53	88	.246	.321	.327	73	-18	2	6	-3	.984	-11	2-151/3-10,S-9	-2.9

■ RAY GARDNER
Gardner, Raymond Vincent b: 10/25/01, Frederick, Md. d: 5/3/68, Frederick, Md. BR/TR, 5'8", 145 lbs. Deb: 4/16/29

1929	Cle-A	82	256	28	67	3	2	1	24	29	16	.262	.337	.301	63	-13	10	13	-5	.952	8	S-82	-0.1
1930	Cle-A	33	13	7	1	0	0	0	1	0	0	.077	.077	.077	-59	-3	0	1	-0	.861	8	S-22/2-5,3-1	0.4
Total	2	115	269	35	68	3	2	1	25	29	16	.253	.326	.290	57	-16	10	14	-5	.945	16	S-104/2-5,3-1	0.3

■ BILLY GARDNER
Gardner, William Frederick "Shotgun" b: 7/19/27, Waterford, Conn. BR/TR, 6', 180 lbs. Deb: 4/22/54 MC

1954	NY-N	62	108	10	23	5	0	1	7	6	19	.213	.261	.287	42	-9	0	1	-1	.987	10	3-30,2-13/S-5	0.0
1955	NY-N	59	187	26	38	10	1	3	17	13	19	.203	.262	.316	52	-13	0	0	0	.940	8	S-38,3-10/2-4	-1.0
1956	Bal-A	144	515	53	119	16	2	11	50	29	53	.231	.281	.334	67	-27	5	5	-2	.974	-12	*2-132,S-25/3-6	-2.9
1957	Bal-A	154	644	79	169	**36**	3	6	55	53	67	.262	.326	.356	92	-8	10	7	-1	**.987**	6	*2-148/S-9	0.9
1958	Bal-A	151	560	32	126	28	2	3	33	34	53	.225	.273	.298	60	-31	2	3	-1	.985	-22	*2-151,S-13	-4.6
1959	Bal-A	140	401	34	87	13	2	6	27	38	61	.217	.286	.304	64	-20	2	1	0	.976	31	*2-139/S-1,3-1	2.0
1960	Was-A	145	592	71	152	26	5	9	56	43	76	.257	.314	.363	83	-14	2	4	-0	.973	-2	*2-145,S-13	-0.5
1961	Min-A	45	154	13	36	9	0	1	11	10	14	.234	.280	.312	55	-10	0	0	0	.973	-4	2-41/3-2	-1.0
	*NY-A	41	99	11	21	5	0	1	2	6	18	.212	.278	.293	56	-6	0	0	0	.952	3	3-33/2-6	-0.3
	Yr	86	253	24	57	14	0	2	13	16	32	.225	.279	.304	56	-16	0	0	0	.975	-1	2-47,3-35	-1.3
1962	NY-A	4	1	0	0	0	0	0	0	0	0	.000	.000	.000	-99	-0	0	0	0	1.000	1	/2-1,3-1	0.0
	Bos-A	53	199	22	54	9	2	0	12	10	39	.271	.310	.337	72	-8	0	0	-1	.963	-8	2-38/3-7,S-4	-1.2
	Yr	57	200	22	54	9	2	0	12	10	40	.270	.308	.335	71	-8	0	0	-1	.963	-7	2-39/3-8,S-4	-1.2
1963	Bos-A	36	84	4	16	2	1	0	1	4	19	.190	.236	.238	32	-8	0	0	0	.989	7	2-21/3-2	0.1
Total	10	1034	3544	356	841	159	18	41	271	246	439	.237	.293	.327	70	-155	19	22	-8	.978	8	2-839,S-108/3-92	-8.5

■ LARRY GARDNER
Gardner, William Lawrence b: 5/13/1886, Enosburg Falls, Vt d: 3/11/76, St.George, Vt. BL/TR, 5'8", 165 lbs. Deb: 6/25/08

1908	Bos-A	3	10	0	3	1	0	0	1	0		.300	.300	.400	124	0	0			.571	-2	/3-3	-0.2
1909	Bos-A	19	37	7	11	1	2	0	5	3		.297	.381	.432	153	2	1			.800	-4	/3-8,S-5	-0.1
1910	Bos-A	113	413	55	117	12	10	2	36	41		.283	.354	.375	125	12	8			.944	-9	*2-113	0.1
1911	Bos-A	138	492	80	140	17	8	4	44	64		.285	.373	.376	110	8	27			.962	24	3-72,2-62	3.1
1912	*Bos-A	143	517	88	163	24	18	3	86	56		.315	.383	.449	131	20	25			.930	-1	*3-143	2.0
1913	Bos-A	131	473	64	133	17	10	2	63	49	34	.281	.347	.359	104	3	18			.943	-16	*3-130	-1.2

YEAR	TM/L	G	AB	R	H	2B	3B	HR	RBI	BB	SO	AVG	OBP	SLG	PRO+	BR/A	SB	CS	SBR	FA	FR	G/POS	TPR
1914	Bos-A	155	553	50	143	23	19	3	68	35	39	.259	.303	.385	107	1	16	23	-9	.942	0	*3-153	-0.3
1915	*Bos-A	127	430	51	111	14	6	1	55	39	24	.258	.327	.326	98	-1	11	12	-4	.933	-7	*3-127	-0.7
1916	*Bos-A	148	493	47	152	19	7	2	62	48	27	.308	.372	.387	128	17	12			.953	-14	*3-147	0.8
1917	Bos-A	146	501	53	133	23	7	1	61	54	37	.265	.341	.345	110	7	16			.937	-7	*3-146	0.3
1918	Phi-A	127	463	50	132	22	6	1	52	43	22	.285	.342	.365	113	7	9			.964	10	*3-127	2.2
1919	Cle-A	139	524	67	157	29	7	2	79	39	29	.300	.352	.393	103	1	7			.946	-6	*3-139	0.1
1920	*Cle-A	154	597	72	185	31	11	3	118	53	25	.310	.367	.414	103	3	3	20	-11	.976	-2	*3-154	-0.2
1921	Cle-A	153	586	101	187	32	14	3	120	65	16	.319	.382	.437	109	9	3	3	-1	.950	-1	*3-152	1.7
1922	Cle-A	137	470	74	134	31	3	2	68	49	21	.285	.355	.377	90	-6	9	8	-2	.951	-5	*3-128	-0.4
1923	Cle-A	52	79	4	20	5	1	0	12	12	7	.253	.352	.342	83	-2	0	1	-1	.962	3	3-19	0.1
1924	Cle-A	38	50	3	10	0	0	0	4	5	1	.200	.273	.200	23	-6	0	1	-1	.875	-4	/3-8,2-6	-0.1
Total	17	1923	6688	866	1931	301	129	27	934	654	282	.289	.355	.384	109	75	165	68		.948	-39	*3-1656,2-181/S-5	6.4

■ ART GARIBALDI
Garibaldi, Arthur Edward   b: 8/20/07, San Francisco, Cal   d: 10/19/67, Sacramento, Cal.   BR/TR, 5'8", 165 lbs.   Deb: 6/20/36

YEAR	TM/L	G	AB	R	H	2B	3B	HR	RBI	BB	SO	AVG	OBP	SLG	PRO+	BR/A	SB	CS	SBR	FA	FR	G/POS	TPR
1936	StL-N	71	232	30	64	12	0	1	20	16	30	.276	.323	.341	79	-7	3			.925	-5	3-46,2-24	-0.9

■ DEBS GARMS
Garms, Debs C. "Tex"   b: 6/26/08, Bangs, Tex.   d: 12/16/84, Glen Rose, Tex.   BL/TR, 5'8.5", 165 lbs.   Deb: 8/10/32

YEAR	TM/L	G	AB	R	H	2B	3B	HR	RBI	BB	SO	AVG	OBP	SLG	PRO+	BR/A	SB	CS	SBR	FA	FR	G/POS	TPR
1932	StL-A	34	134	20	38	7	1	1	8	17	7	.284	.364	.373	86	-2	4	3	-1	.953	-1	O-33	-0.5
1933	StL-A	78	189	35	60	10	2	4	24	30	21	.317	.416	.455	123	7	2	5	-2	.960	-2	O-47	0.0
1934	StL-A	91	232	25	68	14	4	0	31	27	19	.293	.372	.388	89	-4	0	0	0	.942	-3	O-56	-0.8
1935	StL-A	10	15	1	4	0	0	0	0	2	1	.267	.353	.267	59	-1	0	0	0	.800	-0	/O-2	-0.1
1937	Bos-N	125	478	60	124	15	8	2	37	37	33	.259	.311	.337	85	-11	2			.977	-8	O-81,3-36	-2.0
1938	Bos-N	117	428	62	135	19	1	0	47	34	22	.315	.371	.364	114	9	4			.985	-7	O-63,3-54/2-1	0.1
1939	Bos-N	132	513	68	153	24	9	2	37	39	20	.298	.350	.392	107	4	2			.964	-4	O-96,3-37	-0.3
1940	Pit-N	103	358	76	127	23	7	5	57	23	6	.355	.395	.500	147	22	3			.964	-1	3-64,O-19	2.2
1941	Pit-N	83	220	25	58	9	3	3	42	12	12	.264	.331	.373	98	-1	1			.911	-10	3-29,O-24	-1.2
1943	*StL-N	90	249	26	64	10	2	0	22	13	8	.257	.299	.313	74	-9	1			.980	-5	O-47,3-23/S-1	-1.7
1944	*StL-N	73	149	17	30	3	0	0	5	13	8	.201	.265	.221	37	-12	0			1.000	1	O-23,3-21	-2.2
1945	StL-N	74	146	23	49	7	2	0	18	31	3	.336	.452	.411	137	9	0			.956	-10	3-32,O-10	0.0
Total	12	1010	3111	438	910	141	39	17	328	288	161	.293	.355	.379	103	13	18	8		.966	-58	O-501,3-296/S-1,2-1	-6.5

■ PHIL GARNER
Garner, Philip Mason   b: 4/30/49, Jefferson City, Tenn.   BR/TR, 5'10", 177 lbs.   Deb: 9/10/73   MC

YEAR	TM/L	G	AB	R	H	2B	3B	HR	RBI	BB	SO	AVG	OBP	SLG	PRO+	BR/A	SB	CS	SBR	FA	FR	G/POS	TPR
1973	Oak-A	9	5	0	0	0	0	0	0	0	3	.000	.000	.000	-99	-1	0	0	0	1.000	1	/3-9	-0.1
1974	Oak-A	30	28	4	5	1	0	0	1	1	5	.179	.207	.214	23	-3	1	1	-0	.955	4	3-19/S-8,2-3,D-2	0.1
1975	*Oak-A	160	488	46	120	21	5	6	54	30	65	.246	.296	.346	83	-12	4	6	-2	.968	-16	*2-160/S-1	-2.2
1976	Oak-A★	159	555	54	145	29	12	8	74	36	71	.261	.308	.400	111	5	35	13	3	.975	-14	*2-159	0.5
1977	Pit-N	153	585	99	152	35	10	17	77	55	65	.260	.326	.441	101	-0	32	9	4	.971	1	*3-107,2-50,S-12	0.7
1978	Pit-N	154	528	66	138	25	9	10	66	66	71	.261	.349	.400	104	4	27	14	-0	.976	10	2-81,3-81/S-4	1.9
1979	*Pit-N	150	549	76	161	32	8	11	59	55	74	.293	.361	.441	112	10	17	8	0	.981	5	2-83,3-78,S-14	2.2
1980	Pit-N★	151	548	62	142	27	6	5	58	46	53	.259	.319	.358	87	-9	32	7	5	.976	16	2-151/S-1	2.3
1981	Pit-N★	56	181	22	46	6	2	1	20	21	21	.254	.332	.326	84	-3	4	6	-2	.968	-6	2-50	-1.0
	*Hou-N	31	113	13	27	3	1	0	6	15	11	.239	.328	.283	79	-3	6	2	1	.982	0	2-31	-0.0
	Yr	87	294	35	73	9	3	1	26	36	32	.248	.330	.310	82	-6	10	8	-2	.973	-6	2-81	-1.0
1982	Hou-N	155	588	65	161	33	8	13	83	40	92	.274	.323	.423	116	10	24	13	-1	.980	1	*2-136,3-18	1.8
1983	Hou-N	154	567	76	135	24	2	14	79	63	84	.238	.320	.362	94	-5	18	12	-2	.945	4	*3-154	-0.5
1984	Hou-N	128	374	60	104	17	6	4	45	43	63	.278	.359	.388	118	10	3	2	-0	.979	23	3-82,2-35	3.3
1985	Hou-N	135	463	65	124	23	10	6	51	34	72	.268	.321	.400	103	1	4	4	-1	.932	-9	*3-123,2-15	-1.1
1986	*Hou-N	107	313	43	83	14	3	9	41	30	45	.265	.331	.415	108	3	12	6	0	.896	1	3-84/2-7	0.2
1987	Hou-N	43	112	15	25	5	0	3	15	8	20	.223	.275	.348	66	-6	1	1	0	.976	2	3-36/2-2	-0.4
	LA-N	70	126	14	24	4	0	2	8	20	24	.190	.301	.270	54	-8	5	1	1	.923	6	3-46,2-12/S-2	-0.1
	Yr	113	238	29	49	9	0	5	23	28	44	.206	.289	.307	60	-14	6	1	1	.947	8	3-82,2-14/S-2	-0.5
1988	SF-N	15	13	0	2	0	0	0	1	1	3	.154	.214	.154	8	-2	0	1	-1	.000	0	/3-2	-0.2
Total	16	1860	6136	780	1594	299	82	109	738	564	842	.260	.326	.389	100	-10	225	105	4	.974	30	2-975,3-839/S-42,D	7.4

■ RALPH GARR
Garr, Ralph Allen "Road Runner"   b: 12/12/45, Monroe, La.   BL/TR, 5'11", 197 lbs.   Deb: 9/3/68

YEAR	TM/L	G	AB	R	H	2B	3B	HR	RBI	BB	SO	AVG	OBP	SLG	PRO+	BR/A	SB	CS	SBR	FA	FR	G/POS	TPR
1968	Atl-N	11	7	3	2	0	0	0	0	1	0	.286	.375	.286	100	0	1	0	0	.000	0	H	0.0
1969	Atl-N	22	27	6	6	1	0	0	2	2	4	.222	.276	.259	50	-2	1	1	-0	.857	-1	/O-7	-0.4
1970	Atl-N	37	96	18	27	3	0	0	8	5	12	.281	.317	.313	65	-5	5	2	0	1.000	0	O-21	-0.5
1971	Atl-N	154	639	101	219	24	6	9	44	30	68	.343	.374	.441	122	18	30	14	1	.968	16	*O-153	2.9
1972	Atl-N	134	554	87	180	22	0	12	53	25	41	.325	.361	.430	113	9	25	9	2	.962	-4	*O-131	0.1
1973	Atl-N	148	668	94	200	32	6	11	55	22	64	.299	.324	.415	96	-5	35	11	4	.968	1	*O-148	-0.7
1974	Atl-N★	143	606	87	214	24	17	11	54	28	52	.353	.384	.503	141	30	26	16	2	.967	-19	*O-139	0.4
1975	Atl-N	151	625	74	174	26	11	6	31	44	50	.278	.329	.384	94	-6	14	9	-1	.966	6	*O-148	-0.7
1976	Chi-A	136	527	63	158	22	6	4	36	17	41	.300	.324	.387	107	3	14	5	1	.978	-6	*O-125/D-6	-0.8
1977	Chi-A	134	543	78	163	29	7	10	54	27	41	.300	.333	.435	108	5	12	7	1	.987	3	*O-126/D-2	0.1
1978	Chi-A	118	443	67	122	18	9	3	29	24	41	.275	.314	.377	93	-5	7	5	-1	.959	1	*O-109/D-9	-1.0
1979	Chi-A	102	307	34	86	10	2	9	39	17	19	.280	.320	.414	96	-2	2	4	-2	.951	-8	O-67,D-17	-1.4
	Cal-A	6	24	0	3	0	0	0	0	0	3	.125	.125	.125	-33	-4	0	0	0	.000	0	/D-6	-0.5
	Yr	108	331	34	89	10	2	9	39	17	22	.269	.307	.393	87	-7	2	4	-2	.951	-8	/O-67,D-17/H-6	-1.9
1980	Cal-A	21	42	5	8	1	0	0	3	4	6	.190	.261	.214	33	-4	0	0	0	.750	-2	/O-2,D-8	-0.4
Total	13	1317	5108	717	1562	212	64	75	408	246	445	.306	.340	.416	106	33	172	83	2	.968	-11	*O-1176/D-48	-2.9

■ ADRIAN GARRETT
Garrett, Henry Adrian "Pat"   b: 1/3/43, Brooksville, Fla.   BL/TR, 6'3", 185 lbs.   Deb: 4/13/66   FC

YEAR	TM/L	G	AB	R	H	2B	3B	HR	RBI	BB	SO	AVG	OBP	SLG	PRO+	BR/A	SB	CS	SBR	FA	FR	G/POS	TPR
1966	Atl-N	4	3	0	0	0	0	0	0	0	2	.000	.000	.000	-99	-1	0	0	0	.000	-0	/O-1	-0.1
1970	Chi-N	3	3	0	0	0	0	0	0	0	0	.000	.000	.000	-89	-1	0	0	0	.000	-0	H	-0.1
1971	Oak-A	14	21	3	3	0	0	1	2	5	7	.143	.308	.286	70	-1	0	0	0	1.000	-0	/O-5	-0.1
1972	Oak-A	14	11	0	0	0	0	0	0	1	4	.000	.083	.000	-78	-2	0	0	0	1.000	-1	/O-2	-0.3
1973	Chi-N	36	54	7	12	0	0	3	8	4	18	.222	.276	.389	77	-2	1	0	0	1.000	-1	/O-7,C-6	-0.3
1974	Chi-N	10	8	0	0	0	0	0	0	1	1	.000	.111	.000	-64	-2	0	0	0	1.000	0	/C-3,1-1,O-1	-0.1
1975	Chi-N	16	21	1	2	0	0	1	6	1	8	.095	.136	.238	2	-3	0	0	0	1.000	1	/1-4	-0.2
	Cal-A	37	107	17	28	5	0	6	18	14	28	.262	.347	.477	141	5	0	0	1	1.000	-0	D-23,1-10/O-2,C-1	0.5
1976	Cal-A	29	48	4	6	3	0	0	3	5	16	.125	.208	.188	17	-5	0	0	0	.974	-4	C-15/1-1,D-4	-0.9
Total	8	163	276	30	51	8	0	11	37	31	87	.185	.267	.333	71	-11	4	0	1	.959	-5	/D-27,C-25,O-18,1	-1.6

■ WAYNE GARRETT
Garrett, Ronald Wayne   b: 12/3/47, Brooksville, Fla.   BL/TR, 5'11", 183 lbs.   Deb: 4/12/69   F

YEAR	TM/L	G	AB	R	H	2B	3B	HR	RBI	BB	SO	AVG	OBP	SLG	PRO+	BR/A	SB	CS	SBR	FA	FR	G/POS	TPR
1969	*NY-N	124	400	38	87	11	3	1	39	40	75	.218	.293	.268	57	-22	4	2	0	.951	-13	3-72,2-47/S-9	-3.4
1970	NY-N	114	366	74	93	17	4	12	45	81	60	.254	.392	.421	118	12	5	1	1	.944	-19	3-70,2-45/S-1	-0.3
1971	NY-N	56	202	20	43	2	0	1	11	28	31	.213	.312	.238	58	-10	1	3	-2	.967	-4	3-53/2-9	-1.7
1972	NY-N	111	298	41	69	13	3	2	29	70	58	.232	.378	.315	101	4	3	2	-0	.960	2	3-82,2-22	0.7
1973	*NY-N	140	504	76	129	20	3	16	58	72	74	.256	.350	.403	115	10	6	5	-1	.942	11	*3-130/S-9,2-6	1.9
1974	NY-N	151	522	55	117	14	3	13	53	89	96	.224	.339	.337	91	-4	4	6	-2	.955	14	*3-144/S-9	0.7
1975	NY-N	107	274	49	73	8	3	6	34	50	45	.266	.382	.383	118	8	5	4	-1	.966	11	3-94/S-3,2-1	1.9
1976	NY-N	80	251	36	56	8	1	4	26	52	26	.223	.359	.311	97	1	7	5	-1	.948	3	3-64,2-10/S-1	0.4
	Mon-N	59	177	15	43	4	1	2	11	30	20	.243	.353	.311	86	-2	0	2	-1	.982	1	2-54/3-2	0.2
	Yr	139	428	51	99	12	2	6	37	82	46	.231	.356	.311	92	-1	9	7	-2	1.000	4	3-66,2-64/S-1	0.6
1977	Mon-N	68	159	17	43	6	1	2	22	30	18	.270	.389	.358	105	3	1	3	-1	1.000	2	3-49/2-1	0.4
1978	Mon-N	49	69	6	12	0	0	1	5	19	10	.174	.260	.217	35	-6	0	0	0	.969	1	3-13	-0.6
	StL-N	33	63	11	21	4	0	1	10	11	16	.333	.432	.444	148	5	1	0	0	.927	-2	3-19	0.3
	Yr	82	132	17	33	4	0	2	12	19	26	.250	.344	.326	89	-1	1	0	0	.945	-2	3-32	-0.3
Total	10	1092	3285	438	786	107	22	61	340	561	529	.239	.352	.341	95	-4	38	30	-7	.956	7	3-792,2-195/S-32	0.5

YEAR	TM/L	G	AB	R	H	2B	3B	HR	RBI	BB	SO	AVG	OBP	SLG	PRO+	BR/A	SB	CS	SBR	FA	FR	G/POS	TPR

■ GIL GARRIDO
Garrido, Gil Gonzalo b: 6/26/41, Panama City, Pan. BR/TR, 5′8″, 160 lbs. Deb: 4/24/64

1964	SF-N	14	25	1	2	0	0	0	1	2	7	.080	.148	.080	-33	-4	1	0	0	.969	-1	S-14	-0.5
1968	Atl-N	18	53	5	11	0	0	0	2	2	2	.208	.236	.208	34	-1	0	0	0	.987	3	S-17	0.1
1969	*Atl-N	82	227	18	50	5	1	0	10	16	11	.220	.272	.251	47	-16	0	0	0	.973	-11	S-81	-2.1
1970	Atl-N	101	367	38	97	5	4	1	19	15	16	.264	.293	.308	58	-22	0	2	-1	.975	-1	S-80,2-26	-1.3
1971	Atl-N	79	125	8	27	3	0	0	12	15	12	.216	.300	.240	51	-8	0	1	-1	.961	4	S-32,3-28,2-18	0.0
1972	Atl-N	40	75	11	20	1	0	0	7	11	6	.267	.368	.280	79	-1	1	1	-0	.989	1	2-21,S-10/3-3	0.0
Total	6	334	872	81	207	14	5	1	51	61	54	.237	.288	.268	53	-55	2	4	-2	.974	-4	S-234/2-65,3-31	-3.8

■ CECIL GARRIOTT
Garriott, Virgil Cecil b: 8/15/16, Harristown, Ill. d: 2/20/90, Lake Elsinore, Cal BL/TR, 5′8″, 165 lbs. Deb: 9/4/46

1946	Chi-N	6	5	1	0	0	0	0	0	2	.000	.167	.000							.000		H	-0.1

■ FORD GARRISON
Garrison, Robert Ford "Rocky" or "Snapper" b: 8/29/15, Greenville, S.C. BR/TR, 5′10.5″, 180 lbs. Deb: 4/22/43 C

1943	Bos-A	36	129	13	36	5	1	1	11	5	14	.279	.306	.357	92	-2	0	1	-1	.988	-0	O-32	-0.5
1944	Bos-A	13	49	5	12	3	0	0	2	6	4	.245	.327	.306	82	-1	0	0	0	.969	1	O-12	-0.1
	Phi-A	121	449	58	121	13	2	4	37	22	40	.269	.307	.334	84	-10	10	4	1	.987	6	*O-119	-1.0
	Yr	134	498	63	133	16	2	4	39	28	44	.267	.309	.331	84	-11	10	4	1	.985	7	*O-131	-1.1
1945	Phi-A	6	23	3	7	1	0	1	6	4	3	.304	.407	.478	157	2	1	0	0	1.000	0	/O-5	0.2
1946	Phi-A	9	37	1	4	0	0	0	0	6	.108	.108	.108	-40	-7	0	0	0	1.000	-2	/O-8	-1.0
Total	4	185	687	80	180	22	3	6	56	37	67	.262	.302	.329	81	-18	11	5	0	.986	5	O-176	-2.4

■ WEBSTER GARRISON
Garrison, Webster Leotis b: 8/24/65, Marrero, La. BR/TR, 5′11″, 170 lbs. Deb: 8/2/96

1996	Oak-A	5	9	0	0	0	0	0	0	1	0	.000	.100	.000	-75	-2	0	0	0	.875	-1	/2-3,1-1	-0.3

■ HANK GARRITY
Garrity, Francis Joseph b: 2/4/08, Boston, Mass. d: 9/1/62, Boston, Mass. BR/TR, 6′1″, 185 lbs. Deb: 7/26/31

1931	Chi-A	8	14	0	3	1	0	0	2	1	2	.214	.267	.286	48	-1	0	0	0	.941	0	/C-7	-0.1

■ STEVE GARVEY
Garvey, Steven Patrick b: 12/22/48, Tampa, Fla. BR/TR, 5′10″, 192 lbs. Deb: 9/1/69

1969	LA-N	3	3	0	1	0	0	0	0	0	1	.333	.333	.333	94	-0	0	0	0	.000	0	H	0.0
1970	LA-N	34	93	8	25	5	0	1	6	6	17	.269	.313	.355	82	-3	1	1	-0	.943	3	3-27/2-1	0.3
1971	LA-N	81	225	27	51	12	1	7	26	21	33	.227	.293	.382	95	-2	1	2	-1	.939	19	3-79	1.6
1972	LA-N	96	294	36	79	14	2	9	30	19	36	.269	.315	.422	110	3	4	2	0	.902	13	3-85/1-3	1.6
1973	LA-N	114	349	37	106	17	3	8	50	11	42	.304	.331	.438	116	6	0	2	-1	.993	-8	1-76,O-10	-1.0
1974	*LA-N★	156	642	95	200	32	3	21	111	31	66	.312	.346	.469	132	23	5	4	-1	.995	-13	*1-156	-0.2
1975	LA-N★	160	659	85	210	38	6	18	95	33	66	.319	.354	.476	135	27	11	3	2	**.995**	-10	*1-160	0.9
1976	LA-N★	162	631	85	200	37	4	13	80	50	69	.317	.368	.450	134	27	19	8	1	**.998**	-16	*1-162	0.1
1977	*LA-N★	162	646	91	192	25	3	33	115	38	90	.297	.337	.498	121	17	9	6	-1	**.995**	-16	*1-160	-1.0
1978	*LA-N★	162	639	89	**202**	36	9	21	113	40	70	.316	.357	.499	138	29	10	5	0	.994	-9	*1-161	1.1
1979	LA-N★	162	648	92	204	32	1	28	110	37	59	.315	.354	.497	131	25	3	6	-3	.995	-2	*1-162	1.2
1980	LA-N★	163	658	78	**200**	27	1	26	106	36	67	.304	.343	.467	126	21	6	11	-5	.996	-3	*1-162	1.0
1981	*LA-N★	110	431	63	122	23	1	10	64	25	49	.283	.324	.411	111	5	3	5	-2	**.999**	-6	*1-110	-1.1
1982	LA-N	162	625	66	176	35	1	16	86	20	86	.282	.305	.418	103	-0	5	3	-0	.995	1	*1-158	-0.8
1983	SD-N	100	388	76	114	22	0	14	59	29	39	.294	.348	.459	126	12	4	1	1	.994	-11	*1-100	-0.4
1984	*SD-N★	161	617	72	175	27	2	8	86	24	64	.284	.312	.373	92	-8	1	2	-1	**1.000**	-4	*1-159	-2.4
1985	SD-N★	162	654	80	184	34	6	17	81	35	67	.281	.321	.430	110	6	0	0	0	.997	-8	*1-162	-1.3
1986	SD-N	155	557	58	142	22	0	21	81	23	72	.255	.286	.408	91	-9	1	2	-1	.994	-18	*1-148	-4.0
1987	SD-N	27	76	5	16	2	0	1	9	1	10	.211	.231	.276	35	-7	0	0	0	1.000	0	1-20	-0.8
Total	19	2332	8835	1143	2599	440	43	272	1308	479	1003	.294	.333	.446	117	171	83	62	-12	.996	-78	*1-2059,3-191/O2	-5.2

■ ROD GASPAR
Gaspar, Rodney Earl b: 4/3/46, Long Beach, Cal. BB/TR, 5′11″, 165 lbs. Deb: 4/8/69

1969	*NY-N	118	215	26	49	6	1	1	14	25	19	.228	.314	.279	66	-9	7	3	0	.983	-7	O-91	-2.0
1970	NY-N	11	14	4	0	0	0	0	0	1	4	.000	.067	.000	-80	-4	1	0	0	1.000	-1	/O-8	-0.4
1971	SD-N	16	17	1	2	0	0	0	2	3	3	.118	.250	.118	8	-2	1	0	-1	1.000	0	/O-2	-0.3
1974	SD-N	33	14	4	3	0	0	0	1	4	3	.214	.389	.214	75	-0	0	0	0	1.000	-2	O-8,1-2	-0.3
Total	4	178	260	35	54	6	1	1	17	33	29	.208	.302	.250	55	-15	8	4	0	.986	-10	O-109/1-2	-3.0

■ TOM GASTALL
Gastall, Thomas Everett b: 6/13/32, Fall River, Mass. d: 9/20/56, Riviera Beach, Md. BR/TR, 6′2″, 187 lbs. Deb: 6/21/55

1955	Bal-A	20	27	4	4	1	0	0	3	5	.148	.233	.185	15	-3	0	0	0	.967	-1	C-15	-0.4
1956	Bal-A	32	56	3	11	2	0	0	4	3	8	.196	.250	.232	30	-6	0	0	0	1.000	1	C-20	-0.4
Total	2	52	83	7	15	3	0	0	4	6	13	.181	.244	.217	25	-9	0	0	0	.990	0	/C-35	-0.8

■ ED GASTFIELD
Gastfield, Edward b: 8/1/1865, Chicago, Ill. d: 12/1/1899, Chicago, Ill. BR, 5′9.5″, 155 lbs. Deb: 8/13/1884

1884	Det-N	23	82	6	6	1	0	0	2	34	.073	.095	.085	-45	-13				.827	9	C-19/O-2,1-2	-0.3
1885	Det-N	1	3	0	0	0	0	0	0	2	.000	.000	.000	-99	-1				.714	-0	/C-1	-0.1
	Chi-N	1	3	0	0	0	0	0	0	1	.000	.000	.000	-87	-1				1.000	1	/C-1	0.1
	Yr	2	6	0	0	0	0	0	0	3	.000	.000	.000	-93	-1				.889	1	/C-2	0.0
Total	2	25	88	6	6	1	0	0	2	37	.068	.089	.080	-49	-14				.832	10	/C-21,1-2,O-2	-0.3

■ ALEX GASTON
Gaston, Alexander Nathaniel b: 3/12/1893, New York, N.Y. d: 2/8/79, Santa Monica, Cal. BR/TR, 5′9″, 170 lbs. Deb: 9/26/20 F

1920	NY-N	4	10	2	1	0	0	0	1	1	2	.100	.182	.100	-18	-1	0	0	0	.917	-1	/C-3	-0.3
1921	NY-N	20	22	1	5	1	0	0	3	1	9	.227	.261	.364	63	-1	0	0	0	.950	0	C-11	-0.1
1922	NY-N	16	26	1	5	0	0	0	1	0	3	.192	.192	.192	-1	-4	1	0	0	1.000	-0	C-13	-0.3
1923	NY-N	22	39	3	8	2	0	1	5	0	6	.205	.225	.333	46	-3	0	0	0	.957	-0	C-21	-0.3
1926	Bos-A	98	301	37	67	9	0	0	21	21	28	.223	.282	.259	43	-25	0	0	1	.981	-10	C-98	-2.8
1929	Bos-A	55	116	14	26	5	2	2	9	6	8	.224	.262	.353	58	-8	0	0	0	.986	-1	C-49	-0.5
Total	6	215	514	58	112	13	6	3	40	29	56	.218	.266	.284	45	-43	1	0	1	.979	-13	C-195	-4.3

■ CITO GASTON
Gaston, Clarence Edwin b: 3/17/44, San Antonio, Tex. BR/TR, 6′4″, 210 lbs. Deb: 9/14/67 MC

1967	Atl-N	9	25	1	3	0	1	0	1	0	5	.120	.120	.200	-10	-4	1	0	0	.800	-1	/O-7	-0.5
1969	SD-N	129	391	20	90	11	7	2	28	24	117	.230	.276	.309	67	-18	4	4	-1	.959	6	*O-113	-2.1
1970	SD-N★	146	584	92	186	26	9	29	93	41	142	.318	.365	.543	146	34	4	1	1	.975	4	*O-142	3.1
1971	SD-N	141	518	57	118	13	9	17	61	24	121	.228	.265	.386	88	-11	1	0	0	.982	0	*O-133	-1.9
1972	SD-N	111	379	30	102	14	0	7	44	22	76	.269	.313	.361	98	-2	2	0	-1	.977	1	O-94	-0.8
1973	SD-N	133	476	51	119	18	4	16	57	20	88	.250	.282	.405	96	-6	0	1	-1	.947	5	*O-119	-1.0
1974	SD-N	106	267	19	57	11	0	6	33	16	51	.213	.261	.322	65	-14	0	0	0	.992	3	O-63	-1.4
1975	Atl-N	64	141	17	34	6	0	6	15	17	33	.241	.323	.397	95	-1	0	0	0	.974	-1	O-35/1-1	-0.3
1976	Atl-N	69	134	15	39	4	0	4	25	13	21	.291	.354	.410	109	2	1	0	0	.977	-2	O-28/1-2	-0.1
1977	Atl-N	56	85	6	23	4	0	3	21	5	19	.271	.311	.424	85	-2	1	0	0	1.000	0	/O-9,1-5	-0.2
1978	Atl-N	60	118	5	27	1	0	3	20	1	19	.229	.248	.263	38	-10	0	0	0	.957	-4	O-29/1-4	-1.5
	Pit-N	2	2	1	1	0	0	0	0	0	1	.500	.500	.500	172	0	0	0	0	1.000	0	/O-1	0.0
	Yr	62	120	6	28	1	0	3	20	1	20	.233	.252	.267	41	-9	0	0	0	.957	-4	O-30/1-4	-1.5
Total	11	1026	3120	314	799	106	30	91	387	185	693	.256	.300	.397	95	-32	13	7	-0	.970	6	O-773/1-12	-6.7

■ BRENT GATES
Gates, Brent Robert b: 3/14/70, Grand Rapids, Mich. BB/TR, 6′1″, 180 lbs. Deb: 5/5/93

1993	Oak-A	139	535	64	155	29	2	7	69	56	75	.290	.361	.391	109	7	7	3	0	.981	-3	*2-139	0.9
1994	Oak-A	64	233	29	66	11	2	2	24	21	32	.283	.345	.365	91	-3	3	0	1	.974	-17	2-63/1-1	-1.5
1995	Oak-A	136	524	60	133	24	4	5	56	46	84	.254	.314	.344	75	-19	3	3	-1	.982	11	*2-132/1-1,D-3	-0.1
1996	Oak-A	64	247	26	65	19	2	2	30	18	35	.263	.318	.381	79	-8	1	1	-0	.973	-2	2-63	-0.6
Total	4	403	1539	179	419	83	6	16	179	141	226	.272	.336	.369	89	-23	14	7	0	.979	-10	2-397/D-3,1-2	-1.3

■ JOE GATES
Gates, Joseph Daniel b: 10/3/54, Gary, Ind. BL/TR, 5′7″, 175 lbs. Deb: 9/12/78

1978	Chi-A	8	24	6	6	0	0	0	1	4	6	.250	.379	.250	80	-0	1	0	0	.972	-2	/2-8	-0.2

YEAR	TM/L	G	AB	R	H	2B	3B	HR	RBI	BB	SO	AVG	OBP	SLG	PRO+	BR/A	SB	CS	SBR	FA	FR	G/POS	TPR
1979	Chi-A	16	16	5	1	0	1	0	1	2	3	.063	.167	.188	-5	-2	1	1	-0	.966	5	/2-8,3-1,D-1	0.2
Total	2	24	40	11	7	0	1	0	1	2	3	.175	.298	.225	46	-3	2	1	0	.969	3	/2-16,D-1,3-1	0.0

■ MIKE GATES
Gates, Michael Grant b: 9/20/56, Culver City, Cal. BL/TR, 6', 165 lbs. Deb: 5/6/81

YEAR	TM/L	G	AB	R	H	2B	3B	HR	RBI	BB	SO	AVG	OBP	SLG	PRO+	BR/A	SB	CS	SBR	FA	FR	G/POS	TPR
1981	Mon-N	1	2	1	1	0	0	0	1	0	1	.500	.500	1.500	445	1	0	0	0	1.000	-0	/2-1	0.0
1982	Mon-N	36	121	16	28	2	3	0	8	9	19	.231	.285	.298	62	-6	0	0	0	1.000	-9	2-36	-1.5
Total	2	37	123	17	29	2	4	0	9	9	20	.236	.288	.317	68	-5	0	0	0	1.000	-10	/2-37	-1.5

■ FRANK GATINS
Gatins, Frank Anthony b: 3/6/1871, Johnstown, Pa. d: 11/8/11, Johnstown, Pa. Deb: 9/21/1898

YEAR	TM/L	G	AB	R	H	2B	3B	HR	RBI	BB	SO	AVG	OBP	SLG	PRO+	BR/A	SB	CS	SBR	FA	FR	G/POS	TPR
1898	Was-N	17	58	6	13	2	0	0	5	3		.224	.274	.259	53	-4	2			.790	-8	S-17	-1.0
1901	Bro-N	50	197	21	45	7	2	1	21	5		.228	.255	.299	59	-11	6			.919	-9	3-46/S-5	-1.9
Total	2	67	255	27	58	9	2	1	26	8		.227	.259	.290	58	-14	8			.841	-17	/3-46,S-22	-2.9

■ JIM GAUDET
Gaudet, James Jennings b: 6/3/55, New Orleans, La. BR/TR, 6', 185 lbs. Deb: 9/10/78

YEAR	TM/L	G	AB	R	H	2B	3B	HR	RBI	BB	SO	AVG	OBP	SLG	PRO+	BR/A	SB	CS	SBR	FA	FR	G/POS	TPR
1978	KC-A	3	8	0	0	0	0	0	0	0	3	.000	.000	.000	-97	-2	0	0	0	.938	1	/C-3	-0.1
1979	KC-A	3	6	0	1	0	0	0	0	0	0	.167	.167	.167	-10	-1	0	0	0	1.000	1	/C-3	0.0
Total	2	6	14	0	1	0	0	0	0	0	3	.071	.071	.071	-59	-3	0	0	0	.966	2	/C-6	-0.1

■ MIKE GAULE
Gaule, Michael John b: 8/4/1869, Baltimore, Md. d: 1/24/18, Baltimore, Md. BL/TL, 6'2", Deb: 6/15/1889

YEAR	TM/L	G	AB	R	H	2B	3B	HR	RBI	BB	SO	AVG	OBP	SLG	PRO+	BR/A	SB	CS	SBR	FA	FR	G/POS	TPR
1889	Lou-a	1	2	0	0	0	0	0	0	0	1	.000	.000	.000	-99	-1	0			.000	-1	/O-1	-0.1

■ DOC GAUTREAU
Gautreau, Walter Paul "Punk" b: 7/26/01, Cambridge, Mass. d: 8/23/70, Salt Lake City, Ut BR/TR, 5'4", 129 lbs. Deb: 6/22/25

YEAR	TM/L	G	AB	R	H	2B	3B	HR	RBI	BB	SO	AVG	OBP	SLG	PRO+	BR/A	SB	CS	SBR	FA	FR	G/POS	TPR
1925	Phi-A	4	7	0	0	0	0	0	0	0	3	.000	.000	.000	-94	-2	0	0	0	.933	1	/2-4	-0.1
	Bos-N	68	279	45	73	13	3	0	23	35	13	.262	.346	.330	81	-7	11	7	-1	.976	-4	2-68	-1.0
1926	Bos-N	79	266	36	71	9	4	0	8	35	24	.267	.356	.331	94	-1	17			.942	-20	2-74	-1.9
1927	Bos-N	87	236	38	58	12	2	0	20	25	20	.246	.321	.314	76	-8	11			.965	-2	2-57	-0.8
1928	Bos-N	23	18	3	5	0	1	0	1	4	3	.278	.409	.389	116	1	1			.750	-1	/2-4,S-1	0.0
Total	4	261	806	122	207	34	10	0	52	99	63	.257	.341	.324	83	-18	40	7		.960	-25	2-207/S-1	-3.8

■ SID GAUTREAUX
Gautreaux, Sidney Allen "Pudge" b: 5/4/12, Schriever, La. d: 4/19/80, Morgan City, La. BB/TR, 5'8", 190 lbs. Deb: 4/15/36

YEAR	TM/L	G	AB	R	H	2B	3B	HR	RBI	BB	SO	AVG	OBP	SLG	PRO+	BR/A	SB	CS	SBR	FA	FR	G/POS	TPR
1936	Bro-N	75	71	8	19	3	0	0	16	9	7	.268	.358	.310	80	-2	0			.963	-1	C-15	-0.2
1937	Bro-N	11	10	0	1	1	0	0	2	1	1	.100	.182	.200	4	-1	0			.000	0	H	-0.1
Total	2	86	81	8	20	4	0	0	18	10	8	.247	.337	.296	71	-3	0			.963	-1	/C-15	-0.3

■ GAVERN
Gavern Deb: 6/15/1874

YEAR	TM/L	G	AB	R	H	2B	3B	HR	RBI	BB	SO	AVG	OBP	SLG	PRO+	BR/A	SB	CS	SBR	FA	FR	G/POS	TPR
1874	Atl-n	1	4	1	0	0	0	0	0	0	0	.000	.000	.000	-99	-1	0	0	0	.750	2	/2-1	0.0

■ MIKE GAZELLA
Gazella, Michael b: 10/13/1896, Olyphant, Pa. d: 9/11/78, Odessa, Tex. BR/TR, 5'7.5", 165 lbs. Deb: 7/2/23

YEAR	TM/L	G	AB	R	H	2B	3B	HR	RBI	BB	SO	AVG	OBP	SLG	PRO+	BR/A	SB	CS	SBR	FA	FR	G/POS	TPR
1923	NY-A	8	13	2	1	0	0	0	1	2	3	.077	.200	.077	-25	-2	0	0	0	1.000	-1	/S-4,2-3,3-2	-0.3
1926	*NY-A	66	168	21	39	6	0	0	20	25	24	.232	.335	.268	60	-9	2	2	-1	.913	-4	3-45,S-11	-1.0
1927	NY-A	54	115	17	32	8	4	0	9	23	16	.278	.403	.417	117	4	4	1	1	.961	-6	3-44/S-6	0.0
1928	NY-A	32	56	11	13	0	0	0	2	6	7	.232	.317	.232	48	-4	2	1	0	.969	-1	3-16/2-4,S-3	-0.4
Total	4	160	352	51	85	14	4	0	32	56	50	.241	.350	.304	73	-12	8	4	0	.940	-12	3-107/S-24,2-6	-1.7

■ DALE GEAR
Gear, Dale Dudley b: 2/2/1872, Lone Elm, Kan. d: 9/23/51, Topeka, Kan. BR/TR, 5'11", 165 lbs. Deb: 8/15/1896

YEAR	TM/L	G	AB	R	H	2B	3B	HR	RBI	BB	SO	AVG	OBP	SLG	PRO+	BR/A	SB	CS	SBR	FA	FR	G/POS	TPR
1896	Cle-N	4	15	5	6	1	1	0	3	1	1	.400	.438	.600	163	1	0			.857	-1	/P-3,1-1	0.0
1897	Cle-N	7	24	3	4	1	0	0	2		3	.167	.286	.208	30	-2	2			.750	0	/O-6	-0.2
1901	Was-A	58	199	17	47	9	2	0	20		4	.236	.267	.302	54	-13	2			.944	1	O-35,P-24	-1.0
Total	3	69	238	25	57	11	3	0	25	8	1	.239	.267	.311	59	-14	4			.900	0	/O-41,P-27,1-1	-1.2

■ GARY GEARHART
Gearhart, Lloyd William b: 8/10/23, New Lebanon, Ohio BR/TL, 5'11", 180 lbs. Deb: 4/18/47

YEAR	TM/L	G	AB	R	H	2B	3B	HR	RBI	BB	SO	AVG	OBP	SLG	PRO+	BR/A	SB	CS	SBR	FA	FR	G/POS	TPR
1947	NY-N	73	179	26	44	9	0	6	17	17	30	.246	.315	.397	87	-4	1			.961	-1	O-44	-0.7

■ HUCK GEARY
Geary, Eugene Francis Joseph b: 1/22/17, Buffalo, N.Y. d: 1/27/81, Cuba, N.Y. BL/TL, 5'10.5", 170 lbs. Deb: 7/17/42

YEAR	TM/L	G	AB	R	H	2B	3B	HR	RBI	BB	SO	AVG	OBP	SLG	PRO+	BR/A	SB	CS	SBR	FA	FR	G/POS	TPR
1942	Pit-N	9	22	3	5	0	0	0	0	2	4	.227	.292	.227	52	-1	0			.939	0	/S-8	-0.1
1943	Pit-N	46	166	17	25	4	0	1	13	18	6	.151	.234	.193	23	-16	3			.956	-6	S-46	-2.1
Total	2	55	188	20	30	4	0	1	15	20	9	.160	.240	.197	26	-17	3			.954	-6	/S-54	-2.2

■ ELMER GEDEON
Gedeon, Elmer John b: 4/15/17, Cleveland, Ohio d: 4/20/44, St.Pol, France BR/TR, 6'4", 196 lbs. Deb: 9/18/39

YEAR	TM/L	G	AB	R	H	2B	3B	HR	RBI	BB	SO	AVG	OBP	SLG	PRO+	BR/A	SB	CS	SBR	FA	FR	G/POS	TPR
1939	Was-A	5	15	1	3	0	0	0	1	2	5	.200	.294	.200	31	-1	0	0	0	1.000	1	/O-5	-0.1

■ JOE GEDEON
Gedeon, Elmer Joseph b: 12/5/1893, Sacramento, Cal. d: 5/19/41, San Francisco, Cal BR/TR, 6', 167 lbs. Deb: 5/13/13

YEAR	TM/L	G	AB	R	H	2B	3B	HR	RBI	BB	SO	AVG	OBP	SLG	PRO+	BR/A	SB	CS	SBR	FA	FR	G/POS	TPR
1913	Was-A	29	71	3	13	1	3	0	6	1	6	.183	.205	.282	41	-6	3			.929	0	O-15/3-7,2-2,S-2,P	-0.4
1914	Was-A	4	2	0	0	0	0	0	1	0	1	.000	.333	.000	1	-0	0			.667	-1	/O-4	-0.1
1916	NY-A	122	435	50	92	14	4	0	27	40	61	.211	.282	.262	62	-20	14			.955	-10	*2-122	-2.9
1917	NY-A	33	117	15	28	7	0	0	8	7	13	.239	.288	.299	78	-3	4			.983	4	2-31	0.2
1918	StL-A	123	441	39	94	14	3	1	41	27	29	.213	.271	.265	64	-20	7			.977	16	*2-123	0.4
1919	StL-A	120	437	57	111	13	4	0	50	35		.254	.340	.302	79	-11	4			.975	-3	*2-118	-0.8
1920	StL-A	153	606	95	177	33	6	0	61	55	36	.292	.355	.366	89	-9	3	3	-2	.964	-26	*2-153	-3.1
Total	7	584	2109	259	515	82	20	1	171	180	181	.244	.311	.303	75	-69	33	3		.969	-18	2-549/O-19,3-7,SP	-6.7

■ RICH GEDMAN
Gedman, Richard Leo b: 9/26/59, Worcester, Mass. BL/TR, 6', 215 lbs. Deb: 9/7/80

YEAR	TM/L	G	AB	R	H	2B	3B	HR	RBI	BB	SO	AVG	OBP	SLG	PRO+	BR/A	SB	CS	SBR	FA	FR	G/POS	TPR
1980	Bos-A	9	24	2	5	0	0	0	1	0	5	.208	.208	.208	14	-3	0	0	0	.867	-0	/C-2,D-4	-0.3
1981	Bos-A	62	205	22	59	15	0	5	26	9	31	.288	.321	.434	109	2	0	0	0	.990	-2	C-59	0.2
1982	Bos-A	92	289	30	72	17	2	4	26	10	37	.249	.279	.363	71	-12	0	1	-1	.977	-7	C-86	-1.7
1983	Bos-A	81	204	21	60	16	1	2	18	15	37	.294	.345	.412	100	0	0	1	-0	.980	-3	C-68	0.0
1984	Bos-A	133	449	54	121	26	4	24	72	29	72	.269	.315	.506	118	9	0	0	1	.977	-8	*C-125	0.7
1985	Bos-A★	144	498	66	147	30	5	18	80	50	79	.295	.363	.484	124	17	2	0	1	.983	4	*C-139	2.7
1986	*Bos-A★	135	462	49	119	29	0	16	65	37	61	.258	.318	.424	100	-1	1	0	0	.994	10	*C-134	1.8
1987	Bos-A	52	151	11	31	8	0	1	13	10	24	.205	.255	.278	49	-13	0	0	0	.976	-4	C-51	-1.3
1988	*Bos-A	95	299	33	69	14	0	9	39	18	49	.231	.281	.368	77	-10	0	0	0	.992	2	C-93/D-1	-0.1
1989	Bos-A	93	260	24	55	9	0	4	16	23	47	.212	.276	.292	57	-15	0	1	-1	.981	-0	C-91	-1.2
1990	Bos-A	10	15	3	3	0	0	0	0	0	6	.200	.429	.200	78	0	0	0	0	.970	-1	/C-9	0.1
	Hou-N	40	104	4	21	7	0	1	10	15	20	.202	.303	.298	68	-4	0	0	0	1.000	6	C-39	0.4
1991	StL-N	46	94	7	10	4	0	0	8	8	15	.106	.143	.213	-1	-13	0	1	-1	.976	10	C-43	-0.2
1992	StL-N	41	105	5	23	4	0	1	8	11	22	.219	.293	.286	67	-5	0	0	0	.988	11	C-40	0.8
Total	13	1033	3159	331	795	176	12	88	382	236	509	.252	.307	.399	90	-48	3	4	-2	.984	20	C-979/D-5	1.9

■ COUNT GEDNEY
Gedney, Alfred W. b: 5/10/1849, Brooklyn, N.Y. d: 3/26/22, Hackensack, N.J. 5'9", 140 lbs. Deb: 4/27/1872

YEAR	TM/L	G	AB	R	H	2B	3B	HR	RBI	BB	SO	AVG	OBP	SLG	PRO+	BR/A	SB	CS	SBR	FA	FR	G/POS	TPR
1872	Tro-n	9	47	14	20	3	0	3	18	0		.426	.426	.681	232	7	1	0	0	.933	-1	O-9	0.4
	Eck-n	18	71	4	13	1	0	0	7	0	1	.183	.183	.197	20	-6	2	1	0	.911	0	O-18	-0.2
	Yr	27	118	18	33	4	0	3	25	0	1	.280	.280	.390	115	1	3	1	0	.915	-1	O-27	0.2
1873	Mut-n	53	224	41	60	5	5	1	25	7	5	.268	.290	.348	89	-3	1	0	0	.867	15	*O-53	1.0
1874	Ath-n	54	222	49	61	4	1	1	34	7	11	.275	.297	.315	89	-4	2	2	1	.822	-3	*O-51/1-4	-0.4
1875	Mut-n	68	267	30	55	12	2	0	17	0	8	.206	.206	.266	59	-11	2	3	1	.843	12	*O-67/P-2	0.1
Total	4 n	202	831	138	209	25	8	5	101	14	25	.252	.264	.319	83	-17	8	6	-1	.853	25	O-198/1-4,P-2	0.8

■ BILLY GEER
Geer, William Henry Harrison (b: George Harrison Geer) b: 8/13/1849, Syracuse, N.Y. TR, 5'8", 160 lbs. Deb: 10/15/1874

YEAR	TM/L	G	AB	R	H	2B	3B	HR	RBI	BB	SO	AVG	OBP	SLG	PRO+	BR/A	SB	CS	SBR	FA	FR	G/POS	TPR
1874	Mut-n	2	8	0	2	0	0	0	0			.250	.250	.250	59	-0	0			.889	2	/O-2	0.1
1875	NH-n	37	164	20	40	4	1	0	9	1	0	.244	.248	.280	96	0	2	2	-1	.765	3	O-17,2-13/S-6,13	0.2
1878	Cin-N	61	237	31	52	13	2	0	20	10	18	.219	.251	.291	86	-3				.867	-4	*S-60/2-2	-0.4
1880	Wor-N	2	6	0	0	0	0	0	0	0	0	.000	.000	.000	-92	-1				1.000	-1	/O-1,S-1	-0.2
1884	Phi-U	9	36	7	9	2	1	0	0		4	.250	.325	.361	116	-0				.772	1	/S-9	0.1

YEAR	TM/L	G	AB	R	H	2B	3B	HR	RBI	BB	SO	AVG	OBP	SLG	PRO+	BR/A	SB	CS	SBR	FA	FR	G/POS	TPR
	Bro-a	107	391	68	82	15	7	0		38		.210	.281	.284	84	-6				.870	17	*S-107/P-2,2-2	1.1
1885	Lou-a	14	51	2	6	2	0	0	3	2		.118	.167	.157	3	-6				.872	2	S-14	-0.3
Total	2 n	39	172	20	42	4	1	0	10	1	4	.244	.249	.279	93	-0	2	2	-1	.791	5	/O-19,2-13,S-6,31	0.3
Total	4	193	721	108	149	32	10	0	23	54	18	.207	.264	.279	79	-15				.864	15	S-191/2-4,P-2,O-1	0.3

■ LOU GEHRIG
Gehrig, Henry Louis "The Iron Horse" b: 6/19/03, New York, N.Y. d: 6/2/41, Riverdale, N.Y. BL/TL, 6′, 200 lbs. Deb: 6/15/23 H

YEAR	TM/L	G	AB	R	H	2B	3B	HR	RBI	BB	SO	AVG	OBP	SLG	PRO+	BR/A	SB	CS	SBR	FA	FR	G/POS	TPR
1923	NY-A	13	26	6	11	4	1	1	9	2	5	.423	.464	.769	217	4	0	0	0	.933	-1	/1-9	0.3
1924	NY-A	10	12	2	6	1	0	0	5	1	3	.500	.538	.583	190	2	0	0	0	1.000	0	/1-2,O-1	0.1
1925	NY-A	126	437	73	129	23	10	20	68	46	49	.295	.365	.531	127	15	6	3	0	.989	-9	*1-114/O-6	-0.1
1926	*NY-A	155	572	135	179	47	**20**	16	112	105	73	.313	.420	.549	154	46	6	5	-1	.991	-8	*1-155	2.6
1927	*NY-A	155	584	149	218	**52**	18	47	**175**	109	84	.373	.474	.765	224	**107**	10	8	-2	.992	-6	*1-155	8.1
1928	*NY-A	154	562	139	210	47	13	27	**142**	95	69	.374	**.467**	.648	197	81	4	11	-5	.989	-8	*1-154	5.1
1929	NY-A	154	553	127	166	32	10	35	126	122	68	.300	.431	.584	170	61	4	4	-1	.994	-5	*1-154	3.7
1930	NY-A	154	581	143	220	42	17	41	**174**	101	63	.379	.473	.721	207	97	12	14	-5	.989	1	*1-153/O-1	6.9
1931	NY-A	155	619	**163**	**211**	31	15	**46**	**184**	117	56	.341	.446	.662	199	90	17	12	-2	.991	-10	*1-154/O-1	5.8
1932	*NY-A	156	596	138	208	42	9	34	151	108	38	.349	.451	.621	184	77	4	11	-5	.987	-6	*1-156	4.9
1933	NY-A★	152	593	**138**	198	41	12	32	139	92	42	.334	.424	.605	181	68	9	13	-5	.993	-3	*1-152	4.3
1934	NY-A★	154	579	128	210	40	6	**49**	165	109	31	**.363**	**.465**	**.706**	213	98	9	5	-0	.994	-1	*1-153/S-1	**7.8**
1935	NY-A★	149	535	**125**	176	26	10	30	119	**132**	38	.329	**.466**	.583	180	70	8	7	-2	.990	0	*1-149	4.8
1936	*NY-A★	155	579	**167**	205	37	7	**49**	152	**130**	46	.354	**.478**	**.696**	193	89	3	4	-2	.994	1	*1-155	**6.4**
1937	*NY-A★	157	569	138	200	37	9	37	159	**127**	49	.351	**.473**	.643	177	72	4	3	-1	.989	-6	*1-157	4.3
1938	*NY-A★	157	576	115	170	32	6	29	114	107	75	.295	.410	.523	133	30	6	1	1	.991	-1	*1-157	1.2
1939	NY-A†	8	28	2	4	0	0	0	1	5	1	.143	.273	.143	9	-4	0	0	0	.971	-1	/1-8	-0.5
Total	17	2164	8001	1888	2721	534	163	493	1995	1508	790	.340	.447	.632	182	1005	102	101	-30	.991	-60	*1-2137/O-9,S-1	65.7

■ CHARLIE GEHRINGER
Gehringer, Charles Leonard "The Mechanical Man" b: 5/11/03, Fowlerville, Mich. d: 1/21/93, Bloomfield Hills, Mich. BL/TR, 5′11″, 180 lbs. Deb: 9/22/24 CH

YEAR	TM/L	G	AB	R	H	2B	3B	HR	RBI	BB	SO	AVG	OBP	SLG	PRO+	BR/A	SB	CS	SBR	FA	FR	G/POS	TPR
1924	Det-A	5	13	2	6	0	0	0	1	0	2	.462	.462	.462	141	1	1	1	-0	.967	4	/2-5	0.4
1925	Det-A	8	18	3	3	0	0	0	0	2	0	.167	.250	.167	7	-3	0	1	-1	1.000	4	/2-6	0.0
1926	Det-A	123	459	62	127	19	17	1	48	30	42	.277	.322	.399	86	-11	9	7	-2	.973	-10	*2-112/3-6	-1.8
1927	Det-A	133	508	110	161	29	11	4	61	52	31	.317	.383	.441	112	9	17	8	0	.965	20	*2-121	3.1
1928	Det-A	154	603	108	193	29	16	6	74	69	22	.320	.395	.451	120	19	15	9	-1	.962	4	*2-154	2.3
1929	Det-A	155	634	**131**	**215**	**45**	**19**	13	106	64	19	.339	.405	.532	139	36	**27**	9	**3**	**.975**	-3	*2-154	3.9
1930	Det-A	154	610	144	201	47	15	16	98	69	17	.330	.404	.534	133	31	19	15	-3	**.979**	2	*2-154	3.4
1931	Det-A	101	383	67	119	24	5	4	53	29	15	.311	.359	.431	103	1	13	4	2	.979	-1	2-78/1-9	0.6
1932	Det-A	152	618	112	184	44	11	19	107	68	34	.298	.370	.497	118	15	9	8	-2	.967	-1	*2-152	1.8
1933	Det-A★	155	628	103	204	42	6	12	105	68	27	.325	.393	.468	125	23	5	4	-1	.981	7	*2-155	3.6
1934	*Det-A★	154	601	**134**	**214**	50	7	11	127	99	25	.356	.450	.517	149	47	11	8	-2	.981	7	*2-154	5.7
1935	*Det-A★	150	610	123	201	32	8	19	108	79	16	.330	.409	.502	139	36	11	4	1	**.985**	3	*2-149	4.7
1936	Det-A★	154	641	144	227	**60**	12	15	116	83	13	.354	.431	.555	141	43	4	1	1	**.974**	16	*2-154	6.1
1937	Det-A★	144	564	133	209	40	1	14	96	90	25	**.371**	.458	.520	143	41	11	4	1	**.986**	6	*2-142	5.2
1938	Det-A★	152	568	133	174	32	5	20	107	113	21	.306	.425	.486	121	21	14	1	**4**	.976	-2	*2-152	3.0
1939	Det-A	118	406	86	132	29	6	16	86	68	16	.325	.423	.544	135	22	4	3	-1	**.977**	7	*2-107	2.6
1940	*Det-A	139	515	108	161	33	3	10	81	101	17	.313	.428	.447	116	16	10	0	3	.972	-20	*2-138	0.8
1941	Det-A	127	436	65	96	19	4	3	46	95	26	.220	.363	.303	71	-16	1	2	-1	**.982**	-3	*2-116	-1.1
1942	Det-A	45	45	6	12	0	0	1	7	7	4	.267	.365	.333	90	-0	0	0	0	1.000	1	/2-3	0.1
Total	19	2323	8860	1774	2839	574	146	184	1427	1186	372	.320	.404	.480	123	332	181	89	1	.976	33	*2-2206/1-9,3-6	44.4

■ PHIL GEIER
Geier, Philip Louis "Little Phil" b: 11/3/1875, Washington, D.C. d: 9/25/67, Spokane, Wash. BL/TR, 5′7″, 145 lbs. Deb: 8/17/1896

YEAR	TM/L	G	AB	R	H	2B	3B	HR	RBI	BB	SO	AVG	OBP	SLG	PRO+	BR/A	SB	CS	SBR	FA	FR	G/POS	TPR
1896	Phi-N	17	56	12	13	1	0	0	6	6	7	.232	.317	.268	56	-3	3			.813	-2	O-12/2-3,C-2	-0.5
1897	Phi-N	92	316	51	88	6	2	1	35	56		.278	.392	.320	91	-0	19			.932	-7	O-45,2-37/S-6,3-2	-0.7
1900	Cin-N	30	113	18	29	1	4	0	10	7		.257	.306	.336	79	-3	3			.941	0	O-27/3-2	-0.4
1901	Phi-A	50	211	42	49	5	2	0	23	24		.232	.314	.275	61	-11	7			.934	-5	O-50/S-2,3-1	-1.7
	Mil-A	11	39	4	7	1	1	0	1	5		.179	.273	.256	50	-3	4			1.000	-1	/O-8,3-3	-0.4
	Yr	61	250	46	56	6	3	0	24	29		.224	.307	.272	60	-13	11			.941	-6	O-58/3-4,S-2	-2.1
1904	Bos-N	149	580	70	141	17	2	1	27	56		.243	.314	.284	88	-6	18			.933	-3	*O-137/3-7,2-5,S-1	-1.8
Total	5	349	1315	197	327	30	12	2	102	154	7	.249	.332	.294	81	-27	54			.932	-16	O-279/2-45,3-15,SC	-5.5

■ GARY GEIGER
Geiger, Gary Merle b: 4/4/37, Sand Ridge, Ill. d: 4/24/96, Murphysboro, Ill. BL/TR, 6′, 168 lbs. Deb: 4/15/58

YEAR	TM/L	G	AB	R	H	2B	3B	HR	RBI	BB	SO	AVG	OBP	SLG	PRO+	BR/A	SB	CS	SBR	FA	FR	G/POS	TPR
1958	Cle-A	91	195	28	45	3	1	6	27	14	51	.231	.333	.272	70	-7	2	2	-1	.986	4	O-53/3-2,P-1	-0.6
1959	Bos-A	120	335	45	82	10	4	11	48	21	55	.245	.289	.397	83	-9	9	3	1	.989	-10	O-95	-2.3
1960	Bos-A	77	245	32	74	13	6	9	33	23	38	.302	.369	.490	126	9	2	2	-1	1.000	4	O-66	0.9
1961	Bos-A	140	499	82	116	21	6	18	64	87	91	.232	.351	.407	99	1	16	4	2	.988	10	*O-137	0.5
1962	Bos-A	131	466	67	116	18	4	16	54	67	66	.249	.346	.408	99	-0	18	11	-1	.987	4	*O-129	-0.1
1963	Bos-A	121	399	67	105	13	5	16	44	36	63	.263	.329	.441	110	5	9	4	0	.984	14	O-95/1-6	1.4
1964	Bos-A	5	13	5	5	0	1	0	1	2	2	.385	.467	.538	170	1	0	0	0	1.000	-0	/O-4	0.1
1965	Bos-A	24	45	5	9	3	0	1	2	13	10	.200	.379	.333	98	-1	0	3	0	.970	-3	O-16	0.1
1966	Atl-N	78	126	23	33	5	3	4	10	21	29	.262	.372	.444	124	5	4	1	-1	.982	-9	O-49	-0.6
1967	Atl-N	69	117	17	19	1	1	5	20	35		.162	.285	.214	45	-8	1	1	-0	.980	-6	O-38	-1.6
1969	Hou-N	93	125	19	28	4	1	0	16	24	34	.224	.353	.272	79	-2	3	1	-2	.968	-7	O-65	-1.2
1970	Hou-N	5	4	0	1	0	0	0	0	0	1	.250	.250	.250	36	-0	0	0	0	1.000	-1	/O-2	-0.1
Total	12	954	2569	388	633	91	29	77	283	341	466	.246	.339	.394	98	-6	62	29	1	.986	4	O-749/1-6,3-2,P-1	-3.5

■ BILL GEIS
Geis, William J. (b: William J. Geiss) b: 7/15/1858, Chicago, Ill. d: 9/18/24, Chicago, Ill. 5′10″, 164 lbs. Deb: 5/1/1884 F

YEAR	TM/L	G	AB	R	H	2B	3B	HR	RBI	BB	SO	AVG	OBP	SLG	PRO+	BR/A	SB	CS	SBR	FA	FR	G/POS	TPR
1884	Det-N	75	283	22	50	11	4	2	16	6	60	.177	.194	.265	46	-17				.862	-7	2-73/O-1,1-1,P-1	-2.0

■ EMIL GEISS
Geiss, Emil August b: 3/20/1867, Chicago, Ill. d: 10/4/11, Chicago, Ill. BR/TR, 5′11″, 170 lbs. Deb: 5/18/1887 F

YEAR	TM/L	G	AB	R	H	2B	3B	HR	RBI	BB	SO	AVG	OBP	SLG	PRO+	BR/A	SB	CS	SBR	FA	FR	G/POS	TPR
1887	Chi-N	3	12	0	1	0	0	0	0	0	7	.083	.083	.083	-47	-2	0			.571	-1	/2-1,1-1,P-1	-0.3

■ CHARLIE GELBERT
Gelbert, Charles Magnus b: 1/26/06, Scranton, Pa. d: 1/13/67, Easton, Pa. BR/TR, 5′11″, 170 lbs. Deb: 4/16/29

YEAR	TM/L	G	AB	R	H	2B	3B	HR	RBI	BB	SO	AVG	OBP	SLG	PRO+	BR/A	SB	CS	SBR	FA	FR	G/POS	TPR
1929	StL-N	146	512	60	134	29	8	3	65	51	46	.262	.329	.367	71	-23	8			.948	7	*S-146	0.1
1930	*StL-N	139	513	92	156	39	11	3	72	43	41	.304	.360	.441	89	-9	6			.947	9	*S-139	1.3
1931	*StL-N	131	447	61	129	29	5	1	62	54	31	.289	.365	.383	97	-0	7			.959	13	*S-130	2.5
1932	StL-N	122	455	60	122	28	9	1	45	39	30	.268	.330	.376	87	-8	8			.945	2	*S-122	0.3
1935	StL-N	62	168	24	49	7	2	2	17	18		.292	.357	.393	97	-0	0			.978	5	3-37,S-21/2-3	0.6
1936	StL-N	93	280	33	64	15	2	3	27	25	26	.229	.292	.329	67	-13	2			.965	3	3-60,S-28/2-8	-0.2
1937	Cin-N	43	114	12	22	4	0	1	13	15	12	.193	.287	.254	51	-8	1			.968	-2	S-37/2-9,3-1	-0.7
	Det-A	20	47	4	4	2	0	0	1	4		.085	.157	.128	-27	-9	0			.934	-0	S-16	-0.8
1939	Was-A	68	188	36	48	7	5	3	29	30	11	.255	.361	.394	100	0	2	0	0	.970	-3	S-28,3-20/2-1	0.0
1940	Was-A	22	54	7	20	7	1	0	7	4	3	.370	.424	.537	157	5	0	0	0	.920	1	S-12/P-2,2-1	0.3
	Bos-N	30	91	9	18	2	0	0	8	8	16	.198	.263	.220	25	-10	0	0	0	.926	5	3-29/S-1	-0.5
	Yr	52	145	16	38	9	1	0	15	12	19	.262	.323	.338	72	-6	0	0	0	.926	5	S-13/P-2,2-1	-0.2
Total	9	876	2869	398	766	169	43	17	350	290	245	.267	.336	.374	82	-76	34	0		.951	35	S-680,3-147/2-22,P	2.6

■ FRANK GENINS
Genins, C. Frank "Frenchy" b: 11/2/1866, St.Louis, Mo. d: 9/30/22, St.Louis, Mo. TR , Deb: 7/5/1892

YEAR	TM/L	G	AB	R	H	2B	3B	HR	RBI	BB	SO	AVG	OBP	SLG	PRO+	BR/A	SB	CS	SBR	FA	FR	G/POS	TPR
1892	Cin-N	35	110	12	20	4	0	0	7	12	12	.182	.262	.218	46	-7	7			.901	4	S-17,O-14/3-4	-0.2
	StL-N	15	51	5	10	1	0	0	4	1	11	.196	.212	.216	31	-4	3			.821	-8	S-14/O-1	-1.1
	Yr	50	161	17	30	5	0	0	11	13	23	.186	.247	.217	42	-11	10			.868	-3	S-31,O-15/3-4	-1.3
1895	Pit-N	73	252	43	63	8	0	2	24	22	14	.250	.315	.306	64	-13	19			.931	4	O-29,3-16,2-16/S1	-1.8
1901	Cle-A	26	101	15	23	5	0	0	9	8		.228	.284	.277	58	-6	3			.940	1	O-26	-0.6
Total	3	149	514	75	116	18	0	2	44	43	37	.226	.288	.272	56	-30	32			.934	-10	/O-70,S-39,3-20,21	-3.7

YEAR	TM/L	G	AB	R	H	2B	3B	HR	RBI	BB	SO	AVG	OBP	SLG	PRO+	BR/A	SB	CS	SBR	FA	FR	G/POS	TPR

■ **GEORGE GENOVESE**   Genovese, George Michael   b: 2/22/22, Staten Island, N.Y   BL/TR, 5'6.5", 160 lbs.   Deb: 4/29/50

| 1950 | Was-A | 3 | 1 | 1 | 0 | 0 | 0 | 0 | 0 | 1 | 0 | .000 | .500 | .000 | 39 | 0 | 0 | 0 | 0 | .000 | 0 | H | 0.0 |

■ **JIM GENTILE**   Gentile, James Edward "Diamond Jim"   b: 6/3/34, San Francisco, Cal.   BL/TL, 6'4", 215 lbs.   Deb: 9/10/57

1957	Bro-N	4	6	1	1	0	0	1	1	1	1	.167	.286	.667	133	0	0	0	0	1.000	-0	/1-2	0.0
1958	LA-N	12	30	0	4	1	0	0	4	4	6	.133	.235	.167	9	-4	0	0	0	.981	-1	/1-8	-0.6
1960	Bal-A★	138	384	67	112	17	0	21	98	68	72	.292	.407	.500	146	27	0	0	0	.993	-6	*1-124	1.2
1961	Bal-A★	148	486	96	147	25	2	46	141	96	106	.302	.428	.646	189	64	1	1	-0	.989	2	*1-144	5.3
1962	Bal-A★	152	545	80	137	21	1	33	87	77	100	.251	.351	.475	128	21	1	0	0	.988	6	*1-150	1.7
1963	Bal-A	145	496	65	123	16	1	24	72	76	101	.248	.355	.429	123	17	1	0	0	**.995**	7	*1-143	1.9
1964	KC-A	136	439	71	110	10	0	28	71	84	122	.251	.376	.465	128	19	0	0	0	.988	-0	*1-128	1.4
1965	KC-A	38	118	14	29	5	0	10	22	9	26	.246	.305	.542	138	5	0	0	0	.981	-1	1-35	0.2
	Hou-N	81	227	22	55	11	1	7	31	34	72	.242	.353	.392	118	6	0	0	0	.993	2	1-68	0.5
1966	Hou-N	49	144	16	35	6	1	7	18	21	39	.243	.355	.444	129	6	0	0	0	.989	2	1-43	0.6
	Cle-N	33	47	2	6	1	0	2	4	5	18	.128	.212	.277	39	-4	0	0	0	.944	-0	/1-9	-0.5
Total	9	936	2922	434	759	113	6	179	549	475	663	.260	.372	.486	137	157	3	1	0	.990	10	1-854	11.7

■ **SAM GENTILE**   Gentile, Samuel Christopher   b: 10/12/16, Charlestown, Mass.   BL/TR, 5'11", 180 lbs.   Deb: 4/24/43

| 1943 | Bos-N | 8 | 4 | 1 | 1 | 1 | 0 | 0 | 0 | 1 | 0 | .250 | .400 | .500 | 162 | 0 | 0 | 0 | | .000 | 0 | H | 0.0 |

■ **HARVEY GENTRY**   Gentry, Harvey William   b: 5/27/26, Winston-Salem, N.C   BL/TR, 6', 170 lbs.   Deb: 4/14/54   F

| 1954 | NY-N | 5 | 4 | 0 | 1 | 0 | 0 | 0 | 1 | 1 | 0 | .250 | .400 | .250 | 73 | -0 | 0 | 0 | 0 | .000 | 0 | H | 0.0 |

■ **ALEX GEORGE**   George, Alex Thomas M.   b: 9/27/38, Kansas City, Mo.   BL/TR, 5'11.5", 170 lbs.   Deb: 9/16/55

| 1955 | KC-A | 5 | 10 | 0 | 1 | 0 | 0 | 0 | 0 | 1 | 7 | .100 | .182 | .100 | -22 | -2 | 0 | 0 | 0 | .917 | -1 | /S-5 | -0.3 |

■ **GREEK GEORGE**   George, Charles Peter   b: 12/25/12, Waycross, Ga.   BR/TR, 6'2", 200 lbs.   Deb: 6/30/35

1935	Cle-A	2	0	0	0	0	0	0	0	0	0	—	—	—	—	0	0	0	0	1.000	0	/C-1	0.0
1936	Cle-A	23	77	3	15	3	0	0	5	9	16	.195	.279	.234	28	-9	0	0	0	.994	16	C-22	0.7
1938	Bro-N	7	20	0	4	1	0	0	2	0	4	.200	.200	.300	35	-2	0			1.000	2	/C-7	0.0
1941	Chi-N	35	64	4	10	2	0	0	6	2	10	.156	.182	.188	4	-8	0			.973	6	C-18	-0.5
1945	Phi-A	51	138	8	24	4	1	0	11	17	29	.174	.265	.217	41	-10	0	0	0	.972	-6	C-46	-1.5
Total	5	118	299	15	53	9	2	0	24	28	59	.177	.248	.221	29	-29	0	0	<u>0</u>	.983	14	/C-94	-1.3

■ **BILL GEORGE**   George, William M.   b: 1/27/1865, Bellaire, Ohio   d: 8/23/16, Wheeling, W.Va.   BR/TL, 5'8", 165 lbs.   Deb: 5/11/1887

1887	NY-N	13	53	6	9	0	0	0	5	1	6	.170	.185	.170	-1	-7	2			.854	1	P-13/O-1	0.0
1888	*NY-N	9	39	7	9	1	0	1	6	0	2	.231	.231	.333	79	-1	1			1.000	-1	/O-6,P-4	-0.2
1889	NY-N	3	15	1	4	0	0	0	0	0	3	.267	.267	.267	49	-1	1			.875	-0	/O-3	-0.1
	Col-a	5	17	1	4	0	0	0	3	1	1	.235	.278	.235	49	-1	1			.667	-1	/O-4,P-2	-0.2
Total	3	30	124	15	26	1	0	1	14	2	12	.210	.222	.242	36	-10	5			.860	-2	/P-19,O-14	-0.5

■ **BEN GERAGHTY**   Geraghty, Benjamin Raymond   b: 7/19/12, Jersey City, N.J.   d: 6/18/63, Jacksonville, Fla   BR/TR, 5'11", 175 lbs.   Deb: 4/17/36

1936	Bro-N	51	129	11	25	4	0	0	9	8	16	.194	.241	.225	26	-13	4			.922	-7	S-31/2-9,3-5	-1.8
1943	Bos-N	8	1	2	0	0	0	0	0	0	0	.000	.000	.000	-99	-0	0			1.000	1	/2-1,S-1,3-1	0.1
1944	Bos-N	11	16	3	4	0	0	0	0	1	2	.250	.294	.250	52	-1	0			1.000	0	/2-4,3-3	-0.1
Total	3	70	146	16	29	4	0	0	9	9	18	.199	.245	.226	28	-15	4			.922	-6	/S-32,2-14,3-9	-1.8

■ **CRAIG GERBER**   Gerber, Craig Stuart   b: 1/8/59, Chicago, Ill.   BL/TR, 6', 175 lbs.   Deb: 4/11/85

| 1985 | Cal-A | 65 | 91 | 8 | 24 | 1 | 2 | 0 | 6 | 2 | 3 | .264 | .280 | .319 | 64 | -5 | 0 | 3 | -2 | .970 | 19 | S-53/3-9,2-1,D-1 | 1.4 |

■ **WALLY GERBER**   Gerber, Walter "Spooks"   b: 8/18/1891, Columbus, Ohio   d: 6/19/51, Columbus, Ohio   BR/TR, 5'10", 152 lbs.   Deb: 9/23/14

1914	Pit-N	17	54	5	13	1	1	0	5	2	8	.241	.281	.296	75	-2	0			.921	1	S-17	0.0
1915	Pit-N	56	144	8	28	2	0	0	7	9	16	.194	.252	.208	40	-10	6	1	1	.930	2	3-23,S-21/2-2	-0.5
1917	StL-A	14	39	2	12	1	1	0	2	3	2	.308	.357	.385	131	1	1			.939	-2	S-12/2-2	0.0
1918	StL-A	56	171	10	41	4	0	0	10	19	11	.240	.316	.263	77	-4	2			.922	-9	S-56	-1.2
1919	StL-A	140	462	43	105	14	6	1	37	49	36	.227	.308	.290	67	-20	1			.940	-8	*S-140	-2.1
1920	StL-A	154	584	70	163	26	2	2	60	58	32	.279	.346	.341	80	-16	4	13	-7	.939	7	*S-154	-0.2
1921	StL-A	114	436	55	121	12	9	2	48	34	19	.278	.337	.360	73	-18	4	7	-3	.943	-3	*S-113	-1.2
1922	StL-A	153	604	81	161	22	8	1	51	52	34	.267	.326	.334	70	-26	6	4	-1	.944	0	*S-153	-1.1
1923	StL-A	154	605	85	170	26	3	1	62	54	50	.281	.342	.339	75	-21	4	6	-2	.950	6	*S-154	-0.2
1924	StL-A	148	496	61	135	20	4	0	55	43	34	.272	.341	.329	69	-22	4	5	-2	.946	-7	*S-147	-1.4
1925	StL-A	72	246	29	67	13	1	0	19	26	15	.272	.344	.333	69	-11	1	2	-1	.949	5	S-71	-0.6
1926	StL-A	131	411	37	111	8	0	0	42	40	29	.270	.339	.290	62	-21	0	2	-1	.944	3	*S-129	-0.6
1927	StL-A	142	438	44	98	13	9	0	45	35	25	.224	.284	.295	49	-34	3	6	-3	.946	9	*S-141/3-1	-1.3
1928	StL-A	6	18	1	5	1	0	0	1	3		.278	.316	.333	69	-1	0			.783	-2	/S-6	-0.2
	Bos-A	104	300	21	64	6	1	0	28	32	31	.213	.289	.240	41	-25	6	1	1	.955	34	*S-103	1.9
	Yr	110	318	22	69	7	1	0	28	33	34	.217	.291	.245	43	-26	6	1	1	.948	**32**	*S-109	1.7
1929	Bos-A	61	91	6	15	3	1	0	5	8	12	.165	.232	.220	17	-11	1	0	0	.937	-0	S-30,2-22	0.5
Total	15	1522	5099	558	1309	172	46	7	476	465	357	.257	.323	.313	67	-241	43	<u>47</u>		.943	52	*S-1447/2-26,3-24	-7.6

■ **BOB GEREN**   Geren, Robert Peter   b: 9/22/61, San Diego, Cal.   BR/TR, 6'3", 205 lbs.   Deb: 5/17/88

1988	NY-A	10	10	0	1	0	0	0	2	0	3	.100	.250	.100	2	-1	0	0	0	1.000	1	C-10	0.0
1989	NY-A	65	205	26	59	5	1	9	27	12	44	.288	.330	.454	120	5	0	0	0	.991	0	C-60/D-2	0.9
1990	NY-A	110	277	21	59	7	0	8	31	13	73	.213	.261	.325	63	-14	0	0	0	.993	9	*C-107/D-1	0.3
1991	NY-A	64	128	7	28	6	0	2	12	9	31	.219	.270	.289	55	-8	0	0	-1	.989	9	C-63	0.2
1993	SD-N	58	145	8	31	6	0	3	6	13	28	.214	.278	.317	58	-9	0	0	0	.993	4	C-49/1-1,3-1	0.2
Total	5	307	765	62	178	21	1	22	76	49	179	.233	.284	.349	74	-28	0	1	-1	.992	26	C-289/D-3,3-1,1-1	1.2

■ **JOE GERHARDT**   Gerhardt, John Joseph "Move Up Joe"   b: 2/14/1855, Washington, D.C.   d: 3/11/22, Middletown, N.Y.   BR/TR, 6', 160 lbs.   Deb: 9/1/1873   M

1873	Was-n	13	56	6	12	3	0	0	7	0	5	.214	.214	.268	44	-4	0	0	0	.700	-5	S-13	-0.7
1874	Bal-n	14	61	10	19	0	1	0	6	0	0	.311	.311	.344	111	1	0	0	0	.750	3	S-14	0.3
1875	Mut-n	58	252	29	54	7	3	0	20	0	2	.214	.214	.266	62	-10	0	5	-3	.753	-1	3-47,2-13/S-1,O-1	-1.2
1876	Lou-N	65	292	33	76	10	3	2	18	3	5	.260	.268	.336	85	-8				.944	5	*1-54/2-5,S-3,O3	-0.3
1877	Lou-N	59	250	41	76	6	5	1	35	5	8	.304	.318	.380	101	-2				.888	20	*2-57/O-1,S-1,1-1	1.7
1878	Cin-N	60	259	46	77	7	2	0	28	7	14	.297	.316	.340	127	8				.906	5	*2-60	1.6
1879	Cin-N	79	313	22	62	12	3	1	39	3	19	.198	.206	.265	57	-14				.908	3	2-55,3-16/1-8,S-1	-0.3
1881	Det-N	80	297	35	72	13	6	0	36	7	31	.242	.260	.327	80	-7				.908	8	2-79/3-1	0.3
1883	Lou-a	78	319	56	84	11	9	0		14		.263	.294	.354	116	7				.906	20	*2-78,M	2.4
1884	Lou-a	106	404	39	89	7	8	0	40	13		.220	.254	.277	76	-10				.920	27	*2-106	1.8
1885	NY-N	112	399	43	62	12	2	0	33	24	47	.155	.203	.195	30	-30				.911	11	*2-112	-1.4
1886	NY-N	123	426	44	81	11	7	0	40	22	63	.190	.230	.249	45	-28	8			.924	14	*2-123	-0.8
1887	NY-N	1	4	0	0	0	0	0	0	0	0	.000	.000	.000	-99	-1	0			1.000	0	/3-1	-0.1
	NY-a	85	307	40	68	13	2	0	27	24		.221	.280	.277	58	-17	15			.896	15	2-84/3-1	0.3
1890	Bro-a	99	369	34	75	10	4	2	40	30		.203	.270	.268	61	-18	9			.938	37	*2-99	2.1
	StL-a	37	125	15	32	0	0	1	11	9		.256	.321	.280	68	-6	5			.955	5	2-20,3-17,M	0.1
	Yr	136	494	49	107	10	4	3	51	39		.217	.283	.271	63	-24	14			**.940**	**42**	*2-119,3-17	2.2
1891	Lou-a	2	6	0	0	0	0	0	0	1	0	.000	.143	.000	-99	-1	0			.833	-0	/2-2	-0.1
Total	3 n	85	369	45	85	10	4	0	33	0	7	.230	.230	.279	67	-13	0	5	-3	.732	-2	/3-47,S-28,2-13,O-1	-1.6
Total	12	986	3770	448	854	112	51	7	<u>347</u>	162	<u>187</u>	.227	.261	.289	72	-127	37			.913	173	2-880/1-63,3-38,SO	7.0

■ **KEN GERHART**   Gerhart, Harold Kenneth   b: 5/19/61, Charleston, S.C.   BR/TR, 6', 190 lbs.   Deb: 9/14/86

| 1986 | Bal-A | 20 | 69 | 4 | 16 | 2 | 0 | 1 | 7 | 4 | 18 | .232 | .274 | .304 | 58 | -4 | 1 | 1 | -1 | .971 | -3 | O-20 | -0.8 |

YEAR	TM/L	G	AB	R	H	2B	3B	HR	RBI	BB	SO	AVG	OBP	SLG	PRO+	BR/A	SB	CS	SBR	FA	FR	G/POS	TPR
1987	Bal-A	92	284	41	69	10	2	14	34	17	53	.243	.288	.440	92	-4	9	2	2	.973	-6	O-91	-1.1
1988	Bal-A	103	262	27	51	10	1	9	23	21	57	.195	.260	.344	69	-11	7	3	0	.975	-8	O-93/D-3	-2.1
Total	3	215	615	72	136	22	3	24	64	42	128	.221	.274	.384	79	-20	16	6	1	.974	-16	O-204/D-3	-4.0

■ GEORGE GERKEN
Gerken, George Herbert "Pickles"   b: 7/28/03, Chicago, Ill.   d: 10/23/77, Arcadia, Cal.   BR/TR, 5'11.5", 175 lbs.   Deb: 4/19/27

YEAR	TM/L	G	AB	R	H	2B	3B	HR	RBI	BB	SO	AVG	OBP	SLG	PRO+	BR/A	SB	CS	SBR	FA	FR	G/POS	TPR
1927	Cle-A	6	14	1	3	0	0	0	2	1	3	.214	.267	.214	26	-2	0	0	0	.917	0	/O-5	-0.2
1928	Cle-A	38	115	16	26	7	2	0	9	12	22	.226	.305	.348	64	-6	3	3	-1	.940	-1	O-34	-1.0
Total	2	44	129	17	29	7	2	0	11	13	25	.225	.301	.310	60	-8	3	3	-1	.937	-1	/O-39	-1.2

■ JOHNNY GERLACH
Gerlach, John Glenn   b: 5/11/17, Shullsburg, Wis.   BR/TR, 5'9", 165 lbs.   Deb: 9/3/38

YEAR	TM/L	G	AB	R	H	2B	3B	HR	RBI	BB	SO	AVG	OBP	SLG	PRO+	BR/A	SB	CS	SBR	FA	FR	G/POS	TPR
1938	Chi-A	9	25	2	7	0	0	0	1	4	2	.280	.379	.280	66	-1	0	0	0	.949	1	/S-8	0.0
1939	Chi-A	3	2	0	2	0	0	0	0	0	0	1.000	1.000	1.000	402	1	0	0	0	1.000	0	/3-1	0.1
Total	2	12	27	2	9	0	0	0	1	4	2	.333	.419	.333	89	-0	0	0	0	.949	1	/S-8,3-1	0.1

■ DICK GERNERT
Gernert, Richard Edward   b: 9/28/28, Reading, Pa.   BR/TR, 6'3", 210 lbs.   Deb: 4/16/52   C

YEAR	TM/L	G	AB	R	H	2B	3B	HR	RBI	BB	SO	AVG	OBP	SLG	PRO+	BR/A	SB	CS	SBR	FA	FR	G/POS	TPR
1952	Bos-A	102	367	58	89	20	2	19	67	35	83	.243	.317	.463	107	2	4	1	1	.987	-1	1-99	-0.3
1953	Bos-A	139	494	73	125	15	1	21	71	88	82	.253	.371	.415	106	6	0	7	-4	.986	-3	*1-136	-0.6
1954	Bos-A	14	23	2	6	2	0	0	1	6	4	.261	.414	.348	99	0	0	0	0	1.000	-1	/1-6	-0.1
1955	Bos-A	7	20	6	4	2	0	0	1	1	5	.200	.238	.300	40	-2	0	0	0	.974	-0	/1-5	-0.2
1956	Bos-A	106	306	53	89	11	0	16	68	56	57	.291	.404	.484	119	9	1	0	0	.985	-1	O-50,1-37	0.5
1957	Bos-A	99	316	45	75	13	3	14	58	39	62	.237	.327	.430	99	-1	1	1	-0	.989	-2	1-71,O-16	-0.8
1958	Bos-A	122	431	59	102	19	1	20	69	59	78	.237	.331	.425	100	-0	2	0	1	.991	8	*1-114	0.1
1959	Bos-A	117	298	41	78	14	1	11	42	52	49	.262	.371	.426	113	6	1	2	-1	.995	3	1-75,O-25	0.4
1960	Chi-N	52	96	8	24	3	0	0	11	10	19	.250	.321	.281	67	-4	1	0	0	.987	3	1-18/O-5	-0.2
	Det-A	21	50	6	15	4	0	1	5	4	5	.300	.352	.440	110	1	0	0	0	1.000	0	1-13/O-6	-0.2
1961	Det-A	6	5	1	1	0	0	1	1	1	2	.200	.333	.800	187	1	0	0	0	.000	0	H	0.1
	*Cin-N	40	63	4	19	1	0	0	7	7	9	.302	.371	.317	84	-1	0	0	0	.993	3	1-21	-0.2
1962	Hou-N	10	24	1	5	0	0	0	1	5	7	.208	.345	.208	57	-1	0	0	0	1.000	-1	/1-9	-0.2
Total	11	835	2493	357	632	104	8	103	402	363	462	.254	.352	.426	104	15	10	11	-4	.990	9	1-604,O-102	-1.4

■ CESAR GERONIMO
Geronimo, Cesar Francisco (Zorrilla)   b: 3/11/48, ElSeibo, D.R.   BL/TL, 6'2", 170 lbs.   Deb: 4/16/69

YEAR	TM/L	G	AB	R	H	2B	3B	HR	RBI	BB	SO	AVG	OBP	SLG	PRO+	BR/A	SB	CS	SBR	FA	FR	G/POS	TPR
1969	Hou-N	28	8	8	2	1	0	0	0	0	3	.250	.250	.375	74	-0	0	0	0	1.000	-3	/O-9	-0.3
1970	Hou-N	47	37	5	9	0	0	0	2	2	5	.243	.300	.243	49	-3	0	0	0	.920	-6	O-26	-0.9
1971	Hou-N	94	82	13	18	2	2	1	6	5	31	.220	.264	.329	69	-4	2	2	-1	.977	-16	O-64	-2.2
1972	*Cin-N	120	255	32	70	9	7	4	29	24	64	.275	.344	.412	121	7	2	7	-4	.982	-10	*O-106	-1.1
1973	*Cin-N	139	324	35	68	14	3	4	33	23	74	.210	.269	.309	63	-17	5	5	-2	.992	-6	*O-130	-3.0
1974	Cin-N	150	474	73	133	17	8	7	54	46	96	.281	.347	.395	109	5	9	5	0	.987	12	*O-145	1.1
1975	*Cin-N	148	501	69	129	25	5	6	53	48	97	.257	.327	.363	90	-7	13	5	1	.993	14	*O-148	0.2
1976	*Cin-N	149	486	59	149	24	11	2	49	56	95	.307	.385	.424	124	17	22	5	4	.985	4	*O-146	2.0
1977	Cin-N	149	492	54	131	22	4	10	52	35	89	.266	.321	.388	88	-9	10	4	1	.992	12	*O-147	-0.1
1978	Cin-N	122	296	28	67	15	1	5	27	43	67	.226	.330	.334	86	-5	8	3	1	.981	0	*O-115	-0.8
1979	Cin-N	123	356	38	85	17	4	4	38	37	56	.239	.314	.343	79	-10	1	1	-0	.993	7	*O-118	-0.8
1980	Cin-N	103	145	16	37	5	0	2	9	14	24	.255	.321	.331	82	-3	2	1	0	1.000	-18	O-86	-2.5
1981	*KC-A	59	118	14	29	0	2	2	13	11	16	.246	.310	.331	85	-2	6	1	1	.980	-6	O-57	-0.9
1982	KC-A	53	119	14	32	6	3	0	23	8	16	.269	.315	.471	112	-2	2	0	1	1.000	-2	O-44/D-1	0.0
1983	KC-A	38	87	2	18	4	0	0	4	2	13	.207	.242	.253	36	-8	0	1	-1	.986	-1	O-35	-1.1
Total	15	1522	3780	460	977	161	50	51	392	354	746	.258	.327	.368	93	-37	82	40	1	.988	-20	*O-1376/D-1	-10.4

■ LOU GERTENRICH
Gertenrich, Louis Wilhelm   b: 5/4/1875, Chicago, Ill.   d: 10/23/33, Chicago, Ill.   BR/TR, 5'8", 175 lbs.   Deb: 9/15/01

YEAR	TM/L	G	AB	R	H	2B	3B	HR	RBI	BB	SO	AVG	OBP	SLG	PRO+	BR/A	SB	CS	SBR	FA	FR	G/POS	TPR
1901	Mil-A	2	3	1	1	0	0	0	0	0	0	.333	.333	.333	90	-0	0			.000	-0	/O-1	0.0
1903	Pit-N	1	3	0	0	0	0	0	0	0	0	.000	.000	.000	-97	-1	0			1.000	-0	/O-1	-0.1
Total	2	3	6	1	1	0	0	0	0	0	0	.167	.167	.167	-6	-1	0			1.000	-0	/O-2	-0.1

■ DOC GESSLER
Gessler, Harry Homer "Brownie"   b: 12/23/1880, Greensburg, Pa.   d: 12/25/24, Pittsburgh, Pa.   BL/TR, 5'10", 180 lbs.   Deb: 4/23/03   M

YEAR	TM/L	G	AB	R	H	2B	3B	HR	RBI	BB	SO	AVG	OBP	SLG	PRO+	BR/A	SB	CS	SBR	FA	FR	G/POS	TPR
1903	Det-A	29	105	9	25	5	4	0	12	3		.238	.273	.362	92	-1				.974	-2	O-28	-0.5
	Bro-N	49	154	20	38	8	3	0	18	17		.247	.366	.338	104	2	9			.984	-3	O-43	-0.3
1904	Bro-N	104	341	41	99	18	4	2	28	30		.290	.355	.384	131	13	13			.920	-3	O-88/1-2,1	1.0
1905	Bro-N	126	431	44	125	17	4	3	46	38		.290	.366	.369	129	17	26			.973	2	*1-107,O-12	1.5
1906	Bro-N	9	33	3	8	1	2	0	4	3		.242	.324	.394	134	1				.946	1	/1-9	0.2
	*Chi-N	34	83	8	21	3	0	0	10	12		.253	.354	.289	95	0	4			1.000	-1	O-21/1-1	-0.2
	Yr	43	116	11	29	4	2	0	14	15		.250	.346	.319	104	1	7			1.000	-1	O-21,1-10	0.0
1908	Bos-A	135	435	55	134	13	14	3	63	51		.308	**.394**	.423	161	31	19			.950	-7	*O-126	2.1
1909	Bos-A	111	396	57	115	24	1	0	46	31		.290	.354	.356	122	10	16			.933	-4	*O-109	0.6
	Was-A	17	54	10	13	2	1	0	8	12		.241	.406	.315	134	3	4			1.000	-1	O-16/1-1	0.2
	Yr	128	450	67	128	26	2	0	54	43		.284	.361	.351	123	13	20			.940	-2	*O-125/1-1	0.8
1910	Was-A	145	487	58	126	17	12	2	50	62		.259	.361	.355	130	20	18			.953	-3	O-144	1.1
1911	Was-A	128	450	65	127	19	5	4	78	74		.282	.406	.373	120	17	29			.943	-10	*O-126/1-1	0.1
Total	8	880	2969	370	831	127	50	14	363	333		.280	.370	.370	128	113	142			.945	-23	O-713,1-120/2-1	5.8

■ CHARLIE GETTIG
Gettig, Charles Henry   b: 12/1870, Baltimore, Md.   d: 4/11/35, Baltimore, Md.   BR, 5'10", 172 lbs.   Deb: 8/5/1896

YEAR	TM/L	G	AB	R	H	2B	3B	HR	RBI	BB	SO	AVG	OBP	SLG	PRO+	BR/A	SB	CS	SBR	FA	FR	G/POS	TPR
1896	NY-N	6	9	3	3	1	0	0	0	0		.333	.333	.444	107	0				1.000	0	/P-4	0.0
1897	NY-N	22	75	8	15	6	0	0	12	6		.200	.277	.280	49	-6	3			.556	-8	/3-7,2-6,0-3,S-3,P	-1.2
1898	NY-N	64	196	30	49	6	2	0	26	15		.250	.310	.301	78	-6	5			.833	-10	O-21,P-17,2/S31C	-1.4
1899	NY-N	34	97	7	24	3	0	0	9	7		.247	.305	.278	63	-5	4			.833	-4	P-18/3-8,2-3,1-3,0	-0.5
Total	4	126	377	48	91	16	2	0	47	28	0	.241	.302	.294	68	-16	12			.879	-22	/P-42,O-25,23S1C	-3.1

■ TOM GETTINGER
Gettinger, Lewis Thomas Leyton (b: Lewis Thomas Leyton Gittinger)   b: 12/11/1868, Frederick, Md.   d: 7/26/43, Pensacola, Fla.   BL/TL, 5'10", 180 lbs.   Deb: 9/21/1889

YEAR	TM/L	G	AB	R	H	2B	3B	HR	RBI	BB	SO	AVG	OBP	SLG	PRO+	BR/A	SB	CS	SBR	FA	FR	G/POS	TPR
1889	StL-a	4	16	2	7	0	1	2	2	1		.438	.500	.625	194	2				.750	-1	/O-4	0.0
1890	StL-a	58	227	31	54	7	5	3	30	20		.238	.302	.352	81	-8	8			.886	-6	O-58	-1.4
1895	Lou-N	63	260	28	70	11	5	2	32	8	15	.269	.296	.373	77	-10	6			.910	-3	O-63/P-2	-1.5
Total	3	125	503	61	131	18	10	6	64	29	16	.261	.306	.372	82	-16	14			.897	-10	O-125/P-2	-2.9

■ JAKE GETTMAN
Gettman, Jacob John   b: 10/25/1876, Frank, Russia   d: 10/4/56, Denver, Colo.   BB/TL, 5'11", 185 lbs.   Deb: 8/20/1897

YEAR	TM/L	G	AB	R	H	2B	3B	HR	RBI	BB	SO	AVG	OBP	SLG	PRO+	BR/A	SB	CS	SBR	FA	FR	G/POS	TPR
1897	Was-N	36	143	28	45	7	3	3	29	7		.315	.359	.469	118	3	8			.981	-3	O-36	-0.2
1898	Was-N	142	567	75	157	16	5	5	47	29		.277	.319	.349	92	-7	32			.926	2	*O-139/1-3	-1.5
1899	Was-N	19	62	5	13	1	0	0	2	4		.210	.258	.226	93	-1	4			1.000	-1	O-16/1-2	-0.8
Total	3	197	772	108	215	24	8	8	78	40		.278	.322	.361	99	-10	44			.941	-2	O-191/1-5	-2.5

■ GUS GETZ
Getz, Gustave "Gee-Gee"   b: 8/3/1889, Pittsburgh, Pa.   d: 5/28/69, Keansburg, N.J.   BR/TR, 5'11", 165 lbs.   Deb: 8/15/09

YEAR	TM/L	G	AB	R	H	2B	3B	HR	RBI	BB	SO	AVG	OBP	SLG	PRO+	BR/A	SB	CS	SBR	FA	FR	G/POS	TPR
1909	Bos-N	40	148	6	33	2	0	0	9	1		.223	.228	.236	42	-10	2			.934	0	3-36/2-8,S-2	-1.0
1910	Bos-N	54	144	14	28	0	1	0	7	6	10	.194	.232	.208	27	-13	2			.915	3	3-22,2-13/O-8,S-4	-1.1
1914	Bro-N	55	210	13	52	8	1	0	20	2	15	.248	.255	.295	62	-10	9			.949	12	3-55	0.4
1915	Bro-N	130	477	39	123	10	5	2	46	8	14	.258	.275	.312	76	-15	19	15	-3	.951	3	*3-128/S-2	-0.6
1916	*Bro-N	40	96	9	21	1	2	0	8	0	5	.219	.219	.271	49	-6	9			.913	-3	3-20/S-7,1-3	-0.9
1917	Cin-N	7	14	2	4	0	0	0	3	0		.286	.412	.286	121	1				.875	-2	/2-4,3-3	-0.2
1918	Cle-A	6	15	2	2	0	0	0	0	4	1	.133	.350	.200	60	-0				.941	-0	/3-5	-0.1
	Pit-N	7	10	2	2	0	0	0	2	0		.200	.200	.200	21	-1	0			.875	-0	/3-2	0.0
Total	7	339	1114	85	265	22	9	2	93	24	46	.238	.257	.290	60	-56	41	15		.942	18	3-271/2-19,S-15,O1	-3.5

■ CHAPPIE GEYGAN
Geygan, James Edward   b: 6/3/03, Ironton, Ohio   d: 3/15/66, Columbus, Ohio   BR/TR, 5'11", 170 lbs.   Deb: 7/16/24

YEAR	TM/L	G	AB	R	H	2B	3B	HR	RBI	BB	SO	AVG	OBP	SLG	PRO+	BR/A	SB	CS	SBR	FA	FR	G/POS	TPR
1924	Bos-A	33	82	7	21	5	2	0	4	4	16	.256	.307	.366	73	-4	0	2	-1	.952	4	S-32	0.2

YEAR	TM/L	G	AB	R	H	2B	3B	HR	RBI	BB	SO	AVG	OBP	SLG	PRO+	BR/A	SB	CS	SBR	FA	FR	G/POS	TPR
1925	Bos-A	3	11	0	2	0	0	0	0	0	2	.182	.182	.182	-8	-2	0	0	0	.813	-1	/S-3	-0.3
1926	Bos-A	4	10	0	3	0	0	0	0	1	1	.300	.364	.300	77	-0	0	0	0	.800	-1	/3-3	-0.1
Total	3	40	103	7	26	5	2	0	4	5	19	.252	.300	.340	65	-6	0	2	-1	.938	2	/S-35,3-3	-0.2

■ PATSY GHARRITY   Gharrity, Edward Patrick b: 3/13/1892, Parnell, Iowa   d: 10/10/66, Beloit, Wis.   BR/TR, 5′10″, 170 lbs.   Deb: 5/16/16   C

YEAR	TM/L	G	AB	R	H	2B	3B	HR	RBI	BB	SO	AVG	OBP	SLG	PRO+	BR/A	SB	CS	SBR	FA	FR	G/POS	TPR
1916	Was-A	39	92	8	21	5	1	0	9	8	18	.228	.297	.304	81	-5	2			1.000	-3	C-16,1-16	-0.5
1917	Was-A	76	176	15	50	5	0	0	18	14	18	.284	.337	.313	99	-0	7			.980	1	1-46/C-5,O-1	-0.1
1918	Was-A	4	4	0	1	1	0	0	2	0	1	.250	.250	.500	129	-0	0			.000	0	H	0.0
1919	Was-A	111	347	35	94	19	4	2	43	25	39	.271	.325	.366	95	-3	4			.969	-5	C-60,O-33/1-7	-0.5
1920	Was-A	131	428	51	105	18	3	3	44	37	52	.245	.307	.322	69	-20	6	5	-1	.965	-3	*C-121/1-7,O-1	-1.5
1921	Was-A	121	387	62	120	19	8	7	55	45	44	.310	.386	.455	120	12	4	3	-1	.977	-0	*C-115	1.6
1922	Was-A	96	273	40	70	16	6	5	45	36	30	.256	.351	.414	104	2	1	3	-1	.981	3	C-87	0.7
1923	Was-A	93	251	26	52	9	4	3	33	22	27	.207	.276	.311	57	-17	6	2	-1	.986	1	C-35,1-33	-1.5
1929	Was-A	3	2	0	0	0	0	0	0	1	2	.000	.333	.000	-7	-0	0	0	0	.000	0	H	0.0
1930	Was-A	2	1	0	0	0	0	0	0	0	0	.000	.000	.000	-99	-0	0	0	0	1.000	0	/1-1	0.0
Total	10	676	1961	237	513	92	26	20	249	188	231	.262	.331	.366	90	-29	32	13		.974	-7	C-439,1-110/O-35	-1.8

■ JASON GIAMBI   Giambi, Jason Gilbert b: 1/8/71, W.Covina, Cal.   BL/TR, 6′2″, 200 lbs.   Deb: 5/8/95

YEAR	TM/L	G	AB	R	H	2B	3B	HR	RBI	BB	SO	AVG	OBP	SLG	PRO+	BR/A	SB	CS	SBR	FA	FR	G/POS	TPR
1995	Oak-A	54	176	27	45	7	0	6	25	28	31	.256	.367	.398	105	2	2	1	0	.960	-3	3-30,1-26/D-2	-0.2
1996	Oak-A	140	536	84	156	40	1	20	79	51	95	.291	.358	.481	114	11	0	1	-1	.993	-1	1-45,O-45,3-39,D-12	0.5
Total	2	194	712	111	201	47	1	26	104	79	126	.282	.360	.461	112	13	2	2	-1	.993	-1	/1-71,3-69,O-45,D	0.3

■ RAY GIANNELLI   Giannelli, Raymond John b: 2/5/66, Brooklyn, N.Y.   BL/TR, 6′, 195 lbs.   Deb: 5/4/91

YEAR	TM/L	G	AB	R	H	2B	3B	HR	RBI	BB	SO	AVG	OBP	SLG	PRO+	BR/A	SB	CS	SBR	FA	FR	G/POS	TPR
1991	Tor-A	9	24	2	4	1	0	0	0	5	9	.167	.310	.208	45	-2	1	0	0	.923	-2	/3-9	-0.3
1995	StL-N	9	11	0	1	0	0	0	0	3	4	.091	.286	.091	5	-1	0	0	0	1.000	-1	/1-2,O-2	-0.2
Total	2	18	35	2	5	1	0	0	0	8	13	.143	.302	.171	32	-3	1	0	0	.923	-3	/3-9,O-2,1-2	-0.5

■ JOE GIANNINI   Giannini, Joseph Francis b: 9/8/1888, San Francisco, Cal.   d: 9/26/42, San Francisco, Cal.   BL/TR, 5′8″, 155 lbs.   Deb: 8/7/11

YEAR	TM/L	G	AB	R	H	2B	3B	HR	RBI	BB	SO	AVG	OBP	SLG	PRO+	BR/A	SB	CS	SBR	FA	FR	G/POS	TPR
1911	Bos-A	1	2	0	1	1	0	0	0	0		.500	.500	1.000	317	1	0			.500	-0	/S-1	0.0

■ JOHN GIBBONS   Gibbons, John Michael b: 6/8/62, Great Falls, Mont.   BR/TR, 5′11″, 187 lbs.   Deb: 4/11/84

YEAR	TM/L	G	AB	R	H	2B	3B	HR	RBI	BB	SO	AVG	OBP	SLG	PRO+	BR/A	SB	CS	SBR	FA	FR	G/POS	TPR
1984	NY-N	10	31	1	2	0	0	0	1	3	11	.065	.171	.065	-32	-5	0	0	0	.983	-1	/C-9	-0.6
1986	NY-N	8	19	4	9	4	0	1	1	3	5	.474	.545	.842	285	5	0	0	0	1.000	1	/C-8	0.6
Total	2	18	50	5	11	4	0	1	2	6	16	.220	.316	.360	90	-0	0	0	0	.990	-1	/C-17	0.0

■ JAKE GIBBS   Gibbs, Jerry Dean b: 11/7/38, Grenada, Miss.   BL/TR, 6′, 185 lbs.   Deb: 9/11/62

YEAR	TM/L	G	AB	R	H	2B	3B	HR	RBI	BB	SO	AVG	OBP	SLG	PRO+	BR/A	SB	CS	SBR	FA	FR	G/POS	TPR
1962	NY-A	2	0	2	0	0	0	0	0	0	0	—	—	—	—		0	0	0	.000	0	/3-1	0.0
1963	NY-A	4	8	1	2	0	0	0	0	0	1	.250	.250	.250	41	-1	0	0	0	1.000	-1	/C-1	-0.1
1964	NY-A	3	6	1	1	0	0	0	0	0	1	.167	.167	.167	-7	-1	0	0	0	1.000	-1	/C-2	0.0
1965	NY-A	37	68	6	15	1	0	2	7	4	20	.221	.274	.324	70	-3	0	0	0	.991	2	C-21	0.0
1966	NY-A	62	182	19	47	6	0	3	20	19	16	.258	.328	.341	96	-1	3	0	0	.988	4	C-54	0.8
1967	NY-A	116	374	33	87	7	1	4	25	28	57	.233	.293	.289	75	-11	7	6	-2	.975	1	C-99	-0.8
1968	NY-A	124	423	31	90	12	3	3	29	27	68	.213	.270	.277	68	-17	9	8	-2	.991	-4	*C-121	-1.7
1969	NY-A	71	219	18	49	9	2	0	18	23	30	.224	.298	.283	65	-10	3	4	-2	.990	8	C-66	0.0
1970	NY-A	49	153	23	46	9	2	8	26	7	14	.301	.335	.542	146	8	2	0	1	.987	3	C-44	1.4
1971	NY-A	70	206	23	45	0	5	2	21	12	23	.218	.271	.335	76	-8	2	2	-1	.988	-5	C-51	-1.2
Total	10	538	1639	157	382	53	8	25	146	120	231	.233	.291	.321	81	-42	28	22	-5	.986	8	C-459/3-1	-1.6

■ STEVE GIBRALTER   Gibralter, Stephan Benson b: 10/9/72, Dallas, Tex.   BR/TR, 6′, 185 lbs.   Deb: 6/1/95

YEAR	TM/L	G	AB	R	H	2B	3B	HR	RBI	BB	SO	AVG	OBP	SLG	PRO+	BR/A	SB	CS	SBR	FA	FR	G/POS	TPR
1995	Cin-N	4	3	0	1	0	0	0	0	0	0	.333	.333	.333	77	-0	0	0	0	1.000	-1	/O-2	-0.1
1996	Cin-N	2	2	0	0	0	0	0	0	0	2	.000	.000	.000	-99	-1	0	0	0	.000	-1	/O-2	-0.2
Total	2	6	5	0	1	0	0	0	0	0	2	.200	.200	.200	6	-1	0	0	0	.500	-2	/O-4	-0.3

■ CHARLIE GIBSON   Gibson, Charles Ellsworth "Gibby" b: 11/17/1879, Sharon, Pa.   d: 11/22/54, Sharon, Pa.   BR/TR, 6′, 160 lbs.   Deb: 9/23/05

YEAR	TM/L	G	AB	R	H	2B	3B	HR	RBI	BB	SO	AVG	OBP	SLG	PRO+	BR/A	SB	CS	SBR	FA	FR	G/POS	TPR
1905	StL-A	1	3	0	0	0	0	0	0	0		.000	.000	.000	-99	-1	0			1.000	-0	/C-1	-0.1

■ CHARLIE GIBSON   Gibson, Charles Griffin b: 11/21/1899, LaGrange, Ga.   d: 12/18/90, LaGrange, Ga.   BR/TR, 5′8″, 160 lbs.   Deb: 5/30/24

YEAR	TM/L	G	AB	R	H	2B	3B	HR	RBI	BB	SO	AVG	OBP	SLG	PRO+	BR/A	SB	CS	SBR	FA	FR	G/POS	TPR
1924	Phi-A	12	15	1	2	0	0	1	2	0	1	.133	.235	.133	-3	-2	0			.870	-0	C-12	-0.2

■ FRANK GIBSON   Gibson, Frank Gilbert b: 9/27/1890, Omaha, Neb.   d: 4/27/61, Austin, Tex.   BB/TR, 6′0.5″, 172 lbs.   Deb: 4/22/13

YEAR	TM/L	G	AB	R	H	2B	3B	HR	RBI	BB	SO	AVG	OBP	SLG	PRO+	BR/A	SB	CS	SBR	FA	FR	G/POS	TPR
1913	Det-A	23	57	8	8	1	0	2	3	9		.140	.197	.158	4	-7	2			.914	-6	C-19/O-2	-1.3
1921	Bos-N	63	125	14	33	5	4	2	13	3	17	.264	.292	.416	90	-2	0	0	0	.979	1	C-41	0.0
1922	Bos-N	66	164	15	49	7	5	2	20	10	27	.299	.339	.421	99	-1	4	1	1	.981	-1	C-29,1-20	-0.1
1923	Bos-N	41	50	13	15	1	0	0	5	7	7	.300	.386	.320	92	-0	0	2	-1	.923	-2	C-20	-0.2
1924	Bos-N	90	229	25	71	15	6	1	30	10	23	.310	.342	.441	113	3	1	1	-0	.972	2	C-46,1-10/3-2	0.7
1925	Bos-N	104	316	36	88	23	5	2	50	15	28	.278	.313	.402	89	-7	3	3	-1	.968	-2	C-86/1-2	-0.5
1926	Bos-N	24	47	3	16	4	0	0	7	4	6	.340	.392	.426	132	2	0			1.000	0	C-13	0.4
1927	Bos-N	60	167	7	37	1	2	0	19	3	10	.222	.235	.251	33	-16	2			.965	-3	C-47	-1.7
Total	8	471	1155	121	317	57	19	8	146	55	127	.274	.310	.377	86	-28	12	7		.967	-10	C-301/1-32,3-2,O-2	-2.7

■ GEORGE GIBSON   Gibson, George C. "Moon" b: 7/22/1880, London, Ont., Can.   d: 1/25/67, London, Ont., Can.   BR/TR, 5′11.5″, 190 lbs.   Deb: 7/2/05   MC

YEAR	TM/L	G	AB	R	H	2B	3B	HR	RBI	BB	SO	AVG	OBP	SLG	PRO+	BR/A	SB	CS	SBR	FA	FR	G/POS	TPR
1905	Pit-N	46	135	14	24	2	2	2	14	15		.178	.270	.267	59	-7	2			.966	3	C-44	0.0
1906	Pit-N	81	259	8	46	6	1	0	20	16		.178	.225	.208	34	-20	1			.971	-5	C-81	-2.0
1907	Pit-N	113	382	28	84	8	7	3	35	18		.220	.261	.301	75	-12	2			.972	-3	*C-109/1-1	-0.6
1908	Pit-N	143	486	37	111	19	4	2	45	19		.228	.260	.296	78	-14	4			.973	-14	*C-140	-1.7
1909	*Pit-N	150	510	42	135	25	9	2	52	44		.265	.326	.361	104	1	9			.983	3	*C-150	1.9
1910	Pit-N	143	482	53	125	22	6	3	44	47	31	.259	.333	.349	93	-4	7			.984	3	*C-143	1.3
1911	Pit-N	100	311	32	65	12	2	0	19	29	16	.209	.281	.260	50	-21	3			.979	0	C-98	-1.1
1912	Pit-N	95	300	23	72	14	3	2	35	20	21	.240	.290	.327	69	-13	0			.990	-1	C-94	-0.5
1913	Pit-N	48	118	6	33	4	2	0	12	10	8	.280	.341	.347	101	0	2			.986	-9	C-48	-0.5
1914	Pit-N	102	274	19	78	9	5	0	30	27	27	.285	.359	.354	117	7	4			.974	-9	*C-101	0.6
1915	Pit-N	120	351	28	88	15	6	1	30	31	25	.251	.313	.336	98	-1	5	2	0	.965	-1	*C-118	1.8
1916	Pit-N	33	84	4	17	2	2	0	4	3	7	.202	.239	.274	57	-4	0			.989	7	C-29	0.5
1917	NY-N	35	82	1	14	3	0	0	5	7	2	.171	.236	.207	38	-6	1			.986	1	C-35	-0.4
1918	NY-N	4	2	0	1	1	0	0	0	0	0	.500	.500	1.000	360	1	0			1.000	0	/C-4	0.1
Total	14	1213	3776	295	893	142	49	15	345	286	132	.236	.295	.312	81	-94	40	2		.977	-18	*C-1194/1-1	-0.6

■ RUSS GIBSON   Gibson, John Russell b: 5/6/39, Fall River, Mass.   BR/TR, 6′1″, 195 lbs.   Deb: 4/14/67

YEAR	TM/L	G	AB	R	H	2B	3B	HR	RBI	BB	SO	AVG	OBP	SLG	PRO+	BR/A	SB	CS	SBR	FA	FR	G/POS	TPR
1967	*Bos-A	49	138	8	28	7	0	1	15	12	31	.203	.267	.275	56	-7	0	0	-6	1.000	-6	C-48	-1.2
1968	Bos-A	76	231	15	52	11	1	3	20	8	38	.225	.251	.320	68	-9	1	2	-1	.983	-6	C-74/1-1	-0.6
1969	Bos-A	85	287	21	72	9	1	3	27	15	25	.251	.290	.321	67	-13	1	1	-0	.979	-6	C-83	-1.6
1970	SF-N	24	69	3	16	6	0	0	6	9	12	.232	.303	.319	67	-4	0	0	0	.971	2	C-23	-0.4
1971	SF-N	25	57	2	11	1	1	1	7	2	13	.193	.220	.298	46	-4	0	0	0	.965	0	C-22	-0.2
1972	SF-N	5	12	0	2	0	1	0	3	0	4	.167	.167	.333	38	-1	0	0	0	1.000	0	/C-5	-0.2
Total	6	264	794	49	181	34	4	8	78	44	123	.228	.269	.311	64	-38	2	3	-1	.983	-10	C-255/1-1	-4.0

■ KIRK GIBSON   Gibson, Kirk Harold b: 5/28/57, Pontiac, Mich.   BL/TL, 6′3″, 215 lbs.   Deb: 9/8/79

YEAR	TM/L	G	AB	R	H	2B	3B	HR	RBI	BB	SO	AVG	OBP	SLG	PRO+	BR/A	SB	CS	SBR	FA	FR	G/POS	TPR
1979	Det-A	12	38	3	9	3	0	1	4	2	10	.237	.256	.395	70	-2	3	3	-1	1.000	-1	O-10	-0.4
1980	Det-A	51	175	23	46	2	1	9	16	10	45	.263	.306	.440	100	-1	4	7	-3	.992	-2	O-49/D-1	-0.7
1981	Det-A	83	290	41	95	11	3	9	40	18	64	.328	.371	.479	138	14	17	5	2	.973	-4	O-67/D-9	1.0
1982	Det-A	69	266	34	74	16	2	8	35	25	41	.278	.342	.444	113	5	9	7	-2	.994	3	O-64/D-4	0.5
1983	Det-A	128	401	60	91	12	9	15	51	53	96	.227	.323	.414	104	2	14	3	2	.975	-1	D-66,O-54	-0.1

YEAR	TM/L	G	AB	R	H	2B	3B	HR	RBI	BB	SO	AVG	OBP	SLG	PRO+	BR/A	SB	CS	SBR	FA	FR	G/POS	TPR
1984	*Det-A	149	531	92	150	23	10	27	91	63	103	.282	.367	.516	142	30	29	9	3	.954	-9	*O-139/D-6	2.0
1985	Det-A	154	581	96	167	37	5	29	97	71	137	.287	.370	.518	141	33	30	4	7	.963	-7	*O-144/D-8	2.7
1986	Det-A	119	441	84	118	11	2	28	86	68	107	.268	.374	.492	134	22	34	6	7	.990	-9	*O-114/D-4	1.6
1987	*Det-A	128	487	95	135	25	3	24	79	71	117	.277	.375	.489	132	24	26	7	4	.974	5	*O-121/D-4	2.7
1988	*LA-N	150	542	106	157	28	1	25	76	73	120	.290	.381	.483	151	37	31	4	7	.964	8	*O-148	5.0
1989	LA-N	71	253	35	54	8	2	9	28	35	55	.213	.314	.368	96	-1	12	3	2	.980	1	O-70	-0.1
1990	LA-N	89	315	59	82	20	0	8	38	39	65	.260	.347	.400	108	4	26	2	7	.995	5	O-81	1.4
1991	KC-A	132	462	81	109	17	6	16	55	69	103	.236	.343	.403	105	4	18	4	3	.976	-2	O-94,D-30	0.2
1992	Pit-N	16	56	6	11	0	0	2	5	3	12	.196	.237	.304	53	-4	3	1	0	1.000	1	O-13	-0.3
1993	Det-A	116	403	62	105	18	6	13	62	44	87	.261	.339	.432	106	3	15	6	1	.987	-1	D-76,O-32	-0.1
1994	Det-A	98	330	71	91	17	2	23	72	42	69	.276	.363	.548	130	14	4	5	-2	.988	-2	D-56,O-38	0.6
1995	Det-A	70	227	37	59	12	2	9	35	33	61	.260	.361	.449	110	4	9	2	2	.000	-0	D-63/O-1	0.0
Total	17	1635	5798	985	1553	260	54	255	870	718	1285	.268	.355	.463	123	188	284	78	38	.976	-17	*O-1239,D-327	16.0

■ **WHITEY GIBSON**   Gibson, Leighton P.   b: 10/6/1868, Lancaster, Pa.   d: 10/11/07, Talmage, Pa.   TR, 5'9", 178 lbs.   Deb: 5/2/1888

YEAR	TM/L	G	AB	R	H	2B	3B	HR	RBI	BB	SO	AVG	OBP	SLG	PRO+	BR/A	SB	CS	SBR	FA	FR	G/POS	TPR
1888	Phi-a	1	3	0	0	0	0	0	0	0	0	.000	.000	.000	-99	-1	0			1.000	1	/C-1	0.0

■ **JOE GIEBEL**   Giebel, Joseph Henry   b: 11/30/1891, Washington, D.C.   d: 3/17/81, Silver Spring, Md.   BR/TR, 5'10.5", 175 lbs.   Deb: 9/30/13

YEAR	TM/L	G	AB	R	H	2B	3B	HR	RBI	BB	SO	AVG	OBP	SLG	PRO+	BR/A	SB	CS	SBR	FA	FR	G/POS	TPR
1913	Phi-N	1	3	0	1	0	0	0	0	0	1	.333	.333	.333	97	-0	0			1.000	-0	/C-1	0.0

■ **NORM GIGON**   Gigon, Norman Phillip   b: 5/12/38, Teaneck, N.J.   BR/TR, 6', 195 lbs.   Deb: 4/12/67

YEAR	TM/L	G	AB	R	H	2B	3B	HR	RBI	BB	SO	AVG	OBP	SLG	PRO+	BR/A	SB	CS	SBR	FA	FR	G/POS	TPR
1967	Chi-N	34	70	8	12	3	1	1	6	4	14	.171	.237	.286	47	-5	0	0	0	.982	-3	2-12/O-4,3-1	-0.8

■ **BENJI GIL**   Gil, Romar Benjamin (Aguilar)   b: 10/6/72, Tijuana, Mex.   BR/TR, 6'2", 180 lbs.   Deb: 4/5/93

YEAR	TM/L	G	AB	R	H	2B	3B	HR	RBI	BB	SO	AVG	OBP	SLG	PRO+	BR/A	SB	CS	SBR	FA	FR	G/POS	TPR
1993	Tex-A	22	57	3	7	0	0	0	2	5	22	.123	.194	.123	-13	-9	1	2	-1	.954	8	S-22	0.0
1995	Tex-A	130	415	36	91	20	3	9	46	26	147	.219	.267	.347	57	-27	2	4	-2	.974	16	*S-130	-0.1
1996	Tex-A	5	5	0	2	0	0	0	1	1	1	.400	.500	.400	123	0	0	1	-1	.923	1	/S-5	0.0
Total	3	157	477	39	100	20	3	9	49	32	170	.210	.261	.321	50	-36	3	7	-3	.970	25	S-157	-0.1

■ **GUS GIL**   Gil, Tomas Gustavo (Guillen)   b: 4/19/39, Caracas, Venez.   BR/TR, 5'10", 180 lbs.   Deb: 4/11/67

YEAR	TM/L	G	AB	R	H	2B	3B	HR	RBI	BB	SO	AVG	OBP	SLG	PRO+	BR/A	SB	CS	SBR	FA	FR	G/POS	TPR
1967	Cle-A	51	96	11	11	4	0	0	5	9	18	.115	.198	.156	6	-11	0	0	0	1.000	2	2-49/1-1	-0.8
1969	Sea-A	92	221	20	49	7	0	0	17	16	28	.222	.274	.253	49	-15	2	0	1	.942	1	3-38,2-18,S-12	-1.2
1970	Mil-A	64	119	12	22	4	0	1	12	21	12	.185	.307	.244	53	-7	2	0	1	.978	3	2-38,3-14	-0.1
1971	Mil-A	14	32	3	5	1	0	0	3	10	5	.156	.357	.188	59	-1	1	0	0	.977	-0	/2-8,3-6	0.0
Total	4	221	468	46	87	16	0	1	37	56	63	.186	.274	.226	43	-34	5	0	2	.987	7	2-113/3-58,S-12,1-1	-2.1

■ **ANDY GILBERT**   Gilbert, Andrew   b: 7/18/14, Bradenville, Pa.   d: 8/29/92, Davis, Cal.   BR/TR, 6', 203 lbs.   Deb: 9/14/42   C

YEAR	TM/L	G	AB	R	H	2B	3B	HR	RBI	BB	SO	AVG	OBP	SLG	PRO+	BR/A	SB	CS	SBR	FA	FR	G/POS	TPR
1942	Bos-A	6	11	0	1	0	0	0	1	1	3	.091	.167	.091	-26	-2	0	0	0	1.000	-2	/O-5	-0.4
1946	Bos-A	2	1	1	0	0	0	0	0	0	0	.000	.000	.000	-95	-0	0	0	0	.000	-1	/O-1	-0.1
Total	2	8	12	1	1	0	0	0	1	1	3	.083	.154	.083	-31	-2	0	0	0	1.000	-2	/O-6	-0.5

■ **CHARLIE GILBERT**   Gilbert, Charles Mader   b: 7/8/19, New Orleans, La.   d: 8/13/83, New Orleans, La.   BL/TL, 5'9", 165 lbs.   Deb: 4/16/40   F

YEAR	TM/L	G	AB	R	H	2B	3B	HR	RBI	BB	SO	AVG	OBP	SLG	PRO+	BR/A	SB	CS	SBR	FA	FR	G/POS	TPR
1940	Bro-N	57	142	23	35	9	1	2	8	8	13	.246	.287	.366	74	-5	0			.960	-2	O-43	-0.8
1941	Chi-N	39	86	11	24	2	1	0	12	11	6	.279	.361	.326	98	0	1			1.000	-1	O-22	-0.2
1942	Chi-N	74	179	18	33	6	3	0	7	25	24	.184	.284	.251	60	-9	1			.981	0	O-47	-1.1
1943	Chi-N	8	20	1	3	0	0	0	0	3	3	.150	.261	.150	20	-2	1			.000	-1	/O-6	-0.3
1946	Chi-N	15	13	2	1	0	0	0	1	1	4	.077	.143	.077	-38	-2	0			1.000	0	/O-2	-0.3
	Phi-N	88	260	34	63	5	2	1	17	25	18	.242	.314	.288	73	-9	3			1.000	6	O-69	-0.6
	Yr	103	273	36	64	5	2	1	18	26	22	.234	.306	.278	68	-11	3			1.000	6	O-71	-0.9
1947	Phi-N	83	152	20	36	5	2	2	10	13	14	.237	.301	.336	72	-6	1			.961	-0	O-37	-0.7
Total	6	364	852	109	195	27	9	5	55	86	82	.229	.302	.299	70	-33	7			.982	3	O-226	-4.1

■ **BUDDY GILBERT**   Gilbert, Drew Edward   b: 7/26/35, Knoxville, Tenn.   BL/TR, 6'3", 195 lbs.   Deb: 9/9/59

YEAR	TM/L	G	AB	R	H	2B	3B	HR	RBI	BB	SO	AVG	OBP	SLG	PRO+	BR/A	SB	CS	SBR	FA	FR	G/POS	TPR
1959	Cin-N	7	20	4	3	0	0	2	3	4	4	.150	.261	.450	82	-1	0	0	0	1.000	1	/O-6	0.0

■ **TOOKIE GILBERT**   Gilbert, Harold Joseph   b: 4/4/29, New Orleans, La.   d: 6/23/67, New Orleans, La.   BL/TR, 6'2.5", 185 lbs.   Deb: 5/5/50   F

YEAR	TM/L	G	AB	R	H	2B	3B	HR	RBI	BB	SO	AVG	OBP	SLG	PRO+	BR/A	SB	CS	SBR	FA	FR	G/POS	TPR
1950	NY-N	113	322	40	71	12	2	4	32	43	36	.220	.314	.307	64	-16	3			.988	1	*1-111	-1.7
1953	NY-N	70	160	12	27	3	0	3	16	22	21	.169	.269	.244	34	-15	1	0	0	.995	1	1-44	-1.5
Total	2	183	482	52	98	15	2	7	48	65	57	.203	.299	.286	54	-32	4	0		.991	1	1-155	-3.2

■ **HARRY GILBERT**   Gilbert, Harry H.   b: 7/7/1868, Pottstown, Pa.   d: 12/23/09, Pottstown, Pa.   Deb: 6/23/1890   F

YEAR	TM/L	G	AB	R	H	2B	3B	HR	RBI	BB	SO	AVG	OBP	SLG	PRO+	BR/A	SB	CS	SBR	FA	FR	G/POS	TPR
1890	Pit-N	2	8	1	2	0	0	0	0	0	3	.250	.250	.250	52	-1	0			1.000	-1	/2-2	-0.1

■ **JOHN GILBERT**   Gilbert, John G.   b: 1/8/1864, Pottstown, Pa.   d: 11/12/03, Pottstown, Pa.   Deb: 6/23/1890   F

YEAR	TM/L	G	AB	R	H	2B	3B	HR	RBI	BB	SO	AVG	OBP	SLG	PRO+	BR/A	SB	CS	SBR	FA	FR	G/POS	TPR
1890	Pit-N	2	8	0	0	0	0	0	0	0	2	.000	.000	.000	-99	-2	0			1.000	-0	/S-2	-0.2

■ **JACK GILBERT**   Gilbert, John Robert "Jackrabbit"   b: 9/4/1875, Rhinecliff, N.Y.   d: 7/7/41, Albany, N.Y.   Deb: 9/11/1898

YEAR	TM/L	G	AB	R	H	2B	3B	HR	RBI	BB	SO	AVG	OBP	SLG	PRO+	BR/A	SB	CS	SBR	FA	FR	G/POS	TPR
1898	Was-N	2	5	0	1	0	0	0	1	1		.200	.429	.200	82	0	1			.500	-0	/O-2	0.0
	NY-N	1	4	0	1	0	0	0	0	0		.250	.250	.250	45	-0	1			.500	-0	/O-1	-0.1
	Yr	3	9	0	2	0	0	0	1	1		.222	.364	.222	70	-0	2			.500	-1	/O-3	-0.1
1904	Pit-N	25	87	13	21	0	0	0	3	12		.241	.353	.241	82	-1	3			.857	-6	O-25	-0.9
Total	2	28	96	13	23	0	0	0	4	13		.240	.354	.240	81	-1	5			.821	-6	/O-28	-1.0

■ **LARRY GILBERT**   Gilbert, Lawrence William   b: 12/3/1891, New Orleans, La.   d: 2/17/65, New Orleans, La.   BL/TL, 5'9", 158 lbs.   Deb: 4/14/14   F

YEAR	TM/L	G	AB	R	H	2B	3B	HR	RBI	BB	SO	AVG	OBP	SLG	PRO+	BR/A	SB	CS	SBR	FA	FR	G/POS	TPR
1914	*Bos-N	72	224	32	60	6	1	5	25	26	34	.268	.347	.371	114	4	3			.979	-2	O-60	0.1
1915	Bos-N	45	106	11	16	4	0	0	4	11	13	.151	.231	.189	29	-9	4	1	1	.941	-2	O-27	-1.3
Total	2	117	330	43	76	10	1	5	29	37	47	.230	.310	.312	88	-5	7	1		.969	-3	/O-87	-1.2

■ **MARK GILBERT**   Gilbert, Mark David   b: 8/22/56, Atlanta, Ga.   BB/TR, 6', 175 lbs.   Deb: 7/21/85

YEAR	TM/L	G	AB	R	H	2B	3B	HR	RBI	BB	SO	AVG	OBP	SLG	PRO+	BR/A	SB	CS	SBR	FA	FR	G/POS	TPR
1985	Chi-A	7	22	3	6	1	0	0	3	4	3	.273	.385	.318	92	-0	0	0	0	1.000	-1	/O-7	-0.1

■ **PETE GILBERT**   Gilbert, Peter   b: 9/6/1867, Baltic, Conn.   d: 1/1/12, Springfield, Mass.   TR, 5'8", 180 lbs.   Deb: 9/6/1890

YEAR	TM/L	G	AB	R	H	2B	3B	HR	RBI	BB	SO	AVG	OBP	SLG	PRO+	BR/A	SB	CS	SBR	FA	FR	G/POS	TPR
1890	Bal-a	29	100	25	28	2	1	1	18	10		.280	.363	.350	105	1	12			.899	-3	3-29	-0.1
1891	Bal-a	139	513	81	118	15	7	3	72	37	77	.230	.317	.304	77	-16	31			.862	2	*3-139	-0.6
1892	Bal-N	4	15	0	3	0	0	0	0	1	3	.200	.250	.200	35	-1	1			.889	1	/3-4	0.0
1894	Bro-N	6	25	1	2	0	0	0	1	1	3	.080	.148	.080	-47	-6	2			.938	-3	/2-3,3-3	-0.4
	Lou-N	28	108	13	33	3	1	1	14	5	4	.306	.353	.380	82	-3	2			.742	-6	3-28	-0.7
	Yr	34	133	14	35	3	1	1	15	6	7	.263	.315	.323	58	-9	4			.766	-4	3-31/2-3	-1.1
Total	4	206	761	120	184	20	9	5	105	54	87	.242	.321	.311	76	-25	48			.851	-4	3-203/2-3	-1.8

■ **WALLY GILBERT**   Gilbert, Walter John   b: 12/19/1900, Oscoda, Mich.   d: 9/7/58, Duluth, Minn.   BR/TR, 6', 180 lbs.   Deb: 8/18/28

YEAR	TM/L	G	AB	R	H	2B	3B	HR	RBI	BB	SO	AVG	OBP	SLG	PRO+	BR/A	SB	CS	SBR	FA	FR	G/POS	TPR
1928	Bro-N	39	153	26	31	4	0	0	14	8		.203	.274	.229	33	-15	2			.965	-1	3-39	-1.3
1929	Bro-N	143	569	88	173	31	4	3	58	42	29	.304	.359	.388	87	-11	7			.956	7	*3-142	0.2
1930	Bro-N	150	623	92	183	34	5	3	67	47	33	.294	.345	.379	76	-24	7			.944	9	*3-150	-0.6
1931	Bro-N	145	552	60	147	25	6	0	46	39	38	.266	.322	.333	77	-17	3			.948	5	*3-145	-0.3
1932	Cin-N	114	420	35	90	18	2	1	40	20	23	.214	.252	.274	43	-34	2			.929	-6	*3-111	-3.3
Total	5	591	2317	301	624	112	17	7	214	162	131	.269	.322	.341	71	-101	21			.947	17	3-587	-5.0

■ **BILLY GILBERT**   Gilbert, William Oliver   b: 6/21/1876, Tullytown, Pa.   d: 8/8/27, New York, N.Y.   BR/TR, 5'4", 153 lbs.   Deb: 4/25/01

YEAR	TM/L	G	AB	R	H	2B	3B	HR	RBI	BB	SO	AVG	OBP	SLG	PRO+	BR/A	SB	CS	SBR	FA	FR	G/POS	TPR
1901	Mil-A	127	492	77	133	14	7	0	43	31		.270	.320	.327	84	-10	19			.936	-0	*2-127	-0.4
1902	Bal-A	129	445	74	109	12	3	2	38	45		.245	.327	.299	71	-16	38			.907	-5	*S-129	-1.3
1903	NY-N	128	413	62	104	9	0	1	40	41		.252	.348	.281	77	-10	37			.935	11	*2-128	0.5
1904	NY-N	146	478	57	121	13	3	1	54	46		.253	.340	.299	94	-1	33			.946	8	*2-146	1.1

YEAR	TM/L	G	AB	R	H	2B	3B	HR	RBI	BB	SO	AVG	OBP	SLG	PRO+	BR/A	SB	CS	SBR	FA	FR	G/POS	TPR
1905	*NY-N	115	376	45	93	11	3	0	24	41		.247	.331	.293	84	-6	11			.947	25	*2-115	2.1
1906	NY-N	104	307	44	71	6	1	1	27	42		.231	.341	.267	88	-2	22			.940	23	2-98	2.3
1908	StL-N	89	276	12	59	7	0	0	10	20		.214	.274	.239	67	-10	6			.952	6	2-89	-0.5
1909	StL-N	12	29	4	5	0	0	0	1	4		.172	.333	.172	61	-1	1			.922	0	2-12	-0.1
Total	8	850	2816	375	695	72	17	5	237	270		.247	.328	.290	81	-57	167			.942	68	2-715,S-129	3.7

■ ROD GILBREATH
Gilbreath, Rodney Joe b: 9/24/52, Laurel, Miss. BR/TR, 6'2", 185 lbs. Deb: 6/17/72

YEAR	TM/L	G	AB	R	H	2B	3B	HR	RBI	BB	SO	AVG	OBP	SLG	PRO+	BR/A	SB	CS	SBR	FA	FR	G/POS	TPR
1972	Atl-N	18	38	2	9	1	0	0	1	2	10	.237	.293	.263	54	-2	1	1	-0	1.000	3	/2-7,3-4	0.0
1973	Atl-N	29	74	10	21	2	1	0	2	6	10	.284	.346	.338	84	-1	2	1	0	.960	-0	3-22	-0.2
1974	Atl-N	3	6	2	2	0	0	0	0	2	0	.333	.500	.333	131	0	0	0	0	1.000	0	/2-2	0.0
1975	Atl-N	90	202	24	49	3	1	2	16	24	26	.243	.326	.297	71	-7	5	5	-2	.980	4	2-52,3-10/S-1	-0.4
1976	Atl-N	116	383	57	96	11	8	1	32	42	36	.251	.331	.329	83	-8	7	7	-2	.975	7	*2-104/3-7,S-1	0.4
1977	Atl-N	128	407	47	99	15	2	8	43	45	79	.243	.322	.349	71	-16	9	9	-5	.978	3	*2-122/3-1	-1.0
1978	Atl-N	116	326	22	80	13	3	3	31	26	51	.245	.301	.331	69	-14	7	6	-2	.968	3	3-62,2-39	-1.8
Total	7	500	1436	164	356	45	15	14	125	147	212	.248	.322	.329	74	-48	25	29	-10	.978	11	2-326,3-106/S-2	-2.9

■ DON GILE
Gile, Donald Loren "Bear" b: 4/19/35, Modesto, Cal. BR/TR, 6'6", 220 lbs. Deb: 9/25/59

YEAR	TM/L	G	AB	R	H	2B	3B	HR	RBI	BB	SO	AVG	OBP	SLG	PRO+	BR/A	SB	CS	SBR	FA	FR	G/POS	TPR
1959	Bos-A	3	10	1	2	0	1	0	1	0	2	.200	.273	.300	55	-1	0	0	0	1.000	-0	/C-3	-0.1
1960	Bos-A	29	51	6	9	1	1	1	4	1	13	.176	.192	.294	29	-5	0	0	0	1.000	-1	C-15,1-11	-0.7
1961	Bos-A	8	18	2	5	0	0	1	1	1	5	.278	.316	.444	98	-0	0	0	0	.958	-1	/1-6,C-1	-0.1
1962	Bos-A	18	41	3	2	0	0	1	3	3	15	.049	.133	.122	-30	-8	0	0	0	.990	-1	1-14	-0.9
Total	4	58	120	12	18	2	1	3	9	5	35	.150	.197	.258	21	-14	0	0	0	.982	-2	/1-31,C-19	-1.8

■ BRIAN GILES
Giles, Brian Jeffrey b: 4/27/60, Manhattan, Kan. BR/TR, 6'1", 165 lbs. Deb: 9/12/81

YEAR	TM/L	G	AB	R	H	2B	3B	HR	RBI	BB	SO	AVG	OBP	SLG	PRO+	BR/A	SB	CS	SBR	FA	FR	G/POS	TPR
1981	NY-N	9	7	0	0	0	0	0	0	0	0	.000	.000	.000	-99	-2	0	0	0	1.000	3	/2-2,S-2	0.2
1982	NY-N	45	138	14	29	5	0	3	10	12	29	.210	.273	.312	64	-7	6	1	1	.992	15	2-45/S-2	1.2
1983	NY-N	145	400	39	98	15	0	2	27	36	77	.245	.311	.298	70	-16	17	10	-1	.980	15	*2-140,S-12	0.4
1985	Mil-A	34	58	6	10	1	0	1	1	7	16	.172	.262	.241	39	-5	2	1	0	.963	8	S-20,2-13/D-2	0.4
1986	Chi-A	9	11	0	3	0	0	0	1	0	2	.273	.273	.273	48	-1	0	0	0	1.000	4	/2-7,S-1	0.3
1990	Sea-A	45	95	15	22	6	0	4	11	5	24	.232	.336	.421	109	1	2	1	0	.978	7	S-37/2-2,3-1,D-1	1.1
Total	6	287	709	74	162	27	0	10	50	70	151	.228	.300	.309	70	-29	27	13	0	.985	52	2-209/S-74,D-3,3-1	3.6

■ BRIAN GILES
Giles, Brian Stephen b: 1/21/71, ElCajon, Cal. BL/TL, 5'11", 195 lbs. Deb: 9/16/95

YEAR	TM/L	G	AB	R	H	2B	3B	HR	RBI	BB	SO	AVG	OBP	SLG	PRO+	BR/A	SB	CS	SBR	FA	FR	G/POS	TPR
1995	Cle-A	6	9	6	5	3	0	1	3	0	1	.556	.556	.889	265	2	0	0	0	1.000	0	/O-3,D-1	0.2
1996	*Cle-A	51	121	26	43	14	1	5	27	19	13	.355	.443	.612	163	12	3	0	1	1.000	-1	D-21,O-16	0.9
Total	2	57	130	32	48	14	1	6	30	19	14	.369	.450	.631	170	14	3	0	1	1.000	-1	/D-22,O-19	1.1

■ GEORGE GILHAM
Gilham, George Louis b: 9/17/1899, Shamokin, Pa. d: 4/25/37, Lansdowne, Pa. BR/TR, 5'11", 164 lbs. Deb: 9/24/20

YEAR	TM/L	G	AB	R	H	2B	3B	HR	RBI	BB	SO	AVG	OBP	SLG	PRO+	BR/A	SB	CS	SBR	FA	FR	G/POS	TPR
1920	StL-N	1	3	0	0	0	0	0	0	0	1	.000	.000	.000	-99	-1	0	0	0	.750	-1	/C-1	-0.2
1921	StL-N	1	1	0	0	0	0	0	0	0	0	.000	.000	.000	-99	-0	0	0	0	.750	-1	H	0.0
Total	2	2	4	0	0	0	0	0	0	0	1	.000	.000	.000	-99	-1	0	0	0	.750	-1	/C-1	-0.2

■ FRANK GILHOOLEY
Gilhooley, Frank Patrick "Flash" b: 6/10/1892, Toledo, Ohio d: 7/11/59, Toledo, Ohio BL/TR, 5'8", 155 lbs. Deb: 9/18/11

YEAR	TM/L	G	AB	R	H	2B	3B	HR	RBI	BB	SO	AVG	OBP	SLG	PRO+	BR/A	SB	CS	SBR	FA	FR	G/POS	TPR
1911	StL-N	1	0	0	0	0	0	0	0	0	0	—	—	—	—	0	0			.000	-0	/O-1	0.0
1912	StL-N	13	49	5	11	0	0	0	2	3	8	.224	.269	.224	37	-4	0			1.000	-2	O-11	-0.7
1913	NY-A	24	85	10	29	2	1	0	14	4	9	.341	.378	.388	124	2	6			.977	-1	O-24	0.1
1914	NY-A	1	3	0	2	0	0	0	0	1	0	.667	.750	.667	327	1	0			.000	-0	/O-1	0.1
1915	NY-A	1	4	0	0	0	0	0	0	0	1	.000	.000	.000	-99	-1	0			1.000	-0	/O-1	-0.1
1916	NY-A	58	223	40	62	5	3	1	10	37	17	.278	.383	.341	115	6	16			.971	3	O-57	0.6
1917	NY-A	54	165	14	40	6	1	0	8	30	13	.242	.362	.291	99	1	6			.933	-1	O-46	-0.3
1918	NY-A	112	427	59	118	13	5	1	23	53	24	.276	.358	.337	107	5	7			.961	1	*O-111	-0.1
1919	Bos-A	48	112	14	27	4	0	0	1	12	8	.241	.315	.277	71	-4	2			.922	-5	O-33	-1.2
Total	9	312	1068	142	289	30	10	2	58	140	80	.271	.357	.323	102	6	37			.957	-7	O-285	-1.6

■ BERNARD GILKEY
Gilkey, Otis Bernard b: 9/24/66, St.Louis, Mo. BR/TR, 6', 170 lbs. Deb: 9/4/90

YEAR	TM/L	G	AB	R	H	2B	3B	HR	RBI	BB	SO	AVG	OBP	SLG	PRO+	BR/A	SB	CS	SBR	FA	FR	G/POS	TPR
1990	StL-N	18	64	11	19	5	2	1	3	8	5	.297	.375	.484	134	3	6	1	1	.961	3	O-18	0.7
1991	StL-N	81	268	28	58	7	2	5	20	39	33	.216	.318	.313	78	-7	14	8	-1	.994	9	O-74	-0.1
1992	StL-N	131	384	56	116	19	4	7	43	39	52	.302	.368	.427	128	14	18	12	-2	.978	7	*O-111	1.9
1993	StL-N	137	557	99	170	40	5	16	70	56	66	.305	.373	.481	129	23	15	10	-2	.969	3	*O-134/1-3	2.1
1994	StL-N	105	380	52	96	22	6	6	45	39	65	.253	.338	.363	84	-8	15	8	-0	.983	5	*O-102	-0.6
1995	StL-N	121	480	73	143	33	4	17	69	42	70	.298	.361	.490	122	15	12	6	0	.986	10	*O-118	2.0
1996	NY-N	153	571	108	181	44	3	30	117	73	125	.317	.398	.562	161	50	17	9	-0	.982	24	*O-151	6.6
Total	7	746	2704	427	783	170	21	82	367	296	416	.290	.365	.459	123	90	97	54	-3	.981	61	O-708/1-3	12.6

■ BOB GILKS
Gilks, Robert James b: 7/2/1864, Cincinnati, Ohio d: 8/21/44, Brunswick, Ga. BR/TR, 5'8", 178 lbs. Deb: 8/25/1887

YEAR	TM/L	G	AB	R	H	2B	3B	HR	RBI	BB	SO	AVG	OBP	SLG	PRO+	BR/A	SB	CS	SBR	FA	FR	G/POS	TPR
1887	Cle-a	22	83	12	26	2	0	0	13		3	.313	.352	.337	96	-0	5			.881	2	P-13/1-6,O-3,2-1	0.0
1888	Cle-a	119	484	59	111	14	4	1	63		7	.229	.245	.281	70	-17	16			.899	-1	O-87,3-28/S-4,P2	-1.1
1889	Cle-N	53	210	17	50	5	2	0	18	7	20	.238	.273	.281	56	-13	6			1.000	0	O-29,S-13,1-10/2-1	-1.1
1890	Cle-N	130	544	65	116	10	3	0	41	32	38	.213	.265	.243	49	-35	17			.941	1	*O-123/P-4,S-3,2-2	-3.3
1893	Bal-N	15	64	10	17	2	0	0	7	0	3	.266	.277	.297	52	-2	3			.969	3	O-15	-0.2
Total	5	339	1385	163	320	33	9	1	142	49	61	.231	.265	.270	60	-69	47			.937	5	O-257/3-28,PS12	-6.4

■ JIM GILL
Gill, James C. b: St.Louis, Mo. Deb: 6/27/1889

YEAR	TM/L	G	AB	R	H	2B	3B	HR	RBI	BB	SO	AVG	OBP	SLG	PRO+	BR/A	SB	CS	SBR	FA	FR	G/POS	TPR
1889	StL-a	2	8	2	2	1	0	0	1	1	2	.250	.333	.375	90	-0	1			1.000	-0	/O-1,2-1	-0.1

■ JOHNNY GILL
Gill, John Wesley "Patcheye" b: 3/27/05, Nashville, Tenn. d: 12/26/84, Nashville, Tenn. BL/TR, 6'2", 190 lbs. Deb: 8/28/27

YEAR	TM/L	G	AB	R	H	2B	3B	HR	RBI	BB	SO	AVG	OBP	SLG	PRO+	BR/A	SB	CS	SBR	FA	FR	G/POS	TPR
1927	Cle-A	21	60	8	13	3	1		4	7	13	.217	.319	.317	65	-3	1	1	-0	1.000	-2	O-17	-0.6
1928	Cle-A	2	2	0	0	0	0	0	0	0	0	.000	.000	.000	-99	-1	0			.000	0	H	-0.1
1931	Was-A	8	30	2	8	2	1	0	5	1	6	.267	.313	.400	86	-1	0	1	-1	1.000	-1	/O-8	0.1
1934	Was-A	13	53	7	13	3	0	2	7	2	3	.245	.286	.415	82	-2	0	0	0	1.000	-1	O-13	-0.3
1935	Chi-N	3	3	1	2	1	0	0	1	0	1	.333	.333	.667	161	0	0			.000	0	H	0.0
1936	Chi-N	71	174	20	44	8	0	7	28	13	19	.253	.309	.420	92	-2	0			.938	-3	O-41	-0.6
Total	6	118	322	39	79	17	1	10	45	23	43	.245	.306	.398	84	-8	1		2	.968	-2	/O-79	-1.5

■ WARREN GILL
Gill, Warren Darst "Doc" b: 12/21/1878, Ladoga, Ind. d: 11/26/52, Laguna Beach, Cal. BR/TR, 6'1", 175 lbs. Deb: 8/26/08

YEAR	TM/L	G	AB	R	H	2B	3B	HR	RBI	BB	SO	AVG	OBP	SLG	PRO+	BR/A	SB	CS	SBR	FA	FR	G/POS	TPR
1908	Pit-N	27	76	10	17	0	1	0	14	11		.224	.366	.250	97	1	3			1.000	-3	1-25	-0.2

■ SAM GILLEN
Gillen, Samuel (b: Samuel Gilleland) b: 1/1871, Pittsburgh, Pa. d: 5/13/05, Pittsburgh, Pa. 5'8", Deb: 8/19/1893

YEAR	TM/L	G	AB	R	H	2B	3B	HR	RBI	BB	SO	AVG	OBP	SLG	PRO+	BR/A	SB	CS	SBR	FA	FR	G/POS	TPR
1893	Pit-N	3	6	0	0	0	0	0	0	0	1	.000	.000	.000	-99	-2	0			.750	-2	/S-3	-0.2
1897	Phi-N	75	270	32	70	10	3	0	27	35		.259	.353	.319	80	-6	2			.896	-29	S-69/3-6	-3.0
Total	2	78	276	32	70	10	3	0	27	35	1	.254	.346	.312	76	-8	2			.892	-30	/S-72,3-6	-3.2

■ TOM GILLEN
Gillen, Thomas J. b: 5/18/1862, Philadelphia, Pa. d: 1/26/1889, Philadelphia, Pa. 5'8", 160 lbs. Deb: 4/18/1884

YEAR	TM/L	G	AB	R	H	2B	3B	HR	RBI	BB	SO	AVG	OBP	SLG	PRO+	BR/A	SB	CS	SBR	FA	FR	G/POS	TPR
1884	Phi-U	29	116	5	18	2	0	0		1		.155	.162	.172	2	-17				.895	-4	C-27/O-3	-1.7
1886	Det-N	2	10	2	4	0	0	0		1		.400	.400	.400	140	-0				.889	-2	/C-2	-0.1
Total		31	126	7	22	2	0	0		4	1	1	.175	.181	.190	14	-17	0			.895	-6	/C-29,O-3	-1.8

■ CARDEN GILLENWATER
Gillenwater, Carden Edison b: 5/13/18, Riceville, Tenn. BR/TR, 6'1", 178 lbs. Deb: 9/22/40

YEAR	TM/L	G	AB	R	H	2B	3B	HR	RBI	BB	SO	AVG	OBP	SLG	PRO+	BR/A	SB	CS	SBR	FA	FR	G/POS	TPR
1940	StL-N	7	25	1	4	1	0	0	5	0	2	.160	.160	.200	-1	-3	0			1.000	-1	/O-7	-0.5
1943	Bro-N	8	17	1	3	0	0	0	2	2	3	.176	.263	.176	28	-2	0			1.000	-0	/O-4	-0.2
1945	Bos-N	144	517	74	149	20	2	7	72	73	70	.288	.379	.375	110	9	13			.979	24	*O-140	2.5
1946	Bos-N	99	224	30	51	10	1	1	14	39	27	.228	.342	.295	81	-4	3			.979	1	O-78	-0.6

YEAR	TM/L	G	AB	R	H	2B	3B	HR	RBI	BB	SO	AVG	OBP	SLG	PRO+	BR/A	SB	CS	SBR	FA	FR	G/POS	TPR
1948	Was-A	77	221	23	54	10	4	3	21	39	36	.244	.358	.367	96	-1	4	2	0	.974	-1	O-67	-0.5
Total 5		335	1004	129	261	41	7	11	114	153	138	.260	.359	.348	96	-1	20	2		.979	23	O-296	0.7

■ JIM GILLESPIE
Gillespie, James Wheatfield b: 9/1858, Canada BL/TR. Deb: 10/1/1890

YEAR	TM/L	G	AB	R	H	2B	3B	HR	RBI	BB	SO	AVG	OBP	SLG	PRO+	BR/A	SB	CS	SBR	FA	FR	G/POS	TPR
1890	Buf-P	1	3	0	0	0	0	0	0	0	0	.000	.000	.000	-99	-1	0			.250	-0	/O-1	-0.1

■ PAUL GILLESPIE
Gillespie, Paul Allen b: 9/18/20, Sugar Valley, Ga. d: 8/11/70, Anniston, Ala. BL/TR, 6'3", 195 lbs. Deb: 9/11/42

YEAR	TM/L	G	AB	R	H	2B	3B	HR	RBI	BB	SO	AVG	OBP	SLG	PRO+	BR/A	SB	CS	SBR	FA	FR	G/POS	TPR
1942	Chi-N	5	16	3	4	0	0	2	4	1	2	.250	.294	.625	172	1	0			1.000	-1	/C-4	0.0
1944	Chi-N	9	26	2	7	1	0	1	2	3	3	.269	.345	.423	116	1	0			.903	-1	/C-7	0.0
1945	*Chi-N	75	163	12	47	6	0	3	25	18	9	.288	.366	.380	110	3	2			.989	1	C-45/O-1	0.6
Total 3		89	205	17	58	7	0	6	31	22	14	.283	.358	.405	115	4	2			.978	-1	C-56,O-1	0.6

■ PETE GILLESPIE
Gillespie, Peter Patrick b: 11/30/1851, Carbondale, Pa. d: 5/5/10, Carbondale, Pa. BL/TR, 6'1.5", 178 lbs. Deb: 5/1/1880

YEAR	TM/L	G	AB	R	H	2B	3B	HR	RBI	BB	SO	AVG	OBP	SLG	PRO+	BR/A	SB	CS	SBR	FA	FR	G/POS	TPR
1880	Tro-N	82	346	50	84	20	5	2	24	17	35	.243	.278	.347	105					.905	7	*O-82	0.5
1881	Tro-N	84	348	43	96	14	3	0	41	9	24	.276	.294	.333	92	-4				.933	4	*O-84	-0.1
1882	Tro-N	74	298	46	82	5	4	2	33	9	14	.275	.296	.339	108	3				.827	-6	*O-74	-0.2
1883	NY-N	98	411	64	129	23	12	1	62	9	27	.314	.329	.436	131	15				.897	7	*O-98	1.8
1884	NY-N	101	413	75	109	7	4	2	44	19	35	.264	.296	.315	90	-5				.893	-3	*O-101	-0.9
1885	NY-N	102	420	67	123	17	6	0	52	15	32	.293	.317	.362	121	9				**.942**	-4	*O-102	0.2
1886	NY-N	97	396	65	108	13	8	0	58	16	30	.273	.301	.346	95	-3	17			.901	-10	*O-97	-1.4
1887	NY-N	76	295	40	78	9	3	3	37	12	21	.264	.304	.346	84	-6	37			.946	-2	O-76/3-1	-0.8
Total 8		714	2927	450	809	108	45	10	351	106	218	.276	.303	.354	104	11	54			.903	-8	O-714/3-1	-0.9

■ JIM GILLIAM
Gilliam, James William "Junior" b: 10/17/28, Nashville, Tenn. d: 10/8/78, Inglewood, Cal. BB/TR, 5'10.5", 175 lbs. Deb: 4/14/53 C

YEAR	TM/L	G	AB	R	H	2B	3B	HR	RBI	BB	SO	AVG	OBP	SLG	PRO+	BR/A	SB	CS	SBR	FA	FR	G/POS	TPR
1953	*Bro-N	151	605	125	168	31	**17**	6	63	100	38	.278	.383	.415	106	8	21	14	-2	.976	3	*2-149	1.7
1954	Bro-N	146	607	107	171	28	8	13	52	76	30	.282	.364	.418	100	1	8	7	-2	.977	-11	*2-143/O-4	-0.3
1955	*Bro-N	147	538	110	134	20	8	7	40	70	37	.249	.342	.355	83	-12	15	15	-5	.968	-9	2-99,O-46	-2.0
1956	*Bro-N☆	153	594	102	178	23	8	6	43	95	39	.300	.400	.396	107	10	21	9	1	.981	18	*2-102,O-56	3.4
1957	Bro-N	149	617	89	154	26	4	2	37	64	31	.250	.324	.314	66	-28	26	10	2	**.986**	3	*2-148/O-2	-1.2
1958	LA-N	147	555	81	145	25	5	2	43	78	22	.261	.352	.335	81	-13	18	11	-1	.987	8	O-75,3-44,2-32	-0.8
1959	*LA-N★	145	553	91	156	18	4	3	34	**96**	25	.282	.388	.345	91	-3	23	10	1	.958	2	*3-132/2-8,O-3	0.0
1960	LA-N	151	557	96	138	20	2	5	40	96	28	.248	.361	.318	82	-10	12	9	-2	.960	9	*3-130,2-30	0.0
1961	LA-N	144	439	74	107	26	3	4	32	79	34	.244	.359	.344	81	-10	8	4	0	.956	2	3-74,2-71,O-11	-0.2
1962	LA-N	160	588	83	159	24	1	4	43	93	35	.270	.372	.335	97	-3	21	7	1	.981	-14	*2-113,3-90/O-1	0.0
1963	*LA-N	148	525	77	148	27	4	6	49	60	28	.282	.358	.383	122	15	19	5	3	.985	-8	*2-119,3-55	2.2
1964	LA-N	116	334	44	76	8	3	2	27	42	21	.228	.319	.287	78	-9	4	4	-1	.936	-20	3-86,2-25/O-2	-3.1
1965	*LA-N	111	372	54	104	19	4	4	39	53	31	.280	.375	.384	123	13	5	3	0	.960	-13	3-80,O-22/2-5	-0.3
1966	*LA-N	88	235	30	51	9	0	1	16	34	17	.217	.316	.268	70	-9	2	1	0	.953	-12	3-70/1-2,2-2	-2.4
Total 14		1956	7119	1163	1889	304	71	65	558	1036	416	.265	.361	.355	92	-45	203	111	-6	.979	-43	*2-1046,3-761,O/1	-3.0

■ BARNEY GILLIGAN
Gilligan, Andrew Bernard b: 1/3/1856, Cambridge, Mass. d: 4/1/34, Lynn, Mass. BR/TR, 5'6.5", 130 lbs. Deb: 9/25/1875

YEAR	TM/L	G	AB	R	H	2B	3B	HR	RBI	BB	SO	AVG	OBP	SLG	PRO+	BR/A	SB	CS	SBR	FA	FR	G/POS	TPR
1875	Atl-n	2	8	2	2	0	0	0	0	0	0	.250	.250	.250	85	-0	0	0	0	1.000	-1	/C-1,O-1	-0.1
1879	Cle-N	52	205	20	35	6	2	0	11	0	13	.171	.171	.220	28	-15				.870	-0	C-27,O-23/S-2	-1.5
1880	Cle-N	30	99	9	17	4	3	1	13	6	12	.172	.219	.303	77	-2				.969	4	C-23/O-4,S-4	0.3
1881	Pro-N	46	183	19	40	7	2	0	20	9	24	.219	.255	.279	69	-6				.930	-1	C-36,S-10/O-1	-0.5
1882	Pro-N	56	201	32	45	7	6	0	26	4	26	.224	.239	.318	77	-5				.932	10	C-54/S-2	0.6
1883	Pro-N	74	263	34	52	13	3	0	24	26	32	.198	.270	.270	63	-11				.900	10	*C-74	0.3
1884	*Pro-N	82	294	47	72	8	3	1	38	35	41	.245	.325	.313	104	3				.928	17	*C-81/3-1,1-1	2.4
1885	Pro-N	71	252	23	54	7	3	0	12	23	33	.214	.280	.266	80	-4				.872	-3	C-65/S-5,0-1,2-1	-0.1
1886	Was-N	81	273	23	52	9	2	0	17	39	35	.190	.292	.238	66	-9	6			.925	-9	C-71,O-14/S-1,3-1	-0.9
1887	Was-N	28	90	7	18	2	0	1	6	5	18	.200	.242	.256	40	-7	2			.874	4	C-26/S-3,O-1	-0.7
1888	Det-N	1	5	1	1	0	0	0	0	0	1	.200	.200	.200	28	-0				.875	-0	/C-1	-0.0
Total 10		521	1865	215	386	68	23	3	167	147	235	.207	.265	.273	71	-58	8	0		.912	24	C-458/O-44,S321	-0.1

■ GRANT GILLIS
Gillis, Grant b: 1/24/01, Grove Hill, Ala. d: 2/4/81, Thomasville, Ala. BR/TR, 5'10", 165 lbs. Deb: 9/19/27

YEAR	TM/L	G	AB	R	H	2B	3B	HR	RBI	BB	SO	AVG	OBP	SLG	PRO+	BR/A	SB	CS	SBR	FA	FR	G/POS	TPR
1927	Was-A	10	36	8	8	3	1	0	2	2	0	.222	.263	.361	61	-2	0	0	0	1.000	-2	S-10	-0.3
1928	Was-A	24	87	13	22	5	1	0	10	4	5	.253	.309	.333	69	-4	0	1	-1	.910	-13	S-16/2-5,3-3	-1.3
1929	Bos-A	28	73	5	18	4	0	0	11	6	8	.247	.304	.301	58	-5	0	1	-1	.956	-4	2-25	-0.7
Total 3		62	196	26	48	12	2	0	23	12	13	.245	.299	.327	63	-11	0	2	-1	.948	-16	/2-30,S-26,3-3	-2.3

■ JIM GILMAN
Gilman, James Deb: 7/10/1893

YEAR	TM/L	G	AB	R	H	2B	3B	HR	RBI	BB	SO	AVG	OBP	SLG	PRO+	BR/A	SB	CS	SBR	FA	FR	G/POS	TPR
1893	Cle-N	2	7	1	2	0	0	0	1	0	2	.286	.286	.286	49	-1				.667	-1	/3-2	-0.1

■ PIT GILMAN
Gilman, Pitkin Clark b: 3/14/1864, Laporte, Ohio d: 8/17/50, Elyria, Ohio BL/TL, 170 lbs. Deb: 9/18/1884

YEAR	TM/L	G	AB	R	H	2B	3B	HR	RBI	BB	SO	AVG	OBP	SLG	PRO+	BR/A	SB	CS	SBR	FA	FR	G/POS	TPR
1884	Cle-N	2	10	1	1	0	0	0	0	0	3	.100	.100	.100	-36	-2				1.000	0	/O-2	-0.1

■ GROVER GILMORE
Gilmore, Ernest Grover b: 11/1/1888, Chicago, Ill. d: 11/25/19, Sioux City, Iowa BL/TL, 5'9.5", 170 lbs. Deb: 4/18/14

YEAR	TM/L	G	AB	R	H	2B	3B	HR	RBI	BB	SO	AVG	OBP	SLG	PRO+	BR/A	SB	CS	SBR	FA	FR	G/POS	TPR
1914	KC-F	139	530	91	152	25	5	1	32	37	108	.287	.337	.358	93	-14	23			.973	3	*O-132	-1.8
1915	KC-F	119	411	53	117	22	15	1	47	26	50	.285	.347	.418	120	3	19			.979	7	*O-119	0.5
Total 2		258	941	144	269	47	20	2	79	63	158	.286	.341	.385	105	-10	42			.976	10	O-251	-1.3

■ JIM GILMORE
Gilmore, James b: 5/1853, Baltimore, Md. d: 11/18/28, Baltimore, Md. Deb: 4/26/1875

YEAR	TM/L	G	AB	R	H	2B	3B	HR	RBI	BB	SO	AVG	OBP	SLG	PRO+	BR/A	SB	CS	SBR	FA	FR	G/POS	TPR
1875	Was-n	3	12	2	3	0	0	0	0	0	3	.250	.250	.250	77	-0				.667	-1	/C-2,3-1,O-1	-0.1

■ GILROY
Gilroy Deb: 9/7/1874

YEAR	TM/L	G	AB	R	H	2B	3B	HR	RBI	BB	SO	AVG	OBP	SLG	PRO+	BR/A	SB	CS	SBR	FA	FR	G/POS	TPR
1874	Chi-n	8	38	4	8	1	0	0	7	1	3	.211	.231	.237	50	-2				.816	-2	/C-8	-0.3
1875	Ath-n	2	6	0	1	0	0	0	0	0	0	.167	.167	.167	15	-1				.800	1	/C-1,O-1	0.1
Total 2 n		10	44	4	9	1	0	0	7	1	3	.205	.222	.227	45	-3				.814	-1	/C-9,O-1	-0.2

■ TINSLEY GINN
Ginn, Tinsley Rucker b: 9/26/1891, Royston, Ga. d: 8/30/31, Atlanta, Ga. BL/TR, 5'9", 180 lbs. Deb: 6/27/14

YEAR	TM/L	G	AB	R	H	2B	3B	HR	RBI	BB	SO	AVG	OBP	SLG	PRO+	BR/A	SB	CS	SBR	FA	FR	G/POS	TPR
1914	Cle-A	2	1	0	0	0	0	0	0	0	0	.000	.000	.000	-96	-0				.000	0	/O-2	0.0

■ JOE GINSBERG
Ginsberg, Myron Nathan b: 10/11/26, New York, N.Y. BL/TR, 5'11", 180 lbs. Deb: 9/15/48

YEAR	TM/L	G	AB	R	H	2B	3B	HR	RBI	BB	SO	AVG	OBP	SLG	PRO+	BR/A	SB	CS	SBR	FA	FR	G/POS	TPR
1948	Det-A	11	36	7	13	0	0	0	1	3	1	.361	.410	.361	103	1	0	0	0	.943	-2	C-11	0.0
1950	Det-A	36	95	12	22	6	0	0	12	11	6	.232	.318	.295	56	-6	0	0	0	.981	-4	C-31	-0.8
1951	Det-A	102	304	44	79	10	2	8	37	43	21	.260	.355	.385	100	0	0	2	-1	.978	-1	C-95	0.2
1952	Det-A	113	307	29	68	13	2	6	36	51	21	.221	.338	.336	87	-4	1	1	0	.984	-14	*C-101	-1.4
1953	Det-A	18	53	6	16	2	0	0	3	10	1	.302	.422	.340	109	1	0	0	0	.988	0	C-15	0.2
	Cle-A	46	109	10	31	4	0	0	10	14	4	.284	.371	.321	91	-1	0	0	0	.966	-5	C-39	-0.4
	Yr	64	162	16	47	6	0	0	13	24	5	.290	.388	.327	97	-1	0	0	0	.974	-5	C-54	-0.2
1954	Cle-A	3	2	0	1	0	0	0	0	0	0	.500	.667	1.500	473	1	0	0	0	1.000	-0	/C-1	0.1
1956	KC-A	71	195	15	48	8	1	1	12	23	17	.246	.326	.313	69	-8	1	0	0	.989	-2	C-57	-0.9
	Bal-A	15	28	0	2	0	0	0	0	2	4	.071	.133	.071	-48	-6	0	0	0	1.000	-0	C-8	-0.6
	Yr	86	223	15	50	8	1	1	12	25	21	.224	.302	.283	56	-14	1	0	0	.990	-3	C-65	-1.5
1957	Bal-A	85	175	15	48	8	2	0	18	18	19	.274	.349	.360	100	0	0	0	0	.986	1	C-66	0.3
1958	Bal-A	61	109	4	23	1	0	3	16	13	14	.211	.306	.303	72	-4	0	0	0	.994	3	C-39	0.1
1959	Bal-A	65	166	14	30	3	0	1	14	11	13	.181	.273	.211	35	-14	0	0	0	.993	5	C-62	-0.9
1960	Bal-A	14	30	3	3	1	0	0	0	6	6	.100	.270	.133	90	-0	0	0	0	.940	0	C-14	0.1
	Chi-A	28	75	8	19	4	0	0	6	10	8	.253	.349	.307	80	-2	0	0	0	.993	-2	C-25	0.4
	Yr	42	105	11	27	5	0	0	6	15	16	.257	.361	.305	83	-2	0	0	0	.976	-2	C-39	0.5
1961	Chi-A	6	3	0	0	0	0	0	0	0	2	.000	.250	.000	-27	-1	0	0	0	1.000	0	/C-2	0.0
	Bos-A	19	24	1	6	0	0	0	0	2	2	.250	.250	.250	33	-1	0	0	0	1.000	-1	/C-6	-0.3

YEAR	TM/L	G	AB	R	H	2B	3B	HR	RBI	BB	SO	AVG	OBP	SLG	PRO+	BR/A	SB	CS	SBR	FA	FR	G/POS	TPR
	Yr	25	27	1	6	0	0	0	5	1	4	.222	.250	.222	27	-3	0	0	0	1.000	-1	/C-8	-0.3
1962	NY-N	2	5	0	0	0	0	0	0	0	0	.000	.000	.000	-98	-1	0	0	0	1.000	1	/C-2	0.0
Total	13	695	1716	168	414	59	8	20	182	226	135	.241	.334	.320	79	-47	7	5	-1	.983	-17	C-574	-3.9

■ AL GIONFRIDDO

Gionfriddo, Albert Francis b: 3/8/22, Dysart, Pa. BL/TL, 5'6", 165 lbs. Deb: 9/23/44

YEAR	TM/L	G	AB	R	H	2B	3B	HR	RBI	BB	SO	AVG	OBP	SLG	PRO+	BR/A	SB	CS	SBR	FA	FR	G/POS	TPR
1944	Pit-N	4	6	0	1	0	0	0	0	1	1	.167	.286	.167	28	-1	0			1.000	0	/O-1	-0.1
1945	Pit-N	122	409	74	116	18	9	2	42	60	22	.284	.377	.386	108	6	12			.964	-8	*O-106	-0.8
1946	Pit-N	64	102	11	26	2	2	0	10	14	5	.255	.345	.314	85	-2	1			.944	-5	O-33	-0.8
1947	Pit-N	1	1	0	0	0	0	0	0	0	0	.000	.000	.000	-97	-0	0			.000	0	H	-0.6
	*Bro-N	37	62	10	11	2	1	0	6	16	11	.177	.346	.242	57	-3	2			.938	-2	O-17	-0.6
	Yr	38	63	10	11	2	1	0	6	16	11	.175	.342	.238	54	-4	2			.938	-2	O-17	-0.6
Total	4	228	580	95	154	22	12	2	58	91	39	.266	.366	.355	97	0	15			.959	-15	O-157	-2.3

■ TOMMY GIORDANO

Giordano, Thomas Arthur "T-Bone" b: 10/9/25, Newark, N.J. BR/TR, 6', 175 lbs. Deb: 9/11/53

YEAR	TM/L	G	AB	R	H	2B	3B	HR	RBI	BB	SO	AVG	OBP	SLG	PRO+	BR/A	SB	CS	SBR	FA	FR	G/POS	TPR
1953	Phi-A	11	40	6	7	2	0	2	5	5	6	.175	.267	.375	69	-2	0	1	-1	.984	1	2-11	-0.1

■ ED GIOVANOLA

Giovanola, Edward Thomas b: 3/4/69, Los Gatos, Cal. BL/TR, 5'10", 170 lbs. Deb: 9/10/95

YEAR	TM/L	G	AB	R	H	2B	3B	HR	RBI	BB	SO	AVG	OBP	SLG	PRO+	BR/A	SB	CS	SBR	FA	FR	G/POS	TPR
1995	Atl-N	13	14	2	1	0	0	0	0	3	5	.071	.235	.071	-14	-2	0	0	0	1.000	-2	/2-7,3-3,S-1	-0.4
1996	Atl-N	43	82	10	19	2	0	0	7	8	13	.232	.308	.256	48	-6	1	0	0	.983	-2	S-25/3-6,2-5	-1.0
Total	2	56	96	12	20	2	0	0	7	11	18	.208	.296	.229	39	-8	1	0	0	.983	-4	/S-26,2-12,3-9	-1.0

■ JOE GIRARDI

Girardi, Joseph Elliott b: 10/14/64, Peoria, Ill. BR/TR, 5'11", 195 lbs. Deb: 4/4/89

YEAR	TM/L	G	AB	R	H	2B	3B	HR	RBI	BB	SO	AVG	OBP	SLG	PRO+	BR/A	SB	CS	SBR	FA	FR	G/POS	TPR
1989	*Chi-N	59	157	15	39	10	0	1	14	11	26	.248	.306	.331	76	-5	2	1	0	.981	13	C-59	1.2
1990	Chi-N	133	419	36	113	24	2	1	38	17	50	.270	.303	.344	72	-16	8	3	1	.985	-9	*C-133	-1.7
1991	Chi-N	21	47	3	9	2	0	0	6	6	6	.191	.283	.234	45	-3	0	0	0	.972	4	C-21	0.1
1992	Chi-N	91	270	19	73	3	1	1	12	19	38	.270	.321	.300	75	-8	0	2	-1	.991	-4	C-86	-1.0
1993	Col-N	86	310	35	90	14	5	3	31	24	41	.290	.347	.397	85	-7	6	6	-2	.989	-8	C-84	-1.2
1994	Col-N	93	330	47	91	9	4	4	34	21	48	.276	.323	.364	67	-16	3	3	-1	.992	5	C-93	-0.6
1995	*Col-N	125	462	63	121	17	2	8	55	29	76	.262	.308	.359	59	-30	3	3	-1	.988	-4	*C-122	-2.6
1996	*NY-A	124	422	55	124	22	3	2	45	30	55	.294	.348	.374	81	-12	13	4	2	.996	7	*C-120/D-2	0.5
Total	8	732	2417	273	660	101	17	20	235	157	340	.273	.322	.354	72	-97	35	22	-3	.989	4	C-718/D-2	-5.3

■ TONY GIULIANI

Giuliani, Angelo John b: 11/24/12, St.Paul, Minn. BR/TR, 5'11", 175 lbs. Deb: 4/18/36

YEAR	TM/L	G	AB	R	H	2B	3B	HR	RBI	BB	SO	AVG	OBP	SLG	PRO+	BR/A	SB	CS	SBR	FA	FR	G/POS	TPR
1936	StL-A	71	198	17	43	3	0	0	13	11	13	.217	.258	.232	21	-25	0	0	0	.966	5	C-66	-1.5
1937	StL-A	19	53	6	16	1	0	0	3	3	3	.302	.339	.321	67	-3	0	0	0	.986	-0	C-19	-0.2
1938	Was-A	46	115	10	25	3	0	0	8	7	17	.217	.268	.252	33	-12	1	0	0	1.000	-1	C-46	-1.0
1939	Was-A	54	172	30	43	6	2	0	18	4	7	.250	.267	.308	50	-13	0	1	-1	.979	1	C-50	-0.9
1940	Bro-N	1	1	0	0	0	0	0	0	0	0	.000	.000	.000	-94	-0	0	0	0	1.000	0	/C-1	0.0
1941	Bro-N	3	2	0	0	0	0	0	0	0	1	.000	.000	.000	-96	-1	0	0	0	1.000	1	/C-3	0.0
1943	Was-A	49	133	5	30	4	1	0	20	12	14	.226	.290	.271	67	-6	0	1	-1	.962	-5	C-49	-0.5
Total	7	243	674	58	157	18	3	0	69	38	41	.233	.274	.269	42	-59	1	2		.976	6	C-234	-4.1

■ JIM GLADD

Gladd, James Walter b: 10/2/22, Ft.Gibson, Okla. d: 11/8/77, Long Beach, Cal. BR/TR, 6'2", 190 lbs. Deb: 9/9/46

YEAR	TM/L	G	AB	R	H	2B	3B	HR	RBI	BB	SO	AVG	OBP	SLG	PRO+	BR/A	SB	CS	SBR	FA	FR	G/POS	TPR
1946	NY-N	4	11	0	1	0	0	0	0	1	4	.091	.167	.091	-26	-2	0			1.000	4	/C-4	0.2

■ DAN GLADDEN

Gladden, Clinton Daniel b: 7/7/57, San Jose, Cal. BR/TR, 5'11", 180 lbs. Deb: 9/5/83

YEAR	TM/L	G	AB	R	H	2B	3B	HR	RBI	BB	SO	AVG	OBP	SLG	PRO+	BR/A	SB	CS	SBR	FA	FR	G/POS	TPR
1983	SF-N	18	63	6	14	2	0	1	9	5	11	.222	.279	.302	63	-3	4	3	-1	1.000	2	O-18	-0.2
1984	SF-N	86	342	71	120	17	2	4	31	33	37	.351	.411	.447	146	22	31	16	-0	.988	9	O-85	2.9
1985	SF-N	142	502	64	122	15	8	7	41	40	78	.243	.308	.347	87	-9	32	15	1	.975	1	*O-124	-1.3
1986	SF-N	102	351	55	97	16	1	4	29	39	59	.276	.357	.362	104	3	27	10	2	.987	12	O-89	1.4
1987	*Min-A	121	438	69	109	21	2	8	38	38	72	.249	.313	.361	75	-15	25	9	2	.987	6	*O-111/D-4	-1.0
1988	Min-A	141	576	91	155	32	6	11	62	46	74	.269	.327	.403	100	-0	28	8	4	.991	16	*O-140/2-1,3-1,P-1	1.6
1989	Min-A	121	461	69	136	23	3	8	46	23	53	.295	.335	.410	102	1	23	7	3	.966	5	*O-117/P-1,D-2	0.6
1990	Min-A	136	534	64	147	27	6	5	40	26	67	.275	.316	.376	87	-10	25	9	2	.980	12	*O-133/D-2	0.1
1991	*Min-A	126	461	65	114	14	9	6	52	36	60	.247	.309	.356	80	-13	15	9	-1	.988	1	*O-126	-1.6
1992	Det-A	113	417	57	106	20	1	7	42	30	64	.254	.307	.357	85	-9	4	2	0	.987	0	*O-108/D-2	-1.1
1993	Det-A	91	356	52	95	16	2	13	56	21	50	.267	.313	.433	99	-2	8	5	-1	.986	8	O-86/D-5	0.4
Total	11	1197	4501	663	1215	203	40	74	446	337	625	.270	.327	.382	94	-36	222	93	11	.984	73	*O-1137/D-15,P32	1.8

■ BUCK GLADMAN

Gladman, John H. b: 1864, Washington, D.C. Deb: 7/7/1883

YEAR	TM/L	G	AB	R	H	2B	3B	HR	RBI	BB	SO	AVG	OBP	SLG	PRO+	BR/A	SB	CS	SBR	FA	FR	G/POS	TPR
1883	Phi-N	1	4	1	0	0	0	0	0	0	2	.000	.000	.000	-99	-1				1.000	-1	/3-1	-0.1
1884	Was-a	56	224	17	35	5	3	1	9	2	28	.156	.178	.219	33	-16				.796	-3	3-53/O-2,S-1	-1.7
1886	Was-N	44	152	17	21	5	3	1	15	12	30	.138	.201	.230	33	-12	5			.830	-6	3-44	-1.6
Total	3	101	380	35	56	10	6	2	15	15	32	.147	.186	.221	31	-28	5			.812	-10	/3-98,O-2,S-1	-3.4

■ ROLAND GLADU

Gladu, Roland Edouard b: 5/10/11, Montreal, Que., Can d: 7/26/94, Montreal, Que., Can. BL/TR, 5'8.5", 185 lbs. Deb: 4/18/44

YEAR	TM/L	G	AB	R	H	2B	3B	HR	RBI	BB	SO	AVG	OBP	SLG	PRO+	BR/A	SB	CS	SBR	FA	FR	G/POS	TPR
1944	Bos-N	21	66	5	16	2	1	1	7	3	8	.242	.275	.348	72	-3	0			.891	-5	3-15/O-3	-0.8

■ DOUG GLANVILLE

Glanville, Douglas Metunwa b: 8/25/70, Hackensack, N.J. BR/TR, 6'2", 170 lbs. Deb: 6/9/96

YEAR	TM/L	G	AB	R	H	2B	3B	HR	RBI	BB	SO	AVG	OBP	SLG	PRO+	BR/A	SB	CS	SBR	FA	FR	G/POS	TPR
1996	Chi-N	49	83	10	20	5	1	1		3	11	.241	.267	.361	63	-5	2	0	1	.973	-6	O-35	-1.0

■ JACK GLASSCOCK

Glasscock, John Wesley "Pebbly Jack" b: 7/22/1859, Wheeling, W.Va. d: 2/24/47, Wheeling, W.Va. BR/TR, 5'8", 160 lbs. Deb: 5/1/1879 M

YEAR	TM/L	G	AB	R	H	2B	3B	HR	RBI	BB	SO	AVG	OBP	SLG	PRO+	BR/A	SB	CS	SBR	FA	FR	G/POS	TPR
1879	Cle-N	80	325	31	68	9	3	0	29	6	24	.209	.224	.255	58	-14				.919	-6	*2-66,3-14	-1.4
1880	Cle-N	77	296	37	72	13	3	0	27	2	21	.243	.248	.307	89	-3				.891	7	*S-77	0.8
1881	Cle-N	85	335	49	86	9	5	0	33	15	8	.257	.289	.313	94	-2				.911	9	*S-79/2-6	1.2
1882	Cle-N	84	358	60	104	27	9	4	46	13	9	.291	.315	.450	147	18				.900	24	*S-83/3-1	4.1
1883	Cle-N	96	383	67	110	19	6	0	46	13	23	.287	.311	.368	107	3				.922	17	*S-93/2-3	1.9
1884	Cle-N	72	281	45	70	4	4	1	22	25	16	.249	.310	.302	91	-3				.893	27	S-69/2-3,P-2	2.2
	Cin-U	38	172	48	72	9	5	2				.419	.444	.564	189	14				.889	1	S-36/2-2	1.3
1885	StL-N	111	446	66	125	18	3	1	40	29	10	.280	.324	.341	123	12				.917	19	*S-110/2-1	3.1
1886	StL-N	121	486	96	158	29	7	3	40	38	13	.325	.394	.432	154	33	38			.906	14	*S-120/O-1	4.2
1887	Ind-N	122	483	91	142	18	7	0	40	41	8	.294	.361	.360	105	5	62			.906	35	*S-122/P-1	3.5
1888	Ind-N	113	442	63	119	17	3	1	45	14	17	.269	.302	.328	99	-1	48			.901	11	*S-110/2-3,P-1	1.3
1889	Ind-N	134	582	128	205	40	3	7	85	31	10	.352	.390	.467	136	26	57			.915	36	*S-132/2-2,P-1,M	5.9
1890	NY-N	124	512	91	172	32	9	1	66	41	8	.336	.395	.439	143	27	54			.910	22	*S-124	4.9
1891	NY-N	97	369	46	89	12	6	0	55	36	11	.241	.317	.306	85	-6	29			.913	-2	*S-97	-0.3
1892	StL-N	139	566	83	151	27	5	3	44	24	19	.267	.327	.348	110	6	20			.916	6	*S-139,M	1.7
1893	StL-N	48	195	32	56	8	1	1	26	25	3	.287	.382	.354	96	-0	20			.907	-7	S-48	-0.4
	Pit-N	66	293	49	100	7	11	1	74	17	4	.341	.385	.451	124	9	16			.934	12	S-66	2.0
	Yr	114	488	81	156	15	12	2	100	42	7	.320	.384	.412	113	9	36			.923	5	*S-114	1.6
1894	Pit-N	86	332	46	93	10	7	1	63	10	4	.280	.349	.361	72	-15	18			.933	5	S-85	-0.2
1895	Lou-N	18	74	9	25	3	1	1	6	3	1	.338	.387	.446	122	2	1			.900	3	S-13/1-5	0.4
	Was-N	25	100	20	23	5	0	0	16	10	3	.230	.300	.250	43	-8	3			.895	5	S-25	-0.1
	Yr	43	174	29	48	8	1	1	22	13	4	.276	.337	.333	76	-6	4			.897	8	S-38/1-5	0.3
Total	17	1736	7030	1163	2040	313	98	27	825	439	212	.290	.337	.374	112	105	372			.910	240	*S-1628/2-86,31PO	36.1

■ TOMMY GLAVIANO

Glaviano, Thomas Giatano "Rabbit" b: 10/26/23, Sacramento, Cal. BR/TR, 5'9", 175 lbs. Deb: 4/19/49

YEAR	TM/L	G	AB	R	H	2B	3B	HR	RBI	BB	SO	AVG	OBP	SLG	PRO+	BR/A	SB	CS	SBR	FA	FR	G/POS	TPR
1949	StL-N	87	258	32	69	16	1	6	36	41	35	.267	.380	.407	106	4	0			.929	14	3-73/2-7	1.6
1950	StL-N	115	410	92	119	17	2	11	44	90	74	.290	.421	.446	122	17	6			.935	6	*3-106/2-5,S-1	2.1
1951	StL-N	54	104	20	19	4	0	1	4	26	18	.183	.356	.250	66	-4	3	0	1	.972	-3	O-17/2-9	-0.6
1952	StL-N	80	162	30	39	5	3	1	19	27	26	.241	.366	.340	97	0	0	0	0	.934	4	3-52/2-1	0.4

YEAR	TM/L	G	AB	R	H	2B	3B	HR	RBI	BB	SO	AVG	OBP	SLG	PRO+	BR/A	SB	CS	SBR	FA	FR	G/POS	TPR
1953	Phi-N	53	74	17	15	1	2	3	5	24	20	.203	.410	.392	111	2	2	0	1	.892	-2	3-14,2-12/S-1	0.1
Total	5	389	1008	191	259	55	6	24	108	208	173	.257	.395	.395	108	20	11	0		.931	18	3-245/2-34,O-17,S-2	3.6

■ HARRY GLEASON

Gleason, Harry Gilbert b: 3/28/1875, Camden, N.J. d: 10/21/61, Camden, N.J. BR/TR, 5'6", 160 lbs. Deb: 9/27/01 F

YEAR	TM/L	G	AB	R	H	2B	3B	HR	RBI	BB	SO	AVG	OBP	SLG	PRO+	BR/A	SB	CS	SBR	FA	FR	G/POS	TPR
1901	Bos-A	1	1	0	1	0	0	0	0	0	0	1.000	1.000	1.000	464	0	1			.667	1	/3-1	0.1
1902	Bos-A	71	240	30	54	5	5	2	25	10		.225	.265	.313	58	-14	6			.930	-0	3-35,O-23/2-4	-1.5
1903	Bos-A	6	13	3	2	1	0	0	2	0		.154	.154	.231	13	-1	0			.750	-1	/3-2	-0.3
1904	StL-A	46	155	10	33	7	1	0	6	4		.213	.247	.271	68	-6	1			.908	-3	S-20,3-20/2-5,O-1	-0.9
1905	StL-A	150	535	45	116	11	5	1	57	34		.217	.269	.262	72	-17	23			.911	-15	*3-144/2-7	-2.9
Total	5	274	944	88	206	24	11	3	90	48		.218	.263	.276	67	-38	31			.914	-19	3-202/O-24,S-20,2	-5.5

■ JACK GLEASON

Gleason, John Day b: 7/14/1854, St.Louis, Mo. d: 9/4/44, St.Louis, Mo. BR/TR, 170 lbs. Deb: 10/2/1877 F

YEAR	TM/L	G	AB	R	H	2B	3B	HR	RBI	BB	SO	AVG	OBP	SLG	PRO+	BR/A	SB	CS	SBR	FA	FR	G/POS	TPR
1877	StL-N	1	4	0	1	0	0	0	0	1		.250	.250	.250	61	-0				.000	-0	/O-1	-0.1
1882	StL-a	78	331	53	84	10	1	2		27		.254	.310	.308	105	2				.768	2	*3-73/O-6,2-1	0.5
1883	StL-a	9	34	2	8	0	0	0		4		.235	.316	.235	76	-1				.833	0	/O-9,3-1	0.0
	Lou-a	84	355	69	106	11	4	2		25		.299	.345	.369	140	17				.795	-33	*3-83/S-1	-1.5
	Yr	93	389	71	114	11	4	2		29		.293	.342	.357	134	16				.798	-33	3-84/O-9,S-1	-1.5
1884	StL-U	92	395	90	128	30	2	4		23		.324	.361	.441	137	7				.768	-6	*3-92	0.1
1885	StL-N	2	7	0	1	0	0	0	0	0	1	.143	.143	.143	-8	-1				.857	-0	/3-2	-0.1
1886	Phi-a	77	299	39	56	8	7	1	31	16		.187	.255	.271	64	-13	8			.797	-6	3-77	-1.4
Total	6	343	1425	253	384	59	14	9	31	95	2	.269	.320	.349	112	11	8			.781	-43	3-328/O-16,S-1,2-1	-2.5

■ ROY GLEASON

Gleason, Roy William b: 4/9/43, Melrose Park, Ill. BB/TR, 6'5.5", 220 lbs. Deb: 9/3/63

YEAR	TM/L	G	AB	R	H	2B	3B	HR	RBI	BB	SO	AVG	OBP	SLG	PRO+	BR/A	SB	CS	SBR	FA	FR	G/POS	TPR
1963	LA-N	8	1	3	1	0	0	0	0	0	0	1.000	1.000	2.000	795	1	0	0	0	.000	0	H	0.1

■ BILL GLEASON

Gleason, William G. "Will" b: 11/12/1858, St.Louis, Mo. d: 7/21/32, St.Louis, Mo. BR/TR, 5'8", 170 lbs. Deb: 5/2/1882 FU

YEAR	TM/L	G	AB	R	H	2B	3B	HR	RBI	BB	SO	AVG	OBP	SLG	PRO+	BR/A	SB	CS	SBR	FA	FR	G/POS	TPR
1882	StL-a	79	347	63	100	11	6	1		6		.288	.300	.363	118	5				.833	9	*S-79	1.7
1883	StL-a	98	425	81	122	21	5	0		42	15	.287	.311	.393	119	7				.871	-2	*S-98	0.7
1884	StL-a	110	472	97	127	21	7	1		27		.269	.325	.350	116	8				.867	-17	*S-110/3-1	-0.7
1885	*StL-a	112	472	79	119	9	5	3	53	29		.252	.316	.311	94	-3				.869	-42	*S-112	-3.9
1886	*StL-a	125	524	97	141	18	5	0	61	43		.269	.333	.323	101	-0	19			.853	-29	*S-125	-2.5
1887	*StL-a	135	598	135	172	19	1	0	76	41		.288	.342	.323	78	-21	23			.875	-10	*S-135	-2.4
1888	Phi-a	123	499	55	112	10	2	0	61	12		.224	.256	.253	63	-20	27			.858	-14	*S-121/3-1,1-1	-2.9
1889	Lou-a	16	58	6	14	2	0	0	5	4	1	.241	.302	.276	66	-2	1			.822	-3	S-16	-0.4
Total	8	798	3395	613	907	111	35	7	298	177	1	.267	.313	.327	95	-26	70			.860	-106	S-796/3-2,1-1	-10.4

■ KID GLEASON

Gleason, William J. b: 10/26/1866, Camden, N.J. d: 1/2/33, Philadelphia, Pa. BB/TR, 5'7", 158 lbs. Deb: 4/20/1888 FMC

YEAR	TM/L	G	AB	R	H	2B	3B	HR	RBI	BB	SO	AVG	OBP	SLG	PRO+	BR/A	SB	CS	SBR	FA	FR	G/POS	TPR
1888	Phi-N	24	83	4	17	2	0	0	5	3	16	.205	.233	.229	45	-5	3			.841	-3	P-24/O-1	0.0
1889	Phi-N	30	99	11	25	5	0	0	8	8	12	.253	.308	.303	65	-5	4			.862	-1	P-29/O-3,2-2	-0.1
1890	Phi-N	63	224	22	47	3	0	0	17	12	21	.210	.250	.223	37	-18	10			.937	-6	P-60/2-2	-0.1
1891	Phi-N	65	214	31	53	5	2	0	17	20	17	.248	.318	.290	75	-7	6			.896	-6	P-53/O-9,S-4	-0.4
1892	StL-N	66	233	35	50	4	2	3	25	34	21	.215	.315	.288	87	-3	7			.934	3	P-47,O-10/2-9,1-1	-0.3
1893	StL-N	59	199	25	51	6	4	0	20	19	8	.256	.327	.327	74	-8	2			.907	-0	P-48,O-11/S-1	-0.3
1894	StL-N	9	28	3	7	0	1	0	1	2	1	.250	.300	.321	50	-1	0			.885	1	/P-8,1-1	0.0
	*Bal-N	26	86	22	30	5	1	0	17	7	2	.349	.398	.430	95	-1	1			.900	-2	P-21/1-1	0.0
	Yr	35	114	25	37	5	2	0	18	9	3	.325	.374	.404	85	-3	1			.894	-0	P-29/1-2	0.0
1895	*Bal-N	112	421	90	130	14	12	0	74	33	18	.309	.366	.399	95	-4	19			.899	-17	2-85,3-12/P-9,O-4	-1.3
1896	NY-N	133	541	79	162	17	5	4	89	42	13	.299	.352	.372	93	-5	46			.938	3	*2-130/3-3,O-1	0.5
1897	NY-N	131	540	85	172	16	4	1	106	26		.319	.353	.369	93	-5	43			.930	7	*2-129/S-3	0.2
1898	NY-N	150	570	78	126	8	5	0	62	39		.221	.278	.253	54	-34	21			.938	21	*2-144/S-6	-0.3
1899	NY-N	146	576	72	152	14	4	0	59	24		.264	.293	.302	66	-28	29			.946	26	*2-146	0.5
1900	NY-N	111	420	60	104	11	3	1	29	17		.248	.280	.295	62	-22	23			.931	14	*2-111/S-1	-0.3
1901	Det-A	135	547	82	150	16	12	3	75	41		.274	.327	.364	87	-10	32			.925	6	*2-135	0.1
1902	Det-A	118	441	42	109	11	4	1	38	25		.247	.292	.297	62	-22	17			.941	6	*2-118	-1.2
1903	Phi-N	106	412	65	117	19	6	1	49	23		.284	.326	.367	101	-1	12			.959	-4	*2-102/O-4	-0.1
1904	Phi-N	153	587	61	161	23	6	0	42	37		.274	.319	.334	106	3	17			.942	1	*2-152/3-1	0.9
1905	Phi-N	155	608	95	150	17	7	1	50	45		.247	.302	.303	83	-12	16			.947	-8	*2-155	-1.9
1906	Phi-N	135	494	47	112	17	2	0	34	36		.227	.281	.269	71	-17	17			.947	-29	*2-135	-5.1
1907	Phi-N	36	126	11	18	3	0	0	6	7		.143	.200	.167	15	-12	3			.979	-2	2-26/1-4,S-4,O-1	-1.7
1908	Phi-N	2	1	0	0	0	0	0	0	0		.000	.000	.000	-97	-0				1.000	0	/2-1,O-1	0.0
1912	Chi-A	1	2	0	1	0	0	0	0	0		.500	.500	.500	192	0	0			1.000	-0	/2-1	0.0
Total	22	1966	7452	1020	1944	216	80	15	823	500	131	.261	.311	.317	78	-216	328			.938	8	*2-1583,P-299/OS31	-10.8

■ BILLY GLEASON

Gleason, William Patrick b: 9/6/1894, Chicago, Ill. d: 1/9/57, Holyoke, Mass. BR/TR, 5'6.5", 157 lbs. Deb: 9/25/16

YEAR	TM/L	G	AB	R	H	2B	3B	HR	RBI	BB	SO	AVG	OBP	SLG	PRO+	BR/A	SB	CS	SBR	FA	FR	G/POS	TPR
1916	Pit-N	1	2	0	0	0	0	0	0	0	0	.000	.000	.000	-99	-0	0			1.000	-0	/2-1	-0.1
1917	Pit-N	13	42	3	7	1	0	0	0	5	5	.167	.255	.190	36	-3	1			.978	-5	2-13	-0.9
1921	StL-A	26	74	6	19	0	1	0	8	6	6	.257	.329	.284	54	-5	0	1	-1	.960	-5	2-25	-0.9
Total	3	40	118	9	26	1	1	0	8	11	11	.220	.298	.246	47	-8	1		1	.966	-10	/2-39	-1.9

■ JIM GLEESON

Gleeson, James Joseph "Gee Gee" b: 3/5/12, Kansas City, Mo. d: 5/1/96, Kansas City, Mo. BB/TR, 6'1", 191 lbs. Deb: 4/25/36 C

YEAR	TM/L	G	AB	R	H	2B	3B	HR	RBI	BB	SO	AVG	OBP	SLG	PRO+	BR/A	SB	CS	SBR	FA	FR	G/POS	TPR
1936	Cle-A	41	139	26	36	9	2	4	12	18	17	.259	.344	.439	91	-2	2	1	0	.958	-2	O-33	-0.5
1939	Chi-N	111	332	43	74	19	6	4	45	39	46	.223	.308	.352	76	-11	7			.957	-4	O-91	-1.9
1940	Chi-N	129	485	76	152	39	11	5	61	54	52	.313	.389	.470	139	26	4			.983	3	*O-123	2.2
1941	Cin-N	102	301	47	70	10	3	4	34	45	30	.233	.340	.296	80	-6	0			.981	-8	O-84	-2.0
1942	Cin-N	9	20	3	4	0	0	0	2	2	2	.200	.304	.200	49	-1	0			.889	-0	/O-5	-0.2
Total	5	392	1277	195	336	77	19	16	154	158	147	.263	.350	.391	101	5	20	1		.972	-11	O-336	-2.4

■ FRANK GLEICH

Gleich, Frank Elmer "Inch" b: 3/7/1894, Columbus, Ohio d: 3/27/49, Columbus, Ohio BL/TR, 5'11", 175 lbs. Deb: 9/17/19

YEAR	TM/L	G	AB	R	H	2B	3B	HR	RBI	BB	SO	AVG	OBP	SLG	PRO+	BR/A	SB	CS	SBR	FA	FR	G/POS	TPR
1919	NY-A	5	4	0	1	0	0	0	1	1	0	.250	.400	.250	84	-0	0			.000	-2	/O-4	-0.2
1920	NY-A	24	41	6	5	0	0	0	3	6	10	.122	.234	.122	-4	-6	0	0	0	.864	-4	O-15	-1.1
Total	2	29	45	6	6	0	0	0	4	7	10	.133	.250	.133	4	-6	0	0		.826	-7	/O-19	-1.3

■ BOB GLENALVIN

Glenalvin, Robert J. (b: Robert J. Dowling) b: 1/17/1867, Indianapolis, Ind. d: 3/24/44, Detroit, Mich. TR, 5'9", 160 lbs. Deb: 7/12/1890

YEAR	TM/L	G	AB	R	H	2B	3B	HR	RBI	BB	SO	AVG	OBP	SLG	PRO+	BR/A	SB	CS	SBR	FA	FR	G/POS	TPR
1890	Chi-N	66	250	43	67	10	3	4	26	19	31	.268	.337	.380	105	1	30			.928	-14	2-66	-0.9
1893	Chi-N	16	61	11	21	3	0	0	12	7	3	.344	.412	.426	125	2	7			.928	-5	2-16	-0.2
Total	2	82	311	54	88	13	3	4	38	26	34	.283	.352	.389	109	3	37			.928	-19	/2-82	-1.1

■ ED GLENN

Glenn, Edward C. "Mouse" b: 9/19/1860, Richmond, Va. d: 2/10/1892, Richmond, Va. BR/TR, 5'10", 160 lbs. Deb: 8/5/1884

YEAR	TM/L	G	AB	R	H	2B	3B	HR	RBI	BB	SO	AVG	OBP	SLG	PRO+	BR/A	SB	CS	SBR	FA	FR	G/POS	TPR
1884	Ric-a	43	175	26	43	2	4	1		6		.246	.271	.320	93	-1				.833	5	O-43	0.2
1886	Pit-a	71	277	32	53	6	5	0	26	17		.191	.241	.249	54	-15	19			.865	0	O-71	-1.4
1888	KC-a	3	8	0	0	0	0	0	0	0		.000	.200	.000	-32	-1	1			.857	-0	/O-3	-0.1
	Bos-N	20	65	8	10	0	2	0	3	2	8	.154	.203	.215	33	-5	0			.957	2	O-19/3-1	-0.3
Total	3	137	525	66	106	8	11	1	29	24	8	.202	.245	.265	62	-22	20			.867	7	O-136/3-1	-1.6

■ ED GLENN

Glenn, Edward D. b: 10/1875, Ohio d: 12/6/11, Ludlow, Ky. BR/TR, Deb: 9/7/1898

YEAR	TM/L	G	AB	R	H	2B	3B	HR	RBI	BB	SO	AVG	OBP	SLG	PRO+	BR/A	SB	CS	SBR	FA	FR	G/POS	TPR
1898	Was-N	1	4	0	0	0	0	0	0	0	0	.000	.000	.000	-99	-1	0			1.000	-1	/S-1	-0.2
	NY-N	2	4	1	1	0	0	0	0	0	3	.250	.571	.250	142	1	1			.750	-3	/S-2	-0.2
	Yr	3	8	1	1	0	0	0	0	0	3	.125	.364	.125	42	-0	1			.857	-3	/S-3	-0.4
1902	Chi-N	2	7	0	0	0	0	0	0	0	1	.000	.125	.000	-63	-1	0			1.000	-1	/S-2	-0.3
Total	2	5	15	1	1	0	0	0	0	0	4	.067	.263	.067	-2	-2	1			.923	-5	/S-5	-0.7

YEAR	TM/L	G	AB	R	H	2B	3B	HR	RBI	BB	SO	AVG	OBP	SLG	PRO+	BR/A	SB	CS	SBR	FA	FR	G/POS	TPR

■ HARRY GLENN Glenn, Harry Melville "Husky" b: 6/9/1890, Shelburn, Ind. d: 10/12/18, St.Paul, Minn. BR/TR, 6'1", 200 lbs. Deb: 4/14/15

| 1915 | StL-N | 6 | 16 | 1 | 5 | 0 | 0 | 0 | 1 | 3 | 0 | .313 | .421 | .313 | 123 | 1 | | 0 | | .929 | -1 | /C-5 | 0.0 |

■ JOHN GLENN Glenn, John b: 7/10/28, Moultrie, Ga. BR/TR, 6'3", 180 lbs. Deb: 6/16/60

| 1960 | StL-N | 32 | 31 | 4 | 8 | 0 | 1 | 0 | 5 | 0 | 9 | .258 | .258 | .323 | 53 | -2 | 0 | 0 | 0 | 1.000 | -7 | O-28 | -1.0 |

■ JOHN GLENN Glenn, John W. b: 1849, Rochester, N.Y. d: 11/10/1888, Sandy Hill, N.Y. BR/TR, 5'8.5", 169 lbs. Deb: 5/13/1871

1871	Oly-n	26	120	25	37	3	2	0	21	3	1	.308	.325	.367	104	1	1	1	-0	.860	1	*O-26	0.2
1872	Oly-n	9	39	6	6	0	0	0	3	1	0	.154	.175	.154	2	-4	0	1	-1	.800	3	/O-9	-0.1
	Nat-n	1	4	0	2	0	0	0	0	0	0	.500	.500	.500	179	0	0	0		.667	-0	/O-1	0.0
	Yr	10	43	6	8	0	0	0	3	1	0	.186	.205	.186	22	-4	0	1	-1	.791	3	O-10	-0.1
1873	Was-n	39	185	39	49	8	2	1	21	3	0	.265	.277	.346	87	-3	2	1	0	.928	-2	*1-39	-0.2
1874	Chi-n	55	237	33	67	9	0	0	33	5	4	.283	.298	.321	97	-1	2	2	-1	.918	2	1-37,O-19	0.0
1875	Chi-n	69	308	46	75	8	0	0	27	3	6	.244	.251	.269	80	-6	10	2	2	.898	-2	O-44,1-29	-0.5
1876	Chi-N	66	276	55	84	9	2	0	32	12	6	.304	.333	.351	115	2				.881	-2	*O-56,1-15	0.0
1877	Chi-N	50	202	31	46	6	1	0	20	8	16	.228	.257	.267	58	-10				.948	0	O-36,1-14	-1.1
Total	5 n	199	893	149	236	28	4	1	105	15	11	.264	.276	.308	87	-12	15	7	0	.923	0	1-105/O-99	-0.6
Total	2	116	478	86	130	15	3	0	52	20	22	.272	.301	.316	90	-8				.904	-2	/O-92,1-29	-1.1

■ JOE GLENN Glenn, Joseph Charles "Gabby" (b: Joseph Charles Gurzensky) b: 11/19/08, Dickson City, Pa. d: 5/6/85, Tunkhannock, Pa. BR/TR, 5'11", 175 lbs. Deb: 9/15/32

1932	NY-A	6	16	0	2	0	0	0	1	0	5	.125	.222	.125	-8	-3	0	0	0	1.000	-2	/C-5	-0.4
1933	NY-A	5	21	1	3	0	0	0	1	0	3	.143	.143	.143	-26	-4	0	0	0	1.000	-2	/C-5	-0.5
1935	NY-A	17	43	7	10	4	0	0	6	4	1	.233	.298	.326	65	-2	0	0	0	.984	0	C-16	-0.1
1936	NY-A	44	129	21	35	7	0	1	20	20	10	.271	.373	.349	82	-3	3	1	-0	.970	7	C-44	0.1
1937	NY-A	25	53	6	15	2	2	0	4	10	11	.283	.397	.396	100	1	0	0	0	.978	4	C-24	0.4
1938	NY-A	41	123	10	32	5	1	0	25	10	14	.260	.316	.350	67	-6	1	0	0	.974	0	C-40	-0.4
1939	StL-A	88	286	29	78	13	1	4	29	31	40	.273	.344	.367	80	-8	4	4	-1	.968	-13	C-82	-1.7
1940	Bos-A	22	47	3	6	1	0	0	4	5	7	.128	.212	.149	-5	-7	0	0	0	.961	-0	C-19	-0.6
Total	8	248	718	77	181	34	5	5	89	81	91	.252	.330	.334	69	-33	6	5	-1	.972	-10	C-235	-3.2

■ NORM GLOCKSON Glockson, Norman Stanley b: 6/15/1894, Blue Island, Ill. d: 8/5/55, Maywood, Ill. BR/TR, 6'2", 200 lbs. Deb: 9/16/14

| 1914 | Cin-N | 7 | 12 | 0 | 0 | 0 | 0 | 0 | 0 | 1 | 6 | .000 | .077 | .000 | -74 | -3 | 0 | | | .923 | -1 | /C-7 | -0.3 |

■ AL GLOSSOP Glossop, Alban b: 7/23/15, Christopher, Ill. d: 7/2/91, Walnut Creek, Cal. BB/TR, 6', 170 lbs. Deb: 9/23/39

1939	NY-N	10	32	3	6	0	0	1	3	4	2	.188	.278	.281	50	-2	0			.980	0	2-10	-0.1
1940	NY-N	27	91	16	19	3	0	4	8	10	16	.209	.294	.374	82	-2	1			.952	0	2-24	0.0
	Bos-N	60	148	17	35	2	1	3	14	17	22	.236	.315	.324	81	-4	1			.938	6	2-18,3-18/S-1	0.4
	Yr	87	239	33	54	5	1	7	22	27	38	.226	.307	.343	82	-6	2			.947	7	2-42,3-18/S-1	0.4
1942	Phi-N	121	454	33	102	15	1	4	40	29	35	.225	.273	.289	68	-20	3			.961	7	*2-118/3-1	-0.6
1943	Bro-N	87	217	28	37	9	0	3	21	28	27	.171	.268	.253	51	-13	0			.927	-7	S-33,2-24,3-17/O-1	-1.9
1946	Chi-N	4	10	2	0	0	0	0	0	1	3	.000	.231	.000	-32	-2	0			1.000	0	/2-2,S-2	-0.3
Total	5	309	952	99	199	29	2	15	86	89	105	.209	.280	.291	66	-43	5			.954	6	2-196/S-36,3-36,O-1	-2.5

■ BILL GLYNN Glynn, William Vincent b: 7/30/25, Sussex, N.J. BL/TL, 6', 190 lbs. Deb: 9/16/49

1949	Phi-N	8	10	1	2	0	0	0	1	0	0	.200	.200	.200	8	-1	0			1.000	0	/1-1	-0.1
1952	Cle-A	44	92	15	25	5	0	2	7	5	16	.272	.309	.391	101	-0	1	0	0	.973	0	1-32	-0.1
1953	Cle-A	147	411	60	100	14	2	3	30	44	65	.243	.324	.309	74	-14	1	3	-2	.993	6	*1-135/O-2	-1.5
1954	*Cle-A	111	171	19	43	3	2	5	18	12	21	.251	.301	.380	84	-4	3	2	-0	.987	3	1-96/O-1	-0.4
Total	4	310	684	94	170	22	4	10	56	61	105	.249	.315	.336	79	-21	5	5	5	.989	9	1-264/O-3	-2.1

■ JOHN GOCHNAUER Gochnauer, John Peter b: 9/12/1875, Altoona, Pa. d: 9/27/29, Altoona, Pa. BR/TR, 5'9", 160 lbs. Deb: 9/29/01

1901	Bro-N	3	11	1	4	0	0	0	2	1		.364	.417	.364	124	-0	1			1.000	-1	/S-3	0.0
1902	Cle-A	127	459	45	85	16	4	0	37	38		.185	.247	.237	36	-39	7			.933	-3	*S-127	-3.3
1903	Cle-A	134	438	48	81	16	4	0	48	48		.185	.265	.240	53	-24	10			.869	-21	*S-134	-4.1
Total	3	264	908	94	170	32	8	0	87	87		.187	.258	.240	45	-63	18			.901	-24	S-264	-7.4

■ JOHN GODAR Godar, John Michael b: 10/25/1864, Cincinnati, Ohio d: 6/23/49, Park Ridge, Ill. BR/TR, 5'9", 170 lbs. Deb: 7/8/1892

| 1892 | Bal-N | 5 | 14 | 2 | 3 | 0 | 0 | 0 | 1 | 0 | | .214 | .353 | .214 | 71 | -0 | 1 | | | 1.000 | -0 | /O-5 | -0.1 |

■ DANNY GODBY Godby, Danny Ray b: 11/4/46, Logan, W.Va. BR/TR, 6', 185 lbs. Deb: 8/10/74

| 1974 | StL-N | 13 | 13 | 2 | 2 | 0 | 0 | 0 | 1 | 3 | 4 | .154 | .313 | .154 | 34 | -1 | 0 | 0 | 0 | 1.000 | 1 | /O-4 | 0.0 |

■ JOE GODDARD Goddard, Joseph Harold b: 7/23/50, Beckley, W.Va. BR/TR, 5'11", 181 lbs. Deb: 7/31/72

| 1972 | SD-N | 12 | 35 | 0 | 7 | 2 | 0 | 0 | 2 | 5 | 9 | .200 | .300 | .257 | 64 | -2 | 0 | 0 | 0 | .973 | -2 | C-12 | -0.4 |

■ JOHN GODWIN Godwin, John Henry "Bunny" b: 3/10/1877, E.Liverpool, Ohio d: 5/5/56, E.Liverpool, Ohio BR/TR, 6', 190 lbs. Deb: 8/14/05

1905	Bos-A	15	43	4	14	1	0	0	10	3		.326	.408	.349	139	2	3			.950	1	/O-7,2-5	0.3
1906	Bos-A	66	193	11	36	5	1	0	15	6		.187	.215	.207	32	-15	6			.907	2	3-27,S-14,O-10,/21	-1.4
Total	2	81	236	15	50	6	1	0	25	9		.212	.253	.233	53	-13	9			.935	3	/3-27,O-17,S-14,21	-1.1

■ ED GOEBEL Goebel, Edwin b: 9/1/1899, Brooklyn, N.Y. d: 8/12/59, Brooklyn, N.Y. BR/TR, 5'11", 170 lbs. Deb: 5/13/22

| 1922 | Was-A | 37 | 59 | 13 | 16 | 1 | 0 | 1 | 3 | 8 | 16 | .271 | .358 | .339 | 87 | -1 | 1 | 1 | -0 | 1.000 | -1 | O-16 | -0.3 |

■ BILLY GOECKEL Goeckel, William John b: 9/3/1871, Wilkes-Barre, Pa. d: 11/1/22, Philadelphia, Pa. BR/TL, Deb: 8/10/1899

| 1899 | Phi-N | 37 | 141 | 17 | 37 | 3 | 1 | 0 | 16 | 1 | | .262 | .283 | .298 | 61 | -8 | 6 | | | .978 | -3 | 1-36 | -0.9 |

■ JERRY GOFF Goff, Jerry Leroy b: 4/12/64, San Rafael, Cal. BL/TR, 6'3", 205 lbs. Deb: 5/15/90

1990	Mon-N	52	119	14	27	1	0	3	7	21	36	.227	.343	.311	84	-2	0	2	-1	.963	-1	C-38/1-3,3-3	-0.2
1992	Mon-N	3	3	0	0	0	0	0	0	0	3	.000	.000	.000	-99	-1	0	0	0	.000	0	/H	-0.1
1993	Pit-N	14	37	5	11	2	0	2	6	8	9	.297	.422	.514	149	3	0	0	0	.984	-2	C-14	0.1
1994	Pit-N	8	25	0	2	0	0	0	1	0	11	.080	.080	.080	-57	-6	0	0	0	.950	-1	/C-7	-0.7
1995	Hou-N	12	26	2	4	2	0	1	3	4	13	.154	.267	.346	64	-1	0	0	0	1.000	7	C-11	0.5
1996	Hou-N	1	4	1	2	1	0	0	2	0	1	.500	.500	1.250	377	1	0	0	0	1.000	0	/C-1	0.1
Total	6	90	214	22	46	5	0	6	19	33	73	.215	.320	.336	80	-5	0	2	-1	.974	2	/C-71,3-3,1-3	-0.3

■ CHUCK GOGGIN Goggin, Charles Francis b: 7/7/45, Pompano Beach, Fla. BB/TR, 5'11", 175 lbs. Deb: 9/8/72

1972	Pit-N	5	7	0	2	0	0	0	1	0	1	.286	.375	.286	92	-0	0	0	0	1.000	0	/2-1	0.0
1973	Pit-N	1	1	1	1	0	0	0	0	0	0	1.000	1.000	1.000	468	0	0	0	0	1.000	-0	/C-1	0.0
	Atl-N	64	90	18	26	5	0	0	7	9	19	.289	.354	.344	88	-1	0	1	-1	.938	-10	2-19/O-6,S-5,C-1	-1.1
	Yr	65	91	19	27	5	0	0	7	9	19	.297	.360	.352	91	-1	0	1	-1	.938	-10	2-19/O-6,S-5,C-2	-1.1
1974	Bos-A	2	1	0	0	0	0	0	0	0	0	.000	.000	.000	-93	-0	0	0	0	.667	1	/2-2	0.0
Total	3	72	99	19	29	5	0	0	7	10	21	.293	.358	.343	90	-1	0	1	-1	.927	-9	/2-22,O-6,S-5,C-2	-1.1

■ MIKE GOLDEN Golden, Michael Henry b: 9/11/1851, Shirley, Mass. d: 1/11/29, Rockford, Ill. BR/TR, 5'8", 168 lbs. Deb: 5/5/1875

1875	Wes-n	13	46	6	6	0	0	0		1	3	.130	.130	.130	-9	-5	0	0	0	.844	-1	P-13	0.0
	Chi-n	39	155	16	40	3	0	0	14	2	10	.258	.268	.277	89	-2	3	2	-0	.833	-1	O-27,P-14	-0.1
	Yr	52	201	22	46	3	0	0	15	2	13	.229	.236	.244	66	-7	3	2	-0	.833	-1	P-27,O-27	-0.1
1878	Mil-N	55	214	16	44	6	3	0	20	3	35	.206	.217	.262	53	-11				.831	-3	O-39,P-22/1-1	-1.2

■ JONAH GOLDMAN Goldman, Jonah John b: 8/29/06, New York, N.Y. d: 8/17/80, Palm Beach, Fla. BR/TR, 5'7", 170 lbs. Deb: 9/22/28

| 1928 | Cle-A | 7 | 21 | 1 | 5 | 1 | 0 | 0 | 3 | 0 | | .238 | .333 | .286 | 63 | -1 | 0 | 0 | 0 | .878 | 0 | /S-7 | 0.0 |
| 1930 | Cle-A | 111 | 306 | 32 | 74 | 18 | 0 | 1 | 44 | 28 | 25 | .242 | .312 | .310 | 56 | -5 | 3 | 5 | -2 | .945 | 21 | S-93,3-20 | 0.7 |

YEAR	TM/L	G	AB	R	H	2B	3B	HR	RBI	BB	SO	AVG	OBP	SLG	PRO+	BR/A	SB	CS	SBR	FA	FR	G/POS	TPR
1931	Cle-A	30	62	0	8	1	0	0	3	4	6	.129	.182	.145	-12	-10	1	1	-0	.947	14	S-30	0.5
Total	3	148	389	33	87	20	0	1	49	35	31	.224	.293	.283	46	-31	4	6	-2	.941	35	S-130/3-20	1.2

■ **GORDON GOLDSBERRY**   Goldsberry, Gordon Frederick   b: 8/30/27, Sacramento, Cal.   d: 2/23/96, Lake Forest, Cal.   BL/TL, 6′, 170 lbs.   Deb: 4/20/49

YEAR	TM/L	G	AB	R	H	2B	3B	HR	RBI	BB	SO	AVG	OBP	SLG	PRO+	BR/A	SB	CS	SBR	FA	FR	G/POS	TPR
1949	Chi-A	39	145	25	36	3	2	1	13	18	9	.248	.331	.317	74	-5	2	0	1	.990	-1	1-38	-0.6
1950	Chi-A	82	127	19	34	8	2	2	25	26	18	.268	.392	.409	108	2	0	2	-1	.989	3	1-40/O-3	0.4
1951	Chi-A	10	11	4	1	0	0	0	1	2	2	.091	.231	.091	-11	-2	0	0	0	1.000	1	/1-8	0.0
1952	StL-A	86	227	30	52	9	3	3	17	34	37	.229	.330	.335	83	-5	0	2	-1	.983	-3	1-72/O-2	-1.1
Total	4	217	510	78	123	20	7	6	56	80	66	.241	.344	.343	85	-10	2	4	-2	.987	1	1-158/O-5	-1.3

■ **WALT GOLDSBY**   Goldsby, Walton Hugh   b: 12/31/1861, Louisiana   d: 1/11/14, Dallas, Tex.   BL   Deb: 5/28/1884

YEAR	TM/L	G	AB	R	H	2B	3B	HR	RBI	BB	SO	AVG	OBP	SLG	PRO+	BR/A	SB	CS	SBR	FA	FR	G/POS	TPR
1884	StL-a	5	20	2	4	1	0	0	1	0		.200	.200	.200	30	-2				.800	-1	/O-5	-0.2
	Was-a	6	24	4	9	0	0	0	3	1		.375	.400	.375	174	2				.909	1	/O-6	0.2
	Ric-a	11	40	4	9	1	0	0	4	1		.225	.262	.250	69	-1				.737	-1	O-11	-0.2
	Yr	22	84	10	22	1	0	0	8	2		.262	.287	.274	87	-1				.800	-1	O-22	-0.2
1886	Was-N	6	18	0	4	1	0	0	1	2	3	.222	.300	.278	81	-0	0			.818	-1	/O-6	-0.1
1888	Bal-a	45	165	13	39	1	1	0	14	8		.236	.288	.255	76	-4	17			.903	-6	O-45	-1.0
Total	3	73	267	23	65	3	1	0	23	12	3	.243	.289	.262	80	-5	17			.858	-8	/O-73	-1.3

■ **FRED GOLDSMITH**   Goldsmith, Fred Ernest   b: 5/15/1856, New Haven, Conn.   d: 3/28/39, Berkley, Mich.   BR/TR, 6′1″, 195 lbs.   Deb: 10/23/1875   U

YEAR	TM/L	G	AB	R	H	2B	3B	HR	RBI	BB	SO	AVG	OBP	SLG	PRO+	BR/A	SB	CS	SBR	FA	FR	G/POS	TPR
1875	NH-n	1	4	0	2	0	0	0	1	0		.500	.500	.500	285	1	0	0	0	.700	0	/2-1	0.1
1879	Tro-N	9	38	6	9	1	0	0	2	1	3	.237	.256	.263	77	-1				.833	1	/P-8,O-2,1-1	0.0
1880	Chi-N	35	142	24	37	4	2	0	15	2	15	.261	.271	.317	93	-1				.968	1	P-26,O-10/1-4	-0.2
1881	Chi-N	42	158	24	38	3	4	0	16	6	17	.241	.268	.310	78	-4				.863	5	P-39/O-3	0.0
1882	Chi-N	45	183	23	42	11	1	0	19	4	29	.230	.246	.301	71	-6				.939	-2	P-45/1-1	0.0
1883	Chi-N	60	235	38	52	12	3	1	16	4	35	.221	.234	.311	60	-12				.865	1	P-46,O-16/1-2	-0.3
1884	Chi-N	22	81	11	11	2	0	2	6	7	26	.136	.205	.235	35	-6				.774	-3	P-21/O-2	0.0
	Bal-a	4	14	2	2	0	0	0		2		.143	.250	.143	30	-1				.889	1	/P-4,1-1	0.0
Total	6	217	851	128	191	33	10	3	74	26	125	.224	.247	.297	69	-31				.882	4	P-189/O-33,1-9	-0.5

■ **WALLY GOLDSMITH**   Goldsmith, Wallace   b: 1849, Baltimore, Md.   5′7″, 146 lbs.   Deb: 5/4/1871

YEAR	TM/L	G	AB	R	H	2B	3B	HR	RBI	BB	SO	AVG	OBP	SLG	PRO+	BR/A	SB	CS	SBR	FA	FR	G/POS	TPR
1871	Kek-n	19	88	8	18	1	0	0	12	4	2	.205	.239	.216	31	-8	0	0	0	.767	-10	S-14/3-8,C-2	-1.2
1872	Oly-n	9	41	4	10	2	0	0	5	0	0	.244	.244	.293	68	-1	0	0	0	.679	-1	/S-5,2-4	-0.2
1873	Mar-n	1	4	0	0	0	0	0	0	0		.000	.000	.000	-99	-1	0	0	0	.667	-0	/2-1	-0.1
1875	Wes-n	13	51	3	6	0	0	0	1	0	2	.118	.118	.118	-17	-6	0	0	0	.814	-1	3-13	-0.6
Total	4 n	42	184	15	34	3	0	0				.185	.202	.201	24	-16	0	0	0	.694	-13	/3-21,S-19,2-5,C-2	-2.1

■ **LONNIE GOLDSTEIN**   Goldstein, Leslie Elmer   b: 5/13/18, Austin, Tex.   BL/TL, 6′2.5″, 190 lbs.   Deb: 9/11/43

YEAR	TM/L	G	AB	R	H	2B	3B	HR	RBI	BB	SO	AVG	OBP	SLG	PRO+	BR/A	SB	CS	SBR	FA	FR	G/POS	TPR
1943	Cin-N	5	5	1	1	0	0	0	0	2	1	.200	.429	.200	85	0	0			1.000	-0	/1-2	0.0
1946	Cin-N	6	5	1	0	0	0	0	0	1	1	.000	.167	.000	-53	-1	0			.000	-0	H	-0.1
Total	2	11	10	2	1	0	0	0	0	3	2	.100	.308	.100	20	-1	0			1.000	-0	/1-2	-0.1

■ **PURNAL GOLDY**   Goldy, Purnal William   b: 11/28/37, Camden, N.J.   BR/TR, 6′5″, 200 lbs.   Deb: 4/12/62

YEAR	TM/L	G	AB	R	H	2B	3B	HR	RBI	BB	SO	AVG	OBP	SLG	PRO+	BR/A	SB	CS	SBR	FA	FR	G/POS	TPR
1962	Det-A	20	70	8	16	1	1	3	12	0	12	.229	.239	.400	66	-4	0	0	0	.964	-0	O-15	-0.5
1963	Det-A	9	8	1	2	0	0	0	0	0	4	.250	.250	.250	39	-1	0	0	0	.000	0	H	-0.1
Total	2	29	78	9	18	1	1	3	12	0	16	.231	.241	.385	64	-4	0	0	0	.964	-0	/O-15	-0.6

■ **STAN GOLETZ**   Goletz, Stanley "Stash"   b: 5/21/18, Crescent, Ohio   BL/TL, 6′3″, 200 lbs.   Deb: 9/9/41

YEAR	TM/L	G	AB	R	H	2B	3B	HR	RBI	BB	SO	AVG	OBP	SLG	PRO+	BR/A	SB	CS	SBR	FA	FR	G/POS	TPR
1941	Chi-A	5	5	0	3	0	0	0	0	0	2	.600	.600	.600	221	1	0	0	0	.000	0	H	0.1

■ **MIKE GOLIAT**   Goliat, Mike Mitchel   b: 11/5/25, Yatesboro, Pa.   BR/TR, 6′, 180 lbs.   Deb: 8/3/49

YEAR	TM/L	G	AB	R	H	2B	3B	HR	RBI	BB	SO	AVG	OBP	SLG	PRO+	BR/A	SB	CS	SBR	FA	FR	G/POS	TPR
1949	Phi-N	55	189	24	40	6	3	3	19	20	32	.212	.290	.323	66	-9	0			.969	-2	2-50/1-5	-0.9
1950	*Phi-N	145	483	49	113	13	6	13	64	53	75	.234	.314	.366	80	-15	3			.972	-18	*2-145	-2.6
1951	Phi-N	41	138	14	31	2	1	4	15	9	18	.225	.277	.341	66	-7	0	1	-1	.968	-7	2-37/3-2	-1.3
	StL-A	5	11	0	2	0	0	0	1	0	1	.182	.182	.182	-1	-2	0	0	0	1.000	0	/2-2	-0.1
1952	StL-A	3	4	0	0	0	0	0	0	1	1	.000	.200	.000	-40	-1	0	0	0	1.000	1	/2-3	0.0
Total	4	249	825	87	186	21	10	20	99	83	127	.225	.300	.348	73	-33	3	1		.971	-26	2-237/1-5,3-2	-4.9

■ **WALT GOLVIN**   Golvin, Walter George   b: 2/1/1894, Hershey, Neb.   d: 6/11/73, Gardena, Cal.   BL/TL, 6′, 165 lbs.   Deb: 4/15/22

YEAR	TM/L	G	AB	R	H	2B	3B	HR	RBI	BB	SO	AVG	OBP	SLG	PRO+	BR/A	SB	CS	SBR	FA	FR	G/POS	TPR
1922	Chi-N	2	2	0	0	0	0	0	0	0	0	.000	.000	.000	-98	-1	0	0	0	1.000	-0	/1-2	-0.1

■ **CHRIS GOMEZ**   Gomez, Christopher Cory   b: 6/16/71, Los Angeles, Cal.   BR/TR, 6′1″, 183 lbs.   Deb: 7/19/93

YEAR	TM/L	G	AB	R	H	2B	3B	HR	RBI	BB	SO	AVG	OBP	SLG	PRO+	BR/A	SB	CS	SBR	FA	FR	G/POS	TPR
1993	Det-A	46	128	11	32	7	1	0	11	9	17	.250	.304	.320	69	-6	2	2	-1	.963	11	S-29,2-17/D-1	0.6
1994	Det-A	84	296	32	76	19	0	8	53	33	64	.257	.337	.402	89	-5	5	3	-0	.981	-17	S-57,2-30	-1.5
1995	Det-A	123	431	49	96	20	2	11	50	41	96	.223	.295	.355	68	-21	4	1	1	.973	3	S-97,2-31/D-2	-0.6
1996	Det-A	48	128	21	31	5	0	1	16	18	20	.242	.340	.305	65	-6	1	1	-0	.970	3	S-47	0.0
	*SD-N	89	328	32	86	16	1	3	29	39	64	.262	.351	.345	89	-4	2	2	-1	.967	-6	S-89	-0.3
Total	4	390	1311	145	321	67	4	23	159	140	261	.245	.324	.355	78	-41	14	9	-1	.971	-6	S-319/2-78,D-3	-1.8

■ **CHILE GOMEZ**   Gomez, Jose Luis (Gonzales)   b: 5/23/09, Villa Union, Mex.   d: 12/1/92, Nuevo Laredo, Mex.   BR/TR, 5′10″, 165 lbs.   Deb: 7/27/35

YEAR	TM/L	G	AB	R	H	2B	3B	HR	RBI	BB	SO	AVG	OBP	SLG	PRO+	BR/A	SB	CS	SBR	FA	FR	G/POS	TPR
1935	Phi-N	67	222	24	51	3	0	0	16	17	34	.230	.285	.243	39	-19	2			.948	12	S-36,2-32	-0.3
1936	Phi-N	108	332	24	77	4	1	0	28	14	32	.232	.265	.250	36	-30	1			.948	18	2-71,S-40	-0.5
1942	Was-A	25	73	8	14	2	2	0	6	9	7	.192	.280	.274	57	-4	0	1	0	.973	-1	2-23/3-1	-0.4
Total	3	200	627	56	142	9	3	0	50	40	73	.226	.274	.250	39	-53	3	0		.954	29	2-126/S-76,3-1	-1.2

■ **LEO GOMEZ**   Gomez, Leonardo (Velez)   b: 3/2/66, Canovanas, P.R.   BR/TR, 6′, 180 lbs.   Deb: 9/17/90

YEAR	TM/L	G	AB	R	H	2B	3B	HR	RBI	BB	SO	AVG	OBP	SLG	PRO+	BR/A	SB	CS	SBR	FA	FR	G/POS	TPR
1990	Bal-A	12	39	3	9	0	0	0	8	7		.231	.362	.231	71	-1	0	0	0	.886	-2	3-12	-0.3
1991	Bal-A	118	391	40	91	17	2	16	45	40	82	.233	.307	.409	100	-1	1	1	-0	.972	-13	*3-105,D-10/1-3	-1.4
1992	Bal-A	137	468	62	124	24	0	17	64	63	78	.265	.362	.425	117	11	2	3	-1	.951	-13	*3-137	-0.3
1993	Bal-A	71	244	30	48	7	0	10	25	32	60	.197	.297	.348	70	-11	0	1	-1	.951	6	3-70/D-1	-0.5
1994	Bal-A	84	285	46	78	20	0	15	56	41	55	.274	.371	.502	116	7	0	0	-0	.975	2	3-78/1-1,D-5	1.0
1995	Bal-A	53	127	16	30	5	0	4	12	18	23	.236	.340	.370	83	-3	0	1	-1	.978	2	3-44/1-3,D-5	-0.1
1996	Chi-N	136	362	44	86	19	0	17	56	53	94	.238	.346	.431	102	1	1	4	-2	**.972**	-5	*3-124/1-8,S-1	-0.6
Total	7	611	1916	241	466	92	2	79	259	255	399	.243	.340	.417	102	5	4	10	-5	.962	-22	3-570/D-21,1-15,S-1	-2.2

■ **LUIS GOMEZ**   Gomez, Luis (Sanchez)   b: 8/19/51, Guadalajara, Mex.   BR/TR, 5′9″, 150 lbs.   Deb: 4/28/74

YEAR	TM/L	G	AB	R	H	2B	3B	HR	RBI	BB	SO	AVG	OBP	SLG	PRO+	BR/A	SB	CS	SBR	FA	FR	G/POS	TPR
1974	Min-A	82	168	18	35	1	0	0	3	12	16	.208	.261	.214	37	-13	2	3	-1	.960	20	S-74/2-2,D-1	1.2
1975	Min-A	89	72	7	10	0	0	0	5	4	12	.139	.184	.139	-7	-10	0	2	-1	.975	20	S-70/2-6,D-7	1.0
1976	Min-A	38	57	5	11	1	0	0	3	6	3	.193	.233	.211	30	-5	1	0	-0	.988	5	S-24/2-8,3-4,0-1,D	0.4
1977	Min-A	32	65	6	16	4	2	0	11	4	9	.246	.290	.369	79	-2	0	0	-0	.983	4	2-19/S-7,3-4,0-1,D	0.2
1978	Tor-A	153	413	39	92	7	3	0	32	34	41	.223	.282	.254	51	-26	2	10	-5	.976	-10	*S-153	-2.5
1979	Tor-A	59	163	11	39	7	0	0	11	6	17	.239	.266	.282	48	-12	1	0	0	1.000	4	3-22,2-20,S-15	-0.6
1980	Atl-N	121	278	18	53	0	0	0	24	17	27	.191	.240	.212	26	-27	0	4	-2	.968	12	*S-119	-0.8
1981	Atl-N	35	35	4	7	0	0	0	1	6	4	.200	.317	.200	48	-2	0	1	-1	.895	-3	S-21/3-9,2-3,P-1	-0.5
Total	8	609	1251	108	263	20	5	0	90	86	129	.210	.262	.239	40	-98	6	22	-11	.970	54	S-483/2-58,3DOP	-1.6

■ **PRESTON GOMEZ**   Gomez, Pedro (Martinez)   b: 4/20/23, Preston, Cuba   BR/TR, 5′11″, 170 lbs.   Deb: 5/5/44   MC

YEAR	TM/L	G	AB	R	H	2B	3B	HR	RBI	BB	SO	AVG	OBP	SLG	PRO+	BR/A	SB	CS	SBR	FA	FR	G/POS	TPR
1944	Was-A	8	7	2	2	1	0	0	2	0	4	.286	.286	.429	107	0				1.000	-1	/2-2,S-2	-0.1

■ **RANDY GOMEZ**   Gomez, Randell Scott   b: 2/4/57, San Mateo, Cal.   BR/TR, 5′10″, 185 lbs.   Deb: 8/21/84

YEAR	TM/L	G	AB	R	H	2B	3B	HR	RBI	BB	SO	AVG	OBP	SLG	PRO+	BR/A	SB	CS	SBR	FA	FR	G/POS	TPR
1984	SF-N	14	30	0	5	1	0	0	0	8	3	.167	.342	.200	57	-1	0	0	0	.951	3	C-14	0.3

YEAR	TM/L	G	AB	R	H	2B	3B	HR	RBI	BB	SO	AVG	OBP	SLG	PRO+	BR/A	SB	CS	SBR	FA	FR	G/POS	TPR

■ JESSE GONDER Gonder, Jesse Lemar b: 1/20/36, Monticello, Ark. BL/TR, 5'10", 190 lbs. Deb: 9/23/60

1960	NY-A	7	7	1	2	0	0	1	3	1	1	.286	.375	.714	199	1	0	0	0	1.000	1	/C-1	0.2
1961	NY-A	15	12	2	4	1	0	0	3	3	1	.333	.467	.417	146	1	0	0	0	.000	0	H	-0.1
1962	Cin-N	4	4	0	0	0	0	0	0	0	3	.000	.000	.000	-97	-1	0	0	0	.000	0	H	-0.1
1963	Cin-N	31	32	5	10	2	0	3	5	1	12	.313	.333	.656	172	3	0	0	0	1.000	1	/C-7	0.4
	NY-N	42	126	12	38	4	0	3	15	6	25	.302	.333	.405	110	1	1	2	-1	.978	-14	C-31	-1.4
	Yr	73	158	17	48	6	0	6	20	7	37	.304	.333	.456	122	4	1	2	-1	.981	-13	C-38	-1.0
1964	NY-N	131	341	28	92	11	1	7	35	29	65	.270	.331	.370	99	-0	0	0	0	.979	-1	C-97	0.3
1965	NY-N	53	105	6	25	4	0	4	9	11	20	.238	.310	.390	100	-0	0	0	0	.992	-5	C-31	-0.4
	Mil-N	31	53	2	8	2	0	1	5	4	9	.151	.211	.245	28	-5	0	0	0	.989	5	C-13	-0.4
	Yr	84	158	8	33	6	0	5	14	15	29	.209	.277	.342	75	-5	0	0	0	.991	-0	C-44	-0.4
1966	Pit-N	59	160	13	36	3	1	7	16	12	39	.225	.287	.387	85	-3	0	0	0	.978	-2	C-52	-0.2
1967	Pit-N	22	36	4	5	1	0	0	3	5	9	.139	.279	.167	30	-3	0	0	0	.971	-0	C-18	-0.3
Total	8	395	876	73	220	28	2	26	94	72	184	.251	.312	.377	94	-7	1	2	-1	.981	-15	C-250	-1.4

■ DAN GONZALES Gonzales, Daniel David b: 9/30/53, Whittier, Cal. BL/TR, 6'1", 195 lbs. Deb: 4/7/79

1979	Det-A	7	18	1	4	1	0	0	2	0	2	.222	.222	.278	33	-2	1	0	0	1.000	-1	/O-3,D-1	-0.2
1980	Det-A	2	7	1	1	0	0	0	0	0	1	.143	.143	.143	-21	-1	0	0	0	.750	1	/O-1,D-1	-0.1
Total	2	9	25	2	5	1	0	0	2	0	3	.200	.200	.240	18	-3	1	0	0	.857	-1	/O-4,D-2	-0.3

■ LARRY GONZALES Gonzales, Lawrence Christopher b: 3/28/67, West Covina, Cal. BR/TR, 6'3", 200 lbs. Deb: 6/13/93

1993	Cal-A	2	2	0	1	0	0	0	1	1	0	.500	.667	.500	212	0	0	0	0	1.000	-0	/C-2	0.0

■ RENE GONZALES Gonzales, Rene Adrian b: 9/3/60, Austin, Tex. BR/TR, 6'3", 191 lbs. Deb: 7/27/84

1984	Mon-N	29	30	5	7	1	0	0	2	2	5	.233	.303	.267	64	-1	0	0	0	.957	1	S-27	0.0
1986	Mon-N	11	26	1	3	0	0	0	2	2	7	.115	.179	.115	-17	-4	0	2	-1	1.000	2	/S-6,3-5	-0.4
1987	Bal-A	37	60	14	16	2	1	1	7	3	11	.267	.302	.383	82	-2	1	0	0	.963	5	3-29/2-6,S-1	0.4
1988	Bal-A	92	237	13	51	6	0	2	15	13	32	.215	.265	.266	50	-16	2	0	1	.966	15	3-80,2-14/S-2,10	-0.1
1989	Bal-A	71	166	16	36	4	0	1	11	12	30	.217	.270	.259	51	-11	5	3	-0	.978	-1	2-54,3-17/S-1	-1.1
1990	Bal-A	67	103	13	22	3	1	1	12	12	14	.214	.296	.291	67	-4	1	2	-1	.994	9	2-43,3-16/S-9,0-1	0.5
1991	*Tor-A	71	118	16	23	3	0	1	6	12	22	.195	.291	.246	48	-8	0	0	0	.973	10	S-36,3-26,2-11/1-2	0.4
1992	Cal-A	104	329	47	91	17	1	7	38	41	46	.277	.364	.398	113	6	7	4	-0	.954	5	3-53,2-42,1-13/S-8	1.2
1993	Cal-A	118	335	34	84	17	0	2	31	49	45	.251	.348	.319	78	-9	5	5	-2	.956	-0	3-79,1-31/S-5,2P	-1.2
1994	Cle-A	22	23	6	8	1	1	1	5	5	3	.348	.464	.609	173	3	2	0	1	.952	1	3-13/1-4,S-4,2-1	0.6
1995	Cal-A	30	18	1	6	1	0	0	1	0	0	.333	.333	.556	127	1	0	0	0	1.000	5	3-18/2-6,S-1,D-1	0.2
1996	*Tex-A	51	92	19	20	4	0	2	5	10	11	.217	.294	.326	53	-7	0	0	0	.989	-1	1-23,3-15,S-10,2/O	-0.1
Total	12	703	1537	185	367	59	4	19	135	161	230	.239	.316	.319	75	-52	23	16	-3	.957	55	3-351,2-186,S/1ODP	0.4

■ ALEX GONZALEZ Gonzalez, Alexander Scott b: 4/8/73, Miami, Fla. BR/TR, 6', 180 lbs. Deb: 4/4/94

1994	Tor-A	15	53	7	8	3	1	0	1	4	17	.151	.224	.245	21	-6	3	0	1	.918	1	S-15	-0.3
1995	Tor-A	111	367	51	89	19	4	10	42	44	114	.243	.325	.398	88	-7	4	4	-1	.957	-29	S-97/3-9,D-3	-2.7
1996	Tor-A	147	527	64	124	30	5	14	64	45	127	.235	.302	.391	73	-23	16	6	1	.973	23	*S-147	1.4
Total	3	273	947	122	221	52	10	24	107	93	258	.233	.307	.385	76	-36	23	10	1	.964	-6	S-259/3-9,D-3	-1.6

■ TONY GONZALEZ Gonzalez, Andres Antonio (Gonzalez) b: 8/28/36, Central Cunagua, Cuba BL/TR, 5'9", 170 lbs. Deb: 4/12/60

1960	Cin-N	39	99	10	21	5	1	3	14	4	27	.212	.250	.374	67	-5	1	0	0	.957	-4	O-31	-1.0
	Phi-N	78	241	27	72	17	5	6	33	11	47	.299	.337	.485	122	6	2	2	-1	.981	-1	O-67	0.3
	Yr	117	340	37	93	22	6	9	47	15	74	.274	.312	.453	106	2	3	2	-0	.975	-4	O-98	-0.7
1961	Phi-N	126	426	58	118	16	8	12	58	49	66	.277	.360	.437	112	8	15	5	2	.984	-1	*O-118	0.2
1962	Phi-N	118	437	76	132	16	4	20	63	40	82	.302	.372	.494	134	21	17	8	0	1.000	6	*O-114	2.0
1963	Phi-N	155	555	78	170	36	12	4	66	53	68	.306	.375	.436	134	25	13	8	-1	.986	-6	*O-151	1.2
1964	Phi-N	131	421	55	117	25	3	4	40	44	74	.278	.355	.380	108	6	0	5	-3	.996	-6	*O-119	-0.1
1965	Phi-N	108	370	48	109	19	4	13	41	31	52	.295	.354	.457	129	14	3	4	-2	.983	-6	*O-104	0.2
1966	Phi-N	132	384	53	110	20	4	6	40	26	60	.286	.337	.406	105	3	2	6	-3	.986	-1	*O-121	-0.5
1967	Phi-N	149	508	74	172	23	9	9	59	47	58	.339	.400	.472	147	32	10	9	-2	.993	5	*O-143	3.0
1968	Phi-N	121	416	45	110	13	4	3	38	40	42	.264	.339	.337	103	3	6	5	-1	.979	-4	*O-117	-1.0
1969	SD-N	53	182	17	41	4	0	2	8	19	24	.225	.309	.280	69	-7	1	0	0	.975	5	O-49	-0.6
	*Atl-N	89	320	51	94	15	2	10	50	27	22	.294	.358	.447	124	10	3	1	0	.989	2	O-82	0.8
	Yr	142	502	68	135	19	2	12	58	46	46	.269	.340	.386	104	3	4	1	0	.983	6	O-131	0.2
1970	Atl-N	123	430	57	114	18	2	7	55	46	45	.265	.347	.365	86	-8	3	5	-2	.987	-3	O-119	-1.8
	Cal-A	26	92	9	28	2	0	1	12	2	11	.304	.326	.359	92	-1	3	2	-0	.960	-1	O-24	-0.4
1971	Cal-A	111	314	32	77	9	2	3	38	28	28	.245	.313	.315	84	-7	0	1	-1	.987	-6	O-88	-1.9
Total	12	1559	5195	690	1485	238	57	103	615	467	706	.286	.353	.413	114	100	79	61	-13	.987	-12	*O-1447	0.4

■ DENNY GONZALEZ Gonzalez, Denio Mariano (Manzueta) b: 7/22/63, Sabana Grande De Boya, D.R. BR/TR, 5'11", 185 lbs. Deb: 8/6/84

1984	Pit-N	26	82	9	15	3	1	0	4	7	21	.183	.247	.244	38	-7	1	1	-0	1.000	-1	3-11,S-10/O-3	-0.5
1985	Pit-N	35	124	11	28	4	0	4	12	13	27	.226	.299	.355	83	-3	2	4	-2	.894	-4	3-21,O-13/2-6	-1.0
1987	Pit-N	5	7	1	0	0	0	0	0	1	2	.000	.125	.000	-63	-2	0	0	0	1.000	1	/S-1	-0.2
1988	Pit-N	24	32	5	6	1	0	0	1	6	10	.188	.316	.219	57	-2	0	0	0	1.000	-1	S-14/2-4,3-2	-0.1
1989	Cle-A	8	17	3	5	1	0	0	1	0	4	.294	.333	.353	92	-0	0	0	0	.000	-0	/3-1,D-6	-0.1
Total	5	98	262	29	54	9	1	4	18	27	64	.206	.283	.294	62	-13	3	5	-2	.925	-4	/3-35,S-25,O-16,2D	-1.9

■ EUSEBIO GONZALEZ Gonzalez, Eusebio Miguel (Lopez) "Papo" b: 7/13/1892, Havana, Cuba d: 2/14/76, Havana, Cuba BR/TR, 5'10", 165 lbs. Deb: 7/26/18

1918	Bos-A	3	5	2	2	1	0	0	0	1	1	.400	.571	.800	319	1	0			1.000	-1	/S-2,3-1	0.1

■ FERNANDO GONZALEZ Gonzalez, Jose Fernando (Quinones) b: 6/19/50, Arecibo, P.R. BR/TR, 5'10", 170 lbs. Deb: 9/15/72

1972	Pit-N	3	2	0	0	0	0	0	0	0	2	.000	.000	.000	-99	-1	0	0	0	.500	0	/3-1	-0.1
1973	Pit-N	37	49	5	11	0	1	1	5	1	11	.224	.255	.327	62	-3	0	0	0	.923	-1	/3-5	-0.4
1974	KC-A	9	21	1	3	1	0	0	2	0	4	.143	.143	.190	-5	-3	1	0	0	1.000	0	/3-8,D-1	-0.3
	NY-A	51	121	11	26	5	1	1	7	7	7	.215	.258	.298	60	-6	0	0	0	.982	2	2-42/3-7,S-3	-0.2
	Yr	60	142	12	29	6	1	1	9	7	11	.204	.242	.282	50	-9	1	0	0	.982	2	2-42,3-15/S-3,D-1	-0.5
1977	Pit-N	80	181	17	50	10	0	4	27	13	21	.276	.325	.398	90	-2	3	3	-1	.972	-5	3-37,O-16/2-6,S-2	-1.2
1978	Pit-N	9	21	2	4	0	0	0	1	3	4	.190	.227	.238	29	-2	0	0	0	.923	-4	/2-4,3-3	-0.7
	SD-N	101	320	27	80	10	2	2	29	18	32	.250	.290	.313	74	-12	4	4	-1	.982	0	2-94	-0.7
	Yr	110	341	29	84	11	2	2	29	19	35	.246	.286	.308	71	-14	4	4	-1	.981	-3	2-98/3-3	-1.4
1979	SD-N	114	323	22	70	13	3	9	34	18	34	.217	.258	.359	71	-15	0	0	0	.976	-14	*2-103/3-3	-2.3
Total	6	404	1038	85	244	40	7	17	104	58	114	.235	.276	.344	71	-44	8	7	-2	.979	-24	2-249/3-64,O-16,SD	-5.9

■ JOSE GONZALEZ Gonzalez, Jose Rafael (Gutierrez) b: 11/23/64, Puerto Plata, D.R. BR/TR, 6'2", 196 lbs. Deb: 9/2/85

1985	LA-N	23	11	6	3	2	0	0	1	1	3	.273	.333	.455	122	0	1	0	-0	1.000	-6	O-18	-0.6
1986	LA-N	57	93	15	20	5	1	2	6	7	29	.215	.270	.355	76	-3	4	3	-1	.924	-10	O-57	-1.6
1987	LA-N	19	16	2	3	2	0	0	1	1	2	.188	.235	.313	45	-1	5	0	2	1.000	-1	O-14	-0.1
1988	*LA-N	37	24	7	2	1	0	0	2	2	10	.083	.154	.125	-20	-4	3	0	1	.938	-8	O-24	-1.2
1989	LA-N	95	261	31	70	11	2	3	18	23	53	.268	.327	.360	98	-1	9	3	1	.968	-0	O-87	-0.2
1990	LA-N	106	99	15	23	5	3	2	6	6	27	.232	.283	.404	89	-2	3	3	0	1.000	-22	O-81	-2.5
1991	LA-N	42	28	3	0	0	0	0	0	1	9	.000	.067	.000	-82	-7	0	0	0	1.000	-9	O-27	-1.4
	Pit-N	16	20	2	2	2	0	0	1	0	10	.100	.100	.250	-5	-3	0	0	0	1.000	6	O-14	-0.5
	Yr	58	48	5	2	2	0	0	1	1	19	.042	.080	.104	-50	-10	0	0	0	1.000	-8	O-41	-1.9
	Cle-A	33	69	10	11	2	1	4	11	2	15	.159	.284	.261	51	-4	8	0	3	.981	-3	O-32	-0.6
1992	Cal-A	33	55	4	10	2	0	1	6	3	20	.182	.274	.218	39	-4	5	1	-1	1.000	-4	O-22/D-1	-0.9
Total	8	461	676	95	144	30	7	9	42	60	186	.213	.279	.318	69	-29	33	9	5	.972	-62	O-378/D-1	-9.6

JUAN GONZALEZ
Gonzalez, Juan Alberto (Vazquez) b: 10/20/69, Arecibo, P.R. BR/TR, 6'3", 175 lbs. Deb: 9/1/89

YEAR	TM/L	G	AB	R	H	2B	3B	HR	RBI	BB	SO	AVG	OBP	SLG	PRO+	BR/A	SB	CS	SBR	FA	FR	G/POS	TPR
1989	Tex-A	24	60	6	9	3	0	1	7	6	17	.150	.227	.250	34	-5	0	0	0	.964	-2	O-24	-0.7
1990	Tex-A	25	90	11	26	7	1	4	12	2	18	.289	.308	.522	131	3	0	1	-1	1.000	-1	O-16/D-9	0.4
1991	Tex-A	142	545	78	144	34	1	27	102	42	118	.264	.323	.479	121	13	4	4	-1	.981	-19	*O-136/D-4	-1.1
1992	Tex-A	155	584	77	152	24	2	43	109	35	143	.260	.308	.529	135	23	0	1	-1	.975	5	*O-148/D-4	2.4
1993	Tex-A★	140	536	105	166	33	1	46	118	37	99	.310	.369	.632	170	49	4	1	1	.985	5	*O-129,D-10	4.9
1994	Tex-A	107	422	57	116	18	4	19	85	30	66	.275	.333	.472	105	2	6	4	-1	.991	7	*O-107	0.6
1995	Tex-A	90	352	57	104	20	2	27	82	17	66	.295	.328	.594	131	13	0	0	0	1.000	0	D-83/O-5	0.7
1996	*Tex-A	134	541	89	170	33	2	47	144	45	82	.314	.370	.643	140	30	2	0	1	.988	-10	*O-102,D-32	1.9
Total	8	817	3130	480	887	172	13	214	659	214	609	.283	.336	.552	133	127	16	11	-2	.983	-10	O-667,D-142	8.8

JULIO GONZALEZ
Gonzalez, Julio Cesar (Hernandez) b: 12/25/52, Caguas, P.R. BR/TR, 5'11", 165 lbs. Deb: 4/8/77

YEAR	TM/L	G	AB	R	H	2B	3B	HR	RBI	BB	SO	AVG	OBP	SLG	PRO+	BR/A	SB	CS	SBR	FA	FR	G/POS	TPR
1977	Hou-N	110	383	34	94	18	3	1	27	19	45	.245	.288	.316	68	-18	3	3	-1	.921	-26	S-63,2-45	-3.6
1978	Hou-N	78	223	24	52	3	1	1	16	8	31	.233	.263	.269	53	-15	6	1	1	.983	-20	2-54,S-17/3-4	-3.1
1979	Hou-N	68	181	16	45	5	2	0	10	5	14	.249	.280	.298	62	-10	2	1	0	.987	1	2-32,S-21/3-9	-0.5
1980	Hou-N	40	52	5	6	1	0	0	1	1	8	.115	.132	.135	-28	-9	1	0	0	1.000	3	S-16,3-11/2-2	-0.5
1981	StL-N	20	22	2	7	1	0	1	3	1	3	.318	.348	.500	135	1	0	0	0	1.000	1	/S-5,2-4,3-2	0.2
1982	StL-N	42	87	9	21	3	2	1	7	1	24	.241	.258	.356	70	-4	1	1	-0	.907	-1	3-21/2-9,S-1	-0.6
1983	Det-A	12	21	0	3	1	0	0	2	1	7	.143	.182	.190	3	-3	0	0	0	.889	3	/S-6,2-5,3-1	0.1
Total	7	370	969	90	228	32	8	4	66	36	132	.235	.269	.297	59	-58	13	6	0	.976	-39	2-151,S-129/3-48	-8.0

LUIS GONZALEZ
Gonzalez, Luis Emilio b: 9/3/67, Tampa, Fla. BL/TR, 6'2", 180 lbs. Deb: 9/4/90

YEAR	TM/L	G	AB	R	H	2B	3B	HR	RBI	BB	SO	AVG	OBP	SLG	PRO+	BR/A	SB	CS	SBR	FA	FR	G/POS	TPR
1990	Hou-N	12	21	1	4	2	0	0	0	2	5	.190	.261	.286	52	-1	0	0	0	1.000	2	/3-4,1-2	0.1
1991	Hou-N	137	473	51	120	28	9	13	69	40	101	.254	.322	.433	117	9	10	7	-1	.984	13	*O-133	1.9
1992	Hou-N	122	387	40	94	19	3	10	55	24	52	.243	.291	.385	94	-5	7	7	-2	.993	15	*O-111	0.7
1993	Hou-N	154	540	82	162	34	3	15	72	47	83	.300	.367	.457	124	18	20	9	1	.978	20	*O-149	3.5
1994	Hou-N	112	392	57	107	29	4	8	67	49	57	.273	.358	.429	110	6	15	13	-3	.991	12	*O-111	1.2
1995	Hou-N	56	209	35	54	10	4	6	35	18	30	.258	.326	.431	105	1	1	3	-2	.980	2	O-55	0.0
	Chi-N	77	262	34	76	19	4	7	34	39	33	.290	.388	.473	128	12	5	5	-2	.978	10	O-76	1.8
	Yr	133	471	69	130	29	8	13	69	57	63	.276	.361	.454	118	13	6	8	-3	.978	12	*O-131	1.8
1996	Chi-N	146	483	70	131	30	4	15	79	61	49	.271	.358	.443	108	6	9	6	-1	.988	3	*O-139/1-2	0.5
Total	7	816	2767	370	748	171	31	74	411	280	410	.270	.344	.435	112	46	67	50	-10	.985	78	O-774/1-4,3-4	9.7

MIKE GONZALEZ
Gonzalez, Miguel Angel (Cordero) b: 9/24/1890, Havana, Cuba d: 2/19/77, Havana, Cuba BR/TR, 6'1", 200 lbs. Deb: 9/28/12 MC

YEAR	TM/L	G	AB	R	H	2B	3B	HR	RBI	BB	SO	AVG	OBP	SLG	PRO+	BR/A	SB	CS	SBR	FA	FR	G/POS	TPR
1912	Bos-N	1	2	0	0	0	0	0	0	1	1	.000	.333	.000	-5	-0	0			.875	1	/C-1	0.1
1914	Cin-N	95	176	19	41	6	0	0	10	13	16	.233	.293	.267	65	-7	2			.954	10	C-83	0.8
1915	StL-N	51	97	12	22	2	2	0	10	8	9	.227	.306	.289	80	-2	4	2	0	.992	4	C-32/1-8	0.3
1916	StL-N	118	331	33	79	15	4	0	29	28	18	.239	.304	.308	89	-4	5			.981	7	C-93,1-13	1.0
1917	StL-N	106	290	28	76	8	1	1	28	22	24	.262	.316	.307	94	-2	12			.977	0	C-68,1-18/O-1	0.3
1918	StL-N	117	349	33	88	13	4	3	20	39	30	.252	.327	.338	107	3	14			.978	-1	*C-100/O-5,1-2	1.1
1919	NY-N	58	158	18	30	6	0	0	8	20	9	.190	.293	.228	58	-7	3			.962	-2	C-52/1-4	-0.7
1920	NY-N	11	13	1	3	0	0	0	0	3	1	.231	.375	.231	77	-0	1	0	0	1.000	-1	/C-8	0.0
1921	NY-N	13	24	3	9	1	0	0	0	6	0	.375	.400	.417	116	1	0	0	0	.981	0	/1-6,C-2	0.0
1924	StL-N	120	402	34	119	27	1	3	53	24	22	.296	.337	.391	96	-2	1	5	-3	.986	-7	*C-119	-0.4
1925	StL-N	22	71	9	22	3	0	0	4	6	2	.310	.380	.352	86	-1	1	2	-1	.982	4	C-22	0.3
	Chi-N	70	197	26	52	13	1	3	18	13	15	.264	.316	.386	77	-7	2	1	0	.989	1	C-50/1-9	-0.4
	Yr	92	268	35	74	16	1	3	22	19	17	.276	.333	.377	80	-8	3	3	-1	.987	5	C-72/1-9	-0.1
1926	Chi-N	80	253	24	63	13	3	1	23	13	17	.249	.288	.336	67	-12	3			.989	6	C-78	-0.1
1927	Chi-N	39	108	15	26	4	1	1	15	10	8	.241	.311	.324	70	-5	1			.994	9	C-36	0.6
1928	Chi-N	49	158	12	43	9	2	1	21	12	7	.272	.324	.373	83	-4	2			.983	6	C-45	0.8
1929	*Chi-N	60	167	15	40	7	0	0	18	18	14	.240	.317	.257	44	-14	1			.992	6	C-60	-0.3
1931	StL-N	15	19	1	2	0	0	0	3	0	3	.105	.105	.105	-42	-4	0			1.000	-0	/C-4	-0.4
1932	StL-N	17	14	0	2	0	0	0	3	0	2	.143	.143	.143	-22	-2	0			1.000	2	/C-7	-0.1
Total	17	1042	2829	283	717	123	19	13	263	231	198	.253	.314	.324	81	-71	52	10		.980	45	C-868/1-60,O-6	2.9

ORLANDO GONZALEZ
Gonzalez, Orlando Eugene b: 11/15/51, Havana, Cuba BL/TL, 6'2", 180 lbs. Deb: 6/7/76

YEAR	TM/L	G	AB	R	H	2B	3B	HR	RBI	BB	SO	AVG	OBP	SLG	PRO+	BR/A	SB	CS	SBR	FA	FR	G/POS	TPR
1976	Cle-A	28	68	5	17	2	0	0	4	5	7	.250	.301	.279	72	-2	1	2	-1	.992	-2	1-15/O-7,D-2	-0.7
1978	*Phi-N	26	26	1	5	0	0	0	0	1	1	.192	.222	.192	17	-3	0	0	0	1.000	-2	O-11/1-3	-0.6
1980	Oak-A	25	70	10	17	0	0	0	1	9	8	.243	.329	.243	64	-3	0	2	-1	.990	1	1-11/O-2,D-8	-0.4
Total	3	79	164	16	39	2	0	0	5	15	16	.238	.302	.250	59	-8	1	4	-2	.991	-3	/1-29,O-20,D-10	-1.7

PEDRO GONZALEZ
Gonzalez, Pedro (Olivares) b: 12/12/37, San Pedro De Macoris, D.R. BR/TR, 6', 176 lbs. Deb: 4/11/63

YEAR	TM/L	G	AB	R	H	2B	3B	HR	RBI	BB	SO	AVG	OBP	SLG	PRO+	BR/A	SB	CS	SBR	FA	FR	G/POS	TPR
1963	NY-A	14	26	3	5	1	0	0	1	0	5	.192	.192	.231	18	-3	0	1	-1	.963	-1	/2-7	-0.4
1964	*NY-A	80	112	18	31	8	1	0	5	7	22	.277	.331	.366	92	-1	3	4	-2	.992	1	1-31,O-20/3-9,2-6	-0.2
1965	NY-A	7	5	0	2	1	0	0	0	0	0	.400	.400	.600	181	0	0	0	0	.000	0	H	0.1
	Cle-A	116	400	38	101	14	3	5	39	18	57	.253	.290	.340	78	-12	7	4	-0	.980	8	*2-112/O-3,3-2	0.6
	Yr	123	405	38	103	15	3	5	39	18	59	.254	.291	.343	79	-12	7	4	-0	.980	8	*2-112/O-3,3-2	0.7
1966	Cle-A	110	352	21	82	9	2	2	17	15	54	.233	.268	.287	60	-18	8	5	-1	.984	11	*2-104/3-1,O-1	-0.1
1967	Cle-A	80	189	19	43	6	0	1	8	12	36	.228	.277	.275	61	-9	4	6	-2	.971	-5	2-64/1-4,3-4,S-3	-1.4
Total	5	407	1084	99	264	39	6	8	70	52	176	.244	.283	.313	70	-43	22	20	-5	.980	14	2-293/1-35,O-24,3S	-1.4

CHARLIE GOOCH
Gooch, Charles Furman b: 6/5/02, Smyrna, Tenn. d: 5/30/82, Lanham, Md. BR/TR, 5'9", 170 lbs. Deb: 4/18/29

YEAR	TM/L	G	AB	R	H	2B	3B	HR	RBI	BB	SO	AVG	OBP	SLG	PRO+	BR/A	SB	CS	SBR	FA	FR	G/POS	TPR
1929	Was-A	39	57	6	16	2	1	0	5	7	8	.281	.359	.351	83	-1	0	1	-1	.970	-2	/1-7,3-7,S-1	-0.3

JOHNNY GOOCH
Gooch, John Beverley b: 11/9/1897, Smyrna, Tenn. d: 5/15/75, Nashville, Tenn. BB/TR, 5'11", 175 lbs. Deb: 9/9/21 C

YEAR	TM/L	G	AB	R	H	2B	3B	HR	RBI	BB	SO	AVG	OBP	SLG	PRO+	BR/A	SB	CS	SBR	FA	FR	G/POS	TPR
1921	Pit-N	13	38	2	9	0	0	0	3	3	3	.237	.293	.237	41	-3	1	0	0	.985	3	C-13	0.1
1922	Pit-N	105	353	45	116	13	5	1	42	39	15	.329	.403	.397	106	5	1	1	-0	.970	-3	*C-103	0.7
1923	Pit-N	66	202	16	56	10	2	1	20	17	13	.277	.336	.361	82	-5	1			.975	-2	C-66	0.3
1924	Pit-N	70	224	26	65	6	5	0	25	16	12	.290	.343	.362	88	-4	1	3	-2	.988	-6	C-69	-0.7
1925	*Pit-N	79	215	24	64	8	4	0	30	20	16	.298	.357	.372	81	-6	1	0	0	.968	-5	C-76	-0.6
1926	Pit-N	86	218	19	59	15	1	0	42	20	14	.271	.340	.362	85	-4	1			.980	-5	C-80	-0.5
1927	*Pit-N	101	291	22	75	17	2	2	48	19	21	.258	.305	.351	70	-12	0			.974	-4	C-91	-0.4
1928	Pit-N	31	80	7	19	2	1	0	5	3	6	.237	.265	.287	43	-7	0			.957	-4	C-31	-0.1
	Bro-N	42	101	9	32	1	2	0	12	7	9	.317	.361	.366	92	-1	0			.969	-2	C-38	0.0
	Yr	73	181	16	51	3	3	0	17	10	15	.282	.319	.331	70	-8	0			.964	2	C-69	-0.1
1929	Bro-N	1	1	0	0	0	0	0	0	0	0	.000	.000	.000	-99	-0	0			.000	0	H	0.0
	Cin-N	92	287	22	86	13	5	0	34	24	10	.300	.356	.380	86	-6	5			.975	5	C-86	0.6
	Yr	93	288	22	86	13	5	0	34	24	10	.299	.356	.378	86	-6	5			.975	5	C-86	0.6
1930	Cin-N	82	276	29	67	10	3	2	30	27	15	.243	.315	.322	57	-19	0			.955	-5	C-79	-1.5
1933	Bos-A	37	77	6	14	1	1	0	2	11	7	.182	.284	.221	36	-7	0	0	0	.991	-4	C-26	-0.1
Total	11	805	2363	227	662	98	29	7	293	206	141	.280	.342	.355	79	-69	11	5		.973	-2	C-758	-2.2

LEE GOOCH
Gooch, Lee Currin b: 2/23/1890, Oxford, N.C. d: 5/18/66, Raleigh, N.C. BR/TR, 6', 190 lbs. Deb: 8/17/15

YEAR	TM/L	G	AB	R	H	2B	3B	HR	RBI	BB	SO	AVG	OBP	SLG	PRO+	BR/A	SB	CS	SBR	FA	FR	G/POS	TPR
1915	Cle-A	2	2	0	1	0	0	0	0	0	0	.500	.500	.500	196	1	0			.000	0	H	0.0
1917	Phi-A	17	59	4	17	2	0	1	8	4	10	.288	.333	.373	117	1	1	0		.893	-2	O-16	-0.2
Total	2	19	61	4	18	2	0	1	8	4	10	.295	.338	.377	120	1	1	0		.893	-2	/O-16	-0.2

GENE GOOD
Good, Eugene J. b: 12/13/1882, Roxbury, Mass. d: 8/6/47, Boston, Mass. BL/TL, 5'6", 130 lbs. Deb: 4/12/06

YEAR	TM/L	G	AB	R	H	2B	3B	HR	RBI	BB	SO	AVG	OBP	SLG	PRO+	BR/A	SB	CS	SBR	FA	FR	G/POS	TPR
1906	Bos-N	34	119	4	18	0	0	0	0	13		.151	.246	.151	25	-10	2			.873	-2	O-34	-1.6

WILBUR GOOD

Good, Wilbur David "Lefty"   b: 9/28/1885, Punxsutawney, Pa.   d: 12/30/63, Brooksville, Fla.   BL/TL, 5'6", 165 lbs.   Deb: 8/18/05

YEAR	TM/L	G	AB	R	H	2B	3B	HR	RBI	BB	SO	AVG	OBP	SLG	PRO+	BR/A	SB	CS	SBR	FA	FR	G/POS	TPR
1905	NY-A	5	8	2	3	0	0	0	0	0		.375	.375	.375	124	0	0			.889	0	/P-5	0.0
1908	Cle-A	46	154	23	43	1	3	1	14	13		.279	.351	.344	126	5	7			.845	-8	O-42	-0.6
1909	Cle-A	94	318	33	68	6	5	0	17	28		.214	.296	.264	74	-9	13			.953	2	O-80	-1.1
1910	Bos-N	23	86	15	29	5	4	0	11	6	13	.337	.394	.488	150	5	5			.969	5	O-23	0.9
1911	Bos-N	43	165	21	44	9	3	0	15	12	22	.267	.316	.358	82	-5	3			.945	8	O-43	0.1
	Chi-N	58	145	27	39	5	4	2	21	11	17	.269	.329	.400	103	0	10			.928	-5	O-40	-0.7
	Yr	101	310	48	83	14	7	2	36	23	39	.268	.322	.377	92	-4	13			.938	3	O-83	-0.6
1912	Chi-N	39	35	7	5	0	0	0	1	3	7	.143	.211	.143	-2	-5	3			1.000	-3	O-10	-0.8
1913	Chi-N	49	91	11	23	3	2	1	12	11	16	.253	.340	.363	100	0	5			.974	-3	O-26	-0.4
1914	Chi-N	154	580	70	158	24	7	2	43	53	74	.272	.341	.348	105	4	31			.930	-1	*O-154	-0.4
1915	Chi-N	128	498	66	126	18	9	2	27	34	65	.253	.307	.337	95	-2	19	17	-5	.936	-2	*O-125	-1.8
1916	Phi-N	75	136	25	34	4	3	1	15	8	13	.250	.306	.346	96	-1	7			.983	-5	O-46	-0.8
1918	Chi-A	35	148	24	37	9	4	0	11	11	16	.250	.315	.365	104	0	1			.982	4	O-35	0.3
Total	11	749	2364	324	609	84	44	9	187	190	243	.258	.322	.342	98	-7	104	17		.942	-8	O-624/P-5	-5.3

BILL GOODENOUGH

Goodenough, William B.   b: 1863, St.Louis, Mo.   d: 5/24/05, St.Louis, Mo.   6'1", 170 lbs.   Deb: 8/31/1893

YEAR	TM/L	G	AB	R	H	2B	3B	HR	RBI	BB	SO	AVG	OBP	SLG	PRO+	BR/A	SB	CS	SBR	FA	FR	G/POS	TPR
1893	StL-N	10	31	4	5	1	0	0	2	3	4	.161	.297	.194	31	-3	2			.880	-1	O-10	-0.4

MIKE GOODFELLOW

Goodfellow, Michael J.   b: 10/3/1866, Port Jervis, N.Y.   d: 2/12/20, Newark, N.J.   BR/TR, 6', 180 lbs.   Deb: 6/13/1887

YEAR	TM/L	G	AB	R	H	2B	3B	HR	RBI	BB	SO	AVG	OBP	SLG	PRO+	BR/A	SB	CS	SBR	FA	FR	G/POS	TPR
1887	StL-a	1	4	0	0	0	0	0	0	0		.000	.000	.000	-90	-1	0			.800	-0	/C-1	-0.1
1888	Cle-a	68	269	24	66	7	0	0	29	11		.245	.283	.271	80	-6	7			.863	-6	O-62/C-4,1-3,S-1	-1.0
Total	2	69	273	24	66	7	0	0	29	11		.242	.279	.267	77	-7	7			.909	-7	/O-62,C-5,1-3,S-1	-1.1

IVAL GOODMAN

Goodman, Ival Richard "Goodie"   b: 7/23/08, Northview, Mo.   d: 11/25/84, Cincinnati, Ohio   BL/TR, 5'11", 170 lbs.   Deb: 4/16/35

YEAR	TM/L	G	AB	R	H	2B	3B	HR	RBI	BB	SO	AVG	OBP	SLG	PRO+	BR/A	SB	CS	SBR	FA	FR	G/POS	TPR
1935	Cin-N	148	592	86	159	23	18	12	72	35	50	.269	.314	.429	101	-1	14			.960	8	*O-146	0.1
1936	Cin-N	136	489	81	139	15	14	17	71	38	53	.284	.347	.476	128	17	6			.972	3	*O-120	1.4
1937	Cin-N	147	549	86	150	25	12	12	55	55	58	.273	.347	.428	115	11	10			.974	6	*O-141	1.1
1938	Cin-N★	145	568	103	166	27	10	30	92	53	51	.292	.368	.533	149	36	3			.988	5	*O-142	3.7
1939	*Cin-N★	124	470	85	152	37	16	7	84	54	32	.323	.401	.515	144	29	2			.981	7	*O-123	3.1
1940	*Cin-N	136	519	78	134	20	6	12	63	60	54	.258	.335	.389	98	-1	9			.970	-5	*O-135	-1.4
1941	Cin-N	42	149	14	40	5	2	1	12	16	15	.268	.343	.349	95	-1	0			.966	1	O-40	-0.3
1942	Cin-N	87	226	21	55	18	1	0	15	24	32	.243	.319	.332	91	-3	0			.991	0	O-57	-0.5
1943	Chi-N	80	225	31	72	10	5	3	45	24	20	.320	.390	.449	144	13	4			.968	-7	O-61	0.4
1944	Chi-N	62	141	24	37	8	1	1	16	23	15	.262	.377	.355	107	2	0			1.000	-6	O-35	-0.5
Total	10	1107	3928	609	1104	188	85	95	525	382	380	.281	.352	.445	120	104	49			.975	12	O-1000	7.1

JAKE GOODMAN

Goodman, Jacob   b: 9/14/1853, Lancaster, Pa.   d: 3/9/1890, Reading, Pa.   6'1.5",   Deb: 5/2/1878

YEAR	TM/L	G	AB	R	H	2B	3B	HR	RBI	BB	SO	AVG	OBP	SLG	PRO+	BR/A	SB	CS	SBR	FA	FR	G/POS	TPR
1878	Mil-N	60	252	28	62	4	3	1	27	7	33	.246	.266	.298	80	-6				.944	-4	*1-60	-1.1
1882	Pit-a	10	41	5	13	2	2	0	2	9		.317	.349	.463	180	3				.962	1	1-10	0.3
Total	2	70	293	33	75	6	5	1	27	9	33	.256	.278	.321	92	-3				.946	-3	/1-70	-0.8

BILLY GOODMAN

Goodman, William Dale   b: 3/22/26, Concord, N.C.   d: 10/1/84, Sarasota, Fla.   BL/TR, 5'11", 165 lbs.   Deb: 4/19/47   C

YEAR	TM/L	G	AB	R	H	2B	3B	HR	RBI	BB	SO	AVG	OBP	SLG	PRO+	BR/A	SB	CS	SBR	FA	FR	G/POS	TPR
1947	Bos-A	12	11	1	2	0	0	0	1	1	2	.182	.250	.182	20	-1	0	0	0	1.000	0	/O-1	-0.1
1948	Bos-A	127	445	65	138	27	2	1	66	74	44	.310	.414	.387	108	9	5	3	0	.993	-4	*1-117/2-2,3-2	0.4
1949	Bos-A★	122	443	54	132	23	3	0	56	58	21	.298	.382	.363	91	-4	2	0	1	.992	-1	*1-117	-0.6
1950	Bos-A	110	424	91	150	25	3	4	68	52	25	.354	.427	.455	115	11	2	4	-2	.991	-2	O-45,3-27,1-21,/2S	0.4
1951	Bos-A	141	546	92	162	34	4	0	50	79	37	.297	.388	.374	97	-0	7	4	-2	.995	-2	1-62,2-44,O-38,/3-1	-0.4
1952	Bos-A	138	513	79	157	27	3	4	56	48	21	.306	.370	.394	104	4	8	2	1	.975	20	*2-103,1-23/3-5,O-4	3.0
1953	Bos-A★	128	514	73	161	33	5	2	41	57	11	.313	.384	.409	108	7	1	4	-2	.974	-11	*2-112,1-20	0.0
1954	Bos-A	127	489	71	148	25	4	1	36	51	15	.303	.371	.376	95	-3	3		-1	.979	1	*2-72,1-27,O-13,3-12	-0.9
1955	Bos-A	149	599	100	176	31	2	0	52	99	44	.294	.397	.352	94	-1	5	5	-2	.969	-18	*2-143/1-5,O-1	-1.0
1956	Bos-A	105	399	61	117	22	8	2	38	40	22	.293	.358	.404	90	-6	3	5	-2	.966	-11	2-95	-0.3
1957	Bos-A	18	16	1	1	1	0	0	0	2	1	.063	.167	.125	-18	-3	0	0	0	.000	0	H	-0.3
	Bal-A	73	263	36	81	10	3	3	33	21	18	.308	.366	.403	117	6	0	2	-1	.961	-0	3-54/O-9,1-8,2-5,S	-0.4
	Yr	91	279	37	82	11	3	3	33	23	19	.294	.354	.387	106	3	0	2	-1	.961	-10	3-54/O-9,1-8,2-5,S	-0.7
1958	Chi-A	116	425	41	127	15	5	0	40	37	21	.299	.358	.358	100	1	1	0	0	.954	-18	*3-111/1-3,2-1,S-1	-1.7
1959	*Chi-A	104	268	21	67	14	1	1	28	19	20	.250	.304	.321	73	-10	3	0	1	.950	-3	3-74/2-3	-1.1
1960	Chi-A	30	77	5	18	4	0	0	6	12	8	.234	.337	.286	71	-3	0	0	0	.982	3	3-20/2-7	0.1
1961	Chi-A	41	51	4	13	4	0	1	10	7	6	.255	.345	.392	98	-0	0	0	0	.944	-0	/3-7,1-2,2-1	-0.0
1962	Hou-N	82	161	12	41	4	1	0	10	12	11	.255	.306	.292	66	-8	0	0	0	.972	-9	2-31,3-17/1-1	-1.5
Total	16	1623	5644	807	1691	299	44	19	591	669	329	.300	.377	.378	98	-1	37	30	-7	.972	-63	2-624,1-406,3O/S	-4.1

ED GOODSON

Goodson, James Edward   b: 1/25/48, Pulaski, Va.   BL/TR, 6'3", 185 lbs.   Deb: 9/5/70

YEAR	TM/L	G	AB	R	H	2B	3B	HR	RBI	BB	SO	AVG	OBP	SLG	PRO+	BR/A	SB	CS	SBR	FA	FR	G/POS	TPR
1970	SF-N	7	11	1	3	0	0	0	0	0	2	.273	.273	.273	47	-1	0	0	0	.941	0	/1-2	-0.1
1971	SF-N	20	42	4	8	1	0	0	1	2	4	.190	.227	.214	26	-4	0	0	0	1.000	1	1-14	-0.5
1972	SF-N	58	150	15	42	1	1	6	30	8	12	.280	.321	.420	107	1	0	0	0	.991	2	1-42	0.0
1973	SF-N	102	384	37	116	20	1	12	53	15	44	.302	.332	.453	111	4	0	1	-1	.911	-14	3-93	-1.1
1974	SF-N	98	298	25	81	15	0	6	48	18	22	.272	.320	.383	91	-4	1	0	0	.997	-4	1-73/3-8	-1.2
1975	SF-N	39	121	10	25	7	0	1	8	7	14	.207	.250	.289	47	-9	0	1	-1	.993	1	1-16,3-13	-0.9
	Atl-N	47	76	5	16	2	0	1	8	2	8	.211	.231	.276	39	-6	0	0	0	.990	0	1-13/3-1	-0.7
	Yr	86	197	15	41	9	0	2	16	9	22	.208	.243	.284	44	-15	0	1	-1	.992	1	1-29,3-14	-1.6
1976	LA-N	83	118	8	27	4	0	3	17	8	19	.229	.278	.339	76	-4	0	0	0	.833	-4	3-16/1-3,O-2,2-1	-0.9
1977	*LA-N	61	66	3	11	1	0	1	5	3	10	.167	.203	.227	15	-8	0	1	-1	1.000	1	1-13/3-4	-0.9
Total	8	515	1266	108	329	51	2	30	170	63	135	.260	.298	.374	84	-31	1	3	-2	.994	-16	1-176,3-135/O-2,2-1	-6.2

PEP GOODWIN

Goodwin, Claire Vernon   b: 12/19/1891, Pocatello, Idaho   d: 2/15/72, Oakland, Cal.   BL/TR, 5'10.5", 160 lbs.   Deb: 4/16/14

YEAR	TM/L	G	AB	R	H	2B	3B	HR	RBI	BB	SO	AVG	OBP	SLG	PRO+	BR/A	SB	CS	SBR	FA	FR	G/POS	TPR
1914	KC-F	112	374	38	88	15	6	1	32	27	23	.235	.290	.316	68	-24	4			.907	-13	S-67,3-40/1-1	-3.1
1915	KC-F	81	229	22	54	5	1	0	16	15	23	.236	.291	.266	60	-16	6			.906	-8	S-42,2-23	-2.2
Total	2	193	603	60	142	20	7	1	48	42	46	.235	.291	.297	65	-39	10			.907	-20	S-109/3-40,2-23,1-1	-5.3

CURTIS GOODWIN

Goodwin, Curtis La Mar   b: 9/30/72, Oakland, Cal.   BL/TL, 5'11", 180 lbs.   Deb: 6/2/95

YEAR	TM/L	G	AB	R	H	2B	3B	HR	RBI	BB	SO	AVG	OBP	SLG	PRO+	BR/A	SB	CS	SBR	FA	FR	G/POS	TPR
1995	Bal-A	87	289	40	76	11	3	1	24	15	53	.263	.304	.332	64	-15	22	4	4	.990	1	O-84/D-3	-1.1
1996	Cin-N	49	136	20	31	3	0	0	5	19	34	.228	.323	.250	64	-8	15	6	1	.970	-5	O-42	-1.3
Total	2	136	425	60	107	14	3	1	29	34	87	.252	.310	.306	61	-24	37	10	4	.985	-4	O-126/D-3	-2.4

DANNY GOODWIN

Goodwin, Danny Kay   b: 9/2/53, St.Louis, Mo.   BL/TR, 6'1", 195 lbs.   Deb: 9/3/75

YEAR	TM/L	G	AB	R	H	2B	3B	HR	RBI	BB	SO	AVG	OBP	SLG	PRO+	BR/A	SB	CS	SBR	FA	FR	G/POS	TPR
1975	Cal-A	4	10	0	1	0	0	0	0	0	5	.100	.100	.100	-47	-2	0	0	0	.000	0	/D-3	-0.2
1977	Cal-A	35	91	5	19	6	1	1	8	5	19	.209	.250	.330	59	-5	0	0	0	.000	0	D-23	-0.6
1978	Cal-A	24	58	9	16	5	0	2	10	10	13	.276	.382	.466	143	4	0	0	0	1.000	0	D-15	0.3
1979	Min-A	58	159	22	46	8	5	5	27	11	23	.289	.335	.497	117	3	0	0	0	1.000	0	D-51/1-8	0.1
1980	Min-A	55	115	12	23	5	1	1	11	17	32	.200	.303	.270	54	-7	0	0	0	1.000	0	D-38,1-13	-0.8
1981	Min-A	59	151	18	34	6	1	2	17	16	32	.225	.299	.318	73	-5	3	1	0	.992	-2	1-40/O-1,D-5	-1.0
1982	Oak-A	17	52	6	11	2	1	2	8	2	13	.212	.241	.404	77	-2	0	0	0	.000	0	D-15	-0.2
Total	7	252	636	72	150	32	8	13	81	61	137	.236	.303	.373	84	-15	3	1	0	.994	-2	D-150/1-61,O-1	-2.5

TOM GOODWIN

Goodwin, Thomas Jones   b: 7/27/68, Fresno, Cal.   BL/TR, 6'1", 165 lbs.   Deb: 9/1/91

YEAR	TM/L	G	AB	R	H	2B	3B	HR	RBI	BB	SO	AVG	OBP	SLG	PRO+	BR/A	SB	CS	SBR	FA	FR	G/POS	TPR
1991	LA-N	16	7	3	1	0	0	0	0	0	2	.143	.143	.143	-20	-1	1	1	-0	1.000	-1	/O-5	-0.2
1992	LA-N	57	73	15	17	1	1	0	3	6	10	.233	.291	.274	62	-4	7	3	0	1.000	-9	O-45	-1.4
1993	LA-N	30	17	6	5	0	0	0	1	0	4	.294	.333	.353	89	-0	1	2	-1	1.000	0	O-12	-0.5
1994	KC-A	2	2	0	0	0	0	0	0	0	1	.000	.000	.000	-96	-1	0	0	0	1.000	-0	/O-1,D-1	-0.1

YEAR	TM/L	G	AB	R	H	2B	3B	HR	RBI	BB	SO	AVG	OBP	SLG	PRO+	BR/A	SB	CS	SBR	FA	FR	G/POS	TPR
1995	KC-A	133	480	72	138	16	3	4	28	38	72	.287	.346	.358	83	-11	50	18	4	.990	-2	*O-130/D-2	-1.2
1996	KC-A	143	524	80	148	14	4	1	35	39	79	.282	.335	.330	71	-22	66	22	7	.984	-7	*O-136/D-5	-2.5
Total	6	381	1103	176	309	32	8	5	67	84	166	.280	.335	.337	75	-39	125	46	10	.988	-22	O-329/D-8	-5.9

■ RAY GOOLSBY
Goolsby, Raymond Daniel "Ox"   b: 9/5/19, Florala, Ala.   BR/TR, 6'1", 185 lbs.   Deb: 4/18/46

YEAR	TM/L	G	AB	R	H	2B	3B	HR	RBI	BB	SO	AVG	OBP	SLG	PRO+	BR/A	SB	CS	SBR	FA	FR	G/POS	TPR
1946	Was-A	3	4	0	0	0	0	0	0	0	1	1	.000	.200	.000	-43	-1	0	0	0	1.000	-0	/O-1	-0.1

■ GREG GOOSSEN
Goossen, Gregory Bryant   b: 12/14/45, Los Angeles, Cal.   BR/TR, 6'1.5", 210 lbs.   Deb: 9/3/65

YEAR	TM/L	G	AB	R	H	2B	3B	HR	RBI	BB	SO	AVG	OBP	SLG	PRO+	BR/A	SB	CS	SBR	FA	FR	G/POS	TPR
1965	NY-N	11	31	2	9	0	0	1	2	1	5	.290	.313	.387	99	-0	0	0	0	.979	-1	/C-8	-0.1
1966	NY-N	13	32	1	6	2	0	1	5	1	11	.188	.235	.344	60	-2	0	0	0	1.000	-4	C-11	-0.6
1967	NY-N	37	69	2	11	1	0	0	3	4	26	.159	.216	.174	13	-8	0	0	0	.973	-1	C-23	-0.9
1968	NY-N	38	106	4	22	7	0	0	6	10	21	.208	.288	.274	69	-4	0	0	0	.992	2	1-31/C-1	-0.5
1969	Sea-A	52	139	19	43	8	1	10	24	14	29	.309	.385	.597	174	13	1	1	0	.993	2	1-31/O-2	1.3
1970	Mil-A	21	47	3	12	3	0	1	3	10	12	.255	.407	.383	118	2	0	0	0	.990	-1	1-15	-0.1
	Was-A	21	36	2	8	3	0	1		2	8	.222	.263	.306	59	-2	0	0	0	1.000	-0	/O-5,1-2	-0.3
	Yr	42	83	5	20	6	0	1	4	12	20	.241	.351	.349	96	-0	0	0	0	.992	-2	1-17/O-5	-0.4
Total	6	193	460	33	111	24	1	13	44	42	112	.241	.317	.383	99	-1	1	1	0	.992	-5	/1-79,C-43,O-7	-1.2

■ GLEN GORBOUS
Gorbous, Glen Edward   b: 7/8/30, Drumheller, Alberta, Canada   d: 6/12/90, Calgary, Alberta, Canada   BL/TR, 6'2", 175 lbs.   Deb: 4/11/55

YEAR	TM/L	G	AB	R	H	2B	3B	HR	RBI	BB	SO	AVG	OBP	SLG	PRO+	BR/A	SB	CS	SBR	FA	FR	G/POS	TPR
1955	Cin-N	8	18	2	6	3	0	0	4	3	1	.333	.429	.500	137	1	0	0	0	.857	-0	/O-5	0.1
	Phi-N	91	224	25	53	9	1	4	23	21	17	.237	.302	.339	71	-9	0	3	-2	.984	6	O-57	-0.7
	Yr	99	242	27	59	12	1	4	27	24	18	.244	.312	.351	77	-8	0	3	-2	.971	6	O-62	-0.6
1956	Phi-N	15	33	1	6	0	0	0	1	0	1	.182	.182	.182	-2	-5	0	0	0	1.000	-2	/O-8	-0.7
1957	Phi-N	3	2	1	1	1	0	0	1	0	0	.500	.667	1.000	351	1	0	0	0	.000	-0	H	0.1
Total	3	117	277	29	66	13	1	4	29	25	19	.238	.301	.336	70	-12	0	3	-2	.973	4	O-70	-1.2

■ JOE GORDON
Gordon, Joseph Lowell "Flash"   b: 2/18/15, Los Angeles, Cal.   d: 4/14/78, Sacramento, Cal.   BR/TR, 5'10", 180 lbs.   Deb: 4/18/38   MC

YEAR	TM/L	G	AB	R	H	2B	3B	HR	RBI	BB	SO	AVG	OBP	SLG	PRO+	BR/A	SB	CS	SBR	FA	FR	G/POS	TPR
1938	*NY-A	127	458	83	117	24	7	25	97	56	72	.255	.340	.502	109	3	11	3	2	.960	**24**	*2-126	3.2
1939	*NY-A★	151	567	92	161	32	5	28	111	75	57	.284	.370	.506	124	19	11	10	-3	.967	6	*2-151	2.8
1940	NY-A★	155	616	112	173	32	10	30	103	52	57	.281	.340	.511	122	17	18	8	1	.975	14	*2-155	3.9
1941	*NY-A★	156	588	104	162	26	7	24	87	72	80	.276	.358	.466	118	14	10	9	-2	.958	6	*2-131,1-30	2.5
1942	*NY-A★	147	538	88	173	29	4	18	103	79	95	.322	.409	.491	156	41	12	6	0	.966	4	*2-147	5.4
1943	*NY-A☆	152	543	82	135	28	5	17	69	98	75	.249	.365	.413	126	20	4	7	-3	.969	26	*2-152	5.4
1946	NY-A★	112	376	35	79	15	0	11	47	49	72	.210	.308	.338	79	-10	2	5	-2	.974	22	*2-108	1.7
1947	Cle-A★	155	562	89	153	27	6	29	93	62	49	.272	.346	.496	136	24	7	3	0	.978	-4	*2-155	3.1
1948	*Cle-A★	144	550	96	154	21	4	32	124	77	68	.280	.371	.507	136	26	5	2	0	.971	-7	*2-144/S-2	2.7
1949	Cle-A★	148	541	74	136	18	3	20	84	83	33	.251	.355	.407	103	2	5	6	-2	.980	-18	*2-145	-1.1
1950	Cle-A	119	368	59	87	12	1	19	57	56	41	.236	.340	.429	99	-2	4	1	1	.969	-18	*2-105	-1.4
Total	11	1566	5707	914	1530	264	52	253	975	759	702	.268	.357	.466	121	153	89	60	-9	.970	54	*2-1519/1-30,S-2	28.2

■ KEITH GORDON
Gordon, Keith Bradley   b: 1/22/69, Bethesda, Md.   BR/TR, 6'1", 205 lbs.   Deb: 7/9/93

YEAR	TM/L	G	AB	R	H	2B	3B	HR	RBI	BB	SO	AVG	OBP	SLG	PRO+	BR/A	SB	CS	SBR	FA	FR	G/POS	TPR
1993	Cin-N	3	6	0	1	0	0	0	0	0	2	.167	.167	.167	-10	-1	0	0	0	1.000	-0	/O-2	-0.1

■ MIKE GORDON
Gordon, Michael William   b: 9/11/53, Leominster, Mass.   BB/TR, 6'3", 215 lbs.   Deb: 4/7/77

YEAR	TM/L	G	AB	R	H	2B	3B	HR	RBI	BB	SO	AVG	OBP	SLG	PRO+	BR/A	SB	CS	SBR	FA	FR	G/POS	TPR
1977	Chi-N	8	23	0	1	0	0	0	2	2	8	.043	.120	.043	-49	-5	0	0	0	.970	-3	/C-8	-0.8
1978	Chi-N	4	5	0	1	0	0	0	0	3	2	.200	.556	.200	106	0	0	0	0	1.000	-0	/C-4	0.0
Total	2	12	28	0	2	0	0	0	2	5	10	.071	.235	.071	-11	-4	0	0	0	.979	-3	/C-12	-0.8

■ SID GORDON
Gordon, Sidney   b: 8/13/17, Brooklyn, N.Y.   d: 6/17/75, New York, N.Y.   BR/TR, 5'10", 185 lbs.   Deb: 9/11/41

YEAR	TM/L	G	AB	R	H	2B	3B	HR	RBI	BB	SO	AVG	OBP	SLG	PRO+	BR/A	SB	CS	SBR	FA	FR	G/POS	TPR
1941	NY-N	9	31	4	8	1	1	0	2	5	3	.258	.378	.355	105	0				1.000	-1	/O-9	-0.1
1942	NY-N	6	19	4	6	0	1	0	2	3	2	.316	.409	.421	142	1	0			.913	1	/3-6	0.3
1943	NY-N	131	474	50	119	9	11	9	63	43	32	.251	.315	.373	98	-2	2			.941	3	3-53,1-41,O-28,/2-3	-0.2
1946	NY-N	135	450	64	132	15	4	5	45	60	21	.293	.380	.378	115	11	1			.995	1	*O-101,3-30	0.8
1947	NY-N	130	437	57	119	19	8	13	57	50	21	.272	.347	.442	107	4	2			.971	1	*O-124/3-2	-0.2
1948	NY-N☆	142	521	100	156	26	4	30	107	74	39	.299	.390	.537	148	34	8			**.948**	-5	*3-115,O-23	2.7
1949	NY-N★	141	489	87	139	26	2	26	90	95	21	.284	.404	.505	142	32	1			.958	-23	*3-123,O-15/1-1	0.6
1950	Bos-N	134	481	78	146	33	4	27	103	78	31	.304	.403	.557	160	42	2			.990	6	*O-123,3-10	4.1
1951	Bos-N	150	550	96	158	28	1	29	109	80	32	.287	.383	.500	146	35	2	0	1	.984	-4	*O-122,3-34	2.7
1952	Bos-N	144	522	69	151	22	2	25	75	77	40	.289	.384	.483	144	32	0	4	-2	**.996**	4	*O-142/3-2	2.6
1953	Mil-N	140	464	67	127	22	4	19	75	71	40	.274	.372	.461	123	17	1	1	0	.977	-1	*O-137	1.0
1954	Pit-N	131	363	38	111	12	0	12	49	67	24	.306	.414	.438	124	16	0	0	0	.977	-6	O-73,3-40	0.6
1955	Pit-N	16	47	2	8	1	0	0	1	2	6	.170	.204	.191	6	-6	0	0	0	1.000	-0	/3-8,O-4	-0.5
	NY-N	66	144	19	35	6	1	7	25	25	15	.243	.355	.444	110	2	0	0	0	1.000	6	3-31,O-17	0.7
	Yr	82	191	21	43	7	1	7	26	27	21	.225	.321	.382	86	-4	0	0	0	1.000	7	3-39,O-21	0.2
Total	13	1475	4992	735	1415	220	43	202	805	731	356	.283	.377	.466	130	218	19	5		.985	-19	*O-918,3-454/1-42,2	15.1

■ GEORGE GORE
Gore, George F. "Piano Legs"   b: 5/3/1857, Saccarappa, Me.   d: 9/16/33, Utica, N.Y.   BL/TR, 5'11", 195 lbs.   Deb: 5/1/1879   M

YEAR	TM/L	G	AB	R	H	2B	3B	HR	RBI	BB	SO	AVG	OBP	SLG	PRO+	BR/A	SB	CS	SBR	FA	FR	G/POS	TPR
1879	Chi-N	63	266	43	70	17	4	0	32	8	30	.263	.285	.357	104	0				.872	-2	O-54/1-9	-0.4
1880	Chi-N	77	322	70	116	23	2	2	47	21	10	**.360**	**.399**	**.463**	180	26				.879	6	*O-74/1-7	2.8
1881	Chi-N	73	309	**86**	92	18	9	1	44	27	23	.298	.354	.424	137	13				.874	2	*O-72/3-1,1-1	1.2
1882	Chi-N	84	367	**99**	117	15	7	3	51	**29**	21	.319	.369	.422	146	19				.842	6	*O-84	2.1
1883	Chi-N	92	392	105	131	30	9	2	52	27	13	.334	.377	.472	148	21				.867	11	*O-92	2.7
1884	Chi-N	103	422	104	134	18	4	5	34	**61**	26	.318	.404	.415	146	23				.868	2	*O-103	2.0
1885	*Chi-N	109	441	115	138	21	13	5	57	68	25	.313	.405	.454	154	25				.884	-3	*O-109	1.8
1886	*Chi-N	118	444	150	135	20	12	6	63	**102**	30	.304	.438	.444	145	25	23			.876	-3	*O-118	1.7
1887	NY-N	111	459	95	133	16	5	1	49	42	18	.290	.358	.353	103	4	39			.889	1	*O-111	0.3
1888	*NY-N	64	254	37	56	4	4	2	17	30	31	.220	.308	.291	93	-1	11			.836	-9	O-64	-1.2
1889	*NY-N	120	488	132	149	21	7	7	54	84	28	.305	.416	.420	134	26	28			.864	-8	*O-120	1.3
1890	NY-P	93	399	132	127	26	8	10	55	77	23	.318	.432	.499	136	20	28			.877	-12	O-93	0.4
1891	NY-N	130	528	103	150	22	7	2	48	74	34	.284	.379	.364	122	18	19			.909	-6	*O-130	0.7
1892	NY-N	53	193	47	49	11	2	0	11	49	16	.254	.412	.332	128	10	20			.932	1	O-53	0.9
	StL-N	20	73	9	15	0	1	0	4	18	6	.205	.363	.233	85	0	2			.844	-2	O-20,M	-0.2
	Yr	73	266	56	64	11	3	0	15	67	22	.241	.399	.305	116	10	22			.908	-0	O-73	0.7
Total	14	1310	5357	1327	1612	262	94	46	618	717	332	.301	.386	.411	134	231	170			.876	-14	*O-1297/1-17,3-1	16.1

■ BOB GORINSKI
Gorinski, Robert John   b: 1/7/52, Latrobe, Pa.   BR/TR, 6'3", 215 lbs.   Deb: 4/10/77

YEAR	TM/L	G	AB	R	H	2B	3B	HR	RBI	BB	SO	AVG	OBP	SLG	PRO+	BR/A	SB	CS	SBR	FA	FR	G/POS	TPR
1977	Min-A	54	118	14	23	4	1	3	22	5	29	.195	.228	.322	49	-9	1	0	0	.936	-7	O-37/D-9	-1.6

■ HERB GORMAN
Gorman, Herbert Allen   b: 12/18/24, San Francisco, Cal   d: 4/5/53, San Diego, Cal.   BL/TL, 5'11", 180 lbs.   Deb: 4/19/52

YEAR	TM/L	G	AB	R	H	2B	3B	HR	RBI	BB	SO	AVG	OBP	SLG	PRO+	BR/A	SB	CS	SBR	FA	FR	G/POS	TPR
1952	StL-N	1	1	0	0	0	0	0	0	0	0	.000	.000	.000	-99	-0				.000	0	H	0.0

■ HOWIE GORMAN
Gorman, Howard Paul "Lefty"   b: 5/14/13, Pittsburgh, Pa.   d: 4/29/84, Harrisburg, Pa.   BL/TL, 6'2", 160 lbs.   Deb: 8/7/37

YEAR	TM/L	G	AB	R	H	2B	3B	HR	RBI	BB	SO	AVG	OBP	SLG	PRO+	BR/A	SB	CS	SBR	FA	FR	G/POS	TPR
1937	Phi-N	13	19	3	4	1	0	0	1	1	1	.211	.250	.263	37	-2	0			.500	-3	/O-7	-0.5
1938	Phi-N	1	1	0	0	0	0	0	0	0	0	.000	.000	.000	-99	-0	0			.000	0	H	0.0
Total	2	14	20	3	4	1	0	0	1	1	1	.200	.238	.250	30	-2	1			.500	-3	/O-7	-0.5

■ JACK GORMAN
Gorman, John F. "Stooping Jack"   b: 1859, St.Louis, Mo.   d: 9/9/1889, St.Louis, Mo.   Deb: 7/1/1883

YEAR	TM/L	G	AB	R	H	2B	3B	HR	RBI	BB	SO	AVG	OBP	SLG	PRO+	BR/A	SB	CS	SBR	FA	FR	G/POS	TPR
1883	StL-a	1	4	0	0	0	0	0	0	0	0	.000	.000	.000	-95	-0				.667	0	/O-1	
1884	KC-U	33	137	25	38	5	2	0			4	.277	.298	.343	108	-3				.954	0	1-24/O-5,3-4	-0.7
	Pit-a	8	27	3	4	1	0	0			4	.148	.179	.222	30	-2				.750	-2	/P-3,O-3,3-2	-0.3
Total	2	42	168	28	42	5	3	0			5	.250	.272	.315	89	-6				.944	-4	/1-24,O-9,3-6,P-3	-1.0

YEAR	TM/L	G	AB	R	H	2B	3B	HR	RBI	BB	SO	AVG	OBP	SLG	PRO+	BR/A	SB	CS	SBR	FA	FR	G/POS	TPR

■ JOHNNY GORYL — Goryl, John Albert b: 10/21/33, Cumberland, R.I. BR/TR, 5'10", 175 lbs. Deb: 9/20/57 MC

1957	Chi-N	9	38	7	8	2	0	0	1	5	9	.211	.318	.263	59	-2	0	1	-1	.952	-1	/3-9	-0.4
1958	Chi-N	83	219	27	53	9	3	4	14	27	34	.242	.337	.365	85	-4	0	1	-1	.931	11	3-44,2-35	0.8
1959	Chi-N	25	48	1	9	3	1	1	6	5	3	.188	.264	.354	63	-3	1	1	-0	.973	0	2-11/3-4	-0.2
1962	Min-A	37	26	6	5	0	1	2	2	2	6	.192	.250	.500	93	-0	0	0	0	.923	-0	/2-4,S-1	-0.1
1963	Min-A	64	150	29	43	5	3	9	24	15	29	.287	.355	.540	144	9	0	0	0	.958	-9	2-34,3-11/S-7	0.3
1964	Min-A	58	114	9	16	0	2	0	1	10	25	.140	.216	.175	10	-14	1	0	0	.975	2	2-28,3-13	-1.0
Total	6	276	595	79	134	19	10	16	48	64	106	.225	.306	.371	83	-15	2	3	-1	.960	3	2-112/3-81,S-8	-0.6

■ JIM GOSGER — Gosger, James Charles b: 11/6/42, Port Huron, Mich. BL/TL, 5'11", 185 lbs. Deb: 5/4/63

1963	Bos-A	19	16	3	1	0	0	0	0	3	5	.063	.211	.063	-19	-3	0	0	0	.818	-0	/O-4	-0.3
1965	Bos-A	81	324	45	83	15	4	9	35	29	61	.256	.321	.410	100	-0	3	1	0	.975	9	O-81	0.6
1966	Bos-A	40	126	16	32	4	0	5	17	15	20	.254	.333	.405	101	0	0	1	-1	.985	-0	O-32	-0.3
	KC-A	88	272	34	61	14	1	5	27	37	53	.224	.322	.338	93	-2	5	3	-0	.994	1	O-77	-0.5
	Yr	128	398	50	93	18	1	10	44	52	73	.234	.325	.359	96	-1	5	4	-1	.991	0	*O-109	-0.8
1967	KC-A	134	356	31	86	14	5	5	36	53	69	.242	.340	.351	108	5	5	7	-3	.981	-1	*O-113	-0.4
1968	Oak-A	88	150	7	27	1	0	0	5	17	21	.180	.263	.200	44	-10	4	0	1	1.000	-2	O-64	-1.5
1969	Sea-A	39	55	4	6	2	1	1	1	6	11	.109	.197	.236	21	-6	2	1	0	1.000	-3	O-26	-1.1
	NY-N	10	15	0	2	2	0	0	1	1	6	.133	.188	.267	25	-2	0	0	0	1.000	-1	/O-5	-0.3
1970	Mon-N	91	274	38	72	11	2	5	37	35	35	.263	.348	.372	93	-2	5	3	-0	1.000	-3	O-71,1-19	-0.9
1971	Mon-N	51	102	7	16	2	2	0	8	9	17	.157	.232	.216	27	-10	1	1	-0	.952	2	O-23/1-6	-1.4
1973	NY-N	38	92	9	22	1	0	0	10	9	16	.239	.307	.261	60	-5	0	1	-1	1.000	-7	O-35	-1.4
1974	NY-N	26	33	3	3	0	0	0	0	1	9	.091	.167	.091	-27	-6	0	0	0	1.000	-7	O-24	-1.4
Total	10	705	1815	197	411	67	16	30	177	217	316	.226	.311	.331	83	-39	25	18	-3	.985	-17	O-555/1-25	-8.9

■ GOOSE GOSLIN — Goslin, Leon Allen b: 10/16/1900, Salem, N.J. d: 5/15/71, Bridgeton, N.J. BL/TR, 5'11.5", 185 lbs. Deb: 9/16/21 H

1921	Was-A	14	50	8	13	1	1	1	6	6	5	.260	.351	.380	91	-1	0	0	0	1.000	0	O-14	-0.2
1922	Was-A	101	358	44	116	19	7	3	53	25	26	.324	.373	.441	117	8	4	4	-1	.932	-3	O-93	-0.2
1923	Was-A	150	600	86	180	29	**18**	9	99	40	53	.300	.347	.453	115	10	7	2	1	.957	7	*O-149	0.7
1924	*Was-A	154	579	100	199	30	17	12	**129**	68	29	.344	.421	.516	145	39	15	14	-4	.960	5	*O-154	2.9
1925	*Was-A	150	601	116	201	34	**20**	18	113	53	50	.334	.394	.547	140	33	27	8	3	.971	14	*O-150	3.7
1926	Was-A	147	568	105	201	26	15	17	108	63	38	.354	.425	.542	155	45	8	8	-2	.964	19	*O-147	4.9
1927	Was-A	148	581	96	194	37	15	13	120	50	28	.334	.392	.516	136	29	21	6	3	.955	2	*O-148	2.3
1928	Was-A	135	456	80	173	36	10	17	102	48	19	**.379**	.442	.614	176	50	16	3	3	.962	3	*O-142	4.5
1929	Was-A	145	553	82	159	28	7	18	91	66	33	.288	.366	.461	111	8	10	3	1	.968	-4	*O-142	-0.4
1930	Was-A	47	188	34	51	11	5	7	38	19	19	.271	.344	.495	110	2	3	2	-0	.937	-5	O-47	-0.6
	StL-A	101	396	81	129	25	7	30	100	48	35	.326	.400	.652	156	32	14	9	-1	.973	12	*O-101	3.2
	Yr	148	584	115	180	36	12	37	138	67	54	.308	.382	.601	142	34	17	11	-2	.964	7	*O-151	3.1
1931	StL-A	151	591	114	194	42	10	24	105	80	41	.328	.412	.555	147	40	9	6	-1	.960	5	*O-149/3-1	1.2
1932	StL-A	150	572	88	171	28	9	17	104	92	35	.299	.398	.469	117	16	12	9	-2	.951	8	*O-149/3-1	0.5
1933	*Was-A	132	549	97	163	35	10	10	64	42	32	.297	.348	.452	112	7	5	2	0	.965	8	*O-128	0.5
1934	*Det-A	151	614	106	187	38	7	13	100	65	38	.305	.373	.453	112	10	5	4	-1	.953	2	*O-149	0.5
1935	*Det-A	147	590	88	172	34	6	9	109	56	31	.292	.355	.415	102	1	5	4	-1	.965	0	*O-144	-0.5
1936	Det-A★	147	572	122	180	33	8	24	125	85	50	.315	.403	.526	127	24	14	4	2	.955	-5	*O-144	1.4
1937	Det-A	79	181	30	43	11	1	4	35	34	18	.238	.367	.376	86	-3	0	1	-1	.954	-2	O-40/1-1	-0.7
1938	Was-A	38	57	6	9	3	0	0	11	6	6	.158	.262	.316	47	-5	0	0	0	1.000	-1	O-13	-0.6
Total	18	2287	8656	1483	2735	500	173	248	1609	949	585	.316	.387	.500	128	347	175	89	-1	.960	62	*O-2188/1-1,3-1	26.0

■ HOWIE GOSS — Goss, Howard Wayne b: 11/1/34, Wewoka, Okla. BR/TR, 6'4", 204 lbs. Deb: 4/10/62

1962	Pit-N	89	111	19	27	6	0	2	10	9	36	.243	.306	.351	76	-4	5	2	0	.985	-12	O-66	-1.7
1963	Hou-N	133	411	37	86	18	2	9	44	31	128	.209	.265	.328	74	-15	4	6	-2	.993	7	*O-123	-1.8
Total	2	222	522	56	113	24	2	11	54	40	164	.216	.274	.333	75	-19	9	8	-2	.991	-5	O-189	-3.5

■ DICK GOSSETT — Gossett, John Star b: 8/21/1891, Dennison, Ohio d: 10/6/62, Massillon, Ohio BR/TR, 5'11", 185 lbs. Deb: 4/30/13

1913	NY-A	39	105	9	17	2	0	0	9	10	22	.162	.254	.181	28	-9	1			.972	-5	C-38	-1.2
1914	NY-A	10	21	3	3	0	0	0	1	5	5	.143	.333	.143	44	-1	0			.977	-1	C-10	-0.2
Total	2	49	126	12	20	2	0	0	10	15	27	.159	.269	.175	31	-10	1			.973	-6	/C-48	-1.4

■ JULIO GOTAY — Gotay, Julio Enrique (Sanchez) b: 6/9/39, Fajardo, P.R. BR/TR, 6', 180 lbs. Deb: 8/6/60

1960	StL-N	3	8	1	3	0	0	0	0	0	2	.375	.375	.375	98	-0	1	0	0	.750	-2	/S-2,3-1	-0.1
1961	StL-N	10	45	5	11	4	0	0	5	3	5	.244	.292	.333	59	-3	0	0	0	.804	-4	S-10	-0.6
1962	StL-N	127	369	47	94	12	1	2	27	27	47	.255	.316	.309	62	-19	7	3	0	.956	5	*S-120/2-8,O-2,3-1	-0.4
1963	Pit-N	4	2	0	1	0	0	0	0	0	0	.500	.500	.500	188	-0	0	0	0	.667	0	/2-1	0.0
1964	Pit-N	3	2	1	1	0	0	0	0	1	0	.500	.667	.500	235	1	0	0	0	.000	0	H	0.1
1965	Cal-A	40	77	6	19	4	0	1	3	4	9	.247	.284	.338	78	-2	0	0	0	.961	3	2-23/3-9,S-1	0.2
1966	Hou-N	4	5	0	0	0	0	0	0	0	0	.000	.000	.000	-99	-1	0	0	0	1.000	0	/3-1	-0.1
1967	Hou-N	77	234	30	66	10	2	2	15	15	30	.282	.331	.368	103	1	1	1	-0	.971	-4	2-30,S-20/3-3	0.1
1968	Hou-N	75	165	9	41	3	0	1	11	4	21	.248	.271	.285	68	-7	1	2	-1	.982	10	2-48/3-1	0.6
1969	Hou-N	46	81	7	21	5	0	0	9	7	13	.259	.318	.321	81	-2	2	1	0	.987	6	2-16/3-1	0.5
Total	10	389	988	106	257	38	3	6	70	61	127	.260	.309	.323	75	-32	12	7	-1	.944	15	S-153,2-126/3-17,O	0.3

■ CHARLIE GOULD — Gould, Charles Harvey b: 8/21/1847, Cincinnati, Ohio d: 4/10/17, Flushing, N.Y. BR/TR, 6', 172 lbs. Deb: 5/5/1871 M

1871	Bos-n	31	151	38	43	9	2	2	32	3	1	.285	.299	.411	98	-1	6	2	1	.906	-3	*1-30/O-1	-0.1
1872	Bos-n	45	211	40	54	9	**8**	0	33	2	3	.256	.263	.374	89	-4	0	0	0	.933	0	*1-44/O-2	-0.1
1874	Bal-n	33	143	20	32	6	0	0	14	2	1	.224	.234	.266	60	-6	1	0	0	.951	0	1-32/C-1	-0.4
1875	NH-n	27	109	9	29	4	1	0	8	1	2	.266	.273	.321	121	3	0	1	0	.946	-4	1-26/C-1,O-1,M	-0.1
1876	Cin-N	61	258	27	65	7	0	0	11	6	11	.252	.269	.279	97	1				.939	1	*1-61/P-2,M	0.0
1877	Cin-N	24	91	5	25	2	1	0	13	5	5	.275	.313	.319	112	2				.922	-4	1-24/O-1	0.1
Total	4 n	136	614	107	158	28	11	2	87	8	7	.257	.267	.349	90	-8	7	3	0	.934	-6	1-132/O-4,C-2	-0.7
Total	2	85	349	32	90	9	1	0	24	11	16	.258	.281	.289	101	2				.934	0	/1-85,P-2,O-1	0.1

■ NICK GOULISH — Goulish, Nicholas Edward b: 11/13/17, Punxsutawney, Pa. d: 5/15/84, Youngstown, Ohio BL/TL, 6'1", 179 lbs. Deb: 4/19/44

1944	Phi-N	1	1	0	0	0	0	0	0	0	0	.000	.000	.000	-99	-0	0	0	0	.000	0	H	0.0
1945	Phi-N	13	11	4	3	0	0	0	2	1	3	.273	.333	.273	72	-0	0	0	0	1.000	-1	/O-2	-0.1
Total	2	14	12	4	3	0	0	0	2	1	3	.250	.308	.250	58	-1	0	0	0	1.000	-1	/O-2	-0.1

■ CLAUDE GOUZZIE — Gouzzie, Claude b: 1873, France d: 9/21/07, Denver, Colo. BR/TR, 5'9", 170 lbs. Deb: 7/22/03

| 1903 | StL-A | 1 | 1 | 0 | 0 | 0 | 0 | 0 | 0 | 0 | 0 | .000 | .000 | .000 | -99 | -0 | 0 | | | 1.000 | 0 | /2-1 | 0.0 |

■ HANK GOWDY — Gowdy, Henry Morgan b: 8/24/1889, Columbus, Ohio d: 8/1/66, Columbus, Ohio BR/TR, 6'2", 182 lbs. Deb: 9/13/10 MC

1910	NY-N	7	14	1	3	1	0	0	2	0	3	.214	.313	.286	75	-0	1			.943	1	/1-5	0.0
1911	NY-N	4	4	1	1	1	0	0	0	0	2	.250	.500	.500	175	1	0			1.000	-0	/1-2	0.0
	Bos-N	29	97	9	28	4	2	0	16	4	19	.289	.324	.371	87	-2	2			.966	-1	1-26/C-1	-0.3
	Yr	33	101	10	29	5	2	0	16	6	19	.287	.333	.376	92	-1	2			.969	-1	1-28/C-1	-0.3
1912	Bos-N	44	96	16	26	6	1	2	10	16	13	.271	.386	.448	126	4	3			.926	-2	C-22/1-7	0.3
1913	Bos-N	3	5	0	3	1	0	0	2	3	2	.600	.750	.800	336	2				1.000	-1	/C-2	0.1
1914	*Bos-N	128	366	42	89	17	6	3	46	48	40	.243	.337	.347	104	-3	14			.968	-5	*C-115/1-9	0.7
1915	Bos-N	118	316	27	78	15	3	2	30	41	34	.247	.339	.332	108	4	10	4	1	.974	4	*C-114	1.5
1916	Bos-N	118	349	32	88	14	1	1	34	24	33	.252	.311	.307	94	-2	8			.980	5	*C-116	1.0
1917	Bos-N	49	154	12	33	7	0	1	14	15	13	.214	.288	.260	73	-5	2			.969	-1	C-49	-0.2
1919	Bos-N	78	219	18	61	8	1	1	29	19	16	.279	.339	.338	108	5	5			.977	5	C-74/1-1	1.4

YEAR	TM/L	G	AB	R	H	2B	3B	HR	RBI	BB	SO	AVG	OBP	SLG	PRO+	BR/A	SB	CS	SBR	FA	FR	G/POS	TPR
1920	Bos-N	80	214	14	52	11	2	0	18	20	15	.243	.314	.313	84	-4	6	1	1	.980	11	C-74	1.3
1921	Bos-N	64	164	17	49	7	2	2	17	16	11	.299	.368	.402	110	3	2	0	1	.981	-1	C-53	0.4
1922	Bos-N	92	221	23	70	11	1	1	27	24	13	.317	.391	.389	107	3	2	1	0	.971	1	C-72/1-1	0.7
1923	Bos-N	23	48	5	6	1	1	0	5	15	5	.125	.354	.188	48	-3	1	1	-0	.982	-2	C-15	-0.4
	*NY-N	53	122	13	40	6	3	1	18	21	9	.328	.427	.451	133	7	2	0	1	.986	-7	C-43	0.2
	Yr	76	170	18	46	7	4	1	23	36	14	.271	.404	.376	109	4	3	1	0	.985	-10	C-58	-0.2
1924	*NY-N	87	191	25	62	9	1	4	37	26	11	.325	.411	.445	133	10	1	0	0	.982	5	C-78	1.9
1925	NY-N	47	114	14	37	4	3	3	19	12	7	.325	.389	.491	128	5	0	0	0	1.000	1	C-41	0.7
1929	Bos-N	10	16	1	7	0	0	0	3	0	2	.438	.438	.438	122	1	0			1.000	-0	/C-9	0.0
1930	Bos-N	16	25	0	5	1	0	0	2	3	1	.200	.310	.240	37	-3	0			.972	1	C-15	-0.1
Total	17	1050	2735	270	738	124	27	21	322	311	247	.270	.351	.358	105	25	59	7		.975	5	C-893/1-51	9.2

■ BILLY GRABARKEWITZ

Grabarkewitz, Billy Cordell   b: 1/18/46, Lockhart, Tex.   BR/TR, 5'10", 170 lbs.   Deb: 4/22/69

YEAR	TM/L	G	AB	R	H	2B	3B	HR	RBI	BB	SO	AVG	OBP	SLG	PRO+	BR/A	SB	CS	SBR	FA	FR	G/POS	TPR
1969	LA-N	34	65	4	6	1	1	0	5	4	19	.092	.145	.138	-22	-11	0	1	0	.954	-2	S-18/3-6,2-3	-1.2
1970	LA-N★	156	529	92	153	20	8	17	84	95	149	.289	.403	.454	135	30	19	9	0	.959	-1	3-97,S-50,2-20	3.4
1971	LA-N	44	71	9	16	5	0	0	6	19	16	.225	.389	.296	102	1	1	2	-1	1.000	4	2-13,3-10/S-1	0.6
1972	LA-N	53	144	17	24	4	0	4	16	18	53	.167	.268	.278	57	-8	3	0	1	.902	-4	3-24,2-19/S-2	-1.1
1973	Cal-A	61	129	27	21	6	1	3	9	28	27	.163	.316	.295	79	-3	2	2	1	.965	-6	2-18,3-12/S-1,0D	-0.9
	Phi-N	25	66	12	19	2	0	2	7	12	18	.288	.397	.409	121	2	3	1	0	.960	1	2-20/3-3,O-1	0.4
1974	Phi-N	34	30	7	4	0	0	1	2	5	10	.133	.257	.233	36	-3	1	0	0	1.000	1	/O-5,3-1	-0.3
	Chi-N	53	125	21	31	3	2	1	12	21	28	.248	.361	.328	90	-1	1	2	1	.954	1	2-45/S-7,3-6	0.2
	Yr	87	155	28	35	3	2	2	14	26	38	.226	.341	.310	80	-3	4	3	-1	.954	2	2-45/3-7,S-7,0-5	-0.1
1975	Oak-A	6	2	0	0	0	0	0	0	1	0	.000	.000	.000	-99	-1	0	0	0	.833	-0	/2-4,D-1	0.0
Total	7	466	1161	189	274	41	12	28	141	202	321	.236	.354	.364	101	8	33	17		.952	-8	3-159,2-142/SOD	1.1

■ ROD GRABER

Graber, Rodney Blaine   b: 6/20/30, Massillon, Ohio   BL/TL, 5'11", 175 lbs.   Deb: 9/9/58

YEAR	TM/L	G	AB	R	H	2B	3B	HR	RBI	BB	SO	AVG	OBP	SLG	PRO+	BR/A	SB	CS	SBR	FA	FR	G/POS	TPR
1958	Cle-A	4	8	0	1	0	0	0	0	1	2	.125	.222	.125	-2	-1	0	0	0	1.000	-0	/O-2	-0.1

■ JOHNNY GRABOWSKI

Grabowski, John Patrick "Nig"   b: 1/7/1900, Ware, Mass.   d: 5/23/46, Albany, N.Y.   BR/TR, 5'10", 185 lbs.   Deb: 7/11/24

YEAR	TM/L	G	AB	R	H	2B	3B	HR	RBI	BB	SO	AVG	OBP	SLG	PRO+	BR/A	SB	CS	SBR	FA	FR	G/POS	TPR
1924	Chi-A	20	56	10	14	3	0	0	3	2	4	.250	.276	.304	51	-4	0	0	0	.972	1	C-19	-0.2
1925	Chi-A	21	46	5	14	4	1	0	10	2	4	.304	.333	.435	99	-0	0	1	-1	.983	0	C-21	0.0
1926	Chi-A	48	122	6	32	1	1	1	11	4	15	.262	.286	.311	58	-8	0	1	-1	.973	-2	C-38/1-1	-0.8
1927	*NY-A	70	195	29	54	2	4	0	25	20	15	.277	.350	.328	79	-5	0	0	0	.984	0	C-68	-0.1
1928	NY-A	75	202	21	48	7	1	1	21	10	21	.238	.274	.297	51	-15	0	0	0	.987	-2	C-75	-0.7
1929	NY-A	22	59	4	12	1	0	0	2	3	6	.203	.242	.220	21	-7	1	0	0	.943	-0	C-22	-0.5
1931	Det-A	40	136	9	32	7	1	1	14	6	19	.235	.268	.324	53	-10	0	0	0	.984	2	C-39	-0.5
Total	7	296	816	84	206	25	8	3	86	47	84	.252	.295	.314	60	-49	1	2	-1	.979	4	C-282/1-1	-2.8

■ JOE GRACE

Grace, Joseph Laverne   b: 1/5/14, Gorham, Ill.   d: 9/18/69, Murphysboro, Ill.   BL/TR, 6'1", 180 lbs.   Deb: 9/24/38

YEAR	TM/L	G	AB	R	H	2B	3B	HR	RBI	BB	SO	AVG	OBP	SLG	PRO+	BR/A	SB	CS	SBR	FA	FR	G/POS	TPR
1938	StL-A	12	47	9	16	4	0	0	4	2	3	.340	.367	.362	83	-1	0		-1	.933	-2	O-12	-0.4
1939	StL-A	74	207	35	63	11	2	3	22	19	24	.304	.363	.420	98	-1	3	2	-0	.968	-4	O-53	-0.6
1940	StL-A	80	229	45	59	14	2	5	25	26	23	.258	.336	.402	88	-4	2	1	-1	.958	-5	O-51,C-12	-1.1
1941	StL-A	115	362	53	112	17	4	6	60	57	31	.309	.410	.428	118	12	1	3	-2	.983	-2	O-88/C-9	0.3
1946	StL-A	48	161	21	37	7	2	1	13	16	20	.230	.307	.317	71	-6	1	3	-2	.967	1	O-43	-0.9
	Was-A	77	321	39	97	17	4	2	31	24	19	.302	.358	.399	118	7	1	4	-2	.959	4	O-74	0.5
	Yr	125	482	60	134	24	6	3	44	40	39	.278	.341	.371	101	1	2	7	-4	.962	5	*O-117	-0.4
1947	Was-A	78	234	25	58	9	4	3	17	35	15	.248	.348	.359	99	0	1	2	-1	.976	2	O-67	-0.2
Total	6	484	1561	225	442	76	18	20	172	179	135	.283	.362	.393	102	7	9	17	-8	.969	-6	O-388/C-21	-2.4

■ MARK GRACE

Grace, Mark Eugene   b: 6/28/64, Winston-Salem, N.C   BL/TL, 6'2", 190 lbs.   Deb: 5/2/88

YEAR	TM/L	G	AB	R	H	2B	3B	HR	RBI	BB	SO	AVG	OBP	SLG	PRO+	BR/A	SB	CS	SBR	FA	FR	G/POS	TPR
1988	Chi-N	134	486	65	144	23	4	7	57	60	43	.296	.374	.403	118	13	3	3	-1	.987	-4	*1-133	-0.3
1989	*Chi-N	142	510	74	160	28	3	13	79	80	42	.314	.407	.457	136	27	14	7	0	.996	13	*1-142	3.0
1990	Chi-N	157	589	72	182	32	1	9	82	59	54	.309	.377	.413	109	9	15	6	1	.992	27	*1-153	2.5
1991	Chi-N	160	619	87	169	28	5	8	58	70	53	.273	.350	.373	99	0	3	4	-2	.995	20	*1-160	0.9
1992	Chi-N	158	603	72	185	37	5	9	79	72	36	.307	.384	.430	127	23	6	1	1	.998	9	*1-157	2.4
1993	Chi-N★	155	594	86	193	39	4	14	98	71	32	.325	.398	.475	135	31	8	4	0	.997	1	*1-154	1.8
1994	Chi-N	106	403	55	120	23	3	6	44	48	41	.298	.373	.414	106	5	0	1	-1	.993	-5	*1-103	-0.5
1995	Chi-N★	143	552	97	180	**51**	3	16	92	65	46	.326	.399	.516	142	34	6	2	1	.995	4	*1-143	2.4
1996	Chi-N	142	547	88	181	39	1	9	75	62	41	.331	.400	.455	123	20	2	3	-1	.995	7	*1-141	0.9
Total	9	1297	4903	696	1514	300	29	91	664	587	388	.309	.384	.437	122	162	57	31	-2	.995	74	*1-1286	13.1

■ MIKE GRACE

Grace, Michael Lee   b: 6/14/56, Pontiac, Mich.   BR/TR, 6', 175 lbs.   Deb: 4/18/78

YEAR	TM/L	G	AB	R	H	2B	3B	HR	RBI	BB	SO	AVG	OBP	SLG	PRO+	BR/A	SB	CS	SBR	FA	FR	G/POS	TPR
1978	Cin-N	5	3	0	0	0	0	0	0	0	2	.000	.000	.000	-99	-1	0	0	0	1.000	1	/3-2	0.0

■ EARL GRACE

Grace, Robert Earl   b: 2/24/07, Barlow, Ky.   d: 12/22/80, Phoenix, Ariz.   BL/TR, 6', 175 lbs.   Deb: 4/23/29

YEAR	TM/L	G	AB	R	H	2B	3B	HR	RBI	BB	SO	AVG	OBP	SLG	PRO+	BR/A	SB	CS	SBR	FA	FR	G/POS	TPR
1929	Chi-N	27	80	7	20	2	0	2	17	9	7	.250	.333	.338	67	-4	0			1.000	3	C-27	0.1
1931	Chi-N	7	9	2	1	0	0	0	1	4	1	.111	.385	.111	39	-1	0			1.000	-0	/C-2	0.0
	Pit-N	47	150	8	42	6	1	1	20	13	5	.280	.337	.353	87	-3	0			.974	-1	C-45	0.0
	Yr	54	159	10	43	6	1	1	21	17	6	.270	.341	.340	84	-3	0			.976	-1	C-47	0.0
1932	Pit-N	115	390	41	107	17	5	8	55	14	23	.274	.305	.405	91	-6	0			**.998**	-7	*C-114	-0.6
1933	Pit-N	93	291	22	84	13	1	3	44	26	23	.289	.349	.371	106	3	0			.980	1	C-88	0.9
1934	Pit-N	95	289	27	78	17	1	4	24	20	19	.270	.317	.377	83	-7	0			.982	-9	C-83/1-1	-1.2
1935	Pit-N	77	224	19	59	8	1	3	29	32	17	.263	.355	.348	87	-3	1			.990	3	C-69	0.3
1936	Phi-N	86	221	24	55	11	0	4	32	34	20	.249	.352	.353	82	-5	0			.976	-4	C-65	-0.6
1937	Phi-N	80	223	19	47	11	1	6	29	33	15	.211	.313	.345	73	-8	0			.990	-3	C-64	-0.8
Total	8	627	1877	169	493	83	10	31	251	185	130	.263	.331	.367	86	-34	1			.987	-17	C-557/1-1	-1.9

■ JOHN GRADY

Grady, John J.   b: 6/18/1860, Lowell, Mass.   d: 7/15/1893, Lowell, Mass.   5'7", 150 lbs.   Deb: 5/10/1884

YEAR	TM/L	G	AB	R	H	2B	3B	HR	RBI	BB	SO	AVG	OBP	SLG	PRO+	BR/A	SB	CS	SBR	FA	FR	G/POS	TPR
1884	Alt-U	9	36	5	11	3	0	0		2		.306	.342	.389	119	-0				.909	-1	/1-8,O-1	-0.2

■ MIKE GRADY

Grady, Michael William   b: 12/23/1869, Kennett Square, Pa   d: 12/3/43, Kennett Square, Pa.   BR/TR, 5'11", 190 lbs.   Deb: 4/24/1894

YEAR	TM/L	G	AB	R	H	2B	3B	HR	RBI	BB	SO	AVG	OBP	SLG	PRO+	BR/A	SB	CS	SBR	FA	FR	G/POS	TPR
1894	Phi-N	60	190	45	69	13	8	0	40	14	11	.363	.427	.516	130	9	3			.878	-12	C-44,1-11/O-2	0.1
1895	Phi-N	46	123	21	40	3	1	1	23	14	8	.325	.407	.390	106	2	3			.926	-11	C-38/O-5,3-1,1-1	-0.5
1896	Phi-N	71	242	49	77	20	7	1	44	16	19	.318	.382	.471	126	9	10			.942	-7	C-61/3-7	0.7
1897	Phi-N	4	13	1	2	0	0	0	0	1		.154	.214	.154	-2	-2	0			1.000	1	/C-3	-0.1
	StL-N	83	322	48	90	11	3	7	45	26		.280	.352	.398	100	-0	7			.974	-1	1-83/O-1	-0.1
	Yr	87	335	49	92	11	3	7	45	27		.275	.347	.388	96	-2	7			.974	-0	1-83/C-3,O-1	-0.2
1898	NY-N	93	287	64	85	19	5	3	49	38		.296	.399	.429	142	17	20			.944	-1	C-57,0-30/1-7,S-3	0.8
1899	NY-N	86	311	47	104	18	8	2	54	29		.334	.403	.463	142	18	20			.939	-13	C-43,3-35/O-4,1-4	0.8
1900	NY-N	83	251	36	55	8	4	0	29	21		.219	.331	.283	74	-7	9			.932	-14	C-41,1-12,S/3O2	-1.6
1901	Was-A	94	347	57	99	17	10	9	56	27		.285	.351	.470	128	12	14			.975	8	1-59,C-30/O-3	1.5
1904	StL-N	101	323	44	101	15	11	5	43	31		.313	.376	.474	169	26	6			.955	-20	C-77,1-11/2-3,3-1	1.5
1905	StL-N	100	311	41	89	20	7	4	41	33		.286	.360	.434	141	15	15			.956	-11	C-71,1-20	1.2
1906	StL-N	97	280	33	70	11	3	3	27	48		.250	.369	.343	127	11	5			.983	10	C-60,1-38	0.9
Total	11	918	3000	486	881	155	67	35	449	311	40	.294	.374	.425	127	110	114			.946	-95	C-525,1-246/3OS2	5.9

■ FRED GRAFF

Graff, Frederick Gottleib   b: 8/25/1889, Canton, Ohio   d: 10/4/79, Chattanooga, Tenn.   BR/TR, 5'10.5", 164 lbs.   Deb: 5/14/13

YEAR	TM/L	G	AB	R	H	2B	3B	HR	RBI	BB	SO	AVG	OBP	SLG	PRO+	BR/A	SB	CS	SBR	FA	FR	G/POS	TPR
1913	StL-A	4	5	1	2	1	0	0	2	3	3	.400	.625	.600	266	1	0			1.000	-1	/3-4	0.1

■ LOUIS GRAFF

Graff, Louis George "Chappie"   b: 7/25/1866, Philadelphia, Pa.   d: 4/16/55, Bryn Mawr, Pa.   TR,   Deb: 6/23/1890

YEAR	TM/L	G	AB	R	H	2B	3B	HR	RBI	BB	SO	AVG	OBP	SLG	PRO+	BR/A	SB	CS	SBR	FA	FR	G/POS	TPR
1890	Syr-a	1	5	0	2	1	0	0	3	0		.400	.400	.600	217	1	0			.333	-2	/C-1	-0.1

YEAR	TM/L	G	AB	R	H	2B	3B	HR	RBI	BB	SO	AVG	OBP	SLG	PRO+	BR/A	SB	CS	SBR	FA	FR	G/POS	TPR

■ **MILT GRAFF** Graff, Milton Edward b: 12/30/30, Jefferson Center, Pa. BL/TR, 5'7.5", 158 lbs. Deb: 4/16/57 C

1957	KC-A	56	155	16	28	4	3	0	10	15	10	.181	.262	.245	39	-13	2	5	-2	.988	1	2-53	-1.1
1958	KC-A	5	1	0	0	0	0	0	0	0	0	.000	.000	.000	-98	-0				1.000	0	/2-1	0.0
Total	2	61	156	16	28	4	3	0	10	15	10	.179	.260	.244	38	-13	2	5	-2	.988	2	/2-54	-1.1

■ **TONY GRAFFANINO** Graffanino, Anthony Joseph b: 6/6/72, Amityville, N.Y. BR/TR, 6'1", 175 lbs. Deb: 4/19/96

1996	Atl-N	22	46	7	8	1	1	0	2	4	13	.174	.255	.239	30	-5	0	0	0	.969	4	2-18	-0.1

■ **MOONLIGHT GRAHAM** Graham, Archibald Wright b: 11/9/1876, Fayetteville, N.C. d: 8/25/65, Chisholm, Minn. BL/TR, 5'10.5", 170 lbs. Deb: 6/29/05

1905	NY-N	1	0	0	0	0	0	0	0	0	0	—	—	—	—		0		0	.000	-0	/O-1	0.0

■ **SKINNY GRAHAM** Graham, Arthur William b: 8/12/09, Somerville, Mass. d: 7/10/67, Cambridge, Mass. BL/TR, 5'7", 162 lbs. Deb: 9/14/34

1934	Bos-A	13	47	7	11	2	1	0	3	6	13	.234	.321	.319	61	-3	2	2	-1	1.000	-1	O-13	-0.5
1935	Bos-A	8	10	1	3	0	0	0	1	1	3	.300	.364	.300	69	-0	1	0	0	1.000	-1	/O-2	-0.1
Total	2	21	57	8	14	2	1	0	4	7	16	.246	.328	.316	62	-3	3	2	-0	1.000	-2	/O-15	-0.6

■ **BARNEY GRAHAM** Graham, Barney b: Philadelphia, Pa. d: 12/31/1896, Mobile, Ala. Deb: 9/4/1889

1889	Phi-a	4	18	0	3	0	0	0	0	0	0	.167	.167	.167	-5	-2	0			.933	1	/3-4	-0.1

■ **BERNIE GRAHAM** Graham, Bernard W. b: 1860, Beloit, Wis. d: 10/30/1886, Mobile, Ala. BL, Deb: 7/11/1884

1884	CP-U	1	5	2	1	0	0	0		0		.200	.200	.200	22	-1				1.000	-0	/O-1	-0.1
	Bal-U	41	167	21	45	11	0	0		2		.269	.278	.335	77	-10				.814	1	O-40/1-1	-0.8
	Yr	42	172	23	46	11	0	0		2		.267	.276	.331	76	-10				.816	1	O-41/1-1	-0.9

■ **BERT GRAHAM** Graham, Bert "B.G." b: 4/3/1886, Tilton, Ill. d: 6/19/71, Cottonwood, Ariz. BB/TR, 5'11.5", 187 lbs. Deb: 9/9/10

1910	StL-A	8	26	1	3	2	1	0	5	1		.115	.148	.269	32	-2	0			.964	1	/1-5,2-2	-0.1

■ **CHARLIE GRAHAM** Graham, Charles Henry b: 4/25/1878, Santa Clara, Cal. d: 8/29/48, San Francisco, Cal BR/TR, 5'11", 180 lbs. Deb: 4/16/06

1906	Bos-A	30	90	10	21	1	0	1	12	10		.233	.330	.278	91	-0	1			.963	7	C-27	1.0

■ **DAN GRAHAM** Graham, Daniel Jay b: 7/19/54, Ray, Ariz. BL/TR, 6'1", 205 lbs. Deb: 6/8/79

1979	Min-A	2	4	0	0	0	0	0	0	0	0	.000	.000	.000	-96	-1	0	0	0	.000	0	/D-1	-0.1
1980	Bal-A	86	266	32	74	7	1	15	54	14	40	.278	.314	.481	116	4	0	0	0	.981	6	C-73/3-9,O-1,D-2	0.7
1981	Bal-A	55	142	7	25	3	0	2	11	13	32	.176	.245	.239	40	-11	0	0	0	.975	-4	C-40/3-4,D-6	-1.5
Total	3	143	412	39	99	10	1	17	65	27	72	.240	.287	.393	88	-7	0	0	0	.979	-4	C-113/3-13,D-9,O-1	-0.9

■ **TINY GRAHAM** Graham, Dawson Francis b: 9/9/1892, Nashville, Tenn. d: 12/29/62, Nashville, Tenn. BR/TR, 6'2", 185 lbs. Deb: 8/30/14

1914	Cin-N	25	61	5	14	1	0	3	9	3	10	.230	.266	.246	51	-4	1			.961	-2	1-25	-0.6

■ **PEACHES GRAHAM** Graham, George Frederick b: 3/23/1877, Aledo, Ill. d: 7/25/39, Long Beach, Cal. BR/TR, 5'9", 180 lbs. Deb: 9/14/02 F

1902	Cle-A	2	6	0	2	0	0	0	1	1		.333	.429	.333	118	0				1.000	0	/2-1	0.0
1903	Chi-N	1	2	0	0	0	0	0	0	0		.000	.000	.000	-99	-1				1.000	0	/P-1	0.0
1908	Bos-N	75	215	22	59	5	0	0	22	23		.274	.361	.298	112	4	4			.955	-3	C-62/2-5	0.8
1909	Bos-N	92	267	27	64	6	3	0	17	24		.240	.302	.285	79	-7	7			.948	-4	C-76/O-6,S-1,3-1	-0.4
1910	Bos-N	110	291	31	82	13	2	0	21	33	15	.282	.359	.340	100	0	5			.966	-8	C-87/3-2,1-1,O-1	0.1
1911	Bos-N	33	88	7	24	6	1	0	12	14	5	.273	.373	.364	98	0	2			.912	-5	C-26	-0.3
	Chi-N	36	71	6	17	3	0	0	8	11	8	.239	.365	.282	82	-1	2			.972	-5	C-28	-0.4
	Yr	69	159	13	41	9	1	0	20	25	13	.258	.369	.327	92	-1	4			.937	-10	C-54	-0.7
1912	Phi-N	24	59	6	17	1	0	1	4	8	5	.288	.373	.356	94	-0	1			.944	-2	C-19	-0.5
Total	7	373	999	99	265	34	6	1	85	114	33	.265	.347	.314	95	-3	21			.953	-25	C-298/O-7,2-6,31SP	-0.2

■ **JACK GRAHAM** Graham, John Bernard b: 12/24/16, Minneapolis, Minn. BL/TL, 6'2", 200 lbs. Deb: 4/16/46 F

1946	Bro-N	2	5	0	1	0	0	0	0	0	0	.200	.200	.200	14	-1	0			1.000	0	/1-2	-0.1
	NY-N	100	270	34	59	6	4	14	47	23	37	.219	.282	.426	99	-2	1			.949	-1	O-62/1-7	-0.7
	Yr	102	275	34	60	6	4	14	47	23	37	.218	.281	.422	97	-3	1			.949	-1	O-62/1-9	-0.8
1949	StL-A	137	500	71	119	22	1	24	79	61	62	.238	.326	.430	95	-7	0	1	-1	.984	-6	*1-136	-1.4
Total	2	239	775	105	179	28	5	38	126	84	99	.231	.310	.427	96	-9	1	1		.985	-7	1-145/O-62	-2.2

■ **LEE GRAHAM** Graham, Lee Willard b: 9/22/59, Summerfield, Fla. BL/TL, 5'10", 170 lbs. Deb: 9/3/83

1983	Bos-A	5	6	2	0	0	0	0	0	0	0	.000	.000	.000	-93	-2	0	1	-1	1.000	1	/O-3	-0.2

■ **ROY GRAHAM** Graham, Roy Vincent b: 2/22/1895, San Francisco, Cal d: 4/26/33, Manila, Philippines BR/TR, 5'10.5", 175 lbs. Deb: 5/28/22

1922	Chi-A	5	3	0	0	0	0	0	0	0	0	.000	.400	.000	12	-0	0	0	0	1.000	-0	/C-3	0.0
1923	Chi-A	36	82	3	16	2	0	0	6	9	6	.195	.290	.220	36	-7	0	0	0	.949	-7	C-33	-1.3
Total	2	41	85	3	16	2	0	0	6	9	6	.188	.296	.212	35	-8	0	0	0	.950	-7	/C-36	-1.3

■ **WAYNE GRAHAM** Graham, Wayne Leon b: 4/6/37, Yoakum, Tex. BR/TR, 6', 200 lbs. Deb: 4/10/63

1963	Phi-N	10	22	1	4	0	0	0	3	3	1	.182	.280	.182	36	-2	0	0	0	.857	-1	/O-6	-0.3
1964	NY-N	20	33	1	3	1	0	0	0	3	5	.091	.091	.121	-42	-6	0	0	0	1.000	-2	3-11	-0.9
Total	2	30	55	2	7	1	0	0	3	6	6	.127	.172	.145	-9	-8	0	0	0	1.000	-3	/3-11,O-6	-1.2

■ **ALEX GRAMMAS** Grammas, Alexander Peter b: 4/3/26, Birmingham, Ala. BR/TR, 6', 178 lbs. Deb: 4/13/54 MC

1954	StL-N	142	401	57	106	17	4	2	29	40	29	.264	.339	.342	77	-13	6	1	1	.966	30	*S-142/3-1	2.8
1955	StL-N	128	366	32	88	19	2	3	25	33	36	.240	.308	.328	69	-16	4	1	1	.968	7	*S-126	0.1
1956	StL-N	6	12	1	3	0	0	0	1	1	1	.250	.308	.250	52	-1	0	0	0	1.000	0	/S-5	-0.1
	Cin-N	77	140	17	34	11	0	0	16	16	18	.243	.325	.321	70	-6	0	1	-1	.968	4	3-58,S-12/2-5	-0.2
	Yr	83	152	18	37	11	0	0	17	17	19	.243	.324	.316	69	-6	0	1	-1	.968	4	3-58,S-17/2-5	-0.2
1957	Cin-N	73	99	14	30	4	0	0	8	10	6	.303	.367	.343	86	-2	1	3	-2	.966	4	S-42,2-20/3-9	0.1
1958	Cin-N	105	216	25	47	8	0	1	12	34	24	.218	.329	.255	54	-13	2	2	-1	.993	-0	S-61,3-38,2-14	-1.3
1959	StL-N	131	368	43	99	14	2	3	30	38	26	.269	.339	.342	77	-11	3	3	-1	.964	12	*S-130	1.0
1960	StL-N	102	196	20	48	4	1	4	17	12	15	.245	.292	.337	66	-9	0	1	-1	.972	20	S-46,2-38,3-13	0.8
1961	StL-N	89	170	23	36	10	1	0	21	19	21	.212	.295	.282	49	-12	0	1	-1	.960	17	S-65,2-18/3-3	0.8
1962	StL-N	21	18	0	2	0	0	0	1	1	6	.111	.158	.111	-24	-3	0	0	0	.933	1	S-16/2-2	-0.2
	Chi-N	23	60	3	14	3	0	0	3	2	7	.233	.270	.283	47	-4	1	1	-0	1.000	1	S-13/2-3,3-1	-0.2
	Yr	44	78	3	16	3	0	0	4	3	13	.205	.244	.244	29	-8	1	1	-0	.955	3	S-29/2-5,3-1	-0.3
1963	Chi-N	16	27	1	5	0	0	0	3	2	2	.185	.185	.185	7	-3	0	0	0	.955	-3	S-13	-0.7
Total	10	913	2073	236	512	90	10	12	163	206	192	.247	.320	.317	67	-93	17	14	-3	.968	88	S-671,3-123,2-100	3.6

■ **JACK GRANEY** Graney, John Gladstone b: 6/10/1886, St.Thomas, Ont., Can. d: 4/20/78, Louisiana, Mo. BL/TL, 5'9", 180 lbs. Deb: 4/30/08

1908	Cle-A	2										—	—	—	—		0	0		.000	-0	/P-2	0.0
1910	Cle-A	116	454	62	107	13	9	1	31	37		.236	.293	.311	88	-7	18			.949	1	*O-114	-1.3
1911	Cle-A	146	527	84	142	25	5	1	45	66		.269	.363	.342	96	-1	21			.927	4	*O-142	-0.7
1912	Cle-A	78	264	44	64	13	2	0	20	50		.242	.367	.307	90	-1	9			.958	4	O-75	-0.1
1913	Cle-A	148	517	56	138	18	12	3	68	48	55	.267	.335	.366	102	1	27			.970	2	*O-148	-0.5
1914	Cle-A	130	460	63	122	17	10	1	39	67	46	.265	.362	.352	111	6	20	18	-5	.935	5	*O-127	0.2
1915	Cle-A	116	404	42	105	20	7	1	56	59	29	.260	.357	.351	110	6	12	15	-5	.972	5	*O-115	0.0
1916	Cle-A	155	589	106	142	41	14	5	54	102	72	.241	.355	.384	115	12	10			.959	3	*O-154	0.7
1917	Cle-A	146	535	87	122	29	7	3	35	94	49	.228	.348	.325	98	1	16			.959	-7	*O-145	-1.6
1918	Cle-A	70	177	27	42	7	4	0	9	28	19	.237	.351	.322	94	-0	3			.975	-6	O-45	-1.0
1919	Cle-A	128	461	79	108	22	8	1	30	105	39	.234	.380	.323	93	0	7			.961	6	*O-125	-0.3
1920	*Cle-A	62	152	31	45	11	1	0	13	27	21	.296	.412	.382	108	3	4	2	0	.941	-6	O-47	-0.6
1921	Cle-A	68	107	19	32	3	0	2	18	20	9	.299	.414	.383	103	2	1	1	-0	.933	-9	O-32	-0.9

YEAR	TM/L	G	AB	R	H	2B	3B	HR	RBI	BB	SO	AVG	OBP	SLG	PRO+	BR/A	SB	CS	SBR	FA	FR	G/POS	TPR
1922	Cle-A	37	58	6	9	0	0	0	2	9	12	.155	.279	.155	16	-7	0	0	0	.862	-1	O-13	-0.9
Total	14	1402	4705	706	1178	219	79	18	420	712	345	.250	.354	.342	100	16	148	36		.953	-3	*O-1282/P-2	-7.0

■ EDDIE GRANT
Grant, Edward Leslie "Harvard Eddie" b: 5/21/1883, Franklin, Mass. d: 10/5/18, Argonne Forest, France   BL/TR, 5'11.5", 168 lbs.   Deb: 8/4/05

YEAR	TM/L	G	AB	R	H	2B	3B	HR	RBI	BB	SO	AVG	OBP	SLG	PRO+	BR/A	SB	CS	SBR	FA	FR	G/POS	TPR
1905	Cle-A	2	8	1	3	0	0	0				.375	.375	.375	136	0	0			.833	-2	/2-2	-0.2
1907	Phi-N	74	268	26	65	4	3	0	19	10		.243	.272	.280	74	-9	10			.916	-2	3-74	-1.0
1908	Phi-N	147	598	69	146	13	8	0	32	35		.244	.289	.293	83	-12	27			.930	2	*3-134,S-13	-0.5
1909	Phi-N	154	631	75	170	18	4	1	37	35		.269	.311	.315	94	-6	28			.957	3	*3-154	0.3
1910	Phi-N	152	579	70	155	15	5	1	67	39	54	.268	.315	.316	81	-14	25			.935	-10	*3-152	-2.2
1911	Cin-N	136	458	49	102	12	7	1	53	51	47	.223	.301	.286	67	-20	28			.953	-7	*3-122,S-11	-2.5
1912	Cin-N	96	255	37	61	6	1	2	20	18	27	.239	.292	.294	62	-13	11			.948	0	S-56,3-15	-0.9
1913	Cin-N	27	94	12	20	1	0	0	9	11	10	.213	.295	.223	49	-6	7			.929	-4	3-26	-1.0
	*NY-N	27	20	8	4	1	0	0	1	2	2	.200	.273	.250	49	-1	1			1.000	6	/3-5,2-3,S-1	0.5
	Yr	54	114	20	24	2	0	0	10	13	12	.211	.291	.228	49	-7	8			.940	2	3-31/2-3,S-1	-0.5
1914	NY-N	88	282	34	78	7	1	0	29	23	21	.277	.333	.309	94	-2	11			.948	-7	3-52,S-21,2-16	-0.6
1915	NY-N	37	192	18	40	2	1	0	10	9	20	.208	.248	.229	47	-12	5		-2	.970	-5	3-35/2-9,1-1,S-1	-2.0
Total	10	990	3385	399	844	79	30	5	277	233	181	.249	.300	.295	78	-95	153	6		.942	-26	3-769,S-103/2-30,1	-10.1

■ JIMMY GRANT
Grant, James Charles b: 10/6/18, Racine, Wis. d: 7/8/70, Rochester, Minn.   BL/TR, 5'8", 166 lbs.   Deb: 9/8/42

YEAR	TM/L	G	AB	R	H	2B	3B	HR	RBI	BB	SO	AVG	OBP	SLG	PRO+	BR/A	SB	CS	SBR	FA	FR	G/POS	TPR
1942	Chi-A	12	36	0	6	1	1	0	1	5	6	.167	.268	.250	47	-3	0	0	0	.944	1	3-10	-0.2
1943	Chi-A	58	197	23	51	9	2	4	22	18	34	.259	.321	.386	106	1	4	3	-1	.893	3	3-51	0.2
	Cle-A	15	22	3	3	2	0	0	1	4	7	.136	.269	.227	49	-1	0	0	0	.941	2	/3-5	0.0
	Yr	73	219	26	54	11	2	4	23	22	41	.247	.315	.370	101	-0	4	3	-1	.897	3	3-56	0.2
1944	Cle-A	61	99	12	27	4	3	1	12	11	20	.273	.357	.404	122	3	1	0	0	.926	-4	2-20/3-4	0.1
Total	3	146	354	38	87	16	6	5	36	38	67	.246	.322	.367	101	-0	5	3	-0	.907	-0	/3-70,2-20	0.1

■ TOM GRANT
Grant, Thomas Raymond b: 5/28/57, Worcester, Mass.   BL/TR, 6'2", 190 lbs.   Deb: 6/17/83

YEAR	TM/L	G	AB	R	H	2B	3B	HR	RBI	BB	SO	AVG	OBP	SLG	PRO+	BR/A	SB	CS	SBR	FA	FR	G/POS	TPR
1983	Chi-N	16	20	2	3	1	0	0	2	3	4	.150	.261	.200	28	-2	0	0	0	1.000	-2	O-10	-0.4

■ GEORGE GRANTHAM
Grantham, George Farley "Boots" b: 5/20/1900, Galena, Kan. d: 3/16/54, Kingman, Ariz.   BR/TR, 5'10", 170 lbs.   Deb: 9/20/22

YEAR	TM/L	G	AB	R	H	2B	3B	HR	RBI	BB	SO	AVG	OBP	SLG	PRO+	BR/A	SB	CS	SBR	FA	FR	G/POS	TPR
1922	Chi-N	7	23	3	4	1	1	0	3	1	3	.174	.208	.304	30	-2	2	0		1.000	-3	/3-5	-0.4
1923	Chi-N	152	570	81	160	36	8	8	70	71	92	.281	.360	.414	104	4	43	28	-4	.942	1	*2-150	0.3
1924	Chi-N	127	469	85	148	19	6	12	60	55	63	.316	.390	.458	125	18	21	21	-6	.941	1	*2-118/3-6	1.4
1925	*Pit-N	114	359	74	117	24	6	8	52	50	29	.326	.413	.493	122	13	14	4	2	.989	-4	*1-102	0.5
1926	Pit-N	141	449	66	143	27	13	8	70	60	42	.318	.400	.490	131	21	6			.990	-2	*1-132	1.0
1927	*Pit-N	151	531	96	162	33	11	8	66	74	39	.305	.396	.454	119	16	9			.953	-24	*2-124,1-29	-0.6
1928	Pit-N	124	440	93	142	24	9	10	85	59	37	.323	.408	.486	128	19	9			.986	1	*1-119/2-1,3-1	1.0
1929	Pit-N	110	349	85	107	23	10	12	90	93	38	.307	.454	.533	140	26	5			.967	-5	2-76,O-19,1-12	2.1
1930	Pit-N	146	552	120	179	34	14	18	99	81	66	.324	.413	.534	124	25	5			.958	-13	2-141/1-4	1.6
1931	Pit-N	127	465	91	142	26	6	10	46	71	50	.305	.400	.452	130	22	5			.985	-22	1-78,2-51	-0.4
1932	Cin-N	126	493	81	144	29	6	6	39	56	40	.292	.364	.412	112	9	4			.959	-29	*2-115,1-10	-1.5
1933	Cin-N	87	260	32	53	14	3	4	28	38	21	.204	.310	.327	83	-5	4			.948	-11	2-72,1-12	-1.4
1934	NY-N	32	29	5	7	2	0	1	4	8	6	.241	.405	.414	123	1	0			1.000	1	/1-4,3-2	0.1
Total	13	1444	4989	912	1508	292	93	105	712	717	526	.302	.392	.461	121	166	132	53		.949	-109	2-848,1-502/O-19,3	3.7

■ MICKEY GRASSO
Grasso, Newton Michael b: 5/10/20, Newark, N.J. d: 10/15/75, Miami, Fla.   BR/TR, 6', 195 lbs.   Deb: 9/18/46

YEAR	TM/L	G	AB	R	H	2B	3B	HR	RBI	BB	SO	AVG	OBP	SLG	PRO+	BR/A	SB	CS	SBR	FA	FR	G/POS	TPR
1946	NY-N	7	22	1	3	0	0	0	1	0	3	.136	.136	.136	-22	-4	0			.967	0	/C-7	-0.3
1950	Was-A	75	195	25	56	4	1	1	22	25	31	.287	.374	.333	86	-3	1	1	-0	.942	6	C-69	0.5
1951	Was-A	52	175	16	36	3	0	0	14	14	17	.206	.268	.240	39	-15	0	0	0	.967	-2	C-49	-1.5
1952	Was-A	115	361	22	78	9	0	0	27	29	36	.216	.276	.241	46	-26	0	1	0	.970	6	*C-114	-1.5
1953	Was-A	61	196	13	41	7	0	2	22	9	20	.209	.251	.276	43	-16	0	0	0	.984	1	C-59	-1.3
1954	*Cle-A	4	6	1	2	0	0	0	1	1	1	.333	.500	.833	256	1	0	0	0	.833	-1	/C-4	0.1
1955	NY-N	8	2	0	0	0	0	0	0	3	0	.000	.600	.000	77	0	0	0	0	.900	0	/C-8	0.0
Total	7	322	957	78	216	23	1	5	87	81	108	.226	.291	.268	53	-62	2	1		.964	9	C-310	-4.0

■ LEW GRAULICH
Graulich, Lewis b: Camden, N.J.   Deb: 9/17/1891

YEAR	TM/L	G	AB	R	H	2B	3B	HR	RBI	BB	SO	AVG	OBP	SLG	PRO+	BR/A	SB	CS	SBR	FA	FR	G/POS	TPR
1891	Phi-N	7	26	2	8	0	0	0	3	1	2	.308	.333	.308	85	-1				.640	-3	/C-4,1-3	-0.3

■ FRANK GRAVES
Graves, Frank M. b: 11/2/1860, Cincinnati, Ohio   6', 163 lbs.   Deb: 5/10/1886

YEAR	TM/L	G	AB	R	H	2B	3B	HR	RBI	BB	SO	AVG	OBP	SLG	PRO+	BR/A	SB	CS	SBR	FA	FR	G/POS	TPR
1886	StL-N	43	138	7	21	2	0	0	9	4	48	.152	.193	.167	11	-14	11			.885	4	C-41/O-3,P-1	-0.5

■ JOE GRAVES
Graves, Joseph Ebenezer b: 2/26/06, Marblehead, Mass. d: 12/22/80, Salem, Mass.   BR/TR, 5'10", 160 lbs.   Deb: 9/26/26   F

YEAR	TM/L	G	AB	R	H	2B	3B	HR	RBI	BB	SO	AVG	OBP	SLG	PRO+	BR/A	SB	CS	SBR	FA	FR	G/POS	TPR
1926	Chi-N	2	5	0	0	0	0	0	0	0	1	.000	.000	.000	-99	-1	0			.250	-1	/3-2	-0.3

■ SID GRAVES
Graves, Samuel Sidney "Whitey" b: 11/30/01, Marblehead, Mass. d: 12/26/83, Biddeford, Maine   BR/TR, 6', 170 lbs.   Deb: 7/23/27   F

YEAR	TM/L	G	AB	R	H	2B	3B	HR	RBI	BB	SO	AVG	OBP	SLG	PRO+	BR/A	SB	CS	SBR	FA	FR	G/POS	TPR
1927	Bos-N	7	20	5	5	1	1	0	2	0	1	.250	.250	.400	78	-1	1			.857	0	/O-5	-0.1

■ GARY GRAY
Gray, Gary George b: 9/21/52, New Orleans, La.   BR/TR, 6', 203 lbs.   Deb: 6/23/77

YEAR	TM/L	G	AB	R	H	2B	3B	HR	RBI	BB	SO	AVG	OBP	SLG	PRO+	BR/A	SB	CS	SBR	FA	FR	G/POS	TPR
1977	Tex-A	1	2	0	0	0	0	0	0	0	1	.000	.000	.000	-99	-0	0	0	0	.000	-0	/O-1	-0.1
1978	Tex-A	17	50	4	12	0	0	2	6	1	12	.240	.255	.380	76	-2	1	0	0	.000	-0	D-11	-0.2
1979	Tex-A	16	42	4	10	0	0	1	2	2	8	.238	.273	.238	40	-3	1	1	-0	.000	0	D-13	-0.4
1980	Cle-A	28	54	4	8	1	0	2	4	3	14	.148	.193	.278	27	-6	0	0	0	1.000	-2	/1-6,O-6,D-9	-0.8
1981	Sea-A	69	208	27	51	7	1	13	31	4	44	.245	.259	.476	104	-0	2	0	1	.993	-1	1-34,D-15/O-4	-0.5
1982	Sea-A	80	269	26	69	14	2	7	29	24	59	.257	.322	.401	95	-2	1	1	-0	.984	-3	1-60,D-14	-0.8
Total	6	211	625	65	150	23	3	24	71	34	137	.240	.281	.402	86	-14	5	2	0	.988	-7	1-100/D-62,O-11	-2.8

■ REDDY GRAY
Gray, James D.   TR,   Deb: 6/17/1890

YEAR	TM/L	G	AB	R	H	2B	3B	HR	RBI	BB	SO	AVG	OBP	SLG	PRO+	BR/A	SB	CS	SBR	FA	FR	G/POS	TPR
1890	Pit-P	2	9	3	2	0	0	1	3	0	2	.222	.222	.556	114	-1				.813	-1	/2-2	-0.1
	Pit-N	1	3	0	0	0	0	0	0	0	1	.000	.000	.000	-99	-1				.571	-1	/S-1	-0.1
1893	Pit-N	2	9	0	4	1	0	0	2	0	1	.444	.444	.556	168	1	0			.800	-3	/S-2	-0.2
Total	2	5	21	3	6	1	0	1	5	0	4	.286	.286	.476	111	0				.667	-4	/S-3,2-2	-0.4

■ JIM GRAY
Gray, James W. b: 8/7/1862, Pittsburgh, Pa. d: 1/31/38, Allegheny, Pa.   TR,   Deb: 10/9/1884

YEAR	TM/L	G	AB	R	H	2B	3B	HR	RBI	BB	SO	AVG	OBP	SLG	PRO+	BR/A	SB	CS	SBR	FA	FR	G/POS	TPR
1884	Pit-a	1	2	0	1	0	0	0				.500	.500	.500	224	0				.500	-0	/3-1	0.0

■ LORENZO GRAY
Gray, Lorenzo b: 3/4/58, Mound Bayou, Miss.   BR/TR, 6'1", 180 lbs.   Deb: 7/8/82

YEAR	TM/L	G	AB	R	H	2B	3B	HR	RBI	BB	SO	AVG	OBP	SLG	PRO+	BR/A	SB	CS	SBR	FA	FR	G/POS	TPR
1982	Chi-A	17	28	4	8	1	0	0	2		4	.286	.333	.321	81	-1	1	0	0	.864	-3	3-16	-0.4
1983	Chi-A	41	78	18	14	3	0	1	4	8	16	.179	.256	.256	40	-6	1	0	0	.940	2	3-31/D-7	-0.4
Total	2	58	106	22	22	4	0	1	4	8	20	.208	.276	.274	50	-7	2	0	0	.921	-1	/3-47,D-7	-0.8

■ MILT GRAY
Gray, Milton Marshall b: 2/21/14, Louisville, Ky. d: 6/30/69, Quincy, Fla.   BR/TR, 6'1", 170 lbs.   Deb: 5/27/37

YEAR	TM/L	G	AB	R	H	2B	3B	HR	RBI	BB	SO	AVG	OBP	SLG	PRO+	BR/A	SB	CS	SBR	FA	FR	G/POS	TPR
1937	Was-A	2	6	0	0	0	0	0	0	0	0	.000	.000	.000	-99	-2	0	0	0	1.000	0	/C-2	-0.1

■ PETE GRAY
Gray, Peter J. (b: Peter Wyshner) b: 3/6/15, Nanticoke, Pa.   BL/TL, 6'1", 169 lbs.   Deb: 4/17/45

YEAR	TM/L	G	AB	R	H	2B	3B	HR	RBI	BB	SO	AVG	OBP	SLG	PRO+	BR/A	SB	CS	SBR	FA	FR	G/POS	TPR
1945	StL-A	77	234	26	51	6	2	0	13	13	11	.218	.259	.261	49	-15	5	6	-2	.959	1	O-61	-2.1

■ DICK GRAY
Gray, Richard Benjamin b: 7/11/31, Jefferson, Pa.   BR/TR, 5'11", 165 lbs.   Deb: 4/15/58

YEAR	TM/L	G	AB	R	H	2B	3B	HR	RBI	BB	SO	AVG	OBP	SLG	PRO+	BR/A	SB	CS	SBR	FA	FR	G/POS	TPR
1958	LA-N	58	197	25	49	5	6	9	30	19	30	.249	.327	.472	105	1	1	1	-0	.929	14	3-55	1.5
1959	LA-N	21	52	8	8	1	0	2	4	6	12	.154	.241	.288	38	-5	0	0	0	.900	-0	3-11	-0.5
	StL-N	36	51	9	16	1	0	1	6	6	8	.314	.386	.392	101	1	0	3	0	.958	-9	S-13/3-6,2-2,O-1	-0.5
	Yr	57	103	17	24	2	0	3	10	12	20	.233	.313	.340	69	-4	0	1	0	.935	-9	3-17,S-13/2-2,O-1	-1.2
1960	StL-N	9	5	1	0	0	0	0	0	2	2	.000	.286	.000	-13	-1	0	0	0	1.000	1	/2-4,3-1	0.1
Total	3	124	305	43	73	7	6	12	41	33	52	.239	.322	.420	91	-4	1	1	1	.930	6	/3-73,S-13,2-6,O-1	0.4

YEAR	TM/L	G	AB	R	H	2B	3B	HR	RBI	BB	SO	AVG	OBP	SLG	PRO+	BR/A	SB	CS	SBR	FA	FR	G/POS	TPR

■ STAN GRAY Gray, Stanley Oscar "Dolly" b: 12/10/1888, Ladonia, Tex. d: 10/11/64, Snyder, Tex. BR/TR, 6'0.5", 184 lbs. Deb: 9/17/12

| 1912 | Pit-N | 6 | 20 | 4 | 5 | 0 | 1 | 0 | 2 | 0 | 3 | .250 | .250 | .350 | 64 | -1 | 0 | | | 1.000 | -1 | /1-4 | -0.2 |

■ CRAIG GREBECK Grebeck, Craig Allen b: 12/29/64, Johnstown, Pa. BR/TR, 5'8", 160 lbs. Deb: 4/13/90

1990	Chi-A	59	119	7	20	3	1	5	9	8	24	.168	.233	.235	32	-11	0	0	0	.987	8	3-35,S-16/2-6,D-1	-0.2
1991	Chi-A	107	224	37	63	16	3	6	31	38	40	.281	.388	.460	137	12	1	3	-2	.933	-1	3-49,2-36,S-26	1.2
1992	Chi-A	88	287	24	77	21	2	3	35	30	34	.268	.344	.387	106	2	0	3	-2	.980	-4	S-85/3-7,O-2	0.2
1993	*Chi-A	72	190	25	43	5	0	1	12	26	26	.226	.319	.263	61	-10	1	2	-1	.983	14	S-46,2-16,3-14	0.7
1994	Chi-A	35	97	17	30	5	0	0	5	12	5	.309	.391	.361	97	0	0	0	0	.982	-3	2-14,S-14/3-7	-0.1
1995	Chi-A	53	154	19	40	12	0	1	18	21	23	.260	.360	.357	91	-1	0	0	0	.961	6	S-31,3-18/2-8	0.7
1996	Fla-N	50	95	8	20	1	0	1	9	4	14	.211	.250	.253	34	-9	0	0	0	.985	10	2-29/S-2,3-1	0.2
Total	7	464	1166	137	293	63	6	13	119	139	166	.251	.337	.349	89	-16	2	8	-4	.972	29	S-220,3-131,2/OD	2.7

■ DAVID GREEN Green, David Alejandro (Casaya) b: 12/4/60, Managua, Nicaragua BR/TR, 6'3", 170 lbs. Deb: 9/4/81

1981	StL-N	21	34	6	5	1	0	0	2	6	5	.147	.275	.176	29	-3	0	1	-1	.970	-3	O-18	-0.8
1982	*StL-N	76	166	21	47	7	1	2	23	8	29	.283	.320	.373	92	-2	11	3	2	.991	-8	O-68	-1.0
1983	StL-N	146	422	52	120	14	10	8	69	26	76	.284	.327	.422	106	2	34	16	1	.970	-8	*O-136	-0.8
1984	StL-N	126	452	49	121	14	4	15	65	20	105	.268	.300	.416	102	-1	17	9	-0	.991	-5	*1-117,O-14	-1.4
1985	SF-N	106	294	36	73	10	2	5	20	22	58	.248	.303	.347	85	-6	6	5	-1	.987	-3	1-78,O-12	-1.6
1987	StL-N	14	30	4	8	2	1	1	1	2	5	.267	.313	.500	109	0	0	1	-1	.882	-1	O-10/1-3	-0.2
Total	6	489	1398	168	374	48	18	31	180	84	278	.268	.311	.394	97	-9	68	35	-1	.972	-27	O-258,1-198	-5.8

■ DANNY GREEN Green, Edward b: 11/6/1876, Burlington, N.J. d: 11/9/14, Camden, N.J. BL/TR Deb: 8/17/1898

1898	Chi-N	47	188	26	59	4	3	4	27	7		.314	.342	.431	121	4	12			.970	5	O-47	0.5
1899	Chi-N	117	475	90	140	12	11	6	56	35		.295	.352	.404	110	6	18			.947	1	*O-115	-0.1
1900	Chi-N	103	389	63	116	21	5	5	49	17		.298	.339	.416	112	5	28			.938	5	*O-102	-0.2
1901	Chi-N	133	537	82	168	16	12	6	61	40		.313	.364	.421	132	21	31			.932	8	*O-133	1.9
1902	Chi-N	129	481	77	150	16	11	0	62	53		.312	.388	.391	122	17	35			.942	-3	*O-129	0.5
1903	Chi-A	135	499	75	154	26	7	6	62	47		.309	.375	.425	146	29	29			.933	2	*O-133	2.4
1904	Chi-A	147	536	83	142	16	10	2	62	63		.265	.352	.343	125	18	28			.964	1	*O-146	1.2
1905	Chi-A	112	379	56	92	13	6	0	44	53		.243	.345	.309	112	8	11			.914	-11	*O-107	-0.8
Total	8	923	3484	552	1021	124	65	29	423	315		.293	.359	.391	124	108	192			.941	8	O-912	5.4

■ PUMPSIE GREEN Green, Elijah Jerry b: 10/27/33, Oakland, Cal. BB/TR, 6', 175 lbs. Deb: 7/21/59

1959	Bos-A	50	172	30	40	6	3	1	10	29	22	.233	.350	.320	81	-3	4	2	0	.972	4	2-45/S-1	0.4
1960	Bos-A	133	260	36	63	10	3	3	21	44	47	.242	.354	.338	85	-4	3	4	-2	.982	-13	2-69/S-41	-1.3
1961	Bos-A	88	219	33	57	12	3	6	27	42	32	.260	.379	.425	112	5	4	2	0	.940	-5	S-57/2-7	0.5
1962	Bos-A	56	91	12	21	2	1	2	11	11	18	.231	.314	.341	74	-3	1	0	0	.953	-9	2-18/S-5	-1.1
1963	NY-N	17	54	9	15	1	2	1	5	12	13	.278	.409	.426	139	3	0	2	-1	.857	-1	3-16	0.1
Total	5	344	796	119	196	31	12	13	74	138	132	.246	.360	.364	94	-3	12	10	-2	.975	-24	2-139,S-104/3-16	-1.4

■ GARY GREEN Green, Gary Allan b: 1/14/62, Pittsburgh, Pa. BR/TR, 6'3", 175 lbs. Deb: 9/14/86 F

1986	SD-N	13	33	2	7	1	0	0	2	1	11	.212	.235	.242	33	-3	0	0	0	1.000	5	S-13	0.3
1989	SD-N	15	27	4	7	3	0	0	0	1	1	.259	.286	.370	86	-1	0	1	-1	.921	4	S-11/3-1	0.3
1990	Tex-A	62	88	10	19	3	0	0	8	6	18	.216	.266	.250	45	-6	1	1	-0	.972	21	S-58	1.6
1991	Tex-A	8	20	0	3	1	0	0	1	1	6	.150	.190	.200	8	-2	0	0	0	.968	1	/S-8	-0.2
1992	Cin-N	8	12	3	4	1	0	0	0	0	2	.333	.333	.417	108	0	0	0	0	1.000	-1	/S-6,3-1	-0.1
Total	5	106	180	19	40	9	0	0	11	9	38	.222	.259	.272	49	-12	1	2	-1	.970	29	/S-96,3-2	1.9

■ GENE GREEN Green, Gene Leroy b: 6/26/33, Los Angeles, Cal. d: 5/23/81, St.Louis, Mo. BR/TR, 6'2", 205 lbs. Deb: 9/10/57

1957	StL-N	6	15	0	3	1	0	0	2	0	3	.200	.200	.267	23	-2	0	0	0	1.000	-1	/O-3	-0.3
1958	StL-N	137	442	47	124	18	3	13	55	37	84	.281	.338	.423	96	-3	2	1	0	.956	9	O-75,C-48	0.5
1959	StL-N	30	74	8	14	6	0	1	3	5	18	.189	.241	.311	43	-6	0	0	0	.944	4	O-19,C-11	-0.3
1960	Bal-A	1	4	0	1	0	0	0	0	0	0	.250	.250	.250	36	-0	0	0	0	1.000	-0	/O-1	-0.0
1961	Was-A	110	364	52	102	16	3	18	62	35	65	.280	.345	.489	122	10	0	2	-1	.986	-22	C-79,O-21	-0.9
1962	Cle-A	66	143	16	40	4	1	11	28	8	21	.280	.318	.552	133	6	0	0	0	.964	-2	O-33/1-2	0.2
1963	Cle-A	43	78	4	16	3	0	2	7	4	22	.205	.262	.321	63	-4	0	0	0	1.000	-3	O-18	-0.3
	Cin-N	15	31	3	7	1	0	1	3	0	8	.226	.250	.355	70	-1	0	0	0	.932	-2	/C-8	-0.3
Total	7	408	1151	130	307	49	7	46	160	89	185	.267	.322	.441	101	-0	2	3	-1	.963	-16	O-170,C-146/1-2	-1.9

■ JIM GREEN Green, James R. b: Cleveland, Ohio Deb: 7/19/1884

| 1884 | Was-U | 10 | 36 | 4 | 5 | 1 | 0 | 0 | | 0 | | .139 | .139 | .167 | -8 | -6 | | | | .818 | -0 | /3-9,O-1 | -0.5 |

■ JOE GREEN Green, Joseph Henry (a.k.a. Joseph Henry Greene) b: 9/17/1897, Philadelphia, Pa. d: 2/4/72, Bryn Mawr, Pa. BR/TR, 6'2", 170 lbs. Deb: 7/2/24

| 1924 | Phi-A | 1 | 0 | 0 | 0 | 0 | 0 | 0 | 0 | 0 | 0 | .000 | .000 | .000 | -99 | -0 | 0 | 0 | 0 | .000 | 0 | H | 0.0 |

■ LENNY GREEN Green, Leonard Charles b: 1/6/33, Detroit, Mich. BL/TL, 5'11", 170 lbs. Deb: 8/25/57

1957	Bal-A	19	33	2	6	1	1	1	5	1	4	.182	.206	.364	56	-2	0	1	-1	.950	-4	O-15	-0.8
1958	Bal-A	69	91	10	21	4	0	0	4	9	10	.231	.300	.275	63	-5	0	2	-1	.965	-11	O-53	-1.8
1959	Bal-A	27	24	3	7	0	0	1	2	1	3	.292	.346	.417	111	0	0	0	0	1.000	-6	O-23	-0.7
	Was-A	88	190	29	46	6	1	2	15	20	15	.242	.314	.316	74	-7	9	5	-0	.979	-4	O-58	-1.4
	Yr	115	214	32	53	6	1	3	17	21	18	.248	.318	.327	78	-6	9	5	-0	.981	-11	O-81	-2.1
1960	Was-A	127	330	62	97	16	7	5	33	43	25	.294	.385	.430	121	11	21	8	2	.991	-6	*O-100	0.3
1961	Min-A	156	600	92	171	28	7	9	50	81	59	.285	.376	.400	102	4	17	11	-2	.978	-15	*O-153	-2.2
1962	Min-A	158	619	97	168	33	3	14	63	88	63	.271	.369	.402	104	6	8	4	0	.995	-17	*O-156	-2.1
1963	Min-A	145	280	41	67	10	1	4	27	31	21	.239	.319	.325	80	-7	11	5	0	.988	-25	*O-119	-3.8
1964	Min-A	26	15	3	0	0	0	0	0	4	6	.000	.211	.000	-35	-3	1	0	-1	1.000	-2	/O-7	-0.6
	LA-A	39	92	13	23	2	0	2	4	10	8	.250	.330	.337	96	-1	2	0	1	.977	-1	O-23	-0.2
	Bal-A	14	21	0	4	0	0	0	1	7	3	.190	.393	.190	69	-0	1	0	0	1.000	-1	/O-8	0.1
	Yr	79	128	16	27	2	0	2	5	21	17	.211	.327	.273	72	-4	3	1	0	.985	-2	O-38	-0.7
1965	Bos-A	119	373	69	103	24	6	7	24	48	43	.276	.363	.429	117	9	8	2	1	.980	2	O-95	0.8
1966	Bos-A	85	133	18	32	6	0	1	12	15	19	.241	.320	.308	76	-4	0	1	-1	.978	-1	O-27	-0.7
1967	Det-A	58	151	22	42	8	1	1	13	9	17	.278	.319	.364	99	-0	1	1	-0	.983	-4	O-44	-0.7
1968	Det-A	6	4	0	1	0	0	0	1	0	0	.250	.400	.250	97	-0	0	0	0	.000	-1	/O-2	-0.1
Total	12	1136	2956	461	788	138	27	47	253	368	260	.267	.353	.379	99	-2	78	41	-1	.984	-95	O-883	-13.9

■ DICK GREEN Green, Richard Larry b: 4/21/41, Sioux City, Iowa BR/TR, 5'10", 180 lbs. Deb: 9/9/63

1963	KC-A	13	37	5	10	2	0	1	4	2	10	.270	.325	.405	98	-0	0	0	0	.941	2	/S-6,2-4	0.3
1964	KC-A	130	435	48	115	14	5	11	37	27	87	.264	.312	.395	92	-5	3	3	-1	.990	17	*2-120	2.1
1965	KC-A	133	474	64	110	15	1	15	55	50	110	.232	.309	.363	92	-5	6	2	-1	.980	-7	*2-126	-0.2
1966	KC-A	140	507	58	127	24	3	9	62	27	101	.250	.298	.363	92	-6	6	1	0	.979	-1	*2-137/3-2	0.4
1967	KC-A	122	349	26	69	12	4	5	37	30	68	.198	.261	.298	67	-15	6	3	0	.946	-2	3-59,2-50/1-1,S-1	-1.6
1968	Oak-A	76	202	19	47	6	0	6	18	21	41	.233	.308	.351	104	1	3	1	0	.974	13	2-61/C-1,3-1	1.9
1969	Oak-A	136	483	61	133	25	6	12	64	53	94	.275	.357	.427	123	15	2	3	1	**.986**	10	*2-131	3.5
1970	Oak-A	135	384	34	73	7	0	4	29	38	73	.190	.268	.240	43	-30	3	0	1	.978	-6	*2-127/3-5,C-1	-2.0
1971	*Oak-A	144	475	58	116	14	1	12	49	51	83	.244	.321	.354	93	-4	1	1	-0	.986	8	*2-143/S-1	1.6
1972	*Oak-A	26	42	1	12	1	1	0	3	4	8	.286	.348	.357	116	1	0	0	0	.964	2	2-26	-0.2
1973	*Oak-A	133	332	33	87	17	0	3	42	21	63	.262	.310	.340	88	-6	0	3	-1	.988	-9	*2-133/S-1,3-1	-0.9
1974	*Oak-A	100	287	20	61	8	2	2	22	21	50	.213	.269	.275	61	-15	2	2	0	.983	-5	*2-100	-1.8
Total	12	1288	4007	427	960	145	23	80	422	345	785	.240	.305	.347	87	-70	26	20	-4	.983	28	2-1158/3-68,SC1	3.6

YEAR	TM/L	G	AB	R	H	2B	3B	HR	RBI	BB	SO	AVG	OBP	SLG	PRO+	BR/A	SB	CS	SBR	FA	FR	G/POS	TPR

■ SHAWN GREEN   Green, Shawn David   b: 11/10/72, Des Plaines, Ill.   BL/TL, 6'4", 190 lbs.   Deb: 9/28/93

1993	Tor-A	3	6	0	0	0	0	0	0	0	1	.000	.000	.000	-99	-2	0	0	0	1.000	-1	/O-2,D-1	-0.2
1994	Tor-A	14	33	1	3	1	0	0	1	1	8	.091	.118	.121	-38	-7	1	0	0	1.000	-2	O-14	-0.8
1995	Tor-A	121	379	52	109	31	4	15	54	20	68	.288	.328	.509	115	6	1	2	-1	.973	6	*O-109	0.9
1996	Tor-A	132	422	52	118	32	3	11	45	33	75	.280	.343	.448	97	-2	5	1	1	.992	7	*O-127/D-1	0.3
Total	4	270	840	105	230	64	7	26	100	54	152	.274	.326	.460	99	-4	7	3	0	.984	11	O-252/D-2	0.2

■ HANK GREENBERG   Greenberg, Henry Benjamin "Hammerin' Hank"   b: 1/1/11, New York, N.Y.   d: 9/4/86, Beverly Hills, Cal   BR/TR, 6'3.5", 210 lbs.   Deb: 9/14/30   H

1930	Det-A	1	1	0	0	0	0	0	0	0	0	.000	.000	.000	-98	-0	0	0	0	.000	0	H	0.0
1933	Det-A	117	449	59	135	33	3	12	87	46	78	.301	.367	.468	118	11	6	2	1	.988	1	*1-117	0.1
1934	*Det-A	153	593	118	201	**63**	7	26	139	63	93	.339	.404	.600	156	46	9	5	-0	.990	1	*1-153	3.2
1935	*Det-A	152	619	121	203	46	16	**36**	**170**	87	91	.328	.411	.628	171	63	4	3	-1	.992	6	*1-152	4.7
1936	Det-A	12	46	10	16	6	2	1	16	9	6	.348	.455	.630	165	5	1	0	0	.992	1	1-12	0.4
1937	Det-A☆	154	594	137	200	49	14	40	**183**	102	101	.337	.436	.668	171	64	8	3	1	.992	5	*1-154	4.7
1938	Det-A†	155	556	**144**	175	23	4	**58**	146	**119**	92	.315	.438	.683	167	57	7	5	-1	.991	1	*1-155	4.0
1939	Det-A★	138	500	112	156	42	7	33	112	91	95	.312	.420	.622	152	38	8	3	1	**.993**	-1	*1-136	2.1
1940	*Det-A★	148	573	129	195	**50**	8	**41**	**150**	93	75	.340	.433	**.670**	166	55	6	3	0	.954	3	*O-148	4.4
1941	Det-A	19	67	12	18	5	1	2	12	16	12	.269	.410	.463	118	2	1	0	0	.914	-3	O-19	-0.2
1945	*Det-A†	78	270	47	84	20	2	13	60	42	40	.311	.404	.544	164	22	3	1	0	1.000	-6	O-72	1.3
1946	Det-A	142	523	91	145	29	5	**44**	**127**	80	88	.277	.373	.604	160	40	5	1	1	.989	2	*1-140	3.5
1947	Pit-N	125	402	71	100	13	2	25	74	**104**	73	.249	.408	.478	131	21	0	0	0	.992	1	*1-119	1.8
Total	13	1394	5193	1051	1628	379	71	331	1276	852	844	.313	.412	.605	157	422	58	26		.991	15	*1-1138,O-239	30.0

■ AL GREENE   Greene, Altar Alphonse   b: 11/9/54, Detroit, Mich.   BL/TR, 5'11", 190 lbs.   Deb: 7/23/79

| 1979 | Det-A | 29 | 59 | 9 | 8 | 1 | 0 | 3 | 6 | 10 | 15 | .136 | .261 | .305 | 50 | -4 | 0 | 1 | -1 | 1.000 | 0 | D-15/O-6 | -0.5 |

■ CHARLIE GREENE   Greene, Charles Patrick   b: 1/23/71, Miami, Fla.   BR/TR, 6'1", 170 lbs.   Deb: 9/15/96

| 1996 | NY-N | 2 | 1 | 0 | 0 | 0 | 0 | 0 | 0 | 0 | 0 | .000 | .000 | .000 | -99 | -0 | 0 | 0 | 0 | 1.000 | -0 | /C-1 | 0.0 |

■ JUNE GREENE   Greene, Julius Foust   b: 6/25/1899, Ramseur, N.C.   d: 3/19/74, Glendora, Cal.   BL/TR, 6'2.5", 185 lbs.   Deb: 4/20/28

1928	Phi-N	11	6	0	3	0	0	0	0	3	1	.500	.667	.500	202	1	0			1.000	0	/P-1	0.0
1929	Phi-N	21	19	1	4	1	0	0	0	2	4	.211	.286	.263	35	-2	0			1.000	0	/P-5	0.0
Total	2	32	25	1	7	1	0	0	0	5	5	.280	.400	.320	79	-1	0			1.000	1	/P-6	0.0

■ PADDY GREENE   Greene, Patrick Joseph "Patsy" (a.k.a. Patrick Foley In 1902)   b: 3/20/1875, Providence, R.I.   d: 10/20/34, Providence, R.I.   BR/TR, 5'8", 150 lbs.   Deb: 9/10/02

1902	Phi-N	19	65	6	11	1	0	0	1	2		.169	.206	.185	21	-6	2			.912	0	3-19	-0.6
1903	NY-A	4	13	1	4	0	0	0	0	0		.308	.308	.385	100	-0	0			1.000	1	/3-2,S-1	0.1
	Det-A	1	3	0	0	0	0	0	0	0		.000	.000	.000	-99	-1	0			.750	-0	/3-1	-0.1
	Yr	5	16	1	4	0	0	0	0	0		.250	.250	.313	65	-1	0			.933	1	/3-3,S-1	0.0
Total	2	24	81	7	15	2	0	0	1	2		.185	.214	.210	30	-7	2			.916	1	/3-22,S-1	-0.6

■ TODD GREENE   Greene, Todd Anthony   b: 5/8/71, Augusta, Ga.   BR/TR, 5'10", 195 lbs.   Deb: 7/30/96

| 1996 | Cal-A | 29 | 79 | 9 | 15 | 1 | 0 | 2 | 9 | 4 | 11 | .190 | .238 | .278 | 31 | -9 | 2 | 0 | 1 | 1.000 | 1 | C-26/D-1 | -0.5 |

■ WILLIE GREENE   Greene, Willie Louis   b: 9/23/71, Milledgeville, Ga.   BL/TR, 5'11", 180 lbs.   Deb: 9/1/92

1992	Cin-N	29	93	10	25	5	2	2	13	10	23	.269	.340	.430	114	2	0	2	-1	.948	-1	3-25	0.0
1993	Cin-N	15	50	7	8	1	1	2	5	2	19	.160	.192	.340	39	-5	0	0	0	.978	4	S-10/3-5	0.0
1994	Cin-N	16	37	5	8	0	0	3	6	14		.216	.326	.270	58	-2	0	0	0	.958	0	3-13/O-1	-0.2
1995	Cin-N	8	19	1	2	0	0	0	0	1	5	.105	.227	.105	-9	-3	0	0	0	1.000	1	/3-7	0.0
1996	Cin-N	115	287	48	70	5	5	19	63	36	88	.244	.328	.495	114	5	0	1	-1	.927	7	3-73,O-10/1-2,2S	1.1
Total	5	183	486	71	113	13	8	23	84	57	151	.233	.313	.434	97	-3	0	3	-2	.939	11	3-123/O-11,S-11,12	0.7

■ JIM GREENGRASS   Greengrass, James Raymond   b: 10/24/27, Addison, N.Y.   BR/TR, 6'1", 200 lbs.   Deb: 9/9/52

1952	Cin-N	18	68	10	21	2	1	5	24	7	12	.309	.373	.588	163	5	0	0	0	.965	2	O-17	0.6
1953	Cin-N	154	606	86	173	22	7	20	100	47	83	.285	.340	.444	102	1	6	4	-1	.983	8	*O-153	0.2
1954	Cin-N	139	542	79	152	27	4	27	95	41	81	.280	.331	.494	109	5	0	3	-2	.968	5	*O-137	0.2
1955	Cin-N	13	39	1	4	2	0	0	1	9	9	.103	.271	.154	16	-5	0	0	0	1.000	2	O-11	-0.3
	Phi-N	94	323	43	88	20	2	12	37	33	43	.272	.342	.458	112	4	0	2	-1	.988	1	O-83/3-2	0.0
	Yr	107	362	44	92	22	2	12	38	42	52	.254	.333	.425	100	0	0	2	-1	.990	4	O-94/3-2	-0.1
1956	Phi-N	86	215	24	44	9	2	5	25	28	43	.205	.296	.335	71	-9	0	0	0	.991	-2	O-62	-1.4
Total	5	504	1793	243	482	82	16	69	282	165	271	.269	.332	.448	102	5	6	9	-4	.980	17	O-463/3-2	-0.5

■ MIKE GREENWELL   Greenwell, Michael Lewis   b: 7/18/63, Louisville, Ky.   BL/TR, 6', 200 lbs.   Deb: 9/5/85

1985	Bos-A	17	31	7	10	1	0	4	8	3	4	.323	.382	.742	191	4	1	0	0	1.000	-5	O-17	-0.1
1986	*Bos-A	31	35	4	11	2	0	4	5	5	7	.314	.400	.371	111	1	0	0	0	1.000	-1	O-15/D-3	-0.1
1987	Bos-A	125	412	71	135	31	6	19	89	35	40	.328	.389	.570	146	27	5	4	-1	.971	1	O-91,D-15/C-1	2.3
1988	*Bos-A★	158	590	86	192	39	8	22	119	87	38	.325	.420	.531	158	48	16	8	0	.981	7	*O-147,D-11	4.9
1989	Bos-A★	145	578	87	178	36	0	14	95	56	44	.308	.372	.443	121	17	13	5	1	.967	-4	*O-139/D-5	1.0
1990	*Bos-A	159	610	71	181	30	6	14	73	65	43	.297	.368	.434	118	15	8	7	-2	.977	4	*O-159	1.4
1991	Bos-A	147	544	76	163	26	6	9	83	43	35	.300	.354	.419	108	6	15	5	2	.989	6	*O-143/D-1	1.0
1992	Bos-A	49	180	16	42	2	0	2	18	18	19	.233	.310	.278	62	-9	2	3	-1	1.000	1	O-41/D-6	-1.1
1993	Bos-A	146	540	77	170	38	6	13	72	54	46	.315	.381	.480	122	17	5	4	-1	.993	3	*O-134,D-10	1.5
1994	Bos-A	95	327	60	88	25	1	11	45	38	26	.269	.352	.453	101	0	2	2	-1	.993	0	O-84/D-6	0.0
1995	*Bos-A	120	481	67	143	25	4	15	76	38	35	.297	.351	.459	105	3	9	5	-0	.972	6	*O-118/D-2	1.3
1996	Bos-A	77	295	35	87	20	1	7	44	18	27	.295	.340	.441	92	-4	4	3	-0	.973	4	O-76	0.2
Total	12	1269	4623	657	1400	275	38	130	726	460	364	.303	.371	.463	119	124	80	43	-2	.981	18	*O-1164/D-59,C-1	10.7

■ BILL GREENWOOD   Greenwood, William F.   b: 1857, Philadelphia, Pa.   d: 5/2/02, Philadelphia, Pa.   BB/TL, 5'7.5", 180 lbs.   Deb: 9/16/1882

1882	Phi-a	7	30	8	9	1	0	0		1	1	.300	.323	.333	109	-1				.909	-1	/O-7,2-2	-0.1
1884	Bro-a	92	385	52	83	8	3	3			10	.216	.237	.275	66	-14				.900	-8	*2-92/S-1	-1.8
1887	Bal-a	118	495	114	130	16	6	0	65	54		.263	.336	.319	88	-5	71			**.928**	7	*2-117/O-1	0.4
1888	Bal-a	115	409	69	78	13	1	0	29	30		.191	.256	.227	57	-19	46			.913	-22	2-86,S-28/O-1	-3.5
1889	Col-a	118	414	62	93	7	10	3	49	58	71	.225	.327	.312	86	-5	37			.914	-3	*2-118	-0.2
1890	Roc-a	124	437	76	97	11	6	2	41	48		.222	.310	.288	83	-8	40			.921	3	*2-123/S-1	0.1
Total	6	574	2170	381	490	56	26	8	185	201	71	.226	.298	.287	78	-51	194			.916	-26	2-538/S-30,O-9	-5.1

■ BRIAN GREER   Greer, Brian Keith   b: 5/14/59, Lynwood, Cal.   BR/TR, 6'3", 210 lbs.   Deb: 9/13/77

1977	SD-N	1	1	0	0	0	0	0	0	0	1	.000	.000	.000	-99	-0	0	0	0	.000	0	H	0.0
1979	SD-N	4	3	0	0	0	0	0	0	0	1	.000	.000	.000	-99	-1	0	0	0	1.000	-1	/O-4	-0.2
Total	2	5	4	0	0	0	0	0	0	0	2	.000	.000	.000	-99	-1	0	0	0	1.000	-1	/O-4	-0.2

■ ED GREER   Greer, Edward C.   b: 1865, Philadelphia, Pa.   d: 2/4/1890, Philadelphia, Pa.   BR   Deb: 6/24/1885

1885	Bal-a	56	211	32	42	7	0	0	21	8		.199	.235	.232	49	-12				.908	-0	O-47,C-12	-1.2
1886	Bal-a	11	38	2	5	1	0	0	4	2		.132	.175	.158	5	-4	4			.875	-2	/O-9,C-2	-0.5
	Phi-a	71	264	33	51	5	3	1	20	8		.193	.223	.246	46	-17	12			.921	6	O-70/C-1	-1.1
	Yr	82	302	35	56	6	3	1	24	10		.185	.217	.235	41	-21	16			.919	4	O-79/C-3	-1.6
1887	Phi-a	3	11	1	2	0	0	0	0	0		.182	.182	.182	2	-1	2			.857	0	/O-3	-0.1
	Bro-a	91	327	49	83	13	2	2	48	25		.254	.318	.324	78	-9	33			.921	3	O-76,C-16	-0.5
	Yr	94	338	50	85	13	2	2	48	25		.251	.314	.320	76	-11	35			.918	3	O-79,C-16	-0.6
Total	3	232	851	117	183	26	5	3	93	43		.215	.261	.268	58	-44	51			.916	6	O-205/C-31	-3.4

■ RUSTY GREER   Greer, Thurman Clyde b: 1/21/69, Fort Rucker, Ala. BL/TL, 6', 190 lbs. Deb: 5/16/94

YEAR	TM/L	G	AB	R	H	2B	3B	HR	RBI	BB	SO	AVG	OBP	SLG	PRO+	BR/A	SB	CS	SBR	FA	FR	G/POS	TPR
1994	Tex-A	80	277	36	87	16	1	10	46	46	46	.314	.415	.487	132	15	0	0	0	.976	-7	O-73/1-9	0.5
1995	Tex-A	131	417	58	113	21	2	13	61	55	66	.271	.357	.424	100	0	3	1	0	.982	-15	*O-125/1-3	-1.6
1996	*Tex-A	139	542	96	180	41	6	18	100	62	86	.332	.404	.530	125	21	9	0	3	.984	8	O-137/1-1,D-1	2.5
Total	3	350	1236	190	380	78	9	41	207	163	198	.307	.391	.485	118	36	12	1	3	.982	-13	O-335/1-13,D-1	1.4

■ TOMMY GREGG   Gregg, William Thomas b: 7/29/63, Boone, N.C. BL/TL, 6'1", 190 lbs. Deb: 9/14/87

YEAR	TM/L	G	AB	R	H	2B	3B	HR	RBI	BB	SO	AVG	OBP	SLG	PRO+	BR/A	SB	CS	SBR	FA	FR	G/POS	TPR
1987	Pit-N	10	8	3	2	1	0	0	0	0	2	.250	.250	.375	62	-0	0	0	0	1.000	-2	/O-4	-0.2
1988	Pit-N	14	15	4	3	1	0	1	3	1	4	.200	.250	.467	103	-0	0	1	0	1.000	-2	/O-6	-0.3
	Atl-N	11	29	1	10	3	0	0	4	2	2	.345	.387	.448	132	1	0	0	0	1.000	2	/O-7	0.3
	Yr	25	44	5	13	4	0	1	7	3	6	.295	.340	.455	125	1	0	1	-1	1.000	0	O-13	0.0
1989	Atl-N	102	276	24	67	8	0	6	23	18	45	.243	.289	.337	76	-9	3	4	-2	.967	-10	O-48,1-37	-2.5
1990	Atl-N	124	239	18	63	13	1	5	32	20	39	.264	.323	.389	90	-3	4	3	-1	.987	-2	1-50,O-20	-0.9
1991	*Atl-N	72	107	13	20	8	1	1	12	4	24	.187	.275	.308	60	-6	2	2	-1	1.000	-1	O-14,1-13	-0.1
1992	Atl-N	18	19	1	5	0	0	1	1	1	7	.263	.300	.421	96	-0	1	0	0	1.000	-1	/O-4	-0.1
1993	Cin-N	10	12	1	2	0	0	0	0	1	2	.167	.167	.167	-10	-2	0	0	0	1.000	-1	/O-4	-0.3
1995	Fla-N	72	156	20	37	5	0	6	20	16	33	.237	.316	.385	83	-4	3	1	0	.984	-3	O-38/1-2	-0.8
Total	8	433	861	85	209	39	2	20	88	70	156	.243	.303	.362	81	-23	13	11	-3	.981	-20	O-150,1-102	-5.7

■ ED GREMMINGER   Gremminger, Lorenzo Edward "Battleship" b: 3/30/1874, Canton, Ohio d: 5/26/42, Canton, Ohio BR/TR, 6'1", 200 lbs. Deb: 4/21/1895

YEAR	TM/L	G	AB	R	H	2B	3B	HR	RBI	BB	SO	AVG	OBP	SLG	PRO+	BR/A	SB	CS	SBR	FA	FR	G/POS	TPR
1895	Cle-N	20	78	10	21	1	0	0	15	5	13	.269	.313	.282	51	-6	0				.873	-1	3-20	-0.5
1902	Bos-N	140	522	55	134	20	12	1	65	39		.257	.314	.347	103	1	7				.951	3	*3-140	0.6
1903	Bos-N	140	511	57	135	24	9	5	56	31		.264	.313	.376	100	-2	12				.935	16	*3-140	1.5
1904	Det-A	83	309	18	66	13	3	1	28	14		.214	.257	.285	73	-10	3				.950	-16	3-83	-2.6
Total	4	383	1420	140	356	58	24	7	164	89	13	.251	.301	.340	92	-16	22				.940	2	3-383	-1.0

■ BUDDY GREMP   Gremp, Lewis Edward b: 8/5/19, Denver, Col. BR/TR, 6'1", 175 lbs. Deb: 9/13/40

YEAR	TM/L	G	AB	R	H	2B	3B	HR	RBI	BB	SO	AVG	OBP	SLG	PRO+	BR/A	SB	CS	SBR	FA	FR	G/POS	TPR
1940	Bos-N	4	9	0	2	0	0	0	2	0	0	.222	.222	.222	24	-1	0				1.000	-0	/1-3	-0.1
1941	Bos-N	37	75	7	18	3	0	0	10	5	3	.240	.287	.280	63	-4	0				.977	-3	1-21/2-6,C-3	-0.8
1942	Bos-N	72	207	12	45	11	0	3	19	13	21	.217	.267	.314	71	-8	1				.991	0	1-62/3-1	-1.1
Total	3	113	291	19	65	14	0	3	31	18	24	.223	.271	.302	67	-13	1				.988	-3	/1-86,2-6,C-3,3-1	-2.0

■ REDDY GREY   Grey, Romer Carl (b: Romer Carl Gray) b: 4/8/1875, Zanesville, Ohio d: 11/9/34, Altadena, Cal. BL/TL, 5'11", 175 lbs. Deb: 5/28/03

YEAR	TM/L	G	AB	R	H	2B	3B	HR	RBI	BB	SO	AVG	OBP	SLG	PRO+	BR/A	SB	CS	SBR	FA	FR	G/POS	TPR
1903	Pit-N	3	1	1	1	0	0	0	1	0	0	.333	.500	.333	135	0	0				1.000	-0	/O-1	0.0

■ BILL GREY   Grey, William Tobin b: 4/15/1871, Philadelphia, Pa. d: 12/8/32, Philadelphia, Pa. 5'11", 175 lbs. Deb: 5/14/1890

YEAR	TM/L	G	AB	R	H	2B	3B	HR	RBI	BB	SO	AVG	OBP	SLG	PRO+	BR/A	SB	CS	SBR	FA	FR	G/POS	TPR
1890	Phi-N	34	128	20	31	8	4	0	21	6	3	.242	.287	.367	88	-3	5				1.000	-11	O-10/3-8,2-8,C-7,1	-1.1
1891	Phi-N	23	75	11	18	0	0	0	7	3	10	.240	.296	.240	55	-4	3				.804	-6	C-11,0-10/S-3,3-1	-0.8
1895	Cin-N	52	181	24	55	17	4	1	29	15	8	.304	.364	.459	107	1	4				.906	-4	3-27,2-16/S-5,CO	-0.1
1896	Cin-N	46	121	15	25	2	1	0	17	19	11	.207	.314	.240	44	-10	6				.927	1	2-12,C-11/S-8,013	-0.6
1898	Pit-N	137	528	56	121	17	5	0	67	28		.229	.283	.280	63	-26	5				.879	-20	*3-137	-4.2
Total	5	292	1033	126	250	44	14	1	141	71	32	.242	.303	.315	72	-41	23				.879	-40	3-174/2-36,COS1	-6.8

■ BOBBY GRICH   Grich, Robert Anthony b: 1/15/49, Muskegon, Mich. BR/TR, 6'2", 190 lbs. Deb: 6/29/70

YEAR	TM/L	G	AB	R	H	2B	3B	HR	RBI	BB	SO	AVG	OBP	SLG	PRO+	BR/A	SB	CS	SBR	FA	FR	G/POS	TPR
1970	Bal-A	30	95	11	20	1	3	0	6	9	21	.211	.279	.284	55	-6	1	1	-0	.915	2	S-20/2-9,3-1	-0.1
1971	Bal-A	7	30	7	9	0	0	1	6	5	8	.300	.400	.400	128	1	1	0	0	1.000		/S-5,2-2	0.5
1972	Bal-A★	133	460	66	128	21	3	12	50	53	96	.278	.362	.415	127	16	13	6	0	.950	-25	S-81,2-45,1-16/3-8	4.7
1973	*Bal-A	162	581	82	146	29	7	12	50	107	91	.251	.374	.387	116	16	17	9	-0	.995	21	*2-162	4.8
1974	*Bal-A	160	582	92	153	29	6	19	82	90	117	.263	.380	.431	137	31	17	11	-2	.979	9	*2-160	4.8
1975	Bal-A	150	524	81	136	26	4	13	57	107	88	.260	.393	.399	133	28	14	10	-2	.977	24	*2-150	5.8
1976	Bal-A	144	518	93	138	31	4	13	54	86	99	.266	.374	.417	140	28	14	6	1	.985	-1	*2-140/3-2,D-2	3.9
1977	Cal-A	52	181	24	44	6	0	7	23	37	40	.243	.374	.392	114	5	6	6	-2	.983	-3	S-52	0.6
1978	Cal-A	144	487	68	122	16	2	6	42	75	83	.251	.359	.329	98	2	4	3	-1	.983	0	*2-144	1.2
1979	*Cal-A	153	534	78	157	30	5	30	101	59	84	.294	.366	.537	145	33	1	0	0	.984	4	*2-153	4.2
1980	*Cal-A	150	498	60	135	22	2	14	62	84	108	.271	.381	.408	119	16	3	7	-3	.989	3	*2-146/1-3	2.5
1981	Cal-A	100	352	56	107	14	2	22	61	40	71	.304	.381	.543	164	28	2	4	-2	.983	11	*2-100	4.5
1982	*Cal-A	145	506	74	132	28	5	19	65	82	109	.261	.372	.449	124	19	3	3	-1	.986	11	*2-142/D-1	3.6
1983	Cal-A	120	387	65	113	17	0	16	62	76	62	.292	.417	.460	142	26	2	4	-2	.969	16	*2-118/S-1	4.5
1984	Cal-A	116	363	60	93	15	1	18	58	57	70	.256	.360	.452	124	13	2	5	-2	.982	3	2-91,1-25,3-21	1.5
1985	Cal-A	144	479	74	116	17	3	13	53	81	77	.242	.355	.372	100	2	3	5	-2	.997	15	*2-116,1-16,3-15/D	1.8
1986	*Cal-A	98	313	42	84	18	0	9	30	39	54	.268	.355	.412	109	5	1	3	-2	.980	-10	2-87,1-11/3-2	-0.4
Total	17	2008	6890	1033	1833	320	47	224	864	1087	1278	.266	.373	.424	125	264	104	83	-19	.984	80	*2-1765,S-159/13D	44.0

■ TIM GRIESENBECK   Griesenbeck, Carlos Phillipe Timothy b: 12/10/1897, San Antonio, Tex. d: 3/25/53, San Antonio, Tex. BR/TR, 5'10.5", 190 lbs. Deb: 9/11/20

YEAR	TM/L	G	AB	R	H	2B	3B	HR	RBI	BB	SO	AVG	OBP	SLG	PRO+	BR/A	SB	CS	SBR	FA	FR	G/POS	TPR
1920	StL-N	5	3	1	1	0	0	0	0	0	0	.333	.333	.333	95	-0	0	0	0	1.000	0	/C-3	0.0

■ TOM GRIEVE   Grieve, Thomas Alan b: 3/4/48, Pittsfield, Mass. BR/TR, 6'2", 190 lbs. Deb: 7/5/70

YEAR	TM/L	G	AB	R	H	2B	3B	HR	RBI	BB	SO	AVG	OBP	SLG	PRO+	BR/A	SB	CS	SBR	FA	FR	G/POS	TPR
1970	Was-A	47	116	12	23	5	1	3	10	14	38	.198	.290	.336	76	-4	0	0	0	.939	-7	O-39	-1.3
1972	Tex-A	64	142	12	29	2	1	3	11	11	39	.204	.271	.296	72	-5	1	3	-2	.985	-4	O-49	-1.4
1973	Tex-A	66	123	22	38	6	0	7	21	7	25	.309	.351	.528	151	8	0	0	0	1.000	-12	O-59/D-1	-0.6
1974	Tex-A	84	259	30	66	10	4	9	32	20	48	.255	.313	.429	114	4	0	0	0	1.000	4	D-40,O-38/1-1	0.3
1975	Tex-A	118	369	46	102	17	1	14	61	22	74	.276	.317	.442	113	5	0	2	-1	.990	-7	O-63,D-45	-0.6
1976	Tex-A	149	546	57	139	23	3	20	81	35	119	.255	.304	.418	108	3	4	1	1	.983	1	D-96,O-52	0.1
1977	Tex-A	79	236	24	53	9	0	7	30	13	57	.225	.274	.352	68	-11	1	0	0	.976	-6	O-60,D-13	-1.9
1978	NY-N	54	101	5	21	4	0	0	8	9	23	.208	.273	.297	61	-5	0	1	-1	.979	1	O-26/1-2	-0.7
1979	StL-N	9	15	1	3	1	0	0	0	4	1	.200	.368	.267	76	-0	0	0	0	.875	-1	/O-5	-0.1
Total	9	670	1907	209	474	76	10	65	254	135	424	.249	.303	.401	100	-6	7	7	-2	.982	-31	O-391,D-195/1-3	-6.2

■ KEN GRIFFEY   Griffey, George Kenneth Jr. "Junior" b: 11/21/69, Donora, Pa. BL/TL, 6'3", 195 lbs. Deb: 4/3/89 F

YEAR	TM/L	G	AB	R	H	2B	3B	HR	RBI	BB	SO	AVG	OBP	SLG	PRO+	BR/A	SB	CS	SBR	FA	FR	G/POS	TPR
1989	Sea-A	127	455	61	120	23	0	16	61	44	83	.264	.331	.420	107	4	16	7	1	.969	5	*O-127	0.6
1990	Sea-A★	155	597	91	179	28	7	22	80	63	81	.300	.369	.481	134	27	16	11	-2	.980	5	*O-151/D-2	2.2
1991	Sea-A★	154	548	76	179	42	1	22	100	71	82	.327	.405	.527	156	42	18	6	2	.989	9	*O-152/D-1	4.9
1992	Sea-A★	142	565	83	174	39	4	27	103	44	67	.308	.363	.535	148	34	10	5	1	.997	6	*O-137/D-3	3.7
1993	Sea-A★	156	582	113	180	38	3	45	109	96	91	.309	.408	.617	170	58	17	9	0	.991	4	*O-139,D-19/1-1	5.3
1994	Sea-A★	111	433	94	140	24	4	40	90	56	73	.323	.403	.674	168	43	11	3	2	.983	5	*O-103/D-9	4.2
1995	*Sea-A†	72	260	52	67	7	0	17	42	52	53	.258	.379	.481	121	9	4	2	0	.990	10	O-70/D-2	1.5
1996	Sea-A†	140	545	125	165	26	2	49	140	78	104	.303	.397	.628	154	44	16	1	6	.990	16	*O-137/D-5	5.4
Total	8	1057	3985	695	1204	227	21	238	725	504	634	.302	.384	.549	147	261	108	44	6	.986	53	*O-1016/D-41,1-1	27.8

■ KEN GRIFFEY   Griffey, George Kenneth Sr. b: 4/10/50, Donora, Pa. BL/TL, 6', 200 lbs. Deb: 8/25/73 FC

YEAR	TM/L	G	AB	R	H	2B	3B	HR	RBI	BB	SO	AVG	OBP	SLG	PRO+	BR/A	SB	CS	SBR	FA	FR	G/POS	TPR
1973	*Cin-N	25	86	19	33	5	1	3	14	6	10	.384	.424	.570	182	9	4	2	0	1.000	-3	O-21	0.5
1974	Cin-N	88	227	24	57	9	2	2	19	27	43	.251	.333	.361	96	-1	9	4	0	1.000	-1	O-70	-0.4
1975	Cin-N	132	463	95	141	15	9	4	46	67	67	.305	.394	.402	119	14	16	7	1	.967	-5	O-119	0.5
1976	*Cin-N★	148	562	111	189	28	9	6	74	62	65	.336	.403	.450	139	30	34	11	4	.979	-1	O-144	2.8
1977	Cin-N☆	154	585	117	186	35	8	12	57	69	84	.318	.390	.467	126	23	17	8	0	.990	9	*O-147	2.7
1978	Cin-N	158	614	90	177	33	8	10	63	54	70	.288	.346	.417	112	9	23	9	4	.969	4	*O-154	1.2
1979	Cin-N	95	380	62	120	27	4	8	32	36	39	.316	.376	.471	129	15	12	5	1	.984	-3	O-93	0.9
1980	Cin-N	146	544	89	160	28	10	13	85	62	77	.294	.367	.454	128	21	23	13	1	.978	-0	O-138	2.2
1981	Cin-N	101	396	65	123	21	6	2	34	39	26	.311	.374	.409	120	11	12	4	1	.989	10	O-99	2.0
1982	NY-A	127	484	70	134	23	2	12	54	39	58	.277	.331	.407	103	2	10	4	1	.983	7	*O-125	0.6

YEAR	TM/L	G	AB	R	H	2B	3B	HR	RBI	BB	SO	AVG	OBP	SLG	PRO+	BR/A	SB	CS	SBR	FA	FR	G/POS	TPR
1983	NY-A	118	458	60	140	21	3	11	46	34	45	.306	.356	.437	121	13	6	1	1	.992	-2	*1-101/O-14,D-2	0.6
1984	NY-A	120	399	44	109	20	1	7	56	29	32	.273	.324	.381	98	-1	2	2	-1	.974	0	O-82,1-27/D-2	-0.6
1985	NY-A	127	438	68	120	28	4	10	69	41	51	.274	.336	.425	109	5	7	7	-2	.970	5	*O-110/1-1,D-7	0.4
1986	NY-A	59	198	33	60	7	0	9	26	15	24	.303	.355	.475	125	7	2	2	-1	.971	1	O-51/D-2	0.5
	Atl-N	80	292	36	90	15	3	12	32	20	43	.308	.353	.503	126	10	12	7	-1	.986	1	O-77/1-1	0.8
1987	Atl-N	122	399	65	114	24	1	14	64	46	54	.286	.361	.456	109	6	4	7	-3	.995	1	*O-107/1-3	0.0
1988	Atl-N	69	193	21	48	5	0	2	19	17	26	.249	.310	.306	74	-6	1	3	-2	.969	-4	O-42,1-11	-1.5
	Cin-N	25	50	5	14	1	0	2	4	2	5	.280	.308	.420	103	0	0	0	0	.986	-0	1-10	-0.1
	Yr	94	243	26	62	6	0	4	23	19	31	.255	.309	.329	80	-6	1	3	-2	.969	-4	O-42,1-21	-1.6
1989	Cin-N	106	236	26	62	8	3	8	30	29	42	.263	.346	.424	115	5	4	2	0	.987	-8	O-58/1-9	-0.5
1990	Cin-N	46	63	6	13	2	0	1	8	2	5	.206	.242	.286	43	-5	2	1	0	.979	0	/1-9,O-6	-0.5
	Sea-A	21	77	13	29	2	0	3	18	10	3	.377	.448	.519	168	7	0	0	0	.963	-4	O-20	0.5
1991	Sea-A	30	85	10	24	9	1	9	13	13	13	.282	.384	.400	117	2	0	0	0	1.000	-4	O-26/D-1	-0.2
Total	19	2097	7229	1129	2143	364	77	152	859	719	898	.296	.361	.431	118	175	200	83	10	.981	4	*O-1703,1-172/D-14	12.4

■ **ALFREDO GRIFFIN**   Griffin, Alfredo Claudino (b: Alfredo Claudino Baptist (Griffin))
b: 10/6/57, Santo Domingo, D.R.   BB/TR, 5'11", 165 lbs.   Deb: 9/4/76   C

YEAR	TM/L	G	AB	R	H	2B	3B	HR	RBI	BB	SO	AVG	OBP	SLG	PRO+	BR/A	SB	CS	SBR	FA	FR	G/POS	TPR
1976	Cle-A	12	4	0	1	0	0	0	0	0	2	.250	.250	.250	47	-0	0	1	-1	.750	0	/S-6,D-4	0.0
1977	Cle-A	14	41	5	6	1	0	0	3	3	5	.146	.205	.171	4	-5	2	2	-1	.940	-1	S-13/D-1	-0.6
1978	Cle-A	5	4	1	2	1	0	0	0	0	2	.500	.667	.750	301	1	0	0	0	.917	3	/S-2	0.4
1979	Tor-A	153	624	81	179	22	10	2	31	40	59	.287	.335	.364	87	-11	21	16	-3	.956	6	*S-153	0.9
1980	Tor-A	155	653	63	166	26	**15**	2	41	24	58	.254	.285	.349	70	-28	18	23	-8	.955	2	*S-155	-1.7
1981	Tor-A	101	388	30	81	19	6	0	21	17	38	.209	.244	.289	50	-25	8	12	-5	.937	-19	S-97/3-4,2-1	-4.2
1982	Tor-A	162	539	57	130	20	8	1	48	22	48	.241	.271	.314	55	-34	10	8	-2	.968	6	*S-162	-1.4
1983	Tor-A	162	528	62	132	22	9	4	47	27	44	.250	.290	.348	71	-22	8	11	-4	.965	-1	*S-157/2-5,D-1	-1.5
1984	Tor-A★	140	419	53	101	8	2	4	30	4	33	.241	.250	.298	49	-29	11	3	2	.962	-5	*S-115,2-21/D-5	-2.2
1985	Oak-A	162	614	75	166	18	7	2	64	20	50	.270	.293	.332	77	-21	24	9	2	.960	-15	*S-162	-1.8
1986	Oak-A	162	594	74	169	23	6	4	51	35	52	.285	.326	.364	95	-5	33	16	0	.966	-11	*S-162	-0.1
1987	Oak-A	144	494	69	130	23	5	3	60	28	41	.263	.308	.348	79	-15	26	13	0	.963	0	*S-137/2-1	-0.3
1988	*LA-N	95	316	39	63	8	3	1	27	24	30	.199	.260	.253	49	-21	7	5	-1	.965	2	S-93	-1.3
1989	LA-N	136	506	49	125	27	2	0	29	29	57	.247	.288	.308	72	-19	10	7	-1	.975	-3	*S-131	-1.9
1990	LA-N	141	461	38	97	11	3	1	35	29	65	.210	.260	.254	43	-36	6	3	0	.959	10	*S-139	-1.6
1991	LA-N	109	350	27	85	6	2	0	27	22	49	.243	.290	.271	60	-18	5	4	-1	.961	19	*S-109	0.8
1992	*Tor-A	63	150	21	35	7	0	0	10	9	19	.233	.277	.280	54	-9	3	1	0	.981	-1	S-48,2-16	-0.7
1993	*Tor-A	46	95	15	20	3	0	0	3	3	13	.211	.235	.242	28	-10	0	0	0	.960	4	S-20,2-11/3-6	-0.4
Total	18	1962	6780	759	1688	245	78	24	527	338	664	.249	.287	.319	67	-306	192	134	-23	.961	-10	*S-1861/2-55,D-11,3	-17.6

■ **DOUG GRIFFIN**   Griffin, Douglas Lee   b: 6/4/47, South Gate, Cal.   BR/TR, 6', 170 lbs.   Deb: 9/11/70

YEAR	TM/L	G	AB	R	H	2B	3B	HR	RBI	BB	SO	AVG	OBP	SLG	PRO+	BR/A	SB	CS	SBR	FA	FR	G/POS	TPR
1970	Cal-A	18	55	2	7	1	0	0	4	6	5	.127	.213	.145	1	-7	0	0	0	.964	1	2-11/3-8	-0.6
1971	Bos-A	125	483	51	118	23	2	3	27	31	45	.244	.293	.319	68	-20	11	5	0	.986	7	*2-124	-0.3
1972	Bos-A	129	470	43	122	12	1	2	35	45	48	.260	.327	.302	83	-8	9	2	2	.978	2	*2-129	0.3
1973	Bos-A	113	396	43	101	14	5	1	33	21	42	.255	.298	.323	71	-16	7	5	-1	.990	-14	*2-113	-2.5
1974	Bos-A	93	312	35	83	12	4	0	33	28	21	.266	.330	.330	85	-6	2	8	-4	.979	-3	2-91/S-1	-2.0
1975	*Bos-A	100	287	21	69	6	0	1	29	18	29	.240	.290	.272	55	-17	2	2	-1	.967	-10	2-99/S-1	-2.4
1976	Bos-A	49	127	14	24	2	0	0	4	9	14	.189	.248	.205	30	-11	2	1	0	.989	-1	2-44/D-2	-1.1
1977	Bos-A	5	6	0	0	0	0	0	0	0	0	.000	.000	.000	-90	-2	0	0	0	1.000	1	/2-3	-0.1
Total	8	632	2136	209	524	70	12	7	165	158	204	.245	.301	.299	68	-87	33	23	-4	.981	-28	2-614/3-8,D-2,S-2	-8.7

■ **PUG GRIFFIN**   Griffin, Francis Arthur   b: 4/24/1896, Lincoln, Neb.   d: 10/12/51, Colorado Springs, Colo.   BR/TR, 5'11.5", 187 lbs.   Deb: 7/27/17

YEAR	TM/L	G	AB	R	H	2B	3B	HR	RBI	BB	SO	AVG	OBP	SLG	PRO+	BR/A	SB	CS	SBR	FA	FR	G/POS	TPR
1917	Phi-A	18	25	4	5	1	0	1	3	1	9	.200	.231	.360	81	-1	1			1.000	1	/1-3	0.0
1920	NY-N	5	4	0	1	0	0	0	0	1	2	.250	.400	.250	90	0	0	0	0	1.000	-1	/O-2	-0.1
Total	2	23	29	4	6	1	0	1	3	2	11	.207	.258	.345	83	-1	1	0		1.000	-0	/1-3,O-2	-0.1

■ **IVY GRIFFIN**   Griffin, Ivy Moore   b: 11/16/1896, Thomasville, Ala.   d: 8/25/57, Gainesville, Fla.   BL/TR, 5'11", 180 lbs.   Deb: 9/9/19

YEAR	TM/L	G	AB	R	H	2B	3B	HR	RBI	BB	SO	AVG	OBP	SLG	PRO+	BR/A	SB	CS	SBR	FA	FR	G/POS	TPR
1919	Phi-A	17	68	5	20	2	2	0	6	3	10	.294	.333	.382	99	-0	0			.989	4	1-17	0.3
1920	Phi-A	129	467	46	111	15	1	0	20	17	49	.238	.281	.274	47	-36	3	3	-1	.990	5	*1-127/2-2	-3.4
1921	Phi-A	39	103	14	33	4	2	0	13	5	6	.320	.369	.398	95	-1	1	2	-1	.973	-2	1-27	-0.4
Total	3	185	638	65	164	21	5	0	39	25	65	.257	.301	.306	60	-36	4	5		.988	7	1-171/2-2	-3.5

■ **MIKE GRIFFIN**   Griffin, Michael Joseph   b: 3/20/1865, Utica, N.Y.   d: 4/10/08, Utica, N.Y.   BL/TR, 5'7", 160 lbs.   Deb: 4/16/1887   M

YEAR	TM/L	G	AB	R	H	2B	3B	HR	RBI	BB	SO	AVG	OBP	SLG	PRO+	BR/A	SB	CS	SBR	FA	FR	G/POS	TPR
1887	Bal-a	136	532	142	160	32	13	3	94	55		.301	.375	.427	131	24	94			.924	-12	*O-136	0.8
1888	Bal-a	137	542	103	139	21	11	0	46	55		.256	.331	.336	117	12	46			.938	7	*O-137	1.4
1889	Bal-a	137	531	**152**	148	21	14	4	48	91	29	.279	.387	.394	120	17	39			.910	-10	*O-109,S-25/2-5	0.4
1890	Phi-P	115	489	127	140	29	6	6	54	64	19	.286	.377	.407	107	5	30			**.954**	18	*O-115	1.5
1891	Bro-N	134	521	106	139	**36**	9	3	65	57	31	.267	.340	.388	113	8	65			**.960**	26	*O-134	2.6
1892	Bro-N	129	452	103	125	17	11	3	66	68	36	.277	.376	.383	135	21	49			**.986**	13	*O-127/S-2	2.7
1893	Bro-N	95	362	85	103	21	7	6	59	59	23	.285	.396	.431	126	15	30			**.965**	9	*O-93/2-2	1.6
1894	Bro-N	107	402	122	144	28	4	5	75	78	14	.358	.467	.485	140	32	39			.969	7	*O-106	2.4
1895	Bro-N	131	519	140	173	38	7	4	65	93	29	.333	.444	.457	144	41	27			**.969**	14	*O-131/S-1	3.6
1896	Bro-N	122	493	101	152	27	9	4	51	48	25	.308	.380	.424	118	14	23			.961	3	*O-122	0.6
1897	Bro-N	134	534	136	169	25	11	2	56	81		.316	.416	.416	127	26	16			.974	5	*O-134	1.8
1898	Bro-N	134	537	88	161	18	6	2	40	60		.300	.379	.367	114	12	15			**.974**	10	*O-134,M	1.1
Total	12	1511	5914	1405	1753	313	108	42	719	809	**206**	.296	.388	.407	124	228	473			.956	88	*O-1478/S-28,2-7	20.5

■ **THOMAS GRIFFIN**   Griffin, Thomas William   b: 1/1857, Titusville, Pa.   d: 4/17/33, Rockford, Ill.   Deb: 9/27/1884

YEAR	TM/L	G	AB	R	H	2B	3B	HR	RBI	BB	SO	AVG	OBP	SLG	PRO+	BR/A	SB	CS	SBR	FA	FR	G/POS	TPR
1884	Mil-U	11	41	5	9	2	0	0		3		.220	.273	.268	119	-2				.918	-2	1-11	-0.4

■ **SANDY GRIFFIN**   Griffin, Tobias Charles   b: 7/19/1858, Fayetteville, N.Y.   d: 6/5/26, Fayetteville, N.Y.   BR/TR, 5'10", 160 lbs.   Deb: 5/26/1884   M

YEAR	TM/L	G	AB	R	H	2B	3B	HR	RBI	BB	SO	AVG	OBP	SLG	PRO+	BR/A	SB	CS	SBR	FA	FR	G/POS	TPR
1884	NY-N	16	62	7	11	2	0	0	6	1	19	.177	.190	.210	25	-5				.842	-3	O-16	-0.8
1890	Roc-a	107	407	85	125	28	4	5	53	50		.307	.388	.432	153	28	21			.856	-19	*O-107/2-1	0.5
1891	Was-a	20	69	15	19	4	2	0	10	10	3	.275	.398	.391	132	4	2			.939	-3	O-20,M	0.0
1893	StL-N	23	92	9	18	1	1	0	9	16	2	.196	.315	.228	45	-7	2			.906	-2	O-23	-0.8
Total	4	166	630	116	173	35	7	5	78	77	**24**	.275	.361	.376	120	19	25			.873	-27	O-166/2-1	-1.1

■ **BERT GRIFFITH**   Griffith, Bartholomew Joseph "Buck"   b: 3/30/1896, St.Louis, Mo.   d: 5/5/73, Bishop, Cal.   BR/TR, 5'11", 185 lbs.   Deb: 4/13/22

YEAR	TM/L	G	AB	R	H	2B	3B	HR	RBI	BB	SO	AVG	OBP	SLG	PRO+	BR/A	SB	CS	SBR	FA	FR	G/POS	TPR
1922	Bro-N	106	325	45	100	22	8	2	35	5	11	.308	.322	.443	96	-3	5	7	-3	.981	-1	O-77/1-6	-1.2
1923	Bro-N	79	248	23	73	8	4	2	37	13	16	.294	.332	.383	91	-4	1	2	-1	.949	-8	O-62	-1.5
1924	Was-A	6	8	1	1	0	0	0	0	0	1	.125	.125	.125	-37	-2	0	0	0	1.000	0	/O-2	-0.1
Total	3	191	581	69	174	30	12	4	72	18	28	.299	.324	.413	92	-8	6	9	-4	.968	-9	O-141/1-6	-2.8

■ **CLARK GRIFFITH**   Griffith, Clark Calvin "The Old Fox"
b: 11/20/1869, Clear Creek, Mo.   d: 10/27/55, Washington, D.C.   BR/TR, 5'6.5", 156 lbs.   Deb: 4/11/1891   MH

YEAR	TM/L	G	AB	R	H	2B	3B	HR	RBI	BB	SO	AVG	OBP	SLG	PRO+	BR/A	SB	CS	SBR	FA	FR	G/POS	TPR
1891	StL-a	27	77	11	12	1	0	1	8	8	15	.156	.253	.208	28	-8	2			.930	0	P-27	0.0
	Bos-a	10	23	6	4	1	1	1	3	6	5	.174	.367	.435	131	1	1			.778	-1	/P-7,O-3	0.0
	Yr	37	100	17	16	2	1	2	11	14	20	.160	.282	.260	50	-7	3			.909	-1	P-34/O-3	0.0
1893	Chi-N	4	11	1	2	0	0	0	2	0		.182	.182	.182	-3	-2	0			1.000	1	/P-4	0.0
1894	Chi-N	46	142	27	33	5	4	0	15	23	9	.232	.339	.324	58	-10	6			.942	-3	P-36/O-7,S-1	-0.4
1895	Chi-N	43	144	20	46	3	0	1	27	16		.319	.391	.361	89	-2	6			.923	1	P-42/O-1	0.0
1896	Chi-N	38	135	22	36	5	2	1	16	9	7	.267	.313	.356	73	-6	5			.917	1	P-36	0.0
1897	Chi-N	46	162	27	38	8	4	0	21	18		.235	.311	.333	67	-8	2			.947	2	P-41/O-2,S-2,3-1,1	-0.1
1898	Chi-N	38	122	15	20	5	0	0	15	13		.164	.244	.230	36	-10	1			.952	1	P-38	0.0
1899	Chi-N	39	120	15	31	5	0	0	14	14		.258	.346	.300	80	-3	2			.933	6	P-38/S-1	-0.1

YEAR	TM/L	G	AB	R	H	2B	3B	HR	RBI	BB	SO	AVG	OBP	SLG	PRO+	BR/A	SB	CS	SBR	FA	FR	G/POS	TPR
1900	Chi-N	30	95	16	24	4	1	1	7	8		.253	.311	.347	84	-2	2			.917	-1	P-30	0.0
1901	Chi-A	35	89	21	27	3	1	2	14	23		.303	.446	.427	147	7	0			.946	0	P-35,M	0.0
1902	Chi-A	35	92	11	20	3	0	0	8	7		.217	.273	.250	48	-6	0			**1.000**	-2	P-28/O-3,M	-0.1
1903	NY-A	25	69	5	11	4	0	1	7	11		.159	.284	.261	60	-3	0			.983	-3	P-25,M	0.0
1904	NY-A	16	42	2	6	2	0	0	1	4		.143	.217	.190	28	-3	0			.946	-1	P-16,M	0.0
1905	NY-A	26	32	2	7	1	1	0	5	3		.219	.286	.313	80	-1	0			.960	-2	P-25/O-1,M	0.0
1906	NY-A	17	18	0	2	0	0	0	1	3		.111	.238	.111	9	-2	0			1.000	1	P-17,M	0.0
1907	NY-A	5	2	0	0	0	0	0	0	0		.000	.000	.000	-93	-0	0			.800	1	/P-4,M	0.0
1909	Cin-N	1	2	0	0	0	0	0	0	0		.000	.000	.000	-99	-0	0			1.000	1	/P-1,M	0.0
1910	Cin-N	1	0	1	0	0	0	0	0	0	0	—	—	—	—		0			.000	0	RM	0.0
1912	Was-A	1	1	0	0	0	0	0	0	0	0	.000	.000	.000	-99	0	0			.000	1	/P-1,2-1,M	0.0
1913	Was-A	1	1	0	1	1	0	0	1	0	0	1.000	1.000	2.000	758	1	0			.000	-0	/P-1,O-1,M	0.0
1914	Was-A	1	1	0	1	1	0	0	1	0	0	1.000	1.000	2.000	769	1	0	1	-1	.000	-0	/P-1,M	0.0
Total	21	485	1380	202	321	49	17	8	166	166	46	.233	.318	.310	69	-57	22	1		.942		P-453/O-18,S-4,213	-0.7

■ DERRELL GRIFFITH

Griffith, Robert Derrell b: 12/12/43, Anadarko, Okla. BL/TR, 6', 168 lbs. Deb: 9/26/63

YEAR	TM/L	G	AB	R	H	2B	3B	HR	RBI	BB	SO	AVG	OBP	SLG	PRO+	BR/A	SB	CS	SBR	FA	FR	G/POS	TPR
1963	LA-N	1	2	0	0	0	0	0	0	0	0	.000	.000	.000	-99	-1	0	0	0			/2-1	-0.1
1964	LA-N	78	238	27	69	16	2	4	23	5	21	.290	.307	.424	112	2	5	1	1	.769	-12	3-35,O-29	-1.1
1965	LA-N	22	41	3	7	0	0	1	2	0	9	.171	.171	.244	16	-5	0	0	0	1.000	-0	O-11	-0.5
1966	LA-N	23	15	3	1	0	0	0	2	2	3	.067	.176	.067	-32	-3	0	0	0	1.000	-2	/O-7	-0.5
Total	4	124	296	33	77	16	2	5	27	7	33	.260	.280	.378	90	-5	5	1	1	.970	-14	/O-47,3-35,2-1	-2.2

■ TOMMY GRIFFITH

Griffith, Thomas Herman b: 10/26/1889, Prospect, Ohio d: 4/13/67, Cincinnati, Ohio BL/TR, 5'10", 175 lbs. Deb: 8/28/13

YEAR	TM/L	G	AB	R	H	2B	3B	HR	RBI	BB	SO	AVG	OBP	SLG	PRO+	BR/A	SB	CS	SBR	FA	FR	G/POS	TPR
1913	Bos-N	37	127	16	32	4	1	1	12	9	8	.252	.301	.323	77	-4	1			.886	1	O-35	-0.4
1914	Bos-N	16	48	3	5	0	0	0	1	2	6	.104	.140	.104	-27	-7	0			.931	3	O-14	-0.6
1915	Cin-N	160	583	59	179	31	16	4	85	41	34	.307	.355	.436	136	24	6	24	-13	.952	-13	*O-160	-1.0
1916	Cin-N	155	595	50	158	28	7	2	61	36	37	.266	.310	.346	104	2	16			.967	6	*O-155	-0.1
1917	Cin-N	115	363	45	98	18	7	1	45	19	23	.270	.308	.366	111	4	5			.974	6	*O-100	0.5
1918	Cin-N	118	427	47	113	10	4	2	48	39	30	.265	.326	.321	99	0	10			.969	2	*O-118	-0.5
1919	Bro-N	125	484	65	136	18	4	6	57	23	32	.281	.315	.372	104	1	8			.954	-1	*O-125	-0.9
1920	*Bro-N	93	334	41	87	9	4	2	30	15	18	.260	.292	.329	76	-11	3	3	-1	.972	-11	O-92	-3.1
1921	Bro-N	129	455	66	142	21	6	12	71	36	13	.312	.364	.464	113	8	3	3	-1	.972	7	O-124	0.5
1922	Bro-N	99	329	44	104	17	8	4	49	23	10	.316	.361	.453	110	4	7	1	2	.952	4	O-82	0.4
1923	Bro-N	131	481	70	141	21	9	8	66	50	19	.293	.361	.424	109	7	8	2	1	.927	-7	*O-127	-0.9
1924	Bro-N	140	482	43	121	19	5	3	67	34	19	.251	.300	.330	71	-20	0	5	-3	.965	-11	*O-139	-4.3
1925	Bro-N	7	4	2	0	0	0	0	0	3	2	.000	.429	.000	20	-0	1	0	0	1.000	-1	/O-2	-0.1
	Chi-N	76	235	38	67	12	1	7	27	21	11	.285	.348	.434	97	-1	2	4	-2	.937	-3	O-60	-1.0
	Yr	83	239	40	67	12	1	7	27	24	13	.280	.348	.427	96	-2	3	4	-2	.938	-4	O-62	-1.1
Total	13	1401	4947	589	1383	208	72	52	619	351	262	.280	.328	.382	102	6	70	42		.956	-19	*O-1333	-11.3

■ ART GRIGGS

Griggs, Arthur Carle b: 12/10/1883, Topeka, Kan. d: 12/19/38, Los Angeles, Cal. BR/TR, 5'11", 185 lbs. Deb: 5/2/09

YEAR	TM/L	G	AB	R	H	2B	3B	HR	RBI	BB	SO	AVG	OBP	SLG	PRO+	BR/A	SB	CS	SBR	FA	FR	G/POS	TPR
1909	StL-A	108	364	38	102	17	5	0	43	24		.280	.330	.354	125	9	11			.982	-6	1-49,O-41/2-8,S-1	0.1
1910	StL-A	123	416	28	98	22	5	2	30	25		.236	.281	.327	96	-4	11			.878	-1	O-49,2-41,1-17,/S3	-0.8
1911	Cle-A	27	68	7	17	3	2	1	7	5		.250	.301	.397	93	-1	1			.949	-2	2-11/O-4,3-3,1-1	-0.3
1912	Cle-A	89	273	29	83	16	7	0	39	33		.304	.381	.414	123	9	10			.986	1	1-71	0.8
1914	Bro-F	40	112	10	32	6	1	1	15	5	11	.286	.328	.384	94	-3	1			.980	-3	1-27/O-1	-0.7
1915	Bro-F	27	38	4	11	1	0	1	2	3	7	.289	.372	.395	117	0	0			1.000	1	/1-5,O-1	0.1
1918	Det-A	28	99	11	36	8	0	0	16	10	5	.364	.422	.444	168	8	1			.986	-3	1-25	0.5
Total	7	442	1370	127	379	73	20	5	152	105	23	.277	.332	.370	115	19	36			.983	-13	1-195/O-96,2-60,3S	-0.3

■ DENVER GRIGSBY

Grigsby, Denver Clarence b: 3/25/01, Jackson, Ky. d: 11/10/73, Sapulpa, Okla. BL/TR, 5'9", 155 lbs. Deb: 9/1/23

YEAR	TM/L	G	AB	R	H	2B	3B	HR	RBI	BB	SO	AVG	OBP	SLG	PRO+	BR/A	SB	CS	SBR	FA	FR	G/POS	TPR
1923	Chi-N	24	72	8	21	5	2	0	5	5	5	.292	.363	.417	105	1	1	3	-2	1.000	-2	O-22	-0.4
1924	Chi-N	124	411	58	123	18	2	3	48	31	47	.299	.357	.375	95	-2	10	19	-8	.974	3	*O-121	-1.5
1925	Chi-N	51	137	20	35	5	0	0	20	19	12	.255	.346	.292	64	-7	1	1	-0	.966	-1	O-39	-1.0
Total	3	199	620	86	179	28	4	3	73	57	64	.289	.355	.361	89	-8	12	23	-10	.975	0	O-182	-2.9

■ JOHN GRIM

Grim, John Helm b: 8/9/1867, Lebanon, Ky. d: 7/28/61, Indianapolis, Ind BR/TR, 6'2", 175 lbs. Deb: 9/29/1888

YEAR	TM/L	G	AB	R	H	2B	3B	HR	RBI	BB	SO	AVG	OBP	SLG	PRO+	BR/A	SB	CS	SBR	FA	FR	G/POS	TPR
1888	Phi-N	2	7	1	0	0	0	0	1	0		.143	.143	.143	-8	-1	0			.000	-1	/O-1,2-1	-0.1
1890	Roc-a	50	192	30	51	6	9	3	34	7		.266	.299	.422	121	3	14			.851	-7	S-21,C-15/3-8,2O1P	0.0
1891	Mil-a	29	119	14	28	5	1	1	14	2	5	.235	.248	.319	52	-9	1			.926	3	C-16,3-10/2-3	-0.8
1892	Lou-N	97	370	40	90	16	4	1	36	13	24	.243	.280	.316	87	-7	18			.940	-10	C-69,1-11,2/OS3	-1.1
1893	Lou-N	99	415	68	111	19	8	3	54	12	10	.267	.303	.373	86	-10	15			.952	-4	*C-92/1-3,2-2,OS	-0.6
1894	Lou-N	108	410	66	122	27	7	7	70	16	15	.298	.339	.449	95	-5	14			.931	1	C-77,2-24/1-7,3-1	1.0
1895	Bro-N	93	329	54	92	17	5	0	44	13	9	.280	.321	.362	83	-9	9			.947	-0	*C-91/O-1,1-1	-0.3
1896	Bro-N	81	281	32	75	13	1	2	35	12	14	.267	.311	.342	76	-10	7			.939	-1	C-77/1-5	-0.2
1897	Bro-N	80	290	26	72	10	1	0	25	1		.248	.259	.290	47	-23	3			.947	5	C-77	-0.8
1898	Bro-N	52	178	17	50	5	1	0	11	8		.281	.323	.320	85	-4	1			.950	-4	C-52	-0.3
1899	Bro-N	15	47	3	13	1	0	0	7	1		.277	.320	.298	68	-2	0			.966	-0	C-12	0.0
Total	11	706	2638	350	705	119	37	16	330	85	77	.267	.302	.359	82	-76	82			.943	-7	C-578/2-44,1S3OP	-2.4

■ ROY GRIMES

Grimes, Austin Roy "Bummer" b: 9/11/1893, Bergholz, Ohio d: 9/13/54, Guilford Lake, O. BR/TR, 6'1", 176 lbs. Deb: 7/31/20 F

YEAR	TM/L	G	AB	R	H	2B	3B	HR	RBI	BB	SO	AVG	OBP	SLG	PRO+	BR/A	SB	CS	SBR	FA	FR	G/POS	TPR
1920	NY-N	26	57	5	9	3	1	0	5	2	11	.158	.200	.175	8	1			-0	.948	-1	2-21	-0.9

■ ED GRIMES

Grimes, Edward Adelbert b: 9/8/05, Chicago, Ill. d: 10/5/74, Chicago, Ill. BR/TR, 5'10", 165 lbs. Deb: 4/19/31

YEAR	TM/L	G	AB	R	H	2B	3B	HR	RBI	BB	SO	AVG	OBP	SLG	PRO+	BR/A	SB	CS	SBR	FA	FR	G/POS	TPR
1931	StL-A	43	57	9	15	1	2	0	5	8	3	.263	.364	.351	86	-1	1	0	0	.892	-2	3-22/2-4,S-3	-0.2
1932	StL-A	31	68	7	16	0	1	0	13	6	12	.235	.297	.265	44	-6	0	1	-1	.891	2	3-18/2-2,S-1	-0.3
Total	2	74	125	16	31	1	3	0	18	15	15	.248	.329	.304	63	-6	1	1	-0	.891	0	/3-40,2-6,S-4	-0.5

■ OSCAR GRIMES

Grimes, Oscar Ray Jr. b: 4/13/15, Minerva, Ohio d: 5/19/93, Westlake, Ohio BR/TR, 5'11", 178 lbs. Deb: 9/28/38 F

YEAR	TM/L	G	AB	R	H	2B	3B	HR	RBI	BB	SO	AVG	OBP	SLG	PRO+	BR/A	SB	CS	SBR	FA	FR	G/POS	TPR
1938	Cle-A	4	10	2	2	0	1	0	2	2	0	.200	.333	.400	85	-0	0	0	0	1.000	-1	/2-2,1-1	-0.1
1939	Cle-A	119	364	51	98	20	5	4	56	56	61	.269	.368	.385	96	-1	8	3	0	.968	-11	2-48,1-43,S-37/3-3	-1.0
1940	Cle-A	11	13	3	0	0	0	0	0	0	5	.000	.000	.000	-99	-4	0	0	0	.958	0	/1-4,3-1	-0.2
1941	Cle-A	77	244	28	58	9	3	4	24	39	47	.238	.345	.348	88	-4	4	0	1	.995	-5	1-62,2-13/3-1	-1.1
1942	Cle-A	51	84	10	15	2	0	0	2	13	17	.179	.289	.202	42	-6	3		-0	.944	-3	2-24/3-8,1-1,S-1	-0.9
1943	NY-A	9	20	4	3	0	0	0	0	2	6	.150	.261	.150	21	-2	0	0	0	1.000	1	/S-3,1-1	-0.3
1944	NY-A	116	387	44	108	17	8	5	46	59	57	.279	.377	.403	119	11	6	4	-2	.945	-10	3-97,S-20	0.5
1945	NY-A†	142	480	64	127	19	7	4	45	97	73	.265	.395	.358	114	13	7	6	-2	.937	3	*3-141/1-1	1.9
1946	NY-A	14	39	1	8	1	0	0	4	7		.205	.325	.231	27	-4	1	0	0	.895	0	/S-7,2-5	-0.4
	Phi-A	59	191	28	50	5	0	1	20	29	29	.262	.356	.304	86	-2	2	0	1	.958	-12	2-43/3-6,S-4	-1.1
	Yr	73	230	29	58	6	0	1	24	28	36	.252	.336	.291	76	-6	2	0	1	.957	-12	2-48,S-11/3-6	-1.5
Total	9	602	1832	235	469	73	24	18	200	297	303	.256	.363	.352	98	1	30	12	-2	.940	-39	3-257,2-135,1/S	-2.7

■ RAY GRIMES

Grimes, Oscar Ray Sr. b: 9/11/1893, Bergholz, Ohio d: 5/25/53, Minerva, Ohio BR/TR, 5'11", 168 lbs. Deb: 9/24/20 F

YEAR	TM/L	G	AB	R	H	2B	3B	HR	RBI	BB	SO	AVG	OBP	SLG	PRO+	BR/A	SB	CS	SBR	FA	FR	G/POS	TPR
1920	Bos-A	2	4	1	1	0	0	0	1	0		.250	.400	.250	78	-0	0	0	0	1.000	-0	/1-1	0.0
1921	Chi-N	147	530	91	170	38	6	6	79	70	55	.321	.406	.449	126	22	5	8	-3	.993	-5	*1-147	1.1
1922	Chi-N	138	509	99	180	45	12	14	99	75	33	.354	.442	.572	157	45	7	7	-2	.987	-2	*1-138	3.3
1923	Chi-N	64	216	32	71	7	2	2	36	24	17	.329	.401	.407	114	5	5	0	2	.991	-1	1-62	-0.3
1924	Chi-N	51	177	30	53	6	5	5	34	28	15	.299	.401	.475	132	9	4	2	0	.982	-7	1-50	-0.1
1926	Phi-N	32	101	20	30	5	0	0	15	6	12	.297	.343	.347	82	-2	0			.981	0	1-28	-0.4
Total	6	433	1537	269	505	101	25	27	263	204	133	.329	.413	.480	132	79	21	17		.989	-14	1-426	4.2

YEAR	TM/L	G	AB	R	H	2B	3B	HR	RBI	BB	SO	AVG	OBP	SLG	PRO+	BR/A	SB	CS	SBR	FA	FR	G/POS	TPR

■ CHARLIE GRIMM Grimm, Charles John "Jolly Cholly" b: 8/28/1898, St.Louis, Mo. d: 11/15/83, Scottsdale, Ariz. BL/TL, 5'11.5", 173 lbs. Deb: 7/30/16 MC

YEAR	TM/L	G	AB	R	H	2B	3B	HR	RBI	BB	SO	AVG	OBP	SLG	PRO+	BR/A	SB	CS	SBR	FA	FR	G/POS	TPR
1916	Phi-A	12	22	0	2	0	0	0	0	2	4	.091	.167	.091	-24	-3	0			.875	-2	/O-7	-0.6
1918	StL-N	50	141	11	31	7	0	0	12	6	15	.220	.262	.270	64	-6	2			.971	-3	1-42/O-2,3-1	-1.2
1919	Pit-N	14	44	6	14	1	3	0	6	2	4	.318	.348	.477	141	2	1			.968	-3	1-13	-0.1
1920	Pit-N	148	533	38	121	13	7	2	54	30	40	.227	.273	.289	60	-28	7	8	-3	.995	4	*1-148	-3.2
1921	Pit-N	151	562	62	154	21	17	7	71	31	38	.274	.314	.409	88	-11	6	8	-3	.994	-6	*1-150	-2.4
1922	Pit-N	154	593	64	173	28	13	0	76	43	15	.292	.343	.383	86	-12	6	10	-4	.994	-4	*1-154	-2.6
1923	Pit-N	152	563	78	194	29	13	7	99	41	43	.345	.389	.480	125	20	6	9	-4	.995	2	*1-152	1.0
1924	Pit-N	151	542	53	156	25	12	2	63	37	22	.288	.336	.389	92	-6	3	6	-3	.995	-3	*1-151	-2.1
1925	Chi-N	141	519	73	159	29	5	10	76	38	25	.306	.354	.439	100	-1	4	3	-1	.989	0	*1-139	-0.8
1926	Chi-N	147	524	58	145	30	6	8	82	49	25	.277	.342	.403	99	-1	3			.988	-6	*1-147	-1.6
1927	Chi-N	147	543	68	169	29	6	2	74	45	21	.311	.367	.398	105	4	3			.990	-3	*1-147	-0.3
1928	Chi-N	147	547	67	161	25	5	5	62	39	20	.294	.342	.386	91	-7	7			.993	-2	*1-147	-2.2
1929	*Chi-N	120	463	66	138	28	3	10	91	42	25	.298	.358	.436	95	-4	3			.992	0	*1-120	-1.4
1930	Chi-N	114	429	58	124	27	2	6	66	41	26	.289	.359	.403	83	-11	1			.995	1	*1-113	-1.9
1931	Chi-N	146	531	65	176	33	11	4	66	53	29	.331	.393	.458	126	20	1			.993	2	*1-144	0.8
1932	*Chi-N	149	570	66	175	42	2	7	80	35	22	.307	.349	.425	108	6	2			.993	10	*1-149,M	0.5
1933	Chi-N	107	384	38	95	15	2	3	37	23	15	.247	.290	.320	74	-13	1			.996	9	*1-104,M	-1.4
1934	Chi-N	75	267	24	79	8	1	5	47	16	12	.296	.338	.390	96	-2	1			.995	1	1-74,M	-0.6
1935	Chi-N	2	8	0	0	0	0	0	0	0	1	.000	.000	.000	-99	-2	0			1.000	0	/1-2,M	-0.3
1936	Chi-N	39	132	13	33	4	0	1	16	5	8	.250	.277	.303	55	-8	0			1.000	5	1-35,M	-0.6
Total	20	2166	7917	908	2299	394	108	79	1078	578	410	.290	.341	.397	95	-63	57	44		.993	10	*1-2131/O-9,3-1	-21.0

■ MYRON GRIMSHAW Grimshaw, Myron Frederick b: 11/30/1875, St.Johnsville, N.Y d: 12/11/36, Canajoharie, N.Y. BB/TR, 6'1", 173 lbs. Deb: 4/25/05

YEAR	TM/L	G	AB	R	H	2B	3B	HR	RBI	BB	SO	AVG	OBP	SLG	PRO+	BR/A	SB	CS	SBR	FA	FR	G/POS	TPR
1905	Bos-A	85	285	39	68	8	2	4	35	21		.239	.293	.323	94	-2	4			.980	-5	1-74	-1.1
1906	Bos-A	110	428	46	124	16	12	0	48	23		.290	.332	.383	124	11	5			.987	-1	*1-110	0.7
1907	Bos-A	64	181	19	37	7	2	0	33	16		.204	.273	.265	72	-5	6			.980	-6	1-20,O-18/S-2	-1.4
Total	3	259	894	104	229	31	16	4	116	60		.256	.307	.340	104	3	15			.984	-12	1-204/O-18,S-2	-1.8

■ MARQUIS GRISSOM Grissom, Marquis Deon b: 4/17/67, Atlanta, Ga. BR/TR, 5'11", 190 lbs. Deb: 8/22/89

YEAR	TM/L	G	AB	R	H	2B	3B	HR	RBI	BB	SO	AVG	OBP	SLG	PRO+	BR/A	SB	CS	SBR	FA	FR	G/POS	TPR
1989	Mon-N	26	74	16	19	2	0	1	2	12	21	.257	.360	.324	96	0	1	0	0	.943	-4	O-23	-0.5
1990	Mon-N	98	288	42	74	14	2	3	29	27	40	.257	.321	.351	88	-5	22	2	5	.988	-4	O-87	-0.5
1991	Mon-N	148	558	73	149	23	9	6	39	34	89	.267	.310	.373	93	-6	76	17	13	.984	20	*O-138	2.4
1992	Mon-N	159	653	99	180	39	6	14	66	42	81	.276	.324	.418	110	7	78	13	16	.983	7	*O-157	2.8
1993	Mon-N★	157	630	104	188	27	2	19	95	52	76	.298	.355	.438	106	6	53	10	10	.984	15	*O-157	2.3
1994	Mon-N★	110	475	96	137	25	4	11	45	41	66	.288	.346	.427	99	-1	36	6	7	.985	16	*O-109	2.0
1995	*Atl-N	139	551	80	142	23	3	12	42	47	61	.258	.319	.376	80	-16	29	9	3	.994	11	*O-136	-0.5
1996	*Atl-N	158	671	106	207	32	10	23	74	41	73	.308	.351	.489	112	11	28	11	2	.997	9	*O-158	1.7
Total	8	995	3900	616	1096	185	36	89	392	296	507	.281	.334	.415	100	-5	323	68	56	.987	67	O-965	9.7

■ DICK GROAT Groat, Richard Morrow b: 11/4/30, Wilkinsburg, Pa. BR/TR, 5'11.5", 180 lbs. Deb: 6/19/52

YEAR	TM/L	G	AB	R	H	2B	3B	HR	RBI	BB	SO	AVG	OBP	SLG	PRO+	BR/A	SB	CS	SBR	FA	FR	G/POS	TPR
1952	Pit-N	95	384	38	109	6	1	1	29	19	27	.284	.319	.313	74	-13	2	4	-2	.952	1	S-94	-0.7
1955	Pit-N	151	521	45	139	28	2	4	51	38	26	.267	.318	.351	74	-16	0	2	-1	.961	15	*S-149	1.1
1956	Pit-N	142	520	40	142	19	3	0	37	35	25	.273	.319	.321	74	-18	0	3	-2	.954	-3	*S-141/3-2	-0.8
1957	Pit-N	125	501	58	158	30	5	7	54	27	28	.315	.354	.437	114	10	0	1	-1	.968	-1	*S-123/3-2	2.0
1958	Pit-N	151	584	67	175	36	9	3	66	23	32	.300	.331	.408	97	-4	2	2	-1	.975	3	*S-149	1.2
1959	Pit-N★	147	593	74	163	22	7	5	51	32	35	.275	.314	.361	80	-17	0	2	-1	.964	3	*S-145	-0.3
1960	*Pit-N★	138	573	85	186	26	4	2	50	39	35	.325	.372	.394	109	8	0	2	-1	.966	11	*S-136	2.9
1961	Pit-N	148	596	71	164	25	6	6	55	40	44	.275	.322	.367	82	-15	0	4	-2	.957	9	*S-144/3-1	0.4
1962	Pit-N★	161	678	76	199	34	3	2	61	31	61	.294	.327	.361	85	-15	2	1	0	.956	3	*S-161	1.4
1963	StL-N★	158	631	85	201	43	11	6	73	56	58	.319	.380	.450	126	22	3	1	0	.964	-13	*S-158	2.2
1964	*StL-N★	161	636	70	186	35	6	1	70	44	42	.292	.338	.371	92	-6	2	3	-1	.949	-12	*S-160	-0.9
1965	StL-N	153	587	55	149	26	5	0	52	56	50	.254	.320	.315	73	-20	1	1	0	.962	-8	*S-148/3-2	-2.0
1966	Phi-N	155	584	58	152	21	4	3	53	40	38	.260	.313	.320	77	-18	2	1	0	.974	11	*S-139,3-20/1-1	0.6
1967	Phi-N	10	26	3	3	0	0	0	1	4	4	.115	.233	.115	3	-3	0	0	0	.947	2	/S-6	-1.4
	SF-N	34	70	4	12	1	1	0	4	6	7	.171	.237	.214	30	-6	0	0	0	.912	-8	S-24/2-1	-1.4
	Yr	44	96	7	15	1	1	0	5	10	11	.156	.236	.188	23	-9	0	0	0	.925	-5	S-30/2-1	-1.4
Total	14	1929	7484	829	2138	352	67	39	707	490	512	.286	.332	.366	89	-112	14	27	-12	.961	28	*S-1877/3-27,2-1,1	5.7

■ HEINIE GROH Groh, Henry Knight b: 9/18/1889, Rochester, N.Y. d: 8/22/68, Cincinnati, Ohio BR/TR, 5'8", 158 lbs. Deb: 4/12/12 FM

YEAR	TM/L	G	AB	R	H	2B	3B	HR	RBI	BB	SO	AVG	OBP	SLG	PRO+	BR/A	SB	CS	SBR	FA	FR	G/POS	TPR
1912	NY-N	27	48	8	13	2	1	0	3	8	7	.271	.375	.354	97	1	6			.887	3	2-12/S-7,3-6	0.3
1913	NY-N	4	2	0	0	0	0	0	0	0	1	.000	.000	.000	-99	-1	0			1.000	1	/3-2,S-1	0.0
	Cin-N	117	397	51	112	19	5	3	48	38	36	.282	.351	.378	109	5	24			.963	10	*2-113/S-4	1.3
	Yr	121	399	51	112	19	5	3	48	38	37	.281	.349	.376	107	4	24			.963	10	*2-113/S-5,3-2	1.3
1914	Cin-N	139	455	59	131	18	4	2	32	64	28	.288	.391	.358	120	15	24			.936	-7	*2-134/S-2	0.7
1915	Cin-N	160	584	72	170	32	9	3	50	50	33	.291	.354	.390	123	17	12	17	-7	.969	11	*3-131,2-29	2.9
1916	Cin-N	149	553	85	149	24	14	2	28	84	34	.269	.370	.374	132	24	13			.957	19	*3-110,2-33/S-5	5.4
1917	Cin-N	156	599	91	182	39	11	1	53	71	30	.304	.385	.411	150	38	15			.966	8	*3-154/2-2	5.3
1918	Cin-N	126	493	86	158	28	1	1	37	54	24	.320	.395	.396	144	28	11			.969	2	*3-126,M	3.6
1919	*Cin-N	122	448	79	139	17	11	5	63	56	26	.310	.392	.431	151	29	21			.971	-2	*3-121	3.5
1920	Cin-N	145	550	86	164	28	12	0	49	60	29	.298	.375	.393	122	18	16	19	-7	.969	-6	*3-144/S-1	1.3
1921	Cin-N	97	357	54	118	19	6	0	48	36	17	.331	.398	.417	122	13	22	14	-2	.950	1	3-97	1.8
1922	*NY-N	115	426	63	113	21	3	3	51	53	21	.265	.353	.350	81	-10	5	6	-2	.965	-3	*3-110	-0.3
1923	*NY-N	123	465	91	135	22	5	4	48	60	43	.290	.379	.385	103	4	3	4	-2	.975	4	*3-145	1.6
1924	*NY-N	145	559	82	157	32	3	2	46	52	29	.281	.354	.360	94	-3	8	6	-1	.983	3	*3-145	1.0
1925	NY-N	25	65	7	15	4	0	0	4	6	3	.231	.296	.292	53	-5	0	0	0	.909	-6	3-16/2-2	-0.9
1926	NY-N	12	35	2	8	2	0	0	3	2	3	.229	.270	.286	50	-2	0			.950	-1	/3-7	-0.3
1927	*Pit-N	14	35	2	10	1	0	0	3	2	3	.286	.324	.314	67	-2	0			.958	-1	3-12	-0.2
Total	16	1676	6074	918	1774	308	87	26	566	696	345	.292	.373	.384	119	167	180	66		.967	39	*3-1299,2-325/S-20	27.0

■ LEW GROH Groh, Lewis Carl "Silver" b: 10/16/1883, Rochester, N.Y. d: 10/20/60, Rochester, N.Y. BR/TR, Deb: 8/2/19 F

YEAR	TM/L	G	AB	R	H	2B	3B	HR	RBI	BB	SO	AVG	OBP	SLG	PRO+	BR/A	SB	CS	SBR	FA	FR	G/POS	TPR
1919	Phi-A	2	4	0	0	0	0	0	0	0	2	.000	.000	.000	-99	-1	0			1.000	-0	/3-1	-0.1

■ HOWDY GROSKLOSS Groskloss, Howard Hoffman b: 4/9/07, Pittsburgh, Pa. BR/TR, 5'9", 176 lbs. Deb: 6/23/30

YEAR	TM/L	G	AB	R	H	2B	3B	HR	RBI	BB	SO	AVG	OBP	SLG	PRO+	BR/A	SB	CS	SBR	FA	FR	G/POS	TPR
1930	Pit-N	2	3	0	1	0	0	0	0	0	0	.333	.333	.333	62	-0	0			.000	-1	/S-1	-0.1
1931	Pit-N	53	161	13	45	7	2	0	20	11	16	.280	.326	.348	82	-4	0			.981	-1	2-39/S-3	-0.3
1932	Pit-N	17	20	1	2	0	0	0	1	0	3	.100	.100	.100	-47	-4	0			.800	-1	/S-1	-0.5
Total	3	72	184	14	48	7	2	0	21	11	19	.261	.303	.321	68	-8	1			.700	-3	/2-39,S-5	-0.9

■ EMIL GROSS Gross, Emil Michael b: 3/3/1858, Chicago, Ill. d: 8/24/21, Eagle River, Wis. BR/TR, 6', 190 lbs. Deb: 8/13/1879

YEAR	TM/L	G	AB	R	H	2B	3B	HR	RBI	BB	SO	AVG	OBP	SLG	PRO+	BR/A	SB	CS	SBR	FA	FR	G/POS	TPR
1879	Pro-N	30	132	31	46	9	5	0	24	4	8	.348	.368	.492	183	12				.897	-5	C-30	0.7
1880	Pro-N	87	347	43	90	18	3	1	34	16	15	.259	.292	.337	116	6				.866	-14	*C-87	-0.6
1881	Pro-N	51	182	15	50	9	4	1	24	13	11	.275	.323	.385	124	6				.893	-4	C-50/O-1	0.3
1883	Phi-N	57	231	39	71	25	7	1	25	12	18	.307	.342	.489	163	18				.789	-24	C-55/O-2	-0.3
1884	CP-U	23	95	13	34	6	2	4		6		.358	.396	.589	196	8				.860	-3	C-15/O-9	0.6
Total	5	248	987	141	291	67	21	7	107	51	52	.295	.329	.427	146	49				.859	-50	C-237/O-12	0.7

■ TURKEY GROSS Gross, Ewell b: 2/21/1896, Mesquite, Tex. d: 1/11/36, Dallas, Tex. BR/TR, 6', 165 lbs. Deb: 4/14/25

YEAR	TM/L	G	AB	R	H	2B	3B	HR	RBI	BB	SO	AVG	OBP	SLG	PRO+	BR/A	SB	CS	SBR	FA	FR	G/POS	TPR
1925	Bos-A	9	32	2	3	1	0	0	2	2	2	.094	.171	.156	-16	-6	0	0	0	.976	-1	/S-9	-0.5

YEAR	TM/L	G	AB	R	H	2B	3B	HR	RBI	BB	SO	AVG	OBP	SLG	PRO+	BR/A	SB	CS	SBR	FA	FR	G/POS	TPR

■ GREG GROSS   Gross, Gregory Eugene   b: 8/1/52, York, Pa.   BL/TL, 5'11", 175 lbs.   Deb: 9/5/73

YEAR	TM/L	G	AB	R	H	2B	3B	HR	RBI	BB	SO	AVG	OBP	SLG	PRO+	BR/A	SB	CS	SBR	FA	FR	G/POS	TPR
1973	Hou-N	14	39	5	9	2	1	0	1	4	4	.231	.302	.333	76	-1	2	1	0	1.000	1	/O-9	-0.1
1974	Hou-N	156	589	78	185	21	8	0	36	76	39	.314	.393	.377	121	20	12	20	-8	.994	-9	*O-151	-0.5
1975	Hou-N	132	483	67	142	14	10	0	41	63	37	.294	.375	.364	114	11	2	2	-1	.958	5	O-121	1.0
1976	Hou-N	128	426	52	122	12	3	0	27	64	39	.286	.380	.329	112	10	2	6	-3	.978	3	*O-115	0.5
1977	Chi-N	115	239	43	77	10	4	5	32	33	19	.322	.404	.460	118	7	0	1	-1	.991	-8	O-71	-0.4
1978	Chi-N	124	347	34	92	12	7	1	39	33	19	.265	.329	.349	80	-9	3	1	0	.979	-14	*O-111	-2.8
1979	Phi-N	111	174	21	58	6	3	0	15	29	5	.333	.429	.402	124	7	5	2	0	.978	-12	O-73	-0.6
1980	*Phi-N	127	154	19	37	7	2	0	12	24	7	.240	.346	.312	80	-3	1	1	-0	.973	-22	O-91/1-1	-2.9
1981	*Phi-N	83	102	14	23	6	1	0	7	15	5	.225	.325	.304	76	-3	2	2	-1	.982	-7	O-55	-1.2
1982	Phi-N	119	134	14	40	4	0	0	10	19	8	.299	.386	.328	99	1	4	3	-1	.983	-18	O-71	-1.9
1983	*Phi-N	136	245	25	74	12	3	0	29	34	15	.302	.389	.376	114	6	3	5	-2	.991	-28	*O-110/1-1	-2.7
1984	Phi-N	112	202	19	65	9	1	0	16	24	11	.322	.396	.376	116	5	1	0	-0	.986	-4	O-48,1-28	0.0
1985	Phi-N	93	169	21	44	5	2	0	14	32	9	.260	.378	.314	93	-0	1	0	0	1.000	-9	O-52/1-8	-0.8
1986	Phi-N	87	101	11	25	5	0	0	8	21	11	.248	.382	.297	87	-1	1	0	0	1.000	-3	O-27/1-5,P-1	-0.4
1987	Phi-N	114	133	14	38	4	1	1	12	25	12	.286	.403	.353	99	1	0	0	0	1.000	-12	O-50,1-11	-1.2
1988	Phi-N	98	133	10	27	1	0	0	5	16	3	.203	.289	.211	46	-9	0	0	0	1.000	-11	O-37,1-14	-2.3
1989	Hou-N	60	75	2	15	0	0	0	4	11	6	.200	.310	.200	51	-4	0	0	0	.929	-3	O-12/1-6,P-1	-0.8
Total	17	1809	3745	449	1073	130	46	7	308	523	250	.287	.375	.351	103	38	39	44	-15	.982	-148	*O-1204/1-74,P-2	-17.1

■ WAYNE GROSS   Gross, Wayne Dale   b: 1/14/52, Riverside, Cal.   BL/TR, 6'2", 210 lbs.   Deb: 8/21/76

YEAR	TM/L	G	AB	R	H	2B	3B	HR	RBI	BB	SO	AVG	OBP	SLG	PRO+	BR/A	SB	CS	SBR	FA	FR	G/POS	TPR
1976	Oak-A	10	18	0	4	0	0	0	1	2	1	.222	.300	.222	57	-1	0	0	0	.966	-1	/1-3,O-2,D-3	-0.2
1977	Oak-A☆	146	485	66	113	21	1	22	63	86	84	.233	.354	.416	111	9	5	4	-1	.932	-23	*3-145/1-1	-1.7
1978	Oak-A	118	285	18	57	10	2	7	23	40	63	.200	.309	.323	82	-6	0	2	-1	.917	-8	*3-106,1-15	-1.7
1979	Oak-A	138	442	54	99	19	1	14	50	72	62	.224	.334	.367	94	-3	4	3	-1	.943	-10	*3-120,1-18/O-2	-1.5
1980	Oak-A	113	366	45	103	20	3	14	61	44	39	.281	.360	.467	134	17	5	3	-0	.948	-28	3-99,1-10/D-1	-1.3
1981	*Oak-A	82	243	29	50	7	1	10	31	34	28	.206	.308	.366	98	-0	2	1	0	.946	-9	3-73/1-2,D-1	-1.2
1982	Oak-A	129	386	43	97	14	0	9	41	53	50	.251	.345	.358	98	-0	3	1	0	.970	-7	*3-108,1-16/D-1	-1.0
1983	Oak-A	137	339	34	79	18	0	12	44	36	52	.233	.312	.392	98	-1	3	5	-2	.996	-5	1-74,3-67/P-1,D-1	-1.2
1984	Bal-A	127	342	53	74	9	1	22	64	68	67	.216	.348	.442	119	10	1	2	-1	.937	-5	*3-117/1-3,D-1	0.3
1985	Bal-A	103	217	31	51	8	0	11	18	46	48	.235	.369	.424	120	7	1	1	-0	.933	-0	3-67,D-10/1-9	0.5
1986	Oak-A	2	0	0	0	0	0	0	0	1	0	—	.333	.000	-0	-0	0	0	0	/3-1	0		-0.0
Total	11	1106	3125	373	727	126	9	121	396	482	496	.233	.339	.395	106	31	24	22	-6	.941	-96	3-903,1-151/DOP	-9.1

■ GEORGE GROSSART   Grossart, George Albert   b: 4/11/1880, Meadville, Pa.   d: 4/18/02, Pittsburgh, Pa.   Deb: 6/7/01

YEAR	TM/L	G	AB	R	H	2B	3B	HR	RBI	BB	SO	AVG	OBP	SLG	PRO+	BR/A	SB	CS	SBR	FA	FR	G/POS	TPR
1901	Bos-N	7	26	4	3	0	1	0	1	0		.115	.115	.115	-30	-4	0			1.000	0	/O-7	-0.5

■ JERRY GROTE   Grote, Gerald Wayne   b: 10/6/42, San Antonio, Tex.   BR/TR, 5'10", 190 lbs.   Deb: 9/21/63

YEAR	TM/L	G	AB	R	H	2B	3B	HR	RBI	BB	SO	AVG	OBP	SLG	PRO+	BR/A	SB	CS	SBR	FA	FR	G/POS	TPR
1963	Hou-N	3	5	0	1	0	0	0	1	1	3	.200	.333	.200	61	-0	0	0	0	1.000	-1	/C-3	-0.1
1964	Hou-N	100	298	26	54	9	3	3	24	20	75	.181	.242	.262	44	-22	0	2	-1	.985	2	C-98	-1.8
1966	NY-N	120	317	26	75	12	2	3	31	40	81	.237	.328	.315	82	-7	4	3	-1	.981	5	*C-115/3-2	-0.1
1967	NY-N	120	344	25	67	8	0	4	23	14	65	.195	.228	.253	38	-28	2	2	-1	.990	7	*C-119	-2.3
1968	NY-N★	124	404	29	114	18	0	3	31	44	81	.282	.357	.349	112	7	1	5	-3	.994	7	*C-115	2.3
1969	*NY-N	113	365	38	92	12	3	6	40	32	59	.252	.314	.351	84	-8	0	1	-1	.991	19	*C-112	1.8
1970	NY-N	126	415	38	106	14	1	2	34	36	39	.255	.316	.308	68	-18	2	1	0	.991	10	*C-125	-0.2
1971	NY-N	125	403	35	109	25	0	2	35	40	47	.270	.339	.347	96	-1	1	4	-2	.990	5	*C-122	0.7
1972	NY-N	64	205	15	43	5	1	3	21	26	27	.210	.308	.288	72	-7	1	0	0	.998	3	C-59/3-3,O-1	-0.1
1973	*NY-N	84	285	17	73	10	2	1	32	13	23	.256	.291	.316	69	-12	0	1	0	.995	9	C-81/3-2	0.0
1974	NY-N★	97	319	25	82	8	1	5	36	33	33	.257	.331	.335	88	-5	0	1	-1	.988	3	C-94	-0.5
1975	NY-N	119	386	28	114	14	5	2	39	38	23	.295	.360	.373	109	5	0	1	-1	**.995**	6	*C-111	1.6
1976	NY-N	101	323	30	88	14	2	4	28	38	19	.272	.351	.365	110	5	1	2	-1	.993	12	C-95/O-2	1.9
1977	NY-N	42	115	8	31	3	1	0	7	9	12	.270	.333	.313	78	-3	0	0	0	1.000	-2	C-28,3-11	-0.5
	*LA-N	18	27	3	7	0	0	0	4	2	5	.259	.310	.259	55	-2	0	1	-1	1.000	4	C-16/3-2	0.2
	Yr	60	142	11	38	3	1	0	11	11	17	.268	.329	.303	73	-5	0	1	-1	1.000	2	C-44,3-13	-0.3
1978	*LA-N	41	70	5	19	5	0	0	9	10	5	.271	.363	.343	98	0	0	0	0	.985	8	C-32/3-7	0.9
1981	KC-A	22	56	4	17	3	1	1	9	3	2	.304	.350	.446	129	2	1	0	0	1.000	4	C-22	0.7
	LA-N	2	2	0	0	0	0	0	0	0	1	.000	.000	.000	-99	-1	0	0	0	1.000	0	/C-1	0.0
Total	16	1421	4339	352	1092	160	22	39	404	399	600	.252	.326	.326	83	-95	15	23	-15	.991	85	*C-1348/3-27,O-3	4.5

■ JEFF GROTEWOLD   Grotewold, Jeffrey Scott   b: 12/8/65, Madera, Cal.   BL/TR, 6', 215 lbs.   Deb: 4/12/92

YEAR	TM/L	G	AB	R	H	2B	3B	HR	RBI	BB	SO	AVG	OBP	SLG	PRO+	BR/A	SB	CS	SBR	FA	FR	G/POS	TPR
1992	Phi-N	72	65	7	13	2	0	3	5	9	16	.200	.307	.369	91	-1	0	0	0	1.000	-1	/C-2,O-2,1-1	-0.2
1995	KC-A	15	36	4	10	1	0	1	6	9	7	.278	.422	.389	111	1	0	0	0	.750	-0	D-11/1-1	0.0
Total	2	87	101	11	23	3	0	4	11	18	23	.228	.350	.376	99	-0	0	0	0	.833	-2	/D-11,1-2,O-2,C-2	-0.2

■ JOHNNY GROTH   Groth, John Thomas   b: 7/23/26, Chicago, Ill.   BR/TR, 6', 182 lbs.   Deb: 9/5/46

YEAR	TM/L	G	AB	R	H	2B	3B	HR	RBI	BB	SO	AVG	OBP	SLG	PRO+	BR/A	SB	CS	SBR	FA	FR	G/POS	TPR
1946	Det-A	4	9	1	0	0	0	0	0	0	3	.000	.000	.000	-94	-2	0	0	0	1.000	-1	/O-4	-0.4
1947	Det-A	2	4	1	1	0	0	0	0	2	1	.250	.500	.250	109	0	0	0	0	1.000	1	/O-1	0.1
1948	Det-A	6	17	3	8	3	0	1	5	1	1	.471	.500	.824	242	3	0	0	0	.900	0	/O-4	0.3
1949	Det-A	103	348	60	102	19	5	11	73	65	27	.293	.407	.471	132	17	3	7	-3	.966	1	O-99	0.9
1950	Det-A	157	566	95	173	30	8	12	85	95	45	.306	.407	.451	116	16	1	5	-3	.985	-12	*O-157	-0.6
1951	Det-A	118	428	41	128	29	1	3	49	31	32	.299	.349	.393	100	-1	1	1	-0	**.993**	-1	*O-112	-0.5
1952	Det-A	141	524	56	149	22	2	4	51	51	39	.284	.348	.351	96	-3	2	10	-5	.986	0	*O-139	-1.4
1953	StL-A	141	557	65	141	27	4	10	57	42	53	.253	.308	.370	81	-16	2	5	-2	.991	17	*O-141	-0.7
1954	Chi-A	125	422	41	116	20	0	7	60	42	37	.275	.343	.372	93	-4	3	9	-5	.988	-1	*O-125	-1.5
1955	Chi-A	32	77	13	26	7	0	2	11	6	12	.338	.386	.506	135	3	1	0	0	1.000	-0	O-26	0.2
	Was-A	63	183	22	40	4	5	2	17	18	18	.219	.289	.328	69	-9	2	0	1	.984	-1	O-48	-1.1
	Yr	95	260	35	66	11	5	4	28	24	31	.254	.317	.381	89	-5	3	0	1	.989	-1	O-74	-0.9
1956	KC-A	95	244	22	63	13	3	5	37	30	31	.258	.339	.398	94	-2	1	2	-1	1.000	-7	O-84	-1.4
1957	KC-A	55	59	10	15	0	0	0	2	7	6	.254	.333	.254	62	-3	0	0	0	.974	-13	O-50	-0.5
	Det-A	38	103	11	30	10	0	0	16	6	7	.291	.336	.388	95	-1	0	0	0	.991	-16	O-36	-0.5
	Yr	93	162	21	45	10	0	0	18	13	13	.278	.335	.340	83	-4	0	0	0	.991	-16	O-86	-2.2
1958	Det-A	88	146	24	41	5	2	1	11	13	19	.281	.340	.384	92	-2	0	1	-0	.990	-11	O-80	-1.6
1959	Det-A	55	102	12	24	7	1	1	10	7	14	.235	.284	.353	70	-4	0	0	0	.983	-6	O-41	-1.2
1960	Det-A	25	19	3	7	1	0	0	4	3	4	.368	.455	.421	135	1	0	0	0	1.000	-3	/O-8	-0.2
Total	15	1248	3808	480	1064	197	31	60	486	419	329	.279	.353	.395	99	-5	19	42	-20	.987	-40	*O-1155	-11.3

■ ROY GROVER   Grover, Roy Arthur   b: 1/17/1892, Snohomish, Wash.   d: 2/7/78, Milwaukie, Ore.   BR/TR, 5'8", 150 lbs.   Deb: 9/13/16

YEAR	TM/L	G	AB	R	H	2B	3B	HR	RBI	BB	SO	AVG	OBP	SLG	PRO+	BR/A	SB	CS	SBR	FA	FR	G/POS	TPR
1916	Phi-A	20	77	8	21	1	2	0	7	6	10	.273	.325	.338	104	-7	0	5		.952	-7	2-20	-0.7
1917	Phi-A	141	482	45	108	15	7	0	34	43	53	.224	.292	.284	77	-14	12			.960	5	*2-139	-0.2
1919	Phi-A	22	56	8	13	1	0	0	2	5	6	.232	.295	.250	53	-3	0			.915	-6	2-12/3-3	-0.9
	Was-A	24	75	6	14	1	0	0	7	6	10	.187	.256	.187	25	-7	2			.947	-4	2-24	-1.1
	Yr	46	131	14	27	1	0	0	9	11	16	.206	.273	.214	37	-11	2			.936	-10	2-36/3-3	-2.0
Total	3	207	690	67	156	17	9	0	50	60	79	.226	.292	.277	72	-24	19			.956	-12	2-195/3-3	-2.9

■ HARVEY GRUBB   Grubb, Harvey Harrison   b: 9/18/1890, Lexington, N.C.   d: 1/25/70, Corpus Christi, Tex.   BR/TR, 6', 165 lbs.   Deb: 9/27/12

YEAR	TM/L	G	AB	R	H	2B	3B	HR	RBI	BB	SO	AVG	OBP	SLG	PRO+	BR/A	SB	CS	SBR	FA	FR	G/POS	TPR
1912	Cle-A	1	0	0	0	0	0	0	0	0	0	—	1.000	—	187	0	0			1.000	0	/3-1	0.0

■ JOHNNY GRUBB   Grubb, John Maywood   b: 8/4/48, Richmond, Va.   BL/TR, 6'3", 188 lbs.   Deb: 9/10/72

YEAR	TM/L	G	AB	R	H	2B	3B	HR	RBI	BB	SO	AVG	OBP	SLG	PRO+	BR/A	SB	CS	SBR	FA	FR	G/POS	TPR
1972	SD-N	7	21	4	7	1	1	0	1	1	3	.333	.364	.476	147	1	0	1	-1	1.000	0	/O-6	0.1
1973	SD-N	113	389	52	121	22	3	8	37	37	50	.311	.374	.445	137	19	9	3	1	.988	7	*O-102/3-2	2.2
1974	SD-N★	140	444	53	127	20	4	8	42	46	47	.286	.358	.403	118	10	4	0	1	.976	12	*O-122/3-2	1.9

YEAR	TM/L	G	AB	R	H	2B	3B	HR	RBI	BB	SO	AVG	OBP	SLG	PRO+	BR/A	SB	CS	SBR	FA	FR	G/POS	TPR
1975	SD-N	144	553	72	149	36	2	4	38	59	59	.269	.345	.363	103	2	2	7	-4	.991	-4	*O-139	-1.1
1976	SD-N	109	384	54	109	22	1	5	27	65	53	.284	.393	.385	132	19	1	2	-1	.974	-9	O-98/1-9,3-3	0.4
1977	Cle-A	34	93	8	28	3	3	2	14	19	18	.301	.425	.462	146	7	0	3	-2	1.000	-0	O-28/D-4	0.4
1978	Cle-A	113	378	54	100	16	6	14	61	59	60	.265	.367	.450	130	16	5	1	1	.973	5	*O-110	1.8
	Tex-A	21	33	8	13	3	0	1	6	11	5	.394	.545	.576	215	6	1	1	-0	1.000	-1	O-13/D-3	0.5
	Yr	134	411	62	113	19	6	15	67	70	65	.275	.383	.460	137	22	6	2	1	.974	5	*O-123/D-3	2.3
1979	Tex-A	102	289	42	79	14	0	10	37	34	44	.273	.352	.426	110	4	2	4	-2	.986	-8	O-82	-0.8
1980	Tex-A	110	274	40	76	12	1	9	32	42	35	.277	.377	.427	124	10	2	3	-1	.952	-7	O-77/D-8	0.0
1981	Tex-A	67	199	26	46	9	1	3	26	23	25	.231	.317	.332	92	-2	0	3	-2	.990	-4	O-58	-1.0
1982	Tex-A	103	308	35	86	13	3	3	26	39	37	.279	.371	.370	110	6	0	3	-2	.965	-6	O-77,D-18	-0.4
1983	Det-A	57	134	20	34	5	2	4	22	28	17	.254	.390	.410	124	6	0	0	0	1.000	-3	O-26,D-18	0.1
1984	*Det-A	86	176	25	47	5	0	8	17	36	36	.267	.397	.432	130	9	1	0	0	1.000	-6	O-36,D-33	0.2
1985	Det-A	78	155	19	38	7	1	5	25	24	25	.245	.350	.400	106	2	0	1	-1	1.000	-3	D-33,O-18	-0.2
1986	Det-A	81	210	32	70	13	1	13	51	28	28	.333	.417	.590	171	21	0	1	-1	1.000	-2	D-52,O-19	1.6
1987	*Det-A	59	114	9	23	6	0	2	13	15	16	.202	.295	.307	63	-6	0	0	0	1.000	-4	O-31,D-16/3-1	-1.0
Total	16	1424	4154	553	1153	207	29	99	475	566	558	.278	.369	.413	121	130	27	33	-12	.981	-31	*O-1042,D-185/1-9,3	4.7

■ FRANK GRUBE
Grube, Franklin Thomas "Hans" b: 1/7/05, Easton, Pa. d: 7/2/45, New York, N.Y. BR/TR, 5'9", 190 lbs. Deb: 5/12/31

YEAR	TM/L	G	AB	R	H	2B	3B	HR	RBI	BB	SO	AVG	OBP	SLG	PRO+	BR/A	SB	CS	SBR	FA	FR	G/POS	TPR
1931	Chi-A	88	265	29	58	13	2	1	24	22	22	.219	.284	.294	55	-18	2	2	-1	.977	-10	C-81	-2.2
1932	Chi-A	93	277	36	78	16	2	0	31	33	13	.282	.362	.354	92	-2	6	1	1	.957	-2	C-92	-0.2
1933	Chi-A	85	256	23	59	13	0	0	23	38	20	.230	.334	.281	67	-11	1	1	-0	.984	-7	C-83	-1.3
1934	StL-A	65	170	22	49	10	0	0	11	24	11	.288	.379	.347	82	-4	2	1	0	.963	-0	C-55	-0.2
1935	StL-A	3	6	3	2	1	0	0	0	0	1	.333	.333	.500	108	0	0	0	0	1.000	-0	/C-3	0.0
	Chi-A	9	19	1	7	2	0	0	6	3	2	.368	.455	.474	137	1	0	0	0	.944	3	/C-9	0.4
	Yr	12	25	4	9	3	0	0	6	3	3	.360	.429	.480	131	1	0	0	0	.955	3	C-12	0.4
1936	Chi-A	33	93	6	15	2	1	0	11	9	15	.161	.235	.204	9	-14	1	0	0	.991	2	C-32	-0.9
1941	StL-A	18	39	1	6	2	0	1	4	2	4	.154	.195	.205	6	-5	0	0	0	.951	3	C-18	-0.2
Total	7	394	1125	121	274	59	5	1	107	131	88	.244	.326	.308	67	-52	12	5	1	.970	-13	C-373	-4.2

■ KELLY GRUBER
Gruber, Kelly Wayne b: 2/26/62, Houston, Tex. BR/TR, 6', 185 lbs. Deb: 4/20/84

YEAR	TM/L	G	AB	R	H	2B	3B	HR	RBI	BB	SO	AVG	OBP	SLG	PRO+	BR/A	SB	CS	SBR	FA	FR	G/POS	TPR
1984	Tor-A	15	16	1	1	0	0	1	2	0	5	.063	.063	.250	-18	-3	0	0	0	.933	1	3-12/O-2,S-1	-0.1
1985	Tor-A	5	13	0	3	0	0	0	1	0	3	.231	.231	.231	26	-1	0	0	0	1.000	-1	/3-5,2-1	-0.2
1986	Tor-A	87	143	20	28	4	1	5	15	5	27	.196	.223	.343	50	-10	2	5	-2	.940	1	3-42,2-14,D-14,/OS	-0.6
1987	Tor-A	138	341	50	80	14	3	12	36	17	70	.235	.285	.399	77	-12	12	2	2	.948	8	*3-119,S-21/2-7,OD	-0.2
1988	Tor-A	158	569	75	158	33	5	16	81	38	92	.278	.331	.438	113	9	23	5	4	.971	25	*3-156/2-7,O-2,SD	3.7
1989	*Tor-A☆	135	545	83	158	24	4	18	73	30	60	.290	.330	.448	120	12	10	5	0	.945	19	*3-119,O-16/S-1,D-1	3.2
1990	Tor-A★	150	592	92	162	36	6	31	118	48	94	.274	.336	.512	132	23	14	2	3	.953	-3	*3-145/O-6,D-1	2.0
1991	*Tor-A	113	429	58	108	18	2	20	65	31	70	.252	.311	.443	102	0	12	7	-1	.962	4	*3-111/D-2	0.4
1992	*Tor-A	120	446	42	102	16	3	11	43	26	72	.229	.277	.352	72	-18	7	7	-2	.949	-4	*3-120	-2.4
1993	Cal-A	18	65	10	18	3	0	3	9	2	11	.277	.309	.462	101	-0	0	0	0	.938	6	3-17/O-1,D-1	0.0
Total	10	939	3159	431	818	148	24	117	443	197	504	.259	.310	.432	102	-1	80	33	4	.955	64	3-846/O-38,2-29,SD	6.7

■ MARK GRUDZIELANEK
Grudzielanek, Mark James b: 6/30/70, Milwaukee, Wis. BR/TR, 6'1", 185 lbs. Deb: 4/28/95

YEAR	TM/L	G	AB	R	H	2B	3B	HR	RBI	BB	SO	AVG	OBP	SLG	PRO+	BR/A	SB	CS	SBR	FA	FR	G/POS	TPR
1995	Mon-N	78	269	27	66	12	2	1	20	14	47	.245	.300	.316	60	-15	8	3	1	.987	7	S-34,3-31,2-13	-0.4
1996	Mon-N★	153	657	99	201	34	4	6	49	26	83	.306	.341	.397	92	-8	33	7	6	.959	-11	*S-153	0.1
Total	2	231	926	126	267	46	6	7	69	40	130	.288	.329	.374	82	-23	41	10	6	.964	-4	S-187/3-31,2-13	-0.3

■ SIG GRYSKA
Gryska, Sigmund Stanley b: 11/4/15, Chicago, Ill. BR/TR, 5'11.5", 173 lbs. Deb: 9/28/38

YEAR	TM/L	G	AB	R	H	2B	3B	HR	RBI	BB	SO	AVG	OBP	SLG	PRO+	BR/A	SB	CS	SBR	FA	FR	G/POS	TPR
1938	StL-A	7	21	3	10	2	1	0	4	3	3	.476	.542	.667	202	3	0	0	0	.912	1	/S-7	0.4
1939	StL-A	18	49	4	13	2	0	0	8	10	10	.265	.345	.306	66	-2	3	1	0	.873	-4	S-14	-0.5
Total	2	25	70	7	23	4	1	0	12	9	13	.329	.405	.414	107	1	3	1	0	.887	-4	/S-21	-0.1

■ MARV GUDAT
Gudat, Marvin John b: 8/27/05, Goliad, Tex. d: 3/1/54, Los Angeles, Cal. BL/TL, 5'11", 162 lbs. Deb: 5/21/29

YEAR	TM/L	G	AB	R	H	2B	3B	HR	RBI	BB	SO	AVG	OBP	SLG	PRO+	BR/A	SB	CS	SBR	FA	FR	G/POS	TPR
1929	Cin-N	9	10	0	2	0	0	0	0	2	0	.200	.200	.200	-1	-2				.800	-1	/P-7	0.0
1932	*Chi-N	60	94	15	24	4	1	1	15	16	10	.255	.369	.351	96	0			0	.933	-6	O-14/1-8,P-1	-0.7
Total	2	69	104	15	26	4	1	1	15	16	10	.250	.355	.337	87	-1			0	.800	-6	/O-14,1-8,P-8	-0.7

■ MIKE GUERRA
Guerra, Fermin (Romero) b: 10/11/12, Havana, Cuba d: 10/9/92, Miami Beach, Fla. BR/TR, 5'9", 162 lbs. Deb: 9/19/37

YEAR	TM/L	G	AB	R	H	2B	3B	HR	RBI	BB	SO	AVG	OBP	SLG	PRO+	BR/A	SB	CS	SBR	FA	FR	G/POS	TPR
1937	Was-A	1	3	0	0	0	0	0	0	0	2	.000	.000	.000	-99	-1	0	0	0	.750	-1	/C-1	-0.1
1944	Was-A	75	210	29	59	7	2	1	29	13	14	.281	.323	.348	96	-2	8	2	1	.960	-5	C-58/O-1	-0.2
1945	Was-A	56	138	11	29	1	1	1	15	10	12	.210	.268	.254	57	-8	4	1	1	.990	5	C-38	0.0
1946	Was-A	41	83	3	21	2	1	0	4	5	6	.253	.295	.301	71	-3	1	0	0	.938	-2	C-27	-0.4
1947	Phi-A	72	209	20	45	2	2	0	18	10	11	.215	.251	.244	37	-18	1	2	-1	.964	1	C-62	-1.3
1948	Phi-A	53	142	18	30	4	2	1	23	18	13	.211	.300	.289	57	-9	2	3	-1	.973	-0	C-47	-0.7
1949	Phi-A	98	298	41	79	14	1	3	31	37	26	.265	.346	.349	87	-6	3	0	1	.982	-3	C-95	-0.2
1950	Phi-A	87	252	25	71	10	4	2	26	16	12	.282	.325	.377	81	-8	1	0	0	.990	-6	C-78	-1.0
1951	Bos-A	10	32	1	5	0	0	0	2	6	5	.156	.289	.156	21	-3	1	0	0	1.000	-1	C-10/1-1	-0.3
	Was-A	72	214	20	43	2	1	1	20	16	18	.201	.257	.234	34	-20	4	4	-1	.977	-11	C-66	-2.9
	Yr	82	246	21	48	2	1	1	22	22	23	.195	.261	.224	32	-23	5	4	-1	.982	-11	C-76	-3.2
Total	9	565	1581	168	382	42	14	9	168	131	123	.242	.300	.303	65	-77	25	12	0	.975	-20	C-482/O-1	-7.1

■ JUAN GUERRERO
Guerrero, Juan Antonio b: 2/1/67, Los Llanos, D.R. BR/TR, 5'11", 160 lbs. Deb: 4/9/92

YEAR	TM/L	G	AB	R	H	2B	3B	HR	RBI	BB	SO	AVG	OBP	SLG	PRO+	BR/A	SB	CS	SBR	FA	FR	G/POS	TPR
1992	Hou-N	79	125	8	25	4	2	1	14	10	32	.200	.256	.288	59	-7	1	0	0	.980	-7	S-19,3-12/O-3,2-2	-1.4

■ MARIO GUERRERO
Guerrero, Mario Miguel (Abud) b: 9/28/49, Santo Domingo, D.R. BR/TR, 5'10", 155 lbs. Deb: 4/8/73

YEAR	TM/L	G	AB	R	H	2B	3B	HR	RBI	BB	SO	AVG	OBP	SLG	PRO+	BR/A	SB	CS	SBR	FA	FR	G/POS	TPR
1973	Bos-A	66	219	19	51	5	2	0	11	10	21	.233	.273	.274	51	-14	2	1	-1	.974	1	S-46,2-24	-0.8
1974	Bos-A	93	284	18	70	6	2	0	23	13	22	.246	.284	.282	59	-15	3	1	0	.969	-0	S-93	-0.4
1975	StL-N	64	184	17	44	9	0	0	11	10	7	.239	.286	.288	57	-11	0	0	0	.955	6	S-64	0.1
1976	Cal-A	83	268	24	76	12	0	1	18	7	12	.284	.309	.340	96	-2	0	0	0	.973	-12	2-41,S-41/D-7	-0.9
1977	Cal-A	86	244	17	69	8	2	1	28	4	16	.283	.294	.344	76	-8	0	0	0	.985	-2	S-31,D-19,2-12	-0.7
1978	Oak-A	143	505	27	139	18	4	3	38	15	35	.275	.304	.345	87	-10	0	5	-3	.958	-40	*S-142	-3.7
1979	Oak-A	46	166	12	38	5	0	0	18	6	7	.229	.256	.259	42	-14	0	1	0	.952	-4	S-43	-1.4
1980	Oak-A	116	381	32	91	16	2	2	23	19	32	.239	.277	.307	64	-19	3	3	-1	.962	-42	*S-116	-5.0
Total	8	697	2251	166	578	79	12	7	170	84	152	.257	.288	.312	69	-93	8	12	-5	.961	-95	S-576/2-77,D-26	-12.8

■ PEDRO GUERRERO
Guerrero, Pedro b: 6/29/56, San Pedro De Macoris, D.R. BR/TR, 6', 195 lbs. Deb: 9/22/78

YEAR	TM/L	G	AB	R	H	2B	3B	HR	RBI	BB	SO	AVG	OBP	SLG	PRO+	BR/A	SB	CS	SBR	FA	FR	G/POS	TPR
1978	LA-N	5	8	3	5	0	1	0	1	0	0	.625	.625	.875	316	2	0	0	0	1.000	0	/1-4	0.2
1979	LA-N	25	62	7	15	2	0	2	9	1	14	.242	.254	.371	69	-3	2	0	1	1.000	-3	O-12/1-8,3-3	-0.6
1980	LA-N	75	183	27	59	9	1	7	31	12	31	.322	.364	.497	141	9	2	1	0	.987	-6	O-40,2-12/3-3,1-2	0.6
1981	*LA-N★	98	347	46	104	17	2	12	48	34	57	.300	.366	.464	139	17	5	9	-4	.974	-3	O-75,3-21/1-1	1.4
1982	LA-N	150	575	87	175	27	5	32	100	65	89	.304	.380	.536	157	43	22	5	3	.976	2	*O-137,3-24	4.6
1983	*LA-N★	160	584	87	174	28	6	32	103	72	110	.298	.377	.531	150	38	23	7	3	.934	6	*3-157/1-2	4.6
1984	LA-N	144	535	85	162	29	4	16	72	49	105	.303	.362	.462	132	22	9	4	3	.917	-8	3-76,O-58,1-16	0.8
1985	*LA-N†	137	487	99	156	22	2	33	87	83	68	.320	**.425**	**.577**	183	56	12	4	1	.974	8	O-81,3-44,1-12	6.3
1986	LA-N	31	61	7	15	0	0	5	10	7	15	.246	.281	.541	131	6	0	0	0	1.000	-2	O-10/1-4	-0.1
1987	LA-N	152	545	89	184	25	2	27	89	74	85	.338	.421	.539	156	46	9	7	2	.971	1	*O-109,1-40	3.8
1988	LA-N	59	215	24	64	7	1	5	35	25	33	.298	.379	.409	130	9	2	1	0	.895	-13	3-45,1-15/O-2	-0.6
	StL-N	44	149	16	40	7	1	5	30	21	26	.268	.366	.430	126	6	2	0	1	1.000	-7	1-37/O-7	0.1
	Yr	103	364	40	104	14	2	10	65	46	59	.286	.373	.418	128	15	4	1	1	.952	-20	1-52,3-45/O-9	-0.5
1989	StL-N★	162	570	60	177	**42**	1	17	117	79	84	.311	.398	.477	145	35	2	0	1	.990	-14	*1-160	0.9
1990	StL-N	136	498	42	140	31	1	13	80	44	70	.281	.341	.426	109	6	1	0	1	.989	-10	*1-132	-1.5

YEAR	TM/L	G	AB	R	H	2B	3B	HR	RBI	BB	SO	AVG	OBP	SLG	PRO+	BR/A	SB	CS	SBR	FA	FR	G/POS	TPR
1991	StL-N	115	427	41	116	12	1	8	70	37	46	.272	.331	.361	94	-3	4	2	0	.985	-8	*1-112	-1.9
1992	StL-N	43	146	10	32	6	1	1	16	11	25	.219	.274	.295	63	-7	2	2	-1	.988	-7	1-28,O-10	-1.9
Total	15	1536	5392	730	1618	267	29	215	898	609	862	.300	.374	.480	138	277	97	47	1	.988	-49	1-573,O-541,3/2	16.7

■ VLADIMIR GUERRERO
Guerrero, Vladimir b: 2/9/76, Nizao Bani, D.R. BR/TR, 6'2", 158 lbs. Deb: 9/19/96

YEAR	TM/L	G	AB	R	H	2B	3B	HR	RBI	BB	SO	AVG	OBP	SLG	PRO+	BR/A	SB	CS	SBR	FA	FR	G/POS	TPR
1996	Mon-N	9	27	2	5	0	0	1	1	0	3	.185	.185	.296	24	-3	0	0	0	1.000	-1	/O-8	-0.4

■ WILTON GUERRERO
Guerrero, Wilton b: 10/24/74, Don Gregorio, D.R. BR/TR, 5'11", 145 lbs. Deb: 9/3/96

YEAR	TM/L	G	AB	R	H	2B	3B	HR	RBI	BB	SO	AVG	OBP	SLG	PRO+	BR/A	SB	CS	SBR	FA	FR	G/POS	TPR
1996	LA-N	5	2	1	0	0	0	0	0	0	2	.000	.000	.000	-99	-1	0	0	0	.000	0	/H	-0.1

■ OZZIE GUILLEN
Guillen, Oswaldo Jose (Barrios) b: 1/20/64, Ocullare Del Tuy, Venezuela BL/TR, 5'11", 150 lbs. Deb: 4/9/85

YEAR	TM/L	G	AB	R	H	2B	3B	HR	RBI	BB	SO	AVG	OBP	SLG	PRO+	BR/A	SB	CS	SBR	FA	FR	G/POS	TPR
1985	Chi-A	150	491	71	134	21	9	1	33	12	36	.273	.292	.358	74	-18	7	4	-0	.980	12	*S-150	0.6
1986	Chi-A	159	547	58	137	19	4	2	47	12	52	.250	.268	.311	55	-34	8	4	0	.970	14	*S-157/D-1	-0.5
1987	Chi-A	149	560	64	156	22	7	2	51	22	52	.279	.307	.354	73	-22	25	8	3	.975	13	*S-149	0.6
1988	Chi-A†	156	566	58	148	16	7	0	39	25	40	.261	.295	.314	71	-22	25	13	-0	.977	43	*S-156	3.3
1989	Chi-A	155	597	63	151	20	8	1	54	15	48	.253	.271	.318	67	-27	36	17	1	.973	14	*S-155	0.0
1990	Chi-A★	160	516	61	144	21	4	1	58	26	37	.279	.315	.341	85	-11	13	17	-6	.977	3	*S-159	-0.1
1991	Chi-A★	154	524	52	143	20	3	3	49	11	38	.273	.288	.340	75	-19	21	15	-3	.970	-3	*S-149	-1.4
1992	Chi-A	12	40	5	8	4	0	0	7	1	5	.200	.220	.300	45	-3	1	0	0	1.000	1	S-12	-0.1
1993	*Chi-A	134	457	44	128	23	4	4	50	10	41	.280	.296	.374	80	-14	5	4	-1	.972	-12	*S-133	-1.6
1994	Chi-A	100	365	46	105	9	5	1	39	14	35	.288	.314	.348	72	-15	5	4	-1	.959	-23	S-99	-2.9
1995	Chi-A	122	415	50	103	20	3	1	41	13	25	.248	.271	.318	55	-28	6	7	-2	.976	-1	*S-120/D-1	-2.0
1996	Chi-A	150	499	62	131	24	8	4	45	10	27	.263	.277	.367	64	-28	6	5	-1	.981	-24	*S-146/O-2	-3.8
Total	12	1601	5577	634	1488	219	62	20	513	171	436	.267	.289	.339	70	-241	158	98	-11	.974	37	*S-1585/O-2,D-2	-7.9

■ BOBBY GUINDON
Guindon, Robert Joseph b: 9/4/43, Brookline, Mass. BL/TL, 6'2", 185 lbs. Deb: 9/19/64

YEAR	TM/L	G	AB	R	H	2B	3B	HR	RBI	BB	SO	AVG	OBP	SLG	PRO+	BR/A	SB	CS	SBR	FA	FR	G/POS	TPR
1964	Bos-A	5	8	0	1	0	0	0	0	1	4	.125	.222	.250	30	-1	0	0	0	1.000	-0	/1-1,O-1	-0.1

■ BEN GUINEY
Guiney, Benjamin Franklin b: 11/16/1858, Detroit, Mich. d: 12/5/30, Detroit, Mich. BB/TR, 6', 170 lbs. Deb: 9/4/1883

YEAR	TM/L	G	AB	R	H	2B	3B	HR	RBI	BB	SO	AVG	OBP	SLG	PRO+	BR/A	SB	CS	SBR	FA	FR	G/POS	TPR
1883	Det-N	1	5	1	1	0	0	0	0	0	1	.200	.200	.200	23	-0				.000	-1	/O-1	-0.1
1884	Det-N	2	7	0	0	0	0	0	0	0	3	.000	.000	.000	-99	-2				.750	-2	/C-2	-0.3
Total	2	3	12	1	1	0	0	0	0	0	4	.083	.083	.083	-51	-2				.750	-2	/C-2,O-1	-0.4

■ BEN GUINTINI
Guintini, Benjamin John b: 1/13/20, Los Banos, Cal. BR/TR, 6'1.5", 190 lbs. Deb: 4/21/46

YEAR	TM/L	G	AB	R	H	2B	3B	HR	RBI	BB	SO	AVG	OBP	SLG	PRO+	BR/A	SB	CS	SBR	FA	FR	G/POS	TPR
1946	Pit-N	2	3	0	0	0	0	0	0	0	0	.000	.000	.000	-98	-1	0			1.000	0	/O-1	-0.1
1950	Phi-A	3	4	0	0	0	0	0	0	0	1	.000	.000	.000	-99	-1	0	0	0	1.000	0	/O-1	-0.1
Total	2	5	7	0	0	0	0	0	0	0	1	.000	.000	.000	-99	-2	0	0		1.000	0	/O-2	-0.2

■ LOU GUISTO
Guisto, Louis Joseph b: 1/16/1895, Napa, Cal. d: 10/15/89, Napa, Cal. BR/TR, 5'11", 193 lbs. Deb: 9/10/16

YEAR	TM/L	G	AB	R	H	2B	3B	HR	RBI	BB	SO	AVG	OBP	SLG	PRO+	BR/A	SB	CS	SBR	FA	FR	G/POS	TPR
1916	Cle-A	6	19	2	3	0	0	0	2	4	3	.158	.304	.158	37	-1	1			1.000	0	/1-6	-0.2
1917	Cle-A	73	200	9	37	4	2	0	29	25	18	.185	.282	.225	51	-11	3			.989	-1	1-59	-1.6
1921	Cle-A	2	2	0	1	0	0	0	1	0	1	.500	.500	.500	153	0	0	0	0	1.000	0	/1-1	0.0
1922	Cle-A	35	84	7	21	10	1	0	9	2	7	.250	.276	.393	72	-4	0	0	0	.995	4	1-24	-0.4
1923	Cle-A	40	144	17	26	5	0	0	18	15	15	.181	.262	.215	27	-15	1	1	-0	.988	1	1-40	-1.6
Total	5	156	449	35	88	19	3	0	59	46	44	.196	.277	.252	47	-31	5	1		.990	4	1-130	-3.8

■ BRAD GULDEN
Gulden, Bradley Lee b: 6/10/56, New Ulm, Minn. BL/TR, 5'11", 180 lbs. Deb: 9/22/78

YEAR	TM/L	G	AB	R	H	2B	3B	HR	RBI	BB	SO	AVG	OBP	SLG	PRO+	BR/A	SB	CS	SBR	FA	FR	G/POS	TPR
1978	LA-N	3	4	0	0	0	0	0	0	0	2	.000	.000	.000	-99	-1	0	0	0	1.000	1	/C-3	0.0
1979	NY-A	40	92	10	15	4	0	0	6	9	16	.163	.238	.207	21	-10	0	1	-1	.995	11	C-40	0.2
1980	NY-A	2	3	1	1	0	0	1	2	0	0	.333	.333	1.333	340	1	0	0	0	1.000	-1	/C-2	0.0
1981	Sea-A	8	16	0	3	2	0	0	1	0	2	.188	.188	.313	40	-1	0	0	0	1.000	2	/C-6	0.1
1982	Mon-N	5	6	1	0	0	0	0	0	1	1	.000	.143	.000	-56	-1	0	0	0	1.000	1	/C-2	0.0
1984	Cin-N	107	292	31	66	8	2	4	33	33	35	.226	.309	.308	71	-11	2	2	-1	.975	-4	*C-100	-1.2
1986	SF-N	17	22	2	2	0	0	0	1	2	5	.091	.167	.091	-28	-4	0	0	0	1.000	-1	C-10	-0.5
Total	7	182	435	45	87	14	2	5	43	45	61	.200	.278	.276	53	-27	2	3	-1	.982	9	C-163	-1.4

■ TOM GULLEY
Gulley, Thomas Jefferson b: 12/25/1899, Garner, N.C. d: 11/24/66, St.Charles, Ark. BL/TR, 5'11", 178 lbs. Deb: 8/24/23

YEAR	TM/L	G	AB	R	H	2B	3B	HR	RBI	BB	SO	AVG	OBP	SLG	PRO+	BR/A	SB	CS	SBR	FA	FR	G/POS	TPR
1923	Cle-A	2	3	1	1	1	0	0	0	0	0	.333	.333	.667	159	0	0	0	0	1.000	-0	/O-1	0.0
1924	Cle-A	8	20	4	3	0	1	0	1	3	2	.150	.261	.250	32	-2	0	0	0	.933	-2	/O-5	-0.2
1926	Chi-A	16	35	5	8	3	1	0	8	5	2	.229	.325	.371	84	-1	0	0	0	1.000	-2	O-12	-0.3
Total	3	26	58	10	12	4	2	0	9	8	4	.207	.303	.345	61	-3	0	0	0	.971	-2	/O-18	-0.5

■ TED GULLIC
Gullic, Theodore Jasper b: 1/2/07, Koshkonong, Mo. BR/TR, 6'2", 175 lbs. Deb: 4/15/30

YEAR	TM/L	G	AB	R	H	2B	3B	HR	RBI	BB	SO	AVG	OBP	SLG	PRO+	BR/A	SB	CS	SBR	FA	FR	G/POS	TPR
1930	StL-A	92	308	39	77	7	5	4	44	27	43	.250	.310	.344	64	-17	4	0	1	.967	3	O-82/1-3	-1.8
1933	StL-A	104	304	34	74	18	3	5	35	15	38	.243	.281	.372	67	-15	3	1	0	.988	10	O-36,3-33,1-14	-0.6
Total	2	196	612	73	151	25	8	9	79	42	81	.247	.296	.358	65	-33	7	1	2	.975	12	O-118/3-33,1-17	-2.4

■ GLENN GULLIVER
Gulliver, Glenn James b: 10/15/54, Detroit, Mich. BL/TR, 5'11", 175 lbs. Deb: 7/17/82

YEAR	TM/L	G	AB	R	H	2B	3B	HR	RBI	BB	SO	AVG	OBP	SLG	PRO+	BR/A	SB	CS	SBR	FA	FR	G/POS	TPR
1982	Bal-A	50	145	24	29	7	0	1	5	37	18	.200	.363	.269	77	-3	0	0	0	.970	-4	3-50	-0.8
1983	Bal-A	23	47	5	10	3	0	0	2	9	5	.213	.339	.277	73	-1	0	1	-1	1.000	0	3-21	-0.2
Total	2	73	192	29	39	10	0	1	7	46	23	.203	.357	.271	76	-4	0	1	-1	.978	-4	/3-71	-1.0

■ FRED GUNKLE
Gunkle, Frederick W. b: Reading, Pa. Deb: 5/17/1879

YEAR	TM/L	G	AB	R	H	2B	3B	HR	RBI	BB	SO	AVG	OBP	SLG	PRO+	BR/A	SB	CS	SBR	FA	FR	G/POS	TPR
1879	Cle-N	1	3	1	0	0	0	0	0	0	0	.000	.000	.000	-99	-1				1.000	-2	/O-1,C-1	-0.3

■ HY GUNNING
Gunning, Hyland b: 8/6/1888, Maplewood, N.J. d: 3/28/75, Togus, Me. BL/TR, 6'1.5", 189 lbs. Deb: 8/8/11

YEAR	TM/L	G	AB	R	H	2B	3B	HR	RBI	BB	SO	AVG	OBP	SLG	PRO+	BR/A	SB	CS	SBR	FA	FR	G/POS	TPR
1911	Bos-A	4	9	0	1	0	0	0	2	2		.111	.273	.111	9	-1				1.000	-1	/1-4	-0.2

■ TOM GUNNING
Gunning, Thomas Francis b: 3/4/1862, Newmarket, N.H. d: 3/17/31, Fall River, Mass. BR/TR, 5'10", 160 lbs. Deb: 7/26/1884 U

YEAR	TM/L	G	AB	R	H	2B	3B	HR	RBI	BB	SO	AVG	OBP	SLG	PRO+	BR/A	SB	CS	SBR	FA	FR	G/POS	TPR
1884	Bos-N	12	45	4	5	1	1	0	2	1	12	.111	.130	.178	-4	-5				.914	-5	C-12	-0.9
1885	Bos-N	48	174	17	32	3	0	0	15	5	29	.184	.207	.201	34	-12				.877	-7	C-48	-1.5
1886	Bos-N	27	98	15	22	2	1	0	7	3	19	.224	.248	.265	58	-5	3			.892	-5	C-27	-0.6
1887	Phi-N	28	104	22	27	6	1	1	16	5	6	.260	.306	.365	81	-3	18			.895	6	C-28	0.5
1888	Phi-a	23	92	18	18	0	0	0	5	2		.196	.237	.196	40	-6	14			.894	-1	C-23	-0.5
1889	Phi-a	8	24	3	6	1	1	0	1	0	4	.250	.250	.458	101	-0	3			.838	-2	/C-8	-0.1
Total	6	146	537	79	110	12	4	2	46	16	70	.205	.235	.253	50	-32	38			.887	-15	C-146	-3.1

■ JOE GUNSON
Gunson, Joseph Brook b: 3/23/1863, Philadelphia, Pa. d: 11/15/42, Philadelphia, Pa. BR/TR, 5'6", 160 lbs. Deb: 6/14/1884

YEAR	TM/L	G	AB	R	H	2B	3B	HR	RBI	BB	SO	AVG	OBP	SLG	PRO+	BR/A	SB	CS	SBR	FA	FR	G/POS	TPR
1884	Was-U	45	166	15	23	2	0	0		3		.139	.154	.151	-8	-27				.915	10	C-33,O-18	-1.3
1889	KC-a	34	122	15	24	3	1	0	12	3	17	.197	.228	.238	31	-11	2			.862	-6	C-32/O-1,3-1	-1.3
1892	Bal-N	89	314	35	67	10	5	0	32	16	17	.213	.267	.277	63	-15	2			.921	-1	C-67,O-20/1-2,2-1	-1.1
1893	StL-N	40	151	20	41	5	0	0	15	6		.272	.321	.305	66	-7	0			.927	-5	C-35/O-5	-0.1
	Cle-N	21	73	11	19	1	0	0	9	6		.260	.316	.274	54	-5	0			.942	2	C-20	-0.1
	Yr	61	224	31	60	6	0	0	24	12		.268	.320	.295	62	-12	0			.932	5	C-55/O-5	-0.1
Total	4	229	826	96	174	21	6	0	68	34	40	.211	.254	.251	45	-65	4			.912	8	C-187/O-44,1-2,23	-3.9

■ ERNIE GUST
Gust, Ernest Herman Frank "Red" b: 1/24/1888, Bay City, Mich. d: 10/26/45, Maupin, Ore. BR/TR, 6', 170 lbs. Deb: 8/17/11

YEAR	TM/L	G	AB	R	H	2B	3B	HR	RBI	BB	SO	AVG	OBP	SLG	PRO+	BR/A	SB	CS	SBR	FA	FR	G/POS	TPR
1911	StL-A	3	12	0	0	0	0	0	0	0		.000	.000	.000	-99	-3	0			.974	-0	/1-3	-0.4

■ FRANKIE GUSTINE
Gustine, Frank William b: 2/20/20, Hoopeston, Ill. d: 4/1/91, Davenport, Iowa BR/TR, 6', 180 lbs. Deb: 9/13/39 C

YEAR	TM/L	G	AB	R	H	2B	3B	HR	RBI	BB	SO	AVG	OBP	SLG	PRO+	BR/A	SB	CS	SBR	FA	FR	G/POS	TPR
1939	Pit-N	22	70	5	13	3	0	0	3	9	4	.186	.278	.229	38	-6	0			.896	4	3-22	-0.2
1940	Pit-N	133	524	59	147	32	7	1	55	35	39	.281	.328	.374	94	-5	7			.941	-8	*2-130	-0.4
1941	Pit-N	121	463	46	125	24	7	1	46	28	38	.270	.313	.359	89	-8	5			.954	-1	*2-104,3-15	-0.1

YEAR	TM/L	G	AB	R	H	2B	3B	HR	RBI	BB	SO	AVG	OBP	SLG	PRO+	BR/A	SB	CS	SBR	FA	FR	G/POS	TPR
1942	Pit-N	115	388	34	89	11	4	2	35	29	27	.229	.288	.294	68	-16	5			.954	-10	*2-108/S-2,3-2,C-1	-2.1
1943	Pit-N	112	414	40	120	21	3	0	43	32	36	.290	.341	.355	98	-1	12			.938	-6	S-68,2-40/1-1	1.2
1944	Pit-N	127	405	42	93	18	3	2	42	33	41	.230	.288	.304	64	-19	8			.938	-27	*S-116,2-11/3-1	-3.9
1945	Pit-N	128	478	67	134	27	5	2	66	37	33	.280	.335	.370	92	-5	8			.930	-19	*S-104,2-29/C-1	-1.5
1946	Pit-N★	131	495	60	128	23	6	8	52	40	52	.259	.318	.378	95	-5	2			.967	8	*2-113,S-13/3-7	1.2
1947	Pit-N★	156	616	102	183	30	6	9	67	63	65	.297	.364	.409	102	2	5			.944	15	*3-156	1.8
1948	Pit-N★	131	449	68	120	19	2	9	42	42	62	.267	.333	.379	90	-6	5			.947	9	*3-118	0.2
1949	Chi-N	76	261	29	59	13	4	4	27	18	22	.226	.279	.352	70	-12	3			.931	1	3-55,2-16	-1.1
1950	StL-A	9	19	1	3	1	0	0	2	3	8	.158	.273	.211	24	-2	0	1	-1	.857	-0	/3-6	-0.3
Total	12	1261	4582	553	1214	222	47	38	480	369	427	.265	.322	.359	87	-82	60	1		.955	-35	2-551,3-382,S/C1	-6.4

■ BUCKY GUTH
Guth, Charles Henry b: 8/18/47, Baltimore, Md. BR/TR, 6'1", 180 lbs. Deb: 9/12/72

YEAR	TM/L	G	AB	R	H	2B	3B	HR	RBI	BB	SO	AVG	OBP	SLG	PRO+	BR/A	SB	CS	SBR	FA	FR	G/POS	TPR
1972	Min-A	3	3	1	0	0	0	0	0	0	0	.000	.000	.000	-95	-1	0	0		1.000	1	/S-1	0.0

■ CESAR GUTIERREZ
Gutierrez, Cesar Dario "Coca" b: 1/26/43, Coro, Venez. BR/TR, 5'9", 155 lbs. Deb: 4/16/67

YEAR	TM/L	G	AB	R	H	2B	3B	HR	RBI	BB	SO	AVG	OBP	SLG	PRO+	BR/A	SB	CS	SBR	FA	FR	G/POS	TPR
1967	SF-N	18	21	4	3	0	0	0	0	1	4	.143	.217	.143	5	-3	1	0	0	.946	3	S-15/2-1	0.1
1969	SF-N	15	23	4	5	1	0	0	0	6	2	.217	.379	.261	84	-0	1	0	0	.882	-0	/3-7,S-4	0.0
	Det-A	17	49	5	12	1	0	0	0	5	3	.245	.315	.265	61	-2	1	2	-1	.946	1	S-16	0.0
1970	Det-A	135	415	40	101	11	6	0	22	18	39	.243	.276	.299	58	-24	4	3	-1	.957	-18	*S-135	-2.9
1971	Det-A	38	37	8	7	0	0	0	4	0	3	.189	.211	.189	13	-4	0	0		.971	5	S-14/3-5,2-2	0.2
Total	4	223	545	61	128	13	6	0	26	30	51	.235	.279	.281	55	-33	7	5	-1	.955	-9	S-184/3-12,2-3	-2.6

■ JACKIE GUTIERREZ
Gutierrez, Joaquin Fernando b: 6/27/60, Cartagena, Colombia BR/TR, 5'11", 175 lbs. Deb: 9/6/83

YEAR	TM/L	G	AB	R	H	2B	3B	HR	RBI	BB	SO	AVG	OBP	SLG	PRO+	BR/A	SB	CS	SBR	FA	FR	G/POS	TPR
1983	Bos-A	5	10	2	3	0	0	0	0	1	1	.300	.364	.300	79	-0	0	1	-1	.938	0	/S-4	-0.1
1984	Bos-A	151	449	55	118	12	3	2	29	15	49	.263	.287	.316	64	-22	12	5	1	.949	-33	*S-150	-4.2
1985	Bos-A	103	275	33	60	5	2	2	21	12	37	.218	.251	.273	42	-22	10	2	2	.943	5	S-99	-0.7
1986	Bal-A	61	145	8	27	3	0	0	4	3	27	.186	.208	.207	14	-17	3	1	0	.990	7	2-53/3-6,D-1	-0.8
1987	Bal-A	3	1	0	0	0	0	0	0	0	0	.000	.000	.000	-99	-0	0	0	0	.000	0	/2-1,3-1	-0.6
1988	Phi-N	33	77	8	19	4	0	0	9	2	9	.247	.266	.299	61	-4	0	0	0	.919	-2	S-22,3-13	-0.6
Total	6	356	957	106	227	24	5	4	63	33	123	.237	.263	.285	50	-66	25	9	2	.945	-23	S-275/2-54,3-20,D-1	-6.4

■ RICKY GUTIERREZ
Gutierrez, Ricardo b: 5/23/70, Miami, Fla. BR/TR, 6'1", 175 lbs. Deb: 4/13/93

YEAR	TM/L	G	AB	R	H	2B	3B	HR	RBI	BB	SO	AVG	OBP	SLG	PRO+	BR/A	SB	CS	SBR	FA	FR	G/POS	TPR
1993	SD-N	133	438	76	110	10	5	5	26	50	97	.251	.335	.331	78	-13	4	3	-1	.971	-15	*S-117/2-6,0-5,3-4	-1.9
1994	SD-N	90	275	27	66	11	2	1	28	32	54	.240	.324	.305	74	-13	2	6	-3	.925	-8	S-78/2-7	-1.7
1995	Hou-N	52	156	22	43	6	0	0	12	10	33	.276	.323	.314	74	-6	5	0	2	.956	-6	S-44/3-2	-0.6
1996	Hou-N	89	218	28	62	8	1	1	15	23	42	.284	.361	.344	96	-1	6	1	1	.953	-10	S-74/3-6,2-5	-0.4
Total	4	364	1087	153	281	35	8	7	81	115	226	.259	.336	.325	78	-32	17	10	-1	.954	-38	S-313/2-18,3-12,0-5	-4.6

■ DON GUTTERIDGE
Gutteridge, Donald Joseph b: 6/19/12, Pittsburg, Kan. BR/TR, 5'10.5", 165 lbs. Deb: 9/7/36 MC

YEAR	TM/L	G	AB	R	H	2B	3B	HR	RBI	BB	SO	AVG	OBP	SLG	PRO+	BR/A	SB	CS	SBR	FA	FR	G/POS	TPR
1936	StL-N	23	91	13	29	3	4	3	16	1	14	.319	.326	.538	130	3	3			.967	0	3-23	0.4
1937	StL-N	119	447	66	121	26	10	7	61	25	66	.271	.311	.421	95	-4	12			.978	2	*3-105/S-8	0.0
1938	StL-N	142	552	61	141	21	15	6	64	29	49	.255	.293	.397	83	-14	14			.945	0	3-73,S-68	-0.8
1939	StL-N	148	524	71	141	27	4	7	54	27	70	.269	.309	.376	78	-17	5			.934	-18	*3-143/S-2	-3.4
1940	StL-N	69	108	19	29	5	0	3	14	5	15	.269	.301	.398	86	-2	3			.877	-2	3-39	-0.3
1942	StL-A	147	616	90	157	27	11	1	50	59	64	.255	.320	.339	84	-13	16	13	-3	.973	3	*2-145/3-2	-0.5
1943	StL-A	132	538	77	147	35	6	1	36	50	64	.273	.335	.366	103	2	10	9	-2	.958	-31	*2-132	-2.6
1944	*StL-A	148	603	94	148	27	11	3	36	51	63	.245	.304	.342	80	-17	20	8	1	.957	-8	*2-146	-1.6
1945	StL-A	143	543	72	129	24	3	2	49	43	46	.238	.295	.304	70	-21	9	6	-1	.970	-20	*2-128,O-14	-3.7
1946	*Bos-A	22	47	8	11	3	0	1	6	2	7	.234	.265	.362	70	-2	0	0	0	1.000	-1	/2-9,3-8	-0.3
1947	Bos-A	54	131	20	22	2	0	2	5	17	13	.168	.264	.229	35	-11	0			.938	-1	2-20,3-19	-1.2
1948	Pit-N	4	2	0	0	0	0	0	0	0	1	.000	.000	.000	-98	-1	0			.000	0	H	-0.1
Total	12	1151	4202	586	1075	200	64	39	391	309	444	.256	.308	.362	84	-98	95	37		.964	-76	2-580,3-412/S-78,O	-14.1

■ DOUG GWOSDZ
Gwosdz, Douglas Wayne "Eye Chart" b: 6/20/60, Houston, Tex. BR/TR, 5'11", 185 lbs. Deb: 8/17/81

YEAR	TM/L	G	AB	R	H	2B	3B	HR	RBI	BB	SO	AVG	OBP	SLG	PRO+	BR/A	SB	CS	SBR	FA	FR	G/POS	TPR
1981	SD-N	16	24	1	4	2	0	0	3	3	6	.167	.259	.250	48	-2	0	0	0	1.000	2	C-13	0.1
1982	SD-N	7	17	1	3	0	0	0	2	2	1	.176	.263	.176	27	-2	0	0	0	1.000	2	/C-7	0.0
1983	SD-N	39	55	7	6	1	0	1	4	7	19	.109	.210	.182	10	-7	0	0	0	.971	2	C-32	-0.5
1984	SD-N	7	8	0	2	0	0	0	1	2	1	.250	.400	.250	86	-0	0	0	0	.963	2	/C-6	0.2
Total	4	69	104	9	15	3	0	1	8	14	37	.144	.246	.202	27	-10	0	0	0	.981	8	/C-58	-0.2

■ TONY GWYNN
Gwynn, Anthony Keith b: 5/9/60, Los Angeles, Cal. BL/TL, 5'11", 200 lbs. Deb: 7/19/82 F

YEAR	TM/L	G	AB	R	H	2B	3B	HR	RBI	BB	SO	AVG	OBP	SLG	PRO+	BR/A	SB	CS	SBR	FA	FR	G/POS	TPR
1982	SD-N	54	190	33	55	12	2	1	17	14	16	.289	.338	.389	109	2	8	3	1	.991	-6	O-52	-0.5
1983	SD-N	86	304	34	94	12	2	1	37	23	21	.309	.358	.372	106	3	7	4	-0	.994	6	O-81	0.6
1984	*SD-N★	158	606	88	**213**	21	10	5	71	59	23	**.351**	.411	.444	140	34	33	18	-1	.989	16	*O-156	4.5
1985	SD-N★	154	622	90	197	29	5	6	46	45	33	.317	.365	.408	118	15	14	11	-2	.989	17	*O-152	2.5
1986	SD-N★	160	642	**107**	**211**	33	7	14	59	52	35	.329	.382	.467	136	31	37	9	6	.989	20	*O-160	5.2
1987	SD-N★	157	589	119	**218**	36	13	7	54	82	35	**.370**	.450	.511	160	**54**	56	12	10	.981	9	*O-156	6.6
1988	SD-N★	133	521	64	163	22	5	7	70	51	40	**.313**	.374	.415	128	20	26	11	1	.982	3	*O-133	2.1
1989	SD-N★	158	604	82	**203**	27	7	4	62	56	30	**.336**	.393	.424	133	27	40	16	2	.984	11	*O-157	3.9
1990	SD-N★	141	573	79	177	29	10	4	72	44	23	.309	.359	.415	114	9	17	8	0	.985	15	*O-141	2.2
1991	SD-N★	134	530	69	168	27	11	4	62	34	19	.317	.358	.432	118	12	8	8	-2	.990	11	*O-134	1.8
1992	SD-N★	128	520	77	165	27	3	6	41	46	16	.317	.373	.415	121	15	3	6	-3	.982	12	*O-127	2.3
1993	SD-N★	122	489	70	175	41	3	7	59	36	19	.358	.403	.497	137	26	14	1	4	.981	4	*O-121	3.0
1994	SD-N★	110	419	79	**165**	35	1	12	64	48	19	**.394**	.458	.568	171	45	5	0	2	.985	4	*O-106	4.5
1995	SD-N★	135	535	82	**197**	33	1	9	90	35	15	**.368**	.408	.484	139	30	17	5	2	.992	5	*O-133	3.2
1996	*SD-N†	116	451	67	159	27	2	3	50	39	17	**.353**	.405	.441	130	20	11	4	1	.989	-5	*O-111	1.3
Total	15	1946	7595	1140	2560	411	82	90	854	664	361	.337	.392	.448	132	342	296	116	19	.987	120	*O-1920	43.2

■ CHRIS GWYNN
Gwynn, Christopher Karlton b: 10/13/64, Los Angeles, Cal. BL/TL, 6'", 200 lbs. Deb: 8/14/87 F

YEAR	TM/L	G	AB	R	H	2B	3B	HR	RBI	BB	SO	AVG	OBP	SLG	PRO+	BR/A	SB	CS	SBR	FA	FR	G/POS	TPR
1987	LA-N	17	32	2	7	1	0	0	2	1	7	.219	.242	.250	32	-3	0	0	0	1.000	-1	O-10	-0.5
1988	LA-N	12	11	1	2	0	0	0	0	1	2	.182	.250	.182	27	-1	0	0	0	.000	-2	/O-4	-0.3
1989	LA-N	32	68	9	16	4	1	0	7	2	9	.235	.257	.324	66	-3	1	0	0	1.000	-2	O-19	-0.6
1990	LA-N	101	141	19	40	2	1	5	22	7	28	.284	.318	.418	104	0	1	0	-1	1.000	-9	O-44	-1.1
1991	LA-N	94	139	18	35	5	1	5	22	10	23	.252	.301	.410	102	-0	1	0	0	1.000	-5	O-41	-1.0
1992	KC-A	34	84	10	24	3	2	1	7	3	10	.286	.310	.405	96	-1	0	0	0	1.000	-2	O-19/D-2	-0.3
1993	KC-A	103	287	36	86	14	4	1	25	24	34	.300	.356	.387	94	-2	0	1	-1	.994	-9	O-83/1-1,D-5	-0.4
1994	LA-N	58	71	9	19	0	0	3	13	7	7	.268	.333	.394	95	-1	0	0	0	1.000	-2	O-20	-0.6
1995	*LA-N	67	84	8	18	5	1	1	10	6	23	.214	.275	.333	65	-5	0	0	0	1.000	-1	O-17/1-2	-0.6
1996	*SD-N	81	90	8	16	2	1	1	10	10	28	.178	.260	.256	39	-8	0	0	0	1.000	-7	O-29/1-1	-1.5
Total	10	599	1007	119	263	36	11	17	118	71	171	.261	.312	.369	85	-23	2	4	-2	.997	-36	O-286/D-7,1-4	-6.9

■ DICK GYSELMAN
Gyselman, Richard Renald b: 4/6/08, San Francisco, Cal. d: 9/20/90, Seattle, Wash. BR/TR, 6'2", 170 lbs. Deb: 4/20/33

YEAR	TM/L	G	AB	R	H	2B	3B	HR	RBI	BB	SO	AVG	OBP	SLG	PRO+	BR/A	SB	CS	SBR	FA	FR	G/POS	TPR
1933	Bos-N	58	155	10	37	6	2	0	12	7	21	.239	.272	.303	70	-7	0			.926	3	3-42/2-5,S-1	0.2
1934	Bos-N	24	36	7	6	1	1	0	4	2	11	.167	.211	.250	25	-4	0			.739	-2	3-15/2-2	-0.5
Total	2	82	191	17	43	7	3	0	16	9	32	.225	.260	.293	61	-11	0			.901	4	/3-57,2-7,S-1	-0.3

■ BERT HAAS
Haas, Berthold John b: 2/8/14, Naperville, Ill. BR/TR, 5'11", 180 lbs. Deb: 9/9/37

YEAR	TM/L	G	AB	R	H	2B	3B	HR	RBI	BB	SO	AVG	OBP	SLG	PRO+	BR/A	SB	CS	SBR	FA	FR	G/POS	TPR
1937	Bro-N	16	25	2	10	3	0	0	2	1	1	.400	.423	.520	152	2	0			1.000	-1	/O-4,1-3	0.1
1938	Bro-N	1	0	0	0	0	0	0	0	0	0					0	0					H	0.0
1942	Cin-N	154	585	59	140	21	6	6	54	59	54	.239	.310	.326	86	-10	6			.925	-10	*3-146/1-6,O-2	-2.0
1943	Cin-N	101	332	39	87	17	6	4	44	22	26	.262	.308	.386	101	-1	6			.993	9	1-44,3-23,O-18	0.5
1946	Cin-N	140	535	57	141	24	7	3	50	33	42	.264	.310	.351	91	-8	22			.994	0	*1-140/3-6	-1.7

YEAR	TM/L	G	AB	R	H	2B	3B	HR	RBI	BB	SO	AVG	OBP	SLG	PRO+	BR/A	SB	CS	SBR	FA	FR	G/POS	TPR
1947	Cin-N★	135	482	58	138	17	7	3	67	42	27	.286	.346	.369	91	-6	9			.956	-4	O-69,1-53	-1.6
1948	Phi-N	95	333	35	94	9	2	4	34	36	25	.282	.354	.357	95	-2	8			.892	-8	3-54,1-35	-1.1
1949	Phi-N	2	1	0	0	0	0	0	0	1	1	.000	.500	.000	47	0	0			.000	0	H	0.0
	NY-N	54	104	12	27	2	3	1	10	5	8	.260	.294	.365	76	-4	0			.983	-1	1-23,3-11	-0.5
	Yr	56	105	12	27	2	3	1	10	6	9	.257	.297	.362	76	-4	0			.983	-1	1-23,3-11	-0.5
1951	Chi-A	23	43	1	7	0	1	1	2	5	4	.163	.250	.279	44	-4	0	0	0	1.000	-1	1/-7,O-4,3-1	-0.5
Total	9	721	2440	263	644	93	32	22	263	204	188	.264	.323	.355	91	-33	51	0		.991	-17	1-311,3-241/O-97	-6.8

■ BRUNO HAAS   Haas, Bruno Philip "Boon" b: 5/5/1891, Worcester, Mass. d: 6/5/52, Sarasota, Fla. BB/TL, 5'10", 180 lbs. Deb: 6/23/15

| 1915 | Phi-A | 12 | 18 | 1 | 1 | 0 | 0 | 0 | 0 | 1 | 7 | .056 | .105 | .056 | -54 | -3 | 0 | | | .875 | 1 | /P-6,O-3 | -0.2 |

■ EDDIE HAAS   Haas, George Edwin b: 5/26/35, Paducah, Ky. BL/TR, 5'11", 178 lbs. Deb: 9/8/57 MC

1957	Chi-N	14	24	1	5	1	0	0	4	1	5	.208	.240	.250	32	-2	0	0	0	1.000	-1	/O-4	-0.3
1958	Mil-N	9	14	2	5	0	0	0	1	2	1	.357	.438	.357	124	1	0	0	0	1.000	-0	/O-3	0.0
1960	Mil-N	32	32	4	7	2	0	0	1	5	14	.219	.324	.375	98	-0	0	0	0	1.000	-0	/O-4	-0.1
Total	3	55	70	7	17	3	0	1	6	8	20	.243	.321	.329	80	-2	0	0	0	1.000	-2	/O-9	-0.4

■ MULE HAAS   Haas, George William b: 10/15/03, Montclair, N.J. d: 6/30/74, New Orleans, La. BL/TR, 6'1", 175 lbs. Deb: 8/15/25 C

1925	Pit-N	4	3	1	0	0	0	0	0	0	1	.000	.000	.000	-94	-1				1.000	-1	/O-2	-0.2
1928	Phi-A	91	332	41	93	21	4	6	39	23	20	.280	.331	.422	94	-4	2	3	-1	.974	-3	O-82	-1.3
1929	*Phi-A	139	578	115	181	41	9	16	82	34	38	.313	.356	.498	113	9	0	4	-2	.982	2	*O-139	-0.1
1930	*Phi-A	132	532	91	159	33	7	2	68	43	31	.299	.352	.398	86	-11	2	2	-1	.976	12	*O-131	-0.8
1931	*Phi-A	102	440	82	142	29	7	8	56	30	29	.323	.366	.475	113	7	0	0	0	.989	4	*O-102	0.3
1932	Phi-A	143	558	91	170	28	5	6	65	62	49	.305	.376	.405	99	0	1	0	0	.987	7	*O-137	-0.2
1933	Chi-A	146	585	97	168	33	4	1	51	65	41	.287	.360	.362	96	-2	0	5	-3	.983	-5	*O-146	-1.6
1934	Chi-A	106	351	54	94	16	3	2	22	47	22	.268	.354	.348	79	-10	1	0	0	.991	-2	O-89	-1.5
1935	Chi-A	92	327	44	95	22	1	2	40	37	17	.291	.363	.382	90	-4	4	1	1	.989	-1	O-84	-0.7
1936	Chi-A	119	408	75	116	26	2	0	46	64	29	.284	.383	.358	81	-10	1	1	-0	.989	-6	O-96/1-7	-1.9
1937	Chi-A	54	111	8	23	3	3	0	15	16	10	.207	.313	.288	52	-8	1	0	0	.975	0	1-32/O-2	-1.0
1938	Chi-A	40	78	7	16	2	0	0	12	12	10	.205	.311	.231	39	-7	0	0	0	1.000	2	O-12/1-6	-1.0
Total	12	1168	4303	706	1257	254	45	43	496	433	299	.292	.359	.402	93	-41	12	16	-6	.984	5	*O-1022/1-45	-10.0

■ EMIL HABERER   Haberer, Emil Karl b: 2/2/1878, Cincinnati, Ohio d: 10/19/51, Louisville, Ky. BR/TR, 6'1", 204 lbs. Deb: 7/9/01

1901	Cin-N	6	18	2	3	0	1	0	1	0	3	.167	.286	.278	68	-1	0			.545	-2	/3-3,1-2	-0.2
1903	Cin-N	5	13	1	1	0	0	0	0	2		.077	.200	.077	-18	-2	0			.933	-2	/C-4	-0.4
1909	Cin-N	5	16	1	3	1	0	0	2	0		.188	.188	.250	36	-1	0			.895	-2	/C-4	-0.3
Total	3	16	47	4	7	1	1	0	3	5		.149	.231	.213	31	-4	0			.912	-6	/C-8,3-3,1-2	-0.9

■ IRV HACH   Hach, Irvin William "Major" b: 6/6/1873, Louisville, Ky. d: 8/13/36, Louisville, Ky. BR/TR, Deb: 7/1/1897

| 1897 | Lou-N | 16 | 51 | 5 | 11 | 2 | 0 | 0 | 3 | 5 | | .216 | .322 | .255 | 55 | -3 | 1 | | | .889 | -2 | /2-9,3-7 | -0.3 |

■ STAN HACK   Hack, Stanley Camfield "Smiling Stan" b: 12/6/09, Sacramento, Cal d: 12/15/79, Dixon, Ill. BL/TR, 6', 170 lbs. Deb: 4/12/32 MC

1932	*Chi-N	72	178	32	42	5	6	2	19	17	16	.236	.306	.365	80	-5	5			.913	-5	3-51	-0.7
1933	Chi-N	20	60	10	21	3	1	1	2	8	3	.350	.451	.483	167	6	4			.983	6	3-17	1.3
1934	Chi-N	111	402	54	116	16	6	1	21	45	42	.289	.363	.366	98	0	11			.949	-3	*3-109	0.5
1935	*Chi-N	124	427	75	133	23	9	4	64	65	17	.311	.406	.436	125	18	14			.942	11	*3-111/1-7	3.1
1936	Chi-N	149	561	102	167	27	4	6	78	89	39	.298	.396	.392	110	12	17			.950	-12	*3-140,1-11	0.4
1937	Chi-N	154	582	106	173	27	6	2	63	83	42	.297	.388	.375	104	6	16			.968	-9	*3-150/1-4	0.1
1938	*Chi-N★	152	609	109	195	34	11	4	67	94	39	.320	.411	.432	128	28	16			.954	7	*3-152	3.6
1939	Chi-N★	156	641	112	191	28	6	8	56	65	35	.298	.364	.398	103	4	17			.956	-7	*3-156	-0.1
1940	Chi-N	149	603	101	191	38	6	8	40	75	24	.317	.395	.439	132	29	21			.954	14	*3-148/1-1	4.5
1941	Chi-N★	151	586	111	186	33	5	7	45	99	40	.317	.417	.427	143	38	10			.954	-16	*3-150/1-1	2.6
1942	Chi-N	140	553	91	166	36	3	6	39	94	40	.300	.402	.409	143	34	9			.965	-10	*3-139	2.7
1943	Chi-N★	144	533	78	154	24	4	3	35	82	27	.289	.384	.366	119	16	5			.960	-7	*3-136	1.1
1944	Chi-N	98	383	65	108	16	1	3	32	53	21	.282	.369	.352	104	4	5			.939	2	3-75,1-18	0.6
1945	*Chi-N†	150	597	110	193	29	7	2	43	99	30	.323	.420	.405	133	32	12			.975	18	*3-146/1-5	5.2
1946	Chi-N	92	323	55	92	13	4	0	26	83	32	.285	.431	.350	125	17	3			.968	-3	3-90	1.6
1947	Chi-N	76	240	28	65	11	2	0	12	41	19	.271	.377	.333	94	-0	1			.962	7	3-66	0.7
Total	16	1938	7278	1239	2193	363	81	57	642	1092	466	.301	.394	.397	120	238	165			.957	-4	*3-1836/1-47	27.2

■ RICH HACKER   Hacker, Richard Warren b: 10/6/47, Belleville, Ill. BB/TR, 6', 160 lbs. Deb: 7/2/71 C

| 1971 | Mon-N | 16 | 33 | 2 | 4 | 1 | 0 | 0 | 3 | 0 | 12 | .121 | .194 | .152 | -1 | -4 | 0 | 0 | 0 | .984 | 5 | S-16 | 0.2 |

■ JIM HACKETT   Hackett, James Joseph "Sunny Jim" b: 10/1/1877, Jacksonville, Ill. d: 3/28/61, Douglas, Mich. BR/TR, 6'2", 185 lbs. Deb: 9/14/02

1902	StL-N	6	21	2	6	1	0	0	3	1		.286	.348	.333	115	0	1			.833	-1	/P-4,O-2	0.0
1903	StL-N	99	351	24	80	13	8	0	36	19		.228	.272	.311	68	-16	2			.972	-6	1-89/P-7	-2.2
Total	2	105	372	26	86	14	8	0	40	21		.231	.276	.312	70	-15	3			.893	-7	/1-89,P-11,O-2	-2.2

■ MERT HACKETT   Hackett, Mortimer Martin b: 11/11/1859, Cambridge, Mass. d: 2/22/38, Cambridge, Mass. BR/TR, 5'10.5", 175 lbs. Deb: 5/2/1883 F

1883	Bos-N	46	179	20	42	8	6	2	24	1	48	.235	.239	.380	82	-4				.909	-4	C-44/O-4	-0.7
1884	Bos-N	72	268	28	55	13	2	1	20	2	66	.205	.211	.280	53	-14				.928	12	C-71/3-1	0.3
1885	Bos-N	34	115	9	21	7	1	0	4	2	28	.183	.197	.261	49	-6				.901	5	C-34	0.2
1886	KC-N	62	230	18	50	8	3	3	25	4	59	.217	.231	.317	61	-11	1			.926	-17	C-53,O-13	-2.1
1887	Ind-N	42	147	12	35	6	3	2	10	7	24	.238	.282	.361	80	-4	4			.938	-9	C-40/O-2,1-1	-0.8
Total	5	256	939	87	203	42	15	8	83	16	225	.216	.231	.318	65	-40	5			.921	-15	C-242/O-19,1-1,3-1	-3.1

■ WALTER HACKETT   Hackett, Walter Henry b: 8/15/1857, Cambridge, Mass. d: 10/2/20, Cambridge, Mass. Deb: 4/17/1884 F

1884	Bos-U	103	415	71	101	19	0	1		7		.243	.256	.296	68	-28				.855	12	*S-103	-1.3
1885	Bos-N	35	125	8	23	3	0	0	9	3	22	.184	.203	.208	34	-9				.893	-12	2-20,S-15	-1.9
Total	2	138	540	79	124	22	0	1	9	10	22	.230	.244	.276	61	-37				.852	1	S-118/2-20	-3.2

■ KENT HADLEY   Hadley, Kent William b: 12/17/34, Pocatello, Idaho BL/TL, 6'3", 190 lbs. Deb: 9/14/58

1958	KC-A	3	11	1	2	0	0	0	0	0	4	.182	.182	.182	0	-1	0	0	0	1.000	-1	/1-2	-0.2
1959	KC-A	113	288	40	73	11	1	10	39	24	74	.253	.313	.403	93	-1	1	2	-1	.989	-2	1-95	-1.1
1960	NY-A	55	64	8	13	2	0	4	11	6	19	.203	.271	.422	90	-1	0	0	0	.991	-0	1-24	-0.2
Total	3	171	363	49	88	13	1	14	50	30	97	.242	.302	.399	90	-6	1	2	-1	.989	-2	1-121	-1.5

■ BILL HAEFFNER   Haeffner, William Bernhard b: 7/8/1894, Philadelphia, Pa. d: 1/27/82, Springfield, Pa. BR/TR, 5'9", 165 lbs. Deb: 6/29/15

1915	Phi-A	3	4	0	1	0	0	0	0	1		.250	.250	.250	51	-0	0			1.000	-1	/C-3	-0.2
1920	Pit-N	54	175	8	34	4	1	0	14	8	14	.194	.230	.229	31	-15	1	1	-0	.972	-3	C-52	-1.7
1928	NY-N	2	1	0	0	0	0	0	0	0	1	.000	.000	.000	-99	-0	0			.750	1	/C-2	0.0
Total	3	59	180	8	35	4	1	0	14	8	15	.194	.229	.228	30	-16	1	1		.968	-2	/C-57	-1.9

■ CHICK HAFEY   Hafey, Charles James b: 2/12/03, Berkeley, Cal. d: 7/2/73, Calistoga, Cal. BR/TR, 6', 185 lbs. Deb: 8/28/24 H

1924	StL-N	24	91	10	23	5	2	2	22	4	8	.253	.292	.418	90	-2	1	0	0	.927	-1	O-24	-0.4
1925	StL-N	93	358	36	108	25	2	5	57	10	29	.302	.321	.425	87	-8	3	7	-3	.955	-1	O-88	-1.7
1926	*StL-N	78	225	30	61	19	2	4	38	11	36	.271	.311	.427	93	-3	2			.974	-6	O-64	-1.2
1927	*StL-N	103	346	62	114	26	5	18	63	36	45	.329	.401	.590	157	27	12			.980	5	O-94	2.6
1928	*StL-N	138	520	101	175	46	6	27	111	40	53	.337	.386	.604	152	37	8			.965	3	*O-133	2.9
1929	*StL-N	134	517	101	175	47	9	29	125	45	42	.338	.394	.632	148	36	7			.966	3	*O-130	2.7
1930	*StL-N	120	446	108	150	39	12	26	107	46	51	.336	.407	.652	146	31	12			.976	-4	*O-116	1.8
1931	*StL-N	122	450	94	157	35	8	16	95	39	43	.349	.404	.569	153	33	11			.983	-4	*O-118	2.0

YEAR	TM/L	G	AB	R	H	2B	3B	HR	RBI	BB	SO	AVG	OBP	SLG	PRO+	BR/A	SB	CS	SBR	FA	FR	G/POS	TPR
1932	Cin-N	83	253	34	87	19	3	2	36	22	20	.344	.403	.466	137	14	4			.965	-3	O-65	0.7
1933	Cin-N★	144	568	77	172	34	6	7	62	40	44	.303	.351	.421	121	15	3			.987	8	*O-144	1.6
1934	Cin-N	140	535	75	157	29	6	18	67	52	63	.293	.359	.471	123	17	4			.967	4	*O-140	1.5
1935	Cin-N	15	59	10	20	6	1	1	9	4	5	.339	.400	.525	151	4	1			.912	-3	O-15	0.1
1937	Cin-N	89	257	39	67	11	5	9	41	23	42	.261	.324	.447	113	4	2			.971	-2	O-64	0.0
Total 13		1283	4625	777	1466	341	67	164	833	372	477	.317	.372	.526	133	205	70		7	.971	1	*O-1195	12.6
■ BUD HAFEY — Hafey, Daniel Albert b: 8/6/12, Berkeley, Cal. d: 7/27/86, Sacramento, Cal. BR/TR, 6', 185 lbs. Deb: 4/21/35 F																							
1935	Chi-A	2	0	1	0	0	0	0	0	0	0	—	—	—		0	0	0	0	.000	0	R	0.0
	Pit-N	58	184	29	42	11	2	6	16	16	48	.228	.290	.408	83	-5	0			.970	4	O-47	-0.3
1936	Pit-N	39	118	19	25	6	1	4	13	10	27	.212	.273	.381	73	-5	0			.932	0	O-29	-0.6
1939	Cin-N	6	13	1	2	1	0	0	1	1	4	.154	.214	.231	19	-1	1			1.000	-0	/O-4	-0.2
	Phi-N	18	51	3	9	1	0	0	3	3	12	.176	.222	.196	14	-6	1			1.000	1	O-13/P-2	-0.6
	Yr	24	64	4	11	2	0	0	4	4	16	.172	.221	.203	15	-8	2			1.000	0	O-17/P-2	-0.8
Total 3		123	366	53	78	19	3	10	33	30	91	.213	.273	.363	68	-18	2		0	.963	4	/O-93,P-2	-1.7
■ TOM HAFEY — Hafey, Thomas Francis "Heave-O" or "The Arm" b: 7/12/13, Berkeley, Cal. d: 10/2/96, ElCerrito, Cal. BR/TR, 6'1", 180 lbs. Deb: 7/21/39 F																							
1939	NY-N	70	256	37	62	10	1	6	26	10	44	.242	.271	.359	67	-13	1			.960	-0	3-70	-1.2
1944	StL-A	8	14	1	5	2	0	0	2	1	4	.357	.400	.500	148	1	0			1.000	-0	/O-4,1-1	0.1
Total 2		78	270	38	67	12	1	6	28	11	48	.248	.278	.367	72	-12	1		0	.960	-0	/3-70,O-4,1-1	-1.1
■ JOE HAGUE — Hague, Joe Clarence b: 4/25/44, Huntington, W.Va. d: 11/5/94, San Antonio, Tex. BL/TL, 6', 198 lbs. Deb: 9/19/68																							
1968	StL-N	7	17	2	4	0	0	1	1	2	2	.235	.316	.412	119	0	0	0	0	.800	-1	/O-3,1-2	-0.1
1969	StL-N	40	100	8	17	2	1	2	8	12	23	.170	.259	.270	48	-7	0	2	-1	.939	-4	O-17/1-9	-1.1
1970	StL-N	139	451	58	122	16	4	14	68	63	87	.271	.361	.417	106	4	2	1	0	.994	-4	1-82,O-52	-0.9
1971	StL-N	129	380	46	86	9	3	16	54	58	69	.226	.332	.392	100	1	0	3	-2	.996	-3	1-91,O-36	-1.3
1972	StL-N	27	76	8	18	5	1	3	11	17	18	.237	.376	.447	135	4	0	1	-1	1.000	-2	1-22/O-3	0.1
	*Cin-N	69	138	17	34	7	1	4	20	20	18	.246	.342	.399	116	3	1	1	0	1.000	-2	1-22,O-19	-0.1
	Yr	96	214	25	52	12	2	7	31	37	36	.243	.355	.416	124	7	1	2	-1	1.000	-2	1-44,O-22	0.0
1973	Cin-N	19	33	2	5	2	0	0	1	5	5	.152	.263	.212	35	-3	1	0	0	1.000	-1	/O-5,1-4	-0.4
Total 6		430	1195	141	286	41	10	40	163	177	222	.239	.339	.391	101	1	4	8	-4	.996	-11	1-232,O-135	-3.8
■ BILL HAGUE — Hague, William L. (b: William L. Haug) b: 1852, Philadelphia, Pa. BR/TR, 5'9", 164 lbs. Deb: 5/4/1875																							
1875	StL-n	62	260	24	57	2	0	0	22	2	9	.219	.225	.227	63	-8	3	4	-2	.781	3	*3-62/1-1	-0.6
1876	Lou-N	67	294	31	78	8	0	1	22	2	10	.265	.270	.303	77	-10				.754	-26	*3-67/S-1	-3.1
1877	Lou-N	59	263	38	70	7	1	1	24	7	18	.266	.285	.312	75	-10				.843	-19	*3-59	-2.5
1878	Pro-N	62	250	21	51	3	0	0	25	5	34	.204	.220	.216	44	-15				**.925**	19	*3-62	0.7
1879	Pro-N	29	209	20	47	3	1	0	21	3	19	.225	.236	.249	61	-8				.822	5	3-51	-0.3
Total 4		239	1016	110	246	21	2	2	92	17	81	.242	.255	.273	66	-43				.843	-22	3-239/S-1	-5.2
■ DON HAHN — Hahn, Donald Antone b: 11/16/48, San Francisco, Cal. BR/TR, 6'1", 185 lbs. Deb: 4/8/69																							
1969	Mon-N	4	9	0	1	0	0	0	2	0	5	.111	.111	.111	-37	-2	0	0	0	1.000	0	/O-3	-0.2
1970	Mon-N	82	149	22	38	8	0	0	8	27	27	.255	.376	.309	86	-2	4	2	0	.986	-7	O-61	-1.0
1971	NY-N	98	178	16	42	5	1	1	11	21	32	.236	.320	.292	76	-5	2	3	-1	.973	-6	O-80	-1.5
1972	NY-N	17	37	0	6	0	0	0	1	4	12	.162	.244	.162	18	-4	0	0	0	1.000	-0	O-10	-0.7
1973	*NY-N	93	262	22	60	10	0	2	21	22	43	.229	.289	.290	62	-13	0	1	0	.989	-3	O-87	-2.1
1974	NY-N	110	323	34	81	14	1	4	28	37	34	.251	.330	.337	88	-5	2	0	1	.987	-1	*O-106	-1.0
1975	Phi-N	9	5	0	0	0	0	0	0	0	0	.000	.000	.000	-96	-1	0	0	0	1.000	0	/O-7	-0.3
	StL-N	7	8	3	1	0	0	0	0	1	1	.125	.222	.125	-2	-1	0	0	0	1.000	-1	/O-4	-0.2
	SD-N	34	26	7	6	1	2	0	3	10	2	.231	.444	.423	151	1	1	0	0	1.000	-7	O-26	-0.5
	Yr	50	39	10	7	1	2	0	3	11	5	.179	.360	.308	89	-0	1	0	0	1.000	-10	O-37	-1.0
Total 7		454	997	104	235	38	4	7	74	122	158	.236	.321	.303	75	-30	11	6	-0	.985	-29	O-384	-7.5
■ DICK HAHN — Hahn, Richard Frederick b: 7/24/16, Canton, Ohio d: 11/5/92, Orlando, Fla. BR/TR, 5'11", 176 lbs. Deb: 9/7/40																							
1940	Was-A	1	3	0	0	0	0	0	0	0	0	.000	.000	.000	-99	-1	0	0	0	1.000	0	/C-1	-0.1
■ ED HAHN — Hahn, William Edgar b: 8/27/1875, Nevada, Ohio d: 11/29/41, Des Moines, Iowa BL/TR, 160 lbs. Deb: 8/31/05																							
1905	NY-A	43	160	32	51	5	0	0		11	25	.319	.426	.350	132	7	1			.957	2	O-43	0.8
1906	NY-A	11	22	2	2	1	0	0		1	3	.091	.259	.136	23	-2	2			1.000	-1	/O-7	-0.3
	*Chi-A	130	484	80	110	7	5	0		27	69	.227	.335	.262	90	-2	19			.949	-6	*O-130	-1.5
	Yr	141	506	82	112	8	5	0		28	72	.221	.331	.262	86	-4	21			.952	-6	*O-137	-1.8
1907	Chi-A	156	592	87	151	9	7	0		45	84	.255	.359	.294	112	14	17			**.990**	-5	*O-156	0.3
1908	Chi-A	122	447	58	112	12	8	0		21	39	.251	.329	.313	111	7	11			.965	-11	*O-118	-1.1
1909	Chi-A	76	287	30	52	6	0	1		16	31	.181	.268	.213	54	-14	9			.990	-7	O-76	-2.8
1910	Chi-A	15	53	2	6	1	0	0		1	7	.113	.217	.151	16	-5	0			.933	-3	O-15	-1.0
Total 6		553	2045	291	484	42	20	1		122	258	.237	.335	.278	97	5	59			.970	-30	O-545	-5.6
■ ED HAIGH — Haigh, Edward E. b: 2/7/1867, Philadelphia, Pa. d: 2/13/53, Atlantic City, N.J Deb: 8/14/1892																							
1892	StL-N	1	4	0	1	0	0	0	0	0	2	.250	.250	.250	54	-0	0			1.000	1	/O-1	0.0
■ HINKEY HAINES — Haines, Henry Luther b: 12/23/1898, Red Lion, Pa. d: 1/9/79, Sharon Hill, Pa. BR/TR, 5'10", 170 lbs. Deb: 4/20/23																							
1923	*NY-A	28	25	9	4	2	0	0	3	4	5	.160	.276	.240	36	-2	3	1	0	1.000	-3	O-14	-0.5
■ JERRY HAIRSTON — Hairston, Jerry Wayne b: 2/16/52, Birmingham, Ala. BB/TR, 5'10", 180 lbs. Deb: 7/26/73 F																							
1973	Chi-A	60	210	25	57	11	1	0	23	33	30	.271	.373	.333	97	1	0	0	0	.944	2	O-33,1-19/D-8	-0.1
1974	Chi-A	45	109	8	25	7	0	0	8	13	18	.229	.311	.294	73	-4	0	2	-1	.926	-4	O-22,D-10	-1.0
1975	Chi-A	69	219	26	62	8	0	0	23	46	23	.283	.410	.320	107	5	1	0	0	.951	1	O-59/D-8	0.4
1976	Chi-A	44	119	20	27	2	0	0	10	24	19	.227	.357	.277	87	-1	1	1	-0	.973	-3	O-40	-0.6
1977	Chi-A	13	26	3	8	2	0	0	4	5	7	.308	.419	.385	121	1	0	0	0	1.000	-2	O-11	-0.1
	Pit-N	51	52	5	10	2	0	2	6	6	10	.192	.276	.346	64	-3	0	0	0	.923	-4	O-14/2-1	-0.7
1981	Chi-A	9	25	5	7	1	0	1	6	2	4	.280	.357	.440	131	1	0	0	0	.933	0	/O-7	0.0
1982	Chi-A	85	90	11	21	5	0	5	18	9	15	.233	.303	.456	105	0	0	0	0	1.000	-8	O-36/D-2	-0.8
1983	*Chi-A	101	126	17	37	9	1	5	22	23	16	.294	.403	.500	141	8	0	1	-1	.968	-9	O-32/D-4	-0.2
1984	Chi-A	115	227	41	59	13	2	5	19	41	29	.260	.375	.401	110	4	2	1	0	.967	-5	O-37,D-20	-0.2
1985	Chi-A	95	140	9	34	8	0	2	20	29	18	.243	.380	.343	96	1	0	0	0	1.000	-1	D-29/O-5	-0.1
1986	Chi-A	101	225	32	61	15	0	5	26	26	26	.271	.349	.404	101	1	0	0	0	1.000	-3	D-29,1-19,O-11	-0.4
1987	Chi-A	66	126	14	29	8	0	5	20	25	25	.230	.362	.413	102	1	0	0	0	1.000	0	O-13,D-13/1-7	0.0
1988	Chi-A	2	2	0	0	0	0	0	0	0	0	.000	.000	.000	-99	-1	0	0	0	.000	0	/H	-0.1
1989	Chi-A	3	3	1	1	0	0	0	0	1	0	.333	.333	.333	91	-0	0	0	0	.000	0	/D-2	0.0
Total 14		859	1699	216	438	91	6	30	205	282	240	.258	.366	.371	103	15	4	5	-2	.963	-35	O-320,D-125/1-45,2	-3.9
■ JOHNNY HAIRSTON — Hairston, John Louis b: 8/27/44, Birmingham, Ala. BR/TR, 6'2", 200 lbs. Deb: 9/6/69 F																							
1969	Chi-N	3	4	0	1	0	0	0	0	0	2	.250	.250	.250	36	-0	0	0	0	1.000	-1	/C-1,O-1	-0.1
■ SAMMY HAIRSTON — Hairston, Samuel Harding b: 1/20/20, Crawford, Miss. BR/TR, 5'10.5", 187 lbs. Deb: 7/21/51 FC																							
1951	Chi-A	4	5	1	2	1	0	0	1	2	0	.400	.571	.600	222	1	0	0	0	1.000	-1	/C-2	0.0
■ CHET HAJDUK — Hajduk, Chester b: 7/21/18, Chicago, Ill. BR/TR, 6', 195 lbs. Deb: 4/16/41																							
1941	Chi-A	1	1	0	0	0	0	0	0	0	0	.000	.000	.000	-99	-0	0	0	0	.000	0	H	0.0
■ DAVE HAJEK — Hajek, David Vincent b: 10/14/67, Roseville, Cal. BR/TR, 5'10", 165 lbs. Deb: 9/15/95																							
1995	Hou-N	5	2	0	0	0	0	0	0	1	1	.000	.333	.000	-3	-0	1	0	0	.000	0	-0,-0	0.0

YEAR	TM/L	G	AB	R	H	2B	3B	HR	RBI	BB	SO	AVG	OBP	SLG	PRO+	BR/A	SB	CS	SBR	FA	FR	G/POS	TPR
1996	Hou-N	8	10	3	3	1	0	0	0	2	1	.300	.417	.400	128	1	0	0	0	1.000	1	/3-3,2-2	0.2
Total	2	13	12	3	3	1	0	0	0	3	1	.250	.400	.333	105	0	1	0	0	1.000	1	/3-3,2-2	0.2

■ GEORGE HALAS
Halas, George Stanley   b: 2/2/1895, Chicago, Ill.   d: 10/31/83, Chicago, Ill.   BB/TR, 6', 164 lbs.   Deb: 5/6/19

YEAR	TM/L	G	AB	R	H	2B	3B	HR	RBI	BB	SO	AVG	OBP	SLG	PRO+	BR/A	SB	CS	SBR	FA	FR	G/POS	TPR
1919	NY-A	12	22	0	2	0	0	0	0	0	8	.091	.091	.091	-49	-4	0			1.000	-1	/O-6	-0.6

■ JOHN HALDEMAN
Haldeman, John Avery   b: 12/2/1855, Pewee Valley, Ky.   d: 9/17/1899, Louisville, Ky.   BL/TR, 5'10", 175 lbs.   Deb: 7/3/1877

YEAR	TM/L	G	AB	R	H	2B	3B	HR	RBI	BB	SO	AVG	OBP	SLG	PRO+	BR/A	SB	CS	SBR	FA	FR	G/POS	TPR
1877	Lou-N	1	4	0	0	0	0	0	0	0	0	.000	.000	.000	-85	-1				.571	-1	/2-1	-0.2

■ ODELL HALE
Hale, Arvel Odell "Bad News"   b: 8/10/08, Hosston, La.   d: 6/9/80, ElDorado, Ark.   BR/TR, 5'10", 175 lbs.   Deb: 8/1/31

YEAR	TM/L	G	AB	R	H	2B	3B	HR	RBI	BB	SO	AVG	OBP	SLG	PRO+	BR/A	SB	CS	SBR	FA	FR	G/POS	TPR
1931	Cle-A	25	92	14	26	2	4	1	5	8	8	.283	.340	.424	94	-1	2	0	1	.918	-4	3-15,2-10/S-1	-0.3
1933	Cle-A	98	351	49	97	19	8	10	64	30	37	.276	.333	.462	104	0	2	3	-1	.954	3	2-73,3-21	0.8
1934	Cle-A	143	563	82	170	44	6	13	101	48	50	.302	.357	.471	110	7	8	12	-5	.956	26	*2-137/3-5	3.3
1935	Cle-A	150	589	80	179	37	11	16	101	52	55	.304	.361	.486	115	11	15	13	-3	.938	7	*3-149/2-1	1.9
1936	Cle-A	153	620	126	196	50	13	14	87	64	43	.316	.380	.506	116	14	8	5	-1	.946	17	*3-148/2-3	3.1
1937	Cle-A	154	561	74	150	32	4	6	82	56	41	.267	.335	.371	77	-20	9	6	-1	.964	26	3-90,2-64	1.1
1938	Cle-A	130	496	69	138	32	2	8	69	44	39	.278	.338	.399	86	-12	8	1	2	.963	-13	*2-127	-1.4
1939	Cle-A	108	253	36	79	16	2	4	48	25	18	.312	.374	.439	111	4	4	5	-2	.966	-16	2-73/3-2	-0.9
1940	Cle-A	48	50	3	11	3	1	0	6	5	7	.220	.291	.320	60	-3	0	0	0	.700	-1	/3-3	-0.4
1941	Bos-A	12	24	5	5	2	0	1	1	3	4	.208	.296	.417	85	-1	0	0	0	.857	-3	/3-6,2-1	-0.4
	NY-N	41	102	13	20	3	0	0	9	18	13	.196	.317	.225	53	-6	1			.964	1	2-29	-0.3
Total	10	1062	3701	551	1071	240	51	73	573	353	315	.289	.352	.441	100	-6	57	45		.959	42	2-518,3-439/S-1	6.5

■ GEORGE HALE
Hale, George Wagner "Ducky"   b: 8/3/1894, Dexter, Kan.   d: 11/1/45, Wichita, Kan.   BR/TR, 5'10", 160 lbs.   Deb: 8/24/14

YEAR	TM/L	G	AB	R	H	2B	3B	HR	RBI	BB	SO	AVG	OBP	SLG	PRO+	BR/A	SB	CS	SBR	FA	FR	G/POS	TPR
1914	StL-A	6	11	1	2	0	0	0	0	0	3	.182	.182	.182	10	-1	0			.895	-0	/C-6	-0.1
1916	StL-A	4	1	0	0	0	0	0	0	0	1	.000	.500	.000	54	0	0			1.000	0	/C-3	0.0
1917	StL-A	38	61	4	12	2	1	0	8	10	12	.197	.310	.262	78	-1	0			.927	3	C-28	0.3
1918	StL-A	12	30	0	4	1	0	0	1	1	5	.133	.161	.167	-1	-4	0			.981	2	C-11	-0.1
Total	4	60	103	5	18	3	1	0	9	11	21	.175	.261	.223	49	-6	0			.940	5	/C-48	0.1

■ JOHN HALE
Hale, John Steven   b: 8/5/53, Fresno, Cal.   BL/TR, 6'2", 195 lbs.   Deb: 9/8/74

YEAR	TM/L	G	AB	R	H	2B	3B	HR	RBI	BB	SO	AVG	OBP	SLG	PRO+	BR/A	SB	CS	SBR	FA	FR	G/POS	TPR
1974	LA-N	4	4	2	4	1	0	0	2	0	0	1.000	1.000	1.250	549	2	0	0	0	.000	-1	/O-3	0.1
1975	LA-N	71	204	20	43	7	0	6	22	26	51	.211	.306	.333	81	-5	1	2	-1	.977	-7	O-68	-1.7
1976	LA-N	44	91	4	14	2	1	0	8	16	14	.154	.294	.198	42	-6	4	1	1	.983	-4	O-37	-1.2
1977	LA-N	79	108	10	26	4	1	2	11	15	28	.241	.333	.352	84	-2	2	1	0	.986	-16	O-73	-2.0
1978	Sea-A	107	211	24	36	8	0	4	22	34	64	.171	.286	.265	56	-12	3	4	-2	.988	-13	O-98/D-3	-3.0
1979	Sea-A	54	63	6	14	3	0	2	7	12	26	.222	.347	.365	91	-1	0	0	0	1.000	-11	O-42/D-2	-1.2
Total	6	359	681	66	137	25	2	14	72	103	183	.201	.310	.305	72	-24	10	8	-2	.985	-52	O-321/D-5	-9.0

■ BOB HALE
Hale, Robert Houston   b: 11/7/33, Sarasota, Fla.   BL/TL, 5'10", 195 lbs.   Deb: 7/4/55

YEAR	TM/L	G	AB	R	H	2B	3B	HR	RBI	BB	SO	AVG	OBP	SLG	PRO+	BR/A	SB	CS	SBR	FA	FR	G/POS	TPR
1955	Bal-A	67	182	13	65	7	1	0	29	5	19	.357	.378	.407	119	4	0	2	-1	.974	2	1-44	0.3
1956	Bal-A	85	207	18	49	10	1	1	24	11	10	.237	.279	.309	60	-13	0	2	-1	.975	-0	1-51	-1.7
1957	Bal-A	42	44	2	11	0	0	0	7	2	2	.250	.283	.250	50	-3	0	0	0	1.000	-0	/1-5	-0.4
1958	Bal-A	19	20	2	7	2	0	0	3	2	1	.350	.409	.450	144	1	0	0	0	1.000	1	/1-2	0.2
1959	Bal-A	40	54	2	10	3	0	0	7	6	6	.185	.214	.241	25	-6	0	0	0	1.000	-1	/1-8	-0.7
1960	Cle-A	70	70	2	21	7	0	0	12	5	6	.300	.329	.400	99	-0	0	0	0	.944	0	/1-5	0.0
1961	Cle-A	42	36	0	6	0	0	0	6	0	7	.167	.211	.167	2	-5	0	0	0	.000	0	H	-0.5
	NY-A	11	13	2	2	0	0	1	1	0	0	.154	.154	.385	41	-1	0	0	0	1.000	-1	/1-5	-0.1
	Yr	53	49	2	8	0	0	1	7	1	7	.163	.196	.224	12	-6	0	0	0	1.000	-1	/1-5	-0.6
Total	7	376	626	41	171	29	2	2	89	26	51	.273	.305	.335	76	-22	0	4	-2	.977	2	1-120	-2.9

■ SAMMY HALE
Hale, Samuel Douglas   b: 9/10/1896, Glen Rose, Tex.   d: 9/6/74, Wheeler, Tex.   BR/TR, 5'8.5", 160 lbs.   Deb: 4/20/20

YEAR	TM/L	G	AB	R	H	2B	3B	HR	RBI	BB	SO	AVG	OBP	SLG	PRO+	BR/A	SB	CS	SBR	FA	FR	G/POS	TPR
1920	Det-A	76	116	13	34	3	3	1	14	5	15	.293	.322	.397	92	-2	2	0	1	.886	-3	3-16/O-4,2-1	-0.3
1921	Det-A	9	2	2	0	0	0	0	0	0	1	.000	.000	.000	-99	-1	0	1	-1	.000	0	H	-0.1
1923	Phi-A	115	434	68	125	22	8	3	51	17	31	.288	.327	.396	89	-9	8	3	1	.916	-19	*3-107	-1.7
1924	Phi-A	80	261	41	83	14	2	2	17	17	19	.318	.367	.410	99	-1	3	2	-0	.948	-8	3-55/O-5,S-1	-0.4
1925	Phi-A	110	391	62	135	30	11	8	63	17	27	.345	.376	.540	122	11	7	4	-0	.919	-4	3-96/2-1	1.2
1926	Phi-A	111	327	49	92	22	9	4	43	13	36	.281	.311	.440	89	-7	1	4	2	.947	-2	3-77/O-1	-0.6
1927	Phi-A	131	501	77	157	24	8	5	81	32	32	.313	.358	.423	97	-3	11	3	2	.961	1	*3-128	0.5
1928	Phi-A	88	314	38	97	20	9	4	58	9	21	.309	.334	.468	106	1	2	0	1	.932	12	3-79	1.7
1929	Phi-A	101	379	51	105	14	3	1	40	12	18	.277	.303	.338	62	-21	6	2	1	.956	-7	3-99/2-1	-2.3
1930	StL-A	62	190	21	52	8	1	2	25	8	18	.274	.303	.358	65	-10	1	1	-0	.947	-3	3-47	-1.0
Total	10	883	2915	422	880	157	54	30	392	130	218	.302	.336	.424	93	-42	41	20		.939	-33	3-704/O-10,2-3,S-1	-3.0

■ CHIP HALE
Hale, Walter William   b: 12/2/64, San Jose, Cal.   BL/TR, 5'11", 180 lbs.   Deb: 8/27/89

YEAR	TM/L	G	AB	R	H	2B	3B	HR	RBI	BB	SO	AVG	OBP	SLG	PRO+	BR/A	SB	CS	SBR	FA	FR	G/POS	TPR
1989	Min-A	28	67	6	14	3	0	0	4	1	6	.209	.221	.254	31	-6	0	0	0	.980	-3	2-16/3-9,D-2	-0.9
1990	Min-A	1	2	0	0	0	0	0	2	0	1	.000	.000	.000	-94	-1	0	0	0	1.000	1	/2-1	0.1
1993	Min-A	69	186	25	62	6	1	3	27	18	17	.333	.410	.425	124	7	2	1	0	.952	3	2-21,3-19,D-19/1S	0.4
1994	Min-A	67	118	13	31	9	0	1	11	16	14	.263	.356	.364	86	-2	0	2	-1	.964	5	3-21,D-10/1-7,2O	0.1
1995	Min-A	69	103	10	27	4	0	2	18	11	20	.262	.333	.359	80	-3	0	0	0	1.000	1	D-27/2-7,3-5,1-3	-0.4
1996	Min-A	85	87	8	24	5	0	1	16	10	6	.276	.351	.368	80	-2	0	0	0	1.000	1	2-14,D-10/1-6,3O	-0.2
Total	6	319	563	62	158	27	1	7	78	56	64	.281	.353	.369	90	-7	2	3	-1	.969	7	/D-68,2-64,310S	-0.9

■ FRED HALEY
Haley, Frederick   b: 6/18/1853, Wheeling, W.Va.   TR,   Deb: 6/22/1880

YEAR	TM/L	G	AB	R	H	2B	3B	HR	RBI	BB	SO	AVG	OBP	SLG	PRO+	BR/A	SB	CS	SBR	FA	FR	G/POS	TPR
1880	Tro-N	2	7	0	0	0	0	0	0	0		.000	.125	.000	-51	-1				.750	-2	/C-2	-0.3

■ RAY HALEY
Haley, Raymond Timothy "Pat"   b: 1/23/1891, Danbury, Iowa   d: 10/8/73, Bradenton, Fla.   BR/TR, 5'11", 180 lbs.   Deb: 4/21/15

YEAR	TM/L	G	AB	R	H	2B	3B	HR	RBI	BB	SO	AVG	OBP	SLG	PRO+	BR/A	SB	CS	SBR	FA	FR	G/POS	TPR
1915	Bos-A	5	7	2	1	1	0	0	1	0	1	.143	.250	.286	62	-0	0			1.000	0	/C-4	0.0
1916	Bos-A	1	1	0	0	0	0	0	0	0	0	.000	.000	.000	-99	-0	0			.000	0	H	0.0
	Phi-A	34	108	8	25	5	0	0	4	6	19	.231	.278	.278	70	-4	0			.982	6	C-33	0.5
	Yr	35	109	8	25	5	0	0	4	6	20	.229	.275	.275	69	-4	0			.982	6	C-33	0.5
1917	Phi-A	41	98	7	27	2	1	0	11	4	12	.276	.311	.316	93	-1	2			.947	-6	C-34	-0.6
Total	3	81	214	17	53	8	1	0	15	11	32	.248	.291	.294	80	-6	2			.970	1	/C-71	-0.1

■ ALBERT HALL
Hall, Albert   b: 3/7/58, Birmingham, Ala.   BB/TR, 5'11", 155 lbs.   Deb: 9/12/81

YEAR	TM/L	G	AB	R	H	2B	3B	HR	RBI	BB	SO	AVG	OBP	SLG	PRO+	BR/A	SB	CS	SBR	FA	FR	G/POS	TPR
1981	Atl-N	6	2	1	0	0	0	0	0	1	1	.000	.333	.000	1	-0	0	0	0	.000	-1	/O-2	-0.1
1982	Atl-N	5	0	1	0	0	0	0	0	0	0	—	—	—		0	0	0	0	.000	0	/R	0.0
1983	Atl-N	10	8	2	0	0	0	0	0	2	0	.000	.200	.000	-37	-1	1	1	-0	.750	-2	/O-4	-0.4
1984	Atl-N	87	142	25	37	6	1	1	9	10	18	.261	.309	.338	76	-4	6	4	-1	.932	-10	O-66	-1.7
1985	Atl-N	54	47	5	7	0	1	0	3	9	12	.149	.286	.191	34	-4	1	1	0	.900	-4	O-13	-0.8
1986	Atl-N	16	50	6	12	2	0	1	5	6	6	.240	.309	.280	60	-3	8	3	1	.900	-3	O-14	-0.3
1987	Atl-N	92	292	54	83	20	4	3	24	38	36	.284	.367	.411	102	2	33	10	4	.981	3	O-69	0.6
1988	Atl-N	85	231	27	57	7	1	1	15	21	35	.247	.315	.299	73	-7	15	10	-2	.973	2	O-63	-1.0
1989	Pit-N	20	33	4	6	2	1	0	1	3	5	.182	.250	.303	59	-2	3	0	1	.909	-3	O-12	-0.5
Total	9	375	805	125	202	37	8	5	53	89	115	.251	.329	.335	80	-20	67	29	3	.958	-15	O-243	-4.2

■ AL HALL
Hall, Archibald W.   b: Worcester, Mass.   d: 2/10/1885, Warren, Pa.   Deb: 5/1/1879

YEAR	TM/L	G	AB	R	H	2B	3B	HR	RBI	BB	SO	AVG	OBP	SLG	PRO+	BR/A	SB	CS	SBR	FA	FR	G/POS	TPR
1879	Tro-N	67	306	30	79	7	3	0	14	3	13	.258	.265	.301	92	-2				.842	5	*O-67	-0.1
1880	Cle-N	3	8	1	1	0	0	0	0	0	0	.125	.125	.125	-15	-1				1.000	-1	/O-3	-0.2
Total	2	70	314	31	80	7	3	0	14	3	13	.255	.262	.296	90	-3				.843	4	/O-70	-0.3

YEAR	TM/L	G	AB	R	H	2B	3B	HR	RBI	BB	SO	AVG	OBP	SLG	PRO+	BR/A	SB	CS	SBR	FA	FR	G/POS	TPR

■ CHARLIE HALL Hall, Charles Walter "Doc" b: 8/24/1863, Toulon, Ill. d: 6/24/21, Tacoma, Wash. Deb: 5/3/1887

1887	NY-a	3	12	1	1	0	0	0	0	0	2	.083	.214	.083	-16	-2	1			1.000	0	/O-3	-0.1

■ GEORGE HALL Hall, George William b: 3/29/1849, Stepney, England d: 6/11/23, Ridgewood, N.J. BL, 5'7", 142 lbs. Deb: 5/5/1871

1871	Oly-n	32	136	31	40	3	3	2	17	8	0	.294	.333	.404	117	4	2	1	0	.913	7	*O-32	0.8
1872	Bal-n	53	250	69	84	17	6	1	37	3	1	.336	.344	.464	140	10	6	1	1	.836	-3	*O-52/1-1	0.7
1873	Bal-n	35	168	44	58	6	3	0	30	2	0	.345	.353	.417	128	6	0	0	0	.840	2	*O-35	0.6
1874	Bos-n	47	222	58	64	10	8	1	32	1	0	.288	.291	.419	118	3	2	0	1	.811	-2	*O-47	0.2
1875	Ath-n	77	358	71	107	10	12	4	62	3	4	.299	.305	.427	136	10	8	5	-1	.887	4	*O-77/1-1	1.1
1876	Phi-N	60	268	51	98	7	13	5	45	8	4	.366	.384	.545	208	30				.801	-2	*O-60	2.4
1877	Lou-N	61	269	53	87	15	8	0	26	12	19	.323	.352	.439	125	5				**.900**	-6	*O-61	-0.3
Total	5 n	244	1134	273	353	46	32	8	178	17	5	.311	.321	.429	130	32	18	7	1	.861	7	O-243/1-2	3.4
Total	2	121	537	104	185	22	21	5	71	20	23	.345	.368	.492	162	35				.837	-7	O-121	2.1

■ IRV HALL Hall, Irvin Gladstone b: 10/7/18, Alberton, Md. BR/TR, 5'10.5", 160 lbs. Deb: 4/20/43

1943	Phi-A	151	544	37	139	15	4	0	54	22	42	.256	.292	.298	73	-19	10	7	-1	.948	-11	*S-148/2-1,3-1	-2.2
1944	Phi-A	143	559	60	150	20	8	0	45	31	46	.268	.309	.333	85	-12	2	5	-2	.980	-5	2-97,S-40/1-4	-1.2
1945	Phi-A	151	616	62	161	17	5	0	50	35	42	.261	.307	.305	78	-17	3	10	-5	.978	**26**	*2-151	1.4
1946	Phi-A	63	185	19	46	6	2	0	19	9	18	.249	.287	.303	65	-9	1	1	-0	.973	-4	2-40/S-7	-1.1
Total	4	508	1904	178	496	58	19	0	168	97	148	.261	.302	.311	77	-58	16	23	-9	.977	6	2-289,S-195/1-4,3-1	-3.1

■ JIM HALL Hall, James d: 1/30/1886, Brooklyn, N.Y. Deb: 5/20/1872

1872	Atl-n	13	57	9	18	0	1	0	6	1	0	.316	.328	.351	93	-2	0	0	0	.750	-3	2-13	-0.4
1874	Atl-n	2	9	0	1	0	0	0	0	0	0	.111	.111	.111	-32	-2	0	0	0	.857	-1	/2-2,O-1	-0.2
1875	Wes-n	1	3	0	1	0	1	0	1	0	0	.333	.333	1.000	327	1	0	0	0	.000	-1	/O-1	0.0
Total	3 n	16	69	9	20	0	2	0	7	1	0	.290	.300	.348	89	-2	0	0	0	.758	-5	/2-15,O-2	-0.6

■ JIMMIE HALL Hall, Jimmie Randolph b: 3/17/38, Mt.Holly, N.C. BL/TR, 6', 175 lbs. Deb: 4/9/63

1963	Min-A	156	497	88	129	21	5	33	80	63	101	.260	.343	.521	136	23	3	3	-1	.982	-10	*O-143	0.5
1964	Min-A★	149	510	61	144	20	3	25	75	44	112	.282	.341	.480	125	16	5	2	0	.985	13	*O-137	2.4
1965	*Min-A★	148	522	81	149	25	4	20	86	51	79	.285	.350	.464	124	16	14	7	0	.976	-2	*O-141	0.8
1966	Min-A	120	356	52	85	7	4	20	47	33	66	.239	.303	.449	106	2	1	2	-1	.978	-1	*O-103	-0.4
1967	Cal-A	129	401	54	100	8	3	16	55	42	65	.249	.321	.404	117	8	4	1	1	.990	-2	*O-120	0.1
1968	Cal-A	46	126	15	27	3	0	1	8	16	19	.214	.303	.262	75	-3	1	0	0	.981	-4	O-39	-1.0
	Cle-A	53	111	4	22	4	0	1	8	10	19	.198	.264	.261	61	-5	0	0	0	.983	-1	O-29	-0.5
	Yr	99	237	19	49	7	0	2	16	26	38	.207	.285	.262	68	-9	2	0	1	.982	-2	O-68	-1.5
1969	Cle-A	4	10	1	0	0	0	0	0	2	3	.000	.167	.000	-48	-2	1	0	0	1.000	-0	/O-3	-0.2
	NY-A	80	212	21	50	8	5	3	26	19	34	.236	.299	.363	88	-4	8	3	1	.963	-5	O-50/1-7	-1.2
	Yr	84	222	22	50	8	5	3	26	21	37	.225	.292	.347	81	-6	9	3	1	.966	-5	O-53/1-7	-1.4
	Chi-N	11	24	1	5	1	0	0	1	1	5	.208	.240	.250	33	-2	0	0	0	1.000	-1	O-5	-0.4
1970	Chi-N	28	32	2	3	1	0	0	1	4	12	.094	.194	.125	-11	-5	0	0	0	1.000	-2	/O-8	-0.7
	Atl-N	39	47	7	10	2	0	2	4	2	14	.213	.245	.383	62	-3	0	0	0	1.000	-6	O-28	-0.9
	Yr	67	79	9	13	3	0	2	5	6	26	.165	.224	.278	31	-8	0	0	0	1.000	-7	O-36	-1.6
Total	8	963	2848	387	724	100	24	121	391	287	529	.254	.323	.434	112	40	38	18	1	.982	-17	O-806/1-7	-1.5

■ JOE HALL Hall, Joseph Geroy b: 3/6/66, Paducah, Ky. BR/TR, 6', 180 lbs. Deb: 4/5/94

1994	Chi-A	17	28	6	11	3	0	1	5	2	4	.393	.452	.607	173	3	0	0	0	.917	-2	/O-9,D-2	0.1
1995	Det-A	7	15	2	2	0	0	0	0	2	3	.133	.235	.133	-1	-2	0	0	0	1.000	1	/O-5,D-2	-0.1
Total	2	24	43	8	13	3	0	1	5	4	7	.302	.375	.442	112	1	0	0	0	.958	-1	/O-14,D-4	0.0

■ MEL HALL Hall, Melvin b: 9/16/60, Lyons, N.Y. BL/TL, 6'1", 205 lbs. Deb: 9/3/81

1981	Chi-N	10	11	1	1	0	0	1	2	1	4	.091	.167	.364	45	-1	0	0	0	.000	-2	/O-3	-0.3
1982	Chi-N	24	80	6	21	3	2	0	4	5	17	.262	.322	.350	86	-1	0	1	-1	.939	1	O-22	-0.2
1983	Chi-N	112	410	60	116	23	5	17	56	42	101	.283	.354	.488	125	13	6	6	-2	.988	1	*O-112	0.8
1984	Chi-N	48	150	25	42	11	3	4	22	12	23	.280	.333	.473	114	2	2	1	0	.961	-2	O-46	-0.1
	Cle-A	83	257	43	66	13	1	7	30	35	55	.257	.350	.397	104	2	1	1	-0	.993	0	O-69/D-9	0.0
1985	Cle-A	23	66	7	21	6	0	0	12	8	12	.318	.392	.409	121	2	0	1	-1	1.000	-3	O-15/D-5	-0.2
1986	Cle-A	140	442	68	131	29	2	18	77	33	65	.296	.348	.493	128	16	6	6	1	.972	-7	*O-126/D-7	0.6
1987	Cle-A	142	485	57	136	21	1	18	76	20	68	.280	.310	.439	95	-5	5	4	-1	.989	6	*O-122,D-14	-0.5
1988	Cle-A	150	515	69	144	32	4	6	71	28	50	.280	.317	.392	95	-4	7	3	0	.967	-3	*O-141/D-6	-1.1
1989	NY-A	113	361	54	94	9	0	17	58	21	37	.260	.301	.427	104	1	0	0	0	.993	-2	O-75,D-34	-0.4
1990	NY-A	113	360	41	93	23	2	12	46	6	46	.258	.274	.433	95	-5	0	0	0	.973	-6	D-54,O-50	-1.3
1991	NY-A	141	492	67	140	23	2	19	80	26	40	.285	.324	.455	113	7	0	1	-1	.987	-0	*O-120,D-10	0.3
1992	NY-A	152	583	67	163	36	3	15	81	29	53	.280	.315	.429	107	3	4	2	0	.990	6	*O-136,D-11	0.6
1996	SF-N	25	25	3	3	0	0	0	5	1	4	.120	.154	.120	-28	-2	0	0	0	.000	-0	/O-4	-0.6
Total	13	1276	4237	568	1171	229	25	134	620	267	575	.276	.322	.437	107	26	31	22	-4	.981	-13	*O-1041,D-150	-2.3

■ DICK HALL Hall, Richard Wallace b: 9/27/30, St.Louis, Mo. BR/TR, 6'6", 200 lbs. Deb: 4/15/52

1952	Pit-N	26	80	6	11	0	0	0	2	2	17	.138	.159	.150	-14	-12	0	1	-1	.972	0	O-14/3-5	-1.4
1953	Pit-N	7	24	2	4	0	0	0	1	1	3	.167	.200	.167	-3	-4	1	1	-0	.978	11	/2-7	0.7
1954	Pit-N	112	310	38	74	8	4	2	27	33	46	.239	.312	.310	64	-16	3	0	1	.956	-2	*O-102	-2.1
1955	Pit-N	21	40	3	7	1	0	1	3	6	5	.175	.283	.275	50	-3	0	0	0	1.000	-3	P-15/O-3	-0.2
1956	Pit-N	33	29	5	10	0	0	0	1	5	7	.345	.441	.345	118	1	0	0	0	1.000	1	P-19/1-1	0.0
1957	Pit-N	10	1	0	0	0	0	0	0	0	1	.000	.000	.000	-99	-0	0	0	0	.000	-0	/P-8	0.0
1959	Pit-N	2	2	0	0	0	0	0	0	0	1	.000	.000	.000	-99	-1	0	0	0	1.000	-0	/P-2	0.0
1960	KC-A	32	56	5	6	0	0	0	4	4	15	.107	.167	.107	-24	-10	0	0	0	.925	-1	P-29	0.0
1961	Bal-A	30	36	4	5	0	1	0	3	3	13	.139	.205	.139	-6	-5	0	0	0	.970	-1	P-29	0.0
1962	Bal-A	44	24	3	4	1	0	1	4	1	9	.167	.286	.208	38	-2	0	0	0	1.000	-0	P-43	0.0
1963	Bal-A	48	28	7	13	1	0	1	4	0	8	.464	.464	.607	205	4	0	0	0	1.000	1	P-47	0.0
1964	Bal-A	45	16	1	2	0	0	0	1	0	3	.125	.176	.125	-14	-2	0	0	0	1.000	-0	P-45	0.0
1965	Bal-A	49	15	1	5	0	0	0	4	1	4	.333	.412	.467	146	1	0	0	0	.923	-1	P-48	0.0
1966	Bal-A	32	12	0	2	0	0	0	2	0	5	.167	.231	.167	17	-1	0	0	0	1.000	-0	P-32	0.0
1967	Phi-N	48	14	1	1	0	0	0	0	0	5	.071	.071	.071	-58	-3	0	0	0	1.000	-1	P-48	0.0
1968	Phi-N	32	3	0	1	0	0	0	0	0	1	.333	.333	.333	101	-0	0	0	0	1.000	-0	P-32	0.0
1969	*Bal-A	39	7	1	2	0	0	0	0	0	2	.286	.375	.286	86	-0	0	0	0	1.000	-1	P-39	0.0
1970	*Bal-A	32	12	2	1	0	0	0	1	0	3	.083	.083	.083	-53	-2	0	0	0	1.000	-2	P-32	0.0
1971	*Bal-A	27	5	0	2	0	0	0	0	0	0	.400	.400	.600	182	0	0	0	0	.800	-1	P-27	0.0
Total	19	669	714	79	150	15	4	6	61	147		.210	.274	.259	44	-56				.976	0	P-495,O-119/2-7,31	-3.1

■ BOB HALL Hall, Robert Prill b: 12/20/1878, Baltimore, Md. d: 12/1/50, Wellesley, Mass. TR, 5'10", 158 lbs. Deb: 4/18/04

1904	Phi-N	46	163	11	26	4	0	0	17	14		.160	.226	.184	28	-13	5			.843	-10	3-20,S-15,1-11	-2.5
1905	NY-N	1	3	1	1	0	0	0	0	0		.333	.333	.333	97	-0	0			.000	-0	/O-1	0.0
	Bro-N	56	203	21	48	4	1	2	15	11		.236	.279	.296	77	-6	8			.939	6	O-42/2-7,1-3	-0.3
	Yr	57	206	22	49	4	1	2	15	11		.238	.280	.296	77	-6	8			.939	6	O-43/2-7,1-3	-0.3
Total	2	103	369	33	75	8	1	2	32	25		.203	.256	.247	55	-20	13			.968	-5	/O-43,3-20,S-15,12	-2.8

■ RUSS HALL Hall, Robert Russell b: 9/29/1871, Shelbyville, Ky. d: 7/1/37, Los Angeles, Cal. TL, 5'10", 170 lbs. Deb: 4/15/1898

1898	StL-N	39	143	13	35	2	1	0	10	7		.245	.285	.273	59	-8	1			.835	-14	S-35/3-3,O-1	-2.0
1901	Cle-A	1	4	2	2	0	0	0	0	0		.500	.500	.500	185	0	0			.500	-1	/S-1	-0.1
Total	2	40	147	15	37	2	1	0	10	7		.252	.290	.279	62	-7	1			.824	-16	/S-36,3-3,O-1	-2.1

YEAR	TM/L	G	AB	R	H	2B	3B	HR	RBI	BB	SO	AVG	OBP	SLG	PRO+	BR/A	SB	CS	SBR	FA	FR	G/POS	TPR

■ BILL HALL
Hall, William Lemuel b: 7/30/28, Moultrie, Ga. d: 1/1/86, Moultrie, Ga. BL/TR, 5'11", 165 lbs. Deb: 4/18/54

YEAR	TM/L	G	AB	R	H	2B	3B	HR	RBI	BB	SO	AVG	OBP	SLG	PRO+	BR/A	SB	CS	SBR	FA	FR	G/POS	TPR
1954	Pit-N	5	7	0	0	0	0	0	0	0	0	.000	.000	.000	-99	-2	0	0	0	1.000	-0	/C-1	-0.2
1956	Pit-N	1	3	0	0	0	0	0	0	0	1	.000	.000	.000	-99	-1	0	0	0	1.000	1	/C-1	0.0
1958	Pit-N	51	116	15	33	6	0	1	15	15	13	.284	.366	.362	96	-0	0	0	0	.982	7	C-51	0.9
Total	3	57	126	15	33	6	0	1	15	15	15	.262	.340	.333	81	-3	0	0	0	.983	8	/C-53	0.7

■ TOM HALLER
Haller, Thomas Frank b: 6/23/37, Lockport, Ill. BL/TR, 6'4", 195 lbs. Deb: 4/11/61 C

YEAR	TM/L	G	AB	R	H	2B	3B	HR	RBI	BB	SO	AVG	OBP	SLG	PRO+	BR/A	SB	CS	SBR	FA	FR	G/POS	TPR
1961	SF-N	30	62	5	9	1	0	2	8	9	23	.145	.264	.258	41	-5	0	1	-1	1.000	2	C-25	-0.3
1962	*SF-N	99	272	53	71	13	1	18	55	51	59	.261	.385	.515	142	17	1	4	-2	.992	-2	C-91	1.6
1963	SF-N	98	298	32	76	8	1	14	44	34	45	.255	.335	.430	120	8	4	6	-2	.994	-4	C-85/O-7	0.4
1964	SF-N	117	388	43	98	14	3	16	48	55	51	.253	.348	.428	115	9	4	2	0	.989	-1	*C-113/O-3	1.3
1965	SF-N	134	422	40	106	4	3	16	49	47	67	.251	.338	.389	101	1	0	0	0	.987	-5	*C-133	0.4
1966	SF-N☆	142	471	74	113	19	2	27	67	53	74	.240	.345	.461	112	7	1	3	-2	.991	-7	*C-136/1-4	0.8
1967	SF-N★	141	455	54	114	23	5	14	49	62	61	.251	.345	.415	118	12	0	4	-2	.997	3	*C-136/O-1	1.7
1968	LA-N★	144	474	37	135	27	5	4	53	46	76	.285	.351	.388	132	18	1	4	-2	.994	3	*C-139	3.2
1969	LA-N	134	445	46	117	18	3	6	39	48	58	.263	.337	.357	102	1	0	3	-2	.992	-9	*C-132	-0.3
1970	LA-N	112	325	47	93	16	6	10	47	32	35	.286	.354	.465	123	10	3	0	1	.993	-8	*C-106	0.7
1971	LA-N	84	202	23	54	5	0	5	32	25	30	.267	.354	.366	111	3	0	2	-1	.978	4	C-67	0.9
1972	*Det-A	59	121	7	25	5	2	2	13	15	14	.207	.290	.331	82	-2	0	1	-1	1.000	8	C-36	0.7
Total	12	1294	3935	461	1011	153	31	134	504	477	593	.257	.342	.414	114	78	14	30	-14	.992	-20	*C-1199/O-11,1-4	11.1

■ NEWT HALLIDAY
Halliday, Newton Reese b: 6/18/1896, Chicago, Ill. d: 4/6/18, Great Lakes, Ill. BR/TR, 6'1", 175 lbs. Deb: 8/19/16

YEAR	TM/L	G	AB	R	H	2B	3B	HR	RBI	BB	SO	AVG	OBP	SLG	PRO+	BR/A	SB	CS	SBR	FA	FR	G/POS	TPR
1916	Pit-N	1	1	0	0	0	0	0	0	0	1	.000	.000	.000	-99	-0				1.000	0	/1-1	0.0

■ JOCKO HALLIGAN
Halligan, William E. b: 12/8/1868, Avon, N.Y. d: 2/13/45, Buffalo, N.Y. BL, 5'9", 166 lbs. Deb: 5/13/1890

YEAR	TM/L	G	AB	R	H	2B	3B	HR	RBI	BB	SO	AVG	OBP	SLG	PRO+	BR/A	SB	CS	SBR	FA	FR	G/POS	TPR
1890	Buf-P	57	211	28	53	9	2	3	33	20	19	.251	.319	.355	87	-4	7			.824	-5	O-43,C-16	-0.8
1891	Cin-N	61	247	43	77	13	6	3	44	24	25	.312	.375	.449	139	12	5			.856	-3	O-61	0.6
1892	Cin-N	26	101	14	29	4	0	2	12	12	9	.287	.363	.386	128	4	3			.875	-1	O-26	0.2
	Bal-N	46	178	38	47	4	7	2	43	30	24	.264	.376	.399	131	7	8			.861	-7	O-22,1-19/C-5	-0.2
	Yr	72	279	52	76	8	7	4	55	42	33	.272	.372	.394	130	11	11			.869	-8	O-48,1-19/C-5	0.0
Total	3	190	737	123	206	30	15	10	132	86	77	.280	.358	.402	120	19	23			.848	-16	O-152/C-21,1-19	-0.2

■ ED HALLINAN
Hallinan, Edward S. b: 8/23/1888, San Francisco, Cal d: 8/24/40, San Francisco, Cal BR/TR, 5'9", 168 lbs. Deb: 5/13/11

YEAR	TM/L	G	AB	R	H	2B	3B	HR	RBI	BB	SO	AVG	OBP	SLG	PRO+	BR/A	SB	CS	SBR	FA	FR	G/POS	TPR
1911	StL-A	52	169	13	35	3	1	0	14	14		.207	.268	.237	43	-13	4			.902	-6	S-34,2-15/3-3	-1.7
1912	StL-A	29	86	11	19	2	0	0	1	5		.221	.272	.244	50	-6	3			.866	-7	S-26	-1.1
Total	2	81	255	24	54	5	1	0	15	19		.212	.269	.239	45	-19	7			.887	-12	/S-60,2-15,3-3	-2.8

■ JIMMY HALLINAN
Hallinan, James H. b: 5/27/1849, Ireland d: 10/28/1879, Chicago, Ill. BL/TL, 5'9", 172 lbs. Deb: 7/26/1871

YEAR	TM/L	G	AB	R	H	2B	3B	HR	RBI	BB	SO	AVG	OBP	SLG	PRO+	BR/A	SB	CS	SBR	FA	FR	G/POS	TPR
1871	Kek-n	5	25	7	5	0	0	0	2	2	0	.200	.259	.200	34	-2	1	1	-0	.475	-6	/S-5	-0.6
1875	Wes-n	13	51	12	14	2	1	0	3	0	1	.275	.275	.353	110	0	2	2	-1	.742	-5	S-13	-0.5
	Mut-n	44	203	29	58	6	3	3	21	1	2	.286	.289	.389	127	4	2	2	-1	.765	-10	S-43/3-1,O-1	-0.7
	Yr	57	254	41	72	8	4	3	24	1	3	.283	.286	.382	123	5	4	4	-1	.761	-15	S-56/3-1,O-1	-1.2
1876	NY-N	54	240	45	67	7	6	2	36	2	4	.279	.285	.383	139	10				.764	-15	*S-50/2-4,O-2	-0.5
1877	Cin-N	16	73	18	27	1	1	0	7	1	1	.370	.378	.411	167	6				.854	-6	2-16	0.0
	Chi-N	19	89	17	25	4	1	0	11	4	2	.281	.312	.348	96	-1				.800	-2	O-19	-0.3
	Yr	35	162	35	52	5	2	0	18	5	3	.321	.341	.377	124	4				.800	-8	O-19,2-16	-0.3
1878	Chi-N	16	67	14	19	3	0	0	2	5	6	.284	.333	.328	111	1				.789	-4	O-11/2-5	-0.3
	Ind-N	3	12	0	3	2	0	0	1	0	2	.250	.250	.417	134	0				.667	-1	/O-3	0.0
	Yr	19	79	14	22	5	0	0	3	5	8	.278	.321	.342	114	1				.760	-5	O-14/2-5	-0.3
Total	2 n	62	279	48	77	8	4	3	26	3	3	.276	.284	.366	114	3	5	5	-2	.728	-22	/S-61,O-1,3-1	-1.8
Total	3	108	481	94	141	17	8	2	57	12	15	.293	.310	.374	129	16				.783	-28	/S-50,O-35,2-25	-1.1

■ BILL HALLMAN
Hallman, William Harry b: 3/15/1876, Philadelphia, Pa. d: 4/23/50, Philadelphia, Pa. BL/TL, Deb: 4/25/01

YEAR	TM/L	G	AB	R	H	2B	3B	HR	RBI	BB	SO	AVG	OBP	SLG	PRO+	BR/A	SB	CS	SBR	FA	FR	G/POS	TPR
1901	Mil-A	139	549	70	135	27	6	2	47	41		.246	.301	.328	78	-16	12			.905	-2	*O-139	-2.7
1903	Chi-A	63	207	29	43	7	4	0	18	31		.208	.320	.280	85	-2	11			.953	2	O-57	-0.4
1906	Pit-N	23	89	12	24	3	1	1	6	15		.270	.375	.360	124	3	3			.935	-1	O-23	0.1
1907	Pit-N	94	302	39	67	6	2	0	15	33		.222	.305	.255	74	-8	21			.966	-6	O-84	-1.9
Total	4	319	1147	150	269	43	13	3	86	120		.235	.311	.303	82	-24	47			.933	-7	O-303	-4.9

■ BILL HALLMAN
Hallman, William Wilson b: 3/31/1867, Pittsburgh, Pa. d: 9/11/20, Philadelphia, Pa. BR/TR, 5'8", 160 lbs. Deb: 4/23/1888 M

YEAR	TM/L	G	AB	R	H	2B	3B	HR	RBI	BB	SO	AVG	OBP	SLG	PRO+	BR/A	SB	CS	SBR	FA	FR	G/POS	TPR
1888	Phi-N	18	63	5	13	4	1	0	6	1	12	.206	.219	.302	61	-3	1			.898	-7	C-10/2-4,O-3,S-1,3	-0.9
1889	Phi-N	119	462	67	117	21	8	2	60	36	54	.253	.313	.346	77	-16	20			.895	-5	*S-106,2-13/C-1	-0.2
1890	Phi-P	84	356	59	95	16	7	1	37	33	24	.267	.338	.360	84	-9	6			.885	-8	O-34,C-26,2-14,3/S	-1.1
1891	Phi-a	141	587	112	166	21	13	6	69	38	56	.283	.332	.394	104	-0	18			.930	-5	*2-141	0.1
1892	Phi-N	138	586	106	171	27	10	2	84	52	52	.292	.335	.382	117	10	19			.936	-24	*2-138	-1.0
1893	Phi-N	132	596	119	183	28	7	5	76	51	27	.307	.367	.403	105	3	22			.950	-15	*2-120,1-12	-0.7
1894	Phi-N	119	505	107	156	19	7	0	66	36	15	.309	.360	.374	79	-16	36			.930	-19	*2-119	-2.3
1895	Phi-N	124	539	94	169	26	5	1	91	34	20	.314	.359	.386	92	-7	16			.943	6	*2-122/S-3	0.4
1896	Phi-N	120	469	82	150	21	3	2	83	45	23	.320	.382	.390	105	5	16			.945	3	*2-120/P-1	1.2
1897	Phi-N	31	126	16	33	3	0	0	15	8		.262	.326	.286	64	-6	1			.958	-10	2-31	-1.2
	StL-N	79	298	31	66	6	2	0	26	24		.221	.288	.255	45	-23	12			.939	-7	2-77/1-3,M	-1.4
	Yr	110	424	47	99	9	2	0	41	32		.233	.300	.264	51	-29	13			.944	-7	*2-108/1-3	-2.6
1898	Bro-N	134	509	57	124	10	7	2	63	29		.244	.291	.303	70	-20	9			.944	-3	*2-124,3-10	-1.4
1901	Cle-A	5	19	2	4	0	0	0	3	2		.211	.286	.211	41	-1	0			.815	-3	/S-5	-0.4
	Phi-N	123	445	60	82	13	5	0	38	26		.184	.236	.236	36	-36	13			.971	-5	2-90,3-33	-3.7
1902	Phi-N	73	254	14	63	8	4	0	35	14		.248	.287	.311	64	-6	5			.932	-6	3-72	-1.2
1903	Phi-N	63	198	20	42	11	2	0	17	16		.212	.271	.288	61	-10	2			.932	-3	2-22,3-19/1-9,OS	-1.2
Total	14	1503	6012	937	1634	234	81	21	769	425	283	.272	.325	.348	84	-136	200			.940	-88	*2-1135,3-145,S/OC1P	-14.9

■ JIM HALPIN
Halpin, James Nathaniel b: 10/4/1863, England d: 1/4/1893, Boston, Mass. Deb: 6/15/1882

YEAR	TM/L	G	AB	R	H	2B	3B	HR	RBI	BB	SO	AVG	OBP	SLG	PRO+	BR/A	SB	CS	SBR	FA	FR	G/POS	TPR
1882	Wor-N	2	8	0	0	0	0	0	0	0	2	.000	.000	.000	-98	-2				.625	-1	/3-2	-0.3
1884	Was-U	46	168	24	31	3	0	0			2	.185	.194	.202	21	-21				.809	-7	S-39/3-7	-2.5
1885	Det-N	15	54	3	7	2	0	0	1	1	12	.130	.145	.167	1	-6				.846	1	S-15	-0.5
Total	3	63	230	27	38	5	0	0	1		14	.165	.176	.187	12	-28				.821	-8	/S-54,3-9	-3.3

■ AL HALT
Halt, Alva William b: 11/23/1890, Sandusky, Ohio d: 1/22/73, Sandusky, Ohio BR/TR, 6', 180 lbs. Deb: 5/29/14

YEAR	TM/L	G	AB	R	H	2B	3B	HR	RBI	BB	SO	AVG	OBP	SLG	PRO+	BR/A	SB	CS	SBR	FA	FR	G/POS	TPR
1914	Bro-F	80	261	26	61	6	2	3	25	13	39	.234	.270	.307	57	-20	11			.890	-11	S-71/2-3,O-1	-2.7
1915	Bro-F	151	524	41	131	22	7	3	64	39	79	.250	.307	.336	81	-21	20			.930	3	*3-111,S-40	-1.2
1918	Cle-A	26	69	9	12	2	0	0	1	9	12	.174	.269	.203	39	-5	4			.971	-0	3-14/2-4,S-4,1-2	-0.6
Total	3	257	854	76	204	30	9	6	90	61	130	.239	.293	.316	70	-47	35			.933	-9	3-125,S-115/2-7,10	-4.5

■ RALPH HAM
Ham, Ralph A. b: 3/1849, Troy, N.Y. d: 2/13/05, Troy, N.Y. 5'8", 158 lbs. Deb: 5/6/1871

YEAR	TM/L	G	AB	R	H	2B	3B	HR	RBI	BB	SO	AVG	OBP	SLG	PRO+	BR/A	SB	CS	SBR	FA	FR	G/POS	TPR
1871	Rok-n	25	113	25	28	4	3					.248	.254	.283		-6	6	2	1	.723	-5	O-19/3-7,S-2	-0.6

■ CHARLIE HAMBURG
Hamburg, Charles M. (b: Charles M. Hambrick) b: 11/22/1863, Louisville, Ky. d: 5/18/31, Union, N.J. 6', 175 lbs. Deb: 4/18/1890

YEAR	TM/L	G	AB	R	H	2B	3B	HR	RBI	BB	SO	AVG	OBP	SLG	PRO+	BR/A	SB	CS	SBR	FA	FR	G/POS	TPR
1890	*Lou-a	133	485	93	132	22	2	3	77	69		.272	.370	.344	113	11	46			.946	-2	*O-133	0.4

■ JIM HAMBY
Hamby, James Sanford "Cracker" b: 7/29/1897, Wilkesboro, N.C. d: 10/21/91, Springfield, Ill. BR/TR, 6', 170 lbs. Deb: 9/20/26

YEAR	TM/L	G	AB	R	H	2B	3B	HR	RBI	BB	SO	AVG	OBP	SLG	PRO+	BR/A	SB	CS	SBR	FA	FR	G/POS	TPR
1926	NY-N	1	3	0	0	0	0	0	0	0	0	.000	.000	.000	-99	-1	0			.600	-1	/C-1	-0.2
1927	NY-N	21	52	6	10	1	0	0	5	7	7	.192	.288	.231	40	-4	0			.904	-0	C-19	-0.3
Total	2	22	55	6	10	1	0	0	5	7	7	.182	.274	.218	33	-5	1			.885	-1	/C-20	-0.5

YEAR	TM/L	G	AB	R	H	2B	3B	HR	RBI	BB	SO	AVG	OBP	SLG	PRO+	BR/A	SB	CS	SBR	FA	FR	G/POS	TPR

■ BOB HAMELIN
Hamelin, Robert James b: 11/29/67, Elizabeth, N.J. BL/TL, 6', 235 lbs. Deb: 9/12/93

YEAR	TM/L	G	AB	R	H	2B	3B	HR	RBI	BB	SO	AVG	OBP	SLG	PRO+	BR/A	SB	CS	SBR	FA	FR	G/POS	TPR
1993	KC-A	16	49	2	11	3	0	2	5	6	15	.224	.309	.408	86	-1	0	0	0	.986	-0	1-15	-0.2
1994	KC-A	101	312	64	88	25	1	24	65	56	62	.282	.393	.599	145	21	4	3	-1	.992	1	D-70,1-24	1.3
1995	KC-A	72	208	20	35	7	1	7	25	26	56	.168	.279	.313	53	-15	0	1	-1	1.000	1	D-56/1-8	-1.8
1996	KC-A	89	239	31	61	14	1	9	40	54	58	.255	.397	.435	113	7	5	2	0	.984	0	D-47,1-33	0.1
Total	4	278	808	117	195	49	3	42	135	142	191	.241	.361	.465	109	12	9	6	-1	.989	2	D-173/1-80	-0.6

■ DARRYL HAMILTON
Hamilton, Darryl Quinn b: 12/3/64, Baton Rouge, La. BL/TR, 6'1", 180 lbs. Deb: 6/3/88

YEAR	TM/L	G	AB	R	H	2B	3B	HR	RBI	BB	SO	AVG	OBP	SLG	PRO+	BR/A	SB	CS	SBR	FA	FR	G/POS	TPR
1988	Mil-A	44	103	14	19	4	0	1	11	12	9	.184	.276	.252	49	-7	7	3	0	1.000	-1	O-37/D-3	-0.8
1990	Mil-A	89	156	27	46	5	0	1	18	9	12	.295	.333	.346	91	-2	10	3	1	.992	-6	O-72/D-9	-0.8
1991	Mil-A	122	405	64	126	15	6	1	57	33	38	.311	.363	.385	110	6	16	6	1	.996	-10	*O-117	-0.5
1992	Mil-A	128	470	67	140	19	7	5	62	45	42	.298	.360	.400	115	10	41	14	4	1.000	1	*O-124	1.2
1993	Mil-A	135	520	74	161	21	1	9	48	45	62	.310	.368	.406	109	8	21	13	-2	.992	6	*O-129/D-1	0.9
1994	Mil-A	36	141	23	37	10	1	1	13	15	17	.262	.333	.369	77	-5	3	0	1	1.000	-4	O-32/D-4	-0.8
1995	Mil-A	112	398	54	108	20	6	5	44	47	35	.271	.353	.389	88	-7	11	1	3	.989	-2	*O-109/D-2	-0.8
1996	*Tex-A	148	627	94	184	29	4	6	51	54	66	.293	.351	.383	80	-19	15	5	2	1.000	7	*O-147	-1.4
Total	8	814	2820	417	821	123	25	29	304	260	281	.291	.353	.383	95	-16	124	45	10	.996	-9	O-767/D-19	-3.0

■ JEFF HAMILTON
Hamilton, Jeffrey Robert b: 3/19/64, Flint, Mich. BR/TR, 6'3", 207 lbs. Deb: 6/28/86

YEAR	TM/L	G	AB	R	H	2B	3B	HR	RBI	BB	SO	AVG	OBP	SLG	PRO+	BR/A	SB	CS	SBR	FA	FR	G/POS	TPR
1986	LA-N	71	147	22	33	5	0	5	19	2	43	.224	.235	.361	66	-8	0	0	0	.968	11	3-66/S-2	0.3
1987	LA-N	35	83	5	18	3	0	0	1	7	22	.217	.286	.253	45	-6	0	1	-1	.935	9	3-31/S-1	0.2
1988	*LA-N	111	309	34	73	14	2	6	33	10	51	.236	.269	.353	80	-9	0	2	-1	.941	-0	*3-105/S-2,1-1	-1.2
1989	LA-N	151	548	45	134	35	1	12	56	20	71	.245	.275	.378	86	-12	0	0	0	.951	-6	*3-147/P-1,2-1,S-1	-1.8
1990	LA-N	7	24	1	3	0	0	0	1	0	3	.125	.125	.125	-32	-4	0	0	0	1.000	1	/3-7	-0.4
1991	LA-N	41	94	4	21	4	0	1	14	4	21	.223	.255	.298	56	-6	0	0	0	.928	3	3-33/S-1	-0.6
Total	6	416	1205	111	282	61	3	24	124	43	211	.234	.265	.349	74	-45	0	3	-2	.948	15	3-389/S-7,2-1,P1	-3.5

■ TOM HAMILTON
Hamilton, Thomas Ball "Ham" b: 9/29/25, Altoona, Kan. d: 11/29/73, Tyler, Tex. BL/TR, 6'4", 213 lbs. Deb: 9/4/52

YEAR	TM/L	G	AB	R	H	2B	3B	HR	RBI	BB	SO	AVG	OBP	SLG	PRO+	BR/A	SB	CS	SBR	FA	FR	G/POS	TPR
1952	Phi-A	9	10	1	2	1	0	0	1	1	1	.200	.273	.300	56	-1	0	0	0	1.000	-0	/1-5	-0.1
1953	Phi-A	58	56	8	11	2	0	0	5	7	11	.196	.286	.232	40	-5	0	0	0	1.000	-1	/1-7,O-2	-0.6
Total	2	67	66	9	13	3	0	0	6	8	12	.197	.284	.242	42	-5	0	0	0	1.000	-1	/1-12,O-2	-0.7

■ BILLY HAMILTON
Hamilton, William Robert "Sliding Billy" b: 2/16/1866, Newark, N.J. d: 12/16/40, Worcester, Mass. BL/TR, 5'6", 165 lbs. Deb: 7/31/1888 H

YEAR	TM/L	G	AB	R	H	2B	3B	HR	RBI	BB	SO	AVG	OBP	SLG	PRO+	BR/A	SB	CS	SBR	FA	FR	G/POS	TPR
1888	KC-a	35	129	21	34	4	4	0	11	4		.264	.307	.357	106	-0	19			.961	-2	O-35	-0.3
1889	KC-a	137	534	144	161	17	12	3	77	87	41	.301	.413	.395	123	19	111			.857	-7	*O-137	0.7
1890	Phi-N	123	496	133	161	13	9	2	49	83	37	.325	.430	.399	139	29	102			.882	4	*O-123	2.5
1891	Phi-N	133	527	141	179	23	7	2	60	102	28	.340	.453	.421	151	41	111			.907	5	*O-133	3.7
1892	Phi-N	139	554	132	183	21	7	3	53	81	29	.330	.423	.410	153	39	57			.919	14	*O-139	4.3
1893	Phi-N	82	355	110	135	22	7	5	44	63	7	.380	.490	.524	170	40	43			.937	4	O-82	3.3
1894	Phi-N	129	544	192	220	25	15	4	87	126	17	.404	.523	.528	158	65	98			.964	5	*O-129	4.6
1895	Phi-N	123	517	166	201	22	6	7	74	96	30	.389	.490	.495	154	49	97			.913	-1	*O-123	3.1
1896	Bos-N	131	523	152	191	24	9	3	52	110	29	.365	.477	.463	140	36	83			.934	-11	*O-131	1.2
1897	*Bos-N	127	507	152	174	17	5	3	61	105		.343	.461	.414	124	24	66			.962	-3	*O-126	1.0
1898	Bos-N	110	417	110	154	16	5	3	50	87		.369	.480	.453	159	38	54			.904	-15	*O-110	1.4
1899	Bos-N	84	297	63	92	7	1	1	33	72		.310	.446	.350	109	8	19			.952	-2	O-81	-0.1
1900	Bos-N	136	520	103	173	20	5	1	47	107		.333	.449	.396	119	18	32			.947	2	*O-136	0.9
1901	Bos-N	102	348	71	100	11	2	3	38	64		.287	.404	.356	111	8	20			.945	1	O-99	0.1
Total	14	1591	6268	1690	2158	242	94	40	736	1187	218	.344	.455	.432	139	414	912			.926	-5	*O-1584	26.4

■ KEN HAMLIN
Hamlin, Kenneth Lee b: 5/18/35, Detroit, Mich. BR/TR, 5'10", 170 lbs. Deb: 6/17/57

YEAR	TM/L	G	AB	R	H	2B	3B	HR	RBI	BB	SO	AVG	OBP	SLG	PRO+	BR/A	SB	CS	SBR	FA	FR	G/POS	TPR
1957	Pit-N	2	1	0	0	0	0	0	0	0	0	.000	.000	.000	-99	-0	0	0	0	1.000	0	/S-1	0.0
1959	Pit-N	3	8	1	1	0	0	0	0	2	1	.125	.300	.125	19	-1	0	0	0	1.000	-1	/S-3	-0.2
1960	KC-A	140	428	51	96	10	2	2	24	44	48	.224	.298	.271	55	-26	1	1	-0	.955	-41	*S-139	-5.9
1961	LA-A	42	91	4	19	3	0	1	5	11	9	.209	.301	.275	49	-6	0	1	-1	.963	13	S-39	0.8
1962	Was-A	98	292	29	74	12	0	3	22	22	22	.253	.306	.325	70	-12	7	4	-2	.963	-11	S-87/2-2	-1.9
1965	Was-A	117	362	45	99	21	1	4	22	33	45	.273	.336	.370	102	1	8	2	1	.976	-29	2-77,S-47/3-1	-2.0
1966	Was-A	66	158	13	34	7	1	1	16	13	21	.215	.275	.291	63	-7	1	0	0	.963	6	2-50/3-1	0.2
Total	7	468	1340	143	323	53	4	11	89	125	146	.241	.307	.311	71	-52	17	11	-2	.959	-63	S-316,2-129/3-2	-9.0

■ STEVE HAMMOND
Hammond, Steven Benjamin b: 5/9/57, Atlanta, Ga. BL/TR, 6'2", 190 lbs. Deb: 6/28/82 F

YEAR	TM/L	G	AB	R	H	2B	3B	HR	RBI	BB	SO	AVG	OBP	SLG	PRO+	BR/A	SB	CS	SBR	FA	FR	G/POS	TPR
1982	KC-A	46	126	14	29	5	1	1	11	4	18	.230	.254	.310	54	-8	0	1	-1	1.000	3	O-37/D-1	-0.7

■ JACK HAMMOND
Hammond, Walter Charles "Wobby" b: 2/26/1891, Amsterdam, N.Y. d: 3/4/42, Kenosha, Wis. BR/TR, 5'11", 170 lbs. Deb: 4/15/15

YEAR	TM/L	G	AB	R	H	2B	3B	HR	RBI	BB	SO	AVG	OBP	SLG	PRO+	BR/A	SB	CS	SBR	FA	FR	G/POS	TPR
1915	Cle-A	35	84	9	18	2	1	0	4	1	19	.214	.224	.262	44	-6	0	1	-1	.957	-8	2-19	-1.6
1922	Cle-A	1	4	1	1	0	0	0	0	0	0	.250	.250	.250	30	-0	0	0	0	.333	-2	/2-1	-0.2
	Pit-N	9	11	3	3	0	0	0	0	1	0	.273	.333	.273	57	-1	0	0	0	1.000	2	/2-4	0.1
Total	2	45	99	13	22	2	1	0	4	2	19	.222	.238	.263	45	-7	0	1	-1	.943	-8	/2-24	-1.7

■ JEFFREY HAMMONDS
Hammonds, Jeffrey Bryan b: 3/5/71, Plainfield, N.J. BR/TR, 6', 195 lbs. Deb: 6/25/93

YEAR	TM/L	G	AB	R	H	2B	3B	HR	RBI	BB	SO	AVG	OBP	SLG	PRO+	BR/A	SB	CS	SBR	FA	FR	G/POS	TPR
1993	Bal-A	33	105	10	32	8	0	3	19	2	16	.305	.318	.467	104	0	4	0	1	.961	1	O-23/D-8	0.1
1994	Bal-A	68	250	45	74	18	2	8	31	17	39	.296	.346	.480	105	1	5	0	2	.962	1	O-66	0.5
1995	Bal-A	57	178	18	43	9	1	4	23	9	30	.242	.282	.371	67	-9	4	2	0	.989	1	O-46/D-5	-0.8
1996	Bal-A	71	248	38	56	10	1	9	27	23	53	.226	.302	.383	73	-11	3	3	-1	.980	-0	O-70/D-1	-1.3
Total	4	229	781	111	205	45	4	24	100	51	138	.262	.313	.423	86	-19	16	5	2	.973	6	O-205/D-14	-1.5

■ GRANNY HAMNER
Hamner, Granville Wilbur b: 4/26/27, Richmond, Va. d: 9/12/93, Philadelphia, Pa. BR/TR, 5'10", 163 lbs. Deb: 9/14/44 F

YEAR	TM/L	G	AB	R	H	2B	3B	HR	RBI	BB	SO	AVG	OBP	SLG	PRO+	BR/A	SB	CS	SBR	FA	FR	G/POS	TPR
1944	Phi-N	21	77	6	19	1	0	0	5	3	7	.247	.275	.260	53	-5	0			.933	6	S-21	0.3
1945	Phi-N	14	41	3	7	2	0	0	6	1	3	.171	.190	.220	14	-5	0			.861	3	S-13	-0.1
1946	Phi-N	2	7	0	1	0	0	0	0	0	3	.143	.143	.143	-19	-1	0			.857	-1	/S-2	-0.2
1947	Phi-N	2	7	1	2	0	0	0	0	1	0	.286	.375	.286	81	-0	0			1.000	-1	/S-2	0.0
1948	Phi-N	129	446	42	116	21	5	3	48	22	39	.260	.298	.350	76	-16	2			.967	-8	2-87,S-37/3-3	-1.7
1949	Phi-N	154	662	83	174	32	5	6	53	25	47	.263	.290	.353	74	-27	6			.961	-0	*S-154	-1.6
1950	*Phi-N	157	637	78	172	27	5	11	82	39	35	.270	.314	.380	83	-17	2			.944	-5	*S-157	-0.9
1951	Phi-N	150	589	61	150	23	7	9	72	29	32	.255	.290	.363	76	-22	10	5	0	.958	-2	*S-150	-1.3
1952	Phi-N★	151	596	74	164	30	5	17	87	27	51	.275	.307	.428	103	-0	7	3	0	.951	-4	*S-151	0.7
1953	Phi-N★	154	609	90	168	30	8	21	92	32	28	.276	.313	.455	98	-4	2	1	0	.970	-6	2-93,S-71	-0.3
1954	Phi-N★	152	596	83	178	39	11	13	89	53	44	.299	.356	.466	112	10	1	2	-1	.978	-23	*2-152/S-1	-0.3
1955	Phi-N	104	405	57	104	15	4	5	43	41	30	.257	.327	.343	79	-11	0	1	-1	.960	-36	2-82,S-32	-3.9
1956	Phi-N	122	401	42	90	24	3	4	42	30	42	.224	.278	.329	64	-21	2	0	0	.937	-13	*S-110,2-11/P-3	-2.4
1957	Phi-N	133	502	59	114	19	5	10	62	34	42	.227	.276	.345	68	-24	3	1	0	.963	-39	*2-125/S-5,P-1	-5.5
1958	Phi-N	35	133	18	40	7	3	2	18	8	16	.301	.340	.444	107	1	0	1	-1	.984	5	3-22,2-11/S-3	-0.1
1959	Phi-N	21	64	10	19	4	0	2	9	3	6	.297	.348	.453	109	1	0	0	0	.947	-7	S-15/3-1	-0.6
	Cle-A	27	67	4	11	1	1	1	3	1	8	.164	.176	.254	17	-8	0	0	0	.960	-2	S-10/2-7,3-5	-0.9
1962	KC-A	3	0	0	0	0	0	0	0	0	0	—	—	—	—	—	0			1.000	0	/P-3	0.0
Total	17	1531	5839	711	1529	272	62	104	708	351	432	.262	.304	.383	84	-149	35	14		.946	-139	S-934,2-568/3-31,P	-18.8

■ GARVIN HAMNER
Hamner, Wesley Garvin b: 3/18/24, Richmond, Va. BR/TR, 5'11", 172 lbs. Deb: 4/17/45 F

YEAR	TM/L	G	AB	R	H	2B	3B	HR	RBI	BB	SO	AVG	OBP	SLG	PRO+	BR/A	SB	CS	SBR	FA	FR	G/POS	TPR
1945	Phi-N	32	101	12	20	3	0	0	5	7	9	.198	.250	.228	34	-9	2			.962	-4	2-21/S-9,3-1	-1.1

■ IKE HAMPTON
Hampton, Isaac Bernard b: 8/22/51, Camden, S.C. BB/TR, 6'1", 185 lbs. Deb: 9/12/74

YEAR	TM/L	G	AB	R	H	2B	3B	HR	RBI	BB	SO	AVG	OBP	SLG	PRO+	BR/A	SB	CS	SBR	FA	FR	G/POS	TPR
1974	NY-N	4	4	0	0	0	0	0	0	1	0	1	.000	.000	.000	-99	-1	0	0	0	1.000	-0	/C-1	-0.1

YEAR	TM/L	G	AB	R	H	2B	3B	HR	RBI	BB	SO	AVG	OBP	SLG	PRO+	BR/A	SB	CS	SBR	FA	FR	G/POS	TPR
1975	Cal-A	31	66	8	10	3	0	0	4	7	19	.152	.243	.197	28	-6	0	0	0	.947	-5	C-28/S-2,3-1	-1.0
1976	Cal-A	3	2	0	0	0	0	0	0	0	0	.000	.000	.000	-99	-1	0	0	0	1.000	1	/C-2,S-1	0.0
1977	Cal-A	52	44	5	13	1	0	3	9	2	10	.295	.340	.523	137	2	0	0	0	.968	1	C-47/D-2	0.3
1978	Cal-A	19	14	2	3	0	1	1	4	2	7	.214	.313	.571	149	1	1	0	0	.905	1	C-13/1-1,D-4	0.2
1979	Cal-A	4	5	0	2	0	0	0	1	0	1	.400	.400	.400	121	0	0	0	0	1.000	1	/1-2	0.1
Total	6	113	135	15	28	4	1	4	18	11	38	.207	.277	.341	75	-5	1	0	0	.953	-2	/C-91,D-6,1-3,S3	-0.5

■ BERT HAMRIC
Hamric, Odbert Herman b: 3/1/28, Clarksburg, W.Va. d: 8/8/84, Springboro, Ohio BL/TR, 6′, 165 lbs. Deb: 4/24/55

YEAR	TM/L	G	AB	R	H	2B	3B	HR	RBI	BB	SO	AVG	OBP	SLG	PRO+	BR/A	SB	CS	SBR	FA	FR	G/POS	TPR
1955	Bro-N	2	1	0	0	0	0	0	0	0	0	.000	.000	.000	-97	-1	0	0	0	.000	0	H	0.0
1958	Bal-A	8	8	0	1	0	0	0	0	0	6	.125	.125	.125	-33	-1	0	0	0	.000	0	H	-0.2
Total	2	10	9	0	1	0	0	0	0	0	7	.111	.111	.111	-41	-2	0	0	0	.000	0	-0,-0	-0.2

■ RAY HAMRICK
Hamrick, Raymond Bernard b: 8/1/21, Nashville, Tenn. BR/TR, 5′11.5″, 160 lbs. Deb: 8/14/43

YEAR	TM/L	G	AB	R	H	2B	3B	HR	RBI	BB	SO	AVG	OBP	SLG	PRO+	BR/A	SB	CS	SBR	FA	FR	G/POS	TPR
1943	Phi-N	44	160	12	32	3	1	0	9	8	28	.200	.238	.231	37	-13	0			.960	-11	2-31,S-12	-2.4
1944	Phi-N	74	292	22	60	10	1	1	23	23	34	.205	.268	.257	50	-19	1			.948	20	S-74	0.7
Total	2	118	452	34	92	13	2	1	32	31	62	.204	.258	.248	46	-33	1			.946	9	/S-86,2-31	-1.7

■ BUDDY HANCKEN
Hancken, Morris Medlock b: 8/30/14, Birmingham, Ala. BR/TR, 6′1″, 175 lbs. Deb: 5/14/40 C

YEAR	TM/L	G	AB	R	H	2B	3B	HR	RBI	BB	SO	AVG	OBP	SLG	PRO+	BR/A	SB	CS	SBR	FA	FR	G/POS	TPR
1940	Phi-A	1	0	0	0					0	0						0	0	0	1.000	-0	/C-1	0.0

■ FRED HANCOCK
Hancock, Fred James b: 3/28/20, Allenport, Pa. d: 3/12/86, Clearwater, Fla. BR/TR, 5′8″, 170 lbs. Deb: 4/26/49

YEAR	TM/L	G	AB	R	H	2B	3B	HR	RBI	BB	SO	AVG	OBP	SLG	PRO+	BR/A	SB	CS	SBR	FA	FR	G/POS	TPR
1949	Chi-A	39	52	7	7	2	1	0	9	8	9	.135	.262	.212	27	-6	0	1	-1	.978	-3	S-27/3-3,O-1	-0.9

■ GARRY HANCOCK
Hancock, Ronald Garry b: 1/23/54, Tampa, Fla. BL/TL, 6′, 175 lbs. Deb: 7/16/78

YEAR	TM/L	G	AB	R	H	2B	3B	HR	RBI	BB	SO	AVG	OBP	SLG	PRO+	BR/A	SB	CS	SBR	FA	FR	G/POS	TPR
1978	Bos-A	38	80	10	18	3	0	0	4	1	12	.225	.235	.262	36	-7	0	0	0	1.000	-0	O-19,D-13	-0.8
1980	Bos-A	46	115	9	33	6	0	4	19	3	11	.287	.305	.443	97	-1	0	3	-2	.963	-2	O-27,D-12	-0.6
1981	Bos-A	26	45	4	7	3	0	0	3	2	4	.156	.191	.222	18	-5	0	0	0	1.000	-5	/O-8,D-4	-0.5
1982	Bos-A	11	14	3	0	0	0	0	0	1	1	.000	.067	.000	-75	-3	0	0	0	1.000	-5	/O-7	-0.6
1983	Oak-A	101	256	29	70	7	3	8	30	5	13	.273	.290	.418	98	-2	2	0	1	.981	-9	O-67,1-27/D-9	-1.3
1984	Oak-A	51	60	2	13	2	0	0	8	0	1	.217	.217	.250	31	-6	0	0	0	1.000	-5	O-18/1-4,P-1,D-5	-1.1
Total	6	273	570	57	141	21	3	12	64	12	42	.247	.264	.358	71	-23	2	3	-1	.982	-19	O-146/D-43,1-31,P-1	-4.9

■ MIKE HANDIBOE
Handiboe, Aloysius James "Coalyard Mike" b: 7/21/1887, Washington, D.C. d: 1/31/53, Savannah, Ga. BL/TL, 5′10″, 155 lbs. Deb: 9/8/11

YEAR	TM/L	G	AB	R	H	2B	3B	HR	RBI	BB	SO	AVG	OBP	SLG	PRO+	BR/A	SB	CS	SBR	FA	FR	G/POS	TPR
1911	NY-A	5	15	0	1	0	0	0	0	0	2	.067	.176	.067	-29	-3	0			1.000	-0	/O-4	-0.3

■ GENE HANDLEY
Handley, Eugene Louis b: 11/25/14, Kennett, Mo. BR/TR, 5′10.5″, 165 lbs. Deb: 4/16/46 F

YEAR	TM/L	G	AB	R	H	2B	3B	HR	RBI	BB	SO	AVG	OBP	SLG	PRO+	BR/A	SB	CS	SBR	FA	FR	G/POS	TPR
1946	Phi-A	89	251	31	63	8	5	0	21	22	25	.251	.311	.323	78	-3	8	3	1	.947	-17	2-68/3-4,S-1	-2.1
1947	Phi-A	36	90	10	23	2	1	0	8	10	2	.256	.330	.300	74	-3	1	0	0	.973	-5	2-17,3-10/S-1	-0.7
Total	2	125	341	41	86	10	6	0	29	32	27	.252	.316	.317	77	-10	9	3	1	.952	-23	/2-85,3-14,S-2	-2.8

■ LEE HANDLEY
Handley, Lee Elmer "Jeep" b: 7/31/13, Clarion, Iowa d: 4/8/70, Pittsburgh, Pa. BR/TR, 5′7″, 160 lbs. Deb: 4/15/36 F

YEAR	TM/L	G	AB	R	H	2B	3B	HR	RBI	BB	SO	AVG	OBP	SLG	PRO+	BR/A	SB	CS	SBR	FA	FR	G/POS	TPR
1936	Cin-N	24	78	10	24	1	0	2	9	7	16	.308	.365	.397	112	1	3			.926	-0	2-16/3-7	0.2
1937	Pit-N	127	480	59	120	21	12	3	37	37	40	.250	.306	.363	81	-14	5			.950	-14	*2-126/3-1	-1.9
1938	Pit-N	139	570	91	153	25	8	6	51	53	31	.268	.332	.372	93	-6	7			.948	9	*3-136	0.5
1939	Pit-N	101	376	43	107	14	5	1	42	32	20	.285	.341	.356	89	-6	**17**			.936	-10	*3-100	-1.5
1940	Pit-N	98	302	50	85	7	4	1	19	27	16	.281	.340	.341	89	-4	7			.925	1	3-80/2-2	-0.2
1941	Pit-N	124	459	59	132	18	4	0	33	35	22	.288	.338	.344	93	-4	16			.947	-1	*3-114	-0.2
1944	Pit-N	40	86	7	19	2	0	0	5	3	5	.221	.247	.244	37	-7	1			.947	2	2-19,3-11/S-3	-0.4
1945	Pit-N	98	312	39	93	16	2	1	32	20	16	.298	.340	.372	94	-3	7			.947	15	3-79	1.4
1946	Pit-N	116	416	43	99	8	7	1	28	29	20	.238	.289	.298	65	-19	4			.958	13	*3-102/2-3	-0.5
1947	Phi-N	101	277	17	70	10	3	0	42	24	18	.253	.312	.310	68	-12	7			.975	2	3-83/2-3,S-1	-1.0
Total	10	968	3356	418	902	122	45	15	297	267	204	.269	.323	.345	84	-73	68			.949	16	3-713,2-169/S-4	-3.6

■ HARRY HANEBRINK
Hanebrink, Harry Aloysius b: 11/12/27, St.Louis, Mo. d: 9/9/96, Bridgeton, Mo. BL/TR, 6′, 165 lbs. Deb: 5/3/53

YEAR	TM/L	G	AB	R	H	2B	3B	HR	RBI	BB	SO	AVG	OBP	SLG	PRO+	BR/A	SB	CS	SBR	FA	FR	G/POS	TPR
1953	Mil-N	51	80	8	19	1	1	1	8	6	8	.237	.291	.313	61	-5	1	0	0	.979	4	2-21/3-1	0.0
1957	Mil-N	6	7	0	2	0	0	0	0	1	2	.286	.375	.286	87	-0	0	0	0	1.000	1	/3-2	0.1
1958	*Mil-N	63	133	14	25	3	0	4	10	13	9	.188	.270	.301	56	-9	0	1	-1	.982	-0	O-33/3-7	-1.1
1959	Phi-N	57	97	10	25	3	1	1	7	2	12	.258	.273	.340	61	-5	0	0	0	.889	-6	2-15/3-9,O-1	-1.1
Total	4	177	317	32	71	7	2	6	25	22	31	.224	.279	.315	60	-19	1	1	-0	.959	-2	/2-36,O-34,3-19	-2.1

■ FRED HANEY
Haney, Fred Girard "Pudge" b: 4/25/1898, Albuquerque, N.Mex d: 11/9/77, Beverly Hills, Cal. BR/TR, 5′6″, 170 lbs. Deb: 4/18/22 MC

YEAR	TM/L	G	AB	R	H	2B	3B	HR	RBI	BB	SO	AVG	OBP	SLG	PRO+	BR/A	SB	CS	SBR	FA	FR	G/POS	TPR
1922	Det-A	81	213	41	75	7	4	0	25	32	14	.352	.439	.423	129	11	3	8	-4	.937	4	3-53,1-11/S-2	1.2
1923	Det-A	142	503	85	142	13	4	4	67	45	23	.282	.347	.348	85	-10	13	5	1	.955	-2	2-69,3-55,S-16	-0.5
1924	Det-A	86	256	54	79	11	1	1	30	39	13	.309	.400	.371	101	2	7	4	-0	.933	4	3-59/S-4,2-3	0.2
1925	Det-A	114	398	84	111	15	3	1	40	66	29	.279	.384	.332	84	-7	11	1	3	.953	-2	*3-106	0.2
1926	Bos-A	138	462	47	102	15	7	0	52	74	28	.221	.330	.284	63	-23	13	6	0	.957	6	*3-137	-0.8
1927	Bos-A	47	116	23	32	4	1	3	12	25	14	.276	.404	.405	113	3	4	1	0	.936	-2	3-34/O-1	0.3
	Chi-N	4	3	0	0	0	0	0	0	0	0	.000	.000	.000	-99	-1	0			.000	0	H	-0.1
1929	StL-N	10	26	4	3	1	1	0	2	1	2	.115	.179	.231	1	-4	0			.958	3	/3-6	-0.1
Total	7	622	1977	338	544	66	21	8	228	282	123	.275	.368	.342	87	-29	51	25		.949	9	3-450/2-72,S-22,10	1.2

■ TODD HANEY
Haney, Todd Michael b: 7/30/65, Waco, Tex. BR/TR, 5′9″, 165 lbs. Deb: 9/9/92

YEAR	TM/L	G	AB	R	H	2B	3B	HR	RBI	BB	SO	AVG	OBP	SLG	PRO+	BR/A	SB	CS	SBR	FA	FR	G/POS	TPR
1992	Mon-N	7	10	0	3	1	0	0	1	0	0	.300	.300	.400	97	-0	0	0	0	1.000	-0	/2-5	-0.1
1994	Chi-N	17	37	6	6	0	0	1	2	3	3	.162	.244	.243	28	-4	2	1	0	.979	-0	2-11/3-3	-0.4
1995	Chi-N	25	73	11	30	3	0	0	7	11	7	.411	.463	.603	182	9	0	0	0	.978	3	2-17/3-4	0.2
1996	Chi-N	49	82	11	11	1	0	0	3	7	15	.134	.202	.146	-6	-13	1	0	0	.978	7	2-23/3-4,S-3	-0.4
Total	4	98	202	28	50	10	0	3	12	17	29	.248	.309	.342	72	-8	3	1	0	.979	10	/2-56,3-11,S-3	0.3

■ LARRY HANEY
Haney, Wallace Larry b: 11/19/42, Charlottesville, Va BR/TR, 6′2″, 195 lbs. Deb: 7/27/66 FC

YEAR	TM/L	G	AB	R	H	2B	3B	HR	RBI	BB	SO	AVG	OBP	SLG	PRO+	BR/A	SB	CS	SBR	FA	FR	G/POS	TPR
1966	Bal-A	20	56	3	9	1	0	1	3	1	15	.161	.190	.232	21	-6	0	0	0	.985	3	C-20	-0.2
1967	Bal-A	58	164	13	44	11	0	3	20	6	28	.268	.294	.390	101	-0	1	0	0	.991	2	C-57	0.5
1968	Bal-A	38	89	5	21	3	1	1	5	0	19	.236	.236	.326	69	-4	0	0	0	.994	4	C-32	0.2
1969	Sea-A	22	59	3	15	3	0	2	7	6	12	.254	.323	.407	105	0	1	1	-0	.956	-2	C-20	-0.1
	Oak-A	53	86	8	13	4	0	2	12	7	19	.151	.223	.267	38	-7	0	0	0	.994	-0	C-53	-0.7
	Yr	75	145	11	28	7	0	4	19	13	31	.193	.264	.324	66	-7	1	1	-0	.979	-2	C-73	-0.8
1970	Oak-A	2	2	0	0	0	0	0	0	1	0	.000	.500	.000	51	0	0	0	0	1.000	0	/C-1	0.0
1972	Oak-A	5	4	0	0	0	0	0	0	0	1	.000	.000	.000	-99	-1	0	0	0	.800	-1	/C-4,2-1	-0.3
1973	Oak-A	2	2	0	1	0	0	0	1	0	0	.500	.500	.500	192	0	0	0	0	1.000	-0	/C-2	0.0
	StL-N	2	1	0	0	0	0	0	0	0	0	.000	.000	.000	-99	-0	0	0	0	1.000	0	/C-2	0.0
1974	*Oak-A	76	121	12	20	4	0	2	3	8	15	.165	.185	.248	25	-12	0	0	0	.992	10	C-73/3-3,1-2	0.0
1975	Oak-A	47	26	3	5	0	0	1	2	1	4	.192	.222	.308	50	-2	0	0	0	1.000	0	C-43/3-4	0.6
1976	Oak-A	88	177	12	40	6	0	10	13	26	30	.226	.283	.237	56	-10	0	1	0	.974	9	C-87	0.2
1977	Mil-A	63	127	7	29	2	0	0	10	5	30	.228	.258	.244	38	-11	0	0	0	.985	8	C-63	-0.2
1978	Mil-A	4	5	0	1	0	0	0	1	0	1	.200	.200	.200	13	-1	0	0	0	1.000	-0	/C-4	-0.1
Total	12	480	919	68	198	30	1	12	73	44	175	.215	.254	.289	57	-53	2	2	-0	.985	40	C-461/3-7,1-2,2-1	-0.2

■ CHARLIE HANFORD
Hanford, Charles Joseph b: 6/3/1881, Tunstall, England d: 7/19/63, Trenton, N.J. BR/TR, 5′6.5″, 145 lbs. Deb: 4/13/14

YEAR	TM/L	G	AB	R	H	2B	3B	HR	RBI	BB	SO	AVG	OBP	SLG	PRO+	BR/A	SB	CS	SBR	FA	FR	G/POS	TPR
1914	Buf-F	155	597	83	174	28	13	12	90	32	81	.291	.332	.442	107	-5	37			.973	10	*O-155	-0.3
1915	Chi-F	77	179	27	43	4	5	0	22	12	28	.240	.295	.318	77	-9	10			.971	-4	O-43	-1.6
Total	2	232	776	110	217	32	18	12	112	44	109	.280	.323	.414	101	-14	47			.972	6	O-198	-1.9

YEAR	TM/L	G	AB	R	H	2B	3B	HR	RBI	BB	SO	AVG	OBP	SLG	PRO+	BR/A	SB	CS	SBR	FA	FR	G/POS	TPR

■ JAY HANKINS   Hankins, Jay Nelson b: 11/7/35, St.Louis Co., Mo.   BL/TR, 5'7", 170 lbs.   Deb: 4/15/61

YEAR	TM/L	G	AB	R	H	2B	3B	HR	RBI	BB	SO	AVG	OBP	SLG	PRO+	BR/A	SB	CS	SBR	FA	FR	G/POS	TPR
1961	KC-A	76	173	23	32	0	3	3	6	8	17	.185	.225	.272	32	-17	2	0	1	.970	-10	O-65	-2.9
1963	KC-A	10	34	2	6	0	1	1	4	0	3	.176	.176	.324	35	-3	0	1	-1	.952	1	/O-9	-0.4
Total	2	86	207	25	38	0	4	4	10	8	20	.184	.218	.280	32	-20	2	1	0	.967	-10	/O-74	-3.3

■ FRANK HANKINSON   Hankinson, Frank Edward b: 4/29/1856, New York, N.Y. d: 4/5/11, Palisades Park, N.J BR/TR, 5'11", 168 lbs.   Deb: 5/1/1878

YEAR	TM/L	G	AB	R	H	2B	3B	HR	RBI	BB	SO	AVG	OBP	SLG	PRO+	BR/A	SB	CS	SBR	FA	FR	G/POS	TPR
1878	Chi-N	58	240	38	64	8	3	1	27	5	36	.267	.282	.338	96	-2				.875	8	*3-57/P-1	0.8
1879	Chi-N	44	171	14	31	4	0	0	8	2	16	.181	.191	.205	29	-13				.933	6	P-26,O-14/3-5	-0.4
1880	Cle-N	69	263	32	55	7	4	1	19	1	23	.209	.212	.278	66	-9				.844	-12	*3-56,O-12/P-4	-2.0
1881	Tro-N	85	321	34	62	15	0	1	19	10	41	.193	.218	.249	44	-21				.907	7	*3-84/S-1	-1.1
1883	NY-N	94	337	40	74	13	6	2	30	19	38	.220	.261	.312	74	-10				.870	-4	*3-93/O-1	-1.3
1884	NY-N	105	389	44	90	16	7	2	43	23	59	.231	.274	.324	85	-7				.871	-1	*3-105/O-1	-0.6
1885	NY-a	94	362	43	81	12	2	2	44	12		.224	.251	.285	75	-10				.906	18	*3-94/P-1	0.9
1886	NY-a	136	522	66	126	14	5	2	63	49		.241	.306	.299	94	-2	10			.873	25	*3-136	2.3
1887	NY-a	127	512	79	137	29	11	1	71	38		.268	.318	.373	97	-3	19			.864	8	*3-127	0.6
1888	KC-a	37	155	20	27	4	1	1	20	11		.174	.229	.232	45	-10	2			.947	-5	2-13/S-9,O-7,3-7,1	-1.3
Total	10	849	3272	410	747	122	39	13	344	170	211	.228	.267	.301	77	-85	31			.875	50	3-764/O-35,P2S1	-2.1

■ NED HANLON   Hanlon, Edward Hugh b: 8/22/1857, Montville, Conn. d: 4/14/37, Baltimore, Md.   BL/TR, 5'9.5", 170 lbs.   Deb: 5/1/1880   MH

YEAR	TM/L	G	AB	R	H	2B	3B	HR	RBI	BB	SO	AVG	OBP	SLG	PRO+	BR/A	SB	CS	SBR	FA	FR	G/POS	TPR
1880	Cle-N	73	280	30	69	10	3	0	32	11	30	.246	.275	.304	98	-0				.804	-3	*O-69/S-4	-0.5
1881	Det-N	76	305	63	85	14	8	2	28	22	11	.279	.327	.397	122	7				.897	-5	*O-74/S-2	0.1
1882	Det-N	82	347	68	80	18	6	5	38	26	25	.231	.284	.360	105	3				.887	14	*O-82/2-1	1.4
1883	Det-N	100	413	65	100	13	2	1	40	34	44	.242	.300	.291	84	-6				.884	2	*O-90,2-11	-0.4
1884	Det-N	114	450	86	119	18	6	5	39	40	52	.264	.324	.364	124	14				.874	13	*O-114	2.2
1885	Det-N	105	424	93	128	18	8	1	29	47	18	.302	.372	.389	146	23				.863	4	*O-105	2.2
1886	Det-N	126	494	105	116	6	6	4	60	57	39	.235	.314	.296	84	-8	50			.929	-4	*O-126/2-1	-1.4
1887	*Det-N	118	471	79	129	13	7	4	69	30	24	.274	.320	.357	85	-10	69			.904	3	*O-118	-0.8
1888	Det-N	109	459	64	122	6	8	5	39	15	32	.266	.295	.346	104	-3	38			.919	-6	*O-109	-0.7
1889	Pit-N	116	461	81	110	14	10	2	37	58	25	.239	.326	.325	91	-4	53			.919	-3	*O-116,M	-0.8
1890	Pit-P	118	472	106	131	16	6	1	44	80	24	.278	.389	.343	105	9	65			.911	-2	*O-118,M	0.3
1891	Pit-N	119	455	87	121	12	8	0	60	48	30	.266	.341	.327	97	-0	54			.881	-3	*O-119/S-1,M	-0.3
1892	Bal-N	11	43	3	7	1	1	0	2	3	3	.163	.217	.233	35	-3	0			.786	-0	O-11,M	-0.4
Total	13	1267	5074	930	1317	159	79	30	517	471	357	.260	.325	.340	102	25	329			.891	14	*O-1251/2-13,S-7	0.9

■ BILL HANLON   Hanlon, William Joseph "Big Bill" b: 6/24/1876, Los Angeles, Cal. d: 11/23/05, Los Angeles, Cal.   6',   Deb: 4/16/03

YEAR	TM/L	G	AB	R	H	2B	3B	HR	RBI	BB	SO	AVG	OBP	SLG	PRO+	BR/A	SB	CS	SBR	FA	FR	G/POS	TPR
1903	Chi-N	8	21	4	2	0	0	0	2	6		.095	.296	.095	14	-2	1			.980	-0	/1-8	-0.2

■ JOHN HANNA   Hanna, John b: 11/3/1863, Philadelphia, Pa. d: 11/7/30, Philadelphia, Pa.   Deb: 5/23/1884

YEAR	TM/L	G	AB	R	H	2B	3B	HR	RBI	BB	SO	AVG	OBP	SLG	PRO+	BR/A	SB	CS	SBR	FA	FR	G/POS	TPR
1884	Was-a	23	76	8	5	0	0	0		6		.066	.134	.066	-37	-11				.874	0	C-18/O-6	-0.9
	Ric-a	22	67	6	13	2	1	0		0		.194	.206	.254	50	-4				.924	4	C-21/S-1	0.2
	Yr	45	143	14	18	2	1	0		6		.126	.167	.154	6	-14				.900	4	C-39/O-6,S-1	-0.7

■ TRUCK HANNAH   Hannah, James Harrison b: 6/5/1889, Larimore, N.D. d: 4/27/82, Fountain Valley, Cal.   BR/TR, 6'1", 190 lbs.   Deb: 4/15/18

YEAR	TM/L	G	AB	R	H	2B	3B	HR	RBI	BB	SO	AVG	OBP	SLG	PRO+	BR/A	SB	CS	SBR	FA	FR	G/POS	TPR
1918	NY-A	90	250	24	55	6	0	2	21	51	25	.220	.361	.268	88	-1	5			.974	3	C-88	1.0
1919	NY-A	75	227	14	54	8	3	1	20	22	19	.238	.313	.313	76	-7	0			.984	-9	C-73/1-1	-1.0
1920	NY-A	79	259	24	64	11	2	1	25	24	35	.247	.313	.320	66	-13	2	0	1	.961	-6	C-78	-1.2
Total	3	244	736	62	173	25	5	4	66	97	79	.235	.331	.300	76	-21	7	0	0	.973	-11	C-239/1-1	-1.2

■ JACK HANNIFIN   Hannifin, John Joseph b: 2/25/1883, Holyoke, Mass. d: 10/27/45, Northampton, Mass.   BR/TR, 5'11", 167 lbs.   Deb: 4/19/06

YEAR	TM/L	G	AB	R	H	2B	3B	HR	RBI	BB	SO	AVG	OBP	SLG	PRO+	BR/A	SB	CS	SBR	FA	FR	G/POS	TPR
1906	Phi-A	1	1	0	1	0	0	0	0	0		1.000	1.000	1.000	511	0	0			.000	0	H	0.0
	NY-N	10	30	4	6	0	0	0	3	2		.200	.250	.267	60	-1	1			.903	-2	/S-6,3-3,2-1	-0.2
1907	NY-N	56	149	16	34	7	3	1	15	15		.228	.303	.336	97	-1	6			.996	-4	1-29,3-10/S-9,O-2	-0.5
1908	NY-N	1	2	0	0	0	0	0	0	0		.000	.000	.000	-95	-0	0			.000	-0	/O-1	-0.1
	Bos-N	90	257	30	53	6	2	2	22	28		.206	.284	.268	78	-6	7			.930	5	3-35,2-22,S-15/O-7	-0.2
	Yr	91	259	30	53	6	2	2	22	28		.205	.282	.266	77	-6	7			.930	5	3-35,2-22,S-15/O-8	-0.1
Total	3	158	439	50	94	13	6	3	40	45		.214	.289	.292	84	-8	14			.937	0	/3-48,S-30,1-29,2O	-0.8

■ PAT HANNIFIN   Hannifin, Patrick James b: 4/20/1866, Halifax, N.S., Can. d: 11/5/08, Springfield, Mass.   TL ,   Deb: 4/29/1897

YEAR	TM/L	G	AB	R	H	2B	3B	HR	RBI	BB	SO	AVG	OBP	SLG	PRO+	BR/A	SB	CS	SBR	FA	FR	G/POS	TPR
1897	Bro-N	10	20	4	5	0	0	0	2	1		.250	.375	.250	71	-1	4			.867	2	/O-3,2-2	0.1

■ DAVE HANSEN   Hansen, David Andrew b: 11/24/68, Long Beach, Cal.   BL/TR, 6', 180 lbs.   Deb: 9/16/90

YEAR	TM/L	G	AB	R	H	2B	3B	HR	RBI	BB	SO	AVG	OBP	SLG	PRO+	BR/A	SB	CS	SBR	FA	FR	G/POS	TPR
1990	LA-N	5	7	0	1	0	0	0	1	0	3	.143	.143	.143	-22	-1	0	0	0	.500	-1	/3-2	-0.2
1991	LA-N	53	56	3	15	4	0	1	5	2	12	.268	.293	.393	93	-1	1	0	0	1.000	-1	3-21/S-1	0.1
1992	LA-N	132	341	30	73	11	0	6	22	34	49	.214	.287	.299	67	-15	0	2	-1	.968	7	*3-108	-1.0
1993	LA-N	84	105	13	38	3	0	4	30	21	13	.362	.468	.505	170	12	0	1	-1	.927	-1	3-18	1.0
1994	LA-N	40	44	3	15	3	0	0	5	5	5	.341	.408	.409	122	2	0	0	0	.857	-1	/3-7	0.0
1995	*LA-N	100	181	19	52	10	0	1	14	28	28	.287	.386	.359	107	3	0	0	0	.933	-6	3-58	-0.3
1996	*LA-N	80	104	7	23	1	0	0	6	11	22	.221	.296	.231	45	-8	0	0	0	.962	0	3-19/1-8	-0.9
Total	7	494	838	75	217	32	0	12	83	101	132	.259	.340	.340	91	-8	1	3	-2	.954	-1	3-233/1-8,S-1	-1.3

■ DOUG HANSEN   Hansen, Douglas William b: 12/16/28, Los Angeles, Cal.   BR/TR, 6', 180 lbs.   Deb: 9/4/51

YEAR	TM/L	G	AB	R	H	2B	3B	HR	RBI	BB	SO	AVG	OBP	SLG	PRO+	BR/A	SB	CS	SBR	FA	FR	G/POS	TPR
1951	Cle-A	3	0	2	0	0	0	0	0	0	0						0	0	0	.000	0	R	0.0

■ BOB HANSEN   Hansen, Robert Joseph b: 5/26/48, Boston, Mass.   BL/TL, 6', 195 lbs.   Deb: 5/10/74

YEAR	TM/L	G	AB	R	H	2B	3B	HR	RBI	BB	SO	AVG	OBP	SLG	PRO+	BR/A	SB	CS	SBR	FA	FR	G/POS	TPR
1974	Mil-A	58	88	8	26	4	1	2	9	3	16	.295	.319	.432	115	1	2	1	0	1.000	-0	D-18/1-3	0.1
1976	Mil-A	24	61	4	10	1	0	0	4	6	8	.164	.239	.180	24	-6	0	0	0	.000	-0	D-14/1-1	-0.7
Total	2	82	149	12	36	5	1	2	13	9	24	.242	.285	.329	78	-4	2	1	0	1.000	-0	/D-32,1-4	-0.6

■ RON HANSEN   Hansen, Ronald Lavern b: 4/5/38, Oxford, Neb.   BR/TR, 6'3", 200 lbs.   Deb: 4/15/58   C

YEAR	TM/L	G	AB	R	H	2B	3B	HR	RBI	BB	SO	AVG	OBP	SLG	PRO+	BR/A	SB	CS	SBR	FA	FR	G/POS	TPR
1958	Bal-A	12	19	1	0	0	0	0	1	0	7	.000	.050	.000	-90	-5	0	0	0	.943	-0	S-12	-0.5
1959	Bal-A	2	4	0	0	0	0	0	0	1	1	.000	.200	.000	-41	-1	0	0	0	.889	1	/S-2	-0.1
1960	Bal-A★	153	530	72	135	22	5	22	86	69	94	.255	.343	.440	111	8	3	3	-1	.964	6	*S-153	2.5
1961	Bal-A	155	533	51	132	13	2	12	51	66	96	.248	.332	.347	85	-11	1	3	-2	.959	12	*S-149/2-7	1.3
1962	Bal-A	71	196	12	34	7	0	3	17	30	36	.173	.289	.255	51	-13	0	1	-1	.965	4	S-64	-0.5
1963	Chi-A	144	482	55	109	17	2	13	67	78	74	.226	.334	.351	94	-2	1	1	-0	.983	27	*S-144	3.6
1964	Chi-A	158	575	85	150	25	3	20	68	73	73	.261	.350	.419	116	13	1	0	0	.975	16	*S-158	4.3
1965	Chi-A	162	587	61	138	23	4	11	66	60	73	.235	.308	.344	91	-4	1	3	-2	.969	17	*S-161/2-1	2.1
1966	Chi-A	23	74	3	13	1	0	0	4	15	10	.176	.322	.189	55	-4	0	1	-1	.946	3	S-23	0.0
1967	Chi-A	157	498	35	116	20	0	8	51	64	51	.233	.320	.321	94	-3	0	3	-2	*S-157	1.4
1968	Was-A	86	275	28	51	12	0	8	28	35	49	.185	.282	.316	84	-5	0	0	0	.963	2	S-81/3-5	0.5
	Chi-A	40	87	7	20	3	0	1	4	11	12	.230	.316	.299	86	-1	0	1	-1	.959	6	3-29/S-7,2-2	0.6
	Yr	126	362	35	71	15	0	9	32	46	61	.196	.290	.312	84	-7	0	1	-1	.963	7	S-88,3-34/2-2	1.1
1969	Chi-A	85	185	15	48	6	1	2	19	28	25	.259	.328	.335	82	-1	0	1	-1	.967	-3	2-26,1-21/S-8,3-7	-0.4
1970	NY-A	59	91	13	27	4	0	4	14	19	19	.297	.423	.473	155	8	0	1	-1	.983	-3	S-15,3-11/2-1	0.6
1971	NY-A	61	145	6	30	3	0	2	20	9	27	.207	.253	.269	51	-10	0	0	0	.918	-3	3-30/2-9,S-3	-1.3
1972	KC-A	16	30	2	4	0	0	0	2	3	6	.133	.212	.133	-4	-3	0	0	0	.944	3	/S-6,3-4,2-1	0.0
Total	15	1384	4311	446	1007	156	17	106	501	551	643	.234	.323	.351	92	-42	9	14	-6	.968	90	*S-1143/3-86,2-47,1	14.2

■ DON HANSKI   Hanski, Donald Thomas (b: Donald Thomas Hanyzewski) b: 2/27/16, LaPorte, Ind. d: 9/2/57, Worth, Ill.   BL/TL, 5'11", 180 lbs.   Deb: 5/6/43

YEAR	TM/L	G	AB	R	H	2B	3B	HR	RBI	BB	SO	AVG	OBP	SLG	PRO+	BR/A	SB	CS	SBR	FA	FR	G/POS	TPR
1943	Chi-A	9	21	1	5	1	0	0	2	0	5	.238	.238	.286	53	-1	0	1	-1	.952	-0	/1-5,P-1	-0.3
1944	Chi-A	2	1	0	0	0	0	0	0	0	0	.000	.000	.000	-99	-0	0	0	0	.000	-0	/P-2	0.0
Total	2	11	22	1	5	1	0	0	2	0	5	.227	.227	.273	46	-2	0	1	-1	—	-1	/1-5,P-3	-0.3

YEAR	TM/L	G	AB	R	H	2B	3B	HR	RBI	BB	SO	AVG	OBP	SLG	PRO+	BR/A	SB	CS	SBR	FA	FR	G/POS	TPR

■ HARRY HANSON Hanson, Harry Francis b: 1/17/1896, Elgin, Ill. d: 10/5/66, Savannah, Ga. BR/TR, 5'11″, Deb: 7/14/13

| 1913 | NY-A | 1 | 2 | 0 | 0 | 0 | 0 | 0 | 0 | 0 | 0 | .000 | .000 | .000 | -99 | -0 | 0 | | | 1.000 | -0 | /C-1 | -0.1 |

■ JOHN HAPPENNY Happenny, John Clifford "Cliff" b: 5/18/01, Waltham, Mass. d: 12/29/88, Coral Springs, Fla BR/TR, 5'11″, 165 lbs. Deb: 7/2/23

| 1923 | Chi-A | 32 | 86 | 7 | 19 | 5 | 0 | 0 | 10 | 3 | 13 | .221 | .256 | .279 | 41 | -8 | 0 | 0 | 0 | .947 | 5 | 2-19/S-9,3-2 | -0.6 |

■ BILL HARBIDGE Harbidge, William Arthur "Yaller Bill" b: 3/29/1855, Philadelphia, Pa. d: 3/17/24, Philadelphia, Pa. BL/TL, 162 lbs. Deb: 5/15/1875

1875	Har-n	53	208	32	50	3	3	0	26	9	3	.240	.272	.284	89	-3	2	4	-2	.871	-0	C-31,O-13,2-11,/1S	-0.3
1876	Har-N	30	106	11	23	2	1	0	6	3	2	.217	.239	.255	59	-5				.799	1	C-24/O-6,1-2	-0.3
1877	Har-N	41	167	18	37	5	2	0	8	3	6	.222	.235	.275	68	-6				.881	-4	C-32/O-5,2-4,3-1	-0.8
1878	Chi-N	54	240	32	71	12	0	0	37	6	13	.296	.313	.346	109	2				.878	-8	*C-53/O-8	-0.6
1879	Chi-N	4	18	2	2	0	0	0	1	0	5	.111	.111	.111	-25	-2				.571	-1	/O-4	-0.3
1880	Tro-N	9	27	3	10	0	1	0	2	0	3	.370	.370	.444	166	2				.887	0	/C-9,O-1	0.2
1882	Tro-N	32	123	11	23	1	1	0	13	10	17	.187	.248	.211	52	-6				.836	-4	O-23/1-6,C-3	-0.9
1883	Phi-N	73	280	32	62	12	3	0	21	24	20	.221	.283	.286	81	-5				.796	-11	O-44,S-11/2-9,C3	-1.4
1884	Cin-U	82	341	59	95	12	5	2		25		.279	.328	.361	101	-10				.906	5	*O-80/S-3,1-2	-0.6
Total	8	325	1302	168	323	44	13	2	88	71	66	.248	.287	.306	86	-30				.849	-21	O-171,C-128/S213	-4.7

■ SCOTT HARDESTY Hardesty, Scott Durbin b: 1/26/1870, Bellville, Ohio d: 10/29/44, Fostoria, Ohio Deb: 8/17/1899

| 1899 | NY-N | 22 | 72 | 4 | 16 | 0 | 0 | 0 | 4 | 1 | | .222 | .243 | .222 | 29 | -7 | 2 | | | .895 | 2 | S-20/1-2 | -0.3 |

■ PAT HARDGROVE Hardgrove, William Henry b: 5/10/1895, Palmyra, Kan. d: 1/26/73, Jackson, Miss. BR/TR, 5'10″, 158 lbs. Deb: 6/8/18

| 1918 | Chi-A | 2 | 2 | 0 | 0 | 0 | 0 | 0 | 0 | 0 | 0 | .000 | .000 | .000 | -99 | -0 | 0 | | | .000 | 0 | H | -0.1 |

■ LOU HARDIE Hardie, Louis W. b: 8/24/1864, New York, N.Y. d: 3/5/29, Oakland, Cal. 5'11″, 180 lbs. Deb: 5/22/1884

1884	Phi-N	3	8	0	3	2	0	0	0	0	2	.375	.375	.625	219	1				.857	-3	/C-3	-0.1
1886	Chi-N	16	51	4	9	0	0	0	3	4	10	.176	.236	.176	24	-5	1			.964	-0	C-13/O-2,3-1	-0.4
1890	Bos-N	47	185	17	42	8	0	3	17	18	36	.227	.296	.319	73	-7	4			.886	-0	C-25,O-15/3-7,S1	-0.5
1891	Bal-a	15	56	7	13	0	3	0	1	8	8	.232	.328	.339	90	-1	3			1.000	1	O-15	0.0
Total	4	81	300	28	67	10	3	3	21	30	56	.223	.294	.307	71	-12	8			.910	-2	/C-41,O-32,3-8,1S	-1.0

■ BUD HARDIN Hardin, William Edgar b: 6/14/22, Shelby, N.C. BR/TR, 5'10″, 165 lbs. Deb: 4/15/52

| 1952 | Chi-N | 3 | 7 | 1 | 1 | 0 | 0 | 0 | 0 | 0 | 0 | .143 | .143 | .143 | -20 | -1 | 0 | 0 | 0 | 1.000 | 0 | /S-2,2-1 | -0.1 |

■ LOU HARDING Harding, Louis Edward "Jumbo" b: 1865, San Francisco, Cal. 5'9.5″, 213 lbs. Deb: 10/5/1886

| 1886 | StL-a | 1 | 3 | 0 | 1 | 1 | 0 | 0 | 1 | 0 | | .333 | .333 | .667 | 201 | 0 | 0 | | | .889 | 1 | /C-1 | 0.1 |

■ JASON HARDTKE Hardtke, Jason Robert b: 9/15/71, Milwaukee, Wis. BB/TR, 5'10″, 175 lbs. Deb: 9/8/96

| 1996 | NY-N | 19 | 57 | 3 | 11 | 5 | 0 | 0 | 6 | 2 | 12 | .193 | .233 | .281 | 37 | -5 | 0 | 0 | 0 | 1.000 | -2 | 2-18 | -0.6 |

■ CARROLL HARDY Hardy, Carroll William b: 5/18/33, Sturgis, S.Dak. BR/TR, 6', 185 lbs. Deb: 4/15/58

1958	Cle-A	27	49	10	10	3	0	1	6	6	14	.204	.304	.327	75	-2	1	2	-1	1.000	1	O-17	-0.3
1959	Cle-A	32	53	12	11	1	0	0	2	3	7	.208	.250	.226	33	-5	1	1	-0	1.000	1	O-15	-0.5
1960	Cle-A	29	18	7	2	1	0	0	1	2	2	.111	.200	.167	0	-3	0	0	0	1.000	-4	O-17	-0.7
	Bos-A	73	145	26	34	5	2	2	15	17	40	.234	.315	.338	74	-5	3	2	0	.968	-6	O-59	-1.4
	Yr	102	163	33	36	6	2	2	16	19	42	.221	.302	.319	67	-7	3	2	0	.973	-11	O-76	-2.1
1961	Bos-A	85	281	46	74	20	2	2	36	26	53	.263	.330	.381	87	-5	4	2	0	.961	-1	O-76	-1.0
1962	Bos-A	115	362	52	78	13	5	8	36	54	68	.215	.321	.345	77	-11	3	7	-3	.991	1	*O-105	-1.9
1963	Hou-N	15	44	5	10	0	0	3	3	7		.227	.277	.295	69	-2	1	0	0	.947	5	O-10	-0.1
1964	Hou-N	46	157	13	29	1	1	2	12	8	30	.185	.234	.242	36	-13	1	0	0	.990	5	O-41	-1.2
1967	Min-A	11	8	1	3	0	0	0	2	1	1	.375	.444	.750	229	1	0	0	0	.000	-1	/O-4	0.0
Total	8	433	1117	172	251	47	10	17	113	120	222	.225	.304	.330	72	-45	13	14	-5	.981	-5	O-344	-7.1

■ JACK HARDY Hardy, John Doolittle b: 6/23/1877, Cleveland, Ohio d: 10/20/21, Cleveland, Ohio BR/TR, 6', 185 lbs. Deb: 8/29/03

1903	Cle-A	5	19	1	3	1	0	0	1	0	1	.158	.200	.211	24	-2	1			1.000	-1	/O-5	-0.3
1907	Chi-N	1	4	0	1	0	0	0	0	0	0	.250	.250	.250	53	-0	0			.909	0	/C-1	0.0
1909	Was-A	10	24	3	4	0	0	0	4	0	1	.167	.200	.167	17	-2	0			.974	-2	/C-9,2-1	-0.4
1910	Was-A	7	8	1	2	0	0	0	0	0	0	.250	.250	.250	59	-0	0			.933	1	/C-4,O-1	0.0
Total	4	23	55	5	10	1	0	0	5	2		.182	.211	.200	28	-5	1			.953	-2	/C-14,O-6,2-1	-0.7

■ SHAWN HARE Hare, Shawn Robert b: 3/26/67, St.Louis, Mo. BL/TL, 6'2″, 190 lbs. Deb: 9/6/91

1991	Det-A	9	19	0	1	1	0	0	0	2	1	.053	.143	.105	-30	-3	0	0	0	1.000	0	/O-6,D-2	-0.4
1992	Det-A	15	26	0	3	1	0	0	5	2	4	.115	.179	.154	-6	-4	0	0	0	1.000	-2	/O-9,1-4	-0.6
1994	NY-N	22	40	7	9	1	1	0	2	4	11	.225	.295	.300	56	-3	0	0	0	1.000	-0	O-14	-0.3
1995	Tex-A	18	24	2	6	1	0	0	4	4	6	.250	.357	.292	70	-1	0	0	0	1.000	-1	/O-9,1-1,D-3	-0.2
Total	4	64	109	9	19	4	1	0	9	12	22	.174	.256	.229	31	-11	0	0	0	1.000	-3	/O-38,1-5,D-5	-1.5

■ GARY HARGIS Hargis, Gary Lynn b: 11/2/56, Minneapolis, Minn. BR/TR, 5'11″, 165 lbs. Deb: 9/29/79

| 1979 | Pit-N | 1 | 0 | 0 | 0 | 0 | 0 | 0 | | — | — | — | | | | | | 0 | 0 | 0 | .000 | 0 | /R | 0.0 |

■ BUBBLES HARGRAVE Hargrave, Eugene Franklin b: 7/15/1892, New Haven, Ind. d: 2/23/69, Cincinnati, Ohio BR/TR, 5'10.5″, 174 lbs. Deb: 9/18/13 F

1913	Chi-N	3	3	0	1	0	0	0		0	0	.333	.333	.333	90	-0	0			1.000	0	/C-2	0.0
1914	Chi-N	23	36	3	8	2	0	0	2	0	4	.222	.222	.278	48	-2	2			.930	-4	C-16	-0.6
1915	Chi-N	15	19	2	3	0	1	0	2	1	5	.158	.200	.263	40	-1	0			1.000	-1	/C-9	-0.2
1921	Cin-N	93	263	28	76	17	8	1	38	12	15	.289	.327	.426	102	0	4	2	0	.973	-7	C-73	-0.3
1922	Cin-N	98	320	49	101	22	10	7	57	26	18	.316	.371	.512	128	12	7	4	-0	.982	-9	C-87	0.7
1923	Cin-N	118	378	54	126	23	9	10	78	44	22	.333	.419	.521	150	28	4	5	-2	.988	3	*C-109	3.3
1924	Cin-N	98	312	42	94	19	10	3	33	30	20	.301	.370	.455	122	10	2	1	-1	.983	-1	C-91	1.4
1925	Cin-N	87	273	28	82	13	6	3	33	25	23	.300	.361	.414	100	0	4	3	-1	.979	-6	C-84	-0.2
1926	Cin-N	105	326	42	115	22	8	6	62	25	17	**.353**	.406	.525	153	24	2			.988	-12	C-93	1.8
1927	Cin-N	102	305	36	94	18	3	0	35	31	18	.308	.376	.387	108	4	0			**.988**	-10	C-92	0.1
1928	Cin-N	65	190	19	56	12	3	0	23	13	14	.295	.353	.389	95	-1	4			.991	2	C-57	0.5
1930	NY-N	45	108	11	30	7	0	0	9	1	6	.278	.339	.343	77	-4	0	0	0	.992	-5	C-34	-0.6
Total	12	852	2533	314	786	155	58	29	376	217	165	.310	.372	.452	119	70	29	16		.983	-50	C-747	5.9

■ PINKY HARGRAVE Hargrave, William McKinley b: 1/31/1896, New Haven, Ind. d: 10/3/42, Ft.Wayne, Ind. BB/TR, 5'8.5″, 180 lbs. Deb: 5/18/23 F

1923	Was-A	33	59	4	17	2	0	0	5	1	8	.288	.311	.322	70	-3	0	0	0	.917	-4	/3-8,C-5,O-1	-0.6
1924	Was-A	24	33	3	5	1	1	0	5	1	4	.152	.176	.242	8	-5	0	0	0	1.000	-1	/C-8	-0.5
1925	Was-A	5	6	0	3	0	0	0	0	1	2	.500	.571	.500	177	1	0	0	0	1.000	1	/C-1	0.2
	StL-A	67	225	34	64	15	2	8	43	13	13	.284	.326	.476	97	-3	2	0	1	.981	-6	C-62	-0.5
	Yr	72	231	34	67	15	2	8	43	14	15	.290	.333	.476	99	-2	2	0	1	.981	-5	C-63	-0.3
1926	StL-A	92	235	20	66	16	3	7	37	10	38	.281	.319	.464	98	-2	3	0	1	.977	-2	C-58	0.0
1928	Det-A	121	320	38	88	13	5	10	63	32	28	.275	.343	.441	103	1	4	1	0	.977	-14	C-88	-0.5
1929	Det-A	76	185	26	61	12	0	3	26	20	24	.330	.401	.443	117	5	2	2	-1	.973	-1	C-48	0.7
1930	Det-A	55	137	18	39	8	0	5	18	20	12	.285	.380	.453	108	2	2	0	0	.984	-4	C-40	0.2
	Was-A	10	31	3	6	2	2	1	7	3	1	.194	.265	.484	85	-1	0	0	0	1.000	1	/C-9	0.1
	Yr	65	168	21	45	10	2	6	25	23	13	.268	.359	.458	104	1	3	0	0	.987	-3	C-49	0.3
1931	Was-A	40	80	6	26	8	0	1	19	9	12	.325	.393	.463	124	3	1	0	0	.978	-2	C-25	0.2
1932	Bos-N	82	217	20	57	14	3	4	33	24	18	.263	.336	.410	103	1	1			.968	-4	C-73	0.1
1933	Bos-N	45	73	5	13	0	0	0	4	6	9	.178	.241	.178	23	-7	1			.957	1	C-25	-0.2
Total	10	650	1601	177	445	91	16	39	265	140	165	.278	.339	.428	98	-8	17	3		.976	-35	C-442/3-8,O-1	-1.2

YEAR	TM/L	G	AB	R	H	2B	3B	HR	RBI	BB	SO	AVG	OBP	SLG	PRO+	BR/A	SB	CS	SBR	FA	FR	G/POS	TPR
■ **CHARLIE HARGREAVES**			Hargreaves, Charles Russell				b: 12/14/1896, Trenton, N.J.			d: 5/9/79, Neptune, N.J.			BR/TR, 6', 170 lbs.			Deb: 7/15/23							
1923	Bro-N	20	57	5	16	0	0	0	4	1	2	.281	.293	.281	54	-4	0	0	0	.921	-4	C-15	-0.7
1924	Bro-N	15	27	4	11	2	0	0	5	1	1	.407	.429	.481	148	2	0	1	-1	1.000	-1	/C-9	0.0
1925	Bro-N	45	83	9	23	3	1	0	13	6	1	.277	.326	.337	72	-3	1	1	-0	.986	2	C-18/1-2	-0.1
1926	Bro-N	85	208	14	52	13	2	2	23	19	10	.250	.316	.361	83	-5	1			.986	4	C-70	0.2
1927	Bro-N	46	133	9	38	3	1	0	11	14	7	.286	.362	.323	85	-2	1			.985	-1	C-44	0.0
1928	Bro-N	20	61	3	12	2	0	0	5	6	6	.197	.269	.230	32	-6	1			.979	2	C-20	-0.3
	Pit-N	79	260	15	74	8	2	1	32	12	9	.285	.319	.342	70	-11	1			.962	-5	C-77	-1.0
	Yr	99	321	18	86	10	2	1	37	18	15	.268	.309	.321	63	-17	2			.966	-3	C-97	-1.3
1929	Pit-N	102	328	33	88	12	5	1	44	16	12	.268	.306	.345	60	-21	1			.981	2	*C-101	-0.9
1930	Pit-N	11	31	4	7	1	0	0	2	2	1	.226	.273	.258	29	-4	0			1.000	6	C-11	0.3
Total	8	423	1188	96	321	44	11	4	139	77	49	.270	.318	.336	69	-55	6	2		.977	4	C-365/1-2	-2.5
■ **MIKE HARGROVE**			Hargrove, Dudley Michael			b: 10/26/49, Perryton, Tex.			BL/TL, 6', 195 lbs.			Deb: 4/7/74 MC										
1974	Tex-A	131	415	57	134	18	6	4	66	49	42	.323	.400	.424	141	23	0	0	0	.987	9	1-91,D-32/O-6	2.7
1975	Tex-A★	145	519	82	157	22	2	11	62	79	66	.303	.399	.416	132	25	4	3	-1	.964	3	O-96,1-48,D-12	2.1
1976	Tex-A	151	541	80	155	30	1	7	58	97	64	.287	.401	.384	128	24	2	3	-1	.984	1	*1-141/D-5	1.5
1977	Tex-A	153	525	98	160	28	4	18	69	103	59	.305	.424	.476	143	37	2	5	-2	.993	-0	*1-152	2.5
1978	Tex-A	146	494	63	124	24	1	7	40	107	47	.251	.391	.346	109	12	2	5	-2	.987	7	*1-140/D-4	0.8
1979	SD-N	52	125	15	24	5	0	0	8	25	15	.192	.327	.232	59	-6	0	2	-1	.986	0	1-37	-1.2
	Cle-A	100	338	60	110	21	4	10	56	63	40	.325	.438	.500	152	28	2	3	-1	.993	0	O-65,1-28/D-7	2.2
1980	Cle-A	160	589	86	179	22	2	11	85	111	36	.304	.421	.404	127	28	4	2	0	.993	-5	*1-160	1.3
1981	Cle-A	94	322	43	102	21	0	2	49	60	16	.317	.432	.401	143	22	5	4	-1	.989	6	1-88/D-4	2.3
1982	Cle-A	160	591	67	160	26	1	4	65	101	58	.271	.380	.338	100	5	2	2	-1	.996	11	*1-153/D-5	0.7
1983	Cle-A	134	469	57	134	21	4	3	57	78	40	.286	.393	.367	107	8	0	6	-4	.994	12	*1-131/D-1	0.9
1984	Cle-A	133	352	44	94	14	2	2	44	53	38	.267	.363	.335	93	-1	2	1	-1	.991	6	*1-124	-0.3
1985	Cle-A	107	284	31	81	14	1	1	27	39	29	.285	.372	.352	100	1	1	0	0	.991	5	1-85	0.2
Total	12	1666	5564	783	1614	266	28	80	686	965	550	.290	.400	.391	121	205	24	37	-15	.991	52	*1-1378,O-167/D-70	15.7
■ **TIM HARKNESS**			Harkness, Thomas William			b: 12/23/37, Lachine, Que., Can.			BL/TL, 6'2", 182 lbs.			Deb: 9/12/61										
1961	LA-N	5	8	4	4	2	0	0	3	1	1	.500	.636	.750	245	2	1	0	0	1.000	-0	/1-2	0.2
1962	LA-N	92	62	9	16	2	0	2	7	10	20	.258	.370	.387	110	1	1	0	0	1.000	1	1-59	0.2
1963	NY-N	123	375	35	79	12	3	10	41	36	79	.211	.292	.339	80	-10	4	3	-1	.986	16	*1-106	0.2
1964	NY-N	39	117	11	33	2	1	2	13	9	18	.282	.339	.368	101	0	1	1	-0	.993	3	1-32	0.2
Total	4	259	562	59	132	18	4	14	61	58	118	.235	.316	.356	90	-6	7	4	-0	.989	21	1-199	0.8
■ **DICK HARLEY**			Harley, Richard Joseph			b: 9/25/1872, Philadelphia, Pa.			d: 4/3/52, Philadelphia, Pa.			BL/TR, 5'10.5", 165 lbs.			Deb: 6/2/1897						
1897	StL-N	89	330	43	96	6	4	3	35	36		.291	.379	.361	98	1	23			.899	1	*O-89	-0.4
1898	StL-N	142	549	74	135	6	5	0	42	34		.246	.316	.275	68	-22	13			.926	9	*O-141	-2.2
1899	Cle-N	142	567	70	142	15	7	1	50	40		.250	.315	.307	76	-18	15			.924	3	*O-142	-2.2
1900	Cin-N	5	21	2	9	1	0	0	5	1		.429	.455	.476	161	2	4			1.000	-1	/O-5	0.0
1901	Cin-N	133	535	69	146	13	2	4	27	31		.273	.323	.327	95	-3	37			.898	-5	*O-133	-1.7
1902	Det-A	125	491	59	138	9	8	2	44	36		.281	.345	.344	90	-6	20			.930	-2	*O-125	-1.5
1903	Chi-N	104	386	72	89	9	1	0	33	45		.231	.328	.259	70	-13	27			.923	3	*O-103	-1.5
Total	7	740	2879	389	755	59	27	10	236	223		.262	.332	.312	83	-58	139			.918	10	O-738	-9.5
■ **LARRY HARLOW**			Harlow, Larry Duane			b: 11/13/51, Colorado Springs, Colo.			BL/TL, 6'2", 185 lbs.			Deb: 9/20/75								
1975	Bal-A	4	3	1	1	0	0	0	0	1	1	.333	.333	.333	95	-0	0	0	0	1.000	-2	/O-4	-0.2
1977	Bal-A	46	48	4	10	0	1	0	0	5	8	.208	.283	.250	50	-3	6	1	1	.887	-12	O-38	-1.4
1978	Bal-A	147	460	67	112	25	1	8	26	55	72	.243	.326	.354	97	-2	14	11	-2	.979	-5	*O-138/P-1	-1.5
1979	Bal-A	38	41	5	11	1	0	0	1	7	4	.268	.375	.293	86	-0	1	3	-2	.970	-10	O-31/D-1	-1.2
	*Cal-A	62	159	22	37	8	2	0	14	25	34	.233	.344	.308	80	-2	1	3	-2	.975	-2	O-58	-0.9
	Yr	100	200	27	48	9	2	0	15	32	38	.240	.350	.305	81	-4	2	6	-3	.974	-12	O-89/D-1	-2.1
1980	Cal-A	109	301	47	83	13	4	4	27	48	61	.276	.377	.385	112	7	3	2	-0	.976	12	O-94/1-1,D-1	1.5
1981	Cal-A	43	82	13	17	1	0	0	4	16	25	.207	.337	.220	63	-3	1	1	-0	.981	-8	O-39	-1.3
Total	6	449	1094	159	271	48	8	12	72	156	205	.248	.344	.339	94	-5	26	21	-5	.971	-26	O-402/D-2,1-1,P-1	-5.0
■ **BILL HARMAN**			Harman, William Bell			b: 1/2/19, Bridgewater, Va.			BR/TR, 6'4", 200 lbs.			Deb: 6/17/41									
1941	Phi-N	15	14	1	1	0	0	0	0	0	3	.071	.071	.071	-62	-3	0			1.000	-1	/P-5,C-5	-0.2
■ **CHUCK HARMON**			Harmon, Charles Byron			b: 4/23/24, Washington, Ind.			BR/TR, 6'2", 175 lbs.			Deb: 4/17/54								
1954	Cin-N	94	286	39	68	7	3	2	25	17	27	.238	.283	.304	52	-20	7	3	0	.961	4	3-67/1-3	-1.7
1955	Cin-N	96	198	31	50	6	3	5	28	26	24	.253	.348	.389	90	-2	9	9	-3	.935	4	3-39,O-32/1-4	-0.3
1956	Cin-N	13	4	2	0	0	0	0	0	0	0	.000	.000	.000	-94	-1	1	0	0	1.000	-2	/O-6,1-2	-0.3
	StL-N	20	15	2	0	0	0	0	0	2	2	.000	.118	.000	-65	-4	0	0	0	1.000	-6	O-11/1-2,3-1	-0.8
	Yr	33	19	4	0	0	0	0	0	2	2	.000	.095	.000	-70	-5	1	0	0	1.000	-6	O-17/1-4,3-1	-1.1
1957	StL-N	9	3	1	1	0	0	0	1	0	0	.333	.333	1.000	236	1	1	0	0	1.000	-3	/O-8	-0.2
	Phi-N	57	86	14	22	2	1	0	5	1	4	.256	.264	.302	53	-6	7	2	1	1.000	-5	O-25/3-5,1-2	-0.7
	Yr	66	89	16	23	2	1	0	6	1	4	.258	.267	.326	60	-5	8	2	1	1.000	-5	O-33/3-5,1-2	-0.9
Total	4	289	592	90	141	15	8	7	59	46	57	.238	.298	.326	62	-33	25	14	-1	.952	-3	3-112/O-82,1-13	-4.0
■ **TERRY HARMON**			Harmon, Terry Walter			b: 4/12/44, Toledo, Ohio			BR/TR, 6'2", 180 lbs.			Deb: 7/23/67								
1967	Phi-N	2	0	0	0	0	0	0	0	0	0	—	—	—		0	0	0	0	.000	0	R	0.0
1969	Phi-N	87	201	25	48	8	1	0	16	22	31	.239	.323	.289	74	-6	1	2	-1	.968	8	S-38,2-19/3-2	0.7
1970	Phi-N	71	129	16	32	2	4	0	7	12	22	.248	.317	.326	75	-5	6	3	0	.989	-3	S-35,2-14/3-2	-0.4
1971	Phi-N	79	221	27	45	4	2	0	12	20	45	.204	.282	.240	49	-14	3	0	0	.986	8	2-58/S-9,3-3,1-2	-0.7
1972	Phi-N	73	218	35	62	8	2	2	13	29	22	.284	.373	.367	108	4	3	2	0	.996	-1	2-50,S-15/3-5	0.6
1973	Phi-N	72	148	17	31	3	0	0	8	13	14	.209	.278	.230	41	-11	1	0	0	.988	2	2-43,S-19/3-1	-0.7
1974	Phi-N	27	15	5	2	0	0	0	0	3	3	.133	.278	.133	17	-2	0	0	0	1.000	3	/S-7,2-5	0.1
1975	Phi-N	48	72	14	13	1	2	0	5	9	13	.181	.280	.250	46	-5	0	1	0	.989	1	S-25/2-7,3-1	-0.2
1976	*Phi-N	42	61	12	18	4	1	0	4	3	10	.295	.328	.393	101	-0	3	0	1	.960	3	S-19,2-13/3-5	0.6
1977	Phi-N	46	60	13	11	1	0	2	5	6	9	.183	.269	.300	50	-4	0	2	-1	.982	8	2-28,S-16/3-3	0.4
Total	10	547	1125	164	262	31	12	4	72	117	175	.233	.312	.292	69	-44	17	11	29	.989	29	2-237,S-183/3-22,1	1.0
■ **BRIAN HARPER**			Harper, Brian David			b: 10/16/59, Los Angeles, Cal.			BR/TR, 6'2", 195 lbs.			Deb: 9/29/79								
1979	Cal-A	1	2	0	0	0	0	0	0	0	0	.000	.000	.000	-99	-1	0	0	0	.000	0	/D-1	-0.1
1981	Cal-A	4	11	1	3	0	0	0	1	0	0	.273	.273	.273	58	-1	1	0	0	.833	-0	/O-2,D-1	0.0
1982	Pit-N	20	29	4	8	1	0	2	4	1	4	.276	.300	.517	121	1	0	0	0	1.000	-1	/O-8	-0.1
1983	Pit-N	61	131	16	29	4	1	7	20	2	15	.221	.239	.427	79	-4	0	0	0	1.000	-5	O-35/1-1	-1.1
1984	Pit-N	46	112	4	29	4	0	2	11	5	11	.259	.303	.348	82	-3	0	0	0	.981	-2	O-37/C-2	-0.6
1985	*StL-N	43	52	5	13	4	0	1	8	2	8	.250	.278	.327	69	-2	0	0	0	1.000	-4	O-13/3-6,C-2,1-1	-0.7
1986	Det-A	19	36	2	5	1	0	0	4	0	3	.139	.205	.167	3	-5	0	0	0	.929	-2	O-11/C-2,1-2,D-6	-0.7
1987	Oak-A	11	17	1	4	1	0	0	1	0	2	.235	.235	.294	42	-1	0	0	0	.000	-0	/O-1,D-7	-0.2
1988	Min-A	60	166	15	49	11	1	3	20	10	12	.295	.346	.428	112	3	0	4	-3	.991	-7	C-48/3-2,D-5	-0.3
1989	Min-A	126	385	43	125	24	0	8	57	13	16	.325	.356	.449	118	8	2	4	-3	.978	-14	*C-101,D-19/O-3,13	-0.3
1990	Min-A	134	479	61	141	42	3	6	54	19	27	.294	.331	.432	105	2	3	2	-0	.985	2	*C-120,D-11/3-3,1-2	1.1
1991	*Min-A	123	441	54	137	28	1	10	69	14	22	.311	.341	.447	111	5	1	0	-0	.988	-6	*C-119/1-0,1-0,1,D-2	0.5
1992	Min-A	140	502	58	154	25	0	9	73	26	22	.307	.350	.410	109	5	0	2	-1	.984	-7	*C-133/D-2	0.6
1993	Min-A	147	530	52	161	26	1	12	73	29	29	.304	.350	.425	107	5	1	3	-2	.988	-14	*C-134/D-7	-0.3
1994	Mil-A	64	251	23	73	15	0	4	32	9	18	.291	.323	.398	81	-7	0	2	-1	.981	2	D-36,C-25/O-3	-0.7

YEAR	TM/L	G	AB	R	H	2B	3B	HR	RBI	BB	SO	AVG	OBP	SLG	PRO+	BR/A	SB	CS	SBR	FA	FR	G/POS	TPR
1995	Oak-A	2	7	0	0	0	0	0	0	0	1	.000	.000	.000	-99	-2	0	0	0	1.000	-1	/C-2	-0.3
Total	16	1001	3151	339	931	186	7	63	428	133	188	.295	.333	.419	102	2	8	17	-8	.985	-60	C-688,O-114/D31	-3.2

■ GEORGE HARPER

Harper, George Washington b: 6/24/1892, Arlington, Ky. d: 8/18/78, Magnolia, Ark. BL/TR, 5'8", 167 lbs. Deb: 4/15/16

YEAR	TM/L	G	AB	R	H	2B	3B	HR	RBI	BB	SO	AVG	OBP	SLG	PRO+	BR/A	SB	CS	SBR	FA	FR	G/POS	TPR
1916	Det-A	44	56	4	9	1	0	0	3	5	8	.161	.230	.179	22	-5	0			.938	-4	O-14	-1.0
1917	Det-A	47	117	6	24	3	0	0	12	11	15	.205	.290	.231	59	-5	2			.980	-3	O-31	-1.1
1918	Det-A	69	227	19	55	5	2	0	16	18	14	.242	.301	.282	79	-6	3			.956	-1	O-64	-1.2
1922	Cin-N	128	430	67	146	22	8	2	68	35	22	.340	.397	.442	118	13	11	10	-3	.955	1	*O-109	0.3
1923	Cin-N	61	125	14	32	4	2	3	16	11	9	.256	.316	.392	88	-3	0	2	-1	.967	-2	O-29	-0.7
1924	Cin-N	28	74	7	20	3	0	0	3	13	5	.270	.393	.311	92	0	1	3	-2	.964	1	O-22	-0.2
	Phi-N	109	411	68	121	26	6	16	55	38	23	.294	.361	.504	115	8	10	11	-4	.991	3	*O-109	0.0
	Yr	137	485	75	141	29	6	16	58	51	28	.291	.366	.474	113	8	11	14	-5	.986	4	O-131	-0.2
1925	Phi-N	132	495	86	173	35	7	18	97	28	32	.349	.391	.558	128	19	10	8	-2	.971	6	*O-126	1.5
1926	Phi-N	56	194	32	61	6	5	7	38	16	7	.314	.367	.505	126	6	6			.942	-6	O-55	-0.3
1927	NY-N	145	483	85	160	19	6	16	87	84	27	.331	.435	.495	149	37	7			.975	-2	*O-142	2.7
1928	NY-N	19	57	11	13	1	0	2	7	10	4	.228	.353	.351	84	-1	1			.957	2	O-18	0.0
	*StL-N	99	272	41	83	8	2	17	58	51	15	.305	.418	.537	145	19	2			.988	1	O-84	1.4
	Yr	118	329	52	96	9	2	19	65	61	19	.292	.407	.505	135	18	3			.982	3	O-102	1.4
1929	Bos-N	136	457	65	133	25	5	10	68	69	27	.291	.387	.433	108	7	5			.972	-1	O-130	-0.3
Total	11	1073	3398	505	1030	158	43	91	528	389	208	.303	.380	.455	118	90	58	34		.970	-5	O-933	1.1

■ TERRY HARPER

Harper, Terry Joe b: 8/19/55, Douglasville, Ga. BR/TR, 6'4", 195 lbs. Deb: 9/12/80

YEAR	TM/L	G	AB	R	H	2B	3B	HR	RBI	BB	SO	AVG	OBP	SLG	PRO+	BR/A	SB	CS	SBR	FA	FR	G/POS	TPR
1980	Atl-N	21	54	3	10	1	0	3	6	5		.185	.279	.259	49	-4	2	1	0	.968	-2	O-18	-0.6
1981	Atl-N	40	73	9	19	1	0	2	8	11	17	.260	.357	.356	100	0	5	1	1	.976	-2	O-27	-0.1
1982	*Atl-N	48	150	16	43	3	0	2	16	14	28	.287	.352	.347	92	-1	7	4	-0	.987	-0	O-41	-0.3
1983	Atl-N	80	201	19	53	13	1	3	26	20	43	.264	.333	.383	91	-2	6	5	-1	.952	-1	O-60	-0.7
1984	Atl-N	40	102	4	16	3	1	0	8	4	21	.157	.196	.206	12	-12	4	1	1	1.000	4	O-29	-0.9
1985	Atl-N	138	492	58	130	15	2	17	72	44	76	.264	.328	.407	94	-1	9	9	-3	.978	1	*O-131	-0.7
1986	Atl-N	106	265	26	68	12	0	8	30	29	39	.257	.332	.392	94	-2	3	6	-3	.970	-11	O-83	-1.9
1987	Det-A	31	64	4	13	3	0	1	10	9	8	.203	.301	.391	85	-1	1	0	0	.952	-2	D-15,O-14	-0.3
	Pit-N	36	66	8	19	3	0	1	7	7	11	.288	.356	.379	94	-0	0	1	-1	1.000	-3	O-20	-0.4
Total	8	540	1467	147	371	55	5	36	180	144	248	.253	.323	.371	88	-24	37	28	-6	.976	-16	O-423/D-15	-5.9

■ TOMMY HARPER

Harper, Tommy b: 10/14/40, Oak Grove, La. BR/TR, 5'10", 168 lbs. Deb: 4/9/62 C

YEAR	TM/L	G	AB	R	H	2B	3B	HR	RBI	BB	SO	AVG	OBP	SLG	PRO+	BR/A	SB	CS	SBR	FA	FR	G/POS	TPR
1962	Cin-N	6	23	1	4	0	0	0	1	2	6	.174	.240	.174	13	-3	1	0	0	.929	-1	/3-6	-0.4
1963	Cin-N	129	408	67	106	12	3	10	37	44	72	.260	.336	.377	102	2	12	1	3	.983	6	*O-118/3-1	0.5
1964	Cin-N	102	317	42	77	5	2	4	22	39	56	.243	.328	.309	78	-8	24	3	5	.994	5	O-92/3-2	-0.2
1965	Cin-N	159	646	**126**	166	28	3	18	64	78	127	.257	.342	.393	99	1	35	6	7	.983	7	*O-159/3-2,2-1	0.8
1966	Cin-N	149	553	85	154	22	5	5	31	57	85	.278	.349	.363	91	-6	29	10	3	.996	-13	*O-147	-2.4
1967	Cin-N	103	365	55	82	17	3	7	22	43	51	.225	.306	.345	77	-10	23	8	2	.995	7	*O-100	-0.7
1968	Cle-A	130	235	26	51	15	2	6	26	26	56	.217	.298	.374	104	1	11	7	-1	.984	-16	*O-115/2-2	-2.3
1969	Sea-A	148	537	78	126	10	2	9	41	95	90	.235	.351	.311	88	-5	**73**	18	11	.959	-15	2-59,3-59,O-26	-0.6
1970	Mil-A★	154	604	104	179	35	4	31	82	77	107	.296	.380	.522	145	37	38	16	2	.943	-3	*3-128,2-22,O-13	3.6
1971	Mil-A	152	585	79	151	26	3	14	52	65	92	.258	.333	.385	104	3	25	3	6	.975	-19	O-90,3-70/2-1	-1.6
1972	Bos-A	144	556	92	141	29	2	14	49	67	104	.254	.343	.388	111	9	25	7	4	.985	-1	*O-144	0.8
1973	Bos-A	147	566	92	159	23	3	17	71	61	93	.281	.352	.422	111	8	**54**	14	**8**	.985	3	*O-143/D-1	1.2
1974	Bos-A	118	443	66	105	15	3	5	24	46	65	.237	.313	.318	77	-13	28	12	1	.982	-3	O-61,D-51	-1.9
1975	Cal-A	89	285	40	68	10	1	3	31	38	51	.239	.332	.312	89	-3	19	8	1	.992	-2	D-57,1-19/O-9	-0.7
	*Oak-A	34	69	11	22	4	0	2	7	5	9	.319	.373	.464	139	5	7	0	2	.963	-3	1-16/O-9,3-2,D-3	0.1
	Yr	123	354	51	90	14	1	5	38	43	60	.254	.340	.342	99	0	26	8	3	.978	-5	D-60,1-35,O-18,/3-2	-0.6
1976	Bal-A	46	77	8	18	5	0	1	7	10	16	.234	.322	.338	99	0	4	3	-1	1.000	-1	D-27/1-1,O-1	-0.2
Total	15	1810	6269	972	1609	256	36	146	567	753	1080	.257	.340	.379	100	15	408	116	53	.986	-47	*O-1227,3-270,D/21	-4.0

■ TOBY HARRAH

Harrah, Colbert Dale b: 10/26/48, Sissonville, W.Va. BR/TR, 6', 180 lbs. Deb: 9/5/69 MC

YEAR	TM/L	G	AB	R	H	2B	3B	HR	RBI	BB	SO	AVG	OBP	SLG	PRO+	BR/A	SB	CS	SBR	FA	FR	G/POS	TPR
1969	Was-A	8	1	4	0	0	0	0	0	0	0	.000	.000	.000	-99	-0	0	0	0	.000	0	/S-1	0.0
1971	Was-A	127	383	45	88	11	3	2	22	40	48	.230	.303	.290	73	-14	10	9	-2	.955	-7	*S-116/3-7	-1.0
1972	Tex-A†	116	374	47	97	14	3	1	31	34	31	.259	.321	.321	95	-2	16	7	1	.960	-9	*S-106	0.5
1973	Tex-A	118	461	64	120	16	1	10	50	46	49	.260	.330	.364	100	-0	10	3	1	.951	-13	S-76,3-52	-0.2
1974	Tex-A	161	573	79	149	23	2	21	74	50	65	.260	.322	.417	114	9	15	14	-4	.963	-2	*S-158/3-3	2.5
1975	Tex-A☆	151	522	81	153	24	1	20	93	98	71	.293	.406	.458	145	34	23	9	2	.963	14	*S-118,3-28,2-21	**6.2**
1976	Tex-A★	155	584	64	152	21	1	15	67	91	59	.260	.363	.377	114	13	8	5	-1	.955	-0	*S-146/3-5,D-4	3.2
1977	Tex-A	159	539	90	142	25	5	27	87	**109**	73	.263	.397	.479	136	31	27	5	5	.963	-24	*S-159/S-1	1.0
1978	Tex-A	139	450	56	103	17	3	12	59	83	66	.229	.351	.360	100	3	31	8	5	.965	-8	3-91,S-49	0.4
1979	Cle-A	149	527	99	147	25	1	20	77	89	60	.279	.391	.444	124	21	20	9	1	.940	-49	3-127,S-33/D-9	-2.6
1980	Cle-A	160	561	100	150	22	4	11	72	98	60	.267	.383	.380	109	11	17	2	4	.971	2	*3-156/S-2,D-1	1.5
1981	Cle-A	103	361	64	105	12	4	5	44	57	44	.291	.389	.388	126	15	12	1	3	.949	-12	3-101/S-3,D-1	0.4
1982	Cle-A☆	162	602	100	183	29	4	25	78	84	52	.304	.400	.490	144	39	17	3	3	.971	-19	3-159/2-3,S-2	1.9
1983	Cle-A	138	526	81	140	23	1	9	53	75	49	.266	.365	.365	98	1	16	10	-1	**.971**	-11	3-137/2-1,D-1	-1.3
1984	NY-A	88	253	40	55	9	4	1	26	42	28	.217	.333	.296	79	-6	3	1	0	.968	3	3-74/2-4,O-1,D-2	-0.3
1985	Tex-A	126	396	65	107	18	1	9	44	113	60	.270	.437	.389	127	22	11	4	1	.989	-14	*2-122/S-2,D-1	1.4
1986	Tex-A	95	289	36	63	18	2	7	41	44	53	.218	.325	.360	86	-5	2	5	-2	.982	-20	2-93	-2.4
Total	17	2155	7402	1115	1954	307	40	195	918	1153	868	.264	.368	.395	114	171	238	94	15	.963	-167	*3-1099,S-813,2/DO	11.2

■ JOHN HARRELL

Harrell, John Robert b: 11/27/47, Long Beach, Cal. BR/TR, 6'2", 190 lbs. Deb: 10/1/69

YEAR	TM/L	G	AB	R	H	2B	3B	HR	RBI	BB	SO	AVG	OBP	SLG	PRO+	BR/A	SB	CS	SBR	FA	FR	G/POS	TPR
1969	SF-N	2	6	0	3	0	0	0	2	2	1	.500	.625	.500	223	1	0	0	0	1.000	-0	/C-2	0.1

■ BILLY HARRELL

Harrell, William b: 7/18/28, Norristown, Pa. BR/TR, 6'1.5", 180 lbs. Deb: 9/2/55

YEAR	TM/L	G	AB	R	H	2B	3B	HR	RBI	BB	SO	AVG	OBP	SLG	PRO+	BR/A	SB	CS	SBR	FA	FR	G/POS	TPR
1955	Cle-A	13	19	2	8	1	0	1		3	3	.421	.500	.421	144	1	1	0	0	.926	-0	S-11	0.2
1957	Cle-A	22	57	6	15	1	1	1	5	4	7	.263	.311	.368	86	-1	3	1	0	.893	-4	S-14/3-6,2-1	-0.4
1958	Cle-A	101	229	36	50	4	0	7	19	15	36	.218	.272	.328	66	-11	12	2	2	.986	-7	3-46,S-45/2-7,O-1	-1.2
1961	Bos-A	37	37	10	6	2	0	0	1	1	8	.162	.184	.216	6	-5	1	0	0	1.000	9	3-10/S-7,1-3	0.2
Total	4	173	342	54	79	7	1	8	26	23	54	.231	.283	.327	68	-16	17	3	3	.933	-5	/S-77,3-62,2-8,1O	-1.2

■ BUD HARRELSON

Harrelson, Derrel McKinley b: 6/6/44, Niles, Cal. BB/TR, 5'11", 160 lbs. Deb: 9/2/65 MC

YEAR	TM/L	G	AB	R	H	2B	3B	HR	RBI	BB	SO	AVG	OBP	SLG	PRO+	BR/A	SB	CS	SBR	FA	FR	G/POS	TPR
1965	NY-N	19	37	3	4	1	1	0	2		11	.108	.154	.189	-4	-5	0	0	0	.955	4	S-18	-0.1
1966	NY-N	33	99	20	22	2	4	0	4	13	23	.222	.313	.323	79	-3	7	3	0	.993	5	S-29	0.5
1967	NY-N	151	540	59	137	16	4	1	28	48	64	.254	.319	.304	80	-13	12	13	-4	.958	7	*S-149	0.4
1968	NY-N	111	402	38	88	7	3	0	14	29	68	.219	.273	.251	58	-20	4	5	-2	.972	-5	*S-106	-1.8
1969	*NY-N	123	395	42	98	11	6	0	24	54	54	.248	.341	.306	81	-8	1	3	-2	.969	-5	*S-119	-0.2
1970	NY-N★	157	564	72	137	18	8	1	42	95	74	.243	.355	.309	79	-13	23	4	5	.971	-28	*S-156	-1.8
1971	NY-N★	142	547	55	138	16	6	0	32	53	59	.252	.321	.303	79	-14	28	7	4	.978	11	*S-140	2.0
1972	NY-N	115	418	54	90	10	4	1	24	58	57	.215	.315	.266	68	-16	12	4	1	.970	-12	*S-115	-1.0
1973	*NY-N	106	356	35	92	12	3	0	20	48	49	.258	.348	.309	85	-6	5	1	1	.979	-3	*S-103	0.6
1974	NY-N	106	331	48	75	10	0	1	13	71	39	.227	.366	.266	80	-5	9	4	0	.968	16	S-97	2.4
1975	NY-N	34	73	5	16	2	0	0	3	12	13	.219	.329	.247	65	-3	0	0	0	.941	1	S-34	0.0
1976	NY-N	118	359	34	84	12	4	1	26	63	56	.234	.351	.298	91	-2	9	3	1	.962	-5	*S-117	0.8
1977	NY-N	107	269	25	48	9	1	2	12	49	32	.178	.256	.242	57	-6	5	2	0	.984	-2	S-98	-2.0
1978	Phi-N	71	103	16	22	1	0	0	9	18	21	.214	.331	.223	57	-5	5	2	0	.972	15	2-43,S-15	1.3
1979	Phi-N	53	71	7	20	2	0	0	5	13	14	.282	.400	.366	107	1	3	3	-1	.990	6	2-25,S-17/3-9,0-1	0.8
1980	Tex-A	87	180	26	49	8	0	1	9	29	23	.272	.373	.322	95	-0	4	4	-1	.952	11	S-87/2-2	1.7
Total	16	1533	4744	539	1120	136	45	7	267	633	653	.236	.329	.288	75	-136	127	60	2	.969	16	*S-1400/2-70,3-9,O	3.6

YEAR	TM/L	G	AB	R	H	2B	3B	HR	RBI	BB	SO	AVG	OBP	SLG	PRO+	BR/A	SB	CS	SBR	FA	FR	G/POS	TPR

■ KEN HARRELSON
Harrelson, Kenneth Smith "Hawk" b: 9/4/41, Woodruff, S.C. BR/TR, 6'2", 190 lbs. Deb: 6/9/63

YEAR	TM/L	G	AB	R	H	2B	3B	HR	RBI	BB	SO	AVG	OBP	SLG	PRO+	BR/A	SB	CS	SBR	FA	FR	G/POS	TPR
1963	KC-A	79	226	16	52	10	1	6	23	23	58	.230	.301	.363	81	1	1	1	-0	.980	-5	1-34,O-28	-1.5
1964	KC-A	49	139	15	27	5	0	7	12	13	34	.194	.263	.381	74	-5	0	1	-1	.977	3	O-24,1-15	-0.4
1965	KC-A	150	483	61	115	17	3	23	66	66	112	.238	.331	.429	116	10	9	7	-2	.992	-4	*1-125/O-4	-0.2
1966	KC-A	63	210	24	47	5	0	5	22	27	59	.224	.312	.319	85	-4	9	2	2	.985	2	1-58/O-3	-0.4
	Was-A	71	250	25	62	8	1	7	28	26	53	.248	.321	.372	100	-0	4	1	1	.991	-4	1-70	-0.9
	Yr	134	460	49	109	13	1	12	50	53	112	.237	.317	.348	93	-4	13	3	2	.989	-2	*1-128/O-3	-1.3
1967	Was-A	26	79	10	16	0	0	3	10	7	15	.203	.267	.316	75	-3	1	0	0	.996	0	1-23	-0.4
	KC-A	61	174	23	53	11	0	6	30	17	17	.305	.366	.471	151	11	8	2	1	.992	-1	1-45	0.9
	*Bos-A	23	80	9	16	4	1	3	14	5	12	.200	.247	.387	79	-2	1	1	-0	.929	-3	O-23/1-1	-0.8
	Yr	110	333	42	85	15	1	12	54	29	44	.255	.315	.414	115	5	10	3	1	.993	-4	1-69,O-23	-0.3
1968	Bos-A★	150	535	79	147	17	4	35	**109**	69	90	.275	.360	.518	153	34	2	6	-3	**1.000**	8	*O-132,1-19	3.5
1969	Bos-A	10	46	6	10	1	0	3	8	4	6	.217	.280	.435	92	-1	0	1	-1	.991	2	1-10	-0.1
	Cle-A	149	519	83	115	13	4	27	84	95	96	.222	.344	.418	109	7	17	8	0	.985	5	*O-144,1-16	0.3
	Yr	159	565	89	125	14	4	30	92	99	102	.221	.339	.419	107	6	17	9	-0	.985	6	*O-144,1-26	0.2
1970	Cle-A	17	39	3	11	1	0	1	6	4	4	.282	.378	.385	106	0	0	0	0	1.000	1	1-13	0.0
1971	Cle-A	52	161	20	32	2	0	5	14	24	21	.199	.303	.304	66	-7	1	0	0	.988	-1	1-40/O-7	-1.3
Total	9	900	2941	374	703	94	14	131	421	382	577	.239	.328	.414	109	35	53	30	-2	.990	2	1-469,O-365	-1.3

■ ANDY HARRINGTON
Harrington, Andrew Matthew b: 2/12/03, Mountain View, Cal. d: 1/26/79, Boise, Idaho BR/TR, 5'11", 170 lbs. Deb: 4/18/25

YEAR	TM/L	G	AB	R	H	2B	3B	HR	RBI	BB	SO	AVG	OBP	SLG	PRO+	BR/A	SB	CS	SBR	FA	FR	G/POS	TPR
1925	Det-A	1	1	0	0	0	0	0	0	0	0	.000	.000	.000	-99	-0	0	0	0	.000	0	H	0.0

■ MICKEY HARRINGTON
Harrington, Charles Michael b: 10/8/34, Hattiesburg, Miss. BR/TR, 6'4", 205 lbs. Deb: 7/10/63

YEAR	TM/L	G	AB	R	H	2B	3B	HR	RBI	BB	SO	AVG	OBP	SLG	PRO+	BR/A	SB	CS	SBR	FA	FR	G/POS	TPR
1963	Phi-N	1	0	0	0	0	0	0	0	0	0	—	—	—	—	0	0	0	0	.000	0	R	0.0

■ JERRY HARRINGTON
Harrington, Jeremiah Peter b: 8/12/1869, Keokuk, Iowa d: 4/16/13, Keokuk, Iowa BR/TR, 5'11", 220 lbs. Deb: 4/30/1890

YEAR	TM/L	G	AB	R	H	2B	3B	HR	RBI	BB	SO	AVG	OBP	SLG	PRO+	BR/A	SB	CS	SBR	FA	FR	G/POS	TPR
1890	Cin-N	65	236	25	58	7	1	1	23	15	29	.246	.299	.297	74	-8	4				.957	5	C-65	0.3
1891	Cin-N	92	333	25	76	10	5	2	41	19	34	.228	.272	.306	68	-15	4				.908	3	C-92/3-1	-0.8
1892	Cin-N	22	61	6	13	1	0	0	3	6	1	.213	.284	.230	56	-3	0				.989	1	C-22/1-1	-0.1
1893	Lou-N	10	36	4	4	1	0	0	6	3	9	.111	.179	.139	-16	-6	0				.853	-4	C-10	-0.1
Total	4	189	666	60	151	19	6	3	73	43	73	.227	.278	.287	64	-32	8				.932	-1	C-189/1-1,3-1	-1.4

■ JOE HARRINGTON
Harrington, Joseph C. b: 12/21/1869, Fall River, Mass. d: 9/13/33, Fall River, Mass. BR/TR, 5'8.5", 162 lbs. Deb: 9/10/1895

YEAR	TM/L	G	AB	R	H	2B	3B	HR	RBI	BB	SO	AVG	OBP	SLG	PRO+	BR/A	SB	CS	SBR	FA	FR	G/POS	TPR
1895	Bos-N	18	65	21	18	0	2	2	13	7	5	.277	.356	.431	95	-1	3				.912	-1	2-18	0.0
1896	Bos-N	54	198	25	39	5	3	1	25	19	17	.197	.271	.268	40	-18	2				.816	-10	3-49/S-4,2-1	-2.3
Total	2	72	263	46	57	5	5	3	38	26	22	.217	.292	.308	54	-19	5				.901	-10	/3-49,2-19,S-4	-2.3

■ CANDY HARRIS
Harris, Alonzo b: 9/17/47, Selma, Ala. BB/TR, 6', 160 lbs. Deb: 4/13/67

YEAR	TM/L	G	AB	R	H	2B	3B	HR	RBI	BB	SO	AVG	OBP	SLG	PRO+	BR/A	SB	CS	SBR	FA	FR	G/POS	TPR
1967	Hou-N	6	1	0	0	0	0	0	0	0	1	.000	.000	.000	-99	-0	0	0	0	.000	0	H	0.0

■ SPENCER HARRIS
Harris, Anthony Spencer b: 8/12/1900, Duluth, Minn. d: 7/3/82, Minneapolis, Minn. BL/TL, 5'9", 145 lbs. Deb: 4/14/25

YEAR	TM/L	G	AB	R	H	2B	3B	HR	RBI	BB	SO	AVG	OBP	SLG	PRO+	BR/A	SB	CS	SBR	FA	FR	G/POS	TPR
1925	Chi-A	56	92	12	26	2	0	1	13	14	13	.283	.383	.337	89	-1	1	3	-2	.957	-5	O-27	-0.8
1926	Chi-A	80	222	36	56	11	3	2	27	20	15	.252	.317	.356	78	-8	8	3	1	.949	-6	O-63	-1.6
1929	Was-A	6	14	1	3	1	0	0	1	0	3	.214	.214	.286	27	-2	1	0	0	1.000	-1	/O-4	-0.2
1930	Phi-A	22	49	4	9	1	0	0	5	5	2	.184	.259	.204	18	-6	0	0	0	.958	1	O-13	-0.6
Total	4	164	377	53	94	15	3	3	46	39	33	.249	.323	.329	70	-16	10	6	-1	.954	-11	O-107	-3.2

■ GAIL HARRIS
Harris, Boyd Gail b: 10/15/31, Abingdon, Va. BL/TL, 6', 195 lbs. Deb: 6/3/55

YEAR	TM/L	G	AB	R	H	2B	3B	HR	RBI	BB	SO	AVG	OBP	SLG	PRO+	BR/A	SB	CS	SBR	FA	FR	G/POS	TPR
1955	NY-N	79	263	27	61	9	0	12	36	20	46	.232	.291	.403	82	-8	0	0	0	.982	0	1-75	-1.1
1956	NY-N	12	38	2	5	0	1	1	3	1	8	.132	.233	.263	33	-4	0	0	0	.975	0	1-11	-0.4
1957	NY-N	90	225	28	54	7	3	9	31	16	28	.240	.308	.418	93	-3	1	0	0	.985	-2	1-61	-0.8
1958	Det-A	134	451	63	123	18	8	20	83	36	60	.273	.332	.481	113	7	1	2	-1	.986	3	*1-122	0.1
1959	Det-A	114	349	39	77	4	3	9	39	29	49	.221	.292	.327	66	-16	0	1	-1	.992	3	1-93	-2.1
1960	Det-A	8	5	0	0	0	0	0	0	2	1	.000	.286	.000	-15	-1	0	0	0	1.000	0	/1-5	-0.1
Total	6	437	1331	159	320	38	15	51	190	106	194	.240	.306	.406	88	-25	2	3	-1	.986	4	1-367	-4.4

■ CHARLIE HARRIS
Harris, Charles Jenkins b: 10/21/1877, Macon, Ga. d: 3/14/63, Gainesville, Fla. BR/TR, 5'8", 200 lbs. Deb: 5/25/1899

YEAR	TM/L	G	AB	R	H	2B	3B	HR	RBI	BB	SO	AVG	OBP	SLG	PRO+	BR/A	SB	CS	SBR	FA	FR	G/POS	TPR
1899	Bal-N	30	68	16	19	3	0	0	7	14		.279	.319	.324	73	-3	4			.872	-5	3-21/O-3,2-2,S-1	-0.7

■ DAVE HARRIS
Harris, David Stanley "Sheriff" b: 7/14/1900, Summerfield, N.C. d: 9/18/73, Atlanta, Ga. BR/TR, 5'11", 170 lbs. Deb: 4/14/25

YEAR	TM/L	G	AB	R	H	2B	3B	HR	RBI	BB	SO	AVG	OBP	SLG	PRO+	BR/A	SB	CS	SBR	FA	FR	G/POS	TPR
1925	Bos-N	92	340	49	90	8	7	5	36	27	44	.265	.321	.374	84	-9	6	4	-1	.962	8	O-90	-0.7
1928	Bos-N	7	17	2	2	1	0	0	0	2	6	.118	.211	.176	2	-2	0			.833	-1	/O-6	-0.4
1930	Chi-A	33	86	16	21	2	1	5	13	7	22	.244	.309	.465	96	-1	0	0	0	1.000	-0	O-23/2-1	-0.3
	Was-A	73	205	40	65	19	8	4	44	28	35	.317	.399	.546	137	11	6	3	0	.983	1	O-59	0.8
	Yr	106	291	56	86	21	9	9	57	35	57	.296	.373	.522	125	11	6	3	0	.988	1	O-82/2-1	0.5
1931	Was-A	77	231	49	72	14	8	5	50	49	38	.312	.434	.506	146	17	7	6	-2	.950	-2	O-60	0.9
1932	Was-A	81	156	26	51	7	4	6	29	19	34	.327	.400	.538	143	10	4	4	-1	.932	-2	O-34	0.4
1933	*Was-A	82	177	33	46	9	2	5	38	25	26	.260	.358	.418	106	2	3	1	0	.964	-7	O-45/1-6,3-2	-0.7
1934	Was-A	97	235	28	59	14	3	2	37	39	40	.251	.358	.362	89	-3	2	3	-1	.973	-4	O-64/3-5	-0.9
Total	7	542	1447	243	406	74	33	32	247	196	245	.281	.368	.444	112	25	28	21		.963	-8	O-381/3-7,1-6,2-1	-0.9

■ DONALD HARRIS
Harris, Donald b: 11/12/67, Waco, Tex. BR/TR, 6'1", 185 lbs. Deb: 9/4/91

YEAR	TM/L	G	AB	R	H	2B	3B	HR	RBI	BB	SO	AVG	OBP	SLG	PRO+	BR/A	SB	CS	SBR	FA	FR	G/POS	TPR
1991	Tex-A	18	8	4	3	0	1	0	2	1	3	.375	.444	.750	228	1	1	0	0	1.000	-5	O-12/D-3	-0.3
1992	Tex-A	24	33	3	6	1	0	0	0	0	15	.182	.182	.212	10	-4	1	0	0	.974	-4	O-24	-0.8
1993	Tex-A	40	76	10	15	2	0	1	8	5	18	.197	.256	.263	41	-6	0	1	-1	.943	-7	O-38/D-3	-1.5
Total	3	82	117	17	24	3	0	2	11	6	36	.205	.250	.282	46	-9	2	1	0	.959	-16	/O-74,D-6	-2.6

■ FRANK HARRIS
Harris, Frank W. b: 11/2/1858, Pittsburgh, Pa. d: 11/26/39, E.Moline, Ill. BR/TR, Deb: 4/17/1884

YEAR	TM/L	G	AB	R	H	2B	3B	HR	RBI	BB	SO	AVG	OBP	SLG	PRO+	BR/A	SB	CS	SBR	FA	FR	G/POS	TPR
1884	Alt-U	24	95	10	25	2	1	0			3	.263	.286	.305	78	-5				.941	-1	1-17/O-7	-0.7

■ BILLY HARRIS
Harris, James William b: 11/24/43, Hamlet, N.C. BL/TR, 6', 175 lbs. Deb: 6/16/68

YEAR	TM/L	G	AB	R	H	2B	3B	HR	RBI	BB	SO	AVG	OBP	SLG	PRO+	BR/A	SB	CS	SBR	FA	FR	G/POS	TPR
1968	Cle-A	38	94	10	20	5	1	0	3	8	22	.213	.275	.287	71	-3	2	0	1	.970	-1	2-27,3-10/S-1	-0.3
1969	KC-A	5	7	1	2	1	0	0	0	0	1	.286	.286	.429	97	-0	0	0	0	1.000	-0	/2-1	0.0
Total	2	43	101	11	22	6	1	0	3	8	23	.218	.275	.297	73	-3	2	0	1	.971	-1	/2-28,3-10,S-1	-0.3

■ JOHN HARRIS
Harris, John Thomas b: 9/13/54, Portland, Ore. BL/TL, 6'3", 205 lbs. Deb: 9/26/79

YEAR	TM/L	G	AB	R	H	2B	3B	HR	RBI	BB	SO	AVG	OBP	SLG	PRO+	BR/A	SB	CS	SBR	FA	FR	G/POS	TPR
1979	Cal-A	1	2	0	0	0	0	0	0	0	0	.000	.000	.000	-99	-1	0	0	0	1.000	-0	/1-1	-0.1
1980	Cal-A	19	41	8	12	5	0	2	7	4	9	.293	.396	.561	163	4	0	0	-1	1.000	-0	1-10/O-3	-0.4
1981	Cal-A	36	77	5	19	0	0	3	9	6	11	.247	.275	.403	93	-1	0	0	0	.976	-4	1-11,O-10/D-1	-0.6
Total	3	56	120	13	31	5	0	5	16	10	15	.258	.315	.450	115	2	0	0	-1	.987	-4	/1-22,O-13,D-1	-0.5

■ JOE HARRIS
Harris, Joseph "Moon" b: 5/20/1891, Coulters, Pa. d: 12/10/59, Renton, Pa. BR/TR, 5'9", 170 lbs. Deb: 6/9/14

YEAR	TM/L	G	AB	R	H	2B	3B	HR	RBI	BB	SO	AVG	OBP	SLG	PRO+	BR/A	SB	CS	SBR	FA	FR	G/POS	TPR
1914	NY-A	2	1	0	0	0	0	0	0	0	3	1	.000	.800	.000	143	1	0			1.000	-1	/1-1,O-1	0.0
1917	Cle-A	112	369	40	112	22	4	0	65	55	32	.304	.398	.385	129	15	11			.985	10	1-95/O-5,3-2	2.3
1919	Cle-A	62	184	30	69	16	1	1	46	33	21	.375	.472	.489	160	17	2			.988	5	1-46/S-4	1.8
1922	Bos-A	119	408	53	129	30	9	6	54	30	15	.316	.364	.478	119	10	2	6	-3	.953	7	O-83,1-21	0.7
1923	Bos-A	142	483	82	162	28	11	13	76	52	27	.335	.406	.520	142	28	7	3	0	.968	-2	*O-132/1-9	1.7
1924	Bos-A	133	491	82	148	36	9	3	77	81	25	.301	.406	.430	115	14	6	1	-1	.993	6	*1-128/O-3	1.2
1925	Bos-A	8	19	4	3	0	1	1	2	5	5	.158	.333	.421	90	-0	0	0	0	1.000	-1	/1-6	-0.1
	*Was-A	100	300	60	97	21	9	12	59	51	28	.323	.420	.573	156	26	5	3	0	.989	-0	1-58,O-41	1.9
	Yr	108	319	64	100	21	10	13	61	56	33	.313	.424	.564	152	26	5	3	0	.990	-1	1-64,O-41	1.8
1926	Was-A	92	257	43	79	13	9	5	55	37	9	.307	.405	.486	135	14	2	3	-1	.994	-3	1-36,O-35	0.5

YEAR	TM/L	G	AB	R	H	2B	3B	HR	RBI	BB	SO	AVG	OBP	SLG	PRO+	BR/A	SB	CS	SBR	FA	FR	G/POS	TPR
1927	*Pit-N	129	411	57	134	27	9	5	73	48	19	.326	.402	.472	125	15	0			.990	2	*1-116/O-3	0.9
1928	Pit-N	16	23	2	9	2	1	0	2	4	2	.391	.500	.565	171	3	0			1.000	1	/1-6	0.3
	Bro-N	55	89	8	21	6	1	1	8	14	4	.236	.340	.360	84	-2	0			.958	-2	O-16	-0.4
	Yr	71	112	10	30	8	2	1	10	18	6	.268	.374	.402	103	1	0			.958	-0	O-16/1-6	-0.1
Total	10	970	3035	461	963	201	64	47	517	413	188	.317	.404	.472	131	140	36	16		.989	20	1-522,O-319/S-4,3-2	10.8

■ LENNY HARRIS
Harris, Leonard Anthony   b: 10/28/64, Miami, Fla.   BL/TR, 5'10", 195 lbs.   Deb: 9/7/88

YEAR	TM/L	G	AB	R	H	2B	3B	HR	RBI	BB	SO	AVG	OBP	SLG	PRO+	BR/A	SB	CS	SBR	FA	FR	G/POS	TPR
1988	Cin-N	16	43	7	16	1	0	0	8	5	4	.372	.438	.395	135	2	4	1	1	1.000	1	3-10/2-6	0.4
1989	Cin-N	61	188	17	42	4	0	2	11	9	20	.223	.263	.277	52	-12	10	6	-1	.980	1	2-32,S-17,3-16	-1.0
	LA-N	54	147	19	37	6	1	1	15	11	13	.252	.308	.327	83	-3	4	3	-1	1.000	-7	O-21,2-14/3-8,S-1	-1.1
	Yr	115	335	36	79	10	1	3	26	20	33	.236	.283	.299	66	-15	14	9	-1	.975	-5	2-46,3-24,O-21,S-18	-2.1
1990	LA-N	137	431	61	131	16	4	2	29	29	31	.304	.349	.374	102	1	15	10	-2	.959	-8	3-94,2-44/O-2,S-1	-0.7
1991	LA-N	145	429	59	123	16	1	3	38	37	32	.287	.350	.350	100	1	12	3	2	.943	-1	*3-113,2-27,S-20,/O	0.3
1992	LA-N	135	347	28	94	11	0	0	30	24	24	.271	.320	.303	78	-9	19	7	2	.963	17	2-81,3-33,O-15,S-10	1.1
1993	LA-N	107	160	20	38	6	1	2	11	15	15	.237	.303	.325	72	-6	3	1	0	.987	2	2-35,3-17/S-3,O-2	-0.3
1994	Cin-N	66	100	13	31	3	1	0	14	5	13	.310	.343	.360	84	-2	7	2	1	.846	-0	3-15/1-4,O-3,2-2	-0.2
1995	*Cin-N	101	197	32	41	8	3	2	16	14	20	.208	.261	.310	50	-15	10	1	2	.939	-2	3-24,1-23/O-8,2-1	-1.7
1996	Cin-N	125	302	33	86	17	2	5	32	21	31	.285	.333	.404	94	-3	14	6	1	1.000	-7	O-37,3-24,1-16,/2-7	-1.1
Total	9	947	2344	289	639	88	13	17	204	170	203	.273	.324	.343	85	-46	98	40	5	.940	-3	3-354,2-249/OS1	-4.3

■ NED HARRIS
Harris, Robert Ned   b: 7/9/16, Ames, Iowa   d: 12/18/76, W.Palm Beach, Fla.   BL/TL, 5'11", 175 lbs.   Deb: 4/20/41

YEAR	TM/L	G	AB	R	H	2B	3B	HR	RBI	BB	SO	AVG	OBP	SLG	PRO+	BR/A	SB	CS	SBR	FA	FR	G/POS	TPR
1941	Det-A	26	61	11	13	3	1	1	4	6	13	.213	.284	.344	59	-4	1	0	0	1.000	-2	O-12	-0.6
1942	Det-A	121	398	53	108	16	10	9	45	49	35	.271	.351	.430	110	5	5	4	-1	.944	-10	*O-104	-1.1
1943	Det-A	114	354	43	90	14	3	6	32	47	29	.254	.343	.362	99	-0	6	8	-3	.961	-3	O-96	-1.2
1946	Det-A	1	1	0	0	0	0	0	0	0	0	.000	.000	.000	-94	-0	0	0	0	.000	0	H	0.0
Total	4	262	814	107	211	33	14	16	81	102	77	.259	.342	.393	101	1	12	12	-4	.955	-15	O-212	-2.9

■ BUCKY HARRIS
Harris, Stanley Raymond   b: 11/8/1896, Port Jervis, N.Y.   d: 11/8/77, Bethesda, Md.   BR/TR, 5'9.5", 156 lbs.   Deb: 8/28/19   MH

YEAR	TM/L	G	AB	R	H	2B	3B	HR	RBI	BB	SO	AVG	OBP	SLG	PRO+	BR/A	SB	CS	SBR	FA	FR	G/POS	TPR
1919	Was-A	8	28	0	6	2	0	0	4	1	3	.214	.267	.286	56	-2	0			.925	2	/2-8	0.1
1920	Was-A	136	506	76	152	26	6	1	68	44	36	.300	.377	.381	104	5	16	17	-5	.958	-10	*2-134	-0.6
1921	Was-A	154	584	82	169	22	8	0	54	54	39	.289	.367	.354	89	-7	29	9	3	.959	12	2-154	1.1
1922	Was-A	154	602	95	162	24	8	2	40	52	38	.269	.341	.346	84	-14	25	11	1	.970	**26**	*2-154	1.7
1923	Was-A	145	532	60	150	21	13	2	70	50	29	.282	.358	.382	100	0	23	16	-3	.961	19	*2-144/S-1	1.8
1924	*Was-A	143	544	88	146	28	9	1	58	56	41	.268	.344	.358	84	-13	20	10	0	.968	-13	*2-143,M	-2.3
1925	*Was-A	144	551	91	158	30	3	1	66	64	21	.287	.370	.358	87	-9	14	12	-3	.970	3	*2-144,M	-0.6
1926	Was-A	141	537	94	152	39	9	1	63	58	41	.283	.363	.395	100	0	16	11	-2	.963	-1	*2-141,M	-0.8
1927	Was-A	128	475	98	127	20	3	1	55	66	33	.267	.363	.328	81	-11	18	3	4	**.972**	1	*2-128,M	-0.1
1928	Was-A	99	358	34	73	11	5	0	28	27	26	.204	.264	.263	39	-32	5	2	0	.970	11	2-96/3-1,O-1,M	-1.8
1929	Det-A	7	11	3	1	0	0	0	0	2	2	.091	.231	.091	-14	-2	1	0		.900	-2	/2-4,S-1,M	-0.1
1931	Det-A	4	8	1	1	1	0	0	0	1	1	.125	.222	.250	23	-1	0	0	0	1.000	0	/2-3,M	-0.1
Total	12	1263	4736	722	1297	224	64	9	506	472	310	.274	.352	.354	86	-85	167	91		.965	43	*2-1253/S-2,O-1,3-1	-1.7

■ VIC HARRIS
Harris, Victor Lanier   b: 3/27/50, Los Angeles, Cal.   BB/TR, 6', 170 lbs.   Deb: 7/21/72

YEAR	TM/L	G	AB	R	H	2B	3B	HR	RBI	BB	SO	AVG	OBP	SLG	PRO+	BR/A	SB	CS	SBR	FA	FR	G/POS	TPR
1972	Tex-A	61	186	8	26	5	1	0	10	12	39	.140	.192	.177	11	-21	7	3	0	.960	-5	2-58/S-1	-2.0
1973	Tex-A	152	555	71	138	14	7	8	44	55	81	.249	.319	.342	90	-7	13	12	-3	.977	2	*O-113,3-25,2-18	-1.4
1974	Chi-N	62	200	18	39	6	3	0	11	29	26	.195	.297	.255	53	-12	9	3	1	.943	-17	2-56	-2.7
1975	Chi-N	51	56	6	10	0	0	0	5	6	7	.179	.258	.179	22	-6	0	0	0	.900	-2	O-11/3-7,2-5	-0.8
1976	StL-N	97	259	21	59	12	3	1	19	16	55	.228	.275	.309	65	-12	1	2	-1	.945	-8	2-37,O-35,3-12/S-1	-2.1
1977	SF-N	69	165	28	43	12	0	2	14	19	36	.261	.337	.370	90	-2	2	1	0	.973	-10	2-27,S-11/3-9,O-3	-0.9
1978	SF-N	53	100	8	15	4	0	1	11	11	24	.150	.234	.220	29	-10	0	0	0	.934	-7	S-22,2-10/O-6	-1.5
1980	Mil-A	34	89	8	19	4	1	1	7	12	13	.213	.307	.315	73	-3	4	1	1	.967	-2	O-31/3-2,2-1	-0.6
Total	8	579	1610	168	349	57	15	13	121	160	281	.217	.289	.295	65	-73	36	22	-2	.954	-43	2-212,O-199/3-55,S	-12.0

■ CHUCK HARRISON
Harrison, Charles William   b: 4/25/41, Abilene, Tex.   BR/TR, 5'10", 190 lbs.   Deb: 9/15/65

YEAR	TM/L	G	AB	R	H	2B	3B	HR	RBI	BB	SO	AVG	OBP	SLG	PRO+	BR/A	SB	CS	SBR	FA	FR	G/POS	TPR
1965	Hou-N	15	45	2	9	4	0	1	9	8	9	.200	.321	.356	97	-0	0	0	0	.983	0	1-12	-0.1
1966	Hou-N	119	434	52	111	23	2	9	52	37	69	.256	.317	.380	100	-1	2	0	1	.992	4	*1-114	-0.5
1967	Hou-N	70	177	13	43	7	3	2	26	13	30	.243	.295	.350	87	-3	0	0	0	.987	-1	1-59	-0.7
1969	KC-A	75	213	18	47	5	1	3	18	16	20	.221	.278	.296	60	-11	1	2	-1	.993	2	1-55	-1.6
1971	KC-A	49	143	9	31	4	0	2	21	11	19	.217	.273	.287	59	-8	0	0	0	.992	0	1-39	-1.2
Total	5	328	1012	94	241	43	6	17	126	85	147	.238	.299	.343	83	-24	3	2	-0	.991	5	1-279	-4.1

■ BEN HARRISON
Harrison, Leo J.   BR ,   Deb: 9/27/01

YEAR	TM/L	G	AB	R	H	2B	3B	HR	RBI	BB	SO	AVG	OBP	SLG	PRO+	BR/A	SB	CS	SBR	FA	FR	G/POS	TPR
1901	Was-A	1	2	0	0	0	0	0	0	0	1	.000	.333	.000	-2	-0	0			.000	-0	/O-1	-0.1

■ TOM HARRISON
Harrison, Thomas James   b: 1/18/45, Trail, B.C., Canada   BR/TR, 6'3", 200 lbs.   Deb: 5/7/65

YEAR	TM/L	G	AB	R	H	2B	3B	HR	RBI	BB	SO	AVG	OBP	SLG	PRO+	BR/A	SB	CS	SBR	FA	FR	G/POS	TPR
1965	KC-A	2	0	0	0	0	0	0	0	0	0	—	—	—	—	0	0	0	0	.000	-0	/P-1	0.0

■ RIT HARRISON
Harrison, Washington Ritter   b: 9/16/1849, Waterbury, Conn.   d: 11/7/1888, Bridgeport, Conn.   Deb: 5/20/1875

YEAR	TM/L	G	AB	R	H	2B	3B	HR	RBI	BB	SO	AVG	OBP	SLG	PRO+	BR/A	SB	CS	SBR	FA	FR	G/POS	TPR
1875	NH-n	1	4	0	2	1	0	0	1	0	0	.500	.500	.750	376	1	0	1	-1	.333	-2	/C-1,S-1	-0.2

■ SAM HARSHANY
Harshany, Samuel   b: 5/1/10, Madison, Ill.   BR/TR, 6', 180 lbs.   Deb: 9/28/37

YEAR	TM/L	G	AB	R	H	2B	3B	HR	RBI	BB	SO	AVG	OBP	SLG	PRO+	BR/A	SB	CS	SBR	FA	FR	G/POS	TPR
1937	StL-A	5	11	0	1	1	0	0	0	3	0	.091	.286	.182	20	-1	0	0	0	.905	1	/C-4	-0.1
1938	StL-A	11	24	2	7	0	0	0	0	3	2	.292	.370	.292	68	-1	0	0	0	.975	-0	C-10	-0.1
1939	StL-A	42	145	15	35	2	0	0	15	9	8	.241	.290	.255	40	-13	0	1	-1	.994	-2	C-36	-1.2
1940	StL-A	3	1	0	0	0	0	0	0	1	0	.000	.500	.000	41	-0	0	0	0	.000	0	/C-2	0.0
Total	4	61	181	17	43	3	0	0	15	16	10	.238	.303	.254	43	-15	0	1	-1	.983	-2	/C-52	-1.4

■ JACK HARSHMAN
Harshman, John Elvin   b: 7/12/27, San Diego, Cal.   BL/TL, 6'2", 185 lbs.   Deb: 9/16/48

YEAR	TM/L	G	AB	R	H	2B	3B	HR	RBI	BB	SO	AVG	OBP	SLG	PRO+	BR/A	SB	CS	SBR	FA	FR	G/POS	TPR
1948	NY-N	5	8	0	2	0	0	0	1	1	3	.250	.333	.250	60	-0	0			1.000	0	/1-3	0.0
1950	NY-N	9	32	3	4	0	0	2	4	3	6	.125	.200	.313	32	-3	0			.989	0	/1-9	-0.3
1952	NY-N	3	2	0	0	0	0	0	0	0	1	.000	.000	.000	-99	-1	0			1.000	0	/P-2	0.0
1954	Chi-A	36	56	6	8	1	0	2	5	12	21	.143	.294	.268	53	-4	0	0	0	.967	-1	P-35/1-1	0.0
1955	Chi-A	32	60	6	11	1	0	2	8	9	17	.183	.290	.300	57	-4	0	0	0	.970	-8	P-32	0.0
1956	Chi-A	36	71	8	12	1	0	6	19	11	21	.169	.280	.437	86	-2	0	0	0	.886	-2	P-34	0.0
1957	Chi-A	30	45	5	10	1	0	2	5	10	17	.222	.364	.378	102	2	0	0	0	.947	-3	P-30	0.0
1958	Bal-A	47	82	11	16	1	0	6	14	17	22	.195	.333	.427	114	2	0	0	0	.980	1	P-34/O-1	0.0
1959	Bal-A	15	10	3	2	0	0	1	1	2	2	.200	.333	.500	128	0	0	0	0	1.000	1	P-14	0.0
	Bos-A	9	7	1	1	0	0	0	2	2	2	.143	.333	.143	34	-1	0	0	0	1.000	-0	/P-8	0.0
	Cle-A	21	34	3	7	1	0	0	5	5	4	.206	.308	.235	53	-2	0	0	0	1.000	-0	P-13	0.0
	Yr	45	51	7	10	1	0	1	8	9	8	.196	.317	.275	65	-2	0	0	0	1.000	1	P-35	0.0
1960	Cle-A	15	17	0	3	1	0	0	1	0	4	.176	.176	.235	11	-2	0	0	0	1.000	-1	P-15	0.0
Total	10	258	424	46	76	7	0	21	65	72	119	.179	.298	.344	74	-16	0	0	0	.962	-5	P-217/1-13,O-1	-0.3

■ BURT HART
Hart, James Burton   b: 6/28/1870, Brown Co., Minn.   d: 1/29/21, Sacramento, Cal.   BB, 6'3", 200 lbs.   Deb: 6/6/01

YEAR	TM/L	G	AB	R	H	2B	3B	HR	RBI	BB	SO	AVG	OBP	SLG	PRO+	BR/A	SB	CS	SBR	FA	FR	G/POS	TPR
1901	Bal-A	58	206	33	64	3	5	0	23	20		.311	.383	.374	106	2	7			.976	-8	1-58	-0.6

■ HUB HART
Hart, James Henry   b: 2/2/1878, Everett, Mass.   d: 10/10/60, Fort Wayne, Ind.   BL/TR, 5'11", 170 lbs.   Deb: 7/16/05

YEAR	TM/L	G	AB	R	H	2B	3B	HR	RBI	BB	SO	AVG	OBP	SLG	PRO+	BR/A	SB	CS	SBR	FA	FR	G/POS	TPR
1905	Chi-A	11	20	3	2	0	0	0		4	3	.100	.217	.100	2	-2	0			1.000	-2	/C-7	-0.4
1906	Chi-A	17	37	1	6	0	0	0	0	2	5	.162	.205	.162	16	-4	0			.935	-4	C-15	-0.7
1907	Chi-A	29	70	6	19	1	0	0		7	5	.271	.329	.286	100	0	1			.956	-5	C-25	-0.3
Total	3	57	127	10	27	1	0	0	11	10		.213	.275	.220	59	-5	1			.957	-11	/C-47	-1.4

YEAR	TM/L	G	AB	R	H	2B	3B	HR	RBI	BB	SO	AVG	OBP	SLG	PRO+	BR/A	SB	CS	SBR	FA	FR	G/POS	TPR

■ MIKE HART Hart, James Michael b: 12/20/51, Kalamazoo, Mich. BB/TR, 6'3", 185 lbs. Deb: 6/12/80

| 1980 | Tex-A | 5 | 4 | 1 | 1 | 0 | 0 | 0 | 1 | 1 | 1 | .250 | .400 | .250 | 85 | -0 | 0 | 0 | 0 | 1.000 | -1 | /O-2 | -0.1 |

■ JIM RAY HART Hart, James Ray b: 10/30/41, Hookerton, N.C. BR/TR, 5'11", 185 lbs. Deb: 7/7/63

1963	SF-N	7	20	1	4	1	0	0	2	3	6	.200	.360	.250	80	-0	0	0	0	1.000	0	/3-7	0.0
1964	SF-N	153	566	71	162	15	6	31	81	47	94	.286	.345	.498	132	23	5	2	0	.937	4	*3-149/O-6	2.7
1965	SF-N	160	591	91	177	30	6	23	96	47	75	.299	.353	.487	130	23	6	4	-1	.919	-13	*3-144,O-15	0.6
1966	SF-N★	156	578	88	165	23	4	33	93	48	75	.285	.344	.510	130	22	2	5	-2	.941	-5	*3-139,O-17	1.2
1967	SF-N	158	578	98	167	26	7	29	99	77	100	.289	.376	.509	153	40	1	1	-0	.937	-15	3-89,O-72	2.2
1968	SF-N	136	480	67	124	14	3	23	78	46	74	.258	.327	.444	130	17	3	1	-0	.925	-12	3-72,O-65	0.2
1969	SF-N	95	236	27	60	9	0	3	26	28	49	.254	.346	.331	92	-2	0	0	0	.943	-7	O-68/3-3	-1.2
1970	SF-N	76	255	30	72	12	1	8	37	30	29	.282	.365	.431	114	5	0	0	0	.908	-17	3-56,O-18	-1.3
1971	*SF-N	31	39	5	10	0	0	2	5	6	8	.256	.356	.410	118	1	0	1	-1	.833	-1	/3-3,O-3	-0.1
1972	SF-N	24	79	10	24	5	0	5	8	6	10	.304	.360	.557	155	5	0	1	-1	.886	-9	3-20	-0.5
1973	SF-N	5	3	0	0	0	0	0	1	3	1	.000	.500	.000	48	0	0	0	0	.600	0	/3-1	0.0
	NY-A	114	339	29	86	13	2	13	52	36	45	.254	.326	.419	112	5	0	2	-1	.000	0	*D-106	0.1
1974	NY-A	10	19	1	1	0	0	0	3	0	7	.053	.182	.053	-30	-3	0	0	0	.000	0	/D-4	-0.3
Total	12	1125	3783	518	1052	148	29	170	578	380	573	.278	.348	.467	128	136	17	17	-5	.929	-73	3-683,O-264,D-110	3.6

■ MIKE HART Hart, Michael Lawrence b: 2/17/58, Milwaukee, Wis. BL/TL, 5'11", 185 lbs. Deb: 5/8/84

1984	Min-A	13	29	0	5	0	0	0	5	1	2	.172	.200	.172	4	-4	0	1	-1	1.000	1	O-11	-0.4
1987	Bal-A	34	76	7	12	2	0	4	12	6	19	.158	.220	.342	47	-6	1	4	-2	1.000	-2	O-32	-1.0
Total	2	47	105	7	17	2	0	4	17	7	21	.162	.214	.295	35	-10	1	5	-3	1.000	-1	/O-43	-1.4

■ TOM HART Hart, Thomas Henry "Bushy" b: 6/15/1869, Canaan, N.Y. d: 9/17/39, Gardner, Mass. 5'7", 160 lbs. Deb: 4/15/1891

| 1891 | Was-a | 8 | 24 | 1 | 3 | 0 | 0 | 0 | 2 | 2 | 1 | .125 | .192 | .125 | -9 | -3 | 1 | | | 1.000 | 1 | /C-5,O-3 | -0.2 |

■ BILL HART Hart, William Woodrow b: 3/4/13, Wiconisco, Pa. d: 7/29/68, Lykens, Pa. BR/TR, 6', 175 lbs. Deb: 9/18/43

1943	Bro-N	8	19	0	3	0	0	0	1	1	2	.158	.200	.158	4	-2	0			1.000	4	/3-6,S-1	0.2
1944	Bro-N	29	90	8	16	4	2	0	4	9	7	.178	.253	.267	47	-6	1			.941	-8	S-25/3-2	-1.3
1945	Bro-N	58	161	27	37	6	2	3	27	14	21	.230	.291	.348	78	-5	7			.913	-2	3-39/S-8	-0.6
Total	3	95	270	35	56	10	4	3	32	24	30	.207	.272	.307	63	-14	8			.924	-6	/3-47,S-34	-1.7

■ CHUCK HARTENSTEIN Hartenstein, Charles Oscar "Twiggy" b: 5/26/42, Seguin, Tex. BR/TR, 5'11", 165 lbs. Deb: 9/11/65 C

1965	Chi-N	1	0	0	0	0	0	0	0	0	0	—	—	—			0	0	0	.000	0	R	0.0
1966	Chi-N	5	0	0	0	0	0	0	0	0	0	—	—	—			0	0	0	1.000	0	/P-5	0.0
1967	Chi-N	45	16	0	1	0	0	0	1	0	9	.063	.063	.063	-61	-3	0	0	0	.950	0	/P-45	0.0
1968	Chi-N	28	2	0	0	0	0	0	0	0	0	.000	.000	.000	-94	-0	0	0	0	.818	-0	P-28	0.0
1969	Pit-N	56	14	0	1	0	0	0	0	1	8	.071	.133	.071	-42	-3	0	0	0	1.000	1	P-56	0.0
1970	Pit-N	17	1	0	0	0	0	0	0	0	1	.000	.000	.000	-99	-0	0	0	0	.900	1	P-17	0.0
	StL-N	6	2	0	0	0	0	0	0	1	2	.000	.333	.000	-3	-0	0	0	0	1.000	-0	/P-6	0.0
	Yr	23	3	1	0	0	0	0	0	1	2	.000	.250	.000	-27	-1	0	0	0	.923	1	P-23	0.0
	Bos-A	17	2	0	0	0	0	0	0	1	2	.000	.333	.000	-0	-0	0	0	0	1.000	-1	P-17	0.0
1977	Tor-A	13	0	0	0	0	0	0	0	0	0	—	—	—			0	0	0	1.000	0	P-13	0.0
Total	7	188	37	1	2	0	0	0	1	3	21	.054	.125	.054	-47	-7	0	0	0	.952	2	P-187	0.0

■ BRUCE HARTFORD Hartford, Bruce Daniel b: 5/14/1892, Chicago, Ill. d: 5/25/75, Los Angeles, Cal. BR/TR, 6'0.5", 190 lbs. Deb: 6/3/14

| 1914 | Cle-A | 8 | 22 | 5 | 4 | 1 | 0 | 0 | 4 | 4 | 9 | .182 | .308 | .227 | 59 | -1 | | | | .913 | -3 | /S-8 | -0.4 |

■ CHRIS HARTJE Hartje, Christian Henry b: 3/25/15, San Francisco, Cal. d: 6/26/46, Seattle, Wash. BR/TR, 5'10.5", 165 lbs. Deb: 9/9/39

| 1939 | Bro-N | 9 | 16 | 2 | 5 | 1 | 0 | 0 | 5 | 1 | 0 | .313 | .353 | .375 | 92 | -0 | | | | .909 | -2 | /C-8 | -0.2 |

■ GROVER HARTLEY Hartley, Grover Allen "Slick" b: 7/2/1888, Osgood, Ind. d: 10/19/64, Daytona Beach, Fla BR/TR, 5'11", 175 lbs. Deb: 5/13/11 C

1911	NY-N	11	18	1	4	2	0	0	1	1	1	.222	.263	.333	64	-1	1			.962	3	C-10	0.2
1912	NY-N	25	34	3	8	2	1	0	7	0	4	.235	.257	.353	64	-2	2			.960	2	C-25	0.1
1913	NY-N	23	19	4	6	0	0	0	0	1	2	.316	.350	.316	90	-0	4			.978	0	C-21/1-1	0.2
1914	StL-F	86	212	24	61	13	2	1	25	12	26	.288	.329	.382	89	-7	4			.956	-9	C-32,2-13/1-9,30	-1.4
1915	StL-F	120	394	47	108	21	6	1	50	42	21	.274	.356	.365	98	-5	10			.972	-7	*C-113/1-1	-0.4
1916	StL-A	89	222	19	50	8	0	0	12	30	24	.225	.325	.261	80	-4	0			.968	1	C-75	0.1
1917	StL-A	19	13	2	3	0	0	0	0	2	1	.231	.333	.231	75	-0	0			.875	1	/C-4,S-1,3-1	0.1
1924	NY-N	4	7	1	2	1	0	0	1	0	0	.286	.375	.429	118	0	0	0	0	1.000	-0	/C-3	0.1
1925	NY-N	46	95	9	30	1	1	0	8	8	3	.316	.375	.347	89	-1	2	0	1	.974	0	C-37/1-8	0.4
1926	NY-N	13	21	0	1	0	0	0	0	5	0	.048	.231	.048	-22	-4	0			1.000	0	C-13	-0.3
1927	Bos-A	103	244	23	67	11	0	1	31	22	14	.275	.337	.332	76	-8	1	0	0	.967	-13	C-86	-1.5
1929	Cle-A	24	33	2	9	0	1	0	8	2	1	.273	.314	.333	64	-2	0			1.000	0	C-13	-0.4
1930	Cle-A	1	4	0	3	0	0	0	0	0	0	.750	.750	.750	271	1	0			.750	-0	/C-1	0.1
1934	StL-A	5	3	0	1	0	0	0	1	0	0	.333	.500	.667	183	0	0			1.000	0	/C-2	0.1
Total	14	569	1319	135	353	60	11	3	144	127	97	.268	.339	.337	85	-33	29	0		.968	-19	C-435/1-19,23OS	-2.6

■ CHICK HARTLEY Hartley, Walter Scott b: 8/22/1880, Philadelphia, Pa. d: 7/18/48, Philadelphia, Pa. BR/TR, 5'8", 180 lbs. Deb: 6/4/02

| 1902 | NY-N | 1 | 4 | 0 | 0 | 0 | 0 | 0 | 0 | 0 | 0 | .000 | .000 | .000 | -99 | -1 | 0 | | | 1.000 | -0 | /O-1 | -0.1 |

■ FRED HARTMAN Hartman, Frederick Orrin "Dutch" b: 4/25/1868, Allegheny, Pa. d: 11/11/38, McKeesport, Pa. BR/TR, 5'8", 170 lbs. Deb: 7/26/1894

1894	Pit-N	49	182	41	58	4	7	2	20	16	11	.319	.389	.451	103	1	12			.876	-4	3-49	-0.2
1897	StL-N	124	516	67	158	21	8	2	67	26		.306	.350	.390	97	-3	18			.867	-4	*3-124	-0.3
1898	NY-N	123	475	57	129	16	11	2	88	25		.272	.313	.364	97	-3	11			.882	9	*3-123	0.6
1899	NY-N	50	174	25	41	3	5	1	16	12		.236	.318	.328	80	-5	2			.886	-4	3-50	-0.7
1901	Chi-A	120	473	77	146	23	13	3	89	25		.309	.355	.431	120	12	31			.894	-6	*3-119	0.5
1902	StL-N	114	416	30	90	10	3	0	52	14		.216	.251	.255	58	-21	14			.908	-12	*3-105/S-4,1-3	-2.5
Total	6	580	2236	297	622	77	47	10	332	118	11	.278	.326	.368	95	-19	88			.886	-12	3-570/S-4,1-3	-2.4

■ J C HARTMAN Hartman, J C b: 4/15/34, Cottonton, Ala. BR/TR, 6', 175 lbs. Deb: 7/21/62

1962	Hou-N	51	148	11	33	5	0	0	5	4	16	.223	.248	.257	39	-13	1	1	-0	.972	7	S-48	-0.3
1963	Hou-N	39	90	2	11	1	0	0	3	2	13	.122	.151	.133	-19	-14	1	0	0	.950	0	S-32	-1.3
Total	2	90	238	13	44	6	0	0	8	6	29	.185	.211	.210	18	-27	2	1	0	.964	7	/S-80	-1.6

■ GABBY HARTNETT Hartnett, Charles Leo b: 12/20/1900, Woonsocket, R.I. d: 12/20/72, Park Ridge, Ill. BR/TR, 6'1", 195 lbs. Deb: 4/12/22 MCH

1922	Chi-N	31	72	4	14	1	1	0	4	6	8	.194	.256	.236	27	-8	0			.982	6	C-27	-0.1
1923	Chi-N	85	231	28	62	12	2	8	39	25	22	.268	.347	.442	107	2	4	0	1	.994	9	C-39,1-31	0.7
1924	Chi-N	111	354	56	106	17	7	16	67	39	37	.299	.377	.523	137	18	10	2	0	.963	-4	*C-105	2.3
1925	Chi-N	117	398	61	115	28	3	24	67	36	77	.289	.351	.555	126	13	1	5	-3	.958	10	*C-110	2.5
1926	Chi-N	93	284	35	78	25	3	8	41	32	37	.275	.352	.468	118	7	0			.978	5	C-88	1.7
1927	Chi-N	127	449	56	132	32	5	10	80	44	42	.294	.361	.454	117	10	2			.973	4	*C-126	2.3
1928	Chi-N	120	388	61	117	26	9	14	57	65	32	.302	.404	.523	143	25	3			.989	9	*C-118	4.2
1929	*Chi-N	25	22	2	6	2	1	1	9	5	5	.273	.407	.591	144	2	1			1.000	-0	/C-1	0.1
1930	Chi-N	141	508	84	172	31	3	37	122	55	62	.339	.404	.630	144	35	0			.989	2	*C-136	4.4
1931	Chi-N	116	380	53	107	32	1	8	70	52	48	.282	.370	.434	113	8	3			.981	2	*C-105	1.7
1932	Chi-N	121	406	52	110	25	3	12	52	51	59	.271	.354	.436	112	7	0			.989	0	*C-117/1-1	2.0
1933	Chi-N★	140	490	55	135	21	4	16	88	37	51	.276	.326	.433	115	9	1			.989	6	*C-140	2.6
1934	Chi-N★	130	438	58	131	21	4	22	90	37	46	.299	.358	.502	130	18	0			.996	14	*C-129	3.5
1935	*Chi-N★	116	413	67	142	32	6	13	91	41	46	.344	.404	.545	152	30	1			.984	15	*C-110	4.8
1936	Chi-N★	121	424	49	130	25	6	7	64	30	36	.307	.361	.443	113	7	0			.991	9	*C-114	2.1

YEAR	TM/L	G	AB	R	H	2B	3B	HR	RBI	BB	SO	AVG	OBP	SLG	PRO+	BR/A	SB	CS	SBR	FA	FR	G/POS	TPR
1937	Chi-N★	110	356	47	126	21	6	12	82	43	19	.354	.424	.548	156	28	0			.996	1	*C-103	3.3
1938	*Chi-N☆	88	299	40	82	19	1	10	59	48	17	.274	.380	.445	123	10	1			.995	-4	C-83,M	1.1
1939	Chi-N	97	306	36	85	18	2	12	59	37	32	.278	.358	.467	118	7	0			.992	-8	C-86,M	0.4
1940	Chi-N	37	64	3	17	3	0	1	12	8	7	.266	.347	.500	97	-0	0			.951	1	C-22/1-1,M	0.2
1941	NY-N	64	150	20	45	5	0	5	26	12	14	.300	.356	.433	119	4	0			.994	-3	C-34	0.3
Total	20	1990	6432	867	1912	396	64	236	1179	703	697	.297	.370	.489	126	232	28		7	.984	74	*C-1793/1-33	40.1

■ PAT HARTNETT
Hartnett, Patrick J. "Happy" b: 10/20/1863, Boston, Mass. d: 4/10/35, Boston, Mass. 6'1", 175 lbs. Deb: 4/18/1890

YEAR	TM/L	G	AB	R	H	2B	3B	HR	RBI	BB	SO	AVG	OBP	SLG	PRO+	BR/A	SB	CS	SBR	FA	FR	G/POS	TPR
1890	StL-a	14	53	6	10	2	1	0	4	6		.189	.283	.264	54	-3	1			.954	-1	1-14	-0.4

■ GREG HARTS
Harts, Gregory Rudolph b: 4/21/50, Atlanta, Ga. BL/TL, 6', 168 lbs. Deb: 9/15/73

YEAR	TM/L	G	AB	R	H	2B	3B	HR	RBI	BB	SO	AVG	OBP	SLG	PRO+	BR/A	SB	CS	SBR	FA	FR	G/POS	TPR
1973	NY-N	3	2	0	1	0	0	0	0	0	0	.500	.500	.500	181	0	0	0	0	.000		H	0.0

■ TOPSY HARTSEL
Hartsel, Tully Frederick b: 6/26/1874, Polk, Ohio d: 10/14/44, Toledo, Ohio BL/TL, 5'5", 155 lbs. Deb: 9/14/1898

YEAR	TM/L	G	AB	R	H	2B	3B	HR	RBI	BB	SO	AVG	OBP	SLG	PRO+	BR/A	SB	CS	SBR	FA	FR	G/POS	TPR
1898	Lou-N	22	71	11	23	0	0	0	9	11		.324	.422	.324	116	2	2			.931	-2	O-21	-0.1
1899	Lou-N	30	75	8	18	1	1	1	7	11		.240	.345	.320	83	-1	1			.927	-2	O-22	-0.4
1900	Cin-N	18	64	10	21	2	1	2	5	8		.328	.403	.484	148	4	7			.957	-5	O-18	-0.2
1901	Chi-N	140	558	111	187	25	16	7	54	74		.335	.414	.475	164	47	41			.951	-1	*O-140	3.5
1902	Phi-A	137	545	109	154	20	12	5	58	87		.283	.383	.391	110	10	47			.955	-1	*O-137	0.0
1903	Phi-A	98	373	65	116	19	14	5	26	49		.311	.391	.477	152	25	13			.968	-6	O-96	1.4
1904	Phi-A	147	534	79	135	17	12	2	25	75		.253	.347	.341	112	10	19			.959	-4	*O-147	-0.3
1905	*Phi-A	150	538	88	148	22	8	0	28	121		.275	.409	.346	138	31	37			.939	-7	*O-149	1.8
1906	Phi-A	144	533	96	136	21	9	1	30	88		.255	.363	.334	115	13	31			.969	0	*O-144	0.7
1907	Phi-A	143	507	93	142	23	6	3	29	106		.280	.405	.367	143	31	20			.967	-11	*O-143	1.6
1908	Phi-A	129	460	73	112	16	6	0	29	93		.243	.371	.330	120	14	15			.960	-5	*O-129	0.5
1909	Phi-A	83	267	30	72	4	4	1	18	48		.270	.381	.326	121	9	3			.966	-4	O-74	0.3
1910	*Phi-A	90	285	45	63	10	3	0	22	58		.221	.353	.277	99	3	11			.945	-6	O-83	-0.8
1911	Phi-A	25	38	8	9	2	0	0	1	8		.237	.396	.289	94	0	0			.941	1	/O-9	0.1
Total	14	1356	4848	826	1336	182	92	31	341	837		.276	.384	.370	128	199	247			.956	-53	*O-1312	8.1

■ ROY HARTSFIELD
Hartsfield, Roy Thomas "Spec" b: 10/25/25, Chattahoochee, Ga. BR/TR, 5'9", 165 lbs. Deb: 4/28/50 MC

YEAR	TM/L	G	AB	R	H	2B	3B	HR	RBI	BB	SO	AVG	OBP	SLG	PRO+	BR/A	SB	CS	SBR	FA	FR	G/POS	TPR
1950	Bos-N	107	419	62	116	15	2	7	24	27	61	.277	.322	.372	88	-8	7			.949	-24	2-96	-2.8
1951	Bos-N	120	450	63	122	11	2	6	31	41	73	.271	.333	.344	89	-7	7	2	1	.969	-5	*2-114	-0.5
1952	Bos-N	38	107	13	28	4	3	0	4	5	12	.262	.295	.355	82	-3	0	0	0	.950	-6	2-29	-0.7
Total	3	265	976	138	266	30	7	13	59	73	146	.273	.324	.358	88	-18	14	2		.959	-34	2-239	-4.0

■ CLINT HARTUNG
Hartung, Clinton Clarence "Floppy" or "The Hondo Hurricane" b: 8/10/22, Hondo, Tex. BR/TR, 6'4", 215 lbs. Deb: 4/15/47

YEAR	TM/L	G	AB	R	H	2B	3B	HR	RBI	BB	SO	AVG	OBP	SLG	PRO+	BR/A	SB	CS	SBR	FA	FR	G/POS	TPR
1947	NY-N	34	94	13	29	4	3	4	13	3	21	.309	.330	.543	127	3	0			1.000	-2	P-23/O-7	-0.1
1948	NY-N	43	56	5	10	1	1	0	3	7	24	.179	.270	.232	37	-5	0			1.000	-6	P-36	0.0
1949	NY-N	38	63	7	12	0	0	4	7	4	21	.190	.239	.381	64	-4	0			.957	2	P-33	0.0
1950	NY-N	32	43	7	13	2	1	3	10	1	13	.302	.318	.605	136	2	0			.939	3	P-20/O-2,1-1	0.0
1951	*NY-N	21	44	4	9	1	0	2	9	1	9	.205	.222	.227	21	-5	0	0	0	1.000	-2	O-12	-0.8
1952	NY-N	28	78	6	17	2	1	3	8	9	24	.218	.299	.385	88	-1	0	0	0	.932	-1	O-24	-0.3
Total	6	196	378	42	90	10	6	14	43	25	112	.238	.285	.407	84	-10	0			.972	-2	P-112/O-45,1-1	-1.2

■ ROY HARTZELL
Hartzell, Roy Allen b: 7/6/1881, Golden, Colo. d: 11/6/61, Golden, Colo. BL/TR, 5'8.5", 155 lbs. Deb: 4/17/06

YEAR	TM/L	G	AB	R	H	2B	3B	HR	RBI	BB	SO	AVG	OBP	SLG	PRO+	BR/A	SB	CS	SBR	FA	FR	G/POS	TPR
1906	StL-A	113	404	43	86	7	0	0	24	19		.213	.266	.230	58	-19	21			.889	-3	*3-103/S-6,2-2	-2.0
1907	StL-A	60	220	20	52	3	5	0	13	11		.236	.285	.295	85	-4	7			.911	0	3-38,2-12/S-2,0-2	-0.3
1908	StL-A	115	422	41	112	5	6	2	32	19		.265	.302	.320	101	-0	24			.943	-6	0-82,S-18/3-7,2-4	-1.0
1909	StL-A	152	595	64	161	12	5	0	32	29		.271	.312	.308	103	1	14			.940	4	O-85,S-65/2-1	0.3
1910	StL-A	151	542	52	118	13	5	2	30	49		.218	.290	.271	81	-12	18			.929	1	3-89,S-38,O-23	-0.9
1911	NY-A	144	527	67	156	17	11	3	91	63		.296	.375	.387	106	5	22			.936	-12	*3-124,S-12/O-8	-0.5
1912	NY-A	125	416	50	113	10	11	1	38	64		.272	.370	.356	102	2	20			.906	-3	3-56,O-56,S-10/2-2	0.1
1913	NY-A	141	490	60	127	18	1	0	38	67	40	.259	.353	.300	91	-3	26			.942	-0	2-81,O-31,3-21,/S-4	-0.5
1914	NY-A	137	481	55	112	15	9	1	32	68	38	.233	.335	.308	94	-2	22	25	-8	.973	0	*O-128/2-5	-1.8
1915	NY-A	119	387	39	97	11	2	3	60	57	37	.251	.351	.313	99	1	7	19	-9	.963	-3	*O-107/2-5,3-2	-1.7
1916	NY-A	33	64	12	12	1	0	0	7	9	3	.188	.297	.203	49	-4	1			1.000	-6	O-28	-1.2
Total	11	1290	4548	503	1146	112	55	12	397	455	118	.252	.327	.309	93	-33	182	44		.959	-26	O-550,3-440,S2	-9.5

■ LUTHER HARVEL
Harvel, Luther Raymond "Red" b: 9/30/05, Cambria, Ill. d: 4/10/86, Kansas City, Mo. BR/TR, 5'11", 180 lbs. Deb: 7/31/28

YEAR	TM/L	G	AB	R	H	2B	3B	HR	RBI	BB	SO	AVG	OBP	SLG	PRO+	BR/A	SB	CS	SBR	FA	FR	G/POS	TPR
1928	Cle-A	40	136	12	30	6	1	0	14	4	17	.221	.264	.279	42	-11	1	1	-0	.948	-2	O-39	-1.5

■ ZAZA HARVEY
Harvey, Ervin King b: 1/5/1879, Saratoga, Cal. d: 6/3/54, Santa Monica, Cal. BL/TL, 6', 190 lbs. Deb: 5/3/00

YEAR	TM/L	G	AB	R	H	2B	3B	HR	RBI	BB	SO	AVG	OBP	SLG	PRO+	BR/A	SB	CS	SBR	FA	FR	G/POS	TPR
1900	Chi-A	2	3	0	0	0	0	0	0	0		.000	.000	.000	-99	-0	0			1.000	-0	/P-1	0.0
1901	Chi-A	17	40	11	10	3	1	0	3	2		.250	.302	.375	89	-1	0			.930	2	P-16	0.0
	Cle-A	45	170	21	60	5	5	1	24	9		.353	.392	.459	141	9	15			.890	2	O-45	0.7
	Yr	62	210	32	70	8	6	1	27	11		.333	.375	.443	131	9	16			.890	3	O-45,P-16	0.7
1902	Cle-A	12	46	5	16	2	0	0	5	3		.348	.388	.391	121	1	1			1.000	1	O-12	0.1
Total	3	76	259	37	86	10	6	1	32	14		.332	.373	.429	127	9	17			.907	4	/O-57,P-17	0.8

■ ZIGGY HASBROOK
Hasbrook, Robert Lyndon "Ziggy" b: 11/21/1893, Grundy Center, Ia. d: 2/9/76, Garland, Tex. BR/TR, 6'1", 180 lbs. Deb: 9/6/16

YEAR	TM/L	G	AB	R	H	2B	3B	HR	RBI	BB	SO	AVG	OBP	SLG	PRO+	BR/A	SB	CS	SBR	FA	FR	G/POS	TPR
1916	Chi-A	9	8	1	1	0	0	0	0	0	2	.125	.222	.125	4	-1	0			1.000	1	/1-7	0.0
1917	Chi-A	2	1	1	0	0	0	0	0	0	0	.000	.000	.000	-98	-0	0			1.000	1	/2-1	0.0
Total	2	11	9	2	1	0	0	0	0	1	2	.111	.200	.111	-6	-1	0			1.000	1	/1-7,2-1	0.0

■ BILL HASELMAN
Haselman, William Joseph b: 5/25/66, Long Branch, N.J. BR/TR, 6'3", 205 lbs. Deb: 9/3/90

YEAR	TM/L	G	AB	R	H	2B	3B	HR	RBI	BB	SO	AVG	OBP	SLG	PRO+	BR/A	SB	CS	SBR	FA	FR	G/POS	TPR
1990	Tex-A	7	13	0	2	0	0	0	3	1	5	.154	.214	.154	9	-2	0	0	0	1.000	0	/C-1,D-3	-0.1
1992	Sea-A	8	19	1	5	0	0	0	0	0	5	.263	.263	.263	48	-1	0	0	0	1.000	-2	/C-5,O-2	-0.3
1993	Sea-A	58	137	21	35	8	0	5	16	12	19	.255	.320	.423	97	-1	2	1	0	.992	-2	C-49/O-2,D-4	-0.1
1994	Sea-A	38	83	11	16	7	1	1	8	3	19	.193	.230	.337	43	-7	1	0	0	.982	-1	C-33/O-2,D-3	-0.6
1995	*Bos-A	64	152	22	37	6	1	5	23	17	30	.243	.327	.395	84	-4	0	2	-1	.989	7	C-48,D-11/1-1,3-1	0.4
1996	Bos-A	77	237	33	65	13	1	8	34	19	52	.274	.331	.439	89	-4	4	2	0	.994	20	C-69/1-2,D-2	1.8
Total	6	252	641	88	160	34	3	19	84	52	124	.250	.311	.401	81	-19	7	5	-1	.991	22	C-205/D-23,O-6,13	1.1

■ DON HASENMAYER
Hasenmayer, Donald Irvin b: 4/4/27, Roslyn, Pa. BR/TR, 5'10.5", 180 lbs. Deb: 5/2/45

YEAR	TM/L	G	AB	R	H	2B	3B	HR	RBI	BB	SO	AVG	OBP	SLG	PRO+	BR/A	SB	CS	SBR	FA	FR	G/POS	TPR
1945	Phi-N	5	18	1	2	0	0	0	0	2	1	.111	.200	.111	-13	-3	0			.920	3	/2-4,3-1	0.0
1946	Phi-N	6	12	0	1	0	0	0	0	0	2	.083	.083	.167	-31	-2	0			1.000	2	/3-3	0.0
Total	2	11	30	1	3	0	0	0	0	2	3	.100	.156	.133	-19	-5	0			1.000	5	/3-4,2-4	0.0

■ MICKEY HASLIN
Haslin, Michael Joseph b: 10/31/10, Wilkes-Barre, Pa. BR/TR, 5'8", 165 lbs. Deb: 9/7/33

YEAR	TM/L	G	AB	R	H	2B	3B	HR	RBI	BB	SO	AVG	OBP	SLG	PRO+	BR/A	SB	CS	SBR	FA	FR	G/POS	TPR
1933	Phi-N	26	89	3	21	2	0	0	8	2	6	.236	.261	.258	43	-6	1			.956	-4	2-26	-1.0
1934	Phi-N	72	166	28	44	8	2	1	11	16	13	.265	.330	.355	74	-5	3			.941	-3	3-26,2-21/S-4	-0.7
1935	Phi-N	110	407	53	108	17	3	3	52	19	25	.265	.300	.344	66	-20	5			.931	-3	S-87,3-11/2-9	-1.7
1936	Phi-N	16	64	6	22	1	0	1	6	3	5	.344	.373	.391	96	-0	0			.938	-5	2-12/3-5	-0.4
	Bos-N	36	104	14	29	1	2	2	11	5	9	.279	.312	.385	93	-1	0			.892	-5	3-17/2-7	-0.5
	Yr	52	168	20	51	2	2	3	17	8	14	.304	.335	.387	95	-1	0			.854	-10	3-22,2-19	-0.9
1937	NY-N	27	42	8	8	1	0	0	5	4	3	.190	.333	.214	51	-2	1			.920	6	/S-9,2-4,3-4	0.4
1938	NY-N	31	102	13	33	3	0	3	15	4	4	.324	.361	.441	119	-1	2			.902	-3	3-15,2-13	0.1
Total	6	318	974	125	265	33	8	9	109	59	64	.272	.316	.350	74	-34	8			.927	-15	S-100/2-92,3-78	-3.8

■ PETE HASNEY
Hasney, Peter James b: 5/26/1865, England d: 5/24/08, Philadelphia, Pa. Deb: 9/13/1890

YEAR	TM/L	G	AB	R	H	2B	3B	HR	RBI	BB	SO	AVG	OBP	SLG	PRO+	BR/A	SB	CS	SBR	FA	FR	G/POS	TPR
1890	Phi-a	2	7	1	1	1	0	0	0	0	1	.143	.250	.143	16	-1	0			.000	-1	/O-2	-0.2

■ BILL HASSAMAER
Hassamaer, William Louis "Roaring Bill" b: 7/26/1864, St.Louis, Mo. d: 5/29/10, St.Louis, Mo. 6', 180 lbs. Deb: 4/19/1894

YEAR	TM/L	G	AB	R	H	2B	3B	HR	RBI	BB	SO	AVG	OBP	SLG	PRO+	BR/A	SB	CS	SBR	FA	FR	G/POS	TPR
1894	Was-N	118	494	106	159	33	17	4	90	41	20	.322	.375	.482	109	6	16			.916	5	O-68,3-31,2-14,/S-4	0.5
1895	Was-N	85	358	42	100	18	4	1	60	26	13	.279	.328	.360	78	-12	8			.964	-7	O-75/1-9,S-1,3-1	-2.0
	Lou-N	23	96	7	20	2	2	0	14	3	4	.208	.232	.271	31	-10	0			.980	3	1-21/2-1,S-1	-0.5
	Yr	108	454	49	120	20	6	1	74	29	17	.264	.308	.341	69	-22	8			.964	-4	O-75,1-30/S-2,32	-2.5
1896	Lou-N	30	106	8	26	5	0	2	14	14	7	.245	.333	.349	83	-2	1			.976	6	1-29	0.4
Total	3	256	1054	163	305	58	23	7	178	84	44	.289	.342	.408	90	-19	25			.938	7	O-143/1-59,3-32,2S	-1.6

■ BUDDY HASSETT
Hassett, John Aloysius b: 9/5/11, New York, N.Y. BL/TL, 5'11", 180 lbs. Deb: 4/14/36

YEAR	TM/L	G	AB	R	H	2B	3B	HR	RBI	BB	SO	AVG	OBP	SLG	PRO+	BR/A	SB	CS	SBR	FA	FR	G/POS	TPR
1936	Bro-N	156	635	79	197	29	11	3	82	35	17	.310	.350	.405	102	1	5			.983		*1-156	-0.9
1937	Bro-N	137	556	71	169	31	6	1	53	20	19	.304	.334	.387	94	-5	13			.984	9	*1-131/O-7	-1.2
1938	Bro-N	115	335	49	98	11	6	0	40	32	19	.293	.356	.361	95	-1	3			.945	-2	O-71/1-8	-0.7
1939	Bos-N	147	590	72	182	15	3	2	60	29	14	.308	.342	.354	94	-6	13			.985	9	*1-123,O-23	-1.1
1940	Bos-N	124	458	59	107	19	4	0	27	25	16	.234	.273	.293	59	-26	4			.979	7	1-98,O-13	-2.9
1941	Bos-N	118	405	59	120	9	4	1	33	36	15	.296	.354	.346	102	1	10			.991	7	1-99	0.1
1942	*NY-A	132	538	80	153	16	6	5	48	32	16	.284	.323	.364	95	-5	5	5	-2	.991	11	*1-132	-0.3
Total	7	929	3517	469	1026	130	40	12	343	209	116	.292	.333	.362	92	-40	53	5		.985	45	1-747,O-114	-7.0

■ RON HASSEY
Hassey, Ronald William b: 2/27/53, Tucson, Ariz. BL/TR, 6'2", 200 lbs. Deb: 4/23/78 C

YEAR	TM/L	G	AB	R	H	2B	3B	HR	RBI	BB	SO	AVG	OBP	SLG	PRO+	BR/A	SB	CS	SBR	FA	FR	G/POS	TPR
1978	Cle-A	25	74	5	15	0	0	2	9	5	7	.203	.262	.284	54	-5	2	0	1	.993	5	C-24	0.2
1979	Cle-A	75	223	20	64	14	0	4	32	19	19	.287	.342	.404	100	0	1	0	0	.992	1	C-68/1-2,D-1	0.9
1980	Cle-A	130	390	43	124	18	4	8	65	49	16	.318	.395	.446	130	17	0	2	-1	.993	-7	*C-113/1-3,D-7	1.3
1981	Cle-A	61	190	8	44	4	0	1	25	17	11	.232	.301	.268	66	-8	0	1	-1	.991	6	C-56/1-5,D-1	-0.4
1982	Cle-A	113	323	33	81	18	0	5	34	53	32	.251	.358	.353	97	-1	0	3	-2	.993	8	*C-105/1-2,D-2	1.2
1983	Cle-A	117	341	48	92	21	0	6	42	38	35	.270	.346	.384	97	-1	2	2	-1	.995	-3	*C-113/D-1	1.2
1984	Cle-A	48	149	11	38	5	1	0	19	15	26	.255	.323	.302	73	-5	1	0	0	1.000	-1	C-44/1-1,D-1	-0.4
	Chi-N	19	33	5	11	0	0	2	5	4	6	.333	.405	.515	144	2	0	1	-1	1.000	-0	/C-6,1-4	0.1
1985	NY-A	92	267	31	79	16	1	13	42	28	21	.296	.369	.509	141	15	0	1	0	.984	-2	C-69/1-2,D-2	1.6
1986	NY-A	64	191	23	57	14	0	6	29	24	16	.298	.382	.466	131	9	1	1	0	.985	-13	C-51/D-3	-0.2
	Chi-A	49	150	22	53	11	1	3	20	22	11	.353	.439	.500	150	11	0	0	0	1.000	1	D-34,C-11	1.2
	Yr	113	341	45	110	25	1	9	49	46	27	.323	.408	.481	140	20	1	1	0	.988	-12	C-62,D-37	1.0
1987	Chi-A	49	145	15	31	9	0	3	12	17	11	.214	.305	.338	69	-6	0	1	0	1.000	-1	C-24,D-18	-0.4
1988	*Oak-A	107	323	32	83	15	0	7	45	30	42	.257	.328	.368	98	-1	2	0	1	.994	-1	C-91/D-9	0.4
1989	*Oak-A	97	268	29	61	12	0	5	23	24	45	.228	.294	.328	78	-8	1	0	0	.991	7	C-78/1-1,D-2	0.3
1990	*Oak-A	94	254	18	54	7	0	5	22	27	29	.213	.291	.299	68	-11	0	0	0	.997	3	C-59,D-15/1-3	-0.5
1991	Mon-N	52	119	5	27	8	0	1	14	13	16	.227	.302	.319	76	-7	1	0	0	.989	-4	C-34	-0.7
Total	14	1192	3440	348	914	172	7	71	438	385	378	.266	.343	.382	100	7	14	10		.993	10	C-946/D-96,1-23	5.2

■ JOE HASSLER
Hassler, Joseph Frederick b: 4/7/05, Ft.Smith, Ark. d: 9/4/71, Duncan, Okla. BR/TR, 6', 165 lbs. Deb: 5/26/28

YEAR	TM/L	G	AB	R	H	2B	3B	HR	RBI	BB	SO	AVG	OBP	SLG	PRO+	BR/A	SB	CS	SBR	FA	FR	G/POS	TPR
1928	Phi-A	28	34	5	9	2	0	0	3	2	4	.265	.306	.324	64	-2	0	1	-1	.879	1	S-28	0.0
1929	Phi-A	4	4	1	0	0	0	0	0	0	2	.000	.000	.000	-97	-1	0	0	-1	.600	-0	/S-2	-0.1
1930	StL-A	5	8	3	2	0	0	0	1	0	1	.250	.250	.250	26	-1	0	0	0	1.000	1	/S-3	0.1
Total	3	37	46	9	11	2	0	0	4	2	7	.239	.271	.283	43	-4	0	1	-1	.875	2	/S-33	0.0

■ GENE HASSON
Hasson, Charles Eugene b: 7/20/15, Connellsville, Pa BL/TL, 6', 197 lbs. Deb: 9/9/37

YEAR	TM/L	G	AB	R	H	2B	3B	HR	RBI	BB	SO	AVG	OBP	SLG	PRO+	BR/A	SB	CS	SBR	FA	FR	G/POS	TPR
1937	Phi-A	28	98	12	30	6	3	1	14	13	14	.306	.387	.520	129	4	0	0	0	1.000	-2	1-28	-0.1
1938	Phi-A	19	69	10	19	6	2	1	12	12	7	.275	.383	.464	114	2	0	0	0	.958	-4	1-19	-0.4
Total	2	47	167	22	49	12	5	4	26	25	21	.293	.385	.497	123	6	0	0	0	.985	-6	/1-47	-0.5

■ SCOTT HASTINGS
Hastings, Winfield Scott b: 8/10/1847, Hillsboro, Ohio d: 8/14/07, Sawtelle, Cal. BR/TR, 5'8", 161 lbs. Deb: 5/6/1871 M

YEAR	TM/L	G	AB	R	H	2B	3B	HR	RBI	BB	SO	AVG	OBP	SLG	PRO+	BR/A	SB	CS	SBR	FA	FR	G/POS	TPR
1871	Rok-n	25	118	27	30	6	4	0	16	4	2	.254	.267	.373	85	-2	11	2		.856	1	*C-23/2-2,O-2,1M	-0.1
1872	Cle-n	22	115	34	45	4	0	0	16	3	2	.391	.407	.426	165	9	5	1	1	.797	-7	C-12/O-8,2-6,M	0.2
	Bal-n	13	62	16	19	3	1	0	4	1	2	.306	.317	.387	111	0	0	1	-1	.900	4	C-12/2-2,O-1	0.2
	Yr	35	177	50	64	7	1	0	20	4	4	.362	.376	.412	145	9	5	2	0	.851	-3	C-24/O-9,2-8	0.2
1873	Bal-n	30	146	41	41	4	0	0	15	4	1	.281	.300	.308	81	-3	4	2	0	.892	-3	C-19,O-12/2-1	-0.4
1874	Har-n	52	246	60	80	11	2	0	29	5	3	.325	.339	.386	126	6	7	4	-0	.741	-14	C-39,O-26/2-1,S-1	-0.6
1875	Chi-n	65	287	43	73	9	0	0	30	9	14	.254	.277	.286	95	-1	13	11	-3	.815	3	C-46,O-29/2-3	0.0
1876	Lou-N	67	283	36	73	6	1	0	21	5	11	.258	.271	.286	73	-11				.872	-7	*O-65/C-5	-1.7
1877	Cin-N	20	71	7	10	1	0	0	3	3	6	.141	.176	.155	6	-9				.791	-9	C-20/O-1	-1.4
Total	5 n	207	974	221	288	37	7	0	114	24	24	.296	.313	.348	109	10	40	21		.819	-19	C-151/O-78,2-15,S1	-0.7
Total	2	87	354	43	83	7	1	0	24	8	17	.234	.251	.260	61	-18				.872	-17	/O-66,C-25	-3.1

■ MICKEY HATCHER
Hatcher, Michael Vaughn b: 3/15/55, Cleveland, Ohio BR/TR, 6'2", 200 lbs. Deb: 8/3/79 C

YEAR	TM/L	G	AB	R	H	2B	3B	HR	RBI	BB	SO	AVG	OBP	SLG	PRO+	BR/A	SB	CS	SBR	FA	FR	G/POS	TPR
1979	LA-N	33	93	9	25	4	1	1	5	7	12	.269	.327	.366	90	-1	1	3	-2	.974	-1	O-19,3-17	-0.5
1980	LA-N	57	84	4	19	2	0	1	5	2	12	.226	.244	.286	48	-6	0	2	-1	1.000	-5	O-25,3-18	-1.4
1981	Min-A	99	377	36	96	23	2	3	37	15	29	.255	.287	.350	77	-11	3	1	0	.992	4	O-91/1-7,3-2,D-1	-1.2
1982	Min-A	84	277	23	69	13	2	3	26	8	27	.249	.266	.343	65	-13	0	2	-1	.988	8	O-47,D-29/3-5	-1.7
1983	Min-A	106	375	50	119	15	3	9	47	14	19	.317	.344	.445	111	5	2	0	1	.979	6	O-56,D-39/1-7,3-1	0.8
1984	Min-A	152	576	61	174	35	5	5	69	37	34	.302	.346	.406	103	2	2	0	1	.974	13	*O-100,D-37,1-17,/3	1.0
1985	Min-A	116	444	46	125	28	0	3	49	16	23	.282	.310	.365	79	-13	0	0	0	.991	8	O-97,D-11/1-4	-0.9
1986	Min-A	115	317	40	88	13	3	3	32	19	26	.278	.318	.366	84	-7	2	1	0	.971	-3	O-46,D-28,1-22,/3-3	-1.3
1987	LA-N	101	287	27	81	19	1	7	42	20	19	.282	.331	.429	102	0	2	3	-1	.929	-3	3-49,1-37/O-7	-0.4
1988	*LA-N	88	191	22	56	8	0	1	25	7	7	.293	.325	.351	97	0	0	0	0	1.000	1	O-29,1-25/3-3	-0.6
1989	LA-N	94	224	18	66	9	2	2	25	13	16	.295	.336	.379	106	1	1	2	-1	.961	-3	O-48,3-16/1-5,P-1	-0.4
1990	LA-N	85	132	12	28	3	1	0	13	6	12	.212	.252	.250	40	-11	0	0	0	1.000	-4	1-25,3-10,O-10	-1.7
Total	12	1130	3377	348	946	172	20	38	375	164	246	.280	.316	.377	89	-55	11	15	-6	.983	26	O-575,1-149,D3/P	-8.3

■ BILLY HATCHER
Hatcher, William Augustus b: 10/4/60, Williams, Ariz. BR/TR, 5'9", 175 lbs. Deb: 9/10/84

YEAR	TM/L	G	AB	R	H	2B	3B	HR	RBI	BB	SO	AVG	OBP	SLG	PRO+	BR/A	SB	CS	SBR	FA	FR	G/POS	TPR
1984	Chi-N	8	9	1	1	0	0	0	0	1	0	.111	.200	.111	-10	-1	2	0	1	1.000	-0	/O-4	-0.1
1985	Chi-N	53	163	24	40	12	1	2	10	9	18	.245	.293	.368	75	-6	2	4	-2	.988	-3	O-44	-1.2
1986	*Hou-N	127	419	55	108	15	4	6	36	22	52	.258	.303	.356	83	-10	38	14	3	.983	-5	*O-121	-1.7
1987	Hou-N	141	564	96	167	28	3	11	63	42	70	.296	.354	.415	107	6	53	9	11	.986	10	*O-140	2.2
1988	Hou-N	145	530	79	142	25	4	7	52	37	56	.268	.325	.370	103	2	32	13	2	.983	7	*O-142	0.1
1989	Hou-N	108	395	49	90	15	3	3	44	30	53	.228	.284	.304	71	-15	22	6	3	.991	4	*O-104	-1.4
	Pit-N	27	86	10	21	4	0	1	7	0	9	.244	.253	.326	67	-4	2	1	0	1.000	-4	O-20	-0.9
	Yr	135	481	59	111	19	3	4	51	30	62	.231	.279	.308	70	-19	24	7	3	.992	-2	*O-124	-2.3
1990	*Cin-N	139	504	68	139	28	5	5	25	33	42	.276	.328	.381	91	-6	30	10	3	**.997**	8	*O-131	0.1
1991	Cin-N	138	442	45	116	25	3	4	41	26	55	.262	.314	.360	86	-9	11	9	-2	.981	-2	*O-121	-1.6
1992	Cin-N	43	94	10	27	3	0	2	10	5	12	.287	.323	.383	97	-1	0	0	0	.967	-3	O-23	-0.5
	Bos-A	75	315	37	75	16	2	1	23	17	41	.238	.284	.311	62	-16	4	6	-2	.968	-5	O-75	-2.2
1993	Bos-A	136	508	71	146	24	3	9	57	28	46	.287	.338	.400	92	-4	14	7	0	.993	-4	*O-130/2-2	-1.3
1994	Bos-A	44	164	24	40	9	1	1	18	11	14	.244	.295	.329	58	-10	4	1	0	.968	1	O-43/D-1	-1.1
	Phi-N	43	134	15	33	5	1	2	16	9	14	.246	.279	.343	60	-7	8	4	1	1.000	-3	O-40	-1.1
1995	Tex-A	6	12	2	1	1	0	0	1	0	2	.083	.154	.167	-16	-2	0	0	0	1.000	-5	/O-5,D-1	-0.4
Total	12	1233	4339	586	1146	210	30	54	399	267	476	.264	.315	.364	85	-88	218	87	13	.986	-4	*O-1143/D-2,2-2	-10.8

■ FRED HATFIELD
Hatfield, Fred James b: 3/18/25, Lanett, Ala. BL/TR, 6'1", 171 lbs. Deb: 8/31/50 C

YEAR	TM/L	G	AB	R	H	2B	3B	HR	RBI	BB	SO	AVG	OBP	SLG	PRO+	BR/A	SB	CS	SBR	FA	FR	G/POS	TPR
1950	Bos-A	10	12	3	3	0	0	0	2	3	1	.250	.400	.250	63	-1	0	0	0	1.000	3	/3-3	0.2
1951	Bos-A	80	163	23	28	4	2	2	14	22	27	.172	.274	.258	40	-14	1	0	0	.959	21	3-49	0.6
1952	Bos-A	19	25	6	8	1	1	0	3	4	2	.320	.433	.560	162	2	0	3	-2	1.000	4	3-17	0.4
	Det-A	112	441	42	104	12	2	2	25	35	52	.236	.301	.286	63	-21	2	2	-1	.968	14	*3-107/S-9	-1.0

YEAR	TM/L	G	AB	R	H	2B	3B	HR	RBI	BB	SO	AVG	OBP	SLG	PRO+	BR/A	SB	CS	SBR	FA	FR	G/POS	TPR
	Yr	131	466	48	112	13	3	3	28	39	54	.240	.309	.300	69	-19	2	5	-2	**.971**	18	*3-124/S-9	-0.6
1953	Det-A	109	311	41	79	11	1	3	19	40	34	.254	.341	.325	81	-7	3	5	-2	.978	9	3-54,2-28/S-1	0.0
1954	Det-A	81	218	31	64	12	0	2	25	28	24	.294	.386	.376	112	5	4	2	0	.972	-7	2-54,3-15	0.0
1955	Det-A	122	413	51	96	15	3	8	33	61	49	.232	.338	.341	85	-8	3	2	-0	.975	-6	2-92,3-16,S-14	-0.6
1956	Det-A	8	12	2	3	0	0	0	2	2	1	.250	.400	.250	75	-1	0	0	0	1.000	-1	/2-4	-0.1
	Chi-A	106	321	46	84	9	1	7	33	37	36	.262	.352	.361	88	-5	1	0	0	.961	5	*3-100/S-3	0.1
	Yr	114	333	48	87	9	1	7	35	39	37	.261	.354	.357	87	-5	1	0	0	.961	4	*3-100/2-4,S-3	-0.4
1957	Chi-A	69	114	14	23	3	0	0	8	15	20	.202	.321	.228	52	-7	1	0	0	.951	2	3-44	-0.4
1958	Cle-A	3	8	0	1	0	0	0	1	1	1	.125	.222	.125	-2	-1	0	0	0	1.000	1	/3-2	0.0
	Cin-N	3	1	0	0	0	0	0	0	0	0	.000	.000	.000	-95	-0	0	0	0	.000	-0	/2-1,3-1	0.0
Total	9	722	2039	259	493	67	10	25	165	248	247	.242	.334	.321	78	-57	15	14	-4	.962	43	3-408,2-179/S-27	-0.8

■ GIL HATFIELD
Hatfield, Gilbert "Colonel" b: 1/27/1855, Hoboken, N.J. d: 5/27/21, Hoboken, N.J. TR , 5'9.5", 168 lbs. Deb: 9/24/1885 F

YEAR	TM/L	G	AB	R	H	2B	3B	HR	RBI	BB	SO	AVG	OBP	SLG	PRO+	BR/A	SB	CS	SBR	FA	FR	G/POS	TPR
1885	Buf-N	11	30	1	4	1	0	0		0	11	.133	.133	.200	6	-3				.913	-0	/3-8,2-3	-0.3
1887	NY-N	2	7	2	3	1	0	0	3	0	1	.429	.429	.571	184	1	0			1.000	0	/3-2	0.1
1888	*NY-N	28	105	7	19	1	0	0	9	2	18	.181	.211	.190	29	-8	8			.813	-1	3-14,S-13/O-1,2-1	-0.9
1889	NY-N	32	125	21	23	2	0	1	12	9	15	.184	.250	.224	33	-11	9			.858	1	S-24/P-6,3-2	-0.6
1890	NY-P	71	287	32	80	13	6	2	37	17	19	.279	.328	.387	83	-9	12			.842	-19	3-42,S-27/P-3,0-1	-2.0
1891	Was-a	134	500	83	128	11	8	1	48	50	39	.256	.335	.316	90	-5	43			.869	9	*S-105,3-27/P-4,O-3	1.0
1893	Bro-N	34	120	24	35	3	3	2	19	17	5	.292	.388	.417	119	4	9			.875	-7	3-34	-0.2
1895	Lou-N	5	16	3	3	0	0	0	1	1	1	.188	.278	.188	23	-2	0			.889	-1	/3-3,S-2	-0.2
Total	8	317	1190	173	295	31	18	6	129	96	109	.248	.315	.319	79	-34	81			.850	-17	S-171,3-132/PO2	-3.1

■ JOHN HATFIELD
Hatfield, John Van Buskirk b: 7/20/1847, New Jersey d: 2/20/09, Long Island City, N.Y. 5'10", 165 lbs. Deb: 5/18/1871 FM

YEAR	TM/L	G	AB	R	H	2B	3B	HR	RBI	BB	SO	AVG	OBP	SLG	PRO+	BR/A	SB	CS	SBR	FA	FR	G/POS	TPR
1871	Mut-n	33	168	41	43	3	2	0	24	4	0	.256	.273	.298	70	-5	10	3	1	.853	5	*O-24/2-7,3-2	0.1
1872	Mut-n	56	288	76	92	15	1	1	45	9	6	.319	.340	.389	132	13	12	5	1	.847	7	*2-56,M	1.0
1873	Mut-n	52	255	54	78	5	6	2	45	3	2	.306	.314	.399	110	3	2	0	1	.744	-8	*3-45,2-11/O-1,M	-0.4
1874	Mut-n	63	292	47	66	12	1	0	30	7	12	.226	.244	.274	64	-12	4	0	1	.874	-0	*O-58/3-7,P-3,1S	-0.2
1875	Mut-n	1	4	1	2	1	0	0	0	0	0	.500	.500	.750	311	1	0	0	0	1.000	-0	/O-1	0.1
1876	NY-N	1	4	0	1	0	0	0	1	0	0	.250	.250	.250	77	-0	0	0	0	.833	-0	/2-1	0.0
Total	5 n	205	1007	219	281	36	10	3	143	23	20	.279	.295	.344	97	-0	28	8	4	.868	11	/O-84,2-74,3PS1	0.6

■ SCOTT HATTEBERG
Hatteberg, Scott Allen b: 12/14/69, Salem, Ore. BL/TR, 6'1", 185 lbs. Deb: 9/8/95

YEAR	TM/L	G	AB	R	H	2B	3B	HR	RBI	BB	SO	AVG	OBP	SLG	PRO+	BR/A	SB	CS	SBR	FA	FR	G/POS	TPR
1995	Bos-A	2	2	1	1	0	0	0	0	0	1	.500	.500	.500	156	-0	0	0	0	1.000	0	/C-2	0.0
1996	Bos-A	10	11	3	2	1	0	0	0	3	2	.182	.357	.182	60	-1	0	0	0	1.000	2	C-10	0.1
Total	2	12	13	4	3	1	0	0	0	3	3	.231	.375	.308	73	-0	0	0	0	1.000	2	/C-12	0.1

■ GRADY HATTON
Hatton, Grady Edgebert b: 10/7/22, Beaumont, Tex. BL/TR, 5'9", 175 lbs. Deb: 4/16/46 MC

YEAR	TM/L	G	AB	R	H	2B	3B	HR	RBI	BB	SO	AVG	OBP	SLG	PRO+	BR/A	SB	CS	SBR	FA	FR	G/POS	TPR
1946	Cin-N	116	436	56	118	18	3	14	69	66	53	.271	.369	.422	129	17	6			.941	-19	*3-116/O-2	-0.1
1947	Cin-N	146	524	91	147	24	8	16	77	81	50	.281	.377	.448	119	15	7			.938	-8	*3-136	0.7
1948	Cin-N	133	458	58	110	17	2	9	44	72	50	.240	.343	.345	90	-5	7			.932	4	*3-123/2-3,S-2,0-1	-0.2
1949	Cin-N	137	537	71	141	38	5	11	69	62	48	.263	.342	.413	101	0	6			**.975**	-1	*3-136	-0.3
1950	Cin-N	130	438	67	114	17	1	11	54	70	39	.260	.366	.379	96	-1	6			.954	-3	*3-126/2-1,S-1	-0.5
1951	Cin-N	96	331	41	84	9	3	4	37	33	32	.254	.321	.390	76	-11	4	2	0	.972	5	3-87/O-2	-0.9
1952	Cin-N☆	128	433	48	92	14	1	9	57	66	60	.212	.319	.312	76	-13	5	4	-1	**.990**	-17	*2-120	-2.6
1953	Cin-N	83	159	22	37	3	1	2	22	29	24	.233	.351	.396	94	-1	0	1	-1	.991	-11	2-35,1-10/3-5	-1.1
1954	Cin-N	1	1	0	0	0	0	0	0	0	0	.000	.000	.000	-97	-0	0	0	0			H	0.0
	Chi-A	13	30	3	5	1	0	0	3	5	3	.167	.286	.200	34	-3	1	0	0	1.000	-1	3-10/1-3	-0.4
	Bos-A	99	302	40	85	12	3	5	33	58	25	.281	.401	.391	106	4	1	1	-0	.966	5	3-93/1-1,S-1	0.9
	Yr	112	332	43	90	13	3	5	36	63	28	.271	.390	.373	100	1	2	1	0	**.969**	5	*3-103/1-4,S-1	0.5
1955	Bos-A	126	380	48	93	11	4	4	49	76	28	.245	.371	.326	81	-8	0	1	-1	.976	-2	*3-111/2-1	-1.1
1956	Bos-A	5	5	0	2	0	0	0	2	0	0	.400	.400	.400	100	0	0	0	0	.000	0	H	0.0
	StL-N	44	73	10	18	1	2	0	7	13	7	.247	.360	.315	84	-1	1	0	0	.951	6	2-13/3-1	-0.4
	Bal-A	27	61	4	9	1	0	1	3	13	6	.148	.297	.213	40	-5	0	0	0	1.000	-5	2-15,3-12	-0.9
1960	Chi-N	28	38	3	13	0	0	0	7	2	5	.342	.390	.342	104	0	0	0	0	.931	-2	/2-8	-0.1
Total	12	1312	4206	562	1068	166	33	91	533	646	430	.254	.355	.374	96	-10	42	<u>9</u>		.956	-60	3-956,2-196/1OS	-7.0

■ ARTHUR HAUGER
Hauger, John Arthur b: 11/18/1893, Delhi, Ohio d: 8/2/44, Redwood City, Cal BL/TR, 5'11", 168 lbs. Deb: 7/17/12

YEAR	TM/L	G	AB	R	H	2B	3B	HR	RBI	BB	SO	AVG	OBP	SLG	PRO+	BR/A	SB	CS	SBR	FA	FR	G/POS	TPR
1912	Cle-A	15	18	0	1	0	0	0	1	0		.056	.105	.056	-52	-4	0			1.000	-2	/O-5	-0.5

■ ARNOLD HAUSER
Hauser, Arnold George "Peewee" or "Stub" b: 9/25/1888, Chicago, Ill. d: 5/22/66, Aurora, Ill. BR/TR, 5'6", 145 lbs. Deb: 4/21/10

YEAR	TM/L	G	AB	R	H	2B	3B	HR	RBI	BB	SO	AVG	OBP	SLG	PRO+	BR/A	SB	CS	SBR	FA	FR	G/POS	TPR
1910	StL-N	119	375	37	77	7	2	2	36	49	39	.205	.312	.251	67	-14	15			.931	-8	*S-117/3-1	-1.9
1911	StL-N	136	515	61	124	11	8	3	46	26	67	.241	.286	.311	69	-23	24			.918	-15	*S-134/3-2	-2.9
1912	StL-N	133	479	73	124	14	7	1	42	39	69	.259	.319	.324	78	-15	26			.934	10	*S-132	0.6
1913	StL-N	22	45	3	13	0	0	0	9	2	2	.289	.347	.422	121	1	1			.848	-3	/S-8,2-4	-0.2
1915	Chi-F	23	54	6	11	1	0	0	4	5	7	.204	.283	.222	46	-5	2			.851	-3	S-16/3-6	-0.7
Total	5	433	1468	180	349	33	20	6	137	121	184	.238	.305	.300	72	-55	68			.924	-19	S-407/3-9,2-4	-5.1

■ JOE HAUSER
Hauser, Joseph John "Unser Choe" b: 1/12/1899, Milwaukee, Wis. BL/TL, 5'10.5", 175 lbs. Deb: 4/18/22

YEAR	TM/L	G	AB	R	H	2B	3B	HR	RBI	BB	SO	AVG	OBP	SLG	PRO+	BR/A	SB	CS	SBR	FA	FR	G/POS	TPR
1922	Phi-A	111	368	61	119	21	5	9	43	30	37	.323	.378	.481	119	10	1	5	-3	.986	-3	1-94	0.0
1923	Phi-A	146	537	93	165	21	9	17	94	69	52	.307	.398	.475	127	22	6	6	-2	.990	-3	*1-146	0.9
1924	Phi-A	149	562	97	162	31	8	27	115	56	52	.288	.358	.516	123	15	7	5	-1	.993	-3	*1-146	0.2
1926	Phi-A	91	229	31	44	10	0	8	36	39	35	.192	.312	.341	66	-12	1	1	-0	.996	0	1-65	-1.5
1928	Phi-A	95	300	61	78	19	5	16	59	52	45	.260	.369	.517	127	11	4	2	0	.986	-6	1-88	-0.2
1929	Cle-A	37	48	8	12	1	1	3	9	4	8	.250	.321	.500	104	0	0	0	0	.986	1	/1-8	0.0
Total	6	629	2044	351	580	103	28	80	356	250	229	.284	.368	.479	117	46	19	19	-6	.990	-14	1-547	-0.6

■ GEORGE HAUSMANN
Hausmann, George John b: 2/11/16, St.Louis, Mo. BR/TR, 5'5", 145 lbs. Deb: 4/18/44

YEAR	TM/L	G	AB	R	H	2B	3B	HR	RBI	BB	SO	AVG	OBP	SLG	PRO+	BR/A	SB	CS	SBR	FA	FR	G/POS	TPR
1944	NY-N	131	466	70	124	20	4	3	30	40	25	.266	.324	.333	85	-9	3			.960	-7	*2-122	-0.9
1945	NY-N	154	623	98	174	15	8	2	45	73	46	.279	.356	.339	92	-5	7			.968	5	*2-154	1.0
1949	NY-N	16	47	5	6	0	1	0	3	7	6	.128	.241	.170	12	-6	0			.984	-0	2-13	-0.6
Total	3	301	1136	173	304	35	13	3	78	120	77	.268	.338	.329	86	-19	10			.965	-3	2-289	-0.5

■ CHARLIE HAUTZ
Hautz, Charles A. b: 2/5/1852, St.Louis, Mo. d: 1/24/29, St.Louis, Mo. BR , 5'7", 150 lbs. Deb: 5/4/1875

YEAR	TM/L	G	AB	R	H	2B	3B	HR	RBI	BB	SO	AVG	OBP	SLG	PRO+	BR/A	SB	CS	SBR	FA	FR	G/POS	TPR
1875	RS-n	19	83	5	25	0	0	0	4	0	9	.301	.301	.337	134	3	5	1	1	.921	-1	1-19	0.2
1884	Pit-a	7	24	0	5	0	0	0		3		.208	.296	.208	66	-1				.980	0	/1-5,O-2	-0.1

■ ROY HAWES
Hawes, Roy Lee b: 7/5/26, Shiloh, Ill. BL/TL, 6'2", 190 lbs. Deb: 9/23/51

YEAR	TM/L	G	AB	R	H	2B	3B	HR	RBI	BB	SO	AVG	OBP	SLG	PRO+	BR/A	SB	CS	SBR	FA	FR	G/POS	TPR
1951	Was-A	3	6	0	1	0	0	0	0	1	1	.167	.167	.167	-10	-1	0	0	0	1.000	-0	/1-1	-0.1

■ BILL HAWES
Hawes, William Hildreth b: 11/17/1853, Nashua, N.H. d: 6/16/40, Lowell, Mass. BR/TR, 5'10", 155 lbs. Deb: 5/1/1879

YEAR	TM/L	G	AB	R	H	2B	3B	HR	RBI	BB	SO	AVG	OBP	SLG	PRO+	BR/A	SB	CS	SBR	FA	FR	G/POS	TPR
1879	Bos-N	38	155	19	31	3	3	0	9	2	13	.200	.210	.258	52	-8				.828	-3	O-34/C-5	-1.2
1884	Cin-U	79	349	80	97	7	4	4		5		.278	.288	.355	87	-16				.827	-7	O-58,1-21	-2.4
Total	2	117	504	99	128	10	7	4	<u>9</u>	7	<u>13</u>	.254	.264	.325	77	-24				.827	-10	/O-92,1-21,C-5	-3.6

■ THORNY HAWKES
Hawkes, Thorndike Proctor b: 10/15/1852, Danvers, Mass. d: 2/3/29, Danvers, Mass. BR/TR, 5'8", 135 lbs. Deb: 5/1/1879

YEAR	TM/L	G	AB	R	H	2B	3B	HR	RBI	BB	SO	AVG	OBP	SLG	PRO+	BR/A	SB	CS	SBR	FA	FR	G/POS	TPR
1879	Tro-N	64	250	24	52	6	1	0	20	4	14	.208	.220	.240	55	-11				.896	16	*2-64	0.8
1884	Was-a	38	151	16	42	4	2	0		4		.278	.297	.331	118	3				.917	3	2-38/O-2	0.6
Total	2	102	401	40	94	10	3	0	<u>20</u>	8	<u>14</u>	.234	.249	.274	79	-8				.903	19	2-102/O-2	1.4

■ CHICKEN HAWKS
Hawks, Nelson Louis b: 2/3/1896, San Francisco, Cal. d: 5/26/73, San Rafael, Cal. BL/TL, 5'11", 167 lbs. Deb: 4/14/21

YEAR	TM/L	G	AB	R	H	2B	3B	HR	RBI	BB	SO	AVG	OBP	SLG	PRO+	BR/A	SB	CS	SBR	FA	FR	G/POS	TPR
1921	NY-A	41	73	16	21	2	3	2	15	5	12	.288	.333	.479	103	-0	0	1	-1	.970	-2	O-15	-0.3

YEAR	TM/L	G	AB	R	H	2B	3B	HR	RBI	BB	SO	AVG	OBP	SLG	PRO+	BR/A	SB	CS	SBR	FA	FR	G/POS	TPR
1925	Phi-N	105	320	52	103	15	5	5	45	32	33	.322	.387	.447	103	2	3	6	-3	.986	-0	1-90	-0.5
Total	2	146	393	68	124	17	8	7	60	37	45	.316	.377	.453	103		3	7	-3	.986	-2	/1-90,O-15	-0.8

■ HOWIE HAWORTH
Haworth, Homer Howard "Cully"   b: 8/27/1893, Newberg, Ore.   d: 1/28/53, Troutdale, Ore.   BL/TR, 5'10.5", 165 lbs.   Deb: 8/14/15

YEAR	TM/L	G	AB	R	H	2B	3B	HR	RBI	BB	SO	AVG	OBP	SLG	PRO+	BR/A	SB	CS	SBR	FA	FR	G/POS	TPR
1915	Cle-A	7	7	0	1	0	0	0	0	1	2	.143	.333	.143	42	-0	0			.917	-1	/C-5	-0.1

■ JACK HAYDEN
Hayden, John Francis   b: 10/21/1880, Bryn Mawr, Pa.   d: 8/3/42, Haverford, Pa.   BL/TL, 5'9",   Deb: 4/26/01

YEAR	TM/L	G	AB	R	H	2B	3B	HR	RBI	BB	SO	AVG	OBP	SLG	PRO+	BR/A	SB	CS	SBR	FA	FR	G/POS	TPR
1901	Phi-A	51	211	35	56	6	4	0	17	18		.265	.323	.332	78	-6	4			.841	-4	O-50	-1.2
1906	Bos-A	85	322	22	80	6	4	1	14	17		.248	.292	.301	86	-5	6			.973	-1	O-85	-1.2
1908	Chi-N	11	45	3	9	2	0	0	2	1		.200	.217	.244	45	-3	1			1.000	-1	O-11	-0.5
Total	3	147	578	60	145	14	8	1	33	36		.251	.298	.308	80	-14	11			.929	-5	O-146	-2.9

■ CHARLIE HAYES
Hayes, Charles Dewayne   b: 5/29/65, Hattiesburg, Miss.   Deb: 9/11/88

YEAR	TM/L	G	AB	R	H	2B	3B	HR	RBI	BB	SO	AVG	OBP	SLG	PRO+	BR/A	SB	CS	SBR	FA	FR	G/POS	TPR
1988	SF-N	7	11	0	1	0	0	0	0	0	3	.091	.091	.091	-50	-2	0	0	0	1.000	-1	/O-4,3-3	-0.3
1989	SF-N	3	5	0	1	0	0	0	0	0	2	.200	.200	.200	15	-1	0	0	0	1.000	-1	/3-3	-0.1
	Phi-N	84	299	26	77	15	1	8	43	11	49	.258	.284	.395	92	-4	3	1	0	.910	10	3-82	0.7
	Yr	87	304	26	78	15	1	8	43	11	50	.257	.283	.391	91	-5	3	1	0	.911	10	3-85	0.6
1990	Phi-N	152	561	56	145	20	0	10	57	28	91	.258	.296	.348	77	-19	4	4	-1	.957	24	*3-146/1-4,2-1	0.5
1991	Phi-N	142	460	34	106	23	1	12	53	16	75	.230	.258	.363	74	-18	3	3	-1	.958	7	*3-138/S-2	-1.1
1992	NY-N	142	509	52	131	19	2	18	66	28	100	.257	.300	.409	98	-4	3	5	-2	.963	-11	*3-139/1-4	-1.8
1993	Col-N	157	573	89	175	45	2	25	98	43	82	.305	.359	.522	114	9	11	6	-0	.954	4	*3-154/S-1	1.3
1994	Col-N	113	423	46	122	23	4	10	50	36	71	.288	.348	.433	88	-8	3	6	-3	.944	1	*3-110	-1.0
1995	Col-N	141	529	58	146	30	3	11	85	50	88	.276	.343	.406	96	-3	5	1	1	**.963**	-6	*3-141	-0.8
1996	Pit-N	128	459	51	114	21	2	10	62	36	78	.248	.303	.368	74	-18	6	0	2	.950	17	*3-124	0.0
	*NY-A	20	67	7	19	3	0	2	13	1	12	.284	.294	.418	76	-3	0	0	0	1.000	3	3-19	0.0
Total	9	1089	3896	419	1037	199	15	106	527	249	650	.266	.313	.407	89	-69	38	26	-4	.953	47	*3-1059/1-8,O-4,S2	-2.6

■ FRANKIE HAYES
Hayes, Frank Witman "Blimp"   b: 10/13/14, Jamesburg, N.J.   d: 6/22/55, Point Pleasant, N.J.   BR/TR, 6', 185 lbs.   Deb: 9/21/33

YEAR	TM/L	G	AB	R	H	2B	3B	HR	RBI	BB	SO	AVG	OBP	SLG	PRO+	BR/A	SB	CS	SBR	FA	FR	G/POS	TPR
1933	Phi-A	3	5	0	0	0	0	0	0	0	0	.000	.000	.000	-99	-2	0	0	0	.889	0	/C-3	-0.1
1934	Phi-A	92	248	24	56	10	0	6	30	20	44	.226	.286	.339	63	-15	2	1	0	.955	-11	C-89	-2.1
1936	Phi-A	144	505	59	137	25	2	10	67	46	58	.271	.335	.388	79	-17	3	5	-2	.972	-22	*C-143	-3.1
1937	Phi-A	60	188	24	49	11	1	10	38	29	34	.261	.359	.489	114	3	1	0	0	.971	-4	C-56	0.2
1938	Phi-A	99	316	56	92	19	3	11	55	54	51	.291	.396	.475	120	11	2	3	-1	.975	-16	C-90	-0.2
1939	Phi-A☆	124	431	66	122	28	5	20	83	40	55	.283	.348	.510	119	10	4	1	1	.978	-12	*C-114	0.5
1940	Phi-A★	136	465	73	143	23	4	16	70	61	59	.308	.389	.477	126	19	9	3	1	.971	-13	*C-134/1-2	1.5
1941	Phi-A★	126	439	66	123	27	4	12	63	62	56	.280	.369	.442	117	11	2	0	1	.983	-11	*C-123	1.0
1942	Phi-A	21	63	8	15	4	0	0	5	9	8	.238	.333	.302	80	-1	1	1	-0	1.000	-4	C-20	-0.5
	StL-A	56	159	14	40	6	0	2	17	28	39	.252	.364	.327	94	-0	0	0	0	.971	-8	C-51	-0.4
	Yr	77	222	22	55	10	0	2	22	37	47	.248	.355	.320	90	-2	1	1	-0	.979	-12	C-71	-0.9
1943	StL-A	88	250	16	47	7	0	5	30	37	36	.188	.295	.276	66	-10	1	0	0	.983	-9	C-76/1-1	-1.5
1944	Phi-A★	155	581	62	144	18	6	13	78	57	59	.248	.315	.367	96	-4	2	1	-0	.982	11	*C-155/1-1	0.9
1945	Phi-A	32	110	12	25	2	1	3	14	18	14	.227	.336	.345	98	-0	1	0	0	.994	-2	C-32	0.4
	Cle-A†	119	385	39	91	15	6	6	43	53	52	.236	.335	.353	104	2	1	1	-0	.988	2	*C-119	1.2
	Yr	151	495	51	116	17	7	9	57	71	66	.234	.335	.352	103	3	1	1	-0	.989	0	*C-151	1.6
1946	Cle-A★	51	156	11	40	12	0	3	18	21	26	.256	.345	.391	112	3	1	3	-2	.981	-4	C-50	0.3
	Chi-A	53	179	15	38	6	0	2	16	29	33	.212	.322	.279	72	-6	1	1	-0	.979	-3	C-52	-0.7
	Yr	104	335	26	78	18	0	5	34	50	59	.233	.332	.331	90	-4	2	4	-2	.980	-4	*C-102	-0.4
1947	Bos-A	5	13	0	2	0	0	0	1	0	1	.154	.154	.154	-13	-2	0	0	0	.917	1	/C-4	-0.1
Total	14	1364	4493	545	1164	213	32	119	628	564	627	.259	.343	.400	100	1	30	20	-3	.977	-106	*C-1311/1-4	-2.6

■ JACKIE HAYES
Hayes, John J.   b: 6/27/1861, Brooklyn, N.Y.   TR,   Deb: 5/2/1882

YEAR	TM/L	G	AB	R	H	2B	3B	HR	RBI	BB	SO	AVG	OBP	SLG	PRO+	BR/A	SB	CS	SBR	FA	FR	G/POS	TPR
1882	Wor-N	78	326	27	88	22	4	4	54	6	26	.270	.283	.399	113	4				.855	-10	*O-58,C-15/3-5,S-1	-0.5
1883	Pit-a	85	351	41	92	23	5	3		15		.262	.292	.382	121	8				.911	-18	C-62,O-18/S-5,12	-0.5
1884	Pit-a	33	124	11	28	6	1	0		4		.226	.256	.290	77	-3				.912	-1	C-24/1-5,O-3,2-1	-0.2
	Bro-a	16	51	4	12	3	0	0		3		.235	.278	.294	86	-1				.946	6	C-14/O-2	0.6
	Yr	49	175	15	40	9	1	0		7		.229	.262	.291	79	-4				.925	6	C-38/1-5,O-5,2-1	0.4
1885	Bro-a	42	137	10	18	3	0	0		10	5	.131	.179	.153	6	-14				.900	-2	C-42	-1.2
1886	Was-N	26	89	8	17	3	0	3	9	4	23	.191	.226	.326	70	-3	0			.926	-4	C-14,O-12/2-1	-0.6
1887	Bal-a	8	28	2	4	3	0	0		3	0	.143	.143	.250	9	-3				.250	-4	/O-4,3-3,C-1	-0.6
1890	Bro-P	12	42	3	8	0	0	0	5	2	4	.190	.227	.190	11	-5				.867	-3	/O-6,S-3,C-2,2-1	-0.7
Total	7	300	1148	106	267	63	10	10	81	39	53	.233	.260	.331	87	-18				.906	-36	C-174,O-103/1S32	-3.7

■ MIKE HAYES
Hayes, Michael   b: 1853, Cleveland, Ohio   5'7.5", 170 lbs.   Deb: 9/9/1876

YEAR	TM/L	G	AB	R	H	2B	3B	HR	RBI	BB	SO	AVG	OBP	SLG	PRO+	BR/A	SB	CS	SBR	FA	FR	G/POS	TPR
1876	NY-N	5	21	1	3	0	2	0	2	0	0	.143	.143	.333	63	-1				.882	0	/O-5	-0.1

■ JACKIE HAYES
Hayes, Minter Carney   b: 7/19/06, Clanton, Ala.   d: 2/9/83, Birmingham, Ala.   BR/TR, 5'10.5", 165 lbs.   Deb: 8/5/27

YEAR	TM/L	G	AB	R	H	2B	3B	HR	RBI	BB	SO	AVG	OBP	SLG	PRO+	BR/A	SB	CS	SBR	FA	FR	G/POS	TPR
1927	Was-A	10	29	2	7	0	0	0	2	1	2	.241	.267	.241	33	-3	0	0	0	.969	-1	/S-8,3-1	-0.3
1928	Was-A	60	210	30	54	7	3	0	22	5	10	.257	.274	.319	56	-14	3	0	1	.974	8	2-41,S-15/3-2	-0.2
1929	Was-A	123	424	52	117	20	3	2	57	24	29	.276	.316	.351	71	-18	4	5	-2	.945	3	3-63,2-57/S-2	-1.1
1930	Was-A	51	166	25	47	7	2	1	20	7	8	.283	.312	.367	71	-7	2	3	-1	.981	8	2-29/3-9,1-8	0.1
1931	Was-A	38	108	11	24	2	1	0	8	6	4	.222	.263	.259	38	-10	2	0	1	.962	-4	2-19/3-8,S-3	-1.1
1932	Chi-A	117	475	53	122	20	5	2	54	30	28	.257	.302	.333	69	-23	7	4	-0	.967	1	2-97,S-10,3-10	-1.5
1933	Chi-A	138	535	65	138	23	5	2	47	55	36	.258	.331	.331	79	-16	2	3	-1	.981	10	*2-138	0.1
1934	Chi-A	62	226	19	58	9	1	1	31	23	20	.257	.325	.319	65	-12	3	2	-0	.980	-9	2-61	-1.6
1935	Chi-A	89	329	45	88	14	0	4	45	29	15	.267	.327	.347	72	-13	3	1	0	.966	-6	2-85	-1.2
1936	Chi-A	108	417	53	130	34	3	2	84	35	25	.312	.366	.444	96	-4	4	2	0	.979	**17**	2-89,S-13/3-2	1.8
1937	Chi-A	143	573	63	131	27	4	2	79	41	37	.229	.282	.300	47	-47	1	6	-3	.984	21	*2-143	-1.9
1938	Chi-A	62	238	40	78	21	1	2	20	24	6	.328	.389	.445	106	2	3	2	-0	.976	-3	2-61	0.2
1939	Chi-A	72	269	34	67	12	3	0	23	27	10	.249	.320	.316	62	-15	0	3	-2	.974	5	2-69	-0.8
1940	Chi-A	18	41	2	8	0	1	0	1	2	11	.195	.233	.244	23	-5	0	0	0	.981	-0	2-15	-0.4
Total	14	1091	4040	494	1069	196	33	20	493	309	241	.265	.318	.344	70	-184	34	31	-8	.976	52	2-904/3-95,S-51,1-8	-7.9

■ VON HAYES
Hayes, Von Francis   b: 8/31/58, Stockton, Cal.   BL/TR, 6'5", 185 lbs.   Deb: 4/14/81

YEAR	TM/L	G	AB	R	H	2B	3B	HR	RBI	BB	SO	AVG	OBP	SLG	PRO+	BR/A	SB	CS	SBR	FA	FR	G/POS	TPR
1981	Cle-A	43	109	21	28	8	2	1	17	14	10	.257	.352	.394	116	3	8	1	2	.939	1	D-21,O-13/3-5	0.4
1982	Cle-A	150	527	65	132	25	3	14	82	42	63	.250	.311	.389	91	-7	32	13	2	.981	9	*O-139/3-5,1-4	-0.3
1983	*Phi-N	124	351	45	93	9	5	6	32	36	55	.265	.338	.370	97	-1	20	12	-1	.972	-19	*O-103	-2.5
1984	Phi-N	152	561	85	164	27	6	16	67	59	84	.292	.360	.442	124	17	48	13	7	.988	-8	*O-148	1.3
1985	Phi-N	152	570	76	150	30	4	13	70	61	99	.263	.334	.398	101	-6	21	8	2	.984	-6	*O-146	-0.8
1986	Phi-N	158	610	**107**	186	**46**	2	19	98	74	77	.305	.381	.480	131	27	24	12	0	.990	2	*1-134,O-31	1.9
1987	Phi-N	158	556	84	154	36	5	21	84	121	77	.277	.406	.473	128	26	16	7	1	.990	-13	*1-144,O-32	0.3
1988	Phi-N	104	367	43	100	28	2	6	45	49	59	.272	.360	.409	118	9	20	9	1	.990	-1	1-85,O-16/3-3	0.1
1989	Phi-N★	154	540	93	140	27	2	26	78	101	103	.259	.380	.461	139	30	28	7	4	.980	3	*O-128,1-30,3-10	3.4
1990	Phi-N	129	467	70	122	19	3	17	73	87	81	.261	.382	.413	119	15	16	7	1	.979	-0	*O-127	1.8
1991	Phi-N	77	284	43	64	15	1	0	21	31	42	.225	.308	.285	69	-11	9	2	2	.990	11	O-72	-0.7
1992	Cal-A	94	307	35	69	17	4	1	29	37	54	.225	.308	.326	77	-9	11	6	-0	.983	-1	O-85/1-4,D-5	-1.3
Total	12	1495	5249	767	1402	282	36	143	696	712	804	.267	.357	.416	113	101	253	97	18	.983	-20	*O-1040,1-401/D3	4.3

■ BILL HAYES
Hayes, William Ernest   b: 10/24/57, Cheverly, Md.   BR/TR, 6', 195 lbs.   Deb: 9/30/80

YEAR	TM/L	G	AB	R	H	2B	3B	HR	RBI	BB	SO	AVG	OBP	SLG	PRO+	BR/A	SB	CS	SBR	FA	FR	G/POS	TPR
1980	Chi-N	4	9	0	2	1	0	0	0	0	3	.222	.222	.333	49	-1	0	0	0	1.000	-0	/C-3	-0.1
1981	Chi-N	1	0	0	0	0	0	0	0	0	0	—	—	—		0	0			.000	-0	/C-1	-0.0
Total	2	5	9	0	2	1	0	0	0	0	3	.222	.222	.333	49	-1	0	0	0	1.000	-0	/C-4	-0.1

YEAR	TM/L	G	AB	R	H	2B	3B	HR	RBI	BB	SO	AVG	OBP	SLG	PRO+	BR/A	SB	CS	SBR	FA	FR	G/POS	TPR

■ RED HAYWORTH　Hayworth, Myron Claude　b: 5/14/15, High Point, N.C.　BR/TR, 6'1.5", 200 lbs.　Deb: 4/21/44　F

1944	*StL-A	90	270	20	60	11	1	1	25	10	13	.222	.253	.281	50	-18	0	0	0	.967	1	C-87	-1.4
1945	StL-A	56	160	7	31	4	0	0	17	7	6	.194	.228	.219	28	-15	0	2	-1	.992	4	C-55	-1.0
Total	2	146	430	27	91	15	1	1	42	17	19	.212	.243	.258	42	-33	0	2	-1	.976	4	C-142	-2.4

■ RAY HAYWORTH　Hayworth, Raymond Hall　b: 1/29/04, High Point, N.C.　BR/TR, 6', 180 lbs.　Deb: 6/27/26　FC

1926	Det-A	12	11	1	3	0	0	0	5	1	1	.273	.333	.273	59	-1	0	0	0	1.000	-1	/C-8	-0.1
1929	Det-A	14	43	5	11	0	0	0	4	3	8	.256	.304	.256	45	-3	0	0	0	.951	0	C-14	-0.1
1930	Det-A	77	227	24	63	15	4	0	22	20	19	.278	.336	.379	79	-7	0	2	-1	.977	-13	C-76	-1.3
1931	Det-A	88	273	28	70	10	3	0	25	19	27	.256	.307	.315	62	-15	0	1	-1	.973	4	C-88	-0.6
1932	Det-A	109	338	41	99	20	2	2	44	31	22	.293	.354	.382	87	-6	1	1	-0	.991	3	*C-106	0.2
1933	Det-A	134	425	37	104	14	3	1	45	35	28	.245	.302	.299	59	-25	0	0	0	.994	2	*C-133	-1.5
1934	*Det-A	54	167	20	49	5	2	0	27	16	22	.293	.355	.347	82	-4	0	2	-1	.984	7	C-54	0.3
1935	Det-A	51	175	22	54	14	2	0	22	9	14	.309	.342	.411	98	-1	0	0	0	.996	11	C-48	1.1
1936	Det-A	81	250	31	60	10	0	1	30	39	18	.240	.347	.292	59	-15	0	0	0	.988	-4	C-81	-1.4
1937	Det-A	30	78	9	21	2	0	1	8	14	15	.269	.394	.333	83	-1	0	0	0	.992	6	C-28	0.5
1938	Det-A	8	19	1	4	0	0	0	5	3	4	.211	.318	.211	33	-2	1	0	0	.971	2	/C-7	-0.1
	Bro-N	5	4	0	0	0	0	0	0	1	1	.000	.200	.000	-40	-1	0			1.000	1	/C-3	-0.1
1939	Bro-N	21	26	0	4	2	0	0	1	4	7	.154	.267	.231	34	-2	0			1.000	1	C-18	-0.1
	NY-N	5	13	1	3	0	0	0	0	0	1	.231	.231	.231	24	-1	0			1.000	1	/C-5	0.0
	Yr	26	39	1	7	2	0	0	1	4	8	.179	.256	.231	31	-4	0			1.000	2	C-23	-0.1
1942	StL-A	1	1	0	1	0	0	0	0	0	0	1.000	1.000	1.000	456	0	0			.000	0	H	0.0
1944	Bro-N	7	10	0	0	0	0	0	0	2	1	.000	.167	.000	-51	-2	0			1.000	2	/C-6	0.0
1945	Bro-N	2	2	0	0	0	0	0	0	1	0	.000	.333	.000	-3	-0	0			1.000	0	/C-2	0.0
Total	15	699	2062	220	546	92	16	5	238	198	188	.265	.331	.332	71	-87	2	6		.987	20	C-677	-3.1

■ DRUNGO HAZEWOOD　Hazewood, Drungo La Rue　b: 9/2/59, Mobile, Ala.　BR/TR, 6'3", 210 lbs.　Deb: 9/19/80

1980	Bal-A	6	5	1	0	0	0	0	0	0	4	.000	.000	.000	-99	-1	0	0	0	1.000	-1	/O-3	-0.2

■ BOB HAZLE　Hazle, Robert Sidney "Hurricane"　b: 12/9/30, Laurens, S.C.　d: 4/25/92, Columbia, S.C.　BL/TR, 6', 190 lbs.　Deb: 9/8/55

1955	Cin-N	6	13	0	3	0	0	0	0	3	.231	.231	.231	22	-1	0	0	0	1.000	2	/O-3	0.0
1957	*Mil-N	41	134	26	54	12	6	7	27	18	15	.403	.477	.649	214	22	1	3	-2	.906	-5	O-40	1.3
1958	Mil-N	20	56	6	10	0	0	0	5	9	4	.179	.303	.179	34	-5	0	0	0	1.000	-1	O-20	-0.7
	Det-A	43	58	5	14	2	2	2	5	5	13	.241	.302	.379	80	-2	0	0	0	1.000	-2	O-12	-0.4
Total	3	110	261	37	81	14	8	9	37	32	35	.310	.390	.467	135	14	1	3	-2	.951	-7	/O-75	0.2

■ DOC HAZLETON　Hazleton, Willard Carpenter　b: 8/28/1876, Strafford, Vt.　d: 3/10/41, Burlington, Vt.　Deb: 4/17/02

1902	StL-N	7	23	0	3	0	0	0		0	2	.130	.231	.130	12	-2	0			.973	0	/1-7	-0.3

■ FRAN HEALY　Healy, Francis Xavier　b: 9/6/46, Holyoke, Mass.　BR/TR, 6'5", 220 lbs.　Deb: 9/3/69

1969	KC-A	6	10	0	4	1	0	0	0	0	5	.400	.400	.500	149	1	0	0	0	1.000	0	/C-5	0.1
1971	SF-N	47	93	10	26	3	0	2	11	15	24	.280	.380	.376	117	3	1	0	0	.966	-2	C-22	0.2
1972	SF-N	45	99	12	15	4	0	1	8	13	24	.152	.257	.222	37	-8	0	1	-1	.995	7	C-43	-0.1
1973	KC-A	95	279	25	77	15	2	6	34	31	56	.276	.348	.409	104	2	3	4	-2	.979	-3	C-92/D-1	0.1
1974	KC-A	139	445	59	112	24	2	9	53	62	73	.252	.344	.375	101	2	16	8	0	.977	-7	*C-138	0.1
1975	KC-A	56	188	16	48	5	2	2	18	14	19	.255	.307	.335	79	-5	4	3	-1	.982	5	C-51/D-4	-1.1
1976	KC-A	8	24	2	3	0	0	0	1	4	10	.125	.250	.125	12	-3	2	0	1	1.000	0	/C-6,D-1	-0.2
	NY-A	46	120	10	32	3	0	0	9	9	17	.267	.318	.292	80	-3	3	1	0	.983	3	C-31/D-9	0.1
	Yr	54	144	12	35	3	0	0	10	13	27	.243	.306	.264	68	-5	5	1	1	.987	3	C-37,D-10	-0.1
1977	NY-A	27	67	10	15	5	0	0	7	6	13	.224	.288	.299	61	-4	1	0	0	.971	-0	C-26	-0.3
1978	NY-A	1	1	0	0	0	0	0	0	0	0	.000	.000	.000	-99	-0	0			.000	0	/C-1	0.0
Total	9	470	1326	144	332	60	6	20	141	154	242	.250	.329	.350	90	-16	30	17	-1	.980	-8	C-415/D-15	-1.1

■ FRANCIS HEALY　Healy, Francis Xavier Paul　b: 6/29/10, Holyoke, Mass.　BR/TR, 5'9.5", 175 lbs.　Deb: 4/29/30

1930	NY-N	7	2	2	0	0	0	0	0	0	0	.000	.000	.000	-99	-1	0			.000	0	/C-1	-0.1
1931	NY-N	6	7	1	1	0	0	0	0	0	0	.143	.143	.143	-24	-1	0			1.000	0	/C-4	-0.1
1932	NY-N	14	32	5	8	2	0	0	4	2	8	.250	.294	.313	65	-2	0			.960	2	C-11	0.1
1934	StL-N	15	13	1	4	1	0	0	1	0	2	.308	.308	.385	79	-0	0			1.000	1	/C-2,3-1,O-1	0.0
Total	4	42	54	9	13	3	0	0	5	2	10	.241	.268	.296	51	-3	0			.969	3	/C-18,O-1,3-1	-0.1

■ THOMAS HEALY　Healy, Thomas Fitzgerald　b: 10/30/1895, Altoona, Pa.　d: 1/15/74, Cleveland, Ohio　BR/TR, 6', 172 lbs.　Deb: 7/13/15

1915	Phi-A	23	77	11	17	1	0	0	5	6	4	.221	.310	.234	65	-3	0	4	-2	.933	-1	3-17/S-1	0.0
1916	Phi-A	6	23	4	6	1	1	0	2	1	2	.261	.320	.391	119	0	1			.947	-1	/3-6	0.0
Total	2	29	100	15	23	2	1	0	7	7	6	.230	.313	.270	77	-3	1	4		.936	4	/3-23,S-1	0.0

■ CHARLIE HEARD　Heard, Charles　b: 1/30/1872, Philadelphia, Pa.　d: 2/20/45, Philadelphia, Pa.　BR/TR, 6'2", 190 lbs.　Deb: 7/14/1890

1890	Pit-N	12	43	2	8	2	0	0		0	15	.186	.205	.233	31	-4	0			.600	-3	/O-6,P-6	-0.4

■ ED HEARN　Hearn, Edmund　b: 9/17/1888, Ventura, Cal.　d: 9/8/52, Sawtelle, Cal.　BR/TR, 5'9", 160 lbs.　Deb: 6/9/10

1910	Bos-A	2	2	0	0	0	0	0	0	0	0	.000	.000	.000	-98	-0	0			1.000	2	/S-2	0.1

■ ED HEARN　Hearn, Edward John　b: 8/23/60, Stuart, Fla.　BR/TR, 6'3", 215 lbs.　Deb: 5/17/86

1986	NY-N	49	136	16	36	5	0	4	10	12	19	.265	.324	.390	99	-0	0	1	-1	.987	-6	C-45	-0.5
1987	KC-A	6	17	2	5	2	0	0	3	4	2	.294	.429	.412	121	1	0	0	0	1.000	-2	C-5	-0.1
1988	KC-A	7	18	1	4	2	0	0	1	0	1	.222	.222	.333	53	-1	0	0	0	1.000	-0	/C-4,D-2	-0.1
Total	3	62	171	19	45	9	0	4	14	16	22	.263	.326	.386	97	-0	0	1	-1	.989	-8	/C-54,D-2	-0.7

■ HUGHIE HEARNE　Hearne, Hugh Joseph　b: 4/18/1873, Troy, N.Y.　d: 9/22/32, Troy, N.Y.　BR/TR, 5'8", 182 lbs.　Deb: 8/29/01

1901	Bro-N	2	5	1	2	0	0	0		0	0	.400	.400	.400	129	0	0			1.000	0	/C-2	0.0
1902	Bro-N	66	231	22	65	10	0	0	28	16		.281	.336	.325	103	1	3			.966	-10	C-65	-0.2
1903	Bro-N	26	57	8	16	3	2	0	4	3		.281	.328	.404	111	1	2			.960	3	C-17/1-2	0.5
Total	3	94	293	31	83	13	2	0	35	19		.283	.335	.341	105	2	5			.965	-7	/C-84,1-2	0.3

■ JEFF HEARRON　Hearron, Jeffrey Vernon　b: 11/19/61, Long Beach, Cal.　BR/TR, 6'1", 195 lbs.　Deb: 8/25/85

1985	*Tor-A	4	7	1	1	0	0	0	0	0	2	.143	.143	.143	-21	-1	0	0	0	1.000	2	/C-4	0.0
1986	Tor-A	12	23	2	5	1	0	0	4	3	7	.217	.308	.261	55	-1	0	0	0	.980	1	C-12	0.0
Total	2	16	30	2	6	1	0	0	4	3	9	.200	.273	.233	39	-2	0	0	0	.985	2	/C-16	0.0

■ JEFF HEATH　Heath, John Geoffrey　b: 4/1/15, Ft.William, Ont., Canada　d: 12/9/75, Seattle, Wash.　BL/TR, 5'11.5", 200 lbs.　Deb: 9/13/36

1936	Cle-A	12	41	6	14	3	3	1	8	3	4	.341	.386	.634	147	3	1	0	0	1.000	-3	O-12	0.0
1937	Cle-A	20	61	8	14	1	4	0	8	0	9	.230	.230	.377	50	-5	0	1	-1	1.000	-1	O-14	-0.6
1938	Cle-A	126	502	104	172	31	18	21	112	33	55	.343	.383	.602	146	32	3	1	0	.974	1	*O-122	2.6
1939	Cle-A	121	431	64	126	31	7	14	69	41	64	.292	.354	.494	119	10	8	4	0	.964	6	*O-108	1.1
1940	Cle-A	100	356	55	78	16	3	14	50	40	62	.219	.298	.399	81	-11	5	3	-0	.971	2	O-90	-1.4
1941	Cle-A★	151	585	89	199	32	20	24	123	50	69	.340	.396	.586	165	51	18	12	-2	.949	-4	*O-151	3.4
1942	Cle-A	147	568	82	158	37	13	10	76	62	66	.278	.350	.442	130	20	9	9	-3	.980	-4	*O-146	1.2
1943	Cle-A★	118	424	58	116	22	6	18	79	63	58	.274	.369	.481	157	30	5	8	-3	.968	-4	*O-111	1.8
1944	Cle-A†	60	151	20	52	5	2	5	33	18	12	.344	.404	.503	160	12	1	3		.952	-1	O-37	0.9
1945	Cle-A†	102	370	60	113	16	7	15	61	56	39	.305	.398	.508	169	33	3	1	0	.973	-4	*O-101	2.5
1946	Was-A	48	166	23	47	12	3	4	27	36	36	.283	.411	.464	153	13	0	4	-2	.969	-2	O-47	0.6
	StL-A	86	316	46	87	20	4	16	57	37	37	.275	.353	.478	124	10	0	2	-1	.962	-6	O-83	-0.2
	Yr	134	482	69	134	32	7	16	84	73	73	.278	.374	.473	134	22	0	6	-4	.965	-9	*O-130	0.4

YEAR	TM/L	G	AB	R	H	2B	3B	HR	RBI	BB	SO	AVG	OBP	SLG	PRO+	BR/A	SB	CS	SBR	FA	FR	G/POS	TPR
1947	StL-A	141	491	81	123	20	7	27	85	88	87	.251	.366	.485	133	21	2	1	0	.987	-3	*O-140	1.1
1948	Bos-N	115	364	64	116	26	5	20	76	51	46	.319	.404	.582	167	33	2			.991	-2	*O-106	2.6
1949	Bos-N	36	111	17	34	7	0	9	23	15	26	.306	.389	.613	174	11	0			.983	-2	O-31	0.8
Total	14	1383	4937	777	1447	279	102	194	887	593	670	.293	.370	.509	140	262	56	47		.972	-20	*O-1299	16.4

■ KELLY HEATH
Heath, Kelly Mark   b: 9/4/57, Plattsburgh, N.Y.   BR/TR, 5'7", 155 lbs.   Deb: 4/20/82

YEAR	TM/L	G	AB	R	H	2B	3B	HR	RBI	BB	SO	AVG	OBP	SLG	PRO+	BR/A	SB	CS	SBR	FA	FR	G/POS	TPR
1982	KC-A	1	1	0	0	0	0	0	0	0	0	—	—	—	-99	-0	0	0	0	1.000	1	/2-1	0.1

■ MIKE HEATH
Heath, Michael Thomas   b: 2/5/55, Tampa, Fla.   BR/TR, 5'11", 190 lbs.   Deb: 6/3/78

YEAR	TM/L	G	AB	R	H	2B	3B	HR	RBI	BB	SO	AVG	OBP	SLG	PRO+	BR/A	SB	CS	SBR	FA	FR	G/POS	TPR
1978	*NY-A	33	92	6	21	3	1	0	8	4	9	.228	.268	.283	56	-5	0	0	0	.970	3	C-33	-0.2
1979	Oak-A	74	258	19	66	8	0	3	27	17	18	.256	.309	.322	75	-9	1	0	0	.978	-1	O-46,C-22/3-7,D-3	-1.1
1980	Oak-A	92	305	27	74	10	2	1	33	16	28	.243	.280	.298	63	-16	3	3	-1	.986	8	C-47,D-31/O-8	-0.8
1981	*Oak-A	84	301	26	71	7	1	8	30	13	36	.236	.270	.346	80	-9	3	4	-1	.978	4	C-78/O-6	-0.3
1982	Oak-A	101	318	43	77	18	4	3	39	27	36	.242	.301	.352	82	-8	8	3	1	.973	-8	C-90,O-10/3-5	-1.2
1983	Oak-A	96	345	45	97	17	0	6	33	18	59	.281	.319	.383	98	-2	3	4	-2	.973	-10	C-80,O-24/3-2,D-2	-1.1
1984	Oak-A	140	475	49	118	21	5	13	64	26	72	.248	.289	.396	94	-6	7	4	-0	.986	-19	*C-108,O-45/3-2,S-1	-2.1
1985	Oak-A	138	436	71	109	18	6	13	55	41	63	.250	.316	.408	104	2	7	7	-2	.981	-13	*C-112,O-35,3-13	-0.9
1986	StL-N	65	190	19	39	8	1	4	25	23	36	.205	.294	.321	70	-8	2	3	-1	.967	-7	C-63/O-2	-1.2
	Det-A	30	98	11	26	3	0	4	11	4	17	.265	.294	.418	92	-1	4	1	1	.987	-2	C-29/3-1	0.0
1987	*Det-A	93	270	34	76	16	0	8	33	21	42	.281	.340	.430	107	3	1	5	-3	.989	2	C-67,O-24/1-4,3S2	0.5
1988	Det-A	86	219	24	54	7	2	5	18	18	32	.247	.307	.365	91	-3	1	0	0	.984	-1	C-75/O-9	0.1
1989	Det-A	122	396	38	104	16	2	10	43	24	71	.263	.311	.389	98	-2	7	1	2	.986	0	*C-117/3-4,O-3,D-1	0.6
1990	Det-A	122	370	46	100	18	2	7	38	19	71	.270	.313	.386	94	-4	7	6	-2	.980	-2	*C-117/O-3,S-1,D-2	0.0
1991	Atl-N	49	139	4	29	3	1	1	12	7	26	.209	.252	.266	43	-10	0	0	0	.991	-0	C-45	-0.7
Total	14	1325	4212	462	1061	173	27	86	469	278	616	.252	.302	.367	87	-79	54	40	-8	.981	-46	*C-1083,O-215/D31S2	-8.7

■ MICKEY HEATH
Heath, Minor Wilson   b: 10/30/03, Toledo, Ohio   d: 7/30/86, Dallas, Tex.   BL/TL, 6', 175 lbs.   Deb: 4/18/31

YEAR	TM/L	G	AB	R	H	2B	3B	HR	RBI	BB	SO	AVG	OBP	SLG	PRO+	BR/A	SB	CS	SBR	FA	FR	G/POS	TPR
1931	Cin-N	7	26	2	7	0	0	0	2	3	5	.269	.321	.269	64	-1	0			1.000	-0	/1-7	-0.2
1932	Cin-N	39	134	14	27	1	3	0	15	20	23	.201	.310	.246	55	-8	0			.991	2	1-39	-0.9
Total	2	46	160	16	34	1	3	0	18	22	28	.213	.311	.256	57	-9	0			.992	2	/1-46	-1.1

■ TOMMY HEATH
Heath, Thomas George   b: 8/18/13, Akron, Col.   d: 2/26/67, Los Gatos, Cal.   BR/TR, 5'10", 185 lbs.   Deb: 4/23/35

YEAR	TM/L	G	AB	R	H	2B	3B	HR	RBI	BB	SO	AVG	OBP	SLG	PRO+	BR/A	SB	CS	SBR	FA	FR	G/POS	TPR
1935	StL-A	47	93	10	22	3	0	0	9	20	13	.237	.372	.269	65	-4	0	0	0	.982	-2	C-37	-0.4
1937	StL-A	17	43	4	10	0	2	1	3	10	3	.233	.377	.395	94	-0	0	0	0	1.000	-0	C-14	0.0
1938	StL-A	70	194	22	44	13	0	2	22	35	24	.227	.345	.325	69	-9	0	1	-1	.986	7	C-65	0.0
Total	3	134	330	36	76	16	2	3	34	65	40	.230	.357	.318	71	-13	0	1	-1	.987	5	C-116	-0.4

■ BILL HEATH
Heath, William Chris   b: 3/10/39, Yuba City, Cal.   BL/TR, 5'8", 175 lbs.   Deb: 10/3/65

YEAR	TM/L	G	AB	R	H	2B	3B	HR	RBI	BB	SO	AVG	OBP	SLG	PRO+	BR/A	SB	CS	SBR	FA	FR	G/POS	TPR
1965	Chi-A	1	1	0	0	0	0	0	0	0	0	.000	.000	.000	-99	-0	0	0	0	.000	0	H	0.2
1966	Hou-N	55	123	12	37	6	0	0	8	9	11	.301	.353	.350	103	1	1	0	0	.995	-1	C-37	0.2
1967	Hou-N	9	11	0	1	0	0	0	0	4	3	.091	.333	.091	28	-1	0	0	0	1.000	1	/C-5	0.0
	Det-A	20	32	0	4	0	0	0	4	1	4	.125	.152	.125	-17	-5	0	0	0	1.000	1	/C-7	-0.3
1969	Chi-N	27	32	1	5	0	1	0	1	12	4	.156	.386	.219	65	1	0	0	0	.979	0	/C-9	-0.1
Total	4	112	199	13	47	6	1	0	13	26	22	.236	.327	.276	73	-6	1	0	0	.993	1	/C-58	-0.2

■ CLIFF HEATHCOTE
Heathcote, Clifton Earl   b: 1/24/1898, Glen Rock, Pa.   d: 1/19/39, York, Pa.   BL/TL, 5'10.5", 160 lbs.   Deb: 6/4/18

YEAR	TM/L	G	AB	R	H	2B	3B	HR	RBI	BB	SO	AVG	OBP	SLG	PRO+	BR/A	SB	CS	SBR	FA	FR	G/POS	TPR
1918	StL-N	88	348	37	90	12	3	4	32	20	40	.259	.301	.345	100	-1	12			.934	-4	O-87	-1.1
1919	StL-N	114	401	53	112	13	4	1	29	20	41	.279	.315	.339	103	1	27			.967	-3	*O-101/1-2	-1.0
1920	StL-N	133	489	55	139	18	8	3	56	25	31	.284	.320	.372	102	0	21	14	-2	.964	10	*O-129	-0.1
1921	StL-N	62	156	18	38	6	2	0	9	10	9	.244	.293	.308	61	-9	7	5	-1	.926	-8	O-51	-2.1
1922	StL-N	34	98	11	24	5	2	0	14	9	4	.245	.315	.337	71	-4	0	2	-1	.950	2	O-32	-0.5
	Chi-N	76	243	37	68	8	7	1	34	18	15	.280	.330	.383	82	-7	5	2	0	.986	-1	O-60	-1.2
	Yr	110	341	48	92	13	9	1	48	27	19	.270	.325	.370	79	-11	5	4	-1	.971	0	O-92	-1.7
1923	Chi-N	117	393	48	98	14	3	1	27	25	22	.249	.298	.308	60	-23	32	17	-1	.980	4	*O-112	-2.5
1924	Chi-N	113	392	66	121	19	7	0	30	28	28	.309	.356	.393	100	0	26	24	-7	.979	-2	*O-111	-1.6
1925	Chi-N	109	380	57	100	14	5	5	39	39	26	.263	.343	.366	80	-11	15	11	-2	.970	14	O-99	-0.5
1926	Chi-N	139	510	98	141	33	3	10	53	58	30	.276	.353	.412	104	3	18			**.985**	13	*O-133	0.7
1927	Chi-N	83	228	28	67	12	4	2	25	20	16	.294	.359	.408	105	2	6			.987	-8	O-57	0.7
1928	Chi-N	67	137	26	39	8	0	3	18	17	12	.285	.364	.409	103	1	6			.973	-2	O-39	-0.4
1929	*Chi-N	82	224	45	70	17	0	2	31	15	17	.313	.384	.415	98	-0	9			.985	3	O-52	-0.3
1930	Cin-N	70	150	30	39	10	1	9	18	15	15	.260	.343	.520	104	0	4			.986	-2	O-35	-0.3
1931	Cin-N	90	252	24	65	15	5	0	28	32	16	.258	.342	.365	96	-1	5			.989	12	O-59	0.7
1932	Cin-N	8	3	3	0	0	0	0	0	0	0	.000	.000	.000	-99	-1	0			.000	0	H	-0.1
	Phi-N	30	39	7	11	2	0	1	5	3	3	.282	.333	.410	88	-1	0			.962	-0	/1-7	-0.1
	Yr	38	42	10	11	2	0	1	5	3	3	.262	.311	.381	78	-1	0			.962	-0	/1-7	-0.2
Total	15	1415	4443	643	1222	206	55	42	448	367	325	.275	.333	.375	92	-51	191	75		.971	43	*O-1157/1-9	-9.5

■ RICHIE HEBNER
Hebner, Richard Joseph   b: 11/26/47, Boston, Mass.   BL/TR, 6'1", 197 lbs.   Deb: 9/23/68   C

YEAR	TM/L	G	AB	R	H	2B	3B	HR	RBI	BB	SO	AVG	OBP	SLG	PRO+	BR/A	SB	CS	SBR	FA	FR	G/POS	TPR
1968	Pit-N	2	1	0	0	0	0	0	0	0	0	.000	.000	.000	-99	-0	0	0	0	.000	0	H	0.0
1969	Pit-N	129	459	72	138	23	4	8	47	53	53	.301	.383	.420	127	18	4	1	1	.944	0	*3-124/1-1	2.3
1970	*Pit-N	120	420	60	122	24	8	11	46	42	48	.290	.365	.464	123	13	2	3	-1	.940	1	*3-117	1.2
1971	*Pit-N	112	388	50	105	17	8	17	67	32	68	.271	.331	.487	130	14	2	2	-1	.949	-8	*3-108	0.4
1972	Pit-N	124	427	63	128	24	4	19	72	52	54	.300	.384	.508	155	31	0	0	0	.969	-15	*3-121	1.5
1973	Pit-N	144	509	73	138	28	1	25	74	56	60	.271	.348	.477	130	19	0	1	-1	.939	-14	*3-139	0.4
1974	*Pit-N	146	550	97	160	21	6	18	68	60	53	.291	.364	.449	132	23	0	3	-2	.937	-6	*3-141	1.5
1975	Pit-N	128	472	65	116	16	4	15	57	43	48	.246	.322	.392	98	-2	1	3	-2	.946	-15	*3-126	-1.9
1976	Pit-N	132	434	60	108	21	4	8	51	47	39	.249	.328	.366	96	-2	1	3	-2	.953	-10	*3-126	-1.5
1977	*Phi-N	118	397	67	113	17	4	18	62	61	46	.285	.384	.484	125	15	7	8	-3	.991	2	*1-103,3-13/2-1	0.9
1978	*Phi-N	137	435	61	123	22	3	17	71	56	58	.283	.372	.464	131	19	4	7	-3	.994	-2	*1-117,3-19/2-1	0.8
1979	NY-N	136	473	54	127	25	2	10	79	59	59	.268	.359	.393	109	7	3	1	0	.940	-7	*3-134/1-6	-0.1
1980	Det-A	104	341	48	99	10	7	12	82	38	45	.290	.366	.466	123	11	0	3	-2	.998	-5	1-61,3-32/D-5	0.0
1981	Det-A	78	226	19	51	8	2	5	28	27	28	.226	.314	.345	87	-4	2	1	-1	.995	-3	1-61,D-11	-1.2
1982	Det-A	68	179	25	49	6	0	8	18	25	21	.274	.363	.441	119	5	1	1	-0	.990	-2	1-40,D-20	0.4
	Pit-N	25	70	6	21	2	1	2	5	3	12	.300	.347	.414	109	1	0	1	-1	.964	-2	O-21/1-4,3-1	-0.1
1983	Pit-N	78	162	23	43	4	1	5	26	17	28	.265	.339	.395	100	0	0	3	-1	.967	-6	3-40/1-7,O-7	-0.6
1984	*Chi-N	44	81	12	27	3	0	2	8	10	15	.333	.407	.444	127	3	1	0	0	.963	2	3-14/1-3,O-3	0.3
1985	Chi-N	83	120	10	26	3	0	3	22	7	15	.217	.266	.308	54	-7	1	2	-1	.991	-0	1-12/3-7,O-1	-0.9
Total	18	1908	6144	865	1694	273	57	203	890	687	741	.276	.356	.438	120	164	38	40	-13	.946	-85	*3-1262,1-415/DO2	3.3

■ MIKE HECHINGER
Hechinger, Michael Vincent   b: 2/14/1890, Chicago, Ill.   d: 8/13/67, Chicago, Ill.   BR/TR, 6', 175 lbs.   Deb: 9/27/12

YEAR	TM/L	G	AB	R	H	2B	3B	HR	RBI	BB	SO	AVG	OBP	SLG	PRO+	BR/A	SB	CS	SBR	FA	FR	G/POS	TPR
1912	Chi-N	2	3	0	0	0	0	0	0	1	0	.000	.400	.000	14	-0	0			1.000	0	/C-2	0.0
1913	Chi-N	2	2	0	0	0	0	0	0	0	0	.000	.000	.000	-99	-1	0			.000	0	H	-0.1
	Bro-N	9	11	1	2	1	0	0	0	0	2	.182	.182	.273	28	-1	0			1.000	-1	/C-4	-0.2
	Yr	11	13	1	2	1	0	0	0	0	2	.154	.154	.231	9	-2	0			1.000	-1	/C-4	-0.3
Total	2	13	16	1	2	1	0	0	0	2	2	.125	.222	.188	16	-2	0			1.000	-1	/C-6	-0.3

■ GUY HECKER
Hecker, Guy Jackson   b: 4/3/1856, Youngsville, Pa.   d: 12/3/38, Wooster, Ohio   BR/TR, 6', 190 lbs.   Deb: 5/2/1882   MU

YEAR	TM/L	G	AB	R	H	2B	3B	HR	RBI	BB	SO	AVG	OBP	SLG	PRO+	BR/A	SB	CS	SBR	FA	FR	G/POS	TPR
1882	Lou-a	78	340	62	94	14	4	3			5	.276	.287	.368	126	9				.958	5	*1-66,P-13/O-2	0.2
1883	Lou-a	81	332	59	90	6	6	1			5	.271	.297	.334	111	5				.933	4	P-53,O-23,1-10	0.0
1884	Lou-a	78	316	53	94	14	8	4	42		10	.297	.323	.430	150	17				.951	6	*P-75/O-5	0.0
1885	Lou-a	70	297	48	81	9	2	2	35		5	.273	.287	.337	97	-2				.927	3	P-53,1-17/O-3	-0.4

YEAR	TM/L	G	AB	R	H	2B	3B	HR	RBI	BB	SO	AVG	OBP	SLG	PRO+	BR/A	SB	CS	SBR	FA	FR	G/POS	TPR
1886	Lou-a	84	343	76	117	14	5	4	64	32		.341	.402	.446	157	21	25			.875	-6	P-49,1-22,O-17	0.0
1887	Lou-a	91	370	89	118	21	6	4	50	31		.319	.381	.441	126	13	48			.954	-4	1-43,P-34,O-16	-0.4
1888	Lou-a	56	211	32	48	9	2	0	29	11		.227	.285	.289	86	-3	20			.936	-4	1-30,P-26/O-1	-0.9
1889	Lou-a	81	327	42	93	17	5	1	36	18	27	.284	.333	.376	104	1	17			.969	-0	1-65,P-19/O-1	-0.4
1890	Pit-N	86	340	43	77	13	9	0	38	19	17	.226	.285	.318	86	-7	13			.962	1	1-69,P-14/O-7,M	-0.7
Total	9	705	2876	504	812	117	47	19	278	143	44	.282	.324	.376	118	55	123			.934	5	P-336,1-322/O-75	-2.6

■ DANNY HEEP
Heep, Daniel William b: 7/3/57, San Antonio, Tex. BL/TL, 5'11", 185 lbs. Deb: 8/31/79

YEAR	TM/L	G	AB	R	H	2B	3B	HR	RBI	BB	SO	AVG	OBP	SLG	PRO+	BR/A	SB	CS	SBR	FA	FR	G/POS	TPR
1979	Hou-N	14	14	0	2	0	0	0	2	1	4	.143	.200	.143	-5	-2	0	0	0	1.000	1	/O-2	-0.1
1980	*Hou-N	33	87	6	24	8	0	0	6	8	9	.276	.344	.368	107	1	0	0	0	.990	-2	1-22	-0.2
1981	Hou-N	33	96	6	24	3	0	0	11	10	11	.250	.321	.281	76	-3	0	0	0	.990	-3	1-22/O-1	-0.8
1982	Hou-N	85	198	16	47	14	1	4	22	21	31	.237	.314	.379	100	-0	0	2	-1	1.000	-3	O-39,1-16	-0.7
1983	NY-N	115	253	30	64	12	0	8	21	29	40	.253	.332	.395	102	1	3	3	-1	.967	1	O-61,1-14	-0.7
1984	NY-N	99	199	36	46	9	2	1	12	27	22	.231	.326	.312	81	-4	3	1	0	.967	1	O-48,1-10	-0.5
1985	NY-N	95	271	26	76	17	0	7	42	27	27	.280	.348	.421	117	6	2	2	-1	.977	-5	O-78/1-4	-0.2
1986	*NY-N	86	195	24	55	8	2	5	33	30	31	.282	.381	.421	124	7	1	4	-2	.988	-2	O-56	0.1
1987	LA-N	60	98	7	16	4	0	1	9	8	10	.163	.226	.204	16	-12	1	0	0	.962	-1	O-22/1-6	-1.4
1988	*LA-N	95	149	10	36	2	0	0	11	22	13	.242	.343	.255	76	-3	2	1	-1	1.000	-2	O-32,1-12/P-1	-0.7
1989	Bos-A	113	320	36	96	17	0	5	49	29	26	.300	.360	.400	107	3	0	1	-1	1.000	-0	O-75,1-19/D-9	-1.2
1990	*Bos-A	41	69	3	12	1	1	0	8	7	14	.174	.260	.217	33	-6	0	0	0	1.000	-0	O-14/1-5,P-1,D-6	-0.7
1991	Atl-N	14	12	0	5	1	0	0	3	1	4	.417	.462	.500	161	1	0	1	-1	1.000	-0	/1-1,O-1	0.0
Total	13	883	1961	208	503	96	6	30	229	220	242	.257	.334	.357	95	-12	12	14	-5	.986	-34	O-429,1-131/D-15,P	-7.1

■ BERT HEFFERNAN
Heffernan, Bertram Alexander b: 3/3/65, Centereach, N.Y. BL/TR, 5'10", 185 lbs. Deb: 5/13/92

YEAR	TM/L	G	AB	R	H	2B	3B	HR	RBI	BB	SO	AVG	OBP	SLG	PRO+	BR/A	SB	CS	SBR	FA	FR	G/POS	TPR
1992	Sea-A	8	11	0	1	1	0	0	1	0	1	.091	.091	.182	-25	-2	0	0	0	1.000	1	/C-5,D-1	-0.1

■ DON HEFFNER
Heffner, Donald Henry "Jeep" b: 2/8/11, Rouzerville, Pa. d: 8/1/89, Pasadena, Cal. BR/TR, 5'10", 155 lbs. Deb: 4/17/34 MC

YEAR	TM/L	G	AB	R	H	2B	3B	HR	RBI	BB	SO	AVG	OBP	SLG	PRO+	BR/A	SB	CS	SBR	FA	FR	G/POS	TPR
1934	NY-A	72	241	29	63	8	3	0	25	25	18	.261	.331	.320	73	-9	1	1	-0	.971	-8	2-68	-1.3
1935	NY-A	10	36	3	11	3	1	0	8	4	1	.306	.375	.444	118	1	0	0	0	.980	1	2-10	0.1
1936	NY-A	19	48	7	11	2	1	0	6	6	5	.229	.315	.313	57	-3	0	0	0	.971	4	/3-8,2-5,S-3	0.1
1937	NY-A	60	201	23	50	6	5	0	21	19	19	.249	.314	.328	62	-12	1	4	-2	.980	-8	2-38,S-13/3-3,10	-1.7
1938	StL-A	141	473	47	116	23	3	2	69	65	53	.245	.341	.319	67	-23	1	1	-0	.971	-9	*2-141	-2.2
1939	StL-A	110	375	45	100	10	2	1	35	48	39	.267	.350	.312	69	-16	1	7	-4	.944	-5	S-73,2-32	-1.5
1940	StL-A	126	487	52	115	23	2	3	53	39	37	.236	.295	.310	56	-32	5	5	-2	.977	19	*2-125	-0.5
1941	StL-A	110	399	48	93	14	2	0	17	38	27	.233	.303	.278	53	-27	5	6	-2	.974	3	*2-105	-1.9
1942	StL-A	19	36	2	6	2	0	0	3	1	4	.167	.189	.222	15	-4	1	0	0	.906	1	/2-6,1-4	-0.2
1943	StL-A	18	33	2	4	1	0	0	2	2	2	.121	.171	.152	-5	-4	0	0	0	.974	-0	2-13/1-1	-0.5
	Phi-A	52	178	17	37	6	0	0	8	18	12	.208	.284	.242	55	-10	3	2	-0	.978	-10	2-47/1-1	-1.9
	Yr	70	211	19	41	7	0	0	10	20	14	.194	.267	.227	45	-14	3	2	-0	.978	-10	2-60/1-2	-2.4
1944	Det-A	6	19	0	4	1	0	0	1	5	1	.211	.375	.263	80	-0	0	0	0	.962	-1	/2-5	-0.1
Total	11	743	2526	275	610	99	19	6	248	270	218	.241	.317	.303	61	-140	18	26	-10	.973	-13	2-595/S-89,3-11,10	-11.6

■ JIM HEGAN
Hegan, James Edward b: 8/3/20, Lynn, Mass. d: 6/17/84, Swampscott, Mass. BR/TR, 6'2", 195 lbs. Deb: 9/9/41 FC

YEAR	TM/L	G	AB	R	H	2B	3B	HR	RBI	BB	SO	AVG	OBP	SLG	PRO+	BR/A	SB	CS	SBR	FA	FR	G/POS	TPR
1941	Cle-A	16	47	4	15	2	0	1	5	4	7	.319	.373	.426	116	1	0	0	0	.973	-0	C-16	0.2
1942	Cle-A	68	170	10	33	5	0	0	11	11	31	.194	.243	.224	34	-15	1	3	-2	.977	8	C-66	-0.5
1946	Cle-A	88	271	29	64	11	5	0	17	17	44	.236	.284	.314	71	-11	3	1	0	.991	9	C-87	0.0
1947	Cle-A☆	135	378	38	94	14	5	4	42	41	49	.249	.324	.344	88	-6	3	1	0	.989	7	*C-133	0.9
1948	*Cle-A	144	472	60	117	21	6	14	61	48	74	.248	.317	.407	94	-7	6	3	0	.990	21	*C-142	2.3
1949	Cle-A☆	152	468	54	105	19	5	8	55	49	89	.224	.298	.338	69	-23	1	0	0	.990	10	*C-152	-0.3
1950	Cle-A★	131	415	53	91	16	5	14	58	42	52	.219	.291	.383	74	-19	1	0	0	.993	24	*C-129	1.0
1951	Cle-A★	133	416	60	99	17	5	9	43	38	72	.238	.302	.346	79	-13	0	3	-2	.991	11	*C-129	0.1
1952	Cle-A☆	112	333	39	75	17	2	4	41	29	47	.225	.287	.324	75	-13	0	2	-1	.987	7	*C-107	-0.2
1953	Cle-A	112	299	37	65	10	1	9	37	25	41	.217	.280	.346	71	-13	1	2	-1	.976	3	*C-106	-0.7
1954	*Cle-A	139	423	56	99	12	7	11	40	34	48	.234	.291	.374	80	-13	0	1	-1	.994	13	*C-137	0.5
1955	Cle-A	116	304	30	67	5	2	9	40	34	33	.220	.299	.339	69	-14	0	1	-1	.997	7	*C-111	-0.4
1956	Cle-A	122	315	42	70	15	2	6	34	49	54	.222	.327	.340	75	-11	1	1	-0	.985	16	*C-118	0.8
1957	Cle-A	58	148	14	32	7	0	4	15	16	23	.216	.293	.345	74	-5	0	1	-1	1.000	4	C-58	-0.2
1958	Det-A	45	130	14	25	6	0	1	7	10	32	.192	.250	.262	38	-11	0	0	0	.996	1	C-45	-0.8
	Phi-N	25	59	5	13	6	0	0	4	0	13	.220	.270	.322	57	-4	0	0	0	.991	4	C-25	0.1
1959	Phi-N	25	51	1	10	1	0	1	0	5	8	.196	.241	.216	22	-6	0	1	-1	.990	1	C-25	-0.5
	SF-N	21	30	0	4	1	0	0	0	1	10	.133	.161	.167	-13	-5	0	0	0	.975	5	C-21	-0.5
	Yr	46	81	1	14	2	0	1	0	6	18	.173	.212	.198	10	-10	0	2	-1	.983	5	C-46	-0.5
1960	Chi-N	24	43	4	9	2	1	1	5	1	10	.209	.244	.372	67	-2	0	0	0	.977	2	C-22	0.1
Total	17	1666	4772	550	1087	187	46	92	525	456	742	.228	.296	.344	74	-191	15	24	-10	.990	149	*C-1629	2.4

■ MIKE HEGAN
Hegan, James Michael b: 7/21/42, Cleveland, Ohio BL/TL, 6'1", 190 lbs. Deb: 9/13/64 F

YEAR	TM/L	G	AB	R	H	2B	3B	HR	RBI	BB	SO	AVG	OBP	SLG	PRO+	BR/A	SB	CS	SBR	FA	FR	G/POS	TPR
1964	*NY-A	5	5	0	0	0	0	0	0	1	2	.000	.167	.000	-48	-1	0	0	0	1.000	-1	/1-2	0.0
1966	NY-A	13	39	7	8	0	1	0	2	7	11	.205	.326	.256	73	-1	1	1	-0	.991	-0	1-13	-0.3
1967	NY-A	68	118	12	16	4	1	1	3	20	40	.136	.266	.212	44	-8	7	1	2	1.000	1	1-54,O-10	-0.8
1969	Sea-A†	95	267	54	78	9	6	8	37	62	61	.292	.427	.461	151	21	6	5	-1	.955	2	O-64,1-19	1.8
1970	Mil-A	148	476	70	116	21	2	11	52	67	116	.244	.338	.366	93	-3	9	7	-2	.994	11	*1-139/O-8	-0.6
1971	Mil-A	46	122	19	27	1	1	1	11	26	19	.221	.358	.369	107	2	1	1	-0	1.000	4	1-45	0.3
	*Oak-A	65	55	5	13	3	0	0	3	5	13	.236	.300	.291	69	-2	1	0	0	1.000	6	1-47/O-2	-0.1
	Yr	111	177	24	40	7	1	4	14	31	32	.226	.341	.345	96	0	2	1	-0	1.000	6	1-92/O-2	0.2
1972	*Oak-A	98	79	13	26	3	0	1	5	7	20	.329	.384	.430	150	5	1	0	0	1.000	6	1-64/O-3	0.6
1973	Oak-A	75	71	8	13	0	1	5	9	5	17	.183	.237	.254	40	-6	0	0	0	.988	-3	1-56/O-3,D-3	-1.0
	NY-A	37	131	12	36	3	2	6	14	7	34	.275	.312	.466	121	3	1	2	-1	.992	2	1-37	0.2
	Yr	112	202	20	49	3	3	11	19	12	51	.243	.285	.391	93	-3	1	2	-1	.991	-1	1-93/O-3,D-3	-0.8
1974	NY-A	18	53	3	12	2	0	2	9	5	9	.226	.317	.377	101	1	0	0	0	1.000	-0	1-17	-0.1
	Mil-A	89	190	21	45	7	1	7	32	33	34	.237	.350	.395	114	4	0	4	-2	.991	-2	D-37,1-17,O-17	-0.2
	Yr	107	243	24	57	9	1	9	41	38	43	.235	.343	.391	111	4	1	5	-3	.996	-3	D-37,1-34,O-17	-0.3
1975	Mil-A	93	203	19	51	11	0	5	22	31	42	.251	.350	.350	106	2	1	1	-0	.984	-4	O-42,1-27/D-5	-0.4
1976	Mil-A	80	218	30	54	4	3	5	31	25	54	.248	.328	.362	104	1	0	0	0	1.000	-3	D-40,O-20,1-10	-0.4
1977	Mil-A	35	53	8	9	0	2	1	3	10	17	.170	.313	.283	64	-2	0	0	0	1.000	-3	/O-8,1-6,D-7	-0.6
Total	12	965	2080	281	504	73	18	53	229	311	489	.242	.343	.371	103	15	28	21	-4	.995	11	1-553,O-177/D-92	-1.6

■ BOB HEGMAN
Hegman, Robert Hilmer b: 2/26/58, Springfield, Minn. BR/TR, 6'1", 180 lbs. Deb: 8/8/85

YEAR	TM/L	G	AB	R	H	2B	3B	HR	RBI	BB	SO	AVG	OBP	SLG	PRO+	BR/A	SB	CS	SBR	FA	FR	G/POS	TPR
1985	KC-A	1	0	0	0	0	0	0	0	0	0	—	—	—	—	—	0	0	0	.000	0	/2-1	0.0

■ JACK HEIDEMANN
Heidemann, Jack Seale b: 7/11/49, Brenham, Tex. BR/TR, 6', 178 lbs. Deb: 5/2/69

YEAR	TM/L	G	AB	R	H	2B	3B	HR	RBI	BB	SO	AVG	OBP	SLG	PRO+	BR/A	SB	CS	SBR	FA	FR	G/POS	TPR
1969	Cle-A	3	3	0	0	0	0	0	0	0	2	.000	.250	.000	-24	-0	0	0	0	1.000	1	/S-3	0.0
1970	Cle-A	133	445	44	94	14	2	6	37	34	88	.211	.270	.292	52	-29	2	4	-2	.961	-2	*S-132	-1.9
1971	Cle-A	81	240	16	50	7	0	0	9	12	46	.208	.252	.237	36	-20	1	3	-2	.977	-9	S-81	-2.4
1972	Cle-A	10	20	0	3	0	0	0	1	1	2	.150	.190	.150	24	-2	0	0	0	.964	-1	S-10	-0.3
1974	Cle-A	12	11	2	1	0	0	0	0	0	2	.091	.091	.091	-48	-2	0	0	0	1.000	-1	/3-6,S-4,1-1,2-1	-0.3
	StL-N	47	70	8	19	1	0	1	5	5	10	.271	.320	.286	71	-3	0	0	0	.967	-10	S-45/3-1	-1.0
1975	NY-N	61	145	12	31	4	2	1	16	17	26	.214	.296	.290	66	-7	0	1	-1	.951	-3	S-44/3-4,2-1	-1.6
1976	NY-N	5	12	0	1	0	0	0	0	0	0	.083	.083	.083	-56	-2	0	0	0	1.000	0	/S-3,2-1	-0.2
	Mil-A	69	146	11	32	1	0	2	10	7	24	.219	.255	.267	54	-9	2	3	-2	.962	-7	3-40,2-24/D-1	-1.7
1977	Mil-A	5	1	1	0	0	0	0	0	0	0	.000	.500	.000	—	0	0	0	0	1.000	3	/2-1,D-3	0.1
Total	8	426	1093	94	231	27	4	9	75	78	203	.211	.268	.268	49	-73	5	10	-5	.965	-42	S-322/3-51,2-28,D1	-9.3

YEAR	TM/L	G	AB	R	H	2B	3B	HR	RBI	BB	SO	AVG	OBP	SLG	PRO+	BR/A	SB	CS	SBR	FA	FR	G/POS	TPR

■ EMMET HEIDRICK   Heidrick, R. Emmet "Snags"   b: 7/9/1876, Queenstown, Pa.   d: 1/20/16, Clarion, Pa.   BL/TR, 6′, 185 lbs.   Deb: 9/14/1898

YEAR	TM/L	G	AB	R	H	2B	3B	HR	RBI	BB	SO	AVG	OBP	SLG	PRO+	BR/A	SB	CS	SBR	FA	FR	G/POS	TPR
1898	Cle-N	19	76	10	23	2	2	0	8	3		.303	.329	.382	105	0	3			.850	-1	O-19	-0.2
1899	StL-N	146	591	109	194	21	14	2	82	34		.328	.368	.421	114	9	55			.925	4	*O-145	0.2
1900	StL-N	85	339	51	102	6	8	2	45	18		.301	.338	.383	100	-1	22			.959	15	O-83	0.7
1901	StL-N	118	502	94	170	24	12	6	67	21		.339	.366	.470	149	29	32			.945	1	*O-118	2.0
1902	StL-A	110	447	75	129	19	10	3	56	34		.289	.339	.396	105	2	17			.940	2	*O-109/P-1,S-1,3-1	-0.2
1903	StL-A	120	461	55	129	20	15	1	42	19		.280	.310	.429	113	6	19			.954	2	O-119/C-1	0.1
1904	StL-A	133	538	66	147	14	10	1	36	16		.273	.294	.342	107	3	35			.963	11	*O-130	0.7
1908	StL-A	26	93	8	20	2	2	1	6	1		.215	.223	.312	73	-3	3			.957	-1	O-25	-0.6
Total	8	757	3047	468	914	108	73	16	342	146		.300	.333	.399	114	45	186			.946	33	O-748/C-1,3-1,SP	2.7

■ FRANK HEIFER   Heifer, Franklin "Heck"   b: 1/18/1854, Reading, Pa.   d: 8/29/1893, Reading, Pa.   5′10.5″, 175 lbs.   Deb: 6/4/1875

YEAR	TM/L	G	AB	R	H	2B	3B	HR	RBI	BB	SO	AVG	OBP	SLG	PRO+	BR/A	SB	CS	SBR	FA	FR	G/POS	TPR
1875	Bos-n	11	50	11	14	0	3	0	5	0		.280	.280	.400	129	1	0	0	0	.885	-2	/1-9,O-6,P-2	0.0

■ CHINK HEILEMAN   Heileman, John George   b: 8/10/1872, Cincinnati, Ohio   d: 7/19/40, Cincinnati, Ohio   BR/TR, 5′8″, 155 lbs.   Deb: 7/8/01

YEAR	TM/L	G	AB	R	H	2B	3B	HR	RBI	BB	SO	AVG	OBP	SLG	PRO+	BR/A	SB	CS	SBR	FA	FR	G/POS	TPR
1901	Cin-N	5	15	1	2	1	0	0	1	0		.133	.133	.200	-4	-2	0			.667	-1	/3-4,2-1	-0.3

■ HARRY HEILMANN   Heilmann, Harry Edwin "Slug"   b: 8/3/1894, San Francisco, Cal.   d: 7/9/51, Southfield, Mich.   BR/TR, 6′1″, 195 lbs.   Deb: 5/16/14   CH

YEAR	TM/L	G	AB	R	H	2B	3B	HR	RBI	BB	SO	AVG	OBP	SLG	PRO+	BR/A	SB	CS	SBR	FA	FR	G/POS	TPR
1914	Det-A	69	182	25	41	8	1	2	18	22	29	.225	.316	.313	86	-3	1	8	-5	.870	-6	O-31,1-16/2-6	-1.6
1916	Det-A	136	451	57	127	30	11	2	73	42	40	.282	.349	.410	124	12	9			.952	-10	O-77,1-30/2-9	-0.3
1917	Det-A	150	556	57	156	22	11	5	86	41	54	.281	.333	.387	120	11	11			.960	-2	*O-123,1-27	0.2
1918	Det-A	79	286	34	79	10	6	5	39	35	10	.276	.359	.406	136	12	13			.957	-4	O-40,1-37/2-2	0.5
1919	Det-A	140	537	74	172	30	15	8	93	37	41	.320	.366	.477	139	25	7			.979	-10	*1-140	1.1
1920	Det-A	145	543	66	168	28	5	9	89	39	32	.309	.358	.429	111	7	3	7	-3	.985	-1	*1-122,O-22	-0.1
1921	Det-A	149	602	114	**237**	43	14	19	139	53	37	.394	.444	.606	167	60	2	6	-3	.962	-11	*O-147/1-3	3.2
1922	Det-A	118	455	92	162	27	10	21	92	58	28	.356	.432	.598	172	47	8	4	0	.948	-10	*O-115/1-5	2.7
1923	Det-A	144	524	121	211	44	11	18	115	74	40	.403	.481	.632	195	74	9	7	-2	.960	-2	*O-130,1-12	6.2
1924	Det-A	153	570	107	197	45	16	10	114	78	41	.346	.428	.533	149	42	13	5	1	.970	9	*O-147/1-4	3.9
1925	Det-A	150	573	97	225	40	11	13	134	67	27	.393	.457	.569	161	55	6	6	-2	.970	-3	*O-148	3.7
1926	Det-A	141	502	90	184	41	8	9	103	67	19	.367	.445	.534	152	40	6	7	-2	.972	-2	*O-134	2.6
1927	Det-A	141	505	106	201	50	9	14	120	72	16	.398	.475	.616	179	60	11	5	0	.966	-8	*O-135	4.2
1928	Det-A	151	558	83	183	38	10	14	107	57	45	.328	.390	.507	132	25	7	3	0	.971	1	*O-125,1-25	1.6
1929	Det-A	125	453	86	156	41	7	15	120	50	39	.344	.412	.565	148	32	5	6	-2	.966	-9	*O-114/1-2	1.6
1930	Cin-N	142	459	79	153	43	6	19	91	64	50	.333	.416	.577	144	33	2			.955	12	*O-106,1-19	3.1
1932	Cin-N	15	31	3	8	2	0	0	6	0		.258	.258	.323	57	-2	0			.981	-0	/1-6	-0.3
Total	17	2148	7787	1291	2660	542	151	183	1539	856	550	.342	.410	.520	148	532	113	64		.962	-48	*O-1594,1-448/2-17	32.3

■ VAL HEIM   Heim, Val Raymond   b: 11/4/20, Plymouth, Wis.   BL/TR, 5′11″, 170 lbs.   Deb: 8/31/42

YEAR	TM/L	G	AB	R	H	2B	3B	HR	RBI	BB	SO	AVG	OBP	SLG	PRO+	BR/A	SB	CS	SBR	FA	FR	G/POS	TPR
1942	Chi-A	13	45	6	9	1	1	0	7	5	3	.200	.294	.267	60	-2	1	0	0	.958	-1	O-12	-0.4

■ BUD HEINE   Heine, William Henry   b: 9/22/1900, Elmira, N.Y.   d: 9/2/76, Ft.Lauderdale, Fla   BL/TR, 5′8″, 145 lbs.   Deb: 10/1/21

YEAR	TM/L	G	AB	R	H	2B	3B	HR	RBI	BB	SO	AVG	OBP	SLG	PRO+	BR/A	SB	CS	SBR	FA	FR	G/POS	TPR
1921	NY-N	1	2	0	0	0	0	0	0	0	0	.000	.000	.000	-99	-1	0	0	0	1.000	-0	/2-1	-0.1

■ TOM HEINTZELMAN   Heintzelman, Thomas Kenneth   b: 11/3/46, St.Charles, Mo.   BR/TR, 6′1″, 180 lbs.   Deb: 8/12/73   F

YEAR	TM/L	G	AB	R	H	2B	3B	HR	RBI	BB	SO	AVG	OBP	SLG	PRO+	BR/A	SB	CS	SBR	FA	FR	G/POS	TPR
1973	StL-N	23	29	5	9	0	0	0	3	3		.310	.375	.310	92	-0	0	0	0	1.000	1	/2-6	0.1
1974	StL-N	38	74	10	17	4	0	1	6	9	14	.230	.313	.324	79	-2	0	0	0	.978	0	2-28/3-2,S-1	-0.1
1977	SF-N	2	2	0	0	0	0	0	0	0		.000	.000	.000	-99	-1	0	0	0	.000	0	H	-0.1
1978	SF-N	27	35	2	8	1	0	2	6	2	5	.229	.270	.429	96	-0	0	0	0	1.000	3	/2-5,3-3,1-2	0.2
Total	4	90	140	17	34	5	0	3	12	14	22	.243	.312	.343	84	-3	0	0	0	.984	4	/2-39,3-5,1-2,S-1	0.1

■ JACK HEINZMAN   Heinzman, John Peter   b: 9/27/1863, New Albany, Ind.   d: 11/10/14, Louisville, Ky.   BR/TR,   Deb: 10/2/1886

YEAR	TM/L	G	AB	R	H	2B	3B	HR	RBI	BB	SO	AVG	OBP	SLG	PRO+	BR/A	SB	CS	SBR	FA	FR	G/POS	TPR
1886	Lou-a	1	5	1	0	0	0	0	0	0		.000	.000	.000	-95	-1	0			1.000	-0	/1-1	-0.1

■ BOB HEISE   Heise, Robert Lowell   b: 5/12/47, San Antonio, Tex.   BR/TR, 6′, 175 lbs.   Deb: 9/12/67

YEAR	TM/L	G	AB	R	H	2B	3B	HR	RBI	BB	SO	AVG	OBP	SLG	PRO+	BR/A	SB	CS	SBR	FA	FR	G/POS	TPR
1967	NY-N	16	62	7	20	4	0	0	3	3	1	.323	.354	.387	114	1	0	1	-1	.973	2	2-12/S-3,3-2	0.3
1968	NY-N	6	23	3	5	0	0	0	1	1	1	.217	.250	.217	41	-2	0	0	0	.929	-5	/S-6,2-1	-0.8
1969	NY-N	4	10	1	3	1	0	0	0	3	2	.300	.462	.400	140	1	0	0	0	1.000	-3	/S-3	-0.2
1970	SF-N	67	154	15	36	5	1	1	22	5	13	.234	.258	.299	49	-11	0	1	-1	.915	-1	S-33,2-28/3-2	-0.9
1971	SF-N	13	11	2	0	0	0	0	0	0	1	.000	.000	.000	-99	-3	0	0	0	.833	1	S-3,3-2,2-1	-0.3
	Mil-A	68	189	10	48	9	0	0	7	5	15	.254	.281	.291	63	-9	1	1	0	.961	7	S-51,3-11/2-3,0-1	-0.3
1972	Mil-A	95	271	23	72	10	1	0	12	12	14	.266	.302	.310	84	-6	1	1	0	.990	-2	2-49,3-24/S-9	-0.7
1973	Mil-A	49	98	8	20	2	0	0	4	4	4	.204	.235	.224	31	-9	1	0	0	.956	-1	S-29/3-9,1-4,2-4,D	-0.7
1974	StL-N	3	7	0	1	0	0	0	0	0	0	.143	.143	.143	-20	-1	0	0	0	1.000	0	/2-3	0.1
	Cal-A	29	75	7	20	0	0	0	7	0	1	.267	.313	.360	99	-0	0	1	-1	1.000	2	2-17/3-6,S-3	0.2
1975	Bos-A	63	126	12	27	3	0	0	21	4	6	.214	.250	.238	35	-11	0	4	-3	.940	11	3-45,2-14/S-4,1-1	0.1
1976	Bos-A	58	56	5	15	2	0	0	5	1	2	.268	.293	.304	67	-2	0	0	0	.968	2	3-22/S-9,2-1	0.0
1977	KC-A	54	62	11	16	7	1	0	8	5	4	.258	.292	.323	67	-3	0	1	-1	1.000	10	2-21,S-21,3-12/1-1	0.8
Total	11	499	1144	104	283	43	3	1	86	47	77	.247	.281	.293	63	-55	3	7	-3	.945	23	S-174,2-154,3/1DO	-1.8

■ AL HEIST   Heist, Alfred Michael   b: 10/5/27, Brooklyn, N.Y.   BR/TR, 6′2″, 185 lbs.   Deb: 7/17/60   C

YEAR	TM/L	G	AB	R	H	2B	3B	HR	RBI	BB	SO	AVG	OBP	SLG	PRO+	BR/A	SB	CS	SBR	FA	FR	G/POS	TPR
1960	Chi-N	41	102	11	28	5	3	1	6	10	12	.275	.339	.412	106	1	3	1	0	.985	-2	O-33	-0.2
1961	Chi-N	109	321	48	82	14	3	7	37	39	51	.255	.338	.383	90	-4	3	3	-1	.978	0	O-99	-1.0
1962	Hou-N	27	72	4	16	1	0	0	3	3	9	.222	.263	.236	38	-6	0	0	0	.974	-3	O-23	-1.0
Total	3	177	495	63	126	20	6	8	46	52	72	.255	.328	.368	86	-10	6	4	0	.979	-4	O-155	-2.2

■ HEINIE HEITMULLER   Heitmuller, William Frederick   b: 5/25/1883, San Francisco, Cal.   d: 10/8/12, Los Angeles, Cal.   BR/TR, 6′2″, 215 lbs.   Deb: 4/26/09

YEAR	TM/L	G	AB	R	H	2B	3B	HR	RBI	BB	SO	AVG	OBP	SLG	PRO+	BR/A	SB	CS	SBR	FA	FR	G/POS	TPR
1909	Phi-A	64	210	36	60	9	8	0	15	18		.286	.351	.405	136	8	7			.927	-2	O-61	0.5
1910	Phi-A	31	111	11	27	2	2	0	7	7		.243	.288	.297	84	-2	6			.981	-0	O-28	-0.4
Total	2	95	321	47	87	11	10	0	22	25		.271	.330	.368	118	6	13			.943	-2	/O-89	0.1

■ WOODIE HELD   Held, Woodson George   b: 3/25/32, Sacramento, Cal.   BR/TR, 5′11″, 180 lbs.   Deb: 9/5/54

YEAR	TM/L	G	AB	R	H	2B	3B	HR	RBI	BB	SO	AVG	OBP	SLG	PRO+	BR/A	SB	CS	SBR	FA	FR	G/POS	TPR
1954	NY-A	4	3	2	0	0	0	0	0	0	1	.000	.400	.000	17	-0	0	0	0	1.000	-1	/S-4,3-1	-0.1
1957	NY-A	1	1	0	0	0	0	0	0	0	0	.000	.000	.000	-99	-0	0	0	0	.000	0	H	0.0
	KC-A	92	326	48	78	14	3	20	50	37	81	.239	.322	.485	116	6	4	0	1	.996	17	O-92	1.8
	Yr	93	327	48	78	14	3	20	50	37	81	.239	.322	.483	115	5	4	0	1	.996	17	O-92	1.8
1958	KC-A	47	131	13	28	2	0	4	16	10	28	.214	.280	.321	64	-7	0	1	-1	1.000	-3	O-41/3-4,S-1	-1.3
	Cle-A	67	144	12	28	4	1	3	17	15	36	.194	.288	.299	63	-7	1	0	1	.966	-1	O-43,S-14/3-4	-0.9
	Yr	114	275	25	56	6	1	7	33	25	64	.204	.284	.309	64	-14	1	3	-2	.982	-4	O-84,S-15/3-8	-2.2
1959	Cle-A	143	525	82	132	19	3	29	71	46	118	.251	.314	.465	115	9	0	0	0	.962	-9	*S-103,3-40/O-6,2-3	0.7
1960	Cle-A	109	376	45	97	15	1	21	67	44	73	.258	.344	.471	122	11	0	1	-1	.967	9	*S-109	2.7
1961	Cle-A	146	509	67	136	23	5	23	78	69	111	.267	.358	.468	122	16	0	0	0	.960	-14	*S-144	1.4
1962	Cle-A	139	466	55	116	19	5	18	58	73	107	.249	.346	.406	110	8	0	1	-1	.956	-14	*S-133/3-5,O-1	0.7
1963	Cle-A	133	416	61	103	19	4	17	61	61	96	.248	.355	.435	121	13	2	0	1	.982	-3	2-96,O-35/S-5,3-3	1.7
1964	Cle-A	118	364	50	86	13	0	18	49	43	88	.236	.329	.420	107	4	0	0	0	.966	-3	2-52,O-41,3-30	0.6
1965	Was-A	122	332	46	82	14	2	16	54	49	74	.247	.349	.452	128	9	3	0	1	.963	-19	*O-106/3-5,2-4,S-2	-1.1
1966	Bal-A	56	82	6	17	3	1	5	7	12	30	.207	.309	.305	78	-2	0	0	0	.974	-1	O-10/2-5,S-3,3-3	-0.6
1967	Bal-A	26	41	4	6	3	0	1	5	6	12	.146	.286	.293	72	-1	0	1	-1	.974	-1	/2-9,3-5,O-2	0.0
	Cal-A	58	141	15	31	4	0	4	18	18	46	.220	.317	.333	94	-1	0	0	0	.979	-4	3-19,O-17,S-13,2/3	-0.7
	Yr	84	182	19	37	6	0	5	23	24	58	.203	.310	.319	88	-2	0	1	-1			3-24,O-19,S-13,2-12	-0.7
1968	Cal-A	33	45	4	5	1	0	0	0	5	15	.111	.231	.133	13	-5	0	0	0	1.000	-3	/2-5,S-5,3-5,O-3	-0.9
	Chi-A	40	54	5	9	1	0	2	5	5	14	.167	.250	.185	33	-4	0	0	0	1.000	-6	O-33/3-5,2-1	-1.2

YEAR	TM/L	G	AB	R	H	2B	3B	HR	RBI	BB	SO	AVG	OBP	SLG	PRO+	BR/A	SB	CS	SBR	FA	FR	G/POS	TPR
Yr		73	99	9	14	2	0	0	2	10	29	.141	.241	.162	24	-9	0	0	0	1.000	-9	O-36,3-10/2-6,S-5	-2.1
1969	Chi-A	56	63	9	9	2	0	3	6	13	19	.143	.299	.317	69	-3	0	0	0	1.000	-3	O-18/S-3,3-3,2-1	-0.6
Total	14	1390	4019	524	963	150	22	179	559	508	944	.240	.333	.421	109	48	14	11	-2	.960	-56	S-539,O-448,23	2.2

■ HANK HELF
Helf, Henry Hartz b: 8/26/13, Austin, Tex. d: 10/27/84, Austin, Tex. BR/TR, 6'1", 196 lbs. Deb: 5/5/38

YEAR	TM/L	G	AB	R	H	2B	3B	HR	RBI	BB	SO	AVG	OBP	SLG	PRO+	BR/A	SB	CS	SBR	FA	FR	G/POS	TPR
1938	Cle-A	6	13	1	1	0	0	0	1	1	1	.077	.143	.077	-44	-3	0	0	0	.947	0	/C-5	-0.2
1940	Cle-A	1	1	0	0	0	0	0	0	0	0	.000	.000	.000	-99	-0	0	0	0	1.000	0	/C-1	0.0
1946	StL-A	71	182	17	35	11	0	6	21	9	40	.192	.234	.352	59	-11	0	1	-1	.965	12	C-69	0.4
Total	3	78	196	18	36	11	0	6	22	10	41	.184	.227	.332	51	-14	0	1	-1	.964	12	/C-75	0.2

■ ERIC HELFAND
Helfand, Eric James b: 3/25/69, Erie, Pa. BL/TR, 6', 195 lbs. Deb: 9/4/93

YEAR	TM/L	G	AB	R	H	2B	3B	HR	RBI	BB	SO	AVG	OBP	SLG	PRO+	BR/A	SB	CS	SBR	FA	FR	G/POS	TPR
1993	Oak-A	8	13	1	3	0	0	0	1	0	2	.231	.231	.231	26	-1	0	0	0	1.000	4	/C-5	0.2
1994	Oak-A	7	6	1	1	0	0	0	1	0	1	.167	.167	.167	-15	-1	0	0	0	1.000	1	/C-6	0.0
1995	Oak-A	38	86	9	14	2	1	0	7	11	25	.163	.265	.209	27	-9	0	0	0	.994	3	C-36	-0.5
Total	3	53	105	11	18	2	1	0	9	11	27	.171	.256	.210	25	-12	0	0	0	.996	7	/C-47	-0.3

■ TY HELFRICH
Helfrich, Emory Wilbur b: 10/9/1890, Pleasantville, N.J. d: 3/18/55, Pleasantville, N.J BR/TR, 5'10", 178 lbs. Deb: 6/30/15

YEAR	TM/L	G	AB	R	H	2B	3B	HR	RBI	BB	SO	AVG	OBP	SLG	PRO+	BR/A	SB	CS	SBR	FA	FR	G/POS	TPR
1915	Bro-F	43	104	12	25	6	0	0	5	15	21	.240	.336	.298	80	-4	2			.912	-4	2-34/O-1	-0.8

■ HELLINGS
Hellings b: Philadelphia, Pa. Deb: 7/19/1875

YEAR	TM/L	G	AB	R	H	2B	3B	HR	RBI	BB	SO	AVG	OBP	SLG	PRO+	BR/A	SB	CS	SBR	FA	FR	G/POS	TPR
1875	Atl-n	1	4	0	1	0	0	0	0	0	0	.250	.250	.250	85	-0	0	0	0	.750	-0	/2-1	0.0

■ TONY HELLMAN
Hellman, Anthony J. b: 1861, Cincinnati, Ohio d: 3/29/1898, Cincinnati, Ohio Deb: 10/10/1886

YEAR	TM/L	G	AB	R	H	2B	3B	HR	RBI	BB	SO	AVG	OBP	SLG	PRO+	BR/A	SB	CS	SBR	FA	FR	G/POS	TPR
1886	Bal-a	1	3	0	0	0	0	0	0	0	0	.000	.000	.000	-99	-1	0			1.000	1	/C-1	0.0

■ TOMMY HELMS
Helms, Tommy Vann b: 5/5/41, Charlotte, N.C. BR/TR, 5'10", 175 lbs. Deb: 9/23/64 MC

YEAR	TM/L	G	AB	R	H	2B	3B	HR	RBI	BB	SO	AVG	OBP	SLG	PRO+	BR/A	SB	CS	SBR	FA	FR	G/POS	TPR
1964	Cin-N	2	1	0	0	0	0	0	0	0	1	.000	.000	.000	-97	-0	0	0	0	.000	0	H	0.0
1965	Cin-N	21	42	4	16	2	2	0	6	3	7	.381	.435	.524	158	3	1	0	0	.973	-2	/S-8,3-2,2-1	0.3
1966	Cin-N	138	542	72	154	23	1	9	49	24	31	.284	.307	.380	85	-11	3	4	-2	.961	-13	*3-113,2-20	-2.8
1967	Cin-N★	137	497	40	136	27	4	2	35	24	41	.274	.307	.356	80	-13	5	10	-5	.978	-9	2-88,S-46	-1.8
1968	Cin-N★	127	507	35	146	28	2	2	47	12	27	.288	.307	.363	94	-4	5	6	-2	.979	8	*2-127/S-2,3-1	1.1
1969	Cin-N	126	480	38	129	18	1	1	40	18	33	.269	.297	.317	68	-20	4	6	-2	.975	-3	*2-125/S-4	-1.6
1970	*Cin-N	150	575	42	136	21	1	1	45	21	33	.237	.263	.282	46	-44	2	2	-1	.983	1	*2-148,S-12	-3.2
1971	Cin-N	150	547	40	141	26	1	3	52	26	33	.258	.293	.325	76	-18	3	4	-2	.990	14	*2-149	0.8
1972	Hou-N	139	518	45	134	20	5	5	60	24	27	.259	.292	.346	84	-12	4	3	-1	.979	27	*2-139	2.3
1973	Hou-N	146	543	44	156	28	2	4	61	32	21	.287	.327	.368	93	-6	1	1	-0	.988	-1	*2-145	0.1
1974	Hou-N	137	452	32	126	21	1	5	50	23	24	.279	.315	.363	93	-6	5	4	-1	.985	-11	*2-133	-1.2
1975	Hou-N	64	135	7	28	2	0	1	14	10	8	.207	.267	.222	40	-11	0	0	0	.988	-0	2-42/3-3,S-1	0.4
1976	Pit-N	62	87	10	24	5	1	1	13	10	5	.276	.357	.391	111	1	0	0	0	.921	2	3-22,2-11/S-1	0.4
1977	Pit-N	15	12	0	0	0	0	0	0	0	3	.000	.000	.000	-97	-3	0	0	0	1.000	0	H	-0.4
	Bos-A	21	59	5	16	2	0	1	5	4	4	.271	.328	.356	77	-2	0	0	0	1.000	-2	D-13/3-2,2-1	-0.4
Total	14	1435	4997	414	1342	223	21	34	477	231	301	.269	.303	.342	79	-145	33	40	-14	.983	11	*2-1129,3-143/SD	-7.4

■ HEINIE HELTZEL
Heltzel, William Wade b: 12/21/13, York, Pa. BR/TR, 5'10", 150 lbs. Deb: 7/27/43

YEAR	TM/L	G	AB	R	H	2B	3B	HR	RBI	BB	SO	AVG	OBP	SLG	PRO+	BR/A	SB	CS	SBR	FA	FR	G/POS	TPR
1943	Bos-N	29	86	6	13	3	0	0	5	7	13	.151	.215	.186	17	-9	0			.880	-3	3-29	-1.3
1944	Phi-N	11	22	1	4	1	0	0	2	3	3	.182	.280	.227	45	-2	0			.919	-2	S-10	-0.3
Total	2	40	108	7	17	4	0	0	5	9	16	.157	.229	.194	23	-11	0			.880	-5	/3-29,S-10	-1.6

■ ED HEMINGWAY
Hemingway, Edson Marshall b: 5/8/1893, Sheridan, Mich. d: 7/5/69, Grand Rapids, Mich BB/TR, 5'11.5", 165 lbs. Deb: 9/17/14

YEAR	TM/L	G	AB	R	H	2B	3B	HR	RBI	BB	SO	AVG	OBP	SLG	PRO+	BR/A	SB	CS	SBR	FA	FR	G/POS	TPR
1914	StL-A	3	5	0	0	0	0	0	0	1	1	.000	.167	.000	-51	-1	1			1.000	0	/3-3	-0.1
1917	NY-N	7	25	3	8	1	1	0	1	2	1	.320	.370	.440	153	2	2			.958	1	/3-7	0.3
1918	Phi-N	33	108	7	23	4	1	0	12	7	9	.213	.267	.269	59	-5	4			.955	2	/2-25/3-3,1-1	-0.2
Total	3	43	138	10	31	5	2	0	13	10	11	.225	.282	.290	71	-5	7			.952	3	/2-25,3-13,1-1	0.0

■ SCOTT HEMOND
Hemond, Scott Mathew b: 11/18/65, Taunton, Mass. BR/TR, 6', 205 lbs. Deb: 9/9/89

YEAR	TM/L	G	AB	R	H	2B	3B	HR	RBI	BB	SO	AVG	OBP	SLG	PRO+	BR/A	SB	CS	SBR	FA	FR	G/POS	TPR
1989	Oak-A	4	0	2	0							—	—	—		0	0	0	0	.000	0	R	0.0
1990	Oak-A	7	13	0	2	0	0	0	1	0	5	.154	.154	.154	-14	-2	0	0	0	1.000	-1	/3-7,2-1	-0.3
1991	Oak-A	23	23	4	5	0	0	0	1	0	7	.217	.250	.217	32	-2	1	2	-1	.947	5	/C-8,2-7,3-2,S-1,D	0.2
1992	Oak-A	17	27	7	6	1	0	0	1	3	7	.222	.300	.259	61	-1	1	0	0	1.000	-0	/C-8,S-3,3-2,O-2,D	-0.1
	Chi-A	8	13	1	3	1	0	0	1	1	6	.231	.286	.308	67	-1	0	0	0	1.000	-0	/O-2,C-1,3-1,D-4	-0.1
	Yr	25	40	8	9	2	0	0	2	4	13	.225	.295	.275	63	-2	1	0	0	1.000	-1	/C-9,D-5,O-4,S-3,3	-0.2
1993	Oak-A	91	215	31	55	16	0	6	26	32	55	.256	.355	.414	113	4	14	5	1	.991	4	C-75/O-6,1-1,2-1,D	1.3
1994	Oak-A	91	198	23	44	11	0	3	20	16	51	.222	.280	.323	60	-12	7	6	-2	1.000	7	C-39,2-25,3/1OD	-0.4
1995	StL-N	57	118	11	17	1	0	3	9	12	31	.144	.235	.229	23	-13	0	0	0	.985	-1	C-38/2-6	-1.0
Total	7	298	607	79	132	30	0	12	58	65	162	.217	.296	.326	69	-27	23	13	-1	.991	16	C-169/2-40,3DO1S	-0.4

■ DUCKY HEMP
Hemp, William H. b: 12/27/1867, St.Louis, Mo. d: 3/6/23, St.Louis, Mo. Deb: 10/6/1887

YEAR	TM/L	G	AB	R	H	2B	3B	HR	RBI	BB	SO	AVG	OBP	SLG	PRO+	BR/A	SB	CS	SBR	FA	FR	G/POS	TPR
1887	Lou-a	1	3	1	1	1	0	0	0	1		.333	.500	.667	219	1	0			.000	-1	/O-1	0.0
1890	Pit-N	21	81	9	19	0	2	0	4	8	12	.235	.311	.284	83	-1	3			.867	0	/O-21	-0.2
	Syr-a	9	33	1	5	1	0	0	1	0		.152	.176	.182	6	-4	1			.947	2	/O-9	-0.2
Total	2	31	117	11	25	2	2	0	5	9	12	.214	.281	.265	67	-5	4			.877	2	/O-31	-0.4

■ CHARLIE HEMPHILL
Hemphill, Charles Judson "Eagle Eye" b: 4/20/1876, Greenville, Mich. d: 6/22/53, Detroit, Mich. BL/TL, 5'9", 160 lbs. Deb: 6/27/1899 F

YEAR	TM/L	G	AB	R	H	2B	3B	HR	RBI	BB	SO	AVG	OBP	SLG	PRO+	BR/A	SB	CS	SBR	FA	FR	G/POS	TPR
1899	StL-N	11	37	4	9	0	0	1	5	3	6	.243	.364	.324	87	-0	0			.750	-2	O-10	-0.3
	Cle-N	55	202	23	56	3	5	2	23	6		.277	.301	.371	91	-4	3			.859	-8	O-54	-1.4
	Yr	66	239	27	65	3	5	3	26	12		.272	.312	.364	90	-4	3			.837	-10	O-64	-1.7
1901	Bos-A	136	545	71	142	10	10	3	62	39		.261	.312	.332	80	-14	11			.925	-4	*O-136	-2.6
1902	Cle-A	25	94	14	25	0	2	0	11	5		.266	.303	.287	67	-4	4			.860	-1	O-19	-0.6
	StL-A	103	416	67	132	14	11	6	58	44		.317	.383	.447	131	18	23			.952	-3	*O-101/2-2	0.8
	Yr	128	510	81	157	16	11	6	69	49		.308	.363	.418	120	14	27			.935	-3	*O-120/2-2	0.2
1903	StL-A	105	383	36	94	6	3	0	29	23		.245	.292	.300	80	-9	16			.961	2	*O-104	-1.3
1904	StL-A	114	438	47	112	13	2	2	45	35		.256	.311	.308	102	1	23			.926	-2	*O-108/2-1	-0.8
1906	StL-A	154	585	90	169	19	12	4	62	43		.289	.338	.383	131	20	33			.961	1	*O-154	1.4
1907	StL-A	153	603	66	156	20	9	0	38	51		.259	.319	.322	105	3	14			.957	-2	*O-153	-0.5
1908	NY-A	142	505	62	150	12	9	0	44	59		.297	.374	.356	136	22	42			.937	-2	*O-142	1.7
1909	NY-A	73	181	23	44	5	1	0	10	32		.243	.357	.282	101	2	19			.976	-1	O-45	-0.1
1910	NY-A	102	351	45	84	9	0	0	21	55		.239	.350	.288	95	0	19			.971	-4	O-94	-0.7
1911	NY-A	69	201	32	57	4	2	1	15	37		.284	.397	.338	99	2	9			.952	-7	O-55	-0.8
Total	11	1242	4541	580	1230	117	68	22	421	435		.271	.337	.341	106	37	207			.944	-29	*O-1175/2-3	-5.2

■ FRANK HEMPHILL
Hemphill, Frank Vernon b: 5/13/1878, Greenville, Mich. d: 11/16/50, Chicago, Ill. BR/TR, 5'11", 165 lbs. Deb: 4/17/06 F

YEAR	TM/L	G	AB	R	H	2B	3B	HR	RBI	BB	SO	AVG	OBP	SLG	PRO+	BR/A	SB	CS	SBR	FA	FR	G/POS	TPR
1906	Chi-A	13	40	0	3	0	0	0	2	9		.075	.275	.075	11	-3	1			.970	1	O-13	-0.3
1909	Was-A	1	3	0	0	0	0	0	0	0		.000	.000	.000	-99	-1	0			1.000	0	/O-1	-0.1
Total	2	14	43	0	3	0	0	0	2	9		.070	.259	.070	5	-4	1			.971	1	/O-14	-0.4

■ ROLLIE HEMSLEY
Hemsley, Ralston Burdett b: 6/24/07, Syracuse, Ohio d: 7/31/72, Washington, D.C. BR/TR, 5'10", 170 lbs. Deb: 4/13/28 C

YEAR	TM/L	G	AB	R	H	2B	3B	HR	RBI	BB	SO	AVG	OBP	SLG	PRO+	BR/A	SB	CS	SBR	FA	FR	G/POS	TPR
1928	Pit-N	50	133	14	36	2	3	0	18	4	10	.271	.292	.331	60	-8	1			.962	1	C-49	-0.4
1929	Pit-N	88	235	31	68	13	7	0	37	11	22	.289	.321	.404	77	-9	1			.954	8	C-80	0.4
1930	Pit-N	104	324	45	82	19	6	2	45	22	21	.253	.301	.367	60	-21	3			.979	3	C-98	-0.9
1931	Pit-N	10	35	3	6	3	0	1	5	2	7	.171	.237	.257	33	-3	0			1.000	0	C-9	-0.2
	Chi-N	66	204	28	63	17	4	3	31	17	30	.309	.362	.475	121	6	4			.975	6	C-53	1.5
	Yr	76	239	31	69	20	4	3	32	20	33	.289	.344	.444	109	3	4			.978	6	C-62	1.3

YEAR	TM/L	G	AB	R	H	2B	3B	HR	RBI	BB	SO	AVG	OBP	SLG	PRO+	BR/A	SB	CS	SBR	FA	FR	G/POS	TPR
1932	*Chi-N	60	151	27	36	10	3	4	20	10	16	.238	.286	.424	89	-3	2			.974	2	C-47/O-1	0.1
1933	Cin-N	49	116	9	22	8	0	0	7	6	8	.190	.230	.259	40	-9	0			.970	5	C-41	-0.3
	StL-A	32	95	7	23	2	1	1	15	11	12	.242	.321	.316	65	-5	0	0	0	.965	-3	C-27	-0.5
1934	StL-A	123	431	47	133	31	7	2	52	29	37	.309	.355	.427	93	-5	6	2	1	.973	23	*C-114/O-6	2.2
1935	StL-A★	144	504	57	146	32	7	0	48	44	41	.290	.349	.381	85	-11	3	2	-0	.979	10	*C-141	0.5
1936	StL-A☆	116	377	43	99	24	2	2	39	46	30	.263	.343	.353	70	-18	2	3	-1	.969	-11	*C-114	-2.1
1937	StL-A	100	334	30	74	12	3	3	28	25	29	.222	.276	.302	45	-29	0	0	0	.969	-5	C-94/1-2	-2.6
1938	Cle-A	66	203	27	60	11	3	2	28	23	14	.296	.367	.409	96	-1	1	1	-0	.980	15	C-58	1.4
1939	Cle-A☆	107	395	58	104	17	4	2	36	26	26	.263	.309	.342	69	-19	2	4	-2	.984	6	*C-106	-0.8
1940	Cle-A★	119	416	46	111	20	5	4	42	22	25	.267	.304	.368	75	-16	1	3	-2	**.994**	9	*C-117	0.0
1941	Cle-A	98	288	29	69	10	5	2	24	18	19	.240	.284	.330	65	-15	2	0	1	.980	-2	C-96	-0.9
1942	Cin-N	36	115	7	13	1	2	0	7	4	11	.113	.143	.157	-12	-16	0			.982	11	C-34	-0.3
	NY-A	31	85	12	25	3	1	0	15	5	9	.294	.333	.353	95	-1	1	0	0	.991	1	C-29	0.3
1943	NY-A	62	180	12	43	6	3	2	24	13	9	.239	.290	.339	83	-4	0	1	-1	.981	2	C-52	-0.2
1944	NY-A★	81	284	23	76	12	5	2	26	9	13	.268	.290	.366	84	-7	0	2	-1	.983	-2	C-76	-0.6
1946	Phi-N	49	139	7	31	4	1	0	11	9	10	.223	.270	.266	54	-9	0			.977	11	C-45	0.4
1947	Phi-N	2	3	0	1	0	0	0	1	0	0	.333	.333	.333	80	-0	0			1.000	-0	/C-2	0.0
Total	19	1593	5047	562	1321	257	72	31	555	357	395	.262	.311	.360	74	-205	29	18		.978	90	*C-1482/O-7,1-2	-2.8

■ SOLLY HEMUS
Hemus, Solomon Joseph b: 4/17/23, Phoenix, Ariz. BL/TR, 5'9", 175 lbs. Deb: 4/27/49 MC

YEAR	TM/L	G	AB	R	H	2B	3B	HR	RBI	BB	SO	AVG	OBP	SLG	PRO+	BR/A	SB	CS	SBR	FA	FR	G/POS	TPR
1949	StL-N	20	33	8	11	1	0	0	2	7	3	.333	.450	.364	115	1	0			.981	2	2-16	0.3
1950	StL-N	11	15	1	2	1	0	0	0	2	4	.133	.235	.200	15	-2	0			1.000	1	/3-5	-0.1
1951	StL-N	120	420	68	118	18	9	2	32	75	31	.281	.395	.381	109	9	7	7	-2	.965	13	*S-105,2-12	2.8
1952	StL-N	151	570	**105**	153	28	8	15	52	96	55	.268	.392	.425	126	24	1	5	-3	.960	4	*S-148/3-2	3.8
1953	StL-N	154	585	110	163	32	11	14	61	86	40	.279	.382	.443	114	15	2	1	0	.964	7	*S-150/2-3	3.4
1954	StL-N	124	214	43	65	15	3	2	27	55	27	.304	.456	.430	131	14	5	1	1	.944	-20	S-66,3-27,2-12	-0.1
1955	StL-N	96	206	36	50	10	2	5	21	27	24	.243	.336	.383	91	-3	1	1	0	.956	-4	3-43,2-10/S-2	-0.6
1956	StL-N	8	5	1	1	0	0	0	2	1	1	.200	.429	.200	77	-0	0	0	0	.000	0	H	0.0
	Phi-N	78	187	24	54	10	4	5	24	28	21	.289	.401	.465	134	10	1	1	0	.974	-25	2-49/3-1	-1.1
	Yr	86	192	25	55	10	4	5	26	29	22	.286	.402	.458	133	10	1	1	0	.974	-25	2-49/3-1	-1.1
1957	Phi-N	70	108	8	20	6	1	0	5	20	8	.185	.323	.259	61	-5	1	1	0	.980	-3	2-24	-0.8
1958	Phi-N	105	334	53	95	14	3	8	36	51	34	.284	.392	.416	116	10	3	1	0	.969	-14	2-85/3-1	0.2
1959	Phi-N	24	17	2	4	2	0	0	1	8	2	.235	.500	.353	124	1	0	0	0	1.000	1	/2-1,3-1,M	0.2
Total	11	961	2694	459	736	137	41	51	263	456	248	.273	.390	.411	115	75	21	18		.962	-38	S-471,2-212/3-80	7.7

■ DAVE HENDERSON
Henderson, David Lee b: 7/21/58, Merced, Cal. BR/TR, 6'2", 220 lbs. Deb: 4/9/81

YEAR	TM/L	G	AB	R	H	2B	3B	HR	RBI	BB	SO	AVG	OBP	SLG	PRO+	BR/A	SB	CS	SBR	FA	FR	G/POS	TPR
1981	Sea-A	59	126	17	21	3	0	6	13	16	24	.167	.266	.333	69	-5	2	1	0	1.000	-7	O-58	-1.5
1982	Sea-A	104	324	47	82	17	1	14	48	36	67	.253	.328	.441	106	2	2	5	-2	.985	7	*O-101	0.5
1983	Sea-A	137	484	50	130	24	5	17	55	28	93	.269	.310	.444	101	-1	9	3	1	.982	12	O-133/D-3	0.8
1984	Sea-A	112	350	42	98	23	0	14	43	19	56	.280	.321	.466	116	6	5	5	-2	.988	4	O-97,D-10	1.0
1985	Sea-A	139	502	70	121	28	2	14	68	48	104	.241	.311	.388	90	-7	6	1	1	.986	-4	*O-138	-1.5
1986	Sea-A	103	337	51	93	19	4	14	44	37	95	.276	.341	.481	123	10	1	3	-2	.979	5	O-80,D-22	1.0
	*Bos-A	36	51	8	10	3	0	1	3	2	15	.196	.226	.314	45	-4	1	0	0	.981	-5	O-32	-0.9
	Yr	139	388	59	103	22	4	15	47	39	110	.265	.336	.459	113	6	2	3	-1	.980	0	*O-112,D-22	0.1
1987	Bos-A	75	184	30	43	10	0	8	25	22	48	.234	.316	.418	90	-3	1	1	-0	.958	-5	O-64/D-1	-1.0
	SF-N	15	21	2	5	2	0	1	1	8	5	.238	.448	.333	117	1	2	0	1	1.000	-1	/O-9	0.0
1988	*Oak-A	146	507	100	154	38	1	24	94	47	92	.304	.367	.525	152	34	2	4	-2	.982	5	*O-143	3.3
1989	*Oak-A	152	579	77	145	24	3	15	80	54	131	.250	.318	.380	99	-1	8	5	-1	.977	5	*O-149/D-2	-0.1
1990	*Oak-A	127	450	65	122	28	0	20	63	40	105	.271	.332	.467	126	14	3	1	0	.988	5	*O-116/D-6	2.1
1991	Oak-A★	150	572	86	158	33	0	25	85	58	113	.276	.347	.465	130	22	6	6	-2	.997	11	*O-140/2-1,D-7	2.7
1992	Oak-A	20	63	1	9	1	0	0	2	2	16	.143	.169	.159	-8	-9	0	0	0	.950	-3	O-12/D-4	-1.2
1993	Oak-A	107	382	37	84	19	0	20	53	32	113	.220	.280	.427	93	-6	0	3	-2	.991	9	O-76,D-28	-0.2
1994	KC-A	56	198	27	49	14	1	5	31	16	28	.247	.307	.404	78	-7	2	0	1	.962	-0	O-40,D-16	-0.8
Total	14	1538	5130	710	1324	286	17	197	708	465	1105	.258	.322	.436	108	44	50	38	-8	.984	44	*O-1388/D-99,2-1	4.2

■ KEN HENDERSON
Henderson, Kenneth Joseph b: 6/15/46, Carroll, Iowa BB/TR, 6'2", 180 lbs. Deb: 4/23/65

YEAR	TM/L	G	AB	R	H	2B	3B	HR	RBI	BB	SO	AVG	OBP	SLG	PRO+	BR/A	SB	CS	SBR	FA	FR	G/POS	TPR
1965	SF-N	63	73	10	14	1	1	0	7	9	19	.192	.280	.233	45	-5	1	1	-0	.980	-9	O-48	-1.6
1966	SF-N	11	29	4	9	1	1	1	2	3	3	.310	.375	.517	141	2	0	0	0	.917	-3	O-10	-0.2
1967	SF-N	65	179	15	34	3	0	4	14	19	52	.190	.275	.274	58	-9	0	1	-0	.947	-5	O-52	-1.9
1968	SF-N	3	3	1	1	0	0	0	0	0	2	.333	.600	.333	186	1	0	0	0	1.000	-0	/O-2	0.0
1969	SF-N	113	374	42	84	14	4	6	44	42	64	.225	.311	.332	82	-9	6	4	-1	.969	-3	*O-111/3-3	-2.0
1970	SF-N	148	554	104	163	35	3	17	88	87	78	.294	.395	.460	130	26	20	3	6	.966	2	*O-146	2.4
1971	*SF-N	141	504	80	133	26	6	15	65	64	76	.264	.372	.429	128	21	18	3	4	.966	-1	*O-138/1-1	1.7
1972	SF-N	130	439	60	113	21	2	18	51	38	66	.257	.319	.437	112	5	14	7	0	.974	9	*O-123	0.9
1973	Chi-A	73	262	32	68	13	0	6	32	27	49	.260	.331	.378	96	-1	3	4	-2	.972	-1	O-44,D-26	-0.7
1974	Chi-A	162	602	76	176	35	5	20	95	66	112	.292	.364	.467	134	26	12	7	-1	.987	9	*O-162	2.8
1975	Chi-A	140	513	65	129	20	3	9	53	74	65	.251	.350	.355	98	1	5	3	-0	.990	13	*O-137/D-1	0.8
1976	Atl-N	133	435	52	114	19	0	13	61	62	68	.262	.355	.395	106	5	5	7	-3	.987	-12	*O-122	-1.6
1977	Tex-A	75	244	23	63	14	0	5	23	18	42	.258	.317	.377	87	-4	2	1	-0	.983	-6	O-65/D-3	-1.3
1978	NY-N	7	22	2	5	2	0	1	4	4	4	.227	.346	.455	127	1	0	1	-1	1.000	-0	/O-7	0.0
	Cin-N	64	144	10	24	6	1	3	19	23	32	.167	.281	.285	59	-8	0	0	0	1.000	-2	O-38	-1.2
	Yr	71	166	12	29	8	1	4	23	27	36	.175	.290	.307	67	-7	0	1	-1	1.000	-2	O-45	-1.2
1979	Cin-N	10	13	1	3	1	0	0	2	0	2	.231	.231	.308	45	-1	0	0	0	1.000	-0	/O-2	-0.2
	Chi-A	62	81	11	19	2	0	2	8	15	16	.235	.361	.333	83	-1	0	0	0	.950	-6	O-23	-0.8
	Yr	72	94	12	22	3	0	2	10	15	18	.234	.345	.330	79	-2	0	0	0	.955	-6	O-25	-1.0
1980	Chi-A	44	82	7	16	3	0	2	9	17	19	.195	.333	.305	74	-2	0	0	0	.944	-1	O-22	-0.4
Total	16	1444	4553	595	1168	216	26	122	576	589	763	.257	.346	.396	106	45	86	42	1	.977	-19	*O-1252/D-30,3-3,1	-3.3

■ RICKEY HENDERSON
Henderson, Rickey Henley b: 12/25/58, Chicago, Ill. BR/TL, 5'10", 195 lbs. Deb: 6/24/79

YEAR	TM/L	G	AB	R	H	2B	3B	HR	RBI	BB	SO	AVG	OBP	SLG	PRO+	BR/A	SB	CS	SBR	FA	FR	G/POS	TPR
1979	Oak-A	89	351	49	96	13	3	1	26	34	39	.274	.341	.336	88	-5	33	11	3	.973	3	O-88	-0.3
1980	Oak-A★	158	591	111	179	22	4	9	53	117	54	.303	.422	.399	136	37	**100**	26	14	.984	23	*O-157/D-1	6.6
1981	*Oak-A	108	423	**89**	**135**	18	7	6	35	64	68	.319	.411	.437	152	31	**56**	22	4	.979	20	*O-107	5.2
1982	Oak-A	149	536	119	143	24	4	10	51	**116**	94	.267	.399	.382	121	22	**130**	42	14	.977	9	*O-144/D-4	4.0
1983	Oak-A	145	513	105	150	25	7	9	48	**103**	80	.292	.415	.421	139	33	**108**	19	21	.992	9	*O-142/D-1	5.7
1984	Oak-A★	142	502	113	147	27	4	16	58	86	81	.293	.401	.458	147	35	**66**	18	9	.969	4	*O-140	4.7
1985	NY-A★	143	547	**146**	172	28	5	24	72	99	65	.314	.412	.516	159	48	**80**	10	18	.980	16	*O-141/D-1	7.4
1986	NY-A★	153	608	**130**	160	31	5	28	74	89	81	.263	.359	.469	125	21	**87**	18	15	.986	12	*O-146/D-5	4.2
1987	NY-A★	95	358	78	104	17	3	17	37	80	52	.291	.423	.497	144	27	41	8	7	.980	-5	O-69,D-24	3.5
1988	NY-A★	140	554	118	169	30	2	6	50	82	54	.305	.397	.399	125	22	**93**	13	20	.965	10	*O-136/D-3	4.7
1989	NY-A	65	235	41	58	13	1	3	22	56	29	.247	.394	.349	112	7	25	8	3	.993	4	O-65	1.2
	*Oak-A	85	306	72	90	13	2	9	35	70	39	.294	.429	.438	150	25	52	6	12	.985	7	O-82/D-3	4.1
	Yr	150	541	113	148	26	3	12	57	126	68	.274	.413	.399	133	31	**77**	14	15	.988	11	*O-147/D-3	**5.3**
1990	*Oak-A★	136	489	**119**	159	33	3	28	61	97	60	.325	**.441**	.577	**190**	**63**	65	10	14	.983	11	*O-118/D-15	8.2
1991	Oak-A★	134	470	105	126	17	1	18	57	98	73	.268	.402	.423	136	28	**58**	18	7	.970	10	*O-119/D-10	4.1
1992	Oak-A	117	396	77	112	18	3	15	46	95	56	.283	.429	.457	156	25	48	11	5	.984	6	O-108/D-6	**4.7**
1993	Oak-A	90	318	77	104	19	1	17	47	85	46	.327	.472	.553	186	44	31	6	6	.974	9	O-74,D-16	5.3
	*Tor-A	44	163	37	35	3	1	4	12	35	19	.215	.360	.319	84	-2	22	2	5	.975	-2	O-44	0.0
	Yr	134	481	114	139	22	2	21	59	120	65	.289	.435	.474	150	41	53	8	11	.974	7	*O-118,D-16	5.3
1994	Oak-A	87	296	66	77	13	0	6	20	72	45	.260	.413	.365	112	10	22	7	2	.977	6	O-71,D-13	1.3
1995	Oak-A	112	407	67	122	31	1	9	54	72	66	.300	.410	.447	130	21	32	10	8	.988	1	O-90,D-19	2.0

YEAR	TM/L	G	AB	R	H	2B	3B	HR	RBI	BB	SO	AVG	OBP	SLG	PRO+	BR/A	SB	CS	SBR	FA	FR	G/POS	TPR
1996	*SD-N	148	465	110	112	17	2	9	29	125	90	.241	.412	.344	107	13	37	15	2	.975	-3	*O-134	0.9
Total	18	2340	8528	1829	2450	412	59	244	887	1675	1191	.287	.409	.444	137	514	1186	280	188	.979	162	*O-2175,D-121	77.5

■ STEVE HENDERSON
Henderson, Stephen Curtis   b: 11/18/52, Houston, Tex.   BR/TR, 6'2", 190 lbs.   Deb: 6/16/77   C

YEAR	TM/L	G	AB	R	H	2B	3B	HR	RBI	BB	SO	AVG	OBP	SLG	PRO+	BR/A	SB	CS	SBR	FA	FR	G/POS	TPR
1977	NY-N	99	350	67	104	16	6	12	65	43	79	.297	.376	.480	134	17	6	3	0	.980	6	O-97	1.9
1978	NY-N	157	587	83	156	30	9	10	65	60	109	.266	.336	.399	108	6	13	7	-0	.968	16	*O-155	1.6
1979	NY-N	98	350	42	107	16	8	5	39	38	58	.306	.380	.440	128	14	13	5	1	.990	9	O-94	2.1
1980	NY-N	143	513	75	149	17	8	8	58	62	90	.290	.370	.402	119	14	23	12	-0	.981	13	*O-136	2.3
1981	Chi-N	82	287	32	84	9	5	5	35	42	61	.293	.387	.411	121	9	5	7	-3	.951	1	O-77	0.5
1982	Chi-N	92	257	23	60	12	4	2	29	22	64	.233	.294	.335	73	-9	6	5	-1	.956	0	O-70	-1.2
1983	Sea-A	121	436	50	128	32	3	10	54	44	82	.294	.358	.450	116	10	10	14	-5	.970	1	*O-112/D-6	0.2
1984	Sea-A	109	325	42	85	12	3	10	35	38	62	.262	.341	.409	108	4	2	4	-2	.936	-2	O-53,D-51	-0.3
1985	Oak-A	85	193	25	58	8	3	3	31	18	34	.301	.360	.420	122	6	0	0	0	.953	-7	O-58/D-1	-0.2
1986	Oak-A	11	26	2	2	1	0	0	3	0	5	.077	.077	.115	-52	-5	0	0	0	.800	-2	/O-7,D-1	-0.7
1987	Oak-A	46	114	14	33	7	0	3	9	12	19	.289	.357	.430	115	3	0	0	0	.943	-7	O-31/D-9	-0.5
1988	Hou-N	42	46	4	10	2	0	0	5	7	14	.217	.321	.261	72	-1	1	0	0	1.000	6	/O-8,1-1	-0.2
Total	12	1085	3484	459	976	162	49	68	428	386	677	.280	.354	.413	113	66	79	58	-11	.968	29	O-898/D-68,1-1	5.5

■ GEORGE HENDRICK
Hendrick, George Andrew   b: 10/18/49, Los Angeles, Cal.   BR/TR, 6'3", 195 lbs.   Deb: 6/4/71   C

YEAR	TM/L	G	AB	R	H	2B	3B	HR	RBI	BB	SO	AVG	OBP	SLG	PRO+	BR/A	SB	CS	SBR	FA	FR	G/POS	TPR
1971	Oak-A	42	114	8	27	4	1	0	8	3	20	.237	.256	.289	55	-7	0	1	-1	.981	-7	O-36	-1.8
1972	*Oak-A	58	121	10	22	1	1	4	15	3	22	.182	.208	.306	54	-7	3	2	-0	1.000	-7	O-41	-1.8
1973	Cle-A	113	440	64	118	18	0	21	61	25	71	.268	.312	.452	111	4	7	6	-2	.988	-3	*O-110	-0.6
1974	Cle-A★	139	495	65	138	23	1	19	67	33	73	.279	.325	.444	121	11	6	4	-1	.989	3	*O-133/D-1	0.8
1975	Cle-A★	145	561	82	145	21	2	24	86	40	78	.258	.308	.431	107	3	6	7	-2	.983	1	*O-143	-0.5
1976	Cle-A	149	551	72	146	20	3	25	81	51	82	.265	.327	.448	127	17	4	4	-1	.987	3	*O-146/D-3	1.3
1977	SD-N	152	541	75	168	25	2	23	81	61	74	.311	.382	.492	148	35	11	6	0	.983	8	*O-142	3.8
1978	SD-N	36	111	9	27	4	0	3	8	12	16	.243	.317	.360	96	-1	1	1	-0	.986	-0	O-33	-0.3
	StL-N	102	382	55	110	27	1	17	67	28	44	.288	.342	.497	133	15	1	0	0	.996	6	*O-101	1.8
	Yr	138	493	64	137	31	1	20	75	40	60	.278	.335	.467	126	15	2	1	0	.994	6	*O-134	1.5
1979	StL-N	140	493	67	148	27	1	16	75	49	62	.300	.363	.456	121	14	2	3	-1	.993	6	*O-138	1.4
1980	StL-N★	150	572	73	173	33	2	25	109	32	67	.302	.344	.498	128	20	6	1	1	.994	-6	*O-149	0.9
1981	StL-N	101	394	67	112	19	3	18	61	41	44	.284	.358	.485	134	17	4	2	0	.983	-4	*O-101	1.0
1982	*StL-N☆	136	515	65	145	20	5	19	104	37	80	.282	.331	.450	115	9	3	2	0	.980	-2	*O-134	0.3
1983	StL-N☆	144	529	73	168	33	3	18	97	51	76	.318	.380	.493	140	28	3	4	-2	.992	-1	*O-116/1-1	2.1
1984	StL-N	120	441	57	122	28	1	9	69	32	75	.277	.327	.406	108	3	0	2	-1	.990	-1	*O-116/1-1	-0.2
1985	Pit-N	69	256	23	59	15	0	2	25	18	42	.230	.281	.313	66	-12	1	0	0	.971	3	O-65	-1.1
	Cal-A	16	41	5	5	1	0	2	6	4	8	.122	.200	.293	33	-4	0	0	0	1.000	-1	O-12/D-1	-0.5
1986	Cal-A	102	283	45	77	13	1	14	47	26	41	.272	.335	.473	119	7	1	1	-0	.968	-6	O-93/1-7,D-4	-1.3
1987	Cal-A	65	162	14	39	10	0	5	25	14	18	.241	.301	.395	85	-4	0	0	0	.967	-8	O-45/1-9,D-5	-1.3
1988	Cal-A	69	142	12	31	8	1	2	19	12	31	.218	.289	.323	73	-5	0	1	-1	.933	-12	O-24,1-12/D-3	-0.8
Total	18	2048	7129	941	1980	343	27	267	1111	567	1013	.278	.333	.446	117	144	59	47	-11	.985	-17	*O-1813,1-121/D-17	4.3

■ HARVEY HENDRICK
Hendrick, Harvey "Gink"   b: 11/9/1897, Mason, Tenn.   d: 10/29/41, Covington, Tenn.   BL/TR, 6'2", 190 lbs.   Deb: 4/20/23

YEAR	TM/L	G	AB	R	H	2B	3B	HR	RBI	BB	SO	AVG	OBP	SLG	PRO+	BR/A	SB	CS	SBR	FA	FR	G/POS	TPR
1923	*NY-A	37	66	9	18	3	1	3	12	2	8	.273	.294	.485	101	-1	3	0	1	.947	-2	O-13	-0.2
1924	NY-A	40	76	7	20	0	0	1	11	2	7	.263	.291	.303	53	-5	1	0	0	.975	0	O-17	-0.6
1925	Cle-A	25	28	2	8	1	2	0	3	2	5	.286	.355	.464	106	0	0	0	0	1.000	0	/1-3	0.0
1927	Bro-N	128	458	55	142	18	11	4	50	24	40	.310	.350	.424	106	3	29			.969	-16	O-64,1-53/2-1	-2.0
1928	Bro-N	126	425	83	135	15	10	11	59	54	34	.318	.397	.478	129	19	16			.913	3	3-91,O-17	2.5
1929	Bro-N	110	384	69	136	25	6	14	82	31	20	.354	.404	.560	139	22	14			.975	0	0-42,1-39/3-7,S-4	1.5
1930	Bro-N	68	167	29	43	10	1	5	28	20	19	.257	.344	.419	84	-4	2			.947	-3	O-42/1-7	-0.9
1931	Bro-N	1	0	0	0	0	0	0	0	0	0	.000	.000	.000	-99	-0	0			.000	0	H	0.0
	Cin-N	137	530	74	167	32	9	1	75	53	40	.315	.379	.415	121	16	3			.987	-5	*1-137	-0.2
	Yr	138	531	74	167	32	9	1	75	53	40	.315	.379	.414	120	16	3			.987	-5	*1-137	-0.2
1932	StL-N	28	72	8	18	2	0	1	5	5	9	.250	.299	.319	64	-4	0			.862	-3	3-12/O-5	-0.6
	Cin-N	94	398	56	120	30	3	4	40	23	29	.302	.341	.422	107	4	3			.986	-4	1-94	-0.8
	Yr	122	470	64	138	32	3	5	45	28	38	.294	.335	.406	100	-0	3			.986	-7	1-94,3-12/O-5	-1.4
1933	Chi-N	69	189	30	55	13	3	4	23	13	17	.291	.346	.455	128	6	4			.983	-1	1-38/O-8,3-1	0.2
1934	Phi-N	59	116	12	34	8	0	0	19	9	15	.293	.344	.362	79	-3	0			.962	-3	O-12/1-7,3-7	-0.7
Total	11	922	2910	434	896	157	46	48	413	239	243	.308	.364	.443	113	53	75	0		.986	-32	1-378,O-220,3/S2	-1.8

■ ELLIE HENDRICKS
Hendricks, Elrod Jerome   b: 12/22/40, Charlotte Amalie, V.I.   BL/TR, 6'1", 175 lbs.   Deb: 4/13/68   C

YEAR	TM/L	G	AB	R	H	2B	3B	HR	RBI	BB	SO	AVG	OBP	SLG	PRO+	BR/A	SB	CS	SBR	FA	FR	G/POS	TPR
1968	Bal-A	79	183	19	37	8	1	7	23	19	51	.202	.281	.372	96	-1	0	0		.991	-5	C-53	-0.3
1969	*Bal-A	105	295	36	72	5	0	12	38	39	44	.244	.336	.383	100	0	0	1	-1	.998	5	C-87/1-4	1.0
1970	Bal-A	106	322	32	78	9	0	12	41	33	44	.242	.320	.382	92	-4	0	0		.986	-8	C-95	-0.7
1971	*Bal-A	101	316	33	79	14	1	9	42	39	38	.250	.336	.386	105	2	0	0		.985	-8	C-90/1-3	-0.2
1972	Bal-A	33	84	6	13	4	0	0	4	12	19	.155	.260	.202	38	-6	0	1	-1	.986	2	C-28	-0.5
	Chi-N	17	43	7	5	1	0	2	6	13	8	.116	.321	.279	65	-2	0	1	-1	.978	-1	C-16	-0.1
1973	Bal-A	41	101	9	18	5	1	3	15	10	22	.178	.259	.337	67	-5	0	0		.994	0	C-38/D-1	0.1
1974	*Bal-A	66	159	18	33	8	2	3	8	17	25	.208	.287	.340	83	-4	0	0		1.000	-4	C-54/1-1,D-1	-0.7
1975	Bal-A	85	223	32	48	8	2	5	38	34	40	.215	.322	.377	103	1	0	1	-1	.995	-1	C-83	0.3
1976	Bal-A	28	79	2	11	1	0	1	4	7	13	.139	.209	.190	19	-8	0	1	-1	.971	-5	C-27	-1.4
	*NY-A	26	53	6	12	1	0	3	5	3	10	.226	.268	.415	99	-0	0	0		1.000	1	C-18	0.1
	Yr	54	132	8	23	2	0	4	9	10	23	.174	.232	.280	52	-8	0	1	-1	.982	-4	C-45	-1.3
1977	NY-A	10	11	1	3	1	0	1	5	0	2	.273	.273	.636	140	2	0	0		1.000	0	/C-6	0.1
1978	Bal-A	13	18	4	6	1	0	1	3	3	3	.333	.333	.556	186	2	0	0		.955	0	/C-6,P-1,D-1	-0.1
1979	Bal-A	1	1	0	0	0	0	0	0	0	0	.000	.000	.000	-99	-0	0	0		.500	-1	/C-1	-0.1
Total	12	711	1888	205	415	66	6	62	230	229	319	.220	.308	.361	90	-24	1	5	-3	.990	-17	C-602/1-8,D-3,P-1	-2.2

■ JACK HENDRICKS
Hendricks, John Charles   b: 4/9/1875, Joliet, Ill.   d: 5/13/43, Chicago, Ill.   BL/TL, 5'11.5", 160 lbs.   Deb: 6/12/02   M

YEAR	TM/L	G	AB	R	H	2B	3B	HR	RBI	BB	SO	AVG	OBP	SLG	PRO+	BR/A	SB	CS	SBR	FA	FR	G/POS	TPR
1902	NY-N	8	26	1	6	2	0	0		0	2	.231	.286	.308	84	-1	2			.929	0	/O-7	-0.1
	Chi-N	2	7	0	4	0	1	0		0	0	.571	.571	.857	350	2	0			1.000	0	/O-2	0.2
	Yr	10	33	1	10	2	1	0		0	2	.303	.343	.424	138	1	2			.950	1	/O-9	0.1
1903	Was-A	32	112	10	20	1	3	0		4	13	.179	.264	.241	51	-6	3			.891	-4	O-32	-1.3
Total	2	42	145	11	30	3	4	0		4	15	.207	.281	.283	70	-5	5			.909	-3	/O-41	-1.2

■ TIM HENDRYX
Hendryx, Timothy Green   b: 1/31/1891, LeRoy, Ill.   d: 8/14/57, Corpus Christi, Tex.   BR/TR, 5'9", 170 lbs.   Deb: 9/4/11

YEAR	TM/L	G	AB	R	H	2B	3B	HR	RBI	BB	SO	AVG	OBP	SLG	PRO+	BR/A	SB	CS	SBR	FA	FR	G/POS	TPR
1911	Cle-A	4	7	0	2	0	0	0		0	0	.286	.286	.286	59	-0	0			1.000	-1	/3-3	-0.1
1912	Cle-A	23	70	9	17	2	4	1	14	8		.243	.329	.429	113	1	3			1.000	-2	O-22	-0.2
1915	NY-A	13	40	4	8	2	0	1	4	2	2	.200	.289	.250	61	-0	4	3	-2	.968	1	O-12	-0.4
1916	NY-A	15	62	10	18	7	1	0	5	8	6	.290	.380	.435	142	3	4			1.000	-2	O-15	0.1
1917	NY-A	125	393	43	98	14	7	5	44	62	45	.249	.359	.359	118	10	15			.955	5	*O-107	1.0
1918	StL-A	88	219	22	61	14	3	0	33	37	35	.279	.388	.370	133	10	5			.982	-9	O-65	-0.2
1920	Bos-A	99	363	54	119	21	5	0	73	42	27	.328	.400	.413	121	12	7	9	-3	.964	-10	O-98	-0.7
1921	Bos-A	49	137	10	33	8	2	0	22	18	13	.241	.362	.328	79	-3	1	1	-0	.958	-4	O-41	-1.0
Total	8	416	1291	152	356	68	22	7	192	185	128	.276	.368	.374	115	31	26	13		.966	-22	O-360/3-3	-1.5

■ DAVE HENGEL
Hengel, David Lee   b: 12/18/61, Oakland, Cal.   BR/TR, 6', 185 lbs.   Deb: 9/3/86

YEAR	TM/L	G	AB	R	H	2B	3B	HR	RBI	BB	SO	AVG	OBP	SLG	PRO+	BR/A	SB	CS	SBR	FA	FR	G/POS	TPR
1986	Sea-A	21	63	3	12	1	0	1	6	1	13	.190	.215	.254	27	-6	0	0		1.000	-1	D-11/O-8	-0.7
1987	Sea-A	10	19	2	6	0	0	1	4	0	4	.316	.316	.474	100	-0	0	0		.875	-2	/O-7,D-1	-0.2
1988	Sea-A	26	60	3	10	1	0	2	9	1	15	.167	.180	.283	27	-6	0	0		.952	-1	O-12,D-12	-0.8

YEAR	TM/L	G	AB	R	H	2B	3B	HR	RBI	BB	SO	AVG	OBP	SLG	PRO+	BR/A	SB	CS	SBR	FA	FR	G/POS	TPR
1989	Cle-A	12	25	2	3	1	0	0	1	2	4	.120	.185	.160	-2	-3	0	0	0	1.000	-1	/O-9,D-3	-0.4
Total	4	69	167	10	31	3	0	4	18	4	36	.186	.209	.275	31	-16	0	0	0	.962	-5	/O-36,D-27	-2.1

■ **MOXIE HENGLE** Hengle, Emery J. b: 10/7/1857, Chicago, Ill. d: 12/11/24, River Forest, Ill. BR, 5'8", 144 lbs. Deb: 4/20/1884

YEAR	TM/L	G	AB	R	H	2B	3B	HR	RBI	BB	SO	AVG	OBP	SLG	PRO+	BR/A	SB	CS	SBR	FA	FR	G/POS	TPR
1884	CP-U	19	74	9	15	2	1	0			3	.203	.234	.257	49	-7				.840	-7	2-19	-1.2
	StP-U	9	33	2	5	1	1	0			0	.152	.152	.242	32	-6				.923	1	/2-9	-0.4
	Yr	28	107	11	20	3	2	0			3	.187	.209	.252	46	-11				.870	-6	2-28	-1.6
1885	Buf-N	7	26	2	4	0	0	0	0	1	2	.154	.185	.154	10	-3				.864	-3	/2-5,O-3	-0.5
Total	2	35	133	13	24	3	2	0		4	2	.180	.204	.233	38	-15				.869	-9	/2-33,O-3	-2.1

■ **GAIL HENLEY** Henley, Gail Curtice b: 10/15/28, Wichita, Kan. BL/TR, 5'9", 180 lbs. Deb: 4/13/54

YEAR	TM/L	G	AB	R	H	2B	3B	HR	RBI	BB	SO	AVG	OBP	SLG	PRO+	BR/A	SB	CS	SBR	FA	FR	G/POS	TPR
1954	Pit-N	14	30	7	9	1	0	1	2	4		.300	.382	.433	114	1	0	0	0	1.000	-0	/O-9	0.0

■ **BUTCH HENLINE** Henline, Walter John b: 12/20/1894, Ft.Wayne, Ind. d: 10/9/57, Sarasota, Fla. BR/TR, 5'10", 175 lbs. Deb: 4/13/21 U

YEAR	TM/L	G	AB	R	H	2B	3B	HR	RBI	BB	SO	AVG	OBP	SLG	PRO+	BR/A	SB	CS	SBR	FA	FR	G/POS	TPR
1921	NY-N	1	1	0	0	0	0	0	0	0	1	.000	.000	.000	-99	-0	0	0	0	.000	-0	H	0.0
	Phi-N	33	111	8	34	2	0	0	8	2	6	.306	.319	.324	65	-5	1	0	0	.987	9	C-32	0.5
	Yr	34	112	8	34	2	0	0	8	2	7	.304	.316	.321	64	-6	1	0	0	.987	9	C-32	0.5
1922	Phi-N	125	430	57	136	20	4	14	64	36	33	.316	.380	.479	110	6	2	2	-1	.983	2	*C-119	1.2
1923	Phi-N	111	330	45	107	14	3	7	46	37	33	.324	.407	.448	112	7	7	5	-1	.978	-16	C-96/O-1	-0.5
1924	Phi-N	115	289	41	82	18	4	5	35	27	15	.284	.361	.426	98	-1	1	2	-1	.973	-1	C-83/O-2	0.2
1925	Phi-N	93	263	43	80	12	5	8	48	24	16	.304	.380	.479	108	3	3	1	0	.956	-2	C-68/O-1	0.5
1926	Phi-N	99	283	32	80	14	1	2	30	21	18	.283	.339	.360	84	-5	1			.970	-10	C-77/1-4,O-2	-1.1
1927	Bro-N	67	177	12	47	10	3	1	18	17	10	.266	.337	.373	90	-3	3			.947	1	C-60	0.2
1928	Bro-N	55	132	12	28	3	1	2	8	7	8	.212	.302	.295	59	-8	2			.976	-4	C-45	-0.8
1929	Bro-N	27	62	5	15	2	0	1	7	9	9	.242	.338	.323	66	-3	0			.967	1	C-21	-0.1
1930	Chi-A	3	8	1	1	0	0	0	2	0	1	.125	.125	.125	-38	-2	0	0	0	1.000	0	/C-3	-0.1
1931	Chi-A	11	15	2	1	1	0	0	2	0	2	.067	.176	.133	-19	-3	0	0	0	.889	0	/C-4	-0.2
Total	11	740	2101	258	611	96	21	40	268	192	156	.291	.361	.414	96	-15	18	10		.971	-20	C-608/O-6,1-4	-0.2

■ **LES HENNESSEY** Hennessey, Lester Baker b: 12/12/1893, Lynn, Mass. d: 11/20/76, New York, N.Y. BR/TR, 6', 190 lbs. Deb: 6/4/13

YEAR	TM/L	G	AB	R	H	2B	3B	HR	RBI	BB	SO	AVG	OBP	SLG	PRO+	BR/A	SB	CS	SBR	FA	FR	G/POS	TPR
1913	Det-A	14	22	2	3	0	0	0	3	6		.136	.240	.136	11	-2	2			.880	-2	2-10	-0.5

■ **FRITZ HENRICH** Henrich, Frank Wilde b: 5/8/1899, Cincinnati, Ohio d: 5/1/59, Philadelphia, Pa. BL/TL, 5'10", 160 lbs. Deb: 4/21/24

YEAR	TM/L	G	AB	R	H	2B	3B	HR	RBI	BB	SO	AVG	OBP	SLG	PRO+	BR/A	SB	CS	SBR	FA	FR	G/POS	TPR
1924	Phi-N	36	90	4	19	4	0	0	4	2	12	.211	.228	.256	26	-9	0	0	0	.978	-9	O-32	-2.0

■ **BOBBY HENRICH** Henrich, Robert Edward b: 12/24/38, Lawrence, Kan. BR/TR, 6'1", 185 lbs. Deb: 5/3/57

YEAR	TM/L	G	AB	R	H	2B	3B	HR	RBI	BB	SO	AVG	OBP	SLG	PRO+	BR/A	SB	CS	SBR	FA	FR	G/POS	TPR
1957	Cin-N	29	10	8	2	0	0	0	1	1	4	.200	.273	.200	28	-1	0	0	0	.875	0	/S-7,O-6,3-2,2-1	-0.1
1958	Cin-N	5	3	2	0	0	0	0	0	0	2	.000	.000	.000	-95	-1	0	0	0	1.000	1	/S-2	0.0
1959	Cin-N	14	3	3	0	0	0	0	0	0	1	.000	.000	.000	-97	-1	0	0	0	1.000	0	/S-5,3-1	-0.1
Total	3	48	16	13	2	0	0	0	1	1	7	.125	.176	.125	-17	-3	0	0	0	.929	1	/S-14,O-6,3-3,2-1	-0.2

■ **TOMMY HENRICH** Henrich, Thomas David "The Clutch" or "Old Reliable" b: 2/20/13, Massillon, Ohio BL/TL, 6', 180 lbs. Deb: 5/11/37 C

YEAR	TM/L	G	AB	R	H	2B	3B	HR	RBI	BB	SO	AVG	OBP	SLG	PRO+	BR/A	SB	CS	SBR	FA	FR	G/POS	TPR
1937	NY-A	67	206	39	66	14	5	8	42	35	17	.320	.419	.553	142	14	4	0	1	.970	-4	O-59	0.8
1938	*NY-A	131	471	109	127	24	7	22	91	92	32	.270	.391	.490	120	15	6	2	1	.984	-1	*O-130	1.0
1939	NY-A	99	347	64	96	18	4	9	57	51	23	.277	.371	.429	106	3	7	0	2	.991	2	O-76/1-1	0.4
1940	NY-A	90	293	57	90	28	5	10	53	48	30	.307	.408	.539	149	22	1	2	-1	.969	-1	O-76/1-2	1.5
1941	*NY-A	144	538	106	149	27	5	31	85	81	40	.277	.377	.519	137	27	3	1	0	.980	-1	*O-139	1.8
1942	NY-A★	127	483	77	129	30	5	13	67	58	42	.267	.352	.431	122	13	4	4	-1	.987	-1	*O-119/1-7	0.4
1946	NY-A	150	565	92	142	25	4	19	83	87	63	.251	.358	.411	113	11	5	2	0	.992	-2	*O-111,1-41	0.6
1947	*NY-A★	142	550	109	158	35	13	16	98	71	54	.287	.372	.485	139	27	3	2	-0	.983	6	*O-132/1-6	2.7
1948	NY-A★	146	588	138	181	42	14	25	100	76	42	.308	.391	.554	151	40	2	3	-1	.978	-0	*O-102,1-46	3.1
1949	*NY-A☆	115	411	90	118	20	3	24	85	86	34	.287	.416	.526	148	30	2	2	-1	.958	-4	O-61,1-52	2.1
1950	NY-A★	73	151	20	41	6	8	6	34	27	6	.272	.382	.536	137	8	0	1	-1	.987	-5	1-34	0.1
Total	11	1284	4603	901	1297	269	73	183	795	712	383	.282	.382	.491	132	211	37	19	-0	.981	-7	*O-1017,1-189	14.5

■ **OLAF HENRIKSEN** Henriksen, Olaf "Swede" b: 4/26/1888, Kirkerup, Denmark d: 10/17/62, Norwood, Mass. BL/TL, 5'7.5", 158 lbs. Deb: 8/11/11

YEAR	TM/L	G	AB	R	H	2B	3B	HR	RBI	BB	SO	AVG	OBP	SLG	PRO+	BR/A	SB	CS	SBR	FA	FR	G/POS	TPR
1911	Bos-A	27	93	17	34	2	1	0	8	14		.366	.449	.409	141	6	4			.953	-0	O-25	0.4
1912	*Bos-A	44	56	20	18	3	1	0	8	14		.321	.457	.411	142	4	0			.909	-3	O-11	0.1
1913	Bos-A	31	40	8	15	1	0	0	2	7	5	.375	.468	.400	151	3	3			1.000	-1	/O-7	0.2
1914	Bos-A	63	95	16	25	2	1	1	5	22	12	.263	.407	.337	124	4	5	4	-1	.947	-5	O-29	-0.3
1915	Bos-A	73	92	9	18	2	0	0	13	18	7	.196	.333	.261	80	-1	1	5	-0	.967	-4	O-25	-0.9
1916	*Bos-A	68	99	13	20	2	2	0	11	19	15	.202	.331	.263	78	-2	2			1.000	-4	O-31	-0.8
1917	Bos-A	15	12	1	1	0	0	0	1	3	4	.083	.267	.083	7	-1	0			.000	-0	H	-0.1
Total	7	321	487	84	131	12	7	1	48	97	43	.269	.392	.329	112	13	15	9		.966	-17	O-128	-1.4

■ **SNAKE HENRY** Henry, Frederick Marshall b: 7/19/1895, Waynesville, N.C. d: 10/12/87, Wendell, N.C. BL/TL, 6', 170 lbs. Deb: 9/15/22

YEAR	TM/L	G	AB	R	H	2B	3B	HR	RBI	BB	SO	AVG	OBP	SLG	PRO+	BR/A	SB	CS	SBR	FA	FR	G/POS	TPR
1922	Bos-N	18	66	5	13	4	1	0	5	2	8	.197	.221	.288	32	-7	2	2	-1	.995	1	1-18	-0.7
1923	Bos-N	11	9	1	1	0	0	0	2	1	1	.111	.200	.111	-17	-2	0	0	0	.000	0	H	-0.1
Total	2	29	75	6	14	4	1	0	7	3	9	.187	.218	.267	26	-8	2	2	-1	.995	1	/1-18	-0.8

■ **GEORGE HENRY** Henry, George Washington b: 8/10/1863, Philadelphia, Pa. d: 12/30/34, Lynn, Mass. BR/TR, 5'9", 180 lbs. Deb: 4/27/1893

YEAR	TM/L	G	AB	R	H	2B	3B	HR	RBI	BB	SO	AVG	OBP	SLG	PRO+	BR/A	SB	CS	SBR	FA	FR	G/POS	TPR
1893	Cin-N	21	83	11	23	3	0	0	13	11	12	.277	.375	.313	82	-2	2			.965	5	O-21	0.1

■ **JOHN HENRY** Henry, John Michael b: 9/2/1863, Springfield, Mass. d: 6/11/39, Hartford, Conn. TL, Deb: 8/13/1884

YEAR	TM/L	G	AB	R	H	2B	3B	HR	RBI	BB	SO	AVG	OBP	SLG	PRO+	BR/A	SB	CS	SBR	FA	FR	G/POS	TPR
1884	Cle-N	9	26	2	4	0	0	0			12	.154	.154	.154	-3	-3				1.000	0	/P-5,O-4	-0.1
1885	Bal-a	10	34	4	9	3	0	0		3	1	.265	.286	.353	102	0				.931	2	/P-9,O-1	0.0
1886	Was-N	4	14	3	5	0	0	0		0	3	.357	.357	.357	125	0	0			.833	-0	/P-4	0.0
1890	NY-N	37	144	19	35	6	0	0	16	7	12	.243	.283	.285	65	-7	12			.870	-3	O-37	-0.9
Total	4	60	218	28	53	9	0	0	19	8	27	.243	.273	.284	66	-9	12			.867	-3	/O-42,P-18	-1.0

■ **JOHN HENRY** Henry, John Park "Bull" b: 12/26/1889, Amherst, Mass. d: 11/24/41, Fort Huachuca, Ariz. BR/TR, 6', 180 lbs. Deb: 7/8/10

YEAR	TM/L	G	AB	R	H	2B	3B	HR	RBI	BB	SO	AVG	OBP	SLG	PRO+	BR/A	SB	CS	SBR	FA	FR	G/POS	TPR
1910	Was-A	29	87	2	13	1	1	0	5		2	.149	.169	.184	11	-9	2			.989	2	C-18,1-10	-0.7
1911	Was-A	85	261	24	53	5	0	0	21	25		.203	.273	.222	39	-21	8			.969	9	C-51,1-30	-0.7
1912	Was-A	66	191	23	37	4	1	0	9	31		.194	.309	.225	53	-11	10			.977	8	C-65	0.4
1913	Was-A	96	273	26	61	8	1	0	26	30	43	.223	.309	.293	75	-8	5			.982	3	C-96	0.3
1914	Was-A	92	261	22	44	7	0	0	20	37	47	.169	.274	.226	49	-16	7	3	0	.980	4	C-92	-0.2
1915	Was-A	95	277	20	61	9	2	1	22	36	28	.220	.323	.278	78	-6	10	2	2	.972	4	C-94	0.7
1916	Was-A	117	305	28	76	12	3	0	46	49	40	.249	.364	.308	103	8	12			.981	-4	*C-116	0.8
1917	Was-A	65	163	10	31	6	0	0	4	18	24	.190	.302	.227	62	-6	1			.988	0	C-59	-0.1
1918	Bos-N	43	102	6	21	2	0	0	4	10	15	.206	.283	.225	58	-5	0			.964	1	C-38	-0.1
Total	9	688	1920	161	397	54	15	2	171	244	189	.207	.303	.254	65	-79	55	5		.978	31	C-629/1-40	0.4

■ **RON HENRY** Henry, Ronald Baxter b: 8/7/36, Chester, Pa. BR/TR, 6'1", 180 lbs. Deb: 4/15/61

YEAR	TM/L	G	AB	R	H	2B	3B	HR	RBI	BB	SO	AVG	OBP	SLG	PRO+	BR/A	SB	CS	SBR	FA	FR	G/POS	TPR
1961	Min-A	20	28	1	4	0	0	2	3	7		.143	.200	.143	-6	-4	0	0	0	1.000	-1	/C-5,1-1	-0.5
1964	Min-A	22	41	4	5	1	1	2	5	2	17	.122	.163	.341	36	-4	0	0	0	.984	-0	C-13	-0.4
Total	2	42	69	5	9	1	1	2	8	4	24	.130	.178	.261	18	-8	0	0	0	.988	-1	/C-18,1-1	-0.9

■ **BABE HERMAN** Herman, Floyd Caves b: 6/26/03, Buffalo, N.Y. d: 11/27/87, Glendale, Cal. BL/TL, 6'4", 190 lbs. Deb: 4/14/26 C

YEAR	TM/L	G	AB	R	H	2B	3B	HR	RBI	BB	SO	AVG	OBP	SLG	PRO+	BR/A	SB	CS	SBR	FA	FR	G/POS	TPR
1926	Bro-N	137	496	64	158	35	11	11	81	44	65	.319	.375	.500	136	24	8			.986	0	*1-101,O-35	1.5
1927	Bro-N	130	412	65	112	26	9	14	73	39	41	.272	.336	.481	116	8	4			.980	0	*1-105/O-1	0.1
1928	Bro-N	134	486	64	165	37	6	12	91	38	36	.340	.390	.514	136	25	1			.937	-7	*O-127	1.0
1929	Bro-N	146	569	105	217	42	13	21	113	55	45	.381	.436	.612	160	52	21			.941	-17	*O-141/1-2	2.3

YEAR	TM/L	G	AB	R	H	2B	3B	HR	RBI	BB	SO	AVG	OBP	SLG	PRO+	BR/A	SB	CS	SBR	FA	FR	G/POS	TPR
1930	Bro-N	153	614	143	241	48	11	35	130	66	56	.393	.455	.678	171	71	18			.978	-20	*O-153	3.4
1931	Bro-N	151	610	93	191	43	16	18	97	50	65	.313	.365	.525	137	30	17			.960	-1	*O-150	1.9
1932	Cin-N	148	577	87	188	38	19	16	87	60	45	.326	.389	.541	152	42	7			.969	16	*O-146	4.7
1933	Chi-N	137	508	77	147	36	12	16	93	50	57	.289	.353	.502	142	27	6			.957	-5	*O-131	1.5
1934	Chi-N	125	467	65	142	34	5	14	84	35	71	.304	.353	.488	125	15	1			.971	-10	*O-113/1-7	0.0
1935	Pit-N	26	81	8	19	8	1	0	7	3	10	.235	.271	.358	65	-4	0			.958	-3	O-15/1-3	-0.8
	Cin-N	92	349	44	117	23	5	10	58	35	25	.335	.396	.516	147	23	5			.976	-1	O-76,1-14	1.7
	Yr	118	430	52	136	31	6	10	65	38	35	.316	.373	.486	131	19	5			.974	-4	O-91,1-17	0.9
1936	Cin-N	119	380	59	106	25	2	13	71	39	36	.279	.348	.458	123	11	4			.967	-7	O-92/1-4	0.1
1937	Det-A	17	20	2	6	3	0	0	3	1	6	.300	.364	.450	102	0	2	0	1	1.000	-0	/O-2	0.0
1945	Bro-N	37	34	6	9	1	0	1	9	5	7	.265	.359	.382	107	0	0			.000	-1	/O-3	-0.1
Total	13	1552	5603	882	1818	399	110	181	997	520	553	.324	.383	.532	141	323	94	0		.961	-55	*O-1185,1-236	17.3

■ BILLY HERMAN

Herman, William Jennings Bryan b: 7/7/09, New Albany, Ind. d: 9/5/92, W.Palm Beach, Fla. BR/TR, 5'11", 180 lbs. Deb: 8/29/31 MCH

YEAR	TM/L	G	AB	R	H	2B	3B	HR	RBI	BB	SO	AVG	OBP	SLG	PRO+	BR/A	SB	CS	SBR	FA	FR	G/POS	TPR
1931	Chi-N	25	98	14	32	7	0	0	16	13	6	.327	.405	.398	115	3				.939	3	2-25	0.7
1932	*Chi-N	154	656	102	206	42	7	1	51	40	33	.314	.358	.404	105	6	14			.961	17	*2-154	3.0
1933	Chi-N	153	619	82	173	35	2	0	44	45	34	.279	.332	.342	93	-5	5			.956	29	*2-153	3.5
1934	Chi-N★	113	456	79	138	21	6	3	42	34	31	.303	.355	.395	102	2	6			.975	16	*2-111	2.3
1935	*Chi-N★	154	666	113	227	57	6	7	83	42	29	.341	.383	.476	128	26	6			.964	19	*2-154	5.4
1936	Chi-N★	153	632	101	211	57	7	5	93	59	30	.334	.392	.470	128	25	5			.975	15	*2-153	5.0
1937	Chi-N★	138	564	106	189	35	11	8	65	56	22	.335	.396	.479	131	25	2			.954	19	*2-137	5.2
1938	*Chi-N★	152	624	86	173	34	7	1	56	59	31	.277	.342	.359	90	-7	3			.981	25	*2-151	2.6
1939	Chi-N★	156	623	111	191	34	18	7	70	66	31	.307	.378	.453	120	18	9			.967	-3	*2-156	2.3
1940	Chi-N★	135	558	77	163	24	4	5	57	47	30	.292	.347	.376	101	1	1			.974	19	*2-135	2.9
1941	Chi-N	11	36	4	7	0	1	0		9	5	.194	.356	.250	75	-1	0			.898	-5	2-11	-0.5
	*Bro-N★	133	536	77	156	30	4	3	41	58	38	.291	.361	.379	104	4	1			.970	-27	*2-133	-1.4
	Yr	144	572	81	163	30	5	3	41	67	43	.285	.361	.371	103	3	1			.964	-32	*2-144	-1.9
1942	Bro-N★	155	571	76	146	34	2	2	65	72	52	.256	.339	.333	95	-2	6			.973	-11	*2-153/1-3	-0.4
1943	Bro-N★	153	585	76	193	41	2	2	100	66	26	.330	.398	.417	135	28	4			.971	-17	*2-117,3-37	1.9
1946	Bro-N	47	146	24	53	8	4	0	28	26	10	.288	.376	.375	112	4	2			.945	-2	3-29,2-16	0.4
	Bos-N	75	252	32	77	23	1	3	22	43	13	.306	.409	.440	139	14	1			.956	-16	2-44,1-22/3-5	0.0
	Yr	122	436	56	130	31	5	3	50	69	23	.298	.395	.413	128	18	3			.968	-18	2-60,3-34,1-22	0.4
1947	Pit-N	15	47	3	10	4	0	0	6	2	7	.213	.245	.298	42	-4	0			1.000	-9	2-10/1-2,M	-1.2
Total	15	1922	7707	1163	2345	486	82	47	839	737	428	.304	.367	.407	112	138	67			.967	71	*2-1813/3-71,1-27	31.7

■ AL HERMANN

Hermann, Albert Bartel b: 3/28/1899, Milltown, N.J. d: 8/20/80, Lewes, Del. BR/TR, 6', 180 lbs. Deb: 7/17/23

YEAR	TM/L	G	AB	R	H	2B	3B	HR	RBI	BB	SO	AVG	OBP	SLG	PRO+	BR/A	SB	CS	SBR	FA	FR	G/POS	TPR
1923	Bos-N	31	93	2	22	4	0	0	11	0	7	.237	.237	.280	37	-9	3	2	-0	.957	-6	2-15/3-5,1-4	-1.4
1924	Bos-N	1	1	0	0	0	0	0	0	0	0	.000	.000	.000	-99	-0	0	0	0	.000	0	H	0.0
Total	2	32	94	2	22	4	0	0	11	0	8	.234	.234	.277	36	-9	3	2	-0	.957	-6	/2-15,3-5,1-4	-1.4

■ GENE HERMANSKI

Hermanski, Eugene Victor b: 5/11/20, Pittsfield, Mass. BL/TR, 5'11.5", 185 lbs. Deb: 8/15/43

YEAR	TM/L	G	AB	R	H	2B	3B	HR	RBI	BB	SO	AVG	OBP	SLG	PRO+	BR/A	SB	CS	SBR	FA	FR	G/POS	TPR
1943	Bro-N	18	60	6	18	2	1	0	12	11	7	.300	.417	.367	127	3	1			.976	9	O-17	0.5
1946	Bro-N	64	110	15	22	2	2	0	8	17	10	.200	.313	.255	61	-5	2			.938	-7	O-34	-0.6
1947	*Bro-N	79	189	36	52	7	1	7	39	28	7	.275	.377	.434	111	3	5			.982	-7	O-66	-0.6
1948	Bro-N	133	400	63	116	22	7	15	60	64	46	.290	.391	.493	133	19	15			.971	4	*O-119	1.7
1949	*Bro-N	87	224	48	67	13	3	8	42	47	21	.299	.431	.487	140	15	12			.980	-4	O-77	0.8
1950	Bro-N	94	289	36	86	17	3	7	34	36	26	.298	.381	.450	115	7	2			.989	3	O-78	0.7
1951	Bro-N	31	80	8	20	4	0	1	5	10	12	.250	.333	.338	79	-2	0	2	-1	.977	1	O-19	-0.3
	Chi-N	75	231	28	65	12	1	3	20	35	30	.281	.385	.381	105	3	3	0	1	.966	5	O-63	0.6
	Yr	106	311	36	85	16	1	4	25	45	42	.273	.372	.370	98	1	3	2	-0	.969	6	O-82	0.3
1952	Chi-N	99	275	28	70	6	0	4	34	29	32	.255	.330	.320	80	-7	2	0	1	.981	2	O-76	-0.7
1953	Chi-N	18	40	1	6	1	0	0	1	4	7	.150	.227	.175	7	-5	1	0	0	1.000	-2	O-13	-0.7
	Pit-N	41	62	7	11	0	0	1	4	8	14	.177	.282	.226	35	-6	0	0	0	1.000	-0	O-13	-0.6
	Yr	59	102	8	17	1	0	1	5	12	21	.167	.261	.206	24	-11	1	0	0	1.000	-2	O-26	-1.3
Total	9	739	1960	276	533	85	18	46	259	289	212	.272	.372	.404	107	25	43	2		.977	-1	O-575	-0.0

■ REMY HERMOSO

Hermoso, Angel Remigio b: 10/1/46, Carabobo, Venezuela BR/TR, 5'8", 155 lbs. Deb: 9/14/67

YEAR	TM/L	G	AB	R	H	2B	3B	HR	RBI	BB	SO	AVG	OBP	SLG	PRO+	BR/A	SB	CS	SBR	FA	FR	G/POS	TPR
1967	Atl-N	11	26	3	8	0	0	0	2		4	.308	.357	.308	93	-0	1	0	0	.952	1	/S-9,2-2	0.2
1969	Mon-N	28	74	6	12	0	0	0	3	5	10	.162	.225	.162	10	-9	3	1	0	.968	4	2-18/S-6	-0.3
1970	Mon-N	4	1	1	0	0	0	0	0	0	0	.000	.000	.000	-99	-0	0	0	0	1.000	0	/2-1,3-1	0.0
1974	Cle-A	48	122	15	27	3	1	0	5	7	7	.221	.264	.262	52	-8	2	2	-1	.967	7	2-45	0.1
Total	4	91	223	25	47	3	1	0	8	14	21	.211	.261	.233	42	-17	6	3	0	.968	12	/2-66,S-15,3-1	-0.0

■ CARLOS HERNANDEZ

Hernandez, Carlos Alberto (Almeida) b: 5/24/67, San Felix, Venez. BR/TR, 5'11", 185 lbs. Deb: 4/20/90

YEAR	TM/L	G	AB	R	H	2B	3B	HR	RBI	BB	SO	AVG	OBP	SLG	PRO+	BR/A	SB	CS	SBR	FA	FR	G/POS	TPR
1990	LA-N	10	20	2	4	1	0	0	1	0	2	.200	.200	.250	24	-2	0	0	0	1.000	1	C-10	-0.1
1991	LA-N	15	14	1	3	1	0	0	1	0	5	.214	.267	.286	57	-1	0	1	0	.966	1	C-13/3-1	0.0
1992	LA-N	69	173	11	45	4	0	3	17	11	21	.260	.319	.335	87	-3	0	1	-1	.979	2	C-63	0.2
1993	LA-N	50	99	6	25	5	0	2	7	2	11	.253	.267	.364	71	-4	0	0	0	.966	7	C-43	0.4
1994	LA-N	32	64	6	14	2	0	2	6	1	14	.219	.231	.344	51	-5	0	0	0	1.000	5	C-27	0.1
1995	LA-N	45	94	3	14	1	0	2	8	7	25	.149	.216	.223	18	-12	0	0	0	.983	12	C-41	0.2
1996	LA-N	13	14	1	4	0	0	0	0	0	5	.286	.375	.286	84	-0	0	0	0	1.000	2	/C-9	0.2
Total	7	234	478	30	109	14	0	9	40	23	80	.228	.272	.314	62	-27	1	1	0	.981	29	C-206/3-1	1.0

■ CESAR HERNANDEZ

Hernandez, Cesar Dario (Perez) b: 9/28/66, Yamasa, D.R. BR/TR, 6', 160 lbs. Deb: 7/19/92

YEAR	TM/L	G	AB	R	H	2B	3B	HR	RBI	BB	SO	AVG	OBP	SLG	PRO+	BR/A	SB	CS	SBR	FA	FR	G/POS	TPR
1992	Cin-N	34	51	6	14	4	0	0	4	0	10	.275	.275	.353	74	-2	3	1	0	.952	-2	O-18	-0.4
1993	Cin-N	27	24	3	2	0	0	0	1	1	8	.083	.120	.083	-44	-5	1	2	-1	.970	-2	O-23	-0.8
Total	2	61	75	9	16	4	0	0	5	1	18	.213	.224	.267	35	-7	4	3	-1	.963	-5	/O-41	-1.2

■ ENZO HERNANDEZ

Hernandez, Enzo Octavio b: 2/12/49, Valle De Guanape, Venez. BR/TR, 5'8", 155 lbs. Deb: 4/17/71

YEAR	TM/L	G	AB	R	H	2B	3B	HR	RBI	BB	SO	AVG	OBP	SLG	PRO+	BR/A	SB	CS	SBR	FA	FR	G/POS	TPR
1971	SD-N	143	549	58	122	9	4	0	12	54	34	.222	.295	.250	60	-28	21	5	3	.955	-11	*S-143	-1.9
1972	SD-N	114	329	33	64	11	2	1	15	22	25	.195	.245	.249	44	-25	24	3	5	.963	5	*S-107/O-3	-0.1
1973	SD-N	70	247	26	55	2	1	0		17	14	.223	.273	.239	47	-18	15	4	2	.977	-1	S-67	-0.9
1974	SD-N	147	512	55	119	19	2	0	34	38	36	.232	.285	.277	60	-27	37	10	5	.966	-8	S-145	-1.2
1975	SD-N	116	344	37	75	12	2	0	19	26	25	.218	.277	.265	54	-22	20	4	4	.965	8	*S-111	0.0
1976	SD-N	113	340	31	87	13	3	1	24	32	16	.256	.322	.321	89	-5	12	7	-1	.966	4	*S-101	1.1
1977	SD-N	7	3	1	0	0	0	0	0	0	0	.000	.000	.000	-99	-1	0	0	0	1.000	0	/S-7	0.1
1978	LA-N	4	3	0	0	0	0	0	0	0	1	.000	.000	.000	-99	-1	0	0	0	.000	0	/S-2	0.1
Total	8	714	2327	241	522	66	13	2	113	189	151	.224	.284	.266	59	-127	129	33	19	.964	-1	S-683/O-3	-3.0

■ JACKIE HERNANDEZ

Hernandez, Jacinto (Zulueta) b: 9/11/40, Central Tinguaro, Cuba BR/TR, 6', 175 lbs. Deb: 9/14/65

YEAR	TM/L	G	AB	R	H	2B	3B	HR	RBI	BB	SO	AVG	OBP	SLG	PRO+	BR/A	SB	CS	SBR	FA	FR	G/POS	TPR
1965	Cal-A	6	6	2	2	0	0	0	0	0	1	.333	.333	.500	137	0	1	0	0	1.000	-0	/S-2,3-1	0.0
1966	Cal-A	58	23	19	1	0	0	0	2	1	4	.043	.083	.043	-64	-5	1	1	-0	.857	13	3-11/2-8,S-8,0-3	0.9
1967	Min-A	29	28	9	4	0	0	0	3	0	6	.143	.143	.143	-14	-4	0	0	0	.974	0	S-15,3-13	0.3
1968	Min-A	83	199	13	35	3	0	2	17	9	52	.176	.219	.221	32	-16	5	2	0	.927	9	S-79/1-1	-0.1
1969	KC-A	145	504	54	112	14	2	4	40	38	111	.222	.279	.282	57	-29	17	7	1	.954	-15	*S-144	-3.0
1970	KC-A	83	238	14	55	4	2	3	15	10	50	.231	.282	.282	56	-14	1	3	-2	.951	-5	S-77	-1.4
1971	*Pit-N	88	233	30	48	7	3	0	26	17	45	.206	.260	.300	59	-13	0	2	1	.950	12	S-75/3-9	0.6
1972	Pit-N	72	176	12	33	7	1	1	14	9	43	.188	.227	.256	38	-15	1	0	0	.929	17	S-68/3-4	0.9
1973	Pit-N	54	73	8	18	1	2	0	4	12	24	.247	.286	.315	68	-3	1	1	0	.940	17	S-49	1.6
Total	9	618	1480	153	308	37	9	16	121	93	324	.208	.258	.270	49	-99	25	15	2	.945	53	S-517/3-38,2-8,01	-0.2

YEAR	TM/L	G	AB	R	H	2B	3B	HR	RBI	BB	SO	AVG	OBP	SLG	PRO+	BR/A	SB	CS	SBR	FA	FR	G/POS	TPR

■ JOSE HERNANDEZ   Hernandez, Jose Antonio (Figueroa)   b: 7/14/69, Rio Piedras, P.R.   BR/TR, 6'1", 180 lbs.   Deb: 8/9/91

1991	Tex-A	45	98	8	18	2	1	0	4	3	31	.184	.208	.224	20	-11	0	1	-1	.975	9	S-44/3-1	0.0
1992	Cle-A	3	4	0	0	0	0	0	0	0	2	.000	.000	.000	-99	-1	0	0	0	.857	-0	/S-3	-0.1
1994	Chi-N	56	132	18	32	2	3	1	9	8	29	.242	.291	.326	61	-8	2	2	-1	.938	0	3-28,S-21/2-8,0-1	-0.6
1995	Chi-N	93	245	37	60	11	4	13	40	13	69	.245	.283	.482	99	-2	1	0	0	.961	10	S-43,2-29,3-20	1.2
1996	Chi-N	131	331	52	80	14	1	10	41	24	97	.242	.295	.381	76	-12	4	0	1	.948	-7	S-87,3-43/2-1,0-1	-1.1
Total	5	328	810	115	190	29	9	24	94	48	228	.235	.279	.381	73	-33	7	3	0	.958	12	S-198/3-92,2-38,O-2	-0.6

■ KEITH HERNANDEZ   Hernandez, Keith   b: 10/20/53, San Francisco, Cal.   BL/TL, 6', 195 lbs.   Deb: 8/30/74

1974	StL-N	14	34	3	10	1	2	0	2	7	8	.294	.415	.441	141	2	0	0	0	.973	-2	/1-9	0.0
1975	StL-N	64	188	20	47	8	2	3	20	17	26	.250	.312	.362	84	-4	0	1	-1	.996	3	1-56	-0.5
1976	StL-N	129	374	54	108	21	5	7	46	49	53	.289	.376	.428	126	14	4	2	0	.990	16	*1-110	2.4
1977	StL-N	161	560	90	163	41	4	15	91	79	88	.291	.380	.459	126	22	7	7	-2	.992	5	*1-158	1.5
1978	StL-N	159	542	90	138	32	4	11	64	82	68	.255	.355	.389	109	8	13	5	1	.994	3	*1-158	0.3
1979	StL-N★	161	610	**116**	210	**48**	11	11	105	80	78	**.344**	**.421**	.513	152	46	11	6	-0	.995	19	*1-160	5.6
1980	StL-N★	159	595	**111**	191	39	8	16	99	86	73	.321	**.410**	.494	147	40	14	8	-1	.995	5	*1-157	3.6
1981	StL-N	103	376	65	115	27	4	8	48	61	45	.306	.405	.463	142	23	12	5	1	.997	6	1-98/O-3	2.5
1982	*StL-N	160	579	79	173	33	6	7	94	100	67	.299	.404	.413	128	26	19	11	-1	.994	6	*1-158/O-4	2.4
1983	StL-N	55	218	34	62	15	4	3	26	24	30	.284	.355	.431	117	5	1	1	-0	.991	3	1-54	0.5
	NY-N	95	320	43	98	8	3	9	37	64	42	.306	.425	.434	140	21	8	4	0	.993	11	1-90	2.7
	Yr	150	538	77	160	23	7	12	63	88	72	.297	.398	.433	131	26	9	5	-0	.992	14	*1-144	3.2
1984	NY-N★	154	550	83	171	31	0	15	94	97	89	.311	.415	.449	145	37	2	3	-1	.994	18	*1-153	4.6
1985	NY-N	158	593	87	183	34	4	10	91	77	59	.309	.390	.430	132	28	3	3	-1	**.997**	16	*1-157	3.4
1986	*NY-N★	149	551	94	171	34	1	13	83	**94**	69	.310	.414	.446	141	35	2	1	0	**.996**	18	*1-154	4.4
1987	*NY-N★	154	587	87	170	28	2	18	89	81	104	.290	.379	.436	122	20	0	2	-1	.993	18	*1-154	2.5
1988	*NY-N	95	348	43	96	16	0	11	55	31	57	.276	.337	.417	121	9	2	1	0	.998	5	1-93	1.0
1989	NY-N	75	215	18	50	8	0	4	19	27	39	.233	.324	.326	90	-2	0	3	-2	.991	-2	1-58	-1.1
1990	Cle-A	43	130	7	26	2	0	1	8	14	17	.200	.283	.238	47	-9	0	0	0	.994	-2	1-42	-1.4
Total	17	2088	7370	1124	2182	426	60	162	1071	1070	1012	.296	.388	.436	129	320	98	63	-8	.994	148	*1-2014/O-7	34.4

■ LEO HERNANDEZ   Hernandez, Leonardo Jesus   b: 11/6/59, Santa Lucia, Venez.   BR/TR, 5'11", 170 lbs.   Deb: 9/19/82

1982	Bal-A	2	0	0	0	0	0	0	0	0	0	.000	.000	.000	-99	-1	0	0	0	.000	0	/H	-0.1
1983	Bal-A	64	203	21	50	6	1	6	26	12	19	.246	.288	.374	82	-5	1	0	0	.922	-12	3-64	-1.8
1985	Bal-A	12	21	0	1	0	0	0	0	0	4	.048	.048	.048	-76	-5	0	0	0	1.000	-1	/1-1,O-1,D-8	-0.6
1986	NY-A	7	22	2	5	2	0	1	4	1	8	.227	.261	.455	91	-0	0	0	0	1.000	-1	/3-7,2-1	-0.1
Total	4	85	248	23	56	8	1	7	30	13	33	.226	.264	.351	69	-11	1	0	0	.927	-13	/3-71,D-8,2-1,O1	-2.6

■ PEDRO HERNANDEZ   Hernandez, Pedro Julio (b: Pedro Julio Montas (Hernandez))   b: 4/4/59, LaRomana, D.R.   BR/TR, 6'1", 160 lbs.   Deb: 9/8/79

1979	Tor-A	3	0	1	0	0	0	0	0	0	0	—	—	—		0	0	0	0	.000	0	/R	0.0
1982	Tor-A	8	9	1	0	0	0	0	0	0	3	.000	.000	.000	-92	-2	0	0	0	.000	-1	/3-2,O-1,D-3	-0.3
Total	2	11	9	2	0	0	0	0	0	0	3	.000	.000	.000	-92	-2	0	0	0	—	-1	/D-3,3-2,O-1	-0.3

■ TOBY HERNANDEZ   Hernandez, Rafael Tobias (Alvarado)   b: 11/30/58, Calabozo, Venez.   BR/TR, 6'1", 160 lbs.   Deb: 6/22/84

1984	Tor-A	3	2	1	1	0	0	0	0	0	0	.500	.500	.500	171	0	0	0	0	1.000	-1	/C-3	0.0

■ RUDY HERNANDEZ   Hernandez, Rodolfo (Acosta)   b: 10/18/51, Empalme, Mexico   BR/TR, 5'9", 150 lbs.   Deb: 9/6/72

1972	Chi-A	8	21	0	4	0	0	0	1	0	3	.190	.190	.190	13	-2	0	0	0	1.000	1	/S-6	-0.1

■ CHICO HERNANDEZ   Hernandez, Salvador Jose (Ramos)   b: 1/3/16, Havana, Cuba   d: 1/3/86, Havana, Cuba   BR/TR, 6', 195 lbs.   Deb: 4/16/42

1942	Chi-N	47	118	6	27	5	0	0	7	11	13	.229	.295	.271	69	-5	0			.975	-2	C-43	-0.4
1943	Chi-N	43	126	10	34	4	0	0	9	9	9	.270	.324	.302	82	-3	0			.981	-3	C-41	-0.3
Total	2	90	244	16	61	9	0	0	16	20	22	.250	.309	.287	76	-7	0			.978	-5	/C-84	-0.7

■ LARRY HERNDON   Herndon, Larry Darnell   b: 11/3/53, Sunflower, Miss.   BR/TR, 6'3", 195 lbs.   Deb: 9/4/74   C

1974	StL-N	12	1	3	1	0	0	0	0	0	0	1.000	1.000	1.000	465	0	0	0	0	1.000	-0	/O-1	0.0
1976	SF-N	115	337	42	97	11	3	2	23	23	45	.288	.337	.356	94	-2	12	10	-2	.967	-6	*O-110	-1.5
1977	SF-N	49	109	13	26	4	3	1	5	5	20	.239	.278	.358	69	-5	4	2	0	.957	-3	*O-44	-0.9
1978	SF-N	151	471	52	122	15	9	1	32	35	71	.259	.312	.335	84	-11	13	8	-1	.974	4	*O-149	-1.4
1979	SF-N	132	354	35	91	14	5	7	36	29	70	.257	.315	.384	96	-3	8	6	-1	.963	-15	*O-122	-2.3
1980	SF-N	139	493	54	127	17	11	8	49	19	91	.258	.287	.385	88	-10	8	8	-2	.959	-4	*O-122	-2.3
1981	SF-N	96	364	48	105	15	8	5	41	20	55	.288	.327	.415	111	4	15	6	1	.977	5	*O-93	0.8
1982	Det-A	157	614	92	179	21	13	23	88	38	92	.292	.334	.480	120	15	12	9	-2	.983	-5	*O-155/D-3	1.5
1983	Det-A	153	603	88	182	28	9	20	92	46	95	.302	.354	.478	130	23	9	3	1	.951	-3	*O-133,D-19	2.0
1984	*Det-A	125	407	52	114	18	5	7	43	32	63	.280	.336	.400	103	2	6	2	1	.986	-5	*O-117/D-4	-0.5
1985	Det-A	137	442	45	108	12	7	12	37	33	79	.244	.298	.385	86	-9	2	1	0	.976	1	*O-136	-0.8
1986	Det-A	106	283	33	70	13	1	8	37	27	40	.247	.315	.385	90	-4	2	1	0	.988	-5	O-83,D-18	-0.8
1987	*Det-A	89	225	32	73	5	2	9	47	23	35	.324	.387	.520	144	14	1	0	0	.989	-4	O-57,D-23	0.8
1988	Det-A	89	174	16	39	5	0	4	20	23	37	.224	.318	.322	83	-4	0	1	-1	1.000	-2	D-53,O-15	-0.8
Total	14	1537	4877	605	1334	186	76	107	550	353	793	.274	.325	.409	103	11	92	57	-7	.972	-19	*O-1337,D-120	-6.2

■ TOM HERNON   Hernon, Thomas H.   b: 11/4/1866, E.Bridgewater, Mass   d: 2/4/02, New Bedford, Mass.   BR/TR,   Deb: 9/13/1897

1897	Chi-N	4	16	2	1	0	0	0	2	0		.063	.063	.063	-65	-4	1			1.000	0	/O-4	-0.4

■ ED HERR   Herr, Edward Joseph   b: 5/18/1862, St.Louis, Mo.   d: 7/18/43, St.Louis, Mo.   BR/TR, 5'9.5", 179 lbs.   Deb: 4/16/1887

1887	Cle-a	11	44	6	12	2	0	0	6	6		.273	.360	.318	93	-0	2			.729	-3	3-11	-0.2
1888	*StL-a	43	172	21	46	7	1	3	43	11		.267	.323	.372	110	1	9			.872	-9	S-28,O-11/3-4	-0.7
1890	StL-a	12	41	5	9	2	1	0	1	5		.220	.347	.317	84	-1	2			.793	-7	/2-7,O-4,3-1	-0.7
Total	3	66	257	32	67	11	2	3	50	22		.261	.333	.354	102	-0	13			.762	-18	/S-28,3-16,O-15,2-7	-1.6

■ TOM HERR   Herr, Thomas Mitchell   b: 4/4/56, Lancaster, Pa.   BB/TR, 6', 185 lbs.   Deb: 8/13/79

1979	StL-N	14	10	4	2	0	0	0	1	2	2	.200	.333	.200	49	-1	1	0	0	1.000	6	/2-6	0.5
1980	StL-N	76	222	29	55	12	5	0	15	16	21	.248	.301	.347	78	-7	9	2	2	.984	2	2-58,S-14	0.1
1981	StL-N	103	411	50	110	14	9	0	46	39	30	.268	.333	.345	90	-5	23	7	3	**.992**	4	*2-103	0.9
1982	*StL-N	135	493	83	131	19	4	0	36	57	56	.266	.344	.320	86	-7	25	12	0	.987	4	*2-128	0.3
1983	StL-N	89	313	43	101	14	4	2	31	43	27	.323	.406	.412	127	13	8	8	-3	.986	-19	2-86	-0.4
1984	StL-N	145	558	67	154	23	2	4	49	49	56	.276	.337	.346	94	-3	13	7	-0	.992	1	*2-144	0.1
1985	*StL-N★	159	596	97	180	38	3	8	110	80	55	.302	.384	.416	126	23	31	3	8	.985	-31	*2-158	0.6
1986	StL-N	152	559	48	141	30	4	2	61	73	75	.252	.344	.331	88	-7	22	8	2	.988	-22	*2-152	-2.2
1987	*StL-N	141	510	73	134	29	0	2	83	89	62	.263	.353	.331	81	-12	19	4	3	.989	-17	*2-137	-1.9
1988	StL-N	15	50	4	13	0	0	1	3	11	4	.260	.393	.320	106	1	3	0	1	.984	-6	2-15	-0.4
	Min-A	86	304	42	80	16	0	1	21	40	47	.263	.349	.326	88	-4	10	3	1	.988	-8	2-73/S-2,D-3	-0.8
1989	Phi-N	151	561	65	161	25	6	2	37	54	63	.287	.353	.364	105	5	10	7	-1	.990	2	*2-144	1.1
1990	Phi-N	119	447	39	118	21	3	4	50	36	47	.264	.322	.351	85	-9	7	1	2	.991	-3	*2-114	-0.8
	NY-N	27	100	9	25	5	0	1	10	14	11	.250	.342	.330	86	-2	0	0	0	.979	-5	2-26	-0.6
	Yr	146	547	48	143	26	3	5	60	50	58	.261	.326	.347	85	-10	7	1	2	.989	-8	*2-140	-1.4
1991	NY-N	70	155	17	30	7	0	1	14	32	21	.194	.332	.258	68	-5	7	2	1	1.000	4	2-57/O-1	-0.5
	SF-N	32	60	6	15	1	0	1	7	13	7	.250	.384	.300	98	-0	2	0	0	1.000	-6	2-15/3-3	-0.2
	Yr	102	215	23	45	8	0	2	21	45	28	.209	.346	.270	77	-5	9	2	1	1.000	1	2-72/3-3,O-1	-0.2
Total	13	1514	5349	676	1450	254	41	28	574	627	584	.271	.350	.350	95	-18	188	64	18	.989	-94	*2-1416/S-16,3DO	-3.7

YEAR	TM/L	G	AB	R	H	2B	3B	HR	RBI	BB	SO	AVG	OBP	SLG	PRO+	BR/A	SB	CS	SBR	FA	FR	G/POS	TPR

■ JOSE HERRERA Herrera, Jose Concepcion (Ontiveros) "Loco" b: 4/8/42, San Lorenzo, Venez. BR/TR, 5'8", 165 lbs. Deb: 6/3/67

1967	Hou-N	5	4	0	1	0	0	0	1	0	1	.250	.250	.250	45	-0	0	0	0	.000	0	H	0.0
1968	Hou-N	27	100	9	24	5	0	0	7	4	12	.240	.269	.290	69	-4	0	2	-1	.958	-2	O-17/2-7	-0.9
1969	Mon-N	47	126	7	36	5	0	2	12	3	14	.286	.302	.373	88	-2	1	2	-1	.980	-2	O-31/2-2,3-1	-0.7
1970	Mon-N	1	1	0	0	0	0	0	0	0	0	.000	.000	.000	-99	-0	0	0	0	.000	0	H	0.0
Total	4	80	231	16	61	10	0	2	20	7	28	.264	.286	.333	79	-7	1	4	-2	.973	-4	/O-48,2-9,3-1	-1.6

■ JOSE HERRERA Herrera, Jose Ramon (Catalino) b: 8/30/72, Santo Domingo, D.R. BL/TL, 6', 165 lbs. Deb: 8/12/95

1995	Oak-A	33	70	9	17	1	2	0	6	2	11	.243	.303	.314	64	-1	1	3	-2	.956	-3	O-25/D-5	-0.8
1996	Oak-A	108	320	44	86	15	1	6	30	20	59	.269	.318	.378	78	-11	8	2	1	.970	-10	*O-100/D-1	-2.0
Total	2	141	390	53	103	16	3	6	32	26	70	.264	.315	.367	76	-15	9	5	-0	.967	-13	O-125/D-6	-2.8

■ PANCHO HERRERA Herrera, Juan Francisco (Willavicencio) b: 6/16/34, Santiago De Cuba, Cuba BR/TR, 6'3", 220 lbs. Deb: 4/15/58

1958	Phi-N	29	63	5	17	3	0	1	6	7	15	.270	.352	.365	92	-1	1	2	-1	.980	2	3-16,1-11	0.0
1960	Phi-N	145	512	61	144	26	6	17	71	51	136	.281	.352	.455	119	13	2	3	-1	.988	10	*1-134,2-17	1.4
1961	Phi-N	126	400	56	103	17	2	13	51	55	120	.257	.353	.408	102	2	5	1	1	.993	6	*1-115	0.0
Total	3	300	975	122	264	46	8	31	128	113	271	.271	.352	.430	110	15	8	6	-1	.990	18	1-260/2-17,3-16	1.4

■ MIKE HERRERA Herrera, Ramon b: 12/19/1897, Havana, Cuba d: 2/3/78, Havana, Cuba BR/TR, 5'6", 147 lbs. Deb: 9/22/25

1925	Bos-A	10	39	2	15	0	0	0	8	2	2	.385	.415	.385	104	0	1	0		.958	3	2-10	0.4
1926	Bos-A	74	237	20	61	14	1	0	19	15	13	.257	.304	.325	66	-12	0	5	-3	.962	5	2-48,3-16/S-4	-0.8
Total	2	84	276	22	76	14	1	0	27	17	15	.275	.320	.333	72	-12	1	5	-3	.961	8	/2-58,3-16,S-4	-0.4

■ LEFTY HERRING Herring, Silas Clarke b: 3/4/1880, Philadelphia, Pa. d: 2/11/65, Massapequa, N.Y. BL/TL, 5'11", 160 lbs. Deb: 5/16/1899

1899	Was-N	2	1	1	1	0	0	0		0	1	1.000	1.000	1.000	454		0			1.000	0	/P-2	0.0
1904	Was-A	15	46	3	8	1	0	0	2	7		.174	.283	.196	54	-2	0			.991	1	1-10/O-5	-0.2
Total	2	17	47	4	9	1	0	0	2	8		.191	.309	.213	67		0			.991	1	/1-10,O-5,P-2	-0.2

■ ED HERRMANN Herrmann, Edward Martin b: 8/27/46, San Diego, Cal. BL/TR, 6'1", 210 lbs. Deb: 9/1/67 F

1967	Chi-A	2	3	1	2	0	0	1	1	0	0	.667	.750	1.000	429	1	0	0	0	1.000	1	/C-2	0.3
1969	Chi-A	102	290	31	67	8	0	8	31	30	35	.231	.320	.341	81	-7	0	2	-1	.983	-3	C-92	-0.7
1970	Chi-A	96	297	42	84	9	0	19	52	31	41	.283	.356	.505	130	12	0	1	-1	.988	5	C-88	2.0
1971	Chi-A	101	294	32	63	6	0	11	35	44	48	.214	.321	.347	86	-5	0	0	1	.995	9	C-97	0.9
1972	Chi-A	116	354	23	88	9	0	10	40	43	37	.249	.337	.359	105	3	0	0	0	.989	5	*C-112	0.9
1973	Chi-A	119	379	42	85	17	1	10	39	31	55	.224	.295	.354	79	-11	2	4	-2	.984	5	*C-114/D-2	-0.3
1974	Chi-A†	107	367	32	95	13	1	6	39	16	49	.259	.290	.381	90	-6	0	0	0	.987	3	*C-107	0.2
1975	NY-A	80	200	16	51	9	2	6	30	16	23	.255	.310	.410	104	0	0	0	0	.979	7	D-35,C-24	0.8
1976	Cal-A	29	46	5	8	3	0	2	8	7	4	.174	.283	.370	96	-0	0	0	0	.954	-6	C-27	-0.6
	Hou-N	79	265	14	54	8	1	3	25	22	40	.204	.275	.268	60	-14	0	0	0	.987	0	C-79	-1.3
1977	Hou-N	56	158	7	46	7	0	1	17	15	18	.291	.356	.354	100	0	1	1	-0	.990	9	C-49	1.0
1978	Hou-N	16	36	1	4	1	0	0	3	3		.111	.179	.139	-11	-5	0	0	0	1.000	-1	C-14	-0.6
	Mon-N	19	40	1	7	1	0	0	3	1	4	.175	.195	.200	11	-5	0	0	0	.977	-1	C-12	-0.7
	Yr	35	76	2	11	2	0	0	3	4	7	.145	.188	.171	1	-10	0	0	0	.991	-2	C-26	-1.2
Total	11	922	2729	247	654	92	4	80	320	260	361	.240	.312	.364	91	-37	6	8	-3	.987	29	C-817/D-37	2.0

■ JOHN HERRNSTEIN Herrnstein, John Ellett b: 3/31/38, Hampton, Va. BL/TL, 6'3", 215 lbs. Deb: 9/15/62

1962	Phi-N	6	5	0	1	0	0	0	1	1	3	.200	.333	.200	48	-0	0	0	0	.000	0	/O-1	-0.1
1963	Phi-N	15	12	1	2	0	0	1	1	1	5	.167	.231	.417	83	-0	0	0	0	1.000	-1	/O-2,1-1	-0.1
1964	Phi-N	125	303	38	71	12	4	6	25	22	67	.234	.291	.360	83	-7	1	2	-1	.977	-20	O-69,1-68	-3.4
1965	Phi-N	63	85	8	17	2	0	1	5	2	18	.200	.227	.259	37	-7	0	0	0	.984	-3	1-18,O-14	-1.1
1966	Phi-N	4	10	1	1	0	0	0	1	0	7	.100	.100	.100	-44	-2	0	0	0	1.000	-0	/O-2	-0.2
	Chi-N	9	17	3	3	0	0	0	0	3	8	.176	.300	.176	36	-1	0	0	0	.975	-1	/1-4,O-1	-0.3
	Atl-N	17	18	2	4	0	0	0	1	0	7	.222	.222	.222	24	-2	0	0	0	1.000	-1	/O-5	-0.3
	Yr	30	45	5	8	0	0	0	2	3	22	.178	.229	.178	15	-5	0	0	0	1.000	-2	/O-8,1-4	-0.8
Total	5	239	450	52	99	14	4	8	34	29	115	.220	.272	.322	67	-20	1	2	-1	.983	-26	/O-94,1-91	-5.5

■ RICK HERRSCHER Herrscher, Richard Franklin b: 11/3/36, St.Louis, Mo. BR/TR, 6'2.5", 187 lbs. Deb: 8/1/62

| 1962 | NY-N | 35 | 50 | 5 | 11 | 3 | 0 | 1 | 6 | 5 | 11 | .220 | .291 | .340 | 68 | -2 | 0 | 0 | 0 | 1.000 | 2 | 1-10/3-6,0-4,S-3 | 0.0 |

■ EARL HERSH Hersh, Earl Walter b: 5/21/32, Ebbvale, Md. BL/TL, 6', 205 lbs. Deb: 9/4/56

| 1956 | Mil-N | 7 | 13 | 0 | 3 | 0 | 0 | 0 | 0 | 0 | 5 | .231 | .231 | .462 | 85 | -0 | 0 | 0 | 0 | .000 | -1 | /O-2 | -0.2 |

■ MIKE HERSHBERGER Hershberger, Norman Michael b: 10/9/39, Massillon, Ohio BR/TR, 5'10", 175 lbs. Deb: 9/5/61

1961	Chi-A	15	55	9	17	3	0	0	5	2	2	.309	.333	.364	88	-1	1	1	-0	1.000	2	O-13	-0.1
1962	Chi-A	148	427	54	112	14	2	4	46	37	36	.262	.325	.333	78	-13	10	6	-1	.984	-7	*O-135	-2.7
1963	Chi-A	135	476	64	133	26	2	3	45	39	39	.279	.339	.361	98	-1	9	3	1	.976	-5	*O-119	-1.2
1964	Chi-A	141	452	55	104	15	3	2	31	48	47	.230	.310	.290	70	-18	8	6	-1	.984	-8	*O-134	-3.4
1965	KC-A	150	494	43	114	15	5	5	48	37	42	.231	.291	.312	72	-18	7	3	0	.988	4	*O-144	-2.1
1966	KC-A	146	538	55	136	27	1	2	57	47	37	.253	.316	.340	92	-6	13	5	1	.977	12	*O-143	0.1
1967	KC-A	142	480	55	122	25	1	1	49	38	40	.254	.318	.317	91	-5	10	3	1	.982	7	*O-130	-0.3
1968	Oak-A	99	246	23	67	9	2	5	32	21	22	.272	.332	.386	123	6	8	3	1	.978	-7	O-90	-0.4
1969	Oak-A	51	129	11	26	2	1	0	10	10	15	.202	.259	.240	42	-10	1	2	-1	.980	-5	O-35	-1.9
1970	Mil-A	49	98	7	23	5	0	1	6	10	8	.235	.306	.316	71	-4	1	2	-1	.946	-6	O-35	-1.2
1971	Chi-A	74	177	22	46	9	0	2	15	30	23	.260	.379	.345	103	2	6	2	1	.960	-8	O-59	-0.9
Total	11	1150	3572	398	900	150	22	26	344	319	311	.252	.319	.328	85	-66	74	36	1	.980	-21	*O-1037	-14.1

■ WILLARD HERSHBERGER Hershberger, Willard McKee "Bill" b: 5/28/10, Lemoncove, Cal. d: 8/3/40, Boston, Mass. BR/TR, 5'10.5", 167 lbs. Deb: 4/19/38

1938	Cin-N	49	105	12	29	3	1	0	12	5	6	.276	.315	.324	78	-3	1			.960	-1	C-39/2-1	-0.2
1939	*Cin-N	63	174	23	60	9	2	0	32	9	4	.345	.384	.420	115	4	1			.987	-2	C-60	0.5
1940	Cin-N	48	123	6	38	4	2	0	26	6	1	.309	.351	.374	99	-0	0			.985	-2	C-37	0.0
Total	3	160	402	41	127	16	5	0	70	20	16	.316	.356	.381	101	1	2			.980	-5	C-136/2-1	0.3

■ NEAL HERTWECK Hertweck, Neal Charles b: 11/22/31, St.Louis, Mo. BL/TL, 6'1.5", 175 lbs. Deb: 9/27/52

| 1952 | StL-N | 2 | 6 | 0 | 0 | 0 | 0 | 0 | 0 | 1 | 0 | .000 | .143 | .000 | -57 | -1 | 0 | 0 | 0 | 1.000 | -0 | /1-2 | -0.2 |

■ STEVE HERTZ Hertz, Stephen Allan b: 2/26/45, Fairfield, Ohio BR/TR, 6'1", 195 lbs. Deb: 4/21/64

| 1964 | Hou-N | 5 | 4 | 2 | 0 | 0 | 0 | 0 | 0 | 0 | 3 | .000 | .000 | .000 | -99 | -1 | 0 | 0 | 0 | 1.000 | 0 | /3-2 | -0.1 |

■ BUCK HERZOG Herzog, Charles Lincoln b: 7/9/1885, Baltimore, Md. d: 9/4/53, Baltimore, Md. BR/TR, 5'11", 160 lbs. Deb: 4/17/08 M

1908	NY-N	64	160	38	48	6	2	0	11	36		.300	.448	.363	152	13	16			.921	1	2-42,S-12/3-4,O-1	1.6
1909	NY-N	42	130	16	24	2	0	0	8	13		.185	.264	.200	43	-8	2			.914	-2	O-29/2-6,3-4,S-1	-1.3
1910	Bos-N	106	380	51	95	23	3	3	32	30	34	.250	.329	.342	92	-4	13			.915	4	*3-105	0.3
1911	Bos-N	79	294	53	91	19	5	5	41	33	21	.310	.398	.459	129	11	26			.934	8	S-74/3-4	2.4
	*NY-N	69	247	37	66	14	4	1	26	14	19	.267	.325	.368	91	-4	22			.926	10	3-65/2-3,S-1	0.7
	Yr	148	541	90	157	33	9	6	67	47	40	.290	.365	.418	112	8	48			.935	18	S-75,3-69/2-3	3.1
1912	*NY-N	140	482	72	127	20	9	2	47	57	34	.263	.350	.355	90	-6	37			.942	19	*3-140	1.4
1913	*NY-N	96	290	46	83	15	3	3	31	22	12	.286	.349	.390	110	4	23			.947	1	3-84/2-2	0.6
1914	Cin-N	138	498	54	140	14	8	1	40	42	27	.281	.348	.347	104	3	46			.939	31	*S-137/1-2,M	4.7
1915	Cin-N	155	579	61	153	14	10	3	42	34	21	.264	.314	.328	93	-5	35	16	1	.945	31	*S-153/1-2,M	4.2
1916	Cin-N	79	281	30	75	14	2	1	24	21	12	.267	.329	.342	109	3	15	12	-3	.931	-2	S-65,3-12/O-1,M	0.5
	NY-N	77	280	40	73	10	4	0	25	22	24	.261	.326	.325	106	2	19	16	-4	.978	14	2-44,3-27/S-9	2.1
	Yr	156	561	70	148	24	6	1	49	43	36	.264	.327	.333	107	5	34	28	-7	.926	12	S-74,2-44,3-39,/O-1	2.6

YEAR	TM/L	G	AB	R	H	2B	3B	HR	RBI	BB	SO	AVG	OBP	SLG	PRO+	BR/A	SB	CS	SBR	FA	FR	G/POS	TPR
1917	*NY-N	114	417	69	98	10	8	2	31	31	36	.235	.308	.312	93	-3	12			.948	-9	*2-113	-0.6
1918	Bos-N	118	473	57	108	12	6	0	26	29	28	.228	.280	.279	74	-15	10			.961	4	2-99,1-12/S-7	-0.6
1919	Bos-N	73	275	27	77	8	5	1	25	13	11	.280	.327	.356	110	3	16			.953	-14	2-70/1-1	-0.9
	Chi-N	52	193	15	53	4	4	0	17	10	7	.275	.336	.337	102	1	12			.987	-11	2-52	-0.8
	Yr	125	468	42	130	12	9	1	42	23	18	.278	.331	.348	106	4	28			.967	-25	*2-122/1-1	-1.7
1920	Chi-N	91	305	39	59	9	2	0	19	20	21	.193	.261	.236	43	-22	8	9	-3	.938	-6	2-59,3-28/1-1	-3.0
Total	13	1493	5284	705	1370	191	75	20	445	427	307	.259	.329	.335	96	-27	312	53		.954	77	2-490,3-473,S/01	11.3

■ WHITEY HERZOG
Herzog, Dorrel Norman Elvert   b: 11/9/31, New Athens, Ill.   BL/TL, 5'11", 182 lbs.   Deb: 4/17/56   MC

YEAR	TM/L	G	AB	R	H	2B	3B	HR	RBI	BB	SO	AVG	OBP	SLG	PRO+	BR/A	SB	CS	SBR	FA	FR	G/POS	TPR
1956	Was-A	117	421	49	103	13	7	4	35	35	74	.245	.303	.337	69	-20	8	5	-1	.980	1	*O-103/1-5	-2.4
1957	Was-A	36	78	7	13	3	0	0	4	13	12	.167	.301	.205	41	-6		5	-1	.981	-3	O-28	-1.2
1958	Was-A	8	5	0	0	0	0	0	0	1	5	.000	.167	.000	-51	-1	0	0	0	1.000		/O-7	-0.3
	KC-A	88	96	11	23	1	2	0	9	16	21	.240	.348	.292	77	-2	0	3	-2	.968	-10	O-37,1-22	-1.6
	Yr	96	101	11	23	1	2	0	9	17	26	.228	.339	.277	71	-3	0	3	-2	.972	-12	O-44,1-22	-1.9
1959	KC-A	38	123	25	36	7	1	1	9	34	23	.293	.441	.390	129	7	1	0	0	.963	2	O-34/1-1	0.8
1960	KC-A	83	252	43	67	10	2	8	38	40	32	.266	.366	.417	111	4	0	1	-1	.985	1	O-69/1-2	0.1
1961	Bal-A	113	323	39	94	11	6	5	35	50	41	.291	.388	.409	117	9	1	4	-2	1.000	-11	O-98	-0.8
1962	Bal-A	99	263	34	70	13	1	7	35	41	36	.266	.371	.403	116	7	2	3	-1	.978	0	O-70	0.2
1963	Det-A	52	53	5	8	2	1	0	7	11	17	.151	.308	.226	51	-3	0	0	0	.976	-2	/1-7,O-4	-0.5
Total	8	634	1614	213	414	60	20	25	172	241	261	.257	.356	.365	96	-4	13	18	-7	.982	-23	O-450/1-37	-5.7

■ OTTO HESS
Hess, Otto C.   b: 10/10/1878, Bern, Switzerland   d: 2/25/26, Tucson, Ariz.   BL/TL, 6'1", 170 lbs.   Deb: 8/3/02

YEAR	TM/L	G	AB	R	H	2B	3B	HR	RBI	BB	SO	AVG	OBP	SLG	PRO+	BR/A	SB	CS	SBR	FA	FR	G/POS	TPR
1902	Cle-A	7	14	2	1	0	0	0	1		2	.071	.188	.071	-27	-2	0			.870	1	/P-7	0.0
1904	Cle-A	34	100	4	12	2	1	0	5		3	.120	.146	.160	-3	-12	0			.951	-1	P-21,O-12	-0.5
1905	Cle-A	54	173	15	44	8	1	2	13		7	.254	.291	.347	101	-0	2			.950	3	O-28,P-26	0.1
1906	Cle-A	53	154	13	31	5	2	0	11		2	.201	.212	.260	48	-10	3			.949	-3	P-43/O-5	-0.2
1907	Cle-A	19	30	4	4	0	0	0	0		4	.133	.278	.133	31	-2	1			.941	-1	P-17/O-2	-0.1
1908	Cle-A	9	14	0	0	0	0	0	0		1	.000	.067	.000	-78	-3	0			1.000	-1	/P-4,O-4	-0.4
1912	Bos-N	33	94	10	23	4	4	0	10	0	26	.245	.245	.372	66	-5	0			.951	-4	P-33	0.0
1913	Bos-N	35	83	9	26	0	1	2	11	7	15	.313	.367	.410	119	2	0			.945	1	P-29	0.0
1914	Bos-N	31	47	5	11	1	0	1	6	1	11	.234	.250	.319	69	-2	0			.947	1	P-14/1-5	-0.1
1915	Bos-N	5	5	1	2	1	0	0	1	0	2	.400	.400	.600	210	1	0			.800	-0	/P-4,1-1	0.0
Total	10	280	714	63	154	21	9	5	58	27	54	.216	.248	.291	63	-33	4			.941	-3	P-198/O-51,1-6	-1.2

■ TOM HESS
Hess, Thomas (b: Thomas Heslin)   b: 8/15/1875, Brooklyn, N.Y.   d: 12/15/45, Albany, N.Y.   Deb: 6/6/1892

YEAR	TM/L	G	AB	R	H	2B	3B	HR	RBI	BB	SO	AVG	OBP	SLG	PRO+	BR/A	SB	CS	SBR	FA	FR	G/POS	TPR
1892	Bal-N	1	2	0	0	0	0	0	0	0	0	.000	.000	.000	-97	-0	0			.000	0	/C-1	0.0

■ GUS HETLING
Hetling, August Julius   b: 11/21/1885, St.Louis, Mo.   d: 10/13/62, Wichita, Kan.   BR/TR, 5'10", 165 lbs.   Deb: 10/6/06

YEAR	TM/L	G	AB	R	H	2B	3B	HR	RBI	BB	SO	AVG	OBP	SLG	PRO+	BR/A	SB	CS	SBR	FA	FR	G/POS	TPR
1906	Det-A	2	7	0	1	0	0	0	0	0	2	.143	.143	.143	-10	-1	0			1.000	-0	/3-2	-0.1

■ GEORGE HEUBEL
Heubel, George A.   b: 1849, Paterson, N.J.   d: 1/22/1896, Philadelphia, Pa.   5'11.5", 178 lbs.   Deb: 5/20/1871   U

YEAR	TM/L	G	AB	R	H	2B	3B	HR	RBI	BB	SO	AVG	OBP	SLG	PRO+	BR/A	SB	CS	SBR	FA	FR	G/POS	TPR
1871	Ath-n	17	75	18	23	4	2	0	13	2	0	.307	.325	.413	112	1	1	0		.758	1	O-16/1-1	0.2
1872	Oly-n	5	23	2	3	0	0	0	1	0	0	.130	.130	.130	-21	-3	0	0	0	.800	-1	/O-5	-0.3
1876	NY-N	1	4	0	0	0	0	0	0	0	0	.000	.000	.000	-99	-1	0			.750	0	/1-1	0.0
Total	2 n	22	98	20	26	4	2	0	14	2	0	.265	.280	.347	83	-2	1	0	0	.767	0	/O-21,1-1	-0.1

■ JOHNNIE HEVING
Heving, John Aloysius   b: 4/29/1896, Covington, Ky.   d: 12/24/68, Salisbury, N.C.   BR/TR, 6', 175 lbs.   Deb: 9/24/20   F

YEAR	TM/L	G	AB	R	H	2B	3B	HR	RBI	BB	SO	AVG	OBP	SLG	PRO+	BR/A	SB	CS	SBR	FA	FR	G/POS	TPR
1920	StL-A	1	1	0	0	0	0	0	0	0	0	.000	.000	.000	-97	-0	0			.000	0	H	0.0
1924	Bos-A	45	109	15	31	5	1	0	11	10	7	.284	.345	.349	79	-3	0	0	0	.969	4	C-29	-1.0
1925	Bos-A	45	119	14	20	7	0	0	6	12	7	.168	.244	.227	20	-15	0	1	-1	.958	-4	C-34	-1.0
1928	Bos-A	82	158	11	41	7	0	0	11	11	10	.259	.308	.329	69	-7	1	1	-0	.967	-4	C-62	-0.7
1929	Bos-A	76	188	26	60	4	3	0	23	8	7	.319	.354	.372	89	-3	1	2	-1	.988	5	C-55	0.6
1930	Bos-A	75	220	15	61	5	3	0	17	11	14	.277	.312	.327	65	-12	2	0	1	.987	-4	C-71	-0.9
1931	*Phi-A	42	113	8	27	3	2	1	12	6	8	.239	.277	.327	55	-8	0	0	0	.993	2	C-40	-0.3
1932	Phi-A	33	77	14	21	6	1	0	10	7	6	.273	.333	.377	81	-2	0	0	0	1.000	-1	C-28	-0.2
Total	8	399	985	103	261	37	12	1	90	65	59	.265	.312	.330	66	-50	4	4	-1	.981	-4	C-319	-2.3

■ MIKE HEYDON
Heydon, Michael Edward "Ed"   b: 7/15/1874, Missouri   d: 10/13/13, Indianapolis, Ind.   BL/TR, 6',   Deb: 10/12/1898

YEAR	TM/L	G	AB	R	H	2B	3B	HR	RBI	BB	SO	AVG	OBP	SLG	PRO+	BR/A	SB	CS	SBR	FA	FR	G/POS	TPR
1898	Bal-N	3	9	2	1	0	0	0	0	1	2	.111	.333	.111	28	-1	0			.917	-1	/C-3	-0.1
1899	Was-N	3	3	0	0	0	0	0	0	1	0	.000	.400	.000	14	-0	0			.833	-3	/C-2	0.0
1901	StL-N	16	43	2	9	1	1	1	6	1	5	.209	.292	.349	90	-1	2			.941	-3	C-13/O-1	-0.2
1904	Chi-A	4	10	0	1	1	0	0	0	1	1	.100	.250	.200	45	-1	0			1.000	1	/C-4	0.1
1905	Was-A	77	245	20	47	7	1	0	26	21		.192	.261	.265	70	-8	5			.955	12	C-77	1.2
1906	Was-A	49	145	14	23	7	1	0	10	14		.159	.237	.221	46	-9	2			.937	-2	C-49	-0.7
1907	Was-A	62	164	14	30	3	0	0	9	25		.183	.302	.201	66	-5	3			.961	-8	C-57	-0.9
Total	7	214	619	52	111	19	3	1	53	70		.179	.271	.239	64	-24	12			.952	-0	C-205/O-1	-0.6

■ JACK HIATT
Hiatt, Jack E   b: 7/27/42, Bakersfield, Cal.   BR/TR, 6'2", 190 lbs.   Deb: 9/7/64   C

YEAR	TM/L	G	AB	R	H	2B	3B	HR	RBI	BB	SO	AVG	OBP	SLG	PRO+	BR/A	SB	CS	SBR	FA	FR	G/POS	TPR
1964	LA-N	9	16	2	6	0	0	0	2	2	3	.375	.444	.375	145	-1	0	0	0	.889	-1	/C-3,1-2	0.0
1965	SF-N	40	67	5	19	4	0	1	7	12	14	.284	.392	.388	118	2	0	0	0	.987	-2	C-21/1-7	0.2
1966	SF-N	18	23	2	7	2	0	0	1	4	5	.304	.407	.391	120	1	0	0	0	.982	1	/1-7	0.2
1967	SF-N	73	153	24	42	6	0	6	26	27	37	.275	.387	.431	136	8	0	0	0	.990	-1	1-36/C-3,O-2	0.4
1968	SF-N	90	224	14	52	10	2	4	34	41	61	.232	.353	.348	111	5	0	0	0	.994	-1	C-58,1-10	0.8
1969	SF-N	69	194	18	38	4	0	2	34	44	58	.196	.355	.325	93	0	0	0	0	.992	0	C-60/1-3	0.3
1970	Mon-N	17	43	4	14	2	0	2	7	14	14	.326	.491	.372	135	3	0	0	0	.961	-4	C-12/1-2	0.1
	Chi-N	66	178	19	43	12	1	2	22	31	48	.242	.354	.354	81	-5	0	0	0	.990	5	C-63/1-2	0.3
	Yr	83	221	23	57	14	1	2	29	45	62	.258	.383	.357	91	-1	0	0	0	.986	2	C-75/1-4	0.4
1971	Hou-N	69	174	16	48	8	1	1	16	35	39	.276	.403	.351	118	4	0	1	-1	.991	-1	C-65/1-1	0.7
1972	Hou-N	10	25	2	5	3	0	0	0	5	5	.200	.333	.320	88	-0	0	0	0	1.000	-3	C-10	-0.3
	Cal-A	22	45	4	13	0	1	0	5	5	11	.289	.360	.400	133	2	0	0	0	1.000	-8	C-17	-0.7
Total	9	483	1142	110	287	51	4	22	154	224	295	.251	.376	.363	109	24	0	1	-1	.990	-16	C-312/1-70,O-2	1.8

■ PHIL HIATT
Hiatt, Philip Farrell   b: 5/1/69, Pensacola, Fla.   BR/TR, 6'3", 200 lbs.   Deb: 4/7/93

YEAR	TM/L	G	AB	R	H	2B	3B	HR	RBI	BB	SO	AVG	OBP	SLG	PRO+	BR/A	SB	CS	SBR	FA	FR	G/POS	TPR
1993	KC-A	81	238	30	52	12	1	7	36	16	82	.218	.287	.366	70	-11	6	3	0	.909	-1	3-70/D-9	-1.1
1995	KC-A	52	113	11	23	6	0	4	9	8	37	.204	.262	.363	60	-7	1	0	0	.957	-4	O-47/D-2	-1.1
1996	Det-A	7	21	3	4	0	0	1	2	2	11	.190	.261	.286	38	-2	0	0	0	1.000	1	/3-3,O-2,D-1	-0.1
Total	3	140	372	44	79	18	1	12	49	27	130	.212	.278	.360	65	-20	7	3	0	.913	-4	/3-73,O-49,D-12	-2.3

■ JIM HIBBS
Hibbs, James Kerr   b: 9/10/44, Klamath Falls, Ore.   BR/TR, 6', 190 lbs.   Deb: 4/12/67

YEAR	TM/L	G	AB	R	H	2B	3B	HR	RBI	BB	SO	AVG	OBP	SLG	PRO+	BR/A	SB	CS	SBR	FA	FR	G/POS	TPR
1967	Cal-A	3	3	0	0	0	0	0	0	0	0	.000	.000	.000	-99	-1	0			.000	0	H	-0.1

■ EDDIE HICKEY
Hickey, Edward A.   b: 8/18/1872, Cleveland, Ohio   d: 3/25/41, Tacoma, Wash.   Deb: 9/3/01

YEAR	TM/L	G	AB	R	H	2B	3B	HR	RBI	BB	SO	AVG	OBP	SLG	PRO+	BR/A	SB	CS	SBR	FA	FR	G/POS	TPR
1901	Chi-N	10	37	4	6	0	0	0	3	2		.162	.225	.162	14	-4	1			.743	-2	3-10	-0.6

■ MIKE HICKEY
Hickey, Michael Francis   b: 12/25/1871, Chicopee, Mass.   d: 6/11/18, Springfield, Mass   BR/TR, 5'10.5", 150 lbs.   Deb: 9/14/1899

YEAR	TM/L	G	AB	R	H	2B	3B	HR	RBI	BB	SO	AVG	OBP	SLG	PRO+	BR/A	SB	CS	SBR	FA	FR	G/POS	TPR
1899	Bos-N	1	3	0	1	0	0	0	0	0	0	.333	.333	.333	76	-0	0			.889	1	/2-1	0.1

■ CHARLIE HICKMAN
Hickman, Charles Taylor "Cheerful Charlie" or "Piano Legs"   b: 3/4/1876, Taylortown, Dunkard Township, Pa.   d: 4/19/34, Morgantown, W.Va.   BR/TR, 5'11.5", 215 lbs.   Deb: 9/8/1897

YEAR	TM/L	G	AB	R	H	2B	3B	HR	RBI	BB	SO	AVG	OBP	SLG	PRO+	BR/A	SB	CS	SBR	FA	FR	G/POS	TPR
1897	*Bos-N	2	3	1	2	0	0	1	2	0	0	.667	.667	1.667	475	1	0			1.000	0	/P-2	0.0
1898	Bos-N	19	58	4	15	2	0	0	7	1		.259	.283	.293	62	-3	0			1.000	-1	/O-7,1-6,P-6	-0.3
1899	Bos-N	19	63	15	25	2	7	0	15	2		.397	.433	.651	178	6	1			.941	-2	P-11/O-7,1-1	0.1

YEAR	TM/L	G	AB	R	H	2B	3B	HR	RBI	BB	SO	AVG	OBP	SLG	PRO+	BR/A	SB	CS	SBR	FA	FR	G/POS	TPR
1900	NY-N	127	473	65	148	19	17	9	91		17	.313	.359	.482	137	21	10			.842	-4	*3-120/O-7	1.6
1901	NY-N	112	406	44	113	20	6	4	62		15	.278	.315	.387	107	2	5			.904	-7	O-50,S-23,3/P21	-0.6
1902	Bos-A	28	108	13	32	5	2	3	16		3	.296	.339	.463	118	2	1			.939	1	O-27	0.1
	Cle-A	102	426	61	161	31	11	8	94		12	.378	.399	.559	170	37	8			.966	-7	1-98/2-3,P-1	2.7
	Yr	130	534	74	**193**	36	13	11	110		15	.361	.387	.539	159	39	9			.966	-6	1-98,O-27/2-3,P-1	2.8
1903	Cle-A	131	522	64	154	31	11	12	97		17	.295	.325	.466	137	21	14			.972	-7	*1-125/2-7	1.3
1904	Cle-A	86	337	34	97	22	10	4	45		13	.288	.318	.440	142	14	9			.943	-0	2-45,1-40/O-1	1.6
	Det-A	42	144	18	35	6	6	2	22		11	.243	.297	.410	126	4	3			.970	-2	1-39	0.1
	Yr	128	481	52	132	28	16	6	67		24	.274	.312	.437	137	18	12			.969	-3	1-79,2-45/O-1	1.7
1905	Det-A	59	213	21	47	12	3	2	20		12	.221	.278	.333	93	-2	3			.940	3	O-47,1-12	-0.2
	Was-A	88	360	48	112	25	9	2	46		9	.311	.332	.447	152	19	3			.922	8	2-85/1-3	2.9
	Yr	147	573	69	159	37	12	4	66		21	.277	.311	.405	129	16	6			.922	10	2-85,O-47,1-15	2.7
1906	Was-A	120	451	53	128	25	5	9	57		14	.284	.311	.421	135	15	9			.955	-1	O-95,1-18/3-5,2-1	1.0
1907	Was-A	60	198	20	55	9	3	1	23		14	.278	.338	.369	136	8	4			.965	-4	1-30,O-18/2-3,P-1	0.2
	Chi-A	21	23	1	6	2	0	0	1		4	.261	.370	.348	134	1	0			.667	-1	/O-3	0.0
	Yr	81	221	21	61	11	3	1	24		18	.276	.342	.367	135	9	4			.965	-5	1-30,O-21/2-3,P-1	0.2
1908	Cle-A	65	197	16	46	6	1	2	18		9	.234	.271	.305	86	-3	2			.907	-0	O-28,1-20/2-1	-0.6
Total	12	1081	3982	478	1176	217	91	59	614		153	.295	.331	.440	133	144	72			.968	-25	1-394,O-290,23/PS	9.9

■ JIM HICKMAN
Hickman, David James b: 5/19/1894, Johnson City, Tenn. d: 12/30/58, Brooklyn, N.Y. BR/TR, 5'7.5", 170 lbs. Deb: 9/17/15

YEAR	TM/L	G	AB	R	H	2B	3B	HR	RBI	BB	SO	AVG	OBP	SLG	PRO+	BR/A	SB	CS	SBR	FA	FR	G/POS	TPR
1915	Bal-F	20	81	7	17	4	1	1	7	4	14	.210	.256	.321	60	-6	5			.963	4	O-20	-0.3
1916	Bro-N	9	5	3	1	0	0	0	0	2	0	.200	.429	.200	94	0	1			1.000	-1	/O-3	-0.1
1917	Bro-N	114	370	46	81	15	4	6	36	17	66	.219	.253	.330	76	-12	14			.942	7	*O-101	-1.0
1918	Bro-N	53	167	14	39	4	7	1	16	8	31	.234	.281	.359	95	-2	5			.914	-3	O-46	-0.8
1919	Bro-N	57	104	14	20	3	1	0	11	6	17	.192	.236	.240	43	-7	2			.962	-4	O-29	-1.4
Total	5	253	727	84	158	26	13	8	70	37	128	.217	.259	.322	74	-26	27			.941	4	O-199	-3.6

■ JIM HICKMAN
Hickman, James Lucius b: 5/10/37, Henning, Tenn. BR/TR, 6'4", 205 lbs. Deb: 4/14/62

YEAR	TM/L	G	AB	R	H	2B	3B	HR	RBI	BB	SO	AVG	OBP	SLG	PRO+	BR/A	SB	CS	SBR	FA	FR	G/POS	TPR
1962	NY-N	140	392	54	96	18	2	13	46	47	96	.245	.330	.401	94	-4	4	4	-1	.971	1	*O-124	-1.0
1963	NY-N	146	494	53	113	21	6	17	51	44	120	.229	.293	.399	96	-3	0	5	-3	.963	-0	O-82,3-59	-1.2
1964	NY-N	139	409	48	105	14	1	11	57	36	90	.257	.320	.377	98	-1	0	1	-1	.976	-9	*O-113/3-1	-1.6
1965	NY-N	141	369	32	87	18	0	15	40	27	76	.236	.291	.407	98	-2	3	1	0	.965	-8	O-91,1-30,3-14	-1.6
1966	NY-N	58	160	15	38	7	0	4	16	13	34	.237	.299	.356	83	-4	2	1	0	.986	1	O-45,1-17	-0.6
1967	LA-N	65	98	7	16	6	1	0	10	14	28	.163	.268	.245	52	-6	1	1	-0	1.000	-3	O-37/1-2,3-2,P-1	-1.1
1968	Chi-N	75	188	22	42	6	3	5	23	18	38	.223	.295	.367	91	-2	1	0	-0	.975	-4	O-66	-1.1
1969	Chi-N	134	338	38	80	11	2	21	54	47	74	.237	.330	.467	107	2	2	1	0	.981	-14	*O-125	-1.8
1970	Chi-N★	149	514	102	162	33	4	32	115	93	99	.315	.421	.582	148	35	0	1	-1	.974	6	O-79,1-74	3.0
1971	Chi-N	117	383	50	98	13	2	19	60	50	61	.256	.346	.449	108	4	0	1	-1	.982	-4	O-69,1-44	-0.9
1972	Chi-N	115	368	65	100	15	2	17	64	52	64	.272	.365	.462	121	10	3	1	0	.992	7	1-77,O-27	1.1
1973	Chi-N	92	201	27	49	1	2	3	20	42	42	.244	.374	.313	86	-2	1	1	-0	.988	-2	1-51,O-13	-0.9
1974	StL-N	50	60	5	16	0	0	2	4	8	10	.267	.353	.367	102	0	0	0	0	.986	1	1-14/3-1	0.1
Total	13	1421	3974	518	1002	163	25	159	560	491	832	.252	.337	.426	106	28	17	19	-6	.976	-29	O-871,1-309/3-77,P	-7.6

■ BUDDY HICKS
Hicks, Clarence Walter b: 2/15/27, Belvedere, Cal. BB/TR, 5'10", 170 lbs. Deb: 4/17/56

YEAR	TM/L	G	AB	R	H	2B	3B	HR	RBI	BB	SO	AVG	OBP	SLG	PRO+	BR/A	SB	CS	SBR	FA	FR	G/POS	TPR
1956	Det-A	26	47	5	10	2	0	0	5	3	2	.213	.260	.255	36	-4	0	1	-1	1.000	-1	S-16/2-6,3-1	-0.5

■ JIM HICKS
Hicks, James Edward b: 5/18/40, East Chicago, Ind. BR/TR, 6'3", 205 lbs. Deb: 10/2/64

YEAR	TM/L	G	AB	R	H	2B	3B	HR	RBI	BB	SO	AVG	OBP	SLG	PRO+	BR/A	SB	CS	SBR	FA	FR	G/POS	TPR
1964	Chi-A	2	0	0	0	0	0	0	0	0	0	—	—	—	0	0	0	0	0	.000	0	R	0.0
1965	Chi-A	13	19	2	5	1	0	1	2	0	9	.263	.263	.474	112	0	0	0	0	.750	-2	/O-5	-0.2
1966	Chi-A	18	26	3	5	0	1	0	1	1	5	.192	.222	.269	43	-2	0	0	0	1.000	-1	O-10/1-2	-0.4
1969	StL-N	19	44	5	8	0	2	1	3	4	14	.182	.250	.341	64	-2	0	0	0	1.000	-1	O-15	-0.2
	Cal-A	37	48	6	4	0	0	3	8	13	18	.083	.279	.271	57	-3	0	1	-1	1.000	-3	O-10/1-8	-0.8
1970	Cal-A	4	4	0	1	0	0	0	0	0	2	.250	.250	.250	40	-0	0	0	0	.000	0	H	0.0
Total	5	93	141	16	23	1	3	5	14	18	48	.163	.258	.319	64	-7	0	1	-1	.981	-6	/O-40,1-10	-1.6

■ NAT HICKS
Hicks, Nathaniel Woodhull b: 4/19/1845, Hempstead, N.Y. d: 4/21/07, Hoboken, N.J. BR/TR, 6'1", 186 lbs. Deb: 4/22/1872 M

YEAR	TM/L	G	AB	R	H	2B	3B	HR	RBI	BB	SO	AVG	OBP	SLG	PRO+	BR/A	SB	CS	SBR	FA	FR	G/POS	TPR
1872	Mut-n	56	268	55	82	12	6	0	33	5	3	.306	.319	.366	117	7	3	0	1	.875	5	*C-54/O-3	0.8
1873	Mut-n	28	121	12	29	1	2	1	14	7	0	.240	.281	.306	75	-3	2	0	1	.788	4	C-28	0.1
1874	Phi-n	58	266	51	73	8	1	0	30	5	4	.274	.288	.312	89	-4	3	2	-0	.823	6	*C-57/O-4,2-1,M	0.3
1875	Mut-n	62	269	32	67	10	0	0	22	2	10	.249	.255	.286	83	-5	1	0	0	.819	6	*C-60/O-5,M	0.3
1876	NY-N	45	188	20	44	4	1	0	15	3	4	.234	.246	.266	81	-3				.741	-6	C-45	-0.6
1877	Cin-N	8	32	3	6	0	0	0	3	1	2	.188	.212	.188	30	-2				.868	0	/C-8	-0.1
Total	4 n	204	924	150	251	31	5	1	99	19	17	.272	.286	.319	93	-5	9	2	2	.829	22	C-199/O-12,2-1	1.4
Total	2	53	220	23	50	4	1	0	18	4	6	.227	.241	.255	73	-5				.757	-5	/C-53	-0.8

■ JOE HICKS
Hicks, William Joseph b: 4/7/33, Ivy, Va. BL/TR, 6', 180 lbs. Deb: 9/18/59

YEAR	TM/L	G	AB	R	H	2B	3B	HR	RBI	BB	SO	AVG	OBP	SLG	PRO+	BR/A	SB	CS	SBR	FA	FR	G/POS	TPR
1959	Chi-A	6	7	0	3	0	0	0	0	0	1	.429	.500	.429	160	1	0	1	-1	1.000	-0	/O-4	0.0
1960	Chi-A	36	47	3	9	1	0	0	2	6	3	.191	.296	.213	40	-4	0	1	-1	1.000	-4	O-14	-0.9
1961	Was-A	12	29	2	5	0	0	1	1	0	4	.172	.172	.276	18	-3	0	1	-1	1.000	1	/O-7	-0.4
1962	Was-A	102	174	20	39	4	2	6	14	15	34	.224	.286	.374	76	-6	3	1	0	.962	-3	O-42	-1.1
1963	NY-N	56	159	16	36	6	1	5	22	7	31	.226	.272	.371	82	-4	0	3	-3	.966	-2	O-41	-1.0
Total	5	212	416	41	92	11	3	12	39	29	73	.221	.278	.349	72	-17	3	6	-3	.970	-8	O-108	-3.4

■ MAHLON HIGBEE
Higbee, Mahlon Jesse b: 8/16/01, Louisville, Ky. d: 4/7/68, Depauw, Ind. BR/TR, 5'11", 165 lbs. Deb: 9/27/22

YEAR	TM/L	G	AB	R	H	2B	3B	HR	RBI	BB	SO	AVG	OBP	SLG	PRO+	BR/A	SB	CS	SBR	FA	FR	G/POS	TPR
1922	NY-N	3	10	2	4	0	0	1	5	0	2	.400	.400	.700	177	1	0	0	0	1.000	-1	/O-3	0.0

■ HIGBY
Higby Deb: 9/18/1872

YEAR	TM/L	G	AB	R	H	2B	3B	HR	RBI	BB	SO	AVG	OBP	SLG	PRO+	BR/A	SB	CS	SBR	FA	FR	G/POS	TPR
1872	Atl-n	1	4	0	0	0	0	0	0	0	0	.000	.000	.000	-85	-1	0	0	0	.667	0	/O-1	-0.1

■ BILL HIGDON
Higdon, William Travis b: 4/27/24, Camp Hill, Ala. d: 8/30/86, Pascagoula, Miss. BL/TR, 6'1", 193 lbs. Deb: 9/10/49

YEAR	TM/L	G	AB	R	H	2B	3B	HR	RBI	BB	SO	AVG	OBP	SLG	PRO+	BR/A	SB	CS	SBR	FA	FR	G/POS	TPR
1949	Chi-A	11	23	3	7	3	0	0	6		3	.304	.448	.435	139	2	1	0	0	1.000	-1	/O-6	0.1

■ KEVIN HIGGINS
Higgins, Kevin Wayne b: 1/22/67, San Gabriel, Cal. BL/TR, 5'11", 170 lbs. Deb: 5/29/93

YEAR	TM/L	G	AB	R	H	2B	3B	HR	RBI	BB	SO	AVG	OBP	SLG	PRO+	BR/A	SB	CS	SBR	FA	FR	G/POS	TPR
1993	SD-N	71	181	17	40	4	1	0	9	11	14	.221	.295	.254	48	-13	0	1	-1	.983	-3	C-59/3-4,1-3,O-3,2	-1.3

■ MARK HIGGINS
Higgins, Mark Douglas b: 7/9/63, Miami, Fla. BR/TR, 6'2", 210 lbs. Deb: 9/7/89

YEAR	TM/L	G	AB	R	H	2B	3B	HR	RBI	BB	SO	AVG	OBP	SLG	PRO+	BR/A	SB	CS	SBR	FA	FR	G/POS	TPR
1989	Cle-A	6	10	1	1	0	0	0	0	1	6	.100	.182	.100	-18	-2	0	0	0	1.000	1	/1-5	-0.1

■ PINKY HIGGINS
Higgins, Michael Franklin "Mike" b: 5/27/09, Red Oak, Tex. d: 3/21/69, Dallas, Tex. BR/TR, 6'1", 185 lbs. Deb: 6/25/30 M

YEAR	TM/L	G	AB	R	H	2B	3B	HR	RBI	BB	SO	AVG	OBP	SLG	PRO+	BR/A	SB	CS	SBR	FA	FR	G/POS	TPR
1930	Phi-A	14	24	1	6	2	0	0	6	4	0	.250	.357	.333	73	-1	0	0	0	1.000	-2	/3-5,2-2,S-1	-0.3
1933	Phi-A	152	567	85	178	34	12	13	99	61	53	.314	.383	.485	127	22	2	7	-4	.947	-6	3-152	2.0
1934	Phi-A☆	144	543	89	179	37	6	16	90	56	70	.330	.392	.508	136	28	9	2	2	.914	-19	3-144	1.5
1935	Phi-A	133	524	69	155	32	4	23	94	42	62	.296	.350	.504	120	12	6	2	1	.947	-14	3-131	0.4
1936	Phi-A★	146	550	89	159	32	2	12	80	67	61	.289	.366	.420	96	-4	7	4	-0	.941	-14	*3-145	-1.2
1937	Bos-A	153	570	88	172	33	5	9	106	76	51	.302	.385	.425	100	1	2	6	-2	.935	-17	*3-152	-1.3
1938	Bos-A	139	524	77	159	29	5	5	106	71	55	.303	.388	.406	95	-3	10	9	-2	.914	-10	3-138	-1.2
1939	Det-A	132	489	57	135	24	2	8	76	56	41	.276	.353	.380	81	-14	7	4	0	.914	-11	3-130	-2.1
1940	*Det-A	131	480	70	130	24	3	13	76	61	31	.271	.357	.415	91	-7	4	2	0	.928	-13	3-137	-1.4
1941	Det-A	147	526	79	161	28	3	11	73	67	45	.298	.378	.422	101	1	5	4	0	.946	1	3-145	0.5
1942	Det-A	143	499	65	133	34	2	11	90	72	21	.267	.362	.409	108	6	3	7	-3	.926	-14	3-137	-0.9
1943	Det-A	138	512	89	145	20	1	10	84	57	31	.277	.349	.377	104	-7	4	5	-2	.940	-7	3-138	-0.5
1944	Det-A★	148	543	79	161	32	4	7	76	81	34	.297	.392	.409	122	18	4	4	-1	.954	-7	*3-146	1.2

YEAR	TM/L	G	AB	R	H	2B	3B	HR	RBI	BB	SO	AVG	OBP	SLG	PRO+	BR/A	SB	CS	SBR	FA	FR	G/POS	TPR
1946	Det-A	18	60	2	13	3	1	0	8	5	6	.217	.277	.300	58	-3	0	1	-1	.949	-2	3-17	-0.6
	*Bos-A	64	200	18	55	11	1	2	28	24	24	.275	.356	.370	97	-0	0	2	-1	.947	0	3-59	0.0
	Yr	82	260	20	68	14	2	2	36	29	30	.262	.338	.354	88	-4	0	3	-2	.947	-2	3-76	-0.6
Total	14	1802	6636	930	1941	374	51	140	1075	800	590	.292	.370	.428	106	60	61	59	-17	.935	-131	*3-1768/2-2,S-1	-3.9

■ BOB HIGGINS
Higgins, Robert Stone b: 9/23/1886, Fayetteville, Tenn. d: 5/25/41, Chattanooga, Tenn. BR/TR, 5'8", 176 lbs. Deb: 9/13/09

YEAR	TM/L	G	AB	R	H	2B	3B	HR	RBI	BB	SO	AVG	OBP	SLG	PRO+	BR/A	SB	CS	SBR	FA	FR	G/POS	TPR
1909	Cle-A	8	23	0	2	0	0	0	0	0	0	.087	.087	.087	-43	-4	0			1.000	3	/C-8	0.0
1911	Bro-N	4	10	1	3	0	0	0	2	1	0	.300	.364	.300	90	-0	1			.933	0	/C-2,3-1	0.0
1912	Bro-N	1	2	0	0	0	0	0	0	0	0	.000	.000	.000	-99	-1	0			.750	-0	/C-1	-0.1
Total	3	13	35	1	5	0	0	0	2	1	1	.143	.167	.143	-6	-4	1			.970	3	/C-11,3-1	-0.1

■ BILL HIGGINS
Higgins, William Edward b: 9/8/1861, Wilmington, Del. d: 4/25/19, Wilmington, Del. TR, 5'9", 155 lbs. Deb: 8/9/1888

YEAR	TM/L	G	AB	R	H	2B	3B	HR	RBI	BB	SO	AVG	OBP	SLG	PRO+	BR/A	SB	CS	SBR	FA	FR	G/POS	TPR
1888	Bos-N	14	54	5	10	1	0	0	4	1	3	.185	.200	.204	28	-4	1			.906	5	2-14	0.2
1890	StL-a	67	258	39	65	6	2	0	35	24		.252	.316	.291	69	-12	7			.951	13	2-67	0.5
	Syr-a	1	4	1	1	1	0	0	1	0		.250	.250	.500	135	0	0			1.000	1	/2-1	0.1
	Yr	68	262	40	66	7	2	0	36	24		.252	.315	.294	70	-12	7			.952	14	2-68	0.6
Total	2	82	316	45	76	8	2	0	40	25	3	.241	.296	.278	64	-16	8			.943	20	/2-82	0.8

■ BOBBY HIGGINSON
Higginson, Robert Leigh b: 8/18/70, Philadelphia, Pa. BL/TR, 5'11", 180 lbs. Deb: 4/26/95

YEAR	TM/L	G	AB	R	H	2B	3B	HR	RBI	BB	SO	AVG	OBP	SLG	PRO+	BR/A	SB	CS	SBR	FA	FR	G/POS	TPR
1995	Det-A	131	410	61	92	17	5	14	43	62	107	.224	.333	.393	89	-7	6	4	-1	.985	6	*O-123/D-2	-0.5
1996	Det-A	130	440	75	141	35	0	26	81	65	66	.320	.409	.577	147	32	6	3	0	.963	-7	*O-123/D-4	1.9
Total	2	261	850	136	233	52	5	40	124	127	173	.274	.372	.488	119	25	12	7	-1	.974	-1	O-246/D-6	1.4

■ ANDY HIGH
High, Andrew Aird "Handy Andy" b: 11/21/1897, Ava, Ill. d: 2/22/81, Toledo, Ohio BL/TR, 5'6", 155 lbs. Deb: 4/12/22 FC

YEAR	TM/L	G	AB	R	H	2B	3B	HR	RBI	BB	SO	AVG	OBP	SLG	PRO+	BR/A	SB	CS	SBR	FA	FR	G/POS	TPR
1922	Bro-N	153	579	82	164	27	10	6	65	59	26	.283	.354	.396	94	-5	3	12	-6	.958	-5	*3-130,S-22/2-1	-0.4
1923	Bro-N	123	426	51	115	23	9	3	37	47	13	.270	.344	.387	95	-3	4	1	1	.969	-8	3-80,S-45/2-5	0.0
1924	Bro-N	144	582	98	191	26	13	6	61	57	16	.328	.390	.448	128	24	3	6	-3	.964	-10	*2-133,S-17/3-1	1.4
1925	Bro-N	44	115	11	23	4	1	0	6	14	5	.200	.287	.252	40	-10	0	1	-1	.938	-2	2-11,3-11/S-3	-1.4
	Bos-N	60	219	31	63	11	1	4	28	24	2	.288	.361	.402	104	1	3	5	-2	.979	-9	3-60/2-1	-0.6
	Yr	104	334	42	86	15	2	4	34	38	7	.257	.335	.350	80	-10	3	6	-3	.963	-14	3-71,2-12/S-3	-2.0
1926	Bos-N	130	476	55	141	17	10	2	66	39	9	.296	.351	.387	108	5	4			.962	-6	3-81,2-49	0.5
1927	Bos-N	113	384	59	116	19	4	6	46	26	11	.302	.350	.419	114	6	4			.915	-20	3-89/2-8,S-2	-0.9
1928	*StL-N	111	368	58	105	14	3	6	37	37	10	.285	.355	.389	93	-3	2			.935	-19	*3-73,2-19	-1.8
1929	StL-N	146	603	95	178	32	4	10	63	38	18	.295	.340	.411	84	-15	7			**.967**	-19	*3-123,2-22	-2.6
1930	*StL-N	72	215	34	60	12	2	2	29	23	6	.279	.349	.381	74	-9	1			.990	-7	3-48/2-3	-1.1
1931	*StL-N	63	131	20	35	6	1	0	19	24	4	.267	.389	.328	91	-0	0			1.000	-5	3-23,2-19	-0.3
1932	Cin-N	84	191	16	36	4	2	0	12	23	6	.188	.276	.230	39	-16	1			.950	-10	3-46,2-12	-2.3
1933	Cin-N	24	43	4	9	2	0	0	6	5	1	.209	.292	.326	77	-1	0			.966	1	3-11/2-2	-0.4
1934	Phi-N	47	68	4	14	2	0	0	7	9	3	.206	.299	.235	40	-6	0			.906	-2	3-14/2-2	-0.7
Total	13	1314	4400	618	1250	195	65	44	482	425	130	.284	.350	.388	94	-33	33	25		.956	-125	3-790,2-287/S-89	-10.2

■ CHARLIE HIGH
High, Charles Edwin b: 12/1/1898, Ava, Ill. d: 9/11/60, Oak Grove, Ore. BL/TR, 5'9", 170 lbs. Deb: 9/5/19 F

YEAR	TM/L	G	AB	R	H	2B	3B	HR	RBI	BB	SO	AVG	OBP	SLG	PRO+	BR/A	SB	CS	SBR	FA	FR	G/POS	TPR
1919	Phi-A	11	29	2	2	0	0	0	1	3	4	.069	.182	.069	-28	-5	2			.944	-0	/O-9	-0.6
1920	Phi-A	17	65	7	20	2	1	1	6	3	6	.308	.375	.415	108	1	0	2	-1	.882	-1	O-17	-0.2
Total	2	28	94	9	22	2	1	1	7	6	10	.234	.314	.309	68	-4	2	2		.904	-1	/O-26	-0.8

■ HUGH HIGH
High, Hugh Jenken "Bunny" b: 10/24/1887, Pottstown, Pa. d: 11/16/62, St.Louis, Mo. BL/TL, 5'7.5", 155 lbs. Deb: 4/11/13 F

YEAR	TM/L	G	AB	R	H	2B	3B	HR	RBI	BB	SO	AVG	OBP	SLG	PRO+	BR/A	SB	CS	SBR	FA	FR	G/POS	TPR
1913	Det-A	87	183	18	42	6	1	0	16	28	24	.230	.335	.273	80	-4	6			.982	1	O-52	-0.5
1914	Det-A	84	184	25	49	5	3	0	17	26	21	.266	.363	.326	104	2	7	6	-2	.959	-7	O-53	-1.0
1915	NY-A	119	427	51	110	19	7	1	43	62	47	.258	.356	.342	109	6	22	13	-1	**.981**	-1	*O-117	-0.2
1916	NY-A	116	377	44	99	13	4	1	28	47	44	.263	.349	.326	101	1	13			.950	-1	*O-110	-0.6
1917	NY-A	103	365	37	86	11	6	1	19	48	31	.236	.329	.307	93	-2	8			.986	0	*O-100	-0.8
1918	NY-A	7	10	1	0	0	0	0	0	1	1	.000	.091	.000	-71	-2	0			1.000	0	/O-4	-0.2
Total	6	516	1546	176	386	54	21	3	123	212	168	.250	.345	.318	98	2	56	19		.972	-8	O-436	-3.3

■ DICK HIGHAM
Higham, Richard b: 1852, England d: 3/18/05, Chicago, Ill. BL/TR, 5'8.5", 171 lbs. Deb: 6/1/1871 MU

YEAR	TM/L	G	AB	R	H	2B	3B	HR	RBI	BB	SO	AVG	OBP	SLG	PRO+	BR/A	SB	CS	SBR	FA	FR	G/POS	TPR
1871	Mut-n	21	94	21	34	3	1	0	9	2	0	.362	.375	.415	139	6	3	2	-0	.747	-2	2-12/O-8,C-1	0.0
1872	Bal-n	50	245	72	84	10	1	2	38	2	3	.343	.348	.416	128	7	3	5	-2	.847	-3	C-25,O-24/2-5,31	0.1
1873	Mut-n	49	245	57	77	5	4	0	34	2	1	.314	.320	.367	104	1	1	3	-2	.714	-14	O-19,2-18,C-17	-1.1
1874	Mut-n	65	333	58	87	14	3	1	37	4	0	.261	.270	.330	89	-5	5	3	-0	**.852**	8	C-48,O-33/2-1,M	0.3
1875	Chi-n	42	208	44	49	5	3	0	12	1	0	.236	.236	.288	80	-4	6	2	1	.821	-7	C-24,O-14,2-13	-0.8
	Mut-n	15	64	12	25	5	0	0	10	0	1	.391	.391	.469	187	5	0			.739	-3	/C-8,2-6,O-3,1-2	-0.6
	Yr	57	272	56	74	10	3	0	22	1	1	.272	.272	.331	106	1	6	2	1	.802	-10	C-32,2-19,O-17,1-2	-0.6
1876	Har-N	67	312	59	102	21	2	0	35	2	7	.327	.331	.407	134	9				.869	-2	*O-59,C-13/S-1,2-1	0.6
1878	Pro-N	62	281	60	90	22	1	1	29	5	16	.320	.332	.416	145	13				.811	3	*O-62/C-1	1.2
1880	Tro-N	1	5	1	1	0	0	0	0	0	0	.200	.200	.200	34	-0				.000	-2	/O-1,C-1	-0.3
Total	5 n	242	1189	264	356	42	12	3	140	10	5	.299	.305	.362	108	10	18	15	-4	.837	-23	O-123,O-101/213	-1.3
Total	3	130	598	120	193	43	3	1	64	7	23	.323	.331	.410	138	22				.834	-2	O-122/C-15,2-1,S-1	1.5

■ JOHN HILAND
Hiland, John William b: 9/1860, Baltic, R.I. d: 4/10/01, Philadelphia, Pa. BL/TL, 5'8.5", 165 lbs. Deb: 8/20/1885

YEAR	TM/L	G	AB	R	H	2B	3B	HR	RBI	BB	SO	AVG	OBP	SLG	PRO+	BR/A	SB	CS	SBR	FA	FR	G/POS	TPR
1885	Phi-N	3	9	0	0	0	0	0	0	0	0	.000	.000	.000	-99	-2				.833	-2	/2-3	-0.4

■ GEORGE HILDEBRAND
Hildebrand, George Albert b: 9/6/1878, San Francisco, Cal d: 5/30/60, Reseda, Cal. BR/TR, 5'8", 170 lbs. Deb: 4/17/02 U

YEAR	TM/L	G	AB	R	H	2B	3B	HR	RBI	BB	SO	AVG	OBP	SLG	PRO+	BR/A	SB	CS	SBR	FA	FR	G/POS	TPR
1902	Bro-N	11	41	3	9	1	0	0	5	3		.220	.289	.244	64	-2	0			1.000	2	O-11	0.0

■ PALMER HILDEBRAND
Hildebrand, Palmer Marion "Pete" b: 12/23/1884, Shauck, Ohio d: 1/25/60, N.Canton, Ohio BR/TR, 5'10", 170 lbs. Deb: 5/14/13

YEAR	TM/L	G	AB	R	H	2B	3B	HR	RBI	BB	SO	AVG	OBP	SLG	PRO+	BR/A	SB	CS	SBR	FA	FR	G/POS	TPR
1913	StL-N	26	55	3	9	2	0	0	1	1	10	.164	.207	.200	17	-6	1			.968	0	C-22/O-1	-0.5

■ HILDEBRAND
Hildebrand Deb: 8/29/02

YEAR	TM/L	G	AB	R	H	2B	3B	HR	RBI	BB	SO	AVG	OBP	SLG	PRO+	BR/A	SB	CS	SBR	FA	FR	G/POS	TPR
1902	Chi-N	1	4	1	0	0	0	0	0	0	1	.000	.200	.000	-39	-1	0			1.000	-0	/O-1	-0.1

■ BELDEN HILL
Hill, Belden L. b: 8/24/1864, Kewanee, Ill. d: 10/22/34, Cedar Rapids, Iowa BR/TR, 6', Deb: 8/27/1890

YEAR	TM/L	G	AB	R	H	2B	3B	HR	RBI	BB	SO	AVG	OBP	SLG	PRO+	BR/A	SB	CS	SBR	FA	FR	G/POS	TPR
1890	Bal-a	9	30	3	5	0	0	0	2	3		.167	.306	.233	56	-2	6			.857	1	/3-9	0.0

■ DONNIE HILL
Hill, Donald Earl b: 11/12/60, Pomona, Cal. BB/TR, 5'10", 160 lbs. Deb: 7/25/83

YEAR	TM/L	G	AB	R	H	2B	3B	HR	RBI	BB	SO	AVG	OBP	SLG	PRO+	BR/A	SB	CS	SBR	FA	FR	G/POS	TPR
1983	Oak-A	53	158	20	42	7	0	2	15	4	21	.266	.284	.348	77	-5	1	1	-0	.961	0	S-53	-0.1
1984	Oak-A	73	174	21	40	6	0	2	16	5	12	.230	.251	.299	55	-11	1	1	-0	.949	-12	S-66/2-4,3-2,D-2	-1.8
1985	Oak-A	123	393	45	112	13	2	3	48	23	33	.285	.325	.351	92	-5	9	4	0	.973	-41	*2-122	-4.1
1986	Oak-A	108	339	37	96	16	2	4	29	23	38	.283	.329	.378	99	-1	5	2	0	.984	-12	2-68,3-33/S-2,D-3	-1.1
1987	Chi-A	111	410	57	98	14	6	9	46	30	35	.239	.293	.368	72	-17	1	0	0	.987	-29	2-84,3-32/D-1	-4.1
1988	Chi-A	83	221	17	48	14	2	1	20	26	32	.217	.300	.281	64	-11	0	0	0	.975	-11	2-59,3-12/D-5	-1.9
1990	Cal-A	103	352	36	93	18	2	3	32	29	27	.264	.322	.352	90	-5	2	1	0	.990	3	2-60,S-24,3/1PD	0.0
1991	Cal-A	77	209	36	50	8	1	3	30	25	21	.239	.335	.301	77	-5	1	0	0	.971	-3	2-39,S-29/1-3	-0.5
1992	Min-A	25	51	7	15	3	0	0	2	6	6	.294	.368	.353	100	-0	0	1	0	.944	-3	S-10/2-7,3-5,O-1	-0.2
Total	9	756	2307	276	594	91	14	26	228	175	225	.257	.311	.343	81	-59	22	11	0	.980	-107	2-443,S-184,3/D1OP	-13.8

■ GLENALLEN HILL
Hill, Glenallen b: 3/22/65, Santa Cruz, Cal. BR/TR, 6'3", 210 lbs. Deb: 9/1/89

YEAR	TM/L	G	AB	R	H	2B	3B	HR	RBI	BB	SO	AVG	OBP	SLG	PRO+	BR/A	SB	CS	SBR	FA	FR	G/POS	TPR
1989	Tor-A	19	52	4	15	0	0	1	7	3	12	.288	.327	.346	92	-1	2	1	0	.964	-2	O-16/D-3	-0.3
1990	Tor-A	84	260	47	60	11	3	12	32	18	62	.231	.284	.435	95	-3	8	3	1	.983	0	O-60/D-20	-0.4
1991	Tor-A	35	99	14	25	5	2	3	11	6	24	.253	.302	.434	97	-1	2	2	-1	.967	3	D-16,O-13	-0.2
	Cle-A	37	122	15	32	3	0	5	14	16	30	.262	.348	.410	108	1	4	2	0	.978	-1	O-33/D-1	0.0
	Yr	72	221	29	57	8	2	8	25	23	54	.258	.328	.421	103	1	6	4	-1	.975	-0	O-46,D-17	-0.2

YEAR	TM/L	G	AB	R	H	2B	3B	HR	RBI	BB	SO	AVG	OBP	SLG	PRO+	BR/A	SB	CS	SBR	FA	FR	G/POS	TPR
1992	Cle-A	102	369	38	89	16	1	18	49	20	73	.241	.288	.436	102	-1	9	6	-1	.956	2	O-59,D-34	-0.2
1993	Cle-A	66	174	19	39	7	2	5	25	11	50	.224	.274	.374	73	-7	7	3	0	.940	-4	O-39,D-18	-1.2
	Chi-N	31	87	14	30	7	0	10	22	6	21	.345	.387	.770	204	12	1	0	0	.957	1	O-21	1.3
1994	Chi-N	89	269	48	80	12	1	10	38	29	57	.297	.366	.461	115	6	19	6	2	.987	-6	O-78	0.1
1995	SF-N	132	497	71	131	29	4	24	86	39	98	.264	.318	.483	111	6	25	5	5	.959	-1	*O-125	0.5
1996	SF-N	98	379	56	106	26	0	19	67	33	95	.280	.347	.499	125	12	6	3	0	.959	-3	O-98	0.7
Total	8	693	2308	326	607	116	13	107	351	182	522	.263	.320	.464	110	25	83	31	6	.966	-13	O-542/D-92	0.3

■ HERMAN HILL
Hill, Herman Alexander b: 10/12/45, Tuskegee, Ala. d: 12/14/70, Valencia, Venez. BL/TR, 6'2", 190 lbs. Deb: 9/2/69

YEAR	TM/L	G	AB	R	H	2B	3B	HR	RBI	BB	SO	AVG	OBP	SLG	PRO+	BR/A	SB	CS	SBR	FA	FR	G/POS	TPR
1969	Min-A	16	2	4	0	0	0	0	0	0	1	.000	.000	.000	-98	-1	1	2	-1	.000	-1	/O-2	-0.2
1970	Min-A	27	22	8	2	0	0	0	0	0	6	.091	.091	.091	-49	-4	0	0	0	1.000	-2	O-14	-0.7
Total	2	43	24	12	2	0	0	0	0	0	7	.083	.083	.083	-53	-5	1	2	-1	1.000	-3	/O-16	-0.9

■ HUGH HILL
Hill, Hugh Ellis b: 7/21/1879, Ringgold, Ga. d: 9/6/58, Cincinnati, Ohio BL/TR, 5'11.5", 168 lbs. Deb: 5/1/03 F

YEAR	TM/L	G	AB	R	H	2B	3B	HR	RBI	BB	SO	AVG	OBP	SLG	PRO+	BR/A	SB	CS	SBR	FA	FR	G/POS	TPR
1903	Cle-A	1	1	0	0	0	0	0	0	0	0	.000	.000	.000	-99	-0				.000	0	H	0.0
1904	StL-N	23	93	13	21	2	1	3	4	2		.226	.242	.366	91	-2	3			1.000	0	O-23	-0.3
Total	2	24	94	13	21	2	1	3	4	2		.223	.240	.362	89	-2	3			1.000	0	/O-23	-0.3

■ HUNTER HILL
Hill, Hunter Benjamin b: 6/21/1879, Austin, Tex. d: 2/22/59, Austin, Tex. BR/TR, Deb: 7/1/03

YEAR	TM/L	G	AB	R	H	2B	3B	HR	RBI	BB	SO	AVG	OBP	SLG	PRO+	BR/A	SB	CS	SBR	FA	FR	G/POS	TPR
1903	StL-A	86	317	30	77	11	3	0	25	8		.243	.264	.297	70	-12	2			.923	-1	3-86	-1.2
1904	StL-A	58	219	19	47	3	0	0	14	6		.215	.246	.224	54	-12	4			.826	-16	3-56/O-1	-3.0
	Was-A	77	290	18	57	6	1	0	17	11		.197	.228	.224	44	-18	10			.895	-6	3-71/O-5	-2.6
	Yr	135	509	37	104	9	1	0	31	17		.204	.236	.224	48	-30	14			.864	-23	*3-127/O-6	-5.6
1905	Was-A	104	374	37	78	12	1	1	24	32		.209	.278	.254	72	-11	10			.908	-1	*3-103	-0.9
Total	3	325	1200	104	259	32	5	1	80	57		.216	.257	.253	62	-53	26			.895	-24	3-316/O-6	-7.7

■ JESSE HILL
Hill, Jesse Terrill b: 1/20/07, Yates, Mo. d: 8/31/93, Pasadena, Cal. BR/TR, 5'9", 165 lbs. Deb: 4/17/35

YEAR	TM/L	G	AB	R	H	2B	3B	HR	RBI	BB	SO	AVG	OBP	SLG	PRO+	BR/A	SB	CS	SBR	FA	FR	G/POS	TPR
1935	NY-A	107	392	69	115	20	3	4	33	42	32	.293	.362	.390	100	0	14	4	2	.951	2	O-94	0.1
1936	Was-A	85	233	50	71	19	5	0	34	29	23	.305	.384	.429	106	3	11	0	3	.967	-8	O-60	-0.3
1937	Was-A	33	92	24	20	2	1	0	4	13	16	.217	.314	.293	57	-6	2	1	0	.986	-2	O-21	-0.4
	Phi-A	70	242	32	71	12	3	0	37	31	20	.293	.374	.380	92	-2	16	3	3	.954	-5	O-68	-0.6
	Yr	103	334	56	91	14	4	2	41	44	36	.272	.357	.356	82	-8	18	4	3	.964	-3	O-89	-1.0
Total	3	295	959	175	277	53	12	6	108	115	91	.289	.366	.388	95	-5	43	8	8	.959	-8	O-243	-1.2

■ MARC HILL
Hill, Marc Kevin b: 2/18/52, Elsberry, Mo. BR/TR, 6'3", 210 lbs. Deb: 9/28/73 C

YEAR	TM/L	G	AB	R	H	2B	3B	HR	RBI	BB	SO	AVG	OBP	SLG	PRO+	BR/A	SB	CS	SBR	FA	FR	G/POS	TPR
1973	StL-N	1	3	0	0	0	0	0	0	0	1	.000	.000	.000	-99	-1	0	0	0	1.000	0	/C-1	-0.1
1974	StL-N	10	21	2	5	1	0	0	2	4	5	.238	.360	.286	83	-0	0	0	3	1.000	3	/C-9	0.3
1975	SF-N	72	182	14	39	4	0	5	23	25	27	.214	.309	.319	71	-7	0	0	0	.994	1	C-60/3-1	-0.4
1976	SF-N	54	131	11	24	5	0	5	15	10	19	.183	.246	.290	50	-9	0	1	-1	.995	1	C-49/1-1	-0.8
1977	SF-N	108	320	28	80	10	0	9	50	34	34	.250	.322	.366	84	-7	0	1	-1	.989	-3	*C-102	-0.7
1978	SF-N	117	358	20	87	15	1	3	36	45	39	.243	.329	.316	84	-7	1	2	-1	.986	0	*C-116/1-2	-0.5
1979	SF-N	63	169	20	35	3	0	3	15	26	25	.207	.313	.278	67	-7	0	1	-1	.991	-6	C-58/1-1	-1.2
1980	SF-N	17	41	1	7	2	0	0	0	1	7	.171	.190	.220	14	-5	0	0	0	.972	2	C-14	-0.3
	Sea-A	29	70	8	16	2	1	2	9	3	10	.229	.260	.371	70	-3	0	0	0	.991	-0	C-29	-0.3
1981	Chi-A	16	6	0	0	0	0	0	0	0	1	.000	.000	.000	-99	-2	0	0	0	1.000	-0	C-14/1-3,1	-0.1
1982	Chi-A	53	88	9	23	2	0	3	13	6	13	.261	.316	.386	92	-1	0	0	0	.993	6	C-49/1-1,3-1	0.5
1983	Chi-A	58	133	11	30	6	0	1	11	9	24	.226	.275	.293	54	-8	0	1	-1	.991	5	C-55/1-1,D-2	-0.2
1984	Chi-A	77	193	15	45	10	1	5	20	9	26	.233	.275	.373	74	-7	0	1	-1	.991	4	C-72/1-2	-0.1
1985	Chi-A	40	75	5	10	2	0	0	4	12	9	.133	.253	.160	16	-9	0	0	0	.985	9	C-37/3-1	0.1
1986	Chi-A	22	19	2	3	0	0	0	0	1	3	.158	.238	.158	10	-2	0	0	0	1.000	7	C-22	0.5
Total	14	737	1809	146	404	62	3	34	198	185	243	.223	.298	.317	69	-74	1	7	-4	.990	30	C-687/1-9,3-4,D-2	-3.3

■ OLIVER HILL
Hill, Oliver Clinton b: 10/16/12, Powder Springs, Ga. d: 9/20/70, Decatur, Ga. BL/TR, 5'11", 178 lbs. Deb: 4/19/39

YEAR	TM/L	G	AB	R	H	2B	3B	HR	RBI	BB	SO	AVG	OBP	SLG	PRO+	BR/A	SB	CS	SBR	FA	FR	G/POS	TPR
1939	Bos-N	2	2	1	1	1	0	0	0	0	0	.500	.500	1.000	317	1	0			.000	0	H	0.1

■ HOMER HILLEBRAND
Hillebrand, Homer Hiller Henry b: 10/10/1879, Freeport, Ill. d: 1/20/74, Elsinore, Cal. BR/TL, 5'8", 165 lbs. Deb: 4/24/05

YEAR	TM/L	G	AB	R	H	2B	3B	HR	RBI	BB	SO	AVG	OBP	SLG	PRO+	BR/A	SB	CS	SBR	FA	FR	G/POS	TPR
1905	Pit-N	39	110	9	26	3	2	0	7	6		.236	.282	.300	72	-4	1			.978	-3	1-16,P-10/O-7,C-3	-0.6
1906	Pit-N	7	21	1	5	1	0	0	3	1		.238	.273	.286	71	-1	0			1.000	1	/P-7	0.0
1908	Pit-N	1	0	0	0	0	0	0	0	0		—	—	—	—	0	0			.000	-0	/P-1	0.0
Total	3	47	131	10	31	4	2	0	10	7		.237	.281	.298	71	-5	1			1.000	-1	/P-18,1-16,O-7,C-3	-0.6

■ CHUCK HILLER
Hiller, Charles Joseph b: 10/1/34, Johnsburg, Ill. BL/TR, 5'11", 170 lbs. Deb: 4/11/61 C

YEAR	TM/L	G	AB	R	H	2B	3B	HR	RBI	BB	SO	AVG	OBP	SLG	PRO+	BR/A	SB	CS	SBR	FA	FR	G/POS	TPR
1961	SF-N	70	240	38	57	12	1	2	12	32	30	.237	.330	.321	76	-7	4	4	-1	.973	-14	2-67	-1.6
1962	*SF-N	161	602	94	166	22	3	2	48	55	49	.276	.344	.334	84	-12	5	4	-1	.964	-18	*2-161	-1.4
1963	SF-N	111	417	44	93	10	2	6	33	20	23	.223	.262	.300	62	-21	3	2	-0	.963	-15	*2-109	-2.9
1964	SF-N	80	205	21	37	8	1	1	17	17	23	.180	.247	.244	38	-17	1	1	-0	.977	2	2-60/3-1	-1.2
1965	SF-N	7	7	1	1	0	0	1	1	0	1	.143	.143	.571	88	-0	0	0	0	1.000	-1	/2-2	-0.0
	NY-N	100	286	24	68	11	1	5	21	14	24	.238	.276	.336	74	-10	1	1	-0	.959	-12	2-80/O-4,3-2	-1.8
	Yr	107	293	25	69	11	1	6	22	14	25	.235	.273	.341	74	-11	1	1	-0	.959	-13	2-82/O-4,3-2	-1.9
1966	NY-N	108	254	25	71	8	2	2	14	15	22	.280	.332	.350	92	-2	0	0	0	.981	11	2-45,3-14/O-9	1.1
1967	NY-N	25	54	0	5	3	0	0	3	2	11	.093	.125	.148	-22	-9	0	0	0	.968	2	2-14	-0.6
	Phi-N	31	43	4	13	1	0	0	2	4	4	.302	.333	.326	88	-1	0	0	0	.947	-3	/2-6	-0.4
	Yr	56	97	4	18	4	0	0	5	4	15	.186	.218	.227	27	-9	0	0	0	.963	-0	2-20	-1.0
1968	Pit-N	11	13	2	5	1	0	0	1	0	2	.385	.385	.462	155	1	0	0	0	.857	-0	/2-2	0.1
Total	8	704	2121	253	516	76	9	20	152	157	187	.243	.301	.316	72	-78	14	14	-4	.967	-49	2-546/3-17,O-13	-8.8

■ HOB HILLER
Hiller, Harvey Max b: 5/12/1893, E.Mauch Chunk, Pa. d: 12/27/56, Lehighton, Pa. BR/TR, 5'8", 162 lbs. Deb: 4/22/20

YEAR	TM/L	G	AB	R	H	2B	3B	HR	RBI	BB	SO	AVG	OBP	SLG	PRO+	BR/A	SB	CS	SBR	FA	FR	G/POS	TPR
1920	Bos-A	17	29	4	5	1	1	0	2	2	5	.172	.226	.276	34	-3	0	3	-2	.905	1	/3-6,S-5,2-2,0-1	-0.4
1921	Bos-A	1	1	0	0	0	0	0	0	0	0	.000	.000	.000	-99	-0	0			.000	0	H	0.0
Total	2	18	30	4	5	1	1	0	2	2	5	.167	.219	.267	29	-3	0	3	-2	.905	1	/3-6,S-5,2-2,0-1	-0.4

■ ED HILLEY
Hilley, Edward Garfield "Whitey" b: 6/17/1879, Cleveland, Ohio d: 11/14/56, Cleveland, Ohio BR/TR, 5'10.5", 170 lbs. Deb: 9/29/03

YEAR	TM/L	G	AB	R	H	2B	3B	HR	RBI	BB	SO	AVG	OBP	SLG	PRO+	BR/A	SB	CS	SBR	FA	FR	G/POS	TPR
1903	Phi-A	3	1	1	1	0	0	0	0	0	1	.333	.500	.333	147	0	0			.800	-0	/3-1	0.0

■ MACK HILLIS
Hillis, Malcolm David b: 7/23/01, Cambridge, Mass. d: 6/16/61, Cambridge, Mass. BR/TR, 5'10", 165 lbs. Deb: 9/13/24

YEAR	TM/L	G	AB	R	H	2B	3B	HR	RBI	BB	SO	AVG	OBP	SLG	PRO+	BR/A	SB	CS	SBR	FA	FR	G/POS	TPR
1924	NY-A	1	1	1	0	0	0	0	0	0	0	.000	.000	.000	-99	-0	0			.000	0	/2-1	0.0
1928	Pit-N	11	36	6	9	2	3	1	7	0	6	.250	.250	.556	101	-0	1			.973	-1	/2-8,3-1	-0.1
Total	2	12	37	7	9	2	3	1	7	0	6	.243	.243	.541	96	-1	1	0		.973	-1	/2-9,3-1	-0.1

■ PAT HILLY
Hilly, William Edward (b: William Edward Hilgerink) b: 2/24/1887, Fostoria, Ohio d: 7/25/53, Eureka, Mo. BR/TR, 5'11", 180 lbs. Deb: 5/7/14

YEAR	TM/L	G	AB	R	H	2B	3B	HR	RBI	BB	SO	AVG	OBP	SLG	PRO+	BR/A	SB	CS	SBR	FA	FR	G/POS	TPR
1914	Phi-N	8	10	2	3	0	0	0	1	1	5	.300	.364	.300	92	-0	0			1.000	-1	/O-4	-0.1

■ CHARLIE HILSEY
Hilsey, Charles T. b: 3/23/1864, Philadelphia, Pa. d: 10/31/18, Philadelphia, Pa. 5'7", 180 lbs. Deb: 9/27/1883

YEAR	TM/L	G	AB	R	H	2B	3B	HR	RBI	BB	SO	AVG	OBP	SLG	PRO+	BR/A	SB	CS	SBR	FA	FR	G/POS	TPR
1883	Phi-N	3	10	0	1	0	0	0	0		4	.100	.100	.100	-43	-2				.714	-0	/P-3	0.0
1884	Phi-a	6	24	5	5	1	1	0	0			.208	.208	.333	69	-1				.250	-0	/O-3,P-3	-0.1
Total	2	9	34	5	6	1	1	0	4			.176	.176	.265	38	-3				.824	-1	/P-6,O-3	-0.1

■ DAVE HILTON
Hilton, John David b: 9/15/50, Uvalde, Tex. BR/TR, 5'11", 191 lbs. Deb: 9/10/72 C

YEAR	TM/L	G	AB	R	H	2B	3B	HR	RBI	BB	SO	AVG	OBP	SLG	PRO+	BR/A	SB	CS	SBR	FA	FR	G/POS	TPR
1972	SD-N	13	47	2	10	1	2	0	5	3	6	.213	.260	.298	63	-2	0	0	0	.939	-3	3-13	-0.5
1973	SD-N	70	234	21	46	9	0	5	16	19	35	.197	.260	.299	59	-14	2	1	0	.970	-4	3-47,2-23	-1.8
1974	SD-N	74	217	17	52	8	1	1	12	13	28	.240	.283	.309	68	-10	3	5	-2	.948	-5	3-55,2-13	-1.8

YEAR	TM/L	G	AB	R	H	2B	3B	HR	RBI	BB	SO	AVG	OBP	SLG	PRO+	BR/A	SB	CS	SBR	FA	FR	G/POS	TPR
1975	SD-N	4	8	0	0	0	0	0	0	0	0	.000	.000	.000	-99	-2	0	0		.900	1	/3-4	-0.1
Total	4	161	506	40	108	19	3	6	33	35	69	.213	.266	.298	61	-28	6	6	-2	.954	-11	3-119/2-38	-4.2

■ JACK HIMES
Himes, John Herb   b: 9/22/1878, Bryan, Ohio   d: 12/16/49, Joliet, Ill.   BL/TR, 6'2", 180 lbs.   Deb: 9/18/05

YEAR	TM/L	G	AB	R	H	2B	3B	HR	RBI	BB	SO	AVG	OBP	SLG	PRO+	BR/A	SB	CS	SBR	FA	FR	G/POS	TPR
1905	StL-N	12	41	3	6	0	0	0		1		.146	.167	.146	-7	-5	0			1.000	-1	O-11	-0.7
1906	StL-N	40	155	10	42	5	2	0	14	7		.271	.307	.329	102	-0	4			.977	5	O-40	0.3
Total	2	52	196	13	48	5	2	0	14	8		.245	.278	.291	79	-5	4			.981	4	/O-51	-0.4

■ HARRY HINCHMAN
Hinchman, Harry Sibley   b: 8/4/1878, Philadelphia, Pa.   d: 1/19/33, Toledo, Ohio   BB/TR, 5'11", 165 lbs.   Deb: 7/29/07   F

YEAR	TM/L	G	AB	R	H	2B	3B	HR	RBI	BB	SO	AVG	OBP	SLG	PRO+	BR/A	SB	CS	SBR	FA	FR	G/POS	TPR
1907	Cle-A	15	51	3	11	3	1	0	9	5		.216	.286	.314	90	-1	2			.904	4	2-15	0.4

■ BILL HINCHMAN
Hinchman, William White   b: 4/4/1883, Philadelphia, Pa.   d: 2/20/63, Columbus, Ohio   BR/TR, 5'11", 190 lbs.   Deb: 9/24/05   FC

YEAR	TM/L	G	AB	R	H	2B	3B	HR	RBI	BB	SO	AVG	OBP	SLG	PRO+	BR/A	SB	CS	SBR	FA	FR	G/POS	TPR
1905	Cin-N	17	51	10	13	4	1	0	10	13		.255	.415	.373	122	2	4			.905	-3	O-12/3-4,1-1	-0.1
1906	Cin-N	18	54	7	11	1	1	0	1	8		.204	.306	.259	73	-1	2			.963	1	O-16	-0.2
1907	Cle-A	152	514	62	117	19	9	1	50	47		.228	.311	.305	96	-1	15			.958	-5	*O-148/1-4,2-1	-1.3
1908	Cle-A	137	464	55	107	23	8	6	59	38		.231	.301	.353	112	6	9			.975	-6	O-75,S-51/1-4	-0.3
1909	Cle-A	139	457	57	118	20	13	2	53	41		.258	.331	.372	117	9	22			.918	1	*O-131/S-6	0.6
1915	Pit-N	156	577	72	177	33	14	5	77	48	75	.307	.368	.438	146	31	17	17	-5	.969	4	O-156	2.4
1916	Pit-N	152	555	64	175	18	**16**	4	76	54	61	.315	.378	.427	146	30	10			.962	-4	O-124,1-31	2.2
1917	Pit-N	69	244	27	46	5	5	2	29	33	27	.189	.288	.275	70	-8	5			.945	-1	O-48,1-20	-1.4
1918	Pit-N	50	111	10	26	3	0	1	13	15	8	.234	.336	.315	96	-0	1			1.000	-4	O-40/1-3	-0.6
1920	Pit-N	18	16	0	3	0	0	0	1	1	3	.188	.278	.188	34	-1	0	0	0	.000	-1	H	-0.1
Total	10	908	3043	364	793	128	69	20	369	298	174	.261	.336	.368	118	66	85	17		.954	-17	O-750/1-63,S-57,32	1.2

■ HUNKEY HINES
Hines, Henry Fred   b: 9/29/1867, Elgin, Ill.   d: 1/2/28, Rockford, Ill.   BR/TR, 5'7", 165 lbs.   Deb: 5/16/1895

YEAR	TM/L	G	AB	R	H	2B	3B	HR	RBI	BB	SO	AVG	OBP	SLG	PRO+	BR/A	SB	CS	SBR	FA	FR	G/POS	TPR
1895	Bro-N	2	8	3	2	0	0	1	0	0		.250	.400	.250	76	-0	0			1.000	0	/O-2	0.0

■ MIKE HINES
Hines, Michael P.   b: 9/1862, Ireland   d: 3/14/10, New Bedford, Mass.   BR/TL, 5'10", 176 lbs.   Deb: 5/1/1883

YEAR	TM/L	G	AB	R	H	2B	3B	HR	RBI	BB	SO	AVG	OBP	SLG	PRO+	BR/A	SB	CS	SBR	FA	FR	G/POS	TPR
1883	Bos-N	63	231	38	52	13	1	0	16	7	36	.225	.248	.290	61	-11				.887	8	C-59/O-7	0.1
1884	Bos-N	35	132	16	23	3	0	0		3	24	.174	.193	.197	23	-11				.919	6	C-35	-0.2
1885	Bos-N	14	56	11	13	4	0	0	4	4	5	.232	.283	.304	93	-0				.857	-3	O-14	-0.4
	Bro-a	3	13	1	1	0	1	0	1	0		.077	.077	.231	-6	-2				1.000	-1	/C-3	-0.2
	Pro-N	1	3	0	0	0	0	0	0	0	2	.000	.000	.000	-99	-1				.636	-0	/C-1	-0.1
1888	Bos-N	4	16	3	2	0	1	0	2	0		.125	.222	.250	49	-1	0			1.000	-0	/O-3,C-1	-0.1
Total	4	120	451	69	91	20	3	0	26	16	67	.202	.229	.259	51	-25	0			.896	9	/C-99,O-24	-0.9

■ PAUL HINES
Hines, Paul A.   b: 3/1/1852, Washington, D.C.   d: 7/10/35, Hyattsville, Md.   BR/TR, 5'9.5", 173 lbs.   Deb: 4/20/1872

YEAR	TM/L	G	AB	R	H	2B	3B	HR	RBI	BB	SO	AVG	OBP	SLG	PRO+	BR/A	SB	CS	SBR	FA	FR	G/POS	TPR
1872	Nat-n	11	49	9	12	1	0	0	5	0	0	.245	.245	.265	49	-4	0	0	0	.862	-3	/1-9,3-2,C-1	-0.5
1873	Was-n	39	181	33	60	6	3	1	29	1	1	.331	.335	.414	125	6	0	1	-1	.798	-8	*O-36/2-2,C-1	0.4
1874	Chi-n	59	271	47	80	10	2	0	34	4	4	.295	.305	.347	108	2	4	1	1	.877	6	O-50,2-11/S-2	0.7
1875	Chi-n	69	308	45	101	14	4	0	36	1	0	.328	.330	.399	151	15	6	9	-4	.889	9	O-39,2-30/C-1,S-1	1.7
1876	Chi-N	64	305	62	101	**21**	3	2	59	1	3	.331	.333	.439	139	10				**.923**	5	*O-64/2-1	1.2
1877	Chi-N	60	261	44	73	11	7	0	23	1	8	.280	.282	.375	94	-3				.806	-10	O-49,2-11	-1.3
1878	Pro-N	62	257	42	92	13	4	**4**	**50**	2	10	.358	.363	**.486**	178	20				.849	3	O-85	1.8
1879	Pro-N	85	409	81	**146**	25	10	2	52	8	16	.357	.369	.482	181	34				.867	7	*O-75/2-6,1-4	3.3
1880	Pro-N	85	374	64	115	20	2	3	35	13	17	.307	.331	.396	150	19				**.927**	8	*O-75/2-6,1-4	2.4
1881	Pro-N	80	361	65	103	**27**	5	2	31	13	12	.285	.310	.404	125	10				.897	-1	*O-78/2-4,1-1	0.7
1882	Pro-N	84	379	73	117	28	10	4	34	10	14	.309	.326	.467	151	21				.861	1	*O-82/1-2	1.9
1883	Pro-N	97	442	94	132	32	4	4	45	18	23	.299	.326	.416	120	10				.905	7	*O-89/1-9	1.3
1884	*Pro-N	114	490	94	148	**36**	10	3	41	44	28	.302	.360	.435	152	30				.895	2	*O-108/1-7,P-1	2.6
1885	Pro-N	98	411	63	111	20	4	1	35	19	18	.270	.302	.345	114	6				.865	4	*O-92,3-15,1/S2	0.7
1886	Was-N	121	487	80	152	30	8	9	56	35	21	.312	.358	.462	157	33	21			.899	3	*O-92,3-15,1/S2	3.0
1887	Was-N	123	478	83	147	32	5	10	72	48	24	.308	.380	.458	139	27	46			.886	-14	*O-109/1-7,2-5,S-4	0.9
1888	Ind-N	133	513	84	144	26	3	4	58	41	45	.281	.343	.366	124	15	31			.912	-7	*O-125/1-6,S-2	0.4
1889	Ind-N	121	486	77	148	27	1	6	72	49	22	.305	.374	.401	114	10	34			.964	5	*1-109,O-12	0.5
1890	Pit-N	31	121	11	22	1	0	0	9	11	7	.182	.256	.190	34	-10	6			.973	2	1-17,O-14	-0.8
	Bos-N	69	273	41	72	12	3	2	48	32	20	.264	.350	.352	97	-2	9			.881	-12	O-69/1-1	-1.4
	Yr	100	394	52	94	13	3	2	57	43	27	.239	.321	.302	80	-9	15			.871	-10	O-83,1-18	-2.2
1891	Was-a	54	206	25	58	7	5	0	31	21	16	.282	.376	.364	117	6	6			.856	-3	O-47/1-8	0.0
Total	4 n	178	809	134	253	31	9	1	104	6	5	.313	.318	.377	123	19	10	11	-4	.857	11	0-125/2-43,1-9,SC3	2.3
Total	16	1481	6253	1083	1881	368	84	56	751	366	304	.301	.343	.413	133	236	153			.887	-3	*O-1251,1-185/23SP	17.2

■ GORDIE HINKLE
Hinkle, Daniel Gordon   b: 4/3/05, Toronto, Ohio   d: 3/19/72, Houston, Tex.   BR/TR, 6', 185 lbs.   Deb: 4/19/34

YEAR	TM/L	G	AB	R	H	2B	3B	HR	RBI	BB	SO	AVG	OBP	SLG	PRO+	BR/A	SB	CS	SBR	FA	FR	G/POS	TPR
1934	Bos-A	27	75	7	13	6	1	0	9	7	23	.173	.244	.280	33	-8	0	0	0	.992	4	C-26	-0.2

■ GEORGE HINSHAW
Hinshaw, George Addison   b: 10/23/59, Los Angeles, Cal.   BR/TR, 6', 185 lbs.   Deb: 9/19/82

YEAR	TM/L	G	AB	R	H	2B	3B	HR	RBI	BB	SO	AVG	OBP	SLG	PRO+	BR/A	SB	CS	SBR	FA	FR	G/POS	TPR
1982	SD-N	6	15	1	4	0	0	0		3	5	.267	.389	.267	91	0	0	0	0	1.000	0	/O-6	0.0
1983	SD-N	7	16	1	7	1	0	0	4	0	4	.438	.438	.500	165	1	1	0		1.000	-0	/3-5	0.1
Total	2	13	31	2	11	1	0	0	5	3	9	.355	.412	.387	129	1	1	0	0	1.000	0	/O-6,3-5	0.1

■ PAUL HINSON
Hinson, James Paul   b: 5/9/04, Vanleer, Tenn.   d: 9/23/60, Muskogee, Okla.   BR/TR, 5'10", 150 lbs.   Deb: 4/19/28

YEAR	TM/L	G	AB	R	H	2B	3B	HR	RBI	BB	SO	AVG	OBP	SLG	PRO+	BR/A	SB	CS	SBR	FA	FR	G/POS	TPR
1928	Bos-A	3	0	1	0	0	0	0	0	0		—	—	—		0	0	0	0	.000	0	R	0.0

■ CHUCK HINTON
Hinton, Charles Edward   b: 5/3/34, Rocky Mount, N.C.   BR/TR, 6'1", 197 lbs.   Deb: 5/14/61

YEAR	TM/L	G	AB	R	H	2B	3B	HR	RBI	BB	SO	AVG	OBP	SLG	PRO+	BR/A	SB	CS	SBR	FA	FR	G/POS	TPR
1961	Was-A	106	339	51	88	13	5	6	34	40	81	.260	.339	.381	93	-3	22	5	4	.963	0	O-92	-0.4
1962	Was-A	151	542	73	168	25	6	17	75	47	66	.310	.365	.472	124	18	28	10	2	.988	-10	*O-136,2-12/S-1	0.4
1963	Was-A	150	566	80	152	20	12	15	55	64	79	.269	.344	.426	115	11	25	9	2	.989	-1	*O-125,3-19/1-6,S-2	0.6
1964	Was-A★	138	514	71	141	25	7	11	53	57	77	.274	.348	.414	112	8	17	6	2	.985	10	*O-131/3-2	1.4
1965	Cle-A	133	431	59	110	17	6	18	54	53	65	.255	.338	.448	120	11	17	3	3	.966	-9	O-72,1-40,2-23,/3-1	0.3
1966	Cle-A	123	346	48	89	9	3	12	50	35	66	.256	.326	.402	108	3	10	6	-1	.973	-8	*O-104/1-6,2-2	-1.0
1967	Cle-A	147	498	55	122	19	3	10	37	43	100	.245	.306	.355	94	-4	6	8	-3	.976	-13	*O-136/2-5	-2.8
1968	Cal-A	116	267	28	52	10	3	7	23	24	61	.195	.261	.333	82	-6	3	1	0	.987	-6	1-48,O-37,3-13,/2-9	-1.8
1969	Cle-A	94	121	18	31	3	2	4	19	8	22	.256	.308	.388	91	-2	2	0	1	.941	-10	O-40,3-14	-1.2
1970	Cle-A	107	195	24	62	9	0	9	29	25	34	.318	.395	.477	133	9	2	0	-1	.994	-9	1-40,O-35/C-4,23	-0.1
1971	Cle-A	88	147	13	33	5	4	0	14	20	34	.224	.317	.374	87	-2	7	0	0	1.000	-7	1-20,O-20/C-5	-1.2
Total	11	1353	3968	518	1048	152	47	113	443	416	685	.264	.335	.412	108	44	130	50	9	.979	-59	*O-928,1-160/23CS	-5.8

■ JOHN HINTON
Hinton, John Robert "Red"   b: 6/20/1876, Pittsburgh, Pa.   d: 7/19/20, Braddock, Pa.   BR/TR, 6', 200 lbs.   Deb: 6/3/01

YEAR	TM/L	G	AB	R	H	2B	3B	HR	RBI	BB	SO	AVG	OBP	SLG	PRO+	BR/A	SB	CS	SBR	FA	FR	G/POS	TPR
1901	Bos-N	4	13	0	1	0	0	0	0	2		.077	.200	.077	-17	-2	0			.750	-2	/3-4	-0.4

■ TOMMY HINZO
Hinzo, Thomas Lee   b: 6/18/64, San Diego, Cal.   BB/TR, 5'10", 170 lbs.   Deb: 7/16/87

YEAR	TM/L	G	AB	R	H	2B	3B	HR	RBI	BB	SO	AVG	OBP	SLG	PRO+	BR/A	SB	CS	SBR	FA	FR	G/POS	TPR
1987	Cle-A	67	257	31	68	9	3	3	21	10	47	.265	.297	.358	72	-10	9	4	0	.973	-4	2-67	-1.0
1989	Cle-A	18	17	4	0	0	0	0	0	0	6	.000	.105	.000	-67	-4	1	2	-1	.867	0	/2-6,S-1,D-1	-0.4
Total	2	85	274	35	68	9	3	3	21	10	53	.248	.285	.336	64	-14	10	6	-1	.968	-4	/2-73,D-1,S-1	-1.4

■ GENE HISER
Hiser, Gene Taylor   b: 12/11/48, Baltimore, Md.   BL/TL, 5'11", 175 lbs.   Deb: 8/20/71

YEAR	TM/L	G	AB	R	H	2B	3B	HR	RBI	BB	SO	AVG	OBP	SLG	PRO+	BR/A	SB	CS	SBR	FA	FR	G/POS	TPR
1971	Chi-N	17	29	4	6	0	0	0	1	4	8	.207	.303	.207	41	-2	1	0	0	1.000	0	/O-9	-0.2
1972	Chi-N	32	46	2	9	0	0	0	4	6	8	.196	.288	.196	36	-4	1	0	0	1.000	0	O-15	-0.4
1973	Chi-N	100	109	15	19	4	0	0	6	5	33	.174	.256	.220	33	-10	4	5	-2	.980	-18	O-64	-3.2
1974	Chi-N	12	17	2	4	1	0	0	1	0	6	.235	.235	.294	46	-1	0	0	0	1.000	0	/O-8	-0.3
1975	Chi-N	45	62	11	15	3	0	0	6	11	9	.242	.356	.290	77	-1	0	1	-1	1.000	-3	O-18/1-1	-0.5
Total	5	206	263	34	53	7	0	1	18	32	43	.202	.291	.240	46	-18	6	6	-2	.992	-22	O-114/1-1	-4.6

YEAR	TM/L	G	AB	R	H	2B	3B	HR	RBI	BB	SO	AVG	OBP	SLG	PRO+	BR/A	SB	CS	SBR	FA	FR	G/POS	TPR

■ LARRY HISLE
Hisle, Larry Eugene b: 5/5/47, Portsmouth, Ohio BR/TR, 6'2", 195 lbs. Deb: 4/10/68 C

YEAR	TM/L	G	AB	R	H	2B	3B	HR	RBI	BB	SO	AVG	OBP	SLG	PRO+	BR/A	SB	CS	SBR	FA	FR	G/POS	TPR
1968	Phi-N	7	11	1	4	0	0	1	1	4		.364	.417	.455	161	1	0	0	0	1.000	-1	/O-6	0.0
1969	Phi-N	145	482	75	128	23	5	20	56	48	152	.266	.338	.459	125	14	18	8	1	.977	11	*O-140	1.9
1970	Phi-N	126	405	52	83	22	4	10	44	53	139	.205	.302	.353	77	-14	5	5	-2	.978	5	*O-121	-1.6
1971	Phi-N	36	76	7	15	3	0	1	3	6	22	.197	.256	.237	40	-6	1	0	0	.962	-0	O-27	-0.7
1973	Min-A	143	545	88	148	25	6	15	64	64	128	.272	.352	.422	113	10	11	4	1	.975	6	*O-143	1.0
1974	Min-A	143	510	68	146	20	7	19	79	48	112	.286	.357	.465	131	20	12	6	0	.979	-8	*O-137	0.6
1975	Min-A	80	255	37	80	9	2	11	51	27	39	.314	.382	.494	144	15	17	3	3	.976	-7	O-58,D-14	0.8
1976	Min-A	155	581	81	158	19	5	14	96	56	93	.272	.340	.394	112	9	31	18	-2	.984	14	*O-154	1.6
1977	Min-A★	141	546	95	165	36	3	28	119	56	100	.302	.373	.533	146	34	21	10	0	.974	1	*O-134/D-6	2.9
1978	Mil-A★	142	520	96	151	24	0	34	115	66	90	.290	.377	.533	153	36	10	6	-1	.978	-2	O-87,D-51	2.9
1979	Mil-A	26	96	18	27	7	0	3	14	11	19	.281	.355	.448	115	2	1	0	0	1.000	1	D-15,O-10	0.2
1980	Mil-A	17	60	16	17	0	0	6	16	14	7	.283	.427	.583	180	7	0	0	0	.000	0	D-17	0.6
1981	Mil-A	27	87	11	20	4	0	4	11	6	17	.230	.295	.414	108	1	0	0	0	.000	0	D-24	0.0
1982	Mil-A	9	31	7	4	0	0	2	5	5	13	.129	.250	.323	60	-2	0	0	0	.000	0	/D-8	-0.2
Total	14	1197	4205	652	1146	193	32	166	674	462	941	.273	.350	.452	123	126	128	61	2	.978	19	*O-1017,D-135	10.0

■ JIM HITCHCOCK
Hitchcock, James Franklin b: 6/28/11, Inverness, Ala. d: 6/23/59, Montgomery, Ala. BR/TR, 5'11", 175 lbs. Deb: 8/24/38 F

YEAR	TM/L	G	AB	R	H	2B	3B	HR	RBI	BB	SO	AVG	OBP	SLG	PRO+	BR/A	SB	CS	SBR	FA	FR	G/POS	TPR
1938	Bos-N	28	76	2	13	0	0	0	7	2	11	.171	.192	.171	1	-1				.881	-2	S-24/3-2	-1.1

■ BILLY HITCHCOCK
Hitchcock, William Clyde b: 7/31/16, Inverness, Ala. BR/TR, 6'1.5", 185 lbs. Deb: 4/14/42 FMC

YEAR	TM/L	G	AB	R	H	2B	3B	HR	RBI	BB	SO	AVG	OBP	SLG	PRO+	BR/A	SB	CS	SBR	FA	FR	G/POS	TPR
1942	Det-A	85	280	27	59	8	1	0	29	26	21	.211	.280	.246	45	-20	2	2	-1	.944	-3	S-80/3-1	-2.0
1946	Det-A	3	3	0	0	0	0	0	0	1	0	.000	.250	.000	-25	-0	0	0	0	1.000	0	/2-1	0.0
	Was-A	98	354	27	75	8	3	0	25	26	52	.212	.268	.251	48	-25	2	4	-2	.966	-4	S-53,3-46	-2.8
	Yr	101	357	27	75	8	3	0	25	27	52	.210	.268	.249	48	-25	2	4	-3	.966	-3	S-53,3-46/2-1	-2.8
1947	StL-A	80	275	25	61	2	2	1	28	21	34	.222	.277	.255	47	-19	3	0	1	.977	11	2-46,3-17/S-7,1-5	-0.4
1948	Bos-A	49	124	15	37	3	2	1	20	7	9	.298	.341	.387	79	-3	0	0	0	.951	6	2-15,3-15	0.4
1949	Bos-A	55	147	22	30	6	1	0	9	17	11	.204	.291	.259	43	-12	2	3	-1	.993	-8	1-29/2-8	-2.1
1950	Phi-A	115	399	35	109	22	5	1	54	45	32	.273	.347	.361	83	-10	3	1	0	.967	-3	*2-107/S-1	-0.7
1951	Phi-A	77	222	27	68	10	4	1	36	21	23	.306	.371	.401	107	2	2	0	1	.929	7	3-45,2-23/1-1	1.0
1952	Phi-A	119	407	45	100	8	4	1	56	39	45	.246	.318	.292	66	-18	1	1	-0	.942	-1	*3-104,1-13	-2.2
1953	Det-A	22	38	8	8	0	0	0	3	3	3	.211	.268	.211	31	-4	0	0	0	.929	-1	3-12/2-1,S-1	-0.4
Total	9	703	2249	231	547	67	22	5	257	206	230	.243	.310	.299	65	-109	15	11	-2	.938	7	3-240,2-201,S/1	-9.2

■ MYRIL HOAG
Hoag, Myril Oliver b: 3/9/08, Davis, Cal. d: 7/28/71, High Springs, Fla BR/TR, 5'11", 180 lbs. Deb: 4/15/31

YEAR	TM/L	G	AB	R	H	2B	3B	HR	RBI	BB	SO	AVG	OBP	SLG	PRO+	BR/A	SB	CS	SBR	FA	FR	G/POS	TPR
1931	NY-A	44	28	6	4	2	0	0	3	1	8	.143	.172	.214	1	-4	0	0	0	1.000	-7	O-23/3-1	-1.0
1932	*NY-A	46	54	18	20	5	0	1	7	7	13	.370	.443	.519	156	5	1	1	-0	.962	-10	O-35/1-1	-0.6
1934	NY-A	97	251	45	67	8	3	2	34	21	21	.267	.324	.351	79	-8	1	3	-2	.974	-9	O-86	-2.0
1935	NY-A	48	110	13	28	4	1	1	13	12	19	.255	.328	.336	76	-4	4	2	0	.986	-2	O-37/3-1	-0.6
1936	NY-A	45	156	23	47	9	4	3	34	7	16	.301	.343	.468	102	-0	3	1	0	.955	-4	O-39	-0.5
1937	*NY-A	106	362	48	109	19	8	3	46	33	33	.301	.364	.423	97	-2	4	7	-3	.955	-6	O-99	-1.3
1938	*NY-A	85	267	28	74	14	3	0	48	25	31	.277	.344	.352	75	-10	4	3	-1	.965	-4	O-70	-1.6
1939	StL-A★	129	482	58	142	23	4	10	75	24	35	.295	.329	.421	89	-10	9	5	-0	.971	-8	*O-117/P-1	-2.0
1940	StL-A	76	191	20	50	11	0	3	26	13	30	.262	.309	.366	73	-8	2	0	1	.971	-6	O-46	-1.5
1941	StL-A	1	1	0	0	0	0	0	0	0	0	.000	.000	.000	-97	-0	0	0	0	.000	0	H	0.0
	Chi-A	106	380	30	97	13	5	1	44	27	29	.255	.306	.313	65	-19	6	10	-4	.957	-6	O-99	-3.4
	Yr	107	381	30	97	13	5	1	44	27	29	.255	.306	.312	65	-20	6	10	-4	.957	-6	O-99	-3.4
1942	Chi-A	113	412	47	99	18	2	2	37	36	21	.240	.301	.308	73	-15	17	8	0	.972	-4	*O-112	-2.6
1944	Chi-A	17	48	5	11	1	0	0	4	10	1	.229	.362	.250	77	-1	1	3	-2	.969	-1	O-14	-0.4
	Cle-A	67	277	34	79	9	3	1	27	25	23	.285	.347	.350	103	1	6	4	-1	.947	-1	O-66	-0.4
	Yr	84	325	38	90	10	3	1	31	35	24	.277	.349	.335	99	0	7	7	-2	.950	-2	O-80	-0.8
1945	Cle-A	40	128	10	27	5	3	0	3	11	18	.211	.279	.297	70	-5	1	2	-1	.987	0	O-33/P-2	-0.8
Total	13	1020	3147	384	854	141	33	28	401	252	298	.271	.328	.364	83	-80	59	49	-12	.965	-67	O-876/P-3,3-2,1-1	-18.7

■ DON HOAK
Hoak, Donald Albert "Tiger" b: 2/5/28, Roulette, Pa. d: 10/9/69, Pittsburgh, Pa. BR/TR, 6', 175 lbs. Deb: 4/18/54 C

YEAR	TM/L	G	AB	R	H	2B	3B	HR	RBI	BB	SO	AVG	OBP	SLG	PRO+	BR/A	SB	CS	SBR	FA	FR	G/POS	TPR
1954	Bro-N	88	261	41	64	9	5	7	26	25	39	.245	.321	.398	83	-7	8	3	1	.950	4	3-75	-0.3
1955	*Bro-N	94	279	50	67	13	5	5	19	46	50	.240	.350	.362	87	-4	9	5	-0	.960	17	3-78	1.2
1956	Chi-N	121	424	50	91	18	4	5	37	41	46	.215	.285	.311	61	-23	8	3	1	.949	-18	*3-110	-4.1
1957	Cin-N★	149	529	78	155	39	2	19	89	74	54	.293	.384	.482	122	18	8	15	-7	.971	-0	*3-149/2-1	1.4
1958	Cin-N	114	417	51	109	30	0	6	50	43	36	.261	.333	.376	83	-10	3	4	-1	.964	4	*3-112/S-1	-0.8
1959	Pit-N	155	564	60	166	29	5	6	65	71	75	.294	.377	.399	108	9	9	2	2	.961	9	*3-155	2.0
1960	*Pit-N	155	553	97	156	24	9	16	79	74	74	.282	.368	.445	120	17	3	2	-0	.948	4	*3-155	2.0
1961	Pit-N	145	503	72	150	27	5	12	61	73	53	.298	.390	.451	122	18	4	3	-3	.953	-3	*3-143	1.6
1962	Pit-N	121	411	63	99	14	2	5	48	49	49	.241	.323	.350	81	-11	4	2	0	.969	-3	*3-116	-1.2
1963	Pit-N	115	377	35	87	11	3	6	24	27	52	.231	.284	.324	75	-12	5	5	-2	.958	6	*3-106	-0.8
1964	Phi-N	6	4	0	0	0	0	0	0	0	2	.000	.000	.000	-99	-1	0	0	0	.000	0	H	-0.1
Total	11	1263	4322	598	1144	214	44	89	498	523	530	.265	.347	.396	98	-6	64	47	-9	.959	20	*3-1199/S-1,2-1	0.9

■ BILL HOBBS
Hobbs, William Lee "Smokey" b: 5/7/1893, Grants Lick, Ky. d: 1/5/45, Hamilton, Ohio BR/TR, 5'9.5", 155 lbs. Deb: 8/9/13

YEAR	TM/L	G	AB	R	H	2B	3B	HR	RBI	BB	SO	AVG	OBP	SLG	PRO+	BR/A	SB	CS	SBR	FA	FR	G/POS	TPR
1913	Cin-N	4	4	0	0	0	0	0	0	0	3	.000	.000	.000	-99	-1	0			1.000	1	/2-1,3-1	0.0
1916	Cin-N	6	11	1	2	1	0	0	1	2	0	.182	.308	.273	81	-0	1			.947	6	/S-6	0.6
Total	2	10	15	1	2	1	0	0	1	2	3	.133	.235	.200	32	-1	1			.947	6	/S-6,3-1,2-1	0.6

■ DICK HOBLITZEL
Hoblitzel, Richard Carleton "Doc" (b: Richard Carleton Hoblitzell) b: 10/26/1888, Waverly, W.Va. d: 11/14/62, Parkersburg, W.Va. BL/TL, 6', 172 lbs. Deb: 9/5/08

YEAR	TM/L	G	AB	R	H	2B	3B	HR	RBI	BB	SO	AVG	OBP	SLG	PRO+	BR/A	SB	CS	SBR	FA	FR	G/POS	TPR
1908	Cin-N	32	114	8	29	3	2	0	8	7		.254	.309	.316	102	0	2			.985	2	1-32	0.1
1909	Cin-N	142	517	59	159	23	11	4	67	44		.308	.364	.418	144	25	17			.982	-3	*1-142	2.3
1910	Cin-N	155	611	85	170	24	13	4	70	47	32	.278	.332	.380	112	7	28			.984	-8	*1-148/2-7	-0.1
1911	Cin-N	158	622	81	180	19	13	11	91	42	44	.289	.342	.415	116	10	32			.990	2	*1-158	1.2
1912	Cin-N	148	558	73	164	32	12	2	85	48	28	.294	.352	.405	110	7	23			.985	2	*1-147	0.6
1913	Cin-N	137	502	59	143	23	7	3	62	35	26	.285	.334	.376	103	1	18			.988	-5	*1-134	-0.6
1914	Cin-N	78	248	31	52	8	7	0	26	26	26	.210	.287	.298	72	-9	7			.988	-4	1-75	-1.6
	Bos-A	69	229	31	73	10	3	0	33	19	21	.319	.386	.389	133	9	12	12	-4	.979	-5	1-68	-0.1
1915	*Bos-A	124	399	54	113	15	12	2	61	38	26	.283	.351	.396	128	13	9	14	-6	.987	-1	*1-117	0.3
1916	*Bos-A	130	417	57	108	17	1	0	39	47	28	.259	.338	.305	93	-3	10			.989	-1	*1-126	-0.9
1917	Bos-A	120	420	49	108	19	7	1	47	46	22	.257	.336	.343	108	4	12			.990	-8	*1-118	-0.9
1918	Bos-A	25	69	4	11	1	0	0	4	8	3	.159	.266	.174	33	-5	3			.996	1	1-19	-0.6
Total	11	1318	4706	591	1310	194	88	27	593	407	256	.278	.341	.374	111	61	173	26		.987	-29	*1-1284/2-7	-0.3

■ BUTCH HOBSON
Hobson, Clell Lavern b: 8/17/51, Tuscaloosa, Ala. BR/TR, 6'1", 193 lbs. Deb: 9/7/75 M

YEAR	TM/L	G	AB	R	H	2B	3B	HR	RBI	BB	SO	AVG	OBP	SLG	PRO+	BR/A	SB	CS	SBR	FA	FR	G/POS	TPR
1975	Bos-A	2	4	0	1	0	0	0	0	0	2	.250	.250	.250	38	-0	0	0	0	1.000	1	/3-1	0.0
1976	Bos-A	76	269	34	63	7	5	8	34	15	62	.234	.275	.387	82	-7	0	1	-1	.936	-7	3-76	-1.7
1977	Bos-A	159	593	77	157	33	5	30	112	27	162	.265	.301	.489	100	-3	5	4	-1	.946	-28	*3-159	-3.4
1978	Bos-A	147	512	65	128	26	2	17	80	50	122	.250	.317	.408	92	-6	1	0	0	.899	-14	*3-133,D-14	-2.3
1979	Bos-A	146	528	74	138	26	7	28	93	30	78	.261	.301	.496	105	1	3	2	0	.935	-21	*3-142/2-1	-2.1
1980	Bos-A	93	324	35	74	6	0	11	39	25	69	.228	.284	.349	69	-14	1	1	-0	.910	-9	3-57,D-36	-2.6
1981	Cal-A	85	268	27	63	7	4	4	36	35	60	.235	.326	.336	91	-1	1	1	-0	.929	-11	3-83/D-2	-1.7
1982	NY-A	30	58	2	10	2	0	0	3	1	14	.172	.186	.207	8	-7	0	0	0	.951	-1	D-15,1-11	-0.9
Total	8	738	2556	314	634	107	23	98	397	183	569	.248	.300	.423	91	-40	11	9	-2	.926	-90	3-651/D-67,1-11,2-1	-14.7

YEAR	TM/L	G	AB	R	H	2B	3B	HR	RBI	BB	SO	AVG	OBP	SLG	PRO+	BR/A	SB	CS	SBR	FA	FR	G/POS	TPR

■ ED HOCK   Hock, Edward Francis   b: 3/27/1899, Franklin Furnace, Ohio   d: 11/21/63, Portsmouth, Ohio   BL/TL, 5'10.5", 165 lbs.   Deb: 7/8/20

1920	StL-N	1	0	0	0	0	0	0	0	0	0	—	—	—	—	0	0	0	0	.000	-1	/O-1	-0.1
1923	Cin-N	2	0	0	0	0	0	0	0	0	0	—	—	—	—	0	0	0	0	.000	0	R	0.0
1924	Cin-N	16	10	7	1	0	0	0	0	0	2	.100	.182	.100	-23	-2	0	0	0	1.000	-0	/O-2	-0.2
Total	3	19	10	7	1	0	0	0	0	0	2	.100	.182	.100	-23	-2	0	0	0	1.000	-1	/O-3	-0.3

■ ORIS HOCKETT   Hockett, Oris Leon "Brown"   b: 9/29/09, Amboy, Ind.   d: 3/23/69, Torrance, Cal.   BL/TR, 5'9", 182 lbs.   Deb: 9/4/38

1938	Bro-N	21	70	8	23	5	1	8	4	9	.329	.365	.471	126	2	0			.893	-4	O-17	-0.2
1939	Bro-N	9	13	3	3	0	0	0	1	1	1	.231	.286	.231	39	-1	0			1.000	-1	/O-1	-0.1
1941	Cle-A	2	6	0	2	0	0	0	1	2	0	.333	.500	.333	131	0	0			1.000	-1	/O-2	0.0
1942	Cle-A	148	601	85	150	22	7	7	48	45	45	.250	.305	.344	88	-12	12	12	-4	.980	-2	*O-145	-2.6
1943	Cle-A	141	601	70	166	33	4	2	51	45	45	.276	.331	.354	107	4	13	18	-7	.960	1	*O-139	-1.0
1944	Cle-A☆	124	457	47	132	29	5	1	50	35	27	.289	.339	.381	110	5	8	9	-3	.986	-4	*O-110	-0.8
1945	Chi-A	106	417	46	122	23	4	2	55	27	30	.293	.340	.381	112	5	10	9	-2	.982	1	*O-106	-0.1
Total	7	551	2165	259	598	112	21	13	214	159	157	.276	.329	.365	103	3	43	48		.974	-6	O-520	-4.8

■ DENNIS HOCKING   Hocking, Dennis Lee   b: 4/2/70, Torrance, Cal.   BB/TR, 5'10", 180 lbs.   Deb: 9/10/93

1993	Min-A	15	36	7	5	1	0	0	6	8	.139	.262	.167	18	-4	1	0	0	.971	-2	S-12/2-1	-0.5
1994	Min-A	11	31	3	10	3	0	2	0	6	5	.323	.323	.419	89	-1	2	0	1	1.000	1	S-10	0.1
1995	Min-A	9	25	4	5	0	2	0	3	2	2	.200	.259	.360	59	-2	1	0	0	.971	-1	/S-6	0.0
1996	Min-A	49	127	16	25	6	0	1	10	8	24	.197	.244	.268	29	-14	3	3	-1	.985	1	/S-34,O-33,2-3,D1	-1.3
Total	4	84	219	30	45	10	2	1	15	16	38	.205	.260	.283	39	-20	7	3	0	.982	0	/S-34,O-33,2-3,D1	-1.7

■ JOHNNY HODAPP   Hodapp, Urban John   b: 9/26/05, Cincinnati, Ohio   d: 6/14/80, Cincinnati, Ohio   BR/TR, 6', 185 lbs.   Deb: 8/19/25

1925	Cle-A	37	130	12	31	5	1	0	14	11	7	.238	.298	.292	50	-10	2	3	-1	.960	3	3-37	-0.5
1926	Cle-A	3	5	0	1	0	0	0	0	0	1	.200	.200	.200	4	-1	0	0	0	.750	-1	/3-3	-0.1
1927	Cle-A	79	240	25	73	15	3	5	40	14	23	.304	.343	.454	105	1	2	2	-1	.935	1	3-67/1-4	0.3
1928	Cle-A	116	449	51	145	31	6	2	73	20	20	.323	.352	.432	104	2	2	1	0	.944	-2	*3-101,1-13	0.4
1929	Cle-A	90	294	30	96	12	7	4	51	15	14	.327	.361	.456	105	2	3	3	-1	.977	5	2-72	0.8
1930	Cle-A	154	635	111	**225**	51	8	9	121	32	29	.354	.386	.502	119	17	6	5	-1	.970	12	*2-154	3.2
1931	Cle-A	122	468	71	138	19	4	2	56	27	23	.295	.336	.365	80	-14	1	5	-3	.969	16	*2-121	0.7
1932	Cle-A	7	16	2	2	1	0	0	0	0	2	.125	.125	.188	-19	-2	0	0	0	1.000	1	/2-7	-0.4
	Chi-A	68	176	21	40	8	0	3	20	11	3	.227	.273	.324	58	-12	1	0	0	.967	-5	O-31/2-5,3-4	-1.7
	Yr	75	192	23	42	9	0	3	20	11	5	.219	.261	.313	51	-15	1	0	0	.967	-7	O-31,2-12/3-4	-2.1
1933	Bos-A	115	413	55	129	27	5	3	54	33	14	.312	.365	.424	109	5	1	1	-0	.960	3	*2-101,1-10	1.2
Total	9	791	2826	378	880	169	34	28	429	163	136	.311	.350	.425	98	-13	18	20	-7	.967	30	2-460,3-212/O-31,1	3.9

■ MEL HODERLEIN   Hoderlein, Melvin Anthony   b: 6/24/23, Mt.Carmel, Ohio   BB/TR, 5'10", 185 lbs.   Deb: 8/16/51

1951	Bos-A	9	14	1	5	1	1	0	6	2	3	.357	.550	.571	185	1	0	1	-1	1.000	1	/2-3,3-3	0.2
1952	Was-A	72	208	16	56	8	2	0	17	18	22	.269	.333	.327	87	-3	2	0	1	.978	-2	2-58	-0.2
1953	Was-A	23	47	5	9	0	0	0	5	6	9	.191	.283	.191	31	-4	0	0	0	.953	-3	2-11/S-2	-0.7
1954	Was-A	14	25	0	4	1	0	0	1	1	4	.160	.192	.200	8	-3	0	0	0	.939	1	/S-6,2-5	-0.1
Total	4	118	294	22	74	10	3	0	24	31	37	.252	.327	.306	78	-9	2	1	0	.973	-3	/2-77,S-8,3-3	-0.8

■ CHARLIE HODES   Hodes, Charles   b: 1848, New York, N.Y.   d: 2/14/1875, Brooklyn, N.Y.   TR, 5'11.5", 175 lbs.   Deb: 5/8/1871

1871	Chi-n	28	130	32	36	4	1	2	25	7	0	.277	.314	.369	86	-4	3	0	1	.796	3	*C-20,3-10/O-4,S-1	-0.1
1872	Tro-n	13	61	17	15	3	0	0	12	1	0	.246	.258	.295	69	-2	0	0	0	.759	-3	S-5,O-4,C-3,3-1	-0.2
1874	Atl-n	21	81	8	12	3	0	0	7	0	2	.148	.148	.185	7	-7	0	0	0	.786	-4	O-19/C-3,2-3,1-1	-0.9
Total	3 n	62	272	57	63	10	1	2	44	8	2	.232	.254	.298	64	-14	3	0	1	.788	-1	/O-27,C-26,3S21	-1.2

■ BERT HODGE   Hodge, Edward Burton   b: 5/25/17, Knoxville, Tenn.   BL/TR, 5'11", 170 lbs.   Deb: 4/14/42

| 1942 | Phi-N | 8 | 11 | 0 | 2 | 0 | 0 | 0 | 1 | 0 | 1 | .182 | .250 | .182 | 29 | -1 | 0 | | | 1.000 | -1 | /3-2 | -0.2 |

■ GOMER HODGE   Hodge, Harold Morris   b: 4/3/44, Rutherfordton, N.C.   BB/TR, 6'2", 185 lbs.   Deb: 4/6/71

| 1971 | Cle-A | 80 | 83 | 3 | 17 | 3 | 0 | 1 | 9 | 4 | 19 | .205 | .258 | .277 | 47 | -6 | 0 | 0 | 0 | 1.000 | -2 | /1-3,3,3-3,2-2 | -0.8 |

■ GIL HODGES   Hodges, Gilbert Raymond (b: Gilbert Ray Hodge)   b: 4/4/24, Princeton, Ind.   d: 4/2/72, West Palm Beach, Fla   BR/TR, 6'1.5", 200 lbs.   Deb: 10/3/43   M

1943	Bro-N	1	2	0	0	0	0	0	0	1	2	.000	.333	.000	0	-0	1			.600	0	/3-1	0.0
1947	*Bro-N	28	77	9	12	3	1	1	7	14	19	.156	.286	.260	44	-6	0			.958	-2	C-24	-0.7
1948	Bro-N	134	481	48	120	18	5	11	70	43	61	.249	.311	.376	82	-13	7			.986	-4	1-96,C-38	-1.2
1949	*Bro-N★	156	596	94	170	23	4	23	115	66	64	.285	.360	.453	112	10	10			**.995**	-4	*1-156	0.5
1950	Bro-N☆	153	561	98	159	26	2	32	113	73	73	.283	.367	.508	125	20	6			**.994**	1	*1-153	1.6
1951	Bro-N★	158	582	118	156	25	3	40	103	93	99	.268	.374	.527	137	30	9	7	-2	.992	7	*1-158	2.9
1952	*Bro-N☆	153	508	87	129	27	1	32	102	107	90	.254	.386	.500	142	31	2	4	-2	.992	5	*1-153	3.0
1953	*Bro-N★	141	520	101	157	22	7	31	122	75	84	.302	.393	.550	139	31	1	4	-2	.993	8	*1-127,O-24	2.9
1954	Bro-N★	154	579	106	176	23	5	42	130	74	84	.304	.384	.579	142	35	3	3	-1	.995	9	*1-154	3.4
1955	*Bro-N★	150	546	75	158	24	5	27	102	80	91	.289	.383	.500	128	23	2	1	0	.991	1	*1-139,O-16	1.6
1956	*Bro-N	153	550	86	146	29	4	32	87	76	91	.265	.355	.507	119	15	3	3	-1	.992	1	*1-138,O-30/C-1	0.6
1957	Bro-N★	150	579	94	173	28	7	27	98	63	91	.299	.370	.511	122	18	5	3	-0	.990	2	*1-150/3-2,2-1	1.0
1958	LA-N	141	475	68	123	15	1	22	64	52	87	.259	.332	.434	98	-2	8	2	1	.992	1	*1-122,3-15/O-9,C-1	-0.7
1959	*LA-N	124	413	57	114	19	2	25	80	58	92	.276	.369	.513	123	14	3	2	-0	**.992**	0	*1-113/3-4	0.6
1960	LA-N	101	197	22	39	8	1	8	30	26	37	.198	.295	.371	76	-7	0	1	-1	.995	1	1-92,3-10	-1.0
1961	LA-N	109	215	25	52	4	0	8	31	24	43	.242	.318	.372	76	-7	3	1	0	.998	1	*1-100	-1.1
1962	NY-N	54	127	15	32	1	0	9	17	15	27	.252	.331	.472	111	2	0	0	0	.986	-2	1-47	0.3
1963	NY-N	11	22	2	5	0	0	0	3	3	2	.227	.320	.227	60	-1	0	0	0	1.000	1	1-10	0.0
Total	18	2071	7030	1105	1921	295	48	370	1274	943	1137	.273	.361	.487	119	191	63	31		.992	34	*1-1908/O-79,C32	13.7

■ RON HODGES   Hodges, Ronald Wray   b: 6/22/49, Rocky Mount, Va.   BL/TR, 6'1", 185 lbs.   Deb: 6/13/73

1973	*NY-N	45	127	5	33	2	1	0	18	11	19	.260	.319	.299	73	-4	0	1	-1	.992	2	C-40	-0.1
1974	NY-N	59	136	16	30	4	0	4	14	19	11	.221	.316	.338	84	-3	0	0	0	.953	-2	C-44	-0.3
1975	NY-N	9	34	3	7	1	0	2	4	1	6	.206	.229	.412	79	-1	0	0	0	1.000	0	/C-9	-0.1
1976	NY-N	56	155	21	35	6	0	4	24	27	16	.226	.341	.342	100	1	2	0	0	.976	-9	C-52	-0.7
1977	NY-N	66	117	6	31	5	0	0	5	19	17	.265	.317	.325	76	-4	0	2	-1	.992	-0	C-27	-0.5
1978	NY-N	47	102	4	26	4	1	0	7	10	11	.255	.327	.314	83	-2	1	0	0	.982	6	C-30	0.4
1979	NY-N	59	86	4	14	4	0	0	5	19	16	.163	.314	.209	47	-6	0	0	0	.980	1	C-22	-0.4
1980	NY-N	36	42	4	10	2	0	0	5	10	13	.238	.385	.286	92	0	1	1	-0	.982	4	/C-7	0.4
1981	NY-N	35	43	5	13	2	0	1	6	5	8	.302	.375	.419	127	2	1	0	0	1.000	-1	/C-9	0.1
1982	NY-N	80	228	26	56	12	1	5	27	41	40	.246	.361	.373	106	3	4	3	-1	.980	-4	C-74	0.5
1983	NY-N	110	250	20	65	12	0	1	21	49	42	.260	.385	.308	95	1	3	2	-2	.971	-10	C-96	-0.7
1984	NY-N	64	106	5	22	3	0	1	13	23	18	.208	.354	.264	77	-2	1	3	-2	.979	-1	C-35	-0.2
Total	12	666	1426	119	342	56	2	19	147	224	217	.240	.345	.322	88	-16	10	13	-5	.978	-9	C-445	-1.6

■ RALPH HODGIN   Hodgin, Elmer Ralph   b: 2/10/16, Greensboro, N.C.   BL/TR, 5'10", 170 lbs.   Deb: 4/19/39

1939	Bos-N	32	48	4	10	1	0	0	4	3	4	.208	.255	.229	33	-5	0			1.000	-1	/O-9	-0.6
1943	Chi-A	117	407	52	128	22	8	1	50	20	24	.314	.356	.415	123	12	3	5	-2	.945	-7	3-56,O-42	0.2
1944	Chi-A	121	465	56	137	25	7	1	51	21	14	.295	.333	.385	106	3	1	0	0	.942	12	3-82,O-33	1.5
1946	Chi-A	87	258	32	65	10	1	0	25	19	6	.252	.308	.298	73	-9	0	1	-1	.983	-2	O-57	-1.6
1947	Chi-A	59	180	26	53	10	3	1	24	13	4	.294	.332	.400	113	3	1	0	0	.990	1	O-41	0.2
1948	Chi-A	114	331	28	88	11	5	1	34	21	11	.266	.310	.338	75	-13	0	3	-1	.970	4	O-79	-1.4
Total	6	530	1689	198	481	79	24	4	188	97	63	.285	.330	.367	98	-10	5	10		.985	7	O-261,3-138	-1.7

YEAR	TM/L	G	AB	R	H	2B	3B	HR	RBI	BB	SO	AVG	OBP	SLG	PRO+	BR/A	SB	CS	SBR	FA	FR	G/POS	TPR

■ PAUL HODGSON
Hodgson, Paul Joseph Denis   b: 4/14/60, Montreal, Que., Can.   BR/TR, 6'2", 190 lbs.   Deb: 8/31/80

1980	Tor-A	20	41	5	9	0	1	1	5	3	12	.220	.273	.341	64	-2	0	1	-1	1.000	-0	O-11/D-3	-0.3

■ ART HOELSKOETTER
Hoelskoetter, Arthur "Holley" or "Hoss" (a.k.a. Arthur H. Hostetter)
b: 9/30/1882, St.Louis, Mo.   d: 8/3/54, St.Louis, Mo.   BR/TR, 6'2".   Deb: 9/10/05

1905	StL-N	24	83	7	20	2	1	0	5	3		.241	.267	.289	68	-3	1			.972	1	3-20/2-3,P-1	-0.2
1906	StL-N	94	317	21	71	6	3	0	14	4		.224	.238	.262	58	-17	2			.943	-6	3-53,S-16,P-12,O/2	-2.1
1907	StL-N	119	397	21	98	6	3	2	28	27		.247	.298	.292	88	-6	5			.927	10	2-73,1-27/C-8,OP3	0.4
1908	StL-N	62	155	10	36	7	1	0	6	6		.232	.265	.290	81	-4	1			.948	0	C-41/3-2,1-1,2-1	0.0
Total	4	299	952	59	225	21	8	2	53	40		.236	.271	.282	75	-30	9			.924	5	/2-78,3-77,C1OSP	-1.9

■ JACK HOEY
Hoey, John Bernard   b: 11/10/1881, Watertown, Mass.   d: 11/14/47, Waterbury, Conn.   BL/TL, 5'9", 185 lbs.   Deb: 6/27/06

1906	Bos-A	94	361	27	88	8	1	0	24	14		.244	.274	.288	76	-10	10			.915	-8	O-94	-2.5
1907	Bos-A	39	96	7	21	2	1	0	8	1		.219	.227	.260	56	-5	2			.857	-5	O-21	-1.3
1908	Bos-A	13	43	5	7	0	0	0	3	0		.163	.163	.163	6	-4	1			1.000	-0	O-11	-0.6
Total	3	146	500	39	116	10	5	0	35	15		.232	.256	.272	66	-20	13			.913	-13	O-126	-4.4

■ STEW HOFFERTH
Hofferth, Stewart Edward   b: 1/27/13, Logansport, Ind.   d: 3/7/94, Valparaiso, Ind.   BR/TR, 6'2", 195 lbs.   Deb: 4/19/44

1944	Bos-N	66	180	14	36	8	0	1	26	11	5	.200	.246	.261	41	-14	0			.984	1	C-47	-1.2
1945	Bos-N	50	170	13	40	2	0	3	15	14	11	.235	.297	.300	66	-8	1			.980	6	C-45	0.1
1946	Bos-N	20	58	3	12	1	1	0	10	3	6	.207	.248	.259	43	-4	0			1.000	-1	C-15	-0.5
Total	3	136	408	30	88	11	1	4	51	28	22	.216	.268	.277	52	-26	1			.985	6	C-107	-1.6

■ DUTCH HOFFMAN
Hoffman, Clarence Casper "Red"   b: 1/28/04, Freeburg, Ill.   d: 12/6/62, Belleville, Ill.   BR/TR, 6', 175 lbs.   Deb: 4/23/29

1929	Chi-A	107	337	27	87	16	5	3	37	24	28	.258	.307	.362	73	-14	6	3	0	.984	-1	O-88	-2.0

■ DANNY HOFFMAN
Hoffman, Daniel John   b: 3/2/1880, Canton, Conn.   d: 3/14/22, Manchester, Conn.   BL/TL, 5'9", 175 lbs.   Deb: 4/20/03

1903	Phi-A	74	248	29	61	5	7	2	22	6		.246	.267	.347	79	-7	7			.950	0	O-62/P-1	-1.0
1904	Phi-A	53	204	31	61	7	5	3	24	5		.299	.329	.426	131	6	9			.936	0	O-51	0.4
1905	*Phi-A	120	459	66	120	10	10	1	35	33		.261	.312	.333	103	1	**46**			.942	-2	*O-118	-0.7
1906	Phi-A	7	22	4	5	0	0	0	3			.227	.320	.227	70	-1	1			1.000	1	/O-7	0.0
	NY-A	100	320	34	82	10	6	0	23	27		.256	.318	.325	92	-3	32			.938	-9	O-98	-1.8
	Yr	107	342	38	87	10	6	0	23	30		.254	.318	.319	91	-4	33			.943	-8	*O-105	-1.8
1907	NY-A	136	517	81	131	10	3	5	46	42		.253	.325	.313	96	-2	30			.953	8	*O-135	0.1
1908	StL-A	99	363	41	91	9	7	1	25	23		.251	.304	.322	103	1	17			.962	11	O-99	0.9
1909	StL-A	110	387	44	104	6	7	2	26	41		.269	.349	.336	125	12	24			.968	2	*O-110	1.1
1910	StL-A	106	380	20	90	11	5	0	27	34		.237	.306	.292	93	-3	16			.960	1	O-106	-0.8
1911	StL-A	24	81	11	17	3	2	0	7	12		.210	.326	.296	77	-2	3			.908	3	O-23	-0.6
Total	9	829	2981	361	762	71	52	14	235	226		.256	.316	.328	101	4	185			.951	15	O-809/P-1	-1.8

■ TEX HOFFMAN
Hoffman, Edward Adolph   b: 11/30/1893, San Antonio, Tex.   d: 5/19/47, New Orleans, La.   BL/TR, 5'9", 195 lbs.   Deb: 7/11/15

1915	Cle-A	9	13	1	2	0	0	0	1	2	5	.154	.214	.154	10	-1	0			.750	-2	/3-3	-0.3

■ GLENN HOFFMAN
Hoffman, Glenn Edward   b: 7/7/58, Orange, Cal.   BR/TR, 6'2", 190 lbs.   Deb: 4/12/80   F

1980	Bos-A	114	312	37	89	15	4	4	42	19	41	.285	.330	.397	94	-3	2	4	-2	.946	-0	*3-110/S-5,2-2	-0.6
1981	Bos-A	78	242	28	56	10	0	1	20	12	25	.231	.271	.285	57	-13	0	1	-1	.960	5	S-78/3-1	-0.1
1982	Bos-A	150	469	53	98	23	4	7	49	30	69	.209	.264	.311	54	-30	0	4	-2	.972	13	*S-150	-0.6
1983	Bos-A	143	473	56	123	24	1	4	41	30	76	.260	.307	.340	73	-18	1	1	-0	.962	-6	*S-143	-1.0
1984	Bos-A	64	74	8	14	4	0	0	4	5	10	.189	.241	.243	33	-7	0	1	-1	.957	5	S-56/3-4,2-2	0.0
1985	Bos-A	96	279	40	77	17	2	6	34	25	40	.276	.346	.416	103	1	2	2	-1	.975	-1	S-93/2-3,3-3	0.8
1986	Bos-A	12	23	1	5	2	0	0	1	2	3	.217	.280	.304	59	-1	0	0	-0	.923	-2	S-11/3-1	-0.3
1987	Bos-A	21	55	5	11	3	0	0	6	3	9	.200	.267	.255	38	-5	0	0	-0	.984	2	S-16/3-3,2-2	-0.1
	LA-N	40	132	10	29	5	0	0	10	7	23	.220	.270	.258	42	-11	0	1	-1	.966	1	S-40	-0.7
1989	Cal-A	48	104	9	22	3	0	1	3	3	13	.212	.241	.269	44	-8	0	1	-1	.982	3	S-23,3-18/2-4,1D	-0.5
Total	9	766	2163	247	524	106	9	23	204	136	309	.242	.293	.331	68	-94	5	16	-8	.966	21	S-615,3-140/2D1	-3.1

■ IZZY HOFFMAN
Hoffman, Harry C.   b: 1/5/1875, Bridgeport, N.J.   d: 11/13/42, Philadelphia, Pa.   BL/TL, 5'9", 160 lbs.   Deb: 4/14/04

1904	Was-A	10	30	1	3	1	0	0	1	2		.100	.156	.133	8	-4	0			1.000	1	/O-9	-0.4
1907	Bos-N	19	86	17	24	3	1	0	3	6		.279	.326	.337	108	1	2			.897	-2	O-19	-0.2
Total	2	29	116	18	27	4	1	0	4	8		.233	.282	.284	79	-3	2			.939	-1	/O-28	-0.6

■ JOHN HOFFMAN
Hoffman, John Edward "Pork Chop"   b: 10/31/43, Aberdeen, S.D.   BL/TR, 6', 190 lbs.   Deb: 7/30/64

1964	Hou-N	6	15	1	1	0	0	0	0	1	7	.067	.125	.067	-47	-3	0	0	0	1.000	-2	/C-5	-0.5
1965	Hou-N	2	6	1	2	0	0	0	1	0	3	.333	.333	.333	95	-0	0	0	0	1.000	-1	/C-2	-0.1
Total	2	8	21	2	3	0	0	0	1	1	10	.143	.182	.143	-8	-3	0	0	0	1.000	-2	/C-7	-0.6

■ LARRY HOFFMAN
Hoffman, Lawrence Charles   b: 7/18/1878, Chicago, Ill.   d: 12/29/48, Chicago, Ill.   BR/TR,   Deb: 7/9/01

1901	Chi-N	6	22	2	7	1	0	0	6	0		.318	.348	.364	111	0	1			.800	-2	/3-5,2-1	-0.1

■ HICKEY HOFFMAN
Hoffman, Otto Charles   b: 10/27/1856, Cleveland, Ohio   d: 10/27/15, Peoria, Ill.   Deb: 5/10/1879

1879	Cle-N	2	6	0	0	0	0	0		0	3	.000	.000	.000	-99	-1				.857	0	/C-2,O-1	-0.1

■ RAY HOFFMAN
Hoffman, Raymond Lamont   b: 6/14/17, Detroit, Mich.   BL/TR, 6'0.5", 175 lbs.   Deb: 8/30/42

1942	Was-A	7	19	2	1	0	0	0	1	2	1	.053	.100	.053	-57	-4	0	0	0	.815	2	/3-6	-0.2

■ JESSE HOFFMEISTER
Hoffmeister, Jesse H.   b: Toledo, Ohio   TR,   Deb: 7/24/1897

1897	Pit-N	48	188	33	58	6	9	3	36	8		.309	.337	.484	120	4	6			.792	-12	3-48	-0.6

■ SOLLY HOFMAN
Hofman, Arthur Frederick "Circus Solly"   b: 10/29/1882, St.Louis, Mo.   d: 3/10/56, St.Louis, Mo.   BR/TR, 6', 160 lbs.   Deb: 7/28/03

1903	Pit-N	3	2	1	0	0	0	0	0	0		.000	.000	.000	-97	-1	0			.000	-1	/O-2	-0.1
1904	Chi-N	7	26	7	7	0	0	1	4	1		.269	.296	.385	110	0	2			1.000	0	/O-6,S-1	0.0
1905	Chi-N	86	287	43	68	14	4	1	38	20		.237	.289	.324	79	-8	15			.955	4	2-59/1-9,S-9,3-3,O	-0.4
1906	*Chi-N	64	195	30	50	2	3	2	20	20		.256	.326	.328	98	-0	13			.976	-1	O-23,1-21/S-9,23	-0.3
1907	Chi-N	134	470	67	126	11	3	1	36	41		.268	.328	.311	94	-3	29			.938	2	O-69,S-42,1-18/32	-0.4
1908	*Chi-N	120	411	55	100	15	5	2	42	33		.243	.309	.319	96	-2	15			.955	5	O-50,1-37,2-22/3-9	0.2
1909	Chi-N	153	527	60	150	21	4	3	58	53		.285	.351	.351	115	10	20			.965	5	*O-153	1.0
1910	*Chi-N	136	477	83	155	24	16	3	86	65	34	.325	.406	.461	154	33	29			.975	5	*O-110,1-24/3-1	3.4
1911	Chi-N	143	512	66	129	17	2	2	70	66	40	.252	.341	.305	81	-11	30			.968	-6	*O-107,1-36	-2.4
1912	Chi-N	36	125	28	34	11	0	0	18	22	13	.272	.385	.360	105	2	5			.987	4	O-27/1-9	0.4
	Pit-N	17	53	7	15	4	0	2	5	6		.283	.345	.396	104	0	0			1.000	2	O-15	0.2
	Yr	53	178	35	49	15	0	2	20	27	19	.275	.374	.371	105	2	5			.991	6	O-42/1-9	0.6
1913	Pit-N	28	83	11	19	5	2	0	7	8	6	.229	.297	.337	84	-2	3			.964	-1	O-24	-0.4
1914	Bro-F	147	515	65	148	25	12	5	83	54	41	.287	.357	.412	110	-1	34			.951	5	*2-108,1-22,O-21,/S	0.2
1915	Buf-F	109	346	29	81	10	6	0	27	30	28	.234	.295	.298	66	-21	14			.961	1	O-82,1-11/3-4,2S	-2.6
1916	NY-A	6	27	0	8	1	0	0	2	1		.296	.321	.407	116	0	1			1.000	0	/O-6	0.2
	Chi-N	5	16	2	5	0	0	2	2	1		.313	.368	.563	172	1	0			1.000	0	/O-4	0.2
Total	14	1194	4072	554	1095	162	60	19	495	421	171	.269	.340	.352	102	-1	208			.967	26	O-702,2-198,1/S3	-0.8

■ BOBBY HOFMAN
Hofman, Robert George   b: 10/5/25, St.Louis, Mo.   d: 4/5/94, Chesterfield, Mo.   BR/TR, 5'11", 175 lbs.   Deb: 4/19/49   C

1949	NY-N	19	48	4	10	0	0	3	5	6		.208	.296	.208	38	-4	0			.939	-4	2-16	-0.4
1952	NY-N	32	63	11	18	2	2	4	8	10		.286	.375	.476	134	3	0	0	0	.964	3	2-21/3-2,1-1	0.7
1953	NY-N	74	169	21	45	7	2	12	34	12	23	.266	.315	.544	117	3	1	1	-0	.918	2	3-23,2-17	0.5

YEAR	TM/L	G	AB	R	H	2B	3B	HR	RBI	BB	SO	AVG	OBP	SLG	PRO+	BR/A	SB	CS	SBR	FA	FR	G/POS	TPR
1954	NY-N	71	125	12	28	5	0	8	30	17	15	.224	.322	.456	99	-1	0	0	0	.994	-4	1-21,2-10/3-8	-0.5
1955	NY-N	96	207	32	55	7	2	10	28	22	31	.266	.339	.464	110	3	0	2	-1	1.000	-5	1-24,C-19,2-19/3-5	-0.4
1956	NY-N	47	56	1	10	1	0	0	2	6	8	.179	.270	.196	28	-6	0	0	0	1.000	1	/C-7,3-7,1-3,2-2	-0.4
1957	NY-N	2	2	0	0	0	0	0	0	0	1	.000	.000	.000	-99	-1	0	0	0	.000	0	H	-0.1
Total	7	341	670	81	166	22	6	32	101	70	94	.248	.323	.442	100	-2	1	3		.969	-3	/2-85,1-49,3-45,C	-0.6

■ FRED HOFMANN
Hofmann, Fred "Bootnose" b: 6/10/1894, St.Louis, Mo. d: 11/19/64, St.Helena, Cal. BR/TR, 5'11.5", 175 lbs. Deb: 9/26/19 C

YEAR	TM/L	G	AB	R	H	2B	3B	HR	RBI	BB	SO	AVG	OBP	SLG	PRO+	BR/A	SB	CS	SBR	FA	FR	G/POS	TPR
1919	NY-A	1	1	0	0	0	0	0	0	0	0	.000	.000	.000	-99	-0	0			1.000	0	/C-1	0.0
1920	NY-A	15	24	3	7	0	0	0	1	1	2	.292	.346	.292	68	-1	0	0	0	.905	-4	C-14	-0.4
1921	NY-A	23	62	7	11	1	1	1	5	5	13	.177	.250	.274	33	-6	0	0	0	.952	-0	C-18/1-1	-0.6
1922	NY-A	37	91	13	27	5	3	2	10	9	12	.297	.360	.484	116	2	0	0	0	.962	-4	C-29	-0.1
1923	*NY-A	72	238	24	69	10	4	3	26	18	27	.290	.350	.403	96	-2	2	1	0	.979	-3	C-70	-0.2
1924	NY-A	62	166	17	29	6	1	1	11	12	15	.175	.239	.241	24	-19	2	1	0	.991	2	C-54	-1.4
1925	NY-A	3	2	0	0	0	0	0	0	0	0	.000	.000	.000	-99	-1	0	0	0	1.000	0	/C-1	0.0
1927	Bos-A	87	217	20	59	19	1	0	24	21	26	.272	.342	.369	86	-4	2	0	1	.943	-2	C-81	-0.1
1928	Bos-A	78	199	14	45	8	1	0	16	11	25	.226	.270	.276	45	-16	0	1	-1	.982	4	C-71	-0.7
Total	9	378	1000	98	247	49	11	7	93	77	120	.247	.308	.339	68	-48	6	3		.969	-7	C-339/1-1	-3.5

■ HARRY HOGAN
Hogan, Harry S. b: 11/1/1875, Syracuse, N.Y. d: 1/24/34, Syracuse, N.Y. Deb: 8/13/01

YEAR	TM/L	G	AB	R	H	2B	3B	HR	RBI	BB	SO	AVG	OBP	SLG	PRO+	BR/A	SB	CS	SBR	FA	FR	G/POS	TPR
1901	Cle-A	1	4	0	0	0	0	0	0	0	0	.000	.000	.000	-99	-1	0			.000	-0	/O-1	-0.1

■ SHANTY HOGAN
Hogan, James Francis b: 3/21/06, Somerville, Mass. d: 4/7/67, Boston, Mass. BR/TR, 6'1", 240 lbs. Deb: 6/23/25

YEAR	TM/L	G	AB	R	H	2B	3B	HR	RBI	BB	SO	AVG	OBP	SLG	PRO+	BR/A	SB	CS	SBR	FA	FR	G/POS	TPR
1925	Bos-N	9	21	2	6	1	1	0	3	1	3	.286	.318	.429	97	-0	0	0	0	1.000	-1	/O-5	-0.1
1926	Bos-N	4	14	1	4	1	1	0	5	0	0	.286	.286	.500	119	0	0			.852	1	/C-4	0.1
1927	Bos-N	71	229	24	66	17	1	3	32	9	23	.288	.324	.410	104	-0	2			.985	2	C-61	0.6
1928	NY-N	131	411	48	137	25	2	10	71	42	25	.333	.406	.477	129	19	0			.978	-10	*C-124	1.9
1929	NY-N	102	317	19	95	13	0	5	45	25	22	.300	.362	.388	86	-6	1			.979	-4	C-93	-0.2
1930	NY-N	122	389	60	132	26	2	13	75	21	24	.339	.378	.517	116	9	2			.982	-3	C-96	1.3
1931	NY-N	123	396	42	119	17	1	12	65	29	29	.301	.354	.439	115	8	1			**.996**	-0	*C-113	1.5
1932	NY-N	140	502	36	144	18	2	8	77	26	22	.287	.323	.378	90	-7	0			.983	-8	*C-136	-0.7
1933	Bos-N	96	328	15	83	7	0	3	30	13	9	.253	.288	.302	75	-12	0			**.997**	-1	C-95	-0.6
1934	Bos-N	92	279	20	73	5	2	4	34	16	13	.262	.316	.337	81	-8	0			.986	-2	C-90	-0.6
1935	Bos-N	59	163	9	49	8	2	5	25	21	8	.301	.394	.387	120	6	0			.990	-4	C-56	0.4
1936	Was-A	19	65	8	21	4	0	1	7	11	2	.323	.421	.431	117	2	0	1	-1	.989	2	C-19	0.4
1937	Was-A	21	66	4	10	4	0	0	5	6	1	.152	.222	.212	10	-9	0	1	-1	.979	2	C-21	-0.7
Total	13	989	3180	288	939	146	12	61	474	220	188	.295	.348	.406	101	-6	6	2		.985	-26	C-908/O-5	3.2

■ KENNY HOGAN
Hogan, Kenneth Sylvester b: 10/9/02, Cleveland, Ohio d: 1/2/80, Cleveland, Ohio BL/TR, 5'9", 145 lbs. Deb: 10/2/21

YEAR	TM/L	G	AB	R	H	2B	3B	HR	RBI	BB	SO	AVG	OBP	SLG	PRO+	BR/A	SB	CS	SBR	FA	FR	G/POS	TPR
1921	Cin-N	1	2	0	0	0	0	0	0	0	1	.000	.000	.000	-99	-1	0	0	0	.000	-1	/O-1	-0.1
1923	Cle-A	1	0	0	0	0	0	0	0	0	0	—	—	—		0	0	0	0	.000	0	R	0.0
1924	Cle-A	2	1	0	0	0	0	0	0	0	0	.000	.000	.000	-99	-0	0	0	0	.000	0	H	0.0
Total	3	4	3	0	0	0	0	0	0	0	1	.000	.000	.000	-99	-1	0	0	0	—	-1	/O-1	-0.1

■ MARTY HOGAN
Hogan, Martin F. b: 10/15/1869, Wensbury, England d: 8/15/23, Youngstown, Ohio BR, 5'8", 145 lbs. Deb: 8/6/1894

YEAR	TM/L	G	AB	R	H	2B	3B	HR	RBI	BB	SO	AVG	OBP	SLG	PRO+	BR/A	SB	CS	SBR	FA	FR	G/POS	TPR
1894	Cin-N	6	23	4	3	0	0	0	3	1	4	.130	.167	.130	-27	-5	2			.846	-0	/O-6	-0.4
	StL-N	29	100	11	28	3	4	0	13	6	13	.280	.308	.390	67	-6	7			.887	-1	O-29	-0.7
	Yr	35	123	15	31	3	4	0	16	4	17	.252	.281	.341	49	-11	9			.879	-2	O-35	-1.1
1895	StL-N	5	18	2	3	1	0	0	2	3	0	.167	.286	.222	32	-2	2			.833	1	/O-5	-0.1
Total	2	40	141	17	34	4	4	0	18	7	17	.241	.282	.326	47	-12	11			.869	-1	/O-40	-1.2

■ EDDIE HOGAN
Hogan, Robert Edward b: 4/1860, St.Louis, Mo. BR, 5'7", 153 lbs. Deb: 7/5/1882

YEAR	TM/L	G	AB	R	H	2B	3B	HR	RBI	BB	SO	AVG	OBP	SLG	PRO+	BR/A	SB	CS	SBR	FA	FR	G/POS	TPR
1882	StL-a	1	3	1	1	0	0	0				.333	.333	.333	121	0				.333	-1	/P-1	0.0
1884	Mil-U	11	37	6	3	1	0	0		0	7	.081	.227	.108	9	-7				.806	7	O-11	-0.6
1887	NY-a	32	120	22	24	6	1	0	5	30		.200	.373	.267	84	-0	12			.750	-7	O-29/S-4,3-1	-0.6
1888	Cle-a	78	269	60	61	16	6	0	24	50		.227	.368	.331	128	12	30			.896	-5	O-78	0.5
Total	4	122	429	89	89	23	7	0	29	87		.207	.357	.294	108	5	42			.844	-6	O-118/S-4,3-1,P-1	-0.1

■ WILLIE HOGAN
Hogan, William Henry "Happy" b: 9/14/1884, N.San Juan, Cal. d: 9/28/74, San Jose, Cal. BR/TR, 5'10", 175 lbs. Deb: 4/12/11 F

YEAR	TM/L	G	AB	R	H	2B	3B	HR	RBI	BB	SO	AVG	OBP	SLG	PRO+	BR/A	SB	CS	SBR	FA	FR	G/POS	TPR
1911	Phi-A	7	19	1	2	1	0	0	2	0		.105	.105	.158	-27	-3	0			.900	-1	/O-6	-0.3
	StL-A	123	443	53	115	17	8	2	62	43		.260	.328	.348	92	-5	18			.929	13	*O-117/1-5	0.2
	Yr	130	462	54	117	18	8	2	64	43		.253	.320	.340	87	-8	18			.928	13	*O-123/1-5	-0.1
1912	StL-A	108	360	32	77	10	2	1	36	34		.214	.284	.261	58	-19	17			.972	11	*O-100	-1.4
Total	2	238	822	86	194	28	10	3	100	77		.236	.304	.305	75	-28	35			.947	24	O-223/1-5	-1.5

■ BERT HOGG
Hogg, Wilbert George "Sonny" b: 4/21/13, Detroit, Mich. d: 11/5/73, Detroit, Mich. BR/TR, 5'11.5", 162 lbs. Deb: 6/1/34

YEAR	TM/L	G	AB	R	H	2B	3B	HR	RBI	BB	SO	AVG	OBP	SLG	PRO+	BR/A	SB	CS	SBR	FA	FR	G/POS	TPR
1934	Bro-N	2	1	0	0	0	0	0	0	0	0	.000	.000	.000	-99	-0				.000	0	/3-1	0.0

■ GEORGE HOGRIEVER
Hogriever, George C. b: 3/17/1869, Cincinnati, Ohio d: 1/26/61, Appleton, Wis. BR/TR, 5'8", 160 lbs. Deb: 4/24/1895

YEAR	TM/L	G	AB	R	H	2B	3B	HR	RBI	BB	SO	AVG	OBP	SLG	PRO+	BR/A	SB	CS	SBR	FA	FR	G/POS	TPR
1895	Cin-N	69	239	61	65	8	7	2	34	36	17	.272	.374	.389	93	-2	41			.934	2	O-66/2-3	-0.4
1901	Mil-A	54	221	25	52	10	2	0	16	30		.235	.329	.299	79	-5	7			.901	2	O-54	-0.7
Total	2	123	460	86	117	18	9	2	50	66	17	.254	.353	.346	87	-7	48			.920	4	O-120/2-3	-1.1

■ BILL HOHMAN
Hohman, William Henry b: 11/27/03, Brooklyn, Md. d: 10/29/68, Baltimore, Md. BR/TR, 6', 178 lbs. Deb: 8/24/27

YEAR	TM/L	G	AB	R	H	2B	3B	HR	RBI	BB	SO	AVG	OBP	SLG	PRO+	BR/A	SB	CS	SBR	FA	FR	G/POS	TPR
1927	Phi-N	7	18	1	5	0	0	0	0	2	3	.278	.350	.278	69	-1	0			.917	-0	/O-6	-0.1

■ EDDIE HOHNHORST
Hohnhorst, Edward Hicks b: 1/31/1885, Covington, Ky. d: 3/28/16, Covington, Ky. BL/TL, 6'1", 175 lbs. Deb: 9/10/10

YEAR	TM/L	G	AB	R	H	2B	3B	HR	RBI	BB	SO	AVG	OBP	SLG	PRO+	BR/A	SB	CS	SBR	FA	FR	G/POS	TPR
1910	Cle-A	18	63	8	20	3	1	0	6	4		.317	.358	.397	135	2	3			.972	-1	1-18	0.1
1912	Cle-A	15	54	5	11	1	0	0	2	2		.204	.232	.222	29	-5	5			.963	-1	1-15	-0.6
Total	2	33	117	13	31	4	1	0	8	6		.265	.301	.316	83	-3	8			.968	-2	/1-33	-0.5

■ CHRIS HOILES
Hoiles, Christopher Allen b: 3/20/65, Bowling Green, O. BR/TR, 6', 195 lbs. Deb: 4/25/89

YEAR	TM/L	G	AB	R	H	2B	3B	HR	RBI	BB	SO	AVG	OBP	SLG	PRO+	BR/A	SB	CS	SBR	FA	FR	G/POS	TPR
1989	Bal-A	6	9	0	1	1	0	0	1	1	3	.111	.200	.222	19	-1	0	0	0	1.000	1	/C-3,D-3	0.0
1990	Bal-A	23	63	7	12	3	0	1	6	5	12	.190	.250	.286	51	-4	0	0	0	1.000	1	/C-7,1-6,D-7	-0.5
1991	Bal-A	107	341	36	83	15	0	11	31	29	61	.243	.305	.384	93	-4	0	2	-1	**.998**	-14	C-89,D-13/1-2	-1.4
1992	Bal-A	96	310	49	85	10	1	20	40	55	60	.274	.387	.506	145	19	0	2	-1	.994	-10	C-95/D-1	1.4
1993	Bal-A	126	419	80	130	28	0	29	82	69	94	.310	.419	.585	160	37	1	1	-0	.993	-7	*C-124/D-2	4.1
1994	Bal-A	99	332	45	82	10	0	19	53	63	73	.247	.375	.449	106	4	2	0	1	.989	5	C-98	1.5
1995	Bal-A	114	352	53	88	15	1	19	58	67	80	.250	.376	.460	114	9	0	0	0	**.996**	-2	*C-107/D-6	1.4
1996	*Bal-A	127	407	64	105	13	0	25	73	57	97	.258	.362	.474	110	5	1	1	-1	.992	-10	*C-126/1-1	0.4
Total	8	698	2233	334	586	95	2	124	344	346	480	.262	.369	.473	120	66	4	6	-2	.993	-31	C-649/D-32,1-9	6.9

■ AARON HOLBERT
Holbert, Aaron Keith b: 1/9/73, Torrance, Cal. BR/TR, 6', 160 lbs. Deb: 4/14/96 F

YEAR	TM/L	G	AB	R	H	2B	3B	HR	RBI	BB	SO	AVG	OBP	SLG	PRO+	BR/A	SB	CS	SBR	FA	FR	G/POS	TPR
1996	StL-N	1	3	0	0	0	0	0	0	0	0	.000	.000	.000	-99	-1	0	0	0	1.000	-1	/2-1	-0.2

■ RAY HOLBERT
Holbert, Ray Arthur b: 9/25/70, Torrance, Cal. BR/TR, 6', 170 lbs. Deb: 5/2/94 F

YEAR	TM/L	G	AB	R	H	2B	3B	HR	RBI	BB	SO	AVG	OBP	SLG	PRO+	BR/A	SB	CS	SBR	FA	FR	G/POS	TPR
1994	SD-N	5	5	1	1	0	0	0	0	0	4	.200	.200	.200	5	-1	0	0	0	.000	0	/S-1	-0.1
1995	SD-N	63	73	11	13	2	1	2	8	5	20	.178	.277	.315	58	-5	4	0	1	.940	6	S-30/2-7,O-1	0.4
Total	2	68	78	12	14	2	1	2	8	5	24	.179	.273	.308	54	-5	4	0	1	.940	6	/S-31,2-7,O-1	0.3

■ BILL HOLBERT
Holbert, William Henry b: 3/14/1855, Baltimore, Md. d: 3/20/35, Laurel, Md. BR/TR, 197 lbs. Deb: 9/5/1876 MU

YEAR	TM/L	G	AB	R	H	2B	3B	HR	RBI	BB	SO	AVG	OBP	SLG	PRO+	BR/A	SB	CS	SBR	FA	FR	G/POS	TPR
1876	Lou-N	12	43	3	11	0	0	0		0	3	.256	.256	.256	60	-2				.843	7	C-12	0.5
1878	Mil-N	45	173	10	32	2	0	0	12	3	14	.185	.199	.197	28	-13				.818	7	O-30,C-21	-0.7
1879	Syr-N	59	229	11	46	0	0	0	21	1	20	.201	.204	.201	39	-14				.897	-1	*C-56/O-4,M	-1.2

YEAR	TM/L	G	AB	R	H	2B	3B	HR	RBI	BB	SO	AVG	OBP	SLG	PRO+	BR/A	SB	CS	SBR	FA	FR	G/POS	TPR
	Tro-N	4	15	1	4	0	0	0	2	0	1	.267	.267	.267	82	-0				.893	1	/C-4	0.0
	Yr	63	244	12	50	0	0	0	23	1	21	.205	.208	.205	41	-14				.897	0	C-60/O-4	-1.2
1880	Tro-N	60	212	18	40	5	1	0	8	9	18	.189	.222	.222	48	-11				.911	12	*C-58/O-3	0.1
1881	Tro-N	46	180	16	49	3	0	0	14	3	13	.272	.284	.289	77	-5				.918	7	C-43/O-3	0.3
1882	Tro-N	71	251	24	46	5	0	0	23	11	22	.183	.218	.203	38	-16				.892	16	*C-58,3-12/O-3	0.1
1883	NY-a	73	299	26	71	9	1	0		1		.237	.240	.274	62	-13				.920	34	*C-68/O-5,2-1	2.2
1884	*NY-a	65	255	28	53	5	0	0		7		.208	.235	.227	53	-13				.920	21	C-59/O-5,S-1	1.2
1885	NY-a	56	202	13	35	3	0	0	13	8		.173	.205	.188	27	-16				.900	12	C-39,O-13/3-5	0.0
1886	NY-a	48	171	8	35	4	2	0	13	6		.205	.232	.251	54	-9	4			.922	19	C-45/O-3,S-1	1.3
1887	NY-a	69	255	20	58	4	3	0	32	7		.227	.248	.267	46	-19	12			.894	2	C-60/1-8,S-2,2-1	-1.0
1888	Bro-a	15	50	4	6	1	0	0	1	2		.120	.170	.140	-0	-6				.926	2	C-15	-0.2
Total	12	623	2335	182	486	41	7	0	144	58	91	.208	.228	.232	47	-138	16			.907	139	C-538/O-69,31S2	2.6

■ SAMMY HOLBROOK   Holbrook, James Marbury b: 7/17/10, Meridian, Miss. d: 4/10/91, Jackson, Miss. BR/TR, 5'11", 189 lbs. Deb: 4/25/35

YEAR	TM/L	G	AB	R	H	2B	3B	HR	RBI	BB	SO	AVG	OBP	SLG	PRO+	BR/A	SB	CS	SBR	FA	FR	G/POS	TPR
1935	Was-A	52	135	20	35	2	2	2	25	30	16	.259	.408	.348	101	2	0	0	0	.952	-11	C-47	-0.7

■ JOE HOLDEN   Holden, Joseph Francis "Socks" b: 6/4/13, St.Clair, Pa. d: 5/10/96, St.Clair, Pa. BL/TR, 5'8", 175 lbs. Deb: 6/14/34

YEAR	TM/L	G	AB	R	H	2B	3B	HR	RBI	BB	SO	AVG	OBP	SLG	PRO+	BR/A	SB	CS	SBR	FA	FR	G/POS	TPR
1934	Phi-N	10	14	1	1	0	0	0	0	0	2	.071	.071	.071	-54	-3	0			1.000	2	/C-6	-0.1
1935	Phi-N	6	9	0	1	0	0	0	0	0	3	.111	.111	.111	-36	-2	1			1.000	-1	/C-4	-0.2
1936	Phi-N	1	1	0	0	0	0	0	0	0	0	.000	.000	.000	-91	-0	0			.000	0	H	0.0
Total	3	17	24	1	2	0	0	0	0	0	5	.083	.083	.083	-49	-5	1			1.000	2	/C-10	-0.3

■ BILL HOLDEN   Holden, William Paul b: 9/7/1889, Birmingham, Ala. d: 9/14/71, Pensacola, Fla. BR/TR, 6', 170 lbs. Deb: 9/11/13

YEAR	TM/L	G	AB	R	H	2B	3B	HR	RBI	BB	SO	AVG	OBP	SLG	PRO+	BR/A	SB	CS	SBR	FA	FR	G/POS	TPR
1913	NY-A	18	53	6	16	3	1	0	8	8	5	.302	.393	.396	131	0	2			.977	3	O-16	0.4
1914	NY-A	50	165	12	30	3	2	0	12	16	26	.182	.254	.224	44	-11	2	4	-2	.981	-1	O-45	-1.8
	Cin-N	11	28	2	6	0	0	0	1	3	5	.214	.290	.214	49	-2	0			1.000	-2	O-10	-0.4
Total	2	79	246	20	52	6	3	0	21	27	36	.211	.289	.260	64	-11	2	4		.981	0	/O-71	-1.8

■ JIM HOLDSWORTH   Holdsworth, James "Long Jim" b: 7/14/1850, New York, N.Y. d: 3/22/18, New York, N.Y. BR/TR, Deb: 5/14/1872

YEAR	TM/L	G	AB	R	H	2B	3B	HR	RBI	BB	SO	AVG	OBP	SLG	PRO+	BR/A	SB	CS	SBR	FA	FR	G/POS	TPR
1872	Cle-n	22	110	19	33	5	0	0	11	1	2	.300	.306	.345	106	1	3	2	-0	.765	-1	S-22	0.0
	Eck-n	2	7	1	2	0	0	0	0	0	0	.286	.286	.286	90	0	0	0	0	.933	2	/S-2	0.1
	Yr	24	117	20	35	5	0	0	11	1	2	.299	.305	.342	105	1	3	2	-0	.780	1	S-24	0.1
1873	Mut-n	53	233	46	75	4	8	0	28	0	3	.322	.322	.408	116	4	1	0	0	.775	-14	*S-53	-0.8
1874	Phi-n	57	285	60	97	8	9	0	37	1	0	.340	.343	.432	142	12	1	2	-1	.694	-25	3-31,S-21/O-6,21	-1.2
1875	Mut-n	71	324	45	92	12	1	0	23	1	3	.284	.286	.327	107	1	3	3	-1	.780	1	O-45,S-26	0.0
1876	NY-N	52	241	23	64	3	2	0	19	1	2	.266	.269	.295	101	1				.902	1	*O-49/2-3	0.1
1877	Har-N	55	260	26	66	5	2	0	20	2	8	.254	.260	.288	81	-5				.833	-3	*O-55	-0.9
1882	Tro-n	1	3	0	0	0	0	0	0	0	1	.000	.000	.000	-99	-1				1.000	1	/O-1	0.0
1884	Ind-a	5	18	1	2	0	0	0		0	2	.111	.200	.111	4	-2				.929	1	/O-5	0.0
Total	4 n	205	959	171	299	29	18	0	99	3	8	.312	.314	.380	119	18	8	7	-2	.750	-38	S-124/O-51,3-31,21	-1.9
Total	4	113	522	50	132	8	4	0	39	5	11	.253	.260	.284	85	-6				.875	0	O-110/2-3	-0.8

■ WALTER HOLKE   Holke, Walter Henry "Union Man" b: 12/25/1892, St.Louis, Mo. d: 10/12/54, St.Louis, Mo. BB/TL, 6'1.5", 185 lbs. Deb: 10/6/14 C

YEAR	TM/L	G	AB	R	H	2B	3B	HR	RBI	BB	SO	AVG	OBP	SLG	PRO+	BR/A	SB	CS	SBR	FA	FR	G/POS	TPR
1914	NY-N	2	6	0	2	0	0	0	0	0	0	.333	.333	.333	102	-0	0			.950	0	/1-2	0.0
1916	NY-N	34	111	16	39	4	2	0	13	6	16	.351	.390	.423	158	7	10			.997	-0	1-34	0.7
1917	*NY-N	153	527	55	146	12	7	2	55	34	54	.277	.327	.338	107	4	13			.989	-5	*1-153	-0.7
1918	NY-N	88	326	38	82	17	4	1	27	10	26	.252	.276	.337	88	-6	10			.990	5	1-88	-0.5
1919	Bos-N	137	518	48	151	14	6	0	48	21	25	.292	.325	.342	105	2	19			.993	6	*1-136	0.4
1920	Bos-N	144	551	53	162	15	11	3	64	28	31	.294	.329	.377	107	4	4	11	-5	.991	-3	*1-143	-0.8
1921	Bos-N	150	579	60	151	15	10	3	63	17	41	.261	.284	.337	67	-28	8	11	-4	.997	3	*1-150	-3.4
1922	Bos-N	105	395	35	115	9	4	0	46	14	25	.291	.317	.334	71	-17	4	3	-2	.993	-4	*1-105	-2.7
1923	Phi-N	147	562	64	175	31	4	7	70	16	37	.311	.330	.418	86	-13	7	9	-3	.991	-1	*1-146/P-1	-2.4
1924	Phi-N	148	563	60	169	23	6	6	64	25	33	.300	.330	.394	83	-14	3	8	-4	.993	4	*1-148	-2.4
1925	Phi-N	39	86	11	21	5	0	1	17	3	6	.244	.270	.337	50	-7	0	0	0	.994	1	1-23	-0.6
	Cin-N	65	232	24	65	8	4	1	20	17	12	.280	.329	.362	78	-8	1	3	-2	.997	1	1-65	-1.1
	Yr	104	318	35	86	13	4	2	37	20	18	.270	.314	.355	69	-15	1	3	-2	.996	2	1-88	-1.7
Total	11	1212	4456	464	1278	153	58	24	487	191	304	.287	.318	.363	89	-74	81	50		.993	7	*1-1193/P-1	-13.5

■ BILL HOLLAHAN   Hollahan, William James "Happy" b: 11/22/1896, New York, N.Y. d: 11/27/65, New York, N.Y. BR/TR, 5'8", 165 lbs. Deb: 9/27/20

YEAR	TM/L	G	AB	R	H	2B	3B	HR	RBI	BB	SO	AVG	OBP	SLG	PRO+	BR/A	SB	CS	SBR	FA	FR	G/POS	TPR
1920	Was-A	3	4	0	1	0	0	0	1	1	2	.250	.400	.250	77	-0	1	0	0	1.000	0	/3-3	0.1

■ DUTCH HOLLAND   Holland, Robert Clyde b: 10/12/03, Middlesex, N.C. d: 6/16/67, Lumberton, N.C. BR/TR, 6'1", 190 lbs. Deb: 8/16/32

YEAR	TM/L	G	AB	R	H	2B	3B	HR	RBI	BB	SO	AVG	OBP	SLG	PRO+	BR/A	SB	CS	SBR	FA	FR	G/POS	TPR
1932	Bos-N	39	156	15	46	11	1	1	18	12	12	.295	.345	.397	103	1	0			.990	2	O-39	0.0
1933	Bos-N	13	31	3	8	3	0	0	3	3	8	.258	.324	.355	102	0	1			.867	-1	/O-7	-0.2
1934	Cle-A	50	128	19	32	12	1	2	13	13	11	.250	.319	.406	85	-3	0			.957	-4	/O-31	-0.8
Total	3	102	315	37	86	26	2	3	34	28	39	.273	.332	.397	95	-3	1	0		.969	-3	/O-77	-1.0

■ WILL HOLLAND   Holland, Willard A. b: Georgetown, Del. d: 7/19/30, Philadelphia, Pa. 5'10", 180 lbs. Deb: 7/10/1889

YEAR	TM/L	G	AB	R	H	2B	3B	HR	RBI	BB	SO	AVG	OBP	SLG	PRO+	BR/A	SB	CS	SBR	FA	FR	G/POS	TPR
1889	Bal-a	40	143	13	27	1	2	0	16	9	28	.189	.247	.224	34	-13	4			.853	-15	S-39/O-1	-2.2

■ TODD HOLLANDSWORTH   Hollandsworth, Todd Mathew b: 4/20/73, Dayton, Ohio BL/TR, 6'2", 195 lbs. Deb: 4/25/95

YEAR	TM/L	G	AB	R	H	2B	3B	HR	RBI	BB	SO	AVG	OBP	SLG	PRO+	BR/A	SB	CS	SBR	FA	FR	G/POS	TPR
1995	*LA-N	41	103	16	24	2	0	5	13	10	29	.233	.307	.398	92	-2	2	1	0	.938	-3	O-37	-0.5
1996	*LA-N	149	478	64	139	26	4	12	59	41	93	.291	.349	.437	115	9	21	6	3	.978	-3	*O-142	0.6
Total	2	190	581	80	163	28	4	17	72	51	122	.281	.342	.430	111	8	23	7	3	.969	-6	O-179	0.1

■ GARY HOLLE   Holle, Gary Charles b: 8/11/54, Albany, N.Y. BR/TL, 6'6", 210 lbs. Deb: 6/2/79

YEAR	TM/L	G	AB	R	H	2B	3B	HR	RBI	BB	SO	AVG	OBP	SLG	PRO+	BR/A	SB	CS	SBR	FA	FR	G/POS	TPR
1979	Tex-A	5	6	0	1	1	0	0	1	0	1	.167	.286	.333	67	-0	0	0	0	1.000	-0	/1-1	-0.1

■ BUG HOLLIDAY   Holliday, James Wear b: 2/8/1867, St.Louis, Mo. d: 2/15/10, Cincinnati, Ohio BR/TR, 5'11", 151 lbs. Deb: 4/17/1889 U

YEAR	TM/L	G	AB	R	H	2B	3B	HR	RBI	BB	SO	AVG	OBP	SLG	PRO+	BR/A	SB	CS	SBR	FA	FR	G/POS	TPR
1889	Cin-a	135	563	107	181	28	7	19	104	43	59	.321	.372	.497	142	27	46			.923	-7	*O-135	1.4
1890	Cin-N	131	518	93	140	18	14	9	75	49	36	.270	.341	.382	111	7	50			.948	-2	*O-131	0.0
1891	Cin-N	111	442	74	141	21	10	9	84	37	28	.319	.376	.473	145	24	30			.939	-8	*O-111	1.1
1892	Cin-N	152	602	114	176	23	16	13	91	57	59	.292	.354	.449	145	30	43			.933	-4	*O-152/P-1	1.8
1893	Cin-N	126	500	108	155	24	10	5	89	73	22	.310	.401	.428	117	13	32			.944	-10	*O-125/1-1	-0.3
1894	Cin-N	121	511	119	190	24	7	13	119	40	20	.372	.420	.523	121	16	29			.914	-9	*O-119/1-1	0.6
1895	Cin-N	32	127	25	38	2	0	2	20	10	3	.299	.350	.402	90	-2	6			.940	-4	O-32	-0.7
1896	Cin-N	29	84	17	27	4	0	0	8	9	4	.321	.394	.369	95	-0	1			.925	-2	O-16/1-5,S-1,P-1	-0.5
1897	Cin-N	61	195	50	61	9	4	2	20	27		.313	.399	.431	112	3	6			.940	-6	O-42/S-4,2-3,1-3	-0.5
1898	Cin-N	30	106	21	25	5	0	0	7	14		.236	.325	.274	67	-4	5			.969	-2	O-28	-0.8
Total	10	928	3648	728	1134	162	71	65	617	359	211	.311	.376	.448	125	114	248			.935	-45	O-891/1-10,S-5,2P	2.3

■ HOLLY HOLLINGSHEAD   Hollingshead, John Samuel (a.k.a. Samuel John Holly) b: 1/17/1853, Washington, D.C. d: 10/6/26, Washington, D.C. Deb: 4/20/1872 M

YEAR	TM/L	G	AB	R	H	2B	3B	HR	RBI	BB	SO	AVG	OBP	SLG	PRO+	BR/A	SB	CS	SBR	FA	FR	G/POS	TPR
1872	Nat-n	9	44	12	15	1	1	0	6	1	1	.341	.356	.409	115	-0	0	0	0	.778	-3	/2-9	-0.3
1873	Was-n	30	136	25	35	2	1	0	22	0	6	.257	.257	.301	68	-5	0	0	0	.833	2	O-30/2-2	-0.2
1875	Was-n	19	81	8	20	1	0	0	5	1	2	.247	.256	.284	91	-1	2	1	0	.826	2	O-19,M	0.1
Total	3 n	58	261	45	70	4	4	0	33	2	8	.268	.274	.314	83	-7	2	1	0	.831	1	/O-49,2-11	-0.4

■ DAVE HOLLINS   Hollins, David Michael b: 5/25/66, Buffalo, N.Y. BB/TR, 6'1", 195 lbs. Deb: 4/12/90

YEAR	TM/L	G	AB	R	H	2B	3B	HR	RBI	BB	SO	AVG	OBP	SLG	PRO+	BR/A	SB	CS	SBR	FA	FR	G/POS	TPR
1990	Phi-N	72	114	14	21	0	0	5	15	10	28	.184	.256	.316	57	-7	0	0	0	.932	-1	3-30/1-1	-0.9
1991	Phi-N	56	151	18	45	10	2	6	21	17	26	.298	.380	.510	140	10	1	1	-0	.922	-3	3-36/1-6	0.6
1992	Phi-N	156	586	104	158	28	4	27	93	76	110	.270	.372	.469	137	30	9	6	-3	.954	-20	*3-156/1-1	0.9
1993	*Phi-N★	143	543	104	148	30	4	18	93	85	109	.273	.376	.442	120	17	2	3	-1	.914	-29	*3-143	-1.2

YEAR	TM/L	G	AB	R	H	2B	3B	HR	RBI	BB	SO	AVG	OBP	SLG	PRO+	BR/A	SB	CS	SBR	FA	FR	G/POS	TPR
1994	Phi-N	44	162	28	36	7	1	4	26	23	32	.222	.333	.352	77	-5	1	0	0	.887	-15	3-43/O-1	-2.0
1995	Phi-N	65	205	46	47	12	2	7	25	53	38	.229	.399	.410	113	6	1	1	-0	.988	-6	1-61	-0.5
	Bos-A	5	13	2	2	0	0	0	1	4	7	.154	.353	.154	37	-1	0	0	0	1.000	-0	/O-2,D-3	-0.1
1996	Min-A	121	422	71	102	26	0	13	53	71	102	.242	.364	.396	90	-5	6	4	-1	.953	-4	*3-116/S-1,D-3	-0.8
	Sea-A	28	94	17	33	3	0	3	25	13	15	.351	.445	.479	134	6	0	2	-1	.961	2	3-28/1-1	0.6
	Yr	149	516	88	135	29	0	16	78	84	117	.262	.378	.411	98	1	6	6	-2	.955	-2	*3-144/D-3,S-1,1-1	-0.2
Total	7	690	2290	404	592	116	13	83	352	352	467	.259	.369	.429	113	51	20	17	-4	.937	-75	3-552/1-70,D-6,OS	-3.4

■ STAN HOLLMIG
Hollmig, Stanley Ernest "Hondo" b: 1/2/26, Fredericksburg, Tex d: 12/4/81, San Antonio, Tex. BR/TR, 6'2.5", 190 lbs. Deb: 4/19/49

YEAR	TM/L	G	AB	R	H	2B	3B	HR	RBI	BB	SO	AVG	OBP	SLG	PRO+	BR/A	SB	CS	SBR	FA	FR	G/POS	TPR
1949	Phi-N	81	251	28	64	11	6	2	26	20	43	.255	.315	.371	85	-6	1			.958	-6	O-66	-1.4
1950	Phi-N	11	12	1	3	2	0	0	1	0	3	.250	.250	.417	73	-1	0			1.000	-1	/O-3	-0.1
1951	Phi-N	2	2	0	0	0	0	0	0	0	0	.000	.000	.000	-99	-1	0	0	0	.000	-0	H	-0.1
Total	3	94	265	29	67	13	6	2	27	20	46	.253	.310	.370	84	-7	1	0		.959	-6	O-69	-1.6

■ CHARLIE HOLLOCHER
Hollocher, Charles Jacob b: 6/11/1896, St.Louis, Mo. d: 8/14/40, Frontenac, Mo. BL/TR, 5'7", 154 lbs. Deb: 4/16/18

YEAR	TM/L	G	AB	R	H	2B	3B	HR	RBI	BB	SO	AVG	OBP	SLG	PRO+	BR/A	SB	CS	SBR	FA	FR	G/POS	TPR
1918	*Chi-N	131	509	72	**161**	23	6	2	38	47	30	.316	.379	.397	133	21	26			.929	-19	*S-131	0.8
1919	Chi-N	115	430	51	116	14	5	3	26	44	19	.270	.347	.347	108	6	16			.941	6	*S-115	2.0
1920	Chi-N	80	301	53	96	17	2	0	22	41	15	.319	.406	.389	126	12	20	14	-2	.954	9	S-80	2.7
1921	Chi-N	140	558	71	161	28	8	3	37	43	13	.289	.342	.384	91	-6	5	16	-8	**.963**	3	*S-137	0.2
1922	Chi-N	152	592	90	201	37	8	3	69	58	5	.340	.403	.444	116	16	19	29	-12	**.965**	-5	*S-152	1.3
1923	Chi-N	66	260	46	89	14	2	1	28	26	5	.342	.410	.423	120	9	9	10	-3	.963	-9	S-65	0.3
1924	Chi-N	76	286	28	70	12	4	2	21	18	7	.245	.292	.336	67	-14	4	11	-5	.969	-4	S-71	-0.8
Total	7	760	2936	411	894	145	35	14	241	277	94	.304	.370	.392	110	44	99	80		.954	-13	S-751	6.5

■ ED HOLLY
Holly, Edward William (b: Edward William Ruthlavy) b: 7/6/1879, Chicago, Ill. d: 11/27/73, Williamsport, Pa. BR/TR, 5'10", 165 lbs. Deb: 7/18/06

YEAR	TM/L	G	AB	R	H	2B	3B	HR	RBI	BB	SO	AVG	OBP	SLG	PRO+	BR/A	SB	CS	SBR	FA	FR	G/POS	TPR
1906	StL-N	10	34	1	2	0	0	0	7	5		.059	.179	.059	-27	-5	0			.939	-3	S-10	-0.8
1907	StL-N	150	545	55	125	18	3	1	40	36		.229	.283	.279	79	-14	16			.927	11	*S-147/2-3	-2.3
1914	Pit-F	100	350	28	86	9	4	0	26	17	52	.246	.281	.294	57	-27	14			.942	-4	S-94/O-2,2-1	-2.3
1915	Pit-F	16	42	8	11	2	0	0	5	5	6	.262	.354	.310	88	-1	3			.865	-4	S-11/3-3	-0.5
Total	4	276	971	92	224	29	7	1	78	63	58	.231	.282	.278	67	-47	33			.931	1	S-262/2-4,3-3,O-2	-3.6

■ WATTIE HOLM
Holm, Roscoe Albert b: 12/28/01, Peterson, Iowa d: 5/19/50, Everly, Iowa BR/TR, 5'9.5", 160 lbs. Deb: 4/15/24

YEAR	TM/L	G	AB	R	H	2B	3B	HR	RBI	BB	SO	AVG	OBP	SLG	PRO+	BR/A	SB	CS	SBR	FA	FR	G/POS	TPR
1924	StL-N	81	293	40	86	10	4	0	23	8	16	.294	.317	.355	81	-8	1	4	-2	.988	2	O-64/C-9,3-4	-1.3
1925	StL-N	13	58	10	12	1	1	0	2	3	1	.207	.246	.259	28	-6	1	0	0	.976	2	O-13	-0.5
1926	*StL-N	55	144	18	41	5	1	0	21	18	14	.285	.364	.333	85	-2	3			.962	-3	O-39	-0.8
1927	StL-N	110	419	55	120	27	8	3	66	24	29	.286	.327	.411	93	-5	4			.967	-8	O-97/3-9	-1.8
1928	*StL-N	102	386	61	107	24	6	3	47	32	17	.277	.334	.394	88	-7	1			.918	-10	3-83/O-7	-1.3
1929	StL-N	64	176	21	41	5	6	0	14	12	8	.233	.282	.330	50	-14	1			.944	3	O-44/3-1	-1.3
1932	StL-N	11	17	2	3	1	0	0	1	3	1	.176	.333	.235	55	-1	0			1.000	0	O-4	-0.1
Total	7	436	1493	207	410	73	26	6	174	100	86	.275	.322	.370	81	-44	11	4		.970	-15	O-268/3-97,C-9	-7.1

■ BILLY HOLM
Holm, William Frederick Henry b: 7/21/12, Chicago, Ill. d: 7/27/77, East Chicago, Ind BR/TR, 5'10.5", 168 lbs. Deb: 9/24/43

YEAR	TM/L	G	AB	R	H	2B	3B	HR	RBI	BB	SO	AVG	OBP	SLG	PRO+	BR/A	SB	CS	SBR	FA	FR	G/POS	TPR
1943	Chi-N	7	15	0	1	0	0	0	2	4		.067	.176	.067	-29	-2	0			1.000	1	/C-7	-0.1
1944	Chi-N	54	132	10	18	2	0	0	6	16	19	.136	.235	.152	10	-15	1			.979	-2	C-50	-1.6
1945	Bos-A	58	135	12	25	2	1	0	9	21	17	.185	.317	.215	54	-7	1	1	-0	.980	-4	C-57	-0.9
Total	3	119	282	22	44	4	1	0	15	41	40	.156	.272	.177	30	-25	2	1		.981	-4	C-114	-2.6

■ GARY HOLMAN
Holman, Gary Richard b: 1/25/44, Long Beach, Cal. BL/TL, 6'1", 200 lbs. Deb: 6/26/68

YEAR	TM/L	G	AB	R	H	2B	3B	HR	RBI	BB	SO	AVG	OBP	SLG	PRO+	BR/A	SB	CS	SBR	FA	FR	G/POS	TPR
1968	Was-A	75	85	10	25	5	1	0	7	13	15	.294	.388	.376	137	4	0	0	0	1.000	2	1-33,O-10	0.6
1969	Was-A	41	31	1	5	1	0	0	2	4	7	.161	.257	.194	29	-3	0	0	0	1.000	-1	1-11/O-3	-0.5
Total	2	116	116	11	30	6	1	0	9	17	22	.259	.353	.328	107	1	0	0	0	1.000	1	/1-44,O-13	0.1

■ FRED HOLMES
Holmes, Frederick C. b: 7/1/1878, Chicago, Ill. d: 2/13/56, Norwood Park, Ill. BR/TR, Deb: 8/23/03

YEAR	TM/L	G	AB	R	H	2B	3B	HR	RBI	BB	SO	AVG	OBP	SLG	PRO+	BR/A	SB	CS	SBR	FA	FR	G/POS	TPR
1903	NY-A	1	0	0	0	0	0	0	0	1		—	1.000	—	207	0	0			.833	-0	/1-1	0.0
1904	Chi-N	1	3	1	1	1	0	0	0	0	1	.333	.333	.667	206	0	0			1.000	-0	/C-1	0.0
Total	2	3	3	1	1	1	0	0	0	1		.333	.500	.667	255	1	0			1.000	-0	/C-1,1-1	0.0

■ DUCKY HOLMES
Holmes, Howard Elbert b: 7/8/1883, Dayton, Ohio d: 9/18/45, Dayton, Ohio BR/TR, 5'10", 160 lbs. Deb: 4/18/06 U

YEAR	TM/L	G	AB	R	H	2B	3B	HR	RBI	BB	SO	AVG	OBP	SLG	PRO+	BR/A	SB	CS	SBR	FA	FR	G/POS	TPR
1906	StL-N	9	27	2	5	0	0	0	2	2		.185	.267	.185	43	-2	0			.979	-0	/C-9	-0.2

■ DUCKY HOLMES
Holmes, James William b: 1/28/1869, Des Moines, Iowa d: 8/6/32, Truro, Iowa BL/TR, 5'6", 170 lbs. Deb: 8/8/1895

YEAR	TM/L	G	AB	R	H	2B	3B	HR	RBI	BB	SO	AVG	OBP	SLG	PRO+	BR/A	SB	CS	SBR	FA	FR	G/POS	TPR
1895	Lou-N	40	161	33	60	10	2	3	20	12	9	.373	.426	.516	152	13	9			.780	-11	O-29/S-8,3-4,P-2	0.0
1896	Lou-N	47	141	22	38	2	3	0	18	13	5	.270	.360	.319	83	-3	8			.790	-7	O-33/P-2,S-1,2-1	-1.0
1897	Lou-N	2	4	0	0	0	0	0	0	1		.000	.200	.000	-46	-1	0			1.000	1	/S-1	0.0
	NY-N	79	306	51	82	8	6	1	44	18		.268	.317	.343	76	-11	30			.904	-7	O-77/S-1	-2.1
	Yr	81	310	51	82	8	6	1	44	19		.265	.315	.339	75	-12	30			.904	-6	O-77/S-2	-2.1
1898	StL-N	23	101	9	24	1	1	0	2	2		.238	.260	.267	50	-7	4			.900	2	O-22	-0.6
	Bal-N	113	442	54	126	10	9	1	64	23		.285	.333	.355	96	-3	25			.935	4	*O-113	-0.7
	Yr	136	543	63	150	11	10	1	64	25		.276	.320	.339	87	-10	29			.930	6	*O-135	-1.3
1899	Bal-N	138	553	80	177	31	7	4	66	39		.320	.381	.423	114	10	50			.927	6	*O-138	0.5
1901	Det-A	131	537	90	158	28	10	4	62	37		.294	.347	.406	103	1	35			.907	-2	O-131	-0.9
1902	Det-A	92	362	50	93	15	4	2	33	28		.257	.319	.337	80	-9	16			.950	6	O-92	-0.9
1903	Was-A	21	71	13	16	3	1	1	9	4		.225	.286	.338	85	-1	10			.912	1	O-14/3-4,2-2	-0.1
	Chi-A	86	344	53	96	7	5	0	18	25		.279	.335	.328	104	3	25			.965	2	O-82/3-3	0.0
	Yr	107	415	66	112	10	6	1	26	30		.270	.331	.330	101	1	35			.956	3	O-96/3-7,2-2	-0.1
1904	Chi-A	68	251	42	78	11	4	1	19	14		.311	.354	.438	156	15	13			.975	2	O-63	1.5
1905	Chi-A	92	328	42	66	15	2	0	22	19		.201	.258	.259	67	-12	11			.936	-1	O-89	-2.0
Total	10	932	3601	539	1014	142	58	17	374	236	14	.282	.337	.367	99	-5	236			.924	-5	O-883/3-11,S-11,P2	-6.3

■ TOMMY HOLMES
Holmes, Thomas Francis "Kelly" b: 3/29/17, Brooklyn, N.Y. BL/TL, 5'10", 180 lbs. Deb: 4/14/42 M

YEAR	TM/L	G	AB	R	H	2B	3B	HR	RBI	BB	SO	AVG	OBP	SLG	PRO+	BR/A	SB	CS	SBR	FA	FR	G/POS	TPR
1942	Bos-N	141	558	56	155	24	4	4	41	64	10	.278	.353	.357	110	8	2			.990	15	*O-140	1.7
1943	Bos-N	152	629	75	170	33	10	5	41	58	20	.270	.334	.378	107	5	7			.993	8	*O-152	0.5
1944	Bos-N	155	631	93	195	42	6	13	73	61	11	.309	.372	.456	127	22	4			.991	6	*O-155	2.0
1945	Bos-N†	154	636	125	**224**	47	6	28	117	70	9	.352	.420	**.577**	175	62	15			.983	1	*O-154	5.4
1946	Bos-N	149	568	80	176	35	6	9	79	58	14	.310	.377	.424	126	19	7			.987	8	*O-146	2.1
1947	Bos-N	150	618	90	**191**	33	9	9	53	44	16	.309	.360	.416	108	7	3			.989	10	*O-147	0.8
1948	*Bos-N★	139	585	85	190	35	7	6	61	46	20	.325	.375	.439	122	17	1			.983	-3	*O-137	1.3
1949	Bos-N	117	380	47	101	20	4	8	59	39	6	.266	.337	.403	103	1	1			.987	5	*O-103	0.1
1950	Bos-N	105	322	44	96	20	1	9	51	33	8	.298	.370	.450	122	10	0			1.000	0	O-88	0.6
1951	Bos-N	27	29	1	5	2	0	0	4	4	4	.172	.250	.241	35	-3	0	0	0	1.000	-1	/O-3,M	-0.4
1952	*Bro-N	31	36	2	4	1	0	0	1	4	4	.111	.200	.139	-4	-5	0	0	0	1.000	-1	/O-6	-0.6
Total	11	1320	4992	698	1507	292	47	88	581	480	122	.302	.366	.432	122	144	40	0		.989	53	*O-1231	13.5

■ RED HOLT
Holt, James Emmett Madison b: 7/25/1894, Dayton, Tenn. d: 2/2/61, Birmingham, Ala. BL/TL, 5'11", 175 lbs. Deb: 9/5/25

YEAR	TM/L	G	AB	R	H	2B	3B	HR	RBI	BB	SO	AVG	OBP	SLG	PRO+	BR/A	SB	CS	SBR	FA	FR	G/POS	TPR
1925	Phi-A	27	88	13	24	7	0	1	8	12	9	.273	.360	.386	84	-2	0	0	0	.986	0	1-25	-0.3

■ JIM HOLT
Holt, James William b: 5/27/44, Graham, N.C. BL/TR, 6', 195 lbs. Deb: 4/17/68

YEAR	TM/L	G	AB	R	H	2B	3B	HR	RBI	BB	SO	AVG	OBP	SLG	PRO+	BR/A	SB	CS	SBR	FA	FR	G/POS	TPR
1968	Min-A	70	106	9	22	2	1	0	8	4	20	.208	.236	.245	44	-7	0	1	-1	.973	-5	O-38/1-1	-1.6
1969	Min-A	12	14	3	5	1	0	1	2	0	4	.357	.357	.571	153	1	0	0	0	1.000	-2	/O-5,1-1	-0.1
1970	*Min-A	142	319	37	85	9	3	6	40	17	32	.266	.304	.342	77	-10	3	1	0	.995	-11	*O-130/1-2	-2.6
1971	Min-A	126	340	35	88	11	3	1	29	16	28	.259	.294	.318	71	-13	5	0	0	.986	-5	*O-106/1-3	-2.3
1972	Min-A	10	27	6	12	1	1	0	8	0	1	.444	.444	.593	197	3	0	0	0	.917	-3	/O-7,1-1	0.3

YEAR	TM/L	G	AB	R	H	2B	3B	HR	RBI	BB	SO	AVG	OBP	SLG	PRO+	BR/A	SB	CS	SBR	FA	FR	G/POS	TPR
1973	Min-A	132	441	52	131	25	3	11	58	59	43	.297	.343	.442	115	8	0	3	-2	.990	5	*O-102,1-33	0.4
1974	Min-A	79	197	24	50	11	0	0	16	14	16	.254	.307	.310	75	-6	0	0	0	.996	1	1-67/O-5	-0.5
	*Oak-A	30	42	1	6	0	0	0	0	1	9	.143	.182	.143	-6	-6	0	0	0	1.000	1	1-17/D-3	-0.5
	Yr	109	239	25	56	11	0	0	16	15	25	.234	.285	.280	63	-11	0	0	0	.996	6	1-84/O-5,D-3	-1.0
1975	*Oak-A	102	123	7	27	3	0	2	16	11	11	.220	.294	.293	68	-5	0	0	0	.991	1	1-52/O-2,C-1,D-4	-0.6
1976	Oak-A	4	7	0	2	2	0	0	2	1	2	.286	.375	.571	182	1	0	0	0	.000	0	/D-2	0.1
Total	9	707	1616	174	428	64	10	19	177	93	166	.265	.308	.352	84	-35	8	6	-1	.988	-11	O-395,1-177/D-9,C-1	-7.4

■ ROGER HOLT Holt, Roger Boyd b: 4/8/56, Daytona Beach, Fla. BB/TR, 5'11", 165 lbs. Deb: 10/4/80

YEAR	TM/L	G	AB	R	H	2B	3B	HR	RBI	BB	SO	AVG	OBP	SLG	PRO+	BR/A	SB	CS	SBR	FA	FR	G/POS	TPR
1980	NY-A	2	6	0	1	0	0	0	1	1	2	.167	.286	.167	28	-1	0	0	0	1.000	1	/2-2	0.0

■ MARTY HONAN Honan, Martin Weldon b: 4/1871, Chicago, Ill. d: 8/20/08, Chicago, Ill. Deb: 10/3/1890

YEAR	TM/L	G	AB	R	H	2B	3B	HR	RBI	BB	SO	AVG	OBP	SLG	PRO+	BR/A	SB	CS	SBR	FA	FR	G/POS	TPR
1890	Chi-N	1	3	0	0	0	0	0	0	1	0	.000	.000	.000	-96	-1	0			.857	-0	/C-1	-0.1
1891	Chi-N	5	12	1	2	0	0	0	3	1	3	.167	.231	.333	64	-1	0			.963	2	/C-5	0.1
Total	2	6	15	1	2	0	1	0	4	1	5	.133	.188	.267	32	-1	0			.941	1	/C-6	0.0

■ ABIE HOOD Hood, Albie Larrison b: 1/31/03, Sanford, N.C. d: 10/14/88, Chesapeake, Va. BL/TR, 5'7", 152 lbs. Deb: 7/15/25

YEAR	TM/L	G	AB	R	H	2B	3B	HR	RBI	BB	SO	AVG	OBP	SLG	PRO+	BR/A	SB	CS	SBR	FA	FR	G/POS	TPR
1925	Bos-N	5	21	2	6	2	0	1	2	1	0	.286	.318	.524	122	0	0	0	0	.920	-4	/2-5	-0.3

■ WALLY HOOD Hood, Wallace James Sr. b: 2/9/1895, Whittier, Cal. d: 5/2/65, Hollywood, Cal. BR/TR, 5'11.5", 160 lbs. Deb: 4/15/20 F

YEAR	TM/L	G	AB	R	H	2B	3B	HR	RBI	BB	SO	AVG	OBP	SLG	PRO+	BR/A	SB	CS	SBR	FA	FR	G/POS	TPR
1920	Bro-N	7	14	4	2	1	0	0	1	4	4	.143	.333	.214	58	-1	2	0	1	.944	1	/O-5	0.1
	Pit-N	2	1	1	0	0	0	0	0	1	0	.000	.500	.000	50	0	1	0	0	.000	0	H	0.0
	Yr	9	15	5	2	1	0	0	1	5	4	.133	.350	.200	59	-1	3	0	1	.944	1	/O-5	0.1
1921	Bro-N	56	65	16	17	1	2	1	4	9	14	.262	.360	.385	94	-0	2	2	-1	.957	-6	O-20	-0.7
1922	Bro-N	2	0	2	0	0	0	0	0	0	0	—	—	—		0	0	0	0	.000	0	R	0.0
Total	3	67	80	23	19	2	2	1	5	14	18	.237	.358	.350	88	-1	5	2	0	.951	-4	/O-25	-0.6

■ ALEX HOOKS Hooks, Alexander Marcus b: 8/29/06, Edgewood, Tex. d: 6/19/93, Edgewood, Tex. BL/TR, 6'1", 183 lbs. Deb: 4/17/35

YEAR	TM/L	G	AB	R	H	2B	3B	HR	RBI	BB	SO	AVG	OBP	SLG	PRO+	BR/A	SB	CS	SBR	FA	FR	G/POS	TPR
1935	Phi-A	15	44	4	10	3	0	0	4	5	3	.227	.277	.295	48	-3	0	0	0	1.000	0	1-10	-0.4

■ HARRY HOOPER Hooper, Harry Bartholomew b: 8/24/1887, Bell Station, Cal. d: 12/18/74, Santa Cruz, Cal. BL/TR, 5'10", 168 lbs. Deb: 4/16/09 H

YEAR	TM/L	G	AB	R	H	2B	3B	HR	RBI	BB	SO	AVG	OBP	SLG	PRO+	BR/A	SB	CS	SBR	FA	FR	G/POS	TPR
1909	Bos-A	81	255	29	72	3	4	0	12	16		.282	.337	.325	107	2	15			.952	4	O-74	0.4
1910	Bos-A	155	584	81	156	9	10	2	27	62		.267	.346	.327	108	7	40			.938	11	*O-155	1.1
1911	Bos-A	130	524	93	163	20	6	4	45	73		.311	.399	.395	123	19	38			.954	6	*O-130	1.7
1912	*Bos-A	147	590	98	143	20	12	2	53	66		.242	.326	.327	83	-13	29			.964	2	*O-147	-1.9
1913	Bos-A	148	586	100	169	29	12	4	40	60	51	.288	.359	.399	119	14	26			.968	9	*O-147/P-1	1.7
1914	Bos-A	142	530	85	137	23	15	1	41	58	47	.258	.346	.364	110	6	19	14	-3	.973	11	*O-140	0.9
1915	*Bos-A	149	566	90	133	20	13	2	51	89	36	.235	.342	.327	103	4	22	20	-5	.972	11	*O-149	0.2
1916	*Bos-A	151	575	75	156	20	11	1	37	80	35	.271	.361	.350	113	11	27	11	2	.966	8	*O-151	1.4
1917	Bos-A	151	559	89	143	21	11	3	45	80	40	.256	.355	.349	116	13	21			.971	-1	*O-151	0.4
1918	*Bos-A	126	474	81	137	26	13	1	44	75	25	.289	.391	.405	143	26	24			.963	-0	*O-126	2.1
1919	Bos-A	128	491	76	131	25	6	3	49	79	28	.267	.374	.360	113	12	23			.979	5	*O-128	1.3
1920	Bos-A	139	536	91	167	30	17	7	53	88	27	.312	.411	.470	139	32	16	18	-6	.963	7	*O-139	2.2
1921	Chi-A	108	419	74	137	26	6	8	58	55	21	.327	.406	.470	125	17	13	7	-0	.975	-3	*O-108	0.5
1922	Chi-A	152	602	111	183	35	8	11	80	68	33	.304	.379	.444	114	13	16	12	-2	.962	7	*O-149	0.7
1923	Chi-A	145	576	87	166	32	4	10	65	68	22	.288	.370	.410	106	6	18	18	-5	.960	-4	*O-143	-1.3
1924	Chi-A	130	476	107	156	27	10	10	62	65	26	.328	.413	.481	134	25	16	13	-3	.986	11	*O-123	2.3
1925	Chi-A	127	442	62	117	23	5	6	55	54	21	.265	.351	.380	90	-7	12	8	-1	.976	4	*O-124	-1.1
Total	17	2309	8785	1429	2466	389	160	75	817	1136	412	.281	.368	.387	114	188	375	121		.966	91	*O-2284/P-1	12.6

■ MIKE HOOPER Hooper, Michael H. b: 2/7/1850, Baltimore, Md. d: 12/1/17, Baltimore, Md. 5'6", 165 lbs. Deb: 6/27/1873

YEAR	TM/L	G	AB	R	H	2B	3B	HR	RBI	BB	SO	AVG	OBP	SLG	PRO+	BR/A	SB	CS	SBR	FA	FR	G/POS	TPR
1873	Mar-n	3	14	3	3	1	0	0	2	0	0	.214	.214	.286	62	-0	0	0	0	.833	-1	/O-2,C-1	-0.1

■ CHARLIE HOOVER Hoover, Charles E. b: 9/21/1865, Mound City, Ill. BL/TR, 5'8", Deb: 10/9/1888

YEAR	TM/L	G	AB	R	H	2B	3B	HR	RBI	BB	SO	AVG	OBP	SLG	PRO+	BR/A	SB	CS	SBR	FA	FR	G/POS	TPR
1888	KC-a	3	10	0	3	0	0	0	1	0		.300	.300	.300	87	-0				.857	0	/C-3	0.0
1889	KC-a	71	258	44	64	2	5	1	25	29	38	.248	.329	.306	77	-8	9			.916	-4	C-66/3-4,O-3	-0.5
Total	2	74	268	44	67	2	5	1	26	29	38	.250	.328	.306	77	-8	9			.913	-4	/C-69,3-4,O-3	-0.5

■ JOE HOOVER Hoover, Robert Joseph b: 4/15/15, Brawley, Cal. d: 9/2/65, Los Angeles, Cal. BR/TR, 5'11", 175 lbs. Deb: 4/21/43

YEAR	TM/L	G	AB	R	H	2B	3B	HR	RBI	BB	SO	AVG	OBP	SLG	PRO+	BR/A	SB	CS	SBR	FA	FR	G/POS	TPR
1943	Det-A	144	575	78	140	15	8	4	38	36	101	.243	.289	.318	72	-21	6	5	-1	.944	-6	*S-144	-1.9
1944	Det-A	120	441	67	104	20	2	0	29	35	66	.236	.301	.290	66	-19	7	10	-4	.932	15	*S-119/2-1	0.2
1945	*Det-A	74	222	33	57	10	5	1	17	21	35	.257	.324	.360	92	-2	6	2	1	.944	-7	S-68	-0.4
Total	3	338	1238	178	301	45	15	5	84	92	202	.243	.300	.316	73	-43	19	17	-5	.939	3	S-331/2-1	-2.1

■ BUSTER HOOVER Hoover, William J. b: 1863, Philadelphia, Pa. BR/TR, 6'1", 178 lbs. Deb: 4/17/1884

YEAR	TM/L	G	AB	R	H	2B	3B	HR	RBI	BB	SO	AVG	OBP	SLG	PRO+	BR/A	SB	CS	SBR	FA	FR	G/POS	TPR
1884	Phi-U	63	275	76	100	20	8	0		12		.364	.390	.495	180	19				.780	-1	O-37,S-15/1-6,23	1.5
	Phi-N	10	42	6	8	1	0	1	4	4	9	.190	.261	.286	75	-1				.929	-1	O-10	-0.2
1886	Bal-a	40	157	25	34	2	6	0	10	16		.217	.297	.306	91	-1	15			.839	-1	O-40	-0.3
1892	Cin-N	14	51	7	9	0	0	0	2	5	4	.176	.250	.176	30	-4	1			.966	1	O-14	-0.4
Total	3	127	525	114	151	23	14	1	16	37	13	.288	.337	.390	129	12	16			.840	-3	O-101/S-15,2-6,13	0.6

■ DON HOPKINS Hopkins, Donald b: 1/9/52, West Point, Miss. BL/TR, 6', 175 lbs. Deb: 4/8/75

YEAR	TM/L	G	AB	R	H	2B	3B	HR	RBI	BB	SO	AVG	OBP	SLG	PRO+	BR/A	SB	CS	SBR	FA	FR	G/POS	TPR
1975	*Oak-A	82	6	25	1	0	0	0	0	0	2	.167	.375	.167	59	-0	21	9	1	1.000	-2	D-20/O-5R-0	-0.2
1976	Oak-A	3	0	0	0	0	0	0	0	0	0						0	1	-1	.000	0	R	-0.1
Total	2	85	6	25	1	0	0	0	0	0	2	.167	.375	.167	59	-0	21	10	0	1.000	-2	/D-20,O-5	-0.3

■ GAIL HOPKINS Hopkins, Gail Eason b: 2/19/43, Tulsa, Okla. BL/TR, 5'10", 200 lbs. Deb: 6/29/68

YEAR	TM/L	G	AB	R	H	2B	3B	HR	RBI	BB	SO	AVG	OBP	SLG	PRO+	BR/A	SB	CS	SBR	FA	FR	G/POS	TPR
1968	Chi-A	29	37	4	8	2	0	0	6	3		.216	.326	.270	81	-1	0	0	0	1.000	-1	/1-7	-0.2
1969	Chi-A	124	373	52	99	13	3	8	46	50	28	.265	.354	.381	100	1	2	1	0	.994	-3	*1-101	-1.0
1970	Chi-A	116	287	32	82	8	1	6	29	28	19	.286	.351	.383	99	-0	0	0	0	.987	-2	1-77/C-8	-0.8
1971	KC-A	103	295	35	82	16	1	9	47	37	13	.278	.366	.431	126	11	3	1	0	.990	-4	1-83	0.6
1972	KC-A	53	71	1	15	2	0	0	5	7	4	.211	.282	.239	56	-4	0	0	0	.990	-1	1-13/3-1	-0.7
1973	KC-A	74	138	17	34	6	1	2	16	29	15	.246	.385	.348	100	1	1	2	-1	1.000	0	D-36,1-10	0.0
1974	LA-N	15	18	1	4	0	0	0	3	1		.222	.333	.222	60	-1	0	0	0	1.000	0	/C-2,1-2	0.0
Total	7	514	1219	142	324	47	6	25	145	160	83	.266	.355	.376	103	8	6	4	-1	.991	-4	1-293/D-36,C-10,3-1	-2.1

■ BUCK HOPKINS Hopkins, John Winton "Sis" b: 1/3/1883, Grafton, Va. d: 10/2/29, Phoebus, Va. BL/TL, 5'10", 165 lbs. Deb: 7/22/07

YEAR	TM/L	G	AB	R	H	2B	3B	HR	RBI	BB	SO	AVG	OBP	SLG	PRO+	BR/A	SB	CS	SBR	FA	FR	G/POS	TPR
1907	StL-N	15	44	7	6	3	0	0	3	10		.136	.333	.205	71	-1	2			.875	-4	O-15	-0.6

■ MARTY HOPKINS Hopkins, Meredith Hilliard b: 2/22/07, Wolfe City, Tex. d: 11/20/63, Dallas, Tex. BR/TR, 5'11", 175 lbs. Deb: 4/17/34

YEAR	TM/L	G	AB	R	H	2B	3B	HR	RBI	BB	SO	AVG	OBP	SLG	PRO+	BR/A	SB	CS	SBR	FA	FR	G/POS	TPR
1934	Phi-N	10	25	6	3	2	0	0	3	7	5	.120	.313	.200	36	-1	0			1.000	-1	/3-9	-0.3
	Chi-A	67	210	22	45	7	0	2	28	42	26	.214	.348	.276	61	-11	0	3	-2	.957	4	3-63	-0.6
1935	Chi-A	59	144	20	32	3	0	1	17	36	23	.222	.378	.285	72	-5	1	0	0	.960	-7	3-49/2-5	-0.9
Total	2	136	379	48	80	12	0	4	48	85	54	.211	.357	.274	63	-17	1	3		.960	-4	3-121/2-5	-1.8

■ MIKE HOPKINS Hopkins, Michael Joseph "Skinner" b: 11/1/1872, Glasgow, Scotland d: 2/5/52, Pittsburgh, Pa. BR/TR, 5'8", 160 lbs. Deb: 8/24/02

YEAR	TM/L	G	AB	R	H	2B	3B	HR	RBI	BB	SO	AVG	OBP	SLG	PRO+	BR/A	SB	CS	SBR	FA	FR	G/POS	TPR
1902	Pit-N	1	2	0	2	1	0	0	0	0		1.000	1.000	1.500	647	1				1.000	0	/C-1	0.1

■ JOHNNY HOPP Hopp, John Leonard "Hippity" b: 7/18/16, Hastings, Neb. BL/TL, 5'10", 175 lbs. Deb: 9/18/39 C

YEAR	TM/L	G	AB	R	H	2B	3B	HR	RBI	BB	SO	AVG	OBP	SLG	PRO+	BR/A	SB	CS	SBR	FA	FR	G/POS	TPR
1939	StL-N	6	4	0	2	0	0	0	0	1	0	.500	.600	.750	246	1				1.000	0	/1-2	0.1
1940	StL-N	80	152	24	41	7	4	1	14	9	21	.270	.315	.388	88	-3	3			.967	-2	O-39,1-10	-0.6
1941	StL-N	134	445	83	135	25	11	4	50	50	63	.303	.378	.436	121	12	15			.982	1	O-91,1-39	0.6
1942	*StL-N	95	314	41	81	16	7	3	37	36	40	.258	.334	.382	102	1	14			.983	-4	1-88	-0.9

YEAR	TM/L	G	AB	R	H	2B	3B	HR	RBI	BB	SO	AVG	OBP	SLG	PRO+	BR/A	SB	CS	SBR	FA	FR	G/POS	TPR
1943	*StL-N	91	241	33	54	10	2	2	25	24	22	.224	.297	.307	71	-9	8			.950	-2	O-52,1-27	-1.5
1944	*StL-N	139	527	106	177	35	9	11	72	58	47	.336	.404	.499	150	35	15			**.997**	-10	*O-131/1-6	1.9
1945	StL-N	124	446	67	129	22	8	3	44	49	24	.289	.363	.395	108	5	14			.980	-7	*O-104,1-15	-0.7
1946	Bos-N★	129	445	71	148	23	8	3	48	34	34	.333	.386	.440	133	19	21			.981	-1	1-68,O-58	1.2
1947	Bos-N	134	430	74	124	20	2	2	32	58	30	.288	.376	.358	98	1	13			.980	-6	*O-125	-1.1
1948	Pit-N	120	392	64	109	15	12	1	31	40	25	.278	.345	.385	95	-2	5			1.000	1	O-80,1-25	-0.6
1949	Pit-N	20	55	5	12	3	1	0	3	7	3	.218	.306	.309	64	-3	0			.929	-1	/O-7,1-6	-0.4
	Bro-N	8	14	0	0	0	0	0	0	0	3	.000	.000	.000	-96	-4	0			1.000	1	/O-4,1-2	-0.3
	Pit-N	85	316	50	106	11	4	5	36	30	26	.335	.393	.443	121	10	9			.994	-0	1-71/O-9	0.8
	Yr	113	385	55	118	14	5	5	39	37	32	.306	.367	.408	105	3	9			.990	-0	1-79,O-20	0.1
1950	Pit-N	106	318	51	108	24	5	8	47	43	17	.340	.420	.522	141	20	7			.990	-6	1-70/O-7	1.2
	*NY-A	19	27	9	9	2	1	1	8	8	1	.333	.486	.593	180	4	0	1	-1	1.000	-1	1-12/O-6	0.2
1951	*NY-A	46	63	10	13	1	0	2	4	9	11	.206	.306	.317	71	-3	2	0	1	.992	-1	1-25	-0.4
1952	NY-A	15	25	4	4	0	0	0	2	2	3	.160	.250	.160	17	-3	2	0	1	1.000	1	1-12	-0.2
	Det-A	42	46	5	10	1	0	0	3	6	7	.217	.308	.239	53	-3	0	0	0	1.000	-1	/O-4,1-1	-0.4
	Yr	57	71	9	14	1	0	0	5	8	10	.197	.287	.211	41	-5	2	0	1	1.000	-0	1-13/O-4	-0.6
Total	14	1393	4260	698	1262	216	74	46	458	464	378	.296	.368	.414	113	79	128	1		.985	-36	O-717,1-479	-1.1

■ **SHAGS HORAN**   Horan, Joseph Patrick b: 9/6/1895, St.Louis, Mo. d: 2/13/69, Torrance, Cal. BR/TR, 5'10", 170 lbs. Deb: 7/14/24

YEAR	TM/L	G	AB	R	H	2B	3B	HR	RBI	BB	SO	AVG	OBP	SLG	PRO+	BR/A	SB	CS	SBR	FA	FR	G/POS	TPR
1924	NY-A	22	31	4	9	1	0	0	7	1	5	.290	.313	.323	64	-2	0	0	0	1.000	-4	O-14	-0.6

■ **SAM HORN**   Horn, Samuel Lee b: 11/2/63, Dallas, Tex. BL/TL, 6'5", 250 lbs. Deb: 7/25/87

YEAR	TM/L	G	AB	R	H	2B	3B	HR	RBI	BB	SO	AVG	OBP	SLG	PRO+	BR/A	SB	CS	SBR	FA	FR	G/POS	TPR
1987	Bos-A	46	158	31	44	7	0	14	34	17	55	.278	.356	.589	141	9	0	1	-1	.000	0	D-40	0.7
1988	Bos-A	24	61	4	9	0	0	2	8	11	20	.148	.278	.246	46	-4	0	0	0	.000	0	D-16	-0.5
1989	Bos-A	33	54	1	8	2	0	0	4	8	16	.148	.258	.185	25	-5	0	0	0	1.000	-0	D-14/1-2	-0.6
1990	Bal-A	79	246	30	61	13	0	14	45	32	62	.248	.335	.472	127	8	0	0	0	.970	-0	D-63,1-10	0.5
1991	Bal-A	121	317	45	74	16	0	23	61	41	99	.233	.327	.502	131	12	0	0	0	.000	0	*D-102	0.8
1992	Bal-A	63	162	13	38	10	1	5	19	21	60	.235	.326	.401	100	0	0	0	0	.000	0	D-46	-0.2
1993	Cle-A	12	33	8	15	1	0	4	8	1	5	.455	.486	.848	252	7	0	0	0	.000	0	D-11	0.6
1995	Tex-A	11	9	0	1	0	0	0	0	0	6	.111	.200	.111	-16	-2	0	0	0	.000	0	/D-1	-0.2
Total	8	389	1040	132	250	49	1	62	179	132	323	.240	.330	.468	118	25	0	1	-1	.972	-0	D-293/1-12	1.1

■ **BOB HORNER**   Horner, James Robert b: 8/6/57, Junction City, Kan. BR/TR, 6'1", 210 lbs. Deb: 6/16/78

YEAR	TM/L	G	AB	R	H	2B	3B	HR	RBI	BB	SO	AVG	OBP	SLG	PRO+	BR/A	SB	CS	SBR	FA	FR	G/POS	TPR
1978	Atl-N	89	323	50	86	17	1	23	63	24	42	.266	.321	.539	123	8	0	0	0	.956	6	3-89	1.3
1979	Atl-N	121	487	66	153	15	1	33	98	22	74	.314	.348	.552	132	19	0	2	-1	.930	-7	3-82,1-45	0.8
1980	Atl-N	124	463	81	124	14	1	35	89	27	50	.268	.310	.529	126	13	3	1	0	.935	5	*3-121/1-1	1.7
1981	Atl-N	79	300	42	83	10	0	15	42	32	39	.277	.348	.460	125	9	2	3	-1	.938	-15	3-79	-0.9
1982	*Atl-N★	140	499	85	130	24	0	32	97	66	75	.261	.351	.501	131	20	3	5	-2	.970	-17	3-137	-0.3
1983	Atl-N	104	386	75	117	25	1	20	68	50	63	.303	.384	.528	140	21	4	2	0	.958	-13	*3-104/1-1	0.7
1984	Atl-N	32	113	15	31	8	0	3	19	14	17	.274	.354	.425	110	2	0	0	0	.965	-1	3-32	0.1
1985	Atl-N	130	483	61	129	25	3	27	89	50	57	.267	.337	.499	123	14	1	1	-0	1.000	-10	1-87,3-40	-0.3
1986	Atl-N	141	517	70	141	22	0	27	87	52	72	.273	.342	.472	116	10	1	4	-2	.995	-1	*1-139	0.0
1988	StL-N	60	206	15	53	9	1	3	33	32	23	.257	.360	.354	105	2	0	0	0	.990	-1	1-57	-0.3
Total	10	1020	3777	560	1047	169	8	218	685	369	512	.277	.344	.499	125	117	14	18	-7	.946	-50	3-684,1-330	2.8

■ **ROGERS HORNSBY**   Hornsby, Rogers "Rajah" b: 4/27/1896, Winters, Tex. d: 1/5/63, Chicago, Ill. BR/TR, 5'11", 175 lbs. Deb: 9/10/15 MCH

YEAR	TM/L	G	AB	R	H	2B	3B	HR	RBI	BB	SO	AVG	OBP	SLG	PRO+	BR/A	SB	CS	SBR	FA	FR	G/POS	TPR
1915	StL-N	18	57	5	14	2	0	0	4	2	6	.246	.271	.281	67	-2	0	2	-1	.922	9	S-18	-0.2
1916	StL-N	139	495	63	155	17	15	6	65	40	63	.313	.369	.444	150	29	17			.928	-2	3-83,S-45,1-15/2-1	3.5
1917	StL-N	145	523	86	171	24	**17**	8	66	45	34	.327	.385	**.484**	170	42	17			.939	21	*S-144	7.7
1918	StL-N	115	416	51	117	19	11	5	60	40	34	.281	.349	.416	138	18	8			.933	10	*S-109/O-3	3.6
1919	StL-N	138	512	68	163	15	9	8	71	48	41	.318	.384	.430	154	34	17			.933	2	3-72,S-37,2-25,/1-5	4.5
1920	StL-N	149	589	96	218	44	20	9	**94**	60	50	**.370**	**.431**	.559	190	68	12	15	-5	.962	11	*2-149	8.1
1921	StL-N	154	592	**131**	235	44	**18**	21	126	60	48	**.397**	**.458**	.639	191	78	13	13	-4	.969	-3	*2-142/O-6,S-3,3-1	7.1
1922	StL-N	154	623	**141**	250	46	14	**42**	**152**	65	50	**.401**	**.459**	**.722**	210	99	17	12	-2	**.967**	-7	*2-154	8.5
1923	StL-N	107	424	89	163	32	10	17	83	55	29	**.384**	**.459**	.627	188	54	3	7	-3	.962	-17	2-96,1-10	3.3
1924	StL-N	143	536	**121**	227	43	14	25	94	**89**	32	**.424**	**.507**	**.696**	223	97	5	12	-6	.965	-4	*2-143	8.5
1925	StL-N	138	504	133	203	41	10	**39**	**143**	83	39	**.403**	**.489**	**.756**	208	83	5	3	-0	.962	-29	*2-134,M	6.0
1926	*StL-N	134	527	96	167	34	5	11	93	61	39	.317	.388	.463	123	18	3			.962	-29	*2-155,M	-0.8
1927	NY-N	155	568	**133**	205	32	9	26	125	**86**	39	.361	**.448**	.586	176	63	9			.973	-24	*2-140,M	6.9
1928	Bos-N	140	486	99	188	42	7	21	94	**107**	41	**.387**	**.498**	**.632**	204	80	5			.973	1	*2-140,M	5.8
1929	*Chi-N	156	602	**156**	229	47	8	39	149	87	65	.380	.459	**.679**	178	74	2			.973	1	*2-156	7.2
1930	Chi-N	42	104	15	32	5	1	2	18	12	12	.308	.385	.433	96	-0	0			.916	-3	2-25,M	-0.2
1931	Chi-N	100	357	64	118	37	1	16	90	56	23	.331	.421	.574	162	32	1			.951	-15	2-69,3-26,M	2.3
1932	Chi-N	19	58	10	13	2	0	1	7	10	4	.224	.357	.310	82	-1	0			1.000	-4	O-10/3-6,M	-0.5
1933	StL-N	46	83	9	27	6	0	2	21	12	6	.325	.423	.470	147	6	1			.967	-7	2-17	-0.1
	StL-A	11	9	2	3	1	0	1	2	7	1	.333	.455	.778	208	1	0			.000	0	HM	0.1
1934	StL-A	24	23	2	7	2	0	1	11	7	4	.304	.484	.522	147	2	0			1.000	0	/3-1,O-1,M	0.2
1935	StL-A	10	24	1	3	3	0	0	3	3	6	.208	.296	.333	60	-1	0			1.000	-0	/1-1,M	-0.2
1936	StL-A	2	5	1	2	0	0	0	0	1	0	.400	.500	.400	121	0	0			1.000	-0	/1-1,M	-0.2
1937	StL-A	20	56	7	18	3	0	1	11	7	5	.321	.397	.429	107	1	0	0	0	.947	-5	2-17,M	-0.2
Total	23	2259	8173	1579	2930	541	169	301	1584	1038	679	.358	.434	.577	176	874	135	64		.965	-91	*2-1561,S-356,3/10	81.1

■ **JOE HORNUNG**   Hornung, Michael Joseph "Ubbo Ubbo" b: 6/12/1857, Carthage, N.Y. d: 10/30/31, Howard Beach, N.Y. BR/TR, 5'8.5", 164 lbs. Deb: 5/1/1879 U

YEAR	TM/L	G	AB	R	H	2B	3B	HR	RBI	BB	SO	AVG	OBP	SLG	PRO+	BR/A	SB	CS	SBR	FA	FR	G/POS	TPR
1879	Buf-N	78	319	46	85	18	7	0	38	2	27	.266	.271	.367	105	-1				.844	-2	*O-77/1-1	-0.4
1880	Buf-N	85	342	47	91	8	11	1	42	8	29	.266	.283	.363	115	5				.874	-0	*O-67,1-18/2-5,P-1	0.1
1881	Bos-N	83	324	40	78	12	8	2	25	5	25	.241	.252	.346	90	-4				**.948**	12	*O-83	0.6
1882	Bos-N	85	388	67	117	14	11	1	50	2	25	.302	.305	.402	124	10				**.932**	11	*O-84/1-1	1.8
1883	Bos-N	98	446	**107**	124	25	13	8	66	8	54	.278	.291	.446	117	8				**.936**	7	*O-98/3-1	1.2
1884	Bos-N	115	518	119	139	27	10	7	51	17	80	.268	.292	.400	116	8				.916	3	*O-110/1-6	0.8
1885	Bos-N	25	109	14	22	4	1	1	7	1	20	.202	.209	.284	61	-5				.919	-3	O-25	-0.8
1886	Bos-N	94	424	67	109	12	2	4	40	10	62	.257	.274	.309	80	-10	16			**.948**	7	*O-94	-0.5
1887	Bos-N	98	437	85	118	10	6	5	49	17	28	.270	.302	.355	82	-11	41			**.935**	13	*O-98	0.0
1888	Bos-N	107	431	61	103	13	9	1	53	16	39	.239	.269	.318	85	-8	29			.947	-8	*O-107	-1.9
1889	Bal-a	135	533	73	122	13	7	1	78	22	72	.229	.269	.293	59	-30	34			.913	11	*O-134/3-1	-1.9
1890	NY-N	120	513	62	122	18	5	0	65	12	37	.238	.258	.292	60	-28	39			.931	-3	O-77,1-36/3-5,S-2	-3.1
Total	12	1123	4784	788	1230	172	90	31	564	120	498	.257	.277	.350	91	-64	159			.922	49	*O-1054/1-62,32SP	-4.1

■ **TONY HORTON**   Horton, Anthony Darrin b: 12/6/44, Santa Monica, Cal. BR/TR, 6'3", 210 lbs. Deb: 7/31/64

YEAR	TM/L	G	AB	R	H	2B	3B	HR	RBI	BB	SO	AVG	OBP	SLG	PRO+	BR/A	SB	CS	SBR	FA	FR	G/POS	TPR
1964	Bos-A	36	126	9	28	5	0	1	8	3	20	.222	.240	.286	44	-10	0	0	0	1.000	1	O-24/1-8	-1.1
1965	Bos-A	60	163	23	48	8	1	7	23	18	36	.294	.365	.485	131	7	0	2	-1	.980	-1	1-44	0.2
1966	Bos-A	6	22	0	3	0	0	0	2	0	5	.136	.136	.136	-19	-3	0	0	0	1.000	1	/1-6	-0.3
1967	Bos-A	21	39	2	12	3	0	0	9	0	5	.308	.308	.385	96	-0	0	0	0	.929	-1	/1-6	-0.4
	Cle-A	106	363	35	102	13	4	10	44	18	52	.281	.322	.421	117	7	3	0	1	.991	-6	1-94	-0.4
	Yr	127	402	37	114	16	4	10	53	18	57	.284	.321	.418	114	6	3	0	1	.987	-6	*1-100	-0.6
1968	Cle-A	133	477	57	119	29	3	14	59	34	56	.249	.304	.411	117	8	3	3	-1	.989	-0	*1-128	-0.6
1969	Cle-A	159	625	77	174	25	4	27	93	37	91	.278	.321	.461	113	8	3	3	-1	.989	-0	*1-157	-0.6
1970	Cle-A	115	413	48	111	19	3	17	59	30	54	.269	.324	.453	107	3	2	2	-0	.994	3	*1-112	-0.4
Total	7	636	2228	251	597	102	15	76	297	140	319	.268	.315	.430	109	18	12	8	-1	.990	-7	1-555/O-24	-3.4

■ **WILLIE HORTON**   Horton, Willie Watterson b: 10/18/42, Arno, Va. BR/TR, 5'11", 209 lbs. Deb: 9/10/63 C

YEAR	TM/L	G	AB	R	H	2B	3B	HR	RBI	BB	SO	AVG	OBP	SLG	PRO+	BR/A	SB	CS	SBR	FA	FR	G/POS	TPR
1963	Det-A	15	43	6	14	2	1	1	4	0	8	.326	.326	.488	120	1	2	0	1	1.000	-1	/O-9	0.0

YEAR	TM/L	G	AB	R	H	2B	3B	HR	RBI	BB	SO	AVG	OBP	SLG	PRO+	BR/A	SB	CS	SBR	FA	FR	G/POS	TPR
1964	Det-A	25	80	6	13	1	3	1	10	11	20	.162	.272	.287	55	-5	0	0	0	.943	-2	O-23	-0.8
1965	Det-A★	143	512	69	140	20	2	29	104	48	101	.273	.343	.490	132	21	5	9	-4	.988	5	*O-141/3-1	1.6
1966	Det-A	146	526	72	138	22	6	27	100	44	103	.262	.323	.481	125	15	1	1	-0	.979	-4	*O-137	0.6
1967	Det-A	122	401	47	110	20	3	19	67	36	80	.274	.340	.481	137	17	0	0	0	.971	-0	*O-110	1.3
1968	*Det-A★	143	512	68	146	20	2	36	85	49	110	.285	.357	.543	165	38	0	3	-2	.973	0	*O-139	3.4
1969	Det-A	141	508	66	133	17	1	28	91	52	93	.262	.334	.465	116	10	3	3	-1	.972	9	*O-136	1.0
1970	Det-A★	96	371	53	113	18	2	17	69	28	43	.305	.354	.501	133	15	0	1	-1	.982	5	O-96	1.6
1971	Det-A	119	450	64	130	25	1	22	72	37	75	.289	.352	.496	133	18	1	5	-3	.963	-10	*O-118	-0.1
1972	*Det-A	108	333	44	77	9	5	11	36	27	47	.231	.295	.387	99	-1	0	0	0	1.000	-10	*O-98	-1.8
1973	Det-A★	111	411	42	130	19	3	17	53	23	57	.316	.363	.501	132	16	1	4	-2	.942	-10	*O-107/D-1	0.0
1974	Det-A	72	238	32	71	8	1	15	47	21	36	.298	.363	.529	149	14	0	1	-1	.947	-4	O-64/D-1	0.8
1975	Det-A	159	615	62	169	13	1	25	92	44	109	.275	.323	.421	104	2	1	2	-1	.000	0	*D-159	-0.3
1976	Det-A	114	401	40	105	17	0	14	56	49	63	.262	.345	.409	116	8	0	0	0	.000	0	*D-105	0.6
1977	Det-A	1	4	0	1	0	0	0	0	0	0	.250	.250	.250	35	-0	0	0	0	1.000	-0	/O-1	-0.1
	Tex-A	139	519	55	150	23	3	15	75	42	117	.289	.342	.432	108	6	2	3	-1	.938	-1	*D-128,O-10	-0.1
	Yr	140	523	55	151	23	3	15	75	42	117	.289	.342	.430	108	5	2	3	-1	.941	-2	*D-128,O-11	-0.2
1978	Cle-A	50	169	15	42	7	0	5	22	15	25	.249	.314	.379	95	-1	3	0	1	.000	0	D-48	-0.2
	Oak-A	32	102	11	32	8	0	3	19	9	15	.314	.369	.480	145	6	0	1	-1	.333	-1	D-27/O-1	0.4
	Tor-A	33	122	12	25	6	0	3	19	4	29	.205	.230	.328	54	-8	0	0	0	.000	0	D-30	-0.9
	Yr	115	393	38	99	21	0	11	60	28	69	.252	.303	.389	95	-4	3	1	0	.333	-1	*D-105/O-1	-0.7
1979	Sea-A	162	646	77	180	19	5	29	106	42	112	.279	.327	.458	107	5	1	1	-0	.000	0	*D-162	-0.1
1980	Sea-A	97	335	32	74	10	1	8	36	39	70	.221	.300	.328	74	-11	0	4	-2	.000	0	D-92	-1.7
Total	18	2028	7298	873	1993	284	40	325	1163	620	1313	.273	.335	.457	119	166	20	38	-17	.972	-24	*O-1190,D-753/3-1	5.2

■ DWAYNE HOSEY
Hosey, Dwayne Samuel b: 3/11/67, Sharon, Pa. BB/TR, 5'10", 175 lbs. Deb: 9/1/95

YEAR	TM/L	G	AB	R	H	2B	3B	HR	RBI	BB	SO	AVG	OBP	SLG	PRO+	BR/A	SB	CS	SBR	FA	FR	G/POS	TPR
1995	*Bos-A	24	68	20	23	8	1	3	7	8	16	.338	.408	.618	157	6	6	0	2	1.000	-1	O-21/D-1	0.6
1996	Bos-A	28	78	13	17	2	1	1	3	7	17	.218	.282	.333	53	-6	6	3	0	.984	1	O-26/D-2	-0.4
Total	2	52	146	33	40	10	2	4	10	15	33	.274	.342	.466	101	-0	12	3	2	.991	0	/O-47,D-3	0.2

■ STEVE HOSEY
Hosey, Steven Bernard b: 4/2/69, Oakland, Cal. BR/TR, 6'3", 215 lbs. Deb: 8/29/92

YEAR	TM/L	G	AB	R	H	2B	3B	HR	RBI	BB	SO	AVG	OBP	SLG	PRO+	BR/A	SB	CS	SBR	FA	FR	G/POS	TPR
1992	SF-N	21	56	6	14	1	0	1	6	0	15	.250	.250	.321	64	-3	1	1	-0	.960	-2	O-18	-0.6
1993	SF-N	3	2	0	1	1	0	0	1	1	1	.500	.667	1.000	350	1	0	0	0	.000	-0	/O-1	0.0
Total	2	24	58	6	15	2	0	1	7	1	16	.259	.271	.345	77	-2	1	1	-0	.960	-3	/O-19	-0.6

■ TIM HOSLEY
Hosley, Timothy Kenneth b: 5/10/47, Spartanburg, S.C. BR/TR, 5'10", 195 lbs. Deb: 9/8/70

YEAR	TM/L	G	AB	R	H	2B	3B	HR	RBI	BB	SO	AVG	OBP	SLG	PRO+	BR/A	SB	CS	SBR	FA	FR	G/POS	TPR
1970	Det-A	7	12	1	2	0	0	1	2	0	6	.167	.167	.417	55	-1	0	0	0	1.000	0	/C-4	0.1
1971	Det-A	7	16	2	3	0	0	2	6	0	1	.188	.188	.563	102	-0	0	0	0	1.000	-0	/C-4,1-1	0.0
1973	Oak-A	13	14	3	3	0	0	0	2	3	3	.214	.313	.214	53	-1	0	0	0	.952	-1	C-13	-0.2
1974	Oak-A	11	7	3	2	0	0	0	1	1	2	.286	.375	.286	99	0	0	0	0	1.000	0	/C-8,1-1	0.0
1975	Chi-N	62	141	22	36	7	0	6	20	27	25	.255	.382	.433	120	5	1	1	-0	.968	-2	C-53	0.4
1976	Oak-A	37	55	4	9	2	0	1	4	8	12	.164	.270	.255	56	-3	0	0	0	.968	-1	C-37	-0.3
	Chi-N	1	1	0	0	0	0	0	0	0	0	.000	.000	.000	-92	-0	0	0	0	.000	0	H	-0.1
1977	Oak-A	39	78	5	15	0	0	1	10	16	13	.192	.337	.231	59	-4	0	0	0	.955	3	C-19,D-12/1-3	-0.1
1978	Oak-A	13	23	1	7	2	0	0	3	1	6	.304	.360	.391	117	1	0	0	0	.962	1	/C-6,D-1	0.1
1981	Oak-A	18	21	2	2	0	0	1	5	2	5	.095	.174	.238	19	-2	0	0	0	.750	-1	/O-1,1-1,D-4	-0.3
Total	9	208	368	43	79	11	0	12	53	57	73	.215	.326	.342	87	-6	1	1	-0	.968	-1	C-144/D-17,1-6	-0.3

■ CHUCK HOSTETLER
Hostetler, Charles Cloyd b: 9/22/03, McClellandtown, Pa. d: 2/18/71, Fort Collins, Colo BL/TR, 6', 175 lbs. Deb: 4/18/44

YEAR	TM/L	G	AB	R	H	2B	3B	HR	RBI	BB	SO	AVG	OBP	SLG	PRO+	BR/A	SB	CS	SBR	FA	FR	G/POS	TPR
1944	Det-A	90	265	42	79	9	2	0	20	21	31	.298	.350	.347	94	-2	4	4	-1	.985	-2	O-65	-0.6
1945	*Det-A	42	44	3	7	3	0	0	2	7	8	.159	.275	.227	43	-3	0	0	0	.889	-3	/O-8	-0.6
Total	2	132	309	45	86	12	2	0	22	28	39	.278	.338	.330	87	-5	4	4	-1	.979	-2	/O-73	-1.2

■ DAVE HOSTETLER
Hostetler, David Alan b: 3/27/56, Pasadena, Cal. BR/TR, 6'4", 215 lbs. Deb: 9/15/81

YEAR	TM/L	G	AB	R	H	2B	3B	HR	RBI	BB	SO	AVG	OBP	SLG	PRO+	BR/A	SB	CS	SBR	FA	FR	G/POS	TPR
1981	Mon-N	5	6	1	3	0	0	0	1	0	2	.500	.500	1.000	314	1	0	0	0	1.000	-0	/1-2	0.1
1982	Tex-A	113	418	53	97	12	3	22	67	42	113	.232	.304	.433	105	1	2	2	-1	.990	-11	*1-109/D-3	-1.6
1983	Tex-A	94	304	31	67	9	2	11	46	42	103	.220	.325	.372	93	-2	0	2	-1	1.000	-0	D-88/1-2	-0.7
1984	Tex-A	37	82	7	18	2	1	3	10	13	27	.220	.326	.378	91	-1	0	0	0	1.000	1	1-14,D-13	-0.1
1988	Pit-N	6	8	0	2	0	0	0	0	0	3	.250	.250	.250	45	-1	0	0	0	.944	-1	/1-4,C-1	-0.1
Total	5	255	818	92	187	23	6	37	124	97	248	.229	.315	.407	100	-1	2	4	-2	.990	-11	1-131,D-104/C-1	-2.4

■ PETE HOTALING
Hotaling, Peter James "Monkey" b: 12/16/1856, Mohawk, N.Y. d: 7/3/28, Cleveland, Ohio BL/TR, 5'8", 166 lbs. Deb: 5/1/1879

YEAR	TM/L	G	AB	R	H	2B	3B	HR	RBI	BB	SO	AVG	OBP	SLG	PRO+	BR/A	SB	CS	SBR	FA	FR	G/POS	TPR
1879	Cin-N	81	369	64	103	20	9	1	27	12	17	.279	.302	.390	133	13				.843	-0	*O-69/C-8,2-6,3-3	0.9
1880	Cle-N	78	325	40	78	17	8	0	41	10	30	.240	.263	.342	105	2				.896	-2	*O-78/C-2	-0.3
1881	Wor-N	77	317	51	98	15	3	1	35	18	12	.309	.346	.385	123	8				.862	-3	*O-74/C-3	0.3
1882	Bos-N	84	378	64	98	16	5	0	28	16	21	.259	.289	.328	97	-1				.865	2	*O-84	0.1
1883	Cle-N	100	417	54	108	20	8	0	30	12	31	.259	.280	.345	90	-5				.829	1	*O-100	-0.4
1884	Cle-N	102	408	69	99	16	6	3	27	28	50	.243	.291	.333	93	-4				.849	-1	*O-102/2-1	-0.6
1885	Bro-N	94	370	73	95	9	5	1	34	49		.257	.350	.316	111	7				.893	0	*O-94	0.4
1887	Cle-a	126	505	108	151	28	13	3	94	53		.299	.373	.424	126	19	43			.903	1	*O-126	1.4
1888	Cle-a	98	403	67	101	7	6	0	55	26		.251	.307	.298	97	-1	35			.878	-9	*O-98	-1.1
Total	9	840	3492	590	931	148	63	9	371	224	161	.267	.314	.353	108	38	78			.869	-11	O-825/C-13,2-7,3-3	0.7

■ KEN HOTTMAN
Hottman, Kenneth Roger b: 5/7/48, Stockton, Cal. BR/TR, 5'11", 190 lbs. Deb: 9/11/71

YEAR	TM/L	G	AB	R	H	2B	3B	HR	RBI	BB	SO	AVG	OBP	SLG	PRO+	BR/A	SB	CS	SBR	FA	FR	G/POS	TPR
1971	Chi-A	6	16	1	2	0	0	0	0	1	2	.125	.176	.125	-13	-2	0	0	0	1.000	-1	/O-5	-0.4

■ SADIE HOUCK
Houck, Sargent Perry b: 3/1856, Washington, D.C. d: 5/26/19, Washington, D.C. BR/TR, 5'7", 151 lbs. Deb: 5/1/1879

YEAR	TM/L	G	AB	R	H	2B	3B	HR	RBI	BB	SO	AVG	OBP	SLG	PRO+	BR/A	SB	CS	SBR	FA	FR	G/POS	TPR
1879	Bos-N	80	356	69	95	24	9	2	49	4	11	.267	.275	.402	117	6				.814	-8	O-47,S-33	-0.2
1880	Bos-N	12	47	2	7	0	0	0	2	0	6	.149	.149	.149	1	-5				.786	-1	O-12	-0.6
	Pro-N	49	184	27	37	7	7	1	22	3	6	.201	.214	.332	85	-3				.873	-1	O-49	-0.5
	Yr	61	231	29	44	7	7	1	24	3	12	.190	.201	.294	68	-7				.855	-3	O-61	-1.1
1881	Det-N	75	308	43	86	16	6	1	36	6	6	.279	.293	.380	106	1				.868	1	*S-75	0.6
1883	Det-N	101	416	52	105	18	12	0	40	9	18	.252	.268	.353	91	-4				.852	5	*S-101	0.3
1884	Phi-a	108	472	93	140	19	14	0	7			.297	.318	.396	124	10				.893	23	*S-108/2-1	3.1
1885	Phi-a	93	388	74	99	10	9	0	54	10		.255	.286	.327	88	-7				.863	22	*S-93	1.5
1886	Bal-a	61	260	29	50	8	1	0	17	4		.192	.216	.231	41	-18	25			.849	-5	S-55/2-5,O-1	-2.0
	Was-N	52	195	14	42	3	0	0	14	2	28	.215	.223	.231	41	-14	4			.858	-1	S-51/2-1	-1.2
1887	NY-a	10	33	3	5	1	0	0	3	1		.152	.243	.182	20	-3	2			.831	4	S-10/2-1	0.1
Total	8	641	2659	406	666	106	58	4	234	48	75	.250	.269	.338	87	-35	31			.863	39	S-526,O-109/2-8	1.1

■ RALPH HOUK
Houk, Ralph George "Major" b: 8/9/19, Lawrence, Kan. BR/TR, 5'11", 193 lbs. Deb: 4/26/47 MC

YEAR	TM/L	G	AB	R	H	2B	3B	HR	RBI	BB	SO	AVG	OBP	SLG	PRO+	BR/A	SB	CS	SBR	FA	FR	G/POS	TPR
1947	*NY-A	41	92	7	25	3	1	0	12	11	5	.272	.356	.326	91	-1	0	0	0	.987	2	C-41	0.3
1948	NY-A	14	29	3	8	2	0	0	3	0	1	.276	.276	.345	65	-2	0	0	0	1.000	5	C-14	0.3
1949	NY-A	5	7	0	4	0	0	0	1	0	1	.571	.571	.571	203	1	0	0	0	.889	-1	/C-5	0.1
1950	NY-A	10	9	0	1	1	0	0	1	0	2	.111	.111	.222	-17	-2	0	0	0	.929	1	/C-9	-0.1
1951	NY-A	3	5	0	1	0	0	0	0	0	1	.200	.200	.200	9	-1	0	0	0	1.000	1	/C-3	-0.1
1952	*NY-A	9	6	2	2	0	0	0	1	0	1	.333	.429	.333	121	0	0	0	0	.917	1	/C-8	-0.1
1953	NY-A	8	9	0	2	0	0	0	0	0	0	.222	.222	.222	21	-1	0	0	0	1.000	-0	/C-8	-0.1
1954	NY-A	1	1	0	0	0	0	0	0	0	0	.000	.000	.000	-99	-0	0	0	0	.000	0	H	0.0
Total	8	91	158	12	43	6	1	0	20	11	12	.272	.327	.323	79	-6	0	0	0	.981	9	/C-89	0.5

■ FRANK HOUSE
House, Henry Franklin "Pig" b: 2/18/30, Bessemer, Ala. BL/TR, 6'1.5", 190 lbs. Deb: 7/21/50

YEAR	TM/L	G	AB	R	H	2B	3B	HR	RBI	BB	SO	AVG	OBP	SLG	PRO+	BR/A	SB	CS	SBR	FA	FR	G/POS	TPR
1950	Det-A	5	5	1	2	1	0	0	0	0	1	.400	.400	.600	148	0	0	0	0	1.000	0	/C-5	0.0

YEAR	TM/L	G	AB	R	H	2B	3B	HR	RBI	BB	SO	AVG	OBP	SLG	PRO+	BR/A	SB	CS	SBR	FA	FR	G/POS	TPR
1951	Det-A	18	41	3	9	2	0	1	4	6	2	.220	.319	.341	78	-1	1	1	-0	.957	1	C-18	0.0
1954	Det-A	114	352	35	88	12	1	9	38	31	34	.250	.313	.366	87	-7	2	1	0	.992	-1	*C-107	-0.3
1955	Det-A	102	328	37	85	11	1	15	53	22	25	.259	.312	.436	102	-1	0	0	0	.987	2	C-93	0.4
1956	Det-A	94	321	44	77	6	2	10	44	21	19	.240	.293	.364	72	-14	1	1	-0	.986	-6	C-88	-1.7
1957	Det-A	106	348	31	90	9	0	7	36	35	26	.259	.328	.345	82	-8	1	1	-0	.997	9	C-97	0.4
1958	KC-A	76	202	16	51	6	3	4	24	12	13	.252	.298	.371	81	-5	1	0	0	.992	-7	C-55	-1.0
1959	KC-A	98	347	32	82	14	3	1	30	20	23	.236	.282	.303	59	-19	0	3	-2	.982	-8	C-95	-2.5
1960	Cin-N	23	28	0	5	2	0	0	3	0	2	.179	.179	.250	16	-3	0	0	0	1.000	1	/C-8	-0.2
1961	Det-A	17	22	3	5	1	1	0	3	4	2	.227	.346	.364	87	-0	0	0	0	.974	-1	C-14	-0.1
Total	10	653	1994	202	494	64	11	47	235	151	147	.248	.304	.362	80	-60	6	7	-2	.988	-10	C-580	-5.0

■ CHARLIE HOUSEHOLDER
Householder, Charles F.   b: 1856, Harrisburg, Pa.   BR/TR, 5'7", 150 lbs.   Deb: 4/20/1884

YEAR	TM/L	G	AB	R	H	2B	3B	HR	RBI	BB	SO	AVG	OBP	SLG	PRO+	BR/A	SB	CS	SBR	FA	FR	G/POS	TPR
1884	CP-U	83	310	32	74	12	5	1		12		.239	.267	.319	77	-18				.796	-6	3-41,O-40/S-3,P-2	-2.1

■ CHARLIE HOUSEHOLDER
Householder, Charles W.   b: 1856, Harrisburg, Pa.   d: 12/26/08, Harrisburg, Pa.   BL/TL, 5'11", 158 lbs.   Deb: 5/2/1882

YEAR	TM/L	G	AB	R	H	2B	3B	HR	RBI	BB	SO	AVG	OBP	SLG	PRO+	BR/A	SB	CS	SBR	FA	FR	G/POS	TPR
1882	Bal-a	74	307	42	78	10	7	1		4		.254	.264	.342	111	4				.971	3	*1-74/C-3	-0.2
1884	Bro-a	76	273	28	66	15	3	3		12		.242	.279	.352	104	1				.959	-5	1-40,C-31/O-6,2-1	-0.5
Total	2	150	580	70	144	25	10	4		16		.248	.271	.347	108	5				.967	-2	1-114/C-34,O-6,2-1	-0.7

■ ED HOUSEHOLDER
Householder, Edward H.   b: 10/12/1869, Pittsburg, Pa.   d: 7/3/24, Los Angeles, Cal.   TL,   Deb: 4/17/03

YEAR	TM/L	G	AB	R	H	2B	3B	HR	RBI	BB	SO	AVG	OBP	SLG	PRO+	BR/A	SB	CS	SBR	FA	FR	G/POS	TPR
1903	Bro-N	12	43	5	9	0	0	0	9	2		.209	.244	.209	31	-4				.967	1	O-12	-0.4

■ PAUL HOUSEHOLDER
Householder, Paul Wesley   b: 9/4/58, Columbus, Ohio   BB/TR, 6', 180 lbs.   Deb: 8/26/80

YEAR	TM/L	G	AB	R	H	2B	3B	HR	RBI	BB	SO	AVG	OBP	SLG	PRO+	BR/A	SB	CS	SBR	FA	FR	G/POS	TPR
1980	Cin-N	20	45	3	11	1	0	1	7	1	13	.244	.261	.311	59	-3	1	0	0	1.000	-1	O-14	-0.4
1981	Cin-N	23	69	12	19	4	0	2	9	10	16	.275	.367	.420	121	2	3	1	0	1.000	-1	O-19	0.1
1982	Cin-N	138	417	40	88	11	5	9	34	30	77	.211	.267	.326	64	-21	17	11	-2	.992	6	*O-131	-2.0
1983	Cin-N	123	380	40	97	24	4	6	43	44	60	.255	.336	.387	96	-2	12	12	-4	**.991**	-1	*O-112	-0.9
1984	Cin-N	14	12	3	1	1	0	0	0	3	3	.083	.267	.167	23	-1	1	1	-0	1.000	-2	O-10	-0.4
	StL-N	13	14	1	2	0	0	0	0	3	3	.143	.143	.143	-20	-2	0	0	-0	1.000	-3	/O-8	-0.6
	Yr	27	26	4	3	1	0	0	0	3	6	.115	.207	.154	3	-3	1	1	-0	1.000	-5	O-18	-1.0
1985	Mil-A	95	299	41	77	15	0	11	34	27	60	.258	.321	.418	101	0	3	2	-1	.986	-1	O-91/D-3	-0.5
1986	Mil-A	26	78	4	17	3	1	1	16	7	16	.218	.291	.321	64	-4	1	2	-1	1.000	-3	O-22/D-3	-0.8
1987	Hou-N	14	12	2	1	1	0	0	4	2	6	.083	.313	.167	33	-1	0	0	0	1.000	-2	/O-7	-0.3
Total	8	466	1326	146	313	60	11	29	144	126	250	.236	.305	.363	83	-31	36	29	-7	.991	-7	O-414/D-6	-5.8

■ JOHN HOUSEMAN
Houseman, John Franklin   b: 1/10/1870, Holland   d: 11/4/22, Chicago, Ill.   160 lbs.   Deb: 9/11/1894

YEAR	TM/L	G	AB	R	H	2B	3B	HR	RBI	BB	SO	AVG	OBP	SLG	PRO+	BR/A	SB	CS	SBR	FA	FR	G/POS	TPR
1894	Chi-N	4	15	5	6	3	1	0	4	5	3	.400	.571	.733	202	3	2			.950	-0	/S-3,2-1	0.2
1897	StL-N	80	278	34	68	6	6	0	21	28		.245	.329	.309	70	-11	16			.918	-2	2-41,O-33/S-5,3-3	-1.2
Total	2	84	293	39	74	9	7	0	25	33	3	.253	.344	.331	79	-8	18			.916	-3	/2-42,O-33,S-8,3-3	-1.0

■ BEN HOUSER
Houser, Benjamin Franklin   b: 11/30/1883, Shenandoah, Pa.   d: 1/15/52, Augusta, Maine   BL/TL, 6'1", 185 lbs.   Deb: 5/2/10

YEAR	TM/L	G	AB	R	H	2B	3B	HR	RBI	BB	SO	AVG	OBP	SLG	PRO+	BR/A	SB	CS	SBR	FA	FR	G/POS	TPR
1910	Phi-A	34	69	9	13	3	2	0	7	7		.188	.263	.290	74	-2	0			1.000	-0	1-26	-0.3
1911	Bos-N	20	71	11	18	1	0	1	9	8	6	.254	.329	.310	73	-2	2			.988	-3	1-20	-0.2
1912	Bos-N	108	332	38	95	17	3	8	52	22	29	.286	.332	.428	105	1	1			.986	-3	1-83	-0.3
Total	3	162	472	58	126	21	5	9	68	37	35	.267	.322	.390	96	-4	3			.989	-3	1-129	-0.8

■ WAYNE HOUSIE
Housie, Wayne Tyrone   b: 5/20/65, Hampton, Va.   BB/TR, 5'9", 165 lbs.   Deb: 9/17/91

YEAR	TM/L	G	AB	R	H	2B	3B	HR	RBI	BB	SO	AVG	OBP	SLG	PRO+	BR/A	SB	CS	SBR	FA	FR	G/POS	TPR
1991	Bos-A	11	8	2	2	1	0	0	0	1	3	.250	.333	.375	91	-0	1	0	0	1.000	-1	/O-4,D-2	-0.1
1993	NY-N	18	16	2	3	1	0	0	1	1	1	.188	.235	.250	30	-2	0	1	0	1.000	-1	/O-2	-0.2
Total	2	29	24	4	5	2	0	0	1	2	4	.208	.269	.292	51	-2	1	1	0	1.000	-2	/O-6,D-2	-0.3

■ TYLER HOUSTON
Houston, Tyler Sam   b: 1/17/71, Las Vegas, Nev.   BL/TR, 6'2", 210 lbs.   Deb: 4/3/96

YEAR	TM/L	G	AB	R	H	2B	3B	HR	RBI	BB	SO	AVG	OBP	SLG	PRO+	BR/A	SB	CS	SBR	FA	FR	G/POS	TPR
1996	Atl-N	33	27	3	6	2	1	1	4	1	9	.222	.250	.481	83	-1	0	0	0	1.000	0	1-11	-0.1
	Chi-N	46	115	18	39	7	0	2	19	8	18	.339	.382	.452	118	3	3	2	-0	.986	-3	C-27/3-9,2-2,1-1,O	0.1
	Yr	79	142	21	45	9	1	3	27	9	27	.317	.358	.458	110	2	3	2	-0	.986	-3	C-27,1-12/3-9,2O	0.0

■ LEFTY HOUTZ
Houtz, Fred Fritz   b: 9/4/1875, Connersville, Ind.   d: 2/15/59, Wapakoneta, Ohio   BL/TL, 5'10", 170 lbs.   Deb: 7/23/1899

YEAR	TM/L	G	AB	R	H	2B	3B	HR	RBI	BB	SO	AVG	OBP	SLG	PRO+	BR/A	SB	CS	SBR	FA	FR	G/POS	TPR
1899	Cin-N	5	17	1	4	0	1	0	0	4		.235	.381	.353	100	0	1			1.000	4	/O-5	0.4

■ STEVE HOVLEY
Hovley, Stephen Eugene   b: 12/18/44, Ventura, Cal.   BL/TL, 5'10", 188 lbs.   Deb: 6/26/69

YEAR	TM/L	G	AB	R	H	2B	3B	HR	RBI	BB	SO	AVG	OBP	SLG	PRO+	BR/A	SB	CS	SBR	FA	FR	G/POS	TPR
1969	Sea-A	91	329	41	91	14	3	3	20	30	34	.277	.339	.365	98	-1	10	4	1	.989	7	O-84	0.2
1970	Mil-A	40	135	17	38	9	0	0	16	7	11	.281	.366	.348	97	0	5	1	1	.958	-2	O-38	-0.3
	Oak-A	72	100	8	19	1	0	0	1	5	11	.190	.229	.200	20	-11	3	0	1	1.000	-6	O-42	-1.8
	Yr	112	235	25	57	10	0	0	17	22	22	.243	.310	.285	67	-10	8	1	2	.977	-8	O-80	-2.1
1971	Oak-A	24	27	3	3	2	0	0	3	7	9	.111	.314	.185	45	-2	2	0	1	1.000	-1	O-11	-0.2
1972	KC-A	105	196	24	53	5	1	3	24	24	29	.270	.353	.352	111	3	3	3	-1	.982	-5	O-68	-0.5
1973	KC-A	104	232	29	59	12	1	2	24	33	34	.254	.347	.323	83	-4	6	4	-1	.975	-10	O-79,D-15	-1.8
Total	5	436	1019	122	263	39	5	8	88	116	128	.258	.336	.330	88	-14	29	12	-4	.982	-16	O-322/D-15	-4.4

■ CHRIS HOWARD
Howard, Christopher Hugh   b: 2/27/66, San Diego, Cal.   BR/TR, 6'2", 200 lbs.   Deb: 9/15/91

YEAR	TM/L	G	AB	R	H	2B	3B	HR	RBI	BB	SO	AVG	OBP	SLG	PRO+	BR/A	SB	CS	SBR	FA	FR	G/POS	TPR
1991	Sea-A	9	6	1	1	1	0	0	0	1	2	.167	.286	.333	71	-0	0	0	0	1.000	1	/C-9	0.1
1993	Sea-A	4	1	0	0	0	0	0	0	0	0	.000	.000	.000	-99	-0	0	0	0	1.000	1	/C-4	0.0
1994	Sea-A	9	25	2	5	1	0	0	2	1	6	.200	.259	.240	29	-3	0	0	0	1.000	-3	/C-9	-0.5
Total	3	22	32	3	6	2	0	0	2	2	8	.188	.257	.250	33	-3	0	0	0	1.000	-1	/C-22	-0.4

■ DAVE HOWARD
Howard, David Austin "Del"   b: 5/1/1889, Washington, D.C.   d: 1/26/56, Dallas, Tex.   BR/TR, 5'11", 165 lbs.   Deb: 5/8/12

YEAR	TM/L	G	AB	R	H	2B	3B	HR	RBI	BB	SO	AVG	OBP	SLG	PRO+	BR/A	SB	CS	SBR	FA	FR	G/POS	TPR
1912	Was-A	1	0	1	0	0	0	0	0			—	—	—						.000	-0	R	0.0
1915	Bro-F	24	36	5	8	1	0	0	1	1	8	.222	.243	.250	39	-4				.925	3	2-12/O-2,S-1,3-1	-0.1
Total	2	25	36	6	8	1	0	0	1	1	8	.222	.243	.250	39	-4				.925	3	/2-12,O-2,3-1,S-1	-0.1

■ DAVID HOWARD
Howard, David Wayne   b: 2/26/67, Sarasota, Fla.   BB/TR, 6', 165 lbs.   Deb: 4/14/91   F

YEAR	TM/L	G	AB	R	H	2B	3B	HR	RBI	BB	SO	AVG	OBP	SLG	PRO+	BR/A	SB	CS	SBR	FA	FR	G/POS	TPR
1991	KC-A	94	236	20	51	7	0	1	17	16	45	.216	.269	.258	46	-17	3	2	-0	.962	19	S-63,2-26/3-1,OD	0.6
1992	KC-A	74	219	19	49	6	2	1	18	15	43	.224	.274	.283	55	-13	3	4	-2	.976	-0	S-74/O-2	-1.3
1993	KC-A	15	24	5	8	1	0	0	2	2	5	.333	.385	.417	109	0	1	0	0	.927	2	/2-7,S-3,3-2,O-1	0.2
1994	KC-A	46	83	9	19	4	0	1	13	11	23	.229	.319	.313	61	-5	3	2	-0	1.000	4	/3-25,S-15/2-3,OPD	0.2
1995	KC-A	95	255	23	62	13	4	0	19	24	41	.243	.311	.325	65	-13	6	1	-1	.994	15	2-41,S-33,O-30/1D	0.6
1996	KC-A	143	420	51	92	14	5	4	48	40	74	.219	.293	.305	53	-30	5	6	-2	**.982**	19	*S-135/2-3,1-2,O-1	-0.2
Total	6	467	1237	127	281	44	12	7	117	108	231	.227	.292	.299	56	-78	21	15	-3	.977	60	S-323/2-80,O3D1P	0.3

■ DOUG HOWARD
Howard, Douglas Lynn   b: 2/6/48, Salt Lake City, Utah   BR/TR, 6'3", 185 lbs.   Deb: 9/6/72

YEAR	TM/L	G	AB	R	H	2B	3B	HR	RBI	BB	SO	AVG	OBP	SLG	PRO+	BR/A	SB	CS	SBR	FA	FR	G/POS	TPR
1972	Cal-A	11	38	4	10	1	0	0	2	2	3	.263	.300	.289	81	-0	0	0	0	1.000	-1	/O-8,1-1,3-1	-0.2
1973	Cal-A	8	21	2	2	0	0	0	1	1	6	.095	.136	.095	-37	-4	0	0	0	1.000	-0	/O-6,1-1,3-1	-0.5
1974	Cal-A	22	39	5	9	0	1	0	5	2	1	.231	.268	.282	62	-2	1	0	0	1.000	-0	/O-8,1-5,D-3	-0.4
1975	StL-N	17	29	1	6	0	0	0	1	0	5	.207	.207	.310	41	-2	0	0	0	1.000	-1	/1-7	-0.1
1976	Cle-A	39	90	7	19	4	0	0	13	5	13	.211	.245	.256	47	-6	1	1	0	.991	-6	1-32/O-2,D-4	-0.7
Total	5	97	217	19	46	5	1	0	22	7	30	.212	.243	.258	46	-15	2	1	0	.994	-6	/1-46,O-24,D-7,3-2	-1.9

■ ELSTON HOWARD
Howard, Elston Gene   b: 2/23/29, St.Louis, Mo.   d: 12/14/80, New York, N.Y.   BR/TR, 6'2", 200 lbs.   Deb: 4/14/55   C

YEAR	TM/L	G	AB	R	H	2B	3B	HR	RBI	BB	SO	AVG	OBP	SLG	PRO+	BR/A	SB	CS	SBR	FA	FR	G/POS	TPR
1955	*NY-A	97	279	33	81	8	7	10	43	20	36	.290	.340	.477	120	6	0	0	-0	.978	2	O-75/C-9	0.5
1956	*NY-A	98	290	35	76	8	3	5	34	21	30	.262	.314	.362	81	-9	0	1	-1	.990	-5	O-65,C-26	-1.5
1957	*NY-A☆	110	356	33	90	13	4	8	44	16	43	.253	.285	.379	81	-11	2	5	-2	.961	-12	O-71,C-32/1-2	-2.8
1958	*NY-A☆	103	376	45	118	19	5	11	66	22	60	.314	.352	.479	131	14	1	1	-0	.997	-6	C-67,O-24/1-5	1.9
1959	NY-A☆	125	443	59	121	24	6	18	73	20	57	.273	.309	.476	116	7	0	1	-1	.985	-5	1-50,C-43,O-28	0.2

YEAR	TM/L	G	AB	R	H	2B	3B	HR	RBI	BB	SO	AVG	OBP	SLG	PRO+	BR/A	SB	CS	SBR	FA	FR	G/POS	TPR
1960	*NY-A★	107	323	29	79	11	3	6	39	28	43	.245	.305	.353	82	-9	3	0	1	.987	2	C-91/O-1	-0.1
1961	*NY-A★	129	446	64	155	17	5	21	77	28	65	.348	.390	.549	156	33	0	3	-2	.993	7	*C-111/1-9	4.2
1962	*NY-A★	136	494	63	138	23	5	21	91	31	76	.279	.323	.474	115	8	1	1	-0	.995	-1	*C-129	1.2
1963	*NY-A★	135	487	75	140	21	6	28	85	35	68	.287	.343	.528	141	25	0	0	0	.994	-3	*C-132	2.7
1964	*NY-A★	150	550	63	172	27	3	15	84	48	73	.313	.373	.455	127	20	1	1	-0	**.998**	11	*C-146	3.9
1965	NY-A☆	110	391	38	91	15	1	9	45	24	65	.233	.279	.345	77	-13	0	0	0	.991	-5	C-95/1-5,O-1	-1.3
1966	NY-A	126	410	38	105	19	2	6	35	37	65	.256	.319	.356	97	-1	0	0	0	.985	-4	*C-100,1-13	0.0
1967	NY-A	66	199	13	39	6	0	3	17	12	36	.196	.249	.271	56	-11	0	0	0	.984	-1	C-48/1-1	-1.0
	*Bos-A	42	116	9	17	3	0	1	11	9	24	.147	.214	.198	21	-11	0	0	0	.996	2	C-41	-0.8
	Yr	108	315	22	56	9	0	4	28	21	60	.178	.238	.244	42	-23	0	0	0	.990	1	C-89/1-1	-1.8
1968	Bos-A	71	203	22	49	4	0	5	18	22	45	.241	.319	.335	92	-2	1	1	-0	.995	-3	C-68	-0.1
Total	14	1605	5363	619	1471	218	50	167	762	373	786	.274	.325	.427	108	48	9	14	-6	.993	-9	*C-1138,O-265/1-85	7.0

■ FRANK HOWARD
Howard, Frank Oliver "Hondo" or "The Capital Punisher" b: 8/8/36, Columbus, Ohio BR/TR, 6'7", 255 lbs. Deb: 9/10/58 MC

YEAR	TM/L	G	AB	R	H	2B	3B	HR	RBI	BB	SO	AVG	OBP	SLG	PRO+	BR/A	SB	CS	SBR	FA	FR	G/POS	TPR
1958	LA-N	8	29	3	7	1	0	1	2	1	11	.241	.267	.379	66	-1	0	0	0	1.000	0	/O-8	-0.2
1959	LA-N	9	21	2	3	0	1	1	6	2	9	.143	.217	.381	52	-2	0	0	0	1.000	0	/O-6	-0.2
1960	LA-N	117	448	54	120	15	2	23	77	32	108	.268	.321	.464	105	2	0	1	-1	.984	-2	*O-115/1-4	-0.7
1961	LA-N	92	267	36	79	10	2	15	45	21	50	.296	.349	.517	116	5	0	1	-1	.934	-4	O-65/1-7	-0.3
1962	LA-N	141	493	80	146	25	6	31	119	39	108	.296	.349	.560	148	30	1	0	0	.972	2	*O-131	2.5
1963	*LA-N	123	417	58	114	16	1	28	64	33	116	.273	.333	.518	151	25	1	2	-1	.960	-1	*O-111	1.9
1964	LA-N	134	433	60	98	13	2	24	69	51	113	.226	.308	.432	114	7	1	0	0	.979	-7	*O-122	-0.5
1965	Was-A	149	516	53	149	22	6	21	84	55	112	.289	.360	.477	138	25	0	0	0	.981	-8	*O-138	1.2
1966	Was-A	146	493	52	137	19	4	18	71	53	104	.278	.349	.442	127	17	1	1	-0	.982	-2	*O-135	0.9
1967	Was-A	149	519	71	133	20	2	36	89	60	155	.256	.339	.511	154	33	0	1	-1	.986	-7	*O-141/1-4	2.1
1968	Was-A★	158	598	79	164	28	3	**44**	106	54	141	.274	.340	**.552**	172	49	0	0	0	.955	2	*O-107,1-55	4.6
1969	Was-A★	161	592	111	175	17	2	48	111	102	96	.296	.403	.574	180	64	1	0	0	.974	-18	*O-114,1-70	3.7
1970	Was-A★	161	566	90	160	15	1	**44**	**126**	**132**	125	.283	.420	.546	173	61	1	2	-1	.973	-9	*O-120,1-48	4.2
1971	Was-A★	153	549	60	153	25	2	26	83	77	121	.279	.369	.474	146	33	1	0	0	.993	3	*O-100,1-68	2.8
1972	Tex-A	95	287	28	70	9	0	9	31	42	55	.244	.342	.369	117	7	1	0	0	.981	-6	1-66,O-21	-0.6
	Det-A	14	33	1	8	1	0	1	7	4	8	.242	.324	.364	101	0	0	0	0	.952	-1	1-10/O-1	-0.1
	Yr	109	320	29	78	10	0	10	38	46	63	.244	.341	.369	115	7	1	0	0	.978	-7	1-76,O-22	-0.7
1973	Det-A	85	227	26	58	9	1	12	29	24	28	.256	.327	.463	113	3	0	1	-1	.923	-1	D-76/1-2	0.0
Total	16	1895	6488	864	1774	245	35	382	1119	782	1460	.273	.355	.499	143	357	8	9	-3	.975	-57	*O-1435,1-334/D-76	21.3

■ DEL HOWARD
Howard, George Elmer b: 12/24/1877, Kenney, Ill. d: 12/24/56, Seattle, Wash. BL/TR, 6', 180 lbs. Deb: 4/15/05 F

YEAR	TM/L	G	AB	R	H	2B	3B	HR	RBI	BB	SO	AVG	OBP	SLG	PRO+	BR/A	SB	CS	SBR	FA	FR	G/POS	TPR
1905	Pit-N	123	435	56	127	18	5	2	63	27		.292	.345	.370	110	5	19			.978	-7	1-90,O-28/P-1	-0.6
1906	Bos-N	147	545	46	142	19	8	1	54	26		.261	.306	.330	101	-1	17			.911	-12	O-87,2-45,S-14,1-2	-1.8
1907	Bos-N	50	187	20	51	4	2	1	13	11		.273	.330	.332	107	2	11			.969	-3	O-45/2-3	-0.3
	*Chi-N	51	148	10	34	2	2	0	13	6		.230	.269	.270	65	-6	3			.972	-4	1-33/O-8	-1.2
	Yr	101	335	30	85	6	4	1	26	17		.254	.304	.304	88	-5	14			.961	-6	O-53,1-33/2-3	-1.5
1908	*Chi-N	96	315	42	88	7	3	1	26	23		.279	.338	.330	109	3	11			.965	-5	O-81/1-5	-0.6
1909	Chi-N	69	203	25	40	4	2	1	24	18		.197	.282	.251	64	-8	6			.980	-1	1-57	-1.0
Total	5	536	1833	199	482	54	22	6	193	111		.263	.318	.326	98	-5	67			.946	-30	O-249,1-187/2SP	-5.5

■ IVON HOWARD
Howard, Ivon Chester b: 10/12/1882, Kenney, Ill. d: 3/30/67, Medford, Ore. BB/TR, 5'10", 170 lbs. Deb: 4/25/14 F

YEAR	TM/L	G	AB	R	H	2B	3B	HR	RBI	BB	SO	AVG	OBP	SLG	PRO+	BR/A	SB	CS	SBR	FA	FR	G/POS	TPR
1914	StL-A	81	209	21	51	6	2	0	20	28	42	.244	.342	.292	94	-0	14	10	-2	.936	-7	3-34,1-28/O-3,S-1	-1.0
1915	StL-A	113	324	43	90	10	7	2	43	43	48	.278	.368	.370	126	11	29	12	2	.992	5	1-48,3-23,O-17,/2S	1.7
1916	Cle-A	81	246	20	46	11	5	0	23	30	34	.187	.298	.272	68	-9	9			.970	7	2-65/1-7	-0.1
1917	Cle-A	27	39	7	4	0	0	0	0	3	5	.103	.167	.103	-17	-5	1			.833	2	/3-6,2-4,O-4	-0.4
Total	4	302	818	91	191	27	14	2	86	104	129	.233	.331	.308	92	-4	53	22		.990	6	/1-83,2-71,3-63,OS	0.2

■ LARRY HOWARD
Howard, Lawrence Rayford b: 6/6/45, Columbus, Ohio BR/TR, 6'3", 200 lbs. Deb: 8/9/70

YEAR	TM/L	G	AB	R	H	2B	3B	HR	RBI	BB	SO	AVG	OBP	SLG	PRO+	BR/A	SB	CS	SBR	FA	FR	G/POS	TPR
1970	Hou-N	31	88	11	27	6	0	2	16	10	23	.307	.378	.443	124	3	0	0	0	.993	-5	C-26/1-2,O-1	-0.1
1971	Hou-N	24	64	6	15	3	0	2	14	3	17	.234	.269	.375	83	-2	0	1	-1	.992	2	C-22	0.1
1972	Hou-N	54	157	16	35	7	0	2	13	17	30	.223	.299	.306	74	-5	0	0	0	.980	0	C-53/O-1	-0.4
1973	Hou-N	20	48	3	8	3	0	0	4	5	12	.167	.245	.229	32	-4	0	0	0	.989	-1	C-20	-0.5
	Atl-N	4	8	0	1	0	0	0	0	2	3	.125	.300	.125	20	-1	0	0	0	1.000	-0	/C-2	-0.0
	Yr	24	56	3	9	3	0	0	4	7	15	.161	.254	.214	31	-5	0	0	0	.990	-1	C-22	-0.6
Total	4	133	365	36	86	19	0	7	47	37	85	.236	.306	.337	81	-9	0	1	-1	.986	-4	C-123/O-2,1-2	-1.0

■ MATT HOWARD
Howard, Matthew Christopher b: 9/22/67, Fall River, Mass. BR/TR, 5'10", 170 lbs. Deb: 5/17/96

YEAR	TM/L	G	AB	R	H	2B	3B	HR	RBI	BB	SO	AVG	OBP	SLG	PRO+	BR/A	SB	CS	SBR	FA	FR	G/POS	TPR
1996	NY-A	35	54	9	11	1	0	1	7	4	8	.204	.232	.278	28	-6	1	0	0	.976	-5	2-30/3-6	-0.9

■ MIKE HOWARD
Howard, Michael Fredric b: 4/2/58, Seattle, Wash. BB/TR, 6'2", 185 lbs. Deb: 9/12/81

YEAR	TM/L	G	AB	R	H	2B	3B	HR	RBI	BB	SO	AVG	OBP	SLG	PRO+	BR/A	SB	CS	SBR	FA	FR	G/POS	TPR
1981	NY-N	14	24	4	4	1	0	0	3	3	5	.167	.286	.208	43	-2	2	0	1	.952	-1	O-14	-0.2
1982	NY-N	33	39	5	7	0	0	0	3	6	7	.179	.304	.256	59	-2	2	0	1	1.000	-3	O-22/2-3	-0.4
1983	NY-N	1	3	0	1	0	0	0	1	0	1	.333	.333	.333	86	-0	0	0	0	.000	-0	/O-1	0.0
Total	3	48	66	9	12	1	0	0	7	10	14	.182	.299	.242	54	-4	4	0	1	.980	-4	/O-37,2-3	-0.6

■ PAUL HOWARD
Howard, Paul Joseph "Del" b: 5/20/1884, Boston, Mass. d: 8/29/68, Miami, Fla. BR/TR, 5'8", 170 lbs. Deb: 9/16/09

YEAR	TM/L	G	AB	R	H	2B	3B	HR	RBI	BB	SO	AVG	OBP	SLG	PRO+	BR/A	SB	CS	SBR	FA	FR	G/POS	TPR
1909	Bos-A	6	15	2	3	1	0	0	2	3		.200	.368	.267	99	0	0			1.000	-1	/O-6	-0.1

■ STEVE HOWARD
Howard, Steven Bernard b: 12/7/63, Oakland, Cal. BR/TR, 6'2", 205 lbs. Deb: 6/16/90

YEAR	TM/L	G	AB	R	H	2B	3B	HR	RBI	BB	SO	AVG	OBP	SLG	PRO+	BR/A	SB	CS	SBR	FA	FR	G/POS	TPR
1990	Oak-A	21	52	5	12	4	0	0	1	4	17	.231	.286	.308	69	-2	0	0	0	.933	-4	O-14/D-7	-0.7

■ THOMAS HOWARD
Howard, Thomas Sylvester b: 12/11/64, Middletown, Ohio BB/TR, 6'2", 200 lbs. Deb: 7/3/90

YEAR	TM/L	G	AB	R	H	2B	3B	HR	RBI	BB	SO	AVG	OBP	SLG	PRO+	BR/A	SB	CS	SBR	FA	FR	G/POS	TPR
1990	SD-N	20	44	4	12	2	0	0	0	0	11	.273	.273	.318	61	-2	0	1	-1	.950	-2	O-13	-0.5
1991	SD-N	106	281	30	70	12	3	4	22	24	57	.249	.310	.356	84	-6	10	7	-1	.995	3	O-86	-0.6
1992	SD-N	5	3	1	1	0	0	0	0	0	0	.333	.333	.333	88	-0	0	0	0	.000	0	/H	0.0
	Cle-A	117	358	36	99	15	2	2	32	17	60	.277	.309	.346	85	-8	15	8	-0	.990	-7	O-97/D-2	-1.7
1993	Cle-A	74	178	26	42	7	0	3	23	12	42	.236	.284	.326	64	-9	5	1	1	.977	-3	O-47/D-7	-1.2
	Cin-N	38	141	22	39	8	3	4	13	12	21	.277	.333	.461	110	2	5	6	-2	.987	2	O-37	0.1
1994	Cin-N	83	178	24	47	11	0	5	24	10	30	.264	.303	.410	85	-4	4	2	0	.965	-1	O-57	-1.0
1995	*Cin-N	113	281	42	85	15	2	3	26	20	37	.302	.351	.402	98	-1	17	8	0	.985	-9	O-82	-1.0
1996	Cin-N	121	360	50	98	19	10	6	42	17	51	.272	.311	.431	94	-4	6	5	1	.982	-9	*O-103	-1.7
Total	7	677	1824	235	493	89	20	27	182	112	309	.270	.314	.385	88	-33	62	38	-4	.984	-30	O-522/D-9	-7.6

■ WILBUR HOWARD
Howard, Wilbur Leon b: 1/8/49, Lowell, N.C. BB/TR, 6'2", 175 lbs. Deb: 9/4/73

YEAR	TM/L	G	AB	R	H	2B	3B	HR	RBI	BB	SO	AVG	OBP	SLG	PRO+	BR/A	SB	CS	SBR	FA	FR	G/POS	TPR
1973	Mil-A	16	39	3	8	0	0	0	1	2	10	.205	.244	.205	28	-4	0	1	-1	.969	-2	O-12/D-1	-0.2
1974	Hou-N	64	111	19	24	4	0	2	5	5	19	.216	.250	.306	57	-7	4	5	-2	1.000	-4	O-50	-1.5
1975	Hou-N	121	392	62	111	16	8	6	21	21	67	.283	.325	.365	98	-3	32	11	3	.995	1	O-95	-0.2
1976	Hou-N	94	191	26	42	7	2	1	18	7	28	.220	.247	.293	53	-11	7	5	-3	.961	-8	O-63/2-2	-2.3
1977	Hou-N	87	187	22	48	6	0	2	13	5	30	.257	.276	.321	65	-10	11	1	3	.990	-4	O-62/2-4	-1.3
1978	Hou-N	84	148	17	34	4	1	1	13	5	22	.230	.269	.291	61	-8	6	2	1	1.000	-7	O-38/C-3,2-1	-1.7
Total	6	466	1068	149	267	37	11	6	71	45	175	.250	.284	.322	73	-42	60	25	3	.987	-20	O-320/2-7,C-3,D-1	-7.2

■ JIM HOWARTH
Howarth, James Eugene b: 3/7/47, Biloxi, Miss. BL/TL, 5'11", 175 lbs. Deb: 9/5/71

YEAR	TM/L	G	AB	R	H	2B	3B	HR	RBI	BB	SO	AVG	OBP	SLG	PRO+	BR/A	SB	CS	SBR	FA	FR	G/POS	TPR
1971	SF-N	7	13	3	3	1	0	0	2	3	1	.231	.375	.308	97	-0	0	0	0	1.000	-1	/O-6	-0.1
1972	SF-N	74	119	16	28	4	0	1	7	16	18	.235	.326	.294	76	-3	3	2	-0	1.000	-3	O-25/1-4	-0.9
1973	SF-N	65	90	8	18	1	0	0	7	7	8	.200	.258	.233	36	-8	0	0	0	1.000	-5	O-33/1-1	-1.4
1974	SF-N	6	4	0	0	0	0	0	0	0	0	.000	.000	.000	-96	-1	0	0	0	1.000	-0	/O-1	-0.1
Total	4	152	226	27	49	6	1	1	16	26	29	.217	.298	.265	58	-12	3	2	-0	1.000	-9	/O-65,1-5	-2.5

YEAR	TM/L	G	AB	R	H	2B	3B	HR	RBI	BB	SO	AVG	OBP	SLG	PRO+	BR/A	SB	CS	SBR	FA	FR	G/POS	TPR

■ ART HOWE Howe, Arthur Henry b: 12/15/46, Pittsburgh, Pa. BR/TR, 6'2", 190 lbs. Deb: 7/10/74 MC

YEAR	TM/L	G	AB	R	H	2B	3B	HR	RBI	BB	SO	AVG	OBP	SLG	PRO+	BR/A	SB	CS	SBR	FA	FR	G/POS	TPR
1974	*Pit-N	29	74	10	18	4	1	1	5	9	13	.243	.325	.365	96	-0	0	0	0	.937	4	3-20/S-2	0.3
1975	Pit-N	63	146	13	25	9	0	1	10	15	15	.171	.248	.253	40	-12	1	0	0	.938	3	3-42/S-3	-0.9
1976	Hou-N	21	29	0	4	1	0	0	0	6	6	.138	.286	.172	35	-2	0	0	0	.938	2	/3-8,2-2	-0.1
1977	Hou-N	125	413	44	109	23	7	8	58	41	60	.264	.338	.412	110	5	0	1	-1	.985	6	2-96,3-19,S-11	1.7
1978	Hou-N	119	420	46	123	33	3	7	55	34	41	.293	.347	.436	127	14	2	3	-1	.977	-4	*2-107,3-11/1-1	1.7
1979	Hou-N	118	355	32	88	15	2	6	33	36	37	.248	.319	.352	88	-6	3	1	0	.991	6	2-68,3-59/1-3	0.3
1980	*Hou-N	110	321	34	91	12	5	10	46	34	29	.283	.354	.445	132	13	1	0	0	.986	1	1-77,3-25/S-5,2-3	1.1
1981	*Hou-N	103	361	43	107	22	4	3	36	41	23	.296	.368	.404	125	12	1	3	-2	.966	5	3-98/1-2	1.5
1982	Hou-N	110	365	29	87	15	1	5	38	41	45	.238	.317	.326	87	-6	2	0	1	.972	8	3-72,1-35	-0.2
1984	StL-N	89	139	17	30	5	0	2	12	18	18	.216	.306	.295	71	-5	0	2	-1	.979	8	3-45,1-11/2-8,S-5	0.1
1985	StL-N	4	3	0	0	0	0	0	0	0	0	.000	.000	.000	-99	-1	0	0	0	1.000	0	/1-1,3-1	-0.1
Total	11	891	2626	268	682	139	23	43	293	275	287	.260	.332	.379	103	10	10	10	-3	.965	38	3-400,2-284,1/S	5.4

■ SHORTY HOWE Howe, John b: New York, N.Y. Deb: 6/17/1890

YEAR	TM/L	G	AB	R	H	2B	3B	HR	RBI	BB	SO	AVG	OBP	SLG	PRO+	BR/A	SB	CS	SBR	FA	FR	G/POS	TPR
1890	NY-N	19	64	4	11	0	0	0	4	3	2	.172	.221	.172	15	-7	3			.887	3	2-18/3-1	-0.2
1893	NY-N	1	5	1	3	0	0	0	2	0	0	.600	.600	.600	219	1	1			.400	-1	/3-1	0.0
Total	2	20	69	5	14	0	0	0	6	3	2	.203	.247	.203	30	-6	4			.400	2	/2-18,3-2	-0.2

■ HARRY HOWELL Howell, Henry Harry b: 11/14/1876, New Jersey d: 5/22/56, Spokane, Wash. BR/TR, 5'9", Deb: 10/10/1898 U

YEAR	TM/L	G	AB	R	H	2B	3B	HR	RBI	BB	SO	AVG	OBP	SLG	PRO+	BR/A	SB	CS	SBR	FA	FR	G/POS	TPR
1898	Bro-N	2	8	1	2	0	0	0	1	1		.250	.333	.250	68	-0	0			1.000	0	/P-2	0.0
1899	Bal-N	28	82	4	12	2	2	0	3	3		.146	.195	.220	13	-10	0			.940	1	P-28	0.0
1900	*Bro-N	22	42	6	12	2	1	0	6	6		.286	.388	.405	112	1	1			.949	1	P-21	0.0
1901	Bal-A	53	188	26	41	10	5	2	26	5		.218	.242	.356	62	-11	6			.905	-3	P-37/O-9,S-6,1-2,2	-0.5
1902	Bal-A	96	347	42	93	16	11	2	42	18		.268	.312	.395	91	-5	7			.951	-9	P-26,2-26,O3S/1	-1.6
1903	NY-A	40	106	14	23	3	2	1	12	5		.217	.259	.311	66	-4	1			1.000	1	P-25/3-7,S-5,1-1,2	-0.4
1904	StL-A	36	113	9	25	5	2	1	6	4		.221	.261	.327	91	-2	0			.971	9	P-34	0.0
1905	StL-A	42	135	9	26	6	2	1	10	3		.193	.216	.289	63	-6	0			.966	18	P-38/O-3	-0.1
1906	StL-A	35	103	5	13	3	1	0	6	6		.126	.174	.175	10	-11	0			.934	8	P-35	0.0
1907	StL-A	44	114	12	27	5	0	2	7	7		.237	.281	.333	96	-1	2			.982	9	P-42/O-2	0.1
1908	StL-A	41	120	10	22	7	0	1	9	4		.183	.210	.267	54	-6	0			.961	0	P-41	0.0
1909	StL-A	18	34	5	6	1	0	0	3	2		.176	.222	.206	38	-2	0			.938	1	P-10/3-7,O-1	0.0
1910	StL-A	1	2	0	0	0	0	0	0	0		.000	.000	.000	-99	-0	0			1.000	0	/P-1	0.0
Total	13	458	1394	143	302	60	25	11	131	64		.217	.257	.319	69	-59	19			.958	36	P-340/O-33,32S1	-2.5

■ DIXIE HOWELL Howell, Homer Elliott b: 4/24/20, Louisville, Ky. d: 10/5/90, Binghamton, N.Y. BR/TR, 5'11", 195 lbs. Deb: 5/6/47

YEAR	TM/L	G	AB	R	H	2B	3B	HR	RBI	BB	SO	AVG	OBP	SLG	PRO+	BR/A	SB	CS	SBR	FA	FR	G/POS	TPR
1947	Pit-N	76	214	23	59	11	0	4	25	27	34	.276	.357	.383	94	-1	1			.974	-3	C-74	0.0
1949	Cin-N	64	172	17	42	6	1	2	18	8	21	.244	.286	.326	63	-9	0			.987	5	C-56	-0.1
1950	Cin-N	82	224	30	50	9	1	2	22	32	31	.223	.326	.299	65	-11	0			.986	-4	C-81	-1.1
1951	Cin-N	77	207	22	52	6	1	2	18	15	34	.251	.302	.319	66	-10	0	2	-1	.987	4	C-73	-0.5
1952	Cin-N	17	37	4	7	1	1	2	4	3	9	.189	.250	.432	86	-1	0	0	0	.981	1	C-16	0.0
1953	Bro-N	1	1	0	0	0	0	0	0	0	0	.000	.000	.000	-98	-0	0	0	0	.000	0	H	0.0
1955	Bro-N	16	42	2	11	0	0	0	5	1	7	.262	.279	.357	66	-2	0	0	0	.981	-2	C-13	-0.3
1956	Bro-N	7	13	0	3	2	0	0	1	1	3	.231	.286	.385	72	-1	0	0	0	1.000	-0	/C-6	-0.1
Total	8	340	910	98	224	39	4	12	93	87	140	.246	.315	.337	73	-35	1	2		.984	6	C-319	-2.1

■ JACK HOWELL Howell, Jack Robert b: 8/18/61, Tucson, Ariz. BL/TR, 6', 185 lbs. Deb: 5/20/85

YEAR	TM/L	G	AB	R	H	2B	3B	HR	RBI	BB	SO	AVG	OBP	SLG	PRO+	BR/A	SB	CS	SBR	FA	FR	G/POS	TPR
1985	Cal-A	43	137	19	27	4	0	5	18	16	33	.197	.281	.336	68	-6	1	1	-0	.931	-1	3-42	-0.8
1986	*Cal-A	63	151	26	41	14	2	4	21	19	28	.272	.353	.470	123	5	2	0	1	.977	-1	3-39/O-8,D-2	0.4
1987	Cal-A	138	449	64	110	18	5	23	64	57	118	.245	.333	.461	111	7	4	3	-1	.987	-8	O-89,3-48,2-13	-0.5
1988	Cal-A	154	500	59	127	32	2	16	63	46	130	.254	.324	.422	110	6	2	6	-3	.953	-20	*3-152/O-2	-1.8
1989	Cal-A	144	474	56	108	19	4	20	52	52	125	.228	.308	.411	103	1	0	3	-2	.974	23	*3-142/O-4	2.3
1990	Cal-A	105	316	35	72	19	1	8	33	46	61	.228	.328	.370	97	-1	3	0	1	.939	7	*3-102/1-1,S-1	0.8
1991	Cal-A	32	81	11	17	2	0	2	7	11	11	.210	.304	.309	70	-3	1	0	1	.968	-2	2-12/3-8,O-5,1-3,D	-0.2
	SD-N	58	160	24	33	3	1	6	16	18	33	.206	.287	.350	76	-5	0	0	0	.985	6	3-54	0.1
1996	Cal-A	66	126	20	34	5	1	8	21	10	30	.270	.324	.508	108	1	0	1	-0	.884	-2	3-43/1-2,2-1,D-4	-0.2
Total	8	803	2394	314	569	115	16	92	295	275	569	.238	.319	.414	102	4	13	15	-5	.957	5	3-630,O-108/2D1S	0.1

■ RED HOWELL Howell, Murray Donald "Porky" b: 1/29/09, Atlanta, Ga. d: 10/1/50, Travelers Rest, S.C BR/TR, 6', 215 lbs. Deb: 4/24/41

YEAR	TM/L	G	AB	R	H	2B	3B	HR	RBI	BB	SO	AVG	OBP	SLG	PRO+	BR/A	SB	CS	SBR	FA	FR	G/POS	TPR
1941	Cle-A	11	7	0	2	0	0	0	2	2	2	.286	.545	.286	132	1	0	0	0	.000	0	H	0.1

■ PAT HOWELL Howell, Patrick O'Neal b: 8/31/68, Mobile, Ala. BB/TR, 5'11", 155 lbs. Deb: 7/10/92

YEAR	TM/L	G	AB	R	H	2B	3B	HR	RBI	BB	SO	AVG	OBP	SLG	PRO+	BR/A	SB	CS	SBR	FA	FR	G/POS	TPR
1992	NY-N	31	75	9	14	1	0	0	1	2	15	.187	.218	.200	19	-8	4	2	0	1.000	-0	O-28	-1.0

■ ROY HOWELL Howell, Roy Lee b: 12/18/53, Lompoc, Cal. BL/TR, 6'1", 190 lbs. Deb: 9/9/74

YEAR	TM/L	G	AB	R	H	2B	3B	HR	RBI	BB	SO	AVG	OBP	SLG	PRO+	BR/A	SB	CS	SBR	FA	FR	G/POS	TPR
1974	Tex-A	13	44	2	11	1	0	1	3	2	10	.250	.283	.341	81	-1	0	0	0	.906	-2	3-12	-0.3
1975	Tex-A	125	383	43	96	15	2	10	51	39	79	.251	.325	.379	99	-1	2	2	-1	.933	-7	*3-115/D-5	-0.8
1976	Tex-A	140	491	55	124	28	2	8	53	30	106	.253	.297	.367	92	-6	1	0	0	.926	-3	*3-130/D-8	-1.5
1977	Tex-A	7	17	0	0	0	0	0	0	2	4	.000	.105	.000	-68	-4	0	0	0	1.000	-0	/O-2,1-1,3-1,D-2	-0.4
	Tor-A	96	364	41	115	17	1	10	44	42	76	.316	.388	.451	126	14	4	1	1	.953	-7	3-87/D-8	0.7
	Yr	103	381	41	115	17	1	10	44	44	80	.302	.376	.430	117	10	4	1	1	.954	-7	3-88,D-10/O-2,1-1	0.3
1978	Tor-A★	140	551	67	149	28	3	8	61	44	78	.270	.326	.376	95	-4	0	1	-1	.950	11	*3-131/O-5,D-1	0.4
1979	Tor-A	138	511	60	126	28	4	15	72	42	91	.247	.311	.405	90	-8	1	4	-2	.952	-1	*3-133/D-4	-1.2
1980	Tor-A	142	528	51	142	28	9	10	57	50	92	.269	.338	.413	100	-0	0	0	0	.958	-18	*3-138/D-2	-2.0
1981	*Mil-A	76	244	37	58	13	1	6	33	23	39	.238	.309	.373	101	-0	1	0	0	.958	-0	3-53,D-13/1-3,O-1	-0.8
1982	*Mil-A	98	300	31	78	11	2	4	38	21	39	.260	.308	.350	86	-6	2	2	-1	.933	-1	D-84/1-4,O-2	-1.2
1983	Mil-A	69	194	23	54	9	6	1	25	15	29	.278	.330	.448	121	5	1	3	-2	.960	1	D-54/1-2	0.2
1984	Mil-A	68	164	12	38	1	1	4	17	8	32	.232	.284	.348	77	-5	0	1	-1	.907	1	3-46/1-4,D-8	-0.5
Total	11	1112	3791	422	991	183	31	80	454	318	675	.261	.322	.389	97	-17	9	14	-6	.944	-35	3-846,D-189/1-14,O	-7.4

■ BILL HOWERTON Howerton, William Ray "Hopalong" b: 12/12/21, Lompoc, Cal. BL/TR, 5'11", 185 lbs. Deb: 9/11/49

YEAR	TM/L	G	AB	R	H	2B	3B	HR	RBI	BB	SO	AVG	OBP	SLG	PRO+	BR/A	SB	CS	SBR	FA	FR	G/POS	TPR
1949	StL-N	9	13	1	4	1	0	0	1	0	2	.308	.308	.385	81	-0	0			.900	-1	/O-6	-0.2
1950	StL-N	110	313	50	88	20	8	10	59	47	60	.281	.375	.492	120	9	0			.969	-11	O-94	-0.5
1951	StL-N	24	65	10	17	4	1	1	4	10	12	.262	.360	.400	104	1	0	1	-1	.949	1	O-17	0.0
	Pit-N	80	219	29	60	12	2	11	37	26	44	.274	.351	.498	122	6	1	0	-0	.950	-8	O-53/3-4	-0.3
	Yr	104	284	39	77	16	3	12	41	36	56	.271	.353	.475	118	7	1	1	-0	.950	-8	O-70/3-4	-0.3
1952	Pit-N	13	25	3	8	1	0	0	4	6	5	.320	.452	.440	144	2	0	0	0	.900	-2	/O-5,3-1	0.0
	NY-N	11	15	2	1	1	0	0	1	5	9	.067	.222	.133	1	-2	0	0	0	1.000	-0	/O-3	-0.2
	Yr	24	40	5	9	2	0	0	5	11	14	.225	.367	.325	92	-0	0	0	0	.938	-2	/O-8,3-1	-0.2
Total	4	247	650	95	178	39	12	22	106	92	125	.274	.364	.472	117	16	1	1		.958	-22	O-178/3-5	-1.2

■ DANN HOWITT Howitt, Dann Paul John b: 2/13/64, Battle Creek, Mich. BL/TR, 6'5", 205 lbs. Deb: 9/15/89

YEAR	TM/L	G	AB	R	H	2B	3B	HR	RBI	BB	SO	AVG	OBP	SLG	PRO+	BR/A	SB	CS	SBR	FA	FR	G/POS	TPR
1989	Oak-A	3	3	0	0	0	0	0	0	0	2	.000	.000	.000	-99	-1	0	0	0	1.000	-1	/1-1,O-1	-0.1
1990	Oak-A	14	22	3	3	0	1	0	3	1	6	.136	.240	.227	33	-2	0	0	0	1.000	-2	O-11/1-5,3-1	-0.4
1991	Oak-A	21	42	5	7	1	0	1	3	1	12	.167	.186	.262	24	-4	0	0	0	1.000	-4	O-20/1-1	-0.9
1992	Oak-A	22	48	1	6	4	0	0	8	1	12	.125	.208	.188	12	-6	0	0	0	.951	1	O-19/1-4,D-1	-0.6
	Sea-A	13	37	6	10	4	1	1	2	4	8	.270	.325	.514	131	1	1	1	-0	1.000	1	O-11	0.2
	Yr	35	85	7	16	8	1	1	10	5	20	.188	.258	.329	66	-4	1	1	-0	.970	2	O-30/1-4,D-1	-0.4
1993	Sea-A	32	76	6	16	3	1	2	9	4	18	.211	.250	.355	60	-5	0	0	0	1.000	-5	O-29/D-2	-1.0
1994	Chi-A	10	14	4	5	3	0	0	0	0	2	.357	.400	.571	149	1	0	0	0	1.000	-2	/O-7,1-4	-0.1
Total	6	115	242	25	47	11	3	5	22	17	60	.194	.247	.326	57	-15	1	1	-0	.987	-12	/O-98,1-15,D-3,3-1	-2.9

YEAR	TM/L	G	AB	R	H	2B	3B	HR	RBI	BB	SO	AVG	OBP	SLG	PRO+	BR/A	SB	CS	SBR	FA	FR	G/POS	TPR

■ DAN HOWLEY Howley, Daniel Philip "Howling Dan" or "Dapper Dan" b: 10/16/1885, Weymouth, Mass. d: 3/10/44, Weymouth, Mass. BR/TR, 6', 187 lbs. Deb: 5/15/13 MC

1913	Phi-N	26	32	5	4	2	0	0	2	4	4	.125	.222	.188	17	-3	3			.954	1	C-22	-0.2

■ DICK HOWSER Howser, Richard Dalton b: 5/14/36, Miami, Fla. d: 6/17/87, Kansas City, Mo. BR/TR, 5'8", 155 lbs. Deb: 4/11/61 MC

1961	KC-A★	158	611	108	171	29	6	3	45	92	38	.280	.379	.362	97	1	37	9	6	.950	-17	*S-157	0.3
1962	KC-A	83	286	53	68	8	3	6	34	38	8	.238	.329	.350	79	-8	19	2	5	.962	-8	S-72	-0.5
1963	KC-A	15	41	4	8	0	0	0	1	7	3	.195	.313	.195	44	-3	0	0		.957	-4	S-10	-0.6
	Cle-A	49	162	25	40	5	0	1	10	22	18	.247	.337	.296	80	-4	9	3	1	.950	-17	S-44	-1.7
	Yr	64	203	29	48	5	0	1	11	29	21	.236	.332	.276	72	-7	9	3	1	.951	-20	S-54	-2.3
1964	Cle-A	162	637	101	163	23	4	3	52	76	39	.256	.337	.319	84	-11	20	7	2	.974	3	*S-162	0.6
1965	Cle-A	107	307	47	72	8	2	1	6	57	25	.235	.356	.283	83	-4	17	4	3	.977	-6	S-73,2-17	-0.1
1966	Cle-A	67	140	18	32	9	1	2	4	15	23	.229	.303	.350	87	-2	2	4	-2	.986	-7	2-26,S-26	-0.8
1967	NY-A	63	149	18	40	6	0	0	10	25	15	.268	.381	.309	110	3	1	4	-2	.990	-6	2-22,3-12/S-3	-0.4
1968	NY-A	85	150	24	23	2	1	0	3	35	17	.153	.321	.180	57	-6	0	1	-1	.982	5	2-29/3-2,S-1	0.0
Total	8	789	2483	398	617	90	17	16	165	367	186	.248	.348	.318	86	-34	105	34	11	.963	-56	S-548/2-94,3-14	-3.2

■ DUMMY HOY Hoy, William Ellsworth b: 5/23/1862, Houcktown, Ohio d: 12/15/61, Cincinnati, Ohio BL/TR, 5'6", 160 lbs. Deb: 4/20/1888

1888	Was-N	136	503	77	138	10	8	2	29	69	48	.274	.374	.338	136	25	**82**			.897	7	*O-136	2.7
1889	Was-N	127	507	98	139	11	6	0	39	75	30	.274	.374	.320	101	6	35			.890	-4	*O-127	-0.1
1890	Buf-P	122	493	107	147	17	8	1	53	94	36	.298	.418	.371	122	24	39			.912	6	*O-122/2-1	2.0
1891	StL-a	141	567	136	165	14	5	5	66	**119**	25	.291	.424	.360	108	7	59			.909	-1	*O-141	0.2
1892	Was-N	152	593	108	166	19	8	3	75	86	23	.280	.375	.354	124	21	60			.884	-12	*O-152	0.2
1893	Was-N	130	564	106	138	12	6	0	45	66	9	.245	.337	.287	68	-23	48			.892	-1	*O-130	-2.5
1894	Cin-N	126	495	114	148	22	13	5	70	87	18	.299	.414	.426	100	2	27			.896	3	*O-126	-0.3
1895	Cin-N	107	429	93	119	21	3	5	55	52	8	.277	.363	.403	94	-5	50			.883	-3	*O-107	-1.3
1896	Cin-N	121	443	120	132	23	7	4	57	65	13	.298	.403	.409	107	6	50			.946	5	*O-128	0.1
1897	Cin-N	128	497	87	145	24	6	2	42	54		.292	.375	.376	92	-5	37			.934	7	*O-128	-0.6
1898	Lou-N	148	582	104	177	15	16	6	66	49		.304	.367	.416	126	19	37			.946	6	*O-148	1.3
1899	Lou-N	154	633	116	194	17	13	5	49	61		.306	.376	.398	113	12	32			.927	-6	*O-154	-0.5
1901	Chi-A	132	527	112	155	28	11	2	60	**86**		.294	.407	.400	128	25	27			.958	-5	*O-132	1.5
1902	Cin-N	72	279	48	81	15	2	2	20	41		.290	.389	.380	125	10	11			.933	-5	O-72	0.7
Total	14	1796	7112	1426	2044	248	121	40	726	1004	210	.287	.386	.373	109	123	594			.915	7	*O-1795/2-1	2.7

■ KENT HRBEK Hrbek, Kent Alan b: 5/21/60, Minneapolis, Minn. BL/TR, 6'4", 235 lbs. Deb: 8/24/81

1981	Min-A	24	67	5	16	5	0	1	7	5	9	.239	.301	.358	84	-1	0	0	0	1.000	-2	1-13/D-8	-0.4
1982	Min-A★	140	532	82	160	21	4	23	92	54	80	.301	.365	.485	128	20	3	1	0	.993	-0	*1-138/D-2	1.2
1983	Min-A	141	515	75	153	41	5	16	84	57	71	.297	.370	.489	130	21	4	6	-2	.990	-2	*1-137/D-2	0.8
1984	Min-A	149	559	80	174	31	3	27	107	65	87	.311	.387	.522	142	32	1	1	-0	.990	-6	*1-148/D-1	1.7
1985	Min-A	158	593	78	165	31	2	21	93	67	87	.278	.353	.444	110	9	1	1	-0	.995	1	*1-156/D-2	0.0
1986	Min-A	149	550	85	147	27	1	29	91	71	81	.267	.357	.478	122	17	2	2	-1	.992	-2	*1-147/D-1	0.3
1987	*Min-A	143	477	85	136	20	1	34	90	84	60	.285	.392	.545	140	29	5	2	0	.996	-10	*1-137/D-1	0.9
1988	Min-A	143	510	75	159	31	0	25	76	67	54	.312	.392	.520	149	34	0	3	-2	.997	-6	*1-105,D-37	1.6
1989	Min-A	109	375	59	102	17	0	25	84	53	35	.272	.364	.517	136	18	3	0	1	.995	1	1-89,D-18	1.2
1990	Min-A	143	492	61	141	26	0	22	79	69	45	.287	.382	.474	129	20	5	2	0	**.997**	1	*1-120,D-20/3-1	1.2
1991	*Min-A	132	462	72	131	20	1	20	89	67	48	.284	.373	.461	124	16	4	4	-1	.994	4	*1-128	1.0
1992	Min-A	112	394	52	96	20	0	15	58	71	56	.244	.359	.409	111	7	5	2	0	.997	-1	*1-104/D-8	0.5
1993	Min-A	123	392	60	95	11	1	25	83	71	57	.242	.360	.467	120	12	4	2	0	.995	3	*1-115/D-2	0.5
1994	Min-A	81	274	34	74	11	0	10	53	37	28	.270	.350	.420	100	0	0	0	0	.997	-2	1-72/D-4	-0.7
Total	14	1747	6192	903	1749	312	18	293	1086	838	798	.282	.370	.481	127	233	37	26	-5	.994	-21	*1-1609,D-106/3-1	9.3

■ WALT HRINIAK Hriniak, Walter John b: 5/22/43, Natick, Mass. BL/TR, 5'11", 180 lbs. Deb: 9/10/68 C

1968	Atl-N	9	26	4	9	0	0	0	3	0	3	.346	.346	.346	108	0	0	0	0	.967	3	/C-9	0.4
1969	Atl-N	7	7	0	1	0	0	0	0	2	1	.143	.333	.143	38	-0	0	0	0	1.000	-1	/C-6	-0.1
	SD-N	31	66	4	15	0	0	0	1	8	11	.227	.329	.227	61	-3	0	0	0	.981	-2	C-19	-0.4
	Yr	38	73	4	16	0	0	0	1	10	12	.219	.329	.219	58	-4	0	0	0	.982	-3	C-25	-0.5
Total	2	47	99	8	25	0	0	0	4	10	15	.253	.333	.253	71	-3	0	0	0	.977	-0	/C-34	-0.1

■ AL HUBBARD Hubbard, Allen (a.k.a. Al West For 1 Game In 1883) b: 12/9/1860, Westfield, Mass. d: 12/14/30, Newton, Mass. Deb: 9/13/1883

1883	Phi-a	2	6	2	2	0	0	0	2	1		.333	.429	.333	138	-0				.750	-0	/S-1,C-1	0.0

■ GLENN HUBBARD Hubbard, Glenn Dee b: 9/25/57, Hahn Air Force Base, W.Germany BR/TR, 5'7", 180 lbs. Deb: 7/14/78

1978	Atl-N	44	163	15	42	4	0	2	13	10	20	.258	.309	.319	68	-7	2	1	0	.979	3	2-44	0.0
1979	Atl-N	97	325	34	75	12	0	3	29	27	43	.231	.292	.295	56	-19	0	6	-4	.968	5	2-91	-1.3
1980	Atl-N	117	431	55	107	21	3	9	43	49	69	.248	.325	.374	91	-5	7	5	-1	.978	19	*2-117	2.2
1981	Atl-N	99	361	39	85	13	5	6	33	33	59	.235	.303	.349	82	-8	4	2	0	.991	-4	2-98	-0.7
1982	*Atl-N	145	532	75	132	25	1	9	59	59	62	.248	.327	.350	86	-9	4	3	-1	.983	20	*2-144	1.8
1983	Atl-N★	148	517	65	136	24	6	12	70	55	71	.263	.339	.402	97	-2	3	8	-4	.985	22	*2-148	2.4
1984	Atl-N	120	397	53	93	27	2	9	43	55	61	.234	.333	.380	93	-3	4	1	1	.988	20	*2-117	2.2
1985	Atl-N	142	439	51	102	21	0	5	39	56	54	.232	.325	.314	75	-13	4	1	1	.989	**62**	*2-140	5.4
1986	Atl-N	143	408	42	94	16	1	4	36	66	74	.230	.343	.304	76	-11	3	2	-0	.976	**41**	*2-142	3.5
1987	Atl-N	141	443	69	117	33	2	5	38	77	57	.264	.380	.381	98	1	1	1	-0	.986	**28**	*2-139	3.5
1988	*Oak-A	105	294	35	75	12	2	3	33	33	50	.255	.336	.340	93	-2	1	3	-2	.987	-2	*2-104/D-1	0.4
1989	Oak-A	53	131	12	26	6	3	0	12	19	20	.198	.300	.313	76	-4	0	0	0	.968	10	2-48/D-3	0.8
Total	12	1354	4441	545	1084	214	22	70	448	539	640	.244	.330	.349	85	-83	35	35	-11	.983	229	*2-1332/D-4	20.2

■ MIKE HUBBARD Hubbard, Michael Wayne b: 2/16/71, Lynchburg, Va. BR/TR, 6'1", 180 lbs. Deb: 7/13/95

1995	Chi-N	15	23	2	4	0	0	0	1	2	2	.174	.240	.174	12	-3	0	0	0	.971	-1	/C-9	-0.4
1996	Chi-N	21	38	1	4	0	0	1	4	0	15	.105	.105	.184	-25	-7	0	0	0	1.000	-0	C-14	-0.6
Total	2	36	61	3	8	0	0	1	5	2	17	.131	.159	.180	-11	-10	0	0	0	.989	-1	/C-23	-1.0

■ TRENIDAD HUBBARD Hubbard, Trenidad Aviel (b: Trent Hubbard) b: 5/11/64, Chicago, Ill. BR/TR, 5'8", 180 lbs. Deb: 7/7/94

1994	Col-N	18	25	3	7	1	1	3	3	3	4	.280	.357	.520	107	0	0	0	0	1.000	-1	/O-5	-0.1
1995	*Col-N	24	58	13	18	4	0	3	9	8	6	.310	.394	.534	110	0	2	1	0	1.000	-4	O-16	-0.4
1996	Col-N	45	60	12	13	5	1	1	12	9	22	.217	.329	.383	68	-3	2	0	1	1.000	-0	O-19	-0.5
	SF-N	10	29	3	6	0	1	1	2	2	5	.207	.258	.379	68	-1	0	0	0	1.000	1	O-9	0.0
	Yr	55	89	15	19	5	2	2	14	11	27	.213	.307	.382	65	-5	2	0	1	1.000	-0	O-28	-0.5
Total	3	97	172	31	44	10	3	6	26	22	37	.256	.344	.453	88	-4	4	1	1	1.000	-5	/O-49	-1.0

■ KEN HUBBS Hubbs, Kenneth Douglas b: 12/23/41, Riverside, Cal. d: 2/13/64, Provo, Utah BR/TR, 6'2", 175 lbs. Deb: 9/10/61

1961	Chi-N	10	28	4	5	1	1	1	2	0	8	.179	.179	.393	46	-2	0	0	0	1.000	-2	/2-8	-0.3
1962	Chi-N	160	661	90	172	24	9	5	49	35	129	.260	.300	.346	71	-28	3	7	-3	.983	4	*2-159	-1.0
1963	Chi-N	154	566	54	133	19	3	8	47	39	93	.235	.287	.322	71	-21	8	9	-3	.974	20	*2-152	1.1
Total	3	324	1255	148	310	44	13	14	98	74	230	.247	.292	.336	70	-51	11	16	-6	.979	23	2-319	-0.2

■ CLARENCE HUBER Huber, Clarence Bill "Gilly" b: 10/27/1896, Tyler, Tex. d: 2/22/65, Laredo, Tex. BR/TR, 5'10", 165 lbs. Deb: 9/17/20

1920	Det-A	11	42	4	9	2	1	0	5	0	5	.214	.214	.310	39	-4	0	0	0	.907	2	3-11	-0.1
1921	Det-A	1	0	0	0	0	0	0	0	0	0	—	—	—	—	-0	0	0	0	1.000	-0	/3-1	0.0
1925	Phi-N	124	436	46	124	28	5	5	54	17	33	.284	.311	.406	75	-17	3	5	-2	.947	-9	*3-120	-1.9
1926	Phi-N	118	376	45	92	17	7	1	34	42	29	.245	.323	.362	74	-13	9			.956	8	*3-115	0.1
Total	4	254	854	95	225	47	13	6	93	59	67	.263	.313	.370	73	-35	12	<u>5</u>		.948	1	3-247	-1.9

YEAR	TM/L	G	AB	R	H	2B	3B	HR	RBI	BB	SO	AVG	OBP	SLG	PRO+	BR/A	SB	CS	SBR	FA	FR	G/POS	TPR

■ OTTO HUBER   Huber, Otto b: 3/12/14, Garfield, N.J. d: 4/9/89, Passaic, N.J. BR/TR, 5'10", 165 lbs. Deb: 6/10/39

1939	Bos-N	11	22	2	6	1	0	0	3	0	1	.273	.273	.318	63	-1	0			1.000	-0	/2-4,3-4	-0.1

■ DAVE HUDGENS   Hudgens, David Mark b: 12/5/56, Oroville, Cal. BL/TL, 6'2", 210 lbs. Deb: 9/4/83

1983	Oak-A	6	7	0	1	0	0	0	0	0	3	.143	.143	.143	-22	-1	0	0	0	1.000	-0	/1-3,D-1	-0.1

■ JIMMY HUDGENS   Hudgens, James Price b: 8/24/02, Newburg, Mo. d: 8/26/55, St.Louis, Mo. BL/TR, 6', 180 lbs. Deb: 9/14/23

1923	StL-N	6	12	2	3	1	0	0	0	3	3	.250	.400	.333	97	0	0	0		1.000	1	/1-3,2-1	0.1
1925	Cin-N	3	7	0	3	1	1	0	1	1	1	.429	.500	.857	245	2	0	0	0	1.000	0	/1-3	0.1
1926	Cin-N	17	20	2	5	1	0	0	1	1	0	.250	.286	.300	59	-1	0	0		1.000	0	/1-6	-0.1
Total	3	26	39	4	11	3	1	0	1	5	4	.282	.364	.410	107	0	0	0		1.000	1	/1-12,2-1	0.1

■ REX HUDLER   Hudler, Rex Allen b: 9/2/60, Tempe, Ariz. BR/TR, 6'1", 180 lbs. Deb: 9/9/84

1984	NY-A	9	7	2	1	0	0	0	0	0	1	.143	.333	.286	76	-0	0	0	0	1.000	0	/2-9	0.0
1985	NY-A	20	51	4	8	0	1	0	1	1	9	.157	.173	.196	1	-7	0	1	-1	.977	7	2-16/1-1,S-1	0.0
1986	Bal-A	14	1	1	0	0	0	0	0	0	0	.000	.000	.000	-99	-0	1	0	0	.800	1	2-13/3-1	0.1
1988	Mon-N	77	216	38	59	14	2	4	14	10	34	.273	.305	.412	100	-1	29	7	5	.978	-1	2-41,S-27/O-4	0.6
1989	Mon-N	92	155	21	38	7	0	6	13	6	23	.245	.278	.406	92	-2	15	4	2	.958	-14	2-38,O-23,S-18	-1.4
1990	Mon-N	4	3	1	1	0	0	0	0	0	1	.333	.333	.333	87	-0	0	0	0	.000	0	/H	0.0
	StL-N	89	217	30	61	11	2	7	22	12	31	.281	.325	.447	110	2	18	10	-1	.979	0	O-45,2-10/1-6,3S	0.1
	Yr	93	220	31	62	11	2	7	22	12	32	.282	.325	.445	109	2	18	10	-1	.979	0	O-45,2-10/1-6,6S	0.1
1991	StL-N	101	207	21	47	10	2	1	15	10	29	.227	.263	.309	60	-11	12	8	-1	.981	-3	O-58,1-12/2-5	-1.8
1992	StL-N	61	98	17	24	4	0	3	5	2	23	.245	.267	.378	83	-3	2	6	-3	.957	-8	2-16,O-12/1-8	-1.4
1994	Cal-A	56	124	17	37	8	0	8	20	6	28	.298	.331	.556	122	-3	2	2	-1	.971	-2	2-22,O-18/3-4,1D	0.1
1995	Cal-A	84	223	30	59	16	0	6	27	10	48	.265	.311	.417	88	-4	13	0	4	.986	-12	2-52,O-22/1-2,D-3	-1.0
1996	Cal-A	92	302	60	94	20	3	16	40	9	54	.311	.338	.556	123	9	14	5	1	.982	-7	2-53,O-21/1-7,D-8	0.5
Total	11	699	1604	242	429	91	10	51	157	67	285	.267	.302	.432	96	-14	106	43	6	.975	-39	2-275,O-203/S1D3	-4.2

■ JOHNNY HUDSON   Hudson, John Wilson "Mr. Chips" b: 6/30/12, Bryan, Tex. d: 11/7/70, Bryan, Tex. BR/TR, 5'10", 160 lbs. Deb: 6/20/36

1936	Bro-N	6	12	1	2	0	0	0	0	2	1	.167	.286	.167	24	-1	0			.889	-1	/S-4,2-1	-0.2
1937	Bro-N	13	27	3	5	4	0	0	2	3	9	.185	.267	.333	61	-2	0			.867	-4	S-11/2-1	-0.5
1938	Bro-N	135	498	59	130	21	5	2	37	39	36	.261	.315	.335	77	-15	7			.963	-4	*2-132/S-3	-1.2
1939	Bro-N	109	343	46	87	17	3	2	32	30	36	.254	.317	.338	74	-13	5			.959	-18	S-50,2-45/3-1	-2.4
1940	Bro-N	85	179	13	39	4	0	0	19	9	26	.218	.255	.274	43	-14	2			.921	0	S-17,2-13,3-1	-1.0
1941	Chi-N	50	99	8	20	4	0	0	6	3	15	.202	.225	.242	33	-9	3			.907	-1	S-17,2-13,3-10	-0.8
1945	NY-N	28	11	8	0	0	0	0	0	1	1	.000	.083	.000	-75	-3	0			.875	3	/3-5,2-2	0.0
Total	7	426	1169	138	283	50	11	4	96	87	164	.242	.296	.314	65	-56	17			.962	-25	2-221,S-123/3-17	-6.1

■ FRANK HUELSMAN   Huelsman, Frank Elmer b: 6/5/1874, St.Louis, Mo. d: 6/9/59, Affton, Mo. BR/TR, 6'2", 210 lbs. Deb: 10/3/1897

1897	StL-N	2	7	0	2	1	0	0				.286	.286	.429	89	-0	0			.000	-1	/O-2	-0.1
1904	Chi-A	3	6	0	1	1	0	0	0	0		.167	.167	.333	58	-0	0			.000	-1	/O-1	-0.1
	Det-A	4	18	1	6	1	0	0	4	1		.333	.368	.389	144	1	1			1.000	-1	/O-4	0.0
	Chi-A	1	1	0	0	0	0	0	0	0	0	.000	.000	.000	-99	-0	0			.000	0	H	0.0
	StL-A	20	68	6	15	2	1	0	1	6		.221	.303	.279	90	-1	0			1.000	-5	O-18	-0.5
	Was-A	84	303	21	75	19	4	2	30	24		.248	.313	.356	113	5	6			.960	-3	O-84	-0.4
	Yr	112	396	28	97	23	5	2	35	31		.245	.311	.343	110	5	7			.960	-8	*O-107	-1.0
1905	Was-A	121	421	48	114	28	8	3	62	31		.271	.333	.397	136	17	11			.929	-9	*O-116	0.3
Total	3	235	824	76	213	52	13	5	97	62		.258	.322	.371	123	21	18			.941	-17	O-225	-0.8

■ MIKE HUFF   Huff, Michael Kale b: 8/11/63, Honolulu, Hawaii BR/TR, 6'1", 180 lbs. Deb: 8/7/89

1989	LA-N	12	25	4	5	1	0	1	2	3	6	.200	.310	.360	93	-0	0	1	-1	1.000	-0	/O-9	-0.1
1991	Cle-A	51	146	28	35	6	1	2	10	25	30	.240	.366	.336	95	0	11	2	2	.990	-3	O-48/2-2	-0.2
	Chi-A	51	97	14	26	4	1	1	15	12	18	.268	.360	.361	103	1	3	2	-0	.986	-11	O-48/2-2,D-2	-1.1
	Yr	102	243	42	61	10	2	3	25	37	48	.251	.364	.346	98	1	14	4	2	.988	-14	O-96/2-4,D-2	-1.3
1992	Chi-A	60	115	13	24	5	0	0	8	10	24	.209	.278	.252	50	-8	1	2	-1	1.000	-10	O-56/D-1	-2.0
1993	Chi-A	43	44	4	8	2	0	1	6	9	15	.182	.333	.295	72	-1	1	0	0	1.000	-3	O-43	-1.3
1994	Tor-A	80	207	31	63	15	3	3	25	27	27	.304	.392	.449	116	6	2	1	0	.992	-6	O-76	-0.2
1995	Tor-A	61	138	14	32	9	1	1	9	22	21	.232	.342	.333	77	-4	1	0	0	.980	-5	O-55	-1.0
1996	Tor-A	11	29	5	5	0	0	0	1	5	11	.172	.200	.241	11	-4	0	0	0	1.000	-1	/O-9,3-3	-0.5
Total	7	369	801	113	198	42	7	9	75	109	146	.247	.347	.351	88	-11	19	9	0	.991	-48	O-344/2-4,3-3,D-3	-6.4

■ BEN HUFFMAN   Huffman, Benjamin Franklin b: 6/26/14, Rileyville, Va. BL/TR, 5'11.5", 175 lbs. Deb: 4/23/37

1937	StL-A	76	176	18	48	9	0	1	24	10	7	.273	.323	.341	67	-9	1	0	0	.970	-8	C-42	-1.3

■ ED HUG   Hug, Edward Ambrose b: 7/14/1880, Fayetteville, O. d: 5/11/53, Cincinnati, Ohio BR/TR, Deb: 7/6/03

1903	Bro-N	1	0	0	0	0	0	0	0	0	1	—	1.000	—	199	0	0			.000	0	/C-1	0.0

■ MILLER HUGGINS   Huggins, Miller James "Hug" or "Mighty Mite" b: 3/27/1879, Cincinnati, Ohio d: 9/25/29, New York, N.Y. BB/TR, 5'6.5", 140 lbs. Deb: 4/15/04 MH

1904	Cin-N	140	491	96	129	12	7	2	30	88		.263	.377	.328	108	8	13			.945	1	*2-140	1.4
1905	Cin-N	149	564	117	154	11	8	1	38	**103**		.273	.392	.326	103	7	27			.945	**36**	*2-149	4.5
1906	Cin-N	146	545	81	159	11	7	0	26	71		.292	.376	.338	118	14	41			.948	22	*2-146	4.0
1907	Cin-N	156	561	64	139	12	4	1	31	**83**		.248	.346	.289	95	0	28			.961	4	*2-156	-0.1
1908	Cin-N	135	498	65	119	14	5	0	23	58		.239	.321	.287	97	0	30			.959	4	*2-135	0.3
1909	Cin-N	57	159	18	34	3	1	0	6	28		.214	.335	.245	81	-2	11			.933	4	2-31,3-15	0.2
1910	StL-N	151	547	101	145	15	6	1	36	**116**	46	.265	.399	.320	114	18	34			.963	3	*2-151	1.9
1911	StL-N	138	509	106	133	19	2	1	24	96	52	.261	.385	.312	99	5	37			.961	11	*2-136	1.3
1912	StL-N	120	431	82	131	15	4	0	29	87	31	.304	.422	.357	117	16	35			.943	-7	*2-114	0.6
1913	StL-N	121	382	74	109	12	0	0	27	92	49	.285	**.432**	.317	117	17	23			**.977**	0	*2-113,M	1.6
1914	StL-N	148	509	85	134	17	4	1	24	**105**	63	.263	.396	.318	115	16	32			.964	-5	*2-147,M	1.1
1915	StL-N	107	353	57	85	5	2	2	24	74	68	.241	.377	.283	101	5	13	12	-3	.957	4	*2-105,M	0.7
1916	StL-N	18	9	2	3	0	0	0	0	2	3	.333	.500	.333	159	1	0			1.000	5	/2-7,M	0.6
Total	13	1586	5558	948	1474	146	50	9	318	1003	**312**	.265	.382	.314	107	105	324	**12**		.956	78	*2-1530/3-15	18.1

■ ED HUGHES   Hughes, Edward J. b: 10/5/1880, Chicago, Ill. d: 10/11/27, McHenry, Ill. BR/TR, 6'1", 180 lbs. Deb: 8/29/02 F

1902	Chi-A	1	4	0	1	0	0	0	0	0		.250	.250	.250	41	-0	0			.778	0	/C-1	0.0
1905	Bos-A	6	14	2	3	0	0	0	0	0		.214	.214	.214	36	-1	0			.500	-2	/P-6	0.0
1906	Bos-A	2	3	0	0	0	0	0	0	0		.000	.000	.000	-99	-1	0			.750	-0	/P-2	0.0
Total	3	9	21	2	4	0	0	0	0	0		.190	.190	.190	17	-2	0			.571	-2	/P-8,C-1	0.0

■ JOE HUGHES   Hughes, Joseph Thompson b: 2/21/1880, Pardoe, Pa. d: 3/13/51, Cleveland, Ohio BR/TR, 5'10", 165 lbs. Deb: 8/30/02

1902	Chi-N	1	3	0	0	0	0	0	0	0		.000	.000	.000	-99	-1	0			.000	-0	/O-1	-0.1

■ KEITH HUGHES   Hughes, Keith Wills b: 9/12/63, Bryn Mawr, Pa. BL/TL, 6'3", 210 lbs. Deb: 5/19/87

1987	NY-A	4	4	0	0	0	0	0	0	0	0	.000	.000	.000	-99	-1	0	0	0	.000	0	/H	-0.1
	Phi-N	37	76	8	20	2	0	0	10	7	11	.263	.333	.289	65	-4	0	0	0	.963	-2	O-19	-0.6
1988	Bal-A	41	108	10	21	2	0	2	14	16	27	.194	.298	.324	76	-3	1	0	0	.969	0	O-31/D-1	-0.2
1990	NY-N	8	9	0	0	0	0	0	0	0	6	.000	.000	.000	-99	-1	0	0	0	1.000	-0	/O-5	-0.4
1993	Cin-N	3	4	0	0	0	0	0	0	0	0	.000	.000	.000	-99	-1	0	0	0	.000	-0	/O-2	-0.2
Total	4	93	201	18	41	4	0	2	24	23	44	.204	.289	.284	57	-12	1	0	0	.969	-2	/O-57,D-1	-1.5

YEAR	TM/L	G	AB	R	H	2B	3B	HR	RBI	BB	SO	AVG	OBP	SLG	PRO+	BR/A	SB	CS	SBR	FA	FR	G/POS	TPR

■ ROY HUGHES
Hughes, Roy John "Jeep" or "Sage"   b: 1/11/11, Cincinnati, Ohio   d: 3/5/95, Asheville, N.C.   BR/TR, 5'10.5", 167 lbs.   Deb: 4/16/35

YEAR	TM/L	G	AB	R	H	2B	3B	HR	RBI	BB	SO	AVG	OBP	SLG	PRO+	BR/A	SB	CS	SBR	FA	FR	G/POS	TPR
1935	Cle-A	82	266	40	78	15	3	0	14	18	17	.293	.340	.372	83	-7	13	3	2	.987	-1	2-40,S-29/3-1	-0.1
1936	Cle-A	152	638	112	188	35	9	0	63	57	40	.295	.356	.378	81	-19	20	9	1	.973	5	*2-152	-0.2
1937	Cle-A	104	346	57	96	12	6	1	40	40	22	.277	.352	.355	78	-11	11	6	-0	.939	12	3-58,2-32	0.4
1938	StL-A	58	96	16	27	3	0	2	13	12	11	.281	.361	.375	85	-2	3	0	1	.957	4	2-21/3-5,S-2	0.4
1939	StL-A	17	23	6	2	0	0	0	1	4	4	.087	.222	.087	-18	-4	0	0	0	1.000	1	/2-6,S-1	-0.3
	Phi-N	65	237	22	54	5	1	1	16	21	18	.228	.291	.270	53	-15	4			.984	0	2-65	-1.2
1940	Phi-N	1	0	0	0	0	0	0	0	0	0	—	—	—	—	0	0			1.000	-0	/2-1	0.0
1944	Chi-N	126	478	86	137	16	6	1	28	35	30	.287	.337	.351	94	-3	16			.951	11	3-66,S-52	1.3
1945	*Chi-N	69	222	34	58	8	1	0	8	16	18	.261	.311	.306	73	-8	6			.931	-8	S-36,2-21/3-9,1-2	-1.2
1946	Phi-N	89	276	23	65	11	1	0	22	19	15	.236	.287	.283	64	-13	7			.942	-12	S-34,3-31/2-7,1-1	-2.5
Total	9	763	2582	396	705	105	27	5	205	222	175	.273	.332	.340	78	-83	80	18		.980	12	2-345,3-170,S/1	-3.4

■ TERRY HUGHES
Hughes, Terry Wayne   b: 5/13/49, Spartanburg, S.C.   BR/TR, 6'1", 185 lbs.   Deb: 9/2/70

YEAR	TM/L	G	AB	R	H	2B	3B	HR	RBI	BB	SO	AVG	OBP	SLG	PRO+	BR/A	SB	CS	SBR	FA	FR	G/POS	TPR
1970	Chi-N	2	3	0	1	0	0	0	0	0	0	.333	.333	.333	71	-0	0	0	0	.000	-0	/3-1,O-1	0.0
1973	StL-N	11	14	1	3	1	0	0	1	1	4	.214	.267	.286	53	-1	0	0	0	1.000	1	/3-5,1-1	-0.1
1974	Bos-A	41	69	5	14	2	0	1	6	6	18	.203	.286	.275	58	-4	0	0	0	.958	4	3-36/D-1	0.0
Total	3	54	86	6	18	3	0	1	7	7	22	.209	.284	.279	58	-5	0	0	0	.961	3	/3-42,D-1,1-1,O-1	-0.1

■ TOM HUGHES
Hughes, Thomas Franklin   b: 8/6/07, Emmet, Ark.   d: 8/10/89, Beaumont, Tex.   BL/TR, 6'1", 190 lbs.   Deb: 9/9/30

YEAR	TM/L	G	AB	R	H	2B	3B	HR	RBI	BB	SO	AVG	OBP	SLG	PRO+	BR/A	SB	CS	SBR	FA	FR	G/POS	TPR
1930	Det-A	17	59	8	22	2	3	0	5	4	8	.373	.413	.508	130	3	0	1	-1	.897	-3	O-16	-0.2

■ BILL HUGHES
Hughes, William R.   b: 11/25/1866, Blandinsville, Ill.   d: 8/25/43, Santa Ana, Cal.   BL/TL,   Deb: 9/28/1884

YEAR	TM/L	G	AB	R	H	2B	3B	HR	RBI	BB	SO	AVG	OBP	SLG	PRO+	BR/A	SB	CS	SBR	FA	FR	G/POS	TPR
1884	Was-U	14	49	5	6	0	0	0		2		.122	.157	.122	-15	-8				.955	0	/1-9,O-6	-0.8
1885	Phi-a	4	16	3	3	1	1	0	1	1		.188	.278	.375	99	-0				1.000	-0	/O-2,P-2	-0.0
Total	2	18	65	8	9	1	1	0	1	3		.138	.188	.185	15	-8				.813	-0	/1-9,O-8,P-2	-0.8

■ EMIL HUHN
Huhn, Emil Hugo "Hap"   b: 3/10/1892, North Vernon, Ind.   d: 9/5/25, Camden, S.C.   BR/TR, 6', 180 lbs.   Deb: 4/10/15

YEAR	TM/L	G	AB	R	H	2B	3B	HR	RBI	BB	SO	AVG	OBP	SLG	PRO+	BR/A	SB	CS	SBR	FA	FR	G/POS	TPR
1915	New-F	124	415	34	94	18	1	1	41	28	40	.227	.279	.282	61	-29	13			.985	-2	*1-101,C-16	-3.6
1916	Cin-N	37	94	4	24	3	2	0	3	2	11	.255	.271	.330	86	-2	0			.989	-1	C-18,1-14/O-1	-0.1
1917	Cin-N	23	51	2	10	1	2	0	3	2	5	.196	.226	.294	62	-3	1			.969	-2	C-15/1-1	-0.4
Total	3	184	560	40	128	22	5	1	47	32	56	.229	.273	.291	65	-33	14			.986	-3	1-116/C-49,O-1	-4.1

■ BILLY HULEN
Hulen, William Franklin   b: 3/12/1870, Dixon, Cal.   d: 10/2/47, Santa Rosa, Cal.   BL/TL, 5'8", 148 lbs.   Deb: 5/2/1896

YEAR	TM/L	G	AB	R	H	2B	3B	HR	RBI	BB	SO	AVG	OBP	SLG	PRO+	BR/A	SB	CS	SBR	FA	FR	G/POS	TPR
1896	Phi-N	88	339	87	90	18	7	0	38	55	20	.265	.368	.360	93	-2	23			.874	-21	S-73,O-12/2-2	-1.8
1899	Was-N	19	68	10	10	1	0	0	3	10		.147	.256	.162	16	-8	5			.902	-4	S-19	-0.9
Total	2	107	407	97	100	19	7	0	41	65	20	.246	.350	.327	81	-9	28			.880	-25	/S-92,O-12,2-2	-2.7

■ TIM HULETT
Hulett, Timothy Craig   b: 1/12/60, Springfield, Ill.   BR/TR, 6', 185 lbs.   Deb: 9/15/83

YEAR	TM/L	G	AB	R	H	2B	3B	HR	RBI	BB	SO	AVG	OBP	SLG	PRO+	BR/A	SB	CS	SBR	FA	FR	G/POS	TPR
1983	Chi-A	6	5	0	1	0	0	0	0	0	0	.200	.200	.200	10	-1	1	0	0	.875	2	/2-6	0.1
1984	Chi-A	8	1	1	0	0	0	0	0	1	0	.000	.125	.000	-59	-2	1	0	0	1.000	4	/3-4,2-3	0.3
1985	Chi-A	141	395	52	106	19	4	5	37	30	81	.268	.326	.375	88	-6	6	4	-1	.924	8	*3-115,2-28/O-1	0.1
1986	Chi-A	150	520	53	120	16	5	17	44	21	91	.231	.262	.379	70	-23	4	1	1	.951	-6	3-89,2-66	-2.7
1987	Chi-A	68	240	20	52	10	0	7	28	10	41	.217	.248	.346	54	-16	0	2	-1	.953	-3	3-61/2-8	-2.0
1989	Bal-A	33	97	12	27	5	0	3	18	10	17	.278	.346	.423	119	2	0	1	0	.976	-5	2-23,3-11	-0.2
1990	Bal-A	53	153	16	39	7	1	3	16	15	41	.255	.321	.373	97	-1	1	0	0	.961	6	3-24,2-16/D-8	0.6
1991	Bal-A	79	206	29	42	9	0	7	18	13	49	.204	.253	.350	68	-10	0	1	-1	.976	-8	3-39,2-26,D-15,/S-1	-1.8
1992	Bal-A	57	142	11	41	7	2	2	21	10	31	.289	.340	.408	106	1	0	1	-1	.935	10	3-27,D-13,2-10,/S-5	1.0
1993	Bal-A	85	260	40	78	15	0	2	23	23	56	.300	.364	.381	96	-1	1	2	-1	.963	19	3-75/S-8,2-4,D-2	1.7
1994	Bal-A	36	92	11	21	2	1	2	15	12	24	.228	.317	.337	66	-5	0	0	0	.992	13	2-23/3-9,S-6	0.9
1995	StL-N	4	11	0	2	0	0	0	0	0	3	.182	.182	.182	-4	-2	0	0	0	.941	2	/2-2,S-1	0.1
Total	12	720	2128	245	529	90	13	48	220	145	438	.249	.300	.371	80	-62	14	11	-2	.947	43	3-454,2-215/DSO	-1.9

■ DAVID HULSE
Hulse, David Lindsey   b: 2/25/68, San Angelo, Tex.   BL/TL, 5'11", 170 lbs.   Deb: 8/11/92

YEAR	TM/L	G	AB	R	H	2B	3B	HR	RBI	BB	SO	AVG	OBP	SLG	PRO+	BR/A	SB	CS	SBR	FA	FR	G/POS	TPR
1992	Tex-A	32	92	14	28	4	0	0	2	3	18	.304	.326	.348	92	-1	3	1	0	.984	-4	O-31/D-1	-0.5
1993	Tex-A	114	407	71	118	9	10	1	29	26	57	.290	.334	.369	92	-5	29	9	3	.988	-6	*O-112/D-2	-0.9
1994	Tex-A	77	310	58	79	8	4	1	19	21	53	.255	.306	.316	61	-18	18	2	4	.978	-4	O-76/D-1	-1.8
1995	Mil-A	119	339	46	85	11	6	3	47	18	60	.251	.289	.345	61	-20	15	3	3	.984	-26	*O-115	-4.3
1996	Mil-A	81	117	18	26	3	0	0	6	8	16	.222	.272	.248	31	-12	4	1	1	.990	-14	O-68/D-4	-2.5
Total	5	423	1265	207	336	35	20	5	103	76	204	.266	.309	.337	69	-56	69	16	11	.985	-53	O-402/D-8	-10.0

■ RUDY HULSWITT
Hulswitt, Rudolph Edward   b: 2/23/1877, Newport, Ky.   d: 1/16/50, Louisville, Ky.   BR/TR, 5'8.5", 165 lbs.   Deb: 6/16/1899   C

YEAR	TM/L	G	AB	R	H	2B	3B	HR	RBI	BB	SO	AVG	OBP	SLG	PRO+	BR/A	SB	CS	SBR	FA	FR	G/POS	TPR
1899	Lou-N	1	0	0	0	0	0	0	0	0		—	—	—		0	0			.333	-1	/S-1	-0.1
1902	Phi-N	128	497	59	135	11	7	0	38	30		.272	.316	.322	97	-2	12			.917	8	*S-125/3-3	1.4
1903	Phi-N	138	519	56	128	22	9	1	58	28		.247	.288	.329	78	-16	10			.906	-3	*S-138	-1.3
1904	Phi-N	113	406	36	99	11	4	1	36	16		.244	.276	.298	80	-10	8			.912	-13	*S-113	-2.1
1908	Cin-N	119	386	27	88	5	7	1	28	30		.228	.287	.285	85	-7	7			.936	-6	*S-118/2-1	-1.2
1909	StL-N	82	289	21	81	8	3	0	29	19		.280	.329	.329	111	3	7			.930	-6	S-65,2-12	-0.2
1910	StL-N	63	133	9	33	7	2	0	14	13	10	.248	.320	.331	93	-1	5			.854	-13	S-30/2-2	-1.4
Total	7	644	2230	208	564	64	32	3	203	136	10	.253	.299	.314	89	-32		49		.915	-32	S-590/2-15,3-3	-4.9

■ JOHN HUMMEL
Hummel, John Edwin "Silent John"   b: 4/4/1883, Bloomsburg, Pa.   d: 5/18/59, Springfield, Mass.   BR/TR, 5'11", 160 lbs.   Deb: 9/12/05

YEAR	TM/L	G	AB	R	H	2B	3B	HR	RBI	BB	SO	AVG	OBP	SLG	PRO+	BR/A	SB	CS	SBR	FA	FR	G/POS	TPR
1905	Bro-N	30	109	19	29	7	7	0	7	9		.266	.322	.367	114	2	6			.962	0	2-30	0.2
1906	Bro-N	97	286	20	57	6	4	1	21	36		.199	.289	.259	77	-7	10			.953	1	2-50,O-21,1-15	-0.8
1907	Bro-N	107	342	41	80	12	3	3	31	26		.234	.294	.313	98	-2	8			.951	13	2-44,O-33,1-12/S-8	1.0
1908	Bro-N	154	594	51	143	11	12	4	41	34		.241	.284	.320	97	-4	20			.973	8	O-95,2-43/S-9,1-8	0.0
1909	Bro-N	146	542	54	152	15	9	4	52	22		.280	.311	.363	113	5	16			.987	-17	1-54,2-38,S-36,O-17	-1.5
1910	Bro-N	153	578	67	141	21	15	5	74	57	81	.244	.314	.351	97	-4	21			**.965**	-14	*2-153	-2.2
1911	Bro-N	137	477	54	129	21	11	5	58	67	66	.270	.360	.392	115	10	16			**.972**	-5	*2-127/1-4,S-2	0.2
1912	Bro-N	122	411	55	116	21	7	5	54	49	55	.282	.359	.404	113	7	7			.969	-15	2-58,O-44,1-11	-1.1
1913	Bro-N	67	198	20	48	7	7	2	24	13	23	.242	.292	.379	88	-4	4			.938	-1	O-28,S-17/1-6,2-3	-0.4
1914	Bro-N	73	208	25	55	8	9	0	20	16	25	.264	.317	.389	107	1	5			.982	-2	1-36,O-19/2-1,S-1	-0.9
1915	Bro-N	53	100	6	23	2	3	0	8	6	11	.230	.274	.310	75	-3	1	1	-0	1.000	-4	O-21,1-11/S-1	-0.9
1918	NY-A	22	61	9	18	1	2	0	4	11	8	.295	.411	.377	135	3	3			.960	-3	O-15/1-3,2-1	-0.1
Total	12	1161	3906	421	991	128	84	29	394	346	269	.254	.316	.352	103	5	117	1		.963	-40	2-548,O-293,1/S	-5.8

■ AL HUMPHREY
Humphrey, Albert   b: 2/28/1886, Ashtabula, Ohio   d: 5/13/61, Ashtabula, Ohio   BL/TR, 5'11", 180 lbs.   Deb: 9/1/11

YEAR	TM/L	G	AB	R	H	2B	3B	HR	RBI	BB	SO	AVG	OBP	SLG	PRO+	BR/A	SB	CS	SBR	FA	FR	G/POS	TPR
1911	Bro-N	8	27	4	5	0	0	0	3	7		.185	.267	.185	29	-3	0			.923	-2	/O-8	-0.5

■ TERRY HUMPHREY
Humphrey, Terryal Gene   b: 8/4/49, Chickasha, Okla.   BR/TR, 6'3", 190 lbs.   Deb: 9/5/71

YEAR	TM/L	G	AB	R	H	2B	3B	HR	RBI	BB	SO	AVG	OBP	SLG	PRO+	BR/A	SB	CS	SBR	FA	FR	G/POS	TPR
1971	Mon-N	9	26	1	5	1	0	0	1	0	3	.192	.192	.231	19	-3	0	0	0	.981	2	/C-9	0.0
1972	Mon-N	69	215	13	40	8	0	1	9	16	38	.186	.249	.237	38	-17	4	1	1	.986	-3	C-65	-1.9
1973	Mon-N	43	90	5	15	2	0	1	9	5	16	.167	.211	.222	19	-10	0	1	-1	1.000	5	C-35	-0.5
1974	Mon-N	20	52	3	10	3	0	0	3	4	9	.192	.250	.250	38	-4	0	0	0	.990	4	C-17	0.2
1975	Det-A	18	41	0	10	0	0	0	3	4	3	.244	.279	.244	47	-3	0	0	0	1.000	1	C-18	-0.1
1976	Cal-A	71	196	17	48	10	0	1	19	13	30	.245	.308	.311	87	-3	0	1	-0	.980	1	C-71	0.4
1977	Cal-A	123	304	17	69	11	2	2	34	21	58	.227	.286	.283	58	-18	1	1	-0	.989	-0	*C-123	-1.5
1978	Cal-A	53	114	9	25	1	0	0	5	1	8	.219	.270	.228	62	-6	0	1	-1	.978	11	C-52/2-1,3-1	0.5
1979	Cal-A	9	17	2	1	0	0	0	0	1	2	.059	.111	.059	-55	-4	0	0	0	.983	0	/C-9	0.2
Total	9	415	1055	69	223	39	1	6	85	68	175	.211	.268	.267	51	-67	5	6	-2	.986	28	C-399/3-1,2-1	-3.2

YEAR	TM/L	G	AB	R	H	2B	3B	HR	RBI	BB	SO	AVG	OBP	SLG	PRO+	BR/A	SB	CS	SBR	FA	FR	G/POS	TPR

■ MIKE HUMPHREYS   Humphreys, Michael Butler   b: 4/10/67, Dallas, Tex.   BR/TR, 6', 185 lbs.   Deb: 7/29/91

1991	NY-A	25	40	9	8	0	0	0	3	9	7	.200	.347	.200	55	-2	2	0	1	1.000	-2	/O-9,3-6,D-7	-0.3
1992	NY-A	4	10	0	1	0	0	0	0	0	1	.100	.100	.100	-44	-2	0	0	0	1.000	1	/O-2,D-1	-0.1
1993	NY-A	25	35	6	6	2	1	1	6	4	11	.171	.256	.371	69	-2	2	1	0	1.000	-7	O-21/D-3	-0.9
Total	3	54	85	15	15	2	1	1	9	13	19	.176	.286	.259	51	-6	4	1	1	1.000	-8	/O-32,D-11,3-6	-1.3

■ JOHN HUMPHRIES   Humphries, John Henry   b: 11/12/1861, N.Gower, Ont., Can.   d: 11/29/33, Salinas, Cal.   BL/TL, 6', 185 lbs.   Deb: 7/7/1883

1883	NY-N	29	107	5	12	1	0	0	4	1	22	.112	.120	.121	-26	-16				.815	-5	C-20,O-12	-1.8
1884	Was-a	49	193	23	34	2	0	0		9		.176	.217	.187	37	-12				.890	-6	C-35,O-12/1-4	-1.4
	NY-N	20	64	6	6	0	0	0	2	9	19	.094	.205	.094	-2	-7				.896	11	C-20	0.4
Total	2	98	364	34	52	3	0	0	6	19	41	.143	.188	.151	9	-35				.876	-0	/C-75,O-24,1-4	-2.8

■ RANDY HUNDLEY   Hundley, Cecil Randolph   b: 6/1/42, Martinsville, Va.   BR/TR, 6', 175 lbs.   Deb: 9/27/64   FC

1964	SF-N	2	1	1	0	0	0	0	0	0	1	.000	.000	.000	-98	-0	0	0	0	.000	0	/C-2	0.0
1965	SF-N	6	15	0	1	0	0	0	0	0	4	.067	.067	.067	-61	-3	0	0	0	1.000	4	/C-6	0.1
1966	Chi-N	149	526	50	124	22	3	19	63	35	113	.236	.287	.397	87	-10	1	3	-2	.986	-11	*C-149	-1.4
1967	Chi-N	152	539	68	144	25	3	14	60	44	75	.267	.325	.403	102	1	2	4	-2	.996	-12	*C-152	-0.4
1968	Chi-N	160	553	41	125	18	4	7	65	39	69	.226	.282	.311	73	-18	1	0	0	.995	-13	*C-160	-2.3
1969	Chi-N★	151	522	67	133	15	1	18	64	61	90	.255	.336	.391	91	-6	2	3	-1	.992	12	*C-151	1.3
1970	Chi-N	73	250	13	61	5	0	7	36	16	52	.244	.289	.348	62	-14	0	1	-1	.990	-1	C-73	-1.1
1971	Chi-N	9	21	1	7	1	0	0	2	0	2	.333	.333	.381	89	-0	0	0	0	.979	3	/C-8	0.3
1972	Chi-N	114	357	23	78	12	0	5	30	22	62	.218	.264	.294	53	-22	1	0	0	**.995**	7	*C-113	-1.1
1973	Chi-N	124	368	35	83	11	1	10	43	30	51	.226	.284	.342	68	-16	5	6	-2	.993	11	*C-122	-0.3
1974	Min-A	32	88	2	17	2	0	0	3	4	12	.193	.228	.216	27	-8	0	0	0	.965	1	C-28	-0.6
1975	SD-N	74	180	7	37	5	1	2	14	19	29	.206	.285	.278	60	-10	0	0	0	.970	1	/C-51	-0.8
1976	Chi-N	13	18	3	3	0	2	0	1	1	4	.167	.211	.278	35	-2	0	0	0	.923	-0	/C-9	-0.2
1977	Chi-N	2	4	0	0	0	0	0	0	0	1	.000	.000	.000	-90	-1	0	0	0	1.000	0	/C-2	-0.1
Total	14	1061	3442	311	813	118	13	82	381	271	565	.236	.294	.350	76	-109	12	17	-7	.990	0	*C-1026	-6.6

■ TODD HUNDLEY   Hundley, Todd Randolph   b: 5/27/69, Martinsville, Va.   BB/TR, 5'11", 170 lbs.   Deb: 5/18/90   F

1990	NY-N	36	67	8	14	6	0	0	2	6	18	.209	.274	.299	58	-4	0	0	0	.988	2	C-36	-0.1
1991	NY-N	21	60	5	8	0	1	1	7	6	14	.133	.224	.217	25	-6	0	0	0	1.000	-6	C-20	-1.2
1992	NY-N	123	358	32	75	17	0	7	32	19	76	.209	.257	.316	62	-19	3	0	1	.996	2	*C-121	-1.0
1993	NY-N	130	417	40	95	17	2	11	53	23	62	.228	.271	.357	68	-20	1	1	-0	.988	-6	*C-123	-2.0
1994	NY-N	91	291	45	69	10	1	16	42	25	73	.237	.304	.443	93	-4	2	1	0	.990	-4	C-82	-0.3
1995	NY-N	90	275	39	77	11	0	15	51	42	64	.280	.385	.484	131	13	1	0	0	.987	-11	C-89	0.8
1996	NY-N★	153	540	85	140	32	1	41	112	79	146	.259	.357	.550	145	33	1	3	-2	.992	-8	*C-150	3.3
Total	7	644	2008	254	478	93	5	91	299	200	453	.238	.313	.425	99	-6	8	5	-1	.991	-30	C-621	-0.5

■ BERNIE HUNGLING   Hungling, Bernard Herman "Bud"   b: 3/5/1896, Dayton, Ohio   d: 3/30/68, Dayton, Ohio   BR/TR, 6'2", 180 lbs.   Deb: 4/14/22

1922	Bro-N	39	102	9	23	1	2	1	13	6	20	.225	.269	.304	48	-8	2	0	1	.968	1	C-36	-0.4
1923	Bro-N	2	4	0	0	0	0	0	0	0	2	.000	.000	.000	-99	-1	0	1	-1	.667	-1	/C-1	-0.2
1930	StL-A	10	31	4	10	2	0	0	2	5	3	.323	.417	.387	102	0	0	1	-1	1.000	-4	/C-10	-0.3
Total	3	51	137	13	33	3	2	1	15	11	25	.241	.297	.314	57	-9	2	2	-1	.968	-3	/C-47	-0.9

■ BILL HUNNEFIELD   Hunnefield, William Fenton "Wild Bill"   b: 1/5/1899, Dedham, Mass.   d: 8/28/76, Nantucket, Mass.   BB/TR, 5'10", 165 lbs.   Deb: 4/17/26

1926	Chi-A	131	470	81	129	26	4	3	48	37	28	.274	.329	.366	84	-12	24	9	2	.931	-8	S-98,3-17,2-15	-0.7
1927	Chi-A	112	365	45	104	25	1	2	36	25	24	.285	.332	.375	85	-8	15	13	-3	.933	-20	S-79,2-17/3-1	-2.3
1928	Chi-A	94	333	42	98	8	3	2	24	26	24	.294	.351	.354	87	-6	16	6	1	.967	-12	2-82/S-3,3-1	-1.4
1929	Chi-A	47	127	13	23	5	0	0	9	7	4	.181	.224	.220	15	-16	5	2	0	.969	-4	2-29/3-4,S-2	-1.8
1930	Chi-A	31	81	11	22	2	0	1	5	4	9	.272	.314	.333	67	-4	1	1	-0	.932	-1	S-22/1-1	-1.2
1931	Cle-A	21	71	13	17	4	1	0	4	9	4	.239	.325	.324	67	-3	3	1	0	.853	-10	S-21/2-1	-1.0
	Bos-N	11	21	2	6	0	0	0	1	0	2	.286	.286	.286	56	-1				.864	2	/3-5,2-4	0.1
	NY-N	64	196	23	53	5	0	1	17	9	16	.270	.302	.311	67	-9	3			.951	-5	2-56/S-5	-1.1
	Yr	75	217	25	59	5	0	1	18	9	18	.272	.301	.309	66	-10	3			.951	-3	2-60/3-5,S-5	-1.0
Total	6	511	1664	230	452	75	9	9	144	117	111	.272	.322	.344	76	-60	67	32		.925	-67	S-230,2-204/3-28,1	-9.4

■ RANDY HUNT   Hunt, James Randall   b: 1/3/60, Prattville, Ala.   BR/TR, 6', 185 lbs.   Deb: 6/4/85

1985	StL-N	14	19	1	3	0	0	0	1	0	5	.158	.158	.158	-12	-3	0	1	-1	1.000	1	C-13	-0.2
1986	Mon-N	21	48	4	10	0	0	2	5	5	16	.208	.283	.333	70	-2	0	0	0	.960	6	C-21	0.5
Total	2	35	67	5	13	0	0	2	6	5	21	.194	.250	.284	48	-5	0	1	-1	.967	7	/C-34	0.3

■ KEN HUNT   Hunt, Kenneth Lawrence   b: 7/13/34, Grand Forks, N.Dak   BR/TR, 6'1", 205 lbs.   Deb: 9/10/59

1959	NY-A	6	12	2	4	1	0	0	0	0	3	.333	.333	.417	108	0	0	0	0	1.000	0	/O-5	0.0
1960	NY-A	25	22	4	6	2	0	0	1	4	6	.273	.407	.364	117	1	0	0	0	.957	-6	O-24	-0.5
1961	LA-A	149	479	70	122	29	3	25	84	49	120	.255	.329	.484	103	-0	8	2	1	.950	-6	*O-134/2-1	-1.2
1962	LA-A	13	11	4	2	0	0	0	1	1	5	.182	.250	.455	88	-0	1	0	0	.867	-1	/1-3	-0.1
1963	LA-A	59	142	17	26	6	1	5	16	15	49	.183	.261	.345	72	-6	0	1	-1	.972	-6	O-50	-1.6
	Was-A	7	20	1	4	0	0	1	4	2	6	.200	.273	.350	73	-1	0	0	0	1.000	0	/O-5	-0.1
	Yr	66	162	18	30	6	1	6	20	17	55	.185	.263	.346	73	-6	0	1	-1	.976	-6	O-55	-1.7
1964	Was-A	51	96	9	13	4	0	1	4	14	35	.135	.245	.208	28	-9	0	1	-1	1.000	-2	O-37	-1.3
Total	6	310	782	107	177	42	4	33	111	85	222	.226	.306	.417	89	-15	9	4	0	.964	-21	O-255/1-3,2-1	-4.9

■ JOEL HUNT   Hunt, Oliver Joel "Jodie"   b: 10/11/05, Texico, N.Mex.   d: 7/24/78, Teague, Tex.   BR/TR, 5'10", 165 lbs.   Deb: 4/27/31

1931	StL-N	4	1	2	0	0	0	0	0	0	0	.000	.000	.000	-96	-0		0		.000	-1	/O-1	-0.1
1932	StL-N	12	21	0	4	1	0	0	3	4	3	.190	.320	.238	51	-1		0		1.000	0	/O-5	-0.1
Total	2	16	22	2	4	1	0	0	3	4	3	.182	.308	.227	45	-2		0		1.000	-0	/O-6	-0.2

■ DICK HUNT   Hunt, Richard M.   b: 1847, New York   d: 11/20/1895, Brooklyn, N.Y.   5'9", 145 lbs.   Deb: 5/7/1872

| 1872 | Eck-n | 11 | 48 | 11 | 15 | 1 | 1 | 0 | 5 | 1 | 0 | .313 | .327 | .375 | 136 | 3 | 0 | 1 | -1 | .636 | -3 | /O-8,2-3 | -0.1 |

■ RON HUNT   Hunt, Ronald Kenneth   b: 2/23/41, St.Louis, Mo.   BR/TR, 6', 186 lbs.   Deb: 4/16/63

1963	NY-N	143	533	64	145	28	4	10	42	40	50	.272	.338	.396	109	6	5	4	-1	.967	2	*2-142/3-1	2.3
1964	NY-N★	127	475	59	144	19	6	6	42	29	30	.303	.357	.406	117	11	6	2	1	.979	3	*2-109,3-12	1.4
1965	NY-N	57	196	21	47	12	1	1	10	14	19	.240	.310	.327	82	-4	2	7	-4	.979	-5	2-46/3-6	-0.9
1966	NY-N★	132	479	63	138	19	2	3	33	41	34	.288	.358	.355	101	2	8	10	-4	.970	7	*2-123/S-1,3-1	1.5
1967	LA-N	110	388	44	102	17	3	3	33	39	24	.263	.346	.341	107	4	2	1	0	.980	-16	2-90/3-8	-0.6
1968	SF-N	148	529	79	132	19	0	2	28	78	41	.250	.372	.297	103	9	3	2	0	.972	-17	*2-147	-0.3
1969	SF-N	128	478	72	125	23	3	6	41	51	47	.262	.363	.341	100	3	9	2	1	.979	-9	*2-125/3-1	0.6
1970	SF-N	117	367	70	103	17	1	6	41	44	29	.281	.396	.386	111	9	1	2	-1	.968	-2	2-85,3-16	-1.4
1971	Mon-N	152	520	89	145	20	3	5	38	58	41	.279	.403	.358	116	17	5	7	-3	.979	-9	*2-133,3-19	1.7
1972	Mon-N	129	443	56	112	20	0	0	18	51	29	.253	.363	.298	88	-3	2	4	-2	.982	-7	*2-122/3-5	-0.2
1973	Mon-N	113	401	61	124	14	0	0	18	52	19	.309	.419	.344	110	10	10	7	-1	.982	-21	*2-102,3-14	-0.7
1974	Mon-N	115	403	66	108	15	0	0	26	55	17	.268	.375	.305	87	-4	5	5	-2	.941	-14	3-75,2-31/S-1	-2.0
	StL-N	12	23	1	4	0	0	0	0	3	2	.174	.321	.174	42	-2	0	0	0	1.000	-1	/2-5	-0.3
	Yr	127	426	67	112	15	0	0	26	58	19	.263	.372	.300	85	-5	5	5	-2	.941	-16	3-75,2-36/S-1	-2.3
Total	12	1483	5235	745	1429	223	23	39	370	555	382	.273	.369	.347	104	57	65	55	-14	.976	-126	*2-1260,3-158/S-2	1.1

■ BRIAN HUNTER   Hunter, Brian Lee   b: 3/5/71, Portland, Ore.   BR/TR, 6'4", 180 lbs.   Deb: 6/27/94

| 1994 | Hou-N | 6 | 24 | 2 | 6 | 1 | 0 | 0 | 1 | 6 | | .250 | .280 | .292 | 52 | -2 | 2 | 1 | 0 | .938 | 1 | /O-6 | -0.1 |
| 1995 | Hou-N | 78 | 321 | 52 | 97 | 14 | 5 | 2 | 28 | 21 | 52 | .302 | .349 | .396 | 103 | 1 | 24 | 7 | 3 | .955 | 9 | O-74 | 1.0 |

YEAR	TM/L	G	AB	R	H	2B	3B	HR	RBI	BB	SO	AVG	OBP	SLG	PRO+	BR/A	SB	CS	SBR	FA	FR	G/POS	TPR
1996	Hou-N	132	526	74	145	27	2	5	35	17	92	.276	.301	.363	82	-16	35	9	5	.960	9	*O-127	-0.6
Total	3	216	871	128	248	42	7	5	63	39	150	.285	.318	.373	89	-17	61	17	8	.957	18	O-207	0.3

■ BRIAN HUNTER
Hunter, Brian Ronald   b: 3/4/68, Torrance, Cal.   BR/TL, 6′, 195 lbs.   Deb: 5/31/91

YEAR	TM/L	G	AB	R	H	2B	3B	HR	RBI	BB	SO	AVG	OBP	SLG	PRO+	BR/A	SB	CS	SBR	FA	FR	G/POS	TPR
1991	*Atl-N	97	271	32	68	16	1	12	50	17	48	.251	.298	.450	101	-1	0	2	-1	.988	-4	1-85/O-6	-1.1
1992	*Atl-N	102	238	34	57	13	2	14	41	21	50	.239	.301	.487	113	3	1	2	-1	.997	3	1-92/O-6	0.1
1993	Atl-N	37	80	4	11	3	1	0	8	2	15	.138	.159	.200	-5	-12	0	0	0	.994	0	1-29/O-2	-1.3
1994	Pit-N	76	233	28	53	15	1	11	47	15	55	.227	.274	.442	82	-7	0	0	0	.991	-1	1-59/O-5	-1.3
	Cin-N	9	23	6	7	1	0	4	10	2	1	.304	.360	.870	209	3	0	0	0	1.000	-0	/O-5,1-1	0.3
	Yr	85	256	34	60	16	1	15	57	17	56	.234	.282	.480	93	-4	0	0	0	.991	-1	1-60,O-10	-1.0
1995	Cin-N	40	79	9	17	6	0	1	9	11	21	.215	.319	.329	72	-3	2	1	0	.983	0	1-23/O-4	-0.4
1996	Sea-A	75	198	21	53	10	0	7	28	15	43	.268	.332	.424	90	-3	0	1	-1	.991	-2	1-41,O-29/D-2	-0.9
Total	6	436	1122	134	266	64	5	49	193	83	233	.237	.293	.434	90	-20	3	6	-3	.991	-4	1-330/O-57,D-2	-4.6

■ EDDIE HUNTER
Hunter, Edison Franklin   b: 2/6/05, Bellevue, Ky.   d: 3/14/67, Colerain, Ohio   BR/TR, 5′7.5″, 150 lbs.   Deb: 8/5/33

YEAR	TM/L	G	AB	R	H	2B	3B	HR	RBI	BB	SO	AVG	OBP	SLG	PRO+	BR/A	SB	CS	SBR	FA	FR	G/POS	TPR
1933	Cin-N	1	0	0	0	0	0	0	0	0	0	—	—	—		0				.000	0	/3-1	0.0

■ NEWT HUNTER
Hunter, Frederick Creighton   b: 1/5/1880, Chillicothe, Ohio   d: 10/26/63, Columbus, Ohio   BR/TR, 6′, 180 lbs.   Deb: 4/12/11   C

YEAR	TM/L	G	AB	R	H	2B	3B	HR	RBI	BB	SO	AVG	OBP	SLG	PRO+	BR/A	SB	CS	SBR	FA	FR	G/POS	TPR
1911	Pit-N	65	209	35	53	10	6	2	24	25	43	.254	.345	.388	101	0	9			.989	-1	1-61	-0.2

■ GEORGE HUNTER
Hunter, George Henry   b: 7/8/1887, Buffalo, N.Y.   d: 1/11/68, Harrisburg, Pa.   BB/TL, 5′8.5″, 165 lbs.   Deb: 5/4/09   F

YEAR	TM/L	G	AB	R	H	2B	3B	HR	RBI	BB	SO	AVG	OBP	SLG	PRO+	BR/A	SB	CS	SBR	FA	FR	G/POS	TPR
1909	Bro-N	44	123	8	28	7	0	0	8	9		.228	.286	.285	80	-3	1			.871	-4	O-23,P-16	-0.8
1910	Bro-N	1	0	0	0	0	0	0	0	0	0	—	—	—		0	0			.000	-0	/O-1	0.0
Total	2	45	123	8	28	7	0	0	8	9	0	.228	.286	.285	80	-3	1			.871	-5	/O-24,P-16	-0.8

■ BILLY HUNTER
Hunter, Gordon William   b: 6/4/28, Punxsutawney, Pa.   BR/TR, 6′, 180 lbs.   Deb: 4/14/53   MC

YEAR	TM/L	G	AB	R	H	2B	3B	HR	RBI	BB	SO	AVG	OBP	SLG	PRO+	BR/A	SB	CS	SBR	FA	FR	G/POS	TPR
1953	StL-A★	154	567	50	124	18	1	1	37	24	45	.219	.253	.259	38	-50	3	1	0	.970	15	*S-152	-2.4
1954	Bal-A	125	411	28	100	9	5	2	27	21	38	.243	.283	.304	66	-21	5	4	-1	.948	1	*S-124	-1.2
1955	NY-A	98	255	14	58	7	1	3	20	15	18	.227	.270	.298	54	-17	9	2	2	.958	1	S-98	-0.8
1956	NY-A	39	75	8	21	3	4	0	11	2	4	.280	.299	.427	93	-1	0	1	-1	1.000	10	S-32/3-4	0.9
1957	KC-A	116	319	39	61	10	4	8	29	27	43	.191	.261	.323	58	-19	1	2	-1	.974	-5	2-64,S-35,3-17	-1.9
1958	KC-A	22	58	6	9	1	1	2	11	5	7	.155	.222	.310	44	-5	1	1	-0	.933	-3	S-12/2-8,3-1	-0.6
	Cle-A	76	190	21	37	10	2	0	9	17	37	.195	.264	.268	48	-14	4	1	1	.948	1	S-75/3-2	-0.7
	Yr	98	248	27	46	11	3	2	20	22	44	.185	.255	.278	47	-18	5	2	1	.946	-1	S-87/2-8,3-3	-1.3
Total	6	630	1875	166	410	58	18	16	144	111	192	.219	.265	.294	53	-126	23	12	-0	.958	19	S-528/2-72,3-24	-6.7

■ BUDDY HUNTER
Hunter, Harold James   b: 8/9/47, Omaha, Neb.   BR/TR, 5′10″, 170 lbs.   Deb: 7/1/71

YEAR	TM/L	G	AB	R	H	2B	3B	HR	RBI	BB	SO	AVG	OBP	SLG	PRO+	BR/A	SB	CS	SBR	FA	FR	G/POS	TPR
1971	Bos-A	8	9	2	2	1	0	0	2	1		.222	.364	.333	92	-0	0	0	0	1.000	1	/2-6	0.1
1973	Bos-A	13	7	3	3	1	0	0	2	3	1	.429	.636	.571	229	2	0	0	0	1.000	3	/3-3,2-2,D-1	0.5
1975	Bos-A	1	1	0	0	0	0	0	0	0	0	.000	.000	.000	-92	-0	0	0	0	.750	0	/2-1	0.0
Total	3	22	17	5	5	2	0	0	4	4	1	.294	.478	.412	144	1	0	0	0	.968	5	/2-9,3-3,D-1	0.6

■ HERB HUNTER
Hunter, Herbert Harrison   b: 12/25/1896, Boston, Mass.   d: 7/25/70, Orlando, Fla.   BL/TR, 6′0.5″, 165 lbs.   Deb: 4/29/16

YEAR	TM/L	G	AB	R	H	2B	3B	HR	RBI	BB	SO	AVG	OBP	SLG	PRO+	BR/A	SB	CS	SBR	FA	FR	G/POS	TPR
1916	NY-N	21	28	3	7	0	0	1	4	0	5	.250	.250	.357	90	-1	0			1.000	1	/3-6,1-2	0.0
	Chi-N	2	4	0	0	0	0	0	0	0	0	.000	.000	.000	-90	-1	0			.750	0	/3-1	-0.1
	Yr	23	32	3	7	0	0	1	4	0	5	.219	.219	.313	65	-1	0			.941	1	/3-7,1-2	-0.1
1917	Chi-N	3	3	0	0	0	0	0	0	0	0	.000	.000	.000	-93	-1	0			1.000	0	/2-1,3-1	0.0
1920	Bos-A	4	12	2	1	0	0	0	0	1	1	.083	.154	.083	-38	-2	0	0	0	.857	-1	/O-4	-0.3
1921	StL-N	9	2	3	0	0	0	0	0	1	0	.000	.333	.000	-4	-0	0	3	-2	1.000	0	/1-1	-0.2
Total	4	39	49	8	8	0	0	1	4	2	6	.163	.196	.224	24	-5	0	3		.905	0	/3-8,O-4,1-3,2-1	-0.6

■ LEM HUNTER
Hunter, Robert Lemuel   b: 1/16/1863, Warren, Ohio   d: 11/9/56, W.Lafayette, Ohio   Deb: 9/1/1883

YEAR	TM/L	G	AB	R	H	2B	3B	HR	RBI	BB	SO	AVG	OBP	SLG	PRO+	BR/A	SB	CS	SBR	FA	FR	G/POS	TPR
1883	Cle-N	1	4	1	1	0	0	0	0	0	0	.250	.250	.250	53	-0				.000	-1	/O-1,P-1	0.0

■ BILL HUNTER
Hunter, William Ellsworth   b: 7/8/1887, Buffalo, N.Y.   d: 4/10/34, Buffalo, N.Y.   BL/TL, 5′7.5″, 155 lbs.   Deb: 8/6/12   F

YEAR	TM/L	G	AB	R	H	2B	3B	HR	RBI	BB	SO	AVG	OBP	SLG	PRO+	BR/A	SB	CS	SBR	FA	FR	G/POS	TPR
1912	Cle-A	21	55	6	9	2	0	0	2	8	10	.164	.303	.200	43	-4	0			1.000	-0	O-16	-0.5

■ BILL HUNTER
Hunter, William Robert   b: 1855, St.Thomas, Ont., Can.   5′7.5″, 160 lbs.   Deb: 5/2/1884

YEAR	TM/L	G	AB	R	H	2B	3B	HR	RBI	BB	SO	AVG	OBP	SLG	PRO+	BR/A	SB	CS	SBR	FA	FR	G/POS	TPR
1884	Lou-a	2	7	1	1	0	0	0		0		.143	.143	.143	-7	-1				.667	-2	/C-2	-0.3

■ STEVE HUNTZ
Huntz, Stephen Michael   b: 12/3/45, Cleveland, Ohio   BB/TR, 6′1″, 204 lbs.   Deb: 9/19/67

YEAR	TM/L	G	AB	R	H	2B	3B	HR	RBI	BB	SO	AVG	OBP	SLG	PRO+	BR/A	SB	CS	SBR	FA	FR	G/POS	TPR
1967	StL-N	3	6	1	1	0	0	0	1	2	.167	.286	.167	33	-0	0	0	0	1.000	-1	/2-2	-0.2
1969	StL-N	71	139	13	27	4	0	3	13	27	34	.194	.325	.288	73	-4	0	0	0	.945	-6	S-52,2-12/3-6	-0.6
1970	SD-N	106	352	54	77	8	0	11	37	66	69	.219	.344	.335	86	-5	0	3	-2	.958	-12	S-57,3-51	-1.3
1971	Chi-A	35	86	10	18	3	1	2	6	7	9	.209	.269	.337	69	-4	0	0	0	1.000	-1	2-14/S-7,3-6	-0.3
1975	SD-N	22	53	3	8	4	0	0	4	7	8	.151	.250	.226	35	-5	1	0	0	.939	1	3-16/2-2	-0.4
Total	5	237	636	81	131	19	1	16	60	108	122	.206	.322	.314	76	-19	1	3	-2	.955	-18	S-116/3-79,2-30	-2.8

■ DAVE HUPPERT
Huppert, David Blain   b: 4/17/57, South Gate, Cal.   BR/TR, 6′1″, 190 lbs.   Deb: 9/15/83

YEAR	TM/L	G	AB	R	H	2B	3B	HR	RBI	BB	SO	AVG	OBP	SLG	PRO+	BR/A	SB	CS	SBR	FA	FR	G/POS	TPR
1983	Bal-A	2	0	0	0	0	0	0	0	0	0	—	—	—		0	0	0	0	1.000	0	/C-2	0.0
1985	Mil-A	15	21	1	1	0	0	0	2	2	7	.048	.130	.048	-49	-4	0	0	0	.960	2	C-15	-0.2
Total	2	17	21	1	1	0	0	0	2	2	7	.048	.130	.048	-49	-4	0	0	0	.962	2	/C-17	-0.2

■ CLINT HURDLE
Hurdle, Clinton Merrick   b: 7/30/57, Big Rapids, Mich.   BL/TR, 6′3″, 195 lbs.   Deb: 9/18/77

YEAR	TM/L	G	AB	R	H	2B	3B	HR	RBI	BB	SO	AVG	OBP	SLG	PRO+	BR/A	SB	CS	SBR	FA	FR	G/POS	TPR
1977	KC-A	9	26	5	8	0	2	2	7	2	7	.308	.357	.538	139	1	0	0	0	1.000	-0	/O-9	0.1
1978	*KC-A	133	417	48	110	25	5	7	56	56	84	.264	.352	.398	108	5	1	3	-2	.958	-11	O-78,1-52/3-1,D-1	-1.3
1979	KC-A	59	171	16	41	10	3	3	30	28	24	.240	.350	.386	96	-0	0	1	-1	.968	-3	O-50/3-1,D-4	-0.6
1980	*KC-A	130	395	50	116	31	2	10	60	34	61	.294	.353	.458	119	10	0	0	0	.960	-3	*O-126	0.0
1981	*KC-A	28	76	12	25	3	1	4	15	13	10	.329	.427	.553	182	8	0	0	0	1.000	1	O-28	0.8
1982	Cin-N	19	34	2	7	1	0	0	1	2	6	.206	.270	.235	42	-3	0	1	-1	.950	-2	O-17	-0.6
1983	NY-N	13	33	3	6	2	0	0	2	6	10	.182	.229	.242	31	-3	0	0	0	.800	-2	/3-9,O-1	-0.5
1985	NY-N	43	82	7	16	4	0	3	7	13	20	.195	.313	.354	88	-1	0	1	-1	1.000	-2	C-17,O-10	-0.3
1986	StL-N	78	154	18	30	5	1	3	15	26	38	.195	.315	.299	71	-6	0	0	0	.994	-7	1-39,O-10/C-5,3-4	-1.0
1987	NY-N	3	3	1	1	0	0	0	0	0	1	.333	.333	.333	82	-0	0	0	0	1.000	-0	/1-1	0.0
Total	10	515	1391	162	360	81	12	32	193	176	261	.259	.345	.403	106	12	1	6	-3	.965	-23	O-329/1-92,C-22,3D	-3.1

■ JERRY HURLEY
Hurley, Jeremiah   b: 4/1875, New York, N.Y.   d: 12/27/19, New York, N.Y.   BR/TR,   Deb: 9/23/01

YEAR	TM/L	G	AB	R	H	2B	3B	HR	RBI	BB	SO	AVG	OBP	SLG	PRO+	BR/A	SB	CS	SBR	FA	FR	G/POS	TPR
1901	Cin-N	9	21	1	1	0	0	0	0	0	1	.048	.130	.048	-51	-4	1			.938	1	/C-7	-0.3
1907	Bro-N	1	2	0	0	0	0	0	0	1	1	.000	.333	.000	5	-0	0			1.000	0	/C-1	0.0
Total	2	10	23	1	1	0	0	0	0	1	2	.043	.154	.043	-44	-4	1			.943	1	/C-8	-0.3

■ JERRY HURLEY
Hurley, Jeremiah Joseph   b: 6/15/1863, Boston, Mass.   d: 9/17/50, Boston, Mass.   BR/TR, 6′, 190 lbs.   Deb: 5/1/1889

YEAR	TM/L	G	AB	R	H	2B	3B	HR	RBI	BB	SO	AVG	OBP	SLG	PRO+	BR/A	SB	CS	SBR	FA	FR	G/POS	TPR
1889	Bos-N	4	9	0	0	0	0	0	0	0	0	.000	.000	.000	-94	-1	0			.000	-1	/O-1,C-1	-0.2
1890	Pit-P	8	22	5	6	1	0	0	2	2	5	.273	.333	.318	81	-1	0			.906	-0	/C-7,O-1	0.0
1891	Cin-a	24	66	10	14	3	2	0	6	12	13	.212	.333	.318	80	-2	2			.862	-3	C-24/O-1,1-1	-0.3
Total	3	33	92	15	20	4	2	0	8	14	18	.217	.321	.304	72	-3	2			.870	-5	/C-32,O-3,1-1	-0.5

■ DICK HURLEY
Hurley, William H.   b: 1847, Honesdale, Pa.   5′7″, 160 lbs.   Deb: 4/18/1872

YEAR	TM/L	G	AB	R	H	2B	3B	HR	RBI	BB	SO	AVG	OBP	SLG	PRO+	BR/A	SB	CS	SBR	FA	FR	G/POS	TPR
1872	Oly-n	2	7	0	0	0	0	0	0			.000	.000	.000	-99	-2	0	0	0	.667	-0	/O-2	-0.1

■ DON HURST
Hurst, Frank O'Donnell   b: 8/12/05, Maysville, Ky.   d: 12/6/52, Los Angeles, Cal.   BL/TL, 6′, 215 lbs.   Deb: 5/13/28

YEAR	TM/L	G	AB	R	H	2B	3B	HR	RBI	BB	SO	AVG	OBP	SLG	PRO+	BR/A	SB	CS	SBR	FA	FR	G/POS	TPR
1928	Phi-N	107	396	73	113	23	4	19	64	68	40	.285	.391	.508	129	17	3			.989	4	*1-104	1.2
1929	Phi-N	154	589	100	179	29	4	31	125	80	36	.304	.390	.525	117	15	10			.985	5	*1-154	0.4

YEAR	TM/L	G	AB	R	H	2B	3B	HR	RBI	BB	SO	AVG	OBP	SLG	PRO+	BR/A	SB	CS	SBR	FA	FR	G/POS	TPR
1930	Phi-N	119	391	78	128	19	3	17	78	46	22	.327	.401	.522	113	8	6			.984	-3	1-96/O-7	-0.4
1931	Phi-N	137	489	63	149	37	5	11	91	64	28	.305	.386	.468	119	14	8			.986	11	*1-135	1.2
1932	Phi-N	150	579	109	196	41	4	24	**143**	65	27	.339	.412	.547	139	32	10			**.993**	-3	*1-150	1.7
1933	Phi-N	147	550	58	147	27	8	8	76	48	32	.267	.327	.389	92	-6	3			.985	7	*1-142	-1.3
1934	Phi-N	40	130	16	34	9	0	2	21	12	7	.262	.324	.377	77	-4	1			.994	-1	1-34	-0.8
	Chi-N	51	151	13	30	5	0	3	12	8	18	.199	.239	.291	42	-13	0			.986	-2	1-48	-1.8
	Yr	91	281	29	64	14	0	5	33	20	25	.228	.279	.331	60	-16	1			.990	-3	1-82	-2.6
Total	7	905	3275	510	976	190	28	115	610	391	210	.298	.375	.478	113	63	41			.987	19	1-863/O-7	0.2

■ **BUTCH HUSKEY**　Huskey, Robert Leon　b: 11/10/71, Anadarko, Okla.　BR/TR, 6'3", 244 lbs.　Deb: 9/8/93

YEAR	TM/L	G	AB	R	H	2B	3B	HR	RBI	BB	SO	AVG	OBP	SLG	PRO+	BR/A	SB	CS	SBR	FA	FR	G/POS	TPR
1993	NY-N	13	41	2	6	1	0	0	3	1	13	.146	.167	.171	-10	-6	0	0	0	.923	3	3-13	-0.3
1995	NY-N	28	90	8	17	1	0	3	10	10	16	.189	.270	.300	52	-6	1	0	0	.925	5	3-27/O-1	-0.1
1996	NY-N	118	414	43	115	16	2	15	60	27	77	.278	.322	.435	104	1	1	2	-1	.984	-6	1-75,O-40/3-6	-1.3
Total	3	159	545	53	138	18	2	18	74	38	106	.253	.302	.393	87	-12	2	2	-1	.925	2	/1-75,3-46,O-41	-1.7

■ **JEFF HUSON**　Huson, Jeffrey Kent　b: 8/15/64, Scottsdale, Ariz.　BL/TR, 6'3", 180 lbs.　Deb: 9/2/88

YEAR	TM/L	G	AB	R	H	2B	3B	HR	RBI	BB	SO	AVG	OBP	SLG	PRO+	BR/A	SB	CS	SBR	FA	FR	G/POS	TPR
1988	Mon-N	20	42	7	13	2	0	0	3	4	3	.310	.370	.357	105	0	2	1	0	.932	1	S-15/2-2,3-1,O-1	0.2
1989	Mon-N	32	74	1	12	5	0	0	2	6	6	.162	.225	.230	30	-7	3	0	1	.886	4	S-20/2-9,3-1	-0.1
1990	Tex-A	145	396	57	95	12	2	0	28	46	54	.240	.322	.280	70	-15	12	4	1	.960	-13	*S-119,3-36,2-12	-1.9
1991	Tex-A	119	268	36	57	8	3	2	26	39	32	.213	.313	.287	68	-11	8	3	1	.965	-0	*S-116/2-2,3-1	-0.3
1992	Tex-A	123	318	49	83	14	3	4	24	41	43	.261	.347	.362	102	2	18	6	2	.968	-9	S-82,2-47/O-2,D-1	0.0
1993	Tex-A	23	45	3	6	1	1	0	3	0	10	.133	.133	.200	-12	-7	0	0	0	.909	1	S-12/2-5,3-2,D-2	-0.1
1995	Bal-A	66	161	24	40	4	2	1	19	15	20	.248	.316	.317	64	-8	5	4	-1	1.000	2	3-33,2-21/S-1,D-3	-0.6
1996	Bal-A	17	28	5	9	1	0	0	2	1	3	.321	.345	.357	79	-1	0	0	0	.973	1	2-12/3-3,O-1	0.1
Total	8	545	1332	182	315	47	11	7	106	152	171	.236	.317	.304	73	-46	48	18	4	.955	-9	S-365,2-110/3DO	-2.7

■ **CARL HUSTA**　Husta, Carl Lawrence "Sox"　b: 4/8/02, Egg Harbor City, N.J.　d: 11/6/51, Kingston, N.Y.　BR/TR, 5'11", 176 lbs.　Deb: 9/24/25

YEAR	TM/L	G	AB	R	H	2B	3B	HR	RBI	BB	SO	AVG	OBP	SLG	PRO+	BR/A	SB	CS	SBR	FA	FR	G/POS	TPR
1925	Phi-A	6	22	2	3	1	0	0	2	2	3	.136	.208	.136	-11	-4	0	0	0	.976	2	/S-6	-0.1

■ **HARRY HUSTON**　Huston, Harry Emanuel Kress　b: 10/14/1883, Bellefontaine, O.　d: 10/13/69, Blackwell, Okla.　BR/TR, 5'9", 168 lbs.　Deb: 9/3/06

YEAR	TM/L	G	AB	R	H	2B	3B	HR	RBI	BB	SO	AVG	OBP	SLG	PRO+	BR/A	SB	CS	SBR	FA	FR	G/POS	TPR
1906	Phi-N	2	4	0	0	0	0	0	0	0	1	.000	.200	.000	-37	-1	0			1.000	-0	/C-2	-0.1

■ **WARREN HUSTON**　Huston, Warren Llewellyn　b: 10/31/13, Newtonville, Mass.　BR/TR, 6', 170 lbs.　Deb: 6/24/37

YEAR	TM/L	G	AB	R	H	2B	3B	HR	RBI	BB	SO	AVG	OBP	SLG	PRO+	BR/A	SB	CS	SBR	FA	FR	G/POS	TPR
1937	Phi-A	38	54	5	7	3	0	0	3	2	9	.130	.161	.185	-13	-10	0	1	-1	.918	8	2-16,S-15/3-2	-0.1
1944	Bos-N	33	55	7	11	1	0	0	1	8	5	.200	.313	.218	49	-3	0			.979	3	3-20/2-5,S-4	-0.0
Total	2	71	109	12	18	4	0	0	4	10	14	.165	.242	.202	19	-13	0		1	.964	11	/3-22,2-21,S-19	-0.1

■ **JOE HUTCHESON**　Hutcheson, Joseph Johnson "Slug" or "Poodles"　b: 2/5/05, Springtown, Tex.　d: 2/23/93, Tyler, Tex.　BL/TR, 6'2", 200 lbs.　Deb: 7/8/33

YEAR	TM/L	G	AB	R	H	2B	3B	HR	RBI	BB	SO	AVG	OBP	SLG	PRO+	BR/A	SB	CS	SBR	FA	FR	G/POS	TPR
1933	Bro-N	55	184	19	43	4	1	6	21	15	13	.234	.295	.364	91	-2	1			.989	1	O-45	-0.4

■ **ED HUTCHINSON**　Hutchinson, Edwin Forrest　b: 5/19/1867, Pittsburgh, Pa.　d: 7/19/34, Colfax, Cal.　BL/TR, 5'11", 175 lbs.　Deb: 6/17/1890

YEAR	TM/L	G	AB	R	H	2B	3B	HR	RBI	BB	SO	AVG	OBP	SLG	PRO+	BR/A	SB	CS	SBR	FA	FR	G/POS	TPR
1890	Chi-N	4	17	0	1	1	0	0	0	0	0	.059	.059	.118	-47	-3	0			1.000	6	/2-4	0.2

■ **FRED HUTCHINSON**　Hutchinson, Frederick Charles　b: 8/12/19, Seattle, Wash.　d: 11/12/64, Bradenton, Fla.　BL/TR, 6'2", 200 lbs.　Deb: 5/2/39 M

YEAR	TM/L	G	AB	R	H	2B	3B	HR	RBI	BB	SO	AVG	OBP	SLG	PRO+	BR/A	SB	CS	SBR	FA	FR	G/POS	TPR
1939	Det-A	13	34	5	13	1	0	0	6	2	0	.382	.417	.412	105	0	0	0	0	1.000	-0	P-13	0.0
1940	*Det-A	17	30	1	8	1	0	0	2	0	0	.267	.267	.300	43	-3	0	0	0	.900	0	P-17	0.0
1941	Det-A	2	2	0	0	0	0	0	0	0	2	.000	.000	.000	-91	-1	0	0	0	.000	0	H	-0.1
1946	Det-A	40	89	11	28	4	0	0	13	6	1	.315	.358	.360	95	-0	0	0	0	.983	3	P-28	0.0
1947	Det-A	56	106	8	32	5	2	2	15	6	6	.302	.339	.443	113	1	2	0	1	.982	7	P-33	0.0
1948	Det-A	76	112	11	23	1	0	1	12	22	9	.205	.341	.241	55	-6	3	0	1	**1.000**	3	P-33	0.0
1949	Det-A	38	73	12	18	2	1	0	7	8	5	.247	.329	.301	67	-3	1	0	0	.983	2	P-33	0.0
1950	Det-A	44	95	15	31	7	0	0	20	12	3	.326	.407	.400	104	1	0	0	0	.944	3	P-39	0.0
1951	Det-A★	47	85	7	16	2	0	0	7	7	4	.188	.250	.212	26	-9	0	1	-1	.939	2	P-31	0.0
1952	Det-A	17	18	0	1	0	0	0	0	1	1	.056	.190	.056	-29	-3	0	0	0	1.000	2	P-12,M	0.0
1953	Det-A	4	6	1	1	0	0	0	1	0	0	.167	.167	.667	118	0	0	0	0	1.000	-0	/P-3,1-1,M	0.0
Total	11	354	650	71	171	23	3	4	83	66	30	.263	.334	.326	75	-22	6	1	1	.970	15	P-242/1-1	-0.1

■ **ROY HUTSON**　Hutson, Roy Lee　b: 2/27/02, Luray, Mo.　d: 5/20/57, LaMesa, Cal.　BL/TR, 5'9", 165 lbs.　Deb: 9/20/25

YEAR	TM/L	G	AB	R	H	2B	3B	HR	RBI	BB	SO	AVG	OBP	SLG	PRO+	BR/A	SB	CS	SBR	FA	FR	G/POS	TPR
1925	Bro-N	7	8	1	4	0	0	0	1	1	1	.500	.556	.500	177	1	0	0	0	1.000	-1	/O-4	0.0

■ **JIM HUTTO**　Hutto, James Neamon　b: 10/17/47, Norfolk, Va.　BR/TR, 5'11", 195 lbs.　Deb: 4/17/70

YEAR	TM/L	G	AB	R	H	2B	3B	HR	RBI	BB	SO	AVG	OBP	SLG	PRO+	BR/A	SB	CS	SBR	FA	FR	G/POS	TPR
1970	Phi-N	57	92	7	17	2	0	3	12	5	20	.185	.227	.304	42	-8	0	0	0	1.000	-3	O-22,1-12/C-5,3-1	-1.2
1975	Bal-A	4	5	0	0	0	0	0	0	0	2	.000	.000	.000	-99	-1	0	0	0	1.000	-0	/C-3	-0.1
Total	2	61	97	7	17	2	0	3	12	5	22	.175	.216	.289	35	-9	0	0	0	1.000	-3	/O-22,1-12,C-8,3-1	-1.3

■ **TOM HUTTON**　Hutton, Thomas George　b: 4/20/46, Los Angeles, Cal.　BL/TL, 5'11", 180 lbs.　Deb: 9/16/66

YEAR	TM/L	G	AB	R	H	2B	3B	HR	RBI	BB	SO	AVG	OBP	SLG	PRO+	BR/A	SB	CS	SBR	FA	FR	G/POS	TPR
1966	LA-N	3	2	0	0	0	0	0	0	0	0	.000	.000	.000	-99	-1	0	0	0	1.000	-0	/1-3	-0.1
1969	LA-N	16	48	2	13	0	0	0	4	5	7	.271	.340	.271	78	-1	0	0	0	.993	4	1-16	0.2
1972	Phi-N	134	381	40	99	16	2	4	38	56	24	.260	.355	.344	97	0	5	8	-3	.992	4	1-87,O-48	-1.1
1973	Phi-N	106	247	31	65	11	0	5	29	32	31	.263	.348	.368	96	-1	3	1	0	.998	4	1-71	0.0
1974	Phi-N	96	208	32	50	6	3	4	30	30	13	.240	.336	.356	90	-2	2	2	-1	.996	-3	1-39,O-33	-0.9
1975	Phi-N	113	165	24	41	6	0	3	24	27	10	.248	.354	.339	90	-2	2	5	-2	.994	4	1-71,O-12	-0.4
1976	*Phi-N	95	124	15	25	5	1	1	13	27	11	.202	.344	.282	77	-3	1	2	-1	1.000	4	1-72/O-1	-0.2
1977	*Phi-N	107	81	12	25	3	0	2	11	12	10	.309	.398	.420	114	2	1	0	0	.993	1	1-73/O-9	0.2
1978	Tor-A	64	173	19	44	9	2	2	9	19	11	.254	.328	.341	87	-3	2		-1	1.000	-5	O-55/1-9	-1.1
	Mon-N	39	59	4	12	2	1	0	7	10	7	.203	.319	.254	63	-3	0	0	-3	1.000	-3	1-17/O-5	-0.7
1979	Mon-N	86	83	14	21	2	1	1	13	10	7	.253	.333	.337	84	-2	0	0	0	1.000	0	1-25/O-9	-0.1
1980	Mon-N	62	55	2	12	2	0	0	5	4	10	.218	.271	.255	47	-4	0	0	0	1.000	-2	/1-7,O-4,P-1	-0.6
1981	Mon-N	31	29	1	3	0	0	0	1	4	3	.103	.161	.103	-23	-7	0	0	0	1.000	-0	/1-9,O-2	-0.6
Total	12	952	1655	196	410	63	7	22	186	234	140	.248	.341	.334	87	-22	15	21	-8	.995	1	1-499,O-178/P-1	-5.4

■ **HAM HYATT**　Hyatt, Robert Hamilton　b: 11/1/1884, Buncombe Co., N.C.　d: 9/11/63, Liberty Lake, Wash.　BL/TR, 6'1", 185 lbs.　Deb: 4/15/09

YEAR	TM/L	G	AB	R	H	2B	3B	HR	RBI	BB	SO	AVG	OBP	SLG	PRO+	BR/A	SB	CS	SBR	FA	FR	G/POS	TPR
1909	*Pit-N	49	67	9	20	3	4	0	7	3		.299	.329	.463	134	2	1			.933	3	/O-6,1-2	0.5
1910	Pit-N	74	175	19	46	5	6	1	30	8	14	.263	.306	.377	94	-2	3			.986	-2	1-38/O-4	-0.4
1912	Pit-N	46	97	13	28	3	1	0	22	6	8	.289	.330	.340	85	-2	2			.955	-2	O-15/1-3	-0.5
1913	Pit-N	63	81	8	27	6	2	4	16	3	8	.333	.372	.605	184	8	0			1.000	-2	/1-5,O-5	0.7
1914	Pit-N	74	79	2	17	3	1	1	15	7	14	.215	.295	.316	86	-1	0			.980	-2	/1-7,C-1	-0.4
1915	StL-N	106	295	23	79	8	9	2	46	28	24	.268	.337	.376	116	3	6	3		.991	-6	1-64,O-25	-0.4
1918	NY-A	53	131	11	30	8	2	0	10	8	9	.229	.273	.336	82	-4	1			1.000	-1	O-25/1-5	-0.7
Total	7	465	925	85	247	36	23	10	146	63	76	.267	.321	.388	108	6	11	3		.989	-11	1-124/O-80,C-1	-1.2

■ **TIM HYERS**　Hyers, Timothy James　b: 10/3/71, Atlanta, Ga.　BL/TL, 6'1", 185 lbs.　Deb: 4/4/94

YEAR	TM/L	G	AB	R	H	2B	3B	HR	RBI	BB	SO	AVG	OBP	SLG	PRO+	BR/A	SB	CS	SBR	FA	FR	G/POS	TPR
1994	SD-N	52	118	13	30	3	0	0	7	9	15	.254	.307	.280	56	-7	3	0	1	.986	0	1-41/O-2	-0.9
1995	SD-N	6	5	0	0	0	0	0	0	0	1	.000	.000	.000	-99	-1	0	0	0	1.000	-0	1-1	-0.1
1996	Det-A	17	26	1	2	1	0	0	0	4	5	.077	.200	.115	-18	-5	0	0	0	1.000	-0	/1-9,O-1,D-2	-0.5
Total	3	75	149	14	32	4	0	0	7	13	21	.215	.278	.242	37	-14	3	0	1	.987	0	/1-51,O-3,D-2	-1.5

■ **JIM HYNDMAN**　Hyndman, James William　b: 7/1865, Ontario, Canada　Deb: 7/23/1886

YEAR	TM/L	G	AB	R	H	2B	3B	HR	RBI	BB	SO	AVG	OBP	SLG	PRO+	BR/A	SB	CS	SBR	FA	FR	G/POS	TPR
1886	Phi-a	1	4	0	0	0	0	0	0	0	0	.000	.000	.000	-99	-1				1.000	0	/O-1,P-1	-0.1

■ **PAT HYNES**　Hynes, Patrick J.　b: 3/12/1884, St.Louis, Mo.　d: 3/12/07, St.Louis, Mo.　TL,　Deb: 9/27/03

YEAR	TM/L	G	AB	R	H	2B	3B	HR	RBI	BB	SO	AVG	OBP	SLG	PRO+	BR/A	SB	CS	SBR	FA	FR	G/POS	TPR
1903	StL-N	1	3	0	0	0	0	0	0	0	0	.000	.000	.000	-99	-1				.500	-1	/P-1	0.0

YEAR	TM/L	G	AB	R	H	2B	3B	HR	RBI	BB	SO	AVG	OBP	SLG	PRO+	BR/A	SB	CS	SBR	FA	FR	G/POS	TPR
1904	StL-A	66	254	23	60	7	3	0	15	3		.236	.248	.287	74	-8	3			.901	-12	O-63/P-5	-2.5
Total	2	67	257	23	60	7	3	0	15	3		.233	.245	.284	71	-9	3			.857	-12	/O-63,P-6	-2.5

■ RAUL IBANEZ
Ibanez, Raul Javier b: 6/2/72, New York, N.Y. BL/TR, 6'2", 210 lbs. Deb: 8/1/96

YEAR	TM/L	G	AB	R	H	2B	3B	HR	RBI	BB	SO	AVG	OBP	SLG	PRO+	BR/A	SB	CS	SBR	FA	FR	G/POS	TPR
1996	Sea-A	4	5	0	0	0	0	0	0	0	1	.000	.167	.000	-53	-1	0	0	0	.000	0	/D-2	-0.1

■ PETE INCAVIGLIA
Incaviglia, Peter Joseph b: 4/2/64, Pebble Beach, Cal. BR/TR, 6'1", 225 lbs. Deb: 4/8/86

YEAR	TM/L	G	AB	R	H	2B	3B	HR	RBI	BB	SO	AVG	OBP	SLG	PRO+	BR/A	SB	CS	SBR	FA	FR	G/POS	TPR
1986	Tex-A	153	540	82	135	21	2	30	88	55	185	.250	.324	.463	108	5	3	2	-0	.921	-11	*O-114,D-36	-1.0
1987	Tex-A	139	509	85	138	26	4	27	80	48	168	.271	.324	.497	116	11	9	3	1	.945	-3	*O-132/D-6	0.4
1988	Tex-A	116	418	59	104	19	3	22	54	39	153	.249	.323	.467	116	8	6	4	-1	.989	6	O-93,D-21	1.0
1989	Tex-A	133	453	48	107	27	4	21	81	32	136	.236	.295	.453	106	2	5	7	-3	.973	-3	*O-125/D-5	-0.7
1990	Tex-A	153	529	59	123	27	0	24	85	45	146	.233	.304	.420	100	-1	3	4	-2	.974	-0	*O-145/D-2	-0.7
1991	Det-A	97	337	38	72	12	1	11	38	36	92	.214	.291	.353	76	-11	1	3	-2	.973	2	O-54,D-41	-1.4
1992	Hou-N	113	349	31	93	22	1	11	44	25	99	.266	.321	.430	116	6	2	2	-1	.970	4	O-98	0.8
1993	*Phi-N	116	368	60	101	16	3	24	89	21	82	.274	.324	.530	126	11	1	1	-0	.971	-2	O-97	0.7
1994	Phi-N	80	244	28	56	10	1	13	32	16	71	.230	.280	.439	82	-8	1	0		.979	-2	O-63	-1.1
1996	Phi-N	99	269	33	63	7	2	16	42	30	82	.234	.318	.454	98	-1	2	0	1	.969	-3	O-71	-0.6
	*Bal-A	12	33	4	10	2	0	2	9	3	5	.303	.324	.545	116	1	0	0	0	1.000	-0	/O-7,D-4	0.0
Total	10	1211	4049	527	1002	189	21	201	641	347	1221	.247	.313	.453	106	22	33	26	-6	.966	-15	O-999,D-115	-2.6

■ ALEXIS INFANTE
Infante, Fermin Alexis (Carpio) b: 12/4/61, Barquisimeto, Venez. BR/TR, 5'10", 175 lbs. Deb: 9/27/87

YEAR	TM/L	G	AB	R	H	2B	3B	HR	RBI	BB	SO	AVG	OBP	SLG	PRO+	BR/A	SB	CS	SBR	FA	FR	G/POS	TPR
1987	Tor-A	1	0	0	0	0	0	0	0	0							0	0	0	.000	0	/R	0.0
1988	Tor-A	19	15	7	3	0	0	0	0	2	4	.200	.294	.200	41	-1	0	0	0	.909	1	/3-9,S-2,D-7	0.0
1989	Tor-A	20	12	1	2	0	0	0	0	0	1	.167	.167	.167	-6	-2	1	0	0	1.000	4	/S-9,3-4,2-1,D-4	0.3
1990	Atl-N	20	28	3	1	1	0	0	0	0	7	.036	.069	.071	-58	-6	0	0	0	.964	2	2-10/3-4,S-3	-0.2
Total	4	60	55	11	6	1	0	0	0	2	12	.109	.155	.127	-20	-9	1	0	0	.933	9	/3-17,S-14,2-11,D	0.1

■ SCOTTY INGERTON
Ingerton, William John b: 4/19/1886, Peninsula, Ohio d: 6/15/56, Cleveland, Ohio BR/TR, 6'1", 172 lbs. Deb: 4/12/11

YEAR	TM/L	G	AB	R	H	2B	3B	HR	RBI	BB	SO	AVG	OBP	SLG	PRO+	BR/A	SB	CS	SBR	FA	FR	G/POS	TPR
1911	Bos-N	136	521	63	130	24	4	5	61	39	68	.250	.304	.340	74	-20	6			.942	18	3-58,O-43,1-17,2/S	-0.3

■ CHARLIE INGRAHAM
Ingraham, Charles W. b: 4/8/1860, Illinois d: 2/18/06, Chicago, Ill. 5'11", 170 lbs. Deb: 7/4/1883

YEAR	TM/L	G	AB	R	H	2B	3B	HR	RBI	BB	SO	AVG	OBP	SLG	PRO+	BR/A	SB	CS	SBR	FA	FR	G/POS	TPR
1883	Bal-a	1	4	0	1	0	0	0	0	0	0	.250	.250	.250	60	-0				.833	-1	/C-1	-0.1

■ GAREY INGRAM
Ingram, Garey Lamar b: 7/25/70, Columbus, Ga. BR/TR, 5'11", 180 lbs. Deb: 5/15/94

YEAR	TM/L	G	AB	R	H	2B	3B	HR	RBI	BB	SO	AVG	OBP	SLG	PRO+	BR/A	SB	CS	SBR	FA	FR	G/POS	TPR
1994	LA-N	26	78	10	22	1	0	3	8	7	22	.282	.341	.410	101	0	0	0	0	.982	6	2-23	0.7
1995	LA-N	44	55	5	11	2	0	0	3	9	8	.200	.313	.236	52	-4	3	0	1	.750	0	3-12/2-7,O-4	-0.2
Total	2	70	133	15	33	3	0	3	11	16	30	.248	.329	.338	81	-4	3	0	1	.985	6	/2-30,3-12,O-4	0.5

■ MEL INGRAM
Ingram, Melvin David b: 7/4/04, Asheville, N.C. d: 10/28/79, Medford, Ore. BR/TR, 5'11.5", 175 lbs. Deb: 7/24/29

YEAR	TM/L	G	AB	R	H	2B	3B	HR	RBI	BB	SO	AVG	OBP	SLG	PRO+	BR/A	SB	CS	SBR	FA	FR	G/POS	TPR
1929	Pit-N	3	0	1	0	0	0	0	0	0	0					0				.000	0	R	0.0

■ RICCARDO INGRAM
Ingram, Riccardo Benay b: 9/10/66, Douglas, Ga. BR/TR, 6', 205 lbs. Deb: 6/26/94

YEAR	TM/L	G	AB	R	H	2B	3B	HR	RBI	BB	SO	AVG	OBP	SLG	PRO+	BR/A	SB	CS	SBR	FA	FR	G/POS	TPR
1994	Det-A	12	23	3	5	0	0	0	2	1	2	.217	.250	.217	22	-3	0	1	-1	1.000	-0	/O-8,D-1	-0.3
1995	Min-A	4	8	0	1	0	0	0	1	2	1	.125	.300	.125	16	-1	0	0	0	.000	0	/D-3	-0.1
Total	2	16	31	3	6	0	0	0	3	3	3	.194	.265	.194	21	-4	0	1	-1	1.000	-0	/O-8,D-4	-0.4

■ DANE IORG
Iorg, Dane Charles b: 5/11/50, Eureka, Cal. BL/TR, 6', 180 lbs. Deb: 4/9/77 F

YEAR	TM/L	G	AB	R	H	2B	3B	HR	RBI	BB	SO	AVG	OBP	SLG	PRO+	BR/A	SB	CS	SBR	FA	FR	G/POS	TPR
1977	Phi-N	12	30	3	5	1	0	0	2	1	3	.167	.194	.200	6	-4	0	0	0	.986	-0	/1-9	-0.5
	StL-N	30	32	2	10	1	0	0	4	5	4	.313	.405	.344	105	1	0	1	-1	.875	-2	/O-7	-0.2
	Yr	42	62	5	15	2	0	0	6	6	7	.242	.309	.274	58	-4	0	1	-1	.986	-2	/1-9,O-7	-0.7
1978	StL-N	35	85	6	23	4	1	0	4	4	10	.271	.303	.341	81	-2	0	0	0	1.000	0	/O-25	-0.3
1979	StL-N	79	179	12	52	11	1	1	21	12	28	.291	.339	.380	95	-1	1	2	-1	.964	-6	O-39,1-10	-1.0
1980	StL-N	105	251	33	76	23	1	3	36	20	34	.303	.354	.438	116	5	1	1	-0	.991	-3	O-63/1-5,3-1	-0.1
1981	StL-N	75	217	23	71	11	2	2	39	7	9	.327	.348	.424	115	4	2	0	1	.963	-11	O-57/1-8,3-2	-0.9
1982	*StL-N	102	238	17	70	14	1	0	34	23	23	.294	.356	.361	100	1	0	1	-1	.971	-2	O-63,1-10/3-2	-0.7
1983	StL-N	58	116	6	31	9	1	0	11	10	11	.267	.331	.362	92	-1	1	0	0	.974	-3	O-22,1-11	-0.5
1984	StL-N	15	28	3	4	2	0	0	3	2	6	.143	.200	.214	17	-3	0	0	0	1.000	-1	/1-6,O-5	-0.4
	*KC-A	78	235	27	60	16	2	5	30	13	15	.255	.294	.404	90	-4	0	1	-1	.995	-4	1-43,O-22/3-1,D-5	-1.1
1985	*KC-A	64	130	7	29	9	1	1	21	8	16	.223	.268	.331	63	-7	0	1	-0	1.000	-5	O-32/1-2,3-1,D-2	-1.3
1986	SD-N	90	106	10	24	2	1	2	11	2	21	.226	.241	.321	55	-7	0	0	0	1.000	-4	1-10/3-6,O-3,P-2	-0.9
Total	10	743	1647	149	455	103	11	14	216	107	180	.276	.321	.378	92	-19	5	7	-3	.977	-41	O-338,1-114/3DP	-7.9

■ GARTH IORG
Iorg, Garth Ray b: 10/12/54, Arcata, Cal. BR/TR, 5'11", 170 lbs. Deb: 4/9/78 F

YEAR	TM/L	G	AB	R	H	2B	3B	HR	RBI	BB	SO	AVG	OBP	SLG	PRO+	BR/A	SB	CS	SBR	FA	FR	G/POS	TPR
1978	Tor-A	19	49	3	8	0	0	0	3	3	4	.163	.226	.163	11	-6	0	0	0	.966	4	2-18	-0.1
1980	Tor-A	80	222	24	55	10	1	2	14	12	39	.248	.286	.329	65	-11	2	1	0	.988	8	2-32,3-20,O1/SD	-0.2
1981	Tor-A	70	215	17	52	11	0	0	10	7	31	.242	.269	.293	58	-12	2	3	-1	.963	-0	2-46,3-17/S-2,1D	-1.1
1982	Tor-A	129	417	45	119	20	5	1	36	12	38	.285	.312	.365	78	-13	3	2	-0	.946	-4	*3-100,2-30/D-1	-1.8
1983	Tor-A	122	375	40	103	22	5	2	39	13	45	.275	.301	.376	80	-11	7	0	2	.976	-3	3-85,2-39/S-1	-1.1
1984	Tor-A	121	247	24	56	10	3	1	25	5	16	.227	.245	.304	49	-17	1	3	-2	.945	1	*3-112/2-7,S-2,D-1	-1.8
1985	*Tor-A	131	288	33	90	22	1	7	37	21	26	.313	.359	.469	122	8	3	6	-3	.951	11	*3-104,2-23	1.6
1986	Tor-A	137	327	30	85	19	1	3	44	20	47	.260	.305	.352	76	-11	3	0	1	.955	-15	3-90,2-52/S-2	-2.4
1987	Tor-A	122	310	35	65	11	0	4	30	17	52	.210	.264	.284	45	-25	2	2	-1	.982	-13	2-91,3-28/S-1	-3.4
Total	9	931	2450	251	633	125	16	20	238	114	298	.258	.294	.347	72	-96	23	17	-3	.955	-12	3-556,2-338/O1DS	-10.3

■ HAPPY IOTT
Iott, Frederick "Happy Jack" or "Biddo" (b: Frederick Hoyot) b: 7/7/1876, Houlton, Me. d: 2/17/41, Island Falls, Me. BR/TR, 5'10", 175 lbs. Deb: 9/16/03

YEAR	TM/L	G	AB	R	H	2B	3B	HR	RBI	BB	SO	AVG	OBP	SLG	PRO+	BR/A	SB	CS	SBR	FA	FR	G/POS	TPR
1903	Cle-A	3	10	1	2	0	0	0	2	0	3	.200	.333	.200	64	-0	1			.875	-0	/O-3	-0.1

■ HAL IRELAN
Irelan, Harold "Grump" b: 8/5/1890, Burnettsville, Ind. d: 7/16/44, Carmel, Ind. BB/TR, 5'7", 165 lbs. Deb: 4/23/14

YEAR	TM/L	G	AB	R	H	2B	3B	HR	RBI	BB	SO	AVG	OBP	SLG	PRO+	BR/A	SB	CS	SBR	FA	FR	G/POS	TPR
1914	Phi-N	67	165	16	39	8	0	1	16	21	22	.236	.326	.303	82	-3	3			.909	11	2-44/S-3,1-2,3-2	0.8

■ TIM IRELAND
Ireland, Timothy Neal b: 3/14/53, Oakland, Cal. BR/TR, 6', 180 lbs. Deb: 9/20/81

YEAR	TM/L	G	AB	R	H	2B	3B	HR	RBI	BB	SO	AVG	OBP	SLG	PRO+	BR/A	SB	CS	SBR	FA	FR	G/POS	TPR
1981	KC-A	4	0	0	0	0	0	0	0	0	0	—	—	—			0	1	-1	1.000	-0	/1-4	-0.1
1982	KC-A	7	7	1	1	0	0	0	0	0	1	.143	.250	.143	11	-1	0	0	0	1.000	-0	/2-4,O-2,3-1	-0.1
Total	2	11	7	1	1	0	0	0	0	0	1	.143	.250	.143	11	-1	0	0	0	1.000	-0	/2-4,1-4,O-2,3-1	-0.2

■ MONTE IRVIN
Irvin, Monford b: 2/25/19, Columbia, Ala. BR/TR, 6'1", 195 lbs. Deb: 7/8/49 H

YEAR	TM/L	G	AB	R	H	2B	3B	HR	RBI	BB	SO	AVG	OBP	SLG	PRO+	BR/A	SB	CS	SBR	FA	FR	G/POS	TPR
1949	NY-N	36	76	7	17	3	2	0	7	17	11	.224	.366	.316	84	-1	0			1.000	-0	O-10/1-5,3-5	-0.1
1950	NY-N	110	374	61	112	19	5	15	66	52	41	.299	.392	.497	131	18	3			.979	5	1-59,O-49/3-1	1.8
1951	*NY-N	151	558	94	174	19	11	24	121	89	44	.312	.415	.514	147	40	12	2	2	.996	11	*O-112,1-39	4.6
1952	NY-N†	46	126	10	39	2	1	4	21	10	5	.310	.365	.437	120	3	0	1		1.000	-2	O-32	0.0
1953	NY-N	124	444	72	146	21	5	21	97	55	41	.329	.406	.541	142	28	2	0	1	.973	8	*O-113	3.0
1954	*NY-N	135	432	62	113	13	3	19	64	70	23	.262	.367	.438	108	6	7	4	-0	.976	4	*O-128/1-1,3-1	0.5
1955	NY-N	51	150	16	38	7	1	1	17	17	15	.253	.341	.333	80	-4	1	0	0	.961	1	O-45	-0.4
1956	Chi-N	111	339	44	92	13	3	15	50	41	41	.271	.350	.460	118	8	1	0	0	.991	11	O-96	1.5
Total	8	764	2499	366	731	97	31	99	443	351	220	.293	.385	.475	126	98	28	7		.983	38	O-585,1-104/3-7	10.9

■ ED IRVIN
Irvin, William Edward b: 1882, Philadelphia, Pa. d: 2/18/16, Philadelphia, Pa. BR/TR, Deb: 5/18/12

YEAR	TM/L	G	AB	R	H	2B	3B	HR	RBI	BB	SO	AVG	OBP	SLG	PRO+	BR/A	SB	CS	SBR	FA	FR	G/POS	TPR
1912	Det-A	1	3	0	2	0	0	0	0	0	0	.667	.667	2.000	675	-1				.500	-1	/3-1	0.1

■ ARTHUR IRWIN
Irwin, Arthur Albert "Doc" or "Sandy" b: 2/14/1858, Toronto, Ont., Can. d: 7/16/21, At Sea Atlantic Ocean N.Y. To Boston BL/TR, 5'8.5", 158 lbs. Deb: 5/1/1880 FMU

YEAR	TM/L	G	AB	R	H	2B	3B	HR	RBI	BB	SO	AVG	OBP	SLG	PRO+	BR/A	SB	CS	SBR	FA	FR	G/POS	TPR
1880	Wor-N	85	352	53	91	19	4	1	35	11	27	.259	.281	.344	102	-1				.895	31	*S-82/3-3,C-1	3.4

YEAR	TM/L	G	AB	R	H	2B	3B	HR	RBI	BB	SO	AVG	OBP	SLG	PRO+	BR/A	SB	CS	SBR	FA	FR	G/POS	TPR
1881	Wor-N	50	206	27	55	8	2	0	24	7	4	.267	.291	.325	88	-3				.851	-8	S-50	-0.7
1882	Wor-N	84	333	30	73	12	4	0	30	14	34	.219	.251	.279	68	-12				.837	21	3-51,S-33	1.0
1883	Pro-N	98	406	67	116	22	7	0	44	12	38	.286	.306	.374	103	1				.856	-7	*S-94/2-4	-0.4
1884	*Pro-N	102	404	73	97	14	3	2	44	28	52	.240	.289	.304	89	-4				.881	-6	*S-102/P-1	-0.8
1885	Pro-N	59	218	16	39	2	1	0	14	14	29	.179	.228	.197	40	-14				.875	4	S-58/3-1,2-1	-0.8
1886	Phi-N	101	373	51	87	6	6	0	34	35	39	.233	.299	.282	77	-10	24			.891	4	*S-100/3-1	-0.4
1887	Phi-N	100	374	65	95	14	8	2	56	48	26	.254	.344	.350	88	-6	19			.892	-10	*S-100	-1.2
1888	Phi-N	125	448	51	98	12	4	0	28	33	56	.219	.277	.263	69	-15	19			.900	12	*S-122/2-3	0.0
1889	Phi-N	18	73	9	16	5	0	0	10	6	6	.219	.278	.288	54	-5	6			.845	-6	S-18	-0.9
	Was-N	85	313	49	73	10	5	0	32	42	37	.233	.326	.297	80	-7	9			.895	12	S-85/P-1,2-1,M	0.8
	Yr	103	386	58	89	15	5	0	42	48	43	.231	.317	.295	74	-12	15			.888	6	S-103/P-1,2-1	-0.1
1890	Bos-P	96	354	60	92	17	1	0	45	57	29	.260	.364	.314	77	-11	16			.878	3	*S-96	-0.3
1891	Bos-a	6	17	1	2	0	0	0	0	2	1	.118	.286	.118	16	-2	0			.778	-1	/S-1,M	-0.2
1894	Phi-N	1	0	0	0	0	0	0	0	0	0					0	0			.000	0	/S-1,M	0.0
Total	13	1010	3871	552	934	141	45	5	396	309	378	.241	.299	.305	81	-88	93			.881	49	S-947/3-56,2-9,PC	-0.5

■ **CHARLIE IRWIN**   Irwin, Charles Edwin b: 2/15/1869, Clinton, Ill. d: 9/21/25, Chicago, Ill.   BL/TR, 5'10", 160 lbs. Deb: 9/3/1893

YEAR	TM/L	G	AB	R	H	2B	3B	HR	RBI	BB	SO	AVG	OBP	SLG	PRO+	BR/A	SB	CS	SBR	FA	FR	G/POS	TPR
1893	Chi-N	21	82	14	25	6	2	0	13	10	1	.305	.394	.427	120	3	4			.910	-1	S-21	0.2
1894	Chi-N	128	498	84	144	24	9	8	95	63	23	.289	.379	.422	88	-11	35			.822	-11	3-67,S-61	-1.4
1895	Chi-N	3	10	4	2	0	0	0	0	2	1	.200	.333	.200	37	-1	0			.900	-2	/S-3	-0.2
1896	Cin-N	127	476	77	141	16	6	1	67	26	17	.296	.338	.361	79	-16	31			**.931**	7	*3-127	-0.5
1897	Cin-N	134	505	89	146	26	6	0	74	47		.289	.360	.364	86	-11	27			.940	-7	*3-134	-1.2
1898	Cin-N	136	501	77	120	14	5	3	55	31		.240	.297	.305	68	-22	18			.940	14	*3-136	-0.7
1899	Cin-N	90	314	42	73	4	8	1	52	26		.232	.295	.306	64	-16	26			.909	-13	3-78/S-6,2-3,1-1	-2.6
1900	Cin-N	87	333	59	91	15	6	1	44	14		.273	.314	.363	89	-6	9			.931	-11	3-61,S-16/O-6,2-3	-1.4
1901	Cin-N	67	260	25	62	12	2	0	25	14		.238	.285	.300	75	-9	13			.893	4	3-67	-0.4
	Bro-N	65	242	25	52	13	2	0	20	14		.215	.269	.285	59	-13	4			.956	-2	3-65	-1.4
	Yr	132	502	50	114	25	4	0	45	28		.227	.277	.293	67	-21	17			.921	2	*3-132	-1.8
1902	Bro-N	131	458	59	125	14	0	2	43	39		.273	.346	.317	104	4	13			.927	-10	3-130/S-1	-0.6
Total	10	989	3679	555	981	144	46	16	488	286	42	.267	.330	.344	82	-97	180			.921	-32	3-865,S-108/O-6,21	-10.2

■ **JOHN IRWIN**   Irwin, John b: 7/21/1861, Toronto, Ont., Can d: 2/28/34, Boston, Mass.   BL/TR, 5'10", 168 lbs. Deb: 5/31/1882 F

YEAR	TM/L	G	AB	R	H	2B	3B	HR	RBI	BB	SO	AVG	OBP	SLG	PRO+	BR/A	SB	CS	SBR	FA	FR	G/POS	TPR
1882	Wor-N	1	4	0	0	0	0	0	0	0	2	.000	.000	.000	-98	-1				.636	-1	/1-1	-0.2
1884	Bos-U	105	432	81	101	22	6	1		0	15	.234	.260	.319	76	-26				.780	4	*3-105	-1.9
1886	Phi-a	3	13	4	3	1	0	0	1	0		.231	.231	.308	67	-1	0			.714	-1	/S-2,3-1	-0.2
1887	Was-N	8	31	6	11	2	0	2	3	3		.355	.429	.613	196	4	6			.875	-2	/S-5,3-4	0.2
1888	Was-N	37	126	14	28	2	0	0	8	5	18	.222	.263	.294	82	-2	15			.860	1	S-27,3-10	-0.3
1889	Was-N	58	228	42	66	11	4	0	25	25	14	.289	.370	.373	115	6	10			.868	0	3-58	0.7
1890	Buf-P	77	308	62	72	11	4	0	34	43	19	.234	.335	.295	75	-9	18			.883	4	3-64,1-12/2-1	-0.2
1891	Bos-a	19	72	6	16	2	2	0	15	6	9	.222	.282	.306	69	-3	6			.882	0	O-17/3-2,S-1	-0.3
	Lou-a	14	55	7	15	1	1	0	7	5	6	.273	.344	.327	93	-0	1			.795	-7	3-14	-0.6
	Yr	33	127	13	31	3	3	0	22	11	15	.244	.309	.315	80	-4	7			.882	-6	O-17,3-16/S-1	-0.9
Total	8	322	1269	222	312	55	19	3	93	102	74	.246	.308	.326	87	-32	56			.829	-4	3-258/S-35,O-17,12	-2.8

■ **TOMMY IRWIN**   Irwin, Thomas Andrew b: 12/20/12, Altoona, Pa.   BR/TR, 5'11", 165 lbs. Deb: 10/1/38

YEAR	TM/L	G	AB	R	H	2B	3B	HR	RBI	BB	SO	AVG	OBP	SLG	PRO+	BR/A	SB	CS	SBR	FA	FR	G/POS	TPR
1938	Cle-A	3	9	1	1	0	0	0	3	1	.111	.333	.111	16	-1	0	0	0	1.000	0	/S-3	-0.1

■ **WALT IRWIN**   Irwin, Walter Kingsley b: 9/23/1897, Henrietta, Pa. d: 8/18/76, Spring Lake, Mich.   BR/TR, 5'10.5", 170 lbs. Deb: 4/24/21

YEAR	TM/L	G	AB	R	H	2B	3B	HR	RBI	BB	SO	AVG	OBP	SLG	PRO+	BR/A	SB	CS	SBR	FA	FR	G/POS	TPR
1921	StL-N	4	1	1	0	0	0	0	0	1	.000	.000	.000	-99	-0	0	0	0	.000	0	H	0.0

■ **ORLANDO ISALES**   Isales, Orlando (Pizarro) b: 12/22/59, Santurce, P.R.   BR/TR, 5'9", 175 lbs. Deb: 9/11/80

YEAR	TM/L	G	AB	R	H	2B	3B	HR	RBI	BB	SO	AVG	OBP	SLG	PRO+	BR/A	SB	CS	SBR	FA	FR	G/POS	TPR
1980	Phi-N	3	5	1	2	0	0	0	3	1	0	.400	.500	.800	244	1	0	0	0	1.000	-0	/O-2	0.1

■ **FRANK ISBELL**   Isbell, William Frank "Bald Eagle" b: 8/21/1875, Delavan, N.Y. d: 7/15/41, Wichita, Kan.   BL/TR, 5'11", 190 lbs. Deb: 5/1/1898

YEAR	TM/L	G	AB	R	H	2B	3B	HR	RBI	BB	SO	AVG	OBP	SLG	PRO+	BR/A	SB	CS	SBR	FA	FR	G/POS	TPR
1898	Chi-N	45	159	17	37	4	0	0	8	3		.233	.252	.258	46	-11	3			.956	-7	O-28,P-13/3-3,2S	-1.6
1901	Chi-A	137	556	93	143	15	8	3	70	36		.257	.311	.329	79	-15	**52**			.980	13	*1-137/2-2,P-1,S3	-0.3
1902	Chi-A	137	515	62	130	14	4	4	59	14		.252	.276	.318	68	-23	38			.986	10	*1-133/S-4,P-1,C-1	-1.6
1903	Chi-A	138	546	52	132	25	9	2	59	12		.242	.266	.332	82	-13	26			.984	7	*1-117,3-19/2-2,SO	-0.8
1904	Chi-A	96	314	27	66	10	3	1	34	16		.210	.255	.271	69	-11	19			.986	0	1-57,2-27/O-5,S-4	-1.3
1905	Chi-A	94	341	55	101	21	11	2	45	15		.296	.335	.440	151	18	15			.964	-1	2-43,O-41/1-9,S-2	1.6
1906	*Chi-A	143	549	71	153	18	11	0	57	30		.279	.324	.352	115	8	37			.949	-22	*2-132,O-14/P-1,C-1	-1.4
1907	Chi-A	125	486	60	118	19	7	0	41	22		.243	.281	.311	92	-6	22			.957	10	2-119/O-5,P-1,S-1	0.3
1908	Chi-A	84	320	31	79	15	3	1	49	19		.247	.297	.322	103	1	18			.990	2	1-65,2-18	0.1
1909	Chi-A	120	433	43	97	17	6	0	33	23		.224	.265	.291	79	-12	23			.994	1	*1-101/O-9,2-5	-1.3
Total	10	1119	4219	501	1056	158	62	13	455	190		.250	.289	.326	89	-64	253			.986	13	1-619,2-351,O/3PSC	-6.3

■ **MIKE IVIE**   Ivie, Michael Wilson b: 8/8/52, Atlanta, Ga.   BR/TR, 6'3", 205 lbs. Deb: 9/4/71

YEAR	TM/L	G	AB	R	H	2B	3B	HR	RBI	BB	SO	AVG	OBP	SLG	PRO+	BR/A	SB	CS	SBR	FA	FR	G/POS	TPR
1971	SD-N	6	17	0	8	0	0	0	3	1	1	.471	.526	.471	198	2	0	0	0	1.000	-2	/C-6	0.1
1974	SD-N	12	34	1	3	0	0	1	3	2	8	.088	.139	.176	-13	-5	0	0	0	.986	4	1-11	-0.6
1975	SD-N	111	377	36	94	16	2	8	46	20	63	.249	.294	.366	88	-8	4	4	-1	.989	-5	1-78,3-61/C-1	-1.9
1976	SD-N	140	405	51	118	19	5	7	70	30	41	.291	.348	.415	126	12	6	6	-2	.995	1	*1-135/C-2,3-2	0.4
1977	SD-N	134	489	66	133	29	2	9	66	39	57	.272	.328	.395	104	1	3	2	-0	.992	-5	*1-105,3-25	-1.1
1978	SF-N	117	318	34	98	14	3	11	55	27	45	.308	.366	.475	139	16	3	0	1	.995	-10	1-76,O-22	0.2
1979	SF-N	133	402	58	115	18	3	27	89	47	80	.286	.362	.547	155	29	5	1	1	.995	-6	1-98,O-24/3-4,2-1	1.9
1980	SF-N	79	286	21	69	16	1	4	25	19	40	.241	.289	.346	78	-9	1	1	-0	.995	1	1-72	-2.2
1981	SF-N	7	17	1	5	2	0	0	3	0	7	.294	.294	.412	100	0	0	0	0	1.000	1	/1-5	0.0
	Hou-N	19	42	2	10	3	0	0	6	2	11	.238	.273	.310	68	-2	0	0	-1	.989	2	1-10	-0.1
	Yr	26	59	3	15	5	0	0	9	2	12	.254	.279	.339	78	-2	0	0	-1	.992	3	1-15	-0.1
1982	Hou-N	7	6	0	2	0	0	0	0	0	0	.333	.429	.333	125	0	0	0	0	.000	0	/H	0.0
	Det-A	80	259	35	60	12	1	14	38	24	51	.232	.302	.448	102	0	0	0	0	.000	0	D-79	-0.3
1983	Det-A	12	42	4	9	4	0	0	7	2	4	.214	.250	.310	54	-3	0	0	0	1.000	-0	1-12	-0.4
Total	11	857	2694	309	724	145	17	81	411	214	402	.269	.326	.421	113	32	22	16	-3	.993	-31	1-602/3-92,DOC2	-4.0

■ **HANK IZQUIERDO**   Izquierdo, Enrique Roberto (Valdes) b: 3/20/31, Matanzas, Cuba   BR/TR, 5'11", 175 lbs. Deb: 8/9/67

YEAR	TM/L	G	AB	R	H	2B	3B	HR	RBI	BB	SO	AVG	OBP	SLG	PRO+	BR/A	SB	CS	SBR	FA	FR	G/POS	TPR
1967	Min-A	16	26	4	7	2	0	0	2	1	2	.269	.296	.346	83	-1	0	0	0	.986	3	C-16	0.3

■ **RAY JABLONSKI**   Jablonski, Raymond Leo "Jabbo" b: 12/17/26, Chicago, Ill. d: 11/25/85, Chicago, Ill.   BR/TR, 5'10", 183 lbs. Deb: 4/14/53

YEAR	TM/L	G	AB	R	H	2B	3B	HR	RBI	BB	SO	AVG	OBP	SLG	PRO+	BR/A	SB	CS	SBR	FA	FR	G/POS	TPR
1953	StL-N	157	604	64	162	23	5	21	112	34	61	.268	.308	.427	89	-11	2	2	-1	.932	-16	*3-157	-3.0
1954	StL-N★	152	611	80	181	33	3	12	104	49	42	.296	.350	.419	99	-1	9	4	0	.925	-7	*3-149/1-1	-1.1
1955	Cin-N	74	221	28	53	19	0	9	28	13	35	.240	.291	.403	77	-8	0	1	-1	.872	-10	3-28,O-28	-2.0
1956	Cin-N	130	407	42	104	25	1	15	66	37	57	.256	.328	.432	96	-2	2	4	-2	.970	-25	*3-127/2-1	-2.9
1957	NY-N	107	305	37	88	15	1	9	57	31	47	.289	.354	.433	110	5	0	2	-1	.941	-3	3-70/1-6,O-1	0.2
1958	SF-N	82	230	28	53	15	1	12	46	17	50	.230	.289	.461	97	-2	2	0	1	.946	-8	3-57	-0.9
1959	StL-N	60	87	11	22	4	0	3	14	8	19	.253	.316	.402	84	-2	1	0	0	.900	-3	3-19/S-1	-0.5
	KC-A	25	65	4	17	1	0	2	9	3	11	.262	.294	.369	79	-2	0	0	0	.947	-3	3-17	-0.5
1960	KC-A	21	32	3	7	1	0	0	2	4	8	.219	.306	.250	72	-2	0	0	0	.944	0	/3-6	-0.2
Total	8	808	2562	297	687	126	11	83	438	196	330	.268	.324	.423	94	-26	16	13	-3	.936	-75	3-630/O-29,1-7,S2	-10.9

■ **FRED JACKLITSCH**   Jacklitsch, Frederick Lawrence b: 5/24/1876, Brooklyn, N.Y. d: 7/18/37, Brooklyn, N.Y.   BR/TR, 5'9", 180 lbs. Deb: 6/6/00

YEAR	TM/L	G	AB	R	H	2B	3B	HR	RBI	BB	SO	AVG	OBP	SLG	PRO+	BR/A	SB	CS	SBR	FA	FR	G/POS	TPR
1900	Phi-N	5	11	0	2	0	0	0		1		.182	.182	.273	25	-1	0			1.000	-2	/C-3	-0.2
1901	Phi-N	33	120	14	30	4	3	0	24	12		.250	.328	.333	90	-1	2			.971	-1	C-30/3-1	0.1
1902	Phi-N	38	114	8	23	4	0	0	8	9		.202	.278	.237	59	-5	2			.927	-9	C-29/O-1	-1.2

YEAR	TM/L	G	AB	R	H	2B	3B	HR	RBI	BB	SO	AVG	OBP	SLG	PRO+	BR/A	SB	CS	SBR	FA	FR	G/POS	TPR
1903	Bro-N	60	176	31	47	8	3	1	21	33		.267	.389	.364	118	6	4			.975	-9	C-53/2-1,O-1	0.3
1904	Bro-N	26	77	8	18	3	1	0	8	7		.234	.322	.299	94	-0	7			.957	-7	1-11/2-8,C-5	-0.7
1905	NY-A	1	3	1	0	0	0	0	1	1		.000	.250	.000	-17	-0	0			1.000	-0	/C-1	0.0
1907	Phi-N	73	202	19	43	7	0	0	17	27		.213	.312	.248	76	-4	7			.984	11	C-58/1-6,O-1	1.3
1908	Phi-N	37	86	6	19	3	0	0	7	14		.221	.337	.256	87	-1	3			.976	3	C-30	0.6
1909	Phi-N	20	32	6	10	1	1	0	1	10		.313	.476	.406	173	4	1			.964	-2	C-11/2-1	0.3
1910	Phi-N	25	51	7	10	3	0	0	2	5	9	.196	.268	.255	51	-3	0			.989	5	C-13/1-2,2-1,3-1	0.3
1914	Bal-F	122	337	40	93	21	4	2	48	52	66	.276	.376	.380	103	-2	7			**.988**	2	*C-118	1.0
1915	Bal-F	49	135	20	32	9	0	2	13	31	25	.237	.387	.348	104	0	2			.992	-7	C-45/S-1	-0.3
1917	Bos-N	1	0	0	0							—	—	—	—		0			1.000	-0	/C-1	0.0
Total	13	490	1344	160	327	64	12	5	153	201	100	.243	.349	.320	95	-8	35			.978	-14	C-397/1-19,2O3S	1.5

■ CHARLIE JACKSON
Jackson, Charles Herbert "Lefty" b: 2/7/1894, Granite City, Ill. d: 5/27/68, Radford, Va. BL/TL, 5'9", 150 lbs. Deb: 8/20/15

YEAR	TM/L	G	AB	R	H	2B	3B	HR	RBI	BB	SO	AVG	OBP	SLG	PRO+	BR/A	SB	CS	SBR	FA	FR	G/POS	TPR
1915	Chi-A	1	1	0	0	0	0	0	0	1		.000	.000	.000	-97	-0	0			.000	0	H	0.0
1917	Pit-N	41	121	7	29	3	2	0	1	10	22	.240	.303	.298	82	-2	4			.986	0	O-36	-0.4
Total	2	42	122	7	29	3	2	0	1	10	23	.238	.301	.295	80	-3	4			.986	0	/O-36	-0.4

■ CHUCK JACKSON
Jackson, Charles Leo b: 3/19/63, Seattle, Wash. BR/TR, 6' ", 185 lbs. Deb: 5/26/87

YEAR	TM/L	G	AB	R	H	2B	3B	HR	RBI	BB	SO	AVG	OBP	SLG	PRO+	BR/A	SB	CS	SBR	FA	FR	G/POS	TPR
1987	Hou-N	35	71	3	15	3	0	1	6	7	19	.211	.282	.296	55	-5	1	1	-0	.957	-1	3-16,O-13/S-1	-0.6
1988	Hou-N	46	83	7	19	5	1	2	7	7	16	.229	.289	.349	86	-2	1	1	-0	.908	1	3-32/S-3,O-3	-0.1
1994	Tex-A	1	2	0	0	0	0	0	0	0	0	.000	.000	.000	-99	-1	0	0	0	.000	0	/3-1	-0.1
Total	3	82	156	10	34	8	1	2	14	14	35	.218	.282	.321	69	-7	2	2	-1	.928	1	/3-49,O-16,S-4	-0.8

■ DAMIAN JACKSON
Jackson, Damian Jacques b: 8/16/73, Los Angeles, Cal. BR/TR, 5'10", 160 lbs. Deb: 9/12/96

YEAR	TM/L	G	AB	R	H	2B	3B	HR	RBI	BB	SO	AVG	OBP	SLG	PRO+	BR/A	SB	CS	SBR	FA	FR	G/POS	TPR
1996	Cle-A	5	10	2	3	2	0	0	1	1	4	.300	.364	.500	115	0	0	0	0	1.000	2	/S-5	0.3

■ DARRIN JACKSON
Jackson, Darrin Jay b: 8/22/62, Los Angeles, Cal. BR/TR, 6'1", 170 lbs. Deb: 6/17/85

YEAR	TM/L	G	AB	R	H	2B	3B	HR	RBI	BB	SO	AVG	OBP	SLG	PRO+	BR/A	SB	CS	SBR	FA	FR	G/POS	TPR
1985	Chi-N	5	11	0	1	0	0	0	0	0	3	.091	.091	.091	-44	-2	0	0	0	1.000	-1	/O-4	-0.3
1987	Chi-N	7	5	2	4	1	0	0	0	0	0	.800	.800	1.000	359	2	0	0	0	1.000	-2	/O-5	0.0
1988	Chi-N	100	188	29	50	11	3	6	20	5	28	.266	.289	.452	105	0	4	1	1	.983	-10	O-74	-1.1
1989	Chi-N	45	83	7	19	4	0	1	8	6	17	.229	.281	.313	65	-4	1	2	-1	.970	-1	O-39	-0.7
	SD-N	25	87	10	18	3	0	3	12	7	17	.207	.266	.345	73	-3	0	2	-1	.954	2	O-24	-0.3
	Yr	70	170	17	37	7	0	4	20	13	34	.218	.273	.329	68	-7	1	4	-2	.962	1	O-63	-1.0
1990	SD-N	58	113	10	29	3	0	3	9	5	24	.257	.288	.363	77	-4	3	0	1	.985	-5	O-39	-0.9
1991	SD-N	122	359	51	94	12	1	21	49	27	66	.262	.311	.476	117	7	5	3	-0	.992	5	O-98/P-1	1.2
1992	SD-N	155	587	72	146	23	5	17	70	26	106	.249	.285	.392	88	-11	14	3	2	.996	24	*O-153	1.4
1993	Tor-A	46	176	15	38	8	0	5	19	8	53	.216	.250	.347	58	-11	0	4	-2	.989	-2	O-46	-1.4
	NY-A	31	87	4	17	1	0	1	7	2	22	.195	.213	.241	22	-10	0	1	0	1.000	-3	O-26	-0.8
1994	Chi-A	104	369	43	115	17	3	10	51	27	56	.312	.363	.455	111	6	7	1	2	.996	0	*O-102	0.5
Total	9	698	2065	243	531	83	12	67	245	113	392	.257	.299	.406	91	-29	34	14	2	.990	15	O-610/P-1	-2.4

■ GEORGE JACKSON
Jackson, George Christopher "Hickory" b: 10/14/1882, Springfield, Mo. d: 11/25/72, Cleburne, Tex. BR/TR, 6'0.5", 180 lbs. Deb: 8/2/11

YEAR	TM/L	G	AB	R	H	2B	3B	HR	RBI	BB	SO	AVG	OBP	SLG	PRO+	BR/A	SB	CS	SBR	FA	FR	G/POS	TPR
1911	Bos-N	39	147	28	51	11	2	0	25	12	21	.347	.404	.449	128	5	12			.929	-2	O-39	0.1
1912	Bos-N	110	397	55	104	13	5	4	48	38	72	.262	.342	.350	88	-6	22			.943	2	*O-107	-1.0
1913	Bos-N	3	10	2	3	0	0	0	0	0	2	.300	.300	.300	70	-0	0			.875	-0	/O-3	-0.0
Total	3	152	554	85	158	24	7	4	73	50	95	.285	.357	.375	98	-1	34			.938	-0	O-149	-0.9

■ HENRY JACKSON
Jackson, Henry Everett b: 6/23/1861, Union City, Ind. d: 9/14/32, Chicago, Ill. BR/TR, 6'2", 185 lbs. Deb: 9/13/1887

YEAR	TM/L	G	AB	R	H	2B	3B	HR	RBI	BB	SO	AVG	OBP	SLG	PRO+	BR/A	SB	CS	SBR	FA	FR	G/POS	TPR
1887	Ind-N	10	38	1	10	1	0	0	3	0	12	.263	.263	.289	55	-2	2			.933	-1	1-10	-0.4

■ JIM JACKSON
Jackson, James Benner b: 11/28/1877, Philadelphia, Pa. d: 10/9/55, Philadelphia, Pa. BR/TR, Deb: 4/26/01

YEAR	TM/L	G	AB	R	H	2B	3B	HR	RBI	BB	SO	AVG	OBP	SLG	PRO+	BR/A	SB	CS	SBR	FA	FR	G/POS	TPR
1901	Bal-A	99	364	42	91	17	3	2	50	20		.250	.291	.330	69	-16	11			**.971**	3	O-96	-1.9
1902	NY-N	35	110	14	20	5	1	0	13	15		.182	.280	.245	63	-4	6			.897	-2	O-34	-1.0
1905	Cle-A	109	426	59	109	12	4	2	31	34		.256	.317	.317	100	0	15			.951	5	*O-106/3-3	0.0
1906	Cle-A	105	374	44	80	13	2	0	38	38		.214	.290	.259	73	-10	25			.975	-6	*O-104	-2.3
Total	4	348	1274	159	300	47	10	4	132	107		.235	.298	.297	80	-31	57			.959	-1	O-340/3-3	-5.2

■ JOE JACKSON
Jackson, Joseph Jefferson "Shoeless Joe" b: 7/16/1889, Pickens Co., S.C. d: 12/5/51, Greenville, S.C. BL/TR, 6'1", 200 lbs. Deb: 8/25/08

YEAR	TM/L	G	AB	R	H	2B	3B	HR	RBI	BB	SO	AVG	OBP	SLG	PRO+	BR/A	SB	CS	SBR	FA	FR	G/POS	TPR
1908	Phi-A	5	23	0	3	0	0	0				.130	.130	.130	-14	-3	0			.875	-1	/O-5	-0.4
1909	Phi-A	5	17	3	3	0	0	0	3	1		.176	.222	.176	26	-1	0			.833	-0	/O-4	-0.2
1910	Cle-A	20	75	15	29	2	5	1	11	8		.387	.446	.587	220	10	4			.977	0	O-20	1.0
1911	Cle-A	147	571	126	233	45	19	7	83	56		.408	**.468**	.590	192	70	41			.958	8	*O-147	6.8
1912	Cle-A	154	572	121	**226**	44	**26**	3	90	54		.395	.458	.579	190	66	35			.950	13	*O-150	6.9
1913	Cle-A	148	528	109	**197**	**39**	17	7	71	80	26	.373	.460	**.551**	190	**62**	26			.930	2	*O-148	6.0
1914	Cle-A	122	453	61	153	22	13	3	53	41	34	.338	.399	.464	153	28	22	15	-2	.967	2	*O-119	2.4
1915	Cle-A	83	303	42	99	16	9	3	45	28	11	.327	.389	.469	154	19	10	10	-3	.961	-3	O-49,1-30	1.0
	Chi-A	45	158	21	43	4	5	2	36	24	12	.272	.389	.399	129	6	6	10	-4	.947	-2	O-46	-0.2
	Yr	128	461	63	142	20	14	5	81	52	23	.308	.385	.445	145	25	16	20	-7	.953	-5	O-95,1-30	0.8
1916	Chi-A	155	592	91	202	40	**21**	3	78	46	25	.341	.393	.495	165	44	24	14	-1	.975	-1	*O-155	3.6
1917	*Chi-A	146	538	91	162	20	17	5	75	57	25	.301	.375	.429	142	27	13			.984	9	*O-145	3.1
1918	Chi-A	17	65	9	23	2	2	1	20	8	1	.354	.425	.492	175	6	3			1.000	1	O-17	0.5
1919	*Chi-A	139	516	79	181	31	14	7	96	60	10	.351	.422	.506	159	41	9			.967	-4	*O-139	2.9
1920	Chi-A	146	570	105	218	42	**20**	12	121	56	14	.382	.444	.589	172	58	9	12	-5	.965	-1	*O-145	4.1
Total	13	1332	4981	873	1772	307	168	54	785	519	**158**	.356	.423	.517	169	433	202	**61**		.962	23	*O-1289/1-30	37.5

■ KEN JACKSON
Jackson, Kenneth Bernard b: 8/21/63, Shreveport, La. BR/TR, 5'9", 170 lbs. Deb: 9/12/87

YEAR	TM/L	G	AB	R	H	2B	3B	HR	RBI	BB	SO	AVG	OBP	SLG	PRO+	BR/A	SB	CS	SBR	FA	FR	G/POS	TPR
1987	Phi-N	8	16	1	4	2	0	0	2	1	4	.250	.333	.375	85	-0	0	0	0	.955	-1	/S-8	-0.1

■ LOU JACKSON
Jackson, Louis Clarence b: 7/26/35, Riverton, La. d: 5/27/69, Tokyo, Japan BL/TR, 5'10", 168 lbs. Deb: 7/23/58

YEAR	TM/L	G	AB	R	H	2B	3B	HR	RBI	BB	SO	AVG	OBP	SLG	PRO+	BR/A	SB	CS	SBR	FA	FR	G/POS	TPR
1958	Chi-N	24	35	5	6	2	1	1	6	1	9	.171	.194	.371	46	-3	0	1	-1	1.000	-4	O-12	-0.8
1959	Chi-N	6	4	2	1	0	0	0	0	0	2	.250	.250	.250	34	-0	0	0	0	.000	0	H	0.0
1964	Bal-A	4	8	0	3	0	0	0	0	0	2	.375	.375	.375	110	0	0	0	0	1.000	1	O-1	0.1
Total	3	34	47	7	10	2	1	1	7	1	13	.213	.229	.362	55	-3	0	1	-1	1.000	-4	/O-13	-0.7

■ RANDY JACKSON
Jackson, Ransom Joseph "Handsome Ransom" b: 2/10/26, Little Rock, Ark. BR/TR, 6'1.5", 180 lbs. Deb: 5/2/50

YEAR	TM/L	G	AB	R	H	2B	3B	HR	RBI	BB	SO	AVG	OBP	SLG	PRO+	BR/A	SB	CS	SBR	FA	FR	G/POS	TPR
1950	Chi-N	34	111	13	25	4	0	3	6	7	25	.225	.271	.396	74	-5	4			.911	-4	3-27	-0.9
1951	Chi-N	145	557	78	153	24	6	16	76	47	44	.275	.332	.425	101	-1	14	3	2	.956	9	*3-143	0.8
1952	Chi-N	116	379	44	88	8	5	9	34	27	42	.232	.285	.351	75	-14	6	5	-1	.958	-3	*3-104/O-1	-2.0
1953	Chi-N	139	498	61	142	22	8	19	66	42	61	.285	.341	.476	108	5	3	4		.949	3	*3-133	0.5
1954	Chi-N★	126	484	77	132	17	6	19	67	44	55	.273	.336	.450	102	0	2	1	0	.955	-1	*3-124	-0.3
1955	Chi-N★	138	499	73	132	13	7	21	70	58	58	.265	.342	.445	107	5	0	4		.949	-13	*3-134	-1.0
1956	*Bro-N	101	307	37	84	15	7	8	53	28	38	.274	.338	.446	101	0	2	1	0	.993	21	3-80	2.3
1957	Bro-N	48	131	9	26	1	0	2	16	9	20	.198	.250	.252	32	-12	0	1	0	.976	-2	3-34	-1.5
1958	LA-N	35	65	8	12	3	0	1	4	5	10	.185	.243	.277	36	-6	0	0	0	.964	7	3-17	0.1
	Cle-A	29	91	7	22	3	1	2	12	8	18	.242	.266	.429	90	-2	0	0	0	.901	5	3-24	0.4
1959	Cle-A	3	7	0	1	0	0	0	0	0	1	.143	.143	.143	-22	-1	0	0	0	1.000	-1	/3-2	-0.2
	Chi-N	41	74	7	18	5	1	1	9	11	10	.243	.341	.378	92	-1	0	0	0	.941	-3	3-22/O-1	-0.3
Total	10	955	3203	412	835	115	44	103	415	281	382	.261	.322	.421	94	-31	36	**16**		.955	18	3-844/O-2	-2.1

■ REGGIE JACKSON
Jackson, Reginald Martinez b: 5/18/46, Wyncote, Pa. BL/TL, 6', 200 lbs. Deb: 6/9/67 H

YEAR	TM/L	G	AB	R	H	2B	3B	HR	RBI	BB	SO	AVG	OBP	SLG	PRO+	BR/A	SB	CS	SBR	FA	FR	G/POS	TPR
1967	KC-A	35	118	13	21	4	4	1	6	10	46	.178	.271	.305	72	-4	1	1	-0	.933	-2	O-34	-0.9
1968	Oak-A	154	553	82	138	13	6	29	74	50	171	.250	.317	.452	138	23	14	4	2	.959	8	*O-151	2.8

YEAR	TM/L	G	AB	R	H	2B	3B	HR	RBI	BB	SO	AVG	OBP	SLG	PRO+	BR/A	SB	CS	SBR	FA	FR	G/POS	TPR
1969	Oak-A★	152	549	**123**	151	36	3	47	118	114	142	.275	.410	**.608**	190	68	13	5	1	.964	5	*O-150	6.6
1970	Oak-A	149	426	57	101	21	2	23	66	75	135	.237	.361	.458	129	18	26	17	-2	.956	-11	*O-142	-0.2
1971	*Oak-A	150	567	87	157	29	3	32	80	63	161	.277	.355	.508	145	32	16	10	-1	.977	9	*O-145	3.4
1972	*Oak-A	135	499	72	132	25	2	25	75	59	125	.265	.352	.473	152	31	9	8	-2	.971	2	*O-135	2.7
1973	*Oak-A★	151	539	**99**	158	28	2	**32**	**117**	76	111	.293	.387	**.531**	165	46	22	8	2	.971	4	*O-145/D-3	4.6
1974	*Oak-A★	148	506	90	146	25	1	29	93	86	105	.289	.396	.514	**171**	48	25	5	**5**	.968	9	*O-127,D-19	5.6
1975	*Oak-A★	157	593	91	150	39	3	**36**	104	67	133	.253	.332	.511	138	27	17	8	0	.965	9	*O-147/D-9	3.0
1976	Bal-A	134	498	84	138	27	2	27	91	54	108	.277	.353	**.502**	158	34	28	7	4	.964	-1	*O-121,D-11	3.7
1977	*NY-A★	146	525	93	150	39	2	32	110	74	129	.286	.377	.550	151	37	17	3	3	.949	-1	*O-127,D-18	3.3
1978	*NY-A†	139	511	82	140	13	5	27	97	58	133	.274	.358	.477	136	24	14	11	-2	.986	3	*O-104,D-35	1.9
1979	NY-A	131	465	78	138	24	2	29	89	65	107	.297	.385	.544	151	33	9	8	-2	.986	0	*O-125/D-3	3.1
1980	*NY-A★	143	514	94	154	22	4	**41**	111	83	122	.300	.399	.597	172	51	1	2	-1	.962	-2	*O-94,D-46	4.2
1981	*NY-A★	94	334	33	79	17	1	15	54	46	82	.237	.331	.428	119	8	0	3	-2	.974	0	*O-61,D-33	0.3
1982	*Cal-A★	153	530	92	146	17	1	**39**	101	85	156	.275	.378	.532	147	35	4	5	-2	.972	-18	*O-139/D-5	1.2
1983	Cal-A†	116	397	43	77	14	1	14	49	52	140	.194	.294	.340	74	-14	0	2	-1	.986	-5	D-62,O-47	-2.3
1984	Cal-A★	143	525	67	117	17	2	25	81	55	141	.223	.300	.406	94	-5	8	4	0	1.000	0	*D-134/O-3	-0.9
1985	Cal-A	143	460	64	116	27	0	27	85	78	138	.252	.362	.487	130	20	1	2	-1	.944	-9	O-81,D-52	0.7
1986	*Cal-A	132	419	65	101	12	2	18	58	92	115	.241	.381	.408	116	13	1	1	0	.833	-0	*D-121/O-4	1.0
1987	Oak-A	115	336	42	74	14	1	15	43	33	97	.220	.298	.402	89	-6	2	1	0	1.000	0	D-79,O-20	-1.0
Total	21	2820	9864	1551	2584	463	49	563	1702	1375	2597	.262	.358	.490	140	519	228	115	-1	.967	8	*O-2102,D-630	42.8

■ SONNY JACKSON
Jackson, Roland Thomas b: 7/9/44, Washington, D.C. BL/TR, 5'9", 155 lbs. Deb: 9/27/63 C

YEAR	TM/L	G	AB	R	H	2B	3B	HR	RBI	BB	SO	AVG	OBP	SLG	PRO+	BR/A	SB	CS	SBR	FA	FR	G/POS	TPR
1963	Hou-N	1	3	0	0	0	0	0	0	0	1	.000	.000	.000	-99	-1	0	0	0	.833	1	/S-1	0.0
1964	Hou-N	9	23	3	8	1	0	0	1	2	3	.348	.400	.391	131	1	1	0	0	.870	-4	/S-7	-0.2
1965	Hou-N	10	23	1	3	0	0	0	0	1	1	.130	.167	.130	-16	-4	1	1	-0	.969	-1	/S-8,3-1	-0.4
1966	Hou-N	150	596	80	174	6	5	3	25	42	53	.292	.342	.334	95	-3	49	14	6	.951	-13	*S-150	0.4
1967	Hou-N	129	520	67	123	18	3	0	25	36	45	.237	.286	.283	66	-23	22	9	1	.943	-8	*S-128	-1.9
1968	Atl-N	105	358	37	81	8	2	1	19	25	35	.226	.282	.268	66	-14	16	6	1	.952	-17	S-99	-2.4
1969	*Atl-N	98	318	41	76	3	5	1	27	35	33	.239	.318	.289	71	-11	12	7	-1	.961	-23	S-97	-2.6
1970	Atl-N	103	328	60	85	14	3	0	20	45	27	.259	.350	.320	76	-10	11	4	1	.933	-23	S-87	-2.1
1971	Atl-N	149	547	58	141	20	5	2	25	35	45	.258	.304	.324	73	-19	7	6	-2	.980	5	*O-145	-2.7
1972	Atl-N	60	126	20	30	6	3	0	8	7	9	.238	.278	.333	67	-6	1	0	0	.976	-6	S-17,O-10/3-6	-1.0
1973	Atl-N	117	206	29	43	5	2	0	12	22	13	.209	.288	.252	47	-14	6	3	0	.981	-14	O-56,S-36	-2.7
1974	Atl-N	5	7	0	3	0	0	0	0	0	0	.429	.429	.429	134	0	0	1	-1	1.000	1	/O-1	0.0
Total	12	936	3055	396	767	81	28	7	162	250	265	.251	.310	.303	73	-104	126	51	7	.949	-104	S-630,O-212/3-7	-15.6

■ RON JACKSON
Jackson, Ronald Harris b: 10/22/33, Kalamazoo, Mich. BR/TR, 6'7", 225 lbs. Deb: 6/15/54

YEAR	TM/L	G	AB	R	H	2B	3B	HR	RBI	BB	SO	AVG	OBP	SLG	PRO+	BR/A	SB	CS	SBR	FA	FR	G/POS	TPR
1954	Chi-A	40	93	10	26	4	0	4	10	6	20	.280	.337	.452	111	1	2	1	0	.988	-3	1-35	-0.3
1955	Chi-A	40	74	10	15	1	1	2	7	8	22	.203	.280	.324	61	-4	1	0	0	.988	-1	1-29	-0.6
1956	Chi-A	22	56	7	12	3	0	1	4	10	13	.214	.333	.321	73	-2	1	0	0	1.000	1	1-19	-0.2
1957	Chi-A	13	60	4	19	3	0	2	8	1	12	.317	.328	.467	114	1	0	0	0	.992	-1	1-13	-0.1
1958	Chi-A	61	146	19	34	4	0	7	21	18	46	.233	.325	.404	101	0	2	0	1	.997	-2	1-38	-0.3
1959	Chi-A	10	14	3	3	1	0	1	2	1	0	.214	.313	.500	121	0	0	0	0	1.000	-0	/1-5	0.0
1960	Bos-A	10	31	1	7	2	0	0	0	1	6	.226	.250	.290	44	-2	0	0	0	.973	-0	/1-9	-0.3
Total	7	196	474	54	116	18	1	17	52	45	119	.245	.317	.395	92	-6	6	1	1	.992	-6	1-148	-1.8

■ RON JACKSON
Jackson, Ronnie Damien b: 5/9/53, Birmingham, Ala. BR/TR, 6', 205 lbs. Deb: 9/12/75 C

YEAR	TM/L	G	AB	R	H	2B	3B	HR	RBI	BB	SO	AVG	OBP	SLG	PRO+	BR/A	SB	CS	SBR	FA	FR	G/POS	TPR
1975	Cal-A	13	39	2	9	2	0	0	2	2	10	.231	.268	.282	60	-2	1	1	-0	.947	-0	/O-9,3-3,D-1	-0.3
1976	Cal-A	127	410	44	93	18	3	8	40	30	58	.227	.291	.344	91	-6	5	4	-1	.950	1	*3-114/2-7,O-4,D-6	-0.7
1977	Cal-A	106	292	38	71	15	2	8	28	24	42	.243	.303	.390	91	-4	3	2	-0	.990	2	1-43,3-30,D-20/OS	-0.6
1978	Cal-A	105	387	49	115	18	6	6	57	16	31	.297	.340	.421	117	8	2	3	-1	.994	-0	1-75,3-31/O-1,D-1	-0.1
1979	Min-A	159	583	85	158	40	5	14	68	51	59	.271	.339	.429	102	1	3	1	0	.994	11	*1-157/S-1,3-1,O-1	0.3
1980	Min-A	131	396	48	105	29	3	5	42	28	41	.265	.319	.391	87	-7	1	8	-5	.991	-1	*1-119,O-15/3-2,D-1	-1.9
1981	Min-A	54	175	17	46	8	1	1	12	8	11	.263	.306	.383	91	-2	2	1	-0	.988	1	1-36/O-7,3-3,D-6	-0.4
	Det-A	31	95	12	27	8	1	1	12	8	11	.284	.340	.421	114	2	4	1	1	1.000	1	1-29	0.0
	Yr	85	270	29	73	17	1	5	40	18	26	.270	.318	.396	99	-1	6	3	0	.993	1	1-65/O-7,D-6,3-3	-0.4
1982	*Cal-A	53	142	15	47	6	0	2	19	10	12	.331	.383	.415	119	4	0	1	-0	.994	0	1-37/3-9	0.2
1983	Cal-A	102	348	41	80	16	1	8	39	27	33	.230	.291	.351	76	-12	2	2	-1	.957	-2	3-38,1-35,D-16,O-15	-1.4
1984	Cal-A	33	91	5	15	2	1	0	5	7	13	.165	.224	.209	21	-10	0	0	0	.990	-0	1-21/3-9,O-1	-1.1
	Bal-A	12	28	0	8	2	0	0	2	0	4	.286	.286	.357	78	-1	0	0	0	.960	2	3-10	-0.1
	Yr	45	119	5	23	4	1	0	7	7	17	.193	.238	.244	34	-11	0	0	0	.990	1	1-21,3-19/O-1	-1.2
Total	10	926	2986	356	774	165	22	56	342	213	329	.259	.316	.385	94	-29	23	27	-9	.993	14	1-552,3-250/OD2S	-6.1

■ SAM JACKSON
Jackson, Samuel b: 3/24/1849, Ripon, England d: 8/4/1893, Clifton Springs, N.Y. BR/TR, 5'5.5", 160 lbs. Deb: 5/16/1871

YEAR	TM/L	G	AB	R	H	2B	3B	HR	RBI	BB	SO	AVG	OBP	SLG	PRO+	BR/A	SB	CS	SBR	FA	FR	G/POS	TPR
1871	Bos-n	16	76	17	17	5	3	0	11	1	4	.224	.234	.368	68	-3	0	1	-1	.818	-1	2-14/S-1,O-1	-0.4
1872	Atl-n	4	12	0	2	0	0	0	0	0	0	.167	.167	.167	2	-2	0	0	0	.667	-3	/O-3,2-1,3-1	-0.3
Total	2 n	20	88	17	19	5	3	0	11	1	4	.216	.225	.341	58	-5	0	1	-1	.810	-5	/2-15,O-4,3-1,S-1	-0.7

■ TRAVIS JACKSON
Jackson, Travis Calvin "Stonewall" b: 11/2/03, Waldo, Ark. d: 7/27/87, Waldo, Ark. BR/TR, 5'10.5", 160 lbs. Deb: 9/27/22 CH

YEAR	TM/L	G	AB	R	H	2B	3B	HR	RBI	BB	SO	AVG	OBP	SLG	PRO+	BR/A	SB	CS	SBR	FA	FR	G/POS	TPR
1922	NY-N	3	8	1	0	0	0	0	0	0	2	.000	.000	.000	-99	-2	0	0	0	.909	0	/S-3	-0.2
1923	*NY-N	96	327	45	90	12	7	4	37	22	40	.275	.321	.391	88	-6	3	3	-1	.943	-3	S-60,3-31/2-1	-0.3
1924	*NY-N	151	596	81	180	26	8	11	76	21	56	.302	.326	.428	103	1	6	7	-2	.937	-0	*S-151	1.5
1925	NY-N	112	411	51	117	15	2	9	59	24	43	.285	.327	.397	87	-9	8	3	1	.941	3	*S-110	0.6
1926	NY-N	111	385	64	126	24	8	8	51	20	26	.327	.362	.494	130	14	2			.962	1	*S-108/O-1	2.6
1927	NY-N	127	469	67	149	29	4	14	98	32	30	.318	.363	.486	126	16	8			.952	28	*S-124/3-2	5.4
1928	NY-N	150	537	73	145	35	6	14	77	56	46	.270	.339	.436	101	-1	8			.952	28	*S-149	4.3
1929	NY-N	149	551	92	162	21	12	21	94	64	50	.294	.367	.490	111	8	10			**.969**	19	*S-149	4.1
1930	NY-N	116	431	70	146	27	8	13	82	32	25	.339	.386	.529	121	14	6			.956	11	*S-115	3.3
1931	NY-N	145	555	65	172	26	10	5	71	36	23	.310	.353	.420	110	7	13			**.970**	10	*S-145	3.1
1932	NY-N	52	195	23	50	17	1	4	38	13	16	.256	.310	.415	95	-2	1			.925	-5	S-52	-0.2
1933	*NY-N	53	122	11	30	5	0	0	12	8	11	.246	.292	.287	67	-5	2			.890	7	S-21,3-21	0.4
1934	NY-N★	137	523	75	140	26	7	16	101	37	71	.268	.316	.436	102	-0	1			.945	12	*S-130/3-9	1.9
1935	NY-N	128	511	74	154	20	12	9	80	29	26	.301	.340	.440	110	6	3			.947	-3	*3-128	0.4
1936	*NY-N	126	465	41	107	8	1	7	53	18	56	.230	.260	.297	50	-33	0			.952	-1	3-116/S-9	-2.9
Total	15	1656	6086	833	1768	291	86	135	929	412	565	.291	.337	.433	102	71	<u>13</u>			.952	103	*S-1326,3-307/O-1,2	24.0

■ BO JACKSON
Jackson, Vincent Edward b: 11/30/62, Bessemer, Ala. BR/TR, 6'1", 225 lbs. Deb: 9/2/86

YEAR	TM/L	G	AB	R	H	2B	3B	HR	RBI	BB	SO	AVG	OBP	SLG	PRO+	BR/A	SB	CS	SBR	FA	FR	G/POS	TPR
1986	KC-A	25	82	9	17	2	1	2	9	7	34	.207	.286	.329	66	-4	3	1	0	.886	-3	O-23/D-1	-0.7
1987	KC-A	116	396	46	93	17	2	22	53	30	158	.235	.297	.455	93	-5	10	4	1	.955	-7	*O-113/D-1	-1.5
1988	KC-A	124	439	63	108	16	4	25	68	25	146	.246	.288	.472	108	2	27	6	5	.973	-6	*O-121/D-2	-0.5
1989	KC-A★	135	515	86	132	15	6	32	105	39	172	.256	.312	.495	125	14	26	9	2	.967	-7	*O-110,D-24	2.1
1990	KC-A	111	405	74	110	16	1	28	78	44	128	.272	.346	.523	142	21	15	9	0	.952	-8	O-97,D-10	2.6
1991	Chi-A	23	71	8	16	4	0	3	14	12	25	.225	.337	.408	108	1	0	1	-1	.000	0	D-21	-0.1
1993	*Chi-A	85	284	32	66	9	0	16	45	23	106	.232	.290	.433	94	-4	0	2	-1	.989	-3	O-47,D-36	-0.5
1994	Cal-A	75	201	23	56	7	0	13	43	20	72	.279	.347	.507	115	4	1	0	0	.964	-2	O-46/D-9	0.1
Total	8	694	2393	341	598	86	14	141	415	200	841	.250	.311	.474	112	30	82	32	5	.962	12	O-557,D-104	3.0

■ BILL JACKSON
Jackson, William Riley b: 4/4/1881, Pittsburgh, Pa. d: 9/24/58, Peoria, Ill. BL/TL, 5'11.5", 160 lbs. Deb: 4/30/14

YEAR	TM/L	G	AB	R	H	2B	3B	HR	RBI	BB	SO	AVG	OBP	SLG	PRO+	BR/A	SB	CS	SBR	FA	FR	G/POS	TPR
1914	Chi-F	26	25	2	1	0	0	0	1	3	5	.040	.143	.040	-52	-6	0			.917	0	/O-6,1-4	-0.6
1915	Chi-F	50	98	15	16	1	0	1	12	14	15	.163	.268	.204	36	-10	3			.983	0	1-36/O-1	-1.2
Total	2	76	123	17	17	1	0	1	13	17	20	.138	.243	.171	18	-16	3			.984	0	/1-40,O-7	-1.8

YEAR	TM/L	G	AB	R	H	2B	3B	HR	RBI	BB	SO	AVG	OBP	SLG	PRO+	BR/A	SB	CS	SBR	FA	FR	G/POS	TPR

■ SPOOK JACOBS   Jacobs, Forrest Vandergrift   b: 11/4/25, Cheswold, Del.   BR/TR, 5'8.5", 155 lbs.   Deb: 4/13/54

1954	Phi-A	132	508	63	131	11	1	0	26	60	22	.258	.336	.283	71	-18	17	3	3	.974	-19	*2-131	-2.7
1955	KC-A	13	23	7	6	0	0	0	1	3	0	.261	.370	.261	71	-1	1	2	-1	1.000	-3	/2-7	-0.4
1956	KC-A	32	97	13	21	3	0	0	5	15	5	.216	.321	.247	52	-6	4	1	1	.968	-4	2-31	-0.7
	Pit-N	11	37	4	6	2	0	0	1	2	5	.162	.225	.216	20	-4	0	2	-1	.926	-4	2-11	-0.9
Total	3	188	665	87	164	16	1	0	33	80	32	.247	.329	.274	65	-30	22	8	2	.971	-29	2-180	-4.7

■ JAKE JACOBS   Jacobs, Lamar Gary   b: 6/9/37, Youngstown, Ohio   BR/TR, 6', 175 lbs.   Deb: 9/13/60

1960	Was-A	6	2	0	0	0	0	0	0	0	0	.000	.000	.000	-99	-1	0	0	0	.000	0	H	-0.1
1961	Min-A	4	8	0	2	0	0	0	0	0	2	.250	.250	.250	32	-1	0	0	0	1.000	-1	/O-3	-0.2
Total	2	10	10	0	2	0	0	0	0	0	2	.200	.200	.200	7	-1	0	0	0	1.000	-1	/O-3	-0.3

■ MIKE JACOBS   Jacobs, Morris Elmore   b: 12/1877, Louisville, Ky.   d: 3/21/49, Louisville, Ky.   Deb: 7/16/02

1902	Chi-N	5	19	1	4	0	0	0	2	0		.211	.211	.211	31	-2	0			.880	-2	/S-5	-0.3

■ OTTO JACOBS   Jacobs, Otto Albert   b: 4/19/1889, Chicago, Ill.   d: 11/19/55, Chicago, Ill.   BR/TR, 5'9", 180 lbs.   Deb: 6/13/18

1918	Chi-A	29	73	4	15	3	1	0	3	5	8	.205	.256	.274	59	-4	0			.955	-4	C-21	-0.7

■ RAY JACOBS   Jacobs, Raymond F.   b: 1/2/02, Salt Lake City, Utah   d: 4/5/52, Los Angeles, Cal.   BR/TR, 6', 160 lbs.   Deb: 4/20/28

1928	Chi-N	2	2	0	0	0	0	0	0	0	1	.000	.000	.000	-99	-1	0			.000	0	H	-0.1

■ MERWIN JACOBSON   Jacobson, Merwin John William "Jake"   b: 3/7/1894, New Britain, Conn.   d: 1/13/78, Baltimore, Md.   BL/TL, 5'11.5", 165 lbs.   Deb: 9/8/15

1915	NY-N	8	24	0	2	0	0	0	0	1	5	.083	.120	.083	-40	-4	0			.909	0	/O-5	-0.5
1916	Chi-N	4	13	2	3	0	0	0	0	1	0	.231	.286	.231	54	-1	2			1.000	0	/O-4	-0.1
1926	Bro-N	110	288	41	71	9	2	0	23	36	24	.247	.330	.292	70	-11	5			.975	-3	O-86	-1.9
1927	Bro-N	11	6	4	0	0	0	0	0	0	0	.000	.000	.000	-99	-2	0			1.000	-1	/O-3	-0.3
Total	4	133	331	47	76	9	2	0	24	38	34	.230	.309	.269	59	-18	7			.973	-4	/O-98	-2.8

■ BABY DOLL JACOBSON   Jacobson, William Chester   b: 8/16/1890, Cable, Ill.   d: 1/16/77, Orion, Ill.   BR/TR, 6'3", 215 lbs.   Deb: 4/14/15

1915	Det-A	37	65	5	14	6	2	0	4	5	14	.215	.282	.369	90	-1	0	2	-1	.983	-2	1-10/O-7	-0.6
	StL-A	34	115	13	24	6	1	1	9	10	26	.209	.295	.304	82	-3	3	3	-1	.981	-1	O-32	-0.7
	Yr	71	180	18	38	12	3	1	13	15	40	.211	.290	.328	84	-4	3	5	-2	.984	-2	O-39,1-10	-1.3
1917	StL-A	148	529	53	131	23	7	4	55	31	67	.248	.294	.340	97	-4	10			.975	7	*O-131,1-11	-0.5
1919	StL-A	120	455	70	147	31	8	4	51	24	47	.323	.362	.453	125	13	9			.949	1	*O-106/1-8	0.7
1920	StL-A	154	609	97	216	34	14	9	122	46	37	.355	.402	.501	134	29	11	7	-1	.979	5	*O-154/1-1	2.6
1921	StL-A	151	599	90	211	38	14	5	90	42	30	.352	.398	.487	118	15	8	8	-2	.982	5	*O-142,1-11	0.7
1922	StL-A	145	555	88	176	22	16	9	102	46	36	.317	.379	.463	114	11	19	6	2	.969	4	*O-137/1-7	0.7
1923	StL-A	147	592	76	183	29	6	8	81	29	27	.309	.343	.419	95	-6	6	6	-2	.974	9	*O-146	-0.9
1924	StL-A	152	579	103	184	41	12	19	97	35	45	.318	.361	.528	120	13	6	8	-3	.986	16	*O-152	1.5
1925	StL-A	142	540	103	184	30	9	15	76	45	26	.341	.392	.513	122	16	8	11	-4	.965	1	*O-139	0.4
1926	StL-A	50	182	18	52	15	1	2	21	9	14	.286	.319	.412	86	-5	1	2	-1	.964	-6	O-50	-1.5
	Bos-A	98	394	44	120	36	1	6	69	22	22	.305	.344	.447	109	3	4	1	1	.980	-8	O-98	-1.1
	Yr	148	576	62	172	51	2	8	90	31	36	.299	.337	.436	101	-2	5	3	-0	.975	-15	*O-148	-2.6
1927	Bos-A	45	155	11	38	9	3	0	24	5	12	.245	.280	.342	61	-9	1	0	0	.979	1	O-39	-1.0
	Cle-A	32	103	13	26	5	0	0	13	6	4	.252	.300	.301	56	-7	0	0	0	.932	-1	O-31	-0.9
	Phi-A	17	35	3	8	3	0	1	5	0	3	.229	.229	.400	57	-2	0	0	0	1.000	-5	O-14	-0.8
	Yr	94	293	27	72	17	3	1	42	11	19	.246	.280	.334	59	-19	1	0	0	.959	-5	O-84	-2.7
Total	11	1472	5507	787	1714	328	94	83	819	355	410	.311	.357	.450	111	63	86	54		.973	31	*O-1378/1-48	-1.4

■ BROOK JACOBY   Jacoby, Brook Wallace   b: 11/23/59, Philadelphia, Pa.   BR/TR, 5'11", 195 lbs.   Deb: 9/13/81

1981	Atl-N	11	10	0	2	0	0	0	0	0	3	.200	.200	.200	13	-1	0	0	0	1.000	2	/3-3	0.1
1983	Atl-N	4	8	0	0	0	0	0	0	0	1	.000	.000	.000	-93	-2	0	0	0	1.000	-1	/3-2	-0.3
1984	Cle-A	126	439	64	116	19	3	7	40	32	73	.264	.319	.369	88	-7	3	2	-0	.951	-20	*3-126/S-1	-2.9
1985	Cle-A	161	606	72	166	26	3	20	87	48	120	.274	.327	.426	105	3	2	3	-1	.958	-7	*3-161/2-1	-0.7
1986	Cle-A★	158	583	83	168	30	4	17	80	56	137	.288	.349	.441	116	13	2	1	0	.941	-13	*3-158	-0.3
1987	Cle-A	155	540	73	162	26	4	32	69	75	73	.300	.388	.541	142	33	2	3	-1	.946	7	*3-144/1-7,D-4	2.1
1988	Cle-A	152	552	59	133	25	0	9	49	48	101	.241	.303	.335	76	-17	2	3	-1	.975	1	*3-151	-1.9
1989	Cle-A	147	519	49	141	26	5	13	64	62	90	.272	.353	.416	114	10	2	5	-2	.955	-10	*3-134/D-3	-0.1
1990	Cle-A★	155	553	77	162	24	4	14	75	63	58	.293	.367	.427	122	17	1	4	-2	.981	-12	3-99,1-78	-0.2
1991	Cle-A	66	231	14	54	9	1	4	24	16	32	.234	.289	.333	71	-9	0	1	-1	.988	-0	1-55,3-15	-1.3
	Oak-A	56	188	14	40	12	0	0	20	11	22	.213	.260	.277	51	-13	0	0	0	.982	-8	3-52/1-3	-2.1
	Yr	122	419	28	94	21	1	4	44	27	54	.224	.276	.308	63	-22	0	1	-1	.987	-8	3-67,1-58	-3.4
1992	Cle-A	120	291	30	76	7	0	4	36	28	54	.261	.328	.326	85	-5	0	3	-2	.957	3	*3-111,1-10	-0.5
Total	11	1311	4520	535	1220	204	24	120	545	439	764	.270	.337	.405	104	22	16	25	-10	.958	-71	*3-1166,1-153/D2S	-8.1

■ HARRY JACOBY   Jacoby, Harry   b: Philadelphia, Pa.   Deb: 5/2/1882

1882	Bal-a	31	121	17	21	1	0	0			7	.174	.219	.223	53	-5				.776	8	3-19,O-13	0.3
1885	Bal-a	11	43	4	6	2	0	0	1	2		.140	.178	.186	15	-4				.896	-8	2-11	-1.1
Total	2	42	164	21	27	3	1	1	1	9	.165	.208	.213	43	-9				.776	-0	/3-19,O-13,2-11	-0.8

■ JOHN JAHA   Jaha, John Emil   b: 5/27/66, Portland, Ore.   BR/TR, 6'1", 195 lbs.   Deb: 7/9/92

1992	Mil-A	47	133	17	30	3	1	2	10	12	30	.226	.299	.308	72	-5	10	0	3	1.000	-0	1-38/O-1,D-8	-0.4
1993	Mil-A	153	515	78	136	21	0	19	70	51	109	.264	.340	.416	103	2	13	9	-2	.992	9	*1-150/2-1,3-1	-0.3
1994	Mil-A	84	291	45	70	14	0	12	39	32	75	.241	.336	.412	88	-5	3	3	-1	.989	-1	1-73,D-11	-1.4
1995	Mil-A	88	316	59	99	20	2	20	65	36	66	.313	.390	.579	140	18	2	1	0	.997	3	1-81/D-6	1.3
1996	Mil-A	148	543	108	163	28	1	34	118	85	118	.300	.400	.543	128	24	3	1	1	.992	1	1-85,D-63	1.1
Total	5	520	1798	307	498	86	4	87	302	216	398	.277	.364	.474	114	34	31	14	1	.993	10	1-427/D-88,3-1,2O	0.3

■ ART JAHN   Jahn, Arthur Charles   b: 12/2/1895, Struble, Iowa   d: 1/9/48, Little Rock, Ark.   BR/TR, 6', 180 lbs.   Deb: 7/2/25

1925	Chi-N	58	226	30	68	10	8	0	37	11	20	.301	.336	.416	90	-4	2	2	-1	.985	2	O-58	-0.6
1928	NY-N	10	29	7	8	1	0	1	7	2	5	.276	.323	.414	91	-0	0			1.000	1	/O-8	0.0
	Phi-N	36	94	8	21	4	0	0	11	4	11	.223	.270	.266	39	-8	0			.978	-4	O-29	-1.4
	Yr	46	123	15	29	5	0	1	18	6	16	.236	.282	.301	51	-9	0			.985	-3	O-37	-1.4
Total	2	104	349	45	97	15	8	1	55	17	36	.278	.317	.375	76	-13	2			.985	-1	/O-95	-2.0

■ ART JAMES   James, Arthur   b: 8/2/52, Detroit, Mich.   BL/TL, 6', 170 lbs.   Deb: 4/10/75

1975	Det-A	11	40	2	9	2	0	0	1	0	3	.225	.244	.275	44	-3	1	2	-1	1.000	2	O-11	-0.3

■ BERT JAMES   James, Berton Hulon "Jesse"   b: 7/7/1886, Coopertown, Tenn.   d: 1/2/59, Adairville, Ky.   BL/TR, 5'11", 175 lbs.   Deb: 9/18/09

1909	StL-N	6	21	1	6	0	0	0	4			.286	.400	.286	120	1	1	1		.909	0	/O-6	0.1

■ CHARLIE JAMES   James, Charles Wesley   b: 12/22/37, St.Louis, Mo.   BR/TR, 6'1", 195 lbs.   Deb: 8/2/60

1960	StL-N	43	50	5	9	1	0	2	5	1	12	.180	.196	.320	35	-5	0	0	0	.917	-10	O-37	-1.6
1961	StL-N	108	349	43	89	19	2	4	44	15	59	.255	.290	.355	64	-18	2	2	-1	.962	-6	O-90	-3.0
1962	StL-N	129	388	50	107	13	4	8	59	10	58	.276	.301	.392	77	-13	3	4	-2	.988	-10	O-116	-3.0
1963	StL-N	116	347	34	93	14	2	10	45	10	64	.268	.292	.406	91	-5	2	1	0	.994	9	*O-101	-1.0
1964	*StL-N	88	233	24	52	9	5	1	17	11	58	.223	.255	.335	61	-12	0	0	0	.963	-3	O-60	-1.9
1965	Cin-N	26	39	2	8	0	0	2	2	1	9	.205	.225	.205	21	-4	0	0	0	.909	-1	/O-7	-0.5
Total	6	510	1406	158	358	56	9	29	172	48	260	.255	.284	.369	71	-57	7	7	-2	.976	-29	O-411	-11.0

■ CLEO JAMES   James, Cleo Joel   b: 8/31/40, Clarksdale, Miss.   BR/TR, 5'10", 176 lbs.   Deb: 4/15/68

1968	LA-N	10	10	2	2	1	0	0	0	0	6	.200	.200	.300	52	-1	0	0	0	1.000	-0	/O-2	-0.1

YEAR	TM/L	G	AB	R	H	2B	3B	HR	RBI	BB	SO	AVG	OBP	SLG	PRO+	BR/A	SB	CS	SBR	FA	FR	G/POS	TPR
1970	Chi-N	100	176	33	37	7	2	3	14	17	24	.210	.298	.324	59	-10	5	0	2	1.000	-10	O-90	-2.1
1971	Chi-N	54	150	25	43	7	0	2	13	10	16	.287	.355	.373	93	-1	6	2	1	.979	-1	O-48/3-2	-0.4
1973	Chi-N	44	45	9	5	0	0	0	0	1	6	.111	.130	.111	-30	-8	5	0	2	.960	-4	O-22	-1.1
Total	4	208	381	69	87	15	2	5	27	28	52	.228	.300	.318	63	-20	16	2	4	.988	-15	O-162/3-2	-3.7

■ DION JAMES
James, Dion b: 11/9/62, Philadelphia, Pa. BL/TL, 6'1", 170 lbs. Deb: 9/16/83

YEAR	TM/L	G	AB	R	H	2B	3B	HR	RBI	BB	SO	AVG	OBP	SLG	PRO+	BR/A	SB	CS	SBR	FA	FR	G/POS	TPR
1983	Mil-A	11	20	1	2	0	0	0	1	2	2	.100	.182	.100	-22	-3	1	0	0	1.000	-3	/O-9,D-2	-0.7
1984	Mil-A	128	387	52	114	19	5	1	30	32	41	.295	.353	.377	106	4	10	10	-3	.989	-1	*O-118	-0.4
1985	Mil-A	18	49	5	11	1	0	0	3	6	6	.224	.309	.245	54	-3	0	0	0	1.000	-2	O-11/D-3	-0.5
1987	Atl-N	134	494	80	154	37	6	10	61	70	63	.312	.399	.472	124	19	10	8	-2	.996	1	*O-126	1.3
1988	Atl-N	132	386	46	99	17	5	3	30	58	59	.256	.355	.350	98	1	9	9	-3	.987	-12	*O-120	-1.9
1989	Atl-N	63	170	15	44	7	0	1	11	25	23	.259	.357	.318	92	-1	1	3	-2	1.000	-6	O-46/1-8	-0.4
	Cle-A	71	245	26	75	11	0	4	29	24	26	.306	.368	.400	114	5	1	4	-2	.976	9	O-37,D-27/1-2	0.2
1990	Cle-A	87	248	28	68	15	2	1	22	27	23	.274	.348	.363	99	0	5	3	-0	.996	-5	1-35,O-33,D-10	-0.8
1992	NY-A	67	145	24	38	8	0	3	17	22	15	.262	.363	.379	109	2	1	0	0	1.000	-8	*O-46/D-5	-0.6
1993	NY-A	115	343	62	114	21	2	7	36	31	33	.332	.391	.466	134	17	0	0	0	.966	-14	O-103/1-1,D-1	-1.1
1995	*NY-A	85	209	22	60	6	1	2	26	20	16	.287	.349	.354	85	-4	4	1	1	.968	-5	O-29,D-27/1-6	-1.2
1996	NY-A	6	12	1	2	0	0	0	0	1	2	.167	.231	.167	3	-2	1	0	0	1.000	-1	/O-4,D-1	-0.2
Total	11	917	2708	362	781	142	21	32	266	318	307	.288	.365	.392	107	35	43	38	-10	.986	-51	O-682/D-76,1-52	-5.1

■ CHRIS JAMES
James, Donald Chris b: 10/4/62, Rusk, Tex. BR/TR, 6'1", 195 lbs. Deb: 4/23/86

YEAR	TM/L	G	AB	R	H	2B	3B	HR	RBI	BB	SO	AVG	OBP	SLG	PRO+	BR/A	SB	CS	SBR	FA	FR	G/POS	TPR
1986	Phi-N	16	46	5	13	3	0	1	5	1	13	.283	.298	.413	91	-1	0	0	0	1.000	-1	O-11	-0.2
1987	Phi-N	115	358	48	105	20	6	17	54	27	67	.293	.346	.525	123	11	3	1	0	.990	-2	*O-108	0.6
1988	Phi-N	150	566	57	137	24	1	19	66	31	73	.242	.285	.389	90	-9	7	4	-0	.989	-4	*O-116/3-31	-1.8
1989	Phi-N	45	179	14	37	4	0	2	19	4	23	.207	.224	.263	39	-14	3	1	0	.985	-1	O-37,3-11	-1.8
	SD-N	87	303	41	80	13	2	11	46	22	45	.264	.316	.429	111	3	2	1	0	.987	-0	O-79/3-6	0.1
	Yr	132	482	55	117	17	2	13	65	26	68	.243	.283	.367	84	-11	5	2	0	.986	-1	*O-116,3-17	-1.7
1990	Cle-A	140	528	62	158	32	4	12	70	31	71	.299	.343	.443	119	12	4	3	-1	1.000	0	*D-124,O-14	0.7
1991	Cle-A	115	437	31	104	16	2	5	41	18	61	.238	.275	.318	63	-22	3	4	-2	1.000	0	D-60,O-39,1-15	-2.8
1992	SF-N	111	248	25	60	10	4	5	32	14	45	.242	.288	.375	91	-4	2	3	-1	.974	1	O-62	-0.6
1993	Hou-N	65	129	19	33	10	1	6	19	15	34	.256	.338	.488	122	4	2	0	1	.958	-5	O-34	0.6
	Tex-A	8	31	5	11	1	0	3	7	3	6	.355	.412	.677	195	4	0	0	0	1.000	-1	/O-7	0.3
1994	Tex-A	52	133	28	34	8	4	7	19	20	38	.256	.365	.534	128	5	0	0	0	1.000	-6	O-48	-0.1
1995	KC-A	26	58	6	18	3	0	2	7	6	10	.310	.385	.466	118	2	1	0	0	1.000	-0	D-14/O-5	0.1
	Bos-A	16	24	2	4	1	0	0	1	1	4	.167	.200	.208	6	-3	0	0	0	1.000	-0	/O-8,D-6	-0.4
	Yr	42	82	8	22	4	0	2	8	7	14	.268	.333	.390	86	-1	1	0	0	1.000	-1	D-20,O-13	-0.3
Total	10	946	3040	343	794	145	24	90	386	193	490	.261	.310	.413	99	-13	27	17	-2	.987	-12	O-568,D-204/3-48,1	-5.3

■ SKIP JAMES
James, Philip Robert b: 10/21/49, Elmhurst, Ill. BL/TL, 6', 185 lbs. Deb: 9/12/77

YEAR	TM/L	G	AB	R	H	2B	3B	HR	RBI	BB	SO	AVG	OBP	SLG	PRO+	BR/A	SB	CS	SBR	FA	FR	G/POS	TPR
1977	SF-N	10	15	3	4	1	0	0	3	2	3	.267	.353	.333	86	-0	0	0	0	1.000	1	/1-9	0.0
1978	SF-N	41	21	5	2	1	0	0	3	4	5	.095	.240	.143	10	-3	1	0	0	1.000	2	1-27	-0.1
Total	2	51	36	8	6	2	0	0	6	6	8	.167	.286	.222	42	-3	1	0	0	1.000	3	/1-36	-0.1

■ BERNIE JAMES
James, Robert Byrne b: 9/2/05, Angleton, Tex. d: 8/1/94, San Antonio, Tex. BB/TR, 5'9.5", 150 lbs. Deb: 5/6/29

YEAR	TM/L	G	AB	R	H	2B	3B	HR	RBI	BB	SO	AVG	OBP	SLG	PRO+	BR/A	SB	CS	SBR	FA	FR	G/POS	TPR
1929	Bos-N	46	101	12	31	3	2	0	9	9	13	.307	.369	.376	89	-2	3			.940	-9	2-32/O-1	-0.9
1930	Bos-N	8	11	1	2	1	0	0	1	0	1	.182	.182	.273	8	-2	0			.941	0	/2-7	-0.1
1933	NY-N	60	125	22	28	2	1	1	10	8	12	.224	.271	.280	58	-7	5			.948	2	2-26/S-6,3-5	-0.3
Total	3	114	237	35	61	6	3	1	20	17	26	.257	.310	.321	70	-10	8			.944	-7	2-65,S-6,3-5,O-1	-1.3

■ CHARLIE JAMIESON
Jamieson, Charles Devine "Cuckoo" b: 2/7/1893, Paterson, N.J. d: 10/27/69, Paterson, N.J. BL/TL, 5'8.5", 165 lbs. Deb: 9/20/15

YEAR	TM/L	G	AB	R	H	2B	3B	HR	RBI	BB	SO	AVG	OBP	SLG	PRO+	BR/A	SB	CS	SBR	FA	FR	G/POS	TPR
1915	Was-A	17	68	9	19	3	2	0	7	6	9	.279	.338	.382	113	1	0			1.000	4	O-17	0.4
1916	Was-A	64	145	16	36	4	0	0	13	18	18	.248	.331	.276	83	-2	5			.913	-4	O-41/1-4,P-1	-0.9
1917	Was-A	20	35	4	6	2	0	0	2	6	5	.171	.293	.229	60	-2	0			.875	-2	/O-9,P-1	-0.4
	Phi-A	85	345	41	92	6	2	0	27	37	36	.267	.341	.296	96	-1	8			.937	-2	O-92/P-1	-0.8
	Yr	105	380	45	98	8	2	0	29	43	41	.258	.336	.289	92	-2	8			.930	-4	O-92/P-1	-1.2
1918	Phi-A	110	416	50	84	11	2	0	11	54	30	.202	.297	.238	61	-18	11			.970	-5	*O-102/P-5	-2.7
1919	Cle-A	26	17	3	6	2	1	0	2	0	2	.353	.353	.588	153	1	2			.750	-1	/P-4,O-3	0.0
1920	*Cle-A	108	370	69	118	17	7	1	40	41	26	.319	.388	.411	108	5	2	9	-5	.966	-2	*O-98/1-4	-0.8
1921	Cle-A	140	536	94	166	33	10	1	46	67	27	.310	.387	.414	103	4	4	8	-0	.974	-6	*O-137	-1.1
1922	Cle-A	145	567	87	183	29	11	3	57	54	22	.323	.388	.429	112	11	15	9	-1	.978	-8	*O-144/P-2	-0.2
1923	Cle-A	152	644	130	**222**	36	12	2	51	80	37	.345	.422	.447	129	30	18	14	-3	.974	7	*O-152	2.3
1924	Cle-A	143	594	98	213	34	8	3	54	47	15	.359	.407	.458	121	19	21	12	-1	.974	9	*O-139	1.2
1925	Cle-A	138	557	109	165	24	5	4	42	72	26	.296	.380	.379	92	-5	14	18	-7	.955	-7	*O-143	-1.2
1926	Cle-A	143	555	89	166	33	7	2	45	53	22	.299	.361	.395	96	-5	9	7	-2	.960	-0	*O-127	-1.4
1927	Cle-A	127	489	73	151	23	6	0	36	64	14	.309	.394	.380	101	4	7	9	-3	.969	5	*O-137	-0.3
1928	Cle-A	112	433	63	133	18	4	1	37	56	20	.307	.388	.374	100	2	3	12	-6	.984	20	*O-111	0.8
1929	Cle-A	102	364	56	106	22	1	0	26	50	12	.291	.378	.357	87	-5	2	13	-7	.980	-2	O-93	-1.9
1930	Cle-A	103	366	64	110	22	1	1	52	36	20	.301	.368	.374	85	-7	5	2	0	.955	-5	O-95	-1.7
1931	Cle-A	28	43	7	13	2	1	0	4	5	1	.302	.375	.395	97	-0	1	1	-0	.833	-2	/O-7	-0.2
1932	Cle-A	16	16	0	1	0	0	0	0	2	3	.063	.211	.125	-10	-1	0			1.000	1	/O-2	-0.2
Total	18	1779	6560	1062	1990	322	80	18	552	748	385	.303	.378	.385	101	31	131	110		.967	19	*O-1638/P-13,1-8	-9.1

■ VIC JANOWICZ
Janowicz, Victor Felix b: 2/26/30, Elyria, Ohio d: 2/27/96, Columbus, Ohio BR/TR, 5'9", 185 lbs. Deb: 5/31/53

YEAR	TM/L	G	AB	R	H	2B	3B	HR	RBI	BB	SO	AVG	OBP	SLG	PRO+	BR/A	SB	CS	SBR	FA	FR	G/POS	TPR
1953	Pit-N	42	123	10	31	3	1	2	8	7	25	.252	.287	.341	63	-7	0	1	-1	.937	-12	C-35	-1.7
1954	Pit-N	41	73	10	11	3	0	0	2	7	23	.151	.235	.192	13	-9	0	0	0	.904	-3	3-18/O-1	-0.9
Total	2	83	196	20	42	6	1	2	10	12	54	.214	.267	.286	44	-16	0	1	-1	.937	-11	/C-35,3-18,O-1	-2.6

■ RAY JANSEN
Jansen, Raymond William b: 1/16/1889, St.Louis, Mo. d: 3/19/34, St.Louis, Mo. BR/TR, 5'11", 155 lbs. Deb: 9/30/10

YEAR	TM/L	G	AB	R	H	2B	3B	HR	RBI	BB	SO	AVG	OBP	SLG	PRO+	BR/A	SB	CS	SBR	FA	FR	G/POS	TPR
1910	StL-A	1	5	0	4	0	0	0	0	0	0	.800	.800	.800	428	2	0			.700	0	/3-1	0.2

■ HEINIE JANTZEN
Jantzen, Walter C. b: 4/9/1890, Chicago, Ill. d: 4/1/48, Hines, Ill. BR/TR, 5'11.5", 170 lbs. Deb: 6/29/12

YEAR	TM/L	G	AB	R	H	2B	3B	HR	RBI	BB	SO	AVG	OBP	SLG	PRO+	BR/A	SB	CS	SBR	FA	FR	G/POS	TPR
1912	StL-A	31	119	10	22	1	0	2	8	4		.185	.218	.227	28	-11	3			1.000	3	O-31	-1.0

■ HAL JANVRIN
Janvrin, Harold Chandler "Childe Harold" b: 8/27/1892, Haverhill, Mass. d: 3/1/62, Boston, Mass. BR/TR, 5'11.5", 168 lbs. Deb: 7/9/11

YEAR	TM/L	G	AB	R	H	2B	3B	HR	RBI	BB	SO	AVG	OBP	SLG	PRO+	BR/A	SB	CS	SBR	FA	FR	G/POS	TPR
1911	Bos-A	9	27	2	4	1	0	0	1	3		.148	.258	.185	25	-3	0			.733	-2	/3-5,1-4	-0.5
1913	Bos-A	87	276	18	57	5	1	3	25	23	27	.207	.272	.264	56	-16	17			.923	-10	S-48,3-19/2-8,1-6	-2.4
1914	Bos-A	145	492	65	117	18	6	1	51	38	50	.238	.296	.305	81	-12	29	20	-3	.919	-22	2-59,1-57,S-20/3-6	-4.3
1915	*Bos-A	99	316	41	85	9	1	0	37	14	27	.269	.317	.304	88	-5	8	14	-6	.917	-20	S-64,3-20/2-8	-2.8
1916	*Bos-A	117	310	32	69	11	4	0	26	32	32	.223	.299	.284	75	-9	6			.921	-19	S-59,2-39/1-4,3-4	-2.7
1917	Bos-A	55	127	21	25	3	0	0	8	11	13	.197	.266	.220	49	-8	2			.940	-3	2-38,S-10/1-1	-0.5
1919	Was-A	61	208	17	37	4	1	1	13	19	17	.178	.253	.221	34	-18	8			.927	-27	2-56/S-2	-4.6
	StL-N	7	14	1	3	1	0	0	0	2	1	.214	.313	.286	86	-2	0			1.000	0	/2-2,S-1,3-1	-0.2
1920	StL-N	87	270	33	74	8	4	1	28	17	19	.274	.317	.344	93	-3	5	6	-2	.926	-2	S-27,1-25,O-20/2-6	-0.1
1921	StL-N	18	32	5	9	4	0	0	5	1	0	.281	.303	.313	65	-2	1	0	0	.968	-2	/1-9,2-1	-0.1
	Bro-N	44	92	8	18	4	0	0	14	7	6	.196	.253	.239	30	-9	3	1	-0	.922	-4	S-17,2-10/1-8,3-0	-1.3
	Yr	62	124	13	27	8	0	0	19	8	6	.218	.265	.258	49	-11	4	1	0	.927	-3	1-17,S-17,2-11/30	-1.3
1922	Bro-N	30	57	7	17	3	1	0	1	4	4	.298	.344	.386	89	-1	0			.889	-4	2-15/S-4,3-2,1-1,0	-0.4
Total	10	759	2221	250	515	68	18	6	210	171	197	.232	.292	.287	70	-85	79	41		.907	-110	S-252,2-242,1/30	-20.5

■ ROY JARVIS
Jarvis, Leroy Gilbert b: 6/27/26, Shawnee, Okla. d: 1/13/90, Oklahoma City, Okla. BR/TR, 5'9", 160 lbs. Deb: 4/30/44

YEAR	TM/L	G	AB	R	H	2B	3B	HR	RBI	BB	SO	AVG	OBP	SLG	PRO+	BR/A	SB	CS	SBR	FA	FR	G/POS	TPR
1944	Bro-N	1	1	0	0	0	0	0	0	0	1	.000	.000	.000	-99	-0	0			1.000	-0	/C-1	0.0
1946	Pit-N	2	4	0	1	0	0	0	0	0	1	.250	.400	.250	84	-0	0			.800	-0	/C-1	

YEAR	TM/L	G	AB	R	H	2B	3B	HR	RBI	BB	SO	AVG	OBP	SLG	PRO+	BR/A	SB	CS	SBR	FA	FR	G/POS	TPR
1947	Pit-N	18	45	4	7	1	0	1	4	6	5	.156	.255	.244	32	-4	0			.967	-0	C-15	-0.4
Total	3	21	50	4	8	1	0	1	4	7	7	.160	.263	.240	34	-5	0			.955	-1	/C-17	-0.4

■ PAUL JATA
Jata, Paul b: 9/4/49, Astoria, N.Y. BR/TR, 6'1", 190 lbs. Deb: 4/19/72

YEAR	TM/L	G	AB	R	H	2B	3B	HR	RBI	BB	SO	AVG	OBP	SLG	PRO+	BR/A	SB	CS	SBR	FA	FR	G/POS	TPR
1972	Det-A	32	74	8	17	2	0	0	3	7	14	.230	.296	.257	64	-3	0	1	-1	.991	-1	1-12,O-10/C-1	-0.7

■ AL JAVIER
Javier, Ignacio Alfredo (b: Ignacio Alfredo Wilkes (Javier)) b: 2/4/54, San Pedro De Macoris, D.R. BR/TR, 5'11", 170 lbs. Deb: 9/9/76

YEAR	TM/L	G	AB	R	H	2B	3B	HR	RBI	BB	SO	AVG	OBP	SLG	PRO+	BR/A	SB	CS	SBR	FA	FR	G/POS	TPR
1976	Hou-N	8	24	1	5	0	0	0	0	2	5	.208	.269	.208	41	-2	0	0	0	1.000	-2	/O-7	-0.4

■ JULIAN JAVIER
Javier, Manuel Julian (Liranzo) b: 8/9/36, San Francisco De Macoris, D.R. BR/TR, 6'1", 175 lbs. Deb: 5/28/60 F

YEAR	TM/L	G	AB	R	H	2B	3B	HR	RBI	BB	SO	AVG	OBP	SLG	PRO+	BR/A	SB	CS	SBR	FA	FR	G/POS	TPR
1960	StL-N	119	451	55	107	19	8	4	21	21	72	.237	.273	.341	62	-24	19	4	3	.962	5	*2-119	-0.5
1961	StL-N	113	445	58	124	14	3	2	41	30	51	.279	.327	.337	70	-19	11	4	1	.966	-0	*2-113	-0.6
1962	StL-N	155	598	97	157	25	5	7	39	47	73	.263	.317	.356	73	-22	26	9	2	.977	1	*2-151/S-4	-0.4
1963	StL-N★	161	609	82	160	27	9	9	46	24	86	.263	.297	.381	86	-12	18	10	-1	.969	-14	*2-161	-1.2
1964	*StL-N	155	535	66	129	19	5	12	65	30	82	.241	.283	.363	74	-19	9	7	-2	.966	-7	*2-154	-1.6
1965	StL-N	77	229	34	52	6	4	2	23	8	44	.227	.262	.314	56	-13	5	5	-2	.975	-6	2-69	-1.6
1966	StL-N	147	460	52	105	13	5	7	31	26	63	.228	.271	.324	64	-22	11	5	0	.981	2	*2-145	-1.2
1967	*StL-N	140	520	68	146	16	3	14	64	25	92	.281	.315	.404	106	-2	6	7	-2	.965	-19	*2-138	-1.1
1968	*StL-N★	139	519	54	135	25	4	4	52	24	61	.260	.294	.347	93	-5	10	3	1	.976	-24	*2-139	-2.3
1969	StL-N	143	493	59	139	28	2	10	42	40	74	.282	.337	.408	107	4	8	4	0	.967	-18	*2-141	-0.2
1970	StL-N	139	513	62	129	16	3	2	42	24	70	.251	.286	.306	58	-31	6	4	-1	.980	13	*2-137	-0.8
1971	StL-N	90	259	32	67	6	4	3	28	9	33	.259	.289	.347	76	-8	5	1	1	.978	2	2-80/3-1	-0.1
1972	*Cin-N	44	91	3	19	2	0	1	12	6	11	.209	.258	.297	61	-5	1	0	0	.896	-3	3-19/2-5,1-1	-0.8
Total	13	1622	5722	722	1469	216	55	78	506	314	812	.257	.298	.355	78	-174	135	63	3	.972	-68	*2-1552/3-20,S-4,1	-12.4

■ STAN JAVIER
Javier, Stanley Julian Antonio (De Javier) b: 1/9/64, San Francisco De Macoris, D.R. BB/TR, 6', 185 lbs. Deb: 4/15/84 F

YEAR	TM/L	G	AB	R	H	2B	3B	HR	RBI	BB	SO	AVG	OBP	SLG	PRO+	BR/A	SB	CS	SBR	FA	FR	G/POS	TPR
1984	NY-A	7	7	1	1	0	0	0	0	0	1	.143	.143	.143	-22	-1	0	0	0	1.000	-2	/O-5	-0.3
1986	Oak-A	59	114	13	23	8	0	0	8	16	27	.202	.305	.272	63	-6	8	0	2	1.000	-1	O-51/D-2	-0.5
1987	Oak-A	81	151	22	28	3	1	2	9	19	33	.185	.276	.258	46	-12	3	2	-0	.983	-9	O-71/1-6,D-1	-2.2
1988	*Oak-A	125	397	49	102	13	3	2	35	32	63	.257	.316	.320	81	-10	20	1	5	.980	-13	*O-115/1-4,D-2	-2.1
1989	*Oak-A	112	310	42	77	12	3	1	28	31	45	.248	.319	.316	82	-7	12	2	2	.991	-8	*O-107/1-1,2-1	-1.4
1990	Oak-A	19	33	4	8	0	2	0	3	3	6	.242	.306	.364	90	-0	0	0	0	1.000	-2	O-13/D-1	-0.3
	LA-N	104	276	56	84	9	4	3	24	37	44	.304	.387	.399	120	9	15	7	0	1.000	2	O-87	0.9
1991	LA-N	121	176	21	36	5	3	1	11	16	36	.205	.271	.284	57	-10	7	1	2	.986	-14	O-69/1-2	-2.4
1992	LA-N	56	58	6	11	3	0	1	5	6	11	.190	.277	.293	63	-3	1	2	-1	1.000	-7	O-27	-1.2
	Phi-N	74	276	36	72	14	1	0	24	31	43	.261	.340	.319	88	-3	17	1	5	.986	13	O-74	1.3
	Yr	130	334	42	83	17	1	1	29	37	54	.249	.329	.314	84	-6	18	3	4	.987	5	*O-101	0.1
1993	Cal-A	92	237	33	69	10	4	3	28	27	33	.291	.366	.405	104	2	12	2	2	.981	-11	O-64,1-12/2-2,D-1	-0.9
1994	Oak-A	109	419	75	114	23	0	10	44	49	76	.272	.351	.399	101	1	24	7	3	.986	0	*O-108/1-1,3-1	0.2
1995	Oak-A	130	442	81	123	20	2	8	56	49	63	.278	.356	.387	98	-0	36	5	8	1.000	7	*O-124/3-1	1.0
1996	SF-N	71	274	44	74	25	0	2	22	25	51	.270	.336	.383	93	-3	14	2	3	.984	7	O-71	0.5
Total	12	1160	3170	483	822	145	23	33	297	341	532	.259	.334	.351	89	-43	169	32	32	.990	-39	O-986/1-26,D-8,23	-7.4

■ TEX JEANES
Jeanes, Ernest Lee b: 12/19/1900, Maypearl, Tex. d: 4/5/73, Longview, Tex. BR/TR, 6', 176 lbs. Deb: 4/20/21

YEAR	TM/L	G	AB	R	H	2B	3B	HR	RBI	BB	SO	AVG	OBP	SLG	PRO+	BR/A	SB	CS	SBR	FA	FR	G/POS	TPR
1921	Cle-A	5	3	2	2	1	0	0	4	1	0	.667	.750	1.000	338	1	0	0	0	1.000	-1	/O-5	0.0
1922	Cle-A	1	1	0	0	0	0	0	0	1	0	.000	.500	.000	39	0	0	0	0	.000	-1	/P-1,O-1	0.0
1925	Was-A	15	19	2	5	1	0	0	4	3	2	.263	.364	.474	113	0	1	0	0	1.000	0	O-13	-0.5
1926	Was-A	21	30	6	7	2	0	0	3	0	3	.233	.233	.300	39	-3	0	0	0	1.000	-3	O-14	-0.6
1927	NY-N	11	20	5	6	0	0	0	0	2	2	.300	.364	.300	79	-0	0	0	0	1.000	1	/O-6,P-1	0.0
Total	5	53	73	15	20	4	0	0	11	7	7	.274	.338	.370	85	-2	1	0	0	1.000	-9	/O-39,P-2	-1.1

■ HAL JEFFCOAT
Jeffcoat, Harold Bentley b: 9/6/24, W.Columbia, S.C. BR/TR, 5'10.5", 185 lbs. Deb: 4/20/48 F

YEAR	TM/L	G	AB	R	H	2B	3B	HR	RBI	BB	SO	AVG	OBP	SLG	PRO+	BR/A	SB	CS	SBR	FA	FR	G/POS	TPR
1948	Chi-N	134	473	53	132	16	4	4	42	24	68	.279	.315	.355	85	-11	8			.976	9	*O-119	-0.9
1949	Chi-N	108	363	43	89	18	6	2	26	20	48	.245	.286	.344	70	-16	12			.963	7	*O-101	-1.4
1950	Chi-N	66	179	21	42	13	1	2	18	6	23	.235	.259	.352	60	-11	7			.967	-3	O-53	-1.6
1951	Chi-N	113	278	44	76	20	2	4	27	16	23	.273	.315	.403	90	-4	8	4	0	.989	-2	O-87	-0.8
1952	Chi-N	102	297	29	65	17	2	4	30	15	40	.219	.259	.330	61	-16	7	2	1	.996	3	O-95	-1.6
1953	Chi-N	106	183	22	43	3	1	4	22	21	26	.235	.314	.328	66	-9	5	0	2	.973	-17	*O-100	-2.6
1954	Chi-N	56	31	13	8	2	1	1	6	7	6	.258	.281	.484	94	-0	2	0	1	.889	-1	P-43/O-3	-0.1
1955	Chi-N	52	23	3	4	0	1	0	5	1	3	.174	.240	.304	43	-2	0	0	0	.903	1	P-50	0.0
1956	Cin-N	49	54	5	8	2	0	0	5	3	20	.148	.193	.185	2	-7	0	1	-0	.969	3	P-38	0.0
1957	Cin-N	53	69	13	14	3	1	4	11	5	20	.203	.267	.449	82	-2	0	0	0	.958	-1	P-37	0.0
1958	Cin-N	50	9	2	5	0	0	0	0	1	2	.556	.600	.556	198	1	0	0	0	1.000	1	P-49/O-1	0.0
1959	Cin-N	17	1	1	1	0	0	0	0	0	0	1.000	1.000	2.000	655	1	0	0	0	1.000	0	P-17	0.0
	StL-N	12	3	0	0	0	0	0	0	0	3	.000	.000	.000	-94	-1	0	0	0	1.000	0	P-11	0.0
	Yr	29	4	1	1	0	0	0	0	0	3	.250	.250	.500	90	-0	0	0	0	1.000	0	P-28	0.0
Total	12	918	1963	249	487	95	18	26	188	114	289	.248	.291	.355	73	-78	49	7		.978		O-559,P-245	-9.0

■ GREGG JEFFERIES
Jefferies, Gregory Scott b: 8/1/67, Burlingame, Cal. BB/TR, 5'11", 175 lbs. Deb: 9/6/87

YEAR	TM/L	G	AB	R	H	2B	3B	HR	RBI	BB	SO	AVG	OBP	SLG	PRO+	BR/A	SB	CS	SBR	FA	FR	G/POS	TPR
1987	NY-N	6	6	0	3	1	0	0	2	0	0	.500	.500	.667	217	1	0	0	0	.000	0	/H	0.1
1988	*NY-N	29	109	19	35	8	2	6	17	8	10	.321	.368	.596	181	11	5	1	1	.979	-3	3-20,2-10	0.9
1989	NY-N	141	508	72	131	28	2	12	56	39	46	.258	.317	.392	107	3	21	6	3	.975	-31	*2-123,3-20	-2.3
1990	NY-N	153	604	96	171	40	3	15	68	46	40	.283	.339	.434	111	8	11	2	2	.976	-9	*2-118,3-34	0.4
1991	NY-N	136	486	59	132	19	2	9	62	47	38	.272	.338	.374	101	1	26	5	5	.982	-16	2-77,3-51	-0.9
1992	KC-A	152	604	66	172	36	3	10	75	43	29	.285	.333	.404	103	1	19	9	0	.939	-2	*3-146/2-1,D-1	0.0
1993	StL-N★	142	544	89	186	24	3	16	83	62	32	.342	.408	.485	142	34	46	9	8	.993	-11	*1-140/2-1	1.9
1994	StL-N★	103	397	52	129	27	1	12	55	45	26	.325	.395	.489	131	19	12	5	1	.993	-9	*1-102	0.1
1995	Phi-N	114	480	69	147	31	2	11	56	35	45	.306	.353	.448	109	6	9	5	-0	.994	-2	1-59,O-55	-0.4
1996	Phi-N	104	404	59	118	17	3	5	51	36	21	.292	.351	.401	95	-2	20	6	2	.998	6	1-53,O-51	0.0
Total	10	1080	4142	581	1224	231	21	98	525	361	268	.296	.354	.432	114	82	169	48	22	.994	-77	1-354,2-330,3O/D	-0.2

■ REGGIE JEFFERSON
Jefferson, Reginald Jirod b: 9/25/68, Tallahassee, Fla. BL/TL, 6'4", 210 lbs. Deb: 5/18/91

YEAR	TM/L	G	AB	R	H	2B	3B	HR	RBI	BB	SO	AVG	OBP	SLG	PRO+	BR/A	SB	CS	SBR	FA	FR	G/POS	TPR
1991	Cin-N	5	7	1	1	0	0	1	1	1	1	.143	.250	.571	120	0	0	0	0	1.000	0	/1-2	0.0
	Cle-A	26	101	10	20	3	0	2	12	3	22	.198	.221	.287	39	-8	0	0	0	.993	2	1-26	-0.8
1992	Cle-A	24	89	8	30	6	2	1	6	1	17	.337	.352	.483	134	4	0	0	0	.993	1	1-15/D-7	0.3
1993	Cle-A	113	366	35	91	11	2	10	34	28	78	.249	.311	.372	83	-9	1	3	-1	.976	-0	D-88,1-15	-1.6
1994	Sea-A	63	162	24	53	11	0	8	32	17	32	.327	.394	.543	136	4	0	0	0	.981	0	D-32,1-13/O-2	0.6
1995	*Bos-A	46	121	21	35	8	0	5	26	9	24	.289	.338	.479	106	1	0	0	0	1.000	0	D-32/1-7,O-2	0.3
1996	Bos-A	122	386	67	134	30	4	19	74	25	89	.347	.391	.593	139	22	0	0	0	.969	-3	D-49,O-45,1-16	1.2
Total	6	399	1232	166	364	69	8	46	185	84	264	.295	.345	.476	112	17	1	3	-2	.989	-0	D-208/1-94,O-49	-0.4

■ STAN JEFFERSON
Jefferson, Stanley b: 12/4/62, New York, N.Y. BB/TR, 5'11", 175 lbs. Deb: 9/7/86

YEAR	TM/L	G	AB	R	H	2B	3B	HR	RBI	BB	SO	AVG	OBP	SLG	PRO+	BR/A	SB	CS	SBR	FA	FR	G/POS	TPR
1986	NY-N	14	24	6	5	1	0	1	3	2	8	.208	.296	.375	86	-0	0	0	0	1.000	-1	/O-7	-0.1
1987	SD-N	116	422	59	97	8	7	8	29	39	92	.230	.298	.339	71	-18	34	11	4	.987	-10	*O-107	-2.8
1988	SD-N	49	111	16	16	1	2	1	4	9	22	.144	.215	.216	25	-11	5	1	1	1.000	-4	O-38	-1.7
1989	NY-A	10	12	1	1	0	0	0	0	1	4	.083	.083	.083	-54	-2	1	1	-0	1.000	-3	/O-7,D-1	-0.6
	Bal-A	35	127	19	33	7	0	4	20	4	22	.260	.288	.409	97	-1	9	3	1	.988	1	O-32/D-2	0.1
	Yr	45	139	20	34	7	0	4	21	4	26	.245	.271	.381	84	-4	10	4	1	.988	-2	O-39/D-3	-0.5
1990	Bal-A	10	19	1	0	0	0	0	0	2	8	.000	.095	.000	-74	-4	0	0	0	1.000	-2	/O-5,D-1	-0.6
	Cle-A	49	98	21	27	8	0	2	10	8	18	.276	.343	.418	112	2	8	4	0	.985	0	O-34/D-5	0.1
	Yr	59	117	22	27	8	0	2	10	10	26	.231	.302	.350	83	-3	8	4	0	.987	-2	O-39/D-6	-0.5

YEAR	TM/L	G	AB	R	H	2B	3B	HR	RBI	BB	SO	AVG	OBP	SLG	PRO+	BR/A	SB	CS	SBR	FA	FR	G/POS	TPR
1991	Cin-N	13	19	2	1	0	0	0	0	1	3	.053	.100	.053	-54	-4	2	0	1	1.000	-2	/O-5	-0.5
Total	6	296	832	125	180	25	9	16	67	65	177	.216	.279	.326	66	-40	60	20	6	.990	-20	O-235/D-9	-6.1

■ IRV JEFFRIES
Jeffries, Irvine Franklin b: 9/10/05, Louisville, Ky. d: 6/8/82, Louisville, Ky. BR/TR, 5'10", 175 lbs. Deb: 4/30/30

YEAR	TM/L	G	AB	R	H	2B	3B	HR	RBI	BB	SO	AVG	OBP	SLG	PRO+	BR/A	SB	CS	SBR	FA	FR	G/POS	TPR
1930	Chi-A	40	97	14	23	3	0	2	11	3	2	.237	.275	.330	54	-7	1	2	-1	.976	-3	3-20,S-13	-0.8
1931	Chi-A	79	223	29	50	10	6	2	16	14	9	.224	.270	.296	52	-16	3	0	1	.949	2	3-61/2-6,S-5,0-1	-0.9
1934	Phi-N	56	175	28	43	6	0	4	19	15	10	.246	.305	.349	66	-9	2			.962	4	2-52/3-1	-0.2
Total	3	175	495	71	116	19	6	8	46	32	21	.234	.284	.321	58	-32	6	2		.955	3	/3-82,2-58,S-18,0-1	-1.9

■ CHRIS JELIC
Jelic, Christopher John b: 12/16/63, Bethlehem, Pa. BR/TR, 5'11", 180 lbs. Deb: 9/30/90

YEAR	TM/L	G	AB	R	H	2B	3B	HR	RBI	BB	SO	AVG	OBP	SLG	PRO+	BR/A	SB	CS	SBR	FA	FR	G/POS	TPR
1990	NY-N	4	11	2	1	0	0	1	1	0	3	.091	.091	.364	19	-1	0	0	0	1.000	-1	/O-4	-0.3

■ FRANK JELINCICH
Jelincich, Frank Anthony "Jelly" b: 9/3/19, San Jose, Cal. d: 6/27/92, Rochester, Minn. BR/TR, 6'2", 198 lbs. Deb: 9/6/41

YEAR	TM/L	G	AB	R	H	2B	3B	HR	RBI	BB	SO	AVG	OBP	SLG	PRO+	BR/A	SB	CS	SBR	FA	FR	G/POS	TPR
1941	Chi-N	4	8	0	1	0	0	0	2	1	2	.125	.222	.125	-1	-1	0			1.000	-1	/O-2	-0.2

■ GREG JELKS
Jelks, Gregory Dion b: 8/16/61, Cherokee, Ala. BR/TR, 6'2", 190 lbs. Deb: 8/20/87

YEAR	TM/L	G	AB	R	H	2B	3B	HR	RBI	BB	SO	AVG	OBP	SLG	PRO+	BR/A	SB	CS	SBR	FA	FR	G/POS	TPR
1987	Phi-N	10	11	2	1	1	0	0	0	3	4	.091	.286	.182	26	-1	0	0	0	.750	0	/3-4,1-2,O-1	-0.1

■ STEVE JELTZ
Jeltz, Larry Steven b: 5/28/59, Paris, France BB/TR, 5'11", 180 lbs. Deb: 7/17/83

YEAR	TM/L	G	AB	R	H	2B	3B	HR	RBI	BB	SO	AVG	OBP	SLG	PRO+	BR/A	SB	CS	SBR	FA	FR	G/POS	TPR
1983	Phi-N	13	8	0	1	0	1	0	1	1	2	.125	.222	.125	63	-0	0	0	0	1.000	1	/2-4,S-2,3-2	0.0
1984	Phi-N	28	68	7	14	0	1	1	7	7	11	.206	.280	.279	57	-4	2	1	0	.992	11	S-27/3-1	1.0
1985	Phi-N	89	196	17	37	4	1	0	12	26	55	.189	.284	.219	41	-15	1	1	-0	.958	6	S-86	-0.3
1986	Phi-N	145	439	44	96	11	4	0	36	65	97	.219	.321	.262	60	-22	6	3	0	.967	-2	*S-141	-1.1
1987	Phi-N	114	293	37	68	9	6	0	12	39	54	.232	.324	.304	66	-14	1	2	-1	.971	3	*S-114/O-1	-0.3
1988	Phi-N	148	379	39	71	11	4	0	27	59	58	.187	.297	.237	54	-21	3	0	1	.976	-1	*S-148	-1.1
1989	Phi-N	116	263	28	64	7	3	4	25	45	44	.243	.356	.338	99	1	4	2	0	.985	1	S-63,3-30,2-23/O-1	0.7
1990	KC-A	74	103	11	16	4	0	1	6	6	21	.155	.202	.194	11	-12	1	1	-0	.977	9	2-34,S-23,O-13,3D	-0.3
Total	8	727	1749	183	367	46	20	5	130	248	342	.210	.309	.268	61	-86	18	10	-1	.971	28	S-604/2-61,3-36,OD	-1.4

■ JOHN JENKINS
Jenkins, John Robert b: 7/7/1896, Bosworth, Mo. d: 8/3/68, Columbia, Mo. BR/TR, 5'8", 160 lbs. Deb: 8/5/22

YEAR	TM/L	G	AB	R	H	2B	3B	HR	RBI	BB	SO	AVG	OBP	SLG	PRO+	BR/A	SB	CS	SBR	FA	FR	G/POS	TPR
1922	Chi-A	5	3	0	0	0	0	0	1	0	2	.000	.000	.000	-99	-1	0	0	0	.000	-0	/2-1,S-1	-0.1

■ JOE JENKINS
Jenkins, Joseph Daniel b: 10/12/1890, Shelbyville, Tenn. d: 6/21/74, Fresno, Cal. BR/TR, 5'11", 170 lbs. Deb: 4/30/14

YEAR	TM/L	G	AB	R	H	2B	3B	HR	RBI	BB	SO	AVG	OBP	SLG	PRO+	BR/A	SB	CS	SBR	FA	FR	G/POS	TPR
1914	StL-A	19	32	0	4	1	1	0	0	1	11	.125	.152	.219	12	-4	2			.931	-4	/C-9	-0.8
1917	Chi-A	10	9	0	1	0	0	0	2	0	5	.111	.111	.111	-32	-1	0			.000	0	/C-1	-0.2
1919	Chi-A	11	19	0	3	0	0	0	1	1	1	.158	.200	.211	15	-2	1			.824	-2	/C-4	-0.4
Total	3	40	60	0	8	2	1	0	3	2	17	.133	.161	.200	6	-7	3			.891	-6	/C-14	-1.4

■ TOM JENKINS
Jenkins, Thomas Griffith "Tut" b: 4/10/1898, Camden, Ala. d: 5/3/79, Weymouth, Mass. BL/TR, 6'1.5", 174 lbs. Deb: 9/15/25

YEAR	TM/L	G	AB	R	H	2B	3B	HR	RBI	BB	SO	AVG	OBP	SLG	PRO+	BR/A	SB	CS	SBR	FA	FR	G/POS	TPR
1925	Bos-A	15	64	9	19	2	1	0	5	3	4	.297	.338	.359	77	-2	0	0	0	.938	-1	O-15	-0.5
1926	Bos-A	21	50	3	9	1	1	0	6	3	7	.180	.226	.240	22	-6	0	0	0	1.000	-1	O-13	-0.8
	Phi-A	6	23	3	4	2	0	0	0	0	2	.174	.174	.261	12	-3	0	0	0	1.000	-1	/O-6	-0.3
	Yr	27	73	6	13	3	1	0	6	3	9	.178	.211	.247	19	-9	0	0	0	1.000	-1	O-19	-1.1
1929	StL-A	21	22	1	4	0	1	0	4	8		.182	.308	.273	49	-2	0	0	0	1.000	-1	/O-3	-0.3
1930	StL-A	2	8	1	2	1	1	0	3	0	1	.250	.250	.625	110	0	0	0	0	1.000	-0	/O-2	0.0
1931	StL-A	81	230	20	61	7	3	2	25	17	25	.265	.316	.352	73	-9	1	3	-2	.952	-4	O-58	-1.7
1932	StL-A	25	62	5	20	1	0	0	5	1	6	.323	.333	.339	70	-3	0	0	0	.939	-2	O-12	-0.2
Total	6	171	459	42	119	14	6	3	44	28	53	.259	.303	.336	64	-25	1	3	-2	.958	-6	O-109	-3.8

■ ALAMAZOO JENNINGS
Jennings, Alfred Gorden b: 11/30/1850, Newport, Ky. d: 11/2/1894, Cincinnati, Ohio Deb: 8/15/1878 U

YEAR	TM/L	G	AB	R	H	2B	3B	HR	RBI	BB	SO	AVG	OBP	SLG	PRO+	BR/A	SB	CS	SBR	FA	FR	G/POS	TPR
1878	Mil-N	1	2	0	0	0	0	0	0	1	0	.000	.333	.000	16	-0				.429	-2	/C-1	-0.2

■ HUGHIE JENNINGS
Jennings, Hugh Ambrose "Ee-Yah" b: 4/2/1869, Pittston, Pa. d: 2/1/28, Scranton, Pa. BR/TR, 5'8.5", 165 lbs. Deb: 6/1/1891 MCH

YEAR	TM/L	G	AB	R	H	2B	3B	HR	RBI	BB	SO	AVG	OBP	SLG	PRO+	BR/A	SB	CS	SBR	FA	FR	G/POS	TPR
1891	Lou-a	90	360	53	105	10	8	1	58	17	36	.292	.339	.372	105	1	12			.894	7	S-70,1-17/3-3	1.0
1892	Lou-N	152	594	65	132	16	4	2	61	30	30	.222	.270	.273	70	-22	28			.907	15	*S-152	0.0
1893	Lou-N	23	88	6	12	3	0	0	9	3	3	.136	.174	.170	-9	-14	0			.899	6	S-23	-0.6
	Bal-N	16	55	6	14	0	0	1	6	4	3	.255	.339	.309	71	-2	0			.886	-2	S-15/O-1	-0.3
	Yr	39	143	12	26	3	0	1	15	7	6	.182	.240	.224	25	-16	0			.895	4	S-38/O-1	-0.9
1894	*Bal-N	128	501	134	168	28	16	4	109	37	17	.335	.411	.479	109	7	37			.928	33	*S-128	3.6
1895	*Bal-N	131	529	159	204	41	7	4	125	24	17	.386	.444	.512	142	34	53			.940	36	*S-131	6.0
1896	*Bal-N	130	521	125	209	27	9	0	121	19	11	.401	.472	.488	151	42	70			.928	34	*S-130	6.7
1897	*Bal-N	117	439	133	156	26	9	2	79	42		.355	.463	.469	146	35	60			.933	27	*S-115,2-27/O-1	5.4
1898	Bal-N	143	534	135	175	25	11	1	87	78		.328	.454	.421	149	42	28			.929	-0	*S-115/2-27/O-1	4.5
1899	Bro-N	16	41	7	7	0	0	0	6	9		.171	.346	.268	68	-1	4			.825	-1	S-11/1-4	-0.6
	Bal-N	2	8	2	3	0	2	0	4	0		.375	.375	.875	227	1	0			1.000	-1	/2-2	0.0
	Bro-N	51	175	35	57	3	8	0	34	13		.326	.424	.434	133	9	14			.987	-8	1-46/2-1,S-1	0.7
	Yr	69	224	44	67	3	12	0	42	22		.299	.408	.420	124	9	18			.985	-8	1-50,S-12/2-3	0.1
1900	*Bro-N	115	441	61	120	18	6	1	69	31		.272	.348	.347	87	-8	31			.982	5	*1-112/2-2	-0.3
1901	Phi-N	82	302	38	79	21	2	1	39	25		.262	.342	.354	100	1	13			.979	-3	1-80/2-1,S-1	-0.3
1902	Phi-N	78	290	32	79	13	4	1	32	14		.272	.330	.355	111	4	8			.983	2	1-69/S-5,2-4	0.5
1903	Bro-N	6	17	2	4	0	0	0	0	1	1	.235	.316	.235	60	-1	1			1.000	-0	/O-4	-0.1
1907	Det-A	1	4	0	1	0	0	0	2	0		.250	.250	.500	133	0	0			.750	-1	/2-1,S-1,M	-0.1
1909	Det-A	2	4	1	2	0	0	0	2	0		.500	.500	.500	207	0	0			1.000	-0	/1-2,M	0.1
1912	Det-A	1	1	0	0	0	0	0	0	0		.000	.000	.000	-99	-0	0			.000	0	HM	0.0
1918	Det-A	1	1	0	0							—	—	—		—	—			1.000	-0	/1-1,M	0.0
Total	17	1285	4904	994	1527	232	88	18	840	347	117	.311	.390	.406	117	127	359			.922	150	S-899,1-331/203	26.2

■ DOUG JENNINGS
Jennings, James Douglas b: 9/30/64, Atlanta, Ga. BL/TL, 5'10", 175 lbs. Deb: 4/8/88

YEAR	TM/L	G	AB	R	H	2B	3B	HR	RBI	BB	SO	AVG	OBP	SLG	PRO+	BR/A	SB	CS	SBR	FA	FR	G/POS	TPR
1988	Oak-A	71	101	9	21	6	0	1	15	21	28	.208	.355	.297	88	0	0	1	-1	1.000	-3	O-23,1-14/D-2	-0.5
1989	Oak-A	4	4	0	0	0	0	0	0	2	2	.000	.000	.000	-99	-1	0	0	0	1.000	-1	/O-3	-0.2
1990	*Oak-A	64	156	19	30	7	2	2	14	17	48	.192	.280	.301	65	-7	0	3	-2	.984	-8	O-45/1-4,D-8	-1.9
1991	Oak-A	8	9	0	1	0	0	0	0	2	1	.111	.273	.111	11	-1	0	1	-1	1.000	0	/O-6	-0.2
1993	Chi-N	42	52	8	13	3	1	2	8	3	10	.250	.316	.462	107	0	0	0	0	1.000	1	1-10	-0.1
Total	5	189	322	36	65	16	3	5	37	43	90	.202	.307	.317	76	-10	0	5	-3	.991	-13	O-77,1-28,D-10	-2.9

■ ROBIN JENNINGS
Jennings, Robin Christopher b: 4/11/72, Singapore BL/TL, 6'2", 205 lbs. Deb: 4/18/96

YEAR	TM/L	G	AB	R	H	2B	3B	HR	RBI	BB	SO	AVG	OBP	SLG	PRO+	BR/A	SB	CS	SBR	FA	FR	G/POS	TPR
1996	Chi-N	31	58	7	13	5	0	0	4	3	9	.224	.274	.310	53	-4	1	0	0	1.000	0	O-11	-0.3

■ BILL JENNINGS
Jennings, William Lee b: 9/28/25, St.Louis, Mo. BR/TR, 6'2", 175 lbs. Deb: 7/19/51

YEAR	TM/L	G	AB	R	H	2B	3B	HR	RBI	BB	SO	AVG	OBP	SLG	PRO+	BR/A	SB	CS	SBR	FA	FR	G/POS	TPR
1951	StL-A	64	195	20	35	10	2	0	13	26	42	.179	.276	.251	42	-16	1	0	0	.953	-5	S-64	-1.6

■ WOODY JENSEN
Jensen, Forrest Docenus b: 8/11/07, Bremerton, Wash. BL/TL, 5'10.5", 160 lbs. Deb: 4/20/31

YEAR	TM/L	G	AB	R	H	2B	3B	HR	RBI	BB	SO	AVG	OBP	SLG	PRO+	BR/A	SB	CS	SBR	FA	FR	G/POS	TPR
1931	Pit-N	73	267	43	65	5	4	3	17	10	18	.243	.276	.326	62	-15	4			.974	5	O-67	-1.4
1932	Pit-N	7	5	2	0	0	0	0	0	0	2	.000	.000	.000	-99	-1	0			.000	-1	/O-1	-0.2
1933	Pit-N	70	196	29	58	7	3	0	15	8	2	.296	.330	.362	98	-1	1			.980	-0	O-66	-0.3
1934	Pit-N	88	283	34	82	13	4	0	27	4	13	.290	.304	.364	76	-10	2			.993	-3	O-66	-1.4
1935	Pit-N	143	627	97	203	28	7	8	62	15	14	.324	.344	.429	103	-3	9			.977	-4	*O-140	-0.7
1936	Pit-N	153	696	98	197	34	10	10	58	16	19	.283	.305	.404	87	-14	2			.975	1	*O-153	-2.0
1937	Pit-N	124	509	77	142	23	9	5	45	15	29	.279	.301	.389	86	-11	2			.963	-0	*O-120	-1.6
1938	Pit-N	68	125	12	25	4	0	0	10	1	3	.200	.213	.232	22	-13	0			.900	-11	O-38	-2.6
1939	Pit-N	12	12	0	2	0	0	0	0	0	0	.167	.167	.167	-10	-2	0			1.000	0	/O-3	-0.3
Total	9	738	2720	392	774	114	37	26	235	69	100	.285	.307	.382	84	-66	20			.972	-13	O-628	-10.5

YEAR	TM/L	G	AB	R	H	2B	3B	HR	RBI	BB	SO	AVG	OBP	SLG	PRO+	BR/A	SB	CS	SBR	FA	FR	G/POS	TPR

■ JACKIE JENSEN
Jensen, Jack Eugene   b: 3/9/27, San Francisco, Cal.   d: 7/14/82, Charlottesville, Va.   BR/TR, 5'11", 190 lbs.   Deb: 4/18/50

YEAR	TM/L	G	AB	R	H	2B	3B	HR	RBI	BB	SO	AVG	OBP	SLG	PRO+	BR/A	SB	CS	SBR	FA	FR	G/POS	TPR
1950	*NY-A	45	70	13	12	2	2	1	5	7	8	.171	.247	.300	41	-7	4	0	1	.947	-4	O-23	-1.0
1951	NY-A	56	168	30	50	8	1	8	25	18	18	.298	.369	.500	138	8	8	2	1	.974	1	O-48	0.8
1952	NY-A	7	19	3	2	1	1	0	2	4	4	.105	.261	.263	49	-1	1	0	0	1.000	-1	/O-5	-0.3
	Was-A★	144	570	80	163	29	5	10	80	63	40	.286	.360	.407	117	13	17	6	2	.977	6	*O-143	1.5
	Yr	151	589	83	165	30	6	10	82	67	44	.280	.357	.402	115	12	18	6	2	.978	5	*O-148	1.2
1953	Was-A	147	552	87	147	32	8	10	84	73	51	.266	.357	.408	109	7	18	8	1	.983	-4	*O-146	-0.2
1954	Bos-A	152	580	92	160	25	7	25	117	79	52	.276	.365	.472	115	11	22	7		.986	-7	*O-151	0.0
1955	Bos-A★	152	574	95	158	27	6	26	116	89	63	.275	.375	.479	118	14	16	7	1	.977	1	*O-150	0.9
1956	Bos-A	151	578	80	182	23	11	20	97	89	43	.315	.407	.497	123	19	11	3	2	.962	2	*O-151	1.4
1957	Bos-A	145	544	82	153	29	2	23	103	75	66	.281	.370	.469	121	16	8	5	-1	.960	4	*O-144	1.2
1958	Bos-A★	154	548	83	157	31	0	35	122	99	65	.286	.398	.535	144	35	9	4	0	.981	3	*O-153	3.1
1959	Bos-A	148	535	101	148	31	0	28	112	88	67	.277	.379	.492	131	24	20	5	3	.982	15	*O-146	3.4
1961	Bos-A	137	498	64	131	21	2	13	66	66	69	.263	.353	.392	96	-2	9	8	-2	.986	11	*O-131	0.0
Total	11	1438	5236	810	1463	259	45	199	929	750	546	.279	.372	.460	119	138	143	55	10	.977	28	*O-1391	10.8

■ MARCUS JENSEN
Jensen, Marcus C.   b: 12/14/72, Oakland, Cal.   BB/TR, 6'4", 195 lbs.   Deb: 4/14/96

YEAR	TM/L	G	AB	R	H	2B	3B	HR	RBI	BB	SO	AVG	OBP	SLG	PRO+	BR/A	SB	CS	SBR	FA	FR	G/POS	TPR
1996	SF-N	9	19	4	4	1	0	0	4	8	7	.211	.444	.263	96	1	0	0	0	.955	-0	/C-7	0.1

■ DAN JESSEE
Jessee, Daniel Edward   b: 2/22/01, Olive Hill, Ky.   d: 4/30/70, Venice, Fla.   BL/TR, 5'10", 165 lbs.   Deb: 8/14/29

YEAR	TM/L	G	AB	R	H	2B	3B	HR	RBI	BB	SO	AVG	OBP	SLG	PRO+	BR/A	SB	CS	SBR	FA	FR	G/POS	TPR
1929	Cle-A	1	0	0	0	0	0	0	0	0	0	—	—	—			0	0	0	.000	0	R	0.0

■ GARRY JESTADT
Jestadt, Garry Arthur   b: 3/19/47, Chicago, Ill.   BR/TR, 6'2", 188 lbs.   Deb: 9/17/69

YEAR	TM/L	G	AB	R	H	2B	3B	HR	RBI	BB	SO	AVG	OBP	SLG	PRO+	BR/A	SB	CS	SBR	FA	FR	G/POS	TPR
1969	Mon-N	6	6	1	0	0	0	0	1	0	0	.000	.000	.000	-99	-2	0	0	0	.667	-0	/S-1	-0.2
1971	Chi-N	3	3	0	0	0	0	0	0	0	0	.000	.000	.000	-87	-1	0	0	0	.000	0	/3-1	-0.1
	SD-N	75	189	17	55	13	0	0	13	11	24	.291	.330	.360	102	0	1	3	-2	.935	11	3-49,2-23/S-1	1.1
	Yr	78	192	17	55	13	0	0	13	11	24	.286	.325	.354	98	-1	1	3	-2	.935	11	3-50,2-23/S-1	1.0
1972	SD-N	92	256	15	63	5	1	6	22	13	21	.246	.283	.344	83	-7	0	0	0	.944	-17	2-48,3-25/S-3	-2.4
Total	3	176	454	33	118	18	1	6	36	24	45	.260	.297	.344	87	-9	1	3	-2	.942	-7	/3-75,2-71,S-5	-1.6

■ DEREK JETER
Jeter, Derek Sanderson   b: 6/26/74, Pequannock, N.J.   BR/TR, 6'3", 175 lbs.   Deb: 5/29/95

YEAR	TM/L	G	AB	R	H	2B	3B	HR	RBI	BB	SO	AVG	OBP	SLG	PRO+	BR/A	SB	CS	SBR	FA	FR	G/POS	TPR
1995	NY-A	15	48	5	12	4	1	0	7	3	11	.250	.294	.375	73	-2	0	0	0	.962	-1	S-15	-0.2
1996	*NY-A	157	582	104	183	25	6	10	78	48	102	.314	.376	.430	101	2	14	7	0	.969	-3	*S-157	1.3
Total	2	172	630	109	195	29	7	10	85	51	113	.310	.370	.425	99	0	14	7	0	.969	-4	S-172	1.1

■ JOHNNY JETER
Jeter, John   b: 10/24/44, Shreveport, La.   BR/TR, 6'1", 180 lbs.   Deb: 6/14/69   F

YEAR	TM/L	G	AB	R	H	2B	3B	HR	RBI	BB	SO	AVG	OBP	SLG	PRO+	BR/A	SB	CS	SBR	FA	FR	G/POS	TPR
1969	Pit-N	28	29	7	9	1	1	6	3	15	.310	.375	.517	151	2	1	1	-0	1.000	-4	O-20	-0.2
1970	*Pit-N	85	126	27	30	3	2	2	12	13	34	.238	.314	.341	77	-4	9	5	-0	1.000	-8	O-56	-1.4
1971	SD-N	18	75	8	24	4	0	1	3	2	16	.320	.338	.413	120	2	2	0	1	.967	4	O-17	0.6
1972	SD-N	110	326	25	72	4	3	7	21	24	92	.221	.266	.316	70	-14	11	5	0	.987	1	O-91	-1.8
1973	Chi-A	89	300	38	72	14	4	7	26	9	74	.240	.262	.383	77	-10	4	3	-1	.955	-3	O-72/D-3	-1.8
1974	Cle-A	6	17	3	6	1	0	1	1	6	.353	.389	.412	132	1	1	2	-1	.833	-2	/O-6	-0.2
Total	6	336	873	108	213	27	10	18	69	46	237	.244	.284	.360	82	-24	28	16	-1	.975	-11	O-262/D-3	-4.8

■ SHAWN JETER
Jeter, Shawn Darrell   b: 6/28/66, Shreveport, La.   BL/TR, 6'2", 185 lbs.   Deb: 6/13/92   F

YEAR	TM/L	G	AB	R	H	2B	3B	HR	RBI	BB	SO	AVG	OBP	SLG	PRO+	BR/A	SB	CS	SBR	FA	FR	G/POS	TPR
1992	Chi-A	13	18	1	2	0	0	0	0	0	7	.111	.111	.111	-38	-3	0	0	0	.909	-2	/O-8,D-3	-0.5

■ SAM JETHROE
Jethroe, Samuel "Jet"   b: 1/20/18, E.St.Louis, Ill.   BB/TR, 6'1", 178 lbs.   Deb: 4/18/50

YEAR	TM/L	G	AB	R	H	2B	3B	HR	RBI	BB	SO	AVG	OBP	SLG	PRO+	BR/A	SB	CS	SBR	FA	FR	G/POS	TPR
1950	Bos-N	141	582	100	159	28	8	18	58	52	93	.273	.338	.442	110	7	**35**			.969	8	*O-141	0.9
1951	Bos-N	148	572	101	160	29	10	18	65	57	88	.280	.356	.460	127	20	**35**	5	8	.974	7	*O-140	2.9
1952	Bos-N	151	608	79	141	23	7	13	58	68	112	.232	.318	.357	90	-8	28	9	3	.970	-1	*O-151	-0.8
1954	Pit-N	2	1	0	0	0	0	0	0	0	0	.000	.000	.000	-99	-0	0	0	0	1.000	-0	/O-1	-0.1
Total	4	442	1763	280	460	80	25	49	181	177	293	.261	.337	.418	108	18	98	<u>14</u>		.971	19	O-433	2.9

■ NAT JEWETT
Jewett, Nathan W.   b: 12/25/1842, New York, N.Y.   d: 2/23/14, Bronx, N.Y.   5'6", 137 lbs.   Deb: 7/4/1872

YEAR	TM/L	G	AB	R	H	2B	3B	HR	RBI	BB	SO	AVG	OBP	SLG	PRO+	BR/A	SB	CS	SBR	FA	FR	G/POS	TPR
1872	Eck-n	2	8	1	1	0	0	0	0	0	0	.125	.125	.125	-27	-1	0	0	0	.700	-2	/C-2	-0.2

■ HOUSTON JIMENEZ
Jimenez, Alfonso (Gonzalez)   b: 10/30/57, Navojoa, Mexico   BR/TR, 5'8", 144 lbs.   Deb: 6/13/83

YEAR	TM/L	G	AB	R	H	2B	3B	HR	RBI	BB	SO	AVG	OBP	SLG	PRO+	BR/A	SB	CS	SBR	FA	FR	G/POS	TPR
1983	Min-A	36	86	5	15	4	0	0	9	4	11	.174	.211	.256	27	-9	0	1	-1	.969	4	S-36	-0.3
1984	Min-A	108	298	28	60	11	1	0	19	15	34	.201	.240	.245	33	-27	0	1	-1	.959	-5	*S-107	-2.4
1987	Pit-N	5	6	0	0	0	0	0	0	1	2	.000	.143	.000	-58	-1	0	0	0	1.000	1	/2-2,S-2	0.0
1988	Cle-A	9	21	1	1	1	0	0	1	0	2	.048	.048	.048	-71	-5	0	0	0	.973	-5	/2-7,S-2	0.1
Total	4	158	411	34	76	16	2	0	29	20	49	.185	.223	.234	25	-42	0	2	-1	.962	7	S-147/2-9	-2.6

■ ELVIO JIMENEZ
Jimenez, Felix Elvio (Rivera)   b: 1/6/40, San Pedro De Macoris, D.R.   BR/TR, 5'9", 170 lbs.   Deb: 10/4/64   F

YEAR	TM/L	G	AB	R	H	2B	3B	HR	RBI	BB	SO	AVG	OBP	SLG	PRO+	BR/A	SB	CS	SBR	FA	FR	G/POS	TPR
1964	NY-A	1	6	0	2	0	0	0	0	0	0	.333	.333	.333	85	-0	0	0	0	1.000	0	/O-1	0.0

■ MANNY JIMENEZ
Jimenez, Manuel Emilio (Rivera)   b: 11/19/38, San Pedro De Macoris, D.R.   BL/TR, 6'1", 195 lbs.   Deb: 4/11/62   F

YEAR	TM/L	G	AB	R	H	2B	3B	HR	RBI	BB	SO	AVG	OBP	SLG	PRO+	BR/A	SB	CS	SBR	FA	FR	G/POS	TPR
1962	KC-A	139	479	48	144	24	2	11	69	31	34	.301	.357	.428	105	4	0	1	-1	.985	-5	*O-122	-0.9
1963	KC-A	60	157	12	44	9	0	5	15	16	14	.280	.365	.338	93	-1	0	1	-1	.960	1	O-40	-0.2
1964	KC-A	95	204	19	46	7	0	12	38	15	24	.225	.295	.436	97	-1	0	0	0	.939	-4	O-49	-0.7
1966	KC-A	13	35	1	4	0	1	0	4	1	6	.114	.244	.171	22	-3	0	0	0	.909	-2	O-12	-0.7
1967	Pit-N	50	56	3	14	2	0	2	10	1	4	.250	.276	.393	89	-1	0	0	0	1.000	-1	/O-6	-0.3
1968	Pit-N	66	66	7	20	1	1	1	11	6	15	.303	.403	.394	142	4	0	0	0	.857	-1	/O-5	0.3
1969	Chi-N	6	6	0	1	0	0	0	0	2	.167	.167	.167	-6	-1	0	0	0	.000	0	H	-0.1
Total	7	429	1003	90	273	43	4	26	144	75	97	.272	.339	.401	100	0	0	2	-1	.966	-11	O-234	-2.6

■ TOMMY JOHNS
Johns, Thomas Pearce   b: 9/7/1851, Baltimore, Md.   d: 4/13/27, Baltimore, Md.   Deb: 5/14/1873

YEAR	TM/L	G	AB	R	H	2B	3B	HR	RBI	BB	SO	AVG	OBP	SLG	PRO+	BR/A	SB	CS	SBR	FA	FR	G/POS	TPR
1873	Mar-n	1	4	0	0	0	0	0	0	0	0	.000	.000	.000	-99	-1	0	0	0	.000	-1	/O-1	-0.1

■ PETE JOHNS
Johns, William R.   b: 1/17/1889, Cleveland, Ohio   d: 8/9/64, Cleveland, Ohio   BR/TR, 5'10", 165 lbs.   Deb: 8/25/15

YEAR	TM/L	G	AB	R	H	2B	3B	HR	RBI	BB	SO	AVG	OBP	SLG	PRO+	BR/A	SB	CS	SBR	FA	FR	G/POS	TPR
1915	Chi-A	28	100	7	21	2	1	0	11	8	11	.210	.275	.250	56	-6	2	7	-4	.943	4	3-28	-0.5
1918	StL-A	46	89	5	16	1	1	0	11	4	6	.180	.215	.213	30	-8	0			.990	-1	1-10/S-4,3-4,0-4,2	-1.1
Total	2	74	189	12	37	3	2	0	22	12	17	.196	.248	.233	44	-13	2	<u>7</u>		.929	2	/3-32,1-10,0-4,S2	-1.6

■ ABBIE JOHNSON
Johnson, Albert L.   b: 7/26/1872, London, Ont., Can.   5'9.5", 165 lbs.   Deb: 9/1/1896

YEAR	TM/L	G	AB	R	H	2B	3B	HR	RBI	BB	SO	AVG	OBP	SLG	PRO+	BR/A	SB	CS	SBR	FA	FR	G/POS	TPR
1896	Lou-N	25	87	10	20	2	1	0	14	4	6	.230	.264	.276	44	-7	0			.937	-5	2-25	-0.9
1897	Lou-N	48	161	16	39	6	1	0	23	13		.242	.303	.292	59	-9	2			.879	-11	2-33,S-12	-1.6
Total	2	73	248	26	59	8	2	0	37	17	<u>6</u>	.238	.289	.286	54	-16	2			.903	-15	/2-58,S-12	-2.5

■ ALEX JOHNSON
Johnson, Alexander   b: 12/7/42, Helena, Ark.   BR/TR, 6', 205 lbs.   Deb: 7/25/64

YEAR	TM/L	G	AB	R	H	2B	3B	HR	RBI	BB	SO	AVG	OBP	SLG	PRO+	BR/A	SB	CS	SBR	FA	FR	G/POS	TPR
1964	Phi-N	43	109	18	33	7	1	4	18	6	26	.303	.345	.495	135	5	1	2	-1	.980	-1	O-35	0.2
1965	Phi-N	97	262	27	77	9	3	8	28	15	60	.294	.337	.443	120	6	4	4	-1	.966	-5	O-82	-0.2
1966	StL-N	25	86	7	16	0	1	2	6	5	18	.186	.231	.279	41	-7	1	1	-0	.962	-1	O-22	-1.0
1967	StL-N	81	175	20	39	9	2	1	12	9	26	.223	.273	.314	68	-7	6	3	0	.970	0	O-57	-1.0
1968	Cin-N	149	603	79	188	32	6	2	58	26	71	.312	.343	.395	114	10	16	6	1	.947	5	*O-140	0.9
1969	Cin-N	139	523	86	165	18	4	17	88	25	69	.315	.352	.463	122	14	11	8	-2	.927	1	*O-132	0.7
1970	Cal-A★	156	614	85	202	26	6	14	86	35	68	**.329**	.372	.459	133	26	17	2	4	.959	-5	*O-156	2.7
1971	Cal-A	65	242	19	63	8	0	2	21	15	34	.260	.309	.318	84	-6	5	2	0	.926	-6	O-61	-1.5
1972	Cle-A	108	356	31	85	10	1	8	37	22	40	.239	.285	.340	83	-8	6	3	-3	.955	-5	O-95	-2.4
1973	Tex-A	158	624	62	179	26	3	8	68	32	82	.287	.324	.377	101	-1	10	5	0	.987	1	*D-116,O-41	-0.4
1974	Tex-A	114	453	57	132	14	3	4	41	28	59	.291	.338	.362	104	2	20	9	1	.956	6	O-81,D-32	0.4

YEAR	TM/L	G	AB	R	H	2B	3B	HR	RBI	BB	SO	AVG	OBP	SLG	PRO+	BR/A	SB	CS	SBR	FA	FR	G/POS	TPR
	NY-A	10	28	3	6	1	0	1	2	0	3	.214	.214	.357	63	-1	0	0	0	.000	-0	/O-1,D-4	-0.2
	Yr	124	481	60	138	15	3	5	43	28	62	.287	.331	.362	102	1	20	9	1	.956	5	O-82,D-36	0.2
1975	NY-A	52	119	15	31	5	1	1	15	7	21	.261	.302	.345	84	-3	2	3	-1	1.000	-1	D-28/O-7	-0.6
1976	Det-A	125	429	41	115	15	2	6	45	19	49	.268	.302	.354	88	-7	14	10	-2	.954	-3	O-90,D-19	-1.8
Total	13	1322	4623	550	1331	180	33	78	525	244	626	.288	.329	.392	105	22	113	63	-4	.953	-5	O-1000,D-199	-4.2

■ TONY JOHNSON
Johnson, Anthony Clair b: 6/23/56, Memphis, Tenn. BR/TR, 6'3", 145 lbs. Deb: 9/28/81

YEAR	TM/L	G	AB	R	H	2B	3B	HR	RBI	BB	SO	AVG	OBP	SLG	PRO+	BR/A	SB	CS	SBR	FA	FR	G/POS	TPR
1981	Mon-N	2	1	0	0	0	0	0	0	0	0	.000	.000	.000	-99	-0	0	0	0	.000	-0	/O-1	-0.1
1982	Tor-A	70	98	17	23	2	1	3	14	11	26	.235	.312	.367	79	-3	3	13	-7	.979	-2	O-28,D-28	-1.4
Total	2	72	99	17	23	2	1	3	14	11	26	.232	.309	.364	77	-3	3	13	-7	.979	-3	/O-29,D-28	-1.5

■ BOB JOHNSON
Johnson, Bobby Earl b: 7/31/59, Dallas, Tex. BR/TR, 6'3", 195 lbs. Deb: 9/1/81

YEAR	TM/L	G	AB	R	H	2B	3B	HR	RBI	BB	SO	AVG	OBP	SLG	PRO+	BR/A	SB	CS	SBR	FA	FR	G/POS	TPR
1981	Tex-A	6	18	2	5	0	0	2	4	1	3	.278	.316	.611	171	1	0	0	0	1.000	-1	/C-5,1-1	0.1
1982	Tex-A	20	56	4	7	2	0	2	7	3	22	.125	.183	.268	23	-6	0	1	-1	1.000	0	C-14/1-3	-0.6
1983	Tex-A	72	175	18	37	6	1	5	16	16	55	.211	.281	.343	72	-7	3	0	1	1.000	3	C-62,1-10	-0.1
Total	3	98	249	24	49	8	1	9	27	20	80	.197	.262	.345	68	-12	3	1	0	1.000	3	/C-81,1-14	-0.6

■ BRIAN JOHNSON
Johnson, Brian David b: 1/8/68, Oakland, Cal. BR/TR, 6'2", 210 lbs. Deb: 4/5/94

YEAR	TM/L	G	AB	R	H	2B	3B	HR	RBI	BB	SO	AVG	OBP	SLG	PRO+	BR/A	SB	CS	SBR	FA	FR	G/POS	TPR
1994	SD-N	36	93	7	23	4	1	3	16	5	21	.247	.286	.409	81	-3	0	0	0	1.000	2	C-24/1-5	0.1
1995	SD-N	68	207	20	52	9	0	3	29	11	39	.251	.292	.338	68	-10	0	0	0	.993	1	C-55/1-2	-0.5
1996	*SD-N	82	243	18	66	13	1	8	35	4	36	.272	.295	.432	93	-3	0	0	0	.989	1	C-66/1-1,3-1	0.1
Total	3	186	543	45	141	26	2	14	80	20	96	.260	.292	.392	81	-16	0	0	0	.993	4	C-145/1-8,3-1	-0.3

■ CALEB JOHNSON
Johnson, Caleb Clark b: 5/23/1844, Fulton, Ill. d: 3/7/25, Sterling, Ill. Deb: 5/24/1871

YEAR	TM/L	G	AB	R	H	2B	3B	HR	RBI	BB	SO	AVG	OBP	SLG	PRO+	BR/A	SB	CS	SBR	FA	FR	G/POS	TPR
1871	Cle-n	16	67	10	15	1	0	0	7	0	1	.224	.224	.239	35	-5	1	0	0	.736	-5	2-10/O-6	-0.7

■ CHARLIE JOHNSON
Johnson, Charles Cleveland "Home Run" b: 3/12/1885, Slatington, Pa. d: 8/28/40, Marcus Hook, Pa. BL/TL, 5'9", 150 lbs. Deb: 9/21/08

YEAR	TM/L	G	AB	R	H	2B	3B	HR	RBI	BB	SO	AVG	OBP	SLG	PRO+	BR/A	SB	CS	SBR	FA	FR	G/POS	TPR
1908	Phi-N	6	16	2	4	0	1	0	2	1		.250	.333	.375	122	-0	0	0	0	1.000	-0	/O-4	0.0

■ CHARLES JOHNSON
Johnson, Charles Edward b: 7/20/71, Fort Pierce, Fla. BR/TR, 6'2", 215 lbs. Deb: 5/6/94

YEAR	TM/L	G	AB	R	H	2B	3B	HR	RBI	BB	SO	AVG	OBP	SLG	PRO+	BR/A	SB	CS	SBR	FA	FR	G/POS	TPR
1994	Fla-N	4	11	5	5	1	0	1	4	1	4	.455	.500	.818	229	2	0	0	0	1.000	0	/C-4	0.2
1995	Fla-N	97	315	40	79	15	1	11	39	46	71	.251	.353	.410	100	1	0	2	-1	.992	-0	C-97	0.6
1996	Fla-N	120	386	34	84	13	1	13	37	40	91	.218	.294	.358	74	-15	1	0	0	.995	6	*C-120	0.8
Total	3	221	712	79	168	29	2	25	80	87	166	.236	.324	.388	88	-12	1	2	-1	.994	6	C-221	0.8

■ CLIFF JOHNSON
Johnson, Clifford b: 7/22/47, San Antonio, Tex. BR/TR, 6'4", 225 lbs. Deb: 9/13/72

YEAR	TM/L	G	AB	R	H	2B	3B	HR	RBI	BB	SO	AVG	OBP	SLG	PRO+	BR/A	SB	CS	SBR	FA	FR	G/POS	TPR
1972	Hou-N	5	4	0	1	0	0	0	0	2	1	.250	.500	.250	121	0	0	0	0	1.000	1	/C-1	0.1
1973	Hou-N	7	20	6	6	2	0	2	6	1	7	.300	.364	.700	189	2	0	0	0	1.000	-0	/1-5	0.2
1974	Hou-N	83	171	26	39	4	1	10	29	33	45	.228	.362	.439	129	7	0	1	-1	.978	-4	C-28,1-21	0.3
1975	Hou-N	122	340	52	94	16	1	20	65	46	64	.276	.371	.506	152	23	1	0	0	.991	-12	1-47,C-41/O-1	1.0
1976	Hou-N	108	318	36	72	21	2	10	49	62	59	.226	.359	.399	126	12	0	0	0	.977	-12	C-66,O-20,1-16	0.1
1977	Hou-N	51	144	22	43	8	0	10	23	23	30	.299	.409	.563	173	15	0	1	-1	.946	-0	O-34,1-10	1.2
	*NY-A	56	142	24	42	8	0	12	31	20	23	.296	.405	.606	173	15	0	1	-1	1.000	3	D-25,C-15,1-11	1.5
1978	*NY-A	76	174	20	32	9	1	6	19	30	32	.184	.307	.351	87	-3	0	0	0	.975	0	D-39,C-22/1-1	-0.4
1979	NY-A	28	64	11	17	6	0	2	6	10	7	.266	.365	.453	122	2	0	0	0	1.000	-0	D-22/C-4	0.1
	Cle-A	72	240	37	65	10	0	18	61	24	39	.271	.349	.538	135	11	2	0	1	1.000	0	D-62/C-1	0.9
	Yr	100	304	48	82	16	0	20	67	34	46	.270	.353	.520	132	13	2	0	1	1.000	-1	D-84/C-5	1.0
1980	Cle-A	54	174	25	40	3	1	6	28	25	30	.230	.327	.362	88	-3	0	1	-1	1.000	0	D-45	-0.5
	Chi-N	68	196	28	46	8	0	10	34	29	35	.235	.336	.429	104	1	0	0	0	.992	-6	1-46/O-3,C-1	-0.8
1981	*Oak-A	84	273	40	71	8	0	17	59	28	60	.260	.336	.476	138	13	5	3	-0	1.000	-1	D-68/1-9	0.9
1982	Oak-A	73	214	19	51	10	0	7	31	26	41	.238	.326	.383	98	-0	1	2	-1	.987	-1	D-48,1-11	-0.3
1983	Tor-A	142	407	59	108	23	1	22	76	67	69	.265	.376	.489	128	17	0	1	-1	1.000	0	*D-130/1-6	1.1
1984	Tor-A	127	359	51	109	23	1	16	61	50	62	.304	.393	.507	142	21	0	1	-1	1.000	-1	*D-109/1-2	1.7
1985	Tex-A	82	296	31	76	17	1	12	56	31	44	.257	.333	.443	109	3	0	0	0	.000	0	D-82	0.2
	*Tor-A	24	73	4	20	0	0	1	10	9	15	.274	.354	.315	83	-1	0	0	0	.947	-1	D-21/1-3	-0.2
	Yr	106	369	35	96	17	1	13	66	40	59	.260	.337	.417	104	2	0	0	0	.947	-1	*D-103/1-3	0.0
1986	Tor-A	107	336	48	84	12	1	15	55	52	57	.250	.357	.426	109	5	0	1	-1	1.000	0	D-95/1-1	0.3
Total	15	1369	3945	539	1016	188	10	196	699	568	719	.258	.358	.459	125	141	9	12	-5	.993	-33	D-746,1-189,C/O	7.4

■ DARRELL JOHNSON
Johnson, Darrell Dean b: 8/25/28, Horace, Neb. BR/TR, 6'1", 180 lbs. Deb: 4/20/52 MC

YEAR	TM/L	G	AB	R	H	2B	3B	HR	RBI	BB	SO	AVG	OBP	SLG	PRO+	BR/A	SB	CS	SBR	FA	FR	G/POS	TPR
1952	StL-A	29	78	9	22	2	1	0	9	11	4	.282	.371	.333	94	-0	0	0	0	.990	1	C-22	0.2
	Chi-A	22	37	3	4	0	0	0	1	5	9	.108	.214	.108	-8	-5	1	0	0	.955	5	C-21	0.0
	Yr	51	115	12	26	2	1	0	10	16	13	.226	.321	.261	62	-5	1	0	0	.974	6	C-43	0.2
1957	NY-A	21	46	4	10	1	0	1	8	3	10	.217	.280	.304	61	-3	0	0	0	1.000	4	C-20	0.2
1958	NY-A	5	16	1	4	0	0	0	1	0	2	.250	.250	.250	39	-1	0	0	0	1.000	1	/C-4	0.0
1960	StL-N	8	2	0	0	0	0	0	0	1	0	.000	.333	.000	1	-0	0	0	0	1.000	1	/C-8	0.1
1961	Phi-N	21	61	4	14	1	0	0	3	3	8	.230	.277	.246	41	-5	0	0	0	.982	2	C-21	-0.2
	*Cin-N	20	54	3	17	2	0	1	6	1	2	.315	.327	.407	92	-1	0	0	0	1.000	4	C-20	0.4
	Yr	41	115	7	31	3	0	1	9	4	10	.270	.300	.322	65	-6	0	0	0	.991	6	C-41	0.2
1962	Cin-N	2	4	0	0	0	0	0	0	0	0	.000	.333	.000	-2	-0	0	0	0	1.000	2	/C-2	-0.0
	Bal-A	6	22	0	4	0	0	0	0	2	4	.182	.182	.182	-2	-3	0	0	0	1.000	-1	/C-6	-0.4
Total	6	134	320	24	75	6	1	2	28	26	39	.234	.296	.278	57	-19	1	0	0	.988	20	C-124	0.4

■ DAVEY JOHNSON
Johnson, David Allen b: 1/30/43, Orlando, Fla. BR/TR, 6'1", 180 lbs. Deb: 4/13/65 M

YEAR	TM/L	G	AB	R	H	2B	3B	HR	RBI	BB	SO	AVG	OBP	SLG	PRO+	BR/A	SB	CS	SBR	FA	FR	G/POS	TPR
1965	Bal-A	20	47	5	8	3	0	1	5	6	10	.170	.250	.234	38	-4	3	0	1	.929	3	/3-9,2-3,S-2	0.0
1966	*Bal-A	131	501	47	129	20	3	7	56	31	64	.257	.302	.351	88	-8	3	4	-2	.971	2	*2-126/S-3	0.2
1967	Bal-A	148	510	62	126	30	3	10	64	59	82	.247	.330	.376	109	6	4	5	-2	.981	0	*2-144/3-3	1.6
1968	Bal-A★	145	504	50	122	24	4	9	56	44	80	.242	.309	.359	102	1	7	3	0	.978	4	*2-127,S-34	1.6
1969	*Bal-A†	142	511	52	143	34	1	7	57	57	52	.280	.356	.391	108	6	3	4	-2	.984	-3	*2-142/S-2	1.3
1970	*Bal-A★	149	530	68	149	27	1	10	53	66	68	.281	.361	.392	106	6	2	1	0	.990	1	*2-149/S-2	1.9
1971	*Bal-A	142	510	67	144	26	1	18	72	51	55	.282	.353	.443	125	17	3	1	1	.990	10	*2-116	3.0
1972	Bal-A	118	376	31	83	22	3	5	32	52	68	.221	.322	.335	93	-2	1	1	-0	.990	3	*2-116	1.6
1973	Atl-N★	157	559	84	151	25	0	43	99	81	93	.270	.371	.546	140	30	5	3	-0	.966	-3	*2-156	3.7
1974	Atl-N	136	454	56	114	18	0	15	62	75	59	.251	.361	.390	105	5	2	2	-1	.993	7	1-73,2-71	1.0
1975	Atl-N	1	1	0	1	0	0	0	1	0	0	1.000	1.000	2.000	691	1	0	0	0	.000	0	H	0.1
1977	*Phi-N	78	156	23	50	9	1	8	36	23	20	.321	.414	.545	148	11	1	1	-0	1.000	-2	1-43/2-9,3-6	0.8
1978	Phi-N	44	89	14	17	2	0	2	14	10	19	.191	.287	.281	59	-5	0	0	0	.930	-6	2-15/3-9,1-7	-1.1
	Chi-N	24	49	5	15	1	1	2	6	5	9	.306	.393	.490	130	2	0	0	0	.839	-3	3-12	-0.1
	Yr	68	138	19	32	3	1	4	20	15	28	.232	.325	.355	86	-2	0	0	0	.844	-9	3-21,2-15/1-7	-1.2
Total	13	1435	4797	564	1252	242	18	136	609	559	675	.261	.343	.404	110	66	33	25	-5	.980	10	*2-1198,1-123/S3	15.6

■ DERON JOHNSON
Johnson, Deron Roger b: 7/17/38, San Diego, Cal. d: 4/23/92, Poway, Cal. BR/TR, 6'2", 209 lbs. Deb: 9/20/60 C

YEAR	TM/L	G	AB	R	H	2B	3B	HR	RBI	BB	SO	AVG	OBP	SLG	PRO+	BR/A	SB	CS	SBR	FA	FR	G/POS	TPR
1960	NY-A	6	4	0	2	1	0	0	0	0	0	.500	.500	.750	247	1	0	0	0	.750	-0	/3-5	0.1
1961	NY-A	13	19	1	2	0	0	0	0	2	5	.105	.190	.105	-20	-3	0	0	0	1.000	2	/3-8	-0.1
	KC-A	83	283	31	61	11	3	8	42	14	44	.216	.255	.360	61	-16	0	1	-1	.948	3	O-59,3-19/1-3	-1.8
	Yr	96	302	32	63	11	3	8	44	16	49	.209	.251	.344	57	-19	0	1	-1	.948	5	O-59,3-27/1-3	-1.9
1962	KC-A	17	19	1	2	1	0	0	0	3	6	.105	.227	.158	6	-3	0	0	0	1.000	-1	/1-2,3-2,O-2	-0.4
1964	Cin-N	140	477	63	130	24	4	21	79	37	98	.273	.328	.472	118	10	3	0	1	.990	4	*1-131,O-10/3-1	0.7
1965	Cin-N	159	616	92	177	30	7	32	**130**	42	97	.287	.345	.515	129	23	0	4	-2	.948	-12	*3-159	0.5
1966	Cin-N	142	505	75	130	25	3	24	81	39	87	.257	.313	.461	103	1	0	0	0	.980	-8	*O-106,1-71,3-18	-1.5
1967	Cin-N	108	361	39	81	18	1	13	53	22	104	.224	.273	.388	78	-11	0	0	0	.997	-4	1-81,3-24	-2.2
1968	Atl-N	127	342	29	71	11	1	8	33	35	79	.208	.287	.316	81	-8	0	1	-1	.996	-1	1-97,3-21	-1.8

YEAR	TM/L	G	AB	R	H	2B	3B	HR	RBI	BB	SO	AVG	OBP	SLG	PRO+	BR/A	SB	CS	SBR	FA	FR	G/POS	TPR
1969	Phi-N	138	475	51	121	19	4	17	80	60	111	.255	.338	.419	114	9	4	2	0	1.000	-14	O-72,3-50,1-18	-1.0
1970	Phi-N	159	574	66	147	28	3	27	93	72	132	.256	.339	.456	114	10	0	0	0	.995	-11	*1-154/3-3	-1.3
1971	Phi-N	158	582	74	154	29	0	34	95	72	146	.265	.348	.490	135	26	0	1	-1	.995	-4	*1-136,3-22	0.9
1972	Phi-N	96	230	19	49	4	1	9	31	26	69	.213	.301	.357	84	-5	0	1	-1	.982	-4	1-62	-1.5
1973	Phi-N	12	36	3	6	2	0	1	5	5	10	.167	.286	.306	62	-2	0	0	0	.976	-0	1-10	-0.3
	*Oak-A	131	464	61	114	14	2	19	81	59	116	.246	.332	.407	113	8	0	1	-1	.994	-3	*D-107,1-23	0.0
1974	Oak-A	50	174	16	34	1	2	7	23	11	37	.195	.243	.345	72	-7	1	0	0	.991	-2	1-28,D-23	-1.2
	Mil-A	49	152	14	23	3	0	6	18	21	41	.151	.254	.289	56	-9	1	0	0	.833	-0	D-46/1-2	-1.1
	Bos-A	11	25	0	3	0	0	0	2	0	6	.120	.120	.120	-29	-4	0	0	0	.000	-0	/D-8	-0.5
	Yr	110	351	30	60	4	2	13	43	32	84	.171	.240	.305	57	-20	2	0	1	.983	-3	D-69,1-30/H-8	-2.8
1975	Chi-A	148	555	66	129	25	1	18	72	48	117	.232	.295	.378	88	-10	0	1	-1	.994	-4	D-93,1-55	-2.2
	Bos-A	3	10	2	6	0	0	1	3	2	0	.600	.667	.900	313	3	0	0	0	1.000	-1	/1-2,D-1	0.2
	Yr	151	565	68	135	25	1	19	75	50	117	.239	.302	.388	92	-7	0	1	-1	.994	-5	D-94,1-57	-2.0
1976	Bos-A	15	38	3	5	1	1	0	3	5	5	.132	.233	.211	27	-4	0	0	0	1.000	-0	/1-5,D-9	-0.4
Total	16	1765	5941	706	1447	247	33	245	923	585	1318	.244	.313	.420	102	9	11	18	-8	.993	-63	1-880,3-332,DO	-14.9

■ DON JOHNSON

Johnson, Donald Spore "Pep" b: 12/7/11, Chicago, Ill. BR/TR, 6', 170 lbs. Deb: 9/26/43 F

YEAR	TM/L	G	AB	R	H	2B	3B	HR	RBI	BB	SO	AVG	OBP	SLG	PRO+	BR/A	SB	CS	SBR	FA	FR	G/POS	TPR
1943	Chi-N	10	42	5	8	2	0	0	5	4	8	.190	.227	.238	35	-4	0			.957	3	2-10	0.0
1944	Chi-N☆	154	608	50	169	37	1	2	71	28	48	.278	.311	.352	87	-12	8			.947	1	*2-154	-0.3
1945	*Chi-N†	138	557	94	168	23	2	2	58	32	34	.302	.343	.361	98	-2	9			.975	10	*2-138	1.7
1946	Chi-N	83	314	37	76	10	1	1	19	26	39	.242	.306	.290	71	-12	6			.981	-10	2-83	-1.7
1947	Chi-N	120	402	33	104	17	2	3	26	24	45	.259	.302	.333	71	-17	2			.970	-4	*2-108/3-6	-1.4
1948	Chi-N	6	12	0	3	0	0	0	0	0	1	.250	.250	.250	37	-1	1			1.000	-0	/2-2,3-2	-0.3
Total	6	511	1935	219	528	89	6	8	175	112	171	.273	.315	.337	83	-48	26			.966	-2	2-495/3-8	-2.0

■ ED JOHNSON

Johnson, Edwin Cyril b: 3/31/1899, Morganfield, Ky. d: 7/3/75, Morganfield, Ky. BL/TR, 5'9", 160 lbs. Deb: 9/26/20

YEAR	TM/L	G	AB	R	H	2B	3B	HR	RBI	BB	SO	AVG	OBP	SLG	PRO+	BR/A	SB	CS	SBR	FA	FR	G/POS	TPR
1920	Was-A	4	13	1	3	0	0	0	2	3		.231	.375	.231	65	-0	0	0	0	.625	-1	/O-4	-0.1

■ ELMER JOHNSON

Johnson, Elmer Ellsworth "Hickory" b: 6/12/1884, Beard, Ind. d: 10/31/66, Hollywood, Fla. BR/TR, 5'9", 185 lbs. Deb: 4/24/14

YEAR	TM/L	G	AB	R	H	2B	3B	HR	RBI	BB	SO	AVG	OBP	SLG	PRO+	BR/A	SB	CS	SBR	FA	FR	G/POS	TPR
1914	NY-N	11	12	0	2	1	0	0	0	1	3	.167	.231	.250	44	-1	0			.947	-1	C-11	-0.2

■ ERIK JOHNSON

Johnson, Erik Anthony b: 10/11/65, Oakland, Cal. BR/TR, 5'11", 175 lbs. Deb: 7/8/93

YEAR	TM/L	G	AB	R	H	2B	3B	HR	RBI	BB	SO	AVG	OBP	SLG	PRO+	BR/A	SB	CS	SBR	FA	FR	G/POS	TPR
1993	SF-N	4	5	1	2	2	0	0	0	0	1	.400	.400	.800	219	1	0	0	0	1.000	-1	/2-2,3-1,S-1	0.0
1994	SF-N	5	13	0	2	0	0	0	0	0	4	.154	.154	.154	-20	-2	0	0	0	1.000	-1	/2-2,S-1	-0.1
Total	2	9	18	1	4	2	0	0	0	0	5	.222	.222	.333	45	-2	0	0	0	1.000	-0	/2-4,S-2,3-1	-0.1

■ ERNIE JOHNSON

Johnson, Ernest Rudolph b: 4/29/1888, Chicago, Ill. d: 5/1/52, Monrovia, Cal. BL/TR, 5'9", 151 lbs. Deb: 8/5/12 F

YEAR	TM/L	G	AB	R	H	2B	3B	HR	RBI	BB	SO	AVG	OBP	SLG	PRO+	BR/A	SB	CS	SBR	FA	FR	G/POS	TPR
1912	Chi-A	21	42	7	11	0	1	0	5	1		.262	.279	.310	70	-2	0			.984	3	S-16	0.2
1915	StL-F	152	512	58	123	18	10	7	67	46	35	.240	.305	.355	81	-21	32			.942	18	*S-152	0.9
1916	StL-A	74	236	29	54	9	3	0	19	30	23	.229	.323	.292	89	-2	13			.936	-8	S-60,3-12	-0.8
1917	StL-A	80	199	28	49	6	2	2	20	12	16	.246	.296	.327	93	-2	13			.924	11	S-39,2-18,3-14	1.2
1918	StL-A	29	34	7	9	1	0	0	0	2		.265	.286	.294	77	-1	4			.821	-2	S-11/3-1	-0.3
1921	Chi-A	142	613	93	181	28	7	1	51	29	24	.295	.328	.369	78	-21	22	13	-1	.947	18	*S-141	0.9
1922	Chi-A	144	603	85	153	17	3	0	56	40	30	.254	.302	.292	56	-38	21	18	-5	.952	2	*S-141	-2.6
1923	Chi-A	12	53	5	10	2	0	1	3	1	5	.189	.246	.226	25	-6	2	1	0	.922	-0	S-12	-0.5
	*NY-A	19	38	6	17	1	1	0	8	1	1	.447	.462	.605	176	4	0	0	0	.977	-1	S-15/3-1	0.4
	Yr	31	91	11	27	3	1	1	9	4	6	.297	.333	.385	88	-2	2	1	0	.944	-1	S-27/3-1	-0.1
1924	NY-A	64	119	24	42	4	3	2	12	11	7	.353	.412	.597	158	10	1	5	-1	.955	-1	2-27/S-9,3-2	0.5
1925	NY-A	76	170	30	48	5	1	5	17	8	10	.282	.315	.412	85	-5	6	3	0	.955	-10	2-34,S-28/3-2	-1.2
Total	10	813	2619	372	697	91	36	19	256	181	153	.266	.317	.350	80	-84	114	41		.944	29	S-624/2-79,3-32	-1.3

■ FRANK JOHNSON

Johnson, Frank Herbert b: 7/22/42, ElPaso, Tex. BR/TR, 6'1", 155 lbs. Deb: 9/7/66

YEAR	TM/L	G	AB	R	H	2B	3B	HR	RBI	BB	SO	AVG	OBP	SLG	PRO+	BR/A	SB	CS	SBR	FA	FR	G/POS	TPR
1966	SF-N	15	32	2	7	0	0	0	0	2	7	.219	.265	.219	35	-3	0	1	-1	1.000	-3	O-13	-0.8
1967	SF-N	8	10	3	3	0	0	0	0	1		.300	.364	.300	93	-0	0	0	0	.889	-0	/O-3	-0.3
1968	SF-N	67	174	11	33	6	1	7	12	23		.190	.246	.218	40	-12	1	0	0	.944	3	3-36/O-8,S-5,2-3	-1.0
1969	SF-N	7	10	1	2	0	0	0	0	1		.100	.100	.100	-45	-2	0	0	0	1.000	-0	/O-7	-0.3
1970	SF-N	67	161	25	44	1	2	3	31	19	18	.273	.357	.360	94	-1	1	1	0	.979	-2	O-33,1-27	-0.6
1971	SF-N	32	49	4	4	1	0	0	5	3	9	.082	.135	.102	-33	-9	0	0	0	.975	-3	/1-9,O-4	-1.3
Total	6	196	436	47	92	4	2	4	42	50	71	.277	.277	.257	52	-26	2	2	-1	.979	-6	/O-68,1-36,3-36,S2	-4.0

■ HOWARD JOHNSON

Johnson, Howard Michael b: 11/29/60, Clearwater, Fla. BB/TR, 5'11", 178 lbs. Deb: 4/14/82

YEAR	TM/L	G	AB	R	H	2B	3B	HR	RBI	BB	SO	AVG	OBP	SLG	PRO+	BR/A	SB	CS	SBR	FA	FR	G/POS	TPR
1982	Det-A	54	155	23	49	5	0	4	14	16	30	.316	.384	.426	122	5	7	4	-0	.901	-9	3-33,D-10/O-9	-0.5
1983	Det-A	27	66	11	14	0	0	3	5	7	10	.212	.297	.348	79	-2	0	0	0	.851	-6	3-21/D-2	-0.8
1984	*Det-A	116	355	43	88	14	1	12	50	40	67	.248	.326	.394	99	-0	10	6	-1	.944	-18	*3-108/S-9,1-1,OD	-2.0
1985	NY-N	126	389	38	94	18	4	11	46	34	78	.242	.303	.393	96	-3	6	4	0	.941	-13	*3-113/S-7,O-1	-1.8
1986	*NY-N	88	220	30	54	14	0	10	39	31	64	.245	.341	.445	119	5	8	1	2	.903	-2	3-45,S-34/O-1	0.7
1987	NY-N	157	554	93	147	22	1	36	99	83	113	.265	.364	.504	135	27	32	10	4	.938	-18	*3-140,S-38/O-2	1.3
1988	*NY-N	148	495	85	114	21	1	24	68	86	104	.230	.348	.422	126	18	23	7	3	.951	-14	*3-131/S-52	1.0
1989	NY-N★	153	571	**104**	164	41	3	36	101	77	126	.287	.373	.559	171	51	41	8	7	.910	-33	*3-143,S-31	3.0
1990	NY-N	154	590	89	144	37	3	23	90	69	100	.244	.323	.434	107	4	34	8	5	.913	-5	3-92,S-73	1.1
1991	NY-N★	156	564	108	146	34	4	**38**	**117**	78	120	.259	.350	.535	147	33	30	16	-1	.927	-4	*3-104,O-30,S-28	3.2
1992	NY-N	100	350	48	78	19	0	7	43	55	79	.223	.332	.337	91	-3	22	5	4	.981	-4	O-98	-0.6
1993	NY-N	72	235	32	56	8	2	7	26	43	43	.238	.356	.379	98	0	6	4	1	.944	5	3-67	0.5
1994	Col-N	93	227	30	48	10	2	10	40	39	73	.211	.327	.405	77	-8	11	3	2	.979	-2	O-62/1-1	-1.2
1995	Chi-N	87	169	26	33	4	1	7	22	34	42	.195	.333	.355	83	-4	1	1	-0	.926	-8	3-34,O-13/2-8,1S	-1.2
Total	14	1531	4940	760	1229	247	22	228	760	692	1053	.249	.343	.446	118	125	231	77	23	.929	-129	*3-1031,S-273,O/D21	2.9

■ SPUD JOHNSON

Johnson, John Ralph b: 1860, Canada BL/TL, 5'9", 175 lbs. Deb: 4/18/1889

YEAR	TM/L	G	AB	R	H	2B	3B	HR	RBI	BB	SO	AVG	OBP	SLG	PRO+	BR/A	SB	CS	SBR	FA	FR	G/POS	TPR
1889	Col-a	116	459	91	130	14	10	2	79	39	47	.283	.355	.370	112	9	34			.879	-11	O-69,3-44/1-2,S-1	2.2
1890	Col-a	135	538	106	186	23	18	1	**113**	48		.346	.409	.461	168	46	43			.926	-16	*O-135	2.2
1891	Cle-N	80	327	49	84	8	3	1	46	22	23	.257	.319	.309	80	-9	16			.872	-5	O-79/1-1	-1.4
Total	3	331	1324	246	400	45	31	4	238	109	70	.302	.368	.392	125	46	93			.899	-32	O-283/3-44,1-3,S-1	0.6

■ LANCE JOHNSON

Johnson, Kenneth Lance b: 7/6/63, Cincinnati, Ohio BL/TL, 5'10", 160 lbs. Deb: 7/10/87

YEAR	TM/L	G	AB	R	H	2B	3B	HR	RBI	BB	SO	AVG	OBP	SLG	PRO+	BR/A	SB	CS	SBR	FA	FR	G/POS	TPR
1987	*StL-N	33	59	4	13	2	1	0	7	4	6	.220	.270	.288	47	-4	6	1	1	.931	-6	O-25	-0.9
1988	Chi-A	33	124	11	23	4	1	0	6	6	11	.185	.223	.234	28	-12	6	2	1	.970	-4	O-31/D-1	-1.7
1989	Chi-A	50	180	28	54	8	2	0	16	17	24	.300	.360	.367	108	2	16	3	3	.983	0	O-45/D-1	0.4
1990	Chi-A	151	541	76	154	18	9	1	51	33	45	.285	.327	.357	93	-5	36	22	-2	.973	-2	*O-148/D-1	-1.3
1991	Chi-A	159	588	72	161	14	**13**	0	49	26	58	.274	.306	.342	81	-16	26	11	1	.995	13	*O-157	-0.5
1992	Chi-A	157	567	67	158	15	**12**	3	47	34	33	.279	.321	.363	92	-6	41	14	6	.987	16	*O-157	0.3
1993	*Chi-A	147	540	75	168	18	**14**	0	47	36	33	.311	.354	.396	104	3	35	7	6	.980	16	*O-146	2.1
1994	Chi-A	106	412	56	114	11	**14**	3	54	26	23	.277	.323	.393	85	-10	26	6	4	**1.000**	13	*O-103/D-1	0.5
1995	Chi-A	142	607	98	**186**	18	12	10	57	32	31	.306	.342	.425	103	1	40	6	**8**	.991	6	*O-140/D-1	1.1
1996	NY-N★	160	682	117	**227**	31	**21**	9	69	33	40	.333	.365	.479	129	26	50	12	**8**	.971	14	*O-157	4.2
Total	10	1138	4300	604	1258	139	99	26	403	247	304	.293	.332	.389	97	-21	282	84	34	.984	59	*O-1109/D-5	4.2

■ LAMAR JOHNSON

Johnson, Lamar b: 9/2/50, Bessemer, Ala. BR/TR, 6'2", 225 lbs. Deb: 5/18/74

YEAR	TM/L	G	AB	R	H	2B	3B	HR	RBI	BB	SO	AVG	OBP	SLG	PRO+	BR/A	SB	CS	SBR	FA	FR	G/POS	TPR
1974	Chi-A	10	29	1	10	0	0	0	2	0	3	.345	.345	.345	97	-0	0	0	0	1.000	-0	/1-7,D-3	-0.1
1975	Chi-A	8	30	2	6	0	1	1	5	0	4	.200	.226	.400	73	-1	0	0	0	.960	-1	/1-6,D-2	-0.4
1976	Chi-A	82	222	29	71	11	1	4	33	19	37	.320	.379	.432	136	10	2	1	0	.983	-1	D-35,1-34/O-1	0.7
1977	Chi-A	118	374	52	113	12	5	18	65	24	53	.302	.344	.505	128	13	1	1	0	.990	1	D-68,1-45	1.0
1978	Chi-A	148	498	52	136	23	2	8	72	43	46	.273	.333	.376	98	-1	6	5	-1	.992	2	*1-108,D-36	-0.8

YEAR	TM/L	G	AB	R	H	2B	3B	HR	RBI	BB	SO	AVG	OBP	SLG	PRO+	BR/A	SB	CS	SBR	FA	FR	G/POS	TPR
1979	Chi-A	133	479	60	148	29	1	12	74	41	56	.309	.366	.449	118	12	8	2	1	.987	-1	1-94,D-37	0.6
1980	Chi-A	147	541	51	150	26	3	13	81	47	53	.277	.335	.409	103	2	2	3	-1	.990	-1	1-80,D-66	-0.4
1981	Chi-A	41	134	10	37	7	0	1	15	5	14	.276	.302	.351	89	-2	0	2	-1	.989	-2	1-36/D-2	-0.8
1982	Tex-A	105	324	37	84	11	0	7	38	31	40	.259	.326	.358	92	-3	3	5	-2	.982	-2	D-77,1-12	-1.1
Total	9	792	2631	294	755	122	12	64	381	241	307	.287	.342	.415	109	30	22	19	-5	.989	-1	1-422,D-326/O-1	-1.2

■ LARRY JOHNSON
Johnson, Larry Doby b: 8/17/50, Cleveland, Ohio BR/TR, 6', 185 lbs. Deb: 10/3/72

YEAR	TM/L	G	AB	R	H	2B	3B	HR	RBI	BB	SO	AVG	OBP	SLG	PRO+	BR/A	SB	CS	SBR	FA	FR	G/POS	TPR
1972	Cle-A	1	2	0	1	0	0	0	0	0	1	.500	.500	.500	192	0	0	0	0	1.000	0	/C-1	0.1
1974	Cle-A	1	0	1	0	0	0	0	0	0	0	—	—	—	0	0	0	0	0	.000	0	R	0.0
1975	Mon-N	1	3	0	1	0	0	0	1	1	0	.333	.500	.667	212	1	0	0	0	1.000	-0	/C-1	0.0
1976	Mon-N	6	13	0	2	1	0	0	0	0	2	.154	.154	.231	8	-2	0	0	0	1.000	1	/C-5	-0.1
1978	Chi-A	3	8	0	1	1	0	0	0	1	4	.125	.222	.125	0	-1	0	0	0	.857	-0	/C-2,D-1	-0.2
Total	5	12	26	1	5	2	0	0	1	2	8	.192	.250	.269	46	-2	0	0	0	.975	1	/C-9,D-1	-0.2

■ LOU JOHNSON
Johnson, Louis Brown "Slick" b: 9/22/34, Lexington, Ky. BR/TR, 5'11", 175 lbs. Deb: 4/17/60

YEAR	TM/L	G	AB	R	H	2B	3B	HR	RBI	BB	SO	AVG	OBP	SLG	PRO+	BR/A	SB	CS	SBR	FA	FR	G/POS	TPR
1960	Chi-N	34	68	6	14	2	1	0	1	5	19	.206	.270	.265	48	-5	3	1	0	1.000	1	O-25	-0.4
1961	LA-N	1	0	0	0	0	0	0	0	0	0	—	—	—	0	0	0	0	0	.000	-0	/O-1	0.0
1962	Mil-N	61	117	22	33	4	5	2	13	11	27	.282	.349	.453	116	3	6	1	1	1.000	-9	O-55	-0.7
1965	*LA-N	131	468	57	121	24	1	12	58	24	81	.259	.317	.391	105	-2	15	6	1	.985	-3	*O-128	-0.6
1966	*LA-N	152	526	71	143	20	2	17	73	21	75	.272	.317	.414	110	5	8	10	-4	.985	-2	*O-148	-0.7
1967	LA-N	104	330	39	89	14	1	11	41	24	52	.270	.332	.418	124	9	3	3	-1	.976	2	O-91	0.7
1968	Chi-A	62	205	14	50	14	3	1	14	6	23	.244	.289	.356	87	-3	3	1	0	.970	-4	O-57	-1.2
	Cle-A	65	202	25	52	11	1	5	23	9	24	.257	.302	.396	112	2	6	1	1	.989	1	O-57	0.2
1969	Cal-A	67	133	10	27	8	0	0	9	10	19	.203	.274	.263	53	-8	5	1	1	.935	-5	O-44	-1.5
Total	8	677	2049	244	529	97	14	48	232	110	320	.258	.313	.389	103	5	50	24	1	.981	-19	O-606	-4.2

■ MARK JOHNSON
Johnson, Mark Patrick b: 10/17/67, Worcester, Mass. BL/TL, 6'4", 230 lbs. Deb: 4/26/95

YEAR	TM/L	G	AB	R	H	2B	3B	HR	RBI	BB	SO	AVG	OBP	SLG	PRO+	BR/A	SB	CS	SBR	FA	FR	G/POS	TPR
1995	Pit-N	79	221	32	46	6	1	13	28	37	66	.208	.327	.421	94	-2	5	2	0	.986	-4	1-70	-1.2
1996	Pit-N	127	343	55	94	24	0	13	47	44	64	.274	.365	.458	112	6	6	4	-1	.994	5	*1-100/O-1	0.2
Total	2	206	564	87	140	30	1	26	75	81	130	.248	.350	.443	105	4	11	6	-0	.991	1	1-170/O-1	-1.0

■ OTIS JOHNSON
Johnson, Otis L. b: 11/5/1883, Fowler, Ind. d: 11/9/15, Johnson City, N.Y. BB/TR, 5'9", 185 lbs. Deb: 4/12/11

YEAR	TM/L	G	AB	R	H	2B	3B	HR	RBI	BB	SO	AVG	OBP	SLG	PRO+	BR/A	SB	CS	SBR	FA	FR	G/POS	TPR
1911	NY-A	71	209	21	49	9	6	3	36		39	.234	.363	.378	100	1				.907	-9	S-47,2-15/3-3	-0.6

■ PAUL JOHNSON
Johnson, Paul Oscar b: 9/2/1896, N.Grosvenor Dale, Conn. d: 2/14/73, McAllen, Tex. BR/TR, 5'8", 160 lbs. Deb: 9/13/20

YEAR	TM/L	G	AB	R	H	2B	3B	HR	RBI	BB	SO	AVG	OBP	SLG	PRO+	BR/A	SB	CS	SBR	FA	FR	G/POS	TPR
1920	Phi-A	18	72	6	15	0	0	0	5	4	8	.208	.250	.208	22	-8	1	1	-0	.933	-3	O-18	-1.2
1921	Phi-A	48	127	17	40	6	1	2	10	9	17	.315	.360	.417	97	-1	0	2	-1	.969	-5	O-32	-0.8
Total	2	66	199	23	55	6	1	2	15	13	25	.276	.321	.342	71	-9	1	3	-2	.958	-7	/O-50	-2.0

■ RANDY JOHNSON
Johnson, Randall Glenn b: 6/10/56, Escondido, Cal. BR/TR, 6'1", 190 lbs. Deb: 4/27/82

YEAR	TM/L	G	AB	R	H	2B	3B	HR	RBI	BB	SO	AVG	OBP	SLG	PRO+	BR/A	SB	CS	SBR	FA	FR	G/POS	TPR
1982	Atl-N	27	46	5	11	5	0	0	6	6	4	.239	.352	.348	93	-0	0	1	-1	.955	5	2-13/3-4	0.5
1983	Atl-N	86	144	22	36	3	0	1	17	20	27	.250	.345	.292	73	-5	1	3	-2	.991	10	3-53/2-4	0.4
1984	Atl-N	91	294	28	82	13	0	5	30	21	21	.279	.329	.374	91	-4	4	7	-3	.939	5	3-81	-0.3
Total	3	204	484	55	129	21	0	6	53	47	52	.267	.336	.347	85	-8	5	11	-5	.956	20	3-138/2-17	0.6

■ RANDY JOHNSON
Johnson, Randall Stuart b: 8/15/58, Miami, Fla. BL/TL, 6'2", 195 lbs. Deb: 7/5/80

YEAR	TM/L	G	AB	R	H	2B	3B	HR	RBI	BB	SO	AVG	OBP	SLG	PRO+	BR/A	SB	CS	SBR	FA	FR	G/POS	TPR
1980	Chi-A	12	20	0	4	0	0	0	3	2	4	.200	.304	.200	41	-1	0	0	0	.000	-0	/1-1,O-1,D-4	-0.2
1982	Min-A	89	234	26	58	10	0	10	33	30	46	.248	.333	.419	102	1	0	0	0	1.000	-0	D-67/O-2	-0.2
Total	2	101	254	26	62	10	0	10	36	32	50	.244	.331	.402	98	-1	0	0	0	1.000	-1	/D-71,O-3,1-1	-0.4

■ FOOTER JOHNSON
Johnson, Richard Allan "Treads" b: 2/15/32, Dayton, Ohio BL/TL, 5'11", 175 lbs. Deb: 6/22/58

YEAR	TM/L	G	AB	R	H	2B	3B	HR	RBI	BB	SO	AVG	OBP	SLG	PRO+	BR/A	SB	CS	SBR	FA	FR	G/POS	TPR
1958	Chi-N	8	5	1	0	0	0	0	0	0	0	.000	.000	.000	-99	-1	0	0	0	.000	0	H	-0.1

■ BOB JOHNSON
Johnson, Robert Lee "Indian Bob" b: 11/26/06, Pryor, Okla. d: 7/6/82, Tacoma, Wash. BR/TR, 6', 180 lbs. Deb: 4/12/33 F

YEAR	TM/L	G	AB	R	H	2B	3B	HR	RBI	BB	SO	AVG	OBP	SLG	PRO+	BR/A	SB	CS	SBR	FA	FR	G/POS	TPR
1933	Phi-A	142	535	103	155	44	4	21	93	85	74	.290	.387	.505	133	26	8	3	1	.952	2	*O-142	1.9
1934	Phi-A	141	547	111	168	26	6	34	92	58	60	.307	.375	.563	144	33	12	8	-1	.967	10	*O-139	3.3
1935	Phi-A★	147	582	103	174	29	5	28	109	78	76	.299	.384	.510	130	25	2	4	-2	.946	4	*O-147	2.1
1936	Phi-A	153	566	91	165	29	14	25	121	88	71	.292	.389	.525	126	22	6	6	-2	.962	9	*O-131,2-22/1-1	1.7
1937	Phi-A	138	477	91	146	32	6	25	108	98	65	.306	.425	.556	148	37	9	7	-2	.976	9	*O-133/2-2	3.6
1938	Phi-A★	152	563	114	176	27	9	30	113	87	73	.313	.406	.552	142	36	9	8	-2	.963	10	*O-150/2-3,3-1	3.5
1939	Phi-A☆	150	544	115	184	30	9	23	114	99	59	.338	.440	.553	156	49	15	5	2	.967	5	*O-150/2-1	4.7
1940	Phi-A☆	138	512	93	137	25	4	31	103	83	64	.268	.374	.514	130	23	8	2	1	.962	5	*O-136	2.1
1941	Phi-A	149	552	98	152	30	8	22	107	95	75	.275	.385	.478	130	25	6	4	-1	.990	7	*O-122,1-28	2.1
1942	Phi-A★	149	550	78	160	35	7	13	80	82	61	.291	.384	.451	135	26	3	2	-0	.963	5	*O-149	2.4
1943	Was-A★	117	438	65	116	22	8	7	63	64	50	.265	.362	.400	127	16	11	5	0	.996	9	O-88,3-19,1-10	2.2
1944	Bos-A★	144	525	106	170	40	8	17	106	95	67	.324	.431	.528	175	54	2	7	-4	.977	4	*O-142	4.9
1945	Bos-A†	143	529	71	148	27	7	12	74	63	56	.280	.358	.425	124	16	5	3	-0	.975	7	*O-140	1.1
Total	13	1863	6920	1239	2051	396	95	288	1283	1075	851	.296	.393	.506	139	387	96	64	-10	.968	79	*O-1769/1-39,2-28,3	35.6

■ BOB JOHNSON
Johnson, Robert Wallace b: 3/4/36, Omaha, Neb. BR/TR, 5'10", 175 lbs. Deb: 4/19/60

YEAR	TM/L	G	AB	R	H	2B	3B	HR	RBI	BB	SO	AVG	OBP	SLG	PRO+	BR/A	SB	CS	SBR	FA	FR	G/POS	TPR
1960	KC-A	76	146	12	30	4	0	1	9	19	23	.205	.301	.253	51	-10	2	0	1	.947	12	S-30,2-27,3-11	0.6
1961	Was-A	61	224	27	66	13	1	6	28	19	26	.295	.352	.442	113	4	4	2	0	.956	-2	S-57/2-2,3-2	0.6
1962	Was-A	135	466	58	134	20	2	12	43	32	50	.288	.335	.416	102	0	9	6	-1	.944	-4	3-72,S-50/2-3,O-1	0.1
1963	Bal-A	82	254	34	75	10	0	8	32	18	35	.295	.347	.429	120	7	5	1	1	.987	-2	2-50/1-8,S-7,3-5	1.0
1964	Bal-A	93	210	18	52	8	2	3	29	9	37	.248	.277	.348	74	-8	0	0	0	.964	-12	S-18,1-15,2-15/3O	-1.9
1965	Bal-A	87	273	36	66	13	2	5	27	15	34	.242	.284	.359	80	-8	5	2	-0	.996	-11	1-34,S-23,3-13/2-5	-1.9
1966	Bal-A	71	157	13	34	9	1	0	10	12	24	.217	.276	.268	58	-8	2	0	-0	.966	0	2-20,1-17/3-3	-0.9
1967	Bal-A	4	3	1	1	0	0	0	0	1	1	.333	.500	.333	152	0	0	0	0	.000	0	H	-0.1
	NY-N	90	230	26	80	8	3	5	27	12	29	.348	.380	.474	145	13	1	1	-0	.987	-7	2-39,1-23,S-14/3-1	0.8
1968	Cin-N	16	15	2	4	0	0	0	1	1	2	.267	.313	.267	71	-0	0	0	0	.500	-1	/S-2,1-1	-0.1
	Atl-N	59	187	15	49	5	1	0	11	10	20	.262	.299	.299	80	-5	1	1	0	.948	1	3-48/2-4	-0.3
	Yr	75	202	17	53	5	1	0	12	11	22	.262	.300	.297	79	-5	1	1	0	.948	1	3-48/2-4,S-2,1-1	-0.4
1969	StL-N	19	29	1	6	1	0	0	2	2	4	.207	.258	.310	58	-2	0	0	0	.833	-1	/3-4,1-1	-0.3
	Oak-A	51	46	5	23	1	0	1	9	3	4	.343	.380	.402	125	2	1	0	0	1.000	-1	/1-7,2-2	0.2
1970	Oak-A	30	46	6	8	0	1	0	3	2	3	.174	.240	.261	39	-4	2	1	0	.952	1	/3-6,1-1	-0.3
Total	11	874	2307	254	628	88	11	44	230	156	291	.272	.321	.377	95	-18	24	12	0	.956	-26	S-201,2-167,31/O	-2.4

■ RON JOHNSON
Johnson, Ronald David b: 3/23/56, Long Beach, Cal. BR/TR, 6'3", 215 lbs. Deb: 9/12/82

YEAR	TM/L	G	AB	R	H	2B	3B	HR	RBI	BB	SO	AVG	OBP	SLG	PRO+	BR/A	SB	CS	SBR	FA	FR	G/POS	TPR
1982	KC-A	8	14	2	4	2	0	0	4	0	3	.286	.444	.429	141	-0	0	0	0	.976	-0	/1-7	0.0
1983	KC-A	9	27	2	7	0	0	0	3	1	3	.259	.333	.259	66	-1	0	0	0	.971	-1	/1-7,C-2	-0.3
1984	Mon-N	5	5	0	1	0	0	0	1	0	2	.200	.200	.200	13	-1	0	0	0	1.000	-1	/1-2,O-1	-0.1
Total	3	22	46	4	12	2	0	0	8	1	8	.261	.358	.304	85	-2	0	0	0	.974	-2	/1-16,C-2,O-1	-0.4

■ RONDIN JOHNSON
Johnson, Rondin Allen b: 12/16/58, Bremerton, Wash. BB/TR, 5'10", 160 lbs. Deb: 9/3/86

YEAR	TM/L	G	AB	R	H	2B	3B	HR	RBI	BB	SO	AVG	OBP	SLG	PRO+	BR/A	SB	CS	SBR	FA	FR	G/POS	TPR
1986	KC-A	11	31	8	8	1	0	0	2		3	.258	.258	.323	56	-2	0	0	0	1.000	4	2-11	0.2

■ ROY JOHNSON
Johnson, Roy Cleveland b: 2/23/03, Pryor, Okla. d: 9/10/73, Tacoma, Wash. BL/TR, 5'9", 175 lbs. Deb: 4/18/29 F

YEAR	TM/L	G	AB	R	H	2B	3B	HR	RBI	BB	SO	AVG	OBP	SLG	PRO+	BR/A	SB	CS	SBR	FA	FR	G/POS	TPR
1929	Det-A	148	640	128	201	45	14	10	69	67	60	.314	.379	.475	118	17	20	15	-3	.928	14	*O-146	1.7
1930	Det-A	125	462	84	127	30	13	2	35	40	46	.275	.333	.409	85	-11	17	10	-1	.936	4	*O-118	-1.4
1931	Det-A	151	627	107	173	37	19	8	55	72	51	.276	.355	.438	104	3	33	21	-3	.960	15	*O-150	0.5
1932	Det-A	49	195	33	49	14	2	3	22	20	26	.251	.324	.390	81	-6	7	2	1	.929	-0	O-48	-0.7
	Bos-A	94	349	70	104	24	4	11	47	44	41	.298	.378	.484	125	13	13	4	2	.930	-6	O-85	0.3

YEAR	TM/L	G	AB	R	H	2B	3B	HR	RBI	BB	SO	AVG	OBP	SLG	PRO+	BR/A	SB	CS	SBR	FA	FR	G/POS	TPR
	Yr	143	544	103	153	38	6	14	69	64	67	.281	.359	.450	109	7	20	6	2	.930	-5	*O-133	-0.4
1933	Bos-A	133	483	88	151	30	7	10	95	55	36	.313	.387	.466	126	19	13	10	-2	.922	4	*O-125	1.3
1934	Bos-A	143	569	85	182	43	10	7	119	54	36	.320	.379	.467	109	7	11	5	0	.948	-3	*O-137	-0.2
1935	Bos-A	145	553	70	174	33	9	3	66	74	34	.315	.398	.423	105	6	11	12	-4	.944	-2	*O-142	-0.4
1936	*NY-A	63	147	21	39	8	2	1	19	21	14	.265	.361	.367	83	-4	3	1	0	.944	0	O-33	-0.4
1937	NY-A	12	51	5	15	3	0	0	6	3	2	.294	.333	.353	73	-2	1	0	0	.840	-2	O-12	0.2
	Bos-N	85	260	24	72	8	3	3	22	38	29	.277	.369	.365	110	5	5			.965	-1	O-63/3-1	0.2
1938	Bos-N	7	29	2	5	0	0	0	1	1	5	.172	.200	.172	4	-4	1			.769	-2	/O-7	-0.6
Total	10	1155	4359	717	1292	275	83	58	556	489	380	.296	.369	.437	107	43	135	80		.938	22	*O-1066/3-1	-0.1

■ ROY JOHNSON
Johnson, Roy Edward　b: 6/27/59, Parkin, Ark.　BL/TL, 6'4", 205 lbs.　Deb: 7/3/82

YEAR	TM/L	G	AB	R	H	2B	3B	HR	RBI	BB	SO	AVG	OBP	SLG	PRO+	BR/A	SB	CS	SBR	FA	FR	G/POS	TPR
1982	Mon-N	17	32	2	7	2	0	0	2	1	6	.219	.242	.281	45	-2	0	0	0	1.000	-2	O-11	-0.5
1984	Mon-N	16	33	2	5	2	0	1	2	7	10	.152	.300	.303	73	-1	1	0	0	.938	-1	O-10	-0.2
1985	Mon-N	3	5	0	0	0	0	0	0	0	3	.000	.000	.000	-99	-1	0	0	0	.000	-1	/O-3	-0.3
Total	3	36	70	4	12	4	0	1	4	8	19	.171	.256	.271	49	-5	1	0	0	.971	-4	/O-24	-1.0

■ STAN JOHNSON
Johnson, Stanley Lucius　b: 2/12/37, Dallas, Tex.　BL/TL, 5'10", 180 lbs.　Deb: 9/18/60

YEAR	TM/L	G	AB	R	H	2B	3B	HR	RBI	BB	SO	AVG	OBP	SLG	PRO+	BR/A	SB	CS	SBR	FA	FR	G/POS	TPR
1960	Chi-A	5	6	1	1	0	0	1	0	1	1	.167	.167	.667	116	0	0	1	-1	1.000	-1	/O-2	-0.1
1961	KC-A	3	3	1	0	0	0	0	0	2	1	.000	.400	.000	17	-0	0	0	0	.000	-1	/O-2	-0.1
Total	2	8	9	2	1	0	0	1	0	3	2	.111	.273	.444	89	-0	0	1	-1	1.000	-2	/O-4	-0.2

■ TIM JOHNSON
Johnson, Timothy Evald　b: 7/22/49, Grand Forks, N.D.　BL/TR, 6'1", 170 lbs.　Deb: 4/24/73　C

YEAR	TM/L	G	AB	R	H	2B	3B	HR	RBI	BB	SO	AVG	OBP	SLG	PRO+	BR/A	SB	CS	SBR	FA	FR	G/POS	TPR
1973	Mil-A	136	465	39	99	10	2	0	32	29	93	.213	.261	.243	44	-35	6	3	0	.962	-18	*S-135	-3.7
1974	Mil-A	93	245	25	60	7	7	0	25	11	48	.245	.280	.331	76	-8	4	3	-1	.970	-2	S-64,2-26/3-1,0D	-0.3
1975	Mil-A	38	85	6	12	1	0	0	2	6	17	.141	.198	.153	0	-11	3	0	1	1.000	1	2-11,3-11,S-10/1D	-0.8
1976	Mil-A	105	273	25	75	4	3	0	14	19	32	.275	.327	.311	89	-3	4	1	1	.980	-18	*2-100,3-17/1-1,S-1	-1.7
1977	Mil-A	30	33	5	2	1	0	0	2	5	10	.061	.184	.091	-22	-6	1	0	0	.929	3	2-10,3-4,0-1,D	-0.2
1978	Mil-A	3	3	1	0	0	0	0	0	2	0	.000	.000	.000	22	-0	0	0	0	1.000	-1	/S-2	-0.1
	Tor-A	68	79	9	19	2	0	0	3	8	16	.241	.318	.266	65	-3	0	1	-1	.975	5	S-49,2-13	0.4
	Yr	71	82	10	19	2	0	0	3	10	16	.232	.323	.256	63	-4	0	1	-1	.975	4	S-51,2-13	0.3
1979	Tor-A	43	86	6	16	2	1	0	6	8	15	.186	.255	.233	32	-8	0	1	-1	.958	-2	2-25/3-9,1-7	-0.2
Total	7	516	1269	116	283	27	13	0	84	88	231	.223	.276	.265	55	-75	18	9	0	.965	-25	S-267,2-185/31DO	-6.6

■ WALLACE JOHNSON
Johnson, Wallace Darnell　b: 12/25/56, Gary, Ind.　BB/TR, 5'11", 185 lbs.　Deb: 9/8/81

YEAR	TM/L	G	AB	R	H	2B	3B	HR	RBI	BB	SO	AVG	OBP	SLG	PRO+	BR/A	SB	CS	SBR	FA	FR	G/POS	TPR
1981	*Mon-N	11	9	1	2	0	0	0	3	1	1	.222	.300	.444	108	0	1	1	-0	1.000	1	/2-1	0.1
1982	Mon-N	36	57	5	11	0	0	0	2	5	5	.193	.258	.263	45	-4	4	1	1	.952	-6	2-13	-0.9
1983	Mon-N	3	2	1	1	0	0	0	1	0	0	.500	.667	.500	229	1	1	0	0	.000	0	/H	0.1
	SF-N	7	8	0	1	0	0	0	0	1	0	.125	.125	.125	-32	-1	0	0	0	1.000	0	/2-1	-0.1
	Yr	10	10	1	2	0	0	0	1	1	0	.200	.273	.200	34	-1	1	0	0	1.000	1	/2-1	0.0
1984	Mon-N	17	24	3	5	0	0	0	4	5	4	.208	.345	.208	61	-1	0	0	0	.968	0	/1-4	-0.1
1986	Mon-N	61	127	13	36	3	1	1	10	7	9	.283	.321	.346	85	-3	6	3	0	.991	-0	1-27	-0.5
1987	Mon-N	75	85	7	21	5	0	1	14	7	6	.247	.304	.341	69	-4	5	0	2	.972	-1	/1-9	-0.4
1988	Mon-N	86	94	7	29	5	1	0	3	12	15	.309	.387	.383	116	2	2	-0	-1	.989	1	1-13/2-1	0.2
1989	Mon-N	85	114	9	31	3	1	2	17	7	12	.272	.314	.368	93	-1	1	0	0	.972	-1	1-18	-0.4
1990	Mon-N	47	49	6	8	1	0	1	5	9	5	.163	.281	.245	48	-3	1	0	0	1.000	-1	/1-7	-0.5
Total	9	428	569	52	145	17	5	5	59	52	58	.255	.318	.332	81	-15	19	7	2	.983	-7	/1-78,2-16	-2.5

■ WALTER JOHNSON
Johnson, Walter Perry "Barney" or "The Big Train"
b: 11/6/1887, Humboldt, Kan.　d: 12/10/46, Washington, D.C.　BR/TR, 6'1", 200 lbs.　Deb: 8/2/07　MH

YEAR	TM/L	G	AB	R	H	2B	3B	HR	RBI	BB	SO	AVG	OBP	SLG	PRO+	BR/A	SB	CS	SBR	FA	FR	G/POS	TPR
1907	Was-A	14	36	3	4	0	1	0	1	1		.111	.135	.167	-4	-4	0			.893	-2	P-14	0.0
1908	Was-A	36	79	7	13	3	0	0	5	6		.165	.250	.253	69	-3	0			.938	-4	P-36	0.0
1909	Was-A	40	101	6	13	3	0	1	6	1		.129	.137	.188	3	-11	0			.926	-2	P-40	0.0
1910	Was-A	45	137	14	24	6	1	2	12	4		.175	.199	.277	51	-8	2			.950	-1	P-45	0.0
1911	Was-A	42	128	18	30	5	3	1	15	0		.234	.234	.344	62	-7	1			.965	4	P-40	0.0
1912	Was-A	55	144	16	38	6	4	2	20	7		.264	.298	.403	99	-1	2			.964	1	P-50	0.0
1913	Was-A	54	134	12	35	5	6	2	14	5	14	.261	.293	.433	109	0	2			1.000	-0	P-48/O-1	0.0
1914	Was-A	55	136	23	30	4	1	3	16	10	27	.221	.274	.331	79	-4	1	0		.964	2	P-51/O-1	-0.1
1915	Was-A	64	147	14	34	7	4	2	17	8	34	.231	.276	.374	93	-2	0	2	-1	.951	-1	P-47/O-4	-0.2
1916	Was-A	58	142	13	32	2	4	1	7	11	28	.225	.286	.317	82	-4	0			.937	-5	P-48	-0.1
1917	Was-A	57	130	15	33	12	1	0	15	9	30	.254	.312	.362	107	1	0			1.000	-1	P-47	0.0
1918	Was-A	65	150	10	40	4	4	1	18	9	18	.267	.321	.367	109	1	2			.988	-1	P-39/O-4	0.0
1919	Was-A	56	125	13	24	1	3	1	8	12	17	.192	.263	.272	51	-8	1			.988	-1	P-39/O-3	-0.1
1920	Was-A	33	64	6	17	1	3	1	7	3	10	.266	.299	.422	92	-1	0	0	0	.971	-1	P-21	0.0
1921	Was-A	38	111	10	30	7	0	0	10	6	14	.270	.308	.333	67	-6	0	0	0	.982	-3	P-35	0.0
1922	Was-A	43	108	8	22	3	0	1	15	2	12	.204	.218	.259	25	-12	0	0	0	1.000	1	P-41	0.0
1923	Was-A	42	93	11	18	3	3	0	13	4	15	.194	.227	.290	37	-9	0	0	0	.970	-2	P-42	0.0
1924	*Was-A	39	113	18	32	9	0	1	14	3	11	.283	.308	.389	82	-4	0	0	0	1.000	-1	P-38	0.0
1925	*Was-A	36	97	12	42	6	1	2	20	3	6	.433	.455	.577	164	9	0	1	-1	1.000	-4	P-30	0.0
1926	Was-A	35	103	6	20	5	0	1	12	3	11	.194	.217	.272	28	-11	0	0	0	.980	-5	P-33	0.0
1927	Was-A	26	46	6	16	2	0	2	10	3	4	.348	.388	.522	136	2	0	0	0	1.000		P-18	0.0
Total	21	933	2324	241	547	94	41	24	255	110	251	.235	.274	.342	76	-84	13	4		.969	-25	P-802/O-13	-0.4

■ BILL JOHNSON
Johnson, William F. "Sleepy Bill"　b: 9/1862, New Jersey　d: 7/17/42, Chester, Pa.　BL/TL, 140 lbs.　Deb: 6/27/1884

YEAR	TM/L	G	AB	R	H	2B	3B	HR	RBI	BB	SO	AVG	OBP	SLG	PRO+	BR/A	SB	CS	SBR	FA	FR	G/POS	TPR
1884	Phi-U	1	4	0	0	0	0	0	0	0		.000	.000	.000	-99	-1				.000	-0	/O-1	-0.1
1887	Ind-N	11	42	3	8	0	0	0	3	0	6	.190	.209	.190	12	-5	5			.765	-2	O-11	-0.6
1890	Bal-a	24	95	15	28	2	3	0	6	7		.295	.350	.379	110	1	8			.865	2	O-24	0.2
1891	Bal-a	129	480	101	130	13	14	2	79	89	55	.271	.389	.369	116	13	32			.877	6	*O-129	1.2
1892	Bal-N	4	15	2	2	0	0	0	2	2	0	.133	.235	.133	12	-2	0			.667	-1	/O-4	-0.3
Total	5	169	636	121	168	15	17	2	90	98	61	.264	.368	.351	105	6	45			.867	5	O-169	0.4

■ BILL JOHNSON
Johnson, William Lawrence　b: 10/18/1892, Chicago, Ill.　d: 11/3/50, Los Angeles, Cal.　BL/TL, 5'11", 170 lbs.　Deb: 9/22/16

YEAR	TM/L	G	AB	R	H	2B	3B	HR	RBI	BB	SO	AVG	OBP	SLG	PRO+	BR/A	SB	CS	SBR	FA	FR	G/POS	TPR
1916	Phi-A	4	15	1	4	1	0	0	1	0	4	.267	.267	.333	84	-0	0			1.000	-1	/O-4	-0.2
1917	Phi-A	48	109	7	19	2	2	1	8	8	14	.174	.237	.257	51	-7	4			.900	-3	O-30	-1.2
Total	2	52	124	8	23	3	2	1	9	8	18	.185	.241	.266	55	-7	4			.909	-4	/O-34	-1.4

■ BILLY JOHNSON
Johnson, William Russell "Bull"　b: 8/30/18, Montclair, N.J.　BR/TR, 5'10", 180 lbs.　Deb: 4/22/43

YEAR	TM/L	G	AB	R	H	2B	3B	HR	RBI	BB	SO	AVG	OBP	SLG	PRO+	BR/A	SB	CS	SBR	FA	FR	G/POS	TPR
1943	*NY-A	155	592	70	166	24	6	5	94	53	30	.280	.344	.367	107	5	3	5	-2	.966	12	*3-155	1.8
1946	NY-A	85	296	51	77	14	5	4	35	31	42	.260	.334	.382	98	-1	1	0	0	.955	7	3-74	0.8
1947	*NY-A★	132	494	67	141	19	8	10	95	44	47	.285	.351	.417	114	8	1	2	-1	.952	-17	*3-132	-0.9
1948	NY-A	127	446	59	131	20	6	12	64	41	30	.294	.358	.446	114	8	0	0	0	.947	6	*3-118	1.2
1949	*NY-A	113	329	48	82	11	3	8	56	48	44	.249	.348	.374	91	-4	0	0	0	.951	-2	3-81,1-21/2-1	-0.8
1950	*NY-A	108	327	44	85	16	2	6	40	42	30	.260	.346	.376	87	-6	1	0	0	.958	-1	*3-100/1-5	-0.8
1951	NY-A	15	40	5	12	3	0	0	4	7	0	.300	.404	.375	116	1	0	1	-1	.960	-3	3-13	-0.2
	StL-N	124	442	52	116	23	1	14	64	46	49	.262	.340	.414	101	1	5	3	-0	.976	11	*3-124	1.0
1952	StL-N	94	282	23	71	10	2	2	34	34	21	.252	.339	.323	84	-5	3	0	0	.951	2	3-89	-0.5
1953	StL-N	11	5	0	1	1	0	0	1	1	3	.200	.333	.400	90	-0	0	0	0	1.000	2	3-11	0.2
Total	9	964	3253	419	882	141	33	61	487	347	290	.271	.346	.408	102	6	13	11	-3	.959	18	3-897/1-26,2-1	1.8

■ GREG JOHNSTON
Johnston, Gregory Bernard　b: 2/12/55, Los Angeles, Cal.　BL/TL, 6', 175 lbs.　Deb: 7/27/79

YEAR	TM/L	G	AB	R	H	2B	3B	HR	RBI	BB	SO	AVG	OBP	SLG	PRO+	BR/A	SB	CS	SBR	FA	FR	G/POS	TPR
1979	SF-N	42	74	5	15	2	0	1	7	2	17	.203	.224	.270	37	-7	0	0	0	.966	-1	O-17	-0.9
1980	Min-A	14	27	3	5	3	0	0	1	2	4	.185	.241	.296	43	-2	0	0	0	1.000	-3	O-14	-0.5

YEAR	TM/L	G	AB	R	H	2B	3B	HR	RBI	BB	SO	AVG	OBP	SLG	PRO+	BR/A	SB	CS	SBR	FA	FR	G/POS	TPR
1981	Min-A	7	16	2	2	0	0	0	0	2	5	.125	.222	.125	2	-2	0	0	0	1.000	0	/O-6	-0.2
Total	3	63	117	10	22	5	0	1	8	6	26	.188	.228	.256	33	-11	0	0	0	.985	-4	/O-37	-1.6

■ JIMMY JOHNSTON   Johnston, James Harle b: 12/10/1889, Cleveland, Tenn. d: 2/14/67, Chattanooga, Tenn. BR/TR, 5'10", 160 lbs. Deb: 5/3/11 FC

YEAR	TM/L	G	AB	R	H	2B	3B	HR	RBI	BB	SO	AVG	OBP	SLG	PRO+	BR/A	SB	CS	SBR	FA	FR	G/POS	TPR
1911	Chi-A	1	2	0	0	0	0	0		2	0	.000	.000	.000	-99	-1	0			1.000	0	/O-1	-0.1
1914	Chi-N	50	101	9	23	3	2	1	8	4	9	.228	.264	.327	76	-3	3			.929	4	O-28/2-4	0.0
1916	*Bro-N	118	425	58	107	13	8	1	26	35	38	.252	.313	.327	94	-3	22	19	-5	.964	7	*O-106	-0.7
1917	Bro-N	103	330	33	89	10	4	0	25	23	28	.270	.321	.324	96	-1	16			.958	4	O-66,1-14/S-4,23	-0.2
1918	Bro-N	123	484	54	136	16	8	0	27	33	31	.281	.328	.347	106	3	22			.956	8	O-96,1-21/3-4,2-1	0.5
1919	Bro-N	117	405	56	114	11	4	1	23	29	26	.281	.334	.336	100	0	11			.960	-6	2-87,O-14/1-2,S-1	-0.2
1920	*Bro-N	155	635	87	185	17	12	1	52	43	23	.291	.338	.361	98	-2	19	15	-3	.934	-6	*3-146/O-7,S-3	-0.4
1921	Bro-N	152	624	104	203	41	14	5	56	45	26	.325	.372	.460	115	13	28	16	-1	.935	8	*3-150/S-3	3.0
1922	Bro-N	138	567	110	181	20	7	4	49	38	17	.319	.364	.402	98	-1	18	9	0	.947	7	2-62,S-50,3-26	1.3
1923	Bro-N	151	625	111	203	29	11	4	60	53	15	.325	.378	.426	115	14	16	13	-3	.948	19	2-84,S-52,3-14	3.6
1924	Bro-N	86	315	51	94	11	2	2	29	27	10	.298	.356	.365	97	-1	5	6	-2	.939	-4	S-63,3-10/1-4,O-1	0.1
1925	Bro-N	123	431	63	128	13	3	2	43	45	15	.297	.369	.355	88	-6	7	5	-1	.886	-23	3-81,O-20/1-8,S-2	-2.4
1926	Bos-N	23	57	7	14	1	0	1	5	10	3	.246	.358	.316	91	-0	2			.865	4	3-14/2-2,O-1	-0.3
	NY-N	37	69	11	16	0	0	0	5	6	5	.232	.293	.232	43	-5	0			1.000	-5	O-14	-1.1
	Yr	60	126	18	30	1	0	1	10	16	8	.238	.324	.270	64	-6	2			1.000	0	O-15,3-14/2-2	-1.4
Total	13	1377	5070	754	1493	185	75	22	410	391	246	.294	.347	.374	100	7	169	83		.926	10	3-448,O-354,2S/1	3.1

■ JOHNNY JOHNSTON   Johnston, John Thomas b: 3/28/1890, Longview, Tex. d: 3/7/40, San Diego, Cal. BL/TR, 5'11", 172 lbs. Deb: 4/10/13

YEAR	TM/L	G	AB	R	H	2B	3B	HR	RBI	BB	SO	AVG	OBP	SLG	PRO+	BR/A	SB	CS	SBR	FA	FR	G/POS	TPR
1913	StL-A	111	380	37	85	14	4	2	27	42	51	.224	.308	.297	79	-10	11			.965	12	*O-107	-0.3

■ REX JOHNSTON   Johnston, Rex David b: 11/8/37, Colton, Cal. BB/TR, 6'1.5", 202 lbs. Deb: 4/15/64

YEAR	TM/L	G	AB	R	H	2B	3B	HR	RBI	BB	SO	AVG	OBP	SLG	PRO+	BR/A	SB	CS	SBR	FA	FR	G/POS	TPR
1964	Pit-N	14	7	1	0	0	0	0		3	0	.000	.300	.000	-7	-1	0	0	0	1.000	-2	/O-8	-0.3

■ DICK JOHNSTON   Johnston, Richard Frederick b: 4/6/1863, Kingston, N.Y. d: 4/4/34, Detroit, Mich. BR/TR, 5'8", 155 lbs. Deb: 8/12/1884

YEAR	TM/L	G	AB	R	H	2B	3B	HR	RBI	BB	SO	AVG	OBP	SLG	PRO+	BR/A	SB	CS	SBR	FA	FR	G/POS	TPR
1884	Ric-a	39	146	23	41	5	5	2			2	.281	.291	.425	132	5				.865	9	O-37/S-2	1.2
1885	Bos-N	26	111	17	26	6	3	1	23	0	15	.234	.234	.369	96	-1				.842	1	O-26	0.0
1886	Bos-N	109	413	48	99	18	9	1	57	3	70	.240	.245	.334	78	-12	11			.892	17	O-109	0.2
1887	Bos-N	127	507	87	131	13	20	5	77	16	35	.258	.281	.393	85	-12	52			.933	25	*O-127	0.9
1888	Bos-N	135	585	102	173	31	**18**	12	68	15	33	.296	.314	.472	145	27	35			.898	7	*O-135	2.9
1889	Bos-N	132	539	80	123	16	4	5	67	41	60	.228	.285	.301	60	-31	34			.917	-7	*O-132	-3.6
1890	Bos-P	2	9	0	1	0	0	0	0	0	1	.111	.111	.111	-38	-2	0			.800	0	/O-2	-0.1
	NY-P	77	306	37	74	9	7	1	43	18	25	.242	.288	.327	59	-20	7			.897	3	O-76/S-2	-1.6
	Yr	79	315	37	75	9	7	1	43	18	26	.238	.284	.321	56	-22	7			.894	3	O-78/S-2	-1.7
1891	Cin-a	99	376	59	83	11	2	6	51	38	44	.221	.301	.309	68	-18	12			.895	-1	*O-99	-1.9
Total	8	746	2992	453	751	109	68	33	386	133	283	.251	.285	.366	87	-63	151			.903	54	O-743/S-4	-2.0

■ DOC JOHNSTON   Johnston, Wheeler Roger b: 9/9/1887, Cleveland, Tenn. d: 2/17/61, Chattanooga, Tenn. BL/TL, 6', 170 lbs. Deb: 10/3/09 F

YEAR	TM/L	G	AB	R	H	2B	3B	HR	RBI	BB	SO	AVG	OBP	SLG	PRO+	BR/A	SB	CS	SBR	FA	FR	G/POS	TPR
1909	Cin-N	3	10	1	0	0	0	0		1	0	.000	.000	.000	-99	-2	0			1.000	0	/1-3	-0.2
1912	Cle-A	43	164	22	46	7	4	1	11	11		.280	.326	.390	101	-0	8			.991	-2	1-41	-0.3
1913	Cle-A	133	530	74	135	19	12	2	39	35	65	.255	.309	.347	89	-8	19			.989	-1	*1-133	-1.2
1914	Cle-A	103	340	43	83	15	1	0	23	28	46	.244	.311	.294	79	-9	14	9	-1	.987	-7	1-90/O-2	-2.1
1915	Pit-N	147	543	71	144	19	12	5	64	38	40	.265	.328	.372	113	8	26	17	-2	.991	-12	*1-147	-1.1
1916	Pit-N	114	404	33	86	10	10	0	39	20	42	.213	.262	.287	68	-16	17			.987	-2	*1-110	-2.5
1918	Cle-A	74	273	30	62	12	2	0	25	26	19	.227	.301	.286	70	-10	12			.989	4	1-73	-1.8
1919	Cle-A	102	331	42	101	17	3	1	33	25	18	.305	.359	.384	102	1	21			.984	-3	1-98	-0.6
1920	*Cle-A	147	535	68	156	24	10	2	71	28	32	.292	.333	.385	87	-11	13	7	-0	.992	-1	*1-147	-1.5
1921	Cle-A	118	384	53	114	20	7	2	46	29	15	.297	.353	.401	90	-6	2	9	-5	.988	-1	*1-116	-1.3
1922	Phi-A	71	260	41	65	11	7	1	29	24	15	.250	.316	.358	73	-10	7	6	-2	.990	-5	1-65	-2.0
Total	11	1055	3774	478	992	154	68	14	381	264	292	.263	.319	.351	88	-63	139	48		.989	-37	*1-1023/O-2	-14.6

■ FRED JOHNSTON   Johnston, Wilfred Ivy b: 7/9/1899, Charlotte, N.C. d: 7/14/59, Tyler, Tex. BR/TR, 5'11.5", 170 lbs. Deb: 6/29/24

YEAR	TM/L	G	AB	R	H	2B	3B	HR	RBI	BB	SO	AVG	OBP	SLG	PRO+	BR/A	SB	CS	SBR	FA	FR	G/POS	TPR
1924	Bro-N	4	4	1	1	0	0	0	0		1	.250	.250	.250	35	-0	0	0	0	.667	0	/2-1,3-1	0.0

■ JAY JOHNSTONE   Johnstone, John William b: 11/20/45, Manchester, Conn. BL/TR, 6'1", 175 lbs. Deb: 7/30/66

YEAR	TM/L	G	AB	R	H	2B	3B	HR	RBI	BB	SO	AVG	OBP	SLG	PRO+	BR/A	SB	CS	SBR	FA	FR	G/POS	TPR
1966	Cal-A	61	254	35	67	12	4	3	17	11	36	.264	.297	.378	95	-2	3	3	-1	.975	-2	O-61	-0.8
1967	Cal-A	79	230	18	48	7	1	2	10	5	37	.209	.226	.274	49	-15	3	2	-0	.973	2	O-63	-1.8
1968	Cal-A	41	115	11	30	4	1	0	3	7	15	.261	.303	.313	90	-2	2	1	-0	.984	2	O-29	-0.1
1969	Cal-A	148	540	64	146	20	5	10	59	38	75	.270	.324	.381	102	-0	3	9	-5	.983	12	*O-144	-0.5
1970	Cal-A	119	320	34	76	10	5	11	39	24	53	.237	.293	.403	93	-4	1	0	0	.981	-1	*O-100	-1.0
1971	Chi-A	124	388	53	101	14	1	16	40	38	50	.260	.331	.425	109	4	10	5	0	.968	-3	*O-119	-0.4
1972	Chi-A	113	261	27	49	9	0	4	17	25	42	.188	.259	.268	56	-14	2	1	0	.988	-12	O-97	-3.3
1973	Oak-A	23	28	1	3	1	0	0	3	2	4	.107	.167	.143	-13	-4	0	1	-1	1.000	-2	/O-7,2-1,D-4	-0.7
1974	Phi-N	64	200	30	59	10	4	6	30	24	28	.295	.371	.475	130	8	5	5	-2	.968	-7	O-59	-0.3
1975	Phi-N	122	350	50	115	19	2	7	54	42	39	.329	.401	.454	132	16	7	3	0	.976	-2	*O-101	1.1
1976	*Phi-N	129	440	62	140	38	4	5	53	41	39	.318	.379	.457	132	19	5	5	-2	.982	8	*O-122/1-6	2.1
1977	*Phi-N	112	363	64	103	18	4	15	59	38	38	.284	.355	.479	116	8	3	7	-3	1.000	3	O-91,1-19	0.3
1978	Phi-N	35	56	3	10	2	0	0	4	6	9	.179	.258	.214	33	-5	0	2	-1	.988	-1	/1-8,O-7	-0.9
	*NY-A	36	65	6	17	0	0	1	6	4	10	.262	.333	.308	83	-1	0	1	-1	1.000	-3	O-22/D-5	-0.5
1979	NY-A	23	48	7	10	1	0	1	7	2	7	.208	.240	.292	44	-1	0	0	0	1.000	0	O-19/D-3	-0.6
	SD-N	75	201	10	59	8	2	0	32	18	21	.294	.352	.353	99	-0	1	3	-2	.985	-3	O-45,1-22	-0.7
1980	LA-N	109	251	31	77	15	2	2	20	24	29	.307	.372	.406	119	7	3	2	-0	.965	3	O-61	0.6
1981	*LA-N	61	83	8	17	3	0	3	6	7	13	.205	.267	.349	76	-3	0	1	-1	.957	0	O-16/1-2	-0.4
1982	LA-N	21	13	1	1	1	0	0	2	5	2	.077	.333	.154	41	-1	0	0	0	.000	0	H	-0.2
	Chi-N	98	269	39	67	13	1	10	43	40	41	.249	.346	.416	109	4	0	2	-1	.982	1	O-86	0.1
	Yr	119	282	40	68	14	1	10	45	45	43	.241	.346	.404	107	3	0	2	-1	.982	1	O-86	-0.1
1983	Chi-N	86	140	16	36	10	0	6	22	20	24	.257	.362	.436	115	3	1	1	-0	.935	-4	O-44	-0.2
1984	Chi-N	52	73	8	21	2	0	3		7	18	.288	.350	.370	94	-0	0	0	0	1.000	-4	O-15	-0.5
1985	*LA-N	17	15	0	2	1	0	0		2	3	.133	.188	.200	9	-2	0	0	0	.000	0	H	-0.2
Total	20	1748	4703	578	1254	215	38	102	531	429	632	.267	.331	.394	103	10	50	54	-17	.979	-17	*O-1308/1-57,D-12,2	-8.4

■ STAN JOK   Jok, Stanley Edward "Tucker" b: 5/3/26, Buffalo, N.Y. d: 3/6/72, Buffalo, N.Y. BR/TR, 6', 190 lbs. Deb: 4/13/54

YEAR	TM/L	G	AB	R	H	2B	3B	HR	RBI	BB	SO	AVG	OBP	SLG	PRO+	BR/A	SB	CS	SBR	FA	FR	G/POS	TPR
1954	Phi-N	3	3	0	0	0	0	0	0	0		.000	.000	.000	-99	-1	0	0	0	.000	0	H	-0.1
	Chi-A	3	12	1	2	0	0	0		1	2	.167	.231	.167	10	-1	0	0	0	1.000	-0	/3-3	-0.2
1955	Chi-A	6	4	3	1	0	0	1	0	1	2	.250	.400	1.000	260	1	0	0	0	.857	1	/3-3,O-1	0.1
Total	2	12	19	4	3	0	0	1	4	2	5	.158	.238	.316	47	-2	0	0	0	.941	0	/3-6,O-1	-0.2

■ SMEAD JOLLEY   Jolley, Smead Powell "Guinea" or "Smudge" b: 1/14/02, Wesson, Ark. d: 11/17/91, Alameda, Cal. BL/TR, 6'3.5", 210 lbs. Deb: 4/17/30

YEAR	TM/L	G	AB	R	H	2B	3B	HR	RBI	BB	SO	AVG	OBP	SLG	PRO+	BR/A	SB	CS	SBR	FA	FR	G/POS	TPR
1930	Chi-A	152	616	76	193	38	12	16	114	28	52	.313	.346	.492	114	10	3	1	0	.950	-3	*O-151	-0.3
1931	Chi-A	54	110	5	33	11	0	3	28	7	4	.300	.353	.482	125	3	0	0	0	.857	-5	O-23	-0.2
1932	Chi-A	12	42	3	15	3	0	0	7	3	0	.357	.413	.429	127	2	1	0	0	.923	-2	O-11	-0.1
	Bos-A	137	531	57	164	27	5	18	99	27	29	.309	.345	.480	115	9	0	5	-3	.943	-5	*O-126/C-5	-0.6
	Yr	149	573	60	179	30	5	18	106	30	29	.312	.350	.476	116	11	1	5	-3	.942	-8	*O-137/C-5	-0.7
1933	Bos-A	137	531	47	116	32	4	9	65	24	20	.282	.325	.445	103	-0	1	2	0	.955	-4	O-102	-0.9
Total	4	473	1710	188	521	111	21	46	313	89	105	.305	.343	.475	112	24	5	7	-3	.944	-19	O-413/C-5	-2.1

■ JONES   Jones Deb: 5/14/1873

YEAR	TM/L	G	AB	R	H	2B	3B	HR	RBI	BB	SO	AVG	OBP	SLG	PRO+	BR/A	SB	CS	SBR	FA	FR	G/POS	TPR
1873	Mar-n	1	4	0	3	0	0	0	0	1	0	.750	.750	.750	452	2	0	0	0	.800	0	/O-1	0.1

YEAR	TM/L	G	AB	R	H	2B	3B	HR	RBI	BB	SO	AVG	OBP	SLG	PRO+	BR/A	SB	CS	SBR	FA	FR	G/POS	TPR
1874	Bal-n	2	7	0	1	0	0	0	1	0	0	.143	.143	.143	-8	-1	0	0	0	.875	-1	/C-1,O-1	-0.1
Total	2 n	3	11	0	4	0	0	0	2	0	0	.364	.364	.364	140		0	0	0	.800	-0	/O-2,C-1	0.0

■ JONES   Jones b: Johnstown, Pa. Deb: 7/14/1884

YEAR	TM/L	G	AB	R	H	2B	3B	HR	RBI	BB	SO	AVG	OBP	SLG	PRO+	BR/A	SB	CS	SBR	FA	FR	G/POS	TPR
1884	Was-a	4	17	2	5	0	0	0			1	.294	.333	.294	120	0				1.000	-0	/O-4	0.0

■ JONES   Jones Deb: 4/30/1885

YEAR	TM/L	G	AB	R	H	2B	3B	HR	RBI	BB	SO	AVG	OBP	SLG	PRO+	BR/A	SB	CS	SBR	FA	FR	G/POS	TPR
1885	NY-a	1	4	0	1	0	0	0	0	0	0	.250	.250	.250	63	-0				1.000	1	/3-1	0.1

■ ANDRUW JONES   Jones, Andruw Rudolf b: 4/23/77, Willemstad, Curacao BR/TR, 6'1", 170 lbs. Deb: 8/15/96

YEAR	TM/L	G	AB	R	H	2B	3B	HR	RBI	BB	SO	AVG	OBP	SLG	PRO+	BR/A	SB	CS	SBR	FA	FR	G/POS	TPR
1996	*Atl-N	31	106	11	23	7	1	5	13	7	29	.217	.265	.443	78	-4	3	0	1	.975	5	O-29	0.1

■ CHARLIE JONES   Jones, Charles C. "Casey" b: 6/2/1876, Butler, Pa. d: 4/2/47, Two Harbors, Minn. BR/TR, 6'1", Deb: 5/3/01

YEAR	TM/L	G	AB	R	H	2B	3B	HR	RBI	BB	SO	AVG	OBP	SLG	PRO+	BR/A	SB	CS	SBR	FA	FR	G/POS	TPR
1901	Bos-A	10	41	6	6	2	0	0	6	1		.146	.167	.195	0	-6	2			.929	-2	O-10	-0.8
1904	Chi-A	5	17	2	4	0	1	0	1	1		.235	.278	.353	103	-0	0			1.000	1	/O-5	0.1
1905	Was-A	142	544	68	113	18	4	2	41	31		.208	.254	.267	68	-20	24			.971	17	*O-142	-1.2
1906	Was-A	131	497	56	120	11	11	3	42	24		.241	.283	.326	95	-4	34			.961	8	*O-128/2-1	-0.3
1907	Was-A	121	437	48	116	14	10	0	37	22		.265	.304	.343	115	6	26			.967	-1	*O-111/2-5,1-4,S-2	0.1
1908	StL-A	74	263	37	61	11	2	0	17	14		.232	.279	.289	84	-5	14			.963	-1	O-72	-1.0
Total	6	483	1799	217	420	56	28	5	144	93		.233	.276	.304	87	-29	100			.966	21	O-468/2-6,1-4,S-2	-3.1

■ CHARLIE JONES   Jones, Charles F. b: New York, N.Y. Deb: 6/28/1884

YEAR	TM/L	G	AB	R	H	2B	3B	HR	RBI	BB	SO	AVG	OBP	SLG	PRO+	BR/A	SB	CS	SBR	FA	FR	G/POS	TPR
1884	Bro-a	25	90	10	16	1	0	0			5	.178	.221	.189	35	-6				.871	-7	2-13,3-11/O-2	-1.2

■ CHARLEY JONES   Jones, Charles Wesley "Baby" (b: Benjamin Wesley Rippay) b: 4/30/1850, Alamance Co., N.C. BR/TR, 5'11.5", 202 lbs. Deb: 5/4/1875 U

YEAR	TM/L	G	AB	R	H	2B	3B	HR	RBI	BB	SO	AVG	OBP	SLG	PRO+	BR/A	SB	CS	SBR	FA	FR	G/POS	TPR
1875	Wes-n	12	47	4	13	2	4	0	10	0	5	.277	.277	.489	152	2	1	1	-0	.800	-2	O-12	0.0
	Har-n	1	4	1	0	0	0	0	0	0	1	.000	.000	.000	-95	-1	0	0	0	.667	-0	/O-1	-0.1
	Yr	13	51	5	13	2	4	0	10	0	6	.255	.255	.451	133	1	1	1	-0	.778	-2	O-13	-0.1
1876	Cin-N	64	276	40	79	17	4	4	38	7	17	.286	.304	.420	162	19				.857	3	*O-64	1.8
1877	Cin-N	17	69	16	21	3	3	1	10	4	8	.304	.342	.478	175	6				.920	1	1-10/O-8	0.6
	Chi-N	2	8	1	3	1	0	0	2	1	0	.375	.444	.500	176	1				1.000	1	/O-2	0.1
	Cin-N	38	163	36	51	8	7	1	26	10	17	.313	.353	.466	175	14				.838	10	O-38	2.0
	Yr	57	240	53	75	12	10	2	38	15	25	.313	.353	.471	175	21				.845	12	O-48,1-10	**2.7**
1878	Cin-N	61	261	50	81	11	7	3	39	4	17	.310	.321	.441	163	17				.896	6	*O-61	1.9
1879	Bos-N	83	355	**85**	112	22	10	**9**	**62**	**29**	38	.315	.367	.510	182	31				**.933**	7	*O-83	3.5
1880	Bos-N	66	280	44	84	15	3	5	37	11	27	.300	.326	.429	159	17				.826	-4	*O-66	1.0
1883	Cin-a	90	391	84	115	15	12	10	80	20		.294	.328	.471	146	18				.876	2	*O-90	1.7
1884	Cin-a	112	472	107	148	19	17	7	71	37		.314	**.376**	.470	166	34				.887	3	*O-112	3.1
1885	Cin-a	112	487	108	157	19	17	5	35	21		.322	.362	.462	156	29				.891	12	*O-112	3.4
1886	Cin-a	127	500	87	135	22	10	6	68	61		.270	.356	.390	130	17	3			.879	3	*O-127	1.5
1887	Cin-a	41	153	28	48	7	4	2	40	19		.314	.400	.451	134	7	7			.900	-0	O-41	0.5
	NY-a	62	247	30	63	11	3	3	29	12		.255	.306	.360	89	-4	8			.917	4	O-62/P-2,1-1	-0.1
	Yr	103	400	58	111	18	7	5	69	31		.278	.343	.395	107	4	15			.910	4	*O-103/P-2,1-1	0.4
1888	KC-a	6	25	2	4	0	1	0	5	1		.160	.192	.240	36	-2	1			.750	-1	/O-6	-0.1
Total	11	881	3687	728	1101	170	98	56	542	237	124	.299	.347	.443	150	206	19	0		.882	51	O-872/1-11,P-2	20.7

■ CHRIS JONES   Jones, Christopher Carlos b: 12/16/65, Utica, N.Y. BR/TR, 6'2", 205 lbs. Deb: 4/21/91

YEAR	TM/L	G	AB	R	H	2B	3B	HR	RBI	BB	SO	AVG	OBP	SLG	PRO+	BR/A	SB	CS	SBR	FA	FR	G/POS	TPR
1991	Cin-N	52	89	14	26	1	2	2	9	2	31	.292	.308	.416	98	-1	2	1	0	1.000	-5	O-26	-0.6
1992	Hou-N	54	63	7	12	2	1	1	4	7	21	.190	.271	.302	65	-3	3	0	1	.931	-13	O-43	-1.7
1993	Col-N	86	209	29	57	11	4	6	31	10	48	.273	.306	.450	85	-5	9	4	0	.983	-9	O-70	-1.5
1994	Col-N	21	40	6	12	2	1	0	2	1	14	.300	.333	.400	77	-1	0	1	-1	.941	-5	O-14	-0.7
1995	NY-N	79	182	33	51	6	2	8	31	13	45	.280	.332	.467	111	0	2	1	0	.976	-2	O-52/1-5	-0.1
1996	NY-N	89	149	22	36	7	0	4	18	12	42	.242	.307	.369	83	-4	1	0	0	.957	-14	O-66/1-5	-1.8
Total	6	381	732	111	194	29	10	21	92	46	201	.265	.311	.418	90	-12	17	7	1	.971	-48	O-271/1-10	-6.4

■ CHRIS JONES   Jones, Christopher Dale b: 7/13/57, Los Angeles, Cal. BL/TL, 6', 183 lbs. Deb: 6/8/85

YEAR	TM/L	G	AB	R	H	2B	3B	HR	RBI	BB	SO	AVG	OBP	SLG	PRO+	BR/A	SB	CS	SBR	FA	FR	G/POS	TPR
1985	Hou-N	31	25	0	5	0	0	0	1	3	7	.200	.286	.200	39	-2	0	0	0	1.000	-3	O-15	-0.6
1986	SF-N	3	1	0	0	0	0	0	0	0	0	.000	.000	.000	-99	-0	1	0	0	.000	0	/H	0.0
Total	2	34	26	0	5	0	0	0	1	3	7	.192	.276	.192	34	-2	1	0	0	1.000	-3	/O-15	-0.6

■ CLARENCE JONES   Jones, Clarence Woodrow b: 11/7/41, Zanesville, Ohio BL/TL, 6'2", 185 lbs. Deb: 4/20/67 C

YEAR	TM/L	G	AB	R	H	2B	3B	HR	RBI	BB	SO	AVG	OBP	SLG	PRO+	BR/A	SB	CS	SBR	FA	FR	G/POS	TPR
1967	Chi-N	53	135	13	34	7	0	2	16	14	33	.252	.322	.348	88	-2	0	0	0	.978	-4	O-31,1-13	-0.9
1968	Chi-N	5	2	0	0	0	0	0	0	2	1	.000	.500	.000	56	-0	0	0	0	1.000	-0	/1-1	0.0
Total	2	58	137	13	34	7	0	2	16	16	34	.248	.327	.343	88	-2	0	0	0	.979	-4	/O-31,1-14	-0.9

■ CLEON JONES   Jones, Cleon Joseph b: 8/4/42, Plateau, Ala. BR/TL, 6', 200 lbs. Deb: 9/14/63

YEAR	TM/L	G	AB	R	H	2B	3B	HR	RBI	BB	SO	AVG	OBP	SLG	PRO+	BR/A	SB	CS	SBR	FA	FR	G/POS	TPR
1963	NY-N	6	15	1	2	0	0	0	0	0	0	.133	.133	.133	-23	-2	0	0	0	1.000	-1	/O-5	-0.4
1965	NY-N	30	74	2	11	1	0	1	9	2	23	.149	.171	.203	5	-9	1	0	0	1.000	-1	O-23	-1.2
1966	NY-N	139	495	74	136	16	4	8	57	30	62	.275	.320	.372	94	-4	16	8	0	.979	-2	*O-129	-1.3
1967	NY-N	129	411	46	101	10	5	5	30	19	57	.246	.286	.331	77	-13	12	2	2	.977	-6	*O-115	-2.4
1968	NY-N	147	509	63	151	29	4	14	55	31	98	.297	.343	.452	136	21	23	12	-0	.963	-10	*O-139	0.5
1969	*NY-N★	137	483	92	164	25	4	12	75	64	60	.340	.424	.482	150	35	16	8	0	.991	8	*O-122,1-15	3.7
1970	NY-N	134	506	71	140	25	8	10	63	57	87	.277	.356	.417	106	5	12	3	2	.981	12	*O-130	1.2
1971	NY-N	136	505	63	161	24	6	14	69	53	87	.319	.386	.473	144	29	6	5	-1	.981	7	*O-132	3.0
1972	NY-N	106	375	39	92	15	1	5	52	30	83	.245	.308	.331	84	-8	1	6	-3	.986	-1	O-84,1-20	-1.9
1973	*NY-N	92	339	48	88	13	0	11	48	28	51	.260	.322	.395	99	-1	1	1	0	.967	-1	O-92	-0.5
1974	NY-N	124	461	62	130	23	1	13	60	38	79	.282	.345	.421	115	8	3	3	-1	.970	-4	*O-120	0.5
1975	NY-N	21	50	2	12	1	0	0	2	3	6	.240	.283	.260	54	-2	0	0	0	1.000	-3	O-12	-0.7
1976	Chi-A	12	40	2	8	1	0	0	3	5	5	.200	.304	.225	56	-2	0	0	0	1.000	-2	/O-8,D-3	-0.5
Total	13	1213	4263	565	1196	183	33	93	524	360	702	.281	.342	.404	111	56	91	48	-2	.978	6	*O-1111/1-35,D-3	-0.0

■ COBE JONES   Jones, Coburn Dyas b: 8/21/07, Denver, Colo. d: 6/3/69, Denver, Colo. BB/TR, 5'7", 155 lbs. Deb: 9/27/28

YEAR	TM/L	G	AB	R	H	2B	3B	HR	RBI	BB	SO	AVG	OBP	SLG	PRO+	BR/A	SB	CS	SBR	FA	FR	G/POS	TPR
1928	Pit-N	1	2	0	1	0	0	0	0	0	0	.500	.500	.500	156	0	0			1.000	-0	/S-1	0.0
1929	Pit-N	25	63	6	16	5	1	0	4	1	5	.254	.266	.365	53	-5	1			.919	-8	S-15	-1.0
Total	2	26	65	6	17	5	1	0	4	1	5	.262	.273	.369	56	-5	1			.921	-8	/S-16	-1.0

■ DARRYL JONES   Jones, Darryl Lee b: 6/5/51, Meadville, Pa. BR/TR, 5'10", 175 lbs. Deb: 6/6/79 F

YEAR	TM/L	G	AB	R	H	2B	3B	HR	RBI	BB	SO	AVG	OBP	SLG	PRO+	BR/A	SB	CS	SBR	FA	FR	G/POS	TPR
1979	NY-A	18	47	6	12	5	1	0	6	2	7	.255	.286	.404	86	-1	0	0	0	1.000	-1	D-15/O-2	-0.2

■ DAVY JONES   Jones, David Jefferson "Kangaroo" b: 6/30/1880, Cambria, Wis. d: 3/31/72, Mankato, Minn. BL/TR, 5'10", 165 lbs. Deb: 9/15/01

YEAR	TM/L	G	AB	R	H	2B	3B	HR	RBI	BB	SO	AVG	OBP	SLG	PRO+	BR/A	SB	CS	SBR	FA	FR	G/POS	TPR
1901	Mil-A	14	52	12	9	0	0	3	5	11		.173	.328	.346	91	-0	4			.911	1	O-14	0.0
1902	StL-A	15	49	4	11	1	1	0	3	6		.224	.309	.286	67	-2	5			.973	5	O-15	0.1
	Chi-N	64	243	41	74	12	3	0	14	38		.305	.399	.379	144	15	12			.955	-0	O-64	1.0
1903	Chi-N	130	497	64	140	18	3	1	62	53		.282	.352	.336	99	1	15			.970	0	*O-130	-0.6
1904	Chi-N	98	336	44	82	11	5	3	39	41		.244	.330	.333	105	3	14			.932	-10	O-97	-1.3
1906	Det-A	84	323	41	84	12	0		24	41		.260	.347	.310	103	3	21			.981	4	O-83	0.3
1907	*Det-A	126	491	101	134	10	6	0	27	60		.273	.357	.318	111	9	30			.971	13	*O-125	1.9
1908	*Det-A	56	121	17	25	2	1	0	10	13		.207	.284	.240	68	-4	11			.960	2	O-32	-0.3
1909	*Det-A	69	204	44	57	2	2	0	10	28		.279	.369	.309	110	4	12			.982	-2	O-57	-0.1
1910	Det-A	113	377	77	100	6	6	0	24	51		.265	.362	.313	104	4	25			.956	1	*O-101	0.0
1911	Det-A	98	341	78	93	10	0	0	19	41		.273	.354	.302	80	-8	23			.950	-1	O-92	-1.4
1912	Det-A	99	316	54	93	11	1	0	24	38		.294	.370	.323	102	-1	16			.962	-1	O-81	-0.2

YEAR	TM/L	G	AB	R	H	2B	3B	HR	RBI	BB	SO	AVG	OBP	SLG	PRO+	BR/A	SB	CS	SBR	FA	FR	G/POS	TPR
1913	Chi-A	12	21	2	6	0	0	0	0	9	0	.286	.500	.286	132	2	1			.867	-1	/O-9	0.1
1914	Pit-F	97	352	58	96	9	8	2	24	42	16	.273	.355	.361	96	-6	15			.970	8	O-93	-0.3
1915	Pit-F	14	49	6	16	0	1	0	4	6	0	.327	.400	.367	118	1	1			.926	0	O-13	-0.1
Total	14	1089	3772	643	1020	98	40	9	289	478	16	.270	.356	.325	102	22	207			.962	18	*O-1006	-0.9

■ DAX JONES
Jones, Dax Xenos b: 8/4/70, Pittsburgh, Pa. BR/TR, 6', 170 lbs. Deb: 7/11/96

YEAR	TM/L	G	AB	R	H	2B	3B	HR	RBI	BB	SO	AVG	OBP	SLG	PRO+	BR/A	SB	CS	SBR	FA	FR	G/POS	TPR
1996	SF-N	34	58	7	10	0	2	1	7	8	12	.172	.273	.293	51	-4	2	2	-1	1.000	-4	O-33	-1.0

■ FIELDER JONES
Jones, Fielder Allison b: 8/13/1871, Shinglehouse, Pa. d: 3/13/34, Portland, Ore. BL/TR, 5'11", 180 lbs. Deb: 4/18/1896 M

YEAR	TM/L	G	AB	R	H	2B	3B	HR	RBI	BB	SO	AVG	OBP	SLG	PRO+	BR/A	SB	CS	SBR	FA	FR	G/POS	TPR
1896	Bro-N	104	395	82	140	10	8	3	46	48	15	.354	.427	.443	137	24	18			.928	-4	*O-103	1.0
1897	Bro-N	135	548	134	172	15	10	1	49	61		.314	.392	.383	111	12	48			.941	4	*O-135	0.5
1898	Bro-N	146	596	89	181	15	9	1	69	46		.304	.362	.364	108	7	36			.946	-7	*O-144/S-2	-1.0
1899	Bro-N	102	365	75	104	8	2	2	38	54		.285	.390	.334	97	2	18			.946	-3	O-96	-0.8
1900	*Bro-N	136	552	106	171	26	4	4	54	57		.310	.383	.393	108	7	33			.957	0	*O-136	-0.3
1901	Chi-A	133	521	120	162	16	3	2	65	84		.311	.412	.365	120	20	38			.937	1	*O-133	1.0
1902	Chi-A	135	532	98	171	16	5	0	54	57		.321	.390	.370	117	15	33			.972	13	*O-135	1.8
1903	Chi-A	136	530	71	152	18	5	0	45	47		.287	.348	.340	112	9	21			**.985**	0	*O-136	0.1
1904	Chi-A	149	547	72	133	14	5	3	42	53		.243	.316	.303	100	2	25			.977	5	*O-149,M	-0.2
1905	Chi-A	153	568	91	139	17	12	2	38	73		.245	.335	.327	115	12	20			.970	-7	*O-153,M	1.4
1906	*Chi-A	144	496	77	114	22	4	2	34	83		.230	.346	.302	106	8	26			**.988**	8	*O-144,M	1.0
1907	Chi-A	154	559	72	146	18	1	0	47	67		.261	.345	.297	109	9	17			.973	3	*O-154,M	0.6
1908	Chi-A	149	529	92	134	11	7	1	50	86		.253	.366	.306	121	17	26			.968	-2	*O-149,M	1.1
1914	StL-F	5	3	0	1	0	0	0	0	1	0	.333	.500	.333	123	0	0			.000	0	HM	0.0
1915	StL-F	7	6	1	0	0	0	0	0	0	0	.000	.000	.000	-95	-2	0			1.000	-1	/O-3,M	-0.3
Total	15	1788	6747	1180	1920	206	75	21	631	817	15	.285	.368	.347	112	142	359			.964	25	*O-1770/S-2	5.9

■ FRANK JONES
Jones, Frank M. b: 8/25/1858, Princeton, Ill. d: 2/4/36, Marietta, Ohio BL , Deb: 7/2/1884

YEAR	TM/L	G	AB	R	H	2B	3B	HR	RBI	BB	SO	AVG	OBP	SLG	PRO+	BR/A	SB	CS	SBR	FA	FR	G/POS	TPR
1884	Det-N	2	8	0	1	0	0	0	0	0	1	.125	.125	.125	-22	-1				.667	-1	/S-1,O-1	-0.2

■ DEACON JONES
Jones, Grover William b: 4/18/34, White Plains, N.Y. BL/TR, 5'10", 185 lbs. Deb: 9/8/62 C

YEAR	TM/L	G	AB	R	H	2B	3B	HR	RBI	BB	SO	AVG	OBP	SLG	PRO+	BR/A	SB	CS	SBR	FA	FR	G/POS	TPR
1962	Chi-A	18	28	3	9	2	0	0	8	4	6	.321	.406	.393	117	1	0	0	0	.962	-0	/1-6	0.0
1963	Chi-A	17	16	4	3	0	1	1	2	2	2	.188	.316	.500	127	1	0	0	0	1.000	0	/1-1	0.1
1966	Chi-A	5	5	0	2	0	0	0	0	0	0	.400	.400	.400	140	0	0	0	0	.000	0	H	0.0
Total	3	40	49	7	14	2	1	1	10	6	8	.286	.375	.429	122	2	0	0	0	.966	-0	/1-7	0.1

■ HAL JONES
Jones, Harold Marion b: 4/9/36, Louisiana, Mo. BR/TR, 6'2", 194 lbs. Deb: 4/25/61

YEAR	TM/L	G	AB	R	H	2B	3B	HR	RBI	BB	SO	AVG	OBP	SLG	PRO+	BR/A	SB	CS	SBR	FA	FR	G/POS	TPR
1961	Cle-A	12	35	2	6	0	0	0	4	2	12	.171	.216	.343	48	-3	0	0	0	.974	-2	1-10	-0.5
1962	Cle-A	5	16	2	5	1	0	0	1	0	4	.313	.353	.375	99	-0	0	0	0	.969	0	/1-4	0.0
Total	2	17	51	4	11	1	0	0	5	2	16	.216	.259	.353	64	-3	0	0	0	.973	-2	/1-14	-0.5

■ HENRY JONES
Jones, Henry Monroe "Baldy" b: 5/10/1857, New York d: 5/31/55, Manistee, Mich. BB , 5'6", 149 lbs. Deb: 8/20/1884

YEAR	TM/L	G	AB	R	H	2B	3B	HR	RBI	BB	SO	AVG	OBP	SLG	PRO+	BR/A	SB	CS	SBR	FA	FR	G/POS	TPR
1884	Det-N	34	127	24	28	3	1	0	3	16	18	.220	.308	.260	86	-1				.897	-2	2-16,O-11/S-7	-0.3

■ HOWIE JONES
Jones, Howard "Cotton" (b: Howard Painter) b: 3/1/1897, Irwin, Pa. d: 7/15/72, Jeannette, Pa. BL/TL, 5'11", 165 lbs. Deb: 9/5/21

YEAR	TM/L	G	AB	R	H	2B	3B	HR	RBI	BB	SO	AVG	OBP	SLG	PRO+	BR/A	SB	CS	SBR	FA	FR	G/POS	TPR
1921	StL-N	3	2	0	0	0	0	0	0	0	1	.000	.000	.000	-99	-1	0	0	0	.000	-1	/O-1	-0.1

■ DALTON JONES
Jones, James Dalton b: 12/10/43, McComb, Miss. BL/TR, 6'1", 180 lbs. Deb: 4/17/64

YEAR	TM/L	G	AB	R	H	2B	3B	HR	RBI	BB	SO	AVG	OBP	SLG	PRO+	BR/A	SB	CS	SBR	FA	FR	G/POS	TPR
1964	Bos-A	118	374	37	86	16	4	6	39	22	38	.230	.275	.342	67	-17	6	3	0	.959	-8	2-85/S-1,3-1	-1.9
1965	Bos-A	112	367	41	99	13	5	5	37	28	45	.270	.325	.373	92	-4	8	1	0	.930	-3	3-81/2-8	-0.7
1966	Bos-A	115	252	26	59	11	5	4	23	22	27	.234	.303	.365	83	-6	1	2	-1	.962	-15	2-70/3-3	-1.9
1967	*Bos-A	89	159	18	46	6	2	3	25	11	23	.289	.335	.409	110	2	0	1	-1	.912	-4	3-30,2-19/1-1	-0.3
1968	Bos-A	111	354	38	83	13	0	5	29	17	53	.234	.272	.314	72	-12	1	1	-0	.996	-6	1-56,2-26/3-8	-2.5
1969	Bos-A	111	336	50	74	18	3	3	33	39	36	.220	.305	.318	71	-13	1	1	-0	.992	-1	1-81/3-9,2-1	-2.1
1970	Det-A	89	191	29	42	7	0	6	21	33	33	.220	.338	.351	90	-2	1	1	-0	.985	-3	2-35,3-18,1-10	-0.4
1971	Det-A	83	138	15	35	5	0	5	19	11	21	.254	.304	.399	94	-1	1	3	-2	1.000	-7	O-16,3-13/1-3,2-1	-1.1
1972	Det-A	7	7	0	0	0	0	0	0	0	2	.000	.000	.000	-97	-2	0	0	0	.000	0	H	-0.2
	Tex-A	72	151	14	24	2	0	4	19	10	31	.159	.211	.252	39	-12	1	0	0	.979	-7	3-23,2-17/1-7,O-2	-2.1
	Yr	79	158	14	24	2	0	4	19	10	33	.152	.202	.241	33	-14	1	0	0	.979	-7	3-23,2-17/1-7,O-2	-2.3
Total	9	907	2329	268	548	91	19	41	237	191	309	.235	.296	.343	79	-66	20	13	-2	.967	-54	2-262,3-186,1/OS	-13.2

■ JAKE JONES
Jones, James Murrell b: 11/23/20, Epps, La. BR/TR, 6'3", 197 lbs. Deb: 9/20/41

YEAR	TM/L	G	AB	R	H	2B	3B	HR	RBI	BB	SO	AVG	OBP	SLG	PRO+	BR/A	SB	CS	SBR	FA	FR	G/POS	TPR
1941	Chi-A	3	11	0	0	0	0	0	0	0	0	.000	.000	.000	-99	-3	0	0	0	1.000	-1	/1-3	-0.4
1942	Chi-A	7	20	2	3	1	0	0	0	2	2	.150	.227	.200	21	-2	1	0	0	.961	-1	/1-5	-0.3
1946	Chi-A	24	79	10	21	5	1	3	13	6	13	.266	.284	.468	112	0	0	0	0	.986	-3	1-20	-0.4
1947	Chi-A	45	171	15	41	7	1	3	20	13	25	.240	.297	.345	81	-5	1	0	0	.988	-1	1-43	-0.7
	Bos-A	109	404	50	95	14	3	16	76	41	60	.235	.310	.403	91	-6	5	4	-1	.991	-2	*1-109	-1.4
	Yr	154	575	65	136	21	4	19	96	54	85	.237	.306	.386	88	-11	6	4	-1	.990	-3	*1-152	-2.1
1948	Bos-A	36	105	3	21	4	0	1	8	11	26	.200	.276	.267	43	-9	1	0	0	.993	2	1-31	-0.6
Total	5	224	790	80	181	31	5	23	117	69	130	.229	.294	.368	80	-25	8	4	0	.989	-6	1-211	-3.8

■ JIM JONES
Jones, James Tilford "Sheriff" b: 12/25/1876, London, Ky. d: 5/6/53, London, Ky. BR/TR, 5'10", 162 lbs. Deb: 6/29/1897

YEAR	TM/L	G	AB	R	H	2B	3B	HR	RBI	BB	SO	AVG	OBP	SLG	PRO+	BR/A	SB	CS	SBR	FA	FR	G/POS	TPR
1897	Lou-N	2	4	2	1	0	0	0	0	0	1	.250	.400	.500	141	0				.000	-0	/P-1	0.0
1901	NY-N	21	91	10	19	4	3	0	5	4		.209	.250	.319	70	-4	2			.900	3	O-20/P-1	-0.5
1902	NY-N	67	249	16	59	11	1	0	19	13		.237	.275	.289	75	-8	7			.897	-1	O-67	-1.4
Total	3	90	344	28	79	16	4	0	24	18		.230	.270	.299	73	-12	9			.898	2	/O-87,P-2	-1.9

■ JEFF JONES
Jones, Jeffrey Raymond b: 10/22/57, Philadelphia, Pa. BR/TR, 6'2", 200 lbs. Deb: 4/4/83

YEAR	TM/L	G	AB	R	H	2B	3B	HR	RBI	BB	SO	AVG	OBP	SLG	PRO+	BR/A	SB	CS	SBR	FA	FR	G/POS	TPR
1983	Cin-N	16	44	6	10	3	0	0	5	11	13	.227	.393	.295	90	0	2	0	1	1.000	1	O-13/1-1	0.1

■ BINKY JONES
Jones, John Joseph b: 7/11/1899, St.Louis, Mo. d: 5/13/61, St.Louis, Mo. BR/TR, 5'9", 154 lbs. Deb: 4/15/24

YEAR	TM/L	G	AB	R	H	2B	3B	HR	RBI	BB	SO	AVG	OBP	SLG	PRO+	BR/A	SB	CS	SBR	FA	FR	G/POS	TPR
1924	Bro-N	10	37	0	4	1	0	0	2	0	3	.108	.108	.135	-36	-7	0	0	0	.898	-1	S-10	-0.7

■ JOHN JONES
Jones, John William "Skins" b: 5/13/01, Coatesville, Pa. d: 11/3/56, Baltimore, Md. BL/TL, 5'11", 185 lbs. Deb: 9/26/23

YEAR	TM/L	G	AB	R	H	2B	3B	HR	RBI	BB	SO	AVG	OBP	SLG	PRO+	BR/A	SB	CS	SBR	FA	FR	G/POS	TPR
1923	Phi-A	1	4	0	1	0	0	0	0	0	0	.250	.250	.250	31	-0	0	0	0	1.000	0	/O-1	0.0
1932	Phi-A	4	6	0	1	0	0	0	1	0	0	.167	.167	.167	-13	-1	0	0	0	1.000	-0	/O-1	-0.1
Total	2	5	10	0	2	0	0	0	1	0	0	.200	.200	.200	4	-1	0	0	0	1.000	-0	/O-2	-0.1

■ CHIPPER JONES
Jones, Larry Wayne b: 4/24/72, DeLand, Fla. BB/TR, 6'3", 185 lbs. Deb: 9/11/93

YEAR	TM/L	G	AB	R	H	2B	3B	HR	RBI	BB	SO	AVG	OBP	SLG	PRO+	BR/A	SB	CS	SBR	FA	FR	G/POS	TPR
1993	Atl-N	8	3	2	2	1	0	0	0	1	1	.667	.750	1.000	360	1	0	0	0	1.000	1	/S-3	0.2
1995	*Atl-N	140	524	87	139	22	3	23	86	73	99	.265	.355	.450	107	6	8	4	0	.931	3	*3-123,O-20	0.8
1996	*Atl-N★	157	598	114	185	32	5	30	110	87	88	.309	.393	.530	134	31	14	1	4	.947	-23	*3-118,S-38/O-1	1.4
Total	3	305	1125	203	326	55	8	53	196	161	188	.290	.379	.494	123	38	22	5	4	.937	-20	3-241/S-41,O-21	2.4

■ LYNN JONES
Jones, Lynn Morris b: 1/1/53, Meadville, Pa. BR/TR, 5'9", 175 lbs. Deb: 4/13/79 FC

YEAR	TM/L	G	AB	R	H	2B	3B	HR	RBI	BB	SO	AVG	OBP	SLG	PRO+	BR/A	SB	CS	SBR	FA	FR	G/POS	TPR
1979	Det-A	95	213	33	63	4	2	0	26	17	22	.296	.351	.390	96	-1	9	6	-1	.980	-10	O-84/D-6	-1.4
1980	Det-A	30	55	9	14	2	2	0	6	10	5	.255	.369	.364	99	0	1	0	0	1.000	-6	O-17/D-6	-0.1
1981	Det-A	71	174	19	45	5	0	2	19	18	10	.259	.332	.322	86	-3	1	2	-1	.989	-4	O-60/D-4	-1.0
1982	Det-A	58	139	15	31	3	1	0	14	7	14	.223	.260	.259	43	-11	4	0	0	1.000	-5	O-56/D-1	-1.8
1983	Det-A	49	64	9	17	1	2	0	6	6	3	.266	.299	.344	78	-2	1	1	0	.962	-12	O-45	-0.9
1984	*KC-A	47	103	11	31	6	0	1	6	10	4	.301	.333	.388	98	-0	5	1	0	.962	-2	O-45	-1.5
1985	*KC-A	110	152	12	32	7	0	0	9	8	15	.211	.264	.257	43	-12	0	1	0	.983	-24	*O-100/D-2	-3.8
1986	KC-A	67	47	1	6	2	0	0	6	6	5	.128	.226	.170	10	-6	0	0	0	.971	-21	O-62/2-1,D-3	-2.7
Total	8	527	947	109	239	34	5	7	91	73	86	.252	.310	.321	73	-34	13	14	-5	.983	-84	O-455/D-28,2-1	-13.2

YEAR	TM/L	G	AB	R	H	2B	3B	HR	RBI	BB	SO	AVG	OBP	SLG	PRO+	BR/A	SB	CS	SBR	FA	FR	G/POS	TPR

■ MACK JONES   Jones, Mack "Mack The Knife" b: 11/6/38, Atlanta, Ga.   BL/TR, 6'1", 180 lbs.   Deb: 7/13/61

YEAR	TM/L	G	AB	R	H	2B	3B	HR	RBI	BB	SO	AVG	OBP	SLG	PRO+	BR/A	SB	CS	SBR	FA	FR	G/POS	TPR
1961	Mil-N	28	104	13	24	3	2	0	12	12	28	.231	.322	.298	70	-4	4	4	-1	1.000	-2	O-26	-0.9
1962	Mil-N	91	333	51	85	17	4	10	36	44	100	.255	.354	.420	110	5	5	1	1	.973	-8	O-91	-0.7
1963	Mil-N	93	228	36	50	11	4	3	22	26	59	.219	.318	.342	91	-2	8	4	0	.978	-8	O-80	-1.4
1965	Mil-N	143	504	78	132	18	7	31	75	29	122	.262	.314	.510	127	16	8	2	1	.980	-10	*O-133	0.1
1966	Atl-N	118	417	60	110	14	1	23	66	39	85	.264	.338	.468	120	11	16	10	-1	.981	-3	*O-112/1-1	0.2
1967	Atl-N	140	454	72	115	23	4	17	50	64	108	.253	.357	.434	127	17	10	6	-1	.985	-2	*O-126	1.3
1968	Cin-N	103	234	40	59	9	1	10	34	28	46	.252	.337	.427	123	7	2	3	-1	.988	-8	O-60	-0.6
1969	Mon-N	135	455	73	123	23	5	22	79	67	110	.270	.382	.488	142	27	6	7	-2	.959	7	*O-129	2.5
1970	Mon-N	108	271	51	65	11	3	14	32	59	74	.240	.399	.458	129	14	5	3	-0	.968	-4	O-87	0.5
1971	Mon-N	43	91	11	15	3	0	3	9	5	24	.165	.296	.297	68	-4	1	0	0	.952	-2	O-27	-0.6
Total	10	1002	3091	485	778	132	31	133	415	383	756	.252	.349	.444	120	86	65	40	-5	.976	-35	O-871/1-1	0.4

■ RED JONES   Jones, Maurice Morris b: 11/2/14, Timpson, Tex.   d: 6/30/75, Lincoln, Cal.   BL/TR, 6'3", 190 lbs.   Deb: 4/16/40

YEAR	TM/L	G	AB	R	H	2B	3B	HR	RBI	BB	SO	AVG	OBP	SLG	PRO+	BR/A	SB	CS	SBR	FA	FR	G/POS	TPR
1940	StL-N	12	11	0	1	0	0	0	1	1	2	.091	.167	.091	-26	-2	0			1.000	-0	/O-1	-0.2

■ RICKY JONES   Jones, Ricky Miron b: 6/4/58, Tupelo, Miss.   BR/TR, 6'3", 186 lbs.   Deb: 9/3/86

YEAR	TM/L	G	AB	R	H	2B	3B	HR	RBI	BB	SO	AVG	OBP	SLG	PRO+	BR/A	SB	CS	SBR	FA	FR	G/POS	TPR
1986	Bal-A	16	33	2	6	2	0	0	4	6	8	.182	.308	.242	53	-2	0	0	0	1.000	7	2-11/3-6	0.5

■ BOB JONES   Jones, Robert Oliver b: 10/11/49, Elkton, Md.   BL/TL, 6'2", 195 lbs.   Deb: 10/1/74

YEAR	TM/L	G	AB	R	H	2B	3B	HR	RBI	BB	SO	AVG	OBP	SLG	PRO+	BR/A	SB	CS	SBR	FA	FR	G/POS	TPR
1974	Tex-A	2	5	0	0	0	0	0	0	0	1	.000	.000	.000	-99	-1	0	0	0	1.000	0	/O-2	-0.1
1975	Tex-A	9	11	2	1	0	0	0	0	3	3	.091	.286	.091	11	-1	0	0	0	1.000	-1	/O-5,D-1	-0.2
1976	Cal-A	78	166	22	35	6	0	6	17	14	30	.211	.276	.355	90	-3	3	0	1	.990	-5	O-62/D-2	-0.9
1977	Cal-A	14	17	3	3	0	0	1	3	4	5	.176	.333	.353	91	-0	0	0	0	.000	0	/D-6	0.0
1981	Tex-A	10	34	4	9	1	0	3	7	1	7	.265	.286	.559	146	2	0	1	-1	1.000	3	O-10	0.4
1983	Tex-A	41	72	5	16	4	0	1	11	5	17	.222	.291	.319	69	-3	0	2	-1	1.000	0	O-11,D-11/1-1	-0.5
1984	Tex-A	64	143	14	37	4	0	4	22	10	19	.259	.312	.371	85	-3	1	1	-0	1.000	-0	O-22,1-15/D-4	-0.5
1985	Tex-A	83	134	14	30	3	0	5	23	11	30	.224	.288	.351	73	-5	1	0	0	1.000	-7	O-30,D-10/1-4	-1.3
1986	Tex-A	13	21	1	2	0	0	0	3	2	5	.095	.174	.095	-24	-4	0	0	0	.909	-2	/O-9,1-2	-0.6
Total	9	314	603	65	133	17	0	20	86	50	117	.221	.286	.348	78	-18	5	4	-1	.992	-11	O-151/D-34,1-22	-3.7

■ BOB JONES   Jones, Robert Walter "Ducky" b: 12/2/1889, Clayton, Cal.   d: 8/30/64, San Diego, Cal.   BL/TR, 6', 170 lbs.   Deb: 4/11/17

YEAR	TM/L	G	AB	R	H	2B	3B	HR	RBI	BB	SO	AVG	OBP	SLG	PRO+	BR/A	SB	CS	SBR	FA	FR	G/POS	TPR
1917	Det-A	46	77	16	12	1	2	0	2	4	8	.156	.198	.221	28	-7	3			.938	-1	2-18/3-8	-0.8
1918	Det-A	74	287	43	79	14	4	0	21	17	16	.275	.320	.352	107	1	7			.947	-8	3-63/1-6,O-1	-0.7
1919	Det-A	127	439	37	114	18	6	1	57	34	39	.260	.314	.335	84	-10	11			.944	-24	*3-127	-3.0
1920	Det-A	81	265	35	66	6	3	1	18	22	13	.249	.309	.306	65	-13	3	4	-2	.942	-5	3-67/2-5,S-1	-1.6
1921	Det-A	141	554	82	168	23	9	1	72	27	18	.303	.348	.383	87	-11	9	9	-3	.950	10	*3-141	0.6
1922	Det-A	124	455	65	117	10	4	0	44	36	18	.257	.314	.325	69	-21	8	5	-1	**.962**	11	*3-119	-0.2
1923	Det-A	100	372	51	93	15	4	1	40	29	13	.250	.306	.320	66	-19	7	6	-2	.954	5	3-97	-0.6
1924	Det-A	110	393	52	107	27	4	0	47	20	20	.272	.308	.361	73	-17	1	5	-3	.956	-2	*3-106	-1.3
1925	Det-A	50	148	18	35	6	0	0	15	9	5	.236	.280	.277	42	-13	1	1	-0	.985	9	3-46	-0.2
Total	9	853	2990	399	791	120	38	7	316	208	156	.265	.314	.337	75	-109	49	<u>30</u>		.953	-4	3-774/2-23,1-6,SO	-7.8

■ RON JONES   Jones, Ronald Glen b: 6/11/64, Seguin, Tex.   BL/TR, 5'10", 195 lbs.   Deb: 8/26/88

YEAR	TM/L	G	AB	R	H	2B	3B	HR	RBI	BB	SO	AVG	OBP	SLG	PRO+	BR/A	SB	CS	SBR	FA	FR	G/POS	TPR
1988	Phi-N	33	124	15	36	6	1	8	26	2	14	.290	.302	.548	136	5	0	0	0	1.000	2	O-32	0.7
1989	Phi-N	12	31	7	9	0	0	2	4	9	1	.290	.450	.484	167	3	1	0	0	1.000	2	O-12	0.5
1990	Phi-N	24	58	5	16	2	0	3	9	7	9	.276	.373	.466	130	2	0	1	-1	1.000	-1	O-16	0.1
1991	Phi-N	28	26	0	4	2	0	0	3	2	9	.154	.214	.231	25	-3	0	0	0	.000	0	H	-0.4
Total	4	97	239	27	65	10	1	13	40	22	33	.272	.333	.485	128	8	1	1	0	1.000	3	/O-60	0.9

■ ROSS JONES   Jones, Ross A. b: 1/14/60, Miami, Fla.   BR/TR, 6'2", 185 lbs.   Deb: 4/2/84

YEAR	TM/L	G	AB	R	H	2B	3B	HR	RBI	BB	SO	AVG	OBP	SLG	PRO+	BR/A	SB	CS	SBR	FA	FR	G/POS	TPR
1984	NY-N	17	10	2	1	1	0	0	1	0	3	.100	.308	.200	46	-1	0	0	0	.833	1	/S-6,2-1,3-1	0.1
1986	Sea-A	11	21	0	2	0	0	0	0	0	4	.095	.095	.095	-48	-4	0	1	-1	1.000	1	/S-4,2-3,3-2,D-1	-0.4
1987	KC-A	39	114	10	29	4	2	0	10	5	15	.254	.292	.325	62	-6	1	0	0	.974	1	S-36/2-3	-0.2
Total	3	67	145	12	32	5	2	0	11	8	23	.221	.266	.283	46	-11	1	1	-1	.971	3	/S-46,2-7,3-3,D-1	-0.5

■ RUPPERT JONES   Jones, Ruppert Sanderson b: 3/12/55, Dallas, Tex.   BL/TL, 5'10", 175 lbs.   Deb: 8/1/76

YEAR	TM/L	G	AB	R	H	2B	3B	HR	RBI	BB	SO	AVG	OBP	SLG	PRO+	BR/A	SB	CS	SBR	FA	FR	G/POS	TPR
1976	KC-A	28	51	9	11	1	1	1	7	3	16	.216	.259	.333	72	-2	0	2	-1	1.000	-5	O-17/D-3	-0.9
1977	Sea-A★	160	597	85	157	26	8	24	76	55	120	.263	.327	.454	111	8	13	9	-2	.981	22	*O-155/D-4	2.2
1978	Sea-A	129	472	48	111	24	6	6	46	55	85	.235	.315	.337	84	-10	22	6	3	.985	16	*O-128	0.4
1979	Sea-A	162	622	109	166	29	9	21	78	85	78	.267	.358	.444	113	12	33	12	3	.989	14	*O-161	2.1
1980	NY-A	83	328	38	73	11	3	9	42	34	50	.223	.301	.357	81	-9	18	8	1	.988	8	O-82	-0.3
1981	SD-N	105	397	53	99	34	1	4	39	43	66	.249	.323	.370	104	1	7	9	-3	.993	10	*O-104	0.5
1982	SD-N★	116	424	69	120	20	2	12	61	62	90	.283	.376	.425	130	18	18	15	-4	.984	8	*O-114	2.1
1983	SD-N	133	335	42	78	12	3	12	49	35	58	.233	.305	.394	96	-3	11	11	-3	.981	-2	*O-111/1-5	-1.2
1984	*Det-A	79	215	26	61	12	1	12	37	21	47	.284	.347	.516	136	10	2	4	-1	1.000	-5	O-73/D-2	0.2
1985	Cal-A	125	389	66	90	17	2	21	67	57	82	.231	.330	.447	111	6	7	4	0	.995	10	O-73,D-43	1.2
1986	*Cal-A	126	393	73	90	21	3	17	49	64	87	.229	.341	.427	109	6	10	3	1	.981	-12	*O-121	-0.9
1987	Cal-A	85	192	25	47	8	2	8	28	20	38	.245	.316	.432	99	-1	2	1	0	.965	-15	O-66/D-3	-1.6
Total	12	1331	4415	643	1103	215	38	147	579	534	817	.250	.332	.416	106	37	143	84	-8	.986	51	*O-1205/D-55,1-5	3.8

■ JACK JONES   Jones, Ryerson L. "Ri" or "Angel Sleeves" b: Cincinnati, Ohio   TR ,   Deb: 8/13/1883

YEAR	TM/L	G	AB	R	H	2B	3B	HR	RBI	BB	SO	AVG	OBP	SLG	PRO+	BR/A	SB	CS	SBR	FA	FR	G/POS	TPR
1883	Lou-a	2	7	1	0	0	0	0		0		.000	.000	.000	-99	-2				.500	-1	/O-2,S-1	-0.2
1884	Cin-U	69	272	36	71	5	1	2		12		.261	.292	.309	76	-16				.858	2	S-41,2-19,3-10	-1.2
Total	2	71	279	37	71	5	1	2		12		.254	.285	.301	73	-17				.857	1	/S-42,2-19,3-10,O-2	-1.4

■ TERRY JONES   Jones, Terry Lee b: 2/15/71, Birmingham, Ala.   BB/TR, 5'10", 160 lbs.   Deb: 9/9/96

YEAR	TM/L	G	AB	R	H	2B	3B	HR	RBI	BB	SO	AVG	OBP	SLG	PRO+	BR/A	SB	CS	SBR	FA	FR	G/POS	TPR
1996	Col-N	12	10	6	3	0	0	0	1	0	3	.300	.300	.300	46	-1	0	0	0	1.000	-1	/O-4	-0.2

■ TOM JONES   Jones, Thomas b: 1/22/1877, Honesdale, Pa.   d: 6/21/23, Danville, Pa.   BR/TR, 6'1", 195 lbs.   Deb: 8/25/02

YEAR	TM/L	G	AB	R	H	2B	3B	HR	RBI	BB	SO	AVG	OBP	SLG	PRO+	BR/A	SB	CS	SBR	FA	FR	G/POS	TPR
1902	Bal-A	37	159	22	45	8	4	0	14	2		.283	.292	.384	83	-4	1			.955	-2	1-37/2-1	-0.6
1904	StL-A	156	625	53	152	15	10	2	68	15		.243	.270	.309	88	-10	16			.988	0	*1-134,2-23/O-4	-1.4
1905	StL-A	135	504	44	122	16	2	0	48	30		.242	.290	.282	86	-8	5			.985	7	*1-135	-0.6
1906	StL-A	144	539	51	136	22	6	0	30	24		.252	.290	.315	94	-5	27			.985	11	*1-143	0.2
1907	StL-A	155	549	53	137	17	3	0	34	34		.250	.298	.291	88	-7	24			.983	2	*1-155	-1.1
1908	StL-A	155	549	43	135	14	2	1	50	30		.246	.290	.284	86	-8	18			.986	-4	*1-155	-1.5
1909	StL-A	97	337	30	84	9	3	0	29	18		.249	.299	.294	94	-3	13			.989	7	1-95/3-2	0.4
	*Det-A	44	153	13	43	9	0	0	18	5		.281	.317	.340	103	0	9			.984	2	1-44	0.2
	Yr	141	490	43	127	18	3	0	47	23		.259	.305	.308	97	-2	22			.988	9	*1-139/3-2	0.6
1910	Det-A	135	432	32	110	12	4	1	45	35		.255	.325	.308	92	-4	22			.985	-4	*1-135	-0.8
Total	8	1058	3847	341	964	122	34	4	336	193		.251	.294	.303	90	-49	135			.984	22	*1-1033/2-24,O-4,3	-5.2

■ TRACY JONES   Jones, Tracy Donald b: 3/31/61, Hawthorne, Cal.   BR/TR, 6'3", 220 lbs.   Deb: 4/7/86

YEAR	TM/L	G	AB	R	H	2B	3B	HR	RBI	BB	SO	AVG	OBP	SLG	PRO+	BR/A	SB	CS	SBR	FA	FR	G/POS	TPR
1986	Cin-N	46	86	16	30	3	0	2	10	9	5	.349	.411	.453	132	4	7	1	2	1.000	-0	O-24/1-2	0.5
1987	Cin-N	117	359	53	104	17	3	10	44	23	40	.290	.338	.437	99	-1	31	8	5	.990	-3	O-95	-0.3
1988	Cin-N	37	83	9	19	1	0	1	9	3	7	.229	.304	.277	65	-3	9	5	0	.955	-2	O-25	-0.4
	Mon-N	53	141	20	47	5	1	2	15	12	12	.333	.390	.426	128	5	9	6	-1	1.000	-8	O-43	-0.5
	Yr	90	224	29	66	6	1	3	24	20	18	.295	.358	.371	105	2	18	6	2	.980	-10	O-68	-0.9
1989	SF-N	40	97	5	18	4	0	1	12	5	14	.186	.230	.258	23	-8	2	1	1	1.000	2	O-34	-1.9
	Det-A	46	158	17	41	10	0	3	26	16	16	.259	.331	.380	102	1	1	1	-0	.986	-1	O-36/D-8	-0.2
1990	Det-A	50	118	15	27	3	1	4	9	6	13	.229	.283	.381	84	-3	1	1	-0	.952	-2	O-27,D-20	-0.6

YEAR	TM/L	G	AB	R	H	2B	3B	HR	RBI	BB	SO	AVG	OBP	SLG	PRO+	BR/A	SB	CS	SBR	FA	FR	G/POS	TPR
	Sea-A	25	86	8	26	4	0	2	15	3	12	.302	.341	.419	110	1	0	1	-1	1.000	-1	O-18/D-5	-0.1
	Yr	75	204	23	53	8	1	6	24	9	25	.260	.307	.397	95	-2	1	2	-1	.973	-3	O-45,D-25	-0.7
1991	Sea-A	79	175	30	44	8	1	3	24	18	22	.251	.325	.360	89	-2	2	0	1	1.000	-5	D-37,O-36	-0.9
Total	6	493	1303	173	356	56	6	27	164	100	140	.273	.331	.388	96	-7	62	19	7	.988	-31	O-334/D-70,1-2	-4.4

■ **NIPPY JONES**   Jones, Vernal Leroy   b: 6/29/25, Los Angeles, Cal.   d: 10/3/95, Sacramento, Cal.   BR/TR, 6'1", 185 lbs.   Deb: 6/8/46

YEAR	TM/L	G	AB	R	H	2B	3B	HR	RBI	BB	SO	AVG	OBP	SLG	PRO+	BR/A	SB	CS	SBR	FA	FR	G/POS	TPR
1946	*StL-N	16	12	3	4	0	0	0	1	2	2	.333	.429	.333	113	0	0			.800	1	/2-3	0.1
1947	StL-N	23	73	6	18	4	0	1	5	2	10	.247	.267	.342	58	-5	0			.935	-2	2-13/O-2	-0.5
1948	StL-N	132	481	58	122	21	9	10	81	36	45	.254	.307	.397	84	-12	2			.986	-9	*1-128	-2.2
1949	StL-N	110	380	51	114	20	2	8	62	16	20	.300	.330	.426	97	-3	1			.984	-8	1-98	-1.1
1950	StL-N	13	26	0	6	1	0	0	6	3	1	.231	.310	.269	52	-2	0			.983	-1	/1-8	-0.2
1951	StL-N	80	300	20	79	12	0	3	41	9	13	.263	.287	.333	66	-15	1	2	-1	.991	-1	1-71	-2.0
1952	Phi-N	8	30	3	5	0	0	1	5	0	4	.167	.167	.267	19	-3	0	0	0	.976	0	/1-8	-0.3
1957	*Mil-N	30	79	5	21	2	1	2	8	3	7	.266	.293	.392	88	-2	0	0	0	.994	-5	1-20/O-1	-0.3
Total	8	412	1381	146	369	60	12	25	209	71	102	.267	.304	.382	81	-40	4	2		.987	-19	1-333/2-16,O-3	-6.5

■ **BILL JONES**   Jones, William   b: Syracuse, N.Y.   Deb: 5/17/1882

YEAR	TM/L	G	AB	R	H	2B	3B	HR	RBI	BB	SO	AVG	OBP	SLG	PRO+	BR/A	SB	CS	SBR	FA	FR	G/POS	TPR
1882	Bal-a	4	15	1	1	0	0	0		0		.067	.067	.067	-59	-2				1.000	0	/O-2,C-2	-0.2
1884	Phi-U	4	14	2	2	0	0	0		1		.143	.200	.143	6	-2				.862	1	/C-4,O-1	-0.1
Total	2	8	29	3	3	0	0	0		1		.103	.133	.103	-25	-4				.857	1	/C-6,O-3	-0.3

■ **BILL JONES**   Jones, William Dennis "Midget"   b: 4/8/1887, Hartland, N.B., Can.   d: 10/10/46, Boston, Mass.   BL/TR, 5'6.5", 157 lbs.   Deb: 6/20/11

YEAR	TM/L	G	AB	R	H	2B	3B	HR	RBI	BB	SO	AVG	OBP	SLG	PRO+	BR/A	SB	CS	SBR	FA	FR	G/POS	TPR
1911	Bos-N	24	51	6	11	2	1	0	3	15	7	.216	.394	.294	87	-0	1			.867	-1	O-18	-0.2
1912	Bos-N	3	2	0	1	0	0	0	2	0	1	.500	.500	.500	171	0	0			.000	0	H	0.0
Total	2	27	53	6	12	2	1	0	5	15	8	.226	.397	.302	89	-0	1			.867	-1	/O-18	-0.2

■ **TEX JONES**   Jones, William Roderick   b: 8/4/1885, Marion, Kan.   d: 2/26/38, Wichita, Kan.   BR/TR, 6', 192 lbs.   Deb: 4/13/11

YEAR	TM/L	G	AB	R	H	2B	3B	HR	RBI	BB	SO	AVG	OBP	SLG	PRO+	BR/A	SB	CS	SBR	FA	FR	G/POS	TPR
1911	Chi-A	9	31	4	6	1	0	0	4	3		.194	.265	.226	39	-3	1			1.000	3	/1-9	0.0

■ **TIM JONES**   Jones, William Timothy   b: 12/1/62, Sumter, S.C.   BL/TR, 5'10", 172 lbs.   Deb: 7/26/88

YEAR	TM/L	G	AB	R	H	2B	3B	HR	RBI	BB	SO	AVG	OBP	SLG	PRO+	BR/A	SB	CS	SBR	FA	FR	G/POS	TPR
1988	StL-N	31	52	2	14	1	0	0	3	4	10	.269	.321	.269	70	-2	4	1	1	.955	5	/S-9,2-8,3-1	0.4
1989	StL-N	42	75	11	22	6	0	0	7	7	8	.293	.361	.373	107	1	1	0	0	1.000	2	2-12,S-12/3-5,CO	0.4
1990	StL-N	67	128	9	28	7	1	1	12	12	20	.219	.291	.313	66	-6	3	4	-2	.944	3	S-29,2-19/3-6,P-1	-0.4
1991	StL-N	16	24	1	4	2	0	0	2	2	6	.167	.231	.250	35	-2	0	1	-1	1.000	-2	S-14/2-4	-0.5
1992	StL-N	67	145	9	29	4	0	0	3	11	29	.200	.256	.228	39	-11	5	2	0	.972	2	S-34,2-28/3-2,0-1	-0.8
1993	StL-N	29	61	13	16	6	0	0	1	9	8	.262	.366	.361	97	0	2	2	-1	.976	5	S-21/2-7	0.6
Total	6	252	485	45	113	25	1	2	28	45	81	.233	.302	.295	68	-20	15	10	-2	.964	10	S-119/2-78,3OPC	-0.7

■ **WILLIE JONES**   Jones, Willie Edward "Puddin' Head"   b: 8/16/25, Dillon, S.C.   d: 10/18/83, Cincinnati, Ohio   BR/TR, 6'1", 192 lbs.   Deb: 9/10/47

YEAR	TM/L	G	AB	R	H	2B	3B	HR	RBI	BB	SO	AVG	OBP	SLG	PRO+	BR/A	SB	CS	SBR	FA	FR	G/POS	TPR
1947	Phi-N	18	62	5	14	0	1	0	10	7	0	.226	.304	.258	53	-4	2			.909	2	3-17	-0.2
1948	Phi-N	17	60	9	20	2	0	2	9	3	5	.333	.365	.467	126	2	0			.926	3	3-17	0.4
1949	Phi-N	149	532	71	130	35	1	19	77	65	66	.244	.328	.421	102	0	3			.948	-4	*3-145	-0.6
1950	*Phi-N★	157	610	100	163	28	6	25	88	61	40	.267	.337	.456	108	6	5			.954	-6	*3-157	-0.3
1951	Phi-N★	148	564	79	161	28	5	22	81	60	47	.285	.358	.470	123	17	6	2	1	.966	-9	*3-147	0.8
1952	Phi-N	147	541	60	135	12	3	18	72	53	36	.250	.323	.383	96	-3	5	3	-0	**.969**	4	*3-147	-0.3
1953	Phi-N	149	481	61	108	16	2	19	70	85	45	.225	.342	.385	90	-6	1	1	-0	**.975**	3	*3-147	-1.2
1954	Phi-N	142	535	64	145	28	3	12	56	61	54	.271	.346	.402	94	-4	4	1	1	**.968**	-2	*3-141	-0.9
1955	Phi-N	146	516	65	133	20	3	16	81	77	51	.258	.357	.401	103	4	6	2	1	**.960**	-13	*3-146	-0.9
1956	Phi-N	149	520	88	144	20	4	17	78	92	49	.277	.387	.429	121	19	5	4	-1	**.973**	1	*3-149	2.1
1957	Phi-N	133	440	58	96	19	2	9	47	61	41	.218	.313	.332	76	-14	1	0	0	.966	-7	*3-126	-1.9
1958	Phi-N	118	398	52	108	15	1	14	60	49	41	.271	.354	.420	105	4	1	2	-1	**.967**	-13	*3-110/1-1	-1.0
1959	Phi-N	47	160	23	43	9	1	7	24	19	14	.269	.346	.469	113	3	0	0	0	.975	-3	3-46	0.0
	Cle-A	11	18	1	4	1	0	0	1	1	3	.222	.263	.278	51	-1	0	0	0	.929	2	/3-4	0.0
	Cin-N	72	233	33	58	12	1	7	31	28	26	.249	.332	.399	91	-3	0	2	0	.966	-3	3-68	-0.7
1960	Cin-N	79	149	16	40	7	0	3	27	31	16	.268	.394	.376	110	4	1	0	0	.962	-3	3-46/2-1	0.0
1961	Cin-N	9	7	1	0	0	0	0	0	2	3	.000	.222	.000	-34	-1	0	0	0	.000	-0	/3-1	-0.2
Total	15	1691	5826	786	1502	252	33	190	812	755	541	.258	.345	.410	102	20	40	17		.963	-55	*3-1614/2-1,1-1	-4.9

■ **BUBBER JONNARD**   Jonnard, Clarence James   b: 11/23/1897, Nashville, Tenn.   d: 8/23/77, New York, N.Y.   BR/TR, 6'1", 185 lbs.   Deb: 10/1/20   FC

YEAR	TM/L	G	AB	R	H	2B	3B	HR	RBI	BB	SO	AVG	OBP	SLG	PRO+	BR/A	SB	CS	SBR	FA	FR	G/POS	TPR
1920	Chi-A	2	5	0	0	0	0	0	0	0	1	.000	.000	.000	-99	-1	0	0	0	.857	0	/C-1	-0.1
1922	Pit-N	10	21	4	5	0	1	0	2	2	4	.238	.304	.333	64	-1	0	0	0	.974	2	C-10	0.1
1926	Phi-N	19	34	3	4	1	0	0	2	3	4	.118	.189	.147	-8	-5	0	0	0	.949	0	C-15	-0.4
1927	Phi-N	53	143	18	42	6	0	0	14	7	7	.294	.327	.336	77	-5	0	0	0	.967	-9	C-41	-1.1
1929	StL-N	18	31	1	3	0	0	0	2	0	6	.097	.097	.097	-51	-7	0	0	0	.957	1	/C-18	-0.5
1935	Phi-N	1	1	0	0	0	0	0	0	0	1	.000	.000	.000	-91	-0	0	0	0	1.000	-0	/C-1	0.0
Total	6	103	235	26	54	7	1	0	20	12	23	.230	.267	.268	41	-20	0	0		.960	-6	/C-86	-2.0

■ **EDDIE JOOST**   Joost, Edwin David   b: 6/5/16, San Francisco, Cal   BR/TR, 6', 175 lbs.   Deb: 9/11/36   M

YEAR	TM/L	G	AB	R	H	2B	3B	HR	RBI	BB	SO	AVG	OBP	SLG	PRO+	BR/A	SB	CS	SBR	FA	FR	G/POS	TPR
1936	Cin-N	13	26	1	4	0	0	1	2	5		.154	.214	.192	11	-3	0			.947	-1	/S-7,2-5	-0.4
1937	Cin-N	6	12	0	1	0	0	0	1	0		.083	.083	.083	-57	-3	0			.875	0	/2-6	-0.2
1939	Cin-N	42	143	23	36	6	3	0	14	12	15	.252	.310	.336	73	-5	1			.957	-3	2-32/S-6	-0.6
1940	*Cin-N	88	278	24	60	7	2	1	24	32	40	.216	.301	.266	57	-15	4			.960	-1	S-78/2-7,3-4	-0.9
1941	Cin-N	152	537	67	136	25	4	4	40	69	59	.253	.340	.337	91	-5	9			.942	-6	*S-147/2-4,1-2,3-1	0.0
1942	Cin-N	142	562	65	126	30	3	6	41	62	57	.224	.307	.320	84	-11	9			.933	-10	*S-130,2-15	-1.4
1943	Bos-N	124	421	34	78	16	3	2	20	68	60	.185	.299	.252	61	-20	7			.945	13	3-67,2-60/S-1	-0.3
1945	Bos-N	35	141	16	35	7	1	0	9	13	7	.248	.312	.312	73	-5	0			.945	-7	2-19,3-16	-1.1
1947	Phi-A	151	540	76	111	22	3	13	64	114	110	.206	.348	.330	87	-6	6	6	-2	.956	-3	*S-151	-0.3
1948	Phi-A	135	509	99	127	22	16	16	55	119	87	.250	.393	.395	110	11	2	4	-2	.973	5	*S-135	2.1
1949	Phi-A★	144	525	128	138	25	3	23	81	149	80	.263	.429	.453	138	36	2	1	0	.969	6	*S-144	5.2
1950	Phi-A	131	476	79	111	12	3	18	58	103	68	.233	.373	.384	96	-1	5	1	1	.956	-7	*S-131	0.3
1951	Phi-A	140	553	107	160	28	5	19	78	106	70	.289	.402	.461	132	28	10	8	-2	.974	-4	*S-140	3.9
1952	Phi-A☆	146	540	94	132	26	3	20	75	122	94	.244	.388	.415	116	16	5	8	-3	.962	-7	*S-146	1.7
1953	Phi-A	51	177	39	44	6	0	6	15	45	41	.249	.401	.384	109	4	3	2	0	.958	-6	S-51	0.1
1954	Phi-A	19	47	7	17	3	0	2	10	14	10	.362	.474	.489	163	5	0	1	-1	.963	-3	/S-9,3-5,2-1,M	0.2
1955	Bos-A	55	119	15	23	2	0	5	17	17	21	.193	.299	.336	65	-6	0	0	0	.932	5	S-20,2-17/3-2	0.1
Total	17	1574	5606	874	1339	238	35	134	601	1043	827	.239	.361	.366	99	18	61	31		.958	-20	*S-1296,2-166/31	8.4

■ **DUTCH JORDAN**   Jordan, Adolf Otto   b: 1/5/1880, Pittsburgh, Pa.   d: 12/23/72, W.Allegheny, Pa.   BR/TR, 5'10", 185 lbs.   Deb: 4/25/03

YEAR	TM/L	G	AB	R	H	2B	3B	HR	RBI	BB	SO	AVG	OBP	SLG	PRO+	BR/A	SB	CS	SBR	FA	FR	G/POS	TPR
1903	Bro-N	78	267	27	63	11	1	0	21	19		.236	.289	.285	66	-12	9			.928	-14	2-54,3-18/O-4,1-1	-2.3
1904	Bro-N	87	252	21	45	10	2	0	19	13		.179	.258	.234	43	-17	7			.958	-17	2-70,3-11/1-4	-3.5
Total	2	165	519	48	108	21	3	0	40	32		.208	.258	.260	55	-29	16			.945	-31	2-124/3-29,1-5,O-4	-5.8

■ **BUCK JORDAN**   Jordan, Baxter Byerly   b: 1/16/07, Cooleemee, N.C.   d: 3/18/93, Salisbury, N.C.   BL/TR, 6', 170 lbs.   Deb: 9/15/27

YEAR	TM/L	G	AB	R	H	2B	3B	HR	RBI	BB	SO	AVG	OBP	SLG	PRO+	BR/A	SB	CS	SBR	FA	FR	G/POS	TPR
1927	NY-N	5	5	0	1	0	0	0		0	3	.200	.200	.200	7	-1	0			.000	0	H	-0.1
1929	NY-N	2	2	1	1	0	0	0		0	0	.500	.500	1.000	262	0	0			1.000	-0	/1-1	0.0
1931	Was-A	9	18	3	4	2	0	0	1	1	3	.222	.263	.333	56	-1	0	0	0	.978	-1	/1-7	-0.2
1932	Bos-N	49	212	27	68	12	3	2	29	4	5	.321	.333	.434	109	2	1			.991	-1	1-49	-0.3
1933	Bos-N	152	588	77	168	29	9	4	46	34	22	.286	.327	.386	112	7	4			.991	-3	*1-150	-1.1
1934	Bos-N	124	489	68	152	26	9	2	58	35	19	.311	.358	.413	114	9	3			.989	-3	*1-117	-0.4
1935	Bos-N	130	470	62	131	24	5	3	35	19	17	.279	.307	.383	91	-7	3			.983	0	1-95/3-8,O-2	-1.6
1936	Bos-N	138	555	81	179	27	5	3	66	45	22	.323	.375	.405	118	14	2			.993	5	*1-136	0.2
1937	Bos-N	8	8	1	2	0	0	0		0	0	.250	.250	.250	40	-1	0			.000	0	H	-0.1

YEAR	TM/L	G	AB	R	H	2B	3B	HR	RBI	BB	SO	AVG	OBP	SLG	PRO+	BR/A	SB	CS	SBR	FA	FR	G/POS	TPR
	Cin-N	98	316	45	89	14	3	1	28	25	14	.282	.334	.354	92	-4	6			.989	-2	1-76	-1.4
	Yr	106	324	46	91	14	3	1	28	25	14	.281	.332	.352	91	-4	6			.989	-2	1-76	-1.5
1938	Cin-N	9	7	0	2	0	0	0	0	2	0	.286	.444	.286	107	0	0			.000	0	H	0.0
	Phi-N	87	310	31	93	18	1	0	18	17	4	.300	.336	.365	95	-2	1			.973	-4	3-58,1-17	-0.7
	Yr	96	317	31	95	18	1	0	18	19	4	.300	.339	.363	96	-2	1			.973	-4	3-58,1-17	-0.7
Total	10	811	2980	396	890	153	35	17	281	182	109	.299	.340	.391	106	18	20	0		.990	-12	1-648/3-66,O-2	-5.7

■ BRIAN JORDAN
Jordan, Brian O'Neal   b: 3/29/67, Baltimore, Md.   BR/TR, 6'1", 205 lbs.   Deb: 4/8/92

YEAR	TM/L	G	AB	R	H	2B	3B	HR	RBI	BB	SO	AVG	OBP	SLG	PRO+	BR/A	SB	CS	SBR	FA	FR	G/POS	TPR
1992	StL-N	55	193	17	40	9	5	5	22	10	48	.207	.250	.373	77	-7	7	2	1	.991	-1	O-53	-0.8
1993	StL-N	67	223	33	69	10	6	10	44	12	35	.309	.356	.543	139	11	6	6	-2	.973	-3	O-65	0.5
1994	StL-N	53	178	14	46	8	2	5	15	16	40	.258	.323	.410	91	-3	4	3	-1	.991	5	O-46/1-1	0.1
1995	StL-N	131	490	83	145	20	4	22	81	22	79	.296	.340	.488	116	9	24	9	2	.996	4	*O-126	1.1
1996	*StL-N	140	513	82	159	36	1	17	104	29	84	.310	.335	.483	118	12	22	5	4	.994	13	*O-136/1-1	2.5
Total	5	446	1597	229	459	83	17	59	266	89	286	.287	.335	.472	113	24	63	25	4	.991	18	O-426/1-2	3.4

■ SLATS JORDAN
Jordan, Clarence Veasey   b: 9/26/1879, Baltimore, Md.   d: 12/7/53, Catonsville, Md.   BL/TL, 6'1", 190 lbs.   Deb: 9/28/01

YEAR	TM/L	G	AB	R	H	2B	3B	HR	RBI	BB	SO	AVG	OBP	SLG	PRO+	BR/A	SB	CS	SBR	FA	FR	G/POS	TPR
1901	Bal-A	1	3	0	0	0	0	0	0	0	0	.000	.000	.000	-96	-1	0			.867	-1	/1-1	-0.1
1902	Bal-A	1	4	0	0	0	0	0	0	0	0	.000	.000	.000	-96	-1	0			.000	-0	/O-1	-0.1
Total	2	2	7	0	0	0	0	0	0	0	0	.000	.000	.000	-96	-2	0			—	-1	/O-1,1-1	-0.2

■ JIMMY JORDAN
Jordan, James William "Lord"   b: 1/13/08, Tucapau, S.C.   d: 12/4/57, Gastonia, N.C.   BR/TR, 5'9", 157 lbs.   Deb: 4/20/33

YEAR	TM/L	G	AB	R	H	2B	3B	HR	RBI	BB	SO	AVG	OBP	SLG	PRO+	BR/A	SB	CS	SBR	FA	FR	G/POS	TPR
1933	Bro-N	70	211	16	54	12	1	0	17	4	6	.256	.270	.322	71	-8	3			.969	12	S-51,2-11	0.7
1934	Bro-N	97	369	34	98	17	2	0	43	9	32	.266	.285	.322	66	-19	1			.956	-13	S-51,2-41/3-9	-2.6
1935	Bro-N	94	295	26	82	7	0	0	30	9	17	.278	.302	.302	64	-15	3			.983	27	2-46,S-28/3-5	1.6
1936	Bro-N	115	398	26	93	15	1	2	28	15	21	.234	.262	.291	48	-29	1			.970	-17	2-98/S-9,3-6	-3.9
Total	4	376	1273	102	327	51	4	2	118	37	76	.257	.279	.308	60	-71	8			.969	8	2-196,S-139/3-20	-4.2

■ KEVIN JORDAN
Jordan, Kevin Wayne   b: 10/9/69, San Francisco, Cal.   BR/TR, 6'1", 185 lbs.   Deb: 8/8/95

YEAR	TM/L	G	AB	R	H	2B	3B	HR	RBI	BB	SO	AVG	OBP	SLG	PRO+	BR/A	SB	CS	SBR	FA	FR	G/POS	TPR
1995	Phi-N	24	54	6	10	1	0	2	6	2	9	.185	.228	.315	41	-5	0	0	0	.984	6	/2-9,3-1	0.1
1996	Phi-N	43	131	15	37	10	0	3	12	5	20	.282	.314	.427	91	-2	2	1	0	1.000	-2	1-30/2-7,3-1	-0.6
Total	2	67	185	21	47	11	0	5	18	7	29	.254	.289	.395	76	-7	2	1	0	.989	4	/1-30,2-16,3-2	-0.5

■ MIKE JORDAN
Jordan, Michael Henry "Mitty"   b: 2/7/1863, Lawrence, Mass.   d: 9/25/40, Lawrence, Mass.   5'7.5", 155 lbs.   Deb: 8/21/1890

YEAR	TM/L	G	AB	R	H	2B	3B	HR	RBI	BB	SO	AVG	OBP	SLG	PRO+	BR/A	SB	CS	SBR	FA	FR	G/POS	TPR
1890	Pit-N	37	125	8	12	1	0	0	6	15	19	.096	.210	.104	-9	-17	5			.947	2	O-37	-1.4

■ RICKY JORDAN
Jordan, Paul Scott   b: 5/26/65, Richmond, Cal.   BR/TR, 6'5", 210 lbs.   Deb: 7/17/88

YEAR	TM/L	G	AB	R	H	2B	3B	HR	RBI	BB	SO	AVG	OBP	SLG	PRO+	BR/A	SB	CS	SBR	FA	FR	G/POS	TPR
1988	Phi-N	69	273	41	84	15	1	11	43	7	39	.308	.325	.491	128	9	1	1	-0	.992	-5	1-69	-0.3
1989	Phi-N	144	523	63	149	22	3	12	75	23	62	.285	.321	.407	107	-3	4	3	-1	.993	-11	*1-140	-2.1
1990	Phi-N	92	324	32	78	21	0	5	44	13	39	.241	.281	.352	73	-13	2	0	1	.995	-8	1-84	-2.7
1991	Phi-N	101	301	38	82	21	3	9	49	14	49	.272	.309	.452	113	4	0	2	-1	.987	-6	1-72	-0.8
1992	Phi-N	94	276	33	84	19	0	4	34	5	44	.304	.317	.417	106	1	3	0	1	.995	-6	1-54,O-11	-0.8
1993	*Phi-N	90	159	21	46	4	1	5	18	3	32	.289	.327	.421	100	-0	0	0	0	.990	-5	1-33	-0.8
1994	Phi-N	72	220	29	62	14	2	8	37	6	32	.282	.304	.473	96	-2	0	0	0	.993	-8	1-49	-1.4
1996	Sea-A	15	28	4	7	0	0	1	6	1	6	.250	.300	.357	65	-2	0	0	0	1.000	-1	/1-9,D-2	-0.3
Total	8	677	2104	261	592	116	10	55	304	77	303	.281	.311	.424	103	1	10	6	-1	.993	-49	1-510/O-11,D-2	-9.2

■ SCOTT JORDAN
Jordan, Scott Allan   b: 5/27/63, Waco, Tex.   BR/TR, 6', 175 lbs.   Deb: 9/2/88

YEAR	TM/L	G	AB	R	H	2B	3B	HR	RBI	BB	SO	AVG	OBP	SLG	PRO+	BR/A	SB	CS	SBR	FA	FR	G/POS	TPR
1988	Cle-A	7	9	0	1	0	0	0	1	0	3	.111	.111	.111	-37	-2	0	0	0	1.000	-1	/O-6	-0.3

■ TOM JORDAN
Jordan, Thomas Jefferson   b: 9/5/19, Lawton, Okla.   BR/TR, 6'1.5", 195 lbs.   Deb: 9/4/44

YEAR	TM/L	G	AB	R	H	2B	3B	HR	RBI	BB	SO	AVG	OBP	SLG	PRO+	BR/A	SB	CS	SBR	FA	FR	G/POS	TPR
1944	Chi-A	14	45	2	12	1	1	0	3	1	0	.267	.283	.333	77	-2	0	0	0	.947	-1	C-14	-0.2
1946	Chi-A	10	15	1	4	2	1	0	0	1	1	.267	.267	.533	124	0	0	0	0	1.000	1	/C-2	0.1
	Cle-A	14	35	2	7	1	0	1	3	3	1	.200	.263	.314	65	-2	1	1	-0	.974	-4	C-13	-0.8
	Yr	24	50	3	11	3	1	1	3	4	2	.220	.264	.380	83	-2	1	1	-0	.980	-5	C-15	-0.7
1948	StL-A	1	1	0	0	0	0	0	0	0	0	.000	.000	.000	-97	-0	0	0	0	.000	0	H	0.0
Total	3	39	96	5	23	4	2	1	6	4	2	.240	.270	.354	78	-3	1	1	-0	.963	-6	/C-29	-0.9

■ TIM JORDAN
Jordan, Timothy Joseph   b: 2/14/1879, New York, N.Y.   d: 9/13/49, Bronx, N.Y.   BL/TL, 6'1", 170 lbs.   Deb: 8/10/01

YEAR	TM/L	G	AB	R	H	2B	3B	HR	RBI	BB	SO	AVG	OBP	SLG	PRO+	BR/A	SB	CS	SBR	FA	FR	G/POS	TPR
1901	Was-A	6	20	2	4	1	0	0	2	0	3	.200	.304	.250	56	-1	0			.941	-1	/1-6	-0.2
1903	NY-A	2	8	2	1	0	0	0	0	0	0	.125	.125	.125	-23	-1	0			.889	-1	/1-2	-0.2
1906	Bro-N	129	450	67	118	20	8	**12**	78	59		.262	.352	.422	153	27	16			.978	-9	*1-126	1.5
1907	Bro-N	147	485	43	133	15	8	4	53	74		.274	.371	.363	141	25	10			.980	-6	*1-143	1.8
1908	Bro-N	148	515	58	127	18	5	**12**	60	59		.247	.328	.371	128	16	9			.982	-15	*1-146	-0.2
1909	Bro-N	103	330	47	90	20	3	6	36	59		.273	.386	.379	142	19	13			.983	-9	1-95	1.0
1910	Bro-N	5	5	1	1	0	0	1	3	0	2	.200	.200	.800	195	0	0			.000	0	H	0.0
Total	7	540	1813	220	474	74	24	32	232	254	2	.261	.355	.382	139	86	48			.980	-41	1-518	3.7

■ ART JORGENS
Jorgens, Arndt Ludwig   b: 5/18/05, Modum, Norway   d: 3/1/80, Wilmette, Ill.   BR/TR, 5'9", 160 lbs.   Deb: 4/26/29   F

YEAR	TM/L	G	AB	R	H	2B	3B	HR	RBI	BB	SO	AVG	OBP	SLG	PRO+	BR/A	SB	CS	SBR	FA	FR	G/POS	TPR
1929	NY-A	18	34	6	11	3	0	0	4	6	7	.324	.425	.412	125	2	0	2	-1	.979	-0	C-15	0.1
1930	NY-A	16	30	7	11	3	0	0	1	2	4	.367	.406	.467	126	1	0	0	0	.960	-0	C-16	0.2
1931	NY-A	46	100	12	27	1	2	0	14	9	3	.270	.330	.320	76	-3	0	1	-1	.962	-1	C-40	-0.3
1932	NY-A	56	151	13	33	7	1	2	19	14	11	.219	.285	.318	59	-10	0	1	0	.967	0	C-56	-0.6
1933	NY-A	21	50	9	11	3	0	2	13	12	3	.220	.371	.400	111	1	1	0	0	.982	2	C-19	0.4
1934	NY-A	58	183	14	38	6	1	0	20	23	24	.208	.296	.251	45	-15	2	0	1	.984	6	C-56	-0.5
1935	NY-A	36	84	6	20	2	0	0	8	12	10	.238	.333	.262	59	-5	0	0	0	1.000	6	C-33	0.2
1936	NY-A	31	66	5	18	3	1	0	5	2	3	.273	.294	.348	60	-4	0	0	0	.990	-8	C-30	-0.1
1937	NY-A	13	23	3	3	1	0	0	3	2	0	.130	.200	.174	-5	-8	0	0	0	1.000	-6	C-11	-0.3
1938	NY-A	9	17	3	4	0	0	0	2	3	3	.235	.350	.353	77	-1	0	0	0	.923	1	/C-8	0.0
1939	NY-A	3	0	1	0	0	0	0	0	0	0	—	—	—	—	-0	0	0	0	1.000	0	/C-2	0.0
Total	11	307	738	79	176	31	5	4	89	85	73	.238	.317	.310	66	-37	3	3	-1	.978	17	C-286	-0.9

■ PINKY JORGENSEN
Jorgensen, Carl   b: 11/21/14, Laton, Cal.   BR/TR, 6'1", 195 lbs.   Deb: 9/14/37

YEAR	TM/L	G	AB	R	H	2B	3B	HR	RBI	BB	SO	AVG	OBP	SLG	PRO+	BR/A	SB	CS	SBR	FA	FR	G/POS	TPR
1937	Cin-N	6	14	1	4	0	0	0	1	1	2	.286	.333	.286	73	-0	0			.875	0	/O-4	-0.1

■ SPIDER JORGENSEN
Jorgensen, John Donald   b: 11/3/19, Folsom, Cal.   BL/TR, 5'9", 155 lbs.   Deb: 4/15/47

YEAR	TM/L	G	AB	R	H	2B	3B	HR	RBI	BB	SO	AVG	OBP	SLG	PRO+	BR/A	SB	CS	SBR	FA	FR	G/POS	TPR
1947	*Bro-N	129	441	57	121	29	8	5	67	58	45	.274	.360	.410	100	1	4			.949	-5	*3-128	-0.3
1948	Bro-N	31	90	15	27	6	2	1	13	16	13	.300	.411	.444	127	4	1			.887	-6	3-24	-0.3
1949	*Bro-N	53	134	15	36	5	1	1	14	23	13	.269	.376	.343	90	-1	0			.946	-5	3-36	-0.6
1950	Bro-N	2	2	0	0	0	0	0	1	1	0	.000	.333	.000	-4	-0	0			1.000	-0	/3-1	0.0
	NY-N	24	37	5	5	0	0	0	4	5	2	.135	.238	.135	1	-5	0			.913	0	/3-5	-0.4
	Yr	26	39	5	5	0	0	0	5	6	2	.128	.244	.128	1	-6	0			.917	0	/3-6	-0.4
1951	NY-N	28	51	5	12	0	0	2	8	3	2	.235	.291	.353	72	-2	0			1.000	0	O-11/3-1	-0.5
Total	5	267	755	97	201	40	11	9	107	106	75	.266	.359	.384	95	-4	5	0		.940	-17	3-195/O-11	-2.1

■ MIKE JORGENSEN
Jorgensen, Michael   b: 8/16/48, Passaic, N.J.   BL/TL, 6', 195 lbs.   Deb: 9/10/68   M

YEAR	TM/L	G	AB	R	H	2B	3B	HR	RBI	BB	SO	AVG	OBP	SLG	PRO+	BR/A	SB	CS	SBR	FA	FR	G/POS	TPR
1968	NY-N	8	14	0	2	1	0	0	0	0	4	.143	.143	.214	6	-2	0	0	0	1.000	-0	/1-4	-0.2
1970	NY-N	76	87	15	17	3	1	4	9	11	24	.195	.278	.356	69	-4	2	2	-1	.992	3	1-50,O-10	-0.3
1971	NY-N	45	118	16	26	1	1	5	11	11	23	.220	.303	.373	92	-1	1	2	-1	.951	-2	O-31/1-1	-0.6
1972	Mon-N	113	372	48	86	12	3	13	47	53	75	.231	.333	.384	102	1	12	13	-4	.995	0	1-76,O-28	-1.1
1973	Mon-N	138	413	49	95	16	2	9	47	64	49	.230	.338	.344	86	-6	16	7	1	**.995**	4	*1-123,O-11	-1.1
1974	Mon-N	131	287	45	89	16	1	11	59	70	39	.310	.448	.488	153	24	3	5	-2	.998	7	1-91,O-29	2.5
1975	Mon-N	144	445	58	116	18	0	18	67	79	75	.261	.380	.422	117	13	3	3	-1	.994	3	*1-133/O-6	0.7

YEAR	TM/L	G	AB	R	H	2B	3B	HR	RBI	BB	SO	AVG	OBP	SLG	PRO+	BR/A	SB	CS	SBR	FA	FR	G/POS	TPR
1976	Mon-N	125	343	36	87	13	0	6	23	52	48	.254	.352	.344	94	-1	7	1	2	.989	0	1-81,O-41	-0.5
1977	Mon-N	19	20	3	4	1	0	0	0	3	4	.200	.304	.250	52	-1	0	0	0	1.000	1	/1-5	0.0
	Oak-A	66	203	18	50	4	1	8	32	25	44	.246	.335	.394	99	0	3	2	0	.989	1	1-48,O-20/D-2	-0.3
1978	Tex-A	96	97	20	19	3	0	1	9	18	10	.196	.322	.258	65	-4	3	1	0	.994	6	1-78/O-9,D-1	0.1
1979	Tex-A	90	157	21	35	7	0	6	16	14	29	.223	.295	.382	82	-4	0	2	-1	.988	2	1-60,O-20/D-2	-0.6
1980	NY-N	119	321	43	82	11	0	7	43	46	55	.255	.349	.355	100	1	0	3	-2	.995	-1	1-72,O-31	-0.7
1981	NY-N	86	122	8	25	5	2	3	15	12	24	.205	.276	.352	79	-4	4	0	1	.991	1	1-40,O-19	-0.4
1982	NY-N	120	114	16	29	6	0	2	14	21	24	.254	.370	.360	106	2	2	0	1	.991	-3	1-56,O-16	-0.1
1983	NY-N	38	24	5	6	3	0	1	3	2	4	.250	.333	.500	129	1	0	1	-1	1.000	1	1-19	0.1
	Atl-N	57	48	5	12	1	0	1	8	8	8	.250	.357	.333	86	-1	0	0	0	1.000	-0	1-19/O-6	-0.1
	Yr	95	72	10	18	4	0	2	11	10	12	.250	.349	.389	100	0	0	1	-1	1.000	1	1-38/O-6	0.0
1984	Atl-N	31	26	4	7	1	0	0	5	3	7	.269	.345	.308	79	-1	0	0	-1	1.000	-1	/1-8,O-4	-0.3
	StL-N	59	98	5	24	4	2	1	12	10	17	.245	.315	.357	91	-1	0	0	0	.991	2	1-39	-0.1
	Yr	90	124	9	31	5	2	1	17	13	24	.250	.321	.347	87	-2	0	1	-1	.992	0	1-47/O-4	-0.4
1985	*StL-N	72	112	14	22	6	0	0	11	31	27	.196	.375	.250	79	-1	2	1	0	.994	-2	1-49/O-2	-0.6
Total	17	1633	3421	429	833	132	13	95	426	532	589	.243	.349	.373	100	10	58	44	-9	.994	22	*1-1052,O-283/D-5	-3.6

■ TERRY JORGENSEN Jorgensen, Terry Allen b: 9/2/66, Kewaunee, Wis. BR/TR, 6'4", 208 lbs. Deb: 9/10/89

YEAR	TM/L	G	AB	R	H	2B	3B	HR	RBI	BB	SO	AVG	OBP	SLG	PRO+	BR/A	SB	CS	SBR	FA	FR	G/POS	TPR
1989	Min-A	10	23	1	4	1	0	0	2	4	5	.174	.296	.217	44	-2	0	0	0	.958	3	/3-9	0.2
1992	Min-A	22	58	5	18	1	0	0	5	1	11	.310	.355	.328	89	-1	1	2	-1	1.000	2	1-13/3-9,S-2	0.0
1993	Min-A	59	152	15	34	7	0	1	12	10	21	.224	.272	.289	51	-11	1	0	0	.982	8	3-45/1-9,S-6	-0.2
Total	3	91	233	21	56	9	0	1	19	17	37	.240	.295	.292	60	-13	2	2	-1	.975	14	/3-63,1-22,S-8	0.0

■ FELIX JOSE Jose, Domingo Felix Andujar (b: Domingo Felix Andujar (Jose)) b: 5/2/65, Santo Domingo, D.R. BB/TR, 6'1", 190 lbs. Deb: 9/2/88

YEAR	TM/L	G	AB	R	H	2B	3B	HR	RBI	BB	SO	AVG	OBP	SLG	PRO+	BR/A	SB	CS	SBR	FA	FR	G/POS	TPR
1988	Oak-A	8	6	2	2	1	0	0	1	0	1	.333	.333	.500	135	0	1	0	0	1.000	-1	/O-6	0.0
1989	Oak-A	20	57	3	11	2	0	0	5	4	13	.193	.246	.228	36	-5	0	1	-1	.974	-0	O-19	-0.6
1990	Oak-A	101	341	42	90	12	0	8	39	16	65	.264	.307	.370	92	-4	8	2	1	.977	0	O-92/D-7	-0.5
	StL-N	25	85	12	23	4	3	1	13	8	16	.271	.333	.447	112	1	4	4	-1	1.000	2	O-23	-0.2
1991	StL-N★	154	568	69	173	40	6	8	77	50	113	.305	.363	.438	123	18	20	12	-1	.990	4	*O-153	1.8
1992	StL-N	131	509	62	150	22	3	14	75	40	100	.295	.347	.432	123	15	28	12	1	.979	11	*O-127	2.6
1993	KC-A	149	499	64	126	24	3	6	43	36	95	.253	.304	.349	71	-21	31	13	2	.972	-10	*O-144/D-1	-3.2
1994	KC-A	99	366	56	111	28	1	11	55	35	75	.303	.364	.475	110	5	10	12	-4	.980	2	O-98	0.1
1995	KC-A	9	30	2	4	1	0	0	1	2	9	.133	.188	.167	-7	-5	0	0	0	1.000	2	O-7	-0.3
Total	8	696	2461	312	690	134	14	50	309	191	487	.280	.334	.407	102	4	102	56	-3	.981	6	O-669/D-8	-0.3

■ RICK JOSEPH Joseph, Ricardo Emelindo (Harrigan) b: 8/24/39, San Pedro De Macoris, D.R. d: 9/8/79, Santiago, D.R. BR/TR, 6'1", 195 lbs. Deb: 6/18/64

YEAR	TM/L	G	AB	R	H	2B	3B	HR	RBI	BB	SO	AVG	OBP	SLG	PRO+	BR/A	SB	CS	SBR	FA	FR	G/POS	TPR
1964	KC-A	17	54	3	12	2	0	0	3	1	11	.222	.263	.259	45	-4	0	1	-1	.981	-1	1-12/3-3	-0.7
1967	Phi-N	17	41	4	9	2	0	1	5	4	10	.220	.289	.341	79	-1	0	0	0	1.000	1	1-13	0.0
1968	Phi-N	66	155	20	34	5	0	3	12	16	35	.219	.297	.310	82	-3	0	1	-1	.992	1	1-30,3-14/O-1	-0.6
1969	Phi-N	99	264	35	72	15	0	6	37	22	57	.273	.331	.398	106	2	2	1	0	.956	-5	3-58,1-17/2-1	0.8
1970	Phi-N	71	119	7	27	2	1	3	10	6	28	.227	.264	.336	61	-7	0	0	0	.917	-5	O-12,1-10/3-9	-1.3
Total	5	270	633	69	154	26	1	13	65	51	141	.243	.302	.349	85	-13	2	3	-1	.933	2	/3-84,1-82,O-13,2-1	-1.8

■ DUANE JOSEPHSON Josephson, Duane Charles b: 6/3/42, New Hampton, Iowa BR/TR, 6', 195 lbs. Deb: 9/15/65

YEAR	TM/L	G	AB	R	H	2B	3B	HR	RBI	BB	SO	AVG	OBP	SLG	PRO+	BR/A	SB	CS	SBR	FA	FR	G/POS	TPR
1965	Chi-A	4	9	2	1	0	0	0	0	2	4	.111	.273	.111	14	-1	0	0	0	1.000	1	/C-4	0.0
1966	Chi-A	11	38	3	9	1	0	0	3	3	3	.237	.293	.263	65	-2	0	0	0	.974	3	C-11	0.2
1967	Chi-A	62	189	11	45	5	1	1	9	6	24	.238	.262	.291	65	-9	0	3	-2	1.000	-6	C-59	-1.4
1968	Chi-A★	128	434	35	107	16	6	6	45	18	52	.247	.286	.353	92	-5	2	4	-2	.990	12	*C-122	1.5
1969	Chi-A	52	162	19	39	6	2	1	20	13	17	.241	.301	.321	71	-6	0	0	0	.984	-1	C-47	-0.5
1970	Chi-A	96	285	28	90	12	1	4	41	24	28	.316	.364	.407	111	5	0	1	-1	.985	-11	C-84	-0.3
1971	Bos-A	91	306	38	75	14	1	10	39	22	35	.245	.296	.395	88	-6	0	2	-1	.989	-4	C-87	-0.7
1972	Bos-A	26	82	11	22	4	1	1	7	4	11	.268	.310	.378	99	-0	0	2	-1	.980	-1	1-16/C-6	-0.4
Total	8	470	1505	147	388	58	12	23	164	92	174	.258	.305	.358	89	-24	4	10	-5	.989	-7	C-420/1-16	-1.6

■ VON JOSHUA Joshua, Von Everett b: 5/1/48, Oakland, Cal. BL/TL, 5'10", 170 lbs. Deb: 9/2/69

YEAR	TM/L	G	AB	R	H	2B	3B	HR	RBI	BB	SO	AVG	OBP	SLG	PRO+	BR/A	SB	CS	SBR	FA	FR	G/POS	TPR
1969	LA-N	14	8	2	2	0	0	0	0	0	2	.250	.250	.250	43	-1	1	0	0	.800	-2	/O-8	-0.3
1970	LA-N	72	109	23	29	1	3	1	8	6	24	.266	.304	.358	80	-3	2	2	-1	.941	-8	O-41	-1.3
1971	LA-N	11	7	2	0	0	0	0	0	0	1	.000	.000	.000	-99	-2	0	0	0	1.000	-1	/O-5	-0.3
1973	LA-N	75	159	19	40	4	1	2	17	8	29	.252	.292	.327	74	-6	7	2	1	.984	-5	O-46	-1.2
1974	*LA-N	81	124	11	29	5	1	1	16	7	17	.234	.280	.315	69	-5	3	2	-0	.943	-4	O-35	-1.6
1975	SF-N	129	507	75	161	25	10	7	43	32	75	.318	.359	.448	118	11	20	10	0	**.993**	6	*O-117	1.3
1976	SF-N	42	156	13	41	5	2	0	2	4	20	.263	.281	.321	68	-7	1	3	-2	.948	-3	O-35	-1.3
	Mil-A	107	423	44	113	13	5	5	28	18	58	.267	.297	.357	93	-5	8	10	-4	.982	6	*O-105/D-1	-0.8
1977	Mil-A	144	536	58	140	25	7	9	49	21	74	.261	.289	.384	82	-15	12	9	-2	.970	-6	*O-140	-2.8
1979	LA-N	94	142	22	40	7	1	3	14	7	23	.282	.315	.408	97	-1	1	1	-0	.969	-6	O-46	-1.1
1980	SD-N	53	63	8	15	2	1	2	7	5	15	.238	.294	.397	97	-1	0	1	-1	1.000	-2	O-12/1-2	-0.3
Total	10	822	2234	277	610	87	31	30	184	108	338	.273	.307	.380	91	-34	55	40	-8	.975	-31	O-590/1-2,D-1	-9.7

■ TED JOURDAN Jourdan, Theodore Charles b: 9/5/1895, New Orleans, La. d: 9/23/61, New Orleans, La. BL/TL, 6', 175 lbs. Deb: 9/18/16

YEAR	TM/L	G	AB	R	H	2B	3B	HR	RBI	BB	SO	AVG	OBP	SLG	PRO+	BR/A	SB	CS	SBR	FA	FR	G/POS	TPR
1916	Chi-A	3	2	0	0	0	0	0	0	1	1	.000	.333	.000	1	-0	2			.000	-0	H	0.0
1917	Chi-A	17	34	2	5	0	1	0	2	1	3	.147	.171	.206	15	-4	0			.973	-1	1-14	-0.5
1918	Chi-A	7	10	1	1	0	0	0	1	0		.100	.100	.100	-39	-2	0			1.000	-0	/1-2	-0.2
1920	Chi-A	48	150	16	36	5	2	0	8	17	17	.240	.337	.300	70	-6	3	2	-0	.982	-4	1-40	-1.1
Total	4	75	196	19	42	5	3	0	11	19	21	.214	.300	.270	56	-11	5	2		.981	-4	/1-56	-1.8

■ POP JOY Joy, Aloysius C. b: 6/11/1860, Washington, D.C. d: 6/28/37, Washington, D.C. Deb: 6/3/1884

YEAR	TM/L	G	AB	R	H	2B	3B	HR	RBI	BB	SO	AVG	OBP	SLG	PRO+	BR/A	SB	CS	SBR	FA	FR	G/POS	TPR
1884	Was-U	36	130	12	28	0	0	0		2		.215	.227	.215	36	-14				.966	0	1-36	-1.6

■ JOYCE Joyce Deb: 8/14/1886

YEAR	TM/L	G	AB	R	H	2B	3B	HR	RBI	BB	SO	AVG	OBP	SLG	PRO+	BR/A	SB	CS	SBR	FA	FR	G/POS	TPR
1886	Was-N	1	0	0	0	0	0	0	0	0	0	—	—	—	0	0				.000	-0	/O-1	0.0

■ BILL JOYCE Joyce, William Michael "Scrappy Bill" b: 9/21/1865, St.Louis, Mo. d: 5/8/41, St.Louis, Mo. BL/TR, 5'11", 185 lbs. Deb: 4/19/1890 M

YEAR	TM/L	G	AB	R	H	2B	3B	HR	RBI	BB	SO	AVG	OBP	SLG	PRO+	BR/A	SB	CS	SBR	FA	FR	G/POS	TPR
1890	Bro-P	133	489	121	123	18	18	1	78	**123**	77	.252	.413	.368	103	6	43			.811	-11	*3-133	0.0
1891	Bos-a	65	243	76	75	9	15	3	51	63	27	.309	.460	.506	199	29	36			.849	-1	3-64/1-1	2.6
1892	Bro-N	97	372	89	91	15	12	6	45	82	55	.245	.392	.398	144	25	23			.862	-19	3-94/O-3	0.8
1894	Was-N	99	355	103	126	25	14	17	89	87	33	.355	.496	.648	**180**	51	21			.866	-3	*3-99	3.7
1895	Was-N	126	474	110	148	25	13	17	95	**96**	54	.312	.442	.527	151	40	29			.844	-9	*3-126	2.7
1896	Was-N	81	310	85	97	16	10	8	51	67	20	.313	.454	.506	153	28	32			.888	-7	3-48,2-33	2.0
	NY-N	49	165	36	61	9	2	5	43	34	14	.370	.500	.539	179	22	13			.883	0	3-49,M	2.0
	Yr	130	475	121	158	25	12	**13**	94	101	34	.333	.470	.518	162	50	45			.885	-7	3-97,2-33	4.0
1897	NY-N	109	388	109	118	15	13	3	64	78		.304	.441	.433	135	26	33			.852	-1	*3-106/1-2,M	2.3
1898	NY-N	145	508	91	131	20	9	10	91	88		.258	.386	.392	127	22	34			.966	8	*1-130,3-14/2-2,M	2.8
Total	8	904	3304	820	970	152	106	70	607	718	280	.294	.435	.467	144	249	264			.851	-41	3-733,1-133/2-35,O	18.9

■ WALLY JOYNER Joyner, Wallace Keith b: 6/16/62, Atlanta, Ga. BL/TL, 6'2", 190 lbs. Deb: 4/8/86

YEAR	TM/L	G	AB	R	H	2B	3B	HR	RBI	BB	SO	AVG	OBP	SLG	PRO+	BR/A	SB	CS	SBR	FA	FR	G/POS	TPR
1986	*Cal-A★	154	593	82	172	27	3	22	100	57	58	.290	.354	.457	120	16	5	2	0	.989	9	*1-152	1.4
1987	Cal-A	149	564	100	161	33	1	34	117	72	64	.285	.371	.528	140	32	8	2	1	.993	-7	*1-149	1.5
1988	Cal-A	158	597	81	176	31	2	13	85	55	51	.295	.359	.419	120	17	8	2	1	.995	12	*1-156	1.7
1989	Cal-A	159	593	78	167	30	2	16	79	46	58	.282	.340	.420	115	11	3	2	0	**.997**	-4	*1-159	-0.6
1990	Cal-A	83	310	35	83	15	0	8	41	41	34	.268	.355	.394	111	5	2	1	0	.995	2	1-83	0.1
1991	Cal-A	143	551	79	166	34	3	21	96	52	66	.301	.363	.488	133	24	2	0	1	.994	5	*1-141	1.6
1992	KC-A	149	572	66	154	36	2	9	66	55	50	.269	.338	.386	100	-0	11	5	0	.993	14	*1-145/D-4	0.4

YEAR	TM/L	G	AB	R	H	2B	3B	HR	RBI	BB	SO	AVG	OBP	SLG	PRO+	BR/A	SB	CS	SBR	FA	FR	G/POS	TPR
1993	KC-A	141	497	83	145	36	3	15	65	66	67	.292	.378	.467	119	14	5	9	-4	.994	20	*1-140	1.8
1994	KC-A	97	363	52	113	20	3	8	57	47	43	.311	.390	.449	111	7	3	2	-0	.991	3	1-86,D-11	0.0
1995	KC-A	131	465	69	144	28	0	12	83	69	65	.310	.401	.447	119	15	3	2	-0	.998	12	*1-126/D-2	1.4
1996	*SD-N	121	433	59	120	29	1	8	65	69	71	.277	.380	.404	113	10	5	3	-0	.997	4	*1-119	0.2
Total	11	1485	5538	784	1601	319	20	166	854	629	627	.289	.365	.444		151	55	30	-2	.994	66	*1-1456/D-17	9.5

■ FRANK JUDE   Jude, Frank b: 1884, Libby, Minn. d: 5/4/61, Brownsville, Tex. BR/TR, 5'7", 150 lbs. Deb: 7/9/06

YEAR	TM/L	G	AB	R	H	2B	3B	HR	RBI	BB	SO	AVG	OBP	SLG	PRO+	BR/A	SB	CS	SBR	FA	FR	G/POS	TPR
1906	Cin-N	80	308	31	64	6	4	1	31	16		.208	.261	.263	61	-14	7			.965	-3	O-80	-2.4

■ JOE JUDGE   Judge, Joseph Ignatius b: 5/25/1894, Brooklyn, N.Y. d: 3/11/63, Washington, D.C. BL/TL, 5'8.5", 155 lbs. Deb: 9/20/15 C

YEAR	TM/L	G	AB	R	H	2B	3B	HR	RBI	BB	SO	AVG	OBP	SLG	PRO+	BR/A	SB	CS	SBR	FA	FR	G/POS	TPR
1915	Was-A	12	41	7	17	0	0	0	9	4	6	.415	.500	.463	185	5	2	3	-1	.990	-1	1-10/O-2	0.3
1916	Was-A	103	336	42	74	10	8	0	28	54	44	.220	.333	.298	91	-2	18			.986	4	*1-103	-0.3
1917	Was-A	102	393	62	112	15	15	2	30	50	40	.285	.369	.415	141	19	17			.988	-1	*1-100	1.6
1918	Was-A	130	502	56	131	23	7	1	46	49	32	.261	.332	.341	105	2	20			.985	2	*1-130	-0.1
1919	Was-A	135	521	83	150	33	12	2	31	81	35	.288	.386	.409	124	19	23			.988	-4	*1-133	1.1
1920	Was-A	126	493	103	164	19	15	5	51	65	34	.333	.416	.462	136	28	12	12	-4	.992	-8	*1-124	1.3
1921	Was-A	153	622	87	187	26	11	7	72	68	35	.301	.372	.412	105	5	21	6	3	.996	-3	*1-152	0.1
1922	Was-A	148	591	84	174	32	15	10	81	50	20	.294	.355	.450	114	11	5	15	-8	.996	3	*1-147	0.0
1923	Was-A	113	405	56	127	24	6	2	63	58	20	.314	.406	.417	123	16	11	7	-1	.993	8	*1-112	1.6
1924	*Was-A	140	516	71	167	38	9	3	79	53	21	.324	.393	.450	121	16	13	8	-1	.994	4	*1-140	0.4
1925	*Was-A	112	376	65	118	31	5	8	66	55	21	.314	.406	.487	128	17	7	12	-5	.993	3	*1-109	0.9
1926	Was-A	134	453	70	132	25	11	7	92	53	25	.291	.362	.442	113	8	7	5	-1	.994	10	*1-128	0.9
1927	Was-A	137	522	68	161	29	11	2	71	45	22	.308	.366	.418	104	3	10	5	0	.996	-6	*1-136	-1.1
1928	Was-A	153	542	78	166	31	10	3	93	80	19	.306	.396	.417	115	14	16	4	2	.996	1	*1-149	0.4
1929	Was-A	143	543	83	171	35	8	6	71	73	33	.315	.397	.442	115	14	12	5	1	.996	9	*1-142	0.3
1930	Was-A	126	442	83	144	29	11	10	80	60	29	.326	.410	.509	131	22	13	6	0	.998	2	*1-117	1.2
1931	Was-A	35	74	11	21	3	0	0	9	8	8	.284	.354	.324	79	-2	0	0		.994	-0	1-15	-0.2
1932	Was-A	82	291	45	75	16	3	3	29	37	19	.258	.343	.364	84	-6	3	3	-1	.997	1	1-78	-1.1
1933	Bro-N	42	112	7	24	2	1	0	9	7	10	.214	.261	.250	48	-7	1			.989	0	1-28	-1.1
	Bos-A	35	108	20	32	8	1	0	22	13	4	.296	.372	.389	103	1	2	1	0	1.000	-0	1-29	-0.2
1934	Bos-A	10	15	3	5	2	0	0	2	2	1	.333	.412	.467	118	0	1			1.000	0	/1-2	0.0
Total	20	2171	7898	1184	2352	433	159	71	1034	965	478	.298	.378	.420	115	182	213	92		.993	13	*1-2084/O-2	6.0

■ WALLY JUDNICH   Judnich, Walter Franklin b: 1/24/17, San Francisco, Cal d: 7/12/71, Glendale, Cal. BL/TL, 6'1", 205 lbs. Deb: 4/16/40

YEAR	TM/L	G	AB	R	H	2B	3B	HR	RBI	BB	SO	AVG	OBP	SLG	PRO+	BR/A	SB	CS	SBR	FA	FR	G/POS	TPR
1940	StL-A	137	519	97	157	27	7	24	89	54	71	.303	.368	.520	125	18	8	5	-1	.989	-1	*O-133	0.9
1941	StL-A	146	546	90	155	40	6	14	83	80	45	.284	.377	.456	116	13	5	5	-2	.980	3	*O-140	0.5
1942	StL-A	132	457	78	143	22	6	17	82	74	41	.313	.413	.499	153	34	3	2	-0	.991	-2	*O-122	2.5
1946	StL-A	142	511	60	134	23	4	15	72	60	54	.262	.340	.411	104	2	0	4	-2	.995	11	*O-137	0.5
1947	StL-A	144	500	58	129	24	3	18	64	60	62	.258	.338	.426	109	5	2	5	-2	.989	-6	*1-129,O-15	-0.9
1948	*Cle-A	79	218	36	56	13	3	2	29	56	23	.257	.411	.372	112	7	2	3	-2	.970	-8	O-49,1-20	-0.5
1949	Pit-N	10	35	5	8	1	0	0	1	1	2	.229	.250	.257	35	-3	0			1.000	1	/O-8	-0.2
Total	7	790	2786	424	782	150	29	90	420	385	298	.281	.369	.452	119	75	20	24		.988	-2	O-604,1-149	2.8

■ LYLE JUDY   Judy, Lyle Leroy "Punch" b: 11/15/13, Lawrenceville, Ill d: 1/15/91, Ormond Beach, Fla. BR/TR, 5'10", 150 lbs. Deb: 9/17/35

YEAR	TM/L	G	AB	R	H	2B	3B	HR	RBI	BB	SO	AVG	OBP	SLG	PRO+	BR/A	SB	CS	SBR	FA	FR	G/POS	TPR
1935	StL-N	8	11	2	0	0	0	0	0	2	2	.000	.154	.000	-53	-2	2			1.000	1	/2-5	-0.2

■ RED JUELICH   Juelich, John Samuel b: 9/20/16, St.Louis, Mo. d: 12/25/70, St.Louis, Mo. BR/TR, 5'11.5", 170 lbs. Deb: 5/30/39

YEAR	TM/L	G	AB	R	H	2B	3B	HR	RBI	BB	SO	AVG	OBP	SLG	PRO+	BR/A	SB	CS	SBR	FA	FR	G/POS	TPR
1939	Pit-N	17	46	5	11	0	2	0	4	2	4	.239	.271	.326	61	-3	0			.935	-5	2-10/3-2	-0.8

■ GEORGE JUMONVILLE   Jumonville, George Benedict b: 5/16/17, Mobile, Ala. BR/TR, 6', 175 lbs. Deb: 9/13/40

YEAR	TM/L	G	AB	R	H	2B	3B	HR	RBI	BB	SO	AVG	OBP	SLG	PRO+	BR/A	SB	CS	SBR	FA	FR	G/POS	TPR
1940	Phi-N	11	34	0	3	0	0	0	0	6	1	.088	.139	.088	-38	-6	0			.952	-4	S-10/3-1	-1.0
1941	Phi-N	6	7	1	3	0	0	1	2	0	6	.429	.429	.857	266	1	0			1.000	1	/2-1,S-1	0.2
Total	2	17	41	1	6	0	0	1	2	6		.146	.186	.220	12	-5	0			.953	-4	/S-11,2-1,3-1	-0.8

■ ED JURAK   Jurak, Edward James b: 10/24/57, Los Angeles, Cal. BR/TR, 6'2", 185 lbs. Deb: 6/30/82

YEAR	TM/L	G	AB	R	H	2B	3B	HR	RBI	BB	SO	AVG	OBP	SLG	PRO+	BR/A	SB	CS	SBR	FA	FR	G/POS	TPR
1982	Bos-A	12	21	3	7	0	0	0	7	2	4	.333	.391	.333	96	-0	0	0	0	.923	2	3-11/O-1	0.1
1983	Bos-A	75	159	19	44	8	4	0	18	18	25	.277	.354	.377	95	-1	1	2	-1	.943	9	S-38,1-19,3-12,/2D	0.8
1984	Bos-A	47	66	6	16	3	1	1	7	12	12	.242	.359	.364	96	-0	0	2	-1	1.000	4	1-19,2-14/3-9,S-2	0.3
1985	Bos-A	26	13	4	3	0	0	0	0	1	3	.231	.286	.231	42	-1	0	0	0	.833	4	/3-7,S-3,1-1,O-1,D	0.0
1988	Oak-A	3	1	1	0	0	0	0	0	0	0	.000	.000	.000	-99	-0	0	0	0	.000	-0	/3-1,D-1	0.0
1989	SF-N	30	42	2	10	0	0	0	1	5	5	.238	.319	.238	63	-2	0	0	0	.875	-2	/S-6,3-5,2-4,O-2,1	-0.4
Total	6	193	302	35	80	11	5	1	33	38	49	.265	.349	.344	88	-4	1	4	-2	.941	17	/S-49,3-45,12DO	1.0

■ BILLY JURGES   Jurges, William Frederick b: 5/9/08, Bronx, N.Y. BR/TR, 5'11", 175 lbs. Deb: 5/4/31 MC

YEAR	TM/L	G	AB	R	H	2B	3B	HR	RBI	BB	SO	AVG	OBP	SLG	PRO+	BR/A	SB	CS	SBR	FA	FR	G/POS	TPR
1931	Chi-N	88	293	34	59	15	5	0	23	25	41	.201	.264	.287	47	-22	2			.963	11	3-54,2-33/S-3	-0.6
1932	*Chi-N	115	396	40	100	24	4	2	52	19	26	.253	.288	.348	71	-16	1			.964	32	*S-108/3-5	2.4
1933	Chi-N	143	487	49	131	17	6	5	50	26	39	.269	.313	.359	92	-6	3			.958	20	*S-143	2.6
1934	Chi-N	100	358	43	88	15	2	8	33	19	34	.246	.289	.366	76	-13	1			.966	14	S-98	0.7
1935	*Chi-N	146	519	69	125	33	1	1	59	42	39	.241	.304	.314	66	-24	3			.964	30	*S-146	1.3
1936	Chi-N	118	429	51	120	25	1	1	42	23	25	.280	.321	.350	79	-13	4			.960	17	*S-116	1.1
1937	Chi-N☆	129	450	53	134	18	10	1	65	42	21	.298	.365	.389	101	2	2			.975	-7	*S-128	0.3
1938	*Chi-N	137	465	53	114	18	3	1	47	58	53	.245	.335	.303	75	-14	3			.953	-0	*S-136	-0.4
1939	NY-N☆	138	543	84	155	21	11	6	63	47	34	.285	.349	.398	99	-0	3			.965	15	*S-137	2.7
1940	NY-N†	63	214	23	54	3	2	2	36	25	14	.252	.347	.322	85	-3	0			.967	-1	S-63	0.1
1941	NY-N	134	471	50	138	25	2	5	61	47	36	.293	.360	.386	108	7	0			.957	7	*S-134	2.3
1942	NY-N	127	464	45	119	7	1	3	30	43	29	.256	.324	.289	79	-11	1			.978	7	*S-124	0.4
1943	NY-N	136	481	46	110	8	2	4	29	53	38	.229	.310	.279	70	-17	2			.955	1	S-99,3-28	-1.0
1944	NY-N	85	246	28	52	2	1	1	23	23	20	.211	.279	.240	47	-17	4			.961	-0	3-61,S-10/2-1	-1.7
1945	NY-N	61	176	22	57	3	1	3	24	24	11	.324	.405	.403	123	6	2			.937	2	3-44/S-8	1.0
1946	Chi-N	82	221	26	49	9	2	0	17	43	28	.222	.351	.281	82	-3	3			.976	-3	S-73/3-7,2-2	-0.3
1947	Chi-N	14	40	5	8	2	0	1	2	9	9	.200	.347	.325	83	-1	0			.925	-4	S-14	-0.4
Total	17	1816	6253	721	1613	245	55	43	656	568	530	.258	.325	.335	82	-147	36			.964	140	*S-1540,3-199/2-36	10.5

■ JOE JUST   Just, Joseph Erwin (b: Joseph Erwin Juszczak) b: 1/8/16, Milwaukee, Wis. BR/TR, 5'11", 185 lbs. Deb: 5/13/44

YEAR	TM/L	G	AB	R	H	2B	3B	HR	RBI	BB	SO	AVG	OBP	SLG	PRO+	BR/A	SB	CS	SBR	FA	FR	G/POS	TPR
1944	Cin-N	11	11	0	2	0	0	0	0	4	3	.182	.250	.182	24	-1	0			.923	0	C-10	-0.1
1945	Cin-N	14	34	2	5	0	0	0	2	4	7	.147	.237	.147	8	-4	0			.947	-2	C-14	-0.5
Total	2	25	45	2	7	0	0	0	2	8	9	.156	.240	.156	12	-5	0			.941	-1	/C-24	-0.6

■ DAVID JUSTICE   Justice, David Christopher b: 4/14/66, Cincinnati, Ohio BL/TL, 6'3", 195 lbs. Deb: 5/24/89

YEAR	TM/L	G	AB	R	H	2B	3B	HR	RBI	BB	SO	AVG	OBP	SLG	PRO+	BR/A	SB	CS	SBR	FA	FR	G/POS	TPR
1989	Atl-N	16	51	7	12	3	0	1	3	3	9	.235	.291	.353	81	-1	2	1	0	1.000	-1	O-16	-0.3
1990	Atl-N	127	439	76	124	23	2	28	78	64	92	.282	.374	.535	139	23	11	6	-0	.981	-2	1-69,O-61	1.5
1991	*Atl-N	109	396	67	109	25	1	21	87	65	81	.275	.381	.503	138	21	8	8	-2	.968	5	*O-106	2.2
1992	*Atl-N	144	484	78	124	19	5	21	72	79	85	.256	.363	.446	121	14	2	4	-2	.976	14	*O-140	2.5
1993	*Atl-N★	157	585	90	158	15	4	40	120	78	90	.270	.359	.515	129	24	3	5	-2	.985	9	*O-157	2.7
1994	*Atl-N★	104	352	61	110	16	2	19	59	69	45	.313	.428	.531	145	26	2	4	-2	.947	2	*O-102	2.3
1995	Atl-N	120	411	73	104	17	2	24	78	73	68	.253	.368	.479	118	11	4	2	-2	.984	6	*O-120	1.4
1996	Atl-N	40	140	23	45	9	0	6	25	21	22	.321	.414	.514	135	8	1	1	-0	1.000	5	O-40	1.1
Total	8	817	2858	475	786	127	16	160	522	452	492	.275	.377	.499	130	126	33	31	-9	.975	38	O-742/1-69	13.4

■ SKIP JUTZE   Jutze, Alfred Henry b: 5/28/46, Bayside, N.Y. BR/TR, 5'11", 195 lbs. Deb: 9/1/72

YEAR	TM/L	G	AB	R	H	2B	3B	HR	RBI	BB	SO	AVG	OBP	SLG	PRO+	BR/A	SB	CS	SBR	FA	FR	G/POS	TPR
1972	StL-N	21	71	1	17	2	0	0	5	1	16	.239	.250	.268	48	-5	0	1	-1	.964	0	C-17	-0.5
1973	Hou-N	90	278	18	62	6	0	0	18	19	37	.223	.275	.245	45	-20	0	1	-0	.984	-6	C-86	-2.5

YEAR	TM/L	G	AB	R	H	2B	3B	HR	RBI	BB	SO	AVG	OBP	SLG	PRO+	BR/A	SB	CS	SBR	FA	FR	G/POS	TPR
1974	Hou-N	8	13	0	3	0	0	0	1	1	1	.231	.286	.231	48	-1	0	0	0	1.000	-0	/C-7	-0.1
1975	Hou-N	51	93	9	21	2	0	0	6	2	4	.226	.242	.247	39	-8	1	0	0	.988	3	C-47	-0.3
1976	Hou-N	42	92	7	14	2	3	0	6	4	16	.152	.188	.239	22	-10	0	0	0	.986	-0	C-42	-0.8
1977	Sea-A	42	109	10	24	2	0	3	15	7	12	.220	.267	.321	60	-6	0	4	-2	.984	-2	C-40	-1.0
Total	6	254	656	45	141	14	3	3	51	34	86	.215	.255	.259	44	-50	1	6	-3	.983	-3	C-239	-5.2

■ HERB JUUL
Juul, Herbert Victor   b: 2/2/1886, Chicago, Ill.   d: 11/14/28, Chicago, Ill.   BL/TL, 5'11", 150 lbs.   Deb: 7/11/11

YEAR	TM/L	G	AB	R	H	2B	3B	HR	RBI	BB	SO	AVG	OBP	SLG	PRO+	BR/A	SB	CS	SBR	FA	FR	G/POS	TPR
1911	Cin-N	2	2	0	0	0	0	0	0	0	0	.000	.000	.000	-99	-1	0			.000	-0	/P-1	0.0

■ JIM KAAT
Kaat, James Lee   b: 11/7/38, Zeeland, Mich.   BL/TL, 6'4", 217 lbs.   Deb: 8/2/59   C

YEAR	TM/L	G	AB	R	H	2B	3B	HR	RBI	BB	SO	AVG	OBP	SLG	PRO+	BR/A	SB	CS	SBR	FA	FR	G/POS	TPR
1959	Was-A	3	1	0	0	0	0	0	0	0	0	.000	.000	.000	-99	-0	0	0	0	1.000	0	/P-3	0.0
1960	Was-A	13	14	0	2	0	0	0	0	0	6	.143	.143	.143	-23	-2	0	0	0	1.000	0	P-13	0.0
1961	Min-A	47	63	10	15	3	1	0	1	4	13	.238	.294	.317	60	-4	0	0	0	.968	3	P-36	0.0
1962	Min-A☆	48	100	9	18	3	1	1	10	8	40	.180	.241	.260	33	-9	0	0	0	.967	6	P-39	0.0
1963	Min-A	36	61	2	8	1	0	1	8	2	19	.131	.185	.197	7	-8	0	0	0	.984	4	P-31	0.0
1964	Min-A	46	83	11	14	1	0	3	11	11	31	.169	.266	.289	54	-5	0	0	0	.928	3	P-36	0.0
1965	*Min-A	56	93	6	23	4	0	1	9	3	29	.247	.271	.323	65	-4	2	0	1	.929	3	P-45	0.0
1966	Min-A★	47	118	12	23	1	2	1	13	5	41	.195	.228	.280	42	-9	0	0	0	.956	0	P-41	0.0
1967	Min-A	45	99	7	17	3	1	1	4	7	26	.172	.226	.253	38	-8	0	0	0	.952	1	P-42	0.0
1968	Min-A	36	77	7	12	3	0	0	5	2	18	.156	.177	.195	12	-8	0	0	0	.976	-0	P-30	0.0
1969	Min-A	43	87	8	18	8	0	2	10	4	20	.207	.250	.368	69	-4	0	0	0	.826	-3	P-40	0.0
1970	*Min-A	56	76	17	15	1	0	1	8	6	20	.197	.265	.250	42	-6	0	0	0	.935	2	P-45	0.0
1971	Min-A	54	93	6	15	0	0	0	5	2	16	.161	.179	.194	5	-12	2	0	1	.982	-0	P-39	0.0
1972	Min-A	24	45	3	13	1	0	2	4	1	16	.289	.304	.489	127	1	0	1	-1	.923	-0	P-15	0.0
1973	Min-A	31	0	1	0	0	0	0	0	0	0	—	—	—	—	1	0	0	0	.969	-1	P-29	0.0
	Chi-A	7	0	0	0	0	0	0	0	0	0	—	—	—	—	0	0	0	0	1.000	-0	/P-7	
	Yr	38	0	1	0	0	0	0	0	0	0	—	—	—	—	0	0	0	0	.973	-2	P-36	
1974	Chi-A	42	1	0	0	0	0	0	0	0	0	.000	.000	.000	-98	-0	0	0	0	.959	-2	P-42	0.0
1975	Chi-A★	43	0	0	0	0	0	0	0	0	0	—	—	—	—	0	0	0	0	.982	-2	P-43	0.0
1976	*Phi-N	42	79	4	14	3	1	1	8	2	24	.177	.198	.278	33	-7	0	0	0	.949	-3	P-38	0.0
1977	Phi-N	36	53	4	10	3	0	0	2	1	12	.189	.218	.245	23	-6	0	0	0	.897	-2	P-35	0.0
1978	Phi-N	26	48	4	7	1	0	0	2	0	15	.146	.163	.167	-8	-7	0	0	0	1.000	-2	P-26	0.0
1979	Phi-N	3	1	0	0	0	0	0	0	1	1	.000	.500	.000	47	0	0	0	0	1.000	-0	/P-3	0.0
	NY-A	40	0	0	0	0	0	0	0	0	0	—	—	—	—	0	0	0	0	.909	1	P-40	
1980	NY-A	4	0	0	0	0	0	0	0	0	0	—	—	—	—	0	0	0	0	.800	1	P-4	0.0
	StL-N	49	35	4	5	1	0	1	2	2	13	.143	.189	.257	23	-4	1	0	0	.952	-2	P-49	
1981	StL-N	41	8	2	3	1	0	0	2	1	0	.375	.444	.500	163	1	0	0	0	.895	1	P-41	0.0
1982	*StL-N	62	12	0	0	0	0	0	0	1	4	.000	.077	.000	-76	-3	0	0	0	.917	-2	P-62	0.0
1983	StL-N	24	4	0	0	0	0	0	0	0	0	.000	.000	.000	-99	-1	0	0	0	.889	0	P-24	0.0
Total	25	1004	1251	117	232	44	5	16	106	63	367	.185	.229	.267	38	-104	5	1	1	.947	6	P-898	0.0

■ JACK KADING
Kading, John Frederick   b: 11/17/1884, Waukesha, Wis.   d: 6/2/64, Chicago, Ill.   BR/TR, 6'3", 190 lbs.   Deb: 9/12/10

YEAR	TM/L	G	AB	R	H	2B	3B	HR	RBI	BB	SO	AVG	OBP	SLG	PRO+	BR/A	SB	CS	SBR	FA	FR	G/POS	TPR
1910	Pit-N	8	23	5	7	2	1	0	4	4	5	.304	.407	.478	149	1	0			1.000	1	/1-8	0.3
1914	Chi-F★	3	3	0	0	0	0	0	0	0	0	.000	.000	.000	-99	-1	0			.000	0	H	-0.1
Total	2	11	26	5	7	2	1	0	4	4	5	.269	.367	.423	123	1	0			1.000	1	/1-8	0.2

■ JAKE KAFORA
Kafora, Frank Jacob "Tomatoes"   b: 10/16/1888, Chicago, Ill.   d: 3/23/28, Chicago, Ill.   BR/TR, 6', 180 lbs.   Deb: 10/5/13

YEAR	TM/L	G	AB	R	H	2B	3B	HR	RBI	BB	SO	AVG	OBP	SLG	PRO+	BR/A	SB	CS	SBR	FA	FR	G/POS	TPR
1913	Pit-N	1	1	0	0	0	0	0	0	0	1	.000	.500	.000	52	0	0			1.000	-1	/C-1	-0.1
1914	Pit-N	21	23	2	3	0	0	0	0	0	6	.130	.200	.130	-1	-3	0			1.000	-1	C-17	-0.4
Total	2	22	24	3	3	0	0	0	0	0	7	.125	.222	.125	4	-3	0			1.000	-2	/C-18	-0.5

■ IKE KAHDOT
Kahdot, Isaac Leonard "Chief"   b: 10/22/01, Georgetown, Okla.   BR/TR, 5'5", 145 lbs.   Deb: 9/5/22

YEAR	TM/L	G	AB	R	H	2B	3B	HR	RBI	BB	SO	AVG	OBP	SLG	PRO+	BR/A	SB	CS	SBR	FA	FR	G/POS	TPR
1922	Cle-A	4	2	0	0	0	0	0	0	0	1	.000	.000	.000	-99	-1	0	0	0	1.000	1	/3-2	0.0

■ NICK KAHL
Kahl, Nicholas Alexander   b: 4/10/1879, Coulterville, Ill.   d: 7/13/59, Sparta, Ill.   BR/TR, 5'9", 185 lbs.   Deb: 5/2/05

YEAR	TM/L	G	AB	R	H	2B	3B	HR	RBI	BB	SO	AVG	OBP	SLG	PRO+	BR/A	SB	CS	SBR	FA	FR	G/POS	TPR
1905	Cle-A	40	135	16	29	4	1	0	21	4		.215	.248	.259	60	-6	1			.940	-2	2-32/S-1,O-1	-0.9

■ BOB KAHLE
Kahle, Robert Wayne   b: 11/23/15, New Castle, Ind.   d: 12/16/88, Inglewood, Cal.   BR/TR, 6', 170 lbs.   Deb: 4/21/38

YEAR	TM/L	G	AB	R	H	2B	3B	HR	RBI	BB	SO	AVG	OBP	SLG	PRO+	BR/A	SB	CS	SBR	FA	FR	G/POS	TPR
1938	Bos-N	8	3	2	1	0	0	0	0	0	0	.333	.333	.333	93	-0	0			.000	0	H	0.0

■ OWEN KAHN
Kahn, Owen Earle "Jack"   b: 6/5/05, Richmond, Va.   d: 1/17/81, Richmond, Va.   BR/TR, 5'11", 160 lbs.   Deb: 5/24/30

YEAR	TM/L	G	AB	R	H	2B	3B	HR	RBI	BB	SO	AVG	OBP	SLG	PRO+	BR/A	SB	CS	SBR	FA	FR	G/POS	TPR
1930	Bos-N	1	0	1	0	0	0	0	0	0	0	—	—	—	—	0	0			.000	0	R	0.0

■ MIKE KAHOE
Kahoe, Michael Joseph   b: 9/3/1873, Yellow Springs, O   d: 5/14/49, Akron, Ohio   BR/TR, 6', 185 lbs.   Deb: 9/22/1895

YEAR	TM/L	G	AB	R	H	2B	3B	HR	RBI	BB	SO	AVG	OBP	SLG	PRO+	BR/A	SB	CS	SBR	FA	FR	G/POS	TPR
1895	Cin-N	3	4	0	0	0	0	0	0	0		.000	.000	.000	-96	-1	0			1.000	-1	/C-3	-0.1
1899	Cin-N	14	42	2	7	1	1	0	4	0		.167	.167	.238	10	-5	1			.957	4	C-13	-0.1
1900	Cin-N	52	175	18	33	3	3	1	9	4		.189	.215	.257	31	-17	3			.963	5	C-51/S-1	-0.7
1901	Cin-N	4	13	0	4	0	0	0	0	1		.308	.357	.308	100	0	0			1.000	-2	/C-4	-0.2
	Chi-N	67	237	21	53	12	2	1	21	8		.224	.249	.304	62	-12	5			.974	9	C-63/1-6	0.3
	Yr	71	250	21	57	12	2	1	21	9		.228	.255	.304	64	-12	5			.974	7	C-67/1-6	0.1
1902	Chi-N	7	18	0	4	1	0	0	2	0		.222	.222	.278	56	-1	0			.875	-1	/C-4,3-2,S-1	-0.1
	StL-A	55	197	21	48	9	2	2	28	6		.244	.270	.340	69	-9	4			.967	-0	C-53	-0.3
1903	StL-A	77	244	26	46	7	5	0	23	11		.189	.227	.258	46	-16	1			.971	-3	C-71/O-2	-1.2
1904	StL-A	72	236	9	51	6	1	0	12	8		.216	.242	.250	59	-11	4			.968	1	C-69	-0.3
1905	Phi-N	16	51	2	13	2	0	0	4	1		.255	.269	.294	70	-2	1			.975	-0	C-15	-0.1
1907	Chi-N	5	10	0	4	0	0	0	1	0		.400	.400	.400	142	0	0			1.000	-1	/C-3,1-1	-0.1
	Was-A	17	47	3	9	0	1	0	1	0		.191	.191	.213	31	-4	0			.976	0	C-15	-0.2
1908	Was-A	17	27	1	5	1	0	0	0	0		.185	.185	.222	35	-2	0			.983	4	C-11	0.3
1909	Was-A	4	8	0	1	0	0	0	0	0		.125	.125	.125	-22	-1	2			.867	-0	/C-3	-0.1
Total	11	410	1309	103	278	43	14	4	105	39	0	.212	.237	.276	52	-81	21			.968	15	C-378/1-7,O-2,3S	-2.9

■ AL KAISER
Kaiser, Alfred Edward "Deerfoot"   b: 8/3/1886, Cincinnati, Ohio   d: 4/11/69, Cincinnati, Ohio   BR/TR, 5'9", 165 lbs.   Deb: 4/18/11

YEAR	TM/L	G	AB	R	H	2B	3B	HR	RBI	BB	SO	AVG	OBP	SLG	PRO+	BR/A	SB	CS	SBR	FA	FR	G/POS	TPR
1911	Chi-N	26	84	16	21	0	5	0	7	7	12	.250	.308	.369	89	-2	6			.905	-3	O-22	-0.6
	Bos-N	66	197	20	40	5	2	2	15	10	26	.203	.249	.279	44	-15	4			.922	-6	O-58	-2.4
	Yr	92	281	36	61	5	7	2	22	17	38	.217	.267	.306	57	-17	10			.918	-9	O-80	-3.0
1912	Bos-N	4	13	0	0	0	0	0	0	0	3	.000	.000	.000	-98	-4	0			.900	1	/O-4	-0.4
1914	Ind-F	59	187	22	43	10	0	1	16	17	41	.230	.301	.299	58	-14	6			.918	-3	O-50/1-1	-2.0
Total	3	155	481	58	104	15	7	3	38	34	82	.216	.274	.295	53	-34	16			.917	-12	O-134/1-1	-5.4

■ JOHN KALAHAN
Kalahan, John Joseph   b: 9/30/1878, Philadelphia, Pa.   d: 6/20/52, Philadelphia, Pa.   BR/TR, 6', 165 lbs.   Deb: 9/29/03

YEAR	TM/L	G	AB	R	H	2B	3B	HR	RBI	BB	SO	AVG	OBP	SLG	PRO+	BR/A	SB	CS	SBR	FA	FR	G/POS	TPR
1903	Phi-A	1	5	0	0	0	0	0	0	0		.000	.000	.000	-96	-1	0			1.000	-1	/C-1	-0.2

■ CHARLIE KALBFUS
Kalbfus, Charles Henry "Skinny"   b: 12/28/1864, Washington, D.C.   d: 11/18/41, Washington, D.C.   BR/TR, 5'11", 145 lbs.   Deb: 4/18/1884

YEAR	TM/L	G	AB	R	H	2B	3B	HR	RBI	BB	SO	AVG	OBP	SLG	PRO+	BR/A	SB	CS	SBR	FA	FR	G/POS	TPR
1884	Was-U	1	5	1	1	0	0	0		0		.200	.200	.200	22	-1				.000	-0	/O-1	-0.1

■ FRANK KALIN
Kalin, Frank Bruno "Fats" (b: Frank Bruno Kalinkiewicz)   b: 10/3/17, Steubenville, Ohio   d: 1/12/75, Weirton, W.Va.   BR/TR, 6', 200 lbs.   Deb: 9/25/40

YEAR	TM/L	G	AB	R	H	2B	3B	HR	RBI	BB	SO	AVG	OBP	SLG	PRO+	BR/A	SB	CS	SBR	FA	FR	G/POS	TPR
1940	Pit-N	3	3	0	0	0	0	0	0	1	0	.000	.400	.000	19	-0	0			.667	-1	/O-2	-0.1
1943	Chi-A	4	4	0	0	0	0	0	0	0	0	.000	.000	.000	-99	-1	0	0	0	.000	0	H	-0.1
Total	2	7	7	0	0	0	0	0	0	1	0	.000	.222	.000	-34	-1	0			.667	-1	/O-2	-0.2

■ AL KALINE
Kaline, Albert William   b: 12/19/34, Baltimore, Md.   BR/TR, 6'2", 180 lbs.   Deb: 6/25/53   H

YEAR	TM/L	G	AB	R	H	2B	3B	HR	RBI	BB	SO	AVG	OBP	SLG	PRO+	BR/A	SB	CS	SBR	FA	FR	G/POS	TPR
1953	Det-A	30	28	9	7	0	0	1	2	1	5	.250	.300	.357	78	-1	1	0	0	1.000	-7	O-20	-0.8

YEAR	TM/L	G	AB	R	H	2B	3B	HR	RBI	BB	SO	AVG	OBP	SLG	PRO+	BR/A	SB	CS	SBR	FA	FR	G/POS	TPR
1954	Det-A	138	504	42	139	18	3	4	43	22	45	.276	.306	.347	80	-15	9	5	-0	.971	11	*O-135	-1.1
1955	Det-A★	152	588	121	**200**	24	8	27	102	82	57	**.340**	.425	.546	163	53	6	8	-3	.979	7	*O-152	5.0
1956	Det-A★	153	617	96	194	32	10	27	128	70	55	.314	.385	.530	139	33	7	1	2	.984	17	*O-153	4.2
1957	Det-A★	149	577	83	170	29	4	23	90	43	38	.295	.347	.478	120	14	11	9	-2	.985	7	*O-145	1.1
1958	Det-A★	146	543	84	170	34	7	16	85	54	47	.313	.377	.490	127	20	7	4	-0	.994	8	*O-145	3.6
1959	Det-A★	136	511	86	167	19	2	27	94	72	42	.327	.414	**.530**	149	36	10	4	1	.989	11	*O-136	4.0
1960	Det-A★	147	551	77	153	29	4	15	68	65	47	.278	.357	.426	108	7	19	4	3	.987	9	*O-142	1.2
1961	Det-A★	153	586	116	190	**41**	7	19	82	66	42	.324	.396	.515	138	32	14	1	4	.990	12	*O-147/3-1	3.8
1962	Det-A★	100	398	78	121	16	6	29	94	47	39	.304	.379	.593	152	28	4	0	1	.983	12	*O-100	3.4
1963	Det-A★	145	551	89	172	24	3	27	101	54	48	.312	.378	.514	142	31	6	4	-1	.992	-2	*O-140	2.1
1964	Det-A†	146	525	77	154	31	5	17	68	75	51	.293	.385	.469	134	26	4	1	1	.990	11	*O-136	3.2
1965	Det-A★	125	399	72	112	18	2	18	72	72	49	.281	.391	.471	142	24	6	0	2	.985	-4	*O-112/3-1	1.8
1966	Det-A★	142	479	85	138	29	1	29	88	81	66	.288	.396	.534	161	40	5	5	-2	**.993**	5	*O-136	3.9
1967	Det-A†	131	458	94	141	28	2	25	78	83	47	.308	.415	.541	176	46	8	2	1	.983	8	*O-130	5.2
1968	*Det-A	102	327	49	94	14	1	10	53	55	39	.287	.395	.428	145	20	6	4	-1	.978	-1	O-74,1-22	1.5
1969	Det-A	131	456	74	124	17	0	21	69	54	61	.272	.350	.447	117	10	1	2	-1	.966	1	*O-118/1-9	0.3
1970	Det-A	131	467	64	130	24	4	16	71	77	49	.278	.382	.450	127	19	2	2	-1	.988	1	O-91,1-52	1.2
1971	Det-A★	133	405	69	119	19	2	15	54	82	57	.294	.421	.462	144	28	4	6	-2	**1.000**	-6	*O-129/1-5	1.4
1972	*Det-A	106	278	46	87	11	2	10	32	28	33	.313	.380	.475	148	17	1	0	0	.991	-6	O-84,1-11	0.8
1973	Det-A	91	310	40	79	13	0	10	45	29	28	.255	.325	.394	95	-2	4	1	1	1.000	-5	O-63,1-36	-1.2
1974	Det-A★	147	558	71	146	28	2	13	64	65	75	.262	.340	.389	105	4	2	2	-1	.000	-5	*D-146	0.0
Total	22	2834	10116	1622	3007	498	75	399	1583	1277	1020	.297	.379	.480	134	468	137	65	2	.986	103	*O-2488,D-146,1/3	44.6

■ WILLIE KAMM

Kamm, William Edward b: 2/2/1900, San Francisco, Cal. d: 12/21/88, Belmont, Cal. BR/TR, 5'10.5", 170 lbs. Deb: 4/18/23

YEAR	TM/L	G	AB	R	H	2B	3B	HR	RBI	BB	SO	AVG	OBP	SLG	PRO+	BR/A	SB	CS	SBR	FA	FR	G/POS	TPR
1923	Chi-A	149	544	57	159	39	9	6	87	62	82	.292	.366	.430	110	8	18	13	-2	.960	8	*3-149	2.5
1924	Chi-A	147	528	58	134	28	6	6	93	64	59	.254	.337	.364	83	-14	10	9	-2	**.971**	8	*3-146	0.3
1925	Chi-A	152	509	82	142	32	4	6	83	**90**	36	.279	.391	.393	105	7	11	13	-5	**.957**	-0	*3-152	1.2
1926	Chi-A	143	480	63	141	24	10	0	62	77	24	.294	.396	.385	108	9	12	4	1	**.978**	14	*3-142	3.1
1927	Chi-A	148	540	85	146	32	13	0	59	70	18	.270	.354	.378	92	-5	8	9	-3	**.972**	1	*3-146	-0.1
1928	Chi-A	155	552	70	170	30	12	1	84	73	22	.308	.391	.411	112	12	17	9	-0	**.977**	-3	*3-155	1.7
1929	Chi-A	147	523	72	140	33	6	3	63	75	23	.268	.363	.371	90	-6	12	5	1	**.978**	4	*3-145	0.4
1930	Chi-A	112	331	49	89	21	6	3	47	51	20	.269	.368	.396	97	-0	5	4	-1	.939	15	*3-106	1.7
1931	Chi-A	18	59	9	15	4	1	0	9	7	6	.254	.333	.356	86	-1	1	1	-0	.938	2	3-18	0.1
	Cle-A	114	410	68	121	31	4	0	66	64	13	.295	.392	.390	100	2	13	9	-2	.947	1	*3-114	0.8
	Yr	132	469	77	136	35	5	0	75	71	19	.290	.384	.386	99	1	14	10	-2	.945	3	*3-132	0.9
1932	Cle-A	148	524	76	150	34	9	3	83	75	36	.286	.379	.403	96	-2	6	3	0	.967	7	*3-148	1.4
1933	Cle-A	133	447	59	126	17	2	1	47	54	27	.282	.359	.336	81	-10	6	3	0	**.984**	1	*3-131	-0.2
1934	Cle-A	121	386	52	104	23	3	0	42	62	38	.269	.372	.345	84	-7	7	1	2	**.978**	11	*3-118	1.0
1935	Cle-A	6	18	2	6	0	0	0	1	0	1	.333	.333	.333	72	-1	0	1	-1	.875	-2	/3-4	-0.3
Total	13	1693	5851	802	1643	348	85	29	826	824	405	.281	.372	.384	97	-8	126	84	-13	.967	66	*3-1674	13.6

■ ALEX KAMPOURIS

Kampouris, Alexis William b: 11/13/12, Sacramento, Cal. d: 5/29/93, Sacramento, Cal. BR/TR, 5'8", 155 lbs. Deb: 7/31/34

YEAR	TM/L	G	AB	R	H	2B	3B	HR	RBI	BB	SO	AVG	OBP	SLG	PRO+	BR/A	SB	CS	SBR	FA	FR	G/POS	TPR
1934	Cin-N	19	66	6	13	1	0	0	3	3	18	.197	.254	.212	27	-7	2			.946	-1	2-16	-0.7
1935	Cin-N	148	499	46	123	26	5	7	62	32	84	.246	.295	.361	77	-17	8			.957	-1	*2-141/S-6	-0.7
1936	Cin-N	122	355	43	85	10	4	5	46	24	46	.239	.289	.332	72	-15	3			.969	28	*2-119/O-1	1.9
1937	Cin-N	146	458	62	114	21	4	17	71	60	65	.249	.342	.424	112	8	2			.961	3	*2-146	2.0
1938	Cin-N	21	74	13	19	1	0	2	7	10	13	.257	.353	.351	97	-0	0			.973	6	2-21	0.1
	NY-N	82	268	35	66	9	1	5	37	27	50	.246	.318	.343	81	-7	0			.972	13	2-79	1.1
	Yr	103	342	48	85	10	1	7	44	37	63	.249	.325	.345	84	-7	0			.972	14	2-100	1.2
1939	NY-N	74	201	23	50	12	2	5	29	30	41	.249	.349	.403	101	1	0			.973	10	2-62,3-11	1.3
1941	Bro-N	16	51	8	16	4	2	2	9	11	8	.314	.444	.588	181	6	0			.987	2	2-15	0.7
1942	Bro-N	10	21	3	5	2	1	0	3	0	4	.238	.238	.429	92	-0	0			.970	2	2-9	0.2
1943	Bro-N	19	44	9	10	2	0	1	4	7	6	.227	.452	.364	136	4	0			.946	-1	2-18	0.3
	Was-A	51	145	24	30	4	0	2	13	30	25	.207	.361	.276	91	0	7	1	2	.936	-3	3-33,2-10/O-1	-0.1
Total	9	708	2182	272	531	94	20	45	284	244	360	.243	.329	.367	91	-28	22	1		.964	50	2-636/3-44,S-6,0-2	6.1

■ FRANK KANE

Kane, Francis Thomas "Sugar" (a.k.a. Frank Thomas Kiley In 1915)
b: 3/9/1895, Whitman, Mass. d: 12/2/62, Brockton, Mass. BL/TR, 5'11.5", 175 lbs. Deb: 9/13/15

YEAR	TM/L	G	AB	R	H	2B	3B	HR	RBI	BB	SO	AVG	OBP	SLG	PRO+	BR/A	SB	CS	SBR	FA	FR	G/POS	TPR
1915	Bro-F	3	10	2	2	0	1	0	2	0	0	.200	.200	.400	67	-1	0			1.000	1	/O-2	0.0
1919	NY-A	1	1	0	0	0	0	0	0	0	0	.000	.000	.000	-99	-0	0			.000	0	H	0.0
Total	2	4	11	2	2	0	1	0	2	0	0	.182	.182	.364	52	-1	0			1.000	1	/O-2	0.0

■ JIM KANE

Kane, James Joseph "Shamus" b: 11/27/1881, Scranton, Pa. d: 10/2/47, Omaha, Neb. BL/TL, 6'2", 225 lbs. Deb: 4/21/08

YEAR	TM/L	G	AB	R	H	2B	3B	HR	RBI	BB	SO	AVG	OBP	SLG	PRO+	BR/A	SB	CS	SBR	FA	FR	G/POS	TPR
1908	Pit-N	55	145	16	35	3	3	0	22	12		.241	.299	.303	93	-1	5			.966	-2	1-40	-0.4

■ JOHN KANE

Kane, John Francis b: 9/24/1882, Chicago, Ill. d: 1/28/34, St.Anthony, Idaho BR/TR, 5'6", 138 lbs. Deb: 4/11/07

YEAR	TM/L	G	AB	R	H	2B	3B	HR	RBI	BB	SO	AVG	OBP	SLG	PRO+	BR/A	SB	CS	SBR	FA	FR	G/POS	TPR
1907	Cin-N	79	262	40	65	9	4	3	19	22		.248	.325	.347	106	2	20			.959	-1	O-42,3-25/S-6,2-2	0.1
1908	Cin-N	130	455	61	97	11	7	3	23	43		.213	.299	.288	90	-4	30			**.981**	4	*O-127/2-1	-0.6
1909	Chi-N	20	45	6	4	1	0	0	5	2		.089	.146	.111	-20	-6	1			.917	-3	/O-8,S-3,3-3,2-2	-0.4
1910	*Chi-N	32	62	11	15	0	0	1	12	9	10	.242	.338	.290	84	-1	2			1.000	-7	O-18/2-6,3-4,S-2	-0.8
Total	4	261	824	118	181	21	11	7	59	76	10	.220	.303	.297	89	-9		53		.975	-5	O-195/3-32,2-11,S	-1.7

■ JOHN KANE

Kane, John Francis b: 2/19/1900, Chicago, Ill. d: 7/25/56, Chicago, Ill. BB/TR, 5'10.5", 162 lbs. Deb: 9/3/25

YEAR	TM/L	G	AB	R	H	2B	3B	HR	RBI	BB	SO	AVG	OBP	SLG	PRO+	BR/A	SB	CS	SBR	FA	FR	G/POS	TPR
1925	Chi-A	14	56	6	10	1	0	0	3	0	3	.179	.193	.196	-1	-9	0	0	0	.935	1	/S-8,2-6	-0.6

■ TOM KANE

Kane, Thomas Joseph "Sugar" b: 12/15/06, Chicago, Ill. d: 11/26/73, Chicago, Ill. BR/TR, 5'10.5", 160 lbs. Deb: 8/3/38

YEAR	TM/L	G	AB	R	H	2B	3B	HR	RBI	BB	SO	AVG	OBP	SLG	PRO+	BR/A	SB	CS	SBR	FA	FR	G/POS	TPR
1938	Bos-N	2	2	0	0	0	0	0	0	2	0	.000	.500	.000	53	0	0			1.000	-1	/2-2	-0.1

■ JERRY KANE

Kane, William Jeremiah b: 4/1869, Baltimore, Md. d: 6/16/49, E.St.Louis, Ill. BR/TR, 6', 175 lbs. Deb: 5/2/1890

YEAR	TM/L	G	AB	R	H	2B	3B	HR	RBI	BB	SO	AVG	OBP	SLG	PRO+	BR/A	SB	CS	SBR	FA	FR	G/POS	TPR
1890	StL-a	8	25	3	5	0	0	0	2	2		.200	.259	.200	31	-2	0			.907	-1	1-5,C-4	-0.3

■ ROD KANEHL

Kanehl, Roderick Edwin "Hot Rod" b: 4/1/34, Wichita, Kan. BR/TR, 6'1", 180 lbs. Deb: 4/15/62

YEAR	TM/L	G	AB	R	H	2B	3B	HR	RBI	BB	SO	AVG	OBP	SLG	PRO+	BR/A	SB	CS	SBR	FA	FR	G/POS	TPR
1962	NY-N	133	351	52	87	10	2	4	27	23	36	.248	.296	.322	65	-17	8	6	-1	.944	15	2-62,3-30,0-20/1S	0.1
1963	NY-N	109	191	26	46	6	0	1	9	5	26	.241	.268	.288	59	-10	6	3	0	.974	-7	O-58,3-13,2-12/1-3	-1.9
1964	NY-N	98	254	25	59	7	1	1	11	7	18	.232	.256	.280	52	-16	3	1	0	.988	19	2-34,0-25,3-19/1-2	0.4
Total	3	340	796	103	192	23	3	6	47	35	80	.241	.277	.300	60	-44	17	10	-1	.950	27	2-108,O-103/31S	-1.4

■ HEINIE KAPPEL

Kappel, Henry b: 9/1863, Philadelphia, Pa. d: 8/27/05, Philadelphia, Pa. BR/TR, 5'8", 160 lbs. Deb: 5/22/1887 F

YEAR	TM/L	G	AB	R	H	2B	3B	HR	RBI	BB	SO	AVG	OBP	SLG	PRO+	BR/A	SB	CS	SBR	FA	FR	G/POS	TPR
1887	Cin-a	23	78	11	22	3	2	0	15	2		.282	.309	.372	87	-2	3			.667	-3	/3-9,0-7,2-6,S-1	-0.4
1888	Cin-a	36	143	18	37	4	4	1	15	2		.259	.274	.364	98	-1	20			.790	-12	S-25,2-10/3-1	-1.2
1889	Col-a	46	173	25	47	7	5	3	21	21	28	.272	.354	.422	127	6	10			.791	-2	S-23,3-23	0.5
Total	3	105	394	54	106	14	11	4	51	25	28	.269	.318	.391	109	3	33			.796	-17	/S-49,3-33,2-16,0-7	-1.1

■ JOE KAPPEL

Kappel, Joseph b: 4/27/1857, Philadelphia, Pa. d: 7/8/29, Philadelphia, Pa. BR, 5'11", 175 lbs. Deb: 5/26/1884 F

YEAR	TM/L	G	AB	R	H	2B	3B	HR	RBI	BB	SO	AVG	OBP	SLG	PRO+	BR/A	SB	CS	SBR	FA	FR	G/POS	TPR
1884	Phi-N	4	15	1	1	0	0	0	0	0	2	.067	.067	.067	-61	-3				.727	-3	/C-4	-0.5
1890	Phi-a	56	208	29	50	8	1	1	22	20		.240	.310	.303	83	-5	12			.851	-5	O-23,S-18,3-11,/C2	-0.8
Total	2	60	223	30	51	8	1	1	22	20	2	.229	.295	.287	74	-7	12			.773	-8	/O-23,S-18,3-11,C2	-1.3

■ RON KARKOVICE

Karkovice, Ronald Joseph b: 8/8/63, Union, N.J. BR/TR, 6'1", 215 lbs. Deb: 8/17/86

YEAR	TM/L	G	AB	R	H	2B	3B	HR	RBI	BB	SO	AVG	OBP	SLG	PRO+	BR/A	SB	CS	SBR	FA	FR	G/POS	TPR
1986	Chi-A	37	97	13	24	7	0	4	13	9	37	.247	.318	.443	101	-0	1	0	0	.996	14	C-37	1.6
1987	Chi-A	39	85	7	6	2	0	2	7	7	40	.071	.160	.141	-19	-15	3	0	1	.982	10	C-37/D-1	-0.2
1988	Chi-A	46	115	10	20	4	0	3	9	7	30	.174	.228	.287	43	-9	4	2	0	.995	8	C-46	0.2

YEAR	TM/L	G	AB	R	H	2B	3B	HR	RBI	BB	SO	AVG	OBP	SLG	PRO+	BR/A	SB	CS	SBR	FA	FR	G/POS	TPR
1989	Chi-A	71	182	21	48	9	2	3	24	10	56	.264	.309	.385	97	-1	0	0	0	.986	17	C-68/D-2	1.9
1990	Chi-A	68	183	30	45	10	0	6	20	16	52	.246	.310	.399	99	-1	2	0	1	.994	9	C-64/D-2	0.9
1991	Chi-A	75	167	25	41	13	0	5	22	15	42	.246	.311	.413	101	-0	0	0	0	.988	11	C-69/O-1	1.4
1992	Chi-A	123	342	39	81	12	1	13	50	30	89	.237	.304	.392	95	-3	10	4	1	.990		*C-119/O-1	0.8
1993	*Chi-A	128	403	60	92	17	1	20	54	29	126	.228	.290	.424	91	-7	2	2	-1	.994	13	*C-127	1.2
1994	Chi-A	77	207	33	44	9	1	11	29	36	68	.213	.329	.425	94	-2	0	3	-2	.993	-4	C-76	-0.3
1995	Chi-A	113	323	44	70	14	1	13	51	39	84	.217	.311	.387	84	-8	2	3	-1	.991	-7	*C-113	-0.9
1996	Chi-A	111	355	44	78	22	0	10	38	24	93	.220	.271	.366	62	-22	0	0	0	.993	12	*C-111	-0.3
Total	11	888	2459	326	549	117	6	90	317	222	717	.223	.294	.386	83	-67	24	14	-1	.992	86	C-867/D-5,O-2	6.3

■ BILL KARLON Karlon, William John "Hank" b: 1/21/09, Palmer, Mass. d: 12/7/64, Ware, Mass. BR/TR, 6'1", 190 lbs. Deb: 4/28/30

YEAR	TM/L	G	AB	R	H	2B	3B	HR	RBI	BB	SO	AVG	OBP	SLG	PRO+	BR/A	SB	CS	SBR	FA	FR	G/POS	TPR
1930	NY-A	2	5	0	0	0	0	0	0	0	1	.000	.000	.000	-99	-2	0	0	0	1.000	-0	/O-1	-0.2

■ MARTY KAROW Karow, Martin Gregory (b: Martin Gregory Karowsky) b: 7/18/04, Braddock, Pa. d: 4/27/86, Bryan, Texas BR/TR, 5'10.5", 170 lbs. Deb: 6/21/27

YEAR	TM/L	G	AB	R	H	2B	3B	HR	RBI	BB	SO	AVG	OBP	SLG	PRO+	BR/A	SB	CS	SBR	FA	FR	G/POS	TPR
1927	Bos-A	6	10	0	2	1	0	0	0	0	2	.200	.200	.300	29	-1	0	0	0	1.000	0	/S-3,3-2	-0.1

■ ERIC KARROS Karros, Eric Peter b: 11/4/67, Hackensack, N.J. BR/TR, 6'4", 205 lbs. Deb: 9/1/91

YEAR	TM/L	G	AB	R	H	2B	3B	HR	RBI	BB	SO	AVG	OBP	SLG	PRO+	BR/A	SB	CS	SBR	FA	FR	G/POS	TPR
1991	LA-N	14	14	0	1	0	0	0	1	1	6	.071	.133	.143	-23	-2	0	0	0	1.000	—	1-10	-0.3
1992	LA-N	149	545	63	140	30	1	20	88	37	103	.257	.307	.426	107	3	2	4	-2	.993	11	*1-143	0.3
1993	LA-N	158	619	74	153	27	2	23	80	34	82	.247	.289	.409	89	-12	0	1	-1	.992	15	*1-157	-1.0
1994	LA-N	111	406	51	108	21	1	14	46	29	52	.266	.318	.426	98	-3	2	0	1	.991	16	*1-109	0.4
1995	*LA-N	143	551	83	164	29	3	32	105	61	115	.298	.372	.535	149	37	4	4	-1	.995	11	*1-143	2.4
1996	*LA-N	154	608	84	158	29	1	34	111	53	121	.260	.320	.479	117	11	8	0	2	.990	3	*1-154	0.2
Total	6	729	2743	355	724	137	8	123	431	215	480	.264	.320	.454	112	34	16	9	-1	.992	49	1-716	2.0

■ JOHN KARST Karst, John Gottlieb "King" b: 10/15/1893, Philadelphia, Pa. d: 5/21/76, Cape May Court House, N.J. BL/TR, 5'11.5", 175 lbs. Deb: 10/6/15

YEAR	TM/L	G	AB	R	H	2B	3B	HR	RBI	BB	SO	AVG	OBP	SLG	PRO+	BR/A	SB	CS	SBR	FA	FR	G/POS	TPR
1915	Bro-N	1	0	1	0	0	0	0	0	0	0	—	—	—	—	0	0	0	0	1.000	0	/3-1	0.0

■ EDDIE KASKO Kasko, Edward Michael b: 6/27/32, Linden, N.J. BR/TR, 6', 180 lbs. Deb: 4/18/57 M

YEAR	TM/L	G	AB	R	H	2B	3B	HR	RBI	BB	SO	AVG	OBP	SLG	PRO+	BR/A	SB	CS	SBR	FA	FR	G/POS	TPR
1957	StL-N	134	479	59	131	16	5	1	35	33	53	.273	.320	.334	75	-16	6	1	1	.961	-7	*3-120,S-13/2-1	-2.0
1958	StL-N	104	259	20	57	8	1	2	22	21	25	.220	.279	.282	47	-19	1	2	-1	.961	6	S-77,2-12/3-1	-0.8
1959	Cin-N	118	329	39	93	14	1	2	31	14	38	.283	.312	.350	74	-12	2	2	-1	.976	12	S-84,3-31/2-2	0.6
1960	Cin-N	126	479	56	140	21	1	6	51	46	37	.292	.362	.378	101	2	9	9	-3	.966	0	3-86,2-33,S-15	0.3
1961	*Cin-N★	126	469	64	127	22	1	2	27	32	36	.271	.323	.335	74	-17	4	3	-1	.964	-18	*S-112,3-12/2-6	-2.6
1962	Cin-N	134	533	74	148	26	2	4	41	35	44	.278	.328	.356	81	-14	3	3	-1	.941	-8	*3-114,S-21	-2.0
1963	Cin-N	76	199	25	48	9	0	3	10	21	29	.241	.314	.332	83	-4	0	2	-1	.959	-1	3-48,S-15/2-1	-0.5
1964	Hou-N	133	448	45	109	16	1	0	22	37	52	.243	.302	.283	70	-17	6	6	-2	.978	10	*S-128/3-2	-0.1
1965	Hou-N	68	126	18	53	7	1	1	10	11	20	.247	.296	.302	74	-8	1	3	-2	.976	-10	S-59/3-2	-1.7
1966	Bos-A	58	136	11	29	7	0	1	12	15	19	.213	.291	.287	61	-7	1	0	-1	.976	-8	S-20,3-10/2-8	0.3
Total	10	1077	3546	411	935	146	13	22	261	265	353	.264	.318	.331	76	-112	31	31	-9	.971	-9	S-544,3-426/2-63	-8.5

■ RAY KATT Katt, Raymond Frederick b: 5/9/27, New Braunfels, Tex. BR/TR, 6'2", 200 lbs. Deb: 9/16/52 C

YEAR	TM/L	G	AB	R	H	2B	3B	HR	RBI	BB	SO	AVG	OBP	SLG	PRO+	BR/A	SB	CS	SBR	FA	FR	G/POS	TPR
1952	NY-N	9	27	4	6	0	0	0	1	1	5	.222	.250	.222	32	-2	0	0	0	1.000	1	/C-8	-0.1
1953	NY-N	8	29	2	5	1	0	0	1	1	3	.172	.200	.207	6	-4	0	0	0	.975	-1	/C-8	-0.4
1954	NY-N	86	200	26	51	7	1	9	33	19	29	.255	.320	.435	94	-2	1	0	0	.973	-7	C-82	-0.6
1955	NY-N	124	326	27	70	7	2	7	28	22	38	.215	.269	.313	54	-22	0	1	0	.987	-8	*C-122	-2.6
1956	NY-N	37	101	10	23	4	0	7	14	6	16	.228	.278	.475	98	-1	0	1	-1	.978	0	C-37	-0.5
	StL-N	47	158	11	41	4	0	6	20	6	24	.259	.291	.399	83	-4	0	1	-1	.984	-2	C-47	-0.5
	Yr	84	259	21	64	8	0	13	34	12	40	.247	.286	.429	89	-5	0	2	-1	.982	-1	C-84	-0.5
1957	NY-N	72	165	11	38	3	1	2	17	15	35	.230	.302	.297	62	-9	1	0	0	.981	-6	C-68	-1.3
1958	StL-N	19	41	1	7	1	0	1	4	4	6	.171	.244	.268	34	-4	0	0	0	.971	0	C-14	-0.3
1959	StL-N	15	24	0	7	2	0	0	3	1	8	.292	.292	.375	71	-1	0	0	0	.976	-0	C-14	-0.1
Total	8	417	1071	92	248	29	4	32	120	74	164	.232	.285	.356	69	-49	2	2	-1	.981	-22	C-400	-5.9

■ BENNY KAUFF Kauff, Benjamin Michael b: 1/5/1890, Pomeroy, Ohio d: 11/17/61, Columbus, Ohio BL/TL, 5'8", 157 lbs. Deb: 4/20/12

YEAR	TM/L	G	AB	R	H	2B	3B	HR	RBI	BB	SO	AVG	OBP	SLG	PRO+	BR/A	SB	CS	SBR	FA	FR	G/POS	TPR
1912	NY-A	5	11	4	3	0	0	0	2	0	3	.273	.429	.273	96	-1	0			1.000	-1	/O-4	-0.1
1914	Ind-F	154	571	120	211	44	13	8	95	72	55	.370	.447	.534	150	34	75			.953	16	*O-154	4.4
1915	Bro-F	136	483	92	165	23	11	12	83	85	50	.342	.446	.509	170	42	55			.959	15	*O-136	5.3
1916	NY-N	154	552	71	146	22	15	9	74	68	65	.264	.348	.408	139	26	40	26	-4	.962	-2	*O-154	1.9
1917	*NY-N	153	559	89	172	22	4	5	68	59	54	.308	.379	.388	140	28	30			.976	-4	*O-153	1.7
1918	NY-N	67	270	41	85	19	4	2	39	16	30	.315	.355	.437	144	13	9			.952	-1	O-67	1.0
1919	NY-N	135	491	73	136	27	7	10	67	39	45	.277	.334	.422	128	15	21			.950	-3	*O-134	0.4
1920	NY-N	55	157	31	43	12	3	3	26	25	14	.274	.380	.446	138	8	3	7	-3	.960	23	O-51	0.2
Total	8	859	3094	521	961	169	57	49	454	364	313	.311	.389	.450	146	167	234	33		.960	23	O-853	14.8

■ DICK KAUFFMAN Kauffman, Howard Richard b: 6/22/1888, E.Lewisburg, Pa. d: 4/16/48, Mifflinburg, Pa. BB/TR, 6'3", 190 lbs. Deb: 9/17/14

YEAR	TM/L	G	AB	R	H	2B	3B	HR	RBI	BB	SO	AVG	OBP	SLG	PRO+	BR/A	SB	CS	SBR	FA	FR	G/POS	TPR
1914	StL-A	7	15	1	4	1	0	0	2	0	3	.267	.267	.333	83	-0	0	0	0	.967	-1	/1-7	-0.2
1915	StL-A	37	124	9	32	8	2	0	14	5	27	.258	.298	.355	99	-1	0	3	-2	.984	-1	1-32/O-1	-0.5
Total	2	44	139	10	36	9	2	0	16	5	30	.259	.295	.353	97	-1	0	3		.982	-2	/1-39,O-1	-0.7

■ TONY KAUFMANN Kaufmann, Anthony Charles b: 12/16/1900, Chicago, Ill. d: 6/4/82, Elgin, Ill. BR/TR, 5'11", 165 lbs. Deb: 9/23/21 C

YEAR	TM/L	G	AB	R	H	2B	3B	HR	RBI	BB	SO	AVG	OBP	SLG	PRO+	BR/A	SB	CS	SBR	FA	FR	G/POS	TPR
1921	Chi-N	2	5	0	2	1	0	0	0	0	1	.400	.400	.600	161	0	0	0	0	1.000	-1	/P-2	0.0
1922	Chi-N	38	45	4	9	2	1	1	4	2	9	.200	.234	.356	40	-4	0	0	0	.933	-1	P-37	0.0
1923	Chi-N	33	74	10	16	0	2	0	10	7	17	.216	.284	.324	60	-4	0	0	0	.962	-1	P-33	0.0
1924	Chi-N	35	76	6	24	5	0	1	14	3	10	.316	.342	.421	102	0	0	0	0	.981	-1	P-34	0.0
1925	Chi-N	31	78	8	15	7	0	2	13	2	11	.192	.213	.359	42	-7	0	0	0	.981	-0	P-31	0.0
1926	Chi-N	30	60	9	15	1	0	0	7	2	10	.250	.274	.333	62	-3	1			**1.000**	-2	P-26	0.0
1927	Chi-N	9	16	2	5	1	0	0	6	4	4	.313	.450	.500	154	1	0	0	0	1.000	2	/P-9	0.0
	Phi-N	8	7	1	1	0	0	0	2	0	1	.143	.143	.571	83	-0	0	0	0	1.000	-0	/P-5,O-1	0.0
	StL-N	1	0	0	0	0	0	0	—	—	—					0	0			0.000		/P-1	0.0
	Yr	18	23	3	6	1	0	0	8	4	5	.261	.370	.522	136	1	0	0	0	1.000	2	P-15/O-1	0.0
1928	StL-N	5	5	0	0	0	0	0	—	—	—					0	0			1.000	-0	/P-4	0.0
1929	NY-N	39	32	18	1	0	0	0	1	6	4	.031	.184	.031	-43	-7	3			.964	-4	O-16	-1.0
1930	StL-N	2	3	1	1	0	0	0	0	0	0	.333	.500	.333	103	0	0	0	0	1.000	-0	/P-2	0.0
1931	StL-N	20	18	1	2	0	0	0	0	1	3	.111	.158	.111	-26	-3	0	9		.929	-1	P-15/O-1	-0.1
1935	StL-N	7	5	0	1	0	0	0	0	0	1					0	0			1.000		P-3	0.0
Total	12	260	414	62	102	19	1	9	57	28	82	.220	.269	.336	57	-27	4	0		.972	-9	P-202/O-18	-1.1

■ CHARLIE KAVANAGH Kavanagh, Charles Hugh "Silk" b: 6/9/1893, Chicago, Ill. d: 9/6/73, Reedsburg, Wis. BR/TR, 5'9", 165 lbs. Deb: 6/11/14

YEAR	TM/L	G	AB	R	H	2B	3B	HR	RBI	BB	SO	AVG	OBP	SLG	PRO+	BR/A	SB	CS	SBR	FA	FR	G/POS	TPR
1914	Chi-A	6	5	0	1	0	0	0	0	0	2	.200	.333	.200	62	-0	0	0	0	1.000	0	H	0.0

■ LEO KAVANAGH Kavanagh, Leo Daniel b: 8/9/1894, Chicago, Ill. d: 8/10/50, Chicago, Ill. BR/TR, 5'9", 180 lbs. Deb: 4/22/14

YEAR	TM/L	G	AB	R	H	2B	3B	HR	RBI	BB	SO	AVG	OBP	SLG	PRO+	BR/A	SB	CS	SBR	FA	FR	G/POS	TPR
1914	Chi-F	5	11	0	3	0	0	0	1	1	0	.273	.333	.273	70	-1	0			1.000	-1	/S-5	-0.1

■ MARTY KAVANAGH Kavanagh, Martin Joseph b: 6/13/1891, Harrison, N.J. d: 7/28/60, Eloise, Mich. BR/TR, 6', 187 lbs. Deb: 4/18/14

YEAR	TM/L	G	AB	R	H	2B	3B	HR	RBI	BB	SO	AVG	OBP	SLG	PRO+	BR/A	SB	CS	SBR	FA	FR	G/POS	TPR
1914	Det-A	128	439	60	109	21	6	4	35	41	42	.248	.318	.351	98	-2	16	14	-4	.929	-7	*2-115/1-4	-1.5
1915	Det-A	113	332	55	98	14	13	4	49	42	44	.295	.378	.452	141	16	8	8	-2	.987	-15	1-44,2-42/S-2,O3	-0.8
1916	Det-A	58	78	6	11	4	0	0	9	9	15	.141	.239	.192	29	-7	0			1.000	—	O-11/2-3,3-1	-0.8
	Cle-A	19	44	4	11	2	1	1	10	2	5	.250	.283	.409	102	-0	0			.894	-1	/2-9,1-1,3-1	0.0
	Yr	77	122	10	22	6	1	1	15	11	20	.180	.254	.270	55	-7	0			1.000	—	O-11,2-11/3-2,1-1	-0.8
1917	Cle-A	14	14	1	1	0	0	0	1	0	6	.000	.176	.000	-43	-2	1			1.000	—	/O-2	-0.2
1918	Cle-A	13	38	4	8	2	0	0	6	7	7	.211	.348	.263	77	-1	1			.967	-1	1-12	-0.3

YEAR	TM/L	G	AB	R	H	2B	3B	HR	RBI	BB	SO	AVG	OBP	SLG	PRO+	BR/A	SB	CS	SBR	FA	FR	G/POS	TPR
	StL-N	12	44	6	8	1	0	1	8	3	1	.182	.234	.273	56	-2	1			1.000	-2	/O-8,2-4	-0.5
	Det-A	13	44	2	12	0	0	0	9	11	6	.273	.418	.341	135	3	0			.964	-1	1-12	0.1
Total	5	370	1033	138	257	47	20	10	122	118	122	.249	.330	.362	104	4	26	22		.926	-26	2-172/1-73,0-23,3S	-3.4

■ **KAVANAUGH**   Kavanaugh   Deb: 9/11/1872
| 1872 | Eck-n | 5 | 23 | 3 | 6 | 1 | 0 | 0 | | 2 | 0 | 1 | .261 | .261 | .304 | 86 | -0 | 0 | 0 | 0 | .921 | -1 | /1-4,O-2 | 0.0 |

■ **BILL KAY**   Kay, Walter Brocton "King Bill"   b: 2/14/1878, New Castle, Va.   d: 12/3/45, Roanoke, Va.   BL/TR, 6'2", 180 lbs.   Deb: 8/12/07
| 1907 | Was-A | 25 | 60 | 8 | 20 | 1 | 1 | 0 | 7 | 0 | | .333 | .333 | .383 | 139 | 2 | 0 | | | 1.000 | -0 | O-12 | 0.2 |

■ **EDDIE KAZAK**   Kazak, Edward Terrance (b: Edward Terrance Tkaczuk)   b: 7/18/20, Steubenville, O.   BR/TR, 6', 175 lbs.   Deb: 9/29/48
1948	StL-N	6	22	1	6	3	0	0	2	0	2	.273	.273	.409	78	-1	0			.900	1	/3-6	0.0
1949	StL-N★	92	326	43	99	15	3	6	42	29	17	.304	.362	.423	105	2	0			.926	-4	3-80/2-5	-0.2
1950	StL-N	93	207	21	53	2	2	5	23	18	19	.256	.319	.357	74	-8	0			.936	1	3-48	-0.7
1951	StL-N	11	33	2	6	2	0	0	4	5	5	.182	.289	.242	44	-3	0	0	0	.933	-1	3-10	-0.4
1952	StL-N	3	2	1	0	0	0	0	0	0	0	.000	.000	.000	-99	-1	0	0	0	1.000	0	/3-1	0.0
	Cin-N	13	15	1	1	0	0	0	0	0	2	.067	.067	.200	-29	-3	0	0	0	.667	-1	/3-3,1-1	-0.3
	Yr	16	17	2	1	0	0	0	0	0	2	.059	.059	.176	-37	-3	0	0	0	.750	-0	/3-4,1-1	-0.3
Total	5	218	605	69	165	22	6	11	71	52	45	.273	.332	.383	87	-12	0	0		.927	-3	3-148/2-5,1-1	-1.6

■ **TED KAZANSKI**   Kazanski, Theodore Stanley   b: 1/25/34, Hamtramck, Mich.   BR/TR, 6'1", 175 lbs.   Deb: 6/25/53
1953	Phi-N	95	360	39	78	17	5	2	27	26	53	.217	.275	.308	52	-26	1	1	-0	.949	-19	S-95	-3.8
1954	Phi-N	39	104	7	14	2	0	1	8	4	14	.135	.167	.183	-9	-17	0	1	-1	.945	-7	S-38	-2.2
1955	Phi-N	9	12	1	1	0	0	0	1	1	1	.083	.154	.333	25	-1	0	0	0	1.000	1	/S-4,3-4	-0.1
1956	Phi-N	117	379	35	80	11	1	4	34	24	41	.211	.253	.277	43	-31	0	2	-1	.979	-10	*2-116/S-1	-3.5
1957	Phi-N	62	185	15	49	7	1	3	11	17	20	.265	.327	.362	88	-3	1	1	0	.968	-3	3-36,2-22/S-3	-0.4
1958	Phi-N	95	289	21	66	12	3	3	35	22	34	.228	.292	.315	62	-16	2	3	-1	.988	-13	2-59,S-22,3-16	-2.6
Total	6	417	1329	118	288	49	9	14	116	90	163	.217	.270	.299	51	-94	4	8	-4	.981	-51	2-197,S-163/3-56	-12.6

■ **BOB KEARNEY**   Kearney, Robert Henry   b: 10/3/56, San Antonio, Tex.   BR/TR, 6', 190 lbs.   Deb: 9/25/79
1979	SF-N	2	0	0	0	0	0	0	0	1	0	—	1.000	—	211	0	0	0	0	.000	0	/C-1	0.0
1981	Oak-A	1	0	0	0	0	0	0	0	0	0	—	—	—	—	0	0	0	0	.000	0	/C-1	0.0
1982	Oak-A	22	71	7	12	3	0	0	5	3	10	.169	.224	.211	21	-8	0	0	0	.970	5	C-22	-0.2
1983	Oak-A	108	298	33	76	11	0	8	32	21	50	.255	.313	.372	93	-3	1	4	-2	.982	5	*C-101/D-3	0.4
1984	Sea-A	133	431	39	97	24	1	7	43	18	72	.225	.259	.334	64	-22	7	5	-1	.988	5	*C-133	-1.2
1985	Sea-A	108	305	24	74	14	1	6	27	11	59	.243	.278	.354	71	-12	1	1	-0	**.995**	6	*C-108	1.0
1986	Sea-A	81	204	25	49	10	0	6	25	12	35	.240	.282	.377	77	-7	0	2	-1	.989	14	C-79	1.0
1987	Sea-A	24	47	5	8	4	1	0	1	1	9	.170	.188	.298	25	-5	0	0	0	.981	6	C-24	0.2
Total	8	479	1356	131	316	66	3	27	133	67	235	.233	.275	.346	70	-57	9	12	-5	.987	41	C-469/D-3	-0.0

■ **TEDDY KEARNS**   Kearns, Edward Joseph   b: 1/1/1900, Trenton, N.J.   d: 12/21/49, Trenton, N.J.   BR/TR, 5'11", 180 lbs.   Deb: 10/1/20
1920	Phi-A	1	1	0	0	0	0	0	0	0	0	.000	.000	.000	-99	-0	0	0	0	.000	0	H	0.0
1924	Chi-N	4	16	0	4	0	1	0	1	1	1	.250	.294	.375	77	-1	0	0	0	1.000	-0	/1-4	-0.1
1925	Chi-N	3	2	0	1	0	0	0	0	0	0	.500	.500	.500	154	0	0	0	0	1.000	-0	/1-3	0.0
Total	3	8	19	0	5	0	1	0	1	1	1	.263	.300	.368	76	-1	0	0	0	1.000	-0	/1-7	-0.1

■ **TOM KEARNS**   Kearns, Thomas J. "Dasher"   b: 11/9/1859, Rochester, N.Y.   d: 12/7/38, Buffalo, N.Y.   BR/TR, 5'7", 160 lbs.   Deb: 8/26/1880
1880	Buf-N	2	7	0	0	0	0	0		0	0	.000	.000	.000	-98	-1				.667	-1	/C-2	-0.3
1882	Det-N	4	13	2	4	2	0	0		0	4	.308	.308	.462	143	1				.733	-3	/2-4	-0.2
1884	Det-N	21	79	9	16	0	1	0	7	2	10	.203	.222	.228	45	-5				.810	-10	2-21	-1.3
Total	3	27	99	11	20	2	1	0	8	2	14	.202	.218	.242	48	-6				.801	-14	/2-25,C-2	-1.8

■ **EDDIE KEARSE**   Kearse, Edward Paul "Truck"   b: 2/23/16, San Francisco, Cal   d: 7/15/68, Eureka, Cal.   BR/TR, 6'1", 195 lbs.   Deb: 6/13/42
| 1942 | NY-A | 11 | 26 | 2 | 5 | 0 | 0 | 0 | 2 | 3 | 1 | .192 | .276 | .192 | 34 | -2 | 1 | 0 | | 1.000 | 3 | C-11 | 0.2 |

■ **CHICK KEATING**   Keating, Walter Francis   b: 8/8/1891, Philadelphia, Pa.   d: 7/13/59, Philadelphia, Pa.   BR/TR, 5'9.5", 155 lbs.   Deb: 9/26/13
1913	Chi-N	2	5	0	1	1	0	0	0	0	1	.200	.200	.400	69	-0	0			1.000	-1	/S-2	-0.1
1914	Chi-N	20	30	3	3	0	1	0	0	6	9	.100	.250	.167	25	-3	0			.951	5	S-14	-0.2
1915	Chi-N	4	8	1	0	0	0	0	0	0	3	.000	.000	.000	-99	-2	1			.750	-0	/S-2	-0.2
1926	Phi-N	4	2	0	0	0	0	0	0	0	0	.000	.000	.000	-95	-1	0			1.000	-0	/2-2,S-2,3-1	-0.1
Total	4	30	45	4	4	1	1	0	0	6	13	.089	.196	.156	4	-5	1			.903	-1	/S-20,2-2,3-1	-0.6

■ **GREG KEATLEY**   Keatley, Gregory Steven   b: 9/12/53, Princeton, W.Va.   BR/TR, 6'2", 200 lbs.   Deb: 9/27/81
| 1981 | KC-A | 2 | 0 | 0 | 0 | 0 | 0 | 0 | 0 | 0 | 0 | — | — | — | — | 0 | 0 | 0 | 0 | 1.000 | -0 | /C-2 | 0.0 |

■ **PAT KEEDY**   Keedy, Charles Patrick   b: 1/10/58, Birmingham, Ala.   BR/TR, 6'4", 205 lbs.   Deb: 9/10/85
1985	Cal-A	3	4	1	2	1	0	1	0	0	0	.500	.500	1.500	424	2	0	1	-1	.000	-0	/3-2,O-1	0.1
1987	Chi-A	17	41	6	7	1	0	2	2	2	14	.171	.209	.341	42	-4	1	0	0	.943	4	3-11/1-2,2-1,SOD	0.1
1989	Cle-A	9	14	3	3	2	0	0	1	2	5	.214	.313	.357	87	-0	0	0	0	1.000	-0	/O-3,3-2,1-1,S-1,D	0.0
Total	3	29	59	10	12	4	0	3	4	4	19	.203	.254	.424	77	-2	1	1	-0	.929	3	/3-15,O-5,1-3,DS2	0.2

■ **WILLIE KEELER**   Keeler, William Henry "Wee Willie" (b: William Henry O'Kelleher)   b: 3/3/1872, Brooklyn, N.Y.   d: 1/1/23, Brooklyn, N.Y.   BL/TL, 5'4.5", 140 lbs.   Deb: 9/30/1892   H
1892	NY-N	14	53	7	17	3	0	0	6	3	3	.321	.368	.377	128	2	5			.878	-3	3-14	-0.1
1893	NY-N	7	24	5	8	2	1	1	7	5	1	.333	.448	.625	183	3	3			.667	-5	/O-3,2-2,S-2	-0.2
	Bro-N	20	80	14	25	1	1	0	9	4	4	.313	.353	.387	101	0	2			.833	1	3-12/O-8	-0.1
	Yr	27	104	19	33	3	2	2	16	9	5	.317	.377	.442	121	3	5			.833	-6	3-12,O-11/2-2,S-2	-0.3
1894	*Bal-N	129	590	165	219	27	22	5	94	40	6	.371	.427	.517	121	20	32			.938	3	*O-128/2-1	1.1
1895	*Bal-N	131	565	162	213	24	15	4	78	37	12	.377	.419	.494	134	28	47			.946	0	*O-131	1.4
1896	*Bal-N	126	544	153	210	22	13	4	82	37	9	.386	.432	.496	142	33	67			.969	6	*O-126	2.4
1897	*Bal-N	129	564	145	**239**	27	19	0	74	35		**.424**	.464	.539	164	52	64			.970	-2	*O-129	3.4
1898	Bal-N	129	561	126	**216**	7	2	1	44	31		.385	.420	.410	136	26	28			.961	0	*O-128/3-1	1.6
1899	Bro-N	141	570	**140**	216	12	13	1	61	37		.379	.425	.451	137	30	45			.979	5	*O-141	1.5
1900	*Bro-N	136	563	106	**204**	13	12	4	68	30		.362	.402	.449	127	19	41			.940	5	*O-136/2-1	1.3
1901	Bro-N	136	595	123	202	18	12	2	43	21		.339	.365	.420	125	18	23			**.985**	-6	*O-125,3-10/2-3	0.3
1902	Bro-N	133	559	86	186	20	5	0	38	21		.333	.365	.386	131	19	19			**.978**	0	*O-133	1.3
1903	NY-A	132	512	95	160	14	7	0	32	32		.313	.368	.367	114	10	24			.935	-9	*O-128/3-4	-0.8
1904	NY-A	143	543	78	186	14	8	2	40	35		.343	.390	.409	146	28	21			.935	-3	*O-142	1.9
1905	NY-A	149	560	81	169	14	4	4	38	43		.302	.357	.363	115	9	19			.968	-3	*O-137,2-12/3-3	-0.6
1906	NY-A	152	592	96	180	8	3	2	33	40		.304	.353	.338	106	4	23			.987	-2	*O-152	-0.6
1907	NY-A	107	423	50	99	5	2	0	17	15		.234	.265	.255	61	-19	7			.969	-3	*O-107	-2.9
1908	NY-A	91	323	38	85	3	1	1	14	31		.263	.337	.288	102	2	14			.936	-1	O-88	-0.8
1909	NY-A	99	360	44	95	7	5	1	32	24		.264	.327	.319	104	2	10			.968	-5	O-95	-0.8
1910	NY-N	10	10	5	3	0	0	0	1	5		.300	.462	.300	123	1	0			1.000	-0	/O-2	0.0
Total	19	2123	8591	1719	2932	241	145	33	810	524	36	.341	.388	.415	125	286	495			.960	-30	*O-2039/3-44,2-19,S	10.4

■ **BOB KEELY**   Keely, Robert William   b: 8/22/09, St.Louis, Mo.   BR/TR, 6', 175 lbs.   Deb: 7/25/44   C
1944	StL-N	1	0	0	0	0	0	0		0	0	—	—	—		0	0			1.000	-0	/C-1	0.0
1945	StL-N	1	1	0	0	0	0	0	0	0	0	.000	.000	.000	-98	-0	0			1.000	-0	/C-1	0.0
Total	2	2	1	0	0	0	0	0	0	0	0	.000	.000	.000	-98	-0	0			1.000	-0	/C-2	0.0

■ **BILL KEEN**   Keen, William Brown "Buster"   b: 8/16/1892, Oglethorpe, Ga.   d: 7/16/47, South Point, Ohio   BR/TR, 6', 181 lbs.   Deb: 8/8/11
| 1911 | Pit-N | 6 | 7 | 0 | 0 | 0 | 0 | 0 | 0 | 0 | 1 | 4 | .000 | .125 | .000 | -62 | -2 | 0 | | | 1.000 | -0 | /1-1 | -0.2 |

YEAR	TM/L	G	AB	R	H	2B	3B	HR	RBI	BB	SO	AVG	OBP	SLG	PRO+	BR/A	SB	CS	SBR	FA	FR	G/POS	TPR

■ JIM KEENAN   Keenan, James William   b: 2/10/1858, New Haven, Conn.   d: 9/21/26, Cincinnati, Ohio   BR/TR, 5'10", 186 lbs.   Deb: 5/17/1875

YEAR	TM/L	G	AB	R	H	2B	3B	HR	RBI	BB	SO	AVG	OBP	SLG	PRO+	BR/A	SB	CS	SBR	FA	FR	G/POS	TPR
1875	NH-n	5	13	1	1	0	0	0	0	0	0	.077	.077	.077	-53	-2	0	0	0	.800	-3	/C-3,3-2,O-1	-0.5
1880	Buf-N	2	7	1	1	0	0	0	0	1	1	.143	.250	.143	36	-0				.947	3	/C-2	0.2
1882	Pit-a	25	96	10	21	7	0	1		1		.219	.227	.323	87	-1				.906	1	C-22/O-3,S-1	0.1
1884	Ind-a	68	249	36	73	14	4	3	16			.293	.343	.418	151	14				.923	-2	C-59/1-6,O-2,S-2,P	1.5
1885	Cin-a	36	132	16	35	2	2	1	15	8		.265	.307	.333	100	0				.926	-1	C-33/1-4,P-1	0.1
1886	Cin-a	44	148	31	40	4	3	3	24	18		.270	.357	.399	132	6	0			.915	0	C-30/O-7,3-5,1-4,P	0.7
1887	Cin-a	47	174	19	44	4	1	0	17	11		.253	.301	.287	63	-9	7			.934	9	C-38,1-11	0.2
1888	Cin-a	85	313	38	73	9	8	1	40	22		.233	.294	.323	93	-3	9			.946	3	C-69,1-16	0.4
1889	Cin-a	87	300	52	86	10	11	6	60	48	35	.287	.395	.453	137	15	18			.962	1	C-66,1-21/3-1	1.8
1890	Cin-N	54	202	21	28	4	2	3	19	19	36	.139	.216	.223	28	-19	5			.950	4	C-50/1-2,O-1,3-1	-0.9
1891	Cin-N	75	252	30	51	7	5	4	33	33	39	.202	.302	.317	80	-6	2			.974	-4	1-41,C-34/3-1	-0.8
Total	10	523	1873	254	452	61	36	22	208	177	111	.241	.314	.348	99	-4	41		0	.935	14	C-403,1-105/O3PS	3.3

■ GEORGE KEERL   Keerl, George Henry   b: 4/10/1847, Baltimore, Md.   d: 9/13/23, Menominee, Mich.   BR/TR, 5'7", 145 lbs.   Deb: 5/5/1875

YEAR	TM/L	G	AB	R	H	2B	3B	HR	RBI	BB	SO	AVG	OBP	SLG	PRO+	BR/A	SB	CS	SBR	FA	FR	G/POS	TPR
1875	Chi-n	6	23	2	3	0	0	0	3	0	2	.130	.130	.130	-9	-2	0	0	0	.815	-2	/2-6	-0.4

■ JIM KEESEY   Keesey, James Ward   b: 10/27/02, Perryville, Md.   d: 9/5/51, Boise, Idaho   BR/TR, 6'0.5", 170 lbs.   Deb: 9/6/25

YEAR	TM/L	G	AB	R	H	2B	3B	HR	RBI	BB	SO	AVG	OBP	SLG	PRO+	BR/A	SB	CS	SBR	FA	FR	G/POS	TPR
1925	Phi-A	5	5	1	2	0	0	0	1	0	2	.400	.400	.400	97	-0	0	0	0	1.000	-0	/1-2	0.0
1930	Phi-A	11	12	2	3	1	0	0	2	1	2	.250	.308	.333	60	-1				.909	-0	/1-3	-0.1
Total	2	16	17	3	5	1	0	0	3	1	4	.294	.333	.353	71	-1	0	0	0	.923	-1	/1-5	-0.1

■ BILL KEISTER   Keister, William Hoffman "Wagon Tongue"   b: 8/17/1874, Baltimore, Md.   d: 8/19/24, Baltimore, Md.   BL/TR, 5'5.5", 168 lbs.   Deb: 5/20/1896

YEAR	TM/L	G	AB	R	H	2B	3B	HR	RBI	BB	SO	AVG	OBP	SLG	PRO+	BR/A	SB	CS	SBR	FA	FR	G/POS	TPR
1896	Bal-N	15	58	8	14	3	0	0	5	3	5	.241	.302	.293	56	-4	4			.923	-5	/2-8,3-6	-0.7
1898	Bos-N	10	30	5	5	2	0	0	4	0		.167	.167	.233	14	-3	0			1.000	1	/S-4,2-4,O-1	-0.2
1899	Bal-N	136	523	96	172	22	16	3	73	16		.329	.368	.449	117	10	33			.895	-30	S-90,2-46/O-1	-1.0
1900	StL-N	126	497	78	149	26	10	1	72	25		.300	.347	.398	106	3	32			.927	-23	*2-116/S-7,3-3	-1.3
1901	Bal-A	115	442	78	145	20	**21**	2	93	18		.328	.365	.482	128	15	24			.851	-23	*S-112	0.1
1902	Was-A	119	483	82	145	33	9	9	90	14		.300	.329	.462	117	8	27			.912	-1	0-65,2-40,3-14,/S-2	0.2
1903	Phi-N	100	400	53	128	27	7	3	63	14		.320	.352	.445	131	14	11			.940	3	*O-100	1.1
Total	7	621	2433	400	758	133	63	18	400	90	5	.312	.349	.440	116	43	131			.870	-80	S-215,2-214,O/3	-1.8

■ MICKEY KELIHER   Keliher, Maurice Michael   b: 1/11/1890, Washington, D.C.   d: 9/7/30, Washington, D.C.   BL/TL, 6', 175 lbs.   Deb: 9/9/11

YEAR	TM/L	G	AB	R	H	2B	3B	HR	RBI	BB	SO	AVG	OBP	SLG	PRO+	BR/A	SB	CS	SBR	FA	FR	G/POS	TPR
1911	Pit-N	3	7	0	0	0	0	0	0	0	5	.000	.000	.000	-96	-2	0			.875	-0	/1-3	-0.2
1912	Pit-N	2	0	1	0	0	0	0	0	0	0	—	—	—	—	0	0			.000	0	R	0.0
Total	2	5	7	1	0	0	0	0	0	0	5	.000	.000	.000	-96	-2	0			.875	-0	/1-3	-0.2

■ SKEETER KELL   Kell, Everett Lee   b: 10/11/29, Swifton, Ark.   d: 4/19/52   F

YEAR	TM/L	G	AB	R	H	2B	3B	HR	RBI	BB	SO	AVG	OBP	SLG	PRO+	BR/A	SB	CS	SBR	FA	FR	G/POS	TPR
1952	Phi-A	75	213	24	47	8	3	0	17	14	18	.221	.275	.282	53	-14	5	1		.963	-5	2-68	-1.5

■ GEORGE KELL   Kell, George Clyde   b: 8/23/22, Swifton, Ark.   BR/TR, 5'9", 175 lbs.   Deb: 9/28/43   FH

YEAR	TM/L	G	AB	R	H	2B	3B	HR	RBI	BB	SO	AVG	OBP	SLG	PRO+	BR/A	SB	CS	SBR	FA	FR	G/POS	TPR
1943	Phi-A	1	5	1	1	0	1	0	1	0	0	.200	.200	.600	131	0	0	0	0	1.000	0	/3-1	0.0
1944	Phi-A	139	514	51	138	15	3	0	44	22	23	.268	.300	.309	75	-17	5	2	0	.958	-5	*3-139	-2.1
1945	Phi-A	147	567	50	154	30	3	4	56	27	15	.272	.306	.356	92	-8	2	0	1	**.964**	22	*3-147	2.0
1946	Phi-A	26	87	3	26	6	1	0	11	10	6	.299	.378	.391	116	2	0	0		.979	3	3-26	0.6
	Det-A	105	434	67	142	19	9	4	41	30	14	.327	.371	.440	119	10	3	2	-0	.984	5	*3-105/1-1	1.8
	Yr	131	521	70	168	25	10	4	52	40	20	.322	.372	.432	118	12	3	2	-0	**.983**	8	*3-131/1-1	2.4
1947	Det-A★	152	588	75	188	29	5	5	93	61	16	.320	.387	.412	118	16	9	11	-4	.962	16	*3-152	3.1
1948	Det-A☆	92	368	47	112	24	3	2	44	33	15	.304	.369	.402	102	1	2	2	-1	.969	-0	3-92	-0.8
1949	Det-A★	134	522	97	179	38	9	3	59	71	13	**.343**	.424	.467	136	28	7	5	-1	.975	1	*3-134	2.5
1950	Det-A★	157	641	114	**218**	**56**	6	8	101	66	18	.340	.403	.484	122	21	3	3	-1	**.982**	-3	*3-157	1.4
1951	Det-A★	147	598	92	**191**	**36**	3	2	59	61	18	.319	.386	.400	112	12	10	3	-1	**.960**	9	*3-147	2.0
1952	Det-A†	39	152	11	45	8	0	1	17	15	13	.296	.359	.368	102	1	0	1	-0	.959	-2	3-39	-0.3
	Bos-A†	75	276	41	88	15	2	6	40	31	10	.319	.390	.453	124	9	0	0	-0	.959	-7	3-73	0.1
	Yr	114	428	52	133	23	2	7	57	46	23	.311	.379	.423	117	10	0	1	-0	.959	-9	*3-112	-0.2
1953	Bos-A★	134	460	68	141	41	2	12	73	52	22	.307	.383	.483	126	17	5	2	0	**.972**	-14	*3-124/O-7	0.0
1954	Bos-A	26	93	15	24	3	0	0	10	15	3	.258	.361	.290	72	-3	0	0	0	.920	-3	3-25	-0.7
	Chi-A†	71	233	25	66	10	0	5	48	18	12	.283	.335	.391	95	-2	1	1	-0	.996	-11	1-32,3-31/O-2	-1.7
	Yr	97	326	40	90	13	0	5	58	33	15	.276	.343	.362	88	-5	1	1	-0	.936	-14	3-56,1-32/O-2	-2.4
1955	Chi-A	128	429	44	134	24	1	8	81	51	36	.312	.393	.429	118	12	2	2	-1	.976	-19	*3-105,1-24/O-1	-0.9
1956	Chi-A	21	80	7	25	5	0	1	11	8	6	.313	.375	.412	106	1	0	0	0	1.000	-0	3-18/1-4	-0.3
	Bal-A★	102	345	45	90	17	2	8	37	25	31	.261	.316	.391	93	-5	0	1	-1	.974	-7	3-97/1-2,2-1	-1.1
	Yr	123	425	52	115	22	2	9	48	33	37	.271	.328	.395	96	-4	0	1	-1	**.978**	-11	*3-115/1-6,2-1	-1.4
1957	Bal-A★	99	310	28	92	9	0	9	44	25	16	.297	.353	.413	116	6	2	0	0	.979	-0	3-80,1-22	0.3
Total	15	1795	6702	881	2054	385	50	78	870	621	287	.306	.368	.414	111	100	51	36	-6	.969	-29	*3-1692/1-85,O-10,2	5.9

■ DUKE KELLEHER   Kelleher, Albert Aloysius   b: 9/30/1893, New York, N.Y.   d: 9/28/47, Staten Island, N.Y.   TR,   Deb: 8/18/16

YEAR	TM/L	G	AB	R	H	2B	3B	HR	RBI	BB	SO	AVG	OBP	SLG	PRO+	BR/A	SB	CS	SBR	FA	FR	G/POS	TPR
1916	NY-N	1	0	0		0	0	0	0	0	0					0	0			.000	0	/C-1	0.0

■ FRANKIE KELLEHER   Kelleher, Francis Eugene   b: 8/22/16, San Francisco, Cal   d: 4/13/79, Stockton, Cal.   BR/TR, 6'1", 195 lbs.   Deb: 7/18/42

YEAR	TM/L	G	AB	R	H	2B	3B	HR	RBI	BB	SO	AVG	OBP	SLG	PRO+	BR/A	SB	CS	SBR	FA	FR	G/POS	TPR
1942	Cin-N	38	110	13	20	3	1	3	12	16	20	.182	.286	.309	74	-4	0			.986	-0	O-30	-0.5
1943	Cin-N	9	10	1	0	0	0	0	0	2	0	.000	.167	.000	-51	-2	0			1.000	-0	/O-1	-0.2
Total	2	47	120	14	20	3	1	3	12	18	20	.167	.275	.283	64	-6	0			.986	-0	/O-31	-0.7

■ JOHN KELLEHER   Kelleher, John Patrick   b: 9/13/1893, Brookline, Mass.   d: 8/21/60, Brighton, Mass.   BR/TR, 5'11", 150 lbs.   Deb: 7/31/12

YEAR	TM/L	G	AB	R	H	2B	3B	HR	RBI	BB	SO	AVG	OBP	SLG	PRO+	BR/A	SB	CS	SBR	FA	FR	G/POS	TPR
1912	StL-N	8	12	0	4	1	0	0	1	0	2	.333	.333	.417	107	0				1.000	1	/3-3	0.1
1916	Bro-N	2	3	0	0	0	0	0	0	1	0	.000	.000	.000	-97	-1	0			1.000	-1	/S-1,3-1	-0.2
1921	Chi-N	95	301	31	93	11	7	4	47	16	16	.309	.346	.432	104	2	2	5	-2	.947	3	3-37,2-27,1-11,S/O	0.6
1922	Chi-N	63	193	23	50	7	1	0	20	15	14	.259	.316	.306	60	-11	5	7	-3	.932	4	3-46/S-7,1-4	-0.5
1923	Chi-N	66	193	27	59	10	0	6	21	14	9	.306	.353	.451	110	2	2	4	-2	.975	-7	1-22,S-14,3-11,/2-6	-0.5
1924	Bos-N	1	1	0	0	0	0	0	0	0	1	.000	.000	.000	-99	-0	0			.000	0	H	0.0
Total	6	235	703	81	206	29	8	10	89	45	42	.293	.337	.400	92	-8	9	16		.924	-0	/3-98,1-37,2-33,SO	-0.6

■ MICK KELLEHER   Kelleher, Michael Dennis   b: 7/25/47, Seattle, Wash.   BR/TR, 5'9", 176 lbs.   Deb: 9/1/72   C

YEAR	TM/L	G	AB	R	H	2B	3B	HR	RBI	BB	SO	AVG	OBP	SLG	PRO+	BR/A	SB	CS	SBR	FA	FR	G/POS	TPR
1972	StL-N	23	63	5	10	2	1	0	1	6	15	.159	.232	.222	30	-6	0	0	0	.984	5	S-23	0.2
1973	StL-N	43	38	4	7	2	0	0	2	4	11	.184	.279	.237	44	-3	0	0	0	.955	9	S-42	0.8
1974	Hou-N	19	57	4	9	0	0	0	2	5	10	.158	.226	.158	9	-7	1	1	-0	.944	4	S-18	-0.1
1975	StL-N	7	4	0	0	0	0	0	0	0	1	.000	.000	.000	-97	-2	0			.909	4	/S-7	0.1
1976	Chi-N	124	337	28	77	12	1	0	22	15	32	.228	.266	.270	48	-23	0	4	-2	.980	12	*S-101,3-22/2-5	-0.3
1977	Chi-N	63	122	14	28	5	2	0	11	9	12	.230	.288	.303	53	-8	0	0	0	.976	18	2-40,S-14/3-1	1.3
1978	Chi-N	68	95	8	24	0	0	0	6	7	11	.253	.304	.263	53	-6	4	1	-0	1.000	6	3-37,2-17,S-10	1.4
1979	Chi-N	73	142	14	36	4	1	0	7	9	7	.254	.298	.296	57	-8	2	0	1	.966	2	3-32,2-29,S-14	1.6
1980	Chi-N	105	96	12	14	1	1	0	4	7	10	.146	.219	.177	11	-11	1	3	-2	.974	25	2-57,3-31,S-17	1.5
1981	Det-A	61	77	10	17	0	0	0	7	10	7	.221	.286	.273	59	-4	0	0	0	.930	3	3-39,2-11/S-9	0.3
1982	Det-A	2	1	0	0	0	0	0	0	0	0	.000	.000	.000	-99	-0	0			1.000	-0	/2-1,3-1	-0.1
	Cal-A	34	49	9	8	1	0	0	5	5	5	.163	.259	.184	23	-5	1	0		.965	7	S-28/3-6	0.3
	Yr	36	50	9	8	1	0	0	5	5	5	.160	.250	.180	20	-5	1	0		.965	7	S-28/3-7,2-1	0.2
Total	11	622	1081	108	230	32	6	0	65	74	133	.213	.268	.253	43	-82	9	10	-3	.976	128	S-283,3-169,2-160	7.0

■ CHARLIE KELLER   Keller, Charles Ernest "King Kong"   b: 9/12/16, Middletown, Md.   d: 5/23/90, Frederick, Md.   BL/TR, 5'10", 190 lbs.   Deb: 4/22/39   F

YEAR	TM/L	G	AB	R	H	2B	3B	HR	RBI	BB	SO	AVG	OBP	SLG	PRO+	BR/A	SB	CS	SBR	FA	FR	G/POS	TPR
1939	*NY-A	111	398	87	133	21	6	11	83	81	49	.334	.447	.500	144	30	6	3	0	.969	-3	*O-105	2.2

YEAR	TM/L	G	AB	R	H	2B	3B	HR	RBI	BB	SO	AVG	OBP	SLG	PRO+	BR/A	SB	CS	SBR	FA	FR	G/POS	TPR
1940	NY-A★	138	500	102	143	18	15	21	93	**106**	65	.286	.411	.508	142	34	8	2	1	.967	2	*O-136	2.8
1941	*NY-A★	140	507	102	151	24	10	33	122	102	65	.298	.416	.580	163	47	6	4	-1	.980	4	*O-137	4.1
1942	*NY-A	152	544	106	159	24	9	26	108	114	61	.292	.417	.513	164	49	14	2	3	.985	-0	*O-152	4.4
1943	*NY-A†	141	512	97	139	15	11	31	86	**106**	60	.271	.396	.525	**167**	**45**	7	5	-1	.994	4	*O-141	4.3
1945	NY-A	44	163	26	49	7	4	10	34	31	21	.301	.412	.577	178	16	0	2	-1	1.000	4	O-44	1.7
1946	NY-A★	150	538	98	148	29	10	30	101	113	101	.275	.405	.533	158	44	1	4	-2	.979	-1	*O-149	3.5
1947	NY-A†	45	151	36	36	6	1	13	36	41	36	.238	.404	.550	165	14	0	0	0	.967	-2	O-43	1.0
1948	NY-A	83	247	41	66	15	2	6	44	41	25	.267	.372	.417	111	4	1	1	-0	.977	-5	O-66	-0.4
1949	NY-A	60	116	17	29	4	1	3	16	25	15	.250	.392	.379	104	2	2	0	1	.976	-6	O-31	-0.5
1950	Det-A	50	51	7	16	1	3	2	16	13	6	.314	.453	.569	155	5	0	0	0	1.000	-1	/O-6	0.3
1951	Det-A	54	62	6	16	2	0	3	21	11	12	.258	.370	.435	117	2	0	0	0	1.000	-1	/O-8	0.2
1952	NY-A	2	1	0	0	0	0	0	0	0	1	.000	.000	.000	-99	-0	0	0	0	.000	-0	/O-1	-0.1
Total	13	1170	3790	725	1085	166	72	189	760	784	499	.286	.410	.518	152	293	45	23	-0	.980	-4	*O-1019	23.5

■ HAL KELLER
Keller, Harold Kefauver b: 7/7/27, Middletown, Md. BL/TR, 6'1", 200 lbs. Deb: 9/13/49 F

YEAR	TM/L	G	AB	R	H	2B	3B	HR	RBI	BB	SO	AVG	OBP	SLG	PRO+	BR/A	SB	CS	SBR	FA	FR	G/POS	TPR
1949	Was-A	3	3	1	1	0	0	0	0	0	0	.333	.333	.333	78	-0	0	0	0	.000	0	H	0.0
1950	Was-A	11	28	1	6	3	0	1	5	2	2	.214	.267	.429	79	-1	0	0	0	1.000	-2	/C-8	-0.2
1952	Was-A	11	23	2	4	2	0	0	0	1	1	.174	.208	.261	31	-2	0	0	0	.967	-0	C-11	-0.2
Total	3	25	54	4	11	5	0	1	5	3	3	.204	.246	.352	60	-4	0	0	0	.982	-2	/C-19	-0.4

■ FRANK KELLERT
Kellert, Frank William b: 7/6/24, Oklahoma City, Okla. d: 11/19/76, Oklahoma City, Okla. BR/TR, 6'2.5", 185 lbs. Deb: 4/18/53

YEAR	TM/L	G	AB	R	H	2B	3B	HR	RBI	BB	SO	AVG	OBP	SLG	PRO+	BR/A	SB	CS	SBR	FA	FR	G/POS	TPR
1953	StL-A	2	4	0	0	0	0	0	0	0	0	.000	.000	.000	-98	-1	0	0	0	1.000	-1	/1-1	-0.1
1954	Bal-A	10	34	3	7	2	0	0	1	5	4	.206	.308	.265	62	-2	0	0	0	1.000	-1	/1-9	-0.4
1955	*Bro-N	39	80	12	26	4	2	4	19	9	10	.325	.393	.575	149	6	0	1	-1	.983	-0	1-22	0.4
1956	Chi-N	71	129	10	24	3	1	4	17	12	22	.186	.255	.318	54	-9	0	0	0	.991	3	1-27	-0.8
Total	4	122	247	25	57	9	3	8	37	26	36	.231	.304	.389	85	-6	0	1	-1	.990	1	/1-59	-0.9

■ RED KELLETT
Kellett, Donald Stafford b: 7/15/09, Brooklyn, N.Y. d: 11/3/70, Ft.Lauderdale, Fla. BR/TR, 6', 185 lbs. Deb: 7/2/34

YEAR	TM/L	G	AB	R	H	2B	3B	HR	RBI	BB	SO	AVG	OBP	SLG	PRO+	BR/A	SB	CS	SBR	FA	FR	G/POS	TPR
1934	Bos-A	9	9	0	0	0	0	0	0	1	5	.000	.100	.000	-68	-1	0	0	0	.778	1	/S-4,2-2,3-1	-0.1

■ JOE KELLEY
Kelley, Joseph James b: 12/9/1871, Cambridge, Mass. d: 8/14/43, Baltimore, Md. BR/TR, 5'11", 190 lbs. Deb: 7/27/1891 MCH

YEAR	TM/L	G	AB	R	H	2B	3B	HR	RBI	BB	SO	AVG	OBP	SLG	PRO+	BR/A	SB	CS	SBR	FA	FR	G/POS	TPR
1891	Bos-N	12	45	7	11	1	1	0	3	2	7	.244	.277	.311	63	-2	0			.852	-1	O-12	-0.3
1892	Pit-N	56	205	26	49	7	7	0	28	17	21	.239	.297	.341	93	-2	8			.919	2	O-56	-0.3
	Bal-N	10	33	3	7	0	0	0	4	4	7	.212	.316	.212	59	-1	2			.824	-3	O-10	-0.4
	Yr	66	238	29	56	7	7	0	32	21	28	.235	.300	.324	88	-4	10			.908	-1	O-66	-0.7
1893	Bal-N	125	502	120	153	27	16	9	76	77	44	.305	.401	.476	131	22	33			.940	7	*O-125	1.9
1894	*Bal-N	129	507	165	199	48	20	6	111	107	36	.393	.502	.602	158	53	46			.951	7	*O-129	3.5
1895	*Bal-N	131	518	148	189	26	19	10	134	77	29	.365	.456	.546	154	43	54			.964	11	*O-131	3.5
1896	*Bal-N	131	519	148	189	31	19	8	100	91	19	.364	.469	.543	164	53	**87**			.958	4	*O-131	3.8
1897	*Bal-N	131	505	113	183	31	5	5	118	70		.362	.447	.489	147	37	44			.959	-2	*O-130/S-3,3-2	2.2
1898	Bal-N	124	464	71	149	18	15	2	110	56		.321	.398	.438	137	23	24			.969	1	*O-122/3-2	1.4
1899	Bro-N	143	538	108	175	21	14	6	93	70		.325	.410	.450	133	26	31			.977	8	*O-143	2.0
1900	*Bro-N	121	454	90	145	23	17	6	91	53		.319	.398	.485	135	21	26			.959	1	O-77,1-32,3-13	1.4
1901	Bro-N	120	492	77	151	22	12	4	65	40		.307	.363	.425	124	15	18			.975	7	*1-115/3-5	1.9
1902	Bal-N	60	222	50	69	17	7	1	34	34		.311	.405	.464	134	11	12			.973	-0	O-48/3-8,1-5	0.7
	Cin-N	40	156	24	50	9	2	1	12	15		.321	.380	.423	135	6	3			.971	3	O-20,2-10/3-9,SM	0.9
1903	Cin-N	105	383	85	121	22	4	3	45	51		.316	.402	.418	120	10	18			.947	-7	O-67,S-12,2/31M	0.1
1904	Cin-N	123	449	75	126	21	13	0	63	49		.281	.359	.389	119	10	15			.988	0	*1-117/O-6,2-1,M	0.8
1905	Cin-N	90	321	43	89	7	6	1	37	27		.277	.346	.346	96	-2	8			.974	-3	O-85/1-2,M	-0.9
1906	Cin-N	129	465	43	106	19	11	1	53	44		.228	.300	.323	90	-6	9			.966	-5	*O-122/1-3,S-1,3-1	-1.9
1908	Bos-N	73	228	25	59	8	2	2	17	27		.259	.342	.338	119	6	5			.938	-4	O-51,1-11,M	0.1
Total	17	1853	7006	1421	2220	358	194	65	1194	911	<u>163</u>	.317	.402	.451	132	321	443			.955	20	*O-1465,1-291/32S	20.2

■ MIKE KELLEY
Kelley, Michael Joseph b: 12/2/1875, Templeton, Mass. d: 6/6/55, Minneapolis, Minn. BR/TR, 6', 210 lbs. Deb: 7/15/1899

YEAR	TM/L	G	AB	R	H	2B	3B	HR	RBI	BB	SO	AVG	OBP	SLG	PRO+	BR/A	SB	CS	SBR	FA	FR	G/POS	TPR
1899	Lou-N	76	282	48	68	11	2	3	33	21		.241	.307	.326	74	-10	10			.974	-0	1-76	-0.9

■ FRANK KELLIHER
Kelliher, Francis Mortimer "Yucka" b: 5/23/1899, Somerville, Mass. d: 3/4/56, Somerville, Mass. BL/TL, 5'9.5", 175 lbs. Deb: 9/19/19

YEAR	TM/L	G	AB	R	H	2B	3B	HR	RBI	BB	SO	AVG	OBP	SLG	PRO+	BR/A	SB	CS	SBR	FA	FR	G/POS	TPR
1919	Was-A	1	1	0	0	0	0	0	0	0	0	.000	.000	.000	-99	-0	0			.000	0	H	0.0

■ NATE KELLOGG
Kellogg, Nathaniel Monroe b: 9/28/1858, Rochester, Iowa d: 15, 5'9", 175 lbs. Deb: 8/27/1885

YEAR	TM/L	G	AB	R	H	2B	3B	HR	RBI	BB	SO	AVG	OBP	SLG	PRO+	BR/A	SB	CS	SBR	FA	FR	G/POS	TPR
1885	Det-N	5	17	4	2	1	0	0	1	5		.118	.167	.176	11	-2				.783	-2	/S-5	-0.3

■ BILL KELLOGG
Kellogg, William Dearstyne b: 5/25/1884, Albany, N.Y. d: 12/12/71, Baltimore, Md. BR/TR, 5'10", 153 lbs. Deb: 4/14/14

YEAR	TM/L	G	AB	R	H	2B	3B	HR	RBI	BB	SO	AVG	OBP	SLG	PRO+	BR/A	SB	CS	SBR	FA	FR	G/POS	TPR
1914	Cin-N	71	126	14	22	0	1	0	14	28		.175	.262	.190	34	-10	7			.988	-1	1-38,2-11/O-2,3-1	-1.2

■ RED KELLY
Kelly, Albert Michael b: 11/15/1884, Union, Ill. d: 2/4/61, Zephyrhills, Fla. BR/TR, 5'11.5", 165 lbs. Deb: 6/18/10

YEAR	TM/L	G	AB	R	H	2B	3B	HR	RBI	BB	SO	AVG	OBP	SLG	PRO+	BR/A	SB	CS	SBR	FA	FR	G/POS	TPR
1910	Chi-A	14	45	6	7	0	1	0	1	7		.156	.296	.200	58	-2				1.000	-1	O-14	-0.4

■ CHARLIE KELLY
Kelly, Charles H. Deb: 6/14/1883

YEAR	TM/L	G	AB	R	H	2B	3B	HR	RBI	BB	SO	AVG	OBP	SLG	PRO+	BR/A	SB	CS	SBR	FA	FR	G/POS	TPR
1883	Phi-N	2	7	1	1	0	1	0		0	3	.143	.143	.429	71	-0				.700	0	/3-2	0.0
1886	Phi-a	1	3	0	0	0	0	0		0	0	.000	.000	.000	-99	-1	0			.333	-1	/S-1	-0.2
Total	2	3	10	1	1	0	1	0		0	3	.100	.100	.300	19	-1	0			.700	-1	/3-2,S-1	-0.2

■ PAT KELLY
Kelly, Dale Patrick b: 8/27/55, Santa Maria, Cal. BR/TR, 6'3", 210 lbs. Deb: 5/28/80

YEAR	TM/L	G	AB	R	H	2B	3B	HR	RBI	BB	SO	AVG	OBP	SLG	PRO+	BR/A	SB	CS	SBR	FA	FR	G/POS	TPR
1980	Tor-A	3	7	0	2	0	0	0	0	0	0	.286	.286	.286	55	-0	0	0	0	1.000	1	/C-3	0.1

■ GEORGE KELLY
Kelly, George Lange "Highpockets" b: 9/10/1895, San Francisco, Cal. d: 10/13/84, Burlingame, Cal. BR/TR, 6'4", 190 lbs. Deb: 8/18/15 FCH

YEAR	TM/L	G	AB	R	H	2B	3B	HR	RBI	BB	SO	AVG	OBP	SLG	PRO+	BR/A	SB	CS	SBR	FA	FR	G/POS	TPR
1915	NY-N	17	38	2	6	1	0	0	4	1	9	.158	.179	.237	27	-3	0	1	-1	.983	-0	/1-9,O-4	-0.5
1916	NY-N	49	76	4	12	2	1	0	3	6	24	.158	.220	.211	34	-6	1			.981	-3	1-13,O-12/3-1	-1.1
1917	NY-N	11	7	0	0	0	0	0	0	0	3	.000	.000	.000	-99	-2	0			1.000	-1	/O-4,P-1,1-2,1	-0.2
	Pit-N	8	23	2	2	0	0	0	0	1	9	.087	.125	.174	-9	-3	0			.971	-1	/1-8	-0.5
	Yr	19	30	2	2	0	0	0	0	1	12	.067	.097	.133	-30	-5	0			.972	-1	/1-9,O-4,P-1,2-1	-0.7
1919	NY-N	32	107	12	31	6	2	1	14	3	15	.290	.315	.411	119	2	1			.994	-3	1-32	-0.2
1920	NY-N	155	590	69	157	22	11	11	**94**	41	92	.266	.320	.397	106	4	6	16	-8	.994	4	*1-155	-0.4
1921	*NY-N	149	587	95	181	42	9	**23**	122	40	73	.308	.356	.528	131	23	4	12	-6	.990	12	*1-149	2.5
1922	*NY-N	151	592	96	194	33	8	17	107	30	65	.328	.363	.497	119	14	12	3	2	.993	10	*1-151	1.8
1923	*NY-N	145	560	82	172	23	5	16	103	47	64	.307	.362	.452	115	11	14	7	0	.993	-6	*1-145	-0.2
1924	*NY-N	144	571	91	185	37	9	21	**136**	38	52	.324	.371	.531	143	32	7	2	1	.993	-1	1-125,O-14/2-5,3-1	2.3
1925	NY-N	147	586	87	181	29	3	20	99	35	54	.309	.351	.471	112	9	5	2	2	.981	16	*2-108,1-25,O-17	0.7
1926	NY-N	136	499	70	151	24	4	13	80	36	52	.303	.352	.445	115	9	4			**.993**	8	*1-114,2-18	1.1
1927	Cin-N	61	222	27	60	16	5	2	21	11	23	.270	.308	.446	103	-0	1			.992	-3	1-49,2-13/O-2	-0.6
1928	Cin-N	116	402	46	119	33	7	3	58	28	35	.296	.345	.435	104	2	1			.991	9	1-99,O-13	0.2
1929	Cin-N	147	577	73	169	45	9	5	103	33	61	.293	.332	.428	91	-10	7			.993	4	*1-147	-1.9
1930	Cin-N	51	188	18	54	10	1	5	35	7	20	.287	.313	.431	81	-6	1			.993	4	1-50	-0.9
	Chi-N	39	166	22	55	6	1	3	19	7	16	.331	.362	.434	91	-2	0			.998	4	1-39	-0.2
	Yr	90	354	40	109	16	2	8	54	14	36	.308	.336	.432	86	-9	1			.995	5	1-89	-1.1
1932	Bro-N	64	202	23	49	19	1	4	22	22	27	.243	.317	.356	82	-5	0			.984	-2	1-62/O-1	-1.1
Total	16	1622	5993	804	1778	337	76	148	1020	386	694	.297	.342	.452	110	68	65	<u>43</u>		.992	49	*1-1373,2-145/O3P	2.4

■ PAT KELLY
Kelly, Harold Patrick b: 7/30/44, Philadelphia, Pa. BL/TL, 6'1", 185 lbs. Deb: 9/6/67

YEAR	TM/L	G	AB	R	H	2B	3B	HR	RBI	BB	SO	AVG	OBP	SLG	PRO+	BR/A	SB	CS	SBR	FA	FR	G/POS	TPR
1967	Min-A	8	1	1	0	0	0	0	0	0	0	.000	.000	.000	-93	-0	0	0	0	.000	0	H	0.0
1968	Min-A	12	35	2	4	2	0	1	2	3	10	.114	.205	.257	37	-3	0	2	-1	.955	0	O-10	-0.5

YEAR	TM/L	G	AB	R	H	2B	3B	HR	RBI	BB	SO	AVG	OBP	SLG	PRO+	BR/A	SB	CS	SBR	FA	FR	G/POS	TPR
1969	KC-A	112	417	61	110	20	4	8	32	49	70	.264	.348	.388	105	3	40	13	4	.980	12	*O-107	1.4
1970	KC-A	136	452	56	106	16	1	6	38	76	105	.235	.347	.314	84	-8	34	16	1	.963	11	*O-118	-0.2
1971	Chi-A	67	213	32	62	6	3	3	22	36	29	.291	.396	.390	119	7	14	9	-1	.991	1	O-61	0.4
1972	Chi-A★	119	402	57	105	14	7	5	24	55	69	.261	.356	.390	113	8	32	9	4	.968	-2	*O-109	0.6
1973	Chi-A★	144	550	77	154	24	5	1	44	65	91	.280	.358	.347	96	-1	22	15	-2	.978	2	*O-141/D-1	-0.8
1974	Chi-A	122	424	60	119	16	3	4	21	46	58	.281	.354	.361	103	3	18	11	-1	.976	-5	D-67,O-53	-0.7
1975	Chi-A	133	471	73	129	21	7	9	45	58	69	.274	.356	.406	113	9	18	10	-1	**.991**	-3	*O-115,D-14	0.1
1976	Chi-A	107	311	42	79	20	3	5	34	45	45	.254	.354	.386	116	7	15	7	0	.950	-4	D-63,O-26	0.2
1977	Bal-A	120	360	50	92	13	0	10	49	53	75	.256	.357	.375	106	5	25	7	3	.984	-14	*O-109/D-1	-1.0
1978	Bal-A	100	274	38	75	12	1	11	40	34	58	.274	.358	.445	133	12	10	8	-2	.969	-6	O-80/D-2	0.1
1979	*Bal-A	68	153	25	44	11	0	9	25	20	25	.288	.374	.536	147	10	4	5	-2	1.000	-3	O-24,D-18	0.4
1980	Bal-A	89	200	38	52	10	1	3	26	34	54	.260	.368	.365	102	2	16	2	4	1.000	-3	O-36,D-30	0.1
1981	Cle-A	48	75	8	16	4	0	1	16	14	9	.213	.337	.307	88	-1	2	4	-2	1.000	-2	D-18/O-8	-0.6
Total	15	1385	4338	620	1147	189	35	76	418	588	768	.264	.356	.377	107	54	250	118	4	.978	-15	O-997,D-214	-0.5

■ **JIM KELLY**   Kelly, James Robert (Also Played Under Real Name Of Robert John Taggert In 1918)
b: 2/1/1884, Bloomfield, N.J.   d: 4/10/61, Kingsport, Tenn.   BL/TR, 5'10.5", 180 lbs.   Deb: 4/26/14

YEAR	TM/L	G	AB	R	H	2B	3B	HR	RBI	BB	SO	AVG	OBP	SLG	PRO+	BR/A	SB	CS	SBR	FA	FR	G/POS	TPR
1914	Pit-N	32	44	4	10	2	1	0	3	2	3	.227	.261	.318	75	-2	0			1.000	0	/O-7	-0.2
1915	Pit-F	148	524	68	154	12	17	4	50	35	46	.294	.340	.405	110	-2	38			.952	14	*O-148	0.5
1918	Bos-N	35	146	19	48	1	4	0	4	9	9	.329	.376	.390	140	7	4			.955	1	O-35	0.6
Total	3	215	714	91	212	15	22	4	57	46	58	.297	.343	.396	114	3	42			.954	15	O-190	0.9

■ **TOM KELLY**   Kelly, Jay Thomas   b: 8/15/50, Graceville, Minn.   BL/TL, 5'11", 188 lbs.   Deb: 5/11/75   M

YEAR	TM/L	G	AB	R	H	2B	3B	HR	RBI	BB	SO	AVG	OBP	SLG	PRO+	BR/A	SB	CS	SBR	FA	FR	G/POS	TPR
1975	Min-A	49	127	11	23	5	0	1	11	15	22	.181	.268	.244	45	-9	0	0	0	.985	1	1-43/O-2	-1.0

■ **JOHN KELLY**   Kelly, John B.   b: 3/13/1879, Clifton Heights, Pa.   d: 3/19/44, Baltimore, Md.   5'9", 165 lbs.   Deb: 4/11/07

YEAR	TM/L	G	AB	R	H	2B	3B	HR	RBI	BB	SO	AVG	OBP	SLG	PRO+	BR/A	SB	CS	SBR	FA	FR	G/POS	TPR
1907	StL-N	53	197	12	37	5	0	0	6	13		.188	.245	.213	45	-12	7			.968	-1	O-52	-1.7

■ **JOHN KELLY**   Kelly, John Francis "Honest John" or "Father"   b: 3/3/1859, Paterson, N.J.   d: 4/13/08, Paterson, N.J.   BR/TR, 6', 185 lbs.   Deb: 5/1/1882

YEAR	TM/L	G	AB	R	H	2B	3B	HR	RBI	BB	SO	AVG	OBP	SLG	PRO+	BR/A	SB	CS	SBR	FA	FR	G/POS	TPR
1882	Cle-N	30	104	6	14	2	0	0	5	1	24	.135	.143	.154	-5	-12				.800	-14	C-30	-2.3
1883	Bal-a	48	202	18	46	9	2	0		0	3	.228	.239	.292	68	-7				.803	-16	C-38,O-13	-2.0
	Phi-N	1	3	0	0	0	0	0	0	0	2	.000	.000	.000	-99	-1				1.000	1	/O-1	0.0
1884	Cin-U	38	142	23	40	5	1	1		6		.282	.311	.352	93	-5				.865	1	C-37/O-2	-0.3
	Was-U	4	14	1	5	1	0	0		0		.357	.357	.429	142	0				.967	1	/C-3,O-1	0.1
	Yr	42	156	24	45	6	1	1		6		.288	.315	.359	95	-5				.874	1	C-40/O-3	-0.2
Total	3	121	465	48	105	17	3	1	5	10	26	.226	.242	.282	63	-25				.834	-31	C-108/O-17	-4.5

■ **KICK KELLY**   Kelly, John O. "Diamond John"   b: 10/31/1856, New York, N.Y.   d: 3/27/26, Malba, N.Y.   6'0.5", 185 lbs.   Deb: 5/1/1879   MU

YEAR	TM/L	G	AB	R	H	2B	3B	HR	RBI	BB	SO	AVG	OBP	SLG	PRO+	BR/A	SB	CS	SBR	FA	FR	G/POS	TPR
1879	Syr-N	10	36	4	4	1	0	0	2	0	6	.111	.111	.139	-20	-4				.827	-1	/C-8,1-2	-0.5
	Tro-N	6	22	1	5	0	0	0	0	0	1	.227	.227	.227	54	-1				.789	-3	/C-3,O-2,3-1	-0.3
	Yr	16	58	5	9	1	0	0	2	0	5	.155	.155	.172	9	-5				.817	-4	C-11/1-2,O-2,3-1	-0.8

■ **JOE KELLY**   Kelly, Joseph Henry   b: 9/23/1886, Weir City, Kan.   d: 8/16/77, St.Joseph, Mo.   BR/TR, 5'10", 175 lbs.   Deb: 4/14/14

YEAR	TM/L	G	AB	R	H	2B	3B	HR	RBI	BB	SO	AVG	OBP	SLG	PRO+	BR/A	SB	CS	SBR	FA	FR	G/POS	TPR
1914	Pit-N	141	508	47	113	19	9	1	48	39	59	.222	.283	.301	77	-15	21			.946	4	*O-139	-2.0
1916	Chi-N	54	169	18	43	7	1	2	15	9	16	.254	.296	.343	87	-3	10			.953	-1	O-46	-0.7
1917	Bos-N	116	445	41	99	9	8	3	36	26	45	.222	.268	.299	78	-12	21			.946	14	*O-116	-0.6
1918	Bos-N	47	155	20	36	2	4	0	15	6	12	.232	.265	.297	74	-5	12			.933	0	O-45	-0.8
1919	Bos-N	18	64	3	9	1	0	0	3	0	11	.141	.154	.156	-7	-8	2			.943	0	O-16	-1.1
Total	5	376	1341	129	300	38	22	6	117	80	143	.224	.272	.298	75	-44	66			.945	16	O-362	-5.2

■ **JOE KELLY**   Kelly, Joseph James   b: 4/23/1900, New York, N.Y.   d: 11/24/67, Lynbrook, N.Y.   BL/TL, 6', 180 lbs.   Deb: 4/13/26

YEAR	TM/L	G	AB	R	H	2B	3B	HR	RBI	BB	SO	AVG	OBP	SLG	PRO+	BR/A	SB	CS	SBR	FA	FR	G/POS	TPR
1926	Chi-N	65	176	16	59	15	3	0	32	7	11	.335	.361	.455	117	4	0			.953	-5	O-39	-0.3
1928	Chi-N	32	52	3	11	1	0	1	7	1	3	.212	.255	.288	42	-4	0			.974	0	1-10	-0.5
Total	2	97	228	19	70	16	3	1	39	8	14	.307	.336	.417	100	-1	0			.953	-4	/O-39,1-10	-0.8

■ **KING KELLY**   Kelly, Michael Joseph   b: 12/31/1857, Troy, N.Y.   d: 11/8/1894, Boston, Mass.   BR/TR, 5'10", 170 lbs.   Deb: 5/1/1878   MH

YEAR	TM/L	G	AB	R	H	2B	3B	HR	RBI	BB	SO	AVG	OBP	SLG	PRO+	BR/A	SB	CS	SBR	FA	FR	G/POS	TPR
1878	Cin-N	60	237	29	67	7	1	0	27	7	7	.283	.303	.321	116	5				.765	11	*O-47,C-17/3-2	1.3
1879	Cin-N	77	345	78	120	20	12	2	47	8	14	.348	.363	.493	**188**	32				.832	12	3-33,O-29,C-21/2-1	**3.9**
1880	Chi-N	84	344	72	100	17	9	1	60	12	22	.291	.315	.401	133	11				.779	-3	*O-72,C-11/3-8	0.7
1881	Chi-N	82	353	84	114	**27**	3	2	55	16	14	.323	.352	.433	139	15				.841	-3	*O-72,C-11/3-8	1.3
1882	Chi-N	84	377	81	115	**37**	4	1	55	10	27	.305	.323	.432	134	13				.810	3	S-42,O-30,C-12,/31	1.3
1883	Chi-N	98	428	92	109	28	10	3	61	16	35	.255	.282	.388	95	-4				.813	3	*O-82,C-38/2-3,3P	0.0
1884	Chi-N	108	452	**120**	160	28	5	13	95	46	24	.354	**.414**	.524	148	**39**				.794	-6	O-63,C-28,S3/1P2	3.1
1885	*Chi-N	107	438	**124**	126	24	7	9	75	46	24	.288	.355	.436	135	14				.867	3	O-69,C-37/2-6,31	1.8
1886	*Chi-N	118	451	**155**	175	32	11	4	79	83	33	**.388**	**.483**	.534	182	44	53			.811	8	O-56,C-53/1-9,32S	4.5
1887	Bos-N	116	484	120	156	34	11	8	63	55	40	.322	.393	.488	143	29	84			.856	-11	O-61,2-30,C/PS3M	1.7
1888	Bos-N	107	440	85	140	22	11	9	71	31	39	.318	.368	.480	166	32	56			.905	-3	C-76,O-34	3.4
1889	Bos-N	125	507	120	149	**41**	5	9	78	65	40	.294	.376	.448	122	14	68			.848	-9	*O-113,C-23	0.3
1890	Bos-P	89	340	83	111	18	6	4	66	52	22	.326	.419	.450	141	14	51			.915	-3	C-56,S-27/O-6,13PM	1.1
1891	Cin-a	82	283	56	84	15	7	1	53	51	28	.297	.408	.410	123	9	22			.904	14	C-66/3-8,O-7,21PS	2.3
	Bos-a	4	15	2	4	0	0	1	4	0	2	.267	.267	.467	111	-0	1			.950	-1	/C-4	0.0
	Yr	86	298	58	88	15	7	2	57	51	30	.295	.402	.413	123	9	23			.906	13	C-70/3-8,O-7,21PS	2.3
	Bos-N	16	52	7	12	1	0	0	5	6	10	.231	.322	.250	60	-3	6			.844	-3	C-11/O-6	-0.6
1892	*Bos-N	78	281	40	53	7	0	2	41	39	32	.189	.287	.235	54	-16	24			.912	-9	C-72/O-2,3-2,1-2,P	-0.9
1893	NY-N	20	52	9	9	1	0	0	15	6	5	.269	.339	.288	83	-3	3			.895	-4	C-17/O-1	-0.5
Total	16	1455	5894	1357	1813	359	102	69	950	549	418	.308	.368	.438	136	241	368			.820	1	O-750,C-583/3S21P	24.7

■ **MIKE KELLY**   Kelly, Michael Raymond   b: 6/2/70, Los Angeles, Cal.   BR/TR, 6'4", 195 lbs.   Deb: 4/5/94

YEAR	TM/L	G	AB	R	H	2B	3B	HR	RBI	BB	SO	AVG	OBP	SLG	PRO+	BR/A	SB	CS	SBR	FA	FR	G/POS	TPR
1994	Atl-N	30	77	14	21	10	1	2	9	2	17	.273	.300	.506	103	-0	0	1	-1	.962	-5	O-25	-0.6
1995	Atl-N	97	137	26	26	6	1	3	17	11	49	.190	.260	.314	49	-10	7	3	0	.940	-16	O-83	-2.7
1996	Cin-N	19	49	5	9	4	0	1	7	9	11	.184	.333	.327	76	-2	4	0	1	.972	1	O-17	0.0
Total	3	146	263	45	56	20	2	6	33	22	77	.213	.286	.373	70	-12	11	4	1	.953	-20	O-125	-3.3

■ **PAT KELLY**   Kelly, Patrick Franklin   b: 10/14/67, Philadelphia, Pa.   BR/TR, 6', 180 lbs.   Deb: 5/20/91

YEAR	TM/L	G	AB	R	H	2B	3B	HR	RBI	BB	SO	AVG	OBP	SLG	PRO+	BR/A	SB	CS	SBR	FA	FR	G/POS	TPR
1991	NY-A	96	298	35	72	12	4	3	23	15	52	.242	.289	.339	73	-11	12	1	3	.926	7	3-80,2-19	-0.1
1992	NY-A	106	318	38	72	22	2	7	27	25	72	.226	.303	.374	89	-5	8	5	-1	.978	6	*2-101/D-1	0.3
1993	NY-A	127	406	49	111	24	1	7	51	24	68	.273	.322	.389	93	-5	14	11	-2	.978	6	*2-125	0.5
1994	NY-A	93	286	35	80	21	2	3	41	19	51	.280	.335	.399	92	-4	6	5	-1	.978	1	2-93	0.0
1995	*NY-A	89	270	32	64	12	1	4	29	23	65	.237	.309	.333	68	-13	8	1	1	.983	4	2-87/D-1	-0.1
1996	NY-A	13	21	4	3	0	0	0	2	2	9	.143	.217	.143	-6	-3	0	3	-1	.970	1	2-10/D-3	0.1
Total	6	524	1599	193	402	91	10	24	173	108	317	.251	.311	.366	82	-40	48	26	-1	.979	34	2-435/3-80,D-5	0.7

■ **SPEED KELLY**   Kelly, Robert Brown   b: 8/19/1884, Bryan, Ohio   d: 5/6/49, Goshen, Ind.   BR/TR, 6'2", 185 lbs.   Deb: 7/13/09

YEAR	TM/L	G	AB	R	H	2B	3B	HR	RBI	BB	SO	AVG	OBP	SLG	PRO+	BR/A	SB	CS	SBR	FA	FR	G/POS	TPR
1909	Was-A	17	42	3	6	2	1	0	3			.143	.200	.238	40	-3	1			.852	-1	3-10/2-3,O-1	-0.5

■ **ROBERTO KELLY**   Kelly, Roberto Conrado (Gray) "Bobby"   b: 10/1/64, Panama City, Pan.   BR/TR, 6'4", 185 lbs.   Deb: 7/29/87

YEAR	TM/L	G	AB	R	H	2B	3B	HR	RBI	BB	SO	AVG	OBP	SLG	PRO+	BR/A	SB	CS	SBR	FA	FR	G/POS	TPR
1987	NY-A	23	52	12	14	3	0	1	7	5	15	.269	.333	.385	91	-1	9	3	0	.955	-0	O-17/D-2	0.0
1988	NY-A	38	77	9	19	4	1	1	7	3	15	.247	.275	.364	78	-2	5	2	0	.986	-2	O-30/D-3	-0.4
1989	NY-A	137	441	65	133	18	3	9	48	41	89	.302	.369	.417	123	14	35	12	3	.984	1	*O-137	2.1
1990	NY-A	162	641	85	183	32	4	15	61	33	148	.285	.324	.418	106	3	42	17	2	.988	8	*O-160/D-1	1.0
1991	NY-A	126	486	68	130	22	2	20	69	45	77	.267	.336	.444	114	9	32	9	4	.986	-3	*O-125	1.3
1992	NY-A★	152	580	81	158	31	2	10	66	41	96	.272	.325	.384	99	-2	28	5	5	.983	10	*O-146	1.0

YEAR	TM/L	G	AB	R	H	2B	3B	HR	RBI	BB	SO	AVG	OBP	SLG	PRO+	BR/A	SB	CS	SBR	FA	FR	G/POS	TPR
1993	Cin-N★	78	320	44	102	17	3	9	35	17	43	.319	.357	.475	120	9	21	5	3	.995	5	O-77	1.5
1994	Cin-N	47	179	29	54	8	0	3	21	11	35	.302	.352	.397	96	-1	9	8	-2	.992	3	O-47	-0.1
	Atl-N	63	255	44	73	15	3	6	24	24	36	.286	.348	.439	101	0	10	3	1	.985	-2	O-63	-0.1
	Yr	110	434	73	127	23	3	9	45	35	71	.293	.350	.422	99	-0	19	11	-1	.988	1	*O-110	-0.2
1995	Mon-N	24	95	11	26	4	0	1	9	7	14	.274	.337	.347	78	-3	4	3	-1	1.000	-1	O-24	-0.5
	*LA-N	112	409	47	114	19	2	6	48	15	65	.279	.311	.379	89	-8	15	7	0	.969	-4	*O-110	-1.4
	Yr	136	504	58	140	23	2	7	57	22	79	.278	.316	.373	87	-11	19	10	-0	.974	-5	*O-134	-1.9
1996	Min-A	98	322	41	104	17	4	6	47	23	53	.323	.369	.457	108	5	10	2	2	.990	-1	O-93/D-2	0.3
Total	10	1060	3857	536	1110	190	24	87	442	265	686	.288	.340	.417	105	22	220	76	20	.985	27	*O-1029/D-8	4.7

■ VAN KELLY
Kelly, Van Howard b: 3/18/46, Charlotte, N.C. BL/TR, 5'11", 180 lbs. Deb: 6/13/69

YEAR	TM/L	G	AB	R	H	2B	3B	HR	RBI	BB	SO	AVG	OBP	SLG	PRO+	BR/A	SB	CS	SBR	FA	FR	G/POS	TPR
1969	SD-N	73	209	16	51	7	1	3	15	12	24	.244	.285	.330	75	-8	0	1	-1	.971	-3	3-49,2-10	-1.2
1970	SD-N	38	89	9	15	3	0	1	9	15	21	.169	.288	.236	44	-7	0	1	-1	.971	1	3-27/2-1	-0.7
Total	2	111	298	25	66	10	1	4	24	27	45	.221	.286	.302	65	-14	0	2	-1	.971	-3	/3-76,2-11	-1.9

■ BILL KELLY
Kelly, William Henry "Big Bill" b: 12/28/1898, Syracuse, N.Y. d: 4/8/90, Syracuse, N.Y. BR/TR, 6', 190 lbs. Deb: 9/6/20

YEAR	TM/L	G	AB	R	H	2B	3B	HR	RBI	BB	SO	AVG	OBP	SLG	PRO+	BR/A	SB	CS	SBR	FA	FR	G/POS	TPR
1920	Phi-A	9	13	0	3	1	0	0	0	0	2	.231	.231	.308	41	-1	0	0	0	1.000	0	/1-2	-0.1
1928	Phi-N	23	71	6	12	1	1	0	5	7	20	.169	.244	.211	19	-8	0			.991	1	1-23	-0.9
Total	2	32	84	6	15	2	1	0	5	7	22	.179	.242	.226	22	-10	0	0	<u> </u>	.992	2	/1-25	-1.0

■ BILL KELLY
Kelly, William J. b: New York, N.Y. Deb: 5/4/1871

YEAR	TM/L	G	AB	R	H	2B	3B	HR	RBI	BB	SO	AVG	OBP	SLG	PRO+	BR/A	SB	CS	SBR	FA	FR	G/POS	TPR
1871	Kek-n	18	67	16	15	1	1	0	0	0	2	.224	.288	.269	60	-3				.833	1	O-18	-0.1

■ BILLY KELLY
Kelly, William Joseph b: 5/1/1886, Baltimore, Md. d: 6/3/40, Detroit, Mich. BR/TR, 6'0.5", 183 lbs. Deb: 5/2/10

YEAR	TM/L	G	AB	R	H	2B	3B	HR	RBI	BB	SO	AVG	OBP	SLG	PRO+	BR/A	SB	CS	SBR	FA	FR	G/POS	TPR
1910	StL-N	2	2	1	0	0	0	0	1	0	1	.000	.333	.000	-1	-0	0			.000	0	/C-1	0.0
1911	Pit-N	6	8	0	1	0	0	0	0	0	2	.125	.125	.125	-29	-1	0			1.000	1	/C-1	0.0
1912	Pit-N	48	132	20	42	3	2	1	11	2	16	.318	.328	.394	99	-1	8			.990	-9	C-39	-0.6
1913	Pit-N	48	82	11	22	2	2	0	9	2	12	.268	.302	.341	87	-2	1			.960	4	C-40	0.4
Total	4	104	224	32	65	5	4	1	20	5	30	.290	.312	.362	89	-4	9			.977	-5	/C-81	-0.2

■ BILLY KELSEY
Kelsey, George William b: 8/24/1881, Covington, Ohio d: 4/25/68, Springfield, Ohio BR/TR, 5'10", 150 lbs. Deb: 10/4/07

YEAR	TM/L	G	AB	R	H	2B	3B	HR	RBI	BB	SO	AVG	OBP	SLG	PRO+	BR/A	SB	CS	SBR	FA	FR	G/POS	TPR
1907	Pit-N	2	5	1	2	0	0	0	0	0		.400	.400	.400	149	0	0			1.000	-1	/C-2	0.0

■ KEN KELTNER
Keltner, Kenneth Frederick "Butch" b: 10/31/16, Milwaukee, Wis. d: 12/12/91, New Berlin, Wis. BR/TR, 6', 190 lbs. Deb: 10/2/37

YEAR	TM/L	G	AB	R	H	2B	3B	HR	RBI	BB	SO	AVG	OBP	SLG	PRO+	BR/A	SB	CS	SBR	FA	FR	G/POS	TPR
1937	Cle-A	1	1	0	0	0	0	0	1	0	0	.000	.000	.000	-99	-0	0	0	0	1.000	0	/3-1	0.0
1938	Cle-A	149	576	86	159	31	9	26	113	33	75	.276	.319	.497	103	-2	4	3	-1	.956	-10	*3-149	-0.9
1939	Cle-A	154	587	84	191	35	11	13	97	51	41	.325	.379	.489	125	20	6	6	-2	**.974**	6	*3-154	2.4
1940	Cle-A★	149	543	67	138	24	10	15	77	51	56	.254	.322	.418	93	-7	10	5	0	.953	-6	*3-148	-0.9
1941	Cle-A★	149	581	83	156	31	13	23	84	51	56	.269	.330	.485	119	12	2	2	-1	**.971**	23	*3-149	3.5
1942	Cle-A★	152	624	72	179	34	4	6	78	20	36	.287	.312	.383	101	-3	4	3	-1	**.945**	16	*3-151	1.4
1943	Cle-A★	110	427	47	111	31	3	4	39	36	20	.260	.317	.375	109	3	2	2	-1	.969	6	*3-107	1.0
1944	Cle-A★	149	573	74	169	41	9	13	91	53	29	.295	.355	.466	139	26	4	3	-1	.968	15	*3-149	4.4
1946	Cle-A★	116	398	47	96	17	1	13	45	30	38	.241	.294	.387	95	-5	0	3	-2	.965	-2	*3-112	-0.7
1947	Cle-A	151	541	49	139	29	3	11	76	59	45	.257	.331	.383	101	-0	5	4	-1	.972	-9	*3-150	-1.0
1948	*Cle-A★	153	558	91	166	24	4	31	119	89	52	.297	.395	.522	146	36	2	1	0	.969	-1	*3-153	3.3
1949	Cle-A	80	246	35	57	9	2	8	30	38	26	.232	.335	.382	91	-4	0	1	-1	.980	-1	3-69	-0.7
1950	Bos-A	13	28	2	9	2	0	2	3	6		.321	.387	.393	91	-0	0	0	0	.947	-2	/3-8,1-1	-0.2
Total	13	1526	5683	737	1570	308	69	163	852	514	480	.276	.338	.441	113	75	39	33	-8	.965	36	*3-1500/1-1	11.6

■ JOHN KELTY
Kelty, John James "Chief" b: 6/1866, Jersey City, N.J. 5'10", 175 lbs. Deb: 4/19/1890

YEAR	TM/L	G	AB	R	H	2B	3B	HR	RBI	BB	SO	AVG	OBP	SLG	PRO+	BR/A	SB	CS	SBR	FA	FR	G/POS	TPR
1890	Pit-N	59	207	24	49	10	2	1	27	22	42	.237	.322	.319	98	0	10			.898	-3	O-59	-0.4

■ BILL KEMMER
Kemmer, William Edward (b: William Edward Kemmerer) b: 11/15/1873, Pennsylvania d: 6/8/45, Washington, D.C. BR/TR, 6'2", Deb: 6/3/1895

YEAR	TM/L	G	AB	R	H	2B	3B	HR	RBI	BB	SO	AVG	OBP	SLG	PRO+	BR/A	SB	CS	SBR	FA	FR	G/POS	TPR
1895	Lou-N	11	38	5	7	0	0	1	3	2	4	.184	.225	.263	27	-4	0			.809	2	/3-9,1-2	-0.1

■ RUDY KEMMLER
Kemmler, Rudolph (b: Rudolph Kemler) b: 1860, Chicago, Ill. d: 6/20/09, Chicago, Ill. BR/TR, Deb: 7/26/1879

YEAR	TM/L	G	AB	R	H	2B	3B	HR	RBI	BB	SO	AVG	OBP	SLG	PRO+	BR/A	SB	CS	SBR	FA	FR	G/POS	TPR
1879	Pro-N	2	7	0	1	0	0	0	0	0	1	.143	.143	.143	-6	-1				.833	2	/C-2	0.1
1881	Cle-N	1	3	0	0	0	0	0	0	0	1	.000	.000	.000	-99	-1				1.000	1	/C-1	0.0
1882	Cin-a	3	11	0	1	1	0	0	0	0		.091	.091	.182	-10	-1				.909	-1	/C-3,O-1	-0.2
	Pit-a	24	99	7	25	4	0	0		1		.253	.260	.293	90	-1				.920	3	C-23/O-1	0.2
	Yr	27	110	7	26	5	0	0		1		.236	.243	.282	79	-2				.919	1	C-26/O-2	0.0
1883	Col-a	84	318	27	66	6	2	0		13		.208	.239	.239	59	-13				.872	9	*C-82/O-2	-1.5
1884	Col-a	61	211	28	42	3	3	0		15		.199	.252	.242	67	-7				.906	-19	C-58/1-2,O-1	-2.0
1885	Pit-a	18	64	2	13	2	1	0	5	2		.203	.239	.266	60	-3				.870	-3	C-18	-0.3
1886	StL-a	35	123	13	17	2	0	0	6	8		.138	.197	.154	10	-13	0			.914	4	C-32/1-3	-0.5
1889	Col-a	8	26	2	3	0	0	0	3	3	3	.115	.207	.115	-8	-4	0			.930	1	/C-8	-0.2
Total	8	236	862	79	168	18	6	0	11	42	5	.195	.234	.230	52	-42				.894	-22	C-227/1-5,O-5	-4.4

■ STEVE KEMP
Kemp, Steven F b: 8/7/54, San Angelo, Tex. BL/TL, 6', 195 lbs. Deb: 4/7/77

YEAR	TM/L	G	AB	R	H	2B	3B	HR	RBI	BB	SO	AVG	OBP	SLG	PRO+	BR/A	SB	CS	SBR	FA	FR	G/POS	TPR
1977	Det-A	151	552	75	142	29	4	18	88	71	93	.257	.347	.422	103	3	3	3	-1	.981	-3	*O-148	-0.7
1978	Det-A	159	582	75	161	18	4	15	79	97	83	.277	.381	.399	116	16	2	3	-1	.977	8	*O-157	1.6
1979	Det-A★	134	490	88	156	26	3	26	105	68	70	.318	.404	.543	148	34	5	6	-2	.976	6	*O-120,D-11	3.1
1980	Det-A	135	508	88	149	23	4	21	101	69	60	.293	.382	.474	130	22	5	1	1	.995	-6	O-85,D-46	2.4
1981	Det-A	105	372	52	103	18	4	9	49	70	48	.277	.393	.419	129	17	9	3	1	.986	-3	O-92,D-12	1.7
1982	Chi-A	160	580	91	166	23	1	19	98	89	83	.286	.384	.428	121	21	7	7	-2	.976	-7	*O-154/D-2	0.8
1983	NY-A	109	373	53	90	17	3	12	49	41	37	.241	.320	.399	100	-0	1	1	0	.987	-1	*O-101/D-2	-0.2
1984	NY-A	94	313	37	91	12	1	7	41	40	54	.291	.373	.403	119	9	4	1	1	.972	-2	O-75,D-12	0.5
1985	Pit-N	92	236	19	59	13	2	2	21	25	54	.250	.322	.347	88	-4	1	0	0	1.000	-1	O-63	-0.6
1986	Pit-N	13	16	1	3	0	0	1	4	6	4	.188	.350	.375	98	0	1	0	0	1.000	0	/O-4	0.1
1988	Tex-A	16	36	2	8	0	0	2	2	9	2	.222	.263	.222	36	-3	1	0	0	1.000	-2	/O-5,1-1,D-7	-0.4
Total	11	1168	4058	581	1128	179	25	130	634	576	605	.278	.370	.431	119	115	39	24	-3	.982	10	*O-1004/D-92,1-1	8.3

■ FRED KENDALL
Kendall, Fred Lyn b: 1/31/49, Torrance, Cal. BR/TR, 6'1", 190 lbs. Deb: 9/8/69 FC

YEAR	TM/L	G	AB	R	H	2B	3B	HR	RBI	BB	SO	AVG	OBP	SLG	PRO+	BR/A	SB	CS	SBR	FA	FR	G/POS	TPR
1969	SD-N	10	26	2	4	0	0	0	2	1	5	.154	.214	.154	5	-3	0	0	0	1.000	-1	/C-9	-0.4
1970	SD-N	4	5	0	0	0	0	0	1	0	0	.000	.000	.000	-99	-3	0	0	0	1.000	-1	/C-2,1-1,O-1	-0.4
1971	SD-N	49	111	2	19	1	0	1	7	7	16	.171	.220	.207	23	-11	0	0	0	1.000	1	C-39/1-1,3-1	-1.0
1972	SD-N	91	273	18	59	3	4	6	18	11	42	.216	.249	.322	66	-14	0	0	0	.995	3	C-82/1-1	-0.9
1973	SD-N	145	507	39	143	22	3	10	59	30	35	.282	.323	.396	107	3	3	1	0	.984	-17	*C-138	-0.8
1974	SD-N	141	424	32	98	15	2	8	45	49	33	.231	.311	.333	84	-10	0	1	-1	.983	-23	*C-133	-3.0
1975	SD-N	103	286	16	57	9	1	0	24	26	28	.199	.266	.248	46	-21	0	1	0	.977	-8	C-85	-2.7
1976	SD-N	146	456	30	112	17	0	2	39	36	42	.246	.305	.296	77	-14	1	1	-0	.994	-19	*C-146	-3.1
1977	Cle-A	103	317	18	79	13	1	3	39	16	27	.249	.287	.325	69	-14	0	1	-1	.991	-13	*C-102/D-1	-2.5
1978	Bos-A	20	41	3	8	1	0	0	5	2	9	.195	.214	.220	20	-4	0	0	0	1.000	3	1-13/C-5,D-1	-0.2
1979	SD-N	46	102	8	17	2	0	1	6	11	7	.167	.248	.216	29	-10	0	0	0	.977	1	C-40/1-2	-0.5
1980	SD-N	19	24	2	7	0	0	0	2	0	2	.292	.292	.292	67	-1	0	0	0	.938	-2	C-14/1-1	-0.1
Total	12	877	2576	170	603	86	11	31	244	189	240	.234	.288	.312	72	-102	6	5	-2	.987	-71	C-795/1-19,D-2,3O	-15.6

■ JASON KENDALL
Kendall, Jason Daniel b: 6/26/74, San Diego, Cal. BR/TR, 6', 180 lbs. Deb: 4/1/96 F

YEAR	TM/L	G	AB	R	H	2B	3B	HR	RBI	BB	SO	AVG	OBP	SLG	PRO+	BR/A	SB	CS	SBR	FA	FR	G/POS	TPR
1996	Pit-N★	130	414	54	124	23	5	3	42	35	30	.300	.375	.401	102	2	5	2	0	.980	-0	*C-129	1.1

■ AL KENDERS
Kenders, Albert Daniel George b: 4/4/37, Barrington, N.J. BR/TR, 6', 185 lbs. Deb: 8/14/61

YEAR	TM/L	G	AB	R	H	2B	3B	HR	RBI	BB	SO	AVG	OBP	SLG	PRO+	BR/A	SB	CS	SBR	FA	FR	G/POS	TPR
1961	Phi-N	10	23	0	4	1	0	0	1	1	0	.174	.208	.217	13	-3	0	0	0	1.000	-2	C-10	-0.4

YEAR	TM/L	G	AB	R	H	2B	3B	HR	RBI	BB	SO	AVG	OBP	SLG	PRO+	BR/A	SB	CS	SBR	FA	FR	G/POS	TPR

■ EDDIE KENNA   Kenna, Edward Aloysius "Scrap Iron"   b: 9/30/1897, San Francisco, Cal.   d: 8/21/72, San Francisco, Cal   BR/TR, 5'7.5", 150 lbs.   Deb: 6/2/28

YEAR	TM/L	G	AB	R	H	2B	3B	HR	RBI	BB	SO	AVG	OBP	SLG	PRO+	BR/A	SB	CS	SBR	FA	FR	G/POS	TPR
1928	Was-A	41	118	14	35	4	2	1	20	14	8	.297	.376	.390	102	1	1	5	-3	.942	-3	C-33	-0.2

■ ED KENNEDY   Kennedy, Edward   b: 4/1/1856, Carbondale, Pa.   d: 5/20/05, New York, N.Y.   5'6", 150 lbs.   Deb: 5/1/1883

YEAR	TM/L	G	AB	R	H	2B	3B	HR	RBI	BB	SO	AVG	OBP	SLG	PRO+	BR/A	SB	CS	SBR	FA	FR	G/POS	TPR
1883	NY-a	94	356	57	78	6	7	2		17		.219	.255	.292	72	-11				.884	-7	*O-94	-1.7
1884	*NY-a	103	378	49	72	6	2	1		16		.190	.225	.225	49	-20				.915	6	*O-100/S-1,2-1,C-1	-1.5
1885	NY-a	96	349	35	71	8	4	2	21	12		.203	.238	.266	64	-13				.841	2	*O-96	-1.3
1886	Bro-a	6	22	1	4	0	0	0	2	2		.182	.250	.182	36	-2	1			.909	-1	/O-6	-0.2
Total	4	299	1105	142	225	20	13	5	23	47		.204	.239	.259	61	-47	1			.878	0	O-296/C-1,2-1,S-1	-4.7

■ JIM KENNEDY   Kennedy, James Earl   b: 11/1/46, Tulsa, Okla.   BL/TR, 5'9", 160 lbs.   Deb: 6/14/70   F

YEAR	TM/L	G	AB	R	H	2B	3B	HR	RBI	BB	SO	AVG	OBP	SLG	PRO+	BR/A	SB	CS	SBR	FA	FR	G/POS	TPR
1970	StL-N	12	24	1	3	0	0	0	0	0	0	.125	.125	.125	-32	-4	0	0	0	.909	1	/S-7,2-5	-0.3

■ JOHN KENNEDY   Kennedy, John Edward   b: 5/29/41, Chicago, Ill.   BR/TR, 6', 185 lbs.   Deb: 9/5/62

YEAR	TM/L	G	AB	R	H	2B	3B	HR	RBI	BB	SO	AVG	OBP	SLG	PRO+	BR/A	SB	CS	SBR	FA	FR	G/POS	TPR
1962	Was-A	14	42	6	11	0	1	1	3	2	7	.262	.295	.381	81	-1	0	1	-1	.974	0	/S-9,3-2	-0.1
1963	Was-A	36	62	3	11	1	1	0	4	6	22	.177	.261	.226	38	-5	2	0	1	.954	6	3-26/S-2	0.2
1964	Was-A	148	482	55	111	16	4	7	35	29	119	.230	.281	.324	68	-21	3	3	-1	.941	9	*3-106,S-49/2-2	-1.2
1965	*LA-N	104	105	12	18	3	0	1	5	8	33	.171	.243	.229	36	-9	1	0	0	.971	11	3-95/S-5	-0.3
1966	*LA-N	125	274	15	55	9	2	3	24	10	64	.201	.242	.281	49	-20	1	2	-1	.965	13	3-87,S-28,2-15	-0.6
1967	NY-A	78	179	22	35	4	0	1	17	17	35	.196	.269	.235	52	-10	2	1	0	.915	7	S-36,3-34/2-2	-0.1
1969	Sea-A	61	128	18	30	3	1	4	14	14	25	.234	.315	.367	92	-2	4	0	1	.916	-4	S-33,3-23	-0.2
1970	Mil-A	25	55	8	14	2	0	2	6	5	9	.255	.317	.400	96	-1	0	1	-1	.921	-1	2-16/3-5,S-4,1-1	-0.1
	Bos-A	43	129	15	33	7	1	4	17	6	14	.256	.294	.419	88	-2	0	0	0	.960	3	3-33/2-2	0.0
	Yr	68	184	23	47	9	1	6	23	11	23	.255	.301	.413	91	-3	0	1	-1	.962	1	3-38,2-18/S-4,1-1	-0.1
1971	Bos-A	74	272	41	75	12	5	5	22	14	42	.276	.321	.412	99	-1	1	1	-0	.974	-18	2-37,S-33/3-5	-1.3
1972	Bos-A	71	212	22	52	11	1	2	22	18	40	.245	.313	.335	88	-3	1	1	-1	.962	-6	2-32,S-27,3-11	-0.5
1973	Bos-A	67	155	17	28	9	1	1	16	12	45	.181	.249	.271	44	-12	0	0	0	.980	7	2-31,3-24/D-9	-0.3
1974	Bos-A	10	15	3	2	0	0	1	1	1	6	.133	.188	.333	44	-1	0	0	0	.778	-1	/2-6,3-4	-0.2
Total	12	856	2110	237	475	77	17	32	185	142	461	.225	.282	.323	70	-87	14	10	-2	.953	26	3-455,S-226,2/D1	-4.2

■ JOHN KENNEDY   Kennedy, John Irvin   b: 10/12/26, Jacksonville, Fla.   BR/TR, 5'10", 175 lbs.   Deb: 4/22/57

YEAR	TM/L	G	AB	R	H	2B	3B	HR	RBI	BB	SO	AVG	OBP	SLG	PRO+	BR/A	SB	CS	SBR	FA	FR	G/POS	TPR
1957	Phi-N	5	2	1	0	0	0	0	0	0	1	.000	.000	.000	-99	-1	0	0	0	.500	0	/3-2	0.0

■ JUNIOR KENNEDY   Kennedy, Junior Raymond   b: 8/9/50, Fort Gibson, Okla.   BR/TR, 6', 185 lbs.   Deb: 8/9/74   F

YEAR	TM/L	G	AB	R	H	2B	3B	HR	RBI	BB	SO	AVG	OBP	SLG	PRO+	BR/A	SB	CS	SBR	FA	FR	G/POS	TPR
1974	Cin-N	22	19	2	3	0	0	0	0	6	4	.158	.360	.158	49	-1	0	0	0	.909	-1	2-17/3-5	-0.2
1978	Cin-N	89	157	22	40	2	2	0	11	31	28	.255	.381	.293	91	-0	4	1	1	.979	13	2-71/3-4	1.7
1979	Cin-N	83	220	29	60	7	0	1	17	28	31	.273	.355	.318	85	-4	4	3	-1	.980	-1	2-59/S-5,3-4	-0.1
1980	Cin-N	104	337	31	88	16	3	1	34	36	34	.261	.332	.335	87	-5	3	1	0	.988	2	*2-103	0.3
1981	Cin-N	27	44	5	11	1	0	0	5	1	5	.250	.267	.273	52	-3	0	0	0	.980	2	2-16/3-5	0.0
1982	Chi-N	105	242	22	53	3	1	2	25	21	34	.219	.281	.264	52	-15	1	4	-2	.978	13	2-71,S-28/3-7	0.0
1983	Chi-N	17	22	3	3	0	0	0	3	1	6	.136	.174	.136	-12	-3	0	0	0	1.000	2	/2-7,3-4,S-1	-0.1
Total	7	447	1041	114	258	29	6	4	95	124	142	.248	.328	.299	75	-31	12	9	-2	.982	30	2-344/S-34,3-29	1.6

■ DOC KENNEDY   Kennedy, Michael Joseph   b: 8/11/1853, Brooklyn, N.Y.   d: 5/23/20, Grove, N.Y.   BR/TR, 5'9.5", 185 lbs.   Deb: 5/1/1879

YEAR	TM/L	G	AB	R	H	2B	3B	HR	RBI	BB	SO	AVG	OBP	SLG	PRO+	BR/A	SB	CS	SBR	FA	FR	G/POS	TPR
1879	Cle-N	49	193	19	56	8	2	1	18	2	10	.290	.297	.368	119	4				.891	3	C-46/1-4	0.8
1880	Cle-N	66	250	26	50	10	1	0	18	5	12	.200	.216	.248	58	-10				.899	-1	*C-65/O-2	-1.0
1881	Cle-N	39	150	19	47	7	1	0	15	5	13	.313	.335	.373	129	5				.920	5	C-35/O-3,3-1	1.0
1882	Cle-N	1	3	0	1	0	0	0	0	1	0	.333	.500	.333	180	0				.857	3	/C-1	0.3
1883	Buf-N	5	19	3	6	0	0	0	2	2	2	.316	.381	.316	113	0				.583	-2	/O-4,1-1	-0.1
Total	5	160	615	67	160	25	4	1	53	15	37	.260	.278	.319	98	-1				.901	9	C-147/O-9,1-5,3-1	1.0

■ RAY KENNEDY   Kennedy, Raymond Lincoln   b: 5/19/1895, Pittsburgh, Pa.   d: 1/18/69, Casselberry, Fla.   BR/TR, 5'9", 165 lbs.   Deb: 9/8/16

YEAR	TM/L	G	AB	R	H	2B	3B	HR	RBI	BB	SO	AVG	OBP	SLG	PRO+	BR/A	SB	CS	SBR	FA	FR	G/POS	TPR
1916	StL-A	1	1	0	0	0	0	0	0	0	0	.000	.000	.000	-99	-0	0			.000	0	H	0.0

■ BOB KENNEDY   Kennedy, Robert Daniel   b: 8/18/20, Chicago, Ill.   BR/TR, 6'2", 193 lbs.   Deb: 9/14/39   FMC

YEAR	TM/L	G	AB	R	H	2B	3B	HR	RBI	BB	SO	AVG	OBP	SLG	PRO+	BR/A	SB	CS	SBR	FA	FR	G/POS	TPR
1939	Chi-A	3	8	0	2	0	0	0	1	0	0	.250	.250	.250	27	-1	0	0	0	.750	-1	/3-2	-0.2
1940	Chi-A	154	606	74	153	23	3	3	52	42	58	.252	.301	.315	59	-36	3	7	-3	.938	-3	*3-154	-3.8
1941	Chi-A	76	257	16	53	9	3	1	29	17	23	.206	.255	.276	41	-22	5	3	-0	.934	3	3-71	-1.7
1942	Chi-A	113	412	37	95	18	5	0	38	22	41	.231	.270	.299	61	-22	11	7	-1	.956	4	3-96,O-16	-1.9
1946	Chi-A	113	411	43	106	13	5	5	34	24	24	.258	.300	.350	85	-10	6	8	-3	.965	6	O-75,3-29	-1.2
1947	Chi-A	115	428	47	112	19	3	6	48	18	38	.262	.291	.362	84	-11	3	4	-2	.968	-3	*O-106/3-1	-2.2
1948	Chi-A	30	113	4	28	8	1	0	14	4	17	.248	.274	.336	64	-6	0	2	-1	.970	4	O-30	-0.9
	*Cle-A	66	73	10	22	3	2	0	5	4	6	.301	.338	.397	98	-1	0	0	0	1.000	-13	O-50/2-2,1-1	-1.4
	Yr	96	186	14	50	11	3	0	19	8	23	.269	.299	.360	77	-7	0	2	-1	.981	-13	O-80/2-2,1-1	-2.3
1949	Cle-A	121	424	49	117	23	5	9	57	37	40	.276	.334	.417	100	-2	5	5	-2	.990	3	O-98,3-21	-0.6
1950	Cle-A	146	540	79	157	27	5	9	54	53	31	.291	.355	.409	99	-2	3	4	-2	.987	6	*O-144	-0.8
1951	Cle-A	108	321	30	79	15	4	7	29	34	33	.246	.320	.383	95	-3	4	2	0	.968	-1	*O-106	-0.7
1952	Cle-A	22	40	6	12	5	0	1	12	9	5	.300	.429	.425	148	3	1	0	0	1.000	3	O-13/3-3	0.3
1953	Cle-A	100	161	22	38	5	0	3	25	19	11	.236	.320	.323	76	-5	0	2	-1	1.000	-21	O-89	-3.0
1954	Cle-A	1	0	0	0	0	0	0	0	0	0	—	—	—	—	0	0	0	0	.000	-0	/O-1	0.0
	Bal-A	106	323	37	81	13	2	6	45	28	43	.251	.311	.359	90	-6	2	1	0	.938	-6	3-71,O-21	-1.5
	Yr	107	323	37	81	13	2	6	45	28	43	.251	.311	.359	90	-6	2	1	0	.938	-7	3-71,O-22	-1.5
1955	Bal-A	26	70	10	10	1	0	0	5	10	10	.143	.250	.157	12	-9	0	1	-1	1.000	-1	O-14/1-6,3-1	-1.1
	Chi-A	83	214	28	65	10	2	9	43	16	16	.304	.352	.495	122	6	0	2	-1	.938	-12	3-55,O-20/1-3	-0.9
	Yr	109	284	38	75	11	2	9	48	26	26	.264	.326	.412	97	-2	0	3	-2	.938	-13	3-56,O-34/1-9	-2.0
1956	Chi-A	8	13	0	1	0	0	0	0	0	0	.077	.200	.077	-24	-2	0	0	0	1.000	-1	/3-6	-0.3
	Det-A	69	177	17	41	5	0	4	22	24	19	.232	.330	.328	74	-6	2	2	-1	.931	-4	O-29,3-27	-1.0
	Yr	77	190	17	42	5	0	4	22	26	23	.221	.321	.311	67	-2	2	2	-1	.909	-4	3-33,O-29	-1.3
1957	Chi-A	4	2	0	0	0	0	0	0	0	1	.000	.000	.000	-99	-1	0	0	0	.000	0	H	-0.1
	Bro-N	19	31	5	4	1	0	1	4	1	5	.129	.156	.258	8	-4	0	0	0	1.000	-4	/O-9,3-3	-0.9
Total	16	1483	4624	514	1176	196	41	63	514	364	443	.254	.310	.355	80	-142	45	50	-17	.978	-55	O-821,3-540/1-10,2	-23.9

■ SNAPPER KENNEDY   Kennedy, Sherman Montgomery   b: 11/1/1878, Conneaut, Ohio   d: 8/15/45, Pasadena, Tex.   BB/TR, 5'10", 165 lbs.   Deb: 5/1/02

YEAR	TM/L	G	AB	R	H	2B	3B	HR	RBI	BB	SO	AVG	OBP	SLG	PRO+	BR/A	SB	CS	SBR	FA	FR	G/POS	TPR
1902	Chi-N	1	5	0	0	0	0	0	0	0		.000	.000	.000	-99	-1	0			1.000	1	/O-1	-0.1

■ TERRY KENNEDY   Kennedy, Terrence Edward   b: 6/4/56, Euclid, Ohio   BL/TR, 6'3", 220 lbs.   Deb: 9/4/78   F

YEAR	TM/L	G	AB	R	H	2B	3B	HR	RBI	BB	SO	AVG	OBP	SLG	PRO+	BR/A	SB	CS	SBR	FA	FR	G/POS	TPR
1978	StL-N	10	29	0	5	2	0	0	2	4	3	.172	.273	.172	27	-3	0	0	0	.980	0	C-10	-0.3
1979	StL-N	33	109	11	31	7	0	2	17	6	20	.284	.322	.404	96	-1	0	0	0	.993	-4	C-32	-0.4
1980	StL-N	84	248	28	63	12	3	4	34	28	34	.254	.330	.375	93	-2	0	0	0	.967	-3	C-41,O-28	-0.5
1981	SD-N★	101	382	32	115	24	1	2	41	22	53	.301	.342	.385	114	6	0	2	-1	.964	-8	*C-100	0.0
1982	SD-N	153	562	75	166	42	1	21	97	26	91	.295	.332	.486	133	21	1	0	0	.990	-18	*C-139,1-12	0.8
1983	SD-N☆	149	549	47	156	27	2	17	98	51	89	.284	.347	.434	119	13	0	3	-2	.986	-8	*C-143/1-4	1.0
1984	*SD-N	148	530	54	127	16	1	14	57	33	99	.240	.287	.353	79	-16	1	2	-1	.982	-14	*C-147	-2.6
1985	SD-N★	143	532	54	139	27	1	10	74	31	102	.261	.302	.372	89	-9	0	0	0	.986	0	*C-140/1-5	-0.2
1986	SD-N	141	432	46	114	22	1	12	57	37	74	.264	.325	.403	102	0	0	3	-2	.990	0	*C-123	0.6
1987	Bal-A★	143	512	51	128	13	1	18	62	35	112	.250	.299	.385	82	-14	0	0	0	.993	-16	*C-142	-1.7
1988	Bal-A	85	265	20	60	10	0	3	16	15	53	.226	.270	.298	61	-14	0	0	0	.994	-8	C-79	-1.1
1989	*SF-N	125	355	19	85	15	0	5	34	35	56	.239	.308	.324	83	-8	0	1	-1	.986	1	*C-121/1-2	-0.7
1990	SF-N	107	303	25	84	22	0	2	26	31	38	.277	.344	.370	100	0	0	0	0	.991	-12	*C-103	-0.8
1991	SF-N	69	171	12	40	7	1	3	13	11	31	.234	.284	.339	77	-6	0	0	0	.978	-3	C-58/1-2	-0.5
Total	14	1491	4979	474	1313	244	12	113	628	365	855	.264	.316	.386	97	-31	3	11	-7	.985	-100	*C-1378/O-28,1-25	-7.4

YEAR	TM/L	G	AB	R	H	2B	3B	HR	RBI	BB	SO	AVG	OBP	SLG	PRO+	BR/A	SB	CS	SBR	FA	FR	G/POS	TPR

■ ED KENNEDY   Kennedy, William Edward   b: 4/5/1861, Bellevue, Ky.   d: 12/22/12, Cheyenne, Wyoming   BR/TR, 5'7", 160 lbs.   Deb: 5/17/1884

YEAR	TM/L	G	AB	R	H	2B	3B	HR	RBI	BB	SO	AVG	OBP	SLG	PRO+	BR/A	SB	CS	SBR	FA	FR	G/POS	TPR
1884	Cin-U	13	48	6	10	1	1	0		1		.208	.224	.271	46	-5				.857	0	/3-8,S-4,O-1	-0.4

■ JERRY KENNEY   Kenney, Gerald T   b: 6/30/45, St.Louis, Mo.   BL/TR, 6'1", 170 lbs.   Deb: 9/5/67

YEAR	TM/L	G	AB	R	H	2B	3B	HR	RBI	BB	SO	AVG	OBP	SLG	PRO+	BR/A	SB	CS	SBR	FA	FR	G/POS	TPR
1967	NY-A	20	58	4	18	2	0	1	5	10	8	.310	.412	.397	145	4	2	1	0	.952	-4	S-18	0.2
1969	NY-A	130	447	49	115	14	2	2	34	48	36	.257	.331	.311	83	-9	25	14	-1	.975	11	3-83,O-31,S-10	0.1
1970	NY-A	140	404	46	78	10	7	4	35	52	44	.193	.285	.282	60	-22	20	6	2	.960	15	*3-135/2-2	-0.6
1971	NY-A	120	325	50	85	10	3	0	20	56	38	.262	.372	.311	101	3	9	8	-2	.953	11	*3-109/S-5,1-1	1.2
1972	NY-A	50	119	16	25	2	0	0	7	16	13	.210	.304	.227	62	-5	3	0	1	.969	5	S-45/3-1	0.6
1973	Cle-A	5	16	0	4	0	1	0	2	2	0	.250	.333	.375	97	-0	0	0	0	1.000	-2	/2-5	-0.1
Total	6	465	1369	165	325	38	13	7	103	184	139	.237	.329	.299	82	-30	59	29	0	.962	36	3-328/S-78,O-31,21	1.4

■ JOHN KENNEY   Kenney, John   Deb: 5/2/1872

YEAR	TM/L	G	AB	R	H	2B	3B	HR	RBI	BB	SO	AVG	OBP	SLG	PRO+	BR/A	SB	CS	SBR	FA	FR	G/POS	TPR
1872	Atl-n	5	19	0	0				1	0	1	.000	.000	.000	-85	-4	0	0		.692	-2	/2-3,O-3	-0.5

■ JEFF KENT   Kent, Jeffrey Franklin   b: 3/7/68, Bellflower, Cal.   BR/TR, 6'1", 185 lbs.   Deb: 4/12/92

YEAR	TM/L	G	AB	R	H	2B	3B	HR	RBI	BB	SO	AVG	OBP	SLG	PRO+	BR/A	SB	CS	SBR	FA	FR	G/POS	TPR
1992	Tor-A	65	192	36	46	13	1	8	35	20	47	.240	.330	.443	110	2	2	1	0	.915	-3	3-49,2-17/1-3	-0.1
	NY-N	37	113	16	27	8	1	3	15	7	29	.239	.289	.407	97	-1	0	2	-1	.980	8	2-34/3-1,S-1	0.7
1993	NY-N	140	496	65	134	24	0	21	80	30	88	.270	.322	.446	104	2	4	4	-1	.969	-19	*2-127,3-12/S-2	-1.4
1994	NY-N	107	415	53	121	24	5	14	68	23	84	.292	.344	.475	112	6	1	4	2	.976	0	*2-107	0.9
1995	NY-N	125	472	65	131	22	3	20	65	29	89	.278	.330	.464	110	5	3	3	-1	.984	-8	*2-122	0.4
1996	NY-N	89	335	45	97	20	1	9	39	21	56	.290	.333	.436	108	3	4	3	-1	.925	7	3-89	0.0
	*Cle-A	39	102	16	27	7	0	3	16	10	22	.265	.336	.422	90	-2	2	1	0	.992	-5	1-20/2-9,3-6,D-5	0.0
Total	5	602	2125	296	583	118	11	78	318	140	415	.274	.330	.450	107	16	16	18	-6	.977	-12	2-416,3-157/1DS	1.3

■ DICK KENWORTHY   Kenworthy, Richard Lee   b: 4/1/41, Red Oak, Iowa   BR/TR, 5'9", 170 lbs.   Deb: 9/8/62

YEAR	TM/L	G	AB	R	H	2B	3B	HR	RBI	BB	SO	AVG	OBP	SLG	PRO+	BR/A	SB	CS	SBR	FA	FR	G/POS	TPR
1962	Chi-A	3	4	0	0	0	0	0	0	0	3	.000	.000	.000	-99	-1	0	0	0	1.000	1	/2-2	0.0
1964	Chi-A	2	2	0	0	0	0	0	0	0	1	.000	.000	.000	-99	-1	0	0	0	.000	0	H	-0.1
1965	Chi-A	3	1	0	0	0	0	0	0	1	0	.000	.667	.000	113	0	0	0	0	.000	0	H	-0.1
1966	Chi-A	9	25	1	5	0	0	0	0	0	5	.200	.200	.200	16	-3	0	0	0	.875	-3	/3-6	-0.6
1967	Chi-A	50	97	9	22	4	1	4	11	4	17	.227	.265	.412	101	-0	0	2	-1	.971	1	3-35	-0.1
1968	Chi-A	58	122	2	27	2	0	0	2	5	21	.221	.252	.238	49	-8	0	1	-1	.938	4	3-38	-0.4
Total	6	125	251	12	54	6	1	4	13	10	42	.215	.251	.295	63	-12	0	3	-2	.948	4	/3-79,2-2	-1.2

■ BILL KENWORTHY   Kenworthy, William Jennings "Duke"   b: 7/4/1886, Cambridge, Ohio   d: 9/21/50, Eureka, Cal.   BR/TR, 5'7", 165 lbs.   Deb: 8/28/12

YEAR	TM/L	G	AB	R	H	2B	3B	HR	RBI	BB	SO	AVG	OBP	SLG	PRO+	BR/A	SB	CS	SBR	FA	FR	G/POS	TPR
1912	Was-A	12	38	6	9	1	0	0	2	2		.237	.293	.263	59	-2	3			1.000	-0	O-12	-0.3
1914	KC-F	146	545	93	173	40	14	15	91	36	44	.317	.372	.525	148	25	37			.952	21	*2-145	4.5
1915	KC-F	122	396	59	118	30	7	3	52	28	32	.298	.355	.432	126	7	20			.936	-7	*2-108/O-7	0.0
1917	StL-A	5	10	1	1	0	0	0	1	1	1	.100	.182	.100	-14	-1	1			.889	1	/2-4	0.0
Total	4	285	989	159	301	71	21	18	146	67	77	.304	.360	.473	135	28	61			.945	14	2-257/O-19	4.2

■ JOE KEOUGH   Keough, Joseph William   b: 1/7/46, Pomona, Cal.   BL/TL, 6', 185 lbs.   Deb: 8/7/68   F

YEAR	TM/L	G	AB	R	H	2B	3B	HR	RBI	BB	SO	AVG	OBP	SLG	PRO+	BR/A	SB	CS	SBR	FA	FR	G/POS	TPR
1968	Oak-A	34	98	7	21	2	1	2	18	8	11	.214	.274	.316	82	-2	1	0	0	.962	1	O-29/1-1	-0.3
1969	KC-A	70	166	17	31	2	0	1	13	13	13	.187	.254	.199	28	-16	5	2	0	1.000	-3	O-49/1-1	-2.2
1970	KC-A	57	183	28	59	6	2	4	21	23	18	.322	.398	.443	132	8	1	1	-0	.985	2	O-34,1-18	0.7
1971	KC-A	110	351	34	87	14	2	3	30	35	26	.248	.318	.325	83	-8	0	6	-4	.982	6	*O-100	-2.4
1972	KC-A	56	64	8	14	2	0	0	5	8	7	.219	.324	.250	73	-2	2	0	1	1.000	-3	O-16	-0.5
1973	Chi-A	5	1	1	0	0	0	0	0	0	0	.000	.000	.000	-97	-0	0	0	0	.000	0	H	0.0
Total	6	332	863	95	212	26	5	9	81	87	75	.246	.318	.319	82	-19	9	9	-3	.984	6	O-228/1-20	-4.7

■ MARTY KEOUGH   Keough, Richard Martin   b: 4/14/35, Oakland, Cal.   BL/TL, 6', 180 lbs.   Deb: 4/21/56   F

YEAR	TM/L	G	AB	R	H	2B	3B	HR	RBI	BB	SO	AVG	OBP	SLG	PRO+	BR/A	SB	CS	SBR	FA	FR	G/POS	TPR
1956	Bos-A	3	2	1	0	0	0	0	1	0	1	.000	.333	.000	-5	-0	0	0	0	.000	0	H	0.0
1957	Bos-A	9	17	1	1	0	0	0	0	4	3	.059	.238	.059	-14	-3	0	0	0	1.000	0	/O-7	-0.3
1958	Bos-A	68	118	21	26	3	3	1	9	7	29	.220	.264	.322	57	-7	1	1	-0	.974	-5	O-25/1-2	-1.4
1959	Bos-A	96	251	40	61	13	5	7	27	26	40	.243	.321	.418	97	-1	3	1	0	.993	-1	O-69/1-3	-0.6
1960	Bos-A	38	105	15	26	6	1	1	9	8	20	.248	.301	.352	73	-4	2	2	-1	1.000	1	O-29	-0.5
	Cle-A	65	149	19	37	5	0	3	11	9	23	.248	.296	.342	74	-6	2	3	-1	.986	-4	O-42	-1.3
	Yr	103	254	34	63	11	1	4	20	17	31	.248	.298	.346	74	-10	4	5	-2	.992	-3	O-71	-1.8
1961	Was-A	135	390	57	97	18	9	9	34	32	60	.249	.309	.410	92	-6	12	5	1	.978	2	*O-100,1-10	-0.9
1962	Cin-N	111	230	34	64	8	2	7	27	21	31	.278	.349	.422	102	1	3	1	0	.968	-5	O-71,1-29	-0.8
1963	Cin-N	95	172	21	39	8	2	6	21	25	37	.227	.338	.401	109	2	1	4	-2	.992	-3	1-46,O-28	-0.5
1964	Cin-N	109	276	29	71	9	1	9	28	22	58	.257	.314	.395	95	-2	1	2	-1	.991	-6	O-81/1-4	-1.2
1965	Cin-N	62	43	14	5	0	0	0	3	3	14	.116	.191	.116	-10	-6	0	0	0	.988	1	1-32/O-4	-0.7
1966	Atl-N	17	17	1	1	0	0	0	1	1	6	.059	.111	.059	-50	-3	0	0	0	1.000	-2	/1-4,O-3	-0.6
	Chi-N	33	26	3	6	1	0	0	5	5	9	.231	.375	.269	82	-0	1	0	0	1.000	-2	/O-5	-0.2
	Yr	50	43	4	7	1	0	0	6	6	15	.163	.280	.186	32	-4	1	0	0	.667	-3	/O-8,1-4	-0.8
Total	11	841	1796	256	434	71	23	43	176	164	318	.242	.311	.379	86	-35	26	19	-4	.984	-25	O-464,1-130	-9.0

■ JOHN KERINS   Kerins, John Nelson   b: 7/15/1858, Indianapolis, Ind   d: 9/8/19, Louisville, Ky.   BR/TR, 5'10", 177 lbs.   Deb: 5/1/1884   MU

YEAR	TM/L	G	AB	R	H	2B	3B	HR	RBI	BB	SO	AVG	OBP	SLG	PRO+	BR/A	SB	CS	SBR	FA	FR	G/POS	TPR
1884	Ind-a	94	364	58	78	10	3	6		6		.214	.229	.357	76	-10				.972	6	*1-87/C-5,O-5,3-1	-1.3
1885	Lou-a	112	456	65	111	9	16	3	51	20		.243	.281	.353	100	-1				.947	3	*1-96,C-19/O-3,3-1	-0.9
1886	Lou-a	120	487	113	131	19	9	4	50	66		.269	.360	.370	122	12	26			.933	39	C-65,1-47/O-7,S-1	4.6
1887	Lou-a	112	476	101	140	18	19	5	57	38		.294	.349	.443	118	9	49			.970	25	1-74,C-35/O-5	2.4
1888	Lou-a	83	319	38	75	11	4	2	41	25		.235	.297	.313	98	-0	16			.844	2	O-47,C-33/1-4,32M	0.3
1889	Lou-a	2	9	2	3	1	0	0	3	0	1	.333	.333	.444	123	0	0			.500	-1	/O-2,C-1	-0.1
	Bal-a	16	53	7	15	2	0	0	12	2	4	.283	.321	.321	82	-1	2			.981	-2	/1-9,C-4,O-2,S-1	-0.3
	Yr	18	62	9	18	3	0	0	15	2	5	.290	.323	.339	87	-1	2			.981	-2	/1-9,C-5,O-4,S-1	-0.4
1890	StL-a	18	63	8	8	2	0	0	3	8		.127	.225	.159	12	-7	2			.968	1	1-17/C-1,M	-0.6
Total	7	557	2227	392	561	72	51	20	217	165	5	.252	.308	.357	102	2	95			.963	73	1-334,C-163/O3S2	4.4

■ ORIE KERLIN   Kerlin, Orie Milton "Cy"   b: 1/23/1891, Summerfield, La.   d: 10/29/74, Shreveport, La.   BL/TR, 5'7", 149 lbs.   Deb: 6/6/15

YEAR	TM/L	G	AB	R	H	2B	3B	HR	RBI	BB	SO	AVG	OBP	SLG	PRO+	BR/A	SB	CS	SBR	FA	FR	G/POS	TPR
1915	Pit-F	3	0	0	0	0	0	0	0	0	0	.000	.000	.000	-99	-0	0			.000	-0	/C-3	0.0

■ BILL KERN   Kern, William George   b: 2/28/33, Coplay, Pa.   BR/TR, 6'2", 184 lbs.   Deb: 9/19/62

YEAR	TM/L	G	AB	R	H	2B	3B	HR	RBI	BB	SO	AVG	OBP	SLG	PRO+	BR/A	SB	CS	SBR	FA	FR	G/POS	TPR
1962	KC-A	8	16	1	4	0	0	0	1	0	3	.250	.250	.438	77	-1	0	0	0	1.000	1	/O-3	0.0

■ JOE KERNAN   Kernan, Joseph   b: Baltimore, Md.   Deb: 4/14/1873

YEAR	TM/L	G	AB	R	H	2B	3B	HR	RBI	BB	SO	AVG	OBP	SLG	PRO+	BR/A	SB	CS	SBR	FA	FR	G/POS	TPR
1873	Mar-n	2	8	1	3	0	0	0				.375	.375	.375	161	1	0	0	0	.700	1	/2-1,O-1	0.1

■ GEORGE KERNEK   Kernek, George Boyd   b: 1/12/40, Holdenville, Okla.   BL/TL, 6'3", 170 lbs.   Deb: 9/5/65

YEAR	TM/L	G	AB	R	H	2B	3B	HR	RBI	BB	SO	AVG	OBP	SLG	PRO+	BR/A	SB	CS	SBR	FA	FR	G/POS	TPR
1965	StL-N	10	31	6	9	3	0	1	2	2	6	.290	.333	.452	109	0	1	0	0	.972	-0	/1-7	0.0
1966	StL-N	20	50	5	12	0	1	0	4	4	9	.240	.309	.340	65	-2	0	0	0	.984	-0	1-16	-0.3
Total	2	30	81	11	21	3	1	1	6	6	13	.259	.318	.346	82	-2	1	0	0	.980	-0	/1-23	-0.3

■ RUSS KERNS   Kerns, Russell Eldon   b: 11/10/20, Fremont, Ohio   BL/TL, 6', 188 lbs.   Deb: 8/18/45

YEAR	TM/L	G	AB	R	H	2B	3B	HR	RBI	BB	SO	AVG	OBP	SLG	PRO+	BR/A	SB	CS	SBR	FA	FR	G/POS	TPR
1945	Det-A	1	1	0	0	0	0	0	0	0	0	.000	.000	.000	-94	-0	0	0	0	.000	0	H	0.0

■ JOHN KERR   Kerr, John Francis   b: 11/26/1898, San Francisco, Cal.   d: 10/19/93, Long Beach, Cal.   BR/TR, 5'8", 158 lbs.   Deb: 5/1/23

YEAR	TM/L	G	AB	R	H	2B	3B	HR	RBI	BB	SO	AVG	OBP	SLG	PRO+	BR/A	SB	CS	SBR	FA	FR	G/POS	TPR
1923	Det-A	19	42	4	9	1	0	0	4	5		.214	.283	.238	39	-4	0	0		.877	4	S-15	0.1
1924	Det-A	17	11	3	3	0	0	0	0	0		.273	.273	.273	42	-1	0	0		.000	-0	/3-3,O-2	-0.1
1929	Chi-A	127	419	50	108	20	4	1	39	36	24	.258	.310	.332	66	-21	9	8	-2	.971	24	*2-122/S-1	0.6
1930	Chi-A	70	266	37	77	11	6	3	27	21	23	.289	.351	.410	95	-2	4	2	0	.980	-3	2-52,S-20	0.3

YEAR	TM/L	G	AB	R	H	2B	3B	HR	RBI	BB	SO	AVG	OBP	SLG	PRO+	BR/A	SB	CS	SBR	FA	FR	G/POS	TPR
1931	Chi-A	128	444	51	119	17	2	2	50	35	22	.268	.324	.329	77	-15	9	3	1	.968	8	*2-117/3-7,S-1	0.1
1932	Was-A	51	132	14	36	6	1	0	15	13	3	.273	.338	.333	75	-5	3	2	-0	.954	1	2-17,S-14/3-8	-0.3
1933	*Was-A	28	40	5	8	0	0	0	3	3	2	.200	.256	.200	22	-4	0	0	0	.966	3	2-16/3-1	-0.1
1934	Was-A	31	103	8	28	4	0	0	12	8	13	.272	.324	.311	67	-5	1	1	-0	.971	10	3-17,2-13	0.5
Total	8	471	1457	172	388	59	13	6	145	115	92	.266	.323	.337	73	-57	26	16	-2	.970	48	2-337/S-51,3-36,O-2	1.1

■ DOC KERR   Kerr, John Jonas   b: 1/17/1882, Dellroy, Ohio   d: 6/9/37, Baltimore, Md.   BB/TR, 5'10.5", 190 lbs.   Deb: 4/22/14

YEAR	TM/L	G	AB	R	H	2B	3B	HR	RBI	BB	SO	AVG	OBP	SLG	PRO+	BR/A	SB	CS	SBR	FA	FR	G/POS	TPR
1914	Pit-F	42	71	3	17	4	2	1	7	10	13	.239	.333	.394	99	-1	0			.970	1	C-18	0.1
	Bal-F	14	34	4	9	1	1	0	1	1	6	.265	.286	.353	71	-2	1			.979	5	C-13/1-1	0.3
	Yr	56	105	7	26	5	3	1	8	11	19	.248	.319	.381	90	-3	1			.974	5	C-31/1-1	0.4
1915	Bal-F	3	6	1	2	0	0	0	0	1	0	.333	.429	.333	112	0	0			1.000	5	/C-2,1-1	-0.1
Total	2	59	111	8	28	5	3	1	8	12	19	.252	.325	.378	91	-3	1			.975	4	/C-33,1-2	0.3

■ BUDDY KERR   Kerr, John Joseph   b: 11/6/22, Astoria, N.Y.   BR/TR, 6'2", 180 lbs.   Deb: 9/8/43

YEAR	TM/L	G	AB	R	H	2B	3B	HR	RBI	BB	SO	AVG	OBP	SLG	PRO+	BR/A	SB	CS	SBR	FA	FR	G/POS	TPR
1943	NY-N	27	98	14	28	3	0	2	12	8	5	.286	.352	.378	110	1	1			.955	5	S-27	0.8
1944	NY-N	150	548	68	146	31	4	9	63	37	32	.266	.316	.387	97	-3	14			.954	**17**	*S-149	2.6
1945	NY-N	149	546	53	136	20	3	4	40	41	34	.249	.304	.319	72	-21	5			.964	**28**	*S-148	1.9
1946	NY-N	145	497	50	124	20	3	6	40	53	31	.249	.324	.338	87	-8	7			**.982**	6	*S-126,3-18	0.6
1947	NY-N	138	547	73	157	23	5	7	49	36	46	.287	.331	.386	89	-9	2			.977	12	*S-138	1.0
1948	NY-N★	144	496	41	119	16	4	0	46	56	36	.240	.317	.288	64	-23	9			.967	4	*S-143	-1.2
1949	NY-N	90	220	16	46	4	0	0	19	21	23	.209	.284	.227	39	-19	0			.959	6	S-89	-0.8
1950	Bos-N	155	507	45	115	24	6	2	46	50	50	.227	.296	.310	64	-27	0			.965	2	*S-155	-1.3
1951	Bos-N	69	172	18	32	4	0	1	18	22	20	.186	.282	.227	41	-14	0	0	0	.969	13	S-63/2-5	0.3
Total	9	1067	3631	378	903	145	25	31	333	324	280	.249	.312	.328	76	-123	38	0		.967	92	*S-1038/3-18,2-5	3.9

■ MEL KERR   Kerr, John Melville   b: 5/22/03, Souris, Man., Can.   d: 8/9/80, Vero Beach, Fla.   BL/TL, 5'11.5", 155 lbs.   Deb: 9/16/25   C

YEAR	TM/L	G	AB	R	H	2B	3B	HR	RBI	BB	SO	AVG	OBP	SLG	PRO+	BR/A	SB	CS	SBR	FA	FR	G/POS	TPR
1925	Chi-N	1	0	1	0	0	0	0	0	0	0	—	—	—		0	0	0	0	.000	0	R	0.0

■ DAN KERWIN   Kerwin, Daniel Patrick (b: Daniel Patrick Kervin)   b: 7/9/1879, Philadelphia, Pa.   d: 7/13/60, Philadelphia, Pa.   BL/TL, 5'9", 164 lbs.   Deb: 9/27/03

YEAR	TM/L	G	AB	R	H	2B	3B	HR	RBI	BB	SO	AVG	OBP	SLG	PRO+	BR/A	SB	CS	SBR	FA	FR	G/POS	TPR
1903	Cin-N	2	6	1	4	1	0	0	1	2		.667	.778	.833	323		2			.500	-1	*O-2	0.1

■ DON KESSINGER   Kessinger, Donald Eulon   b: 7/17/42, Forrest City, Ark.   BB/TR, 6'1", 175 lbs.   Deb: 9/7/64   FM

YEAR	TM/L	G	AB	R	H	2B	3B	HR	RBI	BB	SO	AVG	OBP	SLG	PRO+	BR/A	SB	CS	SBR	FA	FR	G/POS	TPR
1964	Chi-N	4	12	1	2	0	0	0	1	0	1	.167	.167	.167	-6	-2	0	0	0	1.000	-1	/S-4	-0.3
1965	Chi-N	106	309	19	62	4	3	0	14	20	44	.201	.254	.233	37	-25	1	2	-1	.948	21	*S-105	0.1
1966	Chi-N	150	533	50	146	8	2	1	43	26	46	.274	.308	.302	70	-21	13	7	-0	.951	-10	*S-148	-1.9
1967	Chi-N	145	580	61	134	10	7	0	42	33	80	.231	.277	.272	55	-33	6	13	-6	.973	-3	*S-143	-3.1
1968	Chi-N★	160	655	63	157	14	7	1	32	38	86	.240	.283	.287	67	-25	9	9	-3	.962	18	*S-159	0.8
1969	Chi-N★	158	664	109	181	38	6	4	53	61	70	.273	.335	.366	85	-13	11	8	-2	**.976**	25	*S-157	2.9
1970	Chi-N	154	631	100	168	21	14	1	39	66	59	.266	.338	.349	75	-22	12	6	-0	.972	9	*S-154	0.6
1971	Chi-N★	155	617	77	159	18	6	2	38	52	54	.258	.318	.316	70	-24	15	8	-0	.966	4	*S-154	0.0
1972	Chi-N★	149	577	77	158	20	6	1	39	67	44	.274	.351	.334	87	-8	7	2	-2	.965	8	*S-146	2.0
1973	Chi-N	160	577	52	151	22	3	0	43	57	44	.262	.328	.310	72	-20	6	6	-2	.964	17	*S-158	1.6
1974	Chi-N★	153	599	83	155	20	7	1	42	62	54	.259	.332	.321	80	-15	7	7	-2	.958	-1	*S-150	0.5
1975	Chi-N	154	601	77	146	26	10	0	46	68	47	.243	.321	.319	75	-19	4	7	-3	.967	-2	*S-140,3-13	-1.0
1976	StL-N	145	502	55	120	22	6	1	40	61	51	.239	.323	.313	80	-12	3	0	1	.969	-4	*S-113,2-31/3-2	-0.2
1977	StL-N	59	134	14	32	4	0	0	7	14	26	.239	.311	.269	58	-8	0	0	0	.978	-4	S-26,2-24/3-4	-0.2
	Chi-A	39	119	12	28	3	2	0	11	13	7	.235	.311	.294	66	-5	1	1	-0	.959	-4	S-21,2-13/3-9	-0.7
1978	Chi-A	131	431	35	110	18	1	1	31	36	34	.255	.313	.309	75	-14	2	4	-2	.974	-19	*S-123/2-9	-2.0
1979	Chi-A	56	110	14	22	6	0	1	7	10	12	.200	.267	.282	48	-8	1	0	0	.988	-1	S-54/1-1,2-1,M	-0.4
Total	16	2078	7651	899	1931	254	80	14	527	684	759	.252	.316	.312	72	-274	100	85	-21	.966	61	*S-1955/2-78,3-28,1	-1.1

■ KEITH KESSINGER   Kessinger, Robert Keith   b: 2/19/67, Forrest City, Ark.   BB/TR, 6'2", 185 lbs.   Deb: 9/15/93   F

YEAR	TM/L	G	AB	R	H	2B	3B	HR	RBI	BB	SO	AVG	OBP	SLG	PRO+	BR/A	SB	CS	SBR	FA	FR	G/POS	TPR
1993	Cin-N	11	27	4	7	1	0	1	3	4	4	.259	.355	.407	103	0	0	0	0	.935	-1	S-11	0.0

■ HENRY KESSLER   Kessler, Henry "Lucky"   b: 1847, Brooklyn, N.Y.   d: 1/9/1900, Franklin, Pa.   BR/TR, 5'10", 144 lbs.   Deb: 8/4/1873

YEAR	TM/L	G	AB	R	H	2B	3B	HR	RBI	BB	SO	AVG	OBP	SLG	PRO+	BR/A	SB	CS	SBR	FA	FR	G/POS	TPR
1873	Atl-n	1	5	0	1	0	0	0	1	0	0	.200	.200	.200	21	-0	0	0	0	.882	5	/1-1	0.0
1874	Atl-n	14	56	8	17	1	0	0	4	0	2	.304	.304	.321	114	1	0	0	0	.737	-3	/C-9,2-4,O-4,3-1	-0.1
1875	Atl-n	25	105	17	26	2	0	0	7	1	2	.248	.255	.267	93	-0	0	2	-1	.794	-1	S-18/O-7,C-3,1-1,2	-1.2
1876	Cin-N	59	248	26	64	5	0	0	11	7	10	.258	.278	.278	100	2				.788	-8	S-46,O-16	-0.6
1877	Cin-N	6	20	0	2	0	0	0	2	1		.100	.182	.100	-10	-2				.500	1	/C-5,1-1	-0.7
Total	3 n	40	166	25	44	3	0	0	12	1	4	.265	.269	.283	98	1	0	2	-1	.739	-4	/S-18,C-12,O2,1-3	-0.3
Total	2	65	268	26	66	5	0	0	11	9	11	.246	.271	.265	91	-1				.788	-14	/S-46,O-16,C-5,1-1	-1.3

■ FRED KETCHUM   Ketchum, Frederick L.   b: 7/27/1875, Elmira, N.Y.   d: 3/12/08, Cortland, N.Y.   BL/TR, 5'8", 157 lbs.   Deb: 9/12/1899

YEAR	TM/L	G	AB	R	H	2B	3B	HR	RBI	BB	SO	AVG	OBP	SLG	PRO+	BR/A	SB	CS	SBR	FA	FR	G/POS	TPR
1899	Lou-N	15	61	13	18	1	0	0	5	5		.295	.306	.311	70	-3	2			1.000	-4	O-15	-0.7
1901	Phi-A	5	22	5	5	0	0	0	0	0		.227	.227	.227	25	-2	0			.875	-1	/O-5	-0.3
Total	2	20	83	18	23	1	0	0	7	5		.277	.286	.289	58	-5	2			.960	-5	/O-20	-1.0

■ PHIL KETTER   Ketter, Philip (b: Philip Ketterer)   b: 4/13/1884, St.Louis, Mo.   d: 4/9/65, St.Louis, Mo.   TR,   Deb: 5/23/12

YEAR	TM/L	G	AB	R	H	2B	3B	HR	RBI	BB	SO	AVG	OBP	SLG	PRO+	BR/A	SB	CS	SBR	FA	FR	G/POS	TPR
1912	StL-A	2	6	1	2	0	0	0	0	0	0	.333	.333	.333	94	-0				1.000	-1	/C-2	-0.1

■ SAM KHALIFA   Khalifa, Sam   b: 12/5/63, Fontana, Cal.   BR/TR, 5'11", 170 lbs.   Deb: 6/25/85

YEAR	TM/L	G	AB	R	H	2B	3B	HR	RBI	BB	SO	AVG	OBP	SLG	PRO+	BR/A	SB	CS	SBR	FA	FR	G/POS	TPR
1985	Pit-N	95	320	30	76	14	3	2	31	34	56	.237	.311	.319	77	-9	5	2	0	.967	13	S-95	1.3
1986	Pit-N	64	151	8	28	6	0	0	4	19	28	.185	.276	.225	39	-12	0	2	-1	.961	14	S-60/2-6	0.5
1987	Pit-N	5	17	1	3	0	0	0	2	0	2	.176	.176	.176	-6	-3	0	0	0	.917	-5	/S-5	-0.7
Total	3	164	488	39	107	20	3	2	37	53	86	.219	.296	.285	62	-24	5	4	-1	.964	22	S-160/2-6	1.1

■ HOD KIBBIE   Kibbie, Horace Kent   b: 7/18/03, Ft.Worth, Tex.   d: 10/19/75, Ft.Worth, Tex.   BR/TR, 5'10", 150 lbs.   Deb: 6/13/25

YEAR	TM/L	G	AB	R	H	2B	3B	HR	RBI	BB	SO	AVG	OBP	SLG	PRO+	BR/A	SB	CS	SBR	FA	FR	G/POS	TPR
1925	Bos-N	11	41	5	11	2	0	0	5	6		.268	.348	.317	78	-1	0			.904	-0	/2-8,S-3	-0.1

■ JACK KIBBLE   Kibble, John Westly "Happy"   b: 1/2/1892, Seatonville, Ill.   d: 12/13/69, Roundup, Mont.   BB/TR, 5'9.5", 154 lbs.   Deb: 9/10/12

YEAR	TM/L	G	AB	R	H	2B	3B	HR	RBI	BB	SO	AVG	OBP	SLG	PRO+	BR/A	SB	CS	SBR	FA	FR	G/POS	TPR
1912	Cle-A	5	8	1	0	0	0	0	0	0	0	.000	.111	.000	-65	-2	0			1.000	4	/3-4,2-1	0.2

■ STEVE KIEFER   Kiefer, Steven George   b: 10/18/60, Chicago, Ill.   BR/TR, 6'1", 180 lbs.   Deb: 9/3/84   F

YEAR	TM/L	G	AB	R	H	2B	3B	HR	RBI	BB	SO	AVG	OBP	SLG	PRO+	BR/A	SB	CS	SBR	FA	FR	G/POS	TPR
1984	Oak-A	23	40	7	7	1	2	0	2	2	10	.175	.214	.300	43	-3	2	1	0	.904	1	S-17/3-2,D-3	-0.2
1985	Oak-A	40	66	8	13	1	1	1	10	1	18	.197	.209	.288	37	-6	0	0	0	.881	3	3-34/D-2	-0.3
1986	Mil-A	2	6	0	0	0	0	0	0	0	4	.000	.000	.000	-97	-2	0	0	0	1.000	3	/S-2	0.1
1987	Mil-A	28	99	17	20	4	0	5	17	7	28	.202	.303	.394	69	-5	0	0	0	.966	-3	3-26/2-4	-0.7
1988	Mil-A	7	10	2	3	1	0	1	3	1	2	.300	.462	.700	219	2	0	0	0	1.000	1	/2-4,3-4	0.1
1989	NY-A	5	8	0	1	0	0	0	0	0	5	.125	.125	.125	-30	-1	0	0	0	1.000	-3	/3-5	-0.3
Total	6	105	229	34	44	7	3	7	30	12	68	.192	.239	.341	56	-15	2	1	0	.920	1	/3-71,S-19,2-8,D-5	-1.3

■ BILL KIENZLE   Kienzle, William H.   b: Philadelphia, Pa.   BL/TL,   Deb: 9/15/1882

YEAR	TM/L	G	AB	R	H	2B	3B	HR	RBI	BB	SO	AVG	OBP	SLG	PRO+	BR/A	SB	CS	SBR	FA	FR	G/POS	TPR
1882	Phi-a	9	33	8	11	3	2	0		9	5	.333	.421	.545	200	3				.842	-1	/O-9	0.2
1884	Phi-U	67	299	76	76	13	8	0		21		.254	.303	.351	106	-6				.772	-2	O-67	-0.9
Total	2	76	332	84	87	16	10	0	9	26		.262	.316	.370	116	-3				.781	-3	/O-76	-0.7

■ BROOKS KIESCHNICK   Kieschnick, Michael Brooks   b: 6/6/72, Robstown, Tex.   BL/TR, 6'4", 225 lbs.   Deb: 4/3/96

YEAR	TM/L	G	AB	R	H	2B	3B	HR	RBI	BB	SO	AVG	OBP	SLG	PRO+	BR/A	SB	CS	SBR	FA	FR	G/POS	TPR
1996	Chi-N	25	29	6	10	2	0	1	6	3	8	.345	.406	.517	140	2	0	0	0	.833	-3	/O-8	-0.1

■ PETE KILDUFF   Kilduff, Peter John   b: 4/4/1893, Weir City, Kan.   d: 2/14/30, Pittsburg, Kan.   BR/TR, 5'7", 155 lbs.   Deb: 4/18/17

YEAR	TM/L	G	AB	R	H	2B	3B	HR	RBI	BB	SO	AVG	OBP	SLG	PRO+	BR/A	SB	CS	SBR	FA	FR	G/POS	TPR
1917	NY-N	31	78	12	16	3	0	1	12	4	11	.205	.253	.282	66	-3	2			.954	-2	2-21/S-5,3-1	-0.5
	Chi-N	56	202	23	56	9	5	0	15	12	19	.277	.324	.371	105	-1	11			.920	-14	S-51/2-5	-1.2

YEAR	TM/L	G	AB	R	H	2B	3B	HR	RBI	BB	SO	AVG	OBP	SLG	PRO+	BR/A	SB	CS	SBR	FA	FR	G/POS	TPR
	Yr	87	280	35	72	12	5	1	27	16	30	.257	.304	.346	96	-2	13			.917	-16	S-56,2-26/3-1	-1.7
1918	Chi-N	30	93	7	19	2	2	0	13	7	7	.204	.267	.269	62	-4	1			.935	-3	2-30	-0.6
1919	Chi-N	31	88	5	24	4	2	0	8	10	5	.273	.360	.364	117	2	1			.974	-4	3-14/2-8,S-7	-0.1
	Bro-N	32	73	9	22	3	1	0	8	12	11	.301	.407	.370	132	4	5			.862	-4	3-26/2-1	0.1
	Yr	63	161	14	46	7	3	0	16	22	16	.286	.382	.366	124	6	6			.903	-8	3-40/2-9,S-7	0.0
1920	*Bro-N	141	478	62	130	26	8	0	58	58	43	.272	.351	.360	101	2	2	9	-5	.967	8	*2-134/3-5	1.0
1921	Bro-N	107	372	45	107	15	10	3	45	31	36	.288	.344	.406	94	-3	6	6	-2	.963	13	*2-105/3-1	1.1
Total	5	428	1384	163	374	62	28	4	159	134	132	.270	.338	.364	98	-2	28	<u>15</u>		.963	-7	2-304/S-63,3-47	-0.2

■ JOHN KILEY
Kiley, John Frederick   b: 7/1/1859, Dedham, Mass.   d: 12/18/40, Norwood, Mass.   BL/TL, 5'7", 147 lbs.   Deb: 5/1/1884

YEAR	TM/L	G	AB	R	H	2B	3B	HR	RBI	BB	SO	AVG	OBP	SLG	PRO+	BR/A	SB	CS	SBR	FA	FR	G/POS	TPR
1884	Was-a	14	56	9	12	2	2	0			3	.214	.267	.321	103	0	0			.571	-4	O-14	-0.3
1891	Bos-N	1	2	0	0	0	0	0	0	1	1	.000	.500	.000	45	0	0			1.000	0	/P-1	0.0
Total	2	15	58	9	12	2	2	0	<u>0</u>	4	<u>1</u>	.207	.281	.310	102	0	0			.571	-4	/O-14,P-1	-0.3

■ PAT KILHULLEN
Kilhullen, Joseph Isadore   b: 8/10/1890, Carbondale, Pa.   d: 11/2/22, Oakland, Cal.   BR/TR, 5'9", 175 lbs.   Deb: 6/10/14

YEAR	TM/L	G	AB	R	H	2B	3B	HR	RBI	BB	SO	AVG	OBP	SLG	PRO+	BR/A	SB	CS	SBR	FA	FR	G/POS	TPR
1914	Pit-N	1	1	0	0	0	0	0	0	0	0	.000	.000	.000	-99	-0	0			.000	0	/C-1	0.0

■ HARMON KILLEBREW
Killebrew, Harmon Clayton "Killer"   b: 6/29/36, Payette, Idaho   BR/TR, 5'11", 213 lbs.   Deb: 6/23/54   H

YEAR	TM/L	G	AB	R	H	2B	3B	HR	RBI	BB	SO	AVG	OBP	SLG	PRO+	BR/A	SB	CS	SBR	FA	FR	G/POS	TPR
1954	Was-A	9	13	1	4	1	0	0	3	2	3	.308	.400	.385	122	0	0	0	0	1.000	-2	/2-3	-0.2
1955	Was-A	38	80	12	16	1	0	4	7	9	31	.200	.281	.363	76	-3	0	0	0	.935	5	3-23/2-3	0.2
1956	Was-A	44	99	10	22	2	0	5	13	10	39	.222	.294	.394	80	-3	0	0	0	.951	-0	3-20/2-4	-0.3
1957	Was-A	9	31	4	9	2	0	2	5	2	8	.290	.333	.548	139	1	0	0	0	.947	-1	/3-7,2-1	0.1
1958	Was-A	13	31	2	6	0	0	0	2	0	12	.194	.219	.194	15	-4	0	0	0	1.000	0	/3-9	-0.4
1959	Was-A★	153	546	98	132	20	2	**42**	105	90	116	.242	.356	.516	137	28	3	2	-0	.938	-8	*3-150/O-4	2.0
1960	Was-A	124	442	84	122	19	1	31	80	71	106	.276	.377	.534	145	28	1	0	0	.987	-9	1-71,3-65	1.3
1961	Min-A★	150	541	94	156	20	7	46	122	107	109	.288	.409	.606	159	46	1	2	-1	.987	-10	*1-119,3-45/O-2	2.6
1962	Min-A★	155	552	85	134	21	1	**48**	**126**	106	142	.243	.369	.545	137	29	1	2	-1	.967	-10	*O-151/1-4	0.9
1963	Min-A★	142	515	88	133	18	0	**45**	96	72	105	.258	.353	**.555**	147	32	0	0	0	.987	-3	*O-137	2.2
1964	Min-A★	158	577	95	156	11	1	**49**	111	93	135	.270	.379	.548	153	42	0	0	0	.971	-7	*O-157	2.9
1965	*Min-A★	113	401	78	108	16	1	25	75	72	69	.269	.386	.501	144	25	0	0	0	.988	-9	1-72,3-44/O-1	1.2
1966	Min-A★	162	569	89	160	27	1	39	110	**103**	98	.281	.393	.538	155	42	0	0	-1	.951	-17	*3-107,1-42,O-18	2.0
1967	Min-A★	163	547	105	147	24	1	**44**	113	**131**	111	.269	.413	.558	170	52	1	0	0	.992	-5	*1-160/3-3	3.8
1968	Min-A★	100	295	40	62	7	2	17	40	70	70	.210	.365	.420	131	13	0	0	0	.994	3	1-77,3-11	1.3
1969	*Min-A★	162	555	106	153	20	2	**49**	**140**	**145**	84	.276	**.430**	.584	177	63	8	2	1	.929	-21	*3-105,1-80	3.9
1970	*Min-A★	157	527	96	143	20	1	41	113	128	84	.271	.416	.546	161	48	0	3	-2	.948	-29	*3-138,1-28	1.4
1971	Min-A★	147	500	61	127	19	1	28	**119**	**114**	96	.254	.393	.464	137	28	3	2	-0	.997	-15	1-90,3-64	0.4
1972	Min-A	139	433	53	100	13	2	26	74	94	91	.231	.369	.450	136	22	0	1	-1	.992	11	*1-130	2.5
1973	Min-A	69	248	29	60	9	1	5	32	41	59	.242	.352	.347	94	-1	0	0	0	.998	4	1-57/D-9	-0.1
1974	Min-A	122	333	28	74	7	0	13	54	45	61	.222	.315	.360	91	-4	0	0	0	.992	2	D-57,1-33	-0.6
1975	KC-A	106	312	25	62	13	0	14	44	54	70	.199	.319	.375	90	-3	1	2	-1	1.000	-0	D-92/1-6	-0.9
Total	22	2435	8147	1283	2086	290	24	573	1584	1559	1699	.256	.379	.509	142	482	19	18	-5	.992	-123	1-969,3-791,OD/2	26.4

■ RED KILLEFER
Killefer, Wade Hampton   b: 4/13/1885, Bloomingdale, Mich   d: 9/4/58, Los Angeles, Cal.   BR/TR, 5'9", 175 lbs.   Deb: 9/16/07   F

YEAR	TM/L	G	AB	R	H	2B	3B	HR	RBI	BB	SO	AVG	OBP	SLG	PRO+	BR/A	SB	CS	SBR	FA	FR	G/POS	TPR
1907	Det-A	1	4	0	0	0	0	0	0	0	0	.000	.000	.000	-97	-1	0			1.000	0	/O-1	-0.1
1908	Det-A	28	75	9	16	1	0	0	11	3		.213	.253	.227	54	-4	4			.956	-5	2-16/S-7,3-4	-1.1
1909	Det-A	23	61	6	17	2	2	1	4	3		.279	.343	.426	137	2	2			.912	-1	2-17/O-1	0.1
	Was-A	40	121	11	21	1	0	0	5	13		.174	.265	.182	43	-7	4			.957	-3	O-24/3-6,C-3,2-3,S	-1.2
	Yr	63	182	17	38	3	2	1	9	16		.209	.291	.264	76	-4	6			.957	-4	O-25,2-20/3-6,CS	-1.1
1910	Was-A	106	345	35	79	17	1	0	24	29		.229	.318	.284	93	-1	17			.940	-4	2-88,O-12	-0.9
1914	Cin-N	42	141	16	39	6	1	0	12	20	18	.277	.386	.333	111	3	11			.968	-4	O-37/2-5,3-1	-0.3
1915	Cin-N	155	555	75	151	25	11	1	41	38	33	.272	.340	.362	110	8	12	18	-7	.970	5	*O-150/1-2	-0.3
1916	Cin-N	70	234	29	57	9	1	1	18	21	8	.244	.327	.303	96	-0	7			.966	-2	O-68	-0.6
	NY-N	2	1	0	1	0	0	0	1	0		1.000	1.000	1.000	544	1	0			.000	0	H	0.1
	Yr	72	235	29	58	9	1	1	19	22	8	.247	.332	.306	99	1	7			.966	-2	O-68	-0.5
Total	7	467	1537	181	381	61	16	3	116	128	<u>59</u>	.248	.328	.314	98	0	57	<u>18</u>		.965	-16	O-293,2-129/3SC1	-4.3

■ BILL KILLEFER
Killefer, William Lavier "Reindeer Bill"
b: 10/10/1887, Bloomingdale, Mich   d: 7/3/60, Elsmere, Del.   BR/TR, 5'10.5", 200 lbs.   Deb: 9/13/09   FMC

YEAR	TM/L	G	AB	R	H	2B	3B	HR	RBI	BB	SO	AVG	OBP	SLG	PRO+	BR/A	SB	CS	SBR	FA	FR	G/POS	TPR
1909	StL-A	11	29	0	4	0	0	0	0	1	0	.138	.138	.138	-14	-4	2			.905	2	C-11	-0.1
1910	StL-A	74	193	14	24	2	2	0	7	12		.124	.184	.155	7	-21	4			.938	12	C-73	-0.3
1911	Phi-N	6	16	3	3	0	0	0	2	0	2	.188	.188	.188	5	-2	0			.975	2	/C-6	0.0
1912	Phi-N	85	268	18	60	6	3	1	21	4	14	.224	.241	.280	40	-23	6			.973	17	C-85	0.2
1913	Phi-N	120	360	25	88	14	3	0	24	4	17	.244	.255	.300	56	-21	2			.988	1	*C-118/1-1	0.2
1914	Phi-N	98	299	27	70	10	1	0	27	8	17	.234	.261	.274	56	-17	3			.978	18	C-90	0.9
1915	*Phi-N	105	320	26	76	9	2	0	24	18	14	.237	.287	.278	70	-11	5	3	-0	.972	14	*C-104	1.1
1916	Phi-N	97	286	22	62	5	4	3	27	8	14	.217	.246	.294	63	-13	2			**.985**	-1	C-91	-0.8
1917	Phi-N	125	409	28	112	12	0	1	31	15	21	.274	.306	.303	84	-8	4			**.984**	10	*C-120/O-1	1.3
1918	*Chi-N	104	331	30	77	10	3	0	22	17	10	.233	.276	.281	68	-13	5			.982	9	*C-104	0.6
1919	Chi-N	103	315	17	90	11	0	0	22	15	8	.286	.322	.330	96	-2	5			**.987**	17	*C-100	2.6
1920	Chi-N	62	191	16	42	7	1	0	16	8	5	.220	.280	.267	56	-10	2	2	-1	.977	18	C-61	1.2
1921	Chi-N	45	133	11	43	1	0	0	14	5	7	.323	.357	.331	83	-3	3	3	-1	.964	-1	C-42,M	0.6
Total	13	1035	3150	237	751	86	21	4	240	113	<u>126</u>	.238	.273	.283	63	-147	39	<u>8</u>		.976	131	*C-1005/O-1,1-1	6.6

■ GENE KIMBALL
Kimball, Eugene Boynton   b: 8/31/1850, Rochester, N.Y.   d: 8/2/1882, Rochester, N.Y.   5'10", 160 lbs.   Deb: 5/4/1871

YEAR	TM/L	G	AB	R	H	2B	3B	HR	RBI	BB	SO	AVG	OBP	SLG	PRO+	BR/A	SB	CS	SBR	FA	FR	G/POS	TPR
1871	Cle-n	29	131	18	25	1	0	0	9	3	2	.191	.209	.198	19	-12	5	1	1	.743	-7	2-17/O-9,S-6,3-2	-1.3

■ DICK KIMBLE
Kimble, Richard Lewis   b: 7/27/15, Buchtel, Ohio   BL/TR, 5'9", 160 lbs.   Deb: 8/20/45

YEAR	TM/L	G	AB	R	H	2B	3B	HR	RBI	BB	SO	AVG	OBP	SLG	PRO+	BR/A	SB	CS	SBR	FA	FR	G/POS	TPR
1945	Was-A	20	49	5	12	1	1	0	5		2	.245	.315	.306	88	-1	0	0	0	.950	-3	S-15	-0.3

■ BRUCE KIMM
Kimm, Bruce Edward   b: 6/29/51, Cedar Rapids, Iowa   BR/TR, 5'11", 175 lbs.   Deb: 5/4/76   C

YEAR	TM/L	G	AB	R	H	2B	3B	HR	RBI	BB	SO	AVG	OBP	SLG	PRO+	BR/A	SB	CS	SBR	FA	FR	G/POS	TPR
1976	Det-A	63	152	13	40	8	0	1	6	15	20	.263	.329	.336	91	-1	4	3	-1	.970	4	C-61/D-2	0.4
1977	Det-A	14	25	2	2	1	0	0	1	0	4	.080	.115	.120	-34	-5	0	1	-1	.958	3	C-12/D-2	-0.2
1979	Chi-N	9	11	0	1	0	0	0	0	0	0	.091	.091	.091	-46	-2	0	1	-1	.969	4	/C-9	-0.1
1980	Chi-A	100	251	20	61	10	1	0	19	17	26	.243	.291	.291	60	-13	1	1	-2	.985	-1	C-98	-1.4
Total	4	186	439	35	104	19	1	1	26	32	50	.237	.290	.292	62	-22	5	8	-3	.977	8	C-180/D-4	-1.3

■ WALLY KIMMICK
Kimmick, Walter Lyons   b: 5/30/1897, Turtle Creek, Pa.   d: 7/24/89, Boswell, Pa.   BR/TR, 5'11", 174 lbs.   Deb: 9/13/19

YEAR	TM/L	G	AB	R	H	2B	3B	HR	RBI	BB	SO	AVG	OBP	SLG	PRO+	BR/A	SB	CS	SBR	FA	FR	G/POS	TPR
1919	StL-N	2	1	0	0	0	0	0	0	1	0	.000	.500	.000	61	0	1			1.000	0	/S-1	0.0
1921	Cin-N	3	6	0	1	0	0	0	0	1	0	.167	.167	.167	-12	-1	0	0	0	.667	-0	/3-2	-0.1
1922	Cin-N	39	89	11	22	2	1	0	12	3	12	.247	.272	.292	46	-7	0	0	0	.965	2	S-30/2-3,3-1	-0.3
1923	Cin-N	29	80	11	18	2	1	0	6	5	15	.225	.271	.275	45	-6	3	0	1	.972	8	2-17/3-4,S-1	0.3
1925	Phi-N	70	141	16	43	3	2	1	10	22	26	.305	.399	.376	91	-1	0	1	-2	.904	-3	S-28,3-21,2-13	-0.3
1926	Phi-N	20	28	0	6	2	1	0	2	3	6	.214	.290	.357	70	-1	1			1.000	-2	/1-5,S-4,3-4,2-1	-0.3
Total	6	163	345	39	90	9	5	1	31	34	61	.261	.327	.325	67	-17	4	<u>3</u>		.933	4	/S-64,2-34,3-32,1-5	-0.7

■ JERRY KINDALL
Kindall, Gerald Donald "Slim"   b: 5/27/35, St.Paul, Minn.   BR/TR, 6'2.5", 175 lbs.   Deb: 7/1/56

YEAR	TM/L	G	AB	R	H	2B	3B	HR	RBI	BB	SO	AVG	OBP	SLG	PRO+	BR/A	SB	CS	SBR	FA	FR	G/POS	TPR
1956	Chi-N	32	55	7	9	1	0	0		6	17	.164	.246	.218	27	-6	1	0	0	.956	6	S-18	-0.2
1957	Chi-N	72	181	18	29	3	0	6	12	8	48	.160	.196	.276	25	-19	1	0	0	.920	-4	2-28,3-19/S-9	-2.1
1958	Chi-N	3	6	1	2	0	0	0	1	0	2	.333	.333	.333	29	-1	0	0	0	1.000	1	/2-3	0.1
1960	Chi-N	89	246	17	59	16	2	6	23	9	52	.240	.255	.346	63	-13	4	3	-1	.966	14	2-82/S-2	0.7
1961	Chi-N	96	310	37	75	22	5	9	44	18	89	.242	.288	.419	84	-8	2	5	-1	.950	7	2-50,S-47	0.6
1962	Cle-A	154	530	51	123	21	1	13	55	45	107	.232	.292	.349	74	-20	4	3	-1	.978	21	*2-154	1.6

YEAR	TM/L	G	AB	R	H	2B	3B	HR	RBI	BB	SO	AVG	OBP	SLG	PRO+	BR/A	SB	CS	SBR	FA	FR	G/POS	TPR
1963	Cle-A	86	234	27	48	4	1	5	20	18	71	.205	.268	.295	58	-13	3	1	0	.958	3	S-46,2-37/1-4	-0.5
1964	Cle-A	23	25	5	9	1	0	2	2	7	7	.360	.407	.640	188	3	0	0	0	.989	1	3-23	0.6
	Min-A	62	128	8	19	2	0	1	6	7	44	.148	.199	.188	8	-16	0	0	0	.969	5	2-51/S-7,1-1	-0.9
	Yr	85	153	13	28	3	0	3	8	9	51	.183	.233	.261	37	-13	0	0	0	.969	8	2-51,1-24/S-7	-0.3
1965	Min-A	125	342	41	67	12	1	6	36	36	97	.196	.278	.289	59	-18	2	2	-1	.963	-1	*2-106,3-10/S-3	-1.2
Total	9	742	2057	211	439	83	9	44	198	145	535	.213	.268	.327	62	-111	17	11	-2	.967	50	2-511,S-136/3-29,1	-1.3

■ RALPH KINER
Kiner, Ralph McPherran b: 10/27/22, Santa Rita, N.Mex.   BR/TR, 6'2", 195 lbs.   Deb: 4/16/46 H

YEAR	TM/L	G	AB	R	H	2B	3B	HR	RBI	BB	SO	AVG	OBP	SLG	PRO+	BR/A	SB	CS	SBR	FA	FR	G/POS	TPR
1946	Pit-N	144	502	63	124	17	3	23	81	74	109	.247	.345	.430	116	10	3			.969	1	*O-140	0.5
1947	Pit-N	152	565	118	177	23	4	51	127	98	81	.313	.417	.639	172	57	1			.983	13	*O-152	6.0
1948	Pit-N★	156	555	104	147	19	5	40	123	112	61	.265	.391	.533	145	36	1			.975	7	*O-154	3.4
1949	Pit-N★	152	549	116	170	19	5	54	127	117	61	.310	.432	.658	183	66	6			.979	-1	*O-152	5.6
1950	Pit-N★	150	547	112	149	21	6	47	118	122	79	.272	.408	.590	154	44	2			.965	-3	*O-150	3.4
1951	Pit-N★	151	531	124	164	31	6	42	109	137	57	.309	.452	.627	182	67	2	1	0	.967	-5	O-94,1-58	5.4
1952	Pit-N☆	149	516	90	126	17	2	37	87	110	77	.244	.384	.500	140	30	3	0	1	.970	-6	*O-149	1.9
1953	Pit-N	41	148	27	40	6	1	7	29	25	21	.270	.383	.466	121	5	1	0	0	1.000	1	O-41	0.4
	Chi-N★	117	414	73	117	14	2	28	87	75	67	.283	.394	.529	135	22	1	1	-0	.964	-4	*O-116	1.3
	Yr	158	562	100	157	20	3	35	116	100	88	.279	.391	.512	131	27	2	1	0	.973	-3	*O-157	1.7
1954	Chi-N	147	557	88	159	36	5	22	73	76	90	.285	.373	.487	121	17	2	0	1	.986	-5	O-87	1.1
1955	Cle-A	113	321	56	78	13	0	18	54	65	46	.243	.370	.452	116	8	0	0	0	.986	-5	O-87	-0.1
Total	10	1472	5205	971	1451	216	39	369	1015	1011	749	.279	.398	.548	148	363	22	2		.974	-2	*O-1382/1-58	28.9

■ CHICK KING
King, Charles Gilbert b: 11/10/30, Paris, Tenn.   BR/TR, 6'2", 190 lbs.   Deb: 8/27/54

YEAR	TM/L	G	AB	R	H	2B	3B	HR	RBI	BB	SO	AVG	OBP	SLG	PRO+	BR/A	SB	CS	SBR	FA	FR	G/POS	TPR
1954	Det-A	11	28	4	6	0	1	0	3	3	8	.214	.290	.286	59	-2	0	0	0	.958	1	/O-7	-0.1
1955	Det-A	7	21	3	5	0	0	0	0	1	4	.238	.273	.238	39	-2	0	0	0	.923	-0	/O-6	-0.2
1956	Det-A	7	9	0	2	0	0	0	0	1	4	.222	.300	.222	40	-1	0	0	0	.800	-1	/O-4	-0.2
1958	Chi-N	8	8	1	2	0	0	0	1	3	1	.250	.455	.250	95	-0	0	0	0	1.000	-2	/O-7	-0.2
1959	Chi-N	7	3	3	0	0	0	0	0	0	1	.000	.000	.000	-99	-1	0	0	0	1.000	-1	/O-1	-0.1
	StL-N	5	7	0	3	0	0	0	1	0	2	.429	.429	.429	121	0	0	0	0	1.000	-0	/O-4	0.0
	Yr	12	10	3	3	0	0	0	1	0	3	.300	.300	.300	59	-1	0	0	0	1.000	-0	/O-5	-0.1
Total	5	45	76	11	18	0	1	0	5	8	18	.237	.310	.263	56	-5	0	0	0	.947	-3	/O-29	-0.8

■ LEE KING
King, Edward Lee b: 3/28/1894, Waltham, Mass.   d: 9/7/38, Newton Center, Mass.   BR/TR, 5'10", 160 lbs.   Deb: 6/24/16

YEAR	TM/L	G	AB	R	H	2B	3B	HR	RBI	BB	SO	AVG	OBP	SLG	PRO+	BR/A	SB	CS	SBR	FA	FR	G/POS	TPR
1916	Phi-A	42	144	13	27	1	2	0	8	7	15	.188	.230	.222	38	-11	4			1.000	-10	O-22,S-11/3-5,2-2	-2.5
1919	Bos-N	2	1	0	0	0	0	0	0	0	0	.000	.000	.000	-99	-0	0			.000	0	H	0.0
Total	2	44	145	13	27	1	2	0	8	7	15	.186	.229	.221	37	-12	4			1.000	-10	/O-22,S-11,3-5,2-2	-2.5

■ HAL KING
King, Harold b: 2/1/44, Oviedo, Fla.   BL/TR, 6'1", 200 lbs.   Deb: 9/6/67

YEAR	TM/L	G	AB	R	H	2B	3B	HR	RBI	BB	SO	AVG	OBP	SLG	PRO+	BR/A	SB	CS	SBR	FA	FR	G/POS	TPR
1967	Hou-N	15	44	2	11	1	2	0	6	2	9	.250	.283	.364	87	-1	0	0	0	1.000	-2	C-11	-0.3
1968	Hou-N	27	55	4	8	2	1	0	2	7	16	.145	.242	.218	40	-4	0	0	0	.968	-4	C-19	-0.8
1970	Atl-N	89	204	29	53	8	0	11	30	32	41	.260	.366	.461	113	4	1	0	0	.985	-11	C-62	-0.4
1971	Atl-N	86	198	14	41	9	0	5	19	29	45	.207	.320	.328	79	-5	0	0	0	.983	-2	C-60	-0.5
1972	Tex-A	50	122	12	22	5	0	4	12	25	35	.180	.333	.320	99	1	0	0	0	.970	-7	C-38	-0.6
1973	*Cin-N	35	43	5	8	0	0	4	10	6	10	.186	.286	.465	110	0	0	0	0	1.000	-1	/C-9	0.0
1974	Cin-N	20	17	1	3	1	0	0	3	3	4	.176	.300	.235	52	-1	0	0	0	1.000	0	/C-5	-0.1
Total	7	322	683	67	146	26	3	24	82	104	158	.214	.325	.366	93	-6	1	0	0	.982	-26	C-204	-2.7

■ JIM KING
King, James Hubert b: 8/27/32, Elkins, Ark.   BL/TR, 6', 185 lbs.   Deb: 4/17/55

YEAR	TM/L	G	AB	R	H	2B	3B	HR	RBI	BB	SO	AVG	OBP	SLG	PRO+	BR/A	SB	CS	SBR	FA	FR	G/POS	TPR
1955	Chi-N	113	301	43	77	12	3	11	45	24	39	.256	.315	.425	95	-3	2	1	0	.990	5	O-93	-0.1
1956	Chi-N	118	317	32	79	13	2	15	54	30	40	.249	.316	.445	103	1	1	2	-1	.990	14	O-82	1.0
1957	StL-N	22	35	1	11	0	0	0	2	4	2	.314	.385	.314	89	-0	0	1	-1	1.000	-2	/O-8	-0.3
1958	SF-N	34	56	8	12	2	1	2	8	10	8	.214	.343	.393	96	-0	0	1	-1	1.000	-2	/O-15	-0.3
1961	Was-A	110	263	44	71	12	1	11	46	38	45	.270	.366	.449	118	7	2	1	0	.980	-6	O-91/C-1	-0.2
1962	Was-A	132	333	39	81	15	0	11	35	55	37	.243	.355	.387	101	2	4	2	0	.979	2	*O-101	-0.1
1963	Was-A	136	459	61	106	16	5	24	62	45	43	.231	.301	.444	106	2	3	0	1	.987	1	*O-123	-0.2
1964	Was-A	134	415	46	100	15	1	18	56	55	65	.241	.337	.412	108	5	3	1	0	.973	8	*O-121	0.8
1965	Was-A	120	258	46	55	10	2	14	49	44	50	.213	.339	.430	119	7	1	0	0	.993	-2	O-88	0.3
1966	Was-A	117	310	41	77	14	2	10	30	38	41	.248	.330	.403	111	4	4	0	1	.987	0	O-31/C-1	0.3
1967	Was-A	47	100	10	21	2	1	2	12	15	13	.210	.331	.300	91	-1	1	1	0	.962	-3	O-12	-1.0
	Chi-A	23	50	2	6	1	0	0	2	4	16	.120	.185	.140	-3	0	0	0	0	1.000	-0	/O-1	-0.3
	Cle-A	19	21	2	3	0	0	0	1	2	4	.143	.182	.143	-3	-3	0	0	0	1.000	-0	/O-1	-0.3
	Yr	89	171	14	30	3	2	1	14	20	31	.175	.273	.234	53	-10	1	1	0	.971	-5	O-44/C-1	-1.8
Total	11	1125	2918	374	699	112	19	117	401	363	401	.240	.328	.411	104	15	23	8	2	.984	13	O-851/C-2	-0.6

■ JEFF KING
King, Jeffrey Wayne b: 12/26/64, Marion, Ind.   BR/TR, 6'1", 175 lbs.   Deb: 6/2/89

YEAR	TM/L	G	AB	R	H	2B	3B	HR	RBI	BB	SO	AVG	OBP	SLG	PRO+	BR/A	SB	CS	SBR	FA	FR	G/POS	TPR
1989	Pit-N	75	215	31	42	13	3	5	19	20	34	.195	.270	.353	80	-6	4	2	0	.995	-2	1-46,3-13/2-7,S-1	-1.2
1990	*Pit-N	127	371	46	91	17	1	14	53	21	50	.245	.288	.410	93	-5	3	3	-1	.938	16	*3-115/1-1	1.1
1991	Pit-N	33	109	16	26	1	1	4	18	14	15	.239	.331	.376	100	0	3	1	0	.975	1	3-33	0.1
1992	*Pit-N	130	480	56	111	21	2	14	65	27	56	.231	.275	.371	82	-13	4	6	-2	.953	-4	3-73,1-32,2-32/SO	-2.2
1993	Pit-N	158	611	82	180	35	3	9	98	59	54	.295	.361	.406	105	5	8	6	-1	.964	21	*3-156/2-2,S-2	2.5
1994	Pit-N	94	339	36	89	23	0	5	42	30	38	.263	.322	.375	80	-10	3	0	0	.955	11	3-91/2-1	0.1
1995	Pit-N	122	445	61	118	27	2	18	87	55	63	.265	.347	.456	108	5	7	4	-0	.942	-1	3-84,1-35/2-8,S-2	0.0
1996	Pit-N	155	591	91	160	36	4	30	111	70	95	.271	.350	.497	117	13	15	1	4	.997	-2	1-92,2-71,3-17	1.1
Total	8	894	3161	419	817	173	16	99	493	296	405	.258	.324	.417	99	-10	47	25	4	.984	39	3-582,1-206,2/SO	1.5

■ LEE KING
King, Lee b: 12/26/1892, Hundred, W.Va.   d: 9/16/67, Shinnston, W.Va.   BR/TR, 5'8", 160 lbs.   Deb: 9/20/16

YEAR	TM/L	G	AB	R	H	2B	3B	HR	RBI	BB	SO	AVG	OBP	SLG	PRO+	BR/A	SB	CS	SBR	FA	FR	G/POS	TPR
1916	Pit-N	8	18	0	2	0	0	0	0	0	7	.111	.111	.111	-31	-3	0			.714	-1	/O-8	-0.5
1917	Pit-N	111	381	32	95	14	5	1	35	15	58	.249	.281	.320	81	-9	8			.968	9	*O-102	-0.6
1918	Pit-N	36	112	9	26	3	2	1	11	11	15	.232	.301	.321	87	-2	0			.909	8	O-36	-1.3
1919	NY-N	21	20	5	2	1	0	0	1	1	6	.100	.143	.150	-12	-3	0			.667	-3	/O-7	-0.6
1920	NY-N	93	261	32	72	11	4	7	42	21	38	.276	.335	.429	120	6	3	7	-3	.951	-11	O-84	-1.4
1921	NY-N	39	94	17	21	4	2	0	7	13	6	.223	.324	.309	68	-4	0	0	-0	.921	-5	O-35/1-1	-1.2
	Phi-N	64	216	25	58	19	4	4	32	8	37	.269	.298	.449	88	-5	1	4	-2	.911	-2	O-57	-1.3
	Yr	103	310	42	79	23	6	4	39	21	43	.255	.306	.406	81	-8	1	6	-3	.914	-7	O-92/1-1	-2.5
1922	Phi-N	19	53	8	12	5	1	2	13	8	6	.226	.328	.472	95	-1	0	0	-0	1.000	0	/1-5,O-5	-0.3
	*NY-N	20	34	6	6	3	0	0	2	5	2	.176	.282	.265	41	-3	1	0	0	.961	-2	/O-20/1-5	-0.5
	Yr	39	87	14	18	8	1	2	15	13	8	.207	.310	.391	76	-3	1	0	0	.946	-2	/O-15	-0.2
Total	7	411	1189	134	294	60	18	15	144	82	175	.247	.299	.366	87	-22	16	13		.940	-21	O-349/1-6	-7.4

■ LYNN KING
King, Lynn Paul "Dig" b: 11/28/07, Villisca, Iowa   d: 5/11/72, Atlantic, Iowa   BL/TR, 5'9", 165 lbs.   Deb: 9/21/35

YEAR	TM/L	G	AB	R	H	2B	3B	HR	RBI	BB	SO	AVG	OBP	SLG	PRO+	BR/A	SB	CS	SBR	FA	FR	G/POS	TPR
1935	StL-N	8	22	6	4	0	0	0	2	1	1	.182	.308	.182	34	-2	2			1.000	2	/O-6	0.0
1936	StL-N	78	100	12	19	2	1	0	10	9	14	.190	.257	.230	32	-9	2			.984	-4	/O-34	-1.4
1939	StL-N	89	85	10	20	2	0	0	11	15	3	.235	.350	.259	62	-4	2			.982	-10	/O-44	-1.4
Total	3	175	207	28	43	4	1	0	23	28	18	.208	.302	.237	45	-15	6			.986	-12	/O-84	-2.8

■ MART KING
King, Marshal Ney b: 12/1849, Troy, N.Y.   d: 10/19/11, Troy, N.Y.   TR , 5'9.5", 176 lbs.   Deb: 5/8/1871

YEAR	TM/L	G	AB	R	H	2B	3B	HR	RBI	BB	SO	AVG	OBP	SLG	PRO+	BR/A	SB	CS	SBR	FA	FR	G/POS	TPR
1871	Chi-n	20	101	23	21	3	0	2	16	8	1	.208	.266	.277	51	-8	5	0	2	.786	-3	O-11/C-9,S-3,3-1	-0.6
1872	Tro-n	3	11	0	0	0	0	0	1	0	0	.000	.000	.000	-99	-2	0	0	0	.857	-0	/O-3	-0.2
Total	2 n	23	112	23	21	3	0	2	17	8	1	.188	.242	.250	39	-10	5	0	2	.810	-3	/O-14,C-9,S-3,3-1	-0.8

■ SAM KING
King, Samuel Warren b: 5/17/1852, Peabody, Mass.   d: 8/11/22, Peabody, Mass.   TL, 6', Deb: 5/1/1884

YEAR	TM/L	G	AB	R	H	2B	3B	HR	RBI	BB	SO	AVG	OBP	SLG	PRO+	BR/A	SB	CS	SBR	FA	FR	G/POS	TPR
1884	Was-a	12	45	3	8	2	0	0		1		.178	.213	.222	48	-2				.912	-1	1-12		-0.5

YEAR	TM/L	G	AB	R	H	2B	3B	HR	RBI	BB	SO	AVG	OBP	SLG	PRO+	BR/A	SB	CS	SBR	FA	FR	G/POS	TPR

■ STEVE KING   King, Stephen F.   b: 1842, Troy, N.Y.   d: 7/8/1895, Troy, N.Y.   5'9", 175 lbs.   Deb: 5/9/1871

1871	Tro-n	29	144	45	57	10	6	0	34	1	1	.396	.400	.549	167	12	3	3	-1	.833	3	*O-29	0.9
1872	Tro-n	25	128	33	39	8	0	0	21	1	2	.305	.310	.367	106	1	1	1	-0	.776	1	O-25	0.1
Total	2 n	54	272	78	96	18	6	0	55	2	3	.353	.358	.463	139	12	4	4	-1	.807	4	/O-54	1.0

■ WES KINGDON   Kingdon, Westcott William   b: 7/4/1900, Los Angeles, Cal.   d: 4/19/75, Capistrano, Cal.   BR/TR, 5'8", 148 lbs.   Deb: 6/12/32

| 1932 | Was-A | 18 | 34 | 10 | 11 | 3 | 1 | 0 | 3 | 5 | 2 | .324 | .410 | .471 | 129 | 2 | 0 | 0 | 0 | .929 | -2 | /3-8,S-4 | 0.1 |

■ MIKE KINGERY   Kingery, Michael Scott   b: 3/29/61, St.James, Minn.   BL/TL, 6', 180 lbs.   Deb: 7/7/86

1986	KC-A	62	209	25	54	8	5	3	14	12	30	.258	.299	.388	83	-5	7	3	0	.973	-3	O-59	-1.0
1987	Sea-A	120	354	38	99	25	4	9	52	27	43	.280	.334	.449	100	-0	7	9	-3	.992	10	*O-114/D-4	0.3
1988	Sea-A	57	123	21	25	6	0	1	9	19	23	.203	.315	.276	64	-5	3	1	0	.989	-1	O-44,1-10	-0.7
1989	Sea-A	31	76	14	17	3	0	2	6	7	14	.224	.289	.342	75	-3	1	1	-0	1.000	1	O-23	-0.1
1990	SF-N	105	207	24	61	7	1	0	24	12	19	.295	.336	.338	89	-3	6	1	1	.978	-12	O-95	-1.5
1991	SF-N	91	110	13	20	2	2	0	8	15	21	.182	.280	.236	48	-7	1	0	0	.975	-7	O-38/1-6	-1.5
1992	Oak-A	12	28	3	3	0	0	0	1	1	3	.107	.138	.107	-32	-5	0	0	0	1.000	0	O-10	-0.8
1994	Col-N	105	301	56	105	27	8	4	41	30	26	.349	.411	.532	123	10	5	7	-3	.979	-5	O-98/1-1	0.1
1995	*Col-N	119	350	66	94	18	4	8	37	45	40	.269	.352	.411	78	-13	13	5	1	.979	-11	*O-108/1-5	-2.6
1996	Pit-N	117	276	32	68	12	2	3	27	22	33	.246	.307	.377	68	-13	2	1	0	.985	-8	O-83	-2.3
Total	10	819	2034	292	546	108	26	30	219	191	248	.268	.333	.391	86	-45	45	28	-3	.984	-37	O-672/1-22,D-4	-10.1

■ DAVE KINGMAN   Kingman, David Arthur   b: 12/21/48, Pendleton, Ore.   BR/TR, 6'6", 210 lbs.   Deb: 7/30/71

1971	*SF-N	41	115	17	32	10	2	6	24	9	35	.278	.336	.557	151	7	5	0	2	.981	-4	1-20,O-14	0.3
1972	SF-N	135	472	65	106	17	4	29	83	51	140	.225	.306	.462	114	7	16	6	1	.932	3	3-59,1-56,O-22	0.6
1973	SF-N	112	305	54	62	10	1	24	55	41	122	.203	.302	.479	109	2	8	5	-1	.910	3	3-60,1-46/P-2	0.3
1974	SF-N	121	350	41	78	18	2	18	55	37	125	.223	.303	.440	101	-1	8	8	-2	.983	2	1-91,3-21/O-2	-0.7
1975	NY-N	134	502	65	116	22	1	36	88	34	153	.231	.285	.494	119	7	7	5	-1	.958	4	O-71,1-58,3-12	0.4
1976	NY-N★	123	474	70	113	14	1	37	86	28	135	.238	.288	.506	130	13	7	4	-0	.959	3	*O-111,1-16	1.2
1977	NY-N	58	211	22	44	7	0	9	28	13	66	.209	.264	.370	71	-10	2	3	-0	.974	-2	O-45,1-17	-1.5
	SD-N	56	168	16	40	9	0	11	39	12	48	.238	.297	.488	119	5	3	2	-1	.964	2	O-28,1-13/3-2	0.2
	Yr	114	379	38	84	16	0	20	67	25	114	.222	.279	.422	92	-7	5	5	-2	.970	-0	O-73,1-30/3-2	-1.3
	Cal-A	10	36	4	7	2	0	2	4	1	16	.194	.237	.417	77	-1	0	0	0	.974	-1	/1-8,O-2	-0.2
	NY-A	8	24	5	6	2	0	4	7	2	13	.250	.333	.833	208	3	0	1	-1	1.000	0	/D-6	0.2
	Yr	18	60	9	13	4	0	6	11	3	29	.217	.277	.583	131	2	0	1	-1	.974	-1	/1-8,H-6,O-2	0.0
1978	Chi-N	119	395	65	105	17	4	28	79	39	111	.266	.341	.542	128	13	3	4	-2	.978	0	*O-100/1-6	0.8
1979	Chi-N†	145	532	97	153	19	5	**48**	115	45	131	.288	.348	**.613**	143	28	4	5	0	.954	5	*O-139	2.8
1980	Chi-N★	81	255	31	71	8	0	18	57	21	44	.278	.333	.522	126	8	2	2	-1	.941	1	O-61/1-2	0.6
1981	NY-N	100	353	40	78	11	3	22	59	55	105	.221	.328	.456	122	10	6	0	2	.974	-6	1-56,O-48	0.2
1982	NY-N	149	535	80	109	9	1	**37**	99	59	156	.204	.288	.432	99	-3	4	0	1	.986	-14	*1-143	-2.4
1983	NY-N	100	248	25	49	7	0	13	29	22	57	.198	.266	.383	79	-8	2	1	0	.994	-5	1-50/O-5	-1.7
1984	Oak-A	147	549	68	147	23	1	35	118	44	119	.268	.329	.505	136	24	2	1	0	1.000	-2	*D-139/1-9	1.8
1985	Oak-A	158	592	66	141	16	0	30	91	62	114	.238	.313	.417	105	3	3	2	-0	1.000	-1	*D-149/1-9	-0.2
1986	Oak-A	144	561	70	118	19	0	35	94	33	126	.210	.258	.431	90	-11	3	2	1	.895	-1	*D-140/1-3	-1.6
Total	16	1941	6677	901	1575	240	25	442	1210	608	1816	.236	.305	.478	115	94	85	49	-4	.957	-11	O-648,1-603,D3/P	1.1

■ HARRY KINGMAN   Kingman, Henry Lees   b: 4/3/1892, Tientsin, China   d: 12/27/82, Oakland, Cal.   BL/TL, 6'1.5", 165 lbs.   Deb: 7/1/14

| 1914 | NY-A | 4 | 3 | 0 | 0 | 0 | 0 | 0 | 0 | 1 | 2 | .000 | .250 | .000 | -24 | -0 | 0 | | | 1.000 | -0 | /1-1 | -0.1 |

■ GENE KINGSALE   Kingsale, Eugene Humphrey   b: 8/20/76, Solito, Aruba   BB/TR, 6'3", 170 lbs.   Deb: 9/3/96

| 1996 | Bal-A | 3 | 0 | 0 | 0 | 0 | 0 | 0 | 0 | 0 | 0 | — | — | — | — | | 0 | 0 | 0 | 1.000 | -1 | /O-2 | -0.1 |

■ WALT KINLOCK   Kinlock, Walter   b: 1878, St.Joseph, Mo.   Deb: 8/1/1895

| 1895 | StL-N | 1 | 3 | 0 | 1 | 0 | 0 | 0 | 0 | 0 | 0 | .333 | .333 | .333 | 73 | -0 | 0 | | | 1.000 | -1 | /3-1 | 0.0 |

■ BOB KINSELLA   Kinsella, Robert Francis "Red"   b: 1/5/1899, Springfield, Ill.   d: 12/30/51, Los Angeles, Cal.   BL/TR, 5'9.5", 165 lbs.   Deb: 9/20/19

1919	NY-N	3	9	1	2	0	0	0	0	0	3	.222	.222	.222	34	-1	1			.500	-2	/O-3	-0.3
1920	NY-N	1	3	0	1	0	0	0	1	0	2	.333	.333	.333	93	-0	0	0	0	.500	-1	/O-1	-0.1
Total	2	4	12	1	3	0	0	0	1	0	5	.250	.250	.250	49	-1	1	0		.500	-2	/O-4	-0.4

■ KINSLER   Kinsler   b: Staten Island, N.Y.   Deb: 6/8/1893

| 1893 | NY-N | 1 | 3 | 1 | 0 | 0 | 0 | 0 | 0 | 1 | 1 | .000 | .250 | .000 | -31 | -1 | 0 | | | 1.000 | -1 | /O-1 | -0.1 |

■ TOM KINSLOW   Kinslow, Thomas F.   b: 1/12/1866, Washington, D.C.   d: 2/22/01, Washington, D.C.   BR/TR, 5'10", 160 lbs.   Deb: 6/4/1886

1886	Was-N	3	8	1	2	0	0	0	1	0	1	.250	.250	.250	56	-0	0			1.000	-0	/C-3	0.0
1887	NY-a	2	6	0	0	0	0	0	0	0	0	.000	.000	.000	-99	-2	0			1.000	-0	/C-2	-0.1
1890	Bro-P	64	242	30	64	11	6	4	46	10	22	.264	.299	.409	83	-8	2			.909	11	C-64	0.7
1891	Bro-N	61	228	22	54	6	0	0	33	9	22	.237	.266	.263	55	-13	3			.922	-9	C-61	-1.5
1892	Bro-N	66	246	37	75	6	11	2	40	13	16	.305	.342	.443	142	11	4			.933	5	C-66	1.9
1893	Bro-N	78	312	38	76	8	4	4	45	11	13	.244	.272	.333	63	-18	4			.932	-2	C-76/O-2	-1.1
1894	Bro-N	62	223	39	68	5	6	2	41	20	11	.305	.362	.408	92	-3	4			.907	-9	C-61/1-1	-0.4
1895	Pit-N	19	62	10	14	2	0	0	5	2	2	.226	.250	.258	33	-6	1			.962	-2	C-18	-0.5
1896	Lou-N	8	25	4	7	0	1	0	7	1	5	.280	.308	.360	79	-1	0			.810	-2	/C-5,1-1	-0.2
1898	Was-N	3	9	0	1	0	0	0	1	0	0	.111	.111	.111	-36	-2	0			.800	-1	/C-3,1-1	-0.2
	StL-N	14	53	5	15	2	1	0	4	1	1	.283	.309	.358	89	-1	0			.925	1	C-14	0.1
	Yr	17	62	5	16	2	1	0	4	1	1	.258	.281	.323	72	-3	0			.909	-0	C-17/1-1	-0.1
Total	10	380	1414	186	376	40	29	12	222	67	92	.266	.301	.361	81	-43	18			.923	-7	C-373/1-3,O-2	-1.3

■ WALT KINZIE   Kinzie, Walter Harris   b: 3/1858, Chicago, Ill.   d: 11/5/09,   BR   5'10.5", 161 lbs.   Deb: 7/17/1882

1882	Det-N	13	53	5	5	1	0	0	2	0		.094	.094	.132	-28	-7				.852	-4	S-13	-1.0
1884	Chi-N	19	82	4	13	3	0	2	8	0	13	.159	.159	.268	29	-7				.831	-3	S-17/3-2	-0.8
	StL-a	2	9	0	1	0	0	0	0	0		.111	.111	.111	-26	-1				.727	-3	/2-2	-0.4
Total	2	34	144	9	19	3	1	2	10	0	21	.132	.132	.208	6	-15				.840	-9	/S-30,2-2,3-2	-2.2

■ ED KIPPERT   Kippert, Edward August "Kickapoo"   b: 1/3/1880, Detroit, Mich.   d: 6/3/60, Detroit, Mich.   BR/TR, 5'10.5", 180 lbs.   Deb: 4/14/14

| 1914 | Cin-N | 2 | 2 | 0 | 0 | 0 | 0 | 0 | 0 | 0 | 0 | .000 | .000 | .000 | -97 | -0 | 0 | | | 1.000 | -1 | /O-2 | -0.1 |

■ JIM KIRBY   Kirby, James Herschel   b: 5/5/23, Nashville, Tenn.   BR/TR, 5'11", 175 lbs.   Deb: 5/1/49

| 1949 | Chi-N | 3 | 2 | 0 | 1 | 0 | 0 | 0 | 0 | 0 | 0 | .500 | .500 | .500 | 174 | 0 | 0 | | | .000 | 0 | H | 0.0 |

■ LA RUE KIRBY   Kirby, La Rue   b: 12/30/1889, Eureka, Mich.   d: 6/10/61, Lansing, Mich.   BB/TR, 6', 185 lbs.   Deb: 8/7/12

1912	NY-N	3	5	1	1	0	0	0	0	0		.200	.200	.400	60	-0	0			1.000	0	/P-3	0.0
1914	StL-F	52	195	21	48	6	3	2	18	14	30	.246	.303	.338	71	-11	5			.973	2	O-50	-1.2
1915	StL-F	61	178	15	38	7	2	0	16	17	31	.213	.282	.275	54	-13	3			.969	-3	O-52/P-1	-2.0
Total	3	116	378	37	87	14	5	2	34	31	61	.230	.292	.310	63	-25	8			.971	-1	O-102/P-4	-3.2

■ WAYNE KIRBY   Kirby, Wayne Leonard   b: 1/22/64, Williamsburg, Va.   BL/TR, 5'10", 185 lbs.   Deb: 9/12/91

1991	Cle-A	21	43	4	9	2	0	0	2	2	6	.209	.244	.256	38	-4	1	2	-1	1.000	-1	O-21	-0.6
1992	Cle-A	21	18	9	3	1	0	1	1	3	2	.167	.286	.389	89	-0	0	3	-2	1.000	-0	/O-2,D-4	-0.2
1993	Cle-A	131	458	71	123	19	5	6	60	37	58	.269	.327	.371	88	-8	17	5	2	.983	13	*O-123/D-5	0.4
1994	Cle-A	78	191	33	56	6	0	5	23	13	30	.293	.341	.403	91	-3	11	3	1	.959	-11	O-68/D-2	-1.3
1995	*Cle-A	101	188	29	39	10	2	1	14	13	32	.207	.262	.298	45	-16	10	3	1	.990	-10	O-68/D-7	-2.4
1996	Cle-A	27	16	3	4	1	0	0	1	2	2	.250	.333	.313	65	-1	0	1	-1	1.000	-6	O-18	-0.7

YEAR	TM/L	G	AB	R	H	2B	3B	HR	RBI	BB	SO	AVG	OBP	SLG	PRO+	BR/A	SB	CS	SBR	FA	FR	G/POS	TPR
	*LA-N	65	188	23	51	10	1	1	14	11	17	.271	.335	.351	89	-3	4	2	0	.969	-3	O-53	-0.7
Total	6	444	1102	172	285	49	8	14	115	87	147	.259	.316	.356	79	-34	43	20	1	.980	-18	O-353/D-18	-5.5

■ TOM KIRK
Kirk, Thomas Daniel b: 9/27/27, Philadelphia, Pa. d: 8/1/74, Philadelphia, Pa. BL/TL, 5'10.5", 182 lbs. Deb: 6/24/47

YEAR	TM/L	G	AB	R	H	2B	3B	HR	RBI	BB	SO	AVG	OBP	SLG	PRO+	BR/A	SB	CS	SBR	FA	FR	G/POS	TPR
1947	Phi-A	1	1	0	0	0	0	0	0	0	0	.000	.000	.000	-98	-0	0	0	0	.000	0	H	0.0

■ JAY KIRKE
Kirke, Judson Fabian b: 6/16/1888, Fleischmanns, N.Y d: 8/31/68, New Orleans, La. BL/TR, 6', 195 lbs. Deb: 9/28/10

YEAR	TM/L	G	AB	R	H	2B	3B	HR	RBI	BB	SO	AVG	OBP	SLG	PRO+	BR/A	SB	CS	SBR	FA	FR	G/POS	TPR
1910	Det-A	8	25	3	5	1	0	0	3	1		.200	.231	.240	44	-2	1			.917	-3	/2-7,O-1	-0.5
1911	Bos-N	20	89	9	32	5	5	0	12	2	6	.360	.380	.528	142	4	3			.929	-1	O-14/1-3,2-1,S-1,3	0.3
1912	Bos-N	103	359	53	115	11	4	4	62	9	46	.320	.339	.407	102	-1	7			.903	-2	O-72,3-14/S-2,1-1	-0.5
1913	Bos-N	18	38	3	9	2	0	0	3	1	6	.237	.293	.289	65	-2	0			.923	2	O-13	0.0
1914	Cle-A	67	242	18	66	10	2	1	25	7	30	.273	.296	.343	89	-4	5	10	-5	.974	-0	O-42,1-18	-1.2
1915	Cle-A	87	339	35	105	19	2	2	40	14	21	.310	.346	.395	120	6	5	6	-2	.986	-1	1-87	0.1
1918	NY-N	17	56	1	14	1	0	0	3	1	3	.250	.263	.268	63	-3	0			.978	1	1-16	-0.3
Total	7	320	1148	122	346	49	13	7	148	35	112	.301	.328	.385	103	-0	21	16		.927	-4	O-142,1-125/32S	-2.1

■ WILLIE KIRKLAND
Kirkland, Willie Charles b: 2/17/34, Siluria, Ala. BL/TR, 6'1", 206 lbs. Deb: 4/15/58

YEAR	TM/L	G	AB	R	H	2B	3B	HR	RBI	BB	SO	AVG	OBP	SLG	PRO+	BR/A	SB	CS	SBR	FA	FR	G/POS	TPR
1958	SF-N	122	418	48	108	25	6	14	56	43	69	.258	.335	.447	107	4	3	2	-0	.961	-0	*O-115	-0.3
1959	SF-N	126	463	64	126	22	3	22	68	42	84	.272	.337	.475	116	9	5	3	-0	.969	.1	*O-117	0.4
1960	SF-N	146	515	59	130	21	10	21	65	44	86	.252	.316	.454	115	8	12	7	-1	.978	4	*O-143	0.4
1961	Cle-A	146	525	84	136	22	5	27	95	48	77	.259	.322	.474	113	7	7	0	2	.974	7	*O-138	1.0
1962	Cle-A	137	419	56	84	9	1	21	72	43	62	.200	.275	.377	76	-16	9	1	2	.972	5	*O-125	-2.0
1963	Cle-A	127	427	51	98	13	2	15	47	45	99	.230	.304	.375	90	-4	8	2	1	.984	7	*O-112	-1.0
1964	Bal-A	66	150	14	30	5	0	3	22	17	26	.200	.286	.293	62	-8	5	2	-0	.989	-0	O-58	-1.0
	Was-A	32	102	8	22	6	0	5	13	6	30	.216	.259	.422	86	-2	3	0	-0	.907	-3	O-27	-0.7
	Yr	98	252	22	52	11	0	8	35	23	56	.206	.275	.345	72	-10	3	2	-0	.964	-3	O-85	-1.7
1965	Was-A	123	312	38	72	9	1	14	54	19	65	.231	.275	.401	91	-5	3	2	-0	.987	-6	O-92	-1.6
1966	Was-A	124	163	21	31	2	1	6	17	16	50	.190	.263	.325	68	-7	2	0	1	.983	-12	O-68	-2.1
Total	9	1149	3494	443	837	134	29	148	509	323	648	.240	.307	.422	99	-15	52	19	4	.974	-2	O-995	-6.3

■ ED KIRKPATRICK
Kirkpatrick, Edgar Leon b: 10/8/44, Spokane, Wash. BL/TR, 5'11.5", 195 lbs. Deb: 9/13/62

YEAR	TM/L	G	AB	R	H	2B	3B	HR	RBI	BB	SO	AVG	OBP	SLG	PRO+	BR/A	SB	CS	SBR	FA	FR	G/POS	TPR
1962	LA-A	3	6	0	0	0	0	0	0	2	2	.000	.000	.000	-99	-2	0	0	0	1.000	1	/C-1	-0.1
1963	LA-A	34	77	4	15	5	0	2	7	6	19	.195	.262	.338	71	-3	1	0	0	.986	-0	C-14,O-10	-0.3
1964	LA-A	75	219	20	53	13	3	2	22	23	30	.242	.320	.356	97	-1	2	2	-1	.969	-2	O-63	-0.7
1965	Cal-A	19	73	8	19	5	0	3	8	3	9	.260	.289	.452	110	1	1	2	-1	.969	1	O-19	-0.1
1966	Cal-A	117	312	31	60	7	4	9	44	51	67	.192	.315	.327	87	-4	7	4	-0	.994	-6	*O-102/1-3	-1.6
1967	Cal-A	3	8	0	0	0	0	0	0	0	2	.000	.000	.000	-99	-2	0	0	0	1.000	-2	/C-2,O-1	-0.5
1968	Cal-A	89	161	23	37	4	0	1	15	25	32	.230	.337	.273	90	-1	1	3	-2	.982	5	O-45/C-4,1-2	-1.1
1969	KC-A	120	315	40	81	11	4	14	49	43	42	.257	.352	.451	122	9	3	5	-2	.995	8	O-82/C-8,1-2,3-2,2	1.2
1970	KC-A	134	424	59	97	17	2	18	62	55	65	.229	.319	.406	98	-1	4	4	-1	.978	-8	C-89,O-19,1-16	-0.9
1971	KC-A	120	365	46	80	12	1	9	46	48	60	.219	.313	.332	83	-4	3	4	-2	.992	-1	O-61,C-59	-1.1
1972	KC-A	113	364	43	100	15	1	9	43	51	50	.275	.368	.396	128	14	3	5	-2	.991	-5	*C-108/1-1	1.3
1973	KC-A	126	429	61	113	24	3	6	45	46	48	.263	.336	.375	93	-4	3	7	-3	.990	-5	*O-108,C-14/D-8	-1.7
1974	*Pit-N	116	271	32	67	9	0	6	38	51	30	.247	.370	.347	105	4	1	2	-1	.993	-4	1-59,O-14/C-6	-0.5
1975	*Pit-N	89	144	15	34	5	0	5	16	18	22	.236	.321	.375	93	-1	1	0	0	1.000	1	1-28,O-14	-0.3
1976	Pit-N	83	146	14	34	9	1	0	16	14	15	.233	.300	.295	69	-6	1	0	0	.990	-1	1-25/O-9,3-1	-0.8
1977	Pit-N	21	28	5	4	2	0	1	4	8	6	.143	.333	.321	75	-1	1	0	0	1.000	1	/O-6,1-3,C-1,D-5	-0.4
	Tex-A	20	48	2	9	1	0	0	3	4	11	.188	.250	.208	26	-5	2	0	1	.973	-2	O-22/3-1,D-3	-0.4
	Mil-A	29	77	8	21	4	0	0	6	10	8	.273	.364	.325	89	-1	0	1	-1	.980	-2	O-28/D-8,1-3,C-1,3	-0.8
	Yr	49	125	10	30	5	0	0	9	14	19	.240	.321	.280	65	-6	2	1	0	.989	-5	O-50/D-8,1-3,C-1,3	-0.8
Total	16	1311	3467	411	824	143	18	85	424	456	518	.238	.330	.363	97	-12	34	39	-13	.989	-32	O-577,C-306,1/D32	-8.2

■ ENOS KIRKPATRICK
Kirkpatrick, Enos Claire b: 12/8/1885, Pittsburgh, Pa. d: 4/14/64, Pittsburgh, Pa. BR/TR, 5'10", 175 lbs. Deb: 8/24/12

YEAR	TM/L	G	AB	R	H	2B	3B	HR	RBI	BB	SO	AVG	OBP	SLG	PRO+	BR/A	SB	CS	SBR	FA	FR	G/POS	TPR
1912	Bro-N	32	94	13	18	1	1	0	6	9	15	.191	.269	.223	37	-8	5			.968	6	3-29/S-3	-0.2
1913	Bro-N	48	89	13	22	4	1	1	3	18	18	.247	.287	.348	79	-3	5			.897	-1	S-10/1-8,2-6,3-4	-0.4
1914	Bal-F	55	174	22	44	7	2	2	16	18	30	.253	.330	.351	83	-7	10			.932	-3	3-36,S-11/O-3,1-1	-1.0
1915	Bal-F	68	171	22	41	8	2	0	19	24	15	.240	.337	.310	80	-6	12			.911	-3	3-28,2-21/1-5,S-5	-0.9
Total	4	203	528	70	125	20	6	3	46	54	78	.237	.315	.314	74	-24	32			.936	-2	/3-97,S-29,2-27,10	-2.5

■ JOE KIRRENE
Kirrene, Joseph John b: 10/4/31, San Francisco, Cal. BR/TR, 6'2", 195 lbs. Deb: 10/1/50

YEAR	TM/L	G	AB	R	H	2B	3B	HR	RBI	BB	SO	AVG	OBP	SLG	PRO+	BR/A	SB	CS	SBR	FA	FR	G/POS	TPR
1950	Chi-A	1	4	0	1	0	0	0	0	1		.250	.250	.250	29	-0	0	0	0	1.000	-1	/3-1	-0.1
1954	Chi-A	9	23	4	7	1	0	0	4	5	2	.304	.448	.348	116	1	1	0	0	.947	-2	/3-9	-0.1
Total	2	10	27	4	8	1	0	0	4	5	3	.296	.424	.333	105	1	1	0	0	.952	-3	/3-10	-0.2

■ ERNIE KISH
Kish, Ernest Alexander b: 2/6/18, Washington, D.C. d: 12/21/93, Kirtland, Ohio BL/TR, 5'9.5", 170 lbs. Deb: 7/29/45

YEAR	TM/L	G	AB	R	H	2B	3B	HR	RBI	BB	SO	AVG	OBP	SLG	PRO+	BR/A	SB	CS	SBR	FA	FR	G/POS	TPR
1945	Phi-A	43	110	10	27	5	1	0	10	9	9	.245	.320	.309	83	-2	0	3	-2	.932	-4	O-30	-1.0

■ BILL KISSINGER
Kissinger, William Francis "Shang" b: 8/15/1871, Dayton, Ky. d: 4/20/29, Cincinnati, Ohio BR/TR, 185 lbs. Deb: 5/30/1895

YEAR	TM/L	G	AB	R	H	2B	3B	HR	RBI	BB	SO	AVG	OBP	SLG	PRO+	BR/A	SB	CS	SBR	FA	FR	G/POS	TPR
1895	Bal-N	2	5	1	1	0	0	0	0	0	1	.200	.200	.200	3	-1	0			1.000	-0	/P-2	0.0
	StL-N	33	97	8	24	6	1	0	8	0	11	.247	.247	.330	49	-8	1			.975	-5	P-24/S-4,O-4,3-1	-0.6
	Yr	35	102	9	25	6	1	0	8	0	12	.245	.245	.324	46	-9	1			**.976**	-5	P-26/S-4,O-4,3-1	-0.6
1896	StL-N	23	73	8	22	4	0	0	12	0	4	.301	.301	.356	76	-3	0			.906	0	P-20/O-3,3-1	-0.2
1897	StL-N	14	39	7	13	3	2	0	6	3		.333	.381	.513	137	2	0			.786	-4	/O-7,P-7	-0.1
Total	3	72	214	24	60	13	3	0	26	3	16	.280	.290	.369	73	-9	1			.935	-6	/P-53,O-14,S-4,3-2	-0.9

■ CHRIS KITSOS
Kitsos, Christopher Anestos b: 2/11/28, New York, N.Y. BB/TR, 5'9", 165 lbs. Deb: 4/21/54

YEAR	TM/L	G	AB	R	H	2B	3B	HR	RBI	BB	SO	AVG	OBP	SLG	PRO+	BR/A	SB	CS	SBR	FA	FR	G/POS	TPR
1954	Chi-N	1	0	0	0	0	0	0	0	0		—	—	—		0	0	0	0	1.000	0	/S-1	0.0

■ RON KITTLE
Kittle, Ronald Dale b: 1/5/58, Gary, Indiana BR/TR, 6'4", 220 lbs. Deb: 9/2/82

YEAR	TM/L	G	AB	R	H	2B	3B	HR	RBI	BB	SO	AVG	OBP	SLG	PRO+	BR/A	SB	CS	SBR	FA	FR	G/POS	TPR
1982	Chi-A	20	29	3	7	2	0	1	7	3	12	.241	.313	.414	97	-0	0	0	0	1.000	-2	/O-5,D-3	-0.2
1983	*Chi-A★	145	520	75	132	19	3	35	100	39	150	.254	.316	.504	117	10	8	3	1	.964	-9	*O-139/D-2	-0.3
1984	Chi-A	139	466	67	100	15	0	32	74	49	137	.215	.298	.453	100	-2	3	6	-3	.972	3	*O-124/D-7	-0.5
1985	Chi-A	116	379	51	87	12	0	26	58	31	92	.230	.296	.467	101	-1	1	4	-2	.989	-1	O-57,D-57	-0.8
1986	Chi-A	86	296	34	63	11	0	17	48	28	87	.213	.287	.422	87	-6	2	1	0	1.000	-6	D-62,O-20	-0.6
	NY-A	30	80	9	19	2	0	4	12	7	23	.237	.299	.412	92	-1	2	0	1	1.000	-1	D-24/O-1	-0.1
	Yr	116	376	42	82	13	0	21	60	35	110	.218	.290	.420	89	-7	4	1	1	1.000	-7	D-86,O-21	-0.7
1987	NY-A	59	159	21	44	9	0	12	28	10	36	.277	.324	.535	123	5	0	1	-1	1.000	-5	D-49/O-2	0.3
1988	Cle-A	75	225	31	58	9	0	18	43	16	65	.258	.329	.533	134	9	0	0	0	.000	0	D-63	0.8
1989	Chi-A	51	169	26	51	10	0	11	37	22	42	.302	.383	.556	166	15	0	1	-1	.982	-3	1-27,D-17/O-5	0.8
1990	Chi-A	83	277	29	68	14	0	16	43	24	75	.245	.313	.469	118	5	0	0	0	.987	-4	D-54,1-25	-0.2
	Bal-A	22	61	4	10	2	0	2	3	2	14	.164	.203	.295	39	-5	0	0	0	1.000	-1	D-13/1-5	-0.7
	Yr	105	338	33	78	16	0	18	46	26	91	.231	.293	.438	104	0	0	0	0	.989	-5	D-67,1-30	-0.9
1991	Chi-A	17	47	7	9	0	0	2	7	5	9	.191	.296	.319	72	-2	0	0	0	.982	-1	1-15	-0.4
Total	10	843	2708	356	648	100	3	176	460	236	744	.239	.309	.473	110	28	16	16	-5	.974	-17	O-353,D-351/1-72	-1.9

■ MALACHI KITTRIDGE
Kittridge, Malachi Jeddidah "Jeddidah" b: 10/12/1869, Clinton, Mass. d: 6/23/28, Gary, Ind. BR/TR, 5'7", 170 lbs. Deb: 4/19/1890 M

YEAR	TM/L	G	AB	R	H	2B	3B	HR	RBI	BB	SO	AVG	OBP	SLG	PRO+	BR/A	SB	CS	SBR	FA	FR	G/POS	TPR
1890	Chi-N	96	333	46	67	8	3	3	35	39	53	.201	.287	.270	60	-17	7			.944	2	*C-96	-0.6
1891	Chi-N	79	296	26	62	8	5	2	27	17	28	.209	.252	.291	58	-17	4			.940	-1	C-79	-0.9
1892	Chi-N	69	229	19	41	5	0	0	10	11	27	.179	.217	.201	26	-21	4			.946	15	C-69	-0.1
1893	Chi-N	70	255	32	59	9	5	2	30	17	15	.231	.279	.329	62	-15	3			.939	6	C-70	-0.3
1894	Chi-N	51	168	36	53	8	3	6	25	26	20	.315	.407	.387	88	-3	2			.925	2	C-51	0.3
1895	Chi-N	60	212	30	48	6	3	3	29	16	9	.226	.284	.325	54	-16	6			.976	-2	C-59	-1.0

YEAR	TM/L	G	AB	R	H	2B	3B	HR	RBI	BB	SO	AVG	OBP	SLG	PRO+	BR/A	SB	CS	SBR	FA	FR	G/POS	TPR
1896	Chi-N	65	215	17	48	4	1	1	19	14	14	.223	.274	.265	41	-19	6			.962	1	C-64/P-1	-0.9
1897	Chi-N	79	262	25	53	5	5	1	30	22		.202	.264	.271	40	-24	9			.952	3	C-79	-1.0
1898	Lou-N	86	287	27	70	8	5	1	31	15		.244	.281	.317	73	-11	9			.944	-11	C-86	-1.3
1899	Lou-N	45	129	11	26	2	1	0	12	26		.202	.340	.233	58	-6	3			.974	7	C-43	0.4
	Was-N	44	133	14	20	3	0	0	11	10		.150	.215	.173	7	-17	2			.949	4	C-43	-0.9
	Yr	89	262	25	46	5	1	0	23	36		.176	.280	.202	33	-23	5			.961	11	C-86	-0.5
1901	Bos-N	114	381	24	96	14	0	2	40	32		.252	.312	.304	72	-14	2			**.984**	12	*C-113	1.0
1902	Bos-N	80	255	18	60	7	0	2	30	24		.235	.304	.286	81	-5	4			.981	6	C-72	0.9
1903	Bos-N	32	99	10	21	2	0	0	6	11		.212	.291	.232	52	-6	1			.981	5	C-30	0.2
	Was-A	60	192	8	41	4	1	0	16	10		.214	.252	.245	49	-12	1			.978	-3	C-60	-0.9
1904	Was-A	81	265	11	64	7	0	0	24	8		.242	.266	.268	70	-9	2			.982	4	C-79,M	0.0
1905	Was-A	77	238	16	39	8	0	0	14	15		.164	.213	.197	32	-18	1			.978	4	C-76	-0.7
1906	Was-A	22	68	5	13	0	0	0	3	1		.191	.203	.191	25	-6	0			.946	-2	C-22	-0.7
	Cle-A	5	10	0	1	0	0	0	0	0		.100	.100	.100	-38	-2	0			.938	-1	/C-5	-0.2
	Yr	27	78	5	14	0	0	0	3	1		.179	.190	.179	16	-8	0			.945	-3	C-27	-0.9
Total	16	1215	4027	375	882	108	13	9	390	314	<u>166</u>	.219	.277	.274	56	-236	64			.961	47	*C-1196/P-1	-6.7

■ BOBBY KLAUS

Klaus, Robert Francis b: 12/27/37, Spring Grove, Ill. BR/TR, 5'10", 170 lbs. Deb: 4/21/64 F

YEAR	TM/L	G	AB	R	H	2B	3B	HR	RBI	BB	SO	AVG	OBP	SLG	PRO+	BR/A	SB	CS	SBR	FA	FR	G/POS	TPR
1964	Cin-N	40	93	10	17	5	1	2	6	4	13	.183	.216	.323	48	-7	1	0	0	.972	4	2-18,3-11/S-3	-0.2
	NY-N	56	209	25	51	8	3	2	11	25	30	.244	.325	.340	90	-2	3	4	-2	.986	-4	2-25,3-28/S-5	-0.6
	Yr	96	302	35	68	13	4	4	17	29	43	.225	.293	.334	76	-9	4	4	-1	.981	0	2-43,3-39/S-8	-0.8
1965	NY-N	119	288	30	55	12	0	2	12	45	49	.191	.302	.253	61	-14	1	6	-3	.968	15	2-72,S-28,3-25	0.3
Total	2	215	590	65	123	25	4	6	29	74	92	.208	.298	.295	69	-23	5	10	-5	.973	16	2-115/3-64,S-36	-0.5

■ BILLY KLAUS

Klaus, William Joseph b: 12/9/28, Fox Lake, Ill. BL/TR, 5'10", 165 lbs. Deb: 4/16/52 F

YEAR	TM/L	G	AB	R	H	2B	3B	HR	RBI	BB	SO	AVG	OBP	SLG	PRO+	BR/A	SB	CS	SBR	FA	FR	G/POS	TPR
1952	Bos-N	7	4	3	0	0	0	0	0	1	1	.000	.200	.000	-42	-1	0	0	0	.500	-1	/S-4	-0.2
1953	Mil-N	2	1	0	0	0	0	0	0	1	0	.000	.000	.000	-99	-1	0	0	0	.000	0	H	-0.1
1955	Bos-A	135	541	83	153	26	2	7	60	60	44	.283	.354	.377	89	-8	6	0	2	.955	-7	*S-126/3-8	-0.3
1956	Bos-A	135	520	91	141	29	5	7	59	90	43	.271	.380	.387	92	-5	1	0	0	.945	-4	*3-106,S-26	-0.5
1957	Bos-A	127	477	76	120	18	4	10	42	55	53	.252	.329	.369	85	-9	2	0	1	.961	11	*S-118	1.5
1958	Bos-A	61	88	5	14	4	0	1	5	16	14	.159	.204	.239	20	-10	0	0	0	.883	-6	S-27	-1.6
1959	Bal-A	104	321	33	80	11	0	3	25	51	38	.249	.352	.312	86	-4	2	4	-2	.970	-12	S-59,3-49/2-1	-1.4
1960	Bal-A	46	43	8	9	2	0	1	6	9	9	.209	.346	.326	84	-1	0	0	0	.960	8	2-30,S-12/3-2	0.8
1961	Was-A	91	251	26	57	8	2	1	30	34	34	.227	.314	.359	81	-7	2	2	-1	.961	-5	3-51,S-18/2-1,O-1	-1.0
1962	Phi-N	102	248	30	51	8	2	4	20	29	31	.206	.291	.302	61	-13	1	1	-0	.983	-6	3-53,S-30,2-11	-1.7
1963	Phi-N	11	18	1	1	0	0	0	0	1	4	.056	.105	.056	-53	-4	0	0	0	1.000	-2	/S-5,3-3	-0.6
Total	11	821	2513	357	626	106	15	40	250	331	285	.249	.337	.351	82	-62	14	7	0	.955	-24	S-425,3-272/2-43,O	-5.1

■ OLLIE KLEE

Klee, Ollie Chester "Babe" b: 5/20/1900, Piqua, Ohio d: 2/9/77, Toledo, Ohio BL/TL, 5'9.5", 160 lbs. Deb: 8/10/25

YEAR	TM/L	G	AB	R	H	2B	3B	HR	RBI	BB	SO	AVG	OBP	SLG	PRO+	BR/A	SB	CS	SBR	FA	FR	G/POS	TPR
1925	Cin-N	3	1	0	0	0	0	0	0	0	0	.000	.000	.000	-99	-0	0			.000	-1	/O-1	-0.1

■ CHUCK KLEIN

Klein, Charles Herbert b: 10/7/04, Indianapolis, Ind. d: 3/28/58, Indianapolis, Ind. BL/TR, 6', 185 lbs. Deb: 7/30/28 CH

YEAR	TM/L	G	AB	R	H	2B	3B	HR	RBI	BB	SO	AVG	OBP	SLG	PRO+	BR/A	SB	CS	SBR	FA	FR	G/POS	TPR
1928	Phi-N	64	253	41	91	14	4	11	34	14	22	.360	.396	.577	146	16	0			.978	1	O-63	1.2
1929	Phi-N	149	616	126	219	45	6	**43**	145	54	61	.356	.407	.657	149	44	5			.966	-2	*O-149	2.9
1930	Phi-N	156	648	**158**	250	**59**	8	40	170	54	50	.386	.436	.687	155	55	4			.960	23	*O-156	**5.8**
1931	Phi-N	148	594	**121**	200	34	10	**31**	121	59	49	.337	.398	**.584**	149	39	7			.971	-5	*O-148	2.4
1932	Phi-N	154	650	**152**	**226**	50	15	**38**	137	60	49	.348	.404	**.646**	158	51	**20**			.960	9	*O-154	4.9
1933	Phi-N★	152	606	101	**223**	**44**	7	**28**	120	56	36	**.368**	**.422**	**.602**	168	**52**	15			.986	9	*O-152	**5.5**
1934	Chi-N★	115	435	78	131	27	2	20	80	47	38	.301	.372	.510	136	22	3			.962	-3	*O-110	1.4
1935	*Chi-N	119	434	71	127	14	4	21	73	41	42	.293	.355	.488	123	14	4			.958	-1	*O-111	0.8
1936	Chi-N	29	109	19	32	5	0	5	18	16	14	.294	.384	.477	128	4	0			.917	1	O-29	0.4
	Phi-N	117	492	83	152	30	7	20	86	33	45	.309	.352	.520	120	12	6			.930	-4	*O-117	0.2
	Yr	146	601	102	184	35	7	25	104	49	59	.306	.358	.512	122	16	6			.927	-4	*O-146	0.6
1937	Phi-N	115	406	74	132	20	2	15	57	39	21	.325	.386	.495	127	15	3			.949	-4	*O-102	0.7
1938	Phi-N	129	458	53	113	22	2	8	61	38	30	.247	.304	.356	83	-11	7			.960	-3	O-119	-1.8
1939	Phi-N	25	47	8	9	2	1	1	9	10	4	.191	.333	.340	84	-1	1			1.000	0	O-11/1-1	-0.1
	Pit-N	85	270	37	81	16	4	11	47	26	17	.300	.361	.511	134	12	1			.951	-2	O-66	0.8
	Yr	110	317	45	90	18	5	12	56	36	21	.284	.357	.486	127	11	2			.958	-2	O-77/1-1	0.7
1940	Phi-N	116	354	39	77	16	2	7	37	44	30	.218	.304	.333	79	-10	2			.984	-3	O-96	-1.8
1941	Phi-N	50	73	6	9	0	0	1	3	10	6	.123	.229	.164	12	-8	0			.958	-1	O-14	-0.5
1942	Phi-N	14	14	0	1	0	0	0	0	0	0	.071	.071	.071	-61	-3	0			.000	0	H	-0.3
1943	Phi-N	12	20	0	2	0	0	0	3	0	3	.100	.100	.100	-44	-4	1			.000	-1	/O-2	-0.5
1944	Phi-N	4	7	1	1	0	0	0	0	0	2	.143	.143	.143	-20	-1	0			1.000	1	/O-1	-0.1
Total	17	1753	6486	1168	2076	398	74	300	1201	601	521	.320	.379	.543	135	298	79			.962	16	*O-1600/1-1	21.4

■ LOU KLEIN

Klein, Louis Frank b: 10/22/18, New Orleans, La. d: 6/20/76, Metairie, La. BR/TR, 5'11", 170 lbs. Deb: 4/21/43 MC

YEAR	TM/L	G	AB	R	H	2B	3B	HR	RBI	BB	SO	AVG	OBP	SLG	PRO+	BR/A	SB	CS	SBR	FA	FR	G/POS	TPR
1943	*StL-N	154	627	91	180	28	14	7	62	50	70	.287	.342	.410	112	9	9			.973	-19	*2-126,S-51	-0.1
1945	StL-N	19	57	12	13	4	1	1	6	4	9	.228	.389	.386	113	2	0			.929	-0	/S-7,O-7,3-4,2-2	0.2
1946	StL-N	23	93	12	18	3	0	1	4	7	7	.194	.265	.258	47	-7	1			.975	-3	2-23	-0.9
1949	StL-N	58	114	25	25	6	0	2	12	22	20	.219	.355	.325	80	-3	0			.890	-4	S-21/2-9,3-7	-0.5
1951	Cle-A	2	2	0	0	0	0	0	0	0	0	.000	.000	.000	-99	-1	0	0	0	.000	0	H	-0.1
	Phi-A	49	144	22	33	7	0	5	17	10	12	.229	.279	.382	76	-6	0	0	0	.975	-4	2-42	-0.8
	Yr	51	146	22	33	7	0	5	17	10	12	.226	.276	.377	74	-6	0	0	0	.975	-4	2-42	-0.9
Total	5	305	1037	162	269	48	15	16	101	105	119	.259	.330	.381	97	-6	10	0	<u>0</u>	.975	-30	2-202/S-79,3-11,O-7	-2.2

■ RED KLEINOW

Kleinow, John Peter b: 7/20/1879, Milwaukee, Wis. d: 10/9/29, New York, N.Y. BR/TR, 5'10", 165 lbs. Deb: 5/3/04

YEAR	TM/L	G	AB	R	H	2B	3B	HR	RBI	BB	SO	AVG	OBP	SLG	PRO+	BR/A	SB	CS	SBR	FA	FR	G/POS	TPR
1904	NY-A	68	209	12	43	8	4	0	16	15		.206	.259	.282	68	-8	4			.966	-6	C-62/3-2,O-1	-0.8
1905	NY-A	88	253	23	56	6	3	1	24	20		.221	.284	.281	71	-8	7			.978	-7	C-83/1-3	-0.9
1906	NY-A	96	268	30	59	9	3	0	31	24		.220	.287	.276	69	-9	8			.974	-1	C-95/1-1	-0.2
1907	NY-A	90	269	30	71	6	4	0	26	24		.264	.327	.316	97	-1	5			.970	-6	C-86/1-1	0.2
1908	NY-A	96	279	16	47	3	2	1	13	22		.168	.237	.204	43	-17	5			.973	-4	C-89/2-2	-1.6
1909	NY-A	78	206	24	47	11	4	0	15	25		.228	.315	.320	100	0	7			.966	-3	C-77	0.4
1910	NY-A	6	12	5	5	0	0	0	2	1		.417	.462	.417	166	1	0			1.000	0	/C-5	0.1
	Bos-A	50	147	9	22	1	0	1	8	20		.150	.251	.177	34	-11	3			.968	4	C-49	-0.2
	Yr	56	159	11	27	1	0	1	10	21		.170	.267	.195	44	-10	3			.970	4	C-54	-0.1
1911	Bos-A	8	14	0	3	0	0	0	0	2		.214	.313	.214	48	-1	1			1.000	0	/C-8	0.0
	Phi-N	4	8	0	1	0	0	0	1	0	1	.125	.125	.250	4	-1	0			1.000	-0	/C-4	-0.1
Total	8	584	1665	146	354	45	20	3	135	153	1	.213	.282	.269	79	-54	42			.972	-23	C-558/1-5,2-2,3O	-3.1

■ RYAN KLESKO

Klesko, Ryan Anthony b: 6/12/71, Westminster, Cal. BL/TL, 6'3", 220 lbs. Deb: 9/12/92

YEAR	TM/L	G	AB	R	H	2B	3B	HR	RBI	BB	SO	AVG	OBP	SLG	PRO+	BR/A	SB	CS	SBR	FA	FR	G/POS	TPR
1992	Atl-N	13	14	0	0	0	0	0	0	0	5	.000	.067	.000	-75	-3	0	0	0	1.000	-1	/1-5	-0.4
1993	Atl-N	22	17	3	6	1	0	2	5	3	4	.353	.450	.765	216	3	0	0	0	1.000	-1	/1-3,O-2	0.2
1994	Atl-N	92	245	42	68	13	3	17	47	26	48	.278	.349	.563	130	10	1	0	2	.921	-11	O-74/1-6	-0.2
1995	*Atl-N	107	329	48	102	25	2	23	70	47	72	.310	.399	.608	156	27	5	4	-1	.942	-10	*O-102/1-4	1.3
1996	*Atl-N	153	528	90	149	21	4	34	93	68	129	.282	.366	.530	126	19	6	3	0	.975	-2	*O-144/1-2	1.0
Total	5	387	1133	183	325	60	9	76	216	144	258	.287	.370	.557	134	55	12	7	-1	.955	-26	O-322/1-20	1.9

■ JAY KLEVEN

Kleven, Jay Allen b: 12/2/49, Oakland, Cal. BR/TR, 6'2", 190 lbs. Deb: 6/20/76

YEAR	TM/L	G	AB	R	H	2B	3B	HR	RBI	BB	SO	AVG	OBP	SLG	PRO+	BR/A	SB	CS	SBR	FA	FR	G/POS	TPR
1976	NY-N	2	5	0	1	0	0	0	2	0	1	.200	.200	.200	15	-1	0			1.000	0	/C-2	0.0

YEAR	TM/L	G	AB	R	H	2B	3B	HR	RBI	BB	SO	AVG	OBP	SLG	PRO+	BR/A	SB	CS	SBR	FA	FR	G/POS	TPR

■ LOU KLIMCHOCK   Klimchock, Louis Stephen   b: 10/15/39, Hostetter, Pa.   BL/TR, 5'11", 180 lbs.   Deb: 9/27/58

YEAR	TM/L	G	AB	R	H	2B	3B	HR	RBI	BB	SO	AVG	OBP	SLG	PRO+	BR/A	SB	CS	SBR	FA	FR	G/POS	TPR
1958	KC-A	2	10	2	2	0	0	1	1	0	1	.200	.200	.500	84	-0	0	0	0	1.000	-1	/2-2	-0.1
1959	KC-A	17	66	10	18	1	0	4	13	1	6	.273	.284	.470	101	-0	0	0	0	.949	-4	2-16	-0.3
1960	KC-A	10	10	0	3	0	0	0	0	0	0	.300	.300	.300	62	-1	0	0	0	.000	0	/2-1	-0.1
1961	KC-A	57	121	8	26	4	1	1	16	5	13	.215	.246	.289	42	-10	0	0	0	.976	-5	1-11/O-7,3-6,2-1	-1.7
1962	Mil-N	8	8	0	0	0	0	0	0	0	0	.000	.000	.000	-99	-2	0	0	0	.000	0	H	-0.2
1963	Was-A	9	14	1	2	0	0	0	2	0	1	.143	.143	.143	-20	-2	0	0	0	1.000	1	/2-3	-0.1
	Mil-N	24	46	6	9	1	0	0	1	0	12	.196	.196	.217	19	-5	0	1	-1	.988	0	1-12	-0.6
1964	Mil-N	10	21	3	7	2	0	0	2	1	2	.333	.364	.429	121	1	0	0	0	1.000	-3	/3-4,2-2	-0.2
1965	Mil-N	34	39	3	3	0	0	0	3	2	8	.077	.122	.077	-42	-7	0	0	0	.923	1	/1-4	-0.7
1966	NY-N	5	5	0	0	0	0	0	0	0	3	.000	.000	.000	-99	-1	0	0	0	.000	0	H	-0.1
1968	Cle-A	11	15	0	2	0	0	0	3	1	0	.133	.188	.133	-2	-2	0	0	0	.500	-3	/3-4,1-1,2-1	-0.5
1969	Cle-A	90	258	26	74	13	2	6	26	18	14	.287	.333	.422	107	2	0	0	0	.934	-16	3-56,2-21/C-1	-1.3
1970	Cle-A	41	56	5	9	0	0	1	2	3	9	.161	.217	.214	18	-6	0	0	0	1.000	-1	/1-5,2-5	-0.7
Total	12	318	669	64	155	21	3	13	69	31	71	.232	.267	.330	63	-35	0	1	-1	.906	-30	/3-70,2-52,1-33,OC	-6.6

■ BOBBY KLINE   Kline, John Robert   b: 1/27/29, St.Petersburg, Fla   BR/TR, 6', 179 lbs.   Deb: 4/11/55

YEAR	TM/L	G	AB	R	H	2B	3B	HR	RBI	BB	SO	AVG	OBP	SLG	PRO+	BR/A	SB	CS	SBR	FA	FR	G/POS	TPR
1955	Was-A	77	140	12	31	5	0	0	9	11	27	.221	.288	.257	50	-10	0	0	0	.943	13	S-69/2-4,3-3,P-1	0.7

■ JOHNNY KLING   Kling, John "Noisy"   b: 2/25/1875, Kansas City, Mo.   d: 1/31/47, Kansas City, Mo.   BR/TR, 5'9.5", 160 lbs.   Deb: 9/11/00   FM

YEAR	TM/L	G	AB	R	H	2B	3B	HR	RBI	BB	SO	AVG	OBP	SLG	PRO+	BR/A	SB	CS	SBR	FA	FR	G/POS	TPR
1900	Chi-N	15	51	8	15	3	1	0	7	2		.294	.321	.392	100	-0	0			.901	-2	C-15	-0.1
1901	Chi-N	74	256	26	70	6	3	0	21	9		.273	.301	.320	83	-6	8			.952	-10	C-69/1-1,O-1	-0.9
1902	Chi-N	114	431	49	123	19	3	0	57	29		.285	.330	.343	111	5	24			.974	6	*C-112/S-1	2.4
1903	Chi-N	132	491	67	146	29	13	3	68	22		.297	.330	.428	119	9	23			.969	2	*C-132	2.3
1904	Chi-N	123	452	41	110	18	0	2	46	16		.243	.271	.296	75	-14	7			.974	-12	*C-104,O-10/1-6	-1.5
1905	Chi-N	111	380	26	83	8	6	1	52	28		.218	.272	.279	62	-18	13			.966	0	*C-106/O-4,1-1	-0.7
1906	*Chi-N	107	343	45	107	15	8	2	46	23		.312	.357	.420	134	12	14			**.982**	6	C-96/O-3	2.9
1907	*Chi-N	104	334	44	95	15	8	1	43	27		.284	.342	.386	120	7	9			**.987**	5	C-98/1-2	2.5
1908	*Chi-N	126	424	51	117	23	5	4	59	21		.276	.315	.382	117	7	16			.979	2	*C-117/O-6,1-2	2.2
1910	*Chi-N	91	297	31	80	17	2	2	32	37	27	.269	.354	.360	109	4	3			.979	-5	C-86	0.8
1911	Chi-N	27	80	8	14	3	2	1	5	8	14	.175	.250	.300	53	-5	1			.969	-5	C-25	0.2
	Bos-N	75	241	32	54	8	1	2	24	30	29	.224	.310	.290	63	-12	0			.951	-5	C-71/3-1	-1.0
	Yr	102	321	40	68	11	3	3	29	38	43	.212	.295	.293	61	-17	1			.956	-0	C-96/3-1	-0.8
1912	Bos-N	81	252	26	80	10	3	2	30	15	30	.317	.356	.405	106	2	3			.958	5	C-74,M	1.3
1913	Cin-N	80	209	20	57	7	6	0	23	14	14	.273	.318	.364	95	-2	2			.975	7	C-63	1.1
Total	13	1260	4241	474	1151	181	61	20	513	281	114	.271	.318	.357	100	-11	123			.971	3	*C-1168/O-24,13S	11.5

■ RUDY KLING   Kling, Rudolph A.   b: 3/23/1870, St.Louis, Mo.   d: 3/14/37, St.Louis, Mo.   BR/TR, 5'10", 178 lbs.   Deb: 9/21/02

YEAR	TM/L	G	AB	R	H	2B	3B	HR	RBI	BB	SO	AVG	OBP	SLG	PRO+	BR/A	SB	CS	SBR	FA	FR	G/POS	TPR
1902	StL-N	4	10	1	2	0	0	0	0	4		.200	.429	.200	99	0	1			.842	-2	/S-4	-0.1

■ JOE KLINGER   Klinger, Joseph John   b: 8/2/02, Canonsburg, Pa.   d: 7/31/60, Little Rock, Ark.   BR/TR, 6', 190 lbs.   Deb: 9/13/27

YEAR	TM/L	G	AB	R	H	2B	3B	HR	RBI	BB	SO	AVG	OBP	SLG	PRO+	BR/A	SB	CS	SBR	FA	FR	G/POS	TPR
1927	NY-N	3	5	0	2	0	0	0	0	0	2	.400	.400	.400	115	0	0	0	0	1.000	0	/O-1	0.0
1930	Chi-A	4	8	0	3	0	0	0	1	0	0	.375	.375	.375	94	-0	0	0	0	1.000	-1	/C-2,1-2	-0.1
Total	2	7	13	0	5	0	0	0	2	0	2	.385	.385	.385	102	0	0	0	0	1.000	-1	/1-2,C-2,O-1	-0.1

■ NAP KLOZA   Kloza, John Clarence   b: 9/7/03, Poland   d: 6/11/62, Milwaukee, Wis.   BR/TR, 5'11", 180 lbs.   Deb: 8/16/31

YEAR	TM/L	G	AB	R	H	2B	3B	HR	RBI	BB	SO	AVG	OBP	SLG	PRO+	BR/A	SB	CS	SBR	FA	FR	G/POS	TPR
1931	StL-A	3	7	1	1	0	0	0	0	1	4	.143	.250	.143	5	-1	0	0	0	1.000	-1	/O-3	-0.1
1932	StL-A	19	13	4	2	0	1	0	2	4	4	.154	.353	.308	69	-1	0	0	0	1.000	-1	/O-3	-0.2
Total	2	22	20	5	3	0	1	0	2	5	8	.150	.320	.250	48	-1	0	0	0	1.000	-2	/O-6	-0.3

■ JOE KLUGMANN   Klugmann, Joe   b: 3/26/1895, St.Louis, Mo.   d: 7/18/51, Moberly, Mo.   BR/TR, 5'11", 175 lbs.   Deb: 9/23/21

YEAR	TM/L	G	AB	R	H	2B	3B	HR	RBI	BB	SO	AVG	OBP	SLG	PRO+	BR/A	SB	CS	SBR	FA	FR	G/POS	TPR
1921	Chi-N	6	21	3	6	0	0	0	2	1	2	.286	.348	.286	69	-1	0	1	-1	.969	0	/2-5	-0.1
1922	Chi-N	2	2	0	0	0	0	0	0	0	0	.000	.000	.000	-98	-1	0	0	0	1.000	1	/2-2	0.0
1924	Bro-N	31	79	7	13	2	1	0	3	2	9	.165	.185	.215	7	-10	0	0	0	.929	-1	2-28/S-1	-1.2
1925	Cle-A	38	85	12	28	9	2	0	12	8	4	.329	.387	.482	119	2	3	1	0	.959	-3	2-29/1-4,3-2	0.0
Total	4	77	187	22	47	11	3	0	17	11	15	.251	.296	.342	67	-10	3	2	-0	.947	-3	/2-64,1-4,3-2,S-1	-1.3

■ ELMER KLUMPP   Klumpp, Elmer Edward   b: 8/26/06, St.Louis, Mo.   BR/TR, 6', 184 lbs.   Deb: 4/17/34

YEAR	TM/L	G	AB	R	H	2B	3B	HR	RBI	BB	SO	AVG	OBP	SLG	PRO+	BR/A	SB	CS	SBR	FA	FR	G/POS	TPR
1934	Was-A	12	15	2	2	0	0	0	0	1	1	.133	.188	.133	-17	-3	0	0	0	.889	-1	C-11	-0.3
1937	Bro-N	5	11	0	1	0	0	0	2	1	4	.091	.167	.091	-28	-2	0	0	0	1.000	0	/C-3	-0.1
Total	2	17	26	2	3	0	0	0	2	2	5	.115	.179	.115	-21	-5	0	0	0	.943	-1	/C-14	-0.4

■ BILLY KLUSMAN   Klusman, William F.   b: 3/24/1865, Cincinnati, Ohio   d: 6/24/07, Cincinnati, Ohio   BR/TR, 5'10.5", 185 lbs.   Deb: 6/21/1888

YEAR	TM/L	G	AB	R	H	2B	3B	HR	RBI	BB	SO	AVG	OBP	SLG	PRO+	BR/A	SB	CS	SBR	FA	FR	G/POS	TPR
1888	Bos-N	28	107	9	18	4	0	2	11	5	13	.168	.205	.262	47	-6	3			.914	-9	2-28	-1.4
1890	StL-a	15	65	9	18	4	1	1	11	1	1	.277	.288	.415	94	-1	1			.896	-3	2-15	-0.3
Total	2	43	172	18	36	8	1	3	22	6	13	.209	.236	.320	67	-8	4			.908	-12	/2-43	-1.7

■ TED KLUSZEWSKI   Kluszewski, Theodore Bernard "Big Klu"   b: 9/10/24, Argo, Ill.   d: 3/29/88, Cincinnati, Ohio   BL/TL, 6'2", 225 lbs.   Deb: 4/18/47   C

YEAR	TM/L	G	AB	R	H	2B	3B	HR	RBI	BB	SO	AVG	OBP	SLG	PRO+	BR/A	SB	CS	SBR	FA	FR	G/POS	TPR
1947	Cin-N	9	10	1	1	0	0	0	2	1	2	.100	.182	.100	-23	-2	0	0	0	1.000	-0	/1-2	-0.2
1948	Cin-N	113	379	49	104	23	4	12	57	18	32	.274	.307	.451	107	1	1	1		.990	1	1-98	0.2
1949	Cin-N	136	531	63	164	26	2	8	68	19	24	.309	.333	.411	97	-3	3			.989	-7	*1-134	-1.1
1950	Cin-N	134	538	76	165	37	0	25	111	33	28	.307	.348	.515	123	16	3			.987	-11	*1-131	0.1
1951	Cin-N	154	607	74	157	35	2	13	77	35	33	.259	.301	.387	83	-16	6	2	1	**.997**	-6	*1-154	-2.9
1952	Cin-N	135	497	62	159	24	11	16	86	47	28	.320	.383	.509	146	30	3	3	-1	**.993**	-10	*1-133	1.5
1953	Cin-N★	149	570	97	180	25	0	40	108	55	34	.316	.380	.570	142	34	2	0	1	**.995**	-18	*1-147	1.1
1954	Cin-N★	149	573	104	187	28	3	**49**	**141**	78	35	.326	.410	.642	165	53	0	2	-1	**.996**	-4	*1-149	4.0
1955	Cin-N★	153	612	116	**192**	25	0	47	113	66	40	.314	.384	.585	144	38	1	1	-0	**.995**	-9	*1-153	1.9
1956	Cin-N★	138	517	91	156	14	1	35	102	49	31	.302	.366	.536	130	21	1	0	0	.990	-5	*1-131	0.8
1957	Cin-N	69	127	12	34	7	0	6	21	5	5	.268	.301	.465	95	-1	0	0	0	.989	0	1-23	-0.3
1958	Pit-N	100	301	29	88	13	4	4	37	26	16	.292	.351	.402	101	1	0	0	0	.994	-5	1-72	-0.9
1959	Pit-N	60	122	11	32	10	1	2	17	5	14	.262	.291	.410	85	-3	0	0	0	1.000	-1	1-20	-0.5
	*Chi-A	31	101	11	30	2	1	2	10	9	10	.297	.355	.396	107	1	0	1	-1	1.000	-1	1-29	-0.4
1960	Chi-A	81	181	20	53	9	0	5	39	22	10	.293	.369	.425	116	4	0	1	-1	.997	-6	1-39	-0.1
1961	LA-A	107	263	32	64	11	0	15	39	24	23	.243	.307	.460	91	-4	0	0	0	.989	-5	1-66	-1.4
Total	15	1718	5929	848	1766	290	29	279	1028	492	365	.298	.354	.498	122	169	20	10		.993	-82	*1-1481	1.8

■ MICKEY KLUTTS   Klutts, Gene Ellis   b: 9/20/54, Montebello, Cal.   BR/TR, 5'11", 189 lbs.   Deb: 7/7/76

YEAR	TM/L	G	AB	R	H	2B	3B	HR	RBI	BB	SO	AVG	OBP	SLG	PRO+	BR/A	SB	CS	SBR	FA	FR	G/POS	TPR
1976	NY-A	2	3	0	0	0	0	0	0	0	0	.000	.000	.000	-99	-1	0	0	0	.875	0	/S-2	0.0
1977	NY-A	5	15	3	4	1	0	1	4	2	1	.267	.389	.533	150	1	0	0	0	1.000	1	/3-4,S-1	0.3
1978	NY-A	1	2	1	2	1	0	0	0	0	0	1.000	1.000	1.500	608	2	0	0	0	.750	0	/3-1	0.2
1979	Oak-A	24	73	9	14	2	1	1	4	7	20	.192	.262	.288	51	-5	0	0	0	.882	-2	S-10/2-8,3-6,D-2	-0.7
1980	Oak-A	75	197	20	53	14	0	4	21	13	41	.269	.314	.401	102	-0	0	1	-2	.947	-6	3-62/S-8,2-7,D-1	-0.9
1981	*Oak-A	15	46	9	17	0	0	5	11	2	9	.370	.396	.696	220	7	0	0	0	.957	-5	3-14	0.3
1982	Oak-A	55	157	10	28	9	0	1	14	9	18	.178	.223	.229	26	-16	0	0	0	1.000	0	3-17/D-2	-2.0
1983	Tor-A	22	43	3	11	0	0	0	3	5	11	.256	.289	.465	98	-0	1	0	0	1.000	-16	3-17/D-2	-0.3
Total	8	199	536	49	129	26	1	14	59	34	101	.241	.290	.371	84	-13	1	1	-4	.948	-16	3-153/S-21,2-15,D-5	-3.3

■ CLYDE KLUTTZ   Kluttz, Clyde Franklin   b: 12/12/17, Rockwell, N.C.   d: 5/12/79, Salisbury, N.C.   BR/TR, 6', 198 lbs.   Deb: 4/20/42

YEAR	TM/L	G	AB	R	H	2B	3B	HR	RBI	BB	SO	AVG	OBP	SLG	PRO+	BR/A	SB	CS	SBR	FA	FR	G/POS	TPR
1942	Bos-N	72	210	21	56	10	1	3	31	7	13	.267	.294	.338	86	-4	0			.979	0	C-57	0.0
1943	Bos-N	66	207	13	51	7	0	0	20	15	9	.246	.297	.280	68	-8	0			.973	2	C-55	-0.2
1944	Bos-N	81	229	20	64	12	2	2	19	13	14	.279	.318	.376	91	-3	0			.980	4	C-58	0.4

YEAR	TM/L	G	AB	R	H	2B	3B	HR	RBI	BB	SO	AVG	OBP	SLG	PRO+	BR/A	SB	CS	SBR	FA	FR	G/POS	TPR
1945	Bos-N	25	81	9	24	4	1	0	10	2	6	.296	.313	.370	89	-1	0			.987	-0	C-19	-0.1
	NY-N	73	222	25	62	14	0	4	21	15	10	.279	.331	.396	100	-1	1			.978	-6	C-57	-0.3
	Yr	98	303	34	86	18	1	4	31	17	16	.284	.326	.389	97	-2	1			.981	-6	C-76	-0.4
1946	NY-N	5	8	0	3	0	0	0	1	0	1	.375	.375	.375	112	0	0			.857	-1	/C-2	0.0
	StL-N	52	136	8	36	7	0	0	14	10	10	.265	.315	.316	76	-4	0			.980	2	C-49	0.0
	Yr	57	144	8	39	7	0	0	15	10	11	.271	.318	.319	78	-4	0			.976	1	C-51	0.0
1947	Pit-N	73	232	26	70	9	2	6	42	17	18	.302	.355	.435	106	2	1			.987	3	C-69	0.9
1948	Pit-N	94	271	26	60	12	2	4	20	20	19	.221	.275	.325	61	-15	3			.978	0	C-91	-1.0
1951	StL-A	4	4	2	2	1	0	0	1	1	0	.500	.600	.750	256	1	0	0	0	1.000	1	/C-1	0.2
	Was-A	53	159	15	49	9	0	1	22	20	8	.308	.389	.384	111	3	0	0	0	.968	-7	C-46	-0.2
	Yr	57	163	17	51	10	0	1	23	21	8	.313	.395	.393	115	4	0	0	0	.968	-6	C-47	0.0
1952	Was-A	58	144	7	33	5	0	1	11	12	11	.229	.293	.285	63	-7	0	0	0	.979	-1	C-52	-0.6
Total	9	656	1903	172	510	90	8	19	212	132	119	.268	.318	.354	86	-39	5	0		.978	-3	C-556	-0.9

■ JOE KMAK
Kmak, Joseph Robert   b: 5/3/63, Napa, Cal.   BR/TR, 6', 185 lbs.   Deb: 4/6/93

YEAR	TM/L	G	AB	R	H	2B	3B	HR	RBI	BB	SO	AVG	OBP	SLG	PRO+	BR/A	SB	CS	SBR	FA	FR	G/POS	TPR
1993	Mil-A	51	110	9	24	5	0	0	7	14	13	.218	.317	.264	59	-6	6	2	1	1.000	2	C-50	-0.2
1995	Chi-N	19	53	7	13	3	0	1	6	6	12	.245	.333	.358	84	-1	0	0	0	1.000	-1	C-18/3-1	-0.1
Total	2	70	163	16	37	8	0	1	13	20	25	.227	.323	.294	67	-7	6	2	1	1.000	0	/C-68,3-1	-0.3

■ OTTO KNABE
Knabe, Franz Otto "Dutch"   b: 6/12/1884, Carrick, Pa.   d: 5/17/61, Philadelphia, Pa.   BR/TR, 5'8", 175 lbs.   Deb: 10/3/05   M

YEAR	TM/L	G	AB	R	H	2B	3B	HR	RBI	BB	SO	AVG	OBP	SLG	PRO+	BR/A	SB	CS	SBR	FA	FR	G/POS	TPR
1905	Pit-N	3	10	0	3	1	0	0	2	3		.300	.462	.400	154	1	0			.786	0	/3-3	0.1
1907	Phi-N	129	444	67	113	16	9	1	34	52		.255	.339	.338	114	8	18			.960	1	*2-121/O-5	0.9
1908	Phi-N	151	555	63	121	26	8	0	27	49		.218	.290	.294	84	-10	27			.969	11	*2-151	0.9
1909	Phi-N	113	402	40	94	13	3	0	34	35		.234	.308	.281	82	-8	9			.938	2	*2-110/O-1	-0.3
1910	Phi-N	137	510	73	133	18	4	1	44	47	42	.261	.327	.325	87	-8	15			.954	14	*2-136	0.3
1911	Phi-N	142	528	99	125	15	5	0	42	94	35	.237	.352	.294	80	-10	23			.950	4	*2-142	-1.0
1912	Phi-N	126	426	56	120	11	4	0	46	55	20	.282	.366	.326	85	-7	16			.952	1	*2-123	-0.9
1913	Phi-N	148	571	70	150	25	7	2	53	45	26	.263	.320	.342	85	-11	14			.959	12	*2-148	-0.2
1914	Bal-F	147	469	45	106	26	2	2	42	53	28	.226	.307	.303	65	-30	10			.956	1	*2-144,M	-3.1
1915	Bal-F	103	320	38	81	16	2	1	25	37	16	.253	.334	.325	83	-11	7			.975	7	2-94/O-1,M	-0.3
1916	Pit-N	28	89	4	17	3	1	0	9	6	5	.191	.258	.247	55	-5	1			.962	-0	2-28	-0.5
	Chi-N	51	145	17	40	8	0	0	7	9	18	.276	.327	.331	92	-1	3			.939	6	2-42/S-1,3-1,0-1	0.6
	Yr	79	234	21	57	11	1	0	16	15	24	.244	.300	.299	79	-6	4			.949	5	2-70/S-1,3-1,0-1	0.1
Total	11	1278	4469	572	1103	178	48	8	365	485	191	.247	.325	.313	84	-92	143			.957	64	*2-1239/O-8,3-4,S-1	-4.4

■ COTTON KNAUPP
Knaupp, Henry Antone   b: 8/13/1889, San Antonio, Tex.   d: 7/6/67, New Orleans, La.   BR/TR, 5'9", 165 lbs.   Deb: 8/30/10

YEAR	TM/L	G	AB	R	H	2B	3B	HR	RBI	BB	SO	AVG	OBP	SLG	PRO+	BR/A	SB	CS	SBR	FA	FR	G/POS	TPR
1910	Cle-A	18	59	3	14	3	1	0	11	8		.237	.338	.322	105	1	1			.884	-8	S-18	-0.8
1911	Cle-A	13	39	2	4	1	0	0	0		8	.103	.103	.128	-35	-7	3			.964	2	S-13	-0.5
Total	2	31	98	5	18	4	1	0	11	8	8	.184	.252	.245	48	-6	4			.913	-6	/S-31	-1.3

■ ALAN KNICELY
Knicely, Alan Lee   b: 5/19/55, Harrisonburg, Va.   BR/TR, 6'0.5", 194 lbs.   Deb: 8/12/79

YEAR	TM/L	G	AB	R	H	2B	3B	HR	RBI	BB	SO	AVG	OBP	SLG	PRO+	BR/A	SB	CS	SBR	FA	FR	G/POS	TPR
1979	Hou-N	7	6	0	0	0	0	0	0	2	3	.000	.250	.000	-27	-1	0	0	0	1.000	-2	/C-3,3-1	-0.3
1980	Hou-N	1	1	0	0	0	0	0	0	0	1	.000	.000	.000	-99	-0	0	0	0	.000	0	/H	0.0
1981	Hou-N	7	4	2	4	0	0	2	2	0	1	.571	.571	1.429	477	3	0	0	0	1.000	0	/C-2,O-1	0.3
1982	Hou-N	59	133	10	25	2	0	2	12	14	30	.188	.270	.248	50	-9	0	1	-1	.977	-9	C-23,O-16/3-1	-1.9
1983	Cin-N	59	98	11	22	3	0	2	10	16	28	.224	.333	.316	78	-2	0	2	-1	1.000	-2	C-31/O-8,1-2	-0.5
1984	Cin-N	10	29	0	4	0	0	0	5	3	6	.138	.194	.138	2	-4	0	0	0	.984	0	/1-8,C-1	-0.4
1985	Cin-N	48	158	17	40	9	0	5	26	16	34	.253	.326	.405	98	-0	0	0	0	.968	-14	C-46	-1.3
	Phi-N	7	7	0	0	0	0	0	0	0	4	.000	.000	.000	-97	-2	0	0	0	1.000	-0	/1-1	-0.2
	Yr	55	165	17	40	9	0	5	26	16	38	.242	.310	.388	91	-2	0	0	0	.968	-14	C-46/1-1	-1.5
1986	StL-N	34	82	8	16	3	0	1	6	17	21	.195	.333	.268	68	-3	1	1	-0	.995	-1	1-29/C-2	-0.6
Total	8	228	521	48	111	17	0	12	61	68	128	.213	.306	.315	73	-19	1	4	-2	.979	-26	C-108/1-40,O-25,3-2	-4.9

■ AUSTIN KNICKERBOCKER
Knickerbocker, Austin Jay   b: 10/15/18, Bangall, N.Y.   BR/TR, 5'11", 185 lbs.   Deb: 4/19/47

YEAR	TM/L	G	AB	R	H	2B	3B	HR	RBI	BB	SO	AVG	OBP	SLG	PRO+	BR/A	SB	CS	SBR	FA	FR	G/POS	TPR
1947	Phi-A	21	48	8	12	3	2	0	2	3	4	.250	.294	.396	89	-1	0	1	-1	.943	0	O-14	-0.2

■ BILL KNICKERBOCKER
Knickerbocker, William Hart   b: 12/29/11, Los Angeles, Cal.   d: 9/8/63, Sebastopol, Cal.   BR/TR, 5'11", 170 lbs.   Deb: 4/12/33

YEAR	TM/L	G	AB	R	H	2B	3B	HR	RBI	BB	SO	AVG	OBP	SLG	PRO+	BR/A	SB	CS	SBR	FA	FR	G/POS	TPR
1933	Cle-A	80	279	20	63	16	3	2	32	11	30	.226	.255	.326	51	-21	1	4	-2	.939	2	S-80	-1.5
1934	Cle-A	146	593	82	188	32	5	4	67	24	40	.317	.347	.408	93	-8	2	6	-2	.962	-7	*S-146	-0.7
1935	Cle-A	132	540	77	161	34	0	5	55	27	31	.298	.332	.380	82	-15	2	12	-7	.956	9	*S-128	-0.5
1936	Cle-A	155	618	81	182	35	3	8	73	56	30	.294	.354	.400	85	-15	5	14	-7	.952	-1	*S-155	-1.1
1937	StL-A	121	491	53	128	29	5	4	61	30	32	.261	.303	.365	67	-26	3	0	0	.958	-13	*S-115/2-6	-2.9
1938	NY-A	46	128	15	32	8	3	1	21	11	10	.250	.309	.383	73	-6	2	0	0	.982	-2	2-34/S-3	-0.5
1939	NY-A	6	13	2	2	1	0	0	1	0	0	.154	.154	.231	-3	-2	0	0	0	1.000	2	/2-2,S-2	0.0
1940	NY-A	45	124	17	30	8	1	1	10	14	8	.242	.333	.347	80	-4	0	0	0	.985	-3	S-19,3-17	-0.4
1941	Chi-A	89	343	51	84	23	2	7	29	41	27	.245	.329	.385	89	-6	6	5	-1	.970	-17	2-88	-1.7
1942	Phi-A	87	289	25	73	12	0	1	19	29	30	.253	.323	.304	77	-8	1	2	-1	.964	-12	2-81/S-1	-1.7
Total	10	907	3418	423	943	198	27	28	368	244	238	.276	.326	.374	79	-109	25	46	-20	.955	-42	S-649,2-211/3-17	-11.0

■ LON KNIGHT
Knight, Alonzo P.   b: 6/16/1853, Philadelphia, Pa.   d: 4/23/32, Philadelphia, Pa.   BR/TR, 5'11.5", 165 lbs.   Deb: 9/4/1875   MU

YEAR	TM/L	G	AB	R	H	2B	3B	HR	RBI	BB	SO	AVG	OBP	SLG	PRO+	BR/A	SB	CS	SBR	FA	FR	G/POS	TPR
1875	Ath-n	13	47	5	6	2	0	0	2	0		.128	.128	.170	2	-5	2	0	1	.875	-0	P-13/S-1	-0.1
1876	Phi-N	55	240	32	60	9	3	0	24	2	2	.250	.256	.313	89	-3				.804	-7	P-34,1-13/O-9,2-6	-0.6
1880	Wor-N	49	201	31	48	11	3	0	21	5	8	.239	.257	.323	88	-3				.863	5	O-49	-0.3
1881	Det-N	83	340	67	92	16	3	1	52	23	21	.271	.317	.344	104	1				.890	1	*O-82/2-1,1-1	0.1
1882	Det-N	86	347	39	72	12	6	0	24	16	21	.207	.242	.277	66	-13				.867	2	*O-84/1-2	-1.1
1883	Phi-a	97	429	98	108	23	9	6	53	21		.252	.287	.354	97	-3				.858	0	*O-93/3-3,2-2,M	-0.3
1884	Phi-a	108	484	94	131	18	12	1		10		.271	.287	.364	104	0				.911	11	*O-108/P-2,1-1,M	0.8
1885	Phi-a	29	119	17	25	1	0	1	14	9		.210	.274	.235	58	-6				.921	4	O-29/P-1	-0.2
	Pro-N	25	81	8	13	1	0	0	8	11	17	.160	.261	.173	44	-4				.957	1	O-25/P-1	-0.2
Total	7	532	2241	386	549	91	37	3	196	97	69	.245	.277	.323	90	-30				.887	17	O-479/P-38,1-17,23	-1.7

■ RAY KNIGHT
Knight, Charles Ray   b: 12/28/52, Albany, Ga.   BR/TR, 6'2", 190 lbs.   Deb: 9/10/74   MC

YEAR	TM/L	G	AB	R	H	2B	3B	HR	RBI	BB	SO	AVG	OBP	SLG	PRO+	BR/A	SB	CS	SBR	FA	FR	G/POS	TPR
1974	Cin-N	14	11	1	2	1	0	0	2	1	2	.182	.250	.273	47	-1	0	0	0	1.000	1	3-14	0.0
1977	Cin-N	80	92	8	24	5	1	1	13	9	16	.261	.327	.370	85	-2	1	1	-0	.941	3	3-37,2-17/O-5,S-3	0.3
1978	Cin-N	83	65	7	13	3	0	1	4	3		.200	.235	.292	47	-5	0	0	0	.868	5	3-60/2-4,O-3,1-1,S	0.2
1979	*Cin-N	150	551	64	175	37	4	10	79	38	57	.318	.365	.454	121	16	4	4	-1	.962	-15	*3-149	-0.2
1980	Cin-N★	162	618	71	163	39	7	14	78	36	62	.264	.309	.417	101	-1	2	2	-1	.969	-15	*3-162	-2.1
1981	Cin-N	106	386	43	100	23	1	6	34	33	51	.259	.324	.370	95	-3	1	2	-1	.957	-13	*3-105	-2.2
1982	Hou-N★	158	609	72	179	36	6	6	70	48	58	.294	.350	.402	119	14	2	5	-2	.990	-2	1-96,3-67	0.3
1983	Hou-N	145	507	43	154	36	4	9	70	42	62	.304	.362	.444	130	19	0	3	-2	.993	-11	*1-143	-0.1
1984	Hou-N	88	278	15	62	10	0	2	29	14	30	.223	.263	.281	57	-17	0	0	0	.946	-2	3-54,1-24	-2.4
	NY-N	27	93	13	26	4	0	1	6	7	13	.280	.337	.355	96	-0	0	0	0	.962	-4	3-27/1-3	-0.5
	Yr	115	371	28	88	14	0	3	35	21	43	.237	.282	.299	67	-17	0	0	0	.951	-6	3-81,1-27	-2.9
1985	NY-N	90	271	22	59	12	0	6	36	13	32	.218	.256	.328	64	-14	1	1	-0	.958	-11	3-73/2-2,1-1	-2.7
1986	*NY-N	137	486	51	145	24	2	11	76	40	63	.298	.357	.424	118	11	2	1	0	.948	-11	*3-132/1-1	-0.2
1987	Bal-A	150	563	46	144	24	2	14	65	24	73	.256	.311	.373	82	-15	2	4	-3	.956	10	*3-130,D-14/1-6	-0.7
1988	Det-A	105	299	34	65	12	2	3	33	20	30	.217	.273	.301	63	-15	1	1	-0	.991	-3	1-64,D-25,3-11/O-2	-2.4
Total	13	1495	4829	490	1311	266	27	84	595	343	579	.271	.330	.390	99	-11	14	25	-11	.957	-67	*3-1021,1-339/D2OS	-12.9

■ JOHN KNIGHT
Knight, John Wesley "Schoolboy"   b: 10/6/1885, Philadelphia, Pa.   d: 12/19/65, Walnut Creek, Cal.   BR/TR, 6'2.5", 180 lbs.   Deb: 4/14/05

YEAR	TM/L	G	AB	R	H	2B	3B	HR	RBI	BB	SO	AVG	OBP	SLG	PRO+	BR/A	SB	CS	SBR	FA	FR	G/POS	TPR
1905	Phi-A	88	325	28	66	12	1	3	29	9		.203	.227	.274	58	-16	4			.895	-28	S-79/3-4	-4.8

YEAR	TM/L	G	AB	R	H	2B	3B	HR	RBI	BB	SO	AVG	OBP	SLG	PRO+	BR/A	SB	CS	SBR	FA	FR	G/POS	TPR
1906	Phi-A	74	253	29	49	7	2	3	20	19		.194	.250	.273	62	-11	6			.922	0	3-67/2-7	-1.0
1907	Phi-A	40	139	6	29	7	1	0	12	10		.209	.272	.273	72	-4	1			.862	-0	3-40	-0.4
	Bos-A	98	360	31	78	9	3	2	29	19		.217	.256	.275	70	-13	8			.924	7	3-92/2-4	-0.3
	Yr	138	499	37	107	16	4	2	41	29		.214	.260	.275	71	-17	9			.906	7	*3-132/2-4	-0.7
1909	NY-A	116	360	46	85	8	5	0	40	37		.236	.311	.286	88	-4	15			.901	1	S-76,1-19,2-17/3-3	-0.3
1910	NY-A	117	414	58	129	25	4	3	45	34		.312	.372	.413	138	17	23			.929	-1	S-79,1-23/2-7,30	2.2
1911	NY-A	132	470	69	126	16	7	3	62	42		.268	.342	.351	88	-8	18			.907	3	S-82,1-27,2-21/3-1	0.0
1912	Was-A	32	93	10	15	2	1	0	9	16		.161	.284	.204	40	-7	4			.926	-5	2-27/1-5	-1.2
1913	NY-A	70	250	24	59	10	0	0	24	25	27	.236	.310	.276	72	-9	7			.980	8	1-50,2-21	-0.2
Total	8	767	2664	301	636	96	24	14	270	211	27	.239	.300	.309	84	-55	86			.909	-15	S-316,3-211,12/O	-6.0

■ JOE KNIGHT
Knight, Joseph William "Quiet Joe" b: 9/28/1859, Port Stanley, Ont., Canada d: 10/16/38, Lynhurst, Ont., Canada BL/TL, 5'11", 185 lbs. Deb: 5/16/1884

YEAR	TM/L	G	AB	R	H	2B	3B	HR	RBI	BB	SO	AVG	OBP	SLG	PRO+	BR/A	SB	FA	FR	G/POS	TPR
1884	Phi-N	6	24	2	6	3	0	0	2	0	2	.250	.250	.375	98	-0		.789	-0	/P-6	0.0
1890	Cin-N	127	481	67	150	26	8	4	67	38	33	.312	.367	.424	131	18	17	.925	-6	*O-127	0.6
Total	2	133	505	69	156	29	8	4	69	38	33	.309	.362	.422	130	18	17	.925	-6	O-127/P-6	0.6

■ PETE KNISELY
Knisely, Peter Cole b: 8/11/1887, Waynesburg, Pa. d: 7/1/48, Brownsville, Pa. BR/TR, 5'9", 185 lbs. Deb: 9/4/12

YEAR	TM/L	G	AB	R	H	2B	3B	HR	RBI	BB	SO	AVG	OBP	SLG	PRO+	BR/A	SB	CS	SBR	FA	FR	G/POS	TPR
1912	Cin-N	21	67	10	22	7	3	0	7	4	5	.328	.375	.522	148	4	3			.939	-2	O-13/2-3,S-1	0.1
1913	Chi-N	2	2	0	0	0	0	0	0	0	1	.000	.000	.000	-99	-1				.000	0	H	-0.1
1914	Chi-N	37	69	5	9	1	0	0	5	5	6	.130	.200	.159	7	-8	0			.975	2	O-17	-0.7
1915	Chi-N	64	134	12	33	9	0	0	17	15	18	.246	.331	.313	95	-0	1	2	-1	.940	-7	O-33/2-9	-1.1
Total	4	124	272	27	64	16	4	0	29	24	30	.235	.307	.324	86	-5	4	2		.951	-7	/O-63,2-12,S-1	-1.8

■ CHUCK KNOBLAUCH
Knoblauch, Edward Charles b: 7/7/68, Houston, Tex. BR/TR, 5'9", 175 lbs. Deb: 4/9/91

YEAR	TM/L	G	AB	R	H	2B	3B	HR	RBI	BB	SO	AVG	OBP	SLG	PRO+	BR/A	SB	CS	SBR	FA	FR	G/POS	TPR
1991	*Min-A	151	565	78	159	24	6	1	50	59	40	.281	.354	.350	91	-5	25	5	5	.975	-1	*2-148/S-2	0.2
1992	Min-A★	155	600	104	178	19	6	2	56	88	60	.297	.391	.358	108	10	34	13	2	.992	-16	*2-154/S-1,D-1	0.0
1993	Min-A	153	602	82	167	27	4	2	41	65	44	.277	.357	.346	89	-7	29	11	2	.988	-5	*2-148/S-6,O-1	-0.5
1994	Min-A★	109	445	85	139	45	3	5	51	41	56	.312	.383	.461	116	12	35	6	7	.994	-23	*2-109/S-1	-0.5
1995	Min-A	136	538	107	179	34	8	11	63	78	95	.333	.427	.487	137	33	46	18	3	.985	-8	*2-136/S-2	3.4
1996	Min-A★	153	578	140	197	35	14	13	72	98	74	.341	.452	.517	142	43	45	14	5	.988	-27	*2-151/D-2	2.7
Total	6	857	3328	596	1019	184	41	34	333	429	369	.306	.395	.417	114	85	214	67	24	.986	-81	2-846/S-12,D-3,O-1	5.8

■ MIKE KNODE
Knode, Kenneth Thomson b: 11/8/1895, Westminster, Md. d: 12/20/80, South Bend, Ind. BR/TR, 5'10", 160 lbs. Deb: 6/28/20 F

YEAR	TM/L	G	AB	R	H	2B	3B	HR	RBI	BB	SO	AVG	OBP	SLG	PRO+	BR/A	SB	CS	SBR	FA	FR	G/POS	TPR
1920	StL-N	42	65	11	15	1	1	0	12	5	6	.231	.306	.277	71	-2	0	1	-1	.824	-0	/O-9,2-4,S-2,3-2	-0.4

■ RAY KNODE
Knode, Robert Troxell "Bob" b: 1/28/01, Westminster, Md. d: 4/13/82, Battle Creek, Mich BL/TL, 5'10", 160 lbs. Deb: 6/30/23 F

YEAR	TM/L	G	AB	R	H	2B	3B	HR	RBI	BB	SO	AVG	OBP	SLG	PRO+	BR/A	SB	CS	SBR	FA	FR	G/POS	TPR
1923	Cle-A	22	38	7	11	0	0	2	4	2	4	.289	.325	.447	102	-0	1	0	0	.992	0	1-21	0.0
1924	Cle-A	11	37	6	9	1	0	0	4	3	0	.243	.300	.270	47	-3	2	1	0	.992	1	1-10	-0.2
1925	Cle-A	45	108	13	27	5	0	0	11	10	4	.250	.314	.296	55	-7	3	3	-1	.990	1	1-34	-0.9
1926	Cle-A	31	24	6	8	1	1	0	4	3	4	.333	.407	.458	124	-1	0	0	0	.984	1	1-11	0.1
Total	4	109	207	32	55	7	1	2	23	18	12	.266	.324	.338	70	-9	6	4	-1	.990	2	/1-76	-1.0

■ PUNCH KNOLL
Knoll, Charles Elmer b: 10/7/1881, Evansville, Ind. d: 2/8/60, Evansville, Ind. BR/TR, 5'7.5", 170 lbs. Deb: 4/27/05

YEAR	TM/L	G	AB	R	H	2B	3B	HR	RBI	BB	SO	AVG	OBP	SLG	PRO+	BR/A	SB	FA	FR	G/POS	TPR
1905	Was-A	79	244	24	52	10	5	0	29	9		.213	.247	.295	75	-8	3	.927	-1	O-63/C-5,1-2	-1.3

■ BOBBY KNOOP
Knoop, Robert Frank b: 10/18/38, Sioux City, Iowa BR/TR, 6'1", 170 lbs. Deb: 4/13/64 MC

YEAR	TM/L	G	AB	R	H	2B	3B	HR	RBI	BB	SO	AVG	OBP	SLG	PRO+	BR/A	SB	CS	SBR	FA	FR	G/POS	TPR
1964	LA-A	162	486	42	105	8	1	7	38	46	109	.216	.291	.280	66	-23	3	2	-0	.978	37	*2-161	2.8
1965	Cal-A	142	465	47	125	24	4	7	43	31	101	.269	.315	.383	99	-1	3	2	-0	.971	13	*2-142	2.5
1966	Cal-A★	161	590	54	137	18	11	17	72	43	144	.232	.285	.386	94	-6	1	5	-3	.981	17	*2-161	2.0
1967	Cal-A	159	511	51	125	18	5	9	38	44	156	.245	.306	.352	98	-2	2	2	-1	.986	1	*2-159	1.0
1968	Cal-A	152	494	48	123	20	4	3	39	35	128	.249	.303	.324	93	-5	3	2	-0	.981	16	*2-151	2.2
1969	Cal-A	27	71	5	14	1	0	1	6	13	16	.197	.321	.254	66	-3	1	3	-2	.977	2	2-27	-0.1
	Chi-A	104	345	34	79	14	1	6	41	35	68	.229	.304	.328	73	-12	2	0	1	.985	23	*2-104	2.0
	Yr	131	416	39	93	15	1	7	47	48	84	.224	.307	.315	72	-15	3	3	-1	.984	25	*2-131	1.9
1970	Chi-A	130	402	34	92	13	2	5	36	34	79	.229	.292	.308	63	-20	0	1	-1	.984	35	*2-126	2.5
1971	KC-A	72	161	14	33	8	1	1	11	15	36	.205	.273	.286	59	-9	1	0	0	.968	-1	2-52/3-1	-0.6
1972	KC-A	44	97	8	23	5	0	0	7	9	16	.237	.302	.289	77	-3	0	0	0	.972	8	2-33/3-4	0.7
Total	9	1153	3622	337	856	129	29	56	331	305	833	.236	.298	.334	83	-84	16	17	-5	.980	150	*2-1116/3-5	15.0

■ RANDY KNORR
Knorr, Randy Duane b: 11/12/68, San Gabriel, Cal. BR/TR, 6'2", 205 lbs. Deb: 9/5/91

YEAR	TM/L	G	AB	R	H	2B	3B	HR	RBI	BB	SO	AVG	OBP	SLG	PRO+	BR/A	SB	CS	SBR	FA	FR	G/POS	TPR
1991	Tor-A	3	1	0	0	0	0	0	0	0	1	.000	.500	.000	49	0	0	0		1.000	1	/C-3	0.1
1992	Tor-A	8	19	1	5	0	0	1	2	1	5	.263	.300	.421	96	-0	0	0		1.000	1	/C-8	0.1
1993	*Tor-A	39	101	11	25	3	2	4	20	9	29	.248	.309	.436	97	-1	0	0		1.000	1	C-39	0.0
1994	Tor-A	40	124	20	30	2	0	7	19	10	35	.242	.304	.427	86	-3	0	0		.993	-0	C-40	-0.1
1995	Tor-A	45	132	18	28	8	0	3	16	11	28	.212	.273	.341	59	-8	0	0		.971	-2	C-45	-0.7
1996	Hou-N	37	87	7	17	5	0	1	7	5	18	.195	.247	.287	45	-7	0	1	-1	1.000	6	C-33	0.1
Total	6	172	464	57	105	18	2	16	64	37	116	.226	.286	.377	74	-20	0	1	-1	.990	6	C-168	-0.5

■ GEORGE KNOTHE
Knothe, George Bertram b: 1/12/1898, Bayonne, N.J. d: 7/3/81, Dover, N.J. BR/TR, 5'10", 165 lbs. Deb: 4/25/32 F

YEAR	TM/L	G	AB	R	H	2B	3B	HR	RBI	BB	SO	AVG	OBP	SLG	PRO+	BR/A	SB	FA	FR	G/POS	TPR
1932	Phi-N	6	12	2	1	1	0	0	0	0	0	.083	.083	.167	-31	-2	0	.923	-1	/2-5	-0.3

■ FRITZ KNOTHE
Knothe, Wilfred Edgar b: 5/1/03, Passaic, N.J. d: 3/27/63, Passaic, N.J. BR/TR, 5'10.5", 180 lbs. Deb: 4/12/32 F

YEAR	TM/L	G	AB	R	H	2B	3B	HR	RBI	BB	SO	AVG	OBP	SLG	PRO+	BR/A	SB	FA	FR	G/POS	TPR
1932	Bos-N	89	344	45	82	19	1	1	36	39	37	.238	.318	.308	72	-13	5	.947	-3	3-87	-1.0
1933	Bos-N	44	158	15	36	5	1	1	9	13	25	.228	.291	.304	76	-5	1	.978	-7	3-33/S-9	-1.0
	Phi-N	41	113	10	17	2	0	0	11	6	19	.150	.193	.168	3	-14	2	.949	15	3-32/2-4	0.3
	Yr	85	271	25	53	7	1	1	17	19	44	.196	.251	.247	42	-20	3	.961	8	3-65/S-9,2-4	-0.7
Total	2	174	615	70	135	26	3	2	53	58	81	.220	.289	.281	59	-32	8	.953	5	3-152/S-9,2-4	-1.7

■ JOE KNOTTS
Knotts, Joseph Steven b: 3/3/1884, Greensboro, Pa. d: 9/15/50, Philadelphia, Pa. BR/TR, Deb: 9/18/07

YEAR	TM/L	G	AB	R	H	2B	3B	HR	RBI	BB	SO	AVG	OBP	SLG	PRO+	BR/A	SB	FA	FR	G/POS	TPR
1907	Bos-N	3	8	0	0	0	0	0	0	0	1	.000	.111	.000	-65	-2	0	1.000	-0	/C-3	-0.2

■ ED KNOUFF
Knouff, Edward "Fred" b: 6/1868, Philadelphia, Pa. d: 9/14/1900, Philadelphia, Pa. BR/TR, 210 lbs. Deb: 7/1/1885

YEAR	TM/L	G	AB	R	H	2B	3B	HR	RBI	BB	SO	AVG	OBP	SLG	PRO+	BR/A	SB	FA	FR	G/POS	TPR
1885	Phi-a	14	48	4	9	2	0	0		2	2	.188	.220	.188	28	-4		.867	1	P-14/O-1	0.0
1886	Bal-a	1	3	0	0	0	0	0	0	0	0	.000	.250	.000	-20	-0		1.000	1	/P-1	0.0
1887	Bal-a	9	31	4	9	0	0	0	0	3	1	.290	.313	.290	73	-1	1	.889	-1	/P-9,O-3	-0.1
	StL-a	15	56	4	10	1	2	0	6	1	1	.179	.207	.268	29	-6	1	.800	-2	/O-9,P-6	-0.4
	Yr	24	87	8	19	1	2	0		9	2	.218	.244	.276	43	-7	2	.897	-3	P-15,O-12	-0.5
1888	StL-a	9	31	1	3	0	0	0	1	0	3	.097	.200	.097	-3	-4	1	.842	-3	/P-9	0.0
	Cle-a	2	6	0	1	0	0	0	0	1	0	.167	.286	.333	101	0	0	1.000	1	/P-2,2-1	0.0
	Yr	11	37	1	4	0	0	0	1	1	3	.108	.214	.135	12	-4	1	.880	-1	P-11/2-1	0.0
1889	Phi-a	3	12	3	3	1	0	0	2	1	1	.250	.308	.333	84	-0	1	1.000	1	/P-3	0.0
Total	5	53	187	16	35	3	2	0	14	9	1	.187	.236	.225	35	-15	4	.891	-3	/P-44,O-13,2-1	-0.5

■ JAKE KNOWDELL
Knowdell, Jacob Augustus b: 7/27/1840, Brooklyn, N.Y. 5'7.5", 148 lbs. Deb: 6/20/1874

YEAR	TM/L	G	AB	R	H	2B	3B	HR	RBI	BB	SO	AVG	OBP	SLG	PRO+	BR/A	SB	CS	SBR	FA	FR	G/POS	TPR
1874	Atl-n	24	86	8	12	1	1	0	3	1	3	.140	.149	.174	4	-8	1	0	0	.824	-4	C-21/O-4	-0.9
1875	Atl-n	43	163	17	32	2	0	0	9	1	3	.196	.201	.209	49	-7	0	1	-1	.781	-8	C-33,S-11/O-4,2-1	-1.3
1878	Mil-N	4	14	0	3	1	0	0	2	0	3	.214	.214	.286	59	-1				.875	0	/C-2,O-1,S-1	-0.3
Total	2 n	67	249	25	44	3	1	0	14	2	9	.177	.183	.197	32	-15	1	1	-0	.796	-11	/C-54,S-11,O-8,2-1	-2.2

■ JIMMY KNOWLES
Knowles, James "Darby" b: 9/1856, Toronto, Ont., Can. d: 2/11/12, Jersey City, N.J. 5'9", 160 lbs. Deb: 5/2/1884

YEAR	TM/L	G	AB	R	H	2B	3B	HR	RBI	BB	SO	AVG	OBP	SLG	PRO+	BR/A	SB	FA	FR	G/POS	TPR
1884	Pit-a	46	182	19	42	5	7	0			5	.231	.259	.335	91	-2		.961	-0	1-46	-0.7
	Bro-a	41	153	19	36	5	1	1			3	.235	.255	.301	80	-3		.953	1	1-30,3-11	-0.6

YEAR	TM/L	G	AB	R	H	2B	3B	HR	RBI	BB	SO	AVG	OBP	SLG	PRO+	BR/A	SB	CS	SBR	FA	FR	G/POS	TPR
	Yr	87	335	38	78	10	8	1		8		.233	.257	.319	86	-5				.958	1	1-76,3-11	-1.3
1886	Was-N	115	443	43	94	16	11	3	35	15	73	.212	.238	.318	72	-15	20			.899	28	2-62,3-53	1.5
1887	NY-a	16	60	12	15	1	1	0	6	1		.250	.262	.300	59	-3	6			.934	-3	2-16/3-1	-0.5
1890	Roc-a	123	491	83	138	12	8	5	84	59		.281	.359	.369	124	16	55			.881	7	*3-123	2.4
1892	NY-N	16	59	9	9	1	0	0	7	6	8	.153	.231	.169	22	-5	2			.792	-5	3-15/S-1	-0.9
Total	5	357	1388	185	334	40	28	9	132	89	81	.241	.288	.329	91	-13	83			.861	28	3-203/2-78,1-76,S-1	1.2

■ ANDY KNOX
Knox, Andrew Jackson "Dasher"　b: 1/6/1864, Philadelphia, Pa.　d: 9/14/40, Philadelphia, Pa.　BR/TR,　Deb: 9/19/1890

YEAR	TM/L	G	AB	R	H	2B	3B	HR	RBI	BB	SO	AVG	OBP	SLG	PRO+	BR/A	SB	CS	SBR	FA	FR	G/POS	TPR
1890	Phi-a	21	75	6	19	3	0	0	8	9		.253	.333	.293	87	-1	5			.963	-2	1-21	-0.3

■ CLIFF KNOX
Knox, Clifford Hiram "Bud"　b: 1/7/02, Coalville, Iowa　d: 9/24/65, Oskaloosa, Iowa　BB/TR, 5'11.5", 178 lbs.　Deb: 7/1/24

YEAR	TM/L	G	AB	R	H	2B	3B	HR	RBI	BB	SO	AVG	OBP	SLG	PRO+	BR/A	SB	CS	SBR	FA	FR	G/POS	TPR
1924	Pit-N	6	18	1	4	0	0	0	2	2	0	.222	.300	.222	41	-1	0	0	0	.917	2	/C-6	0.1

■ JOHN KNOX
Knox, John Clinton　b: 7/26/48, Newark, N.J.　BL/TR, 6', 170 lbs.　Deb: 8/1/72

YEAR	TM/L	G	AB	R	H	2B	3B	HR	RBI	BB	SO	AVG	OBP	SLG	PRO+	BR/A	SB	CS	SBR	FA	FR	G/POS	TPR
1972	*Det-A	14	13	1	1	0	0	0	1	0	2	.077	.143	.154	-11	-2	0	0	0	1.000	-4	/2-4	0.2
1973	Det-A	12	32	1	9	1	0	0	3	3	3	.281	.343	.313	80	-1	1	1	-0	1.000	-3	/2-9	-0.3
1974	Det-A	55	88	11	27	1	1	0	6	6	13	.307	.351	.341	96	-0	5	4	-1	.956	8	2-33/3-1,D-2	0.7
1975	Det-A	43	86	8	23	1	0	0	1	11	9	.267	.344	.279	74	-2	1	2	-1	.980	-1	2-23/3-3,D-3	-0.4
Total	4	124	219	21	60	4	1	0	11	20	27	.274	.335	.301	79	-5	7	7	-2	.973	8	/2-69,D-5,3-4	0.2

■ NICK KOBACK
Koback, Nicholas Nicholie　b: 7/19/35, Hartford, Conn.　BR/TR, 6', 187 lbs.　Deb: 7/29/53

YEAR	TM/L	G	AB	R	H	2B	3B	HR	RBI	BB	SO	AVG	OBP	SLG	PRO+	BR/A	SB	CS	SBR	FA	FR	G/POS	TPR
1953	Pit-N	7	16	1	2	0	1	0	0	1	4	.125	.176	.250	10	-2	0	0	0	1.000	-4	/C-6	-0.5
1954	Pit-N	4	10	0	0	0	0	0	0	0	8	.000	.000	.000	-99	-3	0	0	0	1.000	-1	/C-4	-0.3
1955	Pit-N	5	7	0	2	0	0	0	0	0	1	.286	.286	.286	53	-0	0	0	0	1.000	0	/C-2	0.0
Total	3	16	33	1	4	0	1	0	0	1	13	.121	.147	.182	-15	-6	0	0	0	1.000	-6	/C-12	-0.8

■ BARNEY KOCH
Koch, Barnett　b: 3/23/23, Campbell, Neb.　d: 6/6/87, Tacoma, Wash.　BR/TR, 5'8", 140 lbs.　Deb: 7/23/44

YEAR	TM/L	G	AB	R	H	2B	3B	HR	RBI	BB	SO	AVG	OBP	SLG	PRO+	BR/A	SB	CS	SBR	FA	FR	G/POS	TPR
1944	Bro-N	33	96	11	21	2	0	0	1	3	9	.219	.242	.240	37	-8	0			.956	-6	2-29/S-1	-1.3

■ BRAD KOCHER
Kocher, Bradley Wilson　b: 1/16/1888, White Haven, Pa.　d: 1/13/65, White Haven, Pa.　BR/TR, 5'11", 188 lbs.　Deb: 4/24/12

YEAR	TM/L	G	AB	R	H	2B	3B	HR	RBI	BB	SO	AVG	OBP	SLG	PRO+	BR/A	SB	CS	SBR	FA	FR	G/POS	TPR
1912	Det-A	29	63	5	13	3	1	0	9	2		.206	.231	.286	49	-4	0			.904	-3	C-24	-0.6
1915	NY-A	4	11	3	5	0	1	0	2	0	1	.455	.455	.636	243	2	0			1.000	-1	/C-3	0.1
1916	NY-N	34	65	1	7	2	0	0	1	2	10	.108	.134	.138	-17	-9	0			.978	-7	C-30	-1.7
Total	3	67	139	9	25	5	2	0	12	4	11	.180	.203	.245	34	-12	0			.943	-11	/C-57	-2.2

■ PETE KOEGEL
Koegel, Peter John　b: 7/31/47, Mineola, N.Y.　BR/TR, 6'6.5", 230 lbs.　Deb: 9/1/70

YEAR	TM/L	G	AB	R	H	2B	3B	HR	RBI	BB	SO	AVG	OBP	SLG	PRO+	BR/A	SB	CS	SBR	FA	FR	G/POS	TPR
1970	Mil-A	7	8	2	2	0	0	1	1	3		.250	.333	.625	157	1	0	0	0	1.000	0	/O-1	0.0
1971	Mil-A	2	3	0	0	0	0	0	0	0		.000	.400	.000	22	-0	0	0	0	1.000	-0	/1-1	0.0
	Phi-N	12	26	1	6	1	0	0	3	2	7	.231	.286	.269	58	-1	0	0	0	1.000	-1	/C-7,O-1	-0.2
1972	Phi-N	41	49	3	7	2	0	1	6	6	16	.143	.236	.184	20	-5	0	0	0	1.000	-2	/1-8,C-5,3-4,O-2	-0.8
Total	3	62	86	6	15	3	0	1	5	11	28	.174	.268	.244	45	-6	0	0	0	.971	-3	/C-12,1-9,3-4,O-4	-1.0

■ BEN KOEHLER
Koehler, Benard James　b: 1/26/1877, Schoerndorn, Germany　d: 5/21/61, South Bend, Ind.　BR/TR, 5'10.5", 175 lbs.　Deb: 4/23/05

YEAR	TM/L	G	AB	R	H	2B	3B	HR	RBI	BB	SO	AVG	OBP	SLG	PRO+	BR/A	SB	CS	SBR	FA	FR	G/POS	TPR
1905	StL-A	142	536	55	127	14	6	2	47	32		.237	.285	.297	89	-7	22			.969	6	*O-124,1-12/2-6	-0.8
1906	StL-A	66	186	27	41	1	1	0	15	24		.220	.322	.237	79	-3	9			.957	-4	O-52/2-7,S-1,3-1	-1.0
Total	2	208	722	82	168	15	7	2	62	56		.233	.295	.281	87	-10	31			.966	2	O-176/2-13,1-12,3S	-1.8

■ PIP KOEHLER
Koehler, Horace Levering　b: 1/16/02, Gilbert, Pa.　d: 12/8/86, Tacoma, Wash.　BR/TR, 5'10", 165 lbs.　Deb: 4/22/25

YEAR	TM/L	G	AB	R	H	2B	3B	HR	RBI	BB	SO	AVG	OBP	SLG	PRO+	BR/A	SB	CS	SBR	FA	FR	G/POS	TPR
1925	NY-N	12	2	1	0	0	0	0	0	0	0	.000	.000	.000	-99	-1	0	0	0	1.000	-0	/O-3	-0.1

■ BRIAN KOELLING
Koelling, Brian Wayne　b: 6/11/69, Cincinnati, Ohio　BR/TR, 6'1", 185 lbs.　Deb: 8/21/93

YEAR	TM/L	G	AB	R	H	2B	3B	HR	RBI	BB	SO	AVG	OBP	SLG	PRO+	BR/A	SB	CS	SBR	FA	FR	G/POS	TPR
1993	Cin-N	7	15	2	1	0	0	0	0	0	6	.067	.125	.067	-47	-3	0	0	0	.941	1	/2-3,S-2	-0.2

■ LEN KOENECKE
Koenecke, Leonard George　b: 1/18/04, Baraboo, Wis.　d: 9/17/35, Toronto, Ont., Can　BL/TR, 5'11", 180 lbs.　Deb: 4/12/32

YEAR	TM/L	G	AB	R	H	2B	3B	HR	RBI	BB	SO	AVG	OBP	SLG	PRO+	BR/A	SB	CS	SBR	FA	FR	G/POS	TPR
1932	NY-N	42	137	33	35	5	0	4	14	11	13	.255	.320	.380	89	-2	3			.924	-5	O-35	-0.9
1934	Bro-N	123	460	79	147	31	7	14	73	70	38	.320	.411	.509	152	36	8			.994	2	*O-121	3.1
1935	Bro-N	100	325	43	92	13	2	4	27	43	45	.283	.369	.372	102	2	0			.966	-4	O-91	-0.5
Total	3	265	922	155	274	49	9	22	114	124	96	.297	.383	.441	125	36	11			.976	-7	O-247	1.7

■ MARK KOENIG
Koenig, Mark Anthony　b: 7/19/04, San Francisco, Cal.　d: 4/22/93, Willows, Cal.　BB/TR, 6', 180 lbs.　Deb: 9/8/25

YEAR	TM/L	G	AB	R	H	2B	3B	HR	RBI	BB	SO	AVG	OBP	SLG	PRO+	BR/A	SB	CS	SBR	FA	FR	G/POS	TPR
1925	NY-A	28	110	14	23	6	1	0	4	5	4	.209	.243	.282	34	-12	0	1	3	.944	-3	S-28	-1.1
1926	*NY-A	147	617	93	167	26	8	5	62	43	37	.271	.319	.363	79	-21	4	3	-1	.931	-0	*S-141	-0.6
1927	*NY-A	123	526	99	150	20	11	3	62	25	21	.285	.320	.382	84	-14	3	2	-0	.936	14	*S-122	1.2
1928	*NY-A	132	533	89	170	19	10	4	63	32	19	.319	.360	.415	106	4	3	5	-2	.923	-20	*S-125	-0.3
1929	NY-A	116	373	44	109	27	5	3	41	23	17	.292	.335	.416	99	-2	1	1	-0	.911	-13	S-61,3-37/2-1	-0.7
1930	NY-A	21	74	9	17	5	0	0	9	6	5	.230	.296	.297	53	-5	0	0	0	.905	2	S-19	-0.1
	Det-A	76	267	37	64	9	2	1	16	20	15	.240	.295	.300	50	-20	2	0	1	.922	-14	S-70/P-2,3-2,O-1	-2.4
	Yr	97	341	46	81	14	2	1	25	26	20	.238	.295	.299	51	-25	2	0	1	.918	-13	S-89/P-2,3-2,O-1	-2.5
1931	Det-A	106	364	33	92	24	4	1	39	14	12	.253	.282	.349	63	-20	8	2	1	.955	-23	2-55,S-35/P-3	-3.4
1932	*Chi-N	33	102	15	36	5	1	3	11	3	5	.353	.377	.510	137	5	0			.932	10	S-31	1.7
1933	Chi-N	80	218	32	62	12	1	3	25	15	9	.284	.330	.390	105	1	5			.922	5	3-37,S-26/2-2	1.4
1934	Cin-N	151	633	60	172	26	6	1	67	15	24	.272	.289	.336	68	-29	5			.930	8	3-64,S-58,2-26/1-4	-1.6
1935	NY-N	107	396	40	112	12	0	3	37	13	18	.283	.306	.336	74	-15	0			.968	-11	2-64,S-21,3-15	-1.9
1936	*NY-N	42	58	7	16	4	0	1	4	9	3	.276	.373	.397	109	1	0			.905	-3	S-10/2-8,3-3	0.2
Total	12	1162	4271	572	1190	195	49	28	443	222	190	.279	.316	.367	81	-126	31	14		.927	-50	S-747,3-158,2/P10	-8.2

■ HENRY KOHLER
Kohler, Henry C.　b: 5/5/1852, Baltimore, Md.　d: 8/27/34, Baltimore, Md.　Deb: 7/12/1871

YEAR	TM/L	G	AB	R	H	2B	3B	HR	RBI	BB	SO	AVG	OBP	SLG	PRO+	BR/A	SB	CS	SBR	FA	FR	G/POS	TPR
1871	Kek-n	3	12	0	2	0	0	0	1	0	0	.167	.167	.250	17	-1	0	0	0	.000	-0	/C-2,1-2,3-1	-0.1
1873	Mar-n	6	25	2	3	0	0	0	0	1	1	.120	.120	.120	-37	-4	0	0	0	.686	-4	/3-6,C-1,1-1,0-1	-0.6
1874	Bal-n	2	4	0	0	0	0	0	0	0	0	.000	.000	.000	-99	-1	0	0	0	.714	-1	/1-1	-0.1
Total	3 n	11	41	2	5	0	0	0	1	1	1	.122	.122	.146	-24	-6	0	0	0	.700	-5	/3-7,1-4,C-3,O-1	-0.8

■ DICK KOKOS
Kokos, Richard Jerome (b: Richard Jerome Kokoszka)　b: 2/28/28, Chicago, Ill.　d: 4/9/86, Chicago, Ill.　BL/TL, 5'8.5", 170 lbs.　Deb: 7/8/48

YEAR	TM/L	G	AB	R	H	2B	3B	HR	RBI	BB	SO	AVG	OBP	SLG	PRO+	BR/A	SB	CS	SBR	FA	FR	G/POS	TPR
1948	StL-A	71	258	40	77	15	3	4	40	28	32	.298	.374	.426	110	3	4	3	-1	.964	5	O-71	-0.1
1949	StL-A	143	501	80	131	28	1	23	77	66	91	.261	.351	.459	109	4	3	5	-2	.981	8	*O-138	0.3
1950	StL-A	143	490	77	128	27	5	18	67	88	73	.261	.375	.447	106	4	8	5	0	.970	9	*O-127	0.5
1953	StL-A	107	299	41	72	12	0	13	38	56	53	.241	.361	.411	106	3	0	5	-3	.963	-1	O-83	-0.4
1954	Bal-A	11	10	1	2	0	0	1	1	4	3	.200	.429	.500	166	1	0	0	0	1.000	0	/O-1	0.1
Total	5	475	1558	239	410	82	9	59	223	242	252	.263	.365	.441	108	16	15	21	-8	.971	16	O-420	0.4

■ GARY KOLB
Kolb, Gary Alan　b: 3/13/40, Rock Falls, Ill.　BL/TR, 6', 195 lbs.　Deb: 9/7/60

YEAR	TM/L	G	AB	R	H	2B	3B	HR	RBI	BB	SO	AVG	OBP	SLG	PRO+	BR/A	SB	CS	SBR	FA	FR	G/POS	TPR
1960	StL-N	9	3	1	0	0	0	0	0	0	0	.000	.000	.000	-92	-1	0	0	0	1.000	-0	/O-2	-0.1
1962	StL-N	6	14	1	5	0	0	0	1	2	1	.357	.400	.357	96	-0	0	0	0	1.000	-1	/O-6	-0.1
1963	StL-N	75	96	23	26	1	5	3	10	22	26	.271	.407	.479	141	5	2	1	0	.981	-11	O-58/C-1,3-1	0.3
1964	Mil-N	36	64	7	12	2	0	2	6	10	10	.188	.257	.203	31	-6	2	3	-0	1.000	-6	O-14/3-7,2-6,C-2	-1.3
1965	Mil-N	24	27	3	7	0	0	0	1	4	6	.259	.286	.259	54	-2	0	0	0	1.000	-3	O-13	-0.5
	NY-N	40	90	8	15	2	0	1	3	9	28	.167	.194	.222	17	-10	3	1	0	.976	-1	O-29/1-1,3-1	-1.1
	Yr	64	117	11	22	2	0	1	4	13	34	.188	.215	.231	26	-11	3	1	0	.981	-4	O-42/1-1,3-1	-1.7
1968	Pit-N	74	119	16	26	2	0	1	6	11	19	.218	.289	.261	82	-3	2	3	-1	.900	-2	O-25,C-10/3-4,2-1	-0.6
1969	Pit-N	29	37	4	3	1	0	0	1	2	14	.081	.128	.108	-34	-7	0	0	0	1.000	-0	/C-7	-0.7
Total	7	293	450	63	94	9	6	6	29	46	104	.209	.282	.296	65	-21	10	4	1	.965	-23	O-147/C-20,3-13,21	-5.2

YEAR	TM/L	G	AB	R	H	2B	3B	HR	RBI	BB	SO	AVG	OBP	SLG	PRO+	BR/A	SB	CS	SBR	FA	FR	G/POS	TPR

■ DON KOLLOWAY

Kolloway, Donald Martin "Butch" or "Cab"   b: 8/4/18, Posen, Ill.   d: 6/30/94, Blue Island, Ill.   BR/TR, 6'3", 200 lbs.   Deb: 9/16/40

YEAR	TM/L	G	AB	R	H	2B	3B	HR	RBI	BB	SO	AVG	OBP	SLG	PRO+	BR/A	SB	CS	SBR	FA	FR	G/POS	TPR
1940	Chi-A	10	40	5	9	1	0	0	3	0	3	.225	.225	.250	23	-5				.922	4	2-10	-0.5
1941	Chi-A	71	280	33	76	8	3	3	24	6	12	.271	.292	.354	71	-13	11	4	1	.955	-7	2-62/1-4	-1.5
1942	Chi-A	147	601	72	164	**40**	4	3	60	30	39	.273	.311	.368	92	-8	16	14	-4	.966	-9	*2-116,1-33	-1.6
1943	Chi-A	85	348	29	75	14	4	1	33	9	30	.216	.235	.287	53	-22	11	7	-1	.968	-1	2-85	-2.1
1946	Chi-A	123	482	45	135	23	4	3	53	9	29	.280	.293	.363	86	-12	14	6	1	.972	3	2-90,3-31	-0.1
1947	Chi-A	124	485	49	135	25	4	2	35	17	34	.278	.303	.359	87	-11	11	4	1	.962	5	2-99,1-11/3-8	0.1
1948	Chi-A	119	417	60	114	14	4	6	38	18	18	.273	.303	.369	81	-13	2	4	-2	.966	11	2-83,3-18	0.0
1949	Chi-A	4	0	0	0	0	0	0	0	0	1	.000	.000	.000	-99	-1	0	0	0	.000	0	/3-2	-0.1
	Det-A	126	483	71	142	19	3	2	47	49	25	.294	.361	.358	91	-6	7	7	-2	.956	-21	2-62,1-57/3-7	-2.6
	Yr	130	487	71	142	19	3	2	47	49	26	.292	.359	.355	89	-7	7	7	-2	.956	-21	2-62,1-57/3-9	-2.7
1950	Det-A	125	467	55	135	20	4	6	62	29	28	.289	.331	.388	81	-15	1	3	-2	.989	3	*1-118/2-1	-1.5
1951	Det-A	78	212	28	54	7	0	1	17	15	12	.255	.307	.302	65	-10	2	3	-1	.992	6	1-59	-0.8
1952	Det-A	65	173	19	42	9	0	2	21	7	19	.243	.280	.329	69	-8	0	2	-1	.979	-1	1-32/2-8	-1.1
1953	Phi-A	2	1	0	0	0	0	0	0	0	1	.000	.000	.000	-96	-0	0	0	0	.000	0	/3-1	0.0
Total	12	1079	3993	466	1081	180	30	29	393	189	251	.271	.305	.353	80	-124	76	54	-10	.964	-13	2-616,1-314/3-67	-11.8

■ KARL KOLSETH

Kolseth, Karl Dickey "Koley"   b: 12/25/1892, Cambridge, Mass.   d: 5/3/56, Cumberland, Md.   BL/TR, 6', 182 lbs.   Deb: 9/30/15

YEAR	TM/L	G	AB	R	H	2B	3B	HR	RBI	BB	SO	AVG	OBP	SLG	PRO+	BR/A	SB	CS	SBR	FA	FR	G/POS	TPR
1915	Bal-F	6	23	1	6	1	1	0	1	1	0	.261	.292	.391	89	-1	0			.915	-2	/1-6	-0.3

■ FRED KOMMERS

Kommers, Frederick Raymond "Bugs"   b: 3/31/1886, Chicago, Ill.   d: 6/14/43, Chicago, Ill.   BL/TR, 6', 175 lbs.   Deb: 6/25/13

YEAR	TM/L	G	AB	R	H	2B	3B	HR	RBI	BB	SO	AVG	OBP	SLG	PRO+	BR/A	SB	CS	SBR	FA	FR	G/POS	TPR
1913	Pit-N	40	155	14	36	5	4	0	22	10	29	.232	.279	.316	73	-6	1			.979	-2	O-40	-1.0
1914	StL-F	76	244	33	75	9	8	3	41	24	36	.307	.376	.447	117	3	7			.908	-2	O-67	-0.2
	Bal-F	16	42	5	9	1	0	1	1	7	7	.214	.340	.310	75	-2	0			.938	-2	O-12	-0.5
	Yr	92	286	38	84	10	8	4	42	31	43	.294	.371	.427	111	1	7			.911	-3	O-79	-0.7
Total	2	132	441	52	120	15	12	4	64	41	72	.272	.340	.388	99	-5	8			.938	-6	O-119	-1.7

■ BRAD KOMMINSK

Komminsk, Brad Lynn   b: 4/4/61, Lima, Ohio   BR/TR, 6'2", 205 lbs.   Deb: 8/14/83

YEAR	TM/L	G	AB	R	H	2B	3B	HR	RBI	BB	SO	AVG	OBP	SLG	PRO+	BR/A	SB	CS	SBR	FA	FR	G/POS	TPR
1983	Atl-N	19	36	2	8	2	0	0	4	5	7	.222	.317	.278	62	-2	0	1	0	.944	-1	O-13	-0.3
1984	Atl-N	90	301	37	61	10	0	8	36	29	77	.203	.277	.316	62	-15	18	8	1	.993	-2	O-80	-0.5
1985	Atl-N	106	300	52	68	12	3	4	21	38	71	.227	.316	.327	75	-9	10	8	-2	.959	-4	O-92	-1.9
1986	Atl-N	5	5	1	2	0	0	0	1	0	1	.400	.400	.400	115	0	0	1	-1	1.000	-0	/3-2,O-2	-0.1
1987	Mil-N	7	15	0	1	0	0	0	0	1	7	.067	.125	.067	-46	-3	1	0	0	1.000	-0	/O-5,D-1	-0.3
1989	Cle-A	71	198	27	47	8	2	8	33	24	55	.237	.323	.419	106	0	8	2	1	.995	3	O-68	0.4
1990	SF-N	8	5	2	1	0	0	0	0	3	1	.200	.333	.200	52	-0	0	0	0	1.000	-3	/O-7	-0.3
	Bal-A	46	101	18	24	4	0	3	8	14	29	.238	.342	.366	101	0	1	1	-0	1.000	-5	O-40/D-2	-0.5
1991	Oak-A	24	25	1	3	1	0	0	2	2	9	.120	.185	.160	-4	-4	1	0	0	1.000	-6	O-22	-0.9
Total	8	376	986	140	215	37	5	23	105	114	258	.218	.303	.336	75	-31	39	20	-0	.984	-17	O-329/D-3,3-2	-6.0

■ ED KONETCHY

Konetchy, Edward Joseph "Big Ed"   b: 9/3/1885, LaCrosse, Wis.   d: 5/27/47, Ft.Worth, Tex.   BR/TR, 6'2.5", 195 lbs.   Deb: 6/29/07

YEAR	TM/L	G	AB	R	H	2B	3B	HR	RBI	BB	SO	AVG	OBP	SLG	PRO+	BR/A	SB	CS	SBR	FA	FR	G/POS	TPR
1907	StL-N	91	331	34	83	11	8	3	30	26		.251	.317	.360	116	5	13			.975	4	1-91	0.8
1908	StL-N	154	545	46	135	19	12	5	50	38		.248	.309	.354	117	9	16			.986	11	*1-154	2.0
1909	StL-N	152	576	88	165	23	14	4	80	65		.286	.366	.396	145	31	25			.985	5	*1-152	3.7
1910	StL-N	144	520	87	157	23	16	3	78	78	59	.302	.397	.425	145	32	18			**.991**	8	*1-144/P-1	4.1
1911	StL-N	158	571	90	165	**38**	13	6	88	81	63	.289	.384	.433	132	25	27			**.991**	-6	*1-158	1.9
1912	StL-N	143	538	81	169	26	13	8	82	62	66	.314	.389	.455	134	25	25			.991	6	*1-142/O-1	2.8
1913	StL-N	140	504	75	139	18	17	8	68	53	41	.276	.353	.427	124	15	27			**.995**	7	*1-140/P-1	2.2
1914	Pit-N	154	563	56	140	23	9	4	51	32	48	.249	.291	.343	92	-8	20			**.995**	5	*1-154	-0.7
1915	Pit-F	152	576	79	181	31	18	10	93	41	52	.314	.363	.483	138	18	27			**.994**	-0	*1-152	1.5
1916	Bos-N	158	566	76	147	29	13	3	70	43	46	.260	.320	.373	125	13	16			.990	9	*1-158	1.5
1917	Bos-N	130	474	56	129	19	13	2	54	36	40	.272	.330	.380	125	13	16			**.994**	2	*1-129	1.1
1918	Bos-N	119	437	33	103	15	5	2	56	32	35	.236	.291	.307	86	-8	5			**.992**	-2	*1-112/O-6,P-1	-1.6
1919	Bro-N	132	486	46	145	24	9	1	47	29	39	.298	.342	.391	117	10	14			**.994**	7	*1-132	1.3
1920	*Bro-N	131	497	62	153	22	12	5	63	33	18	.308	.352	.431	120	12	3	2	-0	.990	1	*1-130	1.0
1921	Bro-N	55	197	25	53	6	5	3	23	19	21	.269	.336	.396	90	-3	3	3	-1	.987	-1	1-54	-0.6
	Phi-N	72	268	38	86	17	4	8	59	21	17	.321	.379	.504	122	8	3	0	1	.986	6	1-71	1.3
	Yr	127	465	63	139	23	9	11	82	40	38	.299	.361	.458	109	6	6	3	-0	.986	4	*1-125	0.7
Total	15	2085	7649	972	2150	344	181	75	992	689	_545_	.281	.346	.403	122	196	255	_5_		.990	59	*1-2073/O-7,P-3	22.3

■ MIKE KONNICK

Konnick, Michael Aloysius   b: 1/13/1889, Glen Lyon, Pa.   d: 7/9/71, Wilkes-Barre, Pa.   BR/TR, 5'9", 180 lbs.   Deb: 10/3/09

YEAR	TM/L	G	AB	R	H	2B	3B	HR	RBI	BB	SO	AVG	OBP	SLG	PRO+	BR/A	SB	CS	SBR	FA	FR	G/POS	TPR
1909	Cin-N	2	5	0	2	1	0	0	1	0		.400	.400	.600	211	1	0			1.000	-1	/C-2	0.0
1910	Cin-N	1	3	0	0	0	0	0	0	0	1	.000	.250	.000	-27	-0	0			1.000	-1	/S-1	-0.1
Total	2	3	8	0	2	1	0	0	1	1	_0_	.250	.333	.375	117	0	0			1.000	-1	/C-2,S-1	-0.1

■ BRUCE KONOPKA

Konopka, Bruno Bruce   b: 9/16/19, Hammond, Ind.   d: 9/27/96, Denver, Colo.   BL/TL, 6'2", 190 lbs.   Deb: 6/7/42

YEAR	TM/L	G	AB	R	H	2B	3B	HR	RBI	BB	SO	AVG	OBP	SLG	PRO+	BR/A	SB	CS	SBR	FA	FR	G/POS	TPR
1942	Phi-A	5	10	2	3	0	0	0	1	1	0	.300	.364	.300	88	-0	0	0	0	1.000	-0	/1-3	0.0
1943	Phi-A	2	2	0	0	0	0	0	0	0	1	.000	.000	.000	-99	-0	0	0	0	.000	0	H	-0.1
1946	Phi-A	38	93	7	22	4	1	0	9	4	8	.237	.268	.301	59	-5	0	0	0	.994	1	1-20/O-1	-0.6
Total	3	45	105	9	25	4	1	0	10	5	9	.238	.273	.295	59	-6	0	0	0	.995	1	/1-23,O-1	-0.7

■ HARRY KOONS

Koons, Henry M.   b: 1863, Philadelphia, Pa.   BR/TR, 5'8", 174 lbs.   Deb: 4/17/1884

YEAR	TM/L	G	AB	R	H	2B	3B	HR	RBI	BB	SO	AVG	OBP	SLG	PRO+	BR/A	SB	CS	SBR	FA	FR	G/POS	TPR
1884	Alt-U	21	78	8	18	2	1	0		2		.231	.250	.282	60	-6				.866	5	3-21/C-1	-0.1
	CP-U	1	3	0	0	0	0	0		0		.000	.000	.000	-99	-1				.000	0	/3-1	-0.1
	Yr	22	81	8	18	2	1	0		2		.222	.241	.272	54	-7				.866	6	3-22/C-1	-0.2

■ GEORGE KOPACZ

Kopacz, George Felix "Sonny"   b: 2/26/41, Chicago, Ill.   BL/TL, 6'1", 195 lbs.   Deb: 9/18/66

YEAR	TM/L	G	AB	R	H	2B	3B	HR	RBI	BB	SO	AVG	OBP	SLG	PRO+	BR/A	SB	CS	SBR	FA	FR	G/POS	TPR
1966	Atl-N	6	9	1	0	0	0	0	0	1	5	.000	.100	.000	-68	-1	0	0	0	.909	-1	/1-2	-0.3
1970	Pit-N	10	16	1	3	0	0	0	1	0	1	.188	.188	.188	1	-2	0	0	0	1.000	-1	/1-3	-0.3
Total	2	16	25	2	3	0	0	0	1	1	6	.120	.154	.120	-25	-4	0	0	0	.964	-1	/1-5	-0.5

■ WALLY KOPF

Kopf, Walter Henry   b: 7/10/1899, Stonington, Conn.   d: 4/30/79, Hamilton Co., Ohio.   BB/TR, 5'11", 168 lbs.   Deb: 10/1/21   F

YEAR	TM/L	G	AB	R	H	2B	3B	HR	RBI	BB	SO	AVG	OBP	SLG	PRO+	BR/A	SB	CS	SBR	FA	FR	G/POS	TPR
1921	NY-N	2	3	0	1	0	0	0	0	1	1	.333	.500	.333	125	0	0	0	0	1.000	2	/3-2	0.2

■ LARRY KOPF

Kopf, William Lorenz (a.k.a. Fred Brady In 1913)   b: 11/3/1890, Bristol, Conn.   d: 10/15/86, Anderson Twp., O.   BB/TR, 5'9", 160 lbs.   Deb: 9/2/13   F

YEAR	TM/L	G	AB	R	H	2B	3B	HR	RBI	BB	SO	AVG	OBP	SLG	PRO+	BR/A	SB	CS	SBR	FA	FR	G/POS	TPR
1913	Cle-A	6	10	2	3	1	0	0	1	0	0	.300	.300	.400	102	-0	0			.923	2	/2-4,3-1	0.2
1914	Phi-A	37	69	8	13	2	2	0	12	8	14	.188	.300	.275	76	-2	6			.899	1	S-13/3-8,2-5	0.3
1915	Phi-A	118	386	39	87	10	2	1	33	41	45	.275	.314	.269	77	-10	5	9	-4	.920	-8	S-74,3-42/2-2	-1.6
1916	Cin-N	11	40	2	11	2	0	0	5	1	8	.275	.293	.325	92	-1	1			.942	-2	S-11	-0.3
1917	Cin-N	148	573	81	146	19	8	2	26	28	48	.255	.297	.326	95	-5	17			.916	-11	*S-145	-1.0
1919	*Cin-N	135	503	51	136	18	9	0	58	28	27	.270	.313	.326	95	-4	18			.943	-34	*S-135	-3.4
1920	Cin-N	126	458	56	112	15	6	0	59	35	24	.245	.305	.303	76	-13	14	13	-4	.929	-33	S-123/2-2,3-2,O-1	-4.3
1921	Cin-N	107	367	36	80	8	3	1	25	43	20	.218	.310	.264	56	-22	3	14	-8	.947	-15	S-93/2-4,3-3,O-1	-3.6
1922	Bos-N	126	466	59	124	6	3	1	37	16	24	.266	.332	.298	67	-22	0	3	-1	.944	-14	2-78,S-33,3-13	-3.1
1923	Bos-N	39	138	15	38	5	1	0	10	13	6	.275	.338	.312	75	-5	0	3	-1	.905	-8	S-37/2-4	-1.0
Total	10	853	3010	349	750	84	30	5	266	242	214	.249	.312	.302	78	-82	72	_48_		.928	-122	S-664/2-99,3-69,O-2	-17.8

■ MERLIN KOPP

Kopp, Merlin Henry "Manny"   b: 1/2/1892, Toledo, Ohio   d: 5/6/60, Sacramento, Cal.   BB/TR, 5'8", 158 lbs.   Deb: 8/2/15

YEAR	TM/L	G	AB	R	H	2B	3B	HR	RBI	BB	SO	AVG	OBP	SLG	PRO+	BR/A	SB	CS	SBR	FA	FR	G/POS	TPR
1915	Was-A	16	32	2	8	0	0	0		5	5	.250	.351	.250	79	-1	1			.933	-1	/O-9	-0.2
1918	Phi-A	96	363	60	85	7	7	0	18	42	55	.234	.320	.292	84	-6	22			.972	12	O-96	0.0
1919	Phi-A	75	235	34	53	2	4	1	12	42	43	.226	.348	.281	77	-6	16			.924	-2	O-65	-1.3
Total	3	187	630	96	146	9	11	1	30	89	105	.232	.332	.286	81	-12	39			.953	8	O-170	-1.5

YEAR	TM/L	G	AB	R	H	2B	3B	HR	RBI	BB	SO	AVG	OBP	SLG	PRO+	BR/A	SB	CS	SBR	FA	FR	G/POS	TPR

■ JOE KOPPE
Koppe, Joseph (b: Joseph Kopchia) b: 10/19/30, Detroit, Mich. BR/TR, 5'10", 165 lbs. Deb: 8/9/58

YEAR	TM/L	G	AB	R	H	2B	3B	HR	RBI	BB	SO	AVG	OBP	SLG	PRO+	BR/A	SB	CS	SBR	FA	FR	G/POS	TPR
1958	Mil-N	16	9	3	4	0	0	0	0	1	1	.444	.500	.444	167	1	0	0	0	.833	5	/S-3	0.6
1959	Phi-N	126	422	68	110	18	7	7	28	41	80	.261	.329	.386	88	-7	7	7	-2	.954	5	*S-113,2-11	0.6
1960	Phi-N	58	170	13	29	6	1	1	13	23	47	.171	.273	.235	41	-14	3	2	-0	.956	-12	S-55/3-2	-2.3
1961	Phi-N	6	3	1	0	0	0	0	0	0	0	.000	.000	.000	-99	-1	0	0	0	.800	0	/S-5	-0.1
	LA-A	91	338	46	85	12	2	5	40	45	77	.251	.341	.343	75	-12	3	3	-1	.947	-6	S-88/2-3,3-1	-1.0
1962	LA-A	128	375	47	85	16	0	4	40	73	84	.227	.356	.301	81	-7	2	1	0	.957	4	*S-118/2-5,3-4	0.8
1963	LA-A	76	143	11	30	4	1	1	12	9	30	.210	.261	.273	53	-9	0	0	0	.962	8	S-19,3-18,2-14/O-3	0.0
1964	LA-A	54	113	10	29	4	1	0	6	14	16	.257	.339	.310	91	-1	0	0	0	.945	15	S-31,2-13/3-3	1.6
1965	Cal-A	23	33	3	7	1	0	0	3	3	10	.212	.278	.333	75	-1	1	0	0	.979	9	2-10/S-4,3-4	0.9
Total	8	578	1606	202	379	61	12	19	141	209	345	.236	.327	.324	76	-50	16	13	-3	.952	29	S-436/2-56,3-32,O-3	1.1

■ GEORGE KOPSHAW
Kopshaw, George Karl b: 7/5/1895, Passaic, N.J. d: 12/26/34, Lynchburg, Va. BR/TR, 5'11.5", 176 lbs. Deb: 8/4/23

YEAR	TM/L	G	AB	R	H	2B	3B	HR	RBI	BB	SO	AVG	OBP	SLG	PRO+	BR/A	SB	CS	SBR	FA	FR	G/POS	TPR
1923	StL-N	2	5	1	1	0	0	0	0	0	0	.200	.200	.200	56	-0	0	0	0	1.000	-1	/C-1	-0.1

■ STEVE KORCHECK
Korcheck, Stephen Joseph "Hoss" b: 8/11/32, McClellandtown, Pa. BR/TR, 6'1", 205 lbs. Deb: 9/6/54

YEAR	TM/L	G	AB	R	H	2B	3B	HR	RBI	BB	SO	AVG	OBP	SLG	PRO+	BR/A	SB	CS	SBR	FA	FR	G/POS	TPR
1954	Was-A	2	7	0	1	0	0	0	0	0	2	.143	.143	.143	-23	-1	0	0	0	.857	-1	/C-2	-0.2
1955	Was-A	13	36	3	10	2	0	0	2	0	5	.278	.297	.333	73	-1	0	0	0	1.000	1	C-12	0.0
1958	Was-A	21	51	6	4	2	1	0	1	1	16	.078	.096	.157	-32	-9	0	0	0	.975	0	C-20	-0.9
1959	Was-A	22	51	3	8	2	0	0	4	5	13	.157	.232	.196	19	-6	0	0	0	.974	6	C-22	-0.1
Total	4	58	145	12	23	6	1	0	7	6	36	.159	.197	.214	13	-18	0	0	0	.976	7	/C-56	-1.0

■ ART KORES
Kores, Arthur Emil "Dutch" b: 7/22/1886, Milwaukee, Wis. d: 3/26/74, Milwaukee, Wis. BR/TR, 5'9", 167 lbs. Deb: 7/24/15

YEAR	TM/L	G	AB	R	H	2B	3B	HR	RBI	BB	SO	AVG	OBP	SLG	PRO+	BR/A	SB	CS	SBR	FA	FR	G/POS	TPR
1915	StL-F	60	201	18	47	9	2	1	22	21	13	.234	.306	.313	71	-11	6				.960	19	3-60	1.2

■ ANDY KOSCO
Kosco, Andrew John b: 10/5/41, Youngstown, Ohio BR/TR, 6'3", 207 lbs. Deb: 8/13/65

YEAR	TM/L	G	AB	R	H	2B	3B	HR	RBI	BB	SO	AVG	OBP	SLG	PRO+	BR/A	SB	CS	SBR	FA	FR	G/POS	TPR
1965	Min-A	23	55	3	13	4	0	1	6	1	15	.236	.250	.364	69	-2	0	0	0	1.000	0	O-14/1-2	-0.3
1966	Min-A	57	158	11	35	5	0	2	13	7	31	.222	.255	.291	53	-10	0	0	-1	.986	-1	O-40/1-5	-1.4
1967	Min-A	9	28	4	4	1	0	0	4	2	4	.143	.200	.179	12	-3	0	0	0	.923	-0	/O-7	-0.4
1968	NY-A	131	466	47	112	19	1	15	59	16	71	.240	.270	.382	99	-3	2	2	-1	.960	3	O-95,1-28	-0.9
1969	LA-N	120	424	51	105	13	2	19	74	21	66	.248	.285	.422	103	-1	1	1	-1	.981	-6	*O-109/1-3	-1.5
1970	LA-N	74	224	21	51	12	0	8	27	1	40	.228	.231	.388	66	-12	1	1	-0	.981	-2	O-58/1-1	-1.7
1971	Mil-A	98	264	27	60	6	2	10	39	24	57	.227	.292	.379	90	-4	1	3	-2	.988	-3	O-45,1-29,3-12	-1.3
1972	Cal-A	49	142	15	34	4	2	6	13	5	23	.239	.270	.423	110	1	0	0	0	.985	0	O-36	0.0
	Bos-A	17	47	5	10	2	1	3	6	2	9	.213	.260	.489	113	0	0	0	0	1.000	0	O-12	0.0
	Yr	66	189	20	44	6	3	9	19	7	32	.233	.268	.439	111	1	0	0	0	.988	0	O-48	0.0
1973	*Cin-N	47	118	17	33	7	0	9	21	13	26	.280	.351	.568	159	9	0	0	0	1.000	-5	O-36/1-1	0.2
1974	Cin-N	33	37	3	7	0	0	0	5	7	8	.189	.318	.243	59	-2	0	0	0	.846	-2	/3-8,O-1	-0.4
Total	10	658	1963	204	464	75	8	73	267	99	350	.236	.275	.394	92	-28	5	8	-3	.979	-16	O-453/1-69,3-20	-7.7

■ CLEM KOSHOREK
Koshorek, Clement John "Scooter" b: 6/20/25, Royal Oak, Mich. d: 9/8/91, Royal Oak, Mich. BR/TR, 5'4.5", 165 lbs. Deb: 4/15/52

YEAR	TM/L	G	AB	R	H	2B	3B	HR	RBI	BB	SO	AVG	OBP	SLG	PRO+	BR/A	SB	CS	SBR	FA	FR	G/POS	TPR
1952	Pit-N	98	322	27	84	17	0	0	15	26	39	.261	.320	.314	74	-11	4	7	-3	.949	1	S-33,2-27,3-26	-1.0
1953	Pit-N	1	1	0	0	0	0	0	0	0	1	.000	.000	.000	-99	-0	0	0	0	.000	0	H	0.0
Total	2	99	323	27	84	17	0	0	15	26	40	.260	.319	.313	74	-11	4	7	-3	.949	1	/S-33,2-27,3-26	-1.0

■ KEVIN KOSLOFSKI
Koslofski, Kevin Craig b: 9/24/66, Decatur, Ill. BL/TR, 5'8", 165 lbs. Deb: 6/28/92

YEAR	TM/L	G	AB	R	H	2B	3B	HR	RBI	BB	SO	AVG	OBP	SLG	PRO+	BR/A	SB	CS	SBR	FA	FR	G/POS	TPR
1992	KC-A	55	133	20	33	0	2	3	13	12	23	.248	.315	.346	83	-3	2	1	0	.991	-1	O-52	-0.5
1993	KC-A	15	26	4	7	0	0	1	2	4	5	.269	.387	.385	102	0	0	1	-1	1.000	0	O-13/D-1	-0.1
1994	KC-A	2	4	2	1	0	0	0	0	2	1	.250	.500	.250	97	0	0	0	0	.750	0	/O-2	0.0
1996	Mil-A	25	42	5	9	3	2	0	6	4	12	.214	.298	.381	66	-2	0	0	0	.972	-4	O-22/D-1	-0.6
Total	4	97	205	31	50	3	4	4	21	22	41	.244	.326	.356	82	-5	2	2	-1	.983	-5	/O-89,D-2	-1.2

■ MIKE KOSMAN
Kosman, Michael Thomas b: 12/10/17, Hamtramck, Mich. BR/TR, 5'9", 160 lbs. Deb: 4/20/44

YEAR	TM/L	G	AB	R	H	2B	3B	HR	RBI	BB	SO	AVG	OBP	SLG	PRO+	BR/A	SB	CS	SBR	FA	FR	G/POS	TPR
1944	Cin-N	1	0	0	0	0	0	0	0	0	0	—	—	—		0	0			.000	0	R	0.0

■ FRED KOSTER
Koster, Frederick Charles "Fritz" b: 12/21/05, Louisville, Ky. d: 4/24/79, St.Matthews, Ky. BL/TL, 5'10.5", 165 lbs. Deb: 4/27/31

YEAR	TM/L	G	AB	R	H	2B	3B	HR	RBI	BB	SO	AVG	OBP	SLG	PRO+	BR/A	SB	CS	SBR	FA	FR	G/POS	TPR
1931	Phi-N	76	151	21	34	2	2	0	8	14	21	.225	.291	.265	47	-11	4			.923	-4	O-41	-1.7

■ FRANK KOSTRO
Kostro, Frank Jerry b: 8/4/37, Windber, Pa. BR/TR, 6'2", 190 lbs. Deb: 9/2/62

YEAR	TM/L	G	AB	R	H	2B	3B	HR	RBI	BB	SO	AVG	OBP	SLG	PRO+	BR/A	SB	CS	SBR	FA	FR	G/POS	TPR
1962	Det-A	16	41	5	11	3	0	0	3	1	6	.268	.286	.341	66	-2	0	0	0	.967	1	3-11	-0.1
1963	Det-A	31	52	4	12	1	0	0	0	9	13	.231	.344	.250	67	-2	0	0	0	.929	-1	/3-6,1-3,O-3	-0.3
	LA-A	43	99	6	22	2	1	2	10	6	17	.222	.267	.323	68	-4	0	0	0	.960	-2	3-19/1-5,O-3	-0.7
	Yr	74	151	10	34	3	1	2	10	15	30	.225	.295	.298	68	-6	0	0	0	.953	-2	3-25/1-8,O-6	-1.0
1964	Min-A	59	103	10	28	5	0	3	12	4	21	.272	.306	.408	96	-1	0	0	0	.912	-3	3-12/2-7,O-2,1-1	-0.3
1965	Min-A	20	31	2	5	2	0	0	1	4	5	.161	.257	.226	37	-3	0	0	0	.923	-1	/2-7,3-6,O-2	-0.3
1967	Min-A	32	31	4	10	0	0	0	2	8	2	.323	.382	.323	102	0	0	0	0	1.000	-1	/O-3,3-1	-0.1
1968	Min-A	63	108	9	26	4	1	0	9	6	20	.241	.281	.296	71	-4	0	0	0	1.000	-1	O-24/1-5	-0.7
1969	Min-A	2	2	0	0	0	0	0	0	0	1	.000	.000	.000	-98	-1	0	0	0	.000	0	H	-0.1
Total	7	266	467	40	114	17	2	5	37	33	85	.244	.295	.321	74	-16	0	0	0	.926	-8	/3-55,O-37,2-14,1	-2.7

■ BRIAN KOWITZ
Kowitz, Brian Mark b: 8/7/69, Baltimore, Md. BL/TL, 5'10", 180 lbs. Deb: 6/4/95

YEAR	TM/L	G	AB	R	H	2B	3B	HR	RBI	BB	SO	AVG	OBP	SLG	PRO+	BR/A	SB	CS	SBR	FA	FR	G/POS	TPR
1995	Atl-N	10	24	3	4	1	0	0	3	2	4	.167	.259	.208	24	-3	0	1	-1	1.000	-2	/O-8	-0.5

■ ERNIE KOY
Koy, Ernest Anyz "Chief" b: 9/17/09, Sealy, Tex. BR/TR, 6', 200 lbs. Deb: 4/19/38

YEAR	TM/L	G	AB	R	H	2B	3B	HR	RBI	BB	SO	AVG	OBP	SLG	PRO+	BR/A	SB	CS	SBR	FA	FR	G/POS	TPR
1938	Bro-N	142	521	78	156	29	13	11	76	38	76	.299	.352	.468	121	14	15			.984	-1	*O-135/3-1	0.8
1939	Bro-N	125	425	57	118	37	5	8	67	39	64	.278	.338	.445	105	2	11			.962	-0	*O-114	-0.2
1940	Bro-N	24	48	9	11	2	1	1	8	3	8	.229	.275	.375	73	-2	1			1.000	-4	O-19	-0.6
	StL-N	93	348	44	108	19	5	8	52	28	59	.310	.368	.463	121	10	12			.970	-3	O-91	0.3
	Yr	117	396	53	119	21	6	9	60	31	62	.301	.357	.452	115	8	13			.973	-6	*O-110	-0.3
1941	StL-N	13	40	5	8	1	0	2	4	1	12	.200	.220	.375	61	-2	0			1.000	-2	O-12	-0.5
	Cin-N	67	204	24	51	11	2	2	27	14	22	.250	.301	.353	84	-5	1			.990	-1	O-49	-1.0
	Yr	80	244	29	59	12	2	4	31	15	30	.242	.288	.357	80	-7	1			.991	-1	O-61	-1.5
1942	Cin-N	3	2	0	0	0	0	0	0	0	0	.000	.000	.000	-99	-0	0			.000	0	H	-0.1
	Phi-N	91	258	21	63	9	2	4	26	14	50	.244	.283	.349	89	-5	0			.981	-9	O-78	-1.8
	Yr	94	260	21	63	9	2	4	26	14	52	.242	.281	.346	87	-5	0			.981	-9	O-78	-1.9
Total	5	558	1846	238	515	108	29	36	260	137	284	.279	.332	.427	107	11	40			.977	-20	O-498/3-1	-3.1

■ AL KOZAR
Kozar, Albert Kenneth b: 7/5/21, McKees Rocks, Pa. BR/TR, 5'9.5", 173 lbs. Deb: 4/19/48

YEAR	TM/L	G	AB	R	H	2B	3B	HR	RBI	BB	SO	AVG	OBP	SLG	PRO+	BR/A	SB	CS	SBR	FA	FR	G/POS	TPR
1948	Was-A	150	577	61	144	25	8	1	58	66	52	.250	.327	.324	76	-20	4	2	0	.967	-21	*2-149	-3.1
1949	Was-A	105	350	46	94	15	2	4	31	25	23	.269	.321	.357	81	-11	2	1	0	.977	-0	*2-102	-1.4
1950	Was-A	20	55	7	11	1	0	0	3	5	8	.200	.267	.218	27	-6	0	0	0	.962	-0	2-15	-0.6
	Chi-A	10	10	4	3	0	0	1	2	0	3	.300	.300	.600	129	0	0	0	0	1.000	3	/2-4,3-1	0.3
	Yr	30	65	11	14	1	0	1	5	5	11	.215	.271	.277	42	-6	0	0	0	.968	2	2-19/3-1	-0.3
Total	3	285	992	118	252	41	10	6	94	96	86	.254	.321	.334	76	-37	6	3	0	.971	-26	2-270/3-1	-4.8

■ JOE KRACHER
Kracher, Joseph Peter "Jug" b: 11/4/15, Philadelphia, Pa. d: 12/24/81, San Angelo, Tex. BR/TR, 5'11", 185 lbs. Deb: 9/17/39

YEAR	TM/L	G	AB	R	H	2B	3B	HR	RBI	BB	SO	AVG	OBP	SLG	PRO+	BR/A	SB	CS	SBR	FA	FR	G/POS	TPR
1939	Phi-N	5	5	1	1	0	0	0	0	2	1	.200	.429	.200	76	0	0			1.000	-1	/C-2	-0.1

■ CLARENCE KRAFT
Kraft, Clarence Otto "Big Boy" b: 6/9/1887, Evansville, Ind. d: 3/26/58, Fort Worth, Tex. BR/TR, 6', 190 lbs. Deb: 5/1/14

YEAR	TM/L	G	AB	R	H	2B	3B	HR	RBI	BB	SO	AVG	OBP	SLG	PRO+	BR/A	SB	CS	SBR	FA	FR	G/POS	TPR
1914	Bos-N	3	3	0	1	0	0	0	0	0	1	.333	.333	.333	99	-0	0			1.000	0	/1-1	0.0

YEAR	TM/L	G	AB	R	H	2B	3B	HR	RBI	BB	SO	AVG	OBP	SLG	PRO+	BR/A	SB	CS	SBR	FA	FR	G/POS	TPR

■ **ED KRANEPOOL**   Kranepool, Edward Emil   b: 11/8/44, New York, N.Y.   BL/TL, 6'3", 215 lbs.   Deb: 9/22/62

YEAR	TM/L	G	AB	R	H	2B	3B	HR	RBI	BB	SO	AVG	OBP	SLG	PRO+	BR/A	SB	CS	SBR	FA	FR	G/POS	TPR
1962	NY-N	3	6	0	1	1	0	0	0	0	0	1	.167	.167	.333	30	-1	0	0	0	1.000	1	/1-3	0.0
1963	NY-N	86	273	22	57	12	2	2	14	18	50	.209	.258	.289	56	-15	4	2	0	.954	-2	O-55,1-20	-2.3
1964	NY-N	119	420	47	108	19	4	10	45	32	50	.257	.313	.393	100	-1	0	1	-1	.991	3	*1-104/O-6	-0.4
1965	NY-N☆	153	525	44	133	24	4	10	53	39	71	.253	.307	.371	94	-5	1	4	-2	.992	-2	*1-147	-1.8
1966	NY-N	146	464	51	118	15	2	16	57	41	66	.254	.319	.399	100	-0	1	1	-2	.992	5	*1-132,O-11	-0.4
1967	NY-N	141	469	37	126	17	1	10	54	37	51	.269	.323	.373	100	-0	0	4	-2	.992	4	*1-139	-0.7
1968	NY-N	127	373	29	86	13	1	3	20	19	39	.231	.272	.295	70	-14	0	3	-2	.994	5	*1-113/O-2	-2.2
1969	*NY-N	112	353	36	84	9	2	11	49	37	32	.238	.310	.368	88	-6	3	2	0	.993	3	*1-106/O-2	-1.2
1970	NY-N	43	47	2	8	0	0	0	3	5	2	.170	.250	.170	15	-6	0	0	0	1.000	0	/1-8	-0.6
1971	NY-N	122	421	61	118	20	4	14	58	38	33	.280	.341	.447	123	12	0	4	-2	**.998**	-3	*1-108,O-11	-0.3
1972	NY-N	122	327	28	88	15	1	8	34	34	35	.269	.340	.394	111	5	0	0	0	.996	-0	*1-108/O-1	-0.4
1973	*NY-N	100	284	28	68	12	2	1	35	30	28	.239	.312	.306	73	-10	0	0	0	.998	-0	1-51,O-32	-1.5
1974	NY-N	94	217	20	65	11	1	4	24	18	14	.300	.353	.415	116	4	1	0	-1	.977	-6	O-33,1-24	-0.4
1975	NY-N	106	325	42	105	16	0	4	43	27	21	.323	.375	.409	123	10	1	1	0	.997	-0	1-82/O-4	0.4
1976	NY-N	123	415	47	121	17	1	10	49	35	38	.292	.347	.410	121	10	1	0	0	.996	-6	1-86,O-31	-0.2
1977	NY-N	108	281	28	79	17	0	10	40	23	20	.281	.336	.448	113	4	1	4	-2	.984	-5	O-42,1-41	-0.2
1978	NY-N	66	81	7	17	2	0	3	19	8	12	.210	.289	.346	79	-2	0	0	0	1.000	-2	O-12/1-3	-0.5
1979	NY-N	82	155	7	36	5	0	2	17	13	18	.232	.296	.303	66	-7	0	1	-1	1.000	0	1-29/O-8	-1.0
Total	18	1853	5436	536	1418	225	25	118	614	454	581	.261	.319	.377	97	-21	15	27	-12	.994	-1	*1-1304,O-250	-13.7

■ **CHARLIE KRAUSE**   Krause, Charles   b: 10/2/1873, Detroit, Mich.   d: 3/30/48, Eloise, Mich.   TR,   Deb: 7/27/01

YEAR	TM/L	G	AB	R	H	2B	3B	HR	RBI	BB	SO	AVG	OBP	SLG	PRO+	BR/A	SB	CS	SBR	FA	FR	G/POS	TPR
1901	Cin-N	1	4	0	1	0	0	0	0	0	0	.250	.250	.250	48	-0	0			.000	0	/2-1	0.0

■ **DANNY KRAVITZ**   Kravitz, Daniel "Dusty" or "Beak"   b: 12/21/30, Lopez, Pa.   BL/TR, 5'11", 195 lbs.   Deb: 4/17/56

YEAR	TM/L	G	AB	R	H	2B	3B	HR	RBI	BB	SO	AVG	OBP	SLG	PRO+	BR/A	SB	CS	SBR	FA	FR	G/POS	TPR
1956	Pit-N	32	68	6	18	2	2	2	10	5	9	.265	.315	.441	103	0	1	1	-0	.944	0	C-26/3-2	0.1
1957	Pit-N	19	41	2	6	1	0	0	4	2	10	.146	.186	.171	-3	-6	0	0	0	1.000	0	C-15	-0.5
1958	Pit-N	45	100	9	24	3	2	1	5	11	10	.240	.315	.340	76	-3	0	0	0	.967	-6	C-37	-0.8
1959	Pit-N	52	162	18	41	9	1	3	21	5	14	.253	.275	.377	72	-7	0	1	-1	.986	-1	C-45	-0.6
1960	Pit-N	8	6	0	0	0	0	0	0	1	2	.000	.143	.000	-57	-1	0	0	0	1.000	-0	/C-1	-0.1
	KC-A	59	175	17	41	7	2	4	14	11	19	.234	.280	.366	73	-7	0	0	0	.971	-4	C-47	-0.8
Total	5	215	552	52	130	22	7	10	54	35	64	.236	.281	.355	70	-25	1	2	-1	.973	-10	C-171/3-2	-2.7

■ **MIKE KREEVICH**   Kreevich, Michael Andreas   b: 6/10/08, Mt.Olive, Ill.   d: 4/25/94, Pana, Ill.   BR/TR, 5'7.5", 168 lbs.   Deb: 9/7/31

YEAR	TM/L	G	AB	R	H	2B	3B	HR	RBI	BB	SO	AVG	OBP	SLG	PRO+	BR/A	SB	CS	SBR	FA	FR	G/POS	TPR
1931	Chi-N	5	12	0	2	0	0	0	0	0	6	.167	.167	.167	-10	-2	1			1.000	-0	/O-4	-0.2
1935	Chi-A	6	23	3	10	2	0	0	2	1	0	.435	.458	.522	149	2	1	1	-0	1.000	-2	/3-6	-0.1
1936	Chi-A	137	550	99	169	32	11	5	69	61	46	.307	.378	.433	96	-3	10	5	0	.964	-2	*O-133	-0.9
1937	Chi-A	144	583	94	176	29	**16**	12	73	43	45	.302	.350	.468	104	2	10	1	2	**.988**	7	*O-138	0.6
1938	Chi-A★	129	489	73	145	26	12	6	73	55	23	.297	.371	.436	99	-1	13	5	1	.975	4	*O-127	0.0
1939	Chi-A	145	541	85	175	30	8	5	77	59	40	.323	.390	.436	108	8	23	10	1	.975	16	*O-139/3-4	1.8
1940	Chi-A	144	582	86	154	27	10	8	55	34	49	.265	.305	.387	77	-21	15	7	0	.982	12	*O-144	-1.6
1941	Chi-A	121	436	44	101	16	8	0	37	35	26	.232	.289	.305	58	-27	17	5	2	**.994**	0	*O-113	-3.1
1942	Phi-A	116	444	57	113	19	1	1	30	47	13	.255	.326	.309	79	-11	7	9	-3	.981	4	*O-107	-1.7
1943	StL-A	60	161	24	41	6	0	0	10	26	13	.255	.358	.292	89	-1	4	1	1	.993	0	O-51	0.2
1944	*StL-A	105	402	55	121	15	6	5	44	27	24	.301	.348	.405	108	4	3	3	-1	.986	-1	*O-100	-0.3
1945	StL-A	84	295	34	70	11	1	2	21	37	25	.237	.322	.302	78	-8	4	1	1	.991	4	O-81	-0.8
	Was-A	45	158	22	44	5	2	0	23	21	9	.278	.363	.373	124	5	7	5	-1	.971	-2	O-40	0.0
	Yr	129	453	56	114	19	3	2	44	58	36	.252	.337	.327	92	-3	11	6	-0	.985	2	*O-121	-0.8
Total	12	1241	4676	676	1321	221	75	45	514	446	339	.283	.346	.391	92	-54	115	53		.982	46	*O-1177/3-10	-6.1

■ **CHARLIE KREHMEYER**   Krehmeyer, Charles L.   b: 7/5/1863, St.Louis, Mo.   d: 2/10/26, St.Louis, Mo.   BL/TL, 5'11", 179 lbs.   Deb: 7/8/1884

YEAR	TM/L	G	AB	R	H	2B	3B	HR	RBI	BB	SO	AVG	OBP	SLG	PRO+	BR/A	SB	CS	SBR	FA	FR	G/POS	TPR
1884	StL-a	21	70	3	16	0	1	0		5	2	.229	.250	.257	64	-3				.619	-5	O-15/C-7,1-1	-0.7
1885	Lou-a	7	31	4	7	1	1	0		5	1	.226	.250	.323	80	-1				.909	-1	/C-4,O-2,1-1	-0.2
	StL-N	1	3	0	0	0	0	0		0	0	.000	.000	.000	-99	-1				.429	-1	/C-1	-0.1
Total	2	29	104	7	23	1	2	0	10	3	2	.221	.243	.269	64	-4				.571	-7	/O-17,C-12,1-2	-1.1

■ **MICKEY KREITNER**   Kreitner, Albert Joseph   b: 10/10/22, Nashville, Tenn.   BR/TR, 6'3", 190 lbs.   Deb: 9/28/43

YEAR	TM/L	G	AB	R	H	2B	3B	HR	RBI	BB	SO	AVG	OBP	SLG	PRO+	BR/A	SB	CS	SBR	FA	FR	G/POS	TPR
1943	Chi-N	3	8	0	3	0	0	0	2	1	2	.375	.444	.375	140	0	0			1.000	-1	/C-3	0.0
1944	Chi-N	39	85	3	13	2	0	0	1	8	16	.153	.234	.176	17	-9	0			.992	-1	C-39	-0.9
Total	2	42	93	3	16	2	0	0	3	9	18	.172	.252	.194	27	-9	0			.992	-1	/C-42	-0.9

■ **RALPH KREITZ**   Kreitz, Ralph Wesley "Red"   b: 11/13/1885, Plum Creek, Neb.   d: 7/20/41, Portland, Ore.   BR/TR, 5'9.5", 175 lbs.   Deb: 8/1/11

YEAR	TM/L	G	AB	R	H	2B	3B	HR	RBI	BB	SO	AVG	OBP	SLG	PRO+	BR/A	SB	CS	SBR	FA	FR	G/POS	TPR
1911	Chi-A	7	17	0	4	1	0	0	0		2	.235	.316	.294	73	-1	0			1.000	-3	/C-7	-0.3

■ **JIMMY KREMERS**   Kremers, James Edward   b: 10/8/65, Little Rock, Ark.   BL/TR, 6'3", 205 lbs.   Deb: 6/5/90

YEAR	TM/L	G	AB	R	H	2B	3B	HR	RBI	BB	SO	AVG	OBP	SLG	PRO+	BR/A	SB	CS	SBR	FA	FR	G/POS	TPR
1990	Atl-N	29	73	7	8	1	1	1	2	6	27	.110	.177	.192	1	-10	0	0	0	.992	-3	C-27	-1.3

■ **WAYNE KRENCHICKI**   Krenchicki, Wayne Richard   b: 9/17/54, Trenton, N.J.   BL/TR, 6'1", 180 lbs.   Deb: 6/15/79

YEAR	TM/L	G	AB	R	H	2B	3B	HR	RBI	BB	SO	AVG	OBP	SLG	PRO+	BR/A	SB	CS	SBR	FA	FR	G/POS	TPR
1979	Bal-A	16	21	1	4	1	0	0	0	0	0	.190	.190	.238	15	-2	0	0	0	.875	1	/3-7,2-6	-0.1
1980	Bal-A	9	14	1	2	0	0	0	0	1	3	.143	.200	.143	-4	-2	0	0	0	1.000	0	/S-6,2-1,D-1	0.0
1981	Bal-A	33	56	7	12	4	0	0	6	4	9	.214	.267	.286	59	-3	0	0	0	.964	0	S-16/2-7,3-6,D-1	0.3
1982	Cin-N	94	187	19	53	6	1	2	21	13	23	.283	.330	.358	91	-2	5	3	-0	.955	7	3-70/2-9	0.4
1983	Cin-N	51	77	6	21	2	0	0	11	8	4	.273	.349	.299	78	-2	0	0	0	.980	1	3-39/2-1	-0.1
	Det-A	59	133	18	37	7	0	1	16	11	17	.278	.338	.353	93	-1	0	0	0	.934	-8	3-48/2-6,S-6,1-3	-0.9
1984	Cin-N	97	181	18	54	9	2	6	22	19	23	.298	.365	.470	127	6	0	1	-1	.967	3	3-62/1-3,2-3	0.9
1985	Cin-N	90	173	16	47	9	4	0	25	28	20	.272	.373	.393	109	3	0	0	0	.967	3	3-52/2-3	0.7
1986	Mon-N	101	221	21	53	6	2	2	23	22	32	.240	.309	.312	72	-8	2	4	0	.991	1	1-41,3-24/2-1,O-1	-1.2
Total	8	550	1063	107	283	44	5	15	124	106	141	.266	.334	.359	92	-11	7	8	-3	.955	14	3-308/1-47,2SDO	-0.2

■ **CHUCK KRESS**   Kress, Charles Steven   b: 12/9/21, Philadelphia, Pa.   BL/TL, 6', 190 lbs.   Deb: 4/16/47

YEAR	TM/L	G	AB	R	H	2B	3B	HR	RBI	BB	SO	AVG	OBP	SLG	PRO+	BR/A	SB	CS	SBR	FA	FR	G/POS	TPR
1947	Cin-N	11	27	4	4	0	0	0	6	4	4	.148	.303	.148	23	-3	0			.983	1	/1-8	-0.2
1949	Cin-N	27	29	3	6	3	0	0	3	5	5	.207	.281	.310	58	-2	0			.974	0	1-16	-0.2
	Chi-A	97	353	45	98	17	6	1	44	39	44	.278	.349	.368	93	-4	6	7	-2	.994	-0	1-95	-0.7
1950	Chi-A	3	8	0	0	0	0	0	0	0	0	.000	.000	.000	-99	-0	0	0	0	1.000	-0	/1-2	-0.2
1954	Det-A	24	37	4	7	0	1	0	3	1	4	.189	.211	.243	24	-4	0	0	0	.971	-0	/1-7,O-1	-0.5
	Bro-N	13	12	1	1	0	0	0	0	0	2	.083	.083	.083	-55	-3	0	0	0	.500	-1	/1-1	-0.3
Total	4	175	466	57	116	20	7	1	52	49	59	.249	.320	.328	74	-18	6	8		.990	0	1-129/O-1	-2.1

■ **RED KRESS**   Kress, Ralph   b: 1/2/07, Columbia, Cal.   d: 11/29/62, Los Angeles, Cal.   BR/TR, 5'11.5", 165 lbs.   Deb: 9/24/27   C

YEAR	TM/L	G	AB	R	H	2B	3B	HR	RBI	BB	SO	AVG	OBP	SLG	PRO+	BR/A	SB	CS	SBR	FA	FR	G/POS	TPR
1927	StL-A	7	23	3	7	2	1	1	3	3	3	.304	.385	.609	150	2	1			.974	1	/S-7	0.3
1928	StL-A	150	560	78	153	26	10	3	81	48	70	.273	.332	.371	82	-15	5	4	-1	.929	-17	*S-150	-1.4
1929	StL-A	147	557	82	170	38	4	9	107	52	53	.305	.366	.436	102	1	5	8	-3	**.946**	-2	*S-146	1.3
1930	StL-A	154	614	94	192	43	8	16	112	50	56	.313	.366	.487	110	9	3	12	-6	.936	-12	*S-123,3-31	0.6
1931	StL-A	150	605	87	188	46	8	16	114	46	48	.311	.360	.493	118	14	3	16	-9	.936	-11	3-84,O-40,S-38,1-10	0.5
1932	StL-A	14	52	2	9	0	1	2	9	4	6	.173	.232	.327	41	-5	1	1	-0	.909	3	3-14	-0.2
	Chi-A	135	515	83	147	42	4	9	57	47	36	.285	.344	.435	108	5	6	6	-3	.956	11	O-64,S-53,3-19/1-1	1.6
	Yr	149	567	85	156	42	5	11	66	51	42	.275	.336	.425	101	-1	7	4	-0	.956	13	O-64,S-53,3-33/1-1	1.4
1933	Chi-A	129	467	47	116	20	5	10	78	37	40	.248	.304	.377	83	-13	4	4	-1	.978	-1	*1-111/O-8	-2.8
1934	Chi-A	8	14	3	4	1	0	0	3	3	3	.286	.412	.286	108	-0	0	0	0	1.000	-4	/2-3	-0.3
	Was-A	56	171	18	39	4	3	0	24	17	19	.228	.298	.357	71	-8	3	0	0	.993	-1	1-30,O-10/2-6,S3	-1.1
	Yr	64	185	21	43	4	3	0	25	20	22	.232	.307	.351	72	-8	3	0	0	.993	-6	1-30,O-10/2-9,S3	-1.5

YEAR	TM/L	G	AB	R	H	2B	3B	HR	RBI	BB	SO	AVG	OBP	SLG	PRO+	BR/A	SB	CS	SBR	FA	FR	G/POS	TPR
1935	Was-A	84	252	32	75	13	4	2	42	25	16	.298	.361	.405	101	0	3	3	-1	.964	17	S-53/1-5,P-3,O-2,2	1.7
1936	Was-A	109	391	51	111	20	6	8	51	39	25	.284	.349	.427	96	-4	6	0	2	.927	9	S-64,2-33/1-5	1.2
1938	StL-A	150	566	74	171	33	3	7	79	69	47	.302	.378	.408	97	-1	5	4	1	**.965**	-15	*S-150	-0.5
1939	StL-A	13	43	5	12	1	0	0	8	6	2	.279	.367	.302	72	-2	1	0	0	.933	-3	S-13	-0.3
	Det-A	51	157	19	38	7	0	1	22	17	16	.242	.316	.306	55	-10	2	1	0	.959	2	S-25,2-16/3-4	-0.5
	Yr	64	200	24	50	8	0	1	30	23	18	.250	.327	.305	59	-12	3	1	0	.951	-1	S-38,2-16/3-4	-0.8
1940	Det-A	33	99	13	22	3	1	1	11	10	12	.222	.294	.303	50	-7	0	0	0	.924	9	3-17,S-12	0.2
1946	NY-N	1	1	0	0	0	0	0	0	1	0	.000	.500	.000	48	0	0			1.000	1	/P-1	0.0
Total	14	1391	5087	691	1454	298	58	89	799	474	453	.286	.347	.420	96	-35	47	56		.944	-16	S-835,3-170,10/2P	-0.5

■ CHAD KREUTER
Kreuter, Chadden Michael b: 8/26/64, Greenbrae, Cal. BB/TR, 6'2", 190 lbs. Deb: 9/14/88

YEAR	TM/L	G	AB	R	H	2B	3B	HR	RBI	BB	SO	AVG	OBP	SLG	PRO+	BR/A	SB	CS	SBR	FA	FR	G/POS	TPR
1988	Tex-A	16	51	3	14	2	1	1	5	7	13	.275	.362	.412	113	1	0	0	0	.990	2	C-16	0.4
1989	Tex-A	87	158	16	24	3	0	5	9	27	40	.152	.276	.266	52	-10	0	1	-1	.992	12	C-85	0.4
1990	Tex-A	22	22	2	1	1	0	0	2	8	9	.045	.300	.091	14	-2	0	0	0	.977	-1	C-20/D-1	-0.3
1991	Tex-A	3	4	0	0	0	0	0	0	0	1	.000	.000	.000	-99	-1	0	0	0	1.000	1	/C-1	-0.1
1992	Det-A	67	190	22	48	9	0	2	16	20	38	.253	.324	.332	83	-4	0	1	-1	.983	5	C-62/D-1	0.0
1993	Det-A	119	374	59	107	23	3	15	51	49	92	.286	.373	.484	129	16	2	1	0	.988	3	*C-112/1-1,D-2	2.3
1994	Det-A	65	170	17	38	8	1	1	19	28	36	.224	.333	.288	62	-9	0	1	-1	.987	-2	C-64/1-1,O-1	-0.7
1995	Sea-A	26	75	12	17	5	0	1	8	5	22	.227	.293	.333	62	-4	0	0	0	.976	0	C-23	-0.2
1996	Chi-A	46	114	14	25	8	0	3	18	13	29	.219	.310	.368	75	-5	0	0	0	.990	-5	C-38/1-2	-0.6
Total	9	451	1158	145	274	59	4	28	128	157	280	.237	.331	.367	88	-18	2	4	-2	.987	13	C-421/1-4,D-4,O-1	1.5

■ PAUL KRICHELL
Krichell, Paul Bernard b: 12/19/1882, New York, N.Y. d: 6/4/57, New York, N.Y. BR/TR, 5'7", 150 lbs. Deb: 5/12/11

YEAR	TM/L	G	AB	R	H	2B	3B	HR	RBI	BB	SO	AVG	OBP	SLG	PRO+	BR/A	SB	CS	SBR	FA	FR	G/POS	TPR
1911	StL-A	28	82	6	19	3	0	0	8	4		.232	.276	.268	54	-5	2			.943	-2	C-25	-0.4
1912	StL-A	59	161	19	35	6	0	0	8	19		.217	.304	.255	62	-7	2			.959	-1	C-59	-0.3
Total	2	87	243	25	54	9	0	0	16	23		.222	.295	.259	60	-12	4			.955	-3	/C-84	-0.7

■ BILL KRIEG
Krieg, William Frederick b: 1/29/1859, Petersburg, Ill. d: 3/25/30, Chillicothe, Ill. BR/TR, 5'8", 180 lbs. Deb: 4/20/1884

YEAR	TM/L	G	AB	R	H	2B	3B	HR	RBI	BB	SO	AVG	OBP	SLG	PRO+	BR/A	SB	CS	SBR	FA	FR	G/POS	TPR
1884	CP-U	71	279	35	69	15	4	0		11		.247	.276	.330	83	-14				.932	15	C-53,O-20/S-1,1-1	0.4
1885	Chi-N	1	3	0	0	0	0	0	0	0	2	.000	.000	.000	-87	-1				.800	2	/O-1	0.1
	Bro-a	17	60	7	9	4	0	1	5	2		.150	.177	.267	39	-4				.910	-4	C-12/1-5	-0.7
1886	Was-N	27	98	11	25	6	3	1	15	3	12	.255	.277	.408	113	1	2			.975	-1	1-27	-0.3
1887	Was-N	25	95	9	24	4	1	2	17	7	5	.253	.311	.379	95	-1	2			.973	-3	1-16/O-9	-0.4
Total	4	141	535	62	127	29	8	4	37	23	19	.237	.270	.344	85	-18	4			.929	9	/C-65,1-49,O-30,S-1	-0.9

■ KRIEGER
Krieger Deb: 7/28/1884

YEAR	TM/L	G	AB	R	H	2B	3B	HR	RBI	BB	SO	AVG	OBP	SLG	PRO+	BR/A	SB	CS	SBR	FA	FR	G/POS	TPR
1884	KC-U	1	3	0	0	0	0	0		0		.000	.000	.000	-99	-1				.000	-1	/O-1,P-1	-0.1

■ JOHN KRONER
Kroner, John Harold b: 11/13/08, St.Louis, Mo. d: 8/26/68, St.Louis, Mo. BR/TR, 6', 185 lbs. Deb: 9/29/35

YEAR	TM/L	G	AB	R	H	2B	3B	HR	RBI	BB	SO	AVG	OBP	SLG	PRO+	BR/A	SB	CS	SBR	FA	FR	G/POS	TPR
1935	Bos-A	2	4	1	1	0	0	0	0	1	1	.250	.400	.250	67	-0	0	0	0	1.000	-1	/3-2	-0.1
1936	Bos-A	84	298	40	87	17	8	4	62	26	24	.292	.349	.443	89	-6	2	3	-1	.964	-2	2-38,3-28,S-18/O-1	-0.4
1937	Cle-A	86	283	29	67	14	1	2	26	22	25	.237	.292	.314	52	-21	1	1	-0	.969	-3	2-64,3-11	-1.9
1938	Cle-A	51	117	13	29	16	0	1	17	19	6	.248	.353	.410	92	-1	0	1	-1	.974	12	2-31/1-7,3-3,S-1	1.0
Total	4	223	702	83	184	47	9	7	105	68	56	.262	.327	.385	75	-29	3	5	-2	.968	6	2-133/3-44,S-19,1O	-1.4

■ MIKE KRSNICH
Krsnich, Michael b: 9/24/31, W.Allis, Wis. BR/TR, 6'1", 190 lbs. Deb: 4/23/60 F

YEAR	TM/L	G	AB	R	H	2B	3B	HR	RBI	BB	SO	AVG	OBP	SLG	PRO+	BR/A	SB	CS	SBR	FA	FR	G/POS	TPR
1960	Mil-N	4	9	0	3	1	0	0	2	0	0	.333	.333	.444	120	0	0	0	0	1.000	-0	/O-3	0.0
1962	Mil-N	11	12	0	1	1	0	0	2	0	4	.083	.083	.167	-36	-2	0	0	0	1.000	-0	/O-3,1-1,3-1	-0.3
Total	2	15	21	0	4	2	0	0	4	0	4	.190	.190	.286	28	-2	0	0	0	1.000	-0	/O-6,3-1,1-1	-0.3

■ ROCKY KRSNICH
Krsnich, Rocco Peter b: 8/5/27, W.Allis, Wis. BR/TR, 6'1", 174 lbs. Deb: 9/13/49 F

YEAR	TM/L	G	AB	R	H	2B	3B	HR	RBI	BB	SO	AVG	OBP	SLG	PRO+	BR/A	SB	CS	SBR	FA	FR	G/POS	TPR
1949	Chi-A	16	55	7	12	3	1	1	9	6	4	.218	.295	.364	76	-2	1	1	0	.935	4	3-16	0.0
1952	Chi-A	40	91	11	21	7	2	1	15	12	9	.231	.327	.385	97	-0	0	0	0	.959	11	3-37	1.0
1953	Chi-A	64	129	9	26	8	0	1	14	12	11	.202	.270	.287	49	-9	0	2	-1	.929	9	3-57	-0.2
Total	3	120	275	27	59	18	3	3	38	30	24	.215	.294	.335	70	-12	1	3	-2	.942	23	3-110	0.8

■ OTTO KRUEGER
Krueger, Arthur William "Oom Paul" b: 9/17/1876, Chicago, Ill. d: 2/20/61, St.Louis, Mo. BR/TR, 5'7", 165 lbs. Deb: 9/16/1899

YEAR	TM/L	G	AB	R	H	2B	3B	HR	RBI	BB	SO	AVG	OBP	SLG	PRO+	BR/A	SB	CS	SBR	FA	FR	G/POS	TPR
1899	Cle-N	13	44	4	10	1	0	0	2	8		.227	.358	.250	73	-1	1			.763	-2	/3-9,S-2,2-2	-0.3
1900	StL-N	12	35	8	14	3	2	1	3	10		.400	.543	.686	240	8	0			.852	-6	2-12	0.2
1901	StL-N	142	520	77	143	16	12	2	79	50		.275	.353	.363	114	11	19			.881	-9	*3-142	0.3
1902	StL-N	128	467	55	124	7	8	0	46	29		.266	.313	.315	97	-2	14			.897	0	*S-107,3-18	0.6
1903	Pit-N	80	256	42	63	6	8	1	28	21		.246	.323	.344	87	-4	5			.884	-5	S-29,O-28,3-13/2-3	-0.9
1904	Pit-N	86	268	34	52	6	2	1	26	29		.194	.282	.243	61	-12	8			.905	-5	O-33,S-32,3-10	-1.9
1905	Phi-N	46	114	10	21	1	1	0	12	13		.184	.273	.211	47	-7	1			.930	-9	S-23/O-6,3-1	-1.7
Total	7	507	1704	230	427	40	33	5	196	160		.251	.326	.322	94	-7	48			.902	-36	S-193,3-193/O-67,2	-3.7

■ ERNIE KRUEGER
Krueger, Ernest George b: 12/27/1890, Chicago, Ill. d: 4/22/76, Waukegan, Ill. BR/TR, 5'10.5", 185 lbs. Deb: 8/4/13

YEAR	TM/L	G	AB	R	H	2B	3B	HR	RBI	BB	SO	AVG	OBP	SLG	PRO+	BR/A	SB	CS	SBR	FA	FR	G/POS	TPR
1913	Cle-A	5	6	0	0	0	0	0	0	0	2	.000	.000	.000	-97	-1	0			1.000	-0	/C-4	-0.2
1915	NY-A	10	29	3	5	1	0	0	0	0	4	.172	.200	.207	22	-3	0	1	-1	.905	-4	/C-8	-0.7
1917	NY-N	8	10	0	0	0	0	0	0	0	5	.000	.000	.000	-99	-2	0			.857	-2	/C-5	-0.5
	Bro-N	31	81	10	22	2	2	1	6	5	7	.272	.330	.383	115	1	1			.979	1	C-23	0.5
	Yr	39	91	10	22	2	2	1	6	5	11	.242	.296	.341	94	-1	1			.973	-1	C-28	0.0
1918	Bro-N	30	87	4	25	4	2	0	7	4	9	.287	.319	.379	113	1	2			.986	6	C-23	0.9
1919	Bro-N	80	226	24	56	7	4	3	36	19	25	.248	.312	.381	105	1	0			.963	5	C-66	1.4
1920	*Bro-N	52	146	21	42	4	2	1	17	16	13	.288	.358	.363	104	1	2	0	1	.959	-4	C-46	0.1
1921	Bro-N	65	163	18	43	11	4	3	20	14	12	.264	.322	.436	95	-1	2	2	-1	.969	-2	C-52	-0.1
1925	Cin-N	37	88	7	27	4	0	0	7	6	4	.307	.351	.386	90	-1	1	2	-1	.946	-4	C-30	-0.4
Total	8	318	836	87	220	33	14	11	93	64	85	.263	.319	.370	95	-4	12	5		.964	-3	C-257	1.0

■ CHRIS KRUG
Krug, Everett Ben b: 12/25/39, Los Angeles, Cal. BR/TR, 6'4", 200 lbs. Deb: 5/30/65 C

YEAR	TM/L	G	AB	R	H	2B	3B	HR	RBI	BB	SO	AVG	OBP	SLG	PRO+	BR/A	SB	CS	SBR	FA	FR	G/POS	TPR
1965	Chi-N	60	169	16	34	5	0	5	24	13	52	.201	.262	.320	61	-9	0	1	-1	.980	-1	C-58	-0.6
1966	Chi-N	11	28	1	6	1	0	0	1	3	8	.214	.241	.250	36	-2	0	0	0	1.000	3	C-10	0.1
1969	SD-N	8	17	0	1	0	0	0	0	1	6	.059	.111	.059	-53	-3	0	0	0	.938	-1	/C-7	-0.4
Total	3	79	214	17	41	6	0	5	25	15	66	.192	.248	.290	50	-15	0	1	-1	.980	3	/C-75	-0.9

■ GENE KRUG
Krug, Gary Eugene b: 2/12/55, Garden City, Kan. BL/TL, 6'4", 225 lbs. Deb: 4/29/81

YEAR	TM/L	G	AB	R	H	2B	3B	HR	RBI	BB	SO	AVG	OBP	SLG	PRO+	BR/A	SB	CS	SBR	FA	FR	G/POS	TPR
1981	Chi-N	7	5	0	2	0	0	0	0	0	0	.400	.500	.400	151	0	0	0	0	.000	0	/H	0.0

■ HENRY KRUG
Krug, Henry Charles b: 12/4/1876, San Francisco, Cal. d: 1/14/08, San Francisco, Cal BR/TR, Deb: 7/26/02

YEAR	TM/L	G	AB	R	H	2B	3B	HR	RBI	BB	SO	AVG	OBP	SLG	PRO+	BR/A	SB	CS	SBR	FA	FR	G/POS	TPR
1902	Phi-N	53	198	20	45	3	3	0	14	7		.227	.261	.273	65	-9	2			.947	-7	O-28,2-13/S-9,3-6	-1.7

■ MARTY KRUG
Krug, Martin John b: 9/10/1888, Koblenz, Germany d: 6/27/66, Glendale, Cal. BR/TR, 5'9", 165 lbs. Deb: 5/29/12

YEAR	TM/L	G	AB	R	H	2B	3B	HR	RBI	BB	SO	AVG	OBP	SLG	PRO+	BR/A	SB	CS	SBR	FA	FR	G/POS	TPR
1912	Bos-A	24	39	6	12	2	1	0	7	5		.308	.386	.410	122	1	2			.895	-2	/S-13,2-4	0.0
1922	Chi-N	127	450	67	124	23	4	4	60	43	43	.276	.343	.373	82	-11	7	9	-3	.937	-6	*3-104,2-23/S-1	-1.1
Total	2	151	489	73	136	25	5	4	67	48	43	.278	.346	.374	85	-10	9	9		.910	-8	3-104/2-27,S-14	-1.1

■ ART KRUGER
Kruger, Arthur T. b: 3/16/1881, San Antonio, Tex. d: 11/28/49, Honda, Cal. BR/TR, 6', 185 lbs. Deb: 4/11/07

YEAR	TM/L	G	AB	R	H	2B	3B	HR	RBI	BB	SO	AVG	OBP	SLG	PRO+	BR/A	SB	CS	SBR	FA	FR	G/POS	TPR
1907	Cin-N	100	317	25	74	10	9	0	28	18		.233	.285	.322	87	-6	10			.972	0	O-96	-1.0
1910	Cle-A	47	168	14	26	4	0	0	10	15		.155	.237	.202	37	-12	10			.947	2	O-47	-1.4
	Bos-N	1	1	0	0	0	0	0	0	0		.000	.000	.000	-96	-0	0			.000	0	H	0.0
	Cle-A	15	55	5	12	2	1	0	4	5		.218	.295	.291	82	-1	0			.974	2	O-15	0.0
1914	KC-F	122	441	45	114	24	7	4	47	24	59	.259	.297	.372	85	-18	11			.963	-7	*O-120	-3.2

YEAR	TM/L	G	AB	R	H	2B	3B	HR	RBI	BB	SO	AVG	OBP	SLG	PRO+	BR/A	SB	CS	SBR	FA	FR	G/POS	TPR
1915	KC-F	80	240	24	57	9	2	2	26	12	29	.237	.277	.317	70	-14	5			.984	0	O-66	-1.9
Total	4	365	1222	113	283	49	21	6	115	73	88	.232	.281	.321	76	-52	38			.968	-2	O-344	-7.5

■ JOHN KRUK   Kruk, John Martin b: 2/9/61, Charleston, W.Va.   BL/TL, 5'10", 200 lbs.   Deb: 4/7/86

YEAR	TM/L	G	AB	R	H	2B	3B	HR	RBI	BB	SO	AVG	OBP	SLG	PRO+	BR/A	SB	CS	SBR	FA	FR	G/POS	TPR
1986	SD-N	122	278	33	86	16	2	4	38	45	58	.309	.406	.424	132	14	2	4	-2	.981	-5	O-74/1-9	0.5
1987	SD-N	138	447	72	140	14	2	20	91	73	93	.313	.410	.488	142	29	18	10	-1	.996	3	*1-101,O-29	2.3
1988	SD-N	120	378	54	91	17	1	9	44	80	68	.241	.373	.362	114	10	5	3	-0	.995	-1	1-63,O-55	0.2
1989	SD-N	31	76	7	14	0	0	3	6	17	14	.184	.333	.303	83	-1	0	0	0	.962	1	O-27	0.0
	Phi-N	81	281	46	93	13	6	5	38	27	39	.331	.390	.473	146	17	3	0	1	.983	-4	O-72/1-7	1.2
	Yr	112	357	53	107	13	6	8	44	44	53	.300	.377	.437	132	15	3	0	1	.977	-3	O-99/1-7	1.2
1990	Phi-N	142	443	52	129	25	8	7	67	69	70	.291	.387	.431	125	17	10	5	0	.986	-5	O-87,1-61	0.7
1991	Phi-N☆	152	538	84	158	27	6	21	92	67	100	.294	.373	.483	141	29	7	0	2	.997	-1	*1-102,O-52	2.4
1992	Phi-N	144	507	86	164	30	4	10	70	92	88	.323	.428	.458	151	39	3	5	-2	.993	-12	*1-121,O-35	1.8
1993	*Phi-N★	150	535	100	169	33	5	14	85	111	87	.316	.433	.475	145	40	6	2	1	.993	-11	*1-144	1.7
1994	Phi-N	75	255	35	77	17	0	5	38	42	51	.302	.401	.427	113	7	4	1	1	.995	-1	1-69	0.0
1995	Chi-A	45	159	13	49	7	0	2	23	26	33	.308	.405	.390	113	4	0	1	-1	.909	-1	D-42/1-1	0.0
Total	10	1200	3897	582	1170	199	34	100	592	649	701	.300	.400	.446	134	205	58	31	-1	.995	-37	1-678,O-431/D-42	10.8

■ DICK KRYHOSKI   Kryhoski, Richard David b: 3/24/25, Leonia, N.J.   BL/TL, 6'2", 200 lbs.   Deb: 4/19/49

YEAR	TM/L	G	AB	R	H	2B	3B	HR	RBI	BB	SO	AVG	OBP	SLG	PRO+	BR/A	SB	CS	SBR	FA	FR	G/POS	TPR
1949	NY-A	54	177	18	52	10	3	1	27	9	17	.294	.335	.401	94	-2	2	4	-2	.983	-1	1-51	-0.5
1950	Det-A	53	169	20	37	10	0	4	19	8	11	.219	.258	.349	53	-13	0	1	-1	.991	-0	1-47	-1.4
1951	Det-A	119	421	58	121	19	4	12	57	28	29	.287	.335	.437	107	2	1	2	-1	.991	3	*1-112	-0.1
1952	StL-A	111	342	38	83	13	1	11	42	23	42	.243	.296	.383	86	-8	2	0	1	.989	-5	1-86	-1.6
1953	StL-A	104	338	35	94	18	4	16	50	26	33	.278	.333	.497	119	7	0	5	-3	.992	5	1-88	0.6
1954	Bal-A	100	300	32	78	13	2	1	34	19	24	.260	.308	.327	80	-9	0	0	-0	.992	3	1-69	-1.0
1955	KC-A	28	47	2	10	2	0	0	2	6	7	.213	.302	.255	50	-3	0	1	-1	.988	0	1-14	-0.4
Total	7	569	1794	203	475	85	14	45	231	119	163	.265	.315	.403	93	-26	5	13	-6	.990	5	1-467	-4.4

■ TONY KUBEK   Kubek, Anthony Christopher b: 10/12/36, Milwaukee, Wis.   BL/TR, 6'3", 191 lbs.   Deb: 4/20/57

YEAR	TM/L	G	AB	R	H	2B	3B	HR	RBI	BB	SO	AVG	OBP	SLG	PRO+	BR/A	SB	CS	SBR	FA	FR	G/POS	TPR
1957	*NY-A	127	431	56	128	21	3	3	39	24	48	.297	.338	.381	98	-2	6	6	-2	.938	1	O-50,S-41,3-38,/2-1	-0.2
1958	*NY-A☆	138	559	66	148	21	1	2	48	25	57	.265	.297	.317	72	-22	5	4	-1	.961	20	*S-134/O-3,1,-2-1	0.9
1959	NY-A	132	512	67	143	25	7	6	51	24	46	.279	.314	.391	95	-5	3	3	-1	.968	-1	S-67,O-53,3-17,/2-1	-0.3
1960	NY-A	147	568	77	155	25	3	14	62	31	42	.273	.314	.401	98	-4	3	0	1	.968	-4	*S-136,O-29	0.3
1961	*NY-A★	153	617	84	170	38	6	8	46	27	60	.276	.307	.395	91	-10	1	3	-2	.959	13	*S-145	1.3
1962	*NY-A	45	169	28	53	6	1	4	17	12	17	.314	.359	.432	115	3	2	1	0	.954	5	*S-35/O-6	1.2
1963	*NY-A	135	557	72	143	21	3	7	44	28	68	.257	.295	.343	79	-16	4	2	0	.980	10	*S-132/O-1	0.3
1964	NY-A	106	415	46	95	16	3	8	31	26	55	.229	.276	.340	69	-18	4	1	1	.978	-4	S-99	-0.6
1965	NY-A	109	339	26	74	5	3	5	35	20	48	.218	.262	.295	58	-19	1	3	-2	.964	-10	S-93/O-3,1-1	-2.6
Total	9	1092	4167	522	1109	178	30	57	373	217	441	.266	.305	.364	85	-92	29	23	-5	.967	39	S-882,O-145/321	0.3

■ TED KUBIAK   Kubiak, Theodore Rodger b: 5/12/42, New Brunswick, N.J.   BB/TR, 6', 175 lbs.   Deb: 4/14/67

YEAR	TM/L	G	AB	R	H	2B	3B	HR	RBI	BB	SO	AVG	OBP	SLG	PRO+	BR/A	SB	CS	SBR	FA	FR	G/POS	TPR
1967	KC-A	53	102	6	16	2	1	0	5	12	20	.157	.246	.196	33	-8	0	0	0	.984	-3	S-20,2-10/3-5	-1.1
1968	Oak-A	48	120	10	30	5	2	0	8	8	18	.250	.308	.325	96	-1	1	1	-0	.929	-3	2-24,S-12	-0.2
1969	Oak-A	92	305	38	76	9	1	2	27	25	35	.249	.308	.305	75	-10	2	0	1	.976	-9	S-42,2-33	-0.3
1970	Mil-A	158	540	63	136	9	6	4	41	72	51	.252	.340	.313	81	-12	4	9	-4	.989	-17	2-91,S-73	-1.9
1971	Mil-A	89	260	26	59	6	5	3	17	41	31	.227	.332	.323	87	-3	0	5	-3	.971	-3	2-48,S-39	-0.1
	StL-N	32	72	8	18	3	2	1	10	11	12	.250	.349	.389	105	1	1	0	0	.959	1	S-17,2-14	-0.1
1972	Tex-A	46	116	5	26	3	0	0	7	12	12	.224	.302	.250	69	-4	0	1	-1	.990	-3	2-25,S-15/3-1	-0.6
	*Oak-A	51	94	14	17	4	1	0	8	9	11	.181	.252	.245	51	-6	0	0	0	.988	2	2-49/3-1	-0.2
	Yr	97	210	19	43	7	1	0	15	21	23	.205	.280	.248	61	-10	0	1	-1	.989	-1	2-74,S-15/3-2	-0.8
1973	*Oak-A	106	182	15	40	6	1	3	17	12	19	.220	.268	.313	67	-9	1	1	-0	.973	6	2-83,S-26/3-2	0.1
1974	Oak-A	99	220	22	46	3	0	0	18	18	15	.209	.269	.223	46	-15	1	1	-0	.995	-9	2-71,S-19,3-14/D-2	-2.2
1975	Oak-A	20	28	2	7	1	0	0	4	2	2	.250	.300	.286	68	-1	0	0	0	1.000	2	/S-7,3-7,2-6	-0.2
	SD-N	87	196	13	44	5	0	0	14	24	18	.224	.309	.250	60	-10	3	1	0	.954	-2	3-64,2-11/1-1	-0.9
1976	SD-N	96	212	16	50	5	2	0	26	25	28	.236	.316	.278	76	-6	0	3	-2	.971	-9	3-27,2-25/S-6,1-1	-1.7
Total	10	977	2447	238	565	61	21	13	202	271	272	.231	.309	.289	73	-85	13	22	-9	.981	-39	2-490,S-276,3/1D	-9.0

■ JACK KUBISZYN   Kubiszyn, John Henry b: 12/19/36, Buffalo, N.Y.   BR/TR, 5'11", 170 lbs.   Deb: 4/23/61

YEAR	TM/L	G	AB	R	H	2B	3B	HR	RBI	BB	SO	AVG	OBP	SLG	PRO+	BR/A	SB	CS	SBR	FA	FR	G/POS	TPR
1961	Cle-A	25	42	4	9	0	0	0	0	5	8	.214	.250	.214	26	-4	0	0	0	1.000	4	/3-8,S-7,2-2	-0.1
1962	Cle-A	25	59	3	10	2	0	1	2	5	7	.169	.234	.254	32	-6	0	0	0	.964	2	S-18/3-1	-0.2
Total	2	50	101	7	19	2	0	1	2	7	12	.188	.241	.238	30	-10	0	0	0	.969	5	/S-25,3-9,2-2	-0.3

■ GIL KUBSKI   Kubski, Gilbert Thomas b: 10/12/54, Longview, Tex.   BL/TR, 6'3", 185 lbs.   Deb: 9/2/80

YEAR	TM/L	G	AB	R	H	2B	3B	HR	RBI	BB	SO	AVG	OBP	SLG	PRO+	BR/A	SB	CS	SBR	FA	FR	G/POS	TPR
1980	Cal-A	22	63	11	16	1	0	0	5	6	6	.254	.319	.302	73	-2	1	1	-0	1.000	1	O-20	-0.3

■ STEVE KUCZEK   Kuczek, Stanislaw Leo b: 12/28/24, Amsterdam, N.Y.   BR/TR, 6', 160 lbs.   Deb: 9/29/49

YEAR	TM/L	G	AB	R	H	2B	3B	HR	RBI	BB	SO	AVG	OBP	SLG	PRO+	BR/A	SB	CS	SBR	FA	FR	G/POS	TPR
1949	Bos-N	1	1	0	1	1	0	0	0	0	0	1.000	1.000	2.000	723	1	1	0		.000	0	H	0.1

■ BILL KUEHNE   Kuehne, William J. (b: William J. Knelme) b: 10/24/1858, Leipzig, Germany   d: 10/27/21, Sulphur Springs, O   BR/TR, 185 lbs.   Deb: 5/1/1883

YEAR	TM/L	G	AB	R	H	2B	3B	HR	RBI	BB	SO	AVG	OBP	SLG	PRO+	BR/A	SB	CS	SBR	FA	FR	G/POS	TPR
1883	Col-a	95	374	38	85	8	14	1		2		.227	.231	.332	86	-5				.833	-5	*3-69,2-18/S-7,O-3	-0.9
1884	Col-a	110	415	48	98	13	16	5		9		.236	.254	.381	113	6				.881	11	*3-110	1.6
1885	Pit-a	104	411	54	93	9	19	0	43	15		.226	.257	.341	89	-6				.865	-1	*3-97/S-7	-0.5
1886	Pit-a	117	481	73	98	16	17	1	48	19		.204	.237	.314	72	-17	26			.899	-1	O-54,3-47,1-18	-1.8
1887	Pit-N	102	402	68	120	18	15	1	41	14	39	.299	.324	.425	113	6	17			.883	-13	*S-91/3-4,1-4,O-3	-0.5
1888	Pit-N	138	524	60	123	22	11	3	62	9	68	.235	.250	.336	93	-5	34			.910	-5	3-75,S-63	-0.2
1889	Pit-N	97	390	43	96	20	5	5	57	9	36	.246	.263	.362	82	-12	15			.885	-1	3-75,O-13/2-5,S1	-0.9
1890	Pit-P	126	528	66	126	21	12	6	73	28	37	.239	.277	.352	74	-22	19			.850	6	*3-126	-0.9
1891	Col-a	68	261	32	56	9	0	2	22	10	22	.215	.244	.272	50	-18	21			.885	-2	3-68	-1.5
	Lou-a	41	159	28	44	3	1	1	18	8	13	.277	.315	.327	85	-4	10			.904	3	3-41	0.1
	Yr	109	420	60	100	12	1	3	40	18	35	.238	.277	.293	64	-21	31			.893	0	*3-109	-1.4
1892	Lou-N	76	287	22	48	4	5	0	36	13	36	.167	.203	.216	29	-25	6			.874	1	3-76	-2.4
	StL-N	6	24	1	4	0	0	0	0	0	3	.167	.200	.208	25	-2	1			.895	-0	/3-5,S-1	-0.2
	Cin-N	6	24	3	5	1	0	1	4	1	5	.208	.240	.375	87	-1	0			.941	2	/3-4,2-2	0.1
	StL-N	1	4	0	0	0	0	0	0	0	1	.000	.000	.000	-99	-1	0			1.000	0	/3-1	0.0
	Yr	89	339	26	57	5	5	1	40	14	45	.168	.203	.224	32	-29	7			.880	-0	3-86/2-2,S-1	-2.5
Total	10	1087	4284	536	996	145	115	25	404	137	260	.232	.258	.338	82	-105	151			.876	-4	3-798,S-171/O21	-8.0

■ HARVEY KUENN   Kuenn, Harvey Edward b: 12/4/30, W.Allis, Wis.   d: 2/28/88, Peoria, Ariz.   BR/TR, 6'2", 190 lbs.   Deb: 9/6/52   MC

YEAR	TM/L	G	AB	R	H	2B	3B	HR	RBI	BB	SO	AVG	OBP	SLG	PRO+	BR/A	SB	CS	SBR	FA	FR	G/POS	TPR
1952	Det-A	19	80	2	26	2	0	0	8	2	1	.325	.349	.400	107	1	2	1	0	.962	2	S-19	0.4
1953	Det-A★	155	679	94	**209**	33	7	2	48	50	31	.308	.356	.386	101	-1	6	5	-0	.973	-21	*S-155	-0.9
1954	Det-A☆	155	656	81	**201**	28	6	5	48	29	13	.306	.337	.390	100	-1	9	9	-3	.966	3	*S-155	1.2
1955	Det-A	145	620	101	190	**38**	8	8	62	40	27	.306	.349	.423	109	6	8	3	1	.956	-28	*S-141	-0.9
1956	Det-A	146	591	96	196	32	7	12	88	55	34	.332	.391	.470	126	22	9	5	-0	**.968**	-20	*S-141/O-1	1.4
1957	Det-A★	151	624	74	173	30	6	9	44	47	45	.277	.328	.388	92	-7	5	8	-3	.955	-49	*S-136,3-17/1-1	-4.8
1958	Det-A	139	561	73	179	**39**	3	8	54	51	34	.319	.376	.442	116	13	5	10	-5	.984	15	*O-138	1.6
1959	Det-A★	139	561	99	**198**	**42**	7	9	71	48	37	**.353**	.405	.501	140	31	7	2	1	.988	1	*O-137	2.5
1960	Cle-A★	126	474	65	146	24	0	9	54	55	25	.308	.381	.416	119	14	3	0	1	.966	-7	*O-119/3-5	1.0
1961	SF-N	131	471	60	125	22	4	5	46	47	49	.265	.333	.361	87	-8	5	4	-2	.973	-21	O-93,3-32/S-1	-0.5
1962	*SF-N	130	487	73	148	23	5	10	68	49	49	.304	.369	.433	116	12	3	6	-3	.970	-9	*O-105,3-30	-0.5
1963	SF-N	120	417	61	121	6	7	9	31	44	33	.290	.361	.374	113	8	2	1	0	.975	-30	O-64,3-53	-2.7
1964	SF-N	111	351	42	92	16	2	4	22	35	32	.262	.331	.353	91	-4	0	1	-1	.952	-13	O-88,1-11/3-2	-2.3

YEAR	TM/L	G	AB	R	H	2B	3B	HR	RBI	BB	SO	AVG	OBP	SLG	PRO+	BR/A	SB	CS	SBR	FA	FR	G/POS	TPR
1965	SF-N	23	59	4	14	0	0	0	6	10	3	.237	.357	.237	69	-2	3	1	0	1.000	-1	O-14/1-7	-0.4
	Chi-N	54	120	11	26	5	0	0	6	22	13	.217	.338	.258	69	-4	1	0		.975	-3	O-35/1-1	-0.8
	Yr	77	179	15	40	5	0	0	12	32	16	.223	.344	.251	69	-6	4	1	1	.981	-4	O-49/1-8	-1.2
1966	Chi-N	3	3	0	1	0	0	0	0	0	1	.333	.333	.333	85	-0	0	0	0	.000	-0	/O-1	0.0
	Phi-N	86	159	15	47	9	0	0	15	10	16	.296	.337	.352	92	-2	0	0	0	1.000	-6	O-31,1-13/3-1	-1.0
	Yr	89	162	15	48	9	0	0	15	10	17	.296	.337	.352	92	-2	0	0	0	1.000	-7	O-32,1-13/3-1	-1.0
Total	15	1833	6913	951	2092	356	65	87	671	594	404	.303	.359	.408	108	80	68	56	-13	.978	-163	O-826,S-748,3/1	-8.3

■ JOE KUHEL
Kuhel, Joseph Anthony   b: 6/25/06, Cleveland, Ohio   d: 2/26/84, Kansas City, Kan.   BL/TL, 6', 180 lbs.   Deb: 7/31/30   M

YEAR	TM/L	G	AB	R	H	2B	3B	HR	RBI	BB	SO	AVG	OBP	SLG	PRO+	BR/A	SB	CS	SBR	FA	FR	G/POS	TPR
1930	Was-A	18	63	9	18	3	3	0	17	5	6	.286	.348	.429	95	-1	1	0	0	.981	-1	1-16	-0.2
1931	Was-A	139	524	70	141	34	8	8	85	47	45	.269	.335	.410	94	-5	7	5	-1	.991	-7	*1-139	-2.4
1932	Was-A	101	347	52	101	21	5	4	52	32	19	.291	.345	.415	99	-0	5	2	0	.994	-2	1-85	-0.8
1933	*Was-A	153	602	89	194	34	10	11	107	59	48	.322	.385	.467	126	22	17	8	0	.996	-7	*1-153	0.1
1934	Was-A	63	263	49	76	12	3	3	25	30	14	.289	.364	.392	99	-0	2	7	-4	.994	-4	1-63	-1.3
1935	Was-A	151	633	99	165	25	9	2	74	78	44	.261	.345	.338	80	-17	5	4	-1	.991	0	*1-151	-3.3
1936	Was-A	149	588	107	189	42	8	16	118	64	30	.321	.392	.502	126	23	15	7	0	.993	-2	*1-149	0.6
1937	Was-A	136	547	73	155	24	11	6	61	63	39	.283	.357	.400	95	-4	6	3	0	.993	3	*1-136	-1.6
1938	Chi-A	117	412	67	110	27	4	8	51	72	35	.267	.376	.410	95	-2	9	7	-2	.988	-7	*1-111	-2.2
1939	Chi-A	139	546	107	164	24	9	15	56	64	51	.300	.376	.460	110	8	18	5	2	.992	-4	*1-136	-0.7
1940	Chi-A	155	603	111	169	28	8	27	94	87	59	.280	.374	.488	120	18	12	5	1	.988	-5	*1-155	-0.1
1941	Chi-A	153	600	99	150	39	5	12	63	70	55	.250	.331	.392	92	-8	20	5	3	.994	-1	*1-151	-1.6
1942	Chi-A	115	413	60	103	14	4	4	52	60	22	.249	.347	.332	94	-2	22	9	1	.991	-4	*1-113	-1.2
1943	Chi-A	153	531	55	113	21	1	5	46	76	45	.213	.319	.284	77	-13	14	8	-1	.995	1	*1-153	-2.4
1944	Was-A	139	518	90	144	26	7	4	51	68	40	.278	.364	.378	117	13	11	6	-0	.987	-2	*1-138	0.4
1945	Was-A	142	533	73	152	29	13	2	75	79	31	.285	.378	.400	137	27	10	5	0	.989	-6	*1-141	1.2
1946	Was-A	14	20	2	3	0	0	0	2	5	2	.150	.320	.150	36	-1	0	0	0	1.000	-2	/1-5	-0.2
	Chi-A	64	238	24	65	9	3	4	20	21	24	.273	.335	.387	105	1	4	4	-1	.994	-2	1-63	-0.6
	Yr	78	258	26	68	9	3	4	22	26	26	.264	.333	.368	100	-0	4	4	-1	.994	-2	1-68	-0.8
1947	Chi-A	3	3	0	0	0	0	0	0	0	3	.000	.000	.000	-99	-1	0	0	0	.000	-0	H	-0.1
Total	18	2104	7984	1236	2212	412	111	131	1049	980	612	.277	.359	.406	104	56	178	90	-1	.992	-48	*1-2057	-16.4

■ KENNY KUHN
Kuhn, Kenneth Harold   b: 3/20/37, Louisville, Ky.   BL/TR, 5'10.5", 175 lbs.   Deb: 7/7/55

YEAR	TM/L	G	AB	R	H	2B	3B	HR	RBI	BB	SO	AVG	OBP	SLG	PRO+	BR/A	SB	CS	SBR	FA	FR	G/POS	TPR
1955	Cle-A	4	6	0	2	0	0	0	0	1	0	.333	.429	.333	103	0	1	0	0	1.000	-2	/S-4	-0.1
1956	Cle-A	27	22	7	6	1	0	0	2	0	4	.273	.273	.318	54	-1	0	1	-1	1.000	2	S-17/2-5	0.1
1957	Cle-A	40	53	5	9	0	0	0	5	4	9	.170	.228	.170	10	-6	0	0	0	.974	-3	2-14/3-2,S-1	-0.9
Total	3	71	81	12	17	1	0	0	7	5	13	.210	.256	.222	30	-8	1	1	-0	.963	-3	/S-22,2-19,3-2	-1.0

■ WALT KUHN
Kuhn, Walter Charles "Red"   b: 2/2/1884, Fresno, Cal.   d: 6/14/35, Fresno, Cal.   BR/TR, 5'7", 162 lbs.   Deb: 4/18/12

YEAR	TM/L	G	AB	R	H	2B	3B	HR	RBI	BB	SO	AVG	OBP	SLG	PRO+	BR/A	SB	CS	SBR	FA	FR	G/POS	TPR
1912	Chi-A	76	178	16	36	8	0	0	10	20		.202	.286	.242	53	-10	5			.966	9	C-75/2-1	0.4
1913	Chi-A	26	50	5	8	1	0	0	5	13	8	.160	.333	.180	52	-2	1			.980	-2	C-24	-0.3
1914	Chi-A	17	40	4	11	0	0	0	0	8	11	.275	.396	.300	111	1	2	3	-1	.987	-1	C-16	0.0
Total	3	119	268	25	55	9	0	0	15	41	19	.205	.313	.239	62	-12	8	3	-1	.971	6	C-115/2-1	0.1

■ CHARLIE KUHNS
Kuhns, Charles B.   b: 10/27/1877, Freeport, Pa.   d: 7/15/22, Pittsburg, Pa.   5'9", 160 lbs.   Deb: 6/4/1897

YEAR	TM/L	G	AB	R	H	2B	3B	HR	RBI	BB	SO	AVG	OBP	SLG	PRO+	BR/A	SB	CS	SBR	FA	FR	G/POS	TPR
1897	Pit-N	1	3	0	0	0	0	0	0	0	0	.000	.250	.000	-32	-1	0			.667	0	/3-1	0.0
1899	Bos-N	7	18	2	5	0	0	0		3	2	.278	.350	.278	67	-1	0			.813	-1	/S-3,3-3	-0.1
Total	2	8	21	2	5	0	0	0		3	2	.238	.333	.238	38	-1	0			.733	-1	/3-4,S-3	-0.1

■ DUANE KUIPER
Kuiper, Duane Eugene   b: 6/19/50, Racine, Wis.   BL/TR, 6', 175 lbs.   Deb: 9/9/74

YEAR	TM/L	G	AB	R	H	2B	3B	HR	RBI	BB	SO	AVG	OBP	SLG	PRO+	BR/A	SB	CS	SBR	FA	FR	G/POS	TPR
1974	Cle-A	10	22	7	11	4	2	0	4	2	2	.500	.542	.591	228	4	1	1	-0	1.000	1	/2-8	0.5
1975	Cle-A	90	346	42	101	11	1	0	25	30	26	.292	.362	.329	97	-0	19	18	-5	.972	-14	2-87/D-1	-1.5
1976	Cle-A	135	506	47	133	13	6	0	37	30	42	.263	.305	.312	82	-12	10	17	-7	.987	20	*2-128/1-5,D-2	0.9
1977	Cle-A	148	610	62	169	15	8	1	50	37	55	.277	.326	.333	83	-14	11	11	-3	.985	2	*2-148	-0.5
1978	Cle-A	149	547	52	155	18	6	0	43	19	35	.283	.312	.338	84	-12	4	9	-4	.979	-19	*2-149	-2.5
1979	Cle-A	140	479	46	122	9	5	0	39	37	27	.255	.313	.294	65	-23	4	9	-4	.988	-4	*2-140	-2.1
1980	Cle-A	42	149	10	42	5	0	0	9	13	8	.282	.340	.315	80	-4	0	1	-1	.995	-8	2-42	-0.9
1981	Cle-A	72	206	15	53	6	0	0	14	8	13	.257	.285	.286	66	-9	1	1	-1	.983	-5	2-72	-1.1
1982	SF-N	107	218	26	61	9	1	0	17	32	24	.280	.367	.330	100	1	2	2	-1	.978	-7	2-51	-0.4
1983	SF-N	72	176	14	44	2	2	0	14	27	17	.250	.356	.284	82	-3	1	0	-1	.988	-9	2-64	-1.0
1984	SF-N	83	115	8	23	1	0	0	11	12	10	.200	.276	.209	39	-9	0	1	-1	.969	6	2-31/1-1	-0.3
1985	SF-N	9	5	0	3	0	0	0	0	0	0	.600	.667	.600	270	-1	0	0	0	.000	0	/H	0.1
Total	12	1057	3379	329	917	91	29	1	263	248	255	.271	.326	.316	81	-79	52	71	-27	.983	-36	2-920/1-6,D-3	-8.8

■ JEFF KUNKEL
Kunkel, Jeffrey William   b: 3/25/62, W.Palm Beach, Fla.   BR/TR, 6'2", 180 lbs.   Deb: 7/23/84   F

YEAR	TM/L	G	AB	R	H	2B	3B	HR	RBI	BB	SO	AVG	OBP	SLG	PRO+	BR/A	SB	CS	SBR	FA	FR	G/POS	TPR
1984	Tex-A	50	142	13	29	2	3	3	7	2	35	.204	.221	.324	47	-10	4	3	-1	.922	-1	S-48/D-1	-0.9
1985	Tex-A	2	4	1	1	0	0	0	0	0	3	.250	.250	.250	37	-0	0	0	0	1.000	1	/S-2	0.1
1986	Tex-A	8	13	3	3	0	1	0	2	0	2	.231	.231	.462	81	-0	0	0	0	.769	-0	/S-5,D-1	-0.1
1987	Tex-A	15	32	1	7	0	0	1	2	0	10	.219	.242	.313	46	-3	0	1	-1	.955	-7	2-10/3-3,O-3,1SD	0.0
1988	Tex-A	55	154	14	35	8	3	2	15	4	35	.227	.252	.357	67	-7	0	1	-1	.949	-4	2-28,S-19,3/OPD	0.0
1989	Tex-A	108	293	39	79	21	2	8	29	20	75	.270	.323	.437	110	3	3	2	-0	.936	2	S-59,O-30/2-8,3PD	0.8
1990	Tex-A	99	200	17	34	11	1	3	17	11	66	.170	.221	.280	39	-17	2	1	0	.958	9	S-67,3-15,2-13/OD	0.8
1992	Chi-N	20	29	0	4	2	0	1	2	0	8	.138	.138	.207	-3	-4	0	0	0	1.000	-0	/S-6,2-3,O-3	0.0
Total	8	357	867	88	192	44	9	18	73	37	234	.221	.260	.355	69	-38	9	8	-2	.940	22	S-207/2-62,O3DP1	-0.6

■ RUSTY KUNTZ
Kuntz, Russell Jay   b: 2/4/55, Orange, Cal.   BR/TR, 6'3", 190 lbs.   Deb: 9/1/79   C

YEAR	TM/L	G	AB	R	H	2B	3B	HR	RBI	BB	SO	AVG	OBP	SLG	PRO+	BR/A	SB	CS	SBR	FA	FR	G/POS	TPR
1979	Chi-A	5	11	0	1	0	0	0	0	2	4	.091	.231	.091	-9	-2	0	0	0	1.000	1	/O-5	-0.1
1980	Chi-A	36	62	5	14	4	0	0	3	5	13	.226	.284	.290	58	-4	1	0	0	.979	-5	O-34	-0.9
1981	Chi-A	67	55	15	14	2	0	0	4	6	8	.255	.339	.291	85	-1	1	0	0	1.000	-13	O-51/D-5	-1.5
1982	Chi-A	21	26	4	5	1	0	0	3	2	8	.192	.250	.231	33	-2	1	0	0	1.000	-7	O-21	-1.0
1983	Chi-A	28	42	6	11	1	0	1	6	6	13	.262	.354	.286	76	-1	1	0	0	.976	-6	O-27/D-1	-0.7
	Min-A	31	100	13	19	3	0	3	5	12	28	.190	.277	.310	59	-6	0	0	0	.986	-6	O-30	-0.7
	Yr	59	142	19	30	4	0	3	6	18	41	.211	.300	.303	64	-7	1	0	0	.982	-6	O-57/D-1	-1.4
1984	*Det-A	84	140	32	40	12	0	2	22	25	28	.286	.398	.414	126	6	2	2	-1	.987	-16	O-67,D-10	-1.2
1985	Det-A	5	5	0	0	0	0	0	0	0	0	.000	.286	.000	-13	-1	0	1	-1	.000	-0	/1-1,D-3	-0.2
Total	7	277	441	75	104	23	0	5	38	60	106	.236	.330	.322	81	-10	5	3	-0	.988	-46	O-235/D-19,1-1	-6.3

■ WHITEY KUROWSKI
Kurowski, George John   b: 4/19/18, Reading, Pa.   BR/TR, 5'11", 193 lbs.   Deb: 9/23/41

YEAR	TM/L	G	AB	R	H	2B	3B	HR	RBI	BB	SO	AVG	OBP	SLG	PRO+	BR/A	SB	CS	SBR	FA	FR	G/POS	TPR
1941	StL-N	5	9	1	3	2	0	0	0	0	2	.333	.400	.556	157	-1	0			1.000	-1	/3-4	0.0
1942	*StL-N	115	366	51	93	17	3	9	42	33	60	.254	.326	.391	102	0	7			.944	9	*3-104/S-1,O-1	1.1
1943	*StL-N☆	139	522	69	150	24	8	13	70	31	54	.287	.330	.439	116	8	3			.952	1	*3-137/S-2	1.2
1944	*StL-N★	149	555	95	150	25	7	20	87	58	40	.270	.341	.449	119	13	2			.965	4	*3-146/2-9,S-1	1.8
1945	*StL-N†	133	511	84	165	27	3	21	102	45	45	.323	.383	.511	144	28	1			.964	2	*3-131/S-6	3.3
1946	*StL-N★	142	519	76	156	32	5	14	89	72	47	.301	.391	.462	136	25	2			.966	0	*3-138	2.9
1947	*StL-N★	146	513	108	159	27	6	27	104	87	56	.310	.420	.544	148	37	4			.954	-14	*3-141	2.3
1948	StL-N	77	220	34	47	8	0	2	33	42	28	.214	.352	.277	68	-8	0			.939	-11	3-65	-2.0
1949	StL-N	10	14	0	2	0	0	0	3	3	2	.143	.200	.143	-6	-2	0			1.000	-0	/3-2	-0.3
Total	9	916	3229	518	925	162	32	106	529	369	332	.286	.366	.455	124	102	19			.957	-10	3-868/S-10,2-9,O-1	10.3

■ CRAIG KUSICK
Kusick, Craig Robert   b: 9/30/48, Milwaukee, Wis.   BR/TR, 6'3", 232 lbs.   Deb: 9/8/73

YEAR	TM/L	G	AB	R	H	2B	3B	HR	RBI	BB	SO	AVG	OBP	SLG	PRO+	BR/A	SB	CS	SBR	FA	FR	G/POS	TPR
1973	Min-A	15	48	4	12	2	0	0	4	7	9	.250	.357	.292	81	-1	0	0	0	.989	-1	1-11/O-2,D-2	-0.3
1974	Min-A	76	201	36	48	7	1	8	26	35	36	.239	.354	.403	114	4	0	0	0	.996	4	1-75	0.4

YEAR	TM/L	G	AB	R	H	2B	3B	HR	RBI	BB	SO	AVG	OBP	SLG	PRO+	BR/A	SB	CS	SBR	FA	FR	G/POS	TPR
1975	Min-A	57	156	14	37	8	0	6	27	21	23	.237	.346	.404	110	2	0	0	0	.990	1	1-51	0.1
1976	Min-A	109	266	33	69	13	0	11	36	35	44	.259	.348	.432	125	8	5	1	1	.977	3	D-79,1-23	1.0
1977	Min-A	115	268	34	68	12	0	12	45	49	60	.254	.375	.433	121	9	3	1	0	.972	-2	D-85,1-23	0.5
1978	Min-A	77	191	23	33	3	2	4	20	37	38	.173	.310	.272	64	-8	3	2	-0	.987	2	D-35,1-27/O-9	-1.0
1979	Min-A	24	54	8	13	4	0	3	6	3	11	.241	.281	.481	97	-0	0	0	0	1.000	-0	D-12/1-8	-0.1
	Tor-A	24	54	3	11	1	0	2	7	7	7	.204	.306	.333	72	-2	0	0	0	.978	1	1-20/P-1,D-1	-0.2
	Yr	48	108	11	24	5	0	5	13	10	18	.222	.294	.407	85	-3	0	0	0	.983	1	1-28,D-13/P-1	-0.3
Total	7	497	1238	155	291	50	3	46	171	194	228	.235	.345	.392	106	13	11	4	1	.988	8	1-238,D-214/O-11,P	0.4

■ ART KUSNYER
Kusnyer, Arthur William b: 12/19/45, Akron, Ohio BR/TR, 6'2", 198 lbs. Deb: 9/21/70 C

YEAR	TM/L	G	AB	R	H	2B	3B	HR	RBI	BB	SO	AVG	OBP	SLG	PRO+	BR/A	SB	CS	SBR	FA	FR	G/POS	TPR
1970	Chi-A	4	10	0	1	0	0	0	0	0	4	.100	.100	.100	-43	-2	0	0	0	.941	1	/C-3	-0.1
1971	Cal-A	6	13	0	2	0	0	0	0	0	3	.154	.154	.154	-14	-2	0	0	0	.958	1	/C-6	-0.1
1972	Cal-A	64	179	13	37	2	1	2	13	16	33	.207	.276	.263	64	-8	0	0	0	.975	-3	C-63	-0.9
1973	Cal-A	41	64	5	8	2	0	0	3	2	12	.125	.152	.156	-14	-10	0	0	-1	.979	1	C-41	-0.9
1976	Mil-A	15	34	2	4	1	0	0	3	1	5	.118	.167	.147	-8	-5	1	0	0	.938	1	C-14	-0.5
1978	KC-A	9	13	1	3	1	0	1	2	2	4	.231	.333	.538	138	1	0	0	0	.946	3	/C-9	0.4
Total	6	139	313	21	55	6	1	3	21	21	61	.176	.232	.230	37	-26	1	1	-0	.970	2	C-136	-2.1

■ JUL KUSTUS
Kustus, Joseph J. "Joe" or "Kul" b: 9/5/1882, Detroit, Mich. d: 4/27/16, Eloise, Mich. BR/TR, 5'10", Deb: 4/17/09

YEAR	TM/L	G	AB	R	H	2B	3B	HR	RBI	BB	SO	AVG	OBP	SLG	PRO+	BR/A	SB	CS	SBR	FA	FR	G/POS	TPR
1909	Bro-N	53	173	12	25	5	0	1	11	11		.145	.204	.191	23	-16	9			.951	0	O-50	-2.0

■ RANDY KUTCHER
Kutcher, Randy Scott b: 4/20/60, Anchorage, Alaska BR/TR, 5'11", 175 lbs. Deb: 6/19/86

YEAR	TM/L	G	AB	R	H	2B	3B	HR	RBI	BB	SO	AVG	OBP	SLG	PRO+	BR/A	SB	CS	SBR	FA	FR	G/POS	TPR
1986	SF-N	71	186	28	44	9	1	7	16	11	41	.237	.279	.409	92	-3	6	5	-1	.990	-1	O-51,S-13/3-4,2-3	-0.6
1987	SF-N	14	16	7	3	1	1	0	1	1	5	.188	.235	.375	61	-1	1	0	0	1.000	1	/O-6,2-2,3-2,S-1	0.0
1988	Bos-A	19	12	2	2	1	0	0	0	0	2	.167	.167	.250	14	-1	0	1	-1	1.000	0	/O-7,3-2,D-7	-0.2
1989	Bos-A	77	160	28	36	10	3	2	18	11	46	.225	.275	.363	74	-6	3	0	1	.982	-3	O-57/3-6,C-1,D-6	-0.9
1990	*Bos-A	63	74	18	17	4	1	1	5	13	18	.230	.345	.351	91	-1	3	3	-1	1.000	0	O-34,3-11/2-5,D-5	-0.2
Total	5	244	448	83	102	25	6	10	40	36	112	.228	.285	.377	82	-12	13	9	-2	.989	-3	O-155/3-25,DS2C	-1.9

■ JOE KUTINA
Kutina, Joseph Peter b: 1/16/1885, Chicago, Ill. d: 4/13/45, Chicago, Ill. BR/TR, 6'2", 205 lbs. Deb: 9/6/11

YEAR	TM/L	G	AB	R	H	2B	3B	HR	RBI	BB	SO	AVG	OBP	SLG	PRO+	BR/A	SB	CS	SBR	FA	FR	G/POS	TPR
1911	StL-A	26	101	12	26	6	2	3	15	2		.257	.279	.446	105	-0	2			.981	-1	1-26	-0.1
1912	StL-A	69	205	18	42	9	3	1	18	13		.205	.262	.293	61	-11	0			.985	-3	1-51/O-1	-1.5
Total	2	95	306	30	68	15	5	4	33	15		.222	.268	.343	76	-11	2			.984	-4	/1-77,O-1	-1.6

■ AL KVASNAK
Kvasnak, Alexander b: 1/11/21, Sagamore, Pa. BR/TR, 6'1", 170 lbs. Deb: 4/15/42

YEAR	TM/L	G	AB	R	H	2B	3B	HR	RBI	BB	SO	AVG	OBP	SLG	PRO+	BR/A	SB	CS	SBR	FA	FR	G/POS	TPR
1942	Was-A	5	11	3	2	0	0	0	2	1		.182	.308	.182	40	-1	0	0	0	1.000	-0	/O-3	-0.1

■ ANDY KYLE
Kyle, Andrew Ewing b: 10/29/1889, Toronto, Ont., Can. d: 9/6/71, Toronto, Ont., Can. BL/TL, 5'8", 160 lbs. Deb: 9/7/12

YEAR	TM/L	G	AB	R	H	2B	3B	HR	RBI	BB	SO	AVG	OBP	SLG	PRO+	BR/A	SB	CS	SBR	FA	FR	G/POS	TPR
1912	Cin-N	9	21	3	7	1	0	0	4	4	2	.333	.440	.381	129	1	0			1.000	0	/O-7	0.1

■ CHET LAABS
Laabs, Chester Peter b: 4/30/12, Milwaukee, Wis. d: 1/26/83, Warren, Mich. BR/TR, 5'8", 175 lbs. Deb: 5/5/37

YEAR	TM/L	G	AB	R	H	2B	3B	HR	RBI	BB	SO	AVG	OBP	SLG	PRO+	BR/A	SB	CS	SBR	FA	FR	G/POS	TPR
1937	Det-A	72	242	31	58	13	5	8	37	24	66	.240	.308	.434	83	-8	6	2	1	.971	-7	O-62	-1.5
1938	Det-A	64	211	26	50	7	3	7	37	15	52	.237	.288	.398	66	-12	3	2	-0	.971	-1	O-53	-1.4
1939	Det-A	5	16	1	5	1	1	0	2	2	0	.313	.389	.500	117	0	0	0	0	.933	1	/O-5	0.1
	StL-A	95	317	52	95	20	5	10	62	33	62	.300	.368	.489	115	6	4	1	1	.972	-0	O-79	0.3
	Yr	100	333	53	100	21	6	10	64	35	62	.300	.369	.489	115	7	4	1	1	.969	1	O-84	0.4
1940	StL-A	105	218	32	59	11	5	10	40	34	59	.271	.372	.505	122	7	3	3	-1	.969	-7	O-63	-0.3
1941	StL-A	118	392	64	109	23	6	15	59	51	59	.278	.361	.482	117	9	5	2	0	.982	-2	*O-100	0.2
1942	StL-A	144	520	90	143	21	7	27	99	88	88	.275	.380	.498	144	30	0	3	-2	.970	-4	*O-139	1.7
1943	StL-A★	151	580	83	145	27	7	17	85	73	105	.250	.338	.409	115	11	5	7	-3	.976	-4	*O-150	0.2
1944	*StL-A	66	201	28	47	10	2	5	23	29	53	.234	.330	.378	96	-1	3	1	0	1.000	-2	O-55	-0.5
1945	StL-A	35	109	15	26	4	3	1	8	16	17	.239	.352	.358	101	-1	3	1	0	.986	-4	O-35	-0.5
1946	StL-A	80	264	40	69	13	0	16	52	20	50	.261	.316	.492	117	5	3	1	0	.987	1	O-72	0.3
1947	Phi-A	15	32	5	7	1	0	1	6	5	6	.219	.306	.344	79	-1	0	0	0	1.000	1	/O-7	-0.1
Total	11	950	3102	467	813	151	44	117	509	389	595	.262	.346	.452	113	47	32	22	-4	.977	-21	O-820	-1.5

■ COCO LABOY
Laboy, Jose Alberto b: 7/3/39, Ponce, P.R. BR/TR, 5'10", 170 lbs. Deb: 4/8/69

YEAR	TM/L	G	AB	R	H	2B	3B	HR	RBI	BB	SO	AVG	OBP	SLG	PRO+	BR/A	SB	CS	SBR	FA	FR	G/POS	TPR
1969	Mon-N	157	562	53	145	29	1	18	83	40	96	.258	.312	.409	100	-1	0	2	-1	.944	4	*3-156	0.1
1970	Mon-N	137	432	37	86	26	1	5	53	31	81	.199	.256	.299	48	-33	0	2	-1	.946	-4	*3-132/2-3	-3.9
1971	Mon-N	76	151	10	38	4	0	1	14	11	19	.252	.302	.298	70	-6	0	1	-1	.937	1	3-65/2-2	-0.6
1972	Mon-N	28	69	6	18	2	0	3	14	10	16	.261	.354	.420	117	2	0	0	0	.980	2	3-24/2-3,S-2	-0.2
1973	Mon-N	22	33	2	4	1	0	0	2	5	8	.121	.237	.242	32	-3	0	0	0	.889	1	3-20/2-1	-0.2
Total	5	420	1247	108	291	62	2	28	166	97	220	.233	.292	.354	77	-41	0	5	-3	.944	-0	3-397/2-9,S-2	-4.6

■ CANDY LaCHANCE
LaChance, George Joseph b: 2/15/1870, Putnam, Conn. d: 8/18/32, Waterville, Conn. BB/TR, 6'1", 183 lbs. Deb: 8/15/1893

YEAR	TM/L	G	AB	R	H	2B	3B	HR	RBI	BB	SO	AVG	OBP	SLG	PRO+	BR/A	SB	CS	SBR	FA	FR	G/POS	TPR
1893	Bro-N	11	35	1	6	1	0	0	6	2	12	.171	.237	.200	17	-4	0			.654	-6	/C-6,O-5	-0.8
1894	Bro-N	68	257	48	83	13	8	5	52	16	32	.323	.365	.494	114	5	20			.979	-8	1-56,C-10/O-3	-0.2
1895	Bro-N	127	536	99	167	22	8	8	108	29	48	.312	.356	.427	110	7	37			.983	-6	*1-125/O-3	0.3
1896	Bro-N	89	348	60	99	10	13	7	58	23	32	.284	.331	.448	111	-3	17			.986	-3	*1-89	0.1
1897	Bro-N	126	520	86	160	28	16	4	90	15		.308	.333	.446	111	5	26			.978	-4	*1-126	0.1
1898	Bro-N	136	526	62	130	23	7	5	65	31		.247	.299	.346	85	-12	23			.988	-20	1-74,S-48,O-13	-2.9
1899	Bal-N	125	472	65	145	23	10	1	75	21		.307	.350	.405	101	-1	31			.984	-7	*1-125	-0.6
1901	Cle-A	133	548	81	166	22	9	1	75	7		.303	.314	.381	96	-5	11			.979	-3	*1-133	-0.8
1902	Bos-A	138	541	60	151	13	4	6	56	18		.279	.309	.351	80	-15	8			.983	-11	*1-138	-2.8
1903	*Bos-A	141	522	60	134	22	6	1	53	28		.257	.303	.328	85	-10	12			.984	-11	*1-141	-2.4
1904	Bos-A	157	573	55	130	19	5	1	47	23		.227	.265	.283	69	-20	7			**.992**	-14	*1-157	-4.2
1905	Bos-A	12	41	1	6	1	0	0	5	6		.146	.255	.171	36	-3	0			.988	-0	1-12	-0.1
Total	12	1263	4919	678	1377	197	86	39	690	219	124	.280	.318	.379	93	-49	192			.984	-93	*1-1176/S-48,O-24,C	-14.6

■ RENE LACHEMANN
Lachemann, Rene George b: 5/4/45, Los Angeles, Cal. BR/TR, 6', 198 lbs. Deb: 5/4/65 FMC

YEAR	TM/L	G	AB	R	H	2B	3B	HR	RBI	BB	SO	AVG	OBP	SLG	PRO+	BR/A	SB	CS	SBR	FA	FR	G/POS	TPR
1965	KC-A	92	216	20	49	7	1	9	29	12	57	.227	.268	.394	87	-5	0	0	0	.980	2	C-75	0.1
1966	KC-A	7	5	0	1	1	0	0	0	0	1	.200	.200	.400	70	-0	0	0	0	1.000	1	/C-6	0.1
1968	Oak-A	19	60	3	9	1	0	0	4	1	11	.150	.177	.167	70	-7	0	0	0	.967	-6	C-16	-1.5
Total	3	118	281	23	59	9	1	9	33	13	69	.210	.247	.345	70	-12	0	0	0	.978	-3	/C-97	-1.3

■ PETE LaCOCK
LaCock, Ralph Pierre b: 1/17/52, Burbank, Cal. BL/TL, 6'3", 210 lbs. Deb: 9/6/72

YEAR	TM/L	G	AB	R	H	2B	3B	HR	RBI	BB	SO	AVG	OBP	SLG	PRO+	BR/A	SB	CS	SBR	FA	FR	G/POS	TPR
1972	Chi-N	5	6	3	3	0	0	0	4	0	1	.500	.500	.500	167	1	1	0	0	1.000	-1	/O-3	0.0
1973	Chi-N	11	16	1	4	1	0	0	3	1	2	.250	.294	.313	63	-1	0	0	0	1.000	-0	/O-5	-0.1
1974	Chi-N	35	110	9	20	4	1	1	8	12	16	.182	.268	.264	47	-8	0	0	0	.974	-1	O-22,1-11	-0.9
1975	Chi-N	106	249	30	57	8	1	6	30	37	27	.229	.329	.341	82	-5	0	2	-1	.988	1	1-53,O-26	-1.0
1976	Chi-N	106	244	34	54	9	2	8	28	42	37	.221	.338	.373	93	-2	1	4	-2	.975	-4	1-54,O-19	-1.3
1977	*KC-A	88	218	25	66	12	1	3	29	15	25	.303	.350	.408	105	3	2	1	0	.990	1	1-29,D-26,O-12	0.1
1978	KC-A	118	322	44	95	21	2	5	48	21	27	.295	.338	.419	109	3	1	0	0	.993	-6	*1-106	-0.7
1979	KC-A	132	408	54	113	25	4	3	56	37	26	.277	.339	.380	92	-4	2	1	0	**.997**	-9	*1-108,D-16	-1.0
1980	KC-A	114	156	14	32	6	0	1	18	10	24	.205	.287	.263	51	-10	2	1	0	.997	-6	1-86,O-29	-1.5
Total	9	715	1729	214	444	86	11	27	224	182	171	.257	.329	.366	89	-25	8	8	-2	.991	-9	1-447,O-116/D-42	-6.4

■ LEE LACY
Lacy, Leondaus b: 4/10/48, Longview, Tex. BR/TR, 6'1", 175 lbs. Deb: 6/30/72

YEAR	TM/L	G	AB	R	H	2B	3B	HR	RBI	BB	SO	AVG	OBP	SLG	PRO+	BR/A	SB	CS	SBR	FA	FR	G/POS	TPR
1972	LA-N	60	243	34	63	7	3	0	12	19	37	.259	.313	.313	80	-6	5	3	-0	.973	-8	2-58	-1.2
1973	LA-N	57	135	14	28	2	0	0	8	15	34	.207	.287	.222	45	-10	2	3	-1	.965	-1	2-41	-1.0
1974	*LA-N	48	78	13	22	6	0	0	8	2	14	.282	.300	.359	87	-2	2	0	1	.968	-2	2-34/3-1	0.2
1975	LA-N	101	306	44	96	11	5	7	40	22	29	.314	.360	.451	129	11	5	9	-4	.935	-4	2-43,O-43/S-1	0.2

YEAR	TM/L	G	AB	R	H	2B	3B	HR	RBI	BB	SO	AVG	OBP	SLG	PRO+	BR/A	SB	CS	SBR	FA	FR	G/POS	TPR
1976	Atl-N	50	180	25	49	4	2	3	20	6	12	.272	.299	.367	83	-4	2	2	-1	.969	-10	2-44/O-5,3-1	-1.4
	LA-N	53	158	17	42	7	1	0	14	16	13	.266	.333	.323	88	-2	1	2	-1	.979	-1	O-37/3-3,2-2	-0.4
	Yr	103	338	42	91	11	3	3	34	22	25	.269	.316	.346	86	-6	3	4	-2	.970	-10	O-37/3-3,2-2	-1.8
1977	*LA-N	75	169	28	45	7	0	6	21	10	21	.266	.307	.414	92	-2	4	0	1	1.000	-13	O-32,2-22,3-12	-1.3
1978	*LA-N	103	245	29	64	16	4	13	40	27	30	.261	.337	.518	136	11	7	4	-0	.971	-5	O-44,2-24/3-9,S-1	0.5
1979	*Pit-N	84	182	17	45	9	3	5	15	22	36	.247	.332	.412	97	-1	6	1	1	.973	-2	O-41/2-5	-0.3
1980	Pit-N	109	278	45	93	20	4	7	33	28	33	.335	.399	.536	150	19	18	9	0	.984	5	O-88/3-3	2.2
1981	Pit-N	78	213	31	57	11	4	2	10	11	29	.268	.307	.385	92	-3	24	3	5	.977	3	O-63/3-1	0.5
1982	Pit-N	121	359	66	112	16	3	5	31	32	57	.312	.370	.415	116	8	40	15	3	.965	-8	*O-113/3-2	0.0
1983	Pit-N	108	288	40	87	12	3	4	13	22	36	.302	.352	.406	107	-3	31	13	2	1.000	-8	O-98	-0.6
1984	Pit-N	138	474	66	152	26	3	12	70	32	61	.321	.364	.464	131	18	21	11	-0	.996	4	*O-127/2-2	2.0
1985	Bal-A	121	492	69	144	22	4	9	48	39	95	.293	.347	.409	109	6	10	3	1	.984	4	*O-115/D-5	0.7
1986	Bal-A	130	491	77	141	18	0	11	47	37	71	.287	.337	.391	99	-1	4	6	-2	.992	6	*O-120/D-3	-0.1
1987	Bal-A	87	258	35	63	13	3	7	28	32	49	.244	.328	.399	94	-2	3	2	-0	.973	-2	O-80/D-4	-0.3
Total	16	1523	4549	650	1303	207	42	91	458	372	657	.286	.342	.410	108	43	185	86	4	.983	-31	*O-1006,2-275/3DS	-0.3

■ GUY LACY
Lacy, Osceola Guy b: 6/12/1897, Cleveland, Tenn. d: 11/19/53, Cleveland, Tenn. BR/TR, 5'11.5", 170 lbs. Deb: 5/7/26

YEAR	TM/L	G	AB	R	H	2B	3B	HR	RBI	BB	SO	AVG	OBP	SLG	PRO+	BR/A	SB	CS	SBR	FA	FR	G/POS	TPR
1926	Cle-A	13	24	2	4	0	0	1	2	2	2	.167	.259	.292	43	-2	0	0	0	.976	1	2-11/3-2	-0.1

■ HI LADD
Ladd, Arthur Clifford b: 2/9/1870, Willimantic, Conn. d: 5/7/48, Cranston, R.I. BL/TR, 6'4", 180 lbs. Deb: 7/12/1898

YEAR	TM/L	G	AB	R	H	2B	3B	HR	RBI	BB	SO	AVG	OBP	SLG	PRO+	BR/A	SB	CS	SBR	FA	FR	G/POS	TPR
1898	Pit-N	1	1	0	0	0	0	0	0	0		.000	.000	.000	-99	-0	0					H	0.0
	Bos-N	1	4	1	1	0	0	0	0	0		.250	.250	.250	41	-0	0			1.000	-0	/O-1	0.0
	Yr	2	5	1	1	0	0	0	0	0		.200	.200	.200	14	-1	0			1.000	-0	/O-1	0.0

■ STEVE LADEW
Ladew, Stephen b: St.Louis, Mo. Deb: 9/27/1889

YEAR	TM/L	G	AB	R	H	2B	3B	HR	RBI	BB	SO	AVG	OBP	SLG	PRO+	BR/A	SB	CS	SBR	FA	FR	G/POS	TPR
1889	KC-a	2	4	0	0	0	0	0	0	0	3	.000	.000	.000	-95	-1	0			1.000	-0	/O-1,P-1	-0.1

■ JOE LAFATA
Lafata, Joseph Joseph b: 8/3/21, Detroit, Mich. BL/TL, 6', 163 lbs. Deb: 4/17/47

YEAR	TM/L	G	AB	R	H	2B	3B	HR	RBI	BB	SO	AVG	OBP	SLG	PRO+	BR/A	SB	CS	SBR	FA	FR	G/POS	TPR
1947	NY-N	62	95	13	21	1	0	2	18	15	18	.221	.333	.295	68	-4	1			.974	-1	O-19/1-2	-0.6
1948	NY-N	1	1	0	0	0	0	0	0	0	0	.000	.000	.000	-99	-0	0			.000	0	H	0.0
1949	NY-N	64	140	18	33	2	2	3	16	9	23	.236	.282	.343	67	-7	1			.984	-4	1-47	-1.1
Total	3	127	236	31	54	3	2	5	34	24	42	.229	.303	.322	67	-11	2			.985	-5	/1-49,O-19	-1.7

■ FLIP LAFFERTY
Lafferty, Frank Bernard b: 5/4/1854, Scranton, Pa. d: 2/8/10, Wilmington, Del. TR , Deb: 9/15/1876

YEAR	TM/L	G	AB	R	H	2B	3B	HR	RBI	BB	SO	AVG	OBP	SLG	PRO+	BR/A	SB	CS	SBR	FA	FR	G/POS	TPR
1876	Phi-N	1	3	0	0	0	0	0	0	0	0	.000	.000	.000	-99	-1				.750	0	/P-1	0.0
1877	Lou-N	4	17	2	1	1	0	0	0	0	4	.059	.059	.118	-39	-3				.750	-1	/O-4	-0.4
Total	2	5	20	2	1	1	0	0	0	0	4	.050	.050	.100	-46	-3				.750	-1	/O-4,P-1	-0.4

■ TY LaFOREST
LaForest, Byron Joseph b: 4/18/17, Edmundston, N.B., Canada d: 5/5/47, Arlington, Mass. BR/TR, 5'9", 165 lbs. Deb: 8/4/45

YEAR	TM/L	G	AB	R	H	2B	3B	HR	RBI	BB	SO	AVG	OBP	SLG	PRO+	BR/A	SB	CS	SBR	FA	FR	G/POS	TPR
1945	Bos-A	52	204	25	51	7	4	2	16	10	35	.250	.285	.353	83	-5	4	4	-1	.966	1	3-45/O-5	-0.5

■ ROGER LaFRANCOIS
LaFrancois, Roger Victor b: 8/2/54, Norwich, Conn. BL/TR, 6'2", 215 lbs. Deb: 5/27/82

YEAR	TM/L	G	AB	R	H	2B	3B	HR	RBI	BB	SO	AVG	OBP	SLG	PRO+	BR/A	SB	CS	SBR	FA	FR	G/POS	TPR
1982	Bos-A	8	10	1	4	1	0	0	0	0	0	.400	.400	.500	137	0	0	0	0	1.000	-0	/C-8	0.0

■ MIKE LAGA
Laga, Michael Russell b: 6/14/60, Ridgewood, N.J. BL/TL, 6'2", 210 lbs. Deb: 9/1/82

YEAR	TM/L	G	AB	R	H	2B	3B	HR	RBI	BB	SO	AVG	OBP	SLG	PRO+	BR/A	SB	CS	SBR	FA	FR	G/POS	TPR
1982	Det-A	27	88	6	23	9	0	3	11	4	23	.261	.293	.466	104	0	1	0	0	.994	-2	1-19/D-8	-0.3
1983	Det-A	12	21	2	4	0	0	0	2	1	9	.190	.227	.190	17	-2	0	0	0	1.000	0	/1-5,D-6	-0.2
1984	Det-A	9	11	1	6	0	0	0	1	1	2	.545	.583	.545	216	2	0	0	0	1.000	0	/1-4,D-4	0.2
1985	Det-A	9	36	3	6	1	0	2	6	0	9	.167	.167	.361	40	-3	0	0	0	.974	1	/1-4,D-5	-0.3
1986	Det-A	15	45	6	9	1	0	3	8	5	13	.200	.280	.422	88	-1	0	0	0	1.000	-0	1-12/D-2	-0.2
	StL-N	18	46	7	10	4	0	3	8	5	18	.217	.308	.500	120	1	0	0	0	1.000	2	1-16	0.2
1987	StL-N	17	29	4	4	1	0	1	4	2	7	.138	.194	.276	22	-3	0	0	0	.973	1	1-12	-0.3
1988	StL-N	41	100	5	13	0	0	1	4	2	21	.130	.147	.160	-12	-14	0	0	0	1.000	1	1-37	-1.7
1989	SF-N	17	20	1	4	1	0	1	7	1	6	.200	.238	.400	82	-1	0	0	0	1.000	-0	/1-4	-0.1
1990	SF-N	23	27	4	5	1	0	2	4	1	7	.185	.241	.444	88	-1	0	0	0	1.000	1	1-10	0.0
Total	9	188	423	39	84	18	0	16	55	22	115	.199	.242	.355	63	-22	1	0	0	.996	2	1-123/D-25	-2.7

■ JOE LAHOUD
Lahoud, Joseph Michael b: 4/14/47, Danbury, Conn. BL/TL, 6', 202 lbs. Deb: 4/10/68

YEAR	TM/L	G	AB	R	H	2B	3B	HR	RBI	BB	SO	AVG	OBP	SLG	PRO+	BR/A	SB	CS	SBR	FA	FR	G/POS	TPR
1968	Bos-A	29	78	5	15	1	0	1	6	16	16	.192	.330	.244	71	-2	0	2	-1	.926	-3	O-25	-0.9
1969	Bos-A	101	218	32	41	5	0	9	21	40	43	.188	.317	.335	78	-6	2	1	0	.979	-7	O-66/1-1	-1.7
1970	Bos-A	17	49	6	12	1	0	2	5	7	6	.245	.339	.388	93	-0	0	0	0	.963	-2	O-13	0.1
1971	Bos-A	107	256	39	55	9	3	14	32	40	45	.215	.330	.438	108	3	2	2	-1	.993	3	O-69	0.2
1972	Mil-A	111	316	35	75	9	3	12	34	45	54	.237	.332	.399	119	8	3	4	-2	.974	-2	O-97	0.0
1973	Mil-A	96	225	29	46	9	0	5	26	27	36	.204	.304	.311	75	-7	5	5	-2	1.000	2	D-41,O-40	-0.9
1974	Cal-A	127	325	46	88	16	3	13	44	47	57	.271	.366	.458	145	19	4	5	-2	.976	-6	*O-106,D-10	0.8
1975	Cal-A	76	192	21	41	6	2	6	33	48	33	.214	.373	.359	116	6	2	1	0	1.000	-3	D-35,O-29	0.2
1976	Cal-A	42	96	8	17	4	0	0	4	18	16	.177	.319	.219	63	-4	0	0	0	.962	-2	O-26/D-3	-0.7
	Tex-A	38	89	10	20	3	1	1	5	10	16	.225	.307	.315	79	-2	1	0	0	1.000	-2	D-22/O-5	-0.4
	Yr	80	185	18	37	7	1	1	9	28	32	.200	.312	.265	72	-6	1	0	0	.964	-4	O-31,D-25	-1.1
1977	*KC-A	34	65	8	17	5	0	2	8	11	16	.262	.368	.431	116	2	1	0	0	.952	-1	O-15/D-4	0.1
1978	KC-A	13	16	0	2	0	0	0	0	0	2	.125	.125	.125	-29	-3	0	0	0	.000	-0	/O-1,D-1	-0.3
Total	11	791	1925	239	429	68	12	65	218	309	339	.223	.335	.372	103	12	20	20	-6	.979	-19	O-492,D-116/1-1	-3.5

■ DICK LAJESKIE
Lajeskie, Richard Edward b: 1/8/26, Passaic, N.J. d: 8/15/76, Ramsey, N.J. BR/TR, 5'11", 175 lbs. Deb: 9/10/46

YEAR	TM/L	G	AB	R	H	2B	3B	HR	RBI	BB	SO	AVG	OBP	SLG	PRO+	BR/A	SB	CS	SBR	FA	FR	G/POS	TPR
1946	NY-N	6	10	3	2	0	0	0	0	3	2	.200	.429	.200	81	0	0			.964	5	/2-4	0.5

■ NAP LAJOIE
Lajoie, Napoleon "Larry" b: 9/5/1874, Woonsocket, R.I. d: 2/7/59, Daytona Beach, Fla. BR/TR, 6'1", 195 lbs. Deb: 8/12/1896 MH

YEAR	TM/L	G	AB	R	H	2B	3B	HR	RBI	BB	SO	AVG	OBP	SLG	PRO+	BR/A	SB	CS	SBR	FA	FR	G/POS	TPR
1896	Phi-N	39	175	36	57	12	6	4	42	1	11	.326	.330	.543	129	5	7			.995	-3	1-39	0.2
1897	Phi-N	127	545	107	197	40	23	9	127	15		.361	.392	.569	156	39	20			.984	-6	*1-108,O-19/3-2	2.8
1898	Phi-N	147	608	113	197	43	11	6	127	21		.324	.354	.461	139	26	25			.949	-1	*2-146/1-1	3.2
1899	Phi-N	77	312	70	118	19	9	6	70	12		.378	.419	.554	172	29	13			.954	23	2-67/O-5	4.9
1900	Phi-N	102	451	95	152	33	12	7	92	10		.337	.362	.510	140	21	22			.954	30	*2-102/3-1	5.0
1901	Phi-A	131	544	145	232	48	14	14	125	24		.426	.463	.643	196	67	27			.960	29	*2-119,S-12	8.9
1902	Phi-A	1	4	0	1	0	0	0	0	1		.250	.250	.250	37	-0	1			1.000	0	/2-1	-0.1
	Cle-A	86	348	81	132	35	5	7	64	19		.379	.421	.569	180	36	19			.974	30	2-86	6.3
	Yr	87	352	81	133	35	5	7	65	19		.378	.419	.565	178	36	20			.974	29	2-87	6.2
1903	Cle-A	125	485	90	167	41	11	7	93	24		.344	.379	.518	170	39	21			.955	40	*2-122/1-1,3-1	8.4
1904	Cle-A	140	553	92	208	49	15	6	102	27		.376	.413	.552	205	64	29			.962	-1	2-95,S-44/1-2	7.2
1905	Cle-A	65	249	29	82	12	2	2	41	17		.329	.377	.418	150	11	9			.991	9	2-59/1-5,M	1.0
1906	Cle-A	152	602	88	214	48	9	0	91	30		.355	.392	.465	170	46	20			.973	31	*2-130,3-15/S-7,M	8.4
1907	Cle-A	137	509	53	152	30	6	2	63	30		.299	.345	.393	134	18	24			.969	46	*2-128/1-9,M	6.7
1908	Cle-A	157	581	77	168	32	6	2	74	47		.289	.352	.375	136	23	15			.964	49	*2-156/1-1,M	7.8
1909	Cle-A	128	469	56	152	33	7	1	47	35		.324	.378	.431	149	26	13			.959	19	*2-120/1-8,M	4.6
1910	Cle-A	159	591	94	227	51	7	4	76	60		.384	.445	.514	198	66	26			.966	15	*2-149,1-10	8.5
1911	Cle-A	90	315	36	115	20	1	2	60	26		.365	.420	.454	142	18	13			.990	-7	1-41,2-37	1.0
1912	Cle-A	117	448	66	165	34	4	0	90	28		.368	.414	.462	146	26	18			.959	5	2-97,1-20	2.8
1913	Cle-A	137	465	66	156	25	2	1	68	33	17	.335	.398	.404	131	19	17			.970	9	*2-126	2.8
1914	Cle-A	121	419	37	108	14	3	0	50	32	15	.258	.313	.305	83	-9	14	15	-5	.959	8	2-80,1-31	1.0
1915	Phi-A	129	490	40	137	24	5	1	61	11	26	.280	.301	.355	100	-3	10	6	-1	.962	14	*2-110,S-10/1-5,3-2	1.2
1916	Phi-A	113	426	33	105	14	4	2	35	14	26	.246	.272	.312	79	-13	15			.973	30	*2-105/1-5,O-2	2.2
Total	21	2480	9589	1504	3242	657	163	83	1599	516	85	.338	.380	.467	150	558	380	21		.963	367	*2-2035,1-286/SO3	94.2

YEAR	TM/L	G	AB	R	H	2B	3B	HR	RBI	BB	SO	AVG	OBP	SLG	PRO+	BR/A	SB	CS	SBR	FA	FR	G/POS	TPR

■ **EDDIE LAKE**   Lake, Edward Erving "Sparky" b: 3/18/16, Antioch, Cal.   d: 6/7/95, Castro Valley, Cal.   BR/TR, 5'7", 160 lbs.   Deb: 9/26/39

1939	StL-N	2	4	0	1	0	0	0	0	1	0	.250	.400	.250	74	-0	0			.857	-1	/S-2	-0.1
1940	StL-N	32	66	12	14	3	0	2	7	12	17	.212	.342	.348	86	-1	1			.957	-7	2-17/S-6	-0.7
1941	StL-N	45	76	9	8	2	0	0	0	15	22	.105	.253	.132	10	-9	3			.903	6	S-15,3-15/2-5	-0.2
1943	Bos-A	75	216	26	43	10	0	3	16	47	35	.199	.345	.287	84	-2	3	6	-3	.961	3	S-63	0.3
1944	Bos-A	57	126	21	26	5	0	0	8	23	22	.206	.329	.246	66	-5	5	2	0	.927	-5	S-41/P-6,2-3,3-1	-0.7
1945	Bos-A	133	473	81	132	27	1	11	51	106	37	.279	.412	.410	136	27	9	7	-2	.948	19	*S-130/2-1	5.7
1946	Det-A	155	587	105	149	24	1	8	31	103	69	.254	.369	.339	93	-2	15	9	-1	.947	-21	*S-155	-1.6
1947	Det-A	158	602	96	127	19	6	12	46	120	54	.211	.343	.322	83	-11	11	10	-3	.943	-29	*S-158	-3.6
1948	Det-A	64	198	51	52	6	0	2	18	57	20	.263	.427	.323	99	3	3	3	-1	.972	-3	2-45,3-17	0.2
1949	Det-A	94	240	38	47	9	1	1	15	61	33	.196	.359	.254	63	-10	2	8	-4	.959	-10	S-38,2-19,3-18	-2.1
1950	Det-A	20	7	3	0	0	0	0	1	1	3	.000	.125	.000	-64	-2	0	0	0	.000	0	/S-1,3-1	-0.2
Total	11	835	2595	442	599	105	9	39	193	546	312	.231	.366	.323	91	-11	52	45		.947	-48	S-609/2-90,3-52,P-6	-3.0

■ **FRED LAKE**   Lake, Frederick Lovett b: 10/16/1866, Nova Scotia, Can.   d: 11/24/31, Boston, Mass.   BR/TR, 5'10", 170 lbs.   Deb: 5/7/1891   M

1891	Bos-N	5	7	1	1	0	0	0	2	4		.143	.333	.143	36	-1	0			1.000	-0	/C-4,O-1	-0.1
1894	Lou-N	16	42	8	12	2	0	1	10	11	6	.286	.474	.405	122	3	2			.864	-3	/2-6,S-5,C-5	0.0
1897	*Bos-N	19	62	2	15	4	0	0	5	1		.242	.254	.306	45	-5	2			.970	-1	C-18	-0.4
1898	Pit-N	5	13	1	1	0	0	0	1	2		.077	.200	.077	-20	-2	0			1.000	-0	/1-3	-0.2
1910	Bos-N	3	1	0	0	0	0	0	0	1	0	.000	.500	.000	46	-0	0			.000	0	HM	0.0
Total	5	48	125	12	29	6	0	1	16	17	10	.232	.342	.304	68	-5	4			.930	-5	/C-27,2-6,S-5,10	-0.7

■ **STEVE LAKE**   Lake, Steven Michael b: 3/14/57, Inglewood, Cal.   BR/TR, 6'1", 190 lbs.   Deb: 4/9/83

1983	Chi-N	38	85	9	22	4	1	1	7	2	6	.259	.284	.365	75	-3	0	0	0	1.000	4	C-32	0.2
1984	*Chi-N	25	54	4	12	4	0	2	7	0	7	.222	.236	.407	71	-2	0	0	0	.955	6	C-24	-0.1
1985	Chi-N	58	119	5	18	2	0	1	11	3	21	.151	.179	.193	4	-15	1	0	0	.995	6	C-55	-0.8
1986	Chi-N	10	19	4	8	1	0	0	4	1	2	.421	.450	.474	144	1	0	0	0	1.000	-0	C-10	0.1
	StL-N	26	49	4	12	1	0	2	10	2	5	.245	.275	.388	81	-1	0	0	0	.976	1	C-26	0.0
	Yr	36	68	8	20	2	0	2	14	3	7	.294	.324	.412	100	-0	0	0	0	.983	1	C-36	0.1
1987	*StL-N	74	179	19	45	7	2	2	19	10	18	.251	.291	.346	67	-9	0	0	0	.996	-2	C-59	-0.7
1988	StL-N	36	54	5	15	3	0	1	4	3	15	.278	.339	.389	107	1	0	0	0	.983	-1	C-19	0.1
1989	Phi-N	58	155	9	39	5	1	2	14	12	20	.252	.305	.335	83	-3	0	0	0	.990	3	C-55	0.2
1990	Phi-N	29	80	4	20	2	0	0	6	3	12	.250	.286	.275	55	-5	0	0	0	.993	4	C-28	0.0
1991	Phi-N	58	158	12	36	4	1	1	11	2	26	.228	.237	.285	47	-11	0	0	0	.993	-5	C-58	-0.7
1992	Phi-N	20	53	3	13	2	0	1	2	1	8	.245	.259	.340	69	-2	0	0	0	.975	-2	C-17	-0.2
1993	Chi-N	44	120	11	27	6	0	5	13	4	19	.225	.250	.400	72	-1	0	0	0	.985	1	C-41	-0.3
Total	11	476	1125	89	267	41	5	18	108	43	159	.237	.269	.331	64	-56	1	0	0	.989	18	C-424	-2.2

■ **AL LAKEMAN**   Lakeman, Albert Wesley "Moose" b: 12/31/18, Cincinnati, Ohio   d: 5/25/76, Spartanburg, S.C.   BR/TR, 6'2", 195 lbs.   Deb: 4/19/42   C

1942	Cin-N	20	38	0	6	1	0	0	3	2	10	.158	.238	.184	24	-4	0			.970	3	C-17	0.0
1943	Cin-N	22	55	5	14	2	1	0	6	3	11	.255	.293	.327	80	-2	0			1.000	-2	C-21	-0.2
1944	Cin-N	1	1	0	0	0	0	0	0	0	1	.000	.000	.000	-99	-0	0			.000	-0	H	0.0
1945	Cin-N	76	258	22	66	9	4	8	31	17	45	.256	.304	.415	101	-1	0			.963	-11	C-74	-0.7
1946	Cin-N	23	30	0	4	0	0	0	4	2	7	.133	.188	.133	-9	-4	0			1.000	-0	/C-6	-0.5
1947	Cin-N	2	2	0	0	0	0	0	0	0	1	.000	.000	.000	-99	-1	0			.000	-0	H	-0.1
	Phi-N	55	182	11	29	3	0	6	19	5	39	.159	.186	.275	22	-21	0			.995	-5	1-29,C-23	-2.6
	Yr	57	184	11	29	3	0	6	19	5	40	.158	.184	.272	20	-22	0			.995	-5	1-29,C-23	-2.7
1948	Phi-N	32	68	2	11	2	0	1	4	5	22	.162	.219	.235	23	-7	0			1.000	-0	C-22/P-1	-0.8
1949	Bos-N	3	6	0	1	0	0	0	1	0	1	.167	.286	.167	26	-1	0			1.000	1	/1-2	0.0
1954	Det-A	5	4	0	0	0	0	0	0	2	0	.000	.000	.000	-99	-2	0	0	0	1.000	1	/C-4	-0.1
Total	9	239	646	40	131	17	5	15	66	36	137	.203	.248	.314	55	-42	0	0	0	.974	-16	C-167/1-31,P-1	-5.0

■ **TIM LAKER**   Laker, Timothy John b: 11/27/69, Encino, Cal.   BR/TR, 6'3", 195 lbs.   Deb: 8/18/92

1992	Mon-N	28	46	8	10	3	0	4	2	14		.217	.250	.283	51	-3	1	1	-0	.991	5	C-28	0.3
1993	Mon-N	43	86	3	17	2	1	0	7	2	16	.198	.225	.244	24	-9	2	0	1	.987	2	C-43	-0.5
1995	Mon-N	64	141	17	33	8	1	3	20	14	38	.234	.308	.369	75	-5	0	1	-1	.977	3	C-61	0.0
Total	3	135	273	28	60	13	2	3	31	18	68	.220	.273	.315	55	-17	3	2	-0	.982	10	C-132	-0.2

■ **DAN LALLY**   Lally, Daniel J. b: 8/12/1867, Jersey City, N.J.   d: 4/14/36, Milwaukee, Wis.   BR/TR, 5'11.5", 210 lbs.   Deb: 8/19/1891

1891	Pit-N	41	143	24	32	6	2	1	17	16	20	.224	.319	.315	87	-2				.839	-7	O-41	-0.9
1897	StL-N	87	355	56	99	15	5	2	42	9		.279	.310	.366	80	-12	12			.897	2	O-84/1-3	-1.3
Total	2	128	498	80	131	21	7	3	59	25	20	.263	.313	.351	82	-14	12			.886	-4	O-125/1-3	-2.2

■ **RAY LAMANNO**   Lamanno, Raymond Simond b: 11/17/19, Oakland, Cal.   d: 2/9/94, Berkeley, Cal.   BR/TR, 6', 185 lbs.   Deb: 9/11/41

1941	Cin-N	1	0	0	0	0	0	0	0	0	0	—	1.000	—	197	-0	0			1.000	-0	/C-1	0.0
1942	Cin-N	111	371	40	98	12	2	12	43	31	54	.264	.324	.404	113	5	0			.978	-11	*C-104	0.2
1946	Cin-N★	85	239	18	58	12	0	1	30	11	26	.243	.285	.305	70	-10	0			.974	2	C-61	-0.5
1947	Cin-N	118	413	33	106	21	3	5	50	28	39	.257	.307	.358	77	-15	0			.986	-5	*C-109	0.1
1948	Cin-N	127	385	31	93	12	0	0	27	48	32	.242	.329	.273	67	-16	2			.978	-11	*C-125	-2.0
Total	5	442	1408	122	355	57	5	18	150	118	151	.252	.314	.338	82	-36	2			.980	-16	C-400	-2.2

■ **BILL LAMAR**   Lamar, William Harmong "Good Time Bill" b: 3/21/1897, Rockville, Md.   d: 5/24/70, Rockport, Mass.   BL/TR, 6'1", 185 lbs.   Deb: 9/19/17

1917	NY-A	11	42	1	10	0	0	0	3	0	2	.244	.244	.244	48	-3	1			1.000	0	O-11	-0.3
1918	NY-A	28	110	12	25	3	0	0	2	6	2	.227	.267	.255	56	-6	2			.884	-2	O-27	-1.1
1919	NY-A	11	16	1	3	1	0	0	0	2	1	.188	.278	.250	48	-1	1			1.000	-1	/O-3,1-1	-0.2
	Bos-A	48	148	18	43	5	1	0	14	5	9	.291	.314	.338	88	-3	3			.922	-2	O-36	-0.8
	Yr	59	164	19	46	6	1	0	14	7	10	.280	.310	.329	83	-4	4			.926	-3	O-39/1-1	-1.0
1920	*Bro-N	24	44	5	12	4	0	0	4	0	1	.273	.273	.364	79	-1	0	0	0	1.000	-3	/O-12	-0.5
1921	Bro-N	3	3	2	1	0	0	0	0	0	0	.333	.333	.333	74	-0	0	0	0	.000	0	/O-1	-0.1
1924	Phi-A	87	367	68	121	22	5	7	48	18	21	.330	.361	.474	113	5	8	8	-2	.971	4	O-87	0.1
1925	Phi-A	138	568	85	202	39	8	3	77	21	17	.356	.379	.468	107	4	2	6	-3	.953	-3	*O-131	-0.3
1926	Phi-A	116	419	62	119	17	6	5	50	18	15	.284	.315	.389	78	-15	4	5	-2	.954	-3	*O-107	-2.6
1927	Phi-A	84	324	48	97	23	3	4	47	16	10	.299	.334	.426	91	-5	4	8	-4	.952	-3	O-79	-1.6
Total	9	550	2040	303	633	114	23	19	245	86	78	.310	.339	.417	94	-24	25	27		.952	-7	O-494/1-1	-7.4

■ **LAYMON LAMB**   Lamb, Laymon Raymond b: 3/17/1895, Lincoln, Neb.   d: 10/5/55, Fayetteville, Ark.   BR/TR, 5'7", 150 lbs.   Deb: 9/14/20

1920	StL-A	9	24	4	9	2	0	0	4	0	7	.375	.375	.458	116	0	2	0	1	1.000	-2	/O-7	-0.1
1921	StL-A	45	134	18	34	9	2	1	17	4	12	.254	.281	.373	62	-8	0	0	0	.942	-9	3-25/2-7,O-6	-1.5
Total	2	54	158	22	43	11	2	1	21	4	19	.272	.294	.386	70	-8	2	0	1	1.000	-11	/3-25,O-13,2-7	-1.6

■ **PETE LAMER**   Lamer, Pierre b: 12/1873, New York, N.Y.   d: 10/24/31, Brooklyn, N.Y.   TR, 5'10", 170 lbs.   Deb: 9/10/02

1902	Chi-N	2	9	2	2	0	0	0	0	0		.222	.222	.222	38	-1	0			.857	-0	/C-2	-0.1
1907	Cin-N	1	2	0	0	0	0	0	0	0		.000	.000	.000	-96	-0	0			1.000	-0	/C-1	-0.1
Total	2	3	11	2	2	0	0	0	0	0		.182	.182	.182	13	-1	0			.867	-1	/C-3	-0.2

■ **GENE LAMONT**   Lamont, Gene William b: 12/25/46, Rockford, Ill.   BL/TR, 6'1", 195 lbs.   Deb: 9/2/70   MC

1970	Det-A	15	44	3	13	3	1	1	4	2	9	.295	.340	.477	122	1	0	0	0	1.000	1	C-15	0.3
1971	Det-A	7	15	2	1	0	0	0	1	0	6	.067	.067	.067	-60	-3	0	0	0	.952	2	/C-7	-0.1
1972	Det-A	1	0	0	0	0	0	0	0	0	0					0	0	0	0	1.000	-0	/C-1	0.0
1974	Det-A	60	92	9	20	3	0	3	8	7	19	.217	.273	.359	78	-3	0	0	0	.974	8	C-60	0.7

YEAR	TM/L	G	AB	R	H	2B	3B	HR	RBI	BB	SO	AVG	OBP	SLG	PRO+	BR/A	SB	CS	SBR	FA	FR	G/POS	TPR
1975	Det-A	4	8	1	3	1	0	0	1	0	2	.375	.375	.500	139	0	1	0	0	.944	1	/C-4	0.2
Total	5	87	159	15	37	8	1	4	14	9	35	.233	.278	.371	80	-4	1	0	0	.977	12	/C-87	1.1

■ BOBBY LaMOTTE   LaMotte, Robert Eugene b: 2/15/1898, Savannah, Ga. d: 11/2/70, Chatham, Ga.   BR/TR, 5'11", 160 lbs.   Deb: 9/1/20

YEAR	TM/L	G	AB	R	H	2B	3B	HR	RBI	BB	SO	AVG	OBP	SLG	PRO+	BR/A	SB	CS	SBR	FA	FR	G/POS	TPR
1920	Was-A	4	3	0	0	0	0	0	1	0	1	.000	.250	.000	-31	-1	0		0	.750	0	/S-1,3-1	0.0
1921	Was-A	16	41	5	8	0	0	0	2	5	0	.195	.283	.195	25	-5	0		0	.940	2	S-12	-0.2
1922	Was-A	68	214	22	54	10	2	1	23	15	21	.252	.307	.332	70	-10	6	1	1	.954	8	3-62/S-6	0.4
1925	StL-A	97	356	61	97	20	4	2	51	34	22	.272	.338	.368	75	-14	5	5	-2	.926	2	S-93/3-3	-0.3
1926	StL-A	36	79	11	16	4	3	0	9	11	6	.203	.300	.329	61	-5	0	0	0	.919	-2	S-30/3-1	-0.4
Total	5	221	693	99	175	34	9	3	85	66	50	.253	.320	.341	69	-33	11	6	-0	.927	10	S-142/3-67	-0.5

■ KEITH LAMPARD   Lampard, Christopher Keith b: 12/20/45, Warrington, England   BL/TR, 6'2", 197 lbs.   Deb: 9/15/69

YEAR	TM/L	G	AB	R	H	2B	3B	HR	RBI	BB	SO	AVG	OBP	SLG	PRO+	BR/A	SB	CS	SBR	FA	FR	G/POS	TPR
1969	Hou-N	9	12	2	3	0	0	1	2	0	3	.250	.250	.500	108	0	0	0	0	1.000	1	/O-1	0.1
1970	Hou-N	53	72	8	17	8	1	0	5	5	24	.236	.295	.375	82	-2	0	0	0	1.000	-1	O-16/1-2	-0.3
Total	2	62	84	10	20	8	1	1	7	5	27	.238	.289	.393	85	-2	0	0	0	1.000	1	/O-17,1-2	-0.2

■ TOM LAMPKIN   Lampkin, Thomas Michael b: 3/4/64, Cincinnati, Ohio   BL/TR, 5'11", 180 lbs.   Deb: 9/10/88

YEAR	TM/L	G	AB	R	H	2B	3B	HR	RBI	BB	SO	AVG	OBP	SLG	PRO+	BR/A	SB	CS	SBR	FA	FR	G/POS	TPR
1988	Cle-A	4	4	0	0	0	0	0	0	1	0	.000	.200	.000	-38	-1	0	0	0	1.000	-1	/C-3	-0.2
1990	SD-N	26	63	4	14	0	1	1	4	4	9	.222	.269	.302	56	-4	0	1	-1	.971	1	C-20	-0.3
1991	SD-N	38	58	4	11	3	1	0	3	3	9	.190	.230	.276	40	-5	0	0	0	1.000	0	C-11	-0.4
1992	SD-N	9	17	3	4	0	0	0	6	1		.235	.458	.235	100	1	2	0	1	1.000	-2	/C-7,O-1	0.0
1993	Mil-A	73	162	22	32	8	4	4	25	20	26	.198	.286	.321	64	-8	7	3	0	.978	-3	C-60/O-3,D-1	-0.9
1995	SF-N	65	76	8	21	2	0	1	9	9	8	.276	.360	.342	89	-1	2	0	1	1.000	-2	C-17/O-6	-0.1
1996	SF-N	66	177	26	41	8	0	6	29	20	22	.232	.327	.379	89	-3	1	5	-3	.992	7	C-53	0.5
Total	7	281	557	67	123	21	2	12	70	63	75	.221	.308	.330	73	-21	12	9	-2	.987	-1	C-171/O-10,D-1	-1.4

■ RICK LANCELLOTTI   Lancellotti, Richard Anthony b: 7/5/56, Providence, R.I.   BL/TL, 6'3", 195 lbs.   Deb: 8/27/82

YEAR	TM/L	G	AB	R	H	2B	3B	HR	RBI	BB	SO	AVG	OBP	SLG	PRO+	BR/A	SB	CS	SBR	FA	FR	G/POS	TPR
1982	SD-N	17	39	2	7	2	0	0	4	2	8	.179	.220	.231	28	-4	0	0	0	1.000	-2	/1-7,O-3	-0.6
1986	SF-N	15	18	2	4	0	0	2	6	0	7	.222	.222	.556	113	0	0	0	0	1.000	1	/1-1,O-1	0.1
1990	Bos-A	4	8	0	0	0	0	0	1	0	3	.000	.000	.000	-96	-2	0	0	0	1.000	-0	/1-2	-0.2
Total	3	36	65	4	11	2	0	2	11	2	18	.169	.194	.292	35	-6	0	0	0	1.000	-0	/1-10,O-4	-0.7

■ GROVER LAND   Land, Grover Cleveland b: 9/22/1884, Frankfort, Ky. d: 7/22/58, Phoenix, Ariz.   BR/TR, 6', 190 lbs.   Deb: 9/2/08 C

YEAR	TM/L	G	AB	R	H	2B	3B	HR	RBI	BB	SO	AVG	OBP	SLG	PRO+	BR/A	SB	CS	SBR	FA	FR	G/POS	TPR
1908	Cle-A	8	16	1	3	0	0	0	2	0		.188	.188	.188	22	-1	0			.955	-1	/C-8	-0.3
1909	Cle-A	1	4	0	2	0	0	0	1	0		.500	.500	.500	207	0	0			1.000	0	/C-1	0.1
1910	Cle-A	34	111	4	23	0	0	0	7	2		.207	.228	.207	36	-8	1			.982	5	C-33	-0.1
1911	Cle-A	35	107	5	15	1	2	0	10	3		.140	.164	.187	-2	-15	2			.961	1	C-34/1-1	-1.1
1913	Cle-A	17	47	3	11	1	0	0	9	4	1	.234	.321	.255	67	-2	1			.924	1	C-17	0.0
1914	Bro-F	102	335	24	92	6	4	0	29	12	23	.275	.306	.304	67	-20	1			.970	1	C-97	-1.3
1915	Bro-F	96	290	25	75	13	2	0	22	6	20	.259	.279	.317	68	-17	3			.960	-6	C-81	-1.9
Total	7	293	910	62	221	21	6	0	80	27	44	.243	.271	.279	55	-64	14			.964	-2	C-271/1-1	-4.6

■ DOC LAND   Land, William Gilbert (b: Doc Burrell Land) b: 5/14/03, Binnsville, Miss. d: 4/14/86, Livingston, Ala.   BL/TL, 5'11", 165 lbs.   Deb: 10/6/29

YEAR	TM/L	G	AB	R	H	2B	3B	HR	RBI	BB	SO	AVG	OBP	SLG	PRO+	BR/A	SB	CS	SBR	FA	FR	G/POS	TPR
1929	Was-A	1	3	0	0	0	0	0	0	0	0	.000	.250	.000	-30	-1	0			1.000	0	/O-1	-0.1

■ KEN LANDENBERGER   Landenberger, Kenneth Henry "Red" b: 7/29/28, Lyndhurst, Ohio d: 7/28/60, Cleveland, Ohio   BL/TL, 6'3", 200 lbs.   Deb: 9/20/52

YEAR	TM/L	G	AB	R	H	2B	3B	HR	RBI	BB	SO	AVG	OBP	SLG	PRO+	BR/A	SB	CS	SBR	FA	FR	G/POS	TPR
1952	Chi-A	2	5	0	1	0	0	0	0	0	2	.200	.200	.200	11	-1	0	0	0	1.000	0	/1-1	0.0

■ RAFAEL LANDESTOY   Landestoy, Rafael Silvialdo (Santana) b: 5/28/53, Bani, D.R.   BB/TR, 5'10", 165 lbs.   Deb: 8/27/77 C

YEAR	TM/L	G	AB	R	H	2B	3B	HR	RBI	BB	SO	AVG	OBP	SLG	PRO+	BR/A	SB	CS	SBR	FA	FR	G/POS	TPR
1977	*LA-N	15	18	6	5	0	0	0	0	3	2	.278	.381	.278	80	-0	0	0	1	1.000	3	/2-8,S-3	0.3
1978	Hou-N	59	218	18	58	5	1	0	9	8	23	.266	.292	.298	70	-9	7	4	-0	.980	-13	S-50/O-3,2-2	-1.8
1979	Hou-N	129	282	33	76	9	6	0	30	29	24	.270	.340	.344	92	-3	13	4	2	.971	-2	*2-114/S-3	0.2
1980	*Hou-N	149	393	42	97	13	8	0	27	31	37	.247	.307	.328	84	-9	23	12	-0	.991	-6	2-94,S-65/3-3	-0.7
1981	Hou-N	35	74	6	11	1	1	0	4	16	9	.149	.300	.189	43	-5	4	1	1	.966	-4	2-31	-0.8
	Cin-N	12	11	2	2	0	0	0	1	1	0	.182	.250	.182	24	-1	1	0	0	1.000	-0	/2-3	-0.1
	Yr	47	85	8	13	1	1	0	5	17	9	.153	.294	.188	40	-6	5	1	1	.967	-5	2-34	-0.9
1982	Cin-N	73	111	11	21	3	0	1	9	8	14	.189	.250	.243	38	-9	2	0	1	1.000	4	3-21,2-16/O-3,S-2	-0.5
1983	Cin-N	7	5	0	0	0	0	0	0	0	0	.000	.000	.000	-97	-1	0	0	0	1.000	-1	/1-2,3-1,O-1	-0.2
	*LA-N	64	64	6	11	1	1	1	1	3	8	.172	.209	.266	31	-6	0	0	-1	1.000	2	2-14,3-10,O-10,/S-1	-0.5
	Yr	71	69	6	11	1	1	1	1	3	8	.159	.194	.246	21	-7	0	2	-1	1.000	1	2-14,3-11,O-11,/1S	-0.7
1984	LA-N	53	54	10	10	0	0	1	2	1	6	.185	.200	.241	24	-6	2	1	0	.886	1	2-14,3-11/O-5	-0.3
Total	8	596	1230	134	291	32	17	4	83	100	123	.237	.297	.300	70	-50	54	24	1	.976	-17	2-296,S-124/3O1	-4.5

■ JIM LANDIS   Landis, James Henry b: 3/9/34, Fresno, Cal.   BR/TR, 6'1", 180 lbs.   Deb: 4/16/57

YEAR	TM/L	G	AB	R	H	2B	3B	HR	RBI	BB	SO	AVG	OBP	SLG	PRO+	BR/A	SB	CS	SBR	FA	FR	G/POS	TPR
1957	Chi-A	96	274	38	58	11	3	2	16	45	61	.212	.329	.296	72	-10	14	4		.985	4	O-90	-0.9
1958	Chi-A	142	523	72	145	23	7	15	64	52	80	.277	.352	.434	117	12	19	7	2	.986	6	O-142	1.2
1959	*Chi-A	149	515	78	140	26	7	5	60	78	68	.272	.376	.379	109	10	20	9	1	.993	16	*O-148	1.8
1960	Chi-A	148	494	89	125	25	6	10	49	80	84	.253	.367	.389	106	6	23	6	3	.985	13	O-147	1.5
1961	Chi-A	140	534	87	151	18	6	22	85	65	71	.283	.365	.470	123	18	19	5	3	.988	19	*O-139	3.1
1962	Chi-A★	149	534	82	122	21	6	15	61	80	105	.228	.339	.375	92	-5	19	7	2	.995	10	*O-144	-0.2
1963	Chi-A	133	396	56	89	6	6	13	45	47	75	.225	.316	.369	93	-3	8	6	-1	**.993**	1	*O-124	-1.0
1964	Chi-A	106	298	30	62	8	4	1	18	36	64	.208	.306	.272	64	-14	5	0	2	.995	-4	*O-101	-2.1
1965	KC-A	118	364	46	87	15	1	3	36	57	84	.239	.347	.310	90	-3	8	3	1	.985	6	*O-108	-0.2
1966	Cle-A	85	158	23	35	5	1	3	14	20	25	.222	.317	.323	84	-3	2	1	0	1.000	-11	O-61	-1.7
1967	Det-A	25	48	4	10	0	1	2	7	12	8	.208	.349	.333	87	-1	0	1	0	.952	0	O-12	-0.1
	Bos-A	5	7	1	1	0	0	1	1	1	3	.143	.250	.571	126	0	0	0	0	1.000	-1	/O-5	-0.1
	Yr	30	55	5	11	0	1	3	8	13	11	.200	.327	.364	92	-1	0	1	0	.960	-1	O-17	-0.3
	Hou-N	50	143	19	36	11	1	1	14	20	35	.252	.348	.364	107	2	1	1	0	1.000	-1	O-44	-0.1
Total	11	1346	4288	625	1061	169	50	93	467	588	767	.247	.346	.375	100	10	139	51	11	.989	58	*O-1265	1.1

■ KEN LANDREAUX   Landreaux, Kenneth Francis b: 12/22/54, Los Angeles, Cal.   BL/TR, 5'10", 165 lbs.   Deb: 9/11/77

YEAR	TM/L	G	AB	R	H	2B	3B	HR	RBI	BB	SO	AVG	OBP	SLG	PRO+	BR/A	SB	CS	SBR	FA	FR	G/POS	TPR
1977	Cal-A	23	76	6	19	5	1	0	5	5	15	.250	.296	.342	76	-3	1	1	-0	.970	5	O-22	0.1
1978	Cal-A	93	260	37	58	7	5	5	23	20	20	.223	.284	.346	79	-8	7	3	0	.986	-1	O-83/D-1	-1.8
1979	Min-A	151	564	81	172	27	5	15	83	37	57	.305	.352	.450	110	8	10	3	1	.981	-8	*O-147	-0.6
1980	Min-A★	129	484	56	136	23	11	7	62	39	42	.281	.337	.417	98	-2	8	6	-1	.976	-9	*O-120/D-6	-1.7
1981	*LA-N	99	390	48	98	16	4	7	41	25	42	.251	.298	.367	91	-6	18	4	3	**1.000**	-4	O-95	-1.1
1982	LA-N	129	461	71	131	23	7	7	50	39	54	.284	.345	.410	113	8	31	10	3	.986	2	*O-117	1.1
1983	*LA-N	141	481	63	135	25	3	17	66	34	52	.281	.331	.451	115	8	30	11	2	.990	-2	*O-137	0.5
1984	LA-N	134	438	39	110	11	5	11	47	29	35	.251	.299	.374	89	-7	10	6	-1	.986	-16	*O-129	-3.1
1985	*LA-N	147	482	70	129	26	2	12	50	33	37	.268	.316	.405	103	1	15	5	2	.975	-7	*O-140	-1.0
1986	LA-N	103	283	34	74	13	2	4	29	22	39	.261	.317	.364	94	-3	10	5	0	.955	-5	O-85	-1.1
1987	LA-N	115	182	17	37	4	0	6	23	16	28	.203	.271	.357	58	-11	5	3	0	.951	-6	O-63	-1.9
Total	11	1264	4101	522	1099	180	45	91	479	299	421	.268	.320	.400	99	-15	145	60	8	.981	-57	*O-1138/D-7	-10.6

■ HOBIE LANDRITH   Landrith, Hobert Neal b: 3/16/30, Decatur, Ill.   BL/TR, 5'10", 170 lbs.   Deb: 7/30/50 C

YEAR	TM/L	G	AB	R	H	2B	3B	HR	RBI	BB	SO	AVG	OBP	SLG	PRO+	BR/A	SB	CS	SBR	FA	FR	G/POS	TPR
1950	Cin-N	4	14	1	3	0	0	0	1	0	1	.214	.313	.214	41	-1	0			1.000	-1	/C-4	-0.2
1951	Cin-N	4	13	3	5	2	0	0	4	1	0	.385	.429	.462	137	1	0	0	0	1.000	4	/C-4	0.2
1952	Cin-N	15	50	7	13	3	0	0	4	0	4	.260	.260	.340	65	-2	0	0	0	.985	0	C-14	-0.2
1953	Cin-N	52	154	15	37	3	1	3	16	12	8	.240	.299	.331	64	-8	2	0	0	.985	-2	C-47	-0.5
1954	Cin-N	48	81	12	16	0	0	4	7	18	10	.198	.343	.383	86	-1	1	0	0	.986	4	C-42	0.4
1955	Cin-N	43	87	9	22	5	0	4	18	14	12	.253	.330	.425	93	-1	0	0	0	1.000	4	C-27	0.3
1956	Chi-N	111	312	22	69	10	3	4	32	39	38	.221	.310	.311	69	-13	0	2	-1	.975	-3	C-99	-1.3

YEAR	TM/L	G	AB	R	H	2B	3B	HR	RBI	BB	SO	AVG	OBP	SLG	PRO+	BR/A	SB	CS	SBR	FA	FR	G/POS	TPR
1957	StL-N	75	214	18	52	6	0	3	26	25	27	.243	.322	.313	70	-8	1	2	-1	.987	5	C-67	-0.2
1958	StL-N	70	144	9	31	4	0	3	13	26	21	.215	.335	.306	68	-6	0	1	-1	.992	4	C-45	-0.2
1959	SF-N	109	283	30	71	14	0	3	29	43	23	.251	.350	.332	85	-5	1	4	-2	.992	7	*C-109	0.5
1960	SF-N	71	190	18	46	10	0	1	20	23	11	.242	.324	.311	79	-5	1	1	-0	.966	-5	C-70	-0.7
1961	SF-N	43	71	11	17	4	0	2	10	12	7	.239	.349	.380	97	-5	0	0	0	.985	2	C-30	0.1
1962	NY-N	23	45	6	13	3	0	1	7	8	3	.289	.396	.422	118	1	0	0	0	.968	-1	C-21	0.1
	Bal-A	60	167	18	37	4	1	4	17	19	9	.222	.305	.329	75	-6	0	0	0	.982	5	C-60	0.1
1963	Bal-A	2	1	0	0	0	0	0	0	0	0	.000	.000	.000	-99	-0	0	0	0	1.000	-0	/C-1	0.0
	Was-A	42	103	6	18	3	0	1	7	15	12	.175	.280	.233	46	-7	0	0	0	.978	2	C-37	-0.5
	Yr	44	104	6	18	3	0	1	7	15	12	.173	.277	.231	44	-7	0	0	0	.978	2	C-38	-0.5
Total	14	772	1929	179	450	69	5	34	203	253	188	.233	.323	.327	76	-63	5	12		.983	22	C-677	-2.0

■ CED LANDRUM
Landrum, Cedric Bernard b: 9/3/63, Butler, Ala. BL/TR, 5'7", 167 lbs. Deb: 5/28/91

YEAR	TM/L	G	AB	R	H	2B	3B	HR	RBI	BB	SO	AVG	OBP	SLG	PRO+	BR/A	SB	CS	SBR	FA	FR	G/POS	TPR
1991	Chi-N	56	86	28	20	2	1	0	6	10	18	.233	.313	.279	65	-4	27	5	5	.968	-9	O-44	-0.9
1993	NY-N	22	19	2	5	1	0	0	1	0	5	.263	.263	.316	55	-1	0	0	0	.000	-1	/O-3	-0.2
Total	2	78	105	30	25	3	1	0	7	10	23	.238	.304	.286	63	-5	27	5	5	.968	-11	/O-47	-1.1

■ DON LANDRUM
Landrum, Donald Leroy b: 2/16/36, Santa Rosa, Cal. BL/TR, 6', 180 lbs. Deb: 9/28/57

YEAR	TM/L	G	AB	R	H	2B	3B	HR	RBI	BB	SO	AVG	OBP	SLG	PRO+	BR/A	SB	CS	SBR	FA	FR	G/POS	TPR
1957	Phi-N	2	7	1	1	1	0	0	0	2	1	.143	.333	.286	71	-0	0	0	0	1.000	1	/O-2	0.0
1960	StL-N	13	49	7	12	0	1	2	3	4	6	.245	.315	.408	88	-1	3	0	1	1.000	-0	O-13	-0.1
1961	StL-N	28	66	5	11	2	0	1	3	5	14	.167	.225	.242	22	-1	2	0	1	1.000	-0	O-25/2-1	-1.1
1962	StL-N	32	35	11	11	0	0	0	3	3	5	.314	.385	.314	82	-1	2	0	1	1.000	-6	O-26	-0.7
	Chi-N	83	238	29	67	5	5	1	15	30	31	.282	.369	.332	87	-3	9	2	2	.969	-1	O-59	-0.6
	Yr	115	273	40	78	5	5	1	18	34	33	.286	.371	.330	85	-4	11	2	2	.973	-7	O-85	-1.3
1963	Chi-N	84	227	27	55	4	1	1	10	13	42	.242	.295	.282	64	-10	6	3	0	.972	-4	O-57	-1.9
1964	Chi-N	11	11	2	0	0	0	0	0	1	2	.000	.083	.000	-71	-2	0	0	0	1.000	1	/O-1	-0.2
1965	Chi-N	131	425	60	96	20	4	6	34	36	84	.226	.301	.334	77	-13	14	8	-1	.988	-7	*O-115	-1.8
1966	SF-N	72	102	9	19	4	0	1	7	9	18	.186	.259	.255	42	-8	1	1	0	.968	-5	O-54	-1.5
Total	8	456	1160	151	272	36	16	12	75	104	200	.234	.308	.310	69	-45	36	14	2	.982	-16	O-352/2-1	-7.9

■ JESSE LANDRUM
Landrum, Jesse Glenn b: 7/31/12, Crockett, Tex. d: 6/27/83, Beaumont, Tex. BR/TR, 5'11.5", 175 lbs. Deb: 4/26/38

YEAR	TM/L	G	AB	R	H	2B	3B	HR	RBI	BB	SO	AVG	OBP	SLG	PRO+	BR/A	SB	CS	SBR	FA	FR	G/POS	TPR
1938	Chi-A	4	6	0	0	0	0	0	1	0	2	.000	.000	.000	-98	-2	0	0	0	1.000	-1	/2-3	-0.2

■ TITO LANDRUM
Landrum, Terry Lee b: 10/25/54, Joplin, Mo. BR/TR, 5'11", 175 lbs. Deb: 7/23/80

YEAR	TM/L	G	AB	R	H	2B	3B	HR	RBI	BB	SO	AVG	OBP	SLG	PRO+	BR/A	SB	CS	SBR	FA	FR	G/POS	TPR
1980	StL-N	35	77	6	19	2	2	0	7	6	17	.247	.310	.325	75	-3	3	2	-0	.976	-5	O-29	-0.9
1981	StL-N	81	119	13	31	5	4	0	10	6	14	.261	.302	.370	87	-2	4	2	0	1.000	-13	O-67	-1.8
1982	StL-N	79	72	12	20	3	0	2	14	8	18	.278	.358	.403	111	1	0	1	-1	1.000	5	O-56	0.5
1983	StL-N	6	5	0	1	0	1	0	1	0	2	.200	.333	.600	154	0	1	0	0	1.000	-2	/O-5	-0.1
	*Bal-A	26	42	8	13	2	0	1	4	1	11	.310	.326	.429	108	0	2	0	-1	1.000	-6	O-26	-0.7
1984	StL-N	105	173	21	47	9	1	3	26	10	27	.272	.311	.387	98	-1	3	4	-2	.979	-21	O-88	-2.7
1985	*StL-N	85	161	21	45	8	4	2	21	19	30	.280	.356	.429	119	4	1	4	-2	1.000	-11	O-73	-1.0
1986	StL-N	96	205	24	43	7	1	2	17	20	41	.210	.283	.283	57	-12	3	1	0	.993	-4	O-78	-1.8
1987	StL-N	30	50	5	10	1	0	0	6	7	14	.200	.298	.220	39	-4	1	1	-0	1.000	-2	O-23/1-1	-0.7
	LA-N	51	67	8	16	3	0	1	4	3	16	.239	.282	.328	63	-4	1	1	-0	.971	-5	O-31	-0.9
	Yr	81	117	13	26	4	0	1	10	10	30	.222	.289	.282	53	-8	2	2	-1	.987	-7	O-54/1-1	-1.6
1988	Bal-A	13	24	2	3	0	1	0	2	4	6	.125	.250	.208	31	-2	0	0	0	1.000	-3	O-12/D-1	-0.5
Total	9	607	995	120	248	40	12	13	111	85	196	.249	.312	.353	84	-22	17	18	-6	.992	-65	O-488/D-1,1-1	-10.6

■ CHAPPY LANE
Lane, George M. b: Pittsburgh, Pa. BR, 165 lbs. Deb: 5/16/1882

YEAR	TM/L	G	AB	R	H	2B	3B	HR	RBI	BB	SO	AVG	OBP	SLG	PRO+	BR/A	SB	CS	SBR	FA	FR	G/POS	TPR
1882	Pit-a	57	214	26	38	8	2	3			5	.178	.196	.276	60	-8				.974	5	1-43,O-13/C-2	-0.7
1884	Tol-a	57	215	26	49	9	5	1			7	.228	.242	.330	82	-5				.948	4	1-46,O-9,3-2,C-1	-0.6
Total	2	114	429	52	87	17	7	4			7	.203	.219	.303	72	-13				.961	9	/1-89,O-22,C-3,3-2	-1.3

■ HUNTER LANE
Lane, James Hunter "Dodo" b: 7/20/1900, Pulaski, Tenn. d: 9/12/94, Memphis, Tenn. BR/TR, 5'11", 165 lbs. Deb: 5/13/24

YEAR	TM/L	G	AB	R	H	2B	3B	HR	RBI	BB	SO	AVG	OBP	SLG	PRO+	BR/A	SB	CS	SBR	FA	FR	G/POS	TPR
1924	Bos-N	7	15	0	1	0	0	0	0	1	1	.067	.125	.067	-49	-3	0	0	0	.909	-1	/3-4,2-1	-0.4

■ MARVIN LANE
Lane, Marvin b: 1/18/50, Sandersville, Ga. BR/TR, 5'11", 180 lbs. Deb: 9/4/71

YEAR	TM/L	G	AB	R	H	2B	3B	HR	RBI	BB	SO	AVG	OBP	SLG	PRO+	BR/A	SB	CS	SBR	FA	FR	G/POS	TPR
1971	Det-A	8	14	0	2	0	0	0	1	1	3	.143	.200	.143	-1	-2	0	0	0	1.000	-1	/O-6	-0.3
1972	Det-A	8	6	2	0	0	0	0	0	1	0	.000	.000	.000	-97	-1	0	0	0	1.000	-1	/O-3	-0.2
1973	Det-A	6	8	2	2	0	0	0	2	2	2	.250	.400	.625	173	1	0	0	0	1.000	-1	/O-4	0.0
1974	Det-A	50	103	16	24	4	1	2	9	19	24	.233	.352	.350	99	-0	2	0	1	.986	-2	O-46/D-1	-0.3
1976	Det-A	18	48	3	9	1	0	0	5	6	11	.188	.278	.208	42	-3	0	0	1	.960	-2	O-15	-0.6
Total	5	90	179	23	37	5	1	2	17	28	42	.207	.314	.296	74	-5	2	0	1	.983	-8	/O-74,D-1	-1.4

■ DICK LANE
Lane, Richard Harrison b: 6/28/27, Highland Park, Mich. BR/TR, 5'11", 178 lbs. Deb: 6/20/49

YEAR	TM/L	G	AB	R	H	2B	3B	HR	RBI	BB	SO	AVG	OBP	SLG	PRO+	BR/A	SB	CS	SBR	FA	FR	G/POS	TPR
1949	Chi-A	12	42	4	5	0	0	0	4	5	3	.119	.213	.119	-11	-7	0	1	-1	1.000	1	O-11	-0.7

■ DON LANG
Lang, Donald Charles b: 3/15/15, Selma, Cal. BR/TR, 6', 175 lbs. Deb: 7/4/38

YEAR	TM/L	G	AB	R	H	2B	3B	HR	RBI	BB	SO	AVG	OBP	SLG	PRO+	BR/A	SB	CS	SBR	FA	FR	G/POS	TPR
1938	Cin-N	21	50	5	13	3	1	1	11	2	7	.260	.288	.420	95	-1	0			.976	2	3-15/2-1,S-1	0.1
1948	StL-N	117	323	30	87	14	1	4	31	47	38	.269	.364	.356	90	-3	2			.964	9	3-95/2-2	0.5
Total	2	138	373	35	100	17	2	5	42	49	45	.268	.355	.365	91	-4	2			.966	10	3-110/2-3,S-1	0.6

■ BILL LANGE
Lange, William Alexander "Little Eva" b: 6/6/1871, San Francisco, Cal. d: 7/23/50, San Francisco, Cal. BR/TR, 6'1.5", 190 lbs. Deb: 4/27/1893

YEAR	TM/L	G	AB	R	H	2B	3B	HR	RBI	BB	SO	AVG	OBP	SLG	PRO+	BR/A	SB	CS	SBR	FA	FR	G/POS	TPR
1893	Chi-N	117	469	92	132	7	8	8	88	52	20	.281	.358	.380	98	-2	47			.888	2	2-57,O-40/3-8,SC	0.1
1894	Chi-N	111	442	84	145	16	9	6	90	56	18	.328	.405	.446	100	-1	65			.910	4	*O-109/S-2,3-1	-0.3
1895	Chi-N	123	478	120	186	27	16	10	98	55	24	.389	.456	.575	155	38	67			.924	10	*O-121/C-1	3.1
1896	Chi-N	122	469	114	153	21	16	4	92	65	24	.326	.414	.465	128	19	84			.932	10	*O-118	1.6
1897	Chi-N	118	479	119	163	24	14	5	83	48		.340	.406	.480	128	19	**73**			.946	2	*O-111/1-2	1.9
1898	Chi-N	113	442	79	141	16	11	5	69	36		.319	.377	.439	134	18	22			.970	10	O-94,1-14	1.6
1899	Chi-N	107	416	81	135	21	7	1	58	38		.325	.382	.416	122	13	41			.976	12	O-94,1-14	1.6
Total	7	811	3195	689	1055	133	80	39	578	350	86	.330	.401	.459	122	105	399			.942	50	O-716/2-57,1S3C	9.1

■ SAM LANGFORD
Langford, Elton b: 5/21/1899, Briggs, Tex. d: 7/31/93, Plainview, Tex. BL/TR, 6', 180 lbs. Deb: 4/13/26

YEAR	TM/L	G	AB	R	H	2B	3B	HR	RBI	BB	SO	AVG	OBP	SLG	PRO+	BR/A	SB	CS	SBR	FA	FR	G/POS	TPR
1926	Bos-A	1	1	0	0	0	0	0	0	0	0	.000	.000	.000	-99	-0	0	0	0	.000	0	H	0.0
1927	Cle-A	20	67	10	18	5	0	1	7	5	7	.269	.347	.388	90	-1	0	1	-1	1.000	-2	O-20	-0.5
1928	Cle-A	110	427	50	118	17	8	4	50	21	35	.276	.312	.382	81	-13	3	7	-3	.972	-8	*O-107	-3.1
Total	3	131	495	61	136	22	8	5	57	26	42	.275	.316	.382	81	-14	3	8	-4	.976	-11	O-127	-3.6

■ BOB LANGSFORD
Langsford, Robert William (b: Robert Hugo Lankswert) b: 8/5/1865, Louisville, Ky. d: 1/10/07, Louisville, Ky. BR/TR, Deb: 6/18/1899

YEAR	TM/L	G	AB	R	H	2B	3B	HR	RBI	BB	SO	AVG	OBP	SLG	PRO+	BR/A	SB	CS	SBR	FA	FR	G/POS	TPR
1899	Lou-N	1	4	0	0	0	0	0	0	0	0	.000	.000	.000	-99	-0	0	0	0	1.000	-0	/S-1	-0.1

■ HAL LANIER
Lanier, Harold Clifton b: 7/4/42, Denton, N.C. BR/TR, 6'2", 180 lbs. Deb: 6/18/64 FMC

YEAR	TM/L	G	AB	R	H	2B	3B	HR	RBI	BB	SO	AVG	OBP	SLG	PRO+	BR/A	SB	CS	SBR	FA	FR	G/POS	TPR
1964	SF-N	98	383	40	105	16	3	2	28	5	44	.274	.284	.347	75	-13	2	1	0	.979	10	2-98/S-3	0.6
1965	SF-N	159	522	41	118	15	9	0	39	21	67	.226	.256	.289	52	-33	2	1	-5	.976	-5	*2-158/S-11	-2.7
1966	SF-N	149	459	37	106	14	2	3	37	16	49	.231	.257	.290	50	-31	1	0	0	.991	28	*2-112,S-41	0.8
1967	SF-N	151	525	37	112	16	3	0	42	16	61	.213	.239	.255	42	-39	2	1	-1	.974	29	*S-150	0.2
1968	SF-N	151	486	37	100	14	1	0	27	10	12	.206	.225	.239	49	-35	0	2	-1	**.979**	14	*S-150	-0.8
1969	SF-N	150	495	37	113	19	4	1	37	25	26	.228	.265	.251	46	-36	0	1	-1	.969	**29**	*S-150	0.8
1970	SF-N	134	438	33	101	13	1	2	41	21	41	.231	.266	.279	47	-33	1	2	-1	.967	13	*S-130/2-4,1-2	-0.7
1971	*SF-N	109	206	21	48	3	0	1	13	15	26	.233	.285	.286	63	-10	1	0	0	.957	5	3-83,2-13/S-8,1-3	-0.4
1972	NY-A	60	103	5	22	3	0	0	8	0	13	.214	.236	.243	44	-7	0	0	0	.973	9	3-47/S-9,2-3	0.1

YEAR	TM/L	G	AB	R	H	2B	3B	HR	RBI	BB	SO	AVG	OBP	SLG	PRO+	BR/A	SB	CS	SBR	FA	FR	G/POS	TPR
1973	NY-A	35	86	9	18	3	0	0	5	3	10	.209	.244	.244	39	-7	0	0	0	.960	1	S-26/2-8,3-1	-0.4
Total	10	1196	3703	297	843	111	20	8	273	136	436	.228	.256	.275	50	-245	11	11	-3	.971	132	S-655,2-430,3/1	-2.5

■ RIMP LANIER   Lanier, Lorenzo   b: 10/19/48, Tuskegee, Ala.   BL/TR, 5'8", 150 lbs.   Deb: 9/11/71

YEAR	TM/L	G	AB	R	H	2B	3B	HR	RBI	BB	SO	AVG	OBP	SLG	PRO+	BR/A	SB	CS	SBR	FA	FR	G/POS	TPR
1971	Pit-N	6	4	0	0	0	0	0	0	0	1	.000	.200	.000	-39	-1	0	0	0	.000	0	H	-0.1

■ RAY LANKFORD   Lankford, Raymond Lewis   b: 6/5/67, Los Angeles, Cal.   BL/TL, 5'11", 180 lbs.   Deb: 8/21/90

YEAR	TM/L	G	AB	R	H	2B	3B	HR	RBI	BB	SO	AVG	OBP	SLG	PRO+	BR/A	SB	CS	SBR	FA	FR	G/POS	TPR
1990	StL-N	39	126	12	36	10	1	3	12	13	27	.286	.353	.452	119	3	8	2	1	.989	2	O-35	0.6
1991	StL-N	151	566	83	142	23	**15**	9	69	41	114	.251	.303	.392	93	-6	44	20	1	.984	11	*O-149	0.3
1992	StL-N	153	598	87	175	40	6	20	86	72	147	.293	.373	.480	144	35	42	24	-2	.996	10	*O-153	4.3
1993	StL-N	127	407	64	97	17	3	7	45	81	111	.238	.369	.346	95	0	14	14	-4	.978	3	*O-121	-0.4
1994	StL-N	109	416	89	111	25	5	19	57	58	113	.267	.362	.488	121	13	11	10	-3	.978	3	*O-104	1.0
1995	StL-N	132	483	81	134	35	2	25	63	63	110	.277	.363	.513	128	19	24	8	2	.990	7	*O-129	2.5
1996	*StL-N	149	545	100	150	36	8	21	86	79	133	.275	.370	.486	123	19	35	7	6	**.997**	15	*O-144	3.5
Total	7	860	3141	516	845	186	40	104	437	407	755	.269	.356	.453	119	83	178	85	2	.988	51	O-835	11.8

■ RED LANNING   Lanning, Lester Alfred   b: 5/13/1895, Harvard, Ill.   d: 6/13/62, Bristol, Conn.   BL/TL, 5'9", 165 lbs.   Deb: 6/20/16

YEAR	TM/L	G	AB	R	H	2B	3B	HR	RBI	BB	SO	AVG	OBP	SLG	PRO+	BR/A	SB	CS	SBR	FA	FR	G/POS	TPR
1916	Phi-A	19	33	5	6	2	0	0	1	10	9	.182	.372	.242	89	0	0			.909	-4	/O-9,P-6	-0.4

■ CARNEY LANSFORD   Lansford, Carney Ray   b: 2/7/57, San Jose, Cal.   BR/TR, 6'2", 195 lbs.   Deb: 4/8/78   F

YEAR	TM/L	G	AB	R	H	2B	3B	HR	RBI	BB	SO	AVG	OBP	SLG	PRO+	BR/A	SB	CS	SBR	FA	FR	G/POS	TPR
1978	Cal-A	121	453	63	133	23	2	8	52	31	67	.294	.344	.406	115	8	20	9	1	.942	-26	*3-117/S-2,D-1	-1.9
1979	*Cal-A	157	654	114	188	30	5	19	79	39	115	.287	.330	.436	108	6	20	8	1	**.983**	-24	*3-157	-1.8
1980	Cal-A	151	602	87	157	27	3	15	80	50	93	.261	.317	.390	95	-5	14	5	1	.955	-24	*3-150	-3.0
1981	Bos-A	102	399	61	134	23	3	4	52	34	28	**.336**	.391	.439	131	16	15	10	-2	.951	0	3-86,D-16	1.3
1982	Bos-A	128	482	65	145	28	4	11	63	46	48	.301	.364	.444	114	9	9	4	0	.968	-13	*3-114,D-13	-0.6
1983	Oak-A	80	299	43	92	16	2	10	45	22	33	.308	.361	.475	136	14	3	8	-4	.957	-5	3-78/S-1	0.4
1984	Oak-A	151	597	70	179	31	5	14	74	40	62	.300	.347	.439	124	18	9	3	1	.957	-8	*3-151	0.9
1985	Oak-A	98	401	51	111	18	2	13	46	18	27	.277	.314	.429	109	4	2	3	-1	.976	-32	3-97	-3.1
1986	Oak-A	151	591	80	168	16	4	19	72	39	51	.284	.334	.421	112	9	16	7	1	.982	-18	*3-100,1-60/2-1,D-3	-1.5
1987	Oak-A	151	554	89	160	27	4	19	76	60	44	.289	.368	.455	125	20	27	8	3	**.980**	-3	*3-142,1-17/D-4	1.7
1988	*Oak-A★	150	556	80	155	20	2	7	57	35	35	.279	.329	.360	96	-3	29	8	4	**.979**	-12	*3-143/1-9,2-1,D-1	-1.2
1989	*Oak-A	148	551	81	185	28	2	2	52	51	25	.336	.401	.405	132	26	37	15	2	.957	-26	*3-136,1-15/D-3	0.2
1990	*Oak-A	134	507	58	136	15	1	3	50	45	50	.268	.335	.320	88	-7	16	14	-4	**.970**	-21	*3-126/1-5,D-5	-3.2
1991	Oak-A	5	16	0	1	0	0	0	1	0	2	.063	.063	.063	-69	-4	0	0	0	1.000	-1	/3-4,D-1	-0.5
1992	*Oak-A	135	496	65	130	30	1	7	75	43	39	.262	.330	.369	101	0	7	2	1	.965	-23	*3-119,1-18/S-1,D-2	-2.3
Total	15	1862	7158	1007	2074	332	40	151	874	553	719	.290	.346	.411	112	112	224	104	5	.966	-235	*3-1720,1-124/DS2	-14.6

■ JODY LANSFORD   Lansford, Joseph Dale   b: 1/15/61, San Jose, Cal.   BR/TR, 6'5", 225 lbs.   Deb: 7/31/82   F

YEAR	TM/L	G	AB	R	H	2B	3B	HR	RBI	BB	SO	AVG	OBP	SLG	PRO+	BR/A	SB	CS	SBR	FA	FR	G/POS	TPR
1982	SD-N	13	22	6	4	0	0	0	3	6	4	.182	.357	.182	58	-1	0	1	-1	.986	-1	/1-9	-0.3
1983	SD-N	12	8	1	2	0	0	1	2	0	3	.250	.250	.625	140	0	0	0	0	1.000	0	/1-8	0.0
Total	2	25	30	7	6	0	0	1	5	6	7	.200	.333	.300	82	-1	0	1	-1	.988	-1	/1-17	-0.3

■ MIKE LANSING   Lansing, Michael Thomas   b: 4/3/68, Rawlins, Wyo.   BR/TR, 6', 180 lbs.   Deb: 4/7/93

YEAR	TM/L	G	AB	R	H	2B	3B	HR	RBI	BB	SO	AVG	OBP	SLG	PRO+	BR/A	SB	CS	SBR	FA	FR	G/POS	TPR
1993	Mon-N	141	491	64	141	29	1	3	45	46	56	.287	.354	.369	90	-6	23	5	4	.942	6	3-81,S-51,2-25	0.8
1994	Mon-N	106	394	44	105	21	2	5	35	30	37	.266	.329	.368	81	-11	12	8	-1	.983	1	2-82,3-27,S-12	-0.7
1995	Mon-N	127	467	47	119	30	2	10	62	28	65	.255	.301	.392	78	-15	27	4	6	.991	7	*2-127/S-2	0.5
1996	Mon-N	159	641	99	183	40	2	11	53	44	85	.285	.341	.406	94	-6	23	8	2	.985	-10	*2-159/S-2	-0.3
Total	4	533	1993	254	548	120	7	29	195	148	243	.275	.333	.386	87	-38	85	25	11	.986	4	2-393,3-108/S-67	0.3

■ PETE LAPAN   Lapan, Peter Nelson   b: 6/25/1891, Easthampton, Mass   d: 1/5/53, Norwalk, Cal.   BR/TR, 5'7", 165 lbs.   Deb: 9/16/22

YEAR	TM/L	G	AB	R	H	2B	3B	HR	RBI	BB	SO	AVG	OBP	SLG	PRO+	BR/A	SB	CS	SBR	FA	FR	G/POS	TPR
1922	Was-A	11	34	7	11	1	0	1	6	3	4	.324	.378	.441	119	1	1	0	0	.958	-0	C-11	0.2
1923	Was-A	2	2	0	0	0	0	0	0	0	0	.000	.000	.000	-99	-1	0	0	0	.000	0	H	-0.1
Total	2	13	36	7	11	1	0	1	6	3	4	.306	.359	.417	109	0	1	0	0	.958	-0	/C-11	0.1

■ RALPH LaPOINTE   LaPointe, Ralph Robert   b: 1/8/22, Winooski, Vt.   d: 9/13/67, Burlington, Vt.   BR/TR, 5'11", 185 lbs.   Deb: 4/15/47

YEAR	TM/L	G	AB	R	H	2B	3B	HR	RBI	BB	SO	AVG	OBP	SLG	PRO+	BR/A	SB	CS	SBR	FA	FR	G/POS	TPR
1947	Phi-N	56	211	33	65	7	0	0	15	17	15	.308	.362	.355	95	-1	8			.956	-10	S-54	-0.8
1948	StL-N	87	222	27	50	3	0	0	15	18	19	.225	.283	.239	40	-18	1			.965	8	2-44,S-25/3-1	-0.7
Total	2	143	433	60	115	10	0	0	30	35	34	.266	.322	.296	66	-19	9			.955	-2	/S-79,2-44,3-1	-1.5

■ FRANK LaPORTE   LaPorte, Frank Breyfogle "Pot"   b: 2/6/1880, Uhrichsville, Ohio   d: 9/25/39, Newcomerstown, O.   BR/TR, 5'8", 175 lbs.   Deb: 9/29/05

YEAR	TM/L	G	AB	R	H	2B	3B	HR	RBI	BB	SO	AVG	OBP	SLG	PRO+	BR/A	SB	CS	SBR	FA	FR	G/POS	TPR
1905	NY-A	11	40	4	16	1	0	0	12	1		.400	.415	.500	170	3	1			.918	-3	2-11	0.0
1906	NY-A	123	454	60	120	23	9	2	54	22		.264	.300	.368	99	-2	10			.904	-6	*3-114/2-5,O-1	-0.5
1907	NY-A	130	470	56	127	20	11	0	48	27		.270	.317	.360	107	1	10			.896	-11	3-64,O-63/1-1	-0.9
1908	Bos-A	62	156	14	37	1	3	0	15	12		.237	.296	.282	86	-2	3			.950	10	2-27,3-12/O-5	0.8
	NY-A	39	145	7	38	3	4	1	15	8		.262	.301	.359	113	2	3			.934	-3	2-26,O-11	-0.3
	Yr	101	301	21	75	4	7	1	30	20		.249	.298	.319	98	-1	6			.942	6	2-53,O-16,3-12	0.5
1909	NY-A	89	309	35	92	19	3	0	31	18		.298	.340	.379	126	8	5			.938	-15	2-83	-1.0
1910	NY-A	124	432	43	114	14	6	2	67	33		.264	.321	.338	100	-0	16			.959	-11	2-79,O-23,3-15	-1.5
1911	StL-A	136	507	71	159	37	12	2	82	34		.314	.361	.446	130	18	4			.950	-6	*2-133/3-3	0.9
1912	StL-A	80	266	32	83	11	4	1	38	20		.312	.367	.395	122	7	7			.944	-3	2-39,O-32	0.2
	Was-A	40	136	13	42	9	1	0	17	12		.309	.365	.390	115	3	3			.939	3	2-37	0.4
	Yr	120	402	45	125	20	5	1	55	32		.311	.366	.393	120	10	10			.941	0	2-76,O-32	0.6
1913	Was-A	79	242	25	61	5	4	0	18	17	16	.252	.309	.306	78	-7	10			.952	3	3-46,2-13,O-12	-0.5
1914	Ind-F	133	505	86	157	27	12	4	**107**	36	36	.311	.361	.436	105	-4	15			.956	3	*2-132	0.1
1915	New-F	81	273	34	55	11	2	0	36	44	33	.202	.314	.242	68	-16	14			.960	5	2-76	-1.0
Total	11	1194	4212	501	1185	198	79	15	560	288	85	.281	.331	.377	107	12	101			.952	-31	2-731,3-254,O/1	-3.3

■ JACK LAPP   Lapp, John Walker   b: 9/10/1884, Frazer, Pa.   d: 2/6/20, Philadelphia, Pa.   BL/TR, 5'8", 160 lbs.   Deb: 9/11/08

YEAR	TM/L	G	AB	R	H	2B	3B	HR	RBI	BB	SO	AVG	OBP	SLG	PRO+	BR/A	SB	CS	SBR	FA	FR	G/POS	TPR
1908	Phi-A	13	35	4	5	0	1	0	1	5		.143	.268	.200	49	-2	0			.947	-3	C-13	-0.4
1909	Phi-A	21	56	8	19	3	1	0	10	3		.339	.373	.429	150	3	1			.938	1	C-19	0.6
1910	*Phi-A	71	192	18	45	4	4	0	17	20		.234	.310	.286	88	-2	0			.980	6	C-63	1.1
1911	*Phi-A	68	167	35	59	10	3	1	26	24		.353	.435	.467	154	13	4			.972	-6	C-57/1-4	1.2
1912	Phi-A	91	281	26	82	15	6	1	35	19		.292	.337	.399	114	4	3			.958	-14	C-83	-0.2
1913	*Phi-A	82	238	23	54	4	4	1	20	37	26	.227	.336	.290	85	-3	1			.968	-14	C-78/1-1	-1.1
1914	*Phi-A	69	199	22	46	7	2	0	19	31	14	.231	.338	.286	91	-1	1	4	-2	.977	-7	C-67	-0.5
1915	Phi-A	112	312	26	85	16	5	2	31	30	29	.272	.340	.375	118	6	5	2	0	.967	-4	C-89,1-12	0.9
1916	Chi-A	40	101	6	21	0	1	0	8	10	8	.208	.266	.228	48	-6	1			.989	-0	C-34	-0.5
Total	9	567	1581	168	416	59	26	5	166	177	79	.263	.340	.343	105	12	16	6		.969	-39	C-503/1-17	1.1

■ NORM LARKER   Larker, Norman Howard John   b: 12/27/30, Beaver Meadows, Pa.   BL/TL, 6', 200 lbs.   Deb: 4/15/58

YEAR	TM/L	G	AB	R	H	2B	3B	HR	RBI	BB	SO	AVG	OBP	SLG	PRO+	BR/A	SB	CS	SBR	FA	FR	G/POS	TPR
1958	LA-N	99	253	32	70	16	5	4	29	29	21	.277	.358	.427	103	2	1	1	-0	.985	-2	O-43,1-35	-0.4
1959	*LA-N	108	311	37	90	14	1	8	49	26	25	.289	.348	.418	96	-2	0	1	-1	.990	4	1-55,O-30	-0.3
1960	LA-N★	133	440	56	142	26	3	5	78	36	24	.323	.375	.430	112	8	1	0	0	.993	4	*1-119/O-2	0.3
1961	LA-N	97	282	29	76	16	1	6	38	24	22	.270	.329	.387	82	-7	1	0	0	.995	4	1-86/O-1	-1.2
1962	Hou-N	147	506	58	133	19	5	9	63	70	47	.263	.360	.374	105	5	1	1	0	.991	6	*1-135/O-6	0.2
1963	Mil-N	64	147	15	26	6	0	1	14	24	24	.177	.301	.238	58	-7	1	0	0	.991	5	1-42	-0.6
	SF-N	19	14	0	1	0	0	0	2	2	2	.071	.188	.071	-22	-2	0	0	0	.929	-1	1-11	-0.3
	Yr	83	161	15	27	6	0	1	16	26	26	.168	.291	.224	51	-9	1	0	0	.987	4	1-53	-0.9
Total	6	667	1953	227	538	97	15	32	271	211	165	.275	.351	.390	97	-3	5	3	-2	.991	17	1-483/O-82	-2.3

■ BARRY LARKIN   Larkin, Barry Louis   b: 4/28/64, Cincinnati, Ohio   BR/TR, 6', 185 lbs.   Deb: 8/13/86

YEAR	TM/L	G	AB	R	H	2B	3B	HR	RBI	BB	SO	AVG	OBP	SLG	PRO+	BR/A	SB	CS	SBR	FA	FR	G/POS	TPR
1986	Cin-N	41	159	27	45	4	3	3	19	9	21	.283	.321	.403	94	-1	8	0	2	.976	-0	S-36/2-3	0.4

YEAR	TM/L	G	AB	R	H	2B	3B	HR	RBI	BB	SO	AVG	OBP	SLG	PRO+	BR/A	SB	CS	SBR	FA	FR	G/POS	TPR
1987	Cin-N	125	439	64	107	16	2	12	43	36	52	.244	.308	.371	76	-16	21	6	3	.965	-0	*S-119	-0.3
1988	Cin-N★	151	588	91	174	32	5	12	56	41	24	.296	.350	.429	118	13	40	7	8	.960	10	*S-148	4.5
1989	Cin-N☆	97	325	47	111	14	4	4	36	20	23	.342	.383	.446	132	13	10	5	0	.976	16	S-82	3.8
1990	*Cin-N★	158	614	85	185	25	6	7	67	49	49	.301	.360	.396	103	4	30	5	6	.977	20	*S-156	4.3
1991	Cin-N	123	464	88	140	27	4	20	69	55	64	.302	.379	.506	141	26	24	6	4	.976	18	*S-119	5.8
1992	Cin-N	140	533	76	162	32	6	12	78	63	58	.304	.382	.454	132	24	15	4	2	.983	8	*S-140	4.7
1993	Cin-N★	100	384	57	121	20	3	8	51	51	33	.315	.394	.445	125	15	14	1	4	.965	-6	S-99	2.1
1994	Cin-N†	110	427	78	119	23	5	9	52	64	58	.279	.373	.419	107	6	26	2	7	**.980**	2	*S-110	2.4
1995	*Cin-N★	131	496	98	158	29	6	15	66	61	49	.319	.396	.492	133	25	51	5	**12**	.980	-10	*S-130	3.8
1996	Cin-N★	152	517	117	154	32	4	33	89	96	52	.298	.415	.567	157	45	36	10	5	.975	1	*S-151	6.1
Total	11	1328	4946	828	1476	254	48	135	626	545	483	.298	.373	.451	121	154	275	51	52	.974	60	*S-1290/2-3	37.6

■ ED LARKIN Larkin, Edward Francis b: 7/1/1885, Wyalusing, Pa. d: 3/28/34, Wyalusing, Pa. BR/TR, 5'8", Deb: 10/2/09

YEAR	TM/L	G	AB	R	H	2B	3B	HR	RBI	BB	SO	AVG	OBP	SLG	PRO+	BR/A	SB	CS	SBR	FA	FR	G/POS	TPR
1909	Phi-A	2	6	0	1	0	0	0	1		1	.167	.286	.167	42	-0				.769	-2	/C-2	-0.2

■ GENE LARKIN Larkin, Eugene Thomas b: 10/24/62, Flushing, N.Y. BB/TR, 6'3", 212 lbs. Deb: 5/21/87

YEAR	TM/L	G	AB	R	H	2B	3B	HR	RBI	BB	SO	AVG	OBP	SLG	PRO+	BR/A	SB	CS	SBR	FA	FR	G/POS	TPR
1987	*Min-A	85	233	23	62	11	2	4	28	25	31	.266	.342	.382	89	-3	1	4	-2	.989	-2	D-40,1-26	-1.0
1988	Min-A	149	505	56	135	30	2	8	70	68	55	.267	.371	.382	108	8	3	2	-0	.994	-5	D-86,1-60	-0.4
1989	Min-A	136	446	61	119	25	1	6	46	54	57	.267	.358	.368	98	0	5	2	-0	.992	-7	1-67,D-41,O-32	-1.3
1990	Min-A	119	401	46	108	26	4	5	42	42	55	.269	.346	.392	99	0	5	3	-0	1.000	-2	O-47,D-43,1-28	-0.7
1991	*Min-A	98	255	34	73	14	1	2	19	30	21	.286	.364	.373	99	1	2	3	-1	.968	-10	1-47,1-39/2-1,3D	-1.4
1992	Min-A	115	337	38	83	18	1	6	42	28	43	.246	.312	.359	85	-7	7	2	1	.992	-6	1-55,O-43/D-4	-1.7
1993	Min-A	56	144	17	38	7	1	1	19	21	16	.264	.365	.347	92	-1	0	1	-1	1.000	-8	O-28,1-18/3-2,D-3	-1.1
Total	7	758	2321	275	618	131	12	32	266	268	278	.266	.352	.374	97	-2	23	17	-3	.992	-40	1-293,D-221,O/32	-7.6

■ TERRY LARKIN Larkin, Frank S. d: 9/16/1894, Brooklyn, N.Y. BR/TR, Deb: 5/20/1876

YEAR	TM/L	G	AB	R	H	2B	3B	HR	RBI	BB	SO	AVG	OBP	SLG	PRO+	BR/A	SB	CS	SBR	FA	FR	G/POS	TPR
1876	NY-N	1	4	0	0	0	0	0	0	0	0	.000	.000	.000	-99	-1				.500	-0	/P-1	0.0
1877	Har-N	58	228	28	52	6	5	1	18	5	23	.228	.245	.311	83	-4				.885	-1	*P-56/3-2,2-1	0.0
1878	Chi-N	58	226	33	65	9	4	0	32	**17**	17	.288	.337	.363	122	5				.858	-7	*P-56/O-1,3-1	0.1
1879	Chi-N	60	228	26	50	12	2	0	18	8	24	.219	.246	.289	71	-7				.918	-7	*P-58/O-3	-0.1
1880	Tro-N	6	20	1	3	1	0	0	1	3	4	.150	.261	.200	56	-1				1.000	-0	/P-5,O-2,S-1	-0.1
1884	Was-U	17	70	11	17	0	0	0			4	.243	.284	.243	63	-5				.726	-2	3-17	-0.2
	Ric-a	40	139	17	28	1	4	0			9	.201	.265	.266	75	-3				.907	0	2-40	-0.2
Total	6	240	915	116	215	29	15	1	69	46	68	.235	.274	.303	86	-16				.884	-16	P-176/2-41,3-20,OS	-1.1

■ HENRY LARKIN Larkin, Henry E. "Ted" b: 1/12/1860, Reading, Pa. d: 1/31/42, Reading, Pa. BR/TR, 5'10", 175 lbs. Deb: 5/1/1884 M

YEAR	TM/L	G	AB	R	H	2B	3B	HR	RBI	BB	SO	AVG	OBP	SLG	PRO+	BR/A	SB	CS	SBR	FA	FR	G/POS	TPR
1884	Phi-a	85	326	59	90	21	9	3	37	15		.276	.324	.423	133	11				.856	-7	*O-85/2-2	0.2
1885	Phi-a	108	453	114	149	**37**	14	8	88	26		.329	.372	.525	171	34				.882	12	*O-108	3.8
1886	Phi-a	139	565	133	180	**36**	16	2	74	59		.319	**.390**	.450	161	40	32			.866	5	*O-139	3.6
1887	Phi-a	126	497	105	154	22	12	6	88	48		.310	.380	.421	123	16	37			.895	3	O-93,1-23,2-10	1.2
1888	Phi-a	135	546	92	147	28	12	7	101	33		.269	.326	.403	134	20	20			.967	-8	*1-122,2-14	0.1
1889	Phi-a	133	516	105	164	23	12	3	74	63	41	.318	.428	.426	145	36	11			.973	-4	*1-131/3-1,2-1	1.9
1890	Cle-P	125	506	93	167	32	15	5	112	65	18	.330	.419	.482	153	41	5			.978	-8	*1-125/O-1,M	2.1
1891	Phi-a	133	526	94	147	27	14	10	93	66	56	.279	.376	.441	130	19	2			.974	-5	*1-111,O-23	0.6
1892	Was-N	119	464	76	130	13	7	8	96	39	21	.280	.346	.390	126	14	21			.969	1	*1-117/O-2	0.9
1893	Was-N	81	319	54	101	20	3	4	73	50	5	.317	.422	.436	132	17	1			.963	-9	1-81	0.5
Total	10	1184	4718	925	1429	259	114	53	836	484	141	.303	.380	.440	141	247	129			.971	-21	1-710,O-451/2-27,3	14.9

■ BOB LARMORE Larmore, Robert McKahan "Red" b: 12/6/1896, Anderson, Ind. d: 1/15/64, St.Louis, Mo. BR/TR, 5'10.5", 185 lbs. Deb: 5/14/18

YEAR	TM/L	G	AB	R	H	2B	3B	HR	RBI	BB	SO	AVG	OBP	SLG	PRO+	BR/A	SB	CS	SBR	FA	FR	G/POS	TPR
1918	StL-N	4	7	0	2	0	0	0	1	0	2	.286	.286	.286	77	-0				.778	-1	/S-2	-0.1

■ SAM LaROQUE LaRoque, Samuel H. J. b: 2/26/1864, St.Mathias, Que., Canada TR, 5'11", 190 lbs. Deb: 7/30/1888

YEAR	TM/L	G	AB	R	H	2B	3B	HR	RBI	BB	SO	AVG	OBP	SLG	PRO+	BR/A	SB	CS	SBR	FA	FR	G/POS	TPR
1888	Det-N	2	9	1	4	0	0	0	2	1	1	.444	.500	.444	203	1				.789	0	/2-2	0.1
1890	Pit-N	111	434	59	105	20	4	1	40	35	29	.242	.316	.313	95	-2	27			.925	-10	2-78,S-31/1-2,O-1	-0.5
1891	Pit-N	1	4	0	0	0	0	0	0	0	0	.000	.000	.000	-99	-1	0			.714	0	/3-1	-0.1
	Lou-a	10	35	6	11	2	1	1	8	5	8	.314	.429	.514	172	3	1			.875	-3	2-10/1-1	0.0
Total	3	124	482	66	120	22	5	2	50	41	39	.249	.326	.328	101	1	28			.916	-13	/2-90,S-31,1-3,3O	-0.5

■ VIC LaROSE LaRose, Victor Raymond b: 12/23/44, Los Angeles, Cal. BR/TR, 5'11", 180 lbs. Deb: 9/13/68

YEAR	TM/L	G	AB	R	H	2B	3B	HR	RBI	BB	SO	AVG	OBP	SLG	PRO+	BR/A	SB	CS	SBR	FA	FR	G/POS	TPR
1968	Chi-N	4	2	0	0	0	0	0	0	0	0	.000	.333	.000	6	-0	0	0	0	1.000	1	/2-2,S-2	0.1

■ HARRY LaROSS LaRoss, Harry Raymond "Spike" b: 1/2/1888, Easton, Pa. d: 3/22/54, Chicago, Ill. BR/TR, 5'11.5", 170 lbs. Deb: 6/24/14

YEAR	TM/L	G	AB	R	H	2B	3B	HR	RBI	BB	SO	AVG	OBP	SLG	PRO+	BR/A	SB	CS	SBR	FA	FR	G/POS	TPR
1914	Cin-N	22	48	7	11	1	0	0	5	2	10	.229	.260	.250	50	-3	4			.739	-6	O-20	-1.0

■ SWEDE LARSEN Larsen, Erling Adeli b: 11/15/13, Jersey City, N.J. BR/TR, 5'11", 170 lbs. Deb: 6/17/36

YEAR	TM/L	G	AB	R	H	2B	3B	HR	RBI	BB	SO	AVG	OBP	SLG	PRO+	BR/A	SB	CS	SBR	FA	FR	G/POS	TPR
1936	Bos-N	3	1	0	0	0	0	0	0	0	0	.000	.000	.000	-99	-0				1.000	-0	/2-2	-0.1

■ TONY LaRUSSA LaRussa, Anthony b: 10/4/44, Tampa, Fla. BR/TR, 6'1", 190 lbs. Deb: 5/10/63 MC

YEAR	TM/L	G	AB	R	H	2B	3B	HR	RBI	BB	SO	AVG	OBP	SLG	PRO+	BR/A	SB	CS	SBR	FA	FR	G/POS	TPR
1963	KC-A	34	44	4	11	1	1	0	1	7	12	.250	.353	.318	85	-1	0	0	0	.957	2	S-14/2-3	0.2
1968	Oak-A	5	3	0	1	0	0	0	0	0	1	.333	.333	.333	108	0	0	0	0	.000	0	H	0.0
1969	Oak-A	8	8	0	0	0	0	0	0	0	1	.000	.000	.000	-99	-2	0	0	0	.000	0	H	-0.2
1970	Oak-A	52	106	4	21	4	1	0	6	15	19	.198	.303	.255	57	-6	0	0	0	.969	-1	2-44	-0.4
1971	Oak-A	23	8	3	0	0	0	0	0	0	4	.000	.000	.000	-99	-2	0	0	0	.833	4	/2-7,S-4,3-2	0.2
	Atl-N	9	7	1	2	0	0	0		1	1	.286	.375	.286	84	-0	0	0	0	.933	0	/2-9	0.1
1973	Chi-N	1	0	0	0	0	0	0	0	0		.000	.000	.000			0	0	0	.000	0	R	0.0
Total	6	132	176	15	35	5	2	0	7	23	37	.199	.295	.250	54	-11	0	0	0	.963	6	/2-63,S-18,3-2	-0.1

■ AL LARY Lary, Alfred Allen b: 9/26/29, Northport, Ala. BR/TR, 6'3", 185 lbs. Deb: 9/6/54 F

YEAR	TM/L	G	AB	R	H	2B	3B	HR	RBI	BB	SO	AVG	OBP	SLG	PRO+	BR/A	SB	CS	SBR	FA	FR	G/POS	TPR
1954	Chi-N	2	2	0	1	0	0	0	0	0	1	.500	.500	.500	160	0	0	0	0	1.000	-0	/P-1	0.0
1955	Chi-N	4	0	1	0	—	—	—	0	0	0	—	—	—	-99	-0	0	0	0	.000	0	R	0.0
1962	Chi-N	23	6	1	1	0	0	0	0	0	2	.167	.375	.167	49	-0	0	0	0	.857	-0	P-15	0.0
Total	3	29	8	2	2	0	0	0	0	0	2	.250	.400	.250	75	-0	0	0	0	.889	-0	/P-16	0.0

■ LYN LARY Lary, Lynford Hobart "Broadway" b: 1/28/06, Armona, Cal. d: 1/9/73, Downey, Cal. BR/TR, 6', 165 lbs. Deb: 5/11/29

YEAR	TM/L	G	AB	R	H	2B	3B	HR	RBI	BB	SO	AVG	OBP	SLG	PRO+	BR/A	SB	CS	SBR	FA	FR	G/POS	TPR
1929	NY-A	80	236	48	73	9	2	5	26	24	15	.309	.380	.428	115	6	4	1	1	.943	5	3-55,S-14/2-2	1.4
1930	NY-A	117	464	93	134	20	8	3	52	45	40	.289	.357	.386	92	-5	14	2	**3**	.940	-8	*S-113	0.3
1931	NY-A	155	610	100	171	35	9	10	107	88	54	.280	.376	.416	115	15	13	10	-2	.946	9	*S-155	3.4
1932	NY-A	91	280	56	65	14	4	3	39	52	28	.232	.358	.343	87	-4	9	3	1	.941	2	S-80/1-5,2-2,3-2,O	0.5
1933	NY-A	52	127	25	28	3	3	0	13	28	17	.220	.361	.291	79	-3	0	0	0	.938	2	3-28,S-16/1-3,O-1	0.0
1934	NY-A	1	0	0	0	0	0	0	0	1	0	—	1.000	—	189	0	0	0	0	.800	1	/1-1	0.0
	Bos-A	129	419	58	101	20	4	2	54	66	51	.241	.344	.322	68	-19	12	5	1	**.965**	-5	*S-129	-1.5
	Yr	130	419	58	101	20	4	2	54	67	51	.241	.346	.322	68	-19	12	5	1	.965	-5	*S-129/1-1	-1.5
1935	Was-A	39	103	8	20	4	0	0	7	12	10	.194	.278	.233	35	-10	3	0	1	.953	-4	S-30	-1.1
	StL-A	93	371	78	107	25	7	2	35	64	43	.288	.396	.410	104	4	25	4	5	.962	13	S-93	2.5
	Yr	132	474	86	127	29	7	2	42	76	53	.268	.371	.371	90	-5	28	4	**6**	.960	9	*S-123	1.4
1936	StL-A	155	619	112	179	30	6	2	52	117	54	.289	.404	.367	89	-6	**37**	9	**6**	.956	4	*S-155	0.6
1937	Cle-A	156	644	110	187	46	8	8	77	88	64	.290	.378	.421	100	2	18	8	1	.963	6	*S-156	1.7
1938	Cle-A	141	568	94	152	36	4	3	51	88	65	.268	.366	.361	84	-12	23	6	3	.964	-0	*S-141	0.2
1939	Cle-A	3	2	0	0	0	0	0	0	0	0	.000	.000	.000	-99	-1	0	0	0	.000	-0	/S-2	-0.1
	Bro-N	29	31	7	5	1	1	0	1	9	12	.161	.409	.258	80	-0	1			.947	-5	S-12/3-7	0.2
	StL-N	34	75	11	14	3	0	0	9	16	15	.187	.330	.227	49	-5	2			.961	-6	S-30/3-3	-0.8
	Yr	63	106	18	19	4	1	0	10	25	21	.179	.356	.236	59	-5	2			.958	-4	S-42,3-10	-0.6

YEAR	TM/L	G	AB	R	H	2B	3B	HR	RBI	BB	SO	AVG	OBP	SLG	PRO+	BR/A	SB	CS	SBR	FA	FR	G/POS	TPR
1940	StL-A	27	54	5	3	1	1	0	3	4	7	.056	.136	.111	-35	-11	0	0	0	.952	1	S-12/2-1	-0.9
Total	12	1302	4603	805	1239	247	56	38	526	705	470	.269	.369	.372	90	-47	162	49		.956	11	*S-1138/3-95,120	6.5

■ DON LASSETTER
Lassetter, Donald O'Neal   b: 3/27/33, Newnan, Ga.   BR/TR, 6'3", 200 lbs.   Deb: 9/21/57

YEAR	TM/L	G	AB	R	H	2B	3B	HR	RBI	BB	SO	AVG	OBP	SLG	PRO+	BR/A	SB	CS	SBR	FA	FR	G/POS	TPR
1957	StL-N	4	13	2	2	0	1	0	0	1	3	.154	.214	.308	37	-1	0	0	0	1.000	1	/O-3	-0.1

■ JUICE LATHAM
Latham, George Warren "Jumbo"   b: 9/6/1852, Utica, N.Y.   d: 5/26/14, Utica, N.Y.   BR/TR, 5'8", 164 lbs.   Deb: 4/19/1875   M

YEAR	TM/L	G	AB	R	H	2B	3B	HR	RBI	BB	SO	AVG	OBP	SLG	PRO+	BR/A	SB	CS	SBR	FA	FR	G/POS	TPR
1875	Bos-n	16	78	23	21	4	0	0	13	0	2	.269	.269	.321	100	-0	0	0	0	.927	0	1-16	0.0
	NH-n	20	76	6	15	1	0	0	5	0	4	.197	.197	.211	48	-3	6	0	2	.954	3	1-14/S-4,3-3,M	0.1
	Yr	36	154	29	36	5	0	0	18	0	6	.234	.234	.266	78	-3	6	0	2	.941	3	1-30/S-4,3-3	0.1
1877	Lou-N	59	278	42	81	10	6	0	22	5	6	.291	.304	.371	94	-5				.950	2	*1-59	-0.3
1882	Phi-a	74	323	47	92	10	2	0	38	10		.285	.306	.328	102	-1				.972	-0	*1-74,M	-0.9
1883	Lou-a	88	368	60	92	7	6	0		12		.250	.274	.302	92	-2				.956	-3	*1-67,2-14/S-9	-1.0
1884	Lou-a	77	308	31	52	3	3	0	23	8		.169	.197	.198	31	-22				.961	3	*1-76/3-1	-2.7
Total	4	298	1277	180	317	30	17	0	83	35	6	.248	.270	.298	82	-30				.960	1	1-276/2-14,S-9,3-1	-4.9

■ ARLIE LATHAM
Latham, Walter Arlington "The Freshest Man On Earth"   b: 3/15/1860, W.Lebanon, N.H.   d: 11/29/52, Garden City, N.Y.   BR/TR, 5'8", 150 lbs.   Deb: 7/5/1880   MUC

YEAR	TM/L	G	AB	R	H	2B	3B	HR	RBI	BB	SO	AVG	OBP	SLG	PRO+	BR/A	SB	CS	SBR	FA	FR	G/POS	TPR
1880	Buf-N	22	79	9	10	3	1	0	3	1	8	.127	.138	.190	10	-7				.887	-2	S-12,O-10/C-1	-0.8
1883	StL-a	98	406	86	96	12	7	0		18		.236	.269	.300	79	-11				.866	22	*3-98/C-1	0.9
1884	StL-a	110	474	115	130	17	12	1		18		.274	.309	.367	116	7				.864	40	*3-110/C-1	4.2
1885	*StL-a	110	485	84	100	15	3	1	35	18		.206	.242	.256	55	-26				.875	1	*3-109/C-2	-2.1
1886	*StL-a	134	578	152	174	23	8	1	47	55		.301	.368	.374	127	17	60			.827	0	*3-133/2-1	1.8
1887	*StL-a	136	627	163	198	35	10	2	83	45		.316	.366	.413	106	0	129			.877	2	*3-132/2-5,C-2	0.4
1888	*StL-a	133	570	119	151	19	5	2	31	43		.265	.325	.326	98	-4	109			.882	3	*3-133/S-1	0.1
1889	StL-a	118	512	110	126	13	3	4	49	42	30	.246	.317	.307	69	-24	69			.883	9	*3-116/2-3	-0.9
1890	Chi-P	52	214	47	49	7	2	1	20	22	22	.229	.310	.294	59	-13	32			.880	3	3-52	-0.6
	Cin-N	41	164	35	41	6	2	0	15	23	18	.250	.346	.311	92	-1	20			.853	1	3-41/O-1	0.5
1891	Cin-N	135	533	119	145	20	10	7	53	74	35	.272	.372	.386	120	15	87			.879	20	*3-135/C-1	3.7
1892	Cin-N	152	622	111	148	20	4	0	46	60	54	.238	.310	.283	81	-13	66			.883	-5	*3-142/2-9,O-1	-1.2
1893	Cin-N	127	531	101	150	18	6	2	49	62	20	.282	.368	.350	89	-7	57			.892	-11	*3-127	-1.3
1894	Cin-N	129	524	129	164	23	6	4	60	60	24	.313	.393	.403	89	-9	59			.860	-10	*3-127/2-2	-1.5
1895	Cin-N	112	460	93	143	14	6	2	69	42	25	.311	.375	.380	91	-6	48			.861	-16	*3-108/1-3,2-1	-1.6
1896	StL-N	8	35	3	7	0	0	0	5	4	3	.200	.282	.200	29	-3	2			.744	-1	/3-8,M	-0.4
1899	Was-N	6	6	1	1	0	0	0	0	1		.167	.286	.167	26	-1	0			1.000	-0	/O-1,2-1	-0.1
1909	NY-N	4	2	1	0	0	0	0	0	0		.000	.000	.000	-99	-0	0			1.000	1	/2-2	0.0
Total	17	1627	6822	1478	1833	245	85	27	563	588	239	.269	.334	.341	91	-84	739			.870	60	*3-1571/2-24,OSC1	1.1

■ CHICK LATHERS
Lathers, Charles Ten Eyck   b: 10/22/1888, Detroit, Mich.   d: 7/26/71, Petoskey, Mich.   BL/TR, 6', 180 lbs.   Deb: 5/1/10

YEAR	TM/L	G	AB	R	H	2B	3B	HR	RBI	BB	SO	AVG	OBP	SLG	PRO+	BR/A	SB	CS	SBR	FA	FR	G/POS	TPR
1910	Det-A	41	82	4	19	2	0	0	3	8		.232	.300	.256	70	-3	0			.926	5	3-14/2-7,S-4	0.2
1911	Det-A	29	45	5	10	1	0	0	4	5		.222	.314	.244	54	-3	0			.867	-3	/2-9,3-8,S-4,1-3	-0.5
Total	2	70	127	9	29	3	0	0	7	13		.228	.305	.252	64	-5	0			.933	2	/3-22,2-16,S-8,1-3	-0.3

■ TACKS LATIMER
Latimer, Clifford Wesley   b: 11/30/1877, Loveland, Ohio   d: 4/24/36, Loveland, Ohio   BR/TR, 6', 160 lbs.   Deb: 10/1/1898

YEAR	TM/L	G	AB	R	H	2B	3B	HR	RBI	BB	SO	AVG	OBP	SLG	PRO+	BR/A	SB	CS	SBR	FA	FR	G/POS	TPR
1898	NY-N	5	17	1	5	1	0	0	1	0		.294	.294	.353	88	-0	0			.889	-1	/C-4,O-2	-0.1
1899	Lou-N	9	29	3	8	1	0	0	4	2		.276	.323	.310	74	-1	1			.980	3	/C-8,1-1	0.2
1900	Pit-N	4	12	1	4	1	0	0	2	0		.333	.333	.417	106	-0	0			.947	0	/C-4	0.0
1901	Bal-A	1	4	0	1	0	0	0	0	0		.250	.250	.250	37	-0	0			1.000	0	/C-1	-0.1
1902	Bro-N	8	24	0	1	0	0	0	0	0		.042	.042	.042	-74	-5	0			.947	0	/C-8	-0.5
Total	5	27	86	5	19	3	0	0	7	2		.221	.239	.256	41	-7	1			.949	2	/C-25,O-2,1-1	-0.5

■ CHARLIE LAU
Lau, Charles Richard   b: 4/12/33, Romulus, Mich.   d: 3/18/84, Key Colony Beach, Fla.   BL/TR, 6', 190 lbs.   Deb: 9/12/56   C

YEAR	TM/L	G	AB	R	H	2B	3B	HR	RBI	BB	SO	AVG	OBP	SLG	PRO+	BR/A	SB	CS	SBR	FA	FR	G/POS	TPR
1956	Det-A	3	9	1	2	0	0	0	0	0	2	.222	.222	.222	18	-1	0	0	0	1.000	1	/C-3	0.0
1958	Det-A	30	68	8	10	1	2	0	6	12	15	.147	.293	.221	41	-5	0	0	0	.985	1	C-27	-0.4
1959	Det-A	2	6	0	1	0	0	0	0	0	2	.167	.167	.167	-8	-1	0	0	0	1.000	1	/C-2	0.0
1960	Mil-N	21	53	4	10	2	0	0	2	6	10	.189	.271	.226	41	-4	0	0	0	1.000	-3	C-16	0.1
1961	Mil-N	28	82	3	17	5	0	0	5	14	11	.207	.330	.268	65	-4	1	1	-0	.968	-3	C-25	-0.6
	Bal-A	17	47	3	8	0	0	1	4	1	3	.170	.188	.234	12	-6	0	0	0	.990	5	C-17	-0.1
1962	Bal-A	81	197	21	58	11	2	6	37	7	11	.294	.322	.462	115	3	1	0	0	.996	-5	C-56	0.0
1963	Bal-A	29	48	4	9	2	0	0	6	1	5	.188	.204	.229	22	-5	0	0	0	.964	1	/C-8	-0.4
	KC-A	62	187	15	55	11	0	3	26	14	17	.294	.343	.401	102	1	0	0	0	.982	-10	C-50	-0.8
	Yr	91	235	19	64	13	0	3	32	15	22	.272	.316	.366	88	-4	0	0	0	.979	-9	C-58	-1.2
1964	KC-A	43	118	11	32	7	1	2	9	10	18	.271	.328	.398	98	-0	0	0	0	.990	-6	C-35	-0.5
	Bal-A	62	158	16	41	15	1	1	14	17	27	.259	.335	.386	100	-0	0	0	0	.992	-3	C-47	-0.1
	Yr	105	276	27	73	22	2	3	23	27	45	.264	.332	.391	99	-0	0	0	0	.991	-9	C-82	-0.6
1965	Bal-A	68	132	15	39	5	2	2	18	17	18	.295	.376	.409	120	4	0	0	0	.989	-6	C-35	-0.2
1966	Bal-A	18	12	1	6	2	0	0	5	4	1	.500	.625	.583	320	4	0	0	0	.000	0	H	0.4
1967	Bal-A	11	8	0	1	0	0	0	1	1	2	.125	.300	.250	65	-0	0	0	0	.000	0	H	-0.0
	Atl-N	52	45	3	9	1	0	1	5	4	9	.200	.265	.289	59	-2	0	0	0	.000	0	H	-0.3
Total	11	527	1170	105	298	63	9	16	140	109	150	.255	.321	.365	89	-17	3	1	0	.988	-21	C-321	-2.7

■ BILLY LAUDER
Lauder, William   b: 2/23/1874, New York, N.Y.   d: 5/20/33, Norwalk, Conn.   BR/TR, 5'10", 160 lbs.   Deb: 6/25/1898   C

YEAR	TM/L	G	AB	R	H	2B	3B	HR	RBI	BB	SO	AVG	OBP	SLG	PRO+	BR/A	SB	CS	SBR	FA	FR	G/POS	TPR
1898	Phi-N	97	361	42	95	14	7	2	67	19		.263	.300	.357	92	-5	6			.866	-17	3-97	-2.0
1899	Phi-N	151	583	74	156	17	6	3	90	34		.268	.310	.333	79	-18	15			.893	-14	*3-151	-2.7
1901	Phi-A	2	8	1	1	0	0	0	0	0		.125	.125	.125	-29	-1	0			.833	1	/3-2	-0.1
1902	NY-N	125	482	41	114	20	1	1	44	10		.237	.252	.288	67	-20	19			.907	3	*3-121/O-4	-1.8
1903	NY-N	108	395	52	111	13	0	0	53	14		.281	.307	.314	74	-14	19			.908	-7	*3-108	-1.8
Total	5	483	1829	210	477	64	14	6	254	77		.261	.292	.321	77	-58	59			.894	-33	3-479/O-4	-8.4

■ TIM LAUDNER
Laudner, Timothy Jon   b: 6/7/58, Mason City, Iowa   BR/TR, 6'3", 212 lbs.   Deb: 8/28/81

YEAR	TM/L	G	AB	R	H	2B	3B	HR	RBI	BB	SO	AVG	OBP	SLG	PRO+	BR/A	SB	CS	SBR	FA	FR	G/POS	TPR
1981	Min-A	14	43	4	7	2	0	2	5	3	17	.163	.234	.349	62	-2	0	0	0	1.000	-1	C-12/D-2	-0.3
1982	Min-A	93	306	37	78	19	1	7	33	34	74	.255	.329	.392	95	-2	0	2	-1	.976	-15	C-93	-1.4
1983	Min-A	62	168	20	31	9	0	6	18	15	49	.185	.251	.345	60	-10	0	0	0	.986	6	C-57/D-4	-0.2
1984	Min-A	87	262	31	54	16	1	10	35	18	78	.206	.260	.389	73	-10	0	0	0	.978	9	C-81/D-2	0.2
1985	Min-A	72	164	16	39	5	0	7	19	12	45	.238	.294	.396	82	-4	0	1	-1	.969	-6	C-68/1-1	-0.7
1986	Min-A	76	193	21	47	10	0	29	24	56	.244	.336	.451	109	2	1	0	0	.984	-15	C-68	-0.8
1987	*Min-A	113	288	30	55	7	1	16	43	23	80	.191	.253	.389	65	-16	1	0	0	.987	-8	*C-101/1-7,D-2	-1.7
1988	Min-A★	117	375	38	94	18	1	13	54	36	89	.251	.318	.408	99	-1	0	0	0	.992	6	*C-109/1-3,D-4	0.7
1989	Min-A	100	239	24	53	11	1	6	27	25	65	.222	.295	.351	76	-8	1	0	0	.991	6	C-68,D-19,1-11	-0.5
Total	9	734	2038	221	458	97	5	77	263	190	553	.225	.293	.391	83	-50	3	3	-1	.984	-27	C-657/D-33,1-22	-4.7

■ CHUCK LAUER
Lauer, John Charles   b: 1865, Pittsburgh, Pa.   TR,   Deb: 7/17/1884

YEAR	TM/L	G	AB	R	H	2B	3B	HR	RBI	BB	SO	AVG	OBP	SLG	PRO+	BR/A	SB	CS	SBR	FA	FR	G/POS	TPR
1884	Pit-a	13	44	5	5	0	0	0	0	0		.114	.114	.114	-25	-6				.938	-0	O-10/P-3,1-1	-0.5
1889	Pit-N	4	16	2	3	0	0	0	1	0	5	.188	.188	.188	5	-2				.815	1	/C-3,O-1	-0.1
1890	Chi-N	2	8	1	2	1	0	0	2	0		.250	.250	.375	78	-0				.833	0	/C-2	0.0
Total	3	19	68	8	10	1	0	0	3	0	5	.147	.147	.162	-5	-8				.944	-0	/O-11,C-5,P-3,1-1	-0.6

■ BEN LAUGHLIN
Laughlin, Benjamin   Deb: 4/28/1873

YEAR	TM/L	G	AB	R	H	2B	3B	HR	RBI	BB	SO	AVG	OBP	SLG	PRO+	BR/A	SB	CS	SBR	FA	FR	G/POS	TPR
1873	Res-n	12	50	3	12	0	0	0	6	0		.240	.240	.240	47	-3	0	0	0	.725	-1	2-12	-0.3

■ BILL LAUTERBORN
Lauterborn, William Bernard   b: 6/9/1879, Hornell, N.Y.   d: 4/19/65, Andover, N.Y.   BR/TR, 5'6", 140 lbs.   Deb: 9/20/04

YEAR	TM/L	G	AB	R	H	2B	3B	HR	RBI	BB	SO	AVG	OBP	SLG	PRO+	BR/A	SB	CS	SBR	FA	FR	G/POS	TPR
1904	Bos-N	20	69	7	19	2	0	0	2	1		.275	.286	.304	85	-1	1			.943	-3	2-20	-0.4

YEAR	TM/L	G	AB	R	H	2B	3B	HR	RBI	BB	SO	AVG	OBP	SLG	PRO+	BR/A	SB	CS	SBR	FA	FR	G/POS	TPR
1905	Bos-N	67	200	11	37	1	1	0	9	12		.185	.238	.200	32	-17	1			.843	-7	3-29,2-23/S-3,O-2	-2.4
Total	2	87	269	18	56	3	1	0	11	13		.208	.250	.227	45	-18	2			.929	-10	/2-43,3-29,S-3,O-2	-2.8

■ **COOKIE LAVAGETTO**   Lavagetto, Harry Arthur b: 12/1/12, Oakland, Cal. d: 8/10/90, Orinda, Cal. BR/TR, 6', 170 lbs. Deb: 4/17/34 MC

YEAR	TM/L	G	AB	R	H	2B	3B	HR	RBI	BB	SO	AVG	OBP	SLG	PRO+	BR/A	SB	CS	SBR	FA	FR	G/POS	TPR
1934	Pit-N	87	304	41	67	16	3	3	46	32	39	.220	.295	.322	64	-16	6			.961	-14	2-83	-2.4
1935	Pit-N	78	231	27	67	9	4	0	19	18	15	.290	.341	.364	87	-4	1			.951	-11	2-42,3-15	-1.2
1936	Pit-N	60	197	21	48	15	2	2	26	15	13	.244	.300	.371	78	-6	0			.951	-1	2-37,3-13/S-1	-0.5
1937	Bro-N	149	503	64	142	26	6	8	70	74	41	.282	.375	.406	110	9	13			.949	-7	*2-100,3-45	1.0
1938	Bro-N☆	137	487	68	133	34	6	6	79	68	31	.273	.364	.405	109	7	15			.929	-11	*3-132/2-4	-0.2
1939	Bro-N☆	153	587	93	176	28	5	10	87	78	30	.300	.387	.416	112	12	14			.948	-5	*3-149	0.9
1940	Bro-N★	118	448	56	115	21	3	4	43	70	32	.257	.361	.344	90	-4	4			.932	-14	*3-116	-1.5
1941	*Bro-N★	132	441	75	122	24	7	1	78	80	21	.277	.388	.370	109	9	7			.938	-20	*3-120	-0.9
1946	Bro-N	88	242	36	57	9	1	3	27	38	17	.236	.339	.351	86	-3	3			.927	-5	3-67	-0.8
1947	*Bro-N	41	69	6	18	1	0	3	11	12	5	.261	.370	.406	102	0	0			.961	3	3-18/1-3	0.3
Total	10	1043	3509	487	945	183	37	40	486	485	244	.269	.360	.377	98	4	63			.936	-85	3-675,2-266/1-3,S-1	-5.3

■ **MIKE LaVALLIERE**   LaValliere, Michael Eugene b: 8/18/60, Charlotte, N.C. BL/TR, 5'9", 190 lbs. Deb: 9/9/84

YEAR	TM/L	G	AB	R	H	2B	3B	HR	RBI	BB	SO	AVG	OBP	SLG	PRO+	BR/A	SB	CS	SBR	FA	FR	G/POS	TPR
1984	Phi-N	6	7	0	0	0	0	0	0	2	2	.000	.222	.000	-32	-1	0	0	0	1.000	2	/C-6	0.1
1985	StL-N	12	34	2	5	1	0	0	6	7	3	.147	.293	.176	34	-3	0	0	0	1.000	-2	C-12	-0.4
1986	StL-N	110	303	18	71	10	2	3	30	36	37	.234	.318	.310	74	-10	0	1	-1	.988	2	*C-108	-0.3
1987	Pit-N	121	340	33	102	19	0	1	36	43	32	.300	.380	.365	98	1	0	0	0	.992	8	*C-112	1.5
1988	Pit-N	120	352	24	92	18	0	2	47	50	34	.261	.356	.330	99	2	3	2	-0	.987	-0	*C-114	1.0
1989	Pit-N	68	190	15	60	10	0	2	23	29	24	.316	.406	.400	136	10	0	4	-1	.991	-7	C-65	0.6
1990	*Pit-N	96	279	27	72	15	0	3	31	44	20	.258	.363	.344	99	1	0	3	-2	.990	2	*C-95	0.7
1991	*Pit-N	108	336	25	97	11	2	3	41	33	27	.289	.356	.360	103	2	2	1	0	.998	2	*C-105	1.1
1992	*Pit-N	95	293	22	75	13	1	2	29	44	21	.256	.355	.328	95	-0	0	3	-2	.994	-1	C-92/3-1	0.2
1993	Pit-N	1	5	0	1	0	0	0	0	0	0	.200	.200	.200	7	-0	0	0	0	1.000	1	/C-1	0.0
	*Chi-A	37	97	6	25	2	0	0	8	4	14	.258	.287	.278	54	-6	0	1	-1	1.000	4	C-37	-0.1
1994	Chi-A	59	139	6	39	4	0	1	24	20	15	.281	.375	.331	86	-2	0	2	-1	.991	4	C-57	0.4
1995	Chi-A	46	98	7	24	6	0	1	9	5	15	.245	.308	.337	71	-4	0	0	0	.996	6	C-46	0.4
Total	12	879	2473	185	663	109	5	18	294	321	244	.268	.354	.338	94	-11	5	15	-8	.992	21	C-850/3-1	5.2

■ **DOC LAVAN**   Lavan, John Leonard (b: John Leonard Laven) b: 10/28/1890, Grand Rapids, Mich d: 5/29/52, Detroit, Mich. BR/TR, 5'8.5", 151 lbs. Deb: 6/22/13

YEAR	TM/L	G	AB	R	H	2B	3B	HR	RBI	BB	SO	AVG	OBP	SLG	PRO+	BR/A	SB	CS	SBR	FA	FR	G/POS	TPR
1913	StL-A	46	149	8	21	2	1	0	4	10	46	.141	.210	.168	11	-17	3			.899	-5	S-46	-1.9
	Phi-A	5	14	1	1	0	1	0	1	0		.071	.071	.214	-17	-2	0			1.000	0	/S-5	-0.2
	Yr	51	163	9	22	2	2	0	5	10	46	.135	.199	.172	9	-19	3			.906	-5	S-51	-2.1
1914	StL-A	75	239	21	63	7	4	1	21	17	39	.264	.318	.339	101	-0	6	12	-5	.916	-12	*S-74	-1.3
1915	StL-A	157	514	44	112	17	7	1	48	42	83	.218	.281	.284	72	-19	13	19	-8	.913	5	*S-157	-1.0
1916	StL-A	110	343	32	81	13	1	0	19	32	38	.236	.305	.280	80	-9	7			.950	**34**	*S-106	3.4
1917	StL-A	118	355	19	85	8	5	0	30	19	34	.239	.284	.290	78	-10	5			.923	12	*S-110/2-7	0.7
1918	Was-A	117	464	44	129	17	2	0	45	14	21	.278	.302	.323	90	-8	12			.917	-10	*S-117/O-1	-1.4
1919	StL-N	100	356	26	86	12	2	1	25	11	30	.242	.264	.295	72	-13	4			.929	9	S-99	0.2
1920	StL-N	142	516	52	149	21	10	1	63	19	38	.289	.318	.374	102	-0	11	14	-5	.942	16	*S-138	2.4
1921	StL-N	150	560	58	145	23	11	2	82	30	29	.259	.291	.350	70	-25	7	7	-2	.950	**19**	*S-150	0.6
1922	StL-N	89	264	24	60	8	1	0	27	13	10	.227	.271	.265	41	-23	1	3	-2	.937	15	S-82/3-5	-0.1
1923	StL-N	50	111	10	22	6	0	1	12	9	7	.198	.264	.279	44	-9	0	3	-2	.924	1	S-40/3-4,1-3,2-1	-0.7
1924	StL-N	4	6	0	0	0	0	0	0	0	0	.000	.000	.000	-99	-2	0	0	0	1.000	2	/2-2,S-2	0.0
Total	12	1163	3891	338	954	134	45	7	377	209	376	.245	.288	.308	75	-136	71	56		.930	86	*S-1126/2-10,310	0.7

■ **ART LaVIGNE**   LaVigne, Arthur David b: 1/26/1885, Worcester, Mass. d: 7/18/50, Worcester, Mass. BR/TR, 5'10", 162 lbs. Deb: 4/24/14

YEAR	TM/L	G	AB	R	H	2B	3B	HR	RBI	BB	SO	AVG	OBP	SLG	PRO+	BR/A	SB	CS	SBR	FA	FR	G/POS	TPR
1914	Buf-F	51	90	10	14	2	0	0	4	7	25	.156	.216	.178	8	-13	0			.967	6	C-34/1-3	-0.5

■ **JOHNNY LAVIN**   Lavin, John b: Troy, N.Y. 5'11", 175 lbs. Deb: 9/10/1884

YEAR	TM/L	G	AB	R	H	2B	3B	HR	RBI	BB	SO	AVG	OBP	SLG	PRO+	BR/A	SB	CS	SBR	FA	FR	G/POS	TPR
1884	StL-a	16	52	9	11	2	0	0		3		.212	.268	.250	68	-2				.750	-3	O-16	-0.5

■ **RUDY LAW**   Law, Rudy Karl b: 10/7/56, Waco, Tex. BL/TL, 6'1", 165 lbs. Deb: 9/12/78

YEAR	TM/L	G	AB	R	H	2B	3B	HR	RBI	BB	SO	AVG	OBP	SLG	PRO+	BR/A	SB	CS	SBR	FA	FR	G/POS	TPR
1978	LA-N	11	12	2	3	0	0	0	1	1	2	.250	.308	.250	58	-1	3	1	0	1.000	-2	/O-6	-0.3
1980	LA-N	128	388	55	101	5	4	1	23	23	27	.260	.307	.302	72	-14	40	13	4	.988	-1	*O-106	-1.6
1982	Chi-A	121	336	55	107	15	8	3	32	23	41	.318	.362	.438	118	8	36	10	5	.973	-5	O-94/D-3	0.6
1983	*Chi-A	141	501	95	142	20	7	3	34	42	36	.283	.341	.369	92	-5	77	12	16	.994	-4	*O-132/D-3	0.4
1984	Chi-A	136	487	68	122	14	7	6	37	39	42	.251	.310	.345	77	-15	29	17	-2	.985	-2	*O-130	-2.3
1985	Chi-A	125	390	62	101	21	6	4	36	27	40	.259	.312	.374	84	-9	29	6	5	.987	-5	*O-120/D-3	-1.2
1986	KC-A	87	307	42	80	26	5	1	36	29	22	.261	.328	.388	92	-3	14	6	1	.987	-8	O-77/D-2	-1.3
Total	7	749	2421	379	656	101	37	18	199	184	210	.271	.326	.366	88	-38	228	65	29	.986	-27	O-665/D-11	-5.7

■ **VANCE LAW**   Law, Vance Aaron b: 10/1/56, Boise, Idaho BR/TR, 6'2", 190 lbs. Deb: 6/1/80 F

YEAR	TM/L	G	AB	R	H	2B	3B	HR	RBI	BB	SO	AVG	OBP	SLG	PRO+	BR/A	SB	CS	SBR	FA	FR	G/POS	TPR
1980	Pit-N	25	74	11	17	2	2	0	3	3	7	.230	.260	.311	58	-4	2	0	1	.964	-3	2-11/S-8,3-1	-0.6
1981	Pit-N	30	67	1	9	0	1	0	3	2	15	.134	.159	.164	-8	-9	1	1	-0	1.000	5	2-19/S-7,3-2	-0.4
1982	Chi-A	114	359	40	101	20	1	5	54	26	46	.281	.332	.384	96	-2	4	2	0	.953	-3	S-85,3-39,2-10/O-1	0.1
1983	*Chi-A	145	408	55	99	21	5	4	42	51	56	.243	.328	.348	83	-9	3	1	1	.966	5	*3-139/2-3,S-2,OD	-0.5
1984	Chi-A	151	481	60	121	18	2	17	59	41	75	.252	.312	.403	92	-6	4	1	1	.955	-12	*3-137,2-22/O-5,S-4	-1.9
1985	Mon-N	147	519	75	138	30	6	10	52	86	96	.266	.372	.405	124	19	6	5	-1	.985	-1	*2-126,1-20,3-11,/O	2.2
1986	Mon-N	112	360	37	81	17	2	5	44	37	66	.225	.299	.325	73	-13	0	5	0	.993	17	2-94,1-20,3-13/PO	0.5
1987	Mon-N	133	436	52	119	27	1	12	56	51	62	.273	.349	.422	100	0	8	5	0	.980	-5	*2-106,3-22,1-17,/P	-0.6
1988	Chi-N★	151	556	73	163	29	2	11	78	55	79	.293	.360	.412	116	12	1	4	-2	.953	-12	*3-150/O-1	-0.3
1989	*Chi-N	130	408	38	96	22	3	7	42	38	73	.235	.300	.355	81	-10	2	2	0	.949	-18	*3-119/O-1	-3.1
1991	Oak-A	74	134	11	28	7	1	0	9	18	27	.209	.303	.276	65	-6	0	0	0	.951	-6	3-67/S-3,O-3,1-1,P	-1.2
Total	11	1212	3802	453	972	193	26	71	442	408	602	.256	.329	.376	94	-28	34	26	-5	.956	-37	3-700,2-391,S/10PD	-5.8

■ **GARLAND LAWING**   Lawing, Garland Frederick "Knobby" b: 8/29/19, Gastonia, N.C. BR/TR, 6'1", 180 lbs. Deb: 5/29/46

YEAR	TM/L	G	AB	R	H	2B	3B	HR	RBI	BB	SO	AVG	OBP	SLG	PRO+	BR/A	SB	CS	SBR	FA	FR	G/POS	TPR
1946	Cin-N	2	3	0	0	0	0	0	0	0	2	.000	.000	.000	-99	-1	0			.000	-1	/O-1	-0.1
	NY-N	8	12	2	2	0	0	0	0	0	3	.167	.167	.167	-5	-2	0			1.000	-1	/O-4	-0.3
	Yr	10	15	2	2	0	0	0	0	0	5	.133	.133	.133	-24	-2	0			1.000	-1	/O-5	-0.4

■ **TOM LAWLESS**   Lawless, Thomas James b: 12/19/56, Erie, Pa. BR/TR, 5'11", 170 lbs. Deb: 7/15/82

YEAR	TM/L	G	AB	R	H	2B	3B	HR	RBI	BB	SO	AVG	OBP	SLG	PRO+	BR/A	SB	CS	SBR	FA	FR	G/POS	TPR
1982	Cin-N	49	165	19	35	6	0	0	4	9	30	.212	.253	.248	40	-13	16	5	2	.978	7	2-47	-0.2
1984	Cin-N	43	80	10	20	2	0	1	2	8	12	.250	.318	.313	74	-3	6	3	0	1.000	-3	2-23/3-6	-0.5
	Mon-N	11	17	1	3	1	0	0	0	0	6	.176	.176	.235	15	-2	1	0	0	1.000	0	/2-9	-0.1
	Yr	54	97	11	23	3	0	1	2	8	18	.237	.295	.299	66	-4	7	3	0	1.000	-3	2-32/3-6	-0.6
1985	*StL-N	47	58	8	12	1	0	0	2	3	14	.207	.270	.293	58	-3	7	0	3	.971	5	3-13,2-11	0.3
1986	StL-N	46	39	5	11	1	0	0	3	2	9	.282	.317	.308	74	-0	8	1	2	.875	3	3-12/2-7,O-1	0.0
1987	*StL-N	19	25	5	2	0	0	1	2	3	7	.080	.179	.120	-19	-4	1	0	1	1.000	-0	/2-7,3-3,O-1	-0.2
1988	StL-N	54	65	9	10	1	0	0	3	1	16	.154	.236	.262	42	-4	5	0	4	1.000	0	3-24/O-6,2-5,1-1	-0.1
1989	Tor-A	59	70	20	16	1	0	0	3	7	12	.229	.299	.243	55	-4	12	1	3	1.000	0	O-16,3-12,D-12/2C	0.0
1990	Tor-A	15	12	1	1	0	0	0	0	0	2	.083	.083	.083	-52	-2	0	3	-1	.800	1	/3-4,O-2,2-1,D-5	-0.1
Total	8	343	531	78	110	12	0	2	24	41	85	.207	.264	.258	46	-36	53	13	8	.988	20	2-117/3-74,ODC1	-0.7

■ **MIKE LAWLOR**   Lawlor, Michael H. b: 3/11/1854, Troy, N.Y. d: 8/3/18, Troy, N.Y. TR, 6', 180 lbs. Deb: 5/27/1880

YEAR	TM/L	G	AB	R	H	2B	3B	HR	RBI	BB	SO	AVG	OBP	SLG	PRO+	BR/A	SB	CS	SBR	FA	FR	G/POS	TPR
1880	Tro-N	4	9	1	1	0	0	0		0	2	.111	.200	.111	8	-1				.867	1	/C-4	0.0
1884	Was-U	2	7	0	0	0	0	0	0	0	0	.000	.000	.000	-99	-2				1.000	1	/C-2	-0.1
Total	2	6	16	1	1	0	0	0	0	1		.063	.118	.063	-39	-3				.920	2	/C-6	-0.1

YEAR	TM/L	G	AB	R	H	2B	3B	HR	RBI	BB	SO	AVG	OBP	SLG	PRO+	BR/A	SB	CS	SBR	FA	FR	G/POS	TPR

■ **JIM LAWRENCE** Lawrence, James Ross b: 2/12/39, Hamilton, Ont., Can. BL/TR, 6'1", 185 lbs. Deb: 5/30/63

YEAR	TM/L	G	AB	R	H	2B	3B	HR	RBI	BB	SO	AVG	OBP	SLG	PRO+	BR/A	SB	CS	SBR	FA	FR	G/POS	TPR
1963	Cle-A	2	0	0	0	0	0	0	0	0	0	—	—	—	—		0	0	0	.750	0	/C-2	0.0

■ **BILL LAWRENCE** Lawrence, William Henry b: 3/11/06, San Mateo, Cal. BR/TR, 6'4", 194 lbs. Deb: 4/13/32

YEAR	TM/L	G	AB	R	H	2B	3B	HR	RBI	BB	SO	AVG	OBP	SLG	PRO+	BR/A	SB	CS	SBR	FA	FR	G/POS	TPR
1932	Det-A	25	46	10	10	1	0	0	3	5	5	.217	.294	.239	38	-4	0	2	-1	1.000	2	O-15	-0.4

■ **OTIS LAWRY** Lawry, Otis Carroll "Rabbit" b: 11/1/1893, Fairfield, Me. d: 10/23/65, China, Maine BL/TR, 5'8", 133 lbs. Deb: 6/28/16

YEAR	TM/L	G	AB	R	H	2B	3B	HR	RBI	BB	SO	AVG	OBP	SLG	PRO+	BR/A	SB	CS	SBR	FA	FR	G/POS	TPR
1916	Phi-A	41	123	10	25	0	0	0	4	9	21	.203	.263	.203	42	-9	4			.905	-10	2-29/O-5	-2.0
1917	Phi-A	30	55	7	9	1	0	0	1	2	9	.164	.193	.182	15	-6	1			.921	-3	2-17/O-1	-0.9
Total	2	71	178	17	34	1	0	0	5	11	30	.191	.242	.197	34	-14	5			.911	-13	/2-46,O-6	-2.9

■ **MARCUS LAWTON** Lawton, Marcus Dwayne b: 8/18/65, Gulfport, Miss. BB/TR, 6'1", 160 lbs. Deb: 8/11/89 F

YEAR	TM/L	G	AB	R	H	2B	3B	HR	RBI	BB	SO	AVG	OBP	SLG	PRO+	BR/A	SB	CS	SBR	FA	FR	G/POS	TPR
1989	NY-A	10	14	1	3	0	0	0	0	3	3	.214	.214	.214	21	-1	1	0		.818	-2	/O-8,D-1	-0.3

■ **MATT LAWTON** Lawton, Matthew b: 11/3/71, Gulfport, Miss. BL/TR, 5'9", 180 lbs. Deb: 9/5/95 F

YEAR	TM/L	G	AB	R	H	2B	3B	HR	RBI	BB	SO	AVG	OBP	SLG	PRO+	BR/A	SB	CS	SBR	FA	FR	G/POS	TPR
1995	Min-A	21	60	11	19	4	1	1	12	7	11	.317	.414	.467	128	3	1	1	-0	.972	-2	O-19/D-1	0.0
1996	Min-A	79	252	34	65	7	1	6	42	28	28	.258	.342	.365	77	-8	4	4	-1	.985	8	O-75/D-1	-0.3
Total	2	100	312	45	84	11	2	7	54	35	39	.269	.356	.385	87	-5	5	5	-2	.983	6	/O-94,D-2	-0.3

■ **GENE LAYDEN** Layden, Eugene Francis b: 3/14/1894, Pittsburgh, Pa. d: 12/12/84, Pittsburgh, Pa. BL/TL, 5'10", 160 lbs. Deb: 7/29/15

YEAR	TM/L	G	AB	R	H	2B	3B	HR	RBI	BB	SO	AVG	OBP	SLG	PRO+	BR/A	SB	CS	SBR	FA	FR	G/POS	TPR
1915	NY-A	3	7	2	2	0	0	0	0	0	1	.286	.286	.286	71	-0	0	1	-1	.750	-1	/O-2	-0.2

■ **PETE LAYDON** Laydon, Peter John b: 12/30/19, Dallas, Tex. d: 7/18/82, Edna, Tex. BR/TR, 5'11", 185 lbs. Deb: 4/28/48

YEAR	TM/L	G	AB	R	H	2B	3B	HR	RBI	BB	SO	AVG	OBP	SLG	PRO+	BR/A	SB	CS	SBR	FA	FR	G/POS	TPR
1948	StL-A	41	104	11	26	2	1	0	4	6	10	.250	.297	.288	55	-7	4	2	0	.973	-1	O-30	-0.9

■ **HERMAN LAYNE** Layne, Herman b: 2/13/01, New Haven, W.Va. d: 8/27/73, Gallipolis, Ohio BR/TR, 5'11", 165 lbs. Deb: 4/16/27

YEAR	TM/L	G	AB	R	H	2B	3B	HR	RBI	BB	SO	AVG	OBP	SLG	PRO+	BR/A	SB	CS	SBR	FA	FR	G/POS	TPR
1927	Pit-N	11	6	3	0	0	0	0	1	1	0	.000	.143	.000	-55	-1	0			.000	-1	/O-2	-0.3

■ **HILLIS LAYNE** Layne, Ivoria Hillis "Tony" b: 2/23/18, Whitwell, Tenn. BL/TR, 6', 170 lbs. Deb: 9/16/41

YEAR	TM/L	G	AB	R	H	2B	3B	HR	RBI	BB	SO	AVG	OBP	SLG	PRO+	BR/A	SB	CS	SBR	FA	FR	G/POS	TPR
1941	Was-A	13	50	8	14	2	0	0	4	5	4	.280	.333	.320	77	-2	1	1	-0	.953	-1	3-13	-0.1
1944	Was-A	33	87	6	17	2	0	0	8	6	10	.195	.263	.218	40	-7	2	0	1	.949	1	3-18/2-3	-0.5
1945	Was-A	61	147	23	44	5	4	1	14	10	7	.299	.352	.408	132	5	0	1	-1	.956	-5	3-33	0.1
Total	3	107	284	37	75	9	4	1	28	20	22	.264	.321	.335	92	-5	3	2	-0	.953	-5	/3-64,2-3	-0.5

■ **LES LAYTON** Layton, Lester Lee b: 11/18/21, Nardin, Okla. BR/TR, 6', 165 lbs. Deb: 4/24/48

YEAR	TM/L	G	AB	R	H	2B	3B	HR	RBI	BB	SO	AVG	OBP	SLG	PRO+	BR/A	SB	CS	SBR	FA	FR	G/POS	TPR
1948	NY-N	63	91	14	21	4	4	2	12	6	21	.231	.286	.429	90	-2	1			.951	-1	O-20	-0.3

■ **JOHNNY LAZOR** Lazor, John Paul b: 9/9/12, Taylor, Wash. BL/TR, 5'9.5", 180 lbs. Deb: 4/22/43

YEAR	TM/L	G	AB	R	H	2B	3B	HR	RBI	BB	SO	AVG	OBP	SLG	PRO+	BR/A	SB	CS	SBR	FA	FR	G/POS	TPR
1943	Bos-A	83	208	21	47	10	2	0	13	21	25	.226	.297	.293	72	-7	5	6	-2	.979	-3	O-63	-1.6
1944	Bos-A	16	24	0	2	1	0	0	1	0	0	.083	.120	.125	-30	-4	0	0	0	1.000	0	/O-6,C-1	-0.4
1945	Bos-A	101	335	35	104	19	2	5	45	18	17	.310	.346	.424	120	7	3	2	0	.961	-3	O-81	-0.6
1946	Bos-A	23	29	1	4	0	0	1	4	2	11	.138	.194	.241	20	-3	0	0	0	1.000	-2	/O-7	-0.6
Total	4	223	596	57	157	30	4	6	62	42	53	.263	.312	.357	92	-7	8	8	-2	.971	-13	O-157/C-1	-3.2

■ **TONY LAZZERI** Lazzeri, Anthony Michael "Poosh 'Em Up Tony" b: 12/6/03, San Francisco, Cal. d: 8/6/46, San Francisco, Cal. BR/TR, 5'11.5", 170 lbs. Deb: 4/13/26 CH

YEAR	TM/L	G	AB	R	H	2B	3B	HR	RBI	BB	SO	AVG	OBP	SLG	PRO+	BR/A	SB	CS	SBR	FA	FR	G/POS	TPR
1926	*NY-A	155	589	79	162	28	14	18	114	54	96	.275	.338	.462	109	4	16	7	1	.961	-20	*2-149/S-5,3-1	-1.0
1927	*NY-A	153	570	92	176	29	8	18	102	69	82	.309	.383	.482	127	22	22	14	-2	.971	5	*2-113,S-38/3-9	3.1
1928	*NY-A	116	404	62	134	30	11	10	82	43	50	.332	.397	.535	148	27	15	5	2	.956	-11	*2-110	2.0
1929	NY-A	147	545	101	193	37	11	18	106	68	45	.354	.429	.561	164	52	9	10	-3	.969	-4	*2-147	4.8
1930	NY-A	143	571	109	173	34	15	9	121	60	62	.303	.372	.462	115	13	4	4	-1	.971	6	2-77,3-60/S-8,10	2.3
1931	NY-A	135	484	67	129	27	7	8	83	79	80	.267	.371	.401	109	8	18	9	0	.958	-3	2-90,3-39	1.1
1932	*NY-A	142	510	79	153	28	16	15	113	82	64	.300	.399	.506	140	31	11	11	-3	.978	6	*2-134/3-5	3.8
1933	NY-A☆	139	523	94	154	22	12	18	104	73	62	.294	.383	.486	137	28	15	7	0	.968	-14	*2-138	2.1
1934	NY-A	123	438	59	117	24	6	14	67	71	64	.267	.369	.445	117	11	11	1	3	.976	-13	2-92,3-30	0.7
1935	NY-A	130	477	72	130	18	6	13	83	63	75	.273	.361	.417	107	5	11	5	0	.970	-21	*2-118/S-9	-0.6
1936	*NY-A	150	537	82	154	29	6	14	109	97	65	.287	.397	.441	110	11	8	5	-1	.968	-32	*2-148/S-2	-0.6
1937	*NY-A	126	446	56	109	21	3	14	70	71	76	.244	.348	.399	87	-9	7	1	2	.966	-8	*2-125	-0.6
1938	*Chi-N	54	120	21	32	5	0	5	23	22	30	.267	.380	.433	120	4	0			.946	-8	S-25/3-7,2-4,O-1	-0.2
1939	Bro-N	14	39	6	11	2	0	3	6	10	7	.282	.451	.564	165	4	1			.914	0	2-11/3-2	0.5
	NY-N	13	44	7	13	0	0	1	8	7	6	.295	.392	.364	103	1	0			.889	-3	3-13	-0.2
	Yr	27	83	13	24	2	0	4	14	17	13	.289	.422	.458	133	5	1			.897	-2	3-15,2-11	0.3
Total	14	1740	6297	986	1840	334	115	178	1191	869	864	.292	.380	.467	122	213	148	79		.967	-119	*2-1456,3-166/SO1	16.9

■ **FREDDY LEACH** Leach, Frederick b: 11/23/1897, Springfield, Mo. d: 12/10/81, Hagerman, Idaho BL/TR, 5'11", 183 lbs. Deb: 5/24/23

YEAR	TM/L	G	AB	R	H	2B	3B	HR	RBI	BB	SO	AVG	OBP	SLG	PRO+	BR/A	SB	CS	SBR	FA	FR	G/POS	TPR
1923	Phi-N	52	104	5	27	3	0	3	14	3	14	.260	.280	.327	54	-7	1	2	-1	.950	-6	O-26	-1.5
1924	Phi-N	8	28	6	13	2	1	2	7	2	1	.464	.500	.821	221	5	0	0		1.000	-1	/O-7	0.3
1925	Phi-N	65	292	47	91	15	4	5	28	5	21	.312	.323	.442	86	-7	1	2	-1	.952	-2	O-65	-1.4
1926	Phi-N	129	492	73	162	29	7	11	71	16	33	.329	.352	.484	117	10	6			.979	-5	*O-123	0.2
1927	Phi-N	140	536	69	164	30	4	12	83	21	32	.306	.342	.444	108	4	8			.981	14	*O-140	0.9
1928	Phi-N	145	588	83	179	36	11	13	96	30	30	.304	.342	.469	107	4	4			.978	11	*O-120,1-25	0.4
1929	NY-N	113	411	74	119	22	6	6	47	17	14	.290	.324	.431	85	-11	10			.974	-12	O-95	-2.7
1930	NY-N	126	544	90	178	19	13	13	71	22	25	.327	.361	.482	104	2	3			.978	-3	*O-124	-0.8
1931	NY-N	129	515	75	159	30	5	6	61	29	9	.309	.348	.421	109	5	1			.976	-4	*O-125	-0.7
1932	Bos-N	84	223	21	55	9	2	1	29	18	10	.247	.306	.318	71	-9	1			.977	-2	O-50	-1.4
Total	10	991	3733	543	1147	196	53	72	509	163	189	.307	.341	.446	101	-4	32	4		.975	-5	O-875/1-25	-6.7

■ **RICK LEACH** Leach, Richard Max b: 5/4/57, Ann Arbor, Mich. BL/TL, 6', 195 lbs. Deb: 4/30/81

YEAR	TM/L	G	AB	R	H	2B	3B	HR	RBI	BB	SO	AVG	OBP	SLG	PRO+	BR/A	SB	CS	SBR	FA	FR	G/POS	TPR
1981	Det-A	54	83	16	16	3	1	1	11	16	15	.193	.323	.289	75	-2	0	1	-1	1.000	-1	1-32,O-15/D-2	-0.6
1982	Det-A	82	218	23	52	7	2	3	12	21	29	.239	.305	.330	74	-8	4	0	1	.995	-1	1-56,O-14/D-4	-1.0
1983	Det-A	99	242	22	60	17	0	3	26	19	21	.248	.305	.355	83	-6	2	2	-1	.994	-1	1-73,O-13/D-3	-0.7
1984	Tor-A	65	88	11	23	6	2	0	7	8	14	.261	.323	.375	89	-1	0	0	0	1.000	-1	O-23,1-15/P-1,D-6	-0.3
1985	Tor-A	16	35	2	7	1	0	1	4	1	3	.200	.263	.257	42	-3	0	0	0	.987	-0	1-10/O-4	-0.7
1986	Tor-A	110	246	35	76	14	1	5	39	13	24	.309	.344	.435	108	2	0	0	0	.978	-8	D-42,O-39/1-7	-0.7
1987	Tor-A	98	195	26	55	13	1	3	25	25	25	.282	.372	.405	104	3	1	2	-1	.981	-6	O-43,D-30/1-5	-0.6
1988	Tor-A	87	199	21	55	13	1	0	23	18	27	.276	.336	.352	93	-2	1	1	-1	1.000	-4	O-49,D-25/1-4	-0.9
1989	Tex-A	110	239	32	65	14	1	1	23	32	33	.272	.360	.351	100	1	2	1	0	.951	-4	D-44,O-41/1-4	-0.5
1990	SF-N	78	174	24	51	13	0	2	16	21	20	.293	.372	.402	117	3	0	0	-1	.989	-3	O-52/1-7	-0.1
Total	10	799	1719	205	460	100	10	18	183	176	217	.268	.338	.369	94	-11	8	8	-2	.983	-26	O-293,1-213,D/P	-5.7

■ **TOMMY LEACH** Leach, Thomas William b: 11/4/1877, French Creek, N.Y. d: 9/29/69, Haines City, Fla. BR/TR, 5'6.5", 150 lbs. Deb: 9/28/1898

YEAR	TM/L	G	AB	R	H	2B	3B	HR	RBI	BB	SO	AVG	OBP	SLG	PRO+	BR/A	SB	CS	SBR	FA	FR	G/POS	TPR
1898	Lou-N	3	10	0	1	0	0	0	0			.100	.100	.100	-43	-3	0			.727	-0	/3-3,2-1	-0.2
1899	Lou-N	106	406	75	117	10	6	5	57	37		.288	.349	.379	100	-0	19			.908	1	3-80,S-25/2-2	0.3
1900	*Pit-N	51	160	20	34	1	2	1	16	21		.213	.304	.262	57	-9	8			.864	1	3-31/S-8,2-7,O-4	-0.7
1901	Pit-N	98	374	64	114	12	13	2	44	20		.305	.347	.422	119	8	16			.903	9	3-92/S-4	1.7
1902	Pit-N	135	514	97	143	14	**22**	**6**	85	45		.278	.341	.426	132	18	25			.926	13	*3-134	3.3
1903	*Pit-N	127	507	97	151	16	17	7	87	40		.298	.352	.438	121	12	22			.879	7	*3-127	1.9
1904	Pit-N	146	579	92	149	15	12	6	56	45		.257	.316	.335	98	-1	23			.907	**36**	*3-146	4.1
1905	Pit-N	131	499	71	128	10	4	2	53	37		.257	.309	.345	92	-6	17			.988	11	O-71,3-58/2-2,S-2	0.5
1906	Pit-N	133	476	66	136	10	7	1	39	33		.286	.333	.342	106	3	21			.929	2	3-65,O-60/S-1	0.4
1907	Pit-N	149	547	102	166	19	12	4	43	40		.303	.352	.404	135	20	43			.980	11	*O-111,3-33/S-6,2-1	3.1
1908	Pit-N	152	583	93	151	24	16	3	41	54		.259	.324	.381	125	15	24			.937	-4	*3-150/O-2	1.9

YEAR	TM/L	G	AB	R	H	2B	3B	HR	RBI	BB	SO	AVG	OBP	SLG	PRO+	BR/A	SB	CS	SBR	FA	FR	G/POS	TPR
1909	*Pit-N	151	587	**126**	153	29	8	6	43	66		.261	.337	.368	110	6	27			.969	3	*O-138,3-13	0.5
1910	Pit-N	135	529	83	143	24	5	4	52	38	62	.270	.319	.357	92	-7	18			.966	9	*O-131/S-2,2-1	-0.5
1911	Pit-N	108	386	60	92	12	6	3	43	46	50	.238	.323	.324	78	-11	19			.987	2	O-89,S-13/3-1	-1.3
1912	Pit-N	28	97	24	29	4	2	0	19	12	9	.299	.376	.381	109	2	6			.986	4	O-24	0.4
	Chi-N	82	265	50	64	10	3	2	32	55	20	.242	.378	.325	93		14			.975	5	O-73/3-4	0.2
	Yr	110	362	74	93	14	5	2	51	67	29	.257	.377	.340	97	2	20			.978	9	*O-97/3-4	0.6
1913	Chi-N	131	456	**99**	131	23	10	6	32	77	44	.287	.391	.421	132	21	21			**.990**	3	*O-121/3-2	1.9
1914	Chi-N	153	577	80	152	24	9	7	46	79	50	.263	.353	.373	116	13	16			.968	4	*O-136,3-16	1.7
1915	Cin-N	107	335	42	75	7	5	0	17	56	38	.224	.338	.275	85	-4	20	14	-2	.959	-4	O-96	-1.6
1918	Pit-N	30	72	14	14	2	3	0	5	19	5	.194	.363	.306	101	1	2			.952	-2	O-23/S-3	-0.2
Total	19	2156	7959	1355	2143	266	172	63	810	820	278	.269	.340	.370	108	79	361	14		.975	114	*O-1079,3-955/S2	17.4

■ DAN LEAHY
Leahy, Daniel C.   b: 8/8/1870, Knoxville, Tenn.   d: 12/30/03, Knoxville, Tenn.   5'9", 155 lbs.   Deb: 9/2/1896

YEAR	TM/L	G	AB	R	H	2B	3B	HR	RBI	BB	SO	AVG	OBP	SLG	PRO+	BR/A	SB	CS	SBR	FA	FR	G/POS	TPR
1896	Phi-N	2	6	0	2	1	0	0	1	1	2	.333	.429	.500	146	0	0			.857	1	/S-2	0.1

■ TOM LEAHY
Leahy, Thomas Joseph   b: 6/2/1869, New Haven, Conn.   d: 6/11/51, New Haven, Conn.   TR, 168 lbs.   Deb: 5/18/1897

YEAR	TM/L	G	AB	R	H	2B	3B	HR	RBI	BB	SO	AVG	OBP	SLG	PRO+	BR/A	SB	CS	SBR	FA	FR	G/POS	TPR
1897	Pit-N	24	92	10	24	3	3	0	12	7		.261	.320	.359	82	-3	3			.935	-3	O-13/C-6,3-6	-0.5
	Was-N	19	52	12	20	2	1	0	7	9		.385	.529	.462	164	6	6			.727	-4	O-10/3-5,2-3,C-1	0.2
	Yr	43	144	22	44	5	4	0	19	16		.306	.405	.396	114	4	9			.881	-7	O-23,3-11/C-7,2-3	-0.3
1898	Was-N	15	55	10	10	2	0	0	5	8		.182	.297	.218	48	-3	6			.913	0	3-12/2-3	-0.3
1901	Mil-A	33	99	18	24	6	2	0	10	11		.242	.348	.343	97	0	3			.941	-6	C-28/O-2,2-1	-0.2
	Phi-A	5	15	1	5	1	0	0	1	1		.333	.375	.400	110	-1	0			1.000	-1	/O-2,C-1,S-1	0.0
	Yr	38	114	19	29	7	2	0	11	12		.254	.351	.351	99	0	3			.944	-6	C-29/O-4,2-1,S-1	-0.2
1905	StL-N	35	97	3	22	1	3	0	7	8		.227	.286	.299	77	-3	0			.946	-9	C-29	-0.9
Total	4	131	410	54	105	15	9	0	42	44		.256	.348	.337	93	-2	18			.942	-21	/C-65,O-27,3-23,2S	-1.7

■ FRED LEAR
Lear, Frederick Francis "King"   b: 4/7/1894, New York, N.Y.   d: 10/13/55, E.Orange, N.J.   BR/TR, 6'0.5", 180 lbs.   Deb: 6/7/15

YEAR	TM/L	G	AB	R	H	2B	3B	HR	RBI	BB	SO	AVG	OBP	SLG	PRO+	BR/A	SB	CS	SBR	FA	FR	G/POS	TPR
1915	Phi-A	2	5	0	0	0	0	0	0	0	2	.000	.000	.000	-99	-0	0			.600	-0	/3-2	-0.1
1918	Chi-N	2	1	0	0	0	0	0	0	1	0	.000	.500	.000	56	-0	0			.000	0	H	0.0
1919	Chi-N	40	76	8	17	3	1	1	11	8	11	.224	.306	.329	90	-1	2			.990	-2	/1-9,2-9,S-3	-0.3
1920	NY-N	31	87	12	22	0	1	1	7	8	15	.253	.323	.310	83	-2	0	2	-1	.951	-3	3-24/2-1	-0.5
Total	4	75	166	20	39	3	2	2	18	17	28	.235	.314	.313	85	-5	2	2		.924	-5	/3-26,2-10,1-9,S-3	-0.9

■ BILL LEARD
Leard, William Wallace "Wild Bill"   b: 10/14/1885, Oneida, N.Y.   d: 1/15/70, San Francisco, Cal   BR/TR, 5'10", 155 lbs.   Deb: 7/21/17

YEAR	TM/L	G	AB	R	H	2B	3B	HR	RBI	BB	SO	AVG	OBP	SLG	PRO+	BR/A	SB	CS	SBR	FA	FR	G/POS	TPR
1917	Bro-N	3	5	0	0	0	0	0	0	0	0	.000	.000	.000	-97	-1	0					/2-1	-0.1

■ JACK LEARY
Leary, John J.   b: 1858, New Haven, Conn.   TL, 5'11", 186 lbs.   Deb: 8/21/1880

YEAR	TM/L	G	AB	R	H	2B	3B	HR	RBI	BB	SO	AVG	OBP	SLG	PRO+	BR/A	SB	CS	SBR	FA	FR	G/POS	TPR
1880	Bos-N	1	3	1	0	0	0	0	0	0		.000	.250	.000	-7	-0				1.000	1	/O-1,P-1	0.0
1881	Det-N	3	11	2	3	1	1	0	4	1	1	.273	.333	.545	165	1				.833	0	/O-2,P-2	0.1
1882	Pit-a	60	257	32	75	7	3	1			5	.292	.305	.354	128	7				.759	-14	3-33,O-27/P-3,12	-0.6
	Bal-a	4	18	3	4	1	0	0				.222	.222	.278	73	-0				.900	-0	/P-3,O-1	-0.0
	Yr	64	275	35	79	8	3	1			5	.287	.300	.349	124	7				.759	-14	3-33,O-28/P-6,12	-0.6
1883	Lou-a	40	165	16	31	1	3	3			2	.188	.198	.285	58	-7				.816	-1	S-40	-0.7
	Bal-a	3	11	1	2	0	2	0			1	.182	.182	.545	122	0				.727	-1	/2-3	-0.1
	Yr	43	176	17	33	1	5	3			2	.188	.197	.301	62	-7				.816	-2	S-40/2-3	-0.8
1884	Alt-U	8	33	1	3	0	0	0			1	.091	.118	.091	-3	-6				.692	-6	/O-6,P-3,3-1	-0.6
	CP-U	10	40	0	7	1	0	0			1	.175	.175	.200	13	-5				.840	-5	/2-4,3-3,O-3,P-2	-0.3
	Yr	18	73	1	10	1	0	0			1	.137	.149	.151	-9	-12				.625	-5	/O-9,P-5,3-4,2-4	-0.9
Total	5	129	538	56	125	11	9	4			10	1	.232	.246	.309	84	-11				.725	-17	/S-40,O-40,3P21	-2.2

■ JOHN LEARY
Leary, John Louis "Jack"   b: 5/2/1891, Waltham, Mass.   d: 8/18/61, Waltham, Mass.   BR, 5'11.5", 180 lbs.   Deb: 4/14/14

YEAR	TM/L	G	AB	R	H	2B	3B	HR	RBI	BB	SO	AVG	OBP	SLG	PRO+	BR/A	SB	CS	SBR	FA	FR	G/POS	TPR
1914	StL-A	144	533	35	141	28	7	0	45	10	71	.265	.282	.343	91	-9	9	15	-6	.987	-4	*1-130,C-15	-2.4
1915	StL-A	75	227	19	55	10	0	0	15	5	36	.242	.268	.286	69	-10	2	4	-2	.985	-2	1-53,C-11	-1.6
Total	2	219	760	54	196	38	7	0	60	15	107	.258	.278	.326	85	-19	11	19	-8	.987	-7	1-183/C-26	-4.0

■ HAL LEATHERS
Leathers, Harold Langford "Chuck"   b: 12/2/1898, Selma, Cal.   d: 4/12/77, Modesto, Cal.   BL/TR, 5'8", 152 lbs.   Deb: 9/13/20

YEAR	TM/L	G	AB	R	H	2B	3B	HR	RBI	BB	SO	AVG	OBP	SLG	PRO+	BR/A	SB	CS	SBR	FA	FR	G/POS	TPR
1920	Chi-N	9	23	3	7	1	0	1	1	1	1	.304	.333	.478	129	1	1	0		.825	-1	/S-6,2-3	0.1

■ EMIL LEBER
Leber, Emil Bohmiel   b: 5/15/1881, Cleveland, Ohio   d: 11/6/24, Cleveland, Ohio   BR/TR, 5'11", 170 lbs.   Deb: 9/2/05

YEAR	TM/L	G	AB	R	H	2B	3B	HR	RBI	BB	SO	AVG	OBP	SLG	PRO+	BR/A	SB	CS	SBR	FA	FR	G/POS	TPR
1905	Cle-A	2	6	1	0	0	0	0	0	1		.000	.143	.000	-53	-1	0			1.000	-0	/3-2	-0.1

■ BEVO LeBOURVEAU
LeBourveau, De Witt Wiley   b: 8/24/1894, Dana, Cal.   d: 12/9/47, Nevada City, Cal.   BL/TR, 5'11", 175 lbs.   Deb: 9/9/19

YEAR	TM/L	G	AB	R	H	2B	3B	HR	RBI	BB	SO	AVG	OBP	SLG	PRO+	BR/A	SB	CS	SBR	FA	FR	G/POS	TPR
1919	Phi-N	17	63	4	17	0	0	0		10	8	.270	.370	.270	88	-0	2			1.000	2	O-15	0.1
1920	Phi-N	84	261	29	67	7	2	3	12	11	36	.257	.295	.333	76	-8	9	6	-1	.949	3	O-72	-1.2
1921	Phi-N	93	281	42	83	12	5	6	35	29	51	.295	.361	.438	102	1	4	5	-2	.911	-8	O-76	-1.4
1922	Phi-N	74	167	24	45	8	3	2	20	24	29	.269	.368	.389	87	-3	0	3	-1	.920	-3	O-42	-1.0
1929	Phi-A	12	16	1	5	0	1	0	2	5	1	.313	.476	.438	132	1	0	1	-1	1.000	0	/O-3	0.0
Total	5	280	788	100	217	27	11	11	69	79	125	.275	.345	.379	91	-9	15	15		.935	-7	O-208	-3.5

■ AARON LEDESMA
Ledesma, Aaron David   b: 6/3/71, Union City, Cal.   BR/TR, 6'2", 200 lbs.   Deb: 7/2/95

YEAR	TM/L	G	AB	R	H	2B	3B	HR	RBI	BB	SO	AVG	OBP	SLG	PRO+	BR/A	SB	CS	SBR	FA	FR	G/POS	TPR
1995	NY-N	21	33	4	8	0	0	0	3	6	7	.242	.359	.242	64	-1	0	0		.875	-2	3-10/1-2,S-2	-0.3

■ MIKE LEDWITH
Ledwith, Michael   b: Brooklyn, N.Y.   d: 1/2/29, Bronx, N.Y.   Deb: 8/19/1874

YEAR	TM/L	G	AB	R	H	2B	3B	HR	RBI	BB	SO	AVG	OBP	SLG	PRO+	BR/A	SB	CS	SBR	FA	FR	G/POS	TPR
1874	Atl-n	1	4	1	1	0	0	0	0			.250	.250	.250	69	-0	0	0	0	.600	-1	/C-1	-0.1

■ CLIFF LEE
Lee, Clifford Walker   b: 8/4/1896, Lexington, Neb.   d: 8/25/80, Denver, Colo.   BR/TR, 6'1", 175 lbs.   Deb: 5/15/19

YEAR	TM/L	G	AB	R	H	2B	3B	HR	RBI	BB	SO	AVG	OBP	SLG	PRO+	BR/A	SB	CS	SBR	FA	FR	G/POS	TPR
1919	Pit-N	42	112	5	22	2	4	0	2	6	8	.196	.237	.286	55	-6	2			.962	-11	C-28/O-6	-1.7
1920	Pit-N	37	76	9	18	2	2	0	8	4	14	.237	.275	.316	67	-3	0	1	-1	.974	0	C-19/O-2	-1.2
1921	Phi-N	88	286	31	88	14	4	4	29	13	34	.308	.338	.427	94	-3	5	2	-0	.987	-7	1-48,O-27/C-2	-1.2
1922	Phi-N	122	422	65	136	29	6	17	77	32	43	.322	.371	.540	121	11	2	3	-1	.967	-5	O-89,1-18/3-1	-0.1
1923	Phi-N	107	355	54	114	20	4	11	47	20	39	.321	.357	.493	110	3	3	3	-1	.959	-11	O-83,1-16	-1.3
1924	Phi-N	21	56	4	14	3	2	1	7	2	5	.250	.276	.429	77	-2	0	1		1.000	-0	O-13/1-4	-0.4
	Cin-N	6	6	1	2	1	0	0	2	0	2	.333	.333	.500	122	0	0	0		1.000	-0	/O-1	0.0
	Yr	27	62	5	16	4	2	1	9	2	7	.258	.281	.435	82	-2	0	1		1.000	-0	O-14/1-4	-0.4
1925	Cle-A	77	230	43	74	15	6	4	30	24	19	.322	.378	.491	118	6	0	3		.951	-3	O-70	-0.4
1926	Cle-A	21	40	4	7	1	0	1	2	6	8	.175	.283	.275	45	-3	0	0		1.000	-0	/O-9,C-3	-0.4
Total	8	521	1583	216	475	87	28	38	216	104	186	.300	.344	.462	103	6	14	11		.960	-36	O-300/1-86,C-52,3-1	-5.5

■ DEREK LEE
Lee, Derek Gerald   b: 7/28/66, Chicago, Ill.   BL/TR, 6'1", 200 lbs.   Deb: 6/27/93

YEAR	TM/L	G	AB	R	H	2B	3B	HR	RBI	BB	SO	AVG	OBP	SLG	PRO+	BR/A	SB	CS	SBR	FA	FR	G/POS	TPR
1993	Min-A	15	33	3	5	1	0	0	4	1	4	.152	.176	.182	-4	-5	0	0		1.000	-2	O-13	-0.7

■ DUD LEE
Lee, Ernest Dudley (a.k.a. Ernest Dudley ln 1920-21)   b: 8/22/1899, Denver, Colo.   d: 1/7/71, Denver, Colo.   BL/TR, 5'9", 150 lbs.   Deb: 10/3/20

YEAR	TM/L	G	AB	R	H	2B	3B	HR	RBI	BB	SO	AVG	OBP	SLG	PRO+	BR/A	SB	CS	SBR	FA	FR	G/POS	TPR
1920	StL-A	1	2	2	2	0	0	0	0	0	0	1.000	1.000	1.000	418	1	1	0	0	.333	-1	/S-1	0.0
1921	StL-A	72	180	18	30	4	2	0	11	14	34	.167	.235	.211	14	-24	8	4	-0	.922	5	S-31,2-30/3-3	-1.5
1924	Bos-A	94	288	36	73	9	4	0	29	40	24	.253	.350	.313	72	-11	8	4	0	.937	-8	S-90	-0.9
1925	Bos-A	84	255	22	57	7	0	0	19	34	19	.224	.315	.275	51	-19	2	3	-1	.924	17	S-84	0.4
1926	Bos-A	2	7	1	1	0	0	0	0	2	1	.143	.250	.143	4	-1	0	1		1.000	-1	/S-2	-0.2
Total	5	253	732	80	163	20	9	0	60	88	70	.223	.311	.275	50	-54	12	8	-1	.928	12	S-208/2-30,3-3	-2.2

■ HAL LEE
Lee, Harold Burnham "Sheriff"   b: 2/15/05, Ludlow, Miss.   d: 9/4/89, Pascagoula, Miss.   BR/TR, 5'11", 180 lbs.   Deb: 4/19/30

YEAR	TM/L	G	AB	R	H	2B	3B	HR	RBI	BB	SO	AVG	OBP	SLG	PRO+	BR/A	SB	CS	SBR	FA	FR	G/POS	TPR
1930	Bro-N	22	37	5	6	0	0	0	4	4	5	.162	.244	.243	19	-5	0			1.000	-1	O-12	-0.6
1931	Phi-N	44	131	13	29	10	0	2	12	10	18	.221	.282	.344	62	-7	0	5		.967	-1	O-38	-1.1
1932	Phi-N	149	595	76	180	42	10	18	85	36	45	.303	.343	.497	110	7	6			.965	11	*O-148	0.8

YEAR	TM/L	G	AB	R	H	2B	3B	HR	RBI	BB	SO	AVG	OBP	SLG	PRO+	BR/A	SB	CS	SBR	FA	FR	G/POS	TPR
1933	Phi-N	46	167	25	48	12	2	0	12	18	13	.287	.360	.383	100	0	1			.981	1	O-45	-0.1
	Bos-N	88	312	32	69	15	9	1	28	18	26	.221	.266	.337	77	-10	1			.977	2	O-87	-1.4
	Yr	134	479	57	117	27	11	1	40	36	39	.244	.300	.353	87	-9	2			.978	3	*O-132	-1.5
1934	Bos-N	139	521	70	152	23	6	8	79	47	43	.292	.353	.405	111	8	3			.985	5	*O-128/2-4	0.7
1935	Bos-N	112	422	49	128	18	6	0	39	18	25	.303	.333	.374	98	-2	0			.962	6	*O-110	-0.1
1936	Bos-N	152	565	46	143	24	7	3	64	52	50	.253	.318	.336	82	-15	0			.973	6	*O-150	-0.1
Total	7	752	2750	316	755	144	40	33	323	203	225	.275	.326	.392	95	-25	15			.973	16	O-718/2-4	-4.4

■ LEONIDAS LEE
Lee, Leonidas Pyrrhus (b: Leonidas Pyrrhus Funkhouser) b: 12/13/1860, St.Louis, Mo. d: 6/11/12, Hendersonville, N.C. Deb: 7/17/1877

YEAR	TM/L	G	AB	R	H	2B	3B	HR	RBI	BB	SO	AVG	OBP	SLG	PRO+	BR/A	SB	CS	SBR	FA	FR	G/POS	TPR
1877	StL-N	4	18	0	5	1	0	0		0	3	.278	.278	.333	97	-0				.667	-2	/O-4,S-1	-0.2

■ LERON LEE
Lee, Leron b: 3/4/48, Bakersfield, Cal. BL/TR, 6', 196 lbs. Deb: 9/5/69

YEAR	TM/L	G	AB	R	H	2B	3B	HR	RBI	BB	SO	AVG	OBP	SLG	PRO+	BR/A	SB	CS	SBR	FA	FR	G/POS	TPR
1969	StL-N	7	23	3	5	1	0	0	3	0	8	.217	.308	.261	60	-1	0	0	0	1.000	-0	/O-7	-0.2
1970	StL-N	121	264	28	60	13	1	6	23	24	66	.227	.294	.352	71	-11	5	1	1	.969	-5	O-77	-1.8
1971	StL-N	25	28	3	5	1	0	1	2	4	12	.179	.281	.321	68	-1	0	1	-1	.800	-3	/O-8	-0.5
	SD-N	79	256	29	70	20	2	4	21	18	45	.273	.321	.414	115	4	4	5	-2	.920	-4	O-68	-0.5
	Yr	104	284	32	75	21	2	5	23	22	57	.264	.317	.405	108	2	4	6	-2	.914	-6	O-76	-1.0
1972	SD-N	101	370	50	111	23	7	12	47	29	58	.300	.356	.497	151	23	2	5	-2	.975	4	O-96	2.1
1973	SD-N	118	333	36	79	7	2	3	30	33	61	.237	.308	.297	74	-12	4	0	1	.970	2	O-84	-1.2
1974	Cle-A	79	232	18	54	13	0	6	25	15	44	.233	.279	.353	82	-6	3	2	-0	.958	4	O-62/D-2	-0.6
1975	Cle-A	13	23	3	3	1	0	0	0	2	5	.130	.231	.174	16	-3	1	0	0	1.000	-1	/O-5,D-3	-0.3
	LA-N	48	43	2	11	4	0	0	3	2	9	.256	.304	.349	85	-1	0	0	0	1.000	-1	/O-4	-0.3
1976	LA-N	23	45	1	6	0	1	0	1	3	9	.133	.170	.178	-1	-6	0	0	0	1.000	-2	O-10	-0.9
Total	8	614	1617	173	404	83	13	31	152	133	315	.250	.309	.375	95	-15	19	14	-3	.962	-5	O-421/D-5	-4.2

■ MANUEL LEE
Lee, Manuel Lora "Manny" (b: Manuel Lora (Lee)) b: 6/17/65, San Pedro De Macoris, D.R. BB/TR, 5'9", 151 lbs. Deb: 4/10/85

YEAR	TM/L	G	AB	R	H	2B	3B	HR	RBI	BB	SO	AVG	OBP	SLG	PRO+	BR/A	SB	CS	SBR	FA	FR	G/POS	TPR
1985	*Tor-A	64	40	9	8	0	0	0	0	2	9	.200	.238	.200	21	-4	1	4	-2	.971	19	2-38/S-3,5-D-8	1.2
1986	Tor-A	35	78	8	16	0	1	1	7	4	10	.205	.244	.269	39	-7	0	1	-1	.990	4	2-29/S-5/3-2	-0.3
1987	Tor-A	56	121	14	31	2	3	1	11	6	13	.256	.291	.347	67	-6	2	0	1	.966	12	2-27,S-26/D-1	0.8
1988	Tor-A	116	381	38	111	16	3	2	38	26	64	.291	.337	.365	96	-2	3	3	-1	.988	10	2-98/S-23/3-8,D-2	1.2
1989	*Tor-A	99	300	27	78	9	2	3	34	20	60	.260	.306	.333	82	-7	4	2	0	.985	-2	2-40,S-28,3-17,D/O	-0.6
1990	Tor-A	117	391	45	95	12	4	6	41	26	90	.243	.290	.340	74	-14	3	1	0	.993	-10	*2-112/S-9	-2.1
1991	*Tor-A	138	445	41	104	18	3	0	29	24	107	.234	.276	.288	54	-28	7	2	1	.967	-28	*S-138	-4.5
1992	*Tor-A	128	396	49	104	10	1	3	39	50	73	.263	.345	.316	83	-8	6	2	1	.987	-18	*S-128	-1.6
1993	Tex-A	73	205	31	45	3	1	1	12	22	39	.220	.301	.259	54	-12	2	4	-2	.968	4	S-72/D-1	-0.5
1994	Tex-A	95	335	41	93	18	2	2	38	21	66	.278	.320	.361	76	-12	3	1	0	.967	4	S-85,2-13	0.0
1995	StL-N	1	1	1	1	0	0	0	0	0	0	1.000	1.000	1.000	431	0	0	0	0	.800	1	/2-1	0.1
Total	11	922	2693	304	686	88	20	19	249	201	531	.255	.307	.323	73	-100	31	20	-3	.972	-4	S-522,2-358/3DO	-6.3

■ TERRY LEE
Lee, Terry James b: 3/13/62, San Francisco, Cal. BR/TR, 6'5", 215 lbs. Deb: 9/3/90

YEAR	TM/L	G	AB	R	H	2B	3B	HR	RBI	BB	SO	AVG	OBP	SLG	PRO+	BR/A	SB	CS	SBR	FA	FR	G/POS	TPR
1990	Cin-N	12	19	1	4	1	0	0	3	2	2	.211	.286	.263	50	-1	0	0	0	1.000	-1	/1-6	-0.1
1991	Cin-N	3	6	0	0	0	0	0	0	0	2	.000	.000	.000	-96	-2	0	0	0	1.000	1	/1-2	0.0
Total	2	15	25	1	4	1	0	0	3	2	4	.160	.222	.200	17	-3	0	0	0	1.000	2	/1-8	-0.1

■ BILLY LEE
Lee, William Joseph b: 1/9/1892, Bayonne, N.J. d: 1/6/84, West Hazelton, Pa. BR/TR, 5'9", 165 lbs. Deb: 4/15/15

YEAR	TM/L	G	AB	R	H	2B	3B	HR	RBI	BB	SO	AVG	OBP	SLG	PRO+	BR/A	SB	CS	SBR	FA	FR	G/POS	TPR
1915	StL-A	18	59	2	11	1	0	0	4	6	5	.186	.262	.203	41	-4	1	1	-0	1.000	2	O-15/3-1	-0.3
1916	StL-A	7	11	1	2	0	0	0	0	0	2	.182	.250	.182	31	-1	0			1.000	-1	/O-4	-0.2
Total	2	25	70	3	13	1	0	0	4	6	7	.186	.260	.200	39	-5	1	1	1	1.000	1	O-19,3-1	-0.5

■ WATTY LEE
Lee, Wyatt Arnold b: 8/12/1879, Lynch Station, Va. d: 3/6/36, Washington, D.C. BL/TL, 5'10.5", 171 lbs. Deb: 4/30/01

YEAR	TM/L	G	AB	R	H	2B	3B	HR	RBI	BB	SO	AVG	OBP	SLG	PRO+	BR/A	SB	CS	SBR	FA	FR	G/POS	TPR
1901	Was-A	43	129	15	33	6	3	0	12	7		.256	.304	.349	82	-3	0			.948	0	P-36/O-7	-0.2
1902	Was-A	109	391	61	100	21	5	4	45	33		.256	.319	.366	89	-6	8			.916	0	O-96,P-13	-1.1
1903	Was-A	75	231	17	48	8	4	0	13	18		.208	.265	.277	62	-11	5			.930	7	O-47,P-22	-0.6
1904	Pit-N	8	12	1	4	0	1	0	0	0		.333	.333	.500	152	1	0			.889	0	/P-5	0.0
Total	4	235	763	94	185	35	13	4	70	58		.242	.300	.338	80	-20	13			.917	8	O-150/P-76	-1.9

■ GENE LEEK
Leek, Eugene Harold b: 7/15/36, San Diego, Cal. BR/TR, 6', 185 lbs. Deb: 4/22/59

YEAR	TM/L	G	AB	R	H	2B	3B	HR	RBI	BB	SO	AVG	OBP	SLG	PRO+	BR/A	SB	CS	SBR	FA	FR	G/POS	TPR
1959	Cle-A	13	36	7	8	3	0	1	5	2	7	.222	.263	.389	80	-1	0	0	0	.955	-2	3-13/S-1	-0.3
1961	LA-A	57	199	16	45	9	1	5	20	7	54	.226	.260	.357	57	-13	0	1	-1	.958	18	3-49/S-7,O-1	0.6
1962	LA-A	7	14	0	2	0	0	0	0	0	6	.143	.143	.143	-24	-2	0	0	0	1.000	0	/3-4	-0.2
Total	3	77	249	23	55	12	1	6	25	9	67	.221	.254	.349	55	-16	0	1	-1	.959	16	/3-66/S-8,O-1	0.1

■ DAVE LEEPER
Leeper, David Dale b: 10/30/59, Santa Ana, Cal. BL/TL, 5'11", 170 lbs. Deb: 9/10/84

YEAR	TM/L	G	AB	R	H	2B	3B	HR	RBI	BB	SO	AVG	OBP	SLG	PRO+	BR/A	SB	CS	SBR	FA	FR	G/POS	TPR
1984	KC-A	4	6	1	0	0	0	0	0	0	1	.000	.000	.000	-99	-2	0	0	0	1.000	-0	/O-2,D-1	-0.2
1985	KC-A	15	34	1	3	0	0	0	4	1	9	.088	.114	.088	-43	-7	0	0	0	.929	-1	/O-8	-0.8
Total	2	19	40	2	3	0	0	0	4	1	10	.075	.098	.075	-52	-8	0	0	0	.944	-1	/O-10,D-1	-1.0

■ GEORGE LEES
Lees, George Edward b: 2/2/1895, Bethlehem, Pa. d: 1/2/80, Harrisburg, Pa. BR/TR, 5'9", 150 lbs. Deb: 5/7/21

YEAR	TM/L	G	AB	R	H	2B	3B	HR	RBI	BB	SO	AVG	OBP	SLG	PRO+	BR/A	SB	CS	SBR	FA	FR	G/POS	TPR
1921	Chi-A	20	42	3	9	2	0	0	4	0	3	.214	.214	.262	21	-5	0	1	-1	.951	-2	C-16	-0.7

■ JIM LEFEBVRE
Lefebvre, James Kenneth b: 1/7/42, Inglewood, Cal. BB/TR, 6', 185 lbs. Deb: 4/12/65 MC

YEAR	TM/L	G	AB	R	H	2B	3B	HR	RBI	BB	SO	AVG	OBP	SLG	PRO+	BR/A	SB	CS	SBR	FA	FR	G/POS	TPR
1965	*LA-N	157	544	57	136	21	4	12	69	71	92	.250	.339	.369	106		3	5	-2	.970	-12	*2-156	0.5
1966	*LA-N★	152	544	69	149	23	3	24	74	48	72	.274	.336	.460	129	19	1	1	-0	.980	-11	*2-119,3-40	1.7
1967	LA-N	136	494	51	129	18	5	8	50	44	64	.261	.325	.366	106	3	1	5	-3	.955	6	3-92,2-34/1-5	0.8
1968	LA-N	84	286	23	69	12	1	3	31	26	55	.241	.307	.343	102	0	1	0	0	.978	-10	2-62,3-16/O-5,1-3	-0.8
1969	LA-N	95	275	29	65	15	2	4	44	48	37	.236	.352	.349	104	3	2	1	0	.985	4	3-44,2-37/1-6	0.7
1970	LA-N	109	314	33	79	15	1	4	44	29	42	.252	.317	.344	81	-9	1	1	-0	.988	-4	2-70,3-21/1-1	-0.8
1971	LA-N	119	388	40	95	14	2	12	68	39	55	.245	.317	.384	104	0	0	2	-1	.988	-17	2-102/3-7	-0.9
1972	LA-N	70	169	11	34	8	0	5	24	17	30	.201	.274	.337	75	-6	0	0	0	.987	-1	2-33,3-11	-0.6
Total	8	922	3014	313	756	126	18	72	404	322	447	.251	.326	.378	105	18	8	15	-7	.979	-48	2-613,3-231/1-15,O	0.6

■ JOE LEFEBVRE
Lefebvre, Joseph Henry b: 2/22/56, Concord, N.H. BL/TR, 5'10", 175 lbs. Deb: 5/22/80

YEAR	TM/L	G	AB	R	H	2B	3B	HR	RBI	BB	SO	AVG	OBP	SLG	PRO+	BR/A	SB	CS	SBR	FA	FR	G/POS	TPR
1980	*NY-A	74	150	26	34	1	1	8	21	27	30	.227	.345	.407	107	2	0	0	0	.975	-14	O-71	-1.4
1981	SD-N	86	246	31	63	13	4	8	31	35	33	.256	.353	.439	133	11	6	4	-1	.994	4	O-84	1.3
1982	SD-N	102	239	25	57	9	0	4	21	18	50	.238	.295	.326	78	-8	0	0	0	.972	-17	3-39,O-36/C-3	-2.8
1983	SD-N	18	20	1	5	0	0	0	1	2	3	.250	.318	.250	70	-1	0	0	0	1.000	-2	/O-6,3-4,C-2	-0.3
	*Phi-N	101	258	34	80	20	8	8	38	31	46	.310	.390	.543	158	20	5	3	-0	.990	-9	O-74/3-9,C-3	0.9
	Yr	119	278	35	85	20	8	8	39	33	49	.306	.385	.522	151	19	5	3	-0	.990	-11	O-80,3-13/C-5	0.6
1984	Phi-N	52	160	22	40	9	3	0	18	23	37	.250	.351	.363	99	-1	0	2	-1	.966	0	O-47/3-1	-0.2
1986	Phi-N	14	18	0	2	0	0	0	0	3	5	.111	.238	.111	-1	-2	0	0	0	1.000	-0	/O-3	-0.3
Total	6	447	1091	139	281	52	16	31	130	139	204	.258	.346	.414	115	22	11	9	-2	.986	-37	O-321/3-53,C-8	-2.8

■ BILL LEFEBVRE
Lefebvre, Wilfred Henry "Lefty" b: 11/11/15, Natick, R.I. BL/TL, 5'11.5", 180 lbs. Deb: 6/10/38

YEAR	TM/L	G	AB	R	H	2B	3B	HR	RBI	BB	SO	AVG	OBP	SLG	PRO+	BR/A	SB	CS	SBR	FA	FR	G/POS	TPR
1938	Bos-A	1	1	1	1	0	0	0	0	0	0	1.000	1.000	1.000	1048	1	0	0	0	1.000	-0	/P-1	0.0
1939	Bos-A	7	10	3	3	0	0	0	1	2	2	.300	.417	.300	83	1	0	0	0	1.000	-0	/P-5	0.0
1943	Was-A	7	14	0	4	0	0	0	1	1	0	.286	.333	.500	148	1	0	0	0	1.000	-1	/P-6	0.0
1944	Was-A	60	62	4	16	2	1	0	7	15	11	.258	.378	.355	115	1	0	0	0	.933	0	P-24/1-2	0.0
Total	4	75	87	8	24	2	1	0	9	18	13	.276	.382	.414	129	1	0	0	0	.960	-0	/P-36,1-2	0.0

■ AL LEFEVRE
Lefevre, Alfredo Modesto b: 9/16/1898, New York, N.Y. d: 1/21/82, Glen Cove, N.Y. BR/TR, 5'10.5", 160 lbs. Deb: 6/28/20

YEAR	TM/L	G	AB	R	H	2B	3B	HR	RBI	BB	SO	AVG	OBP	SLG	PRO+	BR/A	SB	CS	SBR	FA	FR	G/POS	TPR
1920	NY-N	17	27	5	4	1	0	0	0	0	13	.148	.148	.222	5	-3	0	0	0	1.000	3	/S-9,2-6,3-1	0.0

■ WADE LEFLER
Lefler, Wade Hampton b: 6/5/1896, Cooleemee, N.C. d: 3/6/81, Hickory, N.C. BL/TR, 5'11", 162 lbs. Deb: 4/16/24

YEAR	TM/L	G	AB	R	H	2B	3B	HR	RBI	BB	SO	AVG	OBP	SLG	PRO+	BR/A	SB	CS	SBR	FA	FR	G/POS	TPR
1924	Bos-N	1	1	0	0	0	0	0	0	0	1	.000	.000	.000	-99	-0	0	0	0	.000	0	H	0.0
	Was-A	5	8	0	5	3	0	0	4	0	0	.625	.625	1.000	325	2	0	0	0	1.000	-0	/O-1	0.2
Total	1	6	9	0	5	3	0	0	4	0	0	.556	.556	.889	279	2	0	0	0	1.000	-0	/O-1	0.2

■ RON LeFLORE
LeFlore, Ronald b: 6/16/48, Detroit, Mich. BR/TR, 6', 200 lbs. Deb: 8/1/74

YEAR	TM/L	G	AB	R	H	2B	3B	HR	RBI	BB	SO	AVG	OBP	SLG	PRO+	BR/A	SB	CS	SBR	FA	FR	G/POS	TPR
1974	Det-A	59	254	37	66	8	1	2	13	13	58	.260	.304	.323	78	-7	23	9	2	.935	3	O-59	-0.6
1975	Det-A	136	550	66	142	13	6	8	37	33	139	.258	.303	.347	80	-15	28	20	-4	.973	6	*O-134	-1.9
1976	Det-A★	135	544	93	172	23	8	4	39	51	111	.316	.376	.410	125	18	58	20	5	.973	16	*O-132/D-1	3.5
1977	Det-A	154	652	100	212	30	10	16	57	37	121	.325	.365	.475	121	18	39	19	0	.972	2	*O-152	1.3
1978	Det-A	155	666	**126**	198	30	3	12	62	65	104	.297	.363	.405	113	12	**68**	16	11	.976	9	*O-155	2.6
1979	Det-A	148	600	110	180	22	10	9	57	52	95	.300	.356	.415	104	4	78	14	15	.990	4	*O-113,D-34	1.6
1980	Mon-N	139	521	95	134	21	11	4	39	62	99	.257	.337	.363	95	-2	**97**	19	**18**	.957	5	*O-130	1.6
1981	Chi-A	82	337	46	83	10	4	0	24	28	70	.246	.306	.300	77	-10	36	11	4	.960	-1	O-82	-0.9
1982	Chi-A	91	334	58	96	15	4	4	25	22	91	.287	.331	.392	98	-1	28	14	0	.939	-2	O-83/D-2	-0.7
Total	9	1099	4458	731	1283	172	57	59	353	363	888	.288	.344	.392	103	16	455	142	51	.968	41	*O-1040/D-37	6.5

■ LOU LEGETT
Legett, Louis Alfred "Doc" b: 6/1/01, New Orleans, La. d: 3/6/88, New Orleans, La. BR/TR, 5'10", 166 lbs. Deb: 5/8/29

YEAR	TM/L	G	AB	R	H	2B	3B	HR	RBI	BB	SO	AVG	OBP	SLG	PRO+	BR/A	SB	CS	SBR	FA	FR	G/POS	TPR
1929	Bos-N	39	81	7	13	2	0	0	6	3	18	.160	.190	.185	-7	-14	2			.914	-1	C-28	-1.2
1933	Bos-A	8	5	1	1	0	0	0	1	0	0	.200	.200	.400	56	-0	0	0	0	1.000	1	/C-2	0.0
1934	Bos-A	19	38	4	11	0	0	0	0	2	4	.289	.325	.289	56	-2	0	0	0	.977	-0	C-17	-0.2
1935	Bos-A	2	0	1	0	0	0	0	0	0	0	—	—	—			0			.000		R	0.0
Total	4	68	124	13	25	3	0	0	8	5	22	.202	.233	.226	56	-16	2	0		.938	-1	/C-47	-1.4

■ GREG LEGG
Legg, Gregory Lynn b: 4/21/60, San Jose, Cal. BR/TR, 6'1", 185 lbs. Deb: 4/18/86

YEAR	TM/L	G	AB	R	H	2B	3B	HR	RBI	BB	SO	AVG	OBP	SLG	PRO+	BR/A	SB	CS	SBR	FA	FR	G/POS	TPR
1986	Phi-N	11	20	2	9	1	0	0	1	0	3	.450	.450	.500	156	1	0	0	0	.941	2	/2-4,S-1	0.4
1987	Phi-N	3	2	1	0	0	0	0	0	0	0	.000	.000	.000	-97	-1	0	0	0	1.000	-0	/2-1,S-1,3-1	-0.1
Total	2	14	22	3	9	1	0	0	1	0	3	.409	.409	.455	132	0	0	0	0	.952	2	/2-5,S-2,3-1	0.3

■ MIKE LEHANE
Lehane, Michael Patrick b: 4/15/1865, New York, N.Y. BR, 6'1.5", 180 lbs. Deb: 4/26/1884

YEAR	TM/L	G	AB	R	H	2B	3B	HR	RBI	BB	SO	AVG	OBP	SLG	PRO+	BR/A	SB	CS	SBR	FA	FR	G/POS	TPR
1884	Was-U	3	12	1	4	2	0	0				.333	.333	.500	154	0				.688	-1	/S-3,O-1,3-1	0.0
1890	Col-a	140	512	54	108	19	5	0	56		43	.211	.276	.268	65	-23	13			**.982**	10	*1-140	-1.8
1891	Col-a	137	511	59	110	12	7	1	52	34	77	.215	.268	.272	58	-29	16			**.981**	7	*1-137	-2.5
Total	3	280	1035	114	222	33	12	1	108	77	77	.214	.273	.272	62	-51	29			.982	16	1-277/S-3,3-1,0-1	-4.3

■ PAUL LEHNER
Lehner, Paul Eugene "Peanuts" or "Gulliver" b: 7/1/20, Dolomite, Ala. d: 12/27/67, Birmingham, Ala. BL/TR, 5'9", 165 lbs. Deb: 9/10/46

YEAR	TM/L	G	AB	R	H	2B	3B	HR	RBI	BB	SO	AVG	OBP	SLG	PRO+	BR/A	SB	CS	SBR	FA	FR	G/POS	TPR
1946	StL-A	16	45	6	10	1	2	0	5	1	5	.222	.239	.333	56	-3	0	0	0	.941	-5	O-12	-0.7
1947	StL-A	135	483	59	120	25	9	7	48	28	29	.248	.294	.381	85	-12	5	5	-2	.980	-6	*O-127	-2.7
1948	StL-A	103	333	23	92	15	4	0	46	30	19	.276	.336	.363	84	-8	0	2	-1	.974	-6	O-89/1-2	-2.0
1949	StL-A	104	297	25	68	13	0	3	37	16	20	.229	.271	.303	50	-23	0	2	-1	.987	2	O-56,1-18	-2.5
1950	Phi-A	114	427	48	132	17	5	9	52	32	33	.309	.357	.436	104	1	1	1	-0	.981	6	*O-101	0.3
1951	Phi-A	9	28	1	4	1	0	0	1	5	1	.143	.172	.179	-5	-4	0	0	0	1.000	1	/O-6	-0.3
	Chi-A	23	72	9	15	3	1	0	3	10	4	.208	.305	.278	60	-4	0	0	0	.980	-4	O-20	-0.8
	StL-A	21	67	2	9	5	0	1	2	6	5	.134	.205	.254	23	-8	0	1	-1	1.000	-1	O-18	-1.0
	Cle-A	12	13	2	3	0	0	0	1	1	2	.231	.286	.231	43	-1	0	0	0	1.000	-0	/O-1	-0.1
	Yr	65	180	14	31	9	1	1	7	18	12	.172	.247	.250	35	-17	0	1	-1	.991	-4	O-45	-2.2
1952	Bos-A	3	3	0	2	0	0	0	0	2	0	.667	.800	.667	288	1	0	0	0	1.000	-0	/O-2	0.1
Total	7	540	1768	175	455	80	21	22	197	127	118	.257	.309	.364	78	-60	6	11	-5	.981	-11	O-432/1-20	-9.7

■ CLARENCE LEHR
Lehr, Clarence Emanuel "King" b: 5/16/1886, Escanaba, Mich. d: 1/31/48, Highland Park, Mich. BR/TR, 5'11", 165 lbs. Deb: 5/18/11

YEAR	TM/L	G	AB	R	H	2B	3B	HR	RBI	BB	SO	AVG	OBP	SLG	PRO+	BR/A	SB	CS	SBR	FA	FR	G/POS	TPR
1911	Phi-N	23	27	2	4	0	0	0	2	0	7	.148	.148	.148	-17	-4	0			1.000	-1	/O-5,2-4,S-4	-0.5

■ HANK LEIBER
Leiber, Henry Edward b: 1/17/11, Phoenix, Ariz. d: 11/8/93, Tucson, Ariz. BR/TR, 6'1.5", 205 lbs. Deb: 4/16/33

YEAR	TM/L	G	AB	R	H	2B	3B	HR	RBI	BB	SO	AVG	OBP	SLG	PRO+	BR/A	SB	CS	SBR	FA	FR	G/POS	TPR
1933	NY-N	6	10	1	2	0	0	0	0	0	2	.200	.200	.200	15	-1	0			1.000	1	/O-1	0.0
1934	NY-N	63	187	17	45	5	3	2	25	4	13	.241	.257	.332	58	-12	1			.971	-6	O-51	-1.9
1935	NY-N	154	613	110	203	37	4	22	107	48	29	.331	.389	.512	143	36	0			.965	-15	*O-154	1.5
1936	*NY-N	101	337	44	94	19	7	9	67	37	41	.279	.352	.457	118	8	1			.961	-7	O-86/1-1	-0.3
1937	*NY-N	51	184	24	54	7	3	4	32	15	27	.293	.347	.429	108	2	1			.988	-7	O-46	-0.6
1938	NY-N★	98	360	50	97	18	4	12	65	31	45	.269	.327	.442	109	3	0			.974	-9	O-98	-0.8
1939	Chi-N	112	365	65	113	16	1	24	88	59	42	.310	.411	.556	155	29	1			.977	-4	O-98	2.9
1940	Chi-N†	117	440	68	133	24	2	17	86	45	68	.302	.371	.482	136	21	0			.985	-6	*O-103,1-12	0.9
1941	Chi-N†	53	162	20	35	5	0	7	25	16	25	.216	.291	.377	90	-3	0			.964	-4	O-29,1-15	-1.0
1942	NY-N	58	147	11	32	7	0	4	23	19	27	.218	.315	.340	91	-1	0			.990	-7	O-41/P-1	-0.4
Total	10	813	2805	410	808	137	24	101	518	274	319	.288	.356	.462	122	83	5			.973	-49	O-698/1-28,P-1	0.3

■ NEMO LEIBOLD
Leibold, Harry Loran b: 2/17/1892, Butler, Ind. d: 2/4/77, Detroit, Mich. BL/TR, 5'6.5", 157 lbs. Deb: 4/12/13

YEAR	TM/L	G	AB	R	H	2B	3B	HR	RBI	BB	SO	AVG	OBP	SLG	PRO+	BR/A	SB	CS	SBR	FA	FR	G/POS	TPR
1913	Cle-A	93	286	37	74	11	6	0	12	21	43	.259	.309	.339	87	-5	16			.945	-0	O-74	-1.0
1914	Cle-A	115	402	46	106	13	3	0	32	54	56	.264	.354	.311	96	-0	12	14	-5	.931	9	*O-107	-0.1
1915	Cle-A	57	207	28	53	5	4	0	24	16		.256	.339	.319	95	-1	5	3	-0	.969	9	O-52	0.6
	Chi-A	36	74	10	17	1	0	0	11	15	11	.230	.360	.243	78	-1	1	3	-2	1.000	5	O-22	0.1
	Yr	93	281	38	70	6	4	0	15	39	27	.249	.345	.299	91	-2	6	6	-2	.978	14	O-74	0.7
1916	Chi-A	45	82	5	20	1	2	0	13	7	7	.244	.303	.305	82	-2	7			1.000	-0	*O-24	-0.8
1917	*Chi-A	125	428	59	101	12	6	0	29	74	34	.236	.350	.292	94	-0	27			.961	-1	*O-122	-0.8
1918	Chi-A	116	440	57	110	14	7	0	31	63	32	.250	.344	.314	97	0	13			.979	7	*O-114	0.2
1919	*Chi-A	122	434	81	131	18	2	0	26	72	30	.302	.404	.353	113	11	17			.928	7	*O-122	1.0
1920	Chi-A	108	413	61	91	16	3	1	28	55	30	.220	.316	.281	59	-23	7	15	-7	.977	6	*O-105	-3.2
1921	Bos-A	123	467	88	143	26	6	0	31	41	27	.306	.363	.388	94	-4	13	7	-0	.949	4	*O-117	-0.8
1922	Bos-A	81	271	42	70	8	1	1	18	41	14	.258	.360	.336	76	-8	5	6	-2	.966	6	O-71	-1.0
1923	Bos-A	12	18	1	2	0	0	0	0	1	2	.111	.158	.111	-28	-3	0	1	-1	.909	-3	O-10	-0.7
	Was-A	95	315	68	96	13	4	0	22	53	16	.305	.408	.381	114	9	7	6	-2	.980	1	O-84	0.3
	Yr	107	333	69	98	13	4	1	22	54	18	.294	.396	.356	106	7	7	7	-2	.977	-2	O-94	-0.4
1924	*Was-A	84	246	41	72	6	4	0	20	42	10	.293	.398	.350	97	5	7	5	-1	.994	-3	O-70	-0.6
1925	*Was-A	56	84	14	23	1	4	0	7	8	7	.274	.337	.310	66	-4	1	0	0	.972	-6	O-26/3-1	-1.0
Total	13	1268	4167	638	1109	145	49	3	284	571	335	.266	.357	.327	91	-30	134	60		.961	37	*O-1120/3-1	-7.8

■ ELMER LEIFER
Leifer, Elmer Edwin b: 5/23/1893, Clarington, Ohio d: 9/26/48, Everett, Wash. BL/TR, 5'9.5", 170 lbs. Deb: 9/7/21

YEAR	TM/L	G	AB	R	H	2B	3B	HR	RBI	BB	SO	AVG	OBP	SLG	PRO+	BR/A	SB	CS	SBR	FA	FR	G/POS	TPR
1921	Chi-A	9	10	0	3	0	0	0	4	1	1	.300	.300	.300	54	-1	0	0	0	1.000	-1	/3-1,O-1	-0.1

■ JOHN LEIGHTON
Leighton, John Atkinson b: 10/4/1861, Peabody, Mass. d: 10/31/56, Lynn, Mass. 5'11", 170 lbs. Deb: 7/12/1890

YEAR	TM/L	G	AB	R	H	2B	3B	HR	RBI	BB	SO	AVG	OBP	SLG	PRO+	BR/A	SB	CS	SBR	FA	FR	G/POS	TPR
1890	Syr-a	7	27	6	8	2	0	0		3		.296	.367	.370	131	1	2			.938	-0	/O-7	0.0

■ BILL LEINHAUSER
Leinhauser, William Charles b: 11/4/1893, Philadelphia, Pa. d: 4/14/78, Elkins Park, Pa. BR/TR, 5'10", 150 lbs. Deb: 5/18/12

YEAR	TM/L	G	AB	R	H	2B	3B	HR	RBI	BB	SO	AVG	OBP	SLG	PRO+	BR/A	SB	CS	SBR	FA	FR	G/POS	TPR
1912	Det-A	1	4	0	0	0	0	0	0	0	0	.000	.000	.000	-99	-1	0	0	0	1.000	0	/O-1	-0.1

■ ED LEIP
Leip, Edgar Ellsworth b: 11/29/10, Trenton, N.J. d: 11/24/83, Zephyrhills, Fla. BR/TR, 5'9", 160 lbs. Deb: 9/16/39

YEAR	TM/L	G	AB	R	H	2B	3B	HR	RBI	BB	SO	AVG	OBP	SLG	PRO+	BR/A	SB	CS	SBR	FA	FR	G/POS	TPR
1939	Was-A	9	32	4	11	1	0	0	2		4	.344	.382	.375	102	0	0	1	-1	.951	-1	/2-8	-0.1
1940	Pit-N	3	5	2	1	0	0	0	0		2	.200	.200	.200	11	-1	0	0	0	1.000	-0	/2-2	-0.1
1941	Pit-N	15	25	1	5	0	2	0	3	1	2	.200	.231	.360	65	-1	0	0	0	.889	2	/2-7,3-1	0.1
1942	Pit-N	3	0	0	0	0	0	0	0	0	0	—	—	—						.000	0	R	0.0
Total	4	30	62	7	17	1	2	0	5	3	6	.274	.308	.355	80	-2	0	1		.931	0	/2-17,3-1	-0.1

YEAR	TM/L	G	AB	R	H	2B	3B	HR	RBI	BB	SO	AVG	OBP	SLG	PRO+	BR/A	SB	CS	SBR	FA	FR	G/POS	TPR

■ SCOTT LEIUS Leius, Scott Thomas b: 9/24/65, Yonkers, N.Y. BR/TR, 6'3", 180 lbs. Deb: 9/3/90

1990	Min-A	14	25	4	6	1	0	1	4	2	2	.240	.296	.400	87	-0	0	0	0	1.000	3	S-12/3-1	0.3
1991	*Min-A	109	199	35	57	7	2	5	20	30	35	.286	.380	.417	115	5	5	5	-2	.953	-2	3-79,S-19/O-2	0.3
1992	Min-A	129	409	50	102	18	2	2	35	34	61	.249	.309	.318	73	-14	6	5	-1	.955	4	*3-125,S-10	-1.1
1993	Min-A	10	18	4	3	0	0	0	2	2	4	.167	.250	.167	14	-2	0	0	0	.947	1	/S-9	0.2
1994	Min-A	97	350	57	86	16	1	14	49	37	58	.246	.320	.417	88	-7	2	4	-2	.969	-1	3-95/S-2	-0.9
1995	Min-A	117	372	51	92	16	5	4	45	49	54	.247	.338	.349	79	-11	2	1	0	.945	-4	*3-112/S-7,D-3	-1.4
1996	Cle-A	27	43	3	6	4	0	1	3	2	8	.140	.178	.302	18	-6	0	0	0	1.000	0	/3-8,1-7,2-6,D-1	-0.5
Total	7	503	1416	204	352	62	10	27	158	156	222	.249	.325	.364	82	-35	15	15	-5	.956	5	3-420/S-59,1-7,2DO	-3.1

■ FRANK LEJA Leja, Frank John b: 2/7/36, Holyoke, Mass. d: 5/3/91, Boston, Mass. BL/TL, 6'4", 205 lbs. Deb: 5/1/54

1954	NY-A	12	5	2	1	0	0	0	0	1	1	.200	.200	.200	10	-1	0	0	0	1.000	0	/1-6	-0.1
1955	NY-A	7	2	1	0	0	0	0	0	0	1	.000	.000	.000	-99	-1	0	0	0	1.000	0	/1-2	-0.1
1962	LA-A	7	16	0	0	0	0	0	0	1	6	.000	.059	.000	-85	-4	0	0	0	.953	-0	/1-4	-0.5
Total	3	26	23	3	1	0	0	0	0	1	8	.043	.083	.043	-67	-5	0	0	0	.958	-0	/1-12	-0.7

■ LARRY LeJEUNE LeJeune, Sheldon Aldenbert b: 7/22/1885, Chicago, Ill. d: 4/21/52, Eloise, Mich. BR/TR, 6', 185 lbs. Deb: 5/10/11

1911	Bro-N	6	19	2	3	0	0	0	2	2	8	.158	.238	.158	12	-2	2			.818	-2	/O-6	-0.5
1915	Pit-N	18	65	4	11	0	1	0	2	2	7	.169	.206	.200	23	-6	4	3	-1	.940	2	O-18	-0.6
Total	2	24	84	6	14	0	1	0	4	4	15	.167	.213	.190	21	-8	6	3		.918	1	/O-24	-1.1

■ DON LeJOHN LeJohn, Donald Everett b: 5/13/34, Daisytown, Pa. BR/TR, 5'10", 175 lbs. Deb: 6/30/65

| 1965 | *LA-N | 34 | 78 | 2 | 20 | 2 | 0 | 0 | 7 | 5 | 13 | .256 | .301 | .282 | 70 | -3 | 0 | 1 | -1 | .959 | 1 | 3-26 | -0.4 |

■ JACK LELIVELT Lelivelt, John Frank b: 11/14/1885, Chicago, Ill. d: 1/20/41, Seattle, Wash. BL/TL, 5'11", 175 lbs. Deb: 6/24/09 F

1909	Was-A	91	318	25	93	8	6	0	24	19		.292	.334	.355	124	8	8			.970	8	O-91	1.4
1910	Was-A	110	347	40	92	10	3	0	33	40		.265	.343	.311	110	5	20			.964	4	O-86/1-7	0.6
1911	Was-A	72	225	29	72	12	4	0	22	22		.320	.386	.409	124	8	7			.939	4	O-49/1-7	0.8
1912	NY-A	36	149	12	54	6	7	2	23	4		.362	.383	.537	153	9	7			.963	-1	O-36	0.6
1913	NY-A	18	28	2	6	1	0	0	4	2	2	.214	.267	.286	61	-1	1			1.000	1	/O-5	-0.1
	Cle-A	23	23	0	9	2	0	0	7	0	3	.391	.391	.478	150	1	1			.000	-1	/O-1	0.1
	Yr	41	51	2	15	3	0	0	11	2	5	.294	.321	.373	101	-0	2			1.000	1	/O-6	0.0
1914	Cle-A	34	64	6	21	5	1	0	13	2	10	.328	.348	.438	131	2	3	2	-1	.933	-3	O-13/1-1	-0.3
Total	6	384	1154	114	347	43	22	2	126	89	15	.301	.353	.381	124	31	46	3		.962	13	O-281/1-15	3.1

■ JOHNNIE LeMASTER LeMaster, Johnnie Lee b: 6/19/54, Portsmouth, Ohio BR/TR, 6'2", 167 lbs. Deb: 9/2/75

1975	SF-N	22	74	4	14	4	0	2	9	4	15	.189	.241	.324	53	-5	2	1	0	.967	-1	S-22	-0.4
1976	SF-N	33	100	9	21	3	2	0	9	2	21	.210	.225	.280	42	-8	2	0	1	.937	11	S-31	0.7
1977	SF-N	68	134	13	20	5	1	0	8	13	27	.149	.224	.201	15	-16	2	1	0	.934	7	S-54/3-2	-0.5
1978	SF-N	101	272	23	64	18	3	1	14	21	45	.235	.293	.335	78	-9	6	6	-2	.966	2	S-96/2-2	0.2
1979	SF-N	108	343	42	87	11	2	3	29	25	55	.254	.304	.324	77	-12	9	5	-0	.959	0	*S-106	-0.1
1980	SF-N	135	405	33	87	16	6	3	31	25	57	.215	.260	.306	59	-23	0	1	-1	.957	-14	*S-134	-2.5
1981	SF-N	104	324	27	82	9	1	0	28	24	46	.253	.307	.287	70	-12	3	7	-3	.964	-8	*S-103	-1.5
1982	SF-N	130	436	34	94	14	1	2	30	31	78	.216	.268	.266	50	-29	13	4	2	.963	-8	*S-130	-2.5
1983	SF-N	141	534	81	128	16	1	6	30	60	96	.240	.319	.307	77	-16	39	19	0	.964	-22	*S-139	-2.6
1984	SF-N	132	451	46	98	13	2	4	32	31	97	.217	.268	.282	56	-27	17	5	2	.964	4	*S-129	-0.9
1985	SF-N	12	16	1	0	0	0	0	0	0	5	.000	.059	.000	-86	-4	0	0	0	.955	-1	S-10	-0.5
	Cle-A	11	20	0	3	0	0	0	2	0	6	.150	.150	.150	-18	-3	0	1	0	.949	-5	S-10	0.0
	Pit-N	22	58	4	9	0	0	0	5	6	12	.155	.222	.207	21	-6	1	0	0	.983	13	S-21	0.9
1987	Oak-A	20	24	3	2	0	0	0	1	1	4	.083	.120	.083	-48	-5	0	1	-1	1.000	5	/3-8,S-7,2-5,D-1	0.0
Total	12	1039	3191	320	709	109	19	22	229	241	564	.222	.278	.289	60	-174	94	51	-2	.961	-9	S-992/3-10,2-7,D-1	-9.7

■ STEVE LEMBO Lembo, Stephen Neal b: 11/13/26, Brooklyn, N.Y. d: 12/4/89, Flushing, N.Y. BR/TR, 6'1", 185 lbs. Deb: 9/16/50

1950	Bro-N	5	6	0	1	0	0	0	0	1	0	.167	.286	.167	22	-1	0			1.000	2	/C-5	0.2
1952	Bro-N	2	5	0	1	0	0	0	1	0	1	.200	.200	.200	11	-1	0	0	0	1.000	0	/C-2	0.0
Total	2	7	11	0	2	0	0	0	1	1	1	.182	.250	.182	18	-1	0	0	0	1.000	3	/C-7	0.2

■ MARK LEMKE Lemke, Mark Alan b: 8/13/65, Utica, N.Y. BB/TR, 5'10", 167 lbs. Deb: 9/17/88

1988	Atl-N	16	58	4	13	4	0	0	2	4	5	.224	.274	.293	60	-3	0	2	-1	.970	4	2-16	0.1
1989	Atl-N	14	55	4	10	2	1	2	10	5	7	.182	.250	.364	72	-2	0	1	-1	1.000	-2	2-14	-0.4
1990	Atl-N	102	239	22	54	13	0	0	21	21	22	.226	.288	.280	54	-15	0	1	-1	.989	23	3-45,2-44/S-1	0.9
1991	*Atl-N	136	269	36	63	11	2	2	23	29	27	.234	.309	.312	71	-10	1	2	-1	.978	13	*2-110,3-15	0.4
1992	*Atl-N	155	427	38	97	7	4	6	26	50	39	.227	.308	.304	70	-16	0	3	-2	.984	-10	*2-145	-2.7
1993	*Atl-N	151	493	52	124	19	2	7	49	65	50	.252	.339	.341	82	-11	1	2	-1	.982	6	*2-150	-0.2
1994	Atl-N	104	350	40	103	15	0	3	31	38	37	.294	.363	.363	88	-5	0	3	-2	.994	7	*2-103	0.5
1995	*Atl-N	116	399	42	101	16	5	5	38	44	40	.253	.327	.356	78	-12	2	2	-1	.990	-11	*2-115	-1.6
1996	*Atl-N	135	498	64	127	17	0	5	37	53	48	.255	.327	.319	68	-22	5	2	0	.977	7	*2-133	-0.7
Total	9	929	2788	306	692	104	14	30	237	309	275	.248	.323	.328	74	-97	9	18	-8	.984	38	2-830/3-73,S-1	-3.7

■ CHET LEMON Lemon, Chester Earl b: 2/12/55, Jackson, Miss. BR/TR, 6', 195 lbs. Deb: 9/9/75

1975	Chi-A	9	35	2	9	2	0	0	1	2	6	.257	.297	.314	72	-1	1	0	0	.923	-4	/3-6,O-1,D-2	-0.5
1976	Chi-A	132	451	46	111	15	5	4	38	28	65	.246	.300	.328	83	-0	13	7	-0	.992	11	*O-131	-0.4
1977	Chi-A	150	553	99	151	38	4	19	67	52	88	.273	.347	.459	118	13	8	7	-2	.978	35	*O-149	4.0
1978	Chi-A★	105	357	51	107	24	6	13	55	39	46	.300	.381	.510	147	22	5	9	-4	.983	14	*O-95,D-10	2.8
1979	Chi-A★	148	556	79	177	44	2	17	86	56	68	.318	.394	.496	138	31	7	11	-5	.977	9	*O-147/D-1	2.8
1980	Chi-A	147	514	76	150	32	6	11	51	71	56	.292	.390	.442	128	22	6	6	-2	.981	2	*O-139/2-1,D-6	1.6
1981	Chi-A	94	328	50	99	23	6	9	50	33	49	.302	.388	.491	155	24	5	8	-3	.984	2	O-93	2.0
1982	Det-A	125	436	75	116	20	1	19	52	56	69	.266	.369	.447	122	15	1	4	-2	.984	1	*O-121/D-1	1.0
1983	Det-A	145	491	78	125	21	5	24	69	54	70	.255	.352	.464	126	18	0	7	-4	.988	11	*O-145	2.0
1984	*Det-A★	141	509	77	146	34	6	20	76	51	83	.287	.360	.495	135	24	5	5	-2	.995	16	*O-140/D-1	3.3
1985	Det-A	145	517	69	137	28	4	18	68	45	93	.265	.336	.439	111	7	0	2	-1	.990	11	*O-144	1.2
1986	Det-A	126	403	45	101	21	3	12	53	39	53	.251	.329	.407	99	-0	2	1	0	.985	2	*O-124	-0.1
1987	*Det-A	146	470	75	130	30	3	20	75	70	82	.277	.362	.481	132	23	0	0	0	.992	5	*O-145	2.0
1988	Det-A	144	512	67	135	29	4	17	64	59	65	.264	.348	.436	123	16	1	2	-1	.974	4	*O-144	1.5
1989	Det-A	127	414	45	98	19	2	7	47	46	71	.237	.325	.343	90	-7	0	5	-3	.985	-6	*O-111,D-13	-1.7
1990	Det-A	104	322	39	83	16	4	5	32	48	61	.258	.361	.379	106	4	3	2	-0	.973	6	O-96/D-6	0.8
Total	16	1988	6868	973	1875	396	61	215	884	749	1024	.273	.357	.442	121	203	58	76	-28	.984	116	*O-1925/D-40,3-6,2	22.3

■ JIM LEMON Lemon, James Robert b: 3/23/28, Covington, Va. BR/TR, 6'4", 200 lbs. Deb: 8/20/50 MC

1950	Cle-A	12	34	4	6	1	0	1	3	2	15	.176	.243	.294	38	-3	0	0	0	.824	-2	O-10	-0.5
1953	Cle-A	16	46	5	8	1	0	1	5	3	15	.174	.224	.261	32	-5	0	0	0	.913	-1	O-11/1-2	-0.6
1954	Was-A	37	128	12	30	2	3	2	13	9	34	.234	.285	.344	76	-5	0	0	0	.951	-3	O-33	-1.0
1955	Was-A	10	25	3	5	2	0	0	3	3	4	.200	.286	.400	88	-1	0	0	0	.923	-0	/O-6	-0.1
1956	Was-A	146	538	77	146	21	11	27	96	65	138	.271	.352	.502	123	16	2	4	-2	.963	8	*O-141	1.4
1957	Was-A	137	518	58	147	23	6	17	64	49	94	.284	.349	.450	118	12	1	7	-4	.971	-3	*O-131/1-3	-0.3
1958	Was-A	142	501	65	123	15	9	26	75	50	120	.246	.315	.467	114	8	2	2	-1	.978	0	*O-137	0.1
1959	Was-A	147	531	73	148	18	3	33	100	46	99	.279	.337	.510	130	20	5	5	-0	.969	-3	*O-142	-1.6
1960	Was-A★	148	528	81	142	10	1	38	100	64	114	.269	.359	.568	133	23	0	1	0	.960	-1	*O-145	1.6
1961	Min-A	129	423	57	109	26	1	14	52	44	98	.258	.333	.423	95	-3	1	2	-1	.940	-6	*O-120/1-6	-1.6
1962	Min-A	12	17	1	3	0	0	0	1	5	4	.176	.300	.353	72	-1	0	0	0	1.000	-6	/O-3	-0.2
1963	Min-A	7	17	0	2	0	0	0	1	1	5	.118	.167	.118	-18	-3	0	0	0	.800	-1	/O-4	-0.4

YEAR TM/L	G	AB	R	H	2B	3B	HR	RBI	BB	SO	AVG	OBP	SLG	PRO+	BR/A	SB	CS	SBR	FA	FR	G/POS	TPR
Phi-N	31	59	6	16	2	0	2	6	8	18	.271	.358	.407	121	2	0	0	0	.963	-2	O-18	0.0
Chi-A	36	80	4	16	0	1	1	8	12	32	.200	.304	.262	62	-4	0	0	0	.979	-3	1-25	-0.8
Total 12	1010	3445	446	901	121	35	164	529	363	787	.262	.335	.460	114	57	13	18	-7	.961	-12	O-901/1-30	-1.0

■ **BOB LEMON**   Lemon, Robert Granville b: 9/22/20, San Bernardino, Cal.   BL/TR, 6', 185 lbs.   Deb: 9/9/41   MCH

YEAR TM/L	G	AB	R	H	2B	3B	HR	RBI	BB	SO	AVG	OBP	SLG	PRO+	BR/A	SB	CS	SBR	FA	FR	G/POS	TPR
1941 Cle-A	5	4	0	1	0	0	0	0	0	1	.250	.250	.250	34	-0	0	0	0	1.000	0	/3-1	0.0
1942 Cle-A	5	5	0	0	0	0	0	0	0	3	.000	.000	.000	-99	-1	0	0	0	.500	0	/3-1	-0.1
1946 Cle-A	55	89	9	16	3	0	0	4	7	18	.180	.240	.247	39	-8	0	1	-1	.976	6	P-32,O-12	-0.3
1947 Cle-A	47	56	11	18	4	3	2	5	6	9	.321	.387	.607	179	5	0	0	0	.983	4	P-37/O-2	-0.1
1948 *Cle-A☆	52	119	20	34	9	0	5	21	8	23	.286	.331	.487	119	2	0	0	0	.965	8	P-43	0.0
1949 Cle-A☆	46	108	17	29	6	2	7	19	10	20	.269	.331	.556	135	4	0	0	0	.963	6	P-37	0.0
1950 Cle-A★	72	136	21	37	9	1	6	26	13	25	.272	.340	.485	113	2	0	0	0	.957	5	P-44	0.0
1951 Cle-A★	56	102	11	21	4	1	3	13	9	22	.206	.270	.353	72	-5	0	0	0	.976	4	P-42	0.0
1952 Cle-A★	54	124	14	28	5	0	2	9	4	21	.226	.250	.315	60	-7	0	0	0	.982	7	P-41	0.0
1953 Cle-A☆	51	112	12	26	9	1	2	17	7	20	.232	.277	.384	79	-4	2	0	1	.972	8	P-42	0.0
1954 *Cle-A★	40	98	11	21	4	1	2	10	6	24	.214	.260	.337	61	-6	0	0	0	.963	4	P-36	0.0
1955 Cle-A	49	78	11	19	0	0	1	9	13	16	.244	.352	.282	69	-3	0	0	0	.983	2	P-35	0.0
1956 Cle-A	43	93	8	18	0	0	5	12	9	21	.194	.232	.355	63	-5	0	0	0	.934	4	P-39	0.0
1957 Cle-A	25	46	2	3	1	0	1	1	0	14	.065	.065	.152	-43	-9	0	0	0	1.000	3	P-21	0.0
1958 Cle-A	15	13	1	3	0	0	0	1	1	4	.231	.286	.231	45	-1	0	0	0	1.000	1	P-11	0.0
Total 15	615	1183	148	274	54	9	37	147	93	241	.232	.289	.386	82	-36	2	1	0	.969	62	P-460/O-14,3-2	-0.5

■ **DON LENHARDT**   Lenhardt, Donald Eugene "Footsie" b: 10/4/22, Alton, Ill.   BR/TR, 6'3", 190 lbs.   Deb: 4/18/50   C

YEAR TM/L	G	AB	R	H	2B	3B	HR	RBI	BB	SO	AVG	OBP	SLG	PRO+	BR/A	SB	CS	SBR	FA	FR	G/POS	TPR
1950 StL-A	139	480	75	131	22	6	22	81	90	94	.273	.390	.481	118	13	3	2	-0	.988	-12	1-86,O-39,3-10	-0.2
1951 StL-A	31	103	9	27	3	0	5	18	6	13	.262	.303	.437	95	-1	1	0	0	.982	-2	O-27/1-1	-0.4
Chi-A	64	199	23	53	9	1	10	45	24	25	.266	.351	.472	124	6	1	1	-0	.983	-2	O-53/1-2	0.2
Yr	95	302	32	80	12	1	15	63	30	38	.265	.335	.460	114	5	2	1	-0	.983	-4	O-80/1-3	-0.2
1952 Bos-A	30	105	18	31	4	0	7	24	15	18	.295	.383	.533	142	6	0	1	-1	.981	-2	O-27	0.2
Det-A	45	144	18	27	2	1	3	13	28	18	.188	.320	.278	67	-6	0	1	-1	.989	3	O-43	-0.5
StL-A	18	48	5	13	4	1	1	5	4	8	.271	.327	.458	114	1	0	0	0	1.000	0	O-11/1-2	0.2
Yr	93	297	41	71	10	2	11	42	47	44	.239	.343	.397	102	1	0	2	-1	.988	2	O-81/1-2	-0.3
1953 StL-A	97	303	37	96	15	0	10	35	41	41	.317	.400	.465	131	14	1	2	-1	.969	2	O-77/3-6	1.2
1954 Bal-A	13	33	2	5	1	0	0	1	3	9	.152	.222	.182	12	-4	0	0	0	1.000	0	/O-7,1-2	-0.5
Bos-A	44	66	5	18	4	0	3	17	3	9	.273	.314	.470	101	-0	0	1	0	1.000	-3	O-13/3-1	-0.4
Yr	57	99	7	23	5	0	3	18	6	18	.232	.283	.374	74	-4	0	1	0	1.000	-9	O-20/1-2,3-1	-0.9
Total 5	481	1481	192	401	64	9	61	239	214	235	.271	.365	.450	114	28	6	7	-2	.980	-15	O-297/1-93,3-17	-0.4

■ **PATRICK LENNON**   Lennon, Patrick Orlando b: 4/27/68, Whiteville, N.C.   BR/TR, 6'2", 200 lbs.   Deb: 9/15/91

YEAR TM/L	G	AB	R	H	2B	3B	HR	RBI	BB	SO	AVG	OBP	SLG	PRO+	BR/A	SB	CS	SBR	FA	FR	G/POS	TPR
1991 Sea-A	9	8	2	1	1	0	0	3	1	1	.125	.364	.250	73	-0	0	0	0	1.000	0	/O-1,D-5	0.0
1992 Sea-A	1	2	0	0	0	0	0	0	0	0	.000	.000	.000	-99	-1	0	0	0	1.000	-0	/1-1	-0.1
1996 KC-A	14	30	5	7	3	0	0	1	7	10	.233	.378	.333	84	-0	0	0	0	.947	-1	O-11/D-1	-0.2
Total 3	24	40	7	8	4	0	0	2	10	11	.200	.360	.300	74	-1	0	0	0	.952	-1	/O-12,D-6,1-1	-0.3

■ **BOB LENNON**   Lennon, Robert Albert "Arch" b: 9/15/28, Brooklyn, N.Y.   BL/TL, 6', 200 lbs.   Deb: 9/9/54

YEAR TM/L	G	AB	R	H	2B	3B	HR	RBI	BB	SO	AVG	OBP	SLG	PRO+	BR/A	SB	CS	SBR	FA	FR	G/POS	TPR
1954 NY-N	3	3	0	0	0	0	0	0	0	0	.000	.000	.000	-99	-1	0	0	0	.000	0	H	-0.1
1956 NY-N	26	55	3	10	1	0	1	4	4	17	.182	.237	.200	19	-6	0	0	0	.885	-4	O-21	-1.2
1957 Chi-N	9	21	2	3	1	0	1	3	1	9	.143	.182	.333	35	-2	0	0	0	1.000	-1	/O-4	-0.4
Total 3	38	79	5	13	2	0	1	4	5	26	.165	.214	.228	19	-9	0	0	0	.900	-6	/O-25	-1.7

■ **BILL LENNON**   Lennon, William F. b: 1848, Brooklyn, N.Y.   5'7", 145 lbs.   Deb: 5/4/1871   MU

YEAR TM/L	G	AB	R	H	2B	3B	HR	RBI	BB	SO	AVG	OBP	SLG	PRO+	BR/A	SB	CS	SBR	FA	FR	G/POS	TPR
1871 Kek-n	12	48	5	11	3	0	0	5	1	0	.229	.245	.292	52	-3	1	0	0	.887	-2	C-12/S-2,O-1,M	-0.3
1872 Nat-n	11	54	11	12	1	0	0	6	0	0	.222	.222	.241	36	-5	0	0	0	.765	-5	C-11/1-1	-0.7
1873 Mar-n	5	19	2	4	0	0	0	2	0	0	.211	.211	.211	33	-1	0	0	0	.942	-1	/1-4,C-1,3-1	-0.2
Total 3 n	28	121	18	27	4	0	0	13	1	0	.223	.230	.256	42	-9	1	0	0	.817	-9	/C-24,1-5,S-2,3O	-1.2

■ **ED LENNOX**   Lennox, James Edgar "Eggie" b: 11/3/1885, Camden, N.J.   d: 10/26/39, Camden, N.J.   BR/TR, 5'10", 174 lbs.   Deb: 8/8/06

YEAR TM/L	G	AB	R	H	2B	3B	HR	RBI	BB	SO	AVG	OBP	SLG	PRO+	BR/A	SB	CS	SBR	FA	FR	G/POS	TPR
1906 Phi-A	6	17	1	1	0	0	0	1			.059	.111	.118	-28	-2	0		0	.909	5	/3-6	0.3
1909 Bro-N	126	435	33	114	18	9	2	44	47		.262	.337	.359	120	10	11			.959	-4	*3-121	1.2
1910 Bro-N	110	367	19	95	19	4	3	32	36	39	.259	.333	.357	104	2	2	7		.950	-16	*3-100	-1.2
1912 Chi-N	27	81	13	19	4	1	1	16	12	10	.235	.347	.346	90	-1	1			.934	-5	3-24	-0.6
1914 Pit-F	124	430	71	134	25	10	11	84	71	38	.312	.414	.493	148	24	19			.954	-15	*3-123	1.3
1915 Pit-F	55	53	2	16	3	1	1	9	7	12	.302	.383	.453	136	2	0			1.000	2	/3-3	0.5
Total 6	448	1383	138	379	70	25	18	185	174	99	.274	.361	.400	122	34	38			.953	-32	3-377	1.5

■ **JIM LENTINE**   Lentine, James Matthew b: 7/16/54, Los Angeles, Cal.   BR/TR, 6', 175 lbs.   Deb: 9/3/78

YEAR TM/L	G	AB	R	H	2B	3B	HR	RBI	BB	SO	AVG	OBP	SLG	PRO+	BR/A	SB	CS	SBR	FA	FR	G/POS	TPR
1978 StL-N	8	11	1	2	0	0	0	1	0	0	.182	.250	.182	23	-1	1	0	0	1.000	-0	/O-3	-0.1
1979 StL-N	11	23	2	9	1	0	0		3	6	.391	.462	.435	145	2	0	1	-1	1.000	-0	/O-8	0.1
1980 StL-N	9	10	1	1	0	0	0	1	0	0	.100	.100	.100	-43	-2	0	0	0	1.000	-0	/O-6	-0.4
Det-A	67	161	19	42	8	1	1	17	28	30	.261	.377	.342	96	0	2	1	0	.963	-3	O-55/D-9	
Total 3	95	205	23	54	9	1	1	20	31	38	.263	.368	.332	92	-1	3	2	-0	.969	-5	/O-72,D-9	-0.4

■ **EDDIE LEON**   Leon, Eduardo Antonio b: 8/11/46, Tucson, Ariz.   BR/TR, 6', 175 lbs.   Deb: 9/9/68

YEAR TM/L	G	AB	R	H	2B	3B	HR	RBI	BB	SO	AVG	OBP	SLG	PRO+	BR/A	SB	CS	SBR	FA	FR	G/POS	TPR
1968 Cle-A	6	1	0	0	0	0	0	0	0	0	.000	.000	.000	-99	-0	0	0	0	1.000	3	/S-6	0.3
1969 Cle-A	64	213	20	51	6	0	9	19	19	37	.239	.302	.310	69	-9	2	2	-1	.952	9	S-64	0.6
1970 Cle-A	152	549	58	136	20	4	10	56	47	89	.248	.309	.353	78	-16	1	2	-1	.982	8	*2-141,S-23/3-1	0.5
1971 Cle-A	131	429	35	112	12	2	4	35	34	69	.261	.317	.326	76	-13	3	5	-2	.983	1	*2-107,S-24	-0.4
1972 Cle-A	89	225	14	45	2	1	4	16	20	47	.200	.268	.271	59	-11	0	1	-1	.993	-1	2-36,S-35	-0.8
1973 Chi-A	127	399	37	91	10	3	3	30	34	103	.228	.294	.291	63	-19	1	5	-3	.972	-2	*S-122/2-3	-0.9
1974 Chi-A	31	46	1	5	1	0	0	3	0	12	.109	.146	.130	-20	-7	0	0	0	.962	-2	S-21/2-7,3-2,D-1	0.3
1975 NY-A	1	0	0	0	0	0	0	0	0	0	—	—	—			0	0	0	.000	0	/S-1	
Total 8	601	1862	165	440	51	10	24	159	156	358	.236	.298	.313	69	-76	8	16	-8	.963	25	S-296,2-294/3-3,D-1	-0.4

■ **LEONARD**   Leonard   Deb: 9/12/1892

YEAR TM/L	G	AB	R	H	2B	3B	HR	RBI	BB	SO	AVG	OBP	SLG	PRO+	BR/A	SB	CS	SBR	FA	FR	G/POS	TPR
1892 StL-N	1	0	0	0	0	0	0	0	1	0	—	1.000	—	219	0		1		.000	-0	/O-1	0.0

■ **ANDY LEONARD**   Leonard, Andrew Jackson b: 6/1/1846, County Cavan, Ireland   d: 8/21/03, Boston, Mass.   BR/TR, 5'7", 168 lbs.   Deb: 5/5/1871

YEAR TM/L	G	AB	R	H	2B	3B	HR	RBI	BB	SO	AVG	OBP	SLG	PRO+	BR/A	SB	CS	SBR	FA	FR	G/POS	TPR
1871 Oly-n	31	148	33	43	8	3	0	30	3	1	.291	.305	.385	102	1	14	3	2	.863	-2	2-19,O-11/S-1	0.0
1872 Bos-n	46	240	57	84	7	1	2	43	0	2	.350	.350	.412	127	6	8	5	-1	.828	-4	*O-38/3-6,2-4,S-1	0.1
1873 Bos-n	58	302	81	95	12	7	0	61	4	0	.315	.324	.401	105	-1	5	6	-2	.714	-1	*O-45,2-12/1-2,S-1	-0.2
1874 Bos-n	71	339	68	108	18	4	0	51	2	2	.319	.323	.395	122	6	11	3	1	.807	1	*O-51,2-11,S-11	0.7
1875 Bos-n	80	396	87	127	14	6	1	74	2	6	.321	.344	.394	143	15	14	8	-1	.806	-9	*O-73/S-3,3-3,2-2	1.2
1876 Bos-N	64	303	53	85	10	2	0	27	5	10	.281	.290	.327	103	1				.925	-1	O-35,2-30	-0.8
1877 Bos-N	58	272	46	78	5	0	0	27	5		.287	.300	.305	88	-4				.875	-4	*O-60	-1.3
1878 Bos-N	60	262	41	68	8	5	0	26	8	11	.260	.268	.328	88	-4				.777	-7	*O-60	-1.3
1880 Cin-N	33	133	15	28	3	0	0	17	8	11	.211	.255	.256	75	-3				.833	-12	S-23,3-10	-1.3
Total 5 n	286	1425	326	457	59	21	3	259	11	11	.321	.326	.398	122	28	52	25	1	.778	-7	O-218/2-48,S-17,31	1.8
Total 4	215	970	155	259	26	7	1	87	20	41	.267	.282	.311	91	-11				.856	-23	O-132/S-44,2-30,3	-3.4

■ **JEFFREY LEONARD**   Leonard, Jeffrey b: 9/22/55, Philadelphia, Pa.   BR/TR, 6'2", 200 lbs.   Deb: 9/2/77

YEAR TM/L	G	AB	R	H	2B	3B	HR	RBI	BB	SO	AVG	OBP	SLG	PRO+	BR/A	SB	CS	SBR	FA	FR	G/POS	TPR
1977 LA-N	11	10	1	3	0	1	0	2	1	4	.300	.364	.300	130	-1	0	0	0	1.000	-2	O-10	-0.2
1978 Hou-N	8	26	2	10	2	0	0	4	1	2	.385	.407	.462	154	2	2	0	1	1.000	1	/O-8	0.2
1979 Hou-N	134	411	47	119	15	5	0	47	46	68	.290	.364	.350	102	2	23	10	1	.959	-7	*O-123	-0.8

YEAR	TM/L	G	AB	R	H	2B	3B	HR	RBI	BB	SO	AVG	OBP	SLG	PRO+	BR/A	SB	CS	SBR	FA	FR	G/POS	TPR
1980	*Hou-N	88	216	29	46	7	5	3	20	19	46	.213	.277	.333	75	-8	4	1	1	.979	-2	O-56,1-11	-1.3
1981	Hou-N	7	18	1	3	1	1	0	3	0	4	.167	.167	.333	41	-2	1	0	0	1.000	-0	/1-2,O-2	-0.2
	SF-N	37	127	20	39	11	3	4	26	12	21	.307	.371	.535	158	9	4	2	0	1.000	2	O-28/1-5	1.1
	Yr	44	145	21	42	12	4	4	29	12	25	.290	.348	.510	145	8	5	2	0	1.000	2	O-30/1-7	0.9
1982	SF-N	80	278	32	72	16	1	9	49	19	65	.259	.311	.421	103	1	18	5	2	.958	-5	O-74/1-1	-0.4
1983	SF-N	139	516	74	144	17	7	21	87	35	116	.259	.326	.461	120	11	26	7	4	.975	8	*O-136	1.9
1984	SF-N	136	514	76	155	27	4	21	86	47	123	.302	.360	.484	140	26	17	7	1	.970	6	*O-131	3.0
1985	SF-N	133	507	49	122	20	3	17	62	21	107	.241	.272	.393	88	-11	11	6	-0	.977	3	*O-126	-1.3
1986	SF-N	89	341	48	95	11	3	6	42	20	62	.279	.324	.381	99	-1	16	3	3	.970	3	O-87	0.2
1987	*SF-N★	131	503	70	141	29	4	19	63	21	68	.280	.312	.467	108	3	16	7	1	.966	-4	*O-127	-0.4
1988	SF-N	44	160	12	41	8	1	2	20	9	24	.256	.296	.356	90	-2	7	5	-1	.987	-6	O-43	-0.8
	Mil-A	94	374	45	88	19	0	8	44	16	62	.235	.272	.350	72	-14	10	4	1	.985	3	O-91/D-2	-1.4
1989	Sea-A★	150	566	69	144	20	1	24	93	38	125	.254	.307	.420	100	-2	6	1	1	.982	-7	*D-123,O-26	-0.3
1990	Sea-A	134	478	39	120	20	0	10	75	37	97	.251	.309	.356	84	-10	4	2	0	.983	-8	O-79,D-48	-2.2
Total	14	1415	5045	614	1342	223	37	144	723	342	1000	.266	.316	.411	103	3	163	61	12	.974	-3	*O-1147,D-173/1-19	-2.9

■ JOE LEONARD
Leonard, Joseph Howard b: 11/15/1894, W.Chicago, Ill. d: 5/1/20, Washington, D.C. BL/TR, 5'7.5", 156 lbs. Deb: 5/7/14

YEAR	TM/L	G	AB	R	H	2B	3B	HR	RBI	BB	SO	AVG	OBP	SLG	PRO+	BR/A	SB	CS	SBR	FA	FR	G/POS	TPR
1914	Pit-N	53	126	17	25	2	2	0	4	12	21	.198	.268	.246	56	-7	4			.909	-8	3-38/S-1	-1.5
1916	Cle-A	3	3	1	0	0	0	0	0	0	1	.000	.000	.000	-94	-0	0			1.000	0	/2-1	0.0
	Was-A	42	168	20	46	7	0	0	14	22	23	.274	.358	.315	103	1	4			.952	-8	3-42	-0.5
	Yr	45	170	21	46	7	0	0	14	22	24	.271	.354	.312	101	1	4			.952	-7	3-42/2-1	-0.5
1917	Was-A	99	297	30	57	6	7	0	23	45	40	.192	.302	.259	72	-9	6			.925	-2	3-68,1-19/S-1,O-1	-1.2
1919	Was-A	71	198	26	51	8	3	2	20	20	28	.258	.329	.359	94	-2	3			.944	-9	2-28,3-25/1-4,O-1	-1.0
1920	Was-A	1	0	0	0	0	0	0	0	0	0	—	—	—	—	0	0	0	0	.000	0	R	0.0
Total	5	269	791	94	179	23	12	2	61	99	113	.226	.315	.293	82	-16	17	0		.937	-27	3-173/2-29,1-23,OS	-4.2

■ MARK LEONARD
Leonard, Mark David b: 8/14/64, Mountain View, Cal. BL/TR, 6'1", 195 lbs. Deb: 7/21/90

YEAR	TM/L	G	AB	R	H	2B	3B	HR	RBI	BB	SO	AVG	OBP	SLG	PRO+	BR/A	SB	CS	SBR	FA	FR	G/POS	TPR
1990	SF-N	11	17	3	3	1	0	1	2	3	8	.176	.300	.412	97	-0	0	0	0	1.000	-1	/O-7	-0.1
1991	SF-N	64	129	14	31	7	1	2	14	12	25	.240	.310	.357	90	-2	0	1	-1	1.000	-6	O-34	-0.9
1992	SF-N	55	128	13	30	7	0	4	16	16	31	.234	.333	.383	108	2	0	1	-1	.984	0	O-37	0.1
1993	Bal-A	10	15	1	1	0	0	0	3	3	7	.067	.222	.133	-2	-2	0	0	0	.833	-1	/O-4,D-3	-0.3
1994	SF-N	14	11	2	4	1	0	2	3	2	2	.364	.500	.636	203	2	0	0	0	1.000	-1	/O-2	0.1
1995	SF-N	14	21	4	4	1	1	0	4	5	2	.190	.346	.381	94	-0	0	0	0	1.000	-1	/O-6	-0.1
Total	6	168	321	37	73	18	2	8	41	42	75	.227	.324	.371	97	-1	0	2	-1	.985	-9	/O-90,D-3	-1.2

■ JOHN LEOVICH
Leovich, John Joseph b: 5/5/18, Portland, Ore. BR/TR, 6'0.5", 200 lbs. Deb: 5/1/41

YEAR	TM/L	G	AB	R	H	2B	3B	HR	RBI	BB	SO	AVG	OBP	SLG	PRO+	BR/A	SB	CS	SBR	FA	FR	G/POS	TPR
1941	Phi-A	1	2	0	1	1	0	0	0	0	0	.500	.500	1.000	296	1	0	0	0	.000	-0	/C-1	0.0

■ TED LEPCIO
Lepcio, Thaddeus Stanley b: 7/28/30, Utica, N.Y. BR/TR, 5'10", 177 lbs. Deb: 4/15/52

YEAR	TM/L	G	AB	R	H	2B	3B	HR	RBI	BB	SO	AVG	OBP	SLG	PRO+	BR/A	SB	CS	SBR	FA	FR	G/POS	TPR
1952	Bos-A	84	274	34	72	17	2	5	26	24	41	.263	.329	.394	93	-3	3	3	-1	.972	8	2-57,3-25/S-1	0.6
1953	Bos-A	66	161	17	38	4	2	4	11	17	24	.236	.313	.360	77	-5	0	0	0	.981	17	2-34,S-20,3-11	1.4
1954	Bos-A	116	398	42	102	19	4	11	45	42	62	.256	.332	.384	86	-8	3	4	-2	.971	16	2-80,3-24,S-14	1.2
1955	Bos-A	51	134	19	31	9	0	6	15	12	36	.231	.313	.433	91	-2	1	1	-0	.943	6	3-45	0.3
1956	Bos-A	83	284	34	74	10	0	15	51	30	77	.261	.348	.454	96	-3	1	3	-2	.966	7	2-57,3-22	0.8
1957	Bos-A	79	232	24	56	10	2	9	37	29	61	.241	.328	.418	97	-1	0	0	0	.976	9	2-68	1.3
1958	Bos-A	50	136	10	27	3	0	6	14	12	47	.199	.266	.353	65	-7	0	1	-1	.980	-3	2-40	-0.8
1959	Bos-A	3	3	1	1	1	0	0	0	1	0	.333	.333	.667	160	0	0	0	0	1.000	0	/2-1	0.0
	Det-A	76	215	25	60	8	0	7	24	17	49	.279	.332	.414	98	-1	2	0	1	.951	-6	S-35,2-24,3-11	-0.2
	Yr	79	218	26	61	9	0	7	25	17	51	.280	.332	.417	99	-1	2	0	1	.951	-6	S-35,2-25,3-11	-0.2
1960	Phi-N	69	141	16	32	7	0	2	8	17	41	.227	.319	.319	75	-4	0	3	-2	.942	-5	3-50,S-14/2-5	-1.1
1961	Chi-A	5	2	0	0	0	0	0	0	0	2	.000	.333	.000	-2	-0	0	0	0	.000	-0	/3-1	0.0
	Min-A	47	112	11	19	3	1	7	19	9	31	.170	.231	.402	62	-7	1	0	0	.919	2	3-35,2-22/S-6	-0.3
	Yr	52	114	11	19	3	1	7	19	9	33	.167	.234	.395	62	-7	1	0	0	.895	2	3-36,2-22/S-6	-0.3
Total	10	729	2092	233	512	91	11	69	251	209	471	.245	.319	.398	87	-41	11	15	-6	.972	51	2-388,3-224/S-90	3.2

■ PETE LePINE
LePine, Louis Joseph b: 9/5/1876, Montreal, Que., Can d: 12/3/49, Woonsocket, R.I. BL/TL, 5'10", 142 lbs. Deb: 7/21/02

YEAR	TM/L	G	AB	R	H	2B	3B	HR	RBI	BB	SO	AVG	OBP	SLG	PRO+	BR/A	SB	CS	SBR	FA	FR	G/POS	TPR
1902	Det-A	30	96	8	20	3	2	1	19	8		.208	.276	.313	62	-5	1			1.000	-2	O-19/1-8	-0.7

■ DON LEPPERT
Leppert, Don Eugene "Tiger" b: 11/20/30, Memphis, Tenn. BL/TR, 5'8", 175 lbs. Deb: 4/11/55

YEAR	TM/L	G	AB	R	H	2B	3B	HR	RBI	BB	SO	AVG	OBP	SLG	PRO+	BR/A	SB	CS	SBR	FA	FR	G/POS	TPR
1955	Bal-A	40	70	6	8	0	1	0	2	9	10	.114	.215	.143	-2	-10	1	1	-0	.937	-7	2-35	-1.7

■ DON LEPPERT
Leppert, Donald George b: 10/19/31, Indianapolis, Ind. BR/TR, 6'2", 220 lbs. Deb: 6/18/61 C

YEAR	TM/L	G	AB	R	H	2B	3B	HR	RBI	BB	SO	AVG	OBP	SLG	PRO+	BR/A	SB	CS	SBR	FA	FR	G/POS	TPR
1961	Pit-N	22	60	6	16	2	1	3	5	1	11	.267	.279	.483	97	-1	0	0	0	.968	-2	C-21	0.1
1962	Pit-N	45	139	14	37	6	1	5	18	12	21	.266	.329	.388	92	-2	0	0	1	.989	4	C-44	0.3
1963	Was-A☆	73	211	20	50	11	0	6	24	20	29	.237	.306	.374	90	-3	0	0	-1	.984	-8	C-60	-0.9
1964	Was-A	50	122	6	19	3	0	3	12	11	32	.156	.226	.254	33	-11	0	1	-1	.990	1	C-43	-0.9
Total	4	190	532	46	122	22	2	15	59	44	93	.229	.291	.363	78	-16	0	1	-1	.985	-2	C-168	-1.4

■ DUTCH LERCHEN
Lerchen, Bertram Roe b: 4/4/1889, Detroit, Mich. d: 1/7/62, Detroit, Mich. BR/TR, 5'8", 160 lbs. Deb: 8/14/10 F

YEAR	TM/L	G	AB	R	H	2B	3B	HR	RBI	BB	SO	AVG	OBP	SLG	PRO+	BR/A	SB	CS	SBR	FA	FR	G/POS	TPR
1910	Bos-A	6	15	1	0	0	0	0	0	0	1	.000	.063	.000	-78	-3	0			.929	-3	/S-6	-0.8

■ GEORGE LERCHEN
Lerchen, George Edward b: 12/1/22, Detroit, Mich. BB/TR, 5'11", 175 lbs. Deb: 4/15/52 F

YEAR	TM/L	G	AB	R	H	2B	3B	HR	RBI	BB	SO	AVG	OBP	SLG	PRO+	BR/A	SB	CS	SBR	FA	FR	G/POS	TPR
1952	Det-A	14	32	1	5	1	0	1	3	7	10	.156	.308	.281	64	-1	1	0	0	1.000	-0	/O-7	-0.2
1953	Cin-N	22	17	2	5	1	0	0	2	5	6	.294	.455	.353	113	1	0	0	0	1.000	-0	/O-1	0.0
Total	2	36	49	3	10	2	0	1	5	12	16	.204	.361	.306	82	-1	1	0	0	1.000	-1	/O-8	-0.2

■ WALT LERIAN
Lerian, Walter Irvin "Peck" b: 2/10/03, Baltimore, Md. d: 10/22/29, Baltimore, Md. BR/TR, 5'11", 170 lbs. Deb: 4/16/28

YEAR	TM/L	G	AB	R	H	2B	3B	HR	RBI	BB	SO	AVG	OBP	SLG	PRO+	BR/A	SB	CS	SBR	FA	FR	G/POS	TPR
1928	Phi-N	96	239	28	65	16	2	2	25	41	29	.272	.385	.381	97	1	1			.977	-3	C-74	0.4
1929	Phi-N	105	273	28	61	13	2	6	25	53	37	.223	.354	.352	71	-12	0			**.986**	1	*C-103	-0.3
Total	2	201	512	56	126	29	4	8	50	94	66	.246	.368	.365	83	-11	1			.982	-1	C-177	0.1

■ BRIAN LESHER
Lesher, Brian Herbert b: 3/5/71, Wilrijk, Belgium BR/TL, 6'5", 205 lbs. Deb: 8/25/96

YEAR	TM/L	G	AB	R	H	2B	3B	HR	RBI	BB	SO	AVG	OBP	SLG	PRO+	BR/A	SB	CS	SBR	FA	FR	G/POS	TPR
1996	Oak-A	26	82	11	19	3	0	5	16	5	17	.232	.284	.451	85	-2	0	0	0	.976	-3	O-25/1-1	-0.5

■ ROY LESLIE
Leslie, Roy Reid b: 8/23/1894, Bailey, Tex. d: 4/9/72, Sherman, Tex. BR/TR, 6'1", 175 lbs. Deb: 9/6/17

YEAR	TM/L	G	AB	R	H	2B	3B	HR	RBI	BB	SO	AVG	OBP	SLG	PRO+	BR/A	SB	CS	SBR	FA	FR	G/POS	TPR
1917	Chi-N	7	19	1	4	1	0	0	1	1	5	.211	.250	.211	39	-1				.969	-0	/1-6	-0.2
1919	StL-N	12	24	2	5	0	1	0		4	3	.208	.321	.250	78	-0	0			.957	-0	/1-9	-0.1
1922	Phi-N	141	513	44	139	23	2	6	50	37	49	.271	.320	.359	68	-25	3	7	-3	.990	-4	*1-139	-3.6
Total	3	160	556	47	148	24	2	6	55	42	57	.266	.318	.349	68	-27	4	7		.988	-4	1-154	-3.9

■ SAM LESLIE
Leslie, Samuel Andrew "Sambo" b: 7/26/05, Moss Point, Miss. d: 1/21/79, Pascagoula, Miss. BL/TL, 6', 192 lbs. Deb: 10/6/29

YEAR	TM/L	G	AB	R	H	2B	3B	HR	RBI	BB	SO	AVG	OBP	SLG	PRO+	BR/A	SB	CS	SBR	FA	FR	G/POS	TPR
1929	NY-N	1	0	0	0	0	0	0	0	0	0	.000	.000	.000	-99	-0	0			1.000	-0	/O-1	-0.1
1930	NY-N	2	2	0	1	0	0	0	0	0	1	.500	.500	.500	146	0	0			.000	0	H	0.0
1931	NY-N	53	53	11	16	4	0	3	5	1	2	.302	.315	.547	131	2	3			1.000	0	/1-6	0.2
1932	NY-N	77	75	5	22	0	1	0	15	2	5	.293	.329	.387	94	-1	0			1.000	-0	/1-2	-0.1
1933	NY-N	40	137	21	44	12	3	3	27	12	9	.321	.380	.518	157	10	0			.990	-0	1-35	0.7
	Bro-N	96	364	41	104	11	4	5	46	23	14	.286	.340	.379	110	5	1			.990	-6	1-95	-1.2
	Yr	136	501	62	148	23	7	8	73	35	23	.295	.351	.417	123	15	1			.982	-6	*1-130	-0.5
1934	Bro-N	146	546	75	181	29	6	10	102	66	35	.331	.409	.456	118	32	5			.993	5	*1-138	2.4
1935	Bro-N	142	520	72	160	30	7	5	93	55	19	.308	.379	.421	117	14	4			.989	-0	*1-138	0.0
1936	*NY-N	117	417	49	123	19	5	6	54	23	16	.295	.335	.408	100	-1	0			.991	0	1-99	-1.0
1937	*NY-N	72	191	25	59	7	2	3	30	20	12	.309	.380	.414	114	4	1			.990	3	1-44	0.2

YEAR	TM/L	G	AB	R	H	2B	3B	HR	RBI	BB	SO	AVG	OBP	SLG	PRO+	BR/A	SB	CS	SBR	FA	FR	G/POS	TPR
1938	NY-N	76	154	12	39	7	1	1	16	11	6	.253	.307	.331	75	-5	0			.988	-3	1-32	-1.1
Total	10	822	2460	311	749	123	28	36	389	216	118	.304	.366	.421	117	60	14			.989	-2	1-589/O-1	0.0

■ CHARLIE LETCHAS
Letchas, Charlie b: 10/3/15, Thomasville, Ga. d: 3/14/95, Tampa, Fla. BR/TR, 5'10", 150 lbs. Deb: 9/16/39

YEAR	TM/L	G	AB	R	H	2B	3B	HR	RBI	BB	SO	AVG	OBP	SLG	PRO+	BR/A	SB	CS	SBR	FA	FR	G/POS	TPR
1939	Phi-N	12	44	2	10	2	0	1	3	1	2	.227	.244	.341	57	-3	0			.933	-1	2-12	-0.3
1941	Was-A	2	8	0	1	0	0	0	1	1	1	.125	.222	.125	-6	-1	0	0	0	.800	1	/2-2	-0.2
1944	Phi-N	116	396	29	94	8	0	0	33	32	27	.237	.298	.258	59	-21	0			.968	6	2-47,3-32,S-29	-1.0
1946	Phi-N	6	13	1	3	0	0	0	0	1	1	.231	.286	.231	49	-1	0			1.000	1	/2-4	0.0
Total	4	136	461	32	108	10	0	1	37	35	31	.234	.291	.262	58	-26	0	0	0	.959	5	/2-65,3-32,S-29	-1.5

■ TOM LETCHER
Letcher, Frederick Thomas b: 1/1868, Bryan, Ohio BL, Deb: 9/27/1891

YEAR	TM/L	G	AB	R	H	2B	3B	HR	RBI	BB	SO	AVG	OBP	SLG	PRO+	BR/A	SB	CS	SBR	FA	FR	G/POS	TPR
1891	Mil-a	6	21	3	4	1	0	0	2	0	1	.190	.190	.238	19	-2	1			.857	0	/O-6	-0.2

■ LEUTZ
Leutz, Deb: 5/7/1872

YEAR	TM/L	G	AB	R	H	2B	3B	HR	RBI	BB	SO	AVG	OBP	SLG	PRO+	BR/A	SB	CS	SBR	FA	FR	G/POS	TPR
1872	Eck-n	4	12	1	1	0	0	0	0	0	0	.083	.083	.083	-57	-2	0	0	0	.733	-3	/C-4	-0.4

■ JESSE LEVAN
Levan, Jesse Roy b: 7/15/26, Reading, Pa. BL/TR, 6', 172 lbs. Deb: 9/27/47

YEAR	TM/L	G	AB	R	H	2B	3B	HR	RBI	BB	SO	AVG	OBP	SLG	PRO+	BR/A	SB	CS	SBR	FA	FR	G/POS	TPR
1947	Phi-N	2	9	3	4	0	0	0	1	0	0	.444	.444	.444	142	1	0			1.000	-1	/O-2	0.0
1954	Was-A	7	10	1	3	0	0	0	0	0	0	.300	.300	.300	68	-0	0	0	0	.000	-0	/3-4,1-1	-0.1
1955	Was-A	16	16	1	3	0	0	1	4	0	2	.188	.188	.375	51	-1	0	0	0	.000	0	H	-0.1
Total	3	25	35	5	10	0	0	1	5	0	2	.286	.286	.371	80	-1	0	0		—	-1	/3-4,O-2,1-1	-0.2

■ JIM LEVEY
Levey, James Julius b: 9/13/06, Pittsburgh, Pa. d: 3/14/70, Dallas, Tex. BB/TR, 5'10.5", 154 lbs. Deb: 9/17/30

YEAR	TM/L	G	AB	R	H	2B	3B	HR	RBI	BB	SO	AVG	OBP	SLG	PRO+	BR/A	SB	CS	SBR	FA	FR	G/POS	TPR
1930	StL-A	8	37	7	9	2	0	0	3	3	2	.243	.300	.297	50	-3	0	0	0	.958	2	/S-8	0.0
1931	StL-A	139	498	53	104	19	2	5	38	35	83	.209	.264	.285	43	-42	13	8	-1	.920	-10	*S-139	-3.8
1932	StL-A	152	568	59	159	30	8	4	63	21	48	.280	.310	.382	74	-23	6	4	-1	.939	-18	*S-152	-2.7
1933	StL-A	141	529	43	103	10	4	2	36	26	68	.195	.237	.240	25	-57	4	6	-2	.945	-6	*S-138	-5.4
Total	4	440	1632	162	375	61	14	11	140	85	201	.230	.272	.305	48	-125	23	18	-4	.936	-33	S-437	-11.9

■ CHARLIE LEVIS
Levis, Charles H. b: 6/21/1860, St.Louis, Mo. d: 10/16/26, St.Louis, Mo. BR, Deb: 4/17/1884

YEAR	TM/L	G	AB	R	H	2B	3B	HR	RBI	BB	SO	AVG	OBP	SLG	PRO+	BR/A	SB	CS	SBR	FA	FR	G/POS	TPR
1884	Bal-U	87	373	59	85	11	4	6			3	.228	.234	.327	62	-29				.955	-0	*1-87	-3.6
	Was-U	1	3	0	0	0	0	0				.000	.000	.000	-99	-1				1.000	0	/1-1	-0.1
	Yr	88	376	59	85	11	4	6			3	.226	.232	.324	61	-30				.955	-0	1-88	-3.7
	Ind-a	3	10	0	2	0	0	0				.200	.200	.200	32	-1				1.000	-0	/1-3	-0.1
1885	Bal-a	1	4	2	1	0	0	0				.250	.400	.250	110	0				.889	-0	/1-1	0.0
Total	2	92	390	61	88	11	4	6		0	3	.226	.234	.321	61	-31				.956	-0	/1-92	-3.8

■ JESSE LEVIS
Levis, Jesse b: 4/14/68, Philadelphia, Pa. BL/TR, 5'9", 180 lbs. Deb: 4/24/92

YEAR	TM/L	G	AB	R	H	2B	3B	HR	RBI	BB	SO	AVG	OBP	SLG	PRO+	BR/A	SB	CS	SBR	FA	FR	G/POS	TPR
1992	Cle-A	28	43	2	12	4	0	1	3	0	5	.279	.279	.442	101	-0	0	0	0	.985	1	C-21/D-1	0.1
1993	Cle-A	31	63	7	11	2	0	0	4	2	10	.175	.200	.206	9	-8	0	0	0	.991	4	C-29	-0.6
1994	Cle-A	1	1	0	1	0	0	0	0	0	0	1.000	1.000	1.000	417	0	0	0	0	.000	0	/H	0.0
1995	Cle-A	12	18	1	6	2	0	0	3	1	0	.333	.368	.444	109	0	0	0	0	1.000	0	C-12	0.1
1996	Mil-A	104	233	27	55	6	1	1	21	38	15	.236	.348	.283	59	-14	0	0	0	.998	4	C-90/D-6	-0.5
Total	5	176	358	37	85	14	1	2	31	41	30	.237	.319	.299	59	-21	0	0	0	.995	6	C-152/D-7	-0.9

■ ED LEVY
Levy, Edward Clarence (b: Edward Clarence Whitner) b: 10/28/16, Birmingham, Ala. BR/TR, 6'5.5", 190 lbs. Deb: 4/16/40

YEAR	TM/L	G	AB	R	H	2B	3B	HR	RBI	BB	SO	AVG	OBP	SLG	PRO+	BR/A	SB	CS	SBR	FA	FR	G/POS	TPR
1940	Phi-N	1	3	0	0	0	0	0	0	0	0	.000	.000	.000	-99	-0	0			.000	0	H	0.0
1942	NY-A	13	41	5	5	0	0	0	3	4	5	.122	.200	.122	-9	-6	1			.992	2	1-13	-0.5
1944	NY-A	40	153	12	37	11	2	4	29	6	19	.242	.270	.418	92	-3	1	1	-0	.962	-0	O-36	-0.6
Total	3	54	195	17	42	11	2	4	32	10	24	.215	.254	.354	70	-9	2	1		.962	0	/O-36,1-13	-1.1

■ LEWIS
Lewis b: Brooklyn, N.Y. Deb: 7/12/1890

YEAR	TM/L	G	AB	R	H	2B	3B	HR	RBI	BB	SO	AVG	OBP	SLG	PRO+	BR/A	SB	CS	SBR	FA	FR	G/POS	TPR
1890	Buf-P	1	5	1	1	0	0	0	0	0	0	.200	.200	.200	8	-1	0			.000	0	/O-1,P-1	-0.1

■ ALLAN LEWIS
Lewis, Allan Sydney "The Panamanian Express" b: 12/12/41, Colon, Panama BB/TR, 6', 170 lbs. Deb: 4/11/67

YEAR	TM/L	G	AB	R	H	2B	3B	HR	RBI	BB	SO	AVG	OBP	SLG	PRO+	BR/A	SB	CS	SBR	FA	FR	G/POS	TPR
1967	KC-A	34	6	7	1	0	0	0	0	0	3	.167	.167	.167	-1	-1	14	5	1	.000	0	H	0.0
1968	Oak-A	26	4	9	1	0	0	0	0	0	1	.250	.400	.250	105	-0	8	4	0	.000	-0	/O-1	0.0
1969	Oak-A	12	1	2	0	0	0	0	0	0	0	.000	.000	.000	-99	-0	0	0	0	.000	0	H	0.0
1970	Oak-A	25	8	8	2	0	0	1	1	0	0	.250	.250	.625	139	-0	7	1	2	1.000	-0	/O-2	0.2
1972	*Oak-A	24	10	5	2	1	0	0	2	0	1	.200	.200	.300	50	-1	8	3	1	.900	-1	/O-6	-0.1
1973	*Oak-A	35	0	16	0	0	0	0	0	0	0	—	—	—		0	7	4	-0	1.000	-0	/O-1,D-6	-0.1
Total	6	156	29	47	6	1	0	1	3	0	5	.207	.233	.345	69	-1	44	17	3	.923	-2	/O-10,D-6	0.0

■ DARREN LEWIS
Lewis, Darren Joel b: 8/28/67, Berkeley, Cal. BR/TR, 6', 180 lbs. Deb: 8/21/90

YEAR	TM/L	G	AB	R	H	2B	3B	HR	RBI	BB	SO	AVG	OBP	SLG	PRO+	BR/A	SB	CS	SBR	FA	FR	G/POS	TPR
1990	Oak-A	25	35	4	8	0	0	0	1	4	4	.229	.372	.229	75	-1	2	0	1	1.000	-5	O-23/D-2	-0.5
1991	SF-N	72	222	41	55	5	3	1	15	36	30	.248	.358	.311	93	-1	13	7	-0	1.000	3	O-68	0.1
1992	SF-N	100	320	38	74	8	1	1	18	29	46	.231	.297	.272	66	-14	28	8	4	1.000	8	*O-131	-1.3
1993	SF-N	136	522	84	132	17	7	2	48	30	40	.253	.302	.324	70	-22	46	15	5	1.000	8	*O-131	-1.2
1994	SF-N	114	451	70	116	15	9	4	29	53	50	.257	.341	.357	86	-8	30	13	1	.993	3	*O-113	-0.7
1995	SF-N	74	309	47	78	10	3	1	16	17	37	.252	.304	.314	65	-15	21	7	2	.995	8	O-73	-0.8
	*Cin-N	58	163	19	40	3	0	0	8	17	20	.245	.324	.264	58	-9	11	11	-3	.992	1	O-57	-1.3
	Yr	132	472	66	118	13	3	1	24	34	57	.250	.311	.297	63	-25	32	18	-1	.994	8	*O-130	-2.1
1996	Chi-A	141	337	55	77	12	2	4	53	45	40	.246	.321	.313	66	-17	21	5	3	.990	-11	*O-138	-2.5
Total	7	720	2359	358	580	70	25	13	188	234	267	.246	.321	.313	73	-88	172	66	12	.996	9	O-697/D-2	-8.2

■ FRED LEWIS
Lewis, Frederick Miller b: 10/13/1858, Buffalo, N.Y. d: 6/5/45, Utica, N.Y. BB/TR, 5'10.5", 194 lbs. Deb: 7/2/1881

YEAR	TM/L	G	AB	R	H	2B	3B	HR	RBI	BB	SO	AVG	OBP	SLG	PRO+	BR/A	SB	CS	SBR	FA	FR	G/POS	TPR
1881	Bos-N	27	114	17	25	6	0	0	6	2		.219	.264	.272	72	-3				.837	-2	O-27	-0.6
1883	Phi-N	38	160	21	40	7	0	0	18	4	13	.250	.268	.294	78	-4				.814	1	O-38	-0.3
	StL-a	49	209	37	63	8	4	1	33	1		.301	.305	.392	116	3				.848	-0	O-49	0.2
1884	StL-a	73	300	59	97	25	3	0			16	.323	.366	.427	152	17				.853	3	O-73	1.6
	StL-U	8	30	6	9	1	0	0			3	.300	.364	.333	109	-0				.909	-2	/O-8	-0.2
1885	StL-N	45	181	12	53	9	0	1	27	9	10	.293	.326	.359	130	6				.957	7	O-45	1.1
1886	Cin-a	77	324	72	103	14	6	2	32	20		.318	.365	.417	140	14	8			.884	-2	O-76/3-1	0.9
Total	5	317	1318	224	390	70	13	4	119	60	28	.296	.330	.378	124	32	8			.866	6	O-316/3-1	2.7

■ DUFFY LEWIS
Lewis, George Edward b: 4/18/1888, San Francisco, Cal d: 6/17/79, Salem, N.H. BL/TL, 5'10.5", 165 lbs. Deb: 4/16/10 C

YEAR	TM/L	G	AB	R	H	2B	3B	HR	RBI	BB	SO	AVG	OBP	SLG	PRO+	BR/A	SB	CS	SBR	FA	FR	G/POS	TPR
1910	Bos-A	151	541	64	153	29	7	8	68	32		.283	.328	.407	127	14	10			.944	10	*O-149	1.9
1911	Bos-A	130	469	64	144	32	4	7	86	25		.307	.355	.437	122	12	11			.939	5	*O-125	1.0
1912	*Bos-A	154	581	85	165	36	9	6	109	52		.284	.346	.408	110	5	9			.947	7	*O-154	0.4
1913	Bos-A	149	551	54	164	31	12	0	90	30	55	.298	.336	.397	112	6	12			.960	11	*O-142/P-1,3-1	1.1
1914	Bos-A	146	510	53	142	37	9	2	79	57	41	.278	.357	.398	127	16	22	31	-12	.952	-2	*O-142	-0.4
1915	*Bos-A	152	557	69	162	31	7	2	76	45	63	.291	.348	.382	122	14	14	7	0	.952	-7	*O-152	-0.1
1916	*Bos-A	152	563	56	151	29	5	1	56	33	56	.268	.313	.343	97	-4	16			.970	-1	*O-151	-1.4
1917	Bos-A	150	553	55	167	29	9	1	65	29	54	.302	.342	.392	125	14	8			.972	4	*O-150	1.1
1919	NY-A	141	559	67	152	23	4	7	89	17	42	.272	.293	.365	84	-14	8			.985	-6	*O-141	-3.2
1920	NY-A	107	365	34	99	8	1	4	61	24	32	.271	.320	.332	70	-16	2	8	-4	.961	-2	O-99	-2.9
1921	Was-A	27	102	11	19	4	0	0	18	11	10	.186	.252	.245	29	-11	1	1	-0	.980	-2	O-27	-1.5
Total	11	1459	5351	612	1518	289	68	38	793	352	353	.284	.333	.384	108	36	113	47		.959	16	*O-1432/3-1,P-1	-4.0

■ JACK LEWIS
Lewis, John David b: 2/12/1884, Pittsburgh, Pa. d: 2/25/56, Steubenville, Ohio BR/TR, 5'8", 158 lbs. Deb: 9/16/11

YEAR	TM/L	G	AB	R	H	2B	3B	HR	RBI	BB	SO	AVG	OBP	SLG	PRO+	BR/A	SB	CS	SBR	FA	FR	G/POS	TPR
1911	Bos-N	18	59	7	16	0	0	0	6	7		.271	.368	.271	80	-1	2			.931	-2	2-18	-0.3
1914	Pit-F	117	394	32	92	14	5	1	48	17	46	.234	.276	.302	58	-30	9			.949	9	*2-115/S-1	-2.3

YEAR	TM/L	G	AB	R	H	2B	3B	HR	RBI	BB	SO	AVG	OBP	SLG	PRO+	BR/A	SB	CS	SBR	FA	FR	G/POS	TPR
1915	Pit-F	82	231	24	61	6	5	0	26	8	31	.264	.292	.333	76	-11	7			.962	-2	2-45,S-11/O-6,13	-1.4
Total	3	217	684	63	169	20	10	1	80	32	77	.247	.290	.310	66	-42	18			.951	5	2-178/S-12,O-6,13	-4.0

■ BUDDY LEWIS
Lewis, John Kelly b: 8/10/16, Gastonia, N.C. BL/TR, 6'1", 175 lbs. Deb: 9/16/35

YEAR	TM/L	G	AB	R	H	2B	3B	HR	RBI	BB	SO	AVG	OBP	SLG	PRO+	BR/A	SB	CS	SBR	FA	FR	G/POS	TPR
1935	Was-A	8	28	0	3	0	0	0	2	0	5	.107	.107	.107	-46	-6	0	0	0	.941	-0	/3-6	-0.6
1936	Was-A	143	601	100	175	21	13	6	67	47	46	.291	.347	.399	89	-12	6	6	-2	.933	5	*3-139	-0.3
1937	Was-A	156	668	107	210	32	6	10	79	52	44	.314	.360	.425	104	3	11	5	0	.938	-19	*3-156	-1.0
1938	Was-A★	151	656	122	194	35	9	12	91	58	35	.296	.354	.431	103	1	17	9	-0	.912	-0	*3-151	0.2
1939	Was-A	140	536	87	171	23	**16**	10	75	72	27	.319	.402	.478	134	28	10	9	-2	.933	14	*3-134	3.7
1940	Was-A	148	600	101	190	38	10	6	63	74	36	.317	.393	.443	124	23	15	10	-2	.960	-1	*O-112,3-36	1.5
1941	Was-A	149	569	97	169	29	11	9	72	82	30	.297	.386	.434	122	19	10	7	-1	.972	3	O-96,3-49	1.6
1945	Was-A	69	258	42	86	14	7	2	37	37	15	.333	.423	.465	172	25	1	2	-1	.981	5	O-69	2.5
1946	Was-A	150	582	82	170	28	13	7	45	59	26	.292	.359	.421	125	18	5	3	-0	.970	4	*O-145	1.6
1947	Was-A★	140	506	67	132	15	4	6	48	51	27	.261	.330	.342	89	-7	6	6	-2	.968	1	*O-130	-1.6
1949	Was-A	95	257	25	63	14	4	3	28	41	12	.245	.355	.366	93	-2	2	2	-1	.979	-0	O-67	-0.6
Total	11	1349	5261	830	1563	249	93	71	607	573	303	.297	.368	.420	112	90	83	59	-11	.927	11	3-671,O-619	7.0

■ JOHNNY LEWIS
Lewis, Johnny Joe b: 8/10/39, Greenville, Ala. BL/TR, 6'1", 189 lbs. Deb: 4/14/64 C

YEAR	TM/L	G	AB	R	H	2B	3B	HR	RBI	BB	SO	AVG	OBP	SLG	PRO+	BR/A	SB	CS	SBR	FA	FR	G/POS	TPR
1964	StL-N	40	94	10	22	2	2	2	7	13	23	.234	.327	.362	86	-2	2	2	-1	.966	-1	O-36	-0.4
1965	NY-N	148	477	64	117	15	3	15	45	59	117	.245	.332	.384	105	3	4	7	-3	.975	1	*O-142	-0.5
1966	NY-N	65	166	21	32	6	1	5	20	21	43	.193	.283	.331	72	-6	2	0	1	.988	-3	O-49	-1.1
1967	NY-N	13	34	2	4	1	0	0	2	2	11	.118	.167	.147	-10	-5	0	0	0	1.000	-0	O-10	-0.6
Total	4	266	771	97	175	24	6	22	74	95	194	.227	.314	.359	90	-9	8	9	-3	.977	-3	O-237	-2.6

■ MARK LEWIS
Lewis, Mark David b: 11/30/69, Hamilton, Ohio BR/TR, 6'1", 190 lbs. Deb: 4/26/91

YEAR	TM/L	G	AB	R	H	2B	3B	HR	RBI	BB	SO	AVG	OBP	SLG	PRO+	BR/A	SB	CS	SBR	FA	FR	G/POS	TPR
1991	Cle-A	84	314	29	83	15	1	0	30	15	45	.264	.298	.318	70	-13	2	2	-1	.966	-14	2-50,S-36	-2.4
1992	Cle-A	122	413	44	109	21	0	5	30	25	69	.264	.311	.351	87	-8	4	5	-2	.954	-9	*S-121/3-1	-1.1
1993	Cle-A	14	52	6	13	2	0	1	5	0	7	.250	.250	.346	59	-3	0	0	1	.964	-3	S-13	-0.4
1994	Cle-A	20	73	6	15	5	0	1	8	2	13	.205	.227	.315	38	-7	1	0	0	.902	-7	S-13/3-6,2-1	-1.2
1995	*Cin-N	81	171	25	58	13	1	3	30	21	33	.339	.461	.480	135	9	0	3	-2	.968	2	3-72/2-2,S-2	0.9
1996	Det-A	145	545	69	147	30	3	11	55	42	109	.270	.328	.396	82	-15	6	1	1	.987	-6	*2-144/D-1	-1.0
Total	6	466	1568	179	425	86	5	21	158	105	276	.271	.320	.372	84	-36	16	11	-2	.982	-38	2-197,S-185/3-79,D	-5.2

■ PHIL LEWIS
Lewis, Philip b: 10/7/1883, Pittsburgh, Pa. d: 8/8/59, Port Wentworth, Ga. BR/TR, 6', 195 lbs. Deb: 4/14/05

YEAR	TM/L	G	AB	R	H	2B	3B	HR	RBI	BB	SO	AVG	OBP	SLG	PRO+	BR/A	SB	CS	SBR	FA	FR	G/POS	TPR
1905	Bro-N	118	433	32	110	9	2	3	33	16		.254	.282	.305	81	-11	16			.904	-6	*S-118	-1.6
1906	Bro-N	136	452	40	110	8	4	0	37	43		.243	.309	.279	90	-5	14			.922	-22	*S-135	-2.6
1907	Bro-N	136	475	52	118	11	1	0	30	23		.248	.286	.276	83	-11	16			.938	-20	*S-136	-3.2
1908	Bro-N	118	415	22	91	5	6	1	30	13		.219	.243	.267	66	-17	9			.943	-7	*S-116	-2.6
Total	4	508	1775	146	429	33	13	4	130	95		.242	.281	.282	80	-44	55			.926	-55	S-505	-10.0

■ BILL LEWIS
Lewis, William Henry "Buddy" b: 10/15/04, Ripley, Tenn. d: 10/24/77, Memphis, Tenn. BR/TR, 5'9", 165 lbs. Deb: 6/3/33

YEAR	TM/L	G	AB	R	H	2B	3B	HR	RBI	BB	SO	AVG	OBP	SLG	PRO+	BR/A	SB	CS	SBR	FA	FR	G/POS	TPR
1933	StL-N	15	35	8	14	1	0	1	8	2	3	.400	.432	.514	161	3	0			1.000	1	/C-8	0.4
1935	Bos-N	6	4	1	0	0	0	0	0	1	1	.000	.200	.000	-45	-1	0			.000	0	/C-1	-0.1
1936	Bos-N	29	62	11	19	2	0	0	3	12	7	.306	.419	.339	113	2	0			.967	-4	C-21	-0.1
Total	3	50	101	20	33	3	0	1	11	15	11	.327	.414	.386	124	4	0			.981	-3	/C-30	0.2

■ JIM LEYRITZ
Leyritz, James Joseph b: 12/27/63, Lakewood, Ohio BR/TR, 6', 190 lbs. Deb: 6/8/90

YEAR	TM/L	G	AB	R	H	2B	3B	HR	RBI	BB	SO	AVG	OBP	SLG	PRO+	BR/A	SB	CS	SBR	FA	FR	G/POS	TPR
1990	NY-A	92	303	28	78	13	1	5	25	27	51	.257	.332	.356	92	-3	2	3	-1	.929	-19	3-69,O-14,C-11	-2.3
1991	NY-A	32	77	8	14	3	0	0	4	13	15	.182	.300	.221	46	-5	0	1	-1	.909	-8	3-18/C-5,1-3,D-1	-1.4
1992	NY-A	63	144	17	37	6	0	7	26	14	22	.257	.348	.444	121	4	0	1	-1	.990	7	D-31,C-18/1-2,3O2	0.6
1993	NY-A	95	259	43	80	14	0	14	53	37	59	.309	.411	.525	155	21	0	0	-1	.993	6	1-29,O-28,D-21,C-12	1.2
1994	NY-A	75	249	47	66	12	0	17	58	35	61	.265	.369	.518	130	11	0	0	0	1.000	-3	C-37,D-25,1-10	0.8
1995	*NY-A	77	264	37	71	12	0	7	37	37	73	.269	.375	.394	102	2	1	1	-0	.993	-3	C-46,1-18,D-15	0.8
1996	*NY-A	88	265	23	70	10	0	7	40	30	68	.264	.359	.381	86	-5	2	0	1	.995	-3	C-55,3-13,D/1O2	-0.5
Total		522	1561	203	416	70	1	57	243	193	349	.266	.363	.422	109	25	5	6	-2	.995	-39	C-184,D-105,3/1O2	-1.6

■ CARLOS LEZCANO
Lezcano, Carlos Manuel (Rubio) b: 9/30/55, Arecibo, P.R. BR/TR, 6'2", 185 lbs. Deb: 4/10/80

YEAR	TM/L	G	AB	R	H	2B	3B	HR	RBI	BB	SO	AVG	OBP	SLG	PRO+	BR/A	SB	CS	SBR	FA	FR	G/POS	TPR
1980	Chi-N	42	88	15	18	4	1	3	12	11	29	.205	.300	.375	81	-2	1	2	-1	.948	-4	O-39	-0.8
1981	Chi-N	7	14	1	1	0	0	0	2	0	4	.071	.071	.071	-57	-3	0	0	0	1.000	-1	/O-5	-0.4
Total	2	49	102	16	19	4	1	3	14	11	33	.186	.272	.333	64	-5	1	2	-1	.952	-5	/O-44	-1.2

■ SIXTO LEZCANO
Lezcano, Sixto Joaquin (Curras) b: 11/28/53, Arecibo, P.R. BR/TR, 5'11", 175 lbs. Deb: 9/10/74

YEAR	TM/L	G	AB	R	H	2B	3B	HR	RBI	BB	SO	AVG	OBP	SLG	PRO+	BR/A	SB	CS	SBR	FA	FR	G/POS	TPR
1974	Mil-A	15	54	5	13	2	0	2	9	4	9	.241	.293	.389	95	-0	1	1	-0	.972	2	O-15	0.1
1975	Mil-A	134	429	55	106	19	3	11	43	46	93	.247	.326	.382	99	-1	5	5	-2	.977	-3	*O-129/D-2	-1.0
1976	Mil-A	145	513	53	146	19	5	7	56	51	112	.285	.352	.382	117	11	14	10	-2	.973	8	*O-142/D-3	1.3
1977	Mil-A	109	400	50	109	21	4	21	49	52	78	.273	.359	.503	132	18	6	5	-1	.988	13	*O-108	2.4
1978	Mil-A	132	442	62	129	21	4	15	61	64	83	.292	.383	.459	130	22	3	3	-1	.979	10	*O-127/D-3	2.6
1979	Mil-A	138	473	84	152	29	3	28	101	77	74	.321	.420	.573	165	45	4	3	-1	.986	4	*O-135/D-1	4.0
1980	Mil-A	112	411	51	94	19	3	18	55	39	75	.229	.300	.421	98	-2	1	1	-0	.983	6	*O-108/D-4	-0.1
1981	StL-N	72	214	26	57	8	2	5	28	40	40	.266	.382	.397	117	6	0	1	-0	.973	-4	O-65	0.0
1982	SD-N	138	470	73	136	26	6	16	84	78	69	.289	.393	.472	149	33	2	1	0	.990	16	*O-134	4.6
1983	SD-N	97	317	41	74	11	2	8	49	47	66	.233	.334	.356	95	-2	0	0	-1	.968	5	O-91	0.1
	*Phi-N	18	39	8	11	1	0	0	7	5	9	.282	.364	.308	89	-0	1	0	0	1.000	-1	O-15	-0.1
	Yr	115	356	49	85	12	2	8	56	52	75	.239	.337	.351	94	-2	1	0	-1	.971	5	*O-106	0.0
1984	Phi-N	109	256	36	71	6	2	14	40	38	43	.277	.371	.480	135	12	0	1	-1	.981	-4	O-87	0.9
1985	Pit-N	72	116	16	24	2	0	3	9	35	17	.207	.395	.302	98	-2	0	0	0	.967	-2	O-40	-0.1
Total	12	1291	4134	560	1122	184	34	148	591	576	768	.271	.363	.440	125	143	37	31	-8	.980	52	*O-1196/D-13	14.7

■ STEVE LIBBY
Libby, Stephen Augustus b: 12/8/1853, Scarborough, Me. d: 3/31/35, Milford, Conn. 6'1.5", 168 lbs. Deb: 5/10/1879

YEAR	TM/L	G	AB	R	H	2B	3B	HR	RBI	BB	SO	AVG	OBP	SLG	PRO+	BR/A	SB	CS	SBR	FA	FR	G/POS	TPR
1879	Buf-N	1	2	0	0	0	0	0	0	0	1	.000	.000	.000	-98	-0				1.000	0	/1-1	0.0

■ AL LIBKE
Libke, Albert Walter b: 9/12/18, Tacoma, Wash. BL/TR, 6'4", 215 lbs. Deb: 4/19/45

YEAR	TM/L	G	AB	R	H	2B	3B	HR	RBI	BB	SO	AVG	OBP	SLG	PRO+	BR/A	SB	CS	SBR	FA	FR	G/POS	TPR
1945	Cin-N	130	449	41	127	23	5	4	53	34	62	.283	.336	.383	102	0	6			.963	2	*O-108/P-4,1-2	-0.4
1946	Cin-N	124	431	32	109	22	1	5	42	43	50	.253	.322	.343	92	-5	0			.972	-5	*O-115/P-1	-1.6
Total	2	254	880	73	236	45	6	9	95	77	112	.268	.329	.364	97	-5	6			.967	-3	O-223/P-5,1-2	-2.0

■ FRANKIE LIBRAN
Libran, Francisco (Rosas) b: 5/6/48, Mayaguez, P.R. BR/TR, 6', 168 lbs. Deb: 9/3/69

YEAR	TM/L	G	AB	R	H	2B	3B	HR	RBI	BB	SO	AVG	OBP	SLG	PRO+	BR/A	SB	CS	SBR	FA	FR	G/POS	TPR
1969	SD-N	10	10	1	1	1	0	0	1	1	2	.100	.182	.200	7	-1	0	0	0	1.000	1	/S-9	0.0

■ JOHN LICKERT
Lickert, John Wilbur b: 4/4/60, Pittsburgh, Pa. BR/TR, 5'11", 175 lbs. Deb: 9/19/81

YEAR	TM/L	G	AB	R	H	2B	3B	HR	RBI	BB	SO	AVG	OBP	SLG	PRO+	BR/A	SB	CS	SBR	FA	FR	G/POS	TPR
1981	Bos-A	1	0	0	0	0	0	0	0	0	0	—	—	—			0	0	0	1.000	-0	/C-1	0.0

■ DAVE LIDDELL
Liddell, David Alexander (b: b: 6/15/66, Los Angeles, Cal. BR/TR, 6', 190 lbs. Deb: 6/3/90

YEAR	TM/L	G	AB	R	H	2B	3B	HR	RBI	BB	SO	AVG	OBP	SLG	PRO+	BR/A	SB	CS	SBR	FA	FR	G/POS	TPR
1990	NY-N	1	1	0	1	0	0	0	1	0	0	1.000	1.000	1.000	453		0	0	0	1.000	-0	/C-1	0.0

■ MIKE LIEBERTHAL
Lieberthal, Michael Scott b: 1/18/72, Glendale, Cal. BR/TR, 6', 170 lbs. Deb: 6/30/94

YEAR	TM/L	G	AB	R	H	2B	3B	HR	RBI	BB	SO	AVG	OBP	SLG	PRO+	BR/A	SB	CS	SBR	FA	FR	G/POS	TPR
1994	Phi-N	24	79	6	21	3	1	1	5	3	5	.266	.301	.367	71	-3	1	0	0	.969	-3	C-22	-0.5
1995	Phi-N	16	47	1	12	2	0	1	4	5	5	.255	.327	.298	66	-3	0	0	0	.991	5	C-14	0.1
1996	Phi-N	50	166	21	42	8	0	7	23	10	30	.253	.303	.428	88	-3	0	0	0	.990	0	C-43	0.0
Total	3	90	292	28	75	13	1	8	32	18	40	.257	.307	.390	80	-9	1	0	0	.985	-0	/C-79	-0.4

■ FRED LIESE
Liese, Frederick Richard b: 10/7/1885, Wisconsin d: 6/30/67, Los Angeles, Cal. BL/TL, 5'8", 150 lbs. Deb: 4/14/10

YEAR	TM/L	G	AB	R	H	2B	3B	HR	RBI	BB	SO	AVG	OBP	SLG	PRO+	BR/A	SB	CS	SBR	FA	FR	G/POS	TPR
1910	Bos-N	5	4	0	0	0	0	0	0	0	2	.000	.200	.000	-39	-1	0			.000	0	H	-0.1

YEAR	TM/L	G	AB	R	H	2B	3B	HR	RBI	BB	SO	AVG	OBP	SLG	PRO+	BR/A	SB	CS	SBR	FA	FR	G/POS	TPR

■ GENE LILLARD   Lillard, Robert Eugene   b: 11/12/13, Santa Barbara, Cal   d: 4/12/91, Goleta, Cal.   BR/TR, 5'10.5", 178 lbs.   Deb: 5/8/36   F

1936	Chi-N	19	34	6	7	1	0	0	2	3	8	.206	.270	.235	36	-3				.947	-1	/S-4,3-3	-0.3
1939	Chi-N	23	10	3	1	0	0	0	0	6	3	.100	.438	.100	51	-0			0	1.000	0	P-20	0.0
1940	StL-N	2	0	0	0	0	0	0	0	0	0	—	—	—	—	—				1.000	0	/P-2	0.0
Total	3	44	44	9	8	1	0	0	2	9	11	.182	.321	.205	43	-3			-1	1.000	-1	/P-22,S-4,3-3	-0.3

■ BILL LILLARD   Lillard, William Beverly   b: 1/10/18, Goleta, Cal.   BR/TR, 5'10", 170 lbs.   Deb: 9/11/39   F

1939	Phi-A	7	19	4	6	1	0	0	3	1		.316	.409	.368	102	0	0	0	0	.974	2	/S-7	0.3
1940	Phi-A	73	206	26	49	8	2	1	21	28	28	.238	.332	.311	69	-9	0	1	-1	.921	-18	S-69,2-1	-2.1
Total	2	80	225	30	55	9	2	1	22	31	29	.244	.339	.316	72	-9	0	1	-1	.927	-16	/S-76,2-1	-1.8

■ JIM LILLIE   Lillie, James J. "Grasshopper" (b: James J. Lilly)   b: 7/27/1861, New Haven, Conn.   d: 11/9/1890, Kansas City, Mo.   Deb: 5/17/1883

1883	Buf-N	50	201	25	47	7	3	1	29	1	31	.234	.238	.313	64	-9				.835	-7	O-47/P-3,C-2,S32	-1.4
1884	Buf-N	114	471	68	105	12	5	3	53	5	71	.223	.231	.289	60	-22				.852	16	*O-114/P-2	-0.7
1885	Buf-N	112	430	49	107	13	3	2	30	6	39	.249	.259	.307	60	-11				.862	0	*O-112/S-3,1-1	-1.3
1886	KC-N	114	416	37	73	9	0	0	22	11	80	.175	.197	.197	19	-41	13			.884	11	*O-114/P-1	-3.0
Total	4	390	1518	179	332	41	11	6	134	23	221	.219	.230	.272	54	-82	13			.863	21	O-387/P-6,S-4,C123	-6.4

■ BOB LILLIS   Lillis, Robert Perry   b: 6/2/30, Altadena, Cal.   BR/TR, 5'11", 160 lbs.   Deb: 8/30/58   MC

1958	LA-N	20	69	10	27	1		5	4	2		.391	.432	.507	143	4	1	2	-1	.964	-3	S-19	0.2
1959	LA-N	30	48	7	11	2	0	0	2	2	6	.229	.275	.271	43	-4	0	0	-1	.919	8	S-20	0.5
1960	LA-N	48	60	6	16	4	0	0	6	2	6	.267	.290	.333	66	-3	2	0	1	.982	15	S-23,3-14/2-1	1.3
1961	LA-N	19	9	0	1	0	0	0	1	1	1	.111	.200	.111	-13	-1	0	0		1.000	1	3-12/2-1,S-1	0.0
	StL-N	86	230	24	50	4	0	0	21	7	13	.217	.247	.235	26	-24	3	3	-1	.928	3	S-56,2-24	-1.8
	Yr	105	239	24	51	4	0	0	22	8	14	.213	.245	.230	25	-25	3	3	-1	.924	3	S-99,2-33/3-9	-1.8
1962	Hou-N	129	457	38	114	12	4	1	30	28	23	.249	.293	.300	64	-24	7	3	0	.972	9	*S-124,2-19/3-6	-0.4
1963	Hou-N	147	469	31	93	13	1	1	19	15	35	.198	.230	.237	37	-39	3	4	-2	.957	-5	*S-124,2-19/3-6	-4.0
1964	Hou-N	109	332	31	89	11	2	0	17	11	10	.268	.292	.313	75	-12	4	9	-4	.995	1	2-52,S-43,3-12	-1.0
1965	Hou-N	124	408	34	90	12	1	0	20	20	10	.221	.267	.255	51	-27	2	3	-1	.968	-12	*S-104/3-9,2-6	-3.5
1966	Hou-N	68	164	14	38	6	0	0	11	7	4	.232	.263	.268	52	-11	1	1	-0	.951	-9	2-35,S-18/3-6	-1.8
1967	Hou-N	37	82	3	20	1	0	0	5	1	8	.244	.253	.256	48	-6	0	1	-1	.947	3	S-23/2-3,3-2	-0.2
Total	10	817	2328	198	549	68	9	3	137	99	116	.236	.271	.277	54	-145	23	25	-8	.959	8	S-530,2-174/3-70	-10.7

■ LOU LIMMER   Limmer, Louis   b: 3/10/25, New York, N.Y.   BL/TL, 6'2", 190 lbs.   Deb: 4/22/51

1951	Phi-A	94	214	25	34	9	1	5	30	28	40	.159	.256	.280	44	-17	1	0	0	.988	2	1-58	-1.7
1954	Phi-A	115	316	41	73	10	3	14	32	35	37	.231	.308	.415	96	-3	2	3	-1	.988	2	1-79	-0.6
Total	2	209	530	66	107	19	4	19	62	63	77	.202	.287	.360	75	-20	3	3	-1	.988	4	1-137	-2.3

■ RUFINO LINARES   Linares, Rufino (b: Rufino De La Cruz (Linares))   b: 2/28/51, San Pedro De Macoris, D.R.   BR/TR, 6', 170 lbs.   Deb: 4/10/81

1981	Atl-N	78	253	27	67	9	2	5	25	9	28	.265	.290	.375	85	-6	8	4	0	.963	3	O-60	-0.5
1982	Atl-N	77	191	28	57	7	1	2	17	7	29	.298	.327	.377	92	-2	5	2	0	1.000	1	O-53	-0.3
1984	Atl-N	34	58	4	12	3	0	1	10	6	12	.207	.281	.310	62	-3	0	0	0	.958	1	O-13	-0.3
1985	Cal-A	18	43	7	11	2	0	3	11	2	5	.256	.289	.512	114	1	2	0	1	1.000	-1	D-14/O-2	0.0
Total	4	207	545	66	147	21	3	11	63	24	74	.270	.302	.380	88	-10	15	6	1	.977	4	O-128/D-14	-1.1

■ CARL LIND   Lind, Henry Carl "Hooks"   b: 9/19/03, New Orleans, La.   d: 8/2/46, New York, N.Y.   BR/TR, 6', 160 lbs.   Deb: 9/14/27

1927	Cle-A	12	37	2	5	0	0	0	1	4		.135	.256	.135	4	-5	1	0	0	.969	2	2-11/S-1	-0.3
1928	Cle-A	154	650	102	191	42	4	1	54	36	48	.294	.331	.375	84	-15	8	5	-1	.960	4	*2-154	-0.7
1929	Cle-A	66	225	19	54	8	1	0	13	13	17	.240	.282	.284	44	-19	0	2	-1	.957	16	2-64/3-1	-0.1
1930	Cle-A	24	69	8	17	3	0	0	6	3	7	.246	.278	.290	43	-6	0	1	-1	.940	11	S-22/2-2	0.5
Total	4	256	981	131	267	53	5	1	74	57	79	.272	.313	.339	69	-45	9	8	-2	.960	33	2-231/S-23,3-1	-0.6

■ JACK LIND   Lind, Jackson Hugh   b: 6/8/46, Denver, Col.   BB/TR, 6', 170 lbs.   Deb: 9/10/74

1974	Mil-A	9	17	4	4	2	0	0	1	3	2	.235	.350	.353	103	0	0	0	0	1.000	-0	/S-5,2-4	0.1
1975	Mil-A	17	20	1	1	0	0	0	2	2	12	.050	.136	.050	-45	-4	1	0	0	.919	5	/S-9,3-6,1-1	0.3
Total	2	26	37	5	5	2	0	0	1	5	14	.135	.238	.189	23	-4	1	0	0	.943	5	/S-14,3-6,2-4,1-1	0.3

■ JOSE LIND   Lind, Jose (Salgado) "Chico"   b: 5/1/64, Toa Baja, P.R.   BR/TR, 5'11", 170 lbs.   Deb: 8/28/87

1987	Pit-N	35	143	21	46	8	4	0	11	8	12	.322	.358	.434	108	1	2	1	0	.995	6	2-35	0.9
1988	Pit-N	154	611	82	160	24	4	2	49	42	75	.262	.309	.324	83	-13	15	4	2	.987	3	*2-153	-0.2
1989	Pit-N	153	578	52	134	21	3	2	48	39	64	.232	.283	.289	66	-26	15	1	4	.976	-14	*2-151	-3.3
1990	*Pit-N	152	514	46	134	28	5	1	48	35	52	.261	.309	.340	82	-13	8	0	2	.991	17	*2-152	0.9
1991	*Pit-N	150	502	53	133	16	6	3	54	30	56	.265	.309	.339	83	-11	7	4	-0	.989	23	*2-149	1.5
1992	*Pit-N	135	468	38	110	14	1	0	39	26	29	.235	.277	.269	56	-27	3	1	0	**.992**	12	*2-134	-1.3
1993	KC-A	136	431	33	107	13	2	0	37	13	36	.248	.274	.288	48	-31	3	2	-0	**.994**	-4	*2-136	-3.1
1994	KC-A	85	290	34	78	16	2	1	31	16	34	.269	.307	.348	66	-15	9	5	-0	.988	2	2-84/D-1	-0.9
1995	KC-A	29	97	4	26	3	0	1	6	3	8	.268	.290	.299	53	-7	0	1	-1	.992	-2	2-29	-0.7
	Cal-A	15	43	5	7	2	0	0	1	3	4	.163	.217	.209	12	-6	0	0	0	1.000	-1	2-15	-0.1
	Yr	44	140	9	33	5	0	1	7	6	12	.236	.267	.271	40	-12	0	1	-1	.995	1	2-44	-0.8
Total	9	1044	3677	368	935	145	27	9	324	215	370	.254	.297	.316	70	-148	62	19	7	.988	46	*2-1038/D-1	-6.3

■ EM LINDBECK   Lindbeck, Emerit Desmond   b: 8/27/35, Kewanee, Ill.   BL/TR, 6', 185 lbs.   Deb: 4/22/60

1960	Det-A	2	1	0	0	0	0	0	0	1	0	.000	.500	.000	46	0	0	0	0	.000	0	H	0.0

■ JOHNNY LINDELL   Lindell, John Harlan   b: 8/30/16, Greeley, Colo.   d: 8/27/85, Newport Beach, Cal.   BR/TR, 6'4.5", 217 lbs.   Deb: 4/18/41

1941	NY-A	1	1	0	0	0	0	0	0	0	0	.000	.000	.000	-99	-0	0	0	0	.000	0	H	0.0
1942	NY-A	27	24	1	6	1	0	0	4	0	5	.250	.250	.292	53	-2	0	0	0	.923	-0	P-23	0.0
1943	*NY-A☆	122	441	53	108	17	**12**	4	51	51	55	.245	.329	.365	102	1	2	5	-2	.966	-2	*O-122	-1.0
1944	NY-A	149	594	91	178	33	**16**	18	103	44	56	.300	.351	.500	137	25	5	4	-1	.986	9	*O-149	2.7
1945	NY-A	41	159	26	45	6	3	1	20	17	10	.283	.363	.377	110	2	2	1	0	.982	0	O-41	0.0
1946	NY-A	102	332	41	86	10	5	10	40	32	47	.259	.328	.410	104	1	4	1	1	.982	-5	O-74,1-14	-0.3
1947	*NY-A	127	476	66	131	18	7	11	67	32	70	.275	.322	.412	104	0	1	2	-1	.978	7	*O-118	0.1
1948	NY-A	88	309	58	98	17	2	13	55	35	50	.317	.387	.511	139	16	0	0	0	.994	2	O-79	1.3
1949	*NY-A	78	211	33	51	10	0	6	27	35	22	.242	.350	.374	92	-3	3	0	1	.983	-6	O-65	-1.0
1950	NY-A	7	21	2	4	0	0	0	2	4	2	.190	.320	.190	34	-2	0	0	0	.857	4	/O-6	-0.4
	StL-N	36	113	16	21	5	1	2	16	15	24	.186	.287	.398	74	-5	0	0	0	.984	-2	O-33	-0.8
1953	Pit-N	58	91	11	26	6	1	4	15	16	15	.286	.404	.505	136	5	0	0	0	.962	2	P-27/1-2	0.0
	Phi-N	11	18	3	7	1	0	0	2	6	2	.389	.542	.444	162	3	0	0	0	1.000	0	/P-5,O-2	0.0
	Yr	69	109	14	33	7	1	4	17	22	17	.303	.429	.495	141	8	0	0	0	.964	2	P-32/1-2,O-2	0.0
1954	Phi-N	7	5	0	1	0	0	0	2	3		.200	.429	.200	70	-0	0	0	0	.000	0	H	0.0
Total	12	854	2795	401	762	124	48	72	404	289	366	.273	.344	.429	113	43	17	13		.980	*O-689/P-55,1-16	0.6

■ JIM LINDEMAN   Lindeman, James William   b: 1/10/62, Evanston, Ill.   BR/TR, 6'1", 200 lbs.   Deb: 9/3/86

1986	StL-N	19	55	7	14	1	0	1	6	2	10	.255	.281	.327	68	-3	1	1	0	.992	-1	1-17/3-1,O-1	-0.5
1987	*StL-N	75	207	20	43	13	0	8	28	11	56	.208	.258	.386	67	-11	3	1	0	.976	-1	O-49,1-20	-1.3
1988	StL-N	17	43	3	9	2	0	0	4	1	12	.209	.244	.372	74	-2	0	0	0	.941	-2	O-12/1-3	-0.4
1989	StL-N	73	45	3	5	0	0	0	2	1	6	.111	.167	.133	-13	-7	0	1	0	.989	0	1-42/O-5	-0.7
1990	Det-A	12	32	5	7	2	0	0	3	1	6	.219	.265	.438	92	-1	0	0	0	1.000	0	D-10/1-1,O-1	-0.2
1991	Phi-N	65	95	13	32	5	0	3	12	5	14	.337	.417	.389	129	4	1	1	0	1.000	0	O-30/1-1	0.2
1992	Phi-N	29	39	6	10	1	0	0	4	1	11	.256	.310	.359	89	-1	0	0	0	1.000	-3	/O-9	-0.4
1993	Hou-N	9	23	2	8	1	0	1	6	0	6	.348	.348	.478	123	1	0	0	0	1.000	0	/1-9	0.1

YEAR	TM/L	G	AB	R	H	2B	3B	HR	RBI	BB	SO	AVG	OBP	SLG	PRO+	BR/A	SB	CS	SBR	FA	FR	G/POS	TPR
1994	NY-N	52	137	18	37	8	1	7	20	6	35	.270	.306	.496	106	0	0	0	0	.948	-3	O-33/1-4	-0.3
Total	9	351	676	82	165	34	8	21	89	42	173	.244	.292	.391	83	0	4	3	-1	.970	-14	O-140/1-97,D-10,3-1	-3.9

■ BOB LINDEMANN
Lindemann, John Frederick Mann b: 6/5/1881, Philadelphia, Pa. d: 12/19/51, Williamsport, Pa. BB/TR, 6', 175 lbs. Deb: 8/28/01

YEAR	TM/L	G	AB	R	H	2B	3B	HR	RBI	BB	SO	AVG	OBP	SLG	PRO+	BR/A	SB	CS	SBR	FA	FR	G/POS	TPR
1901	Phi-A	3	9	0	1	0	0	0	0	0		.111	.111	.111	-37	-2	0			.600	-0	/O-3	-0.2

■ WALT LINDEN
Linden, Walter Charles b: 3/27/24, Chicago, Ill. BR/TR, 6'1", 190 lbs. Deb: 4/30/50

YEAR	TM/L	G	AB	R	H	2B	3B	HR	RBI	BB	SO	AVG	OBP	SLG	PRO+	BR/A	SB	CS	SBR	FA	FR	G/POS	TPR
1950	Bos-N	3	5	0	2	1	0	0	1	0	1	.400	.500	.600	201	1	0			1.000	-1	/C-3	0.0

■ CHRIS LINDSAY
Lindsay, Christian Haller "Pinky" or "The Crab"
b: 7/24/1878, Moon Township, Beaver County, Pa. d: 1/25/41, Cleveland, Ohio BR/TR, 6', 190 lbs. Deb: 7/6/05

YEAR	TM/L	G	AB	R	H	2B	3B	HR	RBI	BB	SO	AVG	OBP	SLG	PRO+	BR/A	SB	CS	SBR	FA	FR	G/POS	TPR
1905	Det-A	88	329	38	88	14	1	0	31	18		.267	.315	.316	100	-0	10			.978	-0	1-88	-0.4
1906	Det-A	141	499	59	112	16	2	0	33	45		.224	.293	.265	73	-15	18			.977	-8	*1-122,2-17/3-1	-2.9
Total	2	229	828	97	200	30	3	0	64	63		.242	.301	.285	83	-15	28			.978	-8	1-210/2-17,3-1	-3.3

■ BILL LINDSAY
Lindsay, William Gibbons b: 2/24/1881, Madison, N.C. d: 7/14/63, Greensboro, N.C. BL/TR, 5'10.5", 165 lbs. Deb: 6/21/11

YEAR	TM/L	G	AB	R	H	2B	3B	HR	RBI	BB	SO	AVG	OBP	SLG	PRO+	BR/A	SB	CS	SBR	FA	FR	G/POS	TPR
1911	Cle-A	19	66	6	16	2	0	0	5	1		.242	.265	.273	49	-5	2			.883	2	3-15/2-1	-0.2

■ DOUG LINDSEY
Lindsey, Michael Douglas b: 9/22/67, Austin, Tex. BR/TR, 6'2", 200 lbs. Deb: 10/6/91

YEAR	TM/L	G	AB	R	H	2B	3B	HR	RBI	BB	SO	AVG	OBP	SLG	PRO+	BR/A	SB	CS	SBR	FA	FR	G/POS	TPR
1991	Phi-N	1	3	0	0	0	0	0	0	0	3	.000	.000	.000	-99	-1	0	0	0	1.000	0	/C-1	-0.1
1993	Phi-N	2	2	0	1	0	0	0	0	0	0	.500	.500	.500	171	0	0	0	0	1.000	0	/C-2	0.0
	Chi-A	3	1	0	0	0	0	0	0	0	1	.000	.000	.000	-99	-0	0	0	0	1.000	0	/C-2	0.0
Total	2	5	6	0	1	0	0	0	0	0	4	.167	.167	.167	-8	-1	0	0	0	1.000	1	/C-5	-0.1

■ BILL LINDSEY
Lindsey, William Donald b: 4/12/60, Staten Island, N.Y. BR/TR, 6'3", 195 lbs. Deb: 7/18/87

YEAR	TM/L	G	AB	R	H	2B	3B	HR	RBI	BB	SO	AVG	OBP	SLG	PRO+	BR/A	SB	CS	SBR	FA	FR	G/POS	TPR
1987	Chi-A	9	16	2	3	1	0	0	1	0	3	.188	.188	.188	0	-2	0	0	0	1.000	2	/C-9	0.0

■ CHUCK LINDSTROM
Lindstrom, Charles William b: 9/7/36, Chicago, Ill. BR/TR, 5'11", 175 lbs. Deb: 9/28/58 F

YEAR	TM/L	G	AB	R	H	2B	3B	HR	RBI	BB	SO	AVG	OBP	SLG	PRO+	BR/A	SB	CS	SBR	FA	FR	G/POS	TPR
1958	Chi-A	1	1	1	1	0	1	0	1	0		1.000	1.000	3.000	975	1	0			1.000	-0	/C-1	0.1

■ FREDDY LINDSTROM
Lindstrom, Frederick Charles (b: Frederick Anthony Lindstrom)
b: 11/21/05, Chicago, Ill. d: 10/4/81, Chicago, Ill. BR/TR, 5'11", 170 lbs. Deb: 4/15/24 FH

YEAR	TM/L	G	AB	R	H	2B	3B	HR	RBI	BB	SO	AVG	OBP	SLG	PRO+	BR/A	SB	CS	SBR	FA	FR	G/POS	TPR
1924	*NY-N	52	79	19	20	3	1	0	4	6	10	.253	.314	.316	71	-3	3	1	0	.911	7	2-23,3-11	0.5
1925	NY-N	104	356	43	102	15	12	4	33	22	20	.287	.332	.430	97	-3	5	9	-4	.957	-1	3-96/2-1,S-1	-0.2
1926	NY-N	140	543	90	164	19	9	9	76	39	21	.302	.351	.420	108	5	11			.962	-3	*3-138/O-1	1.1
1927	NY-N	138	562	107	172	36	8	7	58	40	40	.306	.354	.436	111	8	10			.968	1	3-87,O-51	1.0
1928	NY-N	153	646	99	231	39	9	14	107	25	21	.358	.383	.511	131	27	15			.958	15	*3-153	4.8
1929	NY-N	130	549	99	175	23	6	15	91	30	28	.319	.354	.464	101	-0	10			.966	7	*3-128	1.1
1930	NY-N	148	609	127	231	39	7	22	106	48	33	.379	.425	.575	142	41	15			.953	6	*3-148	4.8
1931	NY-N	78	303	38	91	12	6	5	36	26	12	.300	.356	.429	113	5	5			.975	-7	O-73/2-4	-0.6
1932	NY-N	144	595	83	161	26	5	15	92	27	28	.271	.303	.407	91	-9	6			.982	0	*O-128,3-15	-1.6
1933	Pit-N	138	538	70	167	39	10	5	55	33	22	.310	.350	.448	127	18	1			.988	11	*O-130	2.3
1934	Pit-N	97	383	59	111	24	4	4	49	23	21	.290	.333	.405	94	-3	1			.990	-1	O-92	-0.6
1935	*Chi-N	90	342	49	94	22	4	3	62	10	13	.275	.297	.389	82	-9	1			.979	-2	O-50,3-33	-1.1
1936	Bro-N	26	106	12	28	4	0	0	14	5	7	.264	.297	.302	61	-6	1			.982	1	O-26	-0.5
Total	13	1438	5611	895	1747	301	81	103	779	334	276	.311	.351	.449	110	71	84	10		.959	37	3-809,O-551/2-28,S	11.0

■ CARL LINHART
Linhart, Carl James b: 12/14/29, Zborov, Czech. BL/TR, 5'11", 184 lbs. Deb: 8/2/52

YEAR	TM/L	G	AB	R	H	2B	3B	HR	RBI	BB	SO	AVG	OBP	SLG	PRO+	BR/A	SB	CS	SBR	FA	FR	G/POS	TPR
1952	Det-A	3	2	0	0	0	0	0	0	0	0	.000	.000	.000	-99	-1	0	0	0	.000	0	H	-0.1

■ BOB LINTON
Linton, Claud Clarence b: 4/18/03, Emerson, Ark. d: 4/3/80, Destin, Fla. BL/TR, 6', 185 lbs. Deb: 4/26/29

YEAR	TM/L	G	AB	R	H	2B	3B	HR	RBI	BB	SO	AVG	OBP	SLG	PRO+	BR/A	SB	CS	SBR	FA	FR	G/POS	TPR
1929	Pit-N	17	18	0	2	0	0	0	1	1	2	.111	.158	.111	-31	-4	0			1.000	0	/C-8	-0.3

■ LARRY LINTZ
Lintz, Larry b: 10/10/49, Martinez, Cal. BB/TR, 5'9", 150 lbs. Deb: 7/14/73

YEAR	TM/L	G	AB	R	H	2B	3B	HR	RBI	BB	SO	AVG	OBP	SLG	PRO+	BR/A	SB	CS	SBR	FA	FR	G/POS	TPR
1973	Mon-N	52	116	20	29	1	0	0	3	17	18	.250	.351	.259	69	-4	12	4	1	.945	2	2-34,S-15	0.2
1974	Mon-N	113	319	60	76	10	1	0	20	44	50	.238	.334	.276	68	-12	50	7	11	.961	-13	2-67,S-31/3-1	-0.8
1975	Mon-N	46	132	18	26	0	0	0	3	23	18	.197	.316	.197	43	-9	17	9	-0	.970	-6	2-39/S-2	-1.4
	StL-N	27	18	6	5	1	0	0	1	3	2	.278	.381	.333	96	-0	4	0	1	.889	9	/2-6,S-6	1.0
	Yr	73	150	24	31	1	0	0	4	26	20	.207	.324	.213	49	-9	21	9	1	.963	3	2-45/S-8	-0.4
1976	Oak-A	68	1	21	0	0	0	0	0	2	0	.000	.667	.000	111	0	31	11	3	1.000	0	D-19/2-5,O-3	0.3
1977	Oak-A	41	30	11	4	1	0	0	0	8	13	.133	.333	.167	42	-2	13	5	1	1.000	11	2-28/S-2,3-1,D-5	1.0
1978	Cle-A	3	0	1	0	0	0	0	0	0		—	—	—	—	—	1	2	-1	.000	0	R	-0.1
Total	6	350	616	137	140	13	1	0	27	97	101	.227	.336	.252	63	-27	128	38	16	.962	3	2-179/S-56,D-24,O3	0.2

■ PHIL LINZ
Linz, Philip Francis b: 6/4/39, Baltimore, Md. BR/TR, 6'1", 180 lbs. Deb: 4/13/62

YEAR	TM/L	G	AB	R	H	2B	3B	HR	RBI	BB	SO	AVG	OBP	SLG	PRO+	BR/A	SB	CS	SBR	FA	FR	G/POS	TPR
1962	NY-A	71	129	28	37	8	0	1	14	6	17	.287	.319	.372	88	-2	6	2	1	.937	-3	S-21/3-8,2-5,O-2	-0.3
1963	*NY-A	72	186	22	50	9	0	2	12	15	18	.269	.330	.349	91	-2	1	6	-3	.963	1	S-22,3-13,O-12,/2-6	-0.3
1964	*NY-A	112	368	63	92	21	3	5	25	43	61	.250	.332	.364	92	-3	5	4	-2	.952	11	S-55,3-41/2-5,O-3	1.0
1965	NY-A	99	285	37	59	12	1	2	16	30	33	.207	.283	.277	60	-15	2	1	0	.954	11	S-71/3-4,O-4,2-1	0.1
1966	Phi-N	40	70	4	14	3	0	0	6	2	14	.200	.222	.243	29	-7	0	0		.971	1	3-14/S-6,2-3	-0.6
1967	Phi-N	23	18	8	4	2	0	1	5	2	1	.222	.300	.500	124	0	1			.833	-1	/S-7,3-1	-0.1
	Yr	47	76	12	16	4	0	1	6	4	10	.211	.277	.303	66	-3	0	1		.964	-2	2-11/S-8,3-1,O-1	-0.6
1968	NY-N	78	258	19	54	7	0	0	17	10	41	.209	.244	.236	45	-17	1	0		.968	-12	2-71	-0.7
Total	7	519	1372	185	322	64	4	11	96	112	195	.235	.296	.311	72	-49	13	13	-4	.952	6	S-190,2-102/3-82,O	-3.7

■ JOHNNY LIPON
Lipon, John Joseph "Skids" b: 11/10/22, Martins Ferry, O. BR/TR, 6', 175 lbs. Deb: 8/16/42 MC

YEAR	TM/L	G	AB	R	H	2B	3B	HR	RBI	BB	SO	AVG	OBP	SLG	PRO+	BR/A	SB	CS	SBR	FA	FR	G/POS	TPR
1942	Det-A	34	131	9	25	2	0	0	9	7	7	.191	.232	.206	22	-14	1	3	-2	.945	7	S-34	-0.6
1946	Det-A	14	20	4	6	0	0	0	1	5	3	.300	.440	.300	103	0	0	0	0	.933	3	/S-8,3-1	0.4
1948	Det-A	121	458	65	133	18	8	5	52	68	22	.290	.384	.397	105	5	4	4	-1	.970	-12	*S-117/2-1,3-1	-0.1
1949	Det-A	127	439	57	110	14	6	3	59	75	24	.251	.362	.330	84	-8	2	4	-2	.965	4	*S-120	0.2
1950	Det-A	147	601	104	176	27	6	2	63	81	26	.293	.378	.368	89	-8	9	6	-1	.958	9	*S-147	1.1
1951	Det-A	129	487	56	129	15	1	0	38	49	27	.265	.335	.300	72	-18	7	6	-2	.949	-13	*S-125	-2.3
1952	Det-A	39	136	17	30	4	2	0	12	16	6	.221	.303	.279	62	-7	1	1	0	.978	-3	S-39	-0.6
	Bos-A	79	234	25	48	8	1	0	18	32	20	.205	.301	.248	50	-15	1	1	-0	.982	14	S-69/3-7	0.4
	Yr	118	370	42	78	12	3	0	30	48	26	.211	.301	.259	54	-22	2	2	-0	.981	12	*S-108/3-7	-0.2
1953	Bos-A	60	145	18	31	7	0	0	11	17	14	.214	.283	.262	46	-11	1	1		.951	4	S-58	-0.4
	StL-A	7	9	0	2	0	0	0	3	1	3	.222	.222	.222	20	-1	0	1		1.000	-1	/3-6,2-1	-0.2
	Yr	67	154	18	33	7	0	0	14	18	17	.214	.280	.260	44	-12	1	2		.951	3	S-58/3-6,2-1	-0.6
1954	Cin-N	1	1	0	0	0	0	0	0	0		.000	.000	.000	-97	-0	0	0		.000	0	H	0.0
Total	9	758	2661	351	690	95	24	10	266	347	152	.259	.346	.324	79	-77	28	25	-7	.961	13	S-717/3-15,2-2	-2.1

■ NIG LIPSCOMB
Lipscomb, Gerard b: 2/24/11, Rutherfordton, N.C. d: 2/27/78, Huntersville, N.C. BR/TR, 6', 175 lbs. Deb: 4/23/37

YEAR	TM/L	G	AB	R	H	2B	3B	HR	RBI	BB	SO	AVG	OBP	SLG	PRO+	BR/A	SB	CS	SBR	FA	FR	G/POS	TPR
1937	StL-A	36	96	11	31	9	1	0	8	11	10	.323	.398	.438	110		2			.963	2	2-27/P-3,3-1	0.6

■ BOB LIPSKI
Lipski, Robert Peter b: 7/7/38, Scranton, Pa. BL/TR, 6'1", 180 lbs. Deb: 4/28/63

YEAR	TM/L	G	AB	R	H	2B	3B	HR	RBI	BB	SO	AVG	OBP	SLG	PRO+	BR/A	SB	CS	SBR	FA	FR	G/POS	TPR
1963	Cle-A	2	1	0	0	0	0	0	0	0	1	.000	.000	.000	-99	-0	0	0	0	1.000	0	/C-2	0.0

■ NELSON LIRIANO
Liriano, Nelson Arturo (Bonilla) b: 6/3/64, Puerto Plata, D.R. BB/TR, 5'10", 172 lbs. Deb: 8/25/87

YEAR	TM/L	G	AB	R	H	2B	3B	HR	RBI	BB	SO	AVG	OBP	SLG	PRO+	BR/A	SB	CS	SBR	FA	FR	G/POS	TPR
1987	Tor-A	37	158	29	38	6	2	2	10	16	22	.241	.310	.342	71	-6	13	3	3	.995	3	2-37	0.1
1988	Tor-A	99	276	36	73	6	2	3	23	11	40	.264	.298	.333	76	-9	12	5	1	.961	-3	2-80,D-11/3-1	-1.9
1989	*Tor-A	132	418	51	110	26	3	5	53	43	51	.263	.335	.376	102	-5	16	7	1	.980	-18	*2-122/D-5	-1.2
1990	Tor-A	50	170	16	36	7	2	1	15	16	20	.212	.283	.294	61	-9	3	5	-2	.983	-12	2-49	-2.3

YEAR	TM/L	G	AB	R	H	2B	3B	HR	RBI	BB	SO	AVG	OBP	SLG	PRO+	BR/A	SB	CS	SBR	FA	FR	G/POS	TPR
	Min-A	53	185	30	47	5	7	0	13	22	24	.254	.333	.357	87	-3	5	2	0	.968	-15	2-50/S-1,D-2	-1.8
	Yr	103	355	46	83	12	9	1	28	38	44	.234	.310	.327	75	-12	8	7	-2	.975	-28	2-99/D-2,S-1	-4.1
1991	KC-A	10	22	5	9	0	0	0	1	0	2	.409	.409	.409	127	1	0	1	-1	1.000	1	2-10	0.1
1993	Col-N	48	151	28	46	6	3	2	15	18	22	.305	.379	.424	98	-0	6	4	-1	.975	-13	S-35,2-16/3-1	-1.1
1994	Col-N	87	255	39	65	17	5	3	31	42	44	.255	.360	.396	83	-6	0	2	-1	.973	-5	2-79/S-3,3-2	-0.9
1995	Pit-N	107	259	29	74	12	1	5	38	24	34	.286	.351	.398	95	-1	2	2	-1	.981	-18	2-67/3-5,S-1	-1.6
1996	Pit-N	112	217	23	58	14	2	3	30	14	22	.267	.312	.392	82	-6	2	0	1	.984	-6	2-36/3-9,S-5	-1.0
Total	9	735	2111	286	556	99	27	24	229	206	281	.263	.331	.370	86	-39	59	30	-0	.977	-98	2-546/S-45,3-18,D	-11.6

■ JOE LIS
Lis, Joseph Anthony   b: 8/15/46, Somerville, N.J.   BR/TR, 6', 195 lbs.   Deb: 9/5/70

YEAR	TM/L	G	AB	R	H	2B	3B	HR	RBI	BB	SO	AVG	OBP	SLG	PRO+	BR/A	SB	CS	SBR	FA	FR	G/POS	TPR
1970	Phi-N	13	37	1	7	2	0	1	4	5	11	.189	.286	.324	65	-2	0	0	0	.947	0	/O-9	-0.2
1971	Phi-N	59	123	16	26	6	0	6	10	16	43	.211	.312	.407	102	-0	0	1	-1	.978	-3	O-35	-0.5
1972	Phi-N	62	140	13	34	6	0	6	18	30	34	.243	.380	.414	122	5	0	1	-1	.996	1	1-30,O-14	0.3
1973	Min-A	103	253	37	62	11	1	9	25	28	66	.245	.327	.403	101	0	0	2	0	.987	2	1-96/D-1	-0.4
1974	Min-A	24	41	5	8	0	0	0	3	5	12	.195	.298	.195	43	-3	0	0	0	.992	0	1-18	-0.4
	Cle-A	57	109	15	22	3	0	6	16	14	30	.202	.293	.394	97	-1	1	0	0	1.000	-0	1-31/3-9,O-1,D-9	-0.2
	Yr	81	150	20	30	3	0	6	19	19	42	.200	.294	.340	82	-4	1	0	0	.997	-0	1-49/3-9,D-9,O-1	-0.6
1975	Cle-A	9	13	4	4	2	0	1	8	3	3	.308	.471	.923	286	3	0	0	0	1.000	-0	/1-8,D-1	0.3
1976	Cle-A	20	51	4	16	1	0	2	7	8	8	.314	.407	.451	153	4	0	0	0	1.000	-0	1-17/D-1	0.3
1977	Sea-A	9	13	1	3	0	0	0	1	1	2	.231	.286	.231	43	-1	0	0	0	1.000	-1	/1-4,C-1	-0.2
Total	8	356	780	96	182	31	1	32	92	110	209	.233	.334	.399	105	6	1	3	-2	.992	-1	1-204/O-59,D-12,3C	-1.0

■ RICK LISI
Lisi, Riccardo Patrick Emilio   b: 3/17/56, Halifax, N.S., Can.   BR/TR, 6', 175 lbs.   Deb: 5/9/81

YEAR	TM/L	G	AB	R	H	2B	3B	HR	RBI	BB	SO	AVG	OBP	SLG	PRO+	BR/A	SB	CS	SBR	FA	FR	G/POS	TPR
1981	Tex-A	9	16	6	5	0	0	0	1	4	0	.313	.450	.313	130	1	0	1	-1	1.000	-2	/O-8	-0.2

■ PAT LISTACH
Listach, Patrick Alan   b: 9/12/67, Natchitoches, La.   BB/TR, 5'9", 170 lbs.   Deb: 4/8/92

YEAR	TM/L	G	AB	R	H	2B	3B	HR	RBI	BB	SO	AVG	OBP	SLG	PRO+	BR/A	SB	CS	SBR	FA	FR	G/POS	TPR
1992	Mil-A	149	579	93	168	19	6	1	47	55	124	.290	.353	.349	99	1	54	18	5	.966	-7	*S-148/2-1,O-1	1.0
1993	Mil-A	98	356	50	87	15	1	3	30	37	70	.244	.321	.317	73	-13	18	9	0	.975	-16	S-95/O-6	-2.1
1994	Mil-A	16	54	8	16	3	0	0	2	3	8	.296	.333	.352	74	-2	2	1	0	.958	-0	S-16	-0.5
1995	Mil-A	101	334	35	73	8	2	0	25	25	61	.219	.277	.254	37	-31	13	3	2	1.000	-1	2-59,S-36,O-11,/3-2	-2.2
1996	Mil-A	87	317	51	76	16	2	1	33	36	51	.240	.319	.312	57	-20	25	5	5	.982	-0	O-68,2-12/S-7	-1.6
Total	5	451	1640	237	420	61	11	5	137	156	314	.256	.323	.316	71	-65	112	36	12	.968	-25	S-302/O-86,2-72,3-2	-5.0

■ PETE LISTER
Lister, Morris Elmer   b: 7/21/1881, Savanna, Ill.   d: 3/27/47, St.Petersburg, Fla   BR/TR,   Deb: 9/14/07

YEAR	TM/L	G	AB	R	H	2B	3B	HR	RBI	BB	SO	AVG	OBP	SLG	PRO+	BR/A	SB	CS	SBR	FA	FR	G/POS	TPR
1907	Cle-A	22	65	5	18	2	0	0	4	3		.277	.319	.308	99	-0	2			.974	-1	1-22	-0.2

■ SCOTT LITTLE
Little, Dennis Scott   b: 1/19/63, E.St.Louis, Ill.   BR/TR, 6', 198 lbs.   Deb: 7/27/89

YEAR	TM/L	G	AB	R	H	2B	3B	HR	RBI	BB	SO	AVG	OBP	SLG	PRO+	BR/A	SB	CS	SBR	FA	FR	G/POS	TPR
1989	Pit-N	3	4	0	1	0	0	0	0	0	1	.250	.250	.250	45	-0	0	0	0	1.000	1	/O-1	0.1

■ HARRY LITTLE
Little, Harry A.   b: St.Louis, Mo.   TR ,   Deb: 7/16/1877

YEAR	TM/L	G	AB	R	H	2B	3B	HR	RBI	BB	SO	AVG	OBP	SLG	PRO+	BR/A	SB	CS	SBR	FA	FR	G/POS	TPR
1877	StL-N	3	12	2	2	0	0	0	1	6	.167	.231	.167	29	-1					1.000	-0	/O-3	-0.1
	Lou-N	1	3	0	0	0	0	0	0	1	.000	.250	.000	-13	-0					.857	0	/2-1	0.0
	Yr	4	15	2	2	0	0	0	2	7	.133	.235	.133	19	-1					1.000	0	/O-3,2-1	-0.1

■ BRYAN LITTLE
Little, Richard Bryan "Twig"   b: 10/8/59, Houston, Tex.   BB/TR, 5'10", 160 lbs.   Deb: 7/29/82

YEAR	TM/L	G	AB	R	H	2B	3B	HR	RBI	BB	SO	AVG	OBP	SLG	PRO+	BR/A	SB	CS	SBR	FA	FR	G/POS	TPR
1982	Mon-N	29	42	6	9	0	0	0	3	4	6	.214	.283	.214	40	-3	2	1	0	1.000	-2	2-16,S-10	-0.5
1983	Mon-N	106	350	48	91	15	3	1	36	50	22	.260	.356	.329	91	-2	4	5	-2	.968	-32	S-66,2-51	-3.0
1984	Mon-N	85	266	31	65	11	1	0	9	34	19	.244	.332	.293	81	-6	2	3	-1	.982	-22	2-77/S-2	-2.8
1985	Chi-A	73	188	35	47	9	1	2	27	26	21	.250	.350	.340	87	-3	0	1	-1	1.000	-6	2-68/3-2,S-1	-0.7
1986	Chi-A	20	35	3	6	1	0	0	2	4	4	.171	.256	.200	25	-4	0	0	0	.975	5	2-14	0.1
	NY-A	14	41	3	8	1	0	0	0	2	7	.195	.233	.220	24	-4	0	0	0	.983	0	2-26/S-7,3-1	-0.2
	Yr	34	76	6	14	2	0	0	2	6	11	.184	.244	.211	25	-8	0	0	0	.987	5	2-40/S-7,3-1	-0.1
Total	5	327	922	126	226	37	5	3	77	120	79	.245	.336	.306	80	-22	8	10	-4	.987	-56	2-238/S-86,3-3	-7.2

■ JACK LITTLE
Little, William Arthur   b: 3/12/1891, Mart, Tex.   d: 7/27/61, Dallas, Tex.   BR/TR, 5'11", 175 lbs.   Deb: 7/2/12

YEAR	TM/L	G	AB	R	H	2B	3B	HR	RBI	BB	SO	AVG	OBP	SLG	PRO+	BR/A	SB	CS	SBR	FA	FR	G/POS	TPR
1912	NY-A	3	12	2	3	0	0	0	0	1		.250	.357	.250	70	-0	2			1.000	0	/O-3	0.0

■ DENNIS LITTLEJOHN
Littlejohn, Dennis Gerald   b: 10/4/54, Santa Monica, Cal.   BR/TR, 6'2", 200 lbs.   Deb: 7/9/78

YEAR	TM/L	G	AB	R	H	2B	3B	HR	RBI	BB	SO	AVG	OBP	SLG	PRO+	BR/A	SB	CS	SBR	FA	FR	G/POS	TPR
1978	SF-N	2	1	0	0	0	0	0	0	0	0	—	—	—		0	0	0	0	.000	0	/C-2	0.0
1979	SF-N	63	193	15	38	6	1	1	13	21	46	.197	.276	.254	49	-14	0	0	0	.986	5	C-63	-0.6
1980	SF-N	13	29	2	7	1	0	0	2	7	7	.241	.389	.276	91	0	0	0	0	.983	2	C-10	0.2
Total	3	78	222	17	45	7	1	1	15	28	53	.203	.292	.257	55	-14	0	0	0	.985	7	/C-75	-0.4

■ LARRY LITTLETON
Littleton, Larry Marvin   b: 4/3/54, Charlotte, N.C.   BR/TR, 6'1", 185 lbs.   Deb: 4/12/81

YEAR	TM/L	G	AB	R	H	2B	3B	HR	RBI	BB	SO	AVG	OBP	SLG	PRO+	BR/A	SB	CS	SBR	FA	FR	G/POS	TPR
1981	Cle-A	26	23	2	0	0	0	0	0	1	3	6	.000	.115	.000	-65	-5	0	0	0	1.000	-10	O-24	-1.6

■ GREG LITTON
Litton, Jon Gregory   b: 7/13/64, New Orleans, La.   BR/TR, 6', 175 lbs.   Deb: 5/2/89

YEAR	TM/L	G	AB	R	H	2B	3B	HR	RBI	BB	SO	AVG	OBP	SLG	PRO+	BR/A	SB	CS	SBR	FA	FR	G/POS	TPR
1989	*SF-N	71	143	12	36	5	3	4	17	7	29	.252	.291	.413	102	-0	0	2	-1	.953	-5	3-34,2-15/S-9,OC	-0.6
1990	SF-N	93	204	19	50	9	1	4	24	11	45	.245	.287	.314	68	-9	1	0	0	.985	-11	O-56,2-18/S-7,3-5	-2.1
1991	SF-N	59	127	13	23	7	1	1	15	11	25	.181	.252	.276	50	-9	0	2	-1	.989	-2	1-15,2-15,3/SOCP	-0.7
1992	SF-N	68	140	9	32	5	0	4	15	11	33	.229	.285	.350	84	-3	0	1	-1	.992	-3	2-31,3-10/1-8,SO	0.3
1993	Sea-A	72	174	25	52	17	0	3	25	18	30	.299	.368	.448	116	4	0	1	-1	1.000	2	/2-4,1-3,3-2,D-1	-0.3
1994	Bos-A	11	21	2	2	0	0	0	1	0	5	.095	.095	.095	-48	-5	0	0	0	.997	-18	2-100/O-91,31SDCP	-4.6
Total	6	374	809	78	195	43	5	13	97	58	167	.241	.295	.355	81	-22							

■ JACK LITTRELL
Littrell, Jack Napier   b: 1/22/29, Louisville, Ky.   BR/TR, 6', 179 lbs.   Deb: 4/19/52

YEAR	TM/L	G	AB	R	H	2B	3B	HR	RBI	BB	SO	AVG	OBP	SLG	PRO+	BR/A	SB	CS	SBR	FA	FR	G/POS	TPR
1952	Phi-A	4	12	0	0	0	0	0	0	1	2	.000	.333	.000	-2	-0	0	0	0	1.000	0	/S-2,3-1	0.0
1954	Phi-A	9	30	7	9	2	0	1	3	6	3	.300	.417	.467	141	2	0	0	0	.976	-3	/S-9	0.2
1955	KC-A	37	70	7	14	0	1	0	4	4	12	.200	.243	.229	27	-7	0	0	0	.947	-5	S-22/1-6,2-4	-0.6
1957	Chi-N	61	153	8	29	4	2	1	13	9	43	.190	.235	.261	34	-14	1	0	0	.944	-5	S-47/2-6,3-5	-0.9
Total	4	111	255	22	52	6	3	2	17	20	60	.204	.262	.275	45	-20	1	0	0	.949	-13	/S-80,2-10,1-6,3-6	-1.3

■ DANNY LITWHILER
Litwhiler, Daniel Webster   b: 8/31/16, Ringtown, Pa.   BR/TR, 5'10.5", 198 lbs.   Deb: 4/25/40   C

YEAR	TM/L	G	AB	R	H	2B	3B	HR	RBI	BB	SO	AVG	OBP	SLG	PRO+	BR/A	SB	CS	SBR	FA	FR	G/POS	TPR
1940	Phi-N	36	142	10	49	2	2	5	17	3	13	.345	.363	.493	139	7	1			.986	1	O-34	0.6
1941	Phi-N	151	590	72	180	29	6	18	66	39	43	.305	.350	.466	134	23	4			.964	17	*O-150	3.2
1942	Phi-N★	151	591	59	160	25	9	9	56	27	42	.271	.310	.389	109	4	2			1.000	-2	*O-151	-0.6
1943	Phi-N	36	139	23	36	6	0	5	17	11	14	.259	.313	.410	113	1	1			.989	5	O-34	0.3
	*StL-N	80	258	40	72	14	3	7	31	19	31	.279	.327	.438	117	5	1			1.000	1	*O-104	0.8
	Yr	116	397	63	108	20	3	12	48	30	45	.272	.326	.428	115	6	2			.974	-1	*O-136	-0.2
1944	*StL-N	140	492	53	130	25	5	15	82	37	56	.264	.328	.427	109	4	0			.974	0	*O-136	-0.2
1946	StL-N	6	6	0	0	0	0	0	0	1	1	.000	.167	.000	-49	-1	0			.000	0	H	-0.1
	Bos-N	79	247	29	72	12	2	8	38	19	23	.291	.347	.453	125	7	1			.985	-3	O-65/3-2	0.1
	Yr	85	252	29	72	12	2	8	38	20	24	.286	.343	.444	121	6	1			.976	-6	O-66	-1.0
1947	Bos-N	91	226	38	59	7	2	7	31	25	43	.261	.337	.394	96	0	0			1.000	2	/O-8	0.1
1948	Bos-N	13	33	0	9	2	0	0	6	4	2	.273	.385	.333	97	0	0			.988	2	O-83,3-15	1.1
	Cin-N	106	338	51	93	19	2	14	44	48	41	.275	.365	.467	128	13	1			.990	4	O-91,3-15	1.2
	Yr	119	371	51	102	21	2	14	50	52	43	.275	.366	.456	125	13	1			.987	-5	O-82/3-3	0.3
1949	Cin-N	102	292	35	85	18	1	11	48	44	42	.291	.384	.473	127	12	0			.958	-3	O-29	-0.1
1950	Cin-N	54	112	15	29	4	0	6	12	20	26	.259	.371	.455	116	3	0			.933	-1	/O-7	0.0
1951	Cin-N	12	29	3	8	1	0	1	6	5	3	.276	.323	.517	120	1	0			.982	9	O-7	0.0
Total	11	1057	3494	428	982	162	32	107	451	299	377	.281	.342	.438	119	78	11	0		.982	9	O-915/3-20	4.2

YEAR	TM/L	G	AB	R	H	2B	3B	HR	RBI	BB	SO	AVG	OBP	SLG	PRO+	BR/A	SB	CS	SBR	FA	FR	G/POS	TPR

■ PADDY LIVINGSTON
Livingston, Patrick Joseph b: 1/14/1880, Cleveland, Ohio d: 9/19/77, Cleveland, Ohio BR/TR, 5'8", 197 lbs. Deb: 9/2/01 C

YEAR	TM/L	G	AB	R	H	2B	3B	HR	RBI	BB	SO	AVG	OBP	SLG	PRO+	BR/A	SB	CS	SBR	FA	FR	G/POS	TPR
1901	Cle-A	1	2	0	0	0	0	0	0	0		.000	.333	.000	-2	-0	0			1.000	-1	/C-1	-0.1
1906	Cin-N	50	139	8	22	1	4	0	8	12		.158	.259	.223	48	-8	0			.960	3	C-47	-0.1
1909	Phi-A	64	175	15	41	6	4	0	15	15		.234	.323	.314	99	0	4			.969	9	C-64	1.7
1910	Phi-A	37	120	11	25	4	3	0	9	6		.208	.264	.292	75	-4	2			.968	4	C-37	0.4
1911	Phi-A	27	71	9	17	4	0	0	8	7		.239	.316	.296	72	-3	1			.977	5	C-26	0.4
1912	Cle-A	20	47	5	11	2	1	0	3	1		.234	.280	.319	69	-2	0			.976	0	C-14	-0.1
1917	StL-N	7	20	0	4	0	0	0	2	0		.200	.200	.200	23	-2	2			1.000	1	/C-6	-0.1
Total	7	206	574	48	120	17	12	0	45	41	1	.209	.287	.280	73	-18	9			.969	21	C-195	2.1

■ MICKEY LIVINGSTON
Livingston, Thompson Orville b: 11/15/14, Newberry, S.C. d: 4/3/83, Newberry, S.C. BR/TR, 6'1.5", 185 lbs. Deb: 9/17/38

YEAR	TM/L	G	AB	R	H	2B	3B	HR	RBI	BB	SO	AVG	OBP	SLG	PRO+	BR/A	SB	CS	SBR	FA	FR	G/POS	TPR
1938	Was-A	2	4	0	3	2	0	0	1	0	1	.750	.750	1.250	421	2	0	0		.667	-1	/C-2	0.1
1941	Phi-N	95	207	16	42	6	1	0	18	20	38	.203	.276	.242	49	-14	2			.974	-1	C-71/1-1	-1.0
1942	Phi-N	89	239	20	49	6	1	2	22	25	20	.205	.283	.264	64	-11	0			.987	-6	C-78/1-6	-1.2
1943	Phi-N	84	265	25	66	9	2	3	18	19	18	.249	.304	.332	87	-5	1			.988	-2	C-84/1-2	-0.1
	Chi-N	36	111	11	29	5	1	4	16	12	8	.261	.333	.432	122	3	1			1.000	-1	C-31/1-4	0.4
	Yr	120	376	36	95	14	3	7	34	31	26	.253	.313	.362	98	-2	2			.991	-3	*C-115/1-6	0.3
1945	*Chi-N	71	224	19	57	4	2	2	23	19	6	.254	.324	.317	80	-6	2			.990	-1	C-68/1-1	-0.2
1946	Chi-N	66	176	14	45	14	0	2	20	20	19	.256	.338	.369	103	1	0			.981	2	C-56	0.5
1947	Chi-N	19	33	2	7	2	0	0	3	1	5	.212	.235	.273	36	-3	0			1.000	-0	/C-7	-0.3
	NY-N	5	6	0	1	0	0	0	0	1	2	.167	.286	.167	23	-1	0			.800	-0	/C-1	0.0
	Yr	24	39	2	8	2	0	0	3	2	7	.205	.244	.256	34	-4	0			.970	-0	/C-8	-0.3
1948	NY-N	45	99	9	21	4	1	2	12	21	11	.212	.350	.333	85	-1	1			.980	-1	C-42	0.0
1949	NY-N	19	57	6	17	4	0	3	6	2	8	.298	.333	.544	132	2	0			.985	-1	C-19	0.2
	Bos-N	28	64	6	15	2	1	0	6	3	5	.234	.290	.297	61	-4	0			.977	-1	C-22	-0.2
	Yr	47	121	12	32	4	1	4	18	5	13	.264	.310	.413	95	-1	0			.980	-1	C-41	0.0
1951	Bro-N	2	5	0	2	0	0	0	2	1	0	.400	.500	.400	142	0	0	0	0	1.000	-0	/C-2	0.0
Total	10	561	1490	128	354	56	9	19	153	144	141	.238	.310	.326	82	-37	7	0		.984	-11	C-483/1-14	-1.8

■ SCOTT LIVINGSTONE
Livingstone, Scott Louis b: 7/15/65, Dallas, Tex. BL/TR, 6', 190 lbs. Deb: 7/19/91

YEAR	TM/L	G	AB	R	H	2B	3B	HR	RBI	BB	SO	AVG	OBP	SLG	PRO+	BR/A	SB	CS	SBR	FA	FR	G/POS	TPR
1991	Det-A	44	127	19	37	5	0	2	11	10	25	.291	.343	.378	98	-0	2	1	0	.980	1	3-43	0.0
1992	Det-A	117	354	43	100	21	0	4	46	21	36	.282	.323	.376	95	-3	1	3	-2	.962	-6	*3-112	-1.1
1993	Det-A	98	304	39	89	10	2	2	39	19	32	.293	.334	.359	87	-6	1	3	-2	.955	-3	3-62,D-32	-1.1
1994	Det-A	15	23	0	5	1	0	0	1	1	4	.217	.250	.261	32	-2	0	0	0	1.000	0	/1-5,3-1,D-5	-0.2
	SD-N	57	180	11	49	12	1	2	10	6	22	.272	.296	.383	78	-6	2	2	0	.942	-1	3-50	-0.7
1995	SD-N	99	196	26	66	15	0	5	32	15	22	.337	.384	.490	133	9	2	1	0	.991	-2	1-43,3-13/2-4	0.4
1996	*SD-N	102	172	20	51	4	1	2	20	9	22	.297	.331	.366	88	-3	0	1	-1	.993	0	1-22,3-16	-0.5
Total	6	532	1356	158	397	68	4	17	159	81	163	.293	.333	.386	94	-11	8	11	-4	.962	-14	3-297/1-70,D-37,2-4	-3.2

■ ABEL LIZOTTE
Lizotte, Abel b: 4/13/1870, Lewiston, Me. d: 12/4/26, Wilkes-Barre, Pa. 5'8", 174 lbs. Deb: 9/17/1896

YEAR	TM/L	G	AB	R	H	2B	3B	HR	RBI	BB	SO	AVG	OBP	SLG	PRO+	BR/A	SB	CS	SBR	FA	FR	G/POS	TPR
1896	Pit-N	7	29	3	3	0	0	0	3	2		.103	.161	.103	-31	-5	1			.952	1	/1-7	-0.4

■ WINSTON LLENAS
Llenas, Winston Enriquillo (Davila) b: 9/23/43, Santiago, D.R. BR/TR, 5'10", 165 lbs. Deb: 8/15/68 C

YEAR	TM/L	G	AB	R	H	2B	3B	HR	RBI	BB	SO	AVG	OBP	SLG	PRO+	BR/A	SB	CS	SBR	FA	FR	G/POS	TPR
1968	Cal-A	16	39	5	5	1	0	0	1	2	5	.128	.190	.154	6	-4	0	0	0	.800	-3	/3-9	-0.9
1969	Cal-A	34	47	4	8	2	0	0	2	0	10	.170	.204	.213	18	-5	0	0	0	.929	-2	/3-9	-0.8
1972	Cal-A	44	64	3	17	3	0	0	7	3	8	.266	.299	.313	87	-1	0	0	0	.950	-1	3-10/2-2,O-2	-0.3
1973	Cal-A	78	130	16	35	1	0	1	25	10	16	.269	.326	.300	84	-3	0	0	0	1.000	-4	2-20,31/1-0,4,D-4	-0.6
1974	Cal-A	72	138	16	36	6	0	2	17	11	19	.261	.315	.348	96	-1	0	0	0	1.000	-8	O-32,2-15,D-10,3-2	-1.0
1975	Cal-A	56	113	6	21	4	0	0	11	10	11	.186	.252	.221	37	-9	0	1	-1	1.000	-6	2-12,O-10/1-6,3D	-0.6
Total	6	300	531	50	122	17	0	3	61	38	69	.230	.284	.279	66	-24	0	1	-1	1.000	-13	/2-49,O-48,3-44,D1	-4.2

■ MIKE LOAN
Loan, William Joseph b: 9/27/1894, Philadelphia, Pa. d: 11/21/66, Springfield, Pa. BR/TR, 5'11", 185 lbs. Deb: 9/18/12

YEAR	TM/L	G	AB	R	H	2B	3B	HR	RBI	BB	SO	AVG	OBP	SLG	PRO+	BR/A	SB	CS	SBR	FA	FR	G/POS	TPR
1912	Phi-N	1	2	1	1	0	0	0		0	0	.500	.500	.500	163	0	0			1.000	-1	/C-1	0.0

■ BOB LOANE
Loane, Robert Kenneth b: 8/6/14, Berkeley, Cal. BR/TR, 6', 190 lbs. Deb: 7/29/39

YEAR	TM/L	G	AB	R	H	2B	3B	HR	RBI	BB	SO	AVG	OBP	SLG	PRO+	BR/A	SB	CS	SBR	FA	FR	G/POS	TPR
1939	Was-A	3	9	2	0	0	0	0	1	4	4	.000	.308	.000	-16	-1	0	0	0	.909	2	/O-3	0.0
1940	Bos-N	13	22	4	5	3	0	0	1	2	5	.227	.292	.364	84	-1	2			1.000	0	O-10	0.0
Total	2	16	31	6	5	3	0	0	2	6	9	.161	.297	.258	54	-2	2	0		.969	2	/O-13	0.0

■ FRANK LOBERT
Lobert, Frank John b: 11/26/1883, Williamsport, Pa. d: 5/29/32, Pittsburgh, Pa. BR/TR, 6', 180 lbs. Deb: 6/6/14 F

YEAR	TM/L	G	AB	R	H	2B	3B	HR	RBI	BB	SO	AVG	OBP	SLG	PRO+	BR/A	SB	CS	SBR	FA	FR	G/POS	TPR
1914	Bal-F	11	30	3	6	0	1	0	2	0	0	.200	.200	.267	26	-4	0			.870	-2	/3-7,2-1	-0.5

■ HANS LOBERT
Lobert, John Bernard "Honus" b: 10/18/1881, Wilmington, Del. d: 9/14/68, Philadelphia, Pa. BR/TR, 5'9", 170 lbs. Deb: 9/21/03 FMC

YEAR	TM/L	G	AB	R	H	2B	3B	HR	RBI	BB	SO	AVG	OBP	SLG	PRO+	BR/A	SB	CS	SBR	FA	FR	G/POS	TPR
1903	Pit-N	5	13	1	1	1	0	0	0	1		.077	.143	.154	-15	-2	1			.778	-1	/3-3,2-1,S-1	-0.3
1905	Chi-N	14	46	7	9	2	0	0	1	3		.196	.260	.239	47	-3	4			.918	0	3-13/O-1	-0.3
1906	Cin-N	79	268	39	83	5	5	0	19	19		.310	.366	.366	123	7	20			.959	-11	3-35,S-31,2-10/O-1	-0.2
1907	Cin-N	148	537	61	132	9	12	1	41	37		.246	.299	.313	88	-8	30			.941	-18	*S-142/3-5	-2.5
1908	Cin-N	155	570	71	167	17	18	4	63	46		.293	.348	.407	145	27	47			.921	-26	3-99,S-35,O-21	0.6
1909	Cin-N	122	425	50	90	13	5	4	52	48		.212	.304	.294	86	-6	30			.921	-14	*3-122	-1.7
1910	Cin-N	93	314	43	97	6	6	3	40	30	9	.309	.369	.395	128	11	41			.932	-2	3-90	1.2
1911	Phi-N	147	541	94	154	20	9	9	72	66	31	.285	.368	.405	115	11	40			.954	-17	*3-147	-0.4
1912	Phi-N	65	257	37	84	12	5	2	33	19	13	.327	.373	.436	113	4	13			.976	-13	3-64	-0.9
1913	Phi-N	150	573	98	172	28	11	7	55	42	34	.300	.353	.424	117	11	41			.974	-15	*3-145/S-3,2-1	-0.2
1914	Phi-N	135	505	83	139	24	5	1	52	49	32	.275	.343	.349	99	-0	31			.943	-26	*3-133/S-2	-2.3
1915	NY-N	106	386	46	97	18	4	0	38	25	24	.251	.304	.319	94	-3	14	15	-5	.950	-5	*3-103	-1.1
1916	NY-N	48	76	6	17	3	2	0	5	5	8	.224	.272	.316	84	-2	2			.961	2	3-20	0.1
1917	NY-N	50	52	4	10	1	0	1	5	5	5	.192	.276	.269	70	-2	2			.906	-2	3-21	0.0
Total	14	1317	4563	640	1252	159	82	32	482	395	156	.274	.337	.366	109	46	316	15		.944	-142	3-1000,S-214/O-23,2	-8.0

■ HARRY LOCHHEAD
Lochhead, Robert Henry b: 3/29/1876, Stockton, Cal. d: 8/22/09, Stockton, Cal. BR/TR, 5'11", 172 lbs. Deb: 4/16/1899

YEAR	TM/L	G	AB	R	H	2B	3B	HR	RBI	BB	SO	AVG	OBP	SLG	PRO+	BR/A	SB	CS	SBR	FA	FR	G/POS	TPR
1899	Cle-N	148	541	52	129	7	1	1	43	21		.238	.280	.261	52	-35	23			.909	2	*S-146/2-1,P-1	-2.0
1901	Det-A	1	4	2	2	0	0	0	0	0		.500	.600	.500	198	0	0			.857	-0	/S-1	0.0
	Phi-A	9	34	3	3	0	0	0	3	3		.088	.162	.088	-28	-6	0			.757	-8	/S-9	-1.3
	Yr	10	38	5	5	0	0	0	3	3		.132	.214	.132	-3	-5	0			.773	-9	S-10	-1.3
Total	2	158	579	57	134	7	1	1	45	24		.231	.275	.252	48	-40	23			.903	-7	S-156/P-1,2-1	-3.3

■ DON LOCK
Lock, Don Wilson b: 7/27/36, Wichita, Kan. BR/TR, 6'2", 202 lbs. Deb: 7/17/62

YEAR	TM/L	G	AB	R	H	2B	3B	HR	RBI	BB	SO	AVG	OBP	SLG	PRO+	BR/A	SB	CS	SBR	FA	FR	G/POS	TPR
1962	Was-A	71	225	30	57	6	2	12	37	30	63	.253	.341	.458	114	4	4	5	-2	.973	3	O-67	0.1
1963	Was-A	149	531	71	134	20	1	27	82	70	151	.252	.342	.446	119	14	7	3	0	.980	15	*O-146	2.2
1964	Was-A	152	512	73	127	17	4	28	80	79	137	.248	.350	.461	124	17	4	2	0	.987	13	*O-149	2.4
1965	Was-A	143	418	52	90	15	1	16	39	57	115	.215	.317	.371	96	-2	1	3	-2	.969	2	*O-136	-0.7
1966	Was-A	138	386	52	90	13	1	16	48	57	126	.233	.335	.396	110	6	3	4	-2	.977	7	*O-129	0.5
1967	Phi-N	112	313	46	79	13	1	14	51	43	98	.252	.350	.435	123	10	9	5	-0	.973	-2	O-97	0.4
1968	Phi-N	99	248	27	52	7	2	8	34	26	64	.210	.285	.351	90	-3	3	4	-2	.955	-5	O-78	-1.5
1969	Phi-N	4	4	0	0	0	0	0	0	0	1	.000	.000	.000	-99	-1	0	0	0	.000	-0	/O-1	-0.1
	Bos-A	53	58	8	13	1	0	1	2	11	21	.224	.348	.293	77	-1	0	0	0	1.000	-6	O-28/1-4	-0.9
Total	8	921	2695	359	642	92	12	122	373	373	776	.238	.334	.417	111	43	30	29	-8	.976	27	O-831/1-4	2.4

■ MARSHALL LOCKE
Locke, Marshall Pinkney Wilder b: 3/12/1857, Ashland, Ohio d: 3/6/40, Ashland, Ohio Deb: 7/5/1884

YEAR	TM/L	G	AB	R	H	2B	3B	HR	RBI	BB	SO	AVG	OBP	SLG	PRO+	BR/A	SB	CS	SBR	FA	FR	G/POS	TPR
1884	Ind-a	7	29	5	7	1	0	0		5	0	.241	.241	.310	81	-1				.800	-1	/O-7	-0.2

YEAR	TM/L	G	AB	R	H	2B	3B	HR	RBI	BB	SO	AVG	OBP	SLG	PRO+	BR/A	SB	CS	SBR	FA	FR	G/POS	TPR

■ KEITH LOCKHART   Lockhart, Keith Virgil b: 11/10/64, Whittier, Cal. BL/TR, 5'10", 170 lbs. Deb: 4/5/94

1994	SD-N	27	43	4	9	0	0	2	6	4	10	.209	.292	.349	68	-2	1	0	0	1.000	-1	3-13/2-5,S-1,O-1	-0.3
1995	KC-A	94	274	41	88	19	3	6	33	14	21	.321	.363	.478	115	6	8	1	2	.974	-8	2-61,3-17,D-14	0.2
1996	KC-A	138	433	49	118	33	3	7	55	30	40	.273	.323	.411	86	-10	11	6	-0	.975	2	2-84,3-55/D-1	-0.4
Total	3	259	750	94	215	52	6	15	94	48	71	.287	.335	.432	96	-6	20	7	2	.974	-7	2-150/3-85,D-15,OS	-0.5

■ GENE LOCKLEAR   Locklear, Gene b: 7/19/49, Lumberton, N.C. BL/TR, 5'10", 165 lbs. Deb: 4/5/73

1973	Cin-N	29	26	6	5	0	0	0	2	5		.192	.276	.192	34	-2	0	0	0	1.000	-1	/O-5	-0.4
	SD-N	67	154	20	37	6	1	3	25	21	22	.240	.331	.351	97	-1	9	4	0	.952	2	O-37	0.0
	Yr	96	180	26	42	6	1	3	25	23	27	.233	.324	.328	87	-3	9	4	0	.954	1	O-42	-0.4
1974	SD-N	39	74	7	20	3	2	1	3	4	12	.270	.308	.405	103	-0	0	1	-1	1.000	-1	O-12	-0.1
1975	SD-N	100	237	31	76	11	1	5	27	22	26	.321	.381	.439	135	11	4	2	0	.970	-1	O-51	0.9
1976	SD-N	43	67	9	15	3	0	0	8	4	15	.224	.268	.269	57	-4	0	0	0	.952	-1	O-11	-0.5
	NY-A	13	32	2	7	1	0	0	1	2	7	.219	.265	.250	52	-2	0	0	0	1.000	-1	/O-3,D-6	-0.3
1977	NY-A	1	5	1	3	0	0	0	2	0	0	.600	.600	.600	231	1	0	0	0	.667	-0	/O-1	0.1
Total	5	292	595	76	163	24	4	9	66	55	87	.274	.337	.373	105	3	13	7	-0	.962	-0	O-120/D-6	-0.3

■ STU LOCKLIN   Locklin, Stuart Carlton b: 7/22/28, Appleton, Wis. BL/TL, 6'1.5", 190 lbs. Deb: 6/23/55

1955	Cle-A	16	18	4	3	1	0	0	0	3	4	.167	.286	.222	37	-2	0	0	0	1.000	-3	/O-7	-0.4
1956	Cle-A	9	6	0	1	0	0	0	0	0	1	.167	.167	.167	-12	-1	0	0	0	1.000	-0	/O-1	-0.1
Total	2	25	24	4	4	1	0	0	0	3	5	.167	.259	.208	26	-3	0	0	0	1.000	-3	/O-8	-0.5

■ WHITEY LOCKMAN   Lockman, Carroll Walter b: 7/25/26, Lowell, N.C. BL/TR, 6'1", 175 lbs. Deb: 7/5/45 MC

1945	NY-N	32	129	16	44	9	0	3	18	13	10	.341	.410	.481	145	8	1			.961	-4	O-32	0.2
1947	NY-N	2	2	0	1	0	0	0	1	0	0	.500	.500	.500	165	0	0			.000	0	H	0.0
1948	NY-N	146	584	117	167	24	10	18	59	68	63	.286	.361	.454	119	15	8			.987	7	*O-144	1.4
1949	NY-N	151	617	97	186	32	7	11	65	62	31	.301	.368	.429	113	12	12			.973	4	*O-151	0.9
1950	NY-N	129	532	72	157	28	5	6	52	42	29	.295	.349	.400	96	-3	1			.978	5	*O-128	0.1
1951	*NY-N	153	614	85	173	27	7	12	73	50	32	.282	.339	.407	99	-1	4	5	-2	.986	-1	*1-119,O-34	-0.6
1952	NY-N★	154	606	99	176	17	4	13	58	67	52	.290	.363	.396	110	9	2	4	-2	.992	7	*1-154	0.4
1953	NY-N	150	607	85	179	22	9	9	61	52	36	.295	.351	.389	91	-7	3	4	-2	.989	7	*1-120,O-30	-0.8
1954	*NY-N	148	570	73	143	17	3	16	60	59	31	.251	.321	.375	80	-17	2	2	-1	.987	-8	*1-145/O-2	-3.2
1955	NY-N	147	576	76	157	19	0	15	49	39	34	.273	.322	.384	86	-12	3	3	-1	.983	-4	O-81,1-68	-2.4
1956	NY-N	48	169	13	46	7	1	1	10	16	17	.272	.335	.343	83	-4	2	0	0	.960	-1	O-39/1-7	-0.8
	StL-N	70	193	14	48	0	2	0	10	18	8	.249	.313	.269	59	-11	2	2	-1	.955	-8	O-57/1-2	-2.3
	Yr	118	362	27	94	7	3	1	20	34	25	.260	.323	.304	70	-14	2	4	-2	.957	-8	O-96/1-9	-3.1
1957	NY-N	133	456	51	113	9	4	7	30	39	19	.248	.310	.331	73	-17	5	5	-2	.991	-6	*1-102,O-27	-3.3
1958	SF-N	92	122	15	29	5	0	2	7	13	8	.238	.311	.328	71	-5	0	0	0	1.000	-11	O-25,2-15/1-7	-1.6
1959	Bal-A	38	69	7	15	1	1	0	2	8	4	.217	.299	.261	56	-4	0	0	0	.992	-4	1-22/2-5,O-1	-0.8
	Cin-N	52	84	10	22	5	1	0	7	4	6	.262	.295	.345	68	-4	0	0	0	.971	-5	1-20/2-6,3-1,O-1	-0.4
1960	Cin-N	21	10	6	2	0	0	1	1	2	3	.200	.385	.500	138	1	0	0	0	1.000	-0	/1-5	0.1
Total	15	1666	5940	836	1658	222	49	114	563	552	383	.279	.342	.391	95	-40	43	27		.989	-9	1-771,O-752/2-26,3	-13.1

■ SKIP LOCKWOOD   Lockwood, Claude Edward b: 8/17/46, Boston, Mass. BR/TR, 6', 190 lbs. Deb: 4/23/65

1965	KC-A	42	33	4	4	0	0	0	0	7	11	.121	.293	.121	23	-3	0	0	0	1.000	2	/3-7	-0.1
1969	Sea-A	6	7	0	0	0	0	0	0	0	2	.000	.000	.000	-99	-2	0	0	0	1.000	0	/P-6	0.0
1970	Mil-A	27	53	2	12	1	0	1	2	1	11	.226	.241	.302	48	-4	0	0	0	.970	-1	P-27	0.0
1971	Mil-A	36	62	2	5	1	0	1	4	5	20	.081	.149	.145	-17	-10	0	0	0	1.000	-3	P-33	0.0
1972	Mil-A	31	53	3	7	0	0	0	3	0	12	.132	.193	.132	-2	-7	0	1	-1	.958	-3	P-29	0.0
1973	Mil-A	37	0	0	0	0	0	0	0	0	0	—	—	—	—	—	0	0	0	.944	0	P-37	0.0
1974	Cal-A	37	0	0	0	0	0	0	0	0	0	—	—	—	—	0	0	0	0	1.000	0	P-37	0.0
1975	NY-N	24	6	0	1	0	0	0	1	0	0	.167	.167	.167	-8	-1	0	0	0	.800	-1	P-24	0.0
1976	NY-N	56	18	2	6	1	0	0	2	3	0	.333	.400	.389	132	1	0	1	-1	.867	-0	P-56	0.0
1977	NY-N	63	15	1	3	0	0	0	1	0	1	.200	.200	.200	8	-2	0	0	0	.875	-2	P-63	0.0
1978	NY-N	57	11	1	2	1	0	1	1	0	5	.182	.182	.545	100	-0	0	0	0	.900	-2	P-57	0.0
1979	NY-N	28	2	0	0	0	0	0	0	0	1	.000	.000	.000	-99	-1	0	0	0	.800	-1	P-27	0.0
1980	Bos-A	24	0	0	0	0	0	0	0	0	0	—	—	—	—	0	0	0	0	1.000	-1	P-24	0.0
Total	13	468	260	15	40	4	0	3	11	18	66	.154	.214	.204	19	-28	0	2	-1	.947	-11	P-420/3-7	-0.1

■ MILO LOCKWOOD   Lockwood, Milo Hathaway b: 4/7/1858, Solon, Ohio d: 10/9/1897, Economy, Pa. 5'10", 160 lbs. Deb: 4/17/1884

| 1884 | Was-U | 20 | 67 | 9 | 14 | 1 | 0 | 0 | | 8 | | .209 | .293 | .224 | 61 | -5 | | | | .773 | 2 | O-11,P-11/3-3 | -0.2 |

■ DARIO LODIGIANI   Lodigiani, Dario Antonio b: 6/6/16, San Francisco, Cal BR/TR, 5'8", 150 lbs. Deb: 4/18/38 C

1938	Phi-A	93	325	36	91	15	1	6	44	34	25	.280	.361	.388	90	-5	3	0	1	.953	-6	2-80,3-13	-0.5
1939	Phi-A	121	393	46	102	22	4	6	44	42	18	.260	.337	.382	85	-9	2	0	1	.944	3	3-89,2-28	-0.4
1940	Phi-A	1	1	0	0	0	0	0	0	0	0	.000	.000	.000	-99	-0	0	0	0	.000	0	H	0.0
1941	Chi-A	87	322	39	77	19	2	4	40	31	19	.239	.316	.348	76	-11	0	4	-2	.962	6	3-86	-0.5
1942	Chi-A	59	168	9	47	7	0	0	15	18	10	.280	.353	.321	92	-1	3	4	-2	.944	6	3-43/2-7	0.4
1946	Chi-A	44	155	12	38	8	0	0	13	16	14	.245	.324	.297	77	-4	0	0	0	.935	-5	3-44	-0.8
Total	6	405	1364	142	355	71	7	16	156	141	86	.260	.338	.358	84	-31	12	8	-1	.947	3	3-275,2-115	-1.8

■ GEORGE LOEPP   Loepp, George Herbert b: 9/11/01, Detroit, Mich. d: 9/4/67, Los Angeles, Cal. BR/TR, 5'11", 170 lbs. Deb: 8/29/28

1928	Bos-A	15	51	6	9	3	1	0	3	5	12	.176	.250	.275	38	-5	0	0	0	.949	-0	O-14	-0.6
1930	Was-A	50	134	23	37	7	1	0	14	20	9	.276	.382	.343	85	-2	0	4	-2	.958	-5	O-48	-1.1
Total	2	65	185	29	46	10	2	0	17	25	21	.249	.347	.324	73	-7	0	4	-2	.956	-6	/O-62	-1.7

■ KENNY LOFTON   Lofton, Kenneth b: 5/31/67, E.Chicago, Ind. BL/TL, 6', 180 lbs. Deb: 9/14/91

1991	Hou-N	20	74	9	15	1	0	0	0	5	19	.203	.253	.216	35	-6	2	2	0	.977	0	O-20	-0.7
1992	Cle-A	148	576	96	164	15	8	5	42	68	54	.285	.362	.365	106	3	66	12	13	.982	17	*O-143	3.3
1993	Cle-A	148	569	116	185	28	8	1	42	81	83	.325	.410	.408	121	21	70	14	13	.979	13	*O-146	4.1
1994	Cle-A★	112	459	105	160	32	9	12	57	52	56	.349	.417	.536	143	30	60	12	11	.993	8	*O-112	4.2
1995	*Cle-A★	118	481	93	149	22	13	7	53	40	49	.310	.364	.453	110	7	54	15	7	.970	1	*O-114/D-2	1.1
1996	*Cle-A★	154	662	132	210	35	4	14	67	61	82	.317	.375	.446	106	6	75	17	12	.975	10	*O-152	2.2
Total	6	700	2821	551	883	133	42	39	261	307	343	.313	.382	.431	115	65	327	71	56	.980	48	O-687/D-2	14.2

■ DICK LOFTUS   Loftus, Richard Joseph b: 3/7/01, Concord, Mass. d: 1/21/72, Concord, Mass. BL/TR, 6', 155 lbs. Deb: 4/20/24

1924	Bro-N	46	81	18	22	6	0	0	8	7	2	.272	.330	.346	84	-2	1	0	0	1.000	-3	O-29/1-1	-0.6
1925	Bro-N	51	131	16	31	6	0	0	13	5	5	.237	.275	.282	44	-11	2	0	1	.977	-1	O-38	-1.1
Total	2	97	212	34	53	12	0	0	21	12	7	.250	.296	.307	59	-13	3	0	1	.985	-3	/O-67,1-1	-1.7

■ TOM LOFTUS   Loftus, Thomas Joseph b: 11/15/1856, St.Louis, Mo. d: 4/16/10, Dubuque, Iowa BR , 168 lbs. Deb: 8/17/1877 M

1877	StL-N	3	11	2	2	0	0	0	0	0	1	.182	.182	.182	16	-1				.778	2	/O-3	0.0
1883	StL-a	6	22	1	4	0	0	0		2		.182	.250	.182	39	-1				.882	2	/O-6	-0.1
Total	2	9	33	3	6	0	0	0	0	2	1	.182	.229	.182	32	-2				.846	2	/O-9	-0.1

■ JOHNNY LOGAN   Logan, John "Yatcha" b: 3/23/27, Endicott, N.Y. BR/TR, 5'11", 175 lbs. Deb: 4/17/51

1951	Bos-N	62	169	14	37	7	1	0	16	18	13	.219	.298	.272	59	-10	0	0	0	.958	4	S-58	-0.2
1952	Bos-N	117	456	56	129	21	3	4	42	31	33	.283	.334	.368	98	-2	1	2	-1	.972	18	*S-117	2.4
1953	Mil-N	150	611	100	167	27	8	11	73	41	33	.273	.326	.398	93	-7	2	2	-1	.975	21	*S-150	2.3
1954	Mil-N	154	560	66	154	17	7	8	66	51	51	.275	.342	.373	92	-7	2	0	0	.969	14	*S-154	2.1
1955	Mil-N★	154	595	95	177	37	5	13	83	58	58	.297	.364	.442	118	16	3	3	-1	.963	8	*S-154	3.5

YEAR	TM/L	G	AB	R	H	2B	3B	HR	RBI	BB	SO	AVG	OBP	SLG	PRO+	BR/A	SB	CS	SBR	FA	FR	G/POS	TPR
1956	Mil-N	148	545	69	153	27	5	15	46	46	49	.281	.342	.431	113	9	3	0	1	.968	3	*S-148	2.6
1957	*Mil-N☆	129	494	59	135	19	7	10	49	31	49	.273	.321	.401	100	-2	5	0	2	.960	24	*S-129	3.6
1958	*Mil-N★	145	530	54	120	20	0	11	53	40	57	.226	.287	.326	68	-26	1	2	-1	.959	10	*S-144	-0.4
1959	Mil-N☆	138	470	59	137	17	0	13	50	57	45	.291	.372	.411	118	13	1	3	-2	.975	-3	*S-138	2.0
1960	Mil-N	136	482	52	118	14	4	7	42	43	40	.245	.309	.344	82	-12	1	1	-0	.956	2	*S-136	0.0
1961	Mil-N	18	19	0	2	1	0	0	1	1	3	.105	.150	.158	-19	-3	0	0	0	1.000	0	/S-2	-0.2
	Pit-N	27	52	5	12	4	0	0	5	4	8	.231	.286	.308	57	-3	0	0	0	1.000	0	/3-7,S-6	-0.2
	Yr	45	71	5	14	5	0	0	6	5	11	.197	.250	.268	38	-6	0	0	0	.964	0	/S-8,3-7	-0.6
1962	Pit-N	44	80	7	24	3	0	1	12	7	6	.300	.356	.375	96	-0	0	0	0	.980	2	3-19	0.2
1963	Pit-N	81	181	15	42	2	1	0	9	23	27	.232	.325	.254	69	-6	0	0	0	.920	2	S-44/3-4	-0.2
Total	13	1503	5244	651	1407	216	41	93	547	451	472	.268	.331	.378	95	-41	19	13	-2	.965	105	*S-1380/3-30	17.3

■ **PETE LOHMAN**   Lohman, George F. b: 10/21/1864, Lake Elmo, Minn. d: 11/21/28, Los Angeles, Cal. Deb: 5/11/1891

YEAR	TM/L	G	AB	R	H	2B	3B	HR	RBI	BB	SO	AVG	OBP	SLG	PRO+	BR/A	SB	CS	SBR	FA	FR	G/POS	TPR
1891	Was-a	32	109	18	21	1	4	1	11	16	17	.193	.302	.303	76	-3	1			.914	-3	C-21/O-8,3-4,S-1,2	-0.4

■ **HOWARD LOHR**   Lohr, Howard Sylvester b: 6/3/1892, Philadelphia, Pa. d: 6/9/77, Philadelphia, Pa. BR/TR, 6', 165 lbs. Deb: 6/17/14

YEAR	TM/L	G	AB	R	H	2B	3B	HR	RBI	BB	SO	AVG	OBP	SLG	PRO+	BR/A	SB	CS	SBR	FA	FR	G/POS	TPR
1914	Cin-N	18	47	6	10	1	1	0	7	0	8	.213	.213	.277	44	-3	2			.926	-3	O-17	-0.8
1916	Cle-A	3	7	0	1	0	0	0	1	0	1	.143	.143	.143	-13	-1	1			1.000	-1	/O-3	-0.2
Total	2	21	54	6	11	1	1	0	8	0	9	.204	.204	.259	36	-4	3			.933	-4	/O-20	-1.0

■ **JACK LOHRKE**   Lohrke, Jack Wayne "Lucky" b: 2/25/24, Los Angeles, Cal. Deb: 4/18/47

YEAR	TM/L	G	AB	R	H	2B	3B	HR	RBI	BB	SO	AVG	OBP	SLG	PRO+	BR/A	SB	CS	SBR	FA	FR	G/POS	TPR
1947	NY-N	112	329	44	79	12	4	11	35	46	29	.240	.337	.401	95	-3	3			.939	-2	*3-111	-0.4
1948	NY-N	97	280	35	70	15	4	5	31	30	30	.250	.323	.364	85	-6	3			.898	-2	3-50,2-36	-0.6
1949	NY-N	55	180	32	48	11	4	5	22	16	12	.267	.333	.456	110	2	3			.969	4	2-23,3-19,S-15	0.7
1950	NY-N	30	43	4	8	0	0	0	4	4	8	.186	.255	.186	18	-5	0			.958	0	3-16/2-1	-0.5
1951	*NY-N	23	40	3	8	0	0	1	3	10	2	.200	.360	.275	73	-1	0	0	0	.943	-1	3-17/S-1	-0.2
1952	Phi-N	25	29	4	6	0	0	0	1	2	4	.207	.303	.207	44	-2	0	0	0	1.000	1	/S-5,3-3,2-1	-0.1
1953	Phi-N	12	13	3	2	0	0	0	0	1	1	.154	.214	.154	-2	-2	0	0	0	.750	-2	/2-2,S-2,3-1	-0.1
Total	7	354	914	125	221	38	9	22	96	111	86	.242	.327	.375	87	-17	9	0		.928	2	3-217/2-63,S-23	-1.2

■ **ALBERTO LOIS**   Lois, Alberto (b: Alberto Louis (Pie)) b: 5/6/56, Hato Mayor, D.R. BR/TR, 5'9", 175 lbs. Deb: 9/8/78

YEAR	TM/L	G	AB	R	H	2B	3B	HR	RBI	BB	SO	AVG	OBP	SLG	PRO+	BR/A	SB	CS	SBR	FA	FR	G/POS	TPR
1978	Pit-N	3	4	0	1	0	1	0	0	0	1	.250	.250	.750	163	0	0	0	0	1.000	-0	/O-2	0.0
1979	Pit-N	11	0	6	0	0	0	0	0	0	0	—	—	—		0	1	1	-0	.000	0	/R	-0.1
Total	2	14	4	6	1	0	1	0	0	1	.250	.250	.750	163	0	1	1	-0	1.000	-0	/O-2	-0.1

■ **RON LOLICH**   Lolich, Ronald John b: 9/19/46, Portland, Ore. BR/TR, 6'1", 185 lbs. Deb: 7/18/71

YEAR	TM/L	G	AB	R	H	2B	3B	HR	RBI	BB	SO	AVG	OBP	SLG	PRO+	BR/A	SB	CS	SBR	FA	FR	G/POS	TPR
1971	Chi-A	2	8	0	1	0	0	0	0	0	2	.125	.125	.250	4	-1	0	0	0	1.000	-1	/O-2	-0.2
1972	Cle-A	24	80	4	15	1	0	2	8	4	20	.188	.226	.275	47	-5	0	0	0	1.000	-1	O-22	-0.8
1973	Cle-A	61	140	16	32	7	0	2	15	7	27	.229	.265	.321	63	-7	0	2	-1	.909	-4	O-32,D-12	-1.4
Total	3	87	228	20	48	9	0	4	23	11	49	.211	.247	.303	56	-13	0	2	-1	.953	-5	/O-56,D-12	-2.4

■ **SHERM LOLLAR**   Lollar, John Sherman b: 8/23/24, Durham, Ark. d: 9/24/77, Springfield, Mo. BR/TR, 6'1", 185 lbs. Deb: 4/20/46 C

YEAR	TM/L	G	AB	R	H	2B	3B	HR	RBI	BB	SO	AVG	OBP	SLG	PRO+	BR/A	SB	CS	SBR	FA	FR	G/POS	TPR
1946	Cle-A	28	62	7	15	6	0	1	9	5	9	.242	.299	.387	97	-1	0	1	-1	.990	-3	C-24	-0.4
1947	*NY-A	11	32	4	7	0	1	1	6	1	5	.219	.242	.375	71	-1	0	1	-1	1.000	1	/C-9	-0.1
1948	NY-A	22	38	0	8	0	0	0	4	1	6	.211	.231	.211	18	-4	0	0	0	.976	1	C-10	-0.3
1949	StL-A	109	284	28	74	9	1	8	49	32	22	.261	.340	.384	88	-6	0	1	-1	.988	-3	C-93	-0.5
1950	StL-A☆	126	396	55	111	22	3	13	65	64	25	.280	.391	.449	110	7	2	0	1	.995	-2	*C-109	0.7
1951	StL-A	98	310	44	78	21	0	8	44	43	26	.252	.350	.397	99	-0	1	0	0	.989	-2	*C-120	0.2
1952	Chi-A	132	375	35	90	15	0	13	50	54	34	.240	.354	.384	104	3	1	0	0	.989	-2	*C-120	0.7
1953	Chi-A	113	334	46	96	19	0	8	54	47	29	.287	.388	.416	114	8	1	0	0	.994	-2	*C-107/1-1	1.1
1954	Chi-A☆	107	316	31	77	13	0	7	34	37	28	.244	.336	.351	85	-6	0	1	-1	.993	-4	C-93	-0.5
1955	Chi-A☆	138	426	67	111	13	1	16	61	68	34	.261	.375	.408	108	6	2	2	-1	.995	10	*C-136	2.0
1956	Chi-A★	136	450	55	132	28	2	11	75	53	34	.293	.387	.438	116	12	2	0	1	.993	4	*C-132	2.0
1957	Chi-A	101	351	33	90	11	2	11	70	35	24	.256	.346	.393	101	1	2	0	1	.998	-2	C-96	0.4
1958	Chi-A☆	127	421	53	115	16	0	20	84	57	37	.273	.370	.464	128	17	2	1	0	.987	2	*C-116	2.6
1959	*Chi-A★	140	505	63	134	22	3	22	84	55	49	.265	.348	.451	119	13	4	3	-1	.993	10	*C-122,1-24	2.8
1960	Chi-A★	129	421	43	106	23	0	7	46	42	39	.252	.331	.356	87	-7	2	0	1	.995	-2	*C-123	-0.2
1961	Chi-A	116	337	38	95	10	1	7	41	37	22	.282	.363	.380	100	1	0	0	0	.998	-10	*C-107	-0.3
1962	Chi-A	84	220	17	59	12	0	2	26	32	23	.268	.369	.350	95	-0	1	0	0	.991	-8	C-66	-0.6
1963	Chi-A	35	73	4	17	4	0	0	6	8	7	.233	.317	.288	72	-2	0	0	0	.981	-2	C-23/1-2	-0.4
Total	18	1752	5351	623	1415	244	14	155	808	671	453	.264	.359	.402	104	40	20	10	-3	.992	-16	*C-1571/1-27,3-1	9.2

■ **DOUG LOMAN**   Loman, Douglas Edward b: 5/9/58, Bakersfield, Cal. BL/TL, 5'11", 185 lbs. Deb: 9/3/84

YEAR	TM/L	G	AB	R	H	2B	3B	HR	RBI	BB	SO	AVG	OBP	SLG	PRO+	BR/A	SB	CS	SBR	FA	FR	G/POS	TPR
1984	Mil-A	23	76	13	21	4	0	2	12	15	7	.276	.402	.408	130	4	0	2	-1	.967	3	O-23	0.5
1985	Mil-A	24	66	10	14	3	2	0	7	1	12	.212	.224	.318	47	-5	0	0	0	1.000	1	O-20	-0.4
Total	2	47	142	23	35	7	2	2	19	16	19	.246	.327	.366	93	-1	0	2	-1	.981	4	/O-43	0.1

■ **ERNIE LOMBARDI**   Lombardi, Ernesto Natali "Schnozz" or "Bocci" b: 4/6/08, Oakland, Cal. d: 9/26/77, Santa Cruz, Cal. BR/TR, 6'3", 230 lbs. Deb: 4/15/31 H

YEAR	TM/L	G	AB	R	H	2B	3B	HR	RBI	BB	SO	AVG	OBP	SLG	PRO+	BR/A	SB	CS	SBR	FA	FR	G/POS	TPR
1931	Bro-N	73	182	20	54	7	1	4	23	12	12	.297	.340	.412	102	0	1			.984	3	C-50	0.6
1932	Cin-N	118	413	43	125	22	9	11	68	41	19	.303	.371	.479	131	18	0			.963	-11	*C-110	1.3
1933	Cin-N	107	350	30	99	21	1	4	47	16	17	.283	.322	.383	102	0	2			.972	-16	C-95	-1.0
1934	Cin-N	132	417	42	127	19	4	9	62	16	22	.305	.335	.434	107	3	0			.989	-3	C-111	0.5
1935	Cin-N	120	332	36	114	23	3	12	64	16	6	.343	.379	.539	148	21	0			.983	-6	C-82	1.9
1936	Cin-N☆	121	387	42	129	23	2	12	68	19	16	.333	.375	.496	142	21	1			.962	-13	*C-105	1.2
1937	Cin-N☆	120	368	41	123	22	1	9	59	14	17	.334	.362	.473	132	14	1			.973	-18	C-90	0.2
1938	Cin-N★	129	489	60	167	30	1	19	95	40	14	**.342**	.391	.524	154	34	0			.985	-3	*C-123	3.8
1939	*Cin-N★	130	450	43	129	26	2	20	85	35	19	.287	.342	.487	120	11	0			.984	4	*C-120	2.1
1940	*Cin-N★	109	376	50	120	22	0	14	74	31	14	.319	.382	.489	137	19	0			.989	-4	*C-101	2.2
1941	Cin-N	117	398	33	105	12	1	10	60	36	14	.264	.325	.374	96	-2	0			.983	-1	*C-116	0.6
1942	Bos-N★	105	309	32	102	14	0	11	46	37	12	**.330**	.403	.482	162	24	0			.980	-16	C-85	1.5
1943	NY-N★	104	295	19	90	7	0	10	51	43	13	.305	.347	.431	123	8	1			.971	-14	C-73	-0.1
1944	NY-N	117	373	37	95	13	0	10	58	33	25	.255	.317	.370	93	-4	0			.968	-15	*C-100	-1.3
1945	NY-N†	115	368	46	113	7	1	19	70	43	11	.307	.387	.486	140	20	0			.983	0	*C-96	2.7
1946	NY-N	88	238	19	69	4	1	12	39	18	24	.290	.342	.466	129	8	0			.978	1	C-63	1.3
1947	NY-N	48	110	8	31	5	0	4	21	7	9	.282	.325	.436	100	-0	0			.980	-3	C-24	-0.2
Total	17	1853	5855	601	1792	277	27	190	990	430	262	.306	.358	.460	126	195	0		.979	-113	*C-1544	17.3

■ **PHIL LOMBARDI**   Lombardi, Phillip Arden b: 2/20/63, Abilene, Tex. BR/TR, 6'2", 200 lbs. Deb: 4/26/86

YEAR	TM/L	G	AB	R	H	2B	3B	HR	RBI	BB	SO	AVG	OBP	SLG	PRO+	BR/A	SB	CS	SBR	FA	FR	G/POS	TPR
1986	NY-A	20	36	6	10	3	0	2	6	4	7	.278	.366	.528	141	2	0	0	0	.867	-1	/O-8,C-3	0.1
1987	NY-A	5	8	0	1	0	0	0	0	0	2	.125	.125	.125	-34	-2	0	0	0	1.000	-0	/C-3	-0.2
1989	NY-N	18	48	4	11	1	0	1	3	5	8	.229	.302	.313	80	-1	0	0	0	.980	-1	C-16/1-1	-0.2
Total	3	43	92	10	22	4	0	3	9	9	17	.239	.314	.380	95	-1	0	0	0	.975	-2	/C-22,O-8,1-1	-0.3

■ **STEVE LOMBARDOZZI**   Lombardozzi, Stephen Paul b: 4/26/60, Malden, Mass. BR/TR, 6', 175 lbs. Deb: 7/12/85

YEAR	TM/L	G	AB	R	H	2B	3B	HR	RBI	BB	SO	AVG	OBP	SLG	PRO+	BR/A	SB	CS	SBR	FA	FR	G/POS	TPR
1985	Min-A	28	54	10	20	4	1	0	6	6	7	.370	.433	.481	142	3	3	2	-0	.982	11	2-26	1.4
1986	Min-A	156	453	53	103	20	5	8	33	52	76	.227	.308	.347	76	-15	3	4	-1	**.991**	-3	*2-155	-1.2
1987	*Min-A	136	432	51	103	19	3	8	38	33	66	.238	.299	.352	69	-19	5	1	1	.977	-1	*2-133	-1.2
1988	Min-A	103	287	34	60	15	2	3	27	35	48	.209	.296	.307	68	-12	2	5	-2	.986	-7	2-90,S-12/3-5	-1.8
1989	Hou-N	21	37	5	8	3	1	0	3	5	6	.216	.310	.432	100	-0	0	0	0	.922	0	2-18/3-1	0.1
1990	Hou-N	2	1	0	0	0	0	0	0	1	0	.000	.500	.000	52	0	0	0	0	.000	0	/H	0.0
Total	6	446	1264	153	294	61	12	20	107	131	206	.233	.308	.347	76	-42	13	9	-2	.983	1	2-422/S-12,3-6	-2.7

YEAR	TM/L	G	AB	R	H	2B	3B	HR	RBI	BB	SO	AVG	OBP	SLG	PRO+	BR/A	SB	CS	SBR	FA	FR	G/POS	TPR

■ WALTER LONERGAN
Lonergan, Walter E.   b: 9/22/1885, Boston, Mass.   d: 1/23/58, Lexington, Mass.   BR/TR, 5'7", 156 lbs.   Deb: 8/17/11

1911	Bos-A	10	26	2	7	0	0	0	1	1	1	.269	.296	.269	59	-1	1			.935	-1	/2-7,S-1,3-1	-0.2

■ LONG
Long   Deb: 8/29/1888

1888	Lou-a	1	2	0	0	0	0	0	0	0	1	.000	.333	.000	11	-0	0			.000	-0	/O-1	0.0

■ DAN LONG
Long, Daniel W.   b: 8/27/1867, Boston, Mass.   d: 4/30/29, Sausalito, Cal.   Deb: 8/27/1890

1890	Bal-a	21	77	19	12	0	0	0	2	14		.156	.301	.156	33	-6	16			.939	-1	O-21	-0.6

■ HERMAN LONG
Long, Herman C. "Germany" or "Flying Dutchman"   b: 4/13/1866, Chicago, Ill.   d: 9/17/09, Denver, Colo.   BL/TR, 5'8.5", 160 lbs.   Deb: 4/17/1889

1889	KC-a	136	574	137	158	32	6	3	60	64	63	.275	.358	.368	101	-0	89			.874	32	*S-128/2-8,O-1	3.3
1890	Bos-N	101	431	95	108	15	3	8	52	40	34	.251	.320	.355	90	-8	49			.898	1	*S-101	0.8
1891	Bos-N	139	577	129	163	21	12	9	76	80	51	.282	.377	.407	115	9	60			.902	15	*S-139	2.8
1892	*Bos-N	151	646	115	181	33	6	6	78	44	36	.280	.334	.378	105	1	57			.889	14	*S-141,O-12/3-1	1.9
1893	Bos-N	128	552	149	159	22	6	6	58	73	32	.288	.376	.382	94	-6	38			.883	16	*S-123/2-5	1.3
1894	Bos-N	104	475	136	154	28	11	12	79	35	17	.324	.375	.505	103	-2	24			.885	3	*S-98/O-5,2-3	0.5
1895	Bos-N	124	535	109	169	23	10	9	75	31	12	.316	.357	.447	99	-5	35			.891	-7	*S-122/2-2	-0.5
1896	Bos-N	120	501	105	172	26	8	6	100	26	16	.343	.382	.463	115	9	36			.897	10	*S-120	1.9
1897	*Bos-N	107	450	89	145	32	7	3	69	23		.322	.358	.444	105	0	22			.905	-3	*S-107/O-1	-0.3
1898	Bos-N	144	589	99	156	21	10	6	99	39		.265	.311	.365	89	-11	20			.923	1	*S-142/2-2	-0.3
1899	Bos-N	145	578	91	153	30	8	6	100	45		.265	.321	.375	83	-17	20			.929	-10	*S-143/1-2	-1.4
1900	Bos-N	125	486	80	127	19	4	12	66	44		.261	.325	.391	86	-12	20			.937	-6	*S-125	-0.8
1901	Bos-N	138	518	54	112	14	6	3	68	25		.216	.254	.284	51	-34	20			**.946**	-3	*S-138	-2.5
1902	Bos-N	120	439	40	101	11	0	2	44	31		.230	.282	.269	69	-16	24			**.946**	23	*S-107,2-13	1.5
1903	NY-A	22	80	6	15	3	0	0	8	2		.188	.207	.225	28	-7	3			.889	-5	S-22	-1.1
	Det-A	69	239	21	53	12	0	0	23	10		.222	.256	.272	60	-12	11			.879	0	S-38,2-31	-0.9
	Yr	91	319	27	68	15	0	0	31	12		.213	.242	.260	52	-19	14			.883	-4	S-60,2-31	-2.0
1904	Phi-N	1	4	0	1	0	0	0	0	0		.250	.250	.250	56	-0	0			.889	1	/2-1	0.1
Total	16	1874	7674	1455	2127	342	97	91	1055	612	261	.277	.335	.383	93	-110	534			.906	94	*S-1794/2-65,O13	6.6

■ JIMMIE LONG
Long, James Albert   b: 6/29/1898, Ft.Dodge, Iowa   d: 9/14/70, Ft.Dodge, Iowa   BR/TR, 5'11", 160 lbs.   Deb: 9/12/22

1922	Chi-A	3	3	0	0	0	0	0	0	0	1	.000	.250	.000	-30	-1	0	0	0	1.000	-1	/C-2	-0.1

■ JIM LONG
Long, James M.   b: 11/15/1862, Louisville, Ky.   d: 12/12/32, Louisville, Ky.   Deb: 8/9/1891

1891	Lou-a	6	25	5	6	0	0	0	4	3	6	.240	.367	.240	75	-0	1			.857	-1	/O-6	0.0
1893	Bal-N	55	226	31	48	8	1	2	25	16	27	.212	.276	.283	48	-18	23			.893	-1	O-55	-1.8
Total	2	61	251	36	54	8	1	2	29	19	33	.215	.286	.279	51	-18	24			.890	-0	/O-61	-1.8

■ JEOFF LONG
Long, Jeoffrey Keith   b: 10/9/41, Covington, Ky.   BR/TR, 6'1", 200 lbs.   Deb: 7/31/63

1963	StL-N	5	5	0	1	0	0	0	0	0	1	.200	.200	.200	14	-1	0	0	0	.000	0	H	-0.1
1964	StL-N	28	43	5	10	1	0	1	4	6	18	.233	.340	.326	81	-1	0	0	0	.833	-2	/O-4,1-3	-0.3
	Chi-A	23	35	0	5	0	0	1	5	4	15	.143	.231	.143	7	-4	0	0	0	1.000	-1	/1-5,O-5	-0.5
Total	2	56	83	5	16	1	0	2	9	10	34	.193	.287	.241	48	-6	0	0	0	.750	-2	/O-9,1-8	-0.9

■ DALE LONG
Long, Richard Dale   b: 2/6/26, Springfield, Mo.   d: 1/27/91, Palm Coast, Fla.   BL/TL, 6'4", 210 lbs.   Deb: 4/21/51   C

1951	Pit-N	10	12	1	2	0	0	1	1	0	3	.167	.167	.417	50	-1	0	0		1.000	0	/1-1	-0.1
	StL-A	34	105	11	25	5	1	2	11	12	22	.238	.310	.362	79	-3	0	0		.988	-1	1-28/O-1	-0.5
1955	Pit-N★	131	419	59	122	19	13	16	79	48	72	.291	.365	.513	132	19	0	1	-1	.988	6	*1-119	1.7
1956	Pit-N★	148	517	64	136	20	7	27	91	54	85	.263	.333	.485	119	13	0	3		.982	-3	*1-138	0.1
1957	Pit-N	7	22	0	4	1	0	0	5	4	10	.182	.308	.227	48	-2	0	0		1.000	0	/1-7	-0.2
	Chi-N	123	397	55	121	19	0	21	62	52	63	.305	.387	.511	141	23	1	1		.995	-1	*1-104	1.6
	Yr	130	419	55	125	20	0	21	67	56	73	.298	.382	.496	136	22	1	1	-0	.995	-1	*1-111	1.4
1958	Chi-N	142	480	68	130	26	4	20	75	60	64	.271	.361	.467	119	13	0	1		.992	-2	*1-137/C-2	0.4
1959	Chi-N	110	296	34	70	10	3	14	37	31	53	.236	.309	.432	96	-3	0	0		.985	-2	1-85	-0.9
1960	SF-N	37	54	4	9	0	0	3	6	7	7	.167	.262	.333	66	-3	0	0		1.000	0	1-10	-0.3
	*NY-A	26	41	6	15	3	1	3	10	5	6	.366	.435	.707	216	6	0	0		.988	-1	1-11	0.5
1961	Was-A	123	377	52	94	20	4	17	49	39	41	.249	.321	.459	107	3	0	0		.983	-5	1-95	-1.0
1962	Was-A	67	191	17	46	8	0	4	24	18	22	.241	.310	.346	77	-6	5	1		.996	-0	1-51	-0.9
	*NY-A	41	94	12	28	4	0	4	17	18	9	.298	.411	.468	140	6	1	0		.992	1	1-31	0.6
	Yr	108	285	29	74	12	0	8	41	36	31	.260	.345	.386	98	-0	6	1		.995	1	1-82	-0.3
1963	NY-A	14	15	1	3	0	0	0	1	0	3	.200	.250	.200	28	-1	0	0		.917	-1	/1-2	-0.2
Total	10	1013	3020	384	805	135	33	132	467	353	460	.267	.345	.464	116	65	10	8	1	.988	-7	1-819/C-2,O-1	0.8

■ TOM LONG
Long, Thomas Augustus   b: 6/1/1890, Mitchum, Ala.   d: 6/15/72, Mobile, Ala.   BR/TR, 5'10.5", 165 lbs.   Deb: 9/11/11

1911	Was-A	14	48	1	11	0	0	0	5	1		.229	.245	.292	50	-3	4			.875	-2	O-13	-0.6
1912	Was-A	1	1	0	0	0	0	0	0	0		.000	.000	.000	-99	-0	0			.000	0	H	0.0
1915	StL-N	140	507	61	149	21	25	2	61	31	50	.294	.339	.446	137	20	19	15	-3	.927	-4	*O-136	0.7
1916	StL-N	119	403	37	118	11	10	1	33	10	43	.293	.312	.377	112	4	21	14	-2	.945	-8	*O-106	-1.3
1917	StL-N	144	530	49	123	12	14	3	41	37	44	.232	.285	.325	89	-8	21			.919	-19	*O-137	-4.0
Total	5	418	1489	148	401	47	49	6	140	79	137	.269	.309	.379	110	13	65	29		.928	-33	O-392	-5.2

■ TONY LONGMIRE
Longmire, Anthony Eugene   b: 8/12/68, Vallejo, Cal.   BL/TR, 6'1", 197 lbs.   Deb: 9/3/93

1993	*Phi-N	11	13	1	3	0	0	0	1	0	1	.231	.231	.231	24	-1	0	0	0	1.000	0	/O-2	-0.1
1994	Phi-N	69	139	10	33	11	0	0	17	10	27	.237	.293	.317	58	-9	2	1	0	.941	-2	O-32	-1.1
1995	Phi-N	59	104	21	37	7	0	3	19	11	19	.356	.422	.510	143	7	1	1	0	1.000	0	O-23	0.6
Total	3	139	256	32	73	18	0	3	37	21	47	.285	.344	.391	91	-3	3	2	0	.967	-2	/O-57	-0.6

■ JOE LONNETT
Lonnett, Joseph Paul   b: 2/7/27, Beaver Falls, Pa.   BR/TR, 5'10", 180 lbs.   Deb: 4/22/56   C

1956	Phi-N	16	22	2	4	0	0	0	0	7		.182	.250	.182	19	-2	0	0		1.000	0	/C-7	-0.2
1957	Phi-N	67	160	12	27	5	0	5	15	22	39	.169	.273	.294	54	-10	0	0		.997	5	C-65	-0.3
1958	Phi-N	17	50	0	7	2	0	2	2	2	11	.140	.173	.180	-6	-8	0	0		.988	2	C-15	-0.5
1959	Phi-N	43	93	8	16	1	0	1	10	14	17	.172	.287	.215	36	-8	0	1	-1	.983	-6	C-43	-1.3
Total	4	143	325	22	54	8	0	6	27	40	74	.166	.262	.246	37	-29	0	1	-1	.992	0	C-130	-2.3

■ BRUCE LOOK
Look, Bruce Michael   b: 6/9/43, Lansing, Mich.   BL/TR, 5'11", 183 lbs.   Deb: 4/17/68   F

1968	Min-A	59	118	7	29	4	0	0	9	20	24	.246	.355	.280	90	1	0	0	-1	.996	2	C-41	0.3

■ DEAN LOOK
Look, Dean Zachary   b: 7/23/37, Lansing, Mich.   BR/TR, 5'11", 185 lbs.   Deb: 9/22/61   F

1961	Chi-A	3	6	0	0	0	0	0	0	0	2	.000	.000	.000	-99	-2	0	0	0	1.000	0	/O-1	-0.1

■ STAN LOPATA
Lopata, Stanley Edward "Stash"   b: 9/12/25, Delray, Mich.   BR/TR, 6'2", 210 lbs.   Deb: 9/19/48

1948	Phi-N	6	15	2	2	1	0	0	2	1	4	.133	.133	.200	-11	-2	0	0		1.000	0	/C-4	-0.2
1949	Phi-N	83	240	31	65	9	2	8	27	21	44	.271	.330	.425	104	1	1			.973	-3	C-58	0.1
1950	*Phi-N	58	129	10	27	2	2	1	11	22	25	.209	.325	.279	61	-7	1			.974	1	C-51	-0.4
1951	Phi-N	3	5	0	0	0	0	0	0	0	2	.000	.000	.000	-99	-1	0	0		1.000	0	/C-1	-0.1
1952	Phi-N	57	179	25	49	9	1	4	27	36	33	.274	.395	.402	123	7	1	0	1	.987	6	C-55	1.6
1953	Phi-N	81	234	34	56	12	3	8	31	28	39	.239	.321	.419	91	-3	0	1		.987	4	C-80	0.5
1954	Phi-N	86	259	42	75	14	5	14	42	33	37	.290	.372	.544	136	13	1	3	-2	.989	9	C-75/1-1	2.3
1955	Phi-N★	99	303	49	82	9	3	22	58	58	83	.271	.391	.538	146	21	4	1		.995	4	C-66,1-24	2.6
1956	Phi-N☆	146	535	96	143	33	7	32	95	75	93	.267	.358	.535	138	28	5	3		.982	-18	*C-102,1-39	1.3
1957	Phi-N	116	388	50	92	18	2	18	67	66	81	.237	.335	.433	108	4	1	2		.988	-9	*C-108	-0.1
1958	Phi-N	86	258	36	64	9	0	9	33	60	63	.248	.394	.388	109	6	0	1	-1	.987	-9	C-80	0.1

YEAR	TM/L	G	AB	R	H	2B	3B	HR	RBI	BB	SO	AVG	OBP	SLG	PRO+	BR/A	SB	CS	SBR	FA	FR	G/POS	TPR
1959	Mil-N	25	48	0	5	0	0	0	4	3	13	.104	.157	.104	-31	-9	0	0	0	1.000	-3	C-11/1-2	-1.2
1960	Mil-N	7	8	0	1	0	0	0	0	1	3	.125	.222	.125	-2	-1	0	0	0	.944	1	/C-4	0.0
Total	13	853	2601	375	661	116	25	116	397	393	497	.254	.354	.452	115	56	18	11		.986	-15	C-695/1-66	6.5

■ DAVEY LOPES   Lopes, David Earl   b: 5/3/45, E.Providence, R.I.   BR/TR, 5'9", 170 lbs.   Deb: 9/22/72   C

YEAR	TM/L	G	AB	R	H	2B	3B	HR	RBI	BB	SO	AVG	OBP	SLG	PRO+	BR/A	SB	CS	SBR	FA	FR	G/POS	TPR
1972	LA-N	11	42	6	9	4	0	0	1	7	6	.214	.327	.310	84	-1	4	0	1	.964	-2	2-11	-0.1
1973	LA-N	142	535	77	147	13	5	6	37	62	77	.275	.355	.351	101	2	36	16	1	.984	-13	*2-135/O-5,S-2,3-1	-0.2
1974	*LA-N	145	530	95	141	26	3	10	35	66	71	.266	.352	.383	110	8	59	18	7	.965	-22	*2-143	0.0
1975	LA-N	155	618	108	162	24	6	8	41	91	93	.262	.359	.359	104	6	**77**	12	**16**	.979	-23	*2-137,O-24,S-14	0.6
1976	LA-N	117	427	72	103	17	7	4	20	56	49	.241	.335	.342	94	-2	**63**	10	**13**	.964	-20	*2-100,O-19	-0.4
1977	*LA-N	134	502	85	142	19	5	11	53	73	69	.283	.376	.406	110	10	47	12	7	.979	8	*2-130	3.4
1978	*LA-N★	151	587	93	163	25	4	17	58	71	70	.278	.356	.421	117	13	45	4	**11**	.974	3	*2-147/O-2	4.0
1979	LA-N★	153	582	109	154	20	6	28	73	97	88	.265	.373	.464	129	25	44	4	**11**	.981	-34	*2-152	1.2
1980	LA-N★	141	553	79	139	15	3	10	49	58	71	.251	.324	.344	88	-8	23	7	3	.980	-16	*2-140	-1.3
1981	*LA-N★	58	214	35	44	2	0	5	17	22	35	.206	.289	.285	66	-10	20	2	5	.993	-4	2-55	-0.5
1982	Oak-A	128	450	58	109	19	3	11	42	40	51	.242	.305	.371	89	-8	28	12	1	.977	-19	*2-125/O-6	-1.9
1983	Oak-A	147	494	64	137	13	4	17	67	51	61	.277	.347	.423	118	12	22	4	4	.983	-38	*2-123,D-12/O-7,3-5	-1.7
1984	Oak-A	72	230	32	59	11	1	9	36	31	36	.257	.347	.430	122	7	12	0	4	.965	-8	O-42,2-17/3-5,D-9	0.2
	*Chi-N	16	17	5	4	1	0	0	0	6	5	.235	.435	.294	99	0	3	0	1	1.000		/O-9,2-2	-0.1
1985	Chi-N	99	275	52	78	11	0	11	44	46	37	.284	.386	.444	118	8	47	4	12	.991	-12	O-79/3-4,2-1	0.6
1986	Chi-N	59	157	38	47	8	2	6	22	31	16	.299	.421	.490	140	10	17	6	2	.902	-4	3-32,O-22	0.6
	*Hou-N	37	98	11	23	2	1	1	13	12	9	.235	.318	.306	75	-3	8	2	1	1.000		O-19/3-5	0.2
	Yr	96	255	49	70	10	3	7	35	43	25	.275	.383	.420	117	7	25	8	3	1.000	1	O-41,3-37	0.8
1987	Hou-N	47	43	4	10	2	0	1	6	13	8	.233	.411	.349	108	1	7	1	0	.857	-1	/O-5	0.0
Total	16	1812	6354	1023	1671	232	50	155	614	833	852	.263	.351	.388	107	69	557	114	99	.977	-201	*2-1418,O-239/3DS	4.6

■ AL LOPEZ   Lopez, Alfonso Ramon   b: 8/20/08, Tampa, Fla.   BR/TR, 5'11", 165 lbs.   Deb: 9/27/28   MH

YEAR	TM/L	G	AB	R	H	2B	3B	HR	RBI	BB	SO	AVG	OBP	SLG	PRO+	BR/A	SB	CS	SBR	FA	FR	G/POS	TPR
1928	Bro-N	3	12	0	0	0	0	0	0	0	0	.000	.000	.000	-99	-4	0			1.000	-2	/C-3	-0.5
1930	Bro-N	128	421	60	130	20	4	6	57	33	35	.309	.362	.418	89	-7	3			.983	5	*C-126	0.7
1931	Bro-N	111	360	38	97	13	4	0	40	28	33	.269	.324	.328	76	-12	1			.977	-8	*C-105	-1.2
1932	Bro-N	126	404	44	111	18	6	1	43	34	35	.275	.331	.356	87	-7	3			.976	-2	*C-125	-0.2
1933	Bro-N	126	372	39	112	11	4	3	41	21	39	.301	.338	.376	108	4	10			.991	18	*C-124/2-1	3.0
1934	Bro-N★	140	439	50	120	23	2	7	54	49	44	.273	.349	.383	101	1	2			.982	-7	*C-137/2-2,3-2	0.1
1935	Bro-N	128	379	50	95	12	4	3	39	35	36	.251	.316	.327	75	-13	2			.980	6	*C-126	-0.1
1936	Bos-N	128	426	46	103	12	5	7	50	41	41	.242	.311	.343	81	-12	1			.975	10	*C-127/1-1	0.4
1937	Bos-N	105	334	31	68	11	1	3	38	35	57	.204	.281	.275	55	-21	3			.984	8	*C-102	-0.7
1938	Bos-N	71	236	19	63	6	1	1	14	11	24	.267	.305	.314	78	-8	1			.989	3	C-71	-0.1
1939	Bos-N	131	412	32	104	22	1	8	49	40	45	.252	.319	.369	91	-6	1			.986	3	*C-129	0.3
1940	Bos-N	36	119	20	35	3	1	2	17	6	8	.294	.328	.387	102	-0	1			.987	2	C-36	0.4
	Pit-N	59	174	15	45	6	2	1	24	13	13	.259	.310	.333	78	-5	5			.992	4	C-59	0.2
	Yr	95	293	35	80	9	3	3	41	19	21	.273	.317	.355	87	-5	6			**.990**	6	C-95	0.6
1941	Pit-N★	114	317	33	84	9	1	5	43	31	23	.265	.330	.347	91	-3	0			.980	-0	*C-114	0.5
1942	Pit-N	103	289	17	74	8	2	1	26	34	17	.256	.338	.308	88	-3	0			**.995**	3	C-99	0.9
1943	Pit-N	118	372	40	98	9	4	1	39	44	25	.263	.341	.317	88	-5				**.991**	8	*C-116/3-1	1.2
1944	Pit-N	115	331	27	76	12	1	1	34	34	24	.230	.303	.281	62	-16	4			**.984**	4	*C-115	-0.6
1945	Pit-N	91	243	22	53	8	0	0	18	35	12	.218	.317	.251	57	-13	2			.992	5	C-91	-0.1
1946	Pit-N	56	150	13	46	2	0	1	12	23	14	.307	.399	.340	108	3	1			.985	1	C-56	0.7
1947	Cle-A	61	126	9	33	1	0	0	14	9	13	.262	.311	.270	64	-6	1	1	-0	1.000	0	C-57	0.0
Total	19	1950	5916	613	1547	206	43	51	652	556	538	.261	.326	.337	83	-133	46	1		.985	66	*C-1918/3-3,2-3,1-1	4.5

■ ART LOPEZ   Lopez, Arturo (Rodriguez)   b: 6/8/37, Mayaguez, P.R.   BL/TL, 5'9", 170 lbs.   Deb: 4/12/65

YEAR	TM/L	G	AB	R	H	2B	3B	HR	RBI	BB	SO	AVG	OBP	SLG	PRO+	BR/A	SB	CS	SBR	FA	FR	G/POS	TPR
1965	NY-A	38	49	5	7	0	0	0	1	6		.143	.160	.143	-13	-7	0	0	0	.958	-2	O-16	-1.0

■ CARLOS LOPEZ   Lopez, Carlos Antonio (Morales)   b: 9/27/50, Mazatlan, Mexico   BR/TR, 6', 190 lbs.   Deb: 9/17/76

YEAR	TM/L	G	AB	R	H	2B	3B	HR	RBI	BB	SO	AVG	OBP	SLG	PRO+	BR/A	SB	CS	SBR	FA	FR	G/POS	TPR
1976	Cal-A	9	10	1	0	0	0	0	0	2	3	.000	.167	.000	-52	-2	2	0	1	1.000	-1	/O-4,D-1	-0.3
1977	Sea-A	99	297	39	84	18	1	8	34	14	61	.283	.322	.431	104	1	16	4	2	.972	3	O-90/D-2	0.3
1978	Bal-A	129	193	21	46	6	0	4	20	9	34	.238	.276	.332	75	-7	5	7	-3	.988	-25	*O-114/D-1	-3.8
Total	3	237	500	61	130	24	1	12	54	25	98	.260	.301	.384	90	-8	23	11	0	.979	-23	O-208/D-4	-3.8

■ HECTOR LOPEZ   Lopez, Hector Headley (Swainson)   b: 7/9/29, Colon, Panama   BR/TR, 5'11", 182 lbs.   Deb: 5/12/55

YEAR	TM/L	G	AB	R	H	2B	3B	HR	RBI	BB	SO	AVG	OBP	SLG	PRO+	BR/A	SB	CS	SBR	FA	FR	G/POS	TPR
1955	KC-A	128	483	50	140	15	2	15	68	33	58	.290	.339	.422	103	0	1	4	-2	.936	15	3-93,2-36	1.6
1956	KC-A	151	561	91	153	27	3	18	69	63	73	.273	.349	.428	104	2	4	5	-2	.940	1	*3-121,O-20/2-8,S-4	0.3
1957	KC-A	121	391	51	115	19	4	11	35	41	66	.294	.361	.448	118	9	1	6	-3	.937	4	*3-111/2-4,O-3	1.3
1958	KC-A	151	564	84	147	28	4	17	73	49	61	.261	.322	.415	99	-1	2	2	-1	.974	6	2-96,3-55/S-1,O-1	1.2
1959	KC-A	35	135	22	38	10	3	6	24	8	23	.281	.326	.533	129	5	1	0	0	.933	-12	2-33	-0.4
	NY-A	112	406	60	115	16	2	16	69	28	54	.283	.339	.451	119	9	3	1	0	.926	-5	3-76,O-35	0.3
	Yr	147	541	82	153	26	5	22	93	36	77	.283	.336	.471	122	14	4	1	1	.926	-17	3-76,O-35,2-33	-0.1
1960	*NY-A	131	408	66	116	14	6	9	42	46	64	.284	.362	.414	116	9	1	0	0	.976	-0	*O-106/2-5,3-1	0.4
1961	*NY-A	93	243	27	54	7	2	3	22	24	38	.222	.295	.305	64	-13	1	0	0	.977	1	O-72	-1.5
1962	*NY-A	106	335	45	92	19	1	6	48	33	53	.275	.340	.391	99	-0	1	0	0	.984	3	O-84/2-1,3-1	-0.2
1963	*NY-A	130	433	54	108	13	4	14	52	35	71	.249	.306	.395	95	-3	1	2	-1	.957	-3	*O-124/2-1	-1.4
1964	*NY-A	127	285	34	74	9	3	10	34	24	54	.260	.319	.418	101	0	0	1	-0	.971	-13	*O-103/3-1	-1.7
1965	NY-A	111	250	35	74	12	2	7	39	26	61	.296	.326	.492	104	1	1	2	-0	.942	-8	O-75/1-2	-1.0
1966	NY-A	54	117	14	25	4	1	4	16	8	20	.214	.270	.368	84	-3	2	1	-0	.936	-2	O-29	-0.7
Total	12	1450	4644	623	1251	193	37	136	591	418	696	.269	.333	.415	104	17	16	23	-9	.967	-13	O-652,3-459,2/S1	-1.8

■ JAVY LOPEZ   Lopez, Javier Torres   b: 11/5/70, Ponce, P.R.   BR/TR, 6'3", 185 lbs.   Deb: 9/18/92

YEAR	TM/L	G	AB	R	H	2B	3B	HR	RBI	BB	SO	AVG	OBP	SLG	PRO+	BR/A	SB	CS	SBR	FA	FR	G/POS	TPR
1992	*Atl-N	9	16	3	6	2	0	0	2	0	1	.375	.375	.500	137	1	0	0	0	1.000	1	/C-9	0.2
1993	Atl-N	8	16	1	6	1	1	1	2	0	2	.375	.412	.750	201	2	0	0	0	.975	2	/C-7	0.4
1994	Atl-N	80	277	27	68	9	0	13	35	17	61	.245	.301	.419	83	-7	0	2	-1	.995	-9	C-75	-0.1
1995	*Atl-N	100	333	37	105	11	4	14	51	14	57	.315	.347	.498	116	7	0	1	-1	.988	2	C-93	1.4
1996	*Atl-N	138	489	56	138	19	1	23	69	28	84	.282	.325	.466	100	1	1	5	-3	.994	18	*C-135	2.2
Total	5	335	1131	124	323	42	6	51	159	59	205	.286	.327	.469	102	1	1	9	-5	.993	25	C-319	4.1

■ LUIS LOPEZ   Lopez, Luis Antonio   b: 9/1/64, Brooklyn, N.Y.   BR/TR, 6'1", 190 lbs.   Deb: 9/14/90

YEAR	TM/L	G	AB	R	H	2B	3B	HR	RBI	BB	SO	AVG	OBP	SLG	PRO+	BR/A	SB	CS	SBR	FA	FR	G/POS	TPR
1990	LA-N	6	6	0	0	0	0	0	0	0	0	.000	.000	.000	-99	-2	0	0	0	1.000	-0	/1-1	-0.2
1991	Cle-A	35	82	7	18	4	1	0	7	4	9	.220	.264	.293	54	-5	0	0	0	1.000	-2	C-12,1-10/3-1,OD	-0.8
Total	2	41	88	7	18	4	1	0	7	4	9	.205	.247	.273	43	-7	0	0	0	.977	-2	/C-12,1-11,D-6,O3	-1.0

■ LUIS LOPEZ   Lopez, Luis Manuel (Santos)   b: 9/4/70, Cidra, P.R.   BB/TR, 5'11", 175 lbs.   Deb: 9/7/93

YEAR	TM/L	G	AB	R	H	2B	3B	HR	RBI	BB	SO	AVG	OBP	SLG	PRO+	BR/A	SB	CS	SBR	FA	FR	G/POS	TPR
1993	SD-N	17	43	1	5	1	0	0	0	0	8	.116	.116	.140	-31	-8	0	0	0	.983	3	2-15	-0.5
1994	SD-N	77	235	29	65	16	1	2	20	15	39	.277	.328	.379	86	-5	3	2	-0	.941	2	S-43,2-29/3-5	0.1
1996	*SD-N	63	139	10	25	3	0	2	11	9	35	.180	.235	.245	28	-15	0	0	0	.981	-3	S-35,2-22/3-2	-1.4
Total	3	157	417	40	95	20	1	4	32	24	82	.228	.276	.309	55	-27	3	2	-0	.956	2	/S-78,2-66,3-7	-1.8

■ BRIS LORD   Lord, Bristol Robotham "The Human Eyeball"   b: 9/21/1883, Upland, Pa.   d: 11/13/64, Annapolis, Md.   BR/TR, 5'9", 185 lbs.   Deb: 4/21/05

YEAR	TM/L	G	AB	R	H	2B	3B	HR	RBI	BB	SO	AVG	OBP	SLG	PRO+	BR/A	SB	CS	SBR	FA	FR	G/POS	TPR
1905	*Phi-A	66	238	38	57	14	0	0	13	14		.239	.285	.298	83	-5	3			.963	4	O-61	-0.8
1906	Phi-A	118	434	50	101	13	7	1	44	27		.233	.281	.302	80	-10	12			.941	-2	*O-115	-2.0
1907	Phi-A	57	170	12	31	3	0	1	11	14		.182	.249	.218	48	-10	4			.951	4	O-53/P-1	-1.4
1909	Cle-A	69	249	26	67	7	3	1	25	8		.269	.295	.333	94	-2	10			.992	6	O-67	0.1
1910	Cle-A	58	210	23	46	8	7	0	17	12		.219	.268	.324	84	-5	4			.958	4	O-56	-0.4

YEAR	TM/L	G	AB	R	H	2B	3B	HR	RBI	BB	SO	AVG	OBP	SLG	PRO+	BR/A	SB	CS	SBR	FA	FR	G/POS	TPR
	*Phi-A	70	279	53	78	13	11	1	20	23		.280	.337	.416	137	11	6			.980	4	O-70	1.2
	Yr	128	489	76	124	21	18	1	37	35		.254	.307	.376	114	6	10			.972	8	*O-126	0.8
1911	*Phi-A	134	574	92	178	37	11	3	55	35		.310	.355	.429	120	14	15			.963	8	*O-132	1.4
1912	Phi-A	97	378	63	90	12	9	0	25	34		.238	.309	.317	82	-9	15			.942	-0	O-97	-1.4
1913	Bos-N	73	235	22	59	12	1	6	26	8	22	.251	.276	.387	86	-5	7			.914	-10	O-62	-1.9
Total	8	742	2767	379	707	119	49	13	236	175	<u>22</u>	.256	.304	.348	95	-22	74			.957	8	O-713/P-1	-5.2

■ HARRY LORD   Lord, Harry Donald b: 3/8/1882, Porter, Me. d: 8/9/48, Westbrook, Maine BL/TR, 5'10.5", 165 lbs. Deb: 9/25/07 M

YEAR	TM/L	G	AB	R	H	2B	3B	HR	RBI	BB	SO	AVG	OBP	SLG	PRO+	BR/A	SB	CS	SBR	FA	FR	G/POS	TPR
1907	Bos-A	10	38	4	6	1	0	0	3	1		.158	.179	.184	16	-4	1			.919	0	3-10	-0.3
1908	Bos-A	145	560	61	145	15	6	2	37	22		.259	.297	.318	97	-3	23			.902	-10	*3-144	-0.8
1909	Bos-A	136	534	86	166	12	7	0	31	20		.311	.345	.360	120	11	36			.929	-7	*3-134	0.9
1910	Bos-A	77	288	25	72	5	5	1	32	14		.250	.294	.313	88	-5	17			.927	-5	3-70/S-1	-0.9
	Chi-A	44	165	26	49	6	3	0	10	14		.297	.352	.370	131	6	17			.952	-1	3-44	-0.4
	Yr	121	453	51	121	11	8	1	42	28		.267	.315	.333	103	1	34			.935	-16	*3-114/S-1	-1.3
1911	Chi-A	141	561	103	180	18	18	3	61	32		.321	.364	.433	126	18	43			.941	-17	*3-138	0.3
1912	Chi-A	151	570	81	152	19	12	5	54	52		.267	.333	.368	104	2	28			.895	-27	*3-106,O-45	-2.6
1913	Chi-A	150	547	62	144	18	12	1	42	45	39	.263	.327	.346	98	-2	24			.924	-31	*3-150	-3.4
1914	Chi-A	21	69	8	13	1	1	1	3	5	3	.188	.243	.275	57	-4	2	2	-1	.933	-6	3-19/O-1	-1.1
1915	Buf-F	97	359	50	97	12	6	1	21	21	15	.270	.311	.345	83	-14	15			.946	-14	3-92/O-1,M	-2.6
Total	9	972	3691	506	1024	107	70	14	294	226	<u>57</u>	.277	.326	.356	104	6	206	2		.924	-127	3-907/O-47,S-1	-10.9

■ CARLTON LORD   Lord, William Carlton b: 1/7/1900, Philadelphia, Pa. d: 8/15/47, Chester, Pa. BR/TR, 5'11", 170 lbs. Deb: 7/12/23

YEAR	TM/L	G	AB	R	H	2B	3B	HR	RBI	BB	SO	AVG	OBP	SLG	PRO+	BR/A	SB	CS	SBR	FA	FR	G/POS	TPR
1923	Phi-N	17	47	3	11	2	0	0	2	2	3	.234	.265	.277	39	-4	0	1	-1	.833	-1	3-14	-0.4

■ MARK LORETTA   Loretta, Mark David b: 8/14/71, Santa Monica, Cal. BR/TR, 6', 175 lbs. Deb: 9/4/95

YEAR	TM/L	G	AB	R	H	2B	3B	HR	RBI	BB	SO	AVG	OBP	SLG	PRO+	BR/A	SB	CS	SBR	FA	FR	G/POS	TPR
1995	Mil-A	19	50	13	13	3	0	1	3	4	7	.260	.327	.380	79	-2	1	1	-0	.979	-1	S-13/2-4,D-1	-0.2
1996	Mil-A	73	154	20	43	3	0	1	13	14	15	.279	.339	.318	64	-8	2	1	-0	.989	7	2-28,3-23,S-21	0.1
Total	2	92	204	33	56	6	0	2	16	18	22	.275	.336	.333	68	-10	3	2	-0	.980	6	/S-34,2-32,3-23,D-1	-0.1

■ SCOTT LOUCKS   Loucks, Scott Gregory b: 11/11/56, Anchorage, Alaska BR/TR, 6', 178 lbs. Deb: 9/1/80

YEAR	TM/L	G	AB	R	H	2B	3B	HR	RBI	BB	SO	AVG	OBP	SLG	PRO+	BR/A	SB	CS	SBR	FA	FR	G/POS	TPR
1980	Hou-N	8	3	4	1	0	0	0	0	2		.333	.333	.333	94	-0	0	0	0	1.000	-2	/O-4	-0.2
1981	Hou-N	10	7	2	4	0	0	0	0	1	3	.571	.625	.571	254	2	1	0	0	1.000	-2	/O-5	0.0
1982	Hou-N	44	49	6	11	2	0	0	3	3	17	.224	.269	.265	54	-3	4	1	1	.978	-7	O-37	-1.0
1983	Hou-N	7	14	2	3	0	0	0	0	1	4	.214	.267	.214	37	-1	2	2	-1	1.000	-1	/O-6	-0.2
1985	Pit-N	4	7	1	2	2	0	0	1	0	3	.286	.444	.571	184	1	0	0	0	1.000	-1	/O-4	0.0
Total	5	73	80	15	21	4	0	0	4	7	28	.262	.322	.313	83	-2	7	3	0	.985	-10	/O-56	-1.4

■ BALDY LOUDEN   Louden, William P. b: 8/27/1885, Piedmont, W.Va. d: 12/8/35, Piedmont, W.Va. BR/TR, 5'11", 175 lbs. Deb: 9/13/07

YEAR	TM/L	G	AB	R	H	2B	3B	HR	RBI	BB	SO	AVG	OBP	SLG	PRO+	BR/A	SB	CS	SBR	FA	FR	G/POS	TPR
1907	NY-A	4	9	4	1	0	0	0	0	2		.111	.273	.111	21	-1	1			.750	1	/3-3	0.0
1912	Det-A	122	403	57	97	12	4	1	36	58		.241	.352	.298	89	-3	28			.951	23	2-87,3-26/S-5	1.8
1913	Det-A	76	191	28	46	4	5	0	23	24	22	.241	.344	.314	94	-1	6			.906	0	2-30,3-26/S-6,0-5	-0.5
1914	Buf-F	126	431	73	135	11	4	6	63	52	41	.313	.391	.399	113	3	35			.931	-18	*S-115	-0.5
1915	Buf-F	141	469	67	132	18	5	4	48	64	45	.281	.372	.367	106	-1	30			.978	14	2-88,S-27,3-19	1.8
1916	Cin-N	134	439	38	96	16	4	1	32	54	54	.219	.313	.280	85	-6	12			**.968**	17	*2-108,S-23	1.8
Total	6	603	1942	267	507	61	22	12	202	254	162	.261	.355	.334	98	-7	112			.961	37	2-313,S-176/3-74,O	4.9

■ CHARLIE LOUDENSLAGER   Loudenslager, Charles Edward b: 5/21/1881, Baltimore, Md. d: 10/31/33, Baltimore, Md. TR, 5'9", 186 lbs. Deb: 4/15/04

YEAR	TM/L	G	AB	R	H	2B	3B	HR	RBI	BB	SO	AVG	OBP	SLG	PRO+	BR/A	SB	CS	SBR	FA	FR	G/POS	TPR
1904	Bro-N	1	2	0	0	0	0	0	0	0		.000	.000	.000	-99	-0	0			1.000	-1	/2-1	-0.1

■ BILL LOUGHLIN   Loughlin, William H. b: Baltimore, Md. Deb: 5/9/1883

YEAR	TM/L	G	AB	R	H	2B	3B	HR	RBI	BB	SO	AVG	OBP	SLG	PRO+	BR/A	SB	CS	SBR	FA	FR	G/POS	TPR
1883	Bal-a	1	5	0	2	0	0	0	0			.400	.400	.400	154	0				.000	-0	/O-1	0.0

■ LOUGHRAN   Loughran b: New York, N.Y. Deb: 6/6/1884

YEAR	TM/L	G	AB	R	H	2B	3B	HR	RBI	BB	SO	AVG	OBP	SLG	PRO+	BR/A	SB	CS	SBR	FA	FR	G/POS	TPR
1884	NY-N	9	29	4	3	1	1	0	3	7	11	.103	.278	.207	54	-1				.857	-3	/C-9,O-1	-0.3

■ TOM LOVELACE   Lovelace, Thomas Rivers b: 10/19/1897, Wolfe City, Tex. d: 7/12/79, Dallas, Tex. BR/TR, 5'11", 170 lbs. Deb: 9/23/22

YEAR	TM/L	G	AB	R	H	2B	3B	HR	RBI	BB	SO	AVG	OBP	SLG	PRO+	BR/A	SB	CS	SBR	FA	FR	G/POS	TPR
1922	Pit-N	1	0	0	0	0	0	0	0	0	0	.000	.000	.000	-99	-0	0	0	0	.000	0	H	0.0

■ LEN LOVETT   Lovett, Leonard Walker b: 7/17/1852, Lancaster Co., Pa d: 11/18/22, Newark, Del. BR/TR, Deb: 8/4/1873

YEAR	TM/L	G	AB	R	H	2B	3B	HR	RBI	BB	SO	AVG	OBP	SLG	PRO+	BR/A	SB	CS	SBR	FA	FR	G/POS	TPR
1873	Res-n	1	5	1	2	0	0	0	1	0	0	.400	.400	.400	150	0	0	0	0	.500	-0	/P-1	0.0
1875	Cen-n	6	21	2	5	1	0	0	2	1	5	.238	.273	.286	103	0	0	0	0	.700	-1	/O-6	0.0
Total	2 n	7	26	3	7	1	0	0	3	1	5	.269	.296	.308	113	1	0	0	0	.700	-1	/O-6,P-1	0.0

■ MEM LOVETT   Lovett, Merritt Marwood b: 6/15/12, Chicago, Ill. BR/TR, 5'9.5", 165 lbs. Deb: 9/4/33

YEAR	TM/L	G	AB	R	H	2B	3B	HR	RBI	BB	SO	AVG	OBP	SLG	PRO+	BR/A	SB	CS	SBR	FA	FR	G/POS	TPR
1933	Chi-A	1	0	0	0	0	0	0	0	0	0	.000	.000	.000	-99	-0	0	0	0	.000	0	H	0.0

■ JAY LOVIGLIO   Loviglio, John Paul b: 5/30/56, Freeport, N.Y. BR/TR, 5'9", 160 lbs. Deb: 9/2/80

YEAR	TM/L	G	AB	R	H	2B	3B	HR	RBI	BB	SO	AVG	OBP	SLG	PRO+	BR/A	SB	CS	SBR	FA	FR	G/POS	TPR
1980	Phi-N	16	5	7	0	0	0	0	0	1	0	.000	.167	.000	-47	-1	1	2	-1	1.000	1	/2-1	-0.1
1981	Chi-A	14	15	5	4	0	0	0	2	1	1	.267	.313	.267	70	-1	2	2	-1	.786	3	/3-4,2-3,D-2	0.2
1982	Chi-A	15	31	5	6	0	0	0	2	1	4	.194	.219	.194	14	-4	2	1	0	.964	4	2-13/D-2	0.1
1983	Chi-N	1	1	0	0	0	0	0	0	0	0	.000	.000	.000	-95	-0	0	0	0	.000	0	/H	0.0
Total	4	46	52	17	10	0	0	0	4	3	6	.192	.236	.192	21	-5	5	5	-2	.971	9	/2-17,D-4,3-4	0.2

■ JOE LOVITTO   Lovitto, Joseph b: 1/6/51, San Pedro, Cal. BB/TR, 6', 185 lbs. Deb: 4/15/72

YEAR	TM/L	G	AB	R	H	2B	3B	HR	RBI	BB	SO	AVG	OBP	SLG	PRO+	BR/A	SB	CS	SBR	FA	FR	G/POS	TPR
1972	Tex-A	117	330	23	74	9	1	1	19	37	54	.224	.306	.267	75	-10	13	11	-3	.976	4	*O-103	-1.5
1973	Tex-A	26	44	3	6	1	0	0	0	5	7	.136	.224	.159	10	-5	1	0	0	.898	1	3-20/O-3	-0.4
1974	Tex-A	113	283	27	63	9	3	2	26	25	36	.223	.286	.297	69	-11	6	8	-3	.972	-12	*O-107/1-5	-3.2
1975	Tex-A	50	106	17	22	3	0	1	8	10	16	.208	.294	.264	59	-5	2	2	-1	.985	-6	O-38/1-2,C-1,D-2	-1.4
Total	4	306	763	70	165	22	4	4	53	80	113	.216	.292	.271	67	-31	22	21	-6	.975	-14	O-251/3-20,1-7,DC	-6.5

■ TOREY LOVULLO   Lovullo, Salvatore Anthony b: 7/25/65, Santa Monica, Cal. BB/TR, 6'1", 185 lbs. Deb: 9/10/88

YEAR	TM/L	G	AB	R	H	2B	3B	HR	RBI	BB	SO	AVG	OBP	SLG	PRO+	BR/A	SB	CS	SBR	FA	FR	G/POS	TPR
1988	Det-A	12	21	2	8	1	1	1	2	1	2	.381	.409	.667	204	3	0	0	0	1.000	-0	/2-9,3-3	0.3
1989	Det-A	29	87	8	10	2	0	1	4	14	20	.115	.238	.172	18	-9	0	0	0	1.000	-3	1-18,3-11	-1.4
1991	NY-A	22	51	0	9	2	0	0	2	5	7	.176	.250	.216	30	-5	0	0	0	.940	3	3-22	-0.5
1993	Cal-A	116	367	42	92	20	0	6	30	36	49	.251	.319	.354	78	-11	7	6	-2	.981	-24	2-91,3-14/S-9,O1D	-3.3
1994	Sea-A	36	72	9	16	5	0	2	7	9	13	.222	.309	.375	74	-3	1	0	0	1.000	3	2-20/3-5,D-2	0.1
1996	Oak-A	65	82	15	18	4	0	3	9	11	17	.220	.326	.366	81	-4	1	2	-1	1.000	2	1-42,3-11/2-2,SOD	-0.3
Total	6	280	680	76	153	34	1	13	54	76	108	.225	.306	.335	71	-28	9	8	-2	.984	-23	2-122/3-66,1SDO	-5.1

■ FLETCHER LOW   Low, Fletcher b: 4/7/1893, Essex, Mass. d: 6/6/73, Hanover, N.H. BR/TR, 5'10.5", 175 lbs. Deb: 10/7/15

YEAR	TM/L	G	AB	R	H	2B	3B	HR	RBI	BB	SO	AVG	OBP	SLG	PRO+	BR/A	SB	CS	SBR	FA	FR	G/POS	TPR
1915	Bos-N	1	4	1	1	0	1	0	0	0		.250	.250	.750	207	0	0			1.000	-0	/3-1	0.0

■ CHARLIE LOWE   Lowe, Charles b: Baltimore, Md. Deb: 9/28/1872

YEAR	TM/L	G	AB	R	H	2B	3B	HR	RBI	BB	SO	AVG	OBP	SLG	PRO+	BR/A	SB	CS	SBR	FA	FR	G/POS	TPR
1872	Atl-n	7	31	1	5	0	0	0	3	0	2	.161	.161	.161	-0	-4	0	0	0	.820	-1	/2-7	-0.4

■ DICK LOWE   Lowe, Richard Alvern b: 1/28/1854, Evansville, Wis. d: 6/28/22, Janesville, Wis. Deb: 6/26/1884

YEAR	TM/L	G	AB	R	H	2B	3B	HR	RBI	BB	SO	AVG	OBP	SLG	PRO+	BR/A	SB	CS	SBR	FA	FR	G/POS	TPR
1884	Det-N	1	3	0	1	0	0	0	0	1		.333	.333	.333	117	0				.125	-3	/C-1	-0.2

■ BOBBY LOWE   Lowe, Robert Lincoln "Link" b: 7/10/1868, Pittsburgh, Pa. d: 12/8/51, Detroit, Mich. BR/TR, 5'10", 150 lbs. Deb: 4/19/1890 M

YEAR	TM/L	G	AB	R	H	2B	3B	HR	RBI	BB	SO	AVG	OBP	SLG	PRO+	BR/A	SB	CS	SBR	FA	FR	G/POS	TPR
1890	Bos-N	52	207	35	58	13	2	2	21	26	32	.280	.366	.391	112	3	15			.951	-9	S-24,O-15,3-12	-0.4
1891	Bos-N	125	497	92	129	19	5	6	74	53	54	.260	.342	.354	92	-6	43			.927	-6	*O-107,2-17/S-2,3P	-1.5
1892	*Bos-N	124	475	79	115	16	7	3	57	37	47	.242	.308	.324	84	-11	33			.928	13	O-90,3-14,S-13,2-10	-0.4
1893	Bos-N	126	526	130	157	19	5	14	89	55	29	.298	.369	.433	105	0	22			.936	1	*2-121/S-5	0.4

YEAR	TM/L	G	AB	R	H	2B	3B	HR	RBI	BB	SO	AVG	OBP	SLG	PRO+	BR/A	SB	CS	SBR	FA	FR	G/POS	TPR
1894	Bos-N	133	613	158	212	34	11	17	115	50	25	.346	.401	.520	112	8	23			.927	-6	*2-130/S-2,3-1	0.6
1895	Bos-N	99	412	101	122	12	7	7	62	40	16	.296	.370	.410	94	-5	24			.954	15	*2-99	1.2
1896	Bos-N	73	305	59	98	11	4	2	48	20	11	.321	.357	.403	98	-1	15			.965	25	2-73	2.3
1897	*Bos-N	123	499	87	154	24	8	5	106	32		.309	.355	.419	98	-4	16			.952	-4	*2-123	-0.1
1898	Bos-N	147	559	65	152	11	7	4	94	29		.272	.311	.338	82	-15	12			.958	16	*2-145/S-2	1.0
1899	Bos-N	152	559	81	152	5	9	4	88	35		.272	.316	.335	72	-24	17			.954	3	*2-148/S-4	-1.1
1900	Bos-N	127	474	65	132	11	5	3	71	26		.278	.323	.342	74	-18	15			.951	-7	*2-127	-1.8
1901	Bos-N	129	491	47	125	11	1	3	47	17		.255	.284	.299	63	-24	22			.912	-5	*3-111,2-18	-2.7
1902	Chi-N	119	472	41	116	13	3	0	31	11		.246	.270	.286	74	-16	16			.957	26	*2-117/3-2	1.5
1903	Chi-N	32	105	14	28	5	3	0	15	4		.267	.319	.371	99	-0	5			.948	4	2-22/1-6,3-1	0.4
1904	Pit-N	1	1	0	0	0	0	0	0	0		.000	.000	.000	-97	-0	0			.000	0	H	0.0
	Det-A	140	506	47	105	14	6	0	40	17		.208	.236	.259	58	-25	15			.964	-0	*2-140,M	-2.4
1905	Det-A	58	181	17	35	7	2	0	9	13		.193	.255	.254	61	-8	3			.980	-3	O-24,3-22/2-6,S1	-1.2
1906	Det-A	41	145	11	30	3	0	1	12	4		.207	.233	.248	49	-9	3			.915	8	S-19,2-17/3-5	-0.9
1907	Det-A	17	37	2	9	2	0	0	5	4		.243	.317	.297	93	-0	0			.870	-4	3-10/O-4,S-2	-0.5
Total	18	1818	7064	1131	1929	230	85	71	984	473	214	.273	.325	.360	86	-157	302			.951	68	*2-1313,O-240,3/S1P	-4.3

■ JOHN LOWENSTEIN   Lowenstein, John Lee b: 1/27/47, Wolf Point, Mont. BL/TR, 6', 175 lbs. Deb: 9/2/70

YEAR	TM/L	G	AB	R	H	2B	3B	HR	RBI	BB	SO	AVG	OBP	SLG	PRO+	BR/A	SB	CS	SBR	FA	FR	G/POS	TPR
1970	Cle-A	17	43	5	11	3	1	1	6	1	9	.256	.273	.442	89	-1	1	0	0	1.000	-1	2-10/3-2,O-2,S-1	0.4
1971	Cle-A	58	140	15	26	5	0	4	9	16	28	.186	.269	.307	58	-8	1	5	-3	.986	-6	2-29,O-18/S-3	-1.6
1972	Cle-A	68	151	16	32	8	1	6	21	20	43	.212	.304	.397	104	1	2	4	-2	1.000	-2	O-58/1-2	-0.6
1973	Cle-A	98	305	42	89	16	1	6	40	23	41	.292	.341	.410	109	3	5	3	-0	.931	-10	O-51,2-25/3-8,1D	-0.7
1974	Cle-A	140	508	65	123	14	2	8	48	53	85	.242	.316	.325	85	-9	36	17	1	.986	-1	*O-100,3-28,1-12/2	-1.5
1975	Cle-A	91	265	37	64	5	1	12	33	28	28	.242	.314	.404	102	0	15	10	-2	.983	-5	O-36,D-31/3-8,2-2	-0.9
1976	Cle-A	93	229	33	47	8	2	2	14	25	35	.205	.283	.284	67	-9	11	8	-2	.972	-5	O-61,D-11/1-9	-2.0
1977	Cle-A	81	149	24	36	6	1	4	12	21	29	.242	.335	.376	97	-0	1	8	-5	1.000	-3	O-39,D-19/1-1	-1.0
1978	Tex-A	77	176	28	39	8	3	5	21	37	29	.222	.363	.386	110	4	16	3	3	.926	-9	3-25,D-21,O-16	-0.4
1979	*Bal-A	97	197	33	50	8	2	11	34	30	37	.254	.355	.482	128	8	16	4	2	.992	-8	O-72/1-1,3-1,D-3	0.0
1980	Bal-A	104	196	38	61	7	0	6	27	32	29	.311	.408	.413	127	9	7	3	0	.992	-11	O-91/D-3	-0.4
1981	Bal-A	83	189	19	47	7	0	6	20	22	32	.249	.330	.381	105	1	7	6	-2	.990	-12	O-73/D-4	-1.5
1982	Bal-A	122	322	69	103	15	2	24	66	54	59	.320	.419	.602	177	35	7	6	-2	1.000	-7	*O-111	2.4
1983	*Bal-A	122	310	52	87	13	2	15	60	49	55	.281	.381	.481	138	17	2	1	0	.982	-11	O-107/2-1,D-1	0.3
1984	Bal-A	105	270	34	64	13	0	8	28	33	54	.237	.322	.374	94	-2	1	0	0	.971	-8	O-67,D-22/1-2	-1.2
1985	Bal-A	12	26	0	2	0	0	0	2	2	3	.077	.143	.077	-39	-5	0	0	0	1.000	-0	/O-4,D-6	-0.5
Total	16	1368	3476	510	881	137	18	116	441	446	596	.253	.340	.403	108	43	128	78	-8	.984	-96	O-906,D-125/321S	-9.2

■ PEANUTS LOWREY   Lowrey, Harry Lee b: 8/27/18, Culver City, Cal. d: 7/2/86, Inglewood, Cal. BR/TR, 5'8.5", 170 lbs. Deb: 4/14/42 C

YEAR	TM/L	G	AB	R	H	2B	3B	HR	RBI	BB	SO	AVG	OBP	SLG	PRO+	BR/A	SB	CS	SBR	FA	FR	G/POS	TPR
1942	Chi-N	27	58	4	11	4	0	4	4	4	4	.190	.242	.241	43	-4	0			.978	-1	O-19	-0.6
1943	Chi-N	130	480	59	140	25	12	1	63	35	24	.292	.340	.400	115	8	13			.982	14	*O-113,S-16/2-3	1.7
1945	*Chi-N	143	523	72	148	22	7	7	89	48	27	.283	.343	.392	106	4	11			.987	8	*O-138/S-2	0.0
1946	Chi-N★	144	540	75	139	24	5	4	54	56	22	.257	.328	.343	92	-6	10			.979	8	*O-126,3-20	-0.3
1947	Chi-N	115	448	56	126	17	5	5	37	38	26	.281	.339	.375	93	-5	2			.945	9	3-91,O-25/2-6	0.4
1948	Chi-N	129	435	47	128	12	3	2	54	34	31	.294	.347	.349	93	-4	2			.983	-1	*O-103/3-9,2-2,S-1	-1.1
1949	Chi-N	38	111	18	30	5	0	2	10	9	8	.270	.325	.369	88	-2	3			.966	-4	O-31/3-1	-0.8
	Cin-N	89	309	48	85	16	2	2	25	37	11	.275	.354	.359	91	-3	1			.995	8	O-78	0.1
	Yr	127	420	66	115	21	2	4	35	46	19	.274	.347	.362	90	-5	4			.989	4	*O-109/3-1	-0.7
1950	Cin-N	91	264	34	60	14	0	1	11	36	7	.227	.320	.292	62	-14	0			.987	1	O-72/2-1	-1.5
	StL-N	17	56	10	15	0	0	1	4	6	1	.268	.349	.321	74	-2	0			1.000	1	/2-6,3-5,O-4	-0.1
	Yr	108	320	44	75	14	0	2	15	42	8	.234	.325	.297	64	-16	0			.982	2	O-76/2-7,3-5	-1.6
1951	StL-N	114	370	52	112	19	5	5	40	35	12	.303	.366	.422	111	6	0	1	-1	.983	-1	O-85,3-11/2-3	0.1
1952	StL-N	132	374	48	107	18	2	5	48	34	13	.286	.352	.353	96	-1	3	2	-0	.978	-9	*O-106/3-6	-1.5
1953	StL-N	104	182	26	49	9	2	5	27	15	21	.269	.325	.423	93	-2	1	0	0	1.000	-10	O-38,2-10/3-1	-1.2
1954	StL-N	74	61	6	7	1	2	0	5	9	9	.115	.229	.197	12	-8	0	0	0	1.000	-5	O-12	-1.3
1955	Phi-N	54	106	9	20	4	0	0	7	9	10	.189	.239	.226	25	-11	2	0	1	.973	-6	O-28/2-2,1-1	-1.7
Total	13	1401	4317	564	1177	186	45	37	479	403	226	.273	.336	.362	92	-45	48	3		.983	9	O-978,3-144/2S1	-7.8

■ DWIGHT LOWRY   Lowry, Dwight (b: Dwight Lowery) b: 10/23/57, Lumberton, N.C. BL/TR, 6'3", 210 lbs. Deb: 4/3/84

YEAR	TM/L	G	AB	R	H	2B	3B	HR	RBI	BB	SO	AVG	OBP	SLG	PRO+	BR/A	SB	CS	SBR	FA	FR	G/POS	TPR
1984	Det-A	32	45	8	11	2	0	2	7	3	11	.244	.292	.422	95	-0	0	0	0	1.000	5	C-31	0.5
1986	Det-A	56	150	21	46	4	0	3	18	17	19	.307	.392	.393	115	4	0	0	0	.992	-1	C-55/1-1,O-1	0.6
1987	Det-A	13	25	0	5	2	0	0	1	0	6	.200	.200	.280	27	-3	0	0	0	1.000	1	C-12/1-1	-0.2
1988	Min-A	7	7	0	0	0	0	0	0	0	2	.000	.000	.000	-97	-2	0	0	0	1.000	0	/C-5	0.0
Total	4	108	227	29	62	8	0	5	26	20	38	.273	.343	.374	96	-1	0	0	0	.995	7	C-103/1-2,O-1	0.9

■ JOHN LOWRY   Lowry, John D. b: Baltimore, Md. Deb: 6/12/1875

YEAR	TM/L	G	AB	R	H	2B	3B	HR	RBI	BB	SO	AVG	OBP	SLG	PRO+	BR/A	SB	CS	SBR	FA	FR	G/POS	TPR
1875	Was-n	6	22	2	3	0	0	0		1	0	.136	.174	.136	10	-2	0	1	-1	.727	-1	/O-6	-0.3

■ WILLIE LOZADO   Lozado, William b: 5/12/59, New York, N.Y. BR/TR, 6', 166 lbs. Deb: 7/16/84

YEAR	TM/L	G	AB	R	H	2B	3B	HR	RBI	BB	SO	AVG	OBP	SLG	PRO+	BR/A	SB	CS	SBR	FA	FR	G/POS	TPR
1984	Mil-A	43	107	15	29	8	1	0	20	12	23	.271	.345	.411	113	2	0	3	-2	.925	-1	3-36/S-6,2-1,D-1	-0.1

■ STEVE LUBRATICH   Lubratich, Steven George b: 5/1/55, Oakland, Cal. BR/TR, 6', 170 lbs. Deb: 9/27/81

YEAR	TM/L	G	AB	R	H	2B	3B	HR	RBI	BB	SO	AVG	OBP	SLG	PRO+	BR/A	SB	CS	SBR	FA	FR	G/POS	TPR
1981	Cal-A	7	21	2	3	1	0	0	1	0	2	.143	.143	.190	-5	-3	1	0	0	1.000	2	/3-6	-0.1
1983	Cal-A	57	156	12	34	9	0	0	7	4	17	.218	.237	.276	41	-13	0	1	-1	.949	16	S-23,3-22,2-14	0.5
Total	2	64	177	14	37	10	0	0	8	4	19	.209	.227	.266	36	-15	1	1	-0	.988	18	/3-28,S-23,2-14	0.4

■ HAL LUBY   Luby, Hugh Max b: 6/13/13, Blackfoot, Idaho d: 5/4/86, Eugene, Ore. BR/TR, 5'10", 185 lbs. Deb: 9/10/36

YEAR	TM/L	G	AB	R	H	2B	3B	HR	RBI	BB	SO	AVG	OBP	SLG	PRO+	BR/A	SB	CS	SBR	FA	FR	G/POS	TPR
1936	Phi-A	9	38	3	7	1	0	0	3	0	7	.184	.205	.211	3	-6	2	0	1	.880	-4	/2-9	-0.8
1944	NY-N	111	323	30	82	10	2	2	35	52	15	.254	.364	.316	93	-1	2			.943	16	3-65,2-45/1-1	1.9
Total	2	120	361	33	89	11	2	2	38	52	22	.247	.349	.305	83	-7	4	0		.954	12	/3-65,2-54,1-1	1.1

■ JOHNNY LUCADELLO   Lucadello, John b: 2/22/19, Thurber, Tex. BB/TR, 5'11", 160 lbs. Deb: 9/24/38

YEAR	TM/L	G	AB	R	H	2B	3B	HR	RBI	BB	SO	AVG	OBP	SLG	PRO+	BR/A	SB	CS	SBR	FA	FR	G/POS	TPR
1938	StL-A	7	20	1	3	1	0	0	0	0	0	.150	.150	.200	-13	-4	0	0	0	.909	-1	/3-6	-0.5
1939	StL-A	9	30	0	7	2	0	0	4	2	4	.233	.281	.300	48	-4	0	0	0	.912	-4	/2-7	-0.6
1940	StL-A	17	63	15	20	4	2	2	10	6	4	.317	.394	.540	137	3	1	0	0	.968	0	2-16	0.5
1941	StL-A	107	351	58	98	22	4	2	31	48	23	.279	.366	.382	95	-2	5			.962	-16	2-70,S-12/3-6,O-1	-1.1
1946	StL-A	87	210	21	52	7	1	1	15	36	20	.248	.358	.305	82	-4	0	1	-1	.942	-7	3-37,2-19	-1.0
1947	NY-A	12	12	0	1	0	0	0	0	1	5	.083	.154	.083	-33	-2	0	0	0	1.000	-2	/2-5	-0.4
Total	6	239	686	95	181	36	7	5	60	93	56	.264	.353	.359	88	-10	6	3	0	.965	-29	2-117/3-49,S-12,O-1	-3.1

■ RED LUCAS   Lucas, Charles Frederick "The Nashville Narcissus" b: 4/28/02, Columbia, Tenn. d: 7/9/86, Nashville, Tenn. BL/TR, 5'9.5", 170 lbs. Deb: 4/19/23

YEAR	TM/L	G	AB	R	H	2B	3B	HR	RBI	BB	SO	AVG	OBP	SLG	PRO+	BR/A	SB	CS	SBR	FA	FR	G/POS	TPR
1923	NY-N	3	2	0	0	0	0	0	0	0	1	.000	.000	.000	-99	-1	0	0	0	1.000	1	/P-3	0.0
1924	Bos-N	33	33	5	11	1	0	0	5	1	4	.333	.353	.364	96	-0	0	0	0	1.000	1	P-27/3-2	0.0
1925	Bos-N	6	20	1	3	0	0	0	2	1	4	.150	.227	.150	-2	-3	0	0	0	.968	0	/2-6	-0.3
1926	Cin-N	66	76	15	23	4	4	0	14	10	13	.303	.384	.461	130	3	0			1.000	1	P-39/2-1	0.0
1927	Cin-N	80	150	14	47	5	2	0	28	12	10	.313	.368	.373	102	1	0			.983	-6	P-37/2-5,S-3,O-1	-0.4
1928	Cin-N	39	73	8	23	2	1	0	7	4	6	.315	.351	.370	90	-1	0			1.000	-0	P-27	0.0
1929	Cin-N	76	140	15	41	6	0	0	13	15	14	.293	.353	.336	75	-5	1			.949	0	P-32	0.0
1930	Cin-N	80	113	18	38	4	1	2	19	17	4	.336	.423	.442	115	4	1			1.000	-3	P-33	0.0
1931	Cin-N	97	153	15	43	4	0	0	17	12	9	.281	.333	.307	78	-4	0			.984	1	P-29	0.0
1932	Cin-N	76	150	13	43	11	2	0	19	10	9	.287	.329	.387	97	-1	0			.973	-0	P-31	0.0
1933	Cin-N	75	122	14	35	6	1	1	15	12	6	.287	.356	.377	111	2	0			1.000	0	P-29	0.0
1934	Pit-N	68	105	11	23	5	1	0	8	6	16	.219	.261	.286	45	-8	1			.939	-3	P-29	0.0

YEAR	TM/L	G	AB	R	H	2B	3B	HR	RBI	BB	SO	AVG	OBP	SLG	PRO+	BR/A	SB	CS	SBR	FA	FR	G/POS	TPR
1935	Pit-N	47	66	6	21	6	0	0	10	7	11	.318	.392	.409	112	1	0			.968	-1	P-20	0.0
1936	Pit-N	69	108	11	26	4	0	0	14	8	17	.241	.293	.296	58	-6	0			.976	-1	P-27	0.0
1937	Pit-N	59	82	8	22	3	0	0	17	7	6	.268	.326	.305	72	-3	0			1.000	-2	P-20	0.0
1938	Pit-N	33	46	1	5	0	0	0	2	3	2	.109	.163	.109	-24	-8	0			1.000	-1	P-13	0.0
Total	16	907	1439	155	404	61	13	3	190	124	133	.281	.340	.347	84	-29	2	0		.981	-14	P-396/2-12,S-3,3O	-0.7

■ FRED LUCAS   Lucas, Frederick Warrington "Fritz"   b: 1/19/03, Vineland, N.J.   d: 3/11/87, Cambridge, Md.   BR/TR, 5'10", 165 lbs.   Deb: 7/15/35

YEAR	TM/L	G	AB	R	H	2B	3B	HR	RBI	BB	SO	AVG	OBP	SLG	PRO+	BR/A	SB	CS	SBR	FA	FR	G/POS	TPR
1935	Phi-N	20	34	1	9	0	0	0	2	3	6	.265	.324	.265	55	-2	0			.944	-2	O-10	-0.4

■ JOHNNY LUCAS   Lucas, John Charles "Buster"   b: 2/10/03, Glen Carbon, Ill.   d: 10/31/70, Maryville, Ill.   BR/TL, 5'10", 186 lbs.   Deb: 4/15/31

YEAR	TM/L	G	AB	R	H	2B	3B	HR	RBI	BB	SO	AVG	OBP	SLG	PRO+	BR/A	SB	CS	SBR	FA	FR	G/POS	TPR
1931	Bos-A	3	2	0	0	0	0	0	0	0	1	.000	.000	.000	-99	-1	0	0	0	.000	-1	/O-2	-0.2
1932	Bos-A	1	1	0	0	0	0	0	0	0	0	.000	.000	.000	-99	-1	0	0	0	.000	0	H	0.0
Total	2	4	3	0	0	0	0	0	0	0	1	.000	.000	.000	-99	-1	0			—	-1	/O-2	-0.2

■ FRANK LUCE   Luce, Frank Edward   b: 12/6/1896, Spencer, Ohio   d: 2/3/42, Milwaukee, Wis.   BL/TR, 5'11", 180 lbs.   Deb: 9/17/23

YEAR	TM/L	G	AB	R	H	2B	3B	HR	RBI	BB	SO	AVG	OBP	SLG	PRO+	BR/A	SB	CS	SBR	FA	FR	G/POS	TPR
1923	Pit-N	9	12	2	6	0	0	0	3	2	2	.500	.571	.500	181	2	2	1	0	1.000	-2	/O-5	0.0

■ JOE LUCEY   Lucey, Joseph Earl "Scootch"   b: 3/27/1897, Holyoke, Mass.   d: 7/30/80, Holyoke, Mass.   BR/TR, 6', 168 lbs.   Deb: 7/6/20

YEAR	TM/L	G	AB	R	H	2B	3B	HR	RBI	BB	SO	AVG	OBP	SLG	PRO+	BR/A	SB	CS	SBR	FA	FR	G/POS	TPR
1920	NY-A	3	3	0	0	0	0	0	0	0	0	.000	.000	.000	-97	-1	0	0	0	1.000	0	/2-1,S-1	0.0
1925	Bos-A	10	15	0	2	0	0	0	0	0	4	.133	.133	.133	-32	-3	0	0	0	.889	-1	/P-7,S-3	-0.3
Total	2	13	18	0	2	0	0	0	0	0	4	.111	.111	.111	-43	-4	0	0	0	.778	-0	/P-7,S-4,2-1	-0.3

■ FRED LUDERUS   Luderus, Frederick William   b: 9/12/1885, Milwaukee, Wis.   d: 1/5/61, Three Lakes, Wis.   BL/TR, 5'11.5", 185 lbs.   Deb: 9/23/09

YEAR	TM/L	G	AB	R	H	2B	3B	HR	RBI	BB	SO	AVG	OBP	SLG	PRO+	BR/A	SB	CS	SBR	FA	FR	G/POS	TPR
1909	Chi-N	11	37	8	11	1	1	1	9	3		.297	.366	.459	152	2				.950	-2	1-11	0.1
1910	Chi-N	24	54	5	11	1	1	0	3	4	3	.204	.259	.259	52	-3	0			.975	-0	1-17	-0.4
	Phi-N	21	68	10	20	5	2	0	14	9	5	.294	.385	.426	132	3	2			.985	1	1-19	0.4
	Yr	45	122	15	31	6	3	0	17	13	8	.254	.331	.352	98	-0	2			.981	-0	1-36	0.0
1911	Phi-N	146	551	69	166	24	11	16	99	40	76	.301	.353	.472	128	18	6			.985	-2	*1-146	1.6
1912	Phi-N	148	572	77	147	31	5	10	69	44	65	.257	.318	.381	85	-14	8			.990	10	*1-146	-0.6
1913	Phi-N	155	588	67	154	32	7	18	86	34	51	.262	.304	.432	105	0	5			.984	-1	*1-155	0.0
1914	Phi-N	121	443	55	110	16	5	12	55	33	31	.248	.308	.388	100	-2	2			.975	-1	*1-121	-0.3
1915	*Phi-N	141	499	55	157	36	7	7	62	42	36	.315	.376	.457	150	29	9	7	-2	.993	10	*1-141	3.7
1916	Phi-N	146	508	52	143	26	5	5	53	41	32	.281	.341	.374	115	9	8			.982	-2	*1-146	0.3
1917	Phi-N	154	522	57	136	24	4	5	72	65	35	.261	.349	.351	110	8	5			.991	5	*1-154	0.8
1918	Phi-N	125	468	54	135	23	2	5	67	42	33	.288	.351	.378	115	8	4			.988	7	*1-125	1.1
1919	Phi-N	138	509	60	149	30	6	5	49	54	48	.293	.365	.405	123	15	6			.985	10	*1-138	2.2
1920	Phi-N	16	32	1	5	0	0	0	3	6	6	.156	.229	.219	28	-3	0	1	-1	.983	0	/1-7	-0.4
Total	12	1346	4851	570	1344	251	54	84	642	414	421	.277	.340	.403	113	72	55	8		.986	39	*1-1326	8.5

■ BILL LUDWIG   Ludwig, William Lawrence   b: 5/27/1882, Louisville, Ky.   d: 9/5/47, Louisville, Ky.   BR/TR,   Deb: 4/16/08

YEAR	TM/L	G	AB	R	H	2B	3B	HR	RBI	BB	SO	AVG	OBP	SLG	PRO+	BR/A	SB	CS	SBR	FA	FR	G/POS	TPR
1908	StL-N	66	187	15	34	2	2	0	8	16		.182	.246	.214	50	-10	3			.952	-3	C-62	-1.0

■ ROY LUEBBE   Luebbe, Roy John   b: 9/17/1900, Parkersburg, Iowa   d: 8/21/85, Papillion, Neb.   BB/TR, 6', 175 lbs.   Deb: 8/22/25

YEAR	TM/L	G	AB	R	H	2B	3B	HR	RBI	BB	SO	AVG	OBP	SLG	PRO+	BR/A	SB	CS	SBR	FA	FR	G/POS	TPR
1925	NY-A	8	15	1	0	0	0	0	3	2	6	.000	.118	.000	-69	-4				1.000	1	/C-8	-0.2

■ HENRY LUFF   Luff, Henry T.   b: 9/14/1856, Philadelphia, Pa.   d: 10/11/16, Philadelphia, Pa.   5'11", 175 lbs.   Deb: 4/21/1875

YEAR	TM/L	G	AB	R	H	2B	3B	HR	RBI	BB	SO	AVG	OBP	SLG	PRO+	BR/A	SB	CS	SBR	FA	FR	G/POS	TPR
1875	NH-n	38	166	15	45	10	3	2	18	0	5	.271	.271	.404	150	9	3	3	-1	.689	-4	3-30,P-10/O-4,S-1	0.2
1882	Det-N	3	11	1	3	2	0	0	1	0	0	.273	.273	.455	129	0				.667	-1	/2-3,O-1	-0.1
	Cin-a	28	120	16	28	2	0	0	6	2		.233	.246	.283	74	-4				.922	-2	1-27/O-1	-0.8
1883	Lou-a	6	23	1	4	0	0	0	2	0		.174	.174	.174	13	-2				.868	-1	/1-4,O-2	-0.3
1884	Phi-U	26	111	9	30	4	2	0		4		.270	.296	.342	100	-3				.733	-3	0-12/1-6,3-5,2-3	-0.6
	KC-U	5	19	0	1	0	0	0		1		.053	.100	.053	-60	-4				.444	-4	/3-4,O-4	-0.8
	Yr	31	130	9	31	4	2	0		5		.238	.267	.300	78	-7				.706	-7	O-16/3-9,1-6,2-3	-1.4
Total	3	68	284	27	66	8	4	0	9	7	0	.232	.251	.289	73	-13				.911	-12	/1-37,O-20,3-9,2-6	-2.6

■ ROB LUKACHYK   Lukachyk, Robert James   b: 7/24/68, Jersey City, N.J.   BL/TR, 6', 185 lbs.   Deb: 7/5/96

YEAR	TM/L	G	AB	R	H	2B	3B	HR	RBI	BB	SO	AVG	OBP	SLG	PRO+	BR/A	SB	CS	SBR	FA	FR	G/POS	TPR
1996	Mon-N	2	2	0	0	0	0	0	0	0	1	.000	.000	.000	-98	-1	0	0	0	.000	0	/H	-0.1

■ MATT LUKE   Luke, Matthew Clifford   b: 2/26/71, Long Beach, Cal.   BL/TL, 6'5", 220 lbs.   Deb: 4/3/96

YEAR	TM/L	G	AB	R	H	2B	3B	HR	RBI	BB	SO	AVG	OBP	SLG	PRO+	BR/A	SB	CS	SBR	FA	FR	G/POS	TPR
1996	NY-A	1	0	1	0							—	—	—			0	0	0	.000	0	/R	0.0

■ EDDIE LUKON   Lukon, Edward Paul "Mongoose"   b: 8/5/20, Burgettstown, Pa.   BL/TL, 5'10", 168 lbs.   Deb: 8/6/41

YEAR	TM/L	G	AB	R	H	2B	3B	HR	RBI	BB	SO	AVG	OBP	SLG	PRO+	BR/A	SB	CS	SBR	FA	FR	G/POS	TPR
1941	Cin-N	23	86	6	23	3	0	0	6	6	8	.267	.315	.302	74	-3	1			.980	2	O-22	-0.2
1945	Cin-N	2	8	1	1	0	0	0	0	0	1	.125	.125	.125	-31	-1	0			1.000	0	/O-2	-0.2
1946	Cin-N	102	312	31	78	8	8	12	34	26	29	.250	.310	.442	116	4	3			.985	2	O-83	0.3
1947	Cin-N	86	200	26	41	6	1	11	33	28	36	.205	.306	.410	89	-4	0			1.000	-2	O-55	-0.8
Total	4	213	606	64	143	17	9	23	70	60	72	.236	.307	.408	99	-4	4			.989	3	O-162	-0.9

■ MIKE LUM   Lum, Michael Ken-Wai   b: 10/27/45, Honolulu, Hawaii   BL/TL, 6', 180 lbs.   Deb: 9/12/67   C

YEAR	TM/L	G	AB	R	H	2B	3B	HR	RBI	BB	SO	AVG	OBP	SLG	PRO+	BR/A	SB	CS	SBR	FA	FR	G/POS	TPR
1967	Atl-N	9	26	1	6	0	0	0	1	1	4	.231	.259	.231	42	-2	0	1	-1	.944	1	/O-6	-0.2
1968	Atl-N	122	232	22	52	7	3	3	21	14	35	.224	.280	.319	79	-6	3	5	-2	.976	-9	O-95	-2.4
1969	*Atl-N	121	168	20	45	8	0	1	22	16	18	.268	.332	.333	86	-3	0	0	0	.992	-8	O-89	-1.3
1970	Atl-N	123	291	25	74	17	2	7	28	17	43	.254	.307	.390	83	-8	3	2	-0	.988	-3	O-98	-1.5
1971	Atl-N	145	454	56	122	14	1	13	55	47	43	.269	.344	.390	101	1	0	3	-2	.990	9	*O-125/1-1	0.3
1972	Atl-N	123	369	40	84	14	2	9	38	50	52	.228	.325	.350	84	-7	1	4	-2	.976	4	*O-109/1-2	-1.0
1973	Atl-N	138	513	74	151	26	6	16	82	41	89	.294	.354	.462	116	10	2	5	-2	.991	-3	1-84,O-64	-0.4
1974	Atl-N	106	361	50	84	11	2	11	50	45	49	.233	.321	.366	88	-6	0	2	-1	.994	-5	1-60,O-50	-1.9
1975	Atl-N	124	364	32	83	8	4	6	36	39	38	.228	.303	.327	72	-14	2	4	-2	.992	-1	1-60,O-38	-2.3
1976	*Cin-N	84	136	15	31	5	1	3	20	22	24	.228	.340	.346	93	-1	0	1	0	1.000	-6	O-38	-1.0
1977	Cin-N	81	125	14	20	1	0	5	16	9	33	.160	.222	.288	35	-12	0	1	0	1.000	4	O-24/1-8	-1.5
1978	Cin-N	86	146	15	39	7	1	6	23	12	18	.267	.363	.452	126	5	0	0	-0	.987	-1	O-43/1-7	0.3
1979	Atl-N	111	217	27	54	6	0	6	27	18	34	.249	.306	.359	75	-7	0	2	-2	.998	-3	1-51/O-3	-0.9
1980	Atl-N	93	83	7	17	2	0	3	5	18	19	.205	.347	.241	65	-3	0	0	0	1.000	-3	O-19,1-10	-0.7
1981	Atl-N	10	11	1	1	0	0	0	0	2	2	.091	.231	.091	-6	-1	0	0	0	1.000	0	/O-1	-0.1
	Chi-N	41	58	5	14	1	0	2	7	5	5	.241	.313	.362	87	-1	0	0	0	.923	-4	O-14/1-1	-0.6
	Yr	51	69	6	15	1	0	2	7	7	7	.217	.299	.319	72	-2	0	0	0	.938	-4	O-15/1-1	-0.7
Total	15	1517	3554	404	877	128	20	90	431	366	506	.247	.322	.370	89	-54	13	29	-14	.986	-29	O-816,1-284	-15.2

■ HARRY LUMLEY   Lumley, Harry G "Judge"   b: 9/29/1880, Forest City, Pa.   d: 5/22/38, Binghamton, N.Y.   BL/TL, 5'10", 183 lbs.   Deb: 4/14/04   M

YEAR	TM/L	G	AB	R	H	2B	3B	HR	RBI	BB	SO	AVG	OBP	SLG	PRO+	BR/A	SB	CS	SBR	FA	FR	G/POS	TPR
1904	Bro-N	150	577	79	161	23	**18**	**9**	78	41		.279	.331	.428	137	23	30			.955	4	*O-150	1.9
1905	Bro-N	130	505	50	148	19	10	7	47	36		.293	.340	.412	134	19	22			.912	-1	*O-129	1.2
1906	Bro-N	133	484	72	157	23	12	9	61	48		.324	.386	**.477**	**184**	45	35			.949	1	*O-131	4.3
1907	Bro-N	127	454	47	121	23	11	9	66	31		.267	.316	.425	144	19	18			.959	-4	*O-118	1.2
1908	Bro-N	127	440	36	95	13	12	4	39	29		.216	.266	.327	93	-5	4			.955	-5	*O-116	-1.8
1909	Bro-N	55	172	13	43	8	3	0	14	16		.250	.314	.331	104	1	1			.948	2	O-52,M	0.0
1910	Bro-N	8	21	3	3	0	0	0	0	6		.143	.280	.143	25	-2	0			.833	-1	/O-4	-0.3
Total	7	730	2653	300	728	109	66	38	305	204	6	.274	.328	.408	135	99	110			.946	-5	O-700	6.5

■ JERRY LUMPE   Lumpe, Jerry Dean   b: 6/2/33, Lincoln, Mo.   BL/TR, 6'2", 185 lbs.   Deb: 4/17/56   C

YEAR	TM/L	G	AB	R	H	2B	3B	HR	RBI	BB	SO	AVG	OBP	SLG	PRO+	BR/A	SB	CS	SBR	FA	FR	G/POS	TPR
1956	NY-A	20	62	12	16	3	0	1	5		11	.258	.313	.306	66	-3	1	1	-0	.916	3	S-17/3-1	0.1
1957	*NY-A	40	103	15	35	6	2	1	11	9	13	.340	.393	.437	128	4	2	2	-1	.956	-2	3-30/S-6	0.2
1958	*NY-A	81	232	34	59	8	4	3	32	23	21	.254	.324	.362	92	-3	5	2	-1	.943	4	3-65/S-5	0.1

YEAR	TM/L	G	AB	R	H	2B	3B	HR	RBI	BB	SO	AVG	OBP	SLG	PRO+	BR/A	SB	CS	SBR	FA	FR	G/POS	TPR
1959	NY-A	18	45	2	10	0	0	0	2	6	7	.222	.314	.222	52	-3	0	0	0	1.000	2	3-12/S-4,2-1	0.0
	KC-A	108	403	47	98	11	5	3	28	41	32	.243	.313	.318	72	-15	2	1	0	.986	-10	2-61,S-56/3-4	-1.6
	Yr	126	448	49	108	11	5	3	30	47	39	.241	.313	.308	70	-17	2	1	0	.987	-8	2-62,S-60,3-16	-1.6
1960	KC-A	146	574	69	156	19	3	8	53	48	49	.272	.328	.357	85	-12	1	1	-0	.982	-7	*2-134,S-15	-0.5
1961	KC-A	148	569	81	167	29	5	3	54	48	39	.293	.351	.392	96	-3	1	0	0	.979	16	2-147	2.9
1962	KC-A	156	641	89	193	34	10	10	83	44	38	.301	.346	.432	103	2	0	2	-1	.986	-4	*2-156/S-2	1.4
1963	KC-A	157	595	75	161	26	7	5	59	58	44	.271	.334	.363	91	-6	3	2	-0	.988	2	*2-155	1.1
1964	Det-A☆	158	624	75	160	21	6	6	46	50	61	.256	.314	.338	80	-16	2	1	0	.983	-21	*2-158	-2.6
1965	Det-A	145	502	72	129	15	3	4	39	56	34	.257	.335	.323	87	-7	7	0	2	.985	-18	*2-139	-1.2
1966	Det-A	113	385	30	89	14	3	1	26	24	44	.231	.276	.291	62	-19	0	3	-2	.991	-6	2-95	-2.2
1967	Det-A	81	177	19	41	4	0	4	17	16	18	.232	.295	.322	80	-4	0	0	0	.963	-3	2-54/3-6	-0.5
Total	12	1371	4912	620	1314	190	52	47	454	428	411	.268	.327	.356	87	-84	20	15	-3	.984	-44	*2-1100,3-118,S-105	-2.8

■ DON LUND
Lund, Donald Andrew   b: 5/18/23, Detroit, Mich.   BR/TR, 6', 200 lbs.   Deb: 7/3/45   C

YEAR	TM/L	G	AB	R	H	2B	3B	HR	RBI	BB	SO	AVG	OBP	SLG	PRO+	BR/A	SB	CS	SBR	FA	FR	G/POS	TPR
1945	Bro-N	4	3	0	0	0	0	0	0	1	1	.000	.250	.000	-27	-0	0			.000	0	H	0.0
1947	Bro-N	11	20	5	6	2	0	2	5	3	7	.300	.391	.700	178	2	0			1.000	-0	/O-5	0.2
1948	Bro-N	27	69	9	13	4	0	1	5	6	16	.188	.243	.290	42	-6	0			.977	-2	O-25	-0.8
	StL-A	63	161	21	40	7	4	3	25	10	17	.248	.305	.398	84	-5	0	0	0	1.000	-4	O-45	-1.1
1949	Det-A	2	2	0	0	0	0	0	0	0	1	.000	.000	.000	-99	-1	0	0	0	.000	0	H	-0.1
1952	Det-A	8	23	1	7	0	0	0	1	3	3	.304	.385	.304	93	-0	0	1	-1	1.000	0	/O-7	-0.1
1953	Det-A	131	421	51	108	21	4	9	47	39	65	.257	.323	.390	93	-0	5	3	-1	.980	-1	*O-123	-0.9
1954	Det-A	35	54	4	7	2	0	0	3	4	3	.130	.190	.167	-2	-8	1	0	0	.971	-8	O-31	-1.6
Total	7	281	753	91	181	36	8	15	86	65	113	.240	.305	.369	81	-22	5	4		.983	-12	O-236	-4.4

■ GORDY LUND
Lund, Gordon Thomas   b: 2/23/41, Iron Mountain, Mich   BR/TR, 5'11", 170 lbs.   Deb: 8/1/67

YEAR	TM/L	G	AB	R	H	2B	3B	HR	RBI	BB	SO	AVG	OBP	SLG	PRO+	BR/A	SB	CS	SBR	FA	FR	G/POS	TPR
1967	Cle-A	3	8	1	2	1	0	0	0	0	2	.250	.250	.375	82	-0	0	0	0	.667	-2	/S-2	-0.2
1969	Sea-A	20	38	4	10	0	0	0	1	5	7	.263	.349	.263	75	-1	1	1	-0	.927	-1	S-17/2-1,3-1	-0.1
Total	2	23	46	5	12	1	0	0	1	5	9	.261	.333	.283	76	-1	1	1	-0	.902	-2	/S-19,3-1,2-1	-0.3

■ TOM LUNDSTEDT
Lundstedt, Thomas Robert   b: 4/10/49, Davenport, Iowa   BB/TR, 6'4", 195 lbs.   Deb: 8/31/73

YEAR	TM/L	G	AB	R	H	2B	3B	HR	RBI	BB	SO	AVG	OBP	SLG	PRO+	BR/A	SB	CS	SBR	FA	FR	G/POS	TPR
1973	Chi-N	4	5	0	0	0	0	0	0	0	1	.000	.000	.000	-93	-1	0	0	0	1.000	1	/C-4	-0.1
1974	Chi-N	22	32	1	3	0	0	0	0	5	7	.094	.216	.094	-11	-5	0	0	0	.987	2	C-22	-0.3
1975	Min-A	18	28	2	3	0	0	0	1	4	5	.107	.219	.107	-5	-4	0	0	0	1.000	1	C-14/D-2	-0.2
Total	3	44	65	3	6	0	0	0	1	9	13	.092	.203	.092	-15	-10	0	0	0	.993	4	/C-40,D-2	-0.6

■ HARRY LUNTE
Lunte, Harry August   b: 9/15/1892, St.Louis, Mo.   d: 7/27/65, St.Louis, Mo.   BR/TR, 5'11.5", 165 lbs.   Deb: 5/19/19

YEAR	TM/L	G	AB	R	H	2B	3B	HR	RBI	BB	SO	AVG	OBP	SLG	PRO+	BR/A	SB	CS	SBR	FA	FR	G/POS	TPR
1919	Cle-A	26	77	2	15	2	0	0	2	1	7	.195	.215	.221	21	-8	0			.935	-2	S-24	-1.0
1920	*Cle-A	23	71	6	14	0	0	0	7	5	6	.197	.250	.197	19	-8	0	1	-1	.979	3	S-21/2-2	-0.4
Total	2	49	148	8	29	2	0	0	9	6	13	.196	.232	.209	20	-16	0	1		.955	1	/S-45,2-2	-1.4

■ TONY LUPIEN
Lupien, Ulysses John   b: 4/23/17, Chelmsford, Mass.   BL/TL, 5'10.5", 185 lbs.   Deb: 9/12/40

YEAR	TM/L	G	AB	R	H	2B	3B	HR	RBI	BB	SO	AVG	OBP	SLG	PRO+	BR/A	SB	CS	SBR	FA	FR	G/POS	TPR
1940	Bos-A	10	19	5	9	3	2	0	4	1	1	.474	.500	.842	232	4	0	0	0	1.000	-0	/1-8	0.3
1942	Bos-A	128	463	63	130	25	7	3	70	50	20	.281	.351	.384	103	2	10	12	-4	.992	-7	*1-121	-1.7
1943	Bos-A	154	608	65	155	21	9	4	47	54	23	.255	.317	.339	90	-8	16	9	-1	.993	4	*1-153	-1.5
1944	Phi-N	153	597	82	169	23	9	5	52	56	29	.283	.347	.377	107	6	18			.992	1	*1-151	-0.1
1945	Phi-N	15	54	1	17	1	0	0	3	6	3	.315	.383	.333	103	1	2			1.000	3	1-15	0.2
1948	Chi-A	154	617	69	152	19	3	6	54	74	38	.246	.327	.316	74	-23	11	7	-1	.993	-4	*1-154	-2.8
Total	6	614	2358	285	632	92	30	18	230	241	111	.268	.337	.355	94	-19	57	28		.993	-4	1-602	-5.6

■ AL LUPLOW
Luplow, Alvin David   b: 3/13/39, Saginaw, Mich.   BL/TR, 5'11", 180 lbs.   Deb: 9/16/61

YEAR	TM/L	G	AB	R	H	2B	3B	HR	RBI	BB	SO	AVG	OBP	SLG	PRO+	BR/A	SB	CS	SBR	FA	FR	G/POS	TPR
1961	Cle-A	5	18	0	1	0	0	0		2	6	.056	.150	.056	-44	-4	0	0	0	1.000	2	/O-5	-0.3
1962	Cle-A	97	318	54	88	15	3	14	45	36	44	.277	.361	.475	127	12	1	0	0	.960	-3	O-86	0.5
1963	Cle-A	100	295	34	69	6	2	7	27	33	62	.234	.317	.339	85	-6	4	4	-1	.994	-1	O-85	-0.8
1964	Cle-A	19	18	1	2	0	0	0	1	1	8	.111	.158	.111	-24	-3	0	0	0	1.000	-1	/O-5	-0.4
1965	Cle-A	53	45	3	6	2	0	1	4	3	14	.133	.188	.244	22	-5	0	1	-1	1.000	-2	/O-6	-0.7
1966	NY-N	111	334	31	84	9	1	7	31	38	46	.251	.332	.347	91	-3	2	6	-3	.987	-12	*O-101	-2.4
1967	NY-N	41	112	11	23	1	0	3	9	8	19	.205	.264	.295	61	-6	0	0	0	.966	-4	O-33	-1.2
	Pit-N	55	103	13	19	1	0	1	8	6	14	.184	.236	.223	32	-9	1	0	0	.961	3	O-25	-0.8
	Yr	96	215	24	42	2	0	4	17	14	33	.195	.251	.260	47	-15	1	0	0	.963	-1	O-58	-2.0
Total	7	481	1243	147	292	34	6	33	125	127	213	.235	.312	.352	85	-23	8	11	-4	.977	-14	O-346	-6.1

■ SCOTT LUSADER
Lusader, Scott Edward   b: 9/30/64, Chicago, Ill.   BL/TL, 5'10", 165 lbs.   Deb: 9/1/87

YEAR	TM/L	G	AB	R	H	2B	3B	HR	RBI	BB	SO	AVG	OBP	SLG	PRO+	BR/A	SB	CS	SBR	FA	FR	G/POS	TPR
1987	Det-A	23	47	8	15	3	1	1	8	5	7	.319	.385	.489	135	2	1	0	0	.967	-5	O-22/D-1	-0.2
1988	Det-A	16	16	3	1	0	0	0	3	1	4	.063	.118	.250	-0	-2	0	0	0	1.000	-1	/O-4,D-6	-0.4
1989	Det-A	40	103	15	26	4	0	1	8	9	21	.252	.313	.320	81	-3	3	0	1	.933	-6	O-33/D-1	-0.8
1990	Det-A	45	87	13	21	2	0	2	16	12	8	.241	.333	.333	86	-1	0	0	0	.982	-7	O-42/D-2	-0.9
1991	NY-A	11	7	2	1	0	0	0		1	3	.143	.250	.143	12	-1	0	0	0	1.000	-1	/O-4,D-1	-0.2
Total	5	135	260	41	64	9	1	5	36	28	43	.246	.319	.346	86	-5	4	1	1	.961	-20	O-105/D-11	-2.6

■ ERNIE LUSH
Lush, Ernest Benjamin   b: 10/31/1884, Bridgeport, Conn.   d: 2/26/37, Detroit, Mich.   BR/TL,   Deb: 7/20/10   F

YEAR	TM/L	G	AB	R	H	2B	3B	HR	RBI	BB	SO	AVG	OBP	SLG	PRO+	BR/A	SB	CS	SBR	FA	FR	G/POS	TPR
1910	StL-N	1	4	0	0	0	0	0	0	1	1	.000	.200	.000	-42	-0	0			1.000	-0	/O-1	-0.1

■ JOHNNY LUSH
Lush, John Charles   b: 10/8/1885, Williamsport, Pa.   d: 11/18/46, Beverly Hills, Cal   BL/TL, 5'9.5", 165 lbs.   Deb: 4/22/04

YEAR	TM/L	G	AB	R	H	2B	3B	HR	RBI	BB	SO	AVG	OBP	SLG	PRO+	BR/A	SB	CS	SBR	FA	FR	G/POS	TPR
1904	Phi-N	106	369	39	102	22	3	2	42	27		.276	.336	.369	122	9	12			.950	-10	1-62,O-33/P-7	-0.5
1905	Phi-N	6	16	3	5	0	0	0	1	1		.313	.389	.313	114	0	0			.667	-1	/O-3,P-2	-0.1
1906	Phi-N	76	212	28	56	7	1	0	15	14		.264	.310	.307	92	-2	6			.907	5	P-37,O-22/1-2	0.0
1907	Phi-N	17	40	5	8	1	1	0	5	1		.200	.220	.275	56	-2	1			1.000	0	/P-8,O-4	-0.2
	StL-N	27	82	6	23	2	3	0	6	5		.280	.322	.378	123	2	4			.917	-3	P-20/O-7	-0.3
	Yr	44	122	11	31	3	4	0	10	6		.254	.289	.344	101	-0	5			.941	-3	P-28,O-11	-0.5
1908	StL-N	45	89	7	15	2	0	0	2	7		.169	.229	.191	36	-6	1			.926	0	P-38	0.0
1909	StL-N	45	92	11	22	3	0	0	14	6		.239	.293	.293	87	-2	2			.945	-1	P-34/O-3	-0.1
1910	StL-N	47	93	8	21	1	3	0	10	8	11	.226	.287	.301	74	-3	2			.928	-2	P-36	0.0
Total	7	369	993	107	252	40	11	2	94	69	11	.254	.307	.322	98	-4	28			.926	-12	P-182/O-72,1-64	-1.2

■ BILLY LUSH
Lush, William Lucas   b: 11/10/1873, Bridgeport, Conn.   d: 8/28/51, Hawthorne, N.Y.   BB/TR, 5'8", 165 lbs.   Deb: 9/3/1895   F

YEAR	TM/L	G	AB	R	H	2B	3B	HR	RBI	BB	SO	AVG	OBP	SLG	PRO+	BR/A	SB	CS	SBR	FA	FR	G/POS	TPR
1895	Was-N	5	18	2	6	0	0	0	2	2	1	.333	.400	.333	92	-0	0			.692	-2	/O-5	-0.1
1896	Was-N	97	352	74	87	9	11	4	45	66	49	.247	.369	.369	95	-1	28			.885	-2	*O-91/2-3	-0.9
1897	Was-N	3	12	1	0	0	0	0	0	4		.000	.143	.000	-61	-3	0			1.000	1	/O-3	-0.2
1901	Bos-N	27	22	5	5	1	1	0	3	3		.185	.267	.296	58	-2	0			.960	3	/O-7	0.0
1902	Bos-N	120	413	68	92	8	2	1	19	76		.223	.346	.262	87	-2	30			.952	11	*O-116/3-1	0.1
1903	Det-A	119	423	71	116	18	14	1	33	70		.274	.379	.390	135	21	14			.968	12	*O-101,3-12/2-3,S-3	2.8
1904	Cle-A	138	477	76	123	13	8	1	50	72		.258	.359	.325	118	13	12			.959	3	*O-138	0.9
Total	7	489	1722	294	429	49	35	8	152	291	50	.249	.360	.332	107	27	84			.943	25	O-461/3-13,2-6,S-3	2.6

■ CHARLIE LUSKEY
Luskey, Charles Melton   b: 4/6/1876, Washington, D.C.   d: 12/20/62, Bethesda, Md.   BR/TR, 5'7", 165 lbs.   Deb: 9/12/01

YEAR	TM/L	G	AB	R	H	2B	3B	HR	RBI	BB	SO	AVG	OBP	SLG	PRO+	BR/A	SB	CS	SBR	FA	FR	G/POS	TPR
1901	Was-A	11	41	8	8	3	1	0	3	2		.195	.233	.317	52	-3	0			.818	-1	/O-8,C-3	-0.4

■ LUKE LUTENBERG
Lutenberg, Charles William   b: 10/4/1864, Quincy, Ill.   d: 12/24/38, Quincy, Ill.   BR/TR, 6'2", 225 lbs.   Deb: 7/7/1894

YEAR	TM/L	G	AB	R	H	2B	3B	HR	RBI	BB	SO	AVG	OBP	SLG	PRO+	BR/A	SB	CS	SBR	FA	FR	G/POS	TPR
1894	Lou-N	69	250	42	48	10	4	0	23	23	21	.192	.284	.264	35	-27	4			.977	1	1-67/2-2	-1.9

■ LYLE LUTTRELL
Luttrell, Lyle Kenneth   b: 2/22/30, Bloomington, Ill.   d: 7/11/84, Chattanooga, Tenn   BR/TR, 6', 180 lbs.   Deb: 5/15/56

YEAR	TM/L	G	AB	R	H	2B	3B	HR	RBI	BB	SO	AVG	OBP	SLG	PRO+	BR/A	SB	CS	SBR	FA	FR	G/POS	TPR
1956	Was-A	38	122	17	23	5	3	2	9	8	19	.189	.256	.328	53	-9	5	1	1	.939	-7	S-37	-1.1

YEAR	TM/L	G	AB	R	H	2B	3B	HR	RBI	BB	SO	AVG	OBP	SLG	PRO+	BR/A	SB	CS	SBR	FA	FR	G/POS	TPR
1957	Was-A	19	45	4	9	4	0	0	5	3	8	.200	.250	.289	47	-3	0	0	0	.927	-5	S-17	-0.8
Total	2	57	167	21	32	9	3	2	14	11	27	.192	.254	.317	52	-12	5	1	1	.936	-12	/S-54	-1.9

■ RED LUTZ
Lutz, Louis William b: 12/17/1898, Cincinnati, Ohio d: 2/22/84, Cincinnati, Ohio BR/TR, 5'10", 170 lbs. Deb: 5/31/22

YEAR	TM/L	G	AB	R	H	2B	3B	HR	RBI	BB	SO	AVG	OBP	SLG	PRO+	BR/A	SB	CS	SBR	FA	FR	G/POS	TPR
1922	Cin-N	1	1	0	1	1	0	0	0	0	0	1.000	1.000	2.000	669	1	0	0		.000	0	/C-1	0.1

■ JOE LUTZ
Lutz, Rollin Joseph b: 2/18/25, Keokuk, Iowa BL/TL, 6', 195 lbs. Deb: 4/17/51 C

YEAR	TM/L	G	AB	R	H	2B	3B	HR	RBI	BB	SO	AVG	OBP	SLG	PRO+	BR/A	SB	CS	SBR	FA	FR	G/POS	TPR
1951	StL-A	14	36	7	6	0	1	0	2	6	9	.167	.286	.222	38	-3	0	0	0	1.000	-1	1-11	-0.5

■ RUBE LUTZKE
Lutzke, Walter John b: 11/17/1897, Milwaukee, Wis. d: 3/6/38, Granville, Wis. BR/TR, 5'11", 175 lbs. Deb: 4/18/23

YEAR	TM/L	G	AB	R	H	2B	3B	HR	RBI	BB	SO	AVG	OBP	SLG	PRO+	BR/A	SB	CS	SBR	FA	FR	G/POS	TPR
1923	Cle-A	143	511	71	131	20	6	3	65	59	57	.256	.338	.337	78	-16	9	6	-1	.939	17	*3-141/S-2	1.3
1924	Cle-A	106	341	37	83	18	3	0	42	38	46	.243	.328	.314	65	-17	4	0	1	.947	19	*3-103/2-3	1.0
1925	Cle-A	81	238	31	52	9	0	1	16	26	29	.218	.295	.269	44	-20	2	4	-2	.936	-0	3-69,2-10	-1.7
1926	Cle-A	142	475	42	124	28	6	0	59	34	35	.261	.313	.345	71	-21	6	3	0	.960	-1	*3-142	-1.2
1927	Cle-A	100	311	35	78	12	3	0	41	22	29	.251	.307	.309	60	-19	2	1	0	.938	6	3-98	-0.8
Total	5	572	1876	216	468	87	18	4	223	179	196	.249	.319	.321	66	-93	23	14	-2	.945	42	3-553/2-13,S-2	-1.4

■ GREG LUZINSKI
Luzinski, Gregory Michael b: 11/22/50, Chicago, Ill. BR/TR, 6'1", 225 lbs. Deb: 9/9/70 C

YEAR	TM/L	G	AB	R	H	2B	3B	HR	RBI	BB	SO	AVG	OBP	SLG	PRO+	BR/A	SB	CS	SBR	FA	FR	G/POS	TPR
1970	Phi-N	8	12	0	2	0	0	0	0	3	5	.167	.333	.167	39	-1	0	1	-1	1.000	1	/1-3	-0.1
1971	Phi-N	28	100	13	30	8	0	3	15	12	32	.300	.386	.470	141	6	2	0	1	.996	6	1-28	1.1
1972	Phi-N	150	563	66	158	33	5	18	68	42	114	.281	.334	.453	119	12	0	4	-2	.960	1	*O-145/1-2	0.4
1973	Phi-N	161	610	76	174	26	4	29	97	51	135	.285	.347	.484	125	19	3	3	-1	**.993**	-2	*O-159	0.9
1974	Phi-N	85	302	29	82	14	1	7	48	29	76	.272	.335	.394	99	-0	3	0	1	.981	7	O-82	0.3
1975	Phi-N★	161	596	85	179	35	3	34	**120**	89	151	.300	.398	.540	152	43	3	6	-3	.966	-3	*O-159	2.8
1976	*Phi-N★	149	533	74	162	28	1	21	95	50	107	.304	.375	.478	137	26	1	2	-1	.964	-8	*O-144	1.2
1977	*Phi-N★	149	554	99	171	35	3	39	130	80	140	.309	.399	.594	155	43	3	2	-0	.964	-5	*O-148	3.2
1978	*Phi-N★	155	540	85	143	32	2	35	101	100	135	.265	.390	.526	152	40	8	7	-2	.984	-7	*O-154	2.6
1979	Phi-N	137	452	47	114	23	1	18	81	56	103	.252	.347	.427	107	5	3	3	-1	.946	-15	*O-125	-1.7
1980	*Phi-N	106	368	44	84	19	1	19	56	60	100	.228	.346	.440	112	6	3	0	1	.993	-12	*O-105	-0.9
1981	Chi-A	104	378	55	100	15	1	21	62	58	80	.265	.367	.476	144	22	0	0	0	.000	0	*D-103	1.9
1982	Chi-A	159	583	87	170	37	1	18	102	89	120	.292	.391	.451	130	27	1	1	0	.000	0	*D-156	2.1
1983	*Chi-A	144	502	73	128	26	1	32	95	70	117	.255	.358	.502	129	20	2	1	0	1.000	0	*D-139/1-2	1.5
1984	Chi-A	125	412	47	98	13	0	13	58	56	80	.238	.333	.364	89	-5	5	1	1	.000	0	*D-114	-0.7
Total	15	1821	6505	880	1795	344	24	307	1128	845	1495	.276	.366	.478	129	262	37	31	-8	.972	-40	*O-1221,D-512/1-35	14.6

■ MITCH LYDEN
Lyden, Mitchell Scott b: 12/14/64, Portland, Ore. BR/TR, 6'3", 225 lbs. Deb: 6/16/93

YEAR	TM/L	G	AB	R	H	2B	3B	HR	RBI	BB	SO	AVG	OBP	SLG	PRO+	BR/A	SB	CS	SBR	FA	FR	G/POS	TPR
1993	Fla-N	6	10	2	3	0	0	1	1	0	3	.300	.300	.600	127	0	0	0	0	1.000	-1	/C-2	-0.1

■ SCOTT LYDY
Lydy, Donald Scott b: 10/26/68, Mesa, Ariz. BR/TR, 6'5", 195 lbs. Deb: 5/18/93

YEAR	TM/L	G	AB	R	H	2B	3B	HR	RBI	BB	SO	AVG	OBP	SLG	PRO+	BR/A	SB	CS	SBR	FA	FR	G/POS	TPR
1993	Oak-A	41	102	11	23	5	0	2	7	8	33	.225	.288	.333	71	-4	2	0	1	.958	-2	O-38/D-2	-0.6

■ JERRY LYNCH
Lynch, Gerald Thomas b: 7/17/30, Bay City, Mich. BL/TR, 6'1", 189 lbs. Deb: 4/15/54

YEAR	TM/L	G	AB	R	H	2B	3B	HR	RBI	BB	SO	AVG	OBP	SLG	PRO+	BR/A	SB	CS	SBR	FA	FR	G/POS	TPR
1954	Pit-N	98	284	27	68	4	5	6	36	20	43	.239	.292	.373	73	-12	2	2	-1	.965	-4	O-83	-2.0
1955	Pit-N	88	282	43	80	18	6	5	28	22	33	.284	.336	.443	106	2	2	2	-1	.950	-2	O-71/C-2	-0.4
1956	Pit-N	19	19	1	3	0	1	0	0	1	4	.158	.200	.263	24	-2	0	0	0	1.000	-0	/O-1	-0.2
1957	Cin-N	67	124	11	32	4	1	4	13	6	18	.258	.292	.403	79	-4	0	0	0	1.000	-2	O-24/C-2	-0.7
1958	Cin-N	122	420	58	131	20	5	16	68	18	54	.312	.340	.498	112	6	1	4	-2	.970	-7	*O-101	-0.8
1959	Cin-N	117	379	49	102	16	3	17	58	29	50	.269	.323	.462	103	1	2	0	1	.979	2	O-98	-0.2
1960	Cin-N	102	159	23	46	8	2	6	27	16	25	.289	.358	.478	124	5	0	0	0	.913	-4	O-32	0.0
1961	*Cin-N	96	181	33	57	13	2	13	50	27	25	.315	.407	.624	166	17	2	2	-1	.948	-4	O-44	1.0
1962	Cin-N	114	288	41	81	15	4	12	57	24	38	.281	.339	.486	115	5	3	3	-1	.970	-0	O-71	-0.5
1963	Cin-N	22	32	5	8	3	0	2	9	5	5	.250	.294	.531	129	1	0	1	-1	1.000	-1	/O-7	-0.1
	Pit-N	88	237	26	63	6	3	10	36	20	28	.266	.331	.443	120	6	0	1	-1	.960	-6	O-64	-0.4
	Yr	110	269	31	71	9	3	12	45	25	33	.264	.327	.454	121	7	0	1	-1	.962	-7	O-71	-0.5
1964	Pit-N	114	297	35	81	14	2	16	66	26	57	.273	.333	.495	130	11	0	1	-0	.983	-13	O-78	-0.6
1965	Pit-N	73	121	7	34	1	0	5	16	8	26	.281	.331	.413	108	1	0	1	-1	.903	-3	O-26	-0.5
1966	Pit-N	64	56	5	12	1	0	1	5	4	9	.214	.267	.286	54	-3	0	0	0	1.000	-0	/O-4	-0.1
Total	13	1184	2879	364	798	123	34	115	470	224	416	.277	.331	.463	110	34	12	17	-7	.964	-46	O-706/C-4	-5.3

■ HENRY LYNCH
Lynch, Henry W. b: 4/8/1866, Worcester, Mass. d: 11/23/25, Worcester, Mass. BB, 5'7", 143 lbs. Deb: 9/21/1893

YEAR	TM/L	G	AB	R	H	2B	3B	HR	RBI	BB	SO	AVG	OBP	SLG	PRO+	BR/A	SB	CS	SBR	FA	FR	G/POS	TPR
1893	Chi-N	4	14	0	3	2	0	0		2	1	.214	.267	.357	66	-1	0			.833	-1	/O-4	-0.2

■ DANNY LYNCH
Lynch, Matt Dan "Dummy" b: 2/7/26, Dallas, Tex. d: 6/30/78, Plano, Tex. BR/TR, 5'11", 174 lbs. Deb: 9/14/48

YEAR	TM/L	G	AB	R	H	2B	3B	HR	RBI	BB	SO	AVG	OBP	SLG	PRO+	BR/A	SB	CS	SBR	FA	FR	G/POS	TPR
1948	Chi-N	7	7	3	2	0	0	1		1	1	.286	.375	.714	197	1	1			1.000	0	/2-1	0.1

■ MIKE LYNCH
Lynch, Michael Joseph b: 9/10/1875, St.Paul, Minn. d: 4/1/47, Jennings Lodge, Ore TR, 5'10", 155 lbs. Deb: 4/24/02

YEAR	TM/L	G	AB	R	H	2B	3B	HR	RBI	BB	SO	AVG	OBP	SLG	PRO+	BR/A	SB	CS	SBR	FA	FR	G/POS	TPR
1902	Chi-N	7	28	4	4	0	0	0		0	2	.143	.200	.143	6	-3	0			.929	-1	/O-7	-0.5

■ TOM LYNCH
Lynch, Thomas James b: 4/3/1860, Bennington, Vt. d: 3/28/55, Cohoes, N.Y. BL/TR, 5'10.5", 170 lbs. Deb: 8/18/1884 U

YEAR	TM/L	G	AB	R	H	2B	3B	HR	RBI	BB	SO	AVG	OBP	SLG	PRO+	BR/A	SB	CS	SBR	FA	FR	G/POS	TPR
1884	Wil-U	16	58	6	16	3	1	0	5			.276	.333	.362	108	-1				.846	-3	/C-8,O-8,1-1	-0.3
	Phi-N	13	48	7	15	4	2	0	4	5		.313	.365	.479	171	4				.860	-2	C-7,O-7	0.3
1885	Phi-N	13	53	7	10	3	0	1	10	3		.189	.317	.245	86	-0				.838	3	O-13	0.2
Total	2	42	159	20	41	10	3	0	4	19	8	.258	.337	.358	119	3				.887	-2	/O-28,C-15,1-1	0.2

■ WALT LYNCH
Lynch, Walter Edward "Jabber" b: 4/15/1897, Buffalo, N.Y. d: 12/21/76, Daytona Beach, Fla TR, 6', 176 lbs. Deb: 7/8/22

YEAR	TM/L	G	AB	R	H	2B	3B	HR	RBI	BB	SO	AVG	OBP	SLG	PRO+	BR/A	SB	CS	SBR	FA	FR	G/POS	TPR
1922	Bos-A	3	2	1	1	0	0	0	0	1		.500	.500	.500	163	0	0			.500	0	/C-3	0.0

■ BYRD LYNN
Lynn, Byrd "Birdie" b: 3/13/1889, Unionville, Ill. d: 2/5/40, Napa, Cal. BR/TR, 5'11", 165 lbs. Deb: 4/16/16

YEAR	TM/L	G	AB	R	H	2B	3B	HR	RBI	BB	SO	AVG	OBP	SLG	PRO+	BR/A	SB	CS	SBR	FA	FR	G/POS	TPR
1916	Chi-A	31	40	4	9	1	0	0	3	4	7	.225	.311	.250	68	-1	2			.952	8	C-13	0.8
1917	*Chi-A	35	72	7	16	2	0	0	5	7	11	.222	.300	.250	67	-3	1			.959	-2	C-29	-0.3
1918	Chi-A	5	8	0	2	0	0	0	0	2	1	.250	.400	.250	95	0	0			1.000	-1	/C-4	-0.1
1919	*Chi-A	29	66	4	15	4	0	0	4	4	9	.227	.271	.288	57	-4	0			.982	1	C-28	-0.2
1920	Chi-A	16	25	0	8	2	0	0	3	1	3	.320	.346	.480	117	0	0	0	0	1.000	-1	C-14	0.0
Total	5	116	211	15	50	9	1	0	15	18	31	.237	.303	.289	72	-7	3	0		.969	5	/C-88	0.2

■ FRED LYNN
Lynn, Fredric Michael b: 2/3/52, Chicago, Ill. BL/TL, 6'1", 190 lbs. Deb: 9/5/74

YEAR	TM/L	G	AB	R	H	2B	3B	HR	RBI	BB	SO	AVG	OBP	SLG	PRO+	BR/A	SB	CS	SBR	FA	FR	G/POS	TPR
1974	Bos-A	15	43	5	18	2	2	2	10	6	6	.419	.490	.698	226	7	0	0	0	1.000	0	O-12/D-1	0.6
1975	*Bos-A★	145	528	**103**	175	**47**	7	21	105	62	90	.331	.405	**.566**	158	40	10	5	0	.983	13	*O-144	4.7
1976	Bos-A★	132	507	76	159	32	8	10	65	48	67	.314	.374	.467	130	18	14	9	-1	.984	14	*O-128/D-5	2.6
1977	Bos-A	129	497	81	129	29	5	18	76	51	63	.260	.332	.447	98	-2	2	3	-1	.994	8	*O-125/D-1	-0.1
1978	Bos-A	150	541	75	161	33	3	22	82	75	50	.298	.384	.492	131	22	3	6	-3	.984	8	*O-149	2.1
1979	Bos-A★	147	531	116	177	42	1	39	122	82	79	**.333**	.426	**.637**	173	55	2	2	-1	.987	7	*O-143/D-1	5.2
1980	Bos-A★	110	415	67	125	32	3	12	61	58	39	.301	.387	.480	129	18	12	0	4	.994	9	*O-110	2.5
1981	Cal-A★	76	256	28	56	8	1	5	31	38	42	.219	.327	.316	86	-4	1	2	-1	.978	1	O-69	-0.6
1982	*Cal-A★	138	472	89	141	38	1	21	86	58	72	.299	.379	.517	143	28	7	8	-3	.991	-3	*O-133	1.9
1983	Cal-A	117	437	56	119	20	3	22	74	55	83	.272	.356	.483	130	18	2	2	-1	.993	-2	*O-113/D-2	1.2
1984	Cal-A	142	517	84	140	28	4	23	79	77	97	.271	.367	.474	132	23	2	1	-0	.982	-10	*O-140	0.9
1985	Bal-A	124	448	59	118	12	1	23	68	53	100	.263	.343	.449	118	11	7	3	0	.994	2	O-123	0.9
1986	Bal-A	112	397	67	114	13	1	23	67	53	59	.287	.371	.474	137	21	2	2	-1	.994	-0	*O-107/D-1	0.9
1987	Bal-A	111	396	49	100	24	0	23	60	39	72	.253	.321	.487	113	6	3	1	-0	.991	-3	*O-101/D-8	-0.3
1988	Bal-A	87	301	37	76	14	1	11	37	28	66	.252	.316	.482	123	8	0	0	0	.991	0	O-83/D-2	0.6
	Det-A	27	90	9	20	1	0	7	19	5	16	.222	.271	.467	106	0	0	0	0	1.000	0	O-22/D-3	0.0

YEAR	TM/L	G	AB	R	H	2B	3B	HR	RBI	BB	SO	AVG	OBP	SLG	PRO+	BR/A	SB	CS	SBR	FA	FR	G/POS	TPR
	Yr	114	391	46	96	14	1	25	56	33	82	.246	.306	.478	120	8	2	2	-1	.992	1	*O-105/D-5	0.6
1989	Det-A	117	353	44	85	11	1	11	46	47	71	.241	.332	.371	100	1	1	1	-0	.992	-1	O-68,D-46	-0.3
1990	SD-N	90	196	18	47	3	1	6	23	22	44	.240	.320	.357	85	-4	2	0	1	1.000	-4	O-55	-0.9
Total	17	1969	6925	1063	1960	388	43	306	1111	857	1116	.283	.364	.484	129	266	72	54	-11	.988	35	*O-1825/D-70	22.3

■ JERRY LYNN Lynn, Jerome Edward b: 4/14/16, Scranton, Pa. d: 9/25/72, Scranton, Pa. BR/TR, 5'10", 164 lbs. Deb: 9/19/37

YEAR	TM/L	G	AB	R	H	2B	3B	HR	RBI	BB	SO	AVG	OBP	SLG	PRO+	BR/A	SB	CS	SBR	FA	FR	G/POS	TPR
1937	Was-A	1	3	0	2	1	0	0	0	0	0	.667	.667	1.000	329	1	0	0	0	1.000	1	/2-1	0.2

■ RUSS LYON Lyon, Russell Mayo b: 6/26/13, Ball Ground, Ga. d: 12/24/75, Charleston, S.C. BR/TR, 6'1", 230 lbs. Deb: 4/21/44

YEAR	TM/L	G	AB	R	H	2B	3B	HR	RBI	BB	SO	AVG	OBP	SLG	PRO+	BR/A	SB	CS	SBR	FA	FR	G/POS	TPR
1944	Cle-A	7	11	1	2	0	0	0	0	0	1	.182	.250	.182	25	-1	0	0	0	.909	0	/C-3	-0.1

■ BARRY LYONS Lyons, Barry Stephen b: 6/3/60, Biloxi, Miss. BR/TR, 6'1", 205 lbs. Deb: 4/19/86

YEAR	TM/L	G	AB	R	H	2B	3B	HR	RBI	BB	SO	AVG	OBP	SLG	PRO+	BR/A	SB	CS	SBR	FA	FR	G/POS	TPR
1986	NY-N	6	9	1	0	0	0	0	2	1	2	.000	.100	.000	-72	-2	0	0	0	.941	0	/C-3	-0.2
1987	NY-N	53	130	15	33	4	1	4	24	8	24	.254	.307	.392	88	-3	0	0	0	.984	0	C-49	0.0
1988	NY-N	50	91	5	21	7	1	0	11	3	12	.231	.255	.330	70	-4	0	0	0	.979	-2	C-32/1-1	-0.5
1989	NY-N	79	235	15	58	13	0	3	27	11	28	.247	.286	.340	82	-6	0	1	-1	.980	1	C-76	-0.2
1990	NY-N	24	80	8	19	0	0	2	7	2	9	.237	.265	.313	58	-5	0	0	0	.980	3	C-23	0.0
	LA-N	3	5	1	1	0	0	1	2	0	1	.200	.200	.800	166	0	0	0	0	1.000	-1	/C-2	0.0
	Yr	27	85	9	20	0	0	3	9	2	10	.235	.261	.341	65	-4	0	0	0	.980	3	C-25	0.0
1991	LA-N	9	9	0	0	0	0	0	0	0	0	.000	.000	.000	-99	-2	0	0	0	1.000	1	/C-6	-0.1
	Cal-A	2	5	0	1	0	0	0	0	0	0	.200	.200	.200	11	-1	0	0	0	1.000	0	/1-2	-0.1
1995	Chi-A	27	64	8	17	2	0	5	16	4	14	.266	.309	.531	119	1	0	0	0	.987	3	C-16/1-4,D-6	0.4
Total	7	253	628	53	150	26	2	15	89	29	92	.239	.278	.358	78	-20	0	1	-1	.981	6	C-207/1-7,D-6	-0.7

■ DENNY LYONS Lyons, Dennis Patrick Aloysius b: 3/12/1866, Cincinnati, Ohio d: 1/2/29, W.Covington, Ky. BR/TR, 5'10", 185 lbs. Deb: 9/18/1885

YEAR	TM/L	G	AB	R	H	2B	3B	HR	RBI	BB	SO	AVG	OBP	SLG	PRO+	BR/A	SB	CS	SBR	FA	FR	G/POS	TPR
1885	Pro-N	4	16	3	2	1	0	0	1	0	3	.125	.125	.188	-0	-2				.824	1	/3-4	-0.2
1886	Phi-a	32	123	22	26	3	1	0	11	8		.211	.281	.252	67	-5	7			.807	-7	3-32	-0.9
1887	Phi-a	137	570	128	209	43	14	6	102	47		.367	.421	.523	162	47	73			.866	-6	*3-137	3.5
1888	Phi-a	111	456	90	135	22	5	6	83	41		.296	.363	.406	147	25	39			.878	-13	*3-111	1.2
1889	Phi-a	131	510	135	168	36	4	9	82	79	44	.329	.426	.469	157	41	10			.860	9	*3-130/1-1	4.5
1890	Phi-a	88	339	79	120	29	5	4	73	57		.354	**.461**	**.531**	**197**	44	21			.909	3	3-88	4.8
1891	StL-a	120	451	124	142	24	3	11	84	88	58	.315	.445	.455	137	22	9			.871	-6	*3-120	1.8
1892	NY-N	108	389	71	100	16	7	8	51	59	37	.257	.359	.396	130	15	11			.871	-6	*3-108	1.3
1893	Pit-N	131	490	103	150	19	16	3	105	97	29	.306	.430	.429	131	27	19			.918	5	*3-131	2.8
1894	Pit-N	71	254	51	82	14	4	4	50	42	12	.323	.427	.457	114	8	14			.898	7	3-71	1.1
1895	StL-N	33	129	24	38	6	0	2	25	14	5	.295	.377	.388	99	0	3			.894	-5	3-33	-0.3
1896	Pit-N	118	436	77	134	25	4	6	71	67	25	.307	.406	.420	123	17	13			.893	-15	*3-116	0.4
1897	Pit-N	37	131	32	27	6	4	2	17	22		.206	.346	.359	89	-1	5			.989	-1	1-35/3-2	-0.2
Total	13	1121	4294	932	1333	244	69	62	755	621	213	.310	.407	.443	139	237	224			.882	-27	*3-1083/1-36	19.8

■ ED LYONS Lyons, Edward Hoyte "Mouse" b: 5/12/23, Winston-Salem, N.C BR/TR, 5'9", 165 lbs. Deb: 9/15/47 C

YEAR	TM/L	G	AB	R	H	2B	3B	HR	RBI	BB	SO	AVG	OBP	SLG	PRO+	BR/A	SB	CS	SBR	FA	FR	G/POS	TPR
1947	Was-A	7	26	2	4	0	0	0	0	2		.154	.214	.154	3	-3	0	0	0	1.000	4	/2-7	0.1

■ HARRY LYONS Lyons, Harry P. b: 3/25/1866, Chester, Pa. d: 6/30/12, Mauricetown, N.J. BR/TR, 5'10.5", 157 lbs. Deb: 8/29/1887

YEAR	TM/L	G	AB	R	H	2B	3B	HR	RBI	BB	SO	AVG	OBP	SLG	PRO+	BR/A	SB	CS	SBR	FA	FR	G/POS	TPR
1887	Phi-N	1	4	0	0	0	0	0	0	1	0	.000	.200	.000	-38	-1	0			.500	-0	/O-1	-0.1
	*StL-a	2	8	2	1	0	0	0	0	1	0	.125	.125	.125	-27	-1	2			1.000	1	/2-1,O-1	-0.1
1888	*StL-a	123	499	66	97	10	5	4	63	20		.194	.230	.259	51	-30	36			.891	6	*O-122/3-2,S-1,2-1	-2.6
1889	NY-N	5	20	1	2	0	1	0	2	0		.100	.182	.200	7	-3	0			1.000	-0	/O-5	-0.3
1890	Roc-a	133	584	83	152	11	11	3	58	27		.260	.294	.332	91	-9	47			.920	11	*O-132/3-2,C-1,P-1	-0.2
1892	NY-N	96	411	67	98	5	2	0	53	33	29	.238	.297	.260	70	-14	25			.910	3	O-96	-1.5
1893	NY-N	47	187	27	51	5	2	0	21	14	10	.273	.323	.321	71	-8	10			.917	2	O-47	-0.6
Total	6	407	1713	246	401	31	21	7	198	97	35	.234	.277	.289	69	-66	120			.908	21	O-404/3-4,2-2,PCS	-5.4

■ PAT LYONS Lyons, Patrick Jerry b: 3/1860, Canada d: 1/20/14, Springfield, Ohio TR, Deb: 7/21/1890

YEAR	TM/L	G	AB	R	H	2B	3B	HR	RBI	BB	SO	AVG	OBP	SLG	PRO+	BR/A	SB	CS	SBR	FA	FR	G/POS	TPR
1890	Cle-N	11	38	2	2	1	0	0	1	4	4	.053	.143	.079	-36	-7	0			.839	-5	2-11	-1.0

■ STEVE LYONS Lyons, Stephen John b: 6/3/60, Tacoma, Wash. BL/TR, 6'3", 192 lbs. Deb: 4/15/85

YEAR	TM/L	G	AB	R	H	2B	3B	HR	RBI	BB	SO	AVG	OBP	SLG	PRO+	BR/A	SB	CS	SBR	FA	FR	G/POS	TPR
1985	Bos-A	133	371	52	98	14	3	5	30	32	64	.264	.324	.358	83	-8	12	9	-2	.973	-8	*O-114/3-1,S-1,D-5	-2.1
1986	Bos-A	59	124	20	31	7	2	1	14	12	23	.250	.316	.363	84	-3	2	3	-1	.972	-5	O-55	-1.0
	Chi-A	42	123	10	25	2	1	0	6	7	24	.203	.252	.236	33	-11	2	3	-1	.987	1	O-35/3-3,1-1,D-1	-1.2
	Yr	101	247	30	56	9	3	1	20	19	47	.227	.285	.300	58	-14	4	6	-2	.978	-4	O-90/3-3,1-1,D-1	-2.2
1987	Chi-A	76	193	26	54	11	1	1	19	12	37	.280	.322	.363	79	-6	3	1	0	.971	1	3-51,O-15/2-1,D-6	0.4
1988	Chi-A	146	472	59	127	28	3	5	45	32	59	.269	.317	.373	93	-5	1	2	-1	.927	10	*3-128,O-14/2-4,C1	0.3
1989	Chi-A	140	443	51	117	21	3	2	50	35	68	.264	.319	.339	88	-7	9	6	-1	.982	-8	2-70,1-40,30/SCD	-1.7
1990	Chi-A	94	146	22	28	6	1	1	11	10	41	.192	.248	.267	45	-11	1	0	0	.991	-1	1-61,2-15/O-7,3SDP	-1.4
1991	Bos-A	87	212	15	51	10	1	4	17	11	35	.241	.285	.354	70	-9	10	3	1	1.000	-1	O-45,2-16,3/1SDP	-0.8
1992	Atl-N	11	14	0	1	0	1	0	1	1	4	.071	.071	.214	-21	-2	0	0	0	1.000	-2	/O-6,2-2	-0.4
	Mon-N	16	13	2	3	0	0	0	1	3		.231	.286	.231	48	-1	1	2	-1	1.000	-3	/O-8,1-1	-0.4
	Yr	27	27	2	4	0	1	0	2	1	7	.148	.179	.222	13	-3	1	2	-1	1.000	-0	O-14/2-2,1-1	-0.8
	Bos-A	21	28	3	7	1	0	0	2	1		.250	.300	.321	69	-1	1	2	-1	1.000	-0	/1-8,O-5,2-1,D-2	-0.2
1993	Bos-A	28	23	4	10	1	0	0	0	2	5	.130	.200	.174	1	-3	1	2	-1	1.000	-1	O-10/2-9,C-1,13D	-0.5
Total	9	853	2162	264	545	100	17	19	196	156	364	.252	.304	.340	77	-67	42	32	-7	.979	-4	O-334,3-229,21/DSCP	-9.0

■ TERRY LYONS Lyons, Terence Hilbert b: 12/14/08, New Holland, Ohio d: 9/9/59, Dayton, Ohio BR/TR, 6'0.5", 165 lbs. Deb: 4/19/29

YEAR	TM/L	G	AB	R	H	2B	3B	HR	RBI	BB	SO	AVG	OBP	SLG	PRO+	BR/A	SB	CS	SBR	FA	FR	G/POS	TPR
1929	Phi-N	1	0	0	0	0	0	0	0	0	0					0	0			.000	0	/1-1	0.0

■ TED LYONS Lyons, Theodore Amar b: 12/28/1900, Lake Charles, La. d: 7/25/86, Sulphur, La. BB/TR, 5'11", 200 lbs. Deb: 7/2/23 MCH

YEAR	TM/L	G	AB	R	H	2B	3B	HR	RBI	BB	SO	AVG	OBP	SLG	PRO+	BR/A	SB	CS	SBR	FA	FR	G/POS	TPR
1923	Chi-A	9	5	0	1	0	0	0	1	1	3	.200	.333	.200	43	-0	0	0	0	1.000	1	/P-9	0.0
1924	Chi-A	41	77	10	17	0	0	0	6	5	13	.221	.277	.247	37	-7	0	0	0	.902	-3	P-41	0.0
1925	Chi-A	43	97	6	18	3	0	0	7	3	13	.186	.218	.216	11	-13	0	0	0	.957	0	P-43	0.0
1926	Chi-A	41	104	7	22	1	1	0	3	1	10	.212	.219	.240	20	-12	0	0	0	.955	4	P-39	0.0
1927	Chi-A	41	110	16	28	6	2	1	9	6	17	.255	.293	.373	74	-5	0	0	0	.979	0	P-39	0.0
1928	Chi-A	49	91	10	23	2	0	0	8	1	9	.253	.261	.275	41	-8	0	0	0	.920	2	P-39	0.0
1929	Chi-A	40	91	7	20	4	0	0	11	9	13	.220	.290	.264	44	-8	0	0	0	.946	2	P-37/O-1	0.0
1930	Chi-A	57	122	20	38	6	3	1	15	2	18	.311	.323	.434	93	-2	0	0	0	.938	3	P-42	0.0
1931	Chi-A	42	33	6	5	0	0	0	3	2	10	.152	.200	.152	-7	-9	0	0	0	.957	-1	P-22	0.0
1932	Chi-A	49	73	11	19	2	1	0	4	10	4	.260	.308	.356	76	-3	0	0	0	.964	-1	P-33	0.0
1933	Chi-A	51	91	11	26	2	1	1	11	4	6	.286	.316	.363	83	-2	0	1	-1	.983	0	P-36	0.0
1934	Chi-A	29	82	9	20	4	0	0	16	3	19	.244	.278	.293	34	-10	0	0	0	.939	2	P-30	0.0
1935	Chi-A	29	82	5	18	4	0	0	6	3		.220	.256	.268	35	-8	0	0	0	**1.000**	-1	P-23	0.0
1936	Chi-A	26	70	2	11	1	0	0	5	5	12	.157	.213	.157	-7	-12	0	0	0	**1.000**	1	P-26	0.0
1937	Chi-A	23	57	6	12	0	0	0	3	9	14	.211	.318	.211	36	-5	0	0	0	**1.000**	0	P-23	0.0
1938	Chi-A	24	72	9	14	2	0	0	7	2		.194	.216	.222	10	-10	0	0	0	.982	-1	P-23	0.0
1939	Chi-A☆	21	61	5	18	3	0	0	8	5	7	.295	.348	.344	76	-2	0	0	0	.912	-1	P-21	0.0
1940	Chi-A	22	75	4	18	4	0	0	7	2		.240	.260	.293	43	-6	0	0	0	.923	-2	P-22	0.0
1941	Chi-A	22	74	8	20	4	0	0	9	2	6	.270	.289	.297	56	-5	0	0	0	.981	-5	P-22	0.0
1942	Chi-A	20	67	10	16	4	0	0	10	3		.239	.282	.299	65	-3	0	0	0	.980	1	P-20	0.0
1946	Chi-A	5	5	0	0	0	0	0	0	1	3	.000	.067	.000	-83	-3	0	0	0	1.000	0	/P-5,M	0.0
Total	21	705	1563	162	364	49	9	5	149	73	201	.233	.270	.285	44	-130	1	1	-1	.958	11	P-594/O-1	0.0

■ BILL LYONS Lyons, William Allen b: 4/26/58, Alton, Ill. BR/TR, 6'1", 175 lbs. Deb: 7/20/83

YEAR	TM/L	G	AB	R	H	2B	3B	HR	RBI	BB	SO	AVG	OBP	SLG	PRO+	BR/A	SB	CS	SBR	FA	FR	G/POS	TPR
1983	StL-N	42	60	3	10	1	1	0	3	1	11	.167	.180	.217	10	-7	3	2	-0	.985	2	2-23/3-8,S-2	-0.5

YEAR	TM/L	G	AB	R	H	2B	3B	HR	RBI	BB	SO	AVG	OBP	SLG	PRO+	BR/A	SB	CS	SBR	FA	FR	G/POS	TPR
1984	StL-N	46	73	13	16	3	0	0	3	9	13	.219	.305	.260	62	-3	3	1	0	.991	14	2-25,S-11/3-3	1.2
Total	2	88	133	16	26	4	1	0	6	10	24	.195	.252	.241	39	-11	6	3	0	.989	16	/2-48,S-13,3-11	0.7

■ DAD LYTLE
Lytle, Edward Benson "Pop"   b: 3/10/1862, Racine, Wis.   d: 12/21/50, Long Beach, Cal.   BR/TR, 5'11", 160 lbs.   Deb: 8/11/1890

YEAR	TM/L	G	AB	R	H	2B	3B	HR	RBI	BB	SO	AVG	OBP	SLG	PRO+	BR/A	SB	CS	SBR	FA	FR	G/POS	TPR
1890	Chi-N	1	4	1	0	0	0	0	0	0	1	.000	.000	.000	-96	-1	0			1.000	1	/O-1	0.0
	Pit-N	15	55	2	8	1	0	0	8	9	9	.145	.254	.164	25	-5	0			.837	-6	/2-8,O-7	-1.0
	Yr	16	59	3	8	1	0	0	8	9	10	.136	.239	.153	16	-6	0			.824	-5	/O-8,2-8	-1.0

■ JIM LYTTLE
Lyttle, James Lawrence   b: 5/20/46, Hamilton, Ohio   BL/TR, 6', 186 lbs.   Deb: 5/17/69

YEAR	TM/L	G	AB	R	H	2B	3B	HR	RBI	BB	SO	AVG	OBP	SLG	PRO+	BR/A	SB	CS	SBR	FA	FR	G/POS	TPR
1969	NY-A	28	83	7	15	4	0	0	4	4	19	.181	.218	.229	26	-8	1	2	-1	.983	1	O-28	-1.0
1970	NY-A	87	126	20	39	7	1	3	14	10	26	.310	.360	.452	129	5	3	6	-3	.989	-9	O-70	-0.9
1971	NY-A	49	86	7	17	5	0	1	7	8	18	.198	.274	.291	64	-4	0	2	-1	1.000	-3	O-29	-1.0
1972	Chi-A	44	82	8	19	5	2	0	5	1	28	.232	.241	.341	70	-3	0	1	-1	1.000	-2	O-21	-0.7
1973	Mon-N	49	116	12	30	5	1	4	19	9	14	.259	.312	.422	98	-1	0	1	-1	.974	2	O-36	-0.1
1974	Mon-N	25	9	1	3	0	0	0	2	1	3	.333	.400	.333	101	0	0	0	0	1.000	-6	O-18	-0.6
1975	Mon-N	44	55	7	15	4	0	0	6	13	6	.273	.412	.345	107	1	0	1	-1	1.000	-5	O-16	-0.3
1976	Mon-N	42	85	6	23	4	1	1	8	7	13	.271	.326	.376	95	-1	0	0	0	.977	-3	O-29	-0.4
	LA-N	23	68	3	15	3	0	0	5	8	12	.221	.303	.265	63	-3	0	1	-1	1.000	4	O-18	0.0
	Yr	65	153	9	38	7	1	1	13	15	25	.248	.315	.327	81	-4	0	1	-1	.990	2	O-47	-0.4
Total	8	391	710	71	176	37	5	9	70	61	139	.248	.308	.352	86	-14	4	15	-8	.988	-18	O-265	-5.0

■ KEVIN MAAS
Maas, Kevin Christian   b: 1/20/65, Castro Valley, Cal.   BL/TL, 6'3", 195 lbs.   Deb: 6/29/90

YEAR	TM/L	G	AB	R	H	2B	3B	HR	RBI	BB	SO	AVG	OBP	SLG	PRO+	BR/A	SB	CS	SBR	FA	FR	G/POS	TPR
1990	NY-A	79	254	42	64	9	0	21	41	43	76	.252	.367	.535	149	17	1	2	-1	.983	-3	1-57,D-18	0.8
1991	NY-A	148	500	69	110	14	1	23	63	83	128	.220	.336	.390	100	1	5	1	1	.983	-1	*D-109,1-36	-0.6
1992	NY-A	98	286	35	71	12	0	11	35	25	63	.248	.309	.406	99	-1	3	1	0	.986	-3	D-62,1-22	-0.7
1993	NY-A	59	151	20	31	4	0	9	25	24	32	.205	.318	.411	97	-1	1	1	-0	.984	-1	D-31,1-17	-0.4
1995	Min-A	22	57	5	11	4	0	1	5	7	11	.193	.281	.316	55	-4	0	0	0	.936	-2	D-12/1-8	-0.7
Total	5	406	1248	171	287	43	1	65	169	182	310	.230	.332	.422	107	12	10	5	0	.982	-10	D-232,1-140	-1.6

■ JOHN MABRY
Mabry, John Steven   b: 10/17/70, Wilmington, Del.   BL/TR, 6'4", 195 lbs.   Deb: 4/23/94

YEAR	TM/L	G	AB	R	H	2B	3B	HR	RBI	BB	SO	AVG	OBP	SLG	PRO+	BR/A	SB	CS	SBR	FA	FR	G/POS	TPR
1994	StL-N	6	23	2	7	3	0	0	3	2	4	.304	.360	.435	108	0	0	0	0	1.000	1	/O-6	0.1
1995	StL-N	129	388	35	119	21	1	5	41	24	45	.307	.350	.405	99	-1	0	3	-2	.994	2	1-73,O-39	-0.7
1996	*StL-N	151	543	63	161	30	2	13	74	37	84	.297	.345	.431	103	2	3	2	-0	.994	-11	*1-146,O-14	-2.3
Total	3	286	954	100	287	54	3	18	118	63	133	.301	.347	.420	101	1	3	5	-2	.994	-8	1-219/O-59	-2.9

■ HARVEY MacDONALD
Mac Donald, Harvey Forsyth   b: 5/18/1898, New York, N.Y.   d: 10/4/65, Manoa, Pa.   BL/TL, 5'11", 170 lbs.   Deb: 6/12/28

YEAR	TM/L	G	AB	R	H	2B	3B	HR	RBI	BB	SO	AVG	OBP	SLG	PRO+	BR/A	SB	CS	SBR	FA	FR	G/POS	TPR
1928	Phi-N	13	16	0	4	0	0	0	2	2	3	.250	.333	.250	53	-1	0			1.000	-0	/O-2	-0.1

■ MACEY
Macey   b: Columbus, Ohio   Deb: 10/2/1890

YEAR	TM/L	G	AB	R	H	2B	3B	HR	RBI	BB	SO	AVG	OBP	SLG	PRO+	BR/A	SB	CS	SBR	FA	FR	G/POS	TPR
1890	Phi-a	1	1	0	0	0	0	0	0	0	0	.000	.000	.000	-99	-0	0			1.000	-1	/C-1	-0.1

■ MIKE MACFARLANE
Macfarlane, Michael Andrew   b: 4/12/64, Stockton, Cal.   BR/TR, 6'1", 200 lbs.   Deb: 7/23/87

YEAR	TM/L	G	AB	R	H	2B	3B	HR	RBI	BB	SO	AVG	OBP	SLG	PRO+	BR/A	SB	CS	SBR	FA	FR	G/POS	TPR
1987	KC-A	8	19	0	4	1	0	0	3	2	2	.211	.286	.263	46	-1	0	0	0	1.000	-1	/C-8	-0.2
1988	KC-A	70	211	25	56	15	0	4	26	21	37	.265	.335	.393	102	1	0	0	0	.994	-15	C-68	-0.9
1989	KC-A	69	157	13	35	6	0	2	19	7	27	.223	.265	.299	59	-9	0	0	0	.996	2	C-59/D-4	-0.4
1990	KC-A	124	400	37	102	24	4	6	58	25	69	.255	.310	.380	94	-4	1	0	0	.991	-19	*C-112/D-5	-1.7
1991	KC-A	84	267	34	74	18	2	13	41	17	52	.277	.334	.506	128	9	1	0	0	.993	-12	C-69/D-4	0.2
1992	KC-A	129	402	51	94	28	3	17	48	30	89	.234	.311	.445	107	2	1	5	-3	.993	-1	*C-104,D-13	0.4
1993	KC-A	117	388	55	106	27	0	20	67	40	83	.273	.365	.497	122	12	2	5	-2	.985	4	*C-114	1.9
1994	KC-A	92	314	53	80	17	3	14	47	35	71	.255	.362	.462	106	3	1	0	0	.993	4	C-81/D-8	1.1
1995	*Bos-A	115	364	45	82	18	1	15	51	38	78	.225	.322	.404	85	-9	2	1	0	.993	-4	*C-111/D-3	-0.5
1996	KC-A	112	379	58	104	24	2	19	54	31	57	.274	.341	.499	111	5	3	3	-1	.993	-11	C-99/D-9	0.1
Total	10	920	2901	371	737	178	15	110	414	246	565	.254	.331	.440	104	10	11	14	-5	.992	-54	C-825/D-46	0.0

■ ED MacGAMWELL
Mac Gamwell, Edward M.   b: 1/10/1879, Buffalo, N.Y.   d: 5/26/24, Albany, N.Y.   BL/TL,   Deb: 4/14/05

YEAR	TM/L	G	AB	R	H	2B	3B	HR	RBI	BB	SO	AVG	OBP	SLG	PRO+	BR/A	SB	CS	SBR	FA	FR	G/POS	TPR
1905	Bro-N	4	16	0	4	0	0	0	0	1		.250	.294	.250	68	-1	0			.951	-1	/1-4	-0.1

■ KEN MACHA
Macha, Kenneth Edward   b: 9/29/50, Monroeville, Pa.   BR/TR, 6'2", 217 lbs.   Deb: 9/14/74   FC

YEAR	TM/L	G	AB	R	H	2B	3B	HR	RBI	BB	SO	AVG	OBP	SLG	PRO+	BR/A	SB	CS	SBR	FA	FR	G/POS	TPR
1974	Pit-N	5	5	1	3	1	0	0	1	0	0	.600	.600	.800	300	1	0	0	0	1.000	-0	/C-1	0.0
1977	Pit-N	35	95	2	26	4	0	0	11	6	17	.274	.317	.316	68	-4	1	1	-0	.964	-5	3-17,1-11/O-4	-1.0
1978	Pit-N	29	52	5	11	1	1	0	5	12	10	.212	.359	.269	75	-1	2	0	1	.970	-3	3-21	-0.4
1979	Mon-N	25	36	8	10	3	0	0	4	2	9	.278	.333	.417	104	0	0	0	0	1.000	1	3-13/1-2,O-2,C-1	0.1
1980	Mon-N	49	107	10	31	5	1	0	8	11	17	.290	.361	.383	108	1	0	0	0	.910	-5	3-33/1-2,C-1,O-1	-0.6
1981	Tor-A	37	85	4	17	2	0	0	6	8	15	.200	.269	.224	41	-6	1	1	-0	.892	-1	3-19,1-16/C-1,D-2	-0.9
Total	6	180	380	30	98	16	3	1	35	39	68	.258	.330	.324	80	-9	4	4	-1	.938	-13	3-103/1-31,O-7,CD	-2.7

■ MIKE MACHA
Macha, Michael William   b: 2/17/54, Victoria, Tex.   BR/TR, 5'11", 180 lbs.   Deb: 4/20/79   F

YEAR	TM/L	G	AB	R	H	2B	3B	HR	RBI	BB	SO	AVG	OBP	SLG	PRO+	BR/A	SB	CS	SBR	FA	FR	G/POS	TPR
1979	Atl-N	6	13	2	2	0	0	0	1	1	5	.154	.214	.154	2	-2	0	0	0	.769	0	/3-3	-0.1
1980	Tor-A	5	8	0	0	0	0	0	0	1	0	.000	.000	.000	-96	-2	0	0	0	.778	1	/3-2,C-1	-0.2
Total	2	11	21	2	2	0	0	0	1	2	5	.095	.136	.095	-33	-4	0	0	0	.773	1	/3-5,C-1	-0.3

■ ROBERT MACHADO
Machado, Robert Alexis   b: 6/3/73, Caracas, Venez.   BR/TR, 6'1", 205 lbs.   Deb: 7/24/96

YEAR	TM/L	G	AB	R	H	2B	3B	HR	RBI	BB	SO	AVG	OBP	SLG	PRO+	BR/A	SB	CS	SBR	FA	FR	G/POS	TPR
1996	Chi-A	4	6	1	4	1	0	0	2	0	0	.667	.667	.833	292	2	0	0	0	1.000	-1	/C-4	0.1

■ DAVE MACHEMER
Machemer, David Ritchie   b: 5/24/51, St.Joseph, Mo.   BR/TR, 5'11.5", 180 lbs.   Deb: 6/21/78

YEAR	TM/L	G	AB	R	H	2B	3B	HR	RBI	BB	SO	AVG	OBP	SLG	PRO+	BR/A	SB	CS	SBR	FA	FR	G/POS	TPR
1978	Cal-A	10	22	6	6	1	0	1	2	2	1	.273	.333	.455	124	1	0	1	-1	1.000	-2	/2-5,3-3,S-1	-0.2
1979	Det-A	19	26	8	5	1	0	0	3	2	2	.192	.276	.231	37	-2	0	3	-2	.972	5	2-11/O-1,D-1	0.1
Total	2	29	48	14	11	2	0	1	5	4	3	.229	.302	.333	74	-2	0	4	-2	.978	2	/2-16,3-3,D-1,OS	-0.1

■ CONNIE MACK
Mack, Cornelius Alexander "The Tall Tactician" (b: Cornelius Alexander McGillicuddy)
b: 12/22/1862, E.Brookfield, Mass   d: 2/8/56, Philadelphia, Pa.   BR/TR, 6'1", 150 lbs.   Deb: 9/11/1886   FMH

YEAR	TM/L	G	AB	R	H	2B	3B	HR	RBI	BB	SO	AVG	OBP	SLG	PRO+	BR/A	SB	CS	SBR	FA	FR	G/POS	TPR
1886	Was-N	10	36	4	13	1	1	0		1		.361	.361	.472	161	1				.957	9	C-10	1.1
1887	Was-N	82	314	35	63	6	1	0	20	8	17	.201	.228	.226	28	-30	26			.906	3	C-76/O-5,2-2	-1.7
1888	Was-N	85	300	49	56	6	3	0	29	17	18	.187	.249	.273	70	-9	31			.916	5	C-79/O-4,S-1,1-1	0.3
1889	Was-N	98	386	51	113	16	1	0	42	15	12	.293	.333	.339	94	-3	26			.891	5	C-45,O-34,1-22	0.3
1890	Buf-P	123	503	95	134	15	12	0	53	47	13	.266	.353	.344	94	-1	16			.925	-11	*C-112/O-9,1-5	-0.2
1891	Pit-N	75	280	43	60	10	0	0	29	19	11	.214	.286	.250	58	-14	4			.926	9	C-72/1-3	0.0
1892	Pit-N	97	346	39	84	9	4	1	31	21	22	.243	.298	.301	81	-8	11			**.951**	24	C-92/O-3,1-1	2.0
1893	Pit-N	37	133	22	38	3	1	0	15	10	9	.286	.358	.323	83	-3	4			.941	6	C-37	0.5
1894	Pit-N	69	228	32	57	7	1	1	21	20	14	.250	.321	.303	52	-18	8			.947	5	C-69,M	-0.5
1895	Pit-N	14	49	12	15	2	0	0	4	7	1	.306	.404	.347	100	1	1			.962	-2	C-12/1-1,M	-0.8
1896	Pit-N	33	120	9	26	4	1	0	16	5	8	.217	.248	.267	37	-11	0			.974	1	1-28/C-5,M	-0.8
Total	11	723	2695	391	659	79	28	5	265	169	127	.245	.305	.300	72	-98	127			.927	53	C-609/1-61,O-55,2S	1.0

■ DENNY MACK
Mack, Dennis Joseph (b: Dennis Joseph McGee)   b: 1851, Easton, Conn.   d: 4/10/1888, Wilkes-Barre, Pa.   BR/TR, 5'7", 164 lbs.   Deb: 5/6/1871   MU

YEAR	TM/L	G	AB	R	H	2B	3B	HR	RBI	BB	SO	AVG	OBP	SLG	PRO+	BR/A	SB	CS	SBR	FA	FR	G/POS	TPR
1871	Rok-n	25	122	34	30	7	1	0	22	2		.246	.292	.320	79	-2	12	0	4	.936	-1	*1-24/P-3,S-1,O-1	0.3
1872	Ath-n	47	205	68	59	9	1	0	34	**23**	9	.288	.360	.341	116	5	9	5	-0	.948	5	1-26,S-21	0.3
1873	Phi-n	48	205	55	60	5	0	0	20	15	9	.293	.341	.317	93	-2	6	2	1	.936	2	1-42/O-4,S-3,2-1	0.2
1874	Phi-n	56	246	48	51	8	4	0	22	2	3	.207	.214	.272	53	-13	4	0	1	.900	-4	*1-56	-1.0
1876	StL-N	48	180	32	39	5	0	1	7	11	5	.217	.262	.261	79	-3				.886	-8	S-41/2-5,O-2	-1.0
1880	Buf-N	17	59	5	12	0	0	0	6	3	6	.203	.266	.203	60	-2				.940	-2	S-16/2-1	-0.3
1882	Lou-a	72	264	41	48	3	1	0		16		.182	.229	.201	49	-13				.898	-3	S-49,2-24/O-5,M	-1.2

YEAR	TM/L	G	AB	R	H	2B	3B	HR	RBI	BB	SO	AVG	OBP	SLG	PRO+	BR/A	SB	CS	SBR	FA	FR	G/POS	TPR
1883	Pit-a	60	224	26	44	5	3	0			13	.196	.241	.246	60	-9				.844	4	S-38,1-25/2-1	-0.6
Total	4 n	176	778	205	200	29	6	0	93	48	28	.257	.300	.310	85	-12	31	7	5	.926	-9	1-148/S-25,O-5,P2	-0.5
Total	4	197	727	104	143	13	4	1	10	45	12	.197	.244	.230	60	-27				.886	-8	S-144/2-31,1-25,O-7	-3.1

■ EARLE MACK
Mack, Earle Thaddeus (b: Earle Thaddeus McGillicuddy)
b: 2/1/1890, Spencer, Mass. d: 2/4/67, Upper Darby Township, Pa. BL/TR, 5'8", 140 lbs. Deb: 10/5/10 FMC

YEAR	TM/L	G	AB	R	H	2B	3B	HR	RBI	BB	SO	AVG	OBP	SLG	PRO+	BR/A	SB	CS	SBR	FA	FR	G/POS	TPR
1910	Phi-A	1	4	0	2	0	1	0	0	0		.500	.500	1.000	372	1	0			1.000	-1	/C-1	0.1
1911	Phi-A	2	4	0	0	0	0	0	0	0		.000	.000	.000	-99	-1	0			.000	0	/3-2	-0.1
1914	Phi-A	2	8	0	0	0	0	0	1	0	0	.000	.000	.000	-99	-2	1			1.000	0	/1-2	-0.2
Total	3	5	16	0	2	0	1	0	1	0	0	.125	.125	.250	11	-2	1			1.000	-1	/1-2,3-2,C-1	-0.2

■ JOE MACK
Mack, Joe John (b: Joseph John Maciarz) b: 1/4/12, Chicago, Ill. BB/TL, 5'11.5", 185 lbs. Deb: 4/17/45

YEAR	TM/L	G	AB	R	H	2B	3B	HR	RBI	BB	SO	AVG	OBP	SLG	PRO+	BR/A	SB	CS	SBR	FA	FR	G/POS	TPR
1945	Bos-N	66	260	30	60	13	1	3	44	34	39	.231	.320	.323	79	-7	1			.991	0	1-65	-1.1

■ REDDY MACK
Mack, Joseph (b: Joseph McNamara) b: 5/2/1866, Ireland d: 12/30/16, Newport, Ky. 5'8", 182 lbs. Deb: 9/16/1885

YEAR	TM/L	G	AB	R	H	2B	3B	HR	RBI	BB	SO	AVG	OBP	SLG	PRO+	BR/A	SB	CS	SBR	FA	FR	G/POS	TPR
1885	Lou-a	11	41	7	10	1	0	0		5	2	.244	.295	.268	79	-1				.885	0	2-11	0.0
1886	Lou-a	137	483	82	118	23	11	1	56	68		.244	.342	.344	109	5	13			.900	6	*2-137	1.5
1887	Lou-a	128	478	117	147	23	8	1	69	83		.308	.415	.395	124	19	22			.912	5	*2-128	2.3
1888	Lou-a	112	446	77	97	13	5	3	34	52		.217	.320	.289	98	2	18			.907	4	*2-112	0.9
1889	Bal-a	136	519	84	125	24	7	1	87	60	69	.241	.329	.320	84	-11	23			.897	-11	*2-135/O-1	-1.2
1890	Bal-a	26	95	14	27	3	2	0		11	10	.284	.370	.421	127	3	7			.932	1	2-26	0.4
Total	6	550	2062	381	524	87	36	6	262	275	69	.254	.352	.340	104	18	83			.905	5	2-549/O-1	3.9

■ QUINN MACK
Mack, Quinn David b: 9/11/65, Los Angeles, Cal. BL/TL, 5'10", 185 lbs. Deb: 6/16/94 F

YEAR	TM/L	G	AB	R	H	2B	3B	HR	RBI	BB	SO	AVG	OBP	SLG	PRO+	BR/A	SB	CS	SBR	FA	FR	G/POS	TPR
1994	Sea-A	5	21	1	5	3	0	0	2	1	3	.238	.273	.381	65	-1	2	0	1	1.000	-0	/O-4,D-1	-0.1

■ RAY MACK
Mack, Raymond James (b: Raymond James Mickovsky) b: 8/31/16, Cleveland, Ohio d: 5/7/69, Bucyrus, Ohio BR/TR, 6', 200 lbs. Deb: 9/9/38

YEAR	TM/L	G	AB	R	H	2B	3B	HR	RBI	BB	SO	AVG	OBP	SLG	PRO+	BR/A	SB	CS	SBR	FA	FR	G/POS	TPR
1938	Cle-A	2	6	2	2	0	0	0	2	0	1	.333	.333	.667	147	0	0	0	0	1.000	2	/2-2	0.2
1939	Cle-A	36	112	12	17	4	1	1	6	12	19	.152	.240	.232	22	-14	0	2	-1	.976	2	2-34/3-1	-1.0
1940	Cle-A★	146	530	60	150	21	5	12	69	51	77	.283	.346	.409	98	-2	4	2	0	.965	-9	*2-146	-0.1
1941	Cle-A	145	500	54	114	22	4	9	44	54	69	.228	.303	.342	74	-20	8	4	0	.970	-5	*2-145	-1.4
1942	Cle-A	143	481	43	108	14	6	2	45	41	51	.225	.288	.291	67	-22	9	3	1	.969	-4	*2-143	-1.7
1943	Cle-A	153	545	56	120	25	2	7	62	47	61	.220	.285	.312	79	-16	8	3	1	.967	-2	*2-153	-1.0
1944	Cle-A	83	284	24	66	15	3	0	29	28	45	.232	.301	.306	77	-9	4	1	1	.951	10	2-83	0.7
1946	Cle-A	61	171	13	35	6	2	1	9	23	27	.205	.299	.281	67	-7	2	2	-1	.970	1	2-61	-0.4
1947	NY-A	1	0	0	0	0	0	0	0	0	0	—	—	—	—		0	0	0	.000	0	R	0.0
	Chi-N	21	78	9	17	4	0	2	12	5	15	.218	.274	.372	73	-3	0			.965	7	2-21	0.5
Total	9	791	2707	273	629	113	24	34	278	261	365	.232	.301	.332	74	-93	35	17		.966	3	2-788/3-1	-4.2

■ SHANE MACK
Mack, Shane Lee b: 12/7/63, Los Angeles, Cal. BR/TR, 6'", 185 lbs. Deb: 5/25/87 F

YEAR	TM/L	G	AB	R	H	2B	3B	HR	RBI	BB	SO	AVG	OBP	SLG	PRO+	BR/A	SB	CS	SBR	FA	FR	G/POS	TPR
1987	SD-N	105	238	28	57	11	3	4	25	18	47	.239	.301	.361	77	-8	4	6	-2	.982	-8	O-91	-2.0
1988	SD-N	56	119	13	29	3	0	0	12	14	21	.244	.338	.269	78	-3	5	1	1	.983	-3	O-55	-0.6
1990	Min-A	125	313	50	102	10	4	8	44	29	69	.326	.392	.460	129	13	13	4	-2	.988	5	*O-109/D-4	1.3
1991	*Min-A	143	442	79	137	27	8	18	74	34	79	.310	.367	.529	139	22	13	9	-2	.977	-9	*O-140/D-1	0.9
1992	Min-A	156	600	101	189	31	6	16	75	64	106	.315	.395	.467	136	30	26	14	-1	.988	1	*O-155	2.8
1993	Min-A	128	503	66	139	30	4	10	61	41	76	.276	.336	.412	99	-1	15	5	2	.986	14	*O-128	1.1
1994	Min-A	81	303	55	101	21	2	15	61	32	51	.333	.408	.564	147	22	4	1	1	.990	1	O-75/D-4	1.9
Total	7	794	2518	392	754	133	27	71	352	232	449	.299	.368	.458	122	74	80	40	-3	.985	-3	O-753/D-9	5.4

■ PETE MACKANIN
Mackanin, Peter b: 8/1/51, Chicago, Ill. BR/TR, 6'2", 190 lbs. Deb: 7/3/73

YEAR	TM/L	G	AB	R	H	2B	3B	HR	RBI	BB	SO	AVG	OBP	SLG	PRO+	BR/A	SB	CS	SBR	FA	FR	G/POS	TPR
1973	Tex-A	44	90	3	9	2	0	0	2	4	26	.100	.147	.122	-24	-15	0	0	0	.947	2	S-33,3-10	-1.1
1974	Tex-A	2	6	0	1	0	1	0	0	0	2	.167	.167	.500	88	-0	0	0	0	1.000	2	/S-2	0.2
1975	Mon-N	130	448	59	101	19	6	12	44	31	99	.225	.279	.375	77	-16	11	5	0	.966	18	*2-127/S-1,3-1	1.0
1976	Mon-N	114	380	36	85	15	2	8	33	15	66	.224	.257	.337	65	-19	6	2	1	.965	-2	2-100/3-8,S-3,0-1	-1.5
1977	Mon-N	55	85	9	19	2	1	1	6	4	17	.224	.258	.329	58	-5	3	1	0	1.000	3	2-9,S-8,3-5,O-4	-0.1
1978	Phi-N	5	8	0	2	0	0	0	0	0	4	.250	.250	.250	40	-1	0	0	0	1.000	1	/1-1,3-1	-0.1
1979	Phi-N	13	9	2	1	0	0	1	2	1	2	.111	.200	.444	69	-0	0	0	0	1.000	1	/2-2,S-2,3-2	-0.1
1980	Min-A	108	319	31	85	18	0	4	35	14	34	.266	.297	.361	74	-12	6	2	1	.968	16	2-71,S-30/1-4,3D	1.0
1981	Min-A	77	225	21	52	7	1	4	18	7	40	.231	.258	.324	63	-11	1	2	-1	.980	-5	2-31,S-28,1-10,/3D	-1.4
Total	9	548	1570	161	355	63	12	30	141	76	290	.226	.265	.339	65	-79	27	12	1	.968	36	2-340,S-107/31DO	-1.8

■ ERIC MacKENZIE
Mac Kenzie, Eric Hugh b: 8/29/32, Glendon, Alberta, Can. BL/TR, 6', 185 lbs. Deb: 4/23/55

YEAR	TM/L	G	AB	R	H	2B	3B	HR	RBI	BB	SO	AVG	OBP	SLG	PRO+	BR/A	SB	CS	SBR	FA	FR	G/POS	TPR
1955	KC-A	1	1	0	0	0	0	0	0	0	0	.000	.000	.000	-99	-0	0	0	0	.000	-0	/C-1	0.0

■ GORDON MacKENZIE
Mac Kenzie, Henry Gordon b: 7/9/37, St.Petersburg, Fla BR/TR, 5'11", 175 lbs. Deb: 8/13/61 C

YEAR	TM/L	G	AB	R	H	2B	3B	HR	RBI	BB	SO	AVG	OBP	SLG	PRO+	BR/A	SB	CS	SBR	FA	FR	G/POS	TPR
1961	KC-A	11	24	1	3	1	0	0	1	1	6	.125	.160	.125	-22	-4	0	0	0	1.000	-0	/C-7	-0.4

■ FELIX MACKIEWICZ
Mackiewicz, Felix Thaddeus b: 11/20/17, Chicago, Ill. d: 12/20/93, Olivette, Mo. BR/TR, 6'2", 195 lbs. Deb: 9/7/41

YEAR	TM/L	G	AB	R	H	2B	3B	HR	RBI	BB	SO	AVG	OBP	SLG	PRO+	BR/A	SB	CS	SBR	FA	FR	G/POS	TPR
1941	Phi-A	5	14	3	4	0	1	0	0	1	0	.286	.333	.429	103	-0	0	0	0	1.000	-1	/O-3	-0.1
1942	Phi-A	6	14	3	3	2	0	0	2	0	4	.214	.214	.357	59	-1	0	0	0	1.000	0	/O-3	-0.1
1943	Phi-A	9	16	1	1	0	0	0	0	2	8	.063	.167	.063	-32	-3	0	0	0	1.000	0	/O-3	-0.3
1945	Cle-A	120	359	42	98	14	7	2	37	44	41	.273	.356	.368	115	7	5	5	-2	.987	5	*O-112	0.6
1946	Cle-A	78	258	35	67	15	4	0	16	16	32	.260	.305	.349	88	-5	5	1	1	.983	-2	O-72	-1.0
1947	Cle-A	2	5	0	0	0	0	0	0	0	0	.000	.000	.000	-99	-0	0	0	0	1.000	-0	/O-2	-0.2
	Was-A	3	6	1	1	0	0	0	0	0	1	.167	.167	.333	38	-1	0	0	0	1.000	-1	/O-3	-0.2
	Yr	5	11	1	1	0	0	0	0	0	3	.091	.091	.182	-26	-2	0	0	0	1.000	-1	/O-5	-0.4
Total	6	223	672	85	174	32	12	2	55	63	88	.259	.325	.351	97	-3	10	6	-1	.986	2	O-198	-1.3

■ STEVE MACKO
Macko, Steven Joseph b: 9/6/54, Burlington, Iowa d: 11/15/81, Arlington, Tex. BL/TR, 5'10", 160 lbs. Deb: 8/18/79

YEAR	TM/L	G	AB	R	H	2B	3B	HR	RBI	BB	SO	AVG	OBP	SLG	PRO+	BR/A	SB	CS	SBR	FA	FR	G/POS	TPR
1979	Chi-N	19	40	2	9	1	0	0	3	4	8	.225	.295	.250	46	-3	0	0	0	1.000	4	2-10/3-4	0.2
1980	Chi-N	6	20	2	6	2	0	0	2	0	3	.300	.300	.400	87	-0	0	0	0	1.000	1	/S-3,3-2,2-1	0.1
Total	2	25	60	4	15	3	0	0	5	4	11	.250	.297	.300	59	-3	0	0	0	1.000	6	/2-11,3-6,S-3	0.3

■ LONNIE MACLIN
Maclin, Lonnie Lee b: 2/17/67, Clayton, Mo. BL/TL, 5'11", 185 lbs. Deb: 9/7/93

YEAR	TM/L	G	AB	R	H	2B	3B	HR	RBI	BB	SO	AVG	OBP	SLG	PRO+	BR/A	SB	CS	SBR	FA	FR	G/POS	TPR
1993	StL-N	12	13	2	1	0	0	0	0	1	5	.077	.077	.077	-60	-3	1	0	0	1.000	-2	/O-5	-0.4

■ MAX MACON
Macon, Max Cullen b: 10/14/15, Pensacola, Fla. d: 8/5/89, Jupiter, Fla. BL/TL, 6'3", 175 lbs. Deb: 4/21/38

YEAR	TM/L	G	AB	R	H	2B	3B	HR	RBI	BB	SO	AVG	OBP	SLG	PRO+	BR/A	SB	CS	SBR	FA	FR	G/POS	TPR
1938	StL-N	46	36	5	11	0	0	0	3	2	4	.306	.342	.306	75	-1	0			.946	0	P-38/O-1	0.0
1940	Bro-N	2	5	0	5	0	0	0	0	0	0	1.000	1.000	1.000	427	-0	0			.000	-0	/P-2	0.0
1942	Bro-N	26	43	4	12	0	0	1	2	4	5	.279	.311	.372	98	-0	0			.960	0	P-14	0.0
1943	Bro-N	45	55	7	9	0	0	0	6	0	1	.164	.164	.164	-5	-7	1			1.000	0	P-25/1-3	-0.2
1944	Bos-N	106	366	38	100	15	3	0	36	12	23	.273	.296	.355	79	-11	7			.977	-2	1-72,O-22/P-1	-1.8
1947	Bos-N	1	1	0	0	0	0	0	0	0	0	.000	.000	.000	-99	-0	0			1.000	0	/P-1	0.0
Total	6	226	502	54	133	17	4	2	46	18	32	.265	.288	.333	72	-19	9			.965	-2	/P-81,1-75,O-23	-2.0

■ WADDY MacPHEE
Mac Phee, Walter Scott b: 12/23/1899, Brooklyn, N.Y. d: 1/20/80, Charlotte, N.C. BR/TR, 5'8", 140 lbs. Deb: 9/27/22

YEAR	TM/L	G	AB	R	H	2B	3B	HR	RBI	BB	SO	AVG	OBP	SLG	PRO+	BR/A	SB	CS	SBR	FA	FR	G/POS	TPR
1922	NY-N	2	7	2	2	0	0	0	0	1	0	.286	.375	.571	140	0	0	0	0	.889	1	/3-2	0.1

■ JIMMY MACULLAR
Macullar, James F. "Little Mac" b: 1/16/1855, Boston, Mass. d: 4/8/24, Baltimore, Md. BR/TL, 5'6", 155 lbs. Deb: 5/5/1879 MU

YEAR	TM/L	G	AB	R	H	2B	3B	HR	RBI	BB	SO	AVG	OBP	SLG	PRO+	BR/A	SB	CS	SBR	FA	FR	G/POS	TPR
1879	Syr-N	64	246	24	52	9	0	0	13	3	27	.211	.221	.248	61	-9				.864	1	S-37,O-26/2-4,3M	-0.7
1882	Cin-a	79	299	44	70	6	6	0	22	14		.234	.268	.294	76	-5				.922	-0	*O-79	-0.5
1883	Cin-a	14	48	4	8	2	0	0			6	.167	.231	.208	40	-3				.900	-4	O-14/S-1	-0.6
1884	Bal-a	107	360	73	73	16	6	4		36		.203	.290	.314	93	-2				.866	1	*S-107	0.0

YEAR	TM/L	G	AB	R	H	2B	3B	HR	RBI	BB	SO	AVG	OBP	SLG	PRO+	BR/A	SB	CS	SBR	FA	FR	G/POS	TPR
1885	Bal-a	100	320	52	61	7	6	3	26	49		.191	.306	.278	87	-3				.877	0	*S-98/O-2,P-1	-0.1
1886	Bal-a	85	268	49	55	7	1	0	26	49		.205	.332	.239	82	-2	23			.852	-10	S-82/O-2,2-1,P-1	-1.0
Total	6	449	1541	246	319	47	19	7	91	155	27	.207	.285	.276	83	-25	23			.865	-11	S-325,O-123/2-5,P3	-2.9

■ GENE MADDEN
Madden, Eugene b: 6/5/1890, Elm Grove, W.Va. d: 4/6/49, Utica, N.Y. BL/TR, 5'10", 155 lbs. Deb: 4/20/16

YEAR	TM/L	G	AB	R	H	2B	3B	HR	RBI	BB	SO	AVG	OBP	SLG	PRO+	BR/A	SB	CS	SBR	FA	FR	G/POS	TPR
1916	Pit-N	1	1	0	0	0	0	0	0	0	0	.000	.000	.000	-99	-0				.000	0	H	0.0

■ FRANK MADDEN
Madden, Francis A. "Red" b: 10/17/1892, Pittsburgh, Pa. d: 4/30/52, Pittsburgh, Pa. Deb: 7/4/14

YEAR	TM/L	G	AB	R	H	2B	3B	HR	RBI	BB	SO	AVG	OBP	SLG	PRO+	BR/A	SB	CS	SBR	FA	FR	G/POS	TPR
1914	Pit-F	2	2	0	1	0	0	0	1	0	0	.500	.500	.500	174	0		0		.000	0	/C-1	0.0

■ BUNNY MADDEN
Madden, Thomas Francis b: 9/14/1882, Boston, Mass. d: 1/20/54, Cambridge, Mass. BR/TR, 5'10", 190 lbs. Deb: 6/3/09

YEAR	TM/L	G	AB	R	H	2B	3B	HR	RBI	BB	SO	AVG	OBP	SLG	PRO+	BR/A	SB	CS	SBR	FA	FR	G/POS	TPR
1909	Bos-A	10	17	0	4	0	0	0	1	0		.235	.235	.235	48	-1		0		.941	1	/C-7	0.1
1910	Bos-A	14	35	4	13	3	0	0	4	3		.371	.436	.457	175	3		0		.938	-3	C-12	0.1
1911	Bos-A	4	15	2	3	0	0	0	2	2		.200	.294	.200	39	-1		0		1.000	-2	/C-4	-0.3
	Phi-N	28	76	4	21	1	1	0	4	0	13	.276	.276	.316	65	-4		0		.924	3	C-22	0.1
Total	3	56	143	10	41	4	1	0	11	5	13	.287	.315	.329	87	-3		0		.935	-1	/C-45	-0.0

■ TOMMY MADDEN
Madden, Thomas Joseph b: 7/31/1883, Philadelphia, Pa. d: 7/26/30, Philadelphia, Pa. BL/TL, 5'11", 160 lbs. Deb: 9/10/06

YEAR	TM/L	G	AB	R	H	2B	3B	HR	RBI	BB	SO	AVG	OBP	SLG	PRO+	BR/A	SB	CS	SBR	FA	FR	G/POS	TPR
1906	Bos-N	4	15	1	4	0	0	0	0	0		.267	.313	.267	83	-0		0		1.000	-0	/O-4	-0.1
1910	NY-A	1	1	0	0	0	0	0	0	0		.000	.000	.000	-95	-0		0		.000	-0	H	-0.1
Total	2	5	16	1	4	0	0	0	0	0	1	.250	.294	.250	71	-1		0		1.000	-1	/O-4	-0.2

■ CLARENCE MADDERN
Maddern, Clarence James b: 9/26/21, Bisbee, Ariz. d: 8/9/86, Tucson, Ariz. BR/TR, 6'1", 185 lbs. Deb: 9/19/46

YEAR	TM/L	G	AB	R	H	2B	3B	HR	RBI	BB	SO	AVG	OBP	SLG	PRO+	BR/A	SB	CS	SBR	FA	FR	G/POS	TPR
1946	Chi-N	3	3	0	0	0	0	0	0	0	0	.000	.250	.000	-27	-0				1.000	-0	/O-2	-0.1
1948	Chi-N	80	214	16	54	12	1	4	27	10	25	.252	.301	.374	85	-5				.981	-2	O-55	-1.0
1949	Chi-N	10	9	1	3	0	0	1	2	2	0	.333	.455	.667	202	1		0		1.000	-0	/1-1	0.2
1951	Cle-A	11	12	0	2	0	0	0	0	0	1	.167	.167	.167	-10	-2	0	0	0	.667	-0	/O-1	-0.2
Total	4	104	238	17	59	12	1	5	29	12	26	.248	.301	.370	84	-6	0	0		.973	-2	/O-58,1-1	-1.1

■ ELLIOTT MADDOX
Maddox, Elliott b: 12/21/47, East Orange, N.J. BR/TR, 5'11", 181 lbs. Deb: 4/7/70

YEAR	TM/L	G	AB	R	H	2B	3B	HR	RBI	BB	SO	AVG	OBP	SLG	PRO+	BR/A	SB	CS	SBR	FA	FR	G/POS	TPR
1970	Det-A	109	258	30	64	13	4	3	24	30	42	.248	.333	.364	92	-3	2	3	-1	.919	0	3-40,O-37,S-19/2-1	-0.5
1971	Was-A	128	258	38	56	7	2	0	18	51	42	.217	.346	.275	83	-4	10	4	1	.990	-4	*O-103,3-12	-1.0
1972	Tex-A	98	294	40	74	7	2	0	10	49	53	.252	.362	.289	100	2	20	10	0	.990	-4	O-94	0.2
1973	Tex-A	100	172	24	41	1	0	1	17	29	28	.238	.358	.262	80	-3	5	4	-1	.981	-7	O-89/3-7,D-1	-1.4
1974	NY-A	137	466	75	141	26	2	3	45	69	48	.303	.397	.386	128	20	6	5	-1	.986	9	*O-135/2-2,3-1	2.3
1975	NY-A	55	218	36	67	10	3	1	23	21	24	.307	.386	.394	123	8	9	3	1	1.000	-1	O-55/2-1	1.4
1976	*NY-A	18	46	4	10	2	0	0	3	4	3	.217	.280	.261	60	-2	0	1	-1	1.000	-1	O-13/D-2	-0.4
1977	Bal-A	49	107	14	28	7	0	2	9	13	9	.262	.363	.383	110	2	2	2	-1	.990	-4	O-45/3-1	-0.4
1978	NY-N	119	389	43	100	18	2	2	39	71	38	.257	.374	.329	102	4	2	11	-6	.988	-3	O-79,3-43/1-1	-0.9
1979	NY-N	86	224	21	60	13	0	1	12	20	27	.268	.336	.339	88	-3	3	2	-0	.985	-1	O-65,3-11	-0.7
1980	NY-N	130	411	35	101	16	1	4	34	52	44	.246	.339	.319	87	-6	1	9	-5	.956	-3	*3-115/O-4,1-2	-1.6
Total	11	1029	2843	360	742	121	16	18	234	409	358	.261	.361	.334	100	16	60	54	-14	.989	-1	O-719,3-230/S21D	-3.0

■ GARRY MADDOX
Maddox, Garry Lee b: 9/1/49, Cincinnati, Ohio BR/TR, 6'3", 184 lbs. Deb: 4/25/72

YEAR	TM/L	G	AB	R	H	2B	3B	HR	RBI	BB	SO	AVG	OBP	SLG	PRO+	BR/A	SB	CS	SBR	FA	FR	G/POS	TPR
1972	SF-N	125	458	62	122	26	7	12	58	14	97	.266	.294	.432	103	-1	13	6	0	.979	4	*O-121	-0.2
1973	SF-N	144	587	81	187	30	10	11	76	24	73	.319	.352	.460	118	13	24	10	1	.969	8	*O-140	1.6
1974	SF-N	135	538	74	153	31	3	8	50	29	64	.284	.325	.398	97	-4	21	9	1	.986	7	*O-131	-0.2
1975	SF-N	17	52	4	7	1	0	1	4	6	3	.135	.237	.212	24	-5	1	1	-0	1.000	3	O-13	-0.3
	Phi-N	99	374	50	109	25	8	4	46	36	54	.291	.361	.433	115	8	24	3	5	.983	18	O-97	2.7
	Yr	116	426	54	116	26	8	5	50	42	57	.272	.346	.406	104	3	25	4	5	.985	21	*O-110	2.4
1976	*Phi-N	146	531	75	175	37	6	6	68	24	59	.330	.383	.456	133	23	29	12	2	.989	24	*O-144	4.5
1977	*Phi-N	139	571	85	167	27	10	14	74	24	58	.292	.326	.448	101	-1	22	6	3	.977	14	*O-138	1.1
1978	*Phi-N	155	598	62	172	34	3	11	68	39	89	.288	.333	.410	106	3	33	7	6	.983	21	*O-154	2.4
1979	Phi-N	148	548	70	154	28	6	13	61	17	71	.281	.308	.425	95	-6	26	13	0	.996	**27**	*O-140	1.6
1980	Phi-N	143	549	59	142	31	3	11	73	18	52	.259	.282	.386	80	-16	25	5	5	.976	14	*O-143	-0.3
1981	*Phi-N	94	323	37	85	7	1	5	40	17	42	.263	.302	.337	78	-10	9	4	0	.977	9	O-94	-0.3
1982	Phi-N	119	412	39	117	27	2	8	61	12	32	.284	.304	.417	98	-3	7	5	-1	**.992**	7	*O-111	0.1
1983	*Phi-N	97	324	27	89	14	2	4	32	17	31	.275	.313	.367	89	-5	7	6	-2	.977	-0	O-95	-1.0
1984	Phi-N	77	241	29	68	11	0	5	19	13	29	.282	.319	.390	97	-1	3	2	-0	1.000	-0	O-69	-0.4
1985	Phi-N	105	218	22	52	8	1	4	23	13	26	.239	.284	.339	72	-8	0	2	-1	.980	-12	O-94	-2.4
1986	Phi-N	6	7	1	3	0	0	0	1	2	1	.429	.556	.429	169	1	1	0	-0	1.000	-0	/O-3	-0.1
Total	15	1749	6331	777	1802	337	62	117	754	323	781	.285	.323	.413	100	-11	248	92	19	.983	142	*O-1687	8.8

■ JERRY MADDOX
Maddox, Jerry Glenn b: 7/28/53, Whittier, Cal. BR/TR, 6'2", 200 lbs. Deb: 6/3/78

YEAR	TM/L	G	AB	R	H	2B	3B	HR	RBI	BB	SO	AVG	OBP	SLG	PRO+	BR/A	SB	CS	SBR	FA	FR	G/POS	TPR
1978	Atl-N	7	14	1	3	0	0	0	1	1	2	.214	.267	.214	32	-1	0	0	0	.909	-0	/3-5	-0.2

■ ART MADISON
Madison, Arthur b: 1/14/1871, Clarksburg, Mass. d: 1/27/33, N.Adams, Mass. BR/TR, 5'9", 165 lbs. Deb: 9/9/1895

YEAR	TM/L	G	AB	R	H	2B	3B	HR	RBI	BB	SO	AVG	OBP	SLG	PRO+	BR/A	SB	CS	SBR	FA	FR	G/POS	TPR
1895	Phi-N	11	34	6	12	3	0	0	8	1	1	.353	.371	.441	109	0	4			.955	-1	/S-6,2-3,3-2	0.0
1899	Pit-N	42	118	20	32	2	4	0	19	11	1	.271	.338	.356	91	-1	1			.953	-5	2-19,S-15/3-2	-0.4
Total	2	53	152	26	44	5	4	0	27	12	1	.289	.345	.375	95	-1	5			.926	-6	/2-22,S-21,3-4	-0.4

■ SCOTTI MADISON
Madison, Charles Scott b: 9/12/59, Pensacola, Fla. BB/TR, 5'11", 195 lbs. Deb: 7/6/85

YEAR	TM/L	G	AB	R	H	2B	3B	HR	RBI	BB	SO	AVG	OBP	SLG	PRO+	BR/A	SB	CS	SBR	FA	FR	G/POS	TPR
1985	Det-A	6	11	0	0	0	0	0	0	1	2	.000	.154	.000	-54	-2	0	0	0	1.000	-0	/C-1,D-3	-0.2
1986	Det-A	2	7	0	0	0	0	0	1	0	3	.000	.000	.000	-99	-2	0	0	0	.667	-1	/3-1,D-1	-0.3
1987	KC-A	7	15	4	4	3	0	0	0	1	5	.267	.313	.467	100	0	0	0	0	1.000	-0	/1-4,C-3	-0.1
1988	KC-A	16	35	4	6	2	0	0	2	4	5	.171	.256	.229	37	-3	0	1	-2	1.000	-2	/C-4,O-3,1-2,D-4	-0.4
1989	Cin-N	40	98	13	17	7	0	1	8	9	7	.173	.243	.276	46	-7	0	1	-1	1.000	2	3-26	-0.5
Total	5	71	166	21	27	12	0	1	11	15	22	.163	.236	.253	37	-14	0	2	0	.985	-1	/3-27,D-8,C-8,10	-1.5

■ ED MADJESKI
Madjeski, Edward William (b: Edward William Majewski)
b: 7/20/08, Far Rockaway, N.Y. d: 11/11/94, Montgomery, Ohio BR/TR, 5'11", 178 lbs. Deb: 5/2/32

YEAR	TM/L	G	AB	R	H	2B	3B	HR	RBI	BB	SO	AVG	OBP	SLG	PRO+	BR/A	SB	CS	SBR	FA	FR	G/POS	TPR
1932	Phi-A	17	35	4	8	0	0	0	3		6	.229	.289	.229	35	-3	0	0		1.000	2	/C-8	-0.1
1933	Phi-A	51	142	17	40	4	0	0	17	4	21	.282	.301	.310	62	-8	0	0		.958	-4	C-41	-0.9
1934	Phi-A	8	8	1	3	1	0	0	2	0	1	.375	.375	.500	129	0	0	0		1.000	-0	/C-1	-0.4
	Chi-A	85	281	36	62	14	2	5	32	14	31	.221	.260	.338	52	-21	2	0		.973	0	C-79	-1.4
	Yr	93	289	37	65	15	2	5	34	14	32	.225	.263	.343	54	-21	2	0	1	.971	2	C-80	-1.4
1937	NY-N	5	15	0	3	0	0	0	2	0	0	.200	.200	.200	9	-2	0	0		1.000	-2	/C-5	-0.4
Total	4	166	481	58	116	19	2	5	56	21	61	.241	.274	.320	53	-34	2	0		.970	-2	C-134	-2.8

■ BILL MADLOCK
Madlock, Bill b: 1/2/51, Memphis, Tenn. BR/TR, 5'11", 185 lbs. Deb: 9/7/73

YEAR	TM/L	G	AB	R	H	2B	3B	HR	RBI	BB	SO	AVG	OBP	SLG	PRO+	BR/A	SB	CS	SBR	FA	FR	G/POS	TPR
1973	Tex-A	21	77	16	27	5	3	1	5	7	9	.351	.412	.532	171	7	3	2	-0	.918	-6	3-21	0.1
1974	Chi-N	128	453	65	142	21	5	9	54	42	39	.313	.378	.442	124	14	11	7	-1	.946	-12	*3-121	0.1
1975	Chi-N	130	514	77	182	29	7	7	64	42	34	**.354**	.406	.479	139	27	9	7	-2	.943	-11	*3-128	1.5
1976	Chi-N	142	514	68	174	36	1	15	84	56	27	**.339**	.415	.500	146	32	15	11	-2	.961	-20	*3-136	0.9
1977	SF-N	140	533	70	161	28	1	12	46	43	33	.302	.361	.426	111	8	13	10	-2	.949	-17	3-126/2-6	-1.2
1978	SF-N	122	447	76	138	26	3	15	44	48	39	.309	.380	.481	145	26	16	5	-2	.974	-24	*2-114/1-3	1.3
1979	SF-N	69	249	37	65	9	2	3	44	24	22	.261	.311	.398	99	-2	11	3	-2	.976	-14	2-63/1-5	-1.0
	*Pit-N	85	311	48	102	17	3	7	44	34	22	.328	.396	.469	129	13	21	8	2	.969	-6	3-85	0.8
	Yr	154	560	85	167	26	5	14	85	52	41	.298	.359	.438	117	13	32	11	-3	.969	-20	3-85,2-63/1-5	-0.2
1980	Pit-N	137	494	62	137	22	1	10	53	45	33	.277	.343	.399	105	3	16	10	-1	.955	-17	*3-127,1-12	-1.8
1981	Pit-N★	82	279	35	95	23	1	6	45	34	17	**.341**	.418	.495	153	20	18	6	-4	.956	-4	3-78	1.8
1982	Pit-N	154	568	92	181	33	3	19	95	48	39	.319	.376	.488	136	27	18	6	2	.952	-6	*3-146/1-3	1.9

YEAR	TM/L	G	AB	R	H	2B	3B	HR	RBI	BB	SO	AVG	OBP	SLG	PRO+	BR/A	SB	CS	SBR	FA	FR	G/POS	TPR
1983	Pit-N★	130	473	68	153	21	0	12	68	49	24	.323	.389	.444	127	18	3	4	-2	.958	-14	*3-126	0.2
1984	Pit-N	103	403	38	102	16	0	4	44	26	29	.253	.300	.323	75	-14	3	1	0	.942	-8	3-98/1-1	-2.4
1985	Pit-N	110	399	49	100	23	1	10	41	39	42	.251	.325	.388	100	-0	3	3	-1	.940	-16	3-98,1-12	-2.0
	*LA-N	34	114	20	41	4	0	2	15	10	11	.360	.425	.447	149	8	7	1	2	.948	3	3-32	1.2
	Yr	144	513	69	141	27	1	12	56	49	53	.275	.347	.402	110	7	10	4	1	.943	-13	*3-130,1-12	-0.8
1986	LA-N	111	379	38	106	17	0	10	60	30	43	.280	.341	.404	112	6	3	3	-1	.910	-8	*3-101/1-2	-0.6
1987	LA-N	21	61	5	11	1	0	3	7	6	5	.180	.265	.344	61	-4	0	0	0	.912	-4	3-16/1-1	-0.8
	*Det-A	87	326	56	91	17	0	14	50	28	45	.279	.354	.460	119	9	4	3	-1	.989	-2	D-64,1-22/3-1	0.3
Total	15	1806	6594	920	2008	348	34	163	860	605	510	.305	.369	.442	123	200	174	90	-2	.948	-185	*3-1440,2-183/D1	0.3

■ **SAL MADRID**   Madrid, Salvador b: 6/9/20, ElPaso, Tex.   d: 2/24/77, Ft.Wayne, Ind.   BR/TR, 5′9″, 165 lbs.   Deb: 9/17/47

YEAR	TM/L	G	AB	R	H	2B	3B	HR	RBI	BB	SO	AVG	OBP	SLG	PRO+	BR/A	SB	CS	SBR	FA	FR	G/POS	TPR
1947	Chi-N	8	24	0	3	1	0	0	1	1	6	.125	.160	.167	-14	-4	0			.956	4	/S-8	0.0

■ **DAVE MAGADAN**   Magadan, David Joseph b: 9/30/62, Tampa, Fla.   BL/TR, 6′3″, 190 lbs.   Deb: 9/7/86

YEAR	TM/L	G	AB	R	H	2B	3B	HR	RBI	BB	SO	AVG	OBP	SLG	PRO+	BR/A	SB	CS	SBR	FA	FR	G/POS	TPR
1986	NY-N	10	18	3	8	0	0	0	3	1	1	.444	.524	.444	175	2	0	0	0	1.000	1	/1-9	0.3
1987	NY-N	85	192	21	61	13	1	3	24	22	22	.318	.388	.443	126	8	0	0	0	.981	5	3-50,1-13	0.9
1988	*NY-N	112	314	39	87	15	0	1	35	60	39	.277	.396	.334	117	11	0	1	-1	.988	-1	1-71,3-48	0.4
1989	NY-N	127	374	47	107	22	3	4	41	49	37	.286	.370	.393	124	13	1	0	0	.991	3	1-87,3-28	1.0
1990	NY-N	144	451	74	148	28	6	6	72	74	55	.328	.425	.457	143	30	2	1	0	.998	3	*1-113,3-19	2.5
1991	NY-N	124	418	58	108	23	0	4	51	83	50	.258	.384	.342	106	8	1	1	-0	.996	2	*1-122	0.1
1992	NY-N	99	321	33	91	9	1	3	28	56	44	.283	.390	.346	111	8	1	0	0	.941	-13	3-93/1-2	-0.5
1993	Fla-N	66	227	22	65	12	0	4	29	44	30	.286	.404	.392	108	5	0	1	-1	.961	1	3-63/1-2	0.5
	Sea-A	71	228	27	59	11	0	1	21	36	33	.259	.360	.320	83	-4	2	0	1	.991	-1	1-41,3-27/D-2	-0.7
1994	Fla-N	74	211	30	58	7	0	1	17	39	25	.275	.390	.322	86	-2	0	0	0	.958	-5	3-48,1-16	-0.8
1995	Hou-N	127	348	44	109	24	0	2	51	71	56	.313	.430	.399	129	19	2	1	0	.922	-7	*3-100,1-11	1.1
1996	Chi-N	78	169	23	43	10	0	3	17	29	23	.254	.364	.367	92	-1	0	2	-1	.963	-7	3-51,1-10	-0.9
Total	11	1117	3271	421	944	174	11	32	389	566	415	.289	.395	.378	115	95	9	7	-2	.952	-21	3-527,1-497/D-2	3.9

■ **EVER MAGALLANES**   Magallanes, Everado (Espinoza) b: 11/6/65, Chihuahua, Mexico   BL/TR, 5′10″, 165 lbs.   Deb: 5/17/91

YEAR	TM/L	G	AB	R	H	2B	3B	HR	RBI	BB	SO	AVG	OBP	SLG	PRO+	BR/A	SB	CS	SBR	FA	FR	G/POS	TPR
1991	Cle-A	3	2	0	1	0	0	0	0	1	0	.500	.333	.000	1	-0	0	0	0	1.000	-1	/S-2	-0.1

■ **LEE MAGEE**   Magee, Leo Christopher (b: Leopold Christopher Hoernschemeyer) b: 6/4/1889, Cincinnati, Ohio d: 3/14/66, Columbus, Ohio   BB/TR, 5′11″, 165 lbs.   Deb: 7/4/11 M

YEAR	TM/L	G	AB	R	H	2B	3B	HR	RBI	BB	SO	AVG	OBP	SLG	PRO+	BR/A	SB	CS	SBR	FA	FR	G/POS	TPR
1911	StL-N	26	69	9	18	1	1	0	8	8	8	.261	.338	.304	82	-1	4			.975	-2	2-18/S-3	-0.4
1912	StL-N	128	458	60	133	13	8	0	40	39	29	.290	.347	.354	94	-3	16			.956	7	O-85,2-23/1-6,S-1	-0.1
1913	StL-N	137	531	54	142	13	7	2	31	34	30	.267	.314	.330	85	-11	23			.982	13	*O-108,2-22/1-6,S-2	-0.3
1914	StL-N	142	529	59	150	23	4	2	40	42	24	.284	.337	.353	107	4	36			.970	5	*O-102,1-39/2-6	0.4
1915	Bro-F	121	452	87	146	19	10	4	49	22	19	.323	.356	.436	123	6	34			.937	-1	*2-115/1-2,M	0.7
1916	NY-N	131	510	57	131	18	4	3	45	50	31	.257	.324	.325	93	-4	29	25	-6	.975	-1	*O-128/2-2	-1.4
1917	NY-A	51	173	17	38	4	1	0	9	13	18	.220	.278	.254	62	-8	3			.938	-8	O-50	-2.1
	StL-A	36	112	11	19	1	0	0	4	6	6	.170	.212	.179	20	-11	3			.971	-2	3-20/2-6,1-5,O-1	-0.5
	Yr	87	285	28	57	5	1	0	12	19	24	.200	.252	.225	46	-18	6			.938	-2	O-51,3-20/2-6,1-5	-2.6
1918	Cin-N	119	459	61	133	22	13	0	28	28	19	.290	.331	.394	123	11	19			.956	9	*2-114/3-3	3.0
1919	Bro-N	45	181	16	43	7	2	1	7	5	8	.238	.262	.298	67	-8	5			.938	-1	2-36/3-9	-0.7
	Chi-N	79	267	36	78	12	4	1	17	18	16	.292	.339	.378	115	5	14			.978	-6	O-45,S-13,3-10,/2-7	-0.4
	Yr	124	448	52	121	19	6	1	24	23	24	.270	.309	.346	96	-3	19			.978	-7	O-45,2-43,3-19,S-13	-1.1
Total	9	1015	3741	467	1031	133	54	12	277	265	208	.276	.325	.350	98	-20	186	25		.969	27	O-519,2-349/13S	-1.8

■ **SHERRY MAGEE**   Magee, Sherwood Robert b: 8/6/1884, Clarendon, Pa.   d: 3/13/29, Philadelphia, Pa.   BR/TR, 5′11″, 179 lbs.   Deb: 6/29/04 U

YEAR	TM/L	G	AB	R	H	2B	3B	HR	RBI	BB	SO	AVG	OBP	SLG	PRO+	BR/A	SB	CS	SBR	FA	FR	G/POS	TPR
1904	Phi-N	95	364	51	101	15	12	3	57	14		.277	.308	.409	125	9	11			.921	5	O-94/1-1	0.8
1905	Phi-N	155	603	100	180	24	17	5	98	44		.299	.354	.420	135	25	48			.963	10	*O-155	2.8
1906	Phi-N	154	563	77	159	36	8	6	67	52		.282	.348	.407	135	22	55			.982	11	*O-154	2.8
1907	Phi-N	140	503	75	165	28	12	4	85	53		.328	.396	.455	169	40	46			.978	7	*O-139	4.6
1908	Phi-N	143	508	79	144	30	16	2	57	49		.283	.359	.417	143	25	40			.970	4	*O-142	2.3
1909	Phi-N	143	522	60	141	33	14	2	66	43		.270	.339	.398	128	16	38			.970	-6	*O-143	0.4
1910	Phi-N	154	519	110	172	39	17	6	123	94	36	.331	.445	.507	172	51	49			.974	-13	*O-154	3.2
1911	Phi-N	121	445	79	128	32	5	15	94	49	33	.288	.366	.483	135	19	22			.981	3	*O-120	1.6
1912	Phi-N	132	464	79	142	25	9	6	66	55	54	.306	.388	.474	118	12	30			.963	-11	*O-124/1-6	-0.6
1913	Phi-N	138	470	92	144	36	6	11	70	38	36	.306	.369	.479	136	21	23			.968	-10	*O-123/1-4	0.5
1914	Phi-N	146	544	96	171	39	11	15	103	55	42	.314	.380	.509	154	34	25			.940	9	O-67,S-39,1-32,/2-8	4.5
1915	Bos-N	156	571	72	160	34	12	2	87	54	39	.280	.350	.382	130	21	15	12	-3	.981	15	*O-135,1-21	2.9
1916	Bos-N	122	419	44	101	17	5	3	54	44	52	.241	.322	.327	104	3	10			.978	-5	*O-120/1-2,S-1	-1.0
1917	Bos-N	72	246	24	63	8	4	1	29	13	23	.256	.302	.333	100	-0	7			.954	2	O-65/1-2	-0.3
	Cin-N	45	137	17	44	8	4	0	23	16	7	.321	.400	.438	164	11	4			.989	6	O-41/1-2	1.4
	Yr	117	383	41	107	16	8	1	52	29	30	.279	.338	.371	124	10	11			.967	6	*O-106/1-4	1.1
1918	Cin-N	115	400	46	119	15	13	0	76	37	18	.298	.370	.415	142	20	14			.981	-2	1-66,O-38/2-6	1.5
1919	*Cin-N	56	163	11	35	6	1	0	21	26	19	.215	.337	.264	84	-2	4			.990	-3	O-47/2-1,3-1	-0.9
Total	16	2087	7441	1112	2169	425	166	83	1176	736	359	.291	.364	.427	137	324	441	12		.970	16	*O-1861,1-136/S23	26.5

■ **WENDELL MAGEE**   Magee, Wendell Errol b: 8/3/72, Hattiesburg, Miss.   BR/TR, 6′, 225 lbs.   Deb: 8/16/96

YEAR	TM/L	G	AB	R	H	2B	3B	HR	RBI	BB	SO	AVG	OBP	SLG	PRO+	BR/A	SB	CS	SBR	FA	FR	G/POS	TPR
1996	Phi-N	38	142	9	29	7	0	2	14	9	33	.204	.252	.296	43	-12	0	0	0	.978	3	O-37	-1.0

■ **HARL MAGGERT**   Maggert, Harl Vestin b: 2/13/1883, Cromwell, Ind.   d: 1/7/63, Fresno, Cal.   BL/TR, 5′8″, 155 lbs.   Deb: 9/4/07 F

YEAR	TM/L	G	AB	R	H	2B	3B	HR	RBI	BB	SO	AVG	OBP	SLG	PRO+	BR/A	SB	CS	SBR	FA	FR	G/POS	TPR
1907	Pit-N	3	6	1	0	0	0	0	0	0	2	.000	.250	.000	-21	-1	1			1.000	0	/O-2	-0.1
1912	Phi-A	74	242	39	62	8	6	1	13	36		.256	.357	.351	107	2	10			.939	-6	O-61	-0.6
Total	2	77	248	40	62	8	6	1	13	38		.250	.354	.343	104	2	11			.942	-6	/O-63	-0.7

■ **HARL MAGGERT**   Maggert, Harl Warren b: 5/4/14, Los Angeles, Cal.   d: 7/10/86, Citrus Heights, Cal.   BR/TR, 6′, 190 lbs.   Deb: 4/19/38 F

YEAR	TM/L	G	AB	R	H	2B	3B	HR	RBI	BB	SO	AVG	OBP	SLG	PRO+	BR/A	SB	CS	SBR	FA	FR	G/POS	TPR
1938	Bos-N	66	89	12	25	3	0	3	19	10	20	.281	.354	.416	123	4	0			.944	-4	O-10/3-8	0.2

■ **STUBBY MAGNER**   Magner, Edmund Burke b: 2/20/1888, Kalamazoo, Mich.   d: 9/6/56, Chillicothe, Ohio   BR/TR, 5′3″, 135 lbs.   Deb: 7/12/11

YEAR	TM/L	G	AB	R	H	2B	3B	HR	RBI	BB	SO	AVG	OBP	SLG	PRO+	BR/A	SB	CS	SBR	FA	FR	G/POS	TPR
1911	NY-A	13	33	3	7	0	0	0	4	4	4	.212	.297	.212	40	-3	1			.970	-0	/S-6,2-5	-0.3

■ **JOHN MAGNER**   Magner, John T. b: 1855, St.Louis, Mo.   Deb: 7/14/1879 U

YEAR	TM/L	G	AB	R	H	2B	3B	HR	RBI	BB	SO	AVG	OBP	SLG	PRO+	BR/A	SB	CS	SBR	FA	FR	G/POS	TPR
1879	Cin-N	1	4	0	0	0	0	0	0	0	1	.000	.000	.000	-99	-1				.500	-0	/O-1	-0.1

■ **GEORGE MAGOON**   Magoon, George Henry "Maggie" or "Topsy" b: 3/27/1875, St.Albans, Maine   d: 12/6/43, Rochester, N.H.   BR/TR, 5′10″, 160 lbs.   Deb: 6/29/1898

YEAR	TM/L	G	AB	R	H	2B	3B	HR	RBI	BB	SO	AVG	OBP	SLG	PRO+	BR/A	SB	CS	SBR	FA	FR	G/POS	TPR
1898	Bro-N	93	343	35	77	7	0	2	39	30		.224	.293	.254	57	-19	7			.925	13	S-93	-0.1
1899	Bal-N	62	207	26	53	8	3	0	31	26		.256	.353	.324	82	-5	7			.923	5	S-62	0.5
	Chi-N	59	189	24	43	5	1	0	21	24		.228	.333	.265	67	-7	5			.896	6	S-59	0.3
	Yr	121	396	50	96	13	4	0	52	50		.242	.344	.295	75	-12	12			.909	12	*S-121	0.8
1901	Cin-N	127	460	47	116	16	7	1	53	52		.252	.331	.324	97	-1	15			.919	-20	*S-112,2-15	-1.1
1902	Cin-N	45	162	29	44	9	2	0	23	13		.272	.344	.352	105	1	7			.930	4	2-41/S-3	0.7
1903	Cin-N	42	139	6	30	6	0	0	9	19		.216	.314	.259	58	-8	4			.971	6	2-32/3-9	-0.2
	Chi-A	94	334	32	76	11	3	0	25	30		.228	.303	.278	79	-8	9			.936	-21	2-94	-2.6
Total	5	522	1834	199	439	62	16	2	201	194		.239	.321	.294	78	-45	47			.916	-8	S-329,2-182/3-9	-2.5

■ **TOM MAGRANN**   Magrann, Thomas Joseph b: 12/9/63, Hollywood, Fla.   BR/TR, 6′3″, 177 lbs.   Deb: 9/7/89

YEAR	TM/L	G	AB	R	H	2B	3B	HR	RBI	BB	SO	AVG	OBP	SLG	PRO+	BR/A	SB	CS	SBR	FA	FR	G/POS	TPR
1989	Cle-A	9	10	0	0	0	0	0	0	0	4	.000	.000	.000	-98	-3	0	0	0	1.000	3	/C-9	0.1

■ **FREDDIE MAGUIRE**   Maguire, Frederick Edward b: 5/10/1899, Roxbury, Mass.   d: 11/3/61, Boston, Mass.   BR/TR, 5′11″, 155 lbs.   Deb: 9/22/22

YEAR	TM/L	G	AB	R	H	2B	3B	HR	RBI	BB	SO	AVG	OBP	SLG	PRO+	BR/A	SB	CS	SBR	FA	FR	G/POS	TPR
1922	NY-N	5	12	4	4	0	0	0	0	1	0	1	.333	.333	.333	72	-0	1	0	0	.944	2	/2-3	0.1

YEAR	TM/L	G	AB	R	H	2B	3B	HR	RBI	BB	SO	AVG	OBP	SLG	PRO+	BR/A	SB	CS	SBR	FA	FR	G/POS	TPR
1923	*NY-N	41	30	11	6	1	0	0	2	2	4	.200	.250	.233	29	-3	1	0	0	.881	12	2-16/3-1	0.9
1928	Chi-N	140	574	67	160	24	7	1	41	25	38	.279	.312	.350	74	-22	6			.976	51	*2-138	3.1
1929	Bos-N	138	496	54	125	26	8	0	41	19	40	.252	.284	.337	55	-36	8			.971	8	*2-138/S-1	-2.0
1930	Bos-N	146	516	54	138	21	5	0	52	20	22	.267	.297	.328	53	-40	4			.969	-4	*2-146	-3.2
1931	Bos-N	148	492	36	112	18	2	0	26	16	26	.228	.259	.272	45	-39	3			.976	9	*2-148	-2.1
Total	6	618	2120	226	545	90	22	1	163	82	131	.257	.289	.322	57	-140	23	0		.971	77	2-589/S-1,3-1	-3.2

■ JACK MAGUIRE
Maguire, Jack   b: 2/5/25, St.Louis, Mo.   BR/TR, 5'11", 165 lbs.   Deb: 4/18/50

YEAR	TM/L	G	AB	R	H	2B	3B	HR	RBI	BB	SO	AVG	OBP	SLG	PRO+	BR/A	SB	CS	SBR	FA	FR	G/POS	TPR
1950	NY-N	29	40	3	7	2	0	0	3	3	13	.175	.233	.225	21	-5	0			1.000	1	/O-9,1-2	-0.3
1951	NY-N	16	20	6	8	1	1	1	4	2	2	.400	.455	.700	204	3	0	0	0	1.000	-0	/O-8	0.2
	Pit-N	8	5	1	0	0	0	0	0	1	0	.000	.167	.000	-50	-1	0	0	0	1.000	0	/2-1,3-1	0.0
	Yr	24	25	7	8	1	1	1	4	3	2	.320	.393	.560	151	2	0	0	0	1.000	0	/O-8,2-1,3-1	0.2
	StL-A	41	127	15	31	2	1	0	14	12	21	.244	.309	.299	63	-6	1	0	0	.969	-0	O-26/3-5,2-2	-0.7
Total	2	94	192	25	46	5	2	2	21	18	36	.240	.305	.318	66	-9	1	0		.979	2	/O-43,3-6,2-3,1-2	-0.8

■ JIM MAHADY
Mahady, James Bernard   b: 4/22/01, Cortland, N.Y.   d: 8/9/36, Cortland, N.Y.   BR/TR, 5'11", 170 lbs.   Deb: 10/2/21

YEAR	TM/L	G	AB	R	H	2B	3B	HR	RBI	BB	SO	AVG	OBP	SLG	PRO+	BR/A	SB	CS	SBR	FA	FR	G/POS	TPR
1921	NY-N	1	0	0	0	0	0	0	0	0	0	—	—	—		0	0	0	0	1.000	0	/2-1	0.0

■ ART MAHAN
Mahan, Arthur Leo   b: 6/8/13, Somerville, Mass.   BL/TL, 5'11", 178 lbs.   Deb: 4/30/40

YEAR	TM/L	G	AB	R	H	2B	3B	HR	RBI	BB	SO	AVG	OBP	SLG	PRO+	BR/A	SB	CS	SBR	FA	FR	G/POS	TPR
1940	Phi-N	146	544	55	133	24	5	2	39	40	37	.244	.297	.318	73	-21	4			.992	4	*1-145/P-1	-3.1

■ FRANK MAHAR
Mahar, Frank Edward   b: 12/4/1878, Natick, Mass.   d: 12/5/61, Somerville, Mass.   TR, 5'10.5",   Deb: 8/29/02

YEAR	TM/L	G	AB	R	H	2B	3B	HR	RBI	BB	SO	AVG	OBP	SLG	PRO+	BR/A	SB	CS	SBR	FA	FR	G/POS	TPR
1902	Phi-N	1	1	0	0	0	0	0	0	0	0	.000	.000	.000	-99	-0	0			.000	0	H	0.0

■ BILLY MAHARG
Maharg, William Joseph   b: 3/19/1881, Philadelphia, Pa.   d: 11/20/53, Philadelphia, Pa.   BR/TR, 5'4.5", 155 lbs.   Deb: 5/18/12

YEAR	TM/L	G	AB	R	H	2B	3B	HR	RBI	BB	SO	AVG	OBP	SLG	PRO+	BR/A	SB	CS	SBR	FA	FR	G/POS	TPR
1912	Det-A	1	1	0	0	0	0	0	0	0	0	.000	.000	.000	-99	-0	0			1.000	0	/3-1	0.0
1916	Phi-N	1	1	0	0	0	0	0	0	0	0	.000	.000	.000	-97	-0	0			.000	-0	/O-1	-0.1
Total	2	2	2	0	0	0	0	0	0	0	0	.000	.000	.000	-99	-0	0			—	0	/O-1,3-1	-0.1

■ RON MAHAY
Mahay, Ronald Matthew   b: 6/28/71, Crestwood, Ill.   BL/TL, 6'2", 185 lbs.   Deb: 5/21/95

YEAR	TM/L	G	AB	R	H	2B	3B	HR	RBI	BB	SO	AVG	OBP	SLG	PRO+	BR/A	SB	CS	SBR	FA	FR	G/POS	TPR
1995	Bos-A	5	20	3	4	2	0	1	3	1	6	.200	.273	.450	81	-1	0	0	0	1.000	-1	/O-5	-0.1

■ TOM MAHER
Maher, Thomas Francis   b: 7/6/1870, Philadelphia, Pa.   d: 8/25/29, Philadelphia, Pa.   Deb: 4/24/02

YEAR	TM/L	G	AB	R	H	2B	3B	HR	RBI	BB	SO	AVG	OBP	SLG	PRO+	BR/A	SB	CS	SBR	FA	FR	G/POS	TPR
1902	Phi-N	1	0	0	0	0	0	0	0	0	0	—	—	—		0	0			.000	0	R	0.0

■ GREG MAHLBERG
Mahlberg, Gregory John   b: 8/8/52, Milwaukee, Wis.   BR/TR, 5'10", 180 lbs.   Deb: 9/24/78

YEAR	TM/L	G	AB	R	H	2B	3B	HR	RBI	BB	SO	AVG	OBP	SLG	PRO+	BR/A	SB	CS	SBR	FA	FR	G/POS	TPR
1978	Tex-A	1	1	0	0	0	0	0	0	0	0	.000	.000	.000	-99	-0	0			1.000	0	/C-1	0.0
1979	Tex-A	7	17	2	2	0	0	1	1	2	4	.118	.211	.294	35	-2	0	0	0	1.000	-2	/C-7	-0.3
Total	2	8	18	2	2	0	0	1	1	2	4	.111	.200	.278	28	-2	0	0	0	1.000	-2	/C-8	-0.3

■ DAN MAHONEY
Mahoney, Daniel J.   b: 3/20/1864, Springfield, Mass.   d: 2/1/04, Springfield, Mass.   BR/TR, 5'9.5", 165 lbs.   Deb: 8/20/1892

YEAR	TM/L	G	AB	R	H	2B	3B	HR	RBI	BB	SO	AVG	OBP	SLG	PRO+	BR/A	SB	CS	SBR	FA	FR	G/POS	TPR
1892	Cin-N	5	21	1	4	0	1	0	1	1	4	.190	.227	.286	56	-1	0			.943	2	/C-5	0.1
1895	Was-N	6	12	2	2	0	0	0	1	0	0	.167	.167	.167	-14	-2	0			.909	-1	/C-2,1-1	-0.2
Total	2	11	33	3	6	0	1	0	2	1	4	.182	.206	.242	28	-3	0			.949	1	/C-7,1-1	-0.1

■ DANNY MAHONEY
Mahoney, Daniel Joseph   b: 9/6/1888, Haverhill, Mass.   d: 9/28/60, Utica, N.Y.   BR/TR, 5'6.5", 145 lbs.   Deb: 5/15/11

YEAR	TM/L	G	AB	R	H	2B	3B	HR	RBI	BB	SO	AVG	OBP	SLG	PRO+	BR/A	SB	CS	SBR	FA	FR	G/POS	TPR
1911	Cin-N	1	0	0	0	0	0	0	0	0	0	—	—	—		0	0			.000	0	R	0.0

■ MIKE MAHONEY
Mahoney, George W. "Big Mike"   b: 12/5/1873, Boston, Mass.   d: 1/3/40, Boston, Mass.   BR, 6'4", 220 lbs.   Deb: 5/18/1897

YEAR	TM/L	G	AB	R	H	2B	3B	HR	RBI	BB	SO	AVG	OBP	SLG	PRO+	BR/A	SB	CS	SBR	FA	FR	G/POS	TPR
1897	Bos-N	2	2	1	1	0	0	0	1	0	0	.500	.500	.500	155	-0	0			1.000	-0	/C-1,P-1	0.0
1898	StL-N	2	7	0	0	0	0	0	0	0	2	.000	.000	.000	-98	-2	0			.920	-0	/1-2	-0.2
Total	2	4	9	1	1	0	0	0	1	0	2	.111	.111	.111	-36	-2	0			.920	-0	/1-2,P-1,C-1	-0.2

■ JIM MAHONEY
Mahoney, James Thomas "Moe"   b: 5/26/34, Englewood, N.J.   BR/TR, 6', 175 lbs.   Deb: 7/28/59   C

YEAR	TM/L	G	AB	R	H	2B	3B	HR	RBI	BB	SO	AVG	OBP	SLG	PRO+	BR/A	SB	CS	SBR	FA	FR	G/POS	TPR
1959	Bos-A	31	23	10	3	0	0	1	4	3	7	.130	.231	.261	33	-2	0	0	0	.940	10	S-30	0.9
1961	Was-A	43	108	10	26	0	1	0	6	5	23	.241	.274	.259	44	-8	1	2	-1	.968	12	S-31/2-2	0.4
1962	Cle-N	41	74	12	18	4	0	3	5	3	14	.243	.273	.419	86	-2	0	0	0	.964	8	S-23/2-8,3-1	0.8
1965	Hou-N	5	5	0	1	0	0	0	0	0	3	.200	.200	.200	14	-1	0	0	0	1.000	0	/S-5	0.0
Total	4	120	210	32	48	4	1	4	15	11	47	.229	.267	.314	57	-13	1	2	-1	.962	31	/S-89,2-10,3-1	2.1

■ BOB MAIER
Maier, Robert Phillip   b: 9/5/15, Dunellen, N.J.   d: 8/4/93, S.Plainfield, N.J.   BR/TR, 5'8", 180 lbs.   Deb: 4/17/45

YEAR	TM/L	G	AB	R	H	2B	3B	HR	RBI	BB	SO	AVG	OBP	SLG	PRO+	BR/A	SB	CS	SBR	FA	FR	G/POS	TPR
1945	*Det-A	132	486	58	128	25	7	1	34	38	32	.263	.317	.350	88	-8	7	11	-5	.936	-13	*3-124/O-5	-2.4

■ EMIL MAILHO
Mailho, Emil Pierre "Lefty"   b: 12/16/09, Berkeley, Cal.   BL/TL, 5'10", 165 lbs.   Deb: 4/14/36

YEAR	TM/L	G	AB	R	H	2B	3B	HR	RBI	BB	SO	AVG	OBP	SLG	PRO+	BR/A	SB	CS	SBR	FA	FR	G/POS	TPR
1936	Phi-A	21	18	5	1	0	0	0	0	5	3	.056	.261	.056	-18	-3	0	0	0	1.000	-0	/O-1	-0.3

■ CHARLIE MAISEL
Maisel, Charles Louis   b: 4/21/1894, Catonsville, Md.   d: 8/25/53, Baltimore, Md.   BR/TR, 6',   Deb: 10/2/15

YEAR	TM/L	G	AB	R	H	2B	3B	HR	RBI	BB	SO	AVG	OBP	SLG	PRO+	BR/A	SB	CS	SBR	FA	FR	G/POS	TPR
1915	Bal-F	1	4	0	0	0	0	0	0	0	0	.000	.000	.000	-97	-1	0			1.000	0	/C-1	-0.1

■ FRITZ MAISEL
Maisel, Frederick Charles "Flash"   b: 12/23/1889, Catonsville, Md.   d: 4/22/67, Baltimore, Md.   BR/TR, 5'7.5", 170 lbs.   Deb: 8/11/13   F

YEAR	TM/L	G	AB	R	H	2B	3B	HR	RBI	BB	SO	AVG	OBP	SLG	PRO+	BR/A	SB	CS	SBR	FA	FR	G/POS	TPR
1913	NY-A	51	187	33	48	4	3	0	12	34	20	.257	.371	.310	99	1	25			.950	-5	3-51	-0.3
1914	NY-A	150	548	78	134	23	9	2	47	76	69	.239	.334	.325	98	0	74	17	12	.928	-18	*3-148	-0.1
1915	NY-A	135	530	77	149	16	6	4	46	48	35	.281	.342	.357	109	5	51	12	8	.940	-9	*3-134	1.0
1916	NY-A	53	158	18	36	5	0	0	7	20	18	.228	.318	.259	72	-5	4			.980	-5	O-26,3-11/2-4	-1.2
1917	NY-A	113	404	46	80	4	4	0	20	36	18	.198	.267	.228	51	-23	29			.967	-1	*2-100/3-7	-2.2
1918	StL-A	90	284	43	66	4	2	0	16	46	17	.232	.341	.261	84	-3	11			.949	-4	3-79/O-1	-0.6
Total	6	592	2111	295	510	56	24	6	148	260	177	.242	.327	.299	88	-25	194	29		.938	-43	3-430,2-104/O-27	-3.4

■ GEORGE MAISEL
Maisel, George John   b: 3/12/1892, Catonsville, Md.   d: 11/20/68, Baltimore, Md.   BR/TR, 5'10.5", 180 lbs.   Deb: 5/1/13   F

YEAR	TM/L	G	AB	R	H	2B	3B	HR	RBI	BB	SO	AVG	OBP	SLG	PRO+	BR/A	SB	CS	SBR	FA	FR	G/POS	TPR
1913	StL-A	11	18	2	3	2	0	0	1	1	7	.167	.211	.278	44	-1	0			.833	-2	/O-5	-0.4
1916	Det-A	8	5	2	0	0	0	0	0	0	0	.000	.000	.000	-97	-1	0			.857	2	/3-3	0.1
1921	Chi-N	111	393	54	122	7	2	0	43	11	13	.310	.334	.338	78	-12	17	7	1	.978	0	*O-108	-1.8
1922	Chi-N	38	84	9	16	1	1	0	6	8	2	.190	.261	.226	26	-9	1	3	-2	1.000	-2	O-26	-1.4
Total	4	168	500	67	141	10	3	0	50	20	24	.282	.314	.314	66	-23	18	10		.979	-2	O-139/3-3	-3.5

■ HANK MAJESKI
Majeski, Henry "Heeney"   b: 12/13/16, Staten Island, N.Y.   d: 8/9/91, Staten Island, N.Y.   BR/TR, 5'9", 180 lbs.   Deb: 5/17/39

YEAR	TM/L	G	AB	R	H	2B	3B	HR	RBI	BB	SO	AVG	OBP	SLG	PRO+	BR/A	SB	CS	SBR	FA	FR	G/POS	TPR
1939	Bos-N	106	367	35	100	16	1	7	54	18	30	.272	.310	.379	91	-6	2			.945	12	3-99	0.7
1940	Bos-N	3	3	0	0	0	0	0	0	0	0	.000	.000	.000	-99	-1	0			.000	0	H	-0.1
1941	Bos-N	19	55	5	8	5	0	0	3	1	13	.145	.161	.236	11	-7	0			.911	1	3-11	-0.6
1946	NY-A	8	12	1	1	0	1	0	0	0	3	.083	.083	.250	-9	-2	0	0	0	.750	-1	3-2	-0.3
	Phi-A	78	264	25	66	14	3	1	25	26	13	.250	.320	.337	84	-6	3	2	-0	.967	8	3-72	0.3
	Yr	86	276	26	67	14	4	1	25	26	16	.243	.310	.333	80	-7	3	2	-0	.964	7	3-74	0.0
1947	Phi-A	141	479	54	134	26	5	8	72	53	31	.280	.358	.405	110	6	1	0	0	.988	7	*3-134/S-4,2-1	1.5
1948	Phi-A	148	590	88	183	41	4	12	120	48	43	.310	.368	.454	118	13	2	4	-1	.975	1	*3-142/S-8	1.3
1949	Phi-A	114	448	62	124	25	5	9	67	29	23	.277	.326	.417	99	-3	0	1	-1	.957	-4	*3-113	-1.0
1950	Chi-A	122	414	47	128	18	2	6	46	42	34	.309	.377	.406	103	2	1	4	-2	.970	10	*3-112	0.8
1951	Chi-A	12	35	4	9	4	0	0	6	1	0	.257	.278	.371	76	-1	0	0	0	.950	-0	/3-9	-0.2
	Phi-A	89	323	41	92	19	4	5	42	35	24	.285	.358	.411	106	3	1	2	-1	.974	14	3-88	1.4
	Yr	101	358	45	101	23	4	5	48	36	24	.282	.351	.411	104	1	1	2	-1	.972	14	3-97	1.2
1952	Phi-A	34	117	14	30	2	2	2	20	19	10	.256	.365	.359	96	-0	1	1	-1	.976	4	3-34	0.3
	Cle-A	36	54	7	16	2	0	0	9	7	7	.296	.377	.333	106	1	0	0	0	.913	-0	3-11/2-3	0.0
	Yr	70	171	21	46	4	2	2	29	26	17	.269	.369	.351	101	1	1	1	-1	.966	4	3-45/2-3	0.3
1953	Cle-A	50	50	6	15	1	0	2	12	3	8	.300	.352	.440	116	1	0	0	0	1.000	-2	2-10/3-7,O-1	-0.1

YEAR	TM/L	G	AB	R	H	2B	3B	HR	RBI	BB	SO	AVG	OBP	SLG	PRO+	BR/A	SB	CS	SBR	FA	FR	G/POS	TPR
1954	*Cle-A	57	121	10	34	4	0	3	17	7	14	.281	.320	.388	92	-2	0	0	0	.990	4	2-25,3-10	0.4
1955	Cle-A	36	48	3	9	2	0	2	6	8	3	.188	.328	.354	80	-1	0	0	0	1.000	-2	/3-9,2-4	-0.3
	Bal-A	16	41	2	7	1	0	0	2	2	4	.171	.209	.195	10	-5	0	0	0	1.000	-3	/3-8,2-5	-0.9
	Yr	52	89	5	16	3	0	2	8	10	7	.180	.277	.281	50	-6	0	0	0	1.000	-5	3-17/2-9	-1.2
Total	13	1069	3421	404	956	181	27	57	501	299	260	.279	.342	.398	100	-9	10	11		.968	49	3-861/2-48,S-12,O-1	3.2

■ MIKE MAKSUDIAN
Maksudian, Michael Bryant b: 5/28/66, Belleville, Ill. BL/TR, 5'11", 220 lbs. Deb: 9/2/92

YEAR	TM/L	G	AB	R	H	2B	3B	HR	RBI	BB	SO	AVG	OBP	SLG	PRO+	BR/A	SB	CS	SBR	FA	FR	G/POS	TPR
1992	Tor-A	3	3	0	0	0	0	0	0	0	0	.000	.000	.000	-96	-1	0	0	0	.000	0	/1-1	-0.1
1993	Min-A	5	12	2	2	1	0	0	2	4	2	.167	.375	.250	71	-0	0	0	0	1.000	1	/1-4,3-1	0.0
1994	Chi-N	26	26	6	7	2	0	0	4	10	4	.269	.472	.346	120	2	0	1	-1	1.000	1	/1-3,C-2,3-2	0.0
Total	3	34	41	8	9	3	0	0	6	14	6	.220	.418	.293	92	1	0	1	-1	1.000	1	/1-8,3-3,C-2	-0.1

■ JOSE MALAVE
Malave, Jose Francisco b: 5/31/71, Cumana, Venez. BR/TR, 6'2", 212 lbs. Deb: 5/23/96

YEAR	TM/L	G	AB	R	H	2B	3B	HR	RBI	BB	SO	AVG	OBP	SLG	PRO+	BR/A	SB	CS	SBR	FA	FR	G/POS	TPR
1996	Bos-A	41	102	12	24	3	0	4	17	2	25	.235	.257	.382	57	-7	0	0	0	.978	-6	O-38	-1.2

■ CHARLIE MALAY
Malay, Charles Francis b: 6/13/1879, Brooklyn, N.Y. d: 9/18/49, Brooklyn, N.Y. BB/TR, 5'11.5", 175 lbs. Deb: 4/24/05 F

YEAR	TM/L	G	AB	R	H	2B	3B	HR	RBI	BB	SO	AVG	OBP	SLG	PRO+	BR/A	SB	CS	SBR	FA	FR	G/POS	TPR
1905	Bro-N	102	349	33	88	7	2	1	31	22		.252	.300	.292	83	-7	13			.932	-9	2-75,O-25/S-1	-1.8

■ JOE MALAY
Malay, Joseph Charles b: 10/25/05, Brooklyn, N.Y. d: 3/19/89, Bridgeport, Conn. BL/TL, 6', 175 lbs. Deb: 9/7/33 F

YEAR	TM/L	G	AB	R	H	2B	3B	HR	RBI	BB	SO	AVG	OBP	SLG	PRO+	BR/A	SB	CS	SBR	FA	FR	G/POS	TPR
1933	NY-N	8	24	0	3	0	0	0	2	0	0	.125	.125	.125	-29	-4	0			1.000	2	/1-8	-0.3
1935	NY-N	1	1	0	1	0	0	0	0	0	0	1.000	1.000	1.000	447	-0	0			.000	0	H	0.0
Total	2	9	25	0	4	0	0	0	2	0	0	.160	.160	.160	-9	-3	0			1.000	2	/1-8	-0.3

■ CANDY MALDONADO
Maldonado, Candido (Guadarrama) b: 9/5/60, Humacao, P.R. BR/TR, 6', 190 lbs. Deb: 9/7/81

YEAR	TM/L	G	AB	R	H	2B	3B	HR	RBI	BB	SO	AVG	OBP	SLG	PRO+	BR/A	SB	CS	SBR	FA	FR	G/POS	TPR
1981	LA-N	11	12	0	1	0	0	0	0	0	5	.083	.083	.083	-55	-2	0	0	0	1.000	-2	/O-9	-0.5
1982	LA-N	6	4	0	0	0	0	0	0	0	2	.000	.000	.000	-41	-1	0	0	0	1.000	-1	/O-3	-0.1
1983	*LA-N	42	62	5	12	1	1	1	6	5	14	.194	.254	.290	51	-4	0	0	0	1.000	-8	O-33	-1.3
1984	LA-N	116	254	25	68	14	0	5	28	19	29	.268	.321	.382	98	-1	0	3	-2	.955	-16	*O-102/3-4	-2.2
1985	*LA-N	121	213	20	48	7	1	5	19	19	40	.225	.289	.338	77	-7	1	1	-0	.984	-22	*O-113	-3.3
1986	SF-N	133	405	49	102	31	3	18	85	20	77	.252	.292	.477	114	5	4	4	-1	.983	-4	*O-101/3-1	-0.3
1987	*SF-N	118	442	69	129	28	4	20	85	34	78	.292	.351	.509	131	18	8	8	-2	.973	-6	*O-116	0.6
1988	SF-N	142	499	53	127	23	1	12	68	37	89	.255	.315	.377	102	1	6	5	-1	.962	-3	*O-139	-0.8
1989	*SF-N	129	345	39	75	23	0	9	41	37	69	.217	.299	.362	91	-5	4	1	1	.974	-6	*O-116	-1.3
1990	Cle-A	155	590	76	161	32	2	22	95	49	134	.273	.334	.446	117	12	3	5	-2	.993	7	*O-134,D-20	1.3
1991	Mil-A	34	111	11	23	6	0	5	20	13	23	.207	.290	.396	90	-2	1	0	0	.976	-2	O-24	-0.4
	*Tor-A	52	177	26	49	9	0	7	28	23	53	.277	.379	.446	123	6	3	0	1	.990	0	O-52/D-9	0.6
	Yr	86	288	37	72	15	0	12	48	36	76	.250	.345	.427	111	5	4	0	1	.986	-2	O-76/D-9	0.2
1992	*Tor-A	137	489	64	133	25	4	20	66	59	112	.272	.359	.462	123	15	2	2	-1	.978	5	*O-132/D-4	1.7
1993	Chi-N	70	140	8	26	3	0	3	15	13	40	.186	.260	.286	47	-11	0	0	0	.914	-5	O-41	-1.7
	Cle-A	28	81	11	20	2	0	5	20	11	18	.247	.337	.457	112	1	0	1	-1	.976	-3	O-26/D-2	-0.3
1994	Cle-A	42	92	14	18	5	1	5	12	19	31	.196	.333	.435	96	-1	1	1	-0	1.000	-1	D-25/O-5	-0.3
1995	Tor-A	61	160	22	43	13	0	7	25	25	45	.269	.374	.481	121	5	1	1	-0	.988	-8	O-58/D-1	-0.4
	Tex-A	13	30	6	7	3	0	2	5	7	5	.233	.378	.533	131	1	0	1	-1	1.000	-0	O-11	0.0
	Yr	74	190	28	50	16	0	9	30	32	50	.263	.375	.489	123	7	1	2	-1	.990	-8	O-69/D-1	-0.4
Total	15	1410	4106	498	1042	227	17	146	618	391	864	.254	.325	.424	107	31	34	33	-10	.977	-74	*O-1215/D-61,3-5	-8.7

■ JIM MALER
Maler, James Michael b: 8/16/58, New York, N.Y. BR/TR, 6'4", 230 lbs. Deb: 9/3/81

YEAR	TM/L	G	AB	R	H	2B	3B	HR	RBI	BB	SO	AVG	OBP	SLG	PRO+	BR/A	SB	CS	SBR	FA	FR	G/POS	TPR
1981	Sea-A	12	23	1	8	0	0	0	2	2	1	.348	.423	.391	131	1	0	0	0	1.000	-0	/1-5,D-2	0.1
1982	Sea-A	64	221	18	50	8	3	4	26	12	35	.226	.275	.344	67	-10	0	0	0	.991	5	1-57/D-5	-1.0
1983	Sea-A	26	66	5	12	1	0	1	3	5	11	.182	.260	.242	38	-6	0	3	-2	1.000	-1	1-19/D-5	-0.8
Total	3	102	310	24	70	10	3	5	31	19	47	.226	.284	.326	65	-15	0	3	-2	.994	3	/1-81,D-12	-1.7

■ TONY MALINOSKY
Malinosky, Anthony Francis b: 10/5/09, Collinsville, Ill. BR/TR, 5'10.5", 165 lbs. Deb: 4/26/37

YEAR	TM/L	G	AB	R	H	2B	3B	HR	RBI	BB	SO	AVG	OBP	SLG	PRO+	BR/A	SB	CS	SBR	FA	FR	G/POS	TPR
1937	Bro-N	35	79	7	18	2	0	0	3	9	11	.228	.307	.253	53	-5	0			.833	-9	3-13,S-11	-1.4

■ BOBBY MALKMUS
Malkmus, Robert Edward b: 7/4/31, Newark, N.J. BR/TR, 5'9", 180 lbs. Deb: 6/1/57

YEAR	TM/L	G	AB	R	H	2B	3B	HR	RBI	BB	SO	AVG	OBP	SLG	PRO+	BR/A	SB	CS	SBR	FA	FR	G/POS	TPR
1957	Mil-N	13	22	6	2	0	1	0	0	3	3	.091	.200	.182	4	-3	0	0	0	.972	4	/2-7	0.1
1958	Was-A	41	70	5	13	2	1	0	3	4	15	.186	.230	.243	31	-7	0	0	0	.964	8	2-26/3-2,S-1	0.2
1959	Was-A	6	0	0	0	0	0	0	0	0	0	—	—	—		0	0	0	0	.000	0	R	0.0
1960	Phi-N	79	133	16	28	4	1	2	12	11	28	.211	.271	.278	51	-9	2	-1	1.000	7	S-29,2-23,3-12	-0.1
1961	Phi-N	121	342	39	79	8	2	7	31	20	43	.231	.277	.327	61	-20	3	1	-2	.988	16	2-58,S-34,3-25	0.3
1962	Phi-N	8	5	0	1	1	0	0	0	0	1	.200	.200	.400	58	-0	0	0	0	1.000	2	/S-1	0.2
Total	6	268	572	69	123	15	5	8	46	38	90	.215	.266	.301	53	-39	3	5	-2	.982	36	2-114/S-65,3-39	0.7

■ JERRY MALLETT
Mallett, Gerald Gordon b: 9/18/35, Bonne Terre, Mo. BR/TR, 6'5", 208 lbs. Deb: 9/19/59

YEAR	TM/L	G	AB	R	H	2B	3B	HR	RBI	BB	SO	AVG	OBP	SLG	PRO+	BR/A	SB	CS	SBR	FA	FR	G/POS	TPR
1959	Bos-A	4	15	1	4	0	0	0	0	0	0	.267	.313	.267	58	-1	0	0	0	1.000	3	/O-4	0.2

■ LES MALLON
Mallon, Leslie Clyde b: 11/21/05, Sweetwater, Tex. d: 4/17/91, Granbury, Tex. BR/TR, 5'8", 160 lbs. Deb: 4/14/31

YEAR	TM/L	G	AB	R	H	2B	3B	HR	RBI	BB	SO	AVG	OBP	SLG	PRO+	BR/A	SB	CS	SBR	FA	FR	G/POS	TPR
1931	Phi-N	122	375	41	116	19	2	1	45	29	44	.309	.359	.379	91	-4	0			.956	6	2-97/1-5,S-3,3-3	0.8
1932	Phi-N	103	347	44	90	16	2	5	31	28	28	.259	.318	.349	71	-14	1			.955	-31	2-88/3-5	-4.1
1934	Bos-N	42	166	23	49	6	1	0	18	15	12	.295	.354	.343	95	-1	0			.967	-4	2-42	-0.3
1935	Bos-N	116	412	48	113	24	2	2	25	28	37	.274	.322	.357	89	-7	3			.975	-14	2-73,3-36/O-1	-1.3
Total	4	383	1300	156	368	65	5	8	119	100	117	.283	.336	.359	85	-26	4			.962	-43	2-300/3-44,1-5,SO	-4.9

■ BEN MALLONEE
Mallonee, Howard Bennett "Lefty" b: 3/31/1894, Baltimore, Md. d: 2/19/78, Baltimore, Md. BL/TL, 5'6", 150 lbs. Deb: 9/14/21

YEAR	TM/L	G	AB	R	H	2B	3B	HR	RBI	BB	SO	AVG	OBP	SLG	PRO+	BR/A	SB	CS	SBR	FA	FR	G/POS	TPR
1921	Phi-A	7	25	2	6	1	0	0	4	1	2	.240	.269	.280	40	-2	1	0	0	1.000	0	/O-6	-0.2

■ JULE MALLONEE
Mallonee, Julius Norris b: 4/4/1900, Charlotte, N.C. d: 12/26/24, Charlotte, N.C. BL/TL, 6'2", 180 lbs. Deb: 8/4/25

YEAR	TM/L	G	AB	R	H	2B	3B	HR	RBI	BB	SO	AVG	OBP	SLG	PRO+	BR/A	SB	CS	SBR	FA	FR	G/POS	TPR
1925	Chi-A	2	3	1	0	0	0	0	0	1	0	.000	.250	.000	-34	-1	0	0	0	1.000	-0	/O-1	-0.1

■ JIM MALLORY
Mallory, James Baugh "Sunny Jim" b: 9/1/18, Lawrenceville, Va. BR/TR, 6'1", 170 lbs. Deb: 9/8/40

YEAR	TM/L	G	AB	R	H	2B	3B	HR	RBI	BB	SO	AVG	OBP	SLG	PRO+	BR/A	SB	CS	SBR	FA	FR	G/POS	TPR
1940	Was-A	4	12	2	2	0	0	0	1	0	1	.167	.231	.167	5	-2	0	0	0	1.000	1	/O-3	-0.1
1945	StL-N	13	43	3	10	2	0	0	5	0	2	.233	.233	.279	41	-4	0			.923	-2	O-11	-0.6
	NY-N	37	94	10	28	1	0	0	9	6	7	.298	.340	.309	80	-2	1			.979	-0	O-21	-0.4
	Yr	50	137	13	38	3	0	0	14	6	9	.277	.308	.299	68	-6	1			.959	-2	O-32	-1.0
Total	2	54	149	15	40	3	0	0	14	7	10	.268	.301	.289	63	-8	1	0		.964	-1	/O-35	-1.1

■ SHELDON MALLORY
Mallory, Sheldon b: 7/16/53, Argo, Ill. BL/TL, 6'2", 175 lbs. Deb: 4/10/77

YEAR	TM/L	G	AB	R	H	2B	3B	HR	RBI	BB	SO	AVG	OBP	SLG	PRO+	BR/A	SB	CS	SBR	FA	FR	G/POS	TPR
1977	Oak-A	64	126	19	27	4	1	0	5	11	18	.214	.293	.262	53	-8	12	5	1	.977	-3	O-45/1-4,D-7	-1.2

■ HARRY MALMBERG
Malmberg, Harry William "Swede" b: 7/31/26, Fairfield, Ala. d: 10/29/76, San Francisco, Cal BR/TR, 6'1", 170 lbs. Deb: 4/12/55 C

YEAR	TM/L	G	AB	R	H	2B	3B	HR	RBI	BB	SO	AVG	OBP	SLG	PRO+	BR/A	SB	CS	SBR	FA	FR	G/POS	TPR
1955	Det-A	67	208	25	45	5	2	0	19	29	19	.216	.312	.260	56	-12	0	1	-1	.985	6	2-65	-0.2

■ EDDIE MALONE
Malone, Edward Russell b: 6/16/20, Chicago, Ill. BR/TR, 5'10", 175 lbs. Deb: 7/17/49

YEAR	TM/L	G	AB	R	H	2B	3B	HR	RBI	BB	SO	AVG	OBP	SLG	PRO+	BR/A	SB	CS	SBR	FA	FR	G/POS	TPR
1949	Chi-A	55	170	17	46	7	1	0	16	29	19	.271	.377	.353	97	-0	2			.990	-3	C-51	0.0
1950	Chi-A	31	71	2	16	2	0	0	10	10	8	.225	.321	.254	50	-5	0			1.000	0	C-21	-0.2
Total	2	86	241	19	62	9	1	0	26	39	27	.257	.361	.324	83	-5	2	1	0	.993	-2	/C-72	-0.2

■ FERGY MALONE
Malone, Ferguson G. b: 1842, Ireland d: 1/1/05, Seattle, Wash. BR/TR, 5'8", 156 lbs. Deb: 6/3/1871 MU

YEAR	TM/L	G	AB	R	H	2B	3B	HR	RBI	BB	SO	AVG	OBP	SLG	PRO+	BR/A	SB	CS	SBR	FA	FR	G/POS	TPR
1871	Ath-n	27	134	33	46	7	1	0	33	9	1	.343	.385	.433	136	7	9	3	1	.856	9	*C-27	1.0
1872	Ath-n	41	213	46	60	5	0	0	39	4	5	.282	.295	.333	92	-2	3	0	1	.884	4	C-24,1-17	0.2
1873	Phi-n	53	259	59	75	11	2	0	43	14	7	.290	.326	.347	97	-2	2			.898	5	*C-53/S-1,M	0.2
1874	Chi-n	47	223	33	56	5	0	0	29	4	0	.251	.264	.274	72	-7	2	1	0	.820	4	*C-47,M	-0.1

YEAR	TM/L	G	AB	R	H	2B	3B	HR	RBI	BB	SO	AVG	OBP	SLG	PRO+	BR/A	SB	CS	SBR	FA	FR	G/POS	TPR
1875	Phi-n	29	123	15	28	2	1	0	10	1	2	.228	.234	.260	69	-4	1	0	0	.919	-3	1-22/C-6,O-2	-0.6
1876	Phi-N	22	96	14	22	2	0	0	6	0	1	.229	.229	.250	60	-4				.777	-2	C-20/O-3,S-1	-0.5
1884	Phi-U	1	4	0	1	0	0	0		0	0	.250	.250	.250	56	-0				.818	-1	/C-1,M	-0.1
Total	5 n	197	952	186	265	30	7	1	154	32	18	.278	.302	.328	93	-7	17	5	2	.856	19	C-157/1-39,O-2,S-1	0.7
Total	2	23	100	14	23	2	0	0	6	1	1	.230	.230	.250	60	-4				.780	-3	/C-21,O-3,S-1	-0.6

■ LEW MALONE   Malone, Lewis Aloysius b: 3/13/1897, Baltimore, Md. d: 2/17/72, Brooklyn, N.Y. BR/TR, 5'11", 175 lbs. Deb: 5/31/15

YEAR	TM/L	G	AB	R	H	2B	3B	HR	RBI	BB	SO	AVG	OBP	SLG	PRO+	BR/A	SB	CS	SBR	FA	FR	G/POS	TPR
1915	Phi-A	76	201	17	41	4	4	1	17	21	40	.204	.283	.279	70	-8	7	1	2	.919	-4	2-43,3-12/O-4,S-2	-1.0
1916	Phi-A	5	4	1	0	0	0	0	0	1	2	.000	.200	.000	-42	-1	0			1.000	-0	/S-1	-0.1
1917	Bro-N	1	0	1	0	0	0	0	0	0	0	—	—	—	—	0	0			.000	0	R	0.0
1919	Bro-N	51	162	9	33	7	3	0	11	6	18	.204	.232	.284	54	-9	1			.934	-6	3-47/2-2,S-2	-1.6
Total	4	133	367	28	74	11	7	1	28	28	60	.202	.260	.278	62	-18	8	1		.910	-11	/3-59,2-45,S-5,O-4	-2.7

■ JOHN MALONEY   Maloney, John Deb: 9/15/1876

YEAR	TM/L	G	AB	R	H	2B	3B	HR	RBI	BB	SO	AVG	OBP	SLG	PRO+	BR/A	SB	CS	SBR	FA	FR	G/POS	TPR
1876	NY-N	2	7	1	2	0	1	0	2	0	1	.286	.286	.571	206	1				.800	-0	/O-2	0.0
1877	Har-N	1	4	0	1	0	0	0	0	0	0	.250	.250	.250	65	-0				.250	-1	/O-1	-0.1
Total	2	3	11	1	3	0	1	0	2	0	1	.273	.273	.455	152	1				.556	-1	/O-3	-0.1

■ PAT MALONEY   Maloney, Patrick William b: 1/19/1888, Grosvenor Dale, Conn. d: 6/27/79, Pawtucket, R.I. BR/TR, 6', 150 lbs. Deb: 6/19/12

YEAR	TM/L	G	AB	R	H	2B	3B	HR	RBI	BB	SO	AVG	OBP	SLG	PRO+	BR/A	SB	CS	SBR	FA	FR	G/POS	TPR
1912	NY-A	25	79	9	17	1	0	0	4	6		.215	.279	.228	43	-6	3			.926	2	O-20	-0.4

■ BILLY MALONEY   Maloney, William Alphonse b: 6/5/1878, Lewiston, Me. d: 9/2/60, Breckenridge, Tex. BL/TR, 5'10", 177 lbs. Deb: 5/2/01

YEAR	TM/L	G	AB	R	H	2B	3B	HR	RBI	BB	SO	AVG	OBP	SLG	PRO+	BR/A	SB	CS	SBR	FA	FR	G/POS	TPR
1901	Mil-A	86	290	42	85	3	4	0	22	7		.293	.328	.331	87	-5	11			.952	9	C-72/O-8	0.9
1902	StL-A	30	112	8	23	3	0	0	11	6		.205	.258	.232	37	-9	0			.906	-4	O-23/C-7	-1.4
	Cin-N	27	89	13	22	4	0	1	7	2		.247	.272	.326	77	-3	8			.848	-3	O-18/C-7	-0.6
1905	Chi-N	145	558	78	145	17	14	2	56	43		.260	.325	.351	98	-2	59			.954	3	*O-145	-0.6
1906	Bro-N	151	566	71	125	15	7	0	32	49		.221	.286	.272	80	-13	38			.966	11	*O-151	-1.1
1907	Bro-N	144	502	51	115	7	10	0	32	31		.229	.287	.283	86	-9	25			.967	5	*O-144	-1.1
1908	Bro-N	113	359	31	70	5	7	3	17	24		.195	.255	.273	71	-12	14			.947	5	*O-107/C-4	-1.4
Total	6	696	2476	294	585	54	42	6	177	162		.236	.294	.299	83	-53	155			.954	25	O-596/C-90	-5.3

■ FRANK MALZONE   Malzone, Frank James b: 2/28/30, Bronx, N.Y. BR/TR, 5'10", 180 lbs. Deb: 9/17/55

YEAR	TM/L	G	AB	R	H	2B	3B	HR	RBI	BB	SO	AVG	OBP	SLG	PRO+	BR/A	SB	CS	SBR	FA	FR	G/POS	TPR
1955	Bos-A	6	20	2	7	1	0	0	1	0	3	.350	.381	.400	101	0	0	0	0	1.000	2	/3-4	0.2
1956	Bos-A	27	103	15	17	3	1	2	11	9	8	.165	.232	.272	29	-11	1	0	0	.931	1	3-26	-0.9
1957	Bos-A★	153	634	82	185	31	5	15	103	31	41	.292	.326	.427	98	-3	2	1	0	.954	14	*3-153	1.5
1958	Bos-A★	155	627	76	185	30	2	15	87	33	53	.295	.334	.421	100	-1	1	3	-2	.950	17	*3-155	1.6
1959	Bos-A★	154	604	90	169	34	2	19	92	42	49	.280	.328	.437	103	1	6	0	1	.953	8	*3-154	1.1
1960	Bos-A★	152	595	60	161	30	2	14	79	36	42	.271	.317	.398	89	-10	2	3	-1	.948	8	*3-152	-0.5
1961	Bos-A	151	590	74	157	21	4	14	87	44	49	.266	.318	.386	85	-13	1	3	-2	.950	-5	*3-149	-1.8
1962	Bos-A	156	619	74	175	20	3	21	95	35	43	.283	.321	.426	96	-5	0	1	-1	.967	5	*3-156	0.1
1963	Bos-A★	151	580	66	169	25	2	15	71	31	45	.291	.331	.419	105	3	0	2	-1	.964	4	*3-148	0.6
1964	Bos-A☆	148	537	62	142	19	0	13	56	37	43	.264	.314	.372	86	-10	0	0	-0	.959	-0	*3-143	-1.3
1965	Bos-A	106	364	40	87	20	0	3	34	28	38	.239	.295	.319	70	-14	1	1	-0	.969	-3	3-96	-2.1
1966	Cal-A	82	155	6	32	5	0	2	12	10	11	.206	.255	.277	54	-9	0	1	-0	.925	-1	3-35	-1.2
Total	12	1441	5428	647	1486	239	21	133	728	337	434	.274	.318	.399	91	-71	14	14	-4	.955	47	*3-1370	-2.7

■ GUS MANCUSO   Mancuso, August Rodney "Blackie" b: 12/5/05, Galveston, Tex. d: 10/26/84, Houston, Tex. BR/TR, 5'10", 185 lbs. Deb: 4/30/28 FC

YEAR	TM/L	G	AB	R	H	2B	3B	HR	RBI	BB	SO	AVG	OBP	SLG	PRO+	BR/A	SB	CS	SBR	FA	FR	G/POS	TPR
1928	StL-N	11	38	2	7	0	1	0	3	0	5	.184	.184	.237	9	-5	0			.984	4	C-11	0.0
1930	*StL-N	76	227	39	83	17	2	7	59	18	16	.366	.415	.551	127	10	1			.969	1	C-61	1.4
1931	*StL-N	67	187	13	49	16	1	1	23	18	13	.262	.327	.374	85	-4	2			.972	6	C-56	0.6
1932	StL-N	103	310	25	88	23	1	6	43	30	15	.284	.347	.413	100	1	0			.977	8	C-82	1.3
1933	*NY-N	144	481	39	127	17	2	6	56	48	21	.264	.331	.345	95	-2	0			.972	5	*C-142	0.8
1934	NY-N	122	383	32	94	14	0	7	46	27	19	.245	.295	.337	70	-16	0			.977	6	*C-122	-0.4
1935	NY-N★	128	447	33	133	18	2	5	56	30	16	.298	.342	.380	95	-3	1			.972	-5	*C-126	-0.1
1936	*NY-N	139	519	55	156	21	3	9	63	39	28	.301	.351	.405	104	3	0			.977	5	*C-138	1.4
1937	NY-N★	86	287	30	80	17	1	4	39	17	20	.279	.319	.387	90	-4	1			.982	16	C-81	1.5
1938	NY-N	52	158	19	55	8	0	2	15	17	13	.348	.411	.437	132	8	0			.977	4	C-44	1.4
1939	Chi-N	80	251	17	58	10	0	2	17	24	19	.231	.298	.295	59	-14	0			.981	5	C-76	-0.6
1940	Bro-N	60	144	16	33	8	0	0	16	13	7	.229	.293	.285	56	-8	0			.982	7	C-56	0.1
1941	StL-N	106	328	25	75	13	1	2	37	37	19	.229	.309	.293	66	-14	0			.989	11	*C-105	0.4
1942	StL-N	5	13	0	1	0	0	0	1	0	0	.077	.077	.077	-51	-2	0			.917	-1	/C-3	-0.4
	NY-N	39	109	4	21	1	1	0	8	14	7	.193	.285	.220	48	-7	1			.982	3	C-38	-0.2
	Yr	44	122	4	22	1	1	0	9	14	7	.180	.265	.205	38	-9	1			.977	1	C-41	-0.6
1943	NY-N	94	252	11	50	5	0	2	20	28	16	.198	.284	.242	52	-15	0			.974	-0	C-77	-1.1
1944	NY-N	78	195	15	49	4	1	1	25	30	20	.251	.351	.297	84	-3	0			.976	5	C-72	0.5
1945	Phi-N	70	176	11	35	5	0	0	16	28	10	.199	.309	.227	52	-11	2			.988	1	C-70	-0.7
Total	17	1460	4505	386	1194	197	16	53	543	418	264	.265	.328	.351	85	-89	8			.977	75	*C-1360	5.9

■ FRANK MANCUSO   Mancuso, Frank Octavius b: 5/23/18, Houston, Tex. BR/TR, 6', 195 lbs. Deb: 4/18/44 F

YEAR	TM/L	G	AB	R	H	2B	3B	HR	RBI	BB	SO	AVG	OBP	SLG	PRO+	BR/A	SB	CS	SBR	FA	FR	G/POS	TPR
1944	*StL-A	88	244	19	50	11	0	1	24	20	32	.205	.271	.262	50	-16	1	0	0	.953	-6	C-87	-1.8
1945	StL-A	119	365	39	98	13	3	1	38	46	44	.268	.354	.329	94	-2	0	2	-1	.989	-6	*C-115	-0.2
1946	StL-A	87	262	22	63	8	3	3	23	30	31	.240	.323	.328	78	-7	1	0	0	.973	-18	C-85	-2.1
1947	Was-A	43	131	5	30	5	1	0	13	5	11	.229	.257	.282	51	-9	0	0	0	.958	-4	C-35	-1.1
Total	4	337	1002	85	241	37	7	5	98	101	118	.241	.314	.306	74	-34	2	2	-1	.972	-34	C-322	-5.2

■ CARL MANDA   Manda, Carl Alan b: 11/16/1888, Little River, Kan. d: 3/9/83, Artesia, N.Mex. BR/TR, 5'10", 170 lbs. Deb: 9/11/14

YEAR	TM/L	G	AB	R	H	2B	3B	HR	RBI	BB	SO	AVG	OBP	SLG	PRO+	BR/A	SB	CS	SBR	FA	FR	G/POS	TPR
1914	Chi-A	9	15	2	4	0	0	0	1	3		.267	.389	.267	99	0	1			.971	4	/2-7	0.5

■ JIM MANGAN   Mangan, James Daniel b: 9/24/29, San Francisco, Cal. BR/TR, 5'10", 190 lbs. Deb: 4/16/52

YEAR	TM/L	G	AB	R	H	2B	3B	HR	RBI	BB	SO	AVG	OBP	SLG	PRO+	BR/A	SB	CS	SBR	FA	FR	G/POS	TPR
1952	Pit-N	11	13	1	2	0	0	0	2	1	3	.154	.214	.154	-2	-2	0	0	0	.833	-1	/C-4	-0.2
1954	Pit-N	14	26	2	5	0	0	0	2	4	9	.192	.300	.192	32	-2	0	0	0	1.000	0	/C-7	-0.2
1956	NY-N	20	20	2	2	0	0	0	1	4	6	.100	.250	.100	-1	-3	0	0	0	1.000	-0	/C-15	-0.2
Total	3	45	59	5	9	0	0	0	5	9	18	.153	.265	.153	15	-7	0	0	0	.985	-0	/C-26	-0.6

■ ANGEL MANGUAL   Mangual, Angel Luis (Guilbe) b: 3/19/47, Juana Diaz, P.R. BR/TR, 5'10", 180 lbs. Deb: 9/15/69 F

YEAR	TM/L	G	AB	R	H	2B	3B	HR	RBI	BB	SO	AVG	OBP	SLG	PRO+	BR/A	SB	CS	SBR	FA	FR	G/POS	TPR
1969	Pit-N	6	4	1	1	1	0	0	0	0	0	.250	.250	.500	108	0	0	0	0	.000	-1	/O-3	-0.1
1971	*Oak-A	94	287	32	82	8	1	4	30	17	27	.286	.326	.362	97	-2	1	4	-2	.988	-2	O-81	-1.0
1972	*Oak-A	91	272	19	67	13	2	5	32	14	48	.246	.286	.364	97	-2	0	1	-0	.971	-3	O-74	-0.3
1973	*Oak-A	74	192	20	43	4	1	3	13	8	34	.224	.259	.302	61	-11	1	1	-0	.947	-5	O-50,D-14/1-2,2-1	-1.9
1974	*Oak-A	115	365	37	85	14	4	9	43	17	59	.233	.267	.367	87	-8	3	0	1	.961	-7	O-74,D-37/3-1	-1.9
1975	Oak-A	62	109	13	24	3	0	1	6	3	18	.220	.241	.275	47	-8	1	1	-0	.978	-9	O-39,D-15	-1.9
1976	Oak-A	8	12	0	2	1	0	0	1	0	1	.167	.167	.250	22	-1	0	1	-0	1.000	-0	/O-7	-0.4
Total	7	450	1241	122	304	44	8	22	125	59	187	.245	.284	.346	83	-33	6	8	-3	.969	-23	O-328/D-66,1-2,32	-7.5

■ PEPE MANGUAL   Mangual, Jose Manuel (Guilbe) b: 5/23/52, Ponce, P.R. BR/TR, 5'10", 165 lbs. Deb: 9/6/72 F

YEAR	TM/L	G	AB	R	H	2B	3B	HR	RBI	BB	SO	AVG	OBP	SLG	PRO+	BR/A	SB	CS	SBR	FA	FR	G/POS	TPR
1972	Mon-N	8	11	2	3	0	0	0	1	2	3	.273	.333	.273	73	-0	1	1	-1	1.000	-1	/O-3	-0.2
1973	Mon-N	33	62	9	11	2	1	3	7	6	18	.177	.250	.387	71	-3	2	4	-2	.966	-3	O-22	-0.9
1974	Mon-N	23	61	10	19	3	2	0	5	6	12	.311	.364	.361	98	-0	5	4	-0	1.000	-6	O-22	-0.8
1975	Mon-N	140	514	84	126	16	2	9	45	74	115	.245	.345	.337	86	-8	33	11	3	.972	-4	*O-138	-1.5
1976	Mon-N	66	215	34	56	9	1	3	16	50	49	.260	.404	.353	112	6	17	7	1	.968	-6	O-62	0.4
	NY-N	41	102	15	19	5	2	1	9	10	32	.186	.259	.304	63	-5	7	3	0	.985	-2	O-38	-0.9
	Yr	107	317	49	75	14	3	4	25	60	81	.237	.361	.338	99	2	24	10	1	.973	-8	*O-100	-0.5

YEAR	TM/L	G	AB	R	H	2B	3B	HR	RBI	BB	SO	AVG	OBP	SLG	PRO+	BR/A	SB	CS	SBR	FA	FR	G/POS	TPR
1977	NY-N	8	7	1	1	0	0	0	2	1	4	.143	.250	.143	9	-1	0	0	0	.833	-1	/O-4	-0.2
Total	6	319	972	155	235	35	6	16	83	147	238	.242	.345	.340	89	-11	64	26	4	.972	-18	O-289	-3.9

■ GEORGE MANGUS
Mangus, George Graham   b: 5/22/1890, Red Creek, N.Y.   d: 8/10/33, Rutland, Mass.   BL/TR, 5'11.5", 165 lbs.   Deb: 8/20/12

YEAR	TM/L	G	AB	R	H	2B	3B	HR	RBI	BB	SO	AVG	OBP	SLG	PRO+	BR/A	SB	CS	SBR	FA	FR	G/POS	TPR
1912	Phi-N	10	25	2	5	3	0	0	3	1	6	.200	.231	.320	47	-2	0			.750	-1	/O-5	-0.4

■ CLYDE MANION
Manion, Clyde Jennings "Pete"   b: 10/30/1896, Jefferson City, Mo   d: 9/4/67, Detroit, Mich.   BR/TR, 5'11", 175 lbs.   Deb: 5/5/20

YEAR	TM/L	G	AB	R	H	2B	3B	HR	RBI	BB	SO	AVG	OBP	SLG	PRO+	BR/A	SB	CS	SBR	FA	FR	G/POS	TPR
1920	Det-A	32	80	4	22	4	1	0	8	4	7	.275	.318	.350	79	-3	0	0	0	.940	-2	C-30	-0.3
1921	Det-A	12	10	0	2	0	0	0	2	2	2	.200	.385	.200	53	-1	0	0	0	1.000	1	/C-3	0.0
1922	Det-A	42	69	9	19	4	1	0	12	4	6	.275	.315	.362	79	-2	0	1	-1	.932	-2	C-22/1-1	-0.4
1923	Det-A	23	22	0	3	0	0	0	2	2	2	.136	.208	.136	-8	-3	0	0	0	.857	-0	/C-3,1-1	-0.4
1924	Det-A	14	13	1	3	0	0	0	2	1	1	.231	.286	.231	35	-1	0	0	0	.750	-1	/C-3,1-1	-0.2
1926	Det-A	75	176	15	35	4	0	0	14	24	16	.199	.295	.222	36	-16	1	1	-0	.972	-0	C-74	-1.3
1927	Det-A	1	0	0	0	0	0	0	0	1	0	—	1.000	—	174	0	0	0	0	.000	0	H	0.0
1928	StL-A	76	243	25	55	5	1	2	31	15	18	.226	.274	.280	44	-20	3	0	1	.980	12	C-71	-0.1
1929	StL-A	35	111	16	27	2	0	0	11	15	3	.243	.333	.261	53	-7	1	0	0	.976	5	C-34	0.1
1930	StL-A	57	148	12	32	1	0	1	11	24	17	.216	.326	.243	45	-12	0	1	-1	.985	11	C-56	0.3
1932	Cin-N	49	135	7	28	0	0	0	12	14	16	.207	.282	.237	43	-11	0			.970	4	C-47	-0.3
1933	Cin-N	36	84	3	14	1	0	0	3	8	7	.167	.239	.179	21	-8	0			.981	4	C-34	-0.3
1934	Cin-N	25	54	4	10	0	0	0	4	4	7	.185	.241	.185	16	-6	0			1.000	3	C-24	-0.3
Total	13	477	1145	96	250	25	3	3	112	118	102	.218	.293	.253	45	-90	5	3		.973	33	C-401/1-3	-3.3

■ PHIL MANKOWSKI
Mankowski, Philip Anthony   b: 1/9/53, Buffalo, N.Y.   BL/TR, 6', 180 lbs.   Deb: 8/30/76

YEAR	TM/L	G	AB	R	H	2B	3B	HR	RBI	BB	SO	AVG	OBP	SLG	PRO+	BR/A	SB	CS	SBR	FA	FR	G/POS	TPR
1976	Det-A	24	85	9	23	2	1	1	4	4	8	.271	.303	.353	88	-1	0	0	0	.971	2	3-23	0.1
1977	Det-A	94	286	21	79	7	3	3	27	16	41	.276	.319	.353	79	-8	1	2	-1	.964	13	3-85/2-1	0.3
1978	Det-A	88	222	28	61	8	0	4	20	22	28	.275	.346	.365	97	-0	2	3	-1	.972	-1	3-80/D-1	-0.3
1979	Det-A	42	99	11	22	4	0	0	8	10	16	.222	.294	.263	50	-7	0	0	0	.963	-0	3-36/D-1	-0.7
1980	NY-N	8	12	1	2	1	0	0	1	2	4	.167	.286	.250	52	-1	0	0	0	.571	-1	/3-3	-0.2
1982	NY-N	13	35	2	8	1	0	0	4	1	6	.229	.250	.257	42	-3	0	1	-1	.957	-1	3-13	-0.4
Total	6	269	739	72	195	23	4	8	64	55	103	.264	.318	.338	79	-20	3	6	-3	.962	13	3-240/D-2,2-1	-1.2

■ CHARLIE MANLOVE
Manlove, Charles Henry Weeks "Chick"   b: 10/8/1862, Philadelphia, Pa.   d: 2/12/52, Altoona, Pa.   BR/TR, 5'9", 165 lbs.   Deb: 5/31/1884

YEAR	TM/L	G	AB	R	H	2B	3B	HR	RBI	BB	SO	AVG	OBP	SLG	PRO+	BR/A	SB	CS	SBR	FA	FR	G/POS	TPR
1884	Alt-U	2	7	1	3	0	0	0		0	0	.429	.429	.429	158	0				1.000	-1	/C-1,O-1	-0.1
	NY-N	3	10	0	0	0	0	0	0	0	4	.000	.000	.000	-98	-2				.833	-1	/C-3,O-1	-0.3
Total	1	5	17	1	3	0	0	0	0	0	4	.176	.176	.176	9	-2				.880	-2	/C-4,O-2	-0.4

■ GARTH MANN
Mann, Ben Garth "Red"   b: 11/16/15, Brandon, Tex.   d: 9/11/80, Italy, Tex.   BR/TR, 6', 155 lbs.   Deb: 5/14/44

YEAR	TM/L	G	AB	R	H	2B	3B	HR	RBI	BB	SO	AVG	OBP	SLG	PRO+	BR/A	SB	CS	SBR	FA	FR	G/POS	TPR
1944	Chi-N	1	0	1	0	0	0	0	0	0	0	—	—	—	—	0	0	0	0	.000	0	R	0.0

■ FRED MANN
Mann, Fred J.   b: 4/1/1858, Sutton, Vt.   d: 4/6/16, Springfield, Mass.   BL, 5'10.5", 178 lbs.   Deb: 5/1/1882

YEAR	TM/L	G	AB	R	H	2B	3B	HR	RBI	BB	SO	AVG	OBP	SLG	PRO+	BR/A	SB	CS	SBR	FA	FR	G/POS	TPR
1882	Wor-N	19	77	12	18	5	0	0	7	2	15	.234	.253	.299	74	-2				.703	-6	3-18/1-1	-0.8
	Phi-a	29	121	13	28	7	4	0		4		.231	.256	.355	93	-2				.798	-10	3-29	-1.1
1883	Col-a	96	394	61	98	18	13	1		18		.249	.282	.368	117	8				.854	-3	*O-82/1-9,3-6,S-1	0.4
1884	Col-a	99	366	70	101	12	18	7		25		.276	.341	.464	174	31				.857	-6	O-97/2-2	2.1
1885	Pit-a	99	391	60	99	17	6	0	41	31		.253	.318	.327	106	4				.908	-8	*O-116	-0.6
1886	Pit-a	116	440	85	110	16	14	2	60	45		.250	.335	.364	119	11	26			.878	-3	*O-116	0.4
1887	Cle-a	64	259	45	80	15	7	2	41	23		.309	.385	.444	135	13	25			.879	1	O-64	1.0
	Phi-a	55	229	42	63	14	6	0	32	15		.275	.336	.389	102	0	16			.916	-4	O-55	-0.4
Yr	119	488	87	143	29	13	2	73	38		.293	.362	.418	119	13	41			.896	-3	*O-119	0.6
Total	6	577	2277	388	597	104	68	12	181	163	15	.262	.323	.383	122	63	67			.881	-39	O-511/3-56,1-10,2S	1.0

■ JOHNNY MANN
Mann, John Leo   b: 2/4/1898, Fontanet, Ind.   d: 3/31/77, Terre Haute, Ind.   BR/TR, 5'11", 160 lbs.   Deb: 4/18/28

YEAR	TM/L	G	AB	R	H	2B	3B	HR	RBI	BB	SO	AVG	OBP	SLG	PRO+	BR/A	SB	CS	SBR	FA	FR	G/POS	TPR
1928	Chi-A	6	6	0	2	0	0	0	1	0	1	.333	.429	.333	104	0	0	0	0	1.000	0	/3-2	0.0

■ KELLY MANN
Mann, Kelly John   b: 8/17/67, Santa Monica, Cal.   BR/TR, 6'3", 215 lbs.   Deb: 9/4/89

YEAR	TM/L	G	AB	R	H	2B	3B	HR	RBI	BB	SO	AVG	OBP	SLG	PRO+	BR/A	SB	CS	SBR	FA	FR	G/POS	TPR
1989	Atl-N	7	24	1	5	2	0	0		0	6	.208	.240	.292	50	-2	0	0	0	1.000	2	/C-7	0.1
1990	Atl-N	11	28	2	4	1	0	1	2	0	6	.143	.143	.286	14	-3	0	0	0	1.000	-1	C-10	-0.4
Total	2	18	52	3	9	3	0	1	2	0	12	.173	.189	.288	30	-5	0	0	0	1.000	1	/C-17	-0.3

■ LES MANN
Mann, Leslie "Major"   b: 11/18/1893, Lincoln, Neb.   d: 1/14/62, Pasadena, Cal.   BR/TR, 5'9", 172 lbs.   Deb: 4/30/13

YEAR	TM/L	G	AB	R	H	2B	3B	HR	RBI	BB	SO	AVG	OBP	SLG	PRO+	BR/A	SB	CS	SBR	FA	FR	G/POS	TPR
1913	Bos-N	120	407	54	103	24	7	3	51	18	73	.253	.291	.369	86	-9	7			.960	-2	*O-120	-1.7
1914	*Bos-N	126	389	44	96	16	11	4	40	24	50	.247	.292	.375	99	-2	9			.952	13	*O-123	0.6
1915	Chi-F	135	470	74	144	12	19	4	58	36	40	.306	.357	.438	131	10	18			.969	5	*O-130/S-1	1.0
1916	Chi-N	127	415	46	113	13	9	2	29	19	31	.272	.307	.361	95	-3	11	7	-1	.972	-8	*O-115	-1.9
1917	Chi-N	117	444	63	121	19	10	1	44	27	46	.273	.316	.367	101	-0	14			.953	-1	*O-116	-0.7
1918	*Chi-N	129	489	69	141	27	7	2	55	38	45	.288	.342	.384	119	10	21			.961	-3	*O-129	0.0
1919	Chi-N	80	299	31	68	8	8	1	22	11	29	.227	.257	.318	72	-11	12			.982	2	O-78	-1.7
	Bos-N	40	145	15	41	6	4	3	20	9	14	.283	.329	.441	136	6	7			.929	3	O-40	0.6
Yr	120	444	46	109	14	12	4	42	20	43	.245	.281	.358	92	-5	19			.962	4	*O-118	-1.1
1920	Bos-N	115	424	48	117	8	3	32	38	42		.276	.341	.351	104	3	7	7	-2	.980	5	*O-110	-0.5
1921	StL-N	97	256	57	84	12	7	7	30	23	28	.328	.390	.512	140	14	5	5	-2	.969	-2	O-79	0.8
1922	StL-N	84	147	42	51	14	1	2	20	16	12	.347	.415	.497	141	9	0	1	-1	.978	-11	O-57	-0.5
1923	StL-N	38	89	20	33	5	2	5	11	9	5	.371	.434	.640	184	11	0	0	0	.979	-3	O-26	0.6
	Cin-N	8	1	1	0	0	0	0	0	0	0	.000	.000	.000	-99	-0	0	0	0	.000	0	H	0.0
Yr	46	90	21	33	5	2	5	11	9	5	.367	.429	.633	181	10	0	0	0	.979	-3	O-26	0.6
1924	Bos-N	32	102	13	28	7	4	0	10	8	10	.275	.333	.422	105	1	0	1	0	1.000	1	O-28	0.1
1925	Bos-N	60	184	27	63	11	4	2	19	5	11	.342	.373	.478	127	7	6	1	1	.992	-2	O-57	0.4
1926	Bos-N	50	129	23	39	8	2	1	20	9	9	.302	.348	.419	116	2	5			.966	-6	O-46	-0.6
1927	Bos-N	29	66	8	17	3	1	0	4	8	6	.258	.338	.333	87	-1	2			.955	-2	O-24	-0.4
	NY-N	29	67	13	22	4	1	2	10	8	7	.328	.400	.507	142	4	2			1.000	-4	O-22	-0.1
Yr	58	133	21	39	7	2	2	16	16	10	.293	.369	.421	116	3	4			.973	-6	O-46	-0.5
1928	NY-N	82	193	29	51	7	1	2	25	18	9	.264	.330	.342	76	-7	2			.952	-19	O-68	-2.8
Total	16	1498	4716	677	1332	203	106	44	503	324	464	.282	.332	.398	109	43	129	21		.966	-32	*O-1368/S-1	-6.9

■ JIM MANNING
Manning, James H.   b: 1/31/1862, Fall River, Mass.   d: 10/22/29, Edinburg, Tex.   BB/TR, 5'7", 157 lbs.   Deb: 5/16/1884   M

YEAR	TM/L	G	AB	R	H	2B	3B	HR	RBI	BB	SO	AVG	OBP	SLG	PRO+	BR/A	SB	CS	SBR	FA	FR	G/POS	TPR
1884	Bos-N	89	345	52	83	8	6	2	35	19	47	.241	.280	.316	88	-5				.878	1	O-73/S-9,2-9,3-3	-0.4
1885	Bos-N	84	306	34	63	8	9	2	27	19	36	.206	.252	.310	84	-5				.898	9	*O-83/S-1	0.2
	Det-N	20	78	15	21	4	0	1	9	4	10	.269	.305	.359	114	1				.802	-7	S-20	-0.5
Yr	104	384	49	84	12	9	3	36	23	46	.219	.263	.320	90	-4				.898	3	O-83,S-21	-0.3
1886	Det-N	26	97	14	18	2	3	0	7	6	10	.186	.233	.268	51	-6	7			.947	0	O-26/S-1	-0.7
1887	Det-N	13	52	5	10	1	0	0	5	3	6	.192	.276	.212	36	-4	3			.867	-4	O-10/S-3	-0.8
1889	KC-a	132	506	68	103	16	7	3	68	54	61	.204	.297	.281	61	-27	58			.927	-10	O-69,2-63/S-1,3-1	-3.0
Total	5	364	1384	188	298	39	25	8	149	107	168	.215	.278	.297	73	-46	68			.903	-11	O-261/2-72,S-35,3-4	-5.2

■ JACK MANNING
Manning, John E.   b: 12/20/1853, Braintree, Mass.   d: 8/15/29, Boston, Mass.   BR/TR, 5'8.5", 158 lbs.   Deb: 4/23/1873   M

YEAR	TM/L	G	AB	R	H	2B	3B	HR	RBI	BB	SO	AVG	OBP	SLG	PRO+	BR/A	SB	CS	SBR	FA	FR	G/POS	TPR
1873	Bos-n	32	159	29	43	9	2	1	22	1	11	.270	.275	.321	71	-7	1	0	0	.940	-4	1-29/O-5	-0.3
1874	Bal-n	42	174	32	61	8	2	0	18	2	2	.351	.358	.420	149	9	0	0	0	.831	-3	P-22,2-21/S-4,13O	0.0
	Har-n	1	5	1	1	0	0	0	0	0	0	.200	.200	.200	27	-0	0	0	0	.167	-2	/3-1	-0.2
Yr	43	179	33	62	8	2	0	18	2	2	.346	.354	.413	146	9	0	0	0	.831	-4	P-22,2-21/S-4,31OD	-0.2
1875	Bos-n	77	348	71	94	11	3	1	46	2	6	.270	.274	.328	104	1	5	5	-2	.802	-1	*O-65,P-27/1-3,3-1	-0.1
1876	Bos-N	70	288	52	76	13	0	2	25	7	5	.264	.281	.330	101	0				.777	-5	*O-56,P-34/S-1,2-1	-0.5
1877	Cin-N	57	252	47	80	16	1	0	36	5	6	.317	.331	.437	157	16				.742	-13	S-26,1-17,OP/2M	0.2

YEAR	TM/L	G	AB	R	H	2B	3B	HR	RBI	BB	SO	AVG	OBP	SLG	PRO+	BR/A	SB	CS	SBR	FA	FR	G/POS	TPR
1878	Bos-N	60	248	41	63	10	1	0	23	10	16	.254	.283	.302	86	-4				.753	-13	*O-59/P-3	-1.9
1880	Cin-N	48	190	20	41	6	3	2	17	7	15	.216	.244	.311	87	-2				.798	-3	O-47/1-1	-0.6
1881	Buf-N	1	1	0	0	0	0	0	0	0	0	.000	.000	.000	-99	-0				1.000	0	/O-1	0.0
1883	Phi-N	98	420	60	112	31	5	0	37	20	37	.267	.300	.364	110	6				.853	10	*O-98	1.3
1884	Phi-N	104	424	71	115	29	4	5	52	40	67	.271	.334	.394	134	18				.847	-1	*O-104	1.3
1885	Phi-N	107	445	61	114	24	4	3	40	37	27	.256	.313	.348	116	9				.896	-6	*O-107	0.0
1886	Bal-a	137	556	78	124	18	7	1	45	50		.223	.291	.286	83	-10	24			.887	-10	*O-137	-2.0
Total	3 n	152	686	133	199	25	6	1	86	5	22	.290	.295	.348	106	3	6	5	-1	.785	-5	O-71,P-49,12S3	-0.6
Total	9	682	2824	430	725	147	31	13	275	176	173	.257	.301	.345	108	33	24			.844	-40	O-621/P-47,S-27,12	-2.2

■ **RICK MANNING**   Manning, Richard Eugene b: 9/2/54, Niagara Falls, N.Y.   BL/TR, 6′1″, 180 lbs.   Deb: 5/23/75

YEAR	TM/L	G	AB	R	H	2B	3B	HR	RBI	BB	SO	AVG	OBP	SLG	PRO+	BR/A	SB	CS	SBR	FA	FR	G/POS	TPR
1975	Cle-A	120	480	69	137	16	5	3	35	44	62	.285	.348	.358	100	1	19	11	-1	.974	13	*O-118/D-1	0.8
1976	Cle-A	138	552	73	161	24	7	6	43	41	75	.292	.341	.393	116	10	16	10	-1	.987	8	*O-136	1.2
1977	Cle-A	68	252	33	57	7	3	5	18	21	35	.226	.286	.337	71	-10	9	5	-0	.990	5	O-68	-0.8
1978	Cle-A	148	566	65	149	27	3	3	50	38	62	.263	.311	.337	83	-13	12	12	-4	.995	5	*O-144	-1.8
1979	Cle-A	144	560	67	145	12	2	3	51	55	48	.259	.326	.350	71	-21	30	8	4	.986	15	*O-141/D-1	-0.8
1980	Cle-A	140	471	55	110	17	4	3	52	63	66	.234	.326	.306	74	-15	12	6	0	.990	8	*O-139	-1.3
1981	Cle-A	103	360	47	88	15	3	4	33	40	57	.244	.320	.336	90	-4	25	3	6	.987	13	*O-103	1.2
1982	Cle-A	152	562	71	152	18	2	8	44	54	60	.270	.334	.352	89	-7	12	8	-1	.978	5	*O-152	-0.7
1983	Cle-A	50	194	20	54	6	0	1	10	12	22	.278	.320	.325	75	-6	7	3	0	.987	3	O-50	-0.4
	Mil-A	108	375	40	86	14	4	3	33	26	40	.229	.281	.312	68	-17	11	2	2	.991	6	*O-108	-1.2
	Yr	158	569	60	140	20	4	4	43	38	62	.246	.294	.316	71	-23	18	5	2	.990	9	*O-158	-1.6
1984	Mil-A	119	341	53	85	10	5	7	31	34	32	.249	.319	.370	94	-3	5	7	-3	.987	-14	*O-114/D-1	-2.2
1985	Mil-A	79	216	19	47	9	1	2	18	14	19	.218	.265	.296	54	-14	1	0	0	.976	-6	O-74/D-2	-2.1
1986	Mil-A	89	205	31	52	7	3	8	27	17	20	.254	.314	.434	98	-1	5	3	-0	.988	-5	O-83/D-5	-0.8
1987	Mil-A	97	114	21	26	7	1	0	13	12	18	.228	.302	.307	60	-6	4	0	1	.958	-19	O-78/D-2	-2.4
Total	13	1555	5248	664	1349	189	43	56	458	471	616	.257	.319	.341	84	-108	168	78	4	.985	40	*O-1508/D-12	-11.3

■ **TIM MANNING**   Manning, Timothy Edward b: 12/3/1853, Henley-On-The- Thames, England d: 6/11/34, Oak Park, Ill.   BR/TR, 5′10″, 170 lbs.   Deb: 5/1/1882

YEAR	TM/L	G	AB	R	H	2B	3B	HR	RBI	BB	SO	AVG	OBP	SLG	PRO+	BR/A	SB	CS	SBR	FA	FR	G/POS	TPR
1882	Pro-N	21	76	7	8	0	0	0	8	5	13	.105	.160	.105	-13	-9				.787	-10	S-17/C-4	-1.8
1883	Bal-a	35	121	23	26	5	0	0		5	14	.215	.296	.256	77	-3				.913	3	2-35	0.1
1884	Bal-a	91	341	49	70	14	5	2		26		.205	.275	.293	82	-6				.907	-2	*2-91	-0.6
1885	Bal-a	43	157	17	32	8	1	0	16	10		.204	.265	.268	70	-5				.919	3	2-41/3-3	-0.1
	Pro-N	10	35	3	2	1	0	0		1	11	.057	.083	.086	-47	-6				.854	1	S-10	-0.8
Total	4	200	730	99	138	28	6	2	24	56	24	.189	.256	.252	63	-29				.911	-9	2-167/S-27,C-4,3-3	-3.2

■ **DON MANNO**   Manno, Donald D. b: 5/4/15, Williamsport, Pa. d: 3/11/95, Williamsport, Pa.   BR/TR, 6′1″, 190 lbs.   Deb: 9/22/40

YEAR	TM/L	G	AB	R	H	2B	3B	HR	RBI	BB	SO	AVG	OBP	SLG	PRO+	BR/A	SB	CS	SBR	FA	FR	G/POS	TPR
1940	Bos-N	3	7	1	2	0	0	1	4	0	2	.286	.286	.714	177	1	0			1.000	0	/O-2	0.1
1941	Bos-N	22	30	2	5	1	0	0	4	3	7	.167	.242	.200	27	-3	0			1.000	-1	/O-5,3-3,1-1	-0.5
Total	2	25	37	3	7	1	0	1	8	3	9	.189	.250	.297	56	-2	0			1.000	-1	/O-7,3-3,1-1	-0.4

■ **FRED MANRIQUE**   Manrique, Fred Eloy (Reyes) b: 11/5/61, Edo Bolivar, Venez.   BR/TR, 6′1″, 175 lbs.   Deb: 8/23/81

YEAR	TM/L	G	AB	R	H	2B	3B	HR	RBI	BB	SO	AVG	OBP	SLG	PRO+	BR/A	SB	CS	SBR	FA	FR	G/POS	TPR
1981	Tor-A	14	28	1	4	0	0	0	1	0	12	.143	.172	.143	-8	-4	0	1	-1	.949	3	S-11/3-2,D-1	-0.1
1984	Tor-A	10	9	0	3	0	0	0	1	0	1	.333	.333	.333	82	-0	0	0	0	.938	3	/2-9,D-1	0.2
1985	Mon-N	9	13	5	4	1	1	1	1	1	3	.308	.357	.769	219	2	0	0	0	1.000	3	/2-2,S-2,3-1	0.4
1986	StL-N	13	17	2	3	0	0	1	1	1	1	.176	.222	.353	57	-1	1	0	0	1.000	-2	/3-4,2-1	-0.2
1987	Chi-A	115	298	30	77	13	3	4	29	19	69	.258	.305	.362	74	-11	5	3	-0	.984	19	2-92,S-23/D-5	1.1
1988	Chi-A	140	345	43	81	10	6	5	37	21	54	.235	.285	.342	75	-12	6	5	-1	.985	12	*2-129,S-12/D-1	0.4
1989	Chi-A	65	187	23	56	13	1	2	30	9	30	.299	.335	.412	112	3	0	4	-2	.961	-5	2-57/S-2,3-1	-0.3
	Tex-A	54	191	23	55	12	0	2	22	9	33	.288	.320	.382	96	-1	4	1	1	.963	-11	S-37,2-17/3-6,D-1	-0.9
	Yr	119	378	46	111	25	1	4	52	17	63	.294	.327	.397	104	1	4	5	-2	.952	-16	2-74,S-39/3-7,D-1	-1.2
1990	Min-A	69	228	22	54	10	0	5	29	4	35	.237	.256	.346	63	-12	2	0	1	.974	-10	2-67/D-1	-2.0
1991	Oak-A	9	2	2	3	0	0	0	0	0	2	.143	.217	.143	-2	-3	0	0	0	.955	-0	/S-7,2-2	-0.3
Total	9	498	1337	151	340	59	11	20	151	65	239	.254	.293	.360	79	-40	18	14	-3	.976	11	2-376/S-94,3-14,D	-1.7

■ **JOHN MANSELL**   Mansell, John b: 1861, Auburn, N.Y. d: 2/20/25, Romulus, N.Y.   BL, 5′10″, 168 lbs.   Deb: 5/9/1882   F

YEAR	TM/L	G	AB	R	H	2B	3B	HR	RBI	BB	SO	AVG	OBP	SLG	PRO+	BR/A	SB	CS	SBR	FA	FR	G/POS	TPR
1882	Phi-a	31	126	17	30	3	1	0	17	4		.238	.262	.278	73	-4				.791	-4	O-31	-0.7

■ **MIKE MANSELL**   Mansell, Michael R. b: 1/15/1858, Auburn, N.Y. d: 12/4/02, Auburn, N.Y.   BL, 5′11″, 175 lbs.   Deb: 5/1/1879   F

YEAR	TM/L	G	AB	R	H	2B	3B	HR	RBI	BB	SO	AVG	OBP	SLG	PRO+	BR/A	SB	CS	SBR	FA	FR	G/POS	TPR
1879	Syr-N	67	242	24	52	4	2	1	13	5	45	.215	.231	.260	69	-7				.881	15	*O-67	0.5
1880	Cin-N	53	187	22	36	6	2	2	12	4	37	.193	.209	.278	64	-7				.865	12	O-53	0.4
1882	Pit-a	79	347	59	96	18	16	2		7		.277	.291	.438	150	17				.829	3	*O-79	1.8
1883	Pit-a	96	412	90	106	12	13	3		25		.257	.300	.371	120	10				.883	4	*O-96	1.1
1884	Pit-a	27	100	15	14	0	3	1		7		.140	.204	.230	41	-6				.796	-1	O-27	-0.8
	Phi-a	20	70	6	14	1	1	0		5		.200	.253	.243	59	-3				.762	-1	O-20	-0.4
	Ric-a	29	113	21	34	2	5	0		8		.301	.363	.407	153	7				.763	-5	O-29	0.1
	Yr	76	283	42	62	3	9	1		20		.219	.280	.364	89	-3				.775	-7	O-76	-1.1
Total	5	371	1471	237	352	43	42	9	25	61	82	.239	.271	.344	106	11				.854	27	O-371	2.7

■ **TOM MANSELL**   Mansell, Thomas E. "Brick" b: 1/1/1855, Auburn, N.Y. d: 10/6/34, Auburn, N.Y.   BL/TR, 5′8″, 160 lbs.   Deb: 5/1/1879   F

YEAR	TM/L	G	AB	R	H	2B	3B	HR	RBI	BB	SO	AVG	OBP	SLG	PRO+	BR/A	SB	CS	SBR	FA	FR	G/POS	TPR
1879	Tro-N	40	177	29	43	6	1	0	11	3	9	.243	.256	.277	81	-3				.742	-6	O-40	-1.1
	Syr-N	1	4	0	1	0	0	0	0	0	0	.250	.250	.250	74	-0				1.000	-0	/O-1	0.0
	Yr	41	181	29	44	6	1	0	11	3	9	.243	.255	.276	81	-3				.747	-6	O-41	-1.1
1883	Det-N	34	131	22	29	4	1	0	10	8	13	.221	.266	.267	66	-5				.758	-2	O-34/P-1	-0.6
	StL-a	28	112	23	45	8	1	0	24	7		.402	.437	.491	188	10				.786	-6	O-28	0.4
1884	Cin-a	65	266	49	66	4	6	0	23	15		.248	.301	.308	94	-2				.752	-11	O-65	-1.3
	Col-a	23	77	9	15	7	0	0	6	6		.195	.262	.286	85	-1				.667	-4	O-23	-0.5
	Yr	88	343	58	81	11	6	0	29	21		.236	.292	.303	93	-2				.739	-15	O-88	-1.8
Total	3	191	767	132	199	23	11	0	74	39	22	.259	.300	.318	100	-0				.751	-28	O-191/P-1	-3.1

■ **FELIX MANTILLA**   Mantilla, Felix (Lamela) b: 7/29/34, Isabela, P.R.   BR/TR, 6′, 160 lbs.   Deb: 6/21/56

YEAR	TM/L	G	AB	R	H	2B	3B	HR	RBI	BB	SO	AVG	OBP	SLG	PRO+	BR/A	SB	CS	SBR	FA	FR	G/POS	TPR
1956	Mil-N	35	53	9	15	1	1	0	8	3	8	.283	.309	.340	79	-2	0	1	-1	1.000	9	S-15/3-3	0.8
1957	*Mil-N	71	182	28	43	9	1	4	21	14	34	.236	.298	.363	82	-5	2	0	1	.931	6	S-35,2-13/3-7,0-1	0.5
1958	*Mil-N	85	226	37	50	5	1	7	19	20	20	.221	.285	.345	72	-10	2	2	0	.987	-6	O-43,2-21/S-5,3-2	-1.6
1959	Mil-N	103	251	26	54	9	3	3	19	16	31	.215	.268	.271	48	-19	6	1	0	.970	4	2-60,S-23/3-9,O-7	-1.3
1960	Mil-N	63	148	21	38	7	0	3	11	7	16	.257	.295	.365	86	-3	3	1	0	.956	-12	2-26,S-25/O-8	-1.3
1961	Mil-N	45	93	13	20	3	0	1	5	10	16	.215	.298	.280	58	-1	1	1	-0	.933	-1	S-19,2-10,O-10/3-6	-0.9
1962	NY-N	141	466	54	128	17	4	11	59	37	51	.275	.335	.399	94	-4	3	1	0	.948	-7	3-95,S-25,2-14	-0.7
1963	Bos-A	66	178	27	56	8	0	6	15	20	14	.315	.384	.461	131	8	0	1	-0	.965	-5	S-27,O-11/2-5	0.5
1964	Bos-A	133	425	69	123	20	1	30	64	41	46	.289	.357	.553	142	23	0	1	-1	.984	-6	2-82,2-45/3-7,S-6	2.0
1965	Bos-A★	150	534	60	147	17	2	18	92	79	84	.275	.377	.416	118	15	7	3	0	.976	-22	*2-123,O-27/1-2	0.3
1966	Hou-N	77	151	16	33	5	0	6	22	11	32	.219	.280	.371	85	-4	2	0	1	.990	-2	1-14,3-14/2-9,0-1	-0.6
Total	11	969	2707	360	707	97	10	89	330	256	352	.261	.331	.403	100	-6	27	10	2	.977	-44	2-326,S-180,03/1	-1.9

■ **MICKEY MANTLE**   Mantle, Mickey Charles "The Commerce Comet" b: 10/20/31, Spavinaw, Okla. d: 8/13/95, Dallas, Tex.   BB/TR, 5′11″, 198 lbs.   Deb: 4/17/51   CH

YEAR	TM/L	G	AB	R	H	2B	3B	HR	RBI	BB	SO	AVG	OBP	SLG	PRO+	BR/A	SB	CS	SBR	FA	FR	G/POS	TPR
1951	*NY-A	96	341	61	91	11	5	13	65	43	74	.267	.349	.443	117	7	8	7	-2	.959	-6	O-86	-0.3
1952	*NY-A☆	142	549	94	171	37	7	23	87	75	111	.311	.394	.530	166	47	4	1	1	.968	5	*O-141/3-1	4.6
1953	*NY-A★	127	461	105	136	24	3	21	92	79	90	.295	.398	.497	145	30	8	4	1	.982	1	*O-121/S-1	2.7
1954	*NY-A★	146	543	129	163	17	12	27	102	102	107	.300	.411	.525	160	47	5	2	1	.975	-1	*O-144/S-4,2-1	4.1
1955	*NY-A★	147	517	121	158	25	11	37	99	113	97	.306	.433	.611	181	61	8	1	2	.995	8	*O-145/S-2	6.3
1956	*NY-A★	150	533	132	188	22	5	52	130	112	99	.353	.467	.705	213	89	10	1	2	.990	8	*O-144	8.7

YEAR	TM/L	G	AB	R	H	2B	3B	HR	RBI	BB	SO	AVG	OBP	SLG	PRO+	BR/A	SB	CS	SBR	FA	FR	G/POS	TPR
1957	*NY-A★	144	474	**121**	173	28	6	34	94	**146**	75	.365	.515	.665	223	**91**	16	3	3	.979	0	*O-139	**8.6**
1958	*NY-A★	150	519	**127**	158	21	1	**42**	97	**129**	120	.304	.445	.592	**189**	**69**	18	3	4	.977	-0	*O-150	**6.5**
1959	NY-A★	144	541	104	154	23	4	31	75	93	126	.285	.392	.514	152	40	21	3	5	**.995**	8	*O-143	**4.5**
1960	*NY-A★	153	527	**119**	145	17	6	**40**	94	111	125	.275	.402	.558	166	51	14	3	2	.991	-1	*O-150	**4.4**
1961	*NY-A★	153	514	**132**	163	16	6	54	128	**126**	112	.317	.452	**.687**	210	84	12	1	3	.983	4	*O-150	**8.0**
1962	*NY-A★	123	377	96	121	15	1	30	89	**122**	78	.321	**.488**	**.605**	198	61	9	0	3	.978	-6	*O-117	**5.0**
1963	*NY-A†	65	172	40	54	8	0	15	35	40	32	.314	.443	.622	197	24	2	1	0	.990	-2	O-52	2.0
1964	*NY-A★	143	465	92	141	25	2	35	111	99	102	.303	**.426**	.591	177	51	6	3	0	.978	-13	*O-132	3.3
1965	NY-A†	122	361	44	92	12	1	19	46	73	76	.255	.380	.452	136	19	4	1	1	.966	-4	*O-108	1.2
1966	NY-A	108	333	40	96	12	1	23	56	57	76	.288	.392	.538	171	31	1	1	-0	1.000	-7	O-97	2.1
1967	NY-A★	144	440	63	108	17	0	22	55	107	113	.245	.394	.434	150	32	1	1	1	.993	-5	*1-131	2.7
1968	NY-A★	144	435	57	103	14	1	18	54	106	97	.237	.387	.398	143	28	6	2	1	.988	-3	*1-131	1.7
Total	18	2401	8102	1677	2415	344	72	536	1509	1733	1710	.298	.423	.557	173	863	153	38	23	.982	-9	*O-2019,1-262/S23	76.1

■ JEFF MANTO
Manto, Jeffrey Paul b: 8/23/64, Bristol, Pa. BR/TR, 6'3", 210 lbs. Deb: 6/7/90

YEAR	TM/L	G	AB	R	H	2B	3B	HR	RBI	BB	SO	AVG	OBP	SLG	PRO+	BR/A	SB	CS	SBR	FA	FR	G/POS	TPR
1990	Cle-A	30	76	12	17	5	1	2	14	21	18	.224	.392	.395	121	3	0	1	-1	.990	1	1-25/3-5	0.2
1991	Cle-A	47	128	15	27	7	0	2	13	14	22	.211	.308	.313	72	-5	2	0	1	.929	1	3-32,1-14/C-5,O-1	-0.3
1993	Phi-N	8	18	0	1	0	0	0	0	0	3	.056	.105	.056	-56	-4	0	0	0	1.000	-0	/3-6,S-1	-0.4
1995	Bal-A	89	254	31	65	9	0	17	38	24	69	.256	.325	.492	107	2	0	3	-2	.959	-2	3-69,D-13/1-4	-0.3
1996	Bos-A	10	30	5	8	3	1	2	4	3	6	.267	.353	.633	138	2	0	0	-1	.963	0	/2-4,S-4	0.5
	Sea-A	21	54	7	10	3	0	1	4	9	12	.185	.302	.296	52	-1	1	0	-1	.971	0	3-16/O-1,D-2	-0.4
	Bos-A	12	18	3	2	0	0	0	2	5	6	.111	.304	.111	11	-2	0	0	0	.960	4	3-10/1-1	0.1
	Yr	43	102	15	20	6	1	3	10	17	24	.196	.317	.363	70	-5	1	0	-1	.967	4	3-26/2-4,S-4,DO1	0.2
Total	5	217	578	73	130	27	2	24	75	76	136	.225	.323	.403	90	-9	2	5	-2	.955	9	3-138/1-44,DSC2O	-0.6

■ CHUCK MANUEL
Manuel, Charles Fuqua b: 1/4/44, Northfork, W.Va. BL/TR, 6'4", 200 lbs. Deb: 4/8/69 C

YEAR	TM/L	G	AB	R	H	2B	3B	HR	RBI	BB	SO	AVG	OBP	SLG	PRO+	BR/A	SB	CS	SBR	FA	FR	G/POS	TPR
1969	*Min-A	83	164	14	34	6	0	2	24	28	33	.207	.323	.280	69	-6	1	0	0	.967	-6	O-46	-1.4
1970	*Min-A	59	64	4	12	0	0	1	7	6	17	.188	.268	.234	39	-5	0	0	0	1.000	-3	O-11	-0.8
1971	Min-A	18	16	1	2	1	0	0	1	1	8	.125	.176	.188	3	-2	0	0	0	.000	-0	/O-1	-0.3
1972	Min-A	63	122	6	25	5	0	1	4	8	16	.205	.236	.270	48	-8	0	0	0	.977	-1	O-28	-1.1
1974	LA-N	4	3	0	1	0	0	0	1	0	0	.333	.500	.333	142	0	0	0	0	.000	0	H	0.0
1975	LA-N	15	15	0	2	0	0	0	2	0	3	.133	.133	.133	-27	-3	0	0	0	.000	0	H	-0.3
Total	6	242	384	25	76	12	0	4	43	40	77	.198	.277	.260	52	-24	1	0	0	.973	-9	/O-86	-3.9

■ JERRY MANUEL
Manuel, Jerry b: 12/23/53, Hahira, Ga. BB/TR, 6', 165 lbs. Deb: 9/18/75 C

YEAR	TM/L	G	AB	R	H	2B	3B	HR	RBI	BB	SO	AVG	OBP	SLG	PRO+	BR/A	SB	CS	SBR	FA	FR	G/POS	TPR
1975	Det-A	6	18	0	1	0	0	0	0	4	4	.056	.056	.056	-66	-4	0	0	0	.944	3	/2-6	-0.1
1976	Det-A	54	43	4	6	1	0	0	2	3	9	.140	.213	.163	11	-5	1	0	0	.921	10	2-47/S-4,D-1	0.7
1980	Mon-N	7	6	0	0	0	0	0	0	0	2	.000	.000	.000	-99	-2	0	0	0	.941	3	/S-7	0.1
1981	*Mon-N	27	55	10	11	5	0	3	10	6	11	.200	.279	.455	104	-0	0	0	0	.987	-2	2-23/S-2	0.0
1982	SD-N	2	5	0	1	0	1	0	1	1	0	.200	.333	.600	165	0	0	0	0	1.000	0	/2-1,S-1,3-1	-0.1
Total	5	96	127	14	19	6	1	3	13	10	26	.150	.217	.283	42	-10	1	0	0	.949	14	/2-77,S-14,3-1,D-1	0.6

■ FRANK MANUSH
Manush, Frank Benjamin b: 9/18/1883, Tuscumbia, Ala. d: 1/5/65, Laguna Beach, Cal. BR/TR, 5'10.5", 175 lbs. Deb: 8/31/08 F

YEAR	TM/L	G	AB	R	H	2B	3B	HR	RBI	BB	SO	AVG	OBP	SLG	PRO+	BR/A	SB	CS	SBR	FA	FR	G/POS	TPR
1908	Phi-A	23	77	6	12	2	1	0	0	2		.156	.188	.208	27	-6	2			.933	-5	3-20/2-2	-1.2

■ HEINIE MANUSH
Manush, Henry Emmett b: 7/20/01, Tuscumbia, Ala. d: 5/12/71, Sarasota, Fla. BL/TL, 6'1", 200 lbs. Deb: 4/20/23 FCH

YEAR	TM/L	G	AB	R	H	2B	3B	HR	RBI	BB	SO	AVG	OBP	SLG	PRO+	BR/A	SB	CS	SBR	FA	FR	G/POS	TPR
1923	Det-A	109	308	59	103	20	5	4	54	20	21	.334	.406	.471	133	15	3	5	-2	.953	-5	O-79	0.3
1924	Det-A	120	422	83	122	24	8	9	68	27	30	.289	.355	.448	108	3	14	5	1	.979	-6	*O-106/1-1	-0.8
1925	Det-A	99	278	46	84	14	3	5	47	24	21	.302	.362	.428	101	0	8	3	1	.982	-5	O-73	-0.8
1926	Det-A	136	498	95	188	35	8	14	86	31	28	**.378**	.421	.564	153	37	11	5	0	.967	-4	*O-120	2.4
1927	Det-A	151	593	102	177	31	18	6	90	47	29	.298	.354	.442	104	2	12	8	-1	.971	-3	*O-149	-1.1
1928	StL-A	154	638	104	**241**	**47**	20	13	108	39	14	.378	.414	.575	153	46	17	5	2	.992	2	*O-154	3.8
1929	StL-A	142	574	85	204	**45**	10	6	81	43	24	.355	.401	.500	126	22	9	8	-2	.987	-2	*O-141	0.7
1930	StL-A	49	198	26	65	16	4	2	29	5	7	.328	.345	.480	103	0	3	1	0	.990	5	O-48	-0.1
	Was-A	88	356	74	129	33	8	7	65	26	17	.362	.406	.559	141	22	4	3	-1	.988	-2	O-86	1.2
	Yr	137	554	100	194	49	12	9	94	31	24	.350	.385	.531	128	22	7	4	-0	.989	1	*O-134	1.1
1931	Was-A	146	616	110	189	41	11	6	70	36	25	.307	.351	.438	106	4	3	3	-1	.977	-11	*O-143	-1.6
1932	Was-A	149	625	121	214	41	14	14	116	36	29	.342	.383	.520	133	29	7	2	1	.988	-0	*O-150	1.8
1933	*Was-A	153	658	115	**221**	32	**17**	5	95	36	18	.336	.372	.459	120	20	6	4	1	.982	-2	*O-150	0.7
1934	Was-A★	137	556	88	194	42	11	11	89	36	21	.349	.392	.523	140	30	7	3	0	.980	-1	*O-131	2.3
1935	Was-A	119	479	68	131	26	9	4	56	35	17	.273	.328	.390	88	-10	2	0	1	.985	3	*O-111	-1.0
1936	Bos-A	82	313	43	91	15	5	0	45	17	11	.291	.329	.371	69	-16	1	3	-0	.966	-8	O-72	-2.5
1937	Bro-N	132	466	57	155	25	7	4	73	40	24	.333	.389	.442	123	16	6			.970	-12	*O-123	-0.1
1938	Bro-N	17	51	9	12	3	1	0	6	5	4	.235	.304	.333	73	-2	1			1.000	1	O-12	-0.1
	Pit-N	15	13	2	4	1	1	0	4	2	0	.308	.400	.538	155	1	0			.000	0	H	0.1
	Yr	32	64	11	16	4	2	0	10	7	4	.250	.324	.375	90	-1	1			1.000	1	O-12	0.0
1939	Pit-N	10	12	0	0	0	0	0	1	1	1	.000	.077	.000	-79	-2	0			1.000	-0	/O-1	-0.3
Total	17	2008	7654	1287	2524	491	160	110	1183	506	345	.330	.377	.479	121	214	114	58		.979	-50	*O-1845/1-1	5.0

■ KIRT MANWARING
Manwaring, Kirt Dean b: 7/15/65, Elmira, N.Y. BR/TR, 5'11", 185 lbs. Deb: 9/15/87

YEAR	TM/L	G	AB	R	H	2B	3B	HR	RBI	BB	SO	AVG	OBP	SLG	PRO+	BR/A	SB	CS	SBR	FA	FR	G/POS	TPR
1987	SF-N	6	7	0	1	0	0	0	0	1	2	.143	.250	.143	8	-1	0	0	0	.909	-1	/C-6	-0.2
1988	SF-N	40	116	12	29	7	0	1	15	2	21	.250	.281	.336	80	-3	0	1	-1	.979	-2	C-40	-0.4
1989	*SF-N	85	200	14	42	4	2	0	18	11	28	.210	.265	.250	49	-13	2	1	0	.982	-0	C-81	-1.1
1990	SF-N	8	13	0	2	0	1	0	1	0	3	.154	.154	.308	25	-1	0	0	0	1.000	1	/C-8	0.1
1991	SF-N	67	178	16	40	9	0	0	19	9	24	.225	.274	.275	57	-10	1	1	-0	.988	1	C-67	-0.6
1992	SF-N	109	349	24	85	10	5	4	26	29	42	.244	.311	.335	88	-6	2	1	0	.994	1	*C-108	0.0
1993	SF-N	130	432	48	119	15	1	5	49	41	76	.275	.347	.350	90	-5	1	3	-2	**.998**	1	*C-130	0.0
1994	SF-N	97	316	30	79	17	1	1	29	25	50	.250	.311	.320	68	-15	1	1	-0	.993	5	C-97	-0.4
1995	SF-N	118	379	21	95	15	2	4	36	27	72	.251	.317	.332	74	-14	1	0	0	.990	-13	*C-118	-1.9
1996	SF-N	49	145	9	34	6	0	1	14	16	24	.234	.323	.297	68	-6	0	1	-1	.993	1	C-49	-0.3
	Hou-N	37	82	5	18	3	0	0	4	3	16	.220	.264	.256	42	-7	0	0	0	.995	5	C-37	0.0
	Yr	86	227	14	52	9	0	1	18	19	40	.229	.303	.282	59	-13	0	1	-1	.994	6	C-86	-0.3
Total	10	746	2217	179	544	86	12	16	211	163	355	.245	.309	.317	73	-82	8	9	-3	.991	-2	C-741	-4.8

■ CLIFF MAPES
Mapes, Clifford Franklin b: 3/13/22, Sutherland, Neb. BL/TR, 6'3", 205 lbs. Deb: 4/20/48

YEAR	TM/L	G	AB	R	H	2B	3B	HR	RBI	BB	SO	AVG	OBP	SLG	PRO+	BR/A	SB	CS	SBR	FA	FR	G/POS	TPR
1948	NY-A	53	88	19	22	11	1	1	12	6	13	.250	.298	.432	94	-2	1	1	-0	.958	1	O-21	-0.1
1949	*NY-A	111	304	56	75	13	3	7	38	58	50	.247	.369	.378	98	0	6	0	**2**	.976	3	*O-108	0.0
1950	*NY-A	108	356	60	88	14	6	12	61	47	61	.247	.338	.421	96	-3	1	0	0	.950	-7	*O-102	-1.7
1951	NY-A	45	51	6	11	3	1	2	8	4	14	.216	.273	.431	92	-1	0	0	-1	1.000	-9	O-34	-1.0
	StL-A	56	201	32	55	7	2	7	30	26	33	.274	.360	.433	110	3	1	0	0	.983	-1	O-53	-0.1
	Yr	101	252	38	66	10	3	9	38	30	47	.262	.343	.433	109	2	1	0	-1	.986	-10	O-87	-1.1
1952	Det-A	86	193	26	38	7	0	9	23	27	42	.197	.295	.373	84	-5	0	1	-1	.967	-10	O-63	-1.8
Total	5	459	1193	199	289	55	13	38	172	168	213	.242	.338	.406	97	-8	9	2	-0	.969	-23	O-381	-4.7

■ HOWARD MAPLE
Maple, Howard Albert "Mape" b: 7/20/03, Adrian, Mo. d: 11/9/70, Portland, Ore. BL/TR, 5'7", 175 lbs. Deb: 5/19/32

YEAR	TM/L	G	AB	R	H	2B	3B	HR	RBI	BB	SO	AVG	OBP	SLG	PRO+	BR/A	SB	CS	SBR	FA	FR	G/POS	TPR
1932	Was-A	44	41	6	10	0	0	0	7	7	7	.244	.367	.293	74	-1	0			1.000	-3	C-41	-0.3

■ GEORGE MAPPES
Mappes, George Richard "Dick" b: 12/25/1865, St.Louis, Mo. d: 2/20/34, St.Louis, Mo. Deb: 9/23/1885

YEAR	TM/L	G	AB	R	H	2B	3B	HR	RBI	BB	SO	AVG	OBP	SLG	PRO+	BR/A	SB	CS	SBR	FA	FR	G/POS	TPR
1885	Bal-a	6	19	2	4	0	0	0	0	1	5	.211	.300	.316	79	-0				.875	-2	/2-6	-0.2
1886	StL-N	6	14	1	2	0	0	0	0	1	0	.143	.200	.143	6	-2	0			1.000	-1	/C-3,3-2,2-1	-0.2
Total	2	12	33	3	6	0	0	0	0	2	5	.182	.229	.242	48	-2	0			.848	-3	/2-7,C-3,3-2	-0.4

YEAR	TM/L	G	AB	R	H	2B	3B	HR	RBI	BB	SO	AVG	OBP	SLG	PRO+	BR/A	SB	CS	SBR	FA	FR	G/POS	TPR

■ RABBIT MARANVILLE   Maranville, Walter James Vincent   b: 11/11/1891, Springfield, Mass.   d: 1/5/54, New York, N.Y.   BR/TR, 5'5", 155 lbs.   Deb: 9/10/12   MH

1912	Bos-N	26	86	8	18	2	0	0	8	9	14	.209	.292	.233	44	-6	1			.929	5	S-26	0.1
1913	Bos-N	143	571	68	141	13	8	2	48	68	62	.247	.330	.308	81	-12	25			.949	15	*S-143	1.7
1914	*Bos-N	156	586	74	144	23	6	4	78	45	56	.246	.306	.326	88	-9	28			.938	52	*S-156	5.9
1915	Bos-N	149	509	51	124	23	6	2	43	45	65	.244	.308	.324	96	-3	18	12	-2	.941	21	*S-149	3.0
1916	Bos-N	155	604	79	142	16	13	4	38	50	69	.235	.296	.325	94	-5	32	15	1	.947	22	*S-155	2.9
1917	Bos-N	142	561	69	146	19	13	3	43	40	47	.260	.312	.357	111	6	27			.947	14	*S-142	3.0
1918	Bos-N	11	38	3	12	0	1	0	3	4	0	.316	.381	.368	134	2	0			.932	2	S-11	0.4
1919	Bos-N	131	480	44	128	18	10	5	43	36	23	.267	.319	.377	113	7	12			.941	29	*S-131	4.7
1920	Bos-N	134	493	48	131	19	15	1	43	28	24	.266	.305	.371	98	-3	14	11	-2	.948	14	*S-133	2.1
1921	Pit-N	153	612	90	180	25	12	1	70	47	38	.294	.347	.379	90	-8	25	12	0	.962	-11	*S-153	-0.4
1922	Pit-N	155	672	115	198	26	15	0	63	61	43	.295	.355	.378	88	-11	24	13	-1	.961	7	*S-138,2-18	1.0
1923	Pit-N	141	581	78	161	19	9	1	41	42	34	.277	.327	.346	76	-20	14	11	-2	.965	12	*S-141	0.4
1924	Pit-N	152	594	62	158	33	20	2	71	35	53	.266	.307	.399	86	-13	18	14	-3	.973	4	*2-152	-1.0
1925	Chi-N	75	266	37	62	10	3	0	23	29	20	.233	.308	.293	54	-18	6	5	-1	.955	4	S-74,M	-0.7
1926	Bro-N	78	234	32	55	8	5	0	24	26	24	.235	.312	.312	69	-10	7			.948	10	S-60,2-18	0.6
1927	StL-N	9	29	0	7	1	0	0	0	2	2	.241	.290	.276	51	-2	0			.962	3	/S-9	0.2
1928	*StL-N	112	366	40	88	14	10	1	34	36	27	.240	.310	.342	69	-17	3			.969	-5	*S-112/2-2	-0.9
1929	Bos-N	146	560	87	159	26	10	0	55	47	33	.284	.344	.366	79	-18	13			.961	20	*S-145/2-1	1.8
1930	Bos-N	142	558	85	157	26	8	2	43	48	23	.281	.344	.367	75	-22	9			.965	-13	*S-138/3-4	-1.7
1931	Bos-N	145	562	69	146	22	5	0	33	56	34	.260	.329	.317	77	-17	9			.949	-24	*S-137,2-11	-2.7
1932	Bos-N	149	571	67	134	20	4	0	37	46	28	.235	.295	.284	59	-32	4			.975	6	*2-149	-1.9
1933	Bos-N	143	478	46	104	15	4	0	38	36	34	.218	.274	.266	59	-25	2			.971	-27	*2-142	-4.7
1935	Bos-N	23	67	3	10	2	0	0	5	3	3	.149	.186	.179	-2	-10	0			.963	-5	2-20	-1.3
Total	23	2670	10078	1255	2605	380	177	28	884	839	756	.258	.318	.340	82	-246	291	93		.952	155	*S-2153,2-513/3-4	12.5

■ JOHNNY MARCUM   Marcum, John Alfred "Footsie"   b: 9/9/09, Campbellsburg, Ky.   d: 9/10/84, Louisville, Ky.   BL/TR, 5'11", 197 lbs.   Deb: 9/7/33

1933	Phi-A	5	12	2	2	0	0	0	2	1		.167	.286	.167	22	-1	0	0	0	1.000	0	/P-5	0.0
1934	Phi-A	58	112	10	30	4	0	1	13	3	5	.268	.287	.330	61	-7	0	0	1	-1	.949	-7	P-37	0.0
1935	Phi-A	64	119	13	37	2	1	2	17	9	5	.311	.359	.395	96	-1	0	0	0	.896	-3	P-39	0.0
1936	Bos-A	48	88	6	18	3	0	2	7	3	5	.205	.231	.307	30	-10	0	0	0	.950	0	P-31	0.0
1937	Bos-A	51	86	12	23	8	0	0	13	7	4	.267	.323	.360	69	-4	0	0	0	.981	-1	P-37	0.0
1938	Bos-A	19	37	3	5	0	0	0	3	6	9	.135	.256	.135	1	-6	0	0	0	1.000	-1	P-15	0.0
1939	StL-A	16	22	3	10	1	0	0	5	1	2	.455	.478	.500	147	2	0	0	0	1.000	-0	P-12	0.0
	Chi-A	38	57	7	16	0	0	0	12	5	1	.281	.339	.281	58	-3	0	0	0	.941	-1	P-19	0.0
	Yr	54	79	10	26	1	0	0	17	6	3	.329	.376	.342	83	-2	0	0	0	.962	-1	P-31	0.0
Total	7	299	533	56	141	18	1	5	70	36	32	.265	.329	.330	62	-30	0	0	1	-1	.953	-4	P-195	0.0

■ RED MARION   Marion, John Wyeth   b: 3/14/14, Richburg, S.C.   d: 3/13/75, San Jose, Cal.   BR/TR, 6'2", 175 lbs.   Deb: 9/16/35   F

1935	Was-A	4	11	1	2	1	0	1	1	0	2	.182	.182	.167	85	-0	0	0	0	.833	-0	/O-3	-0.1
1943	Was-A	14	17	2	3	0	0	0	1	3	1	.176	.300	.176	42	-1	0	0	0	1.000	-0	/O-4	-0.2
Total	2	18	28	3	5	1	0	1	2	3	3	.179	.258	.321	63	-2	0	0	0	.923	-1	/O-7	-0.3

■ MARTY MARION   Marion, Martin Whiteford "Slats" or "The Octopus"   b: 12/1/17, Richburg, S.C.   BR/TR, 6'2", 170 lbs.   Deb: 4/16/40   FMC

1940	StL-N	125	435	44	121	18	1	3	46	21	34	.278	.311	.345	76	-14	9			.949	-6	*S-125	-1.1
1941	StL-N	155	547	50	138	22	1	3	58	42	48	.252	.308	.320	72	-20	8			.954	7	*S-155	-0.2
1942	*StL-N	147	485	66	134	38	5	0	54	48	50	.276	.343	.375	102	1	8			.960	7	*S-147	1.9
1943	*StL-N★	129	418	38	117	15	3	1	52	32	37	.280	.334	.337	90	-5	1			.970	25	*S-128	3.1
1944	*StL-N★	144	506	50	135	26	2	6	63	43	50	.267	.324	.362	91	-6	1			.972	5	*S-144	1.0
1945	StL-N†	123	430	63	119	27	5	1	59	39	39	.277	.340	.370	95	-3	2			.967	-2	*S-122	0.5
1946	*StL-N★	146	498	51	116	29	4	3	46	59	53	.233	.318	.325	79	-13	1			.973	19	*S-145	1.5
1947	StL-N★	149	540	57	147	19	6	4	74	49	58	.272	.334	.352	79	-16	1			.981	20	*S-141	1.1
1948	StL-N†	144	567	70	143	26	4	4	43	37	54	.252	.298	.333	67	-27	1			.974	9	*S-142	-0.9
1949	StL-N☆	134	515	61	140	31	2	5	70	37	42	.272	.323	.369	81	-14	0			.976	17	*S-134	1.2
1950	StL-N★	106	372	36	92	10	2	4	40	44	55	.247	.327	.317	67	-17	1			.978	-1	*S-101	-1.0
1952	StL-A	67	186	16	46	11	0	2	19	19	17	.247	.320	.339	81	-5	0	2	-1	.980	-7	S-63,M	-0.9
1953	StL-A	3	7	0	0	0	0	0	0	0	0	.000	.000	.000	-98	-2	0	0	0	1.000	-1	/3-2,M	-0.4
Total	13	1572	5506	602	1448	272	37	36	624	470	537	.263	.323	.345	81	-140	35	2		.969	92	*S-1547/3-2	5.8

■ ROGER MARIS   Maris, Roger Eugene (b: Roger Eugene Maras)   b: 9/10/34, Hibbing, Minn.   d: 12/14/85, Houston, Tex.   BL/TR, 6', 204 lbs.   Deb: 4/16/57

1957	Cle-A	116	358	61	84	9	5	14	51	60	79	.235	.346	.405	106	3	8	4	0	.975	5	*O-112	0.3
1958	Cle-A	51	182	26	41	5	1	9	27	17	33	.225	.291	.412	94	-2	4	2	0	.967	5	O-47	0.0
	KC-A	99	401	61	99	14	3	19	53	28	52	.247	.299	.439	99	-2	0	0	0	.975	-4	O-99	-1.2
	Yr	150	583	87	140	19	4	28	80	45	85	.240	.297	.431	97	-4	4	2	0	.972	1	*O-146	-1.2
1959	KC-A★	122	433	69	118	21	7	16	72	58	53	.273	.362	.464	123	14	2	1	0	.975	6	*O-117	1.5
1960	*NY-A★	136	499	98	141	18	7	39	112	70	65	.283	.374	.581	164	42	2	2	-1	.985	3	*O-131	3.8
1961	*NY-A★	161	590	132	159	16	4	61	142	94	67	.269	.376	.620	170	57	0	0	0	.968	-11	*O-160	3.5
1962	*NY-A★	157	590	92	151	34	1	33	100	87	78	.256	.357	.485	128	23	1	0	0	.991	-4	*O-154	1.0
1963	*NY-A	90	312	53	84	14	1	23	53	35	40	.269	.347	.542	146	18	1	0	0	.988	5	O-86	1.7
1964	*NY-A	141	513	86	144	12	2	26	71	62	78	.281	.365	.464	127	19	3	0	0	.996	-0	*O-137	1.4
1965	NY-A	46	155	22	37	7	0	8	27	29	29	.239	.359	.439	126	6	0	0	0	.971	-2	O-43	0.2
1966	NY-A	119	348	37	81	9	2	13	43	36	60	.233	.310	.382	101	0	0	0	0	.993	-7	O-95	-1.1
1967	*StL-N	125	410	64	107	18	7	9	55	52	61	.261	.350	.405	117	10	0	0	0	.991	1	*O-118	0.6
1968	*StL-N	100	310	25	79	18	2	5	45	24	38	.255	.310	.374	106	2	0	0	0	.983	3	O-84	0.6
Total	12	1463	5101	826	1325	195	42	275	851	652	733	.260	.348	.476	128	191	21	9		.983	-3	*O-1383	11.7

■ GENE MARKLAND   Markland, Cleneth Eugene "Mousey"   b: 12/26/19, Detroit, Mich.   BR/TR, 5'10", 160 lbs.   Deb: 4/25/50

| 1950 | Phi-A | 5 | 8 | 2 | 1 | 0 | 0 | 0 | 3 | 0 | .125 | .364 | .125 | 30 | -1 | 0 | 0 | 0 | 1.000 | 0 | /2-5 | -0.1 |

■ HAL MARNIE   Marnie, Harry Sylvester   b: 7/6/18, Philadelphia, Pa.   BR/TR, 6'1", 178 lbs.   Deb: 9/15/40

1940	Phi-N	11	34	4	6	0	0	0	4	4	2	.176	.263	.176	24	-3	0			.984	6	2-11	0.3
1941	Phi-N	61	158	12	38	3	3	0	11	13	25	.241	.298	.297	71	-6	0			.990	5	2-39,S-16/3-3	0.2
1942	Phi-N	24	30	3	5	0	0	0	1	2	.167	.194	.167	6	-4	1			.971	8	2-11/S-7,3-1	0.5
Total	3	96	222	19	49	3	3	0	15	18	29	.221	.279	.261	55	-13	1			.987	19	/2-61,S-23,3-4	1.0

■ FRED MAROLEWSKI   Marolewski, Fred Daniel "Fritz"   b: 10/6/28, Chicago, Ill.   BR/TR, 6'2.5", 205 lbs.   Deb: 9/19/53

| 1953 | StL-N | 1 | 0 | 0 | 0 | 0 | 0 | 0 | 0 | 0 | 0 | — | — | — | | | 0 | 0 | 0 | .000 | 0 | /1-1 | 0.0 |

■ OLLIE MARQUARDT   Marquardt, Albert Ludwig   b: 9/22/02, Toledo, Ohio   d: 2/7/68, Port Clinton, Ohio   BR/TR, 5'9", 156 lbs.   Deb: 4/14/31

| 1931 | Bos-A | 17 | 39 | 4 | 7 | 1 | 0 | 0 | 2 | 3 | 4 | .179 | .238 | .205 | 18 | -5 | 0 | 1 | -1 | .946 | -3 | 2-13/S-1,3-1 | -0.7 |

■ GONZALO MARQUEZ   Marquez, Gonzalo Enrique (Moya)   b: 3/31/46, Carupano, Venez.   d: 12/20/84, Valencia, Venez.   BL/TL, 5'11", 180 lbs.   Deb: 8/11/72

1972	*Oak-A	23	21	2	8	0	0	0	4	3	4	.381	.480	.381	167	2	1	1	-0	.929	-0	/1-2	0.2
1973	Oak-A	23	25	1	6	1	0	0	4	1	3	.240	.240	.280	49	-2	0	0	0	.000	0	/2-2,1-1,O-1,D-1	-0.3
	Chi-N	19	58	5	13	2	0	1	4	3	4	.224	.274	.310	57	-3	0			.994	2	1-18	-0.2
1974	Chi-N	11	11	1	0	0	0	0	0	3	.000	.083	.000	-72	-3	0	0	0	1.000	0	1-1	-0.3
Total	3	76	115	9	27	3	0	1	10	7	14	.235	.290	.287	62	-6	1	1	-0	.989	1	/1-22,2-2,D-1,O-1	-0.6

■ LUIS MARQUEZ   Marquez, Luis Angel (Sanchez) "Canena"   b: 10/28/25, Aguadilla, P.R.   d: 3/1/88, Aguadilla, P.R.   BR/TR, 5'10.5", 174 lbs.   Deb: 4/18/51

| 1951 | Bos-N | 68 | 122 | 19 | 24 | 5 | 1 | 0 | 11 | 10 | 20 | .197 | .274 | .254 | 46 | -9 | 4 | 4 | -1 | 1.000 | -2 | O-43 | -1.4 |
| 1954 | Chi-N | 17 | 12 | 2 | 1 | 0 | 0 | 0 | 0 | 2 | 4 | .083 | .214 | .083 | -19 | -2 | 3 | 0 | 1 | 1.000 | -4 | O-14 | -0.6 |

YEAR TM/L	G	AB	R	H	2B	3B	HR	RBI	BB	SO	AVG	OBP	SLG	PRO+	BR/A	SB	CS	SBR	FA	FR	G/POS	TPR
Pit-N	14	9	3	1	0	0	0	0	4	0	.111	.385	.111	37	-1	0	0	0	1.000	-1	/O-4	-0.2
Yr	31	21	5	2	0	0	0	0	6	4	.095	.296	.095	7	-3	3	0	1	1.000	-5	O-18	-0.8
Total 2	99	143	24	26	5	1	0	11	16	24	.182	.278	.231	40	-12	7	4	-0	1.000	-7	/O-61	-2.2

■ BOB MARQUIS Marquis, Robert Rudolph b: 12/23/24, Oklahoma City, Okla. BL/TL, 6'1", 170 lbs. Deb: 4/17/53

YEAR TM/L	G	AB	R	H	2B	3B	HR	RBI	BB	SO	AVG	OBP	SLG	PRO+	BR/A	SB	CS	SBR	FA	FR	G/POS	TPR
1953 Cin-N	40	44	9	12	1	1	2	3	4	11	.273	.333	.477	107	0	0	0	0	.905	-2	O-10	-0.2

■ ROGER MARQUIS Marquis, Roger Julian "Noonie" b: 4/5/37, Holyoke, Mass. BL/TL, 6', 190 lbs. Deb: 9/25/55

YEAR TM/L	G	AB	R	H	2B	3B	HR	RBI	BB	SO	AVG	OBP	SLG	PRO+	BR/A	SB	CS	SBR	FA	FR	G/POS	TPR
1955 Bal-A	1	1	0	0	0	0	0	0	0	0	.000	.000	.000	-99	-0	0	0	0	.000	-0	/O-1	-0.1

■ LEFTY MARR Marr, Charles W. b: 9/19/1862, Cincinnati, Ohio d: 1/11/12, New Britain, Conn. BL/TL, Deb: 10/3/1886

YEAR TM/L	G	AB	R	H	2B	3B	HR	RBI	BB	SO	AVG	OBP	SLG	PRO+	BR/A	SB	CS	SBR	FA	FR	G/POS	TPR
1886 Cin-a	8	29	2	8	1	0	0		2	1	.276	.323	.379	116	0	1			.696	-1	/O-8	-0.1
1889 Col-a	139	546	110	167	26	**15**	1	75	87	32	.306	.407	.414	141	34	29			.856	12	3-66,O-47,S-26/1C	4.1
1890 Cin-N	130	527	91	157	17	12	1	73	46	29	.298	.361	.381	117	11	44			.930	-11	O-64,3-63/S-3	0.0
1891 Cin-N	72	286	32	74	9	7	0	32	25	15	.259	.323	.339	92	-3	16			.835	-10	O-72	-1.4
Cin-a	14	57	9	11	1	0		4	7	4	.193	.281	.211	38	-5	2			.923	-1	O-14	-0.5
Total 4	363	1445	244	417	54	35	2	186	166	80	.289	.368	.379	118	38	92			.853	-10	O-205,3-129/S1C	2.1

■ ORESTE MARRERO Marrero, Oreste Vilato (Vazquez) b: 10/31/69, Bayamon, P.R. BL/TL, 6', 195 lbs. Deb: 8/12/93

YEAR TM/L	G	AB	R	H	2B	3B	HR	RBI	BB	SO	AVG	OBP	SLG	PRO+	BR/A	SB	CS	SBR	FA	FR	G/POS	TPR
1993 Mon-N	32	81	10	17	5	1	1	4	14	16	.210	.326	.333	74	-3	1	3	-2	.991	-0	1-32	-0.7
1996 LA-N	10	8	2	3	1	0	0	1	1	3	.375	.444	.500	162	1	0	0	0	1.000	-0	/1-1	0.1
Total 2	42	89	12	20	6	1	1	5	15	19	.225	.337	.348	81	-2	1	3	-2	.991	-1	/1-33	-0.6

■ WILLIAM MARRIOTT Marriott, William Earl b: 4/18/1893, Pratt, Kan. d: 8/11/69, Berkeley, Cal. BL/TR, 6', 170 lbs. Deb: 9/6/17

YEAR TM/L	G	AB	R	H	2B	3B	HR	RBI	BB	SO	AVG	OBP	SLG	PRO+	BR/A	SB	CS	SBR	FA	FR	G/POS	TPR
1917 Chi-N	3	6	0	0	0	0	0	0	0	1	.000	.000	.000	-93	-1	0			.667	-0	/O-1	-0.2
1920 Chi-N	14	43	7	12	4	2	0	5	6	5	.279	.367	.465	135	2	1	1	-0	.892	-4	2-14	-0.2
1921 Chi-N	30	38	3	12	1	1	0	7	4	1	.316	.381	.395	105	0	0	1	-1	.826	-1	/2-6,S-1,3-1,O-1	-0.1
1925 Bos-N	103	370	37	99	9	1	1	40	28	26	.268	.322	.305	67	-18	3	8	-4	.928	3	3-89/O-1	-1.2
1926 Bro-N	109	360	39	96	13	9	3	42	17	20	.267	.303	.378	84	-9	12			.927	-3	*3-104	-1.1
1927 Bro-N	6	9	0	1	0	1	0	1	2	2	.111	.273	.333	61	-1	0			.889	1	/3-2	0.0
Total 6	265	826	86	220	27	14	4	95	57	55	.266	.317	.347	78	-27	16	10		.925	-9	3-196/2-20,O-3,S-1	-2.8

■ ARMANDO MARSANS Marsans, Armando b: 10/3/1887, Matanzas, Cuba d: 9/3/60, Havana, Cuba BR/TR, 5'10", 157 lbs. Deb: 7/4/11

YEAR TM/L	G	AB	R	H	2B	3B	HR	RBI	BB	SO	AVG	OBP	SLG	PRO+	BR/A	SB	CS	SBR	FA	FR	G/POS	TPR
1911 Cin-N	58	138	17	36	2	2	0	11	15	11	.261	.346	.304	86	-2	11			.968	-5	O-34/1-1,3-1	-0.9
1912 Cin-N	110	416	59	132	19	7	1	38	20	17	.317	.353	.404	110	5	35			.975	-3	O-98/1-6	-0.3
1913 Cin-N	118	435	49	129	7	6	0	38	17	25	.297	.327	.340	91	-5	37			.963	-5	O-94,1-22/3-2,S-1	-1.5
1914 Cin-N	36	124	16	37	3	0	0	22	14	6	.298	.374	.323	105	1	13			.916	1	O-36	0.0
StL-F	9	40	5	14	0	2	0	2	3	0	.350	.395	.450	123	1	4			.927	0	/2-7,S-2	0.1
1915 StL-F	36	124	16	22	3	0	0	6	14	5	.177	.261	.202	29	-13	5			.975	3	O-35	-1.3
1916 StL-A	151	528	51	134	12	1	1	60	57	41	.254	.333	.286	91	-5	46	26	-2	.977	5	*O-150	-1.0
1917 StL-A	75	257	31	59	12	0	0	20	20	6	.230	.285	.276	74	-8	11			.963	-4	O-67/3-5,2-1	-1.8
NY-A	25	88	10	20	4	0	0	15	8	3	.227	.292	.273	72	-3	6			.974	3	O-25	-0.1
Yr	100	345	41	79	16	0	0	35	28	9	.229	.287	.275	73	-11	17			.967	-1	O-92/3-5,2-1	-1.9
1918 NY-A	37	123	13	29	5	1	0	9	5	3	.236	.266	.293	67	-5	3			.943	-6	O-36	-1.9
Total 8	655	2273	267	612	67	19	2	221	173	117	.269	.325	.318	88	-35	171	26		.967	-11	O-575/1-29,2-8,3S	-8.3

■ FRED MARSH Marsh, Fred Francis b: 1/5/24, Valley Falls, Kan. BR/TR, 5'10", 180 lbs. Deb: 4/19/49

YEAR TM/L	G	AB	R	H	2B	3B	HR	RBI	BB	SO	AVG	OBP	SLG	PRO+	BR/A	SB	CS	SBR	FA	FR	G/POS	TPR
1949 Cle-A	1	0	0	0	0	0	0	0	0	0	—	—	—		0	0	0	0	.000	0	R	0.0
1951 StL-A	130	445	44	108	21	4	4	43	36	56	.243	.299	.335	69	-20	4	4	-1	.928	3	*3-117/S-3,2-2	-1.9
1952 StL-A	11	24	3	5	1	0	0	1	5	4	.208	.345	.250	65	-1	0	1	-1	.963	2	/2-9,S-3	0.1
Was-A	9	24	1	1	0	0	0	1	1	4	.042	.080	.042	-68	-5	0	0	0	1.000	-2	/2-5,O-2	-0.8
StL-A	76	223	25	64	8	1	2	26	22	29	.287	.351	.359	95	-1	3	2	-0	.945	-15	S-57,3-21	-1.4
Yr	96	271	29	70	9	1	2	28	28	37	.258	.328	.321	79	-7	3	3	-1	.945	-15	S-60,3-21,2-14/O-2	-2.1
1953 Chi-A	67	95	22	19	1	0	2	2	13	26	.200	.303	.274	55	-6	0	3	-2	.940	7	3-32,S-17/1-5,2-2	-0.1
1954 Chi-A	62	98	21	30	5	2	0	4	9	16	.306	.364	.398	105	1	4	2	0	.975	18	3-36/S-3,1-2,0-1	1.9
1955 Bal-A	89	303	30	66	7	1	2	19	35	33	.218	.301	.267	58	-18	1	2	0	.983	-15	2-76,3-18,S-16	-2.9
1956 Bal-A	20	24	2	3	0	0	0	0	4	3	.125	.250	.125	2	-3	1	0	0	.929	0	/S-8,3-8,2-5	-0.2
Total 7	465	1236	148	296	43	8	10	96	125	171	.239	.310	.311	69	-54	13	14	-5	.928	-2	3-232,S-107/210	-5.3

■ TOM MARSH Marsh, Thomas Owen b: 12/27/65, Toledo, Ohio BR/TR, 6'2", 180 lbs. Deb: 6/5/92

YEAR TM/L	G	AB	R	H	2B	3B	HR	RBI	BB	SO	AVG	OBP	SLG	PRO+	BR/A	SB	CS	SBR	FA	FR	G/POS	TPR
1992 Phi-N	42	125	7	25	3	2	2	16	2	23	.200	.209	.304	47	-9	0	1	-1	.971	-1	O-35	-1.2
1994 Phi-N	8	18	3	5	1	1	0	3	1	4	.278	.316	.444	93	-0	0	0	0	.889	-1	/O-7	-0.2
1995 Phi-N	43	109	13	32	3	1	3	15	4	25	.294	.319	.422	90	-1	0	1	-1	.939	-0	O-29	-0.3
Total 3	93	252	23	62	7	4	5	34	7	49	.246	.286	.365	71	-11	0	2	-2	.952	-3	/O-71	-1.7

■ CHARLIE MARSHALL Marshall, Charles Anthony (b: Charles Anthony Marczlewicz) b: 8/28/19, Wilmington, Del. BR/TR, 5'10.5", 178 lbs. Deb: 6/14/41

YEAR TM/L	G	AB	R	H	2B	3B	HR	RBI	BB	SO	AVG	OBP	SLG	PRO+	BR/A	SB	CS	SBR	FA	FR	G/POS	TPR
1941 StL-N	1	0	0	0	0	0	0	0	0	0	—	—	—		0				1.000	-0	/C-1	0.0

■ DAVE MARSHALL Marshall, David Lewis b: 1/14/43, Artesia, Cal. BL/TR, 6'1", 190 lbs. Deb: 9/7/67

YEAR TM/L	G	AB	R	H	2B	3B	HR	RBI	BB	SO	AVG	OBP	SLG	PRO+	BR/A	SB	CS	SBR	FA	FR	G/POS	TPR
1967 SF-N	1	0	0	0	—	—	—				—	—	—		0	0	0	0	.000	0	R	0.0
1968 SF-N	76	174	17	46	5	1	6	16	20	37	.264	.344	.322	101	1	2	1	0	.924	-6	O-50	-0.8
1969 SF-N	110	267	32	62	7	1	2	33	40	68	.232	.343	.288	80	-6	1	8	-5	.956	-10	O-87	-2.5
1970 NY-N	92	189	21	46	10	1	6	29	17	43	.243	.306	.402	88	-4	1	1	0	.973	-5	O-43	-0.6
1971 NY-N	100	214	28	51	9	1	3	21	26	54	.238	.326	.332	88	-3	3	1	0	.989	-4	O-64	-0.9
1972 NY-N	72	156	21	39	5	0	4	11	22	28	.250	.346	.359	103	1	3	3	-1	.972	-3	O-42	-0.9
1973 SD-N	39	49	4	14	5	0	0	4	8	9	.286	.397	.388	128	2	0	1	-1	1.000	0	/O-8	0.1
Total 7	490	1049	123	258	41	4	16	114	133	239	.246	.336	.338	92	-8	13	15	-5	.966	-24	O-294	-5.2

■ DOC MARSHALL Marshall, Edward Herbert "Eddie" b: 6/4/06, New Albany, Miss. BR/TR, 5'11", 150 lbs. Deb: 9/28/29

YEAR TM/L	G	AB	R	H	2B	3B	HR	RBI	BB	SO	AVG	OBP	SLG	PRO+	BR/A	SB	CS	SBR	FA	FR	G/POS	TPR
1929 NY-N	5	15	6	6	2	0	0	2	1	0	.400	.438	.533	140	1	0			1.000	-2	/2-5	-0.1
1930 NY-N	78	223	33	69	5	3	0	21	13	9	.309	.350	.359	73	-9	0			.947	-3	S-45,2-17/3-5	-0.6
1931 NY-N	68	194	15	39	6	2	0	10	8	8	.201	.233	.253	31	-19	1			.956	4	2-47,S-11/3-3	-1.2
1932 NY-N	68	226	18	56	8	1	0	28	6	11	.248	.270	.292	52	-15	1			.922	-3	S-63	-1.2
Total 4	219	658	72	170	21	6	0	61	28	28	.258	.291	.309	56	-42	2			.931	-4	S-119/2-69,3-8	-3.1

■ JOE MARSHALL Marshall, Joseph Hanley "Home Run Joe" b: 2/19/1876, Audubon, Minn. d: 9/11/31, Santa Monica, Cal BR/TR, 5'8", 170 lbs. Deb: 9/7/03

YEAR TM/L	G	AB	R	H	2B	3B	HR	RBI	BB	SO	AVG	OBP	SLG	PRO+	BR/A	SB	CS	SBR	FA	FR	G/POS	TPR
1903 Pit-N	10	23	2	6	1	2	0				.261	.261	.478	106	0	0			1.000	-4	/S-3,O-3,2-1	-0.4
1906 StL-N	33	95	2	15	1	2	0	7	6		.158	.216	.211	34	-7	0			.903	-1	O-23/1-4	-1.1
Total 2	43	118	4	21	2	4	0	7	6		.178	.224	.263	50	-7	0			.903	-5	/O-26,1-4,S-3,2-1	-1.5

■ KEITH MARSHALL Marshall, Keith Alan b: 7/2/51, San Francisco, Cal. BR/TR, 6'2", 175 lbs. Deb: 4/7/73

YEAR TM/L	G	AB	R	H	2B	3B	HR	RBI	BB	SO	AVG	OBP	SLG	PRO+	BR/A	SB	CS	SBR	FA	FR	G/POS	TPR
1973 KC-A	8	9	0	2	1	0	0	3	1	4	.222	.300	.333	0	0	0	0	0	1.000	-3	/O-8	-0.3

■ MIKE MARSHALL Marshall, Michael Allen b: 1/12/60, Libertyville, Ill. BR/TR, 6'5", 220 lbs. Deb: 9/7/81

YEAR TM/L	G	AB	R	H	2B	3B	HR	RBI	BB	SO	AVG	OBP	SLG	PRO+	BR/A	SB	CS	SBR	FA	FR	G/POS	TPR
1981 *LA-N	14	25	2	5	1	0	1	3	3	9	.200	.259	.320	66	-1	0	0	0	1.000	-1	/1-3,3-3,O-2	-0.2
1982 LA-N	49	95	10	23	3	0	5	9	13	23	.242	.339	.432	117	2	2	0	1	1.000	-4	O-19,1-13	-0.2
1983 *LA-N	140	465	47	132	17	1	17	65	43	127	.284	.341	.434	117	10	7	3	0	.976	-9	O-109,1-33	-0.1
1984 LA-N☆	134	495	68	127	27	0	21	65	40	93	.257	.316	.438	111	6	4	3	-1	.981	4	*O-118,1-15	0.5
1985 *LA-N	135	518	72	152	27	2	28	95	37	137	.293	.344	.515	141	26	3	10	-5	.991	-0	*O-125/1-7	1.7
1986 LA-N	103	330	47	77	11	0	19	53	27	90	.233	.299	.439	109	2	4	4	-1	.963	-2	*O-97	-0.4
1987 LA-N	104	402	45	118	19	0	16	72	18	79	.294	.330	.460	109	4	0	5	-3	.987	-6	*O-102	-0.8
1988 *LA-N	144	542	63	150	27	4	20	82	24	93	.277	.316	.445	120	11	4	1	1	.966	-1	O-90,1-53	0.4

YEAR	TM/L	G	AB	R	H	2B	3B	HR	RBI	BB	SO	AVG	OBP	SLG	PRO+	BR/A	SB	CS	SBR	FA	FR	G/POS	TPR
1989	LA-N	105	377	41	98	21	1	11	42	33	78	.260	.328	.408	111	5	2	5	-2	.978	-2	*O-102	-0.2
1990	NY-N	53	163	24	39	8	1	6	27	7	40	.239	.283	.411	89	-3	0	2	-1	.993	-1	1-42/O-1	-0.8
	*Bos-A	30	112	10	32	6	1	4	12	4	26	.286	.316	.464	111	1	0	0	0	1.000	1	D-14/1-8,O-8	0.1
1991	Bos-A	22	62	4	18	4	0	1	7	0	19	.290	.290	.403	86	-1	0	0	0	.979	-3	/1-5,O-4,D-7	-0.4
	Cal-A	2	7	0	0	0	0	0	0	0	1	.000	.000	.000	-99	-2	0	0	0	1.000	0	/1-1,D-1	-0.2
	Yr	24	69	4	18	4	0	1	7	0	20	.261	.261	.362	67	-3	0	0	0	.984	-2	/D-8,1-6,O-4	-0.6
Total	11	1035	3593	433	971	173	8	148	530	247	810	.270	.324	.446	115	60	26	33	-12	.978	-21	O-777,1-180/D-22,3	-0.6

■ MAX MARSHALL

Marshall, Milo Max b: 9/18/13, Shenandoah, Iowa BL/TR, 6'1", 180 lbs. Deb: 5/10/42

YEAR	TM/L	G	AB	R	H	2B	3B	HR	RBI	BB	SO	AVG	OBP	SLG	PRO+	BR/A	SB	CS	SBR	FA	FR	G/POS	TPR
1942	Cin-N	131	530	49	135	17	6	7	43	34	38	.255	.301	.349	90	-8	4			.976	-10	*O-129	-2.7
1943	Cin-N	132	508	55	120	11	8	4	39	34	52	.236	.287	.313	74	-18	8			.981	-5	*O-129	-3.2
1944	Cin-N	66	229	36	56	13	2	4	23	21	10	.245	.308	.371	84	-2	3			.965	2	O-59	-0.4
Total	3	329	1267	140	311	41	16	15	105	89	100	.245	.297	.339	84	-28	15			.975	-14	O-317	-6.3

■ JIM MARSHALL

Marshall, Rufus James b: 5/25/31, Danville, Ill. BL/TL, 6'1", 190 lbs. Deb: 4/15/58 MC

YEAR	TM/L	G	AB	R	H	2B	3B	HR	RBI	BB	SO	AVG	OBP	SLG	PRO+	BR/A	SB	CS	SBR	FA	FR	G/POS	TPR
1958	Bal-A	85	191	17	41	4	3	5	19	18	30	.215	.282	.346	76	-7	3	2	-0	1.000	-5	1-52/O-8	-1.5
	Chi-N	26	81	12	22	2	0	5	11	12	13	.272	.372	.481	126	3	1	0	0	.992	-4	1-15,O-11	-0.1
1959	Chi-N	108	294	39	74	10	1	11	40	33	39	.252	.327	.405	95	-2	0	1	-1	.997	1	1-72/O-8	-0.7
1960	SF-N	75	118	19	28	2	2	2	13	17	24	.237	.333	.339	90	-1	0	1	-1	.968	-3	1-28/O-6	-0.7
1961	SF-N	44	36	5	8	0	0	1	7	3	8	.222	.282	.306	58	-2	0	0	0	1.000	-0	/1-4,O-2	-0.2
1962	NY-N	17	32	6	11	1	0	3	4	3	6	.344	.400	.656	175	3	0	0	0	1.000	-0	/1-5,O-1	0.3
	Pit-N	55	100	13	22	5	1	2	12	15	19	.220	.322	.350	80	-3	1	0	0	1.000	1	1-26	-0.3
	Yr	72	132	19	33	6	1	5	16	18	25	.250	.346	.424	103	1	1	0	0	1.000	1	1-31/O-1	0.0
Total	5	410	852	111	206	24	7	29	106	101	139	.242	.323	.388	93	-9	5	4	-1	.994	-10	1-202/O-36	-3.2

■ WILLARD MARSHALL

Marshall, Willard Warren b: 2/8/21, Richmond, Va. BL/TR, 6'1", 205 lbs. Deb: 4/14/42

YEAR	TM/L	G	AB	R	H	2B	3B	HR	RBI	BB	SO	AVG	OBP	SLG	PRO+	BR/A	SB	CS	SBR	FA	FR	G/POS	TPR
1942	NY-N★	116	401	41	103	9	2	11	59	26	20	.257	.307	.372	98	-2	1			.975	-0	*O-107	-0.9
1946	NY-N	131	510	63	144	18	3	13	48	33	29	.282	.327	.406	107	3	3			.978	2	*O-125	-0.2
1947	NY-N★	155	587	102	171	19	6	36	107	67	30	.291	.366	.528	134	26	3			.972	12	*O-155	2.9
1948	NY-N	143	537	72	146	21	8	14	86	64	34	.272	.350	.419	107	5	2			.983	4	*O-142	0.1
1949	NY-N★	141	499	81	153	19	3	12	70	78	20	.307	.401	.429	123	19	4			.974	6	*O-138	1.8
1950	Bos-N	105	298	38	70	10	2	5	40	36	5	.235	.319	.332	77	-10	1			.958	1	O-85	-1.2
1951	Bos-N	136	469	65	132	24	7	11	62	48	18	.281	.351	.433	118	11	0	3	-2	1.000	-8	*O-136	-0.3
1952	Bos-N	21	66	5	15	4	1	2	11	4	4	.227	.271	.409	89	-1	0	0	0	.938	1	O-16	-0.1
	Cin-N	107	397	52	106	23	1	8	46	37	21	.267	.333	.390	100	-0	0	1	-1	.985	2	*O-105	-0.3
	Yr	128	463	57	121	27	2	10	57	41	25	.261	.324	.393	99	-1	0	1	-1	.979	3	*O-121	-0.4
1953	Cin-N	122	357	51	95	14	6	17	62	41	28	.266	.342	.482	111	5	0	0	0	.995	6	O-95	0.8
1954	Chi-A	47	71	4	18	2	0	1	7	11	9	.254	.354	.324	84	-1	0	0	0	.960	-7	O-29	-0.9
1955	Chi-A	22	41	6	7	0	0	0	6	11	3	.171	.370	.171	48	-2	0	0	0	.957	-1	O-12	-0.3
Total	11	1246	4233	583	1160	163	39	130	604	458	219	.274	.347	.423	109	51	14	4		.979	20	O-1145	1.3

■ BILL MARSHALL

Marshall, William Henry b: 2/14/11, Dorchester, Mass. d: 5/5/77, Sacramento, Cal. BR/TR, 5'8.5", 156 lbs. Deb: 6/20/31

YEAR	TM/L	G	AB	R	H	2B	3B	HR	RBI	BB	SO	AVG	OBP	SLG	PRO+	BR/A	SB	CS	SBR	FA	FR	G/POS	TPR
1931	Bos-A	1	0	1	0	0	0	0	0	0	0					0	0			.000	0	R	0.0
1934	Cin-N	6	8	0	1	0	0	0	0	0	2	.125	.125	.125	-34	-1	0			.875	1	/2-2	-0.1
Total	2	7	8	1	1	0	0	0	0	0	2	.125	.125	.125	-34	-1	0	0	0	.875	1	/2-2	-0.1

■ DOC MARSHALL

Marshall, William Riddle b: 9/22/1875, Butler, Pa. d: 12/11/59, Clinton, Ill. BR/TR, 6', 185 lbs. Deb: 4/15/04

YEAR	TM/L	G	AB	R	H	2B	3B	HR	RBI	BB	SO	AVG	OBP	SLG	PRO+	BR/A	SB	CS	SBR	FA	FR	G/POS	TPR
1904	Phi-N	8	20	1	2	0	0	0	0	0	0	.100	.100	.100	-40	-3	0			.944	2	/C-7	-0.1
	NY-N	1	0	0	0	0	0	0	0	0	0	—	—	—	—	0	0			.000	0	/C-1	0.0
	Bos-N	13	43	3	9	0	1	0	2	2	2	.209	.244	.256	56	-2	2			.955	1	C-10/O-1	0.0
	NY-N	10	17	3	6	1	0	0	2	1	1	.353	.389	.412	141	1	0			.955	2	/C-2,O-2,2-1	0.3
	Yr	32	80	7	17	1	1	0	5	3	3	.213	.241	.250	52	-5	2			.952	5	C-20/O-3,2-1	0.2
1906	NY-N	38	102	8	17	3	2	0	7	7	7	.167	.234	.235	45	-7	7			1.000	-2	O-16,C-13/1-2	-0.9
	StL-N	39	123	6	34	4	1	0	10	6	6	.276	.315	.325	104	0	1			.961	9	C-38	1.4
	Yr	77	225	14	51	7	3	0	17	13	13	.227	.278	.284	76	-7	8			.969	7	C-51,O-16/1-2	0.5
1907	StL-N	84	268	19	54	8	2	2	18	12		.201	.246	.269	64	-12	2			.952	5	C-83	0.1
1908	StL-N	6	14	0	1	0	0	0	1	0		.071	.071	.071	-57	-2	0			1.000	0	/C-6	0.6
	Chi-N	12	20	4	6	0	1	0	3	0		.300	.300	.400	118	0	1			1.000	5	/C-4,O-3	0.6
	Yr	18	34	4	7	0	1	0	4	0		.206	.206	.265	49	-2	0			1.000	5	/C-10,O-3	0.6
1909	Bro-N	50	149	7	30	7	1	0	10	6		.201	.232	.262	55	-8	3			.968	-5	C-49/O-1	-1.1
Total	5	261	756	51	159	23	8	2	54	34		.210	.251	.270	64	-34	15			.961	19	C-213/O-23,1-2,2-1	0.3

■ DOC MARTEL

Martel, Leon Alphonse "Marty" b: 1/29/1883, Weymouth, Mass. d: 10/11/47, Washington, D.C. BR/TR, 6', 185 lbs. Deb: 7/6/09

YEAR	TM/L	G	AB	R	H	2B	3B	HR	RBI	BB	SO	AVG	OBP	SLG	PRO+	BR/A	SB	CS	SBR	FA	FR	G/POS	TPR
1909	Phi-N	24	41	1	11	3	1	0	7	4		.268	.333	.390	123	1	0			.974	4	C-12	0.7
1910	Bos-N	10	31	0	4	0	0	0	1	2	3	.129	.182	.129	-9	-4	0			.980	-1	1-10	-0.5
Total	2	34	72	1	15	3	1	0	8	6	3	.208	.269	.278	64	-3	0			.974	4	/C-12,1-10	0.2

■ AL MARTIN

Martin, Albert (a.k.a. Albert May In 1872) Deb: 5/7/1872

YEAR	TM/L	G	AB	R	H	2B	3B	HR	RBI	BB	SO	AVG	OBP	SLG	PRO+	BR/A	SB	CS	SBR	FA	FR	G/POS	TPR
1872	Eck-n	4	18	2	5	0	0	0	2	0	0	.278	.278	.278	84	-0	0	0	0	.636	-3	/2-4	-0.3
1874	Atl-n	7	29	1	4	0	0	0	1	0	1	.138	.138	.138	-13	-3	0	0	0	.646	-2	/2-6,O-1	-0.4
1875	Atl-n	6	26	1	3	0	0	0	1	0	0	.115	.115	.115	-22	-3	0	0	0	.909	-1	/O-6	-0.3
Total	3 n	17	73	4	12	0	0	0	4	0	1	.164	.164	.164	9	-6	0	0	0	.643	-6	/2-10,O-7	-1.0

■ AL MARTIN

Martin, Albert Lee b: 11/24/67, West Covina, Cal. BL/TL, 6'2", 220 lbs. Deb: 7/28/92

YEAR	TM/L	G	AB	R	H	2B	3B	HR	RBI	BB	SO	AVG	OBP	SLG	PRO+	BR/A	SB	CS	SBR	FA	FR	G/POS	TPR
1992	Pit-N	12	12	1	2	0	1	0	2	0	5	.167	.167	.333	39	-1	0	0	0	1.000	-2	/O-7	-0.3
1993	Pit-N	143	480	85	135	26	6	18	64	42	122	.281	.340	.481	117	11	16	9	-1	.975	-10	*O-136	-0.3
1994	Pit-N	82	276	48	79	12	4	9	33	34	56	.286	.369	.457	112	5	15	6	1	.979	2	O-77	0.7
1995	Pit-N	124	439	70	124	25	3	13	41	44	92	.282	.351	.442	105	3	20	11	-1	.977	-3	*O-121	-0.4
1996	Pit-N	155	630	101	189	40	1	18	72	54	116	.300	.357	.452	108	8	38	12	4	.965	-14	*O-152	-0.7
Total	5	516	1837	305	529	103	17	58	212	174	391	.288	.352	.457	110	26	89	38	4	.974	-27	O-493	-1.0

■ BILLY MARTIN

Martin, Alfred Manuel b: 5/16/28, Berkeley, Cal. d: 12/25/89, Johnson City, N.Y. BR/TR, 5'11.5", 165 lbs. Deb: 4/18/50 MC

YEAR	TM/L	G	AB	R	H	2B	3B	HR	RBI	BB	SO	AVG	OBP	SLG	PRO+	BR/A	SB	CS	SBR	FA	FR	G/POS	TPR
1950	NY-A	34	36	10	9	1	0	1	8	3	3	.250	.308	.361	73	-2	0	0	0	.976	-1	2-22/3-1	-0.2
1951	*NY-A	51	58	10	15	1	2	0	2	4	9	.259	.328	.345	85	-1	0	1	-1	.988	16	2-23/S-6,3-2,O-1	1.4
1952	*NY-A	109	363	32	97	13	3	3	33	22	31	.267	.323	.344	91	-5	3	6	-3	.984	18	*2-107	1.6
1953	*NY-A	149	587	72	151	24	6	15	75	43	56	.257	.314	.395	94	-7	6	7	-2	.985	-1	*2-146,S-18	-0.3
1955	*NY-A	20	70	8	21	2	0	1	9	7	8	.300	.364	.371	100	0	1	2	-1	.977	1	2-17/S-3	0.2
1956	*NY-A★	121	458	76	121	24	5	9	49	30	56	.264	.314	.397	90	-9	7	3	0	.980	-14	*2-105,3-16	-1.4
1957	NY-A	43	145	12	35	5	2	1	12	3	14	.241	.262	.324	60	-8	2	1	0	.947	-3	2-26,3-13	-1.0
	KC-A	73	265	33	68	9	3	9	27	12	20	.257	.294	.415	91	-4	7	1	2	.987	-20	2-52,3-20/S-2	-1.9
	Yr	116	410	45	103	14	5	10	39	15	34	.251	.284	.383	80	-12	9	2	2	.973	-23	2-78,3-33/S-2	-2.9
1958	Det-A	131	498	56	127	19	1	7	42	16	62	.255	.282	.339	65	-24	5	3	0	.958	-18	S-88,3-41	-3.5
1959	Cle-A	73	242	37	63	7	0	9	24	8	18	.260	.292	.401	92	-4	0	2	-1	.997	-11	2-67/3-4	-1.1
1960	Cin-N	103	317	34	78	17	1	3	16	27	34	.246	.305	.334	74	-11	0	1	-1	.975	-13	2-97	-1.7
1961	Mil-N	6	6	1	0	0	0	0	0	0	0	.000	.000	.000	-99	-2	0	0	0	.000	0	H	-0.2
	Min-A	108	374	44	92	15	5	6	36	13	42	.246	.277	.361	65	-19	3	2	0	.963	-15	*2-105/S-1	-2.9
Total	11	1021	3419	425	877	137	28	64	333	188	355	.257	.301	.369	81	-96	34	29	-7	.980	-61	2-767,S-118/3-97,O	-10.5

■ PHONNEY MARTIN

Martin, Alphonse Case b: 8/4/1845, New York, N.Y. d: 5/24/33, Hollis, N.Y. 5'7", 148 lbs. Deb: 4/26/1872

YEAR	TM/L	G	AB	R	H	2B	3B	HR	RBI	BB	SO	AVG	OBP	SLG	PRO+	BR/A	SB	CS	SBR	FA	FR	G/POS	TPR
1872	Tro-n	25	117	27	36	2	1	0	14	0	1	.308	.308	.342	98	-0	3			.780	-2	O-25/P-8	-0.1
	Eck-n	18	78	13	12	0	0	0	9	1	2	.154	.165	.154	-2	-8	3	1	0	.806	2	P-10/O-9,M	-0.2
	Yr	43	195	40	48	2	1	0	23	1	3	.246	.250	.267	62	-7	3	1	0	.776	-0	O-34,P-18	-0.3

YEAR	TM/L	G	AB	R	H	2B	3B	HR	RBI	BB	SO	AVG	OBP	SLG	PRO+	BR/A	SB	CS	SBR	FA	FR	G/POS	TPR
1873	Mut-n	31	140	12	31	1	0	0	14	0	4	.221	.221	.229	34	-11	0	1	-1	.680	-7	O-30/P-6	-1.1
Total	2 n	74	335	52	79	3	1	0	37	1	7	.236	.238	.251	50	-19	3	2	-0	.747	-7	/O-64,P-24	-1.4

■ BABE MARTIN
Martin, Boris Michael (b: Boris Michael Martinovich)   b: 3/28/20, Seattle, Wash.   BR/TR, 5'11.5", 194 lbs.   Deb: 9/25/44

YEAR	TM/L	G	AB	R	H	2B	3B	HR	RBI	BB	SO	AVG	OBP	SLG	PRO+	BR/A	SB	CS	SBR	FA	FR	G/POS	TPR
1944	StL-A	2	4	0	3	0	0	0	0	0	0	.750	.750	1.000	376	1	0	0	0	1.000	-0	/O-1	0.1
1945	StL-A	54	185	13	37	5	2	2	16	11	24	.200	.245	.281	50	-12	0	1	-1	.992	6	O-48/1-6	-1.0
1946	StL-A	3	9	0	2	0	0	0	1	1	2	.222	.300	.222	45	-1	0	0	0	1.000	1	/C-2	0.0
1948	Bos-A	4	4	0	2	0	0	0	0	0	0	.500	.500	.500	158	0	0	0	0	.000	0	/C-1	0.0
1949	Bos-A	2	2	0	0	0	0	0	0	0	0	.000	.000	.000	-93	-1	0	0	0	.000	0	/C-1	-0.1
1953	StL-A	4	2	0	0	0	0	0	1	1	0	.000	.333	.000	-4	-0	0	0	0	.000	0	/C-1	0.0
Total	6	69	206	13	44	6	2	2	18	13	27	.214	.260	.291	56	-12	0	1	-1	.992	6	/O-49,1-6,C-5	-1.0

■ FRANK MARTIN
Martin, Frank   b: 2/28/1879, Chicago, Ill.   d: 9/30/24, Chicago, Ill.   Deb: 6/30/1897

YEAR	TM/L	G	AB	R	H	2B	3B	HR	RBI	BB	SO	AVG	OBP	SLG	PRO+	BR/A	SB	CS	SBR	FA	FR	G/POS	TPR
1897	Lou-N	2	8	1	2	0	0	0	0	0		.250	.250	.250	33	-1	0			.813	0	/2-2	0.0
1898	Chi-N	1	4	0	0	0	0	0	0	0		.000	.000	.000	-99	-1	0			1.000	0	/2-1	-0.1
1899	NY-N	17	54	5	14	2	0	0	1	2		.259	.298	.296	66	-3	0			.824	2	3-17	0.0
Total	3	20	66	6	16	2	0	0	1	2		.242	.275	.273	52	-4	0			.870	3	/3-17,2-3	-0.1

■ HERSH MARTIN
Martin, Hershel Ray   b: 9/19/09, Birmingham, Ala.   d: 11/17/80, Cuba, Mo.   BB/TR, 6'2", 190 lbs.   Deb: 4/23/37

YEAR	TM/L	G	AB	R	H	2B	3B	HR	RBI	BB	SO	AVG	OBP	SLG	PRO+	BR/A	SB	CS	SBR	FA	FR	G/POS	TPR
1937	Phi-N	141	579	102	164	35	7	8	49	69	66	.283	.362	.409	101	1	11			.978	5	*O-139	0.1
1938	Phi-N☆	120	466	58	139	36	6	3	39	34	48	.298	.347	.421	113	8	8			.965	1	*O-116	0.5
1939	Phi-N	111	393	59	111	28	5	1	22	42	27	.282	.355	.387	102	2	4			.976	11	O-95	0.9
1940	Phi-N	33	83	10	21	6	1	0	5	9	9	.253	.326	.349	90	-1	1			.979	-0	O-23	-0.2
1944	NY-A	85	328	49	99	12	4	9	47	34	26	.302	.371	.445	128	12	5	2	0	.964	3	O-80	1.1
1945	NY-A	117	408	53	109	18	6	7	53	65	31	.267	.368	.392	115	9	4	1	1	.984	3	O-102	0.8
Total	6	607	2257	331	643	135	29	28	215	253	207	.285	.359	.408	109	31	33	3		.974	22	O-555	3.2

■ JERRY MARTIN
Martin, Jerry Lindsey   b: 5/11/49, Columbia, S.C.   BR/TR, 6'1", 195 lbs.   Deb: 9/7/74   F

YEAR	TM/L	G	AB	R	H	2B	3B	HR	RBI	BB	SO	AVG	OBP	SLG	PRO+	BR/A	SB	CS	SBR	FA	FR	G/POS	TPR
1974	Phi-N	13	14	2	3	1	0	0	1	1	5	.214	.267	.286	52	-1	0	0	0	1.000	-3	O-11	-0.5
1975	Phi-N	57	113	15	24	7	1	2	11	11	16	.212	.288	.345	72	-4	2	1	-1	.979	-3	O-49	-1.0
1976	*Phi-N	130	121	30	30	7	0	2	15	7	28	.248	.289	.355	80	-3	3	2	-0	.975	-30	*O-110/1-1	-3.7
1977	*Phi-N	116	215	34	56	16	3	6	28	18	42	.260	.312	.447	101	0	6	4	-1	.984	-19	*O-106/1-1	-2.2
1978	*Phi-N	128	266	40	72	13	4	9	36	28	65	.271	.342	.451	119	6	9	5	-0	.987	-15	*O-112	-1.3
1979	Chi-N	150	534	74	145	34	5	19	73	38	85	.272	.323	.453	100	-1	2	4	-2	.981	-2	*O-144	-1.1
1980	Chi-N	141	494	57	112	22	5	23	73	38	107	.227	.285	.419	88	-10	8	3	1	.978	-12	*O-129	-2.7
1981	SF-N	72	241	23	58	5	3	4	25	21	52	.241	.309	.336	85	-5	6	2	1	.993	-4	O-64	-1.1
1982	KC-A	147	519	52	138	22	1	15	65	38	138	.266	.318	.399	95	-4	1	1	-0	.980	4	*O-142/D-3	-0.4
1983	KC-A	13	44	4	14	2	0	2	13	1	7	.318	.333	.500	125	1	0	0	0	.957	-2	O-13	-0.1
1984	NY-N	51	91	6	14	1	0	3	6	5	29	.154	.206	.264	32	-9	0	0	0	1.000	-1	O-30/1-3	-1.1
Total	11	1018	2652	337	666	130	17	85	345	207	574	.251	.309	.409	93	-29	38	23	-2	.982	-87	O-910/1-5,D-3	-15.1

■ JACK MARTIN
Martin, John Christopher   b: 4/19/1887, Plainfield, N.J.   d: 7/4/80, Plainfield, N.J.   BR/TR, 5'9", 159 lbs.   Deb: 4/25/12

YEAR	TM/L	G	AB	R	H	2B	3B	HR	RBI	BB	SO	AVG	OBP	SLG	PRO+	BR/A	SB	CS	SBR	FA	FR	G/POS	TPR
1912	NY-A	71	231	30	52	6	1	0	17	37		.225	.347	.260	70	-7	14			.898	3	S-65/3-4,2-1	0.1
1914	Bos-N	33	85	10	18	2	0	0	5	6	7	.212	.264	.235	49	-5	0			.949	0	3-26/1-1,2-1	-0.5
	Phi-N	83	292	26	74	5	3	0	21	27	29	.253	.319	.291	77	-8	6			.930	-3	S-83	-0.4
	Yr	116	377	36	92	7	3	0	26	33	36	.244	.307	.279	71	-13	6			.930	-3	S-83,3-26/1-1,2-1	-0.9
Total	2	187	608	66	144	13	4	0	43	70	36	.237	.323	.271	71	-21	20			.915	-0	S-148/3-30,2-2,1-1	-0.8

■ PEPPER MARTIN
Martin, John Leonard Roosevelt "The Wild Horse Of The Osage"   b: 2/29/04, Temple, Okla.   d: 3/5/65, McAlester, Okla.   BR/TR, 5'8", 170 lbs.   Deb: 4/16/28   C

YEAR	TM/L	G	AB	R	H	2B	3B	HR	RBI	BB	SO	AVG	OBP	SLG	PRO+	BR/A	SB	CS	SBR	FA	FR	G/POS	TPR
1928	*StL-N	39	13	11	4	0	0	0	0	0	2	.308	.400	.308	86	-0	2			1.000	-2	/O-4	-0.2
1930	StL-N	6	1	5	0	0	0	0	0	0	0	.000	.000	.000	-97	-0	0			.000	0	H	0.0
1931	*StL-N	123	413	68	124	32	8	7	75	30	40	.300	.351	.467	114	7	16			.967	-2	*O-110	0.1
1932	StL-N	85	323	47	77	19	6	4	34	30	31	.238	.305	.372	79	-10	9			.976	-1	O-69,3-15	-1.4
1933	StL-N★	145	599	**122**	189	36	12	8	57	67	46	.316	.387	.456	133	27	**26**			.943	-3	*3-145	3.5
1934	*StL-N★	110	454	74	131	25	11	5	49	32	41	.289	.337	.425	96	-3	**23**			.936	-5	*3-107/P-1	-0.3
1935	StL-N★	135	539	121	161	41	6	9	54	33	58	.299	.341	.447	106	4	20			.904	-14	*3-114,O-16	-0.7
1936	StL-N★	143	572	121	177	36	11	11	76	58	66	.309	.371	.469	126	20	**23**			.976	-10	*O-127,3-15/P-1	0.5
1937	StL-N☆	98	339	60	103	27	8	5	38	33	50	.304	.366	.475	124	11	9			.973	11	O-82/3-5	1.9
1938	StL-N	91	269	34	79	18	2	2	38	18	34	.294	.340	.398	97	-1	4			.986	-3	O-62/3-4	-0.6
1939	StL-N	88	281	48	86	17	7	3	37	30	35	.306	.375	.448	113	6	6			.975	-4	O-51,3-22	0.0
1940	StL-N	86	228	28	72	15	4	3	39	22	24	.316	.378	.456	122	7	6			.974	-3	O-63/3-2	-0.2
1944	StL-N	40	86	15	24	4	0	2	4	10	11	.279	.386	.395	118	3	2			.980	-4	O-29	-0.2
Total	13	1189	4117	754	1227	270	75	59	501	369	438	.298	.358	.443	112	70	146			.973	-36	O-613,3-429/P-2	2.8

■ J. C. MARTIN
Martin, Joseph Clifton   b: 12/13/36, Axton, Va.   BL/TR, 6'2", 200 lbs.   Deb: 9/10/59   C

YEAR	TM/L	G	AB	R	H	2B	3B	HR	RBI	BB	SO	AVG	OBP	SLG	PRO+	BR/A	SB	CS	SBR	FA	FR	G/POS	TPR
1959	Chi-A	3	4	0	1	0	0	0	1	0	1	.250	.250	.250	38	-0	0	0	0	.667	-0	/3-2	0.0
1960	Chi-A	7	20	0	2	1	0	0	2	0	6	.100	.100	.150	-34	-4	0	0	0	1.000	-0	/3-5,1-1	-0.4
1961	Chi-A	110	274	26	63	8	3	5	32	21	31	.230	.290	.336	68	-13	1	2	-1	.988	9	1-60,3-36	-0.7
1962	Chi-A	18	26	0	2	0	0	0	2	0	3	.077	.077	.077	-59	-6	0	0	0	1.000	-1	/C-6,1-1,3-1	-0.6
1963	Chi-A	105	259	25	53	11	5	3	28	26	35	.205	.280	.313	67	-11	0	0	0	.983	14	C-98/1-3,3-1	0.6
1964	Chi-A	122	294	23	58	10	1	4	22	16	30	.197	.244	.279	46	-22	0	0	0	.986	8	*C-120	-1.0
1965	Chi-A	119	230	21	60	12	0	2	21	24	29	.261	.336	.339	98	-0	2	1	0	.982	1	*C-112/1-4,3-2	0.4
1966	Chi-A	67	157	13	40	5	3	2	20	14	24	.255	.320	.363	103	0	0	0	0	.982	-1	C-63	0.3
1967	Chi-A	101	252	22	59	12	1	4	22	30	41	.234	.318	.337	97	-1	4	4	-1	.987	3	C-96/1-1	0.6
1968	NY-N	78	244	20	55	9	2	3	21	21	31	.225	.300	.316	84	-4	0	0	0	.994	-3	C-53,1-14	-0.6
1969	*NY-N	66	177	12	37	5	1	4	21	12	32	.209	.259	.316	59	-10	0	0	0	.996	-6	C-48/1-2	-1.5
1970	Chi-N	40	77	11	12	0	1	0	4	20	11	.156	.337	.208	44	-6	0	0	0	.983	2	C-36/1-3	-0.3
1971	Chi-N	47	125	13	33	5	0	2	17	12	16	.264	.338	.352	84	-3	1	1	-0	.996	2	C-43/O-1	0.1
1972	Chi-N	25	50	3	12	3	0	0	7	5	9	.240	.309	.300	67	-2	1	0	0	.970	-3	C-17	-0.5
Total	14	908	2189	189	487	82	12	32	230	201	299	.222	.293	.315	72	-81	9	8	-2	.987	26	C-692/1-89,3-47,O-1	-3.6

■ MIKE MARTIN
Martin, Joseph Michael   b: 12/3/58, Portland, Ore.   BL/TR, 6'2", 193 lbs.   Deb: 8/15/86

YEAR	TM/L	G	AB	R	H	2B	3B	HR	RBI	BB	SO	AVG	OBP	SLG	PRO+	BR/A	SB	CS	SBR	FA	FR	G/POS	TPR
1986	Chi-N	8	13	1	1	1	0	0	2	0	4	.077	.200	.154	-1	-2	0	0	0	1.000	0	/C-8	-0.2

■ JOE MARTIN
Martin, Joseph Samuel "Silent Joe"   b: 1/1/1876, Hollidaysburg, Pa.   d: 5/25/64, Altoona, Pa.   BL/TR, 5'9.5", 155 lbs.   Deb: 4/28/03

YEAR	TM/L	G	AB	R	H	2B	3B	HR	RBI	BB	SO	AVG	OBP	SLG	PRO+	BR/A	SB	CS	SBR	FA	FR	G/POS	TPR
1903	Was-A	35	119	11	27	4	5	0	7	5		.227	.258	.345	78	-3	2			.892	-5	2-15,3-13/O-7	-0.8
	StL-A	44	173	18	37	6	4	0	7	6		.214	.249	.295	64	-8	0			.983	-3	O-38/2-6,3-1	-1.4
	Yr	79	292	29	64	10	9	0	14	11		.219	.252	.315	70	-11	2			.959	-8	O-45,2-21,3-14	-2.2

■ NORBERTO MARTIN
Martin, Norberto Edonal (McDonald)   b: 12/10/66, San Pedro De Macoris, D.R.   BR/TR, 5'10", 175 lbs.   Deb: 9/20/93

YEAR	TM/L	G	AB	R	H	2B	3B	HR	RBI	BB	SO	AVG	OBP	SLG	PRO+	BR/A	SB	CS	SBR	FA	FR	G/POS	TPR
1993	Chi-A	8	14	3	5	0	0	0	2	1	1	.357	.400	.357	108	0	0	0	0	.957	3	/2-5,D-1	0.3
1994	Chi-A	45	131	19	36	7	1	1	16	9	16	.275	.321	.366	78	-4	4	2	0	.982	-6	2-28/S-6,3-5,D-2,D	-0.8
1995	Chi-A	72	160	17	43	7	4	2	17	5	25	.269	.287	.400	80	-5	5	0	2	.950	-3	2-17,O-12,D-10,/3S	-0.5
1996	Chi-A	70	140	30	49	7	0	4	17	12	17	.350	.377	.421	107	5	2	10	2	.943	10	S-24,D-22,2-10,/3-3	1.2
Total	4	195	445	69	133	21	5	4	49	19	59	.299	.329	.396	89	-8	8	19	4	.971	3	/2-60,S-37,D-34,3O	0.2

■ STU MARTIN
Martin, Stuart McGuire   b: 11/17/13, Rich Square, N.C.   BL/TR, 6', 155 lbs.   Deb: 4/14/36

YEAR	TM/L	G	AB	R	H	2B	3B	HR	RBI	BB	SO	AVG	OBP	SLG	PRO+	BR/A	SB	CS	SBR	FA	FR	G/POS	TPR
1936	StL-N☆	92	332	63	99	21	4	6	41	29	27	.298	.356	.440	114	6	17			.949	-13	2-83/S-3	-0.1
1937	StL-N	90	223	34	58	6	1	1	17	32	18	.260	.353	.309	80	-5	3			.946	-6	2-48/1-9,S-1	-0.9
1938	StL-N	114	417	54	116	26	2	1	27	30	28	.278	.328	.357	84	-9	8			.967	-10	2-99	-1.3
1939	Mut-N	120	425	60	114	26	7	3	30	33	40	.268	.325	.384	85	-9	4			**.977**	-3	*2-107/1-1	-0.7

YEAR	TM/L	G	AB	R	H	2B	3B	HR	RBI	BB	SO	AVG	OBP	SLG	PRO+	BR/A	SB	CS	SBR	FA	FR	G/POS	TPR
1940	StL-N	112	369	45	88	12	6	4	32	33	35	.238	.301	.336	71	-14	4			.972	-25	3-73,2-33	-3.8
1941	Pit-N	88	233	37	71	13	2	0	19	10	17	.305	.341	.378	103	1	2			.972	-4	2-53/3-2,1-1	0.0
1942	Pit-N	42	120	16	27	4	2	1	12	8	10	.225	.273	.317	71	-5	1			.979	-11	2-30/1-1,S-1	-1.5
1943	Chi-N	64	118	13	26	4	0	0	5	15	10	.220	.308	.254	64	-5	1			.980	1	2-22/3-8,1-2	-0.3
Total	8	722	2237	322	599	112	24	16	183	190	185	.268	.322	.361	86	-41	36			.966	-71	2-475/3-83,1-14,S-5	-8.6

■ GENE MARTIN
Martin, Thomas Eugene   b: 1/12/47, Americus, Ga.   BL/TR, 6'0.5", 190 lbs.   Deb: 7/28/68

YEAR	TM/L	G	AB	R	H	2B	3B	HR	RBI	BB	SO	AVG	OBP	SLG	PRO+	BR/A	SB	CS	SBR	FA	FR	G/POS	TPR
1968	Was-A	9	11	1	4	1	0	1	1	0	1	.364	.364	.727	232	2	0	0	0	.000	-1	/O-2	0.1

■ JOE MARTIN
Martin, William Joseph "Smokey Joe"   b: 8/28/11, Seymour, Mo.   d: 9/28/60, Buffalo, N.Y.   BR/TR, 5'11.5", 181 lbs.   Deb: 4/27/36

YEAR	TM/L	G	AB	R	H	2B	3B	HR	RBI	BB	SO	AVG	OBP	SLG	PRO+	BR/A	SB	CS	SBR	FA	FR	G/POS	TPR
1936	NY-N	7	15	0	4	1	0	0	4	2	4	.267	.313	.333	75	-1	0			1.000	1	/3-7	0.0
1938	Chi-A	1	0	0	0	0	0	0	0	0	0	—	—	—	—	0	0	0	0	.000	0	R	0.0
Total	2	8	15	0	4	1	0	0	4	2	4	.267	.313	.333	75	-1	0	0	0	1.000	1	/3-7	0.0

■ BILLY MARTIN
Martin, William Lloyd   b: 2/13/1894, Washington, D.C.   d: 9/14/49, Arlington, Va.   BR/TR, 5'8.5", 170 lbs.   Deb: 10/6/14

YEAR	TM/L	G	AB	R	H	2B	3B	HR	RBI	BB	SO	AVG	OBP	SLG	PRO+	BR/A	SB	CS	SBR	FA	FR	G/POS	TPR
1914	Bos-N	1	3	0	0	0	0	0	0	0	0	.000	.000	.000	-99	-1				.500	-1	/S-1	-0.2

■ ANGEL MARTINEZ
Martinez, Angel Sandy (Martinez)   b: 10/3/72, Villa Mella, D.R.   BL/TR, 6'2", 200 lbs.   Deb: 6/24/95

YEAR	TM/L	G	AB	R	H	2B	3B	HR	RBI	BB	SO	AVG	OBP	SLG	PRO+	BR/A	SB	CS	SBR	FA	FR	G/POS	TPR
1995	Tor-A	62	191	12	46	12	0	2	25	7	45	.241	.271	.335	57	-12	0	0	0	.986	-3	C-61	-1.1
1996	Tor-A	76	229	17	52	9	3	3	18	16	58	.227	.289	.332	56	-16	0	0	0	.993	6	C-75	-0.5
Total	2	138	420	29	98	21	3	5	43	23	103	.233	.281	.333	57	-28	0	0	0	.990	3	C-136	-1.6

■ CARLOS MARTINEZ
Martinez, Carlos Alberto Escobar (b: Carlos Alberto Escobar (Martinez))   b: 8/11/64, LaGuaira, Venez.   BR/TR, 6'5", 175 lbs.   Deb: 9/2/88

YEAR	TM/L	G	AB	R	H	2B	3B	HR	RBI	BB	SO	AVG	OBP	SLG	PRO+	BR/A	SB	CS	SBR	FA	FR	G/POS	TPR
1988	Chi-A	17	55	5	9	1	0	0	0	0	12	.164	.164	.182	-3	-7	1	0	0	.909	3	3-15/D-2	-0.5
1989	Chi-A	109	350	44	105	22	0	5	32	21	57	.300	.341	.406	112	5	4	1	1	.912	-6	3-68,1-34,O-10/D-1	-0.9
1990	Chi-A	92	272	18	61	6	5	4	24	10	40	.224	.252	.327	62	-15	0	4	-2	.988	-5	1-82/O-1,D-3	-2.9
1991	Cle-A	72	257	22	73	14	0	5	30	10	43	.284	.316	.397	95	-2	3	2	-0	.968	-4	D-41,1-31	-1.0
1992	Cle-A	69	228	23	60	9	1	5	35	7	21	.263	.288	.377	87	-5	1	2	-1	.996	-5	1-37,3-28/D-4	-1.3
1993	Cle-A	80	262	26	64	10	0	5	31	20	29	.244	.298	.340	71	-11	1	1	-0	.934	-9	3-35,1-22,D-19	-2.2
1995	Cal-A	26	61	7	11	1	0	1	9	6	7	.180	.265	.246	34	-6	0	0	0	.968	2	3-16/1-4,D-2	-0.4
Total	7	465	1485	145	383	63	6	25	161	74	209	.258	.295	.359	81	-41	10	10	-3	.986	-25	1-210,3-162/D-72,O	-8.5

■ CARMELO MARTINEZ
Martinez, Carmelo (Salgado)   b: 7/28/60, Dorado, P.R.   BR/TR, 6'2", 220 lbs.   Deb: 8/22/83

YEAR	TM/L	G	AB	R	H	2B	3B	HR	RBI	BB	SO	AVG	OBP	SLG	PRO+	BR/A	SB	CS	SBR	FA	FR	G/POS	TPR
1983	Chi-N	29	89	8	23	6	0	6	16	4	19	.258	.290	.494	108	0	0	0	0	.992	-0	1-26/3-1,O-1	-0.1
1984	*SD-N	149	488	64	122	28	2	13	66	68	82	.250	.346	.395	108	6	1	3	-2	.976	21	*O-142/1-2	2.2
1985	SD-N	150	514	64	130	28	1	21	72	87	82	.253	.364	.434	124	18	0	4	-3	.978	13	*O-150/1-3	2.5
1986	SD-N	113	244	28	58	10	0	9	25	35	46	.238	.336	.389	101	1	1	1	-0	.978	-0	O-60,1-26/3-1	0.1
1987	SD-N	139	447	59	122	21	2	15	70	70	82	.273	.375	.430	117	12	5	5	-2	.968	-3	O-78,1-65	0.1
1988	SD-N	121	365	48	86	12	0	18	65	35	57	.236	.303	.416	106	2	1	1	-0	.993	10	O-64,1-41	0.7
1989	SD-N	111	267	23	59	12	2	6	39	32	54	.221	.304	.348	86	-5	0	0	0	.982	1	O-65,1-32	-0.7
1990	Phi-N	71	198	23	48	8	0	8	31	29	37	.242	.339	.404	104	1	2	1	0	.994	-5	1-43,O-20	-0.4
	*Pit-N	12	19	3	4	1	0	2	4	1	5	.211	.250	.579	126	0	0	0	0	1.000	0	/1-5,O-2	0.1
	Yr	83	217	26	52	9	0	10	35	30	42	.240	.332	.419	106	2	2	1	0	.995	-2	1-48,O-22	-0.3
1991	Pit-N	11	16	1	4	0	0	0	1	2	2	.250	.294	.250	55	-1	0	0	0	.945	-1	/1-8	-0.2
	KC-A	44	121	17	25	6	0	4	17	22	25	.207	.351	.355	96	2	0	0	-1	.991	1	1-43/D-1	0.1
	Cin-N	53	138	12	32	5	0	6	19	15	37	.232	.307	.399	93	-1	0	0	0	.985	0	1-25,O-16	-0.3
Total	9	1003	2906	350	713	134	7	108	424	404	528	.245	.340	.408	108	35	10	16	-7	.980	41	O-598,1-319/3-2,D-1	3.8

■ TINO MARTINEZ
Martinez, Constantino   b: 12/7/67, Tampa, Fla.   BL/TR, 6'2", 205 lbs.   Deb: 8/20/90

YEAR	TM/L	G	AB	R	H	2B	3B	HR	RBI	BB	SO	AVG	OBP	SLG	PRO+	BR/A	SB	CS	SBR	FA	FR	G/POS	TPR
1990	Sea-A	24	68	4	15	4	0	0	5	9	9	.221	.312	.279	66	-3	0	0	0	1.000	0	1-23	-0.4
1991	Sea-A	36	112	11	23	2	0	4	9	11	24	.205	.276	.330	67	-5	0	0	0	.993	2	1-29/D-5	-0.5
1992	Sea-A	136	460	53	118	19	2	16	66	42	77	.257	.321	.411	103	1	2	1	0	.995	1	1-78,D-47	-0.5
1993	Sea-A	109	408	48	108	25	1	17	60	45	56	.265	.345	.456	112	6	0	3	-2	.997	-3	*1-103/D-6	-0.7
1994	Sea-A	97	329	42	86	21	0	20	61	29	52	.261	.323	.508	108	2	1	2	-1	.997	-2	1-82/D-8	-0.8
1995	*Sea-A★	141	519	92	152	35	3	31	111	62	91	.293	.373	.551	135	26	0	0	0	.993	-3	*1-139/D-1	1.5
1996	*NY-A	155	595	82	174	28	0	25	117	68	85	.292	.367	.466	107	6	2	1	0	.996	-4	*1-151/D-3	-1.1
Total	7	698	2491	332	676	134	6	113	429	266	394	.271	.345	.466	110	34	5	7	-3	.996	-2	1-605/D-70	-2.5

■ DAVE MARTINEZ
Martinez, David   b: 9/26/64, New York, N.Y.   BL/TL, 5'10", 150 lbs.   Deb: 6/15/86

YEAR	TM/L	G	AB	R	H	2B	3B	HR	RBI	BB	SO	AVG	OBP	SLG	PRO+	BR/A	SB	CS	SBR	FA	FR	G/POS	TPR
1986	Chi-N	53	108	13	15	1	1	1	7	6	22	.139	.191	.194	6	-14	4	2	0	.988	-4	O-46	-1.9
1987	Chi-N	142	459	70	134	18	8	8	36	57	96	.292	.373	.418	105	5	16	8	0	.980	1	*O-139	0.2
1988	Chi-N	75	256	27	65	10	1	4	34	21	46	.254	.315	.348	86	-4	7	3	0	.970	-1	O-72	-0.7
	Mon-N	63	191	24	49	3	5	2	12	17	48	.257	.317	.356	89	-3	16	6	1	.992	-5	O-60	-0.8
	Yr	138	447	51	114	13	6	6	46	38	94	.255	.316	.351	87	-7	23	9	2	.979	-5	*O-132	-1.5
1989	Mon-N	126	361	41	99	16	7	3	27	27	57	.274	.325	.382	100	-0	23	4	5	.967	-18	*O-118	-1.8
1990	Mon-N	118	391	60	109	13	5	11	39	24	48	.279	.322	.422	107	2	13	11	-3	.989	-3	*O-108/P-1	-0.5
1991	Mon-N	124	396	47	117	18	5	7	42	20	54	.295	.334	.419	112	5	16	7	1	.982	-1	*O-112	0.4
1992	Cin-N	135	393	47	100	20	5	3	31	42	54	.254	.326	.354	90	-5	12	8	-1	.991	-4	*O-111,1-21	-1.4
1993	SF-N	91	241	28	58	12	1	5	27	27	39	.241	.317	.361	84	-7	6	3	0	.993	-5	O-73	-1.2
1994	SF-N	97	235	23	58	9	3	4	27	21	22	.247	.314	.362	79	-7	3	4	-2	1.000	-5	O-58,1-25	-1.6
1995	Chi-A	119	303	49	93	16	4	5	37	32	41	.307	.375	.436	115	7	8	2	1	.976	-10	O-59,1-47/P-1,D-5	-0.6
1996	Chi-A	146	440	85	140	20	8	10	53	52	52	.318	.394	.468	124	17	15	7	0	.988	-17	*O-121,1-23	-0.6
Total	11	1289	3774	514	1037	156	53	63	372	346	579	.275	.338	.394	99	-2	139	65	3	.984	-69	*O-1077,1-116/D-5,P	-10.2

■ DOMINGO MARTINEZ
Martinez, Domingo Emilio (La Fontaine)   b: 8/4/67, Santo Domingo, D.R.   BR/TR, 6'2", 215 lbs.   Deb: 9/11/92

YEAR	TM/L	G	AB	R	H	2B	3B	HR	RBI	BB	SO	AVG	OBP	SLG	PRO+	BR/A	SB	CS	SBR	FA	FR	G/POS	TPR
1992	Tor-A	7	8	2	5	0	0	1	3	0	1	.625	.625	1.000	333	2	0	0	0	1.000	-1	/1-7	0.2
1993	Tor-A	8	14	2	4	0	0	1	3	1	7	.286	.333	.500	120	0	0	0	0	1.000	1	/1-7,3-1	0.1
Total	2	15	22	4	9	0	0	2	6	1	8	.409	.435	.682	196	1	0	0	0	1.000	0	/1-14,3-1	0.3

■ EDGAR MARTINEZ
Martinez, Edgar   b: 1/2/63, New York, N.Y.   BR/TR, 6'0", 175 lbs.   Deb: 9/12/87

YEAR	TM/L	G	AB	R	H	2B	3B	HR	RBI	BB	SO	AVG	OBP	SLG	PRO+	BR/A	SB	CS	SBR	FA	FR	G/POS	TPR
1987	Sea-A	13	43	6	16	5	0	0	5	2	5	.372	.413	.581	152	3	0	0	0	1.000	1	3-12/D-1	0.4
1988	Sea-A	14	32	0	9	4	0	0	5	4	7	.281	.361	.406	110	0	0	0	0	.929	-4	3-13	-0.4
1989	Sea-A	65	171	20	41	5	0	2	20	17	26	.240	.319	.304	74	-5	2	1	0	.949	-6	3-61	-1.2
1990	Sea-A	144	487	71	147	27	2	11	49	74	62	.302	.399	.433	131	23	1	4	-2	.928	-1	*3-143/D-2	2.1
1991	Sea-A	150	544	98	167	35	1	14	52	84	72	.307	.407	.452	137	31	0	3	-2	.962	3	*3-144/D-2	3.2
1992	Sea-A★	135	528	100	181	46	3	18	73	54	61	.343	.408	.544	164	44	14	4	2	.943	1	*3-103,D-28/1-2	4.6
1993	Sea-A	42	135	20	32	7	0	4	13	28	19	.237	.368	.378	100	1	0	1	0	.889	-4	D-24,3-16	-0.4
1994	Sea-A	89	326	47	93	23	1	13	51	53	42	.285	.390	.482	121	11	6	3	1	.950	5	3-64,D-23	1.5
1995	*Sea-A★	145	511	121	182	52	0	29	113	116	87	.356	.482	.628	184	70	4	3	-1	.800	-1	*D-138/3-4,1-3	5.3
1996	Sea-A★	139	499	121	163	52	2	26	103	123	84	.327	.467	.595	167	58	3	3	-1	.967	-1	*D-134/1-4,3-2	4.1
Total	10	936	3276	604	1031	256	11	117	484	555	465	.315	.420	.507	147	237	30	20	-3	.946	-7	3-562,D-352/1-9	19.2

■ TONY MARTINEZ
Martinez, Gabriel Antonio (Diaz)   b: 3/18/40, Perico, Cuba   d: 8/24/91, Miami, Fla.   BR/TR, 5'10", 165 lbs.   Deb: 4/9/63

YEAR	TM/L	G	AB	R	H	2B	3B	HR	RBI	BB	SO	AVG	OBP	SLG	PRO+	BR/A	SB	CS	SBR	FA	FR	G/POS	TPR
1963	Cle-A	43	141	10	22	4	0	0	8	5	18	.156	.185	.184	4	-18	1	1	-0	.961	-6	S-41	-2.4
1964	Cle-A	9	14	1	3	1	0	0	2	0	2	.214	.214	.286	38	-1	1	1	-0	1.000	4	/2-4,S-1	0.2
1965	Cle-A	4	3	0	0	0	0	0	0	0	0	.000	.000	.000	-99	-1	0	0	0	.000	0	H	-0.1
1966	Cle-A	17	17	2	5	0	0	0	0	1	6	.294	.333	.294	82	-0	1	1	-0	.833	1	/S-5,2-4	0.1
Total	4	73	175	13	30	5	0	0	10	6	26	.171	.199	.200	13	-20	2	3	-1	.958	-1	/S-47,2-8	-2.2

■ BUCK MARTINEZ
Martinez, John Albert   b: 11/7/48, Redding, Cal.   BR/TR, 5'10", 190 lbs.   Deb: 6/18/69

YEAR	TM/L	G	AB	R	H	2B	3B	HR	RBI	BB	SO	AVG	OBP	SLG	PRO+	BR/A	SB	CS	SBR	FA	FR	G/POS	TPR
1969	KC-A	72	205	14	47	6	1	4	23	8	25	.229	.258	.327	62	-11	0	0	0	.972	-1	C-55/O-1	-1.0

YEAR	TM/L	G	AB	R	H	2B	3B	HR	RBI	BB	SO	AVG	OBP	SLG	PRO+	BR/A	SB	CS	SBR	FA	FR	G/POS	TPR
1970	KC-A	6	9	1	1	0	0	0	0	2	1	.111	.273	.111	10	-1	0	0	0	.958	2	/C-5	0.1
1971	KC-A	22	46	3	7	2	0	0	1	5	9	.152	.235	.196	23	-5	0	1	-1	.968	2	C-21	-0.3
1973	KC-A	14	32	2	8	1	0	1	6	4	5	.250	.333	.375	92	-0	0	0	0	.966	-1	C-14	-0.1
1974	KC-A	43	107	10	23	3	1	1	8	14	19	.215	.317	.290	71	-4	0	1	-1	.977	1	C-38	-0.2
1975	KC-A	80	226	15	51	9	2	3	23	21	28	.226	.294	.323	72	-8	1	0	0	.980	-0	C-79	-0.5
1976	*KC-A	95	267	24	61	13	3	5	34	16	45	.228	.272	.356	82	-7	0	0	0	.991	5	C-94	0.1
1977	KC-A	29	80	3	18	4	0	1	9	3	12	.225	.253	.313	53	-5	0	1	-1	.993	3	C-28	-0.3
1978	Mil-A	89	256	26	56	10	1	1	20	14	42	.219	.259	.277	51	-17	1	1	-0	.978	-3	C-89	-1.9
1979	Mil-A	69	196	17	53	8	0	4	26	8	25	.270	.299	.372	80	-6	0	1	-1	.967	-2	C-68/P-1	-0.6
1980	Mil-A	76	219	16	49	9	0	3	17	12	33	.224	.267	.306	58	-13	1	0	0	.985	11	C-76	0.1
1981	Tor-A	45	128	13	29	8	1	4	21	11	16	.227	.293	.398	92	-2	1	0	0	.991	2	C-45	0.2
1982	Tor-A	96	260	26	63	17	0	10	37	24	34	.242	.306	.423	90	-4	1	1	-0	.988	6	C-93	0.4
1983	Tor-A	88	221	27	56	14	0	10	33	29	39	.253	.340	.452	109	3	1	1	-1	.989	-3	C-85	0.2
1984	Tor-A	102	232	24	51	13	1	5	37	29	49	.220	.312	.349	80	-6	0	3	-2	.995	-4	C-98/D-1	-0.9
1985	Tor-A	42	99	11	16	3	0	4	14	10	12	.162	.245	.313	50	-7	0	0	0	.988	4	C-42	-0.2
1986	Tor-A	81	160	13	29	8	0	2	12	20	25	.181	.272	.269	47	-12	0	0	0	.994	-1	C-78/D-1	-1.0
Total	17	1049	2743	245	618	128	10	58	321	230	419	.225	.287	.343	73	-105	5	10	-5	.984	19	*C-1008/D-2,P-1,O-1	-5.9

■ JOSE MARTINEZ
Martinez, Jose (Azcuiz) b: 7/26/42, Cardenas, Cuba BR/TR, 5'10", 190 lbs. Deb: 6/18/69 C

YEAR	TM/L	G	AB	R	H	2B	3B	HR	RBI	BB	SO	AVG	OBP	SLG	PRO+	BR/A	SB	CS	SBR	FA	FR	G/POS	TPR
1969	Pit-N	77	168	20	45	6	0	1	16	9	32	.268	.309	.321	78	-5	1	3	-2	.975	10	2-42,S-20/3-5,O-2	0.7
1970	Pit-N	19	20	1	1	0	0	0	0	1	5	.050	.095	.050	-61	-5	0	0	0	1.000	3	/3-7,2-4,S-1	-0.1
Total	2	96	188	21	46	6	0	1	16	10	37	.245	.286	.293	63	-9	1	3	-2	.966	13	/2-46,S-21,3-12,O-2	0.6

■ MANNY MARTINEZ
Martinez, Manuel (De Jesus) b: 10/3/70, San Pedro De Macoris, D.R. BR/TR, 6'2", 169 lbs. Deb: 6/14/96

YEAR	TM/L	G	AB	R	H	2B	3B	HR	RBI	BB	SO	AVG	OBP	SLG	PRO+	BR/A	SB	CS	SBR	FA	FR	G/POS	TPR
1996	Sea-A	9	17	3	4	2	1	0	3	3	5	.235	.350	.471	105	-0	2	0	1	1.000	0	/O-8	0.1
	Phi-N	13	36	2	8	0	2	0	0	1	11	.222	.263	.333	55	-2	2	1	0	.955	0	O-11	-0.3
Total	1	22	53	5	12	2	3	0	3	4	16	.226	.293	.377	72	-2	4	1	1	.972	0	/O-19	-0.2

■ MARTY MARTINEZ
Martinez, Orlando (Oliva) b: 8/23/41, Havana, Cuba BB/TR, 6'1", 175 lbs. Deb: 5/2/62 MC

YEAR	TM/L	G	AB	R	H	2B	3B	HR	RBI	BB	SO	AVG	OBP	SLG	PRO+	BR/A	SB	CS	SBR	FA	FR	G/POS	TPR
1962	Min-A	37	18	13	3	0	1	0	3	3	4	.167	.286	.278	51	-1	0	0	0	.920	8	S-11/3-1	0.7
1967	Atl-N	44	73	14	21	2	1	0	5	11	11	.288	.388	.342	112	2	0	1	-1	.920	4	S-25/2-9,C-3,3-2,1	0.8
1968	Atl-N	113	356	34	82	5	3	0	12	29	28	.230	.292	.261	67	-14	6	6	-2	.955	-5	S-54,3-37,2-16,C-14	-1.6
1969	Hou-N	78	198	14	61	5	4	0	15	10	21	.308	.341	.374	102	-0	0	0	0	1.000	-9	O-21,S-17,3/CP2	-0.8
1970	Hou-N	75	150	12	33	3	0	0	12	9	22	.220	.264	.240	38	-13	0	0	0	.990	-6	S-29,3-10/C-6,2-4	-1.6
1971	Hou-N	32	62	4	16	3	1	0	4	3	6	.258	.292	.339	80	-2	1	0	0	.968	1	/2-9,S-7,1-4,3-3	0.0
1972	StL-N	9	7	0	3	0	0	0	2	0	1	.429	.429	.429	146	1	0	0	0	1.000	-	/S-3,2-2,3-1	0.1
	Oak-A	22	40	3	5	0	0	0	1	3	6	.125	.186	.125	-7	-5	0	0	0	.944	3	2-17/S-6,3-1	-0.1
	Tex-A	26	41	3	6	1	1	0	3	2	8	.146	.186	.220	21	-4	0	1	-1	.944	-2	/S-5,3-4,2-1	-0.7
	Yr	48	81	6	11	1	1	0	4	5	14	.136	.186	.173	8	-9	0	1	-1	.946	2	2-18,S-11/3-5	-0.8
Total	7	436	945	97	230	19	11	0	57	70	107	.243	.298	.287	70	-37	7	8	-3	.950	-5	S-157/3-74,2CO1P	-3.2

■ PABLO MARTINEZ
Martinez, Pablo Made (Valera) b: 6/29/69, Sabana Grande, D.R. BB/TR, 5'10", 155 lbs. Deb: 7/20/96

YEAR	TM/L	G	AB	R	H	2B	3B	HR	RBI	BB	SO	AVG	OBP	SLG	PRO+	BR/A	SB	CS	SBR	FA	FR	G/POS	TPR
1996	Atl-N	4	2	1	1	0	0	0	0	0	0	.500	.500	.500	156	-0	0	1	-1	1.000	1	/S-1	0.0

■ CHITO MARTINEZ
Martinez, Reyenaldo Ignacio b: 12/19/65, Belize, British Honduras (Belize) BL/TL, 5'10", 180 lbs. Deb: 7/5/91

YEAR	TM/L	G	AB	R	H	2B	3B	HR	RBI	BB	SO	AVG	OBP	SLG	PRO+	BR/A	SB	CS	SBR	FA	FR	G/POS	TPR
1991	Bal-A	67	216	32	58	12	1	13	33	11	51	.269	.304	.514	127	6	1	1	-0	.982	2	O-54/1-1,D-4	0.7
1992	Bal-A	83	198	26	53	10	1	5	25	31	47	.268	.372	.404	114	5	0	1	-1	.973	1	O-52/D-4	0.5
1993	Bal-A	8	15	0	0	0	0	0	0	1	4	.000	.211	.000	-37	-3	0	0	0	1.000	-2	/O-5,D-2	-0.5
Total	3	158	429	58	111	22	2	18	58	46	102	.259	.333	.445	115	8	1	2	-1	.978	2	O-111/D-10,1-1	0.7

■ HECTOR MARTINEZ
Martinez, Rodolfo Hector (Santos) b: 5/11/39, Las Villas, Cuba BR/TR, 5'10", 160 lbs. Deb: 9/30/62

YEAR	TM/L	G	AB	R	H	2B	3B	HR	RBI	BB	SO	AVG	OBP	SLG	PRO+	BR/A	SB	CS	SBR	FA	FR	G/POS	TPR
1962	KC-A	1	1	0	0	0	0	0	0	0	0	.000	.000	.000	-96	-0	0	0	0	.000	0	H	0.0
1963	KC-A	6	14	2	4	0	0	1	3	1	3	.286	.375	.500	135	0	0	1	-1	1.000	0	/O-3	0.0
Total	2	7	15	2	4	0	0	1	3	1	4	.267	.353	.467	120	0	0	1	-1	1.000	0	/O-3	0.0

■ TED MARTINEZ
Martinez, Teodoro Noel (Encarnacion) b: 12/10/47, Central Barahona, D.R. BR/TR, 6', 165 lbs. Deb: 7/18/70

YEAR	TM/L	G	AB	R	H	2B	3B	HR	RBI	BB	SO	AVG	OBP	SLG	PRO+	BR/A	SB	CS	SBR	FA	FR	G/POS	TPR
1970	NY-N	4	16	0	1	0	0	0	0	0	3	.063	.063	.063	-66	-4	0	0	0	1.000	1	/2-4,S-1	-0.3
1971	NY-N	38	125	16	36	5	2	1	10	4	22	.288	.326	.384	102	0	6	0	2	.976	-7	S-23,2-13/3-3,0-1	-0.2
1972	NY-N	103	330	22	74	5	5	1	19	12	49	.224	.254	.279	52	-21	7	4	-0	.994	1	2-47,S-42,0-15,/3-2	-1.5
1973	*NY-N	92	263	34	67	11	0	1	14	13	38	.255	.295	.308	68	-11	3	5	-2	.941	-4	S-44,0-21,3-14,/2-5	-1.4
1974	NY-N	116	334	32	73	15	7	2	43	14	40	.219	.250	.323	61	-19	3	2	0	.952	14	/0-7,2-2,S-1,3-1	0.2
1975	StL-N	16	21	1	4	2	0	0	2	0	9	.190	.190	.286	30	-2	0	0	0	1.000	-0	/O-7,2-2,S-1,3-1	-0.5
	*Oak-A	86	87	7	15	0	0	0	3	2	9	.172	.200	.172	6	-11	1	0	0	.955	4	S-45,2-31,3-14	-0.5
1977	LA-N	67	137	21	41	6	1	1	10	2	20	.299	.309	.380	84	-3	3	4	-2	.992	14	2-27,S-13,3-12	1.1
1978	LA-N	54	55	13	14	1	0	1	5	4	14	.255	.317	.327	80	-1	3	2	0	.912	10	S-17,3-16,2-10	1.0
1979	LA-N	81	112	19	30	5	1	0	8	4	16	.268	.293	.330	71	-5	3	2	-0	.769	-0	3-23,S-21,2-18	-0.4
Total	9	657	1480	165	355	50	16	7	108	55	213	.240	.271	.309	62	-77	29	20	-3	.956	31	S-282,2-168/3-97,O	-2.4

■ JOE MARTY
Marty, Joseph Anton b: 9/1/13, Sacramento, Cal. d: 10/4/84, Sacramento, Cal. BR/TR, 6', 182 lbs. Deb: 4/22/37

YEAR	TM/L	G	AB	R	H	2B	3B	HR	RBI	BB	SO	AVG	OBP	SLG	PRO+	BR/A	SB	CS	SBR	FA	FR	G/POS	TPR
1937	Chi-N	88	290	41	84	17	2	5	44	28	30	.290	.356	.414	104	2	3			.976	-2	O-84	-0.3
1938	*Chi-N	76	235	32	57	8	3	7	35	18	26	.243	.305	.391	88	-4	0			.987	-4	O-68	-1.0
1939	Chi-N	23	76	6	10	1	0	2	10	4	13	.132	.175	.224	6	-10	2			.933	-2	O-21	-1.3
	Phi-N	91	299	32	76	12	6	9	44	24	27	.254	.310	.425	98	-2	1			.974	3	O-79/P-1	-0.2
	Yr	114	375	38	86	13	6	11	54	28	40	.229	.283	.384	79	-13	3			.968	1	*O-100/P-1	-1.5
1940	Phi-N	123	455	60	123	21	8	13	50	17	50	.270	.298	.437	105	0	2			.974	-4	*O-118	-0.3
1941	Phi-N	137	477	60	128	19	3	8	39	51	41	.268	.344	.371	105	4	6			.964	-6	*O-132	-1.1
Total	5	538	1832	223	478	78	22	44	222	142	187	.261	.318	.400	97	-11	14			.972	-9	O-502/P-1	-4.2

■ BOB MARTYN
Martyn, Robert Gordon b: 8/15/30, Weiser, Idaho BL/TR, 6', 176 lbs. Deb: 6/18/57

YEAR	TM/L	G	AB	R	H	2B	3B	HR	RBI	BB	SO	AVG	OBP	SLG	PRO+	BR/A	SB	CS	SBR	FA	FR	G/POS	TPR
1957	KC-A	58	131	10	35	2	4	1	12	11	20	.267	.324	.366	87	-2	1	3	-2	.976	-3	O-49	-1.0
1958	KC-A	95	226	25	59	10	7	2	23	26	36	.261	.337	.394	99	-0	1	4	-2	.967	-5	O-63	-1.0
1959	KC-A	1	1	0	0	0	0	0	0	0	0	.000	.000	.000	-98	-0	0	0	0	.000	0	R	0.0
Total	3	154	358	35	94	12	11	3	35	37	56	.263	.332	.383	94	-3	2	7	-4	.970	-8	O-112	-2.0

■ GARY MARTZ
Martz, Gary Arthur b: 1/10/51, Spokane, Wash. BR/TR, 6'4", 210 lbs. Deb: 7/8/75

YEAR	TM/L	G	AB	R	H	2B	3B	HR	RBI	BB	SO	AVG	OBP	SLG	PRO+	BR/A	SB	CS	SBR	FA	FR	G/POS	TPR
1975	KC-A	1	1	0	0	0	0	0	0	0	0	.000	.000	.000	-97	-0	0	0	0	1.000	-0	/O-1	-0.1

■ JOHN MARZANO
Marzano, John Robert b: 2/14/63, Philadelphia, Pa. BR/TR, 5'11", 197 lbs. Deb: 7/31/87

YEAR	TM/L	G	AB	R	H	2B	3B	HR	RBI	BB	SO	AVG	OBP	SLG	PRO+	BR/A	SB	CS	SBR	FA	FR	G/POS	TPR
1987	Bos-A	52	168	20	41	11	0	5	24	7	41	.244	.287	.399	77	-6	0	1	-1	.986	1	C-52	-0.2
1988	Bos-A	10	29	3	4	1	0	0	1	1	3	.138	.167	.172	-5	-4	0	0	0	1.000	5	C-10	0.2
1989	Bos-A	7	18	5	8	3	0	1	3	0	4	.444	.444	.778	224	3	0	0	0	1.000	0	/C-7	0.3
1990	Bos-A	32	83	8	20	4	0	0	6	5	10	.241	.284	.289	58	-5	0	1	-1	1.000	-4	C-32	0.1
1991	Bos-A	49	114	10	30	6	0	0	9	1	16	.263	.276	.333	64	-6	0	0	0	.985	-2	C-48	-0.6
1992	Bos-A	19	50	4	4	2	1	0	2	2	12	.080	.132	.160	-17	-8	0	0	0	.968	0	C-18/D-1	-0.7
1995	Tex-A	2	6	1	2	0	0	0	0	0	1	.333	.333	.333	72	-0	0	0	0	1.000	0	/C-2	0.0
1996	Sea-A	41	106	8	26	8	0	1	6	7	15	.245	.316	.302	58	-7	0	0	0	.986	-0	C-39	-0.4
Total	8	212	574	59	135	35	1	6	50	23	99	.235	.276	.331	60	-32	0	2	-1	.988	8	C-208/D-1	-1.3

■ CLYDE MASHORE
Mashore, Clyde Wayne b: 5/29/45, Concord, Cal. BR/TR, 5'11", 184 lbs. Deb: 7/11/69

YEAR	TM/L	G	AB	R	H	2B	3B	HR	RBI	BB	SO	AVG	OBP	SLG	PRO+	BR/A	SB	CS	SBR	FA	FR	G/POS	TPR
1969	Cin-N	2	1	0	0	0	0	0	0	0	0	.000	.000	.000	-95	-0	0	0	0	.000	0	H	0.0
1970	Mon-N	13	25	2	4	0	0	1	3	4	11	.160	.276	.280	49	-2	1	0	0	1.000	0	O-10	-0.4
1971	Mon-N	66	114	20	22	5	0	1	7	10	22	.193	.258	.263	48	-8	1	0	0	.967	-11	O-47/3-1	-2.2

YEAR	TM/L	G	AB	R	H	2B	3B	HR	RBI	BB	SO	AVG	OBP	SLG	PRO+	BR/A	SB	CS	SBR	FA	FR	G/POS	TPR
1972	Mon-N	93	176	23	40	7	1	3	23	14	41	.227	.284	.330	73	-6	6	1	1	.988	-13	O-74	-2.2
1973	Mon-N	67	103	12	21	3	0	3	14	15	28	.204	.305	.320	71	-4	4	3	-1	.958	-3	O-44/2-1	-0.9
Total	5	241	419	58	87	15	1	8	47	43	102	.208	.281	.305	64	-20	11	4	1	.974	-28	O-175/2-1,3-1	-5.7

■ DAMON MASHORE
Mashore, Damon Wayne b: 10/31/69, Ponce, P.R. BR/TR, 5'11", 195 lbs. Deb: 6/5/96

YEAR	TM/L	G	AB	R	H	2B	3B	HR	RBI	BB	SO	AVG	OBP	SLG	PRO+	BR/A	SB	CS	SBR	FA	FR	G/POS	TPR
1996	Oak-A	50	105	20	28	7	1	3	12	16	31	.267	.369	.438	107	1	4	0	1	.985	-11	O-48	-0.9

■ PHIL MASI
Masi, Philip Samuel b: 1/6/16, Chicago, Ill. d: 3/29/90, Mt.Prospect, Ill. BR/TR, 5'10", 180 lbs. Deb: 4/23/39

YEAR	TM/L	G	AB	R	H	2B	3B	HR	RBI	BB	SO	AVG	OBP	SLG	PRO+	BR/A	SB	CS	SBR	FA	FR	G/POS	TPR
1939	Bos-N	46	114	14	29	7	2	1	14	9	15	.254	.315	.377	92	-2	0			.960	-3	C-42	-0.3
1940	Bos-N	63	138	11	27	4	1	1	14	14	14	.196	.270	.261	50	-10	0			.966	-1	C-52	-0.7
1941	Bos-N	87	180	17	40	8	2	3	18	16	13	.222	.286	.339	79	-6	4			.978	-7	C-83	-0.8
1942	Bos-N	57	87	14	19	3	1	0	9	12	4	.218	.313	.276	74	-3	2			.961	2	C-39/O-4	0.1
1943	Bos-N	80	238	27	65	9	1	2	28	27	20	.273	.347	.345	102	1	5			.991	-6	C-73	0.0
1944	Bos-N	89	251	33	69	13	5	3	23	31	20	.275	.355	.402	108	3	4			.977	-0	C-63,1-12/3-2	0.6
1945	Bos-N†	114	371	55	101	25	4	7	46	42	32	.272	.348	.418	112	5	9			.980	1	C-95/1-7	1.1
1946	Bos-N★	133	397	52	106	17	5	3	62	55	41	.267	.358	.358	102	2	5			.981	-5	*C-124	0.4
1947	Bos-N★	126	411	54	125	22	4	9	50	47	27	.304	.377	.443	120	12	7			.989	-6	*C-123	1.4
1948	*Bos-N★	113	376	43	95	19	0	5	44	35	26	.253	.318	.343	80	-10	2			.988	1	*C-109	-0.2
1949	Bos-N	37	105	13	22	2	0	0	6	14	10	.210	.303	.229	47	-8	1			.993	-2	C-37	-0.7
	Pit-N	48	135	16	37	6	1	2	13	17	16	.274	.355	.378	94	-1	1			.994	-3	C-44/1-2	0.0
	Yr	85	240	29	59	8	1	2	19	31	26	.246	.332	.313	74	-8	2			.994	-3	C-81/1-2	-0.7
1950	Chi-A	122	377	38	105	17	2	7	55	49	36	.279	.366	.390	96	-2	2	1	0	.996	-1	*C-114	0.2
1951	Chi-A	84	225	24	61	11	2	4	28	32	27	.271	.367	.391	107	3	1	0	0	.979	-5	C-78	0.6
1952	Chi-A	30	63	9	16	1	1	0	5	10	4	.254	.356	.302	84	-1	0	0	0	.956	0	C-25	0.0
Total	14	1229	3468	420	917	164	31	47	417	410	311	.264	.344	.370	97	-14	45	1		.983	-27	*C-1101/1-21,O-4,3	1.7

■ HARRY MASKREY
Maskrey, Harry H. b: 12/21/1861, Mercer, Pa. d: 8/17/30, Mercer, Pa. Deb: 9/21/1882 F

YEAR	TM/L	G	AB	R	H	2B	3B	HR	RBI	BB	SO	AVG	OBP	SLG	PRO+	BR/A	SB	CS	SBR	FA	FR	G/POS	TPR
1882	Lou-a	1	4	0	0	0	0	0		0		.000	.000	.000	-99	-1				.000	-1	/O-1	-0.1

■ LEECH MASKREY
Maskrey, Samuel Leech b: 2/11/1854, Mercer, Pa. d: 4/1/22, Mercer, Pa. BR/TR, 5'8", 150 lbs. Deb: 5/2/1882 F

YEAR	TM/L	G	AB	R	H	2B	3B	HR	RBI	BB	SO	AVG	OBP	SLG	PRO+	BR/A	SB	CS	SBR	FA	FR	G/POS	TPR
1882	Lou-a	76	288	30	65	14	2	0		9		.226	.249	.288	85	-4				.902	-0	*O-76/2-1	-0.4
1883	Lou-a	96	361	50	73	13	8	1		10		.202	.224	.291	70	-11				.914	9	*O-96/S-1	-0.2
1884	Lou-a	105	412	48	103	13	4	0	36	17		.250	.281	.301	94	-2				.896	2	*O-103/3-3,S-1	-0.2
1885	Lou-a	109	423	54	97	8	11	1	46	19		.229	.269	.307	82	-9				.899	-3	*O-108/3-3	-1.3
1886	Lou-a	5	19	1	3	1	0	0	2	1		.158	.200	.211	27	-2	0			.800	-1	/O-5	-0.3
	Cin-a	27	98	7	19	3	1	0	10	5		.194	.240	.245	51	-6	4			.926	1	O-26/3-2	-0.5
	Yr	32	117	8	22	4	1	0	12	6		.188	.234	.239	47	-7	4			.915	0	O-31/3-2	-0.8
Total	5	418	1601	190	360	52	26	2	94	61		.225	.256	.294	80	-33	4			.904	7	O-414/3-8,S-2,2-1	-2.9

■ CHARLIE MASON
Mason, Charles E. b: 6/25/1853, New Orleans, La. d: 10/21/36, Philadelphia, Pa. BR/TR, 175 lbs. Deb: 4/26/1875 M

YEAR	TM/L	G	AB	R	H	2B	3B	HR	RBI	BB	SO	AVG	OBP	SLG	PRO+	BR/A	SB	CS	SBR	FA	FR	G/POS	TPR
1875	Cen-n	12	47	5	11	0	0	0	3	0	1	.234	.234	.234	69	-1	0	0	0	.719	0	O-10/1-2,C-1	-0.1
	Was-n	8	33	2	3	0	0	0	1	0	3	.091	.091	.091	-38	-4	0	0	0	.909	2	/O-8,P-1	-0.2
	Yr	20	80	7	14	0	0	0	4	0	4	.175	.175	.175	23	-6	0	0	0	.796	2	O-18/1-2,C-1,P-1	-0.3
1883	Phi-a	1	2	0	1	0	0	0		0		.500	.500	.500	207	0				.000	-0	/O-1	0.0

■ DON MASON
Mason, Donald Stetson b: 12/20/44, Boston, Mass. BL/TR, 5'11", 160 lbs. Deb: 4/14/66

YEAR	TM/L	G	AB	R	H	2B	3B	HR	RBI	BB	SO	AVG	OBP	SLG	PRO+	BR/A	SB	CS	SBR	FA	FR	G/POS	TPR
1966	SF-N	42	25	8	3	0	0	1	1	0	2	.120	.120	.240	-3	-3	0	1	-1	.905	5	/2-9	0.1
1967	SF-N	4	3	0	0	0	0	0	0	0	0	.000	.000	.000	-99	-1	0	0	0	1.000	1	/2-2	-0.1
1968	SF-N	10	19	3	3	0	0	0	1	1	4	.158	.200	.158	9	-2	1	1	-0	1.000	-1	/2-5,S-4,3-2	-0.4
1969	SF-N	104	250	43	57	4	2	0	13	36	29	.228	.325	.260	67	-10	1	5	-3	.956	10	2-51,3-21/S-7	0.1
1970	SF-N	46	36	4	5	0	0	0	1	5	7	.139	.244	.139	5	-5	0	0	0	.950	2	2-14	-0.3
1971	SD-N	113	344	43	73	12	1	2	11	27	35	.212	.270	.270	57	-20	6	4	-1	.965	-12	2-90/3-3	-2.7
1972	SD-N	9	11	1	2	0	0	0	0	1	1	.182	.250	.182	26	-1	0	0	0	.692	-0	/2-3	-0.1
1973	SD-N	8	8	0	0	0	0	0	0	0	2	.000	.000	.000	-99	-2	0	0	0	.750	1	/2-1	-0.2
Total	8	336	696	102	143	16	3	3	27	70	80	.205	.278	.250	52	-44	8	11	-4	.955	5	2-175/3-26,S-11	-3.5

■ JIM MASON
Mason, James Percy b: 8/14/50, Mobile, Ala. BL/TR, 6'2", 190 lbs. Deb: 9/26/71

YEAR	TM/L	G	AB	R	H	2B	3B	HR	RBI	BB	SO	AVG	OBP	SLG	PRO+	BR/A	SB	CS	SBR	FA	FR	G/POS	TPR
1971	Was-A	3	9	0	3	0	0	0	0	1	3	.333	.400	.333	116	0	0	0	0	.955	-0	/S-3	0.3
1972	Tex-A	46	147	10	29	3	0	0	10	9	39	.197	.248	.218	41	-11	0	0	0	.948	-6	S-32,3-10	-1.4
1973	Tex-A	92	238	23	49	7	2	3	19	24	48	.206	.276	.290	62	-12	0	1	-1	.947	9	S-74,2-19/3-1	0.4
1974	NY-A	152	440	41	110	18	6	5	37	35	87	.250	.305	.352	90	-6	1	2	-1	.964	-4	*S-152	0.8
1975	NY-A	94	223	17	34	3	2	1	16	22	49	.152	.229	.211	25	-22	1	0	0	.955	-10	S-93/2-1	-2.6
1976	*NY-A	93	217	17	39	7	1	1	14	9	37	.180	.212	.235	31	-19	0	1	-0	.966	7	S-93	-0.4
1977	Tor-A	22	79	10	13	3	0	0	2	7	10	.165	.233	.203	20	-9	1	1	-0	.971	-5	S-22	-1.2
	Tex-A	36	55	9	12	3	1	0	7	6	10	.218	.295	.327	69	-2	0	0	0	.976	2	S-32/3-1,D-1	0.6
	Yr	58	134	19	25	6	1	0	9	13	20	.187	.259	.254	40	-11	1	1	-0	.973	-3	S-54/3-1,D-1	-0.6
1978	Tex-A	55	105	10	20	4	0	0	3	5	17	.190	.227	.229	28	-10	0	2	-1	.938	1	S-42,3-11/2-1,D-1	-0.7
1979	Mon-N	40	71	3	13	5	1	0	6	7	16	.183	.256	.282	47	-5	0	2	-1	.966	0	S-33/3-6	-0.4
Total	9	633	1584	140	322	53	12	12	114	124	316	.203	.262	.275	54	-96	2	8	-4	.959	2	S-576/3-29,2-21,D-2	-4.6

■ GORDON MASSA
Massa, Gordon Richard "Moose" or "Duke" b: 9/2/35, Cincinnati, Ohio BL/TR, 6'3", 210 lbs. Deb: 9/24/57

YEAR	TM/L	G	AB	R	H	2B	3B	HR	RBI	BB	SO	AVG	OBP	SLG	PRO+	BR/A	SB	CS	SBR	FA	FR	G/POS	TPR
1957	Chi-N	6	15	2	7	1	0	0	3	4	3	.467	.579	.533	205	3	0	0	0	1.000	-3	/C-6	0.0
1958	Chi-N	2	2	0	0	0	0	0	0	0	2	.000	.000	.000	-99	-1	0	0	0	.000	0	H	-0.1
Total	2	8	17	2	7	1	0	0	3	4	5	.412	.524	.471	172	2	0	0	0	1.000	-3	/C-6	-0.1

■ ROY MASSEY
Massey, Roy Hardee "Red" b: 10/9/1890, Sevierville, Tenn. d: 6/23/54, Atlanta, Ga. BL/TR, 5'11", 170 lbs. Deb: 4/16/18

YEAR	TM/L	G	AB	R	H	2B	3B	HR	RBI	BB	SO	AVG	OBP	SLG	PRO+	BR/A	SB	CS	SBR	FA	FR	G/POS	TPR
1918	Bos-N	66	203	20	59	6	2	0	18	23	20	.291	.363	.340	120	5	1			.954	-3	O-45/3-2,1-1,S-1	0.0

■ BILL MASSEY
Massey, William Harry "Big Bill" b: 1/1871, Philadelphia, Pa. d: 10/9/40, Manila, Philippines BR/TR, 5'11", 168 lbs. Deb: 9/18/1894

YEAR	TM/L	G	AB	R	H	2B	3B	HR	RBI	BB	SO	AVG	OBP	SLG	PRO+	BR/A	SB	CS	SBR	FA	FR	G/POS	TPR
1894	Cin-N	13	53	7	15	3	0	0	5	3	2	.283	.321	.340	57	-4	0			.991	-1	1-10/2-2,3-1	-0.4

■ MIKE MASSEY
Massey, William Herbert b: 9/28/1893, Galveston, Tex. d: 10/17/71, Shreveport, La. BB/TR, 6', 195 lbs. Deb: 4/12/17

YEAR	TM/L	G	AB	R	H	2B	3B	HR	RBI	BB	SO	AVG	OBP	SLG	PRO+	BR/A	SB	CS	SBR	FA	FR	G/POS	TPR
1917	Bos-N	31	91	12	18	0	0	0	2	15	15	.198	.318	.198	63	-3	2			.900	-8	2-25	-1.1

■ DAN MASTELLER
Masteller, Dan Patrick b: 3/17/68, Toledo, Ohio BL/TL, 6', 185 lbs. Deb: 6/23/95

YEAR	TM/L	G	AB	R	H	2B	3B	HR	RBI	BB	SO	AVG	OBP	SLG	PRO+	BR/A	SB	CS	SBR	FA	FR	G/POS	TPR
1995	Min-A	71	198	21	47	12	0	3	21	18	19	.237	.304	.343	68	-9	1	2	-1	.994	-4	1-48,O-22/D-8	-1.8

■ VICTOR MATA
Mata, Victor Jose (Abreu) b: 6/17/61, Santiago, D.R. BR/TR, 6'1", 165 lbs. Deb: 7/22/84

YEAR	TM/L	G	AB	R	H	2B	3B	HR	RBI	BB	SO	AVG	OBP	SLG	PRO+	BR/A	SB	CS	SBR	FA	FR	G/POS	TPR
1984	NY-A	30	70	8	23	5	0	1	6	0	12	.329	.338	.443	119	1	1	1	-0	.942	-6	O-28	-0.5
1985	NY-A	6	7	1	1	0	0	0	0	0	0	.143	.143	.143	-22	-1	0	0	0	1.000	-2	/O-3	-0.3
Total	2	36	77	9	24	5	0	1	6	0	12	.312	.321	.416	106	-1	1	1	-0	.943	-7	/O-31	-0.8

■ TOM MATCHICK
Matchick, John Thomas b: 9/7/43, Hazleton, Pa. BL/TR, 6', 175 lbs. Deb: 9/2/67

YEAR	TM/L	G	AB	R	H	2B	3B	HR	RBI	BB	SO	AVG	OBP	SLG	PRO+	BR/A	SB	CS	SBR	FA	FR	G/POS	TPR
1967	Det-A	8	6	1	1	0	0	0	0	0	0	.167	.167	.167	-1	-1	0	0	0	1.000	0	/S-1	-0.1
1968	*Det-A	80	227	18	46	6	2	3	14	10	46	.203	.249	.286	60	-11	0	2	-1	.950	-14	S-59,2-13/1-6	-2.4
1969	Det-A	94	298	25	72	11	2	6	32	15	51	.242	.278	.292	57	-17	3	0	1	.972	-7	2-47,3-27/S-6,1-2	-2.0
1970	Bos-A	10	14	2	1	0	0	0	1	0	2	.071	.188	.071	-24	-2	0	1	-1	1.000	-1	/3-2,2-1,S-1	-0.4
	KC-A	55	158	11	31	3	0	1	11	6	23	.196	.226	.241	29	-15	0	1	-0	.985	13	S-43,2-10/3-1	0.2
	Yr	65	172	13	32	3	0	1	11	6	25	.186	.222	.227	24	-18	0	2	-1	.985	12	S-44,2-11/3-3	-0.2
1971	Mil-A	42	114	6	25	1	0	1	7	7	23	.219	.264	.254	48	-5	3	2	-0	.979	1	3-41/2-1	-0.8
1972	Bal-A	3	9	0	2	0	0	0	0	0	1	.222	.222	.222	32	-1	0	0	0	.857	-1	/3-3	-0.2
Total	6	292	826	63	178	21	6	4	64	39	148	.215	.255	.270	49	-55	6	6	-2	.967	-8	S-110/3-74,2-72,1-8	-5.7

YEAR	TM/L	G	AB	R	H	2B	3B	HR	RBI	BB	SO	AVG	OBP	SLG	PRO+	BR/A	SB	CS	SBR	FA	FR	G/POS	TPR

■ **MIKE MATHENY**   Matheny, Michael Scott b: 9/22/70, Columbus, Ohio   BR/TR, 6'3", 205 lbs.   Deb: 4/7/94

1994	Mil-A	28	53	3	12	3	0	1	2	3	13	.226	.293	.340	60	-3	0	1	-1	.989	3	C-27	0.0
1995	Mil-A	80	166	13	41	9	1	0	21	12	28	.247	.306	.313	58	-10	2	1	0	.986	5	C-80	-0.2
1996	Mil-A	106	313	31	64	15	2	8	46	14	80	.204	.245	.342	44	-28	3	2	-0	.985	-2	*C-104/D-1	-2.1
Total	3	214	532	47	117	27	3	9	69	29	121	.220	.269	.333	50	-41	5	4	-1	.985	6	C-211/D-1	-2.3

■ **JOE MATHES**   Mathes, Joseph John b: 7/28/1891, Milwaukee, Wis.   d: 12/21/78, St.Louis, Mo.   BB/TR, 6'0.5", 180 lbs.   Deb: 9/19/12

1912	Phi-A	4	14	0	2	0	0	0	0	0		.143	.200	.143	-2	-2	0			.889	-1	/3-4	-0.3
1914	StL-F	26	85	10	25	3	0	0	6	9	11	.294	.362	.329	85	-3	1			.938	-4	2-23	-0.7
1916	Bos-N	2	0	0	0	0	0	0	0	0	0	—	—	—	—		0	0		.000	-1	/2-2	-0.1
Total	3	32	99	10	27	3	0	0	6	9	11	.273	.339	.303	74	-4	1			.921	-6	/2-25,3-4	-1.1

■ **EDDIE MATHEWS**   Mathews, Edwin Lee b: 10/13/31, Texarkana, Tex.   BL/TR, 6'1", 200 lbs.   Deb: 4/15/52   MCH

1952	Bos-N	145	528	80	128	23	5	25	58	59	115	.242	.320	.447	114	8	6	4	-1	.957	-10	*3-142	-0.5
1953	Mil-N★	157	579	110	175	31	8	47	135	99	83	.302	.406	.627	175	64	1	3	-2	.939	3	*3-157	5.8
1954	Mil-N	138	476	96	138	21	4	40	103	113	61	.290	.428	.603	177	57	10	3	1	.966	-3	*3-127,O-10	5.2
1955	Mil-N★	141	499	108	144	23	5	41	101	109	98	.289	.417	.601	175	56	3	4	-2	.952	-4	*3-137	4.9
1956	Mil-N☆	151	552	103	150	21	2	37	95	91	86	.272	.376	.518	146	36	6	0	-2	.944	-12	*3-150	2.8
1957	*Mil-N★	148	572	109	167	28	9	32	94	90	79	.292	.388	.540	157	47	3	1	0	.964	-2	*3-147	4.8
1958	*Mil-N☆	149	546	97	137	18	1	31	77	85	85	.251	.354	.458	123	18	5	0	2	.955	5	*3-149	2.6
1959	Mil-N★	148	594	118	182	16	8	46	114	80	71	.306	.391	.593	172	59	2	1	0	.961	3	*3-148	6.2
1960	Mil-N★	153	548	108	152	19	7	39	124	111	113	.277	.401	.551	170	55	7	3	0	.950	-13	*3-153	4.2
1961	Mil-N★	152	572	103	175	23	6	32	91	93	95	.306	.405	.535	156	48	12	7	-1	.961	-6	*3-151	4.2
1962	Mil-N★	152	536	106	142	25	6	29	90	101	90	.265	.383	.496	138	30	4	2	0	.964	2	*3-140/1-7	3.3
1963	Mil-N	158	547	82	144	27	4	23	84	124	119	.263	.400	.453	147	39	3	4	-2	.968	15	*3-121,O-42	5.3
1964	Mil-N	141	502	83	117	19	1	23	74	85	100	.233	.345	.412	112	9	2	2	-1	.962	7	*3-128/1-7	0.9
1965	Mil-N	156	546	77	137	23	0	32	95	73	110	.251	.342	.469	125	18	1	0	0	.956	9	*3-153	2.6
1966	Atl-N	134	452	72	113	21	4	16	53	63	82	.250	.342	.420	109	6	1	1	-0	.946	-2	*3-127	0.1
1967	Hou-N	101	328	39	78	13	2	10	38	48	65	.238	.337	.381	109	4	2	4	-2	.987	-4	1-79,3-24	-0.7
	Det-A	36	108	14	25	3	0	6	19	15	23	.231	.336	.426	121	3	0	0	0	.933	-2	3-21,1-13	0.0
1968	*Det-A	31	52	4	11	0	0	3	8	8	8	.212	.281	.385	97	-0	0	0	0	.974	-1	/1-6,3-6	0.0
Total	17	2391	8537	1509	2315	354	72	512	1453	1444	1487	.271	.378	.509	145	559	68	39	-3	.956	-20	*3-2181,1-112/O-52	51.6

■ **NELSON MATHEWS**   Mathews, Nelson Elmer b: 7/21/41, Columbia, Ill.   BR/TR, 6'4", 195 lbs.   Deb: 9/9/60   F

1960	Chi-N	3	8	1	2	0	0	0	0	0	2	.250	.250	.250	38	-1	0	0	0	1.000	0	/O-2	-0.1
1961	Chi-N	3	9	0	1	0	0	0	0	0	2	.111	.111	.111	-40	-2	0	0	0	1.000	0	/O-2	-0.2
1962	Chi-N	15	49	5	15	2	0	2	13	5	4	.306	.393	.469	126	2	3	3	-1	.962	-2	O-14	-0.2
1963	Chi-N	61	155	12	24	3	2	4	10	16	48	.155	.234	.277	44	-11	3	4	-2	.979	-2	O-46	-1.9
1964	KC-A	157	573	58	137	27	5	14	60	43	143	.239	.290	.377	82	-14	2	3	-1	.968	9	*O-154	-1.4
1965	KC-A	67	184	17	39	7	7	2	15	24	49	.212	.303	.359	89	-3	0	2	-1	.981	-2	O-57	-0.9
Total	6	306	978	93	218	39	14	22	98	88	248	.223	.289	.359	78	-29	8	12	-5	.972	4	O-275	-4.7

■ **BOBBY MATHEWS**   Mathews, Robert T. b: 11/21/1851, Baltimore, Md.   d: 4/17/1898, Baltimore, Md.   BR/TR, 5'5.5", 140 lbs.   Deb: 5/4/1871   U

1871	Kek-n	19	89	15	24	3	1	0	10	2	0	.270	.286	.326	74	-3	2	1	0	.840	-0	P-19	0.0
1872	Bal-n	50	223	36	50	1	0	0	21	3	2	.224	.235	.229	41	-16	1	1	-0	.780	-6	*P-49/O-8,3-3	-0.3
1873	Mut-n	52	223	40	43	3	0	0	13	10	3	.193	.227	.233	37	-16	1	1	-0	.759	-3	*P-52/O-5	-0.1
1874	Mut-n	65	298	46	72	6	1	0	30	3	3	.242	.249	.268	64	-12	2	0	1	.774	-7	*P-65/3-1,O-1	-0.1
1875	Mut-n	70	264	23	48	6	2	0	15	2	1	.182	.188	.220	39	-16	1	2	-1	.838	-6	*P-70/O-1	0.0
1876	NY-N	56	218	19	40	4	1	0	9	3	2	.183	.195	.211	40	-12				.810	-3	*P-56/O-1	-0.2
1877	Cin-N	15	59	5	10	0	0	0	0	1	0	.169	.183	.169	13	-5				.862	-3	P-15/O-1,S-1	-0.2
1879	Pro-N	43	173	25	35	2	0	1	10	7	12	.202	.233	.231	55	-8				.956	-5	P-27,O-21/3-5	-0.9
1881	Pro-N	16	57	6	11	1	0	0	4	5	6	.193	.258	.211	50	-3				.810	-4	P-14/O-5	-0.2
	Bos-N	19	71	2	12	2	0	0	4	0	5	.169	.169	.197	15	-7				.818	-4	O-18/P-5	-0.9
	Yr	35	128	8	23	3	0	0	8	5	11	.180	.211	.203	32	-10				.811	-9	O-23,P-19	-1.1
1882	Bos-N	45	169	17	38	6	0	0	13	8	18	.225	.260	.260	67	-6				.867	-10	P-34,O-13/S-1	-0.6
1883	Phi-a	45	167	15	31	2	0	0	11	5		.186	.209	.198	29	-13				.874	-2	P-44/O-3	-0.1
1884	Phi-a	49	184	26	34	5	1	0		7		.185	.215	.223	40	-12				.775	-1	P-49/O-1	0.1
1885	Phi-a	48	179	22	30	3	0	0	12	10		.168	.212	.184	24	-16				.881	-0	P-48/O-1	-0.1
1886	Phi-a	24	88	16	21	3	0	0	10	3		.239	.264	.273	67	-3	1			.843	-0	P-24/O-1	-0.1
1887	Phi-a	7	25	5	5	0	0	0		4		.200	.310	.200	44	-2	0			.889	-0	/P-7	-0.0
Total	5 n	256	1097	160	237	19	7	0	89	20	13	.216	.230	.246	49	-64	7	5	-1	.797	-18	P-255/O-15,3-4	-0.5
Total	10	367	1390	158	267	28	2	1	73	53	45	.192	.222	.217	42	-87	1			.845	-30	P-323/O-65,3-5,S-2	-2.9

■ **JIMMY MATHISON**   Mathison, James Michael Ignatius b: 11/11/1878, Baltimore, Md.   d: 7/4/11, Baltimore, Md.   TR ,   Deb: 8/29/02

1902	Bal-A	29	91	12	24	2	1	0	7	9		.264	.368	.308	85	-1	2			.889	-3	3-28/S-1	-0.3

■ **JOHN MATIAS**   Matias, John Roy b: 8/15/44, Honolulu, Hawaii   BL/TL, 5'11", 170 lbs.   Deb: 4/7/70

1970	Chi-A	58	117	7	22	2	0	2	6	3	22	.188	.215	.256	28	-11	1	0	0	.941	-4	O-22,1-18	-1.8

■ **FRANCISCO MATOS**   Matos, Francisco Aguirre (Mancebo) b: 7/23/69, Santo Domingo, D.R.   BR/TR, 6'1", 160 lbs.   Deb: 7/17/94

1994	Oak-A	14	28	1	7	1	0	0	2	1	2	.250	.276	.286	49	-2	1	0	0	.925	1	2-12/D-2	-0.1

■ **C. V. MATTERSON**   Matterson, C. V. b: Ohio   Deb: 6/13/1884

1884	StL-U	1	4	0	0	0	0	0	0	0		.000	.000	.000	-97	-1				.000	-1	/O-1,P-1	-0.1

■ **GARY MATTHEWS**   Matthews, Gary Nathaniel b: 7/5/50, San Fernando, Cal.   BR/TR, 6'3", 190 lbs.   Deb: 9/6/72

1972	SF-N	20	62	11	18	1	1	4	14	7	13	.290	.362	.532	149	4	0	1	-1	.971	-1	O-19	0.2
1973	SF-N	148	540	74	162	22	10	12	58	58	83	.300	.369	.444	119	15	17	5	2	.983	6	*O-145	1.7
1974	SF-N	154	561	87	161	27	6	16	82	70	69	.287	.369	.442	120	16	11	9	-2	.970	5	*O-151	1.2
1975	SF-N	116	425	67	119	22	3	12	58	65	53	.280	.378	.431	119	12	13	4	2	.967	8	*O-113	1.8
1976	SF-N	156	587	79	164	28	4	20	84	75	94	.279	.362	.443	124	19	12	5	1	.975	-3	*O-156	1.1
1977	Atl-N	148	555	89	157	25	5	17	64	67	90	.283	.362	.438	101	1	22	8	-2	.965	8	*O-145	0.6
1978	Atl-N	129	474	75	135	20	5	18	62	61	92	.285	.369	.462	118	11	8	7	-2	.969	-2	*O-127	0.6
1979	Atl-N★	156	631	97	192	34	5	27	90	60	75	.304	.365	.502	125	21	18	6	2	.974	1	*O-156	1.7
1980	Atl-N	155	571	79	159	17	3	19	75	64	93	.278	.328	.419	104	2	12	3	3	.960	-3	*O-143	-0.6
1981	*Phi-N	101	359	62	108	21	3	9	67	59	42	.301	.404	.451	136	19	15	2	3	.963	1	*O-100	2.2
1982	Phi-N	162	616	89	173	31	1	19	83	66	87	.281	.352	.427	114	12	21	4	-4	.966	3	*O-162	1.5
1983	*Phi-N	132	446	66	115	18	2	10	50	69	81	.258	.357	.374	104	4	13	9	-2	.974	-1	O-122	-0.3
1984	*Chi-N	147	491	101	143	21	2	14	82	103	97	.291	.417	.428	126	22	17	5	0	.955	-4	*O-145	1.4
1985	Chi-N	97	298	45	70	12	0	13	40	59	64	.235	.365	.406	104	3	2	0	1	.977	-2	O-85	-0.1
1986	Chi-N	123	370	49	96	11	1	21	46	60	59	.259	.363	.478	121	11	3	4	-0	.940	-8	*O-105	-0.1
1987	Chi-N	44	42	3	11	3	0	4	8	4	11	.262	.326	.333	72	-2	0	0	0	1.000	-0	/O-2	-0.2
	Sea-A	45	119	10	28	1	0	3	15	15	22	.235	.321	.319	67	-5	0	1	-1	.000	-0	D-39	-0.7
Total	16	2033	7147	1083	2011	319	51	234	978	940	1125	.281	.367	.439	116	164	183	74	1	.968	12	*O-1876/D-39	12.0

■ **BOB MATTHEWS**   Matthews, Robert b: Camden, N.J.   Deb: 9/25/1891

1891	Phi-a	1	3	1	1	0	0	0	0	0		.333	.600	.333	163	1	0			.000	-0	/O-1	0.0

■ **WID MATTHEWS**   Matthews, Wid Curry "Matty" b: 10/20/1896, Raleigh, Ill   d: 10/5/65, Hollywood, Cal.   BL/TL, 5'8.5", 155 lbs.   Deb: 4/18/23

1923	Phi-A	129	485	52	133	11	6	1	25	50	27	.274	.343	.328	76	-16	16	16	-5	.947	-8	*O-127	-3.7
1924	Was-A	53	169	25	51	10	4	0	13	11	4	.302	.355	.408	100	-0	3	8	-4	.985	5	O-44	-0.2

YEAR	TM/L	G	AB	R	H	2B	3B	HR	RBI	BB	SO	AVG	OBP	SLG	PRO+	BR/A	SB	CS	SBR	FA	FR	G/POS	TPR
1925	Was-A	10	9	2	4	0	0	0	1	0	1	.444	.444	.444	129	0	0	0	0	1.000	-0	/O-1	0.0
Total	3	192	663	79	188	21	10	1	39	61	32	.284	.348	.350	83	-16	19	24	-9	.957	-4	O-172	-3.9

■ STEVE MATTHIAS   Matthias, Stephen J.   b: 1860, Mitchellville, Md.   BR/TR, 5'8", 160 lbs.   Deb: 4/20/1884

YEAR	TM/L	G	AB	R	H	2B	3B	HR	RBI	BB	SO	AVG	OBP	SLG	PRO+	BR/A	SB	CS	SBR	FA	FR	G/POS	TPR
1884	CP-U	37	142	24	39	7	1	0		5		.275	.299	.338	20	-5				.840	2	S-36/O-2	-0.2

■ BOBBY MATTICK   Mattick, Robert James   b: 12/5/15, Sioux City, Iowa   BR/TR, 5'11", 178 lbs.   Deb: 5/5/38   FM

YEAR	TM/L	G	AB	R	H	2B	3B	HR	RBI	BB	SO	AVG	OBP	SLG	PRO+	BR/A	SB	CS	SBR	FA	FR	G/POS	TPR
1938	Chi-N	1	1	0	1	0	0	0	0	0	0	1.000	1.000	1.000	439	0	0			.000	0	/S-1	0.0
1939	Chi-N	51	178	16	51	12	1	0	23	6	19	.287	.314	.365	80	-5	1			.927	7	S-48	0.6
1940	Chi-N	128	441	30	96	15	0	0	33	19	33	.218	.250	.252	39	-36	5			.946	10	*S-126/3-1	-1.6
1941	Cin-N	20	60	8	11	3	0	0	7	8	7	.183	.279	.233	45	-4	1			.982	0	S-12/3-5,2-1	-0.5
1942	Cin-N	6	10	0	2	1	0	0	0	0	1	.200	.200	.300	45	-1	0			1.000	1	/S-3	0.1
Total	5	206	690	54	161	31	1	0	64	33	60	.233	.269	.281	52	-46	7			.943	17	S-190/3-6,2-1	-1.4

■ WALLY MATTICK   Mattick, Walter Joseph "Chink"   b: 3/12/1887, St.Louis, Mo.   d: 11/5/68, Los Altos, Cal.   BR/TR, 5'10", 180 lbs.   Deb: 4/11/12   F

YEAR	TM/L	G	AB	R	H	2B	3B	HR	RBI	BB	SO	AVG	OBP	SLG	PRO+	BR/A	SB	CS	SBR	FA	FR	G/POS	TPR
1912	Chi-A	90	285	45	74	7	9	1	35	27		.260	.334	.358	101	0	15			.982	-3	O-79	-0.7
1913	Chi-A	71	207	15	39	8	1	0	11	18	16	.188	.253	.237	44	-15	3			.977	2	O-64	-1.7
1918	StL-N	8	14	0	2	0	0	0	1	2	3	.143	.333	.143	49	-1	0			1.000	0	/O-3	0.0
Total	3	169	506	60	115	15	10	1	47	47	19	.227	.302	.302	77	-15	18			.980	-1	O-146	-2.4

■ MIKE MATTIMORE   Mattimore, Michael Joseph   b: 1859, Renovo, Pa.   d: 4/28/31, Butte, Mont.   BL/TL, 5'8.5", 160 lbs.   Deb: 5/3/1887

YEAR	TM/L	G	AB	R	H	2B	3B	HR	RBI	BB	SO	AVG	OBP	SLG	PRO+	BR/A	SB	CS	SBR	FA	FR	G/POS	TPR
1887	NY-N	8	32	5	8	1	0	0	4	0	6	.250	.250	.281	50	2	1			.889	-1	/P-7,O-2	0.0
1888	Phi-a	41	142	22	38	6	5	0	12	12		.268	.333	.380	129	5	16			.915	5	P-26,O-16	0.2
1889	Phi-a	23	73	10	17	1	2	1	8	9	7	.233	.333	.342	94	-0	6			.944	-3	O-12/1-7,P-5	-0.3
	KC-a	19	75	6	12	1	1	0	5	3	16	.160	.192	.200	11	-9	0			.844	-3	O-19/P-1	-0.9
	Yr	42	148	16	29	2	3	1	13	12	23	.196	.265	.270	52	-10	6			.873	-5	O-31/1-7,P-6	-1.2
1890	Bro-a	33	129	14	17	1	1	0	7	16		.132	.238	.155	17	-13	11			.887	-6	P-19,O-14	-0.9
Total	4	124	451	57	92	10	9	1	36	40	29	.204	.278	.273	64	-20	34			.853	-7	/O-63,P-58,1-7	-1.9

■ DON MATTINGLY   Mattingly, Donald Arthur   b: 4/20/61, Evansville, Ind.   BL/TL, 6', 175 lbs.   Deb: 9/8/82

YEAR	TM/L	G	AB	R	H	2B	3B	HR	RBI	BB	SO	AVG	OBP	SLG	PRO+	BR/A	SB	CS	SBR	FA	FR	G/POS	TPR
1982	NY-A	7	12	0	2	0	0	0	1	0	1	.167	.167	.167	-8	-2	0	0	0	1.000	1	/O-6,1-1	-0.1
1983	NY-A	91	279	34	79	15	4	4	32	21	31	.283	.336	.409	108	3	0	0	0	.974	-10	O-48,1-42/2-1	-1.1
1984	NY-A★	153	603	91	**207**	**44**	2	23	110	41	33	**.343**	.386	.537	**159**	46	1	1	-0	**.996**	13	*1-133,O-19	4.9
1985	NY-A★	159	652	107	211	**48**	3	35	**145**	56	41	.324	.379	.567	159	51	2	2	-1	**.995**	-11	*1-159	2.8
1986	NY-A★	162	677	117	**238**	**53**	2	31	113	53	35	.352	.399	**.573**	163	**57**	0	0	0	**.996**	-7	*1-160/3-3,D-1	3.7
1987	NY-A★	141	569	93	186	38	2	30	115	51	38	.327	.383	.559	147	38	1	4	-2	**.996**	-4	*1-140/D-1	2.0
1988	NY-A★	144	599	94	186	37	0	18	88	41	29	.311	.358	.462	129	22	1	0	0	.993	-4	*1-143/O-1,D-1	0.6
1989	NY-A★	158	631	79	191	37	2	23	113	51	30	.303	.351	.477	134	27	3	5	-1	.995	-5	*1-145,D-17/O-1	1.1
1990	NY-A	102	394	40	101	16	0	5	42	28	20	.256	.311	.335	80	-10	1	0	0	.997	-5	1-89,D-13/O-1	-1.2
1991	NY-A	152	587	64	169	35	0	9	68	46	42	.288	.344	.394	103	3	2	0	1	.996	-4	*1-127,D-22	-1.0
1992	NY-A	157	640	89	184	40	0	14	86	39	43	.287	.329	.416	108	5	3	0	0	**.997**	7	*1-143,D-15	0.3
1993	NY-A	134	530	78	154	27	2	17	86	61	42	.291	.366	.445	121	16	0	0	0	**.998**	3	*1-130/D-5	0.3
1994	NY-A	97	372	62	113	20	1	6	51	60	24	.304	.400	.411	114	10	0	0	0	.998	3	1-97	0.4
1995	*NY-A	128	458	59	132	32	2	7	49	40	35	.288	.347	.413	98	-2	0	0	-1	.994	-1	*1-125/D-1	-1.5
Total	14	1785	7003	1007	2153	442	20	222	1099	588	444	.307	.363	.471	128	264	14	9	-1	.996	-19	*1-1634/D-76,O32	11.2

■ RALPH MATTIS   Mattis, Ralph "Matty"   b: 8/24/1890, Roxborough, Pa.   d: 9/13/60, Williamsport, Pa.   BR/TR, 5'11", 172 lbs.   Deb: 4/22/14

YEAR	TM/L	G	AB	R	H	2B	3B	HR	RBI	BB	SO	AVG	OBP	SLG	PRO+	BR/A	SB	CS	SBR	FA	FR	G/POS	TPR
1914	Pit-F	36	85	14	21	4	1	0	8	9	11	.247	.326	.318	77	-1	7			.938	2	O-24	-0.4

■ CLOY MATTOX   Mattox, Cloy Mitchell "Monk"   b: 11/24/02, Leesville, Va.   d: 8/3/85, Danville, Va.   BL/TR, 5'8", 168 lbs.   Deb: 9/1/29   F

YEAR	TM/L	G	AB	R	H	2B	3B	HR	RBI	BB	SO	AVG	OBP	SLG	PRO+	BR/A	SB	CS	SBR	FA	FR	G/POS	TPR
1929	Phi-A	3	6	0	1	0	0	0	1	1	1	.167	.286	.167	19	-1	0	0	0	.875	-0	/C-3	-0.1

■ JIM MATTOX   Mattox, James Powell   b: 12/17/1896, Leesville, Va.   d: 10/12/73, Myrtle Beach, S.C.   BL/TR, 5'9.5", 168 lbs.   Deb: 4/30/22   F

YEAR	TM/L	G	AB	R	H	2B	3B	HR	RBI	BB	SO	AVG	OBP	SLG	PRO+	BR/A	SB	CS	SBR	FA	FR	G/POS	TPR
1922	Pit-N	29	51	11	15	1	1	0	3	1	3	.294	.308	.353	69	-2	0	0	0	.984	1	C-21	-0.1
1923	Pit-N	22	32	4	6	1	1	0	1	0	5	.188	.235	.281	35	-3	0	0	0	.960	1	/C-8	-0.2
Total	2	51	83	15	21	2	2	0	4	1	8	.253	.279	.325	56	-5	0	0	0	.978	2	/C-29	-0.3

■ LEN MATUSZEK   Matuszek, Leonard James   b: 9/27/54, Toledo, Ohio   BL/TR, 6'2", 195 lbs.   Deb: 9/3/81

YEAR	TM/L	G	AB	R	H	2B	3B	HR	RBI	BB	SO	AVG	OBP	SLG	PRO+	BR/A	SB	CS	SBR	FA	FR	G/POS	TPR
1981	Phi-N	13	11	1	3	1	0	0	3	1	3	.273	.429	.364	121	1	0	1	-1	1.000	2	/1-1,3-1	0.1
1982	Phi-N	25	39	1	3	1	0	0	3	1	10	.077	.122	.103	-36	-7	0	1	-1	.750	-2	/3-8,1-3	-1.1
1983	Phi-N	28	80	12	22	6	1	4	16	4	14	.275	.310	.525	129	2	0	1	-1	1.000	-1	1-21	0.0
1984	Phi-N	101	262	40	65	17	1	12	43	39	54	.248	.354	.458	125	9	4	3	-1	.990	-1	1-81/O-1	0.8
1985	Tor-A	62	151	23	32	6	2	2	15	11	24	.212	.265	.318	57	-9	2	1	-1	1.000	0	D-54/1-5	-1.0
	*LA-N	43	63	10	14	2	1	3	13	8	14	.222	.319	.429	111	1	0	1	-1	1.000	-1	O-17,1-10/3-1	-0.2
1986	LA-N	91	199	26	52	7	0	9	28	21	47	.261	.335	.432	118	4	2	2	-1	1.000	-4	O-37,1-31	-0.3
1987	LA-N	16	15	0	1	0	0	0	0	1	4	.067	.125	.067	-49	-3	0	0	0	1.000	0	/1-3	-0.3
Total	7	379	820	113	192	40	5	30	119	88	168	.234	.314	.405	99	-2	8	10	-4	.990	-2	1-155/O-55,D-54,3	-2.0

■ GENE MAUCH   Mauch, Gene William "Skip"   b: 11/18/25, Salina, Kan.   BR/TR, 5'10", 165 lbs.   Deb: 4/18/44   M

YEAR	TM/L	G	AB	R	H	2B	3B	HR	RBI	BB	SO	AVG	OBP	SLG	PRO+	BR/A	SB	CS	SBR	FA	FR	G/POS	TPR
1944	Bro-N	5	15	2	2	0	0	0	2	2	3	.133	.235	.200	24	-1				1.000	-2	/S-5	-0.3
1947	Pit-N	16	30	8	9	0	0	0	1	7	6	.300	.432	.300	95	0				.963	-2	/2-6,S-4	-0.1
1948	Bro-N	12	13	1	2	0	0	0	0	1	4	.154	.214	.154	1	-2	0			.950	1	/2-7,S-1	0.0
	Chi-N	53	138	18	28	3	2	1	7	26	10	.203	.329	.275	68	-5	1			.925	-6	2-26,S-19	-0.9
	Yr	65	151	19	30	3	2	1	7	27	14	.199	.320	.265	62	-7	1			.929	-5	2-33,S-20	-0.9
1949	Chi-N	72	150	15	37	6	4	1	7	21	15	.247	.339	.333	83	-3	3			.971	12	2-25,S-19/3-7	1.0
1950	Bos-N	48	121	17	28	5	0	1	15	14	9	.231	.316	.298	67	-6	1			.968	-1	2-28/3-7,S-5	-0.5
1951	Bos-N	19	20	5	2	0	1	0	1	7	4	.100	.333	.100	24	-2	0			1.000	-0	S-10/3-3,2-2	-0.2
1952	StL-N	7	3	0	0	0	0	0	0	1	2	.000	.250	.000	-25	-0	0			.500	1	/S-2	-0.1
1956	Bos-A	7	25	4	8	1	0	0	1	3	3	.320	.393	.320	80	-1	0			.935	-2	2-6	-0.2
1957	Bos-A	65	222	23	60	10	3	2	28	22	26	.270	.339	.369	88	-3	1	0		.962	-10	2-58	-0.8
Total	9	304	737	93	176	25	7	5	62	104	82	.239	.335	.312	75	-23	6	0		.958	-10	2-158/S-65,3-17	-2.1

■ AL MAUL   Maul, Albert Joseph "Smiling Al"   b: 10/9/1865, Philadelphia, Pa.   d: 5/3/58, Philadelphia, Pa.   BR/TR, 6', 175 lbs.   Deb: 6/20/1884

YEAR	TM/L	G	AB	R	H	2B	3B	HR	RBI	BB	SO	AVG	OBP	SLG	PRO+	BR/A	SB	CS	SBR	FA	FR	G/POS	TPR
1884	Phi-U	1	4	0	0	0	0	0		0	0	.000	.000	.000	-99	-1				1.000	-0	/P-1	0.0
1887	Phi-N	16	56	15	17	2	1	2	4	15	10	.304	.451	.464	146	4	5			.897	-0	/O-8,P-7,1-2	0.3
1888	Pit-N	74	259	21	54	9	4	0	31	21	45	.208	.276	.274	82	-4	9			.975	-1	1-38,O-34/P-3	-0.9
1889	Pit-N	68	257	37	71	6	6	4	44	29	41	.276	.356	.393	121	8	18			.946	11	O-64/P-6	1.3
1890	Pit-P	45	162	31	42	6	2	0	21	22	12	.259	.348	.321	86	-2	5			.904	-3	P-30,O-15/S-1	-0.1
1891	Pit-N	47	149	15	28	3	2	0	14	20	28	.188	.284	.255	59	-7	4			.877	-2	O-40/P-8	-0.9
1893	Was-N	44	134	10	34	8	4	0	22	12	33	.254	.405	.373	110	4	1			.889	1	P-37/O-7	0.1
1894	Was-N	41	124	23	30	3	3	2	20	14	11	.242	.352	.363	75	-5	1			.877	-2	P-28,O-12	-0.1
1895	Was-N	22	72	9	18	5	2	1	16	6	7	.250	.308	.375	76	-3	0			.933	1	P-16/O-4	-0.1
1896	Was-N	8	28	6	8	1	1	0	5	3	2	.286	.355	.393	97	-0	0			.923	-1	/P-8	0.0
1897	Was-N	1	1	0	0	0	0	0	0	0	0	.000	.000	.000	-99	-0	0			1.000	-0	/P-1	0.0
	Bal-N	2	3	0	1	0	0	0	0	0	0	.333	.333	.333	76	-0	0			1.000	-0	/P-2	0.0
	Yr	3	4	0	1	0	0	0	0	0	0	.250	.250	.250	32	-0	0			1.000	-0	/P-3	0.0
1898	Bal-N	29	93	21	19	3	2	0	10	16		.204	.333	.280	75	-3	1			.978	-5	P-28/O-1	0.0
1899	Bro-N	4	11	2	3	0	0	0	1	0		.273	.333	.273	66	-0	0			.900	0	/P-4	0.0
1900	Phi-N	5	15	2	3	0	0	0	2	1		.200	.294	.200	38	-0	0			.917	0	/P-5	0.0
1901	NY-N	3	8	3	3	0	0	0	0	0		.375	.375	.375	122	0	0			1.000	-0	/P-3	0.0
Total	15	410	1376	193	331	45	30	9	179	182	170	.241	.336	.332	91	-12	44			.910	13	P-187,O-185/1-40,S	-0.4

YEAR	TM/L	G	AB	R	H	2B	3B	HR	RBI	BB	SO	AVG	OBP	SLG	PRO+	BR/A	SB	CS	SBR	FA	FR	G/POS	TPR

■ MARK MAULDIN　Mauldin, Marshall Reese　b: 11/5/14, Atlanta, Ga.　d: 9/2/90, Union City, Ga.　BR/TR, 5'11", 170 lbs.　Deb: 9/10/34

| 1934 | Chi-A | 10 | 38 | 3 | 10 | 2 | 0 | 1 | 3 | 0 | 3 | .263 | .263 | .395 | 66 | -2 | 0 | 0 | 0 | .906 | -0 | 3-10 | -0.2 |

■ ROB MAURER　Maurer, Robert John　b: 1/7/67, Evansville, Ind.　BL/TL, 6'3", 210 lbs.　Deb: 9/8/91

1991	Tex-A	13	16	0	1	1	0	0	2	2	6	.063	.211	.125	-5	-2	0	0	0	1.000	1	/1-4,D-2	-0.1
1992	Tex-A	8	9	1	2	0	0	0	1	1	2	.222	.300	.222	50	-1	0	0	0	1.000	0	/1-3,D-1	-0.1
Total	2	21	25	1	3	1	0	0	3	3	8	.120	.241	.160	14	-3	0	0	0	1.000	1	/1-7,D-3	-0.1

■ CARMEN MAURO　Mauro, Carmen Louis　b: 11/10/26, St.Paul, Minn.　BL/TR, 6', 167 lbs.　Deb: 10/1/48

1948	Chi-N	3	5	2	1	0	0	1	1	2	0	.200	.429	.800	235	1	0			1.000	-0	/O-2	0.1
1950	Chi-N	62	185	19	42	4	3	1	10	13	31	.227	.285	.297	54	-12	3			.946	-3	O-49	-1.8
1951	Chi-N	13	29	3	5	1	0	0	3	2	6	.172	.250	.207	24	-3	0	0	0	.900	1	O-6	-0.3
1953	Bro-N	8	9	1	0	0	0	0	0	0	4	.000	.000	.000	-98	-3	0	0	0	1.000	-0	/O-1	-0.3
	Was-A	17	23	1	4	0	1	0	2	1	3	.174	.208	.261	27	-2	0	0	0	1.000	-0	/O-6	-0.3
	Phi-A	64	165	14	44	4	4	0	17	19	21	.267	.342	.339	81	-4	3	4	-2	.969	-1	O-49/3-1	-0.8
	Yr	81	188	15	48	4	5	0	19	20	24	.255	.327	.330	76	-6	3	4	-2	.971	-1	O-55/3-1	-1.1
Total	4	167	416	40	96	9	8	2	33	37	65	.231	.298	.305	61	-23	6	4		.958	-4	O-113/3-1	-3.4

■ BOB MAVIS　Mavis, Robert Henry　b: 4/8/18, Milwaukee, Wis.　BL/TR, 5'7", 160 lbs.　Deb: 9/17/49

| 1949 | Det-A | 1 | 0 | 0 | 0 | | | | | | | — | — | — | — | 0 | 0 | 0 | 0 | .000 | 0 | R | 0.0 |

■ DAL MAXVILL　Maxvill, Charles Dallan　b: 2/18/39, Granite City, Ill.　BR/TR, 5'11", 160 lbs.　Deb: 6/10/62　C

1962	StL-N	79	189	20	42	3	1	1	18	17	39	.222	.290	.265	46	-14	1	2	-1	.962	-2	S-76/3-1	-1.2
1963	StL-N	53	51	12	12	2	0	0	3	6	11	.235	.316	.275	66	-2	0	0	0	.974	7	S-24/2-9,3-3	0.6
1964	*StL-N	37	26	4	6	0	0	0	4	0	7	.231	.231	.231	28	-2	1	0	0	.972	6	2-15,S-13/3-1,0-1	0.4
1965	StL-N	68	89	10	12	2	0	0	10	7	15	.135	.206	.202	14	-10	0	0	0	.993	13	2-49,S-12	0.5
1966	StL-N	134	394	25	96	14	3	0	24	37	61	.244	.312	.294	69	-15	3	0	1	.967	24	*S-128/2-5,O-1	2.1
1967	*StL-N	152	476	37	108	14	4	1	41	48	66	.227	.299	.279	67	-19	0	2	-1	.974	3	*S-148/2-7	-0.4
1968	*StL-N	151	459	51	116	8	5	1	24	52	71	.253	.330	.298	91	-3	0	0	0	.969	-9	*S-151	0.2
1969	StL-N	132	372	27	65	10	2	2	32	44	52	.175	.264	.228	39	-30	1	1	0	.969	21	*S-131	0.4
1970	StL-N	152	399	35	80	5	2	0	28	51	56	.201	.291	.223	39	-33	0	0	0	**.982**	**38**	*S-136,2-22	1.9
1971	StL-N	142	356	31	80	10	1	0	24	43	45	.225	.310	.258	60	-17	1	2	-1	.979	29	*S-140	2.6
1972	StL-N	105	276	22	61	6	1	1	23	31	47	.221	.300	.261	61	-13	0	1	-1	.980	9	S-95,2-11	0.7
	*Oak-A	27	36	2	9	1	0	0	1	1	11	.250	.270	.278	67	-2	0	1	-1	.983	4	2-24/S-4	0.3
1973	Oak-A	29	19	0	4	0	0	0	1	1	3	.211	.250	.211	33	-2	0	0	0	.966	4	S-18,2-11/3-1	0.2
	Pit-N	74	217	19	41	4	3	0	17	22	40	.189	.264	.235	40	-17	0	0	0	.971	1	S-74	-0.5
1974	Pit-N	8	22	3	4	0	0	0	0	2	4	.182	.250	.182	23	-2	0	0	0	.946	1	/S-8	-0.1
	*Oak-A	60	52	3	10	0	0	0	2	8	10	.192	.300	.192	47	-3	0	0	0	1.000	9	2-30,S-29/3-1	0.8
1975	Oak-A	20	10	1	2	0	0	0	0	0	0	.200	.200	.200	59	-1	0	0	0	.955	2	S-20/2-2	0.2
Total	14	1423	3443	302	748	79	24	6	252	370	538	.217	.295	.259	57	-188	7	11	-5	.973	160	*S-1207,2-185/3-7,O	8.7

■ CHARLIE MAXWELL　Maxwell, Charles Richard "Smokey"　b: 4/8/27, Lawton, Mich.　BL/TL, 5'11", 185 lbs.　Deb: 9/20/50

1950	Bos-A	3	8	1	0	0	0	0	0	1	3	.000	.111	.000	-63	-2	0	0	0	1.000	1	/O-2	-0.1
1951	Bos-A	49	80	8	15	1	0	3	12	9	18	.188	.270	.313	52	-6	0	1	-1	.926	-1	O-13	-0.8
1952	Bos-A	8	15	0	1	0	0	0	0	3	11	.067	.222	.133	0	-2	0	0	0	.966	2	/1-3,O-3	-0.1
1954	Bos-A	74	104	9	26	4	1	0	5	12	21	.250	.328	.308	67	-4	3	0	1	1.000	-7	O-27	-1.2
1955	Bal-A	4	4	0	0	0	0	0	0	0	1	.000	.000	.000	-99	-1	0	0	0	.000	0	H	-0.1
	Det-A	55	109	19	29	7	1	7	18	8	20	.266	.328	.541	134	4	0	0	0	.967	2	O-26/1-2	0.5
	Yr	59	113	19	29	7	1	7	18	8	21	.257	.317	.522	126	3	0	0	0	.967	2	O-26/1-2	0.4
1956	Det-A☆	141	500	96	163	14	3	28	87	79	74	.326	.420	.534	150	37	1	1	-0	.987	13	*O-136	4.2
1957	Det-A★	138	492	75	136	23	3	24	82	76	84	.276	.379	.482	130	21	3	2	-0	**.997**	14	*O-137	2.8
1958	Det-A	131	397	56	108	14	4	13	65	64	54	.272	.373	.426	111	7	6	1	-1	.986	-1	*O-114,1-14	0.1
1959	Det-A	145	518	81	130	12	2	31	95	81	91	.251	.359	.461	117	13	0	2	-1	.986	10	*O-136	1.5
1960	Det-A	134	482	70	114	16	5	24	81	58	75	.237	.326	.440	102	1	5	0	2	**.996**	8	*O-120	0.4
1961	Det-A	79	131	11	30	4	2	5	18	20	24	.229	.336	.405	94	-1	0	0	0	.965	2	O-25	-0.1
1962	Det-A	30	67	5	13	2	0	1	9	8	10	.194	.280	.269	47	-5	0	0	0	.966	-1	O-15/1-1	-0.6
	Chi-A	69	206	30	61	8	3	9	43	34	32	.296	.396	.495	139	12	0	0	0	.990	-1	O-56/1-6	0.8
	Yr	99	273	35	74	10	3	10	52	42	42	.271	.368	.440	115	7	0	0	0	.985	-1	O-71/1-7	0.2
1963	Chi-A	71	130	17	30	4	2	3	17	31	21	.231	.379	.362	111	3	0	0	0	1.000	-4	O-24,1-17	-0.2
1964	Chi-A	2	0	0	0	0	0	0	0	0	0	.000	.000	.000	-99	-1	0	0	0	.000	0	H	-0.1
Total	14	1133	3245	478	856	110	26	148	532	484	545	.264	.363	.451	116	77	18	7	1	.988	37	O-834/1-43	7.0

■ CARLOS MAY　May, Carlos　b: 5/17/48, Birmingham, Ala.　BL/TR, 6', 215 lbs.　Deb: 9/6/68　F

1968	Chi-A	17	67	4	12	1	0	1	3	3	15	.179	.214	.194	24	-6	0	0	0	.960	-2	O-17	-1.0
1969	Chi-A★	100	367	62	103	18	2	18	62	58	66	.281	.387	.488	137	19	1	4	-2	.982	-1	*O-100	1.0
1970	Chi-A	150	555	83	158	28	4	12	68	79	96	.285	.377	.414	114	12	12	5	1	.991	1	*O-141/1-7	0.6
1971	Chi-A	141	500	64	147	21	7	7	70	62	61	.294	.379	.406	119	14	16	7	1	.986	-5	*1-130/O-9	-0.3
1972	Chi-A☆	148	523	83	161	26	3	12	68	79	70	.308	.408	.438	149	35	23	14	-2	.983	-1	*O-145/1-5	2.9
1973	Chi-A	149	553	62	148	20	0	20	96	53	73	.268	.337	.412	106	4	8	6	-1	.992	1	D-75,O-70/1-2	0.4
1974	Chi-A	149	551	66	137	19	2	8	58	46	76	.249	.308	.334	82	-12	8	9	-3	.988	6	*O-129,D-13	-1.6
1975	Chi-A	128	454	55	123	19	4	8	53	67	46	.271	.375	.374	111	9	12	7	-1	.989	1	1-63,O-46,D-19	0.3
1976	Chi-A	20	63	7	11	2	0	0	9	9	5	.175	.278	.206	43	-4	4	0	1	1.000	-1	D-10/O-9	-0.5
	*NY-A	87	288	38	80	11	2	3	40	34	32	.278	.364	.361	114	6	1	1	-0	.950	-1	D-71/O-7,1-1	0.4
	Yr	107	351	45	91	13	2	3	43	43	37	.259	.348	.333	101	2	5	1	1	.970	-1	D-81,O-16/1-1	-0.1
1977	NY-A	65	181	21	41	7	1	2	16	17	24	.227	.296	.309	66	-8	0	0	0	1.000	1	D-53/O-4	-1.1
	Cal-A	11	18	0	6	0	0	0	1	5	1	.333	.478	.333	131	1	0	0	0	1.000	-0	/1-3,D-1	0.1
	Yr	76	199	21	47	7	1	2	17	22	25	.236	.315	.312	73	-7	0	0	0	1.000	1	D-54/O-4,1-3	-1.0
Total	10	1165	4120	545	1127	172	23	90	536	512	565	.274	.360	.392	111	70	85	53	-6	.984	0	O-677,D-242,1-211	0.7

■ DAVE MAY　May, David La France　b: 12/23/43, New Castle, Del.　BL/TR, 5'10.5", 186 lbs.　Deb: 7/28/67　F

1967	Bal-A	36	85	12	20	1	1	1	7	6	13	.235	.286	.306	75	-3	0	0	0	.969	-0	O-19	-0.4
1968	Bal-A	84	152	15	29	6	3	0	7	19	27	.191	.285	.270	69	-5	3	3	-1	.984	-11	O-61	-2.2
1969	*Bal-A	78	120	8	29	6	0	3	10	9	23	.242	.300	.367	86	-2	2	1	0	.940	-4	O-40	-0.8
1970	Bal-A	25	31	6	6	0	1	1	6	4	4	.194	.286	.355	75	-1	0	0	0	1.000	-2	/O-9	-0.4
	Mil-A	100	342	36	82	8	1	6	31	44	56	.240	.330	.330	82	-8	8	6	-1	.989	8	O-99	-0.6
	Yr	125	373	42	88	8	2	7	37	48	60	.236	.326	.332	81	-9	8	6	-1	.989	6	*O-108	-1.0
1971	Mil-A	144	501	74	139	20	3	16	65	50	59	.277	.347	.425	119	12	15	9	-1	.975	10	*O-142	1.6
1972	Mil-A	143	500	49	119	20	4	9	45	47	56	.238	.307	.340	94	-4	11	13	-5	.985	15	*O-138	0.0
1973	Mil-A★	156	624	96	189	23	4	25	93	44	78	.303	.354	.472	134	26	6	7	-2	.979	3	*O-152/D-2	2.0
1974	Mil-A	135	477	56	108	15	1	10	42	28	73	.226	.274	.325	72	-18	4	3	-1	.989	-3	*O-121/D-8	-2.8
1975	Atl-N	82	203	28	56	8	0	12	40	25	27	.276	.361	.493	130	8	1	1	-0	.964	-1	O-53	0.5
1976	Atl-N	105	214	27	46	5	3	3	20	26	31	.215	.303	.308	69	-8	5	1	1	.972	-0	O-60	-1.8
1977	Tex-A	120	340	46	82	14	1	7	42	32	43	.241	.314	.350	80	-9	4	3	-1	.969	-4	*O-111/D-5	-1.8
1978	Mil-A	39	77	9	15	4	0	2	11	9	10	.195	.295	.325	74	-3	0	0	0	.944	-1	O-16/D-8	-0.3
	Pit-N											.000	.000	.000	-38	-1	1	0	0	.000	0	H	-0.1
Total	12	1252	3670	462	920	130	20	96	422	344	501	.251	.320	.375	97	-16	60	47	-10	.978	10	*O-1021/D-23	-6.3

■ DERRICK MAY　May, Derrick Brant　b: 7/14/68, Rochester, N.Y.　BL/TR, 6'4", 210 lbs.　Deb: 9/6/90　F

1990	Chi-N	17	61	8	15	3	0	1	11	2	7	.246	.270	.344	63	-3	1	0	0	.972	0	O-17	-0.3
1991	Chi-N	15	22	4	5	2	0	1	3	2	1	.227	.292	.455	102	-0	0	0	0	1.000	-0	/O-7	0.0
1992	Chi-N	124	351	33	96	11	0	8	45	14	40	.274	.307	.373	89	-5	5	3	-0	.969	-11	*O-108	-1.9

YEAR	TM/L	G	AB	R	H	2B	3B	HR	RBI	BB	SO	AVG	OBP	SLG	PRO+	BR/A	SB	CS	SBR	FA	FR	G/POS	TPR
1993	Chi-N	128	465	62	137	25	2	10	77	31	41	.295	.340	.422	104	2	10	3	1	.970	1	*O-122	0.2
1994	Chi-N	100	345	43	98	19	2	8	51	30	34	.284	.341	.420	99	-1	3	2	-0	.994	2	O-92	-0.1
1995	Mil-A	32	113	15	28	3	1	1	9	5	18	.248	.286	.319	54	-8	0	1	-1	.971	-0	O-32	-0.9
	Hou-N	78	206	29	62	15	1	8	41	19	24	.301	.363	.500	134	9	5	0	2	.974	-5	O-55/1-1	0.5
1996	Hou-N	109	259	24	65	12	3	5	33	30	33	.251	.333	.378	96	-2	2	2	-1	.970	4	O-71	0.0
Total	7	603	1822	218	506	90	9	42	270	133	198	.278	.330	.406	98	-7	26	11	1	.975	-7	O-504/1-1	-2.5

■ JERRY MAY

May, Jerry Lee   b: 12/14/43, Staunton, Va.   d: 6/30/96, Swoope, Va.   BR/TR, 6'2.5", 195 lbs.   Deb: 9/19/64

YEAR	TM/L	G	AB	R	H	2B	3B	HR	RBI	BB	SO	AVG	OBP	SLG	PRO+	BR/A	SB	CS	SBR	FA	FR	G/POS	TPR
1964	Pit-N	11	31	1	8	0	0	0	3	3	9	.258	.324	.258	66	-1	0	0	0	.988	4	C-11	0.3
1965	Pit-N	4	2	0	1	0	0	0	1	0	0	.500	.500	.500	182	0	0	0	0	1.000	-0	/C-4	0.0
1966	Pit-N	42	52	6	13	4	0	1	2	2	15	.250	.291	.385	86	-1	0	0	1	.984	8	C-41	0.7
1967	Pit-N	110	325	23	88	13	2	3	22	36	55	.271	.349	.351	100	1	0	0	0	.993	-0	*C-110	0.7
1968	Pit-N	137	416	26	91	15	2	1	33	41	80	.219	.293	.272	72	-14	0	0	0	.988	4	*C-135	-0.1
1969	Pit-N	62	190	21	44	8	0	7	23	9	53	.232	.274	.384	84	-5	1	1	0	.994	-5	C-52	-0.8
1970	Pit-N	51	139	13	29	4	2	1	16	21	25	.209	.317	.288	65	-7	0	0	0	.994	13	C-45	0.8
1971	KC-A	71	218	16	55	13	2	1	24	27	37	.252	.335	.344	93	-1	0	0	0	.997	0	C-71	0.1
1972	KC-A	53	116	10	22	5	1	1	4	14	13	.190	.277	.276	65	-5	0	0	0	.979	-1	C-41	-0.5
1973	KC-A	11	30	4	4	1	1	0	2	3	5	.133	.235	.233	30	-3	0	0	0	.940	-2	C-11	-0.4
	NY-N	4	8	0	2	0	0	0	1	0	1	.250	.333	.250	65	-0	0	0	0	1.000	-1	/C-4	-0.1
Total	10	556	1527	120	357	63	10	15	130	157	293	.234	.310	.318	81	-35	1	2	-1	.990	21	C-525	0.7

■ LEE MAY

May, Lee Andrew   b: 3/23/43, Birmingham, Ala.   BR/TR, 6'3", 205 lbs.   Deb: 9/1/65   FC

YEAR	TM/L	G	AB	R	H	2B	3B	HR	RBI	BB	SO	AVG	OBP	SLG	PRO+	BR/A	SB	CS	SBR	FA	FR	G/POS	TPR
1965	Cin-N	5	4	1	0	0	0	0	0	0	0	.000	.000	.000	-94	-1	0	0	0	.000	0	H	-0.1
1966	Cin-N	25	75	14	25	5	1	2	10	0	14	.333	.333	.507	119	2	0	1	-1	.972	-1	1-16	-0.1
1967	Cin-N	127	438	54	116	29	2	12	57	19	80	.265	.310	.422	97	-3	4	8	-4	.994	2	1-81,O-48	-1.2
1968	Cin-N	146	559	78	162	32	1	22	80	34	100	.290	.337	.469	132	20	4	3	-3	.996	0	*1-122,O-33	0.8
1969	Cin-N★	158	607	85	169	32	3	38	110	45	142	.278	.334	.529	132	23	5	4	-1	.993	0	*1-156/O-7	0.9
1970	*Cin-N	153	605	78	153	34	2	34	94	38	125	.253	.299	.484	106	1	1	1	-0	.993	0	*1-153	-1.2
1971	Cin-N★	147	553	85	154	17	2	39	98	42	135	.278	.334	.532	145	29	3	0	1	.994	-7	*1-143	1.1
1972	Hou-N★	148	592	87	168	31	2	29	98	52	145	.284	.344	.490	137	27	3	1	0	.996	-3	*1-146	1.2
1973	Hou-N	148	545	65	147	24	3	28	105	34	122	.270	.315	.479	117	10	1	1	0	.993	-3	*1-144	-0.5
1974	Hou-N	152	556	59	149	26	0	24	85	17	97	.268	.298	.444	110	3	1	0	0	.994	1	*1-145	-0.5
1975	Bal-A	146	580	67	152	28	3	20	99	36	91	.262	.311	.424	113	7	1	2	1	.993	-1	*1-144/D-2	0.0
1976	Bal-A	148	530	61	137	17	4	25	**109**	41	104	.258	.315	.447	130	17	4	1	1	.996	0	1-94,D-52	0.0
1977	Bal-A	150	585	75	148	16	2	27	99	38	119	.253	.299	.426	101	-2	2	2	-1	.995	-7	*1-110,D-39	-1.7
1978	Bal-A	148	556	56	137	16	1	25	80	31	110	.246	.287	.414	101	-2	5	2	0	.973	-6	*D-140/1-4	-0.7
1979	*Bal-A	124	456	59	116	15	0	19	69	28	100	.254	.299	.412	93	-6	3	4	-2	.913	-1	*D-117/1-2	-1.2
1980	Bal-A	78	222	20	54	10	2	7	31	15	53	.243	.291	.401	88	-4	2	0	1	1.000	-0	D-58/1-7	-0.6
1981	*KC-A	26	55	3	16	3	0	0	8	3	14	.291	.328	.345	95	-0	0	1	-1	1.000	-1	/1-8,D-4	-0.2
1982	KC-A	42	91	12	28	5	2	3	12	14	18	.308	.400	.505	147	6	0	0	0	.989	-2	1-32/D-2	0.3
Total	18	2071	7609	959	2031	340	31	354	1244	487	1570	.267	.315	.459	116	126	39	35	-9	.994	-19	*1-1507,D-414/O-88	-2.7

■ PINKY MAY

May, Merrill Glend   b: 1/18/11, Laconia, Ind.   BR/TR, 5'11.5", 165 lbs.   Deb: 4/21/39   F

YEAR	TM/L	G	AB	R	H	2B	3B	HR	RBI	BB	SO	AVG	OBP	SLG	PRO+	BR/A	SB	CS	SBR	FA	FR	G/POS	TPR
1939	Phi-N	135	464	49	133	27	3	2	62	41	20	.287	.346	.371	95	-3	4			**.956**	8	*3-132	0.7
1940	Phi-N★	136	501	59	147	24	2	1	48	58	33	.293	.371	.355	105	6	2			.954	13	*3-135/S-1	2.1
1941	Phi-N	142	490	46	131	17	4	0	39	55	30	.267	.344	.318	91	-5	2			**.972**	25	*3-140	2.4
1942	Phi-N	115	345	25	82	15	0	0	18	51	17	.238	.338	.281	86	-4	3			.963	17	*3-107	1.5
1943	Phi-N	137	415	31	117	19	2	1	48	56	21	.282	.369	.345	111	8	2			**.963**	11	*3-132	2.2
Total	5	665	2215	210	610	102	11	4	215	261	121	.275	.354	.337	98	2	13			.962	74	3-646/S-1	8.9

■ MILT MAY

May, Milton Scott   b: 8/1/50, Gary, Ind.   BL/TR, 6', 190 lbs.   Deb: 9/8/70   FC

YEAR	TM/L	G	AB	R	H	2B	3B	HR	RBI	BB	SO	AVG	OBP	SLG	PRO+	BR/A	SB	CS	SBR	FA	FR	G/POS	TPR
1970	Pit-N	5	4	1	2	0	0	0	0	0	0	.500	.600	.750	265	1	0	0	0	.000	0	H	0.1
1971	*Pit-N	49	126	15	35	1	0	6	25	9	16	.278	.326	.429	113	2	0	0	0	1.000	3	C-31	0.6
1972	*Pit-N	57	139	12	39	10	0	0	14	10	13	.281	.329	.353	96	-1	0	0	0	.985	5	C-33	0.5
1973	Pit-N	101	283	29	76	8	1	7	31	34	26	.269	.351	.378	105	2	0	1	-1	.973	-6	C-79	-0.1
1974	Hou-N	127	405	47	117	17	4	7	54	39	33	.289	.353	.402	116	8	0	1	-1	**.993**	2	*C-116	1.5
1975	Hou-N	111	386	29	93	15	1	4	52	26	41	.241	.289	.316	73	-15	1	2	-1	.986	1	*C-102	-1.1
1976	Det-A	6	25	2	7	1	0	0	1	0	1	.280	.280	.320	73	-1	0	0	0	1.000	1	/C-6	0.0
1977	Det-A	115	397	32	99	9	3	12	46	26	31	.249	.296	.378	73	-13	0	0	0	.986	1	*C-111	-0.3
1978	Det-A	105	352	24	88	9	0	10	37	27	26	.250	.307	.361	85	-7	0	0	0	.979	1	C-94	-0.4
1979	Det-A	6	11	1	3	2	0	0	3	1	1	.273	.333	.455	107	0	0	0	0	1.000	1	/C-5	0.1
	Chi-A	65	202	23	51	13	0	7	28	14	27	.252	.307	.421	94	-2	0	0	0	.981	1	C-65	0.2
	Yr	71	213	24	54	15	0	7	31	15	28	.254	.309	.423	95	-2	0	0	0	.982	2	C-70	0.2
1980	SF-N	111	358	27	93	16	2	6	50	25	40	.260	.310	.366	90	-5	0	1	-1	.986	-4	*C-103	-0.7
1981	SF-N	97	316	20	98	17	0	2	33	34	29	.310	.377	.383	118	8	1	4	-2	.989	-1	C-93	0.9
1982	SF-N	114	395	29	104	19	0	9	39	28	38	.263	.312	.380	93	-4	0	1	-1	.987	-1	*C-110	-0.2
1983	SF-N	66	186	18	46	8	0	6	20	21	23	.247	.324	.376	96	-1	2	2	-1	.981	-2	C-56	-0.1
	Pit-N	7	12	0	3	0	0	0	0	1	1	.250	.308	.250	55	-1	0	0	0	1.000	2	/C-4	0.1
	Yr	73	198	18	49	8	0	6	20	22	24	.247	.323	.369	94	-2	2	2	-1	.983	0	C-60	0.0
1984	Pit-N	50	96	4	17	3	0	1	8	10	15	.177	.255	.240	40	-8	0	1	-1	.993	-1	C-26	-0.3
Total	15	1192	3693	313	971	147	11	77	443	305	361	.263	.321	.371	93	-37	4	13	-7	.986	14	*C-1034	0.7

■ JOHN MAYBERRY

Mayberry, John Claiborn   b: 2/18/49, Detroit, Mich.   BL/TL, 6'3", 220 lbs.   Deb: 9/10/68   C

YEAR	TM/L	G	AB	R	H	2B	3B	HR	RBI	BB	SO	AVG	OBP	SLG	PRO+	BR/A	SB	CS	SBR	FA	FR	G/POS	TPR
1968	Hou-N	4	9	0	0	0	0	0	0	0	2	.000	.100	.000	-69	-2	0	0	0	1.000	-1	/1-2	-0.3
1969	Hou-N	5	4	0	0	0	0	0	0	1	1	.000	.200	.000	-41	-1	0	0	0	.000	0	H	-0.1
1970	Hou-N	50	148	23	32	3	2	5	14	21	33	.216	.322	.365	87	-3	1	1	-0	.995	3	1-45	-0.3
1971	Hou-N	46	137	16	25	0	1	7	14	13	32	.182	.263	.350	74	-5	0	0	0	.997	-3	1-37	-1.2
1972	KC-A	149	503	65	150	24	3	25	100	78	74	.298	.396	.507	168	43	0	2	-1	**.995**	-0	*1-146	3.3
1973	KC-A★	152	510	87	142	20	2	26	100	**122**	79	.278	**.420**	.478	141	33	3	0	1	.994	-5	*1-149/D-1	1.7
1974	KC-A★	126	427	63	100	13	1	22	69	77	72	.234	.359	.424	118	11	4	2	0	.990	-2	*1-106,D-16	0.2
1975	KC-A	156	554	95	161	38	1	34	106	**119**	73	.291	.419	.547	167	53	5	3	-0	.988	-1	*1-131,D-27	4.6
1976	*KC-A	161	594	76	138	22	6	13	95	82	73	.232	.327	.342	95	-2	3	2	-0	.996	-3	*1-160/D-2	-1.7
1977	*KC-A	153	543	73	125	22	1	23	82	83	86	.230	.340	.401	100	1	1	3	-2	**.995**	-6	*1-145/D-8	-1.5
1978	Tor-A	152	515	51	129	15	2	22	70	60	57	.250	.333	.416	107	3	1	2	-1	.993	-14	*1-139/D-7	-1.9
1979	Tor-A	137	464	61	127	22	1	21	74	69	60	.274	.374	.461	122	16	1	1	-0	.995	-8	*1-135	-0.1
1980	Tor-A	149	501	62	124	19	2	30	82	77	80	.248	.351	.473	118	13	0	0	0	.994	-4	*1-136/D-8	0.0
1981	Tor-A	94	290	34	72	6	1	17	43	44	45	.248	.363	.452	125	10	1	1	-0	.993	-6	1-80,D-10	-0.1
1982	Tor-A	17	33	7	9	0	0	2	3	7	5	.273	.415	.455	127	1	0	0	0	1.000	-1	D-13/1-4	0.0
	NY-A	69	215	20	45	7	0	8	27	28	38	.209	.315	.353	84	-4	0	0	0	.996	-4	1-63/D-4	-1.1
	Yr	86	248	27	54	7	0	10	30	35	43	.218	.329	.367	90	-3	0	0	0	.996	-4	1-67,D-17	-1.1
Total	15	1620	5447	733	1379	211	19	255	879	881	810	.253	.363	.439	122	170	20	17	-4	.994	-49	*1-1478/D-96	1.5

■ LEE MAYE

Maye, Arthur Lee   b: 12/11/34, Tuscaloosa, Ala.   BL/TR, 6'2", 190 lbs.   Deb: 7/17/59

YEAR	TM/L	G	AB	R	H	2B	3B	HR	RBI	BB	SO	AVG	OBP	SLG	PRO+	BR/A	SB	CS	SBR	FA	FR	G/POS	TPR
1959	Mil-N	51	140	17	42	5	1	4	16	7	26	.300	.338	.436	114	2	2	2	-1	.976	1	O-44	0.0
1960	Mil-N	41	83	14	25	6	0	0	2	7	20	.301	.363	.373	110	1	1	0	0	.968	-1	O-19	0.1
1961	Mil-N	110	373	68	101	11	5	14	41	36	50	.271	.340	.440	112	6	10	1	2	.972	-2	O-96	0.0
1962	Mil-N	99	349	40	85	10	0	10	41	25	58	.244	.296	.358	92	-12	9	3	1	.977	1	O-94	-1.6
1963	Mil-N	124	442	67	120	22	7	11	34	36	52	.271	.331	.428	118	10	14	2	3	.983	-8	*O-111	-0.2
1964	Mil-N	153	588	96	179	**44**	5	10	74	34	54	.304	.347	.447	121	16	5	10	-5	.961	-1	*O-135/3-5	0.3
1965	Mil-N	15	53	8	16	2	0	2	5	2	6	.302	.339	.453	120	1	0	0	0	.962	1	O-13	0.2
	Hou-N	108	415	38	104	17	7	3	36	20	37	.251	.287	.347	83	-11	1	5	-3	.953	3	*O-103	-1.6

YEAR	TM/L	G	AB	R	H	2B	3B	HR	RBI	BB	SO	AVG	OBP	SLG	PRO+	BR/A	SB	CS	SBR	FA	FR	G/POS	TPR
	Yr	123	468	46	120	19	7	5	43	22	43	.256	.293	.359	88	-9	1	5	-3	.954	4	*O-116	-1.4
1966	Hou-N	115	358	38	103	12	4	9	36	20	26	.288	.325	.419	113	5	4	3	-1	.949	-1	O-97	-0.1
1967	Cle-A	115	297	43	77	20	4	9	27	26	47	.259	.321	.444	123	8	3	3	-1	.981	-10	O-77/2-1	-0.7
1968	Cle-A	109	299	20	84	13	2	4	26	15	24	.281	.317	.378	112	3	0	0	0	.984	1	O-80/1-1	0.0
1969	Cle-A	43	108	9	27	5	0	1	15	8	15	.250	.308	.324	74	-4	1	0	0	.982	1	O-28	-0.4
	Was-A	71	238	41	69	9	3	9	26	20	25	.290	.345	.466	132	9	1	3	-2	.944	-6	O-65	-0.2
	Yr	114	346	50	96	14	3	10	41	28	40	.277	.333	.422	112	5	2	3	-1	.957	-5	O-93	-0.6
1970	Was-A	96	255	28	67	12	1	7	30	21	32	.263	.321	.400	103	-1	4	2	0	1.000	-8	O-68/3-1	-1.1
	Chi-A	6	6	0	1	0	0	0	1	0	1	.167	.167	.167	-8	-1	0	0	0	.000	0	H	-0.1
	Yr	102	261	28	68	12	1	7	31	21	33	.261	.318	.395	100	-1	4	2	0	1.000	-8	O-68/3-1	-1.2
1971	Chi-A	32	44	6	9	2	0	1	7	5	7	.205	.286	.318	69	-2	0	0	0	1.000	-1	O-10	-0.3
Total	13	1288	4048	533	1109	190	39	94	419	282	481	.274	.324	.410	108	32	59	34	-3	.970	-31	*O-1040/3-6,1-1,2-1	-5.7

■ ED MAYER
Mayer, Edward H.   b: 8/16/1866, Marshall, Ill.   d: 5/18/13, Chicago, Ill.   5'8.5", 155 lbs.   Deb: 4/19/1890

YEAR	TM/L	G	AB	R	H	2B	3B	HR	RBI	BB	SO	AVG	OBP	SLG	PRO+	BR/A	SB	CS	SBR	FA	FR	G/POS	TPR
1890	Phi-N	117	484	49	117	25	5	1	70	22	36	.242	.286	.320	75	-17	20			.878	-4	*3-114/O-4	-1.5
1891	Phi-N	68	268	24	50	2	4	0	31	14	29	.187	.238	.224	34	-23	7			.895	-6	3-31,O-29/S-7,2-1	-2.5
Total	2	185	752	73	167	27	9	1	101	36	65	.222	.269	.286	60	-40	27			.882	-10	3-145/O-33,S-7,2-1	-4.0

■ SAM MAYER
Mayer, Samuel Frankel (b: Samuel Frankel Erskine)   b: 2/28/1893, Atlanta, Ga.   d: 7/1/62, Atlanta, Ga.   BR/TL, 5'10", 164 lbs.   Deb: 9/14/15   F

YEAR	TM/L	G	AB	R	H	2B	3B	HR	RBI	BB	SO	AVG	OBP	SLG	PRO+	BR/A	SB	CS	SBR	FA	FR	G/POS	TPR
1915	Was-A	11	29	5	7	0	0	1	4	4	2	.241	.333	.345	101	0	1	2	-1	1.000	0	/O-9,P-1,1-1	-0.1

■ WALLY MAYER
Mayer, Walter A.   b: 7/8/1890, Cincinnati, Ohio   d: 11/18/51, Minnetonka, Minn.   BR/TR, 5'11", 168 lbs.   Deb: 9/28/11

YEAR	TM/L	G	AB	R	H	2B	3B	HR	RBI	BB	SO	AVG	OBP	SLG	PRO+	BR/A	SB	CS	SBR	FA	FR	G/POS	TPR
1911	Chi-A	1	3	0	0	0	0	0	0	0	2	.000	.400	.000	16	-0	0			.900	-1	/C-1	-0.1
1912	Chi-A	9	9	1	0	0	0	0	0	1	1	.000	.100	.000	-73	-2	0			1.000	-0	/C-6	-0.2
1914	Chi-A	40	85	7	14	3	1	0	5	14	23	.165	.290	.224	55	-4	1	1	-0	.968	5	C-33/3-1	0.3
1915	Chi-A	22	54	3	12	3	1	0	5	5	8	.222	.288	.315	78	-2	0	2	-1	.990	-1	C-20	-0.3
1917	Bos-A	4	12	2	2	0	0	0	1	5	7	.167	.412	.167	78	0	0			.964	2	/C-4	0.2
1918	Bos-A	26	49	7	11	4	0	0	5	7	7	.224	.321	.306	91	0	0			.964	-1	C-23	0.0
1919	StL-A	30	62	2	14	4	1	0	5	8	11	.226	.314	.323	77	-2	0			.959	6	C-25	0.5
Total	7	132	274	22	53	14	3	0	20	42	51	.193	.303	.266	68	-10	1	3		.969	10	C-112/3-1	0.4

■ PADDY MAYES
Mayes, Adair Bushyhead   b: 3/17/1885, Locust Grove, Okla.   d: 5/28/62, Fayetteville, Ark.   BL/TR, 5'11", 160 lbs.   Deb: 6/11/11

YEAR	TM/L	G	AB	R	H	2B	3B	HR	RBI	BB	SO	AVG	OBP	SLG	PRO+	BR/A	SB	CS	SBR	FA	FR	G/POS	TPR
1911	Phi-N	5	5	1	0	0	0	0	0	1	2	.000	.286	.000	-17	-1	0			1.000	-1	/O-2	-0.1

■ BUSTER MAYNARD
Maynard, James Walter   b: 3/25/13, Henderson, N.C.   d: 9/7/77, Durham, N.C.   BR/TR, 5'11", 170 lbs.   Deb: 9/17/40

YEAR	TM/L	G	AB	R	H	2B	3B	HR	RBI	BB	SO	AVG	OBP	SLG	PRO+	BR/A	SB	CS	SBR	FA	FR	G/POS	TPR
1940	NY-N	7	29	6	8	2	2	1	2	2	6	.276	.323	.586	145	2	3			.929	-1	/O-7	0.0
1942	NY-N	89	190	17	47	4	1	4	32	19	19	.247	.319	.342	93	-2	3			.982	-0	O-58,3-10/2-1	-0.4
1943	NY-N	121	393	43	81	8	2	9	32	24	27	.206	.252	.305	60	-21	3			.965	-6	O-74,3-22	-3.4
1946	NY-N	7	4	2	0	0	0	0	0	1	1	.000	.200	.000	-41	-1	0			.750	-1	/O-3	-0.2
Total	4	224	616	68	136	14	5	14	66	46	53	.221	.276	.328	74	-22	6			.967	-8	O-142/3-32,2-1	-4.0

■ CHICK MAYNARD
Maynard, Le Roy Evans   b: 11/2/1896, Turners Falls, Mass.   d: 1/31/57, Bangor, Maine   BL/TR, 5'9", 150 lbs.   Deb: 6/27/22

YEAR	TM/L	G	AB	R	H	2B	3B	HR	RBI	BB	SO	AVG	OBP	SLG	PRO+	BR/A	SB	CS	SBR	FA	FR	G/POS	TPR
1922	Bos-A	12	24	1	3	0	0	0	3	2		.125	.222	.125	-8	-4	0	1	-1	.872	-2	S-12	-0.6

■ BRENT MAYNE
Mayne, Brent Danem   b: 4/19/68, Loma Linda, Cal.   BL/TR, 6'1", 195 lbs.   Deb: 9/18/90

YEAR	TM/L	G	AB	R	H	2B	3B	HR	RBI	BB	SO	AVG	OBP	SLG	PRO+	BR/A	SB	CS	SBR	FA	FR	G/POS	TPR
1990	KC-A	5	13	2	3	0	0	0	1	3	3	.231	.375	.231	74	-0	0	1	-1	.970	1	/C-5	0.0
1991	KC-A	85	231	22	58	8	0	3	31	23	42	.251	.319	.325	78	-7	2	4	-2	.987	4	C-80/D-1	0.0
1992	KC-A	82	213	16	48	10	0	0	18	11	26	.225	.263	.272	49	-15	0	4	-2	.990	2	C-62/3-8,D-1	-1.2
1993	KC-A	71	205	22	52	9	1	2	22	18	31	.254	.317	.337	72	-8	3	2	-0	.995	6	C-68/D-1	0.1
1994	KC-A	46	144	19	37	5	1	2	20	14	27	.257	.323	.347	70	-6	1	0	0	.996	6	C-42/D-3	0.2
1995	KC-A	110	307	23	77	18	1	1	27	25	41	.251	.313	.326	66	-15	0	1	-1	.995	11	*C-103	0.2
1996	NY-N	70	99	12	26	6	0	1	6	12	22	.263	.342	.354	90	-1	0	1	-1	1.000	-4	C-21	-0.5
Total	7	469	1212	113	301	56	3	9	125	106	192	.248	.311	.322	69	-52	6	13	-6	.992	27	C-381/3-8,D-6	-1.2

■ EDDIE MAYO
Mayo, Edward Joseph "Hotshot" (b: Edward Joseph Mayoski)   b: 4/15/10, Holyoke, Mass.   BL/TR, 5'11", 178 lbs.   Deb: 5/22/36   C

YEAR	TM/L	G	AB	R	H	2B	3B	HR	RBI	BB	SO	AVG	OBP	SLG	PRO+	BR/A	SB	CS	SBR	FA	FR	G/POS	TPR
1936	*NY-N	46	141	11	28	4	1	1	8	11	12	.199	.257	.262	40	-12	0			.981	5	3-40	-0.6
1937	Bos-N	65	172	19	39	6	1	1	18	15	20	.227	.293	.291	65	-9	1			.956	-4	3-50	-1.1
1938	Bos-N	8	14	2	3	0	0	0	4	1	0	.214	.267	.429	98	-0	0			.923	2	/3-6,S-2	0.1
1943	Phi-A	128	471	49	103	10	1	0	28	34	32	.219	.278	.244	54	-27	2	0	1	.976	-3	*3-123	-3.0
1944	Det-A	154	607	76	151	18	3	5	63	57	23	.249	.317	.313	76	-18	9	13	-5	.978	29	*2-143,S-11	1.6
1945	*Det-A†	134	501	71	143	24	3	10	54	47	29	.285	.347	.405	111	6	7	7	-2	.980	18	*2-124	3.1
1946	Det-A	51	202	21	51	9	2	0	22	14	12	.252	.301	.317	68	-9	6	2	1	.965	-11	2-49	-1.6
1947	Det-A	142	535	66	149	28	4	6	48	48	28	.279	.338	.379	96	-3	3	7	-3	.983	-23	*2-142	-2.1
1948	Det-A	106	370	35	92	20	1	2	42	30	19	.249	.310	.324	67	-18	1	9	-5	.975	-10	2-86,3-10	-2.7
Total	9	834	3013	350	759	119	16	26	287	257	175	.252	.313	.328	78	-89	29	38		.978	3	2-544,3-229/S-13	-6.3

■ JACKIE MAYO
Mayo, John Lewis   b: 7/26/25, Litchfield, Ill.   BL/TR, 6'1", 190 lbs.   Deb: 9/19/48

YEAR	TM/L	G	AB	R	H	2B	3B	HR	RBI	BB	SO	AVG	OBP	SLG	PRO+	BR/A	SB	CS	SBR	FA	FR	G/POS	TPR
1948	Phi-N	12	35	7	8	1	0	0	3	7	7	.229	.386	.343	101	0	1			1.000	1	O-11	0.1
1949	Phi-N	45	39	3	5	0	0	0	2	4	5	.128	.209	.128	-8	-6	0			.889	-7	O-25	-1.3
1950	*Phi-N	18	36	1	8	3	0	0	3	2	5	.222	.263	.306	50	-3	0			.958	-3	O-15	-0.5
1951	Phi-N	9	7	1	1	0	0	0	0	0	0	.143	.143	.143	-23	-1	0	0	0	1.000	-2	/O-5	-0.3
1952	Phi-N	50	119	13	29	5	1	1	4	12	17	.244	.313	.311	74	-4	1	3	-2	1.000	4	O-27/1-6	-0.3
1953	Phi-N	5	4	0	0	0	0	0	0	0	1	.000	.000	.000	-99	-1	0			.000	0	/O-1	-0.2
Total	6	139	240	25	51	10	1	1	12	25	35	.213	.292	.275	56	-15	2	3		.972	-7	/O-84,1-6	-2.5

■ WILLIE MAYS
Mays, Willie Howard "Say Hey"   b: 5/6/31, Westfield, Ala.   BR/TR, 5'11", 180 lbs.   Deb: 5/25/51   CH

YEAR	TM/L	G	AB	R	H	2B	3B	HR	RBI	BB	SO	AVG	OBP	SLG	PRO+	BR/A	SB	CS	SBR	FA	FR	G/POS	TPR
1951	*NY-N	121	464	59	127	22	5	20	68	57	60	.274	.356	.472	120	12	7	4	-0	.976	11	*O-121	1.9
1952	NY-N	34	127	17	30	2	4	4	23	16	17	.236	.326	.409	102	0	4	1	1	.991	8	O-34	0.7
1954	*NY-N★	151	565	119	195	33	**13**	41	110	66	57	**.345**	.415	**.667**	176	**61**	8	5	-1	.985	16	*O-151	**6.7**
1955	NY-N★	152	580	123	185	18	**13**	**51**	127	79	60	.319	.404	**.659**	176	**62**	24	4	**5**	.982	**20**	*O-152	**7.7**
1956	NY-N★	152	578	101	171	27	8	36	84	68	65	.296	.371	.557	146	37	**40**	10	**6**	.979	12	*O-152	4.7
1957	NY-N★	152	585	112	195	26	**20**	35	97	76	62	.333	.411	**.626**	174	**61**	**38**	19	0	.980	11	*O-150	6.3
1958	SF-N★	152	600	**121**	208	33	11	29	96	78	56	.347	.423	.583	167	58	31	6	6	.980	17	*O-151	7.2
1959	SF-N★	151	575	125	180	43	5	34	104	65	58	.313	.385	.583	157	45	**27**	4	6	.984	7	*O-147	5.0
1960	SF-N★	153	595	107	**190**	29	12	29	103	61	70	.319	.386	.555	164	51	25	10	2	.981	14	*O-152	**5.9**
1961	SF-N★	154	572	**129**	176	32	3	40	123	81	77	.308	.395	.584	162	50	18	9	0	.980	10	*O-153	5.0
1962	*SF-N★	162	621	130	189	36	5	**49**	141	78	85	.304	.385	.615	167	56	18	2	1	.991	14	*O-161	**6.4**
1963	SF-N★	157	596	115	187	32	7	38	103	66	83	.314	.384	.582	176	57	8	3	1	.981	13	*O-157/S-1	6.6
1964	SF-N★	157	578	121	171	21	9	**47**	111	82	72	.296	.384	**.607**	171	54	19	5	3	.984	14	*O-155/1-1,S-1,3-1	6.5
1965	SF-N★	157	558	118	177	21	3	**52**	112	76	71	.317	**.399**	**.645**	184	**61**	9	7	3	.983	16	*O-151	**7.3**
1966	SF-N★	152	552	99	159	29	4	37	103	70	81	.288	.370	.556	149	36	5	1	1	.982	12	*O-150	4.3
1967	SF-N★	141	486	83	128	22	2	22	70	51	92	.263	.336	.453	125	15	6	0	2	.976	-3	*O-142/1-1	1.0
1968	SF-N★	148	498	84	144	20	5	23	79	67	81	.289	.376	.488	158	36	12	6	3	.978	0	*O-108/1-1	3.3
1969	SF-N★	117	403	64	114	17	3	13	58	49	71	.283	.365	.437	126	14	6	2	1	.976	-4	*O-108/1-1	0.2
1970	SF-N★	139	478	94	139	15	2	28	83	79	90	.291	.395	.506	141	29	5	0	2	.975	2	*O-129/1-5	2.6
1971	*SF-N★	136	417	82	113	24	5	18	61	**112**	123	.271	**.429**	.482	160	39	23	3	1	.970	-2	O-84/1-48	3.6
1972	SF-N	19	49	8	9	2	0	0	3	17	5	.184	.394	.224	79	-0	3	0	1	1.000	-1	O-14	-0.1
	NY-N★	69	195	27	52	9	1	8	19	43	43	.267	.402	.446	144	13	1	5	-3	.974	0	O-49,1-11	0.8
	Yr	88	244	35	61	11	1	8	22	60	48	.250	.400	.402	131	13	4	5	-2	.979	-1	O-63,1-11	0.7
1973	*NY-N★	66	209	24	44	10	0	6	25	27	47	.211	.304	.344	81	-6	1	0	0	.991	-5	O-45,1-17	-1.4
Total	22	2992	10881	2062	3283	523	140	660	1903	1464	1526	.302	.387	.557	157	844	338	103	40	.981	180	*O-2842/1-84,S-2,3	92.2

YEAR	TM/L	G	AB	R	H	2B	3B	HR	RBI	BB	SO	AVG	OBP	SLG	PRO+	BR/A	SB	CS	SBR	FA	FR	G/POS	TPR

■ BILL MAZEROSKI Mazeroski, William Stanley "Maz" b: 9/5/36, Wheeling, W.Va. BR/TR, 5'11.5", 183 lbs. Deb: 7/7/56 C

1956	Pit-N	81	255	30	62	8	1	3	14	18	24	.243	.293	.318	66	-12	0	0	0	.981	11	2-81	0.5
1957	Pit-N	148	526	59	149	27	7	8	54	27	49	.283	.319	.407	96	-4	3	3	-1	.978	4	*2-144	1.1
1958	Pit-N★	152	567	69	156	24	6	19	68	25	71	.275	.309	.439	98	-4	1	1	-0	.980	19	*2-152	2.5
1959	Pit-N★	135	493	50	119	15	6	7	59	29	54	.241	.285	.339	66	-25	1	3	-2	.981	-9	*2-133	-2.5
1960	*Pit-N★	151	538	58	147	21	5	11	64	40	50	.273	.325	.392	95	-4	4	0	1	.989	25	*2-151	3.8
1961	Pit-N	152	558	71	148	21	2	13	59	26	55	.265	.302	.380	79	-17	2	1	0	.975	31	*2-152	2.9
1962	Pit-N★	159	572	55	155	24	9	14	81	37	47	.271	.318	.418	95	-5	0	3	-2	.985	41	*2-159	5.0
1963	Pit-N†	142	534	43	131	22	3	8	52	32	46	.245	.288	.343	80	-14	2	0	1	.984	57	*2-138	6.0
1964	Pit-N☆	162	601	66	161	22	8	10	64	29	52	.268	.302	.381	91	-8	1	1	-0	.975	34	*2-162	4.1
1965	Pit-N	130	494	52	134	17	1	6	54	18	34	.271	.300	.346	81	-13	2	1	0	.988	26	*2-127	2.5
1966	Pit-N	162	621	56	163	22	7	16	82	31	62	.262	.299	.398	91	-8	4	3	-1	.992	41	*2-162	4.5
1967	Pit-N★	163	639	62	167	25	3	9	77	30	55	.261	.294	.352	84	-14	1	2	-1	.981	17	*2-163	1.4
1968	Pit-N	143	506	36	127	18	2	3	42	38	38	.251	.306	.312	87	-8	3	4	-2	.981	26	*2-142	2.8
1969	Pit-N	67	227	13	52	7	1	3	25	22	16	.229	.303	.308	73	-8	1	1	-0	.988	14	2-65	1.1
1970	*Pit-N	112	367	29	84	14	0	7	39	27	40	.229	.285	.324	64	-19	2	0	1	.987	24	*2-102	1.3
1971	*Pit-N	70	193	17	49	3	1	1	16	15	8	.254	.308	.295	72	-7	0	0	0	.986	-1	2-46/3-7	-0.5
1972	*Pit-N	34	64	3	12	4	0	0	3	3	5	.188	.224	.250	35	-6	0	0	0	.986	3	2-15/3-3	-0.2
Total	17	2163	7755	769	2016	294	62	138	853	447	706	.260	.302	.367	84	-176	27	23	-6	.983	362	*2-2094/3-10	36.3

■ MEL MAZZERA Mazzera, Melvin Leonard "Mike" b: 1/31/14, Stockton, Cal. BL/TL, 5'11", 180 lbs. Deb: 9/9/35

1935	StL-A	12	30	4	7	2	0	1	2	4	9	.233	.324	.400	82	-1	0	0	0	.950	-1	O-10	-0.2
1937	StL-A	7	7	1	2	2	0	0	0	0	2	.286	.286	.571	110	0	0	0	0	.000	0	H	0.0
1938	StL-A	86	204	33	57	8	2	6	29	12	25	.279	.329	.426	88	-5	1	1	-0	.976	-1	O-47	-0.7
1939	StL-A	33	110	21	33	5	2	3	22	10	20	.300	.364	.464	108	1	0	0	0	.983	0	O-25	0.0
1940	Phi-N	69	156	16	37	5	4	0	13	19	15	.237	.320	.321	80	-4	1			.985	-4	O-42,1-11	-1.0
Total	5	207	507	75	136	22	8	10	66	45	71	.268	.333	.402	90	-8	2	1		.978	-6	O-124/1-11	-1.9

■ LEE MAZZILLI Mazzilli, Lee Louis b: 3/25/55, New York, N.Y. BB/TR, 6'1", 185 lbs. Deb: 9/7/76

1976	NY-N	24	77	9	15	2	0	2	9	14	10	.195	.326	.299	83	-1	5	4	-1	.983	2	O-23	-0.1
1977	NY-N	159	537	66	134	24	3	6	46	72	72	.250	.342	.339	87	-8	22	15	-2	.992	11	*O-156	-0.5
1978	NY-N	148	542	78	148	28	5	16	61	69	82	.273	.356	.432	124	17	20	13	-2	.987	14	*O-144	2.4
1979	NY-N★	158	597	78	181	34	4	15	79	93	74	.303	.397	.449	135	32	34	12	3	.989	8	*O-143,1-15	3.7
1980	NY-N	152	578	82	162	31	4	16	76	82	92	.280	.373	.431	127	23	41	15	3	.983	1	1-92,O-66	2.0
1981	NY-N	95	324	36	74	14	5	6	34	46	53	.228	.328	.358	96	-1	17	7	1	.970	-4	O-89	-0.4
1982	Tex-A	58	195	23	47	8	0	4	17	28	26	.241	.339	.344	93	-1	11	6	0	.945	-3	O-26,D-24	-0.6
	NY-N	37	128	20	34	2	0	6	17	15	15	.266	.347	.422	112	2	2	3	-1	.995	-3	1-23/O-2,D-9	-0.3
	Yr	95	323	43	81	10	0	10	34	43	41	.251	.342	.375	100	1	13	9	2	.949	-4	D-33,O-28,1-23	-0.9
1983	Pit-N	109	246	37	59	9	0	5	24	49	43	.240	.370	.337	95	0	15	5	2	.985	0	O-57/1-7	0.0
1984	Pit-N	111	266	37	63	11	1	4	21	40	42	.237	.339	.331	89	-3	8	1	2	.989	-7	O-74/1-5	-1.1
1985	Pit-N	92	117	20	33	8	0	1	9	29	17	.282	.425	.376	127	6	4	1	1	.986	-1	1-19/O-5	0.5
1986	Pit-N	61	93	18	21	2	1	2	8	26	25	.226	.395	.301	93	3	3	3	-1	1.000	-3	O-18/1-7	-0.4
	*NY-N	39	58	10	16	3	0	2	7	12	11	.276	.417	.431	138	4	1	1	-0	1.000	-1	O-10/1-8	0.2
	Yr	100	151	28	37	5	1	3	15	38	36	.245	.403	.351	109	4	4	4	-1	1.000	-4	O-28,1-15	-0.2
1987	NY-N	88	124	26	38	8	1	3	24	21	14	.306	.407	.460	136	7	5	3	-0	1.000	-6	O-25,1-13	0.0
1988	*NY-N	68	116	9	17	2	0	0	12	12	16	.147	.233	.164	16	-12	4	1	1	1.000	-4	O-18/1-16	-1.9
1989	NY-N	48	60	10	11	2	0	2	7	17	19	.183	.364	.317	101	1	3	0	1	.889	1	O-10/1-8	-0.3
	*Tor-A	28	66	12	15	3	0	4	11	7	16	.227	.400	.455	109	5	2	0	1	.944	-1	D-19/1-2,O-2	0.4
Total	14	1475	4124	571	1068	191	24	93	460	642	627	.259	.361	.385	109	70	197	90	5	.986	4	O-868,1-215/D-52	3.6

■ JIMMY McALEER McAleer, James Robert "Loafer" b: 7/10/1864, Youngstown, Ohio d: 4/29/31, Youngstown, Ohio BR/TR, 6', 175 lbs. Deb: 4/24/1889 M

1889	Cle-N	110	447	66	105	6	6	1	35	30	49	.235	.289	.282	61	-23	37			.955	9	*O-110	-1.5
1890	Cle-P	86	341	58	91	8	7	1	42	37	33	.267	.340	.340	89	-4	21			.940	1	O-86	0.3
1891	Cle-N	136	565	97	135	16	11	1	61	49	47	.239	.305	.312	77	-18	51			.924	5	*O-136	-1.5
1892	*Cle-N	149	571	92	136	26	7	4	70	63	54	.238	.318	.329	92	-6	40			.948	12	*O-149	-0.1
1893	Cle-N	91	350	63	83	5	1	2	41	35	21	.237	.314	.274	54	-24	32			.928	3	*O-91	-2.0
1894	Cle-N	64	253	36	73	15	1	2	40	13	17	.289	.331	.379	68	-14	14			.953	3	O-64	-1.2
1895	*Cle-N	131	528	84	143	17	2	0	68	38	37	.271	.327	.311	61	-31	32			.934	3	*O-131	-3.2
1896	*Cle-N	116	455	70	131	16	4	1	54	47	32	.288	.361	.347	82	-11	24			.958	7	*O-116	-1.2
1897	Cle-N	24	91	6	20	2	0	0	10	7		.220	.283	.242	37	-8	4			.947	-1	O-24	-0.9
1898	Cle-N	106	366	47	87	8	4	1	30	48	46	.238	.331	.246	67	-13	7			.965	3	*O-104/2-2	-1.4
1901	Cle-A	3	7	0	1	0	0	0	0	0	0	.143	.143	.143	-22	-1	0			1.000	-1	/O-2,P-1,3-1,M	-0.2
1902	StL-A	2	3	0	2	0	0	0	0	0	0	.667	.667	.667	274	1	0			.000	-1	/O-2,M	0.0
1907	StL-A	2	0	0	0	0	0	0	0	0	0	—	—	—			0			.000	0	RM	0.0
Total	13	1020	3977	619	1007	114	39	12	469	365	290	.253	.322	.311	72	-153	262			.944	54	*O-1015/2-2,3-1,P-1	-13.2

■ JACK McALEESE McAleese, John James b: 1877, Sharon, Pa. d: 11/15/50, New York, N.Y. BR/TR, 5'8", Deb: 8/10/01

1901	Chi-A	1	1	0	0	0	0	0	0	0	0	.000	.000	.000	-99	-0	0			1.000	0	/P-1	0.0
1909	StL-A	85	267	33	57	7	0	0	12	32		.213	.318	.240	82	-3	18			.910	-3	O-79/3-2	-1.1
Total	2	86	268	33	57	7	0	0	12	32		.213	.317	.239	82	-4	18			.910	-3	/O-79,3-2,P-1	-1.1

■ BILL McALLESTER McAllester, William Lusk b: 12/29/1888, Chattanooga, Tenn. d: 3/3/70, Chattanooga, Tenn. BR/TR, 5'11.5", 170 lbs. Deb: 5/2/13

| 1913 | StL-A | 49 | 85 | 3 | 13 | 4 | 0 | 0 | 6 | 11 | 12 | .153 | .250 | .200 | 33 | -7 | 2 | | | .908 | -4 | C-39 | -0.9 |

■ SPORT McALLISTER McAllister, Lewis William b: 7/23/1874, Austin, Miss. d: 7/17/62, Wyandotte, Mich. BB/TR, 5'11", 180 lbs. Deb: 8/7/1896

1896	Cle-N	8	27	2	6	2	0	0	1	0	2	.222	.250	.296	41	-2	1			.500	-6	/O-4,C-2,P-1	-0.8
1897	Cle-N	43	137	23	30	5	1	0	11	12	5	.219	.287	.270	45	-11	3			.894	-6	O-28/S-4,P-4,1C2	-1.6
1898	Cle-N	17	57	8	13	3	1	0	9	5		.228	.290	.316	75	-2	0			.941	1	/P-9,O-8	0.0
1899	Cle-N	113	418	29	99	6	8	1	31	19		.237	.273	.297	61	-23	5			.943	-15	O-79,C-17/3-7,1SP2	-3.8
1901	Det-A	90	306	45	92	9	4	3	57	15		.301	.344	.386	97	-2	17			.898	-19	C-35,1-28,O-11,3/S	-1.6
1902	Det-A	21	67	8	14	1	0	1	8	2		.209	.243	.269	41	-5	0			1.000	0	/1-5,S-5,2-3,C3O	-0.5
	Bal-A	3	11	0	1	0	0	0	1	1		.091	.167	.091	-26	-2	0			.923	-0	/2-2,1-1	-0.2
	Det-A	45	162	11	34	4	2	0	24	3		.210	.229	.259	34	-14	1			.991	-1	1-21,O-11/C-7,3S	-1.5
	Yr	69	240	19	49	5	2	1	33	6		.204	.230	.254	33	-22	1			.992	-1	1-27,O-12/C-9,S32D	-2.2
1903	Det-A	78	265	31	69	8	2	0	22	10		.260	.297	.306	84	-5	5			.888	-7	S-46,C-18/O-5,31	-0.9
Total	7	418	1450	157	358	38	18	5	164	67	2	.247	.287	.308	67	-68	32			.914	-55	O-147/C-83,1S3P2	-10.9

■ JIM McANANY McAnany, James b: 9/4/36, Los Angeles, Cal. BR/TR, 5'10", 196 lbs. Deb: 9/19/58

1958	Chi-A	5	13	0	0	0	0	0	0	0	0	.000	.000	.000	-99	-4	0			1.000	1	/O-3	-0.3
1959	*Chi-A	67	210	22	58	9	3	0	27	19	26	.276	.339	.348	90	-3	2	1	0	.966	-1	O-67	-0.6
1960	Chi-A	3	2	0	0	0	0	0	0	0	2	.000	.000	.000	-99	-1	0			.000	0	H	-0.1
1961	Chi-N	11	10	1	3	1	0	0	0	1	3	.300	.364	.400	101	0	0			.000	-0	/O-1	0.0
1962	Chi-N	7	6	0	0	0	0	0	0	1	2	.000	.143	.000	-56	-1	0			.000	0	H	-0.1
Total	5	93	241	23	61	10	3	0	27	21	38	.253	.316	.320	75	-8	2	1	0	.968	-1	/O-71	-1.1

■ BUB McATEE McAtee, Michael James "Butch" b: 3/1845, Troy, N.Y. d: 10/18/1876, Troy, N.Y. TR, 5'9", 160 lbs. Deb: 5/8/1871

1871	Chi-n	26	135	34	37	8	2	0	10	5	2	.274	.300	.363	81	-5	5	3	-0	.943	1	*1-26	-0.2
1872	Tro-n	25	129	30	28	3	1	0	15	1	2	.217	.223	.256	46	-8	0	2	-1	.948	1	1-25	-0.5
Total	2 n	51	264	64	65	11	3	0	25	6	4	.246	.263	.311	65	-13	5	5	-2	.945	2	/1-51	-0.7

YEAR	TM/L	G	AB	R	H	2B	3B	HR	RBI	BB	SO	AVG	OBP	SLG	PRO+	BR/A	SB	CS	SBR	FA	FR	G/POS	TPR

■ IKE McAULEY McAuley, James Earl b: 8/19/1891, Wichita, Kan. d: 4/6/28, Des Moines, Iowa BR/TR, 5'9.5", 150 lbs. Deb: 9/10/14

YEAR	TM/L	G	AB	R	H	2B	3B	HR	RBI	BB	SO	AVG	OBP	SLG	PRO+	BR/A	SB	CS	SBR	FA	FR	G/POS	TPR
1914	Pit-N	15	24	3	3	0	0	0	0	0	8	.125	.125	.125	-27	-4	0			.900	1	/S-5,3-3,2-2	-0.3
1915	Pit-N	5	15	0	2	1	0	0	0	0	6	.133	.133	.200	0	-2	0			.917	-3	/S-5	-0.5
1916	Pit-N	4	8	1	2	0	0	0	1	0	1	.250	.250	.250	53	-0	0			.938	1	/S-4	0.0
1917	StL-N	3	7	0	2	0	0	0	1	0	1	.286	.286	.286	78	-0	0			.833	-2	/S-3	-0.3
1925	Chi-N	37	125	10	35	7	2	0	11	11	12	.280	.343	.368	80	-4	1	0	0	.949	-8	S-37	-0.7
Total	5	64	179	14	44	8	2	0	13	11	28	.246	.293	.313	62	-10	1	0		.940	-12	/S-54,3-3,2-2	-1.8

■ GENE McAULIFFE McAuliffe, Eugene Leo b: 2/28/1872, Randolph, Mass. d: 4/29/53, Randolph, Mass. BR/TR, 6'1", 180 lbs. Deb: 8/17/04

YEAR	TM/L	G	AB	R	H	2B	3B	HR	RBI	BB	SO	AVG	OBP	SLG	PRO+	BR/A	SB	CS	SBR	FA	FR	G/POS	TPR
1904	Bos-N	1	2	0	1	0	0	0	0	0		.500	.500	.500	217	0	0			.667	-1	/C-1	0.0

■ DICK McAULIFFE McAuliffe, Richard John b: 11/29/39, Hartford, Conn. BL/TR, 5'11", 176 lbs. Deb: 9/17/60

YEAR	TM/L	G	AB	R	H	2B	3B	HR	RBI	BB	SO	AVG	OBP	SLG	PRO+	BR/A	SB	CS	SBR	FA	FR	G/POS	TPR
1960	Det-A	8	27	2	7	0	1	0	1	2	6	.259	.310	.333	72	-1	0	0	0	.884	1	/S-7	0.1
1961	Det-A	80	285	36	73	12	4	6	33	24	39	.256	.323	.389	87	-6	2	3	-1	.933	-29	S-55,3-22	-3.1
1962	Det-A	139	471	50	124	20	5	12	63	64	76	.263	.351	.403	99	0	4	2	0	.965	-21	2-70,3-49,S-16	-1.2
1963	Det-A	150	568	77	149	18	6	13	61	64	75	.262	.337	.384	98	-1	11	5	0	.963	-24	*S-133,2-15	-1.4
1964	Det-A	162	557	85	134	18	7	24	66	77	96	.241	.336	.427	109	7	8	5	-1	.968	-8	*S-160	1.1
1965	Det-A★	113	404	61	105	13	6	15	54	49	62	.260	.343	.433	118	0	6	9	-4	.956	-15	*S-112	-0.2
1966	Det-A★	124	430	83	118	16	8	23	56	66	80	.274	.375	.509	148	28	5	7	-3	.964	-11	*S-105,3-15	2.5
1967	Det-A★	153	557	92	133	16	7	22	65	105	118	.239	.366	.411	126	21	6	5	-1	.965	-14	*2-145,S-43	1.9
1968	*Det-A	151	570	95	142	24	10	16	56	82	99	.249	.346	.411	125	18	8	7	-2	.986	-20	*2-148/S-5	0.7
1969	Det-A	74	271	49	71	10	5	11	33	47	41	.262	.371	.458	125	10	2	5	-2	.976	-0	2-72	1.4
1970	Det-A	146	530	73	124	21	1	12	50	101	62	.234	.360	.345	95	-0	5	6	-2	.975	-6	*2-127,S-15,3-12	0.4
1971	Det-A	128	477	67	99	16	6	18	57	53	67	.208	.293	.379	86	-10	4	1	1	.987	7	*2-123/S-7	0.9
1972	*Det-A	122	408	47	98	16	3	8	30	59	59	.240	.339	.353	103	3	0	0	0	.975	-7	*2-116/S-3,3-1	0.2
1973	Det-A	106	343	39	94	18	1	12	47	49	52	.274	.366	.437	118	9	0	4	-2	.986	5	*2-102/S-2,D-1	1.7
1974	Bos-A	100	272	32	57	13	1	5	24	39	40	.210	.311	.320	76	-8	2	0	1	.971	-8	2-53,3-40/S-3,D-3	-1.4
1975	Bos-A	7	15	0	2	0	0	0	1	2	1	.133	.188	.133	-7	-2	0	0	0	.769	-2	/3-7	-0.4
Total	16	1763	6185	888	1530	231	71	197	697	882	974	.247	.344	.403	108	78	63	59	-17	.977	-150	2-971,S-666,3/D	3.2

■ GEORGE McAVOY McAvoy, George Robert b: 3/12/1884, E.Liverpool, Ohio Deb: 7/17/14

YEAR	TM/L	G	AB	R	H	2B	3B	HR	RBI	BB	SO	AVG	OBP	SLG	PRO+	BR/A	SB	CS	SBR	FA	FR	G/POS	TPR
1914	Phi-N	1	1	0	0	0	0	0	0	0	0	.000	.000	.000	-94	-0	0			.000	0	H	0.0

■ WICKEY McAVOY McAvoy, James Eugene b: 10/22/1894, Rochester, N.Y. d: 7/6/73, Rochester, N.Y. BR/TR, 5'11", 172 lbs. Deb: 9/29/13

YEAR	TM/L	G	AB	R	H	2B	3B	HR	RBI	BB	SO	AVG	OBP	SLG	PRO+	BR/A	SB	CS	SBR	FA	FR	G/POS	TPR
1913	Phi-A	4	9	0	1	0	0	0	0	0	4	.111	.200	.111	-9	-1	0			1.000	1	/C-4	0.0
1914	Phi-A	8	16	1	2	0	1	0	0	0	4	.125	.125	.250	13	-2	0			.971	1	/C-8	-0.1
1915	Phi-A	68	184	12	35	7	2	0	6	11	32	.190	.236	.250	47	-13	0	2	-1	.931	5	C-64	-0.6
1917	Phi-A	10	24	1	6	1	0	1	4	0	3	.250	.250	.417	105	-0	0			.955	5	/C-8	0.4
1918	Phi-A	83	271	14	66	5	3	0	32	13	23	.244	.283	.284	70	-10	5			.960	5	C-74/P-1,1-1,0-1	0.1
1919	Phi-A	62	170	10	24	5	2	0	11	14	21	.141	.207	.194	13	-20	1			.973	-3	C-57	-1.9
Total	6	235	674	38	134	18	8	1	53	38	87	.199	.245	.254	47	-46	6	2		.954	13	C-215/O-1,1-1,P-1	-2.1

■ ALGIE McBRIDE McBride, Algernon Griggs b: 5/23/1869, Washington, D.C. d: 1/10/56, Georgetown, Ohio BL/TL, 5'9", 152 lbs. Deb: 5/12/1896

YEAR	TM/L	G	AB	R	H	2B	3B	HR	RBI	BB	SO	AVG	OBP	SLG	PRO+	BR/A	SB	CS	SBR	FA	FR	G/POS	TPR
1896	Chi-N	9	29	2	7	1	1	1	7	7	3	.241	.389	.448	116	0	0			.917	0	/O-9	0.0
1898	Cin-N	120	486	94	147	14	12	2	43	51		.302	.383	.393	114	9	16			.959	7	*O-120	0.8
1899	Cin-N	64	251	57	87	12	5	1	23	30		.347	.431	.446	138	15	5			.950	-2	O-64	0.7
1900	Cin-N	112	436	59	120	15	8	4	59	25		.275	.320	.374	94	-5	12			.915	-9	*O-110	-2.0
1901	Cin-N	30	123	19	29	7	0	2	18	7		.236	.282	.341	86	-3	0			.968	-2	O-28	-0.7
	NY-N	68	264	27	74	11	0	2	29	12		.280	.317	.345	95	-2	3			.948	-4	O-65	-1.0
	Yr	98	387	46	103	18	0	4	47	19		.266	.306	.344	92	-4	3			.956	-6	O-93	-1.7
Total	5	403	1589	258	464	60	26	12	179	132	3	.292	.356	.385	108	15	36			.946	-10	O-396	-2.2

■ BAKE McBRIDE McBride, Arnold Ray b: 2/3/49, Fulton, Mo. BL/TR, 6'2", 190 lbs. Deb: 7/26/73

YEAR	TM/L	G	AB	R	H	2B	3B	HR	RBI	BB	SO	AVG	OBP	SLG	PRO+	BR/A	SB	CS	SBR	FA	FR	G/POS	TPR
1973	StL-N	40	63	8	19	3	0	0	5	4	10	.302	.362	.349	98	0	0	1	-1	.976	1	O-17	-0.1
1974	StL-N	150	559	81	173	19	5	6	56	43	57	.309	.372	.394	115	12	30	11	2	.990	14	*O-144	2.3
1975	StL-N	116	413	70	124	10	9	5	36	34	52	.300	.355	.404	107	4	26	8	3	.990	7	*O-107	1.0
1976	StL-N☆	72	272	40	91	13	4	3	24	18	28	.335	.389	.445	135	12	10	5	0	.981	9	O-66	2.0
1977	StL-N	43	122	21	32	5	1	4	20	7	19	.262	.302	.418	93	-2	7	1	0	1.000	-5	O-33	-0.7
	*Phi-N	85	280	55	95	20	5	11	41	25	25	.339	.399	.564	149	19	27	4	6	.986	7	*O-73	2.2
	Yr	128	402	76	127	25	6	15	61	32	44	.316	.371	.520	133	18	36	7	7	.990	-4	*O-106	1.5
1978	*Phi-N	122	472	68	127	20	4	10	49	28	48	.269	.317	.392	96	-3	28	3	7	.996	5	*O-119	0.3
1979	*Phi-N	151	582	82	163	16	12	12	60	41	77	.280	.332	.411	98	-2	25	14	-1	.989	15	*O-147	0.6
1980	*Phi-N	137	554	68	171	33	10	9	87	26	58	.309	.345	.453	115	10	13	10	-2	.990	6	*O-133	0.9
1981	*Phi-N	58	221	26	60	17	1	2	21	11	25	.271	.306	.385	91	-3	5	0	2	.987	-4	O-56	-0.8
1982	Cle-A	27	85	8	31	3	3	0	13	2	12	.365	.379	.471	132	4	2	2	-1	1.000	-2	O-22	0.0
1983	Cle-A	70	220	21	67	8	1	1	18	9	26	.291	.321	.348	81	-6	8	2	1	.977	0	O-46,D-15	-0.7
Total	11	1071	3853	548	1153	167	55	63	430	248	457	.299	.348	.420	109	45	183	63	17	.989	46	O-963/D-15	7.0

■ GEORGE McBRIDE McBride, George Florian b: 11/20/1880, Milwaukee, Wis. d: 7/2/73, Milwaukee, Wis. BR/TR, 5'11", 170 lbs. Deb: 9/12/01 MC

YEAR	TM/L	G	AB	R	H	2B	3B	HR	RBI	BB	SO	AVG	OBP	SLG	PRO+	BR/A	SB	CS	SBR	FA	FR	G/POS	TPR
1901	Mil-A	3	12	0	2	0	0	0	0	1		.167	.231	.167	12	-1	0			1.000	-1	/S-3	-0.2
1905	Pit-N	27	87	9	19	4	0	0	7	6		.218	.277	.264	60	-4	2			.902	-4	3-17/S-8	-0.8
	StL-N	81	281	22	61	1	2	2	34	14		.217	.264	.256	57	-15	10			.938	-2	S-80/1-1	-1.6
	Yr	108	368	31	80	5	2	2	41	20		.217	.267	.258	58	-19	12			.935	-6	S-88,3-17/1-1	-2.4
1906	StL-N	90	313	24	53	8	2	0	13	17		.169	.215	.208	33	-25	5			.944	9	S-90	-1.5
1908	Was-A	155	518	47	120	10	6	0	34	41		.232	.292	.274	92	-4	12			.948	32	*S-155	3.4
1909	Was-A	156	504	38	118	16	0	0	34	36		.234	.294	.266	81	-10	17			.935	11	*S-156	0.4
1910	Was-A	154	514	54	118	19	4	1	55	61		.230	.321	.288	95	-1	11			.939	27	*S-154	3.5
1911	Was-A	154	557	58	131	11	4	0	59	52		.235	.312	.269	64	-26	15			.941	24	*S-154	0.8
1912	Was-A	152	521	56	118	13	7	1	52	38		.226	.288	.284	63	-25	17			.941	31	*S-152	1.9
1913	Was-A	150	499	52	107	18	7	1	52	43	46	.214	.286	.285	66	-22	12			.960	11	*S-150	0.4
1914	Was-A	156	503	49	102	12	4	0	24	43	70	.203	.274	.243	53	-28	12	14	-5	.958	12	*S-156	-1.0
1915	Was-A	146	476	54	97	8	5	0	30	29	60	.204	.251	.252	50	-31	10	5	0	.968	9	*S-146	-1.1
1916	Was-A	139	466	36	106	15	4	1	36	23	58	.227	.271	.283	67	-20	8			.957	13	*S-139	-0.6
1917	Was-A	50	141	6	27	3	0	0	9	10	17	.191	.265	.213	46	-9	1			.943	-1	S-41/3-6,2-2	-0.9
1918	Was-A	18	53	2	7	0	0	0	1	0	11	.132	.132	.132	-21	-8	1			.986	2	S-14/2-2	-0.6
1919	Was-A	15	40	3	9	1	1	0	4	3	6	.225	.256	.275	49	-3	0			.932	1	S-15	-0.2
1920	Was-A	13	41	6	9	1	0	0	3	2	3	.220	.256	.244	34	-4	0	0	0	.966	-3	S-13	-0.6
Total	16	1659	5526	516	1203	140	47	7	447	419	271	.218	.281	.264	65	-236	133	19		.948	169	*S-1626/3-23,2-4,1	1.9

■ JOHN McBRIDE McBride, John F. Deb: 10/12/1890

YEAR	TM/L	G	AB	R	H	2B	3B	HR	RBI	BB	SO	AVG	OBP	SLG	PRO+	BR/A	SB	CS	SBR	FA	FR	G/POS	TPR
1890	Phi-a	1	2	0	0	0	0	0	0	0	0	.000	.000	.000	-99	-1	0			1.000	1	/O-1	0.0

■ TOM McBRIDE McBride, Thomas Raymond b: 11/2/14, Bonham, Tex. BR/TR, 6', 190 lbs. Deb: 4/23/43

YEAR	TM/L	G	AB	R	H	2B	3B	HR	RBI	BB	SO	AVG	OBP	SLG	PRO+	BR/A	SB	CS	SBR	FA	FR	G/POS	TPR
1943	Bos-A	26	96	11	23	3	1	0	7	7	3	.240	.291	.292	70	-2	2	0	1	.984	0	O-24	-0.5
1944	Bos-A	71	216	29	53	7	3	0	24	8	13	.245	.276	.306	67	-10	4	0	1	.992	-1	O-57/1-5	-1.2
1945	Bos-A	100	344	38	105	11	7	1	47	26	17	.305	.354	.387	112	5	2	2	-1	.984	-0	O-81,1-11	-0.1
1946	*Bos-A	61	153	21	46	5	2	0	19	9	6	.301	.340	.359	90	-2	0	1	0	1.000	-7	O-43	-1.2
1947	Bos-a	2	5	0	1	0	0	0	0	0	0	.200	.200	.200	11	-1	0			1.000	1	/O-1	0.0
	Was-A	56	166	19	45	4	0	0	15	15	9	.271	.331	.319	84	-4	3	1	0	.972	-4	O-51/3-1	-1.0
	Yr	58	171	19	46	4	0	0	15	15	9	.269	.328	.316	81	-4	3	1	0	.973	-3	O-52/3-1	-1.0

YEAR	TM/L	G	AB	R	H	2B	3B	HR	RBI	BB	SO	AVG	OBP	SLG	PRO+	BR/A	SB	CS	SBR	FA	FR	G/POS	TPR
1948	Was-A	92	206	22	53	9	1	1	29	28	15	.257	.346	.325	81	-5	2	2	-1	.983	2	O-55	-0.6
Total	6	408	1186	140	326	39	16	2	141	93	63	.275	.328	.340	88	-20	13	6	0	.985	-9	O-312/1-16,3-1	-4.6

■ SWAT McCABE
McCabe, James Arthur b: 11/20/1881, Towanda, Pa. d: 12/9/44, Bristol, Conn. BL/TR, 5'10", Deb: 9/23/09

YEAR	TM/L	G	AB	R	H	2B	3B	HR	RBI	BB	SO	AVG	OBP	SLG	PRO+	BR/A	SB	CS	SBR	FA	FR	G/POS	TPR
1909	Cin-N	3	11	2	6	1	0	0	0	0	0	.545	.545	.636	269	2	1			.625	-1	/O-3	0.1
1910	Cin-N	13	35	3	9	1	0	0	5	1	2	.257	.297	.286	73	-1	0			1.000	1	/O-9	-0.1
Total	2	16	46	5	15	2	0	0	5	1	2	.326	.354	.370	118	1	1			.875	-1	/O-12	0.0

■ JOE McCABE
McCabe, Joseph Robert b: 8/27/38, Indianapolis, Ind. BR/TR, 6', 190 lbs. Deb: 4/18/64

YEAR	TM/L	G	AB	R	H	2B	3B	HR	RBI	BB	SO	AVG	OBP	SLG	PRO+	BR/A	SB	CS	SBR	FA	FR	G/POS	TPR
1964	Min-A	14	19	1	3	0	0	0	2	0	8	.158	.158	.158	-12	-3	0	0	0	1.000	0	C-12	-0.2
1965	Was-A	14	27	1	5	0	0	0	5	8	13	.185	.290	.296	68	-1	1	0	0	.972	-3	C-11	-0.3
Total	2	28	46	2	8	0	0	0	7	8	21	.174	.240	.239	36	-4	1	0	0	.986	-2	/C-23	-0.5

■ BILL McCABE
McCabe, William Francis b: 10/28/1892, Chicago, Ill. d: 9/2/66, Chicago, Ill. BB/TR, 5'9.5", 180 lbs. Deb: 4/16/18

YEAR	TM/L	G	AB	R	H	2B	3B	HR	RBI	BB	SO	AVG	OBP	SLG	PRO+	BR/A	SB	CS	SBR	FA	FR	G/POS	TPR
1918	*Chi-N	29	45	9	8	0	1	0	5	4	7	.178	.245	.222	42	-3	2			.939	5	2-13/O-4	0.3
1919	Chi-N	33	84	8	13	3	1	0	5	9	15	.155	.253	.214	41	-6	3			.950	-1	O-20/S-4,3-1	-0.9
1920	Chi-N	3	2	1	1	0	0	0	0	0	0	.500	.500	.500	184	0	0	0	0	.000	0	H	0.0
	*Bro-N	41	68	10	10	0	0	0	3	2	6	.147	.171	.147	-8	-9	1	2	-1	.882	4	S-13/O-6,2-4,3-3	-0.7
	Yr	44	70	11	11	0	0	0	3	2	6	.157	.181	.157	-2	-9	1	2	-1	.882	4	S-13/O-6,2-4,3-3	-0.7
Total	3	106	199	28	32	3	2	0	13	15	28	.161	.227	.196	26	-18	6	2		.943	8	/O-30,S-17,2-17,3-4	-1.3

■ HARRY McCAFFERY
McCaffery, Harry Charles b: 11/25/1858, St.Louis, Mo. d: 4/19/28, St.Louis, Mo. BR/TR, 5'10.5", 185 lbs. Deb: 6/15/1882 U

YEAR	TM/L	G	AB	R	H	2B	3B	HR	RBI	BB	SO	AVG	OBP	SLG	PRO+	BR/A	SB	CS	SBR	FA	FR	G/POS	TPR
1882	Lou-a	1	4	1	1	0	0	0				.250	.250	.250	73	-0				1.000	-1	/2-1	-0.1
	StL-a	38	153	23	42	8	6	0			3	.275	.288	.405	127	4				.891	4	O-23/2-8,3-7,1-1	0.7
	Yr	39	157	24	43	8	6	0			3	.274	.287	.401	125	4				.891	3	O-23/2-9,3-7,1-1	0.6
1883	StL-a	5	18	0	1	0	0	0		1	1	.056	.105	.056	-44	-3				.889	1	/O-5	-0.2
1885	Cin-a	1	5	0	0	0	0	0				.000	.000	.000	-98	-1				.000	-0	/P-1	0.0
Total	3	45	180	24	44	8	6	0	1		4	.244	.261	.356	101	-0				.891	4	/O-28,2-9,3-7,P1	0.4

■ SPARROW McCAFFREY
McCaffrey, Charles P. b: 1868, Philadelphia, Pa. d: 4/29/1894, Philadelphia, Pa. 120 lbs. Deb: 8/13/1889

YEAR	TM/L	G	AB	R	H	2B	3B	HR	RBI	BB	SO	AVG	OBP	SLG	PRO+	BR/A	SB	CS	SBR	FA	FR	G/POS	TPR
1889	Col-a	2	1	1	1	0	0	0	1	0		1.000	1.000	1.000	495	1	0			.000	0	/C-2	0.1

■ BRIAN McCALL
McCall, Brian Allen "Bam" b: 1/25/43, Kentfield, Cal. BL/TL, 5'10", 170 lbs. Deb: 9/18/62

YEAR	TM/L	G	AB	R	H	2B	3B	HR	RBI	BB	SO	AVG	OBP	SLG	PRO+	BR/A	SB	CS	SBR	FA	FR	G/POS	TPR
1962	Chi-A	4	8	2	3	0	0	2	3	0	2	.375	.375	1.125	287	2	0	0	0	1.000	0	/O-1	0.2
1963	Chi-A	3	7	1	0	0	0	0	0	1	2	.000	.125	.000	-62	-2	0	0	0	1.000	-0	/O-2	-0.2
Total	2	7	15	3	3	0	0	2	3	1	4	.200	.250	.600	126	0	0	0	0	1.000	0	/O-3	-0.2

■ JACK McCANDLESS
McCandless, Scott Cook b: 5/5/1891, Pittsburgh, Pa. d: 8/17/61, Pittsburgh, Pa. BL/TR, 6', 170 lbs. Deb: 9/10/14

YEAR	TM/L	G	AB	R	H	2B	3B	HR	RBI	BB	SO	AVG	OBP	SLG	PRO+	BR/A	SB	CS	SBR	FA	FR	G/POS	TPR
1914	Bal-F	11	31	5	8	0	1	0	3	1	3	.258	.343	.323	79	-1	0			1.000	-0	/O-8	-0.2
1915	Bal-F	117	406	47	87	6	7	5	34	41	99	.214	.296	.302	66	-24	9			.945	3	*O-105	-2.9
Total	2	128	437	52	95	6	8	5	34	41	99	.217	.299	.302	67	-26	9			.948	3	O-113	-3.1

■ EMMETT McCANN
McCann, Robert Emmett b: 3/4/02, Philadelphia, Pa. d: 4/15/37, Philadelphia, Pa. BR/TR, 5'11", 150 lbs. Deb: 4/19/20

YEAR	TM/L	G	AB	R	H	2B	3B	HR	RBI	BB	SO	AVG	OBP	SLG	PRO+	BR/A	SB	CS	SBR	FA	FR	G/POS	TPR
1920	Phi-A	13	34	4	9	1	1	0	3	3	1	.265	.342	.353	84	-1	0		-1	.907	-0	S-11	-0.1
1921	Phi-A	52	157	15	35	5	0	0	15	4	6	.223	.242	.255	27	-17	2	1	0	.949	-0	S-32/3-9,2-2,1-1	-1.4
1926	Bos-A	6	3	0	0	0	0	0	0	1	1	.000	.250	.000	-32	-1	0	0	0	1.000	-0	/S-1,3-1	-0.1
Total	3	71	194	19	44	6	1	0	18	8	8	.227	.261	.268	36	-19	2	2		.939	-1	/S-44,3-10,2-2,1-1	-1.6

■ ROGER McCARDELL
McCardell, Roger Morton b: 8/29/32, Gorsuch Mills, Md. BR/TR, 6', 200 lbs. Deb: 5/8/59

YEAR	TM/L	G	AB	R	H	2B	3B	HR	RBI	BB	SO	AVG	OBP	SLG	PRO+	BR/A	SB	CS	SBR	FA	FR	G/POS	TPR
1959	SF-N	4	4	0	0	0	0	0	0	0	0	.000	.000	.000	-99	-1	0	0	0	1.000	0	/C-3	-0.1

■ BILL McCARREN
McCarren, William Joseph b: 11/4/1895, Fortenia, Pa. d: 9/11/83, Denver, Colo. BR/TR, 5'11.5", 170 lbs. Deb: 5/4/23

YEAR	TM/L	G	AB	R	H	2B	3B	HR	RBI	BB	SO	AVG	OBP	SLG	PRO+	BR/A	SB	CS	SBR	FA	FR	G/POS	TPR
1923	Bro-N	69	216	28	53	10	1	3	27	22	39	.245	.326	.343	79	-6	0	1	-1	.927	-2	3-66/O-1	-0.3

■ ALEX McCARTHY
McCarthy, Alexander George b: 5/12/1888, Chicago, Ill. d: 3/12/78, Salisbury, Md. BR/TR, 5'9", 150 lbs. Deb: 10/7/10

YEAR	TM/L	G	AB	R	H	2B	3B	HR	RBI	BB	SO	AVG	OBP	SLG	PRO+	BR/A	SB	CS	SBR	FA	FR	G/POS	TPR
1910	Pit-N	3	12	1	1	0	1	0	0	0	2	.083	.083	.250	-3	-2	0			.875	0	/S-3	-0.2
1911	Pit-N	50	150	18	36	5	1	2	31	14	24	.240	.305	.327	74	-6	4			.981	-1	S-33,2-11/3-1,0-1	-0.4
1912	Pit-N	111	401	53	111	12	4	1	41	30	26	.277	.332	.334	84	-9	8			.962	3	*2-105/3-4	-0.8
1913	Pit-N	31	74	7	15	5	0	0	10	7	7	.203	.298	.270	66	-3	1			.902	-2	S-12,3-12/2-6	-0.5
1914	Pit-N	57	173	14	26	0	1	1	14	6	17	.150	.192	.179	11	-19	2			.975	11	3-36,2-10/S-6	-0.8
1915	Pit-N	21	49	3	10	1	0	1	3	5	10	.204	.291	.245	64	-2	1	2	-1	.950	1	/2-9,S-5,3-4,1-1	-0.8
	Chi-N	23	72	4	19	3	0	1	9	5	7	.264	.329	.347	105	0	0	3		.972	11	2-12,3-12/S-1	1.2
	Yr	44	121	7	29	3	1	1	9	10	17	.240	.313	.306	88	-1	3	5	-2	.964	12	2-21,3-16/S-6,1-1	1.0
1916	Chi-N	37	107	10	26	2	3	0	6	11	7	.243	.341	.318	93	-0	1			.931	-0	2-34/S-3	-0.2
	Pit-N	50	146	11	29	3	0	0	3	15	10	.199	.282	.219	54	-7	3			.955	-5	S-39/2-7,3-5	-1.2
	Yr	87	253	21	55	5	3	0	9	26	17	.217	.308	.261	72	-7	4			.951	-7	S-42,2-41/3-5	-1.4
1917	Pit-N	49	151	15	33	4	0	0	8	11	13	.219	.276	.245	58	-7	1			.964	7	3-26,2-13/S-9	0.1
Total	8	432	1335	136	306	34	11	5	122	104	123	.229	.295	.282	67	-55	23	5		.957	23	2-207,S-111,3/10	-3.0

■ JERRY McCARTHY
McCarthy, Jerome Francis b: 5/23/23, Brooklyn, N.Y. d: 10/3/65, Oceanside, N.Y. BL/TL, 6'1", 205 lbs. Deb: 6/19/48

YEAR	TM/L	G	AB	R	H	2B	3B	HR	RBI	BB	SO	AVG	OBP	SLG	PRO+	BR/A	SB	CS	SBR	FA	FR	G/POS	TPR
1948	StL-A	2	3	0	1	0	0	0	0	0	0	.333	.333	.333	76	-0	0	0	0	.600	-1	/1-2	-0.1

■ JACK McCARTHY
McCarthy, John Arthur b: 3/26/1869, Gilbertville, Mass. d: 9/11/31, Chicago, Ill. BL/TL, 5'9", 155 lbs. Deb: 8/3/1893

YEAR	TM/L	G	AB	R	H	2B	3B	HR	RBI	BB	SO	AVG	OBP	SLG	PRO+	BR/A	SB	CS	SBR	FA	FR	G/POS	TPR
1893	Cin-N	49	195	28	55	8	3	0	22	22	7	.282	.355	.354	86	-4	6			.887	-1	O-47/1-2	-0.6
1894	Cin-N	40	167	29	45	9	1	0	21	17	6	.269	.348	.335	63	-10	3			.895	2	O-25,1-15	-0.8
1898	Pit-N	137	537	75	155	13	12	4	78	34		.289	.336	.380	107	4	7			.935	4	*O-137	-0.3
1899	Pit-N	138	560	108	171	22	17	3	67	39		.305	.355	.421	113	8	28			.961	-5	*O-138	-0.7
1900	Chi-N	124	503	68	148	16	7	0	48	24		.294	.329	.354	92	-6	22			.944	-1	*O-123	-1.5
1901	Cle-A	86	343	60	110	14	7	0	32	30		.321	.382	.402	123	12	9			.949	-1	O-86	0.4
1902	Cle-A	95	359	45	102	31	5	0	41	24		.284	.329	.398	105	2	12			.944	-5	O-95	-0.9
1903	Cle-A	108	415	47	110	20	8	0	43	19		.265	.299	.352	96	-2	15			.964	-3	*O-108	-1.3
	Chi-N	24	101	11	28	5	0	0	14	4		.277	.305	.327	82	-3	8			.947	-3	O-24	-0.7
1904	Chi-N	115	432	36	114	14	2	0	51	23		.264	.307	.306	89	-6	14			.961	-5	*O-115	-1.8
1905	Chi-N	59	170	16	47	4	3	0	14	10		.276	.320	.335	92	-2	8			.986	-1	O-37/1-6	-0.2
1906	Bro-N	91	322	23	98	13	1	0	35	20		.304	.347	.351	128	9	9			.924	-3	O-86	0.8
1907	Bro-N	25	91	4	20	2	0	0	8	2		.220	.237	.242	54	-5	4			1.000	-0	O-25	-1.2
Total	12	1091	4195	550	1203	171	66	7	474	268	13	.287	.333	.364	100	-3	145			.946	-17	*O-1046/1-23	-8.8

■ JOHNNY McCARTHY
McCarthy, John Joseph b: 1/7/10, Chicago, Ill. d: 9/13/73, Mundelein, Ill. BL/TL, 6'1.5", 185 lbs. Deb: 9/2/34

YEAR	TM/L	G	AB	R	H	2B	3B	HR	RBI	BB	SO	AVG	OBP	SLG	PRO+	BR/A	SB	CS	SBR	FA	FR	G/POS	TPR
1934	Bro-N	17	39	7	7	2	0	1	5	3	2	.179	.220	.308	42	-3	0			.961	1	1-13	-0.3
1935	Bro-N	22	48	9	12	1	1	0	4	2	9	.250	.280	.313	60	-3	1			.982	-3	1-19	-0.7
1936	NY-N	4	16	1	7	0	0	1	2	0	1	.438	.438	.625	185	1	0			.981	0	/1-4	0.3
1937	*NY-N	114	420	53	117	19	3	10	65	24	37	.279	.322	.410	96	-3	2			.987	1	*1-110	-1.3
1938	NY-N	134	470	55	128	13	4	8	59	39	28	.272	.326	.368	91	-6	3			.993	-3	*1-125	-2.4
1939	NY-N	50	80	12	21	6	1	1	11	3	8	.262	.298	.400	85	-2	0			1.000	1	1-12/O-4,P-1	-0.7
1940	NY-N	51	67	6	16	4	0	0	5	2	8	.239	.261	.299	53	-4	0			1.000	-4	1-6	-0.4
1941	NY-N	14	40	1	13	2	0	0	5	3	2	.325	.372	.400	115	1	0			.987	0	/1-8,O-1	0.1
1943	Bos-N	78	313	32	95	24	6	2	33	10	19	.304	.327	.438	122	7	3			.996	1	1-78	0.1
1946	Bos-N	2	7	0	1	0	0	0	0	1	2	.143	.333	.143	37	-0	0			1.000	1	/1-2	-0.1
1948	NY-N	56	50	6	13	2	1	2	12	3	2	.263	.300	.404	88	-1	0			.966	-0	1-6	-0.2
Total	11	542	1557	182	432	72	16	25	209	90	114	.277	.319	.392	95	-14	9			.990	-5	1-383/O-5,P-1	-5.4

YEAR	TM/L	G	AB	R	H	2B	3B	HR	RBI	BB	SO	AVG	OBP	SLG	PRO+	BR/A	SB	CS	SBR	FA	FR	G/POS	TPR
■ JOE McCARTHY			McCarthy, Joseph N.		b: 12/25/1881, Syracuse, N.Y.			d: 1/12/37, Syracuse, N.Y.		BR/TR,		Deb: 9/27/05											
1905	NY-A	1	2	0	0	0	0	0	0	0	0	.000	.000	.000	-90	-0	0			1.000	0	/C-1	0.0
1906	StL-N	15	37	3	9	2	0	0	2	2		.243	.282	.297	84	-1	0			.984	-0	/C-15	0.0
Total	2	16	39	3	9	2	0	0	2	2		.231	.268	.282	74	-1	0			.985	-0	/C-16	0.0

YEAR	TM/L	G	AB	R	H	2B	3B	HR	RBI	BB	SO	AVG	OBP	SLG	PRO+	BR/A	SB	CS	SBR	FA	FR	G/POS	TPR
■ TOMMY McCARTHY			McCarthy, Thomas Francis Michael		b: 7/24/1863, Boston, Mass.			d: 8/5/22, Boston, Mass.		BR/TR, 5'7", 170 lbs.		Deb: 7/10/1884 MH											
1884	Bos-U	53	209	37	45	2	2	0		6		.215	.237	.244	47	-19				.794	-2	O-48/P-7	-1.9
1885	Bos-N	40	148	16	27	2	0	0	11	5	25	.182	.209	.196	33	-11				.865	3	O-40	-0.8
1886	Phi-N	8	27	6	5	2	1	0	3	2	3	.185	.241	.333	73	-1	1			.818	-1	/O-8,P-1	-0.2
1887	Phi-N	18	70	7	13	4	0	0	6	2	5	.186	.219	.243	27	-7	15			.818	-9	/O-8,2-5,S-3,3-2	-1.4
1888	*StL-a	131	511	107	140	20	3	1	68	38		.274	.328	.331	100	-2	93			.932	30	*O-131/P-2	2.2
1889	StL-a	140	604	136	176	24	7	2	63	46	26	.291	.348	.364	91	-12	57			.893	14	*O-140/2-5,P-1	-0.1
1890	StL-a	133	548	137	192	28	9	6	69	66		.350	.430	.467	144	27	**83**			.893	7	*O-102,3-32/2-1,M	2.8
1891	StL-a	136	578	127	179	21	6	8	95	50	19	.310	.375	.408	108	1	37			.895	-1	*O-113,2-14,S/3P	-1.0
1892	*Bos-N	152	603	119	146	19	5	4	63	39	29	.242	.347	.310	91	-6	53			.883	2	*O-152	-1.0
1893	Bos-N	116	462	107	160	28	6	5	111	64	10	.346	.429	.465	128	18	46			.902	3	*O-108/2-7,S-3	1.3
1894	Bos-N	127	539	118	188	21	8	13	126	59	17	.349	.419	.490	110	7	43			.904	11	*O-127/S-2,2-1,P-1	0.7
1895	Bos-N	117	452	90	131	13	2	2	73	72	12	.290	.391	.341	83	-10	18			.885	-10	*O-109/2-9	-2.3
1896	Bro-N	104	377	62	94	8	4	3	47	34	17	.249	.316	.316	71	-15	22			.920	-2	*O-103	-2.2
Total	13	1275	5128	1069	1496	192	53	44	<u>735</u>	537	<u>163</u>	.292	.364	.376	99	-31	468			.897	45	*O-1189/2-39,3SP	-3.1

YEAR	TM/L	G	AB	R	H	2B	3B	HR	RBI	BB	SO	AVG	OBP	SLG	PRO+	BR/A	SB	CS	SBR	FA	FR	G/POS	TPR
■ BILL McCARTHY			McCarthy, William John		b: 2/14/1886, Boston, Mass.			d: 2/4/28, Washington, D.C.		TR ,		Deb: 6/5/05											
1905	Bos-N	1	3	0	0	0	0	0	0	0	0	.000	.000	.000	-99	-1	0			.667	-0	/C-1	-0.1
1907	Cin-N	3	8	1	1	0	0	0	0	0	0	.125	.125	.125	-21	-1	0			1.000	-1	/C-3	-0.2
Total	2	4	11	1	1	0	0	0	0	0	0	.091	.091	.091	-43	-2	0			.842	-1	/C-4	-0.3

YEAR	TM/L	G	AB	R	H	2B	3B	HR	RBI	BB	SO	AVG	OBP	SLG	PRO+	BR/A	SB	CS	SBR	FA	FR	G/POS	TPR
■ FRANK McCARTON			McCarton, Francis		b: 10/6/1854, Middletown, Conn.			d: 6/17/07, New York, N.Y.				Deb: 4/26/1872											
1872	Man-n	19	85	17	28	4	1	0	10	1	3	.329	.337	.400	134	4	0	0		.791	-2	O-19	0.2

YEAR	TM/L	G	AB	R	H	2B	3B	HR	RBI	BB	SO	AVG	OBP	SLG	PRO+	BR/A	SB	CS	SBR	FA	FR	G/POS	TPR
■ DAVID McCARTY			McCarty, David Andrew		b: 11/23/69, Houston, Tex.			BR/TL, 6'5", 215 lbs.		Deb: 5/17/93													
1993	Min-A	98	350	36	75	15	2	2	21	19	80	.214	.257	.286	45	-27	2	6	-3	.959	5	O-67,1-36/D-2	-2.9
1994	Min-A	44	131	21	34	8	2	1	12	7	32	.260	.322	.374	79	-4	2	1	0	.981	1	1-32,O-14	-0.6
1995	Min-A	25	55	10	12	3	1	0	4	4	18	.218	.283	.309	54	-4	0	1	-1	.993	-0	1-18/O-5	-0.8
	SF-N	12	20	1	5	1	0	0	2	2	4	.250	.318	.300	66	-1	1	0	0	.833	-1	/O-4,1-2	0.2
1996	SF-N	91	175	16	38	3	0	6	24	18	43	.217	.297	.337	70	-8	2	1	0	.990	-4	1-51,O-20	-1.5
Total	4	270	731	84	164	30	5	9	63	50	177	.224	.282	.316	59	-44	7	9	-3	.989	-2	1-139,O-110/D-2	-6.0

YEAR	TM/L	G	AB	R	H	2B	3B	HR	RBI	BB	SO	AVG	OBP	SLG	PRO+	BR/A	SB	CS	SBR	FA	FR	G/POS	TPR
■ LEW McCARTY			McCarty, George Lewis		b: 11/17/1888, Milton, Pa.			d: 6/9/30, Reading, Pa.		BR/TR, 5'11.5", 192 lbs.		Deb: 8/30/13											
1913	Bro-N	9	26	1	6	0	0	0	2	2	2	.231	.286	.231	47	-2	0			1.000	0	/C-9	-0.1
1914	Bro-N	90	284	20	72	14	2	1	30	14	22	.254	.293	.327	83	-7	1			.970	1	C-84	0.1
1915	Bro-N	84	276	19	66	9	4	0	19	7	23	.239	.261	.301	68	-11	7	4	-0	.969	-8	C-27,1-17	-1.5
1916	Bro-N	55	150	17	47	6	1	0	13	14	16	.313	.383	.367	127	5	4			.985	-4	C-27,1-17	0.4
	NY-N	25	68	6	27	3	4	0	9	7	9	.397	.453	.559	222	10	0			.993	-0	C-24	1.3
	Yr	80	218	23	74	9	5	0	22	21	25	.339	.405	.427	155	15	4			.989	-3	C-51,1-17	1.7
1917	*NY-N	56	162	15	40	3	2	2	19	14	6	.247	.311	.327	99	-0	1			.979	-3	C-54	0.1
1918	NY-N	86	257	16	69	7	3	0	24	17	13	.268	.321	.319	97	-1	3			.975	-7	C-75	-0.2
1919	NY-N	85	210	17	59	5	4	2	21	18	15	.281	.341	.371	115	4	2			.970	-8	C-59	0.1
1920	NY-N	36	38	2	5	0	0	0	0	4	2	.132	.214	.132	1	-5	2	0	1	1.000	-2	/C-5	-0.2
	StL-N	5	7	0	2	0	0	0	0	0	0	.286	.583	.286	160	1	0	0		1.000	-1	/C-3	0.1
	Yr	41	45	2	7	0	0	0	0	4	2	.156	.296	.156	33	-3	2	0	1	1.000	-3	/C-8	-0.1
1921	StL-N	1	1	0	0	0	0	0	0	0	0	.000	.000	.000	-99	-0	0	0	0	.000	0	H	0.0
Total	9	532	1479	113	393	47	20	5	137	102	109	.266	.318	.335	97	-5	20	4		.975	-28	C-421/1-17	0.1

YEAR	TM/L	G	AB	R	H	2B	3B	HR	RBI	BB	SO	AVG	OBP	SLG	PRO+	BR/A	SB	CS	SBR	FA	FR	G/POS	TPR
■ TIM McCARVER			McCarver, James Timothy		b: 10/16/41, Memphis, Tenn.			BL/TR, 6'1", 195 lbs.		Deb: 9/10/59													
1959	StL-N	8	24	3	4	1	0	0	2		1	.167	.231	.208	19	-3	0	0	0	.971	-2	/C-6	-0.5
1960	StL-N	10	10	3	2	0	0	0	0	0	0	.200	.200	.200	9	-1	0	0	0	1.000	-1	/C-5	-0.1
1961	StL-N	22	67	5	16	2	1	1	6	0	5	.239	.239	.343	47	-5	0	0	0	.969	-2	C-20	-0.6
1963	StL-N	127	405	39	117	12	7	4	51	27	43	.289	.336	.383	97	-1	5	2	0	.994	-0	*C-126	0.3
1964	*StL-N	143	465	53	134	19	3	9	52	40	44	.288	.346	.400	101	1	2	0	1	.987	-9	*C-137	-0.2
1965	StL-N	113	409	48	113	17	2	11	48	30	26	.276	.320	.408	97	-2	5	1	1	**.995**	-4	*C-111	0.1
1966	StL-N★	150	543	50	149	19	**13**	12	68	36	38	.274	.322	.424	105	3	9	6	-1	.992	-4	*C-148	0.8
1967	*StL-N★	138	471	68	139	26	3	14	69	54	32	.295	.374	.452	137	23	8	8	-2	**.997**	4	*C-130	3.4
1968	*StL-N	128	434	35	110	15	6	5	48	26	31	.253	.297	.350	95	-3	4	3	-1	.986	3	*C-109	0.8
1969	StL-N	138	515	46	134	27	3	7	51	49	26	.260	.327	.365	93	-5	4	9	-4	.986	9	*C-136	0.8
1970	Phi-N	44	164	16	47	11	1	4	14	14	16	.287	.346	.439	112	2	0	2	-2	.991	-0	C-44	0.4
1971	Phi-N	134	474	51	132	20	5	8	46	43	26	.278	.340	.392	107	4	5	3	-0	.985	-8	*C-125	0.1
1972	Phi-N	45	152	14	36	8	2	2	14	17	15	.237	.322	.329	83	-3	1	2	-0	.989	-3	C-40	-0.6
	Mon-N	77	239	19	60	5	1	5	20	19	14	.251	.309	.343	84	-5	4	4	-1	.990	-1	C-45,O-14/3-6	-1.1
	Yr	122	391	33	96	13	1	7	34	36	29	.246	.314	.338	83	-8	5	6	-2	.990	-1	C-85,O-14/3-6	-1.1
1973	StL-N	130	331	30	88	16	4	3	49	38	31	.266	.345	.366	97	-1	2	0	1	.986	-6	1-77,C-11	-1.2
1974	StL-N	74	106	13	23	0	1	0	11	22	6	.217	.366	.236	72	-3	0	1	-1	.969	-1	C-21/1-6	-0.4
	Bos-A	11	28	3	7	1	0	0	4	1	1	.250	.344	.286	77	-1	1	0	0	1.000	-1	/C-8,D-2	0.1
1975	Bos-A	12	21	1	8	2	1	0	3	1	3	.381	.409	.571	161	2	0	0	0	.957	-0	/C-7,1-1	0.2
	Phi-N	47	59	6	15	2	0	1	7	14	7	.254	.397	.339	102	1	1	0	0	.984	1	C-10/1-1	0.2
1976	*Phi-N	90	155	26	43	11	2	3	29	35	14	.277	.414	.432	136	9	2	4	-2	1.000	0	C-41/1-2	1.6
1977	*Phi-N	93	169	28	54	13	2	6	30	28	11	.320	.422	.527	146	12	3	5	-2	.988	2	C-42/1-3	1.2
1978	*Phi-N	90	146	18	36	11	1	1	14	28	11	.247	.375	.342	101	2	2	2	-1	.995	2	C-34,1-11	0.3
1979	Phi-N	79	137	13	33	5	1	1	19	12	10	.241	.338	.314	76	-4	0	0	0	.989	3	C-31/O-1	0.0
1980	Phi-N	6	5	2	1	1	0	0	2	1	0	.200	.333	.400	98	-0	0	0	0	1.000	-0	/1-2	0.0
Total	21	1909	5529	590	1501	242	57	97	645	548	422	.271	.340	.388	102	23	61	49	-11	.990	-9	*C-1387,1-103/O3D	6.2

YEAR	TM/L	G	AB	R	H	2B	3B	HR	RBI	BB	SO	AVG	OBP	SLG	PRO+	BR/A	SB	CS	SBR	FA	FR	G/POS	TPR
■ AL McCAULEY			McCauley, Allen A.		b: 3/4/1863, Indianapolis, Ind.			d: 8/24/17, Wayne Twnshp., Ind		BL/TL, 6', 180 lbs.		Deb: 6/21/1884											
1884	Ind-a	17	53	7	10	0	1	0		5	12	.189	.358	.226	97	1				1.000	0	P-10/1-5,O-3	-0.2
1890	Phi-N	112	418	63	102	25	7	1	42	57	38	.244	.346	.344	99	0	8			.973	-6	*1-116	-1.1
1891	Was-a	59	206	36	58	5	8	1	31	30	13	.282	.378	.398	128	8	9			.969	-2	1-59	0.3
Total	3	188	677	106	170	30	16	2	78	99	<u>51</u>	.251	.357	.352	107	9	17			.971	-7	1-180/P-10,O-3	-1.0

YEAR	TM/L	G	AB	R	H	2B	3B	HR	RBI	BB	SO	AVG	OBP	SLG	PRO+	BR/A	SB	CS	SBR	FA	FR	G/POS	TPR
■ JIM McCAULEY			McCauley, James Adelbert		b: 3/24/1863, Stanley, N.Y.			d: 9/14/30, Canandaigua, N.Y.		BL/TR, 6', 180 lbs.		Deb: 9/17/1884											
1884	StL-a	1	2	0	0	0	0	0	0	0	0	.000	.000	.000	-97	-0				.818	-1	/C-1	0.1
1885	Buf-N	24	84	4	15	2	1	0	7	11	12	.179	.274	.226	61	-3				.936	-1	C-21/O-4	-0.2
	Chi-N	3	6	1	1	0	0	0	0	2	3	.167	.375	.167	70	-0				.800	-3	/C-2,O-2	-0.3
	Yr	27	90	5	16	2	1	0	7	13	15	.178	.282	.222	62	-3				.927	-3	C-23/O-6	-0.5
1886	Bro-a	11	30	5	7	1	0	0	3	11		.233	.439	.267	122	2	2			.846	-1	C-11	0.1
Total	3	39	122	10	23	3	1	0	<u>10</u>	24	<u>15</u>	.189	.322	.230	76	-3	2			.893	-3	/C-35,O-6	-0.2

YEAR	TM/L	G	AB	R	H	2B	3B	HR	RBI	BB	SO	AVG	OBP	SLG	PRO+	BR/A	SB	CS	SBR	FA	FR	G/POS	TPR
■ PAT McCAULEY			McCauley, Patrick M.		b: 6/10/1870, Ware, Mass.			d: 1/23/17, Newark, N.J.		TR, 5'10.5", 156 lbs.		Deb: 9/5/1893											
1893	StL-N	5	16	0	1	0	0	0	0	0	0	.063	.063	.063	-67	-4	0			.808	1	/C-5	-0.2
1896	Was-N	26	84	14	21	3	0	3	11	7		.250	.315	.393	86	-2	0			.917	0	C-24/O-1	0.0
1903	NY-A	6	19	0	1	0	0	0	1	0		.053	.053	.053	-64	-4	0			.920	-2	/C-6	-0.6
Total	3	37	119	14	23	3	0	3	12	7	<u>9</u>	.193	.244	.294	44	-10	0			.900	-2	/C-35,O-1	-0.8

YEAR	TM/L	G	AB	R	H	2B	3B	HR	RBI	BB	SO	AVG	OBP	SLG	PRO+	BR/A	SB	CS	SBR	FA	FR	G/POS	TPR

■ **BILL McCAULEY** McCauley, William H. b: 12/20/1869, Washington, D.C. d: 1/27/26, Washington, D.C. Deb: 8/31/1895

| 1895 | Was-N | 1 | 2 | 0 | 0 | 0 | 0 | 0 | 0 | 0 | 0 | .000 | .000 | .000 | -99 | -1 | 0 | | | .714 | 0 | /S-1 | 0.0 |

■ **HARRY McCHESNEY** McChesney, Harry Vincent "Pud" b: 6/1/1880, Pittsburgh, Pa. d: 8/11/60, Pittsburgh, Pa. BR/TR, 5'9", 165 lbs. Deb: 9/17/04

| 1904 | Chi-N | 22 | 88 | 9 | 23 | 6 | 2 | 0 | 11 | 4 | | .261 | .293 | .375 | 106 | 0 | 2 | | | .967 | -2 | O-22 | -0.3 |

■ **PETE McCLANAHAN** McClanahan, Robert Hugh b: 10/24/06, Coldspring, Tex. d: 10/28/87, Mont Belvieu, Tex. BR/TR, 5'9", 170 lbs. Deb: 4/24/31

| 1931 | Pit-N | 7 | 4 | 2 | 2 | 0 | 0 | 0 | 0 | 2 | 0 | .500 | .667 | .500 | 220 | 1 | 0 | | | .000 | 0 | H | 0.1 |

■ **HARVEY McCLELLAN** McClellan, Harvey McDowell "Little Mac" b: 12/22/1894, Cynthiana, Ky. d: 11/6/25, Cynthiana, Ky. BR/TR, 5'9.5", 143 lbs. Deb: 5/31/19

1919	Chi-A	7	12	2	4	0	0	0	1	1	1	.333	.385	.333	102	0	0			1.000	1	/3-3,S-2	0.1
1920	Chi-A	10	18	4	6	1	1	0	5	4	1	.333	.455	.500	153	2	2	0	1	.917	-3	/S-4,3-2	-0.1
1921	Chi-A	63	196	20	35	4	1	1	14	14	18	.179	.237	.224	18	-24	2	3	-1	.968	18	2-21,S-15,O-15/3-5	-0.6
1922	Chi-A	91	301	28	68	17	3	2	28	16	32	.226	.272	.322	55	-21	3	2	-0	.971	-4	3-71/S-8,2-2,O-1	-1.9
1923	Chi-A	141	550	67	129	29	3	1	41	27	44	.235	.270	.304	52	-40	14	11	-2	.958	-18	*S-139/2-2	-4.6
1924	Chi-A	32	85	9	15	3	0	0	9	6	7	.176	.239	.212	17	-11	2	0	1	.938	3	S-21/2-7,3-1,O-1	-0.5
Total	6	344	1162	130	257	54	8	4	98	68	103	.221	.267	.292	46	-94	23	16		.952	-4	S-189/3-82,2-32,O	-7.6

■ **BILL McCLELLAN** McClellan, William Henry b: 3/22/1856, Chicago, Ill. d: 7/3/29, Chicago, Ill. BL/TL, 5'5.5", 156 lbs. Deb: 5/20/1878

1878	Chi-N	48	205	26	46	6	1	0	29	2	13	.224	.232	.263	59	-9				.866	-9	*2-42/S-5,O-1	-1.4
1881	Pro-N	68	259	30	43	3	1	0	16	15	21	.166	.212	.185	26	-21				.855	-8	S-50,O-17/2-1	-2.5
1883	Phi-N	80	326	42	75	21	4	1	33	19	18	.230	.272	.328	89	-3				.849	5	*S-78/O-2,3-1	0.3
1884	Phi-N	111	450	71	116	13	2	3	33	28	43	.258	.301	.316	99	1				.852	-12	*S-111/O-1	-0.9
1885	Bro-a	112	464	85	124	22	7	0	46	28		.267	.317	.345	108	5				.837	-5	3-57,2-55	0.3
1886	Bro-a	141	595	131	152	33	9	1	68	56		.255	.322	.346	108	5	43			.907	5	*2-141	0.4
1887	Bro-a	136	548	109	144	24	6	1	53	80		.263	.363	.334	94	-2	70			.879	-23	*2-136	-1.7
1888	Bro-a	74	278	33	57	7	3	0	21	40		.205	.307	.252	80	-4	13			.905	-7	2-56,O-18	-0.9
	Cle-a	22	72	6	16	0	0	0	5	6		.222	.282	.222	64	-3	6			.875	-4	O-15/2-5,S-2	-0.6
	Yr	96	350	39	73	7	3	0	26	46		.209	.302	.246	77	-7	19			.897	-11	2-61,O-33/S-2	-1.5
Total	8	792	3197	533	773	129	33	6	304	274	95	.242	.305	.308	90	-31	132			.893	-68	2-436,S-246/3-58,O	-7.0

■ **LLOYD McCLENDON** McClendon, Lloyd Glenn b: 1/11/59, Gary, Ind. BR/TR, 5'11", 195 lbs. Deb: 4/6/87

1987	Cin-N	45	72	8	15	5	0	2	13	4	15	.208	.250	.361	57	-5	1	0	0	.981	-2	C-12/1-5,3-1,O-1	-0.6
1988	Cin-N	72	137	9	30	4	0	3	14	15	22	.219	.305	.314	75	-4	4	0	1	1.000	-3	C-23,O-17,1-12/3-2	-0.6
1989	*Chi-N	92	259	47	74	12	1	12	40	37	31	.286	.377	.479	133	12	6	4	-1	.962	-7	O-45,1-28/3-6,C-5	0.1
1990	Cin-N	49	107	5	17	3	0	1	10	14	21	.159	.256	.215	29	-10	1	0	0	.980	1	O-23/C-8,1-8	-1.0
	Pit-N	4	3	1	1	0	0	1	2	0	1	.333	.333	1.333	349	1	0	0	0	.000	-0	/O-1	0.1
	Yr	53	110	6	18	3	0	2	12	14	22	.164	.258	.245	37	-9	1	0	0	.980	1	O-24/C-8,1-8	-0.9
1991	*Pit-N	85	163	24	47	7	0	7	24	18	23	.288	.366	.460	133	7	2	1	0	.966	-7	O-32,1-22/C-2	-0.2
1992	*Pit-N	84	190	26	48	8	1	3	20	28	24	.253	.355	.353	102	1	1	3	-2	.964	-7	O-60,1-18	-0.9
1993	Pit-N	88	181	21	40	11	1	2	19	23	17	.221	.309	.326	70	-7	3	3	-2	.967	-9	O-61/1-6	-2.0
1994	Pit-N	51	92	9	22	4	0	4	12	4	11	.239	.278	.413	76	-4	0	1	-1	.967	-2	O-20/1-2	-0.6
Total	8	570	1204	150	294	54	3	35	154	143	165	.244	.328	.381	94	-9	15	12	-3	.966	-36	O-260,1-101/C-50,3	-5.7

■ **JEFF McCLESKEY** McCleskey, Jefferson Lamar b: 11/6/1891, Americus, Ga. d: 5/11/71, Americus, Ga. BL/TR, 5'11", 160 lbs. Deb: 9/8/13

| 1913 | Bos-N | 2 | 3 | 0 | 0 | 0 | 0 | 0 | 0 | 1 | 0 | .000 | .250 | .000 | -25 | -0 | 0 | | | .750 | -0 | /3-2 | -0.1 |

■ **McCLOSKEY** McCloskey b: Brooklyn, N.Y. Deb: 5/25/1875

| 1875 | Was-n | 11 | 40 | 1 | 7 | 0 | 0 | 0 | 4 | 1 | 2 | .175 | .195 | .175 | 31 | -3 | 0 | 1 | -1 | .673 | -7 | C-11 | -0.9 |

■ **BILL McCLOSKEY** McCloskey, William George b: 5/1854, Pennsylvania 5'8", 155 lbs. Deb: 8/18/1884

| 1884 | Wil-U | 9 | 30 | 0 | 3 | 0 | 0 | 0 | 0 | | | .100 | .100 | .100 | -38 | -6 | | | | .588 | 1 | /O-5,C-5 | -0.4 |

■ **HAL McCLURE** McClure, Harold Murray "Mac" b: 8/8/1859, Lewisburg, Pa. d: 3/1/19, Lewisburg, Pa. BR/TR, 6', 165 lbs. Deb: 5/10/1882

| 1882 | Bos-N | 2 | 6 | 1 | 2 | 0 | 0 | 0 | 0 | 0 | | .333 | .333 | .333 | 115 | 0 | | | | .750 | -0 | /O-2 | 0.0 |

■ **LARRY McCLURE** McClure, Lawrence Ledwith b: 10/3/1885, Wayne, W.Va. d: 8/31/49, Huntington, W.Va. BR/TR, 5'6.5", 130 lbs. Deb: 7/26/10

| 1910 | NY-A | 1 | 1 | 0 | 0 | 0 | 0 | 0 | 0 | 0 | 0 | .000 | .000 | .000 | -95 | -0 | 0 | | | .000 | 0 | /O-1 | 0.0 |

■ **AMBY McCONNELL** McConnell, Ambrose Moses b: 4/29/1883, N.Pownal, Vt. d: 5/20/42, Utica, N.Y. BL/TR, 5'7", 150 lbs. Deb: 4/17/08

1908	Bos-A	140	502	77	140	10	6	2	43	38		.279	.343	.335	117	10	31			.939	-19	*2-126/S-3	-1.2
1909	Bos-A	121	453	61	108	7	8	0	36	34		.238	.300	.289	84	-8	26			.954	15	*2-121	0.5
1910	Bos-A	11	35	6	6	0	0	0	1	5		.171	.310	.171	50	-2	4			.959	-1	2-10	-0.3
	Chi-A	33	120	13	33	2	3	0	5	7		.275	.320	.342	112	1	4			.952	-1	2-32	0.0
	Yr	44	155	19	39	2	3	0	6	12		.252	.318	.303	97	-0	8			.954	-2	2-42	-0.3
1911	Chi-A	104	396	45	111	11	5	1	34	23		.280	.331	.341	90	-5	7			.973	-7	*2-103	-1.4
Total	4	409	1506	202	398	30	22	3	119	107		.264	.324	.319	98	-3	72			.954	-13	2-392/S-3	-2.4

■ **GEORGE McCONNELL** McConnell, George Neely "Slats" b: 9/16/1877, Shelbyville, Tenn. d: 5/10/64, Chattanooga, Tenn. BR/TR, 6'3", 190 lbs. Deb: 4/13/09

1909	NY-A	13	43	4	9	0	1	0	5	1		.209	.227	.256	52	-2	1			.964	2	1-11/P-2	-0.2
1912	NY-A	42	91	11	27	4	2	0	8	4		.297	.333	.385	99	-0	0			.913	5	P-23/1-2	0.0
1913	NY-A	39	67	4	12	2	0	0	5	2	11	.179	.179	.209	13	-7	0			.965	5	P-35/1-1	0.0
1914	Chi-N	1	2	0	0	0	0	0	0	0	1	.000	.000	.000	-99	-0	0			1.000	0	/P-1	0.0
1915	Chi-F	53	125	14	31	6	2	1	18	0	16	.248	.254	.352	74	-7	2			.974	3	P-44	0.0
1916	Chi-N	28	57	2	9	0	0	0	2	4		.158	.200	.158	10	-6	0			.952	2	P-28	0.0
Total	6	176	385	35	88	12	5	1	33	7	32	.229	.248	.294	57	-24	3			.953	16	P-133/1-14	-0.2

■ **SAM McCONNELL** McConnell, Samuel Faulkner b: 6/8/1895, Philadelphia, Pa. d: 6/27/81, Phoenixville, Pa. BL/TR, 5'6.5", 150 lbs. Deb: 4/19/15

| 1915 | Phi-A | 6 | 11 | 1 | 2 | 1 | 0 | 0 | 0 | 1 | 3 | .182 | .250 | .273 | 58 | -1 | 0 | | | .842 | 2 | /3-5 | 0.1 |

■ **DON McCORMACK** McCormack, Donald Ross b: 9/18/55, Omak, Wash. BR/TR, 6'3", 205 lbs. Deb: 9/30/80

1980	Phi-N	2	1	0	1	0	0	0	0	0	0	1.000	1.000	1.000	436	0	0	0	0	1.000	1	/C-2	0.1
1981	Phi-N	3	4	0	1	0	0	0	0	0	0	.250	.250	.250	40	-0	0	0	0	1.000	0	/C-3	0.0
Total	2	5	5	0	2	0	0	0	0	0	0	.400	.400	.400	121	-0	0	0	0	1.000	1	/C-5	0.1

■ **FRANK McCORMICK** McCormick, Frank Andrew "Buck" b: 6/9/11, New York, N.Y. d: 11/21/82, Manhasset, N.Y. BR/TR, 6'4", 205 lbs. Deb: 9/11/34 C

1934	Cin-N	12	16	1	5	2	1	0	5	0	1	.313	.313	.563	132	1	0			.941	-1	/1-2	0.0
1937	Cin-N	24	83	5	27	5	0	0	9	2	7	.325	.341	.386	102	0	1			1.000	1	1-20/2-4,O-1	-0.2
1938	Cin-N★	151	640	89	**209**	40	4	5	106	18	17	.327	.348	.425	115	11	1			.995	-3	*1-151	-1.0
1939	*Cin-N★	156	630	99	**209**	41	4	18	**128**	40	16	.332	.374	.495	131	26	1			**.996**	2	*1-156	1.0
1940	*Cin-N★	155	618	93	191	**44**	3	19	127	52	26	.309	.367	.482	131	25	2			**.995**	1	*1-155	1.1
1941	Cin-N★	154	603	77	162	31	5	17	97	40	13	.269	.318	.421	107	3	2			.995	-1	*1-154	-0.8
1942	Cin-N★	145	564	58	156	24	0	13	89	45	18	.277	.332	.388	111	6	1			.993	6	*1-144	0.3
1943	Cin-N†	126	472	56	143	28	0	8	56	29	15	.303	.345	.413	120	10	2			.995	3	*1-120	0.4
1944	Cin-N☆	153	581	85	177	37	3	20	102	57	17	.305	.371	.482	144	32	7			.992	12	*1-153	3.7
1945	Cin-N†	152	580	68	160	33	0	10	81	56	22	.276	.345	.384	105	4	6			.994	5	*1-151	-0.1
1946	Phi-N★	135	504	46	143	20	2	11	66	36	21	.284	.333	.397	110	4				**.999**	4	*1-134	0.1
1947	Phi-N	15	40	7	9	2	0	0	8	3	2	.225	.279	.350	69	-2	0			.989	-1	1-12	-0.3
	Bos-N	81	212	24	75	18	2	4	43	11	8	.354	.386	.486	133	9	2			.996	-1	1-46	0.7
	Yr	96	252	31	84	20	2	4	51	14	10	.333	.368	.464	123	7	2			.995	-2	1-58	0.4
1948	*Bos-N	75	180	14	45	9	2	4	34	10	9	.250	.289	.389	84	-5	0			.987	0	1-50	-0.3
Total	13	1534	5723	722	1711	334	26	128	951	399	189	.299	.348	.434	118	125	27			.995	31	*1-1448/2-4,O-1	5.0

YEAR	TM/L	G	AB	R	H	2B	3B	HR	RBI	BB	SO	AVG	OBP	SLG	PRO+	BR/A	SB	CS	SBR	FA	FR	G/POS	TPR

■ MOOSE McCORMICK
McCormick, Harry Elwood b: 2/28/1881, Philadelphia, Pa. d: 7/9/62, Lewisburg, Pa. BL/TL, 5'11", 180 lbs. Deb: 4/14/04

YEAR	TM/L	G	AB	R	H	2B	3B	HR	RBI	BB	SO	AVG	OBP	SLG	PRO+	BR/A	SB	CS	SBR	FA	FR	G/POS	TPR
1904	NY-N	59	203	28	54	9	5	1	26	13		.266	.323	.374	110	2	13			.916	-5	O-55	-0.6
	Pit-N	66	238	25	69	10	6	2	23	13		.290	.332	.408	124	6	6			.940	-6	O-66	-0.4
	Yr	125	441	53	123	19	11	3	49	26		.279	.328	.392	118	8	19			.928	-11	*O-121	-1.0
1908	Phi-N	11	22	0	2	0	0	0	2	2		.091	.167	.091	-17	-3	0			1.000	-0	/O-5	-0.4
	NY-N	73	252	31	76	16	3	0	32	4		.302	.315	.389	119	4	6			.901	-11	O-65	-1.1
	Yr	84	274	31	78	16	3	0	34	6		.285	.302	.365	108	1	6			.910	-11	O-70	-1.5
1909	NY-N	110	413	68	120	21	8	3	27	49		.291	.373	.402	138	19	4			.924	-14	*O-110	0.1
1912	*NY-N	42	39	4	13	4	1	0	8	6	9	.333	.422	.487	144	2	1			.667	-3	/O-6,1-1	0.0
1913	*NY-N	57	80	9	22	2	3	0	15	5	13	.275	.318	.375	97	-1	0			.909	-2	O-15	-0.3
Total	5	418	1247	165	356	62	26	6	133	92	22	.285	.340	.391	122	30	30			.920	-40	O-322/1-1	-2.7

■ JIM McCORMICK
McCormick, James Ambrose b: 11/2/1868, Spencer, Mass. d: 2/1/48, Saco, Maine BR/TR, 6'1", 160 lbs. Deb: 9/10/1892

YEAR	TM/L	G	AB	R	H	2B	3B	HR	RBI	BB	SO	AVG	OBP	SLG	PRO+	BR/A	SB	CS	SBR	FA	FR	G/POS	TPR
1892	StL-N	3	11	0	0	0	0	0	1	5		.000	.083	.000	-78	-7	0			1.000	-0	/2-2,3-1	-0.2

■ JERRY McCORMICK
McCormick, John b: Philadelphia, Pa. d: 9/19/05, Philadelphia, Pa. Deb: 5/1/1883

YEAR	TM/L	G	AB	R	H	2B	3B	HR	RBI	BB	SO	AVG	OBP	SLG	PRO+	BR/A	SB	CS	SBR	FA	FR	G/POS	TPR
1883	Bal-a	93	389	40	102	16	6	0		2		.262	.266	.334	89	-6				.799	0	*3-93	-0.5
1884	Phi-U	67	295	41	84	12	2	0		1		.285	.294	.339	99	-9				.811	14	3-54/2-5,O-5,S-3,P	0.4
	Was-U	42	157	23	34	8	2	0		1		.217	.242	.293	57	-13				.792	-6	3-38/S-4	-1.3
	Yr	109	452	64	118	20	4	0		5		.261	.269	.323	84	-22				.806	8	3-92/S-7,2-5,O-5,P	-1.7
Total	2	202	841	104	220	36	10	0		7		.262	.268	.328	86	-28				.802	8	3-185/S-7,O-5,2P	-1.8

■ MIKE McCORMICK
McCormick, Michael J. "Kid" or "Dude" b: 5/1883, Scotland d: 11/18/53, Jersey City, N.J. BR/TR, 5'3", 155 lbs. Deb: 4/14/04

YEAR	TM/L	G	AB	R	H	2B	3B	HR	RBI	BB	SO	AVG	OBP	SLG	PRO+	BR/A	SB	CS	SBR	FA	FR	G/POS	TPR
1904	Bro-N	105	347	28	64	5	4	0	27	43		.184	.278	.222	56	-16	22			.914	-3	*3-104/2-1	-1.7

■ MIKE McCORMICK
McCormick, Myron Winthrop b: 5/6/17, Angels Camp, Cal. d: 4/14/76, Ventura, Cal. BR/TR, 6', 200 lbs. Deb: 4/16/40

YEAR	TM/L	G	AB	R	H	2B	3B	HR	RBI	BB	SO	AVG	OBP	SLG	PRO+	BR/A	SB	CS	SBR	FA	FR	G/POS	TPR
1940	*Cin-N	110	417	48	125	20	0	1	30	13	36	.300	.326	.355	87	-8	8			.986	8	*O-107	-0.6
1941	Cin-N	110	369	52	106	17	3	4	31	30	24	.287	.341	.382	103	1	4			.976	7	*O-101	0.3
1942	Cin-N	40	135	18	32	2	3	1	11	13	7	.237	.304	.319	82	-3	0			.990	1	O-38	-0.4
1943	Cin-N	4	15	0	2	0	0	0	0	2	0	.133	.235	.133	8	-2	0			.909	-0	/O-4	-0.3
1946	Cin-N	23	74	10	16	2	0	0	5	8	4	.216	.293	.243	55	-4	0			1.000	1	O-21	-0.5
	Bos-N	59	164	23	43	6	2	1	16	11	7	.262	.309	.341	83	-4	0			.973	-2	O-48	-0.8
	Yr	82	238	33	59	8	2	1	21	19	11	.248	.304	.311	75	-8	0			.982	-1	O-69	-1.3
1947	Bos-N	92	284	42	81	13	7	3	36	20	21	.285	.332	.412	99	-1	1			.981	-12	O-79	-1.6
1948	*Bos-N	115	343	45	104	22	7	1	39	32	34	.303	.363	.417	112	6	1			.975	-11	*O-100	-1.0
1949	*Bro-N	55	139	17	29	5	1	2	14	14	12	.209	.283	.302	54	-9	1			1.000	-6	O-49	-1.7
1950	NY-N	4	4	0	0	0	0	0	0	0	2	.000	.000	.000	-99	-1	0			.000	0	H	-0.1
	Chi-A	55	138	16	32	4	3	0	10	16	6	.232	.312	.304	60	-8	0	1	-1	.982	-1	O-44	-1.1
1951	Was-A	81	243	31	70	9	3	1	23	29	20	.288	.364	.362	98	-1	2	1	-1	.966	1	O-62	-0.2
Total	10	748	2325	302	640	100	29	14	215	188	173	.275	.330	.361	90	-33	16	3		.980	-14	O-653	-8.0

■ BARRY McCORMICK
McCormick, William J. b: 12/25/1874, Maysville, Ky. d: 1/28/56, Cincinnati, Ohio TR, 5'9", Deb: 9/25/1895 U

YEAR	TM/L	G	AB	R	H	2B	3B	HR	RBI	BB	SO	AVG	OBP	SLG	PRO+	BR/A	SB	CS	SBR	FA	FR	G/POS	TPR
1895	Lou-N	3	12	2	3	0	1	0	0	0	0	.250	.250	.417	75	-1	0			1.000	-2	/S-2,2-1	-0.2
1896	Chi-N	45	168	22	37	3	1	1	23	14	30	.220	.280	.268	43	-14	9			.835	-5	3-35/S-6,2-3,O-1	-1.6
1897	Chi-N	101	419	87	112	8	10	2	55	33		.267	.324	.348	75	-16	44			.851	-3	3-56,S-46/2-1	-1.4
1898	Chi-N	137	530	76	131	15	9	2	78	47		.247	.314	.321	82	-12	15			.888	4	*3-136/S-1,2-1	-0.7
1899	Chi-N	102	376	48	97	15	2	2	52	25		.258	.311	.324	76	-12	14			.941	5	2-99/S-3	-0.1
1900	Chi-N	110	379	35	83	13	5	3	48	38		.219	.292	.303	67	-17	8			.907	-9	S-84,3-21/2-5	-1.7
1901	Chi-N	115	427	45	100	15	6	1	32	31		.234	.288	.304	75	-14	12			.911	0	*S-112/3-3	-0.5
1902	StL-A	139	504	55	124	14	4	3	51	37		.246	.304	.308	71	-19	10			.905	-11	*3-132/S-7,O-1	-2.8
1903	StL-A	61	207	13	45	6	1	1	16	18		.217	.283	.271	69	-7	5			.969	-4	2-28,3-28/S-4	-1.0
	Was-A	63	219	14	47	10	2	0	23	10		.215	.255	.279	59	-11	3			.960	-8	2-63	0.0
	Yr	124	426	27	92	16	3	1	39	28		.216	.269	.275	64	-18	8			.962	-12	2-91,3-28/S-4	-1.0
1904	Was-A	113	404	36	88	11	1	0	39	27		.218	.274	.250	67	-14	9			.938	-1	2-113	-1.4
Total	10	989	3645	433	867	110	42	15	417	280	30	.238	.297	.303	71	-139	130			.885	-17	3-411,2-314,S/O	-11.4

■ BARNEY McCOSKY
McCosky, William Barney b: 4/11/17, Coal Run, Pa. d: 9/6/96, Venice, Fla. BL/TR, 6'1", 184 lbs. Deb: 4/18/39

YEAR	TM/L	G	AB	R	H	2B	3B	HR	RBI	BB	SO	AVG	OBP	SLG	PRO+	BR/A	SB	CS	SBR	FA	FR	G/POS	TPR
1939	Det-A	147	611	120	190	33	14	4	58	70	45	.311	.384	.430	100	1	20	4	4	.986	9	*O-145	0.8
1940	*Det-A	143	589	123	200	39	19	4	57	67	41	.340	.408	.491	120	18	13	9	-2	.983	-1	*O-141	0.8
1941	Det-A	127	494	80	160	25	8	3	55	61	33	.324	.401	.425	108	3	8	3	1	.985	5	*O-122	0.5
1942	Det-A	154	600	75	176	28	11	7	50	68	37	.293	.365	.412	109	7	11	5	0	.981	3	*O-154	0.3
1946	Det-A	25	91	11	18	5	0	1	11	17	9	.198	.324	.286	67	-4	0	0	0	.966	-1	O-24	-0.6
	Phi-A	92	308	33	109	17	4	1	34	43	13	.354	.433	.445	146	21	2	2	-1	.981	-4	O-85	1.3
	Yr	117	399	44	127	22	4	2	45	60	22	.318	.407	.409	127	17	2	2	-1	.978	-4	*O-109	0.7
1947	Phi-A	137	546	77	179	22	7	1	52	57	29	.328	.395	.399	119	16	1	4	-2	.983	4	*O-137	1.1
1948	Phi-A	135	515	95	168	21	5	0	46	68	22	.326	.405	.386	111	11	1	3	-2	.990	-3	*O-134	-0.1
1950	Phi-A	66	179	19	43	10	1	0	11	22	12	.240	.323	.307	63	-10	0	0	0	.987	-5	O-42	-1.6
1951	Phi-A	12	27	4	8	2	0	1	3	4	4	.296	.370	.481	125	1	0	0	0	1.000	-1	/O-7	0.0
	Cin-N	25	50	2	16	3	1	0	11	4	2	.320	.370	.460	120	1	0	0	0	1.000	-3	O-11	-0.2
	Cle-A	31	61	8	13	3	0	0	2	8	5	.213	.304	.262	57	-4	1	0	0	.944	-5	O-19	-0.5
1952	Cle-A	54	80	14	17	4	1	0	3	11	4	.213	.284	.325	74	-3	1	1	0	.984	-1	O-19	-1.0
1953	Cle-A	22	21	3	4	0	0	0	3	1	4	.190	.227	.333	51	-2	0	0	0	.000	0	H	-0.2
Total	11	1170	4172	664	1301	214	71	24	397	497	261	.312	.386	.414	109	62	58	31	-1	.984	-1	*O-1036	0.6

■ WILLIE McCOVEY
McCovey, Willie Lee "Stretch" b: 1/10/38, Mobile, Ala. BL/TL, 6'4", 210 lbs. Deb: 7/30/59 H

YEAR	TM/L	G	AB	R	H	2B	3B	HR	RBI	BB	SO	AVG	OBP	SLG	PRO+	BR/A	SB	CS	SBR	FA	FR	G/POS	TPR
1959	SF-N	52	192	32	68	9	5	13	38	22	35	.354	.431	.656	189	24	2	0	1	.989	-2	1-51	2.0
1960	SF-N	101	260	37	62	15	3	13	51	45	53	.238	.354	.469	130	11	1	1	-0	.985	-3	1-71	0.2
1961	SF-N	106	328	59	89	12	3	18	50	37	60	.271	.354	.491	126	12	1	2	-1	.985	-2	1-84	0.3
1962	*SF-N	91	229	41	67	6	1	20	54	29	35	.293	.372	.590	156	17	3	3	-1	.976	-2	O-57,1-17	1.1
1963	SF-N★	152	564	103	158	19	5	44	102	50	119	.280	.350	.566	161	42	1	1	-0	.942	3	*O-135,1-23	3.9
1964	SF-N	130	364	55	80	14	1	18	54	61	73	.220	.340	.412	108	5	2	6	-6	.935	-6	O-83,1-26	-0.6
1965	SF-N	160	540	93	149	17	4	39	92	88	118	.276	.383	.539	152	39	0	4	-2	.991	-3	*1-156	2.7
1966	SF-N★	150	502	85	148	26	6	36	96	76	100	.295	.394	.586	163	44	2	1	0	.984	-3	*1-145	3.3
1967	SF-N	135	456	73	126	17	4	31	91	71	110	.276	.381	.535	162	37	3	3	-1	.989	-1	*1-127	3.1
1968	SF-N★	148	523	81	153	16	4	36	105	72	71	.293	.383	.545	176	49	4	2	0	.985	-3	*1-146	4.6
1969	SF-N★	149	491	101	157	26	2	45	126	121	66	.320	.458	.656	212	79	0	0	0	.992	-6	*1-148	6.3
1970	SF-N★	152	495	98	143	39	2	39	126	137	75	.289	.446	.612	183	64	0	0	0	.989	13	*1-146	6.2
1971	*SF-N★	105	329	45	91	13	0	18	70	64	57	.277	.401	.480	151	24	-3	2	-5	.983	-2	1-95	1.4
1972	SF-N	81	263	30	56	8	0	14	35	38	45	.213	.317	.403	102	1	0	0	0	.986	-5	1-74	-1.2
1973	SF-N	130	383	52	102	14	3	29	75	105	78	.266	.425	.546	161	35	0	2	-1	.988	1	*1-117	2.8
1974	SD-N	128	344	53	87	19	1	22	63	96	76	.253	.417	.506	164	34	1	0	0	.987	-6	*1-104	2.2
1975	SD-N	122	413	43	104	17	0	23	68	57	80	.252	.347	.460	130	16	1	0	0	.986	-1	*1-115	0.9
1976	SD-N	71	202	20	41	9	0	7	36	21	39	.203	.281	.351	86	-5	0	0	0	.991	5	1-51	-0.4
	Oak-A	11	24	0	5	0	0	0	0	3	4	.208	.296	.208	52	-1	0	0	0	.000	0	/D-9	-0.2
1977	SF-N	141	478	54	134	21	0	28	86	67	106	.280	.369	.500	131	21	3	0	1	.989	-7	*1-136	0.7
1978	SF-N	108	351	32	80	19	2	12	64	36	57	.228	.300	.396	97	-3	1	0	0	.987	-4	1-97	-1.2
1979	SF-N	117	353	34	88	9	0	15	57	36	70	.249	.321	.402	103	3	1	1	0	.987	-1	1-89	-0.9
1980	SF-N	48	113	8	23	8	0	1	16	13	23	.204	.287	.301	67	-5	0	0	0	.992	-2	1-27	-0.9
Total	22	2588	8197	1229	2211	353	46	521	1555	1345	1550	.270	.377	.515	148	540	26	22	-5	.987	-30	*1-2045,O-275/D-9	36.5

YEAR	TM/L	G	AB	R	H	2B	3B	HR	RBI	BB	SO	AVG	OBP	SLG	PRO+	BR/A	SB	CS	SBR	FA	FR	G/POS	TPR

■ ART McCOY
McCoy, Arthur Gray b: 7/1864, Danville, Pa. d: 3/22/04, Danville, Pa. 168 lbs. Deb: 7/8/1889

| 1889 | Was-N | 2 | 6 | 0 | 0 | 0 | 0 | 0 | 2 | 1 | .000 | .250 | .000 | −29 | −1 | 0 | | | .889 | −2 | /2-2 | −0.2 |

■ BENNY McCOY
McCoy, Benjamin Jenison b: 11/9/15, Jenison, Mich. BL/TR, 5'9", 170 lbs. Deb: 9/14/38

1938	Det-A	7	15	2	3	1	0	0	1	2	.200	.250	.267	28	−2	0	0	0	.963	2	/2-6,3-1	0.1
1939	Det-A	55	192	38	58	13	6	1	33	29	26	.302	.394	.448	107	2	3	1	0	.958	−2	2-34,S-16	0.4
1940	Phi-A	134	490	56	126	26	5	7	62	65	44	.257	.345	.373	88	−8	2	2	−1	.951	−16	*2-130/3-1	−1.5
1941	Phi-A	141	517	86	140	12	7	8	61	95	50	.271	.384	.368	102	5	3	3	−1	.963	−13	*2-135	0.1
Total	4	337	1214	182	327	52	18	16	156	190	122	.269	.369	.381	97	−2	8	6	−1	.957	−28	2-305/S-16,3-2	−0.9

■ QUINTON McCRACKEN
McCracken, Quinton Antoine b: 3/16/70, Wilmington, N.C. BB/TR, 5'8", 170 lbs. Deb: 9/17/95

1995	Col-N	3	1	0	0	0	0	0	0	0	1	.000	.000	.000	−78	−0				.000	−0	/O-1	−0.1
1996	Col-N	124	283	50	82	13	6	3	40	32	62	.290	.364	.410	81	−10	17	6	2	.957	−15	O-93	−2.5
Total	2	127	284	50	82	13	6	3	40	32	63	.289	.363	.408	80	−10	17	6	2	.957	−15	/O-94	−2.6

■ TOMMY McCRAW
McCraw, Tommy Lee b: 11/21/40, Malvern, Ark. BL/TL, 6', 183 lbs. Deb: 6/4/63 C

1963	Chi-A	102	280	38	71	11	3	6	33	21	46	.254	.313	.379	94	−2	15	4	2	.993	−1	1-97	−0.5
1964	Chi-A	125	368	47	96	11	5	6	36	32	65	.261	.327	.367	95	−2	15	7	0	.992	−7	1-84,O-36	−1.4
1965	Chi-A	133	273	38	65	12	1	5	21	25	48	.238	.309	.344	91	−4	12	7	−1	.993	−8	1-72,O-64	−1.6
1966	Chi-A	151	389	49	89	16	4	5	48	29	40	.229	.291	.329	83	−9	20	11	−1	.990	−2	*1-121/O-41	−1.9
1967	Chi-A	125	453	55	107	18	3	11	45	33	55	.236	.290	.362	95	−4	24	10	1	.991	11	*1-123/O-6	0.1
1968	Chi-A	136	477	51	112	16	12	9	44	36	58	.235	.295	.375	101	−0	20	5	3	.986	2	*1-135	−0.5
1969	Chi-A	93	240	21	62	12	2	2	25	21	24	.258	.326	.350	85	−5	1	3	2	.989	−10	1-44,O-41	−2.1
1970	Chi-A	129	332	39	73	11	2	6	31	21	50	.220	.275	.319	61	−18	10	5	0	.987	−3	1-59,O-49	−2.6
1971	Was-A	122	207	33	44	6	4	7	25	19	38	.213	.294	.382	96	−2	3	3	−1	.958	−9	O-60,1-30	−1.6
1972	Cle-A	129	391	43	101	13	5	7	33	41	47	.258	.335	.371	106	4	12	10	−2	1.000	−1	O-84,1-38	−0.7
1973	Cal-A	99	264	25	70	7	0	3	24	30	42	.265	.345	.326	97	−0	3	2	−0	1.000	2	O-34,1-25/D-8	−0.2
1974	Cal-A	56	119	21	34	8	0	3	17	12	13	.286	.351	.429	131	4	5	2	1	1.000	2	1-29,O-12/D-3	0.5
	Cle-A	45	112	17	34	8	0	3	17	5	11	.304	.339	.455	128	4	0	1	−1	.990	2	1-38/O-1	0.3
	Yr	101	231	38	68	16	0	6	34	17	24	.294	.345	.442	130	8	5	3	−1	.994	4	1-67,O-13/D-3	0.8
1975	Cle-A	23	51	7	14	1	1	2	5	7	7	.275	.362	.451	129	2	4	1	1	1.000	2	1-16/O-3	0.0
Total	13	1468	3956	484	972	150	42	75	404	332	544	.246	.311	.362	94	−33	143	68	2	.991	−22	1-911,O-431/D-11	−12.2

■ RODNEY McCRAY
McCray, Rodney Duncan b: 9/13/63, Detroit, Mich. BR/TR, 5'10", 175 lbs. Deb: 4/30/90

1990	Chi-A	32	6	8	0	0	0	0	0	1	4	.000	.143	.000	−58	−1	6	0	2	1.000	−5	O-13/D-7	−0.4
1991	Chi-A	17	7	2	2	0	0	0	0	0	2	.286	.286	.286	60	−0	1	1	−0	1.000	−2	/O-8,D-6	−0.2
1992	NY-N	18	1	3	1	0	0	0	1	0	0	1.000	1.000	1.000	475	0	2	0	1	1.000	−3	O-13	−0.3
Total	3	67	14	13	3	0	0	0	1	1	6	.214	.267	.214	36	−1	9	1	2	1.000	−10	/O-34,D-13	−0.9

■ FRANK McCREA
McCrea, Francis William b: 9/6/1896, Jersey City, N.J. d: 2/25/81, Dover, N.J. BR/TR, 5'9", 155 lbs. Deb: 9/26/25

| 1925 | Cle-A | 1 | 5 | 1 | 1 | 0 | 0 | 0 | 0 | 0 | 0 | .200 | .200 | .200 | 2 | −1 | 0 | 0 | 0 | 1.000 | −1 | /C-1 | −0.1 |

■ WALT McCREDIE
McCredie, Walter Henry b: 11/29/1876, Manchester, Iowa d: 7/29/34, Portland, Ore. BL/TR, 6'2", 195 lbs. Deb: 4/20/03

| 1903 | Bro-N | 56 | 213 | 40 | 69 | 5 | 0 | 0 | 20 | 24 | | .324 | .397 | .347 | 116 | 6 | 10 | | | .925 | −4 | O-56 | −0.2 |

■ TOM McCREERY
McCreery, Thomas Livingston b: 10/19/1874, Beaver, Pa. d: 7/3/41, Beaver, Pa. BB/TR, 5'11", 180 lbs. Deb: 6/8/1895

1895	Lou-N	31	108	18	35	3	1	0	10	8	15	.324	.376	.370	99	0	3			.875	−6	O-18/P-8,S-4,3-1,1	−0.7
1896	Lou-N	115	441	87	155	23	21	7	65	42	58	.351	.409	.546	157	35	26			.916	1	*O-111/2-1,P-1	2.2
1897	Lou-N	89	338	55	96	5	6	4	40	38		.284	.356	.370	95	−2	13			.856	−5	*O-89	−1.2
	NY-N	49	177	36	53	8	5	1	27	22		.299	.380	.418	114	4	15			.900	−2	O-45/2-3	−0.1
	Yr	138	515	91	149	13	11	5	67	60		.289	.365	.386	101	2	28			.869	−7	*O-134/2-3	−1.3
1898	NY-N	35	121	15	24	4	3	1	17	19		.198	.307	.306	78	−3	3			.820	−5	O-35	−1.0
	Pit-N	53	190	33	59	5	7	2	20	26		.311	.394	.442	142	11	3			.934	−1	O-51	0.6
	Yr	88	311	48	83	9	10	3	37	45		.267	.360	.389	117	8	6			.901	−6	O-86	−0.4
1899	Pit-N	118	455	76	147	21	9	2	64	47		.323	.390	.422	123	15	11			.911	−7	O-97/S-9,2-7	0.1
1900	Pit-N	43	132	20	29	4	3	1	13	16		.220	.304	.318	71	−5	2			.887	2	O-35/P-1	−0.5
1901	Bro-N	91	335	47	97	11	14	3	53	32		.290	.355	.433	124	10	13			.947	4	O-82/1-4,S-2	0.8
1902	Bro-N	112	430	49	105	8	4	4	57	29		.244	.295	.309	86	−8	16			.979	−1	*1-108/O-4	−1.1
1903	Bro-N	40	141	13	37	5	0	1	10	20		.262	.354	.326	97	0	5			.892	−2	O-38	−0.4
	Bos-N	23	83	15	18	2	1	1	10	9		.217	.293	.301	72	−3	6			.900	−1	O-23	−0.4
	Yr	63	224	28	55	7	3	1	20	29		.246	.332	.317	88	−3	11			.896	−2	O-61	−0.8
Total	9	799	2951	464	855	99	76	26	386	308	73	.290	.359	.401	113	54	116			.905	−22	O-628,1-113/S2P3	−1.7

■ FRANK McCUE
McCue, Frank Aloysius b: 10/4/1898, Chicago, Ill. d: 7/5/53, Chicago, Ill. BB/TR, 5'9", 150 lbs. Deb: 9/15/22

| 1922 | Phi-A | 2 | 5 | 0 | 0 | 0 | 0 | 0 | 0 | 0 | 0 | .000 | .000 | .000 | −97 | −1 | 0 | 0 | 0 | .000 | 0 | /3-2 | −0.1 |

■ CLYDE McCULLOUGH
McCullough, Clyde Edward b: 3/4/17, Nashville, Tenn. d: 9/18/82, San Francisco, Cal. BR/TR, 5'11.5", 180 lbs. Deb: 4/28/40 C

1940	Chi-N	9	26	4	4	1	0	0	5	5	5	.154	.290	.192	36	−2	0			1.000	3	/C-7	0.1
1941	Chi-N	125	418	41	95	9	2	9	53	34	67	.227	.289	.323	75	−15	5			.982	−8	*C-119	−1.3
1942	Chi-N	109	337	39	95	22	1	5	31	25	47	.282	.331	.398	117	6	7			.980	−1	C-97	1.4
1943	Chi-N	87	266	20	63	5	2	2	23	24	33	.237	.302	.293	73	−9	6			.977	−16	C-81	−2.1
1946	Chi-N	95	307	38	88	6	4	3	34	22	39	.287	.338	.417	116	5	2			.991	−2	C-89	0.8
1947	Chi-N	86	234	25	59	12	4	3	30	20	20	.252	.314	.376	86	−5	1			.984	5	C-64	0.5
1948	Chi-N☆	69	172	10	36	4	2	1	7	15	25	.209	.273	.273	50	−12	0			.973	5	C-51	−0.5
1949	Pit-N	91	241	30	57	9	4	4	24	24	30	.237	.316	.349	76	−8	0			.985	6	C-90	0.4
1950	Pit-N	103	279	28	71	16	4	6	34	31	35	.254	.340	.405	92	−3	3			.985	−8	*C-100	−0.7
1951	Pit-N	92	259	26	77	9	2	6	39	27	31	.297	.366	.440	113	5	2	0	1	.988	10	C-87	1.8
1952	Pit-N	66	172	10	40	5	1	1	15	10	18	.233	.283	.291	58	−10	1	0	−1	.981	7	C-61/1-1	−0.1
1953	Chi-N☆	77	229	21	59	7	2	6	23	15	23	.258	.303	.367	72	−10	0	0	0	.987	−3	C-73	−1.0
1954	Chi-N	31	81	9	21	7	0	3	17	5	5	.259	.310	.457	96	−1	0	0	0	.981	−2	C-26/3-3	−0.1
1955	Chi-N	44	81	7	16	0	0	3	10	8	15	.198	.278	.198	29	−8	0	0	0	.989	7	C-37	0.0
1956	Chi-N	14	19	0	4	1	0	0	1	0	5	.211	.211	.263	27	−2	0			1.000	0	/C-7	−0.1
Total	15	1098	3121	308	785	121	28	52	339	265	398	.252	.314	.358	85	−69	27	1		.984	7	C-989/3-3,1-1	−0.9

■ HARRY McCURDY
McCurdy, Harry Henry "Hank" b: 9/15/1899, Stevens Point, Wis. d: 7/21/72, Houston, Tex. BL/TR, 5'11", 187 lbs. Deb: 7/4/22

1922	StL-N	13	27	3	8	2	0	0	5	1	1	.296	.321	.519	119	1	0			.967	−1	/C-9,1-2	0.0
1923	StL-N	67	185	17	49	11	2	0	15	11	11	.265	.306	.346	73	−7	3	1	0	.969	−7	C-58	−1.1
1926	Chi-A	44	86	16	28	7	2	1	16	6	10	.326	.370	.488	127	2	0	1	−1	.974	4	C-25/1-8	0.0
1927	Chi-A	86	262	34	75	19	3	1	27	32	24	.286	.366	.393	99	0	6	4	−1	.972	−3	C-82	0.2
1928	Chi-A	49	103	12	27	10	0	2	13	8	15	.262	.315	.417	92	−2	1	3	−2	.964	−4	C-34	−0.4
1930	Phi-N	80	148	23	49	6	2	1	25	15	12	.331	.393	.419	90	−2	0			.966	−5	C-41	−0.4
1931	Phi-N	66	150	21	43	9	0	1	25	23	16	.287	.382	.367	95	−0	0			.968	−1	C-45	0.1
1932	Phi-N	62	136	13	32	6	1	1	14	17	13	.235	.325	.316	65	−6	0			.974	−1	C-42	−0.5
1933	Phi-N	73	54	9	15	1	0	2	12	16	6	.278	.451	.407	130	3	0			.000	0	/C-2	0.3
1934	Cin-N	3	6	0	0	0	0	0	0	0	0	.000	.000	.000	−99	−2	0			1.000	1	/1-1	−0.1
Total	10	543	1157	148	326	71	12	9	148	129	108	.282	.355	.387	92	−13	12	9		.970	−24	C-338/1-11	−1.9

■ TERRY McDANIEL
McDaniel, Terrence Keith b: 12/6/66, Kansas City, Mo. BR/TR, 5'9", 205 lbs. Deb: 8/31/91

| 1991 | NY-N | 23 | 29 | 3 | 6 | 1 | 0 | 0 | 2 | 1 | 8 | .207 | .233 | .241 | 34 | −3 | 2 | 0 | 1 | 1.000 | −3 | O-14 | −0.5 |

■ RAY McDAVID
McDavid, Ray Darnell b: 7/20/71, San Diego, Cal. BL/TR, 6'3", 190 lbs. Deb: 7/15/94

| 1994 | SD-N | 9 | 28 | 2 | 7 | 0 | 0 | 2 | 1 | 8 | .250 | .276 | .286 | 48 | −2 | 1 | 0 | | 1.000 | −0 | /O-7 | −0.2 |

YEAR	TM/L	G	AB	R	H	2B	3B	HR	RBI	BB	SO	AVG	OBP	SLG	PRO+	BR/A	SB	CS	SBR	FA	FR	G/POS	TPR
1995	SD-N	11	17	2	3	0	0	0	0	2	6	.176	.263	.176	19	-2	1	1	-1	0	1.000	-2	/O-7	-0.4
Total	2	20	45	4	10	1	0	0	2	3	14	.222	.271	.244	37	-4	2	1	0	1.000	-2	/O-14	-0.6

■ RED McDERMOTT
McDermott, Frank A.   b: 11/12/1889, Philadelphia, Pa.   d: 9/11/64, Philadelphia, Pa.   BR/TR, 5'6", 150 lbs.   Deb: 8/6/12

YEAR	TM/L	G	AB	R	H	2B	3B	HR	RBI	BB	SO	AVG	OBP	SLG	PRO+	BR/A	SB	CS	SBR	FA	FR	G/POS	TPR
1912	Det-A	5	15	2	4	1	0	0	0	0	0	.267	.313	.333	87	-0	1			1.000	-0	/O-5	-0.1

■ JOE McDERMOTT
McDermott, Joseph   Deb: 5/4/1871

YEAR	TM/L	G	AB	R	H	2B	3B	HR	RBI	BB	SO	AVG	OBP	SLG	PRO+	BR/A	SB	CS	SBR	FA	FR	G/POS	TPR
1871	Kek-n	2	8	3	2	0	0	0	1	1	1	.250	.333	.250	70	-0	1	0	0	.500	-0	/O-2	0.0
1872	Eck-n	7	32	3	9	3	0	0	3	1	2	.281	.303	.375	126	1	0	0	0	.643	-1	/P-7	0.0
Total	2 n	9	40	6	11	3	0	0	4	2	3	.275	.310	.350	112	1	1	0	0	.643	-1	/P-7,O-2	0.0

■ MICKEY McDERMOTT
McDermott, Maurice Joseph "Maury"   b: 8/29/28, Poughkeepsie, N.Y.   BL/TL, 6'2", 170 lbs.   Deb: 4/24/48   C

YEAR	TM/L	G	AB	R	H	2B	3B	HR	RBI	BB	SO	AVG	OBP	SLG	PRO+	BR/A	SB	CS	SBR	FA	FR	G/POS	TPR
1948	Bos-A	7	8	2	3	1	0	0	0	0	0	.375	.375	.500	125	0	0	0	0	1.000	1	/P-7	0.0
1949	Bos-A	12	33	3	7	3	0	0	6	3	6	.212	.278	.303	50	-2	0	0	0	.941	-0	P-12	0.0
1950	Bos-A	39	44	11	16	5	0	0	12	9	3	.364	.472	.477	131	2	0	0	0	.938	1	P-38	0.0
1951	Bos-A	43	66	8	18	1	1	1		3	14	.273	.314	.364	76	-2	0	1	-1	.950	-0	P-34	0.0
1952	Bos-A	36	62	10	14	1	1	1	7	4	11	.226	.273	.323	60	-3	0	0	0	.944	-0	P-30	0.0
1953	Bos-A	45	93	9	28	8	0	1	13	2	13	.301	.316	.419	92	-1	0	1	-1	.957	1	P-32	0.0
1954	Was-A	54	95	7	19	3	0	0	4	7	12	.200	.255	.232	36	-9	0	0	0	.955	1	P-30	0.0
1955	Was-A	70	95	10	25	4	0	1	10	6	16	.263	.314	.337	79	-3	1	0	0	.943	1	P-31	0.0
1956	*NY-A	46	52	4	11	0	0	1	4	8	13	.212	.317	.269	58	-3	0	0	0	1.000	0	/P-23	0.0
1957	KC-A	58	49	6	12	1	0	4	7	9	16	.245	.362	.510	133	2	0	0	0	.960	-0	P-29/1-2	0.0
1958	Det-A	4	3	0	1	0	0	0	1	0	1	.333	.333	.333	78	-0	0	0	0	.000	-0	/P-2	0.0
1961	StL-N	22	14	1	1	1	0	0	3	0	4	.071	.071	.143	-41	-3	0	0	0	1.000	-0	/P-19	0.0
	KC-A	7	5	0	1	1	0	0	1	1	2	.200	.333	.400	93	-0	0	0	0	.500	-0	/P-4	0.0
Total	12	443	619	71	156	29	2	9	74	52	112	.252	.312	.349	76	-22	1	2	-1	.951	4	P-291/1-2	0.0

■ TERRY McDERMOTT
McDermott, Terrence Michael   b: 3/20/51, Rockville Cen., N.Y   BR/TR, 6'3", 205 lbs.   Deb: 9/12/72

YEAR	TM/L	G	AB	R	H	2B	3B	HR	RBI	BB	SO	AVG	OBP	SLG	PRO+	BR/A	SB	CS	SBR	FA	FR	G/POS	TPR
1972	LA-N	9	23	2	3	0	0	0	0	2	8	.130	.200	.130	-5	-3	0	0	0	1.000	-1	/1-7	-0.5

■ SANDY McDERMOTT
McDermott, Thomas Nathaniel   b: 3/15/1856, Zanesville, Ohio   d: 11/23/22, Mansfield, Ohio   Deb: 6/18/1885

YEAR	TM/L	G	AB	R	H	2B	3B	HR	RBI	BB	SO	AVG	OBP	SLG	PRO+	BR/A	SB	CS	SBR	FA	FR	G/POS	TPR
1885	Bal-a	1	0	0	0	0	0	0	0			—	—	—	—		0			.000	0	/2-1	0.0

■ McDONALD
McDonald   Deb: 5/18/1872

YEAR	TM/L	G	AB	R	H	2B	3B	HR	RBI	BB	SO	AVG	OBP	SLG	PRO+	BR/A	SB	CS	SBR	FA	FR	G/POS	TPR
1872	Eck-n	1	4	0	0	0	0	0	0	0	0	.000	.000	.000	-99	-1	0	0	0	.333	-1	/S-1	-0.2

■ TEX McDONALD
McDonald, Charles E. (b: Charles C. Crabtree)   b: 1/31/1891, Farmersville, Tex.   d: 3/31/43, Houston, Tex.   BL/TR, 5'10", 160 lbs.   Deb: 4/11/12

YEAR	TM/L	G	AB	R	H	2B	3B	HR	RBI	BB	SO	AVG	OBP	SLG	PRO+	BR/A	SB	CS	SBR	FA	FR	G/POS	TPR
1912	Cin-N	61	140	16	36	3	4	1	15	13	24	.257	.329	.357	90	-2	5			.915	-9	S-42	-0.7
1913	Cin-N	11	10	1	3	0	0	0	2	0	1	.300	.300	.300	72	-0	0			.000	0	/S-1	0.0
	Bos-N	62	145	24	52	4	4	0	18	15	17	.359	.422	.441	144	9	4			.869	-1	3-31/2-6,O-1	0.8
	Yr	73	155	25	55	4	4	0	20	15	18	.355	.415	.432	140	8	4			.869	-1	3-31/2-6,S-1,O-1	0.8
1914	Pit-F	67	223	27	71	16	7	3	29	13	23	.318	.361	.493	132	6	9			.925	-3	O-29,2-27/S-5	0.2
	Buf-F	69	250	32	74	13	6	3	32	20	26	.296	.353	.432	111	-0	11			.953	-3	O-61,2-10	-0.6
	Yr	136	473	59	145	29	13	6	61	33	49	.307	.357	.461	121	5	20			.943	-6	O-90,2-37/S-5	-0.4
1915	Buf-F	87	251	31	68	9	6	6	39	27	34	.271	.346	.426	114	1	5			.924	-7	O-65	-1.0
Total	4	357	1019	131	304	45	27	13	135	88	125	.298	.359	.434	118	12	34			.936	-22	O-156/S-48,2-43,3	-1.3

■ JACK McDONALD
McDonald, Daniel   b: 1847, Brooklyn, N.Y.   d: 11/23/1880, Brooklyn, N.Y.   5'11", 154 lbs.   Deb: 5/2/1872

YEAR	TM/L	G	AB	R	H	2B	3B	HR	RBI	BB	SO	AVG	OBP	SLG	PRO+	BR/A	SB	CS	SBR	FA	FR	G/POS	TPR
1872	Atl-n	15	62	9	16	3	1	0	4	0	1	.258	.258	.339	70	-3	0	0	0	.720	-2	O-15	-0.3

■ DAVE McDONALD
McDonald, David Bruce   b: 5/20/43, New Albany, Ind.   BL/TR, 6'3", 215 lbs.   Deb: 9/15/69

YEAR	TM/L	G	AB	R	H	2B	3B	HR	RBI	BB	SO	AVG	OBP	SLG	PRO+	BR/A	SB	CS	SBR	FA	FR	G/POS	TPR
1969	NY-A	9	23	0	5	1	0	0	2	2	5	.217	.280	.261	54	-1	0	1	-1	.960	-1	/1-7	-0.3
1971	Mon-N	24	39	3	4	2	0	1	4	4	14	.103	.186	.231	17	-4	0	0	0	.983	-1	/1-8,O-1	-0.6
Total	2	33	62	3	9	3	0	1	6	6	19	.145	.221	.242	31	-6	0	1	-1	.972	-1	/1-15,O-1	-0.9

■ ED McDONALD
McDonald, Edward C.   b: 10/28/1886, Albany, N.Y.   d: 3/11/46, Albany, N.Y.   BR/TR, 6', 180 lbs.   Deb: 8/5/11

YEAR	TM/L	G	AB	R	H	2B	3B	HR	RBI	BB	SO	AVG	OBP	SLG	PRO+	BR/A	SB	CS	SBR	FA	FR	G/POS	TPR
1911	Bos-N	54	175	28	36	7	3	1	21	40	39	.206	.359	.297	78	-4	11			.955	-6	3-53/S-1	-0.9
1912	Bos-N	121	459	70	119	23	6	2	34	70	91	.259	.363	.349	94	-2	22			.940	-2	*3-118	-0.3
1913	Chi-N	1	0	0	0	0	0	0	0	0	0	—	—	—	—		0	0		.000	0	R	0.0
Total	3	176	634	98	155	30	9	3	55	110	130	.244	.362	.334	89	-6	33			.945	-7	3-171/S-1	-1.2

■ JIM McDONALD
McDonald, James   b: Philadelphia, Pa.   BR/TR, 6', 180 lbs.   Deb: 6/2/02

YEAR	TM/L	G	AB	R	H	2B	3B	HR	RBI	BB	SO	AVG	OBP	SLG	PRO+	BR/A	SB	CS	SBR	FA	FR	G/POS	TPR
1902	NY-N	2	9	0	3	0	0	0	0	0	0	.333	.333	.333	107	0	0	0	0	1.000	-0	/O-2	-0.1

■ JIM McDONALD
McDonald, James A.   b: 8/6/1860, San Francisco, Cal.   d: 9/14/14, San Francisco, Cal.   Deb: 6/20/1884

YEAR	TM/L	G	AB	R	H	2B	3B	HR	RBI	BB	SO	AVG	OBP	SLG	PRO+	BR/A	SB	CS	SBR	FA	FR	G/POS	TPR
1884	Was-U	2	6	0	1	0	0	0			0	.167	.167	.167	1	-1				.700	-1	/C-1,O-1	-0.2
	Pit-a	38	145	11	23	3	0	0			2	.159	.170	.179	14	-13				.795	-6	3-22,O-15/2-1	-1.9
1885	Buf-N	5	14	0	0	0	0	0		0	4	.000	.000	.000	-97	-3				.875	2	/S-4,O-1	-0.1
Total	2	45	165	11	24	3	0	0		0	4	.145	.156	.164	4	-17				.848	-6	/3-22,O-17,S-4,2C	-2.2

■ JOE McDONALD
McDonald, Malcolm Joseph   b: 4/9/1888, Texas   d: 5/30/63, Baytown, Tex.   BR/TR, 5'11", 175 lbs.   Deb: 9/6/10

YEAR	TM/L	G	AB	R	H	2B	3B	HR	RBI	BB	SO	AVG	OBP	SLG	PRO+	BR/A	SB	CS	SBR	FA	FR	G/POS	TPR
1910	StL-A	10	32	4	5	0	0	0		1	1	.156	.182	.156	6	-3	0			.821	-3	3-10	-0.7

■ JIM McDONNELL
McDonnell, James William "Mack"   b: 8/15/22, Gagetown, Mich.   BL/TR, 5'11", 165 lbs.   Deb: 9/23/43

YEAR	TM/L	G	AB	R	H	2B	3B	HR	RBI	BB	SO	AVG	OBP	SLG	PRO+	BR/A	SB	CS	SBR	FA	FR	G/POS	TPR
1943	Cle-A	2	1	1	0	0	0	0	2		1	.000	.667	.000	108	0	0	0	0	1.000	-0	/C-1	0.0
1944	Cle-A	20	43	5	10	0	0	0	4	4	3	.233	.298	.233	55	-2	0	0	0	.900	-2	C-13	-0.4
1945	Cle-A	28	51	3	10	2	0	0	8	2	4	.196	.226	.235	36	-4	0	0	0	.980	8	C-23	0.5
Total	3	50	95	9	20	2	0	0	12	8	8	.211	.272	.232	48	-6	0	0	0	.953	6	/C-37	0.1

■ ED McDONOUGH
McDonough, Edward Sebastian   b: 9/11/1886, Elgin, Ill.   d: 9/2/26, Elgin, Ill.   BR/TR, 6', 160 lbs.   Deb: 8/3/09

YEAR	TM/L	G	AB	R	H	2B	3B	HR	RBI	BB	SO	AVG	OBP	SLG	PRO+	BR/A	SB	CS	SBR	FA	FR	G/POS	TPR
1909	Phi-N	1	1	0	0	0	0	0	0	0	0	.000	.000	.000	-99	-0	0			1.000	-1	/C-1	0.0
1910	Phi-N	5	9	1	1	0	0	0	0	0	1	.111	.111	.111	-34	-2	0			1.000	-1	/C-4	-0.2
Total	2	6	10	1	1	0	0	0	0	0	1	.100	.100	.100	-40	-2	0			1.000	-1	/C-5	-0.2

■ GIL McDOUGALD
McDougald, Gilbert James   b: 5/19/28, San Francisco, Cal   BR/TR, 6'1", 180 lbs.   Deb: 4/20/51

YEAR	TM/L	G	AB	R	H	2B	3B	HR	RBI	BB	SO	AVG	OBP	SLG	PRO+	BR/A	SB	CS	SBR	FA	FR	G/POS	TPR
1951	*NY-A	131	402	72	123	23	4	14	63	56	54	.306	.396	.488	143	25	14	5	1	.949	-16	3-82,2-55	1.2
1952	*NY-A★	152	555	65	146	16	5	11	78	57	73	.263	.336	.369	102	1	6	5	-1	.968	12	*3-117,2-38	1.2
1953	*NY-A	141	541	82	154	27	7	10	83	60	65	.285	.361	.416	113	10	3	4	-2	.953	9	*3-136,2-26	1.2
1954	NY-A	126	394	66	102	22	2	12	48	62	64	.259	.367	.416	118	11	3	4	-2	.989	1	2-92,3-35	1.6
1955	*NY-A	141	533	79	152	10	8	13	53	65	77	.285	.365	.407	109	7	6	4	-1	**.985**	19	*2-126,3-17	3.5
1956	*NY-A☆	120	438	79	136	13	4	13	56	59	59	.311	.407	.443	128	20	3	8	-4	.970	5	S-92,2-31/3-5	2.8
1957	*NY-A★	141	539	87	156	25	**9**	13	62	59	71	.289	.364	.442	121	16	2	5	-2	.976	15	*S-121,2-21/3-7	4.2
1958	NY-A	138	503	69	126	19	1	14	65	59	75	.250	.333	.376	98	-1	6	2	1	.977	-3	*2-115,S-19	0.6
1959	NY-A★	127	434	44	109	16	4	9	34	35	40	.251	.311	.353	85	-9	3	3	-2	.989	5	2-53,S-52,3-25	0.5
1960	*NY-A	119	337	54	87	16	4	8	34	38	45	.258	.339	.401	105	2	2	2	-2	.945	-3	3-84,2-42	0.0
Total	10	1336	4676	697	1291	187	51	112	576	559	623	.276	.358	.410	112	81	45	44	-13	.984	42	2-599,3-508,S-284	16.8

■ ODDIBE McDOWELL
McDowell, Oddibe   b: 8/25/62, Hollywood, Fla.   BL/TL, 5'9", 165 lbs.   Deb: 5/19/85

YEAR	TM/L	G	AB	R	H	2B	3B	HR	RBI	BB	SO	AVG	OBP	SLG	PRO+	BR/A	SB	CS	SBR	FA	FR	G/POS	TPR
1985	Tex-A	111	406	63	97	14	5	18	42	36	85	.239	.304	.431	98	-2	25	7	3	.993	10	*O-103/D-4	0.8
1986	Tex-A	154	572	105	152	24	7	18	49	65	112	.266	.342	.427	105	4	33	15	1	.991	3	*O-148/D-1	0.3
1987	Tex-A	128	407	65	98	26	4	14	52	51	99	.241	.325	.428	97	-2	24	2	6	.989	-2	*O-125	-0.1
1988	Tex-A	120	437	55	108	19	5	6	37	41	89	.247	.315	.355	85	-9	33	10	4	.989	-3	O-113/D-3	-1.2
1989	Cle-A	69	239	33	53	5	2	3	22	25	36	.222	.298	.297	67	-10	12	5	1	.992	6	O-64/D-2	-1.0

YEAR	TM/L	G	AB	R	H	2B	3B	HR	RBI	BB	SO	AVG	OBP	SLG	PRO+	BR/A	SB	CS	SBR	FA	FR	G/POS	TPR
	Atl-N	76	280	56	85	18	4	7	24	27	37	.304	.365	.471	134	12	15	10	-2	.978	5	O-68	1.4
1990	Atl-N	113	305	47	74	14	0	7	25	21	53	.243	.296	.357	74	-11	13	2	3	.971	-6	O-72	-1.6
1994	Tex-A	59	183	34	48	5	1	1	15	28	39	.262	.360	.317	77	-5	14	2	1	.983	-4	O-53/D-2	-0.7
Total	7	830	2829	458	715	125	28	74	266	294	550	.253	.325	.395	94	-23	169	53	19	.987	5	O-746/D-12	-2.1

■ PRYOR McELVEEN
McElveen, Pryor Mynatt "Humpty" b: 11/5/1881, Atlanta, Ga. d: 10/27/51, Pleasant Hill, Tenn. BR/TR, 5'10", 168 lbs. Deb: 4/26/09

YEAR	TM/L	G	AB	R	H	2B	3B	HR	RBI	BB	SO	AVG	OBP	SLG	PRO+	BR/A	SB	CS	SBR	FA	FR	G/POS	TPR
1909	Bro-N	81	258	22	51	8	1	3	25	14		.198	.242	.271	61	-13	6			.938	-5	3-37,O-13,S-10/12	-1.8
1910	Bro-N	74	213	19	48	8	3	1	26	22	47	.225	.307	.305	81	-5	6			.943	-5	3-54/S-6,2-3,C-1	-0.9
1911	Bro-N	16	31	1	6	0	0	0	5	0	3	.194	.194	.194	9	-4	0			.929	-1	/2-5,S-1	-0.5
Total	3	171	502	42	105	16	4	4	56	36	50	.209	.268	.281	67	-22	12			.941	-11	/3-91,S-17,2O1C	-3.2

■ LEE McELWEE
McElwee, Leland Stanford b: 5/23/1894, LaMesa, Cal. d: 2/8/57, Union, Maine BR/TR, 5'10.5", 160 lbs. Deb: 7/3/16

YEAR	TM/L	G	AB	R	H	2B	3B	HR	RBI	BB	SO	AVG	OBP	SLG	PRO+	BR/A	SB	CS	SBR	FA	FR	G/POS	TPR
1916	Phi-A	54	155	9	41	3	0	0	10	8	17	.265	.301	.284	79	-4	0			.883	-2	3-30/O-9,2-3,1-1,S	-0.6

■ FRANK McELYEA
McElyea, Frank b: 8/4/18, Hawthorne Twsp., Ill. d: 4/19/87, Evansville, Ill. BR/TR, 6'6", 221 lbs. Deb: 9/10/42

YEAR	TM/L	G	AB	R	H	2B	3B	HR	RBI	BB	SO	AVG	OBP	SLG	PRO+	BR/A	SB	CS	SBR	FA	FR	G/POS	TPR
1942	Bos-N	7	4	2	0	0	0	0	0	0	0	.000	.000	.000	-99	-1	0			1.000	-0	/O-1	-0.1

■ GUY McFADDEN
McFadden, Guy G. b: 9/3/1872, Topeka, Kan. d: 3/10/11, Topeka, Kan. Deb: 8/24/1895

YEAR	TM/L	G	AB	R	H	2B	3B	HR	RBI	BB	SO	AVG	OBP	SLG	PRO+	BR/A	SB	CS	SBR	FA	FR	G/POS	TPR
1895	StL-N	4	14	1	3	0	0	0	2	0	2	.214	.214	.214	11	-1				.968	-1	/1-4	-0.2

■ LEON McFADDEN
McFadden, Leon b: 4/26/44, Little Rock, Ark. BR/TR, 6'2", 195 lbs. Deb: 9/6/68

YEAR	TM/L	G	AB	R	H	2B	3B	HR	RBI	BB	SO	AVG	OBP	SLG	PRO+	BR/A	SB	CS	SBR	FA	FR	G/POS	TPR
1968	Hou-N	16	47	2	13	1	0	0	1	6	10	.277	.358	.298	101	0	1	0	0	.968	-1	S-16	0.2
1969	Hou-N	44	74	3	13	2	0	0	3	4	9	.176	.218	.203	19	-8	1	2	-1	.944	-3	O-17/S-8	-1.2
1970	Hou-N	2	0	0	0	0	0	0	0	0	0	—	—	—	—	0	0	0	0	.000	0	R	0.0
Total	3	62	121	5	26	3	0	0	4	10	19	.215	.275	.240	50	-8	2	2	-1	.966	-4	/S-24,O-17	-1.0

■ ALEX McFARLAN
McFarlan, Alexander Shepherd b: 11/11/1866, Kentucky d: 3/2/39, Pewee Valley, Ky. Deb: 6/19/1892 F

YEAR	TM/L	G	AB	R	H	2B	3B	HR	RBI	BB	SO	AVG	OBP	SLG	PRO+	BR/A	SB	CS	SBR	FA	FR	G/POS	TPR
1892	Lou-N	14	42	2	7	0	0	0	1	8	11	.167	.300	.167	46	-2	1			.773	-3	O-12/2-2	-0.5

■ CHRIS McFARLAND
McFarland, Christopher b: 8/17/1861, Fall River, Mass. d: 5/24/18, New Bedford, Mass. 5'9", 170 lbs. Deb: 4/19/1884

YEAR	TM/L	G	AB	R	H	2B	3B	HR	RBI	BB	SO	AVG	OBP	SLG	PRO+	BR/A	SB	CS	SBR	FA	FR	G/POS	TPR
1884	Bal-U	3	14	2	3	1	0	0	0			.214	.214	.286	46	-1				.571	-1	/O-3,P-1	-0.2

■ ED McFARLAND
McFarland, Edward William b: 8/3/1874, Cleveland, Ohio d: 11/28/59, Cleveland, Ohio BR/TR, 5'10", 180 lbs. Deb: 7/7/1893

YEAR	TM/L	G	AB	R	H	2B	3B	HR	RBI	BB	SO	AVG	OBP	SLG	PRO+	BR/A	SB	CS	SBR	FA	FR	G/POS	TPR
1893	Cle-N	8	22	5	9	2	1	0	6	1	2	.409	.458	.591	168	2	0			1.000	-4	/O-5,3-2,C-1	-0.1
1896	StL-N	83	290	48	70	13	4	3	36	15	17	.241	.281	.345	67	-15	7			.961	8	C-80/O-2	0.2
1897	StL-N	31	107	14	35	5	2	1	17	8		.327	.374	.439	116	2	2			.965	2	C-23/1-3,0-3,2-1	0.6
	Phi-N	38	130	18	29	3	5	1	16	14		.223	.308	.346	74	-5	2			.951	-2	C-37	-0.2
	Yr	69	237	32	64	8	7	2	33	22		.270	.337	.388	93	-3	4			.957	0	C-60/1-3,0-3,2-1	0.4
1898	Phi-N	121	429	65	121	21	5	3	71	44		.282	.352	.375	113	8	4			.960	-1	*C-121	1.7
1899	Phi-N	96	324	59	108	22	9	2	57	36		.333	.403	.475	146	21	9			.968	13	C-94	3.7
1900	Phi-N	94	344	50	105	14	8	0	38	29		.305	.364	.392	110	5	9			.963	-3	C-93/3-1	0.9
1901	Phi-N	74	295	33	84	14	2	1	32	18		.285	.326	.356	96	-2	11			.970	-4	C-74	0.8
1902	Chi-A	75	246	29	56	9	2	1	25	19		.228	.291	.293	65	-11	8			.967	2	C-69/1-1	-0.2
1903	Chi-A	61	201	15	42	7	2	1	19	14		.209	.264	.279	66	-8	3			.968	-0	C-56/1-1	-0.3
1904	Chi-A	50	160	22	44	11	0	0	20	17		.275	.348	.381	136	7	2			.975	-11	C-49	0.1
1905	Chi-A	80	250	24	70	13	4	0	31	23		.280	.345	.364	130	9	5			.973	6	C-70	2.4
1906	*Chi-A	12	23	0	4	1	0	0	3	3		.174	.269	.217	54	-1	0			.973	-1	/C-7	-0.1
1907	Chi-A	52	138	11	39	9	1	0	8	17		.283	.340	.362	128	4	3			.972	-2	C-43	0.7
1908	Bos-A	19	48	5	10	2	1	0	4	1		.208	.224	.292	66	-2	0			.978	5	C-13	0.3
Total	14	894	3007	398	826	146	49	13	383	254	19	.275	.335	.369	104	13	65			.967	14	C-830/O-10,1-5,32	10.5

■ HERM McFARLAND
McFarland, Hermas Walter b: 3/11/1870, Des Moines, Iowa d: 9/21/35, Richmond, Va. BL/TR, 5'6", 150 lbs. Deb: 4/21/1896

YEAR	TM/L	G	AB	R	H	2B	3B	HR	RBI	BB	SO	AVG	OBP	SLG	PRO+	BR/A	SB	CS	SBR	FA	FR	G/POS	TPR
1896	Lou-N	30	110	11	21	4	1	1	12	9	14	.191	.252	.273	40	-10	4			.833	-3	O-28/C-1	-1.3
1898	Cin-N	19	64	10	18	1	3	0	11	7		.281	.361	.391	108	1	3			.968	-2	O-17	-0.3
1901	Chi-A	132	473	83	130	21	9	4	59	75		.275	.384	.383	116	14	33			.946	5	*O-132	0.8
1902	Chi-A	7	27	5	5	0	0	0	4	2		.185	.241	.185	20	-3	1			1.000	-0	/O-7	-0.4
	Bal-A	61	242	54	78	19	6	3	36	36		.322	.418	.488	144	16	10			.965	6	O-61	1.7
	Yr	68	269	59	83	19	6	3	40	38		.309	.402	.457	133	13	11			.967	6	O-68	1.3
1903	NY-A	103	362	41	88	16	9	5	45	46		.243	.333	.378	106	3	13			.939	-3	*O-103	-0.6
Total	5	352	1278	204	340	61	28	13	167	175	14	.266	.362	.388	110	21	64			.941	2	O-348/C-1	-0.1

■ HOWIE McFARLAND
McFarland, Howard Alexander b: 3/7/11, ElReno, Okla. BR/TR, 6', 175 lbs. Deb: 7/16/45

YEAR	TM/L	G	AB	R	H	2B	3B	HR	RBI	BB	SO	AVG	OBP	SLG	PRO+	BR/A	SB	CS	SBR	FA	FR	G/POS	TPR
1945	Was-A	6	11	0	1	0	0	0	2	0	3	.091	.091	.091	-52	-2	0	0	0	1.000	-0	/O-3	-0.3

■ ORLANDO McFARLANE
McFarlane, Orlando Dejesus (Quesada) b: 6/28/38, Oriente, Cuba BR/TR, 6', 180 lbs. Deb: 4/23/62

YEAR	TM/L	G	AB	R	H	2B	3B	HR	RBI	BB	SO	AVG	OBP	SLG	PRO+	BR/A	SB	CS	SBR	FA	FR	G/POS	TPR
1962	Pit-N	8	23	0	2	0	0	0	1	4		.087	.125	.087	-42	-5	0	0	0	1.000	2	/C-8	-0.2
1964	Pit-N	37	78	5	19	5	0	1	1	4	27	.244	.280	.308	66	-4	0	0	0	.983	-6	C-35/O-1	-0.9
1966	Det-A	49	138	16	35	7	0	5	13	9	46	.254	.304	.413	102	1	0	0	0	.991	-2	C-33	0.0
1967	Cal-A	12	22	0	5	0	0	0	3	1	7	.227	.261	.227	47	-1	0	0	0	.935	-1	/C-6	-0.2
1968	Cal-A	18	31	1	9	0	0	0	2	5	9	.290	.389	.290	112	1	0	0	0	.977	-0	/C-9	0.1
Total	5	124	292	22	70	12	0	5	20	20	93	.240	.291	.332	78	-9	0	0	0	.985	-8	/C-91,O-1	-1.2

■ PATSY McGAFFIGAN
McGaffigan, Mark Andrew b: 9/12/1888, Carlyle, Ill. d: 12/22/40, Carlyle, Ill. BR/TR, 5'8", 140 lbs. Deb: 4/16/17

YEAR	TM/L	G	AB	R	H	2B	3B	HR	RBI	BB	SO	AVG	OBP	SLG	PRO+	BR/A	SB	CS	SBR	FA	FR	G/POS	TPR
1917	Phi-N	19	60	5	10	1	0	0	6	0	7	.167	.167	.183	7	-7	1			.920	-1	S-17/O-1	-0.7
1918	Phi-N	54	192	17	39	3	2	1	8	16	23	.203	.268	.255	56	-10	3			.948	-12	2-53/S-1	-2.1
Total	2	73	252	22	49	4	2	1	14	16	30	.194	.245	.238	45	-16	4			.923	-12	/2-53,S-18,O-1	-2.8

■ EDDIE McGAH
McGah, Edward Joseph b: 9/30/21, Oakland, Cal. BR/TR, 6', 183 lbs. Deb: 4/26/46

YEAR	TM/L	G	AB	R	H	2B	3B	HR	RBI	BB	SO	AVG	OBP	SLG	PRO+	BR/A	SB	CS	SBR	FA	FR	G/POS	TPR
1946	Bos-A	15	37	2	8	1	1	0	1	7	7	.216	.341	.297	75	-1	0	0	0	.981	-2	C-14	-0.3
1947	Bos-A	9	14	1	0	0	0	0	2	3	0	.000	.176	.000	-45	-3	0	0	0	.964	2	/C-7	-0.1
Total	2	24	51	3	8	1	1	0	3	10	7	.157	.295	.216	41	-4	0	0	0	.975	-0	/C-21	-0.4

■ AMBROSE McGANN
McGann, Ambrose b: 1875, Baltimore, Md. 170 lbs. Deb: 5/2/1895

YEAR	TM/L	G	AB	R	H	2B	3B	HR	RBI	BB	SO	AVG	OBP	SLG	PRO+	BR/A	SB	CS	SBR	FA	FR	G/POS	TPR
1895	Lou-N	20	73	9	21	5	2	0	9	8	6	.288	.358	.411	105	1	6			.852	-2	/S-8,3-6,O-5	-0.1

■ DAN McGANN
McGann, Dennis Lawrence "Cap" b: 7/15/1871, Shelbyville, Ky. d: 12/13/10, Louisville, Ky. BB/TR, 6', 190 lbs. Deb: 8/8/1896

YEAR	TM/L	G	AB	R	H	2B	3B	HR	RBI	BB	SO	AVG	OBP	SLG	PRO+	BR/A	SB	CS	SBR	FA	FR	G/POS	TPR
1896	Bos-N	43	171	25	55	6	7	2	30	12	10	.322	.383	.474	118	4	2			.905	-17	2-43	-0.9
1898	Bal-N	145	535	99	161	18	8	5	106	53		.301	.404	.393	126	22	33			.983	2	*1-145	2.1
1899	Bro-N	63	214	49	52	11	4	2	32	21		.243	.362	.360	96	-0	16			.985	2	1-61	0.1
	Was-N	76	280	65	96	9	8	5	58	14		.343	.410	.486	147	18	11			.990	2	1-76	1.8
	Yr	139	494	114	148	20	12	7	90	35		.300	.389	.431	124	18	27			.988	4	*1-137	1.9
1900	StL-N	121	444	79	132	10	4	0	58	32		.297	.376	.387	112	8	26			.990	-1	*1-121/2-1	0.6
1901	StL-N	103	423	73	115	15	9	0	56	19		.272	.333	.392	116	8	17			.984	-3	*1-103	0.4
1902	Bal-A	28	250	40	79	10	4	0	42	19		.316	.378	.420	116	6	17			.987	3	1-68	0.9
	NY-N	61	227	25	68	5	7	0	21	12		.300	.356	.383	129	3	11			.981	5	1-61	0.9
1903	NY-N	129	482	75	130	21	6	3	50	32		.270	.331	.357	92	-5	36			.988	-0	*1-129	-0.7
1904	NY-N	141	517	81	148	22	6	6	71	36		.286	.354	.387	123	14	42			.991	3	*1-141	1.5
1905	*NY-N	136	491	88	147	23	14	5	75	60		.299	.391	.434	143	27	22			.991	4	*1-136	2.9
1906	NY-N	134	451	62	107	14	8	0	37	60		.237	.344	.304	100	2	30			.995	3	*1-133	0.2
1907	NY-N	81	262	29	78	9	1	2	36	29		.298	.383	.363	129	10	7			.994	5	*1-81	1.5
1908	Bos-N	135	475	52	114	8	5	2	55	38		.240	.321	.291	97	0	9			.988	5	*1-121/2-9	0.3
Total	12	1436	5222	842	1482	181	100	42	727	429	10	.284	.364	.381	117	122	282			.989	10	*1-1376/2-53	11.4

YEAR	TM/L	G	AB	R	H	2B	3B	HR	RBI	BB	SO	AVG	OBP	SLG	PRO+	BR/A	SB	CS	SBR	FA	FR	G/POS	TPR

■ CHIPPY McGARR McGarr, James B. b: 5/10/1863, Worcester, Mass. d: 6/6/04, Worcester, Mass. BR/TR, 5'7", 168 lbs. Deb: 7/11/1884 U

1884	CP-U	19	70	10	11	2	0	0		0		.157	.157	.186	4	-10				.905	-6	2-13/O-6	-1.5
1886	Phi-a	71	267	41	71	9	3	2	31	9		.266	.295	.345	99	-1	17			.850	1	S-71	0.0
1887	Phi-a	137	536	93	158	23	6	1	63	23		.295	.326	.366	93	-6	84			.875	-1	*S-137	-0.5
1888	StL-a	34	132	17	31	1	0	0	13	6		.235	.268	.242	58	-7	25			.895	-3	2-33/S-1	-0.7
1889	KC-a	25	108	22	31	3	0	0	16	6	11	.287	.330	.315	79	-3	12			.857	-2	3-11/O-6.2-5,S-3	-0.4
	Bal-a	3	7	1	1	0	0	0	0	1	1	.143	.250	.143	13	-1	0			.583	-2	/S-3	-0.2
	Yr	28	115	23	32	3	0	0	16	7	12	.278	.325	.304	76	-4	12			.857	-4	3-11/O-6,S-6,2-5	-0.6
1890	Bos-N	121	487	68	115	12	7	1	51	34	38	.236	.291	.296	66	-23	39			.933	-2	*3-115/S-5,O-1	-1.8
1893	Cle-N	63	249	38	77	12	0	0	28	20	15	.309	.363	.357	87	-5	24			.886	0	3-63	-0.3
1894	Cle-N	128	523	94	144	24	6	2	74	28	29	.275	.316	.356	59	-36	31			.902	-7	*3-128	-3.3
1895	*Cle-N	112	419	85	111	14	2	2	59	34	33	.265	.322	.322	63	-24	19			.870	-5	3-108/2-4	-2.3
1896	*Cle-N	113	455	68	122	16	4	1	53	22	30	.268	.302	.327	62	-26	16			.924	-7	*3-113/C-1	-2.6
Total	10	826	3253	537	872	116	28	9	388	183	157	.268	.310	.329	71	-144	267			.903	-33	3-538,S-220/20C	-13.6

■ JIM McGARR McGarr, James Vincent "Reds" b: 11/9/1888, Philadelphia, Pa. d: 7/21/81, Miami, Fla. BR/TR, 5'9.5", 170 lbs. Deb: 5/18/12

| 1912 | Det-A | 1 | 4 | 0 | 0 | 0 | 0 | 0 | 0 | | | .000 | .000 | .000 | -99 | -1 | 0 | | | .800 | -0 | /2-1 | -0.2 |

■ DAN McGARVEY McGarvey, Daniel Francis b: 12/2/1887, Philadelphia, Pa. d: 3/7/47, Philadelphia, Pa. Deb: 5/18/12

| 1912 | Det-A | 1 | 3 | 0 | 0 | 0 | 0 | 0 | 0 | | | .000 | .400 | .000 | 18 | -0 | 0 | | | .667 | 0 | /O-1 | 0.0 |

■ JACK McGEACHY McGeachy, John Charles b: 5/23/1864, Clinton, Mass. d: 4/5/30, Cambridge, Mass. BR/TR, 5'8", 165 lbs. Deb: 6/17/1886

1886	Det-N	6	27	3	9	0	1	0	4	0	3	.333	.333	.407	121	1	2			.875	-1	/O-6	0.0
	StL-N	59	226	31	46	12	3	2	24	1	37	.204	.207	.310	59	-11	8			.880	2	O-55/2-2,3-2	-1.0
	Yr	65	253	34	55	12	4	2	28	1	40	.217	.220	.320	66	-10	10			.880	1	O-61/2-2,3-2	-1.0
1887	Ind-N	99	405	69	109	17	3	1	56	5	16	.269	.280	.333	72	-15	27			.894	3	*O-98/3-1,P-1	-0.9
1888	Ind-N	118	452	45	99	15	2	0	30	5	21	.219	.231	.261	56	-23	49			.932	5	*O-117/S-1,P-1	-2.1
1889	Ind-N	113	532	83	142	32	1	2	63	9	39	.267	.282	.342	73	-22	37			.918	9	*O-131/P-3	-1.4
1890	Bro-P	104	443	84	108	24	4	1	65	19	12	.244	.278	.323	57	-30	21			.906	-1	*O-104	-2.8
1891	Phi-a	50	201	24	46	4	3	2	13	6	12	.229	.255	.308	59	-12	9			.910	-4	O-41	-1.1
	Bos-a	41	178	26	45	2	1	1	21	12	8	.253	.304	.292	72	-7	11			.916	-0	O-91	-2.1
	Yr	91	379	50	91	6	4	3	34	18	20	.240	.278	.301	65	-19	20			.916	-4	O-91	-2.1
Total	6	608	2464	345	604	106	18	9	276	57	148	.245	.265	.314	65	-120	164			.909	18	O-602/P-5,3-3,2S	-10.3

■ MIKE McGEARY McGeary, Michael Henry b: 1851, Philadelphia, Pa. BR/TR, 5'7", 138 lbs. Deb: 5/9/1871 M

1871	Tro-n	29	148	42	39	4	0	0	12	6	0	.264	.292	.291	67	-6	20	4	4	.897	-2	*C-26/S-3	-0.3
1872	Ath-n	47	225	68	81	9	2	0	35	2	1	.360	.366	.418	140	10	13	8	-1	.867	7	C-23,S-23/O-1	1.1
1873	Ath-n	52	275	63	83	8	1	0	31	1	1	.302	.304	.338	84	-7	3	6	-3	.805	-5	*S-44,C-13/3-1	-1.1
1874	Ath-n	54	271	61	87	10	2	0	22	1	2	.321	.324	.373	113	2	10	2	2	.837	7	C-28,S-26/O-4	0.8
1875	Phi-n	68	310	71	90	6	2	0	37	1	1	.290	.293	.323	109	2	19	4	3	.743	4	3-27,2-23,S-18/OM	0.7
1876	StL-N	61	276	48	72	3	0	0	30	2	1	.261	.266	.272	84	-4				.889	5	*2-56/C-5,O-1,3-1	0.1
1877	StL-N	57	258	35	65	3	2	0	20	2	6	.252	.258	.279	73	-7				.883	7	2-39,3-19	0.1
1879	Pro-N	85	374	62	103	7	2	0	35	5	13	.275	.285	.305	96	-2				.884	1	*2-73,3-12	0.5
1880	Pro-N	18	59	5	8	0	0	0	1	0	6	.136	.136	.136	-8	-6				.887	3	3-17/2-2,S-1,M	-0.3
	Cle-N	31	111	14	28	2	1	0	6	4	3	.252	.278	.288	94	-1				.887	-4	3-29/O-2	-0.4
	Yr	49	170	19	36	2	1	0	7	4	9	.212	.230	.235	60	-7				.887	-1	3-46/2-2,O-2,S-1	-0.7
1881	Cle-N	11	41	1	9	0	0	0	5	0	6	.220	.220	.220	41	-3				.724	-7	3-11,M	-0.9
1882	Det-N	34	133	14	19	4	1	0	2	2	20	.143	.156	.188	10	-13				.928	8	S-33/2-3	-1.2
Total	5 n	250	1229	305	380	37	7	0	137	11	5	.309	.315	.351	104	0	65	24	5	.808	12	S-114/C-90,3-28,2O	1.2
Total	6	297	1252	179	304	19	6	0	99	15	55	.243	.252	.268	72	-35				.885	13	2-173/3-89,S-34,CO	-1.2

■ DAN McGEE McGee, Daniel Aloysius b: 9/29/11, New York, N.Y. d: 12/4/91, Lakehurst, N.J. BR/TR, 5'8.5", 152 lbs. Deb: 7/14/34

| 1934 | Bos-N | 7 | 22 | 2 | 3 | 0 | 0 | 0 | 1 | 3 | 6 | .136 | .240 | .136 | 4 | -3 | 0 | | | .951 | 3 | /S-7 | 0.0 |

■ FRANK McGEE McGee, Francis De Sales b: 4/28/1899, Columbus, Ohio d: 1/30/34, Columbus, Ohio BR/TR, 5'11.5", 175 lbs. Deb: 9/19/25

| 1925 | Was-A | 2 | 3 | 0 | 0 | 0 | 0 | 0 | 0 | 0 | 1 | .000 | .000 | .000 | -99 | -1 | 0 | 0 | 0 | 1.000 | 0 | /1-2 | -0.1 |

■ PAT McGEE McGee, Patrick b: Philadelphia, Pa. d: 6/21/1889, New York, N.Y. Deb: 9/24/1874

1874	Atl-n	16	65	4	11	0	0	0	6	0	3	.169	.169	.185	15	-5	0	0	0	.795	-1	O-15/S-2,2-1	-0.5
1875	Mut-n	25	95	4	17	2	0	0	9	0	10	.179	.179	.200	30	-7	0	0	0	.848	-2	O-25	-0.7
	Atl-n	18	65	3	10	3	1	0	5	1	4	.154	.167	.231	42	-3	0	0	0	.912	6	O-13/2-6,3-1	0.3
	Yr	43	160	7	27	5	1	0	14	1	14	.169	.174	.213	34	-10	0	0	0	.875	4	O-38/2-6,3-1	-0.4
Total	2 n	59	225	11	38	6	1	0	20	1	17	.169	.173	.204	29	-15	0	0	0	.849	3	/O-53,2-7,S-2,3-1	-0.9

■ WILLIE McGEE McGee, Willie Dean b: 11/2/58, San Francisco, Cal. BB/TR, 6'1", 175 lbs. Deb: 5/10/82

1982	*StL-N	123	422	43	125	12	8	4	56	12	58	.296	.319	.391	97	-3	24	12	0	.958	-9	*O-117	-1.6
1983	StL-N★	147	601	75	172	22	8	5	75	26	98	.286	.314	.374	90	-9	39	8	7	.987	8	*O-145	0.2
1984	StL-N	145	571	82	166	19	11	6	50	29	80	.291	.326	.394	104	2	43	10	7	.985	11	*O-141	1.6
1985	*StL-N★	152	612	114	216	26	18	10	82	34	86	.353	.387	.503	148	38	56	16	7	.978	13	*O-149	5.4
1986	StL-N	124	497	65	127	22	7	7	48	37	82	.256	.306	.370	87	-10	19	16	-4	.991	15	*O-121	-0.2
1987	StL-N★	153	620	76	177	37	11	11	105	24	90	.285	.314	.434	94	-7	16	4	2	.981	9	*O-152/S-1	-0.1
1988	StL-N★	137	562	73	164	24	6	3	50	32	84	.292	.331	.372	100	0	41	6	9	.975	10	*O-135	1.6
1989	StL-N	58	199	23	47	10	2	3	17	10	34	.236	.276	.352	76	-7	8	6	-1	.976	2	O-47	-0.8
1990	StL-N	125	501	76	168	32	5	3	62	38	86	.335	.383	.437	125	17	28	9	3	.957	16	*O-124	3.4
	*Oak-A	29	113	23	31	3	2	0	15	10	18	.274	.333	.336	91	-1	3	0	1	.986	1	O-28/D-1	0.0
1991	SF-N	131	497	67	155	30	3	4	43	34	74	.312	.355	.408	119	12	17	9	0	.978	-2	*O-128	0.4
1992	SF-N	138	474	56	141	20	2	1	36	29	88	.297	.339	.354	102	1	13	4	2	.976	3	*O-119	-0.3
1993	SF-N	130	475	53	143	28	4	4	46	38	67	.301	.354	.389	102	4	10	5	-2	.979	0	*O-126	0.0
1994	SF-N	45	156	19	44	3	0	5	23	15	24	.282	.345	.397	97	-1	3	0	1	.988	0	O-42	0.0
1995	*Bos-A	67	200	32	57	11	3	2	15	9	41	.285	.316	.400	82	-6	5	2	0	.973	-7	O-64	-1.3
1996	*StL-N	123	309	52	95	15	5	2	41	18	60	.307	.350	.417	101	0	5	2	0	.962	-4	O-83/1-6	-0.6
Total	15	1827	6809	929	2028	314	89	73	764	395	1070	.298	.338	.402	104	29	330	113	31	.977	65	*O-1721/1-6,D-1,S-1	8.4

■ DAN McGEEHAN McGeehan, Daniel De Sales b: 6/7/1885, Jeddo, Pa. d: 7/12/55, Hazleton, Pa. BR/TR, 5'6", 135 lbs. Deb: 4/22/11 F

| 1911 | StL-N | 3 | 9 | 0 | 2 | 0 | 0 | 0 | 1 | 0 | 1 | .222 | .222 | .222 | 25 | -1 | 0 | | | .818 | -1 | /2-3 | -0.2 |

■ ED McGHEE McGhee, Warren Edward b: 9/29/24, Perry, Ark. d: 2/13/86, Memphis, Tenn. BR/TR, 5'11", 170 lbs. Deb: 9/20/50

1950	Chi-A	3	6	1	1	0	1	0	0	0	1	.167	.167	.500	67	-0	0	0	0	1.000	-0	/O-1	-0.1
1953	Phi-A	104	358	36	94	11	4	0	29	32	43	.263	.328	.324	74	-13	4	3	-1	.982	7	O-99	-1.0
1954	Phi-A	21	53	5	11	2	0	0	9	4	8	.208	.263	.358	69	-3	0	1	-1	.933	-1	O-13	-0.3
	Chi-A	42	75	12	17	1	0	0	5	12	8	.227	.333	.240	57	-4	5	0	2	.982	-3	O-34	-0.7
	Yr	63	128	17	28	3	0	0	14	16	16	.219	.306	.289	62	-7	5	1	1	.960	-3	O-47	-1.0
1955	Chi-A	26	13	6	1	0	0	0	0	6	1	.077	.368	.077	24	-1	2	0	2	.923	-6	O-17	-0.7
Total	4	196	505	60	124	14	5	3	43	54	61	.246	.322	.311	70	-21	11	5	0	.975	-2	O-164	-2.8

■ BILL McGHEE McGhee, William Mac "Fibber" b: 9/5/05, Shawmut, Ala. d: 3/10/84, Decatur, Ga. BL/TL, 5'10.5", 185 lbs. Deb: 7/5/44

1944	Phi-A	77	287	27	83	12	0	1	19	21	20	.289	.338	.341	96	-2	5			.989	-0	1-75	-0.6
1945	Phi-A	93	250	24	63	6	1	0	19	24	16	.252	.320	.284	76	-7	3	2	-0	.989	-5	O-48/1-8	-1.6
Total	2	170	537	51	146	18	1	1	38	45	36	.272	.329	.315	87	-9	5			.990	-5	/1-83,O-48	-2.2

■ BILL McGILVRAY McGilvray, William Alexander "Big Bill" b: 4/29/1883, Portland, Ore. d: 5/23/52, Denver, Colo. BL/TL, 6', 160 lbs. Deb: 4/17/08

| 1908 | Cin-N | 2 | 2 | 0 | 0 | 0 | 0 | 0 | 0 | 0 | | .000 | .000 | .000 | -99 | -0 | 0 | | | 1.000 | 0 | H | -0.1 |

YEAR	TM/L	G	AB	R	H	2B	3B	HR	RBI	BB	SO	AVG	OBP	SLG	PRO+	BR/A	SB	CS	SBR	FA	FR	G/POS	TPR

■ TIM McGINLEY   McGinley, Timothy S.   b: Philadelphia, Pa.   d: 11/2/1899, Oakland, Cal.   5'9.5", 155 lbs.   Deb: 4/30/1875

1875	Cen-n	13	52	5	12	0	1	0	5	0	4	.231	.231	.269	80	-1	0	0	0	.646	-7	C-12/O-2	-0.6
	NH-n	32	131	13	36	3	1	0	10	0	7	.275	.275	.313	119	3	1	1	-0	.807	-5	C-32,3-2	-0.1
	Yr	45	183	18	48	3	2	0	15	0	11	.262	.262	.301	107	2	1	1	-0	.762	-11	C-44/O-2,3-2	-0.7
1876	Bos-N	9	40	5	6	0	0	0	2	0	1	.150	.150	.150	0	-4				.600	-3	/O-6,C-3	-0.7

■ FRANK McGINN   McGinn, Frank J.   b: 1869, Cincinnati, Ohio   d: 11/19/1897, Cincinnati, Ohio   Deb: 6/9/1890

| 1890 | Pit-N | 1 | 4 | 0 | 0 | 0 | 0 | 0 | 0 | 0 | 0 | .000 | .000 | .000 | -99 | -1 | 0 | | | 1.000 | -0 | /O-1 | -0.1 |

■ RUSS McGINNIS   McGinnis, Russell Brent   b: 6/18/63, Coffeyville, Kan.   BR/TR, 6'3", 225 lbs.   Deb: 6/3/92

1992	Tex-A	14	33	2	8	4	0	0	4	3	7	.242	.306	.364	90	-0	0	0	0	1.000	-3	C-10/1-2,3-2	-0.4
1995	KC-A	3	5	1	0	0	0	0	0	1	1	.000	.167	.000	-51	-1	0	0	0	1.000	-1	/1-1,3-1,O-1	-0.2
Total	2	17	38	3	8	4	0	0	4	4	8	.211	.286	.316	69	-2	0	0	0	1.000	-4	/C-10,3-3,1-3,0-1	-0.6

■ JOHN McGLONE   McGlone, John T.   b: 1864, Brooklyn, N.Y.   d: 11/24/27, Brooklyn, N.Y.   5'10", 165 lbs.   Deb: 10/7/1886

1886	Was-N	4	15	2	1	0	0	0	1	0	3	.067	.067	.067	-63	-3	0			.846	-1	/3-4	-0.4
1887	Cle-a	21	79	14	20	2	1	0	10	7		.253	.337	.304	82	-1	15			.854	1	3-21	0.0
1888	Cle-a	55	203	22	37	1	3	1	22	16		.182	.249	.232	56	-9	26			.787	-6	3-48/O-7	-1.4
Total	3	80	297	38	58	3	4	1	33	23	3	.195	.265	.242	58	-14	41			.810	-7	/3-73,O-7	-1.8

■ ART McGOVERN   McGovern, Arthur John   b: 2/27/1882, St.John, N.B., Can.   d: 11/14/15, Thornton, R.I.   BR/TR, 5'10", 160 lbs.   Deb: 4/21/05

| 1905 | Bos-A | 15 | 44 | 1 | 5 | 1 | 0 | 0 | 1 | 4 | | .114 | .204 | .136 | 9 | -4 | 0 | | | .951 | -1 | C-15 | -0.8 |

■ BEAUTY McGOWAN   McGowan, Frank Bernard   b: 11/8/01, Branford, Conn.   d: 5/6/82, Hamden, Conn.   BL/TR, 5'11", 190 lbs.   Deb: 4/12/22

1922	Phi-A	99	300	36	69	10	5	1	29	40	46	.230	.323	.307	63	-16	6	5	-1	.965	9	O-82	-1.4
1923	Phi-A	95	287	41	73	9	1	1	19	36	25	.254	.340	.303	69	-12	4	3	-1	.971	-0	O-79	-1.7
1928	StL-A	47	168	35	61	13	4	2	18	16	15	.363	.425	.524	143	11	2	1	0	.962	-1	O-47	0.6
1929	StL-A	125	441	62	112	26	6	2	51	61	34	.254	.346	.354	78	-14	5	2	0	.975	7	*O-117	-1.4
1937	Bos-N	9	12	0	1	0	0	0	1	1	2	.083	.154	.083	-37	-2	0			1.000	-1	/O-2	-0.3
Total	5	375	1208	174	316	58	16	6	108	154	122	.262	.347	.351	80	-33	17	11		.970	13	O-327	-4.2

■ JOHN McGRAW   McGraw, John Joseph "Mugsy" or "Little Napoleon"
b: 4/7/1873, Truxton, N.Y.   d: 2/25/34, New Rochelle, N.Y.   BL/TR, 5'7", 155 lbs.   Deb: 8/26/1891   MH

1891	Bal-a	33	115	17	31	3	5	0	14	12	17	.270	.359	.383	111	2	4			.811	-15	S-21/O-9,2-3	-1.0
1892	Bal-N	79	286	41	77	13	2	1	26	32	21	.269	.355	.339	107	3	15			.897	1	O-34,2-34/S-8,3-3	0.4
1893	Bal-N	127	480	123	154	9	10	5	64	101	11	.321	.454	.412	129	27	38			.894	-23	*S-117,O-11	0.7
1894	*Bal-N	124	512	156	174	18	14	1	92	91	12	.340	.451	.436	110	13	78			.892	-2	*3-118/2-6	0.9
1895	*Bal-N	96	388	110	143	13	6	2	48	60	9	.369	.459	.448	131	21	61			.878	9	*3-95/2-1	2.6
1896	*Bal-N	23	77	20	25	2	2	0	14	11	4	.325	.422	.403	116	2	13			.833	-2	3-18/1-1	0.1
1897	*Bal-N	106	391	90	127	15	3	0	48	99		.325	**.471**	.379	126	24	44			.886	-13	*3-105	1.1
1898	Bal-N	143	515	143	176	8	10	0	53	**112**		.342	.475	.396	148	43	43			.900	-12	*3-137/O-3	3.0
1899	Bal-N	117	399	**140**	156	13	3	1	33	**124**		.391	**.547**	.446	165	50	73			.945	2	*3-117,M	4.8
1900	StL-N	99	334	84	115	10	4	2	33	85		.344	**.505**	.416	157	37	29			.909	-9	*3-99	2.5
1901	Bal-A	73	232	71	81	14	9	0	28	61		.349	.508	.487	169	28	24			.890	-20	3-69,M	0.8
1902	Bal-A	20	63	14	18	3	2	1	3	17		.286	.451	.444	143	5	5			.864	-8	3-19,M	-0.3
	NY-N	35	107	13	25	0	0	0	5	26		.234	.401	.234	97	2	7			.926	-3	S-34,M	0.2
1903	NY-N	12	11	2	3	0	0	0	1	1		.273	.467	.273	108	0	1			.000	-2	/2-2,O-2,S-1,3-1,M	-0.2
1904	NY-N	5	12	0	4	0	0	0	0	3		.333	.467	.333	142	1	1			.947	3	/2-2,S-2,M	0.4
1905	NY-N	3	0	0	0							—	—	—	—	—	0	1		.000	-0	/O-1,M	0.0
1906	NY-N	4	2	0	0	0	0	0	0	0		.000	.333	.000	4	-0	0			.000	0	/3-1,M	0.0
Total	16	1099	3924	1024	1309	121	70	13	462	836	74	.334	.466	.410	135	258	436			.898	-92	3-782,S-183/O21	16.0

■ FRED McGRIFF   McGriff, Frederick Stanley   b: 10/31/63, Tampa, Fla.   BL/TL, 6'3", 215 lbs.   Deb: 5/17/86

1986	Tor-A	3	5	1	1	0	0	0	0	0	2	.200	.200	.200	9	-1	0	0	0	1.000	-0	/1-1,D-2	-0.1
1987	Tor-A	107	295	58	73	16	0	20	43	60	104	.247	.376	.505	128	13	3	2	-0	.983	-6	D-90,1-14	0.7
1988	Tor-A	154	536	100	151	35	4	34	82	79	149	.282	.378	.552	156	40	6	1	1	**.997**	-5	*1-153	2.3
1989	*Tor-A	161	551	98	148	27	3	**36**	92	119	132	.269	.402	.525	**162**	**49**	7	4	-0	.989	5	*1-159/D-2	3.5
1990	Tor-A	153	557	91	167	21	1	35	88	94	108	.300	.403	.530	156	43	5	3	-0	.996	9	*1-147/D-6	4.1
1991	SD-N	153	528	84	147	19	1	31	106	105	135	.278	.400	.494	146	35	4	1	1	.990	-11	*1-153	1.5
1992	SD-N★	152	531	79	152	30	4	**35**	104	96	108	.286	.396	.556	164	46	8	6	-1	.991	-5	*1-151	3.5
1993	SD-N	83	302	52	83	11	1	18	46	42	55	.275	.365	.497	126	11	4	3	-1	.983	-6	1-83	-0.2
	*Atl-N	68	255	59	79	18	1	19	55	34	51	.310	.393	.612	163	22	1	0	-1	.992	-1	1-66	1.6
	Yr	151	557	111	162	29	2	37	101	76	106	.291	.378	.549	143	33	5	3	-1	.987	-7	*1-149	1.4
1994	Atl-N★	113	424	81	135	25	1	34	94	50	76	.318	.392	.623	156	34	7	3	0	.994	-5	*1-112	1.8
1995	*Atl-N★	144	528	85	148	27	1	27	93	65	99	.280	.365	.489	119	14	3	6	-3	.996	0	*1-144	-0.2
1996	*Atl-N★	159	617	81	182	37	1	28	107	68	116	.295	.367	.494	118	16	7	3	0	.992	5	*1-158	0.6
Total	11	1450	5129	869	1466	266	18	317	910	812	1135	.286	.386	.530	144	324	55	32	-3	.992	-17	*1-1341,D-100	19.1

■ TERRY McGRIFF   McGriff, Terence Roy   b: 9/23/63, Fort Pierce, Fla.   BR/TR, 6'2", 190 lbs.   Deb: 7/11/87

1987	Cin-N	34	89	6	20	3	0	2	11	8	17	.225	.289	.326	60	-5	0	0	0	.983	4	C-33	0.0
1988	Cin-N	35	96	9	19	3	0	1	4	12	31	.198	.287	.260	56	-5	1	0	0	.990	3	C-32	-0.1
1989	Cin-N	6	11	1	3	0	0	0	2	2	3	.273	.385	.273	88	-0	0	0	0	.929	1	/C-6	0.1
1990	Cin-N	2	4	0	0	0	0	0	0	0	1	.000	.000	.000	-96	-1	0	0	0	1.000	1	/C-1	0.0
	Hou-N	4	5	0	0	0	0	0	0	0	0	.000	.000	.000	-99	-1	0	0	0	.900	-0	/C-4	-0.1
	Yr	6	9	0	0	0	0	0	0	0	1	.000	.000	.000	-99	-2	0	0	0	.938	0	/C-5	-0.1
1993	Fla-N	3	7	0	0	0	0	0	0	0	1	.000	.125	.000	-60	-2	0	0	0	.000	-0	/C-3	-0.2
1994	StL-N	42	114	10	25	6	0	0	13	13	11	.219	.310	.272	55	-7	0	0	0	.991	3	C-39	-0.2
Total	6	126	326	26	67	12	0	3	30	36	65	.206	.288	.270	51	-22	1	0	0	.985	11	C-118	-0.4

■ MARK McGRILLIS   McGrillis, Mark A.   b: 10/22/1872, Philadelphia, Pa.   d: 5/16/35, Philadelphia, Pa.   Deb: 9/17/1892

| 1892 | StL-N | 1 | 3 | 0 | 0 | 0 | 0 | 0 | 0 | 0 | 1 | .000 | .000 | .000 | -99 | -1 | 0 | | | 1.000 | -0 | /3-1 | -0.1 |

■ JOE McGUCKIN   McGuckin, Joseph W.   b: 3/13/1862, Paterson, N.J.   d: 12/31/03, Yonkers, N.Y.   5'8.5", 160 lbs.   Deb: 8/27/1890

| 1890 | Bal-a | 11 | 37 | 2 | 4 | 0 | 0 | 0 | 2 | 6 | | .108 | .250 | .108 | 6 | -4 | 3 | | | .962 | 3 | O-11 | -0.1 |

■ JOHN McGUINNESS   McGuinness, John James   b: 1857, Ireland   d: 12/19/16, Binghamton, N.Y.   5'10.5", 150 lbs.   Deb: 5/6/1876

1876	NY-N	1	4	0	0	0	0	0	0	0	0	.000	.000	.000	-99	-1				.500	-2	/2-1,C-1	-0.2
1879	Syr-N	12	51	7	15	1	1	0	4	0	6	.294	.294	.353	126	-1				.928	-1	1-12	0.1
1884	Phi-U	53	220	25	52	8	1	0		5		.236	.253	.282	67	-15				.959	-0	1-48/2-5,S-1	-1.9
Total	3	66	275	32	67	9	2	0	4	5	6	.244	.257	.291	75	-15				.954	-2	/1-60,2-6,S-1,C-1	-2.0

■ JIM McGUIRE   McGuire, James A.   b: 2/4/1875, Dunkirk, N.Y.   d: 1/26/17, Buffalo, N.Y.   TR   Deb: 9/10/01

| 1901 | Cle-A | 18 | 69 | 4 | 16 | 2 | 0 | 0 | | 3 | | .232 | .232 | .261 | 38 | -6 | 0 | | | .913 | 1 | S-18 | -0.3 |

■ DEACON McGUIRE   McGuire, James Thomas   b: 11/18/1863, Youngstown, Ohio   d: 10/31/36, Duck Lake, Mich.   BR/TR, 6'1", 185 lbs.   Deb: 6/21/1884   MC

1884	Tol-a	45	151	12	28	7	0	1		5		.185	.217	.252	50	-8				.906	-8	C-41/O-4,S-3	-1.2
1885	Det-N	34	121	11	23	4	2	0	9	5	23	.190	.222	.256	54	-6				.920	14	C-31/O-3	1.0
1886	Phi-N	50	167	25	33	7	1	2	18	19	25	.198	.280	.287	72	-5	2			.899	-6	C-49/O-1	-0.5
1887	Phi-N	41	150	22	46	6	6	2	23	11	8	.307	.362	.467	122	5	4			.884	-1	C-41	0.6
1888	Phi-N	12	51	7	17	4	0	2	11	4	9	.333	.382	.490	168	4	0			.800	-5	C-10,3-2	-0.1
	Det-N	3	13	0	0	0	0	0	0	0	4	.000	.000	.000	-99	-3	0			.810	-2	/C-3	-0.5
	Yr	15	64	7	17	4	2	0	11	4	13	.266	.309	.391	117	1	0			.802	-7	C-13/3-2	-0.6

YEAR	TM/L	G	AB	R	H	2B	3B	HR	RBI	BB	SO	AVG	OBP	SLG	PRO+	BR/A	SB	CS	SBR	FA	FR	G/POS	TPR
	Cle-a	26	94	15	24	1	3	1	13	7		.255	.333	.362	126	3	2			.891	-1	C-17/1-6,O-3	0.3
1890	Roc-a	87	331	46	99	16	4	4	53	21		.299	.356	.408	135	14	8			.938	8	C-71,1-15/O-3,P-1	2.4
1891	Was-a	114	413	55	125	22	10	3	66	43	34	.303	.382	.426	137	20	10			.911	-12	*C-98,O-18/3-3,1-1	1.5
1892	Was-N	97	315	46	73	14	4	4	43	61	48	.232	.360	.340	115	8	7			.936	-1	C-89/1-8,O-1	1.2
1893	Was-N	63	237	29	61	14	3	1	26	26	12	.257	.338	.354	86	-5	3			.889	-5	C-50,1-12	-0.5
1894	Was-N	104	425	67	130	18	6	6	78	33	19	.306	.366	.419	92	-6	11			.918	-1	*C-104	0.2
1895	Was-N	132	533	89	179	30	8	10	97	40	18	.336	.388	.478	124	18	16			.936	11	*C-132/S-1	3.3
1896	Was-N	108	389	60	125	25	3	2	70	30	14	.321	.379	.416	110	5	12			.936	4	*C-98/1-1	1.3
1897	Was-N	93	327	51	112	17	7	4	53	21		.343	.386	.474	127	12	9			.947	8	C-73/1-6	2.3
1898	Was-N	131	489	59	131	18	3	1	57	24		.268	.310	.323	82	-12	10			.967	4	C-93,1-37,M	0.0
1899	Was-N	59	199	25	54	3	1	1	12	16		.271	.335	.312	79	-5	3			.973	-4	C-56/1-1	-0.5
	Bro-N	46	157	22	50	12	4	0	23	12		.318	.385	.446	125	5	4			.971	2	C-46	1.0
	Yr	105	356	47	104	15	5	1	35	28		.292	.357	.371	99	0	7			.972	-2	*C-102/1-1	0.5
1900	*Bro-N	71	241	20	69	15	2	0	34	19		.286	.348	.365	91	-3	2			.952	-6	C-69	-0.3
1901	Bro-N	85	301	28	89	16	4	0	40	18		.296	.342	.375	105	2	4			.960	-4	C-81/1-3	0.6
1902	Det-A	73	229	27	52	14	1	2	23	24		.227	.300	.323	71	-9	0			.952	-5	C-70	-0.6
1903	Det-A	72	248	15	62	12	1	0	21	19		.250	.306	.306	87	-4	3			.960	-6	C-69/1-1	-0.2
1904	NY-A	101	322	17	67	12	2	0	20	27		.208	.276	.258	66	-12	2			.970	13	C-97/1-1	1.3
1905	NY-A	72	228	9	50	7	2	0	33	18		.219	.291	.268	69	-8	3			.975	-6	C-71	-0.7
1906	NY-A	51	144	11	43	5	0	0	14	12		.299	.365	.333	108	2	3			.966	-1	C-49/1-1	0.5
1907	NY-A	1	1	0	0	0	0	0	0	0		.000	.000	.000	-93	-0	0			1.000	1	/C-1	0.0
	Bos-A	6	4	1	3	0	0	0	1	0		.750	.750	.750	620	2	0			.000	0	HM	0.2
	Yr	7	5	1	3	0	0	0	1	0		.600	.600	1.200	470	2	0			.000	0	/C-1	0.2
1908	Bos-A	1	1	0	0	0	0	0	0	0		.000	.000	.000	-97	-0	0			.000	0	HM	0.0
	Cle-A	1	4	0	1	1	0	0	2	0		.250	.250	.500	142	0	0			1.000	-0	/1-1	0.0
	Yr	2	5	0	1	1	0	0	2	0		.200	.200	.400	93	0	0			1.000	-0	/1-1	0.0
1910	Cle-A	1	3	0	1	0	0	0	0	0		.333	.500	.333	159	0	0			1.000	-1	/C-1,M	-0.1
1912	Det-A	1	2	0	1	0	0	0	0	0		.500	.500	.500	192	0	0			.714	0	/C-1	0.0
Total	26	1781	6290	770	1748	300	79	45	840	515	214	.278	.341	.372	101	14	117			.938	-16	*C-1611/1-94,O3SP	12.6

■ MICKEY McGUIRE McGuire, M C Adolphus b: 1/18/41, Dayton, Ohio BR/TR, 5'10", 170 lbs. Deb: 9/7/62

YEAR	TM/L	G	AB	R	H	2B	3B	HR	RBI	BB	SO	AVG	OBP	SLG	PRO+	BR/A	SB	CS	SBR	FA	FR	G/POS	TPR
1962	Bal-A	6	4	0	0	0	0	0	0	0		.000	.000	.000	-99	-1	0	0	0	1.000	-0	/S-5	-0.1
1967	Bal-A	10	17	2	4	0	0	0	2	0	2	.235	.235	.235	40	-1	0	0	0	1.000	-2	/2-4	-0.4
Total	2	16	21	2	4	0	0	0	2	0	2	.190	.190	.190	11	-2	0	0	0	1.000	-3	/S-5,2-4	-0.5

■ BILL McGUIRE McGuire, William Patrick b: 2/14/64, Omaha, Neb. BR/TR, 6'3", 205 lbs. Deb: 8/2/88

YEAR	TM/L	G	AB	R	H	2B	3B	HR	RBI	BB	SO	AVG	OBP	SLG	PRO+	BR/A	SB	CS	SBR	FA	FR	G/POS	TPR
1988	Sea-A	9	16	1	3	0	0	0	2	3	2	.188	.316	.188	43	-1	0	0	0	1.000	-0	/C-9	-0.1
1989	Sea-A	14	28	2	5	0	0	1	4	2	6	.179	.233	.286	44	-2	0	0	0	1.000	4	C-14	0.3
Total	2	23	44	3	8	0	0	1	6	5	8	.182	.265	.250	44	-3	0	0	0	1.000	4	/C-23	0.2

■ BILL McGUNNIGLE McGunnigle, William Henry "Gunner" b: 1/1/1855, Boston, Mass. d: 3/9/1899, Brockton, Mass. BR/TR, 5'9", 155 lbs. Deb: 5/2/1879 M

YEAR	TM/L	G	AB	R	H	2B	3B	HR	RBI	BB	SO	AVG	OBP	SLG	PRO+	BR/A	SB	CS	SBR	FA	FR	G/POS	TPR
1879	Buf-N	47	171	22	30	0	1	0	5	5	24	.175	.199	.187	27	-13				.918	1	O-34,P-14	-1.0
1880	Buf-N	7	22	0	4	0	0	0	1	0	4	.182	.182	.182	23	-2				1.000	-0	/P-5,O-3	-0.2
	Wor-N	1	4	0	0	0	0	0	0	0	2	.000	.000	.000	-92	-1				1.000	-1	/O-1	-0.2
	Yr	8	26	0	4	0	0	0	1	0	6	.154	.154	.154	5	-3				1.000	-2	/P-5,O-4	-0.4
1882	Cle-N	1	5	2	1	0	0	0	0	0	2	.200	.200	.200	30	-1				.000	-1	/O-1	-0.1
Total	3	56	202	24	35	0	1	0	6	5	31	.173	.193	.183	25	-16				.900	-1	/O-39,P-19	-1.5

■ MARK McGWIRE McGwire, Mark David b: 10/1/63, Pomona, Cal. BR/TR, 6'5", 225 lbs. Deb: 8/22/86

YEAR	TM/L	G	AB	R	H	2B	3B	HR	RBI	BB	SO	AVG	OBP	SLG	PRO+	BR/A	SB	CS	SBR	FA	FR	G/POS	TPR
1986	Oak-A	18	53	10	10	1	0	3	9	4	18	.189	.259	.377	76	-2	0	1	-1	.833	-3	3-16	-0.6
1987	Oak-A★	151	557	97	161	28	4	**49**	118	71	131	.289	.374	**.618**	168	53	1	1	-0	.992	-7	*1-145/3-8,O-3	3.3
1988	*Oak-A★	155	550	87	143	22	1	32	99	76	117	.260	.354	.478	135	26	0	0	0	.993	-8	*1-154/O-1	0.6
1989	*Oak-A★	143	490	74	113	17	0	33	95	83	94	.231	.345	.467	132	21	1	1	-0	.995	7	*1-154/D-2	1.6
1990	*Oak-A★	156	523	87	123	16	0	39	108	**110**	116	.235	.375	.489	146	35	2	1	0	.997	-5	*1-154/D-2	1.8
1991	Oak-A†	154	483	62	97	22	0	22	75	93	116	.201	.333	.383	103	4	2	1	0	.997	2	*1-152	-0.4
1992	*Oak-A★	139	467	87	125	22	0	42	104	90	105	.268	.391	**.585**	180	50	0	1	-1	.995	-10	*1-139	3.1
1993	Oak-A	27	84	16	28	6	0	9	24	21	19	.333	.472	.726	231	16	0	1	-1	1.000	-1	1-25	1.2
1994	Oak-A	47	135	26	34	3	0	9	25	37	40	.252	.413	.474	140	10	0	0	0	.988	-2	1-40/D-5	0.4
1995	Oak-A†	104	317	75	87	13	0	39	90	88	77	.274	.441	.685	150	51	1	1	-0	.986	-1	1-91,D-10	3.7
1996	Oak-A★	130	423	104	132	21	0	**52**	113	116	112	.312	**.468**	**.730**	**205**	73	0	0	0	.990	-5	*1-109,D-18	5.1
Total	11	1224	4082	725	1053	171	5	329	860	789	945	.258	.384	.544	157	336	7	8	-3	.994	-32	*1-1150/D-37,3-24,O	19.8

■ JIM McHALE McHale, James Bernard "J.B." b: 12/17/1875, Miners Mills, Pa. d: 6/17/59, Los Angeles, Cal. BR/TR, 5'11", 165 lbs. Deb: 4/14/08

YEAR	TM/L	G	AB	R	H	2B	3B	HR	RBI	BB	SO	AVG	OBP	SLG	PRO+	BR/A	SB	CS	SBR	FA	FR	G/POS	TPR
1908	Bos-A	21	67	9	15	2	0	0	7	4		.224	.278	.313	90	-1	4			.970	-2	O-19	-0.4

■ JOHN McHALE McHale, John Joseph b: 9/21/21, Detroit, Mich. BL/TR, 6', 200 lbs. Deb: 5/28/43

YEAR	TM/L	G	AB	R	H	2B	3B	HR	RBI	BB	SO	AVG	OBP	SLG	PRO+	BR/A	SB	CS	SBR	FA	FR	G/POS	TPR
1943	Det-A	4	3	0	0	0	0	0	0	1	1	.000	.250	.000	-23	-0	0	0	0	.000	0	H	0.0
1944	Det-A	1	1	0	0	0	0	0	0	0	0	.000	.000	.000	-95	-0	0	0	0	.000	0	H	0.0
1945	*Det-A	19	14	0	2	0	0	0	1	1	4	.143	.250	.143	14	-1	0	0	0	1.000	0	/1-3	-0.1
1947	Det-A	39	95	10	20	1	0	3	11	7	24	.211	.265	.316	59	-6	1	1	-0	.995	-1	1-25	-0.8
1948	Det-A	1	1	0	0	0	0	0	0	0	0	.000	.000	.000	-97	-0	0	0	0	.000	0	H	0.0
Total	5	64	114	10	22	1	0	3	12	9	29	.193	.258	.281	49	-8	1	1	-0	.995	-1	/1-28	-0.9

■ BOB McHALE McHale, Robert Emmet "Rabbit" b: 2/25/1872, Michigan Bluff, Cal. d: 6/9/52, Sacramento, Cal. Deb: 5/9/1898

YEAR	TM/L	G	AB	R	H	2B	3B	HR	RBI	BB	SO	AVG	OBP	SLG	PRO+	BR/A	SB	CS	SBR	FA	FR	G/POS	TPR
1898	Was-N	11	33	5	6	2	0	1	2	0	7	.182	.270	.242	47	-2	1			.900	-1	/O-9,S-1,1-1	-0.4

■ AUSTIN McHENRY McHenry, Austin Bush "Mac" b: 9/22/1895, Wrightsville, O. d: 11/27/22, Mount Oreb, Ohio BR/TR, 5'11", 152 lbs. Deb: 6/22/18

YEAR	TM/L	G	AB	R	H	2B	3B	HR	RBI	BB	SO	AVG	OBP	SLG	PRO+	BR/A	SB	CS	SBR	FA	FR	G/POS	TPR
1918	StL-N	80	272	32	71	12	6	1	29	21	24	.261	.319	.360	111	3	8			.952	2	O-80	0.0
1919	StL-N	110	371	41	106	19	11	1	47	19	57	.286	.322	.404	125	10	7			.985	1	*O-103	0.4
1920	StL-N	137	504	66	142	19	11	10	65	25	73	.282	.316	.423	115	7	8	11	-4	.952	-1	*O-133	-0.4
1921	StL-N	152	574	92	201	37	8	17	102	38	48	.350	.393	.531	145	36	10	20	-9	.965	7	*O-152	2.3
1922	StL-N	64	238	31	72	18	3	5	43	14	27	.303	.344	.466	112	3	2	2	-1	.935	7	O-61	0.5
Total	5	543	1959	262	592	105	39	34	286	117	229	.302	.343	.448	126	59	35	33		.960	18	O-529	2.8

■ VANCE McHENRY McHenry, Vance Loren b: 7/10/56, Chico, Cal. BR/TR, 5'9", 165 lbs. Deb: 8/13/81

YEAR	TM/L	G	AB	R	H	2B	3B	HR	RBI	BB	SO	AVG	OBP	SLG	PRO+	BR/A	SB	CS	SBR	FA	FR	G/POS	TPR
1981	Sea-A	15	18	3	4	0	0	0	2	1	1	.222	.263	.222	39	-1	0	0	0	.893	0	S-13/D-1	-0.1
1982	Sea-A	3	1	0	0	0	0	0	0	0	0	.000	.000	.000	-97	-0	0	0	0	.500	-0	/S-1,D-1	-0.1
Total	2	18	19	3	4	0	0	0	2	1	1	.211	.250	.211	32	-2	0	0	0	.867	-0	/S-14,D-2	-0.2

■ IRISH McILVEEN McIlveen, Henry Cooke b: 7/27/1880, Belfast, Ireland d: 10/18/60, Lorain, Ohio BL/TL, 5'11.5", 180 lbs. Deb: 7/10/06

YEAR	TM/L	G	AB	R	H	2B	3B	HR	RBI	BB	SO	AVG	OBP	SLG	PRO+	BR/A	SB	CS	SBR	FA	FR	G/POS	TPR
1906	Pit-N	5	5	1	2	0	0	0	0	0	0	.400	.400	.400	143	0	0			1.000	-0	/P-2	0.0
1908	NY-A	44	169	17	36	3	3	0	8	14		.213	.277	.266	76	-4	6			.949	0	O-44	-0.7
1909	NY-A	4	3	0	0	0	0	0	0	0	1	.000	.250	.000	-20	-0	0			.000	0	H	0.0
Total	3	53	177	18	38	3	3	0	8	15		.215	.280	.266	76	-4	6			.949	0	/O-44,P-2	-0.7

■ STUFFY McINNIS McInnis, John Phalen "Jack" b: 9/19/1890, Gloucester, Mass. d: 2/16/60, Ipswich, Mass. BR/TR, 5'9.5", 162 lbs. Deb: 4/12/09 M

YEAR	TM/L	G	AB	R	H	2B	3B	HR	RBI	BB	SO	AVG	OBP	SLG	PRO+	BR/A	SB	CS	SBR	FA	FR	G/POS	TPR
1909	Phi-A	19	46	4	11	0	0	1	4	2		.239	.286	.304	85	-1	0			.886	4	S-14	0.4
1910	Phi-A	38	73	10	22	2	4	0	12	7		.301	.363	.438	152	4	3			.927	-5	S-17/2-5,3-4,O-1	0.0
1911	*Phi-A	126	468	76	150	20	10	3	77	25		.321	.361	.425	121	12	23			.982	-15	1-97,S-24	-0.1
1912	Phi-A	153	568	83	186	25	13	3	101	49		.327	.384	.433	138	28	27			.984	3	*1-153	2.8
1913	*Phi-A	148	543	79	176	30	4	4	90	45	31	.324	.382	.416	137	24	16			**.992**	-2	*1-148	2.3
1914	*Phi-A	149	576	74	181	12	8	1	95	19	27	.314	.341	.368	118	10	25	19	-4	**.995**	0	*1-149	0.2

YEAR	TM/L	G	AB	R	H	2B	3B	HR	RBI	BB	SO	AVG	OBP	SLG	PRO+	BR/A	SB	CS	SBR	FA	FR	G/POS	TPR
1915	Phi-A	119	456	44	143	14	4	0	49	14	17	.314	.337	.362	113	5	8	8	-2	.989	5	*1-119	0.5
1916	Phi-A	140	512	42	151	25	3	1	60	25	19	.295	.331	.361	114	6	7			.992	7	*1-140	0.8
1917	Phi-A	150	567	50	172	19	4	0	44	33	19	.303	.342	.351	113	7	18			.993	2	*1-150	0.4
1918	*Bos-A	117	423	40	115	11	5	0	56	19	10	.272	.306	.322	91	-6	10			.992	4	1-94,3-23	-0.6
1919	Bos-A	120	440	32	134	12	5	1	58	23	11	.305	.341	.361	103	1	8			.995	3	*1-118	-0.1
1920	Bos-A	148	559	50	166	21	3	2	71	18	19	.297	.321	.356	83	-15	6	11	-5	.996	-1	*1-148	-2.4
1921	Bos-A	152	584	72	179	31	10	0	76	21	9	.307	.335	.394	88	-12	2	4	-2	.999	4	*1-152	-1.3
1922	Cle-A	142	537	58	164	28	7	1	78	15	5	.305	.325	.389	85	-13	1	5	-3	.997	-5	*1-140	-2.6
1923	Bos-N	154	607	70	191	23	9	2	95	26	12	.315	.343	.392	97	-3	7	8	-3	.991	4	*1-154	-1.0
1924	Bos-N	146	581	57	169	23	7	1	59	15	6	.291	.311	.360	83	-15	9	3	1	.994	7	*1-146	-1.7
1925	*Pit-N	59	155	19	57	10	4	0	24	17	1	.368	.437	.484	126	7	1	1	-0	.993	1	1-46	0.5
1926	Pit-N	47	127	12	38	6	1	0	13	7	3	.299	.336	.362	83	-3	1			.988	-1	1-40	-0.6
1927	Phi-N	1	0	0	0	0	0	0	0	0	0	—	—	—		0	0			1.000	-0	/1-1,M	0.0
Total	19	2128	7822	872	2405	312	101	20	1062	380	189	.307	.343	.381	106	35	172	59		.993	17	*1-1995/S-55,32O	-2.5

■ TIM McINTOSH

McIntosh, Timothy Allen b: 3/21/65, Minneapolis, Minn. BR/TR, 5'11", 195 lbs. Deb: 9/3/90

YEAR	TM/L	G	AB	R	H	2B	3B	HR	RBI	BB	SO	AVG	OBP	SLG	PRO+	BR/A	SB	CS	SBR	FA	FR	G/POS	TPR
1990	Mil-A	5	5	1	1	0	0	1	1	0	2	.200	.200	.800	168	0	0	0	0	.875	-0	/C-4	0.0
1991	Mil-A	7	11	2	4	1	0	1	1	0	4	.364	.364	.727	199	1	0	0	0	.000	-2	/O-4,1-1,D-2	0.0
1992	Mil-A	35	77	7	14	3	0	0	6	3	9	.182	.232	.221	28	-7	1	3	-2	.983	1	C-14,O-10/1-7,D-3	-0.8
1993	Mil-A	1	0	0	0	0	0	0	0	0	0	—	—	—		0	0			.000	-0	/C-1	0.0
	Mon-N	20	21	2	2	1	0	0	2	0	7	.095	.095	.143	-36	-4	0	0	0	1.000	-3	/O-7,C-5	-0.7
1996	NY-A	3	3	0	0	0	0	0	0	0	0	.000	.000	.000	-98	-1	0	0	0	.000	-0	/C-1,1-1,3-1	-0.1
Total	5	71	117	12	21	5	0	2	10	3	22	.179	.213	.274	34	-11	1	3	-2	.973	-4	/C-25,O-21,1-9,D3	-1.6

■ MATTY McINTYRE

McIntyre, Matthew W. b: 6/12/1880, Stonington, Conn. d: 4/2/20, Detroit, Mich. BL/TL, 5'11", 175 lbs. Deb: 7/3/01

YEAR	TM/L	G	AB	R	H	2B	3B	HR	RBI	BB	SO	AVG	OBP	SLG	PRO+	BR/A	SB	CS	SBR	FA	FR	G/POS	TPR
1901	Phi-A	82	308	38	85	12	4	0	46	30		.276	.346	.341	87	-5	11			.921	-3	O-82	-1.2
1904	Det-A	152	578	74	146	11	10	2	46	44		.253	.310	.317	101	1	11			.959	12	*O-152	0.5
1905	Det-A	131	495	59	130	21	5	0	30	48		.263	.330	.325	107	5	9			.968	17	*O-131	1.7
1906	Det-A	133	493	63	128	19	11	0	39	56		.260	.338	.343	110	7	29			.982	5	*O-133	1.4
1907	Det-A	20	81	6	23	1	1	0	9	7		.284	.341	.321	107	1	3			1.000	3	O-20	0.3
1908	*Det-A	151	569	105	168	24	13	0	28	83		.295	.392	.383	146	32	20			.977	16	*O-151	4.7
1909	*Det-A	125	476	65	116	18	9	1	34	54		.244	.325	.326	101	1	13			.975	-0	*O-122	-0.4
1910	Det-A	83	305	40	72	15	5	0	25	39		.236	.323	.318	94	-2	4			.946	4	O-77	-0.2
1911	Chi-A	146	569	102	184	19	11	1	52	64		.323	.397	.401	127	22	17			.948	-2	*O-146	1.2
1912	Chi-A	49	84	10	14	0	0	0	10	14		.167	.300	.167	36	-6	3			1.000	-1	O-25	-0.8
Total	10	1072	3958	562	1066	140	69	4	319	439		.269	.346	.343	110	57	120			.964	56	*O-1039	7.2

■ OTTO McIVOR

McIvor, Edward Otto b: 7/26/1884, Greenville, Tex. d: 5/4/54, Dallas, Tex. BB/TL, 5'11.5", 175 lbs. Deb: 4/18/11

YEAR	TM/L	G	AB	R	H	2B	3B	HR	RBI	BB	SO	AVG	OBP	SLG	PRO+	BR/A	SB	CS	SBR	FA	FR	G/POS	TPR
1911	StL-N	30	62	11	14	2	1	1	9	14		.226	.333	.339	91	-1	0			.926	-3	O-17	-0.5

■ DAVE McKAY

McKay, David Lawrence b: 3/14/50, Vancouver, B.C., Can BB/TR, 6'1", 195 lbs. Deb: 8/22/75 C

YEAR	TM/L	G	AB	R	H	2B	3B	HR	RBI	BB	SO	AVG	OBP	SLG	PRO+	BR/A	SB	CS	SBR	FA	FR	G/POS	TPR
1975	Min-A	33	125	8	32	4	1	2	16	6	14	.256	.295	.352	81	-3	1	1	-0	.923	2	3-33	-0.2
1976	Min-A	45	138	8	28	2	0	0	8	9	27	.203	.272	.217	43	-9	1	2	-1	.911	-1	3-41/S-2,D-1	-1.3
1977	Tor-A	95	274	18	54	4	3	3	22	7	51	.197	.223	.266	32	-26	2	1	0	.968	7	2-40,3-32,S-20,D-2	-1.6
1978	Tor-A	145	504	59	120	20	8	7	45	20	91	.238	.269	.351	71	-20	4	4	-1	.984	-7	*2-140/S-3,3-2,D-1	-1.8
1979	Tor-A	47	156	19	34	9	0	0	12	7	19	.218	.256	.276	43	-12	1	1	-0	.974	6	2-46/3-2	-0.3
1980	Oak-A	123	295	29	72	16	1	1	29	10	57	.244	.283	.315	60	-13	1	1	-0	.977	-6	2-62,3-54,S-10	-1.6
1981	*Oak-A	79	224	25	59	11	1	4	21	16	43	.263	.318	.375	104	1	4	1	1	.926	-4	3-43,2-38/S-7	-0.1
1982	Oak-A	78	212	25	42	4	1	4	17	11	35	.198	.238	.283	44	-17	6	1	1	.968	-3	2-59,3-16/S-3	-1.7
Total	8	645	1928	191	441	70	15	21	170	86	337	.229	.268	.313	62	-100	20	12	-1	.976	-6	2-385,3-223/S-45,D	-8.6

■ ED McKEAN

McKean, Edwin John "Mack" b: 6/6/1864, Grafton, Ohio d: 8/16/19, Cleveland, Ohio BR/TR, 5'9", 160 lbs. Deb: 4/16/1887

YEAR	TM/L	G	AB	R	H	2B	3B	HR	RBI	BB	SO	AVG	OBP	SLG	PRO+	BR/A	SB	CS	SBR	FA	FR	G/POS	TPR
1887	Cle-a	132	539	97	154	16	13	2	54	60		.286	.358	.375	108	-7	76			.847	-8	*S-123/2-8,O-4	0.1
1888	Cle-a	131	548	94	164	21	15	6	68	28		.299	.340	.425	149	28	52			.909	3	S-78,O-48/2-9,3-1	3.0
1889	Cle-N	123	500	88	159	22	8	4	75	42	25	.318	.375	.418	124	16	35			.907	6	*S-122/2-1	2.5
1890	Cle-N	136	530	95	157	15	14	7	61	87	25	.296	.401	.418	141	31	23			.903	-18	*S-134/2-3	1.9
1891	Cle-N	141	603	115	170	13	12	6	69	64	19	.282	.352	.373	107	4	14			.887	-12	*S-141	0.1
1892	*Cle-N	129	531	76	139	14	10	5	93	49	28	.262	.325	.326	93	-5	19			.862	-45	*S-129	-4.1
1893	Cle-N	125	545	103	169	29	24	4	133	50	12	.310	.372	.473	111	9	16			.902	-4	*S-125	1.0
1894	Cle-N	130	554	116	198	30	15	8	128	49	12	.357	.412	.509	116	13	33			.905	-21	*S-130	0.0
1895	*Cle-N	131	565	131	193	32	17	8	119	45	25	.342	.397	.501	123	17	12			.909	-19	*S-131	0.3
1896	*Cle-N	131	571	100	193	29	12	7	112	45	13	.338	.388	.468	118	13	13			.915	-33	*S-133	-1.3
1897	Cle-N	125	523	83	143	21	14	2	78	40		.273	.330	.379	82	-15	15			.920	-30	*S-125	-3.6
1898	Cle-N	151	604	89	172	23	1	9	94	56		.285	.346	.371	107	5	11			.932	-36	*S-151	-2.2
1899	StL-N	67	277	40	72	7	3	4	33	20		.260	.310	.339	76	-10	4			.886	-17	S-42,1-15,2-10	-2.1
Total	13	1654	6890	1227	2083	272	158	66	1124	635	157	.302	.364	.416	114	115	323			.900	-233	*S-1564/O-52,213	-4.4

■ BILL McKECHNIE

McKechnie, William Boyd "Deacon" b: 8/7/1886, Wilkinsburg, Pa. d: 10/29/65, Bradenton, Fla. BB/TR, 5'10", 160 lbs. Deb: 9/8/07 MCH

YEAR	TM/L	G	AB	R	H	2B	3B	HR	RBI	BB	SO	AVG	OBP	SLG	PRO+	BR/A	SB	CS	SBR	FA	FR	G/POS	TPR
1907	Pit-N	3	8	0	1	0	0	0	0	0	1	.125	.125	.125	-21	-1				1.000	-1	/3-2,2-1	-0.2
1910	Pit-N	71	212	23	46	1	2	0	12	11	23	.217	.256	.241	42	-16	4			.971	8	2-36,S-14/3-8,1-4	-0.8
1911	Pit-N	104	321	40	73	8	7	2	37	28	18	.227	.293	.315	68	-15	9			.975	-0	1-57,2-17,S-12/3-6	-1.5
1912	Pit-N	24	73	8	18	0	1	0	4	5	2	.247	.286	.274	54	-5	2			.978	2	3-13/S-4,2-3,1-2	-0.3
1913	Bos-N	1	4	1	0	0	0	0	0	0	1	.000	.200	.000	-39	-1				1.000	0	/O-1	-0.1
	NY-A	45	112	7	15	0	0	0	8	8	17	.134	.198	.134	-2	-14	2			.950	5	2-28/S-7,3-2	-1.0
1914	Ind-F	149	570	107	173	24	6	2	38	53	36	.304	.368	.377	93	-12	47			.939	23	*3-149	1.6
1915	New-F	127	461	49	113	22	5	1	43	41	31	.251	.316	.328	86	-16	28			.956	2	*3-117/O-1,M	-1.0
1916	NY-N	71	260	22	64	9	1	0	17	7	20	.246	.269	.288	75	-8	7			.940	-3	3-71	-1.1
	Cin-N	37	130	4	36	3	0	0	10	3	12	.277	.293	.300	84	-3	4			.960	-4	3-35	-0.7
	Yr	108	390	26	100	12	1	0	27	10	32	.256	.277	.292	78	-11	11			.947	-8	*3-106	-1.8
1917	Cin-N	48	134	11	34	3	1	0	15	7	7	.254	.296	.291	84	-3	5			.943	-7	2-26,S-13/3-4	-0.9
1918	Pit-N	126	435	34	111	13	9	2	43	24	22	.255	.297	.340	91	-5	12			.966	-6	*3-126	-0.4
1920	Pit-N	40	133	13	29	3	1	1	13	4	7	.218	.241	.278	47	-9	7	4	-0	.943	-1	3-20,S-10/2-6,1-1	-1.0
Total	11	846	2843	319	713	86	33	8	240	190	199	.251	.301	.313	76	-108	127	4		.952	-29	3-553,2-117/1SO	-7.4

■ FRANK McKEE

McKee, Frank b: Philadelphia, Pa. Deb: 6/11/1884

YEAR	TM/L	G	AB	R	H	2B	3B	HR	RBI	BB	SO	AVG	OBP	SLG	PRO+	BR/A	SB	CS	SBR	FA	FR	G/POS	TPR
1884	Was-U	4	17	2	3	0	0	0		1		.176	.222	.176	23	-2				.200	-2	/O-3,3-2,C-1	-0.3

■ RED McKEE

McKee, Raymond Ellis b: 7/20/1890, Shawnee, Ohio d: 8/5/72, Saginaw, Mich. BL/TR, 5'11", 180 lbs. Deb: 4/19/13

YEAR	TM/L	G	AB	R	H	2B	3B	HR	RBI	BB	SO	AVG	OBP	SLG	PRO+	BR/A	SB	CS	SBR	FA	FR	G/POS	TPR
1913	Det-A	68	187	18	53	3	4	1	20	21	21	.283	.359	.358	112	3	7			.950	-5	C-62	0.4
1914	Det-A	34	64	7	12	1	0	0	8	14	16	.188	.342	.234	71	-2	1	2	-1	.964	-6	C-27	-0.7
1915	Det-A	55	106	10	29	5	0	1	17	13	16	.274	.353	.349	105	1	1			.954	-6	C-35	-0.3
1916	Det-A	32	76	3	16	1	0	0	4	6	11	.211	.268	.276	61	-4	0			.955	-5	C-26	-0.7
Total	4	189	433	38	110	10	7	2	49	54	64	.254	.339	.323	95	-1	9	2		.954	-22	C-150	-1.3

■ WALT McKEEL

McKeel, Walt Thomas b: 1/17/72, Wilson, N.C. BR/TR, 6'2", 200 lbs. Deb: 9/14/96

YEAR	TM/L	G	AB	R	H	2B	3B	HR	RBI	BB	SO	AVG	OBP	SLG	PRO+	BR/A	SB	CS	SBR	FA	FR	G/POS	TPR
1996	Bos-A	1	0	0	0	0	0	0	0	0	0	—	—	—		0	0	0	0	.000	0	/C-1	0.0

■ JIM McKEEVER

McKeever, James b: 4/19/1861, St.John, N.B., Can. d: 8/19/1897, Boston, Mass. 5'10", 170 lbs. Deb: 4/17/1884

YEAR	TM/L	G	AB	R	H	2B	3B	HR	RBI	BB	SO	AVG	OBP	SLG	PRO+	BR/A	SB	CS	SBR	FA	FR	G/POS	TPR
1884	Bos-U	16	66	13	9	0	0	0		6		.136	.136	.136	-17	-11				.869	-6	C-12/O-4	-1.4

■ JOHN McKELVEY

McKelvey, John Wellington b: 8/27/1847, Rochester, N.Y. d: 5/31/44, Rochester, N.Y. BR/TR, 5'7.5", 175 lbs. Deb: 4/21/1875

YEAR	TM/L	G	AB	R	H	2B	3B	HR	RBI	BB	SO	AVG	OBP	SLG	PRO+	BR/A	SB	CS	SBR	FA	FR	G/POS	TPR
1875	NH-n	43	188	26	43	3	1	0	10	5	8	.229	.249	.255	86	-1	3	1	0	.656	-8	O-39/3-5	-0.7

YEAR	TM/L	G	AB	R	H	2B	3B	HR	RBI	BB	SO	AVG	OBP	SLG	PRO+	BR/A	SB	CS	SBR	FA	FR	G/POS	TPR

■ RUSS McKELVY McKelvy, Russell Errett b: 9/8/1854, Swissvale, Pa. d: 10/19/15, Omaha, Neb. BR/TR, Deb: 5/1/1878

1878	Ind-N	63	253	33	57	4	3	2	36	5	38	.225	.240	.289	84	-4				.846	6	*O-62/P-4	-0.1
1882	Pit-a	1	4	0	0	0	0	0		0	0	.000	.000	.000	-99	-1				.000	-0	/O-1	-0.1
Total	2	64	257	33	57	4	3	2	36	5	38	.222	.237	.284	81	-4				.846	5	/O-63,P-4	-0.2

■ ED McKENNA McKenna, Edward J. b: St.Louis, Mo. Deb: 7/29/1874

1874	Phi-n	1	4	0	0	0	0	0		0	1	.000	.000	.000	-97	-1	0	0	0	1.000	0	/1-1	-0.1
1877	StL-N	1	5	0	1	0	0	0		0	1	.200	.200	.200	28	-0				1.000	0	/O-1	-0.1
1884	Was-U	32	117	19	22	1	0	0		4		.188	.215	.197	26	-14				.876	-14	C-23,O-10/3-7	-2.3
Total	2	33	122	19	23	1	0	0		4	1	.189	.214	.197	26	-14				.556	-14	/C-23,O-11,3-7	-2.4

■ DAVE McKEOUGH McKeough, David J. b: 12/1/1863, Utica, N.Y. d: 7/11/01, Utica, N.Y. 5'7", 158 lbs. Deb: 4/22/1890

1890	Roc-a	62	218	38	49	5	0	0	20	29		.225	.316	.248	72	-6	14			.929	-4	C-47,S-13/2-2,3-1	-0.5
1891	Phi-a	15	54	4	14	1	1	0	3	8	6	.259	.355	.315	89	-1				.854	-4	C-14/S-1	-0.3
Total	2	77	272	42	63	6	1	0	23	37	6	.232	.324	.261	75	-7	14			.912	-9	/C-61,S-14,2-2,3-1	-0.8

■ RICH McKINNEY McKinney, Charles Richard b: 11/22/46, Piqua, Ohio BR/TR, 5'11", 185 lbs. Deb: 6/26/70

1970	Chi-A	43	119	12	20	5	0	4	17	11	25	.168	.244	.311	50	-8	3	2	-0	.931	9	3-23,S-11	-0.6
1971	Chi-A	114	369	35	100	11	2	8	46	35	37	.271	.337	.377	99	-0	0	0	0	.968	-3	2-67,O-25/3-5	-0.6
1972	NY-A	37	121	10	26	2	0	1	7	7	13	.215	.258	.256	55	-7	1	0	0	.917	-3	3-33	-1.1
1973	Oak-A	48	65	9	16	3	0	1	7	7	4	.246	.319	.338	90	-1	0	0	0	.900	-1	3-17/2-7,O-3,D-6	-0.1
1974	Oak-A	5	7	0	1	0	0	0	0	0	0	.143	.143	.143	-19	-1	0	0	0	1.000	-2	/2-3	-0.4
1975	Oak-A	8	7	0	1	0	0	0	2	1	2	.143	.250	.143	14	-1	0	0	0	1.000	-1	/1-1,D-2	-0.1
1977	Oak-A	86	198	13	35	7	0	6	21	16	43	.177	.238	.303	47	-15	0	1	-1	.978	-4	1-32,D-18/3-7,O2	-2.2
Total	7	341	886	79	199	28	2	20	100	77	124	.225	.289	.328	73	-33	4	3	-1	.911	-17	/3-85,2-80,1ODS	-5.1

■ BOB McKINNEY McKinney, Robert Francis b: 10/4/1875, McSherrystown, Pa. d: 8/19/46, Hanover, Pa. BR/TR, 5'7", 165 lbs. Deb: 7/23/01

1901	Phi-A	2	2	0	0	0	0	0		0		.000	.000	.000	-96	-1						/2-1,3-1	-0.2

■ ALEX McKINNON McKinnon, Alexander J. b: 8/14/1856, Boston, Mass. d: 7/24/1887, Charlestown, Mass BR , 5'11.5", 170 lbs. Deb: 5/1/1884 M

1884	NY-N	116	470	66	128	21	12	4	73	8	62	.272	.285	.394	108	3				.955	-2	*1-116	-1.1
1885	StL-N	100	411	42	121	21	6	1	44	8	31	.294	.308	.382	130	13				**.978**	-2	*1-100,M	-0.1
1886	StL-N	122	491	75	148	24	7	8	72	21	23	.301	.330	.428	138	21	10			.963	-6	*1-119/O-3	0.1
1887	Pit-N	48	200	26	68	16	4	1	30	8	9	.340	.365	.475	140	10	6			.977	-1	1-48	0.7
Total	4	386	1572	209	465	82	29	14	219	45	125	.296	.315	.412	127	48	16			.967	-7	1-383/O-3	-0.4

■ JIM McKNIGHT McKnight, James Arthur b: 6/1/36, Bee Branch, Ark. d: 2/24/94, Van Buren County, Ark. BR/TR, 6'1", 185 lbs. Deb: 9/22/60 F

1960	Chi-N	3	6	0	2	0	0	0	1	0	1	.333	.333	.333	84	-0	0	0	0	.667	-2	/2-1,O-1	-0.2
1962	Chi-N	60	85	6	19	0	1	0	5	2	13	.224	.241	.247	30	-8	0	0	0	.955	3	/3-9,O-5,2-2	-0.6
Total	2	63	91	6	21	0	1	0	6	2	14	.231	.247	.253	34	-8	0	0	0	.875	1	/3-9,O-6,2-3	-0.8

■ JEFF McKNIGHT McKnight, Jefferson Alan b: 2/18/63, Conway, Ark. BB/TR, 6', 170 lbs. Deb: 6/6/89 F

1989	NY-N	6	12	2	3	0	0	0	0	2	3	.250	.357	.250	80	-0	0	0	0	1.000	-3	/2-4,1-1,3-1,S-1	-0.3
1990	Bal-A	29	75	11	15	2	0	1	4	5	17	.200	.259	.267	49	-5	0	0	0	1.000	-3	1-15/O-8,2-5,S-1,D	-0.9
1991	Bal-A	16	41	2	7	1	0	0	2	2	7	.171	.209	.195	13	-5	1	0	0	1.000	-0	/O-7,1-2,D-4	-0.5
1992	NY-N	31	85	10	23	3	1	2	13	2	8	.271	.287	.400	94	-1	0	1	-1	.980	-3	2-14/1-9,3-3,S-3,O	-0.5
1993	NY-N	105	164	19	42	3	1	2	13	13	31	.256	.315	.323	72	-6	0	0	0	.943	-7	S-29,2-15,1-10,/3C	-1.2
1994	NY-N	31	27	1	4	1	0	0	2	4	12	.148	.258	.185	18	-3	0	0	0	1.000	-0	/1-2	-0.3
Total	6	218	404	45	94	10	2	5	34	28	76	.233	.286	.304	63	-21	1	1	-0	.996	-16	/1-39,2-38,SO3DC	-3.7

■ ED McLANE McLane, Edward Cameron b: 8/20/1881, Weston, Mass. d: 8/21/75, Baltimore, Md. 5'10", 179 lbs. Deb: 10/6/07

1907	Bro-N	1	2	0	0	0	0	0	0	0		.000	.333	.000	5	-0				.333	-1	/O-1	-0.1

■ ART McLARNEY McLarney, Arthur James b: 12/20/08, Ft.Worden, Wash. d: 12/20/84, Seattle, Wash. BB/TR, 6', 168 lbs. Deb: 8/23/32

1932	NY-N	9	23	2	3	1	0	0	3	1	3	.130	.167	.174	-8	-4	0			1.000	-1	/S-7	-0.4

■ POLLY McLARRY McLarry, Howard Zell b: 3/25/1891, Leonard, Tex. d: 11/4/71, Bonham, Tex. BL/TR, 6', 185 lbs. Deb: 9/2/12

1912	Chi-A	2	2	0	0	0	0	0	0	0		.000	.000	.000	-99	-1	0			.000	0	H	-0.1
1915	Chi-N	68	127	16	25	3	0	1	12	14	20	.197	.277	.244	56	-6	2	2	-1	.957	3	2-21,1-18	-0.4
Total	2	70	129	16	25	3	0	1	12	14	20	.194	.273	.240	56	-7	2	2		.957	3	/2-21,1-18	-0.5

■ BARNEY McLAUGHLIN McLaughlin, Bernard b: 1857, Ireland d: 2/13/21, Lowell, Mass. BR/TR, Deb: 8/2/1884 F

1884	KC-U	42	162	15	37	7	3	0		9		.228	.269	.309	86	-8				.762	-4	O-24,2-12/P-7,S-2	-1.0
1887	Phi-N	50	205	26	45	8	3	1	26	11	27	.220	.263	.302	53	-13	2			.879	-11	2-50	-2.0
1890	Syr-a	86	329	43	87	8	1	2	40	47		.264	.360	.313	110	7	13			.902	-12	S-86	0.0
Total	3	178	696	84	169	23	7	3	66	67	27	.243	.312	.309	86	-14	15			.900	-27	/S-88,2-62,O-24,P-7	-3.0

■ FRANK McLAUGHLIN McLaughlin, Francis Edward b: 6/19/1856, Lowell, Mass. d: 4/5/17, Lowell, Mass. BR/TR, 5'9", 160 lbs. Deb: 8/9/1882 F

1882	Wor-N	15	55	7	12	0	2	1	4	0	11	.218	.218	.345	76	-2				.760	-3	S-14/O-1	-0.4
1883	Pit-a	29	114	15	25	2	0	1		6		.219	.258	.263	72	-3				.802	-1	S-25/O-4,2-2,P-2	-0.3
1884	Cin-U	16	67	10	16	4	1	2		2		.239	.261	.418	95	-3				.740	-7	S-16	-0.8
	CP-U	15	67	11	16	4	1	0		1		.239	.250	.328	74	-4				.888	5	2-14/S-1,O-1	0.2
	KC-U	32	123	17	28	11	0	1		9		.228	.280	.341	101	-4				.847	-9	2-10,O-10/3-9,SP	-1.1
	Yr	63	257	38	60	19	2	3		12		.233	.268	.358	92	-10				.873	-10	2-24,S-22,O-11,/3P	-1.7
Total	3	107	426	60	97	21	4	5	4	18	11	.228	.259	.331	85	-15				.769	-15	/S-61,2-26,O-16,3P	-2.4

■ JAMES McLAUGHLIN McLaughlin, James b: San Francisco, Cal. Deb: 5/3/1884

1884	Was-U	10	37	3	7	3	0	0				.189	.189	.270	39	-4				.696	-3	/S-9,3-1	-0.6

■ KID McLAUGHLIN McLaughlin, James Anson "Sunshine" b: 4/12/1888, Randolph, N.Y. d: 11/13/34, Allegany, N.Y. BL/TR, 5'8.5", 158 lbs. Deb: 6/30/14

1914	Cin-N	3	2	1	0	0	0	0	0	0	0	.000	.000	.000	-97	-0	0			1.000	-1	/O-2	-0.1

■ JIM McLAUGHLIN McLaughlin, James Robert b: 1/3/02, St.Louis, Mo. d: 12/18/68, Mount Vernon, Ill. BR/TR, 5'8.5", 168 lbs. Deb: 4/18/32

1932	StL-A	1	1	0	0	0	0	0	0	0	0	.000	.000	.000	-95	-0				.000	-0	/3-1	0.0

■ TOM McLAUGHLIN McLaughlin, Thomas b: 3/28/1860, Louisville, Ky. d: 7/21/21, Louisville, Ky. TR , Deb: 7/17/1883

1883	Lou-a	42	146	16	28	1	2	0		5		.192	.219	.226	47	-8				.844	4	S-19,O-17/1-5,32	-0.4
1884	Lou-a	98	335	41	67	11	6	0	21	22		.200	.262	.269	77	-7				.892	19	*S-94/3-4,2-1	1.1
1885	Lou-a	112	411	49	87	13	9	2	41	15		.212	.245	.302	72	-13				.883	1	*2-93,S-19	-0.8
1886	NY-a	74	250	27	34	3	1	0	16	26		.136	.220	.156	19	-22	13			.886	7	S-63,2-10/O-1	-1.2
1891	Was-a	14	41	9	11	0	1	0	3	7	6	.268	.400	.317	111	1	3			.871	-0	S-14	0.2
Total	5	340	1183	142	227	28	19	2	81	75	6	.192	.247	.253	61	-49	16			.886	30	S-209,2-106/O31	-1.1

■ RALPH McLAURIN McLaurin, Ralph Edgar b: 5/23/1885, Kissimmee, Fla. d: 2/11/43, McColl, S.C. Deb: 9/5/08

1908	StL-N	8	22	2	5	0	0	0		0		.227	.227	.227	47	-1	0			.875	-0	/O-6	-0.2

■ LARRY McLEAN McLean, John Bannerman b: 7/18/1881, Fredericton, N.B., Canada d: 3/24/21, Boston, Mass. BR/TR, 6'5", 228 lbs. Deb: 4/26/01

1901	Bos-A	9	19	4	4	1	0	0	2	0		.211	.211	.263	31	-2	1			1.000	0	/1-5	-0.1
1903	Chi-N	1	4	0	0	0	0	0	0	0	1	.000	.200	.000	-42	-1	0			.889	-0	/C-1	-0.1
1904	StL-N	27	84	5	14	2	0	0	4	4		.167	.205	.214	31	-7	1			.954	-2	C-24	-0.7
1906	Cin-N	12	35	3	7	2	0	0	2	4		.200	.282	.257	65	-1	0			.954	-1	C-12	-0.2
1907	Cin-N	113	374	35	108	9	9	0	54	13		.289	.313	.361	107	-3	4			.975	-5	C-89,1-13	0.7
1908	Cin-N	99	309	24	67	9	4	1	28	15		.217	.258	.282	74	-10	2			.963	-6	C-69,1-19	-1.1

YEAR	TM/L	G	AB	R	H	2B	3B	HR	RBI	BB	SO	AVG	OBP	SLG	PRO+	BR/A	SB	CS	SBR	FA	FR	G/POS	TPR
1909	Cin-N	95	324	26	83	12	2	2	36	21		.256	.307	.324	97	-2	1			.978	-6	C-95	0.1
1910	Cin-N	127	423	27	126	14	7	2	71	26	23	.298	.340	.378	114	6	4			.983	-4	*C-119	1.4
1911	Cin-N	107	328	24	94	7	2	0	34	20	18	.287	.330	.320	85	-7	1			.968	8	C-98	1.0
1912	Cin-N	102	333	17	81	15	1	1	27	18	15	.243	.284	.303	63	-18	1			.973	-2	C-98	-1.0
1913	StL-N	48	152	7	41	9	0	0	12	6	9	.270	.297	.329	80	-4				.981	-8	C-42	-0.9
	*NY-N	30	75	3	24	4	0	0	9	4	4	.320	.354	.373	107	1	1			.953	-4	C-28	-0.1
	Yr	78	227	10	65	13	0	0	21	10	13	.286	.316	.344	89	-4	1			.970	-12	C-70	-1.0
1914	NY-N	79	154	8	40	6	0	0	14	4	9	.260	.283	.299	76	-5	4			.973	-4	C-74	-0.5
1915	NY-N	13	33	0	5	0	0	0	4	0	1	.152	.152	.152	-9	-4				.985	2	C-12	-0.2
Total	13	862	2647	183	694	90	26	6	298	136	79	.262	.301	.323	86	-53	20			.973	-29	C-761/1-37	-1.7

■ MARK McLEMORE

McLemore, Mark Tremell b: 10/4/64, San Diego, Cal. BB/TR, 5'11", 195 lbs. Deb: 9/13/86

YEAR	TM/L	G	AB	R	H	2B	3B	HR	RBI	BB	SO	AVG	OBP	SLG	PRO+	BR/A	SB	CS	SBR	FA	FR	G/POS	TPR
1986	Cal-A	5	4	0	0	0	0	0	0	1	2	.000	.200	.000	-40	-1	0		-1	1.000	4	/2-2	0.2
1987	Cal-A	138	433	61	102	13	3	3	41	48	72	.236	.312	.300	66	-20	25	8	3	.974	-5	*2-132/S-6,D-3	-1.6
1988	Cal-A	77	233	38	56	11	2	2	16	25	28	.240	.314	.330	83	-5	13	7	-0	.979	7	2-63/3-5,D-1	0.4
1989	Cal-A	32	103	12	25	3	1	0	14	7	19	.243	.297	.291	68	-4	6	1	1	.966	3	2-27/D-1	0.0
1990	Cal-A	20	48	4	7	2	0	0	2	4	9	.146	.212	.188	13	-6	1	0	1	1.000		/2-8,S-8,D-1	-0.6
	Cle-A	8	12	2	2	0	0	0	0	0	6	.167	.167	.167	-7	-2	0	0	0	1.000	3	/3-4,2-3,D-1	0.1
	Yr	28	60	6	9	2	0	0	2	4	15	.150	.203	.183	9	-7	1	0	1	1.000	2	2-11/S-8,3-4,D-2	-0.5
1991	Hou-N	21	61	6	9	1	0	0	2	6	13	.148	.224	.164	11	-7	0	1	-1	.975	1	2-19	-0.7
1992	Bal-A	101	228	40	56	7	2	0	27	21	26	.246	.309	.294	68	-9	11	5	0	.978	9	2-70,D-17	0.0
1993	Bal-A	148	581	81	165	27	5	4	72	64	92	.284	.356	.368	91	-6	21	15	-3	.987	12	*O-124,2-25/3-4,D-1	-0.1
1994	Bal-A	104	343	44	88	11	1	3	29	51	50	.257	.354	.321	72	-13	20	5	3	.981	-9	2-96/O-7,D-1	-0.8
1995	Tex-A	129	467	73	122	20	5	5	41	59	71	.261	.348	.358	82	-11	21	11	-0	.986	-1	O-73,2-66/D-2	-1.0
1996	*Tex-A	147	517	84	150	23	4	5	46	87	69	.290	.392	.379	90	-5	27	10	2	.985	20	*2-147/O-1	2.4
Total	11	930	3030	445	782	118	23	22	290	373	457	.258	.341	.334	78	-89	145	64	5	.981	48	2-658,O-205/DS3	-1.5

■ RALPH McLEOD

McLeod, Ralph Alton b: 10/19/16, N.Quincy, Mass. BL/TL, 6', 170 lbs. Deb: 9/14/38

YEAR	TM/L	G	AB	R	H	2B	3B	HR	RBI	BB	SO	AVG	OBP	SLG	PRO+	BR/A	SB	CS	SBR	FA	FR	G/POS	TPR
1938	Bos-N	6	7	1	2	1	0	0	0	2		.286	.286	.429	105	-0	0			1.000	-0	/O-1	0.0

■ JIM McLEOD

McLeod, Soule James b: 9/12/08, Jones, La. d: 8/3/81, Little Rock, Ark. BR/TR, 6', 187 lbs. Deb: 5/22/30

YEAR	TM/L	G	AB	R	H	2B	3B	HR	RBI	BB	SO	AVG	OBP	SLG	PRO+	BR/A	SB	CS	SBR	FA	FR	G/POS	TPR
1930	Was-A	18	34	3	9	1	0	0	1	1	5	.265	.306	.294	53	-2	1		-0	1.000	-1	3-10/S-7	-0.2
1932	Was-A	7	0	1	0	0	0	0	0	1	0	—	1.000	—	183	-0	0	0	0	1.000	0	/S-1	0.1
1933	Phi-N	67	232	20	45	6	1	0	15	12	25	.194	.237	.228	30	-21	1			.914	-6	3-67/S-1	-2.5
Total	3	92	266	24	54	7	1	0	16	14	30	.203	.248	.237	33	-23	2	1		.922	-6	/3-77,S-9	-2.6

■ JACK McMAHON

McMahon, John Henry b: 10/15/1869, Waterbury, Conn. d: 12/30/1894, Bridgeport, Conn. BR/TL, 5'10", 165 lbs. Deb: 8/8/1892

YEAR	TM/L	G	AB	R	H	2B	3B	HR	RBI	BB	SO	AVG	OBP	SLG	PRO+	BR/A	SB	CS	SBR	FA	FR	G/POS	TPR
1892	NY-N	40	147	21	33	5	7	1	24	10	9	.224	.278	.374	99	-1	3			.973	-2	1-36/C-5	-0.4
1893	NY-N	11	30	5	10	2	1	0	4	2	0	.333	.375	.467	123	1	0			.891	-1	C-11	0.0
Total	2	51	177	26	43	7	8	1	28	12	9	.243	.295	.390	103	-0	3			.900	-3	/1-36,C-16	-0.4

■ FRANK McMANUS

McManus, Francis E. b: 9/21/1875, Lawrence, Mass. d: 9/1/23, Syracuse, N.Y. TR, 5'10", Deb: 9/14/1899

YEAR	TM/L	G	AB	R	H	2B	3B	HR	RBI	BB	SO	AVG	OBP	SLG	PRO+	BR/A	SB	CS	SBR	FA	FR	G/POS	TPR
1899	Was-N	7	21	3	8	1	0	0	2	2		.381	.435	.429	139	1	3			.931	0	/C-7	0.2
1903	Bro-N	2	7	0	0	0	0	0	0	0		.000	.000	.000	-99	-2	0			.929	1	/C-2	-0.1
1904	Det-A	1	0	0	0	0	0	0	0	0		.000				0	0			.000		/C-4	0.0
	NY-A	4	7	0	0	0	0	0	0	0		.000	.000	.000	-96	-2	0			.900	-1	/C-4	-0.3
	Yr	5	7	0	0	0	0	0	0	0		.000	.000	.000	-97	-2	0			.900	-1	/C-5	-0.3
Total	3	14	35	3	8	1	0	0	2	2		.229	.270	.257	50	-2	3			.925	-2	/C-14	-0.2

■ JIM McMANUS

McManus, James Michael b: 7/20/36, Brookline, Mass. BL/TL, 6'4", 215 lbs. Deb: 9/21/60

YEAR	TM/L	G	AB	R	H	2B	3B	HR	RBI	BB	SO	AVG	OBP	SLG	PRO+	BR/A	SB	CS	SBR	FA	FR	G/POS	TPR
1960	KC-A	5	13	3	4	0	0	1	2	1	2	.308	.357	.538	138	1	0	0	0	1.000	-0	/1-3	0.0

■ MARTY McMANUS

McManus, Martin Joseph b: 3/14/1900, Chicago, Ill. d: 2/18/66, St.Louis, Mo. BR/TR, 5'10.5", 160 lbs. Deb: 9/26/20 M

YEAR	TM/L	G	AB	R	H	2B	3B	HR	RBI	BB	SO	AVG	OBP	SLG	PRO+	BR/A	SB	CS	SBR	FA	FR	G/POS	TPR
1920	StL-A	1	3	0	1	0	0	0	1	0	0	.333	.333	1.000	237	0	0	0	0	.667	-0	/3-1	0.0
1921	StL-A	121	412	49	107	19	8	3	64	27	30	.260	.308	.367	68	-21	5	3	-0	.952	-11	2-96,3-13/1-9,S-2	-2.7
1922	StL-A	154	606	88	189	34	11	11	109	38	41	.312	.358	.459	108	6	9	6	-1	.964	3	*2-153/1-1	1.1
1923	StL-A	154	582	86	180	35	10	15	94	49	50	.309	.367	.481	116	11	14	10	-2	.960	-4	*2-133,1-20	0.8
1924	StL-A	123	442	71	147	23	5	5	80	55	40	.333	.409	.441	112	9	13	9	-2	.972	7	*2-119	1.5
1925	StL-A	154	587	108	169	**44**	8	13	90	73	69	.288	.371	.457	104	2	5	11	-5	.967	4	*2-154/O-1	1.5
1926	StL-A	149	549	102	156	30	10	9	68	55	62	.284	.350	.424	97	-4	5	7	-3	.958	15	3-84,2-61/1-4	1.5
1927	Det-A	108	369	60	99	19	7	9	69	34	38	.268	.332	.431	95	-4	8	7	-2	.960	-2	S-39,2-35,3-22/1-6	-0.1
1928	Det-A	139	500	78	144	37	5	8	73	51	30	.288	.355	.430	104	2	11	13	-5	.955	-9	3-92,1-45/S-2	-0.2
1929	Det-A	154	599	99	168	32	8	18	90	60	52	.280	.347	.451	103	2	16	11	-2	.972	8	*3-150/S-8	1.4
1930	Det-A	132	484	74	155	40	4	9	89	59	28	.320	.396	.475	118	14	**23**	8	2	.906	6	*3-130/S-3,1-1	2.6
1931	Det-A	107	362	39	98	17	3	3	53	49	22	.271	.361	.359	87	-6	7	13		.950	13	3-79,2-21/1-1	1.2
	Bos-A	17	62	8	18	4	0	1	9	8	1	.290	.371	.403	110	1	1	1	-0	1.000	-5	3-11/2-7	0.9
	Yr	124	424	47	116	21	3	4	62	57	23	.274	.362	.366	90	-5	8	14		.956	21	3-90,2-28/1-1	2.1
1932	Bos-A	93	302	39	71	19	4	5	24	36	30	.235	.317	.374	80	-9	1	2	-1	.969	4	2-49,3-30/S-2,1M	0.0
1933	Bos-N	106	366	51	104	30	4	3	36	49	21	.284	.369	.413	108	5	3	0	1	.957	-5	3-76,2-26/1-4,M	0.6
1934	Bos-N	120	435	56	120	18	0	8	47	32	42	.276	.330	.372	95	-4	5			.964	-5	2-73,3-37	-0.3
Total	15	1831	6660	1008	1926	401	88	120	996	675	558	.289	.357	.430	101	5	126	91		.965	44	2-927,3-725/1SO	8.8

■ JIMMY McMATH

McMath, Jimmy Lee b: 8/10/49, Tuscaloosa, Ala. BL/TL, 6'1.5", 195 lbs. Deb: 9/7/68

YEAR	TM/L	G	AB	R	H	2B	3B	HR	RBI	BB	SO	AVG	OBP	SLG	PRO+	BR/A	SB	CS	SBR	FA	FR	G/POS	TPR
1968	Chi-N	6	14	0	2	0	0	0	2	0	6	.143	.143	.143	-13	-2	0	0	0	1.000	0	/O-3	-0.2

■ GEORGE McMILLAN

McMillan, George A. "Reddy" b: Evansville, Ind. 5'8", 175 lbs. Deb: 8/11/1890

YEAR	TM/L	G	AB	R	H	2B	3B	HR	RBI	BB	SO	AVG	OBP	SLG	PRO+	BR/A	SB	CS	SBR	FA	FR	G/POS	TPR
1890	NY-N	10	35	4	5	0	0	0	1	7	4	.143	.286	.143	26	-3	1			.800	-1	O-10	-0.4

■ NORM McMILLAN

McMillan, Norman Alexis "Bub" b: 10/5/1895, Latta, S.C. d: 9/28/??, Marion, S.C. BR/TR, 6', 175 lbs. Deb: 4/12/22

YEAR	TM/L	G	AB	R	H	2B	3B	HR	RBI	BB	SO	AVG	OBP	SLG	PRO+	BR/A	SB	CS	SBR	FA	FR	G/POS	TPR
1922	*NY-A	33	78	7	20	1	2	0	11	6	10	.256	.310	.321	63	-4	4	1	1	.921	-8	O-26/3-5	-1.2
1923	Bos-A	131	459	37	116	24	5	0	42	28	44	.253	.299	.327	64	-25	13	5	1	.942	13	3-67,2-34/S-28	-0.2
1924	StL-A	76	201	25	56	12	2	0	27	12	17	.279	.332	.358	73	-8	6	4	-1	.966	2	2-37,3-19/S-7,1-2	-1.0
1928	Chi-N	49	123	11	27	2	2	1	12	13	19	.220	.299	.293	56	-8				.977	-1	2-19,3-18	-0.7
1929	*Chi-N	124	495	77	134	35	5	5	55	36	43	.271	.324	.392	76	-19	13			.944	6	*3-120	-0.8
Total	5	413	1356	157	353	74	16	6	147	95	133	.260	.313	.352	69	-64	36	10		.944	7	3-229/2-90,S-35,O1	-3.9

■ ROY McMILLAN

McMillan, Roy David b: 7/17/30, Bonham, Tex. BR/TR, 5'11", 170 lbs. Deb: 4/17/51 MC

YEAR	TM/L	G	AB	R	H	2B	3B	HR	RBI	BB	SO	AVG	OBP	SLG	PRO+	BR/A	SB	CS	SBR	FA	FR	G/POS	TPR
1951	Cin-N	85	199	21	42	4	0	1	8	17	26	.211	.273	.246	40	-17	0	0	1	.963	5	S-54,3-12/2-1	-0.9
1952	Cin-N	154	540	60	132	32	2	7	57	45	81	.244	.306	.350	82	-14	4	5	-2	.971	11	*S-154	0.7
1953	Cin-N	155	557	51	130	15	4	5	43	43	52	.233	.290	.302	54	-37	2	4	0	.972	14	*S-155	-1.4
1954	Cin-N	154	588	86	147	21	2	4	42	47	54	.250	.311	.313	61	-33	4	6		.959	6	*S-154	-1.4
1955	Cin-N	151	470	50	126	21	1	1	37	66	53	.268	.366	.328	81	-10	4	4	-1	.969	17	*S-150	1.8
1956	Cin-N★	150	479	51	126	16	7	3	62	76	54	.263	.370	.344	88	-5	4	3	-1	.975	**30**	*S-150	3.7
1957	Cin-N★	151	448	50	122	25	5	1	55	66	44	.272	.373	.357	91	-3	5	3	1	.977	-8	*S-151	0.4
1958	Cin-N	145	398	48	90	18	3	1	25	47	33	.229	.313	.298	60	-22	5	2	1	.980	4	*S-145	-0.6
1959	Cin-N	79	246	38	65	14	2	9	24	27	27	.264	.347	.447	106	2	2	0		.974	-7	S-73	0.2
1960	Cin-N	124	399	42	94	12	2	10	42	35	40	.236	.304	.351	77	-12	1	5		.964	-13	*S-116,2-10	-1.7
1961	Mil-N	154	505	42	111	16	0	7	48	61	56	.220	.309	.293	65	-25	2	4		.975	-0	*S-154	-1.4
1962	Mil-N	137	468	66	115	13	0	12	41	60	53	.246	.338	.350	87	-7	2	3		.972	5	*S-135	0.5
1963	Mil-N	100	320	35	80	10	1	4	29	17	25	.250	.292	.325	78	-9	1	5	-3	.979	-7	S-94	0.2
1964	Mil-N	8	13	1	4	0	0	0	0	0	2	.308	.308	.308	73	-0	0	0		.933	-1	/S-8	-0.1
	NY-N	113	379	30	80	8	2	1	25	14	16	.211	.247	.251	42	-29	3	1	0	.976	-1	*S-111	-2.3

YEAR	TM/L	G	AB	R	H	2B	3B	HR	RBI	BB	SO	AVG	OBP	SLG	PRO+	BR/A	SB	CS	SBR	FA	FR	G/POS	TPR
	Yr	121	392	31	84	8	2	1	27	14	18	.214	.249	.253	43	-30	4	1	1	.975	-2	*S-119	-2.4
1965	NY-N	157	528	44	128	19	2	1	42	24	60	.242	.281	.292	64	-26	1	1	-0	.964	-4	*S-153	-2.0
1966	NY-N	76	220	24	47	9	1	1	12	20	25	.214	.285	.277	59	-12	1	1	-0	.975	6	S-71	-0.1
Total	16	2093	6752	739	1639	253	35	68	594	665	711	.243	.316	.321	72	-259	41	36	-9	.972	66	*S-2028/3-12,2-11	-4.6

■ TOM McMILLAN
McMillan, Thomas Erwin b: 9/13/51, Richmond, Va. BR/TR, 5'9", 165 lbs. Deb: 9/17/77

YEAR	TM/L	G	AB	R	H	2B	3B	HR	RBI	BB	SO	AVG	OBP	SLG	PRO+	BR/A	SB	CS	SBR	FA	FR	G/POS	TPR
1977	Sea-A	2	5	0	0	0	0	0	0	0	0	.000	.000	.000	-99	-1	0	0	0	1.000	-0	/S-2	-0.2

■ TOMMY McMILLAN
McMillan, Thomas Law "Rebel" b: 4/18/1888, Pittston, Pa. d: 7/15/66, Orlando, Fla. BR/TR, 5'5", 130 lbs. Deb: 8/19/08

YEAR	TM/L	G	AB	R	H	2B	3B	HR	RBI	BB	SO	AVG	OBP	SLG	PRO+	BR/A	SB	CS	SBR	FA	FR	G/POS	TPR
1908	Bro-N	43	147	9	35	3	0	0	3	9		.238	.296	.259	80	-3	5			.873	-5	S-29,O-14	-0.9
1909	Bro-N	108	373	18	79	15	1	0	24	20		.212	.254	.257	61	-8	11			.914	-10	*S-105/2-2,3-1	-3.0
1910	Bro-N	23	74	2	13	1	0	0	2	6	10	.176	.237	.189	26	-7	4			.898	-1	S-23	-0.8
	Cin-N	82	248	20	46	0	3	0	13	31	23	.185	.281	.210	46	-16	7			.927	10	*S-82	-0.4
	Yr	105	322	22	59	1	3	0	15	37	33	.183	.271	.205	41	-23	11			.921	8	*S-105	-1.2
1912	NY-A	41	149	24	34	2	0	0	12	15		.228	.303	.242	53	-9	18			.948	-8	S-41	-1.3
Total	4	297	991	73	207	21	4	0	54	81	33	.209	.273	.238	56	-53	45			.917	-15	S-280/O-14,2-2,3-1	-6.4

■ BILLY McMILLON
McMillon, William Edward b: 11/17/71, Otero, N.Mex. BL/TL, 5'11", 172 lbs. Deb: 7/26/96

YEAR	TM/L	G	AB	R	H	2B	3B	HR	RBI	BB	SO	AVG	OBP	SLG	PRO+	BR/A	SB	CS	SBR	FA	FR	G/POS	TPR
1996	Fla-N	28	51	4	11	0	0	0	4	5	14	.216	.286	.216	36	-0	0	0	0	1.000	-2	O-15	-0.6

■ HUGH McMULLEN
McMullen, Hugh Raphael b: 12/16/01, LaCygne, Kan. d: 5/23/86, Whittier, Cal. BB/TR, 6'1", 180 lbs. Deb: 9/19/25

YEAR	TM/L	G	AB	R	H	2B	3B	HR	RBI	BB	SO	AVG	OBP	SLG	PRO+	BR/A	SB	CS	SBR	FA	FR	G/POS	TPR
1925	NY-N	5	15	1	2	1	0	0	0	0	3	.133	.133	.200	-17	-3				1.000	-2	/C-5	-0.4
1926	NY-N	57	91	5	17	2	0	0	6	2	18	.187	.204	.209	11	-11	1			.942	-0	C-56	-0.9
1928	Was-A	1	1	0	0	0	0	0	0	0	1	.000	.000	.000	-99	-0	0	0	0	.000	0	H	0.0
1929	Cin-N	1	1	0	0	0	0	0	0	0		.000	.000	.000	-99	-0	0	0	0	1.000	-0	/C-1	0.0
Total	4	64	108	6	19	3	0	0	6	2	22	.176	.191	.204	5	-15	1	0		.947	-2	/C-62	-1.3

■ KEN McMULLEN
McMullen, Kenneth Lee b: 6/1/42, Oxnard, Cal. BR/TR, 6'3", 195 lbs. Deb: 9/17/62

YEAR	TM/L	G	AB	R	H	2B	3B	HR	RBI	BB	SO	AVG	OBP	SLG	PRO+	BR/A	SB	CS	SBR	FA	FR	G/POS	TPR
1962	LA-N	6	11	0	3	0	0	0	0	0	3	.273	.273	.273	50	-1	0	0	0	1.000	0	/O-2	-0.1
1963	LA-N	79	233	16	55	9	0	5	28	20	46	.236	.299	.339	89	-4	1	2	-1	.933	5	3-71/2-1,O-1	0.2
1964	LA-N	24	67	3	14	0	0	1	2	3	7	.209	.243	.254	43	-5	0	1	-1	.991	-3	1-13/3-4,O-3	-1.0
1965	Was-A	150	555	75	146	18	6	18	54	47	90	.263	.325	.414	110	7	2	0	1	.954	6	*3-142/O-8,1-1	1.0
1966	Was-A	147	524	48	122	19	4	13	54	44	89	.233	.292	.359	87	-9	3	1	1	.951	-1	*3-141/1-8,O-1	-1.4
1967	Was-A	146	563	73	138	22	2	16	67	46	84	.245	.303	.377	104	1	5	3	-0	.965	12	*3-145	1.3
1968	Was-A	151	557	66	138	11	2	20	62	63	66	.248	.327	.382	118	12	1	3	-2	.962	5	*3-145,S-11	1.9
1969	Was-A	158	562	83	153	25	2	19	87	70	103	.272	.354	.425	123	17	4	5	-2	.976	19	*3-154	3.6
1970	Was-A	15	59	5	12	2	0	0	3	5	10	.203	.266	.237	42	-5	0	0	0	.971	-4	*3-15	0.1
	Cal-A	124	422	50	98	9	3	14	61	59	81	.232	.331	.367	96	-5	0	0	0	.959	19	*3-122	0.6
	Yr	139	481	55	110	11	3	14	64	64	91	.229	.323	.351	89	-7	1	0	0	.960	15	*3-137	0.7
1971	Cal-A	160	593	63	148	19	2	21	68	53	74	.250	.314	.395	107	3	1	1	-0	.966	-1	*3-158	0.1
1972	Cal-A	137	472	36	127	18	1	9	34	48	59	.269	.337	.369	116	9	2	2	-1	.970	2	*3-137	1.0
1973	LA-N	42	85	6	21	5	0	5	18	6	13	.247	.297	.482	118	1	0	0	0	.922	5	3-24	0.6
1974	*LA-N	44	60	5	15	1	0	3	12	2	12	.250	.274	.417	95	-1	0	0	0	1.000	-1	/3-7,2-3	-0.1
1975	LA-N	39	46	4	11	1	1	2	14	7	12	.239	.340	.435	119	1	0	0	0	1.000	1	3-11/1-3	0.2
1976	Oak-A	98	186	20	41	6	2	5	23	22	33	.220	.306	.355	97	-1	1	1	-0	.952	-1	3-35,1-26,D-23/O2	-0.5
1977	Mil-A	63	136	11	31	7	1	5	19	15	33	.228	.305	.404	91	-2	0	0	0	.978	2	D-29,1-11/3-7	-0.2
Total	16	1583	5131	568	1273	172	26	156	606	510	815	.248	.318	.383	105	23	20	19	-5	.961	66	*3-1318/1-62,DOS2	7.3

■ FRED McMULLIN
McMullin, Frederick William b: 10/13/1891, Scammon, Kan. d: 11/21/52, Los Angeles, Cal. BR/TR, 5'11", 170 lbs. Deb: 8/27/14

YEAR	TM/L	G	AB	R	H	2B	3B	HR	RBI	BB	SO	AVG	OBP	SLG	PRO+	BR/A	SB	CS	SBR	FA	FR	G/POS	TPR
1914	Det-A	1	1	0	0	0	0	0	0	0	1	.000	.000	.000	-97	-0	0			.667	0	/S-1	0.0
1916	Chi-A	68	187	8	48	3	0	0	10	19	30	.257	.332	.273	81	-4	9			.950	-4	3-63/S-2,2-1	-0.6
1917	*Chi-A	59	194	35	46	2	1	0	12	27	17	.237	.339	.258	81	-3	9			.932	-13	3-52/S-2	-1.7
1918	Chi-A	70	235	32	65	7	0	1	16	25	26	.277	.346	.319	103	2	7			.941	-2	3-69/2-1	0.2
1919	*Chi-A	60	170	31	50	8	4	0	19	11	18	.294	.355	.388	108	2	4			.931	0	3-46/2-5	0.3
1920	Chi-A	46	127	14	25	1	4	0	13	9	13	.197	.255	.268	39	-11	1	1	-0	.962	-5	3-29/2-3,S-1	-1.5
Total	6	304	914	120	234	21	9	1	70	91	105	.256	.333	.302	85	-15	30	1		.942	-24	3-259/2-10,S-6	-3.3

■ JOHN McMULLIN
McMullin, John F. "Lefty" b: 1848, Philadelphia, Pa. d: 4/11/1881, Philadelphia, Pa. BR/TL, 5'9", 160 lbs. Deb: 5/9/1871

YEAR	TM/L	G	AB	R	H	2B	3B	HR	RBI	BB	SO	AVG	OBP	SLG	PRO+	BR/A	SB	CS	SBR	FA	FR	G/POS	TPR
1871	Tro-n	29	136	38	38	0	5	0	32	8	6	.279	.319	.353	92	-1	11	1	3	.871	0	*P-29/S-1	0.0
1872	Mut-n	54	237	48	61	6	1	0	25	11	6	.257	.290	.291	85	-2	8	2	1	.871	0	*O-53/P-3	0.5
1873	Ath-n	52	227	54	62	7	1	0	29	8	4	.273	.298	.313	76	-8	9	1	2	.828	-4	*O-51/P-1	-0.6
1874	Ath-n	55	260	61	90	10	2	2	32	8	12	.346	.366	.423	140	10	4	3	-1	.771	-4	*O-55	-0.1
1875	Phi-n	54	222	33	57	9	4	2	19	5	12	.257	.273	.360	114	3	6	10	-4	.835	-1	*O-54/P-4	-0.1
Total	5 n	244	1082	234	308	32	13	4	137	40	40	.285	.310	.349	103	0	38	17	1	.829	-3	O-213/P-37,S-1	0.2

■ CARL McNABB
McNabb, Carl Mac "Skinny" b: 1/25/17, Stevenson, Ala. BR/TR, 5'9", 155 lbs. Deb: 4/20/45

YEAR	TM/L	G	AB	R	H	2B	3B	HR	RBI	BB	SO	AVG	OBP	SLG	PRO+	BR/A	SB	CS	SBR	FA	FR	G/POS	TPR
1945	Det-A	1	1	0	0	0	0	0	0	0	1	.000	.000	.000	-94	-0	0	0	0	.000	0	H	0.0

■ ERIC McNAIR
McNair, Donald Eric "Boob" b: 4/12/09, Meridian, Miss. d: 3/11/49, Meridian, Miss. BR/TR, 5'8", 160 lbs. Deb: 9/20/29

YEAR	TM/L	G	AB	R	H	2B	3B	HR	RBI	BB	SO	AVG	OBP	SLG	PRO+	BR/A	SB	CS	SBR	FA	FR	G/POS	TPR
1929	Phi-A	4	8	2	4	1	0	0	3	0	0	.500	.500	.625	181	1	1	0	0	1.000	-0	/S-4	0.1
1930	*Phi-A	78	237	27	63	12	2	0	34	9	19	.266	.296	.333	57	-16	5	2	0	.915	-7	S-31,3-29/2-5,O-1	-1.7
1931	*Phi-A	79	280	41	76	10	1	5	33	11	19	.271	.306	.368	72	-12	1	4	-2	.915	-6	3-47,2-16,S-13	-1.4
1932	Phi-A	135	554	87	158	47	3	18	95	28	29	.285	.323	.478	101	-2	8	4	0	.953	-7	*S-133	0.2
1933	Phi-A	89	310	57	81	15	4	7	48	15	32	.261	.302	.403	84	-8	2	1	0	.966	4	S-46,2-27	-0.5
1934	Phi-A	151	599	80	168	20	4	17	82	35	42	.280	.321	.412	91	-10	7	3	-3	.951	4	*S-151	0.0
1935	Phi-A	137	526	55	142	22	2	4	57	35	33	.270	.319	.342	72	-22	3	7	-3	.955	-21	*S-121,3-11/1-2	-3.8
1936	Bos-A	128	494	68	141	36	4	7	74	27	34	.285	.329	.391	73	-22	4	2	0	.966	-12	S-84,2-35,3-11	-2.4
1937	Bos-A	126	455	60	133	29	4	12	76	30	33	.292	.340	.453	94	-5	10	7	-1	.969	-6	*2-106/S-9,3-4,1-1	-0.4
1938	Bos-A	46	96	9	15	1	0	7	9	3	6	.156	.182	.188	-7	-16	0	1	-0	.870	3	S-15,2-14/3-3	-1.2
1939	Chi-A	129	479	62	155	18	5	7	82	38	41	.324	.375	.426	102	1	17	9	-0	.937	4	*3-103,2-19/S-9	0.7
1940	Chi-A	66	251	26	57	13	1	7	31	12	26	.227	.265	.371	62	-15	1	7	-4	.958	-17	2-65/3-1	-3.1
1941	Det-A	23	59	5	11	0	0	3	4	4	4	.186	.250	.203	19	-7	0	0	0	.970	-2	3-11/S-3	-0.9
1942	Det-A	26	68	4	11	2	0	1	4	3	5	.162	.197	.235	20	-7	0	1	-1	.881	-8	S-21	-1.5
	Phi-A	34	103	8	25	2	0	0	4	11	5	.243	.316	.262	64	-5	1	0	0	.952	-6	S-29/2-1	-0.9
	Yr	60	171	13	36	4	0	1	8	14	10	.211	.277	.251	46	-12	1	1	-1	.927	-13	S-50/2-1	-2.4
Total	14	1251	4519	592	1240	229	29	82	633	261	328	.274	.318	.392	80	-146	59	54	-15	.949	-83	S-669,2-288,3/1O	-16.8

■ MIKE McNALLY
McNally, Michael Joseph "Minooka Mike" b: 9/9/1892, Minooka, Pa. d: 5/29/65, Bethlehem, Pa. BR/TR, 5'11", 150 lbs. Deb: 4/21/15

YEAR	TM/L	G	AB	R	H	2B	3B	HR	RBI	BB	SO	AVG	OBP	SLG	PRO+	BR/A	SB	CS	SBR	FA	FR	G/POS	TPR
1915	Bos-A	23	53	7	8	1	0	0	1	4		.151	.196	.189	16	-6	0	2	-1	.891	-7	3-18/2-5	-0.6
1916	*Bos-A	87	135	28	23	0	0	0	9	10	19	.170	.240	.170	20	-13	9			.964	7	2-35,3-14/S-7,O-1	-0.6
1917	Bos-A	42	50	9	15	1	0	0	6	5		.300	.375	.320	113	1	3			.935	6	3-14/S-9,2-6	0.8
1919	Bos-A	33	42	10	11	4	0	0	6	1	2	.262	.279	.357	83	-1	4			.950	9	S-11,3-11/2-3	0.9
1920	Bos-A	93	312	42	80	5	1	0	23	31	24	.256	.326	.279	64	-15	13	10	-2	.930	-3	3-49,2-16	-2.3
1921	*NY-A	71	215	36	56	4	2	1	24	14	15	.260	.306	.312	57	-14	5	6	-4	.974	18	3-42,2-16	0.5
1922	*NY-A	52	143	20	36	2	0	1	18	16	14	.252	.331	.294	63	-7	3	0	1	.983	-0	3-34/2-9,S-4,1-1	-0.4
1923	NY-A	30	38	5	8	0	0	1	3	0	6	.211	.268	.211	27	-4	2	0	0	1.000	5	S-13/3-7,2-5	-0.3
1924	NY-A	49	69	11	17	0	0	0	9	2	7	.246	.316	.246	46	-5	1	1	-0	.985	10	2-25,3-13/S-6	0.4
1925	Was-A	12	21	1	3	1	0	0	1	0	1	.143	.182	.143	-17	-4	0	1	-0	1.000	1	/3-7,S-2,2-1	-0.3
Total	10	492	1078	169	257	16	6	1	85	92	97	.238	.299	.267	54	-69	40	19		.946	41	2-181,3-167/S1O	-1.9

■ GEORGE McNAMARA
McNamara, George Francis b: 1/11/01, Chicago, Ill. d: 6/12/90, Hinsdale, Ill. BL/TR, 6', 175 lbs. Deb: 9/28/22

YEAR	TM/L	G	AB	R	H	2B	3B	HR	RBI	BB	SO	AVG	OBP	SLG	PRO+	BR/A	SB	CS	SBR	FA	FR	G/POS	TPR
1922	Was-A	3	11	3	3	0	0	0	1	1	2	.273	.333	.273	63	-1	0	0	0	1.000	-1	/O-3	-0.1

YEAR	TM/L	G	AB	R	H	2B	3B	HR	RBI	BB	SO	AVG	OBP	SLG	PRO+	BR/A	SB	CS	SBR	FA	FR	G/POS	TPR

■ JIM McNAMARA   McNamara, James Patrick   b: 6/10/65, Nashua, N.H.   BL/TR, 6'4", 210 lbs.   Deb: 4/9/92

1992	SF-N	30	74	6	16	1	0	1	9	6	25	.216	.275	.270	58	-4	0	0	0	.993	-0	C-30	-0.3
1993	SF-N	4	7	0	1	0	0	0	1	0	1	.143	.143	.143	-24	-1	0	0	0	1.000	-0	/C-4	-0.1
Total	2	34	81	6	17	1	0	1	10	6	26	.210	.264	.259	51	-5	0	0	0	.993	-0	/C-34	-0.4

■ DINNY McNAMARA   McNamara, John Raymond   b: 9/16/05, Lexington, Mass.   d: 12/20/63, Arlington, Mass.   BL/TR, 5'9", 165 lbs.   Deb: 7/2/27

1927	Bos-N	11	9	3	0	0	0	0	0	0	3	.000	.000	.000	-99	-3	0			1.000	0	/O-3	-0.2
1928	Bos-N	9	4	2	1	0	0	0	0	0	1	.250	.250	.250	33	-0	0			1.000	0	/O-3	-0.1
Total	2	20	13	5	1	0	0	0	0	0	4	.077	.077	.077	-63	-3	0			1.000	0	/O-6	-0.3

■ BOB McNAMARA   McNamara, Robert Maxey   b: 9/19/16, Denver, Colo.   BR/TR, 5'10", 170 lbs.   Deb: 5/27/39

| 1939 | Phi-A | 9 | 9 | 0 | 2 | 1 | 0 | 0 | 3 | 1 | 1 | .222 | .300 | .333 | 63 | -1 | 0 | 0 | 0 | 1.000 | 0 | /3-5,S-2,1-1,2-1 | 0.0 |

■ TOM McNAMARA   McNamara, Thomas Henry   b: 11/5/1895, Roxbury, Mass.   d: 5/5/74, Danvers, Mass.   BR/TR, 6'2", 200 lbs.   Deb: 6/25/22

| 1922 | Pit-N | 1 | 1 | 0 | 0 | 0 | 0 | 0 | 0 | 0 | 0 | .000 | .000 | .000 | -99 | -0 | 0 | 0 | 0 | .000 | 0 | H | 0.0 |

■ RUSTY McNEALY   McNealy, Robert Lee   b: 8/12/58, Sacramento, Cal.   BL/TL, 5'8", 160 lbs.   Deb: 9/4/83

| 1983 | Oak-A | 15 | 4 | 5 | 0 | 0 | 0 | 0 | 0 | 0 | 0 | .000 | .000 | .000 | -99 | -1 | 0 | 1 | -1 | 1.000 | -2 | /O-5,D-7 | -0.4 |

■ EARL McNEELY   McNeely, George Earl   b: 5/12/1898, Sacramento, Cal.   d: 7/16/71, Sacramento, Cal.   BR/TR, 5'9", 155 lbs.   Deb: 8/9/24   C

1924	*Was-A	43	179	31	59	5	6	0	15	5	21	.330	.355	.425	104	0	3	1	0	.973	-2	O-42	-0.4
1925	*Was-A	122	385	76	110	14	2	3	37	48	54	.286	.378	.356	89	-5	15	16	-5	.975	-2	*O-112/1-1	-1.7
1926	Was-A	124	442	84	134	20	12	0	48	44	28	.303	.373	.403	105	4	18	6	2	.969	-0	*O-118	-0.2
1927	Was-A	73	185	40	51	10	4	0	16	11	13	.276	.320	.373	80	-6	11	4	1	.977	-7	O-47/1-4	-1.4
1928	StL-A	127	496	66	117	27	7	0	44	37	39	.236	.299	.319	61	-29	8	6	-1	.984	7	*O-120	-3.0
1929	StL-A	69	230	27	56	8	1	1	18	7	13	.243	.272	.300	45	-19	2	1	0	.980	7	O-62	-2.8
1930	StL-A	76	235	33	64	19	1	0	20	22	14	.272	.340	.362	75	-9	8	3	1	.939	-5	O-38,1-27	-1.8
1931	StL-A	49	102	12	23	4	0	0	15	9	5	.225	.288	.265	45	-8	4	4	-1	.969	-5	O-37/1-1	-1.5
Total	8	683	2254	369	614	107	33	4	213	183	187	.272	.335	.354	78	-71	69	41	-4	.974	-21	O-576/1-33	-12.8

■ JEFF McNEELY   McNeely, Jeffrey Lavern   b: 10/18/69, Monroe, N.C.   BR/TR, 6'2", 190 lbs.   Deb: 9/5/93

| 1993 | Bos-A | 21 | 37 | 10 | 11 | 1 | 1 | 0 | 1 | 7 | 9 | .297 | .409 | .378 | 106 | 1 | 6 | 0 | 2 | .917 | -3 | O-13/D-3 | 0.0 |

■ NORM McNEIL   McNeil, Norman Francis   b: 10/22/1892, Chicago, Ill.   d: 4/11/42, Buffalo, N.Y.   BR/TR, 5'11", 180 lbs.   Deb: 6/21/19

| 1919 | Bos-A | 5 | 9 | 0 | 3 | 0 | 0 | 0 | 1 | 1 | 0 | .333 | .400 | .333 | 113 | 0 | 0 | | | .818 | -2 | /C-5 | -0.1 |

■ JERRY McNERTNEY   McNertney, Gerald Edward   b: 8/7/36, Boone, Iowa   BR/TR, 6'1", 195 lbs.   Deb: 4/16/64   C

1964	Chi-A	73	186	16	40	5	0	3	23	19	24	.215	.298	.290	66	-8	0	1	0	.987	8	C-69	0.2
1966	Chi-A	44	59	3	13	0	0	1	7	9	6	.220	.303	.220	57	-3	1	1	-0	.969	-3	C-37	0.3
1967	Chi-A	56	123	8	28	6	0	3	13	6	14	.228	.275	.350	87	-2	0	0	0	.996	13	C-52	1.4
1968	Chi-A	74	169	18	37	4	1	3	18	18	29	.219	.302	.308	84	-3	0	0	0	.985	14	C-64/1-1	1.6
1969	Sea-A	128	410	39	99	18	1	8	55	29	63	.241	.292	.349	80	-12	1	0	0	.988	9	*C-122	-0.4
1970	Mil-A	111	296	27	72	11	1	6	22	22	33	.243	.304	.348	79	-9	1	4	-2	.984	-9	C-94,1-13	-1.7
1971	StL-N	56	128	15	37	4	2	4	22	12	14	.289	.350	.445	119	3	0	0	0	.985	-3	C-36	0.2
1972	StL-N	39	48	3	10	3	1	0	9	6	16	.208	.296	.313	74	-2	0	0	0	.982	7	C-10	0.0
1973	Pit-N	9	4	0	1	0	0	0	0	0	0	.250	.250	.250	40	-0	0	0	0	1.000	1	/C-9	0.1
Total	9	590	1423	129	337	51	6	27	163	119	199	.237	.301	.338	81	-36	3	5	-2	.987	33	C-493/1-14	1.7

■ PAT McNULTY   McNulty, Patrick Howard   b: 2/27/1899, Cleveland, Ohio   d: 5/4/63, Hollywood, Cal.   BL/TR, 5'11", 160 lbs.   Deb: 9/5/22

1922	Cle-A	22	59	10	16	2	1	0	5	9	5	.271	.368	.339	85	-1	4	1	1	.956	-3	O-22	-0.5
1924	Cle-A	101	291	46	78	13	5	0	26	33	22	.268	.347	.347	78	-9	10	7	-1	.961	-4	O-75	-1.8
1925	Cle-A	118	373	70	117	18	2	6	43	47	23	.314	.392	.421	105	4	7	7	-2	.965	-2	*O-111	-0.5
1926	Cle-A	48	56	3	14	2	1	0	6	5	9	.250	.311	.321	65	-3	0	1	-1	.909	-2	/O-9	-0.5
1927	Cle-A	19	41	3	13	1	0	0	4	4	3	.317	.378	.341	87	-1	1	2	-1	.906	-1	O-12	-0.2
Total	5	308	820	132	238	36	9	6	84	98	62	.290	.368	.378	91	-10	22	18	-4	.957	-11	O-229	-3.5

■ BILL McNULTY   McNulty, William Francis   b: 8/29/46, Sacramento, Cal.   BR/TR, 6'4", 205 lbs.   Deb: 7/9/69

1969	Oak-A	5	17	0	0	0	0	0	0	0	10	.000	.000	.000	-99	-5	0	0	0	1.000	1	/O-5	-0.4
1972	Oak-A	4	10	0	1	0	0	0	0	2	1	.100	.250	.100	7	-1	0	0	0	.800	-0	/3-3	-0.3
Total	2	9	27	0	1	0	0	0	0	2	11	.037	.103	.037	-61	-6	0	0	0	1.000	-0	/O-5,3-3	-0.7

■ BID McPHEE   McPhee, John Alexander   b: 11/1/1859, Massena, N.Y.   d: 1/3/43, San Diego, Cal.   BR/TR, 5'8", 152 lbs.   Deb: 5/2/1882   M

1882	Cin-a	78	311	43	71	8	7	1	31	11		.228	.255	.309	84	-6				.920	-1	*2-78	-0.5
1883	Cin-a	96	367	61	90	10	10	2	42	18		.245	.281	.343	95	-3				.928	3	*2-96	0.1
1884	Cin-a	112	450	107	125	8	7	5	64	27		.278	.327	.360	118	8				.924	16	*2-112	2.4
1885	Cin-a	110	431	78	114	12	4	0	46	19		.265	.306	.311	94	-3				.936	6	*2-110	0.6
1886	Cin-a	140	560	139	150	23	12	8	70	59		.268	.343	.395	127	16	40			.939	31	*2-140	4.6
1887	Cin-a	129	540	137	156	20	19	2	87	55		.289	.360	.407	111	8	95			.924	26	*2-129	3.0
1888	Cin-a	111	458	88	110	12	10	4	51	43		.240	.312	.336	102	-0	54			.940	31	*2-111	3.3
1889	Cin-a	135	540	109	145	25	7	5	57	60	29	.269	.346	.369	100	-0	63			.946	41	*2-135/3-1	4.0
1890	Cin-N	132	528	125	135	16	22	3	39	82	26	.256	.362	.386	119	14	55			.942	30	*2-132	4.5
1891	Cin-N	138	562	107	144	14	16	6	38	74	35	.256	.345	.370	107	6	33			.954	23	*2-138	3.1
1892	Cin-N	144	573	111	157	19	12	4	60	84	48	.274	.373	.370	127	22	44			.948	25	*2-144	4.5
1893	Cin-N	127	491	101	138	17	11	3	68	94	20	.281	.401	.379	105	7	25			.954	34	*2-127	3.5
1894	Cin-N	126	474	107	144	21	9	5	88	90	23	.304	.420	.418	99	2	33			.945	31	*2-126	2.9
1895	Cin-N	115	432	107	129	24	12	1	75	73	30	.299	.409	.417	109	8	30			.955	15	*2-115	2.3
1896	Cin-N	117	433	81	132	18	7	1	87	51	18	.305	.391	.386	99	-0	48			.978	6	*2-117	1.0
1897	Cin-N	81	282	45	85	13	7	1	39	35		.301	.386	.408	103	1	9			.966	12	2-81	1.5
1898	Cin-N	133	486	72	121	26	9	1	60	66		.249	.341	.346	91	-6	21			.956	-12	*2-130/O-3	-0.9
1899	Cin-N	111	373	60	104	17	7	1	65	40		.279	.360	.370	98	-0	18			.955	-4	*2-105/O-1	0.2
Total	18	2135	8291	1678	2250	303	188	53	1067	981	229	.271	.355	.372	106	72	568			.944	313	*2-2126/O-4,3-1	40.1

■ MART McQUAID   McQuaid, Mortimer Martin   b: 6/28/1861, Chicago, Ill.   d: 3/5/28, Chicago, Ill.   Deb: 8/15/1891

1891	StL-a	4	11	1	4	2	0	1	0	1		.364	.364	.545	139	-0	1			1.000	-1	/2-3,O-1	0.0
1898	Was-N	1	4	0	0	0	0	0	0	0		.000	.000	.000	-99	-1	0			.333	-1	/O-1	-0.2
Total	2	5	15	1	4	2	0	1	0	1		.267	.267	.400	81	-1	1			.333	-1	/2-3,O-2	-0.2

■ JERRY McQUAIG   McQuaig, Gerald Joseph   b: 1/31/12, Douglas, Ga.   BR/TR, 5'11", 183 lbs.   Deb: 8/25/34

| 1934 | Phi-A | 7 | 16 | 2 | 1 | 0 | 0 | 0 | 1 | 2 | 4 | .063 | .167 | .063 | -40 | -3 | 0 | 0 | 0 | .889 | -1 | /O-6 | -0.5 |

■ MOX McQUERY   McQuery, William Thomas   b: 6/28/1861, Garrard Co., Ky.   d: 6/12/1900, Cincinnati, Ohio   6'4",   Deb: 8/20/1884

1884	Cin-U	35	132	31	37	5	0	2		8		.280	.321	.364	99	-4				.978	0	1-35	-0.6
1885	Det-N	70	278	34	76	15	4	0	30	8	29	.273	.294	.388	119	5				.976	5	1-69/O-1	0.2
1886	KC-N	122	449	62	111	27	4	4	38	36	44	.247	.303	.352	93	-5	4			.969	1	*1-122	-1.7
1890	Syr-a	122	461	64	142	17	6	2	55	53		.308	.383	.384	141	25	26			.972	1	*1-122	1.5
1891	Was-a	68	261	40	63	9	4	5	37	18	19	.241	.305	.330	85	-5	3			.977	1	1-68	-0.7
Total	5	417	1581	231	429	73	18	13	160	123	92	.271	.327	.365	110	16	33			.973	7	1-416/O-1	-1.3

■ GLENN McQUILLEN   McQuillen, Glenn Richard "Red"   b: 4/19/15, Strasburg, Va.   d: 6/8/89, Gardenville, Md.   BR/TR, 6', 198 lbs.   Deb: 6/16/38

1938	StL-A	43	116	14	33	4	0	0	13	4	12	.284	.308	.319	57	-8	0	1	-1	.971	-0	O-30	-0.8
1941	StL-A	7	21	4	7	1	2	0	3	1	1	.333	.364	.524	128	1	0	1	-1	.933	-0	/O-6	0.0
1942	StL-A	100	339	40	96	15	12	3	47	10	17	.283	.306	.420	103	-1	1	1	-0	.969	-5	O-77	-1.1

YEAR	TM/L	G	AB	R	H	2B	3B	HR	RBI	BB	SO	AVG	OBP	SLG	PRO+	BR/A	SB	CS	SBR	FA	FR	G/POS	TPR
1946	StL-A	59	166	24	40	3	3	1	12	19	18	.241	.319	.313	73	-6	0	2	-1	.977	-2	O-48	-1.1
1947	StL-A	1	1	0	0	0	0	0	0	0	0	.000	.000	.000	-98	-0	0	0	0	.000	0	H	0.0
Total	5	210	643	82	176	24	16	4	75	34	49	.274	.311	.379	87	-14	1	5	-3	.970	-7	O-161	-3.0

■ GEORGE McQUINN
McQuinn, George Hartley   b: 5/29/10, Arlington, Va.   d: 12/24/78, Alexandria, Va.   BL/TL, 5'11", 165 lbs.   Deb: 4/14/36

YEAR	TM/L	G	AB	R	H	2B	3B	HR	RBI	BB	SO	AVG	OBP	SLG	PRO+	BR/A	SB	CS	SBR	FA	FR	G/POS	TPR
1936	Cin-N	38	134	5	27	3	4	0	13	10	22	.201	.262	.284	50	-10	0			.992	1	1-38	-1.3
1938	StL-A	148	602	100	195	42	7	12	82	58	49	.324	.384	.477	115	13	4	5	-2	.992	-0	*1-148	-0.6
1939	StL-A☆	154	617	101	195	37	13	20	94	65	42	.316	.383	.515	125	22	6	5	-1	.993	10	*1-154	1.3
1940	StL-A	151	594	78	166	39	10	16	84	57	58	.279	.343	.460	104	2	3	3	-1	.992	10	*1-150	-0.3
1941	StL-A	130	495	93	147	28	4	18	80	74	30	.297	.388	.479	124	18	5	4	-1	.995	8	*1-125	1.5
1942	StL-A☆	145	554	86	145	32	5	12	78	60	77	.262	.335	.403	105	3	1	1	-0	.991	1	*1-144	-0.4
1943	StL-A	125	449	53	109	19	2	12	74	56	65	.243	.327	.374	103	1	4	3	-1	.992	2	*1-122	-0.4
1944	*StL-A★	146	516	83	129	26	3	11	85	85	74	.250	.357	.376	103	4	4	1	-0	.994	-5	*1-146	-1.0
1945	StL-A†	139	483	69	134	31	3	7	61	65	51	.277	.364	.398	115	10	1	1	-0	.991	4	*1-136	0.5
1946	Phi-A	136	484	47	109	23	6	6	35	64	62	.225	.317	.316	78	-14	4	2	0	.988	3	*1-134	-1.9
1947	*NY-A★	144	517	84	157	24	3	13	80	78	66	.304	.395	.437	132	24	0	2	-1	.994	-2	*1-142	1.7
1948	NY-A★	94	302	33	75	11	4	11	41	40	38	.248	.336	.421	102	-0	0	2	-1	.993	-1	1-90	-0.3
Total	12	1550	5747	832	1588	315	64	135	794	712	634	.276	.357	.424	109	73	32	31		.992	31	*1-1529	-1.3

■ BRIAN McRAE
McRae, Brian Wesley   b: 8/27/67, Bradenton, Fla.   BB/TR, 6', 175 lbs.   Deb: 8/7/90   F

YEAR	TM/L	G	AB	R	H	2B	3B	HR	RBI	BB	SO	AVG	OBP	SLG	PRO+	BR/A	SB	CS	SBR	FA	FR	G/POS	TPR
1990	KC-A	46	168	21	48	8	3	2	23	9	29	.286	.322	.405	104	0	4	3	-1	1.000	4	O-45	0.2
1991	KC-A	152	629	86	164	28	9	8	64	24	99	.261	.290	.372	81	-17	20	11	-1	.993	4	*O-150	-1.4
1992	KC-A	149	533	63	119	23	5	4	52	42	88	.223	.287	.308	65	-25	18	5	2	.993	10	*O-148	-1.6
1993	KC-A	153	627	78	177	28	9	12	69	37	105	.282	.326	.413	92	-8	23	14	-2	.983	5	*O-110/D-4	-0.8
1994	KC-A	114	436	71	119	22	6	4	40	54	67	.273	.361	.442	87	-7	28	8	4	.988	-6	*O-110/D-4	-1.1
1995	Chi-N	137	580	92	167	38	7	12	48	47	92	.288	.349	.440	108	6	27	10	3	.991	10	*O-137	1.5
1996	Chi-N	157	624	111	172	32	5	17	66	73	84	.276	.362	.425	105	6	37	9	6	.986	1	O-155	0.8
Total	7	908	3597	522	966	179	44	59	362	286	564	.269	.329	.392	91	-45	157	58	12	.990	31	O-898/D-4	-2.4

■ HAL McRAE
McRae, Harold Abraham   b: 7/10/45, Avon Park, Fla.   BR/TR, 5'11", 180 lbs.   Deb: 7/11/68   FMC

YEAR	TM/L	G	AB	R	H	2B	3B	HR	RBI	BB	SO	AVG	OBP	SLG	PRO+	BR/A	SB	CS	SBR	FA	FR	G/POS	TPR
1968	Cin-N	17	51	1	10	1	0	0	2	4	14	.196	.255	.216	40	-4	1	1	-0	.926	-4	2-16	-0.8
1970	*Cin-N	70	165	18	41	6	1	8	23	15	23	.248	.315	.442	100	-1	0	2	-1	.981	-5	O-46/3-6,2-1	-0.9
1971	Cin-N	99	337	39	89	24	2	9	34	11	35	.264	.291	.427	103	-0	3	2	-0	.966	-1	O-91	-0.6
1972	*Cin-N	61	97	9	27	4	0	5	26	2	10	.278	.307	.474	126	3	0	0	-0	.867	-6	O-12,3-11	-0.4
1973	KC-A	106	338	36	79	18	3	9	50	34	38	.234	.315	.385	89	-5	2	2	-1	.963	-4	O-64,D-37/3-2	-1.3
1974	KC-A	148	539	71	167	36	4	15	88	54	68	.310	.373	.475	136	25	11	8	-2	.950	2	D-90,O-56/3-1	2.2
1975	KC-A★	126	480	58	147	38	6	5	71	47	47	.306	.373	.442	126	17	11	8	-2	.986	-1	*O-114,D-12/3-1	0.9
1976	*KC-A★	149	527	75	175	34	5	8	73	64	43	.332	.412	.461	154	38	22	12	-1	.970	-0	*D-117,O-31	3.4
1977	*KC-A	162	641	104	191	54	11	21	92	59	43	.298	.369	.515	137	32	18	14	-3	.958	4	*D-115,O-47	2.7
1978	*KC-A	156	623	90	170	39	5	16	72	51	62	.273	.334	.429	110	7	17	8	0	1.000	5	*D-153/O-3	0.3
1979	KC-A	101	393	55	113	32	4	10	74	38	46	.288	.356	.466	117	9	5	4	-1	1.000	4	*D-100	0.5
1980	*KC-A	124	489	73	145	39	5	14	83	29	56	.297	.346	.483	123	14	10	2	2	1.000	-1	*D-110/O-9	1.1
1981	KC-A	101	389	38	106	23	2	7	36	34	33	.272	.334	.396	111	5	3	4	-2	.909	0	D-97/O-4	0.0
1982	KC-A★	159	613	91	189	46	8	27	133	55	61	.308	.370	.542	146	38	4	4	-1	.500	-1	*D-158/O-1	3.0
1983	KC-A	157	589	84	183	41	6	12	82	50	68	.311	.374	.462	128	23	2	3	-1	.000	0	*D-156	1.6
1984	KC-A	106	317	30	96	13	4	3	42	34	47	.303	.372	.397	112	8	0	1	-1	.000	0	D-94	0.2
1985	*KC-A	112	320	41	83	19	0	14	70	44	45	.259	.351	.450	117	8	0	1	-0	.000	0	D-106	0.5
1986	KC-A	112	278	22	70	14	0	7	37	18	39	.252	.300	.378	81	-8	0	0	0	.000	0	D-75	-0.9
1987	KC-A	18	32	5	10	0	0	1	9	5	1	.313	.405	.500	135	2	0	0	0	.000	0	/D-7	0.1
Total	19	2084	7218	940	2091	484	66	191	1097	648	779	.290	.355	.454	122	210	109	78	-14	.966	-16	*D-1427,O-478/32	11.6

■ McREMER
McRemer   Deb: 6/20/1884

YEAR	TM/L	G	AB	R	H	2B	3B	HR	RBI	BB	SO	AVG	OBP	SLG	PRO+	BR/A	SB	CS	SBR	FA	FR	G/POS	TPR
1884	Was-U	1	3	0	0	0	0	0		0		.000	.000	.000	-99	-1				1.000	0	/O-1	-0.1

■ KEVIN McREYNOLDS
McReynolds, Walter Kevin   b: 10/16/59, Little Rock, Ark.   BR/TR, 6'1", 210 lbs.   Deb: 6/2/83

YEAR	TM/L	G	AB	R	H	2B	3B	HR	RBI	BB	SO	AVG	OBP	SLG	PRO+	BR/A	SB	CS	SBR	FA	FR	G/POS	TPR
1983	SD-N	39	140	15	31	3	1	4	14	12	29	.221	.283	.343	75	-5	2	1	0	.989	0	O-38	-0.7
1984	*SD-N	147	525	68	146	26	6	20	75	34	69	.278	.322	.465	119	11	3	6	-3	.991	18	*O-143	2.3
1985	SD-N	152	564	61	132	24	4	15	75	43	81	.234	.292	.371	85	-12	4	0	1	.993	23	*O-150	0.7
1986	SD-N	158	560	89	161	31	6	26	96	66	83	.287	.364	.504	140	29	8	6	-1	.977	-14	*O-154	1.0
1987	NY-N	151	590	86	163	32	5	29	95	39	70	.276	.322	.495	130	19	14	1	4	.987	9	*O-150	2.0
1988	*NY-N	147	552	82	159	30	2	27	99	38	61	.288	.338	.496	144	28	21	0	6	.985	10	*O-145	4.3
1989	NY-N	148	545	74	148	25	3	22	85	46	74	.272	.329	.450	127	17	15	7	0	.969	15	*O-145	3.0
1990	NY-N	147	521	75	140	23	1	24	82	71	61	.269	.358	.455	122	16	9	2	2	.988	5	*O-144	2.0
1991	NY-N	143	522	65	135	32	1	16	74	49	46	.259	.325	.416	108	4	6	6	-1	.993	-9	*O-141	0.1
1992	KC-A	109	373	45	92	25	0	13	49	67	48	.247	.361	.418	115	9	7	1	2	.986	-3	*O-106/D-1	0.5
1993	KC-A	110	351	44	86	22	4	11	42	37	56	.245	.319	.425	92	-5	2	2	-1	.990	-0	*O-104/D-1	-0.7
1994	NY-N	51	180	23	46	11	2	4	21	20	34	.256	.330	.406	91	-2	0	1	0	1.000	2	O-47	0.0
Total	12	1502	5423	727	1439	284	35	211	807	522	707	.265	.331	.447	116	103	93	32	9	.987	68	*O-1469/D-2	14.5

■ PETE McSHANNIC
McShannic, Peter Robert   b: 3/20/1864, Pittsburgh, Pa.   d: 11/30/46, Toledo, Ohio   BB/TR, 5'7", 190 lbs.   Deb: 9/15/1888

YEAR	TM/L	G	AB	R	H	2B	3B	HR	RBI	BB	SO	AVG	OBP	SLG	PRO+	BR/A	SB	CS	SBR	FA	FR	G/POS	TPR
1888	Pit-N	26	98	5	19	1	0	0	5	1		.194	.218	.204	38	-7	3			.907	-0	3-26	-0.6

■ TRICK McSORLEY
McSorley, John Bernard   b: 12/6/1852, St.Louis, Mo.   d: 2/9/36, St.Louis, Mo.   BR/TR, 5'4", 142 lbs.   Deb: 5/6/1875

YEAR	TM/L	G	AB	R	H	2B	3B	HR	RBI	BB	SO	AVG	OBP	SLG	PRO+	BR/A	SB	CS	SBR	FA	FR	G/POS	TPR
1875	RS-n	15	52	4	11	0	0	0	2			.212	.212	.212	53	-2	3	0	1	.745	1	/3-9,O-7	0.0
1884	Tol-a	21	68	12	17	1	0	0			3	.250	.282	.265	77	-2				.974	1	1-16/O-5,3-1,P-1	-0.2
1885	StL-N	2	6	2	3	1	0	0		1		.500	.667	.667	340	2				.400	-2	/3-2	0.0
1886	StL-a	5	20	1	3	0	0	0	1		1	.150	.150	.300	38	-2	0			.765	-3	/S-5	-0.4
Total	3	28	94	15	23	5	0	0	1	5	1	.245	.283	.298	85	-1	0	0	0	.400	-4	/1-16,S-5,O-5,3P	-0.6

■ PAUL McSWEENEY
McSweeney, Paul A.   b: 4/3/1867, St.Louis, Mo.   d: 8/12/51, St.Louis, Mo.   Deb: 9/20/1891

YEAR	TM/L	G	AB	R	H	2B	3B	HR	RBI	BB	SO	AVG	OBP	SLG	PRO+	BR/A	SB	CS	SBR	FA	FR	G/POS	TPR
1891	StL-a	3	12	2	3	1	0	0	2	0	0	.250	.308	.333	73	-1	1			.643	-2	/2-3,3-1	-0.2

■ JIM McTAMANY
McTamany, James Edward   b: 7/1/1863, Philadelphia, Pa.   d: 4/16/16, Lenni, Pa.   BR/TR, 5'8", 190 lbs.   Deb: 8/15/1885

YEAR	TM/L	G	AB	R	H	2B	3B	HR	RBI	BB	SO	AVG	OBP	SLG	PRO+	BR/A	SB	CS	SBR	FA	FR	G/POS	TPR
1885	Bro-a	35	131	21	36	7	2	1	13	9		.275	.321	.382	121	3				.896	-5	O-35	-0.3
1886	Bro-a	111	418	86	106	23	10	2	56	54		.254	.353	.371	126	14	18			.893	14	*O-111	2.2
1887	Bro-a	134	520	123	134	22	10	1	68	76		.258	.365	.344	97	1	66			.918	8	*O-134	0.5
1888	KC-a	130	516	94	127	12	10	4	41	67		.246	.345	.331	110	7	55			.913	6	*O-130	0.8
1889	Col-a	139	529	113	146	21	7	4	52	116	66	.276	.407	.365	127	27	40			.902	-5	*O-139	1.5
1890	Col-a	125	466	140	120	27	7	1	48	112		.258	.405	.352	132	27	43			.940	2	*O-125	2.2
1891	Col-a	81	304	59	76	17	9	3	35	58	48	.250	.374	.395	127	13	20			.929	-3	O-81	0.6
	Phi-a	58	218	57	49	6	3	1	21	43	44	.225	.365	.321	94	-1	13			.901	1	O-58	-0.2
	Yr	139	522	116	125	23	12	6	56	101	92	.239	.370	.364	112	12	33			.917	-2	*O-139	0.4
Total	7	813	3102	693	794	135	58	19	334	535	158	.256	.373	.355	117	91	255			.913	16	O-813	7.3

■ BILL McTIGUE
McTigue, William Patrick "Rebel"   b: 1/3/1891, Nashville, Tenn.   d: 5/8/20, Nashville, Tenn.   BL/TL, 6'1.5", 175 lbs.   Deb: 5/2/11

YEAR	TM/L	G	AB	R	H	2B	3B	HR	RBI	BB	SO	AVG	OBP	SLG	PRO+	BR/A	SB	CS	SBR	FA	FR	G/POS	TPR
1911	Bos-N	14	12	1	1	0	0	0	1	0	5	.083	.083	.167	-28	-2	0			.875	-1	P-14	0.0
1912	Bos-N	10	13	2	1	0	0	0	0	0	1	.077	.143	.077	-38	-2	0			1.000	0	P-10	0.0
1913	Bos-N	1	0	0	0	0	0	0	0	0	0	—	—	—						.000	0	R	0.0
1916	Det-A	3	1	0	0	0	0	0	1	0	4	.000	.000	.000	-97	-0	0			1.000	0	/P-3	0.0
Total	4	28	26	3	2	0	0	0	2	0	10	.077	.111	.115	-36	-5	0			.957	0	/P-27	0.0

YEAR	TM/L	G	AB	R	H	2B	3B	HR	RBI	BB	SO	AVG	OBP	SLG	PRO+	BR/A	SB	CS	SBR	FA	FR	G/POS	TPR

■ CAL McVEY   McVey, Calvin Alexander   b: 8/30/1850, Montrose, Iowa   d: 8/20/26, San Francisco, Cal   BR/TR, 5'9", 170 lbs.   Deb: 5/5/1871   M

1871	Bos-n	29	153	43	**66**	9	5	0	43	1	2	.431	.435	.556	177	14	6	0	2	.873	1	*C-29/O-5,3-1	1.0
1872	Bos-n	46	237	56	76	10	2	0	41	1	1	.321	.324	.380	110	1		6	1	.869	4	*C-40,O-11/3-1	0.4
1873	Bal-n	38	192	49	73	4	5	2	34	3	2	.380	.390	.484	159	13	1	0	0	.907	-1	C-25/O-6,S-5,213M	0.9
1874	Bos-n	70	343	**91**	**123**	21	6	3	**71**	1	3	.359	.360	.481	158	20	5	2	0	.710	-2	*O-57,C-23	1.6
1875	Bos-n	82	389	89	138	**36**	9	3	**87**	1	5	.355	.356	**.517**	193	33	7	0	2	.949	6	*1-55,O-23,C-16/P	3.4
1876	Chi-N	63	308	62	107	15	0	1	53	2	4	.347	.352	.406	136	9				.959	4	1-55,P-11/C-6,O3	0.9
1877	Chi-N	60	266	58	98	9	7	0	36	8	11	.368	.387	.455	147	12				.859	-13	*C-40,3-17,P/21	0.0
1878	Cin-N	61	271	43	83	10	4	2	28	5	10	.306	.319	.395	147	14				.814	-10	*3-61/C-3,M	0.6
1879	Cin-N	81	354	64	105	18	6	0	55	8	13	.297	.312	.381	134	13				.946	-7	*1-72/O-7,P-3,3CM	0.3
Total	5 n	265	1314	328	476	80	27	8	276	7	13	.362	.366	.482	161	82	25	1	7	.876	1	C-133,O-102/1S23P	7.3
Total	4	265	1199	227	393	52	17	3	172	23	38	.328	.340	.407	140	48				.951	-26	1-128/3-80,CPO2	1.8

■ GEORGE McVEY   McVey, George W.   b: 9/16/1865, Port Jervis, N.Y.   d: 5/3/1896, Quincy, Ill.   BR/TR, 6'1", 185 lbs.   Deb: 9/19/1885

1885	Bro-a	6	21	2	3	0	0	0	1	0	2	.143	.217	.143	15	-2				.967	-0	/1-3,C-3	-0.2

■ BILL McWILLIAMS   McWilliams, William Henry   b: 11/28/10, Dubuque, Iowa   BR/TR, 6', 185 lbs.   Deb: 7/8/31

1931	Bos-A	2	2	0	0	0	0	0	0	0	1	.000	.000	.000	-99	-1	0	0	0	.000	0	H	-0.1

■ BOB MEACHAM   Meacham, Robert Andrew   b: 8/25/60, Los Angeles, Cal.   BB/TR, 6'1", 180 lbs.   Deb: 6/30/83

1983	NY-A	22	51	5	12	2	0	0	4	4	10	.235	.304	.275	63	-2	8	0	2	.929	9	S-18/3-4	1.0
1984	NY-A	99	360	62	91	13	4	2	25	32	70	.253	.319	.328	83	-8	9	5	-0	.955	-12	S-96/2-2	-1.1
1985	NY-A	156	481	70	105	16	2	1	47	54	102	.218	.304	.266	59	-26	25	7	3	.963	-17	*S-155	-2.4
1986	NY-A	56	161	19	36	7	1	0	10	17	39	.224	.309	.280	62	-8	3	6	-3	.948	-5	S-56	-1.0
1987	NY-A	77	203	28	55	11	1	5	21	19	33	.271	.351	.409	102	1	6	5	-1	.961	-1	S-56,2-25/D-1	0.3
1988	NY-A	47	115	18	25	9	0	0	7	14	22	.217	.313	.296	72	-4	7	1	2	.959	-7	S-24,2-21/3-5	-0.8
Total	6	457	1371	202	324	58	8	8	114	140	276	.236	.316	.308	73	-47	58	24	3	.957	-32	S-405/2-48,3-9,D-1	-4.0

■ CHARLIE MEAD   Mead, Charles Richard   b: 4/9/21, Vermilion, Alberta, Canada   BL/TR, 6'1.5", 185 lbs.   Deb: 8/28/43

1943	NY-N	37	146	9	40	6	1	1	13	10	15	.274	.321	.349	93	-2	3			.976	0	O-37	-0.3
1944	NY-N	39	78	5	14	1	0	1	8	5	7	.179	.229	.231	30	-7	0			.981	2	O-23	-0.7
1945	NY-N	11	37	4	10	1	0	1	6	5	2	.270	.357	.378	103	0	0			.962	1	O-11	0.1
Total	3	87	261	18	64	8	1	3	27	20	24	.245	.299	.318	75	-9	3			.975	4	/O-71	-0.9

■ LOUIE MEADOWS   Meadows, Michael Ray   b: 4/29/61, Maysville, N.C.   BL/TL, 5'11", 190 lbs.   Deb: 7/3/86

1986	Hou-N	6	6	1	2	0	0	0	0	0	1	.333	.333	.333	87	-0	1	0	0	.000	-0	/O-1	0.0
1988	Hou-N	35	42	5	8	0	1	2	3	6	8	.190	.292	.381	95	-0	4	2	0	1.000	-4	O-10	0.0
1989	Hou-N	31	51	5	9	0	0	3	10	1	14	.176	.192	.353	55	-3	1	2	-1	1.000	-4	O-14/1-1	-0.9
1990	Hou-N	15	14	3	2	0	0	0	1	2	4	.143	.250	.143	11	-2	0	0	0	1.000	-2	/O-9	-0.4
	Phi-N	15	14	1	1	0	0	0	0	1	2	.071	.133	.071	-42	-7	0	0	0	1.000	-2	/O-4	-0.5
	Yr	30	28	4	3	0	0	0	1	3	6	.107	.194	.107	-15	-4	0	0	0	1.000	-4	O-13	-0.9
Total	4	102	127	15	22	0	1	5	13	10	28	.173	.234	.307	54	-8	6	4	-1	1.000	-9	/O-38,1-1	-1.8

■ PAT MEANEY   Meaney, Patrick J.   b: 7/1871, Philadelphia, Pa.   d: 10/20/22, Philadelphia, Pa.   BR/TR,   Deb: 5/18/12

1912	Det-A	1	2	0	0	0	0	0	0	0	1	.000	.500	.000	48	-0				.833	-0	/S-1	0.0

■ CHARLIE MEARA   Meara, Charles Edward "Goggy"   b: 4/13/1891, New York, N.Y.   d: 2/8/62, Bronx, N.Y.   BL/TR, 5'10", 160 lbs.   Deb: 6/1/14

1914	NY-A	4	7	2	2	0	0	0	1	2	2	.286	.444	.286	120	1	0	1	-1	1.000	-1	/O-3	-0.1

■ PAT MEARES   Meares, Patrick James   b: 9/6/68, Salina, Kan.   BR/TR, 6', 185 lbs.   Deb: 5/5/93

1993	Min-A	111	346	33	87	14	3	0	33	7	52	.251	.268	.309	55	-22	4	5	-2	.961	-1	*S-111	-1.7
1994	Min-A	80	229	29	61	12	1	2	24	14	50	.266	.314	.354	72	-10	5	1	1	.963	2	S-79	0.0
1995	Min-A	116	390	57	105	19	4	12	49	15	68	.269	.315	.431	91	-6	10	4	1	.965	-9	*S-114/O-3	-0.3
1996	Min-A	152	517	66	138	26	7	8	67	17	90	.267	.302	.391	72	-23	9	4	0	.965	-31	*S-150/O-1	-3.7
Total	4	459	1482	185	391	71	15	22	173	53	260	.264	.300	.377	73	-61	28	14	0	.964	-38	S-454/O-4	-5.7

■ RAY MEDEIROS   Medeiros, Ray Antone "Pep"   b: 5/9/26, Oakland, Cal.   BR/TR, 5'10", 163 lbs.   Deb: 4/25/45

1945	Cin-N	1	0	0	0	0	0	0	0	0	0					0				.000	0	R	0.0

■ LUIS MEDINA   Medina, Luis Main   b: 3/26/63, Santa Monica, Cal.   BR/TL, 6'4", 200 lbs.   Deb: 9/2/88

1988	Cle-A	16	51	10	13	0	0	6	8	2	18	.255	.309	.608	146	3	0	0	0	1.000	-0	1-16	0.1
1989	Cle-A	30	83	8	17	1	0	4	8	7	35	.205	.258	.361	72	-3	0	1	-1	.500	-1	D-25/O-3,1-1	-0.6
1991	Cle-A	5	16	0	1	0	0	0	0	7	7	.063	.118	.063	-48	-3	0	0	0	.000	0	/D-5	-0.4
Total	3	51	150	18	31	1	0	10	16	9	60	.207	.261	.413	85	-4	0	1	-1	1.000	-2	/D-30,1-17,O-3	-0.9

■ JOE MEDWICK   Medwick, Joseph Michael "Ducky" or "Muscles"   b: 11/24/11, Carteret, N.J.   d: 3/21/75, St.Petersburg, Fla   BR/TR, 5'10", 187 lbs.   Deb: 9/2/32   H

1932	StL-N	26	106	13	37	12	1	2	12	2	10	.349	.367	.538	136	5	3			.970	-0	O-26	0.4
1933	StL-N	148	595	92	182	40	10	18	98	26	56	.306	.337	.497	129	20	5			.980	8	*O-147	2.1
1934	*StL-N★	149	620	110	198	40	**18**	18	106	21	83	.319	.343	.529	122	16	3			.960	4	*O-149	1.4
1935	StL-N★	154	634	132	224	46	13	23	126	30	59	.353	.386	.576	149	41	4			.965	3	*O-154	3.6
1936	StL-N★	155	636	115	**223**	**64**	13	18	**138**	34	33	.351	.387	.577	157	47	3			.985	14	*O-155	5.3
1937	StL-N★	156	633	**111**	**237**	**56**	10	**31**	**154**	41	50	**.374**	.414	**.641**	179	66	4			**.988**	4	*O-156	6.2
1938	StL-N★	146	590	100	190	**47**	8	21	**122**	42	41	.322	.369	.536	138	29	0			.974	4	*O-144	3.2
1939	StL-N★	150	606	98	201	48	8	14	117	45	44	.332	.380	.507	128	23	6			.976	5	*O-149	2.2
1940	StL-N	37	158	21	48	12	0	3	20	6	8	.304	.329	.437	104	0	0			.988	-0	O-37	-0.2
	Bro-N★	106	423	62	127	18	12	14	66	26	28	.300	.345	.499	123	11	2			.980	5	O-103	1.2
	Yr	143	581	83	175	30	12	17	86	32	36	.301	.341	.482	118	12	2			.982	5	O-140	1.0
1941	*Bro-N★	133	538	100	171	33	10	18	88	38	35	.318	.364	.512	140	26	2			.983	1	*O-131	2.0
1942	Bro-N★	142	553	69	166	37	4	4	96	33	25	.300	.338	.403	115	9	2			.990	-5	*O-140	-0.1
1943	Bro-N	48	173	13	47	10	0	0	25	10	8	.272	.315	.329	86	-3	1			.971	-5	O-42	-1.1
	NY-N	78	324	41	91	20	3	5	45	9	14	.281	.300	.407	103	-1	4			.988	-0	O-74/1-3	0.0
	Yr	126	497	54	138	30	3	5	70	19	22	.278	.306	.380	97	-4	5			.983	-0	*O-116/1-3	-1.1
1944	NY-N★	128	490	64	165	24	3	7	85	38	24	.337	.386	.441	133	21	2			.993	8	*O-122	2.3
1945	NY-N	26	92	14	28	4	3	1	11	2	2	.304	.319	.446	110	1	2			.979	-1	O-23	-0.1
	Bos-N	66	218	17	62	13	0	0	26	12	12	.284	.325	.344	85	-4	2			1.000	-5	O-38,1-15	-0.7
	Yr	92	310	31	90	17	3	1	37	14	14	.290	.323	.374	93	-4	2			.992	-0	O-61,1-15	-0.8
1946	Bro-N	41	77	7	24	4	0	2	18	6	5	.312	.369	.442	128	3	0			1.000	-0	O-18/1-1	-0.1
1947	StL-N	75	150	19	46	12	4	0	28	16	12	.307	.373	.467	117	4	0			1.000	-5	O-43	-0.3
1948	StL-N	20	19	0	4	0	0	0	4	1	1	.211	.250	.211	24	-2	0			.000	-0	/O-1	-0.2
Total	17	1984	7635	1198	2471	540	113	205	1383	437	551	.324	.362	.505	134	310	42			.980	49	*O-1852/1-19	27.1

■ TOMMY MEE   Mee, Thomas William "Judge"   b: 3/18/1890, Chicago, Ill.   d: 5/16/81, Chicago, Ill.   BR/TR, 5'8", 165 lbs.   Deb: 6/14/10

1910	StL-A	8	19	1	3	2	0	1	6	2		.158	.158	.263	34	-2	0			.828	-1	/S-6,2-1,3-1	-0.3

■ DAD MEEK   Meek, Frank J.   b: 3/14/1867, St.Louis, Mo.   d: 12/22/22, St.Louis, Mo.   Deb: 5/10/1889

1889	StL-a	2	2	1	1	0	0	0		0		.500	.500	.500	164	0	1			.667	0	/C-2	0.0
1890	StL-a	4	16	3	5	0	0	0		0		.313	.313	.313	74	-1	1			.913	3	/C-4	0.2
Total	2	6	18	5	6	0	0	0	0	0	0	.333	.333	.333	84	-1	2			.898	3	/C-6	0.2

■ SAMMY MEEKS   Meeks, Samuel Mack   b: 4/23/23, Anderson, S.C.   BR/TR, 5'9", 160 lbs.   Deb: 4/29/48

1948	Was-A	24	33	4	4	1	0	0	1	2	12	.121	.147	.152	-21	-6	0	0	0	.939	-0	S-10/2-1	-0.6
1949	Cin-N	16	36	10	11	2	0	2	6	2	6	.306	.342	.528	128	1	1			1.000	6	/2-8,S-3	0.7

YEAR	TM/L	G	AB	R	H	2B	3B	HR	RBI	BB	SO	AVG	OBP	SLG	PRO+	BR/A	SB	CS	SBR	FA	FR	G/POS	TPR
1950	Cin-N	39	95	7	27	5	0	1	8	6	14	.284	.327	.368	82	-2	1			.951	-4	S-29/3-2	-0.5
1951	Cin-N	23	35	4	8	0	0	0	2	0	4	.229	.229	.229	23	-4	1	0	0	.929	-1	/3-4,S-1	-0.5
Total	4	102	199	25	50	8	0	3	18	9	36	.251	.284	.337	64	-11	3	0		.953	0	/S-43,2-9,3-6	-0.9

■ **DUTCH MEIER** Meier, Arthur Ernst b: 3/30/1879, St.Louis, Mo. d: 3/23/48, Chicago, Ill. BR/TR, 5'10", 175 lbs. Deb: 5/12/06

YEAR	TM/L	G	AB	R	H	2B	3B	HR	RBI	BB	SO	AVG	OBP	SLG	PRO+	BR/A	SB	CS	SBR	FA	FR	G/POS	TPR
1906	Pit-N	82	273	32	70	11	4	0	16	13		.256	.298	.326	90	-4	4			.975	-12	O-52,S-17	-1.9

■ **DAVE MEIER** Meier, David Keith b: 8/8/59, Helena, Mont. BR/TR, 6', 185 lbs. Deb: 4/3/84

YEAR	TM/L	G	AB	R	H	2B	3B	HR	RBI	BB	SO	AVG	OBP	SLG	PRO+	BR/A	SB	CS	SBR	FA	FR	G/POS	TPR
1984	Min-A	59	147	18	35	8	1	0	13	6	9	.238	.273	.306	57	-9	0	1	-1	.978	-4	O-50/3-1,D-4	-1.4
1985	Min-A	71	104	15	27	6	0	1	8	18	12	.260	.374	.346	93	-0	0	6	-4	.987	-9	O-63/D-3	-0.2
1987	Tex-A	13	21	4	6	1	0	0	0	0	4	.286	.286	.333	63	-1	0	0	0	.917	-1	/O-8	-0.1
1988	Chi-N	2	5	0	2	0	0	0	1	0	1	.400	.400	.400	125	0	0	0	0	1.000	1	/3-1	-0.1
Total	4	145	277	37	70	15	1	1	22	24	26	.253	.317	.325	73	-10	0	7	-4	.978	-15	O-121/D-7,3-2	-3.1

■ **WALT MEINERT** Meinert, Walter Henry b: 12/11/1890, New York, N.Y. d: 11/9/58, Decatur, Ill. BL/TL, 5'7.5", 150 lbs. Deb: 9/6/13

YEAR	TM/L	G	AB	R	H	2B	3B	HR	RBI	BB	SO	AVG	OBP	SLG	PRO+	BR/A	SB	CS	SBR	FA	FR	G/POS	TPR
1913	StL-A	4	8	1	3	0	0	0	1	3		.375	.444	.375	144	1	1			1.000	-0	/O-2	0.0

■ **FRANK MEINKE** Meinke, Frank Louis b: 10/18/1863, Chicago, Ill. d: 11/8/31, Chicago, Ill. BR , 5'10.5", 172 lbs. Deb: 5/1/1884 F

YEAR	TM/L	G	AB	R	H	2B	3B	HR	RBI	BB	SO	AVG	OBP	SLG	PRO+	BR/A	SB	CS	SBR	FA	FR	G/POS	TPR
1884	Det-N	92	341	28	56	5	7	6	24	6	89	.164	.179	.273	42	-22				.839	-3	S-51,P-35/O-4,32	-1.3
1885	Det-N	1	3	0	0	0	0	0	0	0	1	.000	.000	.000	-99	-1				1.000	-0	/O-1,P-1	0.0
Total	2	93	344	28	56	5	7	6	24	6	90	.163	.177	.270	41	-22				1.000	-3	/S-51,P-36,O-5,23	-1.3

■ **BOB MEINKE** Meinke, Robert Bernard b: 6/25/1887, Chicago, Ill. d: 12/29/52, Chicago, Ill. BR/TR, 5'10", 135 lbs. Deb: 8/22/10 F

YEAR	TM/L	G	AB	R	H	2B	3B	HR	RBI	BB	SO	AVG	OBP	SLG	PRO+	BR/A	SB	CS	SBR	FA	FR	G/POS	TPR
1910	Cin-N	2	1	0	0	0	0	0	0	0		.000	.500	.000	51	0	0			1.000	1	/S-2	0.1

■ **GEORGE MEISTER** Meister, George B. b: 6/5/1864, Dorzbach, Germany d: 8/24/08, Pittsburgh, Pa. Deb: 8/15/1884

YEAR	TM/L	G	AB	R	H	2B	3B	HR	RBI	BB	SO	AVG	OBP	SLG	PRO+	BR/A	SB	CS	SBR	FA	FR	G/POS	TPR
1884	Tol-a	34	119	9	23	6	0	0		3		.193	.244	.244	58	-5				.817	-9	3-34	-1.4

■ **JOHN MEISTER** Meister, John F. b: 5/10/1863, Allentown, Pa. d: 1/17/23, Philadelphia, Pa. 5'8", 175 lbs. Deb: 8/24/1886

YEAR	TM/L	G	AB	R	H	2B	3B	HR	RBI	BB	SO	AVG	OBP	SLG	PRO+	BR/A	SB	CS	SBR	FA	FR	G/POS	TPR
1886	NY-a	45	186	35	44	7	3	2	21	4		.237	.253	.339	89	-3	1			.906	-8	2-45	-0.8
1887	NY-a	39	157	24	35	6	2	1	21	16		.223	.303	.306	73	-5	9			.930	-9	O-22,2-14/3-3,S-1	-1.2
Total	2	84	343	59	79	13	5	3	42	20		.230	.277	.324	81	-8	10			.905	-17	/2-59,O-22,3-3,S-1	-2.0

■ **KARL MEISTER** Meister, Karl Daniel "Dutch" b: 5/15/1891, Marietta, Ohio d: 8/15/67, Marietta, Ohio BR/TR, 6', 178 lbs. Deb: 8/10/13

YEAR	TM/L	G	AB	R	H	2B	3B	HR	RBI	BB	SO	AVG	OBP	SLG	PRO+	BR/A	SB	CS	SBR	FA	FR	G/POS	TPR
1913	Cin-N	4	7	1	2	0	2	0	4			.286	.286	.429	103	-0	0			.667	-2	/O-4	-0.2

■ **MOXIE MEIXELL** Meixell, Merton Merrill b: 10/18/1887, Lake Crystal, Minn d: 8/17/82, Los Angeles, Cal. BL/TR, 5'10", 168 lbs. Deb: 7/7/12

YEAR	TM/L	G	AB	R	H	2B	3B	HR	RBI	BB	SO	AVG	OBP	SLG	PRO+	BR/A	SB	CS	SBR	FA	FR	G/POS	TPR
1912	Cle-A	3	2	0	1	0	0	0	0			.500	.500	.500	181	0	0			.000	0	/O-1	0.0

■ **MIGUEL MEJIA** Mejia, Miguel b: 3/25/75, San Pedro De Macoris, D.R. BR/TR, 6'1", 155 lbs. Deb: 4/4/96

YEAR	TM/L	G	AB	R	H	2B	3B	HR	RBI	BB	SO	AVG	OBP	SLG	PRO+	BR/A	SB	CS	SBR	FA	FR	G/POS	TPR
1996	*StL-N	45	23	10	2	0	0	0	0	0	10	.087	.087	.087	-54	-5	6	3	0	.933	-6	O-21	-1.1

■ **ROBERTO MEJIA** Mejia, Roberto Antonio (Diaz) b: 4/14/72, Hato Mayor, D.R. BR/TR, 5'11", 160 lbs. Deb: 7/15/93

YEAR	TM/L	G	AB	R	H	2B	3B	HR	RBI	BB	SO	AVG	OBP	SLG	PRO+	BR/A	SB	CS	SBR	FA	FR	G/POS	TPR
1993	Col-N	65	229	31	53	14	5	5	20	13	63	.231	.279	.402	68	-11	4	1	1	.963	7	2-65	-0.2
1994	Col-N	38	116	11	28	8	1	4	15	33		.241	.328	.431	82	-3	0	1	0	.959	-3	2-34	-0.4
1995	Col-N	23	52	5	8	1	0	1	4	0	17	.154	.170	.231	3	-7	0	1	-1	.971	1	2-16	-0.7
Total	3	126	397	47	89	23	6	10	38	28	113	.224	.279	.388	63	-22	7	3	0	.962	5	2-115	-1.3

■ **ROMAN MEJIAS** Mejias, Roman (Gomez) b: 8/9/30, Abreus, Las Villas, Cuba BR/TR, 6', 175 lbs. Deb: 4/13/55

YEAR	TM/L	G	AB	R	H	2B	3B	HR	RBI	BB	SO	AVG	OBP	SLG	PRO+	BR/A	SB	CS	SBR	FA	FR	G/POS	TPR
1955	Pit-N	71	167	14	36	8	1	3	21	9	13	.216	.256	.329	55	-11	1	3	-2	.926	-0	O-44	-1.5
1957	Pit-N	58	142	12	39	7	4	2	15	6	13	.275	.309	.423	97	-1	2	1	-1	1.000	-2	O-42	-0.5
1958	Pit-N	76	157	17	42	3	2	5	19	2	27	.268	.281	.408	82	-5	2	0	1	.973	-1	O-57	-0.7
1959	Pit-N	96	276	28	65	6	1	7	28	21	48	.236	.301	.341	71	-11	1	2	-1	.970	-0	O-85	-1.6
1960	Pit-N	3	1	1	0	0	0	0	0	0	1	.000	.000	.000	-99	-0	0	0	0	.000	0	H	0.0
1961	Pit-N	4	1	1	0	0	0	0	0	0	1	.000	.000	.000	-99	-0	0	0	0	1.000	-1	/O-2	-0.1
1962	Hou-N	146	566	82	162	12	3	24	76	30	83	.286	.329	.445	114	9	12	4	1	.946	-4	*O-142	-0.3
1963	Bos-A	111	357	43	81	18	0	11	39	14	36	.227	.262	.370	72	-14	4	1	1	.973	2	O-86	-1.6
1964	Bos-A	62	101	14	24	3	1	2	4	7	16	.238	.294	.347	74	-4	0	0	0	.962	-3	O-37	-0.8
Total	9	627	1768	212	449	57	12	54	202	89	238	.254	.296	.391	86	-38	22	12	-1	.963	-8	O-495	-7.1

■ **SAM MEJIAS** Mejias, Samuel Elias b: 5/9/52, Santiago, D.R. BR/TR, 6', 170 lbs. Deb: 9/6/76 C

YEAR	TM/L	G	AB	R	H	2B	3B	HR	RBI	BB	SO	AVG	OBP	SLG	PRO+	BR/A	SB	CS	SBR	FA	FR	G/POS	TPR
1976	StL-N	18	21	1	3	1	0	0	2	2	1	.143	.217	.190	16	-2	2	0	1	1.000	-3	O-17	-0.5
1977	Mon-N	74	101	14	23	4	1	3	8	2	17	.228	.243	.376	65	-5	1	0	0	.966	-12	O-56	-1.9
1978	Mon-N	67	56	9	13	1	0	0	6	2	5	.232	.259	.250	43	-4	0	0	0	.949	-14	O-52/P-1	-2.0
1979	Chi-N	31	11	4	2	0	0	0	0	2	5	.182	.308	.182	34	-1	0	0	0	.875	-4	O-23	-0.9
	Cin-N	7	2	1	1	0	0	0	0	0		.500	.500	.500	173	0	0	0	0	1.000	-2	/O-5	-0.2
	Yr	38	13	5	3	0	0	0	0	2	5	.231	.333	.231	53	-1	0	0	0	.889	-10	O-28	-1.1
1980	Cin-N	71	108	16	30	5	1	1	10	6	13	.278	.322	.370	93	-1	4	2	0	.989	-13	O-67	-1.7
1981	Cin-N	66	49	6	14	2	0	1	5	2	9	.286	.314	.327	80	-1	1	0	0	.972	-16	O-58	-1.9
Total	6	334	348	51	86	13	2	4	31	16	51	.247	.282	.330	69	-15	8	2	1	.973	-68	O-278/P-1	-9.1

■ **DUTCH MELE** Mele, Albert Ernest b: 1/11/15, New York, N.Y. d: 2/12/75, Hollywood, Fla. BL/TL, 6'0.5", 195 lbs. Deb: 9/14/37

YEAR	TM/L	G	AB	R	H	2B	3B	HR	RBI	BB	SO	AVG	OBP	SLG	PRO+	BR/A	SB	CS	SBR	FA	FR	G/POS	TPR
1937	Cin-N	6	14	1	2	1	0	0	1	1	1	.143	.200	.214	13	-2	0			1.000	-2	/O-5	-0.4

■ **SAM MELE** Mele, Sabath Anthony b: 1/21/23, Astoria, N.Y. BR/TR, 6'1", 187 lbs. Deb: 4/15/47 MC

YEAR	TM/L	G	AB	R	H	2B	3B	HR	RBI	BB	SO	AVG	OBP	SLG	PRO+	BR/A	SB	CS	SBR	FA	FR	G/POS	TPR
1947	Bos-A	123	453	71	137	14	8	12	73	37	35	.302	.356	.448	114	8	0	3	-2	.992	-3	*O-116/1-1	-0.3
1948	Bos-A	66	180	25	42	12	1	2	25	13	21	.233	.292	.344	66	-9	1	1	-0	.971	-4	O-55	-1.6
1949	Bos-A	18	46	1	9	1	1	0	7	7	14	.196	.302	.261	46	-4	2	0	1	.955	-0	O-11	-0.4
	Was-A	78	264	21	64	12	2	3	25	17	34	.242	.288	.337	67	-14	2	1	0	.966	-8	O-63,1-11	-2.5
	Yr	96	310	22	73	13	3	3	32	24	48	.235	.290	.326	63	-18	4	1	1	.964	-9	O-74,1-11	-2.9
1950	Was-A	126	435	57	119	21	6	12	86	51	40	.274	.351	.432	105	2	2	0	0	.990	-5	O-99,1-16	-0.7
1951	Was-A	143	558	58	153	36	7	5	94	32	31	.274	.315	.391	92	-9	2	3	-1	.993	-4	*O-124,1-15	-1.2
1952	Was-A	9	28	2	12	3	0	2	10	1	2	.429	.448	.750	237	5	0	0	0	.917	-1	/O-7	0.3
	Chi-A	123	423	46	105	18	2	14	59	48	40	.248	.328	.400	101	-0	1	2	-1	1.000	-7	*O-112/1-3	-1.2
	Yr	132	451	48	117	21	2	16	69	49	42	.259	.334	.421	109	4	1	2	-1	.994	-7	*O-119/1-3	-0.9
1953	Chi-A	140	481	64	132	26	8	12	82	58	47	.274	.353	.437	109	5	2	1	0	.996	-8	O-138/1-2	-0.7
1954	Bal-A	72	230	17	55	9	4	5	32	18	26	.239	.294	.378	90	-5	1	0	0	.962	-4	O-62	-1.1
	Bos-A	42	132	22	42	6	0	7	23	12	12	.318	.384	.523	132	5	0	1	-1	.994	-4	1-22,O-13	-0.1
	Yr	114	362	39	97	15	4	12	55	30	38	.268	.327	.431	107	2	1	1	-0	.961	-8	O-75,1-22	-1.2
1955	Bos-A	14	31	1	4	2	0	0	1	0	7	.129	.129	.194	-13	-5	1	0	0	1.000	2	/O-7	-0.3
	Cin-N	35	62	4	13	1	0	2	7	5	13	.210	.279	.323	56	-4	0	0	-1	.960	-3	O-13/1-1	-0.6
1956	Cle-A	57	114	17	29	7	0	4	20	12	20	.254	.325	.421	94	-1	0	0	-1	.969	-0	O-20/1-8	-0.3
Total	10	1046	3437	406	916	168	39	80	544	311	342	.267	.329	.408	97	-26	15	14	-4	.985	-39	O-840/1-79	-10.7

■ **FRANCISCO MELENDEZ** Melendez, Francisco Javier (Villegas) b: 1/25/64, Rio Piedras, P.R. BL/TL, 6', 190 lbs. Deb: 8/26/84

YEAR	TM/L	G	AB	R	H	2B	3B	HR	RBI	BB	SO	AVG	OBP	SLG	PRO+	BR/A	SB	CS	SBR	FA	FR	G/POS	TPR
1984	Phi-N	21	23	0	3	0	0	0	2	1	5	.130	.167	.130	-15	-3	0	0	0	1.000	1	1-10	-0.3
1986	Phi-N	9	8	0	2	0	0	0	0	0	0	.250	.250	.250	37	-1	0	0	0	1.000	-0	/1-2	-0.1
1987	SF-N	12	16	2	5	1	0	1	3	0	3	.313	.313	.500	117	0	0	0	0	1.000	-1	/1-5	0.0
1988	SF-N	23	26	1	5	0	0	0	3	2	2	.192	.276	.192	38	-2	0	0	0	1.000	-1	/1-5	-0.4
1989	Bal-A	9	11	1	3	0	0	0	1	2	2	.273	.333	.273	75	-0	0	0	0	1.000	-1	/1-28,O-1	-0.8
Total	5	74	84	4	18	1	0	1	9	5	14	.214	.258	.250	43	-6	0	0	0	1.000	-1	1-50/O-2	

YEAR	TM/L	G	AB	R	H	2B	3B	HR	RBI	BB	SO	AVG	OBP	SLG	PRO+	BR/A	SB	CS	SBR	FA	FR	G/POS	TPR

■ LUIS MELENDEZ   Melendez, Luis Antonio (Santana) b: 8/11/49, Aibonito, P.R.   BR/TR, 6', 165 lbs.   Deb: 9/7/70

1970	StL-N	21	70	11	21	1	0	0	8	2	12	.300	.319	.314	69	-3	3	0	1	1.000	1	O-18	-0.2
1971	StL-N	88	173	25	39	3	1	0	11	24	29	.225	.320	.254	62	-8	2	0	1	.959	-10	O-66	-2.0
1972	StL-N	118	332	32	79	11	3	5	28	25	34	.238	.293	.334	79	-10	5	4	-1	.959	-6	*O-105	-2.3
1973	StL-N	121	341	35	91	18	1	2	35	27	50	.267	.321	.343	84	-7	2	7	-4	.990	2	O-95	-1.3
1974	StL-N	83	124	15	27	4	3	0	8	11	9	.218	.287	.298	64	-6	2	2	-1	.977	-8	O-46/S-1	-1.6
1975	StL-N	110	291	33	77	8	5	2	27	16	25	.265	.303	.347	77	-9	3	2	-0	.983	-6	O-89	-1.9
1976	StL-N	20	24	0	3	0	0	0	0	3	3	.125	.125	.125	-29	-4	0	0	0	1.000	0	/O-8	-0.5
	SD-N	72	119	15	29	5	0	0	5	3	12	.244	.262	.286	60	-7	1	1	-0	.988	-12	O-60	-2.2
	Yr	92	143	15	32	5	0	0	5	3	15	.224	.240	.259	44	-11	1	1	-0	.990	-13	O-68	-2.7
1977	SD-N	8	3	1	0	0	0	0	0	0	1	.000	.250	.000	-29	-1	0	0	0	1.000	0	/O-2	-0.1
Total	8	641	1477	167	366	50	13	9	122	109	175	.248	.300	.318	73	-54	18	16	-4	.977	-40	O-489/S-1	-12.1

■ SKI MELILLO   Melillo, Oscar Donald "Spinach" b: 8/4/1899, Chicago, Ill.   d: 11/14/63, Chicago, Ill.   BR/TR, 5'8", 150 lbs.   Deb: 4/18/26   C

1926	StL-A	99	385	54	98	18	5	1	30	32	31	.255	.315	.335	66	-19	6	7	-2	.965	8	2-88,3-11	-1.0
1927	StL-A	107	356	45	80	18	2	0	26	25	28	.225	.276	.287	45	-30	3	6	-3	.935	-2	*2-101	-3.0
1928	StL-A	51	132	9	25	0	1	0	9	9	11	.189	.241	.205	18	-16	2	1	-0	.961	4	2-28,3-19	-1.1
1929	StL-A	141	494	57	146	17	10	5	67	29	30	.296	.337	.401	86	-11	11	6	-0	.973	23	*2-141	1.6
1930	StL-A	149	574	62	147	30	10	5	59	23	44	.256	.287	.369	63	-34	15	9	-1	.979	**27**	*2-148	0.0
1931	StL-A	151	617	88	189	34	11	2	75	37	29	.306	.346	.407	94	-6	7	11	-5	.968	**33**	*2-151	2.9
1932	StL-A	154	612	71	148	19	11	3	66	36	42	.242	.286	.324	54	-42	6	6	-2	.981	11	*2-153	-2.4
1933	StL-A	132	496	50	145	23	6	3	79	29	18	.292	.333	.381	83	-12	12	10	-2	**.991**	23	*2-130	1.5
1934	StL-A	144	552	54	133	19	3	2	55	28	27	.241	.279	.297	45	-46	4	6	-2	**.981**	18	*2-141	-2.0
1935	StL-A	19	62	8	13	3	0	0	5	8	4	.210	.300	.258	43	-5	0	0	0	.970	-2	2-18	-0.3
	Bos-A	106	400	45	104	13	2	1	39	38	22	.260	.327	.310	61	-22	3	2	-0	.973	18	*2-105	0.3
	Yr	125	462	53	117	16	2	1	44	46	26	.253	.324	.303	59	-27	3	2	-0	.973	19	*2-123	0.0
1936	Bos-A	98	327	39	74	12	4	0	32	28	16	.226	.287	.287	40	-31	0	0	0	.980	-8	2-93	-2.9
1937	Bos-A	26	56	8	14	2	0	0	6	5	4	.250	.311	.286	50	-4	0	1	-1	.939	-3	2-19/S-2,3-2	-0.7
Total	12	1377	5063	590	1316	210	64	22	548	327	306	.260	.306	.340	64	-279	69	65	-18	.973	151	*2-1316/3-32,S-2	-7.1

■ JOE MELLANA   Mellana, Joseph Peter b: 3/11/05, Oakland, Cal.   d: 11/1/69, Larkspur, Cal.   BR/TR, 5'10", 180 lbs.   Deb: 9/21/27

| 1927 | Phi-A | 4 | 7 | 1 | 2 | 0 | 0 | 0 | 2 | 0 | 1 | .286 | .286 | .286 | 46 | -1 | 0 | 0 | 0 | .889 | 2 | /3-2 | 0.1 |

■ BILL MELLOR   Mellor, William Harpin b: 6/6/1874, Camden, N.J.   d: 11/5/40, Bridgeton, R.I.   BR/TR, 6', 190 lbs.   Deb: 7/28/02

| 1902 | Bal-A | 10 | 36 | 4 | 13 | 3 | 0 | 0 | 5 | 3 | | .361 | .410 | .444 | 131 | 2 | 1 | | | .978 | -1 | 1-10 | 0.0 |

■ PAUL MELOAN   Meloan, Paul B. "Molly" b: 8/23/1888, Paynesville, Mo.   d: 2/11/50, Taft, Cal.   BR/TL, 5'10.5", 175 lbs.   Deb: 8/2/10

1910	Chi-A	65	222	23	54	6	6	0	23	17		.243	.314	.324	104	1	4			.948	3	O-65	0.2
1911	Chi-A	1	3	0	1	0	0	0	1	0		.333	.333	.333	89	-0	0			.000	-1	/O-1	-0.1
	StL-A	64	206	30	54	11	3	3	14	15		.262	.318	.379	98	-1	7			.904	-6	O-54	-1.0
	Yr	65	209	30	55	11	3	3	15	15		.263	.319	.378	98	-1	7			.893	-6	O-55	-1.1
Total	2	130	431	53	109	17	8	3	38	32		.253	.316	.350	101	-0	11			.923	-3	O-120	-0.9

■ DAVE MELTON   Melton, David Olin b: 10/3/28, Pampa, Tex.   BR/TR, 6', 185 lbs.   Deb: 4/17/56

1956	KC-A	3	3	0	1	0	0	0	0	0	0	.333	.333	.333	76	-0	0	0	0	1.000	-1	/O-3	-0.1
1958	KC-A	9	6	0	0	0	0	0	0	0	5	.000	.000	.000	-98	-2	0	0	0	1.000	-0	/O-2	-0.2
Total	2	12	9	0	1	0	0	0	0	0	5	.111	.111	.111	-39	-2	0	0	0	1.000	-1	/O-5	-0.3

■ BILL MELTON   Melton, William Edwin b: 7/7/45, Gulfport, Miss.   BR/TR, 6'2", 200 lbs.   Deb: 5/4/68

1968	Chi-A	34	109	5	29	8	0	2	16	10	32	.266	.328	.394	117	2	1	1	-0	.968	3	3-33	0.6
1969	Chi-A	157	556	67	142	26	2	23	87	56	106	.255	.329	.433	106	4	1	2	-1	.952	7	*3-148,O-11	1.0
1970	Chi-A	141	514	74	135	15	1	33	96	56	107	.263	.345	.488	123	15	2	4	-2	1.000	9	O-71,3-70	1.8
1971	Chi-A☆	150	543	72	146	18	2	**33**	86	61	87	.269	.354	.492	133	23	3	3	-1	.968	27	*3-148	5.1
1972	Chi-A	57	208	22	51	5	0	7	30	23	31	.245	.320	.370	103	1	1	1	-0	.935	3	3-56	0.3
1973	Chi-A	152	560	83	155	29	1	20	87	75	66	.277	.364	.439	121	16	4	4	-1	.953	14	*3-151/D-1	2.9
1974	Chi-A	136	495	63	120	17	0	21	63	59	60	.242	.329	.404	107	5	3	2	-0	.939	-3	*3-123,D-11	0.0
1975	Chi-A	149	512	62	123	16	0	15	70	78	106	.240	.349	.359	99	2	5	4	-1	.945	1	*3-138,D-11	-0.5
1976	Cal-A	118	341	31	71	17	3	6	42	44	53	.208	.302	.328	90	-4	2	0	1	.992	-3	D-51,1-30,3-21	-1.1
1977	Cle-A	50	133	17	32	11	0	0	14	17	21	.241	.336	.323	83	-3	1	3	-2	1.000	1	1-15,D-14,3-13	-0.5
Total	10	1144	3971	496	1004	162	9	160	591	479	669	.253	.340	.419	112	61	23	24	-8	.949	57	3-901/D-88,O-82,1	10.2

■ BOB MELVIN   Melvin, Robert Paul b: 10/28/61, Palo Alto, Cal.   BR/TR, 6'4", 205 lbs.   Deb: 5/25/85

1985	Det-A	41	82	10	18	4	1	0	4	3	21	.220	.247	.293	47	-6	0	0	0	.989	8	C-41	0.3
1986	SF-N	89	268	24	60	14	2	5	25	15	69	.224	.265	.347	71	-12	3	2	-0	.988	7	C-84/3-1	0.0
1987	*SF-N	84	246	31	49	8	0	11	31	17	44	.199	.251	.366	64	-14	0	4	-2	.998	4	C-78/1-1	-0.8
1988	SF-N	92	273	23	64	13	1	8	27	13	46	.234	.267	.377	87	-6	0	2	-1	.984	-8	C-89/1-1	-1.0
1989	Bal-A	85	278	22	67	10	1	1	32	15	53	.241	.280	.295	64	-13	1	4	-2	.991	-9	C-75/D-9	-2.1
1990	Bal-A	93	301	30	73	14	1	5	37	11	53	.243	.269	.346	73	-12	0	1	-1	.997	6	C-76,D-10/1-1	-0.8
1991	Bal-A	79	228	11	57	10	1	1	23	11	46	.250	.285	.307	66	-11	0	0	0	.998	6	C-72/D-4	-0.1
1992	KC-A	32	70	5	22	5	0	0	5	2	15	.314	.360	.386	106	1	0	0	0	1.000	-0	C-21/1-3	0.1
1993	Bos-A	77	176	13	39	7	0	3	23	7	44	.222	.255	.313	49	-13	0	0	0	.994	-8	C-76/1-1	-1.7
1994	NY-A	9	14	2	4	0	0	1	3	0	3	.286	.286	.500	101	-0	0	0	0	1.000	-1	/C-4,1-4,D-1	-0.1
	Chi-A	11	19	3	3	0	0	0	1	1	4	.158	.200	.158	-6	-3	0	0	0	1.000	2	C-11	-0.1
	Yr	20	33	5	7	0	0	1	4	1	7	.212	.235	.303	39	-3	0	0	0	1.000	1	C-15/1-4,D-1	-0.2
Total	10	692	1955	174	456	85	6	35	212	98	396	.233	.270	.337	69	-89	4	13	-7	.993	2	C-627/D-24,1-11,3-1	-6.3

■ MINNIE MENDOZA   Mendoza, Cristobal Rigoberto (Carreras) b: 11/16/33, Ceiba Del Agua, Cuba   BR/TR, 6', 180 lbs.   Deb: 4/9/70   C

| 1970 | Min-A | 16 | 16 | 2 | 3 | 0 | 0 | 0 | 2 | 0 | 1 | .188 | .188 | .188 | 4 | -2 | 0 | 0 | 0 | 1.000 | 0 | /3-5,2-4 | -0.2 |

■ MARIO MENDOZA   Mendoza, Mario (Aizpuru) b: 12/26/50, Chihuahua, Mex.   BR/TR, 5'11", 187 lbs.   Deb: 4/26/74

1974	*Pit-N	91	163	10	36	1	2	0	15	9	35	.221	.262	.252	46	-12	1	1	-0	.964	5	S-87	-0.1
1975	Pit-N	56	50	8	9	1	0	0	3	3	17	.180	.226	.200	19	-5	0	0	0	.952	3	S-53/3-1	0.4
1976	Pit-N	50	92	6	17	5	0	0	12	6	15	.185	.219	.239	30	-9	0	1	-1	.967	12	S-45/3-2,2-1	0.6
1977	Pit-N	70	81	5	16	3	0	0	4	3	10	.198	.226	.235	23	-9	0	0	0	.928	12	S-45,3-19/P-1	0.5
1978	Pit-N	57	55	5	12	1	0	0	3	2	9	.218	.283	.291	58	-3	3	1	0	.980	9	2-21,3-18,S-14	0.8
1979	Sea-A	148	373	26	74	10	3	1	29	9	62	.198	.219	.249	26	-39	3	0	1	.968	28	*S-148	0.2
1980	Sea-A	114	277	27	68	9	2	14	16	42		.245	.287	.310	63	-14	3	4	-2	.959	12	*S-114	0.6
1981	Tex-A	88	229	18	53	6	1	0	22	7	25	.231	.257	.266	54	-14	2	1	0	.970	3	S-88	-0.3
1982	Tex-A	12	17	1	2	0	0	0	0	0	4	.118	.118	.118	-37	-3	0	0	0	.882	2	S-12	-0.1
Total	9	686	1337	106	287	33	9	4	101	52	219	.215	.247	.262	41	-108	12	8	-2	.961	91	S-606/3-40,2-22,P-1	2.6

■ MIKE MENDOZA   Mendoza, Michael Joseph b: 11/26/55, Inglewood, Cal.   BR/TR, 6'5", 215 lbs.   Deb: 9/7/79

| 1979 | Hou-N | 2 | 0 | 0 | 0 | 0 | 0 | 0 | 0 | 0 | 0 | — | — | — | — | — | 0 | 0 | 0 | .000 | 0 | /P-1 | 0.0 |

■ JOCK MENEFEE   Menefee, John b: 1/15/1868, Rowlesburg, W.Va.   d: 3/11/53, Belle Vernon, Pa.   BR/TR, 6', 165 lbs.   Deb: 8/17/1892

1892	Pit-N	2	3	0	0	0	0	0	0	0		.000	.000	.000	-99	-1	0			1.000	0	/O-1,P-1	-0.1
1893	Lou-N	22	73	10	20	2	1	0	12	13	5	.274	.391	.329	100	1	2			.913	3	P-15/O-7	0.1
1894	Lou-N	29	79	7	13	1	0	0	4	8	7	.165	.250	.177	5	-12	2			.940	2	P-28/2-1	0.0
	Pit-N	13	47	6	12	1	0	0	7	3	3	.255	.300	.362	60	-3	2			.909	2	P-13	0.0
	Yr	42	126	13	25	2	0	0	11	11	10	.198	.268	.246	26	-15	4			.928	5	P-41/2-1	0.0
1895	Pit-N	2	0	0	0	0	0	0	0	0							0			.667	0	/P-2	0.0

YEAR	TM/L	G	AB	R	H	2B	3B	HR	RBI	BB	SO	AVG	OBP	SLG	PRO+	BR/A	SB	CS	SBR	FA	FR	G/POS	TPR
1898	NY-N	1	5	0	0	0	0	0	0	0	0	.000	.000	.000	-99	-1	0			.750	0	/P-1	0.0
1900	Chi-N	17	46	5	5	0	0	0	0	4	2	.109	.180	.109	-20	-7	0			.889	-2	P-16	0.0
1901	Chi-N	48	152	19	39	5	3	0	13	8		.257	.327	.329	94	-1	4			.913	-2	O-24,P-21/1-2,2-1	-0.3
1902	Chi-N	65	216	24	50	4	1	0	15	15		.231	.303	.259	76	-5	4			.952	-4	O-23,P-22,1-18,/32	-0.8
1903	Chi-N	22	64	3	13	3	0	0	2	3		.203	.239	.250	40	-5	0			.896	3	P-20/1-2	-0.1
Total	9	221	685	74	152	16	7	0	57	52	15	.222	.295	.266	60	-35	14			.918	3	P-139/O-55,1-22,23	-1.2

■ DENIS MENKE
Menke, Denis John b: 7/21/40, Algona, Iowa BR/TR, 6', 190 lbs. Deb: 4/14/62 C

YEAR	TM/L	G	AB	R	H	2B	3B	HR	RBI	BB	SO	AVG	OBP	SLG	PRO+	BR/A	SB	CS	SBR	FA	FR	G/POS	TPR
1962	Mil-N	50	146	12	28	3	1	2	16	16	38	.192	.280	.267	49	-10	0	1	-1	.980	5	2-20,3-15/S-9,10	-0.4
1963	Mil-N	146	518	58	121	16	4	11	50	37	106	.234	.292	.344	83	-11	6	7	-2	.976	12	S-82,3-51,2-22/10	0.6
1964	Mil-N	151	505	79	143	29	5	20	65	68	77	.283	.373	.479	137	26	4	2	0	.964	2	*S-141,2-15/3-6	4.0
1965	Mil-N	71	181	16	44	13	1	4	18	18	28	.243	.315	.392	97	-1	1	3	-2	.967	-7	S-54/1-8,3-4	-0.7
1966	Atl-N	138	454	55	114	20	4	15	60	71	87	.251	.360	.412	112	9	0	7	-4	.955	-22	*S-106,3-39/1-7	-0.9
1967	Atl-N	129	418	37	95	14	3	7	39	65	62	.227	.335	.325	91	-3	5	7	-3	.965	-23	*S-124/3-3	-1.8
1968	Hou-N	150	542	56	135	23	6	6	56	64	81	.249	.335	.347	107	6	5	8	-3	.982	-17	*2-119,S-35/1-5,3-4	-0.5
1969	Hou-N★	154	553	72	149	25	5	10	90	87	87	.269	.373	.394	115	14	2	7	-4	.956	-9	*S-131,2-23/1-9,3-1	1.7
1970	Hou-N★	154	562	82	171	26	6	13	92	82	80	.304	.398	.441	130	26	6	5	-1	.954	-16	*S-133,2-21/1-5,30	2.6
1971	Hou-N	146	475	57	117	26	3	0	43	59	68	.246	.332	.320	88	-6	4	5	-2	.997	-3	*1-101,3-32,S-17/2	-1.9
1972	*Cin-N	140	447	41	104	19	2	9	50	58	76	.233	.327	.345	97	-1	0	1	-1	.955	1	*3-130,1-11	-0.3
1973	*Cin-N	139	241	38	46	10	0	3	26	69	53	.191	.375	.270	86	-1	1	1	-0	.966	16	*3-123/S-7,2-5,1-1	1.6
1974	Hou-N	30	29	2	3	1	0	0	1	4	10	.103	.212	.138	-1	-4	0	0	0	1.000	3	1-12/3-7,2-3,S-2	-0.1
Total	13	1598	5071	605	1270	225	40	101	606	698	853	.250	.346	.370	104	44	34	54	-22	.961	-58	S-841,3-420,21/O	3.9

■ MIKE MENOSKY
Menosky, Michael William "Leaping Mike" b: 10/16/1894, Glen Campbell, Pa. d: 4/11/83, Detroit, Mich. BL/TR, 5'10", 163 lbs. Deb: 4/18/14

YEAR	TM/L	G	AB	R	H	2B	3B	HR	RBI	BB	SO	AVG	OBP	SLG	PRO+	BR/A	SB	CS	SBR	FA	FR	G/POS	TPR
1914	Pit-F	68	140	26	37	4	1	2	9	16	30	.264	.352	.350	92	-3	5			.942	-3	O-41	-0.8
1915	Pit-F	17	21	3	2	0	0	0	1	2	0	.095	.208	.095	-13	-3	2			.917	-2	/O-9	-0.6
1916	Was-A	11	37	5	6	1	1	0	3	1	10	.162	.184	.243	29	-3	1			.952	1	/O-9	-0.3
1917	Was-A	114	322	46	83	12	10	1	34	45	55	.258	.359	.366	123	10	22			.982	8	O-94	1.4
1919	Was-A	116	342	62	98	15	3	6	39	44	46	.287	.379	.401	120	10	13			.979	0	*O-103	0.4
1920	Bos-A	141	532	80	158	24	9	3	64	65	52	.297	.383	.393	111	10	23	19	-5	.961	-3	*O-141	-0.7
1921	Bos-A	133	477	77	143	18	5	3	45	60	45	.300	.388	.377	99	2	12	6	-0	.970	-4	*O-133	-1.1
1922	Bos-A	126	406	61	115	16	5	3	32	40	33	.283	.355	.369	90	-5	9	5	-0	.977	0	*O-103	-0.7
1923	Bos-A	84	188	22	43	8	4	0	25	22	19	.229	.310	.314	64	-10	5	2	-0	.920	3	O-49	-1.2
Total	9	810	2465	382	685	98	38	18	252	295	290	.278	.364	.370	100	7	90	36		.967	7	O-682	-3.6

■ ED MENSOR
Mensor, Edward "The Midget" b: 11/7/1886, Woodville, Ore. d: 4/20/70, Salem, Ore. BB/TR, 5'6", 145 lbs. Deb: 7/15/12

YEAR	TM/L	G	AB	R	H	2B	3B	HR	RBI	BB	SO	AVG	OBP	SLG	PRO+	BR/A	SB	CS	SBR	FA	FR	G/POS	TPR
1912	Pit-N	39	99	19	26	3	2	0	1	23	12	.263	.402	.333	104	2	10			.955	-2	O-32	-0.2
1913	Pit-N	44	56	9	10	1	0	0	1	8	13	.179	.292	.196	43	-4	2			.971	-1	O-18/2-1,S-1	-0.5
1914	Pit-N	44	89	15	18	2	1	1	6	22	13	.202	.372	.281	99	1	2			.969	2	O-25	0.2
Total	3	127	244	43	54	6	3	1	8	53	38	.221	.367	.283	89	-1	14			.964	-1	/O-75,S-1,2-1	-0.5

■ TED MENZE
Menze, Theodore Charles b: 11/4/1897, St.Louis, Mo. d: 12/23/69, St.Louis, Mo. BR/TR, 5'9", 172 lbs. Deb: 4/23/18

YEAR	TM/L	G	AB	R	H	2B	3B	HR	RBI	BB	SO	AVG	OBP	SLG	PRO+	BR/A	SB	CS	SBR	FA	FR	G/POS	TPR
1918	StL-N	1	3	0	0	0	0	0	0	0	2	.000	.000	.000	-99	-1	0			1.000	-0	/O-1	-0.1

■ RUDY MEOLI
Meoli, Rudolph Bartholomew b: 5/1/51, Troy, N.Y. BL/TR, 5'9", 165 lbs. Deb: 9/9/71

YEAR	TM/L	G	AB	R	H	2B	3B	HR	RBI	BB	SO	AVG	OBP	SLG	PRO+	BR/A	SB	CS	SBR	FA	FR	G/POS	TPR
1971	Cal-A	7	3	0	0	0	0	0	0	0	1	.000	.000	.000	-99	-1	0	0	0	.000	0	H	-0.1
1973	Cal-A	120	305	36	68	12	1	2	23	31	38	.223	.295	.292	70	-12	2	4	-2	.933	-2	S-95,3-13/2-8	-0.5
1974	Cal-A	36	90	9	22	2	0	0	3	8	10	.244	.306	.267	70	-3	2	4	-2	.946	2	3-20/S-8,1-1,2-1	-0.3
1975	Cal-A	70	126	12	27	2	1	0	6	15	20	.214	.298	.246	59	-6	3	0	1	.976	0	S-28,3-15,2-11,/D-3	-0.3
1978	Chi-N	47	29	10	3	0	1	0	2	6	4	.103	.257	.172	20	-3	1	0	0	.900	6	/2-6,3-5	0.4
1979	Phi-N	30	73	2	13	4	1	0	6	9	15	.178	.268	.260	43	-6	1	0	1	.984	5	S-16,2-15/3-1	0.0
Total	6	310	626	69	133	20	4	2	40	69	88	.212	.291	.267	61	-31	10	8	-2	.944	10	S-147/3-54,2-41,D1	-0.8

■ ORLANDO MERCADO
Mercado, Orlando (Rodriguez) b: 11/7/61, Arecibo, P.R. BR/TR, 6', 195 lbs. Deb: 9/13/82

YEAR	TM/L	G	AB	R	H	2B	3B	HR	RBI	BB	SO	AVG	OBP	SLG	PRO+	BR/A	SB	CS	SBR	FA	FR	G/POS	TPR
1982	Sea-A	9	17	1	2	0	0	0	6	0	5	.118	.118	.294	8	-2	0	0	0	1.000	1	/C-8,D-1	-0.1
1983	Sea-A	66	178	10	35	11	2	1	16	14	27	.197	.259	.298	51	-12	2	2	-1	.995	4	C-65	-0.6
1984	Sea-A	30	78	5	17	3	1	0	5	4	12	.218	.265	.282	52	-5	1	0	0	.992	-6	C-29	-1.0
1986	Tex-A	46	102	7	24	3	1	1	7	6	13	.235	.284	.294	56	-6	0	1	-1	.996	16	C-45	1.1
1987	Det-A	10	22	2	3	0	0	0	1	2	0	.136	.208	.136	-6	-3	0	0	0	.980	3	C-10	0.0
	LA-N	7	5	1	3	2	0	0	1	0	0	.600	.667	.800	294	2	0	0	0	1.000	0	/C-7	0.2
1988	Oak-A	16	24	3	3	0	0	0	0	1	6	.125	.222	.250	33	-2	0	0	0	.959	1	C-16	-0.1
1989	Min-A	19	38	1	4	0	0	0	1	4	4	.105	.190	.105	-14	-6	1	0	0	1.000	4	C-19	-0.1
1990	NY-N	42	90	10	19	1	0	3	7	8	11	.211	.290	.322	68	-4	0	0	0	.991	2	C-40	-0.1
	Mon-N	8	8	0	2	1	0	0	0	0	1	.250	.250	.250	39	-1	0	0	0	1.000	3	/C-8	0.2
	Yr	50	98	10	21	1	0	3	7	8	12	.214	.287	.316	66	-5	0	0	0	.992	4	C-48	0.1
Total	8	253	562	40	112	17	4	7	45	42	82	.199	.261	.281	48	-40	4	3	-1	.993	27	C-247/D-1	-0.5

■ ORLANDO MERCED
Merced, Orlando Luis (Villanueva) b: 11/2/66, Hato Rey, P.R. BB/TR, 6', 180 lbs. Deb: 6/27/90

YEAR	TM/L	G	AB	R	H	2B	3B	HR	RBI	BB	SO	AVG	OBP	SLG	PRO+	BR/A	SB	CS	SBR	FA	FR	G/POS	TPR
1990	Pit-N	25	24	3	5	1	0	0	0	1	9	.208	.240	.250	36	-2	0	0	0	.000	-0	/C-1,O-1	-0.3
1991	*Pit-N	120	411	83	113	17	2	10	50	64	81	.275	.374	.399	119	12	8	4	0	.988	-8	*1-105/O-7	-0.2
1992	*Pit-N	134	405	50	100	28	5	6	60	52	63	.247	.336	.385	105	3	5	4	-1	.995	5	*1-114/O-17	-0.5
1993	Pit-N	137	447	68	140	26	4	8	70	77	64	.313	.415	.443	130	23	3	1	-1	.965	3	*O-109,1-42	2.0
1994	Pit-N	108	386	48	105	21	3	9	51	42	58	.272	.345	.412	95	-2	4	1	1	.981	-9	O-68,1-55	-1.6
1995	Pit-N	132	487	75	146	29	4	15	83	52	74	.300	.369	.468	117	12	7	2	1	.976	1	*O-107,1-35	0.9
1996	Pit-N	120	453	69	130	24	1	17	80	51	74	.287	.359	.457	110	7	8	4	0	.988	15	*O-115/1-1	1.8
Total	7	776	2613	396	739	146	19	65	394	339	423	.283	.366	.428	113	52	35	18	-0	.978	8	O-424,1-352/C-1	2.1

■ HENRY MERCEDES
Mercedes, Henry Felipe (Perez) b: 7/23/69, Santo Domingo, D.R. BR/TR, 5'11", 185 lbs. Deb: 4/22/92

YEAR	TM/L	G	AB	R	H	2B	3B	HR	RBI	BB	SO	AVG	OBP	SLG	PRO+	BR/A	SB	CS	SBR	FA	FR	G/POS	TPR
1992	Oak-A	9	5	1	4	0	1	0	1	0	1	.800	.800	1.200	479	2	0	0	0	.875	-0	/C-9	0.2
1993	Oak-A	20	47	5	10	2	0	0	3	2	15	.213	.260	.255	42	-4	1	1	-0	.987	-0	C-18/D-1	-0.4
1995	KC-A	23	43	7	11	2	0	0	9	8	13	.256	.385	.302	81	-1	0	0	0	.986	-3	C-22	-0.2
1996	KC-A	4	4	1	1	0	0	0	0	0	2	.250	.250	.250	28	-0	0	0	0	1.000	-1	/C-4	-0.1
Total	4	56	99	14	26	4	1	0	13	10	30	.263	.342	.323	79	-3	1	1	-0	.981	-4	/C-53,D-1	-0.5

■ LUIS MERCEDES
Mercedes, Luis Roberto (Santana) b: 2/15/68, San Pedro De Macoris, D.R. BR/TR, 6', 180 lbs. Deb: 9/8/91

YEAR	TM/L	G	AB	R	H	2B	3B	HR	RBI	BB	SO	AVG	OBP	SLG	PRO+	BR/A	SB	CS	SBR	FA	FR	G/POS	TPR
1991	Bal-A	19	54	10	11	2	0	0	2	4	12	.204	.259	.241	41	-4	1	0	0	1.000	-2	O-15/D-1	-0.7
1992	Bal-A	23	50	7	7	2	0	0	4	8	9	.140	.271	.180	28	-5	1	0	-1	.956	-2	O-16/D-7	-0.3
1993	Bal-A	10	24	1	7	2	0	0	0	5	4	.292	.414	.375	109	1	1	1	-0	1.000	-0	/O-8,D-2	0.0
	SF-N	18	25	1	4	0	1	0	5	4	7	.160	.250	.240	33	-2	0	1	-1	1.000	-1	/O-5	-0.4
Total	3	70	153	19	29	6	1	0	9	18	25	.190	.287	.242	47	-11	3	2	-2	.976	-2	/O-44,D-10	-1.4

■ WIN MERCER
Mercer, George Barclay b: 6/20/1874, Chester, W.Va. d: 1/12/03, San Francisco, Cal BR/TR, 5'7", 140 lbs. Deb: 4/21/1894

YEAR	TM/L	G	AB	R	H	2B	3B	HR	RBI	BB	SO	AVG	OBP	SLG	PRO+	BR/A	SB	CS	SBR	FA	FR	G/POS	TPR
1894	Was-N	53	165	29	48	5	2	2	29	9	20	.291	.328	.352	73	-8	9			.944	2	P-50/O-4	0.0
1895	Was-N	63	196	26	50	9	1	1	26	12	32	.255	.308	.327	65	-11	7			.874	-8	P-43/S-7,O-5,3-3,2	-0.8
1896	Was-N	49	156	23	38	1	1	1	14	9	18	.244	.302	.282	54	-10	9			.856	1	P-46/O-1	0.0
1897	Was-N	50	139	23	44	2	5	0	19	6		.317	.354	.403	100	-0	7			.858	-1	P-47	0.0
1898	Was-N	80	249	38	80	8	2	1	25	18		.321	.369	.398	120	6	14			.863	-9	P-33,S-23,O-19/32	-0.4
1899	Was-N	108	375	73	112	6	7	1	35	32		.299	.360	.360	99	0	16			.846	-14	3-62,P-23,O-16/S1	-1.6
1900	NY-N	76	248	32	73	4	0	0	27	26		.294	.366	.310	92	-1	15			.931	-2	P-33,3-19,O-14/S2	-0.1
1901	Was-A	51	140	26	42	7	2	0	16	23		.300	.402	.379	119	5	10			.944	-2	P-24,O-16/1-7,S3	-0.1
1902	Det-A	35	100	8	18	2	0	0	6	6		.180	.226	.200	19	-11	1			.935	4	P-35	0.0
Total	9	565	1768	278	505	39	23	7	197	141	70	.286	.344	.346	87	-30	88			.903	-29	P-334/3-90,OS12	-3.4

YEAR	TM/L	G	AB	R	H	2B	3B	HR	RBI	BB	SO	AVG	OBP	SLG	PRO+	BR/A	SB	CS	SBR	FA	FR	G/POS	TPR

■ JOHN MERCER   Mercer, John Locke   b: 6/22/1892, Taylortown, La.   d: 12/22/82, Shreveport, La.   BL/TL, 5'10.5", 155 lbs.   Deb: 6/25/12

1912	StL-N	1	1	0	0	0	0	0	0	0	0	.000	.000	.000	-99	-0	0			.500	-0	/1-1	-0.1

■ ANDY MERCHANT   Merchant, James Anderson   b: 8/30/50, Mobile, Ala.   BL/TR, 5'11", 185 lbs.   Deb: 9/28/75

1975	Bos-A	1	4	1	2	0	0	0	0	1	0	.500	.600	.500	197	1	0	0	0	1.000	-1	/C-1	0.0
1976	Bos-A	2	2	0	0	0	0	0	0	0	2	.000	.000	.000	-89	-0	0	0	0	1.000	-1	/C-1	-0.1
Total	2	3	6	1	2	0	0	0	0	1	2	.333	.429	.333	109	0	0	0	0	1.000	-1	/C-2	-0.1

■ ART MEREWETHER   Merewether, Arthur Francis "Merry"   b: 7/7/02, E.Providence, R.I.   BR/TR, 5'9.5", 155 lbs.   Deb: 7/10/22

1922	Pit-N	1	1	0	0	0	0	0	0	0	0	.000	.000	.000	-99	-0	0	0	0	.000	0	H	0.0

■ FRED MERKLE   Merkle, Frederick Charles   b: 12/20/1888, Watertown, Wis.   d: 3/2/56, Daytona Beach, Fla.   BR/TR, 6'1", 190 lbs.   Deb: 9/21/07   C

1907	NY-N	15	47	0	12	1	0	0	5	1		.255	.271	.277	69	-2	0			.949	-1	1-15	-0.4
1908	NY-N	38	41	6	11	2	1	1	7	4		.268	.333	.439	140	2	0			1.000	-2	1-11/O-5,2-1,3-1	-0.1
1909	NY-N	79	236	15	45	9	1	0	20	16		.191	.245	.237	49	-14	8			.976	-3	1-70/2-1	-2.0
1910	NY-N	144	506	75	148	35	14	4	70	44	59	.292	.353	.441	131	18	23			.981	1	*1-144	1.9
1911	*NY-N	149	541	80	153	24	10	12	84	43	60	.283	.342	.431	112	7	49			.985	15	*1-148	2.1
1912	*NY-N	129	479	82	148	22	6	11	84	42	70	.309	.374	.449	121	13	37			.980	-1	*1-129	1.0
1913	*NY-N	153	563	78	147	30	13	2	69	41	60	.261	.315	.371	95	-5	35			.986	-4	*1-153	-1.1
1914	NY-N	146	512	71	132	25	7	7	63	52	80	.258	.327	.375	112	7	23			.990	3	*1-146	0.7
1915	NY-N	140	505	52	151	25	3	4	62	36	39	.299	.348	.384	129	16	20	15	-3	.989	-1	*1-110,O-30	0.9
1916	NY-N	112	401	45	95	19	3	7	44	33	46	.237	.308	.352	108	3	17			.984	0	*1-112	-0.1
	*Bro-N	23	69	6	16	1	0	0	2	7	4	.232	.312	.246	70	-2	2			.992	-1	1-15/O-4	-0.4
	Yr	135	470	51	111	20	3	7	46	40	50	.236	.308	.336	102	1	19			.985	-1	*1-127/O-4	-0.5
1917	Bro-N	2	8	1	1	1	0	0	0	0	1	.125	.125	.250	13	-1	0			1.000	0	/1-2	-0.1
	Chi-N	146	549	65	146	30	9	3	57	42	60	.266	.323	.370	104	2	13			.983	-3	*1-140/O-6	-0.7
	Yr	148	557	66	147	31	9	3	57	42	61	.264	.320	.368	103	1	13			.983	-3	*1-142/O-6	-0.8
1918	*Chi-N	129	482	55	143	25	5	3	65	35	36	.297	.349	.388	122	12	21			.990	1	*1-129	0.9
1919	Chi-N	133	498	52	133	20	6	3	62	33	35	.267	.315	.349	99	-1	20			.985	-10	*1-132/2-1	-1.7
1920	Chi-N	92	330	33	94	20	4	3	38	24	32	.285	.335	.397	108	3	3	5	-2	.985	-0	1-85/O-1	-0.1
1925	NY-A	7	13	4	5	1	0	0	1	1	1	.385	.429	.462	128	1	0	0	0	1.000	-1	/1-5	-0.1
1926	NY-A	1	2	0	0	0	0	0	0	0	0	.000	.000	.000	-99	-1	0	0	0	1.000	-1	/1-1	-0.1
Total	16	1638	5782	720	1580	290	82	60	733	454	583	.273	.331	.383	109	58	272	20		.985	-5	*1-1547/O-46,2-3,3	0.7

■ ED MERRILL   Merrill, Edward Mason   b: 5/1860, Maysville, Ky.   d: 8/18/24, Chicago, Ill.   5'11", 176 lbs.   Deb: 5/5/1882

1882	Lou-a	1	0	0	0	0	0	0	0	0		—	—	—	—		0			.000	-0	/O-1	0.0
	Wor-N	2	8	0	1	0	0	0	0	0	1	.125	.125	.125	-19	-1				.714	-1	/3-2	-0.1
1884	Ind-a	55	196	14	35	3	1	0		6		.179	.207	.204	35	-13				.900	-4	2-55	-1.5
Total	2	58	204	14	36	3	1	0	4	6	1	.176	.204	.201	33	-14				.900	-5	/2-55,3-2,O-1	-1.6

■ LLOYD MERRIMAN   Merriman, Lloyd Archer "Citation"   b: 8/2/24, Clovis, Cal.   BL/TL, 6', 195 lbs.   Deb: 4/24/49

1949	Cin-N	103	287	35	66	12	5	4	26	21	36	.230	.285	.348	68	-14	2			.969	-1	O-86	-1.7
1950	Cin-N	92	298	44	77	15	3	2	31	30	23	.258	.330	.349	79	-9	6			.989	-4	O-84	-1.6
1951	Cin-N	114	359	34	87	23	2	5	36	31	34	.242	.303	.359	76	-12	8	4	0	.997	9	*O-102	-0.7
1954	Cin-N	73	112	12	30	8	1	0	16	23	10	.268	.406	.357	98	1	3	0	1	.981	-1	O-25	0.0
1955	Chi-A	1	1	0	0	0	0	0	0	0	0	.000	.000	.000	-97	-0	0			.000	0	H	0.0
	Chi-N	72	145	15	31	6	1	1	8	21	21	.214	.313	.290	62	-8	1	0	0	.977	-6	O-47	-1.5
Total	5	455	1202	140	291	64	12	12	117	126	124	.242	.317	.345	75	-42	20	4		.985	-2	O-344	-5.5

■ GEORGE MERRITT   Merritt, George Washington   b: 4/14/1880, Paterson, N.J.   d: 2/21/38, Memphis, Tenn.   TR, 6', 160 lbs.   Deb: 9/6/01

1901	Pit-N	4	11	2	3	0	1	0	0	0		.273	.385	.455	139	1	0			1.000	-0	/P-3	0.0
1902	Pit-N	2	9	2	3	1	0	0	2	0		.333	.333	.444	135	0	0			1.000	1	/O-2	0.1
1903	Pit-N	9	27	4	4	0	1	0	3	2		.148	.233	.222	29	-3	1			.889	-2	/O-7,P-1	-0.4
Total	3	15	47	8	10	1	2	0	5	2		.213	.288	.319	74	-2	1			.929	-1	/O-9,P-4	-0.3

■ HERM MERRITT   Merritt, Herman G.   b: 11/12/1900, Independence, Kan.   d: 5/26/27, Kansas City, Mo.   BR/TR,   Deb: 8/24/21

1921	Det-A	20	46	3	17	1	2	0	6	1	5	.370	.396	.478	123	2	1	0	0	.882	-6	S-17	-0.3

■ JOHN MERRITT   Merritt, John Howard   b: 10/12/1894, Tupelo, Miss.   d: 11/3/55, Tupelo, Miss.   BR/TL, 5'11", 170 lbs.   Deb: 9/27/13

1913	NY-N	1	0	0	0	0	0	0	0	0	0					0	0			.000	-0	/O-1	0.0

■ BILL MERRITT   Merritt, William Henry   b: 7/30/1870, Lowell, Mass.   d: 11/17/37, Lowell, Mass.   BR/TR, 5'7", 160 lbs.   Deb: 8/8/1891

1891	Chi-N	11	42	4	9	1	0	0	4	2	2	.214	.250	.238	42	-3	0			.955	-3	C-11/1-1	-0.5
1892	Lou-N	46	168	22	33	4	2	1	13	11	15	.196	.246	.262	58	-9	3			.940	-3	C-46	-0.8
1893	Bos-N	39	141	30	49	6	3	3	26	13	13	.348	.403	.496	128	5	3			.945	-4	C-37/O-2	0.3
1894	Bos-N	10	26	3	6	1	0	0	6	8	0	.231	.412	.269	62	-1	0			.881	1	/C-8,O-1	-0.2
	Pit-N	36	109	18	30	1	2	1	18	15	7	.275	.363	.349	73	-4	2			.952	-1	C-28/1-4,O-2	-0.2
	Cin-N	29	113	17	37	6	1	1	21	9	3	.327	.387	.425	92	-2	4			.953	-3	C-24/3-3,1-1,O-1	-0.1
	Yr	75	248	38	73	8	3	2	45	32	10	.294	.379	.375	81	-7	6			.941	-3	C-60/1-5,O-4,3-3	-0.4
1895	Cin-N	22	79	9	14	2	0	0	12	6	5	.177	.235	.203	13	-10	2			.955	-1	C-20/2-1	-0.8
	Pit-N	67	239	32	68	5	1	0	27	18	16	.285	.340	.314	73	-10	2			.935	-2	C-63/1-2	-0.4
	Yr	89	318	41	82	7	1	0	39	24	21	.258	.314	.286	57	-20	4			.939	-3	C-83/1-2,2-1	-1.2
1896	Pit-N	77	282	26	82	8	2	1	42	18	10	.291	.336	.344	83	-7	3			.941	2	C-62/3-5,2-3,1-3,S	0.2
1897	Pit-N	62	209	21	55	6	1	1	26	9		.263	.297	.316	64	-11	2			.946	-4	C-53/1-7	-0.8
1899	Bos-N	1	3	0	0	0	0	0	0	1		.000	.333	.000	-5	-0	0			1.000	0	/C-1	0.0
Total	8	400	1410	182	383	40	12	8	195	109	71	.272	.327	.334	75	-52	21			.942	-19	C-353/1-18,3-8,O2S	-3.2

■ JACK MERSON   Merson, John Warren   b: 1/17/22, Elkridge, Md.   BR/TR, 5'11", 175 lbs.   Deb: 9/14/51

1951	Pit-N	13	50	6	18	2	2	1	14	1	7	.360	.373	.540	138	2	0	0	0	.987	2	2-13	0.5
1952	Pit-N	111	398	41	98	20	2	5	38	22	38	.246	.287	.344	72	-15	1	1	-0	.978	-6	2-81,3-27	-1.9
1953	Bos-A	1	4	0	0	0	0	0	0	0	0	.000	.000	.000	-95	-1	0	0	0	.875	0	/2-1	-0.1
Total	3	125	452	47	116	22	4	6	52	23	45	.257	.294	.363	74	-14	1	1		.978	-3	/2-95,3-27	-1.5

■ SAM MERTES   Mertes, Samuel Blair "Sandow"   b: 8/6/1872, San Francisco, Cal.   d: 3/11/45, San Francisco, Cal   BR/TR, 5'10", 185 lbs.   Deb: 6/30/1896

1896	Phi-N	37	143	20	34	4	4	0	14	8	10	.238	.288	.322	61	-8	19			.907	-1	O-35/S-1,2-1	-1.0
1898	Chi-N	83	269	45	80	4	8	1	47	34		.297	.388	.383	121	9	27			.880	2	O-60,S-14/2-4,1-2	0.7
1899	Chi-N	117	426	83	127	13	16	9	81	33		.298	.349	.467	126	13	45			.923	-1	*O-108/1-3,S-1	0.4
1900	Chi-N	127	481	72	142	25	4	7	60	42		.295	.356	.420	114	9	38			.923	-5	O-88,1-33/S-7	-0.2
1901	Chi-A	137	545	94	151	16	17	5	98	52		.277	.347	.396	108	7	46			.940	-6	*2-132/O-5	0.5
1902	Chi-A	129	497	60	140	23	7	1	79	37		.282	.334	.362	97	-2	46			.922	6	*O-120/S-5,CP123	-0.3
1903	NY-N	138	517	100	145	**32**	14	7	**104**	61		.280	.360	.437	122	14	45			**.973**	8	*O-137/C-1,1-1	1.3
1904	NY-N	148	532	83	147	28	11	4	78	54		.276	.346	.393	123	14	47			.956	-1	*O-147/S-1	0.5
1905	*NY-N	150	551	81	154	27	17	5	108	56		.279	.351	.417	126	17	52			.960	-11	*O-150	-0.1
1906	NY-N	71	253	37	60	9	6	1	33	29		.237	.323	.332	102	1	21			.970	1	O-71	-0.1
	StL-N	53	191	20	47	7	4	0	19	16		.246	.304	.325	100	-0	10			.890	-6	O-53	-1.0
	Yr	124	444	57	107	16	10	1	52	45		.241	.315	.329	101	0	31			.938	-5	*O-124	-1.1
Total	10	1190	4405	695	1227	188	108	40	721	422	10	.279	.346	.398	113	73	396			.938	-14	O-974,2-138/1SC3P	0.7

■ LENNIE MERULLO   Merullo, Leonard Richard   b: 5/5/17, Boston, Mass.   BR/TR, 5'11", 168 lbs.   Deb: 9/12/41   F

1941	Chi-N	7	17	3	6	1	0	1	2	0		.353	.421	.412	140	1	1			.968	2	/S-7	0.3
1942	Chi-N	143	515	53	132	23	3	2	37	35	45	.256	.310	.324	89	-8	14			.946	-1	*S-143	0.0
1943	Chi-N	129	453	37	115	18	3	1	25	26	42	.254	.297	.313	78	-14	7			.940	-12	*S-125	-1.8

YEAR	TM/L	G	AB	R	H	2B	3B	HR	RBI	BB	SO	AVG	OBP	SLG	PRO+	BR/A	SB	CS	SBR	FA	FR	G/POS	TPR
1944	Chi-N	66	193	20	41	8	1	1	16	16	18	.212	.276	.280	57	-11	3			.937	2	S-56/1-1	-0.5
1945	*Chi-N	121	394	40	94	18	0	2	37	31	30	.239	.297	.299	68	-17	7			.948	-4	*S-118	-1.3
1946	Chi-N	65	126	14	19	8	0	0	7	11	13	.151	.219	.214	24	-13	2			.946	18	S-44	0.7
1947	Chi-N	108	373	24	90	16	1	0	29	15	26	.241	.274	.290	52	-26	4			.949	7	*S-108	-1.4
Total	7	639	2071	191	497	92	8	6	152	136	174	.240	.291	.301	69	-88	38			.945	11	S-601/1-1	-4.0

■ MATT MERULLO Merullo, Matthew Bates b: 8/4/65, Winchester, Mass. BL/TR, 6'2", 200 lbs. Deb: 4/12/89 F

YEAR	TM/L	G	AB	R	H	2B	3B	HR	RBI	BB	SO	AVG	OBP	SLG	PRO+	BR/A	SB	CS	SBR	FA	FR	G/POS	TPR
1989	Chi-A	31	81	5	18	1	0	1	8	6	14	.222	.276	.272	56	-5	0	1	-1	.973	-4	C-27/D-1	-0.8
1991	Chi-A	80	140	8	32	1	0	5	21	9	18	.229	.275	.343	72	-6	0	0	0	.989	-1	C-27,1-16/D-6	-0.6
1992	Chi-A	24	50	3	9	1	1	0	3	1	8	.180	.212	.240	27	-5	0	0	0	.971	-1	C-16/D-1	-0.5
1993	Chi-A	8	20	1	1	0	0	0	0	0	1	.050	.050	.050	-75	-5	0	0	0	.000	0	/D-6	-0.1
1994	Cle-A	4	10	1	1	0	0	0	0	2	1	.100	.250	.100	-2	0	0	0	0	.957	-0	/C-4	-0.1
1995	Min-A	76	195	19	55	14	1	1	27	14	27	.282	.340	.379	87	-4	0	1	-1	.987	-9	C-46,D-13/1-2	-1.0
Total	6	223	496	37	116	17	2	7	59	32	69	.234	.286	.319	64	-25	0			.981	-14	C-120/D-27,1-18	-3.5

■ STEVE MESNER Mesner, Stephan Mathias b: 1/13/18, Los Angeles, Cal. d: 4/6/81, San Diego, Cal. BR/TR, 5'9", 178 lbs. Deb: 9/23/38

YEAR	TM/L	G	AB	R	H	2B	3B	HR	RBI	BB	SO	AVG	OBP	SLG	PRO+	BR/A	SB	CS	SBR	FA	FR	G/POS	TPR
1938	Chi-N	2	4	2	1	0	0	0	0	1	1	.250	.400	.250	80	-0	0			.667	-1	/S-1	-0.1
1939	Chi-N	17	43	7	12	4	0	0	6	3	4	.279	.340	.372	90	-1	0			.927	1	S-12/2-1,3-1	0.2
1941	StL-N	24	69	8	10	1	0	0	10	5	6	.145	.203	.159	3	-9	0			.958	5	3-22	-0.3
1943	Cin-N	137	504	53	137	26	1	0	52	26	20	.272	.309	.327	85	-11	6			.944	1	*3-130	-0.9
1944	Cin-N	121	414	31	100	17	4	1	47	34	20	.242	.301	.309	75	-14	1			.951	-7	*3-120	-2.1
1945	Cin-N	150	540	52	137	19	1	1	52	52	18	.254	.322	.298	74	-18	4			.971	12	*3-148/2-3	-3.2
Total	6	451	1574	153	397	67	6	2	167	121	69	.252	.308	.306	75	-52	11			.956	10	3-421/S-13,2-4	-3.4

■ BOBBY MESSENGER Messenger, Charles Walter b: 3/19/1884, Bangor, Me. d: 7/10/51, Bath, Maine BB/TR, 5'10.5", 165 lbs. Deb: 8/30/09

YEAR	TM/L	G	AB	R	H	2B	3B	HR	RBI	BB	SO	AVG	OBP	SLG	PRO+	BR/A	SB	CS	SBR	FA	FR	G/POS	TPR
1909	Chi-A	31	112	18	19	1	1	0	0	13		.170	.268	.196	49	-6	7			.950	-2	O-31	-1.0
1910	Chi-A	9	26	7	6	0	1	0	4	4		.231	.375	.308	119	1	3			.846	-0	/O-8	0.0
1911	Chi-A	13	17	4	2	0	0	0	0	3		.118	.250	.235	37	-1	0			.875	-1	/O-4	-0.2
1914	StL-A	1	2	0	0	0	0	0	0	0		.000	.000	.000	-99	-0	0			.000	0	/O-1	-0.1
Total	4	54	157	29	27	1	3	0	4	20	0	.172	.282	.217	57	-7	10			.918	-3	O-44	-1.3

■ TOM MESSITT Messitt, Thomas John b: 7/27/1874, Frankfort, Pa. d: 9/22/34, Chicago, Ill. 5'9", 177 lbs. Deb: 9/14/1899

YEAR	TM/L	G	AB	R	H	2B	3B	HR	RBI	BB	SO	AVG	OBP	SLG	PRO+	BR/A	SB	CS	SBR	FA	FR	G/POS	TPR
1899	Lou-N	3	11	0	1	0	0	0	0			.091	.091	.091	-50	-2	0			1.000	1	/C-3	-0.1

■ AL METCALF Metcalf, Al b: Brooklyn, N.Y. Deb: 5/27/1875

YEAR	TM/L	G	AB	R	H	2B	3B	HR	RBI	BB	SO	AVG	OBP	SLG	PRO+	BR/A	SB	CS	SBR	FA	FR	G/POS	TPR
1875	Mut-n	8	32	2	7	0	0	0	0		3	.219	.219	.219	50	-2	2	0	1	.667	-2	/3-5,O-2,S-1	-0.2

■ SCAT METHA Metha, Frank Joseph b: 12/13/13, Los Angeles, Cal. d: 3/2/75, Fountain Valley, Cal. BR/TR, 5'11", 165 lbs. Deb: 4/22/40

YEAR	TM/L	G	AB	R	H	2B	3B	HR	RBI	BB	SO	AVG	OBP	SLG	PRO+	BR/A	SB	CS	SBR	FA	FR	G/POS	TPR
1940	Det-A	26	37	6	9	2	0	0	8	4	3	.243	.282	.297	46	-3	0	1	-1	.960	4	2-10/3-6	0.0

■ BUD METHENY Metheny, Arthur Beauregard b: 6/1/15, St.Louis, Mo. BL/TL, 5'11", 190 lbs. Deb: 4/27/43

YEAR	TM/L	G	AB	R	H	2B	3B	HR	RBI	BB	SO	AVG	OBP	SLG	PRO+	BR/A	SB	CS	SBR	FA	FR	G/POS	TPR
1943	*NY-A	103	360	51	94	18	2	9	36	39	34	.261	.333	.397	113	5	2	3	-1	.963	-12	O-91	-1.4
1944	NY-A	137	518	72	124	16	1	14	67	56	57	.239	.316	.355	89	-8	5	5	-2	.956	-8	*O-132	-2.6
1945	NY-A	133	509	64	126	18	2	8	53	54	31	.248	.325	.338	88	-7	5	2	0	.984	-6	*O-128	-2.2
1946	NY-A	3	3	0	0	0	0	0	0	0	0	.000	.000	.000	-99	-1	0	0	0	.000	0	H	-0.1
Total	4	376	1390	187	344	52	5	31	156	149	122	.247	.323	.359	94	-11	12	10	-2	.968	-26	O-351	-6.3

■ CATFISH METKOVICH Metkovich, George Michael b: 10/8/20, Angels Camp, Cal. d: 5/17/95, Costa Mesa, Cal. BL/TL, 6'1", 185 lbs. Deb: 7/16/43

YEAR	TM/L	G	AB	R	H	2B	3B	HR	RBI	BB	SO	AVG	OBP	SLG	PRO+	BR/A	SB	CS	SBR	FA	FR	G/POS	TPR
1943	Bos-A	78	321	34	79	14	4	5	27	19	38	.246	.294	.361	90	-5	1	3	-2	.955	-3	O-76/1-2	-1.5
1944	Bos-A	134	549	94	152	28	8	9	59	31	57	.277	.319	.406	108	3	13	4	2	.962	5	O-82,1-50	0.3
1945	Bos-A	138	539	65	140	26	3	5	62	51	70	.260	.331	.347	94	-4	19	6	2	.985	-4	1-97,O-42	-1.6
1946	*Bos-A	86	281	42	69	15	2	4	25	36	39	.246	.333	.356	88	-4	8	3	1	.948	-11	O-81	-1.9
1947	Cle-A	126	473	68	120	22	7	5	40	32	51	.254	.302	.362	86	-11	3	5	-0	.989	1	*O-119/1-1	-1.7
1949	Chi-A	93	338	50	80	9	4	5	45	41	24	.237	.321	.331	75	-13	5	4	-1	.968	-7	O-87	-2.5
1951	Pit-N	120	423	51	124	21	3	7	40	28	23	.293	.338	.378	90	-6	5	2	0	.994	1	O-69,1-37	-0.9
1952	Pit-N	125	373	41	101	18	3	7	41	32	29	.271	.335	.391	98	-1	5	2	0	.988	-7	1-72,O-33	-1.1
1953	Pit-N	26	41	5	6	0	1	1	7	6	3	.146	.255	.268	80	-4	0	0	0	1.000	-6	/1-5,O-4	-0.5
	Chi-N	61	124	19	29	9	0	2	12	16	10	.234	.326	.355	76	-4	2	1	0	1.000	-5	O-38/1-7	-1.0
	Yr	87	165	24	35	9	1	3	19	22	13	.212	.309	.333	66	-8	2	1	0	1.000	-6	O-42,1-12	-1.5
1954	Mil-N	68	123	7	34	5	1	1	15	15	15	.276	.360	.358	94	-1	0	1	0	1.000	1	1-18,O-13	-0.1
Total	10	1055	3585	476	934	167	36	47	373	307	359	.261	.323	.367	91	-49	61	28	2	.976	-28	O-644,1-289	-12.5

■ CHARLIE METRO Metro, Charles (b: Charles Moreskonich) b: 4/28/19, Nanty Glo, Pa. BR/TR, 5'11.5", 178 lbs. Deb: 5/4/43 MC

YEAR	TM/L	G	AB	R	H	2B	3B	HR	RBI	BB	SO	AVG	OBP	SLG	PRO+	BR/A	SB	CS	SBR	FA	FR	G/POS	TPR
1943	Det-A	44	40	12	8	0	0	0		3	6	.200	.256	.200	32	-3	1	1	-0	.966	-2	O-14	-0.6
1944	Det-A	38	78	8	15	0	1	0	5	3	10	.192	.222	.218	25	-8	1	0	0	1.000	-2	O-20	-1.0
	Phi-A	24	40	4	4	0	0	0	1	7	6	.100	.234	.100	-3	-5	0	0	0	1.000	-1	O-11/3-5,2-2	-0.7
	Yr	62	118	12	19	0	1	0	6	10	16	.161	.227	.178	16	-13	1	0	0	1.000	-2	O-31/3-5,2-2	-1.7
1945	Phi-A	65	200	18	42	10	1	3	15	23	33	.210	.291	.315	76	-6	1	1	0	.972	-5	O-57	-1.5
Total	3	171	358	42	69	10	2	3	23	36	55	.193	.266	.257	51	-22	3	2	0	.980	-9	O-102/3-5,2-2	-3.8

■ LENNY METZ Metz, Leonard Raymond b: 7/6/1899, Louisville, Colo. d: 2/24/53, Denver, Colo. BR/TR, 5'10.5", 170 lbs. Deb: 9/11/23

YEAR	TM/L	G	AB	R	H	2B	3B	HR	RBI	BB	SO	AVG	OBP	SLG	PRO+	BR/A	SB	CS	SBR	FA	FR	G/POS	TPR
1923	Phi-N	12	37	4	8	0	0	0	3	4	3	.216	.310	.216	37	-3	0	0	0	.969	1	/2-6,S-6	-0.2
1924	Phi-N	7	7	1	2	0	0	0	1	1	0	.286	.375	.286	71	-0	0	0	0	.846	1	/S-6	-0.2
1925	Phi-N	11	14	1	0	0	0	0	0	0	2	.000	.000	.000	-92	-4	0	0	0	1.000	2	/S-9,2-2	-0.2
Total	3	30	58	6	10	0	0	0	4	5	5	.172	.250	.172	11	-8	0			.951	3	/S-21,2-8	-0.4

■ ROGER METZGER Metzger, Roger Henry b: 10/10/47, Fredericksburg, Tex BB/TR, 6', 165 lbs. Deb: 6/16/70

YEAR	TM/L	G	AB	R	H	2B	3B	HR	RBI	BB	SO	AVG	OBP	SLG	PRO+	BR/A	SB	CS	SBR	FA	FR	G/POS	TPR
1970	Chi-N	1	2	0	0	0	0	0	0	0	0	.000	.000	.000	-89	-1	0	0	0	.833	1	/S-1	0.1
1971	Hou-N	150	562	64	132	14	**11**	0	26	44	50	.235	.295	.299	70	-22	15	6	1	.977	-5	*S-148	-0.7
1972	Hou-N	153	641	84	142	12	3	2	38	60	71	.222	.289	.259	58	-34	23	9	2	.971	5	*S-153	-0.7
1973	Hou-N	154	580	67	145	11	**14**	1	35	39	70	.250	.301	.322	73	-21	10	4	1	**.982**	-19	*S-149	-2.1
1974	Hou-N	143	572	66	145	18	10	0	30	37	73	.253	.299	.320	76	-19	9	7	-2	.976	-11	*S-143	-1.3
1975	Hou-N	127	450	54	102	7	9	2	26	41	39	.227	.291	.296	68	-20	4	5	-2	.977	11	*S-126	0.2
1976	Hou-N	152	481	37	101	13	9	0	29	52	63	.210	.287	.270	65	-23	1	1	-0	**.986**	-3	*S-150/2-2	-0.9
1977	Hou-N	97	269	24	50	9	6	0	16	32	64	.186	.272	.264	49	-20	4	4		.973	-4	S-96/2-1	-1.4
1978	Hou-N	45	123	16	27	4	1	0	6	12	27	.220	.289	.268	61	-6	0	0	0	.964	-4	S-42/2-1	-0.6
	SF-N	75	235	17	61	6	4	0	15	12	47	.260	.296	.294	68	-10	8	1	2	.974	-12	S-74	-1.3
	Yr	120	358	28	88	10	5	0	23	24	74	.246	.293	.285	66	-17	8	1	2	.970	-16	*S-116/2-1	-1.9
1979	SF-N	94	259	24	65	7	4	0	31	23	31	.251	.312	.340	83	-6	11	3	2	.956	2	S-78,2-10/3-1	0.6
1980	SF-N	28	27	5	2	0	0	0	3	2	6	.074	.138	.074	-31	-5	0	0	0	.971	3	S-13/2-1	-0.2
Total	11	1219	4201	453	972	101	71	5	254	355	449	.231	.293	.293	67	-188	83	36	3	.976	-36	*S-1173/2-15,3-1	-8.3

■ WILLIAM METZIG Metzig, William Andrew b: 12/4/18, Ft.Dodge, Iowa BR/TR, 6'1", 180 lbs. Deb: 9/19/44

YEAR	TM/L	G	AB	R	H	2B	3B	HR	RBI	BB	SO	AVG	OBP	SLG	PRO+	BR/A	SB	CS	SBR	FA	FR	G/POS	TPR
1944	Chi-A	5	16	1	2	0	0	0	1	1	4	.125	.176	.125	-13	-2	0	0	0	1.000	2	/2-5	0.0

■ ALEX METZLER Metzler, Alexander b: 1/4/03, Fresno, Cal. d: 11/30/73, Fresno, Cal. BL/TR, 5'9", 167 lbs. Deb: 9/16/25

YEAR	TM/L	G	AB	R	H	2B	3B	HR	RBI	BB	SO	AVG	OBP	SLG	PRO+	BR/A	SB	CS	SBR	FA	FR	G/POS	TPR
1925	Chi-N	9	38	2	7	2	0	0	0	3	1	.184	.244	.237	23	-4	0	0	0	1.000	2	/O-9	-0.3
1926	Phi-A	20	67	8	16	3	0	0	12	7	5	.239	.311	.284	53	-5	1	0	0	1.000	2	O-17	-0.4
1927	Chi-A	143	543	87	173	29	11	3	61	61	39	.319	.396	.429	117	15	15	11	-2	.965	16	*O-134	1.9
1928	Chi-A	139	464	71	141	18	14	3	55	77	26	.304	.410	.422	121	17	16	8	0	.968	-4	*O-134	0.5
1929	Chi-A	146	568	80	156	23	13	2	49	80	45	.275	.367	.371	92	-5	9	5	-0	.960	1	*O-142	-1.3
1930	Chi-A	56	79	12	14	4	0	0	5	11	6	.177	.278	.228	31	-8	0	2	1	.969	-5	O-27	-1.4

YEAR	TM/L	G	AB	R	H	2B	3B	HR	RBI	BB	SO	AVG	OBP	SLG	PRO+	BR/A	SB	CS	SBR	FA	FR	G/POS	TPR
	StL-A	56	209	30	54	6	3	1	23	21	12	.258	.326	.330	65	-11	5	1	1	.951	-5	O-56	-1.8
	Yr	112	288	42	68	10	3	3	28	32	18	.236	.313	.302	57	-19	5	3	0	.955	-10	O-83	-3.2
Total	6	560	1968	290	561	85	41	9	207	260	144	.285	.374	.384	97	-0	46	27	-2	.965	6	O-519	-2.8

■ HENSLEY MEULENS
Meulens, Hensley Filemon Acasio "Bam-Bam" b: 6/23/67, Willemstad, Curacao   BR/TR, 6'4", 200 lbs.   Deb: 8/23/89

YEAR	TM/L	G	AB	R	H	2B	3B	HR	RBI	BB	SO	AVG	OBP	SLG	PRO+	BR/A	SB	CS	SBR	FA	FR	G/POS	TPR
1989	NY-A	8	28	2	5	0	0	0	1	2	8	.179	.233	.179	18	-3	0	1	-1	.875	2	/3-8	-0.1
1990	NY-A	23	83	12	20	7	0	3	10	9	25	.241	.337	.434	113	1	1	0	0	.963	3	O-23	0.4
1991	NY-A	96	288	37	64	8	1	6	29	18	97	.222	.277	.319	64	-14	3	0	1	.967	5	O-73,D-13/1-7	-1.4
1992	NY-A	2	5	1	3	0	0	1	1	1	0	.600	.667	1.200	416	2	0	0	0	1.000	0	/3-2	0.2
1993	NY-A	30	53	8	9	1	1	2	5	8	19	.170	.279	.340	67	-3	0	1	1	1.000	-4	O-24/1-3,3-1	-0.8
Total	5	159	457	60	101	16	2	12	46	38	149	.221	.291	.344	75	-16	4	2	0	.970	3	O-120/D-13,3-11,1	-1.7

■ IRISH MEUSEL
Meusel, Emil Frederick b: 6/9/1893, Oakland, Cal. d: 3/1/63, Long Beach, Cal.   BR/TR, 5'11.5", 178 lbs.   Deb: 10/1/14   FC

YEAR	TM/L	G	AB	R	H	2B	3B	HR	RBI	BB	SO	AVG	OBP	SLG	PRO+	BR/A	SB	CS	SBR	FA	FR	G/POS	TPR
1914	Was-A	1	2	0	0	0	0	0	0	0	0	.000	.000	.000	-96	-0	0			1.000	-0	/O-1	-0.1
1918	Phi-N	124	473	48	132	25	6	4	62	30	21	.279	.323	.383	108	3	18			.972	8	*O-120/2-4	0.6
1919	Phi-N	135	521	65	159	26	7	5	59	15	13	.305	.327	.411	113	7	24			.968	-2	*O-128	-0.4
1920	Phi-N	138	518	75	160	27	8	14	69	32	27	.309	.349	.473	129	17	17	11	-2	.929	-5	*O-129/1-3	0.2
1921	Phi-N	84	343	59	121	21	7	12	51	18	17	.353	.385	.560	136	17	8	4	0	.929	2	O-84	1.2
	*NY-N	62	243	37	80	12	6	2	36	15	12	.329	.373	.453	117	6	5	9	-4	.971	-1	O-62	-0.3
	Yr	146	586	96	201	33	13	14	87	33	29	.343	.380	.515	129	23	13	13	-4	.947	1	*O-146	0.9
1922	*NY-N	154	617	100	204	28	17	16	132	35	33	.331	.369	.509	123	19	12	10	-2	.980	-8	*O-154	-0.3
1923	*NY-N	146	595	102	177	22	14	19	125	38	16	.297	.341	.477	115	10	8	8	-2	.949	-8	*O-145	-0.9
1924	*NY-N	139	549	75	170	26	9	6	102	33	18	.310	.351	.423	109	7	11	7	-1	.967	-7	*O-138	-1.0
1925	NY-N	135	516	82	169	35	8	21	111	26	19	.328	.363	.548	135	24	5	4	-1	.959	0	*O-126	1.4
1926	NY-N	129	449	51	131	25	10	6	65	16	18	.292	.322	.432	103	-0	5			.958	-5	*O-112	-1.3
1927	Bro-N	42	74	7	18	3	1	1	7	11	5	.243	.341	.351	85	-1	0			1.000	-0	O-17	-0.3
Total	11	1289	4900	701	1521	250	93	106	819	269	199	.310	.348	.464	118	107	113	53		.959	-25	*O-1216/2-4,1-3	-1.2

■ BOB MEUSEL
Meusel, Robert William "Long Bob" b: 7/19/1896, San Jose, Cal. d: 11/28/77, Downey, Cal.   BR/TR, 6'3", 190 lbs.   Deb: 4/14/20   F

YEAR	TM/L	G	AB	R	H	2B	3B	HR	RBI	BB	SO	AVG	OBP	SLG	PRO+	BR/A	SB	CS	SBR	FA	FR	G/POS	TPR
1920	NY-A	119	460	75	151	40	7	11	83	20	72	.328	.359	.517	126	14	4	4	-1	.947	-10	O-64,3-45/1-2	-0.0
1921	*NY-A	149	598	104	190	40	16	24	135	34	88	.318	.356	.559	128	20	17	6	2	.934	5	*O-147	1.5
1922	*NY-A	121	473	61	151	26	11	16	84	40	54	.319	.376	.522	129	18	13	8	-1	.950	-0	*O-121	0.9
1923	*NY-A	132	460	93	144	29	10	9	91	31	52	.313	.359	.478	117	9	13	15	-5	.953	-7	*O-121	-1.0
1924	*NY-A	143	579	93	188	40	11	12	120	32	43	.325	.365	.494	120	14	26	14	-1	.951	-7	*O-143/3-2	-0.3
1925	*NY-A	156	624	101	181	34	12	33	138	54	55	.290	.348	.542	125	18	13	14	-5	.985	-9	*O-131,3-27	-0.2
1926	*NY-A	108	413	73	130	22	3	12	81	37	32	.315	.384	.470	120	11	16	17	-5	.960	-6	*O-107	-0.7
1927	*NY-A	135	516	75	174	47	9	8	103	45	58	.337	.393	.510	137	27	24	10	1	.950	-4	*O-131	1.5
1928	*NY-A	131	518	77	154	45	5	11	113	39	56	.297	.349	.467	116	10	6	9	-4	.975	4	*O-131	0.2
1929	NY-A	100	391	46	102	15	3	10	57	17	42	.261	.292	.391	79	-14	1	5	-3	.968	3	O-96	-1.9
1930	Cin-N	113	443	62	128	30	8	10	62	26	63	.289	.330	.460	93	-7	9			.962	-4	O-112	-1.7
Total	11	1407	5475	826	1693	368	95	156	1067	375	619	.309	.356	.497	119	121	142	102		.958	-35	*O-1304/3-74,1-2	-1.7

■ BENNY MEYER
Meyer, Bernhard "Earache" b: 1/1/1888, Hematite, Mo. d: 2/6/74, Festus, Mo.   BR/TR, 5'9", 170 lbs.   Deb: 4/9/13   C

YEAR	TM/L	G	AB	R	H	2B	3B	HR	RBI	BB	SO	AVG	OBP	SLG	PRO+	BR/A	SB	CS	SBR	FA	FR	G/POS	TPR
1913	Bro-N	38	87	12	17	0	1	1	10	10	14	.195	.287	.253	51	-5	8			.943	-2	O-26/C-1	-0.9
1914	Bal-F	143	500	76	152	18	10	5	40	71	53	.304	.395	.410	116	6	23			.916	-11	*O-132/S-4	-1.0
1915	Bal-F	35	120	20	29	2	0	0	5	37	13	.242	.424	.258	91	-0	6			.931	-3	O-34	-0.6
	Buf-F	93	333	37	77	8	6	1	29	40	37	.231	.316	.300	72	-17	9			.947	-6	O-88	-3.0
	Yr	128	453	57	106	10	6	1	34	77	50	.234	.348	.289	78	-17	15			.943	-10	*O-122	-3.6
1925	Phi-N	1	1	1	1	1	0	0	0	0	0	1.000	1.000	2.000	594	1	0	0	0	.000	0	/2-1	0.1
Total	4	310	1041	146	276	29	17	7	84	158	117	.265	.365	.346	99	-15	46	0		.931	-22	O-280/S-4,2-1,C-1	-5.4

■ DAN MEYER
Meyer, Daniel Thomas b: 8/3/52, Hamilton, Ohio   BL/TR, 5'11", 180 lbs.   Deb: 9/14/74

YEAR	TM/L	G	AB	R	H	2B	3B	HR	RBI	BB	SO	AVG	OBP	SLG	PRO+	BR/A	SB	CS	SBR	FA	FR	G/POS	TPR
1974	Det-A	13	50	5	10	1	1	3	7	1	1	.200	.231	.440	86	-1	1	0		.967	1	O-12	-0.1
1975	Det-A	122	470	56	111	17	3	8	47	26	25	.236	.279	.336	70	-19	8	3	1	.950	-0	O-74,1-46	-2.6
1976	Det-A	105	294	37	74	8	4	2	16	17	22	.252	.293	.327	78	-8	10	0	3	.988	-4	O-47,1-19/D-1	-1.3
1977	Sea-A	159	582	75	159	24	4	22	90	43	51	.273	.324	.442	107	5	11	8	-2	.992	1	*1-159	-0.6
1978	Sea-A	123	444	38	101	18	1	8	56	24	39	.227	.267	.327	66	-21	4	1	-1	.989	0	*1-121/O-2,D-1	-3.0
1979	Sea-A	144	525	72	146	21	7	20	74	29	35	.278	.321	.459	106	3	11	7	-1	.936	-14	*3-101,O-31,1-15	-1.4
1980	Sea-A	146	531	56	146	25	6	11	71	31	42	.275	.316	.407	96	-4	3	4	-1	.961	-10	*O-123/3-5,1-4,D-7	-1.9
1981	Sea-A	83	252	26	66	10	1	3	22	10	16	.262	.293	.345	80	-7	4	3	-1	.961	-8	3-49,O-14/1-3,D-3	-1.1
1982	Oak-A	120	383	28	92	17	3	8	59	18	33	.240	.274	.363	77	-13	1	1	0	.990	-6	1-58,D-38,O-11	-2.2
1983	Oak-A	69	169	15	32	9	0	4	13	19	11	.189	.271	.260	50	-11	0	0	0	.987	-6	1-41,D-12,O-11/3-1	-2.0
1984	Oak-A	20	22	1	7	3	1	0	4	0	0	.318	.318	.545	143	0	0	0	0	.944	0	/1-3,D-1	0.1
1985	Oak-A	14	12	2	0	0	0	0	0	1	4	.000	.077	.000	-83	-3	0	0	0	.000	-0	/3-1,O-1,D-1	-0.4
Total	12	1118	3734	411	944	153	31	86	459	219	277	.253	.296	.379	86	-80	61	29	1	.991	-38	1-469,O-326,3/D	-16.5

■ GEORGE MEYER
Meyer, George Francis b: 8/3/09, Chicago, Ill. d: 1/3/92, Hoffman Estates, Ill.   BR/TR, 5'9", 160 lbs.   Deb: 9/3/38

YEAR	TM/L	G	AB	R	H	2B	3B	HR	RBI	BB	SO	AVG	OBP	SLG	PRO+	BR/A	SB	CS	SBR	FA	FR	G/POS	TPR
1938	Chi-A	24	81	10	24	2	2	0	9	11	17	.296	.387	.370	89	-1	3	1	0	.967	6	2-24	0.6

■ DUTCH MEYER
Meyer, Lambert Dalton b: 10/6/15, Waco, Tex.   BR/TR, 5'10.5", 181 lbs.   Deb: 6/23/37

YEAR	TM/L	G	AB	R	H	2B	3B	HR	RBI	BB	SO	AVG	OBP	SLG	PRO+	BR/A	SB	CS	SBR	FA	FR	G/POS	TPR
1937	Chi-N	1	0	0	0	0	0	0	—	—	—	—	—	—	0		0	0		.000	0	R	0.0
1940	Det-A	23	58	12	15	3	0	0	6	4	10	.259	.317	.310	58	-4	2	0	1	.960	0	2-21	-0.2
1941	Det-A	46	153	12	29	9	1	1	14	8	13	.190	.230	.281	31	-16	1	1	-0	.972	6	2-40	-0.7
1942	Det-A	14	52	5	17	3	0	2	9	4	4	.327	.386	.500	137	2	1	1	1	.989	6	2-14	0.9
1945	Cle-A	130	524	71	153	29	8	7	48	40	32	.292	.342	.418	125	15	2	4	-2	.978	-32	*2-130	-1.2
1946	Cle-A	72	207	13	48	5	3	0	16	26	16	.232	.321	.285	75	-7	0	1	-1	.977	-13	2-64	-1.8
Total	6	286	994	113	262	49	12	10	93	82	75	.264	.322	.367	94	-9	5	7		.977	-32	2-269	-3.0

■ LEO MEYER
Meyer, Leo b: 3/29/1888, Iowa d: 9/2/68, Smyrna, Del.   TR,   Deb: 9/27/09

YEAR	TM/L	G	AB	R	H	2B	3B	HR	RBI	BB	SO	AVG	OBP	SLG	PRO+	BR/A	SB	CS	SBR	FA	FR	G/POS	TPR
1909	Bro-N	7	23	1	3	1	0	0	0	0	2	.130	.200	.130	3	-3	0			.882	2	/S-7	-0.1

■ SCOTT MEYER
Meyer, Scott William b: 8/19/57, Evergreen Park, Ill   BR/TR, 6'1", 195 lbs.   Deb: 9/10/78

YEAR	TM/L	G	AB	R	H	2B	3B	HR	RBI	BB	SO	AVG	OBP	SLG	PRO+	BR/A	SB	CS	SBR	FA	FR	G/POS	TPR
1978	Oak-A	8	9	1	1	1	0	0	0	0	4	.111	.111	.222	-9	-1	0	0	0	1.000	-1	/C-7	-0.2

■ JOEY MEYER
Meyer, Tanner Joe b: 5/10/62, Honolulu, Hawaii   BR/TR, 6'3", 260 lbs.   Deb: 4/4/88

YEAR	TM/L	G	AB	R	H	2B	3B	HR	RBI	BB	SO	AVG	OBP	SLG	PRO+	BR/A	SB	CS	SBR	FA	FR	G/POS	TPR
1988	Mil-A	103	327	22	86	18	0	11	45	23	88	.263	.313	.419	102	0	0	1	-1	.986	-0	D-66,1-33	-0.4
1989	Mil-A	53	147	13	33	6	0	7	29	12	36	.224	.283	.408	93	-2	1	0	0	.982	-1	D-31,1-18	-0.4
Total	2	156	474	35	119	24	0	18	74	35	124	.251	.304	.416	100	-2	1	1	-0	.984	-1	/D-97,1-51	-0.8

■ BILLY MEYER
Meyer, William Adam b: 1/14/1892, Knoxville, Tenn. d: 3/31/57, Knoxville, Tenn.   BR/TR, 5'9.5", 170 lbs.   Deb: 9/6/13   M

YEAR	TM/L	G	AB	R	H	2B	3B	HR	RBI	BB	SO	AVG	OBP	SLG	PRO+	BR/A	SB	CS	SBR	FA	FR	G/POS	TPR
1913	Chi-A	1	1	0	1	0	0	0	0	0	0	1.000	1.000	1.000	490	0	0			.857	1	/C-1	0.1
1916	Phi-A	50	138	6	32	2	2	1	12	8	11	.232	.274	.297	75	-5	3			.961	7	C-48	0.6
1917	Phi-A	62	162	9	38	5	1	0	9	7	14	.235	.271	.278	68	-7	0			.962	9	C-55	0.7
Total	3	113	301	15	71	7	3	1	21	15	25	.236	.274	.289	73	-11	3			.960	18	C-104	1.4

■ LEVI MEYERLE
Meyerle, Levi Samuel "Long Levi" b: 7/1845, Philadelphia, Pa. d: 11/4/21, Philadelphia, Pa.   BR/TR, 6'1", 177 lbs.   Deb: 5/20/1871

YEAR	TM/L	G	AB	R	H	2B	3B	HR	RBI	BB	SO	AVG	OBP	SLG	PRO+	BR/A	SB	CS	SBR	FA	FR	G/POS	TPR
1871	Ath-n	26	130	45	64	9	3	4	40	2	1	.492	.500	.700	243	23	4	0	1	.646	-8	*3-26/P-1	0.9
1872	Ath-n	27	146	31	48	10	5	1	31	0	1	.329	.329	.486	147	7	2			.773	5	O-26/3-1	0.9
1873	Phi-n	48	238	53	83	14	4	3	58	2	0	.349	.354	.479	140	10	5	0	2	.743	-6	*3-48/S-1	0.3
1874	Chi-n	53	254	65	100	19	1	1	47	3	4	.394	.401	.488	182	22	3	1	0	.833	-15	2-31,3-14/S-5,O-5	0.5
1875	Phi-n	68	301	55	95	14	8	1	54	0	2	.316	.316	.425	149	13	3			.859	-10	2-36,3-20,1-16	0.3
1876	Phi-N	55	256	46	87	12	6	0	34	3	2	.340	.347	.449	165	17				.791	-3	*3-49/O-3,2-3,P-2	1.3

YEAR	TM/L	G	AB	R	H	2B	3B	HR	RBI	BB	SO	AVG	OBP	SLG	PRO+	BR/A	SB	CS	SBR	FA	FR	G/POS	TPR
1877	Cin-N	27	107	11	35	7	2	0	15	0	4	.327	.327	.430	154	6				.822	1	S-18,2-12/O-1	0.7
1884	Phi-U	3	11	0	1	1	0	0		0		.091	.091	.182	-21	-2				.789	-1	/1-2,O-1	-0.3
Total	5 n	222	1069	249	390	66	21	10	230	7	8	.365	.369	.494	166	76	19	3	4	.704	-35	3-109/2-67,O1SP	2.9
Total	3	85	374	57	123	20	10	0	49	3	6	.329	.334	.436	156	21				.891	-4	/3-49,S-18,2O1P	1.7

■ HENRY MEYERS   Meyers, Henry L. b: 1860, Philadelphia, Pa. d: 6/28/1898, Harrisburg, Pa. Deb: 8/30/1890

YEAR	TM/L	G	AB	R	H	2B	3B	HR	RBI	BB	SO	AVG	OBP	SLG	PRO+	BR/A	SB	CS	SBR	FA	FR	G/POS	TPR
1890	Phi-a	5	19	2	3	0	0	0	1	1		.158	.238	.158	17	-2	2			.684	-3	/3-5	-0.4

■ CHIEF MEYERS   Meyers, John Tortes b: 7/29/1880, Riverside, Cal. d: 7/25/71, San Bernardino, Cal. BR/TR, 5'11", 194 lbs. Deb: 4/16/09

YEAR	TM/L	G	AB	R	H	2B	3B	HR	RBI	BB	SO	AVG	OBP	SLG	PRO+	BR/A	SB	CS	SBR	FA	FR	G/POS	TPR
1909	NY-N	90	220	15	61	10	5	1	30	22		.277	.359	.382	128	7	3			.963	2	C-64	1.6
1910	NY-N	127	365	25	104	18	0	1	62	40	18	.285	.362	.342	106	4	5			.969	5	*C-117	2.0
1911	*NY-N	133	391	48	130	18	9	1	61	25	33	.332	.392	.432	126	14	7			.979	-3	*C-128	2.2
1912	*NY-N	126	371	60	133	16	5	6	54	47	20	.358	.441	.477	147	26	8			.973	-10	*C-122	2.7
1913	*NY-N	120	378	37	118	18	5	3	47	37	22	.312	.387	.410	127	14	7			.967	1	*C-116	2.6
1914	NY-N	134	381	33	109	13	5	1	55	34	25	.286	.357	.354	116	8	4			.970	-12	*C-126	0.6
1915	NY-N	110	289	24	67	10	5	1	26	26	18	.232	.311	.311	94	-2	4	4	-1	.986	-4	C-96	0.0
1916	*Bro-N	80	239	21	59	10	3	0	21	26	15	.247	.336	.314	97	0	2			.984	7	C-74	1.5
1917	Bro-N	47	132	8	28	3	0	0	3	13	7	.212	.283	.235	58	-6	4			.974	-6	C-44	-1.0
	Bos-N	25	68	5	17	4	4	0	4	4	4	.250	.311	.426	133	2	0			1.000	7	C-24	1.2
	Yr	72	200	13	45	7	4	0	7	17	11	.225	.292	.300	82	-4	4			.984	1	C-68	0.2
Total	9	992	2834	276	826	120	41	14	363	274	162	.291	.367	.378	117	67	44	4		.974	-14	C-911	13.4

■ LOU MEYERS   Meyers, Lewis Henry "Crazy Horse" b: 12/9/1859, Cincinnati, Ohio d: 11/30/20, Cincinnati, Ohio BR/TR, 5'11", 165 lbs. Deb: 5/10/1884

YEAR	TM/L	G	AB	R	H	2B	3B	HR	RBI	BB	SO	AVG	OBP	SLG	PRO+	BR/A	SB	CS	SBR	FA	FR	G/POS	TPR
1884	Cin-U	2	3	1	0	0	0	0		1		.000	.250	.000	-17	-1				.667	-2	/C-2,O-1	-0.2

■ MICKEY MICELOTTA   Micelotta, Robert Peter b: 10/20/28, Corona, N.Y. BR/TR, 5'11", 185 lbs. Deb: 4/20/54

YEAR	TM/L	G	AB	R	H	2B	3B	HR	RBI	BB	SO	AVG	OBP	SLG	PRO+	BR/A	SB	CS	SBR	FA	FR	G/POS	TPR
1954	Phi-N	13	3	2	0	0	0	0	0	1	1	.000	.250	.000	-28	-1	0	0	0	1.000	0	/S-1	0.0
1955	Phi-N	4	4	0	0	0	0	0	0	0	0	.000	.000	.000	-99	-1	0	0	0	1.000	0	/S-2	-0.1
Total	2	17	7	2	0	0	0	0	0	1	1	.000	.125	.000	-64	-2	0	0	0	1.000	1	/S-3	-0.1

■ GENE MICHAEL   Michael, Eugene Richard "Stick" b: 6/2/38, Kent, Ohio BB/TR, 6'2", 183 lbs. Deb: 7/15/66 MC

YEAR	TM/L	G	AB	R	H	2B	3B	HR	RBI	BB	SO	AVG	OBP	SLG	PRO+	BR/A	SB	CS	SBR	FA	FR	G/POS	TPR
1966	Pit-N	30	33	9	5	2	1	0	2	0	7	.152	.152	.273	15	-4	0	0	0	.903	5	/S-8,2-2,3-1	0.2
1967	LA-N	98	223	20	45	3	1	0	7	11	30	.202	.246	.224	39	-18	1	3	-2	.950	5	S-83	-1.0
1968	NY-A	61	116	8	23	3	0	1	8	2	23	.198	.218	.250	43	-8	3	2	-0	.939	-1	S-43/P-1	-0.7
1969	NY-A	119	412	41	112	24	4	2	31	43	56	.272	.342	.364	101	1	7	4	1	.968	-1	*S-118	1.3
1970	NY-A	134	435	42	93	16	1	2	38	50	93	.214	.295	.255	56	-26	3	3	-1	.957	7	*S-123/3-4,2-3	-0.9
1971	NY-A	139	456	36	102	15	3	0	35	48	84	.224	.302	.276	69	-18	3	5	-1	.973	17	*S-136	1.6
1972	NY-A	126	391	29	91	7	4	1	32	32	45	.233	.292	.279	73	-13	4	2	0	.969	24	*S-121	3.0
1973	NY-A	129	418	30	94	11	1	3	47	26	51	.225	.270	.278	56	-24	1	3	-2	.965	5	*S-129	-0.5
1974	NY-A	81	177	19	46	9	0	0	13	14	24	.260	.314	.311	82	-4	0	0	0	.970	5	2-45,S-39/3-2	0.5
1975	Det-A	56	145	15	31	3	0	3	13	8	28	.214	.255	.290	51	-9	0	0	0	.938	-4	S-44/2-7,3-4	-1.0
Total		973	2806	249	642	86	12	15	226	234	421	.229	.290	.284	66	-124	22	18	-4	.962	55	S-844/2-57,3-11,P-1	2.5

■ CASS MICHAELS   Michaels, Casimir Eugene (Played In 1943 Under Real Name Of Casimir Eugene Kwietniewski) b: 3/4/26, Detroit, Mich. d: 11/12/82, Grosse Pointe, Mich. BR/TR, 5'11", 175 lbs. Deb: 8/19/43

YEAR	TM/L	G	AB	R	H	2B	3B	HR	RBI	BB	SO	AVG	OBP	SLG	PRO+	BR/A	SB	CS	SBR	FA	FR	G/POS	TPR
1943	Chi-A	2	7	0	0	0	0	0	0	0	0	.000	.000	.000	-99	-2	0	0	0	1.000	-1	/3-2	-0.4
1944	Chi-A	27	68	4	12	4	1	0	5	2	5	.176	.200	.265	33	-6	0	0	0	.930	6	S-21/3-3	0.1
1945	Chi-A	129	445	47	109	8	5	2	54	37	28	.245	.307	.299	78	-12	8	7	-2	.936	10	*S-126/2-1	0.6
1946	Chi-A	91	291	37	75	8	0	1	22	29	36	.258	.333	.296	80	-7	9	3	1	.957	3	2-66,3-13/S-6	0.1
1947	Chi-A	110	355	31	97	15	4	3	34	39	28	.273	.350	.363	102	1	10	5	0	.982	11	2-60,3-44/S-2	1.7
1948	Chi-A	145	484	47	120	12	6	5	56	69	42	.248	.344	.329	82	-11	8	2	1	.957	13	S-85,2-55/O-1	1.0
1949	Chi-A★	154	561	73	173	27	9	6	83	101	50	.308	.417	.421	126	25	5	7	-3	.976	12	*2-154	3.9
1950	Chi-A	36	138	21	43	6	3	4	19	13	8	.312	.375	.486	122	4	0	0	0	.964	-6	2-35	-0.1
	Was-A★	106	388	48	97	8	4	4	47	55	39	.250	.345	.322	75	-14	2	3	-1	.975	7	*2-104	-0.3
	Yr	142	526	69	140	14	7	8	66	68	47	.266	.352	.365	88	-9	2	3	-1	.972	2	*2-139	-0.4
1951	Was-A	138	485	59	125	20	4	4	45	61	41	.258	.342	.340	86	-8	1	1	-0	.964	-23	*2-128	-2.6
1952	Was-A	22	86	10	20	4	1	0	7	7	15	.233	.290	.337	77	-3	0	0	0	.977	1	2-22	-0.1
	StL-A	55	166	21	44	8	2	3	25	23	16	.265	.354	.392	104	1	1	0	0	.916	-3	3-42/2-8	0.1
	Phi-A	55	200	22	50	4	5	1	18	23	11	.250	.330	.335	80	-5	3	0	1	.993	-13	2-55	-1.5
	Yr	132	452	53	114	16	8	5	50	53	42	.252	.332	.356	89	-7	4	0	1	.989	-13	2-85,3-42	-1.5
1953	Phi-A	117	411	53	103	10	0	12	42	51	56	.251	.335	.363	85	-8	7	0	2	.970	-11	*2-110	-1.1
1954	Chi-A	101	282	35	74	13	2	7	44	56	31	.262	.392	.397	113	7	0	1	0	.958	-4	3-91/2-2	0.2
Total	12	1288	4367	508	1142	147	46	53	501	566	406	.262	.349	.353	92	-39	64	32	0	.973	3	2-800,S-240,3/O	1.6

■ RALPH MICHAELS   Michaels, Ralph Joseph b: 5/3/02, Etna, Pa. d: 8/5/88, Monroeville, Pa. BR/TR, 5'10.5", 178 lbs. Deb: 4/16/24

YEAR	TM/L	G	AB	R	H	2B	3B	HR	RBI	BB	SO	AVG	OBP	SLG	PRO+	BR/A	SB	CS	SBR	FA	FR	G/POS	TPR
1924	Chi-N	8	11	0	4	1	0	0	2	0	1	.364	.364	.364	95	-0	0	0	0	.929	1	/S-4	0.1
1925	Chi-N	22	50	10	14	1	0	0	6	6	9	.280	.357	.300	69	-2	1	0	0	.975	3	3-15/1-1,2-1,S-1	0.2
1926	Chi-N	2	0	1	0	0	0	0	0	0	0	—	—	—		0	0	0	0	.000	0	H	0.0
Total	3	32	61	11	18	1	0	0	8	6	10	.295	.358	.311	73	-2	1	0		.933	0	/3-15,S-5,2-1,1,1	0.3

■ ED MICKELSON   Mickelson, Edward Allen b: 9/9/26, Ottawa, Ill. BR/TR, 6'3", 205 lbs. Deb: 9/18/50

YEAR	TM/L	G	AB	R	H	2B	3B	HR	RBI	BB	SO	AVG	OBP	SLG	PRO+	BR/A	SB	CS	SBR	FA	FR	G/POS	TPR
1950	StL-N	5	10	1	1	0	0	0	2	3		.100	.250	.100	-4	-1	0			1.000	1	/1-4	-0.1
1953	StL-A	7	15	1	2	1	0	0	2	2	6	.133	.235	.200	18	-2	0	0	0	1.000	0	/1-3	-0.2
1957	Chi-N	6	12	0	0	0	0	0	0	1	4	.000	.000	.000	-99	-3	0	0	0	1.000	1	/1-2	-0.3
Total	3	18	37	2	3	1	0	0	4	6	10	.081	.171	.108	-23	-7	0	0		1.000	1	/1-9	-0.6

■ EZRA MIDKIFF   Midkiff, Ezra Millington "Salt Rock" b: 11/13/1882, Salt Rock, W.Va. d: 3/20/57, Huntington, W.Va. BL/TR, 5'10", 180 lbs. Deb: 10/5/09

YEAR	TM/L	G	AB	R	H	2B	3B	HR	RBI	BB	SO	AVG	OBP	SLG	PRO+	BR/A	SB	CS	SBR	FA	FR	G/POS	TPR
1909	Cin-N	1	2	0	0	0	0	0	0	0		.000	.000	.000	-99	-0	0			.000	0	/3-1	-0.1
1912	NY-A	21	86	9	21	1	0	0	9	7		.244	.301	.256	56	-5	4			.901	2	3-21	-0.3
1913	NY-A	83	284	22	56	9	1	0	14	12	33	.197	.232	.236	37	-23	9			.957	18	3-76/S-4,2-2	-0.5
Total	3	105	372	31	77	10	1	0	23	19	33	.207	.247	.239	41	-28	13			.942	18	/3-98,S-4,2-2	-0.9

■ ED MIERKOWICZ   Mierkowicz, Edward Frank "Butch" or "Mouse" b: 3/6/24, Wyandotte, Mich. BR/TR, 6'4", 205 lbs. Deb: 8/31/45

YEAR	TM/L	G	AB	R	H	2B	3B	HR	RBI	BB	SO	AVG	OBP	SLG	PRO+	BR/A	SB	CS	SBR	FA	FR	G/POS	TPR
1945	*Det-A	10	15	0	2	2	0	0	2	1	3	.133	.188	.267	29	-1	0	0	0	.000	-1	/O-6	-0.3
1947	Det-A	21	42	6	8	1	0	1	2	1	1	.190	.209	.286	36	-4	0	0	0	.947	-1	O-10	-0.5
1948	Det-A	3	5	0	1	0	0	0	1	2	2	.200	.429	.200	69	-0	0	0	0	1.000	0	/O-1	0.0
1950	StL-N	1	1	0	0	0	0	0	0	0		.000	.000	.000	-95	-0	0			.000	0	H	0.0
Total	4	35	63	6	11	3	0	1	4	4	18	.175	.224	.270	36	-6	1	0		.968	-2	/O-17	-0.8

■ MATT MIESKE   Mieske, Matthew Todd b: 2/13/68, Midland, Mich. BR/TR, 6', 185 lbs. Deb: 5/3/93

YEAR	TM/L	G	AB	R	H	2B	3B	HR	RBI	BB	SO	AVG	OBP	SLG	PRO+	BR/A	SB	CS	SBR	FA	FR	G/POS	TPR
1993	Mil-A	23	58	9	14	3	0	4	14	3	14	.241	.290	.397	84	-2	0	2	-1	.936	-2	O-22	-0.5
1994	Mil-A	84	259	39	67	13	1	10	38	21	62	.259	.322	.432	88	-5	3	5	-2	.976	-3	O-80/D-1	-1.1
1995	Mil-A	117	267	42	67	13	1	12	48	27	45	.251	.329	.442	93	-3	2	4	-2	.979	-3	*O-108/D-2	-1.0
1996	Mil-A	127	374	46	104	24	3	14	64	26	76	.278	.328	.471	94	-5	1	5	-3	.996	1	*O-122	-0.9
Total	4	351	958	136	252	50	5	39	157	78	197	.263	.324	.448	91	-15	6	16	-8	.982	-7	O-332/D-3	-3.5

■ LARRY MIGGINS   Miggins, Lawrence Edward "Irish" b: 8/20/25, Bronx, N.Y. BR/TR, 6'4", 198 lbs. Deb: 10/3/48

YEAR	TM/L	G	AB	R	H	2B	3B	HR	RBI	BB	SO	AVG	OBP	SLG	PRO+	BR/A	SB	CS	SBR	FA	FR	G/POS	TPR
1948	StL-N	1	1	0	0	0	0	0	0	0		.000	.000	.000	-95	-0	0			.000	0	H	0.0
1952	StL-N	42	96	7	22	5	1	2	10	3	19	.229	.253	.365	69	-4	0	1	-1	.967	-4	O-25/1-1	-1.1
Total	2	43	97	8	22	5	1	2	10	3	19	.227	.250	.361	67	-5	0	1		.967	-4	/O-25,1-1	-1.1

JOHN MIHALIC
Mihalic, John Michael   b: 11/13/11, Cleveland, Ohio   d: 4/24/87, Ft.Oglethorpe, Ga.   BR/TR, 5'11", 172 lbs.   Deb: 9/18/35

YEAR	TM/L	G	AB	R	H	2B	3B	HR	RBI	BB	SO	AVG	OBP	SLG	PRO+	BR/A	SB	CS	SBR	FA	FR	G/POS	TPR
1935	Was-A	6	22	4	5	3	0	0	6	2	3	.227	.292	.364	71	-1	1	0	0	.966	-1	/S-6	-0.1
1936	Was-A	25	88	15	21	2	1	0	8	14	14	.239	.343	.284	60	-5	2	1	0	.972	1	2-25	-0.2
1937	Was-A	38	107	13	27	5	2	0	8	17	9	.252	.355	.336	79	-3	2	1	0	.981	4	2-28/S-3	0.3
Total	3	69	217	32	53	10	3	0	22	33	26	.244	.344	.318	70	-9	5	2	0	.977	4	/2-53,S-9	0.0

EDDIE MIKSIS
Miksis, Edward Thomas   b: 9/11/26, Burlington, N.J.   BR/TR, 6'0.5", 185 lbs.   Deb: 6/17/44

YEAR	TM/L	G	AB	R	H	2B	3B	HR	RBI	BB	SO	AVG	OBP	SLG	PRO+	BR/A	SB	CS	SBR	FA	FR	G/POS	TPR
1944	Bro-N	26	91	12	20	2	0	0	11	6	11	.220	.268	.242	45	-7	4			.896	-4	3-15,S-10	-1.0
1946	Bro-N	23	48	3	7	0	0	0	5	3	3	.146	.212	.146	2	-6	0			.970	0	3-13/2-1	-0.6
1947	*Bro-N	45	86	18	23	1	0	4	10	9	8	.267	.337	.419	96	-1	0			1.000	3	2-13,0-11/3-5,S-2	0.3
1948	Bro-N	86	221	28	47	7	1	2	16	19	27	.213	.278	.281	50	-15	5			.967	4	2-54,3-22/S-5	-1.0
1949	*Bro-N	50	113	17	25	5	0	1	6	7	8	.221	.267	.292	48	-8	3			.978	6	3-29/S-4,2-3,1-1	-0.3
1950	Bro-N	51	76	13	19	2	1	2	10	5	10	.250	.296	.382	75	-3	3			.964	5	2-15,S-15/3-7	0.3
1951	Bro-N	19	10	6	2	1	0	0	0	1	2	.200	.333	.300	70	-0	0	0	0	1.000	0	/3-6,2-1	0.2
	Chi-N	102	421	48	112	13	3	4	35	33	36	.266	.319	.340	76	-14	11	5	0	.969	3	*2-102	-0.6
	Yr	121	431	54	114	14	3	4	35	34	38	.265	.320	.339	76	-14	11	5	0	.969	5	*2-103/3-6	-0.4
1952	Chi-N	93	383	44	89	20	1	2	19	20	32	.232	.272	.305	59	-21	4	4	-1	.950	-13	2-54,S-40	-3.1
1953	Chi-N	142	577	61	145	17	6	8	39	33	59	.251	.293	.343	64	-31	13	4	2	.954	-13	2-92,S-53	-3.3
1954	Chi-N	38	99	9	20	3	0	2	3	3	9	.202	.225	.293	33	-10	1	0	0	.961	4	2-21/3-2,O-1	-0.4
1955	Chi-N	131	481	52	113	14	2	9	41	32	55	.235	.283	.328	62	-27	3	6	-3	.989	-3	*O-111,3-18	-3.0
1956	Chi-N	114	356	54	85	10	3	9	27	32	40	.239	.303	.360	79	-11	4	2	0	.975	-3	3-48,O-33,2-19,/S-2	-1.4
1957	StL-N	49	38	3	8	0	0	1	2	7	7	.211	.333	.289	68	-2	0	0	0	1.000	-11	O-31	-1.3
	Bal-A	1	1	0	0	0	0	0	0	0	0	.000	.000	.000	-99	-0	0			.000	0	H	-0.0
1958	Bal-A	3	2	0	0	0	0	0	0	0	1	.000	.000	.000	-99	-1	0	0	0	.000	0	/S-1	-0.1
	Cin-N	69	50	15	7	0	0	0	4	5	5	.140	.218	.140	-7	-1	1	1	-0	1.000	-4	0-32,3-14/2-7,S1	-1.2
Total	14	1042	3053	383	722	95	17	44	228	215	313	.236	.288	.322	62	-164	52	22		.962	-17	2-382,O-219,3S/1	-16.5

HORACE MILAN
Milan, Horace Robert   b: 4/7/1894, Linden, Tenn.   d: 6/29/55, Texarkana, Ark.   BR/TR, 5'9", 175 lbs.   Deb: 8/29/15   F

YEAR	TM/L	G	AB	R	H	2B	3B	HR	RBI	BB	SO	AVG	OBP	SLG	PRO+	BR/A	SB	CS	SBR	FA	FR	G/POS	TPR
1915	Was-A	11	27	6	11	1	1	0	7	8	7	.407	.543	.519	214	5	2			1.000	-3	O-10	0.2
1917	Was-A	31	73	8	21	3	1	0	9	4	9	.288	.342	.356	114	1	4			.932	-4	O-23	-0.4
Total	2	42	100	14	32	4	2	0	16	12	16	.320	.404	.400	144	6	6			.944	-6	/O-33	-0.2

CLYDE MILAN
Milan, Jesse Clyde "Deerfoot"   b: 3/25/1887, Linden, Tenn.   d: 3/3/53, Orlando, Fla.   BL/TR, 5'9", 168 lbs.   Deb: 8/19/07   FMC

YEAR	TM/L	G	AB	R	H	2B	3B	HR	RBI	BB	SO	AVG	OBP	SLG	PRO+	BR/A	SB	CS	SBR	FA	FR	G/POS	TPR
1907	Was-A	48	183	22	51	3	3	0	9	8		.279	.323	.328	117	3	8			.929	4	O-47	0.6
1908	Was-A	130	485	55	116	10	12	1	32	38		.239	.304	.315	110	5	29			.959	9	*O-122	1.1
1909	Was-A	130	400	36	80	12	4	1	15	31		.200	.268	.257	69	-14	10			.972	5	*O-120	-1.6
1910	Was-A	142	531	89	148	17	6	0	16	71		.279	.379	.333	129	22	44			.946	11	*O-142	2.9
1911	Was-A	154	616	109	194	24	8	3	35	74		.315	.395	.394	123	21	58			.957	11	*O-154	2.3
1912	Was-A	154	601	105	184	19	11	1	79	63		.306	.377	.379	116	13	88			.935	8	*O-154	1.3
1913	Was-A	154	579	92	174	18	9	3	54	58	25	.301	.367	.378	116	12	75			.932	-7	*O-154	-0.3
1914	Was-A	115	437	63	129	19	11	1	39	32	26	.295	.346	.396	118	8	38	21	-1	.949	-4	*O-113	-0.2
1915	Was-A	153	573	83	165	13	7	2	66	53	32	.288	.353	.346	107	5	40	19	1	.946	-0	*O-151	-0.2
1916	Was-A	150	565	58	154	18	4	1	45	56	31	.273	.343	.313	98	-0	34	21	-2	.961	17	*O-149	0.7
1917	Was-A	155	579	60	170	15	4	0	48	58	26	.294	.364	.333	114	11	20			.962	-5	*O-153	-0.2
1918	Was-A	128	500	56	146	18	5	0	56	36	14	.290	.344	.346	110	5	26			.972	2	*O-124	0.1
1919	Was-A	88	321	43	92	12	6	0	37	40	16	.287	.371	.361	107	4	11			.953	-3	O-86	-0.5
1920	Was-A	126	506	70	163	22	5	3	41	28	12	.322	.364	.403	106	4	10	12	-4	.971	8	*O-123	-0.2
1921	Was-A	113	406	55	117	19	11	1	40	37	13	.288	.351	.397	95	-4	4	5	-2	.931	2	O-99	-1.0
1922	Was-A	42	74	8	17	5	0	0	5	2	2	.230	.250	.297	44	-6	0	0	0	1.000	1	O-12,M	-0.5
Total	16	1982	7359	1004	2100	240	105	17	617	685	197	.285	.353	.353	109	92	495	78		.953	58	*O-1903	4.2

LARRY MILBOURNE
Milbourne, Lawrence William   b: 2/14/51, Port Norris, N.J.   BB/TR, 6', 165 lbs.   Deb: 4/6/74

YEAR	TM/L	G	AB	R	H	2B	3B	HR	RBI	BB	SO	AVG	OBP	SLG	PRO+	BR/A	SB	CS	SBR	FA	FR	G/POS	TPR
1974	Hou-N	112	136	31	38	2	1	0	9	10	14	.279	.329	.309	83	-3	6	2	1	.974	17	2-87/S-8,O-4	1.7
1975	Hou-N	73	151	17	32	1	2	1	9	6	14	.212	.247	.265	45	-12	1	2	-1	.968	10	2-43/S-22	0.0
1976	Hou-N	59	145	22	36	4	0	0	7	14	10	.248	.319	.276	77	-4	6	1	1	.965	-1	2-32	-0.2
1977	Sea-A	86	242	24	53	10	4	2	21	6	20	.219	.244	.285	44	-19	3	1	0	.982	4	2-41,S-40/3-1,D-1	-0.9
1978	Sea-A	93	234	31	53	6	2	2	20	9	6	.226	.255	.295	55	-14	5	7	-3	.989	16	3-32,S-23,2-15,D-10	0.1
1979	Sea-A	123	356	40	99	13	4	2	26	19	20	.278	.315	.354	79	-11	5	3	-0	.981	-17	S-65,2-49,3-11	-2.0
1980	Sea-A	106	258	31	68	6	6	0	26	19	13	.264	.317	.333	78	-8	7	4	-2	.976	0	2-38,S-34/3-6,D-8	-0.4
1981	*NY-A	61	163	24	51	7	2	1	12	9	14	.313	.353	.399	118	4	2	0	1	.955	-7	S-39,2-14/3-3,D-3	0.2
1982	NY-A	29	27	2	4	1	0	0	0	1	4	.148	.179	.185	0	-4	0	0	-1	.917	1	/S-9,2-3,3-3	-0.3
	Min-A	29	98	9	23	1	1	0	1	7	8	.235	.286	.265	51	-6	1	1	-0	.981	-10	2-26	-1.6
	Cle-A	82	291	29	80	11	4	2	25	12	20	.275	.308	.361	83	-7	2	5	-2	.981	-6	2-63,S-21/3-9,D-1	-1.1
	Yr	125	416	40	107	13	5	2	26	20	32	.257	.295	.327	70	-17	3	7	-3	.979	-15	2-92,S-30,3-12/D-1	-3.0
1983	Phi-N	41	66	3	16	0	1	0	4	4	7	.242	.286	.273	56	-4	2	1	0	.963	1	2-27/S-8,3-3	-0.3
	NY-A	31	70	5	14	4	0	0	2	5	10	.200	.263	.257	46	-5	1	1	-0	1.000	1	2-19/S-6,3-4	-0.1
1984	Sea-A	79	211	22	56	5	1	2	22	10	16	.265	.305	.313	72	-8	0	2	-1	.900	-9	3-40,2-14/S-5,D-6	-1.8
Total	11	989	2448	290	623	71	24	11	184	133	176	.254	.295	.317	70	-101	41	33	-8	.974	1	2-471,S-280,3/DO	-6.7

DON MILES
Miles, Donald Ray   b: 3/13/36, Indianapolis, Ind.   BL/TR, 6'1", 210 lbs.   Deb: 9/9/58

YEAR	TM/L	G	AB	R	H	2B	3B	HR	RBI	BB	SO	AVG	OBP	SLG	PRO+	BR/A	SB	CS	SBR	FA	FR	G/POS	TPR
1958	LA-N	8	22	2	4	0	0	0	0	0	6	.182	.217	.182	7	-3	0	0	0	1.000	2	/O-5	-0.2

DEE MILES
Miles, Wilson Daniel   b: 2/15/09, Kellerman, Ala.   d: 11/2/76, Birmingham, Ala.   BL/TR, 6', 175 lbs.   Deb: 7/7/35

YEAR	TM/L	G	AB	R	H	2B	3B	HR	RBI	BB	SO	AVG	OBP	SLG	PRO+	BR/A	SB	CS	SBR	FA	FR	G/POS	TPR
1935	Was-A	60	215	28	57	5	2	0	29	7	13	.265	.291	.307	57	-14	6	4	-1	.970	-2	O-45	-1.3
1936	Was-A	25	59	8	14	1	1	0	7	1	5	.237	.290	.322	43	-6	0	1	-1	.958	0	O-10	-0.6
1939	Phi-A	106	320	49	96	17	6	1	37	16	17	.300	.331	.400	88	-7	3	4	-2	.968	-7	O-77	-1.6
1940	Phi-A	88	236	26	71	9	6	1	23	8	18	.301	.327	.403	90	-4	1	1	-0	.945	-1	O-50	-0.8
1941	Phi-A	80	170	14	53	7	1	0	15	4	8	.312	.331	.365	86	-4	0	1	-0	1.000	-1	O-35	-0.6
1942	Phi-A	99	346	41	94	12	5	0	22	12	10	.272	.300	.335	79	-11	5	3	-0	.984	-3	O-81	-1.9
1943	Bos-A	45	121	9	26	2	2	0	11	3	3	.215	.234	.264	45	-9	0	2	-1	.968	-1	O-25	-1.3
Total	7	503	1467	175	411	53	24	2	143	50	74	.280	.306	.353	76	-53	15	16	-5	.971	-10	O-323	-8.1

MIKE MILEY
Miley, Michael Wilfred   b: 3/30/53, Yazoo City, Miss.   d: 1/6/77, Baton Rouge, La.   BB/TR, 6'1", 185 lbs.   Deb: 7/6/75

YEAR	TM/L	G	AB	R	H	2B	3B	HR	RBI	BB	SO	AVG	OBP	SLG	PRO+	BR/A	SB	CS	SBR	FA	FR	G/POS	TPR
1975	Cal-A	70	224	17	39	8	0	2	26	16	54	.174	.232	.259	42	-18	0	1	-1	.939	-9	S-70	-2.1
1976	Cal-A	14	38	4	7	2	0	0	4	4	8	.184	.262	.237	50	-2	1	0	-0	.981	-2	S-14	-0.2
Total	2	84	262	21	46	10	0	2	30	20	62	.176	.237	.256	43	-20	1	1	-1	.945	-11	/S-84	-2.3

FELIX MILLAN
Millan, Felix Bernardo (Martinez)   b: 8/21/43, Yabucoa, P.R.   BR/TR, 5'11", 172 lbs.   Deb: 6/2/66

YEAR	TM/L	G	AB	R	H	2B	3B	HR	RBI	BB	SO	AVG	OBP	SLG	PRO+	BR/A	SB	CS	SBR	FA	FR	G/POS	TPR
1966	Atl-N	37	91	20	25	6	0	0	5	2	6	.275	.290	.341	74	-3	3	1	0	.973	-2	2-25/S-1,3-1	-0.4
1967	Atl-N	41	136	13	32	3	3	2	6	4	10	.235	.268	.346	75	-5	0	3	-2	.972	3	2-41	-0.1
1968	Atl-N	149	570	49	165	22	2	1	33	22	26	.289	.323	.340	99	-1	6	6	-2			*2-145	1.0
1969	*Atl-N★	162	652	98	174	23	6	6	57	34	35	.267	.311	.345	83	-15	14	3	2	.980	-16	2-162	-1.6
1970	Atl-N†	142	590	100	183	25	2	2	37	35	23	.310	.354	.380	91	-7	16	5	2	.979	-19	2-142	-1.2
1971	Atl-N★	143	577	65	167	20	4	3	45	37	22	.289	.335	.362	92	-6	11	7	-1	.982	6	2-141	1.2
1972	Atl-N	125	498	46	128	19	3	1	38	23	28	.257	.294	.313	66	-22	6	4	-1	.987	-16	2-120	-3.5
1973	*NY-N	153	638	82	185	23	4	3	37	35	22	.290	.333	.353	91	-7	2	2	-1	.989	-4	2-153	-0.3
1974	NY-N	136	518	50	139	13	3	1	33	31	14	.268	.320	.311	78	-15	5	1	-1	.972	-20	2-134	-2.9
1975	NY-N	162	676	81	191	37	2	1	56	36	28	.283	.330	.348	92	-8	1	6	-3	.972	-25	2-162	-2.8
1976	NY-N	139	531	55	150	25	2	0	35	41	19	.282	.342	.343	101	1	2	4	-2	.977	-24	2-136	-1.8
1977	NY-N	91	314	40	78	21	0	0	21	18	9	.248	.296	.315	67	-15	1	2	-0	.977	-16	2-89	-2.6
Total	12	1480	5791	699	1617	229	38	22	403	318	242	.279	.324	.343	89	-103	67	43	-6	.980	-129	*2-1450/3-1,S-1	-15.0

YEAR	TM/L	G	AB	R	H	2B	3B	HR	RBI	BB	SO	AVG	OBP	SLG	PRO+	BR/A	SB	CS	SBR	FA	FR	G/POS	TPR

■ FRANK MILLARD   Millard, Frank E.   b: 7/4/1865, E.St.Louis, Ill.   d: 7/4/1892, Galveston, Tex.   Deb: 5/4/1890

| 1890 | StL-a | 1 | 1 | 0 | 0 | 0 | 0 | 0 | 0 | 0 | 1 | .000 | .500 | .000 | 42 | 0 | 0 | | | .625 | 1 | /2-1 | 0.0 |

■ DUSTY MILLER   Miller, Charles Bradley   b: 9/10/1868, Oil City, Pa.   d: 9/3/45, Memphis, Tenn.   BL/TR, 5'11.5", 170 lbs.   Deb: 9/23/1889

1889	Bal-a	11	40	4	6	1	1	0	6	2	11	.150	.209	.225	23	-4	3			.636	-7	/S-8,O-3	-1.0
1890	StL-a	26	96	17	21	5	3	0	10	8		.219	.279	.365	78	-4	4			.872	3	O-24/S-3	-0.2
1895	Cin-N	132	529	103	177	31	16	10	112	33	34	.335	.378	.510	123	14	43			.937	11	*O-132	1.2
1896	Cin-N	125	504	91	162	38	12	4	93	33	30	.321	.368	.468	112	6	76			.902	-2	*O-125	-0.5
1897	Cin-N	119	440	83	139	27	1	4	70	48		.316	.393	.409	105	3	29			.929	2	*O-119	-0.3
1898	Cin-N	152	586	99	175	24	12	3	90	38		.299	.351	.396	106	3	32			.929	8	*O-152	0.0
1899	Cin-N	80	323	44	81	12	5	0	37	9		.251	.278	.319	62	-18	18			.927	7	O-80	-1.5
	StL-N	10	39	3	8	1	0	0	3	3		.205	.279	.231	40	-3	1			.875	-1	O-10	-0.4
	Yr	90	362	47	89	13	5	0	40	12		.246	.278	.309	60	-21	19			.921	6	O-90	-1.9
Total	7	655	2557	444	769	139	50	22	421	174	75	.301	.352	.420	102	-3	206			.923	21	O-645/S-11	-2.7

■ BRUCE MILLER   Miller, Charles Bruce   b: 3/4/47, Fort Wayne, Ind.   BR/TR, 6'1", 185 lbs.   Deb: 8/4/73

1973	SF-N	12	21	1	3	0	0	0	2	2	3	.143	.217	.143	2	-3	0	0	0	.900	1	/3-4,2-3,S-1	-0.2
1974	SF-N	73	198	19	55	7	1	0	16	11	15	.278	.319	.323	76	-6	1	1	-0	.938	13	3-41,S-13/2-9	0.8
1975	SF-N	99	309	22	74	6	3	1	31	15	26	.239	.277	.288	55	-19	0	1	-1	.949	10	3-68,2-21/S-6	-0.9
1976	SF-N	12	25	1	4	1	0	0	2	2	5	.160	.222	.200	20	-3	0	0	0	.920	-1	/2-8,3-2	-0.4
Total	4	196	553	43	136	14	4	1	51	30	49	.246	.287	.291	59	-30	1	2	-1	.944	22	3-115/2-41,S-20	-0.7

■ CHARLIE MILLER   Miller, Charles Elmer   b: 1/4/1892, Warrensburg, Mo.   d: 4/23/72, Warrensburg, Mo.   TR   Deb: 9/18/12

| 1912 | StL-A | 1 | 2 | 0 | 0 | 0 | 0 | 0 | 0 | 0 | | .000 | .000 | .000 | -99 | -1 | 0 | | | 1.000 | -0 | /S-1 | -0.1 |

■ CHARLIE MILLER   Miller, Charles Hess   b: 12/30/1877, Conestoga, Pa.   d: 1/13/51, Millersville, Pa.   BR/TR, 6', 190 lbs.   Deb: 10/2/15

| 1915 | Bal-F | 1 | 1 | 0 | 0 | 0 | 0 | 0 | 0 | 0 | 0 | .000 | .000 | .000 | -97 | -0 | 0 | | | | 0 | H | 0.0 |

■ CHUCK MILLER   Miller, Charles Marion   b: 9/18/1889, Woodville, Ohio   d: 6/16/61, Houston, Tex.   BL/TL, 5'8.5", 155 lbs.   Deb: 9/19/13

1913	StL-N	4	12	0	2	0	0	0	1	0	2	.167	.167	.167	-5	-2	0			1.000	-1	/O-3	-0.3
1914	StL-N	36	36	4	7	1	0	0	2	3	9	.194	.256	.222	43	-2	2			1.000	-3	O-14	-0.6
Total	2	40	48	4	9	1	0	0	3	3	11	.188	.235	.208	31	-4	2			1.000	-4	/O-17	-0.9

■ DUSTY MILLER   Miller, Dakin Evans   b: 9/3/1876, Malvern, Iowa   d: 4/19/50, Stockton, Cal.   BL/TR, 5'10", 175 lbs.   Deb: 4/17/02

| 1902 | Chi-N | 51 | 187 | 17 | 46 | 4 | 1 | 0 | 13 | 7 | | .246 | .299 | .278 | 80 | -4 | 10 | | | .955 | 1 | O-51 | -0.7 |

■ DARRELL MILLER   Miller, Darrell Keith   b: 2/26/58, Washington, D.C.   BR/TR, 6'2", 200 lbs.   Deb: 8/14/84

1984	Cal-A	17	41	5	7	0	0	0	4	9		.171	.244	.171	17	-5	0	0	0	.990	-1	1-16/O-1	-0.6
1985	Cal-A	51	48	8	18	2	1	2	7	1	10	.375	.400	.583	166	4	0	1	-1	.952	-11	O-45/C-1,3-1,D-4	-0.7
1986	Cal-A	33	57	6	13	2	1	0	4	4	8	.228	.279	.298	58	-3	0	0	0	1.000	-10	O-23,C-10/D-2	-1.3
1987	Cal-A	53	108	14	26	5	0	4	16	9	13	.241	.311	.398	89	-2	1	0	0	.984	-8	C-33,O-18/3-1,D-1	-0.6
1988	Cal-A	70	140	21	31	4	1	2	7	9	29	.221	.292	.307	70	-6	2	1	0	.987	3	C-53/O-8,D-1	-0.0
Total	5	224	394	54	95	13	3	8	35	27	69	.241	.303	.350	80	-11	3	2	-0	.987	-25	/C-97,O-95,1-16,D3	-3.2

■ BING MILLER   Miller, Edmund John   b: 8/30/1894, Vinton, Iowa   d: 5/7/66, Philadelphia, Pa.   BR/TR, 6', 185 lbs.   Deb: 4/16/21   FC

1921	Was-A	114	420	57	121	28	8	9	71	25	50	.288	.334	.457	105	1	3	-4	-2	.945	2	*O-109	-0.6
1922	Phi-A	143	535	90	179	29	12	21	90	24	42	.335	.371	.551	134	24	10	10	-3	.977	5	*O-139	1.5
1923	Phi-A	123	458	68	137	25	4	12	64	27	34	.299	.344	.450	106	2	9	3	1	.978	-1	*O-119	-0.5
1924	Phi-A	113	398	62	136	22	4	6	62	12	24	.342	.376	.462	114	7	11	5	0	.973	-2	O-94/1-7	-0.1
1925	Phi-A	124	474	78	151	29	10	10	81	19	14	.319	.355	.485	105	1	11	6	-0	.975	-10	*O-115,1-12	-1.6
1926	Phi-A	38	110	13	32	6	2	2	13	11	6	.291	.355	.436	100	-0	4	1	1	1.000	-5	O-34/1-1	-0.6
	StL-A	94	353	60	117	27	5	4	50	22	12	.331	.382	.470	116	8	7	9	-3	.939	4	O-94	0.2
	Yr	132	463	73	149	33	7	6	63	33	18	.322	.376	.462	112	7	11	10	-3	.950	-1	*O-128/1-1	-0.4
1927	StL-A	143	492	83	160	32	7	5	75	30	26	.325	.375	.449	109	6	8	7	-2	.970	4	*O-126	0.1
1928	Phi-A	139	510	76	168	34	7	8	85	27	24	.329	.372	.471	117	12	10	6	-1	.968	-0	*O-133	0.3
1929	*Phi-A	147	556	84	184	32	16	8	93	40	25	.331	.380	.489	118	14	24	9	2	.970	6	*O-145	1.3
1930	*Phi-A	154	585	89	177	38	7	9	100	47	22	.303	.357	.438	96	-4	13	13	-4	.976	5	*O-154	-1.2
1931	*Phi-A	137	534	75	150	43	5	8	77	36	16	.281	.338	.425	94	-6	5	3	-0	.987	6	*O-137	-0.9
1932	Phi-A	95	305	40	90	17	4	7	58	20	11	.295	.343	.446	99	-1	7	3	0	.979	1	O-84	-0.4
1933	Phi-A	67	120	22	33	7	1	2	17	12	7	.275	.346	.400	96	-1	4	2	0	1.000	-6	O-30/1-6	-0.8
1934	Phi-A	81	177	22	43	10	2	1	23	16	14	.243	.309	.339	70	-8	1	0	0	1.000	-3	O-46	-1.2
1935	Bos-A	78	138	18	42	8	1	3	26	10	8	.304	.356	.442	99	-1	0	1	-1	.962	-2	O-29	-0.4
1936	Bos-A	30	47	9	14	2	1	0	6	5	5	.298	.377	.447	97	-0	0	0	0	1.000	-3	O-13	-0.3
Total	16	1820	6212	946	1934	389	96	116	990	383	340	.311	.359	.461	108	52	127	82	-11	.971	2	*O-1601/1-26	-5.2

■ EDDIE MILLER   Miller, Edward Lee   b: 6/29/57, San Pablo, Cal.   BB/TR, 5'9", 175 lbs.   Deb: 9/5/77

1977	Tex-A	17	6	7	2	0	0	0	1	1	1	.333	.429	.333	110	0	3	1	0	1.000	-0	/O-2,D-3	0.0
1978	Atl-N	6	21	5	3	1	0	0	2	2	4	.143	.250	.190	22	-2	3	0	1	1.000	-1	O-5	-0.2
1979	Atl-N	27	113	12	35	1	0	0	5	5	24	.310	.350	.319	78	-3	15	2	3	.988	3	O-27	0.2
1980	Atl-N	11	19	3	3	0	0	0	0	0	5	.158	.158	.158	-11	-3	1	2	-1	1.000	-3	O-9	-0.8
1981	Atl-N	50	134	29	31	3	1	0	7	9	29	.231	.285	.269	56	-8	23	5	4	.985	-1	O-36	-0.7
1982	Det-A	14	25	3	1	0	0	0	0	4	4	.040	.250	.040	-14	-4	0	3	-2	1.000	-0	/O-8,D-1	-0.6
1984	SD-N	13	14	4	4	0	1	1	2	0	4	.286	.286	.643	155	1	4	0	1	1.000	-1	/O-8	0.1
Total	7	138	332	63	79	5	2	1	17	19	71	.238	.297	.274	57	-18	49	13	7	.989	-4	/O-95,D-4	-2.0

■ EDDIE MILLER   Miller, Edward Robert "Eppie"   b: 11/26/16, Pittsburgh, Pa.   BR/TR, 5'9", 180 lbs.   Deb: 9/9/36

1936	Cin-N	5	10	0	1	0	0	0	1	1	1	.100	.182	.100	-24	-2	0			.938	-0	/S-4,2-1	-0.2
1937	Cin-N	36	60	3	9	3	1	0	5	3	8	.150	.190	.233	15	-7	0			.926	7	S-30/3-4	0.1
1939	Bos-N	77	296	32	79	12	2	4	31	16	21	.267	.315	.361	88	-6	4			.970	12	S-77	1.3
1940	Bos-N★	151	569	78	157	33	3	14	79	41	43	.276	.330	.418	111	7	8			**.970**	15	*S-151	3.5
1941	Bos-N★	154	585	54	140	27	3	6	68	35	72	.239	.288	.326	76	-20	8			**.966**	12	*S-154	0.4
1942	Bos-N★	142	534	47	130	28	2	6	47	22	42	.243	.279	.337	81	-15	11			**.983**	4	*S-142	-0.2
1943	Cin-N★	154	576	49	129	26	4	2	71	33	43	.224	.271	.293	64	-28	8			**.979**	27	*S-154	1.1
1944	Cin-N†	155	536	48	112	21	5	4	55	41	41	.209	.266	.289	59	-30	1			.971	12	*S-155	-0.5
1945	Cin-N	115	421	46	100	27	2	13	49	18	38	.238	.275	.404	89	-9	4			**.975**	5	*S-115	0.5
1946	Cin-N†	91	299	30	58	10	0	6	36	25	34	.194	.258	.288	57	-18	5			.970	24	S-88	1.1
1947	Cin-N†	151	545	69	146	**38**	4	19	87	49	40	.268	.333	.457	109	5	5			.972	-5	*S-151	0.7
1948	Phi-N	130	468	45	115	20	1	14	61	19	40	.246	.281	.382	79	-15	1			.966	-14	*S-122	-2.2
1949	Phi-N	85	266	21	55	10	1	6	29	19	21	.207	.294	.320	66	-13	1			.986	-10	2-82/S-1	-2.0
1950	StL-N	64	172	17	39	8	0	3	21	9	21	.227	.307	.326	64	-9	0			.980	14	S-51/2-1	0.8
Total	14	1510	5337	539	1270	263	28	97	640	351	465	.238	.290	.352	80	-160	64			.972	102	*S-1395/2-84,3-4	4.4

■ ED MILLER   Miller, Edwin J. "Big Ed"   b: 11/24/1888, Annville, Pa.   d: 4/17/80, S.Lebanon Twsp, Pa   BR/TR, 6', 180 lbs.   Deb: 6/29/12

1912	StL-A	13	46	4	9	1	0	0	5	2		.196	.245	.217	34	-4	1			.951	-4	/1-8,S-5	-0.8
1914	StL-A	41	58	8	8	0	1	0	4	4	13	.138	.219	.172	18	-6	1	3	-2	.981	-2	/1-8,2-5,O-5,3-2	-1.0
1918	Cle-A	32	96	9	22	4	1	0	3	6	10	.229	.321	.333	89	-1	2			.977	1	1-22/O-4	-0.2
Total	3	86	200	21	39	5	4	0	12	12	23	.195	.275	.260	58	-11	4	3		.972	-5	/1-38,O-9,2-5,S3	-2.0

■ ELMER MILLER   Miller, Elmer   b: 7/28/1890, Sandusky, Ohio   d: 11/28/44, Beloit, Wis.   BR/TR, 6', 175 lbs.   Deb: 4/26/12

1912	StL-N	12	37	5	7	0	0	0	3	4	9	.189	.268	.216	34	-3	1			1.000	0	O-11	-0.4
1915	NY-A	26	83	4	12	1	0	0	3	4	14	.145	.193	.157	5	-10	0			.955	-4	O-26	-1.7
1916	NY-A	43	152	19	34	3	2	0	13	11	18	.224	.280	.289	70	-5	8			.969	5	O-42	-0.4

YEAR	TM/L	G	AB	R	H	2B	3B	HR	RBI	BB	SO	AVG	OBP	SLG	PRO+	BR/A	SB	CS	SBR	FA	FR	G/POS	TPR
1917	NY-A	114	379	43	95	11	3	3	35	40	44	.251	.336	.319	99	1	11			.961	-6	*O-112	-1.2
1918	NY-A	67	202	18	49	9	2	1	22	19	17	.243	.317	.322	91	-2	2			.947	4	O-62	-0.2
1921	*NY-A	56	242	41	72	9	8	4	36	19	16	.298	.356	.450	102	0	2	2	-1	.947	3	O-56	-0.1
1922	NY-A	51	172	31	46	7	2	3	18	11	12	.267	.311	.384	79	-6	2	3	-1	.982	-2	O-51	-1.2
	Bos-A	44	147	16	28	2	3	4	16	5	10	.190	.222	.327	42	-13	3	1	0	.957	-0	O-35	-1.6
	Yr	95	319	47	74	9	5	7	34	16	22	.232	.271	.357	62	-19	5	4	-1	.970	-2	O-86	-2.8
Total 7		413	1414	170	343	43	20	16	151	113	140	.243	.307	.335	80	-40	29	6		.960	-0	O-395	-6.8

■ **ELMER MILLER**   Miller, Elmer Joseph "Lefty" b: 4/17/03, Detroit, Mich. d: 1/8/87, Corona, Cal. BL/TL, 5'11", 189 lbs. Deb: 6/21/29

YEAR	TM/L	G	AB	R	H	2B	3B	HR	RBI	BB	SO	AVG	OBP	SLG	PRO+	BR/A	SB	CS	SBR	FA	FR	G/POS	TPR
1929	Phi-N	31	38	3	9	1	0	1	4	1	5	.237	.256	.342	44	-3	0			.750	2	/P-8,O-4	-0.1

■ **KOHLY MILLER**   Miller, Frank A. b: 1/1874, Cumru Township, Pa. d: 3/29/51, Reading, Pa. Deb: 9/16/1892

YEAR	TM/L	G	AB	R	H	2B	3B	HR	RBI	BB	SO	AVG	OBP	SLG	PRO+	BR/A	SB	CS	SBR	FA	FR	G/POS	TPR
1892	Was-N	1	3	0	0	0	0	0	0	0	1	.000	.000	.000	-99	-1	0			.400	-1	/S-1	-0.2
	StL-N	1	4	0	0	0	0	0	0	0	0	.000	.000	.000	-99	-1	0			.500	-1	/3-1	-0.2
	Yr	2	7	0	0	0	0	0	0	0	1	.000	.000	.000	-99	-2	0			.400	-2	/S-1,3-1	-0.4
1897	Phi-N	3	11	2	2	0	0	0		1	2	.182	.308	.182	32	-1	0			.857	-2	/2-3	-0.3
Total 2		5	18	2	2	0	0	0	1	2	1	.111	.200	.111	-13	-3	0			.857	-5	/2-3,3-1,S-1	-0.7

■ **GEORGE MILLER**   Miller, George C. b: 2/19/1853, Newport, Ky. d: 7/24/29, Norwood, Ohio BR/TR, 5'5", 160 lbs. Deb: 9/6/1877

YEAR	TM/L	G	AB	R	H	2B	3B	HR	RBI	BB	SO	AVG	OBP	SLG	PRO+	BR/A	SB	CS	SBR	FA	FR	G/POS	TPR
1877	Cin-N	11	37	4	6	1	0	0	3	5	2	.162	.262	.189	50	-2				.918	0	C-11	-0.1
1884	Cin-a	6	20	6	5	1	1	0	3	1		.250	.318	.400	127	1				.975	2	/C-6	0.3
Total 2		17	57	10	11	2	1	0	6	6	2	.193	.281	.263	79	-1				.938	2	/C-17	0.2

■ **DOGGIE MILLER**   Miller, George Frederick "Foghorn" or "Calliope"
b: 8/15/1864, Brooklyn, N.Y. d: 4/6/09, Brooklyn, N.Y. BR/TR, 5'6", 145 lbs. Deb: 5/1/1884 M

YEAR	TM/L	G	AB	R	H	2B	3B	HR	RBI	BB	SO	AVG	OBP	SLG	PRO+	BR/A	SB	CS	SBR	FA	FR	G/POS	TPR
1884	Pit-a	89	347	46	78	10	2	0		13		.225	.257	.265	69	-12				.798	-5	O-49,C-36/3,2-1	-1.3
1885	Pit-a	42	166	19	27	3	1	0		13	4	.163	.182	.193	19	-15				.893	-5	C-33/O-6,S-2,3-2	-1.5
1886	Pit-a	83	317	70	80	15	1	2	36	43		.252	.343	.325	110	5	35			.918	-22	C-61,O-23/2-1	-0.9
1887	Pit-N	87	342	58	83	17	4	1	34	35	13	.243	.317	.325	83	-6	33			.928	-22	C-73,O-14/3-1	-1.9
1888	Pit-N	103	404	50	112	17	5	0	36	18	16	.277	.319	.344	121	0	27			.908	-15	C-68,O-32/3-4	0.0
1889	Pit-N	104	422	77	113	25	3	6	56	31	11	.268	.321	.384	107	3	16			.889	-15	C-76,O-27/3-3	0.4
1890	Pit-N	138	549	85	150	24	3	4	66	68	11	.273	.357	.350	120	17	32			.850	1	3-88,O-25,S-13,C/2	2.0
1891	Pit-N	135	548	80	156	19	6	4	57	59	26	.285	.357	.363	113	10	35			.938	-16	C-41,S-37,3-34,O/1	0.1
1892	Pit-N	149	623	103	158	15	12	2	59	69	14	.254	.335	.326	100	1	28			.906	-11	O-76,C-63,S-19/3-2	-0.7
1893	Pit-N	41	154	23	28	6	1	0	17	17	8	.182	.284	.234	49	-13	3			.916	-0	C-40	-0.8
1894	StL-N	127	481	93	163	9	11	8	86	58	14	.339	.414	.453	109	9	17			.832	-14	3-52,C-41,21/OSM	0.0
1895	StL-N	121	490	81	143	15	4	5	74	25	12	.292	.334	.369	82	-13	18			.829	-23	3-46,C-46,O-21/S1	-2.7
1896	Lou-N	98	324	54	89	17	4	1	57	22	16	.275	.334	.361	87	-8	16			.922	-16	C-48,2-25/O-8,31S	-1.4
Total 13		1317	5167	839	1380	192	57	33	567	467	129	.267	.333	.345	97	-12	260			.918	-153	C-636,O-309,3/S21	-8.7

■ **HUGHIE MILLER**   Miller, Hugh Stanley "Cotton" b: 12/28/1887, St.Louis, Mo. d: 12/24/45, Jefferson Barracks, Mo. BR/TR, 6'1.5", 175 lbs. Deb: 6/18/11

YEAR	TM/L	G	AB	R	H	2B	3B	HR	RBI	BB	SO	AVG	OBP	SLG	PRO+	BR/A	SB	CS	SBR	FA	FR	G/POS	TPR
1911	Phi-N	1	0	0	0	0	0	0	0	0	0	—	—	—		0	0			.000	0	R	0.0
1914	StL-F	132	490	51	109	20	5	0	46	27	57	.222	.264	.284	47	-44	4			.990	0	*1-130	-5.0
1915	StL-F	7	6	0	3	1	0	0	3	0	0	.500	.500	.667	216	1	0			1.000	-0	/1-6	0.1
Total 3		140	496	51	112	21	5	0	49	27	57	.226	.267	.288	49	-43	4			.990	-0	1-136	-4.9

■ **JAKE MILLER**   Miller, Jacob George (b: Jacob George Munzing) b: 12/1/1895, Baltimore, Md. d: 8/24/74, Towson, Md. BR/TR, 5'10", 170 lbs. Deb: 7/16/22

YEAR	TM/L	G	AB	R	H	2B	3B	HR	RBI	BB	SO	AVG	OBP	SLG	PRO+	BR/A	SB	CS	SBR	FA	FR	G/POS	TPR
1922	Pit-N	3	11	0	1	0	0	0	0	2	0	.091	.231	.091	-14	-2	1	0	0	.889	0	/O-3	-0.2

■ **HACK MILLER**   Miller, James Eldridge b: 2/13/13, Celeste, Tex. d: 11/21/66, Dallas, Tex. BR/TR, 5'11.5", 215 lbs. Deb: 4/18/44

YEAR	TM/L	G	AB	R	H	2B	3B	HR	RBI	BB	SO	AVG	OBP	SLG	PRO+	BR/A	SB	CS	SBR	FA	FR	G/POS	TPR
1944	Det-A	5	5	1	1	0	0	0	3	1	1	.200	.333	.800	207	1	0	0	0	1.000	0	/C-5	0.1
1945	Det-A	2	4	0	3	0	0	0	1	0	0	.750	.750	.750	315	1	0	0	0	1.000	-0	/C-2	0.1
Total 2		7	9	1	4	0	0	1	4	1	1	.444	.500	.778	250	1	0	0	0	1.000	0	/C-7	0.2

■ **JIM MILLER**   Miller, James McCurdy "Rabbit" b: 10/2/1880, Pittsburgh, Pa. d: 2/7/37, Pittsburgh, Pa. BR/TR, 5'8", 165 lbs. Deb: 9/9/01

YEAR	TM/L	G	AB	R	H	2B	3B	HR	RBI	BB	SO	AVG	OBP	SLG	PRO+	BR/A	SB	CS	SBR	FA	FR	G/POS	TPR
1901	NY-N	18	58	3	8	0			3	6		.138	.219	.138	5	-7	1			.936	-2	2-18	-0.8

■ **JOHN MILLER**   Miller, John Allen b: 3/14/44, Alhambra, Cal. BR/TR, 5'11", 195 lbs. Deb: 9/11/66

YEAR	TM/L	G	AB	R	H	2B	3B	HR	RBI	BB	SO	AVG	OBP	SLG	PRO+	BR/A	SB	CS	SBR	FA	FR	G/POS	TPR
1966	NY-A	6	23	1	2	0	0	1	2	0	9	.087	.087	.217	-16	-3	0	0	0	1.000	-1	/1-3,O-3	-0.5
1969	LA-N	26	38	3	8	1	0	1		2	9	.211	.250	.316	62	-2	0	0	0	1.000	-2	/O-6,1-5,3-2,2-1	-0.5
Total 2		32	61	4	10	1	0	2		2	18	.164	.190	.279	33	-6	0	0	0	1.000	-3	/O-9,1-8,3-2,2-1	-1.0

■ **DOTS MILLER**   Miller, John Barney b: 9/9/1886, Kearny, N.J. d: 9/5/23, Saranac Lake, N.Y. BR/TR, 5'11.5", 170 lbs. Deb: 4/16/09

YEAR	TM/L	G	AB	R	H	2B	3B	HR	RBI	BB	SO	AVG	OBP	SLG	PRO+	BR/A	SB	CS	SBR	FA	FR	G/POS	TPR
1909	*Pit-N	151	560	71	156	31	13	3	87	39		.279	.329	.396	115	8	14			**.953**	-11	*2-150	-0.7
1910	Pit-N	120	444	45	101	13	10	1	48	33	41	.227	.284	.309	69	-19	11			.946	-19	*2-119/1-1,S-1	-4.2
1911	Pit-N	137	470	82	126	17	8	6	78	51	48	.268	.348	.392	99	-1	17			.943	-6	*2-129	-1.0
1912	Pit-N	148	567	74	156	33	12	4	87	37	45	.275	.324	.397	98	-4	18			.985	1	*1-147	-0.5
1913	Pit-N	154	580	75	158	24	20	7	90	37	52	.272	.317	.419	114	8	20			.985	-4	*1-150/S-3	0.2
1914	StL-N	155	573	67	166	27	10	4	88	34	52	.290	.339	.393	119	12	16			.993	4	1-91,S-60/2-5	1.6
1915	StL-N	150	553	73	146	17	10	2	72	43	48	.264	.324	.342	101	1	27	19	-3	.991	4	1-94,2-55/3-9,S-3	0.0
1916	StL-N	143	505	47	120	22	7	1	46	40	49	.238	.300	.315	89	-6	18			.993	2	1-93,2-38,S-21/3-1	-0.6
1917	StL-N	148	544	61	135	15	9	2	45	33	52	.248	.295	.320	91	-6	14			.960	19	2-92,1-46,S-11	1.7
1919	StL-N	101	346	38	80	10	4	1	24	13	23	.231	.265	.292	72	-13	6			.981	4	1-68,2-28	-1.4
1920	Phi-N	98	343	41	87	12	2	1	27	16	17	.254	.289	.309	68	-14	13	6	0	.948	-9	2-59,3-17,S-12/10	-2.1
1921	Phi-N	84	320	37	95	11	3	0	23	15	27	.297	.330	.350	74	-11	3	5	-2	.940	1	3-41,1-38/2-6	-1.1
Total 12		1589	5805	711	1526	232	108	32	715	391	454	.263	.314	.357	95	-46	177	30		.988	-20	1-737,2-681,S/30	-8.1

■ **JOE MILLER**   Miller, Joseph A. b: 2/17/1861, Baltimore, Md. d: 4/23/28, Wheeling, W.Va. BR, 5'9.5", 165 lbs. Deb: 5/1/1884

YEAR	TM/L	G	AB	R	H	2B	3B	HR	RBI	BB	SO	AVG	OBP	SLG	PRO+	BR/A	SB	CS	SBR	FA	FR	G/POS	TPR
1884	Tol-a	105	423	46	101	12	6	1		26		.239	.284	.312	91	-4				.864	1	*S-105	-0.2
1885	Lou-a	98	339	44	62	9	5	0	24	28		.183	.249	.250	55	-17				.891	3	*S-79,3-11/2-8	-1.1
Total 2		203	762	90	163	21	13	1	24	54		.214	.269	.280	75	-21				.876	4	S-184/3-11,2-8	-1.3

■ **JOE MILLER**   Miller, Joseph Wick b: 7/24/1850, Germany d: 8/30/1891, White Bear Lake, Minn. 5'10.5", 169 lbs. Deb: 6/26/1872 M

YEAR	TM/L	G	AB	R	H	2B	3B	HR	RBI	BB	SO	AVG	OBP	SLG	PRO+	BR/A	SB	CS	SBR	FA	FR	G/POS	TPR
1872	Nat-n	1	4	0	1	0	0	0				.250	.250	.250	46	-0				.923	-0	/1-1	0.0
1875	Wes-n	13	50	4	6	1	0	0		0	3	.120	.120	.140	-9	-5				.870	4	2-13	-0.1
	Chi-n	15	54	1	8	0	0	0	1	0		.148	.148	.140	3	-5				.788	-3	2-14/O-1	-0.7
	Yr	28	104	5	14	1	0	0	1	0	10	.135	.135	.144	-3	-10				.832	1	2-27/O-1	-0.8
Total 2 n		29	108	5	15	1	0	0		0	10	.139	.139	.148	-1	-11				.870	1	/2-27,O-1,1-1	-0.8

■ **KEITH MILLER**   Miller, Keith Alan b: 6/12/63, Midland, Mich. BR/TR, 5'11", 180 lbs. Deb: 6/16/87

YEAR	TM/L	G	AB	R	H	2B	3B	HR	RBI	BB	SO	AVG	OBP	SLG	PRO+	BR/A	SB	CS	SBR	FA	FR	G/POS	TPR
1987	NY-N	25	51	14	19	2	2	0	1	2	6	.373	.407	.490	144	5	8	1	2	.967	2	2-16	0.7
1988	NY-N	40	70	9	15	4	1	1	5	6	10	.214	.276	.300	69	-3	0	5	-3	.946	-7	2-16/S-8,3-6,O-1	-1.4
1989	NY-N	57	143	15	33	7	0	1	7	5	27	.231	.262	.301	63	-7	6	0	2	.967	-4	2-23,O-14/S-8,3-2	-0.9
1990	NY-N	88	233	42	60	8	0	1	12	23	46	.258	.329	.305	76	-7	16	3	3	.980	5	O-61,2-11/S-4	0.0
1991	NY-N	98	275	41	77	22	1	4	23	23	44	.280	.347	.411	113	5	14	4	2	.972	0	2-60,O-28/3-2,S-2	0.0
1992	KC-A	106	416	57	118	24	4	4	38	31	46	.284	.354	.389	105	3	16	6	1	.971	-20	2-93,O-16/D-1	-1.4
1993	KC-A	37	108	9	18	4	0	0	8		19	.167	.231	.194	15	-3	3	1	0	.889	-6	3-21/O-4,2-3,D-6	-1.8
1994	KC-A	5	15	1	2	0	0	0				.133	.133	.133	-30	-3	1	0	0	1.000	-0	/O-4,3-2	-0.1
1995	KC-A	9	15	2	5	0	0	1	2	2	4	.333	.412	.533	142	1	0	0	0	1.000	-0	/O-4,D-4	0.1
Total 9		465	1326	190	347	67	8	12	92	100	205	.262	.325	.351	88	-21	63	20	12	.969	-28	2-222,O-132/3SD	-4.1

■ **ED MILLER**   Miller, L. Edward b: Tecumseh, Mich. Deb: 7/18/1884

YEAR	TM/L	G	AB	R	H	2B	3B	HR	RBI	BB	SO	AVG	OBP	SLG	PRO+	BR/A	SB	CS	SBR	FA	FR	G/POS	TPR
1884	Tol-a	8	24	2	6	0	0	0		1	1	.250	.280	.250	72	-1				.615	-1	/O-8	-0.1

YEAR	TM/L	G	AB	R	H	2B	3B	HR	RBI	BB	SO	AVG	OBP	SLG	PRO+	BR/A	SB	CS	SBR	FA	FR	G/POS	TPR
■ **HACK MILLER**				Miller, Lawrence H.			b: 1/1/1894, New York, N.Y.			d: 9/17/71, Oakland, Cal.			BR/TR, 5'9", 195 lbs.		Deb: 9/22/16								
1916	Bro-N	3	3	0	1	0	1	0	1	1	1	.333	.500	1.000	345	1	0			1.000	-1	/O-3	0.0
1918	*Bos-A	12	29	2	8	2	0	0	4	0	4	.276	.276	.345	89	-1	0			1.000	-3	O-10	-0.4
1922	Chi-N	122	466	61	164	28	5	12	78	26	39	.352	.389	.511	128	18	3	3	-1	.959	-3	*O-116	0.6
1923	Chi-N	135	485	74	146	24	2	20	88	27	39	.301	.343	.482	133	9	6	5	-1	.978	6	*O-129	0.4
1924	Chi-N	53	131	17	44	8	1	4	25	8	11	.336	.379	.504	133	6	1	0	0	.948	-4	O-32	0.0
1925	Chi-N	24	86	10	24	3	2	2	9	2	9	.279	.303	.430	84	-2	0	1	-1	.878	-3	O-21	-0.7
Total	6	349	1200	164	387	65	11	38	205	64	103	.322	.361	.490	120	31	10	9		.962	-8	O-311	-0.1
■ **LEMMIE MILLER**			Miller, Lemmie Earl		b: 6/2/60, Dallas, Tex.			BR/TR, 6'1", 190 lbs.		Deb: 5/22/84													
1984	LA-N	8	12	1	2	0	0	0	1	2		.167	.231	.167	13	-1	0	0	0	1.000	-1	/O-5	-0.3
■ **OTTO MILLER**			Miller, Lowell Otto "Moonie"		b: 6/1/1889, Minden, Neb.			d: 3/29/62, Brooklyn, N.Y.			BR/TR, 6', 196 lbs.		Deb: 7/16/10 C									
1910	Bro-N	31	66	5	11	3	0	0	2	2	19	.167	.203	.212	22	-7	1			.987	9	C-28	0.4
1911	Bro-N	25	62	7	13	2	2	0	8	0	4	.210	.210	.306	46	-5	2			.927	-3	C-22	-0.6
1912	Bro-N	98	316	35	88	18	1	1	31	16	50	.278	.325	.351	88	-6	11			.975	13	C-94	1.6
1913	Bro-N	104	320	26	87	11	7	0	26	10	31	.272	.294	.350	81	-9	7			.971	14	*C-103/1-1	1.4
1914	Bro-N	54	169	17	39	6	1	0	9	7	20	.231	.261	.278	59	-9	0			.964	0	C-50/1-1	-0.5
1915	Bro-N	84	254	20	57	4	6	0	25	6	28	.224	.245	.287	60	-13	3			.981	8	C-83	0.2
1916	*Bro-N	73	216	16	55	9	2	1	17	7	29	.255	.281	.329	85	-4	6			.968	4	C-69	0.5
1917	Bro-N	92	274	19	63	5	4	1	17	14	29	.230	.272	.288	70	-10	5			.979	1	C-91	-0.2
1918	Bro-N	75	228	8	44	8	1	0	19	8	20	.193	.230	.228	40	-16	1			.972	4	C-62/1-1	-0.8
1919	Bro-N	51	164	18	37	5	0	0	5	7	14	.226	.257	.256	53	-9	2			.966	5	C-51	-0.3
1920	*Bro-N	90	301	16	87	9	2	0	33	9	18	.289	.312	.332	82	-7	0	5	-3	**.986**	-2	C-89	-0.6
1921	Bro-N	91	286	22	67	8	6	1	27	9	26	.234	.260	.315	50	-21	2	1	0	.972	9	C-91	-0.7
1922	Bro-N	59	180	20	47	11	1	1	23	6	13	.261	.285	.350	63	-10	0	0	0	.968	-3	C-57	-0.4
Total	13	927	2836	229	695	97	33	5	231	104	301	.245	.275	.308	67	-125	40	6		.973	62	C-890/1-3	0.0
■ **KEITH MILLER**			Miller, Neal Keith		b: 3/7/63, Dallas, Tex.		BB/TR, 5'11", 175 lbs.			Deb: 4/23/88													
1988	Phi-N	47	48	4	8	3	0	0	6	5	13	.167	.245	.229	36	-4	0	0	0	1.000	-3	/O-4,3-3,S-1	-0.8
1989	Phi-N	8	10	0	3	1	0	0	0	0	3	.300	.300	.400	98	-0	0	0	0	1.000	-1	/O-2	-0.1
Total	2	55	58	4	11	4	0	0	6	5	16	.190	.254	.259	47	-4	0	0	0	1.000	-4	/O-6,3-3,S-1	-0.9
■ **NORM MILLER**			Miller, Norman Calvin		b: 2/5/46, Los Angeles, Cal.			BL/TR, 5'11", 195 lbs.		Deb: 9/11/65													
1965	Hou-N	11	15	2	3	0	1	0	1	1	7	.200	.250	.333	67	-1	0	0	0	1.000	-0	/O-2	-0.1
1966	Hou-N	11	34	1	5	0	3	0	3	2	8	.147	.194	.235	20	-4	0	0	0	1.000	0	/O-8,3-3	-0.4
1967	Hou-N	64	190	15	39	9	3	1	14	19	42	.205	.278	.300	68	-8	2	0	1	.967	1	O-53	-1.0
1968	Hou-N	79	257	35	61	18	2	6	28	22	48	.237	.310	.393	112	3	6	5	-1	.971	-3	O-74	-0.5
1969	Hou-N	119	409	58	108	21	4	4	50	47	77	.264	.350	.364	102	2	4	4	-1	.984	-1	*O-114	-0.7
1970	Hou-N	90	226	29	54	9	0	4	29	41	33	.239	.358	.332	90	-2	3	1	0	.947	-5	O-72/C-1	-0.9
1971	Hou-N	45	74	5	19	5	0	2	10	5	13	.257	.313	.405	105	0	0	0	0	1.000	-5	O-20/C-1	-0.5
1972	Hou-N	67	107	18	26	4	0	4	13	13	23	.243	.331	.393	107	1	1	0	0	1.000	-4	O-29	-0.4
1973	Hou-N	3	3	0	0	0	0	0	0	0	2	.000	.000	.000	-99	-1	0	0	0	.000	0	/O-1	-0.1
	Atl-N	9	8	2	3	1	0	1	6	3	3	.375	.545	.875	267	2	0	0	0	.667	-0	/O-1	0.2
	Yr	12	11	2	3	1	0	1	6	3	5	.273	.429	.636	181	1	0	0	0	.667	-1	/O-2	0.1
1974	Atl-N	42	41	1	7	1	0	1	5	7	9	.171	.292	.268	55	-2	0	1	0	1.000	-1	/O-4	-0.3
Total	10	540	1364	166	325	68	10	24	159	160	265	.238	.325	.356	95	-9	16	10	-1	.972	-18	O-378/C-2,3-2	-4.7
■ **ORLANDO MILLER**			Miller, Orlando (Salmon)		b: 1/13/69, Changuinola, Pan.			BR/TR, 6'1", 180 lbs.		Deb: 7/8/94													
1994	Hou-N	16	40	3	13	0	1	2	9	2	11	.325	.386	.525	142	2	1	0	0	1.000	-5	S-11/2-3	0.2
1995	Hou-N	92	324	36	85	20	1	5	36	22	71	.262	.319	.377	89	-6	3	4	-2	.964	5	S-89	0.5
1996	Hou-N	139	468	43	120	26	2	15	58	14	116	.256	.293	.417	93	-8	3	7	-3	.958	-12	*S-117,3-29	-1.3
Total	3	247	832	82	218	46	4	22	103	38	199	.262	.308	.406	94	-11	7	11	-5	.962	-8	S-217/3-29,2-3	-0.6
■ **OTTO MILLER**			Miller, Otis Louis		b: 2/2/01, Belleville, Ill.			d: 7/26/59, Belleville, Ill.			BR/TR, 5'10.5", 168 lbs.		Deb: 4/17/27										
1927	StL-A	51	76	8	17	5	0	0	8	5	5	.224	.306	.289	53	-5	0	1	-1	.938	-4	S-35,3-11	-0.8
1930	Bos-A	112	370	49	106	22	5	0	40	26	21	.286	.333	.373	82	-10	2	4	-2	.948	-6	3-83,2-15	-1.1
1931	Bos-A	107	389	38	106	12	1	0	43	15	20	.272	.301	.308	64	-21	1	1	-0	.953	-1	3-75,2-25	-1.5
1932	Bos-A	2	2	0	0	0	0	0	0	0	0	.000	.000	.000	-99	-1	0	0	0	.000	0	H	-0.1
Total	4	272	837	95	229	39	6	0	91	49	46	.274	.315	.335	71	-36	3	6	-3	.949	-11	3-169/2-40,S-35	-3.5
■ **RALPH MILLER**			Miller, Ralph Joseph		b: 2/29/1896, Ft.Wayne, Ind.			d: 3/18/39, Ft.Wayne, Ind.			BR/TR, 6', 190 lbs.		Deb: 4/14/20										
1920	Phi-N	97	338	28	74	14	1	0	28	11	32	.219	.246	.266	45	-24	3	4	-2	.940	0	3-91/1-3,S-2,0-1	-2.3
1921	Phi-N	57	204	19	62	10	0	3	26	6	10	.304	.327	.397	84	-5	3	5	-2	.910	0	S-46,3-10	-0.2
1924	*Was-A	9	15	1	2	0	0	0	0	1	1	.133	.188	.133	-17	-3	0	0	0	.941	0	/2-3	-0.2
Total	3	163	557	48	138	24	1	3	54	18	43	.248	.274	.311	59	-31	6	9	-4	.927	0	3-101/S-48,2-3,10	-2.7
■ **RAY MILLER**			Miller, Raymond Peter		b: 2/12/1888, Pittsburgh, Pa.			d: 4/7/27, Pittsburgh, Pa.			BL/TL, 5'10", 168 lbs.		Deb: 4/14/17										
1917	Cle-A	19	21	1	4	1	0	0	2	4		.190	.414	.238	92	0	0			1.000	1	/1-4	0.2
	Pit-N	6	27	1	4	1	0	0	0	2	6	.148	.207	.185	20	-3	0			1.000	0	/1-6	-0.3
Total	1	25	48	2	8	2	0	0	2	10	6	.167	.310	.208	56	-2	0			1.000	2	/1-10	-0.1
■ **RICK MILLER**			Miller, Richard Alan		b: 4/19/48, Grand Rapids, Mich.			BL/TL, 6', 185 lbs.		Deb: 9/4/71													
1971	Bos-A	15	33	9	11	0	1	1	8	8	8	.333	.463	.576	180	4	0	2	-1	.969	1	O-14	0.3
1972	Bos-A	89	98	13	21	4	1	3	15	11	27	.214	.294	.367	91	-1	0	2	-1	.967	-11	O-75	-1.7
1973	Bos-A	143	441	65	115	17	7	6	43	51	59	.261	.341	.372	95	-2	12	7	-1	.978	-4	*O-137	-1.3
1974	Bos-A	114	280	41	73	8	4	5	22	37	47	.261	.347	.350	94	-1	13	2	3	.989	2	*O-105	0.0
1975	*Bos-A	77	108	21	21	2	1	0	15	21	20	.194	.326	.231	55	-6	3	2	-0	.981	-8	O-65	-1.6
1976	Bos-A	105	269	40	76	15	3	0	27	34	47	.283	.363	.361	100	1	11	10	-3	.991	5	O-82/D-4	0.2
1977	Bos-A	86	189	34	48	9	3	0	24	22	30	.254	.341	.333	76	-6	11	5	0	.992	-7	O-79/D-1	-1.5
1978	Cal-A	132	475	66	125	25	4	1	37	54	70	.263	.343	.339	96	-1	3	13	-7	.989	15	*O-129	0.2
1979	*Cal-A	120	427	60	125	15	5	2	28	50	69	.293	.368	.365	102	3	5	4	-1	.989	10	*O-117/D-2	0.7
1980	Cal-A	129	412	52	113	14	3	2	38	48	71	.274	.351	.337	92	-3	7	3	0	.984	5	O-95	-0.2
1981	Bos-A	97	316	38	92	17	2	2	33	28	28	.291	.351	.377	103	2	3	5	-2	.987	-3	*O-95	-0.7
1982	Bos-A	135	409	50	104	13	2	4	38	40	41	.254	.324	.325	75	-14	5	6	-2	.983	-6	*O-127	-2.5
1983	Bos-A	104	262	41	75	10	2	2	21	28	30	.286	.357	.363	92	-2	3	3	-1	.993	6	O-66/1-2,D-2	-0.5
1984	Bos-A	95	123	17	32	5	1	0	12	17	22	.260	.350	.317	92	-2	1	1	0	.974	-7	/O-31/1-8	-1.1
1985	Bos-A	41	45	5	15	2	0	0	9	5	6	.333	.400	.378	110	-1	1	0	0	1.000	-1	/O-8,D-4	-0.1
Total	15	1482	3887	552	1046	161	35	28	369	454	583	.269	.348	.350	92	-29	78	65	-16	.986	-10	*O-1248/D-13,1-10	-10.0
■ **ROD MILLER**			Miller, Rodney Carter		b: 1/16/40, Portland, Ore.		BL/TR, 5'10", 160 lbs.			Deb: 9/28/57													
1957	Bro-N	1	1	0	0	0	0	0	0	0	1	.000	.000	.000	-91	-0	0	0	0	.000	0	H	0.0
■ **DOC MILLER**			Miller, Roy Oscar		b: 2/4/1883, Chatham, Ontario, Canada			d: 7/31/38, Jersey City, N.J.			BL/TL, 5'10.5", 170 lbs.		Deb: 5/4/10										
1910	Chi-N	1	1	0	0	0	0	0	0	0	0	.000	.000	.000	-99	-0	0	0	0	.000	0	H	0.0
	Bos-N	130	482	48	138	27	4	3	55	33	52	.286	.333	.378	103	0	17			.951	-12	*O-130	-1.9
	Yr	131	483	48	138	27	4	3	55	33	52	.286	.333	.377	102	-0	17			.951	-12	*O-130	-1.9
1911	Bos-N	146	577	69	**192**	36	3	7	91	43	43	.333	.379	.442	120	13	32			.961	2	*O-146	0.8
1912	Bos-N	51	201	26	47	8	1	2	24	14	17	.234	.287	.313	63	-11	6			.948	3	O-50	-1.1
	Phi-N	67	177	24	51	12	5	0	21	9	13	.288	.323	.412	94	-2	3			.986	2	O-40	-0.2
	Yr	118	378	50	98	20	6	2	45	23	30	.259	.303	.360	78	-13	9			.964	5	O-90	-1.3

YEAR	TM/L	G	AB	R	H	2B	3B	HR	RBI	BB	SO	AVG	OBP	SLG	PRO+	BR/A	SB	CS	SBR	FA	FR	G/POS	TPR
1913	Phi-N	69	87	9	30	6	0	0	11	6	6	.345	.400	.414	127	3	2			.800	-4	O-12	-0.1
1914	Cin-N	93	192	8	49	7	2	0	33	16	18	.255	.313	.313	83	-4	4			.976	-4	O-47	-1.1
Total	5	557	1717	184	507	96	15	12	235	121	149	.295	.343	.390	102	-0	64			.958	-13	O-425	-3.6

■ RUDY MILLER   Miller, Rudel Charles b: 7/12/1900, Kalamazoo, Mich. d: 1/22/94, Kalamazoo, Mich. BR/TR, 6'1", 180 lbs. Deb: 9/19/29

YEAR	TM/L	G	AB	R	H	2B	3B	HR	RBI	BB	SO	AVG	OBP	SLG	PRO+	BR/A	SB	CS	SBR	FA	FR	G/POS	TPR
1929	Phi-A	2	4	1	1	0	0	0	1	3	0	.250	.571	.250	115	0	0	0	0	.750	-0	/3-2	0.0

■ TOM MILLER   Miller, Thomas P. "Reddy" b: Philadelphia, Pa. d: 5/29/1876, Philadelphia, Pa. Deb: 10/24/1874

YEAR	TM/L	G	AB	R	H	2B	3B	HR	RBI	BB	SO	AVG	OBP	SLG	PRO+	BR/A	SB	CS	SBR	FA	FR	G/POS	TPR
1874	Ath-n	4	16	1	8	0	0	0		0	0	.500	.500	.500	204	2	0	0	0	.793	0	/C-4,O-1	0.1
1875	StL-n	56	214	18	35	2	0	0	12	1	8	.164	.167	.173	20	-15	2	0	1	.827	-3	*C-53/3-2	-1.4
Total	2 n	60	230	19	43	2	0	0	17	1	8	.187	.190	.196	37	-14	2	0	1	.824	-3	/C-57,3-2,O-1	-1.3

■ TOM MILLER   Miller, Thomas Royall b: 7/5/1897, Powhatan Court House, Va. d: 8/13/80, Richmond, Va. BL/TR, 5'11", 180 lbs. Deb: 7/29/18

YEAR	TM/L	G	AB	R	H	2B	3B	HR	RBI	BB	SO	AVG	OBP	SLG	PRO+	BR/A	SB	CS	SBR	FA	FR	G/POS	TPR
1918	Bos-N	2	2	0	0	0	0	0	0	0	0	.000	.000	.000	-99	-0	1			.000	0	H	-0.1
1919	Bos-N	7	6	2	2	0	0	0	0	0	1	.333	.333	.333	105	0	0			.000	0	H	0.0
Total	2	9	8	2	2	0	0	0	0	0	1	.250	.250	.250	53	-0	1				0	-0,-0	-0.1

■ WARD MILLER   Miller, Ward Taylor "Windy" or "Grump" b: 7/5/1884, Mt.Carroll, Ill. d: 9/4/58, Dixon, Ill. BL/TR, 5'11", 177 lbs. Deb: 4/14/09

YEAR	TM/L	G	AB	R	H	2B	3B	HR	RBI	BB	SO	AVG	OBP	SLG	PRO+	BR/A	SB	CS	SBR	FA	FR	G/POS	TPR
1909	Pit-N	15	56	2	8	0	1	0	4	4	4	.143	.213	.179	20	-5	2			.967	-1	O-14	-0.8
	Cin-N	43	113	17	35	3	1	0	4	6	6	.310	.345	.354	118	2	9			.981	-7	O-26	-0.6
	Yr	58	169	19	43	3	2	0	8	10	10	.254	.300	.296	84	-3	11			.976	-8	O-40	-1.4
1910	Cin-N	81	126	21	30	6	0	0	10	22	13	.238	.356	.286	92	-0	10			.944	-2	O-26	0.0
1912	Chi-N	86	241	45	74	11	4	0	22	26	18	.307	.377	.386	109	4	11			.943	-8	O-64	-0.8
1913	Chi-N	80	203	23	48	5	7	1	16	34	33	.236	.349	.345	98	1	13			.980	3	O-63	0.2
1914	StL-F	121	402	49	118	17	7	4	50	59	36	.294	.397	.400	112	3	18			.953	10	*O-111	0.8
1915	StL-F	154	536	80	164	19	9	1	63	79	39	.306	.400	.381	114	7	33			.963	3	*O-154	0.2
1916	StL-A	146	485	72	129	17	5	1	50	72	76	.266	.371	.328	116	13	25	21	-5	.943	-5	*O-136	-0.6
1917	StL-A	43	82	13	17	1	1	1	2	16	15	.207	.350	.280	96	0	7			.966	-4	O-25	-0.5
Total	8	769	2244	322	623	79	35	8	221	318	230	.278	.375	.355	108	24	128	21		.957	-8	O-619	-2.1

■ WARREN MILLER   Miller, Warren Lemuel "Gitz" b: 7/14/1885, Philadelphia, Pa. d: 8/12/56, Philadelphia, Pa. BL/TL, 5'10", 160 lbs. Deb: 7/29/09

YEAR	TM/L	G	AB	R	H	2B	3B	HR	RBI	BB	SO	AVG	OBP	SLG	PRO+	BR/A	SB	CS	SBR	FA	FR	G/POS	TPR
1909	Was-A	26	51	5	11	0	0	0	1		4	.216	.273	.216	57	-2	0			1.000	-1	O-15	-0.5
1911	Was-A	21	34	3	5	0	0	0	0	1	4	.147	.147	.147	-18	-5	0			.778	-2	/O-9	-0.7
Total	2	47	85	8	16	0	0	0	1		4	.188	.225	.188	25	-8	0			.931	-3	/O-24	-1.2

■ BILL MILLER   Miller, William Alexander b: 5/23/1879, Germany d: 9/8/57, Ashtabula, Ohio BL/TL, 6'2", 170 lbs. Deb: 8/23/02

YEAR	TM/L	G	AB	R	H	2B	3B	HR	RBI	BB	SO	AVG	OBP	SLG	PRO+	BR/A	SB	CS	SBR	FA	FR	G/POS	TPR
1902	Pit-N	1	5	0	1	0	0	0	0		2	.200	.200	.200	23	-0	0			.000	-0	/O-1	-0.1

■ JOE MILLETTE   Millette, Joseph Anthony b: 8/12/66, Walnut Creek, Cal. BR/TR, 6'1", 180 lbs. Deb: 7/16/92

YEAR	TM/L	G	AB	R	H	2B	3B	HR	RBI	BB	SO	AVG	OBP	SLG	PRO+	BR/A	SB	CS	SBR	FA	FR	G/POS	TPR
1992	Phi-N	33	78	5	16	0	0	0	2	5	10	.205	.271	.205	37	-6	1	0	0	.974	10	S-26/3-3,2-1	0.6
1993	Phi-N	10	10	3	2	0	0	0	1	1	2	.200	.273	.200	29	-1	0	0	0	1.000	3	/S-7,3-3	0.3
Total	2	43	88	8	18	0	0	0	4	6	12	.205	.271	.205	36	-7	1	0	0	.978	13	/S-33,3-6,2-1	0.9

■ RALPH MILLIARD   Milliard, Ralph Gregory b: 12/30/73, Willemstad, Curacao BR/TR, 5'11", 170 lbs. Deb: 5/12/96

YEAR	TM/L	G	AB	R	H	2B	3B	HR	RBI	BB	SO	AVG	OBP	SLG	PRO+	BR/A	SB	CS	SBR	FA	FR	G/POS	TPR
1996	Fla-N	24	62	7	10	2	0	0	1	14	16	.161	.316	.194	40	-5	2	0	1	.955	5	2-24	0.2

■ WALLY MILLIES   Millies, Walter Louis b: 10/18/06, Chicago, Ill. d: 2/28/95, Oak Lawn, Ill. BR/TR, 5'10.5", 170 lbs. Deb: 9/23/34

YEAR	TM/L	G	AB	R	H	2B	3B	HR	RBI	BB	SO	AVG	OBP	SLG	PRO+	BR/A	SB	CS	SBR	FA	FR	G/POS	TPR
1934	Bro-N	2	7	0	0	0	0	0	0	0	0	.000	.000	.000	-99	-2	0			1.000	1	/C-2	-0.1
1936	Was-A	74	215	26	67	10	2	0	25	11	8	.312	.345	.377	83	-6	1	0		.968	1	C-72	-0.2
1937	Was-A	59	179	21	40	7	1	0	28	9	15	.223	.261	.274	36	-18	1	0	0	.971	2	C-56	-1.2
1939	Phi-N	84	205	12	48	3	0	0	12	9	5	.234	.270	.249	41	-17	0			.964	-7	C-84	-2.1
1940	Phi-N	26	43	1	3	0	0	0	0	4	4	.070	.149	.070	-39	-8	0			.958	2	C-24	-0.5
1941	Phi-N	1	2	0	0	0	0	0	0	0	0	.000	.000	.000	-99	-1	0			.800	2	/C-1	0.0
Total	6	246	651	60	158	20	3	0	65	33	32	.243	.280	.283	47	-51	2	0		.966	-2	C-239	-4.1

■ JOCKO MILLIGAN   Milligan, John b: 8/8/1861, Philadelphia, Pa. d: 8/29/23, Philadelphia, Pa. BR/TR, 6', 192 lbs. Deb: 5/1/1884

YEAR	TM/L	G	AB	R	H	2B	3B	HR	RBI	BB	SO	AVG	OBP	SLG	PRO+	BR/A	SB	CS	SBR	FA	FR	G/POS	TPR
1884	Phi-a	66	268	39	77	20	3	3		8		.287	.308	.418	126	6				.939	13	C-65/O-1	2.3
1885	Phi-a	67	265	35	71	15	4	2	39	7		.268	.289	.377	103	-0				.935	11	C-61/1-6,O-2	1.4
1886	Phi-a	75	301	52	76	17	3	5	45	21		.252	.301	.379	111	3	18			.919	5	C-40,1-29/O-5,3-2	0.7
1887	Phi-a	95	377	54	114	27	4	2	50	21		.302	.344	.411	110	4	8			.966	3	1-50,C-47/O-1	0.5
1888	*StL-a	63	219	19	55	6	2	5	37	14		.251	.311	.365	105	-0				.941	8	C-58/1-5	1.1
1889	StL-a	72	273	53	100	30	2	12	76	16	19	.366	.408	.623	170	21	2			.933	14	C-66/1-9	3.3
1890	Phi-P	62	234	38	69	9	3	3	57	19	19	.295	.363	.397	101	-0	2			.893	4	C-59/1-3	0.7
1891	Phi-a	118	455	75	138	35	12	11	106	56	51	.303	.397	.505	153	30	2			.939	3	C-87,1-32	3.1
1892	Was-N	88	323	40	89	20	9	4	43	26	24	.276	.335	.430	135	12	2			.947	5	C-59,1-28	1.9
1893	Bal-N	24	102	19	25	5	2	1	19	5	7	.245	.294	.363	73	-5	2			.981	1	1-22/C-1	-0.3
	NY-N	42	147	16	34	5	6	1	25	14	14	.231	.302	.367	77	-6	2			.934	14	C-42	0.9
	Yr	66	249	35	59	10	8	2	44	19	21	.237	.299	.365	76	-10	4			.932	15	C-43,1-22	0.6
Total	10	772	2964	440	848	189	50	49	497	210	134	.286	.341	.433	122	65	41			.930	78	C-585,1-184/O-9,3-2	15.6

■ RANDY MILLIGAN   Milligan, Randy Andre b: 11/27/61, San Diego, Cal. BR/TR, 6'2", 230 lbs. Deb: 9/12/87

YEAR	TM/L	G	AB	R	H	2B	3B	HR	RBI	BB	SO	AVG	OBP	SLG	PRO+	BR/A	SB	CS	SBR	FA	FR	G/POS	TPR
1987	NY-N	3	1	0	0	0	0	0	0	0	1	.000	.000	.000	49	0	0	0	0	.000	0	/H	0.0
1988	Pit-N	40	82	10	18	5	0	3	8	20	24	.220	.379	.390	123	3	1	2	-1	.987	-1	1-25/O-2	0.0
1989	Bal-A	124	365	56	98	23	5	12	45	74	75	.268	.396	.458	144	24	9	5	-0	.995	2	*1-117/D-1	1.7
1990	Bal-A	109	362	64	96	20	1	20	60	88	68	.265	.412	.492	157	31	6	3	0	.990	5	1-98/D-9	2.9
1991	Bal-A	141	483	57	127	17	2	16	70	84	108	.263	.374	.406	121	16	0	5	-3	.990	3	*1-106,D-25/O-9	0.8
1992	Bal-A	137	462	71	111	21	1	11	53	106	81	.240	.386	.361	108	10	0	1	-1	.994	-6	*1-129/D-6	-0.6
1993	Cin-N	83	234	30	64	11	1	6	29	46	49	.274	.395	.406	115	7	0	2	-1	.994	5	1-61/O-9	0.6
	Cle-A	19	47	7	20	7	0	0	7	14	4	.426	.557	.574	206	8	0	0	0	1.000	-1	1-18/D-1	0.6
1994	Mon-N	47	82	10	19	2	0	2	12	21	19	.232	.344	.329	76	-3	0	0	1	.978	2	1-33	-0.3
Total	8	703	2118	305	553	106	10	70	284	447	431	.261	.393	.420	127	97	16	18	-6	.992	9	1-587/D-42,O-20	5.7

■ JACK MILLS   Mills, Abbott Paige b: 10/23/1889, S.Williamstown, Mass. d: 6/3/73, Washington, D.C. BL/TR, 6', 165 lbs. Deb: 7/1/11

YEAR	TM/L	G	AB	R	H	2B	3B	HR	RBI	BB	SO	AVG	OBP	SLG	PRO+	BR/A	SB	CS	SBR	FA	FR	G/POS	TPR
1911	Cle-A	13	17	5	5	0	0	0	1	0	1	.294	.368	.294	85	-0	1			1.000	2	/3-7	0.1

■ CHARLIE MILLS   Mills, Charles b: Brooklyn, N.Y. d: 4/10/1874, Brooklyn, N.Y. 6', Deb: 5/18/1871 U

YEAR	TM/L	G	AB	R	H	2B	3B	HR	RBI	BB	SO	AVG	OBP	SLG	PRO+	BR/A	SB	CS	SBR	FA	FR	G/POS	TPR
1871	Mut-n	32	146	27	36	4	3	0	22	1	0	.247	.252	.315	68	-5	2	0	1	.866	-2	*C-29/O-4,3-1	-0.4
1872	Mut-n	6	31	6	4	0	0	0	2	0	0	.129	.129	.129	-22	-4	0	0	0	.667	-1	/O-4,C-3	-0.4
Total	2 n	38	177	33	40	4	3	0	24	1	0	.226	.230	.282	53	-9	2	0	1	.854	-3	/C-32,O-8,3-1	-0.8

■ BUSTER MILLS   Mills, Colonel Buster "Bus" b: 9/16/08, Ranger, Tex. d: 12/1/91, Arlington, Tex. BR/TR, 5'11.5", 195 lbs. Deb: 4/18/34 MC

YEAR	TM/L	G	AB	R	H	2B	3B	HR	RBI	BB	SO	AVG	OBP	SLG	PRO+	BR/A	SB	CS	SBR	FA	FR	G/POS	TPR
1934	StL-N	29	72	9	17	4	1	1	8	4	11	.236	.295	.361	70	-3	0			1.000	-0	O-18	-0.4
1935	Bro-N	17	56	12	12	2	1	1	7	5	11	.214	.323	.339	80	-1	0			.971	-2	O-17	-0.4
1937	Bos-A	123	505	85	149	25	8	7	58	46	41	.295	.361	.418	92	-6	11	8	-2	.946	-5	*O-120	-1.5
1938	StL-A	123	466	66	133	24	4	3	46	43	46	.285	.350	.373	81	-13	7	8	-3	.964	3	*O-113	-1.5
1940	NY-A	34	63	10	25	3	1	1	15	7	5	.397	.457	.587	176	7	0	0	0	1.000	-2	O-14	0.4
1942	Cle-A	80	195	19	54	4	2	1	26	23	18	.277	.353	.333	99	-0	5	4	-1	.973	2	O-53	-0.2
1946	Cle-A	9	22	1	6	0	0	0	3	3	5	.273	.360	.273	84	-0	0	0	1	1.000	-0	/O-6	-0.2
Total	7	415	1379	200	396	62	19	14	163	131	137	.287	.355	.390	91	-17	23	21		.964	-5	O-341	-3.7

■ EVERETT MILLS   Mills, Everett b: 1/20/1845, Newark, N.J. d: 6/22/08, Newark, N.J. 6'1", 174 lbs. Deb: 5/5/1871 M

YEAR	TM/L	G	AB	R	H	2B	3B	HR	RBI	BB	SO	AVG	OBP	SLG	PRO+	BR/A	SB	CS	SBR	FA	FR	G/POS	TPR
1871	Oly-n	32	157	38	43	6	4	1	24	3	1	.274	.287	.382	95	-0	2	3	-1	.967	3	*1-32	0.2
1872	Bal-n	55	266	55	79	14	2	0	34	3	2	.297	.305	.365	100	-1	0	2	-1	.931	2	*1-55,M	0.1

YEAR	TM/L	G	AB	R	H	2B	3B	HR	RBI	BB	SO	AVG	OBP	SLG	PRO+	BR/A	SB	CS	SBR	FA	FR	G/POS	TPR
1873	Bal-n	54	263	64	87	19	9	0	57	2	1	.331	.336	.471	138	12	1	0	0	.949	2	*1-53/O-1	1.1
1874	Har-n	53	243	39	69	6	1	0	17	4	2	.284	.296	.317	92	-3	0	1	-1	.920	-2	*1-53	-0.4
1875	Har-n	80	342	59	89	8	4	1	48	0	3	.260	.260	.316	94	-3	6	4	-1	.945	-2	*1-80	-0.2
1876	Har-N	63	254	28	66	8	1	0	23	1	3	.260	.263	.299	80	-6				.939	-2	*1-63	-0.9
Total	5 n	274	1271	255	367	53	20	2	180	12	9	.289	.295	.367	104	4	9	10	-3	.941	6	1-273/O-1	0.8

■ FRANK MILLS
Mills, Frank Le Moyne   b: 5/13/1895, Knoxville, Ohio   d: 8/31/83, Youngstown, Ohio   BL/TR, 6', 180 lbs.   Deb: 9/22/14

YEAR	TM/L	G	AB	R	H	2B	3B	HR	RBI	BB	SO	AVG	OBP	SLG	PRO+	BR/A	SB	CS	SBR	FA	FR	G/POS	TPR
1914	Cle-A	4	8	0	1	0	0	0	0	1	2	.125	.222	.125	4	-1	0			.900	-1	/C-2	-0.2

■ BRAD MILLS
Mills, James Bradley   b: 1/19/57, Exeter, Cal.   BL/TR, 6', 195 lbs.   Deb: 6/8/80

YEAR	TM/L	G	AB	R	H	2B	3B	HR	RBI	BB	SO	AVG	OBP	SLG	PRO+	BR/A	SB	CS	SBR	FA	FR	G/POS	TPR
1980	Mon-N	21	60	1	18	1	0	0	8	5	6	.300	.354	.317	88	-1	0	1	-1	.977	-1	3-18	-0.3
1981	*Mon-N	17	21	3	5	1	0	0	1	2	1	.238	.304	.286	67	-1	0	0	0	1.000	-1	/3-7,2-2	-0.1
1982	Mon-N	54	67	6	15	3	0	1	2	5	11	.224	.278	.313	64	-3	0	0	0	.867	-3	3-13	-0.7
1983	Mon-N	14	20	1	5	0	0	0	1	2	3	.250	.318	.250	60	-1	0	0	0	1.000	-1	/3-3,1-1	-0.2
Total	4	106	168	11	43	5	0	1	12	14	21	.256	.313	.304	73	-6	0	1	-1	.959	-5	/3-41,2-2,1-1	-1.3

■ RUPERT MILLS
Mills, Rupert Frank   b: 10/12/1892, Newark, N.J.   d: 7/20/29, Lake Hopatcong, N.J.   BR/TR, 6'2", 185 lbs.   Deb: 6/23/15

YEAR	TM/L	G	AB	R	H	2B	3B	HR	RBI	BB	SO	AVG	OBP	SLG	PRO+	BR/A	SB	CS	SBR	FA	FR	G/POS	TPR
1915	New-F	41	134	12	27	5	1	0	16	6	21	.201	.241	.254	42	-13	6			.976	0	1-37	-1.5

■ BILL MILLS
Mills, William Henry   b: 11/2/20, Boston, Mass.   BR/TR, 5'10", 175 lbs.   Deb: 5/19/44

YEAR	TM/L	G	AB	R	H	2B	3B	HR	RBI	BB	SO	AVG	OBP	SLG	PRO+	BR/A	SB	CS	SBR	FA	FR	G/POS	TPR
1944	Phi-A	5	4	0	1	0	0	0	0	1	1	.250	.400	.250	89	0	0	0	0	.000	0	/C-1	0.0

■ PETE MILNE
Milne, William James   b: 4/10/25, Mobile, Ala.   BL/TR, 6'1", 180 lbs.   Deb: 9/15/48

YEAR	TM/L	G	AB	R	H	2B	3B	HR	RBI	BB	SO	AVG	OBP	SLG	PRO+	BR/A	SB	CS	SBR	FA	FR	G/POS	TPR
1948	NY-N	12	27	0	6	1	0	0	2	1	6	.222	.250	.296	47	-2	0			.867	-2	/O-9	-0.5
1949	NY-N	31	29	5	7	1	0	1	6	3	6	.241	.313	.379	85	-1	0			1.000	-0	/O-1	-0.1
1950	NY-N	4	4	1	1	0	1	0	1	0	1	.250	.250	.750	151	0	0			.000	0	H	0.0
Total	3	47	60	6	14	1	2	1	9	4	13	.233	.281	.367	73	-2	0			.882	-2	/O-10	-0.6

■ BRIAN MILNER
Milner, Brian Tate   b: 11/17/59, Fort Worth, Tex.   BR/TR, 6'2", 200 lbs.   Deb: 6/23/78

YEAR	TM/L	G	AB	R	H	2B	3B	HR	RBI	BB	SO	AVG	OBP	SLG	PRO+	BR/A	SB	CS	SBR	FA	FR	G/POS	TPR
1978	Tor-A	2	9	3	4	0	1	0	2	0	1	.444	.444	.667	204	1	0	0	0	.800	-3	/C-2	-0.1

■ EDDIE MILNER
Milner, Eddie James   b: 5/21/55, Columbus, Ohio   BL/TL, 5'11", 173 lbs.   Deb: 9/2/80

YEAR	TM/L	G	AB	R	H	2B	3B	HR	RBI	BB	SO	AVG	OBP	SLG	PRO+	BR/A	SB	CS	SBR	FA	FR	G/POS	TPR
1980	Cin-N	6	3	1	0	0	0	0	0	0	0	.000	.000	.000	-99	-1	0	0	0	.000	0	/H	-0.1
1981	Cin-N	8	5	0	1	1	0	0	1	1	1	.200	.333	.400	106	0	0	0	0	1.000	-1	/O-4	-0.1
1982	Cin-N	113	407	61	109	23	5	4	31	41	40	.268	.338	.378	98	-1	18	12	-2	.987	-3	*O-107	-0.8
1983	Cin-N	146	502	77	131	23	6	9	33	68	60	.261	.350	.384	100	1	41	12	5	.990	20	*O-139	2.2
1984	Cin-N	117	336	44	78	8	4	7	29	51	50	.232	.337	.342	87	-5	21	13	-2	.983	10	*O-108	0.1
1985	Cin-N	145	453	82	115	19	7	3	33	61	31	.254	.344	.347	89	-5	35	13	3	.983	15	*O-135	0.9
1986	Cin-N	145	424	70	110	22	6	15	47	36	56	.259	.317	.446	104	1	18	11	-1	.990	7	*O-127	0.3
1987	*SF-N	101	214	38	54	14	0	4	19	24	33	.252	.328	.374	90	-3	10	9	-2	.993	-9	O-84	-1.7
1988	Cin-N	23	51	3	9	1	0	0	2	4	9	.176	.236	.196	24	-5	2	2	-1	.968	-3	O-15	-0.7
Total	9	804	2395	376	607	111	28	42	195	286	280	.253	.335	.376	94	-17	145	72	0	.987	38	O-719	0.1

■ JOHN MILNER
Milner, John David "The Hammer"   b: 12/28/49, Atlanta, Ga.   BL/TL, 6', 185 lbs.   Deb: 9/15/71

YEAR	TM/L	G	AB	R	H	2B	3B	HR	RBI	BB	SO	AVG	OBP	SLG	PRO+	BR/A	SB	CS	SBR	FA	FR	G/POS	TPR
1971	NY-N	9	18	1	3	1	0	0	1	0	3	.167	.167	.222	9	-2	0	0	0	1.000	1	/O-3	-0.1
1972	NY-N	117	362	52	86	12	2	17	38	51	74	.238	.333	.423	118	9	2	1	0	.965	-3	O-91,1-10	0.8
1973	*NY-N	129	451	69	108	12	3	23	72	62	84	.239	.333	.432	112	7	1	1	-0	.989	-7	1-95,O-29	-0.9
1974	NY-N	137	507	70	128	19	0	20	63	66	77	.252	.339	.408	110	6	10	2	2	.994	-1	*1-133	-0.2
1975	NY-N	91	220	24	42	11	0	7	29	33	22	.191	.302	.336	81	-6	1	1	-0	.985	-6	O-31,1-29	-0.3
1976	NY-N	127	443	56	120	25	4	15	78	65	53	.271	.364	.447	137	22	0	7	-4	.985	4	*O-112,1-12	1.7
1977	NY-N	131	388	43	99	20	3	12	57	61	55	.255	.356	.415	111	7	6	2	1	.994	-1	1-87,O-22	0.1
1978	Pit-N	108	295	39	80	17	0	6	38	34	25	.271	.347	.390	101	1	5	0	2	1.000	-0	O-69,1-28	-0.3
1979	*Pit-N	128	326	52	90	9	4	16	60	53	37	.276	.379	.475	126	12	3	5	-2	.958	-2	1-64,O-48	0.4
1980	Pit-N	114	238	31	58	6	0	8	34	52	29	.244	.379	.370	108	5	2	2	-1	.991	-5	1-70,O-11	-0.5
1981	Pit-N	34	59	6	14	1	0	2	9	5	3	.237	.297	.356	82	-1	0	0	0	.980	-2	/1-8,O-8	-0.5
	*Mon-N	31	76	6	18	5	0	3	9	12	6	.237	.341	.421	114	1	0	1	-1	.978	-1	1-21	0.1
	Yr	65	135	12	32	6	0	5	18	17	9	.237	.322	.393	100	-0	0	1	-1	.979	-2	1-29/O-8	-0.4
1982	Mon-N	26	28	1	3	0	0	0	2	4	2	.107	.219	.107	-6	-4	0	0	0	1.000	0	/1-5	-0.4
	Pit-N	33	25	5	6	2	0	2	8	6	3	.240	.406	.560	163	2	1	0	0	1.000	-0	/1-1	0.3
	Yr	59	53	6	9	2	0	2	10	10	5	.170	.313	.321	76	-2	1	0	0	1.000	-0	/1-6	-0.1
Total	12	1215	3436	455	855	140	16	131	498	504	473	.249	.347	.413	112	59	31	22	-4	.991	-4	1-547,O-440	0.2

■ MIKE MILOSEVICH
Milosevich, Michael "Mollie"   b: 1/13/15, Zeigler, Ill.   d: 2/3/66, E.Chicago, Ind.   BR/TR, 5'10.5", 172 lbs.   Deb: 4/30/44

YEAR	TM/L	G	AB	R	H	2B	3B	HR	RBI	BB	SO	AVG	OBP	SLG	PRO+	BR/A	SB	CS	SBR	FA	FR	G/POS	TPR
1944	NY-A	94	312	27	77	11	4	0	32	30	37	.247	.313	.308	75	-10	1	2	-1	.954	7	S-91	0.3
1945	NY-A	30	69	5	15	2	0	0	7	6	6	.217	.289	.246	54	-4	0	0	0	.957	1	S-22/2-1	-0.2
Total	2	124	381	32	92	13	4	0	39	36	43	.241	.309	.297	71	-14	1	2	-1	.954	8	S-113/2-1	0.1

■ DON MINCHER
Mincher, Donald Ray   b: 6/24/38, Huntsville, Ala.   BL/TR, 6'3", 213 lbs.   Deb: 4/18/60

YEAR	TM/L	G	AB	R	H	2B	3B	HR	RBI	BB	SO	AVG	OBP	SLG	PRO+	BR/A	SB	CS	SBR	FA	FR	G/POS	TPR
1960	Was-A	27	79	10	19	4	1	2	5	11	11	.241	.333	.392	96	-0	0	1	-1	.977	-4	1-20	-0.7
1961	Min-A	35	101	18	19	5	1	5	11	22	11	.188	.333	.406	91	-1	0	1	-1	.969	-2	1-29	-0.6
1962	Min-A	86	121	20	29	1	1	9	29	34	24	.240	.406	.488	134	7	0	0	0	.978	-1	1-25	0.4
1963	Min-A	82	225	41	58	8	0	17	42	30	51	.258	.353	.520	138	11	0	0	0	.983	-5	1-60	0.4
1964	Min-A	120	287	45	68	12	4	23	56	27	51	.237	.303	.547	130	10	0	0	0	.992	-5	1-76	0.7
1965	*Min-A	128	346	43	87	17	3	22	65	49	73	.251	.348	.509	134	15	1	3	-2	.992	-5	1-99/O-1	0.4
1966	Min-A	139	431	53	108	30	0	14	62	58	68	.251	.342	.418	110	6	3	2	-0	.992	-3	*1-130	0.1
1967	Cal-A★	147	487	81	133	23	3	25	76	69	69	.273	.368	.487	157	35	0	3	-2	.994	-2	*1-142/O-1	2.4
1968	Cal-A	120	399	35	94	12	1	13	48	43	65	.236	.316	.368	111	5	0	2	-1	.991	-1	*1-113	-0.9
1969	Sea-A★	140	427	53	105	14	0	25	78	78	69	.246	.369	.454	131	19	10	11	-4	.995	8	*1-137	1.4
1970	Oak-A	140	463	62	114	18	0	27	74	56	71	.246	.331	.460	120	11	5	4	-1	.990	-4	*1-137	0.1
1971	Oak-A	28	92	9	22	6	1	2	8	20	14	.239	.375	.391	120	3	1	1	-0	.996	3	1-27	0.3
	Was-A	100	323	35	94	15	1	10	45	53	52	.291	.384	.437	143	20	2	1	-0	.990	3	1-88	1.6
	Yr	128	415	44	116	21	2	12	53	73	66	.280	.390	.427	138	23	3	2	-0	.991	6	*1-115	1.9
1972	Tex-A	61	191	23	45	10	0	6	39	46	23	.236	.389	.382	136	11	2	1	-0	.994	6	1-59	1.4
	*Oak-A	47	54	2	8	1	0	0	5	10	16	.148	.290	.167	37	-4	0	2	-2	.988	-1	1-11	-0.7
	Yr	108	245	25	53	11	0	6	44	56	39	.216	.366	.335	115	7	2	3	-0	.993	5	1-70	0.7
Total	13	1400	4026	530	1003	176	16	200	643	606	668	.249	.351	.450	127	149	24	32	-12	.990	2	*1-1138/O-2	6.3

■ ED MINCHER
Mincher, Edward John   b: 1851, Baltimore, Md.   Deb: 5/4/1871

YEAR	TM/L	G	AB	R	H	2B	3B	HR	RBI	BB	SO	AVG	OBP	SLG	PRO+	BR/A	SB	CS	SBR	FA	FR	G/POS	TPR
1871	Kek-n	9	36	4	8	0	0	0	5	0	0	.222	.222	.222	28	-3	1	0		.852	-0	/O-9	-0.2
1872	Nat-n	11	53	5	6	0	0	0	4	0	0	.113	.113	.113	-26	-9	0	0		.837	2	O-11	-0.4
Total	2 n	20	89	9	14	0	0	0	9	0	0	.157	.157	.157	-5	-12	1	0		.842	2	/O-20	-0.6

■ DAN MINNEHAN
Minnehan, Daniel Joseph   b: 11/28/1865, Troy, N.Y.   d: 8/8/29, Troy, N.Y.   BR/TR, 5'10", 145 lbs.   Deb: 9/20/1895

YEAR	TM/L	G	AB	R	H	2B	3B	HR	RBI	BB	SO	AVG	OBP	SLG	PRO+	BR/A	SB	CS	SBR	FA	FR	G/POS	TPR
1895	Lou-N	8	34	6	13	0	0	0	6	1	1	.382	.400	.382	109	1	0			.920	-0	/3-7,O-2	0.0

■ MINNIE MINOSO
Minoso, Saturnino Orestes Armas (Arrieta)   b: 11/29/22, Havana, Cuba   BR/TR, 5'10", 175 lbs.   Deb: 4/19/49   C

YEAR	TM/L	G	AB	R	H	2B	3B	HR	RBI	BB	SO	AVG	OBP	SLG	PRO+	BR/A	SB	CS	SBR	FA	FR	G/POS	TPR
1949	Cle-A	9	16	2	3	0	0	0	1	2	2	.188	.350	.375	94	-0	0	1	-1	1.000	-1	/O-7	-0.2
1951	Cle-A	8	14	3	6	2	0	0	1	1	1	.429	.529	.571	209	2	0			.952	-0	/1-7	0.2
	Chi-A★	138	516	109	167	32	14	10	74	71	41	.324	.419	.498	150	38	31	10	3	.961	-12	O-82,3-68/S-1	2.6
	Yr	146	530	112	173	34	14	10	76	72	42	.326	.422	.500	152	41	31	10	3	.961	-12	O-82,3-68/1-7,S-1	2.8
1952	Chi-A★	147	569	96	160	24	9	13	61	61	46	.281	.375	.424	121	17	22	16	-3	.979	4	*O-143/3-9,S-1	1.2
1953	Chi-A★	151	556	104	174	24	8	15	104	74	43	.313	.410	.466	132	27	25	16	-2	.967	6	*O-147,3-10	2.5

YEAR	TM/L	G	AB	R	H	2B	3B	HR	RBI	BB	SO	AVG	OBP	SLG	PRO+	BR/A	SB	CS	SBR	FA	FR	G/POS	TPR
1954	Chi-A★	153	568	119	182	29	18	19	116	77	46	.320	.416	**.535**	154	43	18	11	-1	.978	13	*O-146/3-9	5.0
1955	Chi-A	139	517	79	149	26	7	10	70	76	43	.288	.390	.424	115	13	19	8	1	.971	12	*O-138/3-2	2.0
1956	Chi-A	151	545	106	172	29	11	21	88	86	40	.316	.430	.525	149	42	12	6	0	.974	3	*O-148/3-8,1-1	3.6
1957	Chi-A★	153	568	96	176	36	5	12	103	79	54	.310	.413	.454	136	32	18	15	-4	.984	6	*O-152/3-1	2.6
1958	Cle-A	149	556	94	168	25	2	24	80	59	53	.302	.384	.484	141	32	14	14	-4	.975	13	*O-147/3-1	3.3
1959	Cle-A★	148	570	92	172	32	0	21	92	54	46	.302	.379	.468	136	29	8	10	-4	.985	16	*O-148	3.4
1960	Chi-A★	154	591	89	**184**	32	4	20	105	52	63	.311	.380	.481	132	27	17	13	-3	.980	5	*O-154	2.0
1961	Chi-A	152	540	91	151	28	3	14	82	67	46	.280	.376	.420	114	13	9	4	0	.956	3	*O-147	0.8
1962	StL-N	39	97	14	19	5	1	0	10	7	17	.196	.271	.278	44	-8	4	0	1	.972	-1	O-27	-0.9
1963	Was-A	109	315	38	72	12	2	4	30	33	38	.229	.317	.317	79	-8	8	6	-1	.955	-5	O-74/3-8	-1.9
1964	Chi-A	30	31	4	7	0	0	0	5	5	3	.226	.351	.323	91	-0	0	0	0	1.000	0	/O-5	-0.1
1976	Chi-A	3	8	0	1	0	0	0	0	0	2	.125	.125	.125	-27	-1	0	0	0	.000	0	/D-3	-0.1
1980	Chi-A	2	2	0	0	0	0	0	0	0	0	.000	.000	.000	-99	-1	0	0	0	.000	0	/H	-0.1
Total	17	1835	6579	1136	1963	336	83	186	1023	814	584	.298	.391	.459	130	297	205	130	-16	.974	62	*O-1665,3-116/1DS	26.0

■ DOUG MIRABELLI

Mirabelli, Douglas Anthony b: 10/18/70, Kingman, Ariz. BR/TR, 6'1", 205 lbs. Deb: 8/27/96

YEAR	TM/L	G	AB	R	H	2B	3B	HR	RBI	BB	SO	AVG	OBP	SLG	PRO+	BR/A	SB	CS	SBR	FA	FR	G/POS	TPR
1996	SF-N	9	18	2	4	1	0	0	1	3	4	.222	.333	.278	66	-1	0	0	0	1.000	-1	/C-8	-0.1

■ WILLY MIRANDA

Miranda, Guillermo (Perez) b: 5/24/26, Velasco, Cuba d: 9/7/96, Baltimore, Md. BB/TR, 5'9.5", 150 lbs. Deb: 5/6/51

YEAR	TM/L	G	AB	R	H	2B	3B	HR	RBI	BB	SO	AVG	OBP	SLG	PRO+	BR/A	SB	CS	SBR	FA	FR	G/POS	TPR
1951	Was-A	7	9	2	4	1	0	0	1	0	1	.444	.444	.444	143	1	0	0	0	.818	-0	/S-2,1-1	0.0
1952	Chi-A	12	8	1	2	1	0	0	0	3	0	.250	.455	.375	131	1	0	0	0	1.000	4	/S-4,3-4,2-1	0.5
	StL-A	7	11	2	1	0	1	0	1	3	1	.091	.286	.273	54	-1	0	0	0	.900	-1	/S-7	-0.1
	Chi-A	58	142	13	31	3	1	0	7	10	14	.218	.275	.254	47	-10	1	0	0	.975	11	S-50/2-1,3-1	0.4
	Yr	77	161	16	34	4	2	0	8	16	15	.211	.287	.261	52	-10	1	0	0	.970	10	S-61/3-5,2-2	0.8
1953	StL-A	17	6	2	1	0	0	0	0	1	1	.167	.286	.167	24	-1	1	1	-0	.933	3	/S-8,3-6	0.3
	NY-A	48	58	12	13	0	0	1	5	5	10	.224	.286	.276	54	-4	1	1	-0	.984	17	S-45	1.4
	Yr	65	64	14	14	0	0	1	5	6	11	.219	.286	.266	51	-4	2	2	-1	.979	20	S-53/3-6	1.7
1954	NY-A	92	116	12	29	4	1	2	12	10	11	.250	.310	.345	82	-3	0	3	-2	.948	16	S-88/2-4,3-1	1.5
1955	Bal-A	153	487	42	124	12	6	1	38	42	58	.255	.315	.310	74	-19	4	3	-1	.958	19	*S-153/2-1	1.2
1956	Bal-A	148	461	38	100	16	4	2	34	46	73	.217	.288	.282	55	-31	3	6	-3	.962	2	*S-147	-2.0
1957	Bal-A	115	314	29	61	3	0	0	20	24	42	.194	.251	.204	28	-31	2	1	0	.966	-3	*S-115	-2.6
1958	Bal-A	102	214	15	43	6	0	1	8	14	25	.201	.250	.243	38	-18	1	1	-0	.962	-2	*S-102	-1.4
1959	Bal-A	65	88	8	14	5	0	0	7	4	5	.159	.221	.216	21	-10	0	0	0	.974	22	S-47,3-11/2-5	1.4
Total	9	824	1914	176	423	50	14	6	132	165	250	.221	.284	.271	54	-126	13	16	-6	.962	88	S-768/3-23,2-12,1-1	0.6

■ JOHN MISSE

Misse, John Beverly b: 5/30/1885, Highland, Kan. d: 3/18/70, St.Joseph, Mo. BR/TR, 5'8", 150 lbs. Deb: 5/26/14

YEAR	TM/L	G	AB	R	H	2B	3B	HR	RBI	BB	SO	AVG	OBP	SLG	PRO+	BR/A	SB	CS	SBR	FA	FR	G/POS	TPR
1914	StL-F	99	306	28	60	8	1	0	22	36	52	.196	.281	.229	38	-31	3			.948	14	2-50,S-43/3-2	-1.4

■ CLARENCE MITCHELL

Mitchell, Clarence Elmer b: 2/22/1891, Franklin, Neb. d: 11/6/63, Grand Island, Neb. BL/TL, 5'11.5", 190 lbs. Deb: 6/2/11 C

YEAR	TM/L	G	AB	R	H	2B	3B	HR	RBI	BB	SO	AVG	OBP	SLG	PRO+	BR/A	SB	CS	SBR	FA	FR	G/POS	TPR
1911	Det-A	5	4	2	2	0	0	0	0	0	1	.500	.600	.500	198	1	0			1.000	-1	/P-5	0.0
1916	Cin-N	56	117	11	28	2	1	0	11	4	6	.239	.264	.274	67	-5	1			.985	-2	P-29/1-9,O-3	-0.5
1917	Cin-N	47	90	13	25	3	0	0	5	5	5	.278	.316	.311	97	-0	0			.982	-0	P-32/1-6,O-5	-0.1
1918	Bro-N	10	24	2	6	1	1	0	2	0	3	.250	.250	.375	90	-0	0			.750	-2	/O-6,1-2,P-1	-0.4
1919	Bro-N	34	49	7	18	1	0	1	2	4	4	.367	.415	.449	156	3	0			.976	1	P-23	0.0
1920	*Bro-N	55	107	9	25	2	2	0	11	8	9	.234	.287	.290	64	-5	1	0		1.000	1	P-19,1-11/O-4	-0.4
1921	Bro-N	46	91	11	24	5	0	0	12	5	4	.264	.316	.319	66	-4	3	1		.945	3	P-37/1-4	0.0
1922	Bro-N	56	155	21	45	6	3	3	28	19	6	.290	.371	.426	106	2	0	0		.992	5	1-42/P-5	0.2
1923	Phi-N	53	78	10	21	3	2	1	9	4	11	.269	.305	.397	75	-3	0	0		.880	-3	P-29	0.0
1924	Phi-N	69	102	7	26	3	0	0	13	2	7	.255	.276	.284	45	-8	1	0		**1.000**	3	P-30	0.0
1925	Phi-N	52	92	7	18	2	0	0	13	5	9	.196	.237	.217	16	-12	2	0	1	**1.000**	4	P-32/1-2	0.0
1926	Phi-N	39	78	8	19	4	0	0	6	5	5	.244	.289	.295	55	-5	0			.986	2	P-28/1-4	0.0
1927	Phi-N	18	42	5	10	2	0	1	6	2	1	.238	.273	.357	67	-2	0			.963	1	P-13	0.0
1928	Phi-N	5	4	0	1	0	0	0	0	0	1	.250	.250	.250	30	-0	0			1.000	-0	/P-3	0.0
	*StL-N	19	56	0	7	1	0	0	1	0	3	.125	.125	.143	-30	-11	0			.982	2	P-19	0.0
	Yr	24	60	0	8	1	0	0	1	0	3	.133	.133	.150	-26	-11	0			.983	3	P-22	0.0
1929	StL-N	26	66	9	18	3	1	0	9	4	6	.273	.348	.348	63	-4	1			.974	-1	P-25	0.0
1930	StL-N	1	2	0	1	0	0	0	0	0	0	.500	.500	.500	138	-0	0			.000	-0	/P-1	0.0
	NY-N	24	47	9	12	1	0	0	1	1	5	.255	.271	.277	33	-5	0			1.000	2	P-24	0.0
	Yr	25	49	9	13	1	0	0	1	1	5	.265	.280	.286	38	-5	0			1.000	2	P-25	0.0
1931	NY-N	27	73	5	16	2	1	0	4	2	4	.219	.240	.288	42	-6	0			.885	-2	P-27	0.0
1932	NY-N	8	10	2	2	0	0	0	0	1	1	.200	.273	.200	30	-1	0			.833	-1	/P-8	0.0
Total	18	650	1287	138	324	41	10	7	133	72	<u>92</u>	.252	.293	.315	64	-65	9	<u>1</u>		.972	14	P-390/1-80,O-18	-1.2

■ FRED MITCHELL

Mitchell, Frederick Francis (b: Frederick Francis Yapp) b: 6/5/1878, Cambridge, Mass. d: 10/13/70, Newton, Mass. BR/TR, 5'9.5", 185 lbs. Deb: 4/27/01 MC

YEAR	TM/L	G	AB	R	H	2B	3B	HR	RBI	BB	SO	AVG	OBP	SLG	PRO+	BR/A	SB	CS	SBR	FA	FR	G/POS	TPR
1901	Bos-A	20	44	5	7	0	2	0	4	2		.159	.196	.250	23	-5	0			.875	-0	P-17/2-2,S-1	-0.1
1902	Bos-A	1	1	0	0	0	0	0	0	0	0	.000	.000	.000	-97	-0	0			.667	0	/P-1	0.0
	Phi-A	19	48	7	9	1	1	0	3	1		.188	.204	.250	24	-5	1			.942	2	P-18/O-1	-0.1
	Yr	20	49	7	9	1	1	0	3	1		.184	.200	.245	22	-5	1			.927	2	P-19/O-1	-0.1
1903	Phi-N	29	95	11	19	4	0	0	10	0		.200	.200	.242	27	-9	0			.857	-3	P-28	0.0
1904	Phi-N	25	82	9	17	3	1	0	3	5		.207	.253	.268	63	-4	1			.981	3	P-13/1-9,3-2,0-1	-0.2
	Bro-N	8	24	3	7	1	1	0	6	1		.292	.346	.417	139	1	0			.906	1	/P-8	0.0
	Yr	33	106	12	24	4	2	0	9	6		.226	.274	.302	80	-3	1			.952	4	P-21/1-9,3-2,0-1	-0.2
1905	Bro-N	27	79	4	15	0	0	0	8	4		.190	.238	.190	30	-7	0			.881	-2	P-12/1-7,3-4,S-1,0	-0.7
1910	NY-A	68	196	16	45	7	2	0	18	9		.230	.274	.286	71	-7	6			.968	-15	C-62	-1.8
1913	Bos-N	4	3	0	1	0	0	0	0	0		.333	.333	.333	89	-0	0			.000	0	/H	0.0
Total	7	201	572	55	120	16	7	0	52	22	<u>2</u>	.210	.245	.262	52	-35	8			.904	-14	/P-97,C-62,13OS2	-2.9

■ JOHNNY MITCHELL

Mitchell, John Franklin b: 8/9/1894, Detroit, Mich. d: 11/4/65, Birmingham, Mich. BB/TR, 5'8", 155 lbs. Deb: 5/21/21

YEAR	TM/L	G	AB	R	H	2B	3B	HR	RBI	BB	SO	AVG	OBP	SLG	PRO+	BR/A	SB	CS	SBR	FA	FR	G/POS	TPR
1921	NY-A	13	42	4	11	1	0	0	2	4		.262	.326	.286	56	-3	1	0		.958	-6	/S-7,2-5	-0.7
1922	NY-A	4	4	1	0	0	0	0	0	0	1	.000	.000	.000	-98	-1	0	0	0	1.000	-1	/S-4	-0.2
	Bos-A	59	203	20	51	4	1	1	8	16	17	.251	.318	.296	61	-11	1	2	-1	.962	-5	S-58	-1.1
	Yr	63	207	21	51	4	1	1	8	16	18	.246	.313	.290	58	-12	1	2	-1	.963	-6	S-62	-1.3
1923	Bos-A	92	347	40	78	15	4	0	19	34	18	.225	.296	.291	55	-23	7	11	-5	.961	-0	S-87/2-5	-1.9
1924	Bro-N	64	243	42	64	10	0	1	16	37	22	.263	.361	.317	86	-3	3	1	0	.951	-1	S-64	0.4
1925	Bro-N	97	336	45	84	8	3	0	18	28	19	.250	.308	.292	55	-22	2	0	1	.947	-4	S-90	-1.5
Total	5	329	1175	152	288	38	8	2	63	119	81	.245	.317	.296	62	-63	14	14	-4	.955	-16	S-310/2-10	-5.0

■ KEITH MITCHELL

Mitchell, Keith Alexander b: 8/6/69, San Diego, Cal. BR/TR, 5'10", 180 lbs. Deb: 7/23/91

YEAR	TM/L	G	AB	R	H	2B	3B	HR	RBI	BB	SO	AVG	OBP	SLG	PRO+	BR/A	SB	CS	SBR	FA	FR	G/POS	TPR
1991	*Atl-N	48	66	11	21	0	0	2	5	8	12	.318	.416	.409	118	2	3	1	0	.970	-7	O-34	-0.5
1994	Sea-A	46	128	21	29	2	0	5	15	18	22	.227	.327	.359	75	-5	0	0	0	.980	-7	O-38/D-6	-1.1
1996	Cin-N	11	15	2	4	1	0	1	3	1	3	.267	.313	.533	119	0	0	0	0	.875	-1	O-5	0.0
Total	3	105	209	34	54	3	0	8	23	27	37	.258	.346	.388	91	-2	3	1	0	.967	-14	/O-77,D-6	-1.6

■ KEVIN MITCHELL

Mitchell, Kevin Darnell b: 1/13/62, San Diego, Cal. BR/TR, 5'11", 210 lbs. Deb: 9/4/84

YEAR	TM/L	G	AB	R	H	2B	3B	HR	RBI	BB	SO	AVG	OBP	SLG	PRO+	BR/A	SB	CS	SBR	FA	FR	G/POS	TPR
1984	NY-N	7	14	0	3	0	0	0	0	0	1	.214	.214	.214	21	-1	0	1	-1	.833	-1	/3-5	-0.3
1986	*NY-N	108	328	51	91	22	2	12	43	33	61	.277	.345	.466	125	10	3	3	-1	.983	-11	O-68,S-24/3-7,1-2	-0.1
1987	SD-N	62	196	19	48	7	1	7	26	20	61	.245	.315	.398	91	-3	0	0	0	.945	4	3-51/O-3	0.0
	*SF-N	69	268	49	82	13	1	15	44	28	27	.306	.376	.530	144	9	6	6	-1	.962	-5	3-68/O-3,S-1	0.9
	Yr	131	464	68	130	20	2	22	70	48	88	.280	.350	.474	121	13	9	6	-1	.954	-2	*3-119/O-6,S-1	0.9
1988	SF-N	148	505	60	127	25	7	19	80	48	85	.251	.323	.442	123	13	5	5	-2	.943	-5	*3-102,O-40	0.5

YEAR	TM/L	G	AB	R	H	2B	3B	HR	RBI	BB	SO	AVG	OBP	SLG	PRO+	BR/A	SB	CS	SBR	FA	FR	G/POS	TPR
1989	*SF-N★	154	543	100	158	34	6	**47**	**125**	87	115	.291	.392	**.635**	**194**	**66**	3	4	-2	.978	7	*O-147/3-2	**7.0**
1990	SF-N★	140	524	90	152	24	2	35	93	58	87	.290	.363	.544	151	35	4	7	-3	.971	7	*O-138	3.6
1991	SF-N	113	371	52	95	13	1	27	69	43	57	.256	.341	.515	142	20	2	3	-1	.970	3	*O-100/1-1	2.0
1992	Sea-A	99	360	48	103	24	0	9	67	35	46	.286	.354	.422	117	8	0	2	-1	1.000	-0	O-69,D-26	0.5
1993	Cin-N	93	323	56	110	21	3	19	64	25	48	.341	.390	.601	160	26	1	0	0	.957	1	O-87	2.6
1994	Cin-N	95	310	57	101	18	1	30	77	59	62	.326	.438	.681	188	41	2	0	1	.972	4	O-89/1-1	4.2
1996	Bos-A	27	92	9	28	4	0	2	13	11	14	.304	.385	.435	98	0	0	0	0	.935	-3	O-21/D-4	-0.3
	Cin-N	37	114	18	37	11	0	6	26	26	16	.325	.450	.579	170	13	0	0	0	.978	-2	O-31/1-3	1.0
Total	11	1152	3948	609	1135	216	24	228	728	473	682	.287	.367	.528	147	245	29	31	-10	.971	-2	O-796,3-235/DS1	21.6

■ **DALE MITCHELL**   Mitchell, Loren Dale b: 8/23/21, Colony, Okla. d: 1/5/87, Tulsa, Okla. BL/TL, 6'1", 195 lbs. Deb: 9/15/46

YEAR	TM/L	G	AB	R	H	2B	3B	HR	RBI	BB	SO	AVG	OBP	SLG	PRO+	BR/A	SB	CS	SBR	FA	FR	G/POS	TPR
1946	Cle-A	11	44	7	19	3	0	0	5	1	2	.432	.444	.500	175	4	1	0	0	1.000	-0	O-11	0.4
1947	Cle-A	123	493	69	156	16	10	1	34	23	14	.316	.347	.396	109	-4	2	5	-2	.977	-9	*O-115	-1.4
1948	*Cle-A	141	608	82	204	30	8	4	56	45	17	.336	.383	.431	119	16	13	18	-7	**.991**	4	*O-140	0.4
1949	Cle-A★	149	640	81	**203**	16	**23**	3	56	43	11	.317	.360	.428	110	7	10	3	1	**.994**	3	*O-149	0.3
1950	Cle-A	130	506	81	156	27	5	3	49	67	21	.308	.390	.399	106	6	3	7	-3	.972	-11	*O-127	-1.3
1951	Cle-A	134	510	83	148	21	7	11	62	53	16	.290	.358	.424	117	11	7	7	-2	.992	-6	*O-124	-0.1
1952	Cle-A★	134	511	61	165	26	3	5	58	52	9	.323	.387	.415	132	22	6	6	-2	.992	-5	*O-128	1.0
1953	Cle-A	134	500	76	150	26	4	13	60	42	20	.300	.354	.446	118	11	3	1	0	.970	-6	*O-125	0.1
1954	*Cle-A	53	60	6	17	1	0	1	6	9	1	.283	.377	.350	98	0	0	0	0	.889	-1	/O-6,1-1	-0.1
1955	Cle-A	61	58	4	15	2	1	0	10	4	3	.259	.306	.328	68	-3	0	0	0	1.000	-1	/1-8,O-3	-0.4
1956	Cle-A	38	30	2	4	0	0	0	6	7	2	.133	.297	.133	17	-3	0	0	0	.000	-0	/O-1	-0.4
	*Bro-N	19	24	3	7	1	0	0	1	0	3	.292	.292	.333	63	-1	0	0	0	1.000	-0	/O-2	-0.2
Total	11	1127	3984	555	1244	169	61	41	403	346	119	.312	.368	.416	114	74	45	47	-15	.985	-32	O-931/1-9	-1.7

■ **MIKE MITCHELL**   Mitchell, Michael Francis b: 12/12/1879, Springfield, Ohio d: 7/16/61, Phoenix, Ariz. BR/TR, 6'1", 185 lbs. Deb: 4/11/07

YEAR	TM/L	G	AB	R	H	2B	3B	HR	RBI	BB	SO	AVG	OBP	SLG	PRO+	BR/A	SB	CS	SBR	FA	FR	G/POS	TPR
1907	Cin-N	148	558	64	163	17	12	3	47	37		.292	.339	.382	121	12	17			.962	22	*O-146/1-2	3.2
1908	Cin-N	119	406	41	90	9	6	1	37	46		.222	.304	.281	89	-4	18			.959	1	*O-118/1-1	-0.9
1909	Cin-N	145	523	83	162	17	**17**	4	86	57		.310	.378	.430	152	31	37			.962	6	*O-145/1-1	3.4
1910	Cin-N	156	583	79	167	16	**18**	5	88	59	56	.286	.356	.401	126	18	35			.958	-3	*O-149/1-7	0.8
1911	Cin-N	142	529	74	154	22	22	2	84	44	34	.291	.348	.427	121	12	35			.971	11	*O-140	1.6
1912	Cin-N	147	552	60	156	14	13	4	78	41	43	.283	.333	.377	97	-4	23			.947	-0	*O-144	-1.1
1913	Chi-N	82	279	37	73	11	6	4	35	32	33	.262	.340	.387	107	3	15			.941	4	O-82	0.3
	Pit-N	54	199	25	54	8	2	1	16	14	15	.271	.319	.347	94	-2	8			.946	7	O-54	0.3
	Yr	136	478	62	127	19	8	5	51	46	48	.266	.331	.370	102	1	23			.943	11	*O-136	0.6
1914	Pit-N	76	273	31	64	11	5	2	23	16	16	.234	.279	.333	86	-6	5			.984	9	O-76	0.0
	Was-A	55	193	20	55	5	3	1	20	22	19	.285	.361	.358	112	3	9	7	-2	.957	4	O-53	0.3
Total	8	1124	4095	514	1138	130	104	27	514	368	**216**	.278	.340	.380	114	64	202	7		.959	61	*O-1107/1-11	7.9

■ **BOBBY MITCHELL**   Mitchell, Robert McKasha b: 2/6/1856, Cincinnati, Ohio d: 5/1/33, Springfield, Ohio BL/TL, 5'5", 135 lbs. Deb: 9/6/1877

YEAR	TM/L	G	AB	R	H	2B	3B	HR	RBI	BB	SO	AVG	OBP	SLG	PRO+	BR/A	SB	CS	SBR	FA	FR	G/POS	TPR
1877	Cin-N	13	49	5	10	3	0	0		5	1	2	.204	.220	.265	59	-2				.920	-1	P-12/O-2	-0.1
1878	Cin-N	13	49	4	12	0	0	0		8	1	4	.245	.260	.245	74	-1				.944	0	/P-9,S-2,O-1	0.0
1879	Cle-N	30	109	11	16	2	2	0		6	0	14	.147	.147	.202	14	-10				.714	-6	P-23/O-9	-0.5
1882	StL-a	1	4	0	0	0	0	0		0	0	0	.000	.000	.000	-96	-1				.000	-1	/O-1,P-1	-0.1
Total	4	57	211	20	38	5	2	0		19	2	20	.180	.188	.223	35	-14				.811	-7	/P-45,O-13,S-2	-0.7

■ **BOBBY MITCHELL**   Mitchell, Robert Van b: 4/7/55, Salt Lake City, Utah BL/TL, 5'10", 170 lbs. Deb: 9/1/80

YEAR	TM/L	G	AB	R	H	2B	3B	HR	RBI	BB	SO	AVG	OBP	SLG	PRO+	BR/A	SB	CS	SBR	FA	FR	G/POS	TPR
1980	LA-N	9	3	1	1	0	0	0	0	1	0	.333	.500	.333	139	0	0	0	0	1.000	-3	/O-8	-0.3
1981	LA-N	10	8	0	1	0	0	0	0	1	4	.125	.222	.125	1	-1	0	0	0	1.000	-3	/O-7	-0.4
1982	Min-A	124	454	48	113	11	6	2	28	54	53	.249	.331	.313	76	-13	8	9	-3	.997	14	*O-121	-0.6
1983	Min-A	59	152	26	35	4	2	1	15	28	21	.230	.354	.303	80	-3	1	1	-0	.990	-3	O-44	-0.8
Total	4	202	617	75	150	15	8	3	43	84	78	.243	.337	.308	76	-17	9	10	-3	.996	5	O-180	-2.1

■ **BOBBY MITCHELL**   Mitchell, Robert Vance b: 10/22/43, Norristown, Pa. BR/TR, 6'4", 190 lbs. Deb: 7/5/70

YEAR	TM/L	G	AB	R	H	2B	3B	HR	RBI	BB	SO	AVG	OBP	SLG	PRO+	BR/A	SB	CS	SBR	FA	FR	G/POS	TPR
1970	NY-A	10	22	1	5	2	0	0	4	2	3	.227	.320	.318	81	-1	0	2	-1	1.000	1	/O-7	-0.1
1971	Mil-A	35	55	7	10	1	1	2	6	6	18	.182	.262	.345	72	-2	0	2	-1	.974	1	O-19	-0.4
1973	Mil-A	47	130	12	29	6	0	5	20	5	32	.223	.252	.385	79	-4	4	1	1	.960	-4	O-20,D-19	-0.9
1974	Mil-A	88	173	27	42	6	2	5	20	18	46	.243	.318	.387	103	0	7	6	-2	.969	-5	D-53,O-26	-0.8
1975	Mil-A	93	229	39	57	14	3	9	41	25	69	.249	.323	.454	117	4	3	4	-2	.992	-4	O-72,D-11	-0.3
Total	5	273	609	86	143	29	6	21	91	56	168	.235	.301	.406	100	-2	14	15	-5	.984	-11	O-144/D-83	-2.5

■ **RALPH MITTERLING**   Mitterling, Ralph "Sarge" b: 4/19/1890, Freeburg, Pa. d: 1/22/56, Pittsburgh, Pa. BR/TR, 5'10", 165 lbs. Deb: 7/7/16

YEAR	TM/L	G	AB	R	H	2B	3B	HR	RBI	BB	SO	AVG	OBP	SLG	PRO+	BR/A	SB	CS	SBR	FA	FR	G/POS	TPR
1916	Phi-A	13	39	1	6	0	0	0	2	3	6	.154	.214	.154	11	-4	0			.944	-2	O-12	-0.8

■ **GEORGE MITTERWALD**   Mitterwald, George Eugene b: 6/7/45, Berkeley, Cal. BR/TR, 6'2", 206 lbs. Deb: 9/15/66 C

YEAR	TM/L	G	AB	R	H	2B	3B	HR	RBI	BB	SO	AVG	OBP	SLG	PRO+	BR/A	SB	CS	SBR	FA	FR	G/POS	TPR
1966	Min-A	3	5	1	1	0	0	0	0	0	0	.200	.200	.200	14	-1	0	0	0	1.000	1	/C-3	0.0
1968	Min-A	11	34	1	7	1	0	0	1	3	8	.206	.270	.235	52	-2	0	0	0	.961	0	C-10	-0.1
1969	*Min-A	69	187	18	48	8	0	5	13	17	47	.257	.329	.380	96	-1	0	1	-1	.987	11	C-63/O-1	1.2
1970	*Min-A	117	369	36	82	12	2	15	46	34	84	.222	.291	.388	84	-9	3	5	-2	.996	24	*C-117	2.0
1971	Min-A	125	388	38	97	13	1	13	44	39	104	.250	.319	.389	97	-2	3	3	-1	.986	-10	*C-120	-0.9
1972	Min-A	64	163	12	30	4	1	9	8	9	37	.184	.227	.239	37	-13	0	1	-1	.984	1	C-61	-0.6
1973	Min-A	125	432	50	112	15	0	16	64	39	111	.259	.328	.405	101	0	3	3	-1	.992	-1	*C-122/D-3	0.5
1974	Chi-N	78	215	17	54	7	0	7	28	14	42	.251	.315	.381	90	-3	1	3	-2	.974	-4	C-68	-0.6
1975	Chi-N	84	200	19	44	4	3	5	26	19	42	.220	.288	.345	72	-8	0	0	0	.976	1	C-59,1-10	-0.8
1976	Chi-N	101	303	19	65	7	0	5	28	16	63	.215	.254	.287	49	-20	1	2	-1	.981	0	C-64,1-25	-2.2
1977	Chi-N	110	340	40	83	22	0	9	38	22	67	.238	.296	.378	72	-15	3	1	0	.989	12	*C-109/1-1	0.1
Total	11	887	2645	251	623	93	7	76	301	222	607	.236	.298	.362	80	-73	14	17	-6	.987	40	*C-796/1-36,D-3,O-1	-1.4

■ **JOHNNY MIZE**   Mize, John Robert "The Big Cat" b: 1/7/13, Demorest, Ga. d: 6/2/93, Demorest, Ga. BL/TR, 6'2", 215 lbs. Deb: 4/16/36 CH

YEAR	TM/L	G	AB	R	H	2B	3B	HR	RBI	BB	SO	AVG	OBP	SLG	PRO+	BR/A	SB	CS	SBR	FA	FR	G/POS	TPR
1936	StL-N	126	414	76	136	30	8	19	93	50	32	.329	.402	.577	162	35	1			.994	3	1-97/O-8	2.5
1937	StL-N★	145	560	103	204	40	7	25	113	56	57	.364	.427	.595	171	55	2			.988	-13	*1-144	2.5
1938	StL-N	149	531	85	179	34	**16**	27	102	74	47	.337	.422	**.614**	172	52	0			.989	-2	*1-140	3.4
1939	StL-N★	153	564	104	197	44	14	**28**	108	92	49	**.349**	.444	**.626**	174	**60**	0			.987	-4	*1-153	3.9
1940	StL-N★	155	579	111	182	31	13	**43**	**137**	82	49	.314	.404	**.636**	173	**56**	7			.990	-7	*1-153	3.4
1941	StL-N★	126	473	67	150	**39**	8	16	100	70	45	.317	.406	.535	153	34	4			.994	3	*1-122	2.8
1942	NY-N★	142	541	97	165	25	7	26	**110**	60	39	.305	.380	**.521**	161	40	3			**.995**	-3	*1-138	3.0
1946	NY-N★	101	377	70	127	18	3	22	70	62	26	.337	.437	.576	185	43	3			.989	5	*1-101	4.4
1947	NY-N★	154	586	**137**	177	26	2	**51**	**138**	74	42	.302	.384	.614	160	48	2			**.996**	9	*1-154	4.9
1948	NY-N★	152	560	110	162	26	4	**40**	125	94	37	.289	.395	.564	156	44	4			.991	4	*1-152	4.6
1949	NY-N★	106	388	59	102	15	0	18	62	50	19	.263	.351	.441	111	6	1			.994	2	*1-101	0.7
	*NY-A	13	23	4	6	1	0	1	2	4	2	.261	.393	.435	119	1	0	0		.980	-0	/1-6	0.8
1950	*NY-A	90	274	43	76	12	0	25	72	29	24	.277	.351	.595	143	14	0	1	-1	.996	-3	1-72	0.8
1951	*NY-A	113	332	37	86	14	1	10	49	36	24	.259	.339	.389	102	1	0	0	0	.994	-4	1-93	-0.7
1952	*NY-A	78	137	9	36	9	0	4	29	11	15	.263	.327	.416	112	2	0	0	0	.987	1	1-27	0.1
1953	*NY-A★	81	104	6	26	3	0	4	27	12	17	.250	.339	.394	101	0	0	0	0	1.000	-0	1-15	-0.1
Total	15	1884	6443	1118	2011	367	83	359	1337	856	524	.312	.397	.562	157	490	28	1		.992	-14	*1-1667/O-8	36.2

■ **JOHN MIZEROCK**   Mizerock, John Joseph b: 12/8/60, Punxsutawney, Pa. BL/TR, 5'11", 190 lbs. Deb: 4/12/83

YEAR	TM/L	G	AB	R	H	2B	3B	HR	RBI	BB	SO	AVG	OBP	SLG	PRO+	BR/A	SB	CS	SBR	FA	FR	G/POS	TPR
1983	Hou-N	33	85	8	13	4	1	0	10	12	15	.153	.265	.229	49	-6	0	0	0	.967	1	C-33	-0.4
1985	Hou-N	15	38	6	9	0	0	0	6	1	7	.237	.293	.342	79	-1	0	0	0	.966	3	C-15	0.3
1986	Hou-N	44	81	9	15	1	1	1	6	24	16	.185	.377	.259	81	-1	0	0	0	.987	4	C-42	0.5

YEAR	TM/L	G	AB	R	H	2B	3B	HR	RBI	BB	SO	AVG	OBP	SLG	PRO+	BR/A	SB	CS	SBR	FA	FR	G/POS	TPR
1989	Atl-N	11	27	1	6	0	0	0	2	0	3	.222	.222	.222	27	-3	0	0	0	1.000	1	C-11	-0.2
Total	4	103	231	24	43	9	2	2	24	38	42	.186	.309	.268	64	-10	0	0	0	.979	8	C-101	0.2

■ BILL MIZEUR
Mizeur, William Francis "Bad Bill" b: 6/22/1897, Nokomis, Ill. d: 8/27/76, Decatur, Ill. BL/TR, 6′, 180 lbs. Deb: 9/30/23

YEAR	TM/L	G	AB	R	H	2B	3B	HR	RBI	BB	SO	AVG	OBP	SLG	PRO+	BR/A	SB	CS	SBR	FA	FR	G/POS	TPR
1923	StL-A	1	1	0	0	0	0	0	0	0	0	.000	.000	.000	-95	-0	0	0	0	.000	0	H	0.0
1924	StL-A	1	1	0	0	0	0	0	0	0	0	.000	.000	.000	-94	-0	0	0	0	.000	0	H	0.0
Total	2	2	2	0	0	0	0	0	0	0	0	.000	.000	.000	-94	-1	0	0	0		0	-0,-0	0.0

■ DAVE MOATES
Moates, David Allan b: 1/30/48, Great Lakes, Ill. BL/TL, 5′9″, 163 lbs. Deb: 9/21/74

YEAR	TM/L	G	AB	R	H	2B	3B	HR	RBI	BB	SO	AVG	OBP	SLG	PRO+	BR/A	SB	CS	SBR	FA	FR	G/POS	TPR
1974	Tex-A	1	0	0	0	0	0	0	0	0	0	—	—	—	—	-0	0	0	0	.000	0	R	0.0
1975	Tex-A	54	175	21	48	9	0	3	14	13	15	.274	.324	.377	99	-1	9	2	2	.984	1	O-51/D-1	0.0
1976	Tex-A	85	137	21	33	7	1	0	13	11	18	.241	.297	.307	75	-4	6	3	0	.991	-10	O-66/D-7	-1.7
Total	3	140	312	42	81	16	1	3	27	24	33	.260	.313	.346	88	-5	15	5	2	.987	-9	O-117/D-8	-1.7

■ DANNY MOELLER
Moeller, Daniel Edward b: 3/23/1885, DeWitt, Iowa d: 4/14/51, Florence, Ala. BB/TR, 5′11″, 165 lbs. Deb: 9/24/07

YEAR	TM/L	G	AB	R	H	2B	3B	HR	RBI	BB	SO	AVG	OBP	SLG	PRO+	BR/A	SB	CS	SBR	FA	FR	G/POS	TPR
1907	Pit-N	11	42	4	12	1	0	0	3	4		.286	.348	.357	119	1	2			.800	-2	O-11	-0.2
1908	Pit-N	36	109	14	21	3	1	0	9	9		.193	.254	.239	57	-5	4			.950	-5	O-27	-1.3
1912	Was-A	132	519	90	143	26	10	6	46	52		.276	.346	.399	112	7	30			.944	10	*O-132	1.0
1913	Was-A	153	589	88	139	15	10	5	42	72	103	.236	.322	.321	86	-9	62			.926	1	*O-153	-1.1
1914	Was-A	151	571	83	143	19	10	1	45	71	89	.250	.341	.324	96	-1	26	25	-7	.930	-1	*O-150	-1.8
1915	Was-A	118	438	65	99	11	10	2	23	59	63	.226	.319	.311	87	-7	32	10	4	.952	-3	*O-116	-1.2
1916	Was-A	78	240	30	59	8	1	1	23	30	35	.246	.335	.300	92	-2	13			.963	2	O-63	-0.4
	Cle-A	25	30	5	2	0	0	0	1	5	6	.067	.200	.067	-19	-4	2			1.000	-2	/O-8,2-1	-0.7
	Yr	103	270	35	61	8	1	1	24	35	41	.226	.319	.274	78	-6	15			.966	-1	O-71/2-1	-1.1
Total	7	704	2538	379	618	83	43	15	192	302	296	.243	.328	.328	93	-20	171	35		.938	5	O-660/2-1	-5.7

■ JOE MOFFETT
Moffett, Joseph W. b: 6/1859, Wheeling, W.Va. 6′, 179 lbs. Deb: 5/6/1884 F

YEAR	TM/L	G	AB	R	H	2B	3B	HR	RBI	BB	SO	AVG	OBP	SLG	PRO+	BR/A	SB	CS	SBR	FA	FR	G/POS	TPR
1884	Tol-a	56	204	17	41	5	3	0		2		.201	.209	.255	49	-12				.957	-5	1-38,3-11/2-4,O-3	-2.0

■ SAM MOFFETT
Moffett, Samuel R. b: 3/14/1857, Wheeling, W.Va. d: 5/5/07, Butte, Mont. BR/TR, 6′, 175 lbs. Deb: 5/15/1884 F

YEAR	TM/L	G	AB	R	H	2B	3B	HR	RBI	BB	SO	AVG	OBP	SLG	PRO+	BR/A	SB	CS	SBR	FA	FR	G/POS	TPR
1884	Cle-N	67	256	26	47	12	2	0	15	8	56	.184	.208	.246	41	-17				.827	6	O-42,P-24/1-2,32	-0.8
1887	Ind-N	11	41	6	5	1	0	0	1	1	6	.122	.143	.146	-20	-7	2			.857	-3	/P-6,O-5	-0.4
1888	Ind-N	10	35	6	4	0	0	0	0	5	4	.114	.225	.114	11	-3	0			.750	-2	/P-7,O-3	-0.2
Total	3	88	332	38	56	13	2	0	16	14	66	.169	.202	.220	30	-27	2			.821	1	/O-50,P-37,1-2,23	-1.4

■ JOHN MOHARDT
Mohardt, John Henry b: 1/21/1898, Pittsburgh, Pa. d: 11/24/61, LaJolla, Cal. BR/TR, 5′10″, 165 lbs. Deb: 4/15/22

YEAR	TM/L	G	AB	R	H	2B	3B	HR	RBI	BB	SO	AVG	OBP	SLG	PRO+	BR/A	SB	CS	SBR	FA	FR	G/POS	TPR
1922	Det-A	5	1	2	1	0	0	0	0	1	0	1.000	1.000	1.000	436	0	1	0	-1	1.000	-1	/O-3	-0.1

■ KID MOHLER
Mohler, Ernest Follette b: 12/13/1874, Oneida, Ill. d: 11/4/61, San Francisco, Cal. BR/TL, 5′4.5″, 145 lbs. Deb: 9/29/1894

YEAR	TM/L	G	AB	R	H	2B	3B	HR	RBI	BB	SO	AVG	OBP	SLG	PRO+	BR/A	SB	CS	SBR	FA	FR	G/POS	TPR
1894	Was-N	3	9	0	1	0	0	0	0	2	4	.111	.273	.111	-5	-2	0			.952	2	/2-3	0.0

■ JOHNNY MOKAN
Mokan, John Leo b: 9/23/1895, Buffalo, N.Y. d: 2/10/85, Buffalo, N.Y. BR/TR, 5′7″, 165 lbs. Deb: 4/15/21

YEAR	TM/L	G	AB	R	H	2B	3B	HR	RBI	BB	SO	AVG	OBP	SLG	PRO+	BR/A	SB	CS	SBR	FA	FR	G/POS	TPR
1921	Pit-N	19	52	7	14	3	2	0	9	5	3	.269	.333	.404	92	-1	0	0	0	.946	0	O-15	-0.1
1922	Pit-N	31	89	9	23	3	1	0	8	9	3	.258	.327	.315	65	-4	0	1	-1	.903	-4	O-23	-1.0
	Phi-N	47	151	20	38	7	1	3	27	16	25	.252	.327	.371	73	-6	1	0	0	.905	-6	O-37/3-2	-1.4
	Yr	78	240	29	61	10	2	3	35	25	28	.254	.327	.350	70	-11	1	1	-1	.905	-10	O-60/3-2	-2.4
1923	Phi-N	113	400	76	125	23	3	10	48	53	31	.313	.401	.460	113	8	6	11	-5	.969	7	*O-105/3-1	0.4
1924	Phi-N	96	366	50	95	15	1	7	44	30	27	.260	.321	.363	74	-14	7	5	-1	.986	-0	O-94	-2.1
1925	Phi-N	75	209	30	69	11	2	6	42	27	9	.330	.417	.488	120	7	3	5	-2	.984	-12	O-68	-1.0
1926	Phi-N	127	456	68	138	23	5	6	62	41	31	.303	.365	.414	104	3	4			.967	-8	*O-123	-1.3
1927	Phi-N	74	213	22	61	13	2	0	33	25	21	.286	.361	.366	94	-1	5			.962	-9	O-63	-1.4
Total	7	582	1936	282	563	98	17	32	273	206	150	.291	.364	.409	97		26	22		.966	-32	O-528/3-3	-7.9

■ FENTON MOLE
Mole, Fenton Le Roy "Muscles" b: 6/14/25, San Leandro, Cal. BL/TL, 6′1.5″, 200 lbs. Deb: 9/1/49

YEAR	TM/L	G	AB	R	H	2B	3B	HR	RBI	BB	SO	AVG	OBP	SLG	PRO+	BR/A	SB	CS	SBR	FA	FR	G/POS	TPR
1949	NY-A	10	27	2	5	2	1	0	3	5	2	.185	.267	.407	58	-2	0	0	0	1.000	1	/1-8	-0.1

■ IZZY MOLINA
Molina, Islay b: 6/3/71, New York, N.Y. BR/TR, 6′, 200 lbs. Deb: 8/15/96

YEAR	TM/L	G	AB	R	H	2B	3B	HR	RBI	BB	SO	AVG	OBP	SLG	PRO+	BR/A	SB	CS	SBR	FA	FR	G/POS	TPR
1996	Oak-A	14	25	0	5	2	0	0	1	1	3	.200	.231	.280	29	-3	0	0	0	1.000	0	C-12/D-1	-0.2

■ BOB MOLINARO
Molinaro, Robert Joseph b: 5/21/50, Newark, N.J. BL/TR, 6′, 190 lbs. Deb: 9/18/75

YEAR	TM/L	G	AB	R	H	2B	3B	HR	RBI	BB	SO	AVG	OBP	SLG	PRO+	BR/A	SB	CS	SBR	FA	FR	G/POS	TPR
1975	Det-A	6	19	2	5	1	0	0	1	1	0	.263	.300	.368	84	-0	0	0	0	1.000	-0	/O-6	-0.1
1977	Det-A	4	4	0	1	1	0	0	0	0	2	.250	.250	.500	94	-0	0	0	0	.000	0	H	0.0
	Chi-A	1	2	0	1	0	0	0	0	0	0	.500	.500	.500	174	0	0	0	0	1.000	-0	/O-1	0.0
	Yr	5	6	0	2	1	0	0	0	0	3	.333	.333	.500	119	0	0	0	0	1.000	-0	/O-1	0.0
1978	Chi-A	105	286	39	75	5	5	6	27	19	12	.262	.315	.378	93	-3	22	6	3	1.000	-7	O-62,D-32	-1.1
1979	Bal-A	8	6	0	0	0	0	0	0	1	3	.000	.143	.000	-60	-1	0	0	0	1.000	-1	/O-5	-0.2
1980	Chi-A	119	344	48	100	16	4	5	36	26	29	.291	.353	.404	107	4	18	7	1	.957	-2	O-49,D-47	-0.1
1981	Chi-A	47	42	7	11	1	1	1	9	8	1	.262	.392	.405	133	2	1	0	0	1.000	-0	/O-2,D-4	0.2
1982	Chi-N	65	66	6	13	3	0	1	12	6	5	.197	.264	.258	45	-5	1	1	-0	1.000	-1	/O-4	-0.7
	Phi-N	19	14	0	4	0	0	0	2	3	1	.286	.412	.286	96	0	1	0	0	.000	-0	H	0.0
	Yr	84	80	6	17	3	0	1	14	9	6	.213	.292	.262	55	-5	2	1	0	1.000	-1	/O-4	-0.7
1983	Phi-N	19	18	1	2	1	0	0	1	3	0	.111	.111	.333	19	-2	0	0	0	.000	0	/D-1	-0.3
	Det-A	8	2	3	0	0	0	0	0	1	1	.000	.333	.000	1	-0	1	1	-0	.000	0	/D-1	-0.1
Total	8	401	803	106	212	25	11	14	90	65	57	.264	.328	.375	95	-6	46	15	5	.980	-12	O-129/D-84	-2.4

■ PAUL MOLITOR
Molitor, Paul Leo b: 8/22/56, St.Paul, Minn. BR/TR, 6′, 185 lbs. Deb: 4/7/78

YEAR	TM/L	G	AB	R	H	2B	3B	HR	RBI	BB	SO	AVG	OBP	SLG	PRO+	BR/A	SB	CS	SBR	FA	FR	G/POS	TPR
1978	Mil-A	125	521	73	142	26	4	6	45	19	54	.273	.303	.372	89	-9	30	12	2	.976	-5	2-91,S-31/3-1,D-2	-0.1
1979	Mil-A	140	584	88	188	27	16	9	62	48	48	.322	.375	.469	126	21	33	13	2	.979	1	*2-122,S-10/D-8	3.3
1980	Mil-A†	111	450	81	137	29	2	9	37	48	48	.304	.375	.438	126	17	34	7	6	.971	-2	2-91,S-12/3-1,D-7	2.8
1981	*Mil-A	64	251	45	67	11	0	2	19	25	29	.267	.341	.335	100	1	10	6	-1	.976	2	O-46,D-16	-0.1
1982	*Mil-A	160	666	136	201	26	8	19	71	69	93	.302	.368	.450	132	29	41	9	7	.942	-1	*3-150/S-4,D-6	3.1
1983	Mil-A	152	608	95	164	28	6	15	47	59	74	.270	.336	.410	113	10	41	8	8	.966	2	*3-146/D-2	1.7
1984	Mil-A	13	46	3	10	1	0	0	6	2	8	.217	.250	.239	38	-4	1	0	0	.933	4	/3-7,D-4	0.0
1985	Mil-A★	140	576	93	171	28	3	10	48	54	80	.297	.358	.408	110	8	21	7	2	.953	-3	*3-135/D-4	0.6
1986	Mil-A	105	437	62	123	24	6	9	55	40	81	.281	.342	.426	104	2	20	5	3	.944	-3	3-91,D-10/O-4	0.5
1987	Mil-A	118	465	114	164	41	5	16	75	69	67	.353	.438	.566	159	42	45	10	8	.947	-10	D-58,3-41,2-19	3.5
1988	Mil-A★	154	609	115	190	34	6	13	60	71	54	.312	.386	.452	132	28	41	10	6	.941	-8	*3-105,D-49/2-1	2.4
1989	Mil-A	155	615	84	194	35	4	11	56	64	67	.315	.384	.439	133	28	27	11	2	.950	4	*3-112,D-28,2-16	3.4
1990	Mil-A	103	418	64	119	27	6	12	45	37	51	.285	.344	.464	125	13	18	3	4	.988	-1	2-60,1-37/3-2,D-4	1.4
1991	Mil-A★	158	665	133	216	32	13	17	75	77	62	.325	.400	.489	148	45	19	8	1	.986	-1	*D-112,1-46	3.6
1992	Mil-A★	158	609	89	195	36	7	12	89	73	66	.320	.396	.461	142	36	31	6	6	.996	-4	*D-108,1-48	3.1
1993	*Tor-A★	160	636	121	211	37	5	22	111	77	71	.332	.406	.509	144	40	22	4	4	.985	-1	*D-137,1-23	3.5
1994	Tor-A★	115	454	86	155	30	4	14	75	55	48	.341	.414	.518	138	27	20	0	6	1.000	0	*D-110/1-5	2.4
1995	Tor-A	130	525	63	142	31	2	15	60	61	57	.270	.352	.423	101	1	12	0	4	.000	0	*D-129	-0.4
1996	Min-A	161	660	99	225	41	8	9	113	56	72	.341	.395	.468	115	16	18	6	0	.993	7	*D-143,1-17	1.9
Total	19	2422	9795	1644	3014	544	105	220	1149	1004	1130	.308	.375	.452	125		351	484	125	70	.950	-20	D-937,3-791,21/SO	35.3

■ FRED MOLLENKAMP
Mollenkamp, Frederick Henry b: 3/15/1890, Cincinnati, Ohio d: 11/1/48, Cincinnati, Ohio Deb: 8/29/14

YEAR	TM/L	G	AB	R	H	2B	3B	HR	RBI	BB	SO	AVG	OBP	SLG	PRO+	BR/A	SB	CS	SBR	FA	FR	G/POS	TPR
1914	Phi-N	3	8	0	1	0	0	0	0	2	0	.125	.300	.125	26	-1	0	0	0	1.000	2	/1-3	0.1

■ FRITZ MOLLWITZ
Mollwitz, Frederick August b: 6/16/1890, Coburg, Germany d: 10/3/67, Bradenton, Fla. BR/TR, 6′2″, 170 lbs. Deb: 9/26/13

YEAR	TM/L	G	AB	R	H	2B	3B	HR	RBI	BB	SO	AVG	OBP	SLG	PRO+	BR/A	SB	CS	SBR	FA	FR	G/POS	TPR
1913	Chi-N	2	7	1	3	0	0	0	0	0	0	.429	.429	.429	145	0	0	0		1.000	-0	/1-2	0.0

YEAR	TM/L	G	AB	R	H	2B	3B	HR	RBI	BB	SO	AVG	OBP	SLG	PRO+	BR/A	SB	CS	SBR	FA	FR	G/POS	TPR
1914	Chi-N	13	20	0	3	0	0	0	1	0	3	.150	.150	.150	-11	-3	1			.962	-1	/1-4,O-1	-0.4
	Cin-N	32	111	12	18	2	0	0	5	3	9	.162	.198	.180	12	-12	2			.991	1	1-32	-1.3
	Yr	45	131	12	21	2	0	0	6	3	12	.160	.191	.176	9	-15	3			.989	0	1-36/O-1	-1.7
1915	Cin-N	153	525	36	136	21	3	1	51	15	49	.259	.281	.316	79	-14	19	11	-1	.996	0	*1-153	-2.2
1916	Cin-N	65	183	12	41	4	4	0	16	5	12	.224	.245	.290	65	-8	6			.981	-1	1-54	-1.2
	Chi-N	33	71	1	19	2	0	0	11	7	6	.268	.333	.296	85	-1	4			.976	-1	1-19/O-6	-0.3
	Yr	98	254	13	60	6	4	0	27	12	18	.236	.271	.291	71	-9	10			.980	-2	1-73/O-6	-1.5
1917	Pit-N	36	140	15	36	1	0	0	12	8	8	.257	.297	.300	81	-3	4			.994	-1	1-36/2-1	-0.6
1918	Pit-N	119	432	43	116	12	7	0	45	23	24	.269	.305	.329	90	-6	23			.990	-0	*1-119	-1.2
1919	Pit-N	56	168	11	29	2	4	0	12	15	18	.173	.249	.232	43	-11	9			.994	-3	1-53/O-1	-1.8
	StL-N	25	83	7	19	3	0	0	5	7	3	.229	.282	.265	71	-3	2			.994	1	1-25	-0.3
	Yr	81	251	18	48	5	4	0	17	22	21	.191	.262	.243	52	-14	11			.994	-3	1-78/O-1	-2.1
Total	7	534	1740	138	420	50	19	1	158	83	132	.241	.278	.294	72	-61	70	11		.991	-6	1-497/O-8,2-1	-9.3

■ BLAS MONACO
Monaco, Blas b: 11/16/15, San Antonio, Tex. BB/TR, 5'11", 170 lbs. Deb: 8/18/37

YEAR	TM/L	G	AB	R	H	2B	3B	HR	RBI	BB	SO	AVG	OBP	SLG	PRO+	BR/A	SB	CS	SBR	FA	FR	G/POS	TPR
1937	Cle-A	5	7	0	2	0	0	0	2	0	2	.286	.375	.571	134	0	0	0	0	1.000	0	/2-3	0.1
1946	Cle-A	12	6	2	0	0	0	0	0	1	1	.000	.143	.000	-62	-1	0	0	0	1.000	0	H	-0.1
Total	2	17	13	2	2	0	0	0	2	1	3	.154	.267	.308	53	-1	0	0	0	1.000	0	/2-3	0.0

■ FREDDIE MONCEWICZ
Moncewicz, Frederick Alfred b: 9/1/03, Brockton, Mass. d: 4/23/69, Brockton, Mass. BR/TR, 5'8.5", 175 lbs. Deb: 6/19/28

YEAR	TM/L	G	AB	R	H	2B	3B	HR	RBI	BB	SO	AVG	OBP	SLG	PRO+	BR/A	SB	CS	SBR	FA	FR	G/POS	TPR
1928	Bos-A	3	1	0	0	0	0	0	0	0	0	.000	.000	.000	-99	-0	0	0	0	1.000	0	/S-2	0.0

■ ALEX MONCHAK
Monchak, Alex b: 12/22/19, Bayonne, N.J. BR/TR, 6', 180 lbs. Deb: 6/22/40 C

YEAR	TM/L	G	AB	R	H	2B	3B	HR	RBI	BB	SO	AVG	OBP	SLG	PRO+	BR/A	SB	CS	SBR	FA	FR	G/POS	TPR
1940	Phi-N	19	14	1	2	0	0	0	0	0	6	.143	.143	.143	-22	-2	1			.833	0	/S-9,2-1	-0.2

■ RICK MONDAY
Monday, Robert James b: 11/20/45, Batesville, Ark. BL/TL, 6'3", 200 lbs. Deb: 9/3/66

YEAR	TM/L	G	AB	R	H	2B	3B	HR	RBI	BB	SO	AVG	OBP	SLG	PRO+	BR/A	SB	CS	SBR	FA	FR	G/POS	TPR
1966	KC-A	17	41	4	4	1	0	2	6	16	.098	.213	.171	12	-5	1	1	-0	.964	-1	O-15	-0.7
1967	KC-A	124	406	52	102	14	6	14	58	42	107	.251	.324	.419	122	10	3	6	-3	.972	15	*O-113	1.9
1968	Oak-A★	148	482	56	132	24	7	8	49	72	143	.274	.373	.402	142	26	14	6	1	.978	-0	*O-144	2.2
1969	Oak-A	122	399	57	108	17	4	12	54	72	100	.271	.389	.424	133	20	12	3	2	.964	-2	*O-119	1.5
1970	Oak-A	112	376	63	109	19	7	10	37	58	99	.290	.388	.457	137	20	17	11	-0	.981	1	*O-109	1.5
1971	*Oak-A	116	355	53	87	9	5	18	56	49	93	.245	.337	.439	121	9	6	9	-4	.984	-0	*O-111	0.1
1972	Chi-N	138	434	68	108	22	5	11	42	78	102	.249	.365	.399	105	5	12	9	-2	.996	-6	*O-134	-0.9
1973	Chi-N	149	554	93	148	24	5	26	56	92	124	.267	.372	.469	123	18	5	12	-6	.973	1	*O-148	0.7
1974	Chi-N	142	538	84	158	19	7	20	58	70	94	.294	.377	.467	130	22	7	9	-3	.984	2	*O-139	1.5
1975	Chi-N	136	491	89	131	29	4	17	60	83	95	.267	.374	.446	121	15	8	3	1	.973	1	*O-131	1.2
1976	Chi-N	137	534	107	145	20	5	32	77	60	125	.272	.347	.507	129	18	5	9	-4	.993	7	*O-103,1-32	1.6
1977	*LA-N	118	392	47	90	13	1	15	48	60	109	.230	.332	.383	91	-4	1	4	-2	.991	-11	O-115/1-3	-2.2
1978	*LA-N★	119	342	54	87	14	1	19	57	49	100	.254	.349	.468	127	12	4	2	-2	.995	-11	O-103/1-1	-0.5
1979	LA-N	12	33	2	10	0	0	2	5	6	.303	.395	.303	94	0	0	0	0	.964	-0	O-10	0.0
1980	LA-N	96	194	35	52	7	1	10	25	28	49	.268	.363	.469	133	9	2	2	-1	.969	-7	O-50	-0.1
1981	*LA-N	66	130	24	41	1	2	11	25	24	42	.315	.426	.608	198	17	1	2	-1	.962	-6	O-41	1.0
1982	*LA-N	104	210	37	54	6	4	11	42	39	51	.257	.376	.481	142	12	2	1	-0	.943	-7	O-57/1-4	0.4
1983	*LA-N	99	178	21	44	7	1	6	20	29	42	.247	.353	.399	108	3	0	0	0	.969	-4	O-44/1-4	-0.3
1984	LA-N	31	47	4	9	2	0	1	7	8	16	.191	.309	.298	72	-2	0	0	0	.987	-1	1-10/O-2	-0.4
Total	19	1986	6136	950	1619	248	64	241	775	924	1513	.264	.362	.443	124	207	98	91	-25	.979	-29	*O-1688/1-54	8.5

■ RAUL MONDESI
Mondesi, Raul Ramon (Avelino) b: 3/12/71, San Cristobal, D.R. BR/TR, 5'11", 202 lbs. Deb: 7/19/93

YEAR	TM/L	G	AB	R	H	2B	3B	HR	RBI	BB	SO	AVG	OBP	SLG	PRO+	BR/A	SB	CS	SBR	FA	FR	G/POS	TPR
1993	LA-N	42	86	13	25	3	1	4	10	4	16	.291	.322	.488	120	2	4	1	-0	.951	-5	O-40	-0.2
1994	LA-N	112	434	63	133	27	8	16	56	16	78	.306	.334	.516	126	13	11	8	-2	.965	2	*O-112	1.1
1995	*LA-N★	139	536	91	153	23	6	26	88	33	96	.285	.332	.496	126	16	27	4	6	.980	14	*O-138	3.2
1996	*LA-N	157	634	98	188	40	7	24	88	32	122	.297	.335	.495	126	20	14	7	0	.967	16	*O-157	3.0
Total	4	450	1690	265	499	93	22	70	242	85	312	.295	.333	.501	126	52	56	20	5	.970	28	O-447	7.1

■ DON MONEY
Money, Donald Wayne "Brooks" b: 6/7/47, Washington, D.C. BR/TR, 6'1", 190 lbs. Deb: 4/10/68

YEAR	TM/L	G	AB	R	H	2B	3B	HR	RBI	BB	SO	AVG	OBP	SLG	PRO+	BR/A	SB	CS	SBR	FA	FR	G/POS	TPR
1968	Phi-N	4	13	1	3	2	0	0	2	2	4	.231	.333	.385	115	0	0	1	-1	1.000	-1	/S-4	-0.1
1969	Phi-N	127	450	41	103	22	2	6	42	43	83	.229	.298	.327	77	-14	1	3	-2	.969	17	*S-126	1.6
1970	Phi-N	120	447	66	132	25	4	14	66	43	68	.295	.366	.463	124	15	4	7	-3	.961	11	*3-119/S-2	2.2
1971	Phi-N	121	439	40	98	22	7	7	38	31	80	.223	.279	.358	79	-13	4	1	1	.953	5	3-68,O-40,2-20	-0.8
1972	Phi-N	152	536	54	119	16	2	15	52	41	92	.222	.280	.343	74	-19	5	7	-3	.978	20	*3-151/S-2	-0.3
1973	Mil-A	145	556	75	158	28	2	11	61	53	56	.284	.350	.401	113	10	22	5	4	.971	-23	*3-124,S-21	-0.8
1974	Mil-A☆	159	629	85	178	32	3	15	65	62	80	.283	.349	.415	120	16	19	6	2	.989	-10	*3-157/2-1,D-1	-0.4
1975	Mil-A	109	405	58	112	16	1	9	43	31	51	.277	.333	.432	114	7	7	9	-3	.951	-21	3-99/S-7	-1.8
1976	Mil-A★	117	439	51	117	18	4	12	62	47	50	.267	.337	.408	120	11	6	5	-1	.958	-4	*3-103,D-10/S-1	0.4
1977	Mil-A†	152	570	86	159	28	3	25	83	57	70	.279	.352	.470	122	17	8	5	-1	.981	-3	*2-116,O-23,3-15/D	1.2
1978	Mil-A★	137	518	88	152	30	2	14	54	48	70	.293	.361	.440	124	16	3	0	1	.994	-2	1-61,2-36,3-25,D/S	1.4
1979	Mil-A	92	350	52	83	20	1	6	38	40	47	.237	.319	.351	81	-9	1	0	0	1.000	-7	D-33,3-26,1-19,2-16	-1.2
1980	Mil-A	86	289	39	74	11	1	17	46	40	36	.256	.348	.498	133	13	0	0	0	.940	0	3-55,1-14,D-14,/2-2	1.1
1981	*Mil-A	60	185	17	40	7	0	2	14	19	27	.216	.293	.286	71	-7	0	0	0	.977	-5	3-56/1-1,D-2	-1.3
1982	*Mil-A	96	275	40	78	14	3	16	55	32	38	.284	.360	.531	150	18	0	2	-1	.923	5	D-66,3-16,1-11,/2-1	1.8
1983	Mil-A	43	114	5	17	5	0	1	8	11	17	.149	.224	.219	24	-12	0	0	0	.980	-8	D-28,3-11/1-2	-0.9
Total	16	1720	6215	798	1623	302	36	176	729	600	866	.261	.330	.406	106	49	80	51	-7	.968	-9	*3-1025,2-192,DS1/O	4.1

■ FRANK MONROE
Monroe, Frank W. b: Hamilton, Ohio Deb: 7/18/1884

YEAR	TM/L	G	AB	R	H	2B	3B	HR	RBI	BB	SO	AVG	OBP	SLG	PRO+	BR/A	SB	CS	SBR	FA	FR	G/POS	TPR
1884	Ind-a	2	8	1	0	0	0	0	0			.000	.000	.000	-99	-2				1.000	-1	/O-1,C-1	-0.3

■ JOHN MONROE
Monroe, John Allen b: 8/24/1898, Farmersville, Tex. d: 6/19/56, Conroe, Tex. BL/TR, 5'10", 160 lbs. Deb: 4/16/21

YEAR	TM/L	G	AB	R	H	2B	3B	HR	RBI	BB	SO	AVG	OBP	SLG	PRO+	BR/A	SB	CS	SBR	FA	FR	G/POS	TPR
1921	NY-N	19	21	4	3	0	1	0	3	3	6	.143	.280	.286	50	-2	0	0	0	.846	2	/2-8,S-1	0.0
	Phi-N	41	133	13	38	4	2	1	8	11	9	.286	.345	.368	82	-3	2	2	-1	.938	5	2-28/3-9	0.3
	Yr	60	154	17	41	4	2	1	11	14	15	.266	.335	.357	79	-4	2	2	-1	.920	7	2-36/3-9,S-1	0.3

■ ED MONTAGUE
Montague, Edward Francis b: 7/24/05, San Francisco, Cal. d: 6/17/88, Daly City, Cal. BR/TR, 5'10", 165 lbs. Deb: 5/14/28

YEAR	TM/L	G	AB	R	H	2B	3B	HR	RBI	BB	SO	AVG	OBP	SLG	PRO+	BR/A	SB	CS	SBR	FA	FR	G/POS	TPR
1928	Cle-A	32	51	12	12	0	1	0	3	6	7	.235	.339	.275	62	-3	1			.914	5	S-15/3-9	0.4
1930	Cle-A	58	179	37	47	5	2	1	16	37	38	.263	.392	.330	82	-3	1	5	-3	.917	-15	S-46,3-13	-1.4
1931	Cle-A	64	193	27	55	8	3	1	26	21	22	.285	.358	.373	87	-3	3	4	-2	.924	16	S-64	1.5
1932	Cle-A	66	192	29	47	5	1	0	24	21	24	.245	.326	.281	55	-12	2	3	-1	.891	-13	S-57,3-11	-2.1
Total	4	220	615	105	161	18	7	2	69	85	91	.262	.357	.324	74	-21	7	12	-5	.912	-7	S-182/3-33	-1.6

■ WILLIE MONTANEZ
Montanez, Guillermo (Naranjo) b: 4/1/48, Catano, P.R. BL/TL, 6'1", 193 lbs. Deb: 4/12/66

YEAR	TM/L	G	AB	R	H	2B	3B	HR	RBI	BB	SO	AVG	OBP	SLG	PRO+	BR/A	SB	CS	SBR	FA	FR	G/POS	TPR
1966	Cal-A	8	12	0	0	0	0	0	0	0	2	.000	.000	.000	-99	-1	0	0	0	1.000	0	/1-2	0.0
1970	Phi-N	18	25	3	6	0	0	0	3	1	4	.240	.269	.240	39	-2	0	0	0	1.000	-1	O-10/1-5	-0.3
1971	Phi-N	158	599	78	153	27	6	30	99	67	105	.255	.333	.471	126	19	4	7	-3	.972	5	*O-158/1-9	1.3
1972	Phi-N	147	531	60	131	39	3	13	64	58	108	.247	.322	.405	103	2	1	3	-2	.985	14	*O-130,1-14	0.8
1973	Phi-N	146	552	69	145	16	5	11	65	46	80	.263	.326	.370	90	-7	2	6	-3	.994	-6	1-99,O-51	-2.7
1974	Phi-N	143	527	55	160	33	4	7	79	32	57	.304	.347	.410	107	4	3	8	-3	.992	1	*1-137/O-1	-1.0
1975	Phi-N	21	84	9	24	8	1	0	4	12	12	.286	.318	.452	108	0	1	0	0	.990	2	1-21	0.1
	SF-N	135	518	52	158	26	2	8	85	45	50	.305	.365	.409	110	7	5	3	-0	.994	-1	*1-134	-0.3
	Yr	156	602	61	182	34	3	10	101	49	62	.302	.359	.415	110	8	6	3	0	.993	0	*1-155	-0.2
1976	SF-N	60	230	22	71	15	2	0	20	15	14	.309	.354	.417	115	4	0	2	-1	.989	4	1-58	0.4
	Atl-N	103	420	52	135	14	0	9	64	21	32	.321	.354	.419	112	6	0	4	-2	.986	-6	*1-103	-1.0
	Yr	163	650	74	206	29	2	9	84	36	46	.317	.354	.418	113	10	0	6	-2	.987	-1	*1-161	-0.6
1977	Atl-N★	136	544	70	156	31	1	20	68	35	60	.287	.330	.458	97	-3	1	1	-0	.992	-4	*1-134	-1.6

YEAR	TM/L	G	AB	R	H	2B	3B	HR	RBI	BB	SO	AVG	OBP	SLG	PRO+	BR/A	SB	CS	SBR	FA	FR	G/POS	TPR
1978	NY-N	159	609	66	156	32	0	17	96	60	92	.256	.324	.392	103	1	9	4	0	.995	3	*1-158	-0.6
1979	NY-N	109	410	36	96	19	0	5	47	25	48	.234	.280	.317	65	-21	0	1	-1	.989	3	*1-108	-2.6
	Tex-A	38	144	19	46	6	0	8	24	8	14	.319	.359	.528	137	7	0	1	-1	.995	1	1-19,D-17	0.6
1980	SD-N	128	481	39	132	12	4	6	63	36	52	.274	.329	.353	96	-3	3	4	-2	.994	1	*1-124	-1.1
	Mon-N	14	19	1	4	0	0	0	1	3	3	.211	.318	.211	50	-1	0	1	-1	1.000	0	/1-4	-0.2
	Yr	142	500	40	136	12	4	6	64	39	55	.272	.328	.348	94	-4	3	5	-2	.994	1	*1-128	-1.3
1981	Mon-N	26	62	6	11	0	1	0	5	4	9	.177	.227	.210	24	-6	0	0	0	.992	1	1-16	-0.6
	Pit-N	29	38	2	10	0	0	1	1	1	2	.263	.282	.342	74	-1	0	-1	0	1.000	1	1-11	-0.3
	Yr	55	100	8	21	0	1	1	6	5	11	.210	.248	.260	43	-7	0	-1	0	.995	0	1-27	-0.9
1982	Pit-N	36	32	4	9	1	0	0	1	3	3	.281	.343	.313	82	-1	0	0	0	1.000	1	/1-2,O-2	-0.1
	Phi-N	18	16	0	1	0	0	0	1	1	3	.063	.118	.063	-47	-3	0	0	0	1.000	1	/1-6	-0.2
	Yr	54	48	4	10	1	0	0	2	4	6	.208	.269	.229	40	-4	0	0	0	1.000	1	/1-8,O-2	-0.4
Total	14	1632	5843	645	1604	279	25	139	802	465	751	.275	.331	.402	101	1	32	42	-16	.992	15	*1-1164,O-352/D-17	-9.5

■ RENE MONTEAGUDO   Monteagudo, Rene (Miranda)   b: 3/12/16, Havana, Cuba   d: 9/14/73, Hialeah, Fla.   BL/TL, 5'7", 165 lbs.   Deb: 9/6/38   F

YEAR	TM/L	G	AB	R	H	2B	3B	HR	RBI	BB	SO	AVG	OBP	SLG	PRO+	BR/A	SB	CS	SBR	FA	FR	G/POS	TPR
1938	Was-A	5	6	0	3	0	0	0	1	0	0	.500	.500	.500	162	1	0	0	0	1.000	-1	/P-5	0.0
1940	Was-A	27	33	4	6	1	0	0	1	1	4	.182	.206	.273	24	-4	0	0	0	.941	-1	P-27	-0.1
1944	Was-A	10	38	2	11	2	0	0	4	0	1	.289	.289	.342	84	-1	0	0	0	.929	-1	/O-9	-0.3
1945	Phi-N	114	193	26	58	6	0	0	15	28	7	.301	.389	.332	104	3	2			.918	-1	O-35,P-14	0.0
Total	4	156	270	32	78	9	1	0	21	29	12	.289	.358	.330	94	-2	2	0		.889	-4	/P-46,O-44	-0.3

■ FELIPE MONTEMAYOR   Montemayor, Felipe Angel "Monty"   b: 2/7/30, Monterrey, Mexico   BL/TL, 6'2", 185 lbs.   Deb: 4/14/53

YEAR	TM/L	G	AB	R	H	2B	3B	HR	RBI	BB	SO	AVG	OBP	SLG	PRO+	BR/A	SB	CS	SBR	FA	FR	G/POS	TPR
1953	Pit-N	28	55	5	6	4	0	0	2	4	13	.109	.210	.182	3	-8	0	0	0	1.000	1	O-12	-0.7
1955	Pit-N	36	95	10	20	1	3	2	8	18	24	.211	.342	.347	85	-2	0	0	0	.957	-5	O-28	-0.8
Total	2	64	150	15	26	5	3	2	10	22	37	.173	.295	.287	55	-10	0	0	0	.974	-5	/O-40	-1.5

■ AL MONTGOMERY   Montgomery, Alvin Atlas   b: 7/3/20, Loving, N.Mex.   d: 4/26/42, Waverly, Va.   BR/TR, 5'10.5", 185 lbs.   Deb: 6/20/41

YEAR	TM/L	G	AB	R	H	2B	3B	HR	RBI	BB	SO	AVG	OBP	SLG	PRO+	BR/A	SB	CS	SBR	FA	FR	G/POS	TPR
1941	Bos-N	42	52	4	10	1	0	0	4	9	8	.192	.323	.212	55	-3	0			.976	-6	C-30	-0.8

■ RAY MONTGOMERY   Montgomery, Raymond James   b: 8/8/69, Bronxville, N.Y.   BR/TR, 6'3", 195 lbs.   Deb: 7/3/96

YEAR	TM/L	G	AB	R	H	2B	3B	HR	RBI	BB	SO	AVG	OBP	SLG	PRO+	BR/A	SB	CS	SBR	FA	FR	G/POS	TPR
1996	Hou-N	12	14	4	3	1	0	1	4	1	5	.214	.267	.500	106	-0	0	0	0	1.000	-2	/O-6	-0.2

■ BOB MONTGOMERY   Montgomery, Robert Edward   b: 4/16/44, Nashville, Tenn.   BR/TR, 6'1", 203 lbs.   Deb: 9/6/70

YEAR	TM/L	G	AB	R	H	2B	3B	HR	RBI	BB	SO	AVG	OBP	SLG	PRO+	BR/A	SB	CS	SBR	FA	FR	G/POS	TPR
1970	Bos-A	22	78	8	14	2	0	1	4	6	20	.179	.247	.244	33	-7	0	0	0	.981	0	C-22	-0.6
1971	Bos-A	67	205	19	49	11	2	2	24	16	43	.239	.304	.341	77	-6	1	0	0	.989	-3	C-66	-0.7
1972	Bos-A	24	77	7	22	1	0	2	7	3	17	.286	.313	.377	99	-0	0	0	0	.985	-2	C-22	-0.2
1973	Bos-A	34	128	18	41	6	2	7	25	7	36	.320	.356	.563	146	7	0	0	0	.974	1	C-33	0.9
1974	Bos-A	88	254	26	64	10	0	4	38	13	50	.252	.291	.339	75	-8	3	0	1	.977	-6	C-79/D-5	-1.1
1975	*Bos-A	62	195	16	44	10	1	2	26	4	37	.226	.245	.318	53	-12	1	1	-0	.987	-5	C-53/1-6,D-3	-1.6
1976	Bos-A	31	93	10	23	3	1	3	13	5	20	.247	.286	.398	88	-2	0	1	-1	.983	-1	C-30/D-1	-0.2
1977	Bos-A	17	40	6	12	2	0	2	7	4	9	.300	.378	.500	123	1	0	0	0	.982	-0	C-15	0.1
1978	Bos-A	10	29	2	7	1	1	0	5	2	12	.241	.290	.345	70	-1	0	0	0	.976	0	C-10	-0.1
1979	Bos-A	32	86	13	30	4	1	0	7	4	24	.349	.378	.419	109	1	1	0	0	.984	-4	C-31	-0.2
Total	10	387	1185	125	306	50	8	23	156	64	268	.258	.300	.372	83	-28	6	2	1	.983	-19	C-361/D-9,1-6	-3.7

■ CHARLIE MONTOYO   Montoyo, Jose Carlos (Diaz)   b: 10/17/65, Florida, P.R.   BR/TR, 5'10", 170 lbs.   Deb: 9/7/93

YEAR	TM/L	G	AB	R	H	2B	3B	HR	RBI	BB	SO	AVG	OBP	SLG	PRO+	BR/A	SB	CS	SBR	FA	FR	G/POS	TPR
1993	Mon-N	4	5	1	2	1	0	0	3	4	0	.400	.400	.600	157	0	0	0	0	.000	0	/2-3	0.0

■ AL MONTREUIL   Montreuil, Allan Arthur   b: 8/23/43, New Orleans, La.   BR/TR, 5'5", 158 lbs.   Deb: 9/1/72

YEAR	TM/L	G	AB	R	H	2B	3B	HR	RBI	BB	SO	AVG	OBP	SLG	PRO+	BR/A	SB	CS	SBR	FA	FR	G/POS	TPR
1972	Chi-N	5	11	0	1	0	0	0	0	1	4	.091	.167	.091	-23	-2	0	0	0	1.000	0	/2-5	-0.2

■ DAN MONZON   Monzon, Daniel Francisco   b: 5/17/46, Bronx, N.Y.   d: 1/21/96, Santo Domingo, D.R.   BR/TR, 5'10", 182 lbs.   Deb: 4/25/72

YEAR	TM/L	G	AB	R	H	2B	3B	HR	RBI	BB	SO	AVG	OBP	SLG	PRO+	BR/A	SB	CS	SBR	FA	FR	G/POS	TPR
1972	Min-A	55	55	13	15	1	0	0	5	8	12	.273	.365	.291	92	-0	1	0	0	.977	9	2-13/3-5,S-3,O-1	1.1
1973	Min-A	39	76	10	17	1	1	0	4	11	9	.224	.330	.263	66	-3	1	0	0	.968	9	2-17,3-14/O-1	0.7
Total	2	94	131	23	32	2	1	0	9	19	21	.244	.344	.275	77	-3	2	0	1	.971	18	/2-30,3-19,S-3,O-2	1.8

■ JOE MOOCK   Moock, Joseph Geoffrey   b: 3/12/44, Plaquemine, La.   BL/TR, 6'1", 180 lbs.   Deb: 9/1/67

YEAR	TM/L	G	AB	R	H	2B	3B	HR	RBI	BB	SO	AVG	OBP	SLG	PRO+	BR/A	SB	CS	SBR	FA	FR	G/POS	TPR
1967	NY-N	13	40	2	9	0	0	0	5	0	7	.225	.225	.275	43	-3	0	0	0	.917	2	3-12	-0.2

■ GEORGE MOOLIC   Moolic, George Henry "Prunes"   b: 3/12/1865, Lawrence, Mass.   d: 2/19/15, Methuen, Mass.   BR/TR, 5'7", 145 lbs.   Deb: 5/1/1886

YEAR	TM/L	G	AB	R	H	2B	3B	HR	RBI	BB	SO	AVG	OBP	SLG	PRO+	BR/A	SB	CS	SBR	FA	FR	G/POS	TPR
1886	Chi-N	16	56	9	8	3	0	0	2	2	17	.143	.172	.196	10	-6	0			.945	3	C-15/O-2	-0.2

■ WALLY MOON   Moon, Wallace Wade   b: 4/3/30, Bay, Ark.   BL/TR, 6', 175 lbs.   Deb: 4/13/54   C

YEAR	TM/L	G	AB	R	H	2B	3B	HR	RBI	BB	SO	AVG	OBP	SLG	PRO+	BR/A	SB	CS	SBR	FA	FR	G/POS	TPR
1954	StL-N	151	635	106	193	29	9	12	76	71	73	.304	.375	.435	109	10	18	10	-1	.978	2	*O-148	0.4
1955	StL-N	152	593	86	175	24	8	19	76	47	65	.295	.350	.459	113	10	11	11	-3	.975	-9	*O-100,1-51	-1.0
1956	StL-N	149	540	86	161	22	11	16	68	80	50	.298	.390	.469	129	24	12	9	-2	.988	0	*O-97,1-52	1.5
1957	StL-N★	142	516	86	152	28	5	24	73	62	57	.295	.371	.508	131	22	5	6	-2	.966	-9	*O-133	0.4
1958	StL-N	108	290	36	69	10	3	7	38	47	30	.238	.344	.366	85	-5	2	3	-1	.984	-8	O-82	-1.9
1959	*LA-N★	145	543	93	164	26	11	19	74	81	64	.302	.396	.495	126	22	15	6	1	.983	-4	*O-143/1-1	1.2
1960	LA-N	138	469	74	140	21	6	13	69	67	53	.299	.387	.452	121	15	6	10	-4	.986	4	*O-127	0.9
1961	LA-N	134	463	79	152	25	3	17	88	89	79	.328	**.438**	.505	137	28	7	5	-1	.970	-9	*O-133	1.5
1962	LA-N	95	244	36	59	9	1	4	31	30	33	.242	.327	.336	84	-5	5	2	0	.981	-2	O-36,1-32	-1.1
1963	LA-N	122	343	41	90	13	2	8	48	45	43	.262	.350	.382	119	9	5	5	-2	.962	-13	O-96	-1.1
1964	LA-N	68	118	8	26	2	1	0	9	12	22	.220	.292	.305	74	-4	1	1	-0	1.000	4	O-23	-0.7
1965	*LA-N	53	89	6	18	3	0	1	11	13	22	.202	.304	.270	67	-4	2	0	1	1.000	-2	O-23	-0.7
Total	12	1457	4843	737	1399	212	60	142	661	644	591	.289	.374	.445	117	123	89	68	-14	.978	-50	*O-1141,1-136	-1.0

■ AL MOORE   Moore, Albert James   b: 8/4/02, Brooklyn, N.Y.   d: 11/29/74, AtSea N.Y.To P.R   BR/TR, 5'10", 174 lbs.   Deb: 9/27/25

YEAR	TM/L	G	AB	R	H	2B	3B	HR	RBI	BB	SO	AVG	OBP	SLG	PRO+	BR/A	SB	CS	SBR	FA	FR	G/POS	TPR
1925	NY-N	2	8	1	1	0	0	0	0	0	2	.125	.222	.125	-9	-1	0	1	-1	1.000	-0	/O-2	-0.2
1926	NY-N	28	81	12	18	4	0	0	10	5	7	.222	.267	.272	46	-6	2			.966	3	O-20	-0.5
Total	2	30	89	12	19	4	0	0	10	5	9	.213	.263	.258	41	-7	2	1		.968	3	/O-22	-0.7

■ JUNIOR MOORE   Moore, Alvin Earl   b: 1/25/53, Waskom, Tex.   BR/TR, 5'11", 185 lbs.   Deb: 8/2/76

YEAR	TM/L	G	AB	R	H	2B	3B	HR	RBI	BB	SO	AVG	OBP	SLG	PRO+	BR/A	SB	CS	SBR	FA	FR	G/POS	TPR
1976	Atl-N	20	26	1	7	1	0	0	2	4	4	.269	.387	.308	93	0	0	0	0	.929	1	/3-6,2-1,O-1	0.1
1977	Atl-N	112	361	41	94	9	3	5	34	33	29	.260	.324	.343	71	-15	4	5	-2	.942	-4	*3-104/2-1	-2.2
1978	Chi-A	24	65	8	19	4	0	0	8	6	7	.292	.352	.323	90	-1	0	0	0	.857	-0	D-12/3-6,O-5	-0.2
1979	Chi-A	88	201	24	53	6	2	1	23	12	20	.264	.305	.328	71	-8	0	2	-1	.966	-9	O-61,D-10/2-2	-2.0
1980	Chi-A	45	121	9	31	4	1	1	10	7	11	.256	.297	.347	72	-5	0	2	-1	.929	-2	3-34/O-3,1-1,D-2	-0.9
Total	5	289	774	83	204	20	7	7	73	62	71	.264	.320	.335	73	-28	5	10	-5	.936	-14	3-150/O-70,D-24,21	-5.2

■ ANSE MOORE   Moore, Ansel Winn   b: 9/22/17, Delhi, La.   d: 10/29/93, Pearl, Miss.   BL/TR, 6'1", 190 lbs.   Deb: 4/17/46

YEAR	TM/L	G	AB	R	H	2B	3B	HR	RBI	BB	SO	AVG	OBP	SLG	PRO+	BR/A	SB	CS	SBR	FA	FR	G/POS	TPR
1946	Det-A	51	134	16	28	4	0	1	8	12	9	.209	.279	.261	48	-7	1	1	-0	.971	1	O-32	-1.1

■ ARCHIE MOORE   Moore, Archie Francis   b: 8/30/41, Upper Darby, Pa.   BL/TL, 6'2", 190 lbs.   Deb: 4/20/64

YEAR	TM/L	G	AB	R	H	2B	3B	HR	RBI	BB	SO	AVG	OBP	SLG	PRO+	BR/A	SB	CS	SBR	FA	FR	G/POS	TPR
1964	NY-A	31	23	4	4	2	0	1	2	9	2	.174	.240	.261	39	-2	0	0	0	1.000	-2	/O-8,1-7	-0.4
1965	NY-A	9	17	1	7	2	0	1	4	4	11	.412	.524	.706	248	2	0	0	0	.889	-0	/O-5	0.3
Total	2	40	40	5	11	4	0	2	6	13	4	.275	.370	.450	128	2	0	0	0	.929	-2	/O-13,1-7	-0.1

■ CHARLEY MOORE   Moore, Charles Wesley   b: 12/1/1884, Jackson Co., Ind.   d: 7/29/70, Portland, Ore.   BR/TR, 5'10", 160 lbs.   Deb: 4/16/12

YEAR	TM/L	G	AB	R	H	2B	3B	HR	RBI	BB	SO	AVG	OBP	SLG	PRO+	BR/A	SB	CS	SBR	FA	FR	G/POS	TPR
1912	Chi-N	5	9	2	2	0	1	0	2	0	1	.222	.222	.444	80	-0	0			.800	1	/S-2,1-2,3-1	0.0

■ CHARLIE MOORE   Moore, Charles William   b: 6/21/53, Birmingham, Ala.   BR/TR, 5'11", 180 lbs.   Deb: 9/8/73

YEAR	TM/L	G	AB	R	H	2B	3B	HR	RBI	BB	SO	AVG	OBP	SLG	PRO+	BR/A	SB	CS	SBR	FA	FR	G/POS	TPR
1973	Mil-A	8	27	0	5	1	0	0	3	2	5	.185	.241	.259	42	-2	0	0	0	.981	3	/C-8	0.1

YEAR	TM/L	G	AB	R	H	2B	3B	HR	RBI	BB	SO	AVG	OBP	SLG	PRO+	BR/A	SB	CS	SBR	FA	FR	G/POS	TPR
1974	Mil-A	72	204	17	50	10	4	0	19	21	34	.245	.316	.333	87	-3	3	4	-2	.985	3	C-61/D-6	0.0
1975	Mil-A	73	241	26	70	20	1	1	29	17	31	.290	.337	.394	106	1	1	5	-3	.960	-6	C-47,O-22/D-1	-0.6
1976	Mil-A	87	241	33	46	7	4	3	16	43	45	.191	.316	.290	80	-5	1	2	-1	.969	-3	C-49,O-28/3-1,D-2	-0.9
1977	Mil-A	138	375	42	93	15	6	5	45	31	39	.248	.307	.360	81	-10	1	7	-4	.980	-7	*C-137	-1.7
1978	Mil-A	96	268	30	72	7	1	5	31	12	24	.269	.300	.358	84	-6	4	2	0	.983	-2	C-95	-0.6
1979	Mil-A	111	337	45	101	16	2	5	38	29	32	.300	.357	.404	105	3	8	5	-1	.979	9	*C-106	1.4
1980	Mil-A	111	320	42	93	13	2	3	30	24	28	.291	.340	.363	96	-2	10	5	0	.989	-15	*C-105	-1.3
1981	*Mil-A	48	156	16	47	8	3	1	9	12	13	.301	.351	.410	125	5	1	4	-2	.970	-0	C-34/O-8,D-6	0.3
1982	*Mil-A	133	456	53	116	22	4	6	45	29	49	.254	.300	.360	86	-10	2	10	-5	.988	5	*O-115,C-20/2-1	-1.2
1983	Mil-A	151	529	65	150	27	6	2	49	55	42	.284	.355	.369	108	7	11	4	1	.978	0	*O-150/C-7,D-1	0.3
1984	Mil-A	70	188	13	44	7	1	2	17	10	26	.234	.276	.314	66	-9	0	4	-2	.984	-3	O-61/C-3	-1.6
1985	Mil-A	105	349	35	81	13	4	0	31	27	53	.232	.289	.292	60	-19	4	0	1	.977	5	*C-102/O-3	-0.8
1986	Mil-A	80	235	24	61	12	3	3	39	21	38	.260	.320	.374	86	-5	5	5	-2	.992	13	C-72/O-4,2-1,D-2	1.0
1987	Tor-A	51	107	15	23	10	1	1	7	13	12	.215	.306	.355	73	-4	0	0	0	.984	6	C-44/O-5	0.4
Total	15	1334	4033	456	1052	187	43	36	408	346	470	.261	.321	.355	89	-59	51	57	-19	.980	9	C-894,O-396/D23	-5.2

■ **DEE MOORE**   Moore, D C   b: 4/6/14, Hedley, Tex.   BR/TR, 5'11", 190 lbs.   Deb: 9/12/36

YEAR	TM/L	G	AB	R	H	2B	3B	HR	RBI	BB	SO	AVG	OBP	SLG	PRO+	BR/A	SB	CS	SBR	FA	FR	G/POS	TPR
1936	Cin-N	6	10	4	4	2	1	0	1	0	3	.400	.400	.800	230	2	0			1.000	-0	/P-2,C-1	0.0
1937	Cin-N	7	13	2	1	0	0	0	0	1	2	.077	.200	.077	-23	-2	0			.931	2	/C-6	0.0
1943	Bro-N	37	79	8	20	3	0	0	12	11	8	.253	.344	.291	84	-1	1			.982	-6	C-15/3-9	-0.7
	Phi-N	37	113	13	27	4	1	1	8	15	8	.239	.328	.319	91	-1	0			.960	-0	C-21/O-6,3-5,1-1	0.0
	Yr	74	192	21	47	7	1	1	20	26	16	.245	.335	.307	88	-2	1			.968	-7	C-36,3-14/O-6,1-1	-0.7
1946	Phi-N	11	13	2	1	0	0	0	1	7	3	.077	.400	.077	41	-0	0			1.000	-0	/C-6,1-2	0.0
Total	4	98	228	29	53	9	2	1	22	34	24	.232	.335	.303	85	-3	1			.962	-5	/C-49,3-14,O-6,1P	-0.7

■ **GENE MOORE**   Moore, Eugene Jr. "Rowdy"   b: 8/26/09, Lancaster, Tex.   d: 3/12/78, Jackson, Miss.   BL/TL, 5'11", 175 lbs.   Deb: 9/19/31   F

YEAR	TM/L	G	AB	R	H	2B	3B	HR	RBI	BB	SO	AVG	OBP	SLG	PRO+	BR/A	SB	CS	SBR	FA	FR	G/POS	TPR
1931	Cin-N	4	14	2	2	1	0	0	1	0	0	.143	.143	.214	-6	-2	0			1.000	-0	/O-3	-0.2
1933	StL-N	11	38	6	15	3	2	0	8	4	10	.395	.452	.579	183	4	1			.967	0	O-10	0.4
1934	StL-N	9	18	2	5	1	0	0	1	2	2	.278	.350	.333	79	-0	0			.923	1	/O-3	0.0
1935	StL-N	3	3	0	0	0	0	0	0	0	1	.000	.000	.000	-96	-1	0			.000	0	H	-0.1
1936	Bos-N	151	637	91	185	38	12	13	67	40	80	.290	.335	.449	117	12	6			.977	15	*O-151	2.0
1937	Bos-N☆	148	561	88	159	29	10	16	70	61	73	.283	.358	.456	132	23	11			.978	14	*O-148	3.1
1938	Bos-N	54	180	27	49	8	3	3	19	16	20	.272	.338	.400	114	3	1			.981	1	O-47	0.2
1939	Bro-N	107	306	45	69	13	6	3	39	40	50	.225	.315	.337	73	-12	4			.961	-6	O-86/1-1	-2.1
1940	Bro-N	10	26	3	7	2	0	0	2	1	3	.269	.296	.346	72	-1	0			1.000	-1	/O-6	-0.2
	Bos-N	103	363	46	106	24	5	5	39	25	32	.292	.338	.405	110	4	2			.986	6	O-94	0.6
	Yr	113	389	49	113	26	5	5	41	26	35	.290	.335	.401	107	3	2			.986	5	*O-100	0.4
1941	Bos-N	129	397	42	108	17	8	5	43	45	37	.272	.349	.393	114	7	5			.968	4	*O-110	0.5
1942	Was-A	1	2	0	0	0	0	0	0	0	1	.000	.000	.000	-99	-1	0	0	0	.000	-1	/O-1	-0.1
1943	Was-A	92	254	41	68	14	3	2	39	39	29	.268	.321	.370	106	1	0	2	-1	.985	0	O-57/1-1	-0.3
1944	*StL-A	110	390	56	93	13	6	6	58	24	37	.238	.284	.349	76	-13	0	5	-3	.968	2	O-98/1-1	-2.1
1945	StL-A	110	354	48	92	16	2	5	50	40	26	.260	.337	.359	97	-1	1	3	-2	.970	-3	*O-100	-1.2
Total	14	1042	3543	497	958	179	53	58	436	317	401	.270	.333	.400	105	24	31	10		.975	32	O-914/1-3	0.5

■ **FERDIE MOORE**   Moore, Ferdinand Depage   b: 2/21/1896, Camden, N.J.   d: 5/6/47, Atlantic City, N.J.   Deb: 10/2/14

YEAR	TM/L	G	AB	R	H	2B	3B	HR	RBI	BB	SO	AVG	OBP	SLG	PRO+	BR/A	SB	CS	SBR	FA	FR	G/POS	TPR
1914	Phi-A	2	4	1	2	0	0	0	1	0	2	.500	.500	.500	209	0	0			.895	-1	/1-2	0.0

■ **GARY MOORE**   Moore, Gary Douglas   b: 2/24/45, Tulsa, Okla.   BR/TL, 5'10", 175 lbs.   Deb: 5/3/70

YEAR	TM/L	G	AB	R	H	2B	3B	HR	RBI	BB	SO	AVG	OBP	SLG	PRO+	BR/A	SB	CS	SBR	FA	FR	G/POS	TPR
1970	LA-N	7	16	2	3	0	2	0	0	0	1	.188	.188	.438	65	-1	1	0	0	1.000	-1	/O-5,1-1	-0.2

■ **EDDIE MOORE**   Moore, Graham Edward   b: 1/18/1899, Barlow, Ky.   d: 2/10/76, Ft.Myers, Fla.   BR/TR, 5'7", 165 lbs.   Deb: 9/25/23

YEAR	TM/L	G	AB	R	H	2B	3B	HR	RBI	BB	SO	AVG	OBP	SLG	PRO+	BR/A	SB	CS	SBR	FA	FR	G/POS	TPR
1923	Pit-N	6	26	6	7	1	0	0	1	2	3	.269	.321	.308	65	-1	1	0	0	.923	-5	/S-6	-0.5
1924	Pit-N	72	209	47	75	8	4	2	13	27	12	.359	.437	.464	139	13	6	7	-2	.988	4	O-35,3-13/2-4	1.3
1925	*Pit-N	142	547	106	163	29	8	6	77	73	26	.298	.383	.413	97	-1	19	7	2	.952	-6	*2-122,O-15/3-3	-0.4
1926	Pit-N	43	132	19	30	8	1	0	19	12	6	.227	.292	.303	57	-8	3			.911	-11	2-24/3-9,S-1	-1.8
	Bos-N	54	184	17	49	3	2	0	15	16	12	.266	.325	.304	77	-6	6			.973	-3	2-39,S-14/3-1	-0.7
	Yr	97	316	36	79	11	3	0	34	28	18	.250	.311	.304	68	-14	9			.950	-14	2-63,S-15,3-10	-2.5
1927	Bos-N	112	411	53	124	14	4	1	32	39	17	.302	.364	.363	103	2	5			.947	-2	3-52,2-39,O-16,S-1	0.3
1928	Bos-N	68	215	27	51	9	0	2	18	19	12	.237	.299	.307	62	-12	7			.958	6	O-54/2-1	-1.0
1929	Bro-N	111	402	48	119	18	6	0	48	44	16	.296	.370	.371	86	-8	3			.955	-18	2-74,S-36/O-2,3-1	-1.6
1930	Bro-N	76	196	24	55	13	1	1	20	21	7	.281	.356	.372	77	-7	1			.991	3	2-23,O-23,S-17,3-1	-0.2
1932	NY-N	37	87	9	23	3	0	1	6	9	6	.264	.340	.333	84	-2	1			.930	3	S-21/3-6,2-5	0.3
1934	Cle-A	27	65	4	10	2	0	0	8	10	4	.154	.267	.185	18	-8	0	0	0	.932	1	2-18/3-3,S-2	-0.6
Total	10	748	2474	360	706	108	26	13	257	272	121	.285	.359	.366	89	-37	52	14		.956	-29	2-349,O-145/S-98,3	-4.9

■ **HARRY MOORE**   Moore, Henry S.   Deb: 4/17/1884

YEAR	TM/L	G	AB	R	H	2B	3B	HR	RBI	BB	SO	AVG	OBP	SLG	PRO+	BR/A	SB	CS	SBR	FA	FR	G/POS	TPR
1884	Was-U	111	461	77	155	23	5	1		19		.336	.363	.414	139	10				.820	-9	*O-105/S-8	-0.1

■ **JACKIE MOORE**   Moore, Jackie Spencer   b: 2/19/39, Jay, Fla.   BR/TR, 6', 180 lbs.   Deb: 4/18/65   MC

YEAR	TM/L	G	AB	R	H	2B	3B	HR	RBI	BB	SO	AVG	OBP	SLG	PRO+	BR/A	SB	CS	SBR	FA	FR	G/POS	TPR
1965	Det-A	21	53	2	5	0	0	0	2	6	12	.094	.186	.094	-17	-8	0	0	0	.985	4	C-20	-0.4

■ **JIMMY MOORE**   Moore, James William   b: 4/24/03, Paris, Tenn.   d: 3/7/86, Memphis, Tenn.   BR/TR, 6'0.5", 187 lbs.   Deb: 8/31/30

YEAR	TM/L	G	AB	R	H	2B	3B	HR	RBI	BB	SO	AVG	OBP	SLG	PRO+	BR/A	SB	CS	SBR	FA	FR	G/POS	TPR
1930	Chi-A	16	39	4	8	2	0	0	6	3	3	.205	.326	.256	52	-3	0	0	0	.900	0	O-11	-0.3
	*Phi-A	15	50	10	19	3	1	2	12	2	4	.380	.404	.560	136	3	1	1	-0	.958	-0	O-13	0.1
	Yr	31	89	14	27	5	1	2	18	5	7	.303	.367	.427	100	0	1	1	-0	.932	0	O-24	-0.2
1931	*Phi-A	49	143	18	32	5	1	2	21	11	13	.224	.284	.315	54	-10	0	1	-1	.973	0	O-36	-1.2
Total	2	80	232	32	59	10	2	4	35	19	20	.254	.316	.358	71	-10	1	2	-1	.958	0	/O-60	-1.4

■ **JERRIE MOORE**   Moore, Jeremiah S.   b: Detroit, Mich.   d: 9/26/1890, Wayne, Mich.   BL, 5'11", 170 lbs.   Deb: 4/17/1884

YEAR	TM/L	G	AB	R	H	2B	3B	HR	RBI	BB	SO	AVG	OBP	SLG	PRO+	BR/A	SB	CS	SBR	FA	FR	G/POS	TPR
1884	Alt-U	20	80	10	25	3	1	1		0		.313	.313	.412	116	-1				.800	-8	C-12/O-9	-0.7
	Cle-N	9	30	1	6	0	0	0	10	0	5	.200	.200	.200	25	-3				.887	-1	/C-9	-0.3
1885	Det-N	6	23	2	4	1	0	0		1	3	.174	.208	.217	38	-2				.800	-3	/C-6	-0.4
Total	2	35	133	13	35	4	1	1	10	1	8	.263	.269	.331	83	-5				.830	-12	/C-27,O-9	-1.4

■ **JOHNNY MOORE**   Moore, John Francis   b: 3/23/02, Waterville, Conn.   d: 4/4/91, Bradenton, Fla.   BL/TR, 5'10.5", 175 lbs.   Deb: 9/15/28

YEAR	TM/L	G	AB	R	H	2B	3B	HR	RBI	BB	SO	AVG	OBP	SLG	PRO+	BR/A	SB	CS	SBR	FA	FR	G/POS	TPR
1928	Chi-N	4	4	0	0	0	0	0	0	0	0	.000	.000	.000	-99	-1	0			.000	0	H	-0.1
1929	Chi-N	37	63	13	18	1	0	2	8	4	6	.286	.338	.397	81	-2	0			.971	-0	O-15	-0.3
1931	Chi-N	39	104	19	25	3	1	2	16	7	5	.240	.288	.346	69	-5	1			.964	1	O-22	-0.5
1932	*Chi-N	119	443	59	135	24	5	13	64	22	38	.305	.342	.470	117	9	4			.983	5	*O-109	0.3
1933	Chi-N	135	514	60	135	19	5	1	49	36	45	.263	.306	.325	81	-12	4			.974	-5	*O-132	-1.6
1934	Cin-N	16	42	5	8	1	0	0	5	3	2	.190	.244	.262	36	-4	0			1.000	0	O-10	-0.4
	Phi-N	116	458	68	157	34	6	11	93	40	18	.343	.397	.515	125	16	7			.981	-1	*O-115	1.7
	Yr	132	500	73	165	35	7	11	98	43	20	.330	.384	.494	120	13	7			.983	6	*O-125	1.3
1935	Phi-N	153	600	84	194	33	4	19	93	45	50	.323	.375	.483	117	14	4			.973	-10	*O-150	-0.1
1936	Phi-N	124	472	85	155	24	3	16	68	26	22	.328	.365	.494	117	10	1			.948	-8	*O-112	-0.2
1937	Phi-N	96	307	46	98	16	2	9	58	18	19	.319	.357	.472	114	5	2			.943	-3	O-72	0.0
1945	Chi-N	7	6	0	1	0	0	0	0	1	1	.167	.286	.167	28	-1	0			.000	0	H	-0.1
Total	10	846	3013	439	926	155	26	73	452	195	176	.307	.352	.449	109	30	23			.970	-7	O-737	-1.3

■ **JO-JO MOORE**   Moore, Joseph Gregg "The Gause Ghost"   b: 12/25/08, Gause, Tex.   BL/TR, 5'11", 155 lbs.   Deb: 9/17/30

YEAR	TM/L	G	AB	R	H	2B	3B	HR	RBI	BB	SO	AVG	OBP	SLG	PRO+	BR/A	SB	CS	SBR	FA	FR	G/POS	TPR
1930	NY-N	3	5	1	1	0	0	0	0	0	1	.200	.200	.200	-3	-1	0			1.000	-0	/O-1	-0.1
1931	NY-N	4	8	0	2	1	0	0	3	0	1	.250	.250	.375	68	-0	1			1.000	0	/O-1	-0.1

YEAR	TM/L	G	AB	R	H	2B	3B	HR	RBI	BB	SO	AVG	OBP	SLG	PRO+	BR/A	SB	CS	SBR	FA	FR	G/POS	TPR
1932	NY-N	86	361	53	110	15	2	2	27	20	18	.305	.341	.374	94	-3	4			.982	-4	O-86	-1.2
1933	*NY-N	132	524	56	153	16	5	0	42	21	27	.292	.323	.342	91	-6	4			.966	3	*O-132	-1.0
1934	NY-N†	139	580	106	192	37	4	15	61	31	23	.331	.370	.486	130	24	5			.954	-10	*O-131	0.8
1935	NY-N★	155	681	108	201	28	9	15	71	53	24	.295	.353	.429	111	10	5			.972	2	*O-155	0.6
1936	*NY-N☆	152	649	110	205	39	7	6	63	37	27	.316	.358	.437	110	9	2			.981	8	*O-149	1.0
1937	*NY-N★	142	580	89	180	37	10	6	57	46	37	.310	.364	.440	116	13	7			.975	-7	*O-140	0.1
1938	NY-N☆	125	506	76	153	23	6	11	56	22	27	.302	.335	.437	110	5	2			.978	-5	*O-114	-0.3
1939	NY-N	138	562	80	151	23	2	10	47	45	15	.269	.324	.370	85	-12	5			.986	3	*O-136	-1.4
1940	NY-N★	138	543	83	150	33	4	6	46	43	30	.276	.337	.385	98	-1	7			.982	-1	*O-133	-1.0
1941	NY-N	121	428	47	117	16	2	7	40	30	15	.273	.322	.369	93	-5	4			.972	-4	O-116	-1.6
Total	12	1335	5427	809	1615	258	53	79	513	348	247	.298	.344	.408	105	33	46			.975	-14	O-1294	-4.2

■ KELVIN MOORE
Moore, Kelvin Orlando   b: 9/26/57, Leroy, Ala.   BR/TL, 6'1", 195 lbs.   Deb: 8/28/81

YEAR	TM/L	G	AB	R	H	2B	3B	HR	RBI	BB	SO	AVG	OBP	SLG	PRO+	BR/A	SB	CS	SBR	FA	FR	G/POS	TPR
1981	*Oak-A	14	47	5	12	0	1	1	3	5	15	.255	.327	.362	103	0	1	0	0	1.000	-1	1-13	-0.1
1982	Oak-A	21	67	6	15	1	1	2	6	3	23	.224	.257	.358	70	-3	0	1	-1	.971	-2	1-20	-0.6
1983	Oak-A	41	124	12	26	4	0	5	16	10	39	.210	.274	.363	78	-4	2	4	-2	.994	-3	1-40	-1.1
Total	3	76	238	23	53	5	2	8	25	18	77	.223	.280	.361	81	-7	3	5	-2	.989	-5	/1-73	-1.8

■ KERWIN MOORE
Moore, Kerwin Lamar   b: 10/29/70, Detroit, Mich.   BB/TR, 6'1", 190 lbs.   Deb: 8/30/96

YEAR	TM/L	G	AB	R	H	2B	3B	HR	RBI	BB	SO	AVG	OBP	SLG	PRO+	BR/A	SB	CS	SBR	FA	FR	G/POS	TPR
1996	Oak-A	22	16	4	1	1	0	0	0	2	6	.063	.167	.125	-26	-3	1	0	0	1.000	-5	O-18/D-2	-0.8

■ MOLLY MOORE
Moore, Maurice   d: 2/24/1881, New York, N.Y.   Deb: 6/30/1875

YEAR	TM/L	G	AB	R	H	2B	3B	HR	RBI	BB	SO	AVG	OBP	SLG	PRO+	BR/A	SB	CS	SBR	FA	FR	G/POS	TPR
1875	Atl-n	21	86	5	19	4	0	0	5	0	4	.221	.221	.267	79	-1	0	1	-1	.747	-5	S-14/1-8,O-2,C23	-0.6

■ RANDY MOORE
Moore, Randolph Edward   b: 6/21/06, Naples, Tex.   d: 6/12/92, Mt.Pleasant, Tex.   BL/TR, 6', 185 lbs.   Deb: 4/12/27

YEAR	TM/L	G	AB	R	H	2B	3B	HR	RBI	BB	SO	AVG	OBP	SLG	PRO+	BR/A	SB	CS	SBR	FA	FR	G/POS	TPR
1927	Chi-A	6	15	0	0	0	0	0	0	0	2	.000	.000	.000	-99	-4	0	0	0	1.000	1	/O-4	-0.4
1928	Chi-A	24	61	6	13	4	1	0	5	3	5	.213	.250	.311	47	-5	0	1	-1	.946	0	O-16	-0.6
1930	Bos-N	83	191	24	55	9	0	2	34	10	13	.288	.323	.366	69	-10	3			.986	-2	O-34,3-13	-1.2
1931	Bos-N	83	192	19	50	8	1	3	34	13	3	.260	.311	.359	83	-5	1			.952	0	O-29,3-22/2-1	-0.5
1932	Bos-N	107	351	41	103	21	2	3	43	15	11	.293	.322	.390	94	-3	1			.987	-7	O-41,3-31,1-22/C-1	-1.3
1933	Bos-N	135	497	64	150	23	7	8	70	40	16	.302	.356	.425	133	20	3			.979	-1	*O-122,1-10	1.3
1934	Bos-N	123	422	55	120	21	2	7	64	40	16	.284	.346	.393	105	3	2			.965	-2	O-72,1-37	-0.4
1935	Bos-N	125	407	42	112	20	4	4	42	26	16	.275	.319	.373	93	-5	1			.950	0	O-78,1-21	-1.0
1936	Bro-N	42	88	4	21	3	0	0	14	8	1	.239	.302	.273	55	-5	0			.964	-4	O-21	-1.0
1937	Bro-N	13	22	3	3	1	0	0	2	3	2	.136	.240	.182	16	-3	0			.889	0	C-10	-0.2
	StL-N	8	7	0	0	0	0	0	0	0	0	.000	.000	.000	-98	-2	0			.000	0	/O-1	-0.2
	Yr	21	29	3	3	1	0	0	2	3	2	.103	.188	.138	-10	-4	0			.889	0	C-10/O-1	-0.4
Total	10	749	2253	258	627	110	17	27	308	158	85	.278	.326	.378	95	-19	11	1		.969	-15	O-418/1-90,3-66,C2	-5.5

■ BOBBY MOORE
Moore, Robert Vincent   b: 10/27/65, Cincinnati, Ohio   BR/TR, 5'9", 165 lbs.   Deb: 9/5/91

YEAR	TM/L	G	AB	R	H	2B	3B	HR	RBI	BB	SO	AVG	OBP	SLG	PRO+	BR/A	SB	CS	SBR	FA	FR	G/POS	TPR
1991	KC-A	18	14	3	5	1	0	0	0	1	2	.357	.400	.429	129	1	3	2	-0	1.000	-4	O-13	-0.4

■ TERRY MOORE
Moore, Terry Bluford   b: 5/27/12, Vernon, Ala.   d: 3/29/95, Collinsville, Ill.   BR/TR, 5'11", 195 lbs.   Deb: 4/16/35   MC

YEAR	TM/L	G	AB	R	H	2B	3B	HR	RBI	BB	SO	AVG	OBP	SLG	PRO+	BR/A	SB	CS	SBR	FA	FR	G/POS	TPR
1935	StL-N	119	456	63	131	34	3	6	53	15	40	.287	.314	.414	90	-7	13			.984	14	*O-117	0.3
1936	StL-N	143	590	85	156	39	4	5	47	37	52	.264	.309	.369	82	-16	9			.977	22	*O-133	0.1
1937	StL-N	115	461	76	123	17	3	5	43	32	41	.267	.317	.349	79	-13	13			.988	14	*O-106	-0.3
1938	StL-N	94	312	49	85	21	3	4	21	46	19	.272	.366	.397	104	3	9			.975	-3	O-75/3-6	0.9
1939	StL-N★	130	417	65	123	25	2	17	77	43	38	.295	.362	.487	119	10	6			**.994**	11	*O-121/P-1	1.7
1940	StL-N★	136	537	92	163	33	4	17	64	42	44	.304	.356	.475	121	14	18			.987	17	*O-133	2.4
1941	StL-N★	122	493	86	145	26	4	6	68	52	31	.294	.364	.400	108	5	3			.984	7	*O-121	0.5
1942	*StL-N★	130	489	80	141	26	3	6	49	56	26	.288	.364	.391	112	8	10			.986	-3	*O-126/3-1	-0.1
1946	*StL-N	91	278	32	73	14	1	3	28	18	26	.263	.312	.353	85	-6	0			.982	1	O-66	-0.8
1947	StL-N	127	460	61	130	17	1	7	45	38	39	.283	.339	.370	84	-10	1			.983	1	*O-120	-1.5
1948	StL-N	91	207	30	48	11	0	4	18	27	12	.232	.321	.343	75	-7	0			.993	-10	O-71	-2.0
Total	11	1298	4700	719	1318	263	28	80	513	406	368	.280	.340	.399	98	-18	82			.985	83	*O-1189/3-7,P-1	1.2

■ SCRAPPY MOORE
Moore, William Allen   b: 12/16/1892, St.Louis, Mo.   d: 10/13/64, Little Rock, Ark.   BR/TR, 5'8", 153 lbs.   Deb: 6/21/17

YEAR	TM/L	G	AB	R	H	2B	3B	HR	RBI	BB	SO	AVG	OBP	SLG	PRO+	BR/A	SB	CS	SBR	FA	FR	G/POS	TPR
1917	StL-A	4	8	1	1	0	0	0	0	1	0	.125	.222	.125	6	-1	0			.750	0	/3-2	-0.1

■ BILL MOORE
Moore, William Henry "Willie"   b: 12/12/01, Kansas City, Mo.   d: 5/24/72, Kansas City, Mo.   BL/TR, 5'11", 170 lbs.   Deb: 9/7/26

YEAR	TM/L	G	AB	R	H	2B	3B	HR	RBI	BB	SO	AVG	OBP	SLG	PRO+	BR/A	SB	CS	SBR	FA	FR	G/POS	TPR
1926	Bos-A	5	18	2	3	0	0	0	0	2	2	.167	.167	.167	-13	-3	0	0	0	1.000	0	/C-5	-0.2
1927	Bos-A	44	69	7	15	2	0	0	4	13	8	.217	.341	.246	56	-4	0	0	0	.938	2	C-42	0.0
Total	2	49	87	9	18	2	0	0	4	13	10	.207	.310	.230	43	-7	0	0	0	.946	2	/C-47	-0.2

■ BILL MOORE
Moore, William Ross   b: 10/10/60, Los Angeles, Cal.   BR/TL, 6'1", 185 lbs.   Deb: 7/19/86

YEAR	TM/L	G	AB	R	H	2B	3B	HR	RBI	BB	SO	AVG	OBP	SLG	PRO+	BR/A	SB	CS	SBR	FA	FR	G/POS	TPR
1986	Mon-N	6	12	0	2	0	0	0	0	0	4	.167	.167	.167	-8	-2	0	0	0	1.000	-1	/1-3,O-1	-0.3

■ ANDRES MORA
Mora, Andres (Ibarra)   b: 5/25/55, Rio Bravo, Mex.   BR/TR, 6', 180 lbs.   Deb: 4/13/76

YEAR	TM/L	G	AB	R	H	2B	3B	HR	RBI	BB	SO	AVG	OBP	SLG	PRO+	BR/A	SB	CS	SBR	FA	FR	G/POS	TPR
1976	Bal-A	73	220	18	48	11	0	6	25	13	49	.218	.262	.350	83	-6	1	0		.951	-2	D-34,O-31	-1.0
1977	Bal-A	77	233	32	57	8	2	13	44	5	53	.245	.264	.464	100	-2	0	0	0	1.000	-9	O-57/3-1,D-5	-1.3
1978	Bal-A	76	229	21	49	8	0	8	14	13	47	.214	.259	.354	75	-9	0	1	-1	.978	1	O-69/D-1	-1.1
1980	Cle-A	9	18	0	2	0	0	0	0	0	6	.111	.111	.111	-39	-3	0	0		1.000	0	/O-3	-0.4
Total	4	235	700	71	156	27	2	27	83	31	149	.223	.258	.383	83	-19	1	1	-0	.978	-10	O-160/D-40,3-1	-3.8

■ JOSE MORALES
Morales, Jose Manuel (Hernandez)   b: 12/30/44, Frederiksted, V.I.   BR/TR, 6', 195 lbs.   Deb: 8/13/73   C

YEAR	TM/L	G	AB	R	H	2B	3B	HR	RBI	BB	SO	AVG	OBP	SLG	PRO+	BR/A	SB	CS	SBR	FA	FR	G/POS	TPR
1973	Oak-A	6	14	0	4	0	0	0	1	1	5	.286	.333	.357	100	-0		1	-1	.000	0	/D-3	-0.1
	Mon-N	5	5	0	2	0	0	0	0	0	0	.400	.400	.400	118	0	0	0	0	.000	0	H	0.0
1974	Mon-N	25	26	3	7	4	0	1	5	1	7	.269	.296	.538	123	1	0	0	0	.800	-1	/C-2	0.0
1975	Mon-N	93	163	18	49	6	1	2	24	14	21	.301	.356	.387	102	0	0	2	-1	.983	4	1-27/O-6,C-5	0.2
1976	Mon-N	104	158	12	50	11	0	4	37	3	20	.316	.337	.462	120	3	0	0	0	.977	1	1-21,C-12	0.4
1977	Mon-N	65	74	3	15	4	1	1	9	5	12	.203	.253	.324	55	-5	0	0	0	1.000	0	/C-8,1-8	-0.7
1978	Min-A	101	242	22	76	13	1	2	38	20	35	.314	.369	.401	114	5	0	1	-1	.000	0	D-77/C-1,1-1,O-1	0.2
1979	Min-A	92	191	21	51	5	1	2	27	14	27	.267	.324	.335	75	-6	0	0	0	1.000	0	D-77/1-1	-0.9
1980	Min-A	97	241	36	73	17	2	8	36	22	19	.303	.364	.490	123	7	0	0	0	1.000	-1	D-86/C-2,1-2	0.4
1981	Bal-A	38	86	6	21	3	0	2	14	3	13	.244	.270	.349	77	-3	0	0	0	1.000	0	D-22/1-3	-0.4
1982	Bal-A	3	3	0	0	0	0	0	0	0	0	.000	.000	.000	-99	-1	0	0	0	.000	0	/H	-0.1
	LA-N	35	30	1	9	0	1	1	8	4	8	.300	.382	.433	131	1	0	0	0	.000	0	H	0.0
1983	*LA-N	47	53	4	15	3	0	3	8	1	11	.283	.296	.509	120	1	0	0	0	.951	0	/1-4	0.1
1984	LA-N	22	19	0	3	1	0	0	2	0	5	.158	.200	.158	2	-2	0	0	0	.000	0	H	0.0
Total	12	733	1305	126	375	68	6	26	207	89	182	.287	.336	.408	102	1	0	4	-2	.981	0	D-265/1-67,C-30,O-7	-1.2

■ JERRY MORALES
Morales, Julio Ruben (Torres)   b: 2/18/49, Yabucoa, P.R.   BR/TR, 5'10", 175 lbs.   Deb: 9/5/69

YEAR	TM/L	G	AB	R	H	2B	3B	HR	RBI	BB	SO	AVG	OBP	SLG	PRO+	BR/A	SB	CS	SBR	FA	FR	G/POS	TPR
1969	SD-N	19	41	5	8	1	0	0	5	2	10	.195	.283	.317	71	-2	0	2	-1	1.000	-1	O-19	-0.4
1970	SD-N	28	58	6	9	0	1	1	4	3	11	.155	.197	.241	17	-7	0	0	0	.926	-5	O-26	-1.3
1971	SD-N	12	17	1	2	0	0	0	1	2	2	.118	.211	.118	-5	-2	0	0	0	1.000	0	/O-7	-0.4
1972	SD-N	115	347	38	83	15	7	4	18	35	54	.239	.309	.357	96	-3	4	6	-2	.987	4	O-96/3-4	-0.6
1973	SD-N	122	388	47	109	23	2	9	34	27	55	.281	.328	.420	115	6	6	5	-1	.991	1	*O-100	0.1
1974	Chi-N	151	534	70	146	21	7	15	82	46	63	.273	.333	.423	106	3	2	12	-7	.979	0	*O-143	-1.7
1975	Chi-N	153	578	62	156	19	0	12	91	50	65	.270	.333	.369	91	-7	3	7	-3	.979	-3	*O-151	-1.7
1976	Chi-N	140	537	66	147	17	0	16	67	41	49	.274	.329	.395	95	-4	3	8	-4	.983	3	*O-136	-1.1
1977	Chi-N★	136	490	54	142	34	5	11	69	43	75	.290	.350	.447	101	1	4	4	-2	.985	-7	*O-128	-1.4
1978	StL-N	130	457	44	109	19	8	4	46	33	44	.239	.291	.341	77	-15	4	4	-1	.977	-0	*O-126	-2.3

YEAR	TM/L	G	AB	R	H	2B	3B	HR	RBI	BB	SO	AVG	OBP	SLG	PRO+	BR/A	SB	CS	SBR	FA	FR	G/POS	TPR
1979	Det-A	129	440	50	93	23	1	14	56	30	56	.211	.265	.364	65	-23	10	4	1	.986	-9	*O-119/D-7	-3.5
1980	NY-N	94	193	19	49	7	1	3	30	13	31	.254	.304	.347	84	-4	2	3	-1	.973	-7	O-63	-1.5
1981	Chi-N	84	245	27	70	6	2	1	25	22	29	.286	.347	.339	91	-2	1	1	-0	.986	-6	O-72	-1.1
1982	Chi-N	65	116	14	33	2	2	4	30	9	7	.284	.336	.440	112	2	1	2	-1	1.000	-5	O-41	-0.5
1983	Chi-N	63	87	11	17	9	0	0	11	7	19	.195	.255	.299	51	-6	0	0	0	1.000	-6	O-29	-1.3
Total	15	1441	4528	516	1173	199	36	95	570	366	567	.259	.316	.382	91	-64	37	57	-23	.983	-44	*O-1256/D-7,3-4	-18.6

■ RICH MORALES
Morales, Richard Angelo b: 9/20/43, San Francisco, Cal. BR/TR, 5'11", 170 lbs. Deb: 8/8/67 C

YEAR	TM/L	G	AB	R	H	2B	3B	HR	RBI	BB	SO	AVG	OBP	SLG	PRO+	BR/A	SB	CS	SBR	FA	FR	G/POS	TPR
1967	Chi-A	8	10	0	0	0	0	0	0	0	2	.000	.000	.000	-99	-2	0	0	0	.944	2	/S-7	-0.1
1968	Chi-A	10	29	2	5	0	0	0	0	2	5	.172	.226	.172	22	-3	0	0	0	.966	2	/S-7,2-5	0.0
1969	Chi-A	55	121	12	26	0	1	0	6	7	18	.215	.269	.231	39	-10	1	0	0	.976	10	2-38,S-13/3-1	0.4
1970	Chi-A	62	112	6	18	2	0	0	2	9	16	.161	.230	.205	20	-12	1	0	0	.967	6	S-24,3-20,2-12	-0.4
1971	Chi-A	84	185	19	45	8	0	2	14	22	26	.243	.336	.319	84	-3	2	3	-1	.976	-1	S-57,3-18/2-3,0-1	0.0
1972	Chi-A	110	287	24	59	7	1	2	20	19	49	.206	.262	.258	54	-16	2	3	-1	.968	-1	S-86,2-16,3-14	-0.9
1973	Chi-A	7	4	1	0	0	0	0	1	1	1	.000	.200	.000	-38	-1	0	0	0	1.000	1	/3-5,2-2	0.0
	SD-N	90	244	9	40	6	1	0	16	27	36	.164	.247	.197	27	-24	0	1	-1	.988	22	2-79,S-10	0.2
1974	SD-N	54	61	8	12	3	0	1	5	8	6	.197	.290	.295	67	-3	1	0	0	.933	7	S-29,2-18/3-6,1-1	0.6
Total	8	480	1053	81	205	26	3	6	64	95	159	.195	.268	.242	46	-74	7	7	-2	.970	47	S-233,2-173/310	-0.2

■ CHARLIE MORAN
Moran, Charles Barthell "Uncle Charlie" b: 2/22/1878, Nashville, Tenn. d: 6/14/49, Horse Cave, Ky. BR/TR, 5'8", 180 lbs. Deb: 9/9/03 U

YEAR	TM/L	G	AB	R	H	2B	3B	HR	RBI	BB	SO	AVG	OBP	SLG	PRO+	BR/A	SB	CS	SBR	FA	FR	G/POS	TPR
1903	StL-N	4	14	2	6	0	0	0	1	0		.429	.429	.429	149	1	1			1.000	-1	/P-3,S-1	0.0
1908	StL-N	21	63	2	11	1	2	0	2	0		.175	.175	.254	38	-5	0			.903	-3	C-16	-0.7
Total	2	25	77	4	17	1	2	0	3	0		.221	.221	.286	61	-4	1			.903	-4	/C-16,P-3,S-1	-0.7

■ CHARLES MORAN
Moran, Charles Vincent b: 3/26/1879, Washington, D.C. d: 4/11/34, Washington, D.C. TR, Deb: 4/29/03

YEAR	TM/L	G	AB	R	H	2B	3B	HR	RBI	BB	SO	AVG	OBP	SLG	PRO+	BR/A	SB	CS	SBR	FA	FR	G/POS	TPR
1903	Was-A	98	373	41	84	14	5	1	24	33		.225	.297	.298	77	-10	8			.943	5	S-96/2-2	-0.1
1904	Was-A	62	243	27	54	10	0	0	7	23		.222	.289	.263	77	-6	7			.919	-13	S-61/3-1	-2.0
	StL-A	82	272	15	47	3	1	0	14	25		.173	.242	.191	40	-18	2			.937	-3	3-81/O-1	-2.0
	Yr	144	515	42	101	13	1	0	21	48		.196	.265	.225	58	-23	9			.938	-16	3-82,S-61/O-1	-4.0
1905	StL-A	27	82	6	16	1	0	0	5	10		.195	.290	.207	62	-3	3			.954	-4	2-20/3-5	-0.7
Total	3	269	970	89	201	28	6	1	50	91		.207	.279	.252	66	-36	20			.935	-15	S-157/3-87,2-22,O-1	-4.8

■ HERBIE MORAN
Moran, John Herbert b: 2/16/1884, Costello, Pa. d: 9/21/54, Clarkson, N.Y. BL/TR, 5'5", 150 lbs. Deb: 4/16/08

YEAR	TM/L	G	AB	R	H	2B	3B	HR	RBI	BB	SO	AVG	OBP	SLG	PRO+	BR/A	SB	CS	SBR	FA	FR	G/POS	TPR
1908	Phi-A	19	59	4	9	0	0	0	4	6		.153	.242	.153	27	-4	1			.952	1	O-19	-0.5
	Bos-N	8	29	3	8	0	0	0	2	2		.276	.364	.276	106	0	1			1.000	2	/O-8	0.3
1909	Bos-N	8	31	8	7	1	0	0	0	5		.226	.333	.258	80	-1	0			1.000	-1	/O-8	-0.1
1910	Bos-N	20	67	11	8	0	0	0	3	13	14	.119	.280	.119	17	-7	6			.958	4	O-20	-0.4
1912	Bro-N	130	508	77	140	18	10	3	40	69	38	.276	.368	.356	102	4	28			.961	8	*O-129	0.5
1913	Bro-N	132	515	71	137	15	5	0	26	45	29	.266	.333	.315	83	-10	21			.950	2	*O-129	-1.4
1914	Cin-N	107	395	43	93	10	5	1	35	41	29	.235	.312	.294	78	-10	26			.954	-5	*O-107	-2.2
	*Bos-N	41	154	24	41	3	1	0	4	17	11	.266	.347	.299	93	-1	4			.940	-8	O-41	-1.1
	Yr	148	549	67	134	13	6	1	39	58	40	.244	.322	.295	82	-11	30			.950	-13	*O-148	-3.3
1915	Bos-N	130	419	59	84	13	5	0	21	66	41	.200	.320	.255	79	-8	16	10	-1	.964	-6	*O-123	-2.3
Total	7	595	2177	300	527	60	26	2	135	264	162	.242	.332	.296	83	-35	103	10		.957	-2	O-584	-7.2

■ PAT MORAN
Moran, Patrick Joseph b: 2/7/1876, Fitchburg, Mass. d: 3/7/24, Orlando, Fla. BR/TR, 5'10", 180 lbs. Deb: 5/15/01 M

YEAR	TM/L	G	AB	R	H	2B	3B	HR	RBI	BB	SO	AVG	OBP	SLG	PRO+	BR/A	SB	CS	SBR	FA	FR	G/POS	TPR
1901	Bos-N	52	180	12	38	5	1	2	18	3		.211	.228	.283	44	-13	3			.973	-5	C-28,1-13/3-4,SO2	-1.6
1902	Bos-N	80	251	22	60	5	5	1	24	17		.239	.303	.311	88	-3	6			.982	1	C-71/1-3,O-1	0.5
1903	Bos-N	109	389	40	102	25	5	2	54	29		.262	.331	.406	114	6	8			.967	19	*C-107/1-1	3.5
1904	Bos-N	113	398	26	90	11	3	4	34	18		.226	.267	.299	77	-11	10			.957	4	C-72,3-39/1-2	0.1
1905	Bos-N	85	267	22	64	11	5	2	22	8		.240	.270	.341	83	-7	3			.986	13	C-78	1.4
1906	*Chi-N	70	226	22	57	13	1	0	35	7		.252	.281	.319	82	-6	3			.979	3	C-61	0.4
1907	*Chi-N	65	198	8	45	5	1	1	19	10		.227	.271	.278	68	-8	5			.973	0	C-59	-0.2
1908	Chi-N	50	150	12	39	5	1	0	12	13		.260	.323	.307	97	-0	5			.968	1	C-45	0.5
1909	Chi-N	77	246	18	54	11	1	1	23	16		.220	.278	.285	73	-8	2			.984	1	C-74	0.0
1910	Phi-N	68	199	13	47	7	1	0	11	17	16	.236	.306	.281	69	-8	6			.989	0	C-56	-0.2
1911	Phi-N	34	103	2	19	0	0	0	8	3	13	.184	.208	.214	18	-11	0			.984	-1	C-32	-1.0
1912	Phi-N	13	26	1	3	1	0	0	1	7		.115	.148	.154	-16	-4	0			.955	-2	C-13	-0.5
1913	Phi-N	1	1	0	0	0	0	0	0	0		.000	.000	.000	-96	-0	0			.000	0	H	0.0
1914	Phi-N	1	0	0	0	0	0	0	0	0		—	—	—	—	0	0			.000	0	/C-1	0.0
Total	14	818	2634	198	618	102	24	18	262	142	36	.235	.283	.312	78	-74	55			.976	34	C-697/3-43,1OS2	2.9

■ AL MORAN
Moran, Richard Alan b: 12/5/38, Detroit, Mich. BR/TR, 6'1.5", 190 lbs. Deb: 4/9/63

YEAR	TM/L	G	AB	R	H	2B	3B	HR	RBI	BB	SO	AVG	OBP	SLG	PRO+	BR/A	SB	CS	SBR	FA	FR	G/POS	TPR
1963	NY-N	119	331	26	64	5	1	1	23	36	60	.193	.274	.230	46	-22	3	7	-3	.951	6	*S-116/3-1	-1.3
1964	NY-N	16	22	2	5	0	0	0	4	2	2	.227	.292	.227	50	-1	0	0	0	.957	4	S-15/3-1	0.3
Total	2	135	353	28	69	5	1	1	27	38	62	.195	.276	.229	46	-23	3	7	-3	.951	10	S-131/3-2	-1.0

■ ROY MORAN
Moran, Roy Ellis "Deedle" b: 9/17/1884, Vincennes, Ind. d: 7/18/66, Atlanta, Ga. BR/TR, 5'8", 155 lbs. Deb: 9/3/12

YEAR	TM/L	G	AB	R	H	2B	3B	HR	RBI	BB	SO	AVG	OBP	SLG	PRO+	BR/A	SB	CS	SBR	FA	FR	G/POS	TPR
1912	Was-A	7	13	1	2	0	0	0	0	8		.154	.476	.154	82	1	3			.889	-0	/O-6	0.0

■ BILL MORAN
Moran, William L. b: 10/10/1869, Joliet, Ill. d: 4/8/16, Joliet, Ill. 175 lbs. Deb: 5/7/1892

YEAR	TM/L	G	AB	R	H	2B	3B	HR	RBI	BB	SO	AVG	OBP	SLG	PRO+	BR/A	SB	CS	SBR	FA	FR	G/POS	TPR
1892	StL-N	24	81	2	11	1	0	0	5	2	12	.136	.157	.148	-8	-11	0			.891	-4	C-22/O-2	-1.3
1895	Chi-N	15	55	8	9	2	1	1	9	3	2	.164	.220	.291	29	-6	2			.827	-2	C-15	-0.5
Total	2	39	136	10	20	3	1	1	14	5	14	.147	.183	.206	10	-17	2			.866	-6	/C-37,O-2	-1.8

■ BILLY MORAN
Moran, William Nelson b: 11/27/33, Montgomery, Ala. BR/TR, 5'11", 185 lbs. Deb: 4/15/58

YEAR	TM/L	G	AB	R	H	2B	3B	HR	RBI	BB	SO	AVG	OBP	SLG	PRO+	BR/A	SB	CS	SBR	FA	FR	G/POS	TPR
1958	Cle-A	115	257	26	58	11	4	1	18	13	23	.226	.263	.280	51	-17	3	2	-0	.960	13	2-74,S-38	0.0
1959	Cle-A	11	17	1	5	0	0	0	2	0	1	.294	.294	.294	64	-1	0	0	0	1.000	-1	/2-6,S-5	-0.1
1961	LA-A	54	173	17	45	7	1	2	22	17	16	.260	.330	.347	73	-7	0	0	0	.966	-5	2-51/S-2	-0.6
1962	LA-A★	160	659	90	186	25	3	17	74	39	80	.282	.326	.407	99	-2	5	1	1	.986	19	*2-160	3.4
1963	LA-A	153	597	67	164	29	5	7	65	31	57	.275	.314	.375	98	-3	1	1	-0	.973	15	*2-151	2.7
1964	LA-A	50	198	26	53	10	1	0	11	13	20	.268	.316	.328	88	-4	1	3	-2	.929	-7	3-47/2-3,S-1	-1.3
	Cle-A	69	151	14	31	6	0	1	10	18	16	.205	.294	.265	57	-8	0	1	-1	.972	3	3-42,2-15/1-2	-0.6
	Yr	119	349	40	84	16	1	1	21	31	36	.241	.306	.301	73	-12	1	4	-2	.947	-4	3-89,2-18/1-2,S-1	-1.9
1965	Cle-A	22	24	1	3	0	0	0	0	2	5	.125	.222	.125	1	-3	0	0	0	1.000	1	/2-7,S-1	-0.2
Total	7	634	2076	242	545	88	10	28	202	133	218	.263	.310	.355	85	-45	10	8	-2	.976	39	2-467/3-89,S-47,1-2	3.3

■ MICKEY MORANDINI
Morandini, Michael Robert b: 4/22/66, Kittanning, Pa. BL/TR, 5'11", 170 lbs. Deb: 9/1/90

YEAR	TM/L	G	AB	R	H	2B	3B	HR	RBI	BB	SO	AVG	OBP	SLG	PRO+	BR/A	SB	CS	SBR	FA	FR	G/POS	TPR
1990	Phi-N	25	79	9	19	4	0	1	3	6	19	.241	.294	.329	71	-3	3	0	1	.990	1	2-25	-0.1
1991	Phi-N	98	325	38	81	11	4	1	20	29	45	.249	.315	.317	79	-9	13	2	3	.986	8	2-97	0.4
1992	Phi-N	127	422	47	112	8	8	3	30	25	64	.265	.306	.344	84	-9	8	3	1	.991	11	*2-124/S-3	0.6
1993	*Phi-N	120	425	57	105	19	9	3	33	34	73	.247	.310	.355	79	-13	13	2	3	.990	-1	*2-111	-0.8
1994	Phi-N	87	274	40	80	16	5	2	26	34	33	.292	.368	.409	103	2	10	5	0	.985	-4	*2-79	0.9
1995	Phi-N★	127	494	65	140	34	6	6	49	42	80	.283	.350	.417	101	1	9	6	-1	.989	-1	*2-122	0.6
1996	Phi-N	140	539	64	135	24	6	3	32	49	87	.250	.323	.334	72	-21	26	5	5	.982	-9	*2-137	-1.6
Total	7	724	2558	320	672	116	39	19	193	219	401	.263	.322	.357	85	-52	82	23	11	.987	14	2-695/S-3	0.0

■ MIKE MORDECAI
Mordecai, Michael Howard b: 12/13/67, Birmingham, Ala. BB/TR, 5'11", 175 lbs. Deb: 5/8/94

YEAR	TM/L	G	AB	R	H	2B	3B	HR	RBI	BB	SO	AVG	OBP	SLG	PRO+	BR/A	SB	CS	SBR	FA	FR	G/POS	TPR
1994	Atl-N	4	4	1	1	0	0	1	3	4		.250	.400	1.000	244	1	0	0	0	1.000	-0	/S-4	0.1
1995	*Atl-N	69	75	10	21	6	0	3	11	9	16	.280	.357	.480	115	2	0	0	0	1.000	-2	2-21/1-9,3-6,S-6,0	0.0
1996	*Atl-N	66	108	12	26	5	0	2	8	9	24	.241	.299	.343	65	-5	0	0	0	.985	-1	2-20,3-10/S-6,1-1	-0.5
Total	3	139	187	23	48	11	0	6	22	19	40	.257	.325	.412	89	-3	0	0	0	.990	-3	/2-41,3-16,S-16,1O	-0.4

RAY MOREHART
Morehart, Raymond Anderson b: 12/2/1899, Near Abner, Tex. d: 1/13/89, Dallas, Tex. BL/TR, 5'9", 157 lbs. Deb: 8/9/24

YEAR	TM/L	G	AB	R	H	2B	3B	HR	RBI	BB	SO	AVG	OBP	SLG	PRO+	BR/A	SB	CS	SBR	FA	FR	G/POS	TPR
1924	Chi-A	31	100	10	20	4	2	0	8	17	7	.200	.316	.280	56	-6	3	1	0	.873	-12	S-27/2-2	-1.4
1926	Chi-A	73	192	27	61	10	3	0	21	11	15	.318	.358	.401	101	-3	0	11	-6	.950	-5	2-48	-0.9
1927	NY-A	73	195	45	50	7	2	1	20	29	18	.256	.353	.328	80	-5	4	4	-1	.945	4	2-53	-0.1
Total	3	177	487	82	131	21	7	1	49	57	40	.269	.347	.347	83	-11	10	16	-7	.946	-13	2-103/S-27	-2.4

DANNY MOREJON
Morejon, Daniel (Torres) b: 7/21/30, Havana, Cuba BR/TR, 6'1", 175 lbs. Deb: 7/11/58

YEAR	TM/L	G	AB	R	H	2B	3B	HR	RBI	BB	SO	AVG	OBP	SLG	PRO+	BR/A	SB	CS	SBR	FA	FR	G/POS	TPR
1958	Cin-N	12	26	4	5	0	0	0	1	9	2	.192	.400	.192	60	-1	1	0	0	1.000	-2	O-11	-0.4

KEITH MORELAND
Moreland, Bobby Keith b: 5/2/54, Dallas, Tex. BR/TR, 6', 200 lbs. Deb: 10/1/78

YEAR	TM/L	G	AB	R	H	2B	3B	HR	RBI	BB	SO	AVG	OBP	SLG	PRO+	BR/A	SB	CS	SBR	FA	FR	G/POS	TPR
1978	Phi-N	1	2	0	0	0	0	0	0	0	0	.000	.000	.000	-99	-1	0	0	0	1.000	0	/C-1	0.0
1979	Phi-N	14	48	3	18	3	2	0	8	3	5	.375	.412	.521	148	3	0	0	0	1.000	-0	C-13	0.3
1980	*Phi-N	62	159	13	50	8	0	4	29	8	14	.314	.347	.440	112	-2	3	1	0	.967	-1	C-39/3-4,O-2	0.3
1981	*Phi-N	61	196	16	50	7	0	6	37	15	13	.255	.311	.383	92	-2	1	2	-1	.982	-7	C-50/3-7,1-2,O-2	-1.0
1982	Chi-N	138	476	50	124	17	2	15	68	46	71	.261	.330	.399	100	0	0	6	-4	.989	-21	O-86,C-44/3-2	-2.7
1983	Chi-N	154	533	76	161	30	3	16	70	68	73	.302	.384	.440	127	20	0	3	-2	.976	-6	*O-151/C-3	0.9
1984	*Chi-N	140	495	59	138	17	3	16	80	34	71	.279	.329	.422	101	-0	1	4	-2	.976	-7	*O-103,1-29/3-8,C-3	-1.5
1985	Chi-N	161	587	74	180	30	3	14	106	68	58	.307	.380	.440	116	13	12	3	2	.976	-9	*O-148,1-12,3-11/C	0.1
1986	Chi-N	156	586	72	159	30	0	12	79	53	48	.271	.332	.384	90	-8	3	6	-3	.980	-9	O-121,3-24,C-13,1	-2.5
1987	Chi-N	153	563	63	150	29	1	27	88	39	66	.266	.314	.465	99	-2	3	3	-1	.934	4	*3-150/1-1	-0.1
1988	SD-N	143	511	40	131	23	0	5	64	40	51	.256	.310	.331	86	-9	2	3	-1	.994	-3	1-73,O-64/3-2	-2.3
1989	Det-A	90	318	34	95	16	0	5	35	27	33	.299	.357	.396	115	6	3	2	-0	1.000	-6	D-51,1-31,3-12/C-1	-0.4
	Bal-A	33	107	11	23	4	0	1	10	4	12	.215	.243	.280	49	-7	0	0	0	.000	0	D-29	-0.8
	Yr	123	425	45	118	20	0	6	45	31	45	.278	.330	.367	99	-1	3	2	-0	1.000	-6	D-80,1-31,3-12/C-1	-1.2
Total	12	1306	4581	511	1279	214	14	121	674	405	515	.279	.339	.411	103	15	28	33	-11	.979	-65	O-677,3-220,C1/D	-9.7

HARRY MORELOCK
Morelock, A. Harry b: 11/1869, Philadelphia, Pa. Deb: 8/21/1891

YEAR	TM/L	G	AB	R	H	2B	3B	HR	RBI	BB	SO	AVG	OBP	SLG	PRO+	BR/A	SB	CS	SBR	FA	FR	G/POS	TPR
1891	Phi-N	4	14	1	1	0	0	0	0	3	3	.071	.235	.071	-9	-2				.824	-4	/S-4	-0.5
1892	Phi-N	1	3	0	0	0	0	0	0	1	0	.000	.250	.000	-23	-0				.600	-1	/3-1	-0.1
Total	2	5	17	1	1	0	0	0	0	4	3	.059	.238	.059	-11	-2				.824	-4	/S-4,3-1	-0.6

JOSE MORENO
Moreno, Jose De Los Santos (b: Jose De Los Santos Mauricio (Moreno)) b: 11/1/57, Santo Domingo, D.R. BB/TR, 6', 175 lbs. Deb: 5/24/80

YEAR	TM/L	G	AB	R	H	2B	3B	HR	RBI	BB	SO	AVG	OBP	SLG	PRO+	BR/A	SB	CS	SBR	FA	FR	G/POS	TPR
1980	NY-N	37	46	6	9	2	1	2	9	3	12	.196	.245	.413	83	-1	1	0	0	.917	0	/2-4,3-4	-0.1
1981	SD-N	34	48	5	11	0	0	1	6	1	6	.229	.245	.271	50	-3	4	1	1	1.000	-0	/O-9,2-1	-0.3
1982	Cal-A	11	3	3	0	0	0	0	0	2	2	.000	.400	.000	21	-0	0	2	-1	1.000	1	/2-2,D-1	0.0
Total	3	82	97	14	20	2	1	2	15	6	20	.206	.252	.330	66	-5	5	3	0	.947	-3	/O-9,2-7,3-4,D-1	-0.4

OMAR MORENO
Moreno, Omar Renan (Quintero) b: 10/24/52, Puerto Armuelles, Panama BL/TL, 6'2", 180 lbs. Deb: 9/6/75

YEAR	TM/L	G	AB	R	H	2B	3B	HR	RBI	BB	SO	AVG	OBP	SLG	PRO+	BR/A	SB	CS	SBR	FA	FR	G/POS	TPR
1975	Pit-N	6	6	1	1	0	0	0	0	1	1	.167	.286	.167	28	-1	1	0	0	.000	-1	/O-1	-0.1
1976	Pit-N	48	122	24	33	4	1	2	12	16	24	.270	.360	.369	106	1	15	5	2	.960	-1	O-42	0.1
1977	Pit-N	150	492	69	118	19	9	7	34	38	102	.240	.296	.358	72	-20	53	16	6	.977	8	*O-147	-1.0
1978	Pit-N	155	515	95	121	15	7	2	33	81	104	.235	.342	.303	78	-12	**71**	22	8	.984	17	*O-152	0.7
1979	*Pit-N	162	695	110	196	21	12	8	69	51	104	.282	.334	.381	90	-9	**77**	21	11	.975	23	*O-162	1.8
1980	Pit-N	162	676	87	168	20	**13**	4	36	57	101	.249	.309	.325	76	-21	96	33	9	.990	27	*O-162	0.9
1981	Pit-N	103	434	62	120	18	8	1	35	26	76	.276	.322	.362	91	-5	39	14	3	.997	10	*O-103	0.3
1982	Pit-N	158	645	82	158	18	9	3	44	44	121	.245	.294	.315	68	-27	60	26	2	.983	13	*O-157	-1.7
1983	Hou-N	97	405	48	98	12	11	0	25	22	72	.242	.283	.326	73	-16	30	13	1	.977	9	O-97	-1.0
	NY-A	48	152	17	38	9	1	1	17	8	31	.250	.287	.342	75	-5	7	3	0	.992	-0	O-48	-0.6
1984	NY-A	117	355	37	92	12	6	4	38	18	48	.259	.297	.361	84	-8	20	11	-1	.985	3	*O-108/D-1	-0.9
1985	NY-A	34	66	12	13	4	1	1	4	1	16	.197	.209	.333	47	-5	1	1	-0	1.000	0	O-26/D-1	-0.6
	KC-A	24	70	9	17	1	3	2	12	3	8	.243	.284	.429	91	-1	0	1	-1	1.000	-3	O-21	-0.6
	Yr	58	136	21	30	5	4	3	16	4	24	.221	.248	.382	70	-6	1	2	-1	1.000	-3	O-47/D-1	-1.2
1986	Atl-N	118	359	46	84	18	6	4	27	36	66	.234	.276	.351	68	-16	17	16	-5	.970	-3	O-97	-2.7
Total	12	1382	4992	699	1257	171	87	37	386	387	885	.252	.308	.343	79	-146	487	182	37	.982	103	*O-1323/D-2	-5.3

CHET MORGAN
Morgan, Chester Collins "Chick" b: 6/6/10, Cleveland, Miss. d: 9/20/91, Pasadena, Tex. BL/TR, 5'9", 160 lbs. Deb: 4/19/35

YEAR	TM/L	G	AB	R	H	2B	3B	HR	RBI	BB	SO	AVG	OBP	SLG	PRO+	BR/A	SB	CS	SBR	FA	FR	G/POS	TPR
1935	Det-A	14	23	2	4	1	0	0	0	5	0	.174	.321	.217	43	-2	0	0	0	.909	0	/O-4	-0.2
1938	Det-A	74	306	50	87	6	1	0	27	20	12	.284	.330	.310	58	-19	5	6	-2	.980	0	O-74	-2.2
Total	2	88	329	52	91	7	1	1	27	25	12	.277	.330	.304	52	-21	5	6	-2	.977	0	/O-78	-2.4

ED MORGAN
Morgan, Edward Carre b: 5/22/04, Cairo, Ill. d: 4/9/80, New Orleans, La. BR/TR, 6'0.5", 180 lbs. Deb: 4/11/28

YEAR	TM/L	G	AB	R	H	2B	3B	HR	RBI	BB	SO	AVG	OBP	SLG	PRO+	BR/A	SB	CS	SBR	FA	FR	G/POS	TPR
1928	Cle-A	76	265	42	83	24	6	4	54	21	17	.313	.366	.494	123	8	5	5	-2	.968	1	1-36,O-21,3-14	0.4
1929	Cle-A	93	318	60	101	19	10	3	37	37	24	.318	.392	.469	116	8	4	3	-1	.908	-11	O-80	-0.8
1930	Cle-A	150	584	122	204	47	11	26	136	62	66	.349	.413	.601	148	41	8	4	0	.987	-3	*1-129,O-19	2.2
1931	Cle-A	131	462	87	162	33	4	11	86	83	46	.351	.451	.511	144	33	4	5	-2	.984	2	*1-117/3-3	2.1
1932	Cle-A	144	532	96	156	32	7	4	68	94	44	.293	.402	.402	102	5	7	6	-2	.985	-8	*1-142/3-1	-1.5
1933	Cle-A	39	121	10	32	3	3	1	13	7	9	.264	.305	.364	73	-5	1	1	-0	.997	1	1-32/O-1	-0.6
1934	Bos-A	138	528	95	141	28	4	3	79	81	46	.267	.367	.352	80	-14	7	1	2	.988	-7	*1-137	-3.0
Total	7	771	2810	512	879	186	45	52	473	385	252	.313	.398	.467	117	76	36	25	-4	.986	-23	1-593,O-121/3-18	-1.2

EDDIE MORGAN
Morgan, Edwin Willis "Pepper" b: 11/19/14, Brady Lake, Ohio d: 6/27/82, Lakewood, Ohio BL/TL, 5'10", 160 lbs. Deb: 4/14/36

YEAR	TM/L	G	AB	R	H	2B	3B	HR	RBI	BB	SO	AVG	OBP	SLG	PRO+	BR/A	SB	CS	SBR	FA	FR	G/POS	TPR
1936	StL-N	8	18	4	5	1	0	1	3	2	4	.278	.350	.444	113	0	0	0	0	.889	-0	/O-4	0.0
1937	Bro-N	31	48	4	9	3	0	0	5	9	7	.188	.316	.250	55	-3	0	0	0	.984	-3	/1-7,O-7	-0.6
Total	2	39	66	8	14	4	0	1	8	11	11	.212	.325	.303	70	-2				.842	-3	/O-11,1-7	-0.6

BILL MORGAN
Morgan, Henry William b: 10/1857, Washington, D.C. Deb: 5/4/1875

YEAR	TM/L	G	AB	R	H	2B	3B	HR	RBI	BB	SO	AVG	OBP	SLG	PRO+	BR/A	SB	CS	SBR	FA	FR	G/POS	TPR
1875	RS-n	19	69	11	18	4	0	0	1	5	4	.261	.311	.319	132	3	2	1	0	.824	-5	O-10/P-7,3-7	-0.2
1878	Mil-N	14	56	2	11	0	0	0	0	5	4	.196	.237	.196	41	-4				.769	-6	O-13/3-3,2-1	-0.9
1882	Pit-a	17	66	10	17	2	0	0		4		.258	.300	.318	114	1				.688	-8	O-11/C-7	-0.6
1884	Ric-a	6	20	0	2	0	0	0		1		.100	.143	.100	-20	-3				.850	-2	/C-3,O-2,2-1	-0.4
	Bal-U	2	9	1	2	0	0	0		0		.222	.300	.222	55	-1				.909	0	/C-1,2-1,O-1	-0.1
Total	3	39	151	13	32	2	1	0	5	9	9	.212	.256	.238	64	-6				.743	-16	/O-27,C-11,2-3,3-3	-2.0

RED MORGAN
Morgan, James Edward b: 10/6/1883, Neola, Iowa d: 3/25/81, New York, N.Y. TR, Deb: 6/20/06

YEAR	TM/L	G	AB	R	H	2B	3B	HR	RBI	BB	SO	AVG	OBP	SLG	PRO+	BR/A	SB	CS	SBR	FA	FR	G/POS	TPR
1906	Bos-A	88	307	20	66	6	3	1	21	16		.215	.270	.264	67	-11	7			.866	-13	3-88	-2.4

JOE MORGAN
Morgan, Joe Leonard b: 9/19/43, Bonham, Tex. BL/TR, 5'7", 160 lbs. Deb: 9/21/63 H

YEAR	TM/L	G	AB	R	H	2B	3B	HR	RBI	BB	SO	AVG	OBP	SLG	PRO+	BR/A	SB	CS	SBR	FA	FR	G/POS	TPR
1963	Hou-N	8	25	5	6	0	1	0	3	5	5	.240	.367	.320	106	0	1	0	0	.909	-3	/2-7	-0.1
1964	Hou-N	10	37	4	7	0	0	0	0	5	7	.189	.302	.189	44	-3	0	1	-1	.949	-0	2-10	-0.3
1965	Hou-N	157	601	100	163	22	12	14	40	**97**	77	.271	.375	.418	132	28	20	9	1	.969	-2	*2-157	4.3
1966	Hou-N†	122	425	60	121	14	8	5	42	89	43	.285	.412	.391	134	25	11	8	-2	.965	-16	2-117	1.6
1967	Hou-N	133	494	73	136	27	11	6	42	81	51	.275	.380	.411	131	22	29	5	**6**	.979	-5	*2-130/O-1	3.4
1968	Hou-N	10	20	6	5	0	0	0	0	7	4	.250	.444	.350	144	2	3	0	1	.882	-4	/2-5,O-1	-0.1
1969	Hou-N	147	535	94	126	18	5	15	43	110	74	.236	.367	.372	110	11	49	14	6	.972	-4	*2-132,O-14	2.5
1970	Hou-N★	144	548	102	147	28	9	8	52	102	55	.268	.384	.396	114	15	42	13	5	.979	11	*2-142	4.1
1971	Hou-N★	160	583	87	149	27	**11**	13	56	88	52	.256	.354	.407	118	15	40	8	5	.977	-4	*2-157	3.5
1972	*Cin-N★	149	552	**122**	161	23	4	16	73	**115**	44	.292	**.419**	.435	152	44	58	17	7	**.990**	-7	*2-149	5.5
1973	*Cin-N★	157	576	116	167	35	2	26	82	111	61	.290	.408	.493	157	48	67	15	**11**	.990	-14	*2-154	6.1
1974	*Cin-N★	149	512	107	150	31	3	22	67	120	69	.293	**.430**	.494	160	47	58	17	8	.982	-13	*2-142	5.6
1975	*Cin-N★	146	498	107	163	27	6	17	94	**132**	52	.327	**.471**	.508	**169**	**55**	67	10	14	**.986**	-7	*2-142	**7.1**
1976	*Cin-N★	141	472	113	151	30	5	27	111	114	41	.320	.453	.576	**186**	**58**	60	9	13	.981	-23	*2-133	5.8

YEAR	TM/L	G	AB	R	H	2B	3B	HR	RBI	BB	SO	AVG	OBP	SLG	PRO+	BR/A	SB	CS	SBR	FA	FR	G/POS	TPR
1977	Cin-N★	153	521	113	150	21	6	22	78	117	58	.288	.420	.478	138	33	49	10	9	**.993**	-18	*2-151	3.5
1978	Cin-N★	132	441	68	104	27	0	13	75	79	40	.236	.354	.385	107	6	19	5	3	.980	-31	*2-124	-1.4
1979	*Cin-N★	127	436	70	109	26	1	9	32	93	45	.250	.383	.376	107	8	28	6	5	.980	-13	*2-121	0.8
1980	*Hou-N	141	461	66	112	17	5	11	49	**93**	47	.243	.370	.373	117	14	24	6	4	.988	-12	*2-130	1.4
1981	SF-N	90	308	47	74	16	1	8	31	66	37	.240	.374	.377	116	9	14	5	1	.991	-11	2-87	0.5
1982	SF-N	134	463	68	134	19	4	14	61	85	60	.289	.402	.438	135	25	24	4	5	.989	-6	*2-120/3-3	3.1
1983	*Phi-N	123	404	72	93	20	1	16	59	89	54	.230	.374	.403	117	12	18	2	4	.971	-2	*2-117	2.1
1984	Oak-A	116	365	50	89	21	0	6	43	66	39	.244	.361	.351	105	5	8	3	1	.977	-31	*2-100/D-5	-2.3
Total	22	2649	9277	1650	2517	449	96	268	1133	1865	1015	.271	.395	.427	133	478	689	162	110	.981	-206	*2-2527/O-16,D-5,3	56.3

■ JOE MORGAN
Morgan, Joseph Michael b: 11/19/30, Walpole, Mass. BL/TR, 5'10", 170 lbs. Deb: 4/14/59 MC

YEAR	TM/L	G	AB	R	H	2B	3B	HR	RBI	BB	SO	AVG	OBP	SLG	PRO+	BR/A	SB	CS	SBR	FA	FR	G/POS	TPR
1959	Mil-N	13	23	2	5	1	0	0	1	2	4	.217	.280	.261	49	-2	0	0	0	.913	-2	/2-7	-0.4
	KC-A	20	21	2	4	0	1	0	3	3	7	.190	.292	.286	58	-1	0	0	0	1.000	-1	/3-2	-0.2
1960	Phi-N	26	83	5	11	2	2	0	2	6	11	.133	.191	.205	8	-11	0	0	0	.971	1	3-24	-1.0
	Cle-A	22	47	6	14	2	0	2	4	6	4	.298	.377	.468	131	2	0	0	0	.889	-2	3-12/O-2	0.0
1961	Cle-A	4	10	0	2	0	0	0		1	3	.200	.273	.200	29	-1	0	0	0	1.000	0	/O-2	-0.1
1964	StL-N	3	3	0	0	0	0	0	0	0	2	.000	.000	.000	-92	-1	0	0	0	.000	0	H	-0.1
Total	4	88	187	15	36	5	3	2	10	18	31	.193	.263	.283	49	-13	0	0	0	.944	-3	/3-38,2-7,O-4	-1.8

■ RAY MORGAN
Morgan, Raymond Caryll b: 6/14/1889, Baltimore, Md. d: 2/15/40, Baltimore, Md. BR/TR, 5'8.5", 155 lbs. Deb: 8/7/11

YEAR	TM/L	G	AB	R	H	2B	3B	HR	RBI	BB	SO	AVG	OBP	SLG	PRO+	BR/A	SB	CS	SBR	FA	FR	G/POS	TPR
1911	Was-A	25	89	11	19	2	0	0	5	4		.213	.247	.236	36	-8	2			.900	-3	3-25	-1.1
1912	Was-A	81	273	40	65	10	7	1	30	29		.238	.318	.337	87	-5	11			.939	-7	2-76/S-4,3-1	-1.3
1913	Was-A	138	481	58	131	19	8	0	57	68	63	.272	.369	.345	107	7	19			.950	-6	*2-134/S-4	-0.1
1914	Was-A	147	491	50	126	22	8	1	49	62	34	.257	.352	.340	104	4	24	17	-3	.948	-9	*2-146	-1.1
1915	Was-A	62	193	21	45	5	4	0	21	30	15	.233	.342	.301	91	-1	6	5	-1	.965	-4	2-57/S-2,3-2	-0.6
1916	Was-A	99	315	41	84	12	4	1	29	59	29	.267	.398	.340	123	13	14			.957	-17	2-82/S-9,1-3,3-1	-0.1
1917	Was-A	101	338	32	90	9	1	1	33	40	29	.266	.346	.308	101	1	7			.961	-8	2-95/3-3	-0.2
1918	Was-A	88	300	25	70	11	1	0	30	28	14	.233	.311	.277	79	-7	4			.959	-5	2-80/O-2	-0.8
Total	8	741	2480	278	630	90	33	4	254	320	184	.254	.348	.322	98	4	87	22		.953	-58	2-670/3-32,S-19,10	-5.3

■ BOBBY MORGAN
Morgan, Robert Morris b: 6/29/26, Oklahoma City, Okla. BR/TR, 5'9", 175 lbs. Deb: 4/18/50

YEAR	TM/L	G	AB	R	H	2B	3B	HR	RBI	BB	SO	AVG	OBP	SLG	PRO+	BR/A	SB	CS	SBR	FA	FR	G/POS	TPR
1950	Bro-N	67	199	38	45	10	3	7	21	32	43	.226	.342	.412	95	-1	0			.969	6	3-52,S-10	0.5
1952	*Bro-N	67	191	36	45	8	0	7	16	46	35	.236	.392	.387	115	6	2	2	-1	.968	3	3-60/2-5,S-4	0.8
1953	*Bro-N	69	196	35	51	6	2	7	33	33	47	.260	.370	.418	103	1	2	2	-1	.920	-2	3-36,S-21	0.0
1954	Phi-N	135	455	58	119	25	2	14	50	70	68	.262	.360	.418	102	2	3	1	0	.954	-22	*S-129/3-8,2-5	-0.9
1955	Phi-N	136	483	61	112	20	2	10	49	73	72	.232	.333	.344	81	-12	6	4	-1	.980	-13	2-88,S-41/3-6,1-1	-1.6
1956	Phi-N	8	25	1	5	0	0	0	1	6	4	.200	.355	.200	56	-1	0	0	0	.857	1	/3-5,2-3	0.0
	StL-N	61	113	14	22	7	0	3	20	15	24	.195	.289	.336	44	-5	0	2	-1	.980	0	2-13,3-11/S-6	-0.5
	Yr	69	138	15	27	7	0	3	21	21	28	.196	.302	.312	65	-7	0	2	-1	.877	1	3-16,2-16/S-6	-0.5
1957	Phi-N	2	0	0	0	0	0	0	0	0	0	—	—	—	—	0	0	0	0	1.000	0	/2-1	0.0
	Chi-N	125	425	43	88	20	2	5	27	52	87	.207	.295	.299	61	-23	5	0	2	.976	8	*2-116,3-12	-0.5
	Yr	127	425	43	88	20	2	5	27	52	87	.207	.295	.299	61	-23	5	0	2	.976	8	*2-117,3-12	-0.5
1958	Chi-N	1	1	0	0	0	0	0	0	0	1	.000	.000	.000	-99	-0	0	0	0	.000	0	H	0.0
Total	8	671	2088	286	487	96	11	53	217	327	381	.233	.339	.366	88	-33	18	11		.978	-18	2-231,S-211,3/1	-2.2

■ VERN MORGAN
Morgan, Vernon Thomas b: 8/8/28, Emporia, Va. d: 11/8/75, Minneapolis, Minn. BL/TR, 6'1", 190 lbs. Deb: 8/10/54 C

YEAR	TM/L	G	AB	R	H	2B	3B	HR	RBI	BB	SO	AVG	OBP	SLG	PRO+	BR/A	SB	CS	SBR	FA	FR	G/POS	TPR
1954	Chi-N	24	64	3	15	2	0	0	2	1	10	.234	.246	.266	33	-6	0	0	0	.895	-3	3-15	-1.1
1955	Chi-N	7	7	1	1	0	0	0	1	3	4	.143	.400	.143	52	-0	0	0	0	.667	-1	/3-2	-0.1
Total	2	31	71	4	16	2	0	0	3	4	14	.225	.267	.254	36	-7	0	0	0	.864	-5	/3-17	-1.2

■ BILL MORGAN
Morgan, William Deb: 8/6/1883

YEAR	TM/L	G	AB	R	H	2B	3B	HR	RBI	BB	SO	AVG	OBP	SLG	PRO+	BR/A	SB	CS	SBR	FA	FR	G/POS	TPR
1883	Pit-a	32	114	12	18	2	1	0	7			.158	.207	.193	31	-8				.825	-2	S-21/O-6,C-5,2-2	-0.8
1884	Was-A	45	162	8	28	1	1	0	8			.173	.216	.191	39	-10				.781	-5	O-31,C-12/2-2,S-2	-1.3
Total	2	77	276	20	46	3	2	0	15			.167	.212	.192	35	-18				.771	-6	/O-37,S-23,C-17,2-4	-2.1

■ MOE MORHARDT
Morhardt, Meredith Goodwin b: 1/16/37, Manchester, Conn. BL/TL, 6'1", 185 lbs. Deb: 9/7/61

YEAR	TM/L	G	AB	R	H	2B	3B	HR	RBI	BB	SO	AVG	OBP	SLG	PRO+	BR/A	SB	CS	SBR	FA	FR	G/POS	TPR
1961	Chi-N	7	18	3	5	0	0	0	3		5	.278	.381	.278	78	-0	0	0	0	.962	-1	/1-7	-0.2
1962	Chi-N	18	16	1	2	0	0	0	2	2	8	.125	.222	.125	-4	-3	0	0	0	.000	0	H	-0.2
Total	2	25	34	4	7	0	0	0	2	5	13	.206	.308	.206	39	-3	0	0	0	.962	-1	/1-7	-0.4

■ GENE MORIARITY
Moriarity, Eugene John b: 1/5/1865, Holyoke, Mass. BL/TL, 5'8", 130 lbs. Deb: 6/18/1884

YEAR	TM/L	G	AB	R	H	2B	3B	HR	RBI	BB	SO	AVG	OBP	SLG	PRO+	BR/A	SB	CS	SBR	FA	FR	G/POS	TPR
1884	Bos-N	4	16	1	1	0	0	0	0		8	.063	.063	.063	-61	-3				.714	-1	/O-4	-0.3
	Ind-a	10	37	4	8	0	2	0	4	0		.216	.216	.324	76	-1				.769	-1	/O-7,P-2,3-1	-0.2
1885	Det-N	11	39	1	1	1	0	0	0		10	.026	.026	.051	-75	-7				.905	2	/O-6,3-4,S-1,P-1	-0.5
1892	StL-N	47	177	20	31	4	1	3	19	4	37	.175	.207	.260	43	-13	7			.820	2	O-47	-1.2
Total	3	72	269	26	41	5	3	3	23	4	55	.152	.174	.227	24	-24	7			.822	2	/O-64,3-5,P-3,S-1	-2.2

■ ED MORIARTY
Moriarty, Edward Jerome b: 10/12/12, Holyoke, Mass. d: 9/29/91, Holyoke, Mass. BR/TR, 5'10.5", 180 lbs. Deb: 6/21/35

YEAR	TM/L	G	AB	R	H	2B	3B	HR	RBI	BB	SO	AVG	OBP	SLG	PRO+	BR/A	SB	CS	SBR	FA	FR	G/POS	TPR
1935	Bos-N	8	34	4	11	2	1	1	1	0	6	.324	.324	.529	136	1	0			.923	-4	/2-8	-0.2
1936	Bos-N	6	6	1	1	0	0	0	1	0	1	.167	.167	.167	-11	-1	0			.000	0	H	-0.1
Total	2	14	40	5	12	2	1	1	1	0	7	.300	.300	.475	114	0	0			.923	-4	/2-8	-0.3

■ GEORGE MORIARTY
Moriarty, George Joseph b: 6/7/1884, Chicago, Ill. d: 4/8/64, Miami, Fla. BR/TR, 6', 185 lbs. Deb: 9/27/03 FMU

YEAR	TM/L	G	AB	R	H	2B	3B	HR	RBI	BB	SO	AVG	OBP	SLG	PRO+	BR/A	SB	CS	SBR	FA	FR	G/POS	TPR
1903	Chi-N	1	5	1	0	0	0	0	0			.000	.000	.000	-99	-1	0			1.000	-0	/3-1	-0.2
1904	Chi-N	4	13	0	0	0	0	0	0		1	.000	.071	.000	-77	-3	0			.778	-0	/3-2,O-2	-0.3
1906	NY-A	65	197	22	46	7	7	0	23	17		.234	.298	.340	90	-3	8			.912	1	3-39,O-15/1-5,2-1	-0.1
1907	NY-A	126	437	51	121	16	5	0	43	25		.277	.320	.336	101	0	28			.899	-10	3-91,1-22/O-9,2S	-0.9
1908	NY-A	101	348	25	82	12	1	0	27	11		.236	.269	.276	76	-9	22			.976	8	1-52,3-28,O-10/2-4	-0.2
1909	*Det-A	133	473	43	129	20	4	1	39	24		.273	.309	.338	100	-1	34			**.939**	2	*3-106,1-24	0.5
1910	Det-A	136	490	53	123	24	3	2	60	33		.251	.308	.324	92	-5	33			.927	-1	*3-134	-0.3
1911	Det-A	130	478	51	116	20	4	1	60	27		.243	.287	.308	63	-25	28			.929	-4	*3-129/1-1	-2.7
1912	Det-A	105	375	38	93	23	1	0	54	26		.248	.316	.315	83	-8	27			.987	-8	1-71,3-33	-1.7
1913	Det-A	105	347	29	83	5	2	0	30	24	25	.239	.302	.265	67	-14	33			.938	-3	3-94/O-7	-1.7
1914	Det-A	132	465	56	118	19	5	1	40	39	27	.254	.318	.323	90	-6	34	15	1	.956	17	*3-126/1-3	1.8
1915	Det-A	31	38	2	8	1	0	0	3	5	7	.211	.318	.237	63	-2	1	1	-0	.875	-0	3-12/1-1,2-1,O-1	-0.2
1916	Chi-A	7	5	1	1	0	0	0	0	2	0	.200	.429	.200	88	1	0			1.000	1	/1-1,3-1	0.1
Total	13	1076	3671	372	920	147	32	5	376	234	59	.251	.303	.312	82	-77	248	16		.931	0	3-796,1-180/O2S	-5.9

■ BILL MORIARTY
Moriarty, William Joseph b: 8/1883, Chicago, Ill. d: 12/25/16, Elgin, Ill. BR/TR, 6'2", 180 lbs. Deb: 4/29/09 F

YEAR	TM/L	G	AB	R	H	2B	3B	HR	RBI	BB	SO	AVG	OBP	SLG	PRO+	BR/A	SB	CS	SBR	FA	FR	G/POS	TPR
1909	Cin-N	6	20	1	4	1	0	0	1	0		.200	.200	.250	40	-1	2			.944	0	/S-6	-0.1

■ BILL MORLEY
Morley, William M. (b: William Morley Jennings) b: 1/23/1890, Holland, Mich. d: 5/14/85, Lubbock, Tex. BR/TR, 5'11", 170 lbs. Deb: 9/8/13

YEAR	TM/L	G	AB	R	H	2B	3B	HR	RBI	BB	SO	AVG	OBP	SLG	PRO+	BR/A	SB	CS	SBR	FA	FR	G/POS	TPR
1913	Was-A	2	1	0	0	0	0	0	0	0		.000	.000	.000	-98	-1	0			.000	0	/2-1	-0.1

■ RUSS MORMAN
Morman, Russell Lee b: 4/28/62, Independence, Mo. BR/TR, 6'4", 215 lbs. Deb: 8/3/86

YEAR	TM/L	G	AB	R	H	2B	3B	HR	RBI	BB	SO	AVG	OBP	SLG	PRO+	BR/A	SB	CS	SBR	FA	FR	G/POS	TPR
1986	Chi-A	49	159	18	40	5	0	4	17	16	36	.252	.328	.358	84	-3	1	0	0	.989	-3	1-47	-0.9
1988	Chi-A	40	75	8	18	2	0	0	3	3	17	.240	.304	.267	51	-5	0	0	0	.981	0	1-22,O-10/D-3	-0.9
1989	Chi-A	33	58	3	13	2	0	0	6	6	16	.224	.297	.259	59	-3	0	0	0	.988	1	1-35/D-1	-0.3
1990	KC-A	12	37	5	10	4	2	1	3	3	3	.270	.325	.568	147	2	0	0	0	1.000	-0	/O-8,1-3,D-1	0.1
1991	KC-A	12	23	1	6	0	0	0	1	1	9	.261	.292	.261	54	-1	0	0	0	1.000	0	/1-8,O-2,D-1	-0.1
1994	Fla-N	13	33	2	7	3	0	1	3	2	8	.212	.278	.364	64	-2	0	0	0	.987	2	/1-8	-0.2
1995	Fla-N	34	72	9	20	2	1	3	7	3	12	.278	.316	.458	101	-0	0	0	0	.955	-2	O-18/1-3	-0.3

YEAR	TM/L	G	AB	R	H	2B	3B	HR	RBI	BB	SO	AVG	OBP	SLG	PRO+	BR/A	SB	CS	SBR	FA	FR	G/POS	TPR
1996	Fla-N	6	6	0	1	1	0	0	0	1	2	.167	.286	.333	65	-0	2	0	1	1.000	-0	/1-2	-0.1
Total	8	203	463	48	115	16	4	9	41	35	100	.248	.307	.359	80	-13	2	0	1	.989	-7	1-128/O-38,D-6	-2.7

■ **JEFF MORONKO**   Moronko, Jeffrey Robert b: 8/17/59, Houston, Tex.   BR/TR, 6'2", 190 lbs.   Deb: 9/1/84

1984	Cle-A	7	19	1	3	1	0	0	3	3	5	.158	.273	.211	35	-2	0	0	0	.895	-0	/3-6,D-1	-0.2
1987	NY-A	7	11	0	1	0	0	0	0	0	2	.091	.167	.091	-29	-2	0	0	0	1.000	-0	/3-3,S-2,O-2	-0.2
Total	2	14	30	1	4	1	0	0	3	3	7	.133	.235	.167	12	-4	0	0	0	.926	-0	/3-9,O-2,S-2,D-1	-0.4

■ **JOHN MORRILL**   Morrill, John Francis "Honest John" b: 2/19/1855, Boston, Mass.   d: 4/2/32, Boston, Mass.   BR/TR, 5'10.5", 155 lbs.   Deb: 4/24/1876 M

1876	Bos-N	66	278	38	73	5	2	0	26	3	5	.263	.270	.295	87	-4				.857	7	2-37,C-23/O-5,1-3	0.3
1877	Bos-N	61	242	47	73	5	1	0	28	6	15	.302	.319	.331	101	0				.864	-9	3-30,1-18,O-11/2-3	-0.8
1878	Bos-N	60	233	26	56	5	1	0	23	5	16	.240	.256	.270	68	-9				.957	2	*1-59/O-1,3-1	-0.8
1879	Bos-N	84	348	56	98	18	5	0	49	14	32	.282	.309	.362	118	6				.878	3	3-51,1-33	0.0
1880	Bos-N	86	342	51	81	16	8	2	44	11	37	.237	.261	.348	108	3				.966	0	1-46,3-40/P-3	0.0
1881	Bos-N	81	311	47	90	19	3	1	39	12	30	.289	.316	.379	123	8				.969	1	*1-74/2-4,P-3,3-2	1.0
1882	Bos-N	83	349	73	101	19	11	2	54	18	29	.289	.324	.424	137	14				.964	-3	*1-76/S-3,2-1,O3PM	0.3
1883	Bos-N	97	404	83	129	33	16	6	68	15	68	.319	.344	.525	155	25				**.974**	-1	*1-81/O-7,3-6,S2PM	1.4
1884	Bos-N	111	438	80	114	19	7	3	61	30	87	.260	.308	.356	109	-5				.971	3	*1-91,2-17/P-7,3OM	-0.2
1885	Bos-N	111	394	74	89	20	7	4	44	64	78	.226	.334	.343	124	14				.969	-2	*1-92,2-17/3-2,M	0.5
1886	Bos-N	117	430	86	106	25	6	7	69	56	81	.247	.333	.381	121	13	9			.895	-3	S-55,1-42,2-20/PM	0.6
1887	Bos-N	127	504	79	141	32	6	12	81	37	86	.280	.330	.438	112	7	19			.984	1	*1-127,M	-0.2
1888	Bos-N	135	486	60	96	18	7	4	39	55	68	.198	.282	.288	81	-9	21			.979	-1	*1-133/2-2,M	-1.3
1889	Was-N	44	146	20	27	5	0	2	16	30	23	.185	.328	.260	70	-5	12			.980	-1	1-40/3-3,2-1,P-1,M	-0.7
1890	Bos-P	2	7	1	1	0	0	0	2	2	1	.143	.333	.143	28	-1	0			.750	-1	/S-1,1-1	-0.1
Total	15	1265	4912	821	1275	239	80	43	643	358	656	.260	.310	.367	111	68	61			.971	22	1-916,3-138,2/SOCP	0.8

■ **DOYT MORRIS**   Morris, Doyt Theodore b: 7/15/16, Stanley, N.C.   d: 7/4/84, Gastonia, N.C.   BR/TR, 6'4", 195 lbs.   Deb: 6/6/37

1937	Phi-A	6	13	0	2	0	0	0	0	0	3	.154	.154	.154	-23	-2	0	0	0	1.000	-0	/O-3	-0.2

■ **E. MORRIS**   Morris, E. b: Trenton, N.J.   Deb: 9/11/1884

1884	Bal-U	1	3	0	0	0	0	0		0		.000	.000	.000	-91	-1				.500	-1	/O-1,P-1	-0.1

■ **JOHN MORRIS**   Morris, John Daniel b: 2/23/61, N.Bellmore, N.Y.   BL/TL, 6'1", 185 lbs.   Deb: 8/5/86

1986	StL-N	39	100	8	24	0	1	1	14	7	15	.240	.290	.290	61	-5	6	2	1	.986	-1	O-31	-0.7
1987	*StL-N	101	157	22	41	6	4	3	23	11	22	.261	.314	.408	88	-3	5	2	0	.989	-15	O-74	-1.8
1988	StL-N	20	38	3	11	2	1	0	3	1	7	.289	.308	.395	99	-0	0	0	0	.857	-5	O-16	-0.6
1989	StL-N	96	117	8	28	4	1	2	14	4	22	.239	.264	.342	70	-5	0	0	0	1.000	-13	O-51	-1.9
1990	StL-N	18	18	0	2	0	0	0	0	3	6	.111	.238	.111	-1	-2	0	0	0	1.000	-2	/O-6	-0.4
1991	Phi-N	85	127	15	28	2	1	1	6	12	25	.220	.293	.276	61	-6	2	0	0	.974	-10	O-57	-1.8
1992	Cal-N	43	57	4	11	1	0	1	3	4	11	.193	.258	.263	46	-4	1	0	0	1.000	-3	O-14/D-6	-0.7
Total	7	402	614	60	145	15	8	8	63	42	108	.236	.288	.326	69	-26	15	4	2	.981	-49	O-249/D-6	-7.9

■ **WALTER MORRIS**   Morris, John Walter b: 1/31/1880, Rockwall, Tex.   d: 8/2/61, Dallas, Tex.   BR/TR, 5'11", Deb: 8/31/08

1908	StL-N	23	73	1	13	1	1	0	2	0		.178	.178	.219	28	-6	1			.938	4	S-23	-0.2

■ **P. MORRIS**   Morris, P. b: Rockford, Ill.   Deb: 5/14/1884

1884	Was-U	1	3	0	0	0	0	0		0		.000	.000	.000	-99	-1				.750	0	/S-1	-0.1

■ **HAL MORRIS**   Morris, William Harold b: 4/9/65, Fort Rucker, Ala.   BL/TL, 6'3", 200 lbs.   Deb: 7/29/88

1988	NY-A	15	20	1	2	0	0	0	0	0	9	.100	.100	.100	-44	-4	0	0	0	1.000	-1	/O-4,D-1	-0.5
1989	NY-A	15	18	2	5	0	0	0	4	1	4	.278	.316	.278	69	-1	0	0	0	1.000	-2	/O-5,1-2,D-1	-0.2
1990	*Cin-N	107	309	50	105	22	3	7	36	21	32	.340	.384	.498	135	14	9	3	1	.995	-8	1-80/O-6	0.9
1991	Cin-N	136	478	72	152	33	1	14	59	46	61	.318	.379	.479	135	22	10	4	1	.992	4	*1-128/O-1	1.9
1992	Cin-N	115	395	41	107	21	3	6	53	45	53	.271	.348	.389	105	3	6	6	-2	**.999**	5	*1-109	-0.1
1993	Cin-N	101	379	48	120	18	0	7	49	34	51	.317	.376	.420	112	7	2	2	5	.994	3	1-98	0.2
1994	Cin-N	112	436	60	146	30	4	10	78	34	62	.335	.389	.491	129	19	6	2	1	**.994**	1	*1-112	1.0
1995	*Cin-N	101	359	53	100	25	2	11	51	29	58	.279	.334	.451	105	2	1	1	-0	.994	5	1-99	-0.2
1996	Cin-N	142	528	82	165	32	4	16	80	50	76	.313	.377	.479	125	19	7	5	-1	.993	-2	*1-140	0.3
Total	9	844	2922	409	902	181	17	71	410	260	406	.309	.369	.455	120	82	41	23	-2	.994	14	1-768/O-16,D-2	3.3

■ **JIM MORRISON**   Morrison, James Forrest b: 9/23/52, Pensacola, Fla.   BR/TR, 5'11", 182 lbs.   Deb: 9/18/77

1977	Phi-N	5	7	3	3	0	0	0	1	1	1	.429	.500	.429	145	1	0	0	0	.875	1	/3-5	0.1
1978	*Phi-N	53	108	12	17	1	1	3	10	10	21	.157	.235	.269	40	-9	1	1	-0	.968	13	2-31/3-3,O-1	0.6
1979	Chi-A	67	240	38	66	14	0	14	35	15	48	.275	.328	.508	122	6	11	3	2	.982	1	2-48,3-29	1.1
1980	Chi-A	162	604	66	171	40	4	15	57	36	74	.283	.332	.424	106	4	9	6	-1	.969	-3	*2-161/S-1,D-1	1.1
1981	Chi-A	90	290	27	68	8	1	10	34	10	29	.234	.265	.372	84	-7	3	2	-0	.956	3	3-87/2-1,D-1	-0.2
1982	Chi-A	51	166	17	37	7	3	7	19	13	15	.223	.279	.428	91	-3	0	1	-1	.914	-14	3-50/D-1	-1.9
	Pit-N	44	86	10	24	4	1	4	15	5	14	.279	.319	.488	119	2	0	2	1	.964	2	3-26/O-2,2-1,S-1	0.4
1983	Pit-N	66	158	16	48	7	2	6	25	9	25	.304	.349	.487	126	5	2	6	-3	.973	3	2-28,3-26/S-7	0.6
1984	Pit-N	100	304	38	87	14	2	11	45	20	52	.286	.332	.454	119	7	0	1	-1	.938	3	3-61,2-26/S-2,1-1	0.7
1985	Pit-N	92	244	17	62	10	0	4	22	8	44	.254	.281	.344	75	-9	3	0	1	.961	1	3-59,2-15/O-1	-0.8
1986	Pit-N	154	537	58	147	35	4	23	88	47	88	.274	.337	.482	120	13	9	8	-2	.946	-13	*3-151/2-1,S-1	-0.5
1987	Pit-N	96	348	41	92	22	1	9	46	27	57	.264	.319	.411	91	-5	8	5	-1	.975	1	3-82,S-17/2-9	-0.4
	*Det-A	34	117	15	24	1	1	4	19	2	26	.205	.225	.333	47	-9	0	1	-1	.962	1	3-16/2-3,S-3,O1D	-0.8
1988	Det-A	24	74	7	16	5	0	1	5	2	13	.216	.216	.284	40	-6	0	2	-1	1.000	-0	D-14/1-4,3-4,O-2,S	-0.8
	Atl-N	51	92	6	14	2	0	2	13	10	13	.152	.235	.239	35	-8	1	0	-1	.933	1	3-20/O-4,P-3	-0.9
Total	12	1089	3375	371	876	170	16	112	435	213	521	.260	.308	.419	98	-18	50	37	-7	.949	2	3-619,2-324/SDO1P	-1.5

■ **JON MORRISON**   Morrison, Jonathan W. b: 1859, London, Ontario, Canada   5'9.5", 167 lbs.   Deb: 8/1/1884

1884	Ind-a	44	182	26	48	6	8	1		7		.264	.306	.401	132	6				.784	3	O-44	0.7
1887	NY-a	9	34	7	4	0	0	0	3	6		.118	.268	.118	10	-4		0		.600	-4	/O-9	-0.7
Total	2	53	216	33	52	6	8	1	3	13		.241	.299	.356	110	3		0		.756	-1	/O-53	0.0

■ **TOM MORRISON**   Morrison, Thomas J. b: 1875, St.Louis, Mo.   5'3", 145 lbs.   Deb: 9/18/1895

1895	Lou-N	6	22	3	6	0	2	0	4	1	1	.273	.304	.455	100	-0	0			1.000	-3	/S-3,3-3	-0.2
1896	Lou-N	8	27	3	4	1	0	0	0	4	4	.148	.258	.185	19	-3	0			.864	-3	/3-5,O-2,S-1	-0.3
Total	2	14	49	6	10	1	2	0	4	5	5	.204	.278	.306	55	-3	0			.839	-3	/3-8,S-4,O-2	-0.5

■ **JACK MORRISSEY**   Morrissey, John Albert "King" b: 5/2/1876, Lansing, Mich.   d: 10/30/36, Lansing, Mich.   BB/TR, 5'10", 160 lbs.   Deb: 9/18/02

1902	Cin-N	12	39	5	11	3	0	0	3	4		.282	.349	.359	108	-2				.941	-2	2-11/O-1	-0.1
1903	Cin-N	29	89	14	22	1	9	0	9	14		.247	.350	.258	67	-4	3			.922	-10	2-17/O-8,S-2	-1.3
Total	2	41	128	19	33	2	1	0	12	18		.258	.349	.289	78	-3	3			.930	-12	/2-28,O-9,S-2	-1.4

■ **JOHN MORRISSEY**   Morrissey, John J. b: 12/30/1856, Janesville, Wis.   d: 4/29/1884, Janesville, Wis.   Deb: 5/2/1881 F

1881	Buf-N	12	47	3	10	2	0	0	3	0	3	.213	.213	.255	47	-3				.865	-2	3-12	-0.4
1882	Det-N	2	7	1	2	0	0	0	0	0	2	.286	.286	.286	84	-0				.714	-1	/3-2	-0.1
Total	2	14	54	4	12	2	0	0	3	0	5	.222	.222	.259	52	-3				.841	-3	/3-14	-0.5

■ **JO-JO MORRISSEY**   Morrissey, Joseph Anselm b: 1/16/04, Warren, R.I.   d: 5/2/50, Worcester, Mass.   BR/TR, 6'1.5", 178 lbs.   Deb: 4/12/32

1932	Cin-N	89	269	15	65	10	1	0	13	14	15	.242	.282	.286	55	-17	2			.967	-9	S-45,2-42,3-12,/O-1	-0.4
1933	Cin-N	148	534	43	123	20	0	0	26	20	22	.230	.261	.268	52	-33	5			.964	-9	2-88,S-63,3-15	-3.5

YEAR	TM/L	G	AB	R	H	2B	3B	HR	RBI	BB	SO	AVG	OBP	SLG	PRO+	BR/A	SB	CS	SBR	FA	FR	G/POS	TPR
1936	Chi-A	17	38	3	7	1	0	0	6	2	3	.184	.225	.211	8	-6	0	0	0	.895	0	/3-9,S-4,2-1	-0.4
Total	3	254	841	61	195	31	1	0	45	36	40	.232	.266	.271	51	-56	7	0		.971	-0	2-131,S-112/3-36,O	-4.3

■ TOM MORRISSEY Morrissey, Thomas J. b: 1861, Janesville, Wis. d: 9/23/41, Janesville, Wis. 5'11", 180 lbs. Deb: 9/27/1884 F

| 1884 | Mil-U | 12 | 47 | 3 | 8 | 2 | 0 | 0 | | 0 | | .170 | .170 | .213 | 28 | -8 | | | | .710 | -1 | 3-12 | -0.8 |

■ BUD MORSE Morse, Newell Obediah b: 9/4/04, Berkeley, Cal. d: 4/6/87, Sparks, Nev. BL/TR, 5'9", 150 lbs. Deb: 9/14/29

| 1929 | Phi-A | 8 | 27 | 1 | 2 | 0 | 0 | 0 | 0 | 0 | 0 | .074 | .074 | .074 | -60 | -6 | 0 | 0 | 0 | .975 | 2 | /2-8 | -0.4 |

■ HAP MORSE Morse, Peter Raymond "Pete" b: 12/6/1886, St.Paul, Minn. d: 6/19/74, St.Paul, Minn. BR/TR, 5'8", 160 lbs. Deb: 4/18/11

| 1911 | StL-N | 4 | 8 | 0 | 0 | 0 | 0 | 0 | 0 | 1 | 2 | .000 | .111 | .000 | -70 | -2 | 0 | | | .750 | -0 | /S-2,O-1 | -0.2 |

■ CHARLIE MORTON Morton, Charles Hazen b: 10/12/1854, Kingsville, Ohio d: 12/9/21, Massillon, Ohio BR/TR, 150 lbs. Deb: 5/2/1882 MU

1882	Pit-a	25	103	12	29	0	3	0		5		.282	.315	.340	127	3				.816	1	O-25/3-3,S-1	0.4
	StL-a	9	32	2	2	0	1	0		2		.063	.118	.125	-17	-4				.708	-4	/2-7,O-3	-0.8
	Yr	34	135	14	31	0	4	0		7		.230	.268	.289	90	-1				.821	-3	O-28/2-7,3-3,S-1	-0.4
1884	Tol-a	32	111	11	18	6	2	0		7		.162	.212	.252	49	-6				.861	-1	3-16,O-15/P-3,2M	-0.5
1885	Det-N	22	79	9	14	1	2	0	3	5	10	.177	.226	.241	51	-4				.750	-2	3-18/S-4,M	-0.2
Total	3	88	325	34	63	7	8	0	3	19	10	.194	.238	.265	66	-11				.841	-3	/O-43,3-37,2-8,SP	-1.1

■ GUY MORTON Morton, Guy Jr. "Moose" b: 11/4/30, Tuscaloosa, Ala. BR/TR, 6'2", 200 lbs. Deb: 9/17/54 F

| 1954 | Bos-A | 1 | 1 | 0 | 0 | 0 | 0 | 0 | 0 | 0 | 1 | .000 | .000 | .000 | -90 | -0 | 0 | 0 | 0 | .000 | 0 | H | 0.0 |

■ BUBBA MORTON Morton, Wycliffe Nathaniel b: 12/13/31, Washington, D.C. BR/TR, 5'10.5", 180 lbs. Deb: 4/19/61

1961	Det-A	77	108	26	31	5	1	2	19	9	25	.287	.347	.407	98	-0	3	1	0	.952	-4	O-30	-0.5
1962	Det-A	90	195	30	51	6	3	4	17	32	32	.262	.366	.385	99	0	1	1	-0	.991	-2	O-62/1-3	-0.4
1963	Det-A	6	11	2	1	0	0	0	2	2	1	.091	.231	.091	-5	-2	0	0	0	.875	-0	/O-3	-0.2
	Mil-N	15	28	1	5	0	0	0	4	2	3	.179	.258	.179	28	-2	0	0	0	1.000	-1	/O-9	-0.4
1966	Cal-A	15	50	4	11	1	0	0	4	2	6	.220	.250	.240	43	-4	1	1	-0	1.000	0	O-14	-0.5
1967	Cal-A	80	201	23	63	9	3	0	32	22	29	.313	.387	.388	135	9	0	3	-2	1.000	-6	O-61	-0.1
1968	Cal-A	81	163	13	44	6	0	1	18	14	18	.270	.343	.325	107	2	2	1	0	.985	-4	O-50/3-1	-0.5
1969	Cal-A	87	172	18	42	10	1	7	32	28	29	.244	.360	.436	128	7	0	0	0	1.000	-0	O-49/1-1	0.5
Total	7	451	928	117	248	37	8	14	128	111	143	.267	.352	.370	106	10	7	7	-2	.988	-17	O-278/1-4,3-1	-2.1

■ WALT MORYN Moryn, Walter Joseph "Moose" b: 4/12/26, St.Paul, Minn. d: 7/21/96, Winfield, Ill. BL/TR, 6'2", 205 lbs. Deb: 6/29/54

1954	Bro-N	48	91	16	25	4	2	1	14	7	11	.275	.333	.429	94	-1	0	0	0	.881	-0	O-20	-0.2
1955	Bro-N	11	19	3	5	1	0	1	3	5	4	.263	.417	.474	132	1	0	0	0	.833	-2	/O-7	-0.1
1956	Chi-N	147	529	69	151	27	3	23	67	50	67	.285	.351	.478	122	16	4	2	0	.983	10	O-141	1.9
1957	Chi-N	149	568	76	164	33	0	19	88	50	90	.289	.349	.447	114	11	0	2	-1	.960	7	*O-147	0.9
1958	Chi-N☆	143	512	77	135	26	7	26	77	62	83	.264	.352	.494	123	16	1	2	-1	.978	5	*O-141	1.3
1959	Chi-N	117	381	41	89	14	1	14	48	44	66	.234	.318	.386	87	-7	0	0	0	.989	0	*O-104	-1.2
1960	Chi-N	38	109	12	32	4	0	2	11	13	19	.294	.369	.385	108	2	2	1	0	.964	0	O-30	0.1
	StL-N	75	200	24	49	4	3	11	35	17	38	.245	.304	.460	97	-1	0	0	0	.990	-3	O-62	-0.7
	Yr	113	309	36	81	8	3	13	46	30	57	.262	.327	.434	101	0	2	1	0	.981	-3	O-92	-0.6
1961	StL-N	17	32	0	4	2	0	0	2	1	5	.125	.152	.188	-10	-5	0	0	0	.889	-1	/O-7	-0.7
	Pit-N	40	65	6	13	1	0	3	9	2	10	.200	.235	.354	53	-5	0	0	0	.950	1	O-11	-0.4
	Yr	57	97	6	17	3	0	3	11	3	15	.175	.208	.299	31	-10	0	0	0	.931	-0	O-18	-1.1
Total	8	785	2506	324	667	116	16	101	354	251	393	.266	.338	.446	108	27	7	7	-2	.972	17	O-670	0.9

■ ROSS MOSCHITTO Moschitto, Rosaire Allen b: 2/15/45, Fresno, Cal. BR/TR, 6'2", 175 lbs. Deb: 4/15/65

1965	NY-A	96	27	12	5	0	0	1	3	0	12	.185	.185	.296	35	-2	0	0	0	.941	-26	O-89	-3.1
1967	NY-A	14	9	1	1	0	0	0	0	1	2	.111	.200	.111	-6	-1	0	0	0	1.000	-2	/O-8	-0.4
Total	2	110	36	13	6	0	0	1	3	1	14	.167	.189	.250	25	-4	0	0	0	.944	-28	/O-97	-3.5

■ LLOYD MOSEBY Moseby, Lloyd Anthony b: 11/5/59, Portland, Ark. BL/TR, 6'3", 200 lbs. Deb: 5/24/80

1980	Tor-A	114	389	44	89	24	1	9	46	25	85	.229	.282	.365	73	-15	4	6	-2	.982	6	*O-104/D-6	-1.6
1981	Tor-A	100	378	36	88	16	2	9	43	24	86	.233	.280	.357	78	-12	11	8	-2	.989	3	*O-100	-1.5
1982	Tor-A	147	487	51	115	20	9	9	52	33	106	.236	.295	.370	74	-18	11	7	-1	.992	-1	*O-145	-2.3
1983	Tor-A	151	539	104	170	31	7	18	81	51	85	.315	.380	.499	132	23	27	8	3	.983	10	*O-147	3.2
1984	Tor-A	158	592	97	166	28	**15**	18	92	78	122	.280	.372	.470	126	22	39	9	6	.990	-17	*O-156	4.0
1985	*Tor-A	152	584	92	151	30	7	18	70	76	91	.259	.348	.426	108	7	37	15	2	.980	1	*O-152	0.5
1986	Tor-A★	152	589	89	149	24	5	21	86	64	122	.253	.332	.418	100	0	32	11	3	.984	3	*O-147/D-3	0.1
1987	Tor-A	155	592	106	167	27	4	26	96	70	124	.282	.360	.473	116	14	39	7	8	.980	-8	*O-153/D-2	0.8
1988	Tor-A	128	472	77	113	17	7	10	42	70	93	.239	.345	.369	99	1	31	8	5	.984	-6	O-125/D-1	-0.4
1989	*Tor-A	135	502	72	111	25	3	11	43	56	101	.221	.307	.349	86	-9	24	7	3	.986	-3	*O-120,D-14	-1.4
1990	Det-A	122	431	64	107	16	5	14	51	48	77	.248	.331	.406	104	2	17	5	2	.983	8	*O-116/D-4	1.0
1991	Det-A	74	260	37	68	15	1	6	35	21	43	.262	.324	.396	97	-1	8	1	2	.955	-1	O-64/D-7	-0.2
Total	12	1588	5815	869	1494	273	66	169	737	616	1135	.257	.334	.414	102	15	280	92	29	.984	28	*O-1529/D-37	2.2

■ ARNIE MOSER Moser, Arnold Robert b: 8/9/15, Houston, Tex. BR/TR, 5'11", 165 lbs. Deb: 6/20/37

| 1937 | Cin-N | 5 | 5 | 0 | 0 | 0 | 0 | 0 | 0 | 0 | 2 | .000 | .000 | .000 | -99 | -1 | 0 | | | .000 | 0 | H | -0.1 |

■ JERRY MOSES Moses, Gerald Braheen b: 8/9/46, Yazoo City, Miss. BR/TR, 6'3", 210 lbs. Deb: 5/9/65

1965	Bos-A	4	4	1	1	0	0	1	0	2		.250	.250	1.000	224	1	0	0	0	.000	0	H	0.1
1968	Bos-A	6	18	2	6	0	0	2	4	1	4	.333	.368	.667	196	2	0	1	-1	.963	-3	/C-6	-0.1
1969	Bos-A	53	135	13	41	9	1	4	17	5	23	.304	.333	.474	117	3	0	1	-1	.981	-5	C-36	-0.2
1970	Bos-A☆	92	315	26	83	18	1	6	35	21	45	.263	.314	.384	85	-7	1	1	-0	.990	2	C-88/O-1	0.0
1971	Cal-A	69	181	12	41	8	2	4	15	10	34	.227	.267	.359	82	-5	0	0	0	.977	5	C-63/O-1	0.1
1972	Cle-A	52	141	9	31	3	0	4	14	11	29	.220	.290	.326	81	-3	0	0	0	.982	1	C-39/1-3	-0.3
1973	NY-A	21	59	5	15	2	0	2	6	2	6	.254	.279	.288	62	-3	0	0	0	1.000	5	C-17/D-1	0.2
1974	Det-A	74	198	19	47	6	3	4	19	7	38	.237	.284	.359	81	-5	0	1	-1	.985	0	C-74	-0.3
1975	SD-N	13	19	1	3	2	0	0	1	2	5	.158	.238	.263	42	-2	0	0	0	.900	-1	/C-5	-0.2
	Chi-A	2	2	1	1	0	0	0	0	0	0	.500	.500	1.500	441	1	0	0	0	1.000	-0	/1-1,D-1	0.1
Total	9	386	1072	89	269	48	8	25	109	63	184	.251	.297	.381	89	-19	1	4	-2	.984	3	C-328/1-4,D-2,O-2	-0.5

■ JOHN MOSES Moses, John William b: 8/9/57, Los Angeles, Cal. BB/TL, 5'10", 170 lbs. Deb: 8/23/82

1982	Sea-A	22	44	7	14	5	1	0	3	6	5	.318	.375	.545	145	3	5	1	1	.947	-4	O-19	-0.1
1983	Sea-A	93	130	19	27	4	1	0	6	12	20	.208	.280	.254	46	-9	11	5	0	.979	-9	O-71,D-10	-1.9
1984	Sea-A	19	35	3	12	1	1	0	2	1	3	.343	.395	.429	129	1	1	0	0	1.000	0	O-19/D-1	-0.3
1985	Sea-A	33	62	4	12	0	0	0	2	1	8	.194	.219	.194	14	-7	5	2	0	1.000	-7	O-29	-1.5
1986	Sea-A	103	399	56	102	16	3	3	34	34	65	.256	.314	.333	76	-13	25	18	-3	.987	2	*O-100/1-16,D-5	-1.8
1987	Sea-A	116	390	58	96	16	4	3	38	29	49	.246	.303	.331	65	-20	23	15	-2	.987	2	*O-100/1-16,D-5	-2.6
1988	Min-A	105	206	33	65	10	3	2	12	15	21	.316	.368	.422	117	5	11	6	0	1.000	-14	O-82/D-2	-1.1
1989	Min-A	129	242	33	68	12	3	1	31	19	23	.281	.336	.368	92	-2	14	7	0	.988	-24	*O-108/1-2,P-1,D-3	-2.8
1990	Min-A	115	172	26	38	9	1	1	14	19	19	.221	.306	.267	58	-9	2	3	-1	1.000	-17	O-85,D-10/1-6,P-2	-3.0
1991	Det-A	13	21	5	1	1	0	0	1	0	3	.048	.130	.095	-36	-4	4	0	1	1.000	-2	O-12	-0.5
1992	Sea-A	21	22	3	3	2	0	0	1	2	10	.136	.296	.182	37	-2	0	0	0	1.000	-4	O-18/D-1	-0.6
Total	11	769	1723	247	438	69	17	11	145	143	226	.254	.315	.333	75	-58	101	57	-4	.990	-86	O-636/D-36,1-31,P-3	-16.2

■ WALLY MOSES Moses, Wallace b: 10/8/10, Uvalda, Ga. d: 10/10/90, Vidalia, Ga. BL/TL, 5'10", 160 lbs. Deb: 4/17/35 C

| 1935 | Phi-A | 85 | 345 | 60 | 112 | 21 | 3 | 5 | 35 | 25 | 18 | .325 | .375 | .446 | 113 | 6 | 3 | 4 | -2 | .943 | 0 | O-80 | 0.2 |
| 1936 | Phi-A | 146 | 585 | 98 | 202 | 35 | 11 | 7 | 66 | 62 | 32 | .345 | .410 | .479 | 121 | 20 | 12 | 6 | 0 | .974 | 3 | *O-144 | 1.5 |

YEAR	TM/L	G	AB	R	H	2B	3B	HR	RBI	BB	SO	AVG	OBP	SLG	PRO+	BR/A	SB	CS	SBR	FA	FR	G/POS	TPR
1937	Phi-A☆	154	649	113	208	48	13	25	86	54	38	.320	.374	.550	132	28	9	7	-2	.958	6	*O-154	2.5
1938	Phi-A	142	589	86	181	29	8	8	49	58	31	.307	.369	.424	101	1	15	5	2	.966	5	*O-139	0.2
1939	Phi-A	115	437	68	134	28	7	3	33	44	23	.307	.370	.423	105	3	7	4	-0	.965	-1	*O-103	-0.1
1940	Phi-A	142	537	91	166	41	9	9	50	75	44	.309	.396	.469	126	22	6	4	-1	.974	4	*O-133	1.8
1941	Phi-A	116	438	78	132	31	4	4	35	62	27	.301	.388	.418	116	12	3	3	-1	.975	9	*O-109	1.3
1942	Chi-A	146	577	73	156	28	4	7	49	74	27	.270	.353	.369	106	5	16	10	-1	.980	7	*O-145	0.3
1943	Chi-A	150	599	82	147	22	**12**	3	48	55	47	.245	.310	.337	89	-9	56	16	8	.979	9	*O-148	0.0
1944	Chi-A	136	535	82	150	26	9	3	34	52	22	.280	.345	.379	108	6	21	7	2	.975	-2	*O-134	-0.1
1945	Chi-A†	140	569	79	168	**35**	15	2	50	69	33	.295	.373	.420	134	25	11	5	0	.977	9	*O-139	2.7
1946	Chi-A	56	168	20	46	9	1	4	16	17	20	.274	.344	.411	115	3	2	2	-1	1.000	-1	O-36	0.0
	*Bos-A	48	175	23	36	11	3	2	17	14	15	.206	.268	.337	65	-9	2	4	-2	.979	-0	O-44	-1.3
	Yr	104	343	43	82	20	4	6	33	31	35	.239	.306	.373	88	-6	4	6	-2	.989	-0	O-80	-1.3
1947	Bos-A	90	255	32	70	18	2	2	27	27	16	.275	.344	.384	95	-2	3	0	1	.974	-3	O-58	-0.7
1948	Bos-A	78	189	26	49	12	1	2	29	21	19	.259	.340	.365	83	-5	5	0	2	.981	-1	O-45	-0.4
1949	Phi-A	110	308	49	85	19	3	1	25	51	19	.276	.381	.367	102	2	1	3	-2	.983	-3	O-92	-0.6
1950	Phi-A	88	265	47	70	16	5	2	21	40	17	.264	.365	.385	94	-2	0	1	-1	.987	5	O-62	-0.7
1951	Phi-A	70	136	17	26	6	0	0	9	21	9	.191	.304	.235	46	-10	2	2	-1	.984	5	O-27	-0.9
Total	17	2012	7356	1124	2138	435	110	89	679	821	457	.291	.364	.416	109	97	174	81	4	.973	51	*O-1792	6.4

■ DOC MOSKIMAN   Moskiman, William Bankhead   b: 12/20/1879, Oakland, Cal.   d: 1/11/53, San Leandro, Cal.   BR/TR, 6', 170 lbs.   Deb: 8/23/10

YEAR	TM/L	G	AB	R	H	2B	3B	HR	RBI	BB	SO	AVG	OBP	SLG	PRO+	BR/A	SB	CS	SBR	FA	FR	G/POS	TPR
1910	Bos-A	5	9	1	1	0	0	0	1	2		.111	.273	.111	20	-1	0			1.000	0	/1-2,O-1	0.0

■ JIM MOSOLF   Mosolf, James Frederick   b: 8/21/05, Puyallup, Wash.   d: 12/28/79, Dallas, Ore.   BL/TR, 5'10", 186 lbs.   Deb: 9/9/29

YEAR	TM/L	G	AB	R	H	2B	3B	HR	RBI	BB	SO	AVG	OBP	SLG	PRO+	BR/A	SB	CS	SBR	FA	FR	G/POS	TPR
1929	Pit-N	8	13	3	6	1	1	0	2	1	1	.462	.500	.692	188	2	0			1.000	0	/O-3	0.2
1930	Pit-N	40	51	16	17	2	1	0	9	8	7	.333	.424	.412	103	1	0			.765	-3	O-12/P-1	-0.3
1931	Pit-N	39	44	7	11	1	0	0	8	8	5	.250	.365	.341	92	-0	0			1.000	-1	/O-4	-0.1
1933	Chi-N	31	82	13	22	5	1	1	9	5	8	.268	.326	.427	104	0	0			.964	1	O-22	0.0
Total	4	118	190	39	56	9	3	2	28	22	21	.295	.374	.405	107	3	0			.929	-4	/O-41,P-1	-0.2

■ JULIO MOSQUERA   Mosquera, Julio Alberto (Cervantes)   b: 1/29/72, Panama City, Panama   BR/TR, 6', 165 lbs.   Deb: 8/17/96

YEAR	TM/L	G	AB	R	H	2B	3B	HR	RBI	BB	SO	AVG	OBP	SLG	PRO+	BR/A	SB	CS	SBR	FA	FR	G/POS	TPR
1996	Tor-A	8	22	2	5	0	0	0	2	0	3	.227	.261	.318	45	-2	0	1	-1	1.000	1	/C-8	-0.1

■ CHARLIE MOSS   Moss, Charles Crosby   b: 3/20/11, Meridian, Miss.   d: 10/9/91, Meridian, Miss.   BR/TR, 5'10", 160 lbs.   Deb: 5/19/34

YEAR	TM/L	G	AB	R	H	2B	3B	HR	RBI	BB	SO	AVG	OBP	SLG	PRO+	BR/A	SB	CS	SBR	FA	FR	G/POS	TPR
1934	Phi-A	10	10	3	2	0	0	0	1	0	0	.200	.200	.200	4	-1	0	0		1.000	-1	/C-6	-0.2
1935	Phi-A	4	3	1	1	0	0	0	1	0		.333	.500	.333	120	0	0	0		.000	0	/C-1	0.0
1936	Phi-A	33	44	2	11	1	1	0	10	6	5	.250	.340	.318	65	-2	1	0		.929	-2	C-19	-0.3
Total	3	47	57	6	14	1	1	0	12	7	5	.246	.328	.298	58	-4	1	0		.935	-2	/C-26	-0.5

■ HOWIE MOSS   Moss, Howard Glenn   b: 10/17/19, Gastonia, N.C.   d: 5/7/89, Baltimore, Md.   BR/TR, 5'11.5", 185 lbs.   Deb: 4/14/42

YEAR	TM/L	G	AB	R	H	2B	3B	HR	RBI	BB	SO	AVG	OBP	SLG	PRO+	BR/A	SB	CS	SBR	FA	FR	G/POS	TPR
1942	NY-N	7	14	0	0	0	0	0	0	0	4	.000	.000	.000	-99	-3	0			1.000	0	/O-3	-0.4
1946	Cin-N	7	26	1	5	0	0	0	1	0	4	.192	.222	.192	19	-3	0			1.000	0	/O-6	-0.3
	Cle-A	8	32	2	2	0	0	0	0	3	9	.063	.143	.063	-44	-6	0	1	-1	.857	0	/3-8	-0.7
Total	2	22	72	3	7	0	0	0	1	3	17	.097	.145	.097	-32	-12	0	<u>1</u>		1.000	0	/O-9,3-8	-1.4

■ LES MOSS   Moss, John Lester   b: 5/14/25, Tulsa, Okla.   BR/TR, 5'11", 205 lbs.   Deb: 9/10/46   MC

YEAR	TM/L	G	AB	R	H	2B	3B	HR	RBI	BB	SO	AVG	OBP	SLG	PRO+	BR/A	SB	CS	SBR	FA	FR	G/POS	TPR
1946	StL-A	12	35	4	13	3	0	0	5	3	5	.371	.436	.457	142	2	1	0	0	.968	-1	C-12	0.4
1947	StL-A	96	274	17	43	5	2	6	27	35	48	.157	.255	.255	41	-22	0	0	0	.983	-5	C-96	-2.3
1948	StL-A	107	335	35	86	12	1	14	46	39	50	.257	.334	.424	98	-2	0	0	0	.988	-9	*C-103	-0.4
1949	StL-A	97	278	28	81	11	0	10	39	49	32	.291	.399	.439	117	8	0	1	-1	.970	-5	C-83	0.7
1950	StL-A	84	222	24	59	6	0	8	34	26	32	.266	.343	.401	87	-5	0	1	-1	.957	-1	C-60	-0.4
1951	StL-A	16	47	5	8	2	0	1	7	6	7	.170	.264	.277	45	-4	0	0	-1	.967	-0	C-12	-0.3
	Bos-A	71	202	18	40	6	0	3	26	25	34	.198	.289	.272	48	-15	0	0	-1	.984	-1	C-69	-1.3
	Yr	87	249	23	48	8	0	4	33	31	42	.193	.285	.273	47	-19	0	0	-1	.981	-1	C-81	-1.6
1952	StL-A	52	118	11	29	3	0	3	12	15	13	.246	.331	.347	86	-2	0	1	-1	.957	-3	C-39	-0.5
1953	StL-A	78	239	21	66	14	1	2	28	18	31	.276	.329	.368	86	-5	0	1	-1	.978	-6	C-71	-0.8
1954	Bal-A	50	126	7	31	3	0	0	5	14	16	.246	.321	.270	68	-5	0	1	-1	.972	-2	C-38	-0.6
1955	Bal-A	29	56	5	19	1	0	2	6	7	4	.339	.413	.464	146	4	0	1	-1	1.000	2	C-17	0.5
	Chi-A	32	59	5	15	2	0	2	7	6	10	.254	.333	.390	91	-0	0		-1	.990	-0	C-32	0.0
	Yr	61	115	10	34	3	0	4	13	13	14	.296	.372	.426	116	3	0	1	-1	.994	-1	C-49	0.5
1956	Chi-A	56	127	20	31	4	0	10	22	18	25	.244	.338	.512	120	3	0	1		.994	-6	C-49	-0.2
1957	Chi-A	42	115	10	31	3	0	2	12	20	18	.270	.378	.348	99	1	0	0		.980	-7	C-39	-0.5
1958	Chi-A	2	1	0	0	0	0	0	0	1	0	.000	.500	.000	51	0	0			.000	0	H	0.0
Total	13	824	2234	210	552	75	4	63	276	282	316	.247	.333	.369	86	-44	1	5	-3	.978	-42	C-720	-5.7

■ JOHNNY MOSTIL   Mostil, John Anthony "Bananas"   b: 6/1/1896, Chicago, Ill.   d: 12/10/70, Midlothian, Ill.   BR/TR, 5'8.5", 168 lbs.   Deb: 6/20/18

YEAR	TM/L	G	AB	R	H	2B	3B	HR	RBI	BB	SO	AVG	OBP	SLG	PRO+	BR/A	SB	CS	SBR	FA	FR	G/POS	TPR
1918	Chi-A	10	33	4	9	2	2	0	4	1	6	.273	.294	.455	125	1	1			.923	-2	/2-9	-0.1
1921	Chi-A	100	326	43	98	21	7	3	42	28	35	.301	.379	.436	109	5	10	12	-4	.946	2	O-91/2-1	-0.5
1922	Chi-A	132	458	74	139	28	14	7	70	38	39	.303	.375	.472	120	13	14	10	-2	.966	5	O-123	0.7
1923	Chi-A	153	546	91	159	37	15	3	64	62	51	.291	.376	.430	113	11	41	16	**3**	.974	22	*O-143/3-5,S-1	2.5
1924	Chi-A	118	385	75	125	22	5	4	49	45	41	.325	.401	.439	120	12	7	11	-5	.974	7	*O-102	0.8
1925	Chi-A	153	605	**135**	181	36	16	2	50	**90**	52	.299	.400	.421	115	16	**43**	20	1	**.985**	7	*O-153	1.3
1926	Chi-A	148	600	120	197	41	15	4	42	79	55	.328	.415	.467	134	32	35	14	**2**	.968	17	*O-147	4.0
1927	Chi-A	13	16	3	2	0	0	0	1	0	1	.125	.176	.125	-21	-3	1	0	0	.857	-2	/O-6	-0.4
1928	Chi-A	133	503	69	136	19	8	0	51	66	54	.270	.360	.340	86	-8	23	21	-6	.976	18	*O-131	-0.5
1929	Chi-A	12	35	9	8	3	0	0	3	6	2	.229	.341	.314	71	-1	1	1	-0	.963	-1	O-11	-0.3
Total	10	972	3507	618	1054	209	82	23	376	415	336	.301	.386	.427	113	78	176	<u>105</u>		.971	72	O-907/2-10,3-5,S-1	7.5

■ ANDY MOTA   Mota, Andres Alberto (Matos)   b: 3/4/66, Santo Domingo, D.R.   BR/TR, 5'10", 180 lbs.   Deb: 8/31/91   F

YEAR	TM/L	G	AB	R	H	2B	3B	HR	RBI	BB	SO	AVG	OBP	SLG	PRO+	BR/A	SB	CS	SBR	FA	FR	G/POS	TPR
1991	Hou-N	27	90	4	17	2	0	1	6	1	17	.189	.198	.244	25	-9	2	0	1	.970	-3	2-27	-1.2

■ JOSE MOTA   Mota, Jose Manuel (Matos)   b: 3/16/65, Santo Domingo, D.R.   BB/TR, 5'9", 155 lbs.   Deb: 5/25/91   F

YEAR	TM/L	G	AB	R	H	2B	3B	HR	RBI	BB	SO	AVG	OBP	SLG	PRO+	BR/A	SB	CS	SBR	FA	FR	G/POS	TPR
1991	SD-N	17	36	4	8	0	0	0	2	2	7	.222	.282	.222	42	-3	0	0	0	.962	0	2-13/S-3	-0.2
1995	KC-A	2	2	0	0	0	0	0	0	0	0	.000	.000	.000	-99	-1	0	0	0	1.000	0	/2-2	0.0
Total	2	19	38	4	8	0	0	0	2	2	7	.211	.268	.211	35	-3	0	0	0	.965	1	/2-15,S-3	-0.2

■ MANNY MOTA   Mota, Manuel Rafael (Geronimo)   b: 2/18/38, Santo Domingo, D.R.   BR/TR, 5'11", 168 lbs.   Deb: 4/16/62   FC

YEAR	TM/L	G	AB	R	H	2B	3B	HR	RBI	BB	SO	AVG	OBP	SLG	PRO+	BR/A	SB	CS	SBR	FA	FR	G/POS	TPR
1962	SF-N	47	74	9	13	0	0	1	9	7	8	.176	.256	.189	22	-8	3	2	-0	1.000	-2	O-27/3-7,2-3	-1.0
1963	Pit-N	59	126	20	34	2	3	0	7	7	18	.270	.313	.333	86	-2	0	2	-1	.953	-5	O-37/2-1	-1.1
1964	Pit-N	115	271	43	75	8	3	5	32	10	31	.277	.310	.384	94	-2	4	1	1	.961	-16	O-93/C-1,2-1	-2.2
1965	Pit-N	121	294	47	82	7	6	4	29	22	32	.279	.333	.384	101	0	2	2	-1	.985	-14	O-95	-1.9
1966	Pit-N	116	322	54	107	16	7	5	46	25	28	.332	.387	.472	137	17	7	7	-2	.994	-11	O-96/3-4	-0.1
1967	Pit-N	120	349	53	112	14	8	4	56	14	46	.321	.351	.441	125	10	3	2	-0	.988	-6	O-99/3-2	-0.3
1968	Pit-N	111	331	35	93	10	2	1	33	20	19	.281	.324	.332	99	-1	4	2	0	.981	-7	O-92/2-1,3-1	-1.4
1969	Mon-N	31	89	6	28	1	1	0	0	6	11	.315	.358	.348	98	-0	1	3	-2	.907	-2	O-22	-0.6
	LA-N	85	294	35	95	6	4	3	30	26	25	.323	.380	.401	128	11	5	4	-1	.969	0	O-80	0.6
	Yr	116	383	41	123	7	5	3	30	32	36	.321	.375	.389	120	11	6	7	-2	.954	-2	*O-102	0.0
1970	LA-N	124	417	63	127	12	6	3	37	47	37	.305	.379	.384	110	7	11	6	-0	.973	0	*O-111/3-1	0.2
1971	LA-N	91	269	24	84	13	5	0	34	20	20	.312	.362	.398	122	8	4	3	-1	.993	-8	O-80	-0.2
1972	LA-N	118	371	57	120	16	5	5	48	22	15	.323	.377	.434	133	16	4	4	-1	.993	-8	O-99	-0.2
1973	LA-N★	89	293	33	92	9	2	0	23	25	12	.314	.370	.365	109	4	1	3	-2	1.000	-6	O-74	-0.7
1974	*LA-N	66	57	5	16	2	0	0	16	5	4	.281	.349	.316	91	-1	0	0	0	1.000	-1	/O-3	-0.2
1975	LA-N	52	49	3	13	1	0	0	10	5	1	.265	.357	.286	84	-1	0	0	0	1.000	-0	/O-5	-0.1

YEAR	TM/L	G	AB	R	H	2B	3B	HR	RBI	BB	SO	AVG	OBP	SLG	PRO+	BR/A	SB	CS	SBR	FA	FR	G/POS	TPR
1976	LA-N	50	52	1	15	3	0	0	13	7	5	.288	.373	.346	107	1	0	0	0	1.000	1	/O-6	0.1
1977	*LA-N	49	38	5	15	1	0	1	4	10	0	.395	.521	.500	176	5	1	1	-0	1.000	-0	/O-1	0.5
1978	LA-N	37	33	2	10	1	0	0	6	3	4	.303	.361	.333	95	-0	0	0	0	.000	0	H	-0.1
1979	LA-N	47	42	1	15	0	0	0	3	3	4	.357	.400	.357	110	1	0	0	0	.000	-0	/O-1	0.0
1980	LA-N	7	7	0	3	0	0	0	2	0	0	.429	.429	.429	143	0	0	0	0	.000	0	/H	0.0
1982	LA-N	1	1	0	0	0	0	0	0	0	0	.000	.000	.000	-99	-0	0	0	0	.000	0	/H	0.0
Total	20	1536	3779	496	1149	125	52	31	438	289	320	.304	.358	.389	112	65	50	42	-10	.979	-87	*O-1021/3-15,2-6,C	-8.4

■ DARRYL MOTLEY
Motley, Darryl De Wayne   b: 1/21/60, Muskogee, Okla.   BR/TR, 5'9", 196 lbs.   Deb: 8/10/81

YEAR	TM/L	G	AB	R	H	2B	3B	HR	RBI	BB	SO	AVG	OBP	SLG	PRO+	BR/A	SB	CS	SBR	FA	FR	G/POS	TPR
1981	KC-A	42	125	15	29	4	0	2	8	7	15	.232	.278	.312	70	-5	1	3	-2	.968	3	O-39	-0.5
1983	KC-A	19	68	9	16	1	2	3	11	2	8	.235	.268	.441	91	-1	2	1	0	.978	1	O-18/D-1	-0.1
1984	*KC-A	146	522	64	148	25	6	15	70	28	73	.284	.321	.441	108	4	10	12	-4	.984	-2	*O-138	-0.6
1985	*KC-A	123	383	45	85	20	1	17	49	18	57	.222	.261	.413	81	-12	6	4	-1	.967	-8	O-114/D-7	-2.4
1986	*KC-A	72	217	22	44	9	1	7	26	11	31	.203	.241	.350	57	-13	0	2	-1	.979	-8	O-66/D-2	-2.4
	Atl-N	5	10	1	2	1	0	0	0	1	1	.200	.273	.300	55	-1	0	0	0	1.000	-0	/O-3	-0.1
1987	Atl-N	6	8	0	0	0	0	0	0	1	1	.000	.000	.000	-95	-2	0	0	0	1.000	-0	/O-2	-0.3
Total	6	413	1333	156	324	60	10	44	159	67	186	.243	.282	.402	86	-30	19	22	-8	.976	-15	O-380/D-10	-6.4

■ BITSY MOTT
Mott, Elisha Matthew   b: 6/12/18, Arcadia, Fla.   BR/TR, 5'8", 155 lbs.   Deb: 4/17/45

YEAR	TM/L	G	AB	R	H	2B	3B	HR	RBI	BB	SO	AVG	OBP	SLG	PRO+	BR/A	SB	CS	SBR	FA	FR	G/POS	TPR
1945	Phi-N	90	289	21	64	8	0	0	22	27	25	.221	.290	.249	52	-18	2			.944	13	S-63,2-27/3-7	0.0

■ CHAD MOTTOLA
Mottola, Charles Edward   b: 10/15/71, Augusta, Ga.   BR/TR, 6'3", 220 lbs.   Deb: 4/22/96

YEAR	TM/L	G	AB	R	H	2B	3B	HR	RBI	BB	SO	AVG	OBP	SLG	PRO+	BR/A	SB	CS	SBR	FA	FR	G/POS	TPR
1996	Cin-N	35	79	10	17	3	0	3	6	6	16	.215	.271	.367	67	-4	2	2	-1	1.000	-2	O-31	-0.7

■ CURT MOTTON
Motton, Curtell Howard   b: 9/24/40, Darnell, La.   BR/TR, 5'7.5", 175 lbs.   Deb: 7/5/67   C

YEAR	TM/L	G	AB	R	H	2B	3B	HR	RBI	BB	SO	AVG	OBP	SLG	PRO+	BR/A	SB	CS	SBR	FA	FR	G/POS	TPR
1967	Bal-A	27	65	5	13	2	0	2	9	5	14	.200	.278	.323	78	-2	0	-1	.973	-1		O-18	-0.3
1968	Bal-A	83	217	27	43	7	0	8	25	31	43	.198	.301	.341	94	-1	1	3	-2	.989	2	O-54	-0.4
1969	*Bal-A	56	89	15	27	6	0	6	21	13	10	.303	.398	.573	167	8	3	1	0	1.000	-3	O-20	0.5
1970	Bal-A	52	84	16	19	3	1	3	19	18	20	.226	.369	.393	109	-2	1	2	-1	1.000	-1	O-21	-0.1
1971	*Bal-A	38	53	13	10	1	0	4	8	10	12	.189	.317	.434	112	1	0	0	0	1.000	-2	O-16	-0.2
1972	Mil-A	6	6	1	1	0	0	1	2	1	2	.167	.286	.667	181	1	0	0	0	.000	-1	/O-3	-0.1
	Cal-A	42	39	6	6	1	0	1	5	12	12	.154	.250	.179	31	-3	0	0	0	1.000	-0	/O-9	-0.4
	Yr	48	45	7	7	1	0	2	7	13	14	.156	.255	.244	52	-3	0	0	0	1.000	-1	O-12	-0.5
1973	Bal-A	5	6	2	2	0	0	1	4	1	1	.333	.429	.833	250	1	0	0	0	.000	-0	/O-1,D-1	0.1
1974	*Bal-A	7	8	0	0	0	0	0	2	2	.000	.200	.000	-40	-1	0	0	0	1.000	-0	/O-2,D-1	-0.2
Total	8	316	567	85	121	20	1	25	89	86	116	.213	.322	.384	105	4	5	7	-3	.991	-5	O-144/D-2	-1.1

■ FRANK MOTZ
Motz, Frank H.   b: 10/1/1868, Freeburg, Pa.   d: 3/18/44, Akron, Ohio   6', 160 lbs.   Deb: 8/27/1890

YEAR	TM/L	G	AB	R	H	2B	3B	HR	RBI	BB	SO	AVG	OBP	SLG	PRO+	BR/A	SB	CS	SBR	FA	FR	G/POS	TPR
1890	Phi-N	1	2	1	0	0	0	0	1	0	.000	.333	.000	-1	-0	1			1.000	0	/1-1	0.0
1893	Cin-N	43	156	16	40	7	1	2	25	19	10	.256	.352	.353	85	-3	3			.981	6	1-43	0.1
1894	Cin-N	18	69	8	14	4	0	0	12	9	1	.203	.304	.261	36	-7	2			.995	4	1-18	-0.3
Total	3	62	227	25	54	11	1	2	37	29	12	.238	.337	.322	68	-11	6			.985	10	/1-62	-0.2

■ ALLIE MOULTON
Moulton, Albert Theodore   b: 1/16/1886, Medway, Mass.   d: 7/10/68, Peabody, Mass.   BR/TR, 5'6", 155 lbs.   Deb: 9/25/11

YEAR	TM/L	G	AB	R	H	2B	3B	HR	RBI	BB	SO	AVG	OBP	SLG	PRO+	BR/A	SB	CS	SBR	FA	FR	G/POS	TPR
1911	StL-A	4	15	4	1	0	0	0	1	4	.067	.263	.067	-6	-2	0			.938	-1	/2-4	-0.3

■ FRANK MOUNTAIN
Mountain, Frank Henry   b: 5/17/1860, Ft.Edward, N.Y.   d: 11/19/39, Schenectady, N.Y.   BR/TR, 5'11", 185 lbs.   Deb: 7/19/1880

YEAR	TM/L	G	AB	R	H	2B	3B	HR	RBI	BB	SO	AVG	OBP	SLG	PRO+	BR/A	SB	CS	SBR	FA	FR	G/POS	TPR
1880	Tro-N	2	9	1	2	0	0	0	0	4	.222	.222	.222	49	-0				1.000	0	/P-2	0.0
1881	Det-N	7	25	0	4	1	1	0	2	8	.160	.222	.280	55	-1				.923	-1	/P-7	0.0
1882	Wor-N	5	16	1	1	0	0	0	0	5	.063	.063	.063	-58	-3				.889	-1	/P-5	0.0
	Phi-a	9	36	5	12	3	0	0	2	.333	.368	.417	147	2				.917	1	/P-8,O-1	0.0
	Wor-N	20	70	8	19	2	2	2	5	18	.271	.301	.443	132	2				.870	-3	P-13/O-6,1-2,S-1	-0.2
1883	Col-a	70	276	36	60	14	5	3	9	.217	.242	.337	92	-2				.848	-2	P-59,O-12	0.0
1884	Col-a	58	210	26	50	7	3	4	9	.238	.283	.357	117	4				.919	2	P-42,O-17	0.0
1885	Pit-a	5	20	1	2	0	1	0	1	1	.100	.143	.200	8	-2				.846	0	/P-5	0.0
1886	Pit-a	18	55	6	8	1	1	0	2	13	.145	.319	.200	64	-2	3			.959	-0	1-16/P-2	-0.3
Total	7	194	717	84	158	28	13	6	13	39	35	.220	.265	.333	96	-2	3			.880	0	P-143/O-36,1-18,S-1	-0.5

■ JAMES MOUTON
Mouton, James Raleigh   b: 12/19/68, Denver, Colo.   BR/TR, 5'9", 175 lbs.   Deb: 4/4/94

YEAR	TM/L	G	AB	R	H	2B	3B	HR	RBI	BB	SO	AVG	OBP	SLG	PRO+	BR/A	SB	CS	SBR	FA	FR	G/POS	TPR
1994	Hou-N	99	310	43	76	11	0	2	16	27	69	.245	.316	.300	65	-16	24	5	4	.982	-5	O-96	-1.8
1995	Hou-N	104	298	42	78	18	2	4	27	25	59	.262	.327	.376	91	-4	25	8	3	1.000	-7	O-94	-1.0
1996	Hou-N	122	300	40	79	15	1	3	34	38	55	.263	.346	.350	93	-3	21	9	1	.971	-4	*O-108	-0.7
Total	3	325	908	125	233	44	3	9	77	90	183	.257	.330	.341	82	-23	70	22	8	.983	-16	O-298	-3.5

■ LYLE MOUTON
Mouton, Lyle Joseph   b: 5/13/69, Lafayette, La.   BR/TR, 6'4", 240 lbs.   Deb: 6/7/95

YEAR	TM/L	G	AB	R	H	2B	3B	HR	RBI	BB	SO	AVG	OBP	SLG	PRO+	BR/A	SB	CS	SBR	FA	FR	G/POS	TPR
1995	Chi-A	58	179	23	54	16	0	5	27	19	46	.302	.375	.475	125	7	1	0	0	.990	-0	O-53/D-2	0.5
1996	Chi-A	87	214	25	63	8	1	7	39	22	50	.294	.366	.439	108	3	3	0	1	.970	-7	O-47,D-28	-0.6
Total	2	145	393	48	117	24	1	12	66	41	96	.298	.370	.455	116	9	4	0	1	.982	-7	O-100/D-30	-0.1

■ RAY MOWE
Mowe, Raymond Benjamin   b: 7/12/1889, Rochester, Ind.   d: 8/14/68, Sarasota, Fla.   BL/TR, 5'7.5", 160 lbs.   Deb: 9/25/13

YEAR	TM/L	G	AB	R	H	2B	3B	HR	RBI	BB	SO	AVG	OBP	SLG	PRO+	BR/A	SB	CS	SBR	FA	FR	G/POS	TPR
1913	Bro-N	5	9	0	1	0	0	0	0	0	1	.111	.200	.111	-10	-1	0			.941	1	/S-2	0.0

■ MIKE MOWREY
Mowrey, Harry Harlan   b: 4/20/1884, Browns Mill, Pa.   d: 3/20/47, Chambersburg, Pa.   BR/TR, 5'10", 180 lbs.   Deb: 9/24/05

YEAR	TM/L	G	AB	R	H	2B	3B	HR	RBI	BB	SO	AVG	OBP	SLG	PRO+	BR/A	SB	CS	SBR	FA	FR	G/POS	TPR
1905	Cin-N	7	30	4	8	1	0	0	6	1	.267	.290	.300	69	-1	0			.759	-0	/3-7	-0.1
1906	Cin-N	21	53	3	17	3	0	0	6	5	.321	.379	.377	130	2	2			.930	4	3-15/2-1,S-1	0.6
1907	Cin-N	138	448	43	113	16	6	1	44	35	.252	.308	.321	93	-4	10			.929	-19	*3-127,S-11	-2.1
1908	Cin-N	77	227	17	50	9	1	0	23	12	.220	.266	.269	73	-7	5			.936	-7	3-56/S-3,O-3,2-1	-1.4
1909	Cin-N	38	115	10	22	5	0	0	5	20	.191	.311	.235	70	-3	2			.947	1	3-22,S-13	-0.2
	StL-N	12	29	3	7	1	0	0	4	4	.241	.333	.276	95	-0	1			.921	-1	/2-7,3-2	-0.1
	Yr	50	144	13	29	6	0	0	9	24	.201	.315	.243	75	-3	3			.948	1	*3-24,S-13/2-7	-0.3
1910	StL-N	143	489	69	138	24	6	2	70	67	38	.282	.375	.368	121	15	21			.927	12	*3-141	3.2
1911	StL-N	137	471	59	126	29	7	0	61	59	46	.268	.355	.359	103	3	15			.944	7	*3-134/S-1	1.1
1912	StL-N	114	408	59	104	13	8	2	50	46	29	.255	.335	.341	87	-7	19			.931	3	*3-108	-0.3
1913	StL-N	132	450	61	117	18	4	0	33	53	40	.260	.342	.318	90	-4	21			.953	16	*3-131	1.4
1914	Pit-N	79	284	24	72	7	5	1	25	22	20	.254	.316	.324	94	-2	8			.960	-2	3-78	-0.2
1915	Pit-F	151	521	56	146	26	6	1	49	66	39	.280	.367	.359	105	-2	40			**.959**	-19	*3-151	-1.6
1916	*Bro-N	144	495	57	121	22	6	0	60	50	60	.244	.320	.313	92	-3	16			**.965**	5	*3-144	0.2
1917	Bro-N	83	271	20	58	9	5	0	25	29	25	.214	.292	.284	75	-7	7			.952	-3	3-80/2-2	-1.0
Total	13	1276	4291	485	1099	183	54	7	461	469	297	.256	.334	.329	96	-21	167			.944	-10	*3-1196/S-29,2-11,O	-0.5

■ JOE MOWRY
Mowry, Joseph Aloysius   b: 4/6/08, St.Louis, Mo.   d: 2/9/94, St.Louis, Mo.   BB/TR, 6', 198 lbs.   Deb: 5/13/33

YEAR	TM/L	G	AB	R	H	2B	3B	HR	RBI	BB	SO	AVG	OBP	SLG	PRO+	BR/A	SB	CS	SBR	FA	FR	G/POS	TPR
1933	Bos-N	86	249	25	55	8	5	0	20	15	22	.221	.273	.293	67	-11	1			.994	1	O-64	-1.5
1934	Bos-N	25	79	9	17	3	0	1	4	3	13	.215	.244	.291	46	-6	0			.976	0	O-20/2-1	-0.7
1935	Bos-N	81	136	17	36	8	1	1	13	11	13	.265	.324	.360	91	-2	0			.970	-7	O-45	-1.0
Total	3	192	464	51	108	19	6	2	37	29	48	.233	.284	.313	71	-19	1			.985	-7	O-129/2-1	-3.2

■ MIKE MOYNAHAN
Moynahan, Michael   b: 1856, Chicago, Ill.   d: 4/9/1899, Chicago, Ill.   BL/TR,   Deb: 8/20/1880

YEAR	TM/L	G	AB	R	H	2B	3B	HR	RBI	BB	SO	AVG	OBP	SLG	PRO+	BR/A	SB	CS	SBR	FA	FR	G/POS	TPR
1880	Buf-N	27	100	12	33	5	1	0	14	6	9	.330	.368	.400	157	6				.862	-6	S-27	0.1
1881	Cle-N	33	135	12	31	5	1	0	8	3	14	.230	.246	.281	69	-5				.883	-2	O-32/3-1	-0.7
	Det-N	1	4	1	1	0	0	0	0	1	.250	.250	.250	55	-0				.857	1	/3-1	0.0
	Yr	34	139	13	32	5	1	0	8	3	15	.230	.246	.281	69	-5				.883	-2	O-32/3-2	-0.7
1883	Phi-a	95	400	90	124	18	10	1	67	31	.310	.360	.412	137	15				.833	0	*S-95	1.5

YEAR	TM/L	G	AB	R	H	2B	3B	HR	RBI	BB	SO	AVG	OBP	SLG	PRO+	BR/A	SB	CS	SBR	FA	FR	G/POS	TPR
1884	Phi-a	1	4	0	0	0	0	0	0	0	0	.000	.000	.000	-94	-1				.000	-0	/O-1	-0.1
	Cle-N	12	45	9	13	2	1	0	6	7	11	.289	.385	.378	136	2				.852	-0	/2-6,S-3,O-3	0.0
Total	4	169	688	124	202	30	13	1	95	47	35	.294	.339	.379	126	17				.837	-9	S-125/O-36,2-6,3-2	1.0

■ HEINIE MUELLER
Mueller, Clarence Francis   b: 9/16/1899, Creve Coeur, Mo.   d: 1/23/75, DeSoto, Mo.   BL/TL, 5'8", 158 lbs.   Deb: 9/25/20

YEAR	TM/L	G	AB	R	H	2B	3B	HR	RBI	BB	SO	AVG	OBP	SLG	PRO+	BR/A	SB	CS	SBR	FA	FR	G/POS	TPR
1920	StL-N	4	22	0	7	1	0	0	1	2	4	.318	.375	.364	117	1	1	0	0	1.000	0	/O-4	0.1
1921	StL-N	55	176	25	62	10	6	1	34	11	22	.352	.397	.494	137	9	2	4	-2	.976	-3	O-54	0.1
1922	StL-N	61	159	20	43	7	2	3	26	14	18	.270	.329	.396	91	-3	2	1	0	.947	-3	O-44	-0.8
1923	StL-N	78	265	39	91	16	9	5	41	18	16	.343	.392	.528	144	16	4	3	-1	.963	2	O-74	1.2
1924	StL-N	92	296	39	78	12	6	2	37	19	16	.264	.312	.365	82	-8	8	7	-2	.962	-2	O-53,1-27	-1.7
1925	StL-N	78	243	33	76	16	4	1	26	17	11	.313	.365	.424	99	-0	0	3	-2	.955	-3	O-72	-0.9
1926	StL-N	52	191	36	51	7	5	3	28	11	6	.267	.330	.403	93	-2	8			.950	-1	O-51	-0.6
	NY-N	85	305	36	76	6	2	4	29	21	17	.249	.300	.321	68	-14	7			.950	5	O-82	-1.5
	Yr	137	496	72	127	13	7	7	57	32	23	.256	.312	.353	78	-16	15			.950	4	*O-133	-2.1
1927	NY-N	84	190	33	55	6	1	3	19	25	12	.289	.384	.379	105	2	2			.944	-7	O-56/1-1	-0.7
1928	Bos-N	42	151	25	34	3	1	0	19	17	9	.225	.316	.258	54	-10	1			.985	6	O-41	-0.6
1929	Bos-N	46	93	10	19	2	1	0	11	12	12	.204	.302	.247	39	-9	-4			1.000	-4	O-24	-1.3
1935	StL-A	16	27	0	5	1	0	0	1	1	4	.185	.214	.222	12	-4	0	0	0	.955	-1	/1-3,O-2	-0.4
Total	11	693	2118	296	597	87	37	22	272	168	147	.282	.342	.389	94	-20	37	18		.960	-11	O-557/1-31	-7.1

■ DON MUELLER
Mueller, Donald Frederick "Mandrake The Magician"   b: 4/14/27, St.Louis, Mo.   BL/TR, 6', 185 lbs.   Deb: 8/2/48   F

YEAR	TM/L	G	AB	R	H	2B	3B	HR	RBI	BB	SO	AVG	OBP	SLG	PRO+	BR/A	SB	CS	SBR	FA	FR	G/POS	TPR
1948	NY-N	36	81	12	29	4	1	1	9	0	3	.358	.358	.469	121	2	0			.973	-1	O-22	0.0
1949	NY-N	51	56	5	13	4	0	0	1	5	6	.232	.295	.304	61	-3	0			1.000	-1	/O-6	-0.4
1950	NY-N	132	525	60	153	15	6	7	84	10	26	.291	.309	.383	80	-16	1			.986	-5	*O-125	-2.5
1951	NY-N	122	469	58	130	10	7	16	69	19	13	.277	.307	.431	95	-5	1	1	-0	.983	-2	*O-115	-1.1
1952	NY-N	126	456	61	128	14	7	12	49	34	24	.281	.333	.421	107	4	2	1	0	.987	-1	*O-120	-0.2
1953	NY-N	131	480	56	160	12	2	6	60	19	13	.333	.360	.404	97	-2	2	0	1	.972	-4	*O-122	-1.0
1954	*NY-N★	153	619	90	**212**	35	8	4	71	22	17	.342	.367	.444	110	-2	8	2	3	-1	.979	-4	*O-153	-0.2
1955	NY-N★	147	605	67	185	21	4	8	83	19	12	.306	.330	.393	91	-8	1	2	-1	.976	-11	*O-146	-2.7
1956	NY-N	138	453	38	122	12	1	5	41	15	7	.269	.293	.333	68	-20	0	1	-1	.989	-9	*O-117	-3.7
1957	NY-N	135	450	45	116	7	1	6	37	13	16	.258	.280	.318	60	-25	2	1	-1	.989	-1	*O-115	-3.3
1958	Chi-A	70	166	7	42	5	0	0	16	11	9	.253	.299	.283	62	-8	0	0	0	.968	-5	O-43	-1.6
1959	Chi-A	4	2	0	0	0	0	0	0	0	0	.000	.500	.500	178	0	0			.000	0	H	0.0
Total	12	1245	4364	499	1292	139	37	65	520	167	146	.296	.324	.390	89	-74	11	8		.982	-38	*O-1084	-16.5

■ HEINIE MUELLER
Mueller, Emmett Jerome   b: 7/20/12, St.Louis, Mo.   d: 10/3/86, Orlando, Fla.   BB/TR, 5'6", 167 lbs.   Deb: 4/19/38

YEAR	TM/L	G	AB	R	H	2B	3B	HR	RBI	BB	SO	AVG	OBP	SLG	PRO+	BR/A	SB	CS	SBR	FA	FR	G/POS	TPR
1938	Phi-N	136	444	53	111	12	4	1	34	64	43	.250	.346	.322	87	-6	2			.967	-27	*2-111,3-21	-2.7
1939	Phi-N	115	341	46	95	19	4	9	43	33	34	.279	.342	.437	111	5	4			.964	-14	2-51,3-17,O-17,S-1	-0.6
1940	Phi-N	97	263	24	65	13	2	3	28	37	23	.247	.344	.346	95	-1	2			.966	-9	2-34,O-31,3-13/1-2	-0.9
1941	Phi-N	93	233	21	53	11	1	1	22	22	24	.227	.302	.296	72	-9	2			.980	-4	2-29,O-21,3-19	-1.2
Total	4	441	1281	144	324	55	11	17	127	156	124	.253	.337	.353	93	-11	10			.968	-54	2-225/3-70,O-69,1S	-5.4

■ RAY MUELLER
Mueller, Ray Coleman "Iron Man"   b: 3/8/12, Pittsburg, Kan.   d: 6/29/94, Lower Paxton Township, Pa.   BR/TR, 5'9", 175 lbs.   Deb: 5/11/35   C

YEAR	TM/L	G	AB	R	H	2B	3B	HR	RBI	BB	SO	AVG	OBP	SLG	PRO+	BR/A	SB	CS	SBR	FA	FR	G/POS	TPR
1935	Bos-N	42	97	10	22	5	0	3	11	3	11	.227	.250	.371	70	-5	0			.978	-2	C-40	-0.5
1936	Bos-N	24	71	5	14	4	0	0	5	5	17	.197	.250	.254	38	-6	0			.986	-4	C-23	-0.9
1937	Bos-N	64	187	21	47	9	2	2	26	18	36	.251	.317	.353	90	-3	1			.995	5	C-57	0.2
1938	Bos-N	83	274	23	65	8	6	4	35	16	28	.237	.282	.354	82	-8	3			.993	-2	C-75	-0.7
1939	Pit-N	86	180	14	42	8	1	2	18	14	22	.233	.289	.322	65	-9	0			.971	-3	C-81	-0.9
1940	Pit-N	4	3	1	1	0	0	0	1	2	0	.333	.600	.333	165	1	0			1.000	1	/C-4	0.1
1943	Cin-N	141	427	50	111	19	4	8	52	56	42	.260	.347	.379	111	7	1			.988	20	*C-140	3.8
1944	Cin-N★	155	555	54	159	24	4	10	73	53	47	.286	.353	.398	115	11	4			.983	-5	*C-155	1.6
1946	Cin-N	114	378	35	96	18	4	8	48	27	37	.254	.309	.386	100	-2	0			**.994**	10	*C-100	1.4
1947	Cin-N	71	192	17	48	11	0	6	33	16	25	.250	.311	.401	88	-4	1			.984	-1	C-55	-0.2
1948	Cin-N	14	34	2	7	1	0	0	2	4	3	.206	.289	.235	45	-3	0			.982	1	C-10	-0.1
1949	Cin-N	32	106	7	29	4	0	1	13	5	13	.274	.319	.340	76	-4	1			1.000	-3	C-31	-0.4
	NY-N	56	170	17	38	2	2	5	23	13	14	.224	.279	.347	67	-8	1			.982	1	C-56	-0.5
	Yr	88	276	24	67	6	2	6	36	18	27	.243	.294	.344	70	-12	2			.988	-2	C-87	-0.9
1950	NY-N	4	11	0	1	1	0	0	0	0	2	.091	.091	.182	-30	-2	0			1.000	2	/C-4	-0.1
	Pit-N	67	156	17	42	7	0	6	24	11	14	.269	.321	.429	92	-2	2			.996	2	C-63	0.2
	Yr	71	167	17	43	8	0	6	24	11	16	.257	.307	.413	85	-4	2			.996	4	C-67	0.2
1951	Bos-N	28	70	8	11	3	1	1	9	7	11	.157	.234	.229	27	-7	0	0	0	1.000	4	C-23	-0.4
Total	14	985	2911	281	733	123	23	56	373	250	322	.252	.314	.368	91	-44	14	0		.988	21	C-917	2.7

■ WALTER MUELLER
Mueller, Walter John   b: 12/6/1894, Central, Mo.   d: 8/16/71, St.Louis, Mo.   BR/TR, 5'8", 160 lbs.   Deb: 5/7/22   F

YEAR	TM/L	G	AB	R	H	2B	3B	HR	RBI	BB	SO	AVG	OBP	SLG	PRO+	BR/A	SB	CS	SBR	FA	FR	G/POS	TPR
1922	Pit-N	32	122	21	33	5	1	2	18	5	7	.270	.305	.377	74	-5	1	0	0	.976	6	O-31	-0.1
1923	Pit-N	40	111	11	34	4	4	0	20	4	6	.306	.336	.414	95	-1	2	2	-1	.941	1	O-26	-0.3
1924	Pit-N	30	50	6	13	1	1	0	8	4	4	.260	.327	.320	73	-2	1	0	0	1.000	-1	O-15	-0.3
1926	Pit-N	19	62	8	15	0	1	0	3	0	2	.242	.242	.274	37	-5	0			.969	0	O-15	-0.6
Total	4	121	345	46	95	10	7	2	49	13	19	.275	.307	.362	74	-13	4	2		.966	7	/O-87	-1.2

■ BILL MUELLER
Mueller, William Lawrence "Hawk"   b: 11/9/20, Bay City, Mich.   BR/TR, 6'1.5", 180 lbs.   Deb: 8/29/42

YEAR	TM/L	G	AB	R	H	2B	3B	HR	RBI	BB	SO	AVG	OBP	SLG	PRO+	BR/A	SB	CS	SBR	FA	FR	G/POS	TPR
1942	Chi-A	26	85	5	14	0	5	12	9			.165	.276	.176	29	-8	2	1	0	.978	7	O-26	-0.2
1945	Chi-A	13	9	3	0	0	0	0	0	2	1	.000	.182	.000	-47	-2	1	0	0	.778	-3	/O-7	-0.4
Total	2	39	94	8	14	1	0	0	5	14	10	.149	.266	.160	22	-9	3	1	0	.960	4	/O-33	-0.6

■ BILL MUELLER
Mueller, William Richard   b: 3/17/71, Maryland Heights, Mo.   BB/TR, 5'11", 175 lbs.   Deb: 4/18/96

YEAR	TM/L	G	AB	R	H	2B	3B	HR	RBI	BB	SO	AVG	OBP	SLG	PRO+	BR/A	SB	CS	SBR	FA	FR	G/POS	TPR
1996	SF-N	55	200	31	66	15	1	0	19	24	26	.330	.404	.415	122	7	0	0	0	.966	-3	3-45/2-8	0.5

■ MIKE MULDOON
Muldoon, Michael D.   b: 1858, Ireland   5'8", 165 lbs.   Deb: 5/1/1882

YEAR	TM/L	G	AB	R	H	2B	3B	HR	RBI	BB	SO	AVG	OBP	SLG	PRO+	BR/A	SB	CS	SBR	FA	FR	G/POS	TPR
1882	Cle-N	84	341	50	84	17	5	6	45	10	28	.246	.268	.378	108	3				.880	3	*3-61,O-23	0.7
1883	Cle-N	98	378	54	86	22	3	0	29	10	39	.228	.247	.302	67	-15				.825	-9	*3-98/O-2	-2.2
1884	Cle-N	110	422	46	101	16	6	2	38	18	67	.239	.270	.320	82	-9				.833	-7	*3-109/O-1,2-1	-1.4
1885	Bal-a	102	410	47	103	20	6	2	52	20		.251	.293	.344	102	1				.870	-3	*3-101/2-1	-0.5
1886	Bal-a	101	381	57	76	13	8	0	23	34		.199	.269	.276	72	-12	12			.912	2	2-57,3-44	-0.5
Total	5	495	1932	254	450	88	28	10	187	92	134	.233	.270	.323	86	-31	12			.846	-14	3-413/2-59,O-26	-3.4

■ TONY MULLANE
Mullane, Anthony John "Count" or "The Apollo Of The Box"   b: 1/20/1859, Cork, Ireland   d: 4/25/44, Chicago, Ill.   BB/TR, 5'10.5", 165 lbs.   Deb: 8/27/1881

YEAR	TM/L	G	AB	R	H	2B	3B	HR	RBI	BB	SO	AVG	OBP	SLG	PRO+	BR/A	SB	CS	SBR	FA	FR	G/POS	TPR
1881	Det-N	5	19	0	5	0	0	0	0	1	0	.263	.263	.263	63	-1				.882	0	/P-5	0.0
1882	Lou-a	77	303	46	78	13	1	0		0	13	.257	.288	.307	107	3				.959	10	*P-55,1-13,O-12,/2	-0.1
1883	StL-a	83	307	38	69	11	6	0	33	13		.225	.256	.300	74	-9				.851	2	P-53,O-30/2-3,1-2	-0.3
1884	Tol-a	95	352	49	97	19	3	3		33		.276	.339	.372	127	11				.885	7	P-67,O-19/1-7,3S2	0.0
1886	Cin-a	91	324	59	73	12	5	0	39	25		.225	.283	.296	78	-9	20			.899	-9	P-63,O-27/1-4,3S2	-0.6
1887	Cin-a	56	199	35	44	6	3	3	23	16		.221	.292	.327	71	-8	20			.944	-2	P-48/O-9	-0.2
1888	Cin-a	51	175	27	44	4	1	0	16	8		.251	.296	.337	97	-1	12			.888	2	P-44/1-4,O-3,2-2	-0.2
1889	Cin-a	63	196	53	58	16	4	0	29	27	21	.296	.387	.418	125	7	24			.920	-1	P-33,3-18,O-12,/1-4	0.3
1890	Cin-N	81	286	41	79	9	8	0	34	39	30	.276	.375	.364	116	7	19			.941	-2	O-28,P-25,3-21,S/1	0.3
1891	Cin-N	64	209	16	31	1	2	0	10	18	33	.148	.229	.172	17	-22	4			.958	-3	P-51,O-12/3-4	-0.6
1892	Cin-N	39	118	14	20	3	1	0	9	8	19	.169	.246	.212	39	-9	4			.926	5	P-37/1-2	0.0
1893	Cin-N	16	52	11	15	2	1	0	6	5	3	.288	.383	.346	92	-0	1			.939	0	P-15/3-1	0.0
	Bal-N	38	114	15	26	2	1	0	14	5	14	.228	.261	.263	39	-10	5			.943	2	P-34/O-2,1-1	-0.1

YEAR	TM/L	G	AB	R	H	2B	3B	HR	RBI	BB	SO	AVG	OBP	SLG	PRO+	BR/A	SB	CS	SBR	FA	FR	G/POS	TPR
	Yr	54	166	26	41	2	1	1	20	10	17	.247	.302	.289	56	-11	6			.942	2	P-49/O-2,3-1,1-1	-0.1
1894	Bal-N	21	53	3	21	3	0	0	9	6	3	.396	.475	.453	120	2	2			.889	-1	P-21	0.0
	Cle-N	4	13	0	1	0	0	0	0	4	2	.077	.294	.077	-6	-2	1			.944	2	/P-4	0.0
	Yr	25	66	3	22	3	0	0	9	10	5	.333	.436	.379	94	-0	3			.911	1	P-25	0.0
Total	13	784	2720	407	661	99	38	8	223	221	114	.243	.307	.316	87	-42	112			.918	18	P-555,O-154/31S2	-1.5

■ GREG MULLEAVY
Mulleavy, Gregory Thomas "Moe"   b: 9/25/05, Detroit, Mich.   d: 2/1/80, Arcadia, Cal.   BR/TR, 5'9", 167 lbs.   Deb: 7/4/30   C

YEAR	TM/L	G	AB	R	H	2B	3B	HR	RBI	BB	SO	AVG	OBP	SLG	PRO+	BR/A	SB	CS	SBR	FA	FR	G/POS	TPR
1930	Chi-A	77	289	27	76	14	5	0	28	20	23	.263	.311	.346	69	-14	5	2	0	.918	-5	S-73	-0.9
1932	Chi-A	1	3	0	0	0	0	0	0	0	0	.000	.000	.000	-99	-1	0	0	0	1.000	0	/2-1	-0.1
1933	Bos-A	1	0	1	0	0	0	0	0	0	0	—	—	—	—	0	0	0	0	.000	0	R	0.0
Total	3	79	292	28	76	14	5	0	28	20	23	.260	.308	.342	67	-15	5	2	0	.918	-5	/S-73,2-1	-1.0

■ MULLEN
Mullen   Deb: 8/17/1872

YEAR	TM/L	G	AB	R	H	2B	3B	HR	RBI	BB	SO	AVG	OBP	SLG	PRO+	BR/A	SB	CS	SBR	FA	FR	G/POS	TPR
1872	Cle-n	1	4	1	0	0	0	0	0	0	0	.000	.000	.000	-99	-1	0	0	0	.400	-0	/O-1	-0.1

■ CHARLIE MULLEN
Mullen, Charles George   b: 3/15/1889, Seattle, Wash.   d: 6/6/63, Seattle, Wash.   BR/TR, 5'10.5", 155 lbs.   Deb: 5/18/10

YEAR	TM/L	G	AB	R	H	2B	3B	HR	RBI	BB	SO	AVG	OBP	SLG	PRO+	BR/A	SB	CS	SBR	FA	FR	G/POS	TPR
1910	Chi-A	41	123	15	24	2	1	0	13	4		.195	.220	.228	42	-8	4			.982	1	1-37/O-2	-0.9
1911	Chi-A	20	59	7	12	2	1	0	5	5		.203	.266	.271	51	-4	1			.969	0	1-20	-0.4
1914	NY-A	93	323	33	84	8	0	0	44	33	55	.260	.332	.285	86	-5	11	17	-7	.994	3	1-93	-1.2
1915	NY-A	40	90	11	24	1	0	0	7	10	12	.267	.340	.278	85	-1	5	2	0	.982	1	1-27	-0.1
1916	NY-A	59	146	11	39	11	1	0	18	9	13	.267	.310	.342	94	-2	7			.943	-4	2-20,1-17/O-6	-0.7
Total	5	253	741	77	183	22	3	0	87	61	80	.247	.306	.285	78	-20	28	19		.988	1	1-194/2-20,O-8	-3.3

■ MOON MULLEN
Mullen, Ford Parker   b: 2/9/17, Olympia, Wash.   BL/TR, 5'9", 165 lbs.   Deb: 4/18/44

YEAR	TM/L	G	AB	R	H	2B	3B	HR	RBI	BB	SO	AVG	OBP	SLG	PRO+	BR/A	SB	CS	SBR	FA	FR	G/POS	TPR
1944	Phi-N	118	464	51	124	9	4	0	31	28	32	.267	.315	.304	77	-14	4			.963	-7	*2-114/3-1	-1.5

■ JOHN MULLEN
Mullen, John   b: Philadelphia, Pa.   BL/TL,   Deb: 9/9/1876

YEAR	TM/L	G	AB	R	H	2B	3B	HR	RBI	BB	SO	AVG	OBP	SLG	PRO+	BR/A	SB	CS	SBR	FA	FR	G/POS	TPR
1876	Phi-N	1	3	0	0	0	0	0	0	0	0	.000	.000	.000	-99	-1				.714	0	/C-1	0.0

■ BILLY MULLEN
Mullen, William John   b: 1/23/1896, St.Louis, Mo.   d: 5/4/71, St.Louis, Mo.   BR/TR, 5'8", 160 lbs.   Deb: 10/2/20

YEAR	TM/L	G	AB	R	H	2B	3B	HR	RBI	BB	SO	AVG	OBP	SLG	PRO+	BR/A	SB	CS	SBR	FA	FR	G/POS	TPR
1920	StL-A	2	4	0	0	0	0	0	0	0	0	.000	.000	.000	-97	-1	0	0	0	1.000	-1	/2-1	-0.2
1921	StL-A	4	4	0	0	0	0	0	0	0	2	.000	.333	.000	-8	-1	0	0	0	1.000	0	/3-2	0.0
1923	Bro-N	4	11	1	3	0	0	0	0	0	0	.273	.273	.273	46	-1	0	0	0	.875	-0	/3-4	-0.1
1926	Det-A	11	13	2	1	0	0	0	0	5	1	.077	.333	.077	11	-1	1	0	0	.875	-0	/3-9	-0.1
1928	StL-A	15	18	2	7	1	0	0	2	3	4	.389	.476	.444	139	1	0	0	0	.867	1	/3-6	0.2
Total	5	36	50	5	11	1	0	0	2	10	6	.220	.350	.240	56	-3	1	0	0	.884	-1	/3-21,2-1	-0.2

■ FREDDIE MULLER
Muller, Frederick William   b: 12/21/07, Newark, Cal.   d: 10/20/76, Davis, Cal.   BR/TR, 5'10", 170 lbs.   Deb: 7/8/33

YEAR	TM/L	G	AB	R	H	2B	3B	HR	RBI	BB	SO	AVG	OBP	SLG	PRO+	BR/A	SB	CS	SBR	FA	FR	G/POS	TPR
1933	Bos-A	15	48	6	9	1	1	0	3	5	5	.188	.264	.250	37	-4	1	0	0	.923	-4	2-14	-0.7
1934	Bos-A	2	1	1	0	0	0	0	0	1	0	.000	.500	.000	36	-0	0	0	0	.800	-0	/2-1,3-1	0.0
Total	2	17	49	7	9	1	1	0	3	6	5	.184	.273	.245	38	-4	1	0	0	.914	-5	/2-15,3-1	-0.7

■ EDDIE MULLIGAN
Mulligan, Edward Joseph   b: 8/27/1894, St.Louis, Mo.   d: 3/15/82, San Rafael, Cal.   BR/TR, 5'9", 152 lbs.   Deb: 9/23/15

YEAR	TM/L	G	AB	R	H	2B	3B	HR	RBI	BB	SO	AVG	OBP	SLG	PRO+	BR/A	SB	CS	SBR	FA	FR	G/POS	TPR
1915	Chi-N	11	22	5	8	1	0	0	2	5	1	.364	.481	.409	170	2	2	2	-1	.907	3	S-10/3-1	0.5
1916	Chi-N	58	189	13	29	3	4	0	9	8	30	.153	.200	.212	24	-17	1			.888	3	S-58	-1.2
1921	Chi-A	151	609	82	153	21	12	1	45	32	53	.251	.293	.330	59	-38	13	18	-7	.955	-13	*3-151/S-1	-4.6
1922	Chi-A	103	372	39	87	14	8	0	31	22	32	.234	.278	.315	55	-26	7	7	-2	.971	-4	3-84/S-7	-1.6
1928	Pit-N	27	43	4	10	2	0	0	1	3	4	.233	.283	.279	45	-3	0			.929	0	/3-6,2-4	-0.3
Total	5	350	1235	143	287	41	24	2	88	70	120	.232	.278	.307	54	-82	23	27		.961	-3	3-242/S-76,2-4	-7.2

■ JOHN MULLIGAN
Mulligan, John   Deb: 6/14/1884

YEAR	TM/L	G	AB	R	H	2B	3B	HR	RBI	BB	SO	AVG	OBP	SLG	PRO+	BR/A	SB	CS	SBR	FA	FR	G/POS	TPR
1884	Was-U	1	4	2	1	0	0	0	0	0	0	.250	.250	.250	54	-0				1.000	1	/3-1	0.1

■ SEAN MULLIGAN
Mulligan, Sean Patrick   b: 4/25/70, Lynwood, Cal.   BR/TR, 6'2", 205 lbs.   Deb: 9/1/96

YEAR	TM/L	G	AB	R	H	2B	3B	HR	RBI	BB	SO	AVG	OBP	SLG	PRO+	BR/A	SB	CS	SBR	FA	FR	G/POS	TPR
1996	SD-N	2	1	0	0	0	0	0	0	0	0	.000	.000	.000	-99	-0	0	0	0	.000	0	/H	0.0

■ GEORGE MULLIN
Mullin, George Joseph "Wabash George"   b: 7/4/1880, Toledo, Ohio   d: 1/7/44, Wabash, Ind.   BR/TR, 5'11", 188 lbs.   Deb: 5/4/02

YEAR	TM/L	G	AB	R	H	2B	3B	HR	RBI	BB	SO	AVG	OBP	SLG	PRO+	BR/A	SB	CS	SBR	FA	FR	G/POS	TPR
1902	Det-A	40	120	20	39	4	3	0	11	8		.325	.367	.408	113	2	1			.921	1	P-35/O-4	-0.1
1903	Det-A	46	126	11	35	9	1	1	12	2		.278	.295	.389	107	1	1			.936	5	P-41/O-1	0.0
1904	Det-A	53	155	14	45	10	2	0	8	10		.290	.337	.381	131	5	1			.936	7	P-45/O-2	-0.1
1905	Det-A	47	135	15	35	4	0	0	12	12		.259	.320	.289	93	-1	4			.962	7	P-44/O-1	0.0
1906	Det-A	50	142	13	32	6	4	0	6	4		.225	.247	.324	76	-4	2			.957	2	P-40/2-1,O-1	-0.1
1907	*Det-A	70	157	16	34	5	3	0	13	12		.217	.276	.287	77	-4	2			.961	4	P-46/1-1	0.0
1908	*Det-A	55	125	13	32	2	1	0	8	7		.256	.306	.328	102	0	2			.973	3	P-39	0.0
1909	*Det-A	53	126	13	27	7	0	0	17	13		.214	.288	.270	73	-4	2			.944	-0	P-40/O-2	-0.1
1910	Det-A	50	129	15	33	6	2	1	11	8		.256	.299	.357	99	-1	1			.944	-3	P-38/O-2	-0.1
1911	Det-A	40	98	4	28	7	2	0	5	10		.286	.352	.398	104	0	1			.941	-2	P-30	0.0
1912	Det-A	38	90	13	25	5	1	0	12	17		.278	.393	.356	118	3	0			.929	0	P-30	0.0
1913	Det-A	12	20	1	7	0	0	0	1	4	1	.350	.458	.350	139	1	0			.952	1	/P-7	0.0
	Was-A	11	21	4	4	0	0	0	0	2	5	.190	.292	.190	41	-1	1			.958	1	P-11	0.0
	Yr	23	41	5	11	0	0	0	1	6	6	.268	.375	.268	89	-0	1			.956	1	P-18	0.0
1914	Ind-F	43	77	11	24	5	3	0	21	11	15	.312	.404	.455	121	1	0			.915	-4	P-36	0.0
1915	New-F	6	10	0	1	0	0	0	2	0	0	.100	.250	.100	0	-1	0			1.000	-1	/P-5	0.0
Total	14	614	1531	163	401	70	23	2	137	122	21	.262	.319	.344	99	-3	18			.947	24	P-487/O-13,1-1,2-1	-0.5

■ HENRY MULLIN
Mullin, Henry J.   b: 4/1862, St.John, N.B., Canada   d: 11/8/27, Beverly, Mass.   BR , 5'9", 160 lbs.   Deb: 6/4/1884

YEAR	TM/L	G	AB	R	H	2B	3B	HR	RBI	BB	SO	AVG	OBP	SLG	PRO+	BR/A	SB	CS	SBR	FA	FR	G/POS	TPR
1884	Was-a	34	120	13	17	3	1	0	8			.142	.195	.183	27	-9				.869	-1	O-34/3-1	-0.9
	Bos-U	2	8	1	0	0	0	0	0			.000	.000	.000	-99	-2				1.000	3	/O-2	0.0
Total	1	36	128	14	17	3	1	0	8			.133	.184	.172	18	-11				.882	2	/O-36,3-1	-0.9

■ JIM MULLIN
Mullin, James Henry   b: 10/16/1883, New York, N.Y.   d: 1/24/25, Philadelphia, Pa.   BR/TR, 5'10", 173 lbs.   Deb: 6/1/04

YEAR	TM/L	G	AB	R	H	2B	3B	HR	RBI	BB	SO	AVG	OBP	SLG	PRO+	BR/A	SB	CS	SBR	FA	FR	G/POS	TPR
1904	Phi-A	22	52	5	14	1	0	1	5	3		.269	.321	.346	106	0	2			.985	-5	/1-7,2-5,S-2,O-1	-0.6
	Was-A	27	102	10	19	2	2	0	4	4		.186	.224	.245	49	-6	3			.981	6	2-27	0.1
	Phi-A	19	58	4	10	0	0	0	4	2		.172	.238	.172	29	-4	2			.984	-1	1-19	-0.6
	Yr	68	212	19	43	3	2	1	13	9		.203	.258	.250	58	-10	7			.965	-0	2-32,1-26/S-2,O-1	-1.1
1905	Was-A	50	163	18	31	7	6	0	13	5		.190	.214	.307	67	-7	5			.928	-3	2-40/1-6	-1.1
Total	2	118	375	37	74	10	8	1	26	14		.197	.236	.275	62	-17	12			.946	-4	/2-72,1-32,S-2,O-1	-2.2

■ PAT MULLIN
Mullin, Patrick Joseph   b: 11/1/17, Trotter, Pa.   BL/TR, 6'2", 190 lbs.   Deb: 9/18/40   C

YEAR	TM/L	G	AB	R	H	2B	3B	HR	RBI	BB	SO	AVG	OBP	SLG	PRO+	BR/A	SB	CS	SBR	FA	FR	G/POS	TPR
1940	Det-A	4	4	0	0	0	0	0	0	0	0	.000	.000	.000	-91	-1	0	0	0	.000	-1	/O-1	-0.2
1941	Det-A	54	220	42	76	11	5	5	23	18	18	.345	.400	.509	126	8	5	1	1	.944	-4	O-51	0.1
1946	Det-A	93	276	34	68	13	4	9	35	25	36	.246	.311	.355	81	-7	3	5	-2	.949	-3	O-75	-1.6
1947	Det-A☆	116	398	62	102	28	6	15	62	63	66	.256	.359	.470	126	13	3	8	-4	.988	8	*O-106	1.2
1948	Det-A★	138	496	91	143	16	11	23	80	77	57	.288	.384	.504	132	22	1	2	-1	.972	0	*O-131	1.3
1949	Det-A	104	310	55	83	16	6	12	59	42	29	.268	.357	.448	112	4	1	2	-1	.989	-4	O-79	-0.4
1950	Det-A	69	142	16	31	5	0	6	23	24	23	.218	.315	.380	75	-6	1	4	-2	1.000	-1	O-32	-0.9
1951	Det-A	110	295	41	83	15	4	12	51	40	38	.281	.367	.481	128	11	2	2	-1	.939	-9	O-83	-0.2
1952	Det-A	97	255	29	64	13	4	7	35	31	30	.251	.332	.424	108	2	4	2	0	.979	-2	O-65	0.2
1953	Det-A	79	97	11	26	4	0	4	17	14	15	.268	.360	.402	107	1	0	1	-0	.944	-2	O-14	-0.2
Total	10	864	2493	381	676	106	43	87	385	330	312	.271	.358	.453	115	47	20	27	-10	.970	-14	O-637	-0.7

■ RANCE MULLINIKS
Mulliniks, Steven Rance   b: 1/15/56, Tulare, Cal.   BL/TR, 6', 170 lbs.   Deb: 6/18/77

YEAR	TM/L	G	AB	R	H	2B	3B	HR	RBI	BB	SO	AVG	OBP	SLG	PRO+	BR/A	SB	CS	SBR	FA	FR	G/POS	TPR
1977	Cal-A	78	271	36	73	13	2	3	21	23	36	.269	.329	.365	93	-3	1	1	-0	.963	2	S-77	0.7

YEAR	TM/L	G	AB	R	H	2B	3B	HR	RBI	BB	SO	AVG	OBP	SLG	PRO+	BR/A	SB	CS	SBR	FA	FR	G/POS	TPR
1978	Cal-A	50	119	6	22	3	1	1	6	8	23	.185	.242	.252	41	-9	2	0	1	.953	2	S-47/D-2	-0.3
1979	Cal-A	22	68	7	10	0	0	1	8	4	14	.147	.205	.191	8	-9	0	0	0	.957	-7	S-22	-1.4
1980	KC-A	36	54	8	14	3	0	0	6	7	10	.259	.344	.315	81	-1	0	0	0	.981	2	S-18,2-14	0.3
1981	KC-A	24	44	6	10	3	0	0	5	2	7	.227	.261	.295	61	-2	0	1	-1	.900	3	2-10/S-7,3-5	0.1
1982	Tor-A	112	311	32	76	25	0	4	35	37	49	.244	.327	.363	82	-8	3	2	-0	.938	-16	*3-102,S-16	-2.5
1983	Tor-A	129	364	54	100	34	3	10	49	57	43	.275	.374	.467	122	12	0	2	-1	.971	-18	*3-116,S-15/2-2	-0.8
1984	Tor-A	125	343	41	111	21	5	3	42	33	44	.324	.385	.440	133	11	2	3	-1	**.968**	-13	*3-119/S-3,2-1	-0.4
1985	*Tor-A	129	366	55	108	26	1	10	57	55	54	.295	.387	.454	126	15	2	0	1	**.971**	-16	*3-119	-0.3
1986	Tor-A	117	348	50	90	22	0	11	45	43	60	.259	.342	.417	103	2	1	1	-0	**.975**	-1	*3-110/2-1,D-5	-0.2
1987	Tor-A	124	332	37	103	28	1	11	44	34	55	.310	.374	.500	127	13	1	1	-0	.927	-6	3-96,D-22/S-1	0.4
1988	Tor-A	119	337	49	101	21	1	12	48	56	57	.300	.399	.475	143	21	1	0	0	1.000	5	*D-108/3-7	1.9
1989	*Tor-A	103	273	25	65	11	2	3	29	34	40	.238	.322	.326	85	-5	0	0	0	.985	1	D-73,3-29	-0.5
1990	Tor-A	57	97	11	28	4	0	2	16	22	19	.289	.420	.392	126	5	2	1	0	.949	-0	3-22,D-10/1-3	0.4
1991	*Tor-A	97	240	27	60	12	1	2	24	44	44	.250	.366	.333	92	-1	0	0	0	1.000	0	D-81/3-5	-0.4
1992	Tor-A	3	2	1	1	0	0	0	1	0	0	.500	.667	.500	221	0	0	0	0	.000	0	/D-2	0.0
Total	16	1325	3569	445	972	226	17	73	435	460	555	.272	.357	.407	107	40	15	12	-3	.961	-68	3-730,D-303,S/21	-3.0

■ **FRAN MULLINS**   Mullins, Francis Joseph b: 5/14/57, Oakland, Cal. BR/TR, 6', 180 lbs. Deb: 9/1/80

YEAR	TM/L	G	AB	R	H	2B	3B	HR	RBI	BB	SO	AVG	OBP	SLG	PRO+	BR/A	SB	CS	SBR	FA	FR	G/POS	TPR
1980	Chi-A	21	62	9	12	4	0	0	3	9	8	.194	.296	.258	53	-4	0	1	-1	.981	-2	3-21	-0.7
1984	SF-N	57	110	8	24	8	0	2	10	9	29	.218	.277	.345	77	-4	3	1	0	.969	9	S-28,3-28/2-4	0.8
1986	Cle-A	28	40	3	7	4	0	0	5	2	11	.175	.214	.275	33	-4	0	0	0	.953	8	2-13,S-11/1-1,D-1	0.4
Total	3	106	212	20	43	16	0	2	18	20	48	.203	.272	.307	61	-11	3	2	-0	.968	15	/3-49,S-39,2-17,D1	0.5

■ **JOE MULVEY**   Mulvey, Joseph H. b: 10/27/1858, Providence, R.I. d: 8/21/28, Philadelphia, Pa. BR/TR, 5'11.5", 178 lbs. Deb: 5/31/1883

YEAR	TM/L	G	AB	R	H	2B	3B	HR	RBI	BB	SO	AVG	OBP	SLG	PRO+	BR/A	SB	CS	SBR	FA	FR	G/POS	TPR
1883	Pro-N	4	16	1	2	1	0	0	2	0	1	.125	.125	.188	-6	-7				.692	-3	/S-4	-0.4
	Phi-N	3	12	2	6	1	0	0	3	0	1	.500	.500	.583	250	2				.750	-1	/3-3	0.1
	Yr	7	28	3	8	2	0	0	5	0	2	.286	.286	.357	96	-0				.692	-3	/S-4,3-3	-0.3
1884	Phi-N	100	401	47	92	11	2	2	32	4	49	.229	.237	.282	66	-15				.834	11	*3-100	-0.3
1885	Phi-N	107	443	74	119	25	6	6	64	3	18	.269	.274	.393	116	6				.848	-7	*3-107	0.1
1886	Phi-N	107	430	71	115	16	10	2	53	15	31	.267	.292	.365	98	-2	27			.879	-19	*3-107/O-1	-1.6
1887	Phi-N	111	474	93	136	21	6	2	78	21	14	.287	.321	.369	86	-10	43			.865	-15	*3-111	-2.0
1888	Phi-N	100	398	37	86	12	3	0	39	9	33	.216	.235	.261	55	-20	18			.891	-14	*3-100	-3.2
1889	Phi-N	129	544	77	157	21	9	6	77	23	25	.289	.319	.393	91	-11	23			.893	-1	*3-129	-0.4
1890	Phi-P	120	519	96	149	26	15	6	87	27	36	.287	.326	.430	99	-5	20			.857	-16	*3-120	-1.3
1891	Phi-a	113	453	62	115	9	13	5	66	17	32	.254	.287	.364	84	-13	11			.894	3	*3-113	-0.5
1892	Phi-N	25	98	19	14	1	1	0	4	9	8	.143	.200	.173	13	-10	2			.883	3	3-25	-0.6
1893	Was-N	55	226	21	53	9	4	0	19	7	8	.235	.264	.310	54	-16	2			.874	5	3-55	-0.8
1895	Bro-N	13	49	8	15	4	1	0	5	2	0	.306	.333	.429	104	0	1			.917	2	3-13	0.2
Total	12	987	4063	598	1059	157	70	29	532	134	257	.261	.287	.355	84	-96	147			.871	-48	3-983/S-4,O-1	-10.7

■ **JERRY MUMPHREY**   Mumphrey, Jerry Wayne b: 9/9/52, Tyler, Tex. BB/TR, 6'2", 185 lbs. Deb: 9/10/74

YEAR	TM/L	G	AB	R	H	2B	3B	HR	RBI	BB	SO	AVG	OBP	SLG	PRO+	BR/A	SB	CS	SBR	FA	FR	G/POS	TPR
1974	StL-N	5	2	2	0	0	0	0	0	0	0	.000	.000	.000	-99	-1	0	0	0	.000	-0	/O-1	-0.1
1975	StL-N	11	16	2	6	2	0	0	1	4	3	.375	.500	.500	172	2	0	0	0	1.000	1	/O-3	0.2
1976	StL-N	112	384	51	99	15	5	1	26	37	53	.258	.325	.331	86	-7	22	6	3	.993	6	O-94	-0.2
1977	StL-N	145	463	73	133	20	10	2	38	47	70	.287	.354	.387	100	1	22	15	-2	.971	-2	*O-133	-0.8
1978	StL-N	125	367	41	96	13	4	2	37	30	40	.262	.319	.335	84	-8	14	10	-2	.995	-8	*O-116	-2.3
1979	StL-N	124	339	53	100	10	3	3	32	26	39	.295	.345	.369	94	-2	8	11	-4	.984	-13	*O-114	-2.4
1980	SD-N	160	564	61	168	24	3	4	59	49	90	.298	.354	.372	109	7	52	5	13	.974	8	*O-153	2.3
1981	*NY-A	80	319	44	98	11	5	6	32	24	27	.307	.356	.429	127	11	14	9	-1	.966	7	O-79	1.5
1982	NY-A	123	477	76	143	24	10	9	68	50	66	.300	.366	.449	124	16	11	3	2	.986	9	*O-123	2.3
1983	NY-A	83	267	41	70	11	4	7	36	28	33	.262	.332	.412	107	3	2	3	-1	.983	7	O-83	0.6
	Hou-N	44	143	17	48	10	2	1	17	22	23	.336	.428	.455	154	11	5	0	2	.990	0	O-43	1.2
1984	Hou-N★	151	524	66	152	20	3	9	83	56	79	.290	.359	.391	119	13	15	7	0	.988	0	*O-137	1.0
1985	Hou-N	130	444	52	123	25	2	8	61	37	57	.277	.333	.396	106	3	6	7	-2	.969	-4	*O-126	-0.3
1986	Chi-N	111	309	37	94	11	2	5	32	26	45	.304	.358	.401	101	1	2	3	-1	.982	-16	O-92	-1.9
1987	Chi-N	118	309	41	103	19	2	13	44	35	47	.333	.401	.534	140	18	1	1	-0	.992	-2	O-85	1.3
1988	Chi-N	63	66	3	9	2	0	0	9	7	16	.136	.219	.167	12	-7	0	0	0	1.000	-1	/O-4	-0.9
Total	15	1585	4993	660	1442	217	55	70	575	478	688	.289	.351	.396	109	61	174	80	4	.981	-3	*O-1386	1.5

■ **JOHN MUNCE**   Munce, John Lewis "Big John" b: 11/18/1857, Philadelphia, Pa. d: 3/15/17, Philadelphia, Pa. 5'8.5", 160 lbs. Deb: 8/19/1884

YEAR	TM/L	G	AB	R	H	2B	3B	HR	RBI	BB	SO	AVG	OBP	SLG	PRO+	BR/A	SB	CS	SBR	FA	FR	G/POS	TPR
1884	Wil-U	7	21	1	4	0	0	0		1		.190	.227	.190	27	-2				.667	-1	/O-7	-0.3

■ **JAKE MUNCH**   Munch, Jacob Ferdinand b: 11/16/1890, Morton, Pa. d: 6/8/66, Lansdowne, Pa. BL/TL, 6'2.5", 170 lbs. Deb: 5/27/18

YEAR	TM/L	G	AB	R	H	2B	3B	HR	RBI	BB	SO	AVG	OBP	SLG	PRO+	BR/A	SB	CS	SBR	FA	FR	G/POS	TPR
1918	Phi-A	22	30	3	8	0	1	0	0	0	5	.267	.267	.333	80	-1	0			.667	-2	/O-3,1-2	-0.3

■ **GEORGE MUNDINGER**   Mundinger, George b: 11/20/1854, New Orleans, La. d: 10/12/10, Covington, La. BR/TR, 6'2", 200 lbs. Deb: 5/9/1884

YEAR	TM/L	G	AB	R	H	2B	3B	HR	RBI	BB	SO	AVG	OBP	SLG	PRO+	BR/A	SB	CS	SBR	FA	FR	G/POS	TPR
1884	Ind-a	3	8	1	2	0	0	0	3	0		.250	.250	.250	65	-0				.750	-3	/C-3	-0.3

■ **BILL MUNDY**   Mundy, William Edward b: 6/28/1889, Salineville, Ohio d: 9/23/58, Kalamazoo, Mich. BL/TL, 5'10", 154 lbs. Deb: 8/17/13

YEAR	TM/L	G	AB	R	H	2B	3B	HR	RBI	BB	SO	AVG	OBP	SLG	PRO+	BR/A	SB	CS	SBR	FA	FR	G/POS	TPR
1913	Bos-A	16	47	4	12	0	0	0	4	4	12	.255	.314	.255	65	-2	0			.952	-2	1-14	-0.5

■ **HORATIO MUNN**   Munn, Horatio B. Deb: 9/6/1875

YEAR	TM/L	G	AB	R	H	2B	3B	HR	RBI	BB	SO	AVG	OBP	SLG	PRO+	BR/A	SB	CS	SBR	FA	FR	G/POS	TPR
1875	Atl-n	1	4	0	0	0	0	0	0	0	0	.000	.000	.000	-99	-1	0	0	0	.833	-0	/2-1	-0.1

■ **JOSE MUNOZ**   Munoz, Jose Luis b: 11/11/67, Chicago, Ill. BB/TR, 5'11", 165 lbs. Deb: 4/7/96

YEAR	TM/L	G	AB	R	H	2B	3B	HR	RBI	BB	SO	AVG	OBP	SLG	PRO+	BR/A	SB	CS	SBR	FA	FR	G/POS	TPR
1996	Chi-A	17	27	7	7	0	0	0	1	4	1	.259	.355	.259	62	-1	0	0	0	.923	-2	/2-7,S-2,3-1,O-1,D	-0.3

■ **NOE MUNOZ**   Munoz, Noe b: 11/11/67, Escatepec, Mexico BR/TR, 6'2", 180 lbs. Deb: 4/30/95

YEAR	TM/L	G	AB	R	H	2B	3B	HR	RBI	BB	SO	AVG	OBP	SLG	PRO+	BR/A	SB	CS	SBR	FA	FR	G/POS	TPR
1995	LA-N	2	1	0	0	0	0	0	0	0	0	.000	.000	.000	-99	-0	0	0	0	1.000	1	/C-2	0.0

■ **PEDRO MUNOZ**   Munoz, Pedro Javier (Gonzalez) b: 9/19/68, Ponce, P.R. BR/TR, 5'11", 170 lbs. Deb: 9/1/90

YEAR	TM/L	G	AB	R	H	2B	3B	HR	RBI	BB	SO	AVG	OBP	SLG	PRO+	BR/A	SB	CS	SBR	FA	FR	G/POS	TPR
1990	Min-A	22	85	13	23	4	1	0	5	2	16	.271	.287	.341	70	-3	3	0	1	.972	-1	O-21/D-1	-0.5
1991	Min-A	51	138	15	39	7	1	7	26	9	31	.283	.331	.500	121	3	3	0	1	.989	0	O-44/D-2	0.4
1992	Min-A	127	418	44	113	16	3	12	71	17	90	.270	.300	.409	94	-5	4	5	-2	.987	-1	*O-122/D-3	-1.0
1993	Min-A	104	326	34	76	11	1	13	38	25	97	.233	.294	.393	82	-9	1	2	-1	.983	-6	*O-102	-1.7
1994	Min-A	75	244	35	72	15	2	11	36	19	67	.295	.351	.508	118	6	0	0	0	.965	-4	O-58,D-12	-0.6
1995	Min-A	104	376	45	113	17	0	18	58	19	86	.301	.339	.489	112	5	0	3	-2	.926	-4	D-77,O-25/1-3	-0.6
1996	Oak-A	34	121	17	31	5	0	6	18	9	31	.256	.308	.446	91	-2	0	0	0	1.000	-3	D-18,O-14	-0.6
Total	7	517	1708	203	467	75	8	67	252	100	418	.273	.317	.444	100	-5	11	10	-3	.980	-19	O-386,D-113/1-3	-4.0

■ **RED MUNSON**   Munson, Clarence Hanford b: 7/31/1883, Cincinnati, Ohio d: 2/19/57, Mishawaka, Ind. TR, Deb: 8/28/05

YEAR	TM/L	G	AB	R	H	2B	3B	HR	RBI	BB	SO	AVG	OBP	SLG	PRO+	BR/A	SB	CS	SBR	FA	FR	G/POS	TPR
1905	Phi-N	9	26	1	3	1	0	0	2	0		.115	.115	.154	-21	-4	0			.857	-1	/C-8	-0.4

■ **JOE MUNSON**   Munson, Joseph Martin Napoleon (b: Joseph Martin Napoleon Carlson)
    b: 11/6/1899, Renovo, Pa. d: 2/24/91, Drexel Hill, Pa. BL/TR, 5'9", 184 lbs. Deb: 9/18/25

YEAR	TM/L	G	AB	R	H	2B	3B	HR	RBI	BB	SO	AVG	OBP	SLG	PRO+	BR/A	SB	CS	SBR	FA	FR	G/POS	TPR
1925	Chi-N	9	35	5	13	3	0	3	3	1		.371	.436	.514	140	2	1	1	-0	1.000	-0	/O-9	0.1
1926	Chi-N	33	101	17	26	2	3	0	15	8	4	.257	.318	.406	93	-1	0			.898	-2	O-28	-0.5
Total	2	42	136	22	39	5	3	3	18	11	5	.287	.349	.434	105	1	1	1	_1_	.922	-2	/O-37	-0.4

■ **THURMAN MUNSON**   Munson, Thurman Lee b: 6/7/47, Akron, Ohio d: 8/2/79, Canton, Ohio BR/TR, 5'11", 191 lbs. Deb: 8/8/69

YEAR	TM/L	G	AB	R	H	2B	3B	HR	RBI	BB	SO	AVG	OBP	SLG	PRO+	BR/A	SB	CS	SBR	FA	FR	G/POS	TPR
1969	NY-A	26	86	6	22	1	2	1	9	10	10	.256	.333	.349	94	-1	0	1	-1	.986	-1	C-25	-0.1
1970	NY-A	132	453	59	137	25	4	6	53	57	56	.302	.389	.415	128	19	5	7	-3	.989	6	*C-125	3.0
1971	NY-A★	125	451	71	113	15	4	10	42	52	65	.251	.337	.368	106	4	6	5	-1	**.998**	-1	*C-117/O-1	0.6

YEAR	TM/L	G	AB	R	H	2B	3B	HR	RBI	BB	SO	AVG	OBP	SLG	PRO+	BR/A	SB	CS	SBR	FA	FR	G/POS	TPR
1972	NY-A	140	511	54	143	16	3	7	46	47	58	.280	.344	.364	115	9	6	7	-2	.977	-5	*C-132	0.9
1973	NY-A★	147	519	80	156	29	4	20	74	64	64	.301	.364	.487	143	28	4	6	-2	.984	6	*C-142/D-1	3.8
1974	NY-A★	144	517	64	135	19	2	13	60	44	66	.261	.320	.381	103	1	2	0	1	.974	2	*C-137/D-4	1.0
1975	NY-A★	157	597	83	190	24	3	12	102	45	52	.318	.343	.429	128	22	3	2	-0	.972	9	*C-130,D-22/1-2,03	3.6
1976	*NY-A★	152	616	79	186	27	1	17	105	29	38	.302	.343	.432	127	19	14	11	-2	.981	-6	*C-121,D-21,0-11	1.4
1977	*NY-A★	149	595	85	183	28	5	18	100	39	55	.308	.352	.462	121	16	5	6	-2	.984	-5	*C-136,D-10	1.3
1978	*NY-A†	154	617	73	183	27	1	6	71	35	70	.297	.337	.373	102	1	2	3	-1	.986	-0	*C-125,D-14,0-13	0.2
1979	NY-A	97	382	42	110	18	3	3	39	32	37	.288	.343	.374	95	-2	1	2	-1	.978	-6	C-88/1-3,D-5	-0.5
Total	11	1423	5344	696	1558	229	32	113	701	438	571	.292	.350	.410	117	117	48	50	-16	.982	-1	*C-1278/D-77,013	15.2

■ JOHN MUNYAN Munyan, John B. b: 11/14/1860, Chester, Pa. d: 2/18/45, Endicott, N.Y. Deb: 7/12/1887

YEAR	TM/L	G	AB	R	H	2B	3B	HR	RBI	BB	SO	AVG	OBP	SLG	PRO+	BR/A	SB	CS	SBR	FA	FR	G/POS	TPR
1887	Cle-a	16	58	9	14	1	1	0	6	3		.241	.279	.293	61	-3	4			.762	-2	O-12/C-3,3-2	-0.4
1890	Col-a	2	7	1	1	0	0	0	0	0		.143	.250	.143	17	-1	0			.667	0	/O-2	-0.1
	StL-a	96	342	61	91	15	7	4	42	32		.266	.341	.386	100	-3	11			.939	-3	C-83/O-7,2-5,3-3,S	0.1
	Yr	98	349	62	92	15	7	4	42	32		.264	.339	.381	99	-4	11			.939	-3	C-83/O-9,2-5,3-3,S	0.0
1891	StL-a	62	182	44	42	4	3	0	20	43	39	.231	.389	.286	81	-4	13			.943	-6	C-45,O-12/S-5,3-3	-0.6
Total	3	176	589	115	148	20	11	4	68	78	39	.251	.351	.343	90	-11	28			.937	-10	C-131/O-33,3-8,S2	-1.0

■ BOBBY MURCER Murcer, Bobby Ray b: 5/20/46, Oklahoma City, Okla BL/TR, 5'11", 180 lbs. Deb: 9/8/65

YEAR	TM/L	G	AB	R	H	2B	3B	HR	RBI	BB	SO	AVG	OBP	SLG	PRO+	BR/A	SB	CS	SBR	FA	FR	G/POS	TPR
1965	NY-A	11	37	2	9	0	1	0	4	5	12	.243	.333	.378	102	0	0	0	0	.932	7	S-11	0.8
1966	NY-A	21	69	3	12	1	1	0	5	4	5	.174	.219	.217	27	-7	2	2	-1	.931	-4	S-18	-1.0
1969	NY-A	152	564	82	146	24	4	26	82	50	103	.259	.323	.454	120	12	7	5	-1	.964	-5	*O-118,3-31	-0.1
1970	NY-A	159	581	95	146	23	3	23	78	87	100	.251	.351	.420	118	14	15	10	-2	.992	10	*O-155	1.5
1971	NY-A	146	529	94	175	25	6	25	94	91	60	.331	**.429**	.543	185	61	14	8	-1	.985	-1	*O-143	**5.5**
1972	NY-A★	153	585	**102**	171	30	7	33	96	63	67	.292	.363	.537	171	49	11	9	-2	.992	10	*O-151	**5.5**
1973	NY-A★	160	616	83	187	29	2	22	95	50	67	.304	.359	.464	135	27	6	7	-2	.985	2	*O-160	1.9
1974	NY-A★	156	606	69	166	25	4	10	88	57	59	.274	.338	.378	108	6	14	5	1	.978	0	*O-156	0.1
1975	SF-N★	147	526	80	157	29	4	11	91	91	45	.298	.404	.432	127	22	9	5	-0	.981	-8	*O-144	0.9
1976	SF-N	147	533	73	138	20	2	23	90	84	78	.259	.364	.433	122	17	12	7	-1	.961	-0	*O-146	1.0
1977	Chi-N	154	554	90	147	18	3	27	89	80	77	.265	.361	.455	106	5	16	7	1	.980	-4	*O-150/2-1,S-1	0.1
1978	Chi-N	146	499	66	140	22	6	9	64	80	57	.281	.380	.403	106	6	14	5	1	.979	-17	*O-138	-1.6
1979	Chi-N	58	190	22	49	4	1	7	22	36	20	.258	.379	.400	103	2	2	3	-1	1.000	3	O-54	0.1
	NY-A	74	264	42	72	12	0	8	33	25	32	.273	.340	.409	103	1	1	1	-0	.983	-6	O-70	-0.6
1980	*NY-A	100	297	41	80	9	1	13	57	34	28	.269	.348	.438	116	7	2	0	1	.955	-9	O-59,D-33	-0.5
1981	*NY-A	50	117	14	31	6	0	6	24	12	15	.265	.333	.470	131	4	0	0	0	.000	0	D-33	0.3
1982	NY-A	65	141	12	32	6	0	7	30	12	15	.227	.292	.418	94	-2	2	1	0	.000	0	D-47	-0.3
1983	NY-A	9	22	2	4	2	0	1	1	1	1	.182	.217	.409	71	-1	0	0	0	.000	0	/D-5	-0.1
Total	17	1908	6730	972	1862	285	45	252	1043	862	841	.277	.361	.445	124	223	127	75	-7	.981	-19	*O-1644,D-118/3S2	12.9

■ SIMMY MURCH Murch, Simeon Augustus b: 11/21/1880, Castine, Me. d: 6/6/39, Exeter, N.H. BR/TR, 6'4", 220 lbs. Deb: 9/20/04

YEAR	TM/L	G	AB	R	H	2B	3B	HR	RBI	BB	SO	AVG	OBP	SLG	PRO+	BR/A	SB	CS	SBR	FA	FR	G/POS	TPR
1904	StL-N	13	51	3	7	1	0	0	1	1		.137	.154	.157	-4	-6	0			.905	-3	/2-6,3-6,S-1	-0.9
1905	StL-N	4	9	0	1	0	0	0	0	0		.111	.111	.111	-35	-1	0			.750	-3	/2-2,S-1	-0.5
1908	Bro-N	6	11	1	2	1	0	0	0	1		.182	.250	.273	70	-0	0			.964	-1	/1-2	-0.1
Total	3	23	71	4	10	2	0	0	1	2		.141	.164	.169	3	-8	0			.880	-6	/2-8,3-6,1-2,S-2	-1.5

■ WILBUR MURDOCH Murdoch, Wilbur Edwin b: 3/14/1875, Avon, N.Y. d: 10/29/41, Los Angeles, Cal. Deb: 8/29/08

YEAR	TM/L	G	AB	R	H	2B	3B	HR	RBI	BB	SO	AVG	OBP	SLG	PRO+	BR/A	SB	CS	SBR	FA	FR	G/POS	TPR
1908	StL-N	27	62	5	16	3	0	0	5	3		.258	.292	.306	96	-0	4			.913	-5	O-16	-0.6

■ TIM MURNANE Murnane, Timothy Hayes b: 6/4/1852, Naugatuck, Conn. d: 2/7/17, Boston, Mass. BL/TR, 5'9.5", 172 lbs. Deb: 4/26/1872 M

YEAR	TM/L	G	AB	R	H	2B	3B	HR	RBI	BB	SO	AVG	OBP	SLG	PRO+	BR/A	SB	CS	SBR	FA	FR	G/POS	TPR
1872	Man-n	24	117	30	42	1	0	0	13	0	1	.359	.359	.368	131	5	1	0	0	.883	-5	1-24	0.1
1873	Ath-n	41	176	53	39	3	0	1	10	8	13	.222	.255	.256	49	-12	7	2	1	.797	-4	O-30,1-10/2-6	-1.0
1874	Ath-n	21	82	11	17	2	0	0	11	1	3	.207	.217	.232	40	-6	0	1	-1	.857	-5	O-14/2-6,1-3	-0.9
1875	Phi-n	69	313	71	85	5	0	1	30	7	7	.272	.287	.297	100	-1	30	9	4	.918	2	1-31,O-26,2-15	0.4
1876	Bos-N	69	308	60	87	4	3	2	34	8	12	.282	.301	.334	109	3				.927	-4	*1-65/O-3,2-1	-0.2
1877	Bos-N	35	140	23	39	7	1	1	15	6	7	.279	.308	.364	107	1				.815	-1	O-30/1-5	-0.1
1878	Pro-N	49	188	35	45	6	1	0	14	8	12	.239	.270	.282	82	-3				.940	1	*1-48/O-1	-0.4
1884	Bos-U	76	311	55	73	5	2	0		22		.235	.285	.264	68	-20				.950	-5	1-63,O-16,M	-2.9
Total	4 n	155	688	165	183	11	0	2	64	16	24	.266	.283	.291	82	-14	38	12	4	.830	-13	/O-70,1-68,2-27	-1.4
Total	4	229	947	173	244	22	7	3	63	44	31	.258	.291	.305	90	-20				.938	-8	1-181/O-50,2-1	-3.6

■ MURPHY Murphy Deb: 8/16/1884

YEAR	TM/L	G	AB	R	H	2B	3B	HR	RBI	BB	SO	AVG	OBP	SLG	PRO+	BR/A	SB	CS	SBR	FA	FR	G/POS	TPR
1884	Bos-U								1			.000	.250	.000	-18	-1				.333	-3	/C-1,O-1	-0.3

■ CLARENCE MURPHY Murphy, Clarence Deb: 6/17/1886

YEAR	TM/L	G	AB	R	H	2B	3B	HR	RBI	BB	SO	AVG	OBP	SLG	PRO+	BR/A	SB	CS	SBR	FA	FR	G/POS	TPR
1886	Lou-a	1	3	0	0	0	0	0	0			.000	.000	.000	-95	-1	0			1.000	0	/O-1	-0.1

■ CONNIE MURPHY Murphy, Cornelius David "Stone Face" b: 11/1/1870, Northfield, Mass. d: 12/14/45, New Bedford, Mass. BL/TR, 5'8", 155 lbs. Deb: 9/17/1893

YEAR	TM/L	G	AB	R	H	2B	3B	HR	RBI	BB	SO	AVG	OBP	SLG	PRO+	BR/A	SB	CS	SBR	FA	FR	G/POS	TPR
1893	Cin-N	6	17	3	3	1	0	0	2	1		.176	.222	.235	21	-2	0			.917	-2	/C-4	-0.3
1894	Cin-N	1	4	0	0	0	0	0	0	1		.000	.000	.000	-46	-1	0			.500	-1	/C-1	-0.2
Total	2	7	21	3	3	1	0	0	2	3		.143	.217	.190	6	-3	0			.857	-3	/C-5	-0.5

■ DALE MURPHY Murphy, Dale Bryan b: 3/12/56, Portland, Ore. BR/TR, 6'5", 215 lbs. Deb: 9/13/76

YEAR	TM/L	G	AB	R	H	2B	3B	HR	RBI	BB	SO	AVG	OBP	SLG	PRO+	BR/A	SB	CS	SBR	FA	FR	G/POS	TPR
1976	Atl-N	19	65	3	17	6	0	0	9	7	9	.262	.333	.354	89	-1	0	0	0	.974	-0	C-19	0.0
1977	Atl-N	18	76	5	24	8	1	2	14	0	8	.316	.316	.526	108	1	0	1	-1	.954	-2	C-18	-0.1
1978	Atl-N	151	530	66	120	14	3	23	79	42	145	.226	.284	.394	80	-16	11	7	-1	.984	4	*1-129,C-21	-2.1
1979	Atl-N	104	384	53	106	7	2	21	57	38	67	.276	.344	.469	111	5	6	4	1	.980	-9	1-76,C-27	-0.6
1980	Atl-N★	156	569	98	160	27	2	33	89	59	133	.281	.350	.510	133	23	9	6	-1	.985	11	*O-154/1-1	2.8
1981	Atl-N	104	369	43	91	12	1	13	50	44	67	.247	.325	.390	100	0	14	5	1	.981	4	*O-103/1-3	0.2
1982	*Atl-N★	162	598	113	168	23	2	36	**109**	93	134	.281	.380	.507	140	33	23	11	0	.979	-1	*O-162	2.9
1983	Atl-N★	162	589	131	178	24	4	36	**121**	90	110	.302	.396	**.540**	146	38	30	4	7	.985	5	*O-160	4.6
1984	Atl-N★	162	607	94	176	32	8	**36**	100	79	134	.290	.374	**.547**	145	36	19	7	2	.987	1	*O-160	3.4
1985	Atl-N★	162	616	**118**	185	32	2	**37**	111	**90**	141	.300	.390	.539	148	40	10	3	1	.980	-5	*O-161	3.3
1986	Atl-N★	160	614	89	163	29	7	29	83	75	141	.265	.347	.477	118	15	7	5	-2	.981	-4	*O-159	0.4
1987	Atl-N	159	566	115	167	27	1	44	105	115	136	.295	.420	.580	154	47	16	6	1	.977	12	*O-159	5.4
1988	Atl-N	156	592	77	134	35	4	24	77	74	125	.226	.314	.421	104	3	3	5	-2	.992	18	*O-156	1.4
1989	Atl-N	154	574	60	131	16	0	20	84	65	142	.228	.309	.361	88	-7	3	2	1	.985	4	*O-151	-0.9
1990	Atl-N	97	349	38	81	14	0	17	55	41	84	.232	.315	.418	94	-3	9	2	2	.981	4	O-97	0.0
	Phi-N	57	214	22	57	9	1	7	28	20	46	.266	.329	.416	104	1	0	1	-1	.992	3	O-55	0.2
	Yr	154	563	60	138	23	1	24	83	61	130	.245	.320	.417	98	-2	9	3	1	.985	7	*O-152	0.2
1991	Phi-N	153	544	66	137	33	1	18	81	48	93	.252	.313	.415	104	2	1	0	0	.983	4	*O-147	0.2
1992	Phi-N	18	62	5	10	1	0	2	7	1	13	.161	.175	.274	25	-6	0	0	0	.950	-3	O-16	-1.1
1993	Col-N	26	42	1	6	1	0	0	3	6	15	.143	.234	.167	8	-6	0	0	0	1.000	-1	/O-13	-0.7
Total	18	2180	7960	1197	2111	350	39	398	1266	986	1748	.265	.346	.469	119	203	161	68	8	.983	45	*O-1853,1-209/C-85	19.3

■ DANNY MURPHY Murphy, Daniel Francis b: 8/11/1876, Philadelphia, Pa. d: 11/22/55, Jersey City, N.J. BR/TR, 5'9", 175 lbs. Deb: 9/17/00 C

YEAR	TM/L	G	AB	R	H	2B	3B	HR	RBI	BB	SO	AVG	OBP	SLG	PRO+	BR/A	SB	CS	SBR	FA	FR	G/POS	TPR
1900	NY-N	22	74	11	20	1	0	0	6	8		.270	.341	.284	77	-2	4			.888	-6	2-22	-0.6
1901	NY-N	5	20	0	4	0	0	0	0	1		.200	.238	.200	29	-2	0			.895	-3	/2-5	-0.4
1902	Phi-A	76	291	46	91	11	1	8	48	13		.313	.351	.416	107	2	12			.963	-12	2-76	-0.6
1903	Phi-A	133	513	66	140	31	11	3	60	13		.273	.295	.382	97	-3	17			.949	-13	*2-133	-1.1
1904	Phi-A	150	557	78	160	30	17	7	77	22		.287	.320	.440	132	18	22			.941	13	*2-150	3.9
1905	*Phi-A	151	537	71	149	34	4	6	71	42		.277	.339	.389	129	17	23			.955	-8	*2-151	1.1
1906	Phi-A	119	448	48	135	28	6	2	60	21		.301	.341	.404	129	14	17			.955	-11	*2-119	0.4

YEAR	TM/L	G	AB	R	H	2B	3B	HR	RBI	BB	SO	AVG	OBP	SLG	PRO+	BR/A	SB	CS	SBR	FA	FR	G/POS	TPR
1907	Phi-A	124	469	51	127	23	3	2	57	30		.271	.317	.345	109	4	11			.965	14	*2-122	1.8
1908	Phi-A	142	525	51	139	28	7	4	66	32		.265	.309	.368	112	5	16			.963	10	O-84,2-56/1-2	1.3
1909	Phi-A	149	541	61	152	28	14	5	69	35		.281	.332	.412	132	18	19			**.977**	-2	*O-149	1.2
1910	*Phi-A	151	560	70	168	28	18	4	64	31		.300	.338	.436	143	24	18			.974	-2	*O-151	1.7
1911	*Phi-A	141	508	104	167	27	11	6	66	50		.329	.398	.461	142	28	22			.961	6	*O-136/2-4	2.6
1912	Phi-A	36	130	27	42	6	2	2	20	16		.323	.401	.446	147	8	8			.891	-6	O-36	0.0
1913	Phi-A	40	59	3	19	5	1	0	6	4	8	.322	.365	.441	139	3	0			1.000	-2	/O-9	0.0
1914	Bro-F	52	161	16	49	9	0	4	32	17	16	.304	.374	.435	121	2	4			.986	1	O-46	0.1
1915	Bro-F	5	6	0	1	0	0	0	0	0	0	.167	.167	.167	-6	-1	0			1.000	-1	/2-1,O-1	-0.2
Total	16	1496	5399	705	1563	289	102	44	702	335	24	.289	.336	.405	124	137	193			.953	-22	2-839,O-612/1-2	11.2

■ DANNY MURPHY
Murphy, Daniel Francis   b: 8/23/42, Beverly, Mass.   BL/TR, 5'11", 185 lbs.   Deb: 6/18/60

YEAR	TM/L	G	AB	R	H	2B	3B	HR	RBI	BB	SO	AVG	OBP	SLG	PRO+	BR/A	SB	CS	SBR	FA	FR	G/POS	TPR
1960	Chi-N	31	75	7	9	2	0	1	6	4	13	.120	.175	.187	-1	-11	0	0	0	.976	-1	O-21	-1.3
1961	Chi-N	4	13	3	5	0	0	2	3	1	5	.385	.429	.846	225	2	0	0	0	1.000	0	/O-4	0.2
1962	Chi-N	14	35	5	7	3	1	0	3	2	9	.200	.243	.343	53	-2	0	0	0	1.000	-3	/O-5	-0.5
1969	Chi-A	17	1	0	0	0	0	0	0	2	0	.000	.667	.000	95	0	0	0	0	1.000	-0	P-17	0.0
1970	Chi-A	51	6	3	2	0	0	1	1	2	2	.333	.500	.833	252	1	0	0	0	.933	-1	P-51	0.0
Total	5	117	130	18	23	5	1	4	13	11	29	.177	.246	.323	53	-9	0	0	0	.947	-4	/P-68,O-30	-1.6

■ DANNY MURPHY
Murphy, Daniel Joseph "Handsome Dan"   b: 9/10/1864, Brooklyn, N.Y.   d: 12/14/15, Brooklyn, N.Y.   156 lbs.   Deb: 4/26/1892

YEAR	TM/L	G	AB	R	H	2B	3B	HR	RBI	BB	SO	AVG	OBP	SLG	PRO+	BR/A	SB	CS	SBR	FA	FR	G/POS	TPR
1892	NY-N	8	26	2	3	0	0	0	0	5	4	.115	.258	.115	14	-2	0			.900	-2	/C-8	-0.4

■ DAVE MURPHY
Murphy, David Francis "Dirty Dave"   b: 5/4/1876, Adams, Mass.   d: 4/8/40, Adams, Mass.   TR ,   Deb: 8/28/05

YEAR	TM/L	G	AB	R	H	2B	3B	HR	RBI	BB	SO	AVG	OBP	SLG	PRO+	BR/A	SB	CS	SBR	FA	FR	G/POS	TPR
1905	Bos-N	3	11	0	2	0	0	0	1	0		.182	.182	.182	9	-1	0			1.000	-1	/S-2,3-1	-0.4

■ DWAYNE MURPHY
Murphy, Dwayne Keith   b: 3/18/55, Merced, Cal.   BL/TR, 6'1", 185 lbs.   Deb: 4/8/78

YEAR	TM/L	G	AB	R	H	2B	3B	HR	RBI	BB	SO	AVG	OBP	SLG	PRO+	BR/A	SB	CS	SBR	FA	FR	G/POS	TPR
1978	Oak-A	60	52	15	10	2	0	0	5	7	14	.192	.288	.231	50	-3	0	1	-1	1.000	-10	O-45/D-5	-1.5
1979	Oak-A	121	388	57	99	10	4	11	40	84	80	.255	.389	.387	116	13	15	11	-2	.988	8	*O-118	1.3
1980	Oak-A	159	573	86	157	18	2	13	68	102	96	.274	.386	.380	119	19	26	15	-1	.990	24	*O-158	3.5
1981	*Oak-A	107	390	58	98	10	3	15	60	73	91	.251	.372	.408	131	18	10	4	1	.985	12	*O-106/D-1	2.8
1982	Oak-A	151	543	84	129	15	1	27	94	94	122	.238	.353	.418	116	14	26	8	3	.983	22	*O-147/S-1,D-1	3.4
1983	Oak-A	130	471	55	107	17	2	17	75	62	105	.227	.317	.380	97	-2	7	5	-1	.979	10	*O-124/D-7	0.3
1984	Oak-A	153	559	93	143	18	2	33	88	74	111	.256	.346	.472	133	24	4	5	-2	.988	21	*O-153	3.8
1985	Oak-A	152	523	77	122	21	3	20	59	84	123	.233	.343	.400	111	9	4	5	-2	.989	9	*O-150	1.1
1986	Oak-A	98	329	50	83	11	3	9	39	56	80	.252	.368	.386	114	8	3	1	0	.993	11	O-97/D-1	1.6
1987	Oak-A	82	219	39	51	7	0	8	35	58	61	.233	.394	.374	113	7	4	1	-0	.984	5	O-79/1-1,2-1	0.3
1988	Det-A	49	144	14	36	5	0	4	19	24	26	.250	.361	.368	109	2	1	1	-0	1.000	1	O-43/D-3	0.2
1989	Phi-N	98	156	20	34	5	0	9	27	29	44	.218	.341	.423	117	4	0	1	0	.986	-6	O-52	-0.4
Total	12	1360	4347	648	1069	139	20	166	609	747	953	.246	.359	.402	116	113	100	61	-7	.987	102	*O-1272/D-18,21S	16.4

■ ED MURPHY
Murphy, Edward Joseph   b: 8/23/18, Joliet, Ill.   d: 12/10/91, Joliet, Ill.   BR/TR, 5'11", 190 lbs.   Deb: 9/10/42

YEAR	TM/L	G	AB	R	H	2B	3B	HR	RBI	BB	SO	AVG	OBP	SLG	PRO+	BR/A	SB	CS	SBR	FA	FR	G/POS	TPR
1942	Phi-N	13	28	2	7	2	0	0	4	2	4	.250	.300	.321	86	-1	0			1.000	-0	/1-8	-0.1

■ TONY MURPHY
Murphy, Francis J.   b: 1863, Brooklyn, N.Y.   5'6", 145 lbs.   Deb: 10/15/1884

YEAR	TM/L	G	AB	R	H	2B	3B	HR	RBI	BB	SO	AVG	OBP	SLG	PRO+	BR/A	SB	CS	SBR	FA	FR	G/POS	TPR
1884	NY-a	1	3	1	1	0	0	0		0		.333	.333	.333	121	0				1.000	-1	/C-1	-0.1

■ FRANK MURPHY
Murphy, Francis Patrick   b: 4/16/1875, N.Tarrytown, N.Y.   d: 11/4/12, Central Islip, N.Y.   Deb: 7/2/01

YEAR	TM/L	G	AB	R	H	2B	3B	HR	RBI	BB	SO	AVG	OBP	SLG	PRO+	BR/A	SB	CS	SBR	FA	FR	G/POS	TPR
1901	Bos-N	45	176	13	46	5	3	1	18	4		.261	.282	.341	73	-7	6			.939	4	O-45	-0.6
	NY-N	35	130	10	21	3	0	0	8	6		.162	.199	.185	12	-15	2			.847	-10	2-23,O-12	-2.5
	Yr	80	306	23	67	8	3	1	26	10		.219	.246	.275	49	-20	8			.940	-6	O-57,2-23	-3.1

■ DUMMY MURPHY
Murphy, Herbert Courtland   b: 12/18/1886, Olney, Ill.   d: 8/10/62, Tallahassee, Fla.   BR/TR, 5'10", 165 lbs.   Deb: 4/14/14

YEAR	TM/L	G	AB	R	H	2B	3B	HR	RBI	BB	SO	AVG	OBP	SLG	PRO+	BR/A	SB	CS	SBR	FA	FR	G/POS	TPR
1914	Phi-N	9	26	1	4	1	0	0	3	0	4	.154	.185	.192	12	-3	0			.864	3	/S-9	0.1

■ HOWARD MURPHY
Murphy, Howard   b: 1/1/1882, Birmingham, Ala.   d: 10/5/26, Fort Worth, Tex.   BL/TR, 5'8.5", 150 lbs.   Deb: 8/4/09

YEAR	TM/L	G	AB	R	H	2B	3B	HR	RBI	BB	SO	AVG	OBP	SLG	PRO+	BR/A	SB	CS	SBR	FA	FR	G/POS	TPR
1909	StL-N	25	60	3	12	0	0	0	3	4		.200	.250	.200	42	-4	1			.925	-2	O-19	-0.7

■ EDDIE MURPHY
Murphy, John Edward   b: 10/2/1891, Hancock, N.Y.   d: 2/21/69, Dunmore, Pa.   BL/TR, 5'9", 155 lbs.   Deb: 8/26/12

YEAR	TM/L	G	AB	R	H	2B	3B	HR	RBI	BB	SO	AVG	OBP	SLG	PRO+	BR/A	SB	CS	SBR	FA	FR	G/POS	TPR
1912	Phi-A	33	142	24	45	4	1	0	6	11		.317	.370	.359	113	3	7			.947	0	O-33	0.1
1913	*Phi-A	137	508	105	150	14	7	1	30	70	44	.295	.391	.356	122	17	21			.942	-12	*O-135	-0.1
1914	*Phi-A	148	573	101	156	12	9	3	43	87	46	.272	.379	.340	121	19	36	32	-8	.941	-5	*O-148	-0.2
1915	Phi-A	68	260	37	60	3	4	0	17	29	15	.231	.315	.273	79	-5	13	3	2	.899	-5	O-58/3-6	-1.3
	Chi-A	70	273	51	86	11	5	0	26	39	12	.315	.410	.392	136	14	20	12	-1	.952	-1	O-70	0.9
	Yr	138	533	88	146	14	9	0	43	68	27	.274	.365	.334	109	8	33	15	1	.933	-6	*O-128/3-6	-0.4
1916	Chi-A	51	105	14	22	5	1	0	4	9	5	.210	.284	.276	68	-4	3			1.000	-3	O-24/3-1	-0.9
1917	Chi-A	53	51	9	16	2	1	0	16	5	1	.314	.386	.392	135	2	4			1.000	-4	/O-9	-0.2
1918	Chi-A	91	286	36	85	9	3	0	23	22	18	.297	.350	.350	110	3	6			.958	-10	O-63/2-8	-1.1
1919	*Chi-A	30	35	8	17	4	0	0	5	7	0	.486	.571	.600	228	7	0			.917	-0	/O-6	0.6
1920	Chi-A	58	118	22	40	2	1	0	19	12	4	.339	.405	.373	107	2	1	3	-2	.886	-2	O-19/3-3	-0.3
1921	Chi-A	6	5	1	1	0	0	0	0	0	0	.200	.200	.200	2	-1	0	0	0	.000	-0	H	-0.1
1926	Pit-N	16	17	3	2	0	0	0	6	3	0	.118	.250	.118	2	-2	0			1.000	-0	/O-3	-0.3
Total	11	761	2373	411	680	66	32	4	195	294	145	.287	.374	.346	114	53	111	50		.942	-39	O-568/3-10,2-8	-2.6

■ JOHN MURPHY
Murphy, John Patrick   b: 1879, New Haven, Conn.   d: 4/20/49, Andover, Mass.   5'7.5", 160 lbs.   Deb: 9/10/02

YEAR	TM/L	G	AB	R	H	2B	3B	HR	RBI	BB	SO	AVG	OBP	SLG	PRO+	BR/A	SB	CS	SBR	FA	FR	G/POS	TPR
1902	StL-N	1	3	1	2	1	0	0	1	1		.667	.750	1.000	457	1	0			1.000	-1	/3-1	0.1
1903	Det-A	5	22	1	4	1	0	0	5	0		.182	.182	.227	23	-2	0			.852	-1	/S-5	-0.3
Total	2	6	25	2	6	2	0	0	6	1		.240	.269	.320	79	-1	0			.852	-2	/S-5,3-1	-0.2

■ LARRY MURPHY
Murphy, Lawrence Patrick   BL ,   Deb: 5/30/1891

YEAR	TM/L	G	AB	R	H	2B	3B	HR	RBI	BB	SO	AVG	OBP	SLG	PRO+	BR/A	SB	CS	SBR	FA	FR	G/POS	TPR
1891	Was-a	101	400	73	106	15	3	1	35	63	27	.265	.372	.325	104	6	29			.874	-5	*O-101	-0.3

■ LEO MURPHY
Murphy, Leo Joseph "Red"   b: 1/7/1889, Terre Haute, Ind.   d: 8/12/60, Racine, Wis.   BR/TR, 6'1", 179 lbs.   Deb: 5/2/15

YEAR	TM/L	G	AB	R	H	2B	3B	HR	RBI	BB	SO	AVG	OBP	SLG	PRO+	BR/A	SB	CS	SBR	FA	FR	G/POS	TPR
1915	Pit-N	31	41	4	4	0	0	0	4	12		.098	.178	.098	-16	-6	0			.932	-3	C-20	-0.9

■ MIKE MURPHY
Murphy, Michael Jerome   b: 8/19/1888, Forestville, Pa.   d: 10/26/52, Johnson City, N.Y.   BR/TR, 5'9", 170 lbs.   Deb: 5/17/12

YEAR	TM/L	G	AB	R	H	2B	3B	HR	RBI	BB	SO	AVG	OBP	SLG	PRO+	BR/A	SB	CS	SBR	FA	FR	G/POS	TPR
1912	StL-N	1	1	0	0	0	0	0	0	0	0	.000	.000	.000	-99	-0	0			.000	-0	/C-1	0.0
1916	Phi-A	14	27	0	3	0	0	0	1	1	3	.111	.143	.111	-25	-4	0			.973	-3	C-12	-0.8
Total	2	15	28	0	3	0	0	0	1	1	3	.107	.138	.107	-28	-4	0			.973	-3	/C-13	-0.8

■ MORGAN MURPHY
Murphy, Morgan Edward   b: 2/14/1867, E.Providence, R.I.   d: 10/3/38, Providence, R.I.   BR/TR, 5'8", 160 lbs.   Deb: 4/22/1890

YEAR	TM/L	G	AB	R	H	2B	3B	HR	RBI	BB	SO	AVG	OBP	SLG	PRO+	BR/A	SB	CS	SBR	FA	FR	G/POS	TPR
1890	Bos-P	68	246	38	56	10	2	2	32	24	31	.228	.301	.309	59	-15	16			.903	4	C-67/S-2,O-1,3-1	-0.5
1891	Bos-a	106	402	60	87	11	4	4	54	36	58	.216	.289	.294	68	-18	17			**.954**	11	*C-104/O-4	0.2
1892	Cin-N	74	234	29	46	8	2	2	24	25	57	.197	.277	.274	68	-9	4			.955	0	C-74	-0.4
1893	Cin-N	57	200	25	47	5	2	1	19	14	35	.235	.295	.285	53	-14	1			.932	-5	C-56/1-1	-1.2
1894	Cin-N	75	255	42	70	9	0	1	37	26	34	.275	.344	.322	59	-17	6			.901	-4	C-74/S-1,3-1	-1.2
1895	Cin-N	25	82	15	22	2	0	0	16	11	8	.268	.355	.293	65	-4	6			.907	-3	C-25	-0.4
1896	StL-N	49	175	12	45	5	2	0	12	6		.257	.290	.309	60	-10	1			.926	-2	C-48	-0.6
1897	StL-N	62	207	13	35	2	0	0	12	6		.169	.196	.179	-1	-30	1			.950	-3	C-53/1-8	-2.4
1898	Pit-N	5	16	0	2	0	0	0	1	2		.125	.176	.125	-14	-2	0			.957	1	/C-5	-0.1
	Phi-N	25	86	6	17	3	0	0	11	6		.198	.258	.233	43	-6	0			.964	0	C-25	-0.4
	Yr	30	102	6	19	3	0	0	13	7		.186	.245	.216	34	-9	0			.963	1	C-30	-0.5
1900	Phi-N	11	36	2	10	3	0	0	3	0		.278	.278	.333	69	-2	0			.980	2	C-11	0.1

YEAR	TM/L	G	AB	R	H	2B	3B	HR	RBI	BB	SO	AVG	OBP	SLG	PRO+	BR/A	SB	CS	SBR	FA	FR	G/POS	TPR
1901	Phi-A	9	28	5	6	1	0	0	6	0		.214	.214	.250	27	-3	1			.929	0	/C-8,1-1	-0.2
Total	11	566	1967	247	443	56	12	10	227	157	237	.225	.287	.281	54	-131	53			.936	2	C-550/1-10,O-5,S3	-7.1

■ PAT MURPHY
Murphy, Patrick J.   b: 1/2/1857, Auburn, Mass.   d: 5/16/27, Worcester, Mass.   TR, 5'10", 160 lbs.   Deb: 9/2/1887

YEAR	TM/L	G	AB	R	H	2B	3B	HR	RBI	BB	SO	AVG	OBP	SLG	PRO+	BR/A	SB	CS	SBR	FA	FR	G/POS	TPR
1887	NY-N	17	56	4	12	2	0	0	4	2	4	.214	.241	.250	38	-5	1			.847	2	C-17	-0.1
1888	*NY-N	28	106	11	18	1	0	0	4	6	11	.170	.214	.179	27	-8	3			.913	3	C-28	-0.3
1889	NY-N	9	28	5	10	1	1	1	4	2	0	.357	.400	.571	170	2	0			.872	-2	/C-9	0.1
1890	NY-N	32	119	14	28	5	1	0	9	14	13	.235	.321	.294	79	-3	3			.905	-5	C-29/O-3,S-1	-0.5
Total	4	86	309	34	68	9	2	1	21	24	28	.220	.278	.272	64	-13	7			.895	-3	/C-83,O-3,S-1	-0.8

■ DICK MURPHY
Murphy, Richard Lee   b: 10/25/31, Cincinnati, Ohio   BL/TL, 5'11", 170 lbs.   Deb: 6/13/54

YEAR	TM/L	G	AB	R	H	2B	3B	HR	RBI	BB	SO	AVG	OBP	SLG	PRO+	BR/A	SB	CS	SBR	FA	FR	G/POS	TPR
1954	Cin-N	6	1	1	0	0	0	0	0	0	1	.000	.000	.000	-97	-0	0	0	0	.000	0	H	0.0

■ BUZZ MURPHY
Murphy, Robert R.   b: 4/26/1895, Denver, Colo.   d: 5/11/38, Denver, Colo.   BL/TL, 5'8.5", 155 lbs.   Deb: 7/14/18

YEAR	TM/L	G	AB	R	H	2B	3B	HR	RBI	BB	SO	AVG	OBP	SLG	PRO+	BR/A	SB	CS	SBR	FA	FR	G/POS	TPR
1918	Bos-N	9	32	6	12	2	3	1	9	3	5	.375	.429	.719	259	6	0			1.000	-2	/O-9	0.4
1919	Was-A	79	252	19	66	7	4	0	28	19	32	.262	.326	.321	83	-5	5			.959	2	O-73	-0.9
Total	2	88	284	25	78	9	7	1	37	22	37	.275	.338	.366	101	0	5			.961	0	/O-82	-0.5

■ BILLY MURPHY
Murphy, William Eugene   b: 5/7/44, Pineville, La.   BR/TR, 6'1", 190 lbs.   Deb: 4/15/66

YEAR	TM/L	G	AB	R	H	2B	3B	HR	RBI	BB	SO	AVG	OBP	SLG	PRO+	BR/A	SB	CS	SBR	FA	FR	G/POS	TPR
1966	NY-N	84	135	15	31	4	1	3	13	7	34	.230	.273	.341	71	-5	1	2	-1	.955	-9	O-57	-1.8

■ WILLIE MURPHY
Murphy, William H. "Gentle Willie"   b: 3/23/1864, Springfield, Mass.   BL, 5'11", 198 lbs.   Deb: 5/1/1884

YEAR	TM/L	G	AB	R	H	2B	3B	HR	RBI	BB	SO	AVG	OBP	SLG	PRO+	BR/A	SB	CS	SBR	FA	FR	G/POS	TPR
1884	Cle-N	42	168	18	38	3	3	1	9	1	23	.226	.231	.298	63	-7				.720	-5	O-42	-1.2
	Was-a	5	21	3	10	0	0	0		1		.476	.542	.476	266	4				.700	-0	/O-4,2-1	0.3
Total	1	47	189	21	48	3	3	1	9	2	23	.254	.269	.317	83	-3				.718	-5	/O-46,2-1	-0.9

■ YALE MURPHY
Murphy, William Henry "Tot" or "Midget"   b: 11/11/1869, Southville, Mass.   d: 2/14/06, Southville, Mass.   BL/TR, 5'3", 125 lbs.   Deb: 4/19/1894

YEAR	TM/L	G	AB	R	H	2B	3B	HR	RBI	BB	SO	AVG	OBP	SLG	PRO+	BR/A	SB	CS	SBR	FA	FR	G/POS	TPR
1894	*NY-N	74	280	64	76	6	2	0	28	51	23	.271	.384	.307	69	-12	28			.898	-11	S-49,O-20/3-3,2-1	-1.7
1895	NY-N	51	184	35	37	6	2	0	16	27	13	.201	.303	.255	46	-14	7			.944	-4	O-33/S-8,3-8,2-1	-1.7
1897	NY-N	5	8	1	0	0	0	0	1	2		.000	.200	.000	-46	-2	0			.800	-2	/S-3,2-2	-0.3
Total	3	130	472	100	113	12	4	0	45	80	36	.239	.350	.282	59	-28	35			.890	-17	/S-60,O-53,3-11,21	-3.7

■ TONY MURRAY
Murray, Anthony Joseph   b: 4/30/04, Chicago, Ill.   d: 3/19/74, Chicago, Ill.   BR/TR, 5'10.5", 154 lbs.   Deb: 10/6/23

YEAR	TM/L	G	AB	R	H	2B	3B	HR	RBI	BB	SO	AVG	OBP	SLG	PRO+	BR/A	SB	CS	SBR	FA	FR	G/POS	TPR
1923	Chi-N	2	4	0	1	0	0	0	0	0	0	.250	.400	.250	75	-0	0	0	0	1.000	-2	/O-2	-0.2

■ EDDIE MURRAY
Murray, Eddie Clarence   b: 2/24/56, Los Angeles, Cal.   BB/TR, 6'2", 200 lbs.   Deb: 4/7/77   F

YEAR	TM/L	G	AB	R	H	2B	3B	HR	RBI	BB	SO	AVG	OBP	SLG	PRO+	BR/A	SB	CS	SBR	FA	FR	G/POS	TPR
1977	Bal-A	160	611	81	173	29	2	27	88	48	104	.283	.336	.470	125	19	0	1	-1	.992	-4	*D-111,1-42/O-3	0.8
1978	Bal-A☆	161	610	85	174	32	3	27	95	70	97	.285	.360	.480	143	34	6	5	-1	.997	1	*1-157/3-3,D-1	2.4
1979	*Bal-A	159	606	90	179	30	2	25	99	72	78	.295	.372	.475	132	27	10	2	2	.994	-1	*1-157/D-2	1.7
1980	Bal-A	158	621	100	186	36	2	32	116	54	71	.300	.357	.519	138	31	7	2	1	.994	-9	*1-154/D-1	1.3
1981	Bal-A★	99	378	57	111	21	2	22	78	40	43	.294	.363	.534	156	26	2	3	-1	.999	10	1-99	3.0
1982	Bal-A★	151	550	87	174	30	1	32	110	70	82	.316	.395	.549	157	43	7	2	1	.997	1	*1-149/D-2	3.6
1983	*Bal-A★	156	582	115	178	30	3	33	111	86	90	.306	.398	.538	158	47	5	1	1	.993	4	*1-153/D-2	4.2
1984	Bal-A★	162	588	97	180	26	3	29	110	107	87	.306	.415	.509	157	50	10	2	2	.992	8	*1-159/D-3	4.9
1985	Bal-A★	156	583	111	173	37	1	31	124	84	68	.297	.387	.523	151	42	5	2	0	.987	13	*1-154/D-2	4.4
1986	Bal-A☆	137	495	61	151	25	1	17	84	78	49	.305	.400	.463	136	27	3	0	1	.989	-3	*1-119,D-16	1.6
1987	Bal-A	160	618	89	171	28	3	30	91	73	80	.277	.353	.477	121	18	1	2	-1	.993	12	*1-156/D-4	1.6
1988	Bal-A	161	603	75	171	27	2	28	84	75	78	.284	.361	.474	136	29	5	2	0	.989	10	*1-103,D-58	2.9
1989	LA-N	160	594	66	147	29	1	20	88	87	85	.247	.346	.401	115	13	7	2	1	.996	13	*1-159/3-2	1.5
1990	LA-N	155	558	96	184	22	3	26	95	82	64	.330	.417	.520	160	48	8	5	1	.992	4	*1-150	4.1
1991	LA-N★	153	576	69	150	23	1	19	96	55	74	.260	.325	.403	106	4	10	3	1	.995	9	*1-149/3-1	0.4
1992	NY-N	156	551	64	144	37	2	16	93	66	74	.261	.340	.423	117	12	4	2	-1	.991	-4	*1-154	-0.3
1993	NY-N	154	610	77	174	28	1	27	100	40	61	.285	.329	.467	112	8	2	2	-1	.988	-1	*1-154	-0.6
1994	Cle-A	108	433	57	110	21	1	17	76	31	53	.254	.304	.425	85	-11	8	4	0	.988	-2	D-82,1-26	-1.8
1995	*Cle-A	113	436	68	141	21	0	21	82	39	65	.323	.379	.516	128	18	5	1	1	.984	3	D-95,1-18	1.2
1996	Cle-A	88	336	33	88	9	1	12	45	34	45	.262	.330	.402	84	-9	3	0	1	1.000	0	D-87/1-1	-1.3
	*Bal-A	64	230	36	59	12	0	10	34	27	42	.257	.335	.439	95	-2	1	0	0	1.000	0	D-62	-0.6
	Yr	152	566	69	147	21	1	22	79	61	87	.260	.332	.417	88	-11	4	0	1			*D-149/1-1	-1.9
Total	20	2971	11169	1614	3218	553	35	501	1899	1318	1490	.288	.364	.478	131	472	109	43	7	.993	63	*1-2413,D-528/3-6,O	35.0

■ ED MURRAY
Murray, Edward Francis   b: 5/8/1895, Mystic, Conn.   d: 11/8/70, Cheyenne, Wyoming   BR/TR, 5'6", 145 lbs.   Deb: 6/24/17

YEAR	TM/L	G	AB	R	H	2B	3B	HR	RBI	BB	SO	AVG	OBP	SLG	PRO+	BR/A	SB	CS	SBR	FA	FR	G/POS	TPR
1917	StL-A	1	1	0	0	0	0	0	0	0	1	.000	.000	.000	-99	-0	0			.000	0	/S-1	0.0

■ GLENN MURRAY
Murray, Glenn Everett   b: 11/23/70, Manning, S.C.   BR/TR, 6'2", 225 lbs.   Deb: 5/10/96

YEAR	TM/L	G	AB	R	H	2B	3B	HR	RBI	BB	SO	AVG	OBP	SLG	PRO+	BR/A	SB	CS	SBR	FA	FR	G/POS	TPR
1996	Phi-N	38	97	8	19	3	0	2	6	7	36	.196	.250	.289	40	-8	1	1	-0	1.000	1	O-27	-0.8

■ JIM MURRAY
Murray, James Oscar   b: 1/16/1878, Galveston, Tex.   d: 4/25/45, Galveston, Tex.   BR/TL, 5'10", 180 lbs.   Deb: 9/2/02

YEAR	TM/L	G	AB	R	H	2B	3B	HR	RBI	BB	SO	AVG	OBP	SLG	PRO+	BR/A	SB	CS	SBR	FA	FR	G/POS	TPR
1902	Chi-N	12	47	3	8	0	0	0	1	2		.170	.204	.170	16	-5	0			1.000	-1	O-12	-0.7
1911	StL-A	31	102	8	19	5	0	3	11	5		.186	.224	.324	54	-7	0			.935	-0	O-25	-0.8
1914	Bos-N	39	112	10	26	4	2	0	12	6	24	.232	.277	.304	73	-4	2			.941	-8	O-32	-1.4
Total	3	82	261	21	53	9	2	3	24	13	24	.203	.244	.287	56	-16	2			.949	-9	/O-69	-2.9

■ MIAH MURRAY
Murray, Jeremiah J.   b: 1/1/1865, Boston, Mass.   d: 1/11/22, Boston, Mass.   BR/TR, 5'11.5", 170 lbs.   Deb: 5/17/1884   U

YEAR	TM/L	G	AB	R	H	2B	3B	HR	RBI	BB	SO	AVG	OBP	SLG	PRO+	BR/A	SB	CS	SBR	FA	FR	G/POS	TPR
1884	Pro-N	8	27	1	5	0	0	0	1	1	8	.185	.214	.185	28	-2				.836	-4	/C-7,O-1,1-1	-0.6
1885	Lou-a	12	43	4	8	0	0	0	3	2		.186	.239	.186	36	-3				.863	1	C-12/1-2	-0.1
1888	Was-N	12	42	1	4	1	0	0	3	1	7	.095	.116	.119	-26	-6	0			.912	-0	/C-10/1-2	-0.5
1891	Was-a	2	8	0	0	0	0	0	0	0		.000	.000	.000	-99	-2	0			1.000	3	/C-2	0.1
Total	4	34	120	6	17	1	0	0	7	4	16	.142	.176	.150	3	-13	0			.884	-1	/C-31,1-5,O-1	-1.1

■ RED MURRAY
Murray, John Joseph   b: 3/4/1884, Arnot, Pa.   d: 12/4/58, Sayre, Pa.   BR/TR, 5'10.5", 190 lbs.   Deb: 6/16/06

YEAR	TM/L	G	AB	R	H	2B	3B	HR	RBI	BB	SO	AVG	OBP	SLG	PRO+	BR/A	SB	CS	SBR	FA	FR	G/POS	TPR
1906	StL-N	46	144	18	37	9	7	1	16	9		.257	.305	.438	137	5	5			.962	-3	O-34/C-7	0.2
1907	StL-N	132	485	46	127	10	10	7	46	24		.262	.301	.367	113	5	23			.935	5	*O-131	0.5
1908	StL-N	154	593	64	167	19	15	7	62	37		.282	.332	.400	140	24	48			.914	-4	*O-154	1.6
1909	NY-N	149	570	74	150	15	12	7	91	45		.263	.319	.368	112	6	48			.947	3	*O-149	0.4
1910	NY-N	149	553	78	153	27	8	4	87	52	51	.277	.345	.376	110	7	57			.948	4	*O-148	0.4
1911	*NY-N	140	488	70	142	27	15	3	78	43	37	.291	.354	.426	114	8	48			.954	-11	*O-131	-0.9
1912	*NY-N	143	549	83	152	26	20	3	92	27	45	.277	.320	.413	97	-5	38			.968	2	*O-143	-1.0
1913	*NY-N	147	520	70	139	21	3	2	59	34	28	.267	.320	.331	85	-10	35			.965	10	*O-147	-0.7
1914	NY-N	86	139	19	31	6	3	0	23	9	7	.223	.270	.309	75	-5	11			1.000	-10	O-49	-1.7
1915	NY-N	45	127	12	28	1	2	3	11	7	15	.220	.261	.331	83	-3	2	4	-1	.959	-1	O-34	-0.7
	Chi-N	51	144	20	43	6	1	0	11	8	8	.299	.342	.354	110	2	6	5	-1	.966	1	O-40/2-1	0.0
	Yr	96	271	32	71	7	3	3	22	15	23	.262	.303	.343	98	-1	8	8	-2	.963	1	O-74/2-1	-0.7
1917	NY-N	22	22	1	1	0	0	0	3	3		.045	.192	.091	-12	-3	0			1.000	-3	O-11/C-1	-0.7
Total	11	1264	4334	555	1170	168	96	37	579	294	194	.270	.323	.379	108	30	321	8		.950	-6	*O-1171/C-8,2-1	-2.6

■ LARRY MURRAY
Murray, Larry   b: 4/1/53, Chicago, Ill.   BB/TR, 5'11", 179 lbs.   Deb: 9/7/74

YEAR	TM/L	G	AB	R	H	2B	3B	HR	RBI	BB	SO	AVG	OBP	SLG	PRO+	BR/A	SB	CS	SBR	FA	FR	G/POS	TPR
1974	NY-A	6	1	1	0	0	0	0	0	0	0	.000	.000	.000	-99	-0	2			1.000	-2	/O-3	-0.3
1975	NY-A	6	1	1	0	0	0	0	0	0	1	.000	.000	.000	-99	-0	0			1.000	-2	/O-4	-0.2
1976	NY-A	3	10	2	1	0	0	0	0	0	2	.100	.182	.100	-16	-1	0			1.000	-2	/O-7	-0.2
1977	Oak-A	90	162	19	29	5	1	2	9	17	36	.179	.257	.253	40	-13	12	3	2	.992	-13	O-78/S-1,D-3	-2.6
1978	Oak-A	11	12	1	1	0	0	0	0	3	2	.083	.267	.083	3	-1	0	0	0	1.000	-1	/O-6	-0.3

YEAR	TM/L	G	AB	R	H	2B	3B	HR	RBI	BB	SO	AVG	OBP	SLG	PRO+	BR/A	SB	CS	SBR	FA	FR	G/POS	TPR
1979	Oak-A	105	226	25	42	11	2	2	20	28	34	.186	.276	.279	53	-15	6	6	-2	.963	-1	O-90/2-3	-2.0
Total	6	226	412	49	73	16	4	3	31	49	74	.177	.265	.257	44	-32	20	10	0	.975	-20	O-188/2-3,D-3,S-1	-5.6

■ RAY MURRAY
Murray, Raymond Lee "Deacon" b: 10/12/17, Spring Hope, N.C. BR/TR, 6'3", 204 lbs. Deb: 4/25/48

YEAR	TM/L	G	AB	R	H	2B	3B	HR	RBI	BB	SO	AVG	OBP	SLG	PRO+	BR/A	SB	CS	SBR	FA	FR	G/POS	TPR
1948	Cle-A	4	4	0	0	0	0	0	0	0	3	.000	.000	.000	-99	-1	0	0	0	.000	0	H	-0.1
1950	Cle-A	55	139	16	38	8	2	1	13	12	13	.273	.331	.381	85	-4	1	0	0	.972	-5	C-45	-0.6
1951	Cle-A	1	1	0	1	0	0	0	1	0	0	1.000	1.000	1.000	468	-1	0	0	0	1.000	1	/C-1	0.1
	Phi-A	40	122	10	26	6	0	0	13	14	8	.213	.294	.262	50	-8	0	0	0	.985	-3	C-39	-0.9
	Yr	41	123	10	27	6	0	0	14	14	8	.220	.299	.268	53	-8	0	0	0	.986	-2	C-40	-0.8
1952	Phi-A	44	136	14	28	5	0	1	10	9	13	.206	.255	.265	42	-11	0	0	0	.995	7	C-42	-0.1
1953	Phi-A	84	268	25	76	14	3	6	41	18	25	.284	.331	.425	99	-1	0	0	0	.989	4	C-78	0.6
1954	Bal-A	22	61	4	15	4	0	1	2	2	5	.246	.270	.344	73	-3	0	0	0	.989	1	C-21	-0.1
Total	6	250	731	69	184	37	6	8	80	55	67	.252	.305	.352	75	-27	1	0	0	.987	6	C-226	-1.1

■ RICH MURRAY
Murray, Richard Dale b: 7/6/57, Los Angeles, Cal. BR/TR, 6'4", 195 lbs. Deb: 6/7/80 F

YEAR	TM/L	G	AB	R	H	2B	3B	HR	RBI	BB	SO	AVG	OBP	SLG	PRO+	BR/A	SB	CS	SBR	FA	FR	G/POS	TPR
1980	SF-N	53	194	19	42	8	2	4	24	11	48	.216	.259	.340	67	-9	2	1	0	.987	0	1-53	-1.3
1983	SF-N	4	10	0	2	0	0	0	1	0	3	.200	.200	.200	11	-1	0	0	0	1.000	-0	/1-3	-0.2
Total	2	57	204	19	44	8	2	4	25	11	51	.216	.256	.333	65	-10	2	1	0	.988	0	/1-56	-1.5

■ BOBBY MURRAY
Murray, Robert Hayes b: 7/4/1894, St.Albans, Vt. d: 1/4/79, Nashua, N.H. BL/TR, 5'7", 155 lbs. Deb: 9/24/23

YEAR	TM/L	G	AB	R	H	2B	3B	HR	RBI	BB	SO	AVG	OBP	SLG	PRO+	BR/A	SB	CS	SBR	FA	FR	G/POS	TPR
1923	Was-A	10	37	2	7	1	0	0	2	1	4	.189	.211	.216	13	-5	1	0	0	1.000	2	3-10	-0.1

■ TOM MURRAY
Murray, Thomas W. b: 1866, Savannah, Ga. Deb: 6/20/1894

YEAR	TM/L	G	AB	R	H	2B	3B	HR	RBI	BB	SO	AVG	OBP	SLG	PRO+	BR/A	SB	CS	SBR	FA	FR	G/POS	TPR
1894	Phi-N	1	2	0	0	0	0	0	0	0	2	.000	.000	.000	-99	-1	0			.833	0	/S-1	0.0

■ BILL MURRAY
Murray, William Allenwood "Dasher" b: 9/6/1893, Vinalhaven, Me. d: 9/14/43, Boston, Mass. BB/TR, 5'11", 165 lbs. Deb: 6/27/17

YEAR	TM/L	G	AB	R	H	2B	3B	HR	RBI	BB	SO	AVG	OBP	SLG	PRO+	BR/A	SB	CS	SBR	FA	FR	G/POS	TPR
1917	Was-A	8	21	2	3	0	1	0	4	2	2	.143	.217	.238	39	-2	1			.889	-2	/2-6,S-1	-0.3

■ IVAN MURRELL
Murrell, Ivan Augustus (Peters) b: 4/24/45, Almirante, Panama BR/TR, 6'2", 196 lbs. Deb: 9/28/63

YEAR	TM/L	G	AB	R	H	2B	3B	HR	RBI	BB	SO	AVG	OBP	SLG	PRO+	BR/A	SB	CS	SBR	FA	FR	G/POS	TPR
1963	Hou-N	2	5	1	1	0	0	0	0	0	0	.200	.200	.200	17	-1	0	0	0	1.000	-0	/O-2	-0.1
1964	Hou-N	10	14	1	2	1	0	0	1	0	6	.143	.143	.214	-1	-2	0	0	0	1.000	-1	/O-5	-0.3
1967	Hou-N	10	29	2	9	0	0	1	1	1	9	.310	.333	.310	88	-0	1	0	0	.846	0	/O-6	-0.1
1968	Hou-N	32	59	3	6	1	1	0	3	1	17	.102	.117	.153	-20	-9	0	0	0	.931	2	O-15	-0.9
1969	SD-N	111	247	19	63	10	6	3	25	11	65	.255	.292	.381	91	-4	3	4	-2	.959	-3	O-72/1-2	-1.2
1970	SD-N	125	347	43	85	9	3	12	35	17	93	.245	.288	.392	84	-10	9	7	-2	.970	-5	*O-101/1-1	-1.2
1971	SD-N	103	255	23	60	6	3	7	24	7	60	.235	.264	.365	82	-8	5	2	0	.978	-5	O-72	-1.1
1972	SD-N	5	7	0	1	0	0	0	1	0	3	.143	.143	.143	-20	-1	0	0	0	1.000	0	/O-1	-0.1
1973	SD-N	93	210	23	48	13	1	9	21	2	52	.229	.236	.429	87	-6	2	0	0	.959	-1	O-37,1-24	-0.9
1974	Atl-N	73	133	11	33	1	1	2	12	5	35	.248	.275	.316	62	-7	0	1	0	.983	-1	O-32,1-13	-1.0
Total	10	564	1306	126	308	41	15	33	123	44	342	.236	.266	.366	77	-46	20	13	-2	.965	-2	O-343/1-40	-6.9

■ DANNY MURTAUGH
Murtaugh, Daniel Edward b: 10/8/17, Chester, Pa. d: 12/2/76, Chester, Pa. BR/TR, 5'9", 165 lbs. Deb: 7/6/41 MC

YEAR	TM/L	G	AB	R	H	2B	3B	HR	RBI	BB	SO	AVG	OBP	SLG	PRO+	BR/A	SB	CS	SBR	FA	FR	G/POS	TPR
1941	Phi-N	85	347	34	76	8	1	0	11	26	31	.219	.275	.248	50	-23	18			.978	2	2-85/S-1	-1.5
1942	Phi-N	144	506	48	122	16	4	0	27	49	39	.241	.311	.289	80	-12	13			.939	4	S-60,3-53,2-32	0.0
1943	Phi-N	113	451	65	123	17	4	1	35	57	23	.273	.357	.335	104	4	4			.974	0	*2-113	1.2
1946	Phi-N	6	19	1	4	1	0	1	3	2	2	.211	.286	.421	102	-0	0			.958	-4	/2-6	-0.4
1947	Bos-N	3	8	0	1	0	0	0	0	1	2	.125	.222	.125	-6	-1	0			1.000	-0	/2-2,3-2	-0.1
1948	Pit-N	146	514	54	149	21	5	1	71	60	40	.290	.365	.356	94	-2	10			.979	1	*2-146	0.7
1949	Pit-N	75	236	16	48	7	2	2	24	29	17	.203	.291	.275	51	-16	2			.975	3	2-74	-1.0
1950	Pit-N	118	367	34	108	20	5	2	37	47	42	.294	.376	.392	99	1	2			.976	3	*2-108	0.8
1951	Pit-N	77	151	9	30	7	0	1	11	16	19	.199	.284	.265	47	-11	0	0	0	.970	-2	2-65/3-3	-1.2
Total	9	767	2599	263	661	97	21	8	219	287	215	.254	.331	.317	81	-61	49	0		.975	10	2-631/S-61,3-58	-1.5

■ TONY MUSER
Muser, Anthony Joseph b: 8/1/47, Van Nuys, Cal. BL/TL, 6'2", 190 lbs. Deb: 9/14/69 C

YEAR	TM/L	G	AB	R	H	2B	3B	HR	RBI	BB	SO	AVG	OBP	SLG	PRO+	BR/A	SB	CS	SBR	FA	FR	G/POS	TPR
1969	Bos-A	2	9	0	1	0	0	0	0	1	1	.111	.200	.111	-10	-1	0	0	0	1.000	1	/1-2	-0.1
1971	Chi-A	11	16	2	5	0	1	0	0	1	1	.313	.353	.438	119	0	0	0	0	.963	0	/1-4	0.1
1972	Chi-A	44	61	6	17	2	2	1	9	2	6	.279	.302	.426	113	1	1	1	-0	.986	-0	1-29/O-1	-0.1
1973	Chi-A	109	309	38	88	14	3	4	30	33	36	.285	.354	.388	105	3	8	4	0	.992	-3	1-89,D-13/O-2	-0.6
1974	Chi-A	103	206	16	60	5	1	1	18	6	22	.291	.315	.340	86	-4	1	4	-2	.998	-4	1-80,D-13	-1.3
1975	Chi-A	43	111	11	27	3	0	0	6	7	8	.243	.288	.270	58	-6	2	1	0	.993	2	1-41	-0.6
	Bal-A	80	82	11	26	3	0	0	11	8	9	.317	.378	.354	115	2	0	0	0	.996	1	1-62	0.2
	Yr	123	193	22	53	6	0	0	17	15	17	.275	.327	.306	83	-4	2	1	0	.994	3	*1-103	-0.4
1976	Bal-A	136	326	25	74	7	1	1	30	21	34	.227	.274	.264	62	-16	1	1	-0	.991	1	*1-109,0-12,D-10	-2.2
1977	Bal-A	120	118	14	27	6	0	0	7	13	16	.229	.305	.280	65	-6	1	2	-1	.992	1	1-77,O-11/D-1	-0.6
1978	Mil-A	15	30	0	4	1	1	0	5	3	5	.133	.212	.233	25	-3	0	0	0	.988	-0	1-12	-0.4
Total	9	663	1268	123	329	41	9	7	117	95	138	.259	.312	.323	82	-30	14	13	-4	.992	-1	1-505/D-37,O-26	-5.6

■ STAN MUSIAL
Musial, Stanley Frank "Stan The Man" b: 11/21/20, Donora, Pa. BL/TL, 6', 175 lbs. Deb: 9/17/41 H

YEAR	TM/L	G	AB	R	H	2B	3B	HR	RBI	BB	SO	AVG	OBP	SLG	PRO+	BR/A	SB	CS	SBR	FA	FR	G/POS	TPR
1941	StL-N	12	47	8	20	4	0	1	7	2	1	.426	.449	.574	175	4	1			1.000	0	O-11	0.4
1942	*StL-N	140	467	87	147	32	10	10	72	62	25	.315	.397	.490	148	28	6			.984	1	*O-135	2.5
1943	*StL-N★	157	617	108	220	48	20	13	81	72	18	.357	.425	.562	176	60	9			.982	11	*O-155	6.4
1944	*StL-N★	146	568	112	197	51	14	12	94	90	28	.347	.440	.549	174	59	7			.987	3	*O-146	5.4
1946	*StL-N★	156	624	124	228	50	20	16	103	73	31	.365	.434	.587	180	65	7			.989	-1	*1-114,O-42	5.7
1947	StL-N★	149	587	113	183	30	13	19	95	80	24	.312	.398	.504	132	28	4			.994	-7	*1-149	1.5
1948	StL-N★	155	611	135	230	46	18	39	131	79	34	.376	.450	.702	196	81	7			.981	-8	*O-155/1-2	6.3
1949	StL-N★	157	612	128	207	41	13	36	123	107	38	.338	.438	.624	174	65	3			.991	-19	*O-156/1-1	3.8
1950	StL-N★	146	555	105	192	41	7	28	109	87	36	.346	.437	.596	161	51	5			.964	-13	O-77,1-69	3.2
1951	StL-N★	152	578	124	205	30	12	32	108	98	40	.355	.449	.614	182	69	4	5	-2	.974	-4	O-91,1-60	6.4
1952	StL-N★	154	578	105	194	42	6	21	91	96	29	.336	.432	.538	167	56	7	7	-2	.987	-7	*O-129,1-25/P-1	4.2
1953	StL-N★	157	593	127	200	53	9	30	113	105	32	.337	.437	.609	169	63	3	4	-2	.984	-9	*O-157	4.4
1954	StL-N★	153	591	120	195	41	9	35	126	103	39	.330	.433	.607	166	60	1	7	-4	.990	-2	*O-152,1-10	4.6
1955	StL-N★	154	562	97	179	30	5	33	108	80	39	.319	.411	.566	156	47	5	4	-1	.992	1	*1-110,O-51	3.8
1956	StL-N★	156	594	87	184	33	6	27	109	75	39	.310	.390	.522	142	36	2	6		.993	6	*1-103,O-53	3.3
1957	StL-N★	134	502	82	176	38	3	29	102	66	34	.351	.428	.612	172	52	1	1	-0	.992	2	*1-130	4.5
1958	StL-N★	135	472	64	159	35	2	17	62	72	26	.337	.426	.528	145	33	0	1	0	.989	8	*1-124	3.4
1959	StL-N★	115	341	37	87	13	2	14	44	60	25	.255	.367	.428	104	3	0	2	-1	.990	2	1-90/O-3	-0.1
1960	StL-N★	116	331	49	91	17	1	17	63	41	34	.275	.358	.486	118	8	1	1	-0	.990	-0	O-59,1-29	0.2
1961	StL-N★	123	372	46	107	22	4	15	70	52	35	.288	.376	.489	116	9	0	0	0	.994	-1	O-103	0.3
1962	StL-N★	135	433	57	143	18	1	19	82	64	46	.330	.420	.508	135	23	3	0	1	.977	-3	*O-119	1.4
1963	StL-N★	124	337	34	86	10	2	12	58	35	43	.255	.329	.404	100	0	2	0	1	.968	-7	O-96	0.3
Total	22	3026	10972	1949	3630	725	177	475	1951	1599	696	.331	.418	.559	157	899	78	31		.984	-38	*O-1890,1-1016/P-1	70.5

■ DANNY MUSSER
Musser, William Daniel b: 9/5/05, Zion, Pa. BL/TR, 5'9.5", 160 lbs. Deb: 9/18/32

YEAR	TM/L	G	AB	R	H	2B	3B	HR	RBI	BB	SO	AVG	OBP	SLG	PRO+	BR/A	SB	CS	SBR	FA	FR	G/POS	TPR
1932	Was-A	1	2	0	1	0	0	0	0	0	0	.500	.500	.500	162	0	0	0	0	.000	0	/3-1	0.0

■ GEORGE MYATT
Myatt, George Edward "Mercury', "Stud" or "Foghorn" b: 6/14/14, Denver, Colo. BL/TR, 5'11", 167 lbs. Deb: 8/16/38 MC

YEAR	TM/L	G	AB	R	H	2B	3B	HR	RBI	BB	SO	AVG	OBP	SLG	PRO+	BR/A	SB	CS	SBR	FA	FR	G/POS	TPR
1938	NY-N	43	170	29	52	2	1	3	10	14	13	.306	.362	.382	104	1	10			.919	7	S-24,3-19	1.1
1939	NY-N	22	53	7	10	2	0	0	3	4	6	.189	.271	.226	35	-5	2			.907	1	3-14	-0.4
1943	Was-A	42	53	11	13	0	0	0	3	13	7	.245	.394	.302	109	1	3	0	1	.930	-1	2-11/S-2,3-2	0.2
1944	Was-A	140	538	86	153	19	6	0	40	54	44	.284	.357	.342	105	1	26	10	2	.957	-22	*2-121,S-15/O-3	-0.8
1945	Was-A	133	490	81	145	17	3	1	39	63	43	.296	.378	.365	127	18	30	11	2	.972	-19	2-94,O-32/3-6,S-1	0.6
1946	Was-A	15	34	7	8	1	0	0	4	2	3	.235	.297	.265	61	-2	1	0	0	.900	-2	/3-7,2-2	-0.4

YEAR	TM/L	G	AB	R	H	2B	3B	HR	RBI	BB	SO	AVG	OBP	SLG	PRO+	BR/A	SB	CS	SBR	FA	FR	G/POS	TPR
1947	Was-A	12	7	1	0	0	0	0	0	4	4	.000	.364	.000	6	-1	0	0	0	1.000	0	/2-1	-0.1
Total	7	407	1345	220	381	44	14	4	99	156	120	.283	.362	.346	108	19	72	22		.962	-35	2-229/3-48,S-42,O	0.2

■ GLENN MYATT
Myatt, Glenn Calvin   b: 7/9/1897, Argenta, Ark.   d: 8/9/69, Houston, Tex.   BL/TR, 5'11", 165 lbs.   Deb: 4/15/20

YEAR	TM/L	G	AB	R	H	2B	3B	HR	RBI	BB	SO	AVG	OBP	SLG	PRO+	BR/A	SB	CS	SBR	FA	FR	G/POS	TPR
1920	Phi-A	70	196	14	49	8	3	0	18	12	22	.250	.293	.321	62	-11	1	3	-2	.900	-5	O-37,C-22	-1.9
1921	Phi-A	44	69	6	14	2	0	0	5	6	7	.203	.267	.232	28	-7	1	0	0	.939	2	C-27	-0.4
1923	Cle-A	92	220	36	63	7	6	3	40	16	18	.286	.338	.414	97	-2	0	2	-1	.934	-8	C-69	-0.8
1924	Cle-A	105	342	55	117	22	7	8	73	33	12	.342	.402	.518	134	16	6	1	1	.978	-15	C-95	0.8
1925	Cle-A	106	358	51	97	15	9	11	54	29	24	.271	.329	.455	97	-4	3	1	0	.973	-18	C-98/O-1	-1.5
1926	Cle-A	56	117	14	29	5	2	0	13	13	13	.248	.323	.325	69	-5	1	0	0	1.000	-1	C-35	-0.4
1927	Cle-A	55	94	15	23	6	0	2	8	12	7	.245	.336	.372	83	-2	1	1	-0	.978	2	C-26	-0.0
1928	Cle-A	58	125	9	36	7	2	1	15	13	13	.288	.355	.400	97	-0	2	0	-1	.967	-9	C-30	-0.8
1929	Cle-A	59	129	14	30	4	1	1	17	7	5	.233	.277	.302	47	-10	0	1	-1	.976	-1	C-41	-0.9
1930	Cle-A	86	265	30	78	23	2	2	37	18	17	.294	.342	.419	88	-5	2	3	-1	.977	-7	C-71	-0.6
1931	Cle-A	65	195	21	48	14	2	1	29	21	13	.246	.319	.354	73	-8	2	1	0	.991	-4	C-53	-0.8
1932	Cle-A	82	252	45	62	12	1	8	46	27	21	.246	.326	.397	81	-8	2	2	-1	.988	-8	C-65	-1.2
1933	Cle-A	40	77	10	18	4	0	0	7	15	8	.234	.372	.286	73	-2	0	1	-1	.965	-1	C-27	-0.2
1934	Cle-A	36	107	18	34	6	1	0	12	13	5	.318	.392	.393	101	1	1	0	0	.980	-1	C-34	0.2
1935	Cle-A	10	36	1	3	1	0	0	2	4	3	.083	.175	.111	-24	-7	0	0	0	1.000	-1	C-10	-0.7
	NY-N	13	18	2	4	0	1	1	6	0	3	.222	.222	.500	90	-0	0			1.000	-1	/C-4	-0.1
1936	Det-A	27	78	5	17	1	0	0	5	9	4	.218	.299	.231	32	-8	0	0	0	1.000	-2	C-27	-0.8
Total	16	1004	2678	346	722	137	37	38	387	248	195	.270	.334	.391	85	-63	20	18		.974	-78	C-734/O-38	-10.1

■ BUDDY MYER
Myer, Charles Solomon   b: 3/16/04, Ellisville, Miss.   d: 10/31/74, Baton Rouge, La.   BL/TR, 5'10.5", 163 lbs.   Deb: 9/26/25

YEAR	TM/L	G	AB	R	H	2B	3B	HR	RBI	BB	SO	AVG	OBP	SLG	PRO+	BR/A	SB	CS	SBR	FA	FR	G/POS	TPR
1925	*Was-A	4	8	1	2	0	0	0	0	0	1	.250	.250	.250	28	-1	0	0	0	1.000	-2	/S-4	-0.3
1926	Was-A	132	434	66	132	18	6	1	62	45	19	.304	.370	.380	98	-0	10	11	-4	.928	-18	*S-118/3-8	-1.0
1927	Was-A	15	51	7	11	1	0	0	7	8	3	.216	.322	.235	47	-4	3	1	0	.933	-3	S-15	-0.4
	Bos-A	133	469	59	135	22	11	2	47	48	15	.288	.359	.394	97	-2	9	5	-0	.940	7	*S-101,3-14,O-10,1/2	1.4
	Yr	148	520	66	146	23	11	2	54	56	18	.281	.355	.379	92	-5	12	6	0	.939	4	*S-116,3-14,O-10/2	1.0
1928	Bos-A	147	536	78	168	26	6	1	44	53	28	.313	.379	.390	104	5	30	16	-1	.967	4	*3-144	1.5
1929	Was-A	141	563	80	169	29	10	3	82	63	33	.300	.373	.403	99	-0	18	7	1	.958	-15	2-88,3-53	-0.7
1930	Was-A	138	541	97	164	18	8	2	61	58	31	.303	.373	.377	90	-6	14	11	-2	.965	-19	*2-134/O-2	-1.8
1931	Was-A	139	591	114	173	33	11	4	56	58	42	.293	.360	.406	100	1	11	14	-5	.984	-17	*2-137	-1.1
1932	Was-A	143	577	120	161	38	16	5	52	69	33	.279	.360	.426	104	4	12	7	-1	.975	-18	*2-139	-0.7
1933	*Was-A	131	530	95	160	29	15	4	61	60	21	.302	.374	.436	115	12	6	8	-3	.978	-1	*2-129	1.4
1934	Was-A	139	524	103	160	33	8	3	57	102	32	.305	.419	.416	121	21	6	4	-2	.975	-13	*2-135	1.4
1935	Was-A☆	151	616	115	215	36	11	5	100	96	40	**.349**	.440	.468	139	41	7	6	-2	.979	8	*2-151	5.4
1936	Was-A	51	156	31	42	5	2	0	15	42	11	.269	.427	.327	94	1	7	2	1	.985	3	2-43	0.8
1937	Was-A☆	125	430	54	126	16	10	1	65	78	41	.293	.407	.384	105	7	2	6	-3	.966	-17	*2-119/O-1	-0.4
1938	Was-A	127	437	79	147	22	4	6	71	93	32	.336	.454	.465	140	33	9	5	-0	**.982**	2	*2-121	3.7
1939	Was-A	83	258	33	78	10	3	1	32	40	18	.302	.396	.376	106	4	4	1	1	.968	-1	2-65	0.7
1940	Was-A	71	210	28	61	14	4	0	29	34	10	.290	.389	.395	111	5	6	3	0	.967	4	2-54	1.1
1941	Was-A	53	107	14	27	3	1	0	9	18	10	.252	.360	.299	80	-2	2	0	1	.982	-8	2-24	-0.8
Total	17	1923	7038	1174	2131	353	130	38	850	965	428	.303	.389	.406	108	120	156	109	-19	.974	-103	*2-1340,S-238,3/O	10.2

■ GEORGE MYERS
Myers, George D.   b: 11/13/1860, Buffalo, N.Y.   d: 12/14/26, Buffalo, N.Y.   BR/TR, 5'8", 170 lbs.   Deb: 5/2/1884

YEAR	TM/L	G	AB	R	H	2B	3B	HR	RBI	BB	SO	AVG	OBP	SLG	PRO+	BR/A	SB	CS	SBR	FA	FR	G/POS	TPR
1884	Buf-N	78	325	34	59	9	2	2	32	13	33	.182	.213	.240	41	-22				.837	-10	C-49,O-34	-2.6
1885	Buf-N	89	326	40	67	7	2	0	19	23	40	.206	.258	.239	60	-14				.899	-6	C-69,O-23	-1.4
1886	StL-N	79	295	26	56	7	3	0	27	18	42	.190	.236	.234	46	-18	6			.928	-13	C-72/O-6,3-1	-2.1
1887	Ind-N	69	235	25	51	8	1	1	20	22	7	.217	.298	.272	62	-11	26			.929	-13	C-50,O-15/1-6,3-1	-1.7
1888	Ind-N	66	248	36	59	9	2	2	16	16	14	.238	.292	.298	87	-3	28			.929	-8	C-47,3-14,O-10/1-1	-0.7
1889	Ind-N	43	149	22	29	3	0	0	12	17	13	.195	.294	.215	42	-11	12			.909	4	O-23,C-18/1-1	-0.5
Total	6	424	1578	183	321	43	8	5	126	109	149	.203	.260	.250	54	-80	72			.901	-46	C-305,O-111/3-16,1	-9.0

■ GREG MYERS
Myers, Gregory Richard   b: 4/14/66, Riverside, Cal.   BL/TR, 6'1", 200 lbs.   Deb: 9/12/87

YEAR	TM/L	G	AB	R	H	2B	3B	HR	RBI	BB	SO	AVG	OBP	SLG	PRO+	BR/A	SB	CS	SBR	FA	FR	G/POS	TPR
1987	Tor-A	7	9	1	1	0	0	0	0	0	3	.111	.111	.111	-40	-2	0	0	0	1.000	2	/C-7	0.0
1989	Tor-A	17	44	0	5	2	0	0	1	2	9	.114	.152	.159	-12	-7	0	1	-1	1.000	2	C-11/D-6	-0.5
1990	Tor-A	87	250	33	59	7	1	5	22	22	33	.236	.298	.332	75	-9	0	1	-1	.993	-0	C-87	-0.5
1991	Tor-A	107	309	25	81	22	0	8	36	21	45	.262	.309	.411	94	-3	0	0	0	.979	-4	*C-104	-0.3
1992	Tor-A	22	61	4	14	6	0	1	13	5	5	.230	.288	.377	81	-2	0	0	0	.991	2	C-18/D-1	0.0
	Cal-A	8	17	0	4	1	0	0	0	0	6	.235	.235	.294	47	-1	0	0	0	1.000	2	/C-8	0.1
	Yr	30	78	4	18	7	0	1	13	5	11	.231	.277	.359	74	-3	0	0	0	.993	2	C-26/D-1	0.1
1993	Cal-A	108	290	27	74	10	0	7	40	17	47	.255	.301	.362	75	-11	3	3	-1	.986	-8	C-97/D-2	-1.5
1994	Cal-A	45	126	10	31	6	0	2	8	10	27	.246	.301	.341	64	-7	0	2	-1	.991	-0	C-41/D-1	-0.7
1995	Cal-A	85	273	35	71	12	2	9	38	17	49	.260	.306	.418	87	-6	0	1	-1	.989	-4	C-61,D-16	-0.7
1996	Min-A	97	329	37	94	22	3	6	47	19	52	.286	.325	.426	86	-8	0	0	0	.985	-12	C-90	-1.2
Total	9	583	1708	172	434	88	6	38	205	113	276	.254	.302	.379	79	-54	3	8	-4	.987	-24	C-524/D-26	-5.3

■ HENRY MYERS
Myers, Henry C.   b: 5/1858, Philadelphia, Pa.   d: 4/18/1895, Philadelphia, Pa.   BR/TR, 5'9", 159 lbs.   Deb: 8/20/1881   M

YEAR	TM/L	G	AB	R	H	2B	3B	HR	RBI	BB	SO	AVG	OBP	SLG	PRO+	BR/A	SB	CS	SBR	FA	FR	G/POS	TPR
1881	Pro-N	1	4	0	0	0	0	0	0	0	2	.000	.000	.000	-99	-1				1.000	-0	/S-1	-0.1
1882	Bal-a	69	294	43	53	3	0	0		0	12	.180	.212	.190	40	-17				.822	-7	*S-68/P-6,M	-1.8
1884	Wil-U	6	24	3	3	0	0	0	0	0		.125	.125	.125	-23	-4				.875	4	/S-5,2-1	0.0
Total	3	76	322	46	56	3	0	0	0	12	2	.174	.204	.183	32	-22				.826	-3	/S-74,P-6,2-1	-1.9

■ HY MYERS
Myers, Henry Harrison   b: 4/27/1889, E.Liverpool, Ohio   d: 5/1/65, Minerva, Ohio   BR/TR, 5'9.5", 175 lbs.   Deb: 8/30/09

YEAR	TM/L	G	AB	R	H	2B	3B	HR	RBI	BB	SO	AVG	OBP	SLG	PRO+	BR/A	SB	CS	SBR	FA	FR	G/POS	TPR
1909	Bro-N	6	22	1	5	1	0	0	6	2		.227	.292	.273	78	-1	1			1.000	-1	/O-6	-0.2
1911	Bro-N	13	43	2	7	1	0	0	2	3		.163	.200	.186	9	-5	1			.889	-2	O-13	-0.8
1914	Bro-N	70	227	35	65	3	9	0	17	7	24	.286	.316	.379	104	0	2			.964	-6	O-60	-0.9
1915	Bro-N	153	605	69	150	21	7	2	46	17	51	.248	.275	.316	77	-18	19	22	-8	.964	7	*O-153	-3.0
1916	*Bro-N	113	412	54	108	12	14	3	36	21	35	.262	.308	.381	108	3	17			.969	1	*O-106	-0.2
1917	Bro-N	120	471	37	126	15	10	1	41	18	25	.268	.294	.348	94	-4	5			.982	-3	O-66,1-22,2-19,3-15	-1.2
1918	Bro-N	107	407	36	104	9	8	4	40	20	26	.256	.292	.346	95	-4	17			.975	13	*O-107	0.3
1919	Bro-N	133	512	62	157	23	**14**	4	**73**	20	34	.307	.339	**.436**	129	16	13			.979	9	*O-131	1.8
1920	*Bro-N	154	582	83	177	36	**22**	4	80	35	54	.304	.345	.462	126	18	9	13	-5	.978	4	*O-152/3-2	0.6
1921	Bro-N	144	549	51	158	14	4	4	68	22	51	.288	.318	.350	74	-20	8	6	-1	.968	6	*O-124,2-21/3-1	-2.4
1922	Bro-N	153	618	82	196	20	6	4	89	13	26	.317	.331	.408	90	-10	9	10	-3	.974	6	*O-152/2-1	-1.8
1923	StL-N	96	330	29	99	18	2	2	48	12	19	.300	.330	.385	90	-5	5	3	-0	.977	6	O-87	-0.4
1924	StL-N	43	124	12	26	5	1	1	15	3	10	.210	.228	.290	39	-11	1	2	-1	.945	-3	O-22,3-12/2-3	-1.6
1925	StL-N	1	1	0	0	0	0	0	0	0	0	.000	.000	.000	-98	-0	0	0	0	.000	0	H	-0.0
	Cin-N	3	6	1	1	1	0	0	0	0	0	.167	.167	.333	25	-1	0	0	0	1.000	-1	/O-3	-0.1
	StL-N	1	1	1	1	0	0	0	0	0	0	1.000	1.000	1.000	403	-0	0	0	0	.000	0	H	-0.1
	Yr	5	8	2	2	1	0	0	0	0	0	.250	.250	.375	58	-1	0	0	0	1.000	-1	/O-3	-0.1
Total	14	1310	4910	555	1380	179	100	32	559	195	358	.281	.312	.378	95	-42	107	56		.972	38	*O-1182/2-44,3-30,1	-9.9

■ BERT MYERS
Myers, James Albert   b: 4/8/1874, Frederick, Md.   d: 10/12/15, Washington, D.C.   BR/TR, 5'10",   Deb: 4/25/1896

YEAR	TM/L	G	AB	R	H	2B	3B	HR	RBI	BB	SO	AVG	OBP	SLG	PRO+	BR/A	SB	CS	SBR	FA	FR	G/POS	TPR
1896	StL-N	122	454	47	116	12	8	0	37	40	32	.256	.320	.317	71	-19	8			.867	-9	*3-121/S-1	-2.1
1898	Was-N	31	110	14	29	1	4	0	13	13		.264	.341	.345	97	-0	2			.835	-3	3-31	-0.3
1900	Phi-N	7	28	5	5	1	0	0	2	3		.179	.258	.214	31	-3	1			.909	2	/3-7	-0.1
Total	3	160	592	66	150	14	12	0	52	56	32	.253	.321	.318	74	-21	11			.863	-10	3-159/S-1	-2.5

YEAR	TM/L	G	AB	R	H	2B	3B	HR	RBI	BB	SO	AVG	OBP	SLG	PRO+	BR/A	SB	CS	SBR	FA	FR	G/POS	TPR

■ AL MYERS
Myers, James Albert "Cod"   b: 10/22/1863, Danville, Ill.   d: 12/24/27, Marshall, Ill.   BR/TR, 5'8.5", 165 lbs.   Deb: 9/27/1884

1884	Mil-U	12	46	6	15	6	0	0		0		.326	.326	.457	249	4				.848	2	2-12	0.6
1885	Phi-N	93	357	25	73	13	2	1	28	11	41	.204	.228	.261	59	-16				.884	-17	*2-93	-2.9
1886	KC-N	118	473	69	131	22	9	4	51	22	42	.277	.309	.387	104	0	3			.913	2	*2-118	0.6
1887	Was-N	105	362	45	84	9	5	2	36	40	26	.232	.312	.301	75	-11	18			.909	-5	2-78,S-27	-1.1
1888	Was-N	132	502	46	104	12	7	2	46	37	46	.207	.270	.271	77	-12	20			.918	-25	*2-132	-3.1
1889	Was-N	46	176	24	46	3	0	0	20	22	7	.261	.347	.278	81	-3	10			.942	3	2-46	0.2
	Phi-N	75	305	52	82	14	2	0	28	36	9	.269	.354	.328	84	-7	8			.853	-8	2-75	-0.9
	Yr	121	481	76	128	17	2	0	48	58	16	.266	.351	.310	83	-10	18			.886	-4	*2-121	-0.7
1890	Phi-N	117	487	95	135	29	7	2	81	57	46	.277	.365	.378	114	9	44			.948	14	*2-117	2.6
1891	Phi-N	135	514	67	118	27	2	2	69	69	46	.230	.331	.302	83	-10	8			.937	-10	*2-135	-1.2
Total	8	833	3222	429	788	135	34	13	359	294	263	.245	.314	.320	88	-45	111			.914	-42	2-806/S-27	-5.2

■ LYNN MYERS
Myers, Lynnwood Lincoln   b: 2/23/14, Enola, Pa.   BR/TR, 5'6.5", 145 lbs.   Deb: 7/13/38   F

1938	StL-N	70	227	18	55	10	2	1	19	9	25	.242	.271	.317	58	-13	9			.944	-1	S-69	-0.9
1939	StL-N	74	117	24	28	6	1	0	10	12	23	.239	.310	.308	63	-6	1			.897	5	S-36,3-13/2-5	0.1
Total	2	144	344	42	83	16	3	1	29	21	48	.241	.285	.314	60	-19	10			.930	4	S-105/3-13,2-5	-0.8

■ HAP MYERS
Myers, Ralph Edward   b: 4/8/1888, San Francisco, Cal.   d: 6/30/67, San Francisco, Cal.   BR/TR, 6'3", 175 lbs.   Deb: 4/16/10

1910	Bos-A	3	6	0	2	0	0	0	0	0	0	.333	.333	.333	106	0	0			1.000	0	/O-2	0.0
1911	StL-A	11	37	4	11	1	0	0	1	1		.297	.316	.324	82	-1	0			.976	-2	1-11	-0.3
	Bos-A	13	38	3	14	2	0	0	0	0	4	.368	.429	.421	139	2	4			.947	-1	1-12	0.1
	Yr	24	75	7	25	3	0	0	1	5		.333	.375	.373	111	1	4			.963	-3	1-23	-0.2
1913	Bos-N	140	524	74	143	20	1	2	50	38	48	.273	.333	.326	87	-8	57			.987	5	*1-135	-0.5
1914	Bro-F	92	305	61	67	10	5	1	29	44	43	.220	.322	.295	69	-17	43			.989	1	1-88	-1.9
1915	Bro-F	118	341	61	98	9	1	1	36	32	39	.287	.352	.328	93	-7	28			.990	1	*1-107	-0.9
Total	5	377	1251	203	335	42	7	4	116	119	130	.268	.338	.322	85	-31	132			.987	4	1-353/O-2	-3.5

■ RICHIE MYERS
Myers, Richard   b: 4/7/30, Sacramento, Cal.   BR/TR, 5'6", 150 lbs.   Deb: 4/21/56

1956	Chi-N	4	1	1	0	0	0	0	0	0	0	.000	.000	.000	-99	-0	0	0	0	.000	0	H	0.0

■ ROD MYERS
Myers, Roderick Demond   b: 1/14/73, Conroe, Tex.   BL/TL, 6', 190 lbs.   Deb: 6/21/96

1996	KC-A	22	63	9	18	7	0	1	11	7	16	.286	.357	.444	104	0	3	2	-0	1.000	-3	O-19	-0.3

■ BILLY MYERS
Myers, William Harrison   b: 8/14/10, Enola, Pa.   d: 4/10/95, Carlisle, Pa.   BR/TR, 5'8", 168 lbs.   Deb: 4/16/35   F

1935	Cin-N	117	445	60	119	15	10	5	36	29	81	.267	.315	.380	89	-8	10			.939	3	*S-112	0.1
1936	Cin-N	98	323	45	87	9	6	6	27	28	56	.269	.328	.390	99	-1	6			.938	8	S-98	1.2
1937	Cin-N	124	335	35	84	13	3	7	43	44	57	.251	.339	.370	97	-1	0			.948	4	*S-121/2-6	1.1
1938	Cin-N	134	442	57	112	18	6	12	47	41	80	.253	.317	.403	99	-1	0			.939	2	*S-123,2-11	1.1
1939	*Cin-N	151	509	79	143	18	6	9	56	71	90	.281	.369	.393	104	5	4			.951	6	*S-151	2.4
1940	*Cin-N	90	282	33	57	14	2	5	30	30	56	.202	.283	.319	65	-14	0			.961	-5	S-88	-1.1
1941	Chi-N	24	63	10	14	1	0	1	4	7	25	.222	.310	.286	71	-2	1			.939	-1	S-19/2-1	0.3
Total	7	738	2399	319	616	88	33	45	243	250	445	.257	.328	.377	93	-22	23			.946	23	S-712/2-18	5.1

■ TIM NAEHRING
Naehring, Timothy James   b: 2/1/67, Cincinnati, Ohio   BR/TR, 6'2", 190 lbs.   Deb: 7/15/90

1990	Bos-A	24	85	10	23	6	0	2	12	8	15	.271	.333	.412	102	0	0	0	0	.918	-1	S-19/3-5,2-1	0.1
1991	Bos-A	20	55	1	6	1	0	0	3	6	15	.109	.197	.127	-8	-8	0	0	0	.956	-1	S-17/3-2,2-1	-0.8
1992	Bos-A	72	186	12	43	8	0	3	14	18	31	.231	.309	.323	72	-7	0	0	0	.992	16	S-30,2-23,3-10/OD	1.1
1993	Bos-A	39	127	14	42	10	0	1	17	10	26	.331	.380	.433	111	2	1	0	0	.973	-4	2-15,D-10/3-9,S-4	-0.1
1994	Bos-A	80	297	41	82	18	1	7	42	30	56	.276	.350	.414	92	-3	1	3	-2	.981	-1	2-49,3-11/1-8,SD	-0.3
1995	*Bos-A	126	433	61	133	27	2	10	57	77	66	.307	.416	.448	121	17	0	2	-1	.954	7	*3-124/D-1	2.0
1996	Bos-A	116	430	77	124	16	0	17	65	49	63	.288	.366	.444	100	0	2	1	0	.963	1	*3-116/2-1	0.1
Total	7	477	1613	216	453	86	3	40	210	198	272	.281	.365	.412	99	1	4	6	-2	.958	16	3-277/2-90,SD10	2.1

■ BILL NAGEL
Nagel, William Taylor   b: 8/19/15, Memphis, Tenn.   d: 10/8/81, Freehold, N.J.   BR/TR, 6'1", 190 lbs.   Deb: 4/20/39

1939	Phi-A	105	341	39	86	19	4	12	39	25	86	.252	.307	.437	90	-7				.944	-15	2-56,3-43/P-1	-1.7
1941	Phi-N	17	56	2	8	1	1	0	6	3	14	.143	.186	.196	8	-7	0			.935	3	2-12/O-2,3-1	-0.3
1945	Chi-A	67	220	21	46	10	3	3	27	15	41	.209	.263	.323	71	-9	3	1	0	.984	-3	1-57/3-1	-1.7
Total	3	189	617	62	140	30	8	15	72	43	141	.227	.281	.374	77	-23	5	2		.942	-15	/2-68,1-57,3-45,OP	-3.7

■ LOU NAGELSEN
Nagelsen, Louis Marcellus (b: Louis Marcellus Nageleisen)   b: 6/29/1887, Piqua, Ohio   d: 10/21/65, Fort Wayne, Ind.   BR/TR, 6'2", 180 lbs.   Deb: 9/10/12

1912	Cle-A	2	3	0	0	0	0	0	0	0	0	.000	.000	.000	-97	-1		0		1.000	-1	/C-2	-0.2

■ RUSS NAGELSON
Nagelson, Russell Charles   b: 9/19/44, Cincinnati, Ohio   BL/TR, 6', 205 lbs.   Deb: 9/11/68

1968	Cle-A	5	3	0	1	0	0	0	2	2	2	.333	.600	.333	192	1	0	0	0	.000	0	H	0.1
1969	Cle-A	12	17	1	6	0	0	0	3	3	3	.353	.450	.353	123	1	0	0	0	1.000	-1	/O-3,1-1	0.0
1970	Cle-A	17	24	3	3	1	0	1	2	3	9	.125	.222	.292	39	-2	0	0	0	1.000	-0	/O-4	-0.3
	Det-A	28	32	5	6	0	0	0	2	5	6	.188	.297	.188	36	-3	0	0	0	1.000	-1	/O-4,1-1	-0.4
	Yr	45	56	8	9	1	0	1	4	8	15	.161	.266	.232	38	-5	0	0	0	1.000	-1	/O-8,1-1	-0.7
Total	3	62	76	9	16	1	0	1	4	13	20	.211	.326	.263	64	-3	0	0	0	1.000	-2	/O-11,1-2	-0.6

■ TOM NAGLE
Nagle, Thomas Edward   b: 10/30/1865, Milwaukee, Wis.   d: 3/9/46, Milwaukee, Wis.   BR/TR, 5'10", 150 lbs.   Deb: 4/22/1890

1890	Chi-N	38	144	21	39	5	1	1	11	7	24	.271	.318	.340	88	-3	4			.939	-7	C-33/O-6	-0.6
1891	Chi-N	8	25	3	3	0	0	0	1	1	3	.120	.154	.120	-20	-4	0			.906	-4	/C-7,O-1	-0.6
Total	2	46	169	24	42	5	1	1	12	8	27	.249	.294	.308	73	-6	4			.935	-11	/C-40,O-7	-1.2

■ BILL NAHORODNY
Nahorodny, William Gerard   b: 8/31/53, Hamtramck, Mich.   BR/TR, 6'2", 200 lbs.   Deb: 9/27/76

1976	Phi-N	3	5	0	1	1	0	0	0	0	0	.200	.200	.400	65	-0	0	0	0	1.000	0	/C-2	0.0
1977	Chi-A	7	23	3	6	1	0	1	4	2	3	.261	.320	.435	104	0	0	0	0	1.000	-1	/C-7	-0.1
1978	Chi-A	107	347	29	82	11	2	8	35	23	52	.236	.288	.349	77	-11	1	0	0	.980	-3	*C-104/1-4,D-1	-1.2
1979	Chi-A	65	179	20	46	10	0	6	29	18	23	.257	.325	.413	98	-1	0	1	-1	.973	-0	C-60/D-3	0.0
1980	Atl-N	59	157	14	38	12	0	5	18	8	21	.242	.287	.414	91	-2	0	2	-1	.990	-7	C-54/1-1	-1.0
1981	Atl-N	14	13	2	3	1	0	0	2	1	3	.231	.286	.308	67	-2	0	0	0	1.000	0	/C-3,1-1	-0.1
1982	Cle-A	39	94	6	21	5	1	4	18	2	9	.223	.240	.426	79	-3	0	0	0	1.000	-3	C-35	-0.6
1983	Det-A	2	1	0	0	0	0	0	0	1	0	.000	.500	.000	53	0	0	0	0	.000	0	/H	0.0
1984	Sea-A	12	25	2	6	0	0	1	3	1	7	.240	.321	.360	89	-0	0	1	-1	.976	-3	C-10/1-1	-0.3
Total	9	308	844	74	203	41	3	25	109	56	118	.241	.292	.385	85	-18	1	4	-2	.983	-17	C-275/1-7,D-4	-3.3

■ FRANK NALEWAY
Naleway, Frank "Chick"   b: 7/5/02, Chicago, Ill.   d: 1/28/49, Chicago, Ill.   BR/TR, 5'9.5", 165 lbs.   Deb: 9/16/24

1924	Chi-A	1	2	0	0	0	0	0	0	1	0	.000	.333	.000	-10	-0	0	0	0	.750	-1	/S-1	-0.1

■ DOC NANCE
Nance, William G. "Kid" (b: Willie G. Cooper)   b: 8/2/1876, Ft. Worth, Tex.   d: 5/28/58, Fort Worth, Tex.   BR/TR, 5'7", 165 lbs.   Deb: 8/19/1897

1897	Lou-N	35	120	25	29	5	3	3	17	20		.242	.355	.408	105	1	3			.986	4	O-35	0.2
1898	Lou-N	22	76	13	24	5	0	1	16	12		.316	.416	.421	142	5	2			.946	2	O-22	0.5
1901	Det-A	132	461	72	129	24	5	3	66	51		.280	.355	.373	98	-1	9			.932	1	*O-132	-0.9
Total	3	189	657	110	182	34	8	7	99	83		.277	.362	.385	104	5	14			.943	6	O-189	-0.2

■ AL NAPLES
Naples, Aloysius Francis   b: 8/29/27, St. George, N.Y.   BR/TR, 5'9", 168 lbs.   Deb: 6/25/49

1949	StL-A	2	7	0	1	1	0	0	0	0	1	.143	.143	.286	12	-1	0	0	0	.875	-1	/S-2	-0.2

YEAR	TM/L	G	AB	R	H	2B	3B	HR	RBI	BB	SO	AVG	OBP	SLG	PRO+	BR/A	SB	CS	SBR	FA	FR	G/POS	TPR

■ DANNY NAPOLEON Napoleon, Daniel b: 1/11/42, Claysburg, Pa. BR/TR, 5'11", 190 lbs. Deb: 4/14/65

1965	NY-N	68	97	5	14	1	1	0	7	8	23	.144	.224	.175	15	-11	0	0	0	.941	1	O-15/3-7	-1.1
1966	NY-N	12	33	2	7	2	0	0	0	1	10	.212	.235	.273	42	-3	0	1	-1	.929	-0	O-10	-0.4
Total	2	80	130	7	21	3	1	0	7	9	33	.162	.227	.200	22	-14	0	1	-1	.938	1	/O-25,3-7	-1.5

■ HAL NARAGON Naragon, Harold Richard b: 10/1/28, Zanesville, Ohio BL/TR, 6', 175 lbs. Deb: 9/23/51 C

1951	Cle-A	3	8	0	2	0	0	0	0	1	0	.250	.400	.250	83	-0	0	0	0	.929	0	/C-2	0.0
1954	*Cle-A	46	101	10	24	2	2	0	12	9	12	.238	.300	.297	63	-5	0	0	0	1.000	-2	C-45	-0.5
1955	Cle-A	57	127	12	41	9	2	1	14	15	8	.323	.394	.449	122	4	1	0	0	.991	-4	C-52	0.2
1956	Cle-A	53	122	11	35	3	1	3	18	13	9	.287	.360	.402	99	-0	0	0	0	.988	-12	C-48	-1.0
1957	Cle-A	57	121	12	31	1	1	0	8	12	9	.256	.328	.281	69	-5	0	0	0	.990	-2	C-39	-0.6
1958	Cle-A	9	9	2	3	0	0	0	0	0	0	.333	.333	.556	144	0	0	0	0	.000	0	H	0.0
1959	Cle-A	14	36	6	10	4	1	0	5	3	2	.278	.333	.444	121	1	0	0	0	1.000	-1	C-10	0.0
	Was-A	71	195	12	47	3	2	0	11	8	9	.241	.275	.277	52	-13	0	1	-1	.993	-2	C-54	-1.2
	Yr	85	231	18	57	7	3	0	16	11	11	.247	.287	.303	63	-12	0	1	-1	.994	-3	C-64	-1.2
1960	Was-A	33	92	7	19	2	0	0	5	8	4	.207	.277	.228	39	-8	0	0	0	.978	-2	C-29	-0.9
1961	Min-A	57	139	10	42	2	1	2	11	4	8	.302	.326	.374	82	-4	0	0	0	.994	-5	C-36	-0.7
1962	Min-A	24	35	1	8	1	0	0	3	1	1	.229	.289	.257	47	-3	0	0	0	1.000	0	/C-9	-0.2
Total	10	424	985	83	262	27	11	6	87	76	62	.266	.323	.334	77	-31	1	1	-1	.991	-29	C-324	-4.9

■ BILL NARLESKI Narleski, William Edward "Cap" b: 6/9/1899, Perth Amboy, N.J. d: 7/22/64, Laurel Springs, N.J. BR/TR, 5'9", 160 lbs. Deb: 4/18/29 F

1929	Bos-A	96	260	30	72	16	1	0	25	21	22	.277	.333	.346	77	-9	4	4	-1	.957	-17	S-51,2-29/3-7	-1.9
1930	Bos-A	39	98	11	23	9	0	0	7	7	5	.235	.306	.327	63	-6	0	0	0	.915	-8	S-19,3-14/2-5	-1.1
Total	2	135	358	41	95	25	1	0	32	28	27	.265	.326	.341	73	-14	4	4	-1	.949	-25	/S-70,2-34,3-21	-3.0

■ JERRY NARRON Narron, Jerry Austin b: 1/15/56, Goldsboro, N.C. BL/TR, 6'3", 205 lbs. Deb: 4/13/79 C

1979	NY-A	61	123	17	21	3	1	4	18	9	26	.171	.227	.309	44	-10	0	0	0	.973	-4	C-56/D-1	-1.3
1980	Sea-A	48	107	7	21	3	0	4	18	13	18	.196	.283	.336	68	-5	0	0	0	.992	-10	C-39/D-1	-1.3
1981	Sea-A	76	203	13	45	5	0	3	17	16	35	.222	.285	.291	64	-9	0	0	0	.996	-14	C-65	-2.3
1983	Cal-A	10	22	1	3	0	0	1	4	1	3	.136	.174	.273	21	-2	0	0	0	.895	-1	/C-6,D-1	-0.3
1984	Cal-A	69	150	9	37	5	0	3	17	8	12	.247	.289	.340	74	-5	0	0	0	.994	-8	C-46/1-7	-1.2
1985	Cal-A	67	132	12	29	4	0	5	14	11	14	.220	.280	.364	75	-5	0	0	0	1.000	2	C-45/1-1,D-7	-0.1
1986	*Cal-A	57	95	5	21	3	1	1	8	9	14	.221	.295	.305	65	-5	0	0	0	.988	1	C-51/D-2	-0.1
1987	Sea-A	4	8	0	0	0	0	0	0	0	2	.000	.000	.000	-95	-2	0	0	0	1.000	-0	/C-3	-0.2
Total	8	392	840	64	177	23	2	21	96	67	127	.211	.272	.318	62	-44	0	0	0	.989	-33	C-311/D-12,1-8	-6.8

■ SAM NARRON Narron, Samuel b: 8/25/13, Middlesex, N.C. BR/TR, 5'10", 180 lbs. Deb: 9/15/35 C

1935	StL-N	4	7	0	3	0	0	0	0	0	0	.429	.429	.429	126	0	0	0	0	1.000	-0	/C-1	0.0
1942	StL-N	10	10	0	4	0	0	0	1	0	0	.400	.400	.400	125	0	0	0	0	1.000	0	/C-2	0.0
1943	*StL-N	10	11	0	1	0	0	0	1	1	2	.091	.167	.091	-24	-2	0	0	0	1.000	1	/C-3	-0.1
Total	3	24	28	0	8	0	0	0	2	1	2	.286	.310	.286	67	-1	0			1.000	1	/C-6	-0.1

■ COTTON NASH Nash, Charles Francis b: 7/24/42, Jersey City, N.J. BR/TR, 6'6", 220 lbs. Deb: 9/1/67

1967	Chi-A	3	1	0	0	0	0	0	0	0	0	.000	.250	.000	-21	-0	0	0	0	.833	-1	/1-3	-0.1
1969	Min-A	6	9	0	2	0	0	0	1	0	2	.222	.300	.222	47	-1	0	0	0	1.000	1	/1-6,O-1	0.0
1970	Min-A	4	4	1	1	0	0	0	2	1	1	.250	.400	.250	82	-0	0	1	-1	1.000	-0	/1-2	-0.1
Total	3	13	16	2	3	0	0	0	3	1	3	.188	.316	.188	45	-1	0	1	-1	.965	0	/1-11,O-1	-0.2

■ KEN NASH Nash, Kenneth Leland (Played One Game In 1912 under name of Costello) b: 7/14/1888, Weymouth, Mass. d: 2/16/77, Epsom, N.H. BB/TR, 5'8", 140 lbs. Deb: 7/4/12

1912	Cle-A	11	23	2	4	0	0	0	3			.174	.269	.174	27	-2	0			.826	-3	/S-8	-0.5
1914	StL-N	24	51	4	14	3	1	0	6	6	10	.275	.351	.373	116	1	0			.875	-6	3-10/2-6,S-3	-0.6
Total	2	35	74	6	18	3	1	0	9	6	10	.243	.325	.311	87	-1	0			.760	-10	/S-11,3-10,2-6	-1.1

■ BILLY NASH Nash, William Mitchell b: 6/24/1865, Richmond, Va. d: 11/15/29, E.Orange, N.J. BR/TR, 5'8.5", 167 lbs. Deb: 8/5/1884 MU

1884	Ric-a	45	166	31	33	8	1	0			12	.199	.281	.361	109	2				.828	8	3-45	0.9
1885	Bos-N	26	94	9	24	4	0	0	11	2	9	.255	.271	.298	87	-1				.864	-4	3-19/2-8	-0.4
1886	Bos-N	109	417	61	117	11	8	1	45	24	28	.281	.320	.353	108	4	16			.863	-5	*3-90,S-17/O-2	0.2
1887	Bos-N	121	475	100	140	24	12	6	94	60	30	.295	.376	.434	124	17	43			.884	9	*3-117/O-5	2.3
1888	Bos-N	135	526	71	149	18	15	4	75	50	46	.283	.350	.397	136	22	20			**.913**	26	*3-105,2-31	**4.9**
1889	Bos-N	128	481	84	132	20	2	3	76	79	44	.274	.379	.343	97	-0	26			.905	12	*3-128/P-1	1.4
1890	Bos-P	129	488	103	130	28	6	5	90	88	43	.266	.383	.379	97	-2	26			.866	18	*3-129/P-1	1.7
1891	Bos-N	140	537	92	148	24	9	5	95	74	50	.276	.369	.382	106	2	28			.900	-12	*3-140	-0.3
1892	*Bos-N	135	526	94	137	25	5	4	95	59	42	.260	.338	.350	99	-2	31			**.898**	24	*3-135/O-1	2.5
1893	Bos-N	128	485	115	141	27	6	10	123	85	29	.291	.399	.433	112	8	30			**.923**	3	*3-128	1.0
1894	Bos-N	132	512	132	148	23	6	8	87	91	23	.289	.393	.404	87	-11	20			**.933**	-4	*3-132	-0.4
1895	Bos-N	132	508	97	147	23	6	10	108	74	19	.289	.383	.417	99	-2	18			.882	-8	*3-132	-0.7
1896	Phi-N	65	227	29	56	9	1	3	30	34	21	.247	.355	.335	83	-4	3			.911	7	3-65,M	0.3
1897	Phi-N	104	337	45	87	20	2	0	39	60		.258	.359	.329	89	-3	4			.919	-3	3-79,S-19/2-4	-0.7
1898	Phi-N	20	70	9	17	2	1	0	9	11		.243	.346	.300	89	-1	0			.958	-1	3-20	-0.1
Total	15	1549	5849	1072	1606	266	87	60	977	803	384	.275	.366	.381	103	29	265			.897	75	*3-1464/2-43,SOP	12.6

■ ROB NATAL Natal, Robert Marcel b: 11/13/65, Long Beach, Cal. BR/TR, 5'11", 190 lbs. Deb: 7/18/92

1992	Mon-N	5	6	0	0	0	0	0	0	0	1	.000	.143	.000	-57	-1	0	0	0	.909	-0	/C-4	-0.2
1993	Fla-N	41	117	3	25	4	1	1	6	6	22	.214	.276	.291	49	-8	1	0	0	1.000	3	C-38	-0.4
1994	Fla-N	10	29	2	8	2	0	0	2	5	5	.276	.382	.345	89	-0	0	0	0	.983	3	C-8	0.3
1995	Fla-N	16	43	2	10	2	1	1	6	1	9	.233	.250	.465	83	-1	0	0	0	.988	-1	C-13	-0.1
1996	Fla-N	44	90	4	12	1	0	1	5	15	31	.133	.257	.167	15	-11	0	1	-1	.976	0	C-43	-0.9
Total	5	116	285	11	55	9	3	4	16	28	68	.193	.274	.277	46	-22	2	1	0	.986	4	C-106	-1.3

■ PETE NATON Naton, Peter Alphonsus b: 9/9/31, Flushing, N.Y. BR/TR, 6'1", 200 lbs. Deb: 6/16/53

| 1953 | Pit-N | 6 | 12 | 2 | 2 | 0 | 0 | 0 | 1 | 2 | 1 | .167 | .286 | .167 | 22 | -1 | 0 | 0 | 0 | 1.000 | -1 | /C-4 | -0.2 |

■ SANDY NAVA Nava, Vincent P. (b: Irwin Sandy) b: 4/12/1850, San Francisco, Cal d: 6/15/06, Baltimore, Md. 5'6", 155 lbs. Deb: 5/5/1882

1882	Pro-N	28	97	15	20	7	0	0	7	1	13	.206	.214	.227	42	-6				.867	-7	C-27/O-1	-1.1
1883	Pro-N	29	100	18	24	4	2	0	16	3	17	.240	.262	.320	74	-3				.813	-4	C-27/O-2	-0.5
1884	Pro-N	34	116	10	11	0	0	0	6	11	35	.095	.173	.095	-14	-15				.887	1	C-27/S-6,2-1	-0.6
1885	Bal-a	8	27	2	5	1	0	0	4	1		.185	.214	.222	39	-2				.825	-5	/C-8	-0.1
1886	Bal-a	2	5	0	1	0	0	0	0	0		.200	.200	.200	26	-0	1			.500	1	/S-1,C-1	-0.1
Total	5	101	345	45	61	7	2	0	33	16	65	.177	.213	.209	33	-26	1			.857	-16	/C-90,S-7,O-3,2-1	-3.3

■ TITO NAVARRO Navarro, Norberto (Rodriguez) b: 9/12/70, Rio Piedras, P.R. BB/TR, 5'10", 165 lbs. Deb: 9/6/93

| 1993 | NY-N | 12 | 17 | 1 | 1 | 0 | 0 | 0 | 0 | 0 | 4 | .059 | .059 | .059 | -69 | -4 | 0 | 0 | 0 | 1.000 | 1 | /S-2 | -0.3 |

■ EARL NAYLOR Naylor, Earl Eugene b: 5/19/19, Kansas City, Mo. d: 1/16/90, Winter Haven, Fla. BR/TR, 6', 190 lbs. Deb: 4/15/42

1942	Phi-N	76	168	9	33	4	1	0	14	11	18	.196	.246	.232	42	-12	1			.984	-5	O-34,P-20	-1.8
1943	Phi-N	33	120	12	21	2	0	3	14	12	16	.175	.256	.267	53	-7	1			.964	6	O-33	-0.3
1946	Bro-N	3	2	1	0	0	0	0	0	0	1	.000	.000	.000	-99	-1	0			.000	0	H	-0.1
Total	3	112	290	22	54	6	1	3	28	23	35	.186	.248	.245	46	-20	2			.971	1	/O-67,P-20	-2.2

■ JACK NEAGLE Neagle, John Henry b: 1/2/1858, Syracuse, N.Y. d: 9/20/04, Syracuse, N.Y. BR/TR, 5'6", 155 lbs. Deb: 7/8/1879

| 1879 | Cin-N | 3 | 12 | 1 | 2 | 0 | 0 | 0 | 2 | 0 | 0 | .167 | .167 | .167 | 11 | -1 | | | | .000 | -1 | /O-2,P-2 | -0.1 |

YEAR	TM/L	G	AB	R	H	2B	3B	HR	RBI	BB	SO	AVG	OBP	SLG	PRO+	BR/A	SB	CS	SBR	FA	FR	G/POS	TPR
1883	Phi-N	18	73	6	12	1	0	0	4	1	9	.164	.176	.178	9	-8				.840	-2	O-12/P-8	-0.5
	Bal-a	9	35	3	10	4	0	0			2	.286	.324	.400	128	1				.769	-3	/P-6,O-5	-0.2
	Pit-a	27	101	14	19	0	1	0			5	.188	.226	.208	43	-6				.839	-3	P-16,O-15	-0.5
	Yr	36	136	17	29	4	1	0			7	.213	.252	.257	66	-5				.818	-6	P-22,O-20	-0.7
1884	Pit-a	43	148	13	22	6	0	0			6	.149	.187	.189	23	-12				.760	-5	P-38/O-6	-0.4
Total	3	100	369	37	65	11	1	0	6	14	9	.176	.208	.211	35	-26				.785	-14	/P-70,O-40	-1.7

■ **CHARLIE NEAL**   Neal, Charles Lenard   b: 1/30/31, Longview, Tex.   d: 11/18/96, Dallas, Tex.   BR/TR, 5'10", 165 lbs.   Deb: 4/17/56

YEAR	TM/L	G	AB	R	H	2B	3B	HR	RBI	BB	SO	AVG	OBP	SLG	PRO+	BR/A	SB	CS	SBR	FA	FR	G/POS	TPR
1956	*Bro-N	62	136	22	39	5	1	2	14	14	19	.287	.353	.382	91	-1	2	2	-1	.972	5	2-51/S-1	0.2
1957	Bro-N	128	448	62	121	13	7	12	62	53	83	.270	.358	.411	96	-1	11	4	1	.949	-3	*S-100,3-23/2-3	0.7
1958	LA-N	140	473	87	120	9	6	22	65	61	91	.254	.345	.438	102	2	7	6	-2	.976	12	*2-132/S-9	2.2
1959	*LA-N★	151	616	103	177	30	11	19	83	43	86	.287	.338	.464	103	2	17	6	2	.989	20	*2-151/S-1	3.5
1960	LA-N★	139	477	60	122	23	2	8	40	48	75	.256	.326	.363	83	-11	5	5	-2	.977	-16	*2-136/S-3	-1.6
1961	LA-N	108	341	40	80	6	1	10	48	30	49	.235	.298	.346	65	-17	3	2	-0	.976	2	*2-104	-0.6
1962	NY-N	136	508	59	132	14	9	11	58	56	90	.260	.333	.388	91	-6	2	8	-4	.970	-8	2-85,S-39,3-12	-0.6
1963	NY-N	72	253	26	57	12	1	3	18	27	49	.225	.302	.316	77	-7	1	2	-1	.961	0	3-66/S-8	-0.8
	Cin-N	34	64	2	10	1	0	0	3	5	15	.156	.217	.172	13	-7	0	1	-1	.927	-2	3-19/2-1,S-1	-1.1
	Yr	106	317	28	67	13	1	3	21	32	64	.211	.286	.287	64	-14	1	3	-2	.955	-2	3-85/S-9,2-1	-1.9
Total	8	970	3316	461	858	113	38	87	391	337	557	.259	.331	.394	90	-47	48	36	-7	.978	7	2-663,S-162,3-120	1.9

■ **OFFA NEAL**   Neal, Theophilus Fountain   b: 6/5/1876, Logan, Ill.   d: 4/12/50, Mt.Vernon, Ill.   BL/TR, 6', 185 lbs.   Deb: 9/30/05

YEAR	TM/L	G	AB	R	H	2B	3B	HR	RBI	BB	SO	AVG	OBP	SLG	PRO+	BR/A	SB	CS	SBR	FA	FR	G/POS	TPR
1905	NY-N	4	13	0	0	0	0	0	0	0	0	.000	.000	.000	-98	-3	0			1.000	-1	/3-3,2-1	-0.4

■ **GREASY NEALE**   Neale, Alfred Earle   b: 11/5/1891, Parkersburg, W.Va.   d: 11/2/73, Lake Worth, Fla.   BL/TR, 6', 170 lbs.   Deb: 4/12/16   C

YEAR	TM/L	G	AB	R	H	2B	3B	HR	RBI	BB	SO	AVG	OBP	SLG	PRO+	BR/A	SB	CS	SBR	FA	FR	G/POS	TPR
1916	Cin-N	138	530	53	139	13	5	0	20	19	79	.262	.295	.306	87	-9	17			.973	11	*O-133	-0.6
1917	Cin-N	121	385	40	113	14	9	3	33	24	36	.294	.343	.400	133	14	25			.979	-5	*O-119	0.4
1918	Cin-N	107	371	57	100	11	11	1	32	24	38	.270	.324	.367	112	5	23			.981	10	*O-102	1.0
1919	*Cin-N	139	500	57	121	10	12	3	54	47	51	.242	.316	.316	93	-3	28			.959	2	*O-138	-1.2
1920	Cin-N	150	530	55	135	10	7	3	46	45	48	.255	.322	.317	85	-9	29	12	2	.987	14	*O-150	-0.4
1921	Phi-N	22	57	7	12	1	0	0	1	14	9	.211	.366	.228	56	-3	3	4	-2	.842	-5	O-16	-1.1
	Cin-N	63	241	39	58	10	5	0	12	22	16	.241	.307	.324	70	-10	9	6	-1	.964	1	O-60	-1.5
	Yr	85	298	46	70	11	5	0	13	36	25	.235	.319	.305	67	-13	12	10	-2	.950	-4	O-76	-2.6
1922	Cin-N	25	43	11	10	2	1	0	2	6	3	.233	.353	.326	77	-1	5	2	0	.864	-4	O-16	-0.5
1924	Cin-N	3	4	0	0	0	0	0	0	0	1	.000	.000	.000	-99	-1	0	0	0	1.000	-0	/O-2	-0.2
Total	8	768	2661	319	688	71	50	8	200	201	281	.259	.319	.332	94	-18	139	24		.972	24	O-736	-4.1

■ **JOE NEALE**   Neale, Joseph Hunt   b: 5/7/1866, Wadsworth, Ohio   d: 12/30/13, Akron, Ohio   BR/TR, 5'8", 153 lbs.   Deb: 6/21/1886

YEAR	TM/L	G	AB	R	H	2B	3B	HR	RBI	BB	SO	AVG	OBP	SLG	PRO+	BR/A	SB	CS	SBR	FA	FR	G/POS	TPR
1886	Lou-a	2	5	0	0	0	0	0	0	0	0	.000	.000	.000	-95	-1	0			1.000	0	/O-2,P-1	-0.1
1887	Lou-a	5	19	3	1	0	0	0	1	3		.053	.182	.053	-32	-3	0			.833	0	/P-5	0.0
1890	StL-a	11	30	4	2	0	0	0	1	3		.067	.152	.067	-31	-5	0			1.000	-2	P-10/O-1	0.0
1891	StL-a	15	51	6	6	0	1	1	8	3	11	.118	.167	.216	8	-7	1			.933	2	P-15	-0.0
Total	4	33	105	13	9	0	1	1	10	9	11	.086	.158	.133	-14	-16	2			.930	0	/P-31,O-3	-0.1

■ **JIM NEALON**   Nealon, James Joseph   b: 12/15/1884, Sacramento, Cal.   d: 4/2/10, San Francisco, Cal.   BR/TR, 6'1.5",   Deb: 4/12/06

YEAR	TM/L	G	AB	R	H	2B	3B	HR	RBI	BB	SO	AVG	OBP	SLG	PRO+	BR/A	SB	CS	SBR	FA	FR	G/POS	TPR
1906	Pit-N	154	556	82	142	21	12	3	83	53		.255	.327	.353	107	4	15			.987	1	*1-154	0.1
1907	Pit-N	105	381	29	98	10	8	0	47	23		.257	.301	.325	95	-3	11			.978	0	*1-104	-0.7
Total	2	259	937	111	240	31	20	3	130	76		.256	.317	.342	102	1	26			.983	1	1-258	-0.6

■ **TOM NEEDHAM**   Needham, Thomas Joseph "Deerfoot"   b: 5/17/1879, Steubenville, Ohio   d: 12/13/26, Steubenville, Ohio   BR/TR, 5'10", 180 lbs.   Deb: 5/12/04

YEAR	TM/L	G	AB	R	H	2B	3B	HR	RBI	BB	SO	AVG	OBP	SLG	PRO+	BR/A	SB	CS	SBR	FA	FR	G/POS	TPR
1904	Bos-N	84	269	18	70	12	3	4	19	11		.260	.292	.372	108	1	3			.945	4	C-77/O-1	1.4
1905	Bos-N	83	271	21	59	6	1	2	17	24		.218	.293	.269	70	-10	3			.949	-8	C-77/O-3,1-2	-1.1
1906	Bos-N	83	285	11	54	8	2	1	12	13		.189	.230	.242	49	-18	3			.962	-7	C-76/2-5,1-2,3-1,O	-2.0
1907	Bos-N	86	260	19	51	6	2	1	19	18		.196	.264	.246	60	-12	4			.967	-11	C-78/1-1	-1.8
1908	NY-N	54	91	8	19	3	0	0	11	12		.209	.339	.242	82	-1	0			.975	7	C-47	1.0
1909	Chi-N	13	28	3	4	0	0	0	0	0		.143	.143	.143	-11	-4	0			.980	1	/C-7	-0.2
1910	*Chi-N	31	76	9	14	3	1	0	10	10	10	.184	.287	.250	57	-4	1			.982	3	C-27/1-1	0.2
1911	Chi-N	27	62	4	12	2	0	0	5	9	14	.194	.315	.226	52	-4	2			.984	6	C-23	0.4
1912	Chi-N	33	90	12	16	5	0	0	7	13		.178	.260	.233	36	-8	3			.994	-1	C-32	-0.6
1913	Chi-N	20	42	5	10	4	1	0	11	4	8	.238	.304	.381	95	-0	0			.962	-1	C-14/1-1	0.5
1914	Chi-N	9	17	3	2	1	0	0	0	0		.118	.167	.176	2	-2	1			.943	1	/C-7	-0.2
Total	11	523	1491	114	311	50	10	8	117	109	49	.209	.274	.272	66	-60	20			.963	-1	C-465/1-7,2-5,03	-2.2

■ **TROY NEEL**   Neel, Troy Lee   b: 9/14/65, Freeport, Tex.   BL/TR, 6'4", 210 lbs.   Deb: 5/30/92

YEAR	TM/L	G	AB	R	H	2B	3B	HR	RBI	BB	SO	AVG	OBP	SLG	PRO+	BR/A	SB	CS	SBR	FA	FR	G/POS	TPR
1992	Oak-A	24	53	8	14	3	0	3	9	5	15	.264	.339	.491	137	2	0	1	-1	.846	-2	/O-9,1-2,D-9	0.0
1993	Oak-A	123	427	59	124	21	0	19	63	49	101	.290	.369	.473	132	19	3	5	-2	.981	-0	D-85,1-34	1.1
1994	Oak-A	83	278	43	74	13	0	15	48	38	61	.266	.358	.475	123	9	2	3	-1	.994	-0	1-45,D-35	0.2
Total	3	230	758	110	212	37	0	37	120	92	177	.280	.363	.475	129	31	5	9	-4	.986	-3	D-129/1-81,O-9	1.3

■ **CAL NEEMAN**   Neeman, Calvin Amandus   b: 2/18/29, Valmeyer, Ill.   BR/TR, 6'1", 192 lbs.   Deb: 4/16/57

YEAR	TM/L	G	AB	R	H	2B	3B	HR	RBI	BB	SO	AVG	OBP	SLG	PRO+	BR/A	SB	CS	SBR	FA	FR	G/POS	TPR
1957	Chi-N	122	415	37	107	17	1	10	39	22	87	.258	.300	.376	81	-11	0	0	0	.990	1	*C-118	-0.6
1958	Chi-N	76	201	30	52	7	0	12	29	21	41	.259	.338	.473	113	3	0	0	0	.992	1	C-71	0.8
1959	Chi-N	44	105	7	17	2	0	3	9	11	23	.162	.241	.267	36	-10	0	0	0	.994	-1	/C-38	-1.0
1960	Chi-N	9	13	0	2	1	0	0	0	0	5	.154	.154	.231	4	-2	0	0	0	1.000	4	/C-9	0.2
	Phi-N	59	160	13	29	6	2	4	13	16	42	.181	.264	.319	59	-9	0	0	0	.979	5	C-52	-0.2
	Yr	68	173	13	31	7	2	4	13	16	47	.179	.257	.312	55	-11	0	0	0	.982	8	C-61	0.0
1961	Phi-N	19	31	0	7	1	0	0	2	4	6	.226	.314	.258	55	-2	1	0	0	.986	2	C-19	0.1
1962	Pit-N	24	50	5	9	1	1	0	5	3	10	.180	.226	.300	40	-4	0	0	0	.983	0	C-24	0.4
1963	Cle-A	9	9	0	0	0	0	0	0	1	5	.000	.100	.000	-70	-2	0	0	0	1.000	3	/C-9	0.1
	Was-A	14	18	1	1	0	0	0	0	1	6	.056	.105	.056	-54	-4	0	0	0	.970	2	C-12	-0.2
	Yr	23	27	1	1	0	0	0	0	2	11	.037	.103	.037	-59	-6	0	0	0	.985	5	C-21	-0.1
Total	7	376	1002	93	224	35	4	30	97	79	221	.224	.286	.356	72	-41	1	0	0	.988	24	C-352	-0.4

■ **DOUG NEFF**   Neff, Douglas Williams   b: 10/8/1891, Harrisonburg, Va.   d: 5/23/32, Cape Charles, Va.   BR/TR, 5'9", 141 lbs.   Deb: 6/26/14

YEAR	TM/L	G	AB	R	H	2B	3B	HR	RBI	BB	SO	AVG	OBP	SLG	PRO+	BR/A	SB	CS	SBR	FA	FR	G/POS	TPR
1914	Was-A	3	2	0	0	0	0	0	0	0	0	.000	.000	.000	-96	-0	0			.889	2	/S-3	0.1
1915	Was-A	30	60	1	10	1	0	0	4	4	6	.167	.219	.183	20	-6	1	2	-1	.867	-4	3-12,2-10/S-7	-1.1
Total	2	33	62	1	10	1	0	0	4	4	6	.161	.212	.177	16	-6	1	2		.900	-2	/3-12,2-10,S-10	-1.0

■ **CY NEIGHBORS**   Neighbors, Flemon Cecil   b: 9/23/1880, Fayetteville, Mo.   d: 5/20/64, Tacoma, Wash.   BR, 5'10", 178 lbs.   Deb: 4/29/08

YEAR	TM/L	G	AB	R	H	2B	3B	HR	RBI	BB	SO	AVG	OBP	SLG	PRO+	BR/A	SB	CS	SBR	FA	FR	G/POS	TPR
1908	Pit-N	1	0	0	0	0	0	0	0	0	0	—	—	—	—	-0	0			.000	-1	/O-1	-0.1

■ **BOB NEIGHBORS**   Neighbors, Robert Otis   b: 11/9/17, Talihina, Okla.   d: 8/8/52, North Korea (Mia)   BR/TR, 5'11", 165 lbs.   Deb: 9/16/39

YEAR	TM/L	G	AB	R	H	2B	3B	HR	RBI	BB	SO	AVG	OBP	SLG	PRO+	BR/A	SB	CS	SBR	FA	FR	G/POS	TPR
1939	StL-A	7	11	3	2	0	1	0	1	0	1	.182	.182	.455	56	-1	0	0	0	.917	-0	/S-5	-0.1

■ **TOMMY NEILL**   Neill, Thomas White   b: 11/7/19, Hartselle, Ala.   d: 9/22/80, Houston, Tex.   BL/TR, 6'2", 200 lbs.   Deb: 9/10/46

YEAR	TM/L	G	AB	R	H	2B	3B	HR	RBI	BB	SO	AVG	OBP	SLG	PRO+	BR/A	SB	CS	SBR	FA	FR	G/POS	TPR
1946	Bos-N	13	45	8	12	2	0	0	7	1		.267	.298	.311	72	-2	0			1.000	-1	O-13	-0.4
1947	Bos-N	7	10	1	2	0	1	0	0	2	1	.200	.333	.400	96	-0	0			1.000	-1	/O-2	-0.1
Total	2	20	55	9	14	2	1	0	7	3		.255	.305	.327	77	-2	0			1.000	-1	/O-15	-0.5

■ **BERNIE NEIS**   Neis, Bernard Edmund   b: 9/26/1895, Bloomington, Ill.   d: 11/29/72, Inverness, Fla.   BB/TR, 5'7", 160 lbs.   Deb: 4/14/20

YEAR	TM/L	G	AB	R	H	2B	3B	HR	RBI	BB	SO	AVG	OBP	SLG	PRO+	BR/A	SB	CS	SBR	FA	FR	G/POS	TPR
1920	*Bro-N	95	249	38	63	11	2	2	22	26	35	.253	.329	.337	89	-3	9	9	-3	.957	-2	O-83	-1.3
1921	Bro-N	102	230	34	59	5	4	4	34	25	41	.257	.332	.365	81	-6	9	7	-2	.946	-6	O-77/2-1	-1.7
1922	Bro-N	61	70	15	16	4	1	1	9	13	8	.229	.349	.357	83	-2	3	2	-0	.897	-5	O-27	-0.7

YEAR	TM/L	G	AB	R	H	2B	3B	HR	RBI	BB	SO	AVG	OBP	SLG	PRO+	BR/A	SB	CS	SBR	FA	FR	G/POS	TPR
1923	Bro-N	126	445	78	122	17	4	5	37	36	38	.274	.330	.364	85	-10	8	8	-2	.941	6	*O-111	-1.2
1924	Bro-N	80	211	43	64	8	3	4	26	27	17	.303	.385	.427	121	7	4	2	0	.937	-4	O-62	-0.1
1925	Bos-N	106	355	47	101	20	2	5	45	38	19	.285	.354	.394	100	-0	8	10	-4	.970	11	O-87	0.1
1926	Bos-N	30	93	16	20	5	2	0	8	8	10	.215	.277	.312	64	-5	4			.925	2	O-23	-0.5
1927	Cle-A	32	96	17	29	9	0	4	18	18	9	.302	.412	.521	140	6	0	1	-1	.978	5	O-29	0.8
	Chi-A	45	76	9	22	5	0	0	11	10	9	.289	.372	.355	92	-1	1	0	0	.927	-3	O-21	-0.4
	Yr	77	172	26	51	14	0	4	29	28	18	.297	.395	.448	120	6	1	1	-0	.962	2	O-50	0.4
Total	8	677	1825	297	496	84	18	25	210	201	186	.272	.346	.379	94	-13	46	39		.950	3	O-520/2-1	-5.0

■ ERNIE NEITZKE   Neitzke, Ernest Fredrich b: 11/13/1894, Toledo, Ohio d: 4/27/77, Sylvania, Ohio BR/TR, 5'10", 180 lbs. Deb: 6/2/21

YEAR	TM/L	G	AB	R	H	2B	3B	HR	RBI	BB	SO	AVG	OBP	SLG	PRO+	BR/A	SB	CS	SBR	FA	FR	G/POS	TPR
1921	Bos-A	11	25	3	6	0	0	0	2	4	4	.240	.345	.240	53	-2	0	0	0	.875	-1	/O-8,P-2	-0.3

■ DAVE NELSON   Nelson, David Earl b: 6/20/44, Fort Sill, Okla. BR/TR, 5'10", 160 lbs. Deb: 4/11/68 C

YEAR	TM/L	G	AB	R	H	2B	3B	HR	RBI	BB	SO	AVG	OBP	SLG	PRO+	BR/A	SB	CS	SBR	FA	FR	G/POS	TPR
1968	Cle-A	88	189	26	44	4	5	0	19	17	35	.233	.300	.307	85	-3	23	7	3	.987	-2	2-59,S-14	0.1
1969	Cle-A	52	123	11	25	0	0	0	6	9	26	.203	.263	.203	31	-11	4	3	-1	.966	4	2-33/O-2	-0.5
1970	Was-A	47	107	5	17	1	0	0	4	7	24	.159	.211	.168	6	-14	2	1	0	.986	1	2-33	-1.1
1971	Was-A	85	329	47	92	11	3	5	33	23	29	.280	.329	.377	105	1	17	8	0	.938	-13	3-84/2-1	-1.3
1972	Tex-A	145	499	60	113	16	3	2	28	67	81	.226	.324	.283	85	-7	51	17	5	.945	-12	*3-119,O-15	-1.8
1973	Tex-A★	142	576	71	165	24	4	7	48	34	78	.286	.326	.378	102	0	43	16	3	.984	-12	*2-140	0.0
1974	Tex-A	121	474	71	112	13	1	3	42	34	72	.236	.293	.287	69	-19	25	13	-0	.969	1	*2-120/D-1	-1.3
1975	Tex-A	28	80	9	17	1	0	2	10	8	10	.213	.292	.300	68	-3	6	0	2	.959	1	2-23/D-1	0.1
1976	*KC-A	78	153	24	36	4	2	1	17	14	26	.235	.299	.307	77	-4	15	5	2	.975	2	2-46,D-22/1-3	0.0
1977	KC-A	27	48	8	9	3	1	0	4	7	11	.188	.291	.292	59	-3	1	3	-2	.926	-2	2-11/D-7	-0.6
Total	10	813	2578	340	630	77	19	20	211	220	392	.244	.307	.312	81	-62	187	73	12	.976	-31	2-466,3-203/DOS1	-6.4

■ ROCKY NELSON   Nelson, Glenn Richard b: 11/18/24, Portsmouth, Ohio BL/TL, 5'11", 178 lbs. Deb: 4/27/49

YEAR	TM/L	G	AB	R	H	2B	3B	HR	RBI	BB	SO	AVG	OBP	SLG	PRO+	BR/A	SB	CS	SBR	FA	FR	G/POS	TPR
1949	StL-N	82	244	28	54	8	4	4	32	11	12	.221	.258	.336	55	-16	1			1.000	-4	1-70	-2.0
1950	StL-N	76	235	27	58	10	4	1	20	26	9	.247	.324	.336	71	-10	4			.992	3	1-70	-0.8
1951	StL-N	9	18	3	4	1	0	0	1	1	0	.222	.263	.278	45	-1	0	0	0	1.000	-1	/1-4,O-1	-0.3
	Pit-N	71	195	29	52	7	4	1	14	10	7	.267	.302	.359	75	-7	1	1	-0	.990	1	1-32/O-12	-0.9
	Yr	80	213	32	56	8	4	1	15	11	7	.263	.299	.352	73	-8	1	1	-0	.991	-0	1-36/O-13	-1.2
	Chi-A	6	5	0	0	0	0	0	0	1	0	.000	.167	.000	-53	-1				.000	0	H	-0.1
1952	*Bro-N	37	39	6	10	1	0	0	3	7	4	.256	.370	.282	82	-1	1			1.000	-1	/1-5	-0.2
1954	Cle-A	4	4	0	0	0	0	0	0	0	1	.000	.000	.000	-98	-1	0			1.000	0	/1-2	-0.1
1956	Bro-N	31	96	7	20	2	0	4	15	4	10	.208	.240	.354	53	-7	0			.991	2	1-25	-0.7
	StL-N	38	56	6	13	5	0	3	8	6	6	.232	.306	.482	108	0	1			1.000	1	1-14/O-8	0.0
	Yr	69	152	13	33	7	0	7	23	10	16	.217	.265	.401	73	-6	1			.993	2	1-39/O-8	-0.7
1959	Pit-N	98	175	31	51	11	0	6	32	23	19	.291	.383	.457	124	6	0			.994	-4	1-56/O-2	0.6
1960	*Pit-N	93	200	34	60	11	1	7	35	24	15	.300	.389	.470	133	10	1	2	-1	.996	1	1-73	0.6
1961	Pit-N	75	127	15	25	5	1	5	13	17	11	.197	.301	.370	77	-4	0	0	0	.996	-1	1-35	-0.7
Total	9	620	1394	186	347	61	14	31	173	130	94	.249	.318	.379	84	-31	7	3		.995	-3	1-386/O-23	-5.2

■ JAMIE NELSON   Nelson, James Victor b: 9/5/59, Clinton, Okla. BR/TR, 5'11", 180 lbs. Deb: 7/21/83

YEAR	TM/L	G	AB	R	H	2B	3B	HR	RBI	BB	SO	AVG	OBP	SLG	PRO+	BR/A	SB	CS	SBR	FA	FR	G/POS	TPR
1983	Sea-A	40	96	9	21	3	0	1	5	13	12	.219	.312	.281	62	-5				.978	3	C-39	0.0

■ CANDY NELSON   Nelson, John W b: c. 1849, Brooklyn, N.Y. d: 9/4/10, Brooklyn, N.Y. BL/TL, 5'6", 145 lbs. Deb: 6/11/1872

YEAR	TM/L	G	AB	R	H	2B	3B	HR	RBI	BB	SO	AVG	OBP	SLG	PRO+	BR/A	SB	CS	SBR	FA	FR	G/POS	TPR
1872	Tro-n	4	20	2	7	0	0	0	4	0	2	.350	.350	.350	114	0	0	0	0	1.000	-1	/O-3,S-1	0.0
	Eck-n	18	76	12	19	2	0	0	8	2	2	.250	.269	.276	80	-1	1	0	0	.818	1	/2-9,O-8,3-3	0.0
	Yr	22	96	14	26	2	0	0	12	2	4	.271	.286	.292	89	-0	1	0	0	.813	1	O-11/2-9,3-3,S-1	0.0
1873	Mut-n	36	168	28	55	4	1	0	22	1	2	.327	.331	.363	107	1	2	0	1	.869	-8	2-27/O-6,3-5,C-1,1	-0.6
1874	Mut-n	65	297	55	73	7	5	0	32	9	5	.246	.268	.303	80	-7	6	0	2	.824	-18	*2-51,S-14/O-1	-2.0
1875	Mut-n	70	276	28	55	7	1	0	23	9	0	.199	.225	.232	56	-13	4	2	0	.855	-0	2-49,3-23/S-2,0-1	-1.2
1878	Ind-N	19	84	12	11	1	0	0	5	5	11	.131	.180	.143	8	-8				.841	-6	S-19	-1.3
1879	Tro-N	28	106	17	28	7	1	0	10	8	4	.264	.316	.349	127	4				.834	8	S-24/O-4	0.8
1881	Wor-N	24	103	13	29	1	0	1	15	5	6	.282	.315	.320	95	-1				.898	2	S-24	0.3
1883	NY-a	97	417	75	127	19	6	0		31		.305	.353	.379	130	13				.875	-5	*S-97	0.9
1884	*NY-a	111	432	114	110	15	3	1		74		.255	.375	.310	129	19				.879	-17	*S-110/2-1	0.3
1885	NY-a	107	420	98	107	12	4	1	30	61		.255	.353	.310	120	15				.892	13	*S-107/3-1	2.6
1886	NY-a	109	413	89	93	7	2	0	23	64		.225	.332	.252	88	-2	14			.855	-8	S-73,O-36	-0.9
1887	NY-a	68	257	61	63	5	1	0	24	48		.245	.380	.272	87	0	29			.895	10	O-37,S-32/2-1	0.8
	NY-N	1	2	0	0	0	0	0	0	0	1	.000	.000	.000	-99	-1	0			.000	0	/3-1	0.0
1890	Bro-a	60	223	44	56	3	2	0	12	35		.251	.365	.283	94	-1	12			.866	-8	S-57/O-4	-0.3
Total	4 n	193	837	125	209	20	7	0	89	21	11	.250	.268	.290	79	-18	13	2	3	.844	-25	2-136/3-31,OS1C	-3.8
Total	9	624	2457	523	624	70	19	3	119	331	22	.254	.349	.302	108	41	55			.875	-15	S-543/O-81,3-2,2-2	3.2

■ LYNN NELSON   Nelson, Lynn Bernard "Line Drive" b: 2/24/05, Sheldon, N.Dak. d: 2/15/55, Kansas City, Mo. BL/TR, 5'10.5", 170 lbs. Deb: 4/18/30

YEAR	TM/L	G	AB	R	H	2B	3B	HR	RBI	BB	SO	AVG	OBP	SLG	PRO+	BR/A	SB	CS	SBR	FA	FR	G/POS	TPR
1930	Chi-N	37	18	0	4	1	1	0	2	0	1	.222	.222	.389	44	-2	0			.966	1	P-37	0.0
1933	Chi-N	29	21	5	5	1	1	0	1	1	3	.238	.273	.381	85	-0				1.000	1	P-24	0.0
1934	Chi-N	2	0	0	0	0	0	0	0	0	0	—	—	—	—	0				.000	-0	/P-2	0.0
1937	Phi-A	74	113	18	40	6	2	4	29	6	13	.354	.387	.549	135	6	1	0	0	1.000	-0	P-30/O-6	0.3
1938	Phi-A	67	112	12	31	0	0	1	15	7	12	.277	.319	.277	52	-8	0			.952	-2	P-32	0.0
1939	Phi-A	40	80	3	15	0	0	0	5	2	13	.188	.217	.213	10	-11	0	1	-1	.950	-1	P-35	0.0
1940	Det-A	19	23	4	8	2	0	0	3	0	6	.348	.348	.478	102	-0	0			1.000	0	P-6	0.0
Total	7	268	367	42	103	10	4	5	55	16	48	.281	.313	.371	74	-16	1	1		.967	1	P-166/O-6	0.3

■ RAY NELSON   Nelson, Raymond "Kell" (b: Raymond Nelson Kellogg) b: 8/4/1875, Holyoke, Mass. d: 1/8/61, Mt.Vernon, N.Y. BR/TR, 5'9", 150 lbs. Deb: 5/6/01

YEAR	TM/L	G	AB	R	H	2B	3B	HR	RBI	BB	SO	AVG	OBP	SLG	PRO+	BR/A	SB	CS	SBR	FA	FR	G/POS	TPR
1901	NY-N	39	130	12	26	2	0	0	7	10		.200	.262	.215	41	-9	3			.885	-3	2-39	-1.1

■ RICKY NELSON   Nelson, Ricky Lee b: 5/8/59, Eloy, Ariz. BL/TR, 6', 200 lbs. Deb: 5/17/83

YEAR	TM/L	G	AB	R	H	2B	3B	HR	RBI	BB	SO	AVG	OBP	SLG	PRO+	BR/A	SB	CS	SBR	FA	FR	G/POS	TPR
1983	Sea-A	98	291	32	74	13	6	3	36	17	50	.254	.295	.371	79	-9	7	4	-0	.971	-8	O-91/D-1	-1.9
1984	Sea-A	9	15	2	3	0	0	1	2	2	4	.200	.294	.400	91	-0	0	0	0	1.000	-0	/O-2,D-3	-0.1
1985	Sea-A★	6	2	2	0	0	0	0	0	0	1	.000	.000	.000	-99	-1	0	0	0	1.000	-1	/O-3	-0.2
1986	Sea-A	10	12	2	2	0	0	0	1	0	4	.167	.167	.167	-9	-2	1	0	0	.667	-0	/O-1,D-5	-0.2
Total	4	123	320	38	79	13	6	4	39	19	59	.247	.289	.363	75	-11	8	4	0	.965	-9	O-97,D-9	-2.4

■ ROB NELSON   Nelson, Robert Augustus b: 5/17/64, Pasadena, Cal. BL/TL, 6'4", 215 lbs. Deb: 9/9/86

YEAR	TM/L	G	AB	R	H	2B	3B	HR	RBI	BB	SO	AVG	OBP	SLG	PRO+	BR/A	SB	CS	SBR	FA	FR	G/POS	TPR
1986	Oak-A	5	9	1	2	1	0	0	0	1	4	.222	.300	.333	78	-0	0	0	0	.800	0	/1-2,D-1	0.0
1987	Oak-A	7	24	1	4	0	0	0	1	0	12	.167	.167	.208	-2	-3	0	0	0	.968	3	/1-7	-0.1
	SD-N	10	11	0	1	0	0	0	1	1	8	.091	.167	.091	-31	-2	0	0	0	1.000	0	/1-2	-0.2
1988	SD-N	7	21	4	4	0	0	1	3	2	11	.190	.261	.333	71	-1	0	0	0	.981	1	/1-5	-0.1
1989	SD-N	42	82	6	16	0	1	3	7	20	29	.195	.353	.329	96	-0	1	3	-2	.991	3	1-31	0.1
1990	SD-N	5	5	0	0	0	0	0	0	0	2	.000	.000	.000	-99	-1	0	0	0	.000	0	/H	-0.2
Total	5	76	152	12	27	1	1	4	11	24	66	.178	.290	.283	62	-8	1	3	-2	.983	6	/1-47,D-1	-0.5

■ TEX NELSON   Nelson, Robert Sidney "Babe" b: 8/7/36, Dallas, Tex. BL/TL, 6'3", 205 lbs. Deb: 6/22/55

YEAR	TM/L	G	AB	R	H	2B	3B	HR	RBI	BB	SO	AVG	OBP	SLG	PRO+	BR/A	SB	CS	SBR	FA	FR	G/POS	TPR
1955	Bal-A	25	31	4	6	0	0	0	7	13		.194	.342	.194	50	-2	0	0	0	.889	0	/O-6,1-2	-0.2
1956	Bal-A	39	68	5	14	2	0	0	5	7	22	.206	.280	.235	40	-6	0	0	0	.939	-3	O-24	-0.9
1957	Bal-A	15	23	2	5	0	2	0	5	1	7	.217	.250	.391	73	-1	0	0	0	1.000	-2	/O-8	-0.2
Total	3	79	122	11	25	2	2	0	11	15	40	.205	.297	.254	52	-8	0	0	0	.938	-5	/O-38,1-2	-1.4

■ TOMMY NELSON   Nelson, Tom Cousineau b: 5/1/17, Chicago, Ill. d: 9/24/73, San Diego, Cal. BR/TR, 5'11.5", 180 lbs. Deb: 4/17/45

YEAR	TM/L	G	AB	R	H	2B	3B	HR	RBI	BB	SO	AVG	OBP	SLG	PRO+	BR/A	SB	CS	SBR	FA	FR	G/POS	TPR
1945	Bos-N	40	121	6	20	2	0	0	6	4	13	.165	.192	.182	4	-16	1			.910	-3	3-20,2-12	-1.8

■ DICK NEN — Nen, Richard Le Roy b: 9/24/39, South Gate, Cal. BL/TL, 6'2", 205 lbs. Deb: 9/18/63 F

YEAR	TM/L	G	AB	R	H	2B	3B	HR	RBI	BB	SO	AVG	OBP	SLG	PRO+	BR/A	SB	CS	SBR	FA	FR	G/POS	TPR
1963	LA-N	7	8	2	1	0	0	1	1	3	3	.125	.364	.500	157	1	0	0	0	1.000	-1	/1-5	0.0
1965	Was-A	69	246	18	64	7	1	6	31	19	47	.260	.316	.370	96	-2	1	2	-1	.993	8	1-65	0.2
1966	Was-A	94	235	20	50	8	0	6	30	28	46	.213	.297	.323	79	-6	0	2	-1	.990	-2	1-76	-1.5
1967	Was-A	110	238	21	52	7	1	6	29	21	39	.218	.282	.332	84	-5	0	1	-1	.995	1	1-65/O-1	-0.9
1968	Chi-N	81	94	8	17	1	1	2	16	6	17	.181	.230	.277	48	-6	0	0	0	.987	-1	1-52	-0.9
1970	Was-A	6	5	1	1	0	0	0	0	0	0	.200	.200	.200	11	-1	0	0	0	1.000	0	/1-1	0.0
Total	6	367	826	70	185	23	3	21	107	77	152	.224	.291	.335	82	-19	1	5	-3	.992	7	1-264/O-1	-3.1

■ JACK NESS — Ness, John Charles b: 11/11/1885, Chicago, Ill. d: 12/3/57, DeLand, Fla. BR/TR, 6'2", 165 lbs. Deb: 5/9/11

YEAR	TM/L	G	AB	R	H	2B	3B	HR	RBI	BB	SO	AVG	OBP	SLG	PRO+	BR/A	SB	CS	SBR	FA	FR	G/POS	TPR
1911	Det-A	12	39	6	6	0	0	0	2	2	-	.154	.195	.154	-2	-5	0			.977	1	1-12	-0.5
1916	Chi-A	75	258	32	69	7	5	1	34	9	32	.267	.310	.345	96	-2	4			.979	-5	1-69	-1.1
Total	2	87	297	38	75	7	5	1	36	11	32	.253	.295	.320	82	-8	4			.978	-4	/1-81	-1.6

■ GRAIG NETTLES — Nettles, Graig b: 8/20/44, San Diego, Cal. BL/TR, 6', 186 lbs. Deb: 9/6/67 FC

YEAR	TM/L	G	AB	R	H	2B	3B	HR	RBI	BB	SO	AVG	OBP	SLG	PRO+	BR/A	SB	CS	SBR	FA	FR	G/POS	TPR
1967	Min-A	3	3	0	1	1	0	0	0	0	0	.333	.333	.667	175	0	0	0	0	.000	0	H	0.0
1968	Min-A	22	76	13	17	2	1	5	8	7	20	.224	.298	.474	125	2	0	0	0	.968	1	O-16/3-5,1-3	0.2
1969	*Min-A	96	225	27	50	9	2	7	26	32	47	.222	.322	.373	92	-2	1	2	-1	.987	-5	O-54,3-21	-1.1
1970	Cle-A	157	549	81	129	13	1	26	62	81	77	.235	.336	.404	99	-1	3	1	0	**.967**	28	*3-154/O-3	2.7
1971	Cle-A	158	598	78	156	18	1	28	86	82	56	.261	.353	.435	112	10	7	4	-0	.973	**42**	*3-158	5.3
1972	Cle-A	150	557	65	141	28	0	17	70	57	50	.253	.327	.395	110	7	2	3	-1	.956	5	*3-150	1.0
1973	NY-A	160	552	65	129	18	0	22	81	78	76	.234	.336	.386	107	6	0	0	0	.953	26	*3-157/D-2	3.1
1974	NY-A	155	566	74	139	21	1	22	75	59	75	.246	.320	.403	109	6	1	0	0	.961	16	*3-154/S-1	2.2
1975	NY-A★	157	581	71	155	24	4	21	91	51	88	.267	.328	.430	115	10	1	3	-2	.964	11	*3-157	1.9
1976	*NY-A★	158	583	88	148	29	2	**32**	93	62	94	.254	.330	.475	135	24	11	6	-0	.965	17	*3-158/S-1	**4.1**
1977	*NY-A★	158	589	99	150	23	4	37	107	68	79	.255	.335	.496	124	18	2	5	-0	.974	-6	*3-156/D-1	1.1
1978	*NY-A★	159	587	81	162	23	2	27	93	59	69	.276	.348	.460	128	21	1	1	-0	.975	-6	*3-159/S-2	1.3
1979	NY-A★	145	521	71	132	15	1	20	73	59	53	.253	.329	.401	98	-2	1	2	-1	.966	9	*3-144	0.5
1980	NY-A★	89	324	52	79	14	0	16	45	42	42	.244	.332	.435	110	4	0	0	0	.960	-1	3-88/S-1	0.0
1981	*NY-A	103	349	46	85	7	1	15	46	47	49	.244	.335	.398	112	6	0	2	-1	.972	8	3-97/D-4	1.2
1982	NY-A	122	405	47	94	11	2	18	55	51	49	.232	.319	.402	98	-1	1	5	-3	.934	8	*3-113/D-3	0.1
1983	NY-A	129	462	56	123	17	3	20	75	51	65	.266	.343	.446	120	12	0	1	-1	.956	1	*3-126/D-1	1.0
1984	*SD-N	124	395	56	90	11	1	20	65	58	55	.228	.334	.413	109	5	0	0	0	.936	-10	*3-119	-0.7
1985	SD-N★	137	440	66	115	23	1	15	61	72	59	.261	.365	.420	121	14	0	0	0	.959	-9	*3-130	0.4
1986	SD-N	126	354	36	77	9	0	16	55	41	62	.218	.302	.379	88	-6	0	1	-1	.941	-2	*3-114	-1.1
1987	Atl-N	112	177	16	37	5	1	5	33	22	25	.209	.296	.350	67	-8	1	0	0	.951	-1	3-40/1-6	-0.9
1988	Mon-N	80	93	5	16	4	0	1	14	9	19	.172	.245	.247	40	-7	0	0	0	.818	-2	3-12/1-5	0.0
Total	22	2700	8986	1193	2225	328	28	390	1314	1088	1209	.248	.332	.421	110	117	32	36	-12	.961	132	*3-2412/O-73,1DS	21.3

■ JIM NETTLES — Nettles, James William b: 3/2/47, San Diego, Cal. BL/TL, 6', 186 lbs. Deb: 9/7/70 F

YEAR	TM/L	G	AB	R	H	2B	3B	HR	RBI	BB	SO	AVG	OBP	SLG	PRO+	BR/A	SB	CS	SBR	FA	FR	G/POS	TPR
1970	Min-A	13	20	3	5	0	0	0	0	1	5	.250	.286	.250	48	-1	0	1	-1	1.000	-2	O-11	-0.5
1971	Min-A	70	168	17	42	5	1	6	24	19	24	.250	.326	.399	101	0	3	2	-0	.986	2	O-62	-0.1
1972	Min-A	102	235	28	48	5	2	4	15	32	52	.204	.302	.294	74	-7	4	3	-1	.982	-1	O-78/1-1	-1.3
1974	Det-A	43	141	20	32	5	1	6	17	15	26	.227	.306	.404	99	-0	3	4	-2	1.000	-1	O-41	-0.5
1979	KC-A	11	23	0	2	0	0	0	1	3	2	.087	.192	.087	-21	-4	0	0	0	1.000	0	/O-8,1-1	-0.4
1981	Oak-A	1	0	0	0	0	0	0	0	0	0	.000	.000	.000	-	-	0	0	0	.000	0	/O-1	0.0
Total	6	240	587	68	129	15	4	16	57	70	109	.220	.305	.341	83	-12	10	10	-3	.988	-3	O-201/1-2	-2.8

■ MORRIS NETTLES — Nettles, Morris b: 1/26/52, Los Angeles, Cal. BL/TL, 6'1", 170 lbs. Deb: 4/26/74

YEAR	TM/L	G	AB	R	H	2B	3B	HR	RBI	BB	SO	AVG	OBP	SLG	PRO+	BR/A	SB	CS	SBR	FA	FR	G/POS	TPR
1974	Cal-A	56	175	27	48	4	0	0	8	16	38	.274	.335	.297	88	-2	20	11	-1	.990	-6	O-54	-1.2
1975	Cal-A	112	294	50	68	11	0	0	23	26	57	.231	.296	.269	65	-13	22	15	-2	.974	-2	O-90/D-9	-2.1
Total	2	168	469	77	116	15	0	0	31	42	95	.247	.311	.279	74	-16	42	26	-3	.980	-8	O-144/D-9	-3.3

■ MILO NETZEL — Netzel, Miles A. b: 5/12/1886, Eldred, Pa. d: 3/18/38, Oxnard, Cal. BL/TL, Deb: 9/16/09

YEAR	TM/L	G	AB	R	H	2B	3B	HR	RBI	BB	SO	AVG	OBP	SLG	PRO+	BR/A	SB	CS	SBR	FA	FR	G/POS	TPR
1909	Cle-A	10	37	2	7	1	0	0	3	3		.189	.250	.216	46	-2	1			.800	-3	/3-6,O-2	-0.6

■ OTTO NEU — Neu, Otto Adam b: 9/24/1894, Springfield, Ohio d: 9/19/32, Kenton, Ohio BR/TR, 5'11", 170 lbs. Deb: 7/10/17

YEAR	TM/L	G	AB	R	H	2B	3B	HR	RBI	BB	SO	AVG	OBP	SLG	PRO+	BR/A	SB	CS	SBR	FA	FR	G/POS	TPR
1917	StL-A	1	0	0	0	0	0	0	0	0	0	—	—	—			0	0		.000	0	/S-1	0.0

■ JOHNNY NEUN — Neun, John Henry b: 10/28/1900, Baltimore, Md. d: 3/28/90, Baltimore, Md. BB/TL, 5'10.5", 175 lbs. Deb: 4/14/25 MC

YEAR	TM/L	G	AB	R	H	2B	3B	HR	RBI	BB	SO	AVG	OBP	SLG	PRO+	BR/A	SB	CS	SBR	FA	FR	G/POS	TPR
1925	Det-A	60	75	15	20	3	3	0	4	9	12	.267	.345	.387	87	-2	2	3	-1	.990	-1	1-13	-0.4
1926	Det-A	97	242	47	72	14	4	0	15	27	26	.298	.370	.388	97	-1	4	7	-3	.993	-3	1-49	-0.9
1927	Det-A	79	204	38	66	9	4	0	27	35	13	.324	.427	.407	116	7	22	7	2	.980	-3	1-53	0.3
1928	Det-A	36	108	15	23	3	1	0	5	7	10	.213	.261	.259	36	-10	2	2	-1	.975	-0	1-25	-1.2
1930	Bos-N	81	212	39	69	12	2	2	23	21	18	.325	.389	.429	101	1	9			.991	-0	1-55	-0.4
1931	Bos-N	79	104	17	23	1	3	0	11	11	14	.221	.302	.288	62	-5	2			.994	-0	1-36	-0.7
Total	6	432	945	171	273	42	17	2	85	110	93	.289	.366	.376	91	-10	41	19		.987	-7	1-231	-3.3

■ ALEXANDER NEVIN — Nevin, Alexander Brown b: 10/3/1850, Allegheny City, Pa. d: 10/10/21, Pensacola, Fla. Deb: 6/17/1873

YEAR	TM/L	G	AB	R	H	2B	3B	HR	RBI	BB	SO	AVG	OBP	SLG	PRO+	BR/A	SB	CS	SBR	FA	FR	G/POS	TPR
1873	Res-n	13	53	7	11	1	2	0	2	0	3	.208	.208	.302	54	-3	0	0	0	.579	-8	3-12/O-1	-0.8

■ PHIL NEVIN — Nevin, Phillip Joseph b: 1/19/71, Fullerton, Cal. BR/TR, 6'2", 180 lbs. Deb: 6/11/95

YEAR	TM/L	G	AB	R	H	2B	3B	HR	RBI	BB	SO	AVG	OBP	SLG	PRO+	BR/A	SB	CS	SBR	FA	FR	G/POS	TPR
1995	Hou-N	18	60	4	7	1	0	0	1	7	13	.117	.221	.133	-4	-9	1	0	0	.933	1	3-16	-0.8
	Det-A	29	96	9	21	3	1	2	12	11	27	.219	.318	.333	70	-4	0	0	0	.963	-0	O-27/D-2	-0.5
1996	Det-A	38	120	15	35	5	0	8	19	8	39	.292	.341	.533	117	3	1	0	0	.943	5	3-24/O-9,C-4,D-1	0.7
Total	2	85	276	28	63	9	1	10	32	26	79	.228	.306	.377	76	-11	2	0	1	.939	5	/3-40,O-36,C-4,D-3	-0.6

■ DON NEWCOMBE — Newcombe, Donald "Newk" b: 6/14/26, Madison, N.J. BL/TL, 6'4", 225 lbs. Deb: 5/20/49

YEAR	TM/L	G	AB	R	H	2B	3B	HR	RBI	BB	SO	AVG	OBP	SLG	PRO+	BR/A	SB	CS	SBR	FA	FR	G/POS	TPR
1949	*Bro-N★	39	96	8	22	0	0	0	10	5	16	.229	.267	.271	43	-8	0			**1.000**	1	P-38	0.0
1950	Bro-N★	40	97	8	24	3	1	1	8	10	19	.247	.318	.330	69	-4	0			.969	-0	P-40	0.0
1951	Bro-N★	40	103	11	23	3	1	0	8	8	9	.223	.286	.272	50	-7	0	0	0	.958	1	P-40	0.0
1954	Bro-N	31	47	6	15	1	0	0	4	4	6	.319	.373	.340	85	-1	0	0	0	.931	-1	P-29	0.0
1955	*Bro-N★	57	117	18	42	9	1	7	23	6	18	.359	.395	.632	163	10	1	0	0	.907	-2	P-34	0.0
1956	*Bro-N	52	111	13	26	6	0	2	16	12	18	.234	.315	.342	71	-4	0	0	0	.985	0	P-38	0.0
1957	Bro-N	34	74	8	17	2	0	1	7	11	11	.230	.329	.297	64	-4	0	1	-1	.964	1	P-28	0.0
1958	LA-N	11	12	2	5	0	0	0	0	0	4	.417	.500	.417	141	1	0	0	0	1.000	0	P-11	0.0
	Cin-N	39	60	9	21	1	0	1	9	8	10	.350	.426	.417	118	2	0	0	0	.950	-2	P-20	0.0
	Yr	50	72	11	26	1	0	1	9	10	12	.361	.439	.417	122	3	0	0	0	**1.000**	-2	P-31	0.0
1959	Cin-N	61	105	10	32	2	0	3	21	17	23	.305	.402	.410	113	3	0	0	0	.978	-1	P-30	0.0
1960	Cin-N	24	36	0	5	1	0	0	2	3	6	.139	.205	.167	3	-5	0	0	0	.895	-1	P-16	0.0
	Cle-A	24	20	1	6	1	0	0	1	1	7	.300	.333	.350	88	-0	0	0	0	.889	-1	P-20	0.0
Total	10	452	878	94	238	33	3	15	108	87	147	.271	.339	.367	85	-17	2	1		.963	-6	P-344	0.0

■ JOHN NEWELL — Newell, John A. b: 1/14/1868, Wilmington, Del. d: 1/28/19, Wilmington, Del. BR/TL, Deb: 7/22/1891

YEAR	TM/L	G	AB	R	H	2B	3B	HR	RBI	BB	SO	AVG	OBP	SLG	PRO+	BR/A	SB	CS	SBR	FA	FR	G/POS	TPR
1891	Pit-N	5	18	1	2	0	0	0	2	0	0	.111	.158	.111	-22	-3	0			.846	-2	/3-5	-0.4

■ T. E. NEWELL — Newell, T. E. b: St.Louis, Mo. Deb: 8/8/1877

YEAR	TM/L	G	AB	R	H	2B	3B	HR	RBI	BB	SO	AVG	OBP	SLG	PRO+	BR/A	SB	CS	SBR	FA	FR	G/POS	TPR
1877	StL-N	1	3	0	0	0	0	0	0	0	0	.000	.000	.000	-99	-1	0			.833	0	/S-1	0.0

■ MARC NEWFIELD — Newfield, Marc Alexander b: 10/19/72, Sacramento, Cal. BR/TR, 6'4", 205 lbs. Deb: 7/6/93

YEAR	TM/L	G	AB	R	H	2B	3B	HR	RBI	BB	SO	AVG	OBP	SLG	PRO+	BR/A	SB	CS	SBR	FA	FR	G/POS	TPR
1993	Sea-A	22	66	6	15	3	0	1	7	2	8	.227	.261	.318	54	-4	0	1	-1	.000	-2	D-15/O-5	-0.7
1994	Sea-A	12	38	3	7	1	0	1	4	2	4	.184	.225	.289	31	-4	0	0	0	1.000	-1	/O-3,D-9	-0.5

YEAR	TM/L	G	AB	R	H	2B	3B	HR	RBI	BB	SO	AVG	OBP	SLG	PRO+	BR/A	SB	CS	SBR	FA	FR	G/POS	TPR
1995	Sea-A	24	85	7	16	3	0	3	14	3	16	.188	.225	.329	42	-8	0	0	0	1.000	-0	O-24	-0.8
	SD-N	21	55	6	17	5	1	1	7	2	8	.309	.333	.491	118	1	0	0	0	1.000	-0	O-19	0.0
1996	SD-N	84	191	27	48	11	0	5	26	16	44	.251	.316	.387	89	-3	1	1	-0	.970	-7	O-51/1-2	-1.2
	Mil-A	49	179	21	55	15	0	7	31	11	26	.307	.361	.508	110	2	0	1	-1	.990	1	O-49	0.1
Total	4	212	614	69	158	38	1	18	89	36	106	.257	.307	.410	84	-16	1	3	-2	.987	-9	O-151/D-24,1-2	-3.1

■ AL NEWMAN
Newman, Albert Dwayne b: 6/30/60, Kansas City, Mo. BB/TR, 5'9", 183 lbs. Deb: 6/14/85

YEAR	TM/L	G	AB	R	H	2B	3B	HR	RBI	BB	SO	AVG	OBP	SLG	PRO+	BR/A	SB	CS	SBR	FA	FR	G/POS	TPR
1985	Mon-N	25	29	7	5	1	0	0	1	3	4	.172	.250	.207	31	-3	2	1	0	1.000	10	2-15/S-2	0.7
1986	Mon-N	95	185	23	37	3	0	1	8	21	20	.200	.282	.232	44	-14	11	11	-3	.967	9	2-59,S-22	-0.6
1987	*Min-A	110	307	44	68	15	5	0	29	34	27	.221	.299	.303	58	-18	15	11	-2	.982	-11	S-55,2-47,3-12/OD	-2.5
1988	Min-A	105	260	35	58	7	0	0	19	29	34	.223	.301	.250	54	-15	12	3	2	.966	-4	3-60,S-28,2-23/D-2	-1.6
1989	Min-A	141	446	62	113	18	2	0	38	59	34	.253	.343	.303	78	-11	25	12	0	.980	-22	2-84,3-37,S-31/OD	-2.9
1990	Min-A	144	388	43	94	14	0	0	30	33	34	.242	.305	.278	60	-20	13	6	0	.993	-2	2-89,S-48,3-28/O-3	-1.8
1991	*Min-A	118	246	25	47	5	0	0	19	23	21	.191	.263	.211	31	-22	4	5	-2	.987	-1	S-55,2-35,3/10D	-2.2
1992	Tex-A	116	246	25	54	5	0	0	12	34	26	.220	.317	.240	60	-12	9	6	-1	.983	12	2-72,3-28,S-20/OD	0.1
Total	8	854	2107	264	476	68	7	1	156	236	212	.226	.306	.266	58	-115	91	55	-6	.984	-10	2-424,S-261,3/DO1	-10.8

■ CHARLIE NEWMAN
Newman, Charles "Decker" b: 11/5/1868, Juda, Wis. d: 11/23/47, San Diego, Cal. BR/TR, Deb: 9/11/1892

YEAR	TM/L	G	AB	R	H	2B	3B	HR	RBI	BB	SO	AVG	OBP	SLG	PRO+	BR/A	SB	CS	SBR	FA	FR	G/POS	TPR
1892	NY-N	3	12	-1	4	0	0	0	1	2	0	.333	.429	.333	133	1	3			.750	-0	/O-3	0.0
	Chi-N	16	61	4	10	0	0	0	2	1	6	.164	.177	.164	3	-7	2			.950	-3	O-16	-1.0
	Yr	19	73	5	14	0	0	0	3	3	6	.192	.224	.192	26	-7	5			.917	-3	O-19	-1.0

■ JEFF NEWMAN
Newman, Jeffrey Lynn b: 9/11/48, Fort Worth, Tex. BR/TR, 6'2", 218 lbs. Deb: 6/30/76 MC

YEAR	TM/L	G	AB	R	H	2B	3B	HR	RBI	BB	SO	AVG	OBP	SLG	PRO+	BR/A	SB	CS	SBR	FA	FR	G/POS	TPR
1976	Oak-A	43	77	5	15	4	0	0	4	4	12	.195	.235	.247	43	-6	0	0	0	.981	6	C-43	0.1
1977	Oak-A	94	162	17	36	9	0	4	15	4	24	.222	.246	.352	61	-9	2	0	1	.970	10	C-94/P-1	0.3
1978	Oak-A	105	268	25	64	7	1	9	32	18	40	.239	.289	.373	90	-5	0	3	-2	.969	-5	C-61,1-36/D-2	-1.2
1979	Oak-A☆	143	516	53	119	17	2	22	71	27	88	.231	.270	.399	82	-15	2	1	0	.977	-1	C-81,1-46/3-7,D-7	-1.5
1980	Oak-A	127	438	37	102	19	1	15	56	25	81	.233	.276	.384	85	-11	3	4	-2	.982	-9	1-60,C-55/3-2,2D	-2.3
1981	*Oak-A	68	216	17	50	12	0	3	15	9	28	.231	.262	.329	73	-8	0	2	-1	.995	2	C-37,1-30	-0.8
1982	Oak-A	72	251	19	50	11	0	6	30	14	49	.199	.242	.315	54	-17	0	1	-1	.989	-1	C-67/1-3,3-1,D-1	-1.6
1983	Bos-A	59	132	11	25	4	0	3	7	10	31	.189	.257	.288	46	-10	0	1	-1	.990	4	C-51/D-6	-0.7
1984	Bos-A	24	63	5	14	2	0	1	3	5	16	.222	.279	.302	58	-4	0	0	0	.992	2	C-24	-0.1
Total	9	735	2123	189	475	85	4	63	233	116	369	.224	.266	.357	73	-84	7	12	-5	.981	7	C-513,1-175/D32P	-7.8

■ PATRICK NEWNAM
Newnam, Patrick Henry b: 12/10/1880, Hempstead, Tex. d: 6/20/38, San Antonio, Tex. BL/TR, 6', 180 lbs. Deb: 5/29/10

YEAR	TM/L	G	AB	R	H	2B	3B	HR	RBI	BB	SO	AVG	OBP	SLG	PRO+	BR/A	SB	CS	SBR	FA	FR	G/POS	TPR
1910	StL-A	103	384	45	83	3	8	2	26	29		.216	.275	.281	79	-10	16			.972	-4	*1-103	-1.6
1911	StL-A	20	62	11	12	4	0	0	5	12		.194	.351	.258	74	-1	4			.986	1	1-20	-0.1
Total	2	123	446	56	95	7	8	2	31	41		.213	.287	.278	78	-11	20			.974	-3	1-123	-1.7

■ SKEETER NEWSOME
Newsome, Lamar Ashby b: 10/18/10, Phenix City, Ala. d: 8/31/89, Columbus, Ga. BR/TR, 5'9", 155 lbs. Deb: 4/19/35

YEAR	TM/L	G	AB	R	H	2B	3B	HR	RBI	BB	SO	AVG	OBP	SLG	PRO+	BR/A	SB	CS	SBR	FA	FR	G/POS	TPR
1935	Phi-A	59	145	18	30	7	1	1	10	5	9	.207	.233	.290	35	-14	2	1	0	.956	8	S-24,2-13/3-4,O-1	-0.5
1936	Phi-A	127	471	41	106	15	2	0	46	25	27	.225	.266	.265	32	-51	13	4	2	.957	7	*S-123/2-2,3-1,0-1	-3.1
1937	Phi-A	122	438	53	111	22	1	1	30	37	22	.253	.312	.315	59	-27	11	5	0	.954	7	*S-122	-1.1
1938	Phi-A	17	48	7	13	4	0	0	7	1	4	.271	.286	.354	61	-3	1	1	-0	.971	1	S-15	-0.1
1939	Phi-A	99	248	22	55	9	1	0	17	19	12	.222	.277	.266	40	-22	5	7	-3	.950	1	S-93/2-2	-1.6
1941	Bos-A	93	227	28	51	6	0	2	17	22	11	.225	.296	.278	51	-16	10	4	1	.958	15	S-69,2-23	0.4
1942	Bos-A	29	95	7	26	6	0	0	9	9	5	.274	.337	.337	87	-2	2	1	0	.925	3	3-12,2-10/S-7	0.2
1943	Bos-A	114	449	48	119	21	2	1	22	21	21	.265	.301	.327	82	-11	5	6	-2	.962	14	S-98,3-15	0.9
1944	Bos-A	136	472	41	114	26	3	0	41	33	21	.242	.291	.309	72	-17	4	3	-1	.963	11	*S-126/2-8,3-1	0.3
1945	Bos-A	125	438	45	127	30	1	1	48	20	15	.290	.332	.370	98	-2	6	3	0	.963	22	2-82,S-33,3-11	2.9
1946	Phi-N	112	375	35	87	10	2	1	23	30	23	.232	.289	.277	63	-18	4			.955	-12	*S-107/2-3,3-2	-2.6
1947	Phi-N	95	310	36	71	8	2	2	22	24	24	.229	.284	.287	54	-21	4			.969	2	S-85/2-6,3-3	-1.5
Total	12	1128	3716	381	910	164	15	9	292	266	194	.245	.293	.304	62	-205	67	35		.959	78	S-902,2-149/3-49,0	-5.8

■ WARREN NEWSON
Newson, Warren Dale b: 7/3/64, Newnan, Ga. BL/TL, 5'7", 190 lbs. Deb: 5/29/91

YEAR	TM/L	G	AB	R	H	2B	3B	HR	RBI	BB	SO	AVG	OBP	SLG	PRO+	BR/A	SB	CS	SBR	FA	FR	G/POS	TPR
1991	Chi-A	71	132	20	39	5	0	4	25	28	34	.295	.419	.424	137	8	2	2	-1	.962	-10	O-50/D-3	-0.3
1992	Chi-A	63	136	19	30	3	0	1	11	37	38	.221	.387	.265	87	-0	3	0	1	1.000	-4	O-50/D-4	-0.4
1993	*Chi-A	26	40	9	12	0	0	2	6	9	12	.300	.429	.450	139	3	0	0	0	1.000	-1	D-10/O-5	0.1
1994	Chi-A	63	102	16	26	5	1	4	14	23		.255	.345	.363	84	-2	1	0	0	.979	-4	O-34/D-3	-0.6
1995	Chi-A	51	85	19	20	0	2	3	9	23	7	.235	.404	.388	112	3	1	1	-0	.978	-1	O-24/D-7	0.1
	*Sea-A	33	72	15	21	2	0	2	6	16	18	.292	.420	.403	114	2	1	0	0	.971	-2	O-23	0.0
	Yr	84	157	34	41	2	2	5	15	39	45	.261	.411	.395	114	5	2	1	-0	.975	-3	O-47/D-7	0.1
1996	*Tex-A	91	235	34	60	14	1	10	31	37	82	.255	.357	.451	96	-2	3	0	1	.992	2	O-66/D-9	0.0
Total	6	398	802	132	208	29	3	24	95	164	234	.259	.386	.393	105	12	11	3	-2	.984	-19	O-252/D-36	-1.1

■ GUS NIARHOS
Niarhos, Constantine Gregory b: 12/6/20, Birmingham, Ala. BR/TR, 6', 165 lbs. Deb: 6/9/46 C

YEAR	TM/L	G	AB	R	H	2B	3B	HR	RBI	BB	SO	AVG	OBP	SLG	PRO+	BR/A	SB	CS	SBR	FA	FR	G/POS	TPR
1946	NY-A	37	40	11	9	1	1	0	2	11	2	.225	.392	.300	94	0	1	0	0	.989	6	C-29	0.8
1948	NY-A	83	228	41	61	12	2	0	19	52	15	.268	.404	.338	99	3	1	3	-2	.990	11	C-82	1.6
1949	*NY-A	32	43	7	12	2	1	0	6	13	8	.279	.456	.372	120	2	0	0	0	1.000	4	C-30	0.7
1950	NY-A	1	0	0	0	0	0	0	0	0	0	—	—	—		0	0			.000	0	R	0.0
	Chi-A	41	105	17	34	4	0	0	16	14	6	.324	.408	.362	101	1	0			.978	8	C-36	1.0
	Yr	42	105	17	34	4	0	0	16	14	6	.324	.408	.362	101	1	0			.978	8	C-36	1.0
1951	Chi-A	66	168	27	43	6	1	0	19	47	9	.256	.419	.310	101	4	4	3	-1	.985	4	C-59	0.9
1952	Bos-A	29	58	4	6	0	0	0	4	12	9	.103	.268	.103	6	-7	0	0	0	.992	6	C-25	0.1
1953	Bos-A	16	35	4	7	1	1	0	2	4	4	.200	.300	.286	56	-2	0	0	-1	.985	4	C-16	0.1
1954	Phi-N	3	5	0	1	0	0	0	0	0	1	.200	.200	.200	5	-1	0	0	0	1.000	1	/C-3	0.0
1955	Phi-N	7	9	1	1	0	0	0	0	0	2	.111	.111	.111	-42	-2	0	0	0	1.000	1	/C-7	-0.1
Total	9	315	691	114	174	26	5	1	59	153	56	.252	.390	.308	89	-2	5	7	-2	.988	45	C-287	5.0

■ SAM NICHOL
Nichol, Samuel Anderson b: 4/20/1869, County Antrim, Ireland d: 4/19/37, Steubenville, Ohio BR/TR, 5'10", 178 lbs. Deb: 10/5/1888

YEAR	TM/L	G	AB	R	H	2B	3B	HR	RBI	BB	SO	AVG	OBP	SLG	PRO+	BR/A	SB	CS	SBR	FA	FR	G/POS	TPR
1888	Pit-N	8	22	3	1	0	0	0	0	2	2	.045	.125	.045	-47	-4	0			.952	0	/O-8	-0.3
1890	Col-a	14	56	7	9	0	0	0	4	2		.161	.190	.161	4	-7	3			.903	3	O-14	-0.4
Total	2	22	78	10	10	0	0	0	4	4	2	.128	.171	.128	-10	-10	3			.923	3	/O-22	-0.7

■ DON NICHOLAS
Nicholas, Donald Leigh b: 10/30/30, Phoenix, Ariz. BL/TR, 5'7", 150 lbs. Deb: 4/16/52

YEAR	TM/L	G	AB	R	H	2B	3B	HR	RBI	BB	SO	AVG	OBP	SLG	PRO+	BR/A	SB	CS	SBR	FA	FR	G/POS	TPR
1952	Chi-A	3	2	0	0	0	0	0	0	0	0	.000	.000	.000	-99	-1	0	0	0	.000	0	H	-0.1
1954	Chi-A	7	0	3	0	0	0	0	0	1	0	—	1.000	.000	185	0	0	1	-1	.000	0	H	0.0
Total	2	10	2	3	0	0	0	0	0	1	0	.000	.333	.000	-2	-0	0	1	-1			-0,-0	-0.1

■ SIMON NICHOLLS
Nicholls, Simon Burdette b: 7/18/1882, Germantown, Md. d: 3/12/11, Baltimore, Md. BL/TR, 5'11.5", 165 lbs. Deb: 9/18/03

YEAR	TM/L	G	AB	R	H	2B	3B	HR	RBI	BB	SO	AVG	OBP	SLG	PRO+	BR/A	SB	CS	SBR	FA	FR	G/POS	TPR
1903	Det-A	2	8	0	3	0	0	0				.375	.375	.375	129	0				.600	-2	/S-2	-0.2
1906	Phi-A	12	44	1	8	1	0	0	1		3	.182	.234	.205	36	-3	0			.965	-2	S-12	-0.6
1907	Phi-A	124	460	75	139	12	2	0	23		24	.302	.338	.337	113	6	13			.930	-20	S-82,2-28,3-13	-1.3
1908	Phi-A	150	550	58	119	17	4	1	31		35	.216	.265	.280	72	-18	14			.913	-20	*S-120,2-23/3-7	-4.1
1909	Phi-A	21	71	10	15	2	1	0	3		3	.211	.243	.268	60	-3	0			.889	1	S-14/3-5,1-1	-0.3
1910	Cle-A	3	3	0	0	0	0	0				—	—	—		0	0			.000	-1	/S-3	-0.0
Total	6	312	1133	144	284	32	6	4	58		65	.251	.292	.300	86	-18	27			.917	-46	S-233/2-51,3-25,1-1	-6.6

■ AL NICHOLS
Nichols, Albert H. b: Brooklyn, N.Y. 5'11", 180 lbs. Deb: 4/24/1875

YEAR	TM/L	G	AB	R	H	2B	3B	HR	RBI	BB	SO	AVG	OBP	SLG	PRO+	BR/A	SB	CS	SBR	FA	FR	G/POS	TPR
1875	Atl-n	32	131	4	20	2	0	0		9	0	.153	.153	.168	13	-10	0	0	0	.785	9	3-32	-0.1
1876	NY-N	57	212	20	38	4	0	0		9	3	.179	.187	.198	33	-14				.779	5	*3-57	-0.6

YEAR	TM/L	G	AB	R	H	2B	3B	HR	RBI	BB	SO	AVG	OBP	SLG	PRO+	BR/A	SB	CS	SBR	FA	FR	G/POS	TPR
1877	Lou-N	6	19	1	4	0	1	0	0	0	2	.211	.211	.316	54	-1				.706	4	/2-3,S-1,3-1,1-1	0.3
Total	2	63	231	21	42	4	1	0	9	2	5	.182	.189	.208	35	-15				.785	9	/3-58,2-3,1-1,S-1	-0.3

■ ART NICHOLS

Nichols, Arthur Francis (b: Arthur Francis Meikle)
b: 7/14/1871, Manchester, N.H.   d: 8/9/45, Willimantic, Conn.   BR/TR, 5'10", 175 lbs.   Deb: 9/16/1898

YEAR	TM/L	G	AB	R	H	2B	3B	HR	RBI	BB	SO	AVG	OBP	SLG	PRO+	BR/A	SB	CS	SBR	FA	FR	G/POS	TPR
1898	Chi-N	14	42	7	12	1	0	0	6	4		.286	.388	.310	101	0			6	.968	1	C-14	0.2
1899	Chi-N	17	47	5	12	2	0	1	11	0		.255	.286	.362	79	-2			3	.931	-1	C-15	-0.2
1900	Chi-N	8	25	1	5	0	0	0	0	3		.200	.286	.200	36	-2			1	.938	-1	/C-7	-0.2
1901	StL-N	93	308	50	75	11	3	1	33	10		.244	.290	.308	77	-9			14	.960	-4	C-47,O-40	-1.0
1902	StL-N	73	251	36	67	12	0	1	31	21		.267	.333	.327	108	3			18	.984	-7	1-56,C-11/O-4	-0.4
1903	StL-N	36	120	13	23	2	0	0	9	12		.192	.281	.208	42	-9			9	.972	-5	1-25/O-7,C-2	-1.4
Total	6	241	793	112	194	28	3	3	90	50		.245	.308	.299	81	-18			51	.952	-17	/C-96,1-81,O-51	-3.0

■ CARL NICHOLS

Nichols, Carl Edward   b: 10/14/62, Los Angeles, Cal.   BR/TR, 6', 208 lbs.   Deb: 9/14/86

YEAR	TM/L	G	AB	R	H	2B	3B	HR	RBI	BB	SO	AVG	OBP	SLG	PRO+	BR/A	SB	CS	SBR	FA	FR	G/POS	TPR
1986	Bal-A	5	5	0	0	0	0	0	0	1	4	.000	.167	.000	-51	-1	0	0	0	1.000	-0	/C-5	-0.1
1987	Bal-A	13	21	4	8	1	0	0	3	1	4	.381	.409	.429	126	1	0	0	0	1.000	-1	C-13	0.2
1988	Bal-A	18	47	2	9	1	0	0	1	3	10	.191	.240	.213	29	-4	0	0	0	.987	6	C-13/O-3	0.2
1989	Hou-N	8	13	0	1	0	0	0	2	0	3	.077	.077	.077	-58	-3	0	0	0	1.000	-0	/C-6	-0.3
1990	Hou-N	32	49	7	10	3	0	0	11	8	11	.204	.328	.265	67	-2	0	0	0	.986	5	C-15/1-3,O-1	0.1
1991	Hou-N	20	51	3	10	3	0	0	1	5	17	.196	.268	.255	51	-3	0	0	0	.971	3	C-17	0.1
Total	6	96	186	16	38	8	0	0	18	18	49	.204	.278	.247	49	-13	0	0	0	.985	12	/C-69,O-4,1-3	0.2

■ ROY NICHOLS

Nichols, Roy   b: 3/3/21, Little Rock, Ark.   BR/TR, 5'11", 155 lbs.   Deb: 5/6/44

YEAR	TM/L	G	AB	R	H	2B	3B	HR	RBI	BB	SO	AVG	OBP	SLG	PRO+	BR/A	SB	CS	SBR	FA	FR	G/POS	TPR
1944	NY-N	11	9	3	2	1	0	0	2	2		.222	.364	.333	97	0	0			1.000	2	/2-1,3-1	0.2

■ REID NICHOLS

Nichols, Thomas Reid   b: 8/5/58, Ocala, Fla.   BR/TR, 5'11", 165 lbs.   Deb: 9/16/80

YEAR	TM/L	G	AB	R	H	2B	3B	HR	RBI	BB	SO	AVG	OBP	SLG	PRO+	BR/A	SB	CS	SBR	FA	FR	G/POS	TPR
1980	Bos-A	12	36	5	8	0	1	0	3	3	8	.222	.282	.278	51	-2	0	1	-1	.962	0	/O-9,D-1	-0.3
1981	Bos-A	39	48	13	9	0	1	0	3	2	6	.188	.220	.229	28	-4	0	1	-1	1.000	-4	O-27/3-1,D-7	-1.0
1982	Bos-A	92	245	35	74	16	1	7	33	14	28	.302	.342	.461	112	3	5	3	-0	.989	-2	O-82/D-4	0.2
1983	Bos-A	100	274	35	78	22	1	6	22	26	36	.285	.353	.438	108	3	7	5	-1	.994	0	O-72,D-18/S-1	-0.1
1984	Bos-A	74	124	14	28	5	1	1	14	12	18	.226	.309	.306	68	-5	2	1	0	.988	-4	O-48/D-1	-1.0
1985	Bos-A	21	32	3	6	1	0	1	3	2	4	.188	.257	.313	53	-2	1	0	0	.933	-2	O-10/2-3,D-4	-0.4
	Chi-A	51	118	20	35	7	1	1	15	15	13	.297	.376	.398	108	2	5	5	-2	1.000	-12	O-48/D-1	-1.2
	Yr	72	150	23	41	8	1	2	18	17	17	.273	.351	.380	96	-0	6	5	-1	.988	-14	O-58/D-5,2-3	-1.6
1986	Chi-A	74	136	9	31	4	0	2	18	11	23	.228	.286	.301	58	-8	5	4	-1	.989	-4	O-53/2-2,D-3	-1.4
1987	Mon-N	77	147	22	39	8	2	4	20	14	13	.265	.333	.429	97	-1	2	1	0	.990	-4	O-59/3-3	-0.5
Total	8	540	1160	156	308	63	8	22	131	99	149	.266	.328	.391	91	-14	27	21	-5	.990	-29	O-408/D-39,2-5,3S	-5.6

■ DAVE NICHOLSON

Nicholson, David Lawrence   b: 8/29/39, St.Louis, Mo.   BR/TR, 6'2", 215 lbs.   Deb: 5/24/60

YEAR	TM/L	G	AB	R	H	2B	3B	HR	RBI	BB	SO	AVG	OBP	SLG	PRO+	BR/A	SB	CS	SBR	FA	FR	G/POS	TPR
1960	Bal-A	54	113	17	21	1	1	5	11	20	55	.186	.308	.345	77	-4	0	2	-1	.982	-5	O-44	-1.1
1962	Bal-A	97	173	25	30	4	1	9	15	27	76	.173	.289	.364	79	-6	3	4	-2	.983	-7	O-80	-1.7
1963	Chi-A	126	449	53	103	11	4	22	70	63	175	.229	.324	.419	108	5	2	1	0	.970	2	*O-123	0.1
1964	Chi-A	97	294	40	60	6	1	13	39	52	126	.204	.330	.364	95	-1	0	2	-1	.972	-2	O-92	-0.9
1965	Chi-A	54	85	11	13	2	1	2	12	9	40	.153	.234	.271	46	-6	0	0	0	1.000	-9	O-36	-1.7
1966	Hou-N	100	280	36	69	8	4	10	31	46	92	.246	.359	.411	122	9	1	1	-0	.968	-3	O-90	0.7
1967	Atl-N	10	25	2	5	0	0	0	1	2	9	.200	.259	.200	34	-2	0	0	0	1.000	-0	/O-7	-0.3
Total	7	538	1419	184	301	32	12	61	179	219	573	.212	.320	.381	97	-4	6	10	-4	.974	-19	O-472	-4.9

■ FRED NICHOLSON

Nicholson, Fred "Shoemaker"   b: 9/1/1894, Honey Grove, Tex.   d: 1/23/72, Kilgore, Tex.   BR/TR, 5'10.5", 173 lbs.   Deb: 4/11/17

YEAR	TM/L	G	AB	R	H	2B	3B	HR	RBI	BB	SO	AVG	OBP	SLG	PRO+	BR/A	SB	CS	SBR	FA	FR	G/POS	TPR
1917	Det-A	13	14	4	4	2	0	0				.286	.333	.357	111	0				1.000	-0	/O-3	-0.1
1919	Pit-N	30	66	8	18	2	1	1	6	6	11	.273	.333	.409	118	1	2			.939	-1	O-17/1-1	-0.1
1920	Pit-N	99	247	33	89	16	7	4	30	18	31	.360	.404	.530	162	19	9	6	-1	.957	2	O-58	1.7
1921	Bos-N	83	245	36	80	11	7	5	41	17	29	.327	.370	.490	133	11	5	4	-1	.983	-4	O-59/1-4,2-2	0.0
1922	Bos-N	78	222	31	56	4	5	2	29	23	24	.252	.336	.342	79	-7	5	7	-3	.915	-4	O-63	-1.7
Total	5	303	794	112	247	34	21	12	107	65	97	.311	.367	.452	124	25	21	17		.950	-11	O-200/1-5,2-2	-0.2

■ OVID NICHOLSON

Nicholson, Ovid Edward   b: 12/30/1888, Salem, Ind.   d: 3/24/68, Salem, Ind.   BL/TR, 5'9.5", 155 lbs.   Deb: 9/17/12

YEAR	TM/L	G	AB	R	H	2B	3B	HR	RBI	BB	SO	AVG	OBP	SLG	PRO+	BR/A	SB	CS	SBR	FA	FR	G/POS	TPR
1912	Pit-N	6	11	2	5	0	0	0	3	1	2	.455	.500	.455	165	1	2			1.000	-1	/O-4	0.0

■ PARSON NICHOLSON

Nicholson, Thomas C. "Deacon"   b: 4/14/1863, Blaine, Ohio   d: 2/28/17, Bellaire, Ohio   6'6", 190 lbs.   Deb: 9/14/1888

YEAR	TM/L	G	AB	R	H	2B	3B	HR	RBI	BB	SO	AVG	OBP	SLG	PRO+	BR/A	SB	CS	SBR	FA	FR	G/POS	TPR
1888	Det-N	24	85	11	22	3	2	1	2	2	6	.259	.284	.388	113	1	6			.935	-2	2-24	0.0
1890	Tol-a	134	523	78	140	16	11	4	72	42		.268	.333	.363	102	-0	46			.929	-8	*2-134/C-1	0.0
1895	Was-N	10	38	7	7	2	1	0	5	7	4	.184	.311	.289	56	-2	6			.797	-2	S-10	-0.3
Total	3	168	646	96	169	20	15	5	86	51	11	.262	.325	.362	100	-2	58			.930	-12	2-158/S-10,C-1	-0.3

■ BILL NICHOLSON

Nicholson, William Beck "Swish"   b: 12/11/14, Chestertown, Md.   d: 3/8/96, Chestertown, Md.   BL/TR, 6', 205 lbs.   Deb: 6/13/36

YEAR	TM/L	G	AB	R	H	2B	3B	HR	RBI	BB	SO	AVG	OBP	SLG	PRO+	BR/A	SB	CS	SBR	FA	FR	G/POS	TPR
1936	Phi-A	11	12	2	0	0	0	0	0	0	5	.000	.000	.000	-99	-4	0	0	0	1.000	-0	/O-1	-0.4
1939	Chi-N	58	220	37	65	12	5	5	38	20	29	.295	.354	.464	116	5	0	0		.955	1	O-58	0.4
1940	Chi-N★	135	491	78	146	27	7	25	98	50	67	.297	.366	.534	148	31	2			.950	-2	*O-123	2.2
1941	Chi-N★	147	532	74	135	26	1	26	98	82	91	.254	.357	.453	132	22	1			.971	6	*O-143	2.0
1942	Chi-N	152	588	83	173	22	11	21	78	76	80	.294	.382	.476	156	42	8			.986	11	*O-151	4.8
1943	Chi-N★	154	608	95	188	30	9	29	128	71	86	.309	.386	.531	166	50	4			.978	6	*O-154	4.9
1944	Chi-N★	156	582	116	167	35	8	33	122	93	71	.287	.391	.545	162	48	3			.979	-3	*O-156	4.2
1945	*Chi-N†	151	559	82	136	28	4	13	88	92	73	.243	.356	.377	106	7	4			.990	1	*O-151	-0.1
1946	Chi-N	105	296	36	65	13	2	8	41	44	44	.220	.325	.358	95	-2	1			.973	-4	O-80	-0.3
1947	Chi-N	148	487	69	119	28	1	26	75	87	85	.244	.364	.466	124	17	1			**.990**	-1	*O-140	0.9
1948	Chi-N	143	494	68	129	24	5	19	67	81	60	.261	.371	.445	125	18	2			.980	-3	*O-136	0.8
1949	Phi-N	98	299	42	70	8	3	11	40	45	53	.234	.344	.391	99	-0	1			.995	3	O-91	-0.1
1950	Phi-N	41	58	3	13	2	1	3	10	8	16	.224	.318	.448	101	-0	0			.952	-2	O-15	-0.3
1951	Phi-N	85	170	23	41	9	2	8	30	25	24	.241	.342	.459	115	3	0	0	1	-1	.987	-3	O-41	-0.1
1952	Phi-N	55	88	17	24	0	0	6	19	14	26	.273	.390	.511	150	3	0	0	0	1.000	-2	O-19	0.4
1953	Phi-N	38	62	12	13	5	1	2	16	12	20	.210	.338	.419	97	-0	0	0	0	1.000	-2	O-12	-0.3
Total	16	1677	5546	837	1484	272	60	235	948	800	828	.268	.365	.465	133	243	27	1		.979	17	O-1471	19.0

■ GEORGE NICOL

Nicol, George Edward   b: 10/17/1870, Barry, Ill.   d: 8/10/24, Milwaukee, Wis.   TL, 5'7", 155 lbs.   Deb: 9/23/1890

YEAR	TM/L	G	AB	R	H	2B	3B	HR	RBI	BB	SO	AVG	OBP	SLG	PRO+	BR/A	SB	CS	SBR	FA	FR	G/POS	TPR
1890	StL-a	3	7	4	2	1	0	0	1	4		.286	.545	.429	164	1	0			1.000	-0	/P-3	0.0
1891	Chi-N	3	6	0	2	0	0	0	3	0	1	.333	.333	.667	189	1	0			1.000	-1	/P-3	0.0
1894	Pit-N	8	20	8	9	1	0	0	3	0	1	.450	.450	.500	130	1	0			.800	-1	/P-8	0.0
	Lou-N	27	108	12	38	6	4	0	19	2	3	.352	.375	.481	113	2	4			.791	-5	O-26/P-1	-0.4
	Yr	35	128	20	47	7	4	0	22	2	4	.367	.386	.484	115	3	4			.791	-6	O-26/P-9	-0.4
Total	3	41	141	24	51	8	5	0	26	6	5	.362	.396	.489	121	4	4			.692	-7	/O-26,P-15	-0.4

■ HUGH NICOL

Nicol, Hugh   b: 1/1/1858, Campsie, Scotland   d: 6/27/21, Lafayette, Ind.   BR/TR, 5'4", 145 lbs.   Deb: 5/3/1881   M

YEAR	TM/L	G	AB	R	H	2B	3B	HR	RBI	BB	SO	AVG	OBP	SLG	PRO+	BR/A	SB	CS	SBR	FA	FR	G/POS	TPR
1881	Chi-N	26	108	13	22	2	0	0		4	12	.204	.232	.222	42	-7				.932	-3	O-26/S-1	-0.4
1882	Chi-N	47	186	19	37	9	1	1	16	7	29	.199	.228	.274	58	-9				.887	10	O-47/S-8	0.1
1883	StL-a	94	368	73	105	13	3	0	39	18		.285	.319	.337	105	1				.916	12	*O-84,2-11	1.1
1884	StL-a	110	442	79	116	14	5	0		22		.262	.302	.317	99	-1				.873	23	*O-87,2-23/S-1,3-1	1.9
1885	*StL-a	112	425	59	88	11	4	0	45	34		.207	.271	.238	59	-20				.888	13	*O-111/3-1	-0.9
1886	StL-a	67	253	44	52	3	0	0	19	26		.206	.280	.253	64	-11	38			.942	-5	O-57/S-8,2-4	-1.4
1887	Cin-a	125	475	122	102	18	2	1	34	86		.215	.341	.267	69	-17	138			.918	-3	*O-125	-1.4
1888	Cin-a	135	548	112	131	10	2	1	35	67		.239	.330	.270	84	-6	103			.957	-3	*O-125,2-12/S-1	-1.1
1889	Cin-a	122	474	82	121	7	8	2	58	54	35	.255	.338	.316	84	-9	80			.918	1	*O-115/2-7,3-3	-0.9

YEAR	TM/L	G	AB	R	H	2B	3B	HR	RBI	BB	SO	AVG	OBP	SLG	PRO+	BR/A	SB	CS	SBR	FA	FR	G/POS	TPR
1890	Cin-N	50	186	28	39	1	4	0	19	19	12	.210	.283	.258	58	-10	24			.921	-6	O-46/S-3,2-1	-1.5
Total	10	888	3465	631	813	91	29	5	272	337	88	.235	.307	.282	78	-88	383			.912	49	O-823/2-58,S-22,3-5	-4.8

■ STEVE NICOSIA

Nicosia, Steven Richard   b: 8/6/55, Paterson, N.J.   BR/TR, 5'10", 185 lbs.   Deb: 7/8/78

YEAR	TM/L	G	AB	R	H	2B	3B	HR	RBI	BB	SO	AVG	OBP	SLG	PRO+	BR/A	SB	CS	SBR	FA	FR	G/POS	TPR
1978	Pit-N	3	5	0	0	0	0	0	0	0	1	.000	.167	.000	-48	-1	0	0	0	1.000	1	/C-1	0.0
1979	*Pit-N	70	191	22	55	16	0	4	13	23	17	.288	.364	.435	112	3	0	2	-1	.991	4	C-65	0.8
1980	Pit-N	60	176	16	38	8	0	1	22	19	16	.216	.296	.278	60	-9	0	1	-1	.984	-1	C-58	-0.9
1981	Pit-N	54	169	21	39	10	1	2	18	13	10	.231	.286	.337	74	-6	3	1	0	.982	1	C-52	-0.4
1982	Pit-N	39	100	6	28	3	0	1	7	11	13	.280	.351	.340	91	-1	0	1	-1	.990	3	C-35/O-3	0.3
1983	Pit-N	21	46	4	6	2	0	1	1	1	7	.130	.149	.239	6	-6	0	0	0	.988	-1	C-15	-0.7
	SF-N	15	33	4	11	0	0	0	6	3	2	.333	.389	.333	105	0	0	0	0	.984	2	/C-9	0.3
	Yr	36	79	8	17	2	0	1	7	4	9	.215	.253	.278	47	-6	0	0	0	.986	1	C-24	-0.4
1984	SF-N	48	132	9	40	11	2	2	19	8	14	.303	.343	.462	129	4	1	1	-0	.985	-5	C-41	0.0
1985	Mon-N	42	71	4	12	2	0	0	1	7	11	.169	.244	.197	26	-7	1	0	0	.988	-5	C-23/1-2	-1.2
	Tor-A	6	15	0	4	0	0	0	1	0	0	.267	.267	.267	46	-1	0	0	0	1.000	1	/C-6	0.0
Total	8	358	938	86	233	52	3	11	88	86	90	.248	.312	.345	82	-23	5	6	-2	.987	-1	C-305/O-3,1-2	-1.8

■ CHARLIE NIEBERGALL

Niebergall, Charles Arthur "Nig"   b: 5/23/1899, New York, N.Y.   d: 8/29/82, Holiday, Fla.   BR/TR, 5'10", 160 lbs.   Deb: 6/17/21

YEAR	TM/L	G	AB	R	H	2B	3B	HR	RBI	BB	SO	AVG	OBP	SLG	PRO+	BR/A	SB	CS	SBR	FA	FR	G/POS	TPR
1921	StL-N	5	6	1	1	0	0	0	0	0	0	.167	.167	.167	-12	-1	0	0	0	1.000	-1	/C-3	-0.1
1923	StL-N	9	28	2	3	1	0	0	1	2	2	.107	.167	.143	-18	-5	0	0	0	1.000	-0	/C-7	-0.5
1924	StL-N	40	58	6	17	6	0	0	7	3	9	.293	.339	.397	98	-0	0	0	0	.951	1	C-34	0.2
Total	3	54	92	9	21	7	0	0	8	5	11	.228	.276	.304	55	-6	0	0	0	.966	1	/C-44	-0.4

■ AL NIEHAUS

Niehaus, Albert Bernard   b: 6/1/1899, Cincinnati, Ohio   d: 10/14/31, Cincinnati, Ohio   BR/TR, 5'11", 175 lbs.   Deb: 4/22/25

YEAR	TM/L	G	AB	R	H	2B	3B	HR	RBI	BB	SO	AVG	OBP	SLG	PRO+	BR/A	SB	CS	SBR	FA	FR	G/POS	TPR
1925	Pit-N	17	64	7	14	8	0	0	7	2	5	.219	.242	.344	45	-6	0	0	0	.962	-1	1-15	-0.7
	Cin-N	51	147	16	44	10	2	0	14	13	10	.299	.360	.395	95	-1	1	4	-2	.988	2	1-45	-0.3
	Yr	68	211	23	58	18	2	0	21	14	15	.275	.326	.379	80	-7	1	4	-2	.981	1	1-60	-1.0

■ BERT NIEHOFF

Niehoff, John Albert   b: 5/13/1884, Louisville, Colo.   d: 12/8/74, Inglewood, Cal.   BR/TR, 5'10.5", 170 lbs.   Deb: 10/4/13   C

YEAR	TM/L	G	AB	R	H	2B	3B	HR	RBI	BB	SO	AVG	OBP	SLG	PRO+	BR/A	SB	CS	SBR	FA	FR	G/POS	TPR
1913	Cin-N	2	8	0	0	0	0	0	0	0	2	.000	.000	.000	-99	-2	0			.917	2	/3-2	0.0
1914	Cin-N	142	484	46	117	16	9	4	49	38	77	.242	.298	.337	86	-9	20			.924	7	*3-134/2-3	0.2
1915	*Phi-N	148	529	61	126	27	2	2	49	30	63	.238	.280	.308	77	-15	21	11	-0	.946	-7	*2-148	-2.3
1916	Phi-N	146	548	65	133	42	4	4	61	37	57	.243	.292	.356	95	-4	20	14	-2	.936	-2	*2-144/3-2	-0.4
1917	Phi-N	114	361	30	92	17	4	2	42	23	29	.255	.303	.341	93	-3	8			.945	18	2-96/1-7,3-6	2.2
1918	StL-N	22	84	5	15	2	0	0	5	3	10	.179	.207	.202	26	-7	2			.975	2	2-22	-0.5
	NY-N	7	23	3	6	0	0	0	1	0	4	.261	.261	.261	60	-1	0			.871	-2	/2-7	-0.4
	Yr	29	107	8	21	2	0	0	6	3	14	.196	.218	.215	33	-9	2			.954	-1	2-29	-0.9
Total	6	581	2037	210	489	104	19	12	207	131	242	.240	.288	.327	84	-42	71	25		.943	18	2-420,3-144/1-7	-1.2

■ MILT NIELSEN

Nielsen, Milton Robert   b: 2/8/25, Tyler, Minn.   BL/TL, 5'11", 190 lbs.   Deb: 9/27/49

YEAR	TM/L	G	AB	R	H	2B	3B	HR	RBI	BB	SO	AVG	OBP	SLG	PRO+	BR/A	SB	CS	SBR	FA	FR	G/POS	TPR
1949	Cle-A	3	9	1	1	0	0	0	0	2	4	.111	.273	.111	4	-1	0	0	0	1.000	-0	/O-3	-0.2
1951	Cle-A	16	6	1	0	0	0	0	0	1	1	.000	.143	.000	-63	-1	0	0	0	1.000	0	H	-0.1
Total	2	19	15	2	1	0	0	0	0	3	5	.067	.222	.067	-22	-3	0	0	0	1.000	-1	/O-3	-0.3

■ BUTCH NIEMAN

Nieman, Elmer Le Roy   b: 2/8/18, Herkimer, Kan.   d: 11/2/93, Topeka, Kan.   BL/TL, 6'2", 195 lbs.   Deb: 5/2/43

YEAR	TM/L	G	AB	R	H	2B	3B	HR	RBI	BB	SO	AVG	OBP	SLG	PRO+	BR/A	SB	CS	SBR	FA	FR	G/POS	TPR
1943	Bos-N	101	335	39	84	15	8	7	46	39	39	.251	.331	.406	114	5	4			.963	1	O-93	0.2
1944	Bos-N	134	468	65	124	16	6	16	65	47	47	.265	.332	.427	108	4	5			.975	-2	*O-126	-0.4
1945	Bos-N	97	247	43	61	15	0	14	56	43	33	.247	.361	.478	131	10	11			.932	0	O-57	0.7
Total	3	332	1050	147	269	46	14	37	167	129	119	.256	.339	.432	116	20	20			.961	-0	O-276	0.5

■ BOB NIEMAN

Nieman, Robert Charles   b: 1/26/27, Cincinnati, Ohio   d: 3/10/85, Corona, Cal.   BR/TR, 5'11", 195 lbs.   Deb: 9/14/51

YEAR	TM/L	G	AB	R	H	2B	3B	HR	RBI	BB	SO	AVG	OBP	SLG	PRO+	BR/A	SB	CS	SBR	FA	FR	G/POS	TPR
1951	StL-A	12	43	6	16	3	1	2	8	3	5	.372	.413	.628	174	4	0	0	0	.962	0	O-11	0.4
1952	StL-A	131	478	66	138	22	6	18	74	46	73	.289	.352	.456	120	12	0	4	-2	.976	1	*O-125	0.5
1953	Det-A	142	508	72	143	32	5	15	69	57	57	.281	.354	.453	118	12	0	3	-2	.979	3	*O-135	0.8
1954	Det-A	91	251	24	66	14	1	8	35	22	32	.263	.322	.422	105	1	0	2	-1	.984	-2	O-62	-0.5
1955	Chi-A	99	272	36	77	11	2	11	53	36	37	.283	.371	.460	119	7	1	0	0	.976	-7	O-78	-0.2
1956	Chi-A	14	40	3	12	1	0	2	4	4	4	.300	.364	.475	118	1	0	1	-1	1.000	1	O-10	0.0
	Bal-A	114	388	60	125	20	6	12	64	86	59	.322	.445	.497	161	38	1	5	-3	.980	7	*O-114	3.5
	Yr	128	428	63	137	21	6	14	68	90	63	.320	.438	.495	156	39	1	6	-3	.982	7	O-124	3.5
1957	Bal-A	129	445	61	123	17	6	13	70	63	66	.276	.369	.429	125	16	4	4	-1	.980	5	*O-120	1.3
1958	Bal-A	105	366	56	119	20	2	16	60	44	57	.325	.391	.522	159	29	2	8	-4	.961	-7	*O-100	1.3
1959	Bal-A	118	360	49	105	18	2	21	60	42	55	.292	.369	.528	146	22	1	2	-1	.973	-0	O-97	1.6
1960	StL-N	81	188	19	54	13	5	4	31	24	31	.287	.374	.473	120	5	0	1	-1	.940	-8	O-55	-0.6
1961	StL-N	6	17	0	8	1	0	0	2	0	0	.471	.471	.529	150	1	0	0	0	1.000	-1	/O-4	0.5
	Cle-A	39	65	2	23	6	0	2	10	7	4	.354	.417	.538	157	5	1	0	0	.960	0	O-12	0.5
1962	Cle-A	2	1	0	0	0	0	0	1	0	1	.000	.000	.000	-99	-0	0	0	0	.000	0	H	0.0
	*SF-N	30	30	1	9	2	0	1	3	1	9	.300	.323	.467	111	0	0	0	0	1.000	-1	/O-3	0.0
Total	12	1113	3452	455	1018	180	32	125	544	435	512	.295	.375	.474	132	154	10	30	-15	.975	-8	O-926	8.6

■ AL NIEMIEC

Niemiec, Alfred Joseph   b: 5/18/11, Meriden, Conn.   d: 10/29/95, Kirkland, Wash.   BR/TR, 5'11", 158 lbs.   Deb: 9/19/34

YEAR	TM/L	G	AB	R	H	2B	3B	HR	RBI	BB	SO	AVG	OBP	SLG	PRO+	BR/A	SB	CS	SBR	FA	FR	G/POS	TPR
1934	Bos-A	9	32	2	7	0	0	0	3	4	2	.219	.286	.219	30	-3	0	0	0	1.000	4	/2-9	0.1
1936	Phi-A	69	203	22	40	3	2	1	20	26	16	.197	.291	.246	35	-21	2	2	-1	.972	10	2-52/S-5	-0.6
Total	2	78	235	24	47	3	2	1	23	29	20	.200	.291	.243	34	-24	2	2	-1	.976	15	/2-61,S-5	-0.5

■ TOM NIETO

Nieto, Thomas Andrew   b: 10/27/60, Downey, Cal.   BR/TR, 6'1", 205 lbs.   Deb: 5/10/84

YEAR	TM/L	G	AB	R	H	2B	3B	HR	RBI	BB	SO	AVG	OBP	SLG	PRO+	BR/A	SB	CS	SBR	FA	FR	G/POS	TPR
1984	StL-N	33	86	7	24	4	0	3	12	5	18	.279	.319	.430	112	1	0	0	0	.994	4	C-32	0.6
1985	*StL-N	95	253	15	57	10	0	3	34	26	37	.225	.305	.281	65	-11	0	2	-1	.990	-4	C-95	-1.3
1986	Mon-N	30	65	5	13	3	1	1	7	6	21	.200	.278	.323	66	-3	0	1	-1	.978	-3	C-30	-0.5
1987	Min-A	41	105	7	21	7	1	1	12	8	24	.200	.276	.314	54	-7	0	0	0	.996	9	C-40/D-1	-0.3
1988	Min-A	24	60	4	4	0	0	0	0	1	17	.067	.097	.067	-52	-12	0	0	0	.991	3	C-24	-0.8
1989	Phi-N	11	20	1	3	0	0	0	6	7	.150	.370	.150	54	-1	0	0	0	1.000	1	C-11	0.3
1990	Phi-N	17	30	1	5	0	0	0	4	3	11	.167	.265	.167	21	-3	0	0	0	.984	1	C-17	0.0
Total	7	251	619	37	127	24	4	5	69	55	135	.205	.281	.281	56	-36	0	3	-2	.991	7	C-249/D-1	-2.0

■ MELVIN NIEVES

Nieves, Melvin Ramos   b: 12/28/71, San Juan, P.R.   BB/TR, 6'2", 186 lbs.   Deb: 9/1/92

YEAR	TM/L	G	AB	R	H	2B	3B	HR	RBI	BB	SO	AVG	OBP	SLG	PRO+	BR/A	SB	CS	SBR	FA	FR	G/POS	TPR
1992	Atl-N	12	19	0	4	1	0	0	1	2	7	.211	.286	.263	53	-1	0	0	0	.727	-1	/O-6	-0.3
1993	SD-N	19	47	4	9	0	0	2	3	3	21	.191	.255	.319	52	-3	0	0	0	.931	-1	/O-15	-0.5
1994	SD-N	10	19	2	5	1	0	1	4	3	10	.263	.364	.474	120	1	0	0	0	1.000	1	/O-6	0.1
1995	SD-N	98	234	32	48	6	1	14	38	19	88	.205	.279	.419	84	-7	2	3	-1	.990	-6	O-79/1-2	-1.5
1996	Det-A	120	431	71	106	23	4	24	60	46	158	.246	.324	.485	102	-1	1	2	-1	.943	4	*O-105,D-11	-0.1
Total	5	259	750	109	172	31	5	41	106	71	284	.229	.306	.448	93	-11	3	5	-2	.950	-3	O-211/D-11,1-2	-2.3

■ TOM NILAND

Niland, Thomas James "Honest Tom"   b: 4/14/1870, Brookfield, Mass.   d: 4/30/50, Lynn, Mass.   BR/TR, 5'11", 160 lbs.   Deb: 4/19/1896

YEAR	TM/L	G	AB	R	H	2B	3B	HR	RBI	BB	SO	AVG	OBP	SLG	PRO+	BR/A	SB	CS	SBR	FA	FR	G/POS	TPR
1896	StL-N	18	68	3	12	0	1	0	3	5	4	.176	.243	.206	20	-8	0			.913	-4	O-13/S-5	-1.1

■ HARRY NILES

Niles, Herbert Clyde   b: 9/10/1880, Buchanan, Mich.   d: 4/18/53, Sturgis, Mich.   BR/TR, 5'8", 175 lbs.   Deb: 4/24/06

YEAR	TM/L	G	AB	R	H	2B	3B	HR	RBI	BB	SO	AVG	OBP	SLG	PRO+	BR/A	SB	CS	SBR	FA	FR	G/POS	TPR
1906	StL-A	142	541	71	124	14	4	2	31	46		.229	.297	.281	85	-9	30			.967	9	*O-108,3-34	-0.5
1907	StL-A	130	492	65	142	9	5	2	35	28		.289	.331	.339	114	7	19			.949	-5	*2-116/O-1	0.1
1908	NY-A	96	362	43	90	14	6	4	24	25		.249	.304	.354	112	4	18			.928	-24	2-85/O-7	-2.4
	Bos-A	17	32	4	8	0	0	1	3	6		.250	.385	.344	133	2	3			1.000	1	/2-8,S-2	0.1
	Yr	113	394	47	98	14	6	5	27	31		.249	.311	.353	114	6	21			.934	-24	2-93/O-7,S-2	-2.3
1909	Bos-A	145	546	64	134	12	5	1	38	39		.245	.311	.291	88	-6	27			.952	-0	*O-117,3-13/S-9,2-5	-1.2

YEAR	TM/L	G	AB	R	H	2B	3B	HR	RBI	BB	SO	AVG	OBP	SLG	PRO+	BR/A	SB	CS	SBR	FA	FR	G/POS	TPR
1910	Bos-A	18	57	6	12	3	0	1	3	4		.211	.262	.316	79	-2	1			.920	-0	O-15	-0.3
	Cle-A	70	240	25	51	6	4	1	18	15		.213	.267	.283	72	-8	9			.975	-4	O-50/S-7,3-5	-1.6
	Yr	88	297	31	63	9	4	2	21	19		.212	.266	.290	73	-10	10			.962	-4	O-65/S-7,3-5	-1.9
Total	5	608	2270	278	561	58	24	12	152	163		.247	.306	.310	95	-12	107			.960	-25	O-298,2-214/3-52,S	-5.8

■ **BILL NILES**   Niles, William E.   b: 1/11/1867, Covington, Ky.   d: 7/3/36, Springfield, Ohio   160 lbs.   Deb: 5/13/1895

YEAR	TM/L	G	AB	R	H	2B	3B	HR	RBI	BB	SO	AVG	OBP	SLG	PRO+	BR/A	SB	CS	SBR	FA	FR	G/POS	TPR
1895	Pit-N	11	37	2	8	0	0	0	5	2		.216	.310	.216	39	-1	2			.930	1	3-10/2-1	-0.2

■ **RABBIT NILL**   Nill, George Charles   b: 7/14/1881, Ft.Wayne, Ind.   d: 5/24/62, Fort Wayne, Ind.   BR/TR, 5'7", 160 lbs.   Deb: 9/27/04

YEAR	TM/L	G	AB	R	H	2B	3B	HR	RBI	BB	SO	AVG	OBP	SLG	PRO+	BR/A	SB	CS	SBR	FA	FR	G/POS	TPR
1904	Was-A	15	48	4	8	0	1	0	3	5		.167	.273	.208	54	-2	0			.878	-4	2-15	-0.6
1905	Was-A	103	319	46	58	7	3	3	31	33		.182	.269	.251	68	-11	12			.897	-2	3-52,2-33/S-6	-1.2
1906	Was-A	89	315	37	74	8	2	0	15	47		.235	.340	.273	97	-2	16			.882	5	S-31,2-25,3-15,O-15	0.8
1907	Was-A	66	215	21	47	7	3	0	25	15		.219	.282	.279	86	-3	6			.962	-4	2-39,O-18/3-1	-0.7
	Cle-A	12	43	5	12	1	0	0	2	3		.279	.326	.302	100	0	2			.815	-4	/3-7,S-4	-0.4
	Yr	78	258	26	59	8	3	0	27	18		.229	.289	.283	88	-3	8			.962	-5	2-39,O-18/3-8,S-4	-1.1
1908	Cle-A	11	23	3	5	0	0	0	1	0		.217	.217	.217	41	-2	0			.833	-0	/S-6,O-3,2-1	-0.1
Total	5	296	963	116	204	23	9	3	77	103		.212	.297	.264	82	-17	36			.943	-6	2-113/3-75,S-47,O	-2.2

■ **DAVE NILSSON**   Nilsson, David Wayne   b: 12/14/69, Brisbane, Queensland, Australia   BL/TR, 6'3", 185 lbs.   Deb: 5/18/92

YEAR	TM/L	G	AB	R	H	2B	3B	HR	RBI	BB	SO	AVG	OBP	SLG	PRO+	BR/A	SB	CS	SBR	FA	FR	G/POS	TPR
1992	Mil-A	51	164	15	38	8	0	4	25	17	18	.232	.304	.354	85	-3	2	2	-1	.992	0	C-46/1-3,D-2	-0.1
1993	Mil-A	100	296	35	76	10	2	7	40	37	36	.257	.339	.375	93	-2	3	6	-3	.981	-9	C-91/1-4,D-4	-0.9
1994	Mil-A	109	397	51	109	28	3	12	69	34	61	.275	.332	.451	95	-4	1	0		.994	-5	C-60,D-43/1-5	-0.7
1995	Mil-A	81	263	41	73	12	1	12	53	24	41	.278	.343	.468	103	0	2	0	1	.981	-2	O-58,D-14/1-7,C-2	-0.3
1996	Mil-A	123	453	81	150	33	2	17	84	57	68	.331	.409	.525	127	20	2	3	-1	.965	-2	O-61,D-40,1-24/C-2	0.9
Total	5	464	1573	223	446	91	8	52	271	169	224	.284	.355	.451	105	10	10	11	-4	.987	-18	O-201,O-119,D/1	-1.1

■ **AL NIXON**   Nixon, Albert Richard "Humpty Dumpty"   b: 4/11/1886, Atlantic City, N.J   d: 11/9/60, Opelousas, La.   BR/TL, 5'7.5", 164 lbs.   Deb: 9/4/15

YEAR	TM/L	G	AB	R	H	2B	3B	HR	RBI	BB	SO	AVG	OBP	SLG	PRO+	BR/A	SB	CS	SBR	FA	FR	G/POS	TPR
1915	Bro-N	14	26	3	6	1	0	0	2	4		.231	.286	.269	67	-1	1	1	-0	1.000	-2	O-14	-0.4
1916	Bro-N	1	2	0	2	0	0	0	0	0		1.000	1.000	1.000	501	1	0			.000	-0	/O-1	0.1
1918	Bro-N	6	11	1	5	0	0	0	0	0		.455	.455	.455	178	1	0			1.000	-0	/O-4	0.1
1921	Bos-N	55	138	25	33	6	3	1	9	7	11	.239	.281	.348	69	-7	3	2	-0	.980	-2	O-43	-1.1
1922	Bos-N	86	318	35	84	14	4	2	22	9	19	.264	.284	.352	66	-17	6	6	-2	.975	1	O-79	-2.2
1923	Bos-N	88	321	53	88	12	4	0	19	24	14	.274	.334	.336	81	-9	2	3	-1	.987	-6	O-80	-0.6
1926	Phi-N	93	311	38	91	18	2	4	41	13	20	.293	.323	.402	90	-5	5			.977	-2	O-88	-1.3
1927	Phi-N	54	154	18	48	7	0	0	18	5	5	.312	.333	.357	84	-4	1			.969	-1	O-44	-0.6
1928	Phi-N	25	64	7	15	2	0	0	6	4	4	.234	.300	.266	47	-5	1			1.000	-0	O-20	-0.6
Total	9	422	1345	180	372	60	13	7	118	66	77	.277	.314	.356	78	-45	19	12		.980	-0	O-373	-6.6

■ **TROT NIXON**   Nixon, Christopher Trotman   b: 4/11/74, Durham, N.C.   BL/TL, 6'1", 195 lbs.   Deb: 9/21/96

YEAR	TM/L	G	AB	R	H	2B	3B	HR	RBI	BB	SO	AVG	OBP	SLG	PRO+	BR/A	SB	CS	SBR	FA	FR	G/POS	TPR
1996	Bos-A	2	4	2	2	1	0	0	0	0	1	.500	.500	.750	203	1	1	0	0	1.000	-0	/O-2	0.1

■ **OTIS NIXON**   Nixon, Otis Junior   b: 1/9/59, Columbus Co., N.C.   BB/TR, 6'2", 180 lbs.   Deb: 9/9/83   F

YEAR	TM/L	G	AB	R	H	2B	3B	HR	RBI	BB	SO	AVG	OBP	SLG	PRO+	BR/A	SB	CS	SBR	FA	FR	G/POS	TPR
1983	NY-A	13	14	2	2	0	0	0	0	1	5	.143	.200	.143	-4	-2	2	0	1	.938	-1	/O-9	-0.2
1984	Cle-A	49	91	16	14	0	0	0	1	8	11	.154	.222	.154	6	-11	12	6	0	1.000	-2	O-46	-1.5
1985	Cle-A	104	162	34	38	4	0	3	9	8	27	.235	.271	.315	60	-9	20	11	-1	.971	-7	O-80,D-11	-1.8
1986	Cle-A	105	95	33	25	4	1	0	8	13	12	.263	.352	.356	88	-1	23	6	3	.969	-23	O-95/D-5	-2.2
1987	Cle-A	19	17	2	1	0	0	0	1	3	4	.059	.200	.059	-26	-4	2	3	-1	1.000	-4	O-17/D-2	-0.8
1988	Mon-N	90	271	47	66	8	2	0	15	28	42	.244	.314	.288	71	-9	46	13	6	.994	-2	O-82	-0.8
1989	Mon-N	126	258	41	56	7	2	0	21	33	36	.217	.306	.260	62	-12	37	12	4	.988	-15	O-98	-2.6
1990	Mon-N	119	231	46	58	6	2	1	20	28	33	.251	.332	.307	80	-6	50	13	7	.994	-9	O-88/S-1	-0.9
1991	Atl-N	124	401	81	119	10	1	0	26	47	40	.297	.373	.327	93	-2	72	21	9	.987	2	*O-115	0.6
1992	*Atl-N	120	456	79	134	14	2	2	22	39	54	.294	.349	.346	92	-4	41	18	2	.991	13	*O-111	0.9
1993	*Atl-N	134	461	77	124	12	3	1	24	61	63	.269	.354	.315	80	-11	47	13	6	.990	4	*O-116	0.1
1994	Bos-A	103	398	60	109	15	1	0	25	55	65	.274	.362	.317	74	-14	42	10	7	.989	2	*O-103	-0.7
1995	Tex-A	139	589	87	174	21	2	0	45	58	85	.295	.359	.338	81	-15	50	21	2	.989	5	*O-138	-1.1
1996	Tor-A	125	496	87	142	15	1	1	29	71	68	.286	.377	.327	80	-12	54	13	8	.994	12	*O-125	0.4
Total	14	1370	3940	692	1062	116	17	8	246	453	545	.270	.345	.314	77	-110	498	160	53	.989	-22	*O-1223/D-18,S-1	-10.6

■ **DONELL NIXON**   Nixon, Robert Donell   b: 12/31/61, Evergreen, N.C.   BR/TR, 6'1", 185 lbs.   Deb: 4/7/87   F

YEAR	TM/L	G	AB	R	H	2B	3B	HR	RBI	BB	SO	AVG	OBP	SLG	PRO+	BR/A	SB	CS	SBR	FA	FR	G/POS	TPR
1987	Sea-A	46	132	17	33	4	0	3	12	13	28	.250	.327	.348	75	-5	21	7	2	1.000	0	O-32/D-6	-0.3
1988	SF-N	59	78	15	27	3	0	0	6	10	12	.346	.420	.385	138	4	11	8	-2	.983	-8	O-46	0.3
1989	*SF-N	95	166	23	44	2	0	1	15	11	30	.265	.311	.295	76	-5	10	3	1	.967	-14	O-64	-2.0
1990	Bal-A	8	20	1	5	2	0	0	2	1	7	.250	.286	.350	79	-1	5	0	2	1.000	-1	/O-4,D-3	0.0
Total	4	208	396	56	109	11	0	4	35	35	77	.275	.337	.333	88	-6	47	18	3	.983	-23	O-146/D-9	-3.0

■ **RUSS NIXON**   Nixon, Russell Eugene   b: 2/19/35, Cleves, Ohio   BL/TR, 6'1", 200 lbs.   Deb: 4/20/57   MC

YEAR	TM/L	G	AB	R	H	2B	3B	HR	RBI	BB	SO	AVG	OBP	SLG	PRO+	BR/A	SB	CS	SBR	FA	FR	G/POS	TPR
1957	Cle-A	62	185	15	52	18	0	2	18	12	12	.281	.325	.362	88	-3	0	1	-1	.984	-6	C-57	-0.8
1958	Cle-A	113	376	42	113	17	4	9	46	13	38	.301	.324	.439	111	4	0	3	-2	.991	-10	*C-101	-0.2
1959	Cle-A	82	258	23	62	10	3	1	29	15	28	.240	.282	.314	66	-12	0	0	0	.985	-7	C-74	-1.6
1960	Cle-A	25	82	6	20	5	0	1	6	6	6	.244	.311	.341	79	-2	0	1	-1	.993	-9	C-25	-0.2
	Bos-A	80	272	24	81	17	3	5	33	13	23	.298	.330	.438	102	0	0	1	-1	.987	-17	C-74	-1.3
	Yr	105	354	30	101	22	3	6	39	19	29	.285	.325	.415	97	-2	0	2	-1	.989	-17	C-99	-1.5
1961	Bos-A	87	242	24	70	12	2	1	19	13	19	.289	.331	.368	84	-5	0	1	-1	.975	-3	C-66	-0.6
1962	Bos-A	65	151	11	42	7	2	1	19	8	14	.278	.314	.371	81	-4	0	0	0	1.000	0	C-38	-0.5
1963	Bos-A	98	287	27	77	18	1	5	30	22	32	.268	.329	.390	98	-1	0	1	0	.992	-10	C-76	-0.8
1964	Bos-A	81	163	10	38	7	1	0	20	14	24	.233	.302	.294	64	-8	0	0	0	.990	-4	C-45	-1.0
1965	Bos-A	59	137	11	37	5	1	1	6	11	6	.270	.341	.339	72	-5	0	0	0	.981	-5	C-38	-1.0
1966	Min-A	51	96	5	25	2	1	0	7	7	13	.260	.317	.302	74	-5	0	0	0	.986	-4	C-32	-0.6
1967	Min-A	74	170	16	40	6	1	1	22	18	29	.235	.309	.300	74	-5	0	0	0	.994	-12	C-69	-1.5
1968	Bos-A	29	85	11	13	1	0	0	6	7	13	.153	.217	.176	19	-8	0	0	0	.994	-5	C-27	-1.3
Total	12	906	2504	225	670	115	19	27	266	154	279	.268	.313	.361	84	-53	0	7	-4	.988	-85	C-722	-11.4

■ **RAY NOBLE**   Noble, Rafael Miguel (Magee)   b: 3/15/19, Central Hatillo, Cuba   BR/TR, 5'11", 210 lbs.   Deb: 4/18/51

YEAR	TM/L	G	AB	R	H	2B	3B	HR	RBI	BB	SO	AVG	OBP	SLG	PRO+	BR/A	SB	CS	SBR	FA	FR	G/POS	TPR
1951	*NY-N	55	141	16	33	6	0	5	26	6	26	.234	.265	.383	72	-6	0	0	0	.974	-5	C-41	-0.9
1952	NY-N	6	5	0	0	0	0	0	0	0	2	.000	.000	.000	-99	-1	0	0	0	1.000	0	/C-5	-0.1
1953	NY-N	46	97	15	20	0	1	4	14	19	14	.206	.353	.351	83	-2	1	0	0	.982	-1	C-41	-0.1
Total	3	107	243	31	53	6	1	9	40	25	41	.218	.299	.362	74	-9	1	0	0	.979	-5	/C-87	-1.1

■ **JUNIOR NOBOA**   Noboa, Milciades Arturo (Diaz)   b: 11/10/64, Azua, D.R.   BR/TR, 5'10", 160 lbs.   Deb: 8/22/84

YEAR	TM/L	G	AB	R	H	2B	3B	HR	RBI	BB	SO	AVG	OBP	SLG	PRO+	BR/A	SB	CS	SBR	FA	FR	G/POS	TPR
1984	Cle-A	23	11	3	4	0	0	0	0	0	2	.364	.364	.364	100	0	1	0	0	1.000	4	2-19/D-1	0.4
1987	Cle-A	39	80	7	18	2	1	0	7	3	6	.225	.253	.275	40	-7	1	0	0	.983	4	2-21/S-8,3-5,D-1	-0.2
1988	Cal-A	21	16	4	1	0	0	0	0	0	0	.063	.063	.063	-67	-4	0	0	0	.967	9	/2-9,S-3,3-2	0.5
1989	Mon-N	21	44	3	10	2	0	0	1	1	3	.227	.244	.227	35	-5	0	0	0	1.000	4	2-13/S-4,3-1	0.4
1990	Mon-N	81	158	15	42	7	0	0	14	7	14	.266	.301	.335	78	-5	4	1	1	1.000	-17	2-31/O-9,3-8,S-7,P	-2.2
1991	Mon-N	67	95	5	23	0	1	0	9	0	5	.242	.250	.305	56	-6	2	3	-1	1.000	-3	/O-7,2-6,3-2,S-2	-1.0
1992	NY-N	46	47	7	7	0	0	0	3	3	8	.149	.216	.149	-5	-6	0	0	0	.977	2	2-16/3-3,S-2	0.0
1994	Oak-A	17	40	3	13	1	0	0	6	2	5	.325	.357	.400	104	0	1	0	0	.943	2	2-14/S-1	0.2
	Pit-N											.000	.000	.000	-99	-1	0	0	0			/S-1	
Total	8	317	493	47	118	13	4	0	33	17	47	.239	.268	.288	54	-31	9	4	0	.981	10	2-129/S-28,3O,D1P	-2.0

■ **PAUL NOCE**   Noce, Paul David   b: 12/16/59, San Francisco, Cal.   BR/TR, 5'10", 175 lbs.   Deb: 6/1/87

YEAR	TM/L	G	AB	R	H	2B	3B	HR	RBI	BB	SO	AVG	OBP	SLG	PRO+	BR/A	SB	CS	SBR	FA	FR	G/POS	TPR
1987	Chi-N	70	180	17	41	6	4	3	14	6	49	.228	.261	.350	58	-11	5	3	-0	.983	19	2-36,S-35/3-2	1.0

YEAR	TM/L	G	AB	R	H	2B	3B	HR	RBI	BB	SO	AVG	OBP	SLG	PRO+	BR/A	SB	CS	SBR	FA	FR	G/POS	TPR
1990	Cin-N	1	1	0	1	0	0	0	0	0	0	1.000	1.000	1.000	434	0	0	0	0	.000	0	/H	0.0
Total	2	71	181	17	42	9	2	3	14	6	49	.232	.265	.354	60	-11	5	3	-0	.983	19	/2-36,S-35,3-2	1.0

■ GEORGE NOFTSKER
Noftsker, George Washington b: 8/24/1859, Shippensburg, Pa. d: 5/8/31, Shippensburg, Pa. BR/TR, 5'8", 135 lbs. Deb: 4/17/1884

YEAR	TM/L	G	AB	R	H	2B	3B	HR	RBI	BB	SO	AVG	OBP	SLG	PRO+	BR/A	SB	CS	SBR	FA	FR	G/POS	TPR
1884	Alt-U	7	25	0	1	0	0	0		0		.040	.040	.040	-75	-6				.818	1	/O-5,C-3	-0.4

■ MATT NOKES
Nokes, Matthew Dodge b: 10/31/63, San Diego, Cal. BL/TR, 6'1", 185 lbs. Deb: 9/3/85

YEAR	TM/L	G	AB	R	H	2B	3B	HR	RBI	BB	SO	AVG	OBP	SLG	PRO+	BR/A	SB	CS	SBR	FA	FR	G/POS	TPR
1985	SF-N	19	53	3	11	2	0	2	5	1	9	.208	.236	.358	67	-3	0	0	0	.977	-1	C-14	-0.3
1986	Det-A	7	24	2	8	1	0	1	2	1	1	.333	.360	.500	132	1	0	0	0	1.000	2	/C-7	0.3
1987	*Det-A★	135	461	69	133	14	2	32	87	35	70	.289	.347	.536	135	22	2	1	0	.992	-9	*C-109,D-19/O-3,3-2	1.8
1988	Det-A	122	382	53	96	18	0	16	53	34	58	.251	.314	.424	109	4	0	1	-1	.989	-3	*C-110/D-4	0.8
1989	Det-A	87	268	15	67	10	0	9	39	17	37	.250	.300	.388	95	-3	1	0	0	.978	-6	C-51,D-33	-0.7
1990	Det-A	44	111	12	30	5	1	3	8	4	14	.270	.308	.414	99	-0	0	0	0	.984	-3	C-24,C-19	-0.3
	NY-A	92	240	21	57	4	0	8	32	20	33	.237	.307	.354	84	-5	2	2	-1	.995	-7	C-46,D-30/O-2	-1.2
	Yr	136	351	33	87	9	1	11	40	24	47	.248	.307	.373	89	-6	2	2	-1	.993	-10	C-65,D-54/O-2	-1.5
1991	NY-A	135	456	52	122	20	0	24	77	25	49	.268	.313	.469	113	6	3	2	-0	.992	-14	*C-130/D-3	-0.1
1992	NY-A	121	384	42	86	9	1	22	59	37	62	.224	.297	.424	101	-1	0	1	-1	.993	-11	*C-111	-0.6
1993	NY-A	76	217	25	54	8	0	10	35	16	31	.249	.306	.424	97	-2	0	0	0	.992	-5	C-56,D-11	-0.4
1994	NY-A	28	79	11	23	3	0	7	19	5	16	.291	.333	.595	138	4	0	0	0	.975	0	C-17/1-4,D-5	0.4
1995	Bal-A	26	49	4	6	1	0	2	6	4	11	.122	.189	.265	16	-6	0	0	0	.989	3	C-16/D-2	-0.2
	Col-N	10	11	1	2	1	0	0	1	0	4	.182	.250	.273	29	-1	0	0	0	.909	-0	/C-3	-0.1
Total	11	902	2735	310	695	96	4	136	422	200	395	.254	.311	.441	106	15	8	7	-2	.990	-53	C-689,D-131/O-5,13	-0.6

■ JOE NOLAN
Nolan, Joseph William b: 5/12/51, St.Louis, Mo. BL/TR, 6', 190 lbs. Deb: 9/21/72

YEAR	TM/L	G	AB	R	H	2B	3B	HR	RBI	BB	SO	AVG	OBP	SLG	PRO+	BR/A	SB	CS	SBR	FA	FR	G/POS	TPR
1972	NY-N	4	10	0	0	0	0	0	0	1	3	.000	.091	.000	-74	-2	0	0	0	.938	-1	/C-3	-0.3
1975	Atl-N	4	4	0	1	0	0	0	0	1	0	.250	.400	.250	80	-0	0	0	0	1.000	-0	/C-1	0.0
1977	Atl-N	62	82	13	23	3	0	3	9	13	12	.280	.379	.427	103	1	1	0	0	1.000	-1	C-19	-0.1
1978	Atl-N	95	213	22	49	7	3	4	22	34	28	.230	.339	.347	83	-4	3	2	-0	.979	-6	C-61	-1.0
1979	Atl-N	89	230	28	57	9	3	4	21	27	28	.248	.335	.365	85	-4	1	3	-2	.983	-7	C-74	-1.1
1980	Atl-N	17	22	2	6	1	0	0	2	2	4	.273	.333	.318	80	-1	0	0	0	1.000	1	/C-6	0.1
	Cin-N	53	154	14	48	7	0	3	24	13	8	.312	.365	.416	117	4	0	0	0	.982	1	C-51	0.7
	Yr	70	176	16	54	8	0	3	26	15	12	.307	.361	.403	112	3	0	0	0	.983	2	C-57	0.8
1981	Cin-N	81	236	25	73	18	1	1	26	24	19	.309	.373	.407	120	7	1	2	-1	.995	-11	C-81	-0.3
1982	Bal-A	77	219	24	51	7	1	6	35	16	35	.233	.285	.356	75	-8	1	1	-0	.978	-3	C-72	-0.9
1983	*Bal-A	73	184	25	51	11	1	5	24	16	31	.277	.342	.429	113	3	0	0	0	.980	-10	C-65	-0.5
1984	Bal-A	35	62	2	18	1	1	1	9	12	10	.290	.405	.387	123	3	0	0	0	.962	-1	D-11/C-6	0.2
1985	Bal-A	31	38	1	5	2	0	0	6	5	5	.132	.233	.184	16	-4	0	0	0	1.000	1	/C-5,D-4	-0.4
Total	11	621	1454	156	382	66	10	27	178	164	183	.263	.340	.378	95	-7	7	8	-3	.984	-37	C-444/D-15	-3.4

■ RED NONNENKAMP
Nonnenkamp, Leo William b: 7/7/11, St.Louis, Mo. BL/TL, 5'11", 165 lbs. Deb: 9/6/33

YEAR	TM/L	G	AB	R	H	2B	3B	HR	RBI	BB	SO	AVG	OBP	SLG	PRO+	BR/A	SB	CS	SBR	FA	FR	G/POS	TPR
1933	Pit-N	1	1	0	0	0	0	0	0	0	1	.000	.000	.000	-99	-0	0			.000	0	H	0.0
1938	Bos-A	87	180	37	51	4	1	0	18	21	13	.283	.358	.317	67	-8	6	1	1	.968	2	O-39/1-5	-0.6
1939	Bos-A	58	75	12	18	2	1	0	5	12	6	.240	.345	.293	62	-4	0	1	-1	.962	-3	O-15	-0.7
1940	Bos-A	9	7	0	0	0	0	0	1	0	4	.000	.125	.000	-62	-2	0	0	0	.000	0	H	-0.2
Total	4	155	263	49	69	6	2	0	24	33	24	.262	.347	.300	62	-14	6	2		.966	-1	/O-54,1-5	-1.5

■ PETE NOONAN
Noonan, Peter John b: 11/24/1881, W.Stockbridge, Mass. d: 2/11/65, Great Barrington, Mass. BR/TR, 6', 180 lbs. Deb: 6/20/04

YEAR	TM/L	G	AB	R	H	2B	3B	HR	RBI	BB	SO	AVG	OBP	SLG	PRO+	BR/A	SB	CS	SBR	FA	FR	G/POS	TPR
1904	Phi-A	39	114	13	23	3	1	2	13	1		.202	.209	.298	56	-6	1			.969	-4	C-22,1-10	-0.9
1906	Chi-N	5	3	0	1	0	0	0	0	0		.333	.333	.333	102	-0	0			1.000	0	/1-1	0.0
	StL-N	44	125	8	21	1	3	1	9	11		.168	.235	.248	53	-7	1			.957	3	C-23,1-16	-0.2
	Yr	49	128	8	22	1	3	1	9	11		.172	.237	.250	54	-7	1			.957	3	C-23,1-17	-0.2
1907	StL-N	74	237	19	53	7	3	1	16	9		.224	.252	.291	73	-9	3			.951	3	C-70	0.1
Total	3	162	479	40	98	11	7	4	38	21		.205	.238	.282	64	-22	5			.955	2	C-115/1-27	-1.0

■ TIM NORDBROOK
Nordbrook, Timothy Charles b: 7/7/49, Baltimore, Md. BR/TR, 6'1", 180 lbs. Deb: 9/13/74

YEAR	TM/L	G	AB	R	H	2B	3B	HR	RBI	BB	SO	AVG	OBP	SLG	PRO+	BR/A	SB	CS	SBR	FA	FR	G/POS	TPR
1974	Bal-A	6	15	4	4	0	0	0	1	2	2	.267	.353	.267	83	-0	1	0	0	1.000	1	/S-5,2-1	0.2
1975	Bal-A	40	34	6	4	0	0	0	0	7	7	.118	.268	.147	21	-3	0	0	0	.970	5	S-37/2-3	0.3
1976	Bal-A	27	22	4	5	0	0	0	3	5	.227	.320	.227	66	-1	0	0	0	1.000	3	2-14,S-12	0.3
	Cal-A	5	8	1	0	0	0	0	0	1	3	.000	.111	.000	-70	-2	1	0	0	.941	2	/S-4,2-1,D-1	0.1
	Yr	32	30	5	5	0	0	0	0	4	8	.167	.265	.167	30	-3	1	0	0	.978	5	S-16,2-15/D-1	0.4
1977	Chi-A	15	20	2	5	0	0	0	1	7	4	.250	.444	.250	95	0	1	0	0	.850	-2	S-11/3-1,D-2	0.0
	Tor-A	24	63	9	11	0	1	0	1	4	11	.175	.224	.206	18	-7	1	0	0	.989	1	S-24	-0.4
	Yr	39	83	11	16	0	1	0	2	11	15	.193	.287	.217	39	-7	2	0	1	.947	-1	S-35/D-2,3-1	-0.4
1978	Tor-A	7	0	1	0	0	0	0	0	0	0	—	1.000	—	200	0	0	0	0	1.000	2	/S-7	0.2
	Mil-A	2	5	0	0	0	0	0	0	1	1	.000	.167	.000	-49	-1	0	0	0	.909	0	/S-2	0.0
	Yr	9	5	1	0	0	0	0	0	1	1	.000	.286	.000	-13	-1	0	0	0	.941	2	/S-9	0.2
1979	Mil-A	2	2	0	1	0	0	0	0	0	0	.500	.500	.500	171	0	0	0	0	1.000	-1	/S-2	0.0
Total	6	128	169	27	30	1	1	0	3	25	33	.178	.287	.195	38	-13	4	0	1	.961	12	S-104/2-19,D-3,3-1	0.7

■ WAYNE NORDHAGEN
Nordhagen, Wayne Oren b: 7/4/48, Thief River Falls, Minn. BR/TR, 6'2", 205 lbs. Deb: 7/16/76

YEAR	TM/L	G	AB	R	H	2B	3B	HR	RBI	BB	SO	AVG	OBP	SLG	PRO+	BR/A	SB	CS	SBR	FA	FR	G/POS	TPR
1976	Chi-A	22	53	6	10	2	0	1	6	2	8	.189	.246	.226	39	-4	0	0	0	1.000	0	O-10/C-5,D-6	-0.4
1977	Chi-A	52	124	16	39	7	3	4	22	2	12	.315	.325	.516	125	4	1	0	0	.944	-10	O-46/C-3,D-2	-0.7
1978	Chi-A	68	206	28	62	16	0	5	35	5	18	.301	.318	.451	113	3	0	1	-1	.941	-8	O-36,D-16,C-12	-0.8
1979	Chi-A	78	193	20	54	15	0	7	25	13	22	.280	.325	.466	111	2	0	0	0	1.000	-0	D-47,O-12/C-5,P-2	-0.9
1980	Chi-A	123	415	45	115	22	4	15	59	14	45	.277	.296	.458	104	0	0	0	0	.969	-5	O-74,D-32	-0.9
1981	Chi-A	65	208	19	64	8	1	6	33	10	25	.308	.342	.442	127	7	0	1	-1	.947	-7	O-60	-0.2
1982	Tor-A	44	115	8	32	3	0	1	14	9	13	.278	.331	.330	75	-4	0	2	-1	1.000	-1	D-32,O-10	-0.7
	Pit-N	1	4	0	2	0	0	0	2	0	1	.500	.500	.500	175	0	0	0	0	1.000	0	/O-1	0.0
	Tor-A	28	70	4	18	1	0	1	9	5	9	.257	.268	.300	51	-5	0	0	0	1.000	0	D-28	-0.6
1983	Chi-N	21	35	1	5	1	0	1	4	0	5	.143	.167	.257	15	-4	0	0	0	1.000	-1	/O-7	-0.6
Total	8	502	1423	147	401	77	8	39	205	54	162	.282	.309	.429	101	-1	1	5	-3	.962	-31	O-256,D-163/C-25,P	-4.9

■ LOU NORDYKE
Nordyke, Louis Ellis b: 8/7/1876, Brighton, Iowa d: 9/27/45, Los Angeles, Cal. BR/TR, 6', 185 lbs. Deb: 4/18/06

YEAR	TM/L	G	AB	R	H	2B	3B	HR	RBI	BB	SO	AVG	OBP	SLG	PRO+	BR/A	SB	CS	SBR	FA	FR	G/POS	TPR
1906	StL-A	25	53	4	13	1	0	0	7	10		.245	.365	.264	102	1	3			.942	-3	1-12	-0.2

■ IRV NOREN
Noren, Irving Arnold b: 11/29/24, Jamestown, N.Y. BL/TL, 6', 190 lbs. Deb: 4/18/50 C

YEAR	TM/L	G	AB	R	H	2B	3B	HR	RBI	BB	SO	AVG	OBP	SLG	PRO+	BR/A	SB	CS	SBR	FA	FR	G/POS	TPR
1950	Was-A	138	542	80	160	27	10	14	98	67	77	.295	.375	.459	118	14	5	2	0	.984	16	*O-121,1-17	2.3
1951	Was-A	129	509	82	142	33	5	8	86	51	35	.279	.345	.411	105	3	10	7	-1	.978	21	*O-126	1.8
1952	Was-A	12	49	4	12	3	1	0	2	6	3	.245	.327	.347	91	-1	1	0	0	1.000	3	O-12	0.2
	*NY-A	93	272	36	64	13	2	5	21	26	34	.235	.314	.353	91	-4	4	2	0	1.000	-7	O-60,1-19	-1.4
	Yr	105	321	40	76	16	3	5	23	32	37	.237	.318	.352	91	-4	5	2	0	1.000	-4	O-72,1-19	-1.2
1953	*NY-A	109	345	55	92	12	6	6	46	42	39	.267	.350	.388	103	1	3	3	-0	.991	-1	O-96	-0.4
1954	NY-A★	125	426	70	136	21	6	12	66	43	38	.319	.383	.481	140	23	4	6	-2	.980	-1	*O-116/1-1	1.5
1955	*NY-A	132	371	49	94	19	1	8	59	43	33	.253	.336	.375	92	-4	3	0	0	.980	-0	*O-126	-0.9
1956	NY-A	29	37	4	8	1	0	0	6	12	7	.216	.408	.243	78	-0	0	0	0	.875	-2	O-10/1-1	-0.3
1957	KC-A	81	160	8	34	8	0	6	11	19	19	.213	.287	.300	54	-10	0	0	0	.990	-2	1-25/O-6	-1.4
	StL-N	17	30	3	11	4	1	0	1	10	4	.367	.441	.667	189	4	0	1	-1	1.000	-2	/O-8	0.1
1958	StL-N	117	178	24	47	9	1	4	22	13	21	.264	.328	.393	87	-3	0	1	-1	.974	-17	O-77	-2.3
1959	StL-N	8	8	0	1	0	0	0	0	0	2	.125	.125	.250	-3	-0	0	0	0	1.000	-0	/O-2,1-1	-0.2
	Chi-N	65	156	27	50	6	0	4	19	13	24	.321	.384	.462	125	6	2	0	1	1.000	3	O-40/1-1	0.8
	Yr	73	164	27	51	6	0	4	19	13	26	.311	.372	.451	118	4	2	0	1	1.000	2	O-42/1-2	0.6

YEAR	TM/L	G	AB	R	H	2B	3B	HR	RBI	BB	SO	AVG	OBP	SLG	PRO+	BR/A	SB	CS	SBR	FA	FR	G/POS	TPR
1960	Chi-N	12	11	0	1	0	0	0	1	3	4	.091	.286	.091	9	-1	0	0	0	.833	-1	/1-1,O-1	-0.2
	LA-N	26	25	1	5	0	0	1	1	1	8	.200	.231	.320	46	-2	0	0	0	.000	-1	H	-0.2
	Yr	38	36	1	6	0	0	1	2	4	12	.167	.250	.250	36	-3	0	0	0	1.000	-1	/1-1,O-1	-0.4
Total	11	1093	3119	443	857	157	35	65	453	335	350	.275	.349	.410	106	23	34	24	-4	.984	10	O-801/1-66	-0.6

■ DAN NORMAN
Norman, Daniel Edmund   b: 1/11/55, Los Angeles, Cal.   BR/TR, 6'2", 195 lbs.   Deb: 9/27/77

YEAR	TM/L	G	AB	R	H	2B	3B	HR	RBI	BB	SO	AVG	OBP	SLG	PRO+	BR/A	SB	CS	SBR	FA	FR	G/POS	TPR
1977	NY-N	7	16	2	4	1	0	0	0	4	2	.250	.400	.313	99	-1	0	0	0	1.000	-1	/O-6	-0.1
1978	NY-N	19	64	7	17	0	1	4	10	2	14	.266	.288	.484	116	1	1	0	0	1.000	-1	O-18	0.0
1979	NY-N	44	110	9	27	3	1	3	11	10	26	.245	.314	.373	90	-2	2	0	1	.967	-0	O-33	-0.3
1980	NY-N	69	92	5	17	1	1	2	9	6	14	.185	.235	.283	45	-7	5	0	2	1.000	-0	O-19	-0.9
1982	Mon-N	53	66	6	14	3	0	2	7	7	20	.212	.288	.348	76	-2	0	1	-1	.969	-6	O-31	-0.9
Total	5	192	348	29	79	8	3	11	37	29	76	.227	.288	.362	81	-10	8	1	2	.981	-11	O-107	-2.2

■ BILL NORMAN
Norman, Henry Willis Patrick   b: 7/16/10, St.Louis, Mo.   d: 4/21/62, Milwaukee, Wis.   BR/TR, 6'2", 190 lbs.   Deb: 8/8/31   MC

YEAR	TM/L	G	AB	R	H	2B	3B	HR	RBI	BB	SO	AVG	OBP	SLG	PRO+	BR/A	SB	CS	SBR	FA	FR	G/POS	TPR
1931	Chi-A	24	55	7	10	2	0	0	6	4	10	.182	.237	.218	22	-6	0	1	-1	.933	-1	O-17	-0.8
1932	Chi-A	13	48	6	11	3	1	0	2	2	3	.229	.260	.333	56	-3	0	0	0	.917	-2	O-13	-0.6
Total	2	37	103	13	21	5	1	0	8	6	13	.204	.248	.272	38	-10	0	1	-1	.928	-3	/O-30	-1.4

■ LES NORMAN
Norman, Leslie Eugene   b: 2/25/69, Warren, Mich.   BR/TR, 6'1", 185 lbs.   Deb: 5/29/95

YEAR	TM/L	G	AB	R	H	2B	3B	HR	RBI	BB	SO	AVG	OBP	SLG	PRO+	BR/A	SB	CS	SBR	FA	FR	G/POS	TPR
1995	KC-A	24	40	6	9	1	0	0	4	6	6	.225	.326	.275	58	-2	0	1	-1	.958	-2	O-17/D-5	-0.5
1996	KC-A	54	49	9	6	0	0	0	6	4	14	.122	.232	.122	-7	-8	1	1	-0	1.000	-7	O-38/D-7	-1.4
Total	2	78	89	15	15	1	0	0	4	12	20	.169	.275	.191	22	-10	1	2	-1	.986	-9	/O-55,D-12	-1.9

■ NELSON NORMAN
Norman, Nelson Augusto   b: 5/23/58, San Pedro De Macoris, D.R.   BB/TR, 6'2", 160 lbs.   Deb: 5/20/78

YEAR	TM/L	G	AB	R	H	2B	3B	HR	RBI	BB	SO	AVG	OBP	SLG	PRO+	BR/A	SB	CS	SBR	FA	FR	G/POS	TPR
1978	Tex-A	23	34	1	9	2	0	0	1	0	5	.265	.265	.324	64	-2	0	0	0	.984	10	S-18/3-6	0.9
1979	Tex-A	147	343	36	76	9	3	0	21	19	41	.222	.262	.265	43	-27	4	1	1	.952	-16	*S-142/2-1	-3.0
1980	Tex-A	17	32	4	7	0	0	0	0	1	1	.219	.242	.219	28	-3	0	1	-1	.943	7	S-17	0.4
1981	Tex-A	7	13	1	3	1	0	0	2	1	2	.231	.286	.308	75	-0	0	0	0	.963	3	/S-5	0.3
1982	Pit-N	3	3	0	0	0	0	0	0	0	0	.000	.000	.000	-97	-1	0	0	0	.000	-1	/2-2,S-1	-0.2
1987	Mon-N	1	4	0	0	0	0	0	0	0	0	.000	.000	.000	-97	-1	0	0	0	.667	-1	/S-1	-0.2
Total	6	198	429	42	95	12	3	0	25	21	50	.221	.258	.263	42	-34	4	2	0	.954	-1	S-184/3-6,2-3	-1.8

■ JIM NORRIS
Norris, James Francis   b: 12/20/48, Brooklyn, N.Y.   BL/TL, 5'10", 175 lbs.   Deb: 4/7/77

YEAR	TM/L	G	AB	R	H	2B	3B	HR	RBI	BB	SO	AVG	OBP	SLG	PRO+	BR/A	SB	CS	SBR	FA	FR	G/POS	TPR
1977	Cle-A	133	440	59	119	23	6	2	37	64	57	.270	.363	.364	102	3	26	17	-2	.982	12	*O-124/1-3	0.8
1978	Cle-A	113	315	41	89	14	5	2	27	42	20	.283	.367	.378	111	6	12	7	-1	.988	0	O-78,D-15/1-6	0.2
1979	Cle-A	124	353	50	87	15	6	3	30	44	35	.246	.330	.348	83	-8	15	10	-2	.982	0	O-93,D-13	-1.3
1980	Tex-A	119	174	23	43	5	0	0	16	23	16	.247	.335	.276	72	-6	6	3	0	1.000	-18	O-82,1-10/D-1	-2.6
Total	4	489	1282	173	338	57	17	7	110	173	128	.264	.351	.351	95	-5	59	37	-5	.985	-5	O-377/D-29,1-19	-2.9

■ LEO NORRIS
Norris, Leo John   b: 5/17/08, Bay St.Louis, Miss   d: 2/13/87, Zachary, La.   BR/TR, 5'11", 165 lbs.   Deb: 4/14/36

YEAR	TM/L	G	AB	R	H	2B	3B	HR	RBI	BB	SO	AVG	OBP	SLG	PRO+	BR/A	SB	CS	SBR	FA	FR	G/POS	TPR
1936	Phi-N	154	581	64	154	27	4	11	76	39	79	.265	.315	.382	79	-18	4			.936	-8	*S-121,2-38	-1.6
1937	Phi-N	116	381	45	98	24	3	9	36	21	53	.257	.296	.407	82	-11	3			.949	-12	2-74,3-24,S-20	-1.7
Total	2	270	962	109	252	51	7	20	112	60	132	.262	.307	.392	80	-29	7			.940	-21	S-141,2-112/3-24	-3.3

■ BILLY NORTH
North, William Alex   b: 5/15/48, Seattle, Wash.   BB/TR, 5'11", 185 lbs.   Deb: 9/3/71

YEAR	TM/L	G	AB	R	H	2B	3B	HR	RBI	BB	SO	AVG	OBP	SLG	PRO+	BR/A	SB	CS	SBR	FA	FR	G/POS	TPR
1971	Chi-N	8	16	3	6	0	0	0	0	4	6	.375	.524	.375	138	1	1	1	-0	1.000	-2	/O-6	-0.1
1972	Chi-N	66	127	22	23	2	3	0	4	13	33	.181	.262	.244	40	-10	6	0	2	.955	-8	O-48	-1.9
1973	Oak-A	146	554	98	158	10	5	5	34	78	89	.285	.376	.348	111	11	53	20	4	.980	24	*O-138/D-6	3.3
1974	*Oak-A	149	543	79	141	20	5	4	33	69	86	.260	.348	.337	105	5	**54**	26	1	.991	18	*O-138/D-8	1.9
1975	*Oak-A	140	524	74	143	17	5	4	43	81	80	.273	.374	.330	103	6	30	12	2	.975	20	*O-138/D-1	2.2
1976	Oak-A	154	590	91	163	20	5	2	31	73	95	.276	.358	.337	109	9	**75**	29	5	.978	6	*O-144/D-8	1.5
1977	Oak-A	56	184	32	48	3	3	1	9	32	25	.261	.376	.326	95	0	17	13	-3	.983	-4	O-52/D-1	-0.8
1978	Oak-A	24	52	5	11	4	0	0	5	9	13	.212	.349	.288	86	-1	3	2	0	1.000	-2	O-17	-0.4
	*LA-N	110	304	54	71	10	0	0	10	65	48	.234	.372	.266	81	-4	27	8	3	.975	-2	*O-103	-0.7
1979	SF-N	142	460	87	119	15	4	5	30	96	84	.259	.388	.341	108	10	58	24	3	.987	9	*O-130	1.0
1980	SF-N	128	415	73	104	12	1	1	19	81	78	.251	.374	.292	90	-1	45	19	2	.982	10	*O-115	0.7
1981	SF-N	46	131	22	29	7	0	1	12	26	28	.221	.354	.298	88	-1	26	8	3	.966	-2	O-37	-0.2
Total	11	1169	3900	640	1016	120	31	20	230	627	665	.261	.366	.323	99	26	395	162	21	.981	61	*O-1066/D-24	6.5

■ HUB NORTHEN
Northen, Hubbard Elwin   b: 8/16/1885, Atlanta, Tex.   d: 10/1/47, Shreveport, La.   BL/TL, 5'8", 175 lbs.   Deb: 9/10/10

YEAR	TM/L	G	AB	R	H	2B	3B	HR	RBI	BB	SO	AVG	OBP	SLG	PRO+	BR/A	SB	CS	SBR	FA	FR	G/POS	TPR
1910	StL-A	26	96	6	19	1	0	0	16	5		.198	.238	.208	42	-6	2			.926	-1	O-26	-1.1
1911	Cin-N	1	0	0	0	0	0	0	0	0		—	—	—	—	0	0			.000	0	H	0.0
	Bro-N	19	76	16	24	2	2	0	1	14	9	.316	.429	.395	137	5	4			.911	2	O-19	0.5
	Yr	20	76	16	24	2	2	0	1	14	9	.316	.429	.395	137	5	4			.911	2	O-19	0.5
1912	Bro-N	118	412	54	116	26	6	3	46	41	46	.282	.352	.396	109	5	8			.950	-7	*O-102	-0.8
Total	3	164	584	76	159	29	8	3	63	60	<u>55</u>	.272	.345	.365	103	3	14			.939	-7	O-147	-1.4

■ RON NORTHEY
Northey, Ronald James   b: 4/26/20, Mahanoy City, Pa.   d: 4/16/71, Pittsburgh, Pa.   BL/TR, 5'10", 195 lbs.   Deb: 4/14/42   FC

YEAR	TM/L	G	AB	R	H	2B	3B	HR	RBI	BB	SO	AVG	OBP	SLG	PRO+	BR/A	SB	CS	SBR	FA	FR	G/POS	TPR
1942	Phi-N	127	402	31	101	13	2	5	31	28	33	.251	.300	.331	89	-7	2			.952	1	*O-109	-1.2
1943	Phi-N	147	586	72	163	31	5	16	68	51	52	.278	.339	.430	127	17	2			.978	3	*O-145	1.4
1944	Phi-N	152	570	72	164	35	9	22	104	67	51	.288	.367	.496	146	33	1			.981	4	*O-151	3.0
1946	Phi-N	128	438	55	109	24	6	16	62	39	59	.249	.313	.441	116	6	1			.971	-6	*O-111	-0.6
1947	Phi-N	13	47	7	12	3	0	0	3	6	3	.255	.340	.319	79	-1	1			1.000	-1	O-13	-0.3
	StL-N	110	311	52	91	19	3	15	63	48	29	.293	.391	.518	133	15	0			.949	-12	O-94/3-2	0.4
	Yr	123	358	59	103	22	3	15	66	54	32	.288	.384	.492	127	14	1			.955	-13	O-107/3-2	-0.3
1948	StL-N	96	246	40	79	10	1	13	64	38	25	.321	.420	.528	147	17	0			.989	-10	O-67	0.4
1949	StL-N	90	265	28	69	18	2	7	50	31	15	.260	.338	.423	98	-1	0			.980	-11	O-73	-1.5
1950	Cin-N	27	77	11	20	5	0	5	15	6		.260	.380	.519	134	4	0			.955	-5	O-24	-0.2
	Chi-A	53	114	11	32	9	0	4	20	10	9	.281	.339	.465	110	1	0			.976	-1	O-27	-0.0
	Yr	80	191	22	52	14	0	9	29	25	15	.272	.356	.487	120	5	0			.969	-6	O-51	-0.2
1952	Chi-A	1	1	0	0	0	0	0	0	0	0	.000	.000	.000	-99	-0	0			.000	0	H	0.0
1955	Chi-A	14	14	1	5	2	0	1	4	3	3	.357	.471	.714	209	2	0	0	0	1.000	-1	/O-2	0.0
1956	Chi-A	53	48	4	17	2	0	3	23	8	1	.354	.446	.583	168	5	0	0	0	1.000	-1	/O-4	0.4
1957	Chi-A	40	27	0	5	1	0	0	7	11	5	.185	.421	.222	80	0	0	0	0	.000	0	H	0.1
	Phi-N	33	26	1	7	0	0	1	6	5	6	.269	.406	.385	118	1	0			.000	0	H	0.1
Total	12	1084	3172	385	874	172	28	108	513	361	297	.276	.352	.450	124	93	7	<u>0</u>		.972	-38	O-820/3-2	1.7

■ SCOTT NORTHEY
Northey, Scott Richard   b: 10/15/46, Philadelphia, Pa.   BR/TR, 6', 175 lbs.   Deb: 9/2/69   F

YEAR	TM/L	G	AB	R	H	2B	3B	HR	RBI	BB	SO	AVG	OBP	SLG	PRO+	BR/A	SB	CS	SBR	FA	FR	G/POS	TPR
1969	KC-A	20	61	11	16	2	2	1	7	7	19	.262	.338	.410	108	1	6	3	0	.973	-0	O-18	-0.1

■ JIM NORTHRUP
Northrup, James Thomas   b: 11/24/39, Breckenridge, Mich.   BL/TR, 6'3", 190 lbs.   Deb: 9/30/64

YEAR	TM/L	G	AB	R	H	2B	3B	HR	RBI	BB	SO	AVG	OBP	SLG	PRO+	BR/A	SB	CS	SBR	FA	FR	G/POS	TPR
1964	Det-A	5	12	1	1	0	0	0	0	0	3	.083	.083	.083	-32	-2	1	0	0	1.000	-1	/O-2	-0.3
1965	Det-A	80	219	20	45	12	3	2	16	12	50	.205	.253	.315	60	-12	1	1	-0	.976	-4	O-54	-1.9
1966	Det-A	123	419	53	111	24	6	16	58	33	52	.265	.325	.465	121	11	4	7	-3	.980	10	*O-113	1.3
1967	Det-A	144	495	63	134	18	6	10	61	43	83	.271	.333	.392	110	6	7	1	2	.972	-20	*O-143	-2.0
1968	*Det-A	154	580	76	153	29	7	21	90	50	87	.264	.326	.447	129	19	4	5	-2	.979	8	*O-151	1.9
1969	Det-A	148	543	79	160	31	5	25	66	52	83	.295	.360	.508	135	23	4	2	0	.985	4	*O-143	2.0
1970	Det-A	139	504	71	132	21	3	24	80	56	78	.262	.336	.458	119	13	3	6	-3	.993	3	*O-136	0.9
1971	Det-A	136	459	72	124	27	2	16	71	60	43	.270	.357	.442	121	13	7	4	0	.981	-20	*O-108,1-32	-1.6
1972	*Det-A	134	426	40	111	15	2	8	42	38	52	.261	.324	.362	101	0	4	4	-1	.978	-16	*O-127/1-2	-2.8
1973	Det-A	119	404	55	124	14	7	12	44	38	41	.307	.368	.465	125	13	2	4	-1	.982	-9	*O-116	-0.2
1974	Det-A	97	376	41	89	12	1	11	42	36	46	.237	.303	.362	88	-6	0	0	0	.973	3	O-97	-0.8

YEAR	TM/L	G	AB	R	H	2B	3B	HR	RBI	BB	SO	AVG	OBP	SLG	PRO+	BR/A	SB	CS	SBR	FA	FR	G/POS	TPR
	Mon-N	21	54	3	13	1	0	2	8	5	9	.241	.305	.370	84	-1	0	0	0	1.000	-2	O-13	-0.4
	Bal-A	8	7	2	4	0	0	1	3	2	1	.571	.667	1.000	386	3	0	0	0	1.000	-1	/O-6,D-1	0.2
1975	Bal-A	84	194	27	53	13	0	5	29	22	22	.273	.353	.418	125	6	0	1	-1	.979	-12	O-58/D-3	-0.8
Total	12	1392	4692	603	1254	218	42	153	610	449	635	.267	.335	.429	115	86	39	38	-11	.981	-57	*O-1267/1-34,D-4	-4.8

■ FRANK NORTON   Norton, Frank Prescott   Deb: 5/5/1871

| 1871 | Oly-n | 1 | 1 | 0 | 0 | 0 | 0 | 0 | 0 | 0 | 1 | .000 | .000 | .000 | -99 | -0 | 0 | 0 | 0 | .000 | -1 | /3-1,O-1 | -0.1 |

■ GREG NORTON   Norton, Gregory Blakemoor b: 7/6/72, San Leandro, Cal. BB/TR, 6'1", 190 lbs. Deb: 8/18/96

| 1996 | Chi-A | 11 | 23 | 4 | 5 | 0 | 0 | 2 | 3 | 4 | 6 | .217 | .333 | .478 | 108 | 0 | 0 | 1 | -1 | .778 | -2 | /S-6,3-2,D-2 | -0.2 |

■ WILLIE NORWOOD   Norwood, Willie b: 11/7/50, Greene County, Ala. BR/TR, 6', 185 lbs. Deb: 4/21/77

1977	Min-A	39	83	15	19	3	0	3	9	6	17	.229	.281	.373	78	-3	6	1	1	.952	-4	O-28/D-5	-0.6
1978	Min-A	125	428	56	109	22	3	8	46	28	64	.255	.305	.376	89	-7	25	10	2	.944	-2	*O-115/D-6	-1.3
1979	Min-A	96	270	32	67	13	3	6	30	20	51	.248	.300	.385	80	-8	9	5	-0	.974	-4	O-71,D-14	-1.5
1980	Min-A	34	73	6	12	2	0	1	8	3	13	.164	.197	.233	16	-8	1	1	-0	1.000	-1	O-17/D-9	-1.1
Total	4	294	854	109	207	40	6	18	93	57	145	.242	.292	.367	79	-26	41	17	2	.959	-12	O-231/D-34	-4.5

■ JOE NOSSEK   Nossek, Joseph Rudolph b: 11/8/40, Cleveland, Ohio BR/TR, 6', 178 lbs. Deb: 4/18/64 C

1964	Min-A	7	1	1	0	0	0	0	0	0	0	.000	.000	.000	-99	-0	0	0	0	.000	-1	/O-2	-0.1
1965	*Min-A	87	170	19	37	9	0	2	16	7	12	.218	.253	.306	55	-10	0	0	1	.970	-6	O-48/3-9	-1.8
1966	Min-A	4	0	0	0	0	0	0	0	0	0	—	—	—	—	0	0	0	0	.000	-1	/O-2	-0.1
	KC-A	87	230	13	60	10	3	1	27	8	21	.261	.286	.343	83	-6	3	2	0	.983	3	O-78/3-1	-0.6
	Yr	91	230	13	60	10	3	1	27	8	21	.261	.286	.343	82	-6	4	2	0	.983	2	O-80/3-1	-0.7
1967	KC-A	87	166	12	34	6	1	0	10	4	26	.205	.224	.253	42	-12	5	0	0	.982	-3	O-63	-1.9
1969	Oak-A	13	6	0	0	0	0	0	0	0	0	.000	.000	.000	-99	-2	0	0	0	1.000	-4	O-12	-0.6
	StL-N	9	5	2	1	0	0	0	0	0	0	.200	.200	.200	12	-1	0	0	0	1.000	-0	/O-1	-0.1
1970	StL-N	1	1	0	0	0	0	0	0	0	0	.000	.000	.000	-98	-0	0	0	0	.000	0	H	0.0
Total	6	295	579	47	132	25	4	3	53	19	72	.228	.254	.301	60	-31	8	2	1	.980	-11	O-206/3-10	-5.2

■ LOU NOVIKOFF   Novikoff, Louis Alexander "The Mad Russian" b: 10/12/15, Glendale, Ariz. d: 9/30/70, South Gate, Cal. BR/TR, 5'10", 185 lbs. Deb: 4/15/41

1941	Chi-N	62	203	22	49	8	0	5	24	11	15	.241	.284	.355	82	-6	0			1.000	-4	O-54	-1.3
1942	Chi-N	128	483	48	145	25	5	7	64	24	28	.300	.337	.416	125	12	3			.964	-2	*O-120	0.4
1943	Chi-N	78	233	22	65	7	3	0	28	18	15	.279	.333	.335	95	-2	0			.980	-8	O-61	-1.4
1944	Chi-N	71	139	15	39	4	2	3	19	10	11	.281	.329	.403	106	1	1			.976	-5	O-29	-0.6
1946	Phi-N	17	23	0	7	1	0	0	3	1	2	.304	.333	.348	96	0	0			1.000	-0	/O-3	-0.1
Total	5	356	1081	107	305	45	10	15	138	64	71	.282	.325	.384	107	6	4			.976	-19	O-267	-2.9

■ RUBE NOVOTNEY   Novotney, Ralph Joseph b: 8/5/24, Streator, Ill. d: 7/16/87, Redondo Beach, Cal. BR/TR, 6', 187 lbs. Deb: 4/29/49

| 1949 | Chi-N | 22 | 67 | 4 | 18 | 2 | 1 | 0 | 6 | 3 | 11 | .269 | .300 | .328 | 70 | -3 | 0 | | | .958 | 0 | C-20 | -0.1 |

■ LES NUNAMAKER   Nunamaker, Leslie Grant b: 1/25/1889, Malcolm, Neb. d: 11/14/38, Hastings, Neb. BR/TR, 6'2", 190 lbs. Deb: 4/28/11

1911	Bos-A	62	183	18	47	4	3	0	19	12		.257	.303	.311	72	-7	1			.972	6	C-59	0.4
1912	Bos-A	35	103	15	26	5	2	0	6	6		.252	.313	.340	82	-3	2			.971	-3	C-35	-0.3
1913	Bos-A	29	65	9	14	5	2	0	9	8	8	.215	.311	.354	92	-1	3			.977	3	C-27	0.5
1914	Bos-A	5	5	0	1	0	0	0	0	1	0	.200	.333	.200	61	-0	0			1.000	0	/C-3,1-1	0.0
	NY-A	87	257	19	68	10	3	0	29	22	34	.265	.327	.350	104	1	11	9	-2	.971	4	C-70/1-5	1.0
	Yr	92	262	19	69	10	3	0	29	23	34	.263	.328	.347	103	1	11	9	-2	.971	5	C-73/1-6	1.0
1915	NY-A	87	249	24	56	6	3	0	17	23	24	.225	.293	.273	70	-9	3	2	-0	.964	-4	C-77/1-2	-0.9
1916	NY-A	91	260	25	77	14	7	0	28	34	21	.296	.380	.404	133	11	4			.983	6	C-79	1.1
1917	NY-A	104	310	22	81	9	2	0	33	21	25	.261	.310	.303	86	-5	5			.976	-4	C-91	-0.3
1918	StL-A	85	274	22	71	9	2	0	22	28	16	.259	.339	.307	98	-0	6			.979	0	C-81/1-1,O-1	0.7
1919	Cle-A	26	56	6	14	1	1	0	7	2	6	.250	.276	.304	59	-3	0			.927	-1	C-16	-0.7
1920	*Cle-A	34	54	10	18	3	0	0	14	4	5	.333	.379	.500	128	2	1	0	0	.963	1	C-17/1-6	0.4
1921	Cle-A	46	131	16	47	7	2	0	25	11	8	.359	.408	.443	115	3	1	1	-0	.970	4	C-46	0.8
1922	Cle-A	25	43	8	13	2	0	0	7	4	3	.302	.362	.349	85	-1	0	0	-0	.936	-2	C-13	-0.3
Total	12	716	1990	194	533	75	30	2	216	176	150	.268	.332	.339	95	-12	36	12		.972	-5	C-614/1-15,O-1	2.4

■ JON NUNNALLY   Nunnally, Jonathan Keith b: 11/9/71, Pelham, N.C. BL/TR, 5'10", 190 lbs. Deb: 4/26/95

1995	KC-A	119	303	51	74	15	6	14	42	51	86	.244	.357	.472	112	5	6	4	-1	.971	-4	*O-107/D-4	-0.2
1996	KC-A	35	90	16	19	5	1	5	17	13	25	.211	.311	.456	93	-1	0	0	0	.968	-1	O-29/D-4	-0.3
Total	2	154	393	67	93	20	7	19	59	64	111	.237	.346	.468	108	4	6	4	-1	.970	-6	O-136/D-8	-0.5

■ EMORY NUSZ   Nusz, Emory Moberly b: 4/2/1866, Frederick, Md. d: 8/3/1893, Point Of Rocks, Md. Deb: 4/26/1884

| 1884 | Was-U | 1 | 4 | 1 | 0 | 0 | 0 | 0 | | 0 | | .000 | .000 | .000 | -99 | -1 | | | | .500 | -0 | /O-1 | -0.1 |

■ DIZZY NUTTER   Nutter, Everett Clarence b: 8/27/1893, Roseville, Ohio d: 7/25/58, Battle Creek, Mich. BL/TR, 5'9", 160 lbs. Deb: 9/7/19

| 1919 | Bos-N | 18 | 52 | 4 | 11 | 0 | 0 | 0 | 3 | 4 | 5 | .212 | .268 | .212 | 47 | -3 | 1 | | | 1.000 | 2 | O-12 | -0.3 |

■ CHARLIE NYCE   Nyce, Charles Reiff (b: Charles Reiff Nice) b: 7/1/1870, Philadelphia, Pa. d: 5/9/08, Philadelphia, Pa. 5'8", 160 lbs. Deb: 5/28/1895

| 1895 | Bos-N | 9 | 35 | 7 | 8 | 5 | 0 | 2 | 9 | 4 | 2 | .229 | .325 | .543 | 113 | 0 | 0 | | | .889 | -1 | /S-9 | 0.0 |

■ CHRIS NYMAN   Nyman, Christopher Curtis b: 6/6/55, Pomona, Cal. BR/TR, 6'4", 200 lbs. Deb: 7/28/82 F

1982	Chi-A	28	65	6	16	1	0	0	2	3	9	.246	.279	.262	50	-4	3	2	-0	.994	0	1-24/O-2	-0.6
1983	Chi-A	21	28	12	8	0	0	2	4	4	7	.286	.394	.500	139	2	2	2	-1	1.000	1	1-10,D-10	0.1
Total	2	49	93	18	24	1	0	2	6	7	16	.258	.317	.333	78	-3	5	4	-1	.996	1	/1-34,D-10,O-2	-0.5

■ NYLS NYMAN   Nyman, Nyls Wallace Rex b: 3/7/54, Detroit, Mich. BL/TR, 6', 170 lbs. Deb: 9/6/74 F

1974	Chi-A	5	14	5	9	2	1	0	4	0	1	.643	.667	.929	347	4	1	0	0	1.000	1	/O-3	0.5
1975	Chi-A	106	327	36	74	6	3	2	28	11	34	.226	.256	.281	51	-21	10	4	1	.958	-4	O-94/D-4	-2.9
1976	Chi-A	8	15	2	2	1	0	0	1	0	5	.133	.133	.200	-3	-2	1	0	0	1.000	-1	/O-7	-0.3
1977	Chi-A	1	1	0	0	0	0	0	0	0	0	.000	.000	.000	-99	-0	0	0	0	.000	0	H	0.0
Total	4	120	357	43	85	9	4	2	33	11	38	.238	.267	.303	60	-19	12	4	1	.962	-4	O-104/D-4	-2.7

■ REBEL OAKES   Oakes, Ennis Telfair b: 12/17/1886, Homer, La. d: 2/29/48, Rocky Springs, Lisbon, La. BL/TR, 5'8", 170 lbs. Deb: 4/14/09 M

1909	Cin-N	120	415	55	112	10	5	3	31	40		.270	.341	.340	112	6	23			.979	-2	*O-113	0.0
1910	StL-N	131	468	50	118	14	6	0	43	38	38	.252	.315	.308	85	-9	18			.939	-7	*O-127	-2.3
1911	StL-N	154	551	69	145	13	6	2	59	41	35	.263	.320	.319	81	-14	25			.961	11	*O-151	-1.1
1912	StL-N	136	495	57	139	19	5	3	58	31	24	.281	.328	.358	90	-8	26			.947	-2	*O-136	-1.6
1913	StL-N	147	539	60	158	14	5	0	49	43	32	.293	.350	.338	98	-0	22			.968	-2	*O-145	-1.0
1914	Pit-F	145	571	82	178	18	10	7	75	35	22	.312	.359	.411	111	-0	28			.960	6	*O-145,M	-0.1
1915	Pit-F	153	580	55	161	24	5	0	82	37	19	.278	.323	.336	86	-19	21			.973	-5	*O-153,M	-3.3
Total	7	986	3619	428	1011	112	42	15	397	265	170	.279	.334	.346	95	-44	163			.961	1	O-970	-9.4

■ PRINCE OANA   Oana, Henry Kauhane b: 1/22/08, Waipahu, Hawaii d: 6/19/76, Austin, Tex. BR/TR, 6'2", 193 lbs. Deb: 4/22/34

1934	Phi-N	6	21	3	5	0	0	1	3	0	1	.238	.238	.286	35	-2	0			1.000	1	/O-4	-0.1
1943	Det-A	20	26	5	10	2	1	0	7	1	2	.385	.407	.654	193	2	0	0	0	.750	-0	P-10	0.0
1945	Det-A	4	5	0	1	0	0	0	1	0	0	.200	.200	.200	15	-1	0	0	0	1.000	0	/P-3	0.0
Total	3	30	52	8	16	2	1	1	11	1	3	.308	.321	.462	108	0	0	0	0	.778	0	/P-13,O-4	-0.1

■ JOHNNY OATES   Oates, Johnny Lane b: 1/21/46, Sylva, N.C. BL/TR, 5'11", 188 lbs. Deb: 9/17/70 MC

| 1970 | Bal-A | 5 | 18 | 2 | 5 | 0 | 1 | 0 | 2 | 2 | 0 | .278 | .350 | .389 | 102 | 0 | 0 | | | .939 | -4 | /C-4 | 0.1 |
| 1972 | Bal-A | 85 | 253 | 20 | 66 | 12 | 1 | 4 | 21 | 28 | 31 | .261 | .335 | .364 | 105 | 2 | 5 | 7 | -3 | .995 | -3 | C-82 | -0.1 |

YEAR	TM/L	G	AB	R	H	2B	3B	HR	RBI	BB	SO	AVG	OBP	SLG	PRO+	BR/A	SB	CS	SBR	FA	FR	G/POS	TPR
1973	Atl-N	93	322	27	80	6	0	4	27	22	31	.248	.299	.304	63	-16	1	4	-2	.981	-6	C-86	-2.1
1974	Atl-N	100	291	22	65	10	0	1	21	23	24	.223	.280	.268	52	-19	2	3	-1	.992	12	C-91	-0.5
1975	Atl-N	8	18	0	4	1	0	0	0	1	4	.222	.263	.278	48	-1	0	0	0	1.000	-0	/C-6	-0.3
	Phi-N	90	269	28	77	14	0	1	25	33	29	.286	.364	.349	95	-1	1	0	0	.990	2	C-82	0.5
	Yr	98	287	28	81	15	0	1	25	34	33	.282	.358	.345	92	-2	1	0	0	.990	1	C-88	0.3
1976	*Phi-N	37	99	10	25	2	0	0	8	8	12	.253	.308	.273	64	-4	0	1	-1	.994	2	C-33	-0.3
1977	*LA-N	60	156	18	42	4	0	3	11	11	11	.269	.317	.353	80	-4	1	0	0	.987	5	C-56	0.2
1978	*LA-N	40	75	5	23	1	0	0	6	5	3	.307	.350	.320	89	-1	0	1	-1	.956	-2	C-24	-0.3
1979	LA-N	26	46	4	6	2	0	0	2	4	1	.130	.200	.174	3	-6	0	1	-1	.975	3	C-20	-0.4
1980	NY-A	39	64	6	12	3	0	1	3	2	3	.188	.224	.281	38	-6	1	2	-1	.991	3	C-39	-0.3
1981	NY-A	10	26	4	5	1	0	0	2	0	2	.192	.250	.231	40	-2	0	0	0	.963	1	C-10	-0.1
Total	11	593	1637	146	410	56	2	14	126	141	149	.250	.311	.313	73	-58	11	19	-8	.987	16	C-533	-3.5

■ SHERMAN OBANDO
Obando, Sherman Omar (Gainor) b: 1/23/70, Bocas Del Toro, Pan. BR/TR, 6'4", 215 lbs. Deb: 4/10/93

YEAR	TM/L	G	AB	R	H	2B	3B	HR	RBI	BB	SO	AVG	OBP	SLG	PRO+	BR/A	SB	CS	SBR	FA	FR	G/POS	TPR
1993	Bal-A	31	92	8	25	2	0	3	15	4	26	.272	.309	.391	83	-2				.929	-1	D-21/O-8	-0.4
1995	Bal-A	16	38	0	10	1	0	0	3	2	12	.263	.300	.289	53	-3	1	0	0	.923	-0	/O-7,D-7	-0.3
1996	Mon-N	89	178	30	44	9	0	8	22	22	48	.247	.333	.433	98	-1	2	0	1	.962	-1	O-47	-0.3
Total	3	136	308	38	79	12	0	11	40	28	86	.256	.322	.403	88	-6	3	0	1	.953	-3	/O-62,D-28	-1.0

■ HENRY OBERBECK
Oberbeck, Henry A. b: 5/17/1858, Missouri d: 8/26/21, St.Louis, Mo. Deb: 5/7/1883

YEAR	TM/L	G	AB	R	H	2B	3B	HR	RBI	BB	SO	AVG	OBP	SLG	PRO+	BR/A	SB	CS	SBR	FA	FR	G/POS	TPR
1883	Pit-a	2	9	1	2	1	0	0		0		.222	.222	.333	80	-0				1.000	0	/1-2	0.0
	StL-a	4	14	0	0	0	0	0		0		.000	.000	.000	-95	-3				.833	1	/O-4	-0.2
	Yr	6	23	1	2	1	0	0		0		.087	.087	.130	-30	-3				.833	1	/O-4,1-2	-0.2
1884	Bal-U	33	125	19	23	4	0	0		3		.184	.203	.216	25	-15				.878	2	O-28/3-8,P-2	-1.2
	KC-U	27	90	7	17	3	0	0		7		.189	.247	.222	50	-8				.823	7	3-15/O-7,P-6,1-3	-0.2
	Yr	60	215	26	40	7	0	0		10		.186	.222	.219	34	-23				.908	9	O-35,3-23/P-8,1-3	-1.2
Total	2	66	238	27	42	8	0	0		10		.176	.210	.210	28	-27				.901	9	/O-39,3-23,P-8,1-5	-1.4

■ KEN OBERKFELL
Oberkfell, Kenneth Ray b: 5/4/56, Highland, Ill. BL/TR, 6', 210 lbs. Deb: 8/22/77

YEAR	TM/L	G	AB	R	H	2B	3B	HR	RBI	BB	SO	AVG	OBP	SLG	PRO+	BR/A	SB	CS	SBR	FA	FR	G/POS	TPR
1977	StL-N	9	9	0	1	0	0	0	1	0	3	.111	.111	.111	-41	-2	0	0	0	1.000	1	/2-6	-0.2
1978	StL-N	24	50	7	6	1	0	0	3	0	1	.120	.170	.140	-13	-8	0	0	0	.987	3	2-17/3-4	-0.4
1979	StL-N	135	369	53	111	19	5	1	35	57	35	.301	.400	.388	115	10	4	1	1	**.985**	-4	*2-117,3-17/S-2	1.4
1980	StL-N	116	422	58	128	27	6	3	46	51	23	.303	.381	.417	118	12	4	4	-1	.989	-8	*2-101,3-16	0.9
1981	StL-N	102	376	43	110	12	6	2	45	37	28	.293	.356	.372	104	3	13	5	1	.956	11	*3-102/S-1	1.3
1982	*StL-N	137	470	55	136	22	5	2	34	40	31	.289	.346	.370	99	0	11	9	-2	**.972**	11	*3-135/2-1	0.6
1983	StL-N	151	488	62	143	26	5	3	38	61	27	.293	.373	.385	110	9	12	6	0	**.960**	3	*3-127,2-32/S-1	1.2
1984	StL-N	50	152	17	47	11	1	0	11	16	10	.309	.379	.395	121	5	1	2	-1	.967	4	3-46/2-2,S-1	0.6
	Atl-N	50	172	21	40	8	1	1	10	15	17	.233	.294	.308	65	-8	1	3	-2	.964	-5	3-45/2-4	-1.6
	Yr	100	324	38	87	19	2	1	21	31	27	.269	.334	.349	90	-4	2	5	-3	.966	-1	3-91/2-6,S-1	-0.8
1985	Atl-N	134	412	30	112	19	4	3	35	51	38	.272	.360	.359	96	-0	1	2	-1	.963	-1	*3-117,2-16	-0.4
1986	Atl-N	151	503	62	136	24	3	5	48	83	40	.270	.376	.360	98	2	7	4	-0	.976	9	*3-130,2-41	1.0
1987	Atl-N	135	508	59	142	29	2	3	48	36	42	.280	.344	.362	83	-11	3	3	-1	.979	-4	*3-126,2-11	-1.8
1988	Atl-N	120	422	42	117	20	4	3	40	32	28	.277	.331	.365	95	-3	4	5	-2	.951	-7	*3-113/2-1	-1.3
	Pit-N	20	54	7	12	2	0	0	2	5	6	.222	.288	.259	59	-3	0	0	0	1.000	-4	2-11/S-3,3-2,1-1	-0.6
	Yr	140	476	49	129	22	4	3	42	37	34	.271	.326	.353	91	-5	4	5	-2	.952	-10	*3-115,2-12/S-3,1-1	-1.9
1989	Pit-N	14	40	2	5	1	0	0	2	2	3	.125	.167	.150	-9	-6	0	0	0	.988	1	/1-9,2-3	-0.7
	*SF-N	83	116	17	37	5	1	2	15	8	8	.319	.373	.431	133	5	0	1	-1	.971	-4	3-38/1-7,2-7	0.0
	Yr	97	156	19	42	6	1	2	17	10	10	.269	.326	.359	97	-1	0	1	-1	.971	-5	3-38,1-16,2-10	-0.7
1990	Hou-N	77	150	10	31	6	1	0	12	15	17	.207	.283	.280	57	-9	1	1	-0	.935	-2	3-24,1-11,2-11	-1.2
1991	Hou-N	53	70	7	16	4	0	0	14	14	8	.229	.357	.286	88	-0	0	0	0	1.000	0	1-13/3-4	-0.1
1992	Cal-A	41	91	6	24	1	0	0	6	6	6	.264	.323	.275	69	-4	0	1	-1	.986	-7	2-21/1-2,D-5	-1.1
Total	16	1602	4874	558	1354	237	44	29	446	546	356	.278	.353	.362	97	-7	62	47	-10	.965	-5	*3-1046,2-402/1SD	-2.2

■ MIKE O'BERRY
O'Berry, Preston Michael b: 4/20/54, Birmingham, Ala. BR/TR, 6'2", 195 lbs. Deb: 4/8/79

YEAR	TM/L	G	AB	R	H	2B	3B	HR	RBI	BB	SO	AVG	OBP	SLG	PRO+	BR/A	SB	CS	SBR	FA	FR	G/POS	TPR
1979	Bos-A	43	59	8	10	1	0	1	4	5	16	.169	.246	.237	29	-6	0	0	0	.957	0	C-43	-0.5
1980	Chi-N	19	48	7	10	1	0	0	5	5	13	.208	.283	.229	41	-4	0	0	0	.982	4	C-19	0.1
1981	Cin-N	55	111	6	20	3	1	1	5	14	19	.180	.272	.252	49	-7	0	0	0	.983	3	C-55	-0.3
1982	Cin-N	21	45	5	10	2	0	0	3	10	13	.222	.364	.267	77	-1	0	0	0	.990	-1	C-21	-0.1
1983	Cal-A	26	60	7	10	1	0	1	5	3	11	.167	.206	.233	21	-7	0	0	0	1.000	-1	C-26	-0.6
1984	NY-A	13	32	3	8	2	0	0	5	2	2	.250	.294	.313	71	-1	0	0	0	1.000	1	C-12/3-1	0.3
1985	Mon-N	20	21	2	4	0	0	0	0	4	3	.190	.320	.190	49	-1	0	0	0	1.000	4	C-20	0.3
Total	7	197	376	38	72	10	1	3	27	43	77	.191	.276	.247	46	-27	0	0	0	.984	10	C-196/3-1	-1.1

■ JIM OBRADOVICH
Obradovich, James Thomas b: 9/13/49, Fort Campbell, Ky. BL/TL, 6'2", 200 lbs. Deb: 9/12/78

YEAR	TM/L	G	AB	R	H	2B	3B	HR	RBI	BB	SO	AVG	OBP	SLG	PRO+	BR/A	SB	CS	SBR	FA	FR	G/POS	TPR
1978	Hou-N	10	17	3	3	0	1	0	2	1	3	.176	.222	.294	47	-1	0	0	0	1.000	-0	/1-3	-0.2

■ CHARLIE O'BRIEN
O'Brien, Charles Hugh b: 5/1/60, Tulsa, Okla. BR/TR, 6'2", 195 lbs. Deb: 6/2/85

YEAR	TM/L	G	AB	R	H	2B	3B	HR	RBI	BB	SO	AVG	OBP	SLG	PRO+	BR/A	SB	CS	SBR	FA	FR	G/POS	TPR
1985	Oak-A	16	11	3	3	1	0	0	1	3	3	.273	.429	.364	129	1	0	0	0	.958	-2	C-16	0.1
1987	Mil-A	10	35	2	7	3	1	0	4	4	4	.200	.282	.343	63	-2	0	1	-1	1.000	6	C-10	0.4
1988	Mil-A	40	118	12	26	6	0	2	9	5	16	.220	.252	.322	59	-7	0	1	-1	.991	12	C-40	0.8
1989	Mil-A	62	188	22	44	10	0	6	35	21	11	.234	.339	.383	104	2	0	0	0	.986	7	C-62	1.1
1990	Mil-A	46	145	11	27	7	2	0	11	11	26	.186	.253	.262	45	-11	0	0	0	.992	5	C-46	-0.3
	NY-N	28	68	6	11	3	0	0	9	10	8	.162	.278	.206	36	-6	0	0	0	.986	9	C-28	0.5
1991	NY-N	69	168	16	31	6	2	0	14	17	25	.185	.275	.256	51	-11	0	2	-1	.991	19	C-67	1.0
1992	NY-N	68	156	15	33	12	0	2	13	16	18	.212	.289	.327	75	-5	0	1	-1	.979	5	C-64	0.2
1993	NY-N	67	188	15	48	11	0	4	23	14	14	.255	.314	.378	85	-4	1	1	-0	.986	11	C-65	1.0
1994	Atl-N	51	152	24	37	11	0	8	28	15	24	.243	.324	.474	102	0	0	0	0	.991	3	C-48	0.5
1995	*Atl-N	67	198	18	45	7	0	9	23	29	40	.227	.343	.399	92	-2	0	1	-1	.992	4	C-64	0.5
1996	Tor-A	109	324	33	77	17	0	13	44	29	68	.238	.332	.410	86	-7	0	1	-1	.995	3	*C-105	0.2
Total	11	633	1751	177	389	94	3	46	210	174	257	.222	.309	.358	79	-52	1	8	-5	.990	83	C-615	6.0

■ EDDIE O'BRIEN
O'Brien, Edward Joseph b: 12/11/30, S.Amboy, N.J. BR/TR, 5'9", 165 lbs. Deb: 4/25/53 FC

YEAR	TM/L	G	AB	R	H	2B	3B	HR	RBI	BB	SO	AVG	OBP	SLG	PRO+	BR/A	SB	CS	SBR	FA	FR	G/POS	TPR
1953	Pit-N	89	261	21	62	5	3	0	14	17	30	.238	.289	.280	50	-19	6	1	1	.935	-14	S-81	-2.6
1955	Pit-N	75	236	26	55	3	1	0	8	18	13	.233	.290	.254	47	-18	4	5	-2	.993	1	O-56/3-7,S-4	-2.1
1956	Pit-N	63	53	17	14	2	0	0	3	2	2	.264	.291	.302	61	-3	1	1	-0	.978	9	S-23/O-6,3-4,2-2,P	0.7
1957	Pit-N	3	4	0	0	0	0	0	0	0	0	.000	.000	.000	-99	-1	0	0	0	1.000	0	/P-3	0.0
1958	Pit-N	1	0	0	0	0	0	0	0	0	0					0	0	0	0	.000	-0	/P-1	0.0
Total	5	231	554	64	131	10	4	0	25	37	45	.236	.288	.269	48	-41	11	7	-1	.942	-4	S-108/O-62,3-11,P2	-4.0

■ MICKEY O'BRIEN
O'Brien, Frank Aloysius b: 9/13/1894, San Francisco, Cal. d: 11/4/71, Monterey Park, Cal. BR/TR, 5'8", 160 lbs. Deb: 4/26/23

YEAR	TM/L	G	AB	R	H	2B	3B	HR	RBI	BB	SO	AVG	OBP	SLG	PRO+	BR/A	SB	CS	SBR	FA	FR	G/POS	TPR
1923	Phi-N	15	21	3	7	2	0	0	2	1	1	.333	.391	.429	104	1	0			.909	0	/C-9	

■ GEORGE O'BRIEN
O'Brien, George Joseph b: 11/4/1889, Cleveland, Ohio d: 3/24/66, Columbus, Ohio BR/TR, 6', 185 lbs. Deb: 8/16/15

YEAR	TM/L	G	AB	R	H	2B	3B	HR	RBI	BB	SO	AVG	OBP	SLG	PRO+	BR/A	SB	CS	SBR	FA	FR	G/POS	TPR
1915	StL-A	3	9	1	2	0	0	0	1	2		.222	.300	.222	59	-0	1			.933	-1	/C-3	-0.1

■ JERRY O'BRIEN
O'Brien, Jeremiah b: 2/2/1864, New York d: 7/4/11, Binghamton, N.Y. Deb: 7/30/1887

YEAR	TM/L	G	AB	R	H	2B	3B	HR	RBI	BB	SO	AVG	OBP	SLG	PRO+	BR/A	SB	CS	SBR	FA	FR	G/POS	TPR
1887	Was-N	1	4	0	0	0	0	0	0	0		.000	.000	.000	-99	-1	0			.714	-0	/2-1	-0.1

■ JOHN O'BRIEN
O'Brien, John E. b: 10/22/1851, Columbus, Ohio d: 12/31/14, Fall River, Mass. TR, 5'11.5", 187 lbs. Deb: 4/19/1884

YEAR	TM/L	G	AB	R	H	2B	3B	HR	RBI	BB	SO	AVG	OBP	SLG	PRO+	BR/A	SB	CS	SBR	FA	FR	G/POS	TPR
1884	Bal-U	18	77	7	19	1	1	0		2		.247	.266	.286	61	-6				.865	0	O-18	-0.5

YEAR	TM/L	G	AB	R	H	2B	3B	HR	RBI	BB	SO	AVG	OBP	SLG	PRO+	BR/A	SB	CS	SBR	FA	FR	G/POS	TPR

■ JOHN O'BRIEN   O'Brien, John J. "Chewing Gum"   b: 7/14/1870, St.John, N.B., Can   d: 5/13/13, Lewiston, Maine   BL/TR, 175 lbs.   Deb: 4/22/1891

YEAR	TM/L	G	AB	R	H	2B	3B	HR	RBI	BB	SO	AVG	OBP	SLG	PRO+	BR/A	SB	CS	SBR	FA	FR	G/POS	TPR
1891	Bro-N	43	167	22	41	4	2	0	26	12	17	.246	.308	.293	76	-5	4			.854	-22	2-43	-2.3
1893	Chi-N	4	14	3	5	0	1	0	1	2		.357	.471	.500	160	1	0			.900	-2	/2-4	0.0
1895	Lou-N	128	539	82	138	10	4	1	50	45	20	.256	.325	.295	65	-26	15			.938	3	*2-125/1-3	-1.4
1896	Lou-N	49	186	24	63	9	1	2	24	13	7	.339	.385	.430	119	5	4			.919	-1	2-49	0.6
	Was-N	73	270	38	72	6	3	4	33	27	12	.267	.344	.356	85	-6	4			.952	3	2-73	0.1
	Yr	122	456	62	135	15	4	6	57	40	19	.296	.361	.386	98	-1	8			.938	2	*2-122	0.7
1897	Was-N	86	320	37	78	12	2	3	45	19		.244	.309	.322	67	-16	6			.942	4	2-86	-0.6
1899	Bal-N	39	135	14	26	4	0	1	17	15		.193	.283	.244	43	-11	4			.966	7	2-39	-0.1
	Pit-N	79	279	26	63	2	4	1	33	21		.226	.285	.272	53	-18	8			.946	3	2-79	-1.0
	Yr	118	414	40	89	6	4	2	50	36		.215	.284	.263	50	-28	12			.953	10	*2-118	-1.1
Total	6	501	1910	246	486	47	17	12	229	154	58	.254	.322	.316	72	-75	45			.936	-6	2-498/1-3	-4.7

■ JACK O'BRIEN   O'Brien, John Joseph   b: 2/5/1873, Watervliet, N.Y.   d: 6/10/33, Watervliet, N.Y.   BL/TR, 6'1", 165 lbs.   Deb: 4/14/1899

YEAR	TM/L	G	AB	R	H	2B	3B	HR	RBI	BB	SO	AVG	OBP	SLG	PRO+	BR/A	SB	CS	SBR	FA	FR	G/POS	TPR
1899	Was-N	127	468	68	132	11	5	6	51	31		.282	.331	.365	92	-6	17			.926	4	*O-121/3-4	-1.0
1901	Was-A	11	45	5	8	0	0	0	5	3		.178	.245	.178	19	-5	2			.929	-0	O-11	-0.5
	Cle-A	92	375	54	106	14	5	0	39	22		.283	.329	.347	91	-4	13			.941	-3	O-92/3-1	-1.3
	Yr	103	420	59	114	14	5	0	44	25		.271	.320	.329	83	-9	15			.939	-3	*O-103/3-1	-1.8
1903	*Bos-A	96	338	44	71	14	4	3	38	21		.210	.262	.302	65	-14	10			.958	-6	O-71,3-11/2-4,S-1	-2.6
Total	3	326	1226	171	317	39	14	9	133	77		.259	.308	.331	82	-29	42			.940	-5	O-295/3-16,2-4,S-1	-5.4

■ JACK O'BRIEN   O'Brien, John K. (b: John K. Bryne)   b: 6/12/1860, Philadelphia, Pa.   d: 11/20/10, Philadelphia, Pa.   BR/TR, 5'10", 184 lbs.   Deb: 5/2/1882

YEAR	TM/L	G	AB	R	H	2B	3B	HR	RBI	BB	SO	AVG	OBP	SLG	PRO+	BR/A	SB	CS	SBR	FA	FR	G/POS	TPR
1882	Phi-a	62	241	44	73	13	3	3	37	13		.303	.339	.419	138	8				**.925**	11	C-45,O-18/3-1,1-1	1.9
1883	Phi-a	94	390	74	113	14	10	3	70	25		.290	.333	.377	119	7				.876	-1	C-58,O-25,3-19/S-1	0.7
1884	Phi-a	36	138	25	39	6	1	1		9		.283	.340	.362	121	3				.930	-0	C-30/O-5,1-1	0.4
1885	Phi-a	62	225	35	60	9	1	2	30	20		.267	.340	.342	109	5				.903	-8	C-43/S-9,1-7,O-3,3	-0.3
1886	Phi-a	105	423	65	107	25	7	0	56	38		.253	.325	.345	109	4	23			.918	-15	C-36,3-27,1S/2O	-0.7
1887	Bro-a	30	123	18	28	4	1	1	17	6		.228	.264	.301	56	-8	8			.839	-2	C-25/O-4,2-1	-1.0
1888	Bal-a	57	196	25	44	11	5	0	18	17		.224	.300	.332	105	1	14			.925	-15	C-37,O-13/1-7	-1.0
1890	Phi-a	109	433	80	113	24	14	4	80	52		.261	.356	.409	128	15	31			.976	4	*1-109/O-1,C-1	1.2
Total	8	555	2169	366	577	106	42	11	308	180		.266	.331	.369	115	34	76			.903	-31	C-275,1-149/O3S2	1.2

■ JOHNNY O'BRIEN   O'Brien, John Thomas   b: 12/11/30, S.Amboy, N.J.   BR/TR, 5'9", 170 lbs.   Deb: 4/19/53   F

YEAR	TM/L	G	AB	R	H	2B	3B	HR	RBI	BB	SO	AVG	OBP	SLG	PRO+	BR/A	SB	CS	SBR	FA	FR	G/POS	TPR
1953	Pit-N	89	279	28	69	13	2	2	22	21	36	.247	.309	.330	67	-13	1	1	-0	.982	-5	2-77/S-1	-1.4
1955	Pit-N	84	278	22	83	15	2	1	25	20	19	.299	.348	.378	94	-2	1	1	-0	.969	5	2-78	0.8
1956	Pit-N	73	104	13	18	1	0	0	3	5	7	.173	.211	.183	7	-13	0	0	0	.959	5	2-53/P-8,S-1	-0.5
1957	Pit-N	34	35	7	11	2	1	0	1	1	4	.314	.368	.429	117	-1	0	0	0	.857	-2	P-16/S-8,2-2	-0.1
1958	Pit-N	3	1	1	0	0	0	0	0	0	0	.000	.000	.000	-99	-0	0	0	0	.000	0	H	0.0
	StL-N	12	2	3	0	0	0	0	0	0	1	.000	.333	.000	-2	-0	0	0	0	1.000	0	/S-5,P-1,2-1	0.0
	Yr	15	3	4	0	0	0	0	0	0	1	.000	.250	.000	-26	-1	0	0	0	1.000	0	/S-5,P-1,2-1	0.0
1959	Mil-N	44	116	16	23	4	0	1	8	11	15	.198	.273	.259	47	-9	0	0	0	.987	-3	2-37	-0.9
Total	6	339	815	90	204	35	5	4	59	59	82	.250	.307	.320	68	-38	2	2	-1	.974	0	2-248/P-25,S-15	-2.1

■ PETE O'BRIEN   O'Brien, Peter J.   b: 6/17/1877, Binghamton, N.Y.   d: 1/31/17, Jersey City, N.J.   BL/TR, 5'7", 170 lbs.   Deb: 9/21/01

YEAR	TM/L	G	AB	R	H	2B	3B	HR	RBI	BB	SO	AVG	OBP	SLG	PRO+	BR/A	SB	CS	SBR	FA	FR	G/POS	TPR
1901	Cin-N	16	54	11	11	1	0	1	3	2		.204	.232	.278	51	-4	0			.889	-2	2-15	-0.5
1906	StL-A	151	524	44	122	9	4	2	57	42		.233	.293	.277	82	-10	25			.933	-41	*2-120,3-20,S-11	-5.5
1907	Cle-A	43	145	9	33	5	2	0	6	7		.228	.263	.290	76	-4	1			.949	-11	2-15,3-12,S-12	-1.7
	Was-A	39	134	6	25	3	1	0	12	12		.187	.259	.224	59	-6	4			.912	4	3-26,S-13/2-1	-0.1
	Yr	82	279	15	58	8	3	0	18	19		.208	.261	.258	68	-10	5			.911	-7	3-38,S-25,2-16	-1.8
Total	3	249	857	60	191	18	7	3	78	63		.223	.279	.271	76	-24	30			.930	-50	2-151/3-58,S-36	-7.8

■ PETE O'BRIEN   O'Brien, Peter James   b: 6/16/1867, Chicago, Ill.   d: 6/30/37, York Township, Du Page County, Ill.   BR/TR, 5'9.5", 165 lbs.   Deb: 4/29/1890

YEAR	TM/L	G	AB	R	H	2B	3B	HR	RBI	BB	SO	AVG	OBP	SLG	PRO+	BR/A	SB	CS	SBR	FA	FR	G/POS	TPR
1890	Chi-N	27	106	15	30	7	0	3	16	5	10	.283	.315	.434	113	1	4			.929	-2	2-27	0.1

■ PETE O'BRIEN   O'Brien, Peter Michael   b: 2/9/58, Santa Monica, Cal.   BL/TL, 6'1", 198 lbs.   Deb: 9/3/82

YEAR	TM/L	G	AB	R	H	2B	3B	HR	RBI	BB	SO	AVG	OBP	SLG	PRO+	BR/A	SB	CS	SBR	FA	FR	G/POS	TPR
1982	Tex-A	20	67	13	16	4	1	4	13	6	8	.239	.301	.507	124	2	1	0	0	1.000	-0	O-11/1-3,D-4	0.1
1983	Tex-A	154	524	53	124	24	5	8	53	58	62	.237	.314	.347	83	-11	5	4	-1	.993	13	*1-133,O-27/D-1	-0.7
1984	Tex-A	142	520	57	149	26	2	18	80	53	50	.287	.353	.448	116	11	3	5	-2	.992	1	*1-141/O-1	0.1
1985	Tex-A	159	573	69	153	34	3	22	92	69	53	.267	.347	.452	115	12	5	10	-5	.995	-6	*1-159	-0.8
1986	Tex-A	156	551	86	160	23	3	23	90	87	66	.290	.387	.468	128	24	4	4	-1	.992	2	*1-155	1.3
1987	Tex-A	159	569	84	163	26	1	23	88	59	61	.286	.354	.457	113	10	0	4	-2	.992	16	*1-158/O-2,D-1	1.2
1988	Tex-A	156	547	57	149	24	1	16	71	72	73	.272	.357	.408	111	9	1	4	-2	.995	13	*1-155/D-1	0.7
1989	Cle-A	155	554	75	144	24	1	12	55	83	48	.260	.358	.372	104	6	3	1	0	.994	3	*1-154/D-1	-0.4
1990	Sea-A	108	366	32	82	18	0	5	27	44	33	.224	.311	.314	74	-12	0	0	0	.995	4	1-97/O-6,D-6	-1.5
1991	Sea-A	152	560	58	139	29	3	17	88	44	61	.248	.304	.402	93	-6	0	1	-1	**.997**	1	*1-132,D-18,O-13	-1.5
1992	Sea-A	134	396	40	88	15	1	14	52	40	27	.222	.294	.371	85	-9	2	1	0	.996	2	1-81,D-36	-1.4
1993	Sea-A	72	210	30	54	7	0	7	27	26	21	.257	.339	.390	94	-2	0	0	0	.988	0	D-52/1-9,O-1	-0.4
Total	12	1567	5437	654	1421	254	21	169	736	641	563	.261	.340	.409	104	34	24	34	-13	.994	49	*1-1377,D-120/O-61	-3.3

■ RAY O'BRIEN   O'Brien, Raymond Joseph   b: 10/31/1892, St.Louis, Mo.   d: 3/31/42, St.Louis, Mo.   BL/TL, 5'9", 175 lbs.   Deb: 6/27/16

YEAR	TM/L	G	AB	R	H	2B	3B	HR	RBI	BB	SO	AVG	OBP	SLG	PRO+	BR/A	SB	CS	SBR	FA	FR	G/POS	TPR
1916	Pit-N	16	57	5	12	2	0	0	1	6		.211	.224	.333	69	-2	0			.864	-1	O-14	-0.4

■ SYD O'BRIEN   O'Brien, Sydney Lloyd   b: 12/18/44, Compton, Cal.   BR/TR, 6'1", 185 lbs.   Deb: 4/15/69

YEAR	TM/L	G	AB	R	H	2B	3B	HR	RBI	BB	SO	AVG	OBP	SLG	PRO+	BR/A	SB	CS	SBR	FA	FR	G/POS	TPR
1969	Bos-A	100	263	47	64	10	5	9	29	15	37	.243	.287	.422	91	-4	2	3	-1	.939	-1	3-53,S-15,2-12	-0.5
1970	Chi-A	121	441	48	109	13	2	8	44	22	62	.247	.286	.340	69	-19	3	3	-1	.938	-6	3-68,2-43/S-5	-2.4
1971	Cal-A	90	251	25	50	8	1	5	21	15	33	.199	.247	.299	58	-15	0	2	-1	.961	-5	S-52/2-7,3-6,1-1,O	-1.2
1972	Cal-A	36	39	10	7	2	0	1	1	6	10	.179	.289	.308	82	-1	0	0	0	.889	1	/3-8,S-4,2-3,1-1	0.0
	Mil-A	31	58	5	12	2	0	1	3	2	13	.207	.233	.293	57	-3	0	1	-1	.852	1	/3-9,2-7	-0.5
	Yr	67	97	15	19	4	0	2	4	8	23	.196	.257	.299	68	-4	0	1	-1	.861	1	3-17,2-10/S-4,1-1	-0.5
Total	4	378	1052	135	242	35	8	24	100	60	155	.230	.274	.347	72	-42	5	9	-4	.934	-8	3-144/S-76,2-72,10	-4.6

■ TOMMY O'BRIEN   O'Brien, Thomas Edward "Obie"   b: 12/19/18, Anniston, Ala.   d: 11/5/78, Anniston, Ala.   BR/TR, 5'11", 195 lbs.   Deb: 4/24/43

YEAR	TM/L	G	AB	R	H	2B	3B	HR	RBI	BB	SO	AVG	OBP	SLG	PRO+	BR/A	SB	CS	SBR	FA	FR	G/POS	TPR
1943	Pit-N	89	232	35	72	12	6	2	26	15	24	.310	.352	.448	126	7	0			.964	-6	O-48/3-9	-0.1
1944	Pit-N	85	156	27	39	6	2	3	20	21	12	.250	.343	.372	97	-0	1			.965	-9	O-48/3-1	-1.2
1945	Pit-N	58	161	23	54	6	5	0	18	9	13	.335	.374	.435	120	4	0			.961	-6	O-45	-0.4
1949	Bos-A	49	125	24	28	5	0	3	10	21	12	.224	.336	.336	73	-5	0	0	0	.984	-1	O-32	-0.8
1950	Bos-A	9	31	0	4	0	0	0	3	3	5	.129	.206	.161	-5	-5	0	0	0	1.000	-1	/O-9	-0.6
	Was-A	3	9	1	1	0	0	0	1	2	0	.111	.200	.111	-20	-2	0	0	0	1.000	1	/O-3	-0.1
	Yr	12	40	1	5	0	0	0	4	4	5	.125	.205	.150	-8	-7	0	0	0	1.000	-0	O-12	-0.7
Total	5	293	714	110	198	30	14	8	78	70	66	.277	.344	.392	100	-1	2	0		.970	-24	O-185/3-10	-3.2

■ TOM O'BRIEN   O'Brien, Thomas H.   b: 6/22/1860, Salem, Mass.   d: 4/21/21, Worcester, Mass.   BR/TR, 6'1", 185 lbs.   Deb: 6/14/1882

YEAR	TM/L	G	AB	R	H	2B	3B	HR	RBI	BB	SO	AVG	OBP	SLG	PRO+	BR/A	SB	CS	SBR	FA	FR	G/POS	TPR
1882	Wor-N	22	89	9	18	1	1	0	7	1	10	.202	.211	.236	42	-6				.789	-2	O-20/2-2,3-1	-0.7
1883	Bal-a	33	138	16	37	6	4	0		5		.268	.294	.370	109	1				.825	-4	2-29/O-4	-0.2
1884	Bos-U	103	449	80	118	31	8	4		12		.263	.282	.394	105	-11				.853	1	*2-99/O-3,1-2,C-1	-0.7
1885	Bal-a	8	33	4	7	1	0	0		3		.212	.257	.303	78	-1				.932	1	/1-6,2-2	-0.2
1887	NY-a	31	129	13	25	3	2	0	18	2		.194	.212	.248	29	-12	10			.963	-2	1-20/O-8,3-2,2-2,P	-1.3
1890	Roc-a	73	273	36	52	6	5	0	31	30		.190	.273	.249	58	-14	6			.971	-4	1-68/2-8	-1.9
Total	6	270	1111	158	257	50	20	4	61	52	10	.231	.267	.323	79	-43	16			.846	-10	2-142/1-96,O3PC	-4.8

TOM O'BRIEN
O'Brien, Thomas J. b: 2/20/1873, Verona, Pa. d: 2/4/01, Phoenix, Ariz. Deb: 5/10/1897

YEAR	TM/L	G	AB	R	H	2B	3B	HR	RBI	BB	SO	AVG	OBP	SLG	PRO+	BR/A	SB	CS	SBR	FA	FR	G/POS	TPR
1897	*Bal-N	50	147	25	37	6	0	0	32	20		.252	.349	.293	70	-6	7			.968	0	1-25,O-24	-0.6
1898	Bal-N	18	60	9	13	0	0	0	14	10		.217	.338	.217	59	-3	0			.833	0	O-16	-0.3
	Pit-N	107	413	53	107	10	8	1	45	25		.259	.318	.329	87	-7	13			.924	-3	O-69,1-21/3-8,2S	-1.4
	Yr	125	473	62	120	10	8	1	59	35		.254	.321	.315	84	-10	13			.911	-3	O-85,1-21/3-8,2S	-1.7
1899	NY-N	150	573	100	170	21	10	6	77	44		.297	.351	.400	109	7	23			.933	-2	*O-127,3-21/S-2,21	-0.4
1900	*Pit-N	102	376	61	109	22	6	3	61	21		.290	.349	.404	107	3	12			.961	-11	1-65,O-25/2-4,S-2	-0.9
Total	4	427	1569	248	436	59	24	10	229	120		.278	.341	.365	97	-6	55			.928	-15	O-261,1-112/32S	-3.6

DARBY O'BRIEN
O'Brien, William D. b: 9/1/1863, Peoria, Ill. d: 6/15/1893, Peoria, Ill. BR/R, 6'1", 186 lbs. Deb: 4/16/1887

YEAR	TM/L	G	AB	R	H	2B	3B	HR	RBI	BB	SO	AVG	OBP	SLG	PRO+	BR/A	SB	CS	SBR	FA	FR	G/POS	TPR
1887	NY-a	127	522	97	157	30	13	5	73	40		.301	.355	.437	126	18	49			.913	6	*O-121,1-10/S-2,3P	1.7
1888	Bro-a	136	532	105	149	27	6	2	65	30		.280	.327	.365	122	12	55			.932	2	*O-136	0.9
1889	*Bro-a	136	567	146	170	30	11	5	80	61	76	.300	.384	.418	128	22	91			.906	-7	*O-136	1.0
1890	*Bro-N	85	350	78	110	28	6	2	63	32	43	.314	.378	.446	139	17	38			.960	4	O-85	1.5
1891	Bro-N	103	395	79	100	18	6	5	57	39	53	.253	.331	.367	104	2	31			.951	2	*O-103	0.0
1892	Bro-N	122	490	72	119	14	5	1	56	29	52	.243	.289	.298	81	-12	57			.956	4	*O-122	-1.3
Total	6	709	2856	577	805	147	47	20	394	231	224	.282	.344	.387	117	58	321			.934	11	O-703/1-10,S-2,P3	3.8

BILLY O'BRIEN
O'Brien, William Smith b: 3/14/1860, Albany, N.Y. d: 5/26/11, Kansas City, Mo. BR, 6', 185 lbs. Deb: 9/27/1884

YEAR	TM/L	G	AB	R	H	2B	3B	HR	RBI	BB	SO	AVG	OBP	SLG	PRO+	BR/A	SB	CS	SBR	FA	FR	G/POS	TPR
1884	StP-U	8	30	1	7	3	0	0	0			.233	.233	.333	129	-2				.840	1	/3-8,P-2	0.0
	KC-U	4	17	2	4	0	0	0	0			.235	.235	.235	49	-2				.714	1	/3-3,1-1	-0.1
	Yr	12	47	3	11	3	0	0	0			.234	.234	.298	92	-3				.795	2	3-11/P-2,1-1	-0.1
1887	Was-N	113	453	71	126	16	12	19	73	21	17	.278	.317	.492	128	15	11			.974	-3	*1-104/O-4,3-4,2-2	0.1
1888	Was-N	133	528	42	119	15	2	9	66	9	70	.225	.238	.313	79	-13	10			.975	-4	*1-132/3-1	-3.0
1889	Was-N	2	8	1	0	0	0	0	0	1	1	.000	.111	.000	-72	-2	0			1.000	-0	/1-2	-0.2
1890	Bro-a	96	388	47	108	25	8	4	67	28		.278	.332	.415	124	10	5			.973	-2	*1-96	0.2
Total	5	356	1424	164	364	59	22	32	206	59	88	.256	.289	.395	108	7	26			.974	-8	1-335/3-16,O-4,2P	-3.0

ALEX OCHOA
Ochoa, Alex b: 3/29/72, Miami Lakes, Fla. BR/TR, 6', 185 lbs. Deb: 9/18/95

YEAR	TM/L	G	AB	R	H	2B	3B	HR	RBI	BB	SO	AVG	OBP	SLG	PRO+	BR/A	SB	CS	SBR	FA	FR	G/POS	TPR
1995	NY-N	11	37	7	11	1	0	0	6	2	10	.297	.333	.324	77	-1	1	0	0	1.000	1	O-10	0.0
1996	NY-N	82	282	37	83	19	3	4	33	17	30	.294	.339	.426	107	2	4	3	-1	.966	3	O-76	0.3
Total	2	93	319	44	94	20	3	4	39	19	40	.295	.338	.414	104	1	5	3	-0	.970	4	/O-86	0.3

WHITEY OCK
Ock, Harold David b: 3/17/12, Brooklyn, N.Y. d: 3/18/75, Mt.Kisco, N.Y. BR/TR, 5'11", 180 lbs. Deb: 9/29/35

YEAR	TM/L	G	AB	R	H	2B	3B	HR	RBI	BB	SO	AVG	OBP	SLG	PRO+	BR/A	SB	CS	SBR	FA	FR	G/POS	TPR
1935	Bro-N	1	3	0	0	0	0	0	0	1	2	.000	.250	.000	-27	-1	0			1.000	-0	/C-1	-0.1

DANNY O'CONNELL
O'Connell, Daniel Francis b: 1/21/27, Paterson, N.J. d: 10/2/69, Clifton, N.J. BR/TR, 6', 180 lbs. Deb: 7/14/50 C

YEAR	TM/L	G	AB	R	H	2B	3B	HR	RBI	BB	SO	AVG	OBP	SLG	PRO+	BR/A	SB	CS	SBR	FA	FR	G/POS	TPR
1950	Pit-N	79	315	39	92	16	1	8	32	24	33	.292	.342	.425	97	-2	7			.977	17	S-65,3-12	2.0
1953	Pit-N	149	588	88	173	26	8	7	55	57	42	.294	.361	.401	99	0	3	4	-2	.958	3	*3-104,2-47	0.6
1954	Mil-N	146	541	61	151	28	4	2	37	38	46	.279	.329	.357	84	-13	3	4	-1	.979	9	*2-103,3-35/1-8,S-1	0.1
1955	Mil-N	124	453	47	102	15	4	6	40	28	43	.225	.278	.316	60	-27	2	2	-1	.981	16	*2-114/3-7,S-1	-0.3
1956	Mil-N	139	498	71	119	17	9	2	42	76	42	.239	.344	.321	86	-8	3	3	-1	.985	-6	*2-138/3-4,S-1	-0.4
1957	Mil-N	48	183	29	43	9	1	1	8	19	20	.235	.314	.311	74	-7	1	0	0	.982	7	2-48	0.4
	NY-N	95	364	57	97	18	3	7	28	33	30	.266	.331	.390	93	-3	8	3	1	.980	6	2-68,3-30	0.9
	Yr	143	547	86	140	27	4	8	36	52	50	.256	.325	.364	87	-10	9	3	1	.981	12	*2-116,3-30	1.3
1958	SF-N	107	306	44	71	12	3	2	23	51	35	.232	.342	.314	77	-9	2	1	0	.986	3	2-104/3-3	0.1
1959	SF-N	34	58	6	11	3	0	0	0	5	15	.190	.254	.241	34	-5	0	1	-1	.927	7	3-26/2-8	0.1
1961	Was-A	138	493	61	128	30	1	1	37	77	62	.260	.363	.331	88	-5	15	5	2	.939	1	3-73,2-61	0.5
1962	Was-A	84	236	24	62	7	2	2	18	23	28	.263	.328	.335	80	-6	5	1	0	.961	-1	3-41,2-22	-0.5
Total	10	1143	4035	527	1049	181	35	39	320	431	396	.260	.335	.351	84	-86	48	22		.980	67	2-713,3-335/S-68,1	3.5

JIMMY O'CONNELL
O'Connell, James Joseph b: 2/11/01, Sacramento, Cal. d: 11/11/76, Bakersfield, Cal. BL/TR, 5'10.5", 175 lbs. Deb: 4/17/23

YEAR	TM/L	G	AB	R	H	2B	3B	HR	RBI	BB	SO	AVG	OBP	SLG	PRO+	BR/A	SB	CS	SBR	FA	FR	G/POS	TPR
1923	*NY-N	87	252	42	63	9	2	6	39	34	32	.250	.351	.373	92	-2	7	3	0	.980	-8	O-64/1-8	-1.4
1924	NY-N	52	104	24	33	4	2	2	18	11	16	.317	.388	.452	128	4	2	1	0	.952	-7	O-29/2-1	-0.4
Total	2	139	356	66	96	13	4	8	57	45	48	.270	.361	.396	102	2	9	4	0	.974	-15	/O-93,1-8,2-1	-1.8

JOHN O'CONNELL
O'Connell, John Charles b: 6/13/04, Berona, Pa. d: 10/17/92, Canton, Ohio BR/TR, 6', 170 lbs. Deb: 8/16/28

YEAR	TM/L	G	AB	R	H	2B	3B	HR	RBI	BB	SO	AVG	OBP	SLG	PRO+	BR/A	SB	CS	SBR	FA	FR	G/POS	TPR
1928	Pit-N	1	1	0	0	0	0	0	0	0	0	.000	.000	.000	-96	-0	0			1.000	1	/C-1	0.0
1929	Pit-N	2	7	1	1	1	0	0	0	1	1	.143	.250	.286	32	-1	0			1.000	-0	/C-2	-0.1
Total	2	3	8	1	1	1	0	0	0	1	1	.125	.222	.250	17	-1	0			1.000	1	/C-3	0.0

JOHN O'CONNELL
O'Connell, John Joseph d: 5/14/08, Derry, N.H. Deb: 8/22/1891

YEAR	TM/L	G	AB	R	H	2B	3B	HR	RBI	BB	SO	AVG	OBP	SLG	PRO+	BR/A	SB	CS	SBR	FA	FR	G/POS	TPR
1891	Bal-a	8	29	2	5	1	0	0	7	3	6	.172	.250	.207	31	-3	2			.938	-3	/S-3,2-3,O-2	-0.5
1902	Det-A	8	22	1	4	0	0	0	0	4	0	.182	.280	.182	29	-2	0			.919	1	/2-6,1-2	-0.1
Total	2	16	51	3	9	1	0	0	7	6	6	.176	.263	.196	30	-5	2			.885	-2	/2-9,S-3,1-2,O-2	-0.6

PAT O'CONNELL
O'Connell, Patrick H. b: 6/10/1861, Bangor, Me. d: 1/24/43, Lewiston, Maine BR/TR, 5'10", 175 lbs. Deb: 7/22/1886

YEAR	TM/L	G	AB	R	H	2B	3B	HR	RBI	BB	SO	AVG	OBP	SLG	PRO+	BR/A	SB	CS	SBR	FA	FR	G/POS	TPR
1886	Bal-a	42	166	20	30	3	2	0	8	11		.181	.236	.223	45	-10	10			.782	-4	O-41/1-1,P-1	-1.4
1890	Bro-a	11	40	7	9	2	1	0	3	7		.225	.340	.325	100	0	3			.830	-1	3-10/1-1	0.0
Total	2	53	206	27	39	5	3	0	11	18		.189	.258	.243	57	-10	13			1.000	-5	/O-41,3-10,1-2,P-1	-1.4

DAN O'CONNOR
O'Connor, Daniel Cornelius b: 8/1868, Guelph, Ont., Canada d: 3/3/42, Guelph, Ont., Canada BL/TR, 6'2", 185 lbs. Deb: 6/3/1890

YEAR	TM/L	G	AB	R	H	2B	3B	HR	RBI	BB	SO	AVG	OBP	SLG	PRO+	BR/A	SB	CS	SBR	FA	FR	G/POS	TPR
1890	Lou-a	6	26	3	12	1	1	0	5	1		.462	.481	.577	217	4	5			1.000	-1	/1-6	0.2

JOHNNY O'CONNOR
O'Connor, John Charles "Bucky" b: 12/1/1891, Cahirciveen, Ire. d: 5/30/82, Bonner Springs, Kan. BR/TR, 5'9", Deb: 9/16/16

YEAR	TM/L	G	AB	R	H	2B	3B	HR	RBI	BB	SO	AVG	OBP	SLG	PRO+	BR/A	SB	CS	SBR	FA	FR	G/POS	TPR
1916	Chi-N	1	0	0	0	0	0	0	0	0	0	—	—	—	—		-0	0			.000	0	/C-1	0.0

JACK O'CONNOR
O'Connor, John Joseph "Rowdy Jack" or "Peach Pie" b: 6/2/1869, St.Louis, Mo. d: 11/14/37, St.Louis, Mo. BR/TR, 5'10", 170 lbs. Deb: 4/20/1887 M

YEAR	TM/L	G	AB	R	H	2B	3B	HR	RBI	BB	SO	AVG	OBP	SLG	PRO+	BR/A	SB	CS	SBR	FA	FR	G/POS	TPR
1887	Cin-a	12	40	4	4	0	0	0		1	2	.100	.143	.150	-31	-7	3			.947	3	/O-7,C-5	-0.3
1888	Cin-a	36	137	14	28	3	1	1	17	6		.204	.243	.263	59	-7	12			.795	-0	O-34/C-2	-0.7
1889	Col-a	107	398	69	107	17	7	4	60	33	37	.269	.331	.377	107	3	26			.955	-1	C-84,O-19/2-4,1-3	0.8
1890	Col-a	121	457	89	148	14	10	2	66	38		.324	.377	.411	142	24	29			.962	10	*C-106/O-9,S-8,23	3.7
1891	Col-a	56	229	28	61	12	3	0	37	11	14	.266	.300	.345	90	-4	10			.878	3	O-40,C-21	-1.0
1892	*Cle-N	140	572	71	142	22	5	1	58	25	48	.248	.282	.309	76	-19	17			.935	9	*O-106,C-34	-1.1
1893	Cle-N	96	384	72	110	23	1	4	75	29	12	.286	.341	.383	87	-9	29			.949	-2	C-56,O-44	-0.7
1894	Cle-N	86	330	67	104	23	7	2	51	15	7	.315	.345	.445	86	-9	15			.942	-7	C-45,O-33/1-7	-0.1
1895	Cle-N	89	340	51	99	14	10	0	58	30	22	.291	.354	.391	87	-8	11			.923	-6	C-47,1-41/3-1	-0.7
1896	*Cle-N	68	256	41	76	11	1	1	43	15	12	.297	.343	.359	81	-9	15			.966	-7	C-37,1-17/O-12	-0.9
1897	Cle-N	103	397	49	115	21	4	2	69	26		.290	.338	.378	84	-10	20			.941	-12	C-52,1-36,C-13	-2.1
1898	Cle-N	131	478	50	119	17	4	1	56	26		.249	.291	.308	72	-18	8			.983	3	1-69,C-48,O-15	-1.1
1899	StL-N	84	289	33	73	5	6	0	43	15		.253	.299	.311	66	-14	7			.943	2	C-57,1-26	-0.7
1900	StL-N	10	32	4	7	0	0	0	6	2		.219	.306	.219	46	-2	0			.957	-1	C-10	-0.2
	*Pit-N	43	147	15	35	4	1	0	19	3		.238	.263	.279	49	-10	5			.944	-9	C-40/1-2	-1.5
	Yr	53	179	19	42	4	1	0	25	5		.235	.271	.268	49	-13	5			.947	-10	C-50/1-2	-1.7
1901	Pit-N	61	202	16	39	7	3	0	22	10		.193	.238	.257	42	-15	2			.978	-1	C-59	-1.0
1902	Pit-N	49	170	13	50	1	1	0	28	3		.294	.306	.341	96	-1	2			.979	-3	C-42/1-6,O-1	-0.8
1903	NY-A	46	212	13	43	9	1	0	12	8		.203	.235	.231	38	-10	4			.988	5	C-63/1-1	-0.9
1904	StL-A	14	47	4	10	1	0	0	4	2		.213	.245	.234	55	-2	0			.943	-4	C-14	-0.6
1906	StL-A	55	174	8	33	0	0	0	11	2		.190	.199	.190	23	-16	4			.990	10	C-51	-0.1
1907	StL-A	25	89	2	14	2	0	0	8	2		.157	.176	.180	13	-9	2			.991	-2	C-25	-1.0

YEAR	TM/L	G	AB	R	H	2B	3B	HR	RBI	BB	SO	AVG	OBP	SLG	PRO+	BR/A	SB	CS	SBR	FA	FR	G/POS	TPR
1910	StL-A	1	0	0	0	0	0	0	0	0		—	—	—	—	0	0			1.000	-0	/C-1,M	0.0
Total	21	1451	5380	713	1417	201	66	19	738	301	152	.263	.307	.336	79	-157	219			.961	-2	C-860,O-372,1/S23	-9.3

■ PADDY O'CONNOR
O'Connor, Patrick Francis b: 8/4/1879, County Kerry, Ireland d: 8/17/50, Springfield, Mass. BR/TR, 5'8", 168 lbs. Deb: 4/17/08 C

YEAR	TM/L	G	AB	R	H	2B	3B	HR	RBI	BB	SO	AVG	OBP	SLG	PRO+	BR/A	SB	CS	SBR	FA	FR	G/POS	TPR
1908	Pit-N	12	16	1	3	0	0	0	2	0		.188	.188	.188	20	-1	0			.889	-2	/C-4	-0.3
1909	*Pit-N	9	16	1	5	1	0	0	3	0		.313	.313	.375	104	-0	0			.700	-2	/C-3,3-1	-0.2
1910	Pit-N	6	4	0	1	0	0	0	0	1	1	.250	.400	.250	85	-0	0			1.000	-0	/C-1	0.0
1914	StL-N	10	9	0	0	0	0	0	0	2	2	.000	.250	.000	-24	-1	0			1.000	-0	/C-7	-0.2
1915	Pit-F	70	219	15	50	10	1	0	16	14	30	.228	.278	.283	58	-16	4			.987	4	C-66	-0.7
1918	NY-A	1	3	0	1	0	0	0	1	0	1	.333	.333	.333	99	-0	0			1.000	-0	/C-1	0.0
Total	6	108	267	17	60	11	1	0	21	17	34	.225	.276	.273	57	-18	4			.979	-0	/C-82,3-1	-1.4

■ KEN O'DEA
O'Dea, James Kenneth b: 3/16/13, Lima, N.Y. d: 12/17/85, Lima, N.Y. BL/TR, 6', 180 lbs. Deb: 4/21/35

YEAR	TM/L	G	AB	R	H	2B	3B	HR	RBI	BB	SO	AVG	OBP	SLG	PRO+	BR/A	SB	CS	SBR	FA	FR	G/POS	TPR
1935	*Chi-N	76	202	30	52	13	2	6	38	26	18	.257	.345	.431	106	2	0			.964	-2	C-63	0.3
1936	Chi-N	80	189	36	58	10	3	2	38	38	18	.307	.423	.423	126	9	0			.979	-3	C-64	0.8
1937	Chi-N	83	219	31	66	7	5	4	32	24	26	.301	.370	.434	113	4	1			.985	-6	C-64	0.1
1938	*Chi-N	86	247	22	65	12	1	3	33	12	18	.263	.297	.356	77	-8	1			.970	4	C-71	-0.1
1939	NY-N	52	97	7	17	1	0	3	11	10	16	.175	.252	.278	42	-8	0			.947	-2	C-30	-0.9
1940	NY-N	48	96	9	23	4	1	0	12	16	15	.240	.348	.302	80	-2	0			.992	2	C-31	0.2
1941	NY-N	59	89	13	19	5	1	3	17	8	20	.213	.278	.393	86	-2	0			1.000	1	C-14	0.0
1942	*StL-N	58	192	22	45	7	1	5	32	17	23	.234	.297	.359	85	-4	0			.979	10	C-49	1.1
1943	*StL-N	71	203	15	57	11	2	3	25	19	25	.281	.345	.399	110	2	0			.989	6	C-56	1.2
1944	*StL-N	85	265	35	66	11	0	6	37	37	29	.249	.343	.374	100	0	1			.994	7	C-69	1.2
1945	StL-N†	100	307	36	78	18	2	4	43	50	31	.254	.359	.365	99	1	0			.995	3	C-91	0.9
1946	StL-N	22	57	2	7	2	0	1	3	8	8	.123	.231	.211	25	-6	0			.991	5	C-22	0.0
	Bos-N	12	32	4	7	0	0	0	2	8	4	.219	.375	.219	70	-1	0			1.000	-1	C-12	-0.1
	Yr	34	89	6	14	2	0	1	5	16	12	.157	.286	.213	41	-7	0			.994	4	C-34	-0.1
Total	12	832	2195	262	560	101	20	40	323	273	251	.255	.338	.374	95	-12	3			.983	26	C-627	4.7

■ PAUL O'DEA
O'Dea, Paul "Lefty" b: 7/3/20, Cleveland, Ohio d: 12/11/78, Cleveland, Ohio BL/TL, 6', 200 lbs. Deb: 4/19/44

YEAR	TM/L	G	AB	R	H	2B	3B	HR	RBI	BB	SO	AVG	OBP	SLG	PRO+	BR/A	SB	CS	SBR	FA	FR	G/POS	TPR
1944	Cle-A	76	173	25	55	9	0	1	13	23	21	.318	.401	.370	126	7	2	2	-1	.949	-5	O-41/P-3,1-3	0.0
1945	Cle-A	87	221	21	52	2	2	1	21	20	26	.235	.299	.276	70	-8	3	0	1	.992	2	O-53/P-1	-0.9
Total	2	163	394	46	107	11	2	1	34	43	47	.272	.345	.317	95	-1	5	2	0	.975	-2	/O-94,P-4,1-3	-0.9

■ HEINIE ODOM
Odom, Herman Boyd b: 10/13/1900, Rusk, Tex. d: 8/31/70, Rusk, Tex. BB/R, 6', 170 lbs. Deb: 4/22/25

YEAR	TM/L	G	AB	R	H	2B	3B	HR	RBI	BB	SO	AVG	OBP	SLG	PRO+	BR/A	SB	CS	SBR	FA	FR	G/POS	TPR
1925	NY-A	1	1	0	1	0	0	0	0	0	0	1.000	1.000	1.000	416	0	0	0	0	1.000	0	/3-1	0.1

■ BLUE MOON ODOM
Odom, Johnny Lee b: 5/29/45, Macon, Ga. BR/TR, 6', 185 lbs. Deb: 9/5/64

YEAR	TM/L	G	AB	R	H	2B	3B	HR	RBI	BB	SO	AVG	OBP	SLG	PRO+	BR/A	SB	CS	SBR	FA	FR	G/POS	TPR
1964	KC-A	5	5	1	0	0	0	0	0	1	4	.000	.167	.000	-47	-1	0	0	0	.800	0	/P-5	0.0
1965	KC-A	1	0	0	0	0	0	0	0	0	0					0	0	0	0	1.000	0	/P-1	0.0
1966	KC-A	17	31	1	3	0	0	0	2	3	16	.097	.176	.097	-20	-5	0	0	0	.970	2	P-14	0.0
1967	KC-A	33	28	4	8	1	0	0	0	1	14	.286	.310	.321	90	-0	0	1	-1	.897	0	P-29	0.0
1968	Oak-A★	42	78	14	17	2	0	1	8	6	29	.218	.282	.282	75	-2	0	0	0	.964	1	P-32	0.0
1969	Oak-A★	43	79	15	21	2	1	5	16	2	24	.266	.293	.506	125	2	0	0	0	.937	1	P-32	0.0
1970	Oak-A	37	54	8	13	2	0	3	7	3	18	.241	.281	.444	100	-0	1	0	0	.929	2	P-29	0.0
1971	Oak-A	37	50	8	8	1	1	1	2	1	24	.160	.192	.260	28	-5	0	0	0	.850	-1	P-25	0.0
1972	*Oak-A	59	66	16	8	1	0	2	2	1	29	.121	.134	.227	7	-8	4	2	0	.873	0	P-31	0.0
1973	*Oak-A	51	1	5	0	0	0	0	0	0	0	.000	.000	.000	-99	-0	1	2	-1	.875	-1	P-30	0.0
1974	*Oak-A	43	0	3	0	0	0	0	0	0	0	—	—	—		0	0	0	0	.821	1	P-34	0.0
1975	Oak-A	8	0	1	0	0	0	0	0	0	0	—	—	—		0	0	0	0	.750	0	/P-7	0.0
	Cle-A	3	0	0	0	0	0	0	0	0	0	—	—	—		0	0	0	0	1.000	0	/P-3	0.0
	Yr	11	0	1	0	0	0	0	0	0	0	—	—	—		0	0	0	0	.800	0	/P-10	0.0
	Atl-N	15	13	0	1	0	0	0	1	0	5	.077	.077	.154	-36	-2	0	0	0	.944	0	P-15	0.0
1976	Chi-A	8	0	0	0	0	0	0	0	0	0	—	—	—		0	0	0	0	.600	-1	/P-8	0.0
Total	13	402	405	76	79	9	2	12	31	19	163	.195	.235	.316	60	-22	6	5	-1	.904	5	P-295	0.0

■ HARRY O'DONNELL
O'Donnell, Harry Herman "Butch" b: 4/2/1894, Philadelphia, Pa. d: 1/31/58, Philadelphia, Pa. BR/TR, 5'8", 175 lbs. Deb: 4/30/27

YEAR	TM/L	G	AB	R	H	2B	3B	HR	RBI	BB	SO	AVG	OBP	SLG	PRO+	BR/A	SB	CS	SBR	FA	FR	G/POS	TPR
1927	Phi-N	16	16	1	1	0	0	0	2	2	1	.063	.167	.063	-36	-3	0			1.000	1	C-12	-0.2

■ JOHN O'DONNELL
O'Donnell, John b: Littlestown, Pa. Deb: 7/16/1884

YEAR	TM/L	G	AB	R	H	2B	3B	HR	RBI	BB	SO	AVG	OBP	SLG	PRO+	BR/A	SB	CS	SBR	FA	FR	G/POS	TPR
1884	Phi-U	1	4	0	1	0	0	0		0		.250	.250	.250	56	-0				.545	-2	/C-1	-0.2

■ LEFTY O'DOUL
O'Doul, Francis Joseph b: 3/4/1897, San Francisco, Cal. d: 12/7/69, San Francisco, Cal. BL/TL, 6', 180 lbs. Deb: 4/29/19

YEAR	TM/L	G	AB	R	H	2B	3B	HR	RBI	BB	SO	AVG	OBP	SLG	PRO+	BR/A	SB	CS	SBR	FA	FR	G/POS	TPR
1919	NY-A	19	16	2	4	0	0	0	1	1	2	.250	.294	.250	53	-1	1			.500	-1	/P-3,O-1	-0.1
1920	NY-A	13	12	2	2	1	0	0	1	1	1	.167	.231	.250	26	-1	0	0	0	.000	-1	/P-2,O-1	-0.1
1922	NY-A	8	9	0	3	1	0	0	4	0	2	.333	.333	.444	99	-0	0	0	0	1.000	0	/P-6	0.0
1923	Bos-A	36	35	2	5	0	0	0	4	2	3	.143	.189	.143	-12	-6	0	0	0	.958	1	P-23/O-1	-0.1
1928	NY-N	114	354	67	113	19	4	8	46	30	8	.319	.372	.463	117	8	9			.962	-12	O-94	-0.9
1929	Phi-N	154	638	152	**254**	35	6	32	122	76	19	**.398**	**.465**	.622	157	58	2			.971	5	*O-154	4.7
1930	Phi-N	140	528	122	202	37	7	22	97	63	21	.383	.453	.604	142	38	3			.953	-5	*O-131	2.0
1931	Bro-N	134	512	85	172	32	11	7	75	48	16	.336	.396	.482	136	26	5			.954	-1	*O-132	1.6
1932	Bro-N	148	595	120	219	32	8	21	90	50	20	**.368**	.423	.555	164	54	11			.979	-5	*O-148	3.9
1933	Bro-N	43	159	14	40	5	1	5	21	15	6	.252	.320	.390	106	1	2			.947	-3	O-41	-0.4
	*NY-N★	78	229	31	70	9	1	9	35	29	17	.306	.388	.472	147	15	1			.974	-6	O-63	0.6
	Yr	121	388	45	110	14	2	14	56	44	23	.284	.361	.438	130	16	3			.962	-8	*O-104	0.2
1934	NY-N	83	177	27	56	4	3	9	46	18	7	.316	.383	.525	144	11	2			.968	-5	O-38	0.4
Total	11	970	3264	624	1140	175	41	113	542	333	122	.349	.413	.532	142	202	36	0		.964	-33	O-804/P-34	11.6

■ FRED ODWELL
Odwell, Frederick William "Fritz" b: 9/25/1872, Downsville, N.Y. d: 8/19/48, Downsville, N.Y. BL/TR, 5'9.5", 160 lbs. Deb: 4/16/04

YEAR	TM/L	G	AB	R	H	2B	3B	HR	RBI	BB	SO	AVG	OBP	SLG	PRO+	BR/A	SB	CS	SBR	FA	FR	G/POS	TPR
1904	Cin-N	129	468	75	133	22	10	1	58	26		.284	.333	.380	110	4	30			.956	14	*O-126/2-1	1.2
1905	Cin-N	130	468	79	113	10	9	**9**	65	26		.241	.293	.359	85	-11	21			.967	4	*O-126	-1.4
1906	Cin-N	58	202	20	45	5	4	0	21	15		.223	.286	.287	76	-6	11			.963	3	O-57	-0.6
1907	Cin-N	94	274	24	74	5	7	0	24	22		.270	.336	.339	107	2	10			.975	5	O-84/2-1	0.5
Total	4	411	1412	198	365	42	30	10	168	89		.258	.313	.352	96	-10	72			.964	26	O-393/2-2	-0.3

■ CHUCK OERTEL
Oertel, Charles Frank "Ducky" or "Snuffy" b: 3/12/31, Coffeyville, Kan. BL/TR, 5'8", 165 lbs. Deb: 9/1/58

YEAR	TM/L	G	AB	R	H	2B	3B	HR	RBI	BB	SO	AVG	OBP	SLG	PRO+	BR/A	SB	CS	SBR	FA	FR	G/POS	TPR
1958	Bal-A	14	12	4	2	0	0	1	1	1	1	.167	.231	.417	78	-0	0	0	0	1.000	-1	/O-2	-0.1

■ RON OESTER
Oester, Ronald John b: 5/5/56, Cincinnati, Ohio BB/TR, 6'2", 190 lbs. Deb: 9/10/78 C

YEAR	TM/L	G	AB	R	H	2B	3B	HR	RBI	BB	SO	AVG	OBP	SLG	PRO+	BR/A	SB	CS	SBR	FA	FR	G/POS	TPR
1978	Cin-N	6	8	1	3	0	0	0	1	0	2	.375	.375	.375	110	-0	0	0	0	1.000	1	/S-6	0.1
1979	Cin-N	6	3	0	0	0	0	0	0	0	1	.000	.000	.000	-99	-1	0	0	0	1.000	1	/S-2	0.0
1980	Cin-N	100	303	40	84	16	2	2	20	26	44	.277	.336	.363	95	-2	6	2	1	.980	-14	2-79,S-17/3-3	-1.0
1981	Cin-N	105	354	45	96	16	7	5	42	42	49	.271	.348	.398	110	5	2	5	-2	.980	5	*2-103/S-9	1.5
1982	Cin-N	151	549	63	143	19	4	9	47	35	82	.260	.305	.359	83	-13	5	6	-2	.972	4	*2-118,S-29,3-13	-0.4
1983	Cin-N	157	549	63	145	23	5	11	58	49	106	.264	.326	.384	93	-6	3	7	-1	.977	-25	*2-154	-2.5
1984	Cin-N	150	553	54	134	26	3	3	38	40	91	.242	.296	.316	69	-23	7	2	1	.980	-16	*2-147/S-1	-3.4
1985	Cin-N	152	526	59	155	26	3	1	34	51	65	.295	.357	.361	97	-1	5	0	2	.989	5	*2-149	1.1
1986	Cin-N	153	523	52	135	23	2	8	44	52	84	.258	.326	.356	84	-11	9	3	2	.978	18	*2-151	1.5
1987	Cin-N	69	237	28	60	9	6	2	23	25	32	.253	.317	.367	77	-8	2	3	-1	.974	6	2-69	0.0
1988	Cin-N	54	150	20	42	7	0	0	10	9	24	.280	.321	.327	83	-3	0	2	-1	.995	2	2-49/S-5	0.0
1989	Cin-N	109	305	23	75	15	0	1	14	32	47	.246	.318	.305	76	-9	3	4	-1	.985	8	*2-102/S-2	0.2

YEAR	TM/L	G	AB	R	H	2B	3B	HR	RBI	BB	SO	AVG	OBP	SLG	PRO+	BR/A	SB	CS	SBR	FA	FR	G/POS	TPR
1990	*Cin-N	64	154	10	46	10	1	0	13	10	29	.299	.341	.377	93	-1	1	2	-1	.982	-8	2-50/3-3	-1.0
Total	13	1276	4214	458	1118	190	33	42	344	369	681	.265	.325	.356	87	-71	40	26	-4	.980	-14	*2-1171/S-71,3-19	-3.9

■ BOB O'FARRELL

O'Farrell, Robert Arthur b: 10/19/1896, Waukegan, Ill. d: 2/20/88, Waukegan, Ill. BR/TR, 5'9.5", 180 lbs. Deb: 9/5/15 M

YEAR	TM/L	G	AB	R	H	2B	3B	HR	RBI	BB	SO	AVG	OBP	SLG	PRO+	BR/A	SB	CS	SBR	FA	FR	G/POS	TPR
1915	Chi-N	2	3	0	1	0	0	0	0	0	0	.333	.333	.333	102	-0	0			.667	-1	/C-2	-0.1
1916	Chi-N	1	0	0	0	0	0	0	0	0	0	—	—	—	—		0	0		.000	-1	/C-1	0.0
1917	Chi-N	3	8	1	3	2	0	0	1	1	0	.375	.444	.625	210	1	1			1.000	-1	/C-3	0.0
1918	*Chi-N	52	113	9	32	7	3	1	14	10	15	.283	.347	.425	132	4	0			.974	-6	C-45	0.1
1919	Chi-N	49	125	11	27	4	2	0	9	7	10	.216	.258	.280	61	-6	2			.965	-4	C-38	-0.7
1920	Chi-N	94	270	29	67	11	4	3	19	34	23	.248	.332	.352	95	-1	1	0	0	.956	-6	C-86	-0.1
1921	Chi-N	96	260	32	65	12	7	4	32	18	14	.250	.299	.396	82	-7	2	0	1	.967	-5	C-90	-0.4
1922	Chi-N	128	392	68	127	18	8	4	60	79	34	.324	.439	.441	125	19	5	3	-0	.977	16	*C-125	3.8
1923	Chi-N	131	452	73	144	25	4	12	84	67	38	.319	.408	.471	131	22	10	3	1	.976	-1	*C-124	2.9
1924	Chi-N	71	183	25	44	6	2	3	28	30	13	.240	.347	.344	85	-3	2	0	1	.984	-2	C-57	-0.1
1925	Chi-N	17	22	2	4	0	1	0	3	2	5	.182	.250	.273	33	-2	0	0	0	1.000	-1	/C-3	-0.3
	StL-N	94	317	37	88	13	2	3	32	46	26	.278	.373	.360	86	-5	0	1	-1	.975	-5	C-92	-0.5
	Yr	111	339	39	92	13	3	3	35	48	31	.271	.365	.354	83	-7	0	1	-1	.975	-6	C-95	-0.8
1926	*StL-N	147	492	63	144	30	9	7	68	61	44	.293	.371	.433	111	8	1			.983	10	*C-146	2.7
1927	StL-N	61	178	19	47	10	1	0	18	23	22	.264	.348	.331	80	-4	3			.979	-0	C-53,M	-0.1
1928	StL-N	16	52	6	11	1	0	0	4	13	9	.212	.369	.231	59	-2	2			.985	0	C-14	-0.1
	NY-N	75	133	23	26	6	0	2	20	34	16	.195	.359	.286	70	-5	0			.988	-1	C-63	-0.2
	Yr	91	185	29	37	7	0	2	24	47	25	.200	.362	.270	67	-7	4			.987	-1	C-77	-0.3
1929	NY-N	91	248	35	76	14	3	4	42	28	30	.306	.384	.435	103	-2	3			.979	-5	C-84	0.3
1930	NY-N	94	249	37	75	16	4	4	54	31	21	.301	.381	.446	101	1	1			.973	0	C-69	0.6
1931	NY-N	85	174	11	39	8	3	1	19	21	23	.224	.311	.322	72	-7	0			.980	1	C-80	-0.2
1932	NY-N	50	67	7	16	3	0	0	8	11	10	.239	.354	.284	76	-2	0			.969	2	C-41	0.1
1933	StL-N	55	163	16	39	4	2	0	20	15	25	.239	.303	.325	76	-5	0			.970	-5	C-50	-0.8
1934	Cin-N	44	123	10	30	8	3	1	9	11	19	.244	.306	.382	85	-3	0			.993	-0	C-42,M	-0.1
	Chi-N	22	67	3	15	3	0	0	5	3	11	.224	.257	.269	42	-6	2			1.000	2	C-22	-0.2
	Yr	66	190	13	45	11	3	1	14	14	30	.237	.289	.342	70	-8	2			.996	2	C-64	-0.3
1935	StL-N	14	10	0	0	0	0	0	0	0	2	.000	.167	.000	-49	-2	0			1.000	1	/C-8	-0.1
Total	21	1492	4101	517	1120	201	58	51	549	547	408	.273	.360	.388	97	-3	35	7		.976	-9	*C-1338	6.2

■ JOSE OFFERMAN

Offerman, Jose Antonio (Dono) b: 11/8/68, San Pedro De Macoris, D.R. BB/TR, 6', 150 lbs. Deb: 8/19/90

YEAR	TM/L	G	AB	R	H	2B	3B	HR	RBI	BB	SO	AVG	OBP	SLG	PRO+	BR/A	SB	CS	SBR	FA	FR	G/POS	TPR
1990	LA-N	29	58	7	9	0	0	1	7	4	14	.155	.210	.207	15	-7	1	0	0	.946	-2	S-27	-0.7
1991	LA-N	52	113	10	22	2	0	0	3	25	32	.195	.345	.212	62	-4	3	2	-0	.945	2	S-50	0.0
1992	LA-N	149	534	67	139	20	8	1	30	57	98	.260	.332	.333	90	-6	23	16	-3	.935	-18	*S-149	-1.7
1993	LA-N	158	590	77	159	21	6	1	62	71	75	.269	.350	.331	88	-8	30	13	1	.950	-1	*S-158	-0.1
1994	LA-N	72	243	27	51	8	4	1	25	38	38	.210	.317	.288	63	-13	2	1	0	.967	-4	S-72	-1.0
1995	*LA-N★	119	429	69	123	14	6	4	33	69	67	.287	.389	.375	113	11	2	7	-4	.932	-10	*S-115	0.2
1996	KC-A	151	561	85	170	33	8	5	47	74	98	.303	.385	.417	106	7	24	10	1	.994	-5	1-96,2-38,S-36/O-1	0.4
Total	7	730	2528	342	673	98	32	13	207	338	422	.266	.354	.346	92	-19	85	49	-4	.943	-39	S-607/1-96,2-38,O-1	-2.3

■ ROWLAND OFFICE

Office, Rowland Johnie b: 10/25/52, Sacramento, Cal. BL/TL, 6', 170 lbs. Deb: 8/5/72

YEAR	TM/L	G	AB	R	H	2B	3B	HR	RBI	BB	SO	AVG	OBP	SLG	PRO+	BR/A	SB	CS	SBR	FA	FR	G/POS	TPR
1972	Atl-N	2	5	1	2	0	0	0	0	1	2	.400	.500	.400	145	0	0	0	0	1.000	0	/O-1	0.0
1974	Atl-N	131	248	20	61	16	1	3	31	16	30	.246	.292	.355	77	-8	5	3	-0	.994	-25	*O-119	-3.8
1975	Atl-N	126	355	30	103	14	1	3	30	23	41	.290	.339	.361	91	-4	2	2	-1	.967	-6	*O-107	-1.6
1976	Atl-N	99	359	51	101	17	1	4	34	37	49	.281	.352	.368	98	-0	2	8	-4	.986	-3	O-92	-1.2
1977	Atl-N	124	428	42	103	13	1	5	39	23	58	.241	.284	.311	53	-28	2	4	-2	.988	7	*O-104/1-1	-2.7
1978	Atl-N	146	404	40	101	13	1	9	40	22	52	.250	.299	.354	73	-15	8	6	-1	.990	-1	*O-136	-2.5
1979	Atl-N	124	277	35	69	14	2	2	37	27	33	.249	.320	.336	74	-10	5	4	-1	.988	-13	O-97	-2.7
1980	Mon-N	116	292	36	78	13	4	6	30	36	39	.267	.348	.401	108	-4	3	3	-1	.987	-11	O-97	-1.2
1981	Mon-N	26	40	4	7	1	0	0	0	4	6	.175	.250	.175	22	-4	0	0	0	.938	-1	/O-15	-0.8
1982	Mon-N	3	3	0	1	1	0	0	0	0	1	.333	.333	.667	170	0	0	0	0	1.000	0	/O-1	0.0
1983	NY-A	2	2	0	0	0	0	0	1	0	0	.000	.000	.000	-99	-1	0	0	0	1.000	-1	/O-2	-0.1
Total	11	899	2413	259	626	101	11	32	242	189	311	.259	.317	.350	79	-66	27	30	-10	.985	-57	O-771/1-1	-16.6

■ JIM OGLESBY

Oglesby, James Dorn b: 8/10/05, Schofield, Mo. d: 9/1/55, Tulsa, Okla. BL/TL, 6', 190 lbs. Deb: 4/14/36

YEAR	TM/L	G	AB	R	H	2B	3B	HR	RBI	BB	SO	AVG	OBP	SLG	PRO+	BR/A	SB	CS	SBR	FA	FR	G/POS	TPR
1936	Phi-A	3	11	0	2	0	0	0	2	2	0	.182	.308	.182	24	-1	0	0	0	1.000	0	/1-3	-0.1

■ BEN OGLIVIE

Oglivie, Benjamin Ambrosio (Palmer) b: 2/11/49, Colon, Panama BL/TL, 6'2", 170 lbs. Deb: 9/4/71

YEAR	TM/L	G	AB	R	H	2B	3B	HR	RBI	BB	SO	AVG	OBP	SLG	PRO+	BR/A	SB	CS	SBR	FA	FR	G/POS	TPR
1971	Bos-A	14	38	2	10	3	0	0	4	0	5	.263	.263	.342	66	-2	0	0	0	.958	1	O-11	-0.1
1972	Bos-A	94	253	27	61	10	2	8	30	18	61	.241	.294	.391	97	-1	1	1	-0	.981	-1	O-65	-0.6
1973	Bos-A	58	147	16	32	9	1	2	9	9	32	.218	.272	.333	66	-7	1	1	-0	.983	0	O-32,D-13	-0.9
1974	Det-A	92	252	28	68	11	3	4	29	34	38	.270	.357	.385	109	4	12	3	2	.947	-5	O-63,1-10/D-4	-0.3
1975	Det-A	100	332	45	95	14	1	9	36	16	62	.286	.323	.416	103	0	11	8	-2	.975	6	O-86/1-5,D-2	0.1
1976	Det-A	115	305	36	87	12	3	15	47	11	44	.285	.317	.492	129	9	9	4	0	.986	1	O-64/1-9,D-1	0.8
1977	Det-A	132	450	63	118	24	2	21	61	40	80	.262	.327	.464	107	3	9	9	-3	.976	7	*O-118/D-2	0.7
1978	Mil-A	128	469	71	142	29	4	18	72	52	69	.303	.372	.497	142	26	11	7	-1	.980	1	O-89,D-27,1-11	2.1
1979	Mil-A	139	514	88	145	30	4	29	81	48	56	.282	.346	.525	131	21	12	5	1	.985	-0	*O-120,D-13/1-9	1.5
1980	Mil-A★	156	592	94	180	26	2	**41**	118	54	71	.304	.367	.563	156	43	11	9	-2	.978	21	*O-152/D-4	5.4
1981	*Mil-A	107	400	53	97	15	2	14	72	37	49	.243	.316	.395	109	4	2	2	-1	.982	-3	*O-101/D-6	-0.3
1982	*Mil-A★	159	602	92	147	22	1	34	102	70	81	.244	.327	.453	119	14	3	5	-2	.982	13	*O-159	2.0
1983	Mil-A★	125	411	49	115	19	3	13	66	60	64	.280	.371	.452	133	20	4	6	-2	.975	6	*O-113/D-8	2.0
1984	Mil-A	131	461	49	121	26	2	12	60	44	56	.262	.328	.384	100	0	6	6	-4	.970	-2	*O-125/D-1	-1.1
1985	Mil-A	101	341	40	99	17	2	10	61	37	51	.290	.363	.440	119	9	2	4	-1	.965	-3	O-91/D-4	0.2
1986	Mil-A	103	346	31	98	20	1	5	53	30	33	.283	.340	.390	95	-2	1	2	-1	.991	-6	O-50,D-42	-0.5
Total	16	1754	5913	784	1615	277	33	235	901	560	852	.273	.340	.450	119	142	87	70	-16	.978	44	*O-1439,D-127/1-44	10.9

■ BRUCE OGRODOWSKI

Ogrodowski, Ambrose Francis "Brusie" b: 2/17/12, Hoytville, Pa. d: 3/5/56, San Francisco, Cal. BR/TR, 5'11", 175 lbs. Deb: 4/14/36

YEAR	TM/L	G	AB	R	H	2B	3B	HR	RBI	BB	SO	AVG	OBP	SLG	PRO+	BR/A	SB	CS	SBR	FA	FR	G/POS	TPR
1936	StL-N	94	237	28	54	15	1	1	20	10	20	.228	.259	.312	66	-16	0			.989	4	C-85	-0.8
1937	StL-N	90	279	37	65	10	3	3	31	11	17	.233	.267	.323	58	-17	2			.984	2	C-87	-1.0
Total	2	184	516	65	119	25	4	4	51	21	37	.231	.263	.318	56	-32	2			.986	6	C-172	-1.8

■ HAL O'HAGEN

O'Hagen, Harry P. b: 9/30/1873, Washington, D.C. d: 1/14/13, Newark, N.J. 6', 173 lbs. Deb: 9/24/1892

YEAR	TM/L	G	AB	R	H	2B	3B	HR	RBI	BB	SO	AVG	OBP	SLG	PRO+	BR/A	SB	CS	SBR	FA	FR	G/POS	TPR
1892	Was-N	1	4	1	1	0	0	0	0	0	2	.250	.250	.250	53	-0	0			1.000	1	/C-1	0.0
1902	Chi-N	31	108	10	21	1	3	0	10	11		.194	.269	.259	65	-4	8			.982	3	1-31	-0.2
	NY-N	4	11	0	1	0	0	0	0	0		.091	.091	.091	-44	-2	0			1.000	-1	/O-4	-0.3
	Cle-A	3	13	2	5	2	0	0	1	0		.385	.385	.538	160	1	2			1.000	1	/1-3	0.1
	NY-N	22	73	5	11	2	1	0	8	2		.151	.195	.205	24	-7	3			.973	-0	1-18/O-4	-0.8
	Yr	57	192	15	33	2	4	0	18	13		.172	.232	.224	45	-13	11			.979	2	1-49/O-8	-1.3
Total	2	61	209	18	39	5	4	0	19	13	2	.187	.241	.249	51	-12	13			.981	3	/1-52,O-8,C-1	-1.2

■ GREG O'HALLORAN

O'Halloran, Gregory Joseph b: 5/21/68, Toronto, Ont., Can. BL/TR, 6'2", 205 lbs. Deb: 5/16/94

YEAR	TM/L	G	AB	R	H	2B	3B	HR	RBI	BB	SO	AVG	OBP	SLG	PRO+	BR/A	SB	CS	SBR	FA	FR	G/POS	TPR
1994	Fla-N	12	11	1	2	0	0	0	1	0	1	.182	.182	.182	-5	-2	0	0	0	1.000	0	/C-1	-0.1

■ KID O'HARA

O'Hara, James Francis b: 12/19/1875, Wilkes-Barre, Pa. d: 12/1/54, Canton, Ohio BB/TR, 5'7.5", 152 lbs. Deb: 9/15/04

YEAR	TM/L	G	AB	R	H	2B	3B	HR	RBI	BB	SO	AVG	OBP	SLG	PRO+	BR/A	SB	CS	SBR	FA	FR	G/POS	TPR
1904	Bos-N	8	29	3	6	0	0	0		0	4	.207	.303	.207	60	-1	1			.923	0	/O-8	-0.2

■ TOM O'HARA

O'Hara, Thomas F. b: 7/13/1885, Waverly, N.Y. d: 6/8/54, Denver, Colo. Deb: 9/19/06

YEAR	TM/L	G	AB	R	H	2B	3B	HR	RBI	BB	SO	AVG	OBP	SLG	PRO+	BR/A	SB	CS	SBR	FA	FR	G/POS	TPR
1906	StL-N	14	53	8	16	1	0	0		5	3	.302	.339	.321	110	1	3			.889	-2	O-14	-0.2

YEAR	TM/L	G	AB	R	H	2B	3B	HR	RBI	BB	SO	AVG	OBP	SLG	PRO+	BR/A	SB	CS	SBR	FA	FR	G/POS	TPR
1907	StL-N	48	173	11	41	2	1	0	5	12		.237	.286	.260	74	-5	1			.943	-1	O-47	-0.9
Total	2	62	226	19	57	3	1	0	5	15		.252	.299	.274	82	-5	4			.930	-3	/O-61	-1.1

■ BILL O'HARA   O'Hara, William Alexander b: 8/14/1883, Toronto, Ont., Can.   d: 6/15/31, Jersey City, N.J.   BL/TR, 5'10",   Deb: 4/15/09

YEAR	TM/L	G	AB	R	H	2B	3B	HR	RBI	BB	SO	AVG	OBP	SLG	PRO+	BR/A	SB	CS	SBR	FA	FR	G/POS	TPR
1909	NY-N	115	360	48	85	9	3	1	30	41		.236	.318	.286	86	-5	31			.978	2	*O-111	-0.8
1910	StL-N	9	20	1	3	0	0	0	2	1	3	.150	.190	.150	-0	-3	0			1.000	-0	/O-4,P-1,1-1	-0.3
Total	2	124	380	49	88	9	3	1	32	42	3	.232	.311	.279	82	-7	31			.979	2	O-115/1-1,P-1	-1.1

■ LEN OKRIE   Okrie, Leonard Joseph b: 7/16/23, Detroit, Mich.   BR/TR, 6', 185 lbs.   Deb: 6/16/48   FC

YEAR	TM/L	G	AB	R	H	2B	3B	HR	RBI	BB	SO	AVG	OBP	SLG	PRO+	BR/A	SB	CS	SBR	FA	FR	G/POS	TPR
1948	Was-A	19	42	1	10	0	1	0	1	1	7	.238	.256	.286	45	-3	0	0	0	.981	2	C-17	-0.1
1950	Was-A	17	27	1	6	0	0	0	2	6	7	.222	.382	.222	61	-1	0	0	0	1.000	1	C-17	0.0
1951	Was-A	5	8	1	1	1	0	0	0	2	1	.125	.300	.250	51	-1	0	0	0	.850	1	/C-5	0.0
1952	Bos-A	1	1	0	0	0	0	0	0	0	1	.000	.000	.000	-93	-0	0	0	0	1.000	-0	/C-1	0.0
Total	4	42	78	3	17	1	1	0	3	9	16	.218	.307	.256	51	-5	0	0	0	.965	4	/C-40	-0.1

■ JIM OLANDER   Olander, James Bentley b: 2/21/63, Tucson, Ariz.   BR/TR, 6'1", 185 lbs.   Deb: 9/20/91

YEAR	TM/L	G	AB	R	H	2B	3B	HR	RBI	BB	SO	AVG	OBP	SLG	PRO+	BR/A	SB	CS	SBR	FA	FR	G/POS	TPR
1991	Mil-A	12	9	2	0	0	0	0	0	2	5	.000	.182	.000	-46	-2	0	0	0	1.000	-2	/O-9,D-2	-0.4

■ DAVE OLDFIELD   Oldfield, David b: 12/18/1864, Philadelphia, Pa.   d: 8/28/39, Philadelphia, Pa.   BB/TL, 5'7", 175 lbs.   Deb: 6/28/1883

YEAR	TM/L	G	AB	R	H	2B	3B	HR	RBI	BB	SO	AVG	OBP	SLG	PRO+	BR/A	SB	CS	SBR	FA	FR	G/POS	TPR
1883	Bal-a	1	4	0	0	0	0	0		0		.000	.000	.000	-97	-1				.667	-1	/C-1	-0.2
1885	Bro-a	10	25	2	8	1	0	0	2	3		.320	.414	.360	145	2				.873	1	C-9,O-2	0.3
1886	Bro-a	14	55	7	13	1	0	0	5	2		.236	.263	.255	62	-2	1			.833	-3	C-13/S-1,O-1	-0.3
	Was-N	21	71	2	10	2	0	0	2	5	15	.141	.197	.169	13	-7	0			.899	-3	C-12/O-9	-0.9
Total	3	46	155	11	31	4	0	0	9	10	15	.200	.253	.226	50	-9	1			.857	-7	/C-35,O-12,S-1	-1.1

■ JOHN OLDHAM   Oldham, John Hardin b: 11/6/32, Salinas, Cal.   BR/TL, 6'3", 198 lbs.   Deb: 9/2/56

YEAR	TM/L	G	AB	R	H	2B	3B	HR	RBI	BB	SO	AVG	OBP	SLG	PRO+	BR/A	SB	CS	SBR	FA	FR	G/POS	TPR
1956	Cin-N	1	0	0	0	0	0	0	0	0	0	—	—	—	—	—	0	0	0	.000	0	R	0.0

■ BOB OLDIS   Oldis, Robert Carl b: 1/5/28, Preston, Iowa   BR/TR, 6'1", 185 lbs.   Deb: 4/28/53   C

YEAR	TM/L	G	AB	R	H	2B	3B	HR	RBI	BB	SO	AVG	OBP	SLG	PRO+	BR/A	SB	CS	SBR	FA	FR	G/POS	TPR
1953	Was-A	7	16	0	4	0	0	0	3	1	2	.250	.294	.250	49	-1	0	0	0	1.000	2	/C-7	0.1
1954	Was-A	11	24	1	8	1	0	0	3	1	3	.333	.360	.375	107	0	0	0	0	.941	-1	/C-8,3-2	0.0
1955	Was-A	6	6	1	0	0	0	0	0	1	0	.000	.143	.000	-62	-1	0	0	0	1.000	0	/C-6	-0.1
1960	*Pit-N	22	20	1	4	1	0	0	1	1	2	.200	.238	.250	34	-2	0	0	0	1.000	3	C-22	0.1
1961	Pit-N	4	5	0	0	0	0	0	0	0	0	.000	.000	.000	-99	-1	0	0	0	1.000	3	/C-4	0.1
1962	Phi-N	38	80	9	21	1	0	1	10	13	10	.262	.366	.313	87	-1	0	1	-1	.987	1	C-30	0.0
1963	Phi-N	47	85	8	19	3	0	0	5	3	5	.224	.250	.259	47	-6	0	0	0	.979	5	C-43	0.0
Total	7	135	236	20	56	6	0	1	22	20	22	.237	.297	.275	60	-12	0	1	-1	.983	12	C-120/3-2	0.2

■ RUBE OLDRING   Oldring, Reuben Henry b: 5/30/1884, New York, N.Y.   d: 9/9/61, Bridgeton, N.J.   BR/TR, 5'10", 186 lbs.   Deb: 10/2/05

YEAR	TM/L	G	AB	R	H	2B	3B	HR	RBI	BB	SO	AVG	OBP	SLG	PRO+	BR/A	SB	CS	SBR	FA	FR	G/POS	TPR
1905	NY-A	8	30	2	9	0	1	1	6	2		.300	.344	.467	140	1	4			.967	5	/S-8	0.7
1906	Phi-A	59	174	15	42	10	1	0	19	2		.241	.263	.310	77	-5	7			.897	2	3-49/S-3,2-2,1-1	-0.2
1907	Phi-A	117	441	48	126	27	8	1	40	7		.286	.305	.390	118	7	29			.974	-9	*O-117	-0.8
1908	Phi-A	116	434	38	96	14	2	1	39	18		.221	.267	.270	70	-15	13			.941	3	*O-116	-2.0
1909	Phi-A	90	326	39	75	13	8	1	39	20		.230	.287	.328	92	-4	17			.963	-1	O-89/1-1	-0.9
1910	Phi-A	134	546	79	168	27	14	4	57	23		.308	.340	.430	142	23	17			.978	-1	*O-134	1.7
1911	*Phi-A	121	495	84	147	11	14	3	59	21		.297	.332	.394	104	1	21			.979	-9	*O-119	-1.4
1912	Phi-A	99	395	61	119	14	5	1	24	10		.301	.324	.370	102	-1	17			.974	-3	O-98	-0.9
1913	*Phi-A	137	538	101	152	27	9	5	71	34	37	.283	.328	.394	113	6	40			.968	-7	*O-131/S-5	-0.6
1914	*Phi-A	119	466	68	129	21	7	3	49	18	35	.277	.308	.371	108	2	14	16	-5	.965	-6	*O-117	-1.7
1915	Phi-A	107	408	49	101	23	3	6	42	22	21	.248	.293	.363	100	-3	11	6	-0	.982	5	O-96/3-8	-0.3
1916	Phi-A	40	146	10	36	8	3	0	14	9	9	.247	.290	.342	95	-2	1			.897	-2	O-40	-0.7
	NY-A	43	158	17	37	8	0	1	12	12	13	.234	.288	.304	76	-5	6			.957	-3	O-43	-1.2
	Yr	83	304	27	73	16	3	1	26	21	22	.240	.289	.322	85	-7	7			.926	-5	O-83	-1.9
1918	Phi-A	49	133	5	31	2	1	0	11	8	10	.233	.282	.263	64	-6	0			.949	-8	O-30/2-2,3-2	-1.8
Total	13	1239	4690	616	1268	205	76	27	471	206	125	.270	.307	.364	103	0	197	22		.966	-35	*O-1130/3-59,S21	-10.1

■ CHARLEY O'LEARY   O'Leary, Charles Timothy b: 10/15/1882, Chicago, Ill.   d: 1/6/41, Chicago, Ill.   BR/TR, 5'7", 165 lbs.   Deb: 4/14/04   C

YEAR	TM/L	G	AB	R	H	2B	3B	HR	RBI	BB	SO	AVG	OBP	SLG	PRO+	BR/A	SB	CS	SBR	FA	FR	G/POS	TPR
1904	Det-A	135	456	39	97	16	3	1	16	21		.213	.254	.254	63	-19	9			.933	6	*S-135	-1.1
1905	Det-A	148	512	47	109	13	5	0	33	29		.213	.259	.242	59	-24	13			.933	-8	*S-148	-3.1
1906	Det-A	128	443	34	97	13	2	0	34	17		.219	.253	.271	62	-20	8			.926	-8	*S-127	-2.6
1907	*Det-A	139	465	61	112	19	1	0	34	32		.241	.286	.286	83	-8	11			.943	-5	*S-138	-1.1
1908	Det-A	65	211	21	53	9	3	0	17	9		.251	.295	.322	96	-1	4			.920	-12	S-64/2-1	-1.4
1909	*Det-A	76	261	29	53	10	5	0	13	6		.203	.224	.241	45	-17	9			.922	-4	3-54,2-15/S-4,O-2	-2.2
1910	Det-A	65	211	23	51	7	1	0	9	9		.242	.276	.284	71	-8	7			.935	1	2-38,S-18/3-6	-0.7
1911	Det-A	74	256	29	68	8	2	0	25	21		.266	.336	.313	77	-7	10			.966	4	2-67/3-6	-0.5
1912	Det-A	3	10	1	2	0	0	0	1	0		.200	.200	.200	15	-1	0			1.000	2	/2-3	0.0
1913	StL-N	121	406	32	88	15	5	0	31	20	34	.217	.260	.278	55	-24	3			.951	-8	*S-103,2-15	-2.5
1934	StL-N	1	1	1	1	0	0	0	0	0	0	1.000	1.000	1.000	385	0	0	0	0	.000	0	H	0.0
Total	11	955	3232	317	731	104	18	3	213	164	34	.226	.270	.272	67	-129	74	0		.935	-32	S-737,2-139/3-66,O	-15.2

■ DAN O'LEARY   O'Leary, Daniel "Hustling Dan" b: 10/22/1856, Detroit, Mich.   d: 6/24/22, Chicago, Ill.   BL, 5'10", 165 lbs.   Deb: 9/3/1879   M

YEAR	TM/L	G	AB	R	H	2B	3B	HR	RBI	BB	SO	AVG	OBP	SLG	PRO+	BR/A	SB	CS	SBR	FA	FR	G/POS	TPR
1879	Pro-N	2	7	1	3	0	0	0	2	0	0	.429	.429	.429	187	1				.000	-1	/O-2	0.0
1880	Bos-N	3	12	1	3	0	0	0	1	0	3	.250	.250	.417	126	0				1.000	-1	/O-3	-0.1
1881	Det-N	2	8	0	0	0	0	0	0	0	2	.000	.000	.000	-96	-2				.714	-1	/O-6	-0.2
1882	Wor-N	6	22	2	4	1	0	0	2	5	5	.182	.333	.227	82	-0				.800	-2	/O-6	-0.2
1884	Cin-U	32	132	14	34	0	2	1		5		.258	.285	.311	74	-8				.862	-2	O-32,M	-0.6
Total	5	45	181	18	44	3	2	1	5	10	10	.243	.283	.298	75	-9				.843	-2	/O-45	-1.1

■ TROY O'LEARY   O'Leary, Troy Franklin b: 8/4/69, Compton, Cal.   BL/TL, 6', 175 lbs.   Deb: 5/9/93

YEAR	TM/L	G	AB	R	H	2B	3B	HR	RBI	BB	SO	AVG	OBP	SLG	PRO+	BR/A	SB	CS	SBR	FA	FR	G/POS	TPR
1993	Mil-A	19	41	3	12	3	0	0	3	5	9	.293	.370	.366	100	0	0	0	0	1.000	-1	O-19	-0.1
1994	Mil-A	27	66	9	18	1	1	2	7	5	11	.273	.333	.409	86	-1	1	1	-0	1.000	-1	O-21/D-1	-0.3
1995	Bos-A	112	399	60	123	31	6	10	49	29	64	.308	.357	.491	114	7	5	3	-0	.976	-5	*O-105/D-3	0.0
1996	Bos-A	149	497	68	129	28	5	15	81	47	80	.260	.328	.427	86	-11	3	2	-0	.971	-26	*O-146	-3.9
Total	4	307	1003	140	282	63	12	27	140	86	165	.281	.342	.449	97	-5	9	6	-1	.977	-33	O-291/D-4	-4.3

■ JOHN OLERUD   Olerud, John Garrett b: 8/5/68, Seattle, Wash.   BL/TL, 6'5", 205 lbs.   Deb: 9/3/89

YEAR	TM/L	G	AB	R	H	2B	3B	HR	RBI	BB	SO	AVG	OBP	SLG	PRO+	BR/A	SB	CS	SBR	FA	FR	G/POS	TPR
1989	Tor-A	6	8	2	3	0	0	0	0	1	3	.375	.375	.375	114	0	0	0	0	1.000	0	/1-5,D-1	0.0
1990	Tor-A	111	358	43	95	15	1	14	48	57	75	.265	.368	.430	120	11	0	2	-1	.986	-1	D-90,1-18	0.5
1991	*Tor-A	139	454	64	116	30	1	17	68	68	84	.256	.360	.438	115	10	0	2	-1	.996	-4	*1-135/D-1	-0.4
1992	*Tor-A	138	458	68	130	28	0	16	66	70	61	.284	.380	.450	126	17	1	0	0	.994	-7	*1-133/D-1	0.6
1993	*Tor-A★	158	551	109	200	54	2	24	107	114	65	.363	.478	.599	186	74	0	2	-1	.992	1	*1-137,D-20	5.8
1994	Tor-A	108	384	47	114	29	2	12	67	61	53	.297	.397	.477	124	15	1	2	-1	.993	2	*1-104/D-3	0.6
1995	Tor-A	135	492	72	143	32	0	8	54	84	54	.291	.398	.404	110	11	0	0	0	.997	-2	*1-133	-0.4
1996	Tor-A	125	398	59	109	25	0	18	61	60	37	.274	.382	.472	114	10	1	2	-1	.998	-1	*1-101,D-15	0.0
Total	8	920	3103	464	910	213	6	109	471	514	430	.293	.399	.471	130	148	3	8	-4	.995	-7	1-766,D-131	6.7

■ FRANK OLIN   Olin, Franklin Walter b: 1/9/1860, Woodford, Vt.   d: 5/21/51, St.Louis, Mo.   BL,   Deb: 7/4/1884

YEAR	TM/L	G	AB	R	H	2B	3B	HR	RBI	BB	SO	AVG	OBP	SLG	PRO+	BR/A	SB	CS	SBR	FA	FR	G/POS	TPR
1884	Was-a	21	83	12	32	4	1	0		7		.386	.433	.458	216	11				.775	-7	2-12,O-11	0.4
	Was-U	1	4	0	0	0	0	0		0		.000	.000	.000	-99	-1				.000	-0	/O-1	-0.1
	Tol-a	26	86	16	22	0	1	1		5		.256	.304	.314	99	-0				.875	0	O-26	0.0
1885	Det-N	1	4	1	2	0	0	0		0	0	.500	.500	.500	224	1				.667	-0	/3-1	0.0
Total	2	49	177	29	56	4	2	1	0	12	0	.316	.363	.379	148	10				.849	-7	/O-38,2-12,3-1	0.3

YEAR	TM/L	G	AB	R	H	2B	3B	HR	RBI	BB	SO	AVG	OBP	SLG	PRO+	BR/A	SB	CS	SBR	FA	FR	G/POS	TPR
■ JOSE OLIVA			Oliva, Jose (Galvez)		b: 3/3/71, San Pedro De Macoris, D.R.			BR/TR, 6'1", 150 lbs.			Deb: 7/1/94												
1994	Atl-N	19	59	9	17	5	0	6	11	7	10	.288	.364	.678	160	5	0	1	-1	.932	2	3-16	0.6
1995	Atl-N	48	109	7	17	4	0	5	12	7	22	.156	.207	.330	38	-10	0	0	0	.902	-1	3-25/1-1	-1.1
	StL-N	22	74	8	9	1	0	2	8	5	24	.122	.198	.216	9	-10	0	0	0	.977	-2	3-18/1-2	-1.3
	Yr	70	183	15	26	5	0	7	20	12	46	.142	.203	.284	26	-20	0	0	0	.933	-3	3-43/1-3	-2.4
Total	2	89	242	24	43	10	0	13	31	19	56	.178	.243	.380	60	-15	0	1	-1	.932	-2	/3-59,1-3	-1.8
■ TONY OLIVA			Oliva, Pedro (Lopez)		b: 7/20/40, Pinar Del Rio, Cuba			BL/TR, 6'2", 190 lbs.			Deb: 9/9/62	C											
1962	Min-A	9	9	3	4	1	0	0	3	3	2	.444	.583	.556	201	2	0	0	0	1.000	-0	/O-2	0.1
1963	Min-A	7	7	0	3	0	0	0	1	0	2	.429	.429	.429	138	0	0	0	0	.000	0	H	0.0
1964	Min-A★	161	672	**109**	**217**	**43**	9	32	94	34	68	**.323**	.361	.557	150	42	12	6	0	.981	5	*O-159	4.1
1965	*Min-A★	149	576	107	**185**	40	5	16	98	55	64	.321	.384	.491	141	31	19	9	0	.964	5	*O-147	3.3
1966	Min-A★	159	622	99	**191**	32	7	25	87	42	72	.307	.356	.502	135	27	13	7	-0	.972	14	*O-159	3.5
1967	Min-A★	146	557	76	161	34	6	17	83	44	61	.289	.350	.463	128	19	11	3	2	.987	12	*O-146	2.7
1968	Min-A★	128	470	54	136	24	5	18	68	45	61	.289	.360	.477	145	25	10	9	-2	.983	8	*O-126	2.7
1969	*Min-A†	153	637	97	**197**	**39**	4	24	101	45	66	.309	.358	.496	134	26	10	13	-5	.982	13	*O-152	2.7
1970	*Min-A★	157	628	96	**204**	**36**	7	23	107	38	67	.325	.366	.514	138	30	5	4	-1	.968	21	*O-157	4.3
1971	Min-A†	126	487	73	164	30	3	22	81	25	44	**.337**	.372	**.546**	152	31	4	1	1	.969	-1	*O-121	2.6
1972	Min-A	10	28	1	9	1	0	0	1	2	5	.321	.367	.357	111	0	0	0	0	.857	-3	/O-9	-0.3
1973	Min-A	146	571	63	166	20	0	16	92	45	44	.291	.347	.410	108	6	0	1	-1	.000	0	*D-142	0.2
1974	Min-A	127	459	43	131	16	2	13	57	27	31	.285	.328	.414	109	4	0	1	-1	.000	0	*D-112	0.1
1975	Min-A	131	455	46	123	10	0	13	58	41	45	.270	.348	.378	104	3	0	1	-1	.000	0	*D-120	-0.1
1976	Min-A	67	123	3	26	3	0	1	16	2	13	.211	.236	.260	44	-9	0	0	0	.000	0	D-32	-1.0
Total	15	1676	6301	870	1917	329	48	220	947	448	645	.304	.356	.476	130	238	86	55	-7	.975	76	*O-1178,D-406	24.9
■ ED OLIVARES			Olivares, Edward (Balzac)		b: 11/5/38, Mayaguez, P.R.			BR/TR, 5'11", 180 lbs.			Deb: 9/16/60	F											
1960	StL-N	3	5	0	0	0	0	0	0	0	3	.000	.000	.000	-92	-1	0	0	0	.500	-0	/3-1	-0.2
1961	StL-N	21	30	2	5	0	0	0	1	0	4	.167	.167	.167	-10	-5	1	0	0	1.000	-2	O-10	-0.7
Total	2	24	35	2	5	0	0	0	1	0	7	.143	.143	.143	-21	-6	1	0	0	1.000	-3	/O-10,3-1	-0.9
■ AL OLIVER			Oliver, Albert		b: 10/14/46, Portsmouth, Ohio			BL/TL, 6', 195 lbs.			Deb: 9/23/68												
1968	Pit-N	4	8	1	1	0	0	0	0	0	4	.125	.125	.125	-25	-1	0	0	0	1.000	0	/O-1	-0.1
1969	Pit-N	129	463	55	132	19	2	17	70	21	38	.285	.334	.445	119	10	8	5	-1	.991	-1	*1-106,O-21	-0.1
1970	*Pit-N	151	551	63	149	33	5	12	83	35	35	.270	.330	.414	100	-1	1	1	-0	.986	1	O-80,1-77	-1.0
1971	*Pit-N	143	529	69	149	31	7	14	64	27	72	.282	.323	.446	116	9	4	3	-1	.981	8	*O-116,1-25	1.0
1972	*Pit-N★	140	565	88	176	27	4	12	89	34	44	.312	.356	.437	127	19	2	4	-2	.985	1	*O-138/1-3	1.1
1973	Pit-N	158	654	90	191	38	7	20	99	22	52	.292	.320	.463	118	12	6	0	2	.964	-2	*O-109,1-50	0.3
1974	Pit-N	147	617	96	198	38	12	11	85	33	58	.321	.360	.475	137	27	10	1	2	.986	7	O-98,1-49	3.0
1975	*Pit-N★	155	628	90	176	39	8	18	84	25	73	.280	.313	.454	112	6	4	2	0	.987	2	*O-153/1-4	0.1
1976	Pit-N★	121	443	62	143	22	5	12	61	26	29	.323	.367	.476	137	20	6	2	1	.984	7	*O-106/1-3	2.4
1977	Pit-N	154	568	75	175	29	6	19	82	40	38	.308	.358	.481	119	15	13	16	-6	.981	0	*O-148	0.3
1978	Tex-A	133	525	65	170	35	5	14	89	31	41	.324	.364	.490	138	24	8	9	-3	.987	6	*O-107,D-26	2.2
1979	Tex-A	136	492	69	159	28	4	12	76	34	34	.323	.372	.470	127	18	4	5	-2	.975	0	*O-119,D-10	1.1
1980	Tex-A★	163	656	96	209	43	3	19	117	39	47	.319	.361	.480	132	27	5	7	-3	.973	4	*O-157/1-1,D-4	2.2
1981	Tex-A★	102	421	53	130	29	1	4	55	24	28	.309	.349	.411	125	12	3	0	1	1.000	-0	*D-101/1-1	1.0
1982	Mon-N★	160	617	90	**204**	**43**	2	22	**109**	61	59	**.331**	.394	.514	149	41	5	2	0	.986	-9	*1-159	2.5
1983	Mon-N★	157	614	70	184	**38**	3	8	84	44	40	.300	.348	.410	110	8	1	3	-2	.990	-1	*1-153/O-1	0.0
1984	SF-N	91	339	27	101	19	2	0	34	20	27	.298	.339	.366	101	0	2	2	-1	.985	-1	1-82	-0.7
	Phi-N	28	93	9	29	7	0	0	14	7	9	.312	.360	.387	108	1	1	2	-1	.987	-3	*1-19/O-5	-0.5
	Yr	119	432	36	130	26	2	0	48	27	36	.301	.343	.370	103	1	3	4	-2	.985	-4	*1-101/O-5	-1.2
1985	LA-N	35	79	1	20	5	0	0	8	5	11	.253	.298	.316	74	-3	1	0	0	.882	-2	O-17	-0.6
	*Tor-A	61	187	20	47	6	1	5	23	7	13	.251	.282	.374	76	-6	0	0	0	1.000	-0	D-59/1-1	-0.6
Total	18	2368	9049	1189	2743	529	77	219	1326	535	756	.303	.348	.451	122	238	84	64	-13	.980	19	*O-1376,1-733,D-200	13.4
■ DAVE OLIVER			Oliver, David Jacob		b: 4/7/51, Stockton, Cal.			BL/TR, 5'11", 175 lbs.			Deb: 9/25/77	C											
1977	Cle-A	7	22	2	7	0	1	0	3	4	0	.318	.444	.409	139	2	0	0	0	.949	1	/2-7	0.2
■ GENE OLIVER			Oliver, Eugene George		b: 3/22/35, Moline, Ill.			BR/TR, 6'2", 225 lbs.			Deb: 6/6/59												
1959	StL-N	68	172	14	42	9	0	6	28	7	41	.244	.274	.401	72	-7	3	2	-0	.955	-5	O-42/C-9,1-5	-1.5
1961	StL-N	22	52	8	14	2	0	4	9	6	10	.269	.367	.538	124	2	0	0	0	1.000	7	C-15/O-1	0.4
1962	StL-N	122	345	42	89	19	1	14	45	50	59	.258	.354	.441	102	1	5	2	0	.991	-4	C-98/O-8,1-3	0.0
1963	StL-N	39	102	10	23	4	0	6	18	13	19	.225	.313	.441	105	1	0	0	0	.981	1	C-35	0.3
	Mil-N	95	296	34	74	12	2	11	47	27	59	.250	.323	.416	112	5	4	4	-1	.985	-14	1-55,O-35/C-2	-1.5
	Yr	134	398	44	97	16	2	17	65	40	78	.244	.321	.422	110	5	4	4	-1	.985	-13	1-55,C-37,O-35	-1.2
1964	Mil-N	93	279	45	77	15	1	13	49	17	41	.276	.320	.477	120	7	3	7	-3	.982	-6	1-76/C-1	-0.6
1965	Mil-N	122	392	56	106	20	0	21	58	36	61	.270	.336	.482	127	13	5	4	-1	.976	1	C-64,1-52/O-1	1.5
1966	Atl-N	76	191	19	37	9	1	8	24	16	43	.194	.256	.377	72	-8	2	0	1	.990	11	C-48/1-5,O-2	0.7
1967	Atl-N	17	51	8	10	2	0	3	6	6	8	.196	.281	.412	97	-0	0	0	0	.968	2	C-14	0.3
	Phi-N	85	263	29	59	16	0	7	34	29	56	.224	.304	.365	90	-4	2	2	-1	.987	-12	C-79/1-2	-1.3
	Yr	102	314	37	69	18	0	10	40	35	64	.220	.300	.373	91	-4	2	2	-1	.984	-10	C-93/1-2	-1.0
1968	Bos-A	16	35	2	5	0	0	1	4	4	12	.143	.250	.143	20	-3	0	0	0	.984	-2	C-10/O-1	-0.5
	Chi-N	8	11	1	4	0	0	1	3	2	4	.364	.500	.364	152	1	0	0	0	1.000	0	/1-2,C-1,O-1	0.1
1969	Chi-N	23	27	0	6	3	0	0	1	0	9	.222	.276	.333	62	-1	0	0	0	1.000	2	/C-6	0.1
Total	10	786	2216	268	546	111	5	93	320	215	420	.246	.317	.427	103	5	24	21	-5	.985	-24	C-382,1-200/O-91	-2.0
■ JOE OLIVER			Oliver, Joseph Melton		b: 7/24/65, Memphis, Tenn.			BR/TR, 6'3", 215 lbs.			Deb: 7/15/89												
1989	Cin-N	49	151	13	41	8	0	3	23	6	28	.272	.304	.384	92	-2	0	0	0	.986	-1	C-47	0.0
1990	*Cin-N	121	364	34	84	23	0	8	52	37	75	.231	.305	.360	79	-11	1	1	-0	**.992**	-1	*C-118	-0.2
1991	Cin-N	94	269	21	58	11	0	11	41	18	53	.216	.265	.379	76	-9	0	0	0	.980	-1	C-90	-0.6
1992	Cin-N	143	485	42	131	25	1	10	57	35	75	.270	.321	.388	97	-2	2	3	-1	.992	-1	*C-141/1-1	0.4
1993	Cin-N	139	482	40	115	28	0	14	75	27	91	.239	.280	.384	76	-18	0	0	0	.992	-9	*C-133,1-12/O-1	-2.0
1994	Cin-N	6	19	1	4	0	0	1	2	5	3	.211	.286	.368	70	-1	0	0	0	.980	2	/C-6	0.1
1995	Mil-A	97	337	43	92	20	0	12	51	27	66	.273	.332	.439	93	-4	2	2	-1	.982	-5	C-91/1-2,D-6	-0.4
1996	Cin-N	106	289	31	70	12	1	11	46	28	54	.242	.313	.405	88	-5	2	2	-1	.992	10	C-97/1-3,O-3	1.0
Total	8	755	2396	225	595	127	2	70	350	180	445	.248	.304	.391	86	-52	7	8	-3	.989	-5	C-723/1-18,D-6,O-4	-1.7
■ NATE OLIVER			Oliver, Nathaniel "Peewee"		b: 12/13/40, St.Petersburg, Fla.			BR/TR, 5'10", 160 lbs.			Deb: 4/9/63												
1963	LA-N	65	163	23	39	2	3	1	9	13	25	.239	.299	.307	80	-4	3	4	-2	.961	5	2-57/S-2	0.4
1964	LA-N	99	321	28	78	9	0	0	21	31	57	.243	.310	.271	70	-12	7	4	-0	.967	-10	2-98/S-1	-1.6
1965	LA-N	8	3	1	3	0	0	0	0	0	0	1.000	1.000	1.000	498	1	1	0	0	1.000	1	/2-2	0.2
1966	*LA-N	80	119	17	23	0	0	0	3	13	17	.193	.278	.210	41	-9	3	3	-1	.977	11	2-68/S-2,3-1	0.4
1967	LA-N	77	232	18	55	6	2	0	7	13	50	.237	.283	.280	67	-10	3	2	-1	.973	-3	2-39,S-32/O-1	-1.5
1968	SF-N	36	73	3	13	2	1	0	1	1	13	.178	.189	.205	18	-7	0	1	-1	.950	1	2-14,S-13/3-1	-0.7
1969	NY-A	1	1	0	0	0	0	0	0	0	0	.000	.000	.000	-99	-0	0	0	0	.000	0	H	0.0
	Chi-N	44	44	15	7	4	0	1	4	1	10	.159	.196	.295	32	-4	1	1	0	1.000	1	2-13	-0.2
Total	7	410	954	107	216	24	5	2	45	72	172	.226	.284	.268	62	-47	17	15	-4	.969	10	2-291/S-50,3-2,O-1	-2.1
■ BOB OLIVER			Oliver, Robert Lee		b: 2/8/43, Shreveport, La.			BR/TR, 6'2", 215 lbs.			Deb: 9/10/65	F											
1965	Pit-N	3	2	1	0	0	0	0	0	0	0	.000	.000	.000	-99	-1	0	0	0	1.000	-0	/O-3	-0.1
1969	KC-A	118	394	43	100	8	4	13	43	21	74	.254	.295	.393	91	-6	5	5	-2	.977	5	O-98,1-12/3-8	-0.9
1970	KC-A	160	612	83	159	24	6	27	99	42	126	.260	.311	.451	108	4	3	3	-1	.993	-8	*1-115,3-46	-1.6

YEAR	TM/L	G	AB	R	H	2B	3B	HR	RBI	BB	SO	AVG	OBP	SLG	PRO+	BR/A	SB	CS	SBR	FA	FR	G/POS	TPR
1971	KC-A	128	373	35	91	12	2	8	52	14	88	.244	.281	.351	79	-12	0	0	0	.988	-0	1-68,O-48/3-2	-2.0
1972	KC-A	16	63	7	17	2	1	1	6	2	12	.270	.292	.381	100	-0	1	0	0	.979	3	O-16	0.3
	Cal-A	134	509	47	137	20	4	19	70	27	97	.269	.310	.436	127	14	4	3	-1	.994	-6	*1-127/O-8	-0.4
	Yr	150	572	54	154	22	5	20	76	29	109	.269	.308	.430	124	13	5	3	-0	.994	-3	*1-127,O-24	-0.1
1973	Cal-A	151	544	51	144	21	1	18	90	33	100	.265	.313	.412	111	5	1	1	-0	.952	-1	3-49,O-47,1-32,D-12	-0.1
1974	Cal-A	110	359	22	89	9	1	8	55	16	51	.248	.282	.345	84	-8	2	1	0	.985	-12	1-57,3-46/O-4,D-1	-2.6
	Bal-A	9	20	1	3	2	0	0	4	0	5	.150	.150	.250	14	-2	1	1	0	.974	1	/1-4,D-1	-0.2
	Yr	119	379	23	92	11	1	8	59	16	56	.243	.275	.340	81	-11	3	2	0	.984	-11	1-61,3-46/O-4,D-2	-2.8
1975	NY-A	18	38	3	5	1	0	0	1	1	9	.132	.154	.158	-12	-6	0	0	0	1.000	-0	/1-8,3-1,D-3	-0.7
Total	8	847	2914	293	745	102	19	94	419	156	562	.256	.298	.400	100	-13	17	14	-3	.991	-19	1-423,O-224,3/D	-8.3

■ TOM OLIVER

Oliver, Thomas Noble "Rebel" b: 1/15/03, Montgomery, Ala. d: 2/26/88, Montgomery, Ala. BR/TR, 6', 168 lbs. Deb: 4/14/30 C

YEAR	TM/L	G	AB	R	H	2B	3B	HR	RBI	BB	SO	AVG	OBP	SLG	PRO+	BR/A	SB	CS	SBR	FA	FR	G/POS	TPR
1930	Bos-A	154	646	86	189	34	2	0	46	42	25	.293	.339	.351	78	-21	6	6	-2	.982	15	*O-154	-1.7
1931	Bos-A	148	586	52	162	35	5	0	70	25	17	.276	.307	.353	77	-21	4	6	-2	.993	13	*O-148	-1.9
1932	Bos-A	122	455	39	120	23	3	0	37	25	12	.264	.305	.327	66	-23	1	6	-3	.983	8	*O-116	-2.4
1933	Bos-A	90	244	25	63	9	1	0	23	13	7	.258	.296	.303	60	-14	1	1	-0	.985	-1	O-86	-1.8
Total	4	514	1931	202	534	101	11	0	176	105	61	.277	.316	.340	73	-79	12	19	-8	.986	35	O-504	-7.8

■ LUIS OLMO

Olmo, Luis Francisco (Rodriguez) (b: Luis Francisco Rodriguez (Olmo)) b: 8/11/19, Arecibo, P.R. BR/TR, 5'11.5", 190 lbs. Deb: 7/23/43

YEAR	TM/L	G	AB	R	H	2B	3B	HR	RBI	BB	SO	AVG	OBP	SLG	PRO+	BR/A	SB	CS	SBR	FA	FR	G/POS	TPR
1943	Bro-N	57	238	39	72	6	4	4	37	8	20	.303	.325	.412	112	2	3			.957	-2	O-57	-0.2
1944	Bro-N	136	520	65	134	20	5	9	85	17	37	.258	.284	.367	84	-13	10			.971	-8	O-64,2-42,3-31	-2.3
1945	Bro-N	141	556	62	174	27	13	10	110	36	33	.313	.356	.462	127	18	15			.971	-9	*O-106,3-31/2-1	0.4
1949	*Bro-N	38	105	15	32	4	1	1	14	5	11	.305	.336	.390	91	-1	2			.950	-4	O-34	-0.7
1950	Bos-N	69	154	23	35	7	1	5	22	18	23	.227	.308	.383	86	-4	3			.974	-9	O-55/3-1	-1.4
1951	Bos-N	21	56	4	11	1	1	0	4	4	4	.196	.250	.250	38	-5	0	1	-1	1.000	-5	O-16	-0.9
Total	6	462	1629	208	458	65	25	29	272	88	128	.281	.319	.405	102	-3	33	1		.968	-34	O-332/3-63,2-43	-5.1

■ BARNEY OLSEN

Olsen, Bernard Charles b: 9/11/19, Everett, Mass. d: 3/30/77, Everett, Mass. BR/TR, 5'11", 179 lbs. Deb: 4/17/41

YEAR	TM/L	G	AB	R	H	2B	3B	HR	RBI	BB	SO	AVG	OBP	SLG	PRO+	BR/A	SB	CS	SBR	FA	FR	G/POS	TPR
1941	Chi-N	24	73	13	21	6	1	1	4	4	11	.288	.325	.438	118	1	0			.947	1	O-23	0.1

■ GREG OLSON

Olson, Gregory William b: 9/6/60, Marshall, Minn. BR/TR, 6', 200 lbs. Deb: 6/27/89

YEAR	TM/L	G	AB	R	H	2B	3B	HR	RBI	BB	SO	AVG	OBP	SLG	PRO+	BR/A	SB	CS	SBR	FA	FR	G/POS	TPR
1989	Min-A	3	2	0	1	0	0	0	0	0	0	.500	.500	.500	171	0	0	0	0	1.000	0	/C-3	0.0
1990	Atl-N★	100	298	36	78	12	1	7	36	30	51	.262	.333	.379	90	-4	1	1	-0	.987	-7	C-97/3-1	-0.5
1991	*Atl-N	133	411	46	99	25	0	6	44	44	48	.241	.319	.345	82	-9	1	1	-0	.995	8	*C-127	0.0
1992	Atl-N	95	302	27	72	14	2	3	27	34	31	.238	.318	.328	78	-8	2	1	0	.998	7	C-94	0.5
1993	*Atl-N	83	262	23	59	10	4	4	24	29	27	.225	.305	.309	64	-13	1	0	0	.988	2	C-81	-1.0
Total	5	414	1275	132	309	61	3	20	131	137	157	.242	.319	.342	79	-34	5	3	-0	.992	2	C-402/3-1	-1.0

■ IVY OLSON

Olson, Ivan Massie b: 10/14/1885, Kansas City, Mo. d: 9/1/65, Inglewood, Cal. BR/TR, 5'10.5", 175 lbs. Deb: 4/12/11 C

YEAR	TM/L	G	AB	R	H	2B	3B	HR	RBI	BB	SO	AVG	OBP	SLG	PRO+	BR/A	SB	CS	SBR	FA	FR	G/POS	TPR
1911	Cle-A	140	545	89	142	20	8	1	50	34		.261	.311	.332	79	-17	20			.909	-16	*S-139/3-1	-2.3
1912	Cle-A	125	467	68	118	13	1	0	33	21		.253	.291	.285	63	-23	16			.917	6	S-56,3-36,2-21,/O-3	-1.3
1913	Cle-A	104	370	47	92	13	3	0	32	22	28	.249	.296	.300	72	-13	7			.953	-1	3-73,1-21/2-1	-1.0
1914	Cle-A	89	310	22	75	6	2	1	20	13	24	.242	.275	.284	65	-14	15	9	-1	.942	12	S-31,2-23,3-19/O1	0.0
1915	Cin-N	63	207	18	48	5	4	0	14	12	13	.232	.274	.295	71	-7	10	6	-1	.938	13	2-39,3-15/1-7	0.6
	Bro-N	18	26	2	2	0	1	0	3	1	0	.077	.111	.154	-20	-4	0			.909	-1	/S-7,2-1,3-1,O-1	-0.5
	Yr	81	233	20	50	5	5	0	17	13	13	.215	.256	.279	61	-11	10	6	-1	.938	12	2-40,3-16/1-7,SO	0.1
1916	*Bro-N	108	351	29	89	13	4	1	38	21	27	.254	.298	.322	88	-5	14			.920	-13	*S-103/2-3,1-1	-1.4
1917	Bro-N	139	580	64	156	18	5	2	38	14	34	.269	.291	.328	87	-10	6			.941	-6	*S-133/3-6	-1.1
1918	Bro-N	126	506	63	121	16	4	1	17	27	18	.239	.286	.292	77	-14	21			.918	-25	*S-126	-3.9
1919	Bro-N	140	590	73	164	14	9	1	36	30	12	.278	.316	.337	94	-4	26			.947	-2	*S-140	0.3
1920	*Bro-N	143	637	71	162	13	11	1	46	20	19	.254	.278	.314	68	-27	4	7	-3	.935	-7	*S-125,2-21	-2.8
1921	Bro-N	151	652	88	174	22	10	3	35	28	26	.267	.301	.345	68	-30	4	9	-4	.943	5	*S-133,2-20	-1.6
1922	Bro-N	136	551	63	150	26	6	1	47	25	10	.272	.306	.347	69	-16	8	5	-1	.960	-6	2-85,S-51	-2.4
1923	Bro-N	82	292	33	76	11	1	1	35	14	10	.260	.296	.315	63	-16	5	0	2	.974	5	2-72/3-4,1-2,S-2	-0.8
1924	Bro-N	10	27	0	6	1	0	0	3	0	1	.222	.300	.259	53	-2	0	0	0	.941	-2	/S-8,2-2	-0.3
Total	14	1574	6111	730	1575	191	69	13	446	285	222	.258	.295	.318	74	-212	156	36		.932	-34	*S-1054,2-288,3/1O	-18.5

■ KARL OLSON

Olson, Karl Arthur "Ole" b: 7/6/30, Kentfield, Cal. BR/TR, 6'3", 205 lbs. Deb: 6/30/51

YEAR	TM/L	G	AB	R	H	2B	3B	HR	RBI	BB	SO	AVG	OBP	SLG	PRO+	BR/A	SB	CS	SBR	FA	FR	G/POS	TPR
1951	Bos-A	5	10	0	1	0	0	0	0	0	3	.100	.100	.100	-42	-2	0	0	0	1.000	-1	/O-5	-0.3
1953	Bos-A	25	57	5	7	2	0	1	6	1	9	.123	.138	.211	-7	-9	0	0	0	.970	-4	O-24	-1.3
1954	Bos-A	101	227	25	59	12	2	1	20	12	23	.260	.297	.344	68	-10	2	1	0	.957	-8	O-78	-2.1
1955	Bos-A	26	48	7	12	1	2	0	1	1	10	.250	.265	.354	60	-3	0	0	0	1.000	-5	O-21	-0.8
1956	Was-A	106	313	34	77	10	2	4	22	28	41	.246	.310	.329	69	-14	1	1	-0	.990	-10	*O-101	-2.8
1957	Was-A	8	12	2	2	0	0	0	0	1	2	.167	.231	.167	10	-1	0	0	0	1.000	-1	/O-6	-0.3
	Det-A	8	14	1	2	0	0	0	1	0	6	.143	.143	.143	-21	-2	0	0	0	1.000	-1	/O-5	-0.4
	Yr	16	26	3	4	0	0	0	1	1	8	.154	.185	.154	-6	-4	0	0	0	1.000	-2	O-11	-0.7
Total	6	279	681	74	160	25	6	6	50	43	94	.235	.281	.316	57	-42	3	2	-0	.979	-28	O-240	-8.0

■ MARV OLSON

Olson, Marvin Clement "Sparky" b: 5/28/07, Gayville, S.Dak. BR/TR, 5'7", 160 lbs. Deb: 9/13/31

YEAR	TM/L	G	AB	R	H	2B	3B	HR	RBI	BB	SO	AVG	OBP	SLG	PRO+	BR/A	SB	CS	SBR	FA	FR	G/POS	TPR
1931	Bos-A	15	53	8	10	1	0	0	5	9	3	.189	.306	.208	40	-4	0	0	0	.963	3	2-15	-0.4
1932	Bos-A	115	403	58	100	14	6	0	25	61	26	.248	.347	.313	74	-14	1	5	-3	.955	-15	*2-106/3-1	-2.4
1933	Bos-A	3	1	1	0	0	0	0	0	0	1	.000	.000	.000	-99	-0	0	0	0	.000	0	/2-1	0.0
Total	3	133	457	67	110	15	6	0	30	70	30	.241	.342	.300	70	-18	1	5	-3	.956	-12	2-122/3-1	-2.4

■ TOM O'MALLEY

O'Malley, Thomas Patrick b: 12/25/60, Orange, N.J. BL/TR, 6', 190 lbs. Deb: 5/8/82

YEAR	TM/L	G	AB	R	H	2B	3B	HR	RBI	BB	SO	AVG	OBP	SLG	PRO+	BR/A	SB	CS	SBR	FA	FR	G/POS	TPR
1982	SF-N	92	291	26	80	12	4	2	27	33	39	.275	.351	.364	100	1	0	3	-2	.965	1	3-83/2-1,S-1	-0.3
1983	SF-N	135	410	40	106	16	1	5	45	52	47	.259	.348	.339	94	-2	2	4	-2	.940	1	*3-117	-0.5
1984	SF-N	13	25	2	3	0	0	0	0	2	2	.120	.185	.120	-13	-4	0	0	0	1.000	-0	/3-7	-0.5
	Chi-N	12	16	0	2	0	0	0	0	3	5	.125	.125	.125	-29	-3	0	0	0	1.000	-2	/3-6	-0.5
1985	Bal-A	8	14	1	1	0	0	0	2	0	2	.071	.071	.286	-8	-2	0	0	0	.833	-1	/3-3	-0.3
1986	Bal-A	56	181	19	46	9	1	1	18	17	21	.254	.318	.320	76	-6	0	1	-1	.938	-1	3-55	-0.9
1987	Tex-A	45	117	10	32	8	0	1	12	15	9	.274	.356	.368	92	-1	0	0	0	.962	-4	3-40/2-1	-0.6
1988	Mon-N	14	27	3	7	2	0	0	2	3	4	.259	.333	.259	69	-1	0	0	0	.905	-1	/3-7	-0.3
1989	NY-N	9	11	2	6	2	0	0	8	0	2	.545	.545	.727	274	2	0	0	0	1.000	-0	/3-3	0.2
1990	NY-N	82	121	14	27	7	0	3	14	11	20	.223	.288	.355	76	-4	0	0	0	.983	2	3-38/1-3	-0.2
Total	9	466	1213	117	310	54	6	13	131	133	151	.256	.332	.340	87	-19	2	8	-4	.951	-5	3-359/1-3,2-2,S-1	-3.6

■ OLLIE O'MARA

O'Mara, Oliver Edward b: 3/8/1891, St.Louis, Mo. d: 10/24/89, Reno, Nev. BR/TR, 5'9", 155 lbs. Deb: 9/8/12

YEAR	TM/L	G	AB	R	H	2B	3B	HR	RBI	BB	SO	AVG	OBP	SLG	PRO+	BR/A	SB	CS	SBR	FA	FR	G/POS	TPR
1912	Det-A	1	4	0	0	0	0	0	0	0		.000	.000	.000	-99	-1	0			.857	0	/S-1	-0.1
1914	Bro-N	67	247	41	65	10	2	1	7	16	26	.263	.316	.332	91	-3	14			.918	-13	S-63	-1.1
1915	Bro-N	149	577	77	141	26	3	0	31	51	40	.244	.308	.300	83	-11	11	12	-4	.906	-34	*S-149	-4.2
1916	*Bro-N	72	193	18	39	5	2	0	15	12	20	.202	.249	.249	52	-11	10			.898	-5	S-51	-1.5
1918	Bro-N	121	450	29	96	8	1	1	24	7	18	.213	.242	.242	48	-28	11			.951	-2	*3-121	-3.1
1919	Bro-N	2	7	1	0	0	0	0	0	0		.000	.000	.000	-98	-2	0			.875	-0	/3-2	-0.2
Total	6	412	1478	166	341	49	8	2	77	86	104	.231	.280	.279	69	-56	46	12		.907	-53	S-264,3-123	-10.2

■ TOM O'MEARA

O'Meara, Thomas Edward b: 12/12/1872, Chicago, Ill. d: 2/16/02, Fort Wayne, Ind. Deb: 9/29/1895

YEAR	TM/L	G	AB	R	H	2B	3B	HR	RBI	BB	SO	AVG	OBP	SLG	PRO+	BR/A	SB	CS	SBR	FA	FR	G/POS	TPR
1895	Cle-N	1	1	1	0	0	0	0	0	0		.000	.500	.000	34	-0	0			.500	-0	/C-1	0.0
1896	Cle-N	12	33	5	5	0	0	0	0	5	7	.152	.263	.152	10	-4	0			.914	-1	/C-9,1-1	-0.4
Total	2	13	34	6	5	0	0	0	0	5	7	.147	.275	.147	12	-4	0			.892	-1	/C-10,1-1	-0.4

■ O'NEAL   O'Neal   Deb: 10/23/1874

YEAR	TM/L	G	AB	R	H	2B	3B	HR	RBI	BB	SO	AVG	OBP	SLG	PRO+	BR/A	SB	CS	SBR	FA	FR	G/POS	TPR
1874	Har-n	1	3	0	0	0	0	0	0	0	1	.000	.000	.000	-95	-1	0	0	0	.667	1	/O-1	0.0

■ DENNY O'NEIL   O'Neil, Dennis   b: 11/22/1866, Holyoke, Mass.   d: 11/15/22, Rushville, Ind.   BL/TL, 6'2.5", 200 lbs.   Deb: 6/18/1893

YEAR	TM/L	G	AB	R	H	2B	3B	HR	RBI	BB	SO	AVG	OBP	SLG	PRO+	BR/A	SB	CS	SBR	FA	FR	G/POS	TPR
1893	StL-N	7	25	3	3	0	0	0	2	4	0	.120	.241	.120	-3	-4	3			.986	-1	/1-7	-0.4

■ MICKEY O'NEIL   O'Neil, George Michael   b: 4/12/1900, St.Louis, Mo.   d: 4/8/64, St.Louis, Mo.   BR/TR, 5'10", 185 lbs.   Deb: 9/12/19   C

YEAR	TM/L	G	AB	R	H	2B	3B	HR	RBI	BB	SO	AVG	OBP	SLG	PRO+	BR/A	SB	CS	SBR	FA	FR	G/POS	TPR
1919	Bos-N	11	28	3	6	0	0	0	1	1	7	.214	.241	.214	39	-2	0			.981	1	C-11	0.2
1920	Bos-N	112	304	19	86	5	4	0	28	21	20	.283	.339	.326	96	-1	4	4	-1	.962	8	*C-105/2-1	1.3
1921	Bos-N	98	277	26	69	9	4	2	29	23	21	.249	.307	.332	73	-11	2	2	-1	.968	8	C-95	0.1
1922	Bos-N	83	251	18	56	5	2	0	26	14	11	.223	.267	.259	38	-23	1	0	0	.978	0	C-79	-1.8
1923	Bos-N	96	306	29	65	7	4	0	20	17	14	.212	.258	.261	39	-27	3	2	-0	.973	14	C-95	-0.9
1924	Bos-N	106	362	32	89	4	1	0	22	14	27	.246	.276	.262	47	-27	4	3	-1	.985	1	*C-106	-2.0
1925	Bos-N	70	222	29	57	6	5	2	30	21	16	.257	.327	.356	81	-6	1	2	-1	.972	-8	C-69	-1.1
1926	Bro-N	75	201	19	42	5	3	0	20	23	8	.209	.293	.264	52	-13	3			.965	-3	C-74	-1.2
1927	Was-A	5	6	0	0	0	0	0	0	0	1	.000	.000	.000	-99	-2	0	0	0	1.000	-0	/C-4	-0.2
	NY-N	16	38	2	5	0	0	0	3	5	2	.132	.233	.132	-0	-5	0			.969	3	C-16	-0.1
Total	9	672	1995	177	475	41	23	4	179	139	127	.238	.292	.288	58	-118	18	13		.972	26	C-654/2-1	-5.7

■ JOHN O'NEIL   O'Neil, John Francis   b: 4/19/20, Shelbiana, Ky.   BR/TR, 5'9", 155 lbs.   Deb: 4/16/46

YEAR	TM/L	G	AB	R	H	2B	3B	HR	RBI	BB	SO	AVG	OBP	SLG	PRO+	BR/A	SB	CS	SBR	FA	FR	G/POS	TPR
1946	Phi-N	46	94	12	25	3	0	0	9	5	12	.266	.303	.298	73	-3	0			.940	4	S-32	0.2

■ FRED O'NEILL   O'Neill, Frederick James "Tip"   b: 1865, London, Ontario, Canada   d: 3/7/1892, London, Ont., Can.   5'7", 142 lbs.   Deb: 5/3/1887

YEAR	TM/L	G	AB	R	H	2B	3B	HR	RBI	BB	SO	AVG	OBP	SLG	PRO+	BR/A	SB	CS	SBR	FA	FR	G/POS	TPR
1887	NY-a	6	26	4	8	1	1	0	3	1		.308	.357	.423	122	1	3			.800	-1	/O-6	-0.1

■ HARRY O'NEILL   O'Neill, Harry Mink   b: 5/8/17, Philadelphia, Pa.   d: 3/6/45, Iwo Jima, Marianas Islands   BR/TR, 6'3", 205 lbs.   Deb: 7/23/39

YEAR	TM/L	G	AB	R	H	2B	3B	HR	RBI	BB	SO	AVG	OBP	SLG	PRO+	BR/A	SB	CS	SBR	FA	FR	G/POS	TPR
1939	Phi-A	1	0	0	0	0	0	0	0	0	0	—	—	—	—	—	0			.000	0	/C-1	0.0

■ TIP O'NEILL   O'Neill, James Edward   b: 5/25/1858, Woodstock, Ont., Canada   d: 12/31/15, Montreal, Que., Can   BR/TR, 6'1.5", 167 lbs.   Deb: 5/5/1883

YEAR	TM/L	G	AB	R	H	2B	3B	HR	RBI	BB	SO	AVG	OBP	SLG	PRO+	BR/A	SB	CS	SBR	FA	FR	G/POS	TPR
1883	NY-N	23	76	8	15	3	0	0	5	3	15	.197	.228	.237	42	-5				.917	-2	P-19/O-7	-0.2
1884	StL-a	78	297	49	82	13	11	3	54	12		.276	.309	.424	132	9				.811	-6	O-64,P-17/1-1	0.0
1885	*StL-a	52	206	44	72	7	4	3	38	13		.350	.399	.466	165	15				.881	-1	O-52	1.1
1886	StL-a	138	579	106	190	28	14	3	107	47		.328	.385	.440	151	32	9			.927	8	*O-138	3.2
1887	*StL-a	124	517	167	225	52	19	14	123	50		.435	.490	.691	205	68	30			.895	-6	*O-124	4.7
1888	*StL-a	130	529	96	177	24	10	5	98	44		.335	.390	.446	151	27	26			.937	-1	*O-130	2.1
1889	StL-a	134	534	123	179	33	8	9	110	72	37	.335	.419	.478	137	23	28			.936	-2	*O-134	1.5
1890	Chi-P	137	577	112	174	20	16	3	75	65	36	.302	.377	.407	105	3	29			.926	-12	*O-137	-1.1
1891	StL-a	129	521	112	167	28	4	10	95	62	33	.321	.402	.447	124	12	25			.935	-13	*O-129	-0.4
1892	Cin-N	109	419	63	105	14	6	2	52	53	25	.251	.339	.327	103	3	14			.922	-3	*O-109	-0.5
Total	10	1054	4255	880	1386	222	92	52	757	421	146	.326	.392	.458	140	188	161			.917	-38	*O-1024/P-36,1-1	10.4

■ JIM O'NEILL   O'Neill, James Leo   b: 2/23/1893, Minooka, Pa.   d: 9/5/76, Chambersburg, Pa.   BR/TR, 5'10.5", 165 lbs.   Deb: 4/15/20   F

YEAR	TM/L	G	AB	R	H	2B	3B	HR	RBI	BB	SO	AVG	OBP	SLG	PRO+	BR/A	SB	CS	SBR	FA	FR	G/POS	TPR
1920	Was-A	86	294	27	85	17	7	1	40	13	30	.289	.324	.405	95	-3	7	3	0	.943	-5	S-80/2-2	-0.2
1923	Was-A	23	33	6	9	1	0	0	3	1	3	.273	.294	.303	60	-2	0	0	0	.946	3	/2-8,3-4,S-1,0-1	0.1
Total	2	109	327	33	94	18	7	1	43	14	33	.287	.321	.394	91	-5	7	3	0	.943	-3	/S-81,2-10,3-4,0-1	-0.1

■ JOHN O'NEILL   O'Neill, John J.   b: New York, N.Y.   TR,   Deb: 9/6/1899

YEAR	TM/L	G	AB	R	H	2B	3B	HR	RBI	BB	SO	AVG	OBP	SLG	PRO+	BR/A	SB	CS	SBR	FA	FR	G/POS	TPR
1899	NY-N	2	7	0	0	0	0	0	0	0		.000	.000	.000	-99	-2	0			.929	1	/C-2	-0.1
1902	NY-N	2	8	0	0	0	0	0	0	0	0	.000	.000	.000	-99	-2	0			.933	1	/C-2	-0.1
Total	2	4	15	0	0	0	0	0	0	0	0	.000	.000	.000	-99	-4	0			.931	2	/C-4	-0.2

■ JACK O'NEILL   O'Neill, John Joseph   b: 1/10/1873, Galway, Ireland   d: 6/29/35, Scranton, Pa.   BR/TR, 5'10", 165 lbs.   Deb: 4/21/02   F

YEAR	TM/L	G	AB	R	H	2B	3B	HR	RBI	BB	SO	AVG	OBP	SLG	PRO+	BR/A	SB	CS	SBR	FA	FR	G/POS	TPR
1902	StL-N	63	192	13	27	1	1	0	12	13		.141	.214	.156	15	-19	2			.973	1	C-59	-1.3
1903	StL-N	75	246	23	58	9	1	0	27	13		.236	.288	.280	64	-11	11			.972	16	C-74	1.1
1904	Chi-N	51	168	8	36	5	0	1	19	6		.214	.258	.262	61	-8	1			.981	5	C-49	0.2
1905	Chi-N	53	172	16	34	4	2	0	12	8		.198	.277	.244	54	-10	6			.974	7	C-50	0.3
1906	Bos-N	61	167	14	30	5	1	0	4	12		.180	.243	.222	46	-10				.971	12	C-48/1-2,O-1	0.6
Total	5	303	945	74	185	24	5	1	74	52		.196	.258	.235	49	-58	20			.974	40	C-280/1-2,O-1	0.9

■ MIKE O'NEILL   O'Neill, Michael Joyce (a.k.a. Michael Joyce In 1901)   b: 9/7/1877, Galway, Ireland   d: 8/12/59, Scranton, Pa.   BR/TR, 5'11", 185 lbs.   Deb: 9/20/01   F

YEAR	TM/L	G	AB	R	H	2B	3B	HR	RBI	BB	SO	AVG	OBP	SLG	PRO+	BR/A	SB	CS	SBR	FA	FR	G/POS	TPR
1901	StL-N	6	15	3	6	0	0	0	2	3		.400	.526	.400	179	2	0			.875	-1	/P-5	0.0
1902	StL-N	51	135	21	43	5	3	2	15	2		.319	.333	.444	145	6	0			.920	-0	P-36/O-3	0.0
1903	StL-N	41	110	12	25	2	2	0	6	8		.227	.303	.282	69	-4	3			.882	-1	P-19,O-13	-0.3
1904	StL-N	30	91	9	21	7	2	0	16	5		.231	.286	.352	101	-0	1			.910	1	P-25/O-3	0.1
1907	Cin-N	9	29	5	2	0	2	0	2	2		.069	.129	.207	5	-3	1			.864	-0	/O-9	-0.5
Total	5	137	380	50	97	14	9	2	41	20		.255	.306	.355	102	-0	4			.907	-1	/P-85,O-28	-0.8

■ PAUL O'NEILL   O'Neill, Paul Andrew   b: 2/25/63, Columbus, Ohio   BL/TL, 6'4", 205 lbs.   Deb: 9/3/85

YEAR	TM/L	G	AB	R	H	2B	3B	HR	RBI	BB	SO	AVG	OBP	SLG	PRO+	BR/A	SB	CS	SBR	FA	FR	G/POS	TPR
1985	Cin-N	5	12	1	4	1	0	0	1	0	2	.333	.333	.417	103	0	0	0	0	1.000	1	/O-2	0.1
1986	Cin-N	3	2	0	0	0	0	0	0	1	0	.000	.333	.000	-0	-0	0	0	0	.000	0	/H	0.0
1987	Cin-N	84	160	24	41	14	1	7	28	18	29	.256	.331	.469	109	2	2	1	0	.949	-3	O-42/1-2,P-1	-0.3
1988	Cin-N	145	485	58	122	25	3	16	73	38	65	.252	.309	.414	102	0	8	6	-1	.984	1	*O-118,1-21	-0.6
1989	Cin-N	117	428	49	118	24	2	15	74	46	64	.276	.349	.446	122	12	20	5	3	.983	4	*O-115	1.7
1990	*Cin-N	145	503	59	136	28	0	16	78	53	103	.270	.342	.421	104	3	13	11	-3	.993	6	*O-150	0.4
1991	Cin-N★	152	532	71	136	36	0	28	91	73	107	.256	.347	.481	126	18	12	7	-1	.994	13	*O-150	2.8
1992	Cin-N	148	496	59	122	19	1	14	66	77	85	.246	.350	.373	102	3	6	3	0	.997	15	*O-143	1.7
1993	NY-A	141	498	71	155	34	1	20	75	44	69	.311	.369	.504	137	25	2	4	-2	.992	-11	*O-138/D-2	0.8
1994	NY-A★	103	368	68	132	25	1	21	83	72	56	.359	.464	.603	179	47	5	4	-1	.995	2	O-99/D-4	4.1
1995	*NY-A★	127	460	82	138	30	4	22	96	71	76	.300	.395	.526	138	27	1	2	-1	.987	-4	*O-121/D-4	1.7
1996	*NY-A	150	546	89	165	35	1	19	91	102	76	.302	.416	.474	122	22	0	1	-1	1.000	0	*O-146/1-1,D-3	2.3
Total	12	1320	4490	631	1269	271	14	178	756	595	733	.283	.369	.468	124	158	69	44	-6	.991	31	*O-1215/1-24,D-13,P	14.7

■ PEACHES O'NEILL   O'Neill, Philip Bernard   b: 8/30/1879, Anderson, Ind.   d: 8/2/55, Anderson, Ind.   BR/TR, 5'11", 165 lbs.   Deb: 4/16/04

YEAR	TM/L	G	AB	R	H	2B	3B	HR	RBI	BB	SO	AVG	OBP	SLG	PRO+	BR/A	SB	CS	SBR	FA	FR	G/POS	TPR
1904	Cin-N	8	15	0	4	0	0	0	1	1		.267	.313	.267	73	-0	0			.900	-3	/C-5,1-1	-0.4

■ STEVE O'NEILL   O'Neill, Stephen Francis   b: 7/6/1891, Minooka, Pa.   d: 1/26/62, Cleveland, Ohio   BR/TR, 5'10", 165 lbs.   Deb: 9/18/11   FMC

YEAR	TM/L	G	AB	R	H	2B	3B	HR	RBI	BB	SO	AVG	OBP	SLG	PRO+	BR/A	SB	CS	SBR	FA	FR	G/POS	TPR
1911	Cle-A	9	27	1	4	1	0	0	1	4		.148	.281	.185	31	-2	2			.986	4	/C-9	0.2
1912	Cle-A	69	215	17	49	4	0	0	14	12		.228	.247	.247	47	-15	2			.961	9	C-68	0.0
1913	Cle-A	80	234	19	69	13	3	0	29	10	24	.295	.329	.376	103	9	5			.973	3	C-80	1.0
1914	Cle-A	87	269	28	68	12	2	0	20	15	35	.253	.292	.312	79	-8	1	3	-2	.956	0	C-82/1-1	-0.2
1915	Cle-A	121	386	32	91	14	2	2	34	26	41	.236	.293	.298	75	-13	2	3	-1	.968	5	*C-115	0.1
1916	Cle-A	130	378	30	89	23	0	0	29	24	33	.235	.288	.296	71	-14	5			.971	5	*C-128	-0.5
1917	Cle-A	129	370	21	68	10	2	0	29	41	55	.184	.272	.222	47	-23	1			.980	1	*C-127	-1.3
1918	Cle-A	114	359	34	87	8	7	1	35	48	22	.242	.343	.312	89	-4	5			.983	0	*C-113	0.8
1919	Cle-A	125	398	46	115	35	5	2	47	48	21	.289	.373	.427	117	9	4			.977	-7	*C-123	1.3
1920	*Cle-A	149	489	63	157	39	5	3	55	69	39	.321	.408	.440	121	17	3	5	-2	.976	-5	*C-148	2.0
1921	Cle-A	106	335	39	108	22	9	1	50	57	22	.322	.424	.403	110	8	0	1	-1	.976	-5	*C-105	1.6
1922	Cle-A	133	392	33	122	27	4	2	65	73	25	.311	.423	.416	118	15	2	2	-1	.974	-14	*C-130	0.6
1923	Cle-A	113	330	31	82	12	0	0	50	64	34	.248	.374	.285	75	-9	0	4	-2	.968	-12	*C-111	-1.7
1924	Bos-A	106	307	29	73	16	1	1	38	63	23	.238	.371	.293	73	-10	0	2	-1	.970	6	C-92	-0.5
1925	NY-A	35	91	7	26	5	0	1	13	10	3	.286	.363	.374	89	-1	0	0	0	.946	3	C-31	0.3

YEAR	TM/L	G	AB	R	H	2B	3B	HR	RBI	BB	SO	AVG	OBP	SLG	PRO+	BR/A	SB	CS	SBR	FA	FR	G/POS	TPR
1927	StL-A	74	191	14	44	7	0	1	22	20	6	.230	.303	.283	51	-14	0	3	-2	.983	1	C-60	-1.0
1928	StL-A	10	24	4	7	1	0	0	6	8	0	.292	.485	.333	115	1	0	0	0	.958	-4	C-10	-0.2
Total	17	1590	4795	448	1259	248	34	13	537	592	383	.263	.349	.337	88	-61	30	23		.972	-6	*C-1532/1-1	3.0

■ BILL O'NEILL
O'Neill, William John   b: 1/22/1880, St.John, N.B., Can.   d: 7/20/20, Woodhaven, N.Y.   BB/TR, 5'11", 175 lbs.   Deb: 5/7/04

YEAR	TM/L	G	AB	R	H	2B	3B	HR	RBI	BB	SO	AVG	OBP	SLG	PRO+	BR/A	SB	CS	SBR	FA	FR	G/POS	TPR
1904	Bos-A	17	51	7	10	1	0	0	5	2		.196	.226	.216	38	-4	0			.933	-2	/O-9,S-2	-0.7
	Was-A	95	365	33	89	10	1	1	16	22		.244	.294	.285	85	-6	22			.893	-12	O-93/2-3	-2.6
	Yr	112	416	40	99	11	1	1	21	24		.238	.286	.276	79	-10	22			.896	-14	*O-102/2-3,S-2	-3.3
1906	*Chi-A	94	330	37	82	4	1	1	21	22		.248	.301	.276	83	-6	19			.949	-6	O-93	-1.8
Total	2	206	746	77	181	15	2	2	42	46		.243	.293	.276	81	-15	41			.919	-20	O-195/2-3,S-2	-5.1

■ RALPH ONIS
Onis, Manuel Dominguez "Curly"   b: 10/24/08, Tampa, Fla.   d: 1/4/95, Tampa, Fla.   BR/TR, 5'9", 180 lbs.   Deb: 4/27/35

YEAR	TM/L	G	AB	R	H	2B	3B	HR	RBI	BB	SO	AVG	OBP	SLG	PRO+	BR/A	SB	CS	SBR	FA	FR	G/POS	TPR
1935	Bro-N	1	1	0	1	0	0	0	0	0	0	1.000	1.000	1.000	449	0				.500	-0	/C-1	0.0

■ EDDIE ONSLOW
Onslow, Edward Joseph   b: 2/17/1893, Meadville, Pa.   d: 5/8/81, Dennison, Ohio   BL/TL, 6', 170 lbs.   Deb: 8/7/12   F

YEAR	TM/L	G	AB	R	H	2B	3B	HR	RBI	BB	SO	AVG	OBP	SLG	PRO+	BR/A	SB	CS	SBR	FA	FR	G/POS	TPR
1912	Det-A	36	128	11	29	1	2	1	13	3		.227	.250	.289	56	-8	3			.972	-3	1-35	-1.2
1913	Det-A	17	55	7	14	1	0	0	8	5	9	.255	.328	.273	77	-1	1			.990	-1	1-17	-0.3
1918	Cle-A	2	6	0	1	0	0	0	0	0	1	.167	.167	.167	1	-1	0			.000	-1	/O-1	-0.2
1927	Was-A	9	18	1	4	1	0	0	1	1	0	.222	.263	.278	41	-2	0	0	0	1.000	0	/1-5	-0.2
Total	4	64	207	19	48	3	2	1	22	9	10	.232	.271	.280	59	-12	4	0		.979	-5	/1-57,O-1	-1.9

■ JACK ONSLOW
Onslow, John James   b: 10/13/1888, Scottdale, Pa.   d: 12/22/60, Concord, Mass.   BR/TR, 5'11", 180 lbs.   Deb: 5/2/12   FMC

YEAR	TM/L	G	AB	R	H	2B	3B	HR	RBI	BB	SO	AVG	OBP	SLG	PRO+	BR/A	SB	CS	SBR	FA	FR	G/POS	TPR
1912	Det-A	36	69	7	11	1	0	0	4	10		.159	.284	.174	33	-6	1			.948	1	C-35/O-1	-0.2
1917	NY-N	9	8	1	2	1	0	0	0	0		.250	.333	.375	121	0	0			.929	-0	/C-9	0.0
Total	2	45	77	8	13	2	0	0	4	10	1	.169	.289	.195	41	-5	1			.947	0	/C-44,O-1	-0.2

■ STEVE ONTIVEROS
Ontiveros, Steven Robert   b: 10/26/51, Bakersfield, Cal.   BB/TR, 6', 185 lbs.   Deb: 8/5/73

YEAR	TM/L	G	AB	R	H	2B	3B	HR	RBI	BB	SO	AVG	OBP	SLG	PRO+	BR/A	SB	CS	SBR	FA	FR	G/POS	TPR
1973	SF-N	24	33	3	8	4	0	0	5	4	7	.242	.324	.333	79	-1	0	0	0	1.000	1	/1-5,O-1	0.0
1974	SF-N	120	343	45	91	15	1	4	33	57	41	.265	.375	.350	99	2	0	4	0	.929	-3	3-75,1-19/O-2	-0.6
1975	SF-N	108	325	21	94	16	0	3	31	55	44	.289	.395	.366	108	6	2	0	1	.923	-2	3-89/O-8,1-4	0.5
1976	SF-N	59	74	8	13	3	0	0	5	6	11	.176	.247	.216	31	-7	0	0	0	1.000	-5	/3-7,O-7,1-4	-1.3
1977	Chi-N	156	546	54	163	32	3	10	68	81	69	.299	.392	.423	107	7	3	3	-1	.955	-2	*3-155	0.3
1978	Chi-N	82	276	34	67	14	4	1	22	34	33	.243	.326	.333	75	-9	0	2	-1	.965	10	3-77/1-1	-0.1
1979	Chi-N	152	519	58	148	28	2	4	57	58	68	.285	.365	.370	92	-4	0	1	-1	.941	-4	*3-142/1-1	-1.1
1980	Chi-N	31	77	7	16	3	0	1	3	14	17	.208	.330	.286	68	-3	0	0	0	.929	-1	3-24	-0.4
Total	8	732	2193	230	600	111	10	24	224	309	290	.274	.367	.366	94	-8	5	6	-2	.944	-9	3-569/1-34,O-18	-2.7

■ JOSE OQUENDO
Oquendo, Jose Manuel (Contreras)   b: 7/4/63, Rio Piedras, P.R.   BB/TR, 5'10", 160 lbs.   Deb: 5/2/83

YEAR	TM/L	G	AB	R	H	2B	3B	HR	RBI	BB	SO	AVG	OBP	SLG	PRO+	BR/A	SB	CS	SBR	FA	FR	G/POS	TPR
1983	NY-N	120	328	29	70	7	1	1	17	19	60	.213	.261	.244	41	-26	8	9	-3	.960	6	*S-116	-1.4
1984	NY-N	81	189	23	42	5	0	0	10	15	26	.222	.286	.249	52	-12	10	1	2	.972	2	S-67	-0.3
1986	StL-N	76	138	20	41	4	1	0	13	15	20	.297	.366	.341	97	-0	2	3	-1	.956	-6	S-29,2-21/3-1,O-1	-0.5
1987	*StL-N	116	248	43	71	9	1	1	24	54	29	.286	.414	.335	99	3	4	4	-1	1.000	5	O-46,2-32,S/3P	0.5
1988	StL-N	148	451	36	125	10	1	7	46	52	40	.277	.352	.350	101	2	4	6	-2	.997	8	2-69,3-47,S10/PC	1.1
1989	StL-N	163	556	59	162	28	7	1	48	79	59	.291	.380	.372	112	12	3	5	-2	.994	20	*2-156/S-7,1-1	3.8
1990	StL-N	156	469	38	118	17	5	1	37	74	46	.252	.354	.316	85	-7	1	1	-0	.996	-1	*2-150/S-4	-0.5
1991	StL-N	127	366	37	88	11	4	1	26	67	46	.240	.359	.301	87	-5	1	2	-1	.988	15	*2-118,S-22/1-3,P-1	1.5
1992	StL-N	14	35	3	9	3	1	0	3	6	5	.257	.367	.400	115	1	0	0	0	1.000	1	/2-9,S-5	0.1
1993	StL-N	46	73	7	15	0	0	0	4	12	8	.205	.318	.205	44	-5	0	0	0	.988	14	S-22,2-16	1.0
1994	StL-N	55	129	13	34	2	2	0	9	21	16	.264	.367	.310	80	-3	1	1	-0	.945	8	S-28,2-16	-0.6
1995	StL-N	88	220	19	46	8	2	2	17	35	21	.209	.318	.300	64	-11	1	1	-0	.981	6	2-62,S-24/3-2,O-1	-0.1
Total	12	1190	3202	339	821	104	24	14	254	448	376	.256	.349	.317	85	-49	35	33	-9	.992	63	2-649,S-364/O31PC	4.6

■ TOM ORAN
Oran, Thomas   b: 1845,   d: 9/22/1886, St.Louis, Mo.   Deb: 5/4/1875

YEAR	TM/L	G	AB	R	H	2B	3B	HR	RBI	BB	SO	AVG	OBP	SLG	PRO+	BR/A	SB	CS	SBR	FA	FR	G/POS	TPR
1875	RS-n	19	81	7	15	3	1	0	10	1	1	.185	.195	.247	58	-3	3	2	-0	.633	-4	O-19/S-1	-0.6

■ ERNIE ORAVETZ
Oravetz, Ernest Eugene   b: 1/24/32, Johnstown, Pa.   BB/TL, 5'4", 145 lbs.   Deb: 4/11/55

YEAR	TM/L	G	AB	R	H	2B	3B	HR	RBI	BB	SO	AVG	OBP	SLG	PRO+	BR/A	SB	CS	SBR	FA	FR	G/POS	TPR
1955	Was-A	100	263	24	71	5	1	0	25	26	19	.270	.338	.297	76	-8	1	2	-1	.967	-3	O-57	-1.5
1956	Was-A	88	137	20	34	3	2	0	11	27	20	.248	.372	.299	79	-3	1	0	0	.946	-2	O-31	-0.6
Total	2	188	400	44	105	8	3	0	36	53	39	.262	.350	.298	77	-11	2	2	-1	.961	-5	/O-88	-2.1

■ TONY ORDENANA
Ordenana, Antonio (Rodriguez) "Mosquito"   b: 10/30/18, Guanabacoa, Havana, Cuba   d: 9/29/88, Miami, Fla.   BR/TR, 5'9", 158 lbs.   Deb: 10/3/43

YEAR	TM/L	G	AB	R	H	2B	3B	HR	RBI	BB	SO	AVG	OBP	SLG	PRO+	BR/A	SB	CS	SBR	FA	FR	G/POS	TPR
1943	Pit-N	1	4	0	2	0	0	0	3	0	0	.500	.500	.500	183	0	0			1.000	1	/S-1	0.1

■ REY ORDONEZ
Ordonez, Reynaldo   b: 11/11/72, Havana, Cuba   BR/TR, 5'9", 160 lbs.   Deb: 4/1/96

YEAR	TM/L	G	AB	R	H	2B	3B	HR	RBI	BB	SO	AVG	OBP	SLG	PRO+	BR/A	SB	CS	SBR	FA	FR	G/POS	TPR
1996	NY-N	151	502	51	129	12	4	1	30	22	53	.257	.290	.303	61	-29	1	3	-2	.962	2	*S-150	-1.4

■ JOE ORENGO
Orengo, Joseph Charles   b: 11/29/14, San Francisco, Cal   d: 7/24/88, San Francisco, Cal.   BR/TR, 6', 185 lbs.   Deb: 4/18/39

YEAR	TM/L	G	AB	R	H	2B	3B	HR	RBI	BB	SO	AVG	OBP	SLG	PRO+	BR/A	SB	CS	SBR	FA	FR	G/POS	TPR
1939	StL-N	7	3	0	0	0	0	0	0	0	1	.000	.000	.000	-94	-1	0			.667	-0	/S-7	-0.1
1940	StL-N	129	415	58	119	23	4	7	56	65	90	.287	.383	.412	113	9	9			.952	5	2-77,3-34,S-19	2.1
1941	NY-N	77	252	23	54	11	2	4	25	28	49	.214	.298	.321	73	-9	1			.958	18	3-59/S-9,2-6	1.2
1943	NY-N	83	266	28	58	8	2	6	29	36	46	.218	.311	.331	85	-5	1			.992	4	1-82	-0.5
	Bro-N	7	15	1	3	2	0	0	1	4	2	.200	.368	.333	103	0	0			1.000	0	/3-6	0.0
	Yr	90	281	29	61	10	2	6	30	40	48	.217	.315	.331	86	-5	1			.992	4	1-82/3-6	-0.5
1944	Det-A	46	154	14	31	10	0	0	10	20	29	.201	.297	.266	58	-8	1	1	-0	.903	6	S-29,3-11/1-5,2-2	0.0
1945	Chi-A	17	15	5	1	0	0	0	0	3	2	.067	.222	.067	-15	-2	0	0	0	.923	1	/3-7,2-1	-0.1
Total	6	366	1120	130	266	54	8	17	122	156	219	.237	.332	.346	88	-16	12	1		.957	34	3-117/1-87,2-86,S	2.6

■ GEORGE ORME
Orme, George William   b: 9/16/1891, Lebanon, Ind.   d: 3/16/62, Indianapolis, Ind.   BR/TR, 5'10", 160 lbs.   Deb: 9/14/20

YEAR	TM/L	G	AB	R	H	2B	3B	HR	RBI	BB	SO	AVG	OBP	SLG	PRO+	BR/A	SB	CS	SBR	FA	FR	G/POS	TPR
1920	Bos-A	4	6	4	2	0	0	0	1	3	0	.333	.556	.333	146	1	0	0	0	1.000	0	/O-3	0.1

■ JESS ORNDORFF
Orndorff, Jesse Walworth Thayer   b: 1/15/1881, Chicago, Ill.   d: 9/28/60, Cardiff-By-The- Sea, Cal.   BB/TR, 6', 168 lbs.   Deb: 4/18/07

YEAR	TM/L	G	AB	R	H	2B	3B	HR	RBI	BB	SO	AVG	OBP	SLG	PRO+	BR/A	SB	CS	SBR	FA	FR	G/POS	TPR
1907	Bos-N	5	17	0	2	0	0	0	0	0		.118	.118	.118	-26	-2	0			.900	-2	/C-5	-0.5

■ FRANK O'ROURKE
O'Rourke, James Francis "Blackie"   b: 11/28/1894, Hamilton, Ont., Can   d: 5/14/86, Chatham, N.J.   BR/TR, 5'10.5", 165 lbs.   Deb: 6/12/12

YEAR	TM/L	G	AB	R	H	2B	3B	HR	RBI	BB	SO	AVG	OBP	SLG	PRO+	BR/A	SB	CS	SBR	FA	FR	G/POS	TPR
1912	Bos-N	61	196	11	24	7	3	1	16	11	50	.122	.177	.148	-10	-30	1			.915	-7	S-59/3-1	-3.3
1917	Bro-N	64	198	18	47	7	1	0	15	14	25	.237	.294	.283	75	-6	11			.954	7	3-58	0.3
1918	Bro-N	4	12	0	2	0	0	0	2	1	3	.167	.231	.167	22	-1	0			.857	1	/2-2,O-1	0.0
1920	Was-A	14	54	8	16	1	0	0	5	2	5	.296	.321	.315	71	-2	2	1	0	.952	3	S-13/3-1	0.3
1921	Was-A	123	444	51	104	17	8	3	54	26	56	.234	.287	.329	60	-29	6	7	-2	.922	-7	*S-122	-2.5
1922	Bos-A	67	216	28	57	14	3	1	17	20	28	.264	.335	.370	84	-5	6	6	-2	.909	-12	S-49,3-20	-1.2
1924	Det-A	47	181	28	50	11	2	0	19	12	19	.276	.332	.359	79	-6	7	4	-0	.970	11	2-40/S-7	0.6
1925	Det-A	124	482	88	141	40	7	5	57	32	37	.293	.350	.436	100	-2	5	8	-3	.971	15	*2-118/3-6	1.1
1926	Det-A	111	363	43	88	16	1	1	41	35	33	.242	.321	.300	62	-20	8	6	-1	.936	10	3-60,2-41,S-10	-0.6
1927	StL-A	140	538	85	144	25	3	6	39	64	43	.268	.338	.331	77	-16	18	8	1	.955	11	*3-121,2-16/1-3	-2.0
1928	StL-A	99	391	54	103	24	3	0	62	21	19	.263	.303	.348	68	-18	10	2	2	.954	-9	3-96/S-2	-2.0
1929	StL-A	154	585	81	147	23	9	6	62	41	28	.251	.306	.332	65	-34	14	7	0	.943	-18	*3-151/2-3,S-2	-4.3
1930	StL-A	115	400	52	107	13	4	1	41	35	30	.268	.326	.333	65	-21	11	1	0	.946	10	3-84,S-23/1-3	-0.5
1931	StL-A	8	9	0	2	0	0	0	0	1	0	.222	.222	.222	17	-1	1	1	-0	1.000	0	/S-2,1-1	-0.1
Total	14	1131	4069	547	1032	196	42	16	430	314	377	.254	.315	.333	68	-189	100	59		.949	16	3-598,S-289,2/1O	-12.0

■ JIM O'ROURKE
O'Rourke, James Henry "Orator Jim"   b: 9/1/1850, Bridgeport, Conn.   d: 1/8/19, Bridgeport, Conn.   BR/TR, 5'8", 185 lbs.   Deb: 4/26/1872   FMUH

YEAR	TM/L	G	AB	R	H	2B	3B	HR	RBI	BB	SO	AVG	OBP	SLG	PRO+	BR/A	SB	CS	SBR	FA	FR	G/POS	TPR
1872	Man-n	23	101	25	31	4	1	0	12	2	0	.307	.320	.366	117	3	1	0	0	.729	-2	S-16/C-8,3-2	0.0
1873	Bos-n	57	280	79	98	19	3	1	48	14	1	.350	.381	.450	135	10	4	2	0	.916	1	1-32,O-22/C-9	0.9

YEAR	TM/L	G	AB	R	H	2B	3B	HR	RBI	BB	SO	AVG	OBP	SLG	PRO+	BR/A	SB	CS	SBR	FA	FR	G/POS	TPR
1874	Bos-n	70	331	82	104	15	8	**5**	61	4	5	.314	.322	.453	138	12	**11**	1	**3**	.943	1	*1-70	1.2
1875	Bos-n	75	358	97	106	13	7	**6**	72	9	6	.296	.313	.422	148	16	17	5	2	.800	-5	O-45,3-27/1-6,C-1	1.2
1876	Bos-N	70	312	61	104	17	3	2	43	15	17	.327	.358	.420	156	18				.856	-3	*O-68/1-2,C-1	1.3
1877	Bos-N	61	265	**68**	96	14	4	0	23	**20**	9	.362	**.407**	.445	162	19				.846	-0	*O-60/1-1	1.4
1878	Bos-N	60	255	44	71	17	7	1	29	5	21	.278	.292	.412	120	4				.860	4	*O-57/1-2,C-2	0.4
1879	Pro-N	81	362	69	126	19	9	1	46	13	10	.348	.371	.459	174	28				.785	-9	*O-56,1-20/C-5,3-3	1.5
1880	Bos-N	86	363	71	100	20	11	**6**	45	21	8	.275	.315	.441	158	22				.907	-3	O-37,1-19,S-17,3/C	1.8
1881	Buf-N	83	348	71	105	21	7	0	30	27	18	.302	.352	.402	139	16				.821	-20	*3-56,O-18/C-8,S1M	-0.2
1882	Buf-N	84	370	62	104	15	6	2	37	13	13	.281	.305	.370	114	5				.866	-0	O-81/S-2,C-2,3M	0.4
1883	Buf-N	94	436	102	143	29	8	1	38	15	13	.328	.350	.438	135	17				.866	-12	O-61,C-33/3-8,SPM	0.6
1884	Buf-N	108	467	119	**162**	33	7	5	63	35	17	**.347**	.392	.480	167	35				.894	-9	*O-86,1-18,C/P3M	2.0
1885	NY-N	112	477	119	143	21	**16**	5	42	40	21	.300	.354	.442	158	31				.940	-16	O-112/C-8	1.2
1886	NY-N	105	440	106	136	26	6	1	34	39	21	.309	.365	.402	132	17	14			.926	8	O-63,C-47/1-2	2.6
1887	NY-N	103	397	73	113	15	13	3	88	36	11	.285	.352	.411	116	10	46			.890	-9	C-40,3-38,O-28/2-2	0.4
1888	*NY-N	107	409	50	112	16	6	4	50	24	30	.274	.319	.372	121	10	25			.960	-1	O-87,C-15/1-4,3-2	0.7
1889	*NY-P	128	502	89	161	36	7	3	81	40	34	.321	.372	.438	126	16	33			.893	-8	*O-128/C-1	0.4
1890	NY-P	111	478	112	172	37	5	9	115	33	20	.360	.410	.459	135	20	23			.930	5	*O-111	1.6
1891	NY-N	136	555	92	164	28	7	5	95	26	29	.295	.334	.398	118	10	19			.906	-1	O-126,C-14	0.6
1892	NY-N	115	448	62	136	28	5	0	56	30	30	.304	.354	.388	127	14	16			.913	-10	*O-111/C-4,1-1	-0.1
1893	Was-N	129	547	75	157	22	5	2	95	49	26	.287	.354	.356	92	-6	15			.927	5	O-87,1-33/C-9,M	-0.4
1904	NY-N	1	4	1	1	0	0	0	0	0	0	.250	.250	.250	52	-0	0			.800	-1	/C-1	-0.1
Total	4 n	225	1070	283	339	51	19	12	193	24	9	.317	.335	.434	138	40	33	8	5	.934	-5	1-108/O-67,3-29,CS	3.3
Total	19	1774	7435	1446	2304	414	132	50	1010	481	348	.310	.355	.421	143	286	191			.898	-80	*O-1377,C-209,31/SP2	16.1

■ CHARLIE O'ROURKE
O'Rourke, James Patrick b: 6/22/37, Walla Walla, Wash. BR/TR, 6'2", 195 lbs. Deb: 6/16/59

YEAR	TM/L	G	AB	R	H	2B	3B	HR	RBI	BB	SO	AVG	OBP	SLG	PRO+	BR/A	SB	CS	SBR	FA	FR	G/POS	TPR
1959	StL-N	2	2	0	0	0	0	0	0	0	0	.000	.000	.000	-94	-0	0	0	0	.000	0	H	-0.1

■ QUEENIE O'ROURKE
O'Rourke, James Stephen b: 12/26/1883, Bridgeport, Conn. d: 12/22/55, Sparrows Point, Md BR/TR, 5'7", 150 lbs. Deb: 8/15/08 F

YEAR	TM/L	G	AB	R	H	2B	3B	HR	RBI	BB	SO	AVG	OBP	SLG	PRO+	BR/A	SB	CS	SBR	FA	FR	G/POS	TPR
1908	NY-A	34	108	5	25	1	0	0	3	4		.231	.259	.241	62	-5	4			1.000	-6	O-14,S-11/2-4,3-3	-1.3

■ JOHN O'ROURKE
O'Rourke, John b: 8/23/1849, Bridgeport, Conn. d: 6/23/11, Boston, Mass. BL/TL, 6', 190 lbs. Deb: 5/1/1879 F

YEAR	TM/L	G	AB	R	H	2B	3B	HR	RBI	BB	SO	AVG	OBP	SLG	PRO+	BR/A	SB	CS	SBR	FA	FR	G/POS	TPR
1879	Bos-N	72	317	69	108	17	11	6	**62**	8	32	.341	.357	**.521**	181	26				.882	2	*O-71	2.3
1880	Bos-N	81	313	30	86	22	8	3	36	18	32	.275	.314	.425	153	17				.871	5	*O-81	1.9
1883	NY-a	77	315	49	85	19	5	2		21		.270	.315	.381	118	6				.856	-3	*O-76/1-1	0.1
Total	3	230	945	148	279	58	24	11	**98**	47	64	.295	.329	.442	150	49				.871	4	O-228/1-1	4.3

■ JOE O'ROURKE
O'Rourke, Joseph Leo Jr. b: 10/28/04, Philadelphia, Pa. d: 6/27/90, Philadelphia, Pa. BL/TR, 5'7", 145 lbs. Deb: 4/19/29 F

YEAR	TM/L	G	AB	R	H	2B	3B	HR	RBI	BB	SO	AVG	OBP	SLG	PRO+	BR/A	SB	CS	SBR	FA	FR	G/POS	TPR
1929	Phi-N	3	3	0	0	0	0	0	0	0	1	.000	.000	.000	-94	-1	0			.000	0	H	-0.1

■ PATSY O'ROURKE
O'Rourke, Joseph Leo Sr. b: 4/13/1881, Philadelphia, Pa. d: 4/18/56, Philadelphia, Pa. BR/TR, 5'7", 160 lbs. Deb: 4/16/08 F

YEAR	TM/L	G	AB	R	H	2B	3B	HR	RBI	BB	SO	AVG	OBP	SLG	PRO+	BR/A	SB	CS	SBR	FA	FR	G/POS	TPR
1908	StL-N	53	164	8	32	4	2	0	16	14		.195	.263	.244	65	-6	2			.860	-7	S-53	-1.5

■ TOM O'ROURKE
O'Rourke, Thomas Joseph b: 10/1865, New York, N.Y. d: 7/19/29, New York, N.Y. TR, 5'9", 158 lbs. Deb: 5/11/1887

YEAR	TM/L	G	AB	R	H	2B	3B	HR	RBI	BB	SO	AVG	OBP	SLG	PRO+	BR/A	SB	CS	SBR	FA	FR	G/POS	TPR
1887	Bos-N	22	78	12	12	3	0	0	10	7	6	.154	.233	.192	19	-8	4			.777	-5	C-21/O-1,3-1	-1.0
1888	Bos-N	20	74	3	13	0	0	0	4	1	9	.176	.187	.176	16	-7	2			.881	1	C-20/O-1	-0.4
1890	NY-N	2	7	1	0	0	0	0	0	1	0	.000	.125	.000	-63	-1				.864	1	/C-2	0.0
	Syr-a	41	153	16	33	8	0	0	12	12		.216	.277	.268	68	-6	2			.907	-12	C-40/O-1-1	-1.3
Total	3	85	312	32	58	11	0	0	26	21	15	.186	.242	.221	39	-23	8			.867	-15	/C-83,O-2,1-1,3-1	-2.7

■ TIM O'ROURKE
O'Rourke, Timothy Patrick "Voiceless Tim" b: 5/18/1864, Chicago, Ill. d: 4/20/38, Seattle, Wash. BL/TR, 5'10", 170 lbs. Deb: 5/27/1890

YEAR	TM/L	G	AB	R	H	2B	3B	HR	RBI	BB	SO	AVG	OBP	SLG	PRO+	BR/A	SB	CS	SBR	FA	FR	G/POS	TPR
1890	Syr-a	87	332	48	94	13	6	1	46	36		.283	.360	.367	128	13	22			.866	-11	3-87	0.4
1891	Col-a	34	136	22	38	1	3	0	12	15	7	.279	.359	.331	104	1	9			.879	9	3-34	0.3
1892	Bal-N	63	239	40	74	8	4	0	35	24	19	.310	.373	.377	123	7	12			.869	-14	S-58/O-4,3-1	-0.4
1893	Bal-N	31	135	22	49	4	1	0	19	12	4	.363	.423	.407	119	4	5			.980	-4	O-25/3-5,S-1	-0.1
	Lou-N	92	352	80	99	8	4	0	53	77	15	.281	.421	.327	108	11	22			.865	-21	S-60,O-26/3-6	-0.6
	Yr	123	487	102	148	12	5	0	72	89	19	.304	.422	.349	112	16	27			.861	-25	S-61,O-51,3-11	-0.7
1894	Lou-N	55	220	46	61	3	3	0	27	23	9	.277	.351	.318	67	-11	9			.977	-1	1-30,O-18/S-3,32	-1.0
	StL-N	18	71	10	20	4	1	0	10	8	3	.282	.354	.366	74	-3	2			.861	-2	3-18	-0.4
	Was-N	7	25	4	5	2	1	0	2	2	1	.200	.259	.360	50	-2	0			.909	1	/2-4,S-3	-0.1
	Yr	80	316	60	86	9	5	0	39	33	13	.272	.345	.332	67	-16	11			.977	-2	1-30,3-21,O-18/S2	-1.5
Total	5	387	1510	272	440	43	23	1	204	197	58	.291	.380	.352	105	20	81			.861	-51	3-154/S-125/O12	-1.9

■ DAVE ORR
Orr, David L. b: 9/29/1859, New York, N.Y. d: 6/3/15, Brooklyn, N.Y. BR/TR, 5'11", 250 lbs. Deb: 5/17/1883 M

YEAR	TM/L	G	AB	R	H	2B	3B	HR	RBI	BB	SO	AVG	OBP	SLG	PRO+	BR/A	SB	CS	SBR	FA	FR	G/POS	TPR
1883	NY-a	1	4	1	1	1	0	0	0	0		.250	.250	.500	130	0				1.000	0	/1-1	0.0
	NY-N	1	3	0	0	0	0	0	0	0	1	.000	.000	.000	-99	-1				1.000	0	/O-1	-0.1
	NY-a	12	46	5	15	3	3	2	11	0		.326	.326	.652	198	5				.938	-2	1-12	0.2
1884	*NY-a	110	458	82	**162**	32	13	9	112	5		.354	.362	.539	**195**	45				.960	-5	*1-110/O-3	2.4
1885	NY-a	107	444	76	152	29	**21**	6	77	8		.342	.358	.543	**197**	47				.966	-3	*1-107/P-3	2.7
1886	NY-a	136	571	93	**193**	25	**31**	7	91	17		.338	.363	**.527**	186	52	16			**.981**	-0	*1-136	3.1
1887	NY-a	84	345	63	127	25	10	2	66	22		.368	.408	.516	164	29	17			.969	-1	1-81/O-3,M	1.6
1888	Bro-a	99	394	57	120	20	5	1	59	7		.305	.330	.388	130	12	11			.979	4	*1-99	0.6
1889	Col-a	134	560	70	183	31	12	4	87	9	38	.327	.340	.446	129	18	12			.983	9	*1-134	1.5
1890	Bro-P	107	464	89	172	32	13	6	124	30	11	.371	.414	.534	144	25	10			.972	-5	*1-107	1.2
Total	8	791	3289	536	1125	198	108	37	**627**	98	50	.342	.366	.502	163	231	66			.973	-3	1-787/O-7,P-3	13.2

■ BILLY ORR
Orr, William John b: 4/22/1891, San Francisco, Cal d: 3/10/67, St.Helena, Cal. BR/TR, 5'11", 168 lbs. Deb: 5/3/13

YEAR	TM/L	G	AB	R	H	2B	3B	HR	RBI	BB	SO	AVG	OBP	SLG	PRO+	BR/A	SB	CS	SBR	FA	FR	G/POS	TPR
1913	Phi-A	30	67	6	13	1	1	0	7	4	10	.194	.239	.239	41	-5	2			.967	-2	S-16/1-3,3-3,2-2	-0.6
1914	Phi-A	10	24	3	4	1	1	0	1	2	5	.167	.231	.292	59	-1	1	1	-0	.810	-4	/S-6,3-1	-0.6
Total	2	40	91	9	17	2	2	0	8	6	15	.187	.237	.253	46	-6	2	1		.927	-6	/S-22,3-4,1-3,2-2	-1.2

■ ERNIE ORSATTI
Orsatti, Ernest Ralph b: 9/8/02, Los Angeles, Cal. d: 9/4/68, Canoga Park, Cal. BL/TL, 5'7.5", 154 lbs. Deb: 9/4/27

YEAR	TM/L	G	AB	R	H	2B	3B	HR	RBI	BB	SO	AVG	OBP	SLG	PRO+	BR/A	SB	CS	SBR	FA	FR	G/POS	TPR
1927	StL-N	27	92	15	29	6	0	0	12	11	12	.315	.388	.457	122	-1	2			.922	-1	O-26	0.1
1928	*StL-N	27	69	10	21	6	0	3	15	10	11	.304	.400	.522	137	4	0			1.000	-2	O-17/1-5	0.1
1929	StL-N	113	346	64	115	21	7	3	39	33	43	.332	.394	.466	110	6	7			.974	4	O-77,1-10	0.4
1930	*StL-N	48	131	24	42	15	5	1	15	12	18	.321	.382	.466	100	0	1			.985	4	1-22,O-11	0.1
1931	*StL-N	70	158	27	46	16	6	0	19	14	16	.291	.349	.468	113	3	1			.988	-5	O-45/1-1	-0.5
1932	StL-N	101	375	44	126	27	4	4	44	18	29	.336	.368	.456	117	9	5			.976	-9	O-96/1-1	-0.6
1933	StL-N	120	436	55	130	21	6	0	38	33	33	.298	.348	.374	101	1	14			.986	-2	*O-107/1-3	-0.4
1934	*StL-N	105	337	39	101	14	4	0	31	27	31	.300	.353	.365	87	-5	6			.986	-2	O-90	-1.1
1935	StL-N	90	221	28	53	9	3	0	24	18	25	.240	.297	.321	64	-11	10			.975	-5	O-60	-1.8
Total	9	701	2165	306	663	129	39	10	237	176	218	.306	.360	.416	102	8	46			.979	-14	O-529/1-42	-3.7

■ JOHN ORSINO
Orsino, John Joseph "Horse" b: 4/22/38, Teaneck, N.J. BR/TR, 6'3", 215 lbs. Deb: 7/14/61

YEAR	TM/L	G	AB	R	H	2B	3B	HR	RBI	BB	SO	AVG	OBP	SLG	PRO+	BR/A	SB	CS	SBR	FA	FR	G/POS	TPR
1961	SF-N	25	83	5	23	3	2	4	13	3	13	.277	.310	.506	116	1	0	0	0	.959	-3	C-25	0.0
1962	*SF-N	18	48	4	13	2	0	0	4	5	11	.271	.340	.313	78	-1	0	0	0	.963	-2	*C-16	-0.2
1963	Bal-A	116	379	53	103	18	1	19	56	38	53	.272	.352	.475	134	17	2	3	-1	.990	-7	*C-109/1-3	1.4
1964	Bal-A	81	248	21	55	10	0	8	23	24	55	.222	.293	.359	81	-7	0	1		.976	1	C-66/1-5	-0.4
1965	Bal-A	77	232	30	54	10	2	9	28	23	51	.233	.315	.409	102	1	1			.987	-8	C-62/1-5	-0.4
1966	Was-A	14	23	1	4	0	0	0	1	1	4	.174	.174	.217	12	-3				1.000	-0	/1-5,C-2	-0.3
1967	Was-A	1	1	0	0	0	0	0	0	0	0	.000	.000	.000	-99	-0	0			.000	0	H	-0.3
Total	7	332	1014	114	252	44	5	40	123	92	191	.249	.321	.420	106	8	3	3	-1	.982	-18	C-280/1-18	0.1

YEAR	TM/L	G	AB	R	H	2B	3B	HR	RBI	BB	SO	AVG	OBP	SLG	PRO+	BR/A	SB	CS	SBR	FA	FR	G/POS	TPR

■ JOE ORSULAK
Orsulak, Joseph Michael b: 5/31/62, Glen Ridge, N.J. BL/TL, 6'1", 186 lbs. Deb: 9/1/83

YEAR	TM/L	G	AB	R	H	2B	3B	HR	RBI	BB	SO	AVG	OBP	SLG	PRO+	BR/A	SB	CS	SBR	FA	FR	G/POS	TPR
1983	Pit-N	7	11	0	2	0	0	0	1	0	2	.182	.182	.182	1	-1	0	1	-1	1.000	0	/O-4	-0.2
1984	Pit-N	32	67	12	17	1	2	0	3	1	7	.254	.275	.328	69	-3	3	1	0	1.000	1	O-25	-0.5
1985	Pit-N	121	397	54	119	14	6	0	21	26	27	.300	.344	.365	100	-0	24	11	1	.976	-0	*O-115	-0.3
1986	Pit-N	138	401	60	100	19	6	2	19	28	38	.249	.300	.342	75	-14	24	11	1	.981	-5	*O-120	-2.2
1988	Bal-A	125	379	48	109	21	3	8	27	23	30	.288	.333	.422	113	6	9	8	-2	.979	-6	*O-117	-0.5
1989	Bal-A	123	390	59	111	22	5	7	55	41	35	.285	.356	.421	122	11	5	3	-0	.985	7	*O-109/D-5	1.5
1990	Bal-A	124	413	49	111	14	3	11	57	46	48	.269	.343	.397	110	6	6	8	-3	.989	11	*O-109/D-5	1.1
1991	Bal-A	143	486	57	135	22	1	5	43	28	45	.278	.322	.358	92	-6	6	2	1	.997	10	*O-132/D-2	0.2
1992	Bal-A	117	391	45	113	18	3	4	39	28	34	.289	.343	.381	100	0	5	4	-1	.983	4	*O-110/D-1	0.1
1993	NY-N	134	409	59	116	15	4	8	35	28	25	.284	.333	.399	96	-3	5	4	-1	.978	-6	*O-114/1-4	-1.2
1994	NY-N	96	292	39	76	3	0	8	42	16	21	.260	.305	.353	72	-12	4	2	0	.979	-8	O-90/1-6	-2.3
1995	NY-N	108	290	41	82	19	2	1	37	19	35	.283	.329	.372	87	-5	1	3	-2	.965	-8	O-86/1-1	-1.7
1996	Fla-N	120	217	23	48	6	1	2	19	16	36	.221	.275	.286	50	-16	1	1	-0	.956	-3	O-59/1-2	-2.0
Total	13	1388	4143	546	1139	174	36	56	398	300	385	.275	.327	.375	94	-37	93	59	-8	.982	-6	*O-1190/1-13,D-13	-8.0

■ JORGE ORTA
Orta, Jorge (Nunez) b: 11/26/50, Mazatlan, Mexico BL/TR, 5'10", 175 lbs. Deb: 4/15/72

YEAR	TM/L	G	AB	R	H	2B	3B	HR	RBI	BB	SO	AVG	OBP	SLG	PRO+	BR/A	SB	CS	SBR	FA	FR	G/POS	TPR
1972	Chi-A	51	124	20	25	3	1	3	11	6	37	.202	.244	.315	64	-6	3	3	-1	.958	-0	S-18,2-14/3-9	-0.5
1973	Chi-A	128	425	46	113	9	10	6	40	37	87	.266	.326	.376	94	-3	8	8	-2	.969	-27	*2-122/S-1	-2.6
1974	Chi-A	139	525	73	166	31	2	10	67	40	88	.316	.368	.440	128	19	9	5	-0	.971	-13	*2-123,D-10/S-3	1.2
1975	Chi-A†	140	542	64	165	26	10	11	83	48	67	.304	.365	.450	128	19	16	9	-1	.978	-12	*2-135/D-2	1.4
1976	Chi-A	158	636	74	174	29	8	14	72	38	77	.274	.320	.410	112	8	24	8	2	.971	2	O-77,3-49,D-31	0.8
1977	Chi-A	144	564	71	159	27	8	11	84	46	49	.282	.338	.417	105	3	4	4	-1	.970	-47	*2-139	-3.5
1978	Chi-A	117	420	45	115	19	2	13	53	42	39	.274	.345	.421	114	8	1	2	-1	.984	-22	*2-114/D-2	-0.7
1979	Chi-A	113	325	49	85	18	3	11	46	44	33	.262	.351	.437	111	5	1	5	-3	.978	-11	D-62,2-41	-0.8
1980	Cle-A☆	129	481	78	140	18	3	10	64	71	44	.291	.384	.407	116	13	6	5	-1	.982	13	*O-120/D-7	2.0
1981	Cle-A	88	338	50	92	14	3	5	34	21	43	.272	.317	.376	100	-0	4	3	-1	.994	4	O-86	0.0
1982	LA-N	86	115	13	25	5	0	2	8	12	13	.217	.297	.313	73	-4	0	1	-1	.947	1	O-17	-0.4
1983	Tor-A	103	245	30	58	6	3	10	38	19	29	.237	.292	.408	85	-6	1	2	-1	1.000	-3	D-70,O-17	-1.2
1984	*KC-A	122	403	50	120	23	7	9	50	28	39	.298	.346	.457	119	10	0	1	-1	.980	-3	D-83,O-26/2-1	0.4
1985	*KC-A	110	300	32	80	21	1	4	45	22	28	.267	.321	.383	92	-4	2	1	0	.000	0	D-85	-0.5
1986	KC-A	106	336	35	93	14	2	9	46	23	34	.277	.323	.411	96	-2	0	3	-2	.000	0	D-87	-0.6
1987	KC-A	21	50	3	9	4	0	2	4	3	8	.180	.226	.380	55	-3	0	0	0	.000	0	D-12	-0.4
Total	16	1755	5829	733	1619	267	63	130	745	500	715	.278	.338	.412	108	56	79	60	-12	.974	-118	2-689,D-451,O/3S	-5.4

■ FRANK ORTENZIO
Ortenzio, Frank Joseph b: 2/24/51, Fresno, Cal. BR/TR, 6'2", 215 lbs. Deb: 9/9/73

YEAR	TM/L	G	AB	R	H	2B	3B	HR	RBI	BB	SO	AVG	OBP	SLG	PRO+	BR/A	SB	CS	SBR	FA	FR	G/POS	TPR
1973	KC-A	9	25	1	7	2	0	1	6	2	6	.280	.333	.480	118	0	0	0	0	.983	1	/1-7,D-1	0.1

■ AL ORTH
Orth, Albert Lewis "Smiling Al" or "The Curveless Wonder" b: 9/5/1872, Tipton, Ind. d: 10/8/48, Lynchburg, Va. BL/TR, 6', 200 lbs. Deb: 8/15/1895 U

YEAR	TM/L	G	AB	R	H	2B	3B	HR	RBI	BB	SO	AVG	OBP	SLG	PRO+	BR/A	SB	CS	SBR	FA	FR	G/POS	TPR
1895	Phi-N	11	45	8	16	4	0	1	13	1	6	.356	.370	.511	125	1	0			.842	-2	P-11	0.0
1896	Phi-N	25	82	12	21	3	3	1	13	3	11	.256	.282	.402	80	-3	2			.901	1	P-25	0.0
1897	Phi-N	53	152	26	50	7	4	1	17	3		.329	.342	.447	110	1	5			.929	0	P-36/O-6	0.0
1898	Phi-N	39	123	17	36	6	4	1	14	3		.293	.310	.431	117	2	1			.959	1	P-32/O-1	0.1
1899	Phi-N	22	62	5	13	3	1	1	5	1		.210	.222	.339	55	-4	2			.793	-4	P-21/O-1	0.0
1900	Phi-N	39	129	6	40	4	1	1	21	2		.310	.326	.380	95	-1	2			.943	1	P-33/O-3	0.0
1901	Phi-N	41	128	14	36	6	0	1	15	3		.281	.303	.352	88	-2	3			.945	1	P-35/O-4	-0.1
1902	Was-A	56	175	20	38	3	2	2	10	9		.217	.255	.291	51	-12	2			.923	-0	P-38,O-13/1-1,S-1	-0.4
1903	Was-A	55	162	19	49	9	7	0	11	4		.302	.323	.444	126	4	3			.920	-2	P-36/S-7,O-4,1-2	-0.1
1904	Was-A	31	102	7	22	3	1	0	11	1		.216	.238	.265	60	-5	2			.816	-2	O-18,P-10	-0.8
	NY-A	24	64	6	19	1	1	0	7	0		.297	.308	.344	101	-0	2			.968	1	P-20/O-2	0.0
	Yr	55	166	13	41	4	2	0	18	1		.247	.265	.295	76	-5	4			.969	-2	P-30,O-20	-0.8
1905	NY-A	55	131	13	24	3	1	1	6	4		.183	.213	.244	40	-9	2			.940	-0	P-40/1-1,O-1	-0.1
1906	NY-A	47	135	12	37	2	2	1	17	6		.274	.305	.341	93	-1	1			.934	2	P-45/O-1	0.1
1907	NY-A	44	105	11	34	6	0	1	13	4		.324	.355	.410	133	3	1			.920	2	P-36/O-1	0.0
1908	NY-A	38	69	4	20	1	2	0	4	2		.290	.310	.362	117	1	1			.909	-1	P-21	0.0
1909	NY-A	22	34	3	9	0	1	0	5	5		.265	.359	.324	115	1	1			1.000	-2	/2-6,P-1	-0.1
Total	15	602	1698	183	464	61	30	12	184	51	17	.273	.298	.366	91	-24	30			.932	-5	P-440/O-55,S-8,21	-1.4

■ JUNIOR ORTIZ
Ortiz, Adalberto Colon b: 10/24/59, Humacao, P.R. BR/TR, 5'11", 176 lbs. Deb: 9/20/82

YEAR	TM/L	G	AB	R	H	2B	3B	HR	RBI	BB	SO	AVG	OBP	SLG	PRO+	BR/A	SB	CS	SBR	FA	FR	G/POS	TPR
1982	Pit-N	7	15	1	3	1	0	0	0	1	3	.200	.250	.267	43	-1	0	0	0	1.000	1	/C-7	0.0
1983	Pit-N	5	8	1	1	0	0	0	0	1	0	.125	.222	.125	-1	-1	0	0	0	1.000	1	/C-4	-0.1
	NY-N	68	185	10	47	5	0	0	12	3	34	.254	.270	.281	53	-12	1	0	0	.965	1	C-67	-0.9
	Yr	73	193	11	48	5	0	0	12	4	34	.249	.268	.275	51	-13	1	0	0	.967	1	C-71	-1.0
1984	NY-N	40	91	6	18	3	0	0	11	5	15	.198	.240	.231	33	-8	0	0	0	.980	-4	C-32	-1.1
1985	Pit-N	23	72	4	21	2	0	1	5	3	17	.292	.320	.361	91	-1	1	0	0	.985	-1	C-23	0.1
1986	Pit-N	49	110	11	37	6	0	0	14	9	13	.336	.387	.417	112	2	0	1	-1	.983	-1	C-36	0.3
1987	Pit-N	75	192	16	52	8	1	1	22	15	23	.271	.324	.339	75	-7	0	2	-1	.975	2	C-72	-0.4
1988	Pit-N	49	118	8	33	6	0	2	18	9	9	.280	.341	.381	109	1	1	4	-2	.983	-2	C-40	0.0
1989	Pit-N	91	230	16	50	6	1	1	22	20	20	.217	.286	.265	61	-12	2	2	-1	.995	-10	C-84	-2.0
1990	Min-A	71	170	18	57	7	1	0	18	12	16	.335	.386	.388	110	3	0	4	-2	1.000	1	C-68/D-3	0.5
1991	*Min-A	61	134	9	28	5	1	0	11	15	12	.209	.293	.261	52	-8	0	1	-1	.995	-0	C-60	-0.7
1992	Cle-A	86	244	20	61	7	0	0	24	12	23	.250	.296	.279	63	-12	1	3	-2	.989	-1	C-86	-1.1
1993	Cle-A	95	249	19	55	13	0	0	20	11	26	.221	.268	.273	46	-19	1	0	0	.990	11	C-95	-0.4
1994	Tex-A	29	76	3	21	2	0	0	9	5	11	.276	.329	.303	65	-4	0	1	-1	.992	-1	C-28	-0.4
Total	13	749	1894	142	484	71	4	5	186	121	222	.256	.306	.305	69	-78	8	18	-8	.986	-4	C-702/D-3	-6.1

■ JAVIER ORTIZ
Ortiz, Javier Victor b: 1/22/63, Boston, Mass. BR/TR, 6'4", 220 lbs. Deb: 6/15/90

YEAR	TM/L	G	AB	R	H	2B	3B	HR	RBI	BB	SO	AVG	OBP	SLG	PRO+	BR/A	SB	CS	SBR	FA	FR	G/POS	TPR
1990	Hou-N	30	77	7	21	5	1	1	10	12	11	.273	.371	.403	116	2	1	1	-0	.978	-3	O-25	-0.2
1991	Hou-N	47	83	7	23	4	1	1	5	14	14	.277	.381	.386	123	3	0	0	0	1.000	-3	O-24	0.0
Total	2	77	160	14	44	9	2	2	15	26	25	.275	.376	.394	120	5	1	1	-0	.987	-6	/O-49	-0.2

■ JOSE ORTIZ
Ortiz, Jose Luis (Irizarry) b: 6/25/47, Ponce, P.R. BR/TR, 5'9.5", 155 lbs. Deb: 9/4/69

YEAR	TM/L	G	AB	R	H	2B	3B	HR	RBI	BB	SO	AVG	OBP	SLG	PRO+	BR/A	SB	CS	SBR	FA	FR	G/POS	TPR
1969	Chi-A	16	11	0	3	1	0	0	2	1	0	.273	.333	.364	90	-0	0	0	0	1.000	-2	/O-8	-0.3
1970	Chi-A	15	24	4	8	1	0	0	2	4	2	.333	.407	.375	113	1	0	0	0	1.000	-1	/O-8	-0.2
1971	Chi-N	36	88	10	26	7	1	0	3	4	10	.295	.347	.398	96	-0	2	2	-1	1.000	-2	O-30	-0.5
Total	3	67	123	14	37	9	1	0	7	6	12	.301	.358	.390	99	0	2	2	-0	1.000	-3	/O-46	-0.6

■ LUIS ORTIZ
Ortiz, Luis Alberto (Galarza) b: 5/25/70, Santo Domingo, D.R. BR/TR, 6', 190 lbs. Deb: 8/31/93

YEAR	TM/L	G	AB	R	H	2B	3B	HR	RBI	BB	SO	AVG	OBP	SLG	PRO+	BR/A	SB	CS	SBR	FA	FR	G/POS	TPR
1993	Bos-A	9	12	0	3	0	0	0	1	0	2	.250	.250	.250	33	-1	0	0	0	1.000	0	/3-5,D-3	-0.1
1994	Bos-A	7	18	3	3	2	0	0	6	1	5	.167	.211	.278	23	-2	0	0	0	.000	0	/D-6	-0.2
1995	Tex-A	41	108	10	25	5	2	1	18	6	18	.231	.272	.343	57	-7	0	1	-1	.867	-5	3-35/D-3	-1.2
1996	Tex-A	3	7	1	2	0	1	1	2	0	1	.286	.286	1.000	192	1	0	0	0	.000	0	/D-1	0.1
Total	4	60	145	14	33	7	3	2	26	7	26	.228	.267	.359	58	-9	0	1	-1	.875	-4	/3-40,D-13	-1.4

■ ROBERTO ORTIZ
Ortiz, Roberto Gonzalo (Nunez) b: 6/30/15, Camaguey, Cuba d: 9/15/71, Miami, Fla. BR/TR, 6'4", 200 lbs. Deb: 9/6/41 F

YEAR	TM/L	G	AB	R	H	2B	3B	HR	RBI	BB	SO	AVG	OBP	SLG	PRO+	BR/A	SB	CS	SBR	FA	FR	G/POS	TPR
1941	Was-A	22	79	10	26	1	2	1	19	7	10	.329	.354	.430	112	1	0	1	-1	.860	-2	O-21	-0.2
1942	Was-A	20	42	4	7	1	3	1	4	5	11	.167	.271	.405	89	-1	0	0	0	.941	-1	/O-9	-0.1
1943	Was-A	4	4	0	1	0	0	0	0	0	0	.250	.250	.250	48	-0	0	1	-1	1.000	0	/O-1	-0.1
1944	Was-A	85	316	36	80	11	4	5	35	19	47	.253	.312	.361	96	-2	4	1	1	.949	-3	O-80	-1.0
1949	Was-A	40	129	12	36	2	3	0	12	9	12	.279	.326	.326	74	-5	0	0	0	.946	-1	O-32	-0.8
1950	Was-A	39	75	4	17	2	1	0	8	7	12	.227	.301	.280	52	-5	0	0	0	1.000	-3	O-19	-0.8

YEAR	TM/L	G	AB	R	H	2B	3B	HR	RBI	BB	SO	AVG	OBP	SLG	PRO+	BR/A	SB	CS	SBR	FA	FR	G/POS	TPR
	Phi-A	6	14	1	1	0	0	0	3	0	3	.071	.071	.071	-65	-3	0	0	0	1.000	-1	/O-3	-0.4
	Yr	45	89	5	18	2	1	0	11	7	15	.202	.268	.247	34	-9	0	0	0	1.000	-3	O-22	-1.2
Total	6	213	659	67	168	18	10	8	78	43	95	.255	.310	.349	84	-16	4	3	-1	.942	-10	O-165	-3.5

■ JOHN ORTON
Orton, John Andrew   b: 12/8/65, Santa Cruz, Cal.   BR/TR, 6'1", 195 lbs.   Deb: 8/20/89

YEAR	TM/L	G	AB	R	H	2B	3B	HR	RBI	BB	SO	AVG	OBP	SLG	PRO+	BR/A	SB	CS	SBR	FA	FR	G/POS	TPR
1989	Cal-A	16	39	4	7	1	0	0	4	2	17	.179	.220	.205	21	-4	0	0	0	.988	5	C-16	0.1
1990	Cal-A	31	84	8	16	5	0	1	6	5	31	.190	.244	.286	49	-6	0	1	-1	.987	1	C-31	-0.4
1991	Cal-A	29	69	7	14	4	0	0	3	10	17	.203	.313	.261	60	-3	0	1	-1	.994	9	C-28/D-1	0.6
1992	Cal-A	43	114	11	25	3	0	2	12	7	32	.219	.276	.298	61	-6	1	1	-0	.981	8	C-43	0.4
1993	Cal-A	37	95	5	18	5	0	1	4	7	24	.189	.252	.274	40	-8	1	2	-1	.980	5	C-35/O-1	-0.2
Total	5	156	401	35	80	18	0	4	29	31	121	.200	.265	.274	49	-28	2	5	-2	.985	28	C-153/O-1,D-1	0.5

■ OSSIE ORWOLL
Orwoll, Oswald Christian   b: 11/17/1900, Portland, Ore.   d: 5/8/67, Decorah, Iowa   BL/TL, 6', 174 lbs.   Deb: 4/13/28

YEAR	TM/L	G	AB	R	H	2B	3B	HR	RBI	BB	SO	AVG	OBP	SLG	PRO+	BR/A	SB	CS	SBR	FA	FR	G/POS	TPR
1928	Phi-A	64	170	28	52	13	2	0	22	16	24	.306	.366	.406	100	0	3	1	0	.983	-1	1-34,P-27	-0.3
1929	Phi-A	30	51	6	13	2	1	0	6	2	11	.255	.283	.333	56	-3	0	0	0	1.000	-2	P-12/O-9	-0.4
Total	2	94	221	34	65	15	3	0	28	18	35	.294	.347	.389	90	-3	3	1	0	.970	-3	/P-39,1-34,O-9	-0.7

■ FRED OSBORN
Osborn, Wilfred Pearl "Ossie"   b: 11/28/1883, Nevada, Ohio   d: 9/2/54, Upper Sandusky, O.   BL/TR, 5'9", 178 lbs.   Deb: 6/8/07

YEAR	TM/L	G	AB	R	H	2B	3B	HR	RBI	BB	SO	AVG	OBP	SLG	PRO+	BR/A	SB	CS	SBR	FA	FR	G/POS	TPR
1907	Phi-N	56	163	22	45	2	3	0	9	3		.276	.298	.325	97	-1	4			1.000	-4	O-36/1-1	-0.7
1908	Phi-N	152	555	62	148	19	12	2	44	30		.267	.305	.355	107	3	16			.969	-2	*O-152	-0.2
1909	Phi-N	58	189	14	35	4	1	0	19	12		.185	.238	.217	41	-13	6			.979	10	O-54	-0.6
Total	3	266	907	98	228	25	16	2	72	45		.251	.290	.321	91	-12	26			.975	8	O-242/1-1	-1.5

■ FRED OSBORNE
Osborne, Frederick W.   b: Hampton, Iowa   TL,   Deb: 7/14/1890

YEAR	TM/L	G	AB	R	H	2B	3B	HR	RBI	BB	SO	AVG	OBP	SLG	PRO+	BR/A	SB	CS	SBR	FA	FR	G/POS	TPR
1890	Pit-N	41	168	24	40	8	3	1	14	6	18	.238	.269	.339	87	-4	0			.828	1	O-35/P-8	-0.3

■ BOBO OSBORNE
Osborne, Lawrence Sidney   b: 10/12/35, Chattahoochee, Ga.   BL/TR, 6'1", 205 lbs.   Deb: 6/27/57 F

YEAR	TM/L	G	AB	R	H	2B	3B	HR	RBI	BB	SO	AVG	OBP	SLG	PRO+	BR/A	SB	CS	SBR	FA	FR	G/POS	TPR
1957	Det-A	11	27	4	4	1	0	0	3	3	7	.148	.233	.185	15	-3	0	0	0	1.000	-1	/O-5,1-4	-0.4
1958	Det-A	2	2	0	0	0	0	0	0	0	0	.000	.000	.000	-93	-1	0	0	0	.000	0	H	-0.1
1959	Det-A	86	209	27	40	7	1	3	21	16	41	.191	.256	.278	44	-16	1	0	0	.983	-1	1-56/O-1	-2.1
1961	Det-A	71	93	8	20	7	0	2	13	20	15	.215	.354	.355	88	-1	1	0	0	.957	-2	/3-8,1-11	-0.4
1962	Det-A	64	74	12	17	1	0	0	7	16	25	.230	.374	.243	68	-3	0	0	0	.857	-2	3-13/1-7,C-1	-0.4
1963	Was-A	125	358	42	76	14	1	12	44	49	83	.212	.312	.358	87	-6	0	0	0	.988	-3	1-81,3-16	-1.3
Total	6	359	763	93	157	30	2	17	86	104	171	.206	.306	.317	71	-29	2	0	1	.987	-9	1-159/3-37,O-6,C-1	-4.7

■ KEITH OSIK
Osik, Keith Richard   b: 10/22/68, Port Jefferson, N.Y.   BR/TR, 6', 185 lbs.   Deb: 4/5/96

YEAR	TM/L	G	AB	R	H	2B	3B	HR	RBI	BB	SO	AVG	OBP	SLG	PRO+	BR/A	SB	CS	SBR	FA	FR	G/POS	TPR
1996	Pit-N	48	140	18	41	14	1	1	14	14	22	.293	.361	.429	104	1	1	0	0	.977	-3	C-41/3-2,O-2	0.1

■ HARRY OSTDIEK
Ostdiek, Henry Girard   b: 4/12/1881, Ottumwa, Iowa   d: 5/6/56, Minneapolis, Minn.   BR/TR, 5'11", 185 lbs.   Deb: 9/10/04

YEAR	TM/L	G	AB	R	H	2B	3B	HR	RBI	BB	SO	AVG	OBP	SLG	PRO+	BR/A	SB	CS	SBR	FA	FR	G/POS	TPR
1904	Cle-A	7	18	1	3	0	1	0	3	3		.167	.318	.278	90	-0	1			.946	-0	/C-7	0.0
1908	Bos-A	1	3	0	0	0	0	0	0	0		.000	.000	.000	-97	-1	0			.889	0	/C-1	0.0
Total	2	8	21	1	3	0	1	0	3	3		.143	.280	.238	65	-1	1			.935	0	/C-8	0.0

■ CHAMP OSTEEN
Osteen, James Champlin   b: 2/24/1877, Hendersonville, N.C.   d: 12/14/62, Greenville, S.C.   BL/TR, 5'8", 150 lbs.   Deb: 9/18/03

YEAR	TM/L	G	AB	R	H	2B	3B	HR	RBI	BB	SO	AVG	OBP	SLG	PRO+	BR/A	SB	CS	SBR	FA	FR	G/POS	TPR
1903	Was-A	10	40	4	8	0	2	0	4	2		.200	.256	.300	65	-2	0			.938	1	S-10	0.0
1904	NY-A	28	107	15	21	1	4	2	9	1		.196	.218	.336	71	-4	0			.930	2	3-17/S-8,1-4	-0.6
1908	StL-N	29	112	2	22	4	0	0	11	0		.196	.204	.232	41	-8	0			.847	-6	S-17,3-12	-1.6
1909	StL-N	16	45	6	9	1	0	0	7	7		.200	.308	.222	69	-1	1			.879	-6	S-16	-0.8
Total	4	83	304	27	60	6	6	2	31	10		.197	.233	.276	60	-15	1			.890	-13	/S-51,3-29,1-4	-3.0

■ RED OSTERGARD
Ostergard, Roy Lund   b: 5/16/1896, Denmark, Wis.   d: 1/13/77, Hemet, Cal.   BR/TR, 5'10.5", 175 lbs.   Deb: 6/14/21

YEAR	TM/L	G	AB	R	H	2B	3B	HR	RBI	BB	SO	AVG	OBP	SLG	PRO+	BR/A	SB	CS	SBR	FA	FR	G/POS	TPR
1921	Chi-A	12	11	2	4	0	0	0	0	0	0	.364	.364	.364	87	0	0	0	0	.000	0	H	0.0

■ CHARLIE OSTERHOUT
Osterhout, Charles H.   b: 1856, Syracuse, N.Y.   d: 5/21/33, Syracuse, N.Y.   TR,   Deb: 6/23/1879

YEAR	TM/L	G	AB	R	H	2B	3B	HR	RBI	BB	SO	AVG	OBP	SLG	PRO+	BR/A	SB	CS	SBR	FA	FR	G/POS	TPR
1879	Syr-N	2	8	0	0	0	0	0	0	0	0	.000	.000	.000	-99	-2				1.000	0	/O-1,C-1	-0.2

■ BRIAN OSTROSSER
Ostrosser, Brian Leonard   b: 6/17/49, Hamilton, Ont., Can   BL/TR, 6', 175 lbs.   Deb: 8/5/73

YEAR	TM/L	G	AB	R	H	2B	3B	HR	RBI	BB	SO	AVG	OBP	SLG	PRO+	BR/A	SB	CS	SBR	FA	FR	G/POS	TPR
1973	NY-N	4	5	0	0	0	0	0	0	0	2	.000	.000	.000	-99	-1	0	0	0	1.000	-0	/S-4	-0.2

■ JOHNNY OSTROWSKI
Ostrowski, John Thaddeus   b: 10/17/17, Chicago, Ill.   d: 11/13/92, Chicago, Ill.   BR/TR, 5'10.5", 170 lbs.   Deb: 9/24/43

YEAR	TM/L	G	AB	R	H	2B	3B	HR	RBI	BB	SO	AVG	OBP	SLG	PRO+	BR/A	SB	CS	SBR	FA	FR	G/POS	TPR
1943	Chi-N	10	29	2	6	0	1	0	3	3	8	.207	.303	.276	69	-1	0			1.000	-2	/O-5,3-4	-0.4
1944	Chi-N	8	13	2	2	1	0	0	2	1	4	.154	.214	.231	25	-1	0			.500	1	/O-2	-0.2
1945	Chi-N	7	10	4	3	2	0	0	1	0	1	.300	.300	.500	123	0	0			.750	2	/3-4	-0.1
1946	Chi-N	64	160	20	34	4	2	3	12	20	31	.213	.300	.319	77	-5	1			.934	1	3-50/2-1	-0.3
1948	Bos-A	1	1	0	0	0	0	0	0	0	0	.000	.000	.000	-95	-0	0	0	0	.000	0	H	0.0
1949	Chi-A	49	158	19	42	9	4	5	31	15	41	.266	.333	.468	115	2	4	3	-1	.944	-4	O-41/3-8	-0.4
1950	Chi-A	21	45	9	10	1	0	2	2	9	8	.222	.364	.422	104	0	0	0	0	1.000	-0	O-14	-0.1
	Was-A	55	141	16	32	2	1	4	23	20	31	.227	.327	.340	75	-6	2	0	1	.947	-0	O-45	-0.6
	Chi-A	1	4	1	2	1	0	0	0	0	1	.500	.500	.750	223	0	0	0	0	1.000	-0	/O-1	0.0
	Yr	77	190	26	44	4	2	6	25	29	40	.232	.339	.368	85	-4	2	0	1	.958	-2	O-60	-0.7
Total	7	216	561	73	131	20	9	14	74	68	125	.234	.321	.376	89	-10	7		3	.950	-9	O-108/3-66,2-1	-2.1

■ REGGIE OTERO
Otero, Regino Jose (Gomez)   b: 9/7/15, Havana, Cuba   d: 10/21/88, Hialeah, Fla.   BL/TR, 6', 165 lbs.   Deb: 9/2/45 C

YEAR	TM/L	G	AB	R	H	2B	3B	HR	RBI	BB	SO	AVG	OBP	SLG	PRO+	BR/A	SB	CS	SBR	FA	FR	G/POS	TPR
1945	Chi-N	14	23	1	9	2	0	0	1	1	0	.391	.440	.391	135	1	0			.967	0	/1-8	0.1

■ RICKY OTERO
Otero, Ricardo (Figueroa)   b: 4/15/72, Vega Baja, P.R.   BB/TR, 5'7", 150 lbs.   Deb: 4/26/95

YEAR	TM/L	G	AB	R	H	2B	3B	HR	RBI	BB	SO	AVG	OBP	SLG	PRO+	BR/A	SB	CS	SBR	FA	FR	G/POS	TPR
1995	NY-N	35	51	5	7	2	0	0		3	10	.137	.185	.176	-4	-8	2	1	0	1.000	-2	O-23	-1.0
1996	Phi-N	104	411	54	112	11	7	2	32	34	30	.273	.331	.348	77	-13	16	10	-1	.985	13	*O-100	-0.4
Total	2	139	462	59	119	13	7	2	33	37	40	.258	.315	.329	69	-21	18	11	-1	.986	10	O-123	-1.4

■ AMOS OTIS
Otis, Amos Joseph   b: 4/26/47, Mobile, Ala.   BR/TR, 5'11", 166 lbs.   Deb: 9/6/67 C

YEAR	TM/L	G	AB	R	H	2B	3B	HR	RBI	BB	SO	AVG	OBP	SLG	PRO+	BR/A	SB	CS	SBR	FA	FR	G/POS	TPR
1967	NY-N	19	59	6	13	2	0	0	1	5	13	.220	.292	.254	59	-3	0	4	-2	1.000	-2	O-16/3-1	-0.9
1969	NY-N	48	93	6	14	3	1	0	4	6	27	.151	.202	.204	14	-11	1	0	0	1.000	-2	O-35/3-3	-1.5
1970	KC-A★	159	620	91	176	**36**	9	11	58	68	67	.284	.356	.424	114	12	33	2	9	.990	14	*O-159	2.7
1971	KC-A★	147	555	80	167	26	4	15	79	40	74	.301	.350	.443	125	16	**52**	8	11	.990	20	*O-144	4.2
1972	KC-A†	143	540	75	158	28	2	11	54	50	59	.293	.358	.413	129	19	28	12	1	.992	9	*O-137	2.6
1973	KC-A★	148	583	89	175	21	4	26	93	49	47	.300	.369	.484	129	21	13	9	-2	.986	3	*O-135,D-14	1.6
1974	KC-A	146	552	87	157	31	9	12	73	58	67	.284	.355	.438	120	14	18	5	2	.986	10	*O-143/D-2	2.1
1975	KC-A	132	470	87	116	26	6	9	46	66	48	.247	.344	.385	103	3	39	11	5	.988	10	*O-130	0.5
1976	*KC-A★	153	592	93	165	**40**	2	18	86	55	100	.279	.345	.444	129	21	26	7	4	.992	-5	*O-152	1.4
1977	*KC-A	142	478	85	120	20	8	17	78	71	88	.251	.348	.433	110	8	23	7	3	.990	2	*O-140	0.6
1978	*KC-A	141	486	74	145	30	7	22	96	66	54	.298	.387	.525	150	33	32	8	5	**.995**	10	*O-136/D-1	4.2
1979	*KC-A	151	577	100	170	28	6	18	90	68	92	.295	.372	.444	117	14	30	5	7	**.992**	5	*O-146/D-4	1.9
1980	*KC-A	107	394	56	99	18	3	10	53	39	70	.251	.323	.383	92	-4	16	1	4	.988	7	*O-105	0.2
1981	*KC-A	99	372	49	100	22	3	9	57	31	59	.269	.328	.417	114	6	16	7	1	.993	11	O-97/D-1	1.4
1982	KC-A	125	475	73	136	25	3	11	88	37	65	.286	.340	.421	108	5	9	5	-0	.997	-1	*O-125	0.0
1983	KC-A	98	336	35	93	14	1	4	41	27	63	.261	.313	.357	84	-8	5	2	0	.996	3	O-96/D-1	-0.7
1984	Pit-N	40	97	6	16	4	0	0	10	7	15	.165	.221	.206	21	-10	0	0	0	.964	2	O-32	-1.0
Total	17	1998	7299	1092	2020	374	66	193	1007	757	1008	.277	.347	.425	114	136	341	93	47	.991	87	*O-1928/D-23,3-4	19.3

■ BILL OTIS
Otis, Paul Franklin   b: 12/24/1889, Scituate, Mass.   d: 12/15/90, Duluth, Minn.   BL/TR, 5'10.5", 150 lbs.   Deb: 7/4/12

YEAR	TM/L	G	AB	R	H	2B	3B	HR	RBI	BB	SO	AVG	OBP	SLG	PRO+	BR/A	SB	CS	SBR	FA	FR	G/POS	TPR
1912	NY-A	4	17	1	1	0	0	0	2	3		.059	.200	.059	-24	-3	0			.917	1	/O-4	-0.2

YEAR	TM/L	G	AB	R	H	2B	3B	HR	RBI	BB	SO	AVG	OBP	SLG	PRO+	BR/A	SB	CS	SBR	FA	FR	G/POS	TPR

■ MEL OTT
Ott, Melvin Thomas "Master Melvin" b: 3/2/09, Gretna, La. d: 11/21/58, New Orleans, La. BL/TR, 5'9", 170 lbs. Deb: 4/27/26 MH

YEAR	TM/L	G	AB	R	H	2B	3B	HR	RBI	BB	SO	AVG	OBP	SLG	PRO+	BR/A	SB	CS	SBR	FA	FR	G/POS	TPR
1926	NY-N	35	60	7	23	2	0	0	4	1	9	.383	.393	.417	120	2	1			.913	1	O-10	0.2
1927	NY-N	82	163	23	46	7	3	1	19	13	9	.282	.335	.380	91	-2	2			.982	-7	O-32	-1.1
1928	NY-N	124	435	69	140	26	4	18	77	52	36	.322	.397	.524	138	24	3			.970	-3	*O-115/2-5,3-1	1.4
1929	NY-N	150	545	138	179	37	2	42	151	113	38	.328	.449	.635	166	59	6			.973	9	*O-149/2-1	5.2
1930	NY-N	148	521	122	182	34	5	25	119	103	35	.349	.458	.578	152	48	9			.969	6	*O-146	3.8
1931	NY-N	138	497	104	145	23	8	29	115	80	44	.292	.392	.545	153	38	10			.981	8	*O-137	3.6
1932	NY-N	154	566	119	180	30	8	38	123	100	39	.318	.424	.601	175	63	6			.984	2	*O-154	5.3
1933	*NY-N	152	580	98	164	36	1	23	103	75	48	.283	.367	.467	139	30	1			.983	-14	*O-152	0.9
1934	NY-N★	153	582	119	190	29	10	35	135	85	43	.326	.415	.591	170	58	0			.974	-9	*O-153	4.1
1935	NY-N★	152	593	113	191	33	6	31	114	82	58	.322	.407	.555	159	50	7			.990	7	*O-137,3-15	4.9
1936	NY-N★	150	534	120	175	28	6	33	135	111	41	.328	.448	.588	179	63	6			.985	-3	*O-148	5.2
1937	*NY-N★	151	545	99	160	28	2	31	95	102	69	.294	.408	.523	149	40	7			.939	0	3-60,O-91	3.7
1938	NY-N★	150	527	116	164	23	6	36	116	118	47	.311	.442	.583	178	61	2			.957	1	*3-113,O-37	6.1
1939	NY-N★	125	396	85	122	23	2	27	80	100	50	.308	.449	.581	173	45	2			.973	-5	O-96,3-20	3.6
1940	NY-N★	151	536	89	155	27	3	19	79	100	50	.289	.407	.457	137	31	6			.982	2	*O-111,3-42	2.8
1941	NY-N★	148	525	89	150	29	0	27	90	100	68	.286	.403	.495	149	37	5			.968	5	*O-145	3.3
1942	NY-N★	152	549	118	162	21	0	30	93	109	61	.295	.415	.497	165	49	6			.990	-1	*O-152,M	4.2
1943	NY-N★	125	380	65	89	12	2	18	47	95	48	.234	.391	.418	133	20	7			.975	1	*O-111/3-1,M	1.5
1944	NY-N★	120	399	91	115	16	4	26	82	90	47	.288	.423	.544	171	41	2			.986	-4	*O-103/3-4,M	3.2
1945	NY-N†	135	451	73	139	23	0	21	79	71	41	.308	.411	.499	150	32	1			.983	-4	*O-118,M	2.2
1946	NY-N	31	68	2	5	1	0	1	4	8	15	.074	.171	.132	-13	-10	0			1.000	-1	O-16,M	-1.3
1947	NY-N	4	4	0	0	0	0	0	0	0	0	.000	.000	.000	-99	-1	0			.000	0	HM	-0.1
Total	22	2730	9456	1859	2876	488	72	511	1860	1708	896	.304	.414	.533	155	776	89			.980	-10	*O-2313,3-256/2-6	62.7

■ ED OTT
Ott, Nathan Edward b: 7/11/51, Muncy, Pa. BL/TR, 5'10", 198 lbs. Deb: 6/10/74 C

YEAR	TM/L	G	AB	R	H	2B	3B	HR	RBI	BB	SO	AVG	OBP	SLG	PRO+	BR/A	SB	CS	SBR	FA	FR	G/POS	TPR
1974	Pit-N	7	5	1	0	0	0	0	0	0	1	.000	.000	.000	-99	-1	0	0	0	1.000	-1	/O-2	-0.2
1975	Pit-N	5	5	0	1	0	0	0	0	0	0	.200	.200	.200	11	-1	0	0	0	1.000	-1	/C-2	-0.1
1976	Pit-N	27	39	2	12	2	0	0	5	3	5	.308	.357	.359	103	0	0	0	0	1.000	1	/C-8	0.0
1977	Pit-N	104	311	40	82	14	3	7	38	32	41	.264	.336	.395	93	-3	7	7	-2	.982	-5	C-90	-0.8
1978	Pit-N	112	379	49	102	18	4	9	38	27	56	.269	.318	.409	97	-2	4	1	1	.975	-9	C-97/O-4	-0.8
1979	*Pit-N	117	403	49	110	20	2	7	51	26	62	.273	.317	.385	86	-8	0	1	-1	.994	-3	*C-116	-0.7
1980	Pit-N	120	392	35	102	14	0	8	41	33	47	.260	.318	.357	87	-7	1	6	-3	.983	-4	C-117/O-3	-1.0
1981	Cal-A	75	258	20	56	8	1	2	22	17	42	.217	.268	.279	58	-14	2	1	0	.979	1	C-72	-1.1
Total	8	567	1792	196	465	76	10	33	195	138	254	.259	.314	.368	86	-36	14	16	-5	.983	-21	C-502/O-9	-4.7

■ BILLY OTT
Ott, William Joseph b: 11/23/40, New York, N.Y. BB/TR, 6'1", 180 lbs. Deb: 9/4/62

YEAR	TM/L	G	AB	R	H	2B	3B	HR	RBI	BB	SO	AVG	OBP	SLG	PRO+	BR/A	SB	CS	SBR	FA	FR	G/POS	TPR
1962	Chi-N	12	28	3	4	0	0	1	2	2	10	.143	.200	.250	19	-3	0	0	0	1.000	-0	/O-7	-0.4
1964	Chi-N	20	39	4	7	3	0	1	3	3	10	.179	.238	.256	38	-3	0	1	-1	1.000	-2	O-10	-0.6
Total	2	32	67	7	11	3	0	1	5	5	20	.164	.222	.254	30	-6	0	1	-1	1.000	-2	/O-17	-1.0

■ JOE OTTEN
Otten, Joseph G. b: Murphysboro, Ill. TR , Deb: 7/5/1895

YEAR	TM/L	G	AB	R	H	2B	3B	HR	RBI	BB	SO	AVG	OBP	SLG	PRO+	BR/A	SB	CS	SBR	FA	FR	G/POS	TPR
1895	StL-N	26	87	8	21	0	0	0	8	5	8	.241	.283	.241	36	-8	2			.947	-4	C-24/O-2	-0.8

■ BILLY OTTERSON
Otterson, William John b: 5/4/1862, Pittsburgh, Pa. d: 9/21/40, Pittsburgh, Pa. BR/TR, 5'7", 124 lbs. Deb: 9/4/1887

YEAR	TM/L	G	AB	R	H	2B	3B	HR	RBI	BB	SO	AVG	OBP	SLG	PRO+	BR/A	SB	CS	SBR	FA	FR	G/POS	TPR
1887	Bro-a	30	100	16	20	4	1	2	15	8		.200	.259	.320	60	-6	8			.859	1	S-30	-0.4

■ PHIL OUELLETTE
Ouellette, Philip Roland b: 11/10/61, Salem, Ore. BB/TR, 6', 190 lbs. Deb: 9/10/86

YEAR	TM/L	G	AB	R	H	2B	3B	HR	RBI	BB	SO	AVG	OBP	SLG	PRO+	BR/A	SB	CS	SBR	FA	FR	G/POS	TPR
1986	SF-N	10	23	1	4	0	0	0	0	3	3	.174	.269	.174	26	-2	0	0	0	1.000	0	/C-9	-0.2

■ JOHNNY OULLIBER
Oulliber, John Andrew b: 2/24/11, New Orleans, La. d: 12/26/80, New Orleans, La. BR/TR, 5'11", 165 lbs. Deb: 7/25/33

YEAR	TM/L	G	AB	R	H	2B	3B	HR	RBI	BB	SO	AVG	OBP	SLG	PRO+	BR/A	SB	CS	SBR	FA	FR	G/POS	TPR
1933	Cle-A	22	75	9	20	1	0	0	3	4	5	.267	.313	.280	55	-5	0	0	0	1.000	-3	O-18	-0.9

■ CHINK OUTEN
Outen, William Austin b: 6/17/05, Mt.Holly, N.C. d: 9/11/61, Durham, N.C. BL/TR, 6', 200 lbs. Deb: 4/16/33

YEAR	TM/L	G	AB	R	H	2B	3B	HR	RBI	BB	SO	AVG	OBP	SLG	PRO+	BR/A	SB	CS	SBR	FA	FR	G/POS	TPR
1933	Bro-N	93	153	20	38	10	0	4	17	20	15	.248	.335	.392	112	3	1			.982	-13	C-56	-0.9

■ JIMMY OUTLAW
Outlaw, James Paulus b: 1/20/13, Orme, Tenn. BR/TR, 5'8", 168 lbs. Deb: 4/20/37

YEAR	TM/L	G	AB	R	H	2B	3B	HR	RBI	BB	SO	AVG	OBP	SLG	PRO+	BR/A	SB	CS	SBR	FA	FR	G/POS	TPR
1937	Cin-N	49	165	18	45	7	3	0	11	3	31	.273	.290	.352	77	-6	2			.914	4	3-41	-0.1
1938	Cin-N	4	0	1	0	0	0	0	0	0	0	—	—	—	—	0	0			.000	0	R	0.0
1939	Bos-N	65	133	15	35	2	0	0	5	10	14	.263	.315	.278	65	-6	1			.964	-3	O-39/3-2	-1.1
1943	Det-A	20	67	8	18	1	0	1	6	8	4	.269	.347	.343	91	-1	0	0	0	1.000	0	O-16	-0.1
1944	Det-A	139	535	69	146	20	6	3	57	41	40	.273	.327	.350	88	-8	7	8	-3	.964	-3	*O-137	-2.2
1945	*Det-A	132	446	56	121	16	5	0	34	45	33	.271	.338	.330	88	-6	6	7	-2	.967	-4	*O-105,3-21	-1.8
1946	Det-A	92	299	36	78	14	2	2	31	29	24	.261	.328	.341	82	-7	5	4	-1	1.000	-8	O-43,3-38	-1.8
1947	Det-A	70	127	20	29	7	1	0	15	21	14	.228	.338	.299	76	-4	3	1	0	.983	0	O-37/3-9	-1.2
1948	Det-A	74	198	33	56	12	0	0	25	31	15	.283	.383	.343	91	-1	0	1	-1	.920	1	3-47,O-13	-0.2
1949	Det-A	5	4	1	1	0	0	0	0	1	1	.250	.250	.250	32	-0	0	0	0	.000	0	H	0.0
Total	10	650	1974	257	529	79	17	6	184	188	176	.268	.333	.334	85	-39	24	21		.972	-19	O-390,3-158	-8.5

■ MICKEY OWEN
Owen, Arnold Malcolm b: 4/4/16, Nixa, Mo. BR/TR, 5'10", 190 lbs. Deb: 5/2/37 C

YEAR	TM/L	G	AB	R	H	2B	3B	HR	RBI	BB	SO	AVG	OBP	SLG	PRO+	BR/A	SB	CS	SBR	FA	FR	G/POS	TPR
1937	StL-N	80	234	17	54	4	2	0	20	15	13	.231	.277	.265	47	-17	1			.974	-3	C-78	-1.6
1938	StL-N	122	397	45	106	25	2	4	36	32	14	.267	.325	.370	86	-8	2			.980	1	*C-116	-0.1
1939	StL-N	131	344	32	89	18	2	3	35	43	28	.259	.344	.349	82	-8	6			.982	4	*C-126	0.2
1940	StL-N	117	307	27	81	16	2	0	27	34	13	.264	.341	.329	81	-7	4			.980	6	*C-113	0.2
1941	*Bro-N★	128	386	32	89	15	2	1	44	34	14	.231	.296	.288	62	-19	1			.995	6	*C-128	-0.3
1942	Bro-N★	133	421	53	109	16	3	0	44	44	17	.259	.330	.311	81	-6	10			.987	5	*C-133	0.9
1943	Bro-N☆	106	365	31	95	11	2	0	54	25	15	.260	.309	.301	77	-11	4			.987	-6	*C-100/3-3,S-1	-1.0
1944	Bro-N☆	130	461	43	126	20	3	1	42	36	17	.273	.326	.336	88	-7	4			.979	-11	*C-125/2-1	-1.1
1945	Bro-N	24	84	5	24	9	0	1	10	11	2	.286	.368	.393	113	2	0			.963	-3	C-24	0.0
1949	Chi-N	62	198	15	54	9	3	2	18	12	13	.273	.318	.379	88	-4	0			.969	-1	C-59	-0.1
1950	Chi-N	86	259	22	63	11	2	2	21	13	16	.243	.282	.309	56	-17	2			.978	3	C-86	-1.0
1951	Chi-N	58	125	10	23	6	0	0	15	19	13	.184	.292	.232	42	-10	1	0	0	.969	8	C-57	0.0
1954	Bos-A	32	68	6	16	3	0	1	11	9	6	.235	.325	.324	70	-3	0	1	-1	.989	-2	C-30	-0.5
Total	13	1209	3649	338	929	163	21	14	378	326	181	.255	.318	.322	76	-114	36	1		.982	3	*C-1175/3-3,2-1,S-1	-4.4

■ DAVE OWEN
Owen, Dave b: 4/25/58, Cleburne, Tex. BB/TR, 6'2", 170 lbs. Deb: 9/6/83 F

YEAR	TM/L	G	AB	R	H	2B	3B	HR	RBI	BB	SO	AVG	OBP	SLG	PRO+	BR/A	SB	CS	SBR	FA	FR	G/POS	TPR
1983	Chi-N	16	22	1	2	0	0	0	2	2	7	.091	.167	.182	-3	-3	1	0	0	1.000	4	S-14/3-3	0.1
1984	Chi-N	47	93	8	18	2	2	1	10	8	15	.194	.272	.290	53	-6	1	2	-1	.969	1	S-35/3-6,2-4	-0.4
1985	Chi-N	22	19	6	7	0	0	0	4	1	5	.368	.400	.368	105	0	1	1	-0	.917	2	/S-7,3-7,2-4	0.2
1988	KC-A	7	5	0	0	0	0	0	0	0	3	.000	.000	.000	-99	-1	0	0	0	.941	1	/S-7	0.3
Total	4	92	139	15	27	2	3	1	16	11	30	.194	.263	.273	47	-10	3	3	-1	.969	10	/S-63,3-16,2-8	0.2

■ LARRY OWEN
Owen, Lawrence Thomas b: 5/31/55, Cleveland, Ohio BR/TR, 5'11", 185 lbs. Deb: 8/14/81

YEAR	TM/L	G	AB	R	H	2B	3B	HR	RBI	BB	SO	AVG	OBP	SLG	PRO+	BR/A	SB	CS	SBR	FA	FR	G/POS	TPR
1981	Atl-N	13	16	0	0	0	0	0	0	1	4	.000	.059	.000	-80	-4	0	0	0	.964	2	C-10	-0.2
1982	Atl-N	2	3	1	1	1	0	0	0	0	1	.333	.333	.667	167	0	0	0	0	1.000	-0	/C-2	0.0
1983	Atl-N	17	17	0	2	0	0	0	3	0	4	.118	.118	.118	-32	-3	0	1	-1	.970	1	C-16	-0.3
1985	Atl-N	26	71	7	17	3	0	2	12	8	17	.239	.316	.366	85	-1	0	0	0	.966	3	C-25	0.2
1987	KC-A	76	164	17	31	6	1	5	14	16	51	.189	.261	.317	51	-12	0	1	0	.983	19	C-75	1.0
1988	KC-A	37	81	5	17	1	0	1	1	9	17	.210	.304	.259	59	-4	0	1	-1	.989	5	C-37	0.3
Total	6	171	352	30	68	11	0	8	30	34	98	.193	.268	.273	51	-24	0	3	-1	.980	29	C-165	1.0

YEAR	TM/L	G	AB	R	H	2B	3B	HR	RBI	BB	SO	AVG	OBP	SLG	PRO+	BR/A	SB	CS	SBR	FA	FR	G/POS	TPR

■ MARV OWEN   Owen, Marvin James "Freck"   b: 3/22/06, Agnew, Cal.   d: 6/22/91, Mountain View, Cal.   BR/TR, 6'1", 175 lbs.   Deb: 4/16/31

1931	Det-A	105	377	35	84	11	6	3	39	29	38	.223	.282	.308	53	-26	2	2	-1	.937	1	S-37,3-37,1-27,/2-4	-2.0
1933	Det-A	138	550	77	144	24	9	2	65	44	56	.262	.321	.349	76	-19	2	2	-1	.944	-11	*3-136	-2.1
1934	*Det-A	154	565	79	179	34	9	8	96	59	37	.317	.385	.451	115	13	3	3	-1	.956	-7	*3-154	1.0
1935	*Det-A	134	483	52	127	24	5	2	71	43	37	.263	.326	.346	76	-17	1	4	-2	.958	-10	*3-131	-2.3
1936	Det-A	154	583	72	172	20	4	9	105	53	41	.295	.361	.389	85	-13	9	6	-1	.952	-4	*3-153/1-2	-1.1
1937	Det-A	107	396	48	114	22	5	1	45	41	24	.288	.358	.376	83	-10	3	4	-2	**.970**	0	*3-106	-0.8
1938	Chi-A	141	577	84	162	23	6	6	55	45	31	.281	.337	.373	76	-22	6	4	-1	.948	0	*3-140	-1.8
1939	Chi-A	58	194	22	46	9	0	0	15	16	15	.237	.302	.284	49	-15	4	5	-2	.953	-2	3-55	-1.7
1940	Bos-A	20	57	4	12	0	0	0	6	8	4	.211	.308	.211	36	-5	0	0	0	.962	2	/3-9,1-8	-0.4
Total	9	1011	3782	473	1040	167	44	31	497	338	283	.275	.339	.367	80	-114	30	30	-9	.953	-30	3-921/1-37,S-37,2-4	-11.2

■ SPIKE OWEN   Owen, Spike Dee   b: 4/19/61, Cleburne, Tex.   BB/TR, 5'10", 170 lbs.   Deb: 6/25/83   F

1983	Sea-A	80	306	36	60	11	3	2	21	24	44	.196	.259	.271	44	-23	10	6	-1	.970	0	S-80	-1.6
1984	Sea-A	152	530	67	130	18	8	3	43	46	63	.245	.309	.326	77	-16	16	8	0	.977	16	*S-151	1.5
1985	Sea-A	118	352	41	91	10	6	6	37	34	27	.259	.324	.372	89	-5	11	5	0	.975	**30**	*S-117	3.5
1986	Sea-A	112	402	46	99	22	6	0	35	34	42	.246	.307	.331	73	-15	1	3	-2	.972	34	*S-112	2.7
	*Bos-A	42	126	21	23	2	1	1	10	17	9	.183	.285	.238	44	-10	3	1	0	.976	-2	S-42	-0.7
	Yr	154	528	67	122	24	7	1	45	51	51	.231	.301	.309	66	-24	4	4	-1	.973	**32**	*S-154	2.0
1987	Bos-A	132	437	50	113	17	7	2	48	53	43	.259	.340	.343	80	-12	11	8	-2	.975	-14	*S-130	-1.5
1988	*Bos-A	89	257	40	64	14	1	5	18	27	27	.249	.325	.370	90	-3	0	1	-1	.967	-1	S-76/D-7	0.1
1989	Mon-N	142	437	52	102	17	4	6	41	76	44	.233	.351	.332	95	-0	3	2	-0	**.979**	11	*S-142	2.2
1990	Mon-N	149	453	55	106	24	5	5	35	70	60	.234	.337	.342	91	-4	8	6	-1	**.989**	-12	*S-148	-0.8
1991	Mon-N	139	424	39	108	22	8	3	26	42	61	.255	.323	.366	95	-3	2	6	-3	.986	8	*S-133	1.1
1992	Mon-N	122	386	52	104	16	3	7	40	50	30	.269	.353	.381	109	5	9	4	0	.982	-10	*S-116	0.4
1993	NY-A	103	334	41	78	16	2	2	20	29	30	.234	.295	.311	65	-16	3	2	-0	.968	10	S-96/D-2	0.4
1994	Cal-A	82	268	30	83	17	2	3	37	49	17	.310	.418	.422	116	9	2	8	-4	.956	-15	3-70/S-5,1-4,2-1,D	0.4
1995	Cal-A	82	218	17	50	9	3	1	28	14	22	.229	.288	.312	57	-14	3	2	-0	.945	-18	S-29,S-25,2-16	-2.8
Total	13	1544	4930	587	1211	215	59	46	439	569	519	.246	.326	.341	83	-107	82	62	-13	.977	51	*S-1373/3-99,2D1	4.5

■ J OWENS   Owens, Claude Jayhawk   b: 2/10/69, Cincinnati, Ohio   BR/TR, 6'1", 200 lbs.   Deb: 6/6/93

1993	Col-N	33	86	12	18	5	0	3	6	6	30	.209	.277	.372	62	-5	1	0	0	.957	1	C-32	-0.2
1994	Col-N	6	12	4	3	1	0	0	1	3	3	.250	.400	.417	97	0	0	0	0	1.000	1	/C-6	0.1
1995	*Col-N	18	45	7	11	2	0	4	12	2	15	.244	.292	.556	91	-1	0	0	0	.988	2	C-16	0.2
1996	Col-N	73	180	31	43	9	1	4	17	27	56	.239	.341	.367	67	-10	4	1	1	.974	-3	C-68	-0.8
Total	4	130	323	54	75	16	2	11	36	38	104	.232	.321	.396	71	-16	5	1	1	.973	1	C-122	-0.7

■ ERIC OWENS   Owens, Eric Blake   b: 2/3/71, Danville, Va.   BR/TR, 6'1", 185 lbs.   Deb: 6/6/95

1995	Cin-N	2	2	0	2	0	0	0	1	0	0	1.000	1.000	1.000	432	1	0	0	0	.000	0	/3-2	0.1
1996	Cin-N	88	205	26	41	6	0	0	9	23	38	.200	.284	.229	38	-18	16	2	4	.986	-5	O-52/2-6,3-5	-2.0
Total	2	90	207	26	43	6	0	0	10	23	38	.208	.290	.237	41	-17	16	2	4	1.000	-5	/O-52,3-7,2-6	-1.9

■ FRANK OWENS   Owens, Frank Walter "Yip"   b: 1/26/1886, Toronto, Ont., Can.   d: 7/2/58, Minneapolis, Minn.   BR/TR, 6', 170 lbs.   Deb: 9/11/05

1905	Bos-A	1	2	0	0	0	0	0	0	0	0	.000	.000	.000	-99	-0	0			1.000	0	/C-1	-0.1
1909	Chi-A	64	174	12	35	4	1	0	17	8		.201	.245	.236	54	-9	3			.959	-6	C-57	-1.2
1914	Bro-F	58	184	15	51	7	3	2	20	9	16	.277	.314	.380	89	-6	2			.967	-14	C-58	-1.7
1915	Bal-F	99	334	32	84	14	7	3	28	17	34	.251	.290	.362	80	-15	4			.976	2	C-99	-0.6
Total	4	222	694	59	170	25	11	5	65	34	50	.245	.284	.334	77	-30	9			.969	-19	C-215	-3.6

■ JACK OWENS   Owens, Furman Lee   b: 5/6/08, Converse, S.C.   d: 11/14/58, Greenville, S.C.   BR/TR, 6'1", 186 lbs.   Deb: 9/21/35

1935	Phi-A	2	8	0	2	0	0	0	1	0	1	.250	.250	.250	30	-1	0	0	0	.900	-0	/C-2	-0.1

■ RED OWENS   Owens, Thomas Llewellyn   b: 11/1/1874, Pottsville, Pa.   d: 8/20/52, Harrisburg, Pa.   BR/TR,   Deb: 7/28/1899

1899	Phi-N	8	21	0	1	0	0	0	1	2		.048	.130	.048	-52	-4	0			.914	-1	/2-8	-0.4
1905	Bro-N	43	168	14	36	6	2	1	20	6		.214	.241	.292	63	-8	1			.929	4	2-43	-0.4
Total	2	51	189	14	37	6	2	1	21	8		.196	.228	.265	49	-13	1			.927	3	/2-51	-0.8

■ HENRY OXLEY   Oxley, Henry Havelock   b: 1/4/1858, Covehead, P.E.I., Canada   d: 10/12/45, Somerville, Mass.   5'11", 163 lbs.   Deb: 7/30/1884

1884	NY-N	2	4	0	0	0	0	0	0	1	2	.000	.200	.000	-31	-1				.900	1	/C-2	0.0
	NY-a	1	3	0	0	0	0	0	0	0		.000	.000	.000	-99	-0				.889	0	/C-1	0.0
Total	1	3	7	0	0	0	0	0	0	1	2	.000	.125	.000	-56	-1				.895	1	/C-3	0.0

■ ANDY OYLER   Oyler, Andrew Paul "Pepper"   b: 5/5/1880, Newville, Pa.   d: 10/24/70, E.Pennsboro Twsp., Pa.   BR/TR, 5'6.5", 138 lbs.   Deb: 5/8/02

1902	Bal-A	27	77	9	17	1	0	1	6	8		.221	.318	.273	62	-4	3			.947	-8	3-20/O-3,S-2,2-1	-1.1

■ RAY OYLER   Oyler, Raymond Francis   b: 8/4/38, Indianapolis, Ind.   d: 1/26/81, Seattle, Wash.   BR/TR, 5'11", 165 lbs.   Deb: 4/18/65

1965	Det-A	82	194	22	36	6	0	5	13	21	61	.186	.265	.294	58	-11	1	0	-1	.955	6	S-57,2-11/1-1,3-1	-0.1
1966	Det-A	71	210	16	36	8	1	1	9	23	62	.171	.263	.252	48	-14	0	0	0	.965	15	S-69	0.6
1967	Det-A	148	367	33	76	14	2	1	29	37	91	.207	.283	.264	61	-17	0	2	-1	.964	15	*S-146	0.9
1968	*Det-A	111	215	13	29	6	1	1	12	20	59	.135	.215	.186	22	-20	0	2	-1	.977	9	*S-111	-0.5
1969	Sea-A	106	255	24	42	5	0	7	22	31	80	.165	.260	.267	48	-18	1	2	-1	.965	9	*S-106	-0.1
1970	Cal-A	24	24	2	2	0	0	0	1	3	6	.083	.185	.083	-24	-4	0	0	0	1.000	-1	S-13/3-2	-0.5
Total	6	542	1265	110	221	39	6	15	86	135	359	.175	.259	.251	48	-84	2	6	-3	.966	52	S-502/2-11,3-3,1-1	0.3

■ CHARLIE PABOR   Pabor, Charles Henry   b: 9/24/1846, New York, N.Y.   d: 4/23/13, New Haven, Conn.   BL/TL, 5'8", 155 lbs.   Deb: 5/4/1871   M

1871	Cle-n	29	142	24	42	2	4	0	18	1	3	.296	.301	.366	96	-0	1	0	0	.773	-5	*O-28/P-7,M	-0.3
1872	Cle-n	21	92	12	19	0	0	0	7	0	0	.207	.207	.207	29	-7	0	0	0	.863	-4	*O-20/P-2	-0.4
1873	Atl-n	55	228	36	82	8	3	0	42	6	3	.360	.376	.421	153	16	2	0	1	.807	-4	*O-55	1.1
1874	Phi-n	17	77	11	17	0	1	0	1	0	0	.221	.221	.247	48	-4	0	1	-1	.553	-1	O-17	-0.5
1875	Atl-n	42	153	14	36	2	2	0	11	1	1	.235	.240	.275	90	-1	0	0	0	.803	1	O-42/P-1,M	0.1
	NH-n	6	23	4	8	0	0	0	2	0	1	.348	.348	.522	227	3	0	0	0	.818	-1	/O-6,M	0.2
	Yr	48	176	18	44	2	2	0	13	1	2	.250	.254	.307	108	2	0	0	0	.804	-0	O-48/P-1	0.3
Total	5 n	170	715	101	204	12	12	0	81	8	8	.285	.293	.336	102	7	3	1	0	.787	-11	O-168/P-10	0.2

■ ED PABST   Pabst, Edward D. A.   b: 1868, St.Louis, Mo.   d: 6/19/40, St.Louis, Mo.   5'11", 170 lbs.   Deb: 9/26/1890

1890	Phi-a	8	25	7	10	2	0	0	3	5		.400	.500	.480	193	3	3			.963	4	/O-8	0.6
	StL-a	4	14	1	2	0	0	0	0	0		.143	.143	.286	23	-2	0			1.000	1	/O-4	0.0
	Yr	12	39	8	12	2	0	0	3	5		.308	.386	.410	131	1	3			.972	5	O-12	0.6

■ JIM PACIOREK   Paciorek, James Joseph   b: 6/7/60, Detroit, Mich.   BR/TR, 6'3", 203 lbs.   Deb: 4/9/87   F

1987	Mil-A	48	101	16	23	5	0	2	10	12	20	.228	.310	.337	69	-4	1	0	0	.980	-4	1-21,3-15/O-5,D-2	-0.9

■ JOHN PACIOREK   Paciorek, John Francis   b: 2/11/45, Detroit, Mich.   BR/TR, 6'2", 200 lbs.   Deb: 9/29/63   F

1963	Hou-N	1	3	4	3	0	0	0	3	2	0	1.000	1.000	1.000	509	2	0	0	0	1.000	0	/O-1	0.2

■ TOM PACIOREK   Paciorek, Thomas Marian   b: 11/2/46, Detroit, Mich.   BR/TR, 6'4", 215 lbs.   Deb: 9/12/70   F

1970	LA-N	8	9	2	2	1	0	0	0	0	3	.222	.300	.333	73	-0	0	0	0	1.000	-1	/O-3	-0.1
1971	LA-N	2	2	0	1	0	0	0	0	0	0	.500	.500	.500	196	0	0	0	0	1.000	0	/O-1	0.0
1972	LA-N	11	47	4	12	4	0	1	6	1	7	.255	.271	.404	92	-1	0	0	0	.979	1	/1-6,O-6	0.0
1973	LA-N	96	195	26	51	8	0	5	18	11	35	.262	.304	.379	92	-3	3	3	-1	.979	-15	O-77/1-4	-2.2
1974	*LA-N	85	175	23	42	8	1	6	24	10	32	.240	.285	.371	86	-4	4	3	-2	.944	-16	O-77/1-1	-2.5
1975	LA-N	62	145	14	28	8	0	1	5	11	29	.193	.250	.269	46	-11	4	3	-1	.972	-9	O-54	-2.4

YEAR	TM/L	G	AB	R	H	2B	3B	HR	RBI	BB	SO	AVG	OBP	SLG	PRO+	BR/A	SB	CS	SBR	FA	FR	G/POS	TPR
1976	Atl-N	111	324	39	94	10	4	4	36	19	57	.290	.335	.383	97	-1	2	3	-1	.983	-12	O-84,1-12/3-1	-2.0
1977	Atl-N	72	155	20	37	8	0	3	15	6	46	.239	.267	.348	57	-10	1	0	0	.984	-2	1-32/O-9,3-1	-1.3
1978	Atl-N	5	9	2	3	0	0	0	0	0	1	.333	.333	.333	78	-0	0	0	0	1.000	-0	/1-2	-0.1
	Sea-A	70	251	32	75	20	3	4	30	15	39	.299	.338	.450	121	6	2	2	-1	.980	-3	O-54,D-12/1-3	0.0
1979	Sea-A	103	310	38	89	23	4	6	42	28	62	.287	.356	.445	113	5	6	4	-1	1.000	-0	O-75,1-15	-0.1
1980	Sea-A	126	418	44	114	19	1	15	59	17	67	.273	.303	.431	98	-3	3	2	-0	1.000	-3	O-60,1-36,D-23	-1.0
1981	Sea-A★	104	405	50	132	28	2	14	66	35	50	.326	.385	.509	150	25	13	10	-2	.974	6	*O-103	2.7
1982	Chi-A	104	382	49	119	27	4	11	55	24	53	.312	.366	.490	133	17	3	3	-1	.993	-1	*1-102/O-6	0.9
1983	*Chi-A	115	420	65	129	32	3	9	63	25	58	.307	.350	.462	117	9	6	1	1	1.000	-10	1-67,O-55/D-2	-0.5
1984	Chi-A	111	363	35	93	21	2	4	29	25	69	.256	.311	.358	81	-9	6	0	2	.993	-13	1-67,O-41	-2.5
1985	Chi-A	46	122	14	30	2	0	0	9	8	22	.246	.298	.262	53	-8	2	0	1	.970	-2	O-23,D-12/1-6	-1.0
	NY-N	46	116	14	33	3	1	1	11	6	14	.284	.325	.353	92	-1	1	0	0	1.000	-5	O-29/1-8	-0.7
1986	Tex-A	88	213	17	61	7	0	4	22	3	41	.286	.306	.376	82	-5	1	3	-2	.967	-1	O-25,1-23,3-21,/SD	-1.0
1987	Tex-A	27	60	6	17	3	0	2	13	2	19	.283	.306	.383	105	0	0	1	-1	1.000	-0	1-12,O-12/D-3	-0.1
Total	18	1392	4121	494	1162	232	30	86	503	245	704	.282	.328	.415	102	6	55	38	-6	.979	-89	O-794,1-396/D3S	-13.9

■ FRANKIE PACK
Pack, Frank b: 4/10/28, Morristown, Tenn. BL/TR, 6', 190 lbs. Deb: 6/5/49

YEAR	TM/L	G	AB	R	H	2B	3B	HR	RBI	BB	SO	AVG	OBP	SLG	PRO+	BR/A	SB	CS	SBR	FA	FR	G/POS	TPR
1949	StL-A	1	1	0	0	0	0	0	0	0	1	.000	.000	.000	-96	-0	0	0	0	.000	0	H	0.0

■ DICK PADDEN
Padden, Richard Joseph "Brains" b: 9/17/1870, Martins Ferry, O. d: 10/31/22, Martins Ferry, O. BR/TR, 5'10", 165 lbs. Deb: 7/15/1896

YEAR	TM/L	G	AB	R	H	2B	3B	HR	RBI	BB	SO	AVG	OBP	SLG	PRO+	BR/A	SB	CS	SBR	FA	FR	G/POS	TPR
1896	Pit-N	61	219	33	53	4	8	2	24	14	9	.242	.294	.361	75	-9	8			.931	-12	2-61	-1.5
1897	Pit-N	134	517	84	146	16	10	2	58	38		.282	.350	.364	92	-5	18			.941	2	*2-134	0.3
1898	Pit-N	128	463	61	119	7	6	2	43	35		.257	.335	.311	87	-7	11			.947	-2	*2-128	0.0
1899	Was-N	134	451	66	125	20	7	2	61	24		.277	.337	.366	94	-4	27			.913	8	S-85,2-48	1.2
1901	StL-N	123	489	71	125	17	7	2	62	31		.256	.335	.331	92	-5	26			.950	1	*2-115/S-8	0.1
1902	StL-A	117	413	54	109	26	3	1	40	30		.264	.327	.349	89	-6	11			**.967**	18	*2-117	1.5
1903	StL-A	29	94	7	19	3	0	0	6	9		.202	.306	.234	65	-3	5			.955	2	2-29	0.4
1904	StL-A	132	453	42	108	19	4	0	36	40		.238	.325	.298	104	4	23			.959	-9	*2-132	-0.2
1905	StL-A	16	58	5	10	1	1	0	4	3		.172	.213	.224	41	-4	3			.950	2	2-16	-0.4
Total	9	874	3157	423	814	113	46	11	334	224	9	.258	.326	.333	90	-39	132			.950	11	2-780/S-93	1.4

■ TOM PADDEN
Padden, Thomas Francis b: 10/6/08, Manchester, N.H. d: 6/10/73, Manchester, N.H. BR/TR, 5'11.5", 170 lbs. Deb: 5/29/32

YEAR	TM/L	G	AB	R	H	2B	3B	HR	RBI	BB	SO	AVG	OBP	SLG	PRO+	BR/A	SB	CS	SBR	FA	FR	G/POS	TPR
1932	Pit-N	47	118	13	31	6	1	0	10	9	7	.263	.315	.331	75	-4				.985	-1	C-43	-0.3
1933	Pit-N	30	90	5	19	2	0	0	8	2	6	.211	.237	.233	35	-8	0			.984	8	C-27	0.0
1934	Pit-N	82	237	27	76	12	2	0	22	30	23	.321	.399	.388	109	5	3			.978	-5	C-76	0.3
1935	Pit-N	97	302	35	82	9	1	1	30	48	26	.272	.371	.318	84	-4	1			.966	14	C-94	1.4
1936	Pit-N	88	281	22	70	9	2	1	31	22	41	.249	.304	.306	63	-14	0			.976	2	C-87	-0.8
1937	Pit-N	35	98	14	28	2	0	0	8	13	11	.286	.369	.306	85	-1	1			.983	6	C-34	0.6
1943	Phi-N	17	41	5	12	0	0	0	1	2	6	.293	.341	.293	87	-1	0			1.000	4	C-16	0.4
	Was-A	3	3	1	0	0	0	0	0	1	0	.000	.250	.000	-25	-0	0	0	0	1.000	0	/C-2	0.0
Total	7	399	1170	122	318	40	6	2	110	127	121	.272	.345	.321	80	-28	5	0		.977	27	C-379	1.6

■ DEL PADDOCK
Paddock, Delmar Harold b: 6/8/1887, Volga, S.Dak. d: 2/6/52, Remer, Minn. BL/TR, 5'9", 165 lbs. Deb: 4/14/12

YEAR	TM/L	G	AB	R	H	2B	3B	HR	RBI	BB	SO	AVG	OBP	SLG	PRO+	BR/A	SB	CS	SBR	FA	FR	G/POS	TPR
1912	Chi-A	1	1	0	0	0	0	0	0	0	0	.000	.000	.000	-99	-0	0			.000	0	H	0.0
	NY-A	46	156	26	45	5	3	1	14	23		.288	.393	.378	114	4	9			.894	-7	3-41/2-2,O-1	-0.3
	Yr	47	157	26	45	5	3	1	14	23		.287	.391	.376	113	3	9			.894	-7	3-41/2-2,O-1	-0.3

■ DON PADGETT
Padgett, Don Wilson b: 12/5/11, Caroleen, N.C. d: 12/9/80, High Point, N.C. BL/TR, 6', 190 lbs. Deb: 4/23/37

YEAR	TM/L	G	AB	R	H	2B	3B	HR	RBI	BB	SO	AVG	OBP	SLG	PRO+	BR/A	SB	CS	SBR	FA	FR	G/POS	TPR
1937	StL-N	123	446	62	140	22	6	10	74	30	43	.314	.357	.457	117	10	4			.955	3	*O-109	0.9
1938	StL-N	110	388	59	105	26	5	8	65	18	28	.271	.303	.425	93	-5	0			.962	5	O-71,1-16/C-6	-0.4
1939	StL-N	92	233	38	93	15	3	5	53	18	11	.399	.444	.554	157	19	1			.978	-3	C-61/1-6	1.8
1940	StL-N	93	240	24	58	15	1	0	41	26	14	.242	.321	.387	89	-4	1			.962	-8	C-72/1-2	-0.7
1941	StL-N	107	324	39	80	18	0	5	44	21	16	.247	.293	.349	75	-11	0			.959	-9	O-62,C-18/1-2	-2.4
1946	Bro-N	19	30	2	5	1	0	1	9	4	7	.167	.265	.300	59	-2	0			1.000	-1	C-10	-0.3
	Bos-N	44	98	6	25	3	0	2	21	5	4	.255	.291	.347	80	-3	0			.939	-6	C-26	-0.8
	Yr	63	128	8	30	4	0	3	30	9	11	.234	.285	.336	75	-5	0			.954	-7	C-36	-1.1
1947	Phi-N	75	158	14	50	8	1	0	24	16	5	.316	.383	.380	107	2	0			.962	-7	C-39	-0.3
1948	Phi-N	36	74	3	17	3	0	0	7	3	2	.230	.260	.270	44	-6	0			.957	-4	C-19	-0.9
Total	8	699	1991	247	573	111	16	37	338	141	130	.288	.336	.415	101	1	6			.962	-32	C-251,O-242/1-26	-3.1

■ ERNIE PADGETT
Padgett, Ernest Kitchen "Red" b: 3/1/1899, Philadelphia, Pa. d: 4/15/57, E.Orange, N.J. BR/TR, 5'8", 155 lbs. Deb: 10/3/23

YEAR	TM/L	G	AB	R	H	2B	3B	HR	RBI	BB	SO	AVG	OBP	SLG	PRO+	BR/A	SB	CS	SBR	FA	FR	G/POS	TPR
1923	Bos-N	4	11	3	2	0	0	0	0	2	0	.182	.308	.182	33	-1	0	0	0	.947	2	/S-2,2-1	0.1
1924	Bos-N	138	502	42	128	25	9	1	46	37	56	.255	.310	.347	79	-15	4	9	-4	.967	-10	*3-113,2-29	-2.1
1925	Bos-N	86	256	31	78	9	7	0	29	14	14	.305	.341	.395	96	-2	3	5	-2	.964	-20	2-47,S-18/3-7	-2.1
1926	Cle-A	36	62	7	13	0	1	0	6	8	3	.210	.300	.242	42	-5	1	0	0	.930	2	3-29/S-2	-0.2
1927	Cle-A	7	7	1	2	0	0	0	0	0	2	.286	.286	.286	48	-1	0	0	0	1.000	-0	/2-4	-0.1
Total	5	271	838	84	223	34	17	1	81	61	75	.266	.318	.351	80	-24	8	14	-6	.957	-26	3-149/2-81,S-22	-4.4

■ DENNIS PAEPKE
Paepke, Dennis Ray b: 4/17/45, Long Beach, Cal. BR/TR, 6', 202 lbs. Deb: 6/2/69

YEAR	TM/L	G	AB	R	H	2B	3B	HR	RBI	BB	SO	AVG	OBP	SLG	PRO+	BR/A	SB	CS	SBR	FA	FR	G/POS	TPR
1969	KC-A	12	27	2	3	1	0	0	0	2	3	.111	.172	.148	-10	-2	0	0	0	1.000	-1	/C-8	-0.1
1971	KC-A	60	152	11	31	6	0	2	14	8	29	.204	.244	.283	49	-10	0	0	0	.994	-3	C-32,O-17	-1.5
1972	KC-A	2	6	0	0	0	0	0	0	1	2	.000	.143	.000	-55	-1	0	0	0	.842	1	/C-2	0.0
1974	KC-A	6	12	0	2	0	0	0	1	1	2	.167	.231	.167	15	-1	0	1	-1	1.000	-1	/C-4,O-1	-0.3
Total	4	80	197	13	36	7	0	2	14	12	36	.183	.230	.249	36	-17	0	1		.984	-1	/C-46,O-18	-1.9

■ ANDY PAFKO
Pafko, Andrew "Handy Andy" or "Pruschka" b: 2/25/21, Boyceville, Wis. BR/TR, 6', 190 lbs. Deb: 9/24/43 C

YEAR	TM/L	G	AB	R	H	2B	3B	HR	RBI	BB	SO	AVG	OBP	SLG	PRO+	BR/A	SB	CS	SBR	FA	FR	G/POS	TPR
1943	Chi-N	13	58	7	22	4	0	0	10	2	5	.379	.400	.431	142	3	1			1.000	-2	O-13	0.0
1944	Chi-N	128	469	47	126	16	2	6	62	28	23	.269	.315	.350	87	-8	2			.983	15	*O-123	0.0
1945	*Chi-N†	144	534	64	159	24	12	12	110	45	36	.298	.361	.455	129	19	5			**.995**	8	*O-140	1.5
1946	Chi-N	65	234	18	66	6	4	3	39	27	15	.282	.366	.380	114	5	4			.978	11	O-64	1.3
1947	Chi-N★	129	513	68	155	25	7	13	66	31	39	.302	.346	.454	115	9	4			.985	7	*O-127	0.9
1948	Chi-N★	142	548	82	171	30	2	26	101	50	50	.312	.375	.516	145	32	3			.938	13	*3-139	4.3
1949	Chi-N★	144	519	79	146	29	2	18	69	63	33	.281	.369	.449	121	16	4			.987	-7	O-98,3-49	0.4
1950	Chi-N★	146	514	95	156	24	8	36	92	69	32	.304	.397	.591	158	43	4			.978	-1	O-144	3.5
1951	Chi-N	49	178	26	47	5	3	12	35	17	10	.264	.342	.528	128	6	1	1	-0	.992	2	O-48	0.6
	Bro-N	84	277	42	69	11	0	18	58	35	27	.249	.350	.484	120	7	1	4	-2	.993	-2	O-76	0.1
	Yr	133	455	68	116	16	3	30	93	52	37	.255	.347	.501	123	14	2	5	-2	.993	-0	O-124	0.7
1952	*Bro-N	150	551	76	158	17	5	19	85	64	48	.287	.367	.455	121	16	4	3	-1	.988	-7	*O-139,3-13	0.3
1953	Mil-N	140	516	70	153	23	4	17	72	37	33	.297	.347	.455	114	9	2	1	0	.976	-4	*O-139	0.1
1954	Mil-N	138	510	61	146	22	4	14	69	37	36	.286	.339	.427	105	2	1	2	-1	.969	-8	*O-138	-0.8
1955	Mil-N	86	252	29	67	3	5	5	34	7	23	.266	.297	.377	81	-7	1	2	-1	.980	-8	O-58,3-17	-1.9
1956	Mil-N	45	93	15	24	5	0	2	9	10	13	.258	.330	.376	95	-1	0	0	0	.978	-5	O-37	-0.7
1957	*Mil-N	83	220	31	61	6	1	8	27	10	22	.277	.312	.423	102	-0	1	0	0	.982	-6	O-69	-0.9
1958	*Mil-N	95	164	17	39	7	1	3	23	15	17	.238	.309	.348	80	-5	0	0	0	1.000	-4	O-93	-2.2
1959	Mil-N	71	142	17	31	8	1	2	15	14	15	.218	.293	.324	70	-6	0	0	0	.978	-12	O-64	-2.0
Total	17	1852	6292	844	1796	264	62	213	976	561	477	.285	.351	.449	118	141	38	13		.984	-21	*O-1570,3-213	4.5

■ JOSE PAGAN
Pagan, Jose Antonio (Rodriguez) b: 5/5/35, Barceloneta, P.R. BR/TR, 5'9", 165 lbs. Deb: 8/4/59 C

YEAR	TM/L	G	AB	R	H	2B	3B	HR	RBI	BB	SO	AVG	OBP	SLG	PRO+	BR/A	SB	CS	SBR	FA	FR	G/POS	TPR
1959	SF-N	31	46	7	8	1	0	0	2	1	8	.174	.208	.196	9	-6	1	0	0	.900	3	3-18/S-5,2-3	-0.2
1960	SF-N	18	49	8	14	2	2	0	2	2	6	.286	.300	.408	97	-0	2	2	-1	.917	-8	S-11/3-1	-0.9
1961	SF-N	134	434	38	110	15	2	5	46	31	45	.253	.306	.332	72	-18	8	5	-1	.964	-19	*S-132/O-4	-2.6

YEAR	TM/L	G	AB	R	H	2B	3B	HR	RBI	BB	SO	AVG	OBP	SLG	PRO+	BR/A	SB	CS	SBR	FA	FR	G/POS	TPR
1962	*SF-N	164	580	73	150	25	6	7	57	47	77	.259	.315	.359	82	-15	13	9	-2	**.973**	-25	*S-164	-2.7
1963	SF-N	148	483	46	113	12	1	6	39	26	67	.234	.279	.300	67	-20	10	7	-1	.970	-18	*S-143/2-1,O-1	-3.2
1964	SF-N	134	367	33	82	10	1	1	28	35	66	.223	.293	.264	57	-20	5	4	-1	.958	-18	*S-132/O-8	-3.3
1965	SF-N	26	83	10	17	4	0	0	5	8	9	.205	.275	.253	48	-6	1	0	0	.941	-5	S-26	-1.0
	Pit-N	42	38	6	9	1	0	0	1	1	7	.237	.275	.263	52	-2	1	0	0	.923	8	3-15/S-7	0.6
	Yr	68	121	16	26	5	0	0	6	9	16	.215	.275	.256	50	-8	2	0	1	.923	3	S-33,3-15	-0.4
1966	Pit-N	109	368	44	97	15	6	4	54	13	38	.264	.296	.370	84	-8	0	2	-1	.949	3	3-83,S-18/2-3,O-3	-0.8
1967	Pit-N	81	211	17	61	6	2	1	19	10	28	.289	.330	.351	95	-1	1	1	-0	.938	10	3-25,O-23,S-16/2C	0.9
1968	Pit-N	80	163	24	36	7	1	4	21	11	32	.221	.282	.350	90	-2	2	3	-1	.924	5	3-30,O-19/S-8,21	-0.9
1969	Pit-N	108	274	29	78	11	4	9	42	17	46	.285	.329	.453	119	6	1	0	0	.954	-4	3-44,O-23/2-1	0.2
1970	*Pit-N	95	230	21	61	14	1	7	29	20	24	.265	.324	.426	101	-0	1	1	-0	.957	-3	3-53/O-4,1-1,2-1	-0.4
1971	*Pit-N	57	158	16	38	1	0	5	15	16	25	.241	.314	.342	86	-3	0	0	0	.980	-1	3-41/O-3,1-2	-0.6
1972	Pit-N	53	127	11	32	9	0	3	8	5	17	.252	.286	.394	93	-2	0	0	0	.899	-8	3-32/O-2	-1.1
1973	Phi-N	46	78	4	16	5	0	0	5	1	15	.205	.215	.269	33	-7	0	1	-1	.958	-1	3-16/1-5,O-2,2-1	-1.0
Total	15	1326	3689	387	922	138	26	52	372	244	510	.250	.300	.344	79	-105	46	35	-7	.963	-91	S-662,3-358/O21C	-17.0

■ MIKE PAGE　Page, Michael Randy　b: 7/12/40, Woodruff, S.C.　BL/TR, 6'2.5", 210 lbs.　Deb: 6/30/68

YEAR	TM/L	G	AB	R	H	2B	3B	HR	RBI	BB	SO	AVG	OBP	SLG	PRO+	BR/A	SB	CS	SBR	FA	FR	G/POS	TPR
1968	Atl-N	20	28	1	5	0	0	0	1	1	9	.179	.207	.179	16	-3	0	0	0	1.000	-1	/O-6	-0.5

■ MITCHELL PAGE　Page, Mitchell Otis　b: 10/15/51, Los Angeles, Cal.　BL/TR, 6'2", 205 lbs.　Deb: 4/9/77

YEAR	TM/L	G	AB	R	H	2B	3B	HR	RBI	BB	SO	AVG	OBP	SLG	PRO+	BR/A	SB	CS	SBR	FA	FR	G/POS	TPR
1977	Oak-A	145	501	85	154	28	8	21	75	78	95	.307	.407	.521	153	39	42	5	**10**	.954	7	*O-133/D-8	4.9
1978	Oak-A	147	516	62	147	25	7	17	70	53	95	.285	.356	.459	135	23	23	19	-5	.973	-1	*O-114,D-33	1.2
1979	Oak-A	133	478	51	118	11	2	9	42	52	93	.247	.325	.335	83	-11	17	16	-5	1.000	0	*D-126/O-4	-2.0
1980	Oak-A	110	348	58	85	10	4	17	51	35	87	.244	.315	.443	113	5	14	7	0	.000	0	*D-101	0.1
1981	Oak-A	34	92	9	13	1	0	4	13	7	29	.141	.202	.283	40	-7	2	1	0	.000	0	D-29	-0.9
1982	Oak-A	31	78	14	20	5	0	4	7	7	24	.256	.333	.474	124	2	3	4	-2	.000	0	D-24	-0.6
1983	Oak-A	57	79	16	19	3	0	1	6	10	22	.241	.341	.278	77	-2	3	3	-1	1.000	-2	D-34,O-10	-0.6
1984	Pit-N	16	12	2	4	1	0	0	3	4	4	.333	.467	.417	150	1	0	0	0	.000	0	H	0.1
Total	8	673	2104	297	560	84	21	72	259	245	449	.266	.348	.429	118	50	104	55	-2	.963	3	D-355,O-261	2.8

■ KARL PAGEL　Pagel, Karl Douglas　b: 3/29/55, Madison, Wis.　BL/TL, 6'2", 190 lbs.　Deb: 9/21/78

YEAR	TM/L	G	AB	R	H	2B	3B	HR	RBI	BB	SO	AVG	OBP	SLG	PRO+	BR/A	SB	CS	SBR	FA	FR	G/POS	TPR
1978	Chi-N	2	0	0	0	0	0	0	0	0	2	.000	.000	.000	-89	-0	0	0	0	.000	0	H	-0.1
1979	Chi-N	1	1	0	0	0	0	0	0	0	1	.000	.000	.000	-91	-0	0	0	0	.000	0	/H	0.0
1981	Cle-A	14	15	3	4	0	2	1	4	4	1	.267	.421	.733	230	1	0	0	0	1.000	2	/1-6,D-1	0.4
1982	Cle-A	23	18	3	3	0	0	0	2	7	11	.167	.400	.167	63	-0	0	0	0	.970	-1	/1-10/D-1	-0.1
1983	Cle-A	8	20	1	6	0	0	0	1	0	5	.300	.300	.300	63	-1	0	0	0	.000	-1	/O-1,D-5	-0.2
Total	5	48	56	7	13	0	2	1	7	11	20	.232	.358	.357	99	-0	0	0	0	.985	1	/1-16,D-7,O-1	0.0

■ JIM PAGLIARONI　Pagliaroni, James Vincent "Pag"　b: 12/8/37, Dearborn, Mich.　BR/TR, 6'4", 210 lbs.　Deb: 8/13/55

YEAR	TM/L	G	AB	R	H	2B	3B	HR	RBI	BB	SO	AVG	OBP	SLG	PRO+	BR/A	SB	CS	SBR	FA	FR	G/POS	TPR
1955	Bos-A	1	0	0	0	0	0	0	0	0	0	—	—	—	—	-0	0	0	0	.000	0	/C-1	0.0
1960	Bos-A	28	62	7	19	5	2	2	9	13	11	.306	.434	.548	158	6	0	0	0	.990	-3	C-18	0.4
1961	Bos-A	120	376	50	91	17	0	16	58	55	74	.242	.345	.415	100	0	1	1	-0	.984	-4	*C-108	0.2
1962	Bos-A	90	260	39	67	14	0	11	37	36	55	.258	.359	.438	110	4	2	1	0	.987	-3	*C-73	0.4
1963	Pit-N	92	252	27	58	5	0	11	26	36	57	.230	.331	.381	104	2	0	1	0	.988	4	C-85	1.0
1964	Pit-N	97	302	33	89	12	3	10	36	41	56	.295	.383	.454	135	15	1	0	0	.992	1	C-96	2.1
1965	Pit-N	134	403	42	108	15	4	17	65	41	84	.268	.340	.432	115	8	0	0	0	.994	3	*C-131	1.1
1966	Pit-N	123	374	37	88	20	0	11	49	50	71	.235	.332	.377	96	-1	0	5	-3	**.997**	-14	*C-118	-1.1
1967	Pit-N	44	100	4	20	1	1	0	9	16	26	.200	.316	.230	59	-5	0	0	0	.984	-0	C-38	-0.3
1968	Oak-A	66	199	19	49	4	0	6	20	24	42	.246	.333	.357	115	4	0	0	0	.997	-9	C-63	-0.1
1969	Oak-A	14	27	1	4	1	0	1	2	5	12	.148	.303	.296	71	-1	0	0	0	.981	2	/C-7	0.1
	Sea-A	40	110	10	29	4	1	5	14	13	16	.264	.341	.455	123	3	0	0	0	.988	-6	C-29/1-2,O-1	-0.2
	Yr	54	137	11	33	5	1	6	16	18	18	.241	.333	.423	113	2	0	0	0	.987	-4	C-36/1-2,O-1	-0.1
Total	11	849	2465	269	622	98	7	90	326	330	494	.252	.346	.407	109	35	4	7	-3	.991	-36	C-767/1-2,O-1	3.6

■ MIKE PAGLIARULO　Pagliarulo, Michael Timothy　b: 3/15/60, Medford, Mass.　BL/TR, 6'1", 205 lbs.　Deb: 7/7/84

YEAR	TM/L	G	AB	R	H	2B	3B	HR	RBI	BB	SO	AVG	OBP	SLG	PRO+	BR/A	SB	CS	SBR	FA	FR	G/POS	TPR
1984	NY-A	67	201	24	48	15	3	7	34	15	46	.239	.292	.448	105	1	0	0	0	.955	6	3-67	0.6
1985	NY-A	138	380	55	91	16	2	19	62	45	86	.239	.326	.442	111	5	0	0	0	.951	-17	*3-134	-1.3
1986	NY-A	149	504	71	120	24	3	28	71	54	120	.238	.317	.464	111	6	4	1	1	.953	6	*3-143/S-2	1.0
1987	NY-A	150	522	76	122	26	3	32	87	53	111	.234	.307	.479	105	2	1	3	-2	.959	4	*3-147/1-1	0.3
1988	NY-A	125	444	46	96	20	1	15	67	37	104	.216	.280	.367	80	-13	1	0	0	.943	-9	*3-124	-1.4
1989	NY-A	74	223	19	44	10	0	4	16	19	43	.197	.266	.296	59	-12	1	1	-0	.936	-4	3-69/D-1	-1.7
	SD-N	50	148	12	29	7	0	3	14	18	39	.196	.287	.304	69	-6	2	0	1	.936	0	3-49	-0.5
1990	SD-N	128	398	29	101	23	2	7	38	39	66	.254	.325	.374	91	-5	1	3	-2	.955	2	3-116	-0.4
1991	*Min-A	121	365	38	102	20	0	6	36	21	55	.279	.324	.384	91	-5	1	2	-1	.965	12	*3-118/2-1	0.7
1992	Min-A	42	105	10	21	4	0	0	9	1	17	.200	.215	.238	26	-10	1	0	0	.962	3	3-37/D-1	-0.8
1993	Min-A	83	253	31	74	16	4	3	23	18	34	.292	.351	.423	107	2	6	6	-2	.984	3	3-79	0.1
	Bal-A	33	117	24	38	9	0	6	21	8	15	.325	.373	.556	140	6	0	0	0	.937	-1	3-28/1-4	0.5
	Yr	116	370	55	112	25	4	9	44	26	49	.303	.358	.465	118	9	6	6	-2	.969	-1	*3-107/1-4	0.6
1995	Tex-A	86	241	27	56	16	0	4	27	15	49	.232	.280	.349	61	-14	0	0	0	.963	5	3-68,1-11	-1.0
Total	11	1246	3901	462	942	206	18	134	505	343	785	.241	.308	.407	93	-43	18	16	-4	.955	15	*3-1179/1-16,DS2	-3.9

■ TOM PAGNOZZI　Pagnozzi, Thomas Alan　b: 7/30/62, Tucson, Ariz.　BR/TR, 6', 190 lbs.　Deb: 4/12/87

YEAR	TM/L	G	AB	R	H	2B	3B	HR	RBI	BB	SO	AVG	OBP	SLG	PRO+	BR/A	SB	CS	SBR	FA	FR	G/POS	TPR
1987	*StL-N	27	48	8	9	1	0	2	9	4	13	.188	.250	.333	52	-3	1	0	0	1.000	-4	C-25/1-1	-0.6
1988	StL-N	81	195	17	55	9	0	0	15	11	32	.282	.320	.328	86	-4	0	4	0	.971	-2	C-28,1-28/3-5	-0.6
1989	StL-N	52	80	3	12	2	0	0	3	6	19	.150	.218	.175	13	-9	0	0	0	.982	-3	C-38/1-2,3-1	-1.2
1990	StL-N	69	220	20	61	15	0	2	23	14	37	.277	.323	.373	91	-3	1	1	-0	.989	10	C-63/1-2	-1.0
1991	StL-N	140	459	38	121	24	5	2	57	36	63	.264	.323	.351	89	-7	9	13	-5	*C-139/1-3	-1.1		
1992	StL-N★	139	485	33	121	26	3	7	44	28	64	.249	.292	.359	86	-10	2	5	-2	**.999**	-16	*C-138	-2.3
1993	StL-N	92	330	31	85	15	1	7	41	19	30	.258	.300	.373	80	-10	1	0	0	.991	-12	C-92	-1.7
1994	StL-N	70	243	21	66	12	1	7	40	21	39	.272	.330	.416	94	-2	0	0	0	.998	-7	C-70/1-1	-0.5
1995	StL-N	62	219	17	47	14	1	2	15	11	31	.215	.255	.315	50	-16	0	1	-1	.995	-7	C-61	-1.4
1996	*StL-N	119	407	48	110	23	0	13	55	24	78	.270	.314	.423	92	-6	4	1	1	.990	-0	*C-116/1-1	0.2
Total	10	851	2686	236	687	141	11	42	302	174	406	.256	.304	.363	82	-70	18	21	-7	.992	-44	C-770/1-38,3-6	-8.2

■ REY PALACIOS　Palacios, Robert Rey　b: 11/8/62, Brooklyn, N.Y.　BR/TR, 5'10", 190 lbs.　Deb: 9/8/88

YEAR	TM/L	G	AB	R	H	2B	3B	HR	RBI	BB	SO	AVG	OBP	SLG	PRO+	BR/A	SB	CS	SBR	FA	FR	G/POS	TPR
1988	KC-A	5	11	2	1	0	0	0	1	0	6	.091	.091	.091	-48	-2	0	0	0	1.000	1	/C-3,3-1,D-1	-0.1
1989	KC-A	55	47	12	8	2	0	1	8	2	14	.170	.220	.277	39	-4	0	1	-1	.958	4	3-21,1-18,C-13/OD	-0.1
1990	KC-A	41	56	8	13	3	0	2	9	5	24	.232	.295	.393	92	-1	2	2	-1	.992	4	C-27/1-7,3-3,O-1	0.4
Total	3	101	114	22	22	5	0	3	17	7	42	.193	.246	.316	57	-7	2	3	-1	.994	9	/C-43,1-25,3-25,DO	0.2

■ ERV PALICA　Palica, Ervin Martin (b: Ervin Martin Pavliecivich)
b: 2/9/28, Lomita, Cal.　d: 5/29/82, Huntington Beach, Cal.　BR/TR, 6'1.5", 180 lbs.　Deb: 4/21/45

YEAR	TM/L	G	AB	R	H	2B	3B	HR	RBI	BB	SO	AVG	OBP	SLG	PRO+	BR/A	SB	CS	SBR	FA	FR	G/POS	TPR
1945	Bro-N	2	0	0	0	0	0	0	0	0	0	—	—	—		0	0	0	0	.000	0	R	0.0
1947	Bro-N	3	0	0	0	0	0	0	0	0	0	—	—	—		-0	0	0	0	.000	0	/P-3	0.0
1948	Bro-N	45	39	6	5	1	1	0	3	4	12	.128	.209	.205	12	-5	0	0	0	1.000	-1	P-41	0.0
1949	*Bro-N	49	19	2	3	1	0	0	2	0	8	.158	.238	.211	20	-4	0	0	0	.875	-0	P-49	0.0
1950	Bro-N	48	68	4	15	0	0	1	8	4	6	.221	.221	.324	40	-6	2			.889	-4	P-43	0.0
1951	Bro-N	20	13	1	2	0	0	0	0	2	5	.154	.267	.154	16	-1	0	0	0	1.000	1	P-19	0.0
1953	Bro-N	4	1	0	1	0	0	0	0	0	0	1.000	1.000	1.000	414	-0	0	0	0	1.000	0	/P-4	0.0
1954	Bro-N	28	16	2	4	1	0	0	1	1	4	.250	.294	.313	56	-1	0	0	0	.875	-2	P-25	0.0
1955	Bal-A	33	55	3	13	1	0	0	3	4	18	.236	.288	.255	50	-4	0	0	0	.905	-1	P-33	0.0

YEAR	TM/L	G	AB	R	H	2B	3B	HR	RBI	BB	SO	AVG	OBP	SLG	PRO+	BR/A	SB	CS	SBR	FA	FR	G/POS	TPR
1956	Bal-A	30	32	4	5	0	0	0	0	0	10	.156	.156	.156	-19	-6	0	0	0	.917	-0	P-29	0.0
Total	10	262	243	22	48	8	1	1	17	13	63	.198	.238	.251	31	-24	2	0		.921	-7	P-246	0.0

■ ORLANDO PALMEIRO
Palmeiro, Orlando b: 1/19/69, Hoboken, N.J. BL/TR, 5'11", 155 lbs. Deb: 7/1/95

YEAR	TM/L	G	AB	R	H	2B	3B	HR	RBI	BB	SO	AVG	OBP	SLG	PRO+	BR/A	SB	CS	SBR	FA	FR	G/POS	TPR
1995	Cal-A	15	20	3	7	0	0	0	1	1	1	.350	.381	.350	93	-0	0	0	0	1.000	-2	/O-7,D-1	-0.2
1996	Cal-A	50	87	6	25	6	1	0	6	8	13	.287	.361	.379	89	-1	0	1	-1	1.000	-8	O-31/D-4	-0.9
Total	2	65	107	9	32	6	1	0	7	9	14	.299	.364	.374	90	-1	0	1	-1	1.000	-9	/O-38,D-5	-1.1

■ RAFAEL PALMEIRO
Palmeiro, Rafael (Corrales) b: 9/24/64, Havana, Cuba BL/TL, 6', 180 lbs. Deb: 9/8/86

YEAR	TM/L	G	AB	R	H	2B	3B	HR	RBI	BB	SO	AVG	OBP	SLG	PRO+	BR/A	SB	CS	SBR	FA	FR	G/POS	TPR
1986	Chi-N	22	73	9	18	4	0	3	12	4	6	.247	.295	.425	89	-1	1	1	-0	.900	-0	O-20	-0.2
1987	Chi-N	84	221	32	61	15	1	14	30	20	26	.276	.339	.543	124	7	2	2	-1	1.000	-4	O-45,1-18	0.0
1988	Chi-N★	152	580	75	178	41	5	8	53	38	34	.307	.353	.436	120	14	12	2	2	.983	4	*O-147/1-5	1.7
1989	Tex-A	156	559	76	154	23	4	8	64	63	48	.275	.355	.374	104	4	4	3	-1	.991	10	*1-147/D-6	0.2
1990	Tex-A	154	598	72	**191**	35	6	14	89	40	59	.319	.365	.468	131	24	3	3	-1	.995	-1	*1-146/D-6	1.1
1991	Tex-A★	159	631	115	203	**49**	3	26	88	68	72	.322	.393	.532	156	48	4	3	-1	.992	-4	*1-157/D-2	3.3
1992	Tex-A	159	608	84	163	27	4	22	85	72	83	.268	.352	.434	124	20	2	3	-1	.995	-14	*1-156/D-2	2.2
1993	Tex-A	160	597	**124**	176	40	2	37	105	73	85	.295	.371	.554	153	43	22	3	5	.997	16	*1-160	4.8
1994	Bal-A	111	436	82	139	32	0	23	76	54	63	.319	.396	.550	134	22	7	3	0	.996	-2	*1-111	0.9
1995	Bal-A	143	554	89	172	30	2	39	104	62	65	.310	.380	.583	145	35	3	1	0	.997	9	*1-142	2.8
1996	*Bal-A	162	626	110	181	40	2	39	142	95	96	.289	.385	.546	134	32	8	0	2	.995	5	*1-159/D-3	2.2
Total	11	1462	5483	868	1636	336	29	233	848	589	637	.298	.371	.498	133	248	68	24	6	.995	46	*1-1201,O-212/D-19	19.0

■ DEAN PALMER
Palmer, Dean William b: 12/27/68, Tallahassee, Fla. BR/TR, 6'1", 175 lbs. Deb: 9/1/89

YEAR	TM/L	G	AB	R	H	2B	3B	HR	RBI	BB	SO	AVG	OBP	SLG	PRO+	BR/A	SB	CS	SBR	FA	FR	G/POS	TPR
1989	Tex-A	16	19	0	2	2	0	0	1	0	12	.105	.105	.211	-13	-3	0	0	0	.667	-0	/3-6,S-1,O-1,D-6	-0.3
1991	Tex-A	81	268	38	50	9	2	15	37	32	98	.187	.281	.403	88	-5	0	2	-1	.944	-10	3-50,O-29/D-5	-1.7
1992	Tex-A	152	541	74	124	25	0	26	72	62	154	.229	.313	.420	107	4	10	4	1	.945	-10	*3-150	-0.6
1993	Tex-A	148	519	88	127	31	2	33	96	53	154	.245	.324	.503	123	15	11	10	-3	.922	-12	*3-148/S-1	0.0
1994	Tex-A	93	342	50	84	14	2	19	59	26	89	.246	.303	.465	94	-4	3	4	-2	.912	-2	3-91	-0.7
1995	Tex-A	36	119	30	40	6	0	9	24	21	21	.336	.451	.613	170	13	1	1	-0	.948	1	3-36	1.2
1996	*Tex-A	154	582	98	163	26	2	38	107	59	145	.280	.351	.527	110	7	2	0	1	.953	-24	*3-154/D-1	-1.5
Total	7	680	2390	378	590	113	8	140	396	253	673	.247	.326	.477	110	26	27	21	-5	.935	-58	3-635/O-30,D-12,S-2	-3.6

■ EDDIE PALMER
Palmer, Edwin Henry "Baldy" b: 6/1/1893, Petty, Tex. d: 1/9/83, Marlow, Okla. BR/TR, 5'9.5", 175 lbs. Deb: 9/6/17

YEAR	TM/L	G	AB	R	H	2B	3B	HR	RBI	BB	SO	AVG	OBP	SLG	PRO+	BR/A	SB	CS	SBR	FA	FR	G/POS	TPR
1917	Phi-A	16	52	7	11	1	0	0	5	7	7	.212	.305	.231	65	-2				.898	0	3-13/S-1	-0.2

■ JOE PALMISANO
Palmisano, Joseph b: 11/19/02, West Point, Ga. d: 11/5/71, Albuquerque, N.Mex. BR/TR, 5'8", 160 lbs. Deb: 5/31/31

YEAR	TM/L	G	AB	R	H	2B	3B	HR	RBI	BB	SO	AVG	OBP	SLG	PRO+	BR/A	SB	CS	SBR	FA	FR	G/POS	TPR
1931	Phi-A	19	44	5	10	2	0	0	4	6	3	.227	.320	.273	54	-1	0	0	0	.960	-2	C-16/2-1	-0.3

■ STAN PALYS
Palys, Stanley Francis b: 5/1/30, Blakely, Pa. BR/TR, 6'2", 190 lbs. Deb: 9/20/53

YEAR	TM/L	G	AB	R	H	2B	3B	HR	RBI	BB	SO	AVG	OBP	SLG	PRO+	BR/A	SB	CS	SBR	FA	FR	G/POS	TPR
1953	Phi-N	2	2	0	0	0	0	0	0	0	1	.000	.333	.000	-4	-0	0	0	0	.000	-0	/O-1	-0.1
1954	Phi-N	2	4	0	1	0	0	0	0	0	1	.250	.400	.250	74	-0	0	0	0	1.000	-0	/O-1	0.0
1955	Phi-N	15	52	8	15	3	0	1	8	6	5	.288	.362	.404	105	0	1	0	0	1.000	-0	O-15	0.0
	Cin-N	79	222	29	51	14	0	7	30	12	35	.230	.272	.387	69	-11	1	1	-0	.992	2	O-55/1-1	-1.1
	Yr	94	274	37	66	17	0	8	38	18	40	.241	.290	.391	75	-10	2	1	0	.993	2	O-70/1-1	-1.1
1956	Cin-N	40	53	5	12	0	0	2	5	8	13	.226	.305	.340	69	-2	0	0	0	.929	-2	O-10	-0.5
Total	4	138	333	42	79	17	0	10	43	26	54	.237	.294	.378	74	-13	2	1	0	.988	-1	/O-82,1-1	-1.7

■ JIM PANKOVITS
Pankovits, James Franklin b: 8/6/55, Pennington Gap, Va. BR/TR, 5'10", 195 lbs. Deb: 5/27/84

YEAR	TM/L	G	AB	R	H	2B	3B	HR	RBI	BB	SO	AVG	OBP	SLG	PRO+	BR/A	SB	CS	SBR	FA	FR	G/POS	TPR
1984	Hou-N	53	81	6	23	7	0	1	14	2	20	.284	.301	.407	105	0	2	1	0	.925	-5	2-15/S-4/O-3	-0.5
1985	Hou-N	75	172	24	42	3	0	4	14	17	29	.244	.316	.331	84	-4	1	0	0	.983	0	O-33,2-21/S-1,3-1	-0.4
1986	*Hou-N	70	113	12	32	6	1	1	7	11	25	.283	.347	.381	103	1	1	1	-0	.969	3	2-26/O-5,C-1	0.4
1987	Hou-N	50	61	7	14	2	0	1	8	6	13	.230	.299	.311	64	-3	2	0	1	1.000	5	/2-9,O-6,3-4	0.2
1988	Hou-N	68	140	13	31	7	1	2	12	8	28	.221	.273	.329	75	-5	2	1	0	.939	-2	2-31,3-11/1-2	-0.7
1990	Bos-A	2	0	0	0	0	0	0	0	0	0	—	—	—			0	0	0	.000	0	/2-2	0.0
Total	6	318	567	62	142	25	2	9	55	44	115	.250	.308	.349	86	-11	8	3	1	.961	1	2-104/O-47,3S1C	-1.0

■ KEN PAPE
Pape, Kenneth Wayne b: 10/1/51, San Antonio, Tex. BR/TR, 5'11", 195 lbs. Deb: 5/17/76

YEAR	TM/L	G	AB	R	H	2B	3B	HR	RBI	BB	SO	AVG	OBP	SLG	PRO+	BR/A	SB	CS	SBR	FA	FR	G/POS	TPR
1976	Tex-A	21	23	7	5	1	0	1	4	3	2	.217	.357	.391	117	1	0	1	-1	.968	4	/S-6,3-4,2-1,D-3	0.5

■ STAN PAPI
Papi, Stanley Gerard b: 2/4/51, Fresno, Cal. BR/TR, 6', 178 lbs. Deb: 4/11/74

YEAR	TM/L	G	AB	R	H	2B	3B	HR	RBI	BB	SO	AVG	OBP	SLG	PRO+	BR/A	SB	CS	SBR	FA	FR	G/POS	TPR
1974	StL-N	8	4	0	1	0	0	0	1	0	0	.250	.250	.250	40	-0	0	0	0	1.000	1	/S-7,2-1	0.0
1977	Mon-N	13	43	5	10	2	1	0	4	1	9	.233	.250	.326	55	-3	1	0	0	.952	-5	3-10/S-2,2-1	-0.7
1978	Mon-N	67	152	15	35	11	0	2	11	10	28	.230	.287	.303	65	-7	0	0	0	.976	-3	S-22,3-15/2-5	-0.8
1979	Bos-A	50	117	9	22	8	0	1	6	5	20	.188	.221	.282	33	-11	0	0	0	.982	13	2-26,S-21/D-1	0.4
1980	Bos-A	1	0	0	0	0	0	0	0	0	0	—	—	—			0	0	0	.000	0	/3-1	0.0
	Det-A	46	114	12	27	3	4	3	17	5	24	.237	.269	.412	82	-3	0	0	0	.973	-2	2-31,3-11/S-5,1-1	-0.4
	Yr	47	114	12	27	3	4	3	17	5	24	.237	.269	.412	82	-3	0	0	0	.973	-2	2-31,3-12/S-5,1-1	-0.4
1981	Det-A	40	93	8	19	2	1	3	12	3	18	.204	.229	.344	61	-5	1	0	0	.941	-1	3-32/1-1,2-1,O-1,D	-0.7
Total	6	225	523	49	114	26	6	7	51	24	99	.218	.255	.331	60	-30	2	0	1	.931	3	/3-69,2-65,SD10	-2.2

■ ERIK PAPPAS
Pappas, Erik Daniel b: 4/25/66, Chicago, Ill. BR/TR, 6', 190 lbs. Deb: 4/19/91

YEAR	TM/L	G	AB	R	H	2B	3B	HR	RBI	BB	SO	AVG	OBP	SLG	PRO+	BR/A	SB	CS	SBR	FA	FR	G/POS	TPR
1991	Chi-N	7	17	1	3	0	0	0	2	1	5	.176	.222	.176	13	-2	0	0	0	1.000	1	/C-6	0.0
1993	StL-N	82	228	25	63	12	0	1	28	35	35	.276	.373	.342	95	-0	1	3	-2	.982	5	C-63,O-16/1-2	0.6
1994	StL-N	15	44	8	4	1	0	0	5	10	13	.091	.273	.114	6	-6	0	0	0	.955	-4	C-15	-1.0
Total	3	104	289	34	70	13	0	1	35	46	53	.242	.348	.298	76	-8	1	3	-2	.978	2	/C-84,O-16,1-2	-0.4

■ CRAIG PAQUETTE
Paquette, Craig Harold b: 3/28/69, Long Beach, Cal. BR/TR, 6', 190 lbs. Deb: 6/1/93

YEAR	TM/L	G	AB	R	H	2B	3B	HR	RBI	BB	SO	AVG	OBP	SLG	PRO+	BR/A	SB	CS	SBR	FA	FR	G/POS	TPR
1993	Oak-A	105	393	35	86	20	4	12	46	14	108	.219	.246	.382	70	-19	4	2	0	.950	-9	*3-104/O-1,D-1	-2.7
1994	Oak-A	14	49	0	7	2	0	0	0	0	14	.143	.143	.184	-18	-9	1	0	0	1.000	1	3-14	-0.7
1995	Oak-A	105	283	42	64	13	1	13	49	12	88	.226	.260	.417	77	-11	5	2	0	.935	-12	3-75,O-20/S-8,1-3	-2.2
1996	KC-A	118	429	61	111	15	1	22	67	23	101	.259	.300	.452	89	-9	5	3	-0	.891	-1	3-51,O-47,1-19,S/D	-2.1
Total	4	342	1154	138	268	50	6	47	162	49	311	.232	.265	.408	76	-48	15	7	0	.938	-32	3-244/O-68,1-22,SD	-7.7

■ AL PARDO
Pardo, Alberto Judas b: 9/8/62, Oviedo, Spain BB/TR, 6'2", 187 lbs. Deb: 7/3/85

YEAR	TM/L	G	AB	R	H	2B	3B	HR	RBI	BB	SO	AVG	OBP	SLG	PRO+	BR/A	SB	CS	SBR	FA	FR	G/POS	TPR
1985	Bal-A	34	75	3	10	1	0	0	1	3	15	.133	.167	.147	-14	-12	0	0	0	.979	3	C-29	-0.7
1986	Bal-A	16	51	3	7	1	0	1	3	0	14	.137	.137	.216	-6	-7	0	0	0	.987	-2	/C-14/D-1	-0.9
1988	Phi-N	2	2	0	0	0	0	0	0	0	2	.000	.000	.000	-98	-0	0	0	0	1.000	-0	/C-2	-0.1
1989	Phi-N	1	1	0	0	0	0	0	0	0	0	.000	.000	.000	-99	-0	0	0	0	1.000	-0	/C-1	0.0
Total	4	53	129	6	17	2	0	1	4	3	31	.132	.152	.171	-12	-20	0	0	0	.982	1	/C-46,D-1	-1.7

■ JOHNNY PAREDES
Paredes, Johnny Alfonso (Isambert) b: 9/2/62, Maracaibo, Venez. BR/TR, 5'11", 165 lbs. Deb: 4/29/88

YEAR	TM/L	G	AB	R	H	2B	3B	HR	RBI	BB	SO	AVG	OBP	SLG	PRO+	BR/A	SB	CS	SBR	FA	FR	G/POS	TPR
1988	Mon-N	35	91	6	17	2	0	1	10	9	17	.187	.282	.242	49	-6	5	2	0	.976	0	2-28/O-1	-0.5
1990	Det-A	6	8	2	1	0	0	0	1	0	5	.125	.222	.125	-0	-1	0	0	0	.917	1	/2-4	0.0
	Mon-N	3	6	0	2	1	0	0	1	1	0	.333	.429	.500	161	1	0	0	0	.889	1	/2-2	0.1
1991	Det-A	16	18	4	6	0	0	0	0	1	5	.333	.368	.333	84	-0	1	1	-0	.958	4	/2-7,3-1,S-1,D-2	0.3
Total	3	60	123	12	26	3	0	1	11	11	18	.211	.292	.260	56	-7	6	3	0	.965	6	/2-41,D-2,S-1,3O	-0.1

■ FREDDY PARENT
Parent, Frederick Alfred b: 11/25/1875, Biddeford, Me. d: 11/2/72, Sanford, Maine BR/TR, 5'7", 154 lbs. Deb: 7/14/1899

YEAR	TM/L	G	AB	R	H	2B	3B	HR	RBI	BB	SO	AVG	OBP	SLG	PRO+	BR/A	SB	CS	SBR	FA	FR	G/POS	TPR
1899	StL-N	2	8	0	1	0	0	0				.125	.125	.125	-31	-1	0			.889	-1	/2-2	-0.2
1901	Bos-A	138	517	87	158	23	9	4	59	41		.306	.367	.408	117	12	16			.918	-0	*S-138	2.1
1902	Bos-A	138	567	91	156	31	8	3	62	24		.275	.309	.374	86	-12	16			.932	4	*S-138	0.4
1903	*Bos-A	139	560	83	170	31	17	4	80	13		.304	.326	.441	122	13	24			.930	9	*S-139	2.8

YEAR	TM/L	G	AB	R	H	2B	3B	HR	RBI	BB	SO	AVG	OBP	SLG	PRO+	BR/A	SB	CS	SBR	FA	FR	G/POS	TPR
1904	Bos-A	155	591	85	172	22	9	6	77	28		.291	.330	.389	120	12	20			.929	-8	*S-155	1.0
1905	Bos-A	153	602	55	141	16	5	0	33	47		.234	.296	.277	81	-12	25			.920	-11	*S-153	-2.1
1906	Bos-A	149	600	67	141	14	10	1	49	31		.235	.277	.297	80	-15	16			.933	-7	*S-143/2-6	-1.9
1907	Bos-A	114	409	51	113	19	5	1	26	22		.276	.321	.355	116	7	12			.978	-2	O-47,S-43/3-7,2-5	0.5
1908	Chi-A	119	391	28	81	7	5	0	35	50		.207	.300	.251	81	-6	9			.930	5	*S-118	0.1
1909	Chi-A	136	472	61	123	10	5	0	30	46		.261	.335	.303	106	5	32			.929	17	S-98,O-38/2-1	2.4
1910	Chi-A	81	258	23	46	6	1	1	16	29		.178	.266	.221	55	-13	14			.970	-3	O-62,2-11/S-4,3-1	-2.0
1911	Chi-A	3	9	2	4	1	0	0	3	2		.444	.545	.556	214	2	0			1.000	1	/2-3	0.2
Total	12	1327	4984	633	1306	180	74	20	471	333		.262	.315	.340	99	-8	184			.927	4	*S-1129,O-147/23	2.9

■ MARK PARENT
Parent, Mark Alan b: 9/16/61, Ashland, Ore. BR/TR, 6'5", 224 lbs. Deb: 9/20/86

YEAR	TM/L	G	AB	R	H	2B	3B	HR	RBI	BB	SO	AVG	OBP	SLG	PRO+	BR/A	SB	CS	SBR	FA	FR	G/POS	TPR
1986	SD-N	8	14	1	2	0	0	0	0	1	3	.143	.200	.143	-4	-2	0	0	0	.889	-1	/C-3	-0.3
1987	SD-N	12	25	0	2	0	0	0	2	0	9	.080	.080	.080	-60	-6	0	0	0	1.000	0	C-10	-0.5
1988	SD-N	41	118	9	23	3	0	6	15	6	23	.195	.234	.373	73	-5	0	0	0	.986	5	C-36	0.3
1989	SD-N	52	141	12	27	4	0	7	21	8	34	.191	.235	.369	70	-6	1	0	0	1.000	6	C-41/1-1	0.2
1990	SD-N	65	189	13	42	11	0	3	16	16	29	.222	.283	.328	67	-9	1	0	0	.992	8	C-60	0.3
1991	Tex-A	3	1	0	0	0	0	0	0	0	1	.000	.000	.000	-99	-0	0	0	0	1.000	1	/C-3	0.0
1992	Bal-A	17	34	4	8	1	0	2	4	3	7	.235	.316	.441	107	0	0	0	0	.988	4	C-16	0.5
1993	Bal-A	22	54	7	14	2	0	4	12	3	14	.259	.298	.519	110	0	0	0	0	.989	-1	C-21/D-1	0.0
1994	Chi-N	44	99	8	26	4	0	3	16	13	24	.263	.354	.394	96	-0	0	1	-1	.976	4	C-37	0.4
1995	Pit-N	69	233	25	54	9	0	15	33	23	62	.232	.301	.464	96	-2	0	0	0	.990	-10	C-67	-0.7
	Chi-N	12	32	5	8	2	0	3	5	3	7	.250	.314	.594	135	1	0	0	0	1.000	2	C-10	0.4
	Yr	81	265	30	62	11	0	18	38	26	69	.234	.302	.479	101	-1	0	0	0	.992	-7	C-77	-0.3
1996	Det-A	38	104	13	25	6	0	7	17	3	27	.240	.262	.500	87	-3	0	0	0	.994	-4	C-33/1-1	-0.4
	*Bal-A	18	33	4	6	1	0	2	6	2	10	.182	.229	.394	54	-3	0	0	0	.987	2	C-18	0.0
	Yr	56	137	17	31	7	0	9	23	5	37	.226	.254	.474	79	-5	0	0	0	.992	-2	C-51/1-1	-0.4
Total	11	401	1077	101	237	43	0	52	147	81	250	.220	.276	.405	81	-33	2	1	0	.990	17	C-355/1-2,D-1	0.2

■ KELLY PARIS
Paris, Kelly Jay b: 10/17/57, Encino, Cal. BR/TR, 6', 180 lbs. Deb: 9/1/82

YEAR	TM/L	G	AB	R	H	2B	3B	HR	RBI	BB	SO	AVG	OBP	SLG	PRO+	BR/A	SB	CS	SBR	FA	FR	G/POS	TPR
1982	StL-N	12	29	1	3	0	0	0	1	0	7	.103	.103	.103	-42	-5	0	0	0	.867	2	/3-5,S-4	-0.3
1983	Cin-N	56	120	13	30	6	0	0	7	15	22	.250	.338	.300	75	-3	8	2	1	1.000	-3	3-16,2-10/S-7,1-3	-0.4
1985	Bal-A	5	9	0	0	0	0	0	0	0	0	.000	.000	.000	-99	-2	0	0	0	.857	-0	/2-2,D-2	-0.3
1986	Bal-A	5	10	0	2	0	0	0	0	0	3	.200	.200	.200	9	-1	0	0	1	.857	1	/3-3,D-2	-0.1
1988	Chi-A	14	44	6	11	0	0	3	6	0	7	.250	.250	.455	93	-1	0	1	0	1.000	-0	/1-9,3-4,D-1	-0.1
Total	5	92	212	20	46	6	0	3	14	15	39	.217	.272	.288	54	-13	8	3	1	.944	1	/3-28,1-12,2-12,SD	-1.2

■ TONY PARISSE
Parisse, Louis Peter b: 6/25/11, Philadelphia, Pa. d: 6/2/56, Philadelphia, Pa. BR/TR, 5'10", 165 lbs. Deb: 9/22/43

YEAR	TM/L	G	AB	R	H	2B	3B	HR	RBI	BB	SO	AVG	OBP	SLG	PRO+	BR/A	SB	CS	SBR	FA	FR	G/POS	TPR
1943	Phi-A	6	17	0	3	0	0	0	1	2	2	.176	.263	.176	30	-1	0	0	0	1.000	0	/C-5	-0.1
1944	Phi-A	4	4	0	0	0	0	0	0	0	1	.000	.000	.000	-99	-1	0	0	0	.500	-1	/C-2	-0.2
Total	2	10	21	0	3	0	0	0	1	2	3	.143	.217	.143	6	-1	0	0	0	.960	-0	/C-7	-0.3

■ ACE PARKER
Parker, Clarence McKay b: 5/17/12, Portsmouth, Va. BR/TR, 6', 180 lbs. Deb: 4/24/37

YEAR	TM/L	G	AB	R	H	2B	3B	HR	RBI	BB	SO	AVG	OBP	SLG	PRO+	BR/A	SB	CS	SBR	FA	FR	G/POS	TPR
1937	Phi-A	38	94	8	11	0	1	2	13	4	17	.117	.153	.202	-11	-17	0	0	0	.905	-5	S-19/2-9,O-5	-1.9
1938	Phi-A	56	113	12	26	5	0	0	12	10	16	.230	.293	.274	44	-10	1	2	-1	.972	-5	S-26/2-9,3-9	-1.3
Total	2	94	207	20	37	5	1	2	25	14	33	.179	.231	.242	19	-26	1	2	-1	.934	-10	/S-45,2-18,3-9,O-5	-3.2

■ PAT PARKER
Parker, Clarence Perkins b: 5/22/1893, Somerville, Mass. d: 3/21/67, Claremont, N.H. BR/TR, 5'7", 160 lbs. Deb: 8/10/15

YEAR	TM/L	G	AB	R	H	2B	3B	HR	RBI	BB	SO	AVG	OBP	SLG	PRO+	BR/A	SB	CS	SBR	FA	FR	G/POS	TPR
1915	StL-A	3	6	0	1	0	0	0	0	1	0	.167	.167	.167	-0	-1	0	1	-1	1.000	0	/O-2	-0.2

■ DAVE PARKER
Parker, David Gene b: 6/9/51, Calhoun, Miss. BL/TR, 6'5", 230 lbs. Deb: 7/12/73

YEAR	TM/L	G	AB	R	H	2B	3B	HR	RBI	BB	SO	AVG	OBP	SLG	PRO+	BR/A	SB	CS	SBR	FA	FR	G/POS	TPR
1973	Pit-N	54	139	17	40	9	4	4	14	2	27	.288	.308	.453	111	1	1	1	-0	.964	0	O-39	0.0
1974	*Pit-N	73	220	27	62	10	3	4	29	10	53	.282	.322	.409	107	1	3	3	-1	.964	1	O-49/1-6	-0.1
1975	*Pit-N	148	558	75	172	35	10	25	101	38	89	.308	.358	.541	148	33	8	6	-1	.972	11	*O-141	3.7
1976	Pit-N	138	537	82	168	28	10	13	90	30	80	.313	.351	.475	132	20	19	7	2	.956	7	*O-134	2.5
1977	Pit-N★	159	637	107	**215**	**44**	8	21	88	58	107	**.338**	.399	.531	143	39	17	19	-6	.965	33	*O-158/2-1	5.8
1978	Pit-N	148	581	102	194	32	12	30	117	57	92	**.334**	.395	**.585**	163	48	20	7	2	.960	8	*O-147	**5.3**
1979	*Pit-N★	158	622	109	193	45	7	25	94	67	101	.310	.385	.526	140	34	20	4	4	.960	9	*O-158	4.0
1980	Pit-N★	139	518	71	153	31	1	17	79	25	69	.295	.330	.458	116	9	10	7	-1	.965	4	*O-130	0.7
1981	Pit-N★	67	240	29	62	14	3	9	48	9	25	.258	.291	.454	106	0	6	2	1	.941	-2	O-60	-0.4
1982	Pit-N	73	244	41	66	19	3	6	29	22	45	.270	.333	.447	113	4	7	5	-1	.957	-1	O-63	-0.3
1983	Pit-N	144	552	68	154	29	4	12	69	28	89	.279	.314	.411	97	-4	12	9	-2	.973	7	*O-142	-0.3
1984	Cin-N	156	607	73	173	28	0	16	94	41	89	.285	.331	.410	103	1	11	10	-3	.974	5	*O-151	-0.1
1985	Cin-N★	160	635	88	198	**42**	4	34	**125**	52	80	.312	.367	.551	146	37	5	13	-6	.972	13	*O-159	3.9
1986	Cin-N	162	637	89	174	31	3	31	116	56	126	.273	.333	.477	116	12	1	6	-3	.970	-2	*O-159	0.1
1987	Cin-N	153	589	77	149	28	0	26	97	44	104	.253	.314	.433	91	-9	7	3	0	.967	8	*O-142/1-9	-0.5
1988	*Oak-A	101	377	43	97	18	1	12	55	32	70	.257	.315	.406	104	1	0	1	-1	.953	-3	D-61,O-34/1-1	-0.2
1989	*Oak-A	144	553	56	146	27	0	22	97	38	91	.264	.313	.432	112	6	0	0	0	1.000	0	*D-140/O-1	0.3
1990	Mil-A☆	157	610	71	176	30	3	21	92	41	102	.289	.337	.451	119	14	4	7	-3	.960	-1	*D-153/1-3	0.5
1991	Cal-A	119	466	45	108	22	2	11	56	29	91	.232	.281	.358	76	-16	3	2	-0	.000	0	*D-119	-2.2
	Tor-A	13	36	2	12	4	0	0	3	4	7	.333	.400	.444	128	1	0	1	-1	.000	0	D-11	0.0
	Yr	132	502	47	120	26	2	11	59	33	98	.239	.290	.365	80	-15	3	3	-1	.000	0	*D-130	-2.2
Total	19	2466	9358	1272	2712	526	75	339	1493	683	1537	.290	.342	.471	121	233	154	113	-22	.965	98	*O-1867,D-484/12	23.0

■ DIXIE PARKER
Parker, Douglas Woolley b: 4/24/1895, Forest Home, Ala. d: 5/15/72, Tuscaloosa, Ala. BL/TR, 5'11", 160 lbs. Deb: 7/28/23

YEAR	TM/L	G	AB	R	H	2B	3B	HR	RBI	BB	SO	AVG	OBP	SLG	PRO+	BR/A	SB	CS	SBR	FA	FR	G/POS	TPR
1923	Phi-N	4	5	0	1	0	0	0	1	0	1	.200	.200	.200	5	-1	0	0	0	.500	-1	/C-2	-0.1

■ SALTY PARKER
Parker, Francis James b: 7/8/13, E.St.Louis, Ill. d: 7/27/92, Houston, Tex. BR/TR, 6', 173 lbs. Deb: 8/13/36 MC

YEAR	TM/L	G	AB	R	H	2B	3B	HR	RBI	BB	SO	AVG	OBP	SLG	PRO+	BR/A	SB	CS	SBR	FA	FR	G/POS	TPR
1936	Det-A	11	25	6	7	2	0	0	4	2	3	.280	.333	.360	71	-1	0	2	-1	.906	3	/S-7,1-2	0.1

■ WES PARKER
Parker, Maurice Wesley b: 11/13/39, Evanston, Ill. BB/TL, 6'1", 180 lbs. Deb: 4/19/64

YEAR	TM/L	G	AB	R	H	2B	3B	HR	RBI	BB	SO	AVG	OBP	SLG	PRO+	BR/A	SB	CS	SBR	FA	FR	G/POS	TPR
1964	LA-N	124	214	26	55	7	1	3	10	14	46	.257	.306	.341	88	-4	5	4	-1	.971	-10	O-69,1-31	-1.8
1965	*LA-N	154	542	80	129	24	7	8	51	75	95	.238	.336	.352	101	2	13	7	-0	.997	-1	*1-154/O-1	-0.8
1966	*LA-N	156	475	67	120	17	5	12	51	69	83	.253	.353	.385	114	11	7	3	0	.992	1	*1-140,O-14	0.3
1967	LA-N	139	413	56	102	16	5	5	31	65	83	.247	.359	.346	112	9	10	5	0	.996	5	*1-112,O-18	0.7
1968	LA-N	135	468	42	112	22	2	3	27	49	87	.239	.314	.314	96	-2	4	6	-2	.999	0	*1-114,O-28	-1.5
1969	LA-N	132	471	76	131	23	4	13	68	56	46	.278	.357	.427	128	17	4	1	1	.995	0	*1-128/O-2	0.8
1970	LA-N	161	614	84	196	47	4	10	111	79	70	.319	.397	.458	134	31	8	2	1	.996	4	*1-161	2.2
1971	LA-N	157	533	69	146	24	1	6	62	63	63	.274	.352	.356	107	6	6	1	1	.996	3	*1-148,O-18	-0.3
1972	LA-N	130	427	45	119	14	3	4	59	62	43	.279	.371	.354	110	8	3	5	-2	.997	1	*1-120/O-5	-0.3
Total	9	1288	4157	548	1110	194	32	64	470	532	615	.267	.353	.375	112	78	60	34	-2	.996	4	*1-1108,O-155	-0.7

■ RICK PARKER
Parker, Richard Alan b: 3/20/63, Kansas City, Mo. BR/TR, 6', 185 lbs. Deb: 5/4/90

YEAR	TM/L	G	AB	R	H	2B	3B	HR	RBI	BB	SO	AVG	OBP	SLG	PRO+	BR/A	SB	CS	SBR	FA	FR	G/POS	TPR
1990	SF-N	54	107	19	26	5	0	2	14	10	15	.243	.314	.346	84	-2	6	1	0	.978	-10	O-35/2-2,3-1,S-1	-1.2
1991	SF-N	13	14	0	1	0	0	0	0	1	5	.071	.133	.071	-42	-3	0	0	0	1.000	-1	/O-4	-0.4
1993	Hou-N	45	45	11	15	3	0	0	4	3	8	.333	.375	.400	112	1	1	2	-1	1.000	-5	O-16/2-1,S-1	-0.5
1994	NY-N	8	16	1	1	0	0	0	0	1	6	.063	.063	.063	-68	-0	0	0	0	1.000	0	/O-6	-0.4
1995	LA-N	27	29	3	8	0	0	0	4	2	4	.276	.323	.276	66	-1	1	1	-0	1.000	-2	O-21/3-2,S-2	-0.4
1996	LA-N	16	14	2	4	0	0	0	2	1	2	.286	.333	.357	90	-0	1	0	0	1.000	-1	/O-4	-0.1
Total	6	163	225	36	55	9	0	2	24	16	36	.244	.300	.311	69	-10	9	4	0	.990	-19	/O-86,S-4,3-3,2-3	-3.0

■ BILLY PARKER
Parker, William David b: 1/14/47, Hayneville, Ala. BR/TR, 5'8", 168 lbs. Deb: 9/9/71

YEAR	TM/L	G	AB	R	H	2B	3B	HR	RBI	BB	SO	AVG	OBP	SLG	PRO+	BR/A	SB	CS	SBR	FA	FR	G/POS	TPR
1971	Cal-A	20	70	4	16	0	1	1	6	2	20	.229	.250	.300	59	-4	1	1	-0	.958	-1	2-20	-0.4

YEAR	TM/L	G	AB	R	H	2B	3B	HR	RBI	BB	SO	AVG	OBP	SLG	PRO+	BR/A	SB	CS	SBR	FA	FR	G/POS	TPR
1972	Cal-A	36	80	11	17	2	0	2	8	9	17	.213	.292	.313	85	-2	0	2	-1	.951	-0	3-21/2-9,O-5,S-1	-0.4
1973	Cal-A	38	102	14	23	2	1	0	7	8	23	.225	.279	.265	61	-5	0	1	-1	.959	-3	2-32/S-3,D-1	-0.7
Total	3	94	252	29	56	4	2	3	21	19	60	.222	.279	.290	68	-11	1	4	-2	.963	-5	/2-61,3-21,O-5,SD	-1.5

■ FRANK PARKINSON
Parkinson, Frank Joseph "Parky" b: 3/23/1895, Dickson City, Pa. d: 7/4/60, Trenton, N.J. BR/TR, 5'11", 175 lbs. Deb: 4/13/21

YEAR	TM/L	G	AB	R	H	2B	3B	HR	RBI	BB	SO	AVG	OBP	SLG	PRO+	BR/A	SB	CS	SBR	FA	FR	G/POS	TPR
1921	Phi-N	108	391	36	99	20	2	5	32	13	81	.253	.277	.353	61	-23	3	4	-2	.931	9	*S-105/3-1	-0.5
1922	Phi-N	141	545	86	150	18	6	15	70	55	93	.275	.344	.413	86	-12	3	4	-2	.963	31	*2-139	2.0
1923	Phi-N	67	219	21	53	12	0	3	28	13	31	.242	.288	.338	58	-14	0	4	-2	.950	3	2-37,S-15,3-11	-1.1
1924	Phi-N	62	156	14	33	7	0	1	19	14	28	.212	.281	.276	44	-12	3	1	0	.952	7	3-28,S-21,2-10	-0.2
Total	4	378	1311	157	335	57	8	24	149	95	233	.256	.308	.366	69	-61	9	13	-5	.962	50	2-186,S-141/3-40	0.2

■ ART PARKS
Parks, Artie William b: 11/1/11, Paris, Ark. d: 12/6/89, Little Rock, Ark. BL/TR, 5'9", 170 lbs. Deb: 9/25/37

YEAR	TM/L	G	AB	R	H	2B	3B	HR	RBI	BB	SO	AVG	OBP	SLG	PRO+	BR/A	SB	CS	SBR	FA	FR	G/POS	TPR
1937	Bro-N	7	16	2	5	2	0	0	0	2	2	.313	.389	.438	122	1	0			1.000	0	/O-4	0.0
1939	Bro-N	71	239	27	65	13	2	1	19	28	14	.272	.348	.356	86	-4	2			.977	-4	O-65	-1.0
Total	2	78	255	29	70	15	2	1	19	30	16	.275	.351	.361	89	-3	2			.978	-4	/O-69	-1.0

■ DEREK PARKS
Parks, Derek Gavin b: 9/29/68, Covina, Cal. BR/TR, 6', 205 lbs. Deb: 9/11/92

YEAR	TM/L	G	AB	R	H	2B	3B	HR	RBI	BB	SO	AVG	OBP	SLG	PRO+	BR/A	SB	CS	SBR	FA	FR	G/POS	TPR
1992	Min-A	7	6	1	2	0	0	0	1	1	1	.333	.500	.333	133	0	0	0	0	1.000	1	/C-7	0.2
1993	Min-A	7	20	3	4	0	0	1	1	1	2	.200	.238	.200	19	-2	0	0	0	.970	-0	/C-7	-0.2
1994	Min-A	31	89	6	17	6	0	1	9	4	20	.191	.242	.292	37	-9	0	1	-1	.993	-3	C-31	-1.0
Total	3	45	115	10	23	6	0	1	10	6	23	.200	.258	.278	40	-10	0	1	-1	.989	-2	/C-45	-1.0

■ BILL PARKS
Parks, William Robert b: 6/4/1849, Easton, Pa. d: 10/10/11, Easton, Pa. BR/TR, 5'8", 150 lbs. Deb: 4/26/1875 M

YEAR	TM/L	G	AB	R	H	2B	3B	HR	RBI	BB	SO	AVG	OBP	SLG	PRO+	BR/A	SB	CS	SBR	FA	FR	G/POS	TPR
1875	Was-n	27	111	13	20	0	0	0	6	1	1	.180	.188	.180	29	-7	1	1	-0	.836	3	O-17,P-14,M	-0.1
	Phi-n	2	6	0	1	0	0	0	0	0	1	.167	.167	.167	16	-1	0	0	-0	.500	-1	/P-2,O-2	0.0
	Yr	29	117	13	21	0	0	0	6	1	2	.179	.186	.179	29	-8	1	1	-0	.833	3	O-19,P-16	-0.1
1876	Bos-N	1	4	0	0	0	0	0	0	0	0	.000	.000	.000	-98	-1				.750	-0	/O-1	-0.1

■ SAM PARRILLA
Parrilla, Samuel (Monge) b: 6/12/43, Santurce, P.R. d: 2/9/94, Brooklyn, N.Y. BR/TR, 5'11", 185 lbs. Deb: 4/11/70

YEAR	TM/L	G	AB	R	H	2B	3B	HR	RBI	BB	SO	AVG	OBP	SLG	PRO+	BR/A	SB	CS	SBR	FA	FR	G/POS	TPR
1970	Phi-N	11	16	0	2	1	0	0	1	0	4	.125	.176	.188	-3	-2	0	0	0	1.000	0	/O-3	-0.2

■ LANCE PARRISH
Parrish, Lance Michael b: 6/15/56, Clairton, Pa. BR/TR, 6'3", 220 lbs. Deb: 9/5/77

YEAR	TM/L	G	AB	R	H	2B	3B	HR	RBI	BB	SO	AVG	OBP	SLG	PRO+	BR/A	SB	CS	SBR	FA	FR	G/POS	TPR
1977	Det-A	12	46	10	9	2	0	3	7	5	12	.196	.275	.435	85	-1	0	0	0	1.000	2	C-12	0.1
1978	Det-A	85	288	37	63	11	3	14	41	11	71	.219	.255	.424	85	-7	0	0	0	.987	5	C-79	-0.1
1979	Det-A	143	493	65	136	26	3	19	65	49	105	.276	.344	.456	110	6	6	7	-2	.989	5	*C-142	1.4
1980	Det-A★	144	553	79	158	34	6	24	82	31	109	.286	.327	.499	120	13	6	4	-1	.990	-5	*C-121,D-16/1-5,O-5	1.1
1981	Det-A	96	348	39	85	18	2	10	46	34	52	.244	.312	.394	98	-1	2	3	-1	.993	-2	C-90/D-5	-0.1
1982	Det-A★	133	486	75	138	19	2	32	87	40	99	.284	.340	.529	134	21	3	4	-2	.989	9	*C-132/O-1	3.3
1983	Det-A★	155	605	80	163	42	3	27	114	44	106	.269	.320	.483	120	15	1	3	-2	.995	0	*C-131,D-27	1.8
1984	*Det-A★	147	578	75	137	16	2	33	98	41	120	.237	.290	.443	100	-2	2	3	-1	.991	1	*C-127,D-22	0.4
1985	Det-A†	140	549	64	150	27	1	28	98	41	90	.273	.324	.479	118	12	2	6	-3	.993	-6	*C-120,D-22	0.9
1986	Det-A★	91	327	53	84	6	1	22	62	38	83	.257	.343	.483	122	10	0	0	0	.989	2	C-85/D-6	1.7
1987	Phi-N	130	466	42	114	21	0	17	67	47	104	.245	.315	.399	85	-10	0	1	-1	.989	-3	*C-127	-0.5
1988	Phi-N★	123	424	44	91	17	2	15	60	47	93	.215	.296	.370	88	-7	0	0	0	.988	-4	*C-117/1-1	-0.2
1989	Cal-A	124	433	48	103	12	1	17	50	42	104	.238	.308	.388	97	-3	1	1	-0	.993	-2	*C-122/D-2	0.2
1990	Cal-A	133	470	54	126	14	0	24	70	46	107	.268	.340	.451	122	13	2	2	-1	.993	10	*C-131/1-4,D-1	3.1
1991	Cal-A	119	402	38	87	12	0	19	51	35	117	.216	.287	.388	85	-9	0	1	-1	.997	0	*C-111/1-3,D-5	-0.3
1992	Cal-A	24	83	7	19	2	0	4	11	5	22	.229	.273	.398	85	-2	0	0	0	.975	-5	C-22/D-2	-0.6
	Sea-A	69	192	19	45	11	1	8	21	19	48	.234	.307	.427	103	0	1	1	-0	.995	-4	C-34,1-16,D-14	-0.4
	Yr	93	275	26	64	13	1	12	32	24	70	.233	.297	.418	98	-2	1	1	-0	.987	-9	C-56,D-16,1-16	-1.0
1993	Cle-A	10	20	2	4	1	0	1	2	4	5	.200	.333	.400	97	-0	1	1	-0	.950	4	C-10	0.4
1994	Pit-N	40	126	10	34	5	0	3	16	18	28	.270	.366	.381	94	-1	1	1	-0	.988	-2	C-38/1-1	-0.1
1995	Tor-A	70	178	15	36	4	0	4	22	15	52	.202	.268	.320	53	-13	0	0	0	1.000	0	C-67/D-1	-0.6
Total	19	1988	7067	856	1782	305	27	324	1070	612	1527	.252	.315	.440	105	33	28	37	-14	.991	15	*C-1818,D-123/1O	12.1

■ LARRY PARRISH
Parrish, Larry Alton b: 11/10/53, Winter Haven, Fla. BR/TR, 6'3", 215 lbs. Deb: 9/6/74

YEAR	TM/L	G	AB	R	H	2B	3B	HR	RBI	BB	SO	AVG	OBP	SLG	PRO+	BR/A	SB	CS	SBR	FA	FR	G/POS	TPR
1974	Mon-N	25	69	9	14	5	0	1	4	6	19	.203	.286	.275	54	-4	0	0	0	.986	8	3-24	0.3
1975	Mon-N	145	532	50	146	32	5	10	65	28	74	.274	.316	.410	96	-5	4	5	-2	.919	-3	*3-143/2-1,S-1	-1.0
1976	Mon-N	154	543	65	126	28	5	11	61	41	91	.232	.288	.363	81	-15	2	6	-3	.945	5	*3-153	-1.6
1977	Mon-N	123	402	50	99	19	2	11	46	37	71	.246	.316	.386	90	-6	2	4	-2	.936	-9	*3-115	-1.9
1978	Mon-N	144	520	68	144	39	4	15	70	32	103	.277	.321	.454	116	9	2	3	-1	.947	-8	*3-139	0.0
1979	Mon-N★	153	544	83	167	39	2	30	82	41	101	.307	.358	.551	146	32	5	1	1	.947	-9	*3-153	2.2
1980	Mon-N	126	452	55	115	27	3	15	72	36	80	.254	.315	.427	105	2	2	6	-3	.949	-8	*3-124	-1.1
1981	*Mon-N	97	349	41	85	19	3	8	44	28	73	.244	.300	.384	92	-5	0	0	0	.935	-17	3-95	-2.6
1982	Tex-A	128	440	59	116	15	0	17	62	30	84	.264	.314	.414	104	1	5	2	0	.962	-7	*O-124/3-3,D-2	-0.9
1983	Tex-A	145	555	76	151	26	4	26	88	46	91	.272	.331	.474	121	14	0	0	0	.962	-5	*O-132,D-13	0.5
1984	Tex-A	156	613	72	175	42	1	22	101	42	116	.285	.337	.465	116	12	2	4	-2	.982	4	O-81,D-63,3-12	1.0
1985	Tex-A	94	346	44	86	11	1	17	51	33	77	.249	.316	.434	101	0	0	2	-1	.991	-3	O-69,D-22/3-2	-0.6
1986	Tex-A	129	464	67	128	22	1	28	94	52	114	.276	.351	.509	127	17	3	1	0	.935	-5	D-98,3-30	0.9
1987	Tex-A★	152	557	79	149	22	1	32	100	49	154	.268	.330	.483	112	8	3	1	0	.918	-9	*D-122,3-28/O-1	-0.4
1988	Tex-A	68	248	22	47	9	1	7	26	20	79	.190	.256	.319	58	-14	0	0	0	.000	0	D-67	-1.6
	*Bos-A	52	158	10	41	5	0	7	26	8	32	.259	.299	.424	96	-1	0	1	-1	.988	3	1-36,D-14	-0.2
	Yr	120	406	32	88	14	1	14	52	28	111	.217	.272	.360	73	-15	0	1	-1	.988	3	D-81,1-36	-1.8
Total	15	1891	6792	850	1789	360	33	256	992	529	1359	.263	.321	.439	106	45	30	36	-13	.941	-62	*3-1021,O-407,D/1S2	-7.0

■ TOM PARROTT
Parrott, Thomas William "Tacky Tom" b: 4/10/1868, Portland, Ore. d: 1/1/32, Dundee, Ore. BR/TR, 5'10.5", 170 lbs. Deb: 6/18/1893 F

YEAR	TM/L	G	AB	R	H	2B	3B	HR	RBI	BB	SO	AVG	OBP	SLG	PRO+	BR/A	SB	CS	SBR	FA	FR	G/POS	TPR
1893	Chi-N	7	27	4	7	1	0	0	3	1	2	.259	.286	.296	56	-2	0			.800	-1	/P-4,3-2,2-1	-0.1
	Cin-N	24	68	5	13	1	1	1	9	1	9	.191	.203	.279	27	-8	0			.915	1	P-22/O-1	-0.1
	Yr	31	95	9	20	2	1	1	12	2	11	.211	.227	.284	35	-9	0			.906	-0	P-26/3-2,2-1,O-1	-0.2
1894	Cin-N	68	229	51	74	12	6	4	40	17	10	.323	.372	.480	101	-1	4			.929	5	P-41,O-13,1/S32	0.1
1895	Cin-N	64	201	35	69	13	7	3	41	11	8	.343	.377	.522	125	6	10			.922	1	P-41,1-14/O-9	0.0
1896	StL-N	118	474	62	138	13	12	7	70	11	24	.291	.307	.414	93	-8	12			.951	13	*O-108/P-7,1-6	-0.2
Total	4	281	999	157	301	40	26	15	163	41	53	.301	.329	.438	96	-12	26			.940	19	O-131,P-115/132S	-0.3

■ JIGGS PARROTT
Parrott, Walter Edward b: 7/14/1871, Portland, Ore. d: 4/16/1898, Phoenix, Ariz. 5'11", 160 lbs. Deb: 7/11/1892 F

YEAR	TM/L	G	AB	R	H	2B	3B	HR	RBI	BB	SO	AVG	OBP	SLG	PRO+	BR/A	SB	CS	SBR	FA	FR	G/POS	TPR
1892	Chi-N	78	333	38	67	8	5	2	22	8	30	.201	.222	.273	49	-22	7			.891	-2	3-78	-2.0
1893	Chi-N	110	455	54	111	10	9	1	65	13	25	.244	.267	.312	54	-32	25			.904	9	*3-99/2-7,O-4	-1.7
1894	Chi-N	124	517	82	128	17	9	3	64	16	35	.248	.274	.333	43	-51	30			.931	-6	*2-123/3-1	-4.0
1895	Chi-N	3	4	0	1	0	0	0	0	0	0	.250	.250	.250	27	-0	0			.000	-2	/O-1,S-1,1-1	-0.2
Total	4	315	1309	174	307	35	23	6	151	37	90	.235	.258	.310	48	-105	62			.899	-1	3-178,2-130/O-5,1S	-7.9

■ CASEY PARSONS
Parsons, Casey Robert b: 4/14/54, Wenatchee, Wash. BL/TR, 6'1", 180 lbs. Deb: 5/31/81

YEAR	TM/L	G	AB	R	H	2B	3B	HR	RBI	BB	SO	AVG	OBP	SLG	PRO+	BR/A	SB	CS	SBR	FA	FR	G/POS	TPR
1981	Sea-A	36	22	6	5	1	0	1	5	1	4	.227	.240	.409	105	-0	0	0	0	1.000	-5	O-24/1-1	-0.5
1983	Chi-A	8	5	1	1	0	0	0	2	1	0	.200	.429	.200	77	-0	0	0	0	1.000	-1	/O-3,D-2	-0.1
1984	Chi-A	1	1	0	0	0	0	0	0	0	0	.000	.000	.000	-96	-0	0	0	0	.000	0	/H	0.0
1987	Cle-A	18	25	2	4	1	0	1	3	1	7	.160	.160	.280	13	-3	0	0	0	1.000	-6	/O-2,1-1,D-5	-0.4
Total	4	63	53	9	10	2	0	3	10	3	11	.189	.259	.321	57	-3	0	0	0	1.000	-6	/O-29,D-7,1-2	-1.0

■ DIXIE PARSONS
Parsons, Edward Dixon b: 5/12/16, Talladega, Ala. d: 10/31/91, Longview, Tex. BR/TR, 6'2", 180 lbs. Deb: 8/16/39

YEAR	TM/L	G	AB	R	H	2B	3B	HR	RBI	BB	SO	AVG	OBP	SLG	PRO+	BR/A	SB	CS	SBR	FA	FR	G/POS	TPR
1939	Det-A	5	1	0	0	0	0	0	0	0	0	.000	.500	.000	36	-0	0	0	0	1.000	0	/C-4	0.0
1942	Det-A	63	188	8	37	4	0	2	11	13	22	.197	.249	.250	37	-16	1	0	0	.981	10	C-62	-0.2

YEAR	TM/L	G	AB	R	H	2B	3B	HR	RBI	BB	SO	AVG	OBP	SLG	PRO+	BR/A	SB	CS	SBR	FA	FR	G/POS	TPR
1943	Det-A	40	106	2	15	3	0	0	4	6	16	.142	.188	.170	4	-13	0	0	0	.975	5	C-40	-0.6
Total	3	108	295	10	52	7	0	2	15	20	39	.176	.229	.220	26	-29	1	0	0	.979	15	C-106	-0.8

■ JOHN PARSONS
Parsons, John S. b: Napoleon, Ohio 5'6", 138 lbs. Deb: 10/15/1884

YEAR	TM/L	G	AB	R	H	2B	3B	HR	RBI	BB	SO	AVG	OBP	SLG	PRO+	BR/A	SB	CS	SBR	FA	FR	G/POS	TPR
1884	Cin-a	1	3	0	0	0	0	0		0	0	.000	.000	.000	-95	-1				1.000	-1	/O-1	-0.1

■ ROY PARTEE
Partee, Roy Robert b: 9/7/17, Los Angeles, Cal. BR/TR, 5'10", 180 lbs. Deb: 4/23/43

YEAR	TM/L	G	AB	R	H	2B	3B	HR	RBI	BB	SO	AVG	OBP	SLG	PRO+	BR/A	SB	CS	SBR	FA	FR	G/POS	TPR
1943	Bos-A	96	299	30	84	14	2	0	31	39	33	.281	.368	.341	106	4	0	0	0	.983	-6	C-91	0.4
1944	Bos-A	89	280	18	68	12	0	2	41	37	29	.243	.333	.307	85	-5	0	1	-1	.989	-6	C-85	-0.7
1946	*Bos-A	40	111	13	35	5	2	0	9	13	14	.315	.387	.396	113	2	0	0	0	.974	-6	C-38	-0.2
1947	Bos-A	60	169	14	39	2	0	0	16	18	23	.231	.305	.243	50	-11	0	0	0	.975	-1	C-54	-0.9
1948	StL-A	82	231	14	47	8	1	0	17	25	21	.203	.284	.247	41	-19	2	2	-1	.982	1	C-76	-1.5
Total	5	367	1090	89	273	41	5	2	114	132	120	.250	.334	.303	78	-29	2	3	-1	.982	-18	C-344	-2.9

■ STEVE PARTENHEIMER
Partenheimer, Harold Philip b: 8/30/1891, Greenfield, Mass. d: 6/16/71, Mansfield, Ohio BR/TR, 5'8.5", 145 lbs. Deb: 6/18/13 F

YEAR	TM/L	G	AB	R	H	2B	3B	HR	RBI	BB	SO	AVG	OBP	SLG	PRO+	BR/A	SB	CS	SBR	FA	FR	G/POS	TPR
1913	Det-A	1	2	0	0	0	0	0		0	0	.000	.333	.000	-1	-0				.750	0	/3-1	0.0

■ JAY PARTRIDGE
Partridge, James Bugg b: 11/15/02, Mountville, Ga. d: 1/14/74, Nashville, Tenn. BL/TR, 5'11", 160 lbs. Deb: 4/12/27

YEAR	TM/L	G	AB	R	H	2B	3B	HR	RBI	BB	SO	AVG	OBP	SLG	PRO+	BR/A	SB	CS	SBR	FA	FR	G/POS	TPR
1927	Bro-N	146	572	72	149	17	6	7	40	20	36	.260	.289	.348	70	-26	9			.938	-16	*2-140	-3.6
1928	Bro-N	37	73	18	18	0	1	0	12	13	6	.247	.368	.274	71	-2	2			.908	-5	2-18/3-2	-0.7
Total	2	183	645	90	167	17	7	7	52	33	42	.259	.299	.340	70	-28	11			.935	-20	2-158/3-2	-4.3

■ BEN PASCHAL
Paschal, Benjamin Edwin b: 10/13/1895, Enterprise, Ala. d: 11/10/74, Charlotte, N.C. BR/TR, 5'11", 185 lbs. Deb: 8/16/15

YEAR	TM/L	G	AB	R	H	2B	3B	HR	RBI	BB	SO	AVG	OBP	SLG	PRO+	BR/A	SB	CS	SBR	FA	FR	G/POS	TPR
1915	Cle-A	9	9	0	1	0	0	0	0	0	3	.111	.111	.111	-33	-33	0			.000	0	H	-0.2
1920	Bos-A	9	28	5	10	0	0	0	5	5	2	.357	.455	.357	122	1	1	0	0	1.000	0	/O-7	0.1
1924	NY-A	4	12	2	3	1	0	0	3	1	0	.250	.308	.333	65	-1	0	0	0	1.000	-0	/O-4	-0.1
1925	NY-A	89	247	49	89	16	5	12	56	22	29	.360	.417	.611	161	22	14	9	-1	.953	-4	O-66	1.2
1926	*NY-A	96	258	46	74	12	3	7	32	26	35	.287	.354	.438	107	2	7	6	-2	.935	-3	O-74	-0.7
1927	NY-A	50	82	16	26	9	2	2	16	4	10	.317	.349	.549	134	3	0	2	-1	.976	-5	O-27	-0.3
1928	NY-A	65	79	12	25	6	1	1	15	8	11	.316	.379	.456	122	3	1	0	0	1.000	-6	O-25	-0.3
1929	NY-A	42	72	13	15	3	0	2	11	6	3	.208	.269	.333	58	-5	1	1	-0	.951	-1	O-20	-0.7
Total	8	364	787	143	243	47	11	24	138	72	93	.309	.369	.488	123	24	24	18		.953	-19	O-223	-1.0

■ JOHNNY PASEK
Pasek, John Paul b: 6/25/05, Niagara Falls, N.Y. d: 3/13/76, Niagara Falls, N.Y BR/TR, 5'10", 175 lbs. Deb: 7/28/33

YEAR	TM/L	G	AB	R	H	2B	3B	HR	RBI	BB	SO	AVG	OBP	SLG	PRO+	BR/A	SB	CS	SBR	FA	FR	G/POS	TPR
1933	Det-A	28	61	6	15	4	0	0	4	7	7	.246	.324	.311	68	-3	2	0	1	.989	-1	C-28	-0.1
1934	Chi-A	4	9	1	3	0	0	0	0	1	1	.333	.400	.333	88	-0	0	0	0	1.000	-0	/C-4	0.0
Total	2	32	70	7	18	4	0	0	4	8	8	.257	.333	.314	70	-3	2	0	1	.990	-1	/C-32	-0.1

■ DODE PASKERT
Paskert, George Henry b: 8/28/1881, Cleveland, Ohio d: 2/12/59, Cleveland, Ohio BR/TR, 5'11", 165 lbs. Deb: 9/21/07

YEAR	TM/L	G	AB	R	H	2B	3B	HR	RBI	BB	SO	AVG	OBP	SLG	PRO+	BR/A	SB	CS	SBR	FA	FR	G/POS	TPR
1907	Cin-N	16	50	10	14	4	0	1	8	2		.280	.333	.420	130	2	2			.973	1	O-16	0.2
1908	Cin-N	118	395	40	96	14	4	1	36	27		.243	.298	.306	96	-2	25			.953	2	*O-116	-0.2
1909	Cin-N	104	322	49	81	7	4	0	33	34		.252	.327	.298	95	-1	23			.968	0	O-82/1-6	-0.5
1910	Cin-N	144	506	63	152	21	5	2	46	70	60	.300	.389	.374	128	20	51			.957	14	*O-139/1-2	2.9
1911	Phi-N	153	560	96	153	18	5	4	47	70	70	.273	.358	.345	96	-2	28			.979	8	O-153	-0.2
1912	Phi-N	145	540	102	170	37	5	2	43	91	67	.315	.420	.413	120	19	36			.967	5	*O-141/2-2,3-1	1.6
1913	Phi-N	124	454	83	119	21	9	4	29	65	69	.262	.358	.374	105	4	12			.972	18	*O-120	1.7
1914	Phi-N	132	451	59	119	25	6	3	44	56	68	.264	.349	.366	106	4	23			.958	12	*O-128/S-4	1.1
1915	*Phi-N	109	328	51	80	17	4	3	39	35	38	.244	.319	.348	100	0	9	6	-1	.970	-2	O-92/1-5	-0.8
1916	Phi-N	149	555	82	155	30	7	8	46	54	76	.279	.346	.402	125	17	22	21	-6	.983	1	*O-146/S-1	0.5
1917	Phi-N	141	546	78	137	27	11	4	43	62	63	.251	.331	.363	108	6	19			**.984**	1	*O-138	-0.4
1918	*Chi-N	127	461	69	132	24	3	3	59	53	49	.286	.362	.371	121	13	20			.980	-3	*O-121/3-6	0.4
1919	Chi-N	88	270	21	53	11	3	2	29	28	33	.196	.274	.281	67	-11	7			.969	-6	O-80	-2.4
1920	Chi-N	139	487	57	136	22	10	5	71	64	58	.279	.366	.396	117	12	16	14	-4	.956	1	*O-137	0.2
1921	Cin-N	27	92	8	16	1	1	0	4	4	8	.174	.208	.207	11	-12	0	2	-1	.984	1	O-24	-1.4
Total	15	1716	6017	868	1613	279	77	42	577	715	659	.268	.350	.361	108	70	293	43		.969	52	*O-1633/1-13,3S2	2.5

■ KEVIN PASLEY
Pasley, Kevin Patrick b: 7/22/53, Bronx, N.Y. BR/TR, 6', 185 lbs. Deb: 10/2/74

YEAR	TM/L	G	AB	R	H	2B	3B	HR	RBI	BB	SO	AVG	OBP	SLG	PRO+	BR/A	SB	CS	SBR	FA	FR	G/POS	TPR
1974	LA-N	1	0	0	0	0	0	0	0	0	0	—	—	—			0	0	0	1.000	-0	/C-1	0.0
1976	LA-N	23	52	4	12	2	0	0	2	3	7	.231	.273	.269	55	-3	0	0	0	.971	5	C-23	0.2
1977	LA-N	3	3	0	1	0	0	0	0	0	0	.333	.333	.333	80	-0	0	0	0	1.000	1	/C-2	0.0
	Sea-A	4	13	1	5	0	0	0	2	1	2	.385	.429	.385	125	1	0	0	0	1.000	-2	/C-4	-0.1
1978	Sea-A	25	54	3	13	5	0	1	3	2	4	.241	.268	.389	83	-1	0	0	0	1.000	-0	/C-25	-0.1
Total	4	55	122	8	31	7	0	1	9	6	13	.254	.289	.336	76	-4	0	0	0	.986	3	/C-55	0.0

■ DAN PASQUA
Pasqua, Daniel Anthony b: 10/17/61, Yonkers, N.Y. BL/TL, 6', 203 lbs. Deb: 5/30/85

YEAR	TM/L	G	AB	R	H	2B	3B	HR	RBI	BB	SO	AVG	OBP	SLG	PRO+	BR/A	SB	CS	SBR	FA	FR	G/POS	TPR
1985	NY-A	60	148	17	31	3	1	9	25	16	38	.209	.291	.426	96	-1	0	0	0	1.000	1	O-37,D-14	-0.1
1986	NY-A	102	280	44	82	17	0	16	45	47	78	.293	.400	.525	151	21	0	0	1	.987	-2	O-81/1-5,D-3	1.7
1987	NY-A	113	318	42	74	7	1	17	42	40	99	.233	.320	.421	96	-2	0	2	-1	.985	-2	O-74,D-20,1-12	-0.8
1988	Chi-A	129	422	48	96	16	2	20	50	46	100	.227	.308	.417	101	0	1	0	0	**.996**	7	*O-112/1-7,D-2	0.4
1989	Chi-A	73	246	26	61	9	1	11	47	25	58	.248	.320	.427	111	3	1	2	-1	.993	2	O-66/D-5	0.2
1990	Chi-A	112	325	43	89	27	3	13	58	37	66	.274	.352	.495	137	16	1	1	-0	.962	0	D-57,O-43	1.3
1991	Chi-A	134	417	71	108	22	5	18	66	62	86	.259	.359	.465	129	17	2	1	-1	.991	-8	1-83,O-59/D-8	0.3
1992	Chi-A	93	265	26	56	16	1	6	33	36	57	.211	.308	.347	84	-5	0	1	-1	.963	-2	O-81/1-5,D-1	-1.0
1993	*Chi-A	78	176	22	36	10	1	5	20	26	51	.205	.307	.358	80	-5	2	2	-1	.984	-3	O-37,1-32/D-6	-1.0
1994	Chi-A	21	23	2	5	2	0	2	4	0	9	.217	.217	.565	95	-2	0	0	0	.867	-1	/O-5,1-3	-0.1
Total	10	905	2620	341	638	129	15	117	390	335	642	.244	.333	.438	112	42	7	10	-4	.984	-8	O-595,1-147,D-116	0.9

■ MIKE PASQUELLA
Pasquella, Michael John "Toney" (b: Michael John Pasquariello) b: 11/7/1898, Philadelphia, Pa. d: 4/5/65, Bridgeport, Conn. BR/TR, 5'11", 167 lbs. Deb: 7/9/19

YEAR	TM/L	G	AB	R	H	2B	3B	HR	RBI	BB	SO	AVG	OBP	SLG	PRO+	BR/A	SB	CS	SBR	FA	FR	G/POS	TPR
1919	Phi-N	1	1	1	1	0	0	0	0	0	0	1.000	1.000	1.000	469	0	0			.000	0	/1-1	0.0
	StL-N	1	1	0	0	0	0	0	0	0	0	.000	.000	.000	-99	-0	0			.000	0	H	0.0
	Yr	2	2	1	1	0	0	0	0	0	0	.500	.500	.500	200	0	0			.000	0	/1-1	0.0

■ CLIFF PASTORNICKY
Pastornicky, Clifford Scott b: 11/18/58, Seattle, Wash. BR/TR, 5'10", 170 lbs. Deb: 6/14/83

YEAR	TM/L	G	AB	R	H	2B	3B	HR	RBI	BB	SO	AVG	OBP	SLG	PRO+	BR/A	SB	CS	SBR	FA	FR	G/POS	TPR
1983	KC-A	10	32	4	4	0	0	2	5	0	3	.125	.125	.313	16	-4	0	0	0	.929	-0	3-10	-0.4

■ BOB PATE
Pate, Robert Wayne b: 12/3/53, Los Angeles, Cal. BR/TR, 6'3.5", 200 lbs. Deb: 6/2/80

YEAR	TM/L	G	AB	R	H	2B	3B	HR	RBI	BB	SO	AVG	OBP	SLG	PRO+	BR/A	SB	CS	SBR	FA	FR	G/POS	TPR
1980	Mon-N	23	39	3	10	2	0	0	5	3	6	.256	.310	.308	73	-1	0	1	-1	1.000	-4	O-18	-0.6
1981	Mon-N	8	6	0	2	0	0	0	0	2	0	.333	.429	.333	117	-0	0	0	0	1.000	-2	/O-5	-0.2
Total	2	31	45	3	12	2	0	0	5	5	6	.267	.327	.311	79	-1	0	1	-1	1.000	-5	/O-23	-0.8

■ FREDDIE PATEK
Patek, Frederick Joseph "The Flea" b: 10/9/44, Seguin, Tex. BR/TR, 5'5", 148 lbs. Deb: 6/3/68

YEAR	TM/L	G	AB	R	H	2B	3B	HR	RBI	BB	SO	AVG	OBP	SLG	PRO+	BR/A	SB	CS	SBR	FA	FR	G/POS	TPR
1968	Pit-N	61	208	31	53	4	2	6	18	12	37	.255	.302	.322	89	-3	18	7	1	.976	-1	S-52/O-5,3-1	0.2
1969	Pit-N	147	460	48	110	9	1	5	32	53	86	.239	.319	.296	75	-14	15	8	-0	.954	-2	*S-146	-0.2
1970	*Pit-N	84	237	42	58	10	5	1	19	29	46	.245	.327	.342	81	-6	8	2	1	.971	11	S-65	1.3
1971	KC-A	147	591	86	158	21	**11**	6	36	44	80	.267	.323	.371	97	-3	49	14	6	.968	10	*S-147	3.4
1972	KC-A†	136	518	59	110	25	4	0	32	47	64	.212	.282	.276	67	-21	33	7	6	.971	**30**	*S-136	3.8
1973	KC-A	135	501	82	117	19	5	5	45	54	63	.234	.312	.321	73	-18	36	14	2	.966	**35**	*S-135	3.8
1974	KC-A	149	537	72	121	18	4	3	38	77	69	.225	.326	.298	76	-15	33	15	1	.967	4	*S-149	1.0
1975	KC-A	148	483	58	110	14	5	5	45	42	65	.228	.292	.308	68	-20	32	7	5	.959	-7	*S-136/D-1	-0.7
1976	*KC-A★	144	432	58	104	19	3	1	43	50	63	.241	.322	.306	84	-8	51	15	6	.962	-6	*S-143/D-1	1.0
1977	*KC-A	154	497	72	130	26	6	5	60	41	84	.262	.324	.368	88	-8	**53**	13	8	.958	-19	*S-154	-0.2

YEAR	TM/L	G	AB	R	H	2B	3B	HR	RBI	BB	SO	AVG	OBP	SLG	PRO+	BR/A	SB	CS	SBR	FA	FR	G/POS	TPR
1978	*KC-A★	138	440	54	109	23	1	2	46	42	56	.248	.315	.318	76	-13	38	11	5	.949	-25	*S-137	-1.7
1979	KC-A	106	306	30	77	17	0	1	37	16	42	.252	.295	.317	64	-15	11	12	-4	.955	-29	S-104	-3.7
1980	Cal-A	86	273	41	72	10	5	5	34	15	26	.264	.304	.392	92	-4	7	6	-2	.953	-18	S-81	-1.5
1981	Cal-A	27	47	3	11	1	1	0	5	2	1	.234	.250	.298	57	-3	1	0	0	.983	2	2-16/3-7,S-3	0.0
Total	14	1650	5530	736	1340	216	55	41	490	523	787	.242	.311	.324	79	-151	385	131	37	.962	-15	*S-1588/2-16,3OD	6.5

■ BOB PATRICK Patrick, Robert Lee b: 10/27/17, Ft.Smith, Ark. BR/TR, 6'2", 190 lbs. Deb: 9/20/41

YEAR	TM/L	G	AB	R	H	2B	3B	HR	RBI	BB	SO	AVG	OBP	SLG	PRO+	BR/A	SB	CS	SBR	FA	FR	G/POS	TPR
1941	Det-A	5	7	2	2	0	0	0	0	0	1	.286	.286	.286	47	-1	0	0	0	.750	-1	/O-3	-0.2
1942	Det-A	4	8	1	2	1	0	1	3	1	0	.250	.333	.750	185	1	0	0	0	1.000	-0	/O-3	0.0
Total	2	9	15	3	4	1	0	1	3	1	1	.267	.313	.533	118	0	0	0	0	.889	-1	/O-6	-0.2

■ HARRY PATTEE Pattee, Harry Ernest b: 1/17/1882, Charlestown, Mass. d: 7/17/71, Lynchburg, Va. BL/TR, 5'8", 149 lbs. Deb: 4/14/08

YEAR	TM/L	G	AB	R	H	2B	3B	HR	RBI	BB	SO	AVG	OBP	SLG	PRO+	BR/A	SB	CS	SBR	FA	FR	G/POS	TPR
1908	Bro-N	80	264	19	57	5	2	0		26	25	.216	.286	.250	74	-7	24			.964	12	2-74	0.5

■ DAN PATTERSON Patterson, Daniel Thomas b: 1846, New York, N.Y. TL, 5'9", 143 lbs. Deb: 5/18/1871

YEAR	TM/L	G	AB	R	H	2B	3B	HR	RBI	BB	SO	AVG	OBP	SLG	PRO+	BR/A	SB	CS	SBR	FA	FR	G/POS	TPR
1871	Mut-n	32	151	31	31	2	0	0	13	1	0	.205	.211	.219	26	-13	2	1	0	.824	-2	*O-31/2-2	-0.9
1872	Eck-n	12	47	5	9	2	0	0	4	0	1	.191	.191	.234	36	-3	0	0	0	.882	2	O-11/1-1	0.0
1874	Mut-n	1	5	1	2	0	0	0	2	0	0	.400	.400	.400	153	0	0	0	0	1.000	-0	/1-1,O-1	0.0
1875	Atl-n	12	45	4	9	0	0	0	4	0	0	.200	.200	.200	45	-2	1	0	0	.636	-6	2-7,O-7	-0.7
Total	4 n	57	248	41	51	4	0	0	23	1	1	.206	.209	.222	33	-17	3	1	0	.833	-7	/O-50,2-9,1-2	-1.6

■ HAM PATTERSON Patterson, Hamilton b: 10/13/1877, Belleville, Ill. d: 11/25/45, E.St.Louis, Ill. BR/TR, 6'2", 185 lbs. Deb: 5/18/09 F

YEAR	TM/L	G	AB	R	H	2B	3B	HR	RBI	BB	SO	AVG	OBP	SLG	PRO+	BR/A	SB	CS	SBR	FA	FR	G/POS	TPR
1909	StL-A	17	49	2	10	0	0	0	5	0		.204	.204	.224	38	-4	1			1.000	-1	/1-6,O-6	-0.6
	Chi-A	1	3	2	0	0	0	0	0	1		.000	.250	.000	-21	-0	0			1.000	1	/1-1	0.0
	Yr	18	52	4	10	1	0	0	5	1		.192	.208	.212	35	-4	1			1.000	-0	/1-7,O-6	-0.6

■ HANK PATTERSON Patterson, Henry Joseph Colquit b: 7/17/07, San Francisco, Cal. d: 9/30/70, Panorama City, Cal. BR/TR, 5'11.5", 170 lbs. Deb: 9/5/32

YEAR	TM/L	G	AB	R	H	2B	3B	HR	RBI	BB	SO	AVG	OBP	SLG	PRO+	BR/A	SB	CS	SBR	FA	FR	G/POS	TPR
1932	Bos-A	1	1	0	0	0	0	0	0	0	0	.000	.000	.000	-99	-0	0	0	0	.000	0	/C-1	0.0

■ JOHN PATTERSON Patterson, John Allen b: 2/11/67, Key West, Fla. BB/TR, 5'9", 160 lbs. Deb: 4/6/92

YEAR	TM/L	G	AB	R	H	2B	3B	HR	RBI	BB	SO	AVG	OBP	SLG	PRO+	BR/A	SB	CS	SBR	FA	FR	G/POS	TPR
1992	SF-N	32	103	10	19	1	1	0	4	5	24	.184	.229	.214	28	-10	5	1	1	.960	6	2-22/O-5	-0.3
1993	SF-N	16	16	1	3	0	0	1	2	0	5	.188	.188	.375	48	-1	0	1	-1	1.000	0	H	-0.3
1994	SF-N	85	240	36	57	10	1	3	32	16	43	.237	.315	.325	70	-10	13	3	2	.979	-9	2-63	-1.5
1995	SF-N	95	205	27	42	5	3	1	14	14	41	.205	.294	.273	52	-14	4	2	0	.983	-6	2-53	-1.7
Total	4	228	564	74	121	16	5	5	52	35	113	.215	.289	.287	56	-35	22	7	2	.977	-9	2-138/O-5	-3.8

■ CLAIRE PATTERSON Patterson, Lorenzo Claire b: 10/5/1887, Arkansas City, Kan. d: 3/28/13, Mojave, Cal. BL/TR, 6' ", 180 lbs. Deb: 9/5/09

YEAR	TM/L	G	AB	R	H	2B	3B	HR	RBI	BB	SO	AVG	OBP	SLG	PRO+	BR/A	SB	CS	SBR	FA	FR	G/POS	TPR
1909	Cin-N	4	8	0	1	0	0	0	0	0		.125	.125	.125	-23	-1	0			1.000	-0	/O-2	-0.2

■ MIKE PATTERSON Patterson, Michael Lee b: 1/26/58, Santa Monica, Cal. BL/TR, 5'10", 170 lbs. Deb: 4/15/81

YEAR	TM/L	G	AB	R	H	2B	3B	HR	RBI	BB	SO	AVG	OBP	SLG	PRO+	BR/A	SB	CS	SBR	FA	FR	G/POS	TPR
1981	Oak-A	12	23	4	8	1	1	0	1	2	5	.348	.400	.478	160	2	0	1	-1	1.000	-1	/O-5,D-2	0.0
	NY-A	4	9	2	2	0	2	0	0	0	0	.222	.222	.667	150	0	0	0	0	1.000	-1	/O-4	0.0
	Yr	16	32	6	10	1	3	0	1	2	5	.313	.353	.531	158	2	0	1	-1	1.000	-1	/O-9,D-2	0.0
1982	NY-A	11	16	3	3	1	0	1		2	6	.188	.278	.438	94	-0	1	0	0	1.000	-3	/O-9,D-1	-0.3
Total	2	27	48	9	13	2	3	1	2	4	11	.271	.327	.500	135	2	1	1	-0	1.000	-5	/O-18,D-3	-0.3

■ PAT PATTERSON Patterson, William Jennings Bryan b: 1/29/01, Belleville, Ill. d: 10/1/77, St.Louis, Mo. BR/TR, 6', 175 lbs. Deb: 4/14/21 F

YEAR	TM/L	G	AB	R	H	2B	3B	HR	RBI	BB	SO	AVG	OBP	SLG	PRO+	BR/A	SB	CS	SBR	FA	FR	G/POS	TPR
1921	NY-N	23	35	5	14	0	0	1	5	2	5	.400	.432	.486	142	2	0	1	-1	.970	4	3-14/S-7	0.6

■ GEORGE PATTISON Pattison, George Deb: 4/24/1884

YEAR	TM/L	G	AB	R	H	2B	3B	HR	RBI	BB	SO	AVG	OBP	SLG	PRO+	BR/A	SB	CS	SBR	FA	FR	G/POS	TPR
1884	Phi-U	2	7	0	1	0	0	0		0	0	.143	.143	.143	-14	-1				.500	-0	/O-2	-0.1

■ GENE PATTON Patton, Gene Tunney b: 7/8/26, Coatesville, Pa. BL/TR, 5'10", 165 lbs. Deb: 6/17/44

YEAR	TM/L	G	AB	R	H	2B	3B	HR	RBI	BB	SO	AVG	OBP	SLG	PRO+	BR/A	SB	CS	SBR	FA	FR	G/POS	TPR
1944	Bos-N	1	0	0	0	0	0	0	0	0	0	—	—	—			0	0		.000	0	R	0.0

■ BILL PATTON Patton, George William b: 10/7/12, Cornwall, Pa. d: 3/15/86, Philadelphia, Pa. BR/TR, 6'2", 180 lbs. Deb: 6/29/35

YEAR	TM/L	G	AB	R	H	2B	3B	HR	RBI	BB	SO	AVG	OBP	SLG	PRO+	BR/A	SB	CS	SBR	FA	FR	G/POS	TPR
1935	Phi-A	9	10	1	3	1	0	0	2	2	3	.300	.417	.400	113	0				1.000	0	/C-3	0.1

■ TOM PATTON Patton, Thomas Allen b: 9/5/35, Honey Brook, Pa. BR/TR, 5'9.5", 185 lbs. Deb: 4/30/57

YEAR	TM/L	G	AB	R	H	2B	3B	HR	RBI	BB	SO	AVG	OBP	SLG	PRO+	BR/A	SB	CS	SBR	FA	FR	G/POS	TPR
1957	Bal-A	1	2	0	0	0	0	0	0	0	2	.000	.000	.000	-99	-1	0	0	0	1.000	1	/C-1	0.1

■ LOU PAUL Paul, Louis BR/TR, Deb: 9/5/1876

YEAR	TM/L	G	AB	R	H	2B	3B	HR	RBI	BB	SO	AVG	OBP	SLG	PRO+	BR/A	SB	CS	SBR	FA	FR	G/POS	TPR
1876	Phi-N	3	12	2	2	1	0	0	0	0	0	.167	.167	.250	37	-1				.643	-2	/C-3	-0.3

■ CARLOS PAULA Paula, Carlos (Conill) b: 11/28/27, Havana, Cuba d: 4/25/83, Miami, Fla. BR/TR, 6'3", 195 lbs. Deb: 9/6/54

YEAR	TM/L	G	AB	R	H	2B	3B	HR	RBI	BB	SO	AVG	OBP	SLG	PRO+	BR/A	SB	CS	SBR	FA	FR	G/POS	TPR
1954	Was-A	9	24	2	4	1	0	0	2	2	4	.167	.231	.208	22	-3	0	0	0	1.000	1	/O-6	-0.2
1955	Was-A	115	351	34	105	20	7	6	45	17	43	.299	.333	.447	115	5	2	3	-1	.941	-2	O-85	-0.2
1956	Was-A	33	82	8	15	2	1	3	13	8	15	.183	.256	.341	56	-6	0	2	-1	.974	-1	O-20	-0.9
Total	3	157	457	44	124	23	8	9	60	27	62	.271	.315	.416	99	-3	2	5	-2	.950	-2	O-111	-1.3

■ GENE PAULETTE Paulette, Eugene Edward b: 5/26/1891, Centralia, Ill. d: 2/8/66, Little Rock, Ark. BR/TR, 6', 150 lbs. Deb: 6/16/11

YEAR	TM/L	G	AB	R	H	2B	3B	HR	RBI	BB	SO	AVG	OBP	SLG	PRO+	BR/A	SB	CS	SBR	FA	FR	G/POS	TPR
1911	NY-N	10	12	1	2	0	0	0	1	0	1	.167	.167	.167	-6	-2	0			.938	-1	/1-7,S-1,3-1	-0.3
1916	StL-A	5	4	1	2	0	0	0	0	1	1	.500	.600	.500	242	1	0			.000	0	H	0.1
1917	StL-A	12	22	3	4	0	0	0	0	3	3	.182	.280	.182	43	-1	0			.982	0	/1-5,2-3,3-1	-0.1
	StL-N	95	332	32	88	21	7	0	34	16	16	.265	.330	.370	109	2	9			.993	-1	1-93	0.0
1918	StL-N	125	461	33	126	15	3	0	52	27	16	.273	.316	.319	97	-2	11			.983	5	1-97,S-12/2-7,O3P	0.0
1919	StL-N	43	144	11	31	6	0	0	11	9	6	.215	.261	.257	60	-7	4			.990	2	1-35/S-3	-0.7
	Phi-N	67	243	20	63	8	3	1	31	19	10	.259	.316	.329	88	-3	10			.957	0	2-58,O-10/1-1	-0.1
	Yr	110	387	31	94	14	3	1	42	28	16	.243	.296	.302	78	-10	14			.957	2	2-58,1-36,O-10,S-3	-0.8
1920	Phi-N	143	562	59	162	16	6	1	36	33	16	.288	.332	.343	90	-7	9	8	-2	.988	6	*1-139/S-2	-0.6
Total	6	500	1780	160	478	66	19	2	165	108	69	.269	.314	.330	92	-19	43	8		.988	11	1-377/2-68,SO3P	-2.0

■ SI PAUXTIS Pauxtis, Simon Francis b: 7/20/1885, Pittston, Pa. d: 3/13/61, Philadelphia, Pa. BR/TR, 6' ", 175 lbs. Deb: 9/18/09

YEAR	TM/L	G	AB	R	H	2B	3B	HR	RBI	BB	SO	AVG	OBP	SLG	PRO+	BR/A	SB	CS	SBR	FA	FR	G/POS	TPR
1909	Cin-N	4	8	2	1	1	0	0	2	1		.125	.222	.125	8	-1	0			1.000	-1	/C-4	-0.2

■ DON PAVLETICH Pavletich, Donald Stephen b: 7/13/38, Milwaukee, Wis. BR/TR, 5'11", 209 lbs. Deb: 4/20/57

YEAR	TM/L	G	AB	R	H	2B	3B	HR	RBI	BB	SO	AVG	OBP	SLG	PRO+	BR/A	SB	CS	SBR	FA	FR	G/POS	TPR
1957	Cin-N	1	1	0	0	0	0	0	0	0	0	.000	.000	.000	-93	-0	0	0	0	.000	0	H	0.0
1959	Cin-N	1	0	1	0	0	0	0	0	0	0	—	—	—			0	0	0	.000	0	R	0.0
1962	Cin-N	34	63	7	14	3	0	1	7	8	18	.222	.310	.317	67	-3	0	0	0	1.000	1	1-25/C-2	-0.3
1963	Cin-N	71	183	18	38	11	0	5	18	17	12	.208	.275	.350	76	-6	0	0	0	.991	-3	1-57,C-13	-1.1
1964	Cin-N	34	91	12	22	4	0	5	11	10	17	.242	.317	.451	109	1	0	0	0	.983	-3	C-27/1-1	-0.1
1965	Cin-N	68	191	25	61	11	1	8	32	23	27	.319	.395	.513	144	11	1	1	-0	.986	-2	C-54/1-9	1.1
1966	Cin-N	83	235	29	69	13	2	12	38	18	37	.294	.346	.519	126	8	1	0	0	.975	-10	C-55,1-10	0.1
1967	Cin-N	74	231	25	55	14	3	6	34	21	38	.238	.313	.403	93	-2	2	1	0	.986	-5	C-66/1-6,3-1	-0.4
1968	Cin-N	46	98	11	28	9	1	8		23	20	.286	.382	.398	117	2	1	0	0	1.000	0	1-22/C-5	0.1
1969	Chi-A	78	188	26	46	12	0	6	33	28	45	.245	.343	.404	103	1	0	0	0	.974	-6	C-51,1-13	-0.4
1970	Bos-A	32	65	4	9	1	0	0	6	10	15	.138	.253	.185	21	-7	0	0	0	1.000	1	1-16,C-10	-0.7
1971	Bos-A	16	27	5	7	3	0	1	6	5	8	.259	.375	.407	113	1	0	0	0	.973	-2	C-8	-0.1
Total	12	536	1373	163	349	73	8	46	193	148	237	.254	.330	.420	103	6	5	2	0	.983	-31	C-291,1-159/3-1	-1.8

■ TED PAWELEK Pawelek, Theodore John "Porky" b: 8/15/19, Chicago Heights, Ill. d: 2/12/64, Chicago Heights, Ill. BL/TR, 5'10.5", 202 lbs. Deb: 9/13/46

YEAR	TM/L	G	AB	R	H	2B	3B	HR	RBI	BB	SO	AVG	OBP	SLG	PRO+	BR/A	SB	CS	SBR	FA	FR	G/POS	TPR
1946	Chi-N	4	4	0	1	1	0	0		0	0	.250	.250	.500	112	0	1	0		1.000	-0	/C-1	0.0

YEAR	TM/L	G	AB	R	H	2B	3B	HR	RBI	BB	SO	AVG	OBP	SLG	PRO+	BR/A	SB	CS	SBR	FA	FR	G/POS	TPR
■ STAN PAWLOSKI			Pawloski, Stanley Walter		b: 9/6/31, Wanamie, Pa.			BR/TR, 6'1", 175 lbs.			Deb: 9/24/55											
1955	Cle-A	2	8	0	1	0	0	0	0	0	2	.125	.125	.125	-31	-1	0	0	0	1.000	1	/2-2	0.0
■ FRED PAYNE			Payne, Frederick Thomas		b: 9/2/1880, Camden, N.Y.		d: 1/16/54, Camden, N.Y.		BR/TR, 5'10", 162 lbs.		Deb: 4/21/06											
1906	Det-A	72	222	23	60	5	5	0	20	13		.270	.316	.338	102	0	4			.966	-1	C-47,O-17	0.4
1907	*Det-A	53	169	17	28	2	2	0	14	7		.166	.221	.201	34	-13	4			.981	3	C-46/O-5	-0.7
1908	Det-A	20	45	3	3	0	0	0	2	3		.067	.176	.067	-20	-6				.954	-3	C-17/O-1	-0.9
1909	Chi-A	32	82	8	20	2	0	0	12	5		.244	.295	.268	82	-2	0			.987	-2	C-27/O-3	-0.1
1910	Chi-A	91	252	17	56	5	4	0	19	11		.222	.260	.274	70	-9	6			.974	-5	C-78/O-2	-0.7
1911	Chi-A	66	133	14	27	2	1	1	19	8		.203	.259	.256	45	-10	6			.963	-4	C-56	-1.0
Total	6	334	903	82	194	16	12	1	86	47		.215	.265	.262	64	-39	21			.972	-11	C-271/O-28	-3.0
■ GEORGE PAYNTER			Paynter, George Washington (b: George Washington Paner)																				
			b: 7/6/1871, Cincinnati, Ohio		d: 10/1/50, Cincinnati, Ohio		BR/TR, 5'9", 125 lbs.		Deb: 8/12/1894														
1894	StL-N	1	4	0	0	0	0	0	1	0		.000	.200	.000	-48	-1	1			1.000	1	/O-1	0.0
■ JOHNNY PEACOCK			Peacock, John Gaston		b: 1/10/10, Fremont, N.C.		d: 10/17/81, Wilson, N.C.		BL/TR, 5'11", 165 lbs.		Deb: 9/23/37											
1937	Bos-A	9	32	3	10	2	1	0	6	1	0	.313	.333	.438	89	-1	0	0	0	.980	1	/C-9	0.1
1938	Bos-A	72	195	29	59	7	1	1	39	17	4	.303	.358	.364	78	-6	4	1	1	.984	-9	C-57/1-1,O-1	-1.1
1939	Bos-A	92	274	33	76	11	4	0	36	29	11	.277	.347	.347	75	-10	1	1	-0	.972	-8	C-84	-1.2
1940	Bos-A	63	131	20	37	4	1	0	13	23	10	.282	.390	.328	85	-2	1	1	-0	.994	-6	C-48	-0.6
1941	Bos-A	79	261	28	74	20	1	0	27	21	3	.284	.339	.368	85	-6	2	1	-0	.988	-4	C-70	-0.3
1942	Bos-A	88	286	17	76	7	3	0	25	21	11	.266	.316	.311	74	-10	1	1	-0	.988	-6	C-82	-1.0
1943	Bos-A	48	114	7	23	3	1	0	7	10	9	.202	.266	.246	49	-7	1	1	-0	.972	-1	C-32	-0.7
1944	Bos-A	4	4	0	0	0	0	0	0	0	0	.000	.000	.000	-99	-1	0	0	0	1.000	0	/C-2	-0.1
	Phi-N	83	253	21	57	9	3	0	21	31	15	.225	.310	.285	70	-9				.990	1	C-73/2-1	-0.4
1945	Phi-N	33	74	6	15	0	0	0	6	6	0	.203	.262	.284	53	-5	1			.969	-5	C-23	-0.9
	Bro-N	48	110	11	28	5	1	0	14	24	10	.255	.388	.318	98	1	2			.975	1	C-38	0.3
	Yr	81	184	17	43	11	1	0	20	30	10	.234	.341	.304	82	-4	3			.973	-5	C-61	-0.6
Total	9	619	1734	175	455	74	16	1	194	183	73	.262	.333	.325	76	-56	14	6		.983	-37	C-518/2-1,O-1,1-1	-5.9
■ ELIAS PEAK			Peak, Elias		b: 5/23/1859, Philadelphia, Pa.		d: 12/17/16, Philadelphia, Pa.		Deb: 4/19/1884														
1884	Bos-U	1	3	2	2	0	0	0		1		.667	.750	.667	338	1				1.000	-0	/O-1	0.1
	Phi-U	54	215	35	42	6	4	0		7		.195	.221	.260	49	-20				.825	-6	2-47/O-5,S-2	-2.2
	Yr	55	218	37	44	6	4	0		8		.202	.230	.266	54	-19				.825	-6	2-47/O-6,S-2	-2.1
■ HARRY PEARCE			Pearce, Harry James		b: 7/12/1889, Philadelphia, Pa.		d: 1/8/42, Philadelphia, Pa.		BR/TR, 5'9", 158 lbs.		Deb: 10/2/17											
1917	Phi-N	7	16	2	4	3	0	0	2	0	4	.250	.294	.438	118	0				.967	5	/S-4	0.5
1918	Phi-N	60	164	16	40	3	2	0	18	9	31	.244	.295	.287	73	-5	5			.944	5	2-46/S-2,1-1,3-1	0.3
1919	Phi-N	68	244	24	44	3	3	0	9	8	27	.180	.209	.217	26	-22	6			.948	-1	2-43,S-23/3-2	-2.2
Total	3	135	424	42	88	9	5	0	29	17	62	.208	.247	.252	48	-27	11			.946	9	/2-89,S-29,3-3,1-1	-1.4
■ DICKEY PEARCE			Pearce, Richard J.		b: 2/29/1836, Brooklyn, N.Y.		d: 10/12/08, Wareham, Mass.		BR/TR, 5'3.5", 161 lbs.		Deb: 5/18/1871	MU										
1871	Mut-n	33	163	31	44	5	0	0	20	4	1	.270	.287	.301	76	-3	0	0	0	.793	-7	*S-33	-0.6
1872	Mut-n	44	206	32	40	1	1	1	23	4	1	.194	.210	.223	35	-14	1	1	-0	.839	-5	*S-42/O-2,M	-1.0
1873	Atl-n	55	262	42	72	5	0	1	26	8	2	.275	.296	.305	88	-1	2	0	1	.780	-1	*S-55/1-1,2-1	0.2
1874	Atl-n	56	255	48	75	1	0	0	25	6	1	.294	.310	.298	109	4	1	0	0	.845	9	*S-56/3-2,2-1	0.9
1875	StL-n	70	311	51	77	6	3	0	29	7	7	.248	.264	.286	100	2	8	3	1	.830	13	*S-70/P-2,M	1.1
1876	StL-N	25	102	12	21	1	0	0	10	3	5	.206	.229	.216	51	-5				.902	5	S-23/O-1,2-1	0.0
1877	StL-N	8	29	1	5	0	0	0	4	1	4	.172	.200	.172	19	-3				.950	5	/S-8	0.0
Total	5 n	258	1197	204	308	18	4	2	123	29	12	.257	.275	.284	84	-12	12	4	1	.818	19	S-256/P-2,3-2,2O1	0.6
Total	2	33	131	13	26	1	0	0	14	4	9	.198	.222	.206	44	-7				.914	7	/S-31,2-1,O-1	0.0
■ DUCKY PEARCE			Pearce, William C.		b: 3/17/1885, Corning, Ohio		d: 5/22/33, Brownstown, Ind.		BR/TR, 6'1", 185 lbs.		Deb: 7/1/08											
1908	Cin-N	2	2	0	0	0	0	0	0	0		.000	.000	.000	-99	-0	0			1.000	1	/C-2	0.1
1909	Cin-N	2	2	0	0	0	0	0	0	0		.000	.000	.000	-99	-0	0			1.000	-0	/C-2	-0.1
Total	2	4	4	0	0	0	0	0	0	0		.000	.000	.000	-99	-1	0			1.000	1	/C-4	0.0
■ ALBIE PEARSON			Pearson, Albert Gregory		b: 9/12/34, Alhambra, Cal.		BL/TL, 5'5", 141 lbs.		Deb: 4/14/58														
1958	Was-A	146	530	63	146	25	5	3	33	64	31	.275	.356	.358	99	1	7	8	-3	.980	6	*O-141	-0.4
1959	Was-A	25	80	9	15	1	0	0	2	14	3	.188	.309	.200	43	-6	1	1	-0	.974	-2	O-21	-1.0
	Bal-A	80	138	22	32	4	2	0	6	13	5	.232	.298	.290	64	-7	4	0	1	.987	-7	O-50	-1.4
	Yr	105	218	31	47	5	2	0	8	27	8	.216	.302	.257	56	-13	5	1	1	.983	-9	O-71	-2.4
1960	Bal-A	48	82	17	20	2	0	1	6	17	3	.244	.374	.305	87	-1	4	0	1	.975	-5	O-32	-0.6
1961	LA-A	144	427	92	123	21	3	7	41	96	40	.288	.422	.400	109	9	11	3	2	.956	-1	*O-113	0.3
1962	LA-A	160	614	**115**	160	29	6	5	42	95	36	.261	.361	.352	96	-1	15	6	1	.989	9	*O-160	-0.1
1963	LA-A★	154	578	92	176	26	5	6	47	92	37	.304	.403	.398	133	30	17	10	-1	.983	7	*O-148	2.9
1964	LA-A	107	265	34	59	5	1	2	16	35	22	.223	.316	.272	72	-9	6	4	-1	.978	-4	O-66	-1.7
1965	Cal-A	122	360	41	100	17	2	4	21	51	17	.278	.370	.369	114	8	12	1	3	.988	-4	*O-101	0.4
1966	Cal-A	2	3	0	0	0	0	0	0	0	0	.000	.000	.000	-99	-1	0	0	0	.000	-0	/O-1	-0.1
Total	9	988	3077	485	831	130	24	28	214	477	195	.270	.370	.355	102	24	77	33	3	.980	1	O-833	-1.7
■ CHARLIE PECHOUS			Pechous, Charles Edward		b: 10/5/1896, Chicago, Ill.		d: 9/13/80, Kenosha, Wis.		BR/TR, 6', 170 lbs.		Deb: 9/14/15											
1915	Chi-F	18	51	4	9	3	0	0	4	4	15	.176	.236	.235	35	-5	1			.938	-1	3-18	-0.6
1916	Chi-N	22	69	5	10	1	1	0	4	3	21	.145	.181	.188	12	-7	1			.940	8	3-22	0.2
1917	Chi-N	13	41	2	10	0	0	0	1	2	9	.244	.295	.244	61	-2	1			1.000	-2	/3-7,S-5	-0.4
Total	3	53	161	11	29	4	1	0	9	9	45	.180	.228	.217	32	-14	3			.947	6	/3-47,S-5	-0.8
■ HAL PECK			Peck, Harold Arthur		b: 4/20/17, Big Bend, Wis.		d: 4/13/95, Milwaukee, Wis.		BL/TL, 5'11", 175 lbs.		Deb: 5/13/43											
1943	Bro-N	1	1	0	0	0	0	0	0	0	0	.000	.000	.000	-99	-0	0			.000	0	H	0.0
1944	Phi-A	2	8	0	2	0	0	0	1	0	2	.250	.250	.250	44	-1	0	2	-1	1.000	0	/O-2	-0.2
1945	Phi-A	112	449	51	124	22	9	5	39	37	28	.276	.331	.399	112	5	5	3	-0	.943	-9	*O-110	-1.1
1946	Phi-A	48	150	14	37	8	2	1	11	16	14	.247	.319	.367	92	-2	1	2	-1	.981	-3	O-35	-0.8
1947	Cle-A	114	392	58	115	18	2	8	44	27	31	.293	.342	.411	112	5	8	4	-1	.983	-7	O-97	-0.8
1948	*Cle-A	45	63	12	18	5	0	0	8	4	8	.286	.328	.333	78	-2	1	0	0	1.000	0	/O-9	-0.4
1949	Cle-A	33	29	1	9	1	0	0	9	3	3	.310	.375	.345	93	-0	0	1	-1	1.000	-1	/O-2	-0.1
Total	7	355	1092	136	305	52	13	15	112	87	86	.279	.334	.392	106	5	10	10		.965	-21	O-255	-3.4
■ ROGER PECKINPAUGH			Peckinpaugh, Roger Thorpe		b: 2/5/1891, Wooster, Ohio		d: 11/17/77, Cleveland, Ohio		BR/TR, 5'10.5", 165 lbs.		Deb: 9/15/10	M									
1910	Cle-A	15	45	1	9	0	0	0	6	1		.200	.234	.200	36	-3	3			.906	-6	S-14	-1.0
1912	Cle-A	70	236	18	50	4	1	1	22	16		.212	.262	.250	45	-17	11			.924	-2	S-68	-1.4
1913	Cle-A	1	0	1	0	0	0	0	0	0		—	—	—	—		0			.000	0	H	0.0
	NY-A	95	340	35	91	10	7	1	32	24	47	.268	.316	.347	94	-4	19			.931	-6	S-93	-0.1
	Yr	96	340	36	91	10	7	1	32	24	47	.268	.316	.347	94	-4	19			.931	-6	S-93	-0.1
1914	NY-A	157	570	55	127	14	6	3	51	51	73	.223	.288	.284	72	-20	38	17	1	.956	3	*S-157,M	-0.3
1915	NY-A	142	540	67	119	18	7	5	44	49	72	.220	.289	.307	79	-16	19	12	-2	.942	11	*S-142	0.5
1916	NY-A	145	552	65	141	22	8	4	58	62	50	.255	.332	.346	101	1	18			.946	-1	*S-145	1.1
1917	NY-A	148	543	63	141	17	0	41	64	46		.260	.340	.330	103	3	17			.934	10	*S-148	2.2
1918	NY-A	122	446	59	103	15	3	0	43	43	41	.231	.303	.278	74	-14	12			.961	25	*S-122	1.8
1919	NY-A	122	453	89	138	20	2	7	33	59	37	.305	.390	.404	122	15	10			.943	-8	*S-121	5.1
1920	NY-A	139	534	109	144	26	6	8	54	72	47	.270	.356	.386	93	-5	8	12	-5	.962	3	*S-137	0.6
1921	*NY-A	149	577	128	166	25	7	8	71	84	44	.288	.380	.397	96	-1	2	2	-1	.948	-5	*S-149	0.7

YEAR	TM/L	G	AB	R	H	2B	3B	HR	RBI	BB	SO	AVG	OBP	SLG	PRO+	BR/A	SB	CS	SBR	FA	FR	G/POS	TPR
1922	Was-A	147	520	62	132	14	4	2	48	55	36	.254	.329	.308	70	-22	11	6	-0	.951	20	*S-147	1.3
1923	Was-A	154	568	73	150	18	4	2	62	64	30	.264	.340	.320	78	-17	10	8	-2	.948	**23**	*S-154	1.9
1924	*Was-A	155	523	72	142	20	5	2	73	72	45	.272	.360	.340	84	-11	9	6	-1	.963	9	*S-155	1.3
1925	*Was-A	126	422	67	124	16	4	4	64	49	23	.294	.367	.379	91	-5	13	4	2	.952	-16	*S-124/1-1	-0.5
1926	Was-A	57	147	19	35	4	1	1	14	28	12	.238	.360	.299	75	-4	3	0	1	.960	-1	S-46/1-1	0.0
1927	Chi-A	68	217	23	64	6	3	0	23	21	6	.295	.360	.350	87	-4	2	3	-1	.964	-1	S-60	0.0
Total	17	2012	7233	1006	1876	256	75	48	739	814	<u>609</u>	.259	.336	.335	87	-122	205	<u>70</u>		.949	97	*S-1982/1-2	13.2

■ BILL PECOTA
Pecota, William Joseph b: 2/16/60, Redwood City, Cal. BR/TR, 6'2", 195 lbs. Deb: 9/19/86

YEAR	TM/L	G	AB	R	H	2B	3B	HR	RBI	BB	SO	AVG	OBP	SLG	PRO+	BR/A	SB	CS	SBR	FA	FR	G/POS	TPR
1986	KC-A	12	29	3	6	2	0	0	2	3	3	.207	.303	.276	58	-2	0	2	-1	.974	6	3-12/S-2,D-4	0.3
1987	KC-A	66	156	22	43	5	1	3	14	15	25	.276	.343	.378	89	-2	5	0	2	.977	7	S-36,3-17,2-15/D-1	0.9
1988	KC-A	90	178	25	37	3	3	1	15	18	34	.208	.288	.275	58	-10	7	2	1	.976	11	S-41,3-21,1/OD2C	0.4
1989	KC-A	65	83	21	17	4	2	3	5	7	9	.205	.275	.434	91	-1	5	0	2	.988	6	S-29,O-15,2/31D	0.5
1990	KC-A	87	240	43	58	15	2	5	20	33	39	.242	.336	.383	102	1	8	5	-1	.986	6	2-50,S-21,3/O1D	0.9
1991	KC-A	125	398	53	114	23	2	6	45	41	45	.286	.356	.399	108	5	16	7	1	.983	-13	*3-102,2-34/S1DOP	-0.6
1992	NY-N	117	269	28	61	13	0	2	26	25	40	.227	.295	.297	69	-11	9	3	1	.926	10	3-48,S-39,2-38/P1	0.2
1993	*Atl-N	72	62	17	20	2	1	0	5	2	5	.323	.344	.387	94	-1	1	1	-0	1.000	1	3-23/2-4,O-1	0.1
1994	Atl-N	64	112	11	24	5	0	2	16	16	16	.214	.313	.313	62	-6	1	0	0	.974	7	3-31/2-1,O-1	0.2
Total	9	698	1527	223	380	72	11	22	148	160	216	.249	.324	.354	87	-26	52	20	4	.968	39	3-272,S-177,2/O1DPC	2.9

■ LES PEDEN
Peden, Leslie Earl "Gooch" b: 9/17/23, Azle, Tex. BR/TR, 6'1.5", 212 lbs. Deb: 4/17/53 C

YEAR	TM/L	G	AB	R	H	2B	3B	HR	RBI	BB	SO	AVG	OBP	SLG	PRO+	BR/A	SB	CS	SBR	FA	FR	G/POS	TPR
1953	Was-A	9	28	4	7	1	0	1	1	4	3	.250	.344	.393	101	-0	0	0	0	1.000	-1	/C-8	0.0

■ STU PEDERSON
Pederson, Stuart Russell b: 1/28/60, Palo Alto, Cal. BL/TL, 6', 185 lbs. Deb: 9/8/85

YEAR	TM/L	G	AB	R	H	2B	3B	HR	RBI	BB	SO	AVG	OBP	SLG	PRO+	BR/A	SB	CS	SBR	FA	FR	G/POS	TPR
1985	LA-N	8	4	1	0	0	0	0	1	0	2	.000	.000	.000	-1	-0	0	0	0	1.000	-1	/O-5	-0.3

■ JORGE PEDRE
Pedre, Jorge Enrique b: 10/12/66, Culver City, Cal. BR/TR, 5'11", 210 lbs. Deb: 9/7/91

YEAR	TM/L	G	AB	R	H	2B	3B	HR	RBI	BB	SO	AVG	OBP	SLG	PRO+	BR/A	SB	CS	SBR	FA	FR	G/POS	TPR
1991	KC-A	10	19	2	5	1	1	0	3	3	5	.263	.364	.421	116	0	0	0	0	.971	-0	/C-9,1-1	0.1
1992	Chi-N	4	4	0	0	0	0	0	0	0	1	.000	.000	.000	-98	-1	0	0	0	1.000	-1	/C-4	-0.2
Total	2	14	23	2	5	1	1	0	3	3	6	.217	.308	.348	81	-1	0	0	0	.973	-1	/C-13,1-1	-0.1

■ AL PEDRIQUE
Pedrique, Alfredo Jose (Garcia) b: 8/11/60, Aragua, Venez. BR/TR, 6' ", 155 lbs. Deb: 4/14/87

YEAR	TM/L	G	AB	R	H	2B	3B	HR	RBI	BB	SO	AVG	OBP	SLG	PRO+	BR/A	SB	CS	SBR	FA	FR	G/POS	TPR
1987	NY-N	5	6	1	0	0	0	0	1	2	0	.000	.143	.000	-61	-1	0	0	0	1.000	1	/S-4,2-1	0.0
	Pit-N	88	246	23	74	10	1	3	27	18	27	.301	.356	.362	90	-3	5	4	-1	.968	-12	S-76/3-3,2-2	-0.9
	Yr	93	252	24	74	10	1	3	27	19	29	.294	.350	.353	87	-4	5	4	-1	.969	-10	S-80/2-3,3-3	-0.9
1988	Pit-N	50	128	7	23	5	0	0	4	8	17	.180	.234	.219	31	-11	0	0	0	.974	2	S-46/3-5	-0.7
1989	Det-A	31	69	1	14	3	0	0	5	2	15	.203	.225	.246	34	-6	0	0	0	.960	8	3-12,S-12/2-8	0.2
Total	3	174	449	32	111	18	1	3	36	29	61	.247	.299	.298	64	-22	5	4	-1	.971	-1	S-138/3-20,2-11	-1.4

■ CHICK PEDROES
Pedroes, Charles P. b: 10/27/1869, Chicago, Ill. d: 8/6/27, Chicago, Ill. Deb: 8/21/02

YEAR	TM/L	G	AB	R	H	2B	3B	HR	RBI	BB	SO	AVG	OBP	SLG	PRO+	BR/A	SB	CS	SBR	FA	FR	G/POS	TPR
1902	Chi-N	2	6	0	0	0	0	0	0	0		.000	.000	.000	-99	-1	0			1.000	-0	/O-2	-0.2

■ HOMER PEEL
Peel, Homer Hefner b: 10/10/02, Port Sullivan, Tex BR/TR, 5'9.5", 170 lbs. Deb: 9/13/27

YEAR	TM/L	G	AB	R	H	2B	3B	HR	RBI	BB	SO	AVG	OBP	SLG	PRO+	BR/A	SB	CS	SBR	FA	FR	G/POS	TPR
1927	StL-N	2	2	0	0	0	0	0	0	0	1	.000	.000	.000	-97	-1	0			.000	-1	/O-1	-0.1
1929	Phi-N	53	156	16	42	12	1	0	19	12	7	.269	.329	.359	66	-8	1			.990	-2	O-39/1-1	-1.2
1930	StL-N	26	73	9	12	2	0	0	10	3	4	.164	.197	.192	-5	-12	0			.968	-4	O-21	-1.6
1933	*NY-N	84	148	16	38	1	1	1	12	14	10	.257	.325	.297	80	-3	0			.962	-12	O-45	-1.8
1934	NY-N	21	41	7	8	0	0	1	3	1	2	.195	.214	.268	29	-4	0			.929	-3	O-10	-0.7
Total	5	186	420	48	100	15	2	2	44	30	24	.238	.294	.298	53	-29	1			.974	-22	O-116/1-1	-5.4

■ JACK PEERSON
Peerson, Jack Chiles b: 8/28/10, Brunswick, Ga. d: 10/23/66, Ft.Walton Beach, Fla. BR/TR, 5'11", 175 lbs. Deb: 9/7/35

YEAR	TM/L	G	AB	R	H	2B	3B	HR	RBI	BB	SO	AVG	OBP	SLG	PRO+	BR/A	SB	CS	SBR	FA	FR	G/POS	TPR
1935	Phi-A	10	19	3	6	1	0	0	1	1	1	.316	.350	.368	87	-0	0	1	0	.952	0	/S-4	0.0
1936	Phi-A	8	34	7	11	1	0	1	5	0	3	.324	.324	.412	82	-1	0	1	-1	.942	4	/S-7,2-1	0.2
Total	2	18	53	10	17	2	0	1	6	1	4	.321	.333	.396	84	-1	0	1	-1	.945	4	/S-11,2-1	0.2

■ CHARLIE PEETE
Peete, Charles "Mule" b: 2/22/29, Franklin, Va. d: 11/27/56, Caracas, Venez. BL/TR, 5'9.5", 190 lbs. Deb: 7/17/56

YEAR	TM/L	G	AB	R	H	2B	3B	HR	RBI	BB	SO	AVG	OBP	SLG	PRO+	BR/A	SB	CS	SBR	FA	FR	G/POS	TPR
1956	StL-N	23	52	3	10	2	2	0	6	6	10	.192	.288	.308	60	-3	0	2	-1	1.000	-1	O-21	-0.7

■ MONTE PEFFER
Peffer, Monte (b: Montague Pfeiffer) b: 10/8/1891, New York, N.Y. d: 9/27/41, New York, N.Y. BR/TR, 5'4.5", 147 lbs. Deb: 9/29/13

YEAR	TM/L	G	AB	R	H	2B	3B	HR	RBI	BB	SO	AVG	OBP	SLG	PRO+	BR/A	SB	CS	SBR	FA	FR	G/POS	TPR
1913	Phi-A	1	3	0	0	0	0	0	0	1	0	.000	.250	.000	-26	-0	0			.800	-0	/S-1	-0.1

■ JULIO PEGUERO
Peguero, Julio Cesar b: 9/7/68, San Isidro, D.R. BB/TR, 6', 160 lbs. Deb: 4/8/92

YEAR	TM/L	G	AB	R	H	2B	3B	HR	RBI	BB	SO	AVG	OBP	SLG	PRO+	BR/A	SB	CS	SBR	FA	FR	G/POS	TPR
1992	Phi-N	14	9	3	2	0	0	0	0	3	3	.222	.417	.222	86	0	0	0	0	1.000	-5	O-14	-0.5

■ STEVE PEGUES
Pegues, Steven Antone b: 5/21/68, Pontotoc, Miss. BR/TR, 6'2", 190 lbs. Deb: 7/6/94

YEAR	TM/L	G	AB	R	H	2B	3B	HR	RBI	BB	SO	AVG	OBP	SLG	PRO+	BR/A	SB	CS	SBR	FA	FR	G/POS	TPR
1994	Cin-N	11	10	1	3	0	0	0	1	3	.300	.364	.300	76	-0	0	0	0	.833	-1	/O-4	-0.1	
	Pit-N	7	26	1	10	2	0	0	2	1	0	.385	.407	.462	124	1	1	0	0	1.000	-1	/O-7	0.0
	Yr	18	36	2	13	2	0	0	2	4	5	.361	.395	.417	112	1	1	0	0	.929	-2	O-11	-0.1
1995	Pit-N	82	171	17	42	8	0	6	16	4	36	.246	.267	.398	71	-8	1	2	-1	.954	-5	O-53	-1.4
Total	2	100	207	19	55	10	0	6	18	6	41	.266	.290	.401	78	-7	2	2	-1	.950	-7	/O-64	-1.5

■ HEINIE PEITZ
Peitz, Henry Clement b: 11/28/1870, St.Louis, Mo. d: 10/23/43, Cincinnati, Ohio BR/TR, 5'11", 165 lbs. Deb: 10/15/1892 FC

YEAR	TM/L	G	AB	R	H	2B	3B	HR	RBI	BB	SO	AVG	OBP	SLG	PRO+	BR/A	SB	CS	SBR	FA	FR	G/POS	TPR
1892	StL-N	1	3	0	0	0	0	0	0	0	0	.000	.000	.000	-99	-1	0			1.000	-0	/C-1	-0.1
1893	StL-N	96	362	53	92	12	9	1	45	54	20	.254	.353	.345	86	-7	12			.948	9	C-74,S-11,O-10/1-5	0.6
1894	StL-N	99	338	52	89	19	9	3	49	43	21	.263	.348	.399	80	-12	14			.897	4	3-47,C-39,1-14,/P-1	-0.3
1895	StL-N	90	334	44	95	14	12	2	65	42		.284	.345	.416	97	-2	9			.937	1	C-71,1-11,3-10	0.5
1896	Cin-N	68	211	33	63	12	5	2	34	30	15	.299	.384	.431	108	2	7			.968	1	C-67	0.9
1897	Cin-N	77	266	35	78	11	7	1	44	18		.293	.340	.398	89	-5	3			**.979**	7	C-71/P-2	0.8
1898	Cin-N	105	330	49	90	15	5	1	43	35		.273	.348	.358	96	-2	9			.945	-3	*C-101	0.5
1899	Cin-N	93	290	45	79	13	2	1	43	45		.272	.374	.341	95	-0	11			.977	-7	C-91/P-1	0.5
1900	Cin-N	91	294	34	75	14	1	2	34	20		.255	.318	.330	81	-8	5			.958	6	C-80/1-8	0.5
1901	Cin-N	82	269	24	82	13	5	1	24	23		.305	.364	.401	130	11	3			.982	2	C-49,2-21/3-6,1-2	1.8
1902	Cin-N	112	387	54	122	23	7	1	60	24		.315	.369	.406	127	12	7			.919	-2	2-48,C-47/1-6,3-6	1.7
1903	Cin-N	105	358	45	93	15	3	0	42	37		.260	.331	.318	77	-11	7			.970	-2	C-78,1-11/3-9,2-4	-0.5
1904	Cin-N	84	272	32	66	13	2	0	30	14		.243	.282	.316	78	-8	1			.975	4	C-64,1-18/3-1	0.3
1905	Pit-N	88	278	18	62	10	0	0	27	24		.223	.289	.259	62	-13	2			.965	-11	C-87/2-1	-1.5
1906	Pit-N	40	125	13	30	8	0	0	20	13		.240	.321	.304	91	-1	1			.979	-8	C-38	0.3
1913	StL-N	3	4	1	1	0	0	0	0	0	0	.250	.250	.750	182	-0	0			.625	-2	/C-2,O-1	-0.1
Total	16	1234	4121	532	1117	191	66	16	560	409	<u>76</u>	.271	.342	.361	92	-46	91			.963	14	C-960/3-79,120SP	5.9

■ JOE PEITZ
Peitz, Joseph b: 11/8/1869, St.Louis, Mo. d: 12/4/19, St.Louis, Mo. Deb: 7/5/1894 F

YEAR	TM/L	G	AB	R	H	2B	3B	HR	RBI	BB	SO	AVG	OBP	SLG	PRO+	BR/A	SB	CS	SBR	FA	FR	G/POS	TPR
1894	StL-N	7	26	10	11	2	1	0		1		.423	.531	.731	202	5	2			.818	1	/O-7	0.3

■ EDDIE PELLAGRINI
Pellagrini, Edward Charles b: 3/13/18, Boston, Mass. BR/TR, 5'9", 165 lbs. Deb: 4/22/46

YEAR	TM/L	G	AB	R	H	2B	3B	HR	RBI	BB	SO	AVG	OBP	SLG	PRO+	BR/A	SB	CS	SBR	FA	FR	G/POS	TPR
1946	Bos-A	22	71	7	15	3	1	2	4	3	18	.211	.253	.366	68	-3	1	0	0	.891	-0	3-14/S-9	-0.3
1947	Bos-A	74	231	29	47	8	1	4	19	23	35	.203	.281	.299	57	-14	2	2	-1	.926	-6	3-42,S-26	-2.0
1948	StL-A	105	290	31	69	8	2	7	27	34	40	.238	.320	.307	65	-14	1	2	-1	.964	**24**	S-98	1.3
1949	StL-A	79	235	26	56	8	1	2	15	14	24	.238	.284	.306	54	-16	2	1	0	.961	-9	S-76	-0.4
1951	Phi-N	86	197	31	46	4	5	5	30	23	26	.234	.326	.381	91	-3	5	1	1	.990	-17	2-53/S-8,3-6	-1.6
1952	Cin-N	46	100	15	17	2	0	1	4	11	20	.170	.231	.220	26	-10	1	0	0	.983	10	2-22/1-8,S-1,3-1	0.1
1953	Pit-N	78	174	16	44	3	2	1	19	14	20	.253	.309	.362	75	-7	1	1	-0	.972	-4	2-31,3-12/S-3	-0.9
1954	Pit-N	73	125	12	27	2	1	0	16	16	21	.216	.290	.264	46	-8	0	0	0	.968	2	3-31/2-7,S-1	-0.8
Total	8	563	1423	167	321	42	13	20	133	128	201	.226	.295	.316	62	-76	13	7	-0	.956	15	S-222,2-113,3/1	-4.6

YEAR	TM/L	G	AB	R	H	2B	3B	HR	RBI	BB	SO	AVG	OBP	SLG	PRO+	BR/A	SB	CS	SBR	FA	FR	G/POS	TPR

■ LOUIS PELOUZE Pelouze, Louis H. BR/TR, 5'8", 170 lbs. Deb: 7/24/1886

| 1886 | StL-N | 1 | 3 | 0 | 0 | 0 | 0 | 0 | 0 | 0 | 2 | .000 | .000 | .000 | -99 | -1 | 0 | | | 1.000 | 0 | /O-1 | 0.0 |

■ DAN PELTIER Peltier, Daniel Edward b: 6/30/68, Clifton Park, N.Y. BL/TL, 6'1", 200 lbs. Deb: 6/26/92

1992	Tex-A	12	24	1	4	0	0	0	2	0	3	.167	.167	.167	-7	-3	0	0	0	.857	-3	O-10	-0.7
1993	Tex-A	65	160	23	43	7	1	1	17	20	27	.269	.354	.344	92	-1	0	4	-2	.950	-7	O-55/1-5	-1.1
1996	SF-N	31	59	3	15	2	0	0	9	7	9	.254	.333	.288	69	-2	0	0	0	1.000	-1	1-13/O-1	-0.5
Total	3	108	243	27	62	9	1	1	28	27	39	.255	.332	.313	77	-7	0	4	-2	.943	-11	/O-66,1-18	-2.3

■ JOHN PELTZ Peltz, John b: 4/23/1861, New Orleans, La. d: 2/27/06, New Orleans, La. BR/TR, Deb: 5/1/1884

1884	Ind-a	106	393	40	86	13	17	3			7	.219	.236	.361	95	-3				.818	4	*O-106	-0.1
1888	Bal-a	1	4	1	1	0	0	0	0	0		.250	.250	.250	62	-0	1			.500	-0	/O-1	-0.1
1890	Bro-a	98	384	55	87	9	6	1	33	32		.227	.289	.289	73	-13	10			.904	3	*O-98	-1.2
	Syr-a	5	17	2	3	1	1	0	2	3		.176	.300	.353	103	0	0			.857	0	/O-5	0.0
	Tol-a	20	73	8	18	2	2	0	13	3		.247	.286	.329	79	-2	7			.886	-2	O-20	-0.4
	Yr	123	474	65	108	12	9	1	48	38		.228	.289	.297	75	-16	17			.900	1	*O-123	-1.6
Total	3	230	871	106	195	25	26	4	48	45		.224	.266	.326	84	-18	18			.865	5	O-230	-1.8

■ BROCK PEMBERTON Pemberton, Brock b: 11/5/53, Tulsa, Okla. BB/TL, 6'3", 190 lbs. Deb: 9/10/74

1974	NY-N	11	22	0	4	0	0	0	0	0	3	.182	.182	.182	2	-3	0	1	-1	1.000	1	/1-4	-0.3
1975	NY-N	2	2	0	0	0	0	0	0	0	1	.000	.000	.000	-99	-1	0	0	0	.000	0	H	-0.1
Total	2	13	24	0	4	0	0	0	0	0	4	.167	.167	.167	-7	-3	0	1	-1	1.000	1	/1-4	-0.4

■ RUDY PEMBERTON Pemberton, Rudy Hector (Perez) b: 12/17/69, San Pedro De Macoris, D.R. BR/TR, 6'1", 185 lbs. Deb: 4/26/95

1995	Det-A	12	30	3	9	3	1	0	3	1	5	.300	.344	.467	109	0	0	0	0	1.000	-0	/O-8,D-3	0.0
1996	Bos-A	13	41	11	21	8	0	1	10	2	4	.512	.556	.780	225	8	3	1	0	1.000	-3	O-13	0.4
Total	2	25	71	14	30	11	1	1	13	3	9	.423	.468	.648	178	8	3	1	0	1.000	-4	/O-21,D-3	0.4

■ BERT PENA Pena, Adalberto (Rivera) b: 7/11/59, Santurce, P.R. BR/TR, 5'11", 165 lbs. Deb: 9/14/81

1981	Hou-N	4	2	0	1	0	0	0	0	0	0	.500	.500	.500	194	0	0	0	0	1.000	0	/S-3	0.0
1983	Hou-N	4	8	0	1	0	0	0	0	2	2	.125	.300	.125	23	-1	0	0	0	1.000	-1	/S-4	-0.2
1984	Hou-N	24	39	3	8	1	0	1	4	3	8	.205	.262	.308	64	-2	0	0	0	.956	6	S-21	0.5
1985	Hou-N	20	29	7	8	2	0	0	4	1	6	.276	.300	.345	82	-1	0	0	0	1.000	-1	/3-7,S-6,2-2	-0.1
1986	Hou-N	15	29	3	6	0	0	0	2	5	5	.207	.324	.241	60	-1	0	0	0	.907	5	S-10/3-2,2-1	0.1
1987	Hou-N	21	46	5	7	0	0	0	0	2	7	.152	.204	.152	-4	-7	0	0	0	.982	-1	S-19/3-1	-0.7
Total	6	88	153	18	31	4	0	1	10	13	28	.203	.269	.248	45	-12	0	0	0	.953	5	/S-63,3-10,2-3	-0.4

■ TONY PENA Pena, Antonio Francisco (Padilla) b: 6/4/57, Monte Cristi, D.R. BR/TR, 6', 181 lbs. Deb: 9/1/80 F

1980	Pit-N	8	21	1	9	1	1	0	1	0	4	.429	.429	.571	174	2	0	1	-1	.952	2	/C-6	0.3
1981	Pit-N	66	210	16	63	9	1	2	17	8	23	.300	.329	.381	98	-1	1	2	-1	.985	2	C-64	0.2
1982	Pit-N★	138	497	53	147	28	4	11	63	17	57	.296	.324	.435	107	3	2	5	-2	.982	-7	*C-137	0.0
1983	Pit-N	151	542	51	163	22	3	15	70	31	73	.301	.339	.435	110	6	6	7	-2	.992	-0	*C-149	1.1
1984	Pit-N★	147	546	77	156	27	2	15	78	36	79	.286	.334	.425	112	8	12	8	-1	.991	13	*C-146	2.8
1985	Pit-N★	147	546	53	136	27	2	10	59	29	67	.249	.287	.361	81	-15	12	8	-1	.988	9	*C-146/1-1	0.0
1986	Pit-N★	144	510	56	147	26	2	10	52	53	69	.288	.356	.435	107	6	9	10	-3	.981	5	*C-139/1-4	1.7
1987	*StL-N	116	384	40	82	13	4	5	44	36	54	.214	.283	.307	55	-25	6	1	-1	.988	-1	*C-112/1-4,O-2	-1.7
1988	StL-N	149	505	55	133	23	1	10	51	33	60	.263	.310	.372	94	-4	6	2	1	.994	6	*C-142/1-3	1.3
1989	StL-N★	141	424	36	110	17	2	4	37	35	33	.259	.319	.337	85	-8	5	3	-0	.997	11	*C-134/O-1	1.0
1990	*Bos-A	143	491	62	129	19	1	7	56	43	71	.263	.323	.348	84	-10	8	6	-1	.995	11	*C-142/1-1	0.8
1991	Bos-A	141	464	45	107	23	2	5	48	37	53	.231	.291	.321	66	-21	8	3	-1	.995	9	*C-140	-0.4
1992	Bos-A	133	410	39	99	21	1	1	38	24	61	.241	.285	.305	61	-21	3	1	-2	.993	11	*C-132	-0.3
1993	Bos-A	126	304	20	55	11	0	4	19	25	46	.181	.248	.257	34	-29	1	3	-2	.995	22	*C-125/D-1	-0.3
1994	Cle-A	40	112	18	33	8	1	2	10	9	11	.295	.347	.438	100	-0	0	1	-1	.996	5	C-40	0.6
1995	*Cle-A	91	263	25	69	15	0	5	28	14	44	.262	.302	.376	74	-10	1	0	-1	.987	10	C-91	0.5
1996	*Cle-A	67	174	14	34	4	0	1	27	15	25	.195	.259	.236	26	-20	0	1	-1	.992	7	C-67	-0.8
Total	17	1948	6403	661	1672	294	27	107	698	445	830	.261	.311	.366	84	-140	80	63	-14	.990	114	*C-1912/1-13,O-3,D	6.8

■ GERONIMO PENA Pena, Geronimo (Martinez) b: 3/29/67, Distrito Nacional, D.R. BB/TR, 6'1", 170 lbs. Deb: 9/5/90

1990	StL-N	18	45	5	11	2	0	0	2	4	14	.244	.320	.289	69	-2	1	1	-0	.982	-1	2-11	-0.3
1991	StL-N	104	185	38	45	8	3	5	17	18	45	.243	.327	.400	103	1	15	5	2	.976	-3	2-83/O-4	0.0
1992	StL-N	62	203	31	62	12	1	7	31	24	37	.305	.392	.478	150	14	13	8	-1	.984	8	2-57	2.3
1993	StL-N	74	254	34	65	19	2	5	30	25	71	.256	.332	.406	98	-1	13	5	1	.966	-1	2-64	0.2
1994	StL-N	83	213	33	54	13	1	11	34	24	54	.254	.346	.479	114	4	9	1	2	.990	-5	2-59/3-1	1.4
1995	StL-N	32	101	20	27	6	1	1	8	16	30	.267	.373	.376	98	-0	3	2	-0	.976	-2	2-25	-0.1
1996	Cle-A	5	9	1	1	0	0	1	2	1	4	.111	.200	.444	57	-1	0	0	0	.000	0	/3-3,2-1	-0.1
Total	7	378	1010	162	265	60	8	30	124	112	255	.262	.349	.427	111	16	54	22	3	.978	7	2-300/3-4,O-4	3.4

■ ROBERTO PENA Pena, Roberto Cesar "Baby" (b: Roberto Cesar Zapata (Pena)) b: 4/17/37, Santo Domingo, D.R. d: 7/23/82, Santiago, D.R. BR/TR, 5'8", 175 lbs. Deb: 4/12/65

1965	Chi-N	51	170	17	37	5	1	2	12	16	19	.218	.293	.294	64	-8	1	2	-1	.930	-10	S-50	-1.6
1966	Chi-N	6	17	0	3	2	0	0	1	0	4	.176	.176	.294	28	-2	0	0	0	.957	0	/S-5	-0.2
1968	Phi-N	138	500	56	130	13	2	1	38	34	63	.260	.310	.300	84	-9	3	5	-2	.954	6	*S-133	1.0
1969	SD-N	139	472	44	118	16	3	4	30	21	63	.250	.286	.322	73	-18	0	3	-2	.977	-23	S-65,2-33,3-27,1-12	-3.7
1970	Oak-A	19	58	4	15	1	0	0	3	3	4	.259	.295	.276	61	-3	1	1	-0	.961	-1	S-12/3-5	-0.4
	Mil-A	121	416	36	99	19	1	6	42	25	45	.238	.284	.310	63	-21	3	5	-2	.981	-16	S-99,2-15/1-7	-2.8
	Yr	140	474	40	114	20	1	6	45	28	49	.241	.286	.306	63	-24	4	6	-2	.979	-17	*S-111,2-15/1-7,3-5	-3.2
1971	Mil-A	113	274	17	65	9	1	2	28	15	37	.237	.279	.325	71	-11	2	1	-0	.996	-5	1-50,3-37,S-23,2-1	-1.8
Total	6	587	1907	174	467	65	10	13	154	114	235	.245	.291	.310	72	-72	10	17	-7	.962	-49	S-387/1-69,3-69,2	-9.4

■ ELMER PENCE Pence, Elmer Clair b: 8/17/1900, Valley Springs, Cal. d: 9/17/68, San Francisco, Cal. BR/TR, 6', 185 lbs. Deb: 8/23/22

| 1922 | Chi-A | 1 | 0 | 0 | 0 | 0 | 0 | 0 | 0 | 0 | 0 | — | — | — | — | | 0 | 0 | 0 | 1.000 | -0 | /O-1 | 0.0 |

■ JIM PENDLETON Pendleton, James Edward b: 1/7/24, St.Charles, Mo. d: 3/20/96, Houston, Tex. BR/TR, 6', 185 lbs. Deb: 4/17/53

1953	Mil-N	120	251	48	75	12	4	7	27	7	36	.299	.323	.462	108	2	6	5	-1	.961	-13	*O-105/S-7	-1.4
1954	Mil-N	71	173	20	38	3	1	1	16	4	21	.220	.237	.266	33	-17	2	4	-2	.950	-4	O-50	-2.3
1955	Mil-N	8	10	0	0	0	0	0	0	0	2	.000	.000	.000	-99	-3	0	0	0	1.000	0	/S-1,3-1,O-1	-0.3
1956	Mil-N	14	11	0	0	0	0	0	0	1	3	.000	.083	.000	-80	-3	0	0	0	1.000	0	/S-3,3-2,1-1,2-1	-0.3
1957	Pit-N	46	59	9	18	1	1	0	9	9	14	.305	.406	.356	110	1	0	1	-0	.917	-3	O-9,3-2,S-1	-0.2
1958	Pit-N	3	3	0	1	0	0	0	0	0	0	.333	.333	.333	79	-0	0	0	0	.000	0	H	-0.0
1959	Cin-N	65	113	13	29	5	2	3	9	8	18	.257	.311	.354	75	-4	3	0	1	.971	-0	O-24,3-16/S-3	-0.4
1962	Hou-N	117	321	30	79	12	2	8	36	14	57	.246	.282	.371	79	-11	0	0	-0	.963	-6	O-90/1-8,3-3,S-2	-2.1
Total	8	444	941	120	240	30	8	19	97	43	151	.255	.292	.365	76	-35	11	6	-0	.959	-26	O-279/3-24,S-17,12	-7.0

■ TERRY PENDLETON Pendleton, Terry Lee b: 7/16/60, Los Angeles, Cal. BB/TR, 5'9", 180 lbs. Deb: 7/18/84

1984	StL-N	67	262	37	85	16	3	1	33	16	32	.324	.363	.420	123	7	20	5	3	.943	9	3-66	1.9
1985	*StL-N	149	559	56	134	16	3	5	69	37	75	.240	.287	.306	66	-25	17	12	-2	.965	23	*3-149	-0.7
1986	StL-N	159	578	56	138	26	5	1	59	34	59	.239	.282	.306	63	-30	24	6	4	.962	24	*3-156/O-1	-0.5
1987	*StL-N	159	583	82	167	29	4	12	96	70	74	.286	.365	.412	103	4	19	12	-2	.949	16	*3-158	1.6
1988	StL-N	110	391	44	99	20	2	6	53	21	51	.253	.295	.361	86	-7	3	4	-1	.963	1	*3-101	0.3
1989	StL-N	162	613	83	162	28	5	13	74	44	81	.264	.314	.390	97	-3	9	5	-0	.971	30	*3-161	2.9
1990	StL-N	121	447	46	103	20	2	6	58	30	58	.230	.280	.324	66	-21	7	5	-1	.947	7	*3-117	-1.5
1991	*Atl-N	153	586	94	187	34	8	22	86	43	70	.319	.367	.517	138	28	10	2	2	.950	28	*3-148	5.9

YEAR	TM/L	G	AB	R	H	2B	3B	HR	RBI	BB	SO	AVG	OBP	SLG	PRO+	BR/A	SB	CS	SBR	FA	FR	G/POS	TPR
1992	*Atl-N★	160	640	98	**199**	39	1	21	105	37	67	.311	.349	.473	123	18	5	2	0	.960	13	*3-158	3.3
1993	*Atl-N	161	633	81	172	33	1	17	84	36	97	.272	.314	.408	91	-10	5	1	1	.959	12	*3-161	0.4
1994	Atl-N	77	309	25	78	18	3	7	30	12	57	.252	.280	.398	73	-13	2	0	1	.950	6	3-77	-0.6
1995	Fla-N	133	513	70	149	32	1	14	78	38	84	.290	.342	.439	104	2	1	2	-1	.952	0	*3-129	0.1
1996	Fla-N	111	406	30	102	20	1	7	58	26	75	.251	.301	.357	76	-15	0	2	-1	.961	7	*3-108	-0.9
	*Atl-N	42	162	21	33	6	0	4	17	15	36	.204	.271	.315	51	-12	2	1	0	.938	1	3-41	-1.1
	Yr	153	568	51	135	26	1	11	75	41	111	.238	.292	.345	68	-27	2	3	-1	.955	8	*3-149	-2.0
Total	13	1764	6682	823	1808	337	39	136	900	459	916	.271	.319	.394	93	-77	124	58	2	.957	187	*3-1730/O-1	11.0

■ SHANNON PENN
Penn, Shannon Dion   b: 9/11/69, Cincinnati, Ohio   BB/TR, 5'10", 160 lbs.   Deb: 4/28/95

YEAR	TM/L	G	AB	R	H	2B	3B	HR	RBI	BB	SO	AVG	OBP	SLG	PRO+	BR/A	SB	CS	SBR	FA	FR	G/POS	TPR
1995	Det-A	3	9	0	3	0	0	0	0	1	2	.333	.400	.333	94	-0	0	0	0	.864	2	/2-3	0.2
1996	Det-A	6	14	0	1	0	0	0	1	0	3	.071	.071	.071	-64	-3	0	0	0	.000	-0	/O-1,D-4	-0.4
Total	2	9	23	0	4	0	0	0	1	1	5	.174	.208	.174	-1	-3	0	0	0	.864	1	/D-4,2-3,O-1	-0.2

■ WILL PENNYFEATHER
Pennyfeather, William Nathaniel   b: 5/25/68, Perth Amboy, N.J.   BR/TR, 6'2", 195 lbs.   Deb: 6/27/92

YEAR	TM/L	G	AB	R	H	2B	3B	HR	RBI	BB	SO	AVG	OBP	SLG	PRO+	BR/A	SB	CS	SBR	FA	FR	G/POS	TPR
1992	Pit-N	15	9	2	2	0	0	0	0	0	0	.222	.222	.222	26	-1	0	0	0	1.000	-4	O-10	-0.5
1993	Pit-N	21	34	4	7	1	0	0	2	0	6	.206	.206	.235	18	-4	0	1	-1	1.000	-5	O-17	-1.0
1994	Pit-N	4	3	0	0	0	0	0	0	0	0	.000	.000	.000	-99	-1	0	0	0	.000	-0	/O-1	-0.1
Total	3	40	46	6	9	1	0	0	2	0	6	.196	.196	.217	11	-6	0	1	-1	1.000	-9	/O-28	-1.6

■ JIMMY PEOPLES
Peoples, James Elsworth   b: 10/8/1863, Big Beaver, Mich.   d: 8/29/20, Detroit, Mich.   TR, 5'8", 200 lbs.   Deb: 5/29/1884   U

YEAR	TM/L	G	AB	R	H	2B	3B	HR	RBI	BB	SO	AVG	OBP	SLG	PRO+	BR/A	SB	CS	SBR	FA	FR	G/POS	TPR
1884	Cin-a	69	267	28	45	2	2	1	16	6		.169	.187	.202	26	-22				.829		S-47,C-14,O-10/31	-1.9
1885	Cin-a	7	22	1	4	0	0	0	1	6		.182	.217	.182	27	-2				.826	-1	/C-5,P-2,O-1	-0.2
	Bro-a	41	151	21	30	4	1	3	15	5		.199	.229	.258	53	-8				.895	-2	C-37/S-2,1-1,3-1,O	-0.6
	Yr	48	173	22	34	4	1	1	16	6		.197	.228	.249	50	-10				.889	-4	C-42/P-2,O-2,S13	-0.8
1886	Bro-a	93	340	43	74	7	3	3	38	20		.218	.261	.282	70	-12	20			.879	19	C-76,S-14/O-8,3-1	1.2
1887	Bro-a	73	268	36	68	14	2	1	38	16		.254	.306	.332	77	-9	22			.853	-5	C-57/O-8,S-4,1-4,2	-0.8
1888	Bro-a	32	103	15	20	5	3	0	17	8		.194	.259	.301	79	-2	10			.904	10	C-25/S-5,O-2	0.9
1889	Col-a	29	100	13	23	6	2	1	16	6	8	.230	.274	.360	84	-3				.922	-4	C-22/O-5,2-2,S-1	-0.4
Total	6	344	1251	157	264	38	13	7	141	62	8	.211	.252	.279	62	-58	55			.886	15	C-236/S-73,O123P	-1.8

■ JOE PEPITONE
Pepitone, Joseph Anthony "Pepi"   b: 10/9/40, Brooklyn, N.Y.   BL/TL, 6'2", 200 lbs.   Deb: 4/10/62   C

YEAR	TM/L	G	AB	R	H	2B	3B	HR	RBI	BB	SO	AVG	OBP	SLG	PRO+	BR/A	SB	CS	SBR	FA	FR	G/POS	TPR
1962	NY-A	63	138	14	33	3	2	7	17	3	21	.239	.255	.442	86	-4	1	1	-0	1.000	-9	O-32,1-16	-1.5
1963	*NY-A★	157	580	79	157	16	3	27	89	23	63	.271	.307	.448	109	5	3	5	-2	.995	4	*1-143,O-16	0.0
1964	*NY-A★	160	613	71	154	12	3	28	100	24	63	.251	.283	.418	90	-10	2	1	0	.988	-6	*1-155,O-30	-2.4
1965	NY-A★	143	531	51	131	18	3	18	62	43	59	.247	.306	.394	98	-2	4	2	0	**.997**	-1	*1-115,O-41	-1.4
1966	NY-A	152	585	85	149	21	4	31	83	29	58	.255	.292	.463	118	10	4	3	-1	.995	1	*1-119,O-55	0.1
1967	NY-A	133	501	45	126	18	3	13	64	34	62	.251	.303	.377	104	1	1	3	-2	.976	6	*O-123/1-6	-0.2
1968	NY-A	108	380	41	93	9	3	15	56	37	45	.245	.313	.403	119	8	8	2	1	.980	-6	O-92,1-12	-0.3
1969	NY-A	135	513	49	124	16	3	27	70	30	42	.242	.285	.442	105	-1	8	6	-1	.995	-6	*1-132	-1.9
1970	Hou-N	75	279	44	70	9	5	14	35	18	28	.251	.299	.470	107	1	5	2	0	.995	-1	1-50,O-28	-0.5
	Chi-N	56	213	38	57	9	2	12	44	15	15	.268	.314	.498	102	1	0	2	-1	.992	2	O-56,1-13	-0.3
	Yr	131	492	82	127	18	7	26	79	33	43	.258	.306	.482	105	1	5	4	-1	.989	1	O-84,1-63	-0.8
1971	Chi-N	115	427	50	131	19	4	16	61	24	41	.307	.349	.482	117	8	1	2	-1	.990	-3	1-95,O-23	-0.6
1972	Chi-N	66	214	23	56	5	0	8	21	13	22	.262	.313	.397	91	-3	1	2	-1	.997	-0	1-66	-0.9
1973	Chi-N	31	112	16	30	3	0	3	18	8	6	.268	.322	.375	86	-2	3	1	0	.985	-1	1-28	-0.4
	Atl-N	3	11	0	4	0	0	0	1	1	1	.364	.417	.364	110	0	0	0	0	.963	-1	/1-3	-0.1
	Yr	34	123	16	34	3	0	3	19	9	7	.276	.331	.374	88	-2	3	1	0	.983	-1	1-31	-0.5
Total	12	1397	5097	606	1315	158	35	219	721	302	526	.258	.303	.432	105	12	41	32	-7	.993	-21	*1-953,O-496	-10.4

■ HENRY PEPLOSKI
Peploski, Henry Stephen "Pep"   b: 9/15/05, Garlin, Poland   d: 1/28/82, Dover, N.J.   BL/TR, 5'9", 155 lbs.   Deb: 9/19/29   F

YEAR	TM/L	G	AB	R	H	2B	3B	HR	RBI	BB	SO	AVG	OBP	SLG	PRO+	BR/A	SB	CS	SBR	FA	FR	G/POS	TPR
1929	Bos-N	6	10	1	2	0	0	0	1	1	3	.200	.273	.200	20	-1	0			1.000	-0	/3-2	-0.1

■ PEPPER PEPLOSKI
Peploski, Joseph Aloysius   b: 9/12/1891, Brooklyn, N.Y.   d: 7/13/72, New York, N.Y.   BR/TR, 5'8", 155 lbs.   Deb: 6/24/13   F

YEAR	TM/L	G	AB	R	H	2B	3B	HR	RBI	BB	SO	AVG	OBP	SLG	PRO+	BR/A	SB	CS	SBR	FA	FR	G/POS	TPR
1913	Det-A	2	4	1	2	0	0	0	0	0	0	.500	.500	.500	196	0	0			1.000	-1	/3-2	0.0

■ DON PEPPER
Pepper, Donald Hoyte   b: 10/8/43, Saratoga Sprgs., N.Y   BL/TR, 6'4.5", 215 lbs.   Deb: 9/10/66

YEAR	TM/L	G	AB	R	H	2B	3B	HR	RBI	BB	SO	AVG	OBP	SLG	PRO+	BR/A	SB	CS	SBR	FA	FR	G/POS	TPR
1966	Det-A	4	3	0	0	0	0	0	0	0	1	.000	.000	.000	-98	-1	0	0	0	1.000	-0	/1-1	-0.1

■ RAY PEPPER
Pepper, Raymond Watson   b: 8/5/05, Decatur, Ala.   d: 3/24/96, Belle Mina, Ala.   BR/TR, 6'2", 195 lbs.   Deb: 4/15/32

YEAR	TM/L	G	AB	R	H	2B	3B	HR	RBI	BB	SO	AVG	OBP	SLG	PRO+	BR/A	SB	CS	SBR	FA	FR	G/POS	TPR
1932	StL-N	21	57	3	14	2	1	0	7	5	13	.246	.306	.316	66	-3	1			.971	-0	O-17	-0.4
1933	StL-N	3	9	2	2	0	0	1	2	0	1	.222	.222	.556	110	0				1.000	-0	/O-2	0.0
1934	StL-A	148	564	71	168	24	6	7	101	29	67	.298	.333	.399	81	-17	1	4	-2	.963	5	*O-136	-1.9
1935	StL-A	92	261	20	66	15	3	4	37	20	32	.253	.300	.379	73	-11	0	2	-1	.982	-3	O-57	-1.6
1936	StL-A	75	124	13	35	5	0	2	23	5	23	.282	.310	.371	66	-7	0	2	-1	.941	-2	O-18	-1.0
Total	5	339	1015	109	285	46	10	14	170	59	136	.281	.321	.387	77	-38	2	8		.967	-1	O-230	-4.9

■ JACK PERCONTE
Perconte, John Patrick   b: 8/31/54, Joliet, Ill.   BL/TR, 5'10", 160 lbs.   Deb: 9/13/80

YEAR	TM/L	G	AB	R	H	2B	3B	HR	RBI	BB	SO	AVG	OBP	SLG	PRO+	BR/A	SB	CS	SBR	FA	FR	G/POS	TPR
1980	LA-N	14	17	2	4	0	0	0	2	2	1	.235	.316	.235	57	-1	3	0	1	1.000	3	/2-9	0.4
1981	LA-N	8	9	2	2	0	1	0	1	2	2	.222	.364	.444	133	0	1	1	-0	1.000	5	/2-2	0.5
1982	Cle-A	93	219	27	52	4	4	0	15	22	25	.237	.307	.292	66	-10	9	3	1	.976	8	2-82/D-2	0.2
1983	Cle-A	14	26	1	7	1	0	0	6	3	1	.269	.387	.308	91	-0	3	1	0	.950	8	2-13	0.8
1984	Sea-A	155	612	93	180	24	4	0	31	57	47	.294	.359	.346	97	-0	29	6	5	.981	0	*2-150	1.1
1985	Sea-A	125	485	60	128	17	7	2	23	50	36	.264	.336	.340	85	-9	31	2	8	.986	0	*2-125	0.4
1986	Chi-A	24	73	6	16	1	0	0	4	11	10	.219	.321	.233	52	-4	2	0	1	.990	-7	2-24	-1.0
Total	7	433	1441	191	389	47	16	2	76	149	123	.270	.342	.329	86	-23	78	13	16	.982	18	2-405/D-2	2.4

■ TONY PEREZ
Perez, Atanasio (Rigal)   b: 5/14/42, Camaguey, Cuba   BR/TR, 6'2", 205 lbs.   Deb: 7/26/64   FMC

YEAR	TM/L	G	AB	R	H	2B	3B	HR	RBI	BB	SO	AVG	OBP	SLG	PRO+	BR/A	SB	CS	SBR	FA	FR	G/POS	TPR
1964	Cin-N	12	25	1	2	1	0	0	1	3	9	.080	.179	.120	-14	-4	0	0	0	.981	-1	/1-6	-0.6
1965	Cin-N	104	281	40	73	14	4	12	47	21	67	.260	.316	.466	110	3	0	2	-1	.989	-2	1-93	-0.5
1966	Cin-N	99	257	25	68	10	4	4	39	14	44	.265	.308	.381	83	-6	1	0	0	.989	-5	1-75	-1.6
1967	Cin-N	156	600	78	174	28	7	26	102	33	102	.290	.331	.490	119	13	0	3	-2	.963	-22	*3-139,1-18/2-1	-1.5
1968	Cin-N★	160	625	93	176	25	7	18	92	51	92	.282	.342	.430	123	17	3	2	-0	.952	5	*3-160	2.6
1969	Cin-N★	160	629	103	185	31	2	37	122	63	131	.294	.360	.526	138	30	4	2	0	.937	1	*3-160	3.3
1970	*Cin-N★	158	587	107	186	28	6	40	129	83	134	.317	.405	.589	162	52	8	3	1	.923	-7	*3-153/1-8	4.3
1971	Cin-N	158	609	72	164	22	3	25	91	51	120	.269	.327	.438	117	12	4	1	1	.959	7	*3-148,1-44	1.8
1972	*Cin-N	136	515	64	146	33	7	21	90	55	121	.283	.353	.497	148	30	4	2	0	.993	-1	*1-136	1.4
1973	*Cin-N	151	564	73	177	33	3	27	101	74	117	.314	.396	.527	162	47	3	1	0	.991	-4	*1-151	3.3
1974	Cin-N★	158	596	81	158	28	2	28	101	61	112	.265	.335	.460	123	16	1	3	-2	**.996**	-6	*1-157	-0.1
1975	*Cin-N★	137	511	74	144	28	3	20	109	54	101	.282	.354	.466	124	15	1	2	-1	.993	-5	*1-132	0.1
1976	*Cin-N★	139	527	77	137	32	6	19	91	50	88	.260	.330	.452	117	10	10	5	0	.996	-4	*1-136	-0.2
1977	Mon-N	154	559	71	158	32	6	19	91	63	111	.283	.357	.463	122	17	4	3	-1	.992	9	*1-148	1.6
1978	Mon-N	148	544	63	158	38	3	14	78	38	104	.290	.339	.449	120	13	2	0	1	.991	-1	*1-145	0.4
1979	Mon-N	132	489	58	132	29	4	13	73	38	82	.270	.326	.425	104	2	2	5	-1	.991	-6	*1-129	-1.3
1980	Bos-A	151	585	73	161	31	3	25	105	41	93	.275	.324	.467	108	5	1	0	0	.993	-1	*1-137,D-13	-0.4
1981	Bos-A	84	306	35	77	11	3	9	39	27	66	.252	.312	.395	97	-2	0	2	0	.993	0	1-56,D-23	-0.6
1982	Bos-A	69	196	18	51	14	2	6	31	19	48	.260	.326	.444	103	1	0	1	-1	.857	0	D-46/1-2	-0.2
1983	*Phi-N	91	253	18	61	11	2	6	43	19	57	.241	.319	.372	92	-3	1	0	0	.998	1	1-69	-0.5
1984	Cin-N	71	137	9	33	6	1	2	15	11	21	.241	.297	.343	76	-4	0	0	0	.990	-2	1-31	-0.8
1985	Cin-N	72	183	25	60	8	0	6	33	22	22	.328	.400	.470	136	9	0	2	-1	.995	-2	1-50	0.4
1986	Cin-N	77	200	14	51	12	1	2	29	25	25	.255	.338	.355	87	-3	1	0	0	.984	-3	1-55	-1.0
Total	23	2777	9778	1272	2732	505	79	379	1652	925	1867	.279	.344	.463	122	270	49	33	-5	.992	-54	*1-1778,3-760/D2	9.9

YEAR	TM/L	G	AB	R	H	2B	3B	HR	RBI	BB	SO	AVG	OBP	SLG	PRO+	BR/A	SB	CS	SBR	FA	FR	G/POS	TPR

■ DANNY PEREZ   Perez, Daniel   b: 2/26/71, ElPaso, Tex.   BR/TR, 5'10", 188 lbs.   Deb: 6/30/96

| 1996 | Mil-A | 4 | 4 | 0 | 0 | 0 | 0 | 0 | 0 | 0 | 0 | .000 | .000 | .000 | -95 | -1 | 0 | 0 | 0 | 1.000 | -0 | /O-3 | -0.1 |

■ EDDIE PEREZ   Perez, Eduardo   b: 5/4/68, Ciudad Ojeda, Venez.   BR/TR, 6'1", 175 lbs.   Deb: 9/10/95

1995	Atl-N	7	13	1	4	1	0	1	4	0	2	.308	.308	.615	132	0	0	0	0	1.000	3	/C-5,1-1	0.3
1996	*Atl-N	68	156	19	40	9	1	4	17	8	19	.256	.297	.404	78	-5	0	0	0	.993	-0	C-54/1-7	-0.3
Total	2	75	169	20	44	10	1	5	21	8	21	.260	.298	.420	82	-5	0	0	0	.993	3	/C-59,1-8	0.0

■ EDUARDO PEREZ   Perez, Eduardo Atanasio   b: 9/11/69, Cincinnati, Ohio   BR/TR, 6'4", 215 lbs.   Deb: 7/27/93   F

1993	Cal-A	52	180	16	45	6	2	4	30	9	39	.250	.293	.372	75	-7	5	4	-1	.962	10	3-45/D-3	0.3
1994	Cal-A	38	129	10	27	7	0	5	16	12	29	.209	.277	.380	66	-7	3	0	1	.997	-3	1-38	-1.2
1995	Cal-A	29	71	9	12	4	1	1	7	12	9	.169	.306	.296	58	-4	0	2	-1	.883	1	3-23/D-1	-0.4
1996	Cin-N	18	36	8	8	0	0	3	5	5	9	.222	.317	.472	106	0	0	0	0	1.000	2	/1-8,3-3	0.1
Total	4	137	416	43	92	17	3	13	58	38	86	.221	.293	.370	72	-18	8	6	-1	.939	10	/3-71,1-46,D-4	-1.2

■ MARTY PEREZ   Perez, Martin Roman   b: 2/28/47, Visalia, Cal.   BR/TR, 5'11", 160 lbs.   Deb: 9/9/69

1969	Cal-A	13	13	3	3	0	0	0	0	0	2	.231	.333	.231	63	-1	0	0	0	1.000	6	/S-7,2-2,3-2	0.6
1970	Cal-A	3	3	0	0	0	0	0	1	0	0	.000	.000	.000	-99	-1	0	0	0	.833	1	/S-2	0.0
1971	Atl-N	130	410	28	93	15	3	4	32	25	44	.227	.273	.307	60	-22	1	2	-1	.955	-14	*S-126/2-1	-2.3
1972	Atl-N	141	479	33	109	13	1	1	28	30	55	.228	.277	.265	50	-31	0	3	-2	.957	-34	*S-141	-5.2
1973	Atl-N	141	501	66	125	15	5	8	57	49	66	.250	.319	.347	79	-14	2	3	-1	.962	-9	*S-139	-0.8
1974	Atl-N	127	447	51	116	20	5	2	34	35	51	.260	.315	.340	80	-12	2	0	1	.985	-5	*2-102,S-14/3-6	-1.5
1975	Atl-N	120	461	50	127	14	2	2	34	37	44	.275	.329	.328	80	-12	0	1	0	.985	-8	*2-116/S-7	-1.5
1976	Atl-N	31	96	12	24	4	0	1	6	8	9	.250	.308	.323	74	-3	0	0	0	.976	-2	2-18,S-17/3-2	-0.3
	SF-N	93	332	37	86	13	1	2	26	30	28	.259	.320	.322	80	-8	3	4	-2	.979	7	2-89/S-5	0.3
	Yr	124	428	49	110	17	1	3	32	38	37	.257	.318	.322	79	-11	3	4	-2	.978	5	*2-107,S-22/3-2	0.0
1977	NY-A	1	4	0	2	0	0	0	0	0	1	.500	.500	.500	175	0	0	0	0	1.000	1	/3-1	0.1
	Oak-A	115	373	32	86	14	5	2	23	29	65	.231	.291	.311	65	-18	1	3	-2	.974	-0	*2-105,3-12/S-4	-1.3
	Yr	116	377	32	88	14	5	2	23	29	66	.233	.293	.313	66	-17	1	3	-2	.974	1	*2-105,3-13/S-4	-1.2
1978	Oak-A	16	12	1	0	0	0	0	0	0	5	.000	.000	.000	-99	-3	0	0	0	1.000	2	3-11/S-3,2-1	-0.1
Total	10	931	3131	313	771	108	22	22	241	245	369	.246	.303	.316	70	-124	11	17	-7	.958	-59	S-465,2-434/3-34	-12.0

■ NEIFI PEREZ   Perez, Neifi Neftali (Diaz)   b: 2/2/75, Villa Mella, D.R.   BB/TR, 6', 175 lbs.   Deb: 8/31/96

| 1996 | Col-N | 17 | 45 | 4 | 7 | 0 | 0 | 0 | 3 | 0 | 8 | .156 | .156 | .200 | -6 | -7 | 2 | 2 | -1 | .972 | -0 | S-14/2-4 | -0.7 |

■ ROBERT PEREZ   Perez, Robert Alexander (Jimenez)   b: 6/4/69, Bolivar, Venez.   BR/TR, 6'3", 205 lbs.   Deb: 7/20/94

1994	Tor-A	4	8	0	1	0	0	0	0	0	1	.125	.125	.125	-35	-2	0	0	0	1.000	-0	/O-4	-0.2
1995	Tor-A	17	48	2	9	2	0	1	3	0	5	.188	.188	.292	22	-6	0	0	0	1.000	-0	O-15	-0.6
1996	Tor-A	86	202	30	66	10	0	2	21	8	17	.327	.355	.406	91	-3	3	0	1	.983	-9	O-79/D-2	-1.1
Total	3	107	258	32	76	12	0	3	24	8	23	.295	.318	.376	75	-10	3	0	1	.987	-9	/O-98,D-2	-1.9

■ TOMAS PEREZ   Perez, Tomas Orlando   b: 12/29/73, Barquismeto, Venez.   BB/TR, 5'11", 165 lbs.   Deb: 5/3/95

1995	Tor-A	41	98	12	24	3	1	1	8	7	18	.245	.295	.327	62	-6	0	1	-1	.954	1	S-31/2-7,3-1	-0.3
1996	Tor-A	91	295	24	74	13	4	1	19	25	29	.251	.312	.332	63	-17	1	2	-1	.970	12	2-75,3-11/S-5	-0.1
Total	2	132	393	36	98	16	5	2	27	32	47	.249	.308	.331	62	-22	1	3	-2	.972	12	/2-82,S-36,3-12	-0.4

■ TONY PEREZCHICA   Perezchica, Antonio Llamas (Gonzales)   b: 4/20/66, Mexicali, Mex.   BR/TR, 5'11", 165 lbs.   Deb: 9/7/88

1988	SF-N	7	8	1	1	0	0	0	1	2	1	.125	.300	.125	27	-1	0	0	0	1.000	-1	/2-6	-0.2
1990	SF-N	4	3	1	1	0	0	0	0	0	2	.333	.500	.333	139	0	0	0	0	1.000	-2	/2-2,S-2	-0.1
1991	SF-N	23	48	2	11	4	1	0	3	2	12	.229	.260	.354	73	-4	0	1	-1	.947	-3	S-13/2-6	-0.5
	Cle-A	17	22	4	8	2	0	0	3	2	5	.364	.440	.455	147	2	0	0	0	1.000	-1	/S-6,3-3,2-2,D-1	0.1
1992	Cle-A	18	20	2	2	1	0	0	1	2	6	.100	.182	.150	-6	-3	0	0	0	.875	-1	/3-9,2-4,S-4,D-1	-0.4
Total	4	69	101	10	23	7	1	0	5	10	26	.228	.297	.317	74	-4	0	1	-1	.944	-8	/S-25,2-20,3-12,D-2	-1.1

■ BRODERICK PERKINS   Perkins, Broderick Phillip   b: 11/23/54, Pittsburg, Cal.   BL/TL, 5'10", 180 lbs.   Deb: 7/7/78

1978	SD-N	62	217	14	52	14	1	2	33	5	29	.240	.257	.341	71	-10	4	0	1	.993	3	1-59	-0.9
1979	SD-N	57	87	8	23	0	0	8	8	12	.264	.326	.264	67	-4	0	0	0	.982	-1	1-28	-0.5
1980	SD-N	43	100	18	37	9	0	2	14	11	10	.370	.432	.520	175	10	2	1	0	.988	-4	1-20,O-10	0.5
1981	SD-N	92	254	27	71	18	3	2	40	14	16	.280	.317	.398	110	2	0	4	-2	.997	-3	1-80/O-3	-0.7
1982	SD-N	125	347	32	94	10	4	2	34	26	20	.271	.327	.340	92	-4	2	1	0	.994	-1	1-98,O-11	-1.0
1983	Cle-A	79	184	23	50	10	0	0	24	9	19	.272	.306	.326	71	-7	1	5	-3	.991	0	1-19,O-17,D-16	-1.1
1984	Cle-A	58	66	5	13	1	0	0	4	3	10	.197	.284	.212	39	-5	0	0	0	1.000	-0	D-10/1-2	-0.6
Total	7	516	1255	127	340	62	8	8	157	80	116	.271	.317	.352	90	-18	9	11	-4	.993	-4	1-306/O-41,D-26	-4.3

■ CY PERKINS   Perkins, Ralph Foster   b: 2/27/1896, Gloucester, Mass.   d: 10/2/63, Philadelphia, Pa.   BR/TR, 5'10.5", 158 lbs.   Deb: 9/25/15   MC

1915	Phi-A	7	20	2	4	1	0	0	3	3	.200	.304	.250	68	-1	0			.920	1	/C-6	0.0
1917	Phi-A	6	18	1	3	0	0	0	2	1	.167	.250	.167	28	-1	0			.978	4	/C-6	0.3
1918	Phi-A	68	218	9	41	4	1	1	14	8	15	.188	.217	.229	34	-18	1			.990	12	C-60	-0.1
1919	Phi-A	101	305	22	77	12	7	2	29	27	22	.252	.313	.357	87	-6	2			.971	7	C-87/S-8	1.0
1920	Phi-A	148	492	40	128	24	6	5	52	28	35	.260	.300	.364	75	-19	5	6	-2	.979	**23**	*C-146/2-1	1.1
1921	Phi-A	141	538	58	155	31	4	12	73	32	32	.288	.329	.428	91	-9	5	9	-4	.971	5	*C-141	0.0
1922	Phi-A	148	505	58	135	20	6	6	69	40	30	.267	.322	.366	77	-17	1	7	-4	.984	-4	*C-141	-1.7
1923	Phi-A	143	500	53	135	34	5	2	65	65	30	.270	.356	.370	90	-6	1	3	-2	.971	-7	*C-137	-0.8
1924	Phi-A	128	392	31	95	19	4	0	32	31	20	.242	.304	.311	58	-25	3	4	-2	.983	-0	*C-128	-1.8
1925	Phi-A	65	140	21	43	10	1	0	18	26	6	.307	.426	.400	104	2	0			.980	11	C-58/3-1	1.4
1926	Phi-A	63	148	14	43	6	0	1	18	14	8	.291	.371	.331	80	-2	1			.984	9	C-55	0.6
1927	Phi-A	59	137	11	35	7	2	1	15	12	8	.255	.315	.358	70	-6	0			.979	1	C-54/1-1	-0.4
1928	Phi-A	19	29	1	5	0	0	0	1	1	1	.172	.200	.172	-1	-4	0	1		.982	4	C-19	-0.1
1929	Phi-A	38	76	4	16	4	0	0	9	5	4	.211	.259	.263	34	-4	0			.990	2	C-38	-0.4
1930	Phi-A	20	38	1	6	2	0	0	4	2	3	.158	.200	.211	4	-6	0			.964	0	C-19/1-1	-0.4
1931	NY-A	16	47	3	12	1	0	0	7	1	4	.255	.286	.277	51	-3	0			1.000	-5	C-16	-0.7
1934	Det-A	1	1	0	0	0	0	0	0	0	0	.000	.000	.000	-99	-0	0			.000	0	H	0.0
Total	17	1171	3604	329	933	175	35	30	409	301	221	.259	.319	.352	75	-131	18	34		.978	62	*C-1111/S-8,1-2,32	-2.0

■ SAM PERLOZZO   Perlozzo, Samuel Benedict   b: 3/4/51, Cumberland, Md.   BR/TR, 5'9", 170 lbs.   Deb: 9/13/77   C

1977	Min-A	10	24	6	7	0	0	0	2	0	3	.292	.346	.458	119	1	0	0	0	1.000	-3	2-10/3-1	-0.2
1979	SD-N	2	2	0	0	0	0	0	0	0	0	.000	.333	.000	-1	-0	0	0	0	.500	-1	/2-2	-0.2
Total	2	12	26	6	7	0	0	0	2	3	.269	.345	.423	110	0	0	0	0	.967	-5	/2-12,3-1	-0.4

■ JOHN PERRIN   Perrin, John Stephenson   b: 2/4/1898, Escanaba, Mich.   d: 6/24/69, Detroit, Mich.   BL/TR, 5'9", 160 lbs.   Deb: 7/11/21

| 1921 | Bos-A | 4 | 13 | 3 | 3 | 0 | 0 | 1 | 0 | 0 | 3 | .231 | .231 | .231 | 19 | -2 | 0 | | | 1.000 | -2 | /O-4 | -0.3 |

■ NIG PERRINE   Perrine, John Grover   b: 1/14/1885, Clinton, Wis.   d: 8/13/48, Kansas City, Mo.   BR/TR, 5'9", 160 lbs.   Deb: 4/11/07

| 1907 | Was-A | 44 | 146 | 13 | 25 | 4 | 1 | 0 | 15 | 13 | .171 | .253 | .212 | 53 | -7 | 10 | | | .946 | -3 | 2-24,S-18/3-2 | -1.2 |

■ GEORGE PERRING   Perring, George Wilson   b: 8/13/1884, Sharon, Wis.   d: 8/20/60, Beloit, Wis.   BR/TR, 6', 190 lbs.   Deb: 4/25/08

1908	Cle-A	89	310	23	67	8	5	0	19	16	.216	.255	.274	72	-10	8			.928	-6	S-48,3-41	-1.6
1909	Cle-A	88	283	26	63	10	9	0	20	19	.223	.258	.322	87	-5	6			.932	3	3-67,S-11/2-4	0.5
1910	Cle-A	39	122	14	27	6	3	0	8	3	.221	.240	.320	74	-4	3			.931	2	3-33/1-4	-0.1
1914	KC-F	144	496	68	138	28	10	2	69	59	39	.278	.355	.387	106	-3	7			.934	9	*3-101,1-41/P-1,S-1	0.8
1915	KC-F	153	553	67	143	23	7	7	67	57	30	.259	.329	.363	99	-10	10			.958	15	*3-102,1-31,2-31/S	0.9
Total	5	513	1764	198	438	75	34	9	183	154	69	.248	.311	.345	93	-32	34			.939	26	3-344/1-76,S-61,2P	0.4

YEAR	TM/L	G	AB	R	H	2B	3B	HR	RBI	BB	SO	AVG	OBP	SLG	PRO+	BR/A	SB	CS	SBR	FA	FR	G/POS	TPR

■ BOYD PERRY
Perry, Boyd Glenn b: 3/21/14, Snow Camp, N.C. d: 6/29/90, Burlington, N.C. BR/TR, 5'10", 158 lbs. Deb: 5/23/41

1941	Det-A	36	83	9	15	5	0	0	11	10	9	.181	.269	.241	32	-8	1	0	0	.974	-0	S-25,2-11	-0.6

■ CLAY PERRY
Perry, Clayton Shields b: 12/18/1881, Rice Lake, Wis. d: 1/16/54, Rice Lake, Wis. BR/TR, 5'10.5", 175 lbs. Deb: 9/2/08

1908	Det-A	7	17	0	2	0	0	0	0	0		.118	.167	.118	-7	-2	0			.850	0	/3-7	-0.2

■ GERALD PERRY
Perry, Gerald June b: 10/30/60, Savannah, Ga. BL/TR, 6', 190 lbs. Deb: 8/11/83

1983	Atl-N	27	39	5	14	2	0	1	6	5	4	.359	.432	.487	144	2	0	1	-1	.982	-2	/1-7,O-1	-0.1
1984	Atl-N	122	347	52	92	12	2	7	47	61	38	.265	.378	.372	104	4	15	12	-3	.988	-8	1-64,O-53	-1.2
1985	Atl-N	110	238	22	51	5	0	3	13	23	28	.214	.284	.273	53	-15	9	5	-0	.985	-0	1-55/O-1	-1.9
1986	Atl-N	29	70	6	19	2	0	2	11	8	4	.271	.346	.386	96	-0	0	1	-1	.889	-5	O-21/1-1	-0.7
1987	Atl-N	142	533	77	144	35	2	12	74	48	63	.270	.332	.411	91	-7	42	16	3	.990	-10	*1-136/O-7	-2.4
1988	Atl-N★	141	547	61	164	29	1	8	74	36	49	.300	.344	.400	108	5	29	14	0	.988	-1	*1-141	-0.6
1989	Atl-N	72	266	24	67	11	0	4	21	32	28	.252	.339	.338	92	-2	10	6	-1	.987	1	1-72	-0.7
1990	KC-A	133	465	57	118	22	2	8	57	39	56	.254	.316	.361	90	-6	17	4	3	.986	2	D-68,1-51	-0.7
1991	StL-N	109	242	29	58	8	4	6	36	22	34	.240	.303	.380	90	-3	15	8	-0	.989	-4	1-61/O-5	-1.1
1992	StL-N	87	143	13	34	8	0	1	18	15	23	.238	.314	.315	81	-3	3	6	-3	.987	-4	1-29	-1.2
1993	StL-N	96	98	21	33	5	0	4	16	18	23	.337	.440	.510	157	9	1	1	-0	.976	-1	1-15/O-1	0.6
1994	StL-N	60	77	12	25	7	0	3	18	15	12	.325	.435	.532	153	7	1	1	-0	.990	-2	1-13	0.4
1995	StL-N	65	79	4	13	4	0	0	5	6	12	.165	.224	.215	16	-10	0	0	-0	1.000	-1	1-11	-1.1
Total	13	1193	3144	383	832	150	11	59	396	328	374	.265	.336	.376	95	-20	142	75	-2	.988	-32	1-656/O-89,D-68	-10.7

■ HERB PERRY
Perry, Herbert Edward b: 9/15/69, Live Oak, Fla. BR/TR, 6'2", 210 lbs. Deb: 5/3/94

1994	Cle-A	4	9	1	1	0	0	0	1	3	1	.111	.385	.111	36	-1	0	0	0	1.000	1	/1-2,3-2	0.0
1995	*Cle-A	52	162	23	51	13	1	3	23	13	28	.315	.380	.463	116	4	1	3	-2	1.000	0	1-45/3-1,D-6	-0.1
1996	Cle-A	7	12	1	1	1	0	0	0	1	2	.083	.154	.167	-19	-2	1	0	0	1.000	0	/1-5,3-1	-0.2
Total	3	63	183	25	53	14	1	3	24	17	31	.290	.366	.426	103	1	2	3	-1	1.000	1	/1-52,D-6,3-4	-0.3

■ BOB PERRY
Perry, Melvin Gray b: 9/14/34, New Bern, N.C. BR/TR, 6'2", 180 lbs. Deb: 5/17/63

1963	LA-A	61	166	16	42	9	0	3	14	9	31	.253	.303	.361	91	-2	1	1	-0	.946	-7	O-55	-1.3
1964	LA-A	70	221	19	61	8	1	3	16	14	52	.276	.319	.362	99	-1	1	1	-0	.975	-4	O-62	-0.9
Total	2	131	387	35	103	17	1	6	30	23	83	.266	.312	.362	95	-4	2	2	-1	.962	-11	O-117	-2.2

■ HANK PERRY
Perry, William Henry "Socks" b: 7/28/1886, Howell, Mich. d: 7/18/56, Pontiac, Mich. BL/TR, 5'11", 190 lbs. Deb: 4/12/12

1912	Det-A	13	36	3	6	1	0	0	3			.167	.231	.194	23	-4	0			1.000	2	/O-7	-0.2

■ JOHNNY PESKY
Pesky, John Michael (b: John Michael Paveskovich) b: 9/27/19, Portland, Ore. BL/TR, 5'9", 168 lbs. Deb: 4/14/42 MC

1942	Bos-A	147	620	105	205	29	9	2	51	42	36	.331	.375	.416	118	14	12	7	-1	.955	18	*S-147	4.1
1946	*Bos-A★	153	621	115	208	43	4	2	55	65	29	.335	.401	.427	124	22	9	8	-2	.969	12	*S-153	4.2
1947	Bos-A	155	638	106	207	27	8	0	39	72	22	.324	.393	.392	110	11	12	9	-2	.976	-11	*S-133,3-22	0.5
1948	Bos-A	143	565	124	159	26	6	3	55	99	32	.281	.394	.365	98	2	3	5	-2	.951	6	*3-141	0.4
1949	Bos-A	148	604	111	185	27	7	2	69	100	19	.306	.408	.384	103	6	8	4	0	.970	21	*3-148	2.4
1950	Bos-A	127	490	112	153	22	6	1	49	104	31	.312	.437	.388	103	7	2	1	0	.974	22	*3-116/S-8	2.5
1951	Bos-A	131	480	93	150	20	6	3	41	84	15	.313	.417	.398	110	10	2	2	-1	.961	9	*S-106,3-11/2-5	2.5
1952	Bos-A	25	67	10	10	2	0	0	2	15	5	.149	.313	.179	36	-5	0	3	-2	.917	-6	3-19/S-2	-1.4
	Det-A	69	177	26	45	4	0	1	9	41	11	.254	.394	.294	93	1	1	2	-1	.952	-6	S-41,2-22/3-3	-0.2
	Yr	94	244	36	55	6	0	1	11	56	16	.225	.372	.262	77	-5	1	5	-3	.953	-11	S-43,3-22,2-22	-1.6
1953	Det-A	103	308	43	90	22	1	2	24	27	10	.292	.353	.390	102	1	3	7	-3	.991	-14	2-73	-1.2
1954	Det-A	20	17	5	3	0	0	0	1	3	1	.176	.300	.353	80	-1	0	0	-0	.000	0	H	-0.1
	Was-A	49	158	17	40	4	3	1	10	9	7	.253	.298	.316	72	-6	1	1	-0	.979	-8	2-37/S-1	-1.3
	Yr	69	175	22	43	4	3	1	10	13	8	.246	.298	.320	72	-7	1	1	-0	.979	-8	2-37/S-1	-1.4
Total	10	1270	4745	867	1455	226	50	17	404	662	218	.307	.394	.386	106	62	53	49	-14	.964	43	S-591,3-460,2-137	12.4

■ ROBERTO PETAGINE
Petagine, Roberto Antonio (Guerra) b: 6/7/71, Nueva Esparta, Venez. BL/TL, 6'1", 170 lbs. Deb: 4/4/94

1994	Hou-N	8	7	0	0	0	0	0	0	3	3	.000	.125	.000	-67	-2	0	0	0	1.000	-0	/1-2	-0.2
1995	SD-N	89	124	15	29	8	0	3	17	26	41	.234	.367	.371	99	1	0	0	0	.996	1	1-51/O-2	-0.1
1996	NY-N	50	99	10	23	3	0	4	17	9	27	.232	.315	.384	89	-2	0	2	-1	.996	3	1-40	-0.3
Total	3	147	230	25	52	11	0	7	34	36	71	.226	.338	.365	90	-3	0	2	-1	.996	3	/1-93,O-2	-0.6

■ BILL PETERMAN
Peterman, William David b: 3/20/21, Philadelphia, Pa. BR/TR, 6'2", 185 lbs. Deb: 4/26/42

1942	Phi-N	1	1	0	1	0	0	0	0	0	0	1.000	1.000	1.000	512	0				.000	0	/C-1	0.1

■ JOHN PETERS
Peters, John Paul b: 4/8/1850, Louisiana, Mo. d: 1/4/24, St.Louis, Mo. BR/TR, 5'7", 180 lbs. Deb: 5/23/1874

1874	Chi-n	55	239	39	69	10	1	0	25	2	11	.289	.295	.343	103	1	2	2	-1	.799	4	S-36,2-19	0.1
1875	Chi-n	69	297	40	85	16	2	0	34	0	3	.286	.286	.354	120	5	12	6	0	.871	10	*S-65/2-6	1.1
1876	Chi-N	66	316	70	111	14	2	1	47	3	2	.351	.357	.418	141	11				.932	-1	*S-66/P-1	0.8
1877	Chi-N	60	265	45	84	10	3	0	41	1	7	.317	.320	.377	106	0				.883	19	*S-60	1.8
1878	Mil-N	55	246	33	76	6	1	0	22	5	8	.309	.323	.341	111	2				.853	5	2-34,S-22	0.9
1879	Chi-N	83	379	45	93	13	3	1	31	1	19	.245	.247	.298	74	-11				.837	-8	*S-83	-1.4
1880	Pro-N	86	359	30	82	5	0	0	24	5	15	.228	.239	.242	66	-12				.900	-1	*S-86	-0.7
1881	Buf-N	54	229	21	49	8	1	0	25	3	12	.214	.224	.258	52	-12				.869	7	*S-53/O-1	-0.2
1882	Pit-a	78	333	46	96	10	1	0		4		.288	.297	.324	115	5				.883	6	*S-77/2-1	1.3
1883	Pit-a	8	28	3	3	0	0	0		0		.107	.107	.107	-32	-4				.818	3	/S-8	-0.1
1884	Pit-a	1	4	0	0	0	0	0		0		.000	.000	.000	-98	-1				.667	-1	/S-1	-0.2
Total	2 n	124	536	79	154	26	2	1	59	2	14	.287	.290	.349	112	6	14	8	-1	.846	14	S-101/2-25	1.2
Total	9	491	2159	293	594	66	10	2	190	22	63	.275	.282	.318	94	-23				.881	28	S-456/2-35,O-1,P-1	2.2

■ JOHN PETERS
Peters, John William "Big Pete" or "Shotgun" b: 7/14/1893, Kansas City, Kan. d: 2/21/32, Kansas City, Mo. BR/TR, 6', 192 lbs. Deb: 5/1/15

1915	Det-A	1	3	0	0	0	0	0	0	0	1	.000	.000	.000	-95	-1	0			1.000	-1	/C-1	-0.1
1918	Cle-A	1	1	0	0	0	0	0	0	1		.000	.500	.000	46	0	0			.500	-1	/C-1	-0.1
1921	Phi-N	55	155	7	45	4	0	3	23	6	13	.290	.329	.374	79	-5	1	0	0	.933	-13	C-44	-1.5
1922	Phi-N	55	143	15	35	9	1	4	24	9	18	.245	.308	.406	75	-6	0	1	-1	.953	-5	C-39	-0.9
Total	4	112	302	22	80	13	1	7	47	16	33	.265	.317	.384	76	-11	1	1		.934	-18	/C-85	-2.4

■ RICK PETERS
Peters, Richard Devin b: 11/21/55, Lynwood, Cal. BB/TR, 5'9", 170 lbs. Deb: 9/8/79

1979	Det-A	12	19	3	5	0	0	0	2	5	3	.263	.417	.263	85	-0	0	0	0	.000	-1	/3-3,2-2,O-1,D-3	-0.1
1980	Det-A	133	477	79	139	19	7	2	42	54	48	.291	.363	.373	102	-0	13	7	-0	.977	-0	*O-109,D-11	-0.2
1981	Det-A	63	207	26	53	7	0	0	15	29	28	.256	.353	.319	91	-1	1	6	-3	.991	3	O-38,D-19	-0.3
1983	Oak-A	55	178	20	51	7	0	0	20	12	21	.287	.335	.326	88	-3	4	9	-4	.986	5	O-47/D-8	-0.4
1986	Oak-A	44	38	7	7	1	0	0	1	7	7	.184	.311	.211	49	-2	2	2	-1	1.000	-0	O-27/2-1	-0.9
Total	5	307	919	135	255	34	10	2	80	107	107	.277	.358	.343	95	-3	20	24	-8	.983	1	O-222/D-41,2-3,3-3	-1.9

■ RUSTY PETERS
Peters, Russell Dixon b: 12/14/14, Roanoke, Va. BR/TR, 5'11", 170 lbs. Deb: 4/14/36

1936	Phi-A	45	119	12	26	3	2	3	16	4	28	.218	.244	.353	47	-11	1	1	-0	.898	1	S-25,3-10/O-2,2-1	-0.8
1937	Phi-A	116	339	39	88	17	6	3	43	41	59	.260	.339	.372	80	-10	4	4	-1	.966	-13	2-70,3-31,S-13	-1.8
1938	Phi-A	2	7	0	0	0	0	0	0	0	1	.000	.000	.000	-99	-2				.714	-2	/S-2	-0.4
1940	Cle-A	30	71	5	17	3	0	0	7	4	14	.239	.280	.338	61	-4	0	0	0	.922	-0	/2-9,S-6,3-6,1-1	-0.3
1941	Cle-A	29	63	6	13	1	0	2	8	7	10	.206	.286	.238	42	-5	0	0	0	.891	3	S-11/3-9,2-3	-0.3
1942	Cle-A	34	58	6	13	5	1	0	4	4	7	.224	.290	.345	70	-3	0	0	0	.944	2	S-24/2-1,3-1	0.0
1943	Cle-A	79	215	22	47	6	2	1	19	18	29	.219	.282	.279	69	-9	1			.913	-6	3-46,S-14/2-6,O-2	-1.5
1944	Cle-A	88	282	23	63	13	3	0	24	15	35	.223	.268	.301	65	-14	2			.976	-3	2-63,S-13/3-8	-1.4
1946	Cle-A	9	21	0	6	0	0	0	1	2	3	.286	.318	.286	74	-1	0			1.000	0	/S-7	-0.1

YEAR	TM/L	G	AB	R	H	2B	3B	HR	RBI	BB	SO	AVG	OBP	SLG	PRO+	BR/A	SB	CS	SBR	FA	FR	G/POS	TPR
1947	StL-A	39	47	10	16	4	0	0	2	6	8	.340	.415	.426	131	2	0	0	0	.955	7	2-13/S-2	1.0
Total	10	471	1222	123	289	53	16	8	117	98	199	.236	.295	.326	69	-57	9	9	-3	.966	-13	2-166,S-117,3/O1	-5.6

■ BUDDY PETERSON   Peterson, Carl Francis   b: 4/23/25, Portland, Ore.   BR/TR, 5'9.5", 170 lbs.   Deb: 9/14/55

YEAR	TM/L	G	AB	R	H	2B	3B	HR	RBI	BB	SO	AVG	OBP	SLG	PRO+	BR/A	SB	CS	SBR	FA	FR	G/POS	TPR
1955	Chi-A	6	21	7	6	1	0	0	2	3	1	.286	.400	.333	96	-1	0	0	0	.962	-1	/S-6	0.0
1957	Bal-A	7	17	1	3	2	0	0	0	2	2	.176	.263	.294	55	-1	0	0	0	.963	-1	/S-7	-0.2
Total	2	13	38	8	9	3	0	0	2	5	3	.237	.341	.316	80	-1	0	0	0	.962	-2	/S-13	-0.2

■ CAP PETERSON   Peterson, Charles Andrew   b: 8/15/42, Tacoma, Wash.   d: 5/16/80, Tacoma, Wash.   BR/TR, 6'2", 195 lbs.   Deb: 9/12/62

YEAR	TM/L	G	AB	R	H	2B	3B	HR	RBI	BB	SO	AVG	OBP	SLG	PRO+	BR/A	SB	CS	SBR	FA	FR	G/POS	TPR
1962	SF-N	4	6	1	1	0	0	0	0	0	1	.167	.286	.167	25	-1	0	0	0	1.000	-1	/S-2	-0.1
1963	SF-N	22	54	7	14	2	0	1	2	2	13	.259	.286	.352	83	-1	0	0	0	.917	-7	/2-8,3-5,O-3,S-1	-0.8
1964	SF-N	66	74	8	15	1	1	1	8	3	20	.203	.234	.284	44	-5	0	0	0	1.000	-3	O-10/1-2,2-1,3-1	-0.9
1965	SF-N	63	105	14	26	7	0	3	15	10	16	.248	.313	.400	97	-1	0	0	0	1.000	-4	O-27	-0.5
1966	SF-N	89	190	13	45	6	1	2	19	11	32	.237	.282	.311	63	-9	2	0	1	1.000	-3	O-51/1-2	-1.4
1967	Was-A	122	405	35	97	17	2	8	46	32	61	.240	.300	.351	95	-3	0	3	-2	.970	-4	*O-101	-1.0
1968	Was-A	94	226	20	46	8	1	3	18	18	31	.204	.265	.282	70	-9	2	1	0	1.000	-4	O-53	-1.4
1969	Cle-A	76	110	8	25	3	0	1	14	24	18	.227	.370	.282	82	-1	0	0	0	.977	-2	O-30/3-4	-0.5
Total	8	536	1170	106	269	44	5	19	122	101	195	.230	.294	.325	80	-30	4	4	-1	.983	-18	O-275/3-10,2-9,1S	-6.6

■ HARDY PETERSON   Peterson, Harding William   b: 10/17/29, Perth Amboy, N.J.   BR/TR, 6', 205 lbs.   Deb: 5/5/55

YEAR	TM/L	G	AB	R	H	2B	3B	HR	RBI	BB	SO	AVG	OBP	SLG	PRO+	BR/A	SB	CS	SBR	FA	FR	G/POS	TPR
1955	Pit-N	32	81	7	20	6	0	1	10	7	7	.247	.315	.358	79	-2	0	0	0	.965	6	C-31	0.4
1957	Pit-N	30	73	10	22	2	1	2	11	9	10	.301	.378	.438	122	2	0	1	-1	.985	2	C-30	0.4
1958	Pit-N	2	6	0	2	0	0	0	0	1	0	.333	.429	.333	108	0	0	0	0	1.000	-0	/C-2	0.0
1959	Pit-N	2	1	0	0	0	0	0	0	0	0	.000	.000	.000	-99	-0	0	0	0	1.000	1	/C-2	0.0
Total	4	66	161	17	44	8	1	3	21	17	17	.273	.334	.391	99	-0	0	1	-1	.976	7	/C-65	0.8

■ BOB PETERSON   Peterson, Robert A.   b: 7/16/1884, Philadelphia, Pa.   d: 11/27/62, Evesham, N.J.   BR/TR, 6'1", 160 lbs.   Deb: 4/18/06

YEAR	TM/L	G	AB	R	H	2B	3B	HR	RBI	BB	SO	AVG	OBP	SLG	PRO+	BR/A	SB	CS	SBR	FA	FR	G/POS	TPR
1906	Bos-A	39	118	10	24	1	1	1	9	11		.203	.277	.254	67	-4	1			.899	-7	C-30/2-3,1-2,O-1	-0.9
1907	Bos-A	4	13	1	1	0	0	0	0	0		.077	.077	.077	-51	-2	0			1.000	0	/C-4	-0.2
Total	2	43	131	11	25	1	1	1	9	11		.191	.259	.237	56	-6	1			.910	-7	/C-34,2-3,1-2,O-1	-1.1

■ TED PETOSKEY   Petoskey, Frederick Lee   b: 1/5/11, St.Charles, Mich.   BR/TR, 5'11.5", 183 lbs.   Deb: 9/9/34

YEAR	TM/L	G	AB	R	H	2B	3B	HR	RBI	BB	SO	AVG	OBP	SLG	PRO+	BR/A	SB	CS	SBR	FA	FR	G/POS	TPR
1934	Cin-N	6	7	0	0	0	0	0	1	0	5	.000	.000	.000	-99	-2	0			1.000	1	/O-2	-0.1
1935	Cin-N	4	5	0	2	0	0	0	0	0	1	.400	.400	.400	119	-0	1			1.000	-1	/O-2	-0.1
Total	2	10	12	0	2	0	0	0	1	0	6	.167	.167	.167	-11	-2	1			1.000	0	/O-4	-0.2

■ GENO PETRALLI   Petralli, Eugene James   b: 9/25/59, Sacramento, Cal.   BL/TR, 6'2", 185 lbs.   Deb: 9/4/82

YEAR	TM/L	G	AB	R	H	2B	3B	HR	RBI	BB	SO	AVG	OBP	SLG	PRO+	BR/A	SB	CS	SBR	FA	FR	G/POS	TPR
1982	Tor-A	16	44	3	16	2	0	0	1	4	6	.364	.417	.409	117	1	0	0	0	.981	-2	C-12/3-3	-0.1
1983	Tor-A	6	4	0	0	0	0	0	0	1	1	.000	.200	.000	-37	-1	0	0	0	1.000	0	/C-5,D-1	0.0
1984	Tor-A	3	3	0	0	0	0	0	0	0	1	.000	.000	.000	-97	-1	0	0	0	1.000	0	/C-1,D-1	0.0
1985	Tex-A	42	100	7	27	2	0	1	11	8	12	.270	.330	.290	71	-4	1	0	0	.990	2	C-41	0.0
1986	Tex-A	69	137	17	35	9	3	2	18	5	14	.255	.282	.409	83	-4	3	0	1	.988	-8	C-41,3-15/2-2,D-2	-0.9
1987	Tex-A	101	202	28	61	11	2	7	31	27	29	.302	.390	.480	129	9	0	2	-1	.995	-0	C-63,3-17/1-5,2OD	1.0
1988	Tex-A	129	351	35	99	14	2	7	36	41	52	.282	.360	.393	108	5	0	1	-1	.981	-1	C-85/D-23/3-9,12	0.9
1989	Tex-A	70	184	18	56	7	0	4	23	17	24	.304	.369	.408	117	4	0	0	0	.989	-12	C-49,D-16	-0.6
1990	Tex-A	133	325	28	83	13	1	0	21	50	49	.255	.360	.302	87	-4	0	1	-1	.991	-4	*C-118/3-7,2-3	-0.2
1991	Tex-A	87	199	21	54	8	1	2	20	21	25	.271	.341	.352	94	-1	2	1	0	.972	-10	C-66/3-7,D-5	-0.8
1992	Tex-A	94	192	11	38	12	0	1	18	20	34	.198	.274	.276	56	-11	0	0	0	.990	3	C-54,D-14/3-4,2-2	-0.6
1993	Tex-A	59	133	16	32	5	0	1	13	22	17	.241	.348	.301	79	-3	2	0	1	.990	-7	C-39/2-1,3-1,D-2	-0.7
Total	12	809	1874	184	501	83	9	24	192	216	263	.267	.346	.360	95	-9	8	6	-1	.987	-37	C-574/D-66,321O	-2.0

■ RICO PETROCELLI   Petrocelli, Americo Peter   b: 6/27/43, Brooklyn, N.Y.   BR/TR, 6', 185 lbs.   Deb: 9/21/63

YEAR	TM/L	G	AB	R	H	2B	3B	HR	RBI	BB	SO	AVG	OBP	SLG	PRO+	BR/A	SB	CS	SBR	FA	FR	G/POS	TPR
1963	Bos-A	1	4	0	1	1	0	0	0	0	1	.250	.250	.500	101	-0	0	0	0	.833	-0	/S-1	0.0
1965	Bos-A	103	323	38	75	15	2	13	33	36	71	.232	.311	.412	98	-1	0	2	-1	.958	10	S-93	1.5
1966	Bos-A	139	522	58	124	20	1	18	59	41	99	.238	.297	.383	85	-11	1	1	-0	.954	1	*S-127/3-5	0.1
1967	*Bos-A★	142	491	53	127	24	2	17	66	49	93	.259	.332	.420	112	7	2	4	-2	.970	3	*S-141	2.3
1968	Bos-A	123	406	41	95	17	2	12	46	31	73	.234	.295	.374	95	-3	0	1	-1	**.978**	11	*S-117/1-1	2.2
1969	Bos-A★	154	535	92	159	32	2	40	97	98	68	.297	.407	.589	167	48	3	5	-2	**.981**	5	*S-153/3-1	**6.9**
1970	Bos-A	157	583	82	152	31	3	29	103	67	82	.261	.339	.473	114	10	1	1	-0	.970	-10	*S-141,3-18	1.7
1971	Bos-A	158	553	82	139	24	4	28	89	91	108	.251	.359	.461	122	17	0	0	1	**.976**	-1	*3-156	1.7
1972	Bos-A	147	521	62	125	15	2	15	75	74	91	.240	.341	.363	104	4	0	1	-1	.970	-1	3-146	0.1
1973	Bos-A	100	356	44	87	13	1	13	45	47	64	.244	.334	.396	99	-0	0	0	0	.980	5	3-99	0.4
1974	Bos-A	129	454	53	121	23	1	15	76	48	74	.267	.339	.421	110	5	1	0	0	.962	-19	*3-116/D-9	-1.4
1975	*Bos-A	115	402	31	96	15	1	7	59	41	66	.239	.314	.333	76	-12	0	0	0	.960	-18	*3-113/D-1	-3.4
1976	Bos-A	85	240	17	51	7	1	3	24	34	36	.213	.310	.287	67	-9	0	5	-3	.967	-4	3-73/2-5,1-1,S-1,D	-1.8
Total	13	1553	5390	653	1352	237	22	210	773	661	926	.251	.336	.420	108	55	10	22	-10	.969	-18	S-774,3-727/D21	10.3

■ PAT PETTEE   Pettee, Patrick E.   b: 1/10/1863, Natick, Mass.   d: 10/9/34, Natick, Mass.   BR/TR, 5'10", 170 lbs.   Deb: 4/8/1891

YEAR	TM/L	G	AB	R	H	2B	3B	HR	RBI	BB	SO	AVG	OBP	SLG	PRO+	BR/A	SB	CS	SBR	FA	FR	G/POS	TPR
1891	Lou-a	2	5	1	0	0	0	0	0	3	1	.000	.375	.000	9	-0	1			.818	-1	/2-2	-0.1

■ NED PETTIGREW   Pettigrew, Jim Ned   b: 8/25/1881, Honey Grove, Tex.   d: 8/20/52, Duncan, Okla.   BR/TR, 5'11", 175 lbs.   Deb: 4/23/14

YEAR	TM/L	G	AB	R	H	2B	3B	HR	RBI	BB	SO	AVG	OBP	SLG	PRO+	BR/A	SB	CS	SBR	FA	FR	G/POS	TPR
1914	Buf-F	2	2	0	0	0	0	0	0	0	0	.000	.000	.000	-98	-1	0			.000	0	H	-0.1

■ JOE PETTINI   Pettini, Joseph Paul   b: 1/26/55, Wheeling, W.Va.   BR/TR, 5'9", 165 lbs.   Deb: 7/10/80

YEAR	TM/L	G	AB	R	H	2B	3B	HR	RBI	BB	SO	AVG	OBP	SLG	PRO+	BR/A	SB	CS	SBR	FA	FR	G/POS	TPR
1980	SF-N	63	190	19	44	3	1	1	9	17	33	.232	.295	.274	61	-10	5	6	0	.955	-13	S-42,3-18/2-8	-1.9
1981	SF-N	35	29	3	2	1	0	0	2	4	5	.069	.182	.103	-18	-4	1	0	0	.920	4	2-12,S-12/3-9	0.0
1982	SF-N	29	39	5	8	1	0	0	3	2	4	.205	.262	.231	39	-3	0	1	-1	.934	-1	S-26/3-1	-0.3
1983	SF-N	61	86	11	16	0	1	0	7	9	11	.186	.263	.209	33	-8	4	1	1	.949	11	S-26,2-14,3-12	0.5
Total	4	188	344	38	70	5	2	1	20	33	53	.203	.273	.238	45	-25	10	4	1	.943	2	S-106/3-40,2-34	-1.7

■ GARY PETTIS   Pettis, Gary George   b: 4/3/58, Oakland, Cal.   BB/TR, 6'1", 165 lbs.   Deb: 9/13/82

YEAR	TM/L	G	AB	R	H	2B	3B	HR	RBI	BB	SO	AVG	OBP	SLG	PRO+	BR/A	SB	CS	SBR	FA	FR	G/POS	TPR
1982	Cal-A	10	5	5	1	0	0	1	0	0	2	.200	.200	.800	159	0	0	0	0	1.000	-2	/O-8	-0.2
1983	Cal-A	22	85	19	25	2	3	3	6	7	15	.294	.348	.494	130	3	8	3	1	.982	2	O-21	0.5
1984	Cal-A	140	397	63	90	11	6	2	29	60	115	.227	.330	.300	77	-10	48	17	4	.983	-1	*O-134	-0.9
1985	Cal-A	125	443	67	114	10	8	1	32	62	125	.257	.349	.323	86	-7	56	9	11	.990	17	*O-122	1.7
1986	*Cal-A	154	539	93	139	23	4	5	58	69	132	.258	.342	.343	88	-7	50	13	7	.985	21	*O-153/D-1	1.6
1987	Cal-A	133	394	49	82	13	2	1	17	52	124	.208	.302	.259	53	-26	24	5	4	.980	6	*O-131	-1.9
1988	Det-A	129	458	65	96	14	4	3	36	47	85	.210	.285	.277	60	-24	44	10	7	.987	10	*O-126/D-2	0.8
1989	Det-A	119	444	77	114	8	6	1	18	84	106	.257	.375	.309	97	2	43	15	4	.988	5	*O-119	0.8
1990	Tex-A	136	423	66	101	16	8	3	31	57	118	.239	.335	.360	88	-5	38	15	2	.993	-4	*O-128/D-2	-1.9
1991	Tex-A	137	282	37	61	7	5	0	19	54	91	.216	.342	.277	75	-8	29	13	1	.977	-11	*O-126/D-3	-1.9
1992	SD-N	30	30	0	6	0	0	0	0	9	11	.200	.250	.233	37	-2	1	0	0	.952	-3	O-14	-0.6
	Det-A	48	129	27	26	4	3	1	12	27	34	.202	.340	.302	81	-2	7	3	0	.993	5	O-46	0.3
Total	11	1183	3629	568	855	109	49	21	259	521	958	.236	.333	.310	80	-86	354	104	44	.986	54	*O-1128/D-8	-1.8

■ BOB PETTIT   Pettit, Robert Henry   b: 7/19/1861, Williamstown, Mass.   d: 11/1/10, Derby, Conn.   BL/TR, 5'9", 160 lbs.   Deb: 9/3/1887

YEAR	TM/L	G	AB	R	H	2B	3B	HR	RBI	BB	SO	AVG	OBP	SLG	PRO+	BR/A	SB	CS	SBR	FA	FR	G/POS	TPR
1887	Chi-N	32	138	29	36	3	3	2	12	8	15	.261	.301	.370	76	-6	16			.894	-1	O-32/C-1,P-1	-0.6
1888	Chi-N	43	163	23	43	1	4	4	23	7	9	.264	.288	.393	104	0	7			.931	-4	O-43	-0.5
1891	Mil-a	21	80	10	14	4	0	1	5	7	7	.175	.267	.262	43	-7	2			.932	-7	/2-9,O-7,3-6	-1.2
Total	3	96	387	62	93	8	7	7	40	22	31	.240	.288	.351	79	-13	25			.919	-11	/O-82,2-9,3-6,PC	-2.3

YEAR	TM/L	G	AB	R	H	2B	3B	HR	RBI	BB	SO	AVG	OBP	SLG	PRO+	BR/A	SB	CS	SBR	FA	FR	G/POS	TPR

■ MARTY PEVEY
Pevey, Marty Ashley b: 12/25/62, Savannah, Ga. BL/TR, 6'1", 185 lbs. Deb: 5/16/89

| 1989 | Mon-N | 13 | 41 | 2 | 9 | 1 | 1 | 0 | 3 | 0 | 8 | .220 | .220 | .293 | 45 | -3 | 0 | 0 | 0 | .985 | -2 | C-11/O-1 | -0.5 |

■ LARRY PEZOLD
Pezold, Lorenz Johannes b: 6/22/1893, New Orleans, La. d: 10/22/57, Baton Rouge, La. BR/TR, 5'9.5", 175 lbs. Deb: 7/27/14

| 1914 | Cle-A | 23 | 71 | 4 | 16 | 0 | 1 | 0 | 5 | 9 | 6 | .225 | .313 | .254 | 68 | -3 | 2 | 3 | -1 | .827 | -1 | 3-20/O-1 | -0.5 |

■ FRED PFEFFER
Pfeffer, Nathaniel Frederick "Fritz" or "Dandelion" b: 3/17/1860, Louisville, Ky. d: 4/10/32, Chicago, Ill. BR/TR, 5'10.5", 184 lbs. Deb: 5/1/1882 M

1882	Tro-N	85	330	26	72	7	4	1	43	1	24	.218	.221	.273	60	-14				.857	11	*S-83/2-2	0.1
1883	Chi-N	96	371	41	87	22	7	1	45	8	50	.235	.251	.340	73	-13				.887	17	*2-79,S-18/3-1,1-1	0.5
1884	Chi-N	112	467	105	135	10	10	25	101	25	47	.289	.325	.514	147	22				.903	**46**	*2-112/P-1	**6.1**
1885	*Chi-N	112	469	90	113	12	7	5	73	26	47	.241	.281	.328	84	-12				.893	25	*2-109/P-5,O-1	1.7
1886	*Chi-N	118	474	88	125	17	8	7	95	36	46	.264	.316	.378	96	-6	30			.903	7	*2-118/1-1	0.5
1887	Chi-N	123	479	95	133	21	6	16	89	34	20	.278	.327	.447	100	-4	57			.917	25	*2-123/O-2	2.0
1888	Chi-N	135	517	90	129	22	10	8	57	32	38	.250	.297	.377	106	2	64			.931	**38**	*2-135	4.4
1889	Chi-N	134	531	85	121	15	7	7	77	53	51	.228	.302	.322	71	-22	45			.943	19	*2-134	0.4
1890	Chi-P	124	499	86	128	21	8	5	80	44	23	.257	.319	.361	78	-18	27			.916	24	*2-124	1.1
1891	Lou-N	137	498	93	123	12	9	7	77	79	60	.247	.353	.349	105	5	40			.921	25	*2-137	3.2
1892	Lou-N	124	470	78	121	14	9	2	76	67	36	.257	.353	.338	119	13	27			.933	12	*2-116,1-10/P-1,M	2.5
1893	Lou-N	125	508	85	129	29	12	3	75	51	18	.254	.322	.376	92	-7	32			.939	6	*2-125	0.2
1894	Lou-N	104	409	68	126	12	14	5	59	30	14	.308	.357	.443	99	-2	31			.937	12	*2-90,S-15/P-1	1.1
1895	Lou-N	11	45	8	13	1	0	0	5	5	3	.289	.360	.311	79	-1	2			.742	-3	/S-5,2-3,1-3	-0.3
1896	NY-N	4	14	1	2	0	0	0	4	1	1	.143	.200	.143	5	-2	0			.760	-1	/2-4	-0.3
	Chi-N	94	360	45	88	16	7	2	52	23	20	.244	.294	.344	65	-20	22			.947	9	*2-94	-0.4
	Yr	98	374	46	90	16	7	2	56	24	21	.241	.292	.337	63	-21	22			.939	8	2-98	-0.7
1897	Chi-N	32	114	10	26	0	1	0	11	12		.228	.304	.246	48	-8	5			.883	-6	2-32	-1.1
Total	16	1670	6555	1094	1671	231	119	94	1019	527	<u>498</u>	.255	.312	.369	92	-86	382			.920	266	*2-1537,S-121/1P03	21.7

■ BOBBY PFEIL
Pfeil, Robert Raymond b: 11/13/43, Passaic, N.J. BR/TR, 6'1", 180 lbs. Deb: 6/26/69

1969	NY-N	62	211	20	49	9	0	0	10	7	27	.232	.260	.275	49	-14	0	1	-1	.976	-4	3-49,2-11/O-2	-1.9
1971	Phi-N	44	70	5	19	3	0	2	9	6	9	.271	.329	.400	106	0	1	1	-0	1.000	-2	3-15/C-4,O-3,12S	-0.2
Total	2	106	281	25	68	12	0	2	19	13	36	.242	.278	.306	63	-14	1	2	-1	.980	-6	/3-64,2-12,O-5,CS1	-2.1

■ GEORGE PFISTER
Pfister, George Edward b: 9/4/18, Bound Brook, N.J. BR/TR, 6', 200 lbs. Deb: 9/27/41 C

| 1941 | Bro-N | 1 | 2 | 0 | 0 | 0 | 0 | 0 | 0 | 0 | 0 | .000 | .000 | .000 | -96 | -1 | 0 | | | .000 | 0 | /C-1 | -0.1 |

■ MONTE PFYL
Pfyl, Meinhard Charles b: 5/11/1884, St.Louis, Mo. d: 10/18/45, San Francisco, Cal BL/TL, 6'3", 190 lbs. Deb: 7/30/07

| 1907 | NY-N | 1 | 0 | 0 | 0 | 0 | 0 | 0 | 0 | 0 | 0 | — | — | — | -0 | 0 | 0 | | | .000 | 0 | /1-1 | 0.0 |

■ ART PHELAN
Phelan, Arthur Thomas "Dugan" b: 8/14/1887, Niantic, Ill. d: 12/27/64, Ft.Worth, Tex. BR/TR, 5'8", 160 lbs. Deb: 6/25/10

1910	Cin-N	23	42	7	9	0	0	0	4	7	6	.214	.327	.214	61	-2	5			1.000	-2	/3-8,2-5,O-3,S-1	-0.4
1912	Cin-N	130	461	56	112	9	11	3	54	46	37	.243	.314	.330	79	-14	25			.924	-2	*3-127/2-3	-1.4
1913	Chi-N	91	261	41	65	11	6	2	35	29	26	.249	.331	.360	97	-1	8			.931	-8	2-46,3-38/S-1	-0.9
1914	Chi-N	25	46	5	13	2	1	0	3	4	3	.283	.340	.370	111	1	0			.905	-0	/3-7,2-3,S-2	0.1
1915	Chi-N	133	448	41	98	16	7	3	35	55	42	.219	.307	.306	86	-7	12	9	-2	.939	-2	*3-110,2-24	-0.6
Total	5	402	1258	150	297	38	25	8	131	141	114	.236	.317	.325	85	-23	50	<u>9</u>		.931	-14	3-290/2-81,S-4,O-3	-3.2

■ DAN PHELAN
Phelan, Daniel T. b: 7/23/1864, Thomaston, Conn. d: 12/7/45, West Haven, Conn. Deb: 4/18/1890

| 1890 | Lou-a | 8 | 32 | 4 | 8 | 1 | 1 | 0 | 4 | 0 | | .250 | .250 | .344 | 77 | -1 | 1 | | | .975 | 0 | /1-8 | -0.1 |

■ DICK PHELAN
Phelan, James Dickson b: 12/10/1854, Towanda, Pa. d: 2/13/31, San Antonio, Tex. BR , Deb: 4/17/1884

1884	Bal-U	101	402	63	99	13	3	3		12		.246	.268	.316	69	-28				.872	-9	*2-100/3-5,O-1	-3.0
1885	Buf-N	4	16	2	2	0	0	1	3	0	3	.125	.125	.313	37	-1				.808	-1	/2-4	-0.2
	StL-N	2	4	1	1	1	0	0	1	0	2	.250	.250	.500	147	0				1.000	-1	/3-2	0.0
	Yr	6	20	3	3	1	0	1	4	0	5	.150	.150	.350	58	-1				.808	-2	/2-4,3-2	-0.2
Total	2	107	422	66	102	14	3	4	<u>4</u>	12	<u>5</u>	.242	.263	.318	69	-29				.869	-10	2-104/3-7,O-1	-3.2

■ NEALY PHELPS
Phelps, Cornelius Carman b: 11/19/1840, New York, N.Y. d: 2/12/1885, New York, N.Y. Deb: 7/1/1871

1871	Kek-n	1	3	0	0	0	0	0	0	0	0	.000	.250	.000	-20	-0	0	0	0	.889	-0	/1-1	0.0
1873	Mut-n	1	6	0	0	0	0	0	0	0	1	.000	.000	.000	-99	-1	0	0	0	1.000	-0	/1-1,O-1	-0.1
1874	Mut-n	6	24	5	3	0	0	0	2	0	0	.125	.125	.125	-19	-3	0	0	0	.818	1	/O-6	-0.1
1875	Mut-n	2	6	1	2	1	0	0	0	0	0	.333	.333	.500	176	0	0	0	0	1.000	-1	/O-2	0.1
1876	NY-N	1	3	0	0	0	0	0	0	0	1	.000	.000	.000	-99	-1	0	0	0	.667	-0	/O-1	-0.1
	Phi-N	1	4	0	0	0	0	0	0	0	0	.000	.000	.000	-99	-1	0	0	0	.571	-1	/C-1	-0.2
	Yr	2	7	0	0	0	0	0	0	0	1	.000	.000	.000	-99	-1	0	0	0	.667	-1	/O-1,C-1	-0.3
Total	4 n	10	39	6	5	1	0	0	2	1	1	.128	.150	.154	-3	-5	0	0	0	.857	2	/O-9,1-2	-0.1

■ ED PHELPS
Phelps, Edward Jaykill "Yaller" b: 3/3/1879, Albany, N.Y. d: 1/31/42, E.Greenbush, N.Y. BR/TR, 5'11", 185 lbs. Deb: 9/3/02

1902	Pit-N	18	61	5	13	1	0	0	6	4		.213	.284	.230	56	-3	2			.968	-6	C-13/1-5	-0.8
1903	*Pit-N	81	273	32	77	7	3	2	31	17		.282	.358	.352	94	-2	2			.980	-8	C-76/1-3	-0.3
1904	Pit-N	94	302	29	73	5	3	0	28	15		.242	.289	.278	73	-9	2			.964	-11	C-91/1-1	-1.1
1905	Cin-N	44	156	18	36	5	3	0	18	12		.231	.306	.301	73	-5	4			.949	-6	C-44	-0.7
1906	Cin-N	12	40	3	11	0	2	1	5	3		.275	.326	.450	136	1	2			.987	-1	C-12	0.2
	Pit-N	43	118	9	28	3	1	0	12	9		.237	.302	.280	78	-3	1			.971	-3	C-40	-0.3
	Yr	55	158	12	39	3	3	1	17	12		.247	.308	.323	93	-2	3			.975	-4	C-52	-0.1
1907	Pit-N	43	113	11	24	1	0	0	12	9		.212	.282	.221	57	-5	1			.979	-3	C-35/1-1	-0.6
1908	Pit-N	34	64	3	15	2	0	0	11	2		.234	.269	.328	90	-1	0			.977	-0	C-20	0.0
1909	StL-N	104	306	43	76	13	0	0	22	39		.248	.350	.297	108	5	7			.954	-9	C-83	0.3
1910	StL-N	93	270	25	71	4	2	0	37	36	29	.263	.356	.293	93	-1	9			.976	-15	C-80	-0.9
1912	Bro-N	52	111	8	32	4	0	0	23	16	15	.288	.388	.378	114	3	1			.976	-4	C-32	0.1
1913	Bro-N	15	18	0	4	0	0	0	1	2		.222	.263	.222	38	-1	0			.875	-2	/C-4	-0.3
Total	11	633	1832	186	460	45	20	3	205	163	46	.251	.325	.302	89	-22	31			.968	-69	C-530/1-10	-4.4

■ BABE PHELPS
Phelps, Ernest Gordon "Blimp" b: 4/19/08, Odenton, Md. d: 12/10/92, Odenton, Md. BL/TR, 6'2", 225 lbs. Deb: 9/17/31

1931	Was-A	3	3	0	1	0	0	0	0	0	0	.333	.333	.333	75	-0	0	0	0	.000	0	H	0.0
1933	Chi-N	3	7	0	2	0	0	0	2	0	1	.286	.286	.286	64	-0	0			1.000	1	/C-2	0.0
1934	Chi-N	44	70	7	20	5	2	2	12	1	8	.286	.296	.500	111	1	0			.981	-2	C-18	-0.1
1935	Bro-N	47	121	17	44	7	2	5	22	9	10	.364	.408	.579	165	11	0			.957	-2	C-34	1.0
1936	Bro-N	115	319	36	117	23	2	5	57	27	18	.367	.421	.498	145	21	1			.977	-16	C-98/O-1	0.9
1937	Bro-N	121	409	42	128	37	3	7	58	25	28	.313	.357	.469	121	11	2			.971	-7	*C-111	1.0
1938	Bro-N†	66	208	33	64	12	2	5	46	23	15	.308	.379	.457	126	8	2			.980	-4	C-55	0.6
1939	Bro-N★	98	323	33	92	21	2	6	42	24	24	.285	.336	.418	98	-1	0			.980	2	C-92	0.5
1940	Bro-N★	118	370	47	109	24	5	13	61	30	27	.295	.349	.492	122	10	2			.977	-9	C-99/1-1	0.8
1941	Bro-N	16	30	3	7	3	0	2	4	3	3	.233	.258	.533	114	1	0			.971	-1	C-11	0.0
1942	Pit-N	95	257	21	73	11	1	9	41	20	24	.284	.345	.440	126	8	0			.959	-3	C-72	1.1
Total	11	726	2117	239	657	143	19	54	345	160	157	.310	.362	.472	124	67	9	<u>0</u>		.974	-41	C-592/1-1,O-1	5.8

■ KEN PHELPS
Phelps, Kenneth Allen b: 8/6/54, Seattle, Wash. BL/TL, 6'1", 209 lbs. Deb: 9/20/80

1980	KC-A	3	4	0	0	0	0	0	0	0	0	.000	.000	.000	-99	-1	0	0	0	1.000	-0	/1-2	-0.1
1981	KC-A	21	22	1	3	0	0	1	1	1	13	.136	.174	.227	15	-2	0	0	0	1.000	-0	/1-2,D-4	-0.2
1982	Mon-N	10	8	0	2	0	0	0	0	0	3	.250	.333	.250	64	-0	0	0	0	.000	0	H	-0.1
1983	Sea-A	50	127	16	30	4	1	7	16	13	25	.236	.307	.449	101	0	0	0	0	1.000	2	1-22,D-19	0.0

YEAR	TM/L	G	AB	R	H	2B	3B	HR	RBI	BB	SO	AVG	OBP	SLG	PRO+	BR/A	SB	CS	SBR	FA	FR	G/POS	TPR
1984	Sea-A	101	290	52	70	9	0	24	51	61	73	.241	.382	.521	149	21	3	3	-1	.987	-1	D-84/1-9	1.6
1985	Sea-A	61	116	18	24	3	0	9	24	24	33	.207	.382	.466	118	3	2	0	1	1.000	-0	D-25/1-8	0.3
1986	Sea-A	125	344	69	85	16	4	24	64	88	96	.247	.409	.526	151	28	2	3	-1	.983	-4	1-55,D-52	1.8
1987	Sea-A	120	332	68	86	13	1	27	68	80	75	.259	.414	.548	145	24	1	1	-0	1.000	-0	*D-114/1-1	1.9
1988	Sea-A	72	190	37	54	8	0	14	32	51	35	.284	.438	.547	167	19	1	0	0	.952	0	D-68/1-3	1.8
	NY-A	45	107	17	24	5	0	10	22	19	26	.224	.341	.551	147	6	0	0	0	.000	-0	D-24/1-9	0.6
	Yr	117	297	54	78	13	0	24	54	70	61	.263	.405	.549	160	26	1	0	0	.952	-0	D-92/1-4	2.4
1989	NY-A	86	185	26	46	3	0	7	29	27	47	.249	.344	.378	105	2	0	0	0	.980	-1	D-55/1-8	-0.1
	*Oak-A	11	9	0	1	1	0	0	0	4	0	.111	.385	.222	78	-0	0	0	0	.000	-0	/1-1,D-1	0.0
	Yr	97	194	26	47	4	0	7	29	31	47	.242	.347	.371	104	2	0	0	0	.980	-1	D-56/1-9	-0.1
1990	Oak-A	32	59	6	11	2	0	1	6	12	10	.186	.324	.271	71	-2	0	0	0	.964	0	D-15/1-5	-0.2
	Cle-A	24	61	4	7	0	0	0	0	10	11	.115	.239	.115	2	-8	1	0	0	1.000	-0	1-14/D-6	-0.9
	Yr	56	120	10	18	2	0	1	6	22	21	.150	.282	.192	36	-10	1	0	0	.992	0	D-21,1-19	-1.1
Total	11	761	1854	308	443	64	7	123	313	390	449	.239	.377	.480	132	89	10	7	-1	.987	-4	D-467,1-131	6.4

■ **DAVE PHILLEY**   Philley, David Earl   b: 5/16/20, Paris, Tex.   BB/TR, 6', 188 lbs.   Deb: 9/6/41

YEAR	TM/L	G	AB	R	H	2B	3B	HR	RBI	BB	SO	AVG	OBP	SLG	PRO+	BR/A	SB	CS	SBR	FA	FR	G/POS	TPR
1941	Chi-A	7	9	4	2	1	0	0	0	3	3	.222	.417	.333	102	0	0	0	0	.000	-1	/O-2	-0.1
1946	Chi-A	17	68	10	24	2	3	0	17	4	4	.353	.389	.471	145	4	5	0	2	.983	5	O-17	1.0
1947	Chi-A	143	551	55	142	25	11	2	45	35	39	.258	.303	.354	85	-13	21	16	-3	.986	2	*O-133/3-4	-2.2
1948	Chi-A	137	488	51	140	28	3	5	42	50	33	.287	.353	.387	100	-0	8	10	-4	.978	15	*O-128	0.4
1949	Chi-A	146	598	84	171	20	8	0	44	54	51	.286	.347	.346	86	-12	13	4	2	.977	2	*O-145	-1.6
1950	Chi-A	156	619	69	150	21	5	14	80	52	57	.242	.302	.360	71	-30	6	3	0	.980	1	*O-154	-3.3
1951	Chi-A	7	25	0	6	2	0	0	2	2	3	.240	.296	.320	68	-1	0	0	0	.938	-0	/O-6	-0.2
	Phi-A	125	468	71	123	18	7	7	59	63	38	.263	.354	.376	95	-2	9	6	-1	.978	-0	*O-120/3-2	-0.6
	Yr	132	493	71	129	20	7	7	61	65	41	.262	.351	.373	94	-3	9	6	-1	.976	2	*O-126/3-2	-0.8
1952	Phi-A	151	586	80	154	25	4	7	59	71	59	.263	.334	.355	86	-10	11	4	1	.991	3	*O-149/3-2	-0.3
1953	Phi-A	157	620	80	188	30	9	9	59	51	35	.303	.358	.424	106	5	13	5	1	.981	-4	*O-157/3-1	-0.4
1954	*Cle-A	133	452	48	102	13	3	12	60	57	48	.226	.312	.347	79	-13	2	4	-2	.984	-4	*O-129	-2.5
1955	Cle-A	43	104	15	31	4	2	2	9	12	10	.298	.371	.433	111	2	0	2	-1	1.000	-3	O-34	-0.3
	Bal-A	83	311	50	93	13	6	4	41	34	38	.299	.368	.418	119	8	1	2	-1	.970	-7	O-82/3-2	-0.3
	Yr	126	415	65	124	17	5	8	50	46	48	.299	.369	.422	116	9	1	4	-2	.976	-9	*O-116/3-2	-0.6
1956	Bal-A	32	117	13	24	4	2	1	17	18	13	.205	.311	.299	67	-6	3	1	0	.935	-4	O-31/3-5	-1.1
	Chi-A	86	279	44	74	14	2	4	47	28	27	.265	.334	.373	85	-6	1	3	-2	.978	-9	1-51,O-30	-2.0
	Yr	118	396	57	98	18	4	5	64	46	40	.247	.327	.351	80	-11	4	4	-2	.965	-13	O-61,1-51/3-5	-3.1
1957	Chi-A	22	71	9	23	4	0	0	9	4	10	.324	.360	.380	102	0	1	1	-0	.975	1	O-17/1-2	-0.1
	Det-A	65	173	15	49	8	1	2	16	7	16	.283	.311	.376	85	-4	3	1	0	.996	1	1-27,O-12/3-1	-0.5
	Yr	87	244	24	72	12	1	2	25	11	26	.295	.325	.377	90	-4	4	2	0	.965	2	O-29,1-29/3-1	-0.6
1958	Phi-N	91	207	30	64	11	4	3	31	15	20	.309	.359	.444	113	4	1	1	-0	1.000	-4	O-24,1-18	-0.2
1959	Phi-N	99	254	32	74	18	2	7	37	18	27	.291	.341	.461	109	3	0	0	0	1.000	1	O-34,1-24	0.1
1960	Phi-N	14	15	2	5	2	0	0	4	3	2	.333	.444	.467	149	1	0	0	0	.000	-2	/O-3,1-2	-0.1
	SF-N	39	61	5	10	0	0	1	7	6	14	.164	.239	.213	26	-6	0	0	0	.941	-4	O-10/3-3	-0.8
	Yr	53	76	7	15	2	0	1	11	9	16	.197	.282	.263	53	-5	0	0	0	.941	-3	O-13/3-3,1-2	-0.9
	Bal-A	14	34	6	9	2	1	1	5	4	5	.265	.342	.471	119	1	1	0	0	1.000	-0	/O-8,3-1	0.0
1961	Bal-A	99	144	13	36	9	2	1	23	10	20	.250	.299	.361	78	-5	2	0	1	1.000	-6	O-25/1-1	-1.1
1962	Bos-A	38	42	3	6	2	0	0	4	5	3	.143	.250	.190	20	-5	0	0	0	1.000	-0	/O-4	-0.5
Total	18	1904	6296	789	1700	276	72	84	729	594	551	.270	.335	.377	91	-86	101	63	-8	.981	-0	*O-1454,1-125/3-21	-16.7

■ **ADOLFO PHILLIPS**   Phillips, Adolfo Emilio (Lopez)   b: 12/16/41, Bethania, Panama   BR/TR, 6', 177 lbs.   Deb: 9/2/64

YEAR	TM/L	G	AB	R	H	2B	3B	HR	RBI	BB	SO	AVG	OBP	SLG	PRO+	BR/A	SB	CS	SBR	FA	FR	G/POS	TPR
1964	Phi-N	13	13	4	3	0	0	0	0	3	3	.231	.375	.231	76	-0	0	0	0	1.000	-0	/O-4	-0.1
1965	Phi-N	41	87	14	20	0	0	3	5	5	34	.230	.272	.379	83	-2	3	3	-1	1.000	-4	O-32	-0.8
1966	Phi-N	2	3	1	0	0	0	0	0	0	0	.000	.000	.000	-99	-1	0	0	0	1.000	-0	/O-1	-0.1
	Chi-N	116	416	68	109	29	1	16	36	43	135	.262	.348	.452	119	11	32	15	1	.978	12	*O-111	1.9
	Yr	118	419	69	109	29	1	16	36	43	135	.260	.346	.449	118	10	32	15	1	.979	12	*O-112	1.8
1967	Chi-N	144	448	66	120	20	7	17	70	80	93	.268	.386	.458	134	23	24	10	1	.981	15	*O-141	3.4
1968	Chi-N	143	439	49	106	20	5	13	33	47	90	.241	.322	.399	108	5	9	7	-2	.979	6	*O-141	0.3
1969	Chi-N	28	49	5	11	3	1	0	1	16	15	.224	.424	.327	100	1	3	2	-2	.956	-3	O-25	-0.4
	Mon-N	58	199	25	43	4	4	4	7	19	62	.216	.288	.337	74	-7	6	5	-1	.981	-1	O-53	-1.3
	Yr	86	248	30	54	7	5	4	8	35	77	.218	.319	.335	80	-6	7	8	-3	.973	-3	O-78	-1.7
1970	Mon-N	92	214	36	51	6	3	6	21	36	51	.238	.353	.379	96	-0	7	1	2	.985	-6	O-75	-0.8
1972	Cle-A	12	7	2	0	0	0	0	0	2	2	.000	.222	.000	-29	-1	0	0	0	1.000	-3	O-10	-0.4
Total	8	649	1875	270	463	86	21	59	173	251	485	.247	.344	.410	110	27	82	44	-2	.980	17	O-593	1.7

■ **J. R. PHILLIPS**   Phillips, Charles Gene   b: 4/29/70, West Covina, Cal.   BL/TL, 6'1", 185 lbs.   Deb: 9/3/93

YEAR	TM/L	G	AB	R	H	2B	3B	HR	RBI	BB	SO	AVG	OBP	SLG	PRO+	BR/A	SB	CS	SBR	FA	FR	G/POS	TPR
1993	SF-N	11	16	1	5	1	1	1	4	0	5	.313	.313	.688	164	1	0	0	0	.971	0	/1-5	0.1
1994	SF-N	15	38	1	5	0	0	1	3	1	13	.132	.154	.211	-7	-6	1	0	0	.989	1	1-10	-0.5
1995	SF-N	92	231	27	45	9	0	9	28	19	69	.195	.256	.351	60	-14	1	1	-0	.993	-2	1-79/O-1	-2.2
1996	SF-N	15	25	3	5	0	0	2	5	1	13	.200	.231	.440	75	-1	0	0	0	.981	-1	1-10	-0.2
	Phi-N	35	79	9	12	5	0	5	10	10	38	.152	.256	.405	69	-4	0	0	0	.957	3	O-15,1-11	-0.2
	Yr	50	104	12	17	5	0	7	15	11	51	.163	.250	.413	71	-5	0	0	0	.992	3	1-21,O-15	-0.4
Total	4	168	389	41	72	15	1	18	50	31	138	.185	.247	.368	61	-24	2	1	0	.992	2	1-115/O-16	-3.0

■ **DAMON PHILLIPS**   Phillips, Damon Roswell "Dee"   b: 6/8/19, Corsicana, Tex.   BR/TR, 6', 176 lbs.   Deb: 7/19/42

YEAR	TM/L	G	AB	R	H	2B	3B	HR	RBI	BB	SO	AVG	OBP	SLG	PRO+	BR/A	SB	CS	SBR	FA	FR	G/POS	TPR
1942	Cin-N	28	84	4	17	2	1	0	7	5	7	.202	.264	.226	44	-6	0			.964	7	S-27	0.3
1944	Bos-N	140	489	35	126	30	1	1	53	28	34	.258	.301	.329	74	-17	1			.932	-4	3-90,S-60	-1.6
1946	Bos-N	2	2	0	1	0	0	0	0	0	0	.500	.500	.500	182	0				.000	0	H	0.0
Total	3	170	575	39	144	32	1	1	59	35	39	.250	.296	.315	70	-23	1			.956	3	/3-90,S-87	-1.3

■ **EDDIE PHILLIPS**   Phillips, Edward David   b: 2/17/01, Worcester, Mass.   d: 1/26/68, Buffalo, N.Y.   BR/TR, 6', 178 lbs.   Deb: 5/4/24

YEAR	TM/L	G	AB	R	H	2B	3B	HR	RBI	BB	SO	AVG	OBP	SLG	PRO+	BR/A	SB	CS	SBR	FA	FR	G/POS	TPR
1924	Bos-N	3	3	0	0	0	0	0	0	0	2	.000	.000	.000	-99	-1	0	0	0	1.000	0	/C-1	-0.1
1929	Det-A	68	221	24	52	13	1	2	21	20	16	.235	.302	.330	62	-13	0	1	-1	.967	-5	C-63	-1.2
1931	Pit-N	106	353	30	82	18	3	7	44	41	49	.232	.317	.360	82	-9	1			.986	-7	*C-103	-0.8
1932	NY-A	9	31	4	9	1	0	2	4	2	3	.290	.333	.516	123	1	0	0	0	1.000	1	/C-9	0.2
1934	Was-A	56	169	6	33	6	1	2	16	26	24	.195	.306	.278	54	-12	1	0	0	.984	-7	C-53	-1.5
1935	Cle-A	70	220	18	60	16	1	1	41	15	21	.273	.319	.368	76	-8	0	0	0	.980	-8	C-69	-1.3
Total	6	312	997	82	236	54	6	14	126	104	115	.237	.312	.345	72	-41	3	1		.980	-27	C-298	-4.7

■ **EDDIE PHILLIPS**   Phillips, Howard Edward   b: 7/8/31, St.Louis, Mo.   BB/TR, 6'1", 180 lbs.   Deb: 9/10/53

YEAR	TM/L	G	AB	R	H	2B	3B	HR	RBI	BB	SO	AVG	OBP	SLG	PRO+	BR/A	SB	CS	SBR	FA	FR	G/POS	TPR
1953	StL-N	9	0	4	0	0	0	0	0	0	0	—	—	—		0	0	0	0	.000	0	R	0.0

■ **JACK PHILLIPS**   Phillips, Jack Dorn "Stretch"   b: 9/6/21, Clarence, N.Y.   BR/TR, 6'4", 193 lbs.   Deb: 8/22/47

YEAR	TM/L	G	AB	R	H	2B	3B	HR	RBI	BB	SO	AVG	OBP	SLG	PRO+	BR/A	SB	CS	SBR	FA	FR	G/POS	TPR
1947	*NY-A	16	36	5	10	0	1	1	2	3	5	.278	.333	.417	109	-0	0	0	0	.986	-2	1-10	-0.2
1948	NY-A	1	2	0	0	0	0	0	0	0	0	.000	.000	.000	-99	-1	0	0	0	.889	-0	/1-1	-0.1
1949	NY-A	45	91	16	28	4	1	1	10	12	9	.308	.388	.407	110	2	0	0	0	.977	-1	1-38	-0.1
	Pit-N	18	56	16	13	3	1	0	3	4	6	.232	.283	.321	60	-3	1			1.000	-1	1-16/3-1	-0.3
1950	Pit-N	69	208	25	61	7	6	5	34	20	17	.293	.355	.457	108	2	1			.986	2	1-54/3-3,P-1	0.3
1951	Pit-N	70	156	12	37	7	3	0	12	15	17	.237	.304	.321	66	-7	2	1	-1	.991	-1	1-53/3-4	-1.1
1952	Pit-N	1	1	0	0	0	0	0	0	0	0	.000	.000	.000	-97	-0	0	0	0	1.000	-1	/1-1	0.0
1955	Det-A	55	117	15	37	6	1	1	20	10	12	.316	.370	.444	121	3	1	0	0	.992	-1	1-35/3-3	0.0
1956	Det-A	67	224	31	66	13	2	1	20	21	19	.295	.355	.384	95	-2	1	1	-0	.981	-1	1-56/2-1,O-1	-0.7
1957	Det-A	1	1	1	1	0	0	0	0	0	0	.000	.000	.000	-97	-0	0	0	0	.000	0	H	0.0
Total	9	343	892	111	252	42	16	9	101	85	86	.283	.345	.396	95	-6	5	3		.986	-6	1-264/3-11,O-1,2P	-2.1

YEAR	TM/L	G	AB	R	H	2B	3B	HR	RBI	BB	SO	AVG	OBP	SLG	PRO+	BR/A	SB	CS	SBR	FA	FR	G/POS	TPR

■ BUBBA PHILLIPS
Phillips, John Melvin b: 2/24/28, West Point, Miss. d: 6/22/93, Hattiesburg, Miss. BR/TR, 5'9", 180 lbs. Deb: 4/30/55

YEAR	TM/L	G	AB	R	H	2B	3B	HR	RBI	BB	SO	AVG	OBP	SLG	PRO+	BR/A	SB	CS	SBR	FA	FR	G/POS	TPR
1955	Det-A	95	184	18	43	4	0	3	23	14	20	.234	.295	.304	63	-10	2	1	0	.992	-1	O-65/3-4	-1.3
1956	Chi-A	67	99	16	27	6	0	2	11	6	12	.273	.321	.394	87	-2	1	-1	-1	1.000	-1	O-35/3-2	-0.5
1957	Chi-A	121	393	38	106	13	3	7	42	28	32	.270	.323	.372	89	-6	5	3	-0	.958	16	3-97,O-20	1.0
1958	Chi-A	84	260	26	71	10	0	5	30	15	14	.273	.315	.369	89	-4	3	0	1	.954	7	3-47,O-37	0.2
1959	*Chi-A	117	379	43	100	27	1	5	40	27	28	.264	.320	.380	92	-4	1	1	-0	.951	3	*3-100,O-23	-0.3
1960	Cle-A	113	304	34	63	14	1	4	33	14	37	.207	.252	.299	50	-22	1	0	0	.953	-8	3-85,O-25/S-1	-3.2
1961	Cle-A	143	546	64	144	23	1	18	72	29	61	.264	.307	.408	92	-8	1	0	0	.958	-18	*3-143	-2.5
1962	Cle-A	148	562	53	145	26	0	10	54	20	55	.258	.292	.358	76	-20	4	0	1	.977	-15	*3-145/O-3,2-1	-3.3
1963	Det-A	128	464	42	114	11	2	5	45	19	42	.246	.281	.310	63	-22	6	2	1	.961	1	*3-117/O-5	-2.2
1964	Det-A	46	87	14	22	1	0	3	6	10	13	.253	.340	.368	92	-1	0	0	0	.983	2	3-22/O-1	0.0
Total	10	1062	3278	348	835	135	8	62	356	182	314	.255	.300	.358	79	-100	25	11	1	.960	-16	3-762,O-214/2-1,S-1	-12.1

■ JACK PHILLIPS
Phillips, John Stephen b: 5/24/19, St.Louis, Mo. d: 6/16/58, St.Louis, Mo. BR/TR, 6'1", 185 lbs. Deb: 7/13/45

YEAR	TM/L	G	AB	R	H	2B	3B	HR	RBI	BB	SO	AVG	OBP	SLG	PRO+	BR/A	SB	CS	SBR	FA	FR	G/POS	TPR
1945	NY-N	2	2	1	1	0	0	0	0	0	0	.500	.500	.500	176	0	0			1.000	-0	/P-1	0.0

■ TONY PHILLIPS
Phillips, Keith Anthony b: 4/25/59, Atlanta, Ga. BB/TR, 5'10", 160 lbs. Deb: 5/10/82

YEAR	TM/L	G	AB	R	H	2B	3B	HR	RBI	BB	SO	AVG	OBP	SLG	PRO+	BR/A	SB	CS	SBR	FA	FR	G/POS	TPR
1982	Oak-A	40	81	11	17	2	2	0	8	12	26	.210	.326	.284	73	-3	2	3	-1	.953	-5	S-39	-0.5
1983	Oak-A	148	412	54	102	12	3	4	35	48	70	.248	.329	.320	85	-8	16	5	2	.941	1	*S-101,2-63/3-4,D-1	0.5
1984	Oak-A	154	451	62	120	24	3	4	37	42	86	.266	.329	.359	97	-2	10	6	-1	.941	-11	S-91,2-90/O-1	-0.4
1985	Oak-A	42	161	23	45	12	2	4	17	13	34	.280	.333	.453	122	4	3	2	-0	.980	-0	3-31,2-24	0.4
1986	Oak-A	118	441	76	113	14	5	5	52	76	82	.256	.369	.345	103	5	15	10	-2	.976	1	2-88,3-30/O-4,SD	0.7
1987	Oak-A	111	379	48	91	20	0	10	46	57	76	.240	.339	.372	95	-2	7	6	-2	.974	-3	2-87,3-11/S-9,OD	-0.1
1988	*Oak-A	79	212	32	43	8	4	2	17	36	50	.203	.321	.307	80	-5	0	2	-1	.913	-20	3-32,O-31,2S/1D	-2.6
1989	*Oak-A	143	451	48	118	15	6	4	47	58	66	.262	.350	.348	101	2	3	8	-4	.985	-24	2-84,3-49,S-17,O/1	-2.3
1990	Det-A	152	573	97	144	23	5	8	55	99	85	.251	.365	.351	100	4	19	9	0	.931	6	*3-104,2-47,S/OD	1.3
1991	Det-A	146	564	87	160	28	4	17	72	79	95	.284	.375	.438	122	19	10	5	0	.992	6	O-56,3-46,2-36,DS	2.5
1992	Det-A	159	606	114	167	32	3	10	64	114	93	.276	.391	.388	118	20	12	10	-2	.968	-2	O-69,2-57,D-34,3/S	2.0
1993	Det-A	151	566	113	177	27	0	7	57	132	102	.313	.446	.398	130	33	16	11	-2	.969	-1	*O-108,2-51/3-1,D-4	2.9
1994	Det-A	114	438	91	123	19	3	19	61	95	105	.281	.411	.468	126	20	13	5	1	.980	7	*O-104,2-12/D-6	2.4
1995	Cal-A	139	525	119	137	21	1	27	61	113	135	.261	.395	.459	122	21	13	10	-2	.924	4	3-88,O-48/D-2	2.2
1996	Chi-A	153	581	119	161	29	3	12	63	125	132	.277	.408	.399	111	17	13	8	-1	.981	16	*O-150/2-2,1-1	2.4
Total	15	1849	6441	1094	1718	286	44	133	692	1099	1237	.267	.376	.387	110	126	152	100	-14	.982	-19	2-668,O-597,3S/D1	11.2

■ MARR PHILLIPS
Phillips, Marr B. b: 6/16/1857, Pittsburgh, Pa. d: 4/1/28, Pittsburgh, Pa. BR, 5'6.5", 164 lbs. Deb: 5/1/1884

YEAR	TM/L	G	AB	R	H	2B	3B	HR	RBI	BB	SO	AVG	OBP	SLG	PRO+	BR/A	SB	CS	SBR	FA	FR	G/POS	TPR
1884	Ind-a	97	413	41	111	18	8	0		5		.269	.279	.351	107	3				.862	14	*S-97	1.6
1885	Det-N	33	139	13	29	5	0	0	17	0	13	.209	.209	.245	46	-8				.881	2	S-33	-0.5
	Pit-a	4	15	1	4	0	0	0	2	2		.267	.353	.267	99	0				.875	-1	/S-4	-0.1
1890	Roc-a	64	257	18	53	8	0	0	34	16		.206	.261	.237	51	-16	10			.918	6	S-64	-0.6
Total	3	198	824	73	197	31	8	0	53	23	13	.239	.263	.296	79	-21	10			.884	21	S-198	0.4

■ MIKE PHILLIPS
Phillips, Michael Dwaine b: 8/19/50, Beaumont, Tex. BL/TR, 6'1", 185 lbs. Deb: 4/15/73

YEAR	TM/L	G	AB	R	H	2B	3B	HR	RBI	BB	SO	AVG	OBP	SLG	PRO+	BR/A	SB	CS	SBR	FA	FR	G/POS	TPR
1973	SF-N	63	104	18	25	3	4	1	9	6	17	.240	.288	.375	79	-3	0	3	-2	.931	-0	3-28,S-20/2-7	-0.4
1974	SF-N	100	283	19	62	6	1	2	20	14	37	.219	.258	.269	45	-21	4	5	-2	.909	4	3-34,2-30,S-23	-1.6
1975	SF-N	10	31	3	6	0	0	0	1	6	4	.194	.324	.194	44	-2	1	0	0	.969	-4	/2-6,3-6	0.2
	NY-N	116	383	31	98	10	7	1	28	25	47	.256	.303	.326	78	-12	3	0	1	.944	1	*S-115/2-1	0.1
	Yr	126	414	34	104	10	7	1	29	31	51	.251	.305	.316	76	-14	4	0	1	.944	-3	*S-115/2-7,3-6	0.3
1976	NY-N	87	262	30	67	4	6	4	29	25	29	.256	.321	.363	99	-1	2	2	-1	.955	-9	S-53,2-19,3-10	-0.4
1977	NY-N	38	86	5	18	2	1	1	3	2	15	.209	.244	.291	45	-7	0	1	0	1.000	-5	S-24/3-9,2-4	-1.1
	StL-N	48	87	17	21	3	2	0	9	9	13	.241	.320	.322	74	-3	1	0	0	.971	5	2-31/S-5,3-5	0.4
	Yr	86	173	22	39	5	3	1	12	11	28	.225	.283	.306	60	-10	1	1	0	.973	1	2-35,S-29,3-14	-0.7
1978	StL-N	76	164	14	44	8	1	1	28	13	25	.268	.330	.348	91	-2	0	0	0	.971	-1	2-55,S-10/3-1	0.1
1979	StL-N	44	97	10	22	3	1	1	6	10	9	.227	.306	.309	68	-4	0	0	0	.973	13	S-25,2-16/3-1	1.1
1980	StL-N	63	128	13	30	5	0	0	7	9	17	.234	.285	.273	55	-3	0	0	0	.971	13	S-37/2-9,3-8	0.9
1981	SD-N	14	29	1	6	0	1	0	0	0	3	.207	.207	.276	39	-2	1	0	0	.979	4	/2-9,S-1	0.2
	*Mon-N	34	55	5	12	2	0	0	4	5	15	.218	.283	.255	53	-3	0	1	-1	.974	0	S-26/2-6	-0.2
	Yr	48	84	6	18	2	1	0	4	5	18	.214	.258	.262	49	-6	1	1	-1	.974	4	S-27,2-15	0.0
1982	Mon-N	14	8	0	1	0	0	0	0	0	1	.125	.125	.125	-29	-1	0	0	0	1.000	1	2-10/S-2	0.1
1983	Mon-N	5	2	0	0	0	0	0	0	0	0	.000	.000	.000	-99	-1	0	0	0	.000	-1	/S-3,3-2	-0.2
Total	11	712	1719	166	412	46	24	11	145	124	234	.240	.294	.314	70	-70	12	12	-4	.956	29	S-344,2-203,3-104	-0.8

■ DICK PHILLIPS
Phillips, Richard Eugene b: 11/24/31, Racine, Wis. BL/TR, 6', 180 lbs. Deb: 4/15/62 C

YEAR	TM/L	G	AB	R	H	2B	3B	HR	RBI	BB	SO	AVG	OBP	SLG	PRO+	BR/A	SB	CS	SBR	FA	FR	G/POS	TPR
1962	SF-N	5	3	1	0	0	0	0	1	1	1	.000	.250	.000	-27	-1	0	0	0	1.000	-0	/1-1	-0.1
1963	Was-A	124	321	33	76	8	0	10	32	29	35	.237	.304	.355	84	-7	1	0	0	.994	4	1-68/2-5,3-4	-0.6
1964	Was-A	109	234	17	54	6	1	2	23	27	22	.231	.313	.291	70	-9	1	2	-1	.994	2	1-61/3-4	-1.1
1966	Was-A	25	37	3	6	0	0	0	4	2	5	.162	.225	.162	13	-4	0	0	0	1.000	-1	/1-5	-0.5
Total	4	263	595	54	136	14	1	12	60	59	63	.229	.302	.316	74	-20	2	2	-1	.995	5	1-135/3-8,2-5	-2.3

■ BILL PHILLIPS
Phillips, William B. b: 1857, St.John, N.B., Canada d: 10/7/1900, Chicago, Ill. BR/TR, 202 lbs. Deb: 5/1/1879

YEAR	TM/L	G	AB	R	H	2B	3B	HR	RBI	BB	SO	AVG	OBP	SLG	PRO+	BR/A	SB	CS	SBR	FA	FR	G/POS	TPR
1879	Cle-N	81	365	58	99	15	4	0	29	2	20	.271	.275	.334	101	0				.954	-5	*1-75,C-11/O-2	-0.6
1880	Cle-N	85	334	41	85	14	10	1	36	6	29	.254	.268	.365	115	5				.963	2	*1-85	-0.1
1881	Cle-N	85	357	51	97	18	10	1	44	5	19	.272	.282	.387	114	5				.966	-1	*1-85	-0.3
1882	Cle-N	78	335	40	87	17	7	4	47	7	18	.260	.275	.388	114	5				.971	3	*1-78/C-1	-0.1
1883	Cle-N	97	382	42	94	29	8	2	40	8	49	.246	.262	.380	93	-3				.967	-2	*1-97	-1.4
1884	Cle-N	111	464	58	128	25	12	3	46	18	93	.276	.303	.401	115	7				.959	-2	*1-111	-0.7
1885	Bro-a	99	391	65	118	16	11	3	63	27		.302	.364	.422	147	21		13		**.973**	0	*1-99	0.8
1886	Bro-a	141	585	68	160	26	15	0	72	33		.274	.313	.369	113	5	13			.978	-2	*1-141	-1.1
1887	Bro-a	132	533	82	142	34	11	2	101	45		.266	.330	.383	97	-3	16			**.982**	4	*1-132	-1.0
1888	KC-a	129	509	57	120	20	10	1	56	27		.236	.284	.320	88	-9	10			.980	3	*1-129	-1.7
Total	10	1038	4255	562	1130	214	98	17	534	178	215	.266	.299	.374	109	35	39			.971	1	*1-1032/C-12,O-2	-6.2

■ BILL PHYLE
Phyle, William Joseph b: 6/25/1875, Duluth, Minn. d: 8/6/53, Los Angeles, Cal. TR, Deb: 9/17/1898

YEAR	TM/L	G	AB	R	H	2B	3B	HR	RBI	BB	SO	AVG	OBP	SLG	PRO+	BR/A	SB	CS	SBR	FA	FR	G/POS	TPR
1898	Chi-N	4	9	1	1	0	0	0	2			.111	.273	.111	11	-1	0			.800	-1	/P-3	0.0
1899	Chi-N	10	34	2	6	0	0	0	1	0		.176	.176	.176	-3	-5	0			.935	1	P-10	0.0
1901	NY-N	25	66	4	12	2	0	0	3	2		.182	.206	.212	22	-7	0			.903	3	P-24/S-1	-0.1
1906	StL-N	22	73	6	13	3	1	0	4	5		.178	.231	.247	51	-4	2			.935	2	3-21	-0.2
Total	4	61	182	17	32	5	1	0	8	9		.176	.215	.214	28	-17	2			.907	3	/P-37,3-21,S-1	-0.2

■ MIKE PIAZZA
Piazza, Michael Joseph b: 9/4/68, Norristown, Pa. BR/TR, 6'3", 200 lbs. Deb: 9/1/92

YEAR	TM/L	G	AB	R	H	2B	3B	HR	RBI	BB	SO	AVG	OBP	SLG	PRO+	BR/A	SB	CS	SBR	FA	FR	G/POS	TPR
1992	LA-N	21	69	5	16	3	0	1	7	4	12	.232	.284	.319	71	-3	0	0	0	.990	-2	C-16	-0.4
1993	LA-N★	149	547	81	174	24	2	35	112	46	86	.318	.370	.561	155	41	3	4	-2	.989	5	*C-146/1-1	5.1
1994	LA-N★	107	405	64	129	18	0	24	92	33	65	.319	.371	.541	143	24	1	0	0	.985	-12	*C-104	1.7
1995	*LA-N★	112	434	82	150	17	0	32	93	39	80	.346	.401	.606	**177**	46	1	0	0	.990	-9	*C-112	4.4
1996	*LA-N★	148	547	87	184	16	0	36	105	81	93	.336	.423	.563	171	58	0	3	-2	.992	-5	C-146	5.9
Total	5	537	2002	319	653	78	2	128	409	203	336	.326	.390	.559	159	165	5	10	-5	.989	-22	C-524/1-1	16.7

■ ROB PICCIOLO
Picciolo, Robert Michael b: 2/4/53, Santa Monica, Cal. BR/TR, 6'2", 185 lbs. Deb: 4/9/77 C

YEAR	TM/L	G	AB	R	H	2B	3B	HR	RBI	BB	SO	AVG	OBP	SLG	PRO+	BR/A	SB	CS	SBR	FA	FR	G/POS	TPR
1977	Oak-A	148	419	35	84	12	3	2	22	9	55	.200	.219	.258	30	-41	1	4	-2	.966	7	*S-148	-2.3
1978	Oak-A	78	93	16	21	1	0	2	7	2	13	.226	.242	.301	55	-6	1	1	-0	.958	12	S-41,2-19,3-13	0.9
1979	Oak-A	115	348	37	88	9	2	5	18	3	45	.253	.261	.328	61	-20	2	1	-0	.964	-3	*S-105/2-6,3-4,O-1	-1.2
1980	Oak-A	95	271	32	65	9	2	1	25	2	18	.240	.245	.343	64	-15	1	1	-0	.977	-23	S-49,2-47/O-1	-3.1

YEAR	TM/L	G	AB	R	H	2B	3B	HR	RBI	BB	SO	AVG	OBP	SLG	PRO+	BR/A	SB	CS	SBR	FA	FR	G/POS	TPR
1981	*Oak-A	82	179	23	48	5	3	4	13	5	22	.268	.292	.397	102	-0	0	1	-1	.981	-15	S-82	-1.0
1982	Oak-A	18	49	3	11	1	0	0	3	1	10	.224	.240	.245	35	-4	1	0	0	.979	3	S-18	0.1
	Mil-A	22	21	7	6	1	0	0	1	1	4	.286	.318	.333	84	-0	0	0	0	1.000	2	2-11/S-6,D-1	0.1
	Yr	40	70	10	17	2	0	0	4	2	14	.243	.264	.271	50	-5	1	0	0	.973	5	S-24,2-11/D-1	0.2
1983	Mil-A	14	27	2	6	3	0	0	1	0	4	.222	.222	.333	55	-2	0	0	0	1.000	0	/S-7,2-3,2-3,2-1-1,D	0.1
1984	Cal-A	87	119	18	24	6	0	1	9	0	21	.202	.202	.277	31	-11	0	1	-1	.974	13	S-66,3-13/2-9,O-1	0.3
1985	Oak-A	71	102	19	28	2	0	1	8	2	17	.275	.288	.324	73	-4	3	2	-0	.889	7	3-19,2-17,1-13,D/S	0.3
Total	9	730	1628	192	381	56	10	17	109	25	254	.234	.247	.312	55	-103	9	11	-4	.970	6	S-531,2-111/31DO	-5.7

■ NICK PICCIUTO

Picciuto, Nicholas Thomas   b: 8/27/21, Newark, N.J.   BR/TR, 5'8.5", 165 lbs.   Deb: 5/11/45

YEAR	TM/L	G	AB	R	H	2B	3B	HR	RBI	BB	SO	AVG	OBP	SLG	PRO+	BR/A	SB	CS	SBR	FA	FR	G/POS	TPR
1945	Phi-N	36	89	7	12	6	0	0	6	6	17	.135	.189	.202	9	-11	0			.839	-6	3-30/2-4	-1.6

■ VAL PICINICH

Picinich, Valentine John   b: 9/8/1896, New York, N.Y.   d: 12/5/42, Nobleboro, Maine   BR/TR, 5'9", 165 lbs.   Deb: 7/25/16   C

YEAR	TM/L	G	AB	R	H	2B	3B	HR	RBI	BB	SO	AVG	OBP	SLG	PRO+	BR/A	SB	CS	SBR	FA	FR	G/POS	TPR
1916	Phi-A	40	118	8	23	3	1	0	5	6	33	.195	.234	.237	44	-9	1			.967	-0	C-37	-0.7
1917	Phi-A	2	6	0	2	0	0	0	0	1	2	.333	.429	.333	135	0	0			.786	-1	/C-2	-0.1
1918	Was-A	47	148	13	34	3	3	0	12	9	25	.230	.274	.291	72	-6	0			.960	-2	C-46	-0.4
1919	Was-A	80	212	18	58	12	3	3	22	17	43	.274	.330	.401	106	1	6			.978	15	C-69	2.1
1920	Was-A	48	133	14	27	6	2	3	14	9	33	.203	.259	.346	61	-8	0	0	0	.978	9	C-45	0.4
1921	Was-A	45	141	10	39	9	0	0	12	16	21	.277	.354	.340	82	-3	0	3	-2	.966	3	C-45	0.0
1922	Was-A	76	210	16	48	2	0	1	19	23	33	.229	.311	.305	64	-11	1	0	0	.976	7	C-76	0.0
1923	Bos-A	87	268	33	74	21	1	2	31	46	32	.276	.386	.384	103	3	3	5	-2	.957	-2	C-81	0.3
1924	Bos-A	69	161	25	44	6	3	1	24	29	19	.273	.394	.366	97	-0	5	1	1	.951	-4	C-52	0.0
1925	Bos-A	90	251	31	64	21	0	1	25	33	21	.255	.344	.351	77	-9	2	0	1	.968	-8	C-74/1-2	-1.1
1926	Cin-N	89	240	33	63	16	1	2	31	29	22	.262	.342	.363	92	-2	4			.967	-0	C-86	0.2
1927	Cin-N	65	173	16	44	8	3	0	12	24	15	.254	.345	.335	85	-3	3			.980	5	C-61	0.6
1928	Cin-N	96	324	29	98	15	1	7	35	20	25	.302	.343	.420	100	-1	1			.983	-3	C-93	0.4
1929	Bro-N	93	273	28	71	16	6	4	31	34	24	.260	.342	.407	86	-6	3			.979	-4	C-85	-0.2
1930	Bro-N	23	46	4	10	3	0	0	3	5	6	.217	.294	.283	41	-4	1			.944	-2	C-22	-0.4
1931	Bro-N	24	45	5	12	4	0	1	4	4	9	.267	.327	.422	100	-0	1			.967	1	C-15	0.1
1932	Bro-N	41	70	8	18	6	0	1	11	4	8	.257	.297	.386	84	-2	0			.985	-2	C-24	-0.3
1933	Bro-N	6	6	1	1	1	0	0	0	0	1	.167	.167	.333	42	-0	0			.889	0	/C-6	0.0
	Pit-N	16	52	6	13	4	0	1	7	5	10	.250	.316	.385	99	-0	0			.982	-3	C-16	-0.2
	Yr	22	58	7	14	5	0	1	7	5	11	.241	.302	.379	95	-0	0			.969	-3	C-22	-0.2
Total	18	1037	2877	298	743	166	26	26	298	314	382	.258	.334	.361	84	-60	31	9		.970	11	C-935/1-2	0.7

■ CHARLIE PICK

Pick, Charles Thomas   b: 4/10/1888, Brookneal, Va.   d: 6/26/54, Lynchburg, Va.   BL/TR, 5'10", 160 lbs.   Deb: 9/20/14

YEAR	TM/L	G	AB	R	H	2B	3B	HR	RBI	BB	SO	AVG	OBP	SLG	PRO+	BR/A	SB	CS	SBR	FA	FR	G/POS	TPR
1914	Was-A	10	23	0	9	0	0	0	1	4	4	.391	.481	.391	157	2	1	2	-1	.833	-0	/O-7	0.0
1915	Was-A	3	2	0	0	0	0	0	0	0	0	.000	.000	.000	-98	-0	0			.000	0	H	-0.1
1916	Phi-A	121	398	29	96	10	3	0	20	40	24	.241	.315	.281	83	-8	25	16	-2	.899	4	*3-108/O-8	-0.3
1918	*Chi-N	29	89	13	29	4	1	0	12	14	4	.326	.417	.393	144	5	7			.964	-0	2-20/3-8	0.7
1919	Chi-N	75	269	27	65	8	6	0	18	14	12	.242	.292	.316	82	-6	17			.946	12	2-71/3-3	1.0
	Bos-N	34	114	12	29	1	1	1	7	7	5	.254	.325	.307	94	-0	4			.924	-2	2-21/3-5,O-3,1-2	-0.2
	Yr	109	383	39	94	9	7	1	25	21	17	.245	.302	.313	86	-6	21			.942	10	2-92/3-8,O-3,1-2	0.8
1920	Bos-N	95	383	34	105	16	6	2	28	23	11	.274	.320	.363	100	-0	10	16	-7	.952	0	2-94	-0.4
Total	6	367	1278	115	333	39	17	3	86	102	60	.261	.323	.325	95	-8	64	34		.949	14	2-206,3-124/O-18,1	0.7

■ EDDIE PICK

Pick, Edgar Everett   b: 5/7/1899, Attleboro, Mass.   d: 5/13/67, Santa Monica, Cal.   BB/TR, 6', 185 lbs.   Deb: 9/13/23

YEAR	TM/L	G	AB	R	H	2B	3B	HR	RBI	BB	SO	AVG	OBP	SLG	PRO+	BR/A	SB	CS	SBR	FA	FR	G/POS	TPR
1923	Cin-N	9	8	2	3	0	0	0	2	3	3	.375	.545	.375	150	1	0	0	0	1.000	-1	/O-4	-0.1
1924	Cin-N	3	2	0	0	0	0	0	0	0	1	.000	.000	.000	-99	-1	0	0	0	1.000	-0	/O-1	-0.1
1927	Chi-N	54	181	23	31	5	2	2	15	20	26	.171	.254	.254	36	-16	0			.910	-6	3-49/2-1,O-1	-2.0
Total	3	66	191	25	34	5	2	2	17	23	30	.178	.266	.257	40	-16	0	0	0	.912	-8	/3-49,O-6,2-1	-2.2

■ OLLIE PICKERING

Pickering, Oliver Daniel   b: 4/9/1870, Olney, Ill.   d: 1/20/52, Vincennes, Ind.   BL/TR, 5'11", 170 lbs.   Deb: 8/9/1896

YEAR	TM/L	G	AB	R	H	2B	3B	HR	RBI	BB	SO	AVG	OBP	SLG	PRO+	BR/A	SB	CS	SBR	FA	FR	G/POS	TPR
1896	Lou-N	45	165	28	50	6	4	1	22	12	11	.303	.350	.406	103	0	13			.901	3	O-45	0.0
1897	Lou-N	63	246	34	62	5	2	1	20	25		.252	.326	.301	68	-11	20			.937	5	O-62	-0.9
	Cle-N	46	182	33	64	5	2	1	22	11		.352	.392	.418	108	2	18			.950	-0	O-46/2-1	-0.1
	Yr	109	428	67	126	10	4	2	42	36		.294	.353	.350	86	-8	38			.943	4	*O-108/2-1	-1.0
1901	Cle-A	137	547	102	169	25	6	0	40	58		.309	.383	.377	116	15	36			.949	15	*O-137	1.7
1902	Cle-A	69	293	46	75	5	2	3	26	19		.256	.306	.317	76	-9	22			.979	-2	O-64/1-2	-1.6
1903	Phi-A	137	512	93	144	13	6	1	36	53		.281	.353	.346	105	2	40			.970	-4	O-135	0.0
1904	Phi-A	124	455	56	103	10	3	0	30	45		.226	.299	.262	74	-12	17			.939	-0	*O-121	-2.2
1907	StL-A	151	576	63	159	15	10	0	60	35		.276	.321	.337	110	6	15			.949	-11	*O-151	-1.2
1908	Was-A	113	373	45	84	7	4	2	30	28		.225	.285	.282	92	-5	13			.940	-8	O-98	-1.7
Total	8	885	3349	500	910	96	39	9	286	286	11	.272	.334	.332	97	-8	194			.949	5	O-859/1-2,2-1	-6.0

■ URBANE PICKERING

Pickering, Urbane Henry "Pick"   b: 6/3/1899, Hoxie, Kan.   d: 5/13/70, Modesto, Cal.   BR/TR, 5'10", 180 lbs.   Deb: 4/18/31

YEAR	TM/L	G	AB	R	H	2B	3B	HR	RBI	BB	SO	AVG	OBP	SLG	PRO+	BR/A	SB	CS	SBR	FA	FR	G/POS	TPR
1931	Bos-A	103	341	48	86	13	4	9	52	33	53	.252	.318	.393	91	-5	3	4	-2	.967	-2	3-74,2-16	-0.3
1932	Bos-A	132	457	47	119	28	5	2	40	39	71	.260	.320	.357	77	-16	3	4	-2	.941	-7	*3-126/C-1	-1.5
Total	2	235	798	95	205	41	9	11	92	72	124	.257	.319	.372	83	-21	6	8	-3	.951	-9	3-200/2-16,C-1	-1.8

■ DAVE PICKETT

Pickett, David T.   b: 5/26/1874, Brookline, Mass.   d: 4/22/50, Easton, Mass.   5'7.5", 170 lbs.   Deb: 7/21/1898

YEAR	TM/L	G	AB	R	H	2B	3B	HR	RBI	BB	SO	AVG	OBP	SLG	PRO+	BR/A	SB	CS	SBR	FA	FR	G/POS	TPR
1898	Bos-N	14	43	3	12	1	0	0	3	6		.279	.380	.302	91	-0	2			.955	-2	O-14	-0.3

■ JOHN PICKETT

Pickett, John Thomas   b: 2/20/1866, Chicago, Ill.   d: 7/4/22, Chicago, Ill.   BR/TR,   Deb: 6/6/1889

YEAR	TM/L	G	AB	R	H	2B	3B	HR	RBI	BB	SO	AVG	OBP	SLG	PRO+	BR/A	SB	CS	SBR	FA	FR	G/POS	TPR
1889	KC-a	53	201	20	45	7	0	0	12	11	21	.224	.271	.259	48	-14	7			.900	-16	O-28,3-14,2-11	-2.6
1890	Phi-P	100	407	82	114	7	9	4	64	40	17	.280	.347	.371	90	-7	12			.893	-22	*2-100	-1.8
1892	Bal-N	36	141	13	30	2	3	1	12	7	10	.213	.260	.291	65	-6	2			.915	-5	2-36	-1.0
Total	3	189	749	115	189	16	12	5	88	58	48	.252	.311	.326	75	-27	21			.900	-42	2-147/O-28,3-14	-5.4

■ TY PICKUP

Pickup, Clarence William   b: 10/29/1897, Philadelphia, Pa.   d: 8/2/74, Philadelphia, Pa.   BR/TR, 6', 180 lbs.   Deb: 4/30/18

YEAR	TM/L	G	AB	R	H	2B	3B	HR	RBI	BB	SO	AVG	OBP	SLG	PRO+	BR/A	SB	CS	SBR	FA	FR	G/POS	TPR
1918	Phi-N	1	1	0	1	0	0	0	0	0	0	1.000	1.000	1.000	478	0	0			1.000	-0	/O-1	0.0

■ GRACIE PIERCE

Pierce, Grayson S.   b: New York, N.Y.   d: 8/28/1894, New York, N.Y.   BR/TR,   Deb: 5/2/1882   U

YEAR	TM/L	G	AB	R	H	2B	3B	HR	RBI	BB	SO	AVG	OBP	SLG	PRO+	BR/A	SB	CS	SBR	FA	FR	G/POS	TPR
1882	Lou-a	9	33	3	10	1	0	0		1		.303	.324	.333	129	1				.864	1	/2-9	0.2
	Bal-a	41	151	8	30	2	1	0		4		.199	.214	.225	52	-7				.796	-10	2-38/O-3,S-1	-1.5
	Yr	50	184	11	40	3	1	0		4		.217	.234	.245	66	-6				.808	-9	2-47/O-3,S-1	-1.3
1883	Col-a	11	41	5	7	0	0	0		0		.171	.171	.171	11	-4				.744	-1	/2-6,O-5	-0.4
	NY-N	18	62	3	5	0	0	0	2	1	9	.081	.095	.113	-37	-10				.850	-2	O-18/2-1	-1.1
1884	NY-a	5	20	2	5	1	0	0		0		.250	.250	.300	81	-0				1.000	-5	/O-3,2-3	-0.5
Total	3	84	307	21	57	4	2	0	2	5	9	.186	.199	.212	36	-20				.795	-17	/2-57,O-29,S-1	-3.3

■ JACK PIERCE

Pierce, Lavern Jack   b: 6/2/48, Laurel, Miss.   BL/TR, 6', 210 lbs.   Deb: 4/27/73

YEAR	TM/L	G	AB	R	H	2B	3B	HR	RBI	BB	SO	AVG	OBP	SLG	PRO+	BR/A	SB	CS	SBR	FA	FR	G/POS	TPR
1973	Atl-N	11	20	1	1	0	0	0	0	2	8	.050	.095	.050	-55	-4	0	0	0	1.000	1	/1-6	-0.4
1974	Atl-N	6	9	1	1	0	0	0	0	0	1	.111	.200	.111	-11	-1	0	0	0	.958	0	/1-2	-0.1
1975	Det-A	53	170	19	40	6	1	8	22	20	40	.235	.323	.424	105	1	0	0	0	.971	-4	1-49	-0.7
Total	3	70	199	20	42	6	1	8	22	22	48	.211	.296	.372	83	-5	0	0	0	.973	-3	/1-57	-1.2

■ MAURY PIERCE

Pierce, Maurice   b: Baltimore, Md.   Deb: 4/23/1884

YEAR	TM/L	G	AB	R	H	2B	3B	HR	RBI	BB	SO	AVG	OBP	SLG	PRO+	BR/A	SB	CS	SBR	FA	FR	G/POS	TPR
1884	Was-U	2	7	0	1	0	0	0		0	4	.143	.143	.143	-14	-1				.778	0	/3-2	-0.1

■ ANDY PIERCY

Piercy, Andrew J.   b: 8/1856, San Jose, Cal.   d: 12/27/32, San Jose, Cal.   TR,   Deb: 5/12/1881

YEAR	TM/L	G	AB	R	H	2B	3B	HR	RBI	BB	SO	AVG	OBP	SLG	PRO+	BR/A	SB	CS	SBR	FA	FR	G/POS	TPR
1881	Chi-N	2	8	1	2	0	0	0	0	0	1	.250	.250	.250	55	-0				.750	-1	/3-1,2-1	-0.2

YEAR	TM/L	G	AB	R	H	2B	3B	HR	RBI	BB	SO	AVG	OBP	SLG	PRO+	BR/A	SB	CS	SBR	FA	FR	G/POS	TPR

■ **JIM PIERSALL** Piersall, James Anthony b: 11/14/29, Waterbury, Conn. BR/TR, 6′, 175 lbs. Deb: 9/7/50 C

YEAR	TM/L	G	AB	R	H	2B	3B	HR	RBI	BB	SO	AVG	OBP	SLG	PRO+	BR/A	SB	CS	SBR	FA	FR	G/POS	TPR
1950	Bos-A	6	7	4	2	0	0	0	0	4	0	.286	.545	.286	107	0	0	0	0	1.000	1	/O-2	0.1
1952	Bos-A	56	161	28	43	8	0	1	16	28	26	.267	.379	.335	93	-1	3	3	-1	.928	-6	S-30,O-22/3-1	-0.7
1953	Bos-A	151	585	76	159	21	9	3	52	41	52	.272	.329	.354	80	-16	11	10	-3	.987	16	*O-151	-0.9
1954	Bos-A★	133	474	77	135	24	2	8	38	36	42	.285	.339	.395	90	-7	5	1	1	.985	0	*O-126	-1.1
1955	Bos-A	149	515	68	146	25	5	13	62	67	52	.283	.368	.427	104	3	6	1	1	.993	13	*O-147	1.1
1956	Bos-A★	155	601	91	176	**40**	6	14	87	58	48	.293	.356	.449	99	-2	7	7	-2	**.991**	18	*O-155	0.5
1957	Bos-A	151	609	103	159	27	5	19	63	62	54	.261	.333	.415	98	-2	14	6	1	.990	13	*O-151	0.2
1958	Bos-A	130	417	55	99	13	5	8	48	42	43	.237	.307	.350	75	-14	12	2	2	.985	9	*O-125	-0.9
1959	Cle-A	100	317	42	78	13	2	4	30	25	31	.246	.305	.338	79	-9	6	3	0	.982	0	O-91/3-1	-1.3
1960	Cle-A	138	486	70	137	12	4	18	66	24	38	.282	.316	.434	104	0	18	5	2	.992	10	*O-134	0.7
1961	Cle-A	121	484	81	156	26	7	6	40	43	46	.322	.380	.442	122	15	8	2	1	**.991**	16	*O-120	2.5
1962	Was-A	135	471	38	115	20	4	4	31	39	53	.244	.302	.329	70	-20	12	7	-1	**.997**	7	*O-132	-2.1
1963	Was-A	29	94	9	23	1	0	1	5	6	11	.245	.290	.287	63	-5	4	0	1	1.000	1	O-25	-0.4
	NY-N	40	124	13	24	4	1	1	10	10	14	.194	.254	.266	49	-8	1	2	-1	1.000	-2	O-38	-1.4
	LA-N	20	52	4	16	1	0	0	4	5	5	.308	.368	.327	103	0	0	1	-1	1.000	-2	O-18	-0.4
1964	LA-A	87	255	28	80	11	0	2	13	16	32	.314	.354	.380	116	5	5	3	-0	1.000	-6	O-72	-0.5
1965	Cal-A	53	112	10	30	5	2	2	12	5	15	.268	.305	.402	101	-0	2	2	-1	.984	-4	O-41	-0.6
1966	Cal-A	75	123	14	26	5	0	0	14	13	19	.211	.287	.252	58	-6	1	2	-1	.973	-10	O-63	-2.1
1967	Cal-A	5	3	0	0	0	0	0	0	2	0	.000	.000	.000	-99	-1	0	0	0	1.000	-0	/O-1	-0.1
Total	17	1734	5890	811	1604	256	52	104	591	524	583	.272	.334	.386	92	-66	115	57	0	.990	73	*O-1614/S-30,3-2	-7.4

■ **DAVE PIERSON** Pierson, David P. b: 8/20/1855, Wilkes-Barre, Pa. d: 11/11/22, Trenton, N.J. BR/TR, 5′7″, 142 lbs. Deb: 4/25/1876 F

| 1876 | Cin-N | 57 | 233 | 33 | 55 | 4 | 1 | 0 | 13 | 1 | 9 | .236 | .239 | .262 | 78 | -4 | | | | .760 | -2 | C-31,O-30/S-1,32P | -0.5 |

■ **DICK PIERSON** Pierson, Edmund Dana b: 10/24/1857, Wilkes-Barre, Pa. d: 7/20/22, Newark, N.J. TR , Deb: 6/23/1885 F

| 1885 | NY-a | 3 | 9 | 1 | 1 | 0 | 0 | 0 | 0 | 2 | | .111 | .273 | .111 | 27 | -1 | | | | .682 | -2 | /2-3 | -0.2 |

■ **TONY PIET** Piet, Anthony Francis (b: Anthony Francis Pietruszka) b: 12/7/06, Berwick, Pa. d: 12/1/81, Hinsdale, Ill. BR/TR, 6′, 175 lbs. Deb: 8/15/31

1931	Pit-N	44	167	22	50	12	4	0	24	13	24	.299	.354	.419	108	2	10			.987	-4	2-44/S-1	0.0
1932	Pit-N	154	574	66	162	25	8	7	85	46	56	.282	.343	.390	98	-1	19			.970	-28	*2-154	-2.0
1933	Pit-N	107	362	45	117	21	5	1	42	19	28	.323	.367	.417	124	11	12			.955	-5	2-97	1.2
1934	Cin-N	106	421	58	109	20	5	1	38	23	44	.259	.307	.337	74	-15	6			.934	-10	3-51,2-49	-2.0
1935	Cin-N	6	5	2	1	1	0	0	2	0	0	.200	.200	.400	59	-0	0			1.000	-0	/O-1	-0.1
	Chi-A	77	292	47	87	17	5	3	27	33	27	.298	.375	.421	103	2	2	1	0	.975	4	2-59,3-17	1.0
1936	Chi-A	109	352	69	96	15	2	7	42	66	44	.273	.400	.386	92	-2	15	5	2	.966	6	2-68,3-32	0.9
1937	Chi-A	100	332	34	78	15	1	4	38	32	36	.235	.314	.322	61	-20	14	6	1	.939	2	3-86,2-13	-1.4
1938	Det-A	41	80	9	17	6	0	0	14	15	11	.213	.351	.287	58	-5	2	4	-2	.919	1	3-18/2-1	-0.6
Total	8	744	2585	352	717	132	30	23	312	247	274	.277	.350	.378	91	-29	80	16		.967	-37	2-485,3-204/O-1,S-1	-3.0

■ **SANDY PIEZ** Piez, Charles William b: 10/13/1892, New York, N.Y. d: 12/29/30, Atlantic City, N.J BR/TR, 5′10″, 170 lbs. Deb: 4/17/14

| 1914 | NY-N | 37 | 8 | 9 | 3 | 0 | 1 | 0 | 3 | 0 | 1 | .375 | .375 | .625 | 202 | 1 | 4 | | | 1.000 | -1 | /O-5 | 0.0 |

■ **JOE PIGNATANO** Pignatano, Joseph Benjamin b: 8/4/29, Brooklyn, N.Y. BR/TR, 5′10″, 180 lbs. Deb: 4/28/57 C

1957	Bro-N	8	14	0	3	1	0	0	1	0	5	.214	.214	.286	30	-1	0	0	0	1.000	3	/C-6	0.2
1958	LA-N	63	142	18	31	4	0	9	17	16	26	.218	.306	.437	91	-2	4	1	1	1.000	10	C-57	1.0
1959	*LA-N	52	139	17	33	4	1	1	11	21	15	.237	.346	.302	69	-5	1	0	0	.997	7	C-49	0.4
1960	LA-N	58	90	11	21	4	0	2	9	15	17	.233	.343	.344	83	-2	1	0	-1	.984	15	C-40	1.5
1961	KC-A	92	243	31	59	10	3	4	22	36	42	.243	.350	.358	88	-3	2	2	-1	.979	1	C-83/3-2	0.1
1962	SF-N	7	5	2	1	0	0	0	0	4	0	.200	.556	.200	114	1	0	0	0	1.000	-1	/C-7	0.0
	NY-N	27	56	2	13	2	0	2	2	11	11	.232	.259	.268	41	-5	0	0	0	.991	4	C-25	0.0
	Yr	34	61	4	14	2	0	2	2	11	11	.230	.299	.262	51	-4	0	0	0	.992	4	C-32	0.0
Total	6	307	689	81	161	25	4	16	62	94	116	.234	.332	.351	80	-18	8	4	0	.990	39	C-267/3-2	3.2

■ **JAY PIKE** Pike, Jacob Emanuel b: Brooklyn, N.Y. BL/TL, Deb: 8/27/1877 F

| 1877 | Har-N | 1 | 4 | 0 | 1 | 0 | 0 | 0 | 0 | 0 | 0 | .250 | .250 | .250 | 65 | -0 | | | | .000 | -1 | /O-1 | -0.1 |

■ **JESS PIKE** Pike, Jess Willard b: 7/31/15, Dustin, Okla. d: 3/28/84, San Diego, Cal. BL/TR, 6′3″, 175 lbs. Deb: 4/18/46

| 1946 | NY-N | 16 | 41 | 4 | 7 | 1 | 1 | 1 | 6 | 6 | 9 | .171 | .277 | .317 | 68 | -1 | | | | .929 | -2 | O-10 | -0.5 |

■ **LIP PIKE** Pike, Lipman Emanuel b: 5/25/1845, New York, N.Y. d: 10/10/1893, Brooklyn, N.Y. BL/TL, 5′8″, 158 lbs. Deb: 5/9/1871 FM

1871	Tro-n	28	130	43	49	10	7	**4**	39	5	7	.377	.400	.654	194	15	3	2	-0	.850	1	O-18/2-7,1-4,M	1.0
1872	Bal-n	56	288	67	84	15	5	**6**	**60**	3	6	.292	.299	.441	119	5	8	1	2	.875	-13	O-25,2-24/3-9	-0.6
1873	Bal-n	56	286	71	90	14	8	**4**	50	7	4	.315	.334	.462	134	11	8	1	2	.704	-3	*O-56/2-2	0.9
1874	Har-n	52	234	58	83	**22**	5	1	51	5	0	.355	.368	**.504**	168	16	3	1	0	.856	14	O-27,S-20/2-7,3M	2.3
1875	StL-n	70	312	61	108	22	12	0	44	3	8	.346	.352	.494	**210**	34	25	10	2	.885	-2	*O-64,2-10/3-2,S-1	2.9
1876	StL-N	63	282	55	91	19	10	1	50	8	9	.323	.341	.472	178	23				.896	-4	*O-62/2-2	1.6
1877	Cin-N	58	262	45	78	12	4	**4**	23	9	7	.298	.321	.420	148	15				.802	-3	O-38,2-22/S-2,M	1.0
1878	Cin-N	31	145	28	47	5	1	0	11	4	9	.324	.342	.372	149	8				.824	-4	O-31	0.2
	Pro-N	5	22	4	5	0	1	0	4	1	1	.227	.261	.318	90	-0				.788	-3	/2-5	-0.3
	Yr	36	167	32	52	5	2	0	15	5	10	.311	.331	.365	140	7				.824	-7	O-31/2-5	-0.1
1881	Wor-N	5	18	1	2	0	0	0	0	4	3	.111	.273	.111	24	-1		0		.647	-1	/O-5	-0.2
1887	NY-a	1	4	0	0	0	0	0	0	0	0	.000	.000	.000	-99	-1	0			1.000	0	/O-1	-0.1
Total	5 n	262	1250	300	414	83	37	15	244	23	25	.331	.343	.493	160	81	47	15	6	.835	-3	O-190/2-50,S-21,31	6.5
Total	5	163	733	133	223	36	16	5	88	26	29	.304	.328	.417	152	43	0			.833	-15	O-137/2-29,S-2	2.2

■ **AL PILARCIK** Pilarcik, Alfred James b: 7/3/30, Whiting, Ind. BL/TL, 5′10″, 180 lbs. Deb: 7/13/56

1956	KC-A	69	239	28	60	10	4	4	22	30	32	.251	.335	.351	81	-6	9	2	2	.976	5	O-67	-0.5
1957	Bal-A	142	407	52	113	16	3	9	49	53	28	.278	.366	.398	116	10	14	7	0	.996	0	*O-126	0.4
1958	Bal-A	141	379	40	92	21	0	4	24	42	37	.243	.322	.306	78	-11	7	3	0	.986	-14	*O-119	-3.1
1959	Bal-A	130	273	37	77	12	1	6	30	30	25	.282	.355	.366	101	1	9	3	1	.978	-16	*O-106	-1.7
1960	Bal-A	104	194	30	48	9	1	4	17	15	16	.247	.315	.345	79	-6	0	2	-1	1.000	-11	O-75	-2.0
1961	KC-A	35	60	9	12	1	1	0	9	6	7	.200	.273	.250	40	-5	1	0	0	1.000	-1	O-21	-0.7
	Chi-A	47	62	9	11	1	0	1	6	9	5	.177	.282	.242	42	-5	1	1	-0	.944	-0	O-17	-0.6
	Yr	82	122	18	23	1	1	1	15	15	12	.189	.277	.246	41	-10	2	1	0	.971	-1	O-38	-1.3
Total	6	668	1614	205	413	66	7	22	143	185	150	.256	.336	.346	89	-22	41	18	2	.986	-39	O-531	-8.2

■ **ANDY PILNEY** Pilney, Antone James b: 1/19/13, Frontenac, Kan. d: 9/15/96, Kenner, La. BR/TR, 5′11″, 174 lbs. Deb: 6/12/36

| 1936 | Bos-N | 3 | 2 | 0 | 0 | 0 | 0 | 0 | 0 | 0 | 1 | .000 | .000 | .000 | -99 | -1 | 0 | | | .000 | 0 | H | -0.1 |

■ **BABE PINELLI** Pinelli, Ralph Arthur (b: Rinaldo Angelo Paolinelli)
b: 10/18/1895, San Francisco, Cal. d: 10/22/84, Daly City, Cal. BR/TR, 5′9″, 165 lbs. Deb: 8/3/18 U

1918	Chi-A	24	78	7	18	1	1	1	7	7	8	.231	.302	.308	83	-2	3			.847	-7	3-24	-0.9
1920	Det-A	102	284	33	65	9	3	0	21	25	16	.229	.296	.282	55	-18	6	8	-3	.954	20	3-74,S-18/2-1	0.3
1922	Cin-N	156	547	77	167	19	7	1	72	48	37	.305	.368	.371	93	-4	17	22	-8	.945	21	*3-156	1.9
1923	Cin-N	117	423	44	117	14	5	0	51	27	29	.277	.320	.333	74	-16	10	14	-5	.938	9	*3-116	-0.2
1924	Cin-N	144	510	61	156	16	7	0	70	32	32	.306	.353	.365	94	-4	23	17	-3	.956	**27**	*3-143	3.1
1925	Cin-N	130	492	68	139	33	6	2	49	22	28	.283	.316	.386	80	-15	8	19	-9	.945	1	*3-109,S-17	0.6
1926	Cin-N	71	207	26	46	7	0	0	24	15	5	.222	.284	.295	58	-12	2			.978	1	3-40,S-27/2-3	-0.7
1927	Cin-N	30	76	11	15	2	0	1	4	6	7	.197	.265	.263	43	-6	2			.968	-1	3-15/S-9,2-5	-0.6
Total	8	774	2617	327	723	101	33	5	298	182	162	.276	.328	.346	79	-77	71	80		.947	91	3-677/S-71,2-9	3.5

YEAR	TM/L	G	AB	R	H	2B	3B	HR	RBI	BB	SO	AVG	OBP	SLG	PRO+	BR/A	SB	CS	SBR	FA	FR	G/POS	TPR

■ LOU PINIELLA Piniella, Louis Victor b: 8/28/43, Tampa, Fla. BR/TR, 6'2", 198 lbs. Deb: 9/4/64 MC

YEAR	TM/L	G	AB	R	H	2B	3B	HR	RBI	BB	SO	AVG	OBP	SLG	PRO+	BR/A	SB	CS	SBR	FA	FR	G/POS	TPR
1964	Bal-A	4	1	0	0	0	0	0	0	0	0	.000	.000	.000	-99	-0	0	0	0	.000	0	H	0.0
1968	Cle-A	6	5	1	0	0	0	0	1	0	0	.000	.000	.000	-99	-1	0	0	0	1.000	-0	/O-2	-0.2
1969	KC-A	135	493	43	139	21	6	11	68	33	56	.282	.331	.416	107	3	2	4	-2	.977	15	*O-129	1.0
1970	KC-A	144	542	54	163	24	5	11	88	35	42	.301	.345	.424	111	7	3	6	-3	.984	4	*O-139/1-1	0.2
1971	KC-A	126	448	43	125	21	5	3	51	21	43	.279	.314	.368	94	-5	5	3	-0	.986	5	*O-115	-1.1
1972	KC-A★	151	574	65	179	33	4	11	72	34	59	.312	.359	.441	138	25	7	2	1	.976	3	*O-150	2.5
1973	KC-A	144	513	53	128	28	1	9	69	30	65	.250	.294	.361	77	-16	5	7	-3	.986	-5	*O-128/D-9	-3.1
1974	NY-A	140	518	71	158	26	0	9	70	32	58	.305	.348	.407	119	12	1	8	-5	.989	11	*O-130/1-1,D-6	1.4
1975	NY-A	74	199	7	39	4	1	0	22	16	22	.196	.266	.226	41	-15	0	0	0	.986	-3	O-46,D-12	-2.0
1976	*NY-A	100	327	36	92	16	6	3	38	18	34	.281	.323	.349	110	3	0	1	-1	.982	2	O-49,D-38	0.1
1977	*NY-A	103	339	47	112	19	3	12	45	20	31	.330	.369	.510	138	17	2	1	-1	.975	-4	O-51,D-43/1-1	0.9
1978	*NY-A	130	472	67	148	34	5	6	69	34	36	.314	.362	.445	129	17	3	1	0	.969	2	*O-103,D-23	1.5
1979	NY-A	130	461	49	137	22	2	11	69	17	31	.297	.325	.425	103	1	3	2	-0	.982	3	*O-112,D-16	-0.1
1980	*NY-A	116	321	39	92	18	0	2	27	29	20	.287	.346	.361	96	-1	0	2	-1	.971	-7	*O-104/D-7	-1.3
1981	*NY-A	60	159	16	44	9	0	5	18	13	9	.277	.331	.428	119	4	0	1	-1	.986	1	O-36,D-19	0.2
1982	NY-A	102	261	33	80	17	1	6	37	18	18	.307	.354	.448	120	7	0	1	-1	1.000	-1	D-55,O-40	0.2
1983	NY-A	53	148	19	43	9	1	2	16	11	12	.291	.344	.405	109	2	1	1	-0	.959	-2	O-43/D-1	-0.1
1984	NY-A	29	86	8	26	1	0	1	6	7	5	.302	.355	.407	115	2	0	0	0	1.000	1	O-24/D-2	0.2
Total	18	1747	5867	651	1705	305	41	102	766	368	541	.291	.336	.409	109	61	32	41	-15	.981	21	*O-1401,D-231/1-3	0.3

■ ED PINKHAM Pinkham, Edward b: 1849, Brooklyn, N.Y. TL, 5'7", 142 lbs. Deb: 5/8/1871

YEAR	TM/L	G	AB	R	H	2B	3B	HR	RBI	BB	SO	AVG	OBP	SLG	PRO+	BR/A	SB	CS	SBR	FA	FR	G/POS	TPR
1871	Chi-n	24	95	27	25	5	5	1	18	3	.263	.381	.453	125	2	5	2	0	.754	9	3-18/O-8,P-3	0.7

■ GEORGE PINKNEY Pinkney, George Burton b: 1/11/1862, Orange Prairie, Ill. d: 11/10/26, Peoria, Ill. BR/TR, 5'7", 160 lbs. Deb: 8/16/1884

YEAR	TM/L	G	AB	R	H	2B	3B	HR	RBI	BB	SO	AVG	OBP	SLG	PRO+	BR/A	SB	CS	SBR	FA	FR	G/POS	TPR
1884	Cle-N	36	144	18	45	9	0	0	16	10	7	.313	.357	.375	126	4				.848	-8	2-25,S-11	-0.3
1885	Bro-a	110	447	77	124	16	5	0	42	27		.277	.328	.336	109	5				.904	-11	2-57,3-51/S-3	-0.2
1886	Bro-a	141	597	119	156	22	7	0	37	70		.261	.339	.322	106	6	32			.858	-16	*3-141/P-1	-0.6
1887	Bro-a	138	580	133	155	26	4	3	69	61		.267	.343	.348	92	-6	59			.890	13	*3-136/S-2	0.8
1888	Bro-a	143	575	134	156	18	8	4	52	66		.271	.358	.351	128	21	51			.898	-26	*3-143	-0.2
1889	*Bro-a	138	545	103	134	25	7	4	82	59	43	.246	.327	.339	90	-7	47			.897	-8	*3-138	-0.9
1890	*Bro-N	126	485	115	150	20	9	7	83	80	19	.309	.411	.431	145	30	47			.933	-15	*3-126	1.8
1891	Bro-N	135	501	80	137	19	6	2	71	67	32	.273	.367	.347	109	8	44			.904	-20	*3-130/S-5	-0.5
1892	StL-N	78	290	31	50	3	2	0	25	36	26	.172	.268	.197	43	-19	4			.888	-8	3-78	-2.2
1893	Lou-N	118	446	64	105	12	6	1	62	50	8	.235	.323	.296	71	-17	12			.923	-2	3-118	-1.4
Total	10	1163	4610	874	1212	170	56	21	539	526	135	.263	.345	.338	103	26	296			.897	-99	*3-1061/2-82,S-21,P	-3.7

■ VADA PINSON Pinson, Vada Edward b: 8/11/38, Memphis, Tenn. d: 10/21/95, Oakland, Cal. BL/TL, 5'11", 181 lbs. Deb: 4/15/58 C

YEAR	TM/L	G	AB	R	H	2B	3B	HR	RBI	BB	SO	AVG	OBP	SLG	PRO+	BR/A	SB	CS	SBR	FA	FR	G/POS	TPR
1958	Cin-N	27	96	20	26	7	0	1	8	11	18	.271	.352	.375	88	-1	2	1	0	1.000	2	O-27	-0.1
1959	Cin-N★	154	648	131	205	47	9	20	84	55	98	.316	.371	.509	128	25	21	6	3	.984	20	*O-154	3.9
1960	Cin-N★	154	652	107	187	37	12	20	61	47	96	.287	.339	.472	117	14	32	12	2	.981	9	*O-154	1.9
1961	*Cin-N	154	607	101	208	34	8	16	87	39	63	.343	.383	.504	131	27	23	10	1	.976	19	*O-153	3.7
1962	Cin-N	155	619	107	181	31	7	23	100	45	68	.292	.344	.477	114	11	26	8	3	.989	7	*O-152	1.2
1963	Cin-N	162	652	96	204	37	14	22	106	36	80	.313	.350	.514	141	32	27	8	3	.979	9	*O-162	3.8
1964	Cin-N	156	625	99	166	23	11	23	84	42	99	.266	.317	.448	109	6	8	2	1	.972	4	*O-156	0.4
1965	Cin-N	159	669	97	204	34	10	22	94	43	81	.305	.353	.484	125	21	21	8	2	.992	15	*O-159	3.1
1966	Cin-N	156	618	70	178	35	6	16	76	34	83	.288	.329	.442	103	2	18	10	-1	.964	5	*O-154	-0.1
1967	Cin-N	158	650	90	187	28	13	18	66	26	86	.288	.318	.454	106	4	26	8	3	.986	5	*O-157	0.4
1968	Cin-N	130	499	60	135	29	6	5	48	32	59	.271	.315	.383	102	1	17	11	-2	.978	-1	*O-123	-0.9
1969	StL-N	132	495	58	126	22	6	10	70	35	63	.255	.308	.384	92	-6	4	4	-1	.996	1	*O-124	-1.4
1970	Cle-A	148	574	74	164	28	6	24	82	28	69	.286	.322	.481	113	8	7	6	-2	.982	5	*O-141/1-7	0.4
1971	Cle-A	146	566	60	149	23	4	11	35	21	58	.263	.297	.376	82	-14	25	6	4	.978	4	*O-141/1-3	-1.5
1972	Cal-A	136	484	56	133	24	2	7	49	30	54	.275	.324	.376	114	7	17	6	2	.991	-5	*O-134/1-1	-0.3
1973	Cal-A	124	466	56	121	14	6	8	57	20	55	.260	.290	.367	91	-8	5	5	-2	.965	-4	*O-120	-1.9
1974	KC-A	115	406	46	112	18	2	6	41	21	45	.276	.315	.374	92	-5	21	5	3	.980	-5	*O-110/1-1,D-2	-1.2
1975	KC-A	103	319	38	71	14	5	4	22	10	21	.223	.251	.335	63	-17	5	6	-2	.993	-3	O-82/1-4,D-5	-2.6
Total	18	2469	9645	1366	2757	485	127	256	1170	574	1196	.286	.330	.442	110	106	305	122	18	.981	87	*O-2403/1-16,D-7	8.8

■ WALLY PIPP Pipp, Walter Clement b: 2/17/1893, Chicago, Ill. d: 1/11/65, Grand Rapids, Mich BL/TL, 6'1", 180 lbs. Deb: 6/29/13

YEAR	TM/L	G	AB	R	H	2B	3B	HR	RBI	BB	SO	AVG	OBP	SLG	PRO+	BR/A	SB	CS	SBR	FA	FR	G/POS	TPR
1913	Det-A	12	31	3	5	0	3	0	5	2	6	.161	.235	.355	73	-1	0			.977	-1	1-10	-0.2
1915	NY-A	136	479	59	118	20	13	4	60	66	81	.246	.339	.367	112	7	18	7	1	.992	3	*1-134	0.8
1916	NY-A	151	545	70	143	20	14	12	93	54	82	.262	.331	.417	122	12	16			.992	6	*1-148	1.3
1917	NY-A	155	587	82	143	29	12	9	70	60	66	.244	.320	.380	112	7	11			.990	4	*1-155	0.7
1918	NY-A	91	349	48	106	15	9	2	44	22	34	.304	.345	.415	127	9	11			.988	0	1-91	0.7
1919	NY-A	138	523	74	144	23	10	7	50	39	42	.275	.330	.398	103	1	9			.991	1	*1-138	-0.3
1920	NY-A	153	610	109	171	30	14	11	76	48	54	.280	.339	.430	99	-3	4	10	-5	.991	0	*1-153	-1.1
1921	*NY-A	153	588	96	174	35	9	8	97	45	28	.296	.347	.427	94	-6	17	10	-1	.991	-4	*1-153	-1.4
1922	*NY-A	152	577	96	190	32	10	9	90	56	32	.329	.392	.466	120	18	7	12	-5	.993	-5	*1-152	0.1
1923	*NY-A	144	569	79	173	19	8	6	108	36	28	.304	.352	.397	95	-5	6	13	-6	.994	-4	*1-144	-2.1
1924	NY-A	153	589	88	174	30	19	9	114	51	36	.295	.352	.457	108	4	12	5	1	.994	2	*1-153	-0.3
1925	NY-A	62	178	19	41	6	3	3	24	13	12	.230	.286	.348	61	-11	3	3	-1	.991	4	1-47	-1.0
1926	Cin-N	155	574	72	167	22	15	6	99	49	26	.291	.352	.413	108	6	8			.992	2	*1-155	-0.1
1927	Cin-N	122	443	49	115	19	6	2	41	32	11	.260	.309	.343	77	-15	2			.996	0	*1-114	-2.2
1928	Cin-N	95	272	30	77	11	3	2	26	23	13	.283	.341	.368	87	-5	1			.989	1	1-72	-1.0
Total	15	1872	6914	974	1941	311	148	90	997	596	551	.281	.341	.408	104	18	125	60		.992	9	*1-1819	-6.1

■ JIM PIRIE Pirie, James Moir b: 3/31/1853, Ontario, Canada d: 6/2/34, Dundas, Ont., Can. 5'8", 169 lbs. Deb: 9/25/1883

YEAR	TM/L	G	AB	R	H	2B	3B	HR	RBI	BB	SO	AVG	OBP	SLG	PRO+	BR/A	SB	CS	SBR	FA	FR	G/POS	TPR
1883	Phi-N	5	19	1	3	0	0	0	0	0	2	.158	.158	.158	-4	-2				.577	-4	/S-5	-0.6

■ GREG PIRKL Pirkl, Gregory Daniel b: 8/7/70, Long Beach, Cal. BR/TR, 6'5", 225 lbs. Deb: 8/13/93

YEAR	TM/L	G	AB	R	H	2B	3B	HR	RBI	BB	SO	AVG	OBP	SLG	PRO+	BR/A	SB	CS	SBR	FA	FR	G/POS	TPR
1993	Sea-A	7	23	1	4	1	0	0	4	0	4	.174	.174	.304	25	-2	0	0	0	1.000	1	/1-5,D-2	-0.2
1994	Sea-A	19	53	7	14	3	0	6	11	1	12	.264	.291	.660	133	2	0	0	0	.983	-1	D-10/1-7	0.0
1995	Sea-A	10	17	2	4	0	0	1	0	1	7	.235	.278	.235	35	-2	0	0	0	1.000	1	/1-6,D-1	-0.1
1996	Sea-A	7	21	2	4	1	0	1	1	0	3	.190	.190	.381	40	-2	0	0	0	1.000	0	/1-2,D-3	-0.2
	Bos-A	2	2	0	0	0	0	0	0	0	1	.000	.000	.000	-97	-1	0	0	0	.000	0	/H	-0.1
	Yr	9	23	2	4	1	0	1	1	0	4	.174	.174	.348	27	-3	0	0	0	1.000	0	/D-3,1-2	-0.3
Total	4	45	116	12	26	4	0	8	16	2	27	.224	.244	.466	77	-5	0	0	0	.994	0	/1-20,D-16	-0.6

■ JIM PISONI Pisoni, James Pete b: 8/14/29, St.Louis, Mo. BR/TR, 5'10", 169 lbs. Deb: 9/25/53

YEAR	TM/L	G	AB	R	H	2B	3B	HR	RBI	BB	SO	AVG	OBP	SLG	PRO+	BR/A	SB	CS	SBR	FA	FR	G/POS	TPR
1953	StL-A	3	12	1	1	0	0	0	1	0	5	.083	.083	.333	8	-2	0	0	0	1.000	-0	/O-3	-0.2
1956	KC-A	10	30	4	8	0	0	2	5	2	8	.267	.313	.467	103	-0	0	0	0	.966	0	/O-9	0.4
1957	KC-A	44	97	14	23	2	2	3	12	10	17	.237	.321	.392	92	-1	0	0	0	.989	-3	O-44	-0.6
1959	Mil-N	9	24	4	4	1	0	0	2	2	6	.167	.231	.208	20	-3	0	0	0	.941	-1	O-9	-0.4
	NY-A	17	17	2	3	0	1	0	1	1	9	.176	.222	.294	42	-1	0	0	0	1.000	0	O-15	-0.4
1960	NY-A	20	9	1	1	0	0	1	1	2	1	.111	.200	.111	-14	-2	0	0	0	.938	-5	O-18	-0.7
Total	5	103	189	26	40	3	3	6	20	16	47	.212	.280	.354	71	-8	0	0	0	.978	-7	/O-98	-1.9

■ ALEX PITKO Pitko, Alexander "Spunk" b: 11/22/14, Burlington, N.J. BR/TR, 5'10", 180 lbs. Deb: 9/11/38

YEAR	TM/L	G	AB	R	H	2B	3B	HR	RBI	BB	SO	AVG	OBP	SLG	PRO+	BR/A	SB	CS	SBR	FA	FR	G/POS	TPR
1938	Phi-N	7	19	2	6	1	0	0	2	3		.316	.409	.368	118	1	1			.889	-2	/O-7	-0.1
1939	Was-A	4	8	0	1	0	0	0	1	1	3	.125	.222	.125	-10	-1	0			1.000	-1	/O-3	-0.2
Total	2	11	27	2	7	1	0	0	3	4	6	.259	.355	.296	80	-1	1		0	.917	-3	/O-10	-0.3

YEAR	TM/L	G	AB	R	H	2B	3B	HR	RBI	BB	SO	AVG	OBP	SLG	PRO+	BR/A	SB	CS	SBR	FA	FR	G/POS	TPR

■ JAKE PITLER Pitler, Jacob Albert b: 4/22/1894, New York, N.Y. d: 2/3/68, Binghamton, N.Y. BR/TR, 5'8", 150 lbs. Deb: 5/30/17 C

1917	Pit-N	109	382	39	89	8	5	0	23	30	24	.233	.297	.280	75	-11	6			**.966**	-12	*2-106/O-3	-1.9
1918	Pit-N	2	1	1	0	0	0	0	0	1	0	.000	.500	.000	55	0	2			.667	0	/2-1	0.1
Total	2	111	383	40	89	8	5	0	23	31	24	.232	.298	.279	75	-11	8			.962	-11	2-107/O-3	-1.8

■ CHRIS PITTARO Pittaro, Christopher Francis b: 9/16/61, Trenton, N.J. BB/TR, 5'11", 170 lbs. Deb: 4/8/85

1985	Det-A	28	62	10	15	3	1	0	7	5	13	.242	.299	.323	71	-2	1	1	-0	.881	-1	3-22/2-4,D-1	-0.3
1986	Min-A	11	21	0	2	0	0	0	0	0	8	.095	.095	.095	-47	-4	0	0	0	.969	2	/2-8,S-4	-0.2
1987	Min-A	14	12	6	4	0	0	0	0	1	0	.333	.385	.333	90	-0	1	0	0	1.000	3	/2-8,D-2	0.2
Total	3	53	95	16	21	3	1	0	7	6	21	.221	.267	.274	48	-7	2	1	0	.968	4	/3-22,2-20,S-4,D-3	-0.3

■ PINKY PITTINGER Pittinger, Clarke Alonzo b: 2/24/1899, Hudson, Mich. d: 11/4/77, Ft.Lauderdale, Fla. BR/TR, 5'10", 160 lbs. Deb: 4/15/21

1921	Bos-A	40	91	6	18	1	0	0	5	4	13	.198	.232	.209	13	-12	3	2	-0	.985	3	O-27/3-3,S-2,2-1	-1.0
1922	Bos-A	66	186	16	48	3	0	0	7	9	10	.258	.299	.274	51	-13	2	5	-2	.920	5	3-33,S-29	-0.6
1923	Bos-A	60	177	15	38	5	0	0	15	5	10	.215	.236	.243	26	-19	3	1	0	.959	-11	2-42,S-10/3-3	-2.8
1925	Chi-N	59	173	21	54	7	2	0	15	12	7	.312	.364	.376	88	-3	5	4	-1	.940	4	S-24,3-24	0.4
1927	Cin-N	31	84	17	23	5	0	1	10	2	5	.274	.291	.369	78	-3	4			.963	3	2-20/S-9,3-2	0.1
1928	Cin-N	40	38	12	9	0	1	0	4	0	1	.237	.237	.289	37	-4	2			.892	8	S-12/2-4,3-4	0.5
1929	Cin-N	77	210	31	62	11	0	0	27	5	4	.295	.318	.348	68	-11	8			.956	2	S-50/3-8,2-4	-0.2
Total	7	373	959	118	252	32	3	1	83	37	50	.263	.294	.306	55	-64	27	12		.938	13	S-136/3-77,2-71,O	-3.6

■ JOE PITTMAN Pittman, Joseph Wayne b: 1/1/54, Houston, Tex. BR/TR, 6'1", 180 lbs. Deb: 4/25/81

1981	*Hou-N	52	135	11	38	4	2	0	7	11	16	.281	.336	.341	97	-1	4	4	-1	.980	-9	2-35/3-4	-1.0
1982	Hou-N	15	10	1	2	1	0	0	0	0	2	.200	.200	.300	41	-1	0	0	0	1.000	0	/3-3,O-1	-0.1
	SD-N	55	118	16	30	2	0	0	7	9	13	.254	.307	.271	66	-5	8	3	1	.964	-3	2-30,S-13	-0.6
	Yr	70	128	16	32	3	0	0	7	9	15	.250	.299	.273	65	-6	8	3	1	.964	-2	2-30,S-13/3-3,O-1	-0.7
1984	SF-N	17	22	2	5	0	0	0	2	0	6	.227	.227	.227	29	-2	1	1	-0	.900	-2	/S-6,2-5,3-2	-0.5
Total	3	139	285	29	75	7	2	0	16	20	37	.263	.311	.302	77	-9	13	8	-1	.974	-14	/2-70,S-19,3-9,O-1	-2.2

■ GAYLEN PITTS Pitts, Gaylen Richard b: 6/6/46, Wichita, Kan. BR/TR, 6'1", 175 lbs. Deb: 5/12/74 C

1974	Oak-A	18	41	4	10	3	0	0	3	5	4	.244	.326	.317	92	-0	0	0	0	.909	0	3-11/2-6,1-1	0.0
1975	Oak-A	10	3	1	1	1	0	0	1	0	0	.333	.333	.667	181	-0	0	0	0	.800	0	/3-6,S-2,2-1	0.2
Total	2	28	44	5	11	4	0	0	4	5	4	.250	.327	.341	98	-0	0	0	0	.895	2	/3-17,2-7,S-2,1-1	0.2

■ HERMAN PITZ Pitz, Herman b: 7/18/1865, Brooklyn, N.Y. d: 9/3/24, Far Rockaway, N.Y. 5'6", 140 lbs. Deb: 4/18/1890

1890	Bro-a	61	189	26	26	0	0	0	6	45		.138	.312	.138	34	-13	25			.885	-7	C-34,3-16/O-9,S2	-1.4
	Syr-a	29	95	17	21	0	0	0	3	13		.221	.321	.221	67	-3	14			.929	-5	C-27/S-1,O-1	-0.5
	Yr	90	284	43	47	0	0	0	9	58		.165	.315	.165	44	-16	39			.906	-12	C-61,3-16,O-10,/S2	-1.9

■ PHIL PLANTIER Plantier, Phillip Alan b: 1/27/69, Manchester, N.H. BL/TR, 6', 175 lbs. Deb: 8/21/90

1990	Bos-A	14	15	1	2	1	0	0	3	4	6	.133	.350	.200	55	-1	0	0	0	.000	-0	/O-1,D-4	-0.1
1991	Bos-A	53	148	27	49	7	1	11	35	23	38	.331	.424	.615	175	15	1	0	0	.976	-0	O-40/D-5	1.4
1992	Bos-A	108	349	46	86	19	0	7	30	44	83	.246	.334	.361	89	-5	2	3	-1	.975	2	O-76,D-23	-0.6
1993	SD-N	138	462	67	111	20	1	34	100	61	124	.240	.338	.509	121	13	4	5	-2	.990	14	*O-134	2.2
1994	SD-N	96	341	44	75	21	0	18	41	36	91	.220	.304	.440	93	-5	0	1	0	.988	6	O-91	0.0
1995	Hou-N	22	68	12	17	2	0	4	15	11	19	.250	.363	.456	123	2	0	0	0	.962	-3	O-20	-0.1
	SD-N	54	148	21	38	4	0	5	19	17	29	.257	.333	.385	92	-2	1	1	-0	.958	4	O-39	0.1
	Yr	76	216	33	55	6	0	9	34	28	48	.255	.343	.407	101	1	1	1	-0	.959	2	O-59	0.0
1996	Oak-A	73	231	29	49	8	1	7	31	28	56	.212	.305	.346	67	-12	2	2	-1	.973	4	O-68/D-1	-0.9
Total	7	558	1762	247	427	82	3	86	274	224	446	.242	.334	.439	104	7	13	12	-3	.980	27	O-469/D-33	2.0

■ DON PLARSKI Plarski, Donald Joseph b: 11/9/29, Chicago, Ill. d: 12/29/81, St.Louis, Mo. BR/TR, 5'6", 160 lbs. Deb: 7/20/55

| 1955 | KC-A | 8 | 11 | 0 | 1 | 0 | 0 | 0 | 0 | 0 | 2 | .091 | .091 | .091 | -50 | -2 | 1 | 0 | 0 | 1.000 | -2 | /O-6 | -0.4 |

■ ELMO PLASKETT Plaskett, Elmo Alexander b: 6/27/38, Frederiksted, V.I. BR/TR, 5'10", 195 lbs. Deb: 9/8/62

1962	Pit-N	7	14	2	4	0	0	1	3	1	3	.286	.333	.500	120	0	0	0	0	1.000	-1	/C-4	-0.1
1963	Pit-N	10	21	1	3	0	0	0	2	0	5	.143	.143	.143	-17	-3	0	0	0	1.000	-2	/C-5,3-1	-0.5
Total	2	17	35	3	7	0	0	1	5	1	8	.200	.222	.286	41	-3	0	0	0	1.000	-3	/C-9,3-1	-0.6

■ WHITEY PLATT Platt, Mizell George b: 8/21/20, W.Palm Beach, Fla. d: 7/27/70, W.Palm Beach, Fla BR/TR, 6'2", 195 lbs. Deb: 9/16/42

1942	Chi-N	4	16	1	1	0	0	0	2	0	3	.063	.063	.063	-66	-3	0			1.000	0	/O-4	-0.4
1943	Chi-N	20	41	2	7	3	0	0	2	1	7	.171	.190	.244	25	-4	0			.952	-3	O-14	-0.9
1946	Chi-A	84	247	28	62	8	5	3	32	17	34	.251	.307	.360	89	-4	1	7	-4	.971	-3	O-61	-1.5
1948	StL-A	123	454	57	123	22	10	7	82	39	51	.271	.331	.410	94	-6	1	4	-2	.948	-6	*O-114	-2.0
1949	StL-A	102	244	29	63	8	2	3	29	24	27	.258	.325	.344	74	-10	0	1	-1	.986	0	O-59/1-2	-1.2
Total	5	333	1002	117	256	41	17	13	147	81	122	.255	.314	.369	83	-27	2	12		.964	-12	O-252/1-2	-6.0

■ AL PLATTE Platte, Alfred Frederick Joseph b: 4/13/1890, Grand Rapids, Mich. d: 8/29/76, Grand Rapids, Mich BL/TL, 5'7", 160 lbs. Deb: 9/1/13

| 1913 | Det-A | 9 | 18 | 1 | 2 | 1 | 0 | 0 | 1 | 1 | 1 | .111 | .158 | .167 | -5 | -2 | 0 | | | .800 | -1 | /O-5 | -0.4 |

■ RANCE PLESS Pless, Rance b: 12/6/25, Greeneville, Tenn. BR/TR, 6', 145 lbs. Deb: 4/21/56

| 1956 | KC-A | 48 | 85 | 4 | 23 | 3 | 1 | 0 | 10 | 13 | 10 | .271 | .354 | .329 | 81 | -2 | 0 | 1 | | 1.000 | 2 | 1-15/3-5 | -0.1 |

■ HERB PLEWS Plews, Herbert Eugene b: 6/14/28, Helena, Mont. BL/TR, 5'11", 160 lbs. Deb: 4/18/56

1956	Was-A	91	256	24	69	10	7	1	25	26	40	.270	.339	.375	88	-4	1	2	-1	.947	-3	2-66/S-5,3-2	-0.4
1957	Was-A	104	329	51	89	19	4	1	26	28	39	.271	.331	.362	90	-4	0	3	-2	.979	-15	2-79,3-11/S-4	-1.5
1958	Was-A	111	380	46	98	12	6	2	29	17	45	.258	.291	.337	74	-14	2	3	-1	.976	-21	2-64,3-36	-3.3
1959	Was-A	27	40	4	9	0	0	0	2	3	5	.225	.279	.225	40	-3	0	1		.971	1	/2-6	-0.2
	Bos-A	13	12	0	1	1	0	0	0	4	4	.083	.083	.167	-32	-2	0	0		.833	1	/2-2	-0.1
	Yr	40	52	4	10	1	0	0	2	7	9	.192	.236	.212	24	-5	0	1		.951	2	/2-8	-0.3
Total	4	346	1017	125	266	42	17	4	82	74	133	.262	.314	.348	80	-28	3	9	-5	.967	-36	2-217/3-49,S-9	-5.5

■ WALTER PLOCK Plock, Walter S. b: 7/2/1869, Philadelphia, Pa. d: 4/28/1900, Richmond, Va. 6'3", 180 lbs. Deb: 8/21/1891

| 1891 | Phi-N | 2 | 5 | 2 | 2 | 0 | 0 | 0 | 0 | 0 | 1 | .400 | .500 | .400 | 159 | 0 | 0 | | | .000 | -1 | /O-2 | -0.1 |

■ BILL PLUMMER Plummer, William Francis b: 3/21/47, Oakland, Cal. BR/TR, 6'1", 200 lbs. Deb: 4/19/68 MC

1968	Chi-N	2	2	0	0	0	0	0	0	0	1	.000	.000	.000	-94	-0	0	0	0	1.000	0	/C-1	0.0
1970	Cin-N	4	8	0	1	0	0	0	0	0	2	.125	.222	.125	-4	-1	0	0	0	.857	-2	/C-4	-0.3
1971	Cin-N	10	19	0	0	0	0	0	0	0	4	.000	.000	.000	-99	-5	0	0	0	1.000	0	/C-4,3-2	-0.5
1972	Cin-N	38	102	8	19	4	0	2	9	9	20	.186	.217	.284	44	-8	0	0	0	.994	0	C-36/1-1,3-1	-0.7
1973	Cin-N	50	119	8	18	3	0	2	11	18	26	.151	.268	.227	41	-9	1	0	0	.994	-1	C-42/3-5	-0.9
1974	Cin-N	50	120	7	27	7	0	2	10	6	21	.225	.262	.333	67	-6	1	0	0	.974	5	C-49/3-1	0.1
1975	Cin-N	65	159	17	29	7	1	0	19	24	28	.182	.297	.245	51	-10	0	0	0	.990	-3	C-63	-1.1
1976	Cin-N	56	153	16	38	6	1	4	19	14	36	.248	.311	.379	93	-2	0	1	0	.977	6	C-54	0.5
1977	Cin-N	51	117	10	16	5	0	1	7	17	34	.137	.246	.205	22	-13	0	1	0	.986	-1	C-50	-1.3
1978	Sea-A	41	93	6	20	5	0	1	7	12	19	.215	.305	.333	80	-2	1	0	0	.978	-5	C-40	-0.7
Total	10	367	892	72	168	37	3	14	82	95	191	.188	.269	.279	53	-57	4	3	-1	.984	0	C-343/3-9,1-1	-4.9

■ BIFF POCOROBA Pocoroba, Biff b: 7/25/53, Burbank, Cal. BB/TR, 5'10", 180 lbs. Deb: 4/25/75

1975	Atl-N	67	188	15	48	7	1	1	22	20	11	.255	.327	.319	77	-5	0	0	0	.970	-4	C-62	-0.8
1976	Atl-N	54	174	16	42	7	0	0	14	19	12	.241	.316	.282	66	-7	1	0	0	.978	4	C-54	-0.1
1977	Atl-N	113	321	46	93	24	1	8	44	57	27	.290	.398	.445	113	7	3	4	-2	.989	2	*C-100	1.1

YEAR	TM/L	G	AB	R	H	2B	3B	HR	RBI	BB	SO	AVG	OBP	SLG	PRO+	BR/A	SB	CS	SBR	FA	FR	G/POS	TPR
1978	Atl-N★	92	289	21	70	8	0	6	34	29	14	.242	.316	.332	73	-10	0	3	-2	.990	1	C-79	-1.0
1979	Atl-N	28	38	6	12	4	0	0	4	7	0	.316	.422	.421	122	1	1	1	-0	.933	0	/C-7	0.2
1980	Atl-N	70	83	7	22	4	0	2	8	11	11	.265	.351	.386	102	0	1	0	0	.934	-1	C-10	0.1
1981	Atl-N	57	122	4	22	4	0	0	8	12	15	.180	.265	.213	36	-10	0	0	0	.938	-5	3-21/C-9	-1.6
1982	*Atl-N	56	120	5	33	7	0	2	22	13	12	.275	.351	.383	101	0	0	0	0	.988	-4	C-36/3-2	-0.3
1983	Atl-N	55	120	11	32	6	0	2	16	12	7	.267	.333	.367	87	-2	0	0	0	.983	-3	C-34	-0.3
1984	Atl-N	4	2	1	0	0	0	0	0	0	0	.000	.500	.000	48	0	0	0	0	.000	0	/H	0.0
Total	10	596	1457	132	374	71	2	21	172	182	109	.257	.342	.351	86	-25	6	8	-3	.982	-9	C-391/3-23	-2.7

■ MIKE POEPPING
Poepping, Michael Harold b: 8/7/50, Little Falls, Minn. BR/TR, 6'6", 230 lbs. Deb: 9/6/75

YEAR	TM/L	G	AB	R	H	2B	3B	HR	RBI	BB	SO	AVG	OBP	SLG	PRO+	BR/A	SB	CS	SBR	FA	FR	G/POS	TPR
1975	Min-A	14	37	0	5	1	0	0	1	5	7	.135	.238	.162	15	-4	0	0	0	.950	-2	O-13	-0.7

■ JIMMY POFAHL
Pofahl, James Willard b: 6/18/17, Faribault, Minn. d: 9/14/84, Owatonna, Minn. BR/TR, 5'11", 185 lbs. Deb: 4/16/40

YEAR	TM/L	G	AB	R	H	2B	3B	HR	RBI	BB	SO	AVG	OBP	SLG	PRO+	BR/A	SB	CS	SBR	FA	FR	G/POS	TPR
1940	Was-A	119	406	34	95	23	5	2	36	37	55	.234	.298	.330	67	-21	2	0	1	.952	-5	*S-112/2-4	-1.5
1941	Was-A	22	75	9	14	3	2	0	6	10	11	.187	.282	.280	52	-5	1	0	0	.934	-4	S-21	-0.7
1942	Was-A	84	283	22	59	7	2	0	28	29	30	.208	.282	.247	50	-18	4	3	-1	.956	1	S-49,2-15,3-14	-1.5
Total	3	225	764	65	168	33	9	2	70	76	96	.220	.290	.295	59	-44	7	3	0	.951	-8	S-182/2-19,3-14	-3.7

■ JOHN POFF
Poff, John William b: 10/23/52, Chillicothe, Ohio BL/TL, 6'2", 190 lbs. Deb: 9/8/79

YEAR	TM/L	G	AB	R	H	2B	3B	HR	RBI	BB	SO	AVG	OBP	SLG	PRO+	BR/A	SB	CS	SBR	FA	FR	G/POS	TPR
1979	Phi-N	12	19	2	2	1	0	0	1	1	4	.105	.150	.158	-15	-3	0	0	0	.875	-0	/O-4,1-1	-0.4
1980	Mil-A	19	68	7	17	1	2	1	7	3	7	.250	.282	.368	79	-2	0	0	0	1.000	-1	/O-7,1-3,D-7	-0.3
Total	2	31	87	9	19	2	2	1	8	4	11	.218	.253	.322	57	-5	0	0	0	.957	-1	/O-11,D-7,1-4	-0.7

■ AARON POINTER
Pointer, Aaron Elton "Hawk" b: 4/19/42, Little Rock, Ark. BR/TR, 6'2", 185 lbs. Deb: 9/22/63

YEAR	TM/L	G	AB	R	H	2B	3B	HR	RBI	BB	SO	AVG	OBP	SLG	PRO+	BR/A	SB	CS	SBR	FA	FR	G/POS	TPR
1963	Hou-N	2	5	0	1	0	0	0	0	0	0	.200	.200	.200	17	-1	0	0	0	1.000	-0	/O-1	-0.1
1966	Hou-N	11	26	5	9	1	0	1	5	5	6	.346	.469	.500	182	3	1	1	-0	1.000	2	O-11	0.4
1967	Hou-N	27	70	6	11	4	0	1	10	13	26	.157	.298	.257	62	-3	1	0	0	.951	1	O-22	-0.3
Total	3	40	101	11	21	5	0	2	15	18	33	.208	.339	.317	91	-0	2	1	0	.966	3	/O-34	0.0

■ HUGH POLAND
Poland, Hugh Reid b: 1/19/13, Tompkinsville, Ky. d: 3/30/84, Guthrie, Ky. BL/TR, 5'11.5", 185 lbs. Deb: 4/22/43

YEAR	TM/L	G	AB	R	H	2B	3B	HR	RBI	BB	SO	AVG	OBP	SLG	PRO+	BR/A	SB	CS	SBR	FA	FR	G/POS	TPR
1943	NY-N	4	12	1	1	0	0	0	2	1	0	.083	.154	.250	16	-1	0			.889	-2	/C-4	-0.3
	Bos-N	44	141	5	27	7	0	0	13	4	11	.191	.214	.241	32	-13	0			.973	-2	C-38	-1.3
	Yr	48	153	6	28	7	1	0	15	5	11	.183	.209	.242	30	-14	0			.969	-4	C-42	-1.6
1944	Bos-N	8	23	1	3	1	0	0	2	0	1	.130	.130	.174	-14	-3	0			.939	1	/C-6	-0.2
1946	Bos-N	4	6	0	1	1	0	0	0	0	0	.167	.167	.333	40	-1	0			1.000	0	/C-2	0.0
1947	Phi-N	4	8	0	0	0	0	0	0	0	0	.000	.000	.000	-99	-2	0			1.000	-1	/C-2	-0.2
	Cin-N	16	18	1	6	0	0	0	2	1	4	.333	.368	.389	102	0	0			.667	-1	/C-3	-0.1
	Yr	20	26	1	6	0	0	0	2	1	4	.231	.259	.269	41	-2	0			.867	-1	/C-5	-0.3
1948	Cin-N	3	3	0	1	0	0	0	0	0	0	.333	.333	.333	84	-0	0			.000	0	H	0.0
Total	5	83	211	8	39	10	1	0	19	6	16	.185	.207	.242	28	-20	0			.958	-4	/C-55	-2.1

■ MARK POLHEMUS
Polhemus, Mark S. "Humpty Dumpty" b: 10/4/1862, Brooklyn, N.Y. d: 11/12/23, Lynn, Mass. 5'6.5", 185 lbs. Deb: 7/13/1887

YEAR	TM/L	G	AB	R	H	2B	3B	HR	RBI	BB	SO	AVG	OBP	SLG	PRO+	BR/A	SB	CS	SBR	FA	FR	G/POS	TPR
1887	Ind-N	20	75	6	18	1	0	0	8	2	9	.240	.260	.253	45	-5	4			.744	0	O-20	-0.5

■ GUS POLIDOR
Polidor, Gustavo Adolfo (Gonzalez) b: 10/26/61, Caracas, Venezuela d: 4/28/95, Caracas, Venezuela BR/TR, 6', 170 lbs. Deb: 9/7/85

YEAR	TM/L	G	AB	R	H	2B	3B	HR	RBI	BB	SO	AVG	OBP	SLG	PRO+	BR/A	SB	CS	SBR	FA	FR	G/POS	TPR
1985	Cal-A	2	1	1	1	0	0	0	0	0	0	1.000	1.000	1.000	452	0	0	0	0	1.000	0	/S-1,O-1	0.0
1986	Cal-A	6	19	1	5	1	0	0	1	1	0	.263	.300	.316	69	-1	0	0	0	1.000	0	/2-4,S-1,3-1	-0.1
1987	Cal-A	63	137	12	36	3	0	2	15	2	15	.263	.279	.328	62	-8	0	0	0	.983	-6	S-46,3-11/2-3	-1.0
1988	Cal-A	54	81	4	12	3	0	0	4	3	11	.148	.179	.185	2	-11	0	0	0	.984	0	S-25,3-22/2-3,D-1	-1.0
1989	Mil-A	79	175	15	34	7	0	0	14	6	18	.194	.230	.234	31	-16	3	0	1	.923	3	3-30,2-29,S-21,/D-2	-1.1
1990	Mil-A	18	15	0	1	0	0	0	1	0	1	.067	.067	.067	-63	-3	0	0	0	1.000	2	3-14/2-2,S-2	-0.2
1993	Fla-A	7	6	0	1	1	0	0	0	2	1	.167	.167	.333	28	-1	0	0	0	.000	-0	/2-1,3-1	0.0
Total	7	229	434	33	90	15	0	2	35	12	47	.207	.234	.256	35	-38	3	0	1	.970	-1	/S-96,3-79,2-42,DO	-3.5

■ NICK POLLY
Polly, Nicholas (b: Nicholas Joseph Polachanin) b: 4/18/17, Chicago, Ill. d: 1/17/93, Chicago, Ill. BR/TR, 5'11", 190 lbs. Deb: 9/11/37

YEAR	TM/L	G	AB	R	H	2B	3B	HR	RBI	BB	SO	AVG	OBP	SLG	PRO+	BR/A	SB	CS	SBR	FA	FR	G/POS	TPR
1937	Bro-N	10	18	2	4	0	0	0	2	2	2	.222	.222	.222	21	-2	0			.850	2	/3-7	0.0
1945	Bos-A	4	7	0	1	0	0	0	1	0	1	.143	.143	.143	-17	-1	0	0	0	1.000	-0	/3-2	-0.1
Total	2	14	25	2	5	0	0	0	3	0	1	.200	.200	.200	11	-3	0	0	0	.870	2	/3-9	-0.1

■ LUIS POLONIA
Polonia, Luis Andrew (Almonte) b: 10/12/64, Santiago, D.R. BL/TL, 5'8", 155 lbs. Deb: 4/24/87

YEAR	TM/L	G	AB	R	H	2B	3B	HR	RBI	BB	SO	AVG	OBP	SLG	PRO+	BR/A	SB	CS	SBR	FA	FR	G/POS	TPR
1987	Oak-A	125	435	78	125	16	10	4	49	32	64	.287	.336	.398	100	-0	29	7	5	.979	-1	*O-104,D-18	-0.1
1988	*Oak-A	84	288	51	84	11	4	2	27	21	40	.292	.340	.378	104	2	24	9	2	.988	1	O-76/D-2	0.2
1989	Oak-A	59	206	31	59	6	4	1	17	9	15	.286	.316	.369	96	-2	13	4	2	.985	5	O-55	0.3
	NY-A	66	227	39	71	11	2	2	29	16	29	.313	.363	.405	118	5	9	4	0	.982	8	O-53/D-9	0.8
	Yr	125	433	70	130	17	6	3	46	25	44	.300	.341	.388	108	4	22	8	2	.984	8	*O-108/D-9	1.1
1990	NY-A	11	22	2	7	0	0	0	3	0	1	.318	.318	.318	78	-1	0	0	0	.000	0	/D-4	0.0
	Cal-A	109	381	50	128	7	9	2	32	25	42	.336	.378	.417	125	13	20	14	2	.980	-11	O-85,D-11	0.3
	Yr	120	403	52	135	7	9	2	35	25	43	.335	.375	.412	122	12	21	14	2	.980	-5	O-85,D-11/H-4	0.3
1991	Cal-A	150	604	92	179	28	8	2	50	52	74	.296	.353	.379	103	-8	48	23	1	.981	1	*O-143/D-4	0.1
1992	Cal-A	149	577	83	165	17	4	0	35	45	64	.286	.339	.329	87	-9	51	21	3	.980	7	O-99,D-47	-0.8
1993	Cal-A	152	576	75	156	17	6	1	32	48	53	.271	.329	.326	74	-20	55	24	2	.983	8	*O-141/D-4	-1.2
1994	NY-A	95	350	62	109	21	6	1	36	37	36	.311	.384	.414	110	6	20	12	-1	.976	2	O-84/D-2	0.5
1995	NY-A	67	238	37	62	9	3	2	15	25	29	.261	.331	.349	78	-7	10	4	1	1.000	5	O-64/D-1	-0.3
	*Atl-N	28	53	6	14	7	0	0	2	3	9	.264	.304	.396	80	-2	3	0	1	1.000	-4	O-15	-0.5
1996	Bal-A	58	175	25	42	4	1	2	14	10	20	.240	.285	.309	51	-13	5	6	0	.983	-2	O-34,D-18	-1.7
	*Atl-N	22	31	3	13	0	0	0	2	1	3	.419	.438	.419	121	1	1	1	-0	.800	-2	/O-7	-0.1
Total	10	1175	4163	634	1214	154	57	19	343	324	479	.292	.345	.370	95	-23	292	129	10	.982	14	O-960,D-120	-2.5

■ CARLOS PONCE
Ponce, Carlos Antonio (Diaz) b: 2/7/59, Rio Piedras, P.R. BR/TR, 5'10", 170 lbs. Deb: 8/14/85

YEAR	TM/L	G	AB	R	H	2B	3B	HR	RBI	BB	SO	AVG	OBP	SLG	PRO+	BR/A	SB	CS	SBR	FA	FR	G/POS	TPR
1985	Mil-A	21	62	4	10	2	0	1	5	1	9	.161	.175	.242	13	-7	0	0	0	1.000	-0	1-10/O-6,D-3	-0.9

■ RALPH POND
Pond, Ralph Benjamin b: 5/4/1888, Eau Claire, Wis. d: 9/8/47, Cleveland, Ohio Deb: 6/8/10

YEAR	TM/L	G	AB	R	H	2B	3B	HR	RBI	BB	SO	AVG	OBP	SLG	PRO+	BR/A	SB	CS	SBR	FA	FR	G/POS	TPR
1910	Bos-A	1	4	0	1	0	0	0		0	0	.250	.250	.250	55	-0	1			.000	-1	/O-1	-0.1

■ HARLIN POOL
Pool, Harold G "Samson" b: 3/12/08, Lakeport, Cal. d: 2/15/63, Rodeo, Cal. BL/TR, 5'10", 195 lbs. Deb: 5/30/34

YEAR	TM/L	G	AB	R	H	2B	3B	HR	RBI	BB	SO	AVG	OBP	SLG	PRO+	BR/A	SB	CS	SBR	FA	FR	G/POS	TPR
1934	Cin-N	99	358	38	117	22	5	2	50	17	18	.327	.369	.433	117	8	3			.953	0	O-94	0.4
1935	Cin-N	28	68	8	12	6	2	0	11	2	2	.176	.200	.324	39	-6	0			.962	-3	O-18	-1.0
Total	2	127	426	46	129	28	7	2	61	19	20	.303	.343	.415	105	2	3			.954	-3	O-112	-0.6

■ ED POOLE
Poole, Edward I. b: 9/7/1874, Canton, Ohio d: 3/11/19, Malvern, Ohio BR/TR, 5'10", 175 lbs. Deb: 10/6/00

YEAR	TM/L	G	AB	R	H	2B	3B	HR	RBI	BB	SO	AVG	OBP	SLG	PRO+	BR/A	SB	CS	SBR	FA	FR	G/POS	TPR
1900	Pit-N	2	4	1	2	0	1	1		3	0	.500	.500	1.750	504	2	0			.500	-0	/O-1,P-1	0.0
1901	Pit-N	26	78	6	16	4	0	1		4	4	.205	.244	.295	54	-5	1			.933	-2	P-12,O-12/2-1,3-1	-0.5
1902	Pit-N	1	4	0	1	0	0	0		0	0	.250	.250	.250	52	-0	0			.667	-0	/P-1	0.0
	Cin-N	17	61	7	7	2	0	0		1	0	.115	.115	.148	-8	-8	0			.929	-0	P-16/O-1	-0.1
	Yr	18	65	7	8	2	0	0		1	0	.123	.123	.154	-13	-9	0			**.976**	-1	P-17/O-1	-0.1
1903	Cin-N	25	70	7	17	1	0	0		7	2	.243	.264	.257	44	-5	0			.929	2	P-25	0.0
1904	Bro-N	25	62	3	8	1	0	0		2	6	.129	.129	.145	-16	-8	0			.973	3	P-25	0.0
Total	5	96	279	24	51	8	2	2		15	6	.183	.200	.240	29	-25	1			.954	3	/P-80,O-14,3-1,2-1	-0.6

■ JIM POOLE
Poole, James Robert "Easy" b: 5/12/1895, Taylorsville, N.C. d: 1/2/75, Hickory, N.C. BL/TR, 6', 175 lbs. Deb: 4/14/25

YEAR	TM/L	G	AB	R	H	2B	3B	HR	RBI	BB	SO	AVG	OBP	SLG	PRO+	BR/A	SB	CS	SBR	FA	FR	G/POS	TPR
1925	Phi-A	133	480	65	143	29	8	3	67	27	37	.298	.338	.423	86	-12	5	4	-1	.982	-7	*1-123	-2.5
1926	Phi-A	112	361	49	106	23	5	8	63	23	25	.294	.339	.452	99	-2	4	3	-1	.992	0	*1-101/O-1	-0.8

YEAR	TM/L	G	AB	R	H	2B	3B	HR	RBI	BB	SO	AVG	OBP	SLG	PRO+	BR/A	SB	CS	SBR	FA	FR	G/POS	TPR
1927	Phi-A	38	99	4	22	2	0	0	10	9	6	.222	.287	.242	36	-9	0	0	0	.993	0	1-31	-1.0
Total	3	283	940	118	271	54	13	13	140	59	68	.288	.333	.415	86	-23	9	7	-2	.987	-7	1-255/O-1	-4.3

■ RAY POOLE   Poole, Raymond Herman   b: 1/16/20, Salisbury, N.C.   BL/TR, 6′, 180 lbs.   Deb: 9/9/41

YEAR	TM/L	G	AB	R	H	2B	3B	HR	RBI	BB	SO	AVG	OBP	SLG	PRO+	BR/A	SB	CS	SBR	FA	FR	G/POS	TPR
1941	Phi-A	2	2	0	0	0	0	0	0	0	1	.000	.000	.000	-99	-1	0	0	0	.000	0	H	-0.1
1947	Phi-A	13	13	1	3	0	0	0	1	1	4	.231	.286	.231	44	-1	0	0	0	.000	0	H	-0.1
Total	2	15	15	1	3	0	0	0	1	1	5	.200	.250	.200	25	-2	0	0	0		0	-0,-0	-0.2

■ TOM POORMAN   Poorman, Thomas Iverson   b: 10/14/1857, Lock Haven, Pa.   d: 2/18/05, Lock Haven, Pa.   BL/TR, 5′7″, 135 lbs.   Deb: 5/5/1880

YEAR	TM/L	G	AB	R	H	2B	3B	HR	RBI	BB	SO	AVG	OBP	SLG	PRO+	BR/A	SB	CS	SBR	FA	FR	G/POS	TPR
1880	Buf-N	19	70	5	11	1	0	0	1	0	13	.157	.157	.171	11	-6				.879	-2	P-11,O-10	-0.6
	Chi-N	7	25	3	5	1	2	0	0	0	2	.200	.200	.400	92	-0				.778	-2	/O-7,P-2	-0.1
	Yr	26	95	8	16	2	2	0	1	0	15	.168	.168	.232	33	-6				.750	-4	O-17,P-13	-0.7
1884	Tol-a	94	382	56	89	8	7	0			10	.233	.254	.291	75	-11				.845	4	*O-93/P-1	-0.8
1885	Bos-N	56	227	44	54	5	3	3	25	7	32	.238	.261	.326	92	-2				.867	-2	O-56	-0.6
1886	Bos-N	88	371	72	97	16	6	3	41	19	52	.261	.297	.361	103	1	31			.902	6	*O-88	0.4
1887	Phi-a	135	585	140	155	18	19	4	61	35		.265	.317	.381	94	-6	88			.911	3	*O-135/2-2,P-1	-1.3
1888	Phi-a	97	383	76	87	16	6	2	44	31		.227	.294	.316	96	-1	46			.898	-10	*O-97	-1.3
Total	6	496	2043	396	498	65	43	12	172	102	99	.244	.285	.335	90	-26	165			.885	-4	O-486/P-15,2-2	-3.5

■ DAVE POPE   Pope, David   b: 6/17/25, Talladega, Ala.   BL/TR, 5′10.5″, 170 lbs.   Deb: 7/1/52

YEAR	TM/L	G	AB	R	H	2B	3B	HR	RBI	BB	SO	AVG	OBP	SLG	PRO+	BR/A	SB	CS	SBR	FA	FR	G/POS	TPR
1952	Cle-A	12	34	9	10	1	1	1	4	1	7	.294	.314	.471	124	1	0	0	0	1.000	-4	O-10	-0.1
1954	*Cle-A	60	102	21	30	2	1	4	13	10	22	.294	.357	.451	118	2	2	1	0	1.000	-4	O-29	-0.2
1955	Cle-A	35	104	17	31	5	0	6	22	12	31	.298	.376	.519	134	5	0	0	0	.954	-3	O-31	0.1
	Bal-A	86	222	21	55	8	4	1	30	16	34	.248	.304	.333	77	-8	5	2	0	1.000	-8	O-73	-1.9
	Yr	121	326	38	86	13	4	7	52	28	65	.264	.328	.393	97	-2	5	2	0	.986	-11	*O-104	-1.8
1956	Bal-A	12	19	1	3	0	0	0	1	0	7	.158	.200	.158	-5	-3	0	0	0	1.000	-1	/O-4	-0.4
	Cle-A	25	70	6	17	3	1	0	3	1	12	.243	.254	.314	48	-5	0	0	0	1.000	-1	O-18	-0.7
	Yr	37	89	7	20	3	1	0	4	1	19	.225	.242	.281	38	-8	0	0	0	1.000	-2	O-22	-1.1
Total	4	230	551	75	146	19	7	12	73	40	113	.265	.319	.390	92	-9	7	3	0	.990	-18	O-165	-3.2

■ PAUL POPOVICH   Popovich, Paul Edward   b: 8/18/40, Flemington, W.Va.   BB/TR, 6′, 175 lbs.   Deb: 4/19/64

YEAR	TM/L	G	AB	R	H	2B	3B	HR	RBI	BB	SO	AVG	OBP	SLG	PRO+	BR/A	SB	CS	SBR	FA	FR	G/POS	TPR
1964	Chi-N	1	1	0	1	0	0	0	0	0	0	1.000	1.000	1.000	447	0	0	0	0	.000	0	H	0.0
1966	Chi-N	2	6	0	0	0	0	0	0	0	2	.000	.000	.000	-99	-0	0	0	0	.889	-1	/2-2	-0.3
1967	Chi-N	49	159	18	34	4	0	2	9	12	.214	.265	.239	43	-11	0	1	-1	.967	-4	S-31,2-17/3-2	-1.3
1968	LA-N	134	418	35	97	8	1	2	25	29	37	.232	.283	.270	72	-15	1	3	-2	.983	3	2-89,S-45/3-7	-0.5
1969	LA-N	28	50	5	10	0	0	0	4	1	4	.200	.216	.200	18	-5	0	0	0	.985	0	2-23/S-3	-0.4
	Chi-N	60	154	26	48	6	0	1	14	18	14	.312	.387	.370	100	1	0	1	-1	.974	-6	2-25/S-7,3-6,0-1	-0.4
	Yr	88	204	31	58	6	0	1	18	19	18	.284	.348	.328	85	-4	0	1	-1	.978	-6	2-48,S-10/3-6,0-1	-0.8
1970	Chi-N	78	186	22	47	5	1	4	20	18	18	.253	.326	.355	73	-7	0	1	-1	.990	-6	2-22,S-17,3-16	-1.0
1971	Chi-N	89	226	24	49	7	1	4	28	14	17	.217	.262	.310	54	-14	0	1	-1	.985	4	2-40,3-16/S-1	-0.9
1972	Chi-N	58	129	8	25	3	2	1	11	12	8	.194	.262	.271	47	-9	0	1	-1	.981	19	2-36/S-8,3-1	1.2
1973	Chi-N	99	280	24	66	6	3	2	24	18	27	.236	.284	.300	58	-16	3	2	-0	.981	26	2-84/S-9,3-1	1.5
1974	*Pit-N	59	83	9	18	2	1	0	5	5	10	.217	.261	.265	49	-6	0	0	0	.962	-1	2-12,S-10	-0.6
1975	Pit-N	25	40	5	8	1	0	0	1	3	2	.200	.273	.225	40	-3	0	0	0	1.000	-3	/2-8,S-8	-0.6
Total	11	682	1732	176	403	42	9	14	134	127	151	.233	.288	.292	62	-87	4	10	-5	.982	31	2-358,S-139/3-49,O	-3.3

■ GEORGE POPPLEIN   Popplein, George J.   b: 8/1/1840, Baltimore, Md.   d: 3/31/01, Baltimore, Md.   Deb: 7/11/1873

YEAR	TM/L	G	AB	R	H	2B	3B	HR	RBI	BB	SO	AVG	OBP	SLG	PRO+	BR/A	SB	CS	SBR	FA	FR	G/POS	TPR
1873	Mar-n	1	4	0	0	0	0	0	0	0	0	.000	.000	.000	-99	-1				.500	-1	/S-1,O-1	-0.2

■ TOM POQUETTE   Poquette, Thomas Arthur   b: 10/30/51, Eau Claire, Wis.   BL/TR, 5′10″, 175 lbs.   Deb: 9/1/73

YEAR	TM/L	G	AB	R	H	2B	3B	HR	RBI	BB	SO	AVG	OBP	SLG	PRO+	BR/A	SB	CS	SBR	FA	FR	G/POS	TPR
1973	KC-A	21	28	4	6	1	0	0	3	1	4	.214	.267	.250	43	-2	1	1	-0	.870	-4	O-20	-0.7
1976	*KC-A	104	344	43	104	18	10	2	34	29	31	.302	.363	.430	131	13	6	5	-1	.979	-8	O-98/D-2	0.1
1977	*KC-A	106	342	43	100	23	6	2	33	19	21	.292	.339	.412	103	1	1	4	-2	1.000	2	O-96	-0.6
1978	*KC-A	80	204	16	44	9	4	0	30	14	9	.216	.266	.338	67	-9	2	0	1	.955	4	O-63/D-1	-0.7
1979	KC-A	21	26	1	5	0	0	0	3	1	4	.192	.222	.192	13	-3	0	0	0	1.000	-2	O-10	-0.5
	Bos-A	63	154	14	51	9	0	2	23	8	7	.331	.354	.429	110	2	2	2	-1	.949	-7	O-43/D-4	-0.6
	Yr	84	180	15	56	9	0	2	26	9	11	.311	.354	.394	97	-1	2	2	-1	.954	-9	O-53/D-4	-1.1
1981	Bos-A	3	2	0	0	0	0	0	0	0	0	.000	.000	.000	-94	-0	0	0	0	.000	-1	/O-2	-0.2
	Tex-A	30	64	2	10	1	0	0	7	5	1	.156	.229	.172	18	-7	1	1	-1	.963	-3	O-18	-1.2
	Yr	33	66	2	10	1	0	0	7	5	1	.152	.222	.167	14	-7	1	1	-1	.963	-4	O-20	-1.4
1982	KC-A	24	62	4	9	1	0	0	5	3	7	.145	.209	.161	3	-8	1	0	0	.957	-1	O-23	-0.9
Total	7	452	1226	127	329	62	18	10	136	80	84	.268	.321	.373	92	-13	13	13	-4	.971	-24	O-373/D-7	-5.3

■ DAN PORTER   Porter, Daniel Edward   b: 10/17/31, Decatur, Ill.   BL/TL, 6′, 164 lbs.   Deb: 8/16/51

YEAR	TM/L	G	AB	R	H	2B	3B	HR	RBI	BB	SO	AVG	OBP	SLG	PRO+	BR/A	SB	CS	SBR	FA	FR	G/POS	TPR
1951	Was-A	13	19	2	4	0	0	0	1	1	0	.211	.286	.211	36	-2	0	0	0	1.000	-0	/O-3	-0.2

■ DARRELL PORTER   Porter, Darrell Ray   b: 1/17/52, Joplin, Mo.   BL/TR, 6′, 193 lbs.   Deb: 9/2/71

YEAR	TM/L	G	AB	R	H	2B	3B	HR	RBI	BB	SO	AVG	OBP	SLG	PRO+	BR/A	SB	CS	SBR	FA	FR	G/POS	TPR
1971	Mil-A	22	70	4	15	2	0	1	9	9	20	.214	.304	.329	80	-2	2	2	-1	.977	2	C-22	0.1
1972	Mil-A	18	56	2	7	1	0	1	2	5	21	.125	.210	.196	22	-5	0	0	0	.976	5	C-18	0.0
1973	Mil-A	117	350	50	89	19	2	16	67	57	85	.254	.360	.457	133	16	5	2	0	.977	-4	C-90,D-19	1.7
1974	Mil-A☆	131	432	59	104	15	4	12	56	50	88	.241	.326	.377	103	2	8	7	-2	.978	-3	*C-117/D-9	0.2
1975	Mil-A	130	409	66	95	12	5	18	60	89	77	.232	.376	.418	123	16	2	5	-2	.979	-2	*C-124/D-2	1.7
1976	Mil-A	119	389	43	81	14	1	5	32	51	61	.208	.302	.288	75	-12	2	0	1	.975	-5	*C-111/D-2	-1.4
1977	*KC-A	130	425	61	117	21	3	16	60	53	70	.275	.357	.452	118	11	1	0	0	.982	5	*C-125/D-1	1.5
1978	*KC-A★	150	520	77	138	27	6	18	78	75	75	.265	.360	.444	122	16	5	5	-3	.988	-6	*C-145/D-4	1.1
1979	KC-A★	157	533	101	155	23	10	20	112	121	65	.291	.429	.484	143	38	3	4	-2	.982	-2	*C-141,D-15	3.8
1980	*KC-A★	118	418	51	104	14	2	7	51	69	50	.249	.358	.342	92	-2	1	1	-0	.978	2	C-81,D-34	0.1
1981	StL-N	61	174	22	39	10	2	6	31	39	32	.224	.369	.408	117	9	5	1	2	.979	-5	C-52	0.4
1982	*StL-N	120	373	46	86	18	5	12	48	66	66	.231	.349	.402	109	6	1	1	-0	.983	-5	*C-111	0.4
1983	StL-N	145	443	57	116	24	3	15	66	68	94	.262	.365	.431	120	13	1	3	-2	.989	-7	*C-133	1.0
1984	StL-N	127	422	56	98	16	3	11	68	60	79	.232	.335	.363	98	0	5	3	-0	.984	-12	*C-122	-0.6
1985	StL-N	84	240	30	53	12	2	10	36	41	48	.221	.347	.412	109	3	6	1	1	.990	-2	C-82	0.7
1986	Tex-A	68	155	21	41	6	0	12	29	22	51	.265	.360	.535	136	8	1	1	-0	.994	2	C-25,D-19	1.1
1987	Tex-A	85	130	19	31	3	0	7	21	30	43	.238	.389	.423	115	4	0	0	0	1.000	-0	D-35/C-7,1-5	0.3
Total	17	1782	5539	765	1369	237	48	188	826	905	1025	.247	.357	.409	118	116	39	37	-11	.982	-38	*C-1506,D-140/1-5	12.1

■ IRV PORTER   Porter, Irving Marble   b: 5/17/1888, Lynn, Mass.   d: 2/20/71, Lynn, Mass.   BB/TR, 5′9″, 155 lbs.   Deb: 8/20/14

YEAR	TM/L	G	AB	R	H	2B	3B	HR	RBI	BB	SO	AVG	OBP	SLG	PRO+	BR/A	SB	CS	SBR	FA	FR	G/POS	TPR
1914	Chi-A	4	4	1	1	0	0	0	0	1		.250	.250	.250	51	-0	0			1.000	-0	/O-1	-0.1

■ JAY PORTER   Porter, J W "J W"   b: 1/17/33, Shawnee, Okla.   BR/TR, 6′2″, 180 lbs.   Deb: 7/30/52

YEAR	TM/L	G	AB	R	H	2B	3B	HR	RBI	BB	SO	AVG	OBP	SLG	PRO+	BR/A	SB	CS	SBR	FA	FR	G/POS	TPR
1952	StL-A	33	104	12	26	4	1	2	7	10	10	.250	.316	.308	72	-4	4	0	1	.973	-1	O-29/3-2	-0.5
1955	Det-A	24	55	6	13	2	0	0	3	8	15	.236	.333	.273	66	-2	1	0	0	1.000	-3	/1-6,C-4,O-4	-0.6
1956	Det-A	14	21	0	2	0	0	0	3	2	6	.095	.095	.095	-49	-4	0	0	0	1.000	-1	/C-2,O-2	-0.5
1957	Det-A	58	140	14	35	8	0	4	18	14	20	.250	.323	.350	82	-3	0	0	0	.953	-3	O-27,C-12/1-3	-0.8
1958	Cle-A	40	85	13	17	1	0	4	19	9	23	.200	.284	.353	76	-3	1	0	0	1.000	-3	C-20/1-4,3-1	-0.5
1959	Was-A	37	106	8	24	4	0	1	10	11	16	.226	.305	.292	65	-5	0	0	0	.993	-1	C-34/1-2	-0.5
	StL-N	23	33	5	7	3	1	0	2	1	4	.212	.257	.394	66	-2	0	0	0	1.000	0	C-19/1-1	-0.1
Total	6	229	544	58	124	22	1	6	62	53	96	.228	.301	.316	68	-24	4	0	1	.990	-12	/C-91,O-62,1-16,3-3	-3.5

■ MATTHEW PORTER   Porter, Matthew Sheldon   b: Kansas City, Mo.   Deb: 6/27/1884   M

YEAR	TM/L	G	AB	R	H	2B	3B	HR	RBI	BB	SO	AVG	OBP	SLG	PRO+	BR/A	SB	CS	SBR	FA	FR	G/POS	TPR
1884	KC-U	3	12	1	1	1	0	0		0		.083	.083	.167	-30	-2				.750	1	/O-3,M	-0.1

YEAR	TM/L	G	AB	R	H	2B	3B	HR	RBI	BB	SO	AVG	OBP	SLG	PRO+	BR/A	SB	CS	SBR	FA	FR	G/POS	TPR

■ DICK PORTER   Porter, Richard Twilley "Wiggles" or "Twitches"   b: 12/30/01, Princess Anne, Md.   d: 9/24/74, Philadelphia, Pa.   BL/TR, 5'10", 170 lbs.   Deb: 4/16/29

YEAR	TM/L	G	AB	R	H	2B	3B	HR	RBI	BB	SO	AVG	OBP	SLG	PRO+	BR/A	SB	CS	SBR	FA	FR	G/POS	TPR
1929	Cle-A	71	192	26	63	16	5	1	24	17	14	.328	.386	.479	117	5	3	5	-2	.941	-5	O-28,2-20	-0.3
1930	Cle-A	119	480	100	168	43	8	4	57	55	31	.350	.420	.498	127	21	3	3	-1	.962	-4	*O-118	0.7
1931	Cle-A	114	414	82	129	24	3	1	38	56	36	.312	.395	.391	102	3	6	9	-4	.970	-6	*O-109/2-1	-1.3
1932	Cle-A	146	621	106	191	42	8	4	60	64	43	.308	.373	.420	99	-1	2	4	-2	.982	-11	*O-145	-2.1
1933	Cle-A	132	499	73	133	19	6	0	41	51	42	.267	.335	.329	73	-19	4	4	-1	**.996**	-1	*O-124	-2.6
1934	Cle-A	13	44	9	10	2	1	1	6	4	5	.227	.292	.386	73	-2	0	0	0	1.000	-1	O-10	-0.4
	Bos-A	80	265	30	80	13	6	0	56	21	15	.302	.355	.396	87	-5	5	2	0	.940	-6	O-65	-1.2
	Yr	93	309	39	90	15	7	1	62	25	20	.291	.346	.395	85	-7	5	2	0	.947	-7	O-75	-1.6
Total	6	675	2515	426	774	159	37	11	282	268	186	.308	.376	.414	99	2	23	27	-9	.973	-35	O-599/2-21	-7.2

■ BOB PORTER   Porter, Robert Lee   b: 7/22/59, Yuma, Ariz.   BL/TL, 5'10", 180 lbs.   Deb: 5/13/81

YEAR	TM/L	G	AB	R	H	2B	3B	HR	RBI	BB	SO	AVG	OBP	SLG	PRO+	BR/A	SB	CS	SBR	FA	FR	G/POS	TPR
1981	Atl-N	17	14	2	4	1	0	0	4	2	1	.286	.375	.357	106	0	0	0	0	.000	0	/H	0.0
1982	Atl-N	24	27	1	3	0	0	0	0	1	9	.111	.143	.111	-27	-5	0	0	0	1.000	-1	/O-4,1-1	-0.6
Total	2	41	41	3	7	1	0	0	4	3	10	.171	.227	.195	19	-4	0	0	0	1.000	-1	/O-4,1-1	-0.6

■ JORGE POSADA   Posada, Jorge Rafael (Villeta)   b: 8/17/71, Santurce, P.R.   BB/TR, 6'2", 190 lbs.   Deb: 9/4/95

YEAR	TM/L	G	AB	R	H	2B	3B	HR	RBI	BB	SO	AVG	OBP	SLG	PRO+	BR/A	SB	CS	SBR	FA	FR	G/POS	TPR
1995	*NY-A	1	0	0	0	0	0	0	0	0	0	—	—	—	—	0	0	0	0	1.000	-0	/C-1	0.0
1996	NY-A	8	14	1	1	0	0	0	0	1	6	.071	.133	.071	-45	-3	0	0	0	1.000	1	/C-4,D-3	-0.1
Total	2	9	14	1	1	0	0	0	0	1	6	.071	.133	.071	-45	-3	0	0	0	1.000	1	/C-5,D-3	-0.1

■ LEO POSADA   Posada, Leopoldo Jesus (Hernandez)   b: 4/15/36, Havana, Cuba   BR/TR, 5'11", 175 lbs.   Deb: 9/21/60

YEAR	TM/L	G	AB	R	H	2B	3B	HR	RBI	BB	SO	AVG	OBP	SLG	PRO+	BR/A	SB	CS	SBR	FA	FR	G/POS	TPR
1960	KC-A	10	36	8	13	0	2	1	2	3	7	.361	.410	.556	158	3	1	0	0	1.000	-2	/O-9	0.1
1961	KC-A	116	344	37	87	10	4	7	53	36	84	.253	.331	.366	85	-7	0	0	0	.973	-3	*O-102	-1.5
1962	KC-A	29	46	6	9	1	1	0	3	7	14	.196	.302	.261	51	-3	0	0	0	1.000	0	O-11	-0.4
Total	3	155	426	51	109	11	7	8	58	46	105	.256	.334	.371	87	-8	1	0	0	.976	-5	O-122	-1.8

■ SCOTT POSE   Pose, Scott Vernon   b: 2/11/67, Davenport, Iowa   BL/TR, 5'11", 165 lbs.   Deb: 4/5/93

YEAR	TM/L	G	AB	R	H	2B	3B	HR	RBI	BB	SO	AVG	OBP	SLG	PRO+	BR/A	SB	CS	SBR	FA	FR	G/POS	TPR
1993	Fla-N	15	41	0	8	2	0	0	3	2	4	.195	.233	.244	26	-4	2	-1		1.000	-3	O-10	-0.9

■ LEW POST   Post, Lewis G.   b: 4/12/1875, Woodland, Mich.   d: 8/21/44, Chicago, Ill.   Deb: 9/21/02

YEAR	TM/L	G	AB	R	H	2B	3B	HR	RBI	BB	SO	AVG	OBP	SLG	PRO+	BR/A	SB	CS	SBR	FA	FR	G/POS	TPR
1902	Det-A	3	12	1	1	0	0	0	2	0		.083	.083	.083	-53	-2	0			.800	-1	/O-3	-0.3

■ SAM POST   Post, Samuel Gilbert   b: 11/17/1896, Richmond, Va.   d: 3/31/71, Portsmouth, Va.   BL/TL, 6'1.5", 170 lbs.   Deb: 4/22/22

YEAR	TM/L	G	AB	R	H	2B	3B	HR	RBI	BB	SO	AVG	OBP	SLG	PRO+	BR/A	SB	CS	SBR	FA	FR	G/POS	TPR
1922	Bro-N	9	25	3	7	0	0	0	4	0	4	.280	.308	.280	53	-1	2	1	0	.982	-1	/1-8	-0.3

■ WALLY POST   Post, Walter Charles   b: 7/9/29, St.Wendelin, Ohio   d: 1/6/82, St.Henry, Ohio   BR/TR, 6'1", 203 lbs.   Deb: 9/18/49

YEAR	TM/L	G	AB	R	H	2B	3B	HR	RBI	BB	SO	AVG	OBP	SLG	PRO+	BR/A	SB	CS	SBR	FA	FR	G/POS	TPR
1949	Cin-N	6	8	1	2	0	0	0	0	0	3	.250	.250	.250	34	-1	0			.750	-1	/O-3	-0.2
1951	Cin-N	15	41	6	9	3	0	1	7	3	4	.220	.273	.366	69	-2	0	0	0	.963	1	/O-9	-0.2
1952	Cin-N	19	58	5	9	1	0	2	7	4	20	.155	.222	.276	37	-5	0	0	0	1.000	2	O-16	-0.4
1953	Cin-N	11	33	3	8	1	0	1	4	4	6	.242	.324	.364	78	-1	1	0	0	.960	1	O-11	-0.1
1954	Cin-N	130	451	46	115	21	3	18	83	26	70	.255	.300	.435	86	-11	2	2	-1	.957	5	*O-116	-1.1
1955	Cin-N	154	601	116	186	33	3	40	109	60	102	.309	.374	.574	139	32	7	4	-0	.978	3	*O-154	2.6
1956	Cin-N	143	539	94	134	25	3	36	83	37	124	.249	.302	.506	105	2	6	0	0	.969	12	*O-136	0.9
1957	Cin-N	134	467	68	114	26	2	20	74	33	84	.244	.294	.437	87	-10	2	2	-1	.985	10	*O-124	-0.7
1958	Phi-N	110	379	51	107	21	3	12	62	32	74	.282	.343	.449	109	4	0	2	-1	.952	8	O-91	0.6
1959	Phi-N	132	468	62	119	17	6	22	94	36	101	.254	.312	.457	100	-1	0	2	-0	.992	5	*O-120	0.1
1960	Phi-N	34	84	11	24	6	1	2	12	9	24	.286	.355	.452	119	2	0	0	0	1.000	1	O-22	0.2
	Cin-N	77	249	36	70	14	0	17	38	28	51	.281	.354	.542	139	13	0	2	-1	.985	4	O-67	1.3
	Yr	111	333	47	94	20	1	19	50	37	75	.282	.354	.520	134	15	0	2	-1	.989	5	O-89	1.5
1961	*Cin-N	99	282	44	83	16	3	20	57	22	61	.294	.348	.585	140	15	0	1	-1	.959	1	O-81	1.1
1962	Cin-N	109	285	43	75	10	3	17	62	32	67	.263	.342	.498	118	7	1	0	0	.935	-4	O-90	-0.1
1963	Cin-N	5	7	1	0	0	0	0	0	1	4	.000	.125	.000	-59	-1	0	0	0	1.000	0	/O-1	-0.1
	Min-A	21	47	6	9	0	1	2	6	2	17	.191	.224	.362	60	-3	0	0	0	1.000	-2	O-12	-0.5
1964	Cle-A	5	8	1	0	0	0	0	0	3	4	.000	.273	.000	-16	-1	0	0	0	.667	-1	/O-2	-0.2
Total	15	1204	4007	594	1064	194	28	210	699	331	813	.266	.325	.485	109	39	19	13		.970	46	*O-1055	3.2

■ MIKE POTTER   Potter, Michael Gary   b: 5/16/51, Montebello, Cal.   BR/TR, 6'1", 195 lbs.   Deb: 9/6/76

YEAR	TM/L	G	AB	R	H	2B	3B	HR	RBI	BB	SO	AVG	OBP	SLG	PRO+	BR/A	SB	CS	SBR	FA	FR	G/POS	TPR
1976	StL-N	9	16	0	0	0	0	0	1	0	6	.000	.059	.000	-82	-4	0	0	0	1.000	0	/O-4	-0.4
1977	StL-N	5	7	0	0	0	0	0	0	0	2	.000	.000	.000	-99	-2	0	0	0	.000	-0	/O-1	-0.2
Total	2	14	23	0	0	0	0	0	1	0	8	.000	.042	.000	-87	-6	0	0	0	1.000	-0	/O-5	-0.6

■ JOHN POTTS   Potts, John Frederick "Fred"   b: 2/6/1887, Tipp City, Ohio   d: 9/5/62, Cleveland, Ohio   BL/TR, 5'7", 165 lbs.   Deb: 4/18/14

YEAR	TM/L	G	AB	R	H	2B	3B	HR	RBI	BB	SO	AVG	OBP	SLG	PRO+	BR/A	SB	CS	SBR	FA	FR	G/POS	TPR
1914	KC-F	41	102	14	27	4	0	1	9	25	13	.265	.414	.333	110	1	7			.933	-4	O-31	-0.4

■ DAN POTTS   Potts, Vivian   b: 1/1869, Bristol, Pa.   Deb: 10/3/1892

YEAR	TM/L	G	AB	R	H	2B	3B	HR	RBI	BB	SO	AVG	OBP	SLG	PRO+	BR/A	SB	CS	SBR	FA	FR	G/POS	TPR
1892	Was-N	1	4	0	1	0	0	0	0	0	1	.250	.250	.250	53	-0	0			1.000	1	/C-1	0.0

■ KEN POULSEN   Poulsen, Ken Sterling   b: 8/4/47, Van Nuys, Cal.   BL/TR, 6'1", 190 lbs.   Deb: 7/3/67

YEAR	TM/L	G	AB	R	H	2B	3B	HR	RBI	BB	SO	AVG	OBP	SLG	PRO+	BR/A	SB	CS	SBR	FA	FR	G/POS	TPR
1967	Bos-A	5	5	0	1	1	0	0	0	0	2	.200	.200	.400	68	-0	0	0	0	.667	-1	/3-2,S-1	-0.1

■ ALONZO POWELL   Powell, Alonzo Sidney   b: 12/12/64, San Francisco, Cal.   BR/TR, 6'2", 190 lbs.   Deb: 4/6/87

YEAR	TM/L	G	AB	R	H	2B	3B	HR	RBI	BB	SO	AVG	OBP	SLG	PRO+	BR/A	SB	CS	SBR	FA	FR	G/POS	TPR
1987	Mon-N	14	41	3	8	3	0	0	4	5	17	.195	.283	.268	46	-3	0	0	0	1.000	-1	O-11	-0.5
1991	Sea-A	57	111	16	24	6	1	3	12	11	24	.216	.293	.369	82	-3	0	2	-1	.960	-9	O-40/1-7,D-7	-1.4
Total	2	71	152	19	32	9	1	3	16	16	41	.211	.290	.342	71	-6	0	2	-1	.968	-10	/O-51,D-7,1-7	-1.9

■ JAKE POWELL   Powell, Alvin Jacob   b: 7/15/08, Silver Spring, Md   d: 11/4/48, Washington, D.C.   BR/TR, 5'11.5", 180 lbs.   Deb: 8/3/30

YEAR	TM/L	G	AB	R	H	2B	3B	HR	RBI	BB	SO	AVG	OBP	SLG	PRO+	BR/A	SB	CS	SBR	FA	FR	G/POS	TPR
1930	Was-A	3	4	1	0	0	0	0	0	0	1	.000	.000	.000	-99	-1	0	0	0	1.000	-0	/O-2	-0.1
1934	Was-A	9	35	6	10	2	0	0	1	4	2	.286	.359	.343	85	-1	1	1	-0	.955	1	/O-9	0.0
1935	Was-A	139	551	88	172	26	10	6	98	37	37	.312	.360	.428	107	4	15	7	0	.976	0	*O-136/2-2	0.0
1936	Was-A	53	210	40	62	11	5	1	30	18	21	.295	.357	.410	94	-2	10	4	1	.951	-7	O-53	-1.0
	*NY-A	87	328	62	99	13	3	7	48	33	30	.302	.366	.424	98	-1	16	7	1	.976	0	O-84	-0.3
	Yr	140	538	102	161	24	8	8	78	51	51	.299	.362	.418	96	-4	26	11	1	.967	-7	*O-137	-1.3
1937	*NY-A	97	365	54	96	22	3	4	45	25	36	.263	.314	.364	70	-17	7	5	-1	.981	0	O-94	-1.9
1938	*NY-A	45	164	27	42	12	1	2	20	15	20	.256	.326	.378	76	-6	3	1	0	.978	-3	O-43	-0.9
1939	NY-A	31	86	12	21	4	1	1	9	3	8	.244	.270	.349	58	-6	1	2	-1	.983	0	O-23	-0.7
1940	NY-A	12	27	3	5	0	2	0	1	4	1	.185	.214	.185	5	-4	0	0	0	1.000	0	/O-7	-0.4
1943	Was-A	37	132	14	35	10	2	0	20	5	13	.265	.297	.371	99	-1	3	5	-2	.978	2	O-33	-0.5
1944	Was-A	96	367	29	88	9	1	1	37	16	26	.240	.272	.278	60	-20	7	2	1	.980	-1	O-90/3-1	-2.5
1945	Was-A	31	98	4	19	2	0	0	8	3	8	.194	.216	.214	40	-8	1	1	-0	.950	-1	O-27	-1.2
	Phi-N	44	173	10	40	5	0	1	14	6	18	.231	.265	.277	52	-11	1			.986	-4	O-44	-1.5
Total	11	688	2540	353	689	116	26	22	327	173	219	.271	.320	.363	81	-75	65	35		.975	-9	O-645/2-2,3-1	-11.1

■ ABNER POWELL   Powell, Charles Abner "Ab"   b: 12/15/1860, Shenandoah, Pa.   d: 8/7/53, New Orleans, La.   BL/TR, 5'7", 160 lbs.   Deb: 8/4/1884

YEAR	TM/L	G	AB	R	H	2B	3B	HR	RBI	BB	SO	AVG	OBP	SLG	PRO+	BR/A	SB	CS	SBR	FA	FR	G/POS	TPR
1884	Was-U	48	191	36	54	10	5	0		3		.283	.294	.387	108	-4				.875	-2	O-30,P-18/3-2,S2	-0.6
1886	Bal-a	11	39	4	7	2	1	0	7	1		.179	.200	.282	52	-2	4			.917	1	/P-7,O-4	-0.2
	Cin-a	19	74	13	17	1	1	0	8	4		.230	.269	.270	67	-3	0			.760	-1	O-13/S-6,P-4	-0.3
	Yr	30	113	17	24	3	2	0	15	5		.212	.246	.274	62	-5	4			.735	1	O-17,P-11/S-6	-0.4
Total	2	78	304	53	78	13	7	0	15	8		.257	.276	.345	91	-9	4			.817	-1	/O-47,P-29,S-7,32	-1.0

YEAR	TM/L	G	AB	R	H	2B	3B	HR	RBI	BB	SO	AVG	OBP	SLG	PRO+	BR/A	SB	CS	SBR	FA	FR	G/POS	TPR

■ HOSKEN POWELL
Powell, Hosken b: 5/14/55, Selma, Ala. BL/TL, 6'1", 185 lbs. Deb: 4/5/78

1978	Min-A	121	381	55	94	20	2	3	31	45	31	.247	.326	.333	84	-7	11	5	0	.983	-1	*O-117	-1.3
1979	Min-A	104	338	49	99	17	3	2	36	33	25	.293	.361	.379	96	-1	5	1	1	.977	-2	O-93/D-5	-0.6
1980	Min-A	137	485	58	127	17	5	6	35	32	46	.262	.312	.355	76	-16	14	3	2	.968	7	*O-129	-1.1
1981	Min-A	80	264	30	63	11	3	2	25	17	31	.239	.287	.326	71	-10	7	4	-0	.970	-2	O-64/D-8	-1.1
1982	Tor-A	112	265	43	73	13	4	3	26	12	23	.275	.307	.389	82	-7	4	4	-1	.974	-9	O-75,D-19	-2.0
1983	Tor-A	40	83	6	14	0	0	1	7	5	8	.169	.216	.205	16	-10	2	0	1	.981	-4	O-33/1-1,D-1	-1.3
Total	6	594	1816	241	470	78	17	17	160	144	164	.259	.316	.349	79	-50	43	17	3	.975	-8	O-511/D-33,1-1	-7.4

■ JIM POWELL
Powell, James Edwin b: 8/30/1859, Richmond, Va. d: 11/20/29, Butte, Mont. 5'10", 170 lbs. Deb: 8/5/1884

| 1884 | Ric-a | 41 | 151 | 23 | 37 | 8 | 4 | 0 | | 7 | | .245 | .296 | .351 | 112 | 2 | | | | .943 | 1 | 1-41 | -0.2 |

■ BOOG POWELL
Powell, John Wesley b: 8/17/41, Lakeland, Fla. BL/TR, 6'4", 240 lbs. Deb: 9/26/61

1961	Bal-A	4	13	0	1	0	0	0	1	0	2	.077	.077	.077	-61	-3	0	0	0	1.000	-1	/O-3	-0.4
1962	Bal-A	124	400	44	97	13	2	15	53	38	79	.243	.311	.398	95	-4	1	1	-0	.969	-7	*O-112/1-1	-1.8
1963	Bal-A	140	491	67	130	22	2	25	82	49	87	.265	.331	.470	126	16	1	2	-1	.969	-8	*O-121,1-23	0.1
1964	Bal-A	134	424	74	123	17	0	39	99	76	91	.290	.400	.606	176	44	0	0	0	.974	4	*O-124/1-5	4.4
1965	Bal-A	144	472	54	117	20	2	17	72	71	93	.248	.351	.407	112	9	1	1	-0	.992	3	1-78,O-71	0.6
1966	*Bal-A	140	491	78	141	18	0	34	109	67	125	.287	.374	.532	159	38	0	4	-2	.989	-7	*1-136	2.1
1967	Bal-A	125	415	53	97	14	1	13	55	55	94	.234	.326	.366	105	3	1	3	-2	.986	-4	*1-114	-1.0
1968	Bal-A★	154	550	60	137	21	1	22	85	73	97	.249	.340	.411	127	18	7	1	2	.990	-5	*1-149	0.4
1969	*Bal-A★	152	533	83	162	25	0	37	121	72	76	.304	.388	.559	161	42	1	1	-0	.995	-2	*1-144	3.0
1970	*Bal-A★	154	526	82	156	28	0	35	114	104	80	.297	.417	.549	163	48	1	0	-0	.992	-2	*1-145	3.3
1971	*Bal-A†	128	418	59	107	19	0	22	92	82	64	.256	.383	.459	139	24	1	0	0	.995	-3	*1-124	1.1
1972	Bal-A	140	465	53	117	20	1	21	81	65	92	.252	.348	.434	129	17	4	0	1	.988	-3	*1-133	0.5
1973	*Bal-A	114	370	52	98	13	1	11	54	85	64	.265	.402	.395	126	17	0	2	-1	.989	2	*1-111	0.9
1974	*Bal-A	110	344	37	91	13	1	12	45	52	58	.265	.361	.413	126	13	0	1	-1	.996	1	*1-102/D-1	0.7
1975	Cle-A	134	435	64	129	18	0	27	86	59	72	.297	.382	.524	154	31	1	3	-2	.997	-2	*1-121/D-5	2.0
1976	Cle-A	95	293	29	63	9	0	9	33	41	43	.215	.311	.338	91	-3	1	1	-0	.987	1	1-89	-0.9
1977	LA-N	50	41	0	10	2	0	0	5	12	9	.244	.415	.244	82	-0	0	0	0	.938	-1	/1-4	-0.1
Total	17	2042	6681	889	1776	270	11	339	1187	1001	1226	.266	.364	.462	134	310	20	21	-7	.991	-33	*1-1479,O-431/D-6	14.9

■ MARTIN POWELL
Powell, Martin J. b: 3/25/1856, Fitchburg, Mass. d: 2/5/1888, Fitchburg, Mass. BL/TL, 6', 170 lbs. Deb: 6/18/1881

1881	Det-N	55	219	47	74	9	4	1	38	15	9	.338	.380	.429	148	12				.947	-3	1-55/C-1	0.4
1882	Det-N	80	338	44	81	13	0	0	29	19	27	.240	.280	.278	80	-7				.940	-5	*1-80	-1.9
1883	Det-N	101	421	76	115	17	5	1	48	28	23	.273	.318	.344	106	5				.950	-3	1-101	-0.7
1884	Cin-U	43	185	46	59	4	2	1		13		.319	.364	.378	116	-1				.940	-2	1-43	-0.8
1885	Phi-a	19	75	5	12	0	3	0	5	1		.160	.192	.240	34	-6				.973	-0	1-19	-0.8
Total	5	298	1238	218	341	43	14	3	120	76	59	.275	.318	.340	104	2				.947	-13	1-298/C-1	-3.8

■ PAUL POWELL
Powell, Paul Ray b: 3/19/48, San Angelo, Tex. BR/TR, 5'11", 185 lbs. Deb: 4/7/71

1971	Min-A	20	31	7	5	0	0	1	2	3	12	.161	.235	.258	38	-3	0	0	0	1.000	-2	O-15	-0.6
1973	LA-N	2	1	0	0	0	0	0	0	0	1	.000	.000	.000	-99	-0	0	0	0			/O-1	-0.1
1975	LA-N	8	10	2	2	1	0	0	0	1	2	.200	.273	.300	61	-1	0	0	0	.955	1	/C-7,O-1	-0.1
Total	3	30	42	9	7	1	0	1	2	4	15	.167	.239	.262	41	-3	0	0	0	1.000	-2	/O-17,C-7	-0.7

■ RAY POWELL
Powell, Raymond Reath "Rabbit" b: 11/20/1888, Siloam Springs, Ark. d: 10/16/62, Chillicothe, Mo. BL/TR, 5'9", 160 lbs. Deb: 4/16/13

1913	Det-A	2	0	0	0	0	0	0	0	0	0	—	—	—			0	0		.000	0	/O-1	0.0
1917	Bos-N	88	357	42	97	10	4	4	30	24	54	.272	.318	.356	113	5	12			.976	9	O-88	0.9
1918	Bos-N	53	188	31	40	7	5	0	20	29	30	.213	.321	.303	95	-0	2			.949	-0	O-53	-0.4
1919	Bos-N	123	470	51	111	12	12	2	33	41	79	.236	.303	.326	93	-4	16			.951	1	*O-122	-1.3
1920	Bos-N	147	609	69	137	12	12	6	29	44	83	.225	.282	.314	74	-21	10	18	-8	.956	5	*O-147	-3.8
1921	Bos-N	149	624	114	191	25	18	12	74	58	85	.306	.369	.462	125	22	6	17	-8	.954	3	*O-149	0.5
1922	Bos-N	142	550	82	163	22	11	6	37	59	66	.296	.369	.409	105	5	3	12	-6	.980	12	*O-136	0.0
1923	Bos-N	97	338	57	102	20	4	7	38	45	36	.302	.385	.420	117	10	1	6	-3	.941	-4	O-84	-0.3
1924	Bos-N	74	188	21	49	9	1	1	15	21	28	.261	.338	.335	85	-4	1	3	-2	.947	4	O-46	-0.4
Total	9	875	3324	467	890	117	67	35	276	321	461	.268	.336	.375	102	11	51	56		.959	29	O-826	-4.8

■ LEROY POWELL
Powell, Robert Leroy b: 10/17/33, Flint, Mich. BR/TR, 6'1", 190 lbs. Deb: 9/16/55

1955	Chi-A	1	0	0	0	0	0	0	0	0	0	—	—	—			0	0	0	.000	0	R	0.0
1957	Chi-A	1	0	1	0	0	0	0	0	0	0	—	—	—			0	0	0	.000	0	R	0.0
Total	2	2	0	1	0	0	0	0	0	0	0	—	—	—			0	0	0		0	-0,-0	0.0

■ TOM POWER
Power, Thomas E. b: San Francisco, Cal. d: 2/25/1898, San Francisco, Cal 5'11", 164 lbs. Deb: 8/27/1890

| 1890 | Bal-a | 38 | 125 | 11 | 26 | 3 | 1 | 0 | 6 | 13 | | .208 | .293 | .248 | 57 | -7 | 6 | | | .960 | -4 | 1-26,2-12 | -1.0 |

■ VIC POWER
Power, Victor Pellot (b: Victor Felipe Pellot (Pove)) b: 11/1/27, Arecibo, P.R. BR/TR, 5'11", 195 lbs. Deb: 4/13/54

1954	Phi-A	127	462	36	118	17	5	8	38	19	19	.255	.288	.366	78	-16	2	1	0	.985	10	*O-101,1-21/S-1,3-1	-1.1
1955	KC-A★	147	596	91	190	34	10	19	76	35	27	.319	.357	.505	128	20	0	2	-1	.993	14	*1-144	2.4
1956	KC-A★	127	530	77	164	21	5	14	63	24	16	.309	.341	.447	106	3	2	2	-1	.993	8	*O-124,1-2	0.8
1957	KC-A	129	467	48	121	15	1	14	42	19	21	.259	.292	.385	82	-13	3	2	-0	.998	12	*1-113/O-6,2-4	-0.8
1958	KC-A	52	205	35	62	13	4	4	27	7	3	.302	.325	.463	112	3	1	1	-0	.992	6	1-50/2-1	0.5
	Cle-A	93	385	63	122	24	6	12	53	13	11	.317	.341	.504	133	15	2	1	0	.977	6	3-42,1-41,2-27/SO	2.1
	Yr	145	590	98	184	37	10	16	80	20	14	.312	.336	.490	125	17	3	2	-0	.992	11	1-91,3-42,2-28/SO	2.6
1959	Cle-A★	147	595	102	172	31	6	10	60	40	22	.289	.336	.412	108	5	9	13	-5	.995	10	*1-121,2-21/3-7	0.4
1960	Cle-A★	147	580	69	167	26	3	10	84	24	20	.288	.316	.395	94	-7	9	5	-0	.996	21	*1-147/S-5,3-4	0.3
1961	Cle-A	147	563	64	151	34	4	5	63	38	16	.268	.316	.369	85	-13	4	3	-1	.994	18	*1-141/2-7	-0.7
1962	Min-A	144	611	80	177	28	2	16	63	22	35	.290	.318	.421	93	-7	3	1	-0	.993	9	*1-142/2-2	-0.6
1963	Min-A	138	541	65	146	28	2	10	52	22	24	.270	.298	.384	88	-9	3	1	-0	.992	-1	*1-124,2-18/3-5	-1.4
1964	Min-A	19	45	6	10	2	0	0	1	1	3	.222	.239	.267	40	-4	0	0	0	.990	1	1-12/2-1	-0.3
	LA-A	68	221	17	55	6	0	3	13	8	14	.249	.278	.317	72	-9	1	1	-0	1.000	2	1-48,3-28/2-5	-0.9
	Yr	87	266	23	65	8	0	3	14	9	17	.244	.272	.308	66	-13	1	1	-0	.998	4	1-60,3-28/2-6	-1.2
	Phi-N	18	48	1	10	4	0	0	3	2	3	.208	.240	.292	50	-3	0	0	0	.993	1	1-17	-0.3
1965	Cal-A	124	197	11	51	7	1	1	20	5	13	.259	.281	.320	72	-8	2	2	-1	.996	6	*1-107/2-6,3-2	-0.5
Total	12	1627	6046	765	1716	290	49	126	658	279	247	.284	.317	.411	97	-43	45	35	-7	.994	123	*1-1304,2-139,O/3S	-0.1

■ MIKE POWERS
Powers, Ellis Foree b: 3/2/06, Toddspoint, Ky. d: 12/2/83, Louisville, Ky. BL/TL, 6'1", 185 lbs. Deb: 8/19/32

1932	Cle-A	14	33	4	6	4	0	0	5	2	2	.182	.229	.303	34	-3	0	0	0	.917	-2	/O-8	-0.5
1933	Cle-A	24	47	6	13	2	1	0	2	6	6	.277	.358	.362	87	-1	2	1	0	.952	-2	O-11	-0.3
Total	2	38	80	10	19	6	1	0	7	8	8	.237	.307	.338	65	-4	2	1	0	.939	-3	/O-19	-0.8

■ JOHN POWERS
Powers, John Calvin b: 7/8/29, Birmingham, Ala. BL/TR, 6', 190 lbs. Deb: 9/24/55

1955	Pit-N	2	4	0	1	0	0	0	0	0	0	.250	.250	.250	34	-0	0	0	0	1.000	-0	/O-2	0.0
1956	Pit-N	11	21	0	1	0	0	0	1	4	9	.048	.091	.048	-63	-5	0	0	0	1.000	-0	/O-8	-0.5
1957	Pit-N	20	35	7	10	3	0	2	5	7	4	.286	.419	.543	161	3	0	0	0	1.000	-0	/O-9	0.3
1958	Pit-N	57	82	6	15	1	0	2	8	8	19	.183	.256	.268	40	-7	0	0	0	1.000	-1	O-14	-0.8
1959	Cin-N	43	43	8	11	2	1	2	6	3	11	.256	.319	.488	108	0	0	0	0	1.000	-1	/O-4	-0.1
1960	Bal-A	10	18	3	2	0	0	0	0	3	1	.111	.238	.111	-2	-3	0	0	0	.833	-1	/O-4	-0.4
	Cle-A	8	12	2	2	1	1	0	2	0	3	.167	.286	.417	90	-0	0	0	0	1.000	-1	/O-5	-0.1
	Yr	18	30	5	4	1	1	0	2	3	4	.133	.257	.233	34	-3	0	0	0	.929	-1	/O-9	-0.5
Total	6	151	215	26	42	7	2	6	14	22	48	.195	.282	.330	64	-11	0	0	0	.986	-2	/O-44	-1.6

YEAR	TM/L	G	AB	R	H	2B	3B	HR	RBI	BB	SO	AVG	OBP	SLG	PRO+	BR/A	SB	CS	SBR	FA	FR	G/POS	TPR

■ LES POWERS   Powers, Leslie Edwin b: 11/5/09, Seattle, Wash. d: 11/13/78, Santa Monica, Cal.   BL/TL, 6′, 175 lbs. Deb: 9/17/38

1938	NY-N	2	3	0	0	0	0	0	0	0	1	.000	.000	.000	-99	-1	0			.000	0	H	-0.1
1939	Phi-N	19	52	7	18	1	1	0	2	4	6	.346	.393	.404	118	1	0			.983	-2	1-13	-0.2
Total	2	21	55	7	18	1	1	0	2	4	7	.327	.373	.382	106	1	0			.983	-2	/1-13	-0.3

■ DOC POWERS   Powers, Michael Riley b: 9/22/1870, Pittsfield, Mass. d: 4/26/09, Philadelphia, Pa.   BR/TR, Deb: 6/12/1898

1898	Lou-N	34	99	13	27	4	3	1	19	5		.273	.308	.404	105	0	1			.962	-3	C-22/1-6,O-1	-0.1
1899	Lou-N	49	169	15	35	8	2	0	22	6		.207	.239	.278	42	-14	1			.942	-8	C-38/1-7	-1.7
	Was-N	14	38	3	10	2	0	0	3	1		.263	.282	.316	65	-2	0			.942	-0	C-12/1-1	-0.1
	Yr	63	207	18	45	10	2	0	25	7		.217	.247	.285	46	-16	1			.942	-8	C-50/1-8	-1.8
1901	Phi-A	116	431	53	108	26	5	1	47	18		.251	.292	.341	72	-17	10			.952	-5	*C-111/1-3	-1.0
1902	Phi-A	71	246	35	65	7	1	2	39	14		.264	.312	.325	74	-9	3			.950	5	C-68/1-3	0.3
1903	Phi-A	75	247	19	56	11	1	0	23	5		.227	.242	.279	54	-14	1			.982	-2	C-66/1-7	-1.0
1904	Phi-A	57	184	11	35	3	0	0	11	6		.190	.220	.207	33	-14	3			.965	-5	C-56/O-1	-1.0
1905	*Phi-A	21	60	6	10	0	0	0	5	0		.167	.180	.167	10	-6	2			.928	3	C-21	-0.1
	NY-A	11	33	3	6	1	0	0	2	1		.182	.206	.212	29	-3	0			.975	-0	/1-7,C-4	-0.3
	*Phi-A	19	61	2	8	0	0	0	5	3		.131	.172	.131	-3	-7	2			.991	-5	C-19	-1.2
	Yr	51	154	11	24	1	0	0	12	4		.156	.182	.162	9	-16	4			.957	-2	C-44/1-7	-1.6
1906	Phi-A	58	185	5	29	1	0	0	7	1		.157	.170	.162	4	-20	2			.974	9	C-57/1-1	-0.6
1907	Phi-A	59	159	9	29	3	0	0	9	7		.182	.217	.201	33	-12	1			.983	14	C-59	0.7
1908	Phi-A	62	172	8	31	6	1	0	7	5		.180	.217	.227	41	-11	1			.967	7	C-60/1-2	0.1
1909	Phi-A	1	4	1	1	0	0	0	0	0		.250	.250	.250	57	-0	0			1.000	0	/C-1	0.0
Total	11	647	2088	183	450	72	13	4	199	72		.216	.248	.268	51	-129	27			.965	12	C-594/1-37,O-2	-6.4

■ PHIL POWERS   Powers, Phillip B. "Grandmother" b: 7/26/1854, New York, N.Y. d: 12/22/14, New York, N.Y.   BR/TR, 5′7″, 166 lbs. Deb: 8/31/1878 U

1878	Chi-N	8	31	2	5	1	1	0		2		.161	.188	.258	42	-2				.930	5	/C-8	0.3
1880	Bos-N	37	126	11	18	5	0	0	10	5	15	.143	.176	.183	22	-10				.851	-5	C-37/O-2	-1.4
1881	Cle-N	5	15	1	1	0	0	0	0	1	2	.067	.125	.067	-40	-2				.955	-1	/C-4,3-1	-0.3
1882	Cin-a	16	60	4	13	1	1	0	5	3		.217	.254	.267	72	-2				.921	3	C-10/1-5,O-1	0.1
1883	Cin-a	30	114	16	28	1	4	0	8	3		.246	.265	.325	84	-2				.893	-2	C-17,O-13	-0.3
1884	Cin-a	34	130	10	18	1	0	0	8	5		.138	.170	.146	4	-14				.891	5	C-31/O-2,1-2	-0.6
1885	Cin-a	15	60	6	16	2	0	0	7	0		.267	.267	.300	77	-2				.833	-3	C-15	-0.3
	Bal-a	9	34	6	4	1	0	0	2	1		.118	.143	.147	-8	-4				.844	-4	/C-8,O-1	-0.7
	Yr	24	94	12	20	3	0	0	9	1		.213	.221	.245	47	-6				.837	-7	C-23/O-1	-1.0
Total	7	154	570	56	103	12	6	0	42	19	22	.181	.207	.223	40	-37				.877	-2	C-130/O-19,1-7,3-1	-3.2

■ CARL POWIS   Powis, Carl Edgar "Jug" b: 1/11/28, Philadelphia, Pa.   BR/TR, 6′, 185 lbs. Deb: 4/15/57

| 1957 | Bal-A | 15 | 41 | 4 | 8 | 3 | 1 | 0 | 2 | 7 | 9 | .195 | .327 | .317 | 82 | -1 | 2 | 0 | 1 | .909 | -1 | O-13 | -0.2 |

■ ARQUIMEDEZ POZO   Pozo, Arquimedez (Ortiz) b: 8/24/73, Santo Domingo, D.R.   BR/TR, 5′10″, 160 lbs. Deb: 9/12/95

1995	Sea-A	1	1	0	0	0	0	0	0	0	0	.000	.000	.000	-99	-0	0	0	0	1.000	0	/2-1	0.0
1996	Bos-A	21	58	4	10	3	1	1	11	2	10	.172	.213	.310	29	-6	1	0	0	.930	3	2-10,3-10	-0.3
Total	2	22	59	4	10	3	1	1	11	2	10	.169	.210	.305	27	-7	1	0	0	.932	3	/2-11,3-10	-0.3

■ JOHNNY PRAMESA   Pramesa, John Steven b: 8/28/25, Barton, Ohio d: 9/9/96, Los Angeles, Cal.   BR/TR, 6′2″, 210 lbs. Deb: 4/24/49

1949	Cin-N	17	25	2	6	1	0	1	2	3		.240	.321	.400	91	-0	0			.966	-1	C-13	-0.1
1950	Cin-N	74	228	14	70	10	1	5	30	19	15	.307	.363	.425	106	2	0			.981	0	C-73	0.5
1951	Cin-N	72	227	12	52	5	2	6	22	5	17	.229	.246	.348	57	-14	0			.968	-7	C-63	-1.9
1952	Chi-N	22	46	1	13	1	0	1	5	4	4	.283	.340	.370	96	-0	0			.958	1	C-17	0.0
Total	4	185	526	29	141	17	3	13	59	31	41	.268	.310	.386	84	-13	0			.973	-6	C-166	-1.3

■ DEL PRATT   Pratt, Derrill Burnham b: 1/10/1888, Walhalla, S.C. d: 9/30/77, Texas City, Tex.   BR/TR, 5′11″, 175 lbs. Deb: 4/11/12

1912	StL-A	152	570	76	172	26	15	5	69	36		.302	.348	.426	125	16	24			.943	14	*2-122,S-21/O-8,3-1	2.8
1913	StL-A	155	592	60	175	31	13	2	87	40	57	.296	.341	.402	121	13	37			.951	5	*2-146/1-9	1.6
1914	StL-A	158	584	85	165	34	13	5	65	50	45	.283	.341	.411	131	19	37	28	-6	.944	-2	*2-152/O-5,S-1	1.2
1915	StL-A	159	602	61	175	31	11	3	78	26	43	.291	.323	.394	119	10	32	23	-4	.965	12	*2-158	2.0
1916	StL-A	158	596	64	159	35	12	5	**103**	54	56	.267	.331	.391	123	14	26	17	-2	.966	22	*2-158	4.2
1917	StL-A	123	450	40	111	22	8	1	53	33	36	.247	.301	.338	98	-2	18			.959	15	*2-119/1-2	2.0
1918	NY-A	126	477	65	131	19	7	2	55	35	26	.275	.327	.356	104	1	12			.969	12	*2-126	2.3
1919	NY-A	140	527	69	154	27	7	4	56	36	24	.292	.342	.393	105	3	22			.969	**28**	*2-140	3.8
1920	NY-A	154	574	84	180	37	8	4	97	50	24	.314	.372	.427	107	6	12	10	-2	.971	12	*2-154	2.0
1921	Bos-A	135	521	80	169	36	10	5	102	44	10	.324	.348	.461	116	12	8	10	-4	.961	-1	*2-134	1.0
1922	Bos-A	154	607	73	183	44	7	6	86	53	20	.301	.361	.427	106	5	7	10	-4	.966	-13	*2-154	-0.8
1923	Det-A	101	297	43	92	18	3	0	40	25	9	.310	.375	.391	104	2	6	1	1	.947	-10	2-60,1-17,3-12	-0.6
1924	Det-A	121	429	56	130	32	3	1	77	31	10	.303	.353	.399	95	-2	6	9	-4	.948	-2	2-65,1-51/3-4,O-1	-1.1
Total	13	1836	6826	856	1996	392	117	43	968	513	360	.292	.345	.403	112	94	247	108		.960	91	*2-1688/1-79,S30	20.4

■ FRANK PRATT   Pratt, Francis Bruce "Truckhorse" b: 8/24/1897, Blocton, Ala. d: 3/8/74, Centreville, Ala.   BL/TR, 5′9.5″, 155 lbs. Deb: 5/13/21

| 1921 | Chi-A | 1 | 1 | 0 | 0 | 0 | 0 | 0 | 0 | 0 | 0 | .000 | .000 | .000 | -99 | -0 | 0 | 0 | 0 | .000 | 0 | H | 0.0 |

■ LARRY PRATT   Pratt, Lester John b: 10/8/1886, Gibson City, Ill. d: 1/8/69, Peoria, Ill.   BR/TR, 6′ ″, 183 lbs. Deb: 9/19/14

1914	Bos-A	5	4	0	0	0	0	0	0	0	4	.000	.000	.000	-99	-1	0			.923	2	/C-5	0.1
1915	Bro-F	20	49	5	9	1	0	1	2	2	18	.184	.216	.265	35	-5	2			.949	-1	C-17	-0.5
	New-F	5	4	2	2	2	0	0	3	3	1	.500	.714	1.000	403	2	2			1.000	-1	/C-3	0.2
	Yr	25	53	7	11	3	0	1	2	5	19	.208	.276	.321	69	-3	4			.953	-2	C-20	-0.3
Total	2	30	57	7	11	3	0	1	2	5	23	.193	.258	.298	58	-4	4			.949	0	/C-25	-0.2

■ TOM PRATT   Pratt, Thomas J. b: 1/26/1844, Chelsea, Mass. d: 9/28/08, Philadelphia, Pa.   TL, 5′7.5″, 150 lbs. Deb: 10/18/1871 U

| 1871 | Ath-n | 1 | 6 | 2 | 2 | 0 | 0 | 0 | 1 | 0 | 0 | .333 | .333 | .333 | 93 | -0 | 0 | 0 | 0 | .786 | -1 | /1-1 | 0.0 |

■ TODD PRATT   Pratt, Todd Alan b: 2/9/67, Bellevue, Neb.   BR/TR, 6′3″, 195 lbs. Deb: 7/29/92

1992	Phi-N	16	46	6	13	1	0	2	10	4	12	.283	.340	.435	118	1	0	0	0	.972	-1	C-11	0.1
1993	*Phi-N	33	87	8	25	6	0	5	13	5	19	.287	.333	.529	128	3	0	0	0	.989	5	C-26	0.9
1994	Phi-N	28	102	10	20	6	1	2	9	12	29	.196	.281	.333	58	-6	0	1	-1	1.000	-4	C-28	-0.6
1995	Chi-N	25	60	3	8	2	0	0	4	6	21	.133	.212	.167	2	-9	0	0	0	.981	7	C-25	0.0
Total	4	102	295	27	66	15	1	9	36	27	81	.224	.291	.373	75	-11	0	1	-1	.988	10	/C-90	0.4

■ MEL PREIBISCH   Preibisch, Melvin Adolphus "Primo" b: 11/23/14, Sealy, Tex. d: 4/12/80, Sealy, Tex.   BR/TR, 5′11″, 185 lbs. Deb: 9/17/40

1940	Bos-N	11	40	3	9	2	0	0	5	2	4	.225	.262	.275	51	-3	0			1.000	1	O-11	-0.3
1941	Bos-N	5	4	0	0	0	0	0	0	1	2	.000	.200	.000	-42	-1	0			1.000	-1	/O-2	-0.2
Total	2	16	44	3	9	2	0	0	5	3	6	.205	.255	.250	42	-3	0			1.000	1	/O-13	-0.5

■ BOBBY PRESCOTT   Prescott, George Bertrand b: 3/27/31, Colon, Panama   BR/TR, 5′11″, 180 lbs. Deb: 6/17/61

| 1961 | KC-A | 10 | 12 | 0 | 1 | 0 | 0 | 0 | 0 | 0 | 6 | .083 | .214 | .083 | -17 | -2 | 0 | 0 | 0 | .000 | -1 | /O-2 | -0.3 |

■ JIM PRESLEY   Presley, James Arthur b: 10/23/61, Pensacola, Fla.   BR/TR, 6′1″, 200 lbs. Deb: 6/24/84

1984	Sea-A	70	251	27	57	12	1	10	36	6	63	.227	.248	.402	78	-9	1	1	-0	.958	-3	3-69/D-1	-1.3
1985	Sea-A	155	570	71	157	33	1	28	84	44	100	.275	.328	.484	118	13	2	2	-1	.961	7	*3-154	1.7
1986	Sea-A☆	155	616	83	163	33	4	27	107	32	172	.265	.305	.463	105	2	0	4	-2	.965	6	*3-155	0.2
1987	Sea-A	152	575	78	142	23	6	24	88	38	157	.247	.298	.433	86	-13	2	0	1	.953	11	*3-148/S-4,D-1	-0.3
1988	Sea-A	150	544	50	125	26	0	14	62	36	114	.230	.283	.355	74	-20	3	5	-2	.940	-13	*3-146/D-4	-3.6
1989	Sea-A	117	390	42	92	20	1	12	41	21	107	.236	.275	.385	82	-11	0	0	0	.924	-4	3-90,1-30/D-1	-1.6

YEAR TM/L	G	AB	R	H	2B	3B	HR	RBI	BB	SO	AVG	OBP	SLG	PRO+	BR/A	SB	CS	SBR	FA	FR	G/POS	TPR
1990 Atl-N	140	541	59	131	34	1	19	72	29	130	.242	.284	.414	85	-13	1	1	-0	.930	-3	*3-133,1-17	-1.7
1991 SD-N	20	59	13	8	0	0	1	5	4	16	.136	.203	.186	10	-7	0	1	-1	.923	-3	3-16	-1.2
Total 8	959	3546	413	875	181	14	135	495	210	859	.247	.292	.420	90	-57	9	14	-6	.949	-2	3-911/1-47,D-7,S-4	-7.8

■ WALT PRESTON
Preston, Walter B. b: 1870, Richmond, Va. BL/TR, 6', 175 lbs. Deb: 4/18/1895

YEAR TM/L	G	AB	R	H	2B	3B	HR	RBI	BB	SO	AVG	OBP	SLG	PRO+	BR/A	SB	CS	SBR	FA	FR	G/POS	TPR
1895 Lou-N	50	197	42	55	6	4	1	24	17	17	.279	.366	.365	95	-1	11			.893	-7	O-26,3-25	-0.7

■ JIM PRICE
Price, Jimmie William b: 10/13/41, Harrisburg, Pa. BR/TR, 6', 195 lbs. Deb: 4/11/67

YEAR TM/L	G	AB	R	H	2B	3B	HR	RBI	BB	SO	AVG	OBP	SLG	PRO+	BR/A	SB	CS	SBR	FA	FR	G/POS	TPR
1967 Det-A	44	92	9	24	4	0	2	8	4	10	.261	.292	.304	74	-3	0	0	0	.974	0	C-24	-0.2
1968 *Det-A	64	132	12	23	4	0	3	13	13	14	.174	.253	.273	58	-7	0	0	0	.996	2	C-42	-0.3
1969 Det-A	72	192	21	45	8	0	9	28	18	20	.234	.300	.417	95	-2	0	0	0	.989	4	C-51	0.4
1970 Det-A	52	132	12	24	4	0	5	15	21	23	.182	.294	.326	70	-5	0	0	0	.979	-1	C-38	-0.5
1971 Det-A	29	54	4	13	2	0	1	7	6	3	.241	.328	.333	84	-1	0	0	0	.981	1	C-25	0.1
Total 5	261	602	58	129	22	0	18	71	62	70	.214	.290	.341	78	-18	0	0	0	.985	5	C-180	-0.5

■ JACKIE PRICE
Price, John Thomas Reid "Johnny" b: 11/13/12, Winborn, Miss. d: 10/2/67, San Francisco, Cal. BL/TR, 5'10.5", 150 lbs. Deb: 8/18/46

YEAR TM/L	G	AB	R	H	2B	3B	HR	RBI	BB	SO	AVG	OBP	SLG	PRO+	BR/A	SB	CS	SBR	FA	FR	G/POS	TPR
1946 Cle-A	7	13	1	3	0	0	0	0	0	0	.231	.231	.231	31	-1	0	0	0	.947	2	/S-4	0.0

■ JOE PRICE
Price, Joseph Preston "Lumber" b: 4/10/1897, Milligan College, Tenn. d: 1/15/61, Washington, D.C. BR/TR, 6'1.5", 187 lbs. Deb: 9/5/28

YEAR TM/L	G	AB	R	H	2B	3B	HR	RBI	BB	SO	AVG	OBP	SLG	PRO+	BR/A	SB	CS	SBR	FA	FR	G/POS	TPR
1928 NY-N	1	1	0	0	0	0	0	0	0	1	.000	.000	.000	-99	-0	0	0	0	.000	-1	/O-1	-0.1

■ BOB PRICHARD
Prichard, Robert Alexander b: 10/21/17, Paris, Tex. d: 9/25/91, Abilene, Tex. BL/TL, 6'1", 195 lbs. Deb: 6/14/39

YEAR TM/L	G	AB	R	H	2B	3B	HR	RBI	BB	SO	AVG	OBP	SLG	PRO+	BR/A	SB	CS	SBR	FA	FR	G/POS	TPR
1939 Was-A	26	85	8	20	5	0	0	8	19	16	.235	.375	.294	79	-2	0	2	-1	.992	-1	1-26	-0.6

■ JERRY PRIDDY
Priddy, Gerald Edward b: 11/9/19, Los Angeles, Cal. d: 3/3/80, N.Hollywood, Cal. BR/TR, 5'11.5", 180 lbs. Deb: 4/17/41

YEAR TM/L	G	AB	R	H	2B	3B	HR	RBI	BB	SO	AVG	OBP	SLG	PRO+	BR/A	SB	CS	SBR	FA	FR	G/POS	TPR
1941 NY-A	56	174	18	37	7	0	1	26	18	16	.213	.290	.270	50	-13	4	2	0	.968	9	2-31,3-14,1-10	-0.2
1942 *NY-A	59	189	23	53	9	2	2	28	31	27	.280	.385	.381	118	6	0	1	-1	.944	5	3-35,1-11/2-8,S-3	1.1
1943 Was-A	149	560	68	152	31	3	4	62	67	76	.271	.350	.359	112	9	5	5	-2	.971	4	*2-134,S-15/3-1	2.2
1946 Was-A	138	511	54	130	22	8	6	58	57	73	.254	.332	.364	100	-0	9	3	1	.962	2	*2-138	1.2
1947 Was-A	147	505	42	108	20	3	3	49	62	79	.214	.301	.283	65	-24	7	6	-2	.980	-2	*2-146	-1.8
1948 StL-A	151	560	96	166	40	9	8	79	86	71	.296	.391	.443	118	16	6	5	-1	.968	24	*2-146	4.4
1949 StL-A	145	544	83	158	26	4	11	63	80	81	.290	.382	.414	106	5	5	3	-0	.968	-3	*2-145	0.8
1950 Det-A	157	618	104	171	26	6	13	75	95	95	.277	.376	.401	96	-3	2	7	-4	.981	31	*2-157	3.0
1951 Det-A	154	584	73	152	22	6	8	57	69	73	.260	.338	.360	88	-9	4	3	-1	.980	10	*2-154/S-1	0.7
1952 Det-A	75	279	37	79	23	3	4	20	42	29	.283	.399	.430	124	10	1	8	-5	.968	-1	2-75	0.8
1953 Det-A	65	196	14	46	6	2	1	24	17	19	.235	.299	.301	63	-10	1	1	-0	.977	4	2-45,1-11/3-2	-0.5
Total 11	1296	4720	612	1252	232	46	61	541	624	639	.265	.353	.373	97	-13	44	44	-13	.973	82	*2-1179/3-52,1-32,S	11.7

■ CURTIS PRIDE
Pride, Curtis John b: 12/17/68, Washington, D.C. BL/TR, 6', 205 lbs. Deb: 9/14/93

YEAR TM/L	G	AB	R	H	2B	3B	HR	RBI	BB	SO	AVG	OBP	SLG	PRO+	BR/A	SB	CS	SBR	FA	FR	G/POS	TPR
1993 Mon-N	10	9	3	4	1	1	1	5	0	3	.444	.444	1.111	288	2	1	0	0	1.000	-0	/O-2	0.2
1995 Mon-N	48	63	10	11	1	0	2	2	5	16	.175	.235	.190	13	-8	3	2	-0	.920	-4	O-24	-1.2
1996 Det-A	95	267	52	80	17	5	10	31	31	63	.300	.372	.513	122	9	11	6	-0	.967	-3	O-48,D-31	0.2
Total 3	153	339	65	95	19	6	11	38	36	82	.280	.349	.469	106	3	15	8	-0	.958	-8	/O-74,D-31	-0.8

■ JOHNNY PRIEST
Priest, John Gooding b: 6/23/1886, St.Joseph, Mo. d: 11/4/79, Washington, D.C. BR/TR, 5'11", 170 lbs. Deb: 5/30/11

YEAR TM/L	G	AB	R	H	2B	3B	HR	RBI	BB	SO	AVG	OBP	SLG	PRO+	BR/A	SB	CS	SBR	FA	FR	G/POS	TPR
1911 NY-A	8	21	2	3	0	0	0		2	2	.143	.250	.143	10	-2	3			.824	-3	/2-5,3-2	-0.6
1912 NY-A	2	2	1	1	0	0	0		1	0	.500	.500	.500	176	0	0			.000	0	H	0.0
Total 2	10	23	3	4	0	0	0		3	2	.174	.269	.174	23	-2	3			.824	-3	/2-5,3-2	-0.6

■ TOM PRINCE
Prince, Thomas Albert b: 8/13/64, Kankakee, Ill. BR/TR, 5'11", 185 lbs. Deb: 9/22/87

YEAR TM/L	G	AB	R	H	2B	3B	HR	RBI	BB	SO	AVG	OBP	SLG	PRO+	BR/A	SB	CS	SBR	FA	FR	G/POS	TPR
1987 Pit-N	4	9	1	2	1	0	1	2	0	2	.222	.222	.667	123	0	0	0	0	1.000	1	/C-4	0.1
1988 Pit-N	29	74	3	13	2	0	0	6	4	15	.176	.218	.203	22	-7	0	0	0	.983	-2	C-28	-0.9
1989 Pit-N	21	52	1	7	4	0	0	5	6	12	.135	.224	.212	26	-5	1	1	-0	.960	-3	C-21	-0.5
1990 Pit-N	4	10	1	1	0	0	0	0	1	2	.100	.182	.100	-21	-2	0	1	-1	1.000	0	/C-3	-0.2
1991 Pit-N	26	34	4	9	3	0	1	2	7	3	.265	.405	.441	140	2	0	0	0	.984	1	C-19/1-1	0.4
1992 Pit-N	27	44	1	4	2	0	0	5	6	9	.091	.200	.136	-3	-6	1	1	-0	.977	3	C-19/3-1	-0.3
1993 Pit-N	66	179	14	35	14	0	2	24	13	38	.196	.276	.307	56	-11	1	1	-0	.984	-1	C-59	-0.9
1994 LA-N	3	6	2	2	0	0	0	1	1	3	.333	.429	.333	109	0	0	0	0	1.000	0	/C-3	0.0
1995 LA-N	18	40	3	8	2	1	1	4	4	10	.200	.273	.375	75	-2	0	1	-0	.988	0	C-17	-0.1
1996 LA-N	40	64	6	19	6	0	1	11	6	15	.297	.375	.438	124	2	0	0	0	.994	9	C-35	1.2
Total 10	238	512	36	100	34	1	6	60	48	109	.195	.277	.301	60	-28	3	4	-2	.984	12	C-208/3-1,1-1	-1.2

■ WALTER PRINCE
Prince, Walter Farr b: 5/9/1861, Amherst, N.H. d: 3/2/38, Bristol, N.H. BL/TR, 5'9", 150 lbs. Deb: 8/7/1883

YEAR TM/L	G	AB	R	H	2B	3B	HR	RBI	BB	SO	AVG	OBP	SLG	PRO+	BR/A	SB	CS	SBR	FA	FR	G/POS	TPR
1883 Lou-a	4	11	1	2	0	0	0	0	0	0	.182	.182	.182	19	-1				.500	-2	/O-2,1-2,S-1	-0.3
1884 Det-N	7	21	0	3	0	0	0	1	3	4	.143	.250	.143	29	-2				.375	-3	/O-7	-0.5
Was-a	43	166	22	36	3	2	1		13		.217	.286	.277	95	0				.940	-6	1-43	-0.9
Was-U	1	4	0	1	0	0	0				.250	.250	.250	54	-0				.818	-1	/1-1	-0.1
Total 2	55	202	23	42	3	2	1	1	16	4	.208	.276	.257	83	-2				.935	-11	/1-46,O-9,S-1	-1.8

■ BUDDY PRITCHARD
Pritchard, Harold William b: 1/25/36, South Gate, Cal. BR/TR, 6'1", 195 lbs. Deb: 4/21/57

YEAR TM/L	G	AB	R	H	2B	3B	HR	RBI	BB	SO	AVG	OBP	SLG	PRO+	BR/A	SB	CS	SBR	FA	FR	G/POS	TPR
1957 Pit-N	23	11	1	1	0	0	0	0	0	4	.091	.091	.091	-53	-2	0	0	0	.947	5	S-10/2-3	0.2

■ CHRIS PRITCHETT
Pritchett, Christopher Davis b: 1/31/70, Merced, Cal. BL/TR, 6'4", 185 lbs. Deb: 9/6/96

YEAR TM/L	G	AB	R	H	2B	3B	HR	RBI	BB	SO	AVG	OBP	SLG	PRO+	BR/A	SB	CS	SBR	FA	FR	G/POS	TPR
1996 Cal-A	5	13	1	2	0	0	0	1	0	3	.154	.154	.154	-22	-2	0	0	0	1.000	-0	/1-5	-0.3

■ GEORGE PROESER
Proeser, George "Yatz" b: 5/30/1864, Cincinnati, Ohio d: 10/13/41, New Burlington, O. BL/TL, 5'10", 190 lbs. Deb: 9/15/1888

YEAR TM/L	G	AB	R	H	2B	3B	HR	RBI	BB	SO	AVG	OBP	SLG	PRO+	BR/A	SB	CS	SBR	FA	FR	G/POS	TPR
1888 Cle-a	7	23	5	7	2	0	1	6		10	.304	.333	.391	136	1	0			.846	-1	/P-7	0.0
1890 Syr-a	13	53	11	13	1	1	1	6		10	.245	.365	.358	126	2	1			.895	-2	O-13	0.0
Total 2	20	76	16	20	3	1	2	7		11	.263	.356	.368	129	3	1			.895	-3	/O-13,P-7	0.0

■ JAKE PROPST
Propst, William Jacob b: 3/10/1895, Kennedy, Ala. d: 2/24/67, Columbus, Miss. BL/TR, 5'10", 165 lbs. Deb: 8/7/23

YEAR TM/L	G	AB	R	H	2B	3B	HR	RBI	BB	SO	AVG	OBP	SLG	PRO+	BR/A	SB	CS	SBR	FA	FR	G/POS	TPR
1923 Was-A	1	1	0	0	0	0	0	0	0	0	.000	.000	.000	-99	-0	0	0	0	.000	0	H	0.0

■ DOC PROTHRO
Prothro, James Thompson b: 7/16/1893, Memphis, Tenn. d: 10/14/71, Memphis, Tenn. BR/TR, 5'10.5", 170 lbs. Deb: 9/26/20 M

YEAR TM/L	G	AB	R	H	2B	3B	HR	RBI	BB	SO	AVG	OBP	SLG	PRO+	BR/A	SB	CS	SBR	FA	FR	G/POS	TPR
1920 Was-A	6	13	2	5	0	0	0	2	0	4	.385	.385	.385	107	0	0	0	0	1.000	-1	/S-2,3-2	0.0
1923 Was-A	6	8	2	2	0	0	0	3	1		.250	.333	.500	124	0	0	0	0	1.000	0	/3-6	0.3
1924 Was-A	46	159	17	53	11	5	0	24	15	11	.333	.394	.465	125	6	4	4	-1	.915	-11	3-45	-0.3
1925 Bos-A	119	415	44	130	23	3	0	51	52	21	.313	.390	.383	97	0	9	11	-4	.945	-6	*3-108/S-3	-0.2
1926 Cin-N	3	5	1	1	0	1	0	1	1	1	.200	.333	.600	151	0	0	0	0	1.000	0	/3-2	0.0
Total 5	180	600	66	191	34	10	0	81	69	40	.318	.390	.408	105	6	13	15	-0	.940	-14	3-163/S-5	-0.2

■ EARL PRUESS
Pruess, Earl Henry "Gibby" b: 4/2/1895, Chicago, Ill. d: 8/28/79, Branson, Mo. BR/TR, 5'10.5", 170 lbs. Deb: 9/15/20

YEAR TM/L	G	AB	R	H	2B	3B	HR	RBI	BB	SO	AVG	OBP	SLG	PRO+	BR/A	SB	CS	SBR	FA	FR	G/POS	TPR
1920 StL-A	1	0	1	0	0	0	0	0	1	0	—	1.000	—	176	0	1	0	0	1.000	0	/O-1	0.1

■ JIM PRUETT
Pruett, James Calvin b: 12/16/17, Nashville, Tenn. BR/TR, 5'10", 178 lbs. Deb: 9/26/44

YEAR TM/L	G	AB	R	H	2B	3B	HR	RBI	BB	SO	AVG	OBP	SLG	PRO+	BR/A	SB	CS	SBR	FA	FR	G/POS	TPR
1944 Phi-A	3	4	1	1	0	0	0	0	1	0	.250	.500	.250	119	0	0	0	0	1.000	1	/C-2	0.1
1945 Phi-A	6	9	1	2	0	0	0	2	1	2	.222	.300	.222	53	-1	0	1	-1	1.000	1	/C-4	-0.1
Total 2	9	13	2	3	0	0	0	2	2	2	.231	.375	.231	77	-0	0	1	-1	1.000	1	/C-6	0.0

■ RON PRUITT
Pruitt, Ronald Ralph b: 10/21/51, Flint, Mich. BR/TR, 6', 185 lbs. Deb: 6/25/75

YEAR TM/L	G	AB	R	H	2B	3B	HR	RBI	BB	SO	AVG	OBP	SLG	PRO+	BR/A	SB	CS	SBR	FA	FR	G/POS	TPR
1975 Tex-A	14	17	2	3	0	0	0	0	1	5	.176	.222	.176	14	-2	0	0	0	1.000	-1	C-13/O-1	-0.3
1976 Cle-A	47	86	7	23	1	1	0	5	16	8	.267	.382	.302	103	1	2	3	-1	1.000	0	O-26/C-6,3-6,1-1,D	0.2
1977 Cle-A	78	219	29	63	10	2	2	32	28	22	.288	.373	.379	109	4	2	3	-1	.972	-8	O-69/C-4,3-1,D-4	-0.7

YEAR	TM/L	G	AB	R	H	2B	3B	HR	RBI	BB	SO	AVG	OBP	SLG	PRO+	BR/A	SB	CS	SBR	FA	FR	G/POS	TPR
1978	Cle-A	71	187	17	44	6	1	6	17	16	20	.235	.296	.374	88	-3	2	1	0	.984	-6	C-48,O-16/3-2,D-5	-1.0
1979	Cle-A	64	166	23	47	7	0	2	21	19	21	.283	.357	.361	94	-1	2	0	1	.957	-5	O-29,D-14,C-11,/3-3	-0.6
1980	Cle-A	23	36	1	11	1	0	0	4	4	6	.306	.375	.333	95	-0	0	0		1.000	0	/O-6,3-2,D-2	0.0
	Chi-A	33	70	8	21	2	0	2	11	8	7	.300	.372	.414	116	2	0	0		1.000	-1	O-11/C-5,3-3,1,D	0.0
	Yr	56	106	9	32	3	0	2	15	12	13	.302	.373	.387	109	2	0	0		1.000	-1	O-17/D-9,3-5,C-5,1	0.0
1981	Cle-A	5	9	0	0	0	0	0	0	1	2	.000	.100	.000	-70	-2	0	0		1.000	-1	/O-3,C-1,D-1	-0.3
1982	SF-N	5	4	1	2	1	0	0	2	1	1	.500	.600	.750	276	1	0	0		1.000	0	/C-1,O-1	0.1
1983	SF-N	1	1	0	0	0	0	0	0	0	0	.000	.000	.000	-99	-0	0	0		0		/H	0.0
Total	9	341	795	88	214	28	4	12	92	94	90	.269	.348	.360	97	-1	8	7	-2	.977	-20	O-162/C-89,D-37,31	-2.6

■ GREG PRYOR
Pryor, Gregory Russell b: 10/2/49, Marietta, Ohio BR/TR, 6', 186 lbs. Deb: 6/4/76

YEAR	TM/L	G	AB	R	H	2B	3B	HR	RBI	BB	SO	AVG	OBP	SLG	PRO+	BR/A	SB	CS	SBR	FA	FR	G/POS	TPR
1976	Tex-A	5	8	2	3	0	0	0	1	0	1	.375	.375	.375	118	0	0	0	0	1.000	0	/2-3,S-1,3-1	0.1
1978	Chi-A	82	222	27	58	11	0	2	15	11	18	.261	.299	.338	78	-7	3	1	0	.966	6	2-35,S-28,3-20	0.4
1979	Chi-A	143	476	60	131	23	3	3	34	35	41	.275	.327	.355	84	-10	3	4	-2	.961	-5	*S-119,2-25,3-22	-0.3
1980	Chi-A	122	338	32	81	18	4	1	29	12	35	.240	.270	.325	63	-18	2	2	-1	.975	22	S-76,3-41/2-5,D-1	1.1
1981	Chi-A	47	76	4	17	1	0	0	6	6	8	.224	.298	.237	57	-4	0	0	0	.931	4	3-27,S-13/2-5	0.0
1982	KC-A	73	152	23	41	10	1	2	12	10	20	.270	.315	.388	92	-2	2	0	1	.951	8	3-40,2-15,1-14,/S-7	0.6
1983	KC-A	68	115	9	25	4	0	1	14	7	8	.217	.262	.278	49	-8	0	0	0	.958	11	3-60/1-6,2-3	0.2
1984	*KC-A	123	270	32	71	11	1	4	25	12	28	.263	.302	.356	80	-7	0	3	-2	.970	17	*3-105,2-22/S-2,1D	0.8
1985	*KC-A	63	114	8	25	3	0	1	3	8	12	.219	.270	.272	49	-8	0	1	-0	.946	2	3-26,2-20,S-13/1D	-0.5
1986	KC-A	63	112	7	19	4	0	0	7	3	14	.170	.191	.205	8	-14	1	1	-0	.935	6	3-35,S-17,2-12/1-1	-0.9
Total	10	789	1883	204	471	85	9	14	146	104	185	.250	.293	.327	70	-78	11	12	-4	.952	71	3-377,S-276,2/1D	1.5

■ GEORGE PUCCINELLI
Puccinelli, George Lawrence "Pooch" or "Count"
b: 6/22/07, San Francisco, Cal. d: 4/16/56, San Francisco, Cal BR/TR, 6'0.5", 190 lbs. Deb: 7/17/30

YEAR	TM/L	G	AB	R	H	2B	3B	HR	RBI	BB	SO	AVG	OBP	SLG	PRO+	BR/A	SB	CS	SBR	FA	FR	G/POS	TPR
1930	*StL-N	11	16	5	9	1	0	3	8	0	1	.563	.563	1.188	298	5	0			1.000	-1	/O-3	0.3
1932	StL-N	31	108	17	30	8	0	3	11	12	13	.278	.350	.435	107	1	1			.942	2	O-30	0.2
1934	StL-N	10	26	4	6	1	0	2	5	1	8	.231	.286	.500	92	-1	0	0		.941	1	/O-6	0.0
1936	Phi-A	135	457	83	127	30	3	11	78	65	70	.278	.369	.429	98	-1	2	3	-1	.948	0	*O-117	-0.6
Total	4	187	607	109	172	40	3	19	102	78	92	.283	.367	.453	105	4	3	3		.947	2	O-156	-0.1

■ KIRBY PUCKETT
Puckett, Kirby b: 3/14/61, Chicago, Ill. BR/TR, 5'8", 210 lbs. Deb: 5/8/84

YEAR	TM/L	G	AB	R	H	2B	3B	HR	RBI	BB	SO	AVG	OBP	SLG	PRO+	BR/A	SB	CS	SBR	FA	FR	G/POS	TPR
1984	Min-A	128	557	63	165	12	5	0	31	16	69	.296	.321	.336	78	-16	14	7	0	.993	30	*O-128	1.0
1985	Min-A	161	691	80	199	29	13	4	74	41	87	.288	.332	.385	90	-9	21	12	-1	.984	21	*O-161	0.6
1986	Min-A★	161	680	119	223	37	6	31	96	34	99	.328	.366	.537	138	34	20	12	-1	.986	11	*O-160	3.8
1987	*Min-A★	157	624	96	207	32	5	28	99	32	91	.332	.370	.534	131	26	12	7	-1	.986	5	*O-147/D-8	2.5
1988	Min-A★	158	657	109	234	42	5	24	121	23	83	.356	.380	.545	151	42	6	7	-2	.994	20	*O-158	5.4
1989	Min-A★	159	635	75	215	45	4	9	85	41	59	.339	.381	.465	129	23	11	4	1	.991	18	*O-157/D-2	3.9
1990	Min-A★	146	551	82	164	40	3	12	80	57	73	.298	.364	.446	119	14	5	4	-1	.989	8	*O-141/2-1,3-1,SD	1.7
1991	*Min-A★	152	611	92	195	29	6	15	89	31	78	.319	.356	.460	118	14	11	5	0	.985	4	*O-152	1.5
1992	Min-A★	160	639	104	210	38	4	19	110	44	97	.329	.377	.490	137	30	17	7	1	.993	6	*O-149/2-2,3-2,SD	3.4
1993	Min-A★	156	622	89	184	39	3	22	89	47	93	.296	.349	.474	119	16	8	6	-1	.994	4	*O-139,D-17	1.4
1994	Min-A★	108	439	79	139	32	3	20	112	28	47	.317	.362	.540	130	18	6	3	0	.986	8	O-95,D-13	2.1
1995	Min-A★	137	538	83	169	39	0	23	99	56	89	.314	.382	.515	130	24	3	2	-0	.981	1	*O-109,D-28/2-1,3S	1.8
Total	12	1783	7244	1071	2304	414	57	207	1085	450	965	.318	.363	.477	123	216	134	76	-5	.989	137	*O-1696/D-81,32S	29.1

■ JOHN PUHL
Puhl, John G. b: 1/10/1876, Brooklyn, N.Y. d: 8/24/1900, Bayonne, N.J. Deb: 10/13/1898

YEAR	TM/L	G	AB	R	H	2B	3B	HR	RBI	BB	SO	AVG	OBP	SLG	PRO+	BR/A	SB	CS	SBR	FA	FR	G/POS	TPR
1898	NY-N	2	9	1	2	0	0	0	1	0		.222	.222	.222	28	-1	0			.667	-1	/3-2	-0.1
1899	NY-N	1	2	0	0	0	0	0	0	0		.000	.333	.000	-6	-0	0			.667	-0	/3-1	0.0
Total	2	3	11	1	2	0	0	0	1	0		.182	.250	.182	24	-1	0			.667	-1	/3-3	-0.1

■ TERRY PUHL
Puhl, Terry Stephen b: 7/8/56, Melville, Sask., Can BL/TR, 6'2", 200 lbs. Deb: 7/12/77

YEAR	TM/L	G	AB	R	H	2B	3B	HR	RBI	BB	SO	AVG	OBP	SLG	PRO+	BR/A	SB	CS	SBR	FA	FR	G/POS	TPR
1977	Hou-N	60	229	40	69	13	5	0	10	30	31	.301	.385	.402	122	8	10	1	2	.992	3	O-59	1.1
1978	Hou-N☆	149	585	87	169	25	6	3	35	48	46	.289	.347	.368	108	6	32	14	1	.992	15	*O-148	1.6
1979	Hou-N	157	600	87	172	22	4	8	49	58	46	.287	.353	.377	105	5	30	22	-4	1.000	3	*O-152	-0.3
1980	*Hou-N	141	535	75	151	24	5	13	55	60	52	.282	.359	.419	126	19	27	11	2	.991	14	*O-135	3.0
1981	*Hou-N	96	350	43	88	19	4	3	28	31	19	.251	.319	.354	96	-2	22	4	4	1.000	5	O-88	0.3
1982	Hou-N	145	507	64	133	17	9	8	50	51	49	.262	.332	.379	106	4	17	9	-0	.989	-6	*O-138	-0.7
1983	Hou-N	137	465	66	136	25	7	8	44	36	48	.292	.346	.428	121	12	24	11	1	.991	-4	*O-124	0.5
1984	Hou-N	132	449	66	135	19	7	9	55	59	45	.301	.383	.434	139	24	13	8	1	.986	-4	*O-126	1.9
1985	Hou-N	57	194	34	55	14	3	2	18	23	18	.284	.347	.418	116	4	6	2	1	1.000	-6	O-53	0.3
1986	Hou-N	81	172	17	42	10	0	3	14	15	24	.244	.305	.355	84	-4	3	2	-0	1.000	-4	O-47	-1.0
1987	Hou-N	90	122	9	28	5	0	2	15	11	16	.230	.293	.320	65	-6	1	1	-0	.980	-6	O-40	-1.3
1988	Hou-N	113	234	42	71	7	2	3	19	35	30	.303	.396	.389	131	11	22	4	4	.983	-7	O-78	0.7
1989	Hou-N	121	354	41	96	25	4	0	27	45	39	.271	.355	.364	110	6	9	8	-2	1.000	-2	*O-103/1-3	-0.1
1990	Hou-N	37	41	5	12	1	0	0	8	5	7	.293	.383	.317	98	0	1	2	-1	1.000	-2	/O-8,1-1	-0.3
1991	KC-A	15	9	1	2	0	0	0	0	3	2	.222	.333	.222	57	-1	0	0	0	1.000	-0	/O-1,D-2	-0.1
Total	15	1531	4855	676	1361	226	56	62	435	505	507	.280	.351	.388	113	84	217	99	6	.993	8	*O-1300/1-4,D-2	5.6

■ RICH PUIG
Puig, Richard Gerald b: 3/16/53, Tampa, Fla. BL/TR, 5'10", 165 lbs. Deb: 9/13/74

YEAR	TM/L	G	AB	R	H	2B	3B	HR	RBI	BB	SO	AVG	OBP	SLG	PRO+	BR/A	SB	CS	SBR	FA	FR	G/POS	TPR
1974	NY-N	4	11	0	0	0	0	0	0	0	1	.000	.091	.000	-74	-2	0	0	0	.923	2	/2-3,3-1	-0.3

■ LUIS PUJOLS
Pujols, Luis Bienvenido (Toribio) b: 11/18/55, Santiago, D.R. BR/TR, 6'1", 195 lbs. Deb: 9/22/77 C

YEAR	TM/L	G	AB	R	H	2B	3B	HR	RBI	BB	SO	AVG	OBP	SLG	PRO+	BR/A	SB	CS	SBR	FA	FR	G/POS	TPR
1977	Hou-N	6	15	0	1	0	0	0	0	0	5	.067	.067	.067	-70	-4	0	0	0	1.000	0	/C-6	-0.4
1978	Hou-N	56	153	11	20	8	1	1	11	12	45	.131	.199	.216	17	-18	0	0	0	.981	0	C-55/1-1	-1.8
1979	Hou-N	26	75	7	17	2	1	0	8	2	14	.227	.247	.280	46	-6	0	0	0	.993	1	C-26	-0.4
1980	*Hou-N	78	221	15	44	6	1	0	20	13	29	.199	.247	.235	38	-19	0	0	0	.990	-3	C-75/3-1	-2.1
1981	*Hou-N	40	117	5	28	3	1	1	14	10	17	.239	.299	.308	76	-4	1	0	0	.995	-1	C-39	-0.3
1982	Hou-N	65	176	8	35	6	2	4	15	10	40	.199	.242	.324	62	-10	0	3	-2	.991	5	C-64	-0.5
1983	Hou-N	40	87	4	17	2	0	0	12	5	14	.195	.239	.218	29	-8	0	0	0	.971	5	C-39	-0.3
1984	KC-A	4	4	0	1	0	0	0	1	0	2	.200	.200	.200	11	-1	0	0	0	1.000	0	/C-4	0.0
1985	Tex-A	1	2	0	2	0	0	0	0	0	0	1.000	1.000	1.000	444	0	0	0	0	1.000	-0	/C-1	0.0
Total	9	316	850	50	164	27	6	6	81	52	164	.193	.241	.260	43	-68	1	3	-2	.987	6	C-309/3-1,1,1-1	-5.8

■ HARVEY PULLIAM
Pulliam, Harvey Jerome b: 10/20/67, San Francisco, Cal. BR/TR, 6', 210 lbs. Deb: 8/10/91

YEAR	TM/L	G	AB	R	H	2B	3B	HR	RBI	BB	SO	AVG	OBP	SLG	PRO+	BR/A	SB	CS	SBR	FA	FR	G/POS	TPR
1991	KC-A	18	33	4	9	1	0	3	9	3	9	.273	.333	.576	146	2	0	0	0	.917	-2	O-15	0.0
1992	KC-A	4	5	2	1	1	0	0	0	0	3	.200	.333	.400	102	0	0	0	0	1.000	0	/O-1,D-2	0.0
1993	KC-A	27	62	7	16	5	0	1	6	2	14	.258	.292	.387	76	-2	0	0	0	.971	-5	O-26	-0.8
1995	Col-N	5	5	1	2	1	0	1	3	0	2	.400	.400	1.200	234	1	0	0	0	1.000	0	/O-1	0.1
1996	Col-N	10	15	2	2	0	0	0	3	0	6	.133	.133	.133	0	0	0	0	0	1.000	-0	/O-3	-0.3
Total	5	64	120	16	30	8	0	5	13	5	34	.250	.302	.442	91	-2	0	0	0	.954	-7	/O-46,D-2	-1.0

■ BLONDIE PURCELL
Purcell, William Aloysius b: Paterson, N.J. BR/TR, 5'9.5", 159 lbs. Deb: 5/1/1879 M

YEAR	TM/L	G	AB	R	H	2B	3B	HR	RBI	BB	SO	AVG	OBP	SLG	PRO+	BR/A	SB	CS	SBR	FA	FR	G/POS	TPR
1879	Syr-N	63	277	32	72	6	3	0	25	3	13	.260	.268	.303	99	0				.773	-13	O-47,P-22/C-1	-1.2
	Cin-N	12	50	10	11	0	0	0	4	0	3	.220	.220	.220	48	-3				.750	1	O-10/P-2	-0.2
	Yr	75	327	42	83	6	3	0	29	3	16	.254	.261	.291	91	-3				.767	-13	O-57,P-24/C-1	-1.4
1880	Cin-N	77	325	48	95	13	6	1	24	5	16	.292	.303	.378	131	10				.814	-2	O-55,P-25/S-1	0.4
1881	Cle-N	20	80	3	14	2	1	0	4	5	8	.175	.224	.225	44	-5				.786	-2	O-20	-0.7
	Buf-N	30	113	15	33	7	2	0	17	8	8	.292	.339	.389	130	4				.706	-6	O-25/P-9	-0.3
	Yr	50	193	18	47	9	3	0	21	13	16	.244	.291	.321	95	-1				.748	-8	O-45/P-9	-1.0
1882	Buf-N	84	380	79	105	18	6	2	40	14	27	.276	.302	.371	113	5				.820	-5	*O-82/P-6	-0.1

YEAR	TM/L	G	AB	R	H	2B	3B	HR	RBI	BB	SO	AVG	OBP	SLG	PRO+	BR/A	SB	CS	SBR	FA	FR	G/POS	TPR
1883	Phi-N	97	425	70	114	20	5	1	32	13	26	.268	.290	.346	101	2				.777	5	3-46,O-44,P-11,M	0.4
1884	Phi-N	103	428	67	108	11	7	1	31	29	30	.252	.300	.318	99	1				.874	-0	*O-103/P-1	-0.1
1885	Phi-a	66	304	71	90	15	5	0	22	16		.296	.337	.378	119	5				.858	-1	O-66/P-1	0.2
	Bos-N	21	87	9	19	1	1	0	3	3	15	.218	.244	.253	63	-3				.840	-3	O-21	-0.7
1886	Bal-a	26	85	17	19	0	1	0	8	17		.224	.365	.247	96	1	13			.867	-1	O-26/S-1,P-1	0.0
1887	Bal-a	140	567	101	142	25	8	4	96	46		.250	.318	.344	90	-7	88			.925	-4	*O-140/P-1	-1.0
1888	Bal-a	101	406	53	96	9	4	2	39	27		.236	.289	.293	89	-5	16			.906	-6	*O-100/S-2,1-1	-1.2
	Phi-a	18	66	10	11	3	1	0	6	5		.167	.236	.242	54	-3	10			.903	-0	O-17/3-1	-0.2
	Yr	119	472	63	107	12	5	2	45	32		.227	.281	.286	84	-8	26			.905	-6	*O-117/S-2,1-1,3-1	-1.5
1889	Phi-a	129	507	72	160	19	7	0	85	50	27	.316	.383	.381	119	14	22			.903	-10	*O-129	0.1
1890	Phi-a	110	463	110	128	28	3	2	59	43		.276	.343	.363	111	6	48			.949	-1	*O-110	0.1
Total	12	1097	4563	767	1217	177	60	13	495	284	170	.267	.314	.340	103	22	197			.869	-49	O-995/P-79,3S1C	-4.6

■ PID PURDY
Purdy, Everett Virgil b: 6/15/04, Beatrice, Neb. d: 1/16/51, Beatrice, Neb. BL/TR, 5'6", 150 lbs. Deb: 9/7/26

YEAR	TM/L	G	AB	R	H	2B	3B	HR	RBI	BB	SO	AVG	OBP	SLG	PRO+	BR/A	SB	CS	SBR	FA	FR	G/POS	TPR
1926	Chi-A	11	33	5	6	2	1	0	6	2	1	.182	.229	.303	39	-3	0	1	-1	1.000	0	/O-9	-0.4
1927	Cin-N	18	62	15	22	2	4	1	12	4	3	.355	.412	.565	164	5	0			.946	-3	O-16	0.1
1928	Cin-N	70	223	32	69	11	1	0	25	23	13	.309	.377	.368	97	-0	1			.966	0	O-61	-0.4
1929	Cin-N	82	181	22	49	7	5	1	16	19	8	.271	.350	.381	85	-4	2			.978	-1	O-42	-0.7
Total	4	181	499	74	146	22	11	2	59	48	25	.293	.362	.393	97	-2	3	1		.969	-4	O-128	-1.4

■ JESSE PURNELL
Purnell, Jesse Rhoades b: 5/11/1881, Glenside, Pa. d: 7/4/66, Philadelphia, Pa. BL/TR, 5'5.5", 140 lbs. Deb: 10/1/04

YEAR	TM/L	G	AB	R	H	2B	3B	HR	RBI	BB	SO	AVG	OBP	SLG	PRO+	BR/A	SB	CS	SBR	FA	FR	G/POS	TPR
1904	Phi-N	7	19	2	2	0	0	0		1	4	.105	.292	.105	25	-1				.864	-1	/3-7	-0.2

■ BILLY PURTELL
Purtell, William Patrick b: 1/6/1886, Columbus, Ohio d: 3/17/62, Bradenton, Fla. BR/TR, 5'9", 170 lbs. Deb: 4/16/08

YEAR	TM/L	G	AB	R	H	2B	3B	HR	RBI	BB	SO	AVG	OBP	SLG	PRO+	BR/A	SB	CS	SBR	FA	FR	G/POS	TPR
1908	Chi-A	26	69	3	9	2	0	0	3	2		.130	.155	.159	2	-7	2			.940	6	3-25	0.0
1909	Chi-A	103	361	34	93	9	3	0	40	19		.258	.302	.299	94	-3	14			.929	5	3-71,2-32	0.4
1910	Chi-A	102	368	21	82	5	3	1	36	21		.223	.272	.261	70	-13	5			.907	4	*3-102	-0.7
	Bos-A	49	168	15	35	1	2	1	15	18		.208	.289	.256	69	-6	2			.908	-5	3-41/S-8	-1.0
	Yr	151	536	36	117	6	5	2	51	39		.218	.278	.259	70	-19	7			.907	-1	*3-143/S-8	-1.7
1911	Bos-A	27	82	5	23	5	3	0	7	1		.280	.298	.415	99	-1	1			.867	-1	3-15/2-3,S-3,0-1	-0.1
1914	Det-A	28	76	4	13	4	0	0	3	2	7	.171	.203	.224	27	-7	0	2	-1	.946	1	3-16/S-2,2-1	-0.9
Total	5	335	1124	82	255	26	11	2	104	63	7	.227	.275	.275	73	-37	24	2		.915	9	3-270/2-36,S-13,0-1	-2.3

■ ED PUTMAN
Putman, Eddy William b: 9/25/53, Los Angeles, Cal. BR/TR, 6'1", 190 lbs. Deb: 9/7/76

YEAR	TM/L	G	AB	R	H	2B	3B	HR	RBI	BB	SO	AVG	OBP	SLG	PRO+	BR/A	SB	CS	SBR	FA	FR	G/POS	TPR
1976	Chi-N	5	7	0	3	0	0	0	0	0	0	.429	.429	.429	132	0	0	0	0	1.000	0	/C-3,1-1	0.0
1978	Chi-N	17	25	2	5	0	0	0	3	4	6	.200	.310	.200	40	-2	0	0	0	.950	-0	/3-8,1-3,C-2	-0.2
1979	Det-N	21	39	4	9	3	0	2	4	4	12	.231	.302	.462	99	-0	0	1	0	1.000	1	C-16/1-5	-0.2
Total	3	43	71	6	17	3	0	2	7	8	18	.239	.316	.366	81	-2	0	1	0	1.000	1	/C-21,1-9,3-8	-0.2

■ PAT PUTNAM
Putnam, Patrick Edward b: 12/3/53, Bethel, Vt. BL/TR, 6'1", 214 lbs. Deb: 9/2/77

YEAR	TM/L	G	AB	R	H	2B	3B	HR	RBI	BB	SO	AVG	OBP	SLG	PRO+	BR/A	SB	CS	SBR	FA	FR	G/POS	TPR
1977	Tex-A	11	26	3	8	4	0	0	3	1	4	.308	.333	.462	113	0	0	1	-1	1.000	-1	/1-7,D-3	-0.1
1978	Tex-A	20	46	4	7	1	0	1	2	2	5	.152	.188	.239	19	-5	0	0	0	1.000	0	D-12/1-4	-0.6
1979	Tex-A	139	426	57	118	19	2	18	64	23	50	.277	.323	.458	109	4	1	6	-3	.994	3	1-96,D-32	-0.5
1980	Tex-A	147	410	42	108	16	2	13	55	36	49	.263	.323	.407	102	0	0	2	-1	.992	5	*1-137/3-1,D-1	-0.3
1981	Tex-A	95	297	33	79	17	2	8	35	17	38	.266	.306	.418	113	3	4	2	0	.993	3	1-94/O-3	0.2
1982	Tex-A	43	122	14	28	8	0	2	9	10	18	.230	.293	.344	78	-4	0	2	-1	.990	1	1-39/3-1,O-1	-0.6
1983	Sea-A	144	469	58	126	23	2	19	67	39	57	.269	.329	.448	107	4	2	1	0	.994	4	*1-125,D-11	0.2
1984	Sea-A	64	155	11	31	6	0	2	16	12	27	.200	.257	.277	49	-11	3	0	1	1.000	6	D-30,O-13/1-6	-1.3
	Min-A	14	38	1	3	1	0	0	4	4	12	.079	.167	.105	-22	-6	0	0	0	.000	0	D-11	-0.7
	Yr	78	193	12	34	7	0	2	20	16	39	.176	.239	.244	34	-17	3	0	1	1.000	6	D-41,O-13/1-6	-2.0
Total	8	677	1989	223	508	95	8	63	255	144	260	.255	.309	.406	96	-14	10	14	-5	.993	10	1-508,D-100/O-17,3	-3.9

■ JIM PYBURN
Pyburn, James Edward b: 11/1/32, Fairfield, Ala. BR/TR, 6', 190 lbs. Deb: 4/17/55

YEAR	TM/L	G	AB	R	H	2B	3B	HR	RBI	BB	SO	AVG	OBP	SLG	PRO+	BR/A	SB	CS	SBR	FA	FR	G/POS	TPR
1955	Bal-A	39	98	5	20	2	0	0	7	8	24	.204	.271	.265	48	-7	1	1	-0	1.000	-5	3-33/O-1	-1.3
1956	Bal-A	84	156	23	27	3	3	2	11	17	26	.173	.254	.269	41	-14	4	1	1	.975	-11	O-77	-2.6
1957	Bal-A	35	40	8	9	0	0	1	2	9	6	.225	.367	.300	90	-0	1	0	0	1.000	-2	O-28/C-1	-0.3
Total	3	158	294	36	56	5	3	3	20	34	56	.190	.277	.272	51	-21	6	2	1	.982	-18	O-106/3-33,C-1	-4.2

■ EDDIE PYE
Pye, Robert Edward b: 2/13/67, Columbia, Tenn. BR/TR, 5'10", 175 lbs. Deb: 6/3/94

YEAR	TM/L	G	AB	R	H	2B	3B	HR	RBI	BB	SO	AVG	OBP	SLG	PRO+	BR/A	SB	CS	SBR	FA	FR	G/POS	TPR
1994	LA-N	7	10	2	1	0	0	0	1	4	.100	.182	.100	-26	-2	0	0	0	1.000	2	/2-3,S-3	0.1
1995	LA-N	7	8	0	0	0	0	0	0	0	4	.000	.000	.000	-99	-2	0	0	0	.000	0	/3-2	-0.2
Total	2	14	18	2	1	0	0	0	0	1	8	.056	.105	.056	-61	-4	0	0	0	1.000	2	/S-3,2-3,3-2	-0.1

■ FRANKIE PYTLAK
Pytlak, Frank Anthony b: 7/30/08, Buffalo, N.Y. d: 5/8/77, Buffalo, N.Y. BR/TR, 5'7.5", 160 lbs. Deb: 4/22/32

YEAR	TM/L	G	AB	R	H	2B	3B	HR	RBI	BB	SO	AVG	OBP	SLG	PRO+	BR/A	SB	CS	SBR	FA	FR	G/POS	TPR
1932	Cle-A	12	29	5	7	1	1	0	4	3	2	.241	.333	.345	71	-1	0	0	1.000	3	C-12	0.2
1933	Cle-A	80	248	36	77	10	6	2	33	17	10	.310	.355	.423	101	-0	3	4	-2	1.000	11	C-69	1.2
1934	Cle-A	91	289	46	75	12	4	0	35	36	11	.260	.352	.329	75	-10	11	2	2	.989	-10	C-88	-1.3
1935	Cle-A	55	149	14	44	6	1	1	12	11	4	.295	.348	.369	84	-3	3	2	0	.984	-1	C-48	-0.2
1936	Cle-A	75	224	35	72	15	4	0	31	24	11	.321	.394	.424	101	1	5	2	0	.996	-6	C-58	-0.1
1937	Cle-A	125	397	60	125	15	6	1	44	52	15	.315	.404	.390	100	3	16	5	2	.986	10	*C-115	1.9
1938	Cle-A	113	364	46	112	14	7	1	43	36	15	.308	.376	.393	95	-2	9	5	-0	.987	-8	C-99	-0.4
1939	Cle-A	63	183	20	49	2	5	0	14	20	5	.268	.343	.333	76	-6	4	1	1	1.000	3	C-51	0.0
1940	Cle-A	62	149	16	21	2	1	0	16	17	5	.141	.234	.168	6	-21	10	0	-1	.996	7	C-58/O-1	-1.0
1941	Bos-A	106	336	36	91	23	1	2	39	28	9	.271	.329	.363	81	-9	5	7	-3	.991	-4	C-91	-0.4
1945	Bos-A	9	17	1	2	0	0	0	0	3	0	.118	.250	.118	8	-2	1	0	0	1.000	1	/C-6	-0.1
1946	Bos-A	4	14	1	2	0	0	0	0	0	0	.143	.143	.143	-19	-2	0	0	0	1.000	2	/C-4	-0.1
Total	12	795	2399	316	677	100	36	7	272	247	97	.282	.355	.363	84	-53	56	29	-1	.991	12	C-699/O-1	-0.2

■ TIM PYZNARSKI
Pyznarski, Timothy Matthew b: 2/4/60, Chicago, Ill. BR/TR, 6'2", 195 lbs. Deb: 9/14/86

YEAR	TM/L	G	AB	R	H	2B	3B	HR	RBI	BB	SO	AVG	OBP	SLG	PRO+	BR/A	SB	CS	SBR	FA	FR	G/POS	TPR
1986	SD-N	15	42	3	10	1	0	0	4	11	.238	.319	.262	63	-2	2	0	1	.977	-0	1-13	-0.3

■ JIM QUALLS
Qualls, James Robert b: 10/9/46, Exeter, Cal. BB/TR, 5'10", 158 lbs. Deb: 4/10/69

YEAR	TM/L	G	AB	R	H	2B	3B	HR	RBI	BB	SO	AVG	OBP	SLG	PRO+	BR/A	SB	CS	SBR	FA	FR	G/POS	TPR
1969	Chi-N	43	120	12	30	5	3	0	9	2	14	.250	.268	.342	62	-6	2	1	0	1.000	-3	O-35/2-4	-1.2
1970	Mon-N	9	9	1	1	0	0	0	1	0	1	.111	.111	.111	-40	-2	0	0	0	1.000	-1	/2-2,O-2	-0.3
1972	Chi-A	11	10	0	0	0	0	0	0	0	1	.000	.000	.000	-98	-2	0	0	0	1.000	-1	/O-1	-0.3
Total	3	63	139	13	31	5	3	0	10	2	16	.223	.239	.302	46	-10	2	1	0	1.000	-4	/O-38,2-6	-1.8

■ MEL QUEEN
Queen, Melvin Douglas b: 3/26/42, Johnson City, N.Y. BL/TR, 6'1", 197 lbs. Deb: 4/13/64 FC

YEAR	TM/L	G	AB	R	H	2B	3B	HR	RBI	BB	SO	AVG	OBP	SLG	PRO+	BR/A	SB	CS	SBR	FA	FR	G/POS	TPR
1964	Cin-N	48	95	7	19	2	0	2	12	4	19	.200	.232	.284	43	-7	0	1	-1	.977	1	O-20	-0.8
1965	Cin-N	5	3	0	0	0	0	0	0	0	0	.000	.000	.000	-94	-1	0	0	0	1.000	0	/O-1	-0.1
1966	Cin-N	56	55	4	7	1	0	0	5	10	12	.127	.262	.145	16	-6	0	0	0	1.000	-4	O-32/P-7	-1.1
1967	Cin-N	49	81	6	17	4	0	0	5	4	10	.210	.247	.259	40	-6	2	0	0	.941	-2	P-31	0.0
1968	Cin-N	10	8	2	1	0	0	0	0	0	5	.125	.222	.125	6	-1	0	0	0	1.000	0	/P-5	0.0
1969	Cin-N	2	6	0	1	0	0	0	1	0	1	.167	.167	.167	-6	-1	0	0	0	1.000	0	/P-2	0.0
1970	Cal-A	37	16	1	4	0	0	0	1	0	3	.250	.250	.250	40	-1	0	0	0	1.000	-1	P-34	0.0
1971	Cal-A	45	8	0	0	0	0	0	0	1	0	.000	.111	.000	-71	-2	0	0	0	.900	-1	P-44	0.0
1972	Cal-A	17	2	0	0	0	0	0	1	1	0	.000	.333	.000	5	-0	0	0	0	1.000	0	P-17	0.0
Total	9	269	274	20	49	7	0	2	25	21	50	.179	.237	.226	30	-25	2	1	0	.951	-7	P-140/O-53	-2.0

■ BILLY QUEEN
Queen, William Eddleman "Doc" b: 11/28/28, Gastonia, N.C. BR/TR, 6'1", 185 lbs. Deb: 4/13/54

YEAR	TM/L	G	AB	R	H	2B	3B	HR	RBI	BB	SO	AVG	OBP	SLG	PRO+	BR/A	SB	CS	SBR	FA	FR	G/POS	TPR
1954	Mil-N	3	2	0	0	0	0	0	0	0	2	.000	.000	.000	-99	-1	0	0	0	1.000	-0	/O-1	-0.1

YEAR	TM/L	G	AB	R	H	2B	3B	HR	RBI	BB	SO	AVG	OBP	SLG	PRO+	BR/A	SB	CS	SBR	FA	FR	G/POS	TPR
■ GEORGE QUELLICH			Quellich, George William b: 2/10/06, Johnsville, Cal. d: 8/31/58, Johnsville, Cal. BR/TR, 6'1", 180 lbs. Deb: 8/1/31																				
1931	Det-A	13	54	6	12	5	0	1	11	3	4	.222	.263	.370	63	-3	1	0	0	1.000	1	O-13	-0.2
■ JOE QUEST			Quest, Joseph L. b: 11/16/1852, New Castle, Pa. d: 11/14/24, San Diego, Cal. BR/TR, 5'6", 150 lbs. Deb: 8/30/1871 U																				
1871	Cle-n	3	13	1	3	1	0	0	2	1	0	.231	.286	.308	75	-2	0	0	0	.571	-2	/2-2,S-1	-0.2
1878	Ind-N	62	278	45	57	3	2	0	13	12	24	.205	.238	.230	63	-10				.876	2	*2-62	-0.4
1879	Chi-N	83	334	38	69	16	1	0	22	9	33	.207	.227	.260	57	-16				**.925**	14	*2-83	0.4
1880	Chi-N	82	300	37	71	12	1	0	27	8	16	.237	.256	.283	78	-7				.895	4	*2-80/S-2,3-1	0.1
1881	Chi-N	78	293	35	72	6	0	1	26	2	9	.246	.251	.276	63	-13				**.929**	6	*2-77/S-1	-0.4
1882	Chi-N	42	159	24	32	5	2	0	15	8	16	.201	.240	.258	57	-8				.879	-5	2-41/S-1	-1.1
1883	Det-N	37	137	22	32	8	2	0	15	10	18	.234	.286	.321	88	-1				.897	0	2-37	-0.1
	StL-a	19	78	12	20	3	1	0	10	1		.256	.266	.321	83	-2				.890	-6	2-19	-0.7
1884	StL-a	81	310	46	64	9	5	0		19		.206	.257	.268	69	-11				.894	-9	*2-81	-1.7
	Pit-a	12	43	2	9	3	0	0		0		.209	.227	.279	63	-2				.938	0	/2-7,S-5	-0.1
	Yr	93	353	48	73	12	5	0		19		.207	.253	.269	68	-12				.898	-9	2-88/S-5	-1.8
1885	Det-N	55	200	24	39	8	2	0	21	14	25	.195	.248	.255	63	-8				.898	-2	2-39,S-15/O-1	-0.8
1886	Phi-a	42	150	14	31	4	1	0	10	20		.207	.300	.247	71	-4	5			.847	3	S-41/2-2	-0.2
Total	9	593	2282	299	496	77	17	1	159	103	<u>161</u>	.217	.252	.267	67	-81	5	<u>0</u>		.902	5	2-528/S-65,O-1,3-1	-5.0
■ HAL QUICK			Quick, James Harold "Blondie" b: 10/4/17, Rome, Ga. d: 3/9/74, Swansea, Ill. BR/TR, 5'10.5", 163 lbs. Deb: 9/7/39																				
1939	Was-A	12	41	3	10	1	0	0	2	1	1	.244	.279	.268	44	-4	1	0		.927	1	S-10	-0.1
■ FRANK QUILICI			Quilici, Francis Ralph "Guido" b: 5/11/39, Chicago, Ill. BR/TR, 6', 175 lbs. Deb: 7/18/65 MC																				
1965	*Min-A	56	149	16	31	5	1	0	7	15	33	.208	.280	.255	51	-9	1	1	-0	.990	3	2-52/S-4	-0.3
1967	Min-A	23	19	2	2	1	0	0	3	4		.105	.227	.158	14	-2	0	0	0	1.000	1	2-13/3-8,S-1	-0.1
1968	Min-A	97	229	22	56	11	4	1	22	21	45	.245	.311	.341	93	-2	0	0	0	1.000	17	2-48,3-40/S-6,1-1	2.0
1969	Min-A	118	144	19	25	3	1	2	12	12	22	.174	.237	.250	36	-13	2	0	1	.935	24	3-84,2-36/S-1	1.5
1970	*Min-A	111	141	19	32	3	0	2	12	15	16	.227	.301	.291	63	-7	0	2	-1	.987	15	2-73,3-27/S-1	1.0
Total	5	405	682	78	146	23	6	5	53	66	120	.214	.284	.287	63	-33	3	3	-1	.993	60	2-222,3-159/S-13,1	4.1
■ LEE QUILLEN			Quillen, Leon Abner b: 5/5/1882, North Branch, Minn. d: 5/14/65, St.Paul, Minn. BR/TR, 5'10", 165 lbs. Deb: 9/30/06																				
1906	Chi-A	4	9	1	3	0	0	0		0		.333	.333	.333	112	0	1			.600	-2	/S-3	-0.2
1907	Chi-A	49	151	17	29	5	0	0	14	10		.192	.256	.225	56	-7	8			.871	0	3-48	-0.6
Total	2	53	160	18	32	5	0	0	14	10		.200	.260	.231	59	-7	9			.871	-2	/3-48,S-3	-0.8
■ QUINLAN		Quinlan Deb: 9/7/1874																					
1874	Phi-n	1	4	0	1	0	0	0	1	0		.250	.250	.250	59	-0	0	0	0	1.000	0	/S-1	
■ FRANK QUINLAN			Quinlan, Francis Patrick b: 3/9/1869, Marlborough, Mass. d: 5/4/04, Brockton, Mass. Deb: 10/5/1891																				
1891	Bos-a	2	5	0	0	0	0	0	0	0	2	.000	.000	.000	-99	-1	0			1.000	-1	/C-1,O-1	-0.2
■ FINNERS QUINLAN			Quinlan, Thomas Finners b: 10/21/1887, Scranton, Pa. d: 2/17/66, Scranton, Pa. BL/TL, 5'8", 154 lbs. Deb: 9/6/13																				
1913	StL-N	13	50	1	8	0	0	0	1	1		.160	.176	.160	-4	-7	0			.897	2	O-12	-0.6
1915	Chi-A	42	114	11	22	3	0	0	7	4	11	.193	.270	.219	45	-8	3	4	-2	1.000	-2	O-32	-1.3
Total	2	55	164	12	30	3	0	0	8	5	20	.183	.243	.201	31	-14	3	<u>4</u>		.961	0	/O-44	-1.9
■ TOM QUINLAN			Quinlan, Thomas Raymond b: 3/27/68, St.Paul, Minn. BR/TR, 6'3", 200 lbs. Deb: 9/4/90																				
1990	Tor-A	1	2	0	1	0	0	0	0	0		.500	.667	.500	227	1	0	0	0	1.000	-0	/3-1	0.0
1992	Tor-A	13	15	2	1	1	0	0	2	2	9	.067	.176	.133	-12	-2	0	0	0	.909	-1	3-13	-0.3
1994	Phi-N	24	35	6	7	2	0	1	3	3	13	.200	.263	.343	55	-2	0	0	0	.966	2	3-20	-0.1
1996	Min-A	4	6	0	0	0	0	0	0	0	4	.000	.000	.000	-98	-2	0	0	0	.667	-1	/3-4	-0.2
Total	4	42	58	8	9	3	0	1	5	5	26	.155	.234	.259	30	-6	0	0	0	.932	0	/3-38	-0.6
■ FRANK QUINN			Quinn, Frank J. b: 1876, Grand Rapids, Mich. d: 2/17/20, Camden, Ind. 5'8", Deb: 8/9/1899																				
1899	Chi-N	12	34	6	6	0	1	0	1	6		.176	.300	.235	49	-2	1			.909	-4	O-10/2-1	-0.6
■ JOHN QUINN			Quinn, John Edward "Pick" b: 9/12/1885, Framingham, Mass. d: 4/9/56, Marlboro, Mass. BR/TR, 5'11", 150 lbs. Deb: 10/9/11																				
1911	Phi-N	1	2	0	0	0	0	0	0	0		.000	.000	.000	-99	-1	0			1.000	-0	/C-1	-0.1
■ JOE QUINN			Quinn, Joseph C. b: 8/1849, Chicago, Ill. d: 1/2/09, Chicago, Ill. 5'8.5", 148 lbs. Deb: 7/26/1871																				
1871	Kek-n	5	17	8	4	0	0	0	2	4	0	.235	.381	.235	81	-0	3	1	0	.964	2	/C-5	0.1
1877	Chi-N	4	14	1	1	0	0	0	0	1	0	.071	.133	.071	-30	-2				.667	0	/O-4	-0.2
■ JOE QUINN			Quinn, Joseph J. b: 12/25/1864, Sydney, Australia d: 11/12/40, St.Louis, Mo. BR/TR, 5'7", 158 lbs. Deb: 4/26/1884 M																				
1884	StL-U	103	429	74	116	21	1	0		9		.270	.285	.324	81	-22				.945	-1	*1-100/O-3,S-1	-3.1
1885	StL-N	97	343	27	73	8	2	0	15	9	38	.213	.233	.248	59	-15				.875	-6	O-57,3-31,1-11	-2.2
1886	StL-N	75	271	33	63	11	3	1	21	8	31	.232	.254	.306	75	-8	12			.895	-3	O-48,2-15/1-7,3S	-0.9
1888	Bos-N	38	156	19	47	8	3	4	29	2	5	.301	.310	.468	143	7	12			.914	-7	2-38	0.1
1889	Bos-N	112	444	57	116	13	5	2	69	25	21	.261	.308	.327	73	-17	24			.860	-29	S-63,2-47/3-2	-3.5
1890	Bos-P	130	509	87	153	19	8	7	82	44	29	.301	.359	.411	99	-4	29			**.942**	15	*2-130	1.5
1891	Bos-N	124	508	70	122	8	10	3	63	28	28	.240	.288	.313	67	-25	24			.938	-23	*2-124	-3.8
1892	*Bos-N	143	532	63	116	14	1	1	59	35	40	.218	.275	.254	55	-30	17			**.951**	2	*2-143	-2.4
1893	StL-N	135	547	68	126	18	6	0	71	33	7	.230	.279	.285	50	-41	24			.942	-30	*2-135	-5.6
1894	StL-N	106	405	59	116	18	1	4	61	24	8	.286	.328	.365	67	-23	25			.952	21	*2-106	0.3
1895	StL-N	134	543	84	169	19	9	2	74	36	9	.311	.356	.390	94	-5	22			.946	-2	*2-134,M	0.0
1896	StL-N	48	191	19	40	6	1	0	17	9	5	.209	.252	.267	39	-17	8			.956	2	2-48	-1.1
	*Bal-N	24	82	22	27	1	1	0	5	6	1	.329	.375	.366	94	-1	6			.951	-3	/2-8,O-8,3-5,S-1	-0.3
	Yr	72	273	41	67	7	2	1	22	15	6	.245	.290	.297	56	-18	14			.955	-1	2-56/O-8,3-5,S-1	-1.4
1897	Bal-N	75	285	33	74	11	4	1	45	13		.260	.299	.337	68	-14	12			.946	9	3-37,S-21,2-11,/O1	-0.3
1898	Bal-N	12	32	5	8	1	0	0	5	1		.250	.273	.281	58	-2	0			.893	0	/3-8,2-1,O-1	-0.1
	StL-N	103	375	35	94	10	5	0	36	24		.251	.301	.304	72	-14	13			.962	-1	2-62,S-41/O-1	-0.9
	Yr	115	407	40	102	11	5	0	41	25		.251	.299	.302	71	-16	13			.960	-0	2-63,S-41/3-8,O-2	-0.9
1899	Cle-N	147	615	73	176	24	6	0	72	21		.286	.312	.345	86	-13	22			**.962**	3	*2-147,M	-0.2
1900	StL-N	22	80	12	21	2	0	1	11	10		.262	.344	.325	86	-1	4			.933	-2	2-14/S-6,3-1	-0.8
	Cin-N	74	266	18	73	5	2	0	25	16		.274	.316	.308	74	-9	7			.950	-18	2-74	-2.2
	Yr	96	346	30	94	7	2	1	36	26		.272	.323	.312	77	-10	11			.947	-26	2-88/S-6,3-1	-3.0
1901	Was-A	66	266	33	67	11	2	2	34	11		.252	.287	.331	72	-10	7			.954	-14	2-66	-2.0
Total	17	1768	6879	891	1797	228	70	29	794	364	<u>214</u>	.261	.302	.327	74	-265	268			.946	-91	*2-1303,S-135,O1/3	-27.4
■ PADDY QUINN		Quinn, Paddy Deb: 5/4/1875																					
1875	Wes-n	11	43	4	14	0	0	0	5	0	1	.326	.326	.349	127	1	0	1	-1	.861	1	C-10/O-1	0.1
	Har-n	5	13	1	3	0	0	0	1	1	3	.231	.286	.231	78	-0	0	1	-1	.833	-0	/C-3,O-3	-0.1
	Chi-n	17	61	12	14	0	0	0	1	0	2	.230	.230	.230	59	-2	1	1	-0	.778	-5	C-11,O-10	-0.7
	Yr	33	117	17	31	0	0	0	7	1	6	.265	.271	.274	87	-2	1	3	-2	.826	-5	C-24,O-14	-0.7
■ PADDY QUINN			Quinn, Patrick b: Boston, Mass. d: 3/1893, 5'8", 162 lbs. Deb: 9/9/1875																				
1875	Atl-n	2	8	2	1	0	0	0	0	0	0	.125	.125	.125	-15	-1	0	0	0	.800	-3	/O-2,S-1	-0.3
1881	Bos-N	1	4	0	0	0	0	0	0	0	0	.000	.000	.000	-99	-1				1.000	-0	/1-1	-0.1
	Wor-N	2	7	0	1	0	0	0	1	1	2	.143	.250	.143	25	-1				.714	0	/C-2	-0.3
	Yr	3	11	0	1	0	0	0	1	1	2	.091	.167	.091	-16	-1				.714	-3	/C-2,1-1	-0.4

YEAR	TM/L	G	AB	R	H	2B	3B	HR	RBI	BB	SO	AVG	OBP	SLG	PRO+	BR/A	SB	CS	SBR	FA	FR	G/POS	TPR

■ TOM QUINN　Quinn, Thomas Oscar　b: 4/25/1864, Annapolis, Md.　d: 7/24/32, Pittsburgh, Pa.　BR/TR, 5'8", 180 lbs.　Deb: 9/2/1886

YEAR	TM/L	G	AB	R	H	2B	3B	HR	RBI	BB	SO	AVG	OBP	SLG	PRO+	BR/A	SB	CS	SBR	FA	FR	G/POS	TPR
1886	Pit-a	3	11	1	0	0	0	0	0	0		.000	.000	.000	-99	-2	1			.929	-2	/C-3	-0.3
1889	Bal-a	55	194	18	34	2	1	1	15	19	22	.175	.252	.211	32	-17	6			.925	8	C-55	-0.4
1890	Pit-P	55	207	23	44	4	3	1	15	17	8	.213	.282	.275	54	-13	1			.888	-4	C-55	-1.0
Total	3	113	412	42	78	6	4	2	30	36	30	.189	.261	.238	40	-33	8			.910	2	C-113	-1.7

■ LUIS QUINONES　Quinones, Luis Raul　b: 4/28/62, Ponce, P.R.　BB/TR, 5'11", 175 lbs.　Deb: 5/27/83

YEAR	TM/L	G	AB	R	H	2B	3B	HR	RBI	BB	SO	AVG	OBP	SLG	PRO+	BR/A	SB	CS	SBR	FA	FR	G/POS	TPR
1983	Oak-A	19	42	5	8	2	1	0	4	1	4	.190	.209	.286	37	-4	1	1	-0	1.000	1	/2-6,3-4,0-4,S-3,D	-0.3
1986	SF-N	71	106	13	19	1	3	0	11	3	17	.179	.209	.245	26	-11	3	1	0	.922	-7	S-33,3-31/2-8	-1.7
1987	Chi-N	49	101	12	22	6	0	0	8	10	16	.218	.288	.277	49	-7	0	0	0	.965	-7	S-28/2-4,3-1	-1.2
1988	Cin-N	23	52	4	12	3	0	1	1	2	11	.231	.259	.346	70	-2	1	1	-0	.974	1	S-10/2-4,3-4	-0.1
1989	Cin-N	97	340	43	83	13	4	12	34	25	46	.244	.302	.412	99	-1	2	4	-2	.979	-5	2-53,3-50/S-5	-0.7
1990	*Cin-N	83	145	10	35	7	0	2	17	13	29	.241	.308	.331	73	-5	1	0	0	.981	9	3-22,2-13/S-9,1-1	0.5
1991	Cin-N	97	212	15	47	4	3	4	20	21	31	.222	.298	.325	72	-8	1	2	-1	.975	-4	2-33,3-19/S-5	-1.2
1992	Min-A	3	5	0	1	0	0	0	1	0	0	.200	.200	.200	12	-1	0	0	0	.714	-0	/3-1,S-1,D-1	-0.1
Total	8	442	1003	102	227	36	11	19	106	75	154	.226	.285	.341	72	-39	9	9	-3	.937	-11	3-132,2-121/SDO1	-4.8

■ REY QUINONES　Quinones, Rey Francisco (Santiago)　b: 11/11/63, Rio Piedras, P.R.　BR/TR, 5'11", 160 lbs.　Deb: 5/17/86

YEAR	TM/L	G	AB	R	H	2B	3B	HR	RBI	BB	SO	AVG	OBP	SLG	PRO+	BR/A	SB	CS	SBR	FA	FR	G/POS	TPR
1986	Bos-A	62	190	26	45	12	1	2	15	19	26	.237	.316	.342	79	-5	3	2	-0	.940	-8	S-62	-0.8
	Sea-A	36	122	6	23	4	0	0	7	5	31	.189	.220	.221	21	-13	1	1	-0	.945	1	S-36	-1.0
	Yr	98	312	32	68	16	1	2	22	24	57	.218	.280	.295	56	-19	4	3	-1	.942	-7	S-98	-1.8
1987	Sea-A	135	478	55	132	18	2	12	56	26	71	.276	.319	.397	84	-11	1	3	-2	.959	-10	*S-135	-1.0
1988	Sea-A	140	499	63	124	30	3	12	52	23	71	.248	.286	.393	84	-12	0	3	-2	.963	3	*S-135/D-4	0.0
1989	Sea-A	7	19	2	2	0	0	0	0	1	1	.105	.150	.105	-26	-3	0	0	0	.889	-2	/S-7	-0.5
	Pit-N	71	225	21	47	11	0	3	29	15	40	.209	.261	.298	62	-12	0	2	-1	.934	-11	S-69	-2.0
Total	4	451	1533	173	373	75	6	29	159	89	240	.243	.290	.357	74	-56	5	11	-5	.952	-27	S-444/D-4	-5.3

■ CARLOS QUINTANA　Quintana, Carlos Narcis (Hernandez)　b: 8/26/65, Estado Miranda, Venez.　BR/TR, 6', 175 lbs.　Deb: 9/16/88

YEAR	TM/L	G	AB	R	H	2B	3B	HR	RBI	BB	SO	AVG	OBP	SLG	PRO+	BR/A	SB	CS	SBR	FA	FR	G/POS	TPR
1988	Bos-A	5	6	1	2	0	0	0	2	2	3	.333	.500	.333	133	0	0	0	0	1.000	-0	/O-3,D-1	0.0
1989	Bos-A	34	77	6	16	5	0	0	6	7	12	.208	.274	.273	51	-5	0	0	0	.926	-5	*1-148/O-3	-1.0
1990	*Bos-A	149	512	56	147	28	0	7	67	52	74	.287	.355	.383	102	2	1	2	-1	.987	15	*1-148/O-3	0.5
1991	Bos-A	149	478	69	141	21	1	11	71	61	66	.295	.377	.412	113	10	1	0	0	.993	7	*1-138,O-13/D-1	0.9
1993	Bos-A	101	303	31	74	5	0	1	19	31	52	.244	.318	.271	57	-18	1	0	0	.991	-1	1-53,O-51	-2.2
Total	5	438	1376	163	380	59	1	19	165	153	207	.276	.351	.362	93	-11	3	2	-0	.990	15	1-340/O-91,D-9	-1.8

■ MARSHALL QUINTON　Quinton, Marshall J.　b: Philadelphia, Pa.　5'11", 190 lbs.　Deb: 8/7/1884

YEAR	TM/L	G	AB	R	H	2B	3B	HR	RBI	BB	SO	AVG	OBP	SLG	PRO+	BR/A	SB	CS	SBR	FA	FR	G/POS	TPR
1884	Ric-a	26	94	12	22	5	0	0		0		.234	.242	.287	73	-3				.878	-9	C-14,O-10/S-2	-1.0
1885	Phi-a	7	29	6	6	1	0	0	4	1		.207	.258	.241	55	-2				.869	-2	/C-7	-0.3
Total	2	33	123	18	28	6	0	0	4	1		.228	.246	.276	68	-4				.874	-11	/C-21,O-10,S-2	-1.3

■ JAMIE QUIRK　Quirk, James Patrick　b: 10/22/54, Whittier, Cal.　BL/TR, 6'4", 200 lbs.　Deb: 9/4/75　C

YEAR	TM/L	G	AB	R	H	2B	3B	HR	RBI	BB	SO	AVG	OBP	SLG	PRO+	BR/A	SB	CS	SBR	FA	FR	G/POS	TPR
1975	KC-A	14	39	2	10	0	0	1	5	2	7	.256	.293	.333	75	-1	0	0	0	.909	0	O-10/3-2,D-1	-0.1
1976	*KC-A	64	114	11	28	6	0	1	15	7	22	.246	.259	.325	70	-5	0	0	0	1.000	-1	D-19,S-12,3-11/1-2	-0.6
1977	Mil-A	93	221	16	48	14	1	3	13	8	47	.217	.251	.330	57	-14	0	1	-1	.950	0	D-53,O-10/3-8	-1.6
1978	KC-A	17	29	3	6	2	0	0	2	5	4	.207	.324	.276	68	-1	0	0	0	.926	2	3-10/S-2,D-1	0.1
1979	KC-A	51	79	8	24	6	1	1	11	5	13	.304	.353	.443	111	1	0	0	0	.944	-1	/C-9,S-5,3-3,D-9	0.1
1980	KC-A	62	163	13	45	5	0	5	21	7	24	.276	.310	.399	92	-2	3	2	-0	.929	-1	3-28,C-15/O-7,1D	-0.3
1981	KC-A	46	100	8	25	7	0	0	10	6	17	.250	.299	.320	79	-3	0	2	-1	.985	-3	C-22/3-8,2-1,O-1	-0.7
1982	KC-A	36	78	8	18	3	0	1	6	3	15	.231	.259	.308	55	-5	0	0	0	1.000	0	C-29/1-6,3-1,O-1	-0.3
1983	StL-N	48	86	3	18	2	1	2	11	6	27	.209	.269	.326	64	-4	0	0	0	.929	-5	C-22/3-7,S-1	-0.9
1984	Chi-A	3	2	0	0	0	0	0	0	0	2	.000	.000	.000	-96	-1	0	0	0	1.000	0	/3-1	-0.1
	Cle-A	1	1	1	1	0	0	0	1	0	0	1.000	1.000	4.000	1189	1	0	0	0	.000	0	/C-1	0.1
	Yr	4	3	1	1	0	0	0	1	0	2	.333	.333	1.333	324	1	0	0	0	1.000	0	/3-1,C-1	0.0
1985	*KC-A	19	57	3	16	3	1	0	4	2	9	.281	.305	.368	83	-1	0	0	0	.986	-3	C-17/1-1	-0.3
1986	KC-A	80	219	24	47	10	0	8	26	17	41	.215	.274	.370	72	-9	0	1	-1	.989	11	C-41,3-24/1-6,O-1	0.3
1987	KC-A	109	296	24	70	17	0	5	33	28	56	.236	.311	.345	72	-12	1	0	0	.986	-4	*C-108/S-1	-0.8
1988	KC-A	84	196	22	47	7	1	8	25	28	41	.240	.338	.408	107	2	1	5	-3	.982	14	C-79/1-1,3-1	1.8
1989	NY-A	13	24	0	2	0	0	0	0	3	5	.083	.185	.083	-22	-4	0	1	-1	1.000	0	/C-6,S-1,D-1	-0.3
	Oak-A	9	10	1	2	0	0	1	1	0	4	.200	.200	.500	95	-0	0	0	0	.500	0	/3-3,C-2,1-1,O-1	-0.1
	Bal-A	25	51	5	11	2	0	0	9	9	11	.216	.333	.255	70	-2	0	0	0	1.000	5	C-24	0.4
	Yr	47	85	6	15	2	0	1	10	12	20	.176	.278	.235	47	-6	0	1	-1	1.000	6	C-32/3-3,S-1,D10	0.0
1990	*Oak-A	56	121	12	34	5	1	3	26	14	34	.281	.360	.413	121	4	0	0	0	.977	-2	C-37/1-8,3-8,O-1,D	0.4
1991	Oak-A	76	203	16	53	4	0	1	17	16	28	.261	.321	.296	76	-6	0	3	-2	.982	6	C-54/1-8,3-1,D-1	0.0
1992	*Oak-A	78	177	13	39	7	1	2	16	11	28	.220	.296	.305	72	-7	0	0	0	.973	5	C-59/1-9,3-2,D-1	0.1
Total	18	984	2266	193	544	100	7	43	247	177	435	.240	.300	.347	78	-68	5	16	-8	.982	28	C-525,3-118/D1OS2	-2.8

■ BRIAN RAABE　Raabe, Brian Charles　b: 11/5/67, New Ulm, Minn.　BR/TR, 5'9", 177 lbs.　Deb: 9/17/95

YEAR	TM/L	G	AB	R	H	2B	3B	HR	RBI	BB	SO	AVG	OBP	SLG	PRO+	BR/A	SB	CS	SBR	FA	FR	G/POS	TPR
1995	Min-A	6	14	4	3	0	0	0	1	1	0	.214	.267	.214	27	-1	0	0	0	1.000	-1	/2-4,3-2	-0.2
1996	Min-A	7	9	0	2	0	0	0	1	0	1	.222	.222	.222	13	-1	0	0	0	.857	-1	/3-6,2-1	-0.2
Total	2	13	23	4	5	0	0	0	2	1	1	.217	.250	.217	21	-3	0	0	0	.857	-1	/3-8,2-5	-0.4

■ JOHN RABB　Rabb, John Andrew　b: 6/23/60, Los Angeles, Cal.　BR/TR, 6'1", 180 lbs.　Deb: 9/4/82

YEAR	TM/L	G	AB	R	H	2B	3B	HR	RBI	BB	SO	AVG	OBP	SLG	PRO+	BR/A	SB	CS	SBR	FA	FR	G/POS	TPR
1982	SF-N	2	2	0	1	0	0	0	0	0	1	.500	.500	1.500	441	1	0	0	0	1.000	-0	/O-1	0.1
1983	SF-N	40	104	10	24	9	0	1	14	9	17	.231	.292	.346	79	-3	1	0	0	.973	4	C-31/O-2	0.3
1984	SF-N	54	82	10	16	1	0	3	9	10	33	.195	.283	.317	71	-3	1	1	-0	.988	-6	1-13/O-8,C-6	-0.6
1985	Atl-N	3	2	0	0	0	0	0	0	0	0	.000	.000	.000	-94	-1	0	0	0	.000	-0	/O-1	-0.1
1988	Sea-A	9	14	2	5	2	0	0	4	0	2	.357	.357	.500	131	1	0	0	0	1.000	0	/O-2,1-1,D-5	0.1
Total	5	108	204	22	46	12	1	4	27	19	53	.225	.291	.353	81	-6	2	1	0	.966	2	/C-37,1-14,O-14,D-5	-0.2

■ JOE RABBITT　Rabbitt, Joseph Patrick　b: 1/16/1900, Frontenac, Kan.　d: 12/5/69, Norwalk, Conn.　BL/TR, 5'10", 165 lbs.　Deb: 9/15/22

YEAR	TM/L	G	AB	R	H	2B	3B	HR	RBI	BB	SO	AVG	OBP	SLG	PRO+	BR/A	SB	CS	SBR	FA	FR	G/POS	TPR
1922	Cle-A	2	3	1	1	0	0	0	0	0	0	.333	.333	.333	74	-0	0	0	0	.000	-1	/O-1	-0.1

■ MARV RACKLEY　Rackley, Marvin Eugene　b: 7/25/21, Seneca, S.C.　BL/TL, 5'10", 170 lbs.　Deb: 4/15/47

YEAR	TM/L	G	AB	R	H	2B	3B	HR	RBI	BB	SO	AVG	OBP	SLG	PRO+	BR/A	SB	CS	SBR	FA	FR	G/POS	TPR
1947	Bro-N	18	9	2	2	0	0	0	2	1	0	.222	.300	.222	39	-1	0			1.000	0	/O-2	0.0
1948	Bro-N	88	281	55	92	13	5	0	15	19	25	.327	.364	.409	107	3	8			.949	-5	O-74	-0.6
1949	*Bro-N	9	9	2	4	0	0	0	1	1	0	.444	.500	.556	175	1	0			1.000	0	/O-3	0.1
	Pit-N	11	35	5	11	2	0	0	2	0	3	.314	.351	.371	92	-0	1			1.000	0	/O-8	-0.1
	*Bro-N	54	141	23	41	4	1	1	14	13	8	.291	.351	.355	86	-2	1			.986	-8	O-44	-1.2
	Yr	74	185	30	56	7	1	1	17	16	11	.303	.358	.368	91	-2	2			.990	-8	O-55	-1.2
1950	Cin-N	5	2	0	1	0	0	0	1	0	0	.500	.500	.500	163	0	0			.000	0	H	0.0
Total	4	185	477	87	151	20	6	1	35	36	36	.317	.365	.390	100	0	10			.966	-13	O-131	-1.8

■ CHARLEY RADBOURN　Radbourn, Charles Gardner "Old Hoss"　b: 12/11/1854, Rochester, N.Y.　d: 2/5/1897, Bloomington, Ill.　BR/TR, 5'9", 168 lbs.　Deb: 5/5/1880　H

YEAR	TM/L	G	AB	R	H	2B	3B	HR	RBI	BB	SO	AVG	OBP	SLG	PRO+	BR/A	SB	CS	SBR	FA	FR	G/POS	TPR
1880	Buf-N	6	21	1	3	0	0	0		0	1	.143	.143	.143	-3	-2				.900	4	/O-3,2-3	0.2
1881	Pro-N	72	270	27	59	9	0	0	28	10	15	.219	.246	.252	58	-12				.906	-2	P-41,O-25,S-13	-0.9
1882	Pro-N	83	326	30	78	11	0	1	32	12	22	.239	.266	.282	76	-8				.912	1	P-55,O-31/S-1	-0.2
1883	Pro-N	89	381	59	108	11	3	3	48	14	16	.283	.309	.352	98	-1				.920	2	*P-76,O-20/1-2	-0.3
1884	*Pro-N	87	361	48	83	7	1	1	37	26	42	.230	.282	.263	74	-10				.892	-6	*P-75/O-7,1-5,S2	-0.3
1885	Pro-N	66	249	34	58	9	1	0	21	36	27	.233	.330	.285	104	3				.937	0	P-49,O-16/2-2	-0.3
1886	Bos-N	66	253	30	60	5	1	2	22	17	36	.237	.285	.289	78	-6	5			.924	1	P-58/O-6	-0.2

YEAR	TM/L	G	AB	R	H	2B	3B	HR	RBI	BB	SO	AVG	OBP	SLG	PRO+	BR/A	SB	CS	SBR	FA	FR	G/POS	TPR
1887	Bos-N	51	175	25	40	2	2	1	24	18	21	.229	.308	.280	64	-8	6			.848	-4	P-50/O-2	-0.1
1888	Bos-N	24	79	6	17	1	0	0	6	3	14	.215	.262	.228	56	-4	4			.895	-1	P-24	0.0
1889	Bos-N	35	122	17	23	1	0	1	13	9	19	.189	.256	.221	32	-11	3			.975	1	P-33/O-2,3-1	-0.1
1890	Bos-P	45	154	20	39	6	0	0	16	9	20	.253	.299	.292	55	-11	7			.935	0	P-41/O-4,1-1	-0.2
1891	Cin-N	29	96	11	17	2	2	0	10	4	11	.177	.225	.240	35	-8	1			.880	-3	P-26/O-2,3-1	-0.1
Total	12	653	2487	308	585	64	11	9	259	158	244	.235	.283	.281	72	-78	26			.913	-6	P-528,O-118/S123	-2.5

■ JOHN RADCLIFF
Radcliff, John Y. b: 6/29/1848, Philadelphia, Pa. d: 7/26/11, Ocean City, N.J. 5'6", 140 lbs. Deb: 5/20/1871

YEAR	TM/L	G	AB	R	H	2B	3B	HR	RBI	BB	SO	AVG	OBP	SLG	PRO+	BR/A	SB	CS	SBR	FA	FR	G/POS	TPR
1871	Ath-n	28	145	47	44	7	5	0	22	6	1	.303	.331	.421	116	3	5	1		.804	3	*S-28	0.5
1872	Bal-n	56	297	71	86	13	4	1	44	0	2	.290	.290	.370	97	-3	3	3	-1	.771	-4	*S-50/3-6,2-1	-0.5
1873	Bal-n	45	245	59	70	7	0	0	33	3	2	.286	.294	.314	81	-5	0	0	0	.762	-1	3-24,S-23/2-1	-0.5
1874	Phi-n	23	103	20	25	7	0	1	14	2	0	.243	.257	.340	87	-2	1	1	-0	.800	-3	O-15/2-4,S-3,3-1	-0.4
1875	Cen-n	5	23	2	4	0	0	0	1	0	0	.174	.208	.174	37	-1	0	0		.651	-1	/S-5	-0.2
Total	5 n	157	813	199	229	34	9	2	113	12	5	.282	.292	.353	93	-8				.764	-5	S-109/3-33,O-15,21	-1.1

■ RIP RADCLIFF
Radcliff, Raymond Allen b: 1/19/06, Kiowa, Okla. d: 5/23/62, Enid, Okla. BL/TR, 5'10", 170 lbs. Deb: 9/17/34

YEAR	TM/L	G	AB	R	H	2B	3B	HR	RBI	BB	SO	AVG	OBP	SLG	PRO+	BR/A	SB	CS	SBR	FA	FR	G/POS	TPR
1934	Chi-A	14	56	7	15	2	1	0	5	0	2	.268	.268	.339	54	-4	1	0	0	.946	1	O-14	-0.3
1935	Chi-A	146	623	95	178	28	8	10	68	53	21	.286	.346	.404	91	-9	4	4	-1	.968	-18	*O-142	-3.1
1936	Chi-A★	138	618	120	207	31	7	8	82	44	12	.335	.381	.447	100	-0	6	3	-0	.936	-17	*O-132	-2.0
1937	Chi-A	144	584	105	190	38	10	4	79	53	25	.325	.383	.445	108	8	6	1	1	.966	-4	*O-139	0.0
1938	Chi-A	129	503	64	166	23	6	5	81	36	17	.330	.376	.429	99	-1	5	7	-3	.979	-1	O-99,1-23	-0.9
1939	Chi-A	113	397	49	105	25	2	2	53	26	21	.264	.313	.353	68	-20	4	5	-1	.970	-10	O-78,1-20	-3.3
1940	StL-A	150	584	83	**200**	33	9	7	81	47	20	.342	.392	.466	119	17	6	4	-0	.973	-6	*O-139/1-4	0.2
1941	StL-A	19	71	12	20	2	2	2	14	10	1	.282	.370	.451	112	1	1	1	-0	1.000	-2	O-14/1-3	-0.2
	Det-A	96	379	47	120	14	5	3	40	19	13	.317	.351	.404	90	-6	4	4	-1	.970	-5	O-87	-1.7
	Yr	115	450	59	140	16	7	5	54	29	14	.311	.354	.411	94	-5	5	5	-2	.974	-8	*O-101/1-3	-1.9
1942	Det-A	62	144	13	36	5	0	1	20	9	6	.250	.294	.306	64	-7	0	1	-1	.978	-0	O-24/1-4	-1.0
1943	Det-A	70	115	3	30	4	0	0	10	13	3	.261	.341	.296	81	-2	1	1	-0	1.000	0	O-19/1-1	-0.4
Total	10	1081	4074	598	1267	205	50	42	533	310	141	.311	.362	.417	96	-23	40	30	-6	.967	-62	O-887/1-55	-12.7

■ DAVE RADER
Rader, David Martin b: 12/26/48, Claremore, Okla. BL/TR, 5'11", 165 lbs. Deb: 9/5/71

YEAR	TM/L	G	AB	R	H	2B	3B	HR	RBI	BB	SO	AVG	OBP	SLG	PRO+	BR/A	SB	CS	SBR	FA	FR	G/POS	TPR
1971	SF-N	3	4	0	0	0	0	0	0	0	0	.000	.000	.000	-99	-1	0	0	0	1.000	-0	/C-1	-0.1
1972	SF-N	133	459	44	119	14	1	6	41	29	31	.259	.308	.333	81	-12	1	2	-1	.985	-13	*C-127	-2.2
1973	SF-N	148	462	59	106	15	4	9	41	63	22	.229	.330	.338	82	-10	0	0	0	.991	-12	*C-148	-1.7
1974	SF-N	113	323	26	94	16	2	1	26	31	21	.291	.353	.362	96	-1	0	0	0	.984	-9	*C-109	-0.6
1975	SF-N	98	292	39	85	19	0	5	31	32	30	.291	.363	.394	106	3	1	0	0	.984	-9	*C-94	0.4
1976	SF-N	88	255	25	67	15	0	1	22	27	21	.263	.333	.333	87	-4	2	0	0	.984	-9	C-81	-1.0
1977	StL-N	66	114	15	30	7	1	1	16	9	14	.263	.317	.368	85	-3	1	0	0	.976	4	C-38	0.2
1978	Chi-N	116	305	29	62	13	3	3	36	34	26	.203	.285	.295	56	-18	1	1	-0	.977	-13	*C-114	-3.1
1979	Phi-N	31	54	3	11	1	1	1	5	6	7	.204	.283	.315	61	-3	0	0	0	.932	-4	C-25	-0.6
1980	Bos-A	50	137	14	45	11	0	3	17	14	12	.328	.391	.474	129	4	1	1	-0	.981	3	C-34/D-9	0.9
Total	10	846	2405	254	619	107	12	30	235	245	180	.257	.329	.349	86	-43	8	4	0	.983	-56	C-771/D-9	-7.8

■ DON RADER
Rader, Donald Russell b: 9/5/1893, Wolcott, Ind. d: 6/26/83, Walla Walla, Wash. BL/TR, 5'10", 164 lbs. Deb: 7/25/13

YEAR	TM/L	G	AB	R	H	2B	3B	HR	RBI	BB	SO	AVG	OBP	SLG	PRO+	BR/A	SB	CS	SBR	FA	FR	G/POS	TPR
1913	Chi-A	4	3	1	1	1	0	0	0	0	0	.333	.333	.667	193	0	0			.000	-1	/3-1,O-1	0.0
1921	Phi-N	9	32	4	9	2	0	0	3	5	0	.281	.343	.344	76	-1	0	0	0	1.000	-6	/S-9	-0.6
Total	2	13	35	5	10	3	0	0	3	5		.286	.342	.371	84	-1	0	0		1.000	-6	/S-9,O-1,3-1	-0.6

■ DOUG RADER
Rader, Douglas Lee "Rojo" or "The Red Rooster" b: 7/30/44, Chicago, Ill. BR/TR, 6'3", 215 lbs. Deb: 7/31/67 MC

YEAR	TM/L	G	AB	R	H	2B	3B	HR	RBI	BB	SO	AVG	OBP	SLG	PRO+	BR/A	SB	CS	SBR	FA	FR	G/POS	TPR
1967	Hou-N	47	162	24	54	10	4	2	26	7	31	.333	.368	.481	146	9	0	3	-2	.972	-1	1-36/3-7	0.5
1968	Hou-N	98	333	42	89	16	4	6	43	31	51	.267	.332	.393	119	8	2	2	-1	.930	1	3-86/1-5	0.9
1969	Hou-N	155	569	62	140	25	3	11	83	62	103	.246	.327	.359	94	-5	1	5	-3	.945	14	*3-154/1-4	0.8
1970	Hou-N	156	576	90	145	25	3	25	87	57	102	.252	.323	.436	106	3	3	2	-0	**.966**	24	*3-154/1-1	2.5
1971	Hou-N	135	484	51	118	21	4	12	56	40	112	.244	.306	.378	95	-4	5	1	1	.946	2	*3-135	-0.3
1972	Hou-N	152	553	70	131	24	7	22	90	57	120	.237	.314	.425	110	6	5	5	-2	.958	18	*3-152	2.2
1973	Hou-N	154	574	79	146	26	0	21	89	46	97	.254	.313	.409	99	-2	4	3	-1	.945	-5	*3-152	-0.9
1974	Hou-N	152	533	61	137	27	3	17	78	60	131	.257	.337	.415	114	9	7	2	1	.965	5	*3-152	1.4
1975	Hou-N	129	448	41	100	23	2	12	48	42	101	.223	.297	.364	89	-9	5	4	-1	**.971**	8	*3-124/S-2	-0.2
1976	SD-N	139	471	45	121	22	4	9	55	55	102	.257	.338	.378	112	7	3	4	-2	.955	14	*3-137	1.9
1977	SD-N	52	170	19	46	8	3	5	27	33	40	.271	.392	.441	137	10	0	1	-1	.961	1	3-51	0.7
	Tor-A	96	313	47	75	18	2	13	40	38	65	.240	.328	.435	104	2	2	1	0	.966	4	3-45,D-34/1-7,O-1	0.0
Total	11	1465	5186	631	1302	245	39	155	722	528	1055	.251	.325	.403	106	34	37	33	-9	.956	82	*3-1349/1-53,DSO	9.8

■ PAUL RADFORD
Radford, Paul Revere "Shorty" b: 10/14/1861, Roxbury, Mass. d: 2/21/45, Boston, Mass. BR/TR, 5'6", 148 lbs. Deb: 5/1/1883

YEAR	TM/L	G	AB	R	H	2B	3B	HR	RBI	BB	SO	AVG	OBP	SLG	PRO+	BR/A	SB	CS	SBR	FA	FR	G/POS	TPR
1883	Bos-N	72	258	46	53	6	3	0	14	9	26	.205	.232	.252	46	-16				.836	-5	*O-72	-1.9
1884	*Pro-N	97	355	56	70	11	2	1	29	25	43	.197	.250	.248	59	-16				.882	5	*O-96/P-2	-1.1
1885	Pro-N	105	371	55	90	12	5	0	32	33	43	.243	.304	.302	101	2				.852	1	*O-88,S-16/P-3,2-1	0.0
1886	KC-N	122	493	78	113	17	5	0	35	58	48	.229	.310	.284	77	-13	39			.890	10	*O-92,S-30/2-1	0.6
1887	NY-a	128	486	127	129	15	5	4	45	**106**	37	.265	.403	.342	114	17	73			.833	-2	S-76,O-37,2-18/P-2	1.3
1888	Bro-a	90	308	48	67	9	3	2	29	35		.218	.305	.286	90	-2	33			.944	9	O-88/2-2	0.4
1889	Cle-N	136	487	94	116	21	5	1	46	91	37	.238	.365	.308	91	-1	30			.942	-0	*O-136/3-1	-0.6
1890	Cle-P	122	466	98	136	24	12	2	62	82	28	.292	.406	.408	128	24	25			.895	8	O-80,S-36/3-7,2P	2.5
1891	Bos-a	133	456	102	118	11	5	0	65	96	36	.259	.393	.305	102	7	55			.906	20	*S-131/O-4,P-1	2.9
1892	Was-N	137	510	93	130	19	4	1	37	86	47	.255	.366	.314	109	10	35			.933	-7	O-62,3-54,S-20,2/2-2	0.3
1893	Was-N	124	464	87	106	18	3	2	34	104	42	.228	.378	.293	82	-6	32			.901	7	*O-123/2-1,P-1	-0.8
1894	Was-N	95	325	61	78	13	5	0	49	65	23	.240	.378	.311	70	-13	24			.852	-0	S-47,2-25,O-24	-0.8
Total	12	1361	4979	945	1206	176	57	13	462	790	**373**	.242	.351	.308	92	-8	346			.901	46	O-902,S-356/32P	2.3

■ JACK RADTKE
Radtke, Jack William b: 4/14/13, Denver, Colo. BB/TR, 5'7", 160 lbs. Deb: 8/1/36

YEAR	TM/L	G	AB	R	H	2B	3B	HR	RBI	BB	SO	AVG	OBP	SLG	PRO+	BR/A	SB	CS	SBR	FA	FR	G/POS	TPR
1936	Bro-N	33	31	8	3	0	0	0	2	4	9	.097	.200	.097	-18	-5	3			1.000	5	2-14/3-5,S-4	0.0

■ JACK RAFTER
Rafter, John Cornelius b: 2/20/1875, Troy, N.Y. d: 1/5/43, Troy, N.Y. BR/TR, 5'8", 165 lbs. Deb: 9/24/04

YEAR	TM/L	G	AB	R	H	2B	3B	HR	RBI	BB	SO	AVG	OBP	SLG	PRO+	BR/A	SB	CS	SBR	FA	FR	G/POS	TPR
1904	Pit-N	1	3	0	0	0	0	0	0	0		.000	.000	.000	-97	-1	0			1.000	0	/C-1	-0.1

■ TOM RAFTERY
Raftery, Thomas Francis b: 10/5/1881, Boston, Mass. d: 12/31/54, Boston, Mass. BR/TR, 5'10.5", 175 lbs. Deb: 4/18/09

YEAR	TM/L	G	AB	R	H	2B	3B	HR	RBI	BB	SO	AVG	OBP	SLG	PRO+	BR/A	SB	CS	SBR	FA	FR	G/POS	TPR
1909	Cle-A	8	32	6	7	2	1	0	0	4		.219	.306	.344	101	0	1			1.000	-1	/O-8	-0.1

■ TOM RAGLAND
Ragland, Thomas b: 6/16/46, Talladega, Ala. BR/TR, 5'10", 155 lbs. Deb: 4/5/71

YEAR	TM/L	G	AB	R	H	2B	3B	HR	RBI	BB	SO	AVG	OBP	SLG	PRO+	BR/A	SB	CS	SBR	FA	FR	G/POS	TPR
1971	Was-A	10	23	1	4	0	0	0	0	0	5	.174	.208	.174	10	-3	0	0	0	1.000	-1	2-10	-0.3
1972	Tex-A	25	58	3	10	2	0	0	2	5	11	.172	.238	.207	35	-5	0	1	-1	.982	3	2-13/3-5,S-3	-0.9
1973	Cle-A	67	183	16	47	7	1	0	12	8	31	.257	.292	.306	67	-8	2	3	-1	.984	13	2-65/S-2	0.7
Total	3	102	264	20	61	9	1	0	14	13	47	.231	.272	.273	56	-15	2	4	-2	.985	10	/2-88,S-5,3-5	0.5

■ LARRY RAINES
Raines, Lawrence Glenn Hope b: 3/9/30, St.Albans, W.Va. d: 1/28/78, Lansing, Mich. BR/TR, 5'10", 165 lbs. Deb: 4/16/57

YEAR	TM/L	G	AB	R	H	2B	3B	HR	RBI	BB	SO	AVG	OBP	SLG	PRO+	BR/A	SB	CS	SBR	FA	FR	G/POS	TPR
1957	Cle-A	96	244	39	64	14	0	2	16	19	40	.262	.318	.344	82	-6	5	5	0	.922	-5	3-27,S-25,2-10/O-8	-0.9
1958	Cle-A	7	9	1	0	0	0	0	0	0	5	.000	.000	.000	-99	-2	0	1	-1	.933	4	/2-2	0.0
Total	2	103	253	40	64	14	0	2	16	19	45	.253	.308	.332	76	-9	5	5	-0	.963	-2	/3-27,S-25,2-12,O-8	-0.9

■ TIM RAINES
Raines, Timothy "Rock" b: 9/16/59, Sanford, Fla. BB/TR, 5'8", 178 lbs. Deb: 9/11/79

YEAR	TM/L	G	AB	R	H	2B	3B	HR	RBI	BB	SO	AVG	OBP	SLG	PRO+	BR/A	SB	CS	SBR	FA	FR	G/POS	TPR
1979	Mon-N	6	0	3	0	0	0	0	0	0	0	—	—	—		0	2	0	1	1.000	0	/R	0.0
1980	Mon-N	15	20	5	1	0	0	0	0	6	5	.050	.269	.050	-6	-3	5	0	2	1.000	2	/2-7,O-1	0.1
1981	*Mon-N★	88	313	61	95	13	7	5	37	45	31	.304	.394	.438	134	15	**71**	11	**15**	.976	2	O-81/2-1	3.1

YEAR	TM/L	G	AB	R	H	2B	3B	HR	RBI	BB	SO	AVG	OBP	SLG	PRO+	BR/A	SB	CS	SBR	FA	FR	G/POS	TPR
1982	Mon-N★	156	647	90	179	32	8	4	43	75	83	.277	.354	.369	101	2	78	16	14	.992	3	*O-120,2-36	1.8
1983	Mon-N★	156	615	133	183	32	8	11	71	97	70	.298	.395	.429	129	27	90	14	19	.988	16	*O-154/2-7	5.8
1984	Mon-N★	160	622	106	192	38	9	8	60	87	69	.309	.395	.437	140	35	75	10	17	.988	10	*O-160/2-2	5.8
1985	Mon-N★	150	575	115	184	30	13	11	41	81	60	.320	.407	.475	155	44	70	9	16	.993	10	*O-146	6.6
1986	Mon-N★	151	580	91	194	35	10	9	62	78	60	.334	.415	.476	155	39	70	9	16	.979	11	*O-147	6.2
1987	Mon-N★	139	530	123	175	34	8	18	68	90	52	.330	.431	.526	148	40	50	5	12	.987	16	*O-139	6.1
1988	Mon-N	109	429	66	116	19	7	12	48	53	44	.270	.353	.431	119	11	33	7	6	.988	7	*O-108	2.2
1989	Mon-N	145	517	76	148	29	6	9	60	93	48	.286	.398	.418	132	25	41	9	7	.996	3	*O-139	3.3
1990	Mon-N	130	457	65	131	11	5	9	62	70	43	.287	.385	.392	119	14	49	16	5	.976	-1	*O-123	1.6
1991	Chi-A	155	609	102	163	20	6	5	50	83	68	.268	.360	.345	98	2	51	15	6	.990	10	*O-133,D-19	1.4
1992	Chi-A	144	551	102	162	22	9	7	54	81	48	.294	.384	.405	123	19	45	6	10	.994	11	*O-129,D-14	4.0
1993	*Chi-A	115	415	75	127	16	4	16	54	64	35	.306	.402	.480	139	25	21	7	2	**1.000**	-1	*O-112	2.3
1994	Chi-A	101	384	80	102	15	5	10	52	61	43	.266	.368	.409	102	2	13	0	4	.981	4	O-96	0.7
1995	Chi-A	133	502	81	143	25	4	12	67	70	52	.285	.376	.422	112	11	13	2	3	.980	1	*O-107,D-22	0.9
1996	*NY-A	59	201	45	57	10	0	9	33	34	29	.284	.390	.468	113	5	10	1	2	.988	-1	O-50/D-2	0.4
Total	18	2112	7967	1419	2352	381	109	155	862	1168	838	.295	.388	.429	126	315	787	137	154	.988	105	*O-1945/D-57,2-53	52.3

■ JOHN RAINEY

Rainey, John Paul b: 7/26/1864, Birmingham, Mich. d: 11/11/12, Detroit, Mich. BL/TR, 5'10", 164 lbs. Deb: 8/25/1887

YEAR	TM/L	G	AB	R	H	2B	3B	HR	RBI	BB	SO	AVG	OBP	SLG	PRO+	BR/A	SB	CS	SBR	FA	FR	G/POS	TPR
1887	NY-N	17	58	6	17	3	0	0	12	5	6	.293	.349	.345	98	0	0			.818	-3	3-17	-0.2
1890	Buf-P	42	166	29	39	5	1	1	20	24	15	.235	.349	.295	79	-3	12			.870	0	O-28/S-7,3-6,2-2	-0.3
Total	2	59	224	35	56	8	1	1	32	29	21	.250	.349	.308	84	-3	12			.827	-3	/O-28,3-23,S-7,2-2	-0.5

■ GARY RAJSICH

Rajsich, Gary Louis b: 10/28/54, Youngstown, Ohio BL/TL, 6'2", 210 lbs. Deb: 4/9/82 F

YEAR	TM/L	G	AB	R	H	2B	3B	HR	RBI	BB	SO	AVG	OBP	SLG	PRO+	BR/A	SB	CS	SBR	FA	FR	G/POS	TPR
1982	NY-N	80	162	17	42	8	3	2	12	17	40	.259	.333	.383	100	0	1	3	-2	1.000	-2	O-35/1-2	-0.5
1983	NY-N	11	36	5	12	3	0	1	3	3	1	.333	.400	.500	149	2	0	0	0	1.000	-0	1-10	0.2
1984	StL-N	7	7	1	1	0	0	0	2	2	1	.143	.333	.143	39	-0	0	0	0	1.000	-0	/1-3	-0.1
1985	SF-N	51	91	5	15	6	0	0	10	17	22	.165	.296	.231	52	-5	0	1	-1	.990	-1	1-23	-0.9
Total	4	149	296	28	70	17	3	3	27	39	64	.236	.329	.345	90	-3	1	4	-2	.994	-4	/1-38,O-35	-1.3

■ DOC RALSTON

Ralston, Samuel Beryl b: 8/3/1885, Pierpont, Ohio d: 8/29/50, Lancaster, Pa. BR/TR, 6', 185 lbs. Deb: 9/8/10

YEAR	TM/L	G	AB	R	H	2B	3B	HR	RBI	BB	SO	AVG	OBP	SLG	PRO+	BR/A	SB	CS	SBR	FA	FR	G/POS	TPR
1910	Was-A	21	73	4	15	1	0	0	6	2	13	.205	.256	.219	51	-4	2			.976	2	O-21	-0.4

■ BOB RAMAZZOTTI

Ramazzotti, Robert Louis b: 1/16/17, Elanora, Pa. BR/TR, 5'8.5", 175 lbs. Deb: 4/20/46

YEAR	TM/L	G	AB	R	H	2B	3B	HR	RBI	BB	SO	AVG	OBP	SLG	PRO+	BR/A	SB	CS	SBR	FA	FR	G/POS	TPR
1946	Bro-N	62	120	10	25	4	0	0	7	9	13	.208	.264	.242	43	-9	0			.939	5	3-30,2-16	-0.3
1948	Bro-N	4	3	0	0	0	0	0	0	0	1	.000	.000	.000	-97	-1	0			1.000	0	/3-2,2-1	-0.1
1949	Bro-N	5	13	1	2	0	0	1	3	0	3	.154	.154	.385	38	-1	0			.833	-1	/3-3	-0.2
	Chi-N	65	190	14	34	3	1	0	6	5	33	.179	.200	.205	9	-24	9			.972	6	3-36,S-12/2-4	-1.8
	Yr	70	203	15	36	3	1	1	9	5	36	.177	.197	.217	11	-26	9			.965	5	3-39,S-12/2-4	-2.0
1950	Chi-N	61	145	19	38	3	3	1	6	4	16	.262	.331	.345	66	-7	3			.961	-2	2-31,3-10/S-3	-0.8
1951	Chi-N	73	158	13	39	5	2	1	15	10	23	.247	.292	.323	64	-8	0	0	0	.950	13	S-51/2-6,3-1	0.7
1952	Chi-N	50	183	26	52	5	3	1	12	14	21	.284	.338	.361	93	-2	3	1	0	.979	-2	2-50	-0.1
1953	Chi-N	26	39	3	6	2	0	0	4	3	4	.154	.214	.205	10	-5	0	0	0	.911	-0	2-18	-0.4
Total	7	346	851	86	196	22	9	4	53	45	107	.230	.271	.291	52	-58	15	1		.966	18	2-126/3-82,S-66	-3.1

■ MANNY RAMIREZ

Ramirez, Manuel Aristides (Onelcida) b: 5/30/72, Brooklyn, N.Y. BR/TR, 6', 190 lbs. Deb: 9/2/93

YEAR	TM/L	G	AB	R	H	2B	3B	HR	RBI	BB	SO	AVG	OBP	SLG	PRO+	BR/A	SB	CS	SBR	FA	FR	G/POS	TPR
1993	Cle-A	22	53	5	9	1	0	2	5	2	8	.170	.200	.302	33	0	0	0	0	1.000	0	D-20/O-1	-0.6
1994	Cle-A	91	290	51	78	22	0	17	60	42	72	.269	.361	.521	124	10	4	2	0	.994	-1	O-84/D-5	0.7
1995	*Cle-A★	137	484	85	149	26	1	31	107	75	112	.308	.406	.558	146	33	6	6	-2	.978	-4	*O-131/D-5	2.2
1996	*Cle-A	152	550	94	170	45	3	33	112	85	104	.309	.404	.582	145	39	8	5	-1	.970	8	*O-149/D-3	3.8
Total	4	402	1377	235	406	94	4	83	284	204	296	.295	.389	.550	137	77	18	13	-2	.978	4	O-365/D-33	6.1

■ MARIO RAMIREZ

Ramirez, Mario (Torres) b: 9/12/57, Yauco, P.R. BR/TR, 5'9", 159 lbs. Deb: 4/25/80

YEAR	TM/L	G	AB	R	H	2B	3B	HR	RBI	BB	SO	AVG	OBP	SLG	PRO+	BR/A	SB	CS	SBR	FA	FR	G/POS	TPR
1980	NY-N	18	24	2	5	0	0	0	0	1	7	.208	.240	.208	27	-2	0	0	0	1.000	3	/S-7/2-4,3-3	0.1
1981	SD-N	13	13	1	1	0	0	0	1	1	2	.077	.200	.077	-21	-2	0	0	0	1.000	4	/S-2,3-2	0.2
1982	SD-N	13	23	1	4	1	0	0	1	2	4	.174	.240	.217	30	-2	0	0	0	.963	-4	/S-8,2-1,3-1	0.0
1983	SD-N	55	107	11	21	6	3	0	12	20	23	.196	.328	.308	80	-2	0	0	0	.985	-2	S-38/3-1	-0.2
1984	*SD-N	48	59	12	7	1	0	2	9	13	14	.119	.278	.237	46	-4	0	0	0	.971	-1	S-33/3-6,2-2	-0.3
1985	SD-N	37	60	6	17	0	0	2	5	3	11	.283	.317	.383	97	-0	0	0	0	.918	-5	S-27/2-7	-0.4
Total	6	184	286	33	55	8	3	4	28	41	64	.192	.296	.283	64	-13	0	0	0	.970	-6	S-115/2-14,3-13	-0.6

■ MILT RAMIREZ

Ramirez, Milton (Barboza) b: 4/2/50, Mayaguez, P.R. BR/TR, 5'9", 150 lbs. Deb: 4/11/70

YEAR	TM/L	G	AB	R	H	2B	3B	HR	RBI	BB	SO	AVG	OBP	SLG	PRO+	BR/A	SB	CS	SBR	FA	FR	G/POS	TPR
1970	StL-N	62	79	8	15	2	1	0	3	8	9	.190	.264	.241	36	-7	0	1	-1	.923	10	S-59/3-1	0.5
1971	StL-N	4	11	2	3	0	0	0	0	1	0	.273	.385	.273	86	-0	0	0	0	.947	-1	/S-4	-0.1
1979	Oak-A	28	62	4	10	3	1	0	3	3	8	.161	.200	.210	11	-8	0	0	0	.923	-5	3-12,2-11/S-8	-1.2
Total	3	94	152	14	28	5	2	0	6	13	18	.184	.248	.230	30	-15	0	1	-1	.920	4	/S-71,3-13,2-11	-0.8

■ ORLANDO RAMIREZ

Ramirez, Orlando (Leal) b: 12/18/51, Cartagena, Colombia BR/TR, 5'10", 175 lbs. Deb: 7/6/74

YEAR	TM/L	G	AB	R	H	2B	3B	HR	RBI	BB	SO	AVG	OBP	SLG	PRO+	BR/A	SB	CS	SBR	FA	FR	G/POS	TPR
1974	Cal-A	31	86	4	14	0	0	0	7	6	23	.163	.217	.163	11	-10	2	1	0	.956	5	S-31	-0.1
1975	Cal-A	44	100	10	24	4	1	0	6	11	22	.240	.315	.300	80	-2	9	6	-1	.905	0	S-40	0.0
1976	Cal-A	30	70	3	14	1	0	0	5	6	13	.200	.263	.214	44	-5	3	2	-0	.966	4	S-30	0.1
1977	Cal-A	25	13	6	1	0	0	0	0	1	6	.077	.077	.077	-60	-3	1	0	0	1.000	8	/2-5,S-3,D-1	0.6
1979	Cal-A	13	12	1	0	0	0	0	0	1	6	.000	.143	.000	-60	-3	1	0	0	.844	4	S-10/D-1	0.2
Total	5	143	281	24	53	5	1	0	16	24	65	.189	.255	.214	37	-23	16	9	-1	.931	22	S-114/2-5,D-2	0.8

■ RAFAEL RAMIREZ

Ramirez, Rafael Emilio (Peguero) b: 2/18/58, San Pedro De Macoris, D.R. BR/TR, 6', 185 lbs. Deb: 8/4/80

YEAR	TM/L	G	AB	R	H	2B	3B	HR	RBI	BB	SO	AVG	OBP	SLG	PRO+	BR/A	SB	CS	SBR	FA	FR	G/POS	TPR
1980	Atl-N	50	165	17	44	6	1	2	11	2	33	.267	.292	.352	76	-5	2	1	0	.949	-10	S-46	-1.1
1981	Atl-N	95	307	30	67	16	2	2	20	24	47	.218	.277	.303	63	-15	7	3	0	.942	-2	S-95	-0.8
1982	*Atl-N	157	609	74	169	24	4	10	52	36	49	.278	.321	.379	91	-7	27	14	-0	.956	17	*S-157	2.4
1983	Atl-N	152	622	82	165	13	5	7	58	36	48	.265	.307	.368	89	-9	16	12	-2	.949	8	*S-152	1.2
1984	Atl-N☆	145	591	51	157	22	4	2	48	26	70	.266	.298	.327	70	-23	14	17	-6	.959	-3	*S-145	-2.0
1985	Atl-N	138	568	54	141	25	4	5	58	20	63	.248	.274	.333	65	-27	2	6	-3	.954	9	*S-133	-0.9
1986	Atl-N	134	496	57	119	21	1	8	33	21	60	.240	.275	.335	64	-25	19	8	1	.952	13	S-86,3-57/O-3	-0.4
1987	Atl-N	56	179	22	47	12	0	1	21	8	16	.263	.302	.346	68	-8	6	3	0	.946	-6	S-38,3-12	-1.1
1988	Hou-N	155	566	51	156	30	6	6	59	18	61	.276	.302	.378	98	-4	3	2	0	.965	-10	*S-154	-0.2
1989	Hou-N	151	537	46	132	20	2	6	54	29	64	.246	.284	.324	76	-18	3	1	0	.945	-41	*S-149	-5.1
1990	Hou-N	132	445	44	116	19	3	2	37	24	46	.261	.300	.330	75	-15	10	5	0	.953	-18	*S-129	-2.5
1991	Hou-N	101	233	17	55	10	0	1	20	13	40	.236	.276	.292	64	-12	3	1	0	.953	-14	S-45,2-27/3-2	-1.1
1992	Hou-N	73	176	17	44	6	0	1	13	7	24	.250	.283	.301	68	-8	0	0	0	.961	-6	S-57/3-1	-1.1
Total	13	1539	5494	562	1432	224	31	53	484	264	621	.261	.297	.342	77	-177	112	75	-11	.953	-64	*S-1386/3-72,2-27,O	-14.1

■ DOMINGO RAMOS

Ramos, Domingo Antonio (De Ramos) b: 3/29/58, Santiago, D.R. BR/TR, 5'10", 155 lbs. Deb: 9/8/78

YEAR	TM/L	G	AB	R	H	2B	3B	HR	RBI	BB	SO	AVG	OBP	SLG	PRO+	BR/A	SB	CS	SBR	FA	FR	G/POS	TPR
1978	NY-A	1	0	0	0	0	0	0	0	0	0	—	—	—		0	0	0	0	.000	0	/S-1	0.0
1980	Tor-A	5	16	0	2	0	0	0	0	0	3	.125	.222	.125	-2	-2	0	0	0	1.000	0	/2-2,S-2,D-1	-0.2
1982	Sea-A	8	26	3	4	2	0	0	1	3	2	.154	.241	.231	30	-3	0	0	0	.920	-5	/S-8	-0.8
1983	Sea-A	53	127	14	36	4	2	0	10	7	12	.283	.326	.362	86	0	3	1	0	.948	8	S-28/2-8,3-8,D-2	0.8
1984	Sea-A	59	81	6	15	2	0	0	5	8	13	.185	.233	.210	24	-8	2	2	0	.911	9	3-38,S-13/1-5,2-3	-1.5
1985	Sea-A	75	168	19	33	6	1	0	15	17	23	.196	.270	.250	43	-13	0	1	-1	.951	-8	S-36,2-20,1-14/3-7	-1.8
1986	Sea-A	49	99	8	18	2	0	0	5	8	15	.182	.250	.202	25	-10	0	1	-1	.966	13	S-21,2-16/3-8,D-2	0.3
1987	Sea-A	42	103	9	32	6	1	0	9	6	32	.311	.336	.427	96	-1	0	1	-1	.925	7	S-25/3-7,2-6,D-2	0.7
1988	Cle-A	22	46	7	12	1	0	0	5	5	8	.261	.320	.283	68	-2	0	0	0	1.000	2	2-11/1-5,S-4,3-2	0.0
	Cal-A	10	15	3	2	0	0	0	0	0	7	.133	.133	.133	-26	-2	0	0	0	1.000	-0	/3-8,O-1	-0.3
	Yr	32	61	10	14	1	0	0	5	5	15	.230	.277	.246	47	-4	0	0	0	1.000	2	2-11,3-10/1-5,S,O	-0.3

YEAR	TM/L	G	AB	R	H	2B	3B	HR	RBI	BB	SO	AVG	OBP	SLG	PRO+	BR/A	SB	CS	SBR	FA	FR	G/POS	TPR
1989	*Chi-N	85	179	18	47	6	2	1	19	17	23	.263	.333	.335	85	-3	1	1	-0	.959	3	S-42,3-30	0.2
1990	Chi-N	98	226	22	60	5	0	2	17	27	29	.265	.346	.314	77	-6	0	2	-1	.932	-15	3-66,S-21/2-1	-2.1
Total	11	507	1086	109	261	34	2	8	85	92	138	.240	.304	.297	64	-53	6	9	-4	.955	7	S-201,3-174/21DO	-3.7

■ CHUCHO RAMOS
Ramos, Jesus Manuel (Garcia) b: 4/12/18, Maturin, Venez. d: 9/2/77, Caracas, Venez. BR/TL, 5'10.5", 167 lbs. Deb: 5/7/44

YEAR	TM/L	G	AB	R	H	2B	3B	HR	RBI	BB	SO	AVG	OBP	SLG	PRO+	BR/A	SB	CS	SBR	FA	FR	G/POS	TPR
1944	Cin-N	4	10	1	5	1	0	0	0	0	0	.500	.500	.600	217	-1				1.000	-1	/O-3	0.0

■ JOHN RAMOS
Ramos, John Joseph b: 8/6/65, Tampa, Fla. BR/TR, 6', 190 lbs. Deb: 9/18/91

YEAR	TM/L	G	AB	R	H	2B	3B	HR	RBI	BB	SO	AVG	OBP	SLG	PRO+	BR/A	SB	CS	SBR	FA	FR	G/POS	TPR
1991	NY-A	10	26	4	8	1	0	0	3	1	3	.308	.333	.346	88	-0	0	0	0	1.000	0	/C-5,D-4	0.0

■ PEDRO RAMOS
Ramos, Pedro (Guerra) "Pete" b: 4/28/35, Pinar Del Rio, Cuba BB/TR, 6', 185 lbs. Deb: 4/11/55

YEAR	TM/L	G	AB	R	H	2B	3B	HR	RBI	BB	SO	AVG	OBP	SLG	PRO+	BR/A	SB	CS	SBR	FA	FR	G/POS	TPR
1955	Was-A	59	38	6	3	0	0	0	0	2	18	.079	.125	.079	-47	-8	0	1	-1	.964	-1	P-45	0.0
1956	Was-A	56	44	9	9	0	2	0	2	2	16	.205	.239	.295	40	-4	0	1	-1	1.000	-0	P-37	0.0
1957	Was-A	56	76	6	13	0	0	1	10	2	27	.171	.192	.211	10	-9	0	0	0	1.000	-0	P-43	0.0
1958	Was-A	53	88	9	21	1	0	0	10	0	33	.239	.239	.250	35	-8	0	0	0	.982	-1	P-43	0.0
1959	Was-A☆	45	75	7	11	1	1	1	2	4	38	.147	.190	.227	14	-9	1	0	0	1.000	-1	P-37	0.0
1960	Was-A	53	86	6	10	3	0	2	4	1	36	.116	.126	.221	-8	-13	0	0	0	1.000	0	P-43	0.0
1961	Min-A	53	93	8	16	1	0	3	11	3	42	.172	.206	.280	27	-10	0	0	0	.955	-3	P-42	0.0
1962	Cle-A	39	68	6	10	3	0	3	8	1	29	.147	.171	.324	31	-7	0	0	0	.962	0	P-37	0.0
1963	Cle-A	54	55	13	6	0	0	3	7	3	32	.109	.155	.273	17	-6	0	0	0	.963	-2	P-36	0.0
1964	Cle-A	44	39	6	7	0	0	2	2	2	22	.179	.220	.333	52	-3	0	0	0	.960	-1	P-36	0.0
	NY-A	13	5	0	0	0	0	0	0	0	0	.000	.000	.000	-98	-1	0	0	0	1.000	-1	P-13	0.0
	Yr	57	44	6	7	0	0	2	2	2	24	.159	.196	.295	34	-4	0	0	0	.960	-2	P-49	0.0
1965	NY-A	65	12	0	1	0	0	0	0	0	8	.083	.083	.083	-53	-2	0	0	0	.895	-1	P-65	0.0
1966	NY-A	52	13	0	2	0	0	0	0	0	5	.154	.154	.154	-12	-2	0	0	0	.952	-0	P-52	0.0
1967	Phi-N	6	1	0	0	0	0	0	0	0	0	.000	.000	.000	-99	-0	0	0	0	1.000	1	/P-6	0.0
1969	Pit-N	5	1	0	0	0	0	0	0	0	0	.000	.000	.000	-99	-0	0	0	0	1.000	-0	/P-5	0.0
	Cin-N	38	8	0	0	0	0	0	0	1	4	.000	.111	.000	-63	-2	0	0	0	1.000	-0	/P-38	0.0
	Yr	43	9	0	0	0	0	0	0	1	5	.000	.100	.000	-67	-2	0	0	0	1.000	-0	/P-43	0.0
1970	Was-A	5	1	0	0	0	0	0	0	0	0	.000	.500	.000	52	0	0	0	0	1.000	-0	/P-4	0.0
Total	15	696	703	76	109	9	3	15	56	22	316	.155	.183	.240	14	-85	2	2	-1	.977	-9	P-582	0.0

■ BOBBY RAMOS
Ramos, Roberto b: 11/5/55, Havana, Cuba BR/TR, 5'11", 208 lbs. Deb: 9/26/78

YEAR	TM/L	G	AB	R	H	2B	3B	HR	RBI	BB	SO	AVG	OBP	SLG	PRO+	BR/A	SB	CS	SBR	FA	FR	G/POS	TPR
1978	Mon-N	2	4	0	0	0	0	0	0	0	0	.000	.000	.000	-99	-1	0	0	0	1.000	-0	/C-1	-0.1
1980	Mon-N	13	32	5	5	2	0	0	2	5	5	.156	.270	.219	38	-3	0	0	0	.964	0	C-12	-0.2
1981	Mon-N	26	41	4	8	1	0	1	3	3	5	.195	.250	.293	53	-3	0	0	0	.974	4	C-23	0.1
1982	NY-A	4	11	1	1	0	0	1	2	0	3	.091	.091	.364	18	-1	0	0	0	1.000	-1	/C-4	0.0
1983	Mon-N	27	61	2	14	3	1	0	5	8	11	.230	.329	.311	79	-2	0	0	0	.984	4	C-25	0.4
1984	Mon-N	31	83	8	16	1	0	2	5	6	13	.193	.247	.277	49	-6	0	0	0	.982	7	C-31	0.2
Total	6	103	232	20	44	7	1	4	17	22	38	.190	.263	.280	53	-15	0	0	0	.980	15	/C-96	0.4

■ FERNANDO RAMSEY
Ramsey, Fernando David (Ramsey) b: 12/20/65, Rainbow, Panama BR/TR, 6'1", 175 lbs. Deb: 9/7/92

YEAR	TM/L	G	AB	R	H	2B	3B	HR	RBI	BB	SO	AVG	OBP	SLG	PRO+	BR/A	SB	CS	SBR	FA	FR	G/POS	TPR
1992	Chi-N	18	25	0	3	0	0	0	2	0	6	.120	.120	.120	-31	-4	0	0	0	1.000	-4	O-15	-1.0

■ MIKE RAMSEY
Ramsey, Michael James b: 7/8/60, Thomson, Ga. BB/TL, 6'", 170 lbs. Deb: 4/6/87

YEAR	TM/L	G	AB	R	H	2B	3B	HR	RBI	BB	SO	AVG	OBP	SLG	PRO+	BR/A	SB	CS	SBR	FA	FR	G/POS	TPR
1987	LA-N	48	125	18	29	4	2	0	12	10	32	.232	.289	.296	57	-8	2	4	-2	.973	-3	O-43	-1.4

■ MIKE RAMSEY
Ramsey, Michael Jeffrey b: 3/29/54, Roanoke, Va. BB/TR, 6'1", 170 lbs. Deb: 9/4/78

YEAR	TM/L	G	AB	R	H	2B	3B	HR	RBI	BB	SO	AVG	OBP	SLG	PRO+	BR/A	SB	CS	SBR	FA	FR	G/POS	TPR
1978	StL-N	12	5	4	1	0	0	0	0	0	1	.200	.200	.200	12	-1	0	0	0	.909	4	/S-4	0.3
1980	StL-N	59	126	11	33	8	0	0	8	3	17	.262	.279	.341	70	-5	0	0	0	.960	-2	2-24,S-20/3-8	-0.3
1981	StL-N	47	124	19	32	3	0	0	9	8	16	.258	.303	.282	65	-5	4	0	1	.966	13	2-35/3-5,2-1,0-1	1.1
1982	*StL-N	112	256	18	59	8	2	1	21	22	34	.230	.294	.289	63	-12	6	5	-1	.963	8	2-43,3-28,S-22/O-2	-0.2
1983	StL-N	97	175	25	46	4	3	1	16	12	23	.263	.314	.337	80	-5	4	2	0	.968	3	2-66,S-20/3-8,0-1	0.0
1984	StL-N	21	15	1	1	1	0	0	0	0	6	.067	.125	.133	-28	-3	0	0	0	1.000	0	/2-7,S-7,3-1	0.2
	Mon-N	37	70	2	15	1	0	0	3	0	13	.214	.214	.229	26	-7	0	0	0	.975	1	S-26,2-12	-0.4
	Yr	58	85	3	16	2	0	0	3	1	16	.188	.198	.212	16	-10	0	0	0	.978	5	S-33,2-19/3-1	-0.2
1985	LA-N	9	15	1	2	1	0	0	2	4	1	.133	.235	.200	24	-2	0	0	0	.923	-1	/S-4,2-2	-0.1
Total	7	394	786	81	189	26	6	2	57	48	111	.240	.286	.296	63	-39	14	7	0	.964	33	2-155,S-138/3-50,O	0.6

■ BILL RAMSEY
Ramsey, William Thrace "Square Jaw" b: 10/20/20, Osceola, Ark. BR/TR, 6', 175 lbs. Deb: 4/19/45

YEAR	TM/L	G	AB	R	H	2B	3B	HR	RBI	BB	SO	AVG	OBP	SLG	PRO+	BR/A	SB	CS	SBR	FA	FR	G/POS	TPR
1945	Bos-N	78	137	16	40	8	0	1	12	4	22	.292	.326	.372	93	-2	1			.963	-7	O-43	-1.0

■ DICK RAND
Rand, Richard Hilton b: 3/7/31, South Gate, Cal. BR/TR, 6'2", 185 lbs. Deb: 9/16/53

YEAR	TM/L	G	AB	R	H	2B	3B	HR	RBI	BB	SO	AVG	OBP	SLG	PRO+	BR/A	SB	CS	SBR	FA	FR	G/POS	TPR
1953	StL-N	9	31	3	9	1	0	0	1	2	6	.290	.333	.323	72	-1	0	0	0	.984	3	/C-9	0.2
1955	StL-N	3	10	1	3	0	0	0	3	1	1	.300	.364	.600	150	1	0	1	-1	1.000	-2	/C-3	-0.1
1957	Pit-N	60	105	7	23	2	1	1	9	11	24	.219	.293	.286	58	-6	0	0	0	.973	0	C-57	-0.5
Total	3	72	146	11	35	3	1	2	13	14	31	.240	.306	.315	68	-7	0	1	-1	.977	2	/C-69	-0.4

■ JOE RANDA
Randa, Joseph Gregory b: 12/18/69, Milwaukee, Wis. BR/TR, 5'11", 190 lbs. Deb: 4/30/95

YEAR	TM/L	G	AB	R	H	2B	3B	HR	RBI	BB	SO	AVG	OBP	SLG	PRO+	BR/A	SB	CS	SBR	FA	FR	G/POS	TPR
1995	KC-A	34	70	6	12	2	0	1	5	6	17	.171	.237	.243	25	-8	0	1	-0	.949	2	3-22/2-9,D-2	-0.6
1996	KC-A	110	337	36	102	24	1	6	47	26	47	.303	.354	.433	100	0	13	4	2	.951	-4	3-92,2-15/1-7,D-1	-0.2
Total	2	144	407	42	114	26	1	7	52	32	64	.280	.334	.400	87	-8	13	5	1	.951	-2	3-114/2-24,1-7,D-3	-0.8

■ SAP RANDALL
Randall, James Odell b: 8/19/60, Mobile, Ala. BB/TR, 5'11", 195 lbs. Deb: 8/2/88

YEAR	TM/L	G	AB	R	H	2B	3B	HR	RBI	BB	SO	AVG	OBP	SLG	PRO+	BR/A	SB	CS	SBR	FA	FR	G/POS	TPR
1988	Chi-A	4	12	1	0	0	0	0	0	1	3	.000	.143	.000	-57	-3	0	0	0	1.000	0	/1-2,O-1,D-1	-0.3

■ NEWT RANDALL
Randall, Newton J. b: 2/3/1880, New Lowell, Ont., Canada d: 5/3/55, Duluth, Minn. BR/TR, 5'10", Deb: 4/18/07

YEAR	TM/L	G	AB	R	H	2B	3B	HR	RBI	BB	SO	AVG	OBP	SLG	PRO+	BR/A	SB	CS	SBR	FA	FR	G/POS	TPR
1907	Chi-N	22	78	6	16	4	2	0	4	8		.205	.279	.308	79	-2	2			.904	1	O-21	-0.2
	Bos-N	75	258	16	55	6	3	0	15	19		.213	.285	.260	71	-8	4			.920	-8	O-73	-2.1
	Yr	97	336	22	71	10	5	0	19	27		.211	.284	.271	73	-10	6			.915	-7	O-94	-2.3

■ BOB RANDALL
Randall, Robert Lee b: 6/10/48, Norton, Kan. BR/TR, 6'3", 180 lbs. Deb: 4/13/76 C

YEAR	TM/L	G	AB	R	H	2B	3B	HR	RBI	BB	SO	AVG	OBP	SLG	PRO+	BR/A	SB	CS	SBR	FA	FR	G/POS	TPR
1976	Min-A	153	475	55	127	18	4	1	34	28	38	.267	.319	.328	88	-7	3	5	-2	.969	-4	*2-153	-0.4
1977	Min-A	103	306	36	73	11	0	0	22	15	25	.239	.290	.294	60	-17	1	4	-2	.985	10	*2-101/1-3,1-3,D-1	-0.4
1978	Min-A	119	330	36	89	11	3	0	21	24	22	.270	.331	.321	82	-7	5	3	-0	.983	10	*2-116/3-2,D-1	1.0
1979	Min-A	80	199	25	49	7	0	0	14	15	17	.246	.299	.281	55	-12	2	2	-1	.983	7	2-71/3-7,S-1,0-1	-0.3
1980	Min-A	5	15	2	3	0	0	0	1	0	0	.200	.250	.267	39	-1	0	0	0	.909	-0	/3-4,2-1	-0.1
Total	5	460	1325	154	341	50	9	1	91	83	102	.257	.311	.311	74	-44	11	14	-5	.979	22	2-442/3-14,D-2,OS1	-0.0

■ LEN RANDLE
Randle, Leonard Shenoff b: 2/12/49, Long Beach, Cal. BB/TR, 5'10", 169 lbs. Deb: 6/16/71

YEAR	TM/L	G	AB	R	H	2B	3B	HR	RBI	BB	SO	AVG	OBP	SLG	PRO+	BR/A	SB	CS	SBR	FA	FR	G/POS	TPR
1971	Was-A	75	215	27	47	11	0	2	13	24	56	.219	.300	.298	74	-7	1	1	-0	.967	5	2-66	0.3
1972	Tex-A	74	249	23	48	13	0	2	21	13	51	.193	.236	.269	52	-15	4	5	-2	.952	1	2-65/S-4,O-2	-1.5
1973	Tex-A	10	29	3	6	1	1	1	1	0	2	.207	.207	.414	74	-1	0	2	-1	.964	-2	/2-5,O-2	-0.5
1974	Tex-A	151	520	65	157	17	4	1	49	29	43	.302	.341	.356	103	2	26	17	-2	.935	1	3-89,2-40,O-21,/SD	0.1
1975	Tex-A	156	601	85	166	24	7	4	57	57	80	.276	.343	.359	99	0	16	19	-7	.973	15	2-79,O-66,3/CSD	1.0
1976	Tex-A	142	539	53	121	11	6	1	51	46	63	.224	.288	.273	63	-24	30	15	0	.971	-4	*2-113,O-30/3-2,D-1	-2.3
1977	NY-N	136	513	78	156	22	7	5	27	65	70	.304	.384	.404	117	14	33	21	-3	.961	-7	*3-110,2-20/O-6,S-1	0.5
1978	NY-N	132	437	53	102	16	8	2	35	64	57	.233	.333	.320	86	-7	14	11	-2	.967	-7	*3-124/2-5	-0.5
1979	NY-A	20	39	2	7	0	0	0	3	3	2	.179	.238	.179	15	-5	1	1	-0	1.000	-0	O-11/D-2	-0.5
1980	Chi-N	130	489	57	135	19	6	5	39	50	55	.276	.344	.370	93	-8	49	19	13	.929	-7	*3-111,2-17/O-6	-1.4
1981	Sea-A	82	273	22	63	9	1	4	25	17	22	.231	.278	.315	68	-11	11	6	-3	.986	7	3-59,2-21/O-5,S-3	-0.4

YEAR	TM/L	G	AB	R	H	2B	3B	HR	RBI	BB	SO	AVG	OBP	SLG	PRO+	BR/A	SB	CS	SBR	FA	FR	G/POS	TPR
1982	Sea-A	30	46	10	8	2	0	0	1	4	4	.174	.240	.217	26	-5	2	2	-1	.964	6	D-13/3-9,2-6	0.0
Total	12	1138	3950	488	1016	145	40	27	322	372	505	.257	.323	.335	87	-63	156	112	-20	.953	9	3-521,2-437,O/DSC	-6.5

■ WILLIE RANDOLPH

Randolph, Willie Larry   b: 7/6/54, Holly Hill, S.C.   BR/TR, 5'11", 166 lbs.   Deb: 7/29/75   C

YEAR	TM/L	G	AB	R	H	2B	3B	HR	RBI	BB	SO	AVG	OBP	SLG	PRO+	BR/A	SB	CS	SBR	FA	FR	G/POS	TPR
1975	*Pit-N	30	61	9	10	1	0	0	3	7	6	.164	.250	.180	21	-6	1	0	0	.962	4	2-14/3-1	-0.2
1976	*NY-A†	125	430	59	115	15	4	1	40	58	39	.267	.358	.328	103	4	37	12	4	.974	15	*2-124	3.2
1977	*NY-A★	147	551	91	151	28	11	4	40	64	53	.274	.351	.387	102	3	13	6	0	.980	5	*2-147	1.9
1978	NY-A	134	499	87	139	18	6	3	42	82	51	.279	.385	.357	112	12	36	7	7	.978	-8	*2-134	2.1
1979	NY-A	153	574	98	155	15	13	5	61	95	39	.270	.376	.368	104	7	33	12	3	.985	9	*2-153	2.9
1980	*NY-A★	138	513	99	151	23	7	7	46	**119**	45	.294	.429	.407	133	31	30	5	6	.976	-7	*2-138	3.8
1981	*NY-A★	93	357	59	83	14	3	2	24	57	24	.232	.338	.305	88	-4	14	5	1	.977	-2	2-93	0.1
1982	*NY-A	144	553	85	155	21	4	3	36	75	35	.280	.369	.349	100	3	16	9	-1	.981	-3	*2-142/D-1	0.7
1983	NY-A	104	420	73	117	21	1	2	38	53	32	.279	.361	.348	100	2	12	4	1	.979	3	*2-104	1.1
1984	NY-A	142	564	86	162	24	2	2	31	86	42	.287	.382	.348	108	10	10	6	-1	.985	-3	*2-143	1.1
1985	NY-A	143	497	75	137	21	2	5	40	85	39	.276	.386	.356	107	9	16	9	-1	.972	-12	*2-139/D-1	0.5
1986	NY-A	141	492	76	136	15	2	5	50	94	49	.276	.396	.346	105	9	15	2	3	.981	-2	*2-119/D-1	2.4
1987	NY-A	120	449	96	137	24	2	7	67	82	25	.305	.415	.414	122	19	11	1	3	.981	-2	*2-110	0.1
1988	NY-A	110	404	43	93	20	1	2	34	55	39	.230	.325	.300	77	-11	8	4	0	.988	8	*2-140	0.7
1989	LA-N★	145	549	62	155	18	0	2	36	71	51	.282	.369	.326	102	0	7	6	-2	.987	-1	2-26	-0.1
1990	LA-N	26	96	15	26	4	0	1	9	13	9	.271	.364	.344	98	0	1	0	0	.969	-2	2-26	-1.4
	*Oak-A	93	292	37	75	9	3	1	21	32	21	.257	.332	.318	86	-5	6	1	1	.982	-12	2-84/D-6	
1991	Mil-A	124	431	60	141	14	3	0	54	75	38	.327	.427	.374	127	20	4	2	0	.969	10	*2-121/D-2	3.3
1992	NY-N	90	286	29	72	11	1	2	15	40	34	.252	.352	.318	90	-1	1	3	-2	.977	-14	2-79	-1.6
Total	18	2202	8018	1239	2210	316	65	54	687	1243	675	.276	.375	.351	105	105	271	94	25	.980	0	*2-2152/D-11,3-1	23.1

■ MERRITT RANEW

Ranew, Merritt Thomas   b: 5/10/38, Albany, Ga.   BL/TR, 5'10", 180 lbs.   Deb: 4/13/62

YEAR	TM/L	G	AB	R	H	2B	3B	HR	RBI	BB	SO	AVG	OBP	SLG	PRO+	BR/A	SB	CS	SBR	FA	FR	G/POS	TPR
1962	Hou-N	71	218	26	51	6	8	4	24	14	43	.234	.289	.390	87	-5	2	2	-1	.980	-6	C-58	-0.9
1963	Chi-N	78	154	18	52	8	1	3	15	9	32	.338	.382	.461	134	7	1	0	0	.980	-5	C-37/1-9	0.3
1964	Chi-N	16	33	0	3	0	0	0	1	2	6	.091	.167	.091	-24	-5	0	0	0	1.000	2	/C-9	-0.3
	Mil-N	9	17	1	2	0	0	0	1	0	3	.118	.118	.118	-33	-3	0	1	-1	1.000	-1	/C-3	-0.5
	Yr	25	50	1	5	0	0	0	2	2	9	.100	.151	.100	-27	-8	0	1	-1	1.000	1	C-12	
1965	Cal-A	41	91	12	19	4	0	1	10	7	22	.209	.265	.286	58	-5	0	0	0	.988	-10	C-13/O-3,3-1	-1.5
1969	Sea-A	54	81	11	20	2	0	0	4	10	14	.247	.330	.272	71	-3	3	3	-1	.969	-6	C-44/1-9,0-3,3-1	-0.9
Total	5	269	594	68	147	20	9	8	54	42	120	.247	.304	.352	83	-14	3	3	-1	.982	-25	C-144/1-9,0-3,3-1	-3.8

■ JEFF RANSOM

Ransom, Jeffrey Dean   b: 11/11/60, Fresno, Cal.   BR/TR, 5'11", 185 lbs.   Deb: 9/5/81

YEAR	TM/L	G	AB	R	H	2B	3B	HR	RBI	BB	SO	AVG	OBP	SLG	PRO+	BR/A	SB	CS	SBR	FA	FR	G/POS	TPR
1981	SF-N	5	15	2	4	1	0	0	1	1	1	.267	.313	.333	85	-0	0	0	0	1.000	2	/C-5	0.2
1982	SF-N	15	44	5	7	0	0	0	3	6	7	.159	.260	.159	20	-5	0	0	0	.988	2	C-14	-0.3
1983	SF-N	6	20	3	4	0	0	1	3	4	7	.200	.333	.350	92	-0	0	0	0	.946	-2	/C-6	-0.1
Total	3	26	79	10	15	1	0	1	7	11	15	.190	.289	.241	50	-5	0	0	0	.980	2	/C-25	-0.2

■ EARL RAPP

Rapp, Earl Wellington   b: 5/20/21, Corunna, Mich.   d: 2/13/92, Swedesboro, N.J.   BL/TR, 6'2", 185 lbs.   Deb: 4/28/49

YEAR	TM/L	G	AB	R	H	2B	3B	HR	RBI	BB	SO	AVG	OBP	SLG	PRO+	BR/A	SB	CS	SBR	FA	FR	G/POS	TPR
1949	Det-A	1	0	0	0	0	0	0	0	1	0	—	1.000	—	175	0	0	0	0	.000	0	H	0.0
	Chi-A	19	54	3	14	1	1	0	11	5	6	.259	.322	.315	71	-2	1	1	-0	.974	2	O-13	-0.1
	Yr	20	54	3	14	1	1	0	11	6	6	.259	.333	.315	74	-2	1	1	-0	.974	2	O-13	-0.1
1951	NY-N	13	11	0	1	0	0	0	1	2	3	.091	.231	.091	-10	-2	0	0	0	.000	0	H	-0.2
	StL-N	26	98	14	32	5	3	2	14	11	11	.327	.394	.500	137	5	1	0	0	.979	0	O-25	0.4
1952	StL-A	30	49	3	7	4	0	0	8	4	8	.143	.143	.224	1	-7	0	0	0	1.000	-1	/O-7	-0.8
	Was-A	46	67	7	19	6	0	0	9	6	13	.284	.351	.373	105	0	0	0	0	.917	-2	O-10	-0.2
	Yr	76	116	10	26	10	0	0	13	6	21	.224	.268	.310	61	-6	0	0	0	.958	-3	O-17	-1.0
Total	3	135	279	27	73	16	4	2	39	25	41	.262	.325	.369	89	-5	1	0	0	.973	-0	/O-55	-0.9

■ GOLDIE RAPP

Rapp, Joseph Aloysius   b: 2/6/1892, Cincinnati, Ohio   d: 7/1/66, LaMesa, Cal.   BB/TR, 5'10", 165 lbs.   Deb: 4/13/21

YEAR	TM/L	G	AB	R	H	2B	3B	HR	RBI	BB	SO	AVG	OBP	SLG	PRO+	BR/A	SB	CS	SBR	FA	FR	G/POS	TPR
1921	NY-N	58	181	21	39	9	1	0	15	15	13	.215	.276	.276	46	-14	3	11	-6	.941	13	3-56	-0.3
	Phi-N	52	202	28	56	7	1	0	10	14	8	.277	.324	.337	70	-9	7	-2		.950	-2	3-50/2-1	-1.0
	Yr	110	383	49	95	16	2	1	25	29	21	.248	.301	.308	59	-22	9	18	-8	.945	10	*3-106/2-1	-1.3
1922	Phi-N	119	502	58	127	26	3	0	38	32	29	.253	.299	.317	54	-35	6	12	-5	.948	5	*3-117/S-2	-2.5
1923	Phi-N	47	179	27	47	5	0	1	10	14	14	.263	.320	.307	59	-10	1	1	-0	.947	-1	3-45	-0.7
Total	3	276	1064	134	269	47	5	2	73	75	64	.253	.303	.312	57	-68	16	31	-14	.947	14	3-268/S-2,2-1	-4.5

■ BILL RARIDEN

Rariden, William Angel "Bedford Bill"   b: 2/4/1888, Bedford, Ind.   d: 8/28/42, Bedford, Ind.   BR/TR, 5'10", 168 lbs.   Deb: 8/12/09

YEAR	TM/L	G	AB	R	H	2B	3B	HR	RBI	BB	SO	AVG	OBP	SLG	PRO+	BR/A	SB	CS	SBR	FA	FR	G/POS	TPR
1909	Bos-N	13	42	1	6	1	0	0	1	4		.143	.217	.167	18	-4	1			.912	-3	C-13	-0.7
1910	Bos-N	49	137	15	31	5	1	1	14	12	22	.226	.293	.299	70	-5	1			.962	3	C-49	0.2
1911	Bos-N	70	246	22	56	9	0	0	21	21	18	.228	.288	.264	51	-16	3			.952	1	C-65/3-3,2-1	-0.8
1912	Bos-N	79	247	27	55	3	1	1	14	18	35	.223	.281	.255	46	-18	3			.964	-5	C-73	-1.6
1913	Bos-N	95	246	31	58	9	2	3	30	30	21	.236	.324	.325	84	-5	3			.976	-0	C-87	0.2
1914	Ind-F	131	396	44	93	15	5	0	47	61	43	.235	.337	.298	67	-23	12			.981	20	*C-130	0.9
1915	New-F	142	444	49	120	30	7	0	46	60	29	.270	.361	.369	112	1	8			.978	23	*C-142	3.8
1916	NY-N	120	351	23	78	9	3	0	29	55	32	.222	.333	.274	92	-1	4			.972	-9	*C-119	-0.1
1917	*NY-N	101	266	20	72	10	1	0	25	42	17	.271	.372	.316	116	7	3			.971	-17	*C-100	-0.3
1918	NY-N	69	183	15	41	5	1	0	15	15	15	.224	.283	.262	68	-7	1			**.984**	-9	C-63	-1.3
1919	*Cin-N	74	218	16	47	6	3	1	24	17	19	.216	.275	.284	70	-8	2	0	1	.983	3	C-70	0.1
1920	Cin-N	39	101	9	25	3	0	0	10	5	0	.248	.283	.277	62	-5	2	0	0	.972	-0	C-37	-0.3
Total	12	982	2877	272	682	105	24	6	272	340	<u>251</u>	.237	.320	.298	78	-83	47	<u>0</u>		.973	8	C-948/3,3,2-1	0.1

■ MORRIE RATH

Rath, Morris Charles   b: 12/25/1886, Mobeetie, Tex.   d: 11/18/45, Upper Darby, Pa.   BL/TR, 5'8.5", 160 lbs.   Deb: 9/28/09

YEAR	TM/L	G	AB	R	H	2B	3B	HR	RBI	BB	SO	AVG	OBP	SLG	PRO+	BR/A	SB	CS	SBR	FA	FR	G/POS	TPR
1909	Phi-A	7	26	4	7	1	0	0	3	2		.269	.387	.308	117	1	1			.846	2	/S-4,3-2	0.3
1910	Phi-A	18	26	3	4	0	0	0	1	5		.154	.290	.154	40	-2	0			.950	-2	3-11/2-3	-0.4
	Cle-A	24	67	5	13	3	0	0	0	10		.194	.299	.239	68	-2	2			.950	2	3-22/S-1	0.1
	Yr	42	93	8	17	3	0	0	1	15		.183	.296	.215	60	-4	2			.950	0	3-33/2-3,S-1	-0.3
1912	Chi-A	157	591	104	161	10	2	1	19	95		.272	.380	.301	98	5	30			**.963**	18	*2-157	1.9
1913	Chi-A	92	295	37	59	2	0	0	12	46	22	.200	.310	.207	52	-16	22			.962	-2	2-86	-2.0
1919	*Cin-N	138	537	77	142	13	1	1	29	64	24	.264	.343	.298	96	0	17			.974	13	*2-138	2.2
1920	Cin-N	129	506	61	135	7	4	0	28	36	24	.267	.319	.308	82	-11	10	11	-4	**.977**	-7	*2-126/3-1,O-1	-1.9
Total	6	565	2048	291	521	36	7	4	92	258	<u>70</u>	.254	.342	.285	86	-25	82	<u>11</u>		.970	25	2-510/3-36,S-5,0-1	0.4

■ GENE RATLIFF

Ratliff, Kelly Eugene   b: 9/28/45, Macon, Ga.   BR/TR, 6'5", 185 lbs.   Deb: 5/15/65

YEAR	TM/L	G	AB	R	H	2B	3B	HR	RBI	BB	SO	AVG	OBP	SLG	PRO+	BR/A	SB	CS	SBR	FA	FR	G/POS	TPR
1965	Hou-N	4	4	0	0	0	0	0	0	0	4	.000	.000	.000	-99	-1	0	0	0	.000	0	H	-0.1

■ PAUL RATLIFF

Ratliff, Paul Hawthorne   b: 1/23/44, San Diego, Cal.   BL/TR, 6'2", 190 lbs.   Deb: 4/14/63

YEAR	TM/L	G	AB	R	H	2B	3B	HR	RBI	BB	SO	AVG	OBP	SLG	PRO+	BR/A	SB	CS	SBR	FA	FR	G/POS	TPR
1963	Min-A	10	21	2	4	1	0	1	3	2	7	.190	.292	.381	85	-0	0	0	0	.976	2	/C-7	0.2
1970	*Min-A	69	149	19	40	7	2	5	22	15	51	.268	.363	.443	119	4	0	0	0	.980	-15	C-53	-1.0
1971	Min-A	21	44	3	7	1	0	2	6	4	17	.159	.229	.318	52	-3	0	0	0	1.000	1	C-15	-0.2
	Mil-A	23	41	3	7	1	0	3	7	5	21	.171	.277	.415	95	-0	0	0	0	.966	-1	C-13	-0.1
	Yr	44	85	6	14	2	0	5	13	9	38	.165	.253	.365	72	-3	0	0	0	.985	0	C-28	-0.3
1972	Mil-A	22	42	1	3	0	1	0	4	2	23	.071	.114	.143	-25	-6	0	0	0	1.000	0	C-13	-1.0
Total	4	145	297	28	61	10	3	11	42	28	119	.205	.293	.374	86	-6	0	0	0	.983	-16	C-101	-2.1

■ TOMMY RAUB

Raub, Thomas Jefferson   b: 12/1/1870, Raubsville, Pa.   d: 2/16/49, Phillipsburg, N.J.   BR/TR, 5'10", 155 lbs.   Deb: 5/3/03

YEAR	TM/L	G	AB	R	H	2B	3B	HR	RBI	BB	SO	AVG	OBP	SLG	PRO+	BR/A	SB	CS	SBR	FA	FR	G/POS	TPR
1903	Chi-N	36	84	6	19	3	2	0	7	5		.226	.278	.310	69	-4	3			.900	-4	C-12/1-6,0-5,3-4	-0.7
1906	StL-N	24	78	9	22	2	4	0	2	4		.282	.325	.410	135	3	2			.957	-4	C-22	0.1
Total	2	60	162	15	41	5	6	0	9	9		.253	.301	.358	99	-1	5			.940	-8	/C-34,1-6,0-5,3-4	-0.6

YEAR	TM/L	G	AB	R	H	2B	3B	HR	RBI	BB	SO	AVG	OBP	SLG	PRO+	BR/A	SB	CS	SBR	FA	FR	G/POS	TPR

■ BOB RAUDMAN   Raudman, Robert Joyce "Shorty" b: 3/14/42, Erie, Pa. BL/TL, 5'9.5", 185 lbs. Deb: 9/13/66

YEAR	TM/L	G	AB	R	H	2B	3B	HR	RBI	BB	SO	AVG	OBP	SLG	PRO+	BR/A	SB	CS	SBR	FA	FR	G/POS	TPR
1966	Chi-N	8	29	1	7	2	0	0	2	1	4	.241	.267	.310	59	-2	0	0	0	.909	0	/O-8	-0.2
1967	Chi-N	8	26	0	4	0	0	0	1	1	4	.154	.185	.154	-2	-3	0	0	0	.875	0	/O-8	-0.4
Total	2	16	55	1	11	2	0	0	3	2	8	.200	.228	.236	30	-5	0	0	0	.889	0	/O-16	-0.6

■ JOHNNY RAWLINGS   Rawlings, John William "Red" b: 8/17/1892, Bloomfield, Iowa d: 10/16/72, Inglewood, Cal. BR/TR, 5'8", 158 lbs. Deb: 4/14/14

YEAR	TM/L	G	AB	R	H	2B	3B	HR	RBI	BB	SO	AVG	OBP	SLG	PRO+	BR/A	SB	CS	SBR	FA	FR	G/POS	TPR
1914	Cin-N	33	60	9	13	1	0	0	8	6	8	.217	.288	.233	54	-3	1			.885	0	3-10/2-7,S-5	-0.3
	KC-F	61	193	19	41	3	0	0	15	22	25	.212	.296	.228	46	-17	6			.937	17	S-61	0.5
1915	KC-F	120	399	40	86	9	2	2	24	27	40	.216	.269	.263	52	-32	17			.926	-4	*S-120	-3.0
1917	Bos-N	122	371	37	95	9	4	2	31	38	32	.256	.337	.318	107	4	12			.977	11	2-96,S-17/3-1,O-1	2.3
1918	Bos-N	111	410	32	85	7	3	0	21	30	31	.207	.265	.239	56	-21	10			.956	2	S-71,2-20,O-18	-1.8
1919	Bos-N	77	275	30	70	8	2	1	16	16	20	.255	.298	.309	86	-5	10			.961	-12	2-58,O-10/S-5	-1.7
1920	Bos-N	5	3	0	0	0	0	0	2	0	1	.000	.000	.000	-99	-1	0	0	0	1.000	-1	/2-1	-0.1
	Phi-N	98	384	39	90	19	2	3	30	22	25	.234	.278	.318	67	-16	9	6	-1	.970	-2	2-97	-1.7
	Yr	103	387	39	90	19	2	3	32	22	26	.233	.276	.315	67	-17	9	6	-1	.970	-2	2-98	-1.8
1921	Phi-N	60	254	20	74	14	2	1	16	8	12	.291	.318	.374	76	-9	4	5	-2	.954	5	2-60	-0.4
	*NY-N	86	307	40	82	8	1	1	30	18	19	.267	.316	.300	66	-14	4	4	-1	.970	-2	2-86/S-1	-1.5
	Yr	146	561	60	156	22	3	2	46	26	31	.278	.317	.339	71	-23	8	9	-3	.963	3	*2-146/S-1	-1.9
1922	NY-N	88	308	46	87	13	8	1	30	23	15	.282	.342	.386	87	-6	7	6	-2	.984	-4	2-77/3-5	-0.9
1923	Pit-N	119	461	53	131	18	4	1	45	25	29	.284	.322	.347	75	-17	9	0	3	.958	-8	*2-119	-2.0
1924	Pit-N	3	3	0	1	0	0	0	2	0	0	.333	.333	.333	78	-0	0	0	-1	.000	0	H	0.0
1925	Pit-N	36	110	17	31	7	0	2	13	8	8	.282	.336	.400	82	-3	0	1	-1	.981	3	2-29	0.0
1926	Pit-N	61	181	27	42	6	0	0	20	14	10	.232	.287	.265	47	-13	3			.970	-3	2-59	-1.5
Total	12	1080	3719	409	928	122	28	14	303	257	275	.250	.303	.309	71	-153	92	22		.968	3	2-709,S-280/O-29,3	-12.1

■ IRV RAY   Ray, Irving Burton "Stubby" b: 1/22/1864, Harrington, Me. d: 2/21/48, Harrington, Me. BL/TR, 5'6", 165 lbs. Deb: 7/7/1888

YEAR	TM/L	G	AB	R	H	2B	3B	HR	RBI	BB	SO	AVG	OBP	SLG	PRO+	BR/A	SB	CS	SBR	FA	FR	G/POS	TPR
1888	Bos-N	50	206	26	51	3	4	2	26	6	11	.248	.272	.316	85	-4	7			.879	-11	S-48/2-3	-1.4
1889	Bos-N	9	33	8	10	1	0	0	2	4	0	.303	.378	.333	94	-0	1			.875	-4	/S-5,3-4	-0.4
	Bal-a	26	106	20	36	4	1	0	17	7	6	.340	.397	.396	124	3	12			.784	-7	S-20/O-6	-0.3
1890	Bal-a	38	139	28	50	6	2	1	20	15		.360	.433	.453	154	9	11			.894	-10	S-38	0.2
1891	Bal-a	103	418	72	116	17	5	0	58	54	18	.278	.366	.342	102	2	28			.885	-14	O-64,S-40	-1.0
Total	4	226	902	154	263	30	11	3	123	86	35	.292	.360	.359	109	11	59			.863	-46	S-151/O-70,3-4,2-3	-2.9

■ JOHNNY RAY   Ray, John Cornelius b: 3/1/57, Chouteau, Okla. BB/TR, 5'11", 185 lbs. Deb: 9/2/81

YEAR	TM/L	G	AB	R	H	2B	3B	HR	RBI	BB	SO	AVG	OBP	SLG	PRO+	BR/A	SB	CS	SBR	FA	FR	G/POS	TPR
1981	Pit-N	31	102	10	25	11	0	0	6	6	9	.245	.287	.353	78	-3	0	0	0	.987	2	2-31	0.0
1982	Pit-N	162	647	79	182	30	7	7	63	36	34	.281	.320	.382	93	-7	16	7	1	.977	8	*2-162	1.1
1983	Pit-N	151	576	68	163	38	7	5	53	35	26	.283	.324	.399	97	-3	18	9	0	.983	17	*2-151	2.2
1984	Pit-N	155	555	75	173	38	6	6	67	37	31	.312	.358	.434	122	15	11	6	-0	.984	-9	2-149	1.1
1985	Pit-N	154	594	67	163	33	3	7	70	46	24	.274	.328	.375	97	-3	13	9	-2	.976	-15	*2-151	-1.4
1986	Pit-N	155	579	67	174	33	0	7	78	58	47	.301	.367	.394	107	7	6	9	-4	.993	5	*2-151	1.5
1987	Pit-N	123	472	48	129	19	3	5	54	41	36	.273	.331	.358	82	-12	4	2	0	.981	-4	*2-119	-0.2
	Cal-A	30	127	16	44	11	0	0	15	3	10	.346	.362	.433	113	2	0	0	0	.986	-1	2-29/D-1	0.3
1988	Cal-A★	153	602	75	184	42	7	6	83	36	38	.306	.349	.420	120	15	4	1	1	.972	-7	*2-104,O-40/D-6	1.1
1989	Cal-A	134	530	52	153	16	3	5	62	36	30	.289	.334	.358	97	-2	6	3	0	.984	4	2-130	0.6
1990	Cal-A	105	404	47	112	23	6	3	43	19	44	.277	.310	.371	91	-6	2	3	-1	.987	12	*2-100/D-1	0.7
Total	10	1353	5188	604	1502	294	36	53	594	353	329	.290	.336	.391	101	4	80	49	-5	.982	20	*2-1277/O-40,D-8	7.0

■ LARRY RAY   Ray, Larry Dale b: 3/11/58, Madison, Ind. BL/TR, 6'1", 195 lbs. Deb: 9/10/82

YEAR	TM/L	G	AB	R	H	2B	3B	HR	RBI	BB	SO	AVG	OBP	SLG	PRO+	BR/A	SB	CS	SBR	FA	FR	G/POS	TPR
1982	Hou-N	5	6	0	1	0	0	0	1	0	0	.167	.167	.167	-7	-1	0	0	0	1.000	-0	/O-1	-0.1

■ FLOYD RAYFORD   Rayford, Floyd Kinnard b: 7/27/57, Memphis, Tenn. BR/TR, 5'10", 195 lbs. Deb: 4/17/80

YEAR	TM/L	G	AB	R	H	2B	3B	HR	RBI	BB	SO	AVG	OBP	SLG	PRO+	BR/A	SB	CS	SBR	FA	FR	G/POS	TPR
1980	Bal-A	8	18	1	4	0	0	1	0	0	5	.222	.222	.222	22	-2	0	0	0	.900	0	/3-4,2-1,D-1	-0.2
1982	Bal-A	34	53	7	7	0	0	0	5	6	14	.132	.220	.302	42	-4	0	1	-1	.898	5	3-27/C-2,D-2	-0.1
1983	StL-N	56	104	5	22	4	0	3	14	10	27	.212	.281	.337	70	-4	1	0	0	.883	-4	3-33	-0.9
1984	Bal-A	86	250	24	64	14	0	4	27	12	51	.256	.298	.360	83	-6	0	3	-2	.991	11	C-66,3-22/1-1	0.5
1985	Bal-A	105	359	55	110	21	1	18	48	10	69	.306	.325	.521	131	13	3	1	0	.972	-2	3-78,C-29/D-1	1.2
1986	Bal-A	81	210	15	37	4	0	8	19	15	50	.176	.231	.310	46	-16	0	0	0	.912	4	3-72,C-10/D-1	-1.3
1987	Bal-A	20	50	5	11	0	0	2	3	2	9	.220	.250	.340	56	-3	0	0	0	.980	6	C-17/3-1,D-1	0.4
Total	7	390	1044	112	255	43	1	38	117	55	225	.244	.284	.397	86	-23	4	5	-2	.931	21	3-237,C-124/D-6,12	-0.4

■ FRED RAYMER   Raymer, Frederick Charles b: 11/12/1875, Leavenworth, Kan. d: 6/11/57, Los Angeles, Cal. BR/TR, 5'11", 185 lbs. Deb: 4/24/01

YEAR	TM/L	G	AB	R	H	2B	3B	HR	RBI	BB	SO	AVG	OBP	SLG	PRO+	BR/A	SB	CS	SBR	FA	FR	G/POS	TPR
1901	Chi-N	120	463	41	108	14	2	0	43	11		.233	.257	.272	56	-27	18			.881	-17	3-82,S-29/1-5,2-3	-4.1
1904	Bos-N	114	419	28	88	12	3	1	27	13		.210	.236	.260	55	-23	17			.958	7	*2-114	-1.4
1905	Bos-N	137	498	26	105	14	2	0	31	8		.211	.232	.247	44	-35	15			.949	-18	*2-134/1-1,O-1	-5.5
Total	3	371	1380	95	301	40	7	1	101	32		.218	.242	.259	51	-85	50			.954	-28	2-251/3-82,S-29,10	-11.0

■ HARRY RAYMOND   Raymond, Harry H. "Jack" b: 2/20/1862, Utica, N.Y. d: 3/21/25, San Diego, Cal. 5'9", 179 lbs. Deb: 9/9/1888

YEAR	TM/L	G	AB	R	H	2B	3B	HR	RBI	BB	SO	AVG	OBP	SLG	PRO+	BR/A	SB	CS	SBR	FA	FR	G/POS	TPR
1888	Lou-a	32	123	8	26	2	0	0	13	1		.211	.218	.228	44	-8	7			.884	-1	3-31/O-1	-0.8
1889	Lou-a	130	515	58	123	12	9	0	47	19	45	.239	.270	.297	63	-26	19			.886	-1	*3-129/O-1,P-1	-1.9
1890	*Lou-a	123	521	91	135	7	4	2	51	22		.259	.293	.299	76	-17	18			.874	-2	*3-119/S-4	-1.3
1891	Lou-a	14	59	4	12	2	0	0	2	5	6	.203	.288	.237	51	-4	3			.898	5	S-14	0.2
1892	Pit-N	12	49	4	4	0	1	0	2	4	8	.082	.151	.122	-17	-7	1			.867	-2	3-12	-0.8
	Was-N	4	15	2	1	0	0	0	0	3	2	.067	.222	.067	-12	-2	1			.783	1	/3-4	-0.1
	Yr	16	64	6	5	0	1	0	2	7	10	.078	.169	.109	-15	-9	2			.838	-1	3-16	-0.9
Total	5	315	1282	167	301	23	14	2	115	54	61	.235	.270	.279	62	-63	49			.878	1	3-295/S-18,O-2,P-1	-4.7

■ LOU RAYMOND   Raymond, Louis Anthony (b: Louis Anthony Raymondjack) b: 12/11/1894, Buffalo, N.Y. d: 5/2/79, Rochester, N.Y. BR/TR, 5'10.5", 187 lbs. Deb: 5/2/19

YEAR	TM/L	G	AB	R	H	2B	3B	HR	RBI	BB	SO	AVG	OBP	SLG	PRO+	BR/A	SB	CS	SBR	FA	FR	G/POS	TPR
1919	Phi-N	1	2	0	1	0	0	0	0	0	0	.500	.500	.500	188	0	0			.000	0	/2-1	0.0

■ AL REACH   Reach, Alfred James b: 5/25/1840, London, England d: 1/14/28, Atlantic City, N.J. BL/TL, 5'6", 155 lbs. Deb: 5/20/1871 FM

YEAR	TM/L	G	AB	R	H	2B	3B	HR	RBI	BB	SO	AVG	OBP	SLG	PRO+	BR/A	SB	CS	SBR	FA	FR	G/POS	TPR
1871	Ath-n	26	133	43	47	7	6	0	34	5	6	.353	.377	.496	150	9	2	0	1	.844	-0	*2-26	0.4
1872	Ath-n	24	118	21	23	0	0	0	11	4	0	.195	.221	.195	29	-9	1	1	-0	.943	4	O-20/1-4	-0.3
1873	Ath-n	13	73	13	16	5	1	0	9	0	0	.219	.219	.315	53	-5	2	0	1	.881	5	/2-9,O-7	0.0
1874	Ath-n	14	55	8	7	2	0	0	1	0	0	.127	.127	.164	-7	-7	0	0	0	.732	4	O-14	-0.2
1875	Ath-n	3	14	4	4	1	0	0	1	0	0	.286	.286	.357	110	-2	2	1	0	1.000	-2	/O-2,2-1	-0.1
Total	5 n	80	393	89	97	15	7	0	57	9	10	.247	.264	.321	73	-12	7	2	1	.857	11	/O-43,2-36,1-4	-0.2

■ BOB REACH   Reach, Robert b: 8/28/1843, Williamsburg, N.Y. d: 5/19/22, Springfield, Mass. 5'5", 155 lbs. Deb: 4/23/1872 F

YEAR	TM/L	G	AB	R	H	2B	3B	HR	RBI	BB	SO	AVG	OBP	SLG	PRO+	BR/A	SB	CS	SBR	FA	FR	G/POS	TPR
1872	Oly-n	2	8	1	2	0	0	0	0	0	0	.250	.250	.250	57	-0	0	0	0	.727	-1	/S-2	-0.1
1873	Was-n	1	5	1	1	0	0	0	0	0	0	.200	.200	.200	20	-0	0	0	0	.500	-1	/S-1	-0.1
Total	2 n	3	13	2	3	0	0	0	0	0	0	.231	.231	.231	42	-1	0	0	0	.632	-2	/S-3	-0.2

■ RANDY READY   Ready, Randy Max b: 1/8/60, Fremont, Cal. BR/TR, 5'11", 180 lbs. Deb: 9/4/83

YEAR	TM/L	G	AB	R	H	2B	3B	HR	RBI	BB	SO	AVG	OBP	SLG	PRO+	BR/A	SB	CS	SBR	FA	FR	G/POS	TPR
1983	Mil-A	12	37	8	15	3	2	1	6	6	3	.405	.488	.676	234	7	0	1	-1	1.000	0	/3-4,D-6	0.6
1984	Mil-A	37	123	13	23	8	1	0	6	14	19	.187	.270	.325	66	-6	0	3	0	.946	3	3-36	-0.3
1985	Mil-A	48	181	29	48	9	5	1	21	14	23	.265	.321	.387	93	-2	0	0	0	.989	4	O-37/3-7,2-3,D-2	0.1
1986	Mil-A	23	79	8	15	4	0	1	4	7	8	.190	.273	.278	49	-6	2	0	0	.950	-4	O-11/2-7,3-3,D-1	-0.9
	SD-N	1	3	0	0	0	0	0	0	0	0	.000	.000	.000	-99	-0	0	0	0	.667	-0	/3-1	-0.0
1987	SD-N	124	350	69	108	26	6	12	54	67	44	.309	.424	.520	154	30	7	3	0	.912	2	3-52,2-51,O-16	3.2
1988	SD-N	114	331	43	88	16	2	7	39	39	38	.266	.349	.390	114	2	6	2	1	.952	-10	3-57,2-26,O-16	-0.3
1989	SD-N	28	67	4	17	3	2	0	4	12		.254	.359	.313	94	-0	2	0	1	.963	1	3-18/2-2,O-1	0.2

YEAR	TM/L	G	AB	R	H	2B	3B	HR	RBI	BB	SO	AVG	OBP	SLG	PRO+	BR/A	SB	CS	SBR	FA	FR	G/POS	TPR
	Phi-N	72	187	33	50	11	1	8	21	31	31	.267	.377	.465	140	10	4	3	-1	.962	-6	O-36,3-14/2-7	0.4
	Yr	100	254	37	67	13	2	8	26	42	31	.264	.372	.425	127	10	4	3	-1	.962	-4	O-37,3-32/2-9	0.6
1990	Phi-N	101	217	26	53	9	1	1	26	29	35	.244	.336	.309	79	-5	3	2	-0	1.000	-6	O-30,2-28	-1.2
1991	Phi-N	76	205	32	51	10	1	1	20	47	25	.249	.391	.322	104	4	2	1	0	.989	-7	2-66	-0.2
1992	*Oak-A	61	125	17	25	2	0	3	17	25	23	.200	.333	.288	80	-3	1	0	0	1.000	-3	O-24,D-24/3-7,12	-0.7
1993	Mon-N	40	134	22	34	8	1	1	10	23	8	.254	.367	.351	89	-1	2	1	0	.968	3	2-28,1-13/3-3	0.0
1994	Phi-N	17	42	5	16	1	0	1	3	6	6	.381	.480	.476	147	3	0	1	-1	1.000	-3	2-11/3-1	0.0
1995	Phi-N	23	29	3	4	0	0	0	3	3	6	.138	.219	.138	-3	-4	0	1	-1	.967	-0	/1-3,2-1	-0.6
Total	13	777	2110	312	547	107	21	40	239	326	276	.259	.362	.387	108	33	27	15	-1	.979	-27	2-234,3-203,O/D1	0.4

■ LEROY REAMS Reams, Leroy b: 8/11/43, Pine Bluff, Ark. BL/TR, 6'2", 175 lbs. Deb: 5/7/69

YEAR	TM/L	G	AB	R	H	2B	3B	HR	RBI	BB	SO	AVG	OBP	SLG	PRO+	BR/A	SB	CS	SBR	FA	FR	G/POS	TPR
1969	Phi-N	1	1	0	0	0	0	0	0	0	1	.000	.000	.000	-99	-0	0	0	0	.000	0	H	0.0

■ PHIL REARDON Reardon, Philip Michael b: 10/3/1883, Brooklyn, N.Y. d: 9/28/20, Brooklyn, N.Y. BR/TR, Deb: 9/19/06

YEAR	TM/L	G	AB	R	H	2B	3B	HR	RBI	BB	SO	AVG	OBP	SLG	PRO+	BR/A	SB	CS	SBR	FA	FR	G/POS	TPR
1906	Bro-N	5	14	0	1	0	0	0	0	0	0	.071	.133	.071	-39	-2	0			.917	1	/O-4	-0.2

■ ART REBEL Rebel, Arthur Anthony b: 3/4/15, Cincinnati, Ohio BL/TL, 5'8", 180 lbs. Deb: 4/19/38

YEAR	TM/L	G	AB	R	H	2B	3B	HR	RBI	BB	SO	AVG	OBP	SLG	PRO+	BR/A	SB	CS	SBR	FA	FR	G/POS	TPR
1938	Phi-N	7	9	2	2	0	0	0	1	1	1	.222	.300	.222	47	-1	0			1.000	-1	/O-3	-0.1
1945	StL-N	26	72	12	25	4	0	0	5	6	4	.347	.397	.403	120	2	1			.976	2	O-18	0.3
Total	2	33	81	14	27	4	0	0	6	7	5	.333	.386	.383	112	1	1			.978	1	/O-21	0.2

■ JEFF REBOULET Reboulet, Jeffrey Allen b: 4/30/64, Dayton, Ohio BR/TR, 6', 167 lbs. Deb: 5/12/92

YEAR	TM/L	G	AB	R	H	2B	3B	HR	RBI	BB	SO	AVG	OBP	SLG	PRO+	BR/A	SB	CS	SBR	FA	FR	G/POS	TPR
1992	Min-A	73	137	15	26	7	1	1	16	23	26	.190	.311	.277	64	-6	3	2	-0	.971	21	S-36,3-22,2-13/OD	1.6
1993	Min-A	109	240	33	62	8	0	1	15	35	37	.258	.357	.304	79	-5	5	5	-2	.982	13	S-62,3-35,2-11/OD	-0.9
1994	Min-A	74	189	28	49	11	1	3	23	18	23	.259	.327	.376	81	-5	0	0	0	.963	-7	S-42,2-14,1/3OD	-0.9
1995	Min-A	87	216	39	63	11	4	0	23	27	34	.292	.373	.398	101	1	1	2	-1	.993	10	S-39,3-22,1-17,2/C	1.1
1996	Min-A	107	234	20	52	9	0	0	23	25	34	.222	.300	.261	43	-20	4	2	0	.987	-5	S-37,3-36,21/OD	-2.2
Total	5	450	1016	135	252	46	2	9	100	128	154	.248	.336	.324	73	-36	13	11	-2	.978	30	S-216,3-121/21ODC	0.5

■ JOHN RECCIUS Reccius, John b: 10/29/1859, Louisville, Ky. d: 9/1/30, Louisville, Ky. 5'6.5", Deb: 5/2/1882 F

YEAR	TM/L	G	AB	R	H	2B	3B	HR	RBI	BB	SO	AVG	OBP	SLG	PRO+	BR/A	SB	CS	SBR	FA	FR	G/POS	TPR
1882	Lou-a	74	266	46	63	12	3	1		23		.237	.298	.316	113	5				.857	-3	*O-65,P-13	0.2
1883	Lou-a	18	63	10	9	2	0	0	3	7		.143	.229	.175	34	-4				.833	-1	O-18/P-1	-0.5
Total	2	92	329	56	72	14	3	1		30		.219	.284	.289	98	1				.851	-4	/O-83,P-14	-0.3

■ PHIL RECCIUS Reccius, Phillip b: 6/7/1862, Louisville, Ky. d: 2/15/03, Louisville, Ky. 5'9", 163 lbs. Deb: 9/25/1882 F

YEAR	TM/L	G	AB	R	H	2B	3B	HR	RBI	BB	SO	AVG	OBP	SLG	PRO+	BR/A	SB	CS	SBR	FA	FR	G/POS	TPR
1882	Lou-a	4	15	0	2	0	0	0		0		.133	.133	.133	-10	-2				.778	-0	/O-4	-0.2
1883	Lou-a	1	3	1	1	1	0	0				.333	.333	.667	231	0				1.000	-0	/O-1	0.0
1884	Lou-a	73	263	23	63	9	2	3	21		5	.240	.267	.323	96	-1				.845	-2	3-51,P-18,S-10	-0.2
1885	Lou-a	102	402	57	97	8	10	1	38		13	.241	.267	.318	84	-8				.829	-2	*3-97/P-7	-0.7
1886	Lou-a	5	13	4	4	1	1	0	2		3	.308	.471	.538	204	2	0			.889	1	/O-5,P-1	0.2
1887	Lou-a	11	37	9	9	2	0	0	4		8	.243	.391	.297	92	2	0	3		.926	-2	O-10/S-1	0.1
	Cle-a	62	229	23	47	6	3	0	29		24	.205	.295	.258	56	-12	9			.877	8	3-62/P-1	-0.2
	Yr	73	266	32	56	8	3	0	33		32	.211	.309	.263	62	-12	12			.877	10	3-62,O-10/S-1,P-1	-0.2
1888	Lou-a	2	9	0	2	1	0	0	4		1	.222	.300	.333	105	0	0			.750	-2	3-2	-0.1
1890	Roc-a	1	4	0	0	0	0	0				.000	.000	.000	-99	-1	0	0		.000	-0	/O-1	-0.1
Total	8	261	975	117	225	28	16	4	99		54	.231	.280	.305	81	-21	12			.848	5	3-212/P-27,O-21,S	-1.3

■ JOHNNY REDER Reder, John Anthony b: 9/24/09, Lublin, Poland d: 4/12/90, Fall River, Mass. BR/TR, 6', 184 lbs. Deb: 4/16/32

YEAR	TM/L	G	AB	R	H	2B	3B	HR	RBI	BB	SO	AVG	OBP	SLG	PRO+	BR/A	SB	CS	SBR	FA	FR	G/POS	TPR
1932	Bos-A	17	37	4	5	1	0	0	3	6	6	.135	.256	.162	11	-5	0	0	0	.990	0	1-10/3-1	-0.5

■ BUCK REDFERN Redfern, George Howard b: 4/7/02, Asheville, N.C. d: 9/8/64, Asheville, N.C. BR/TR, 5'11", 165 lbs. Deb: 4/11/28

YEAR	TM/L	G	AB	R	H	2B	3B	HR	RBI	BB	SO	AVG	OBP	SLG	PRO+	BR/A	SB	CS	SBR	FA	FR	G/POS	TPR
1928	Chi-A	86	261	22	61	6	3	0	35	12	19	.234	.267	.280	44	-21	8	2	1	.953	6	2-45,S-33/3-1	-0.9
1929	Chi-A	21	46	0	6	0	0	0	3	3	3	.130	.184	.130	-18	-8	1	1	-0	.967	-5	2-11/3-5,S-4	-1.2
Total	2	107	307	22	67	6	3	0	38	15	22	.218	.255	.257	35	-29	9	3	1	.955	1	/2-56,S-37,3-6	-2.1

■ JOE REDFIELD Redfield, Joseph Randall b: 1/14/61, Doylestown, Pa. BR/TR, 6'2", 190 lbs. Deb: 6/4/88

YEAR	TM/L	G	AB	R	H	2B	3B	HR	RBI	BB	SO	AVG	OBP	SLG	PRO+	BR/A	SB	CS	SBR	FA	FR	G/POS	TPR
1988	Cal-A	1	2	0	0	0	0	0	0	0	0	.000	.000	.000	-99	-1	0	0	0	1.000	0	/3-1	0.0
1991	Pit-N	11	18	1	2	0	0	0	0	4	1	.111	.273	.111	12	-2	0	1	-1	.917	-1	/3-9	-0.3
Total	2	12	20	1	2	0	0	0	0	4	1	.100	.250	.100	2	-3	0	1	-1	.923	-0	/3-10	-0.3

■ GLENN REDMON Redmon, Glenn Vincent b: 1/11/48, Detroit, Mich. BR/TR, 5'11", 180 lbs. Deb: 9/8/74

YEAR	TM/L	G	AB	R	H	2B	3B	HR	RBI	BB	SO	AVG	OBP	SLG	PRO+	BR/A	SB	CS	SBR	FA	FR	G/POS	TPR
1974	SF-N	7	17	0	4	3	0	0	4	1	3	.235	.278	.412	87	-0	0	0	0	.955	-1	/2-4	-0.1

■ BILLY REDMON Redmon, William T. b: Brooklyn, N.Y. BL/TL, Deb: 5/4/1875

YEAR	TM/L	G	AB	R	H	2B	3B	HR	RBI	BB	SO	AVG	OBP	SLG	PRO+	BR/A	SB	CS	SBR	FA	FR	G/POS	TPR
1875	RS-n	19	82	12	16	2	0	0	1	2	7	.195	.214	.220	56	-3	3	0	1	.837	5	S-19/C-2	0.2
1877	Cin-N	3	12	1	3	1	0	0	3	1	1	.250	.308	.333	115	0	2			.833	2	/S-3	-0.1
1878	Mil-N	48	187	16	43	8	0	0	21	8	13	.230	.262	.273	71	-6				.785	-17	S-39/O-7,3-3,C-1	-2.1
Total	2	51	199	17	46	9	0	0	24	9	14	.231	.264	.276	73	-6				.791	-16	/S-42,O-7,3-3,C-1	-1.9

■ HARRY REDMOND Redmond, Harry John b: 9/13/1887, Cleveland, Ohio d: 7/10/60, Cleveland, Ohio BR/TR, 5'8", 170 lbs. Deb: 9/7/09

YEAR	TM/L	G	AB	R	H	2B	3B	HR	RBI	BB	SO	AVG	OBP	SLG	PRO+	BR/A	SB	CS	SBR	FA	FR	G/POS	TPR
1909	Bro-N	6	19	3	0	0	0	0	1	0	0	.000	.000	.000	-99	-4	0			.892	3	/2-5	-0.1

■ WAYNE REDMOND Redmond, Howard Wayne b: 11/25/45, Athens, Ala. BR/TR, 5'10", 165 lbs. Deb: 9/7/65

YEAR	TM/L	G	AB	R	H	2B	3B	HR	RBI	BB	SO	AVG	OBP	SLG	PRO+	BR/A	SB	CS	SBR	FA	FR	G/POS	TPR
1965	Det-A	4	4	1	0	0	0	0	0	1	1	.000	.200	.000	-38	-1	0	0	0	1.000	-0	/O-2	-0.1
1969	Det-A	5	3	0	0	0	0	0	0	0	2	.000	.000	.000	-96	-1	0	0	0	.000	0	H	-0.1
Total	2	9	7	1	0	0	0	0	0	1	3	.000	.125	.000	-60	-1	0	0	0	1.000	-0	/O-2	-0.2

■ JACK REDMOND Redmond, John McKittrick "Red" b: 9/3/10, Florence, Ariz. d: 7/27/68, Garland, Tex. BL/TR, 5'11", 185 lbs. Deb: 4/22/35

YEAR	TM/L	G	AB	R	H	2B	3B	HR	RBI	BB	SO	AVG	OBP	SLG	PRO+	BR/A	SB	CS	SBR	FA	FR	G/POS	TPR
1935	Was-A	22	34	8	6	1	0	1	7	3	1	.176	.243	.294	40	-3	0	0	0	.978	2	C-15	-0.1

■ GARY REDUS Redus, Gary Eugene b: 11/1/56, Athens, Ala. BR/TR, 6'1", 185 lbs. Deb: 9/7/82

YEAR	TM/L	G	AB	R	H	2B	3B	HR	RBI	BB	SO	AVG	OBP	SLG	PRO+	BR/A	SB	CS	SBR	FA	FR	G/POS	TPR
1982	Cin-N	20	83	12	18	3	2	1	7	5	21	.217	.261	.337	65	-4	11	2	2	.970	1	O-20	-0.2
1983	Cin-N	125	453	90	112	20	9	17	51	71	111	.247	.353	.444	115	10	39	14	3	.972	9	*O-120	1.9
1984	Cin-N	123	394	69	100	21	3	7	22	52	71	.254	.342	.376	97	-1	48	11	8	.967	-2	*O-114	0.3
1985	Cin-N	101	246	51	62	14	6	4	28	44	52	.252	.368	.415	113	5	48	12	7	.986	-10	O-85	0.1
1986	Phi-N	90	340	62	84	22	4	11	33	47	78	.247	.344	.432	109	4	25	7	3	.980	10	O-89	1.5
1987	Chi-A	130	475	78	112	26	6	12	48	69	90	.236	.333	.392	89	-7	52	11	9	.979	4	*O-123/D-4	0.1
1988	Chi-A	77	262	42	69	10	4	6	34	33	52	.263	.350	.401	110	4	26	2	7	.987	1	O-68/D-2	0.9
	Pit-N	30	71	12	14	2	0	2	4	15	19	.197	.345	.310	90	-0	5	2	0	.957	2	O-19	0.1
1989	Pit-N	98	279	42	79	18	6	6	33	40	51	.283	.375	.462	143	16	25	6	4	.987	0	1-72,O-16	1.5
1990	*Pit-N	96	227	32	56	18	2	6	23	33	38	.247	.347	.419	114	5	11	5	0	.988	2	1-72/O-7	-0.1
1991	*Pit-N	98	252	45	62	12	2	7	24	28	39	.246	.329	.393	104	1	17	3	3	.990	-11	1-47,O-33	-1.1
1992	*Pit-N	76	176	26	45	7	3	3	12	17	25	.256	.321	.381	99	-0	11	4	1	1.000	-4	1-36,O-15	-0.6
1993	Tex-A	77	222	28	64	12	4	6	31	23	35	.288	.355	.459	122	4	4	4	-1	.981	-8	O-61/1-5,2-1,D-1	-0.4
1994	Tex-A	18	33	2	9	1	0	0	2	4	6	.273	.351	.303	71	-1	0	0	0	1.000	-2	/O-7,1-5	-0.3
Total	13	1159	3513	591	886	183	51	90	352	481	688	.252	.345	.410	107	39	322	83	47	.974	-12	O-777,1-237/D-7,2-1	3.7

■ BOB REECE Reece, Robert Scott b: 1/5/51, Sacramento, Cal. BR/TR, 6'1", 190 lbs. Deb: 4/22/78

YEAR	TM/L	G	AB	R	H	2B	3B	HR	RBI	BB	SO	AVG	OBP	SLG	PRO+	BR/A	SB	CS	SBR	FA	FR	G/POS	TPR
1978	Mon-N	9	11	2	2	1	0	0	3	0	4	.182	.182	.273	26	-1	0	0	0	.947	1	/C-9	0.0

■ DARREN REED Reed, Darren A. Douglass b: 10/16/65, Ojai, Cal. BR/TR, 6'1", 190 lbs. Deb: 5/1/90

YEAR	TM/L	G	AB	R	H	2B	3B	HR	RBI	BB	SO	AVG	OBP	SLG	PRO+	BR/A	SB	CS	SBR	FA	FR	G/POS	TPR
1990	NY-N	26	39	5	8	4	1	2		3	11	.205	.262	.436	89	-1	1	0	0	.955	-1	O-14	-0.2
1992	Mon-N	42	81	10	14	2	0	5	10	6	23	.173	.239	.383	74	-3	0	0	0	1.000	-3	O-29	-0.7

YEAR	TM/L	G	AB	R	H	2B	3B	HR	RBI	BB	SO	AVG	OBP	SLG	PRO+	BR/A	SB	CS	SBR	FA	FR	G/POS	TPR
	Min-A	14	33	2	6	2	0	0	4	2	11	.182	.229	.242	31	-3	0	0	0	1.000	-2	O-13/D-1	-0.6
Total	2	82	153	17	28	8	1	6	16	11	45	.183	.242	.366	68	-7	1	0	0	.987	-6	/O-56,D-1	-1.5

■ **HUGH REED**   Reed, Hugh   b: 1837, Chicago, Ill.   d: 11/3/1883, Chicago, Ill.   Deb: 8/26/1874

YEAR	TM/L	G	AB	R	H	2B	3B	HR	RBI	BB	SO	AVG	OBP	SLG	PRO+	BR/A	SB	CS	SBR	FA	FR	G/POS	TPR
1874	Bal-n	1	4	0	0	0	0	0	0	0	0	.000	.000	.000	-99	-1	0	0	0	1.000	-1	/O-1	-0.1

■ **JEFF REED**   Reed, Jeffrey Scott   b: 11/12/62, Joliet, Ill.   BL/TR, 6'2", 190 lbs.   Deb: 4/5/84

YEAR	TM/L	G	AB	R	H	2B	3B	HR	RBI	BB	SO	AVG	OBP	SLG	PRO+	BR/A	SB	CS	SBR	FA	FR	G/POS	TPR
1984	Min-A	18	21	3	3	3	0	0	1	2	6	.143	.217	.286	36	-2	0	0	0	.977	2	C-18	0.1
1985	Min-A	7	10	2	2	0	0	0	0	0	3	.200	.200	.200	9	-1	0	0	0	1.000	-0	/C-7	-0.1
1986	Min-A	68	165	13	39	6	1	2	9	16	19	.236	.308	.321	70	-7	1	0	0	.994	8	C-64	0.5
1987	Mon-N	75	207	15	44	11	0	1	21	12	20	.213	.259	.280	42	-17	0	1	-1	.970	-4	C-74	-1.8
1988	Mon-N	43	123	10	27	3	2	0	9	13	22	.220	.294	.276	62	-6	1	0	0	.995	-0	C-39	-0.1
	Cin-N	49	142	10	33	6	0	1	7	15	19	.232	.306	.296	71	-5	0	0	0	.993	5	C-49	0.4
	Yr	92	265	20	60	9	2	1	16	28	41	.226	.300	.287	66	-11	1	0	0	.994	8	C-88	0.3
1989	Cin-N	102	287	16	64	11	0	3	23	34	46	.223	.310	.293	71	-10	0	0	0	.988	-5	C-99	-1.1
1990	*Cin-N	72	175	12	44	8	1	3	16	24	26	.251	.342	.360	89	-2	0	0	0	.987	2	C-70	0.3
1991	Cin-N	91	270	20	72	15	2	3	31	23	38	.267	.327	.370	92	-3	0	1	-1	.991	-0	C-89	0.0
1992	Cin-N	15	25	2	4	0	0	0	2	1	4	.160	.192	.160	1	-3	0	0	0	1.000	-0	/C-6	-0.3
1993	SF-N	66	119	10	31	3	0	6	12	16	22	.261	.348	.437	112	2	0	1	-1	1.000	3	C-37	0.6
1994	SF-N	50	103	11	18	3	0	1	7	11	21	.175	.254	.233	30	-11	0	0	0	.993	-4	C-33	-1.3
1995	SF-N	66	113	12	30	2	0	0	9	20	17	.265	.376	.283	79	-2	0	0	0	.995	3	C-42	0.3
1996	Col-N	116	341	34	97	20	1	8	37	43	65	.284	.368	.419	83	-10	2	2	-1	.982	-12	*C-111	-1.5
Total	13	838	2101	170	508	91	7	28	184	230	328	.242	.319	.332	73	-78	4	5	-2	.988	-0	C-738	-4.0

■ **JODY REED**   Reed, Jody Eric   b: 7/26/62, Tampa, Fla.   BR/TR, 5'9", 170 lbs.   Deb: 9/12/87

YEAR	TM/L	G	AB	R	H	2B	3B	HR	RBI	BB	SO	AVG	OBP	SLG	PRO+	BR/A	SB	CS	SBR	FA	FR	G/POS	TPR
1987	Bos-A	9	30	4	9	1	1	0	8	4	0	.300	.382	.400	105	0	1	1	-0	1.000	5	/S-4,2-3,3-1	0.5
1988	*Bos-A	109	338	60	99	23	1	1	28	45	21	.293	.382	.376	109	6	1	3	-2	.971	3	S-94,2-11/3-4,D-1	1.5
1989	Bos-A	146	524	76	151	42	2	3	40	73	44	.288	.379	.382	111	10	4	5	-2	.967	1	S-77,2-70/3-4,D-1	1.7
1990	*Bos-A	155	598	70	173	**45**	0	5	51	75	65	.289	.372	.390	108	9	4	4	-1	.990	-6	*2-119,S-50/D-1	0.8
1991	Bos-A	153	618	87	175	42	2	5	60	60	53	.283	.350	.382	98	-1	6	5	-1	.982	5	*2-152/S-6	0.2
1992	Bos-A	143	550	64	136	27	1	3	40	62	44	.247	.324	.316	75	-17	7	8	-3	.982	**24**	*2-142/D-1	0.7
1993	LA-N	132	445	48	123	21	2	2	31	38	40	.276	.335	.346	88	-7	1	3	-2	**.993**	19	*2-132	1.4
1994	Mil-N	108	399	48	108	22	0	2	37	57	34	.271	.365	.341	80	-10	1	2	-1	**.995**	11	*2-106	0.4
1995	SD-N	131	445	58	114	18	1	4	40	59	38	.256	.350	.328	83	-9	6	4	-1	.994	18	*2-130/S-5	1.6
1996	*SD-N	146	495	45	121	20	0	2	49	59	53	.244	.329	.297	70	-20	2	5	-2	.987	4	*2-145	-0.9
Total	10	1232	4442	560	1209	261	10	27	384	532	392	.272	.354	.354	92	-41	37	42	-14	.988	81	*2-1009,S-236/3DO	7.9

■ **JACK REED**   Reed, John Burwell   b: 2/2/33, Silver City, Miss.   BR/TR, 6', 185 lbs.   Deb: 4/23/61

YEAR	TM/L	G	AB	R	H	2B	3B	HR	RBI	BB	SO	AVG	OBP	SLG	PRO+	BR/A	SB	CS	SBR	FA	FR	G/POS	TPR
1961	*NY-A	28	13	4	2	0	0	0	1	1	1	.154	.214	.154	0	-2	0	0	0	.933	-9	O-27	-1.1
1962	NY-A	88	43	17	13	2	1	1	4	4	7	.302	.362	.465	125	1	2	1	0	.941	-23	O-75	-2.2
1963	NY-A	106	73	18	15	3	1	0	1	9	14	.205	.293	.274	60	-4	5	1	1	1.000	-21	O-89	-2.6
Total	3	222	129	39	30	5	2	1	6	14	22	.233	.308	.326	76	-4	7	2	1	.972	-53	O-191	-5.9

■ **MILT REED**   Reed, Milton D.   b: 7/4/1890, Atlanta, Ga.   d: 7/27/38, Atlanta, Ga.   BL/TR, 5'9.5", 150 lbs.   Deb: 9/9/11

YEAR	TM/L	G	AB	R	H	2B	3B	HR	RBI	BB	SO	AVG	OBP	SLG	PRO+	BR/A	SB	CS	SBR	FA	FR	G/POS	TPR
1911	StL-N	1	0	0	0	0	0	0	0	0	0	.000	.000	.000	-99	-0	0			.000	0	H	0.0
1913	Phi-N	13	24	4	6	1	0	0	0	1	5	.250	.280	.292	61	-1	1			.900	-4	/S-9,2-3	-0.5
1914	Phi-N	44	107	10	22	2	1	0	2	10	13	.206	.280	.243	52	-6	4			.887	-17	S-22,2-11/3-1	-2.5
1915	Bro-F	10	31	2	9	1	1	0	2	2	0	.290	.353	.387	109	-0	2			.864	-5	S-10	-0.5
Total	4	68	163	16	37	4	2	0	4	13	18	.227	.292	.276	63	-8	7			.880	-26	/S-41,2-14,3-1	-3.5

■ **TED REED**   Reed, Ralph Edwin   b: 10/18/1890, Beaver, Pa.   d: 2/16/59, Beaver, Pa.   BR/TR, 5'11", 190 lbs.   Deb: 9/10/15

YEAR	TM/L	G	AB	R	H	2B	3B	HR	RBI	BB	SO	AVG	OBP	SLG	PRO+	BR/A	SB	CS	SBR	FA	FR	G/POS	TPR
1915	New-F	20	77	5	20	1	2	0	4	2	7	.260	.287	.325	76	-4	1			.863	-3	3-20	-0.7

■ **BILLY REED**   Reed, William Joseph   b: 11/12/22, Shawano, Wis.   BL/TR, 5'10.5", 175 lbs.   Deb: 4/15/52

YEAR	TM/L	G	AB	R	H	2B	3B	HR	RBI	BB	SO	AVG	OBP	SLG	PRO+	BR/A	SB	CS	SBR	FA	FR	G/POS	TPR
1952	Bos-N	15	52	4	13	0	0	0	0	0	5	.250	.264	.250	45	-4	0	0	0	.931	-7	2-14	-1.0

■ **ICICLE REEDER**   Reeder, James Edward   b: 1865, Cincinnati, Ohio   BR, 6',   Deb: 6/24/1884

YEAR	TM/L	G	AB	R	H	2B	3B	HR	RBI	BB	SO	AVG	OBP	SLG	PRO+	BR/A	SB	CS	SBR	FA	FR	G/POS	TPR
1884	Cin-a	3	14	0	2	0	0	0		0			.143	.143	.143	-6	-2				1.000	-0	/O-3	-0.2
	Was-U	3	12	0	2	0	0	0		0			.167	.167	.167	1	-2				.500	-1	/O-3	-0.3
Total	1	6	26	0	4	0	0	0		0			.154	.154	.154	-3	-3				.714	-1	/O-6	-0.5

■ **NICK REEDER**   Reeder, Nicholas (b: Nicholas Herchenroeder)   b: 3/22/1867, Louisville, Ky.   d: 9/26/1894, Louisville, Ky.   BR/TR, 5'9", 189 lbs.   Deb: 4/11/1891

YEAR	TM/L	G	AB	R	H	2B	3B	HR	RBI	BB	SO	AVG	OBP	SLG	PRO+	BR/A	SB	CS	SBR	FA	FR	G/POS	TPR
1891	Lou-a	1	2	0	0	0	0	0	0	0	1	.000	.000	.000	-99	-1	0			1.000	-0	/3-1	-0.1

■ **RANDY REESE**   Reese, Andrew Jackson   b: 2/7/04, Tupelo, Miss.   d: 1/10/66, Tupelo, Miss.   BR/TR, 5'11", 180 lbs.   Deb: 4/15/27

YEAR	TM/L	G	AB	R	H	2B	3B	HR	RBI	BB	SO	AVG	OBP	SLG	PRO+	BR/A	SB	CS	SBR	FA	FR	G/POS	TPR
1927	NY-N	97	355	43	94	14	2	4	21	13	52	.265	.298	.349	73	-14	5			.912	-1	3-64,O-16/1-1	-1.3
1928	NY-N	109	406	61	125	18	4	6	44	13	24	.308	.331	.416	94	-5	7			.941	-10	O-64,2-26/1-6,S3	-1.7
1929	NY-N	58	209	36	55	11	3	0	21	15	19	.263	.316	.344	64	-12	8			.960	1	2-44/O-8,3-4	-0.9
1930	NY-N	67	172	26	47	4	2	4	25	10	12	.273	.313	.390	70	-9	1			.957	-3	O-32,3-10/1-1	-1.2
Total	4	331	1142	166	321	47	11	14	111	51	107	.281	.315	.378	78	-39	21			.954	-14	O-120/3-84,2-70,1S	-5.1

■ **PEE WEE REESE**   Reese, Harold Henry   b: 7/23/18, Ekron, Ky.   BR/TR, 5'9", 175 lbs.   Deb: 4/23/40   CH

YEAR	TM/L	G	AB	R	H	2B	3B	HR	RBI	BB	SO	AVG	OBP	SLG	PRO+	BR/A	SB	CS	SBR	FA	FR	G/POS	TPR
1940	Bro-N	84	312	58	85	8	4	5	28	45	42	.272	.366	.372	98	0	15			.960	-14	S-83	-0.7
1941	*Bro-N	152	595	76	136	23	5	2	46	68	56	.229	.311	.294	68	-24	10			.946	8	*S-151	-0.5
1942	Bro-N	151	564	87	144	24	5	3	53	82	55	.255	.350	.332	98	1	15			.959	17	*S-151	2.9
1946	Bro-N†	152	542	79	154	16	10	5	60	87	71	.284	.384	.378	116	14	10			.966	-4	*S-152	2.1
1947	*Bro-N★	142	476	81	135	24	4	12	73	**104**	67	.284	.414	.426	119	17	7			.966	-2	*S-142	2.2
1948	Bro-N★	151	566	96	155	31	4	9	75	79	63	.274	.363	.390	100	2	25			.962	10	*S-149	2.1
1949	*Bro-N★	155	617	**132**	172	27	3	16	73	116	59	.279	.396	.410	112	15	26			**.977**	2	*S-155	2.7
1950	Bro-N★	141	531	97	138	21	5	11	52	91	62	.260	.369	.380	96	-1	17			.963	2	*S-134/3-7	1.1
1951	Bro-N★	154	616	94	176	20	8	10	84	81	57	.286	.371	.393	103	5	20	14	-2	.953	-8	*S-154	0.6
1952	*Bro-N★	149	559	94	152	18	8	6	58	86	59	.272	.369	.365	103	5	**30**	5	6	.969	-11	*S-145	1.1
1953	*Bro-N☆	140	524	108	142	25	7	13	61	82	61	.271	.374	.420	104	5	22	6	3	.966	-1	*S-135	1.7
1954	Bro-N☆	141	554	98	171	35	8	10	69	90	62	.309	.408	.455	121	20	8	5	-2	.965	-4	*S-140	2.7
1955	*Bro-N★	145	553	99	156	29	4	10	61	78	60	.282	.374	.403	103	5	8	7	-2	.965	-13	*S-142	0.2
1956	*Bro-N★	147	572	85	147	19	2	9	46	56	69	.257	.324	.344	74	-20	13	4	2	.965	-9	*S-136,3-12	-1.7
1957	Bro-N	103	330	33	74	3	1	1	29	39	32	.224	.308	.248	47	-23	5	2	0	.943	10	3-75,S-23	-1.0
1958	LA-N	59	147	21	33	7	2	4	17	26	15	.224	.341	.381	88	-2	1	2	-1	.929	-8	S-22,3-21	-0.9
Total	16	2166	8058	1338	2170	330	80	126	885	1210	890	.269	.366	.377	98	19	232	45		.962	-25	*S-2014,3-115	14.6

■ **JIMMIE REESE**   Reese, James Herman (b: James Herman Soloman)   b: 10/1/01, New York, N.Y.   d: 7/13/94, Santa Ana, Cal.   BL/TR, 5'11.5", 165 lbs.   Deb: 4/19/30   C

YEAR	TM/L	G	AB	R	H	2B	3B	HR	RBI	BB	SO	AVG	OBP	SLG	PRO+	BR/A	SB	CS	SBR	FA	FR	G/POS	TPR
1930	NY-A	77	188	44	65	14	2	3	18	11	9	.346	.382	.489	125	7	1	1	-0	.974	-9	2-48/3-5	-0.1
1931	NY-A	65	245	41	59	10	2	3	26	17	10	.241	.293	.335	68	-12	2	3	-1	.972	5	2-61	-0.4
1932	StL-N	90	309	38	82	15	4	2	26	20	19	.265	.314	.333	72	-12	4			.979	9	2-77	0.1
Total	3	232	742	123	206	39	8	8	70	48	37	.278	.324	.373	84	-17	7	4		.975	4	2-186/3-5	-0.4

■ **RICH REESE**   Reese, Richard Benjamin   b: 9/29/41, Leipsic, Ohio   BL/TL, 6'3", 200 lbs.   Deb: 9/4/64

YEAR	TM/L	G	AB	R	H	2B	3B	HR	RBI	BB	SO	AVG	OBP	SLG	PRO+	BR/A	SB	CS	SBR	FA	FR	G/POS	TPR
1964	Min-A	10	7	0	0	0	0	0	0	0	0	.000	.000	.000	-99	-2	0	0	0	1.000	0	/1-1	-0.2
1965	Min-A	14	7	0	2	0	0	0	0	0	2	.286	.444	.429	143	1	0	0	0	1.000	-0	/1-6,O-1	-0.2
1966	Min-A	3	3	0	0	0	0	0	0	0	0	.000	.000	.333	0	5			-0	.000	0	H	0.0
1967	Min-A	95	101	13	25	5	0	4	20	8	17	.248	.303	.416	102	0	0	0	0	.990	-1	1-36,O-10	-0.2
1968	Min-A	126	332	40	86	15	2	4	28	18	36	.259	.303	.352	93	-3	3	1	0	.991	-2	1-87,O-15	-1.2

YEAR	TM/L	G	AB	R	H	2B	3B	HR	RBI	BB	SO	AVG	OBP	SLG	PRO+	BR/A	SB	CS	SBR	FA	FR	G/POS	TPR
1969	*Min-A	132	419	52	135	24	4	16	69	23	57	.322	.365	.513	140	21	1	5	-3	.993	-4	*1-117/O-5	0.6
1970	*Min-A	153	501	63	131	15	5	10	56	48	70	.261	.335	.371	93	-4	5	4	-1	.992	-2	*1-146	-1.9
1971	Min-A	120	329	40	72	8	3	10	39	20	35	.219	.274	.353	74	-12	7	4	-0	.994	-3	1-95/O-9	-2.4
1972	Min-A	132	197	23	43	3	2	5	26	25	27	.218	.306	.330	85	-3	0	1	-1	.988	3	1-98,O-13	-0.5
1973	Det-A	59	102	10	14	1	0	2	4	7	17	.137	.193	.206	11	-12	0	0	0	1.000	-3	1-37,O-21	-1.8
	Min-A	22	23	7	4	1	1	1	3	6	6	.174	.345	.435	114	1	0	0	0	1.000	-1	1-17	0.1
	Yr	81	125	17	18	2	1	3	7	13	23	.144	.225	.248	31	-12	0	0	0	1.000	-2	1-54,O-21	-1.7
Total	10	866	2020	248	512	73	17	52	245	158	270	.253	.314	.384	95	-15	16	15	-4	.992	-10	1-640/O-74	-7.5

■ BOBBY REEVES
Reeves, Robert Edwin "Gunner" b: 6/24/04, Hill City, Tenn. d: 6/4/93, Chattanooga, Tenn. BR/TR, 5'11", 170 lbs. Deb: 6/9/26

YEAR	TM/L	G	AB	R	H	2B	3B	HR	RBI	BB	SO	AVG	OBP	SLG	PRO+	BR/A	SB	CS	SBR	FA	FR	G/POS	TPR
1926	Was-A	20	49	4	11	0	1	0	7	6	9	.224	.321	.265	56	-3	1	1	-0	.940	1	3-16/2-1,S-1	-0.1
1927	Was-A	112	380	37	97	11	5	1	39	21	53	.255	.296	.318	60	-23	3	1	0	.923	-7	S-96,3-12/2-2	-1.8
1928	Was-A	102	353	44	107	16	8	3	42	24	47	.303	.351	.419	102	1	4	8	-4	.908	-4	*3-131/2-2,S-2,1-1	0.2
1929	Bos-A	140	460	60	114	19	2	2	28	60	57	.248	.343	.311	71	-18	7	8	-3	.912	1	3-62,S-15,2-11	-1.4
1930	Bos-A	92	272	41	59	7	4	2	18	50	36	.217	.345	.294	66	-12	6	2	1	.895	-8	S-66,2-22/3-8,0-1	-0.2
1931	Bos-A	36	84	11	14	2	2	0	1	14	16	.167	.293	.238	43	-7	0	1	-1	.912	-8	2-29/P-1	-1.3
Total	6	502	1598	203	402	55	22	8	135	175	218	.252	.331	.329	65	-62	21	21	-6	.906	-11	3-229,S-180/2P10	-4.6

■ RUDY REGALADO
Regalado, Rudolph Valentino b: 5/21/30, Los Angeles, Cal. BR/TR, 6'1", 185 lbs. Deb: 4/13/54

YEAR	TM/L	G	AB	R	H	2B	3B	HR	RBI	BB	SO	AVG	OBP	SLG	PRO+	BR/A	SB	CS	SBR	FA	FR	G/POS	TPR
1954	*Cle-A	65	180	21	45	5	0	2	24	19	16	.250	.335	.311	76	-5	0	2	-1	.967	-5	3-50/2-2	-1.3
1955	Cle-A	10	26	2	7	2	0	0	5	2	4	.269	.321	.346	77	-1	0	0	0	.955	2	/3-8,2-1	0.1
1956	Cle-A	16	47	4	11	1	0	0	2	4	1	.234	.308	.255	49	-3	0	0	0	.783	-7	3-14/1-1	-1.0
Total	3	91	253	27	63	8	0	2	31	25	21	.249	.329	.304	71	-10	0	2	-1	.944	-10	/3-72,2-3,1-1	-2.2

■ JOE REGAN
Regan, Joseph Charles b: 7/12/1872, Seymour, Conn. d: 11/18/48, Hartford, Conn. BR/TR, 6'1", Deb: 9/21/1898

YEAR	TM/L	G	AB	R	H	2B	3B	HR	RBI	BB	SO	AVG	OBP	SLG	PRO+	BR/A	SB	CS	SBR	FA	FR	G/POS	TPR
1898	NY-N	2	5	1	1	0	0	0	2	0	0	.200	.200	.200	15	-1	0			1.000	-1	/O-2	-0.1

■ BILL REGAN
Regan, William Wright b: 1/23/1899, Pittsburgh, Pa. d: 6/11/68, Pittsburgh, Pa. BR/TR, 5'10", 155 lbs. Deb: 6/2/26

YEAR	TM/L	G	AB	R	H	2B	3B	HR	RBI	BB	SO	AVG	OBP	SLG	PRO+	BR/A	SB	CS	SBR	FA	FR	G/POS	TPR
1926	Bos-A	108	403	40	106	21	3	4	34	23	37	.263	.309	.360	76	-15	6	3	0	.965	17	*2-106	0.5
1927	Bos-A	129	468	43	128	37	10	2	66	26	51	.274	.315	.408	88	-10	10	10	-3	.960	3	*2-121	-0.6
1928	Bos-A	138	511	53	135	30	6	7	75	21	40	.264	.296	.387	80	-17	9	6	1	.963	9	*2-137/O-1	0.6
1929	Bos-A	104	371	38	107	27	7	1	54	22	38	.288	.328	.407	90	-6	7	5	-1	.962	-16	2-91,3-10/1-1	-1.8
1930	Bos-A	134	507	54	135	35	10	3	53	26	60	.266	.303	.393	78	-19	5	4	2	.963	-10	*2-127/3-2	-2.0
1931	Pit-N	28	104	8	21	8	0	1	10	5	19	.202	.239	.308	46	-8	2			.944	5	2-28	-0.7
Total	6	641	2364	236	632	158	36	18	292	122	245	.267	.306	.387	81	-75	38	**26**		.962	8	2-610/3-12,1-1,0-1	-4.6

■ TONY REGO
Rego, Antone (b: Antone Do Rego) b: 10/31/1897, Wailuku, Hawaii d: 1/6/78, Tulsa, Okla. BR/TR, 5'4", 165 lbs. Deb: 6/21/24

YEAR	TM/L	G	AB	R	H	2B	3B	HR	RBI	BB	SO	AVG	OBP	SLG	PRO+	BR/A	SB	CS	SBR	FA	FR	G/POS	TPR
1924	StL-A	24	59	5	13	1	0	0	5	1	3	.220	.233	.237	20	-7	0	0	0	.972	-2	C-23	-0.6
1925	StL-A	20	32	5	13	2	1	0	3	3	2	.406	.472	.531	147	2	0	0	0	.979	2	C-19	0.5
Total	2	44	91	10	26	3	1	0	8	4	5	.286	.323	.341	66	-5	0	0	0	.975	-0	/C-42	-0.1

■ WALLY REHG
Rehg, Walter Phillip b: 8/31/1888, Summerfield, Ill. d: 4/5/46, Burbank, Cal. BR/TR, 5'8", 160 lbs. Deb: 4/14/12

YEAR	TM/L	G	AB	R	H	2B	3B	HR	RBI	BB	SO	AVG	OBP	SLG	PRO+	BR/A	SB	CS	SBR	FA	FR	G/POS	TPR
1912	Pit-N	8	9	1	0	0	0	0	0	0	1	.000	.000	.000	-99	-2	0			1.000	-1	/O-2	-0.3
1913	Bos-A	30	101	13	28	3	2	0	9	2	7	.277	.291	.347	84	-2	4			.943	-3	O-26	-0.7
1914	Bos-A	88	151	14	33	4	2	0	11	18	11	.219	.306	.272	74	-5	5	8	-3	.980	-5	O-43	-1.6
1915	Bos-A	5	5	2	1	0	0	0	0	0	1	.200	.200	.200	20	-1	1			1.000	-0	/O-1	0.0
1917	Bos-N	87	341	48	92	12	6	1	31	24	32	.270	.320	.349	111	4	13			.956	-5	O-86	-0.6
1918	Bos-N	40	133	6	32	5	1	1	12	5	14	.241	.268	.316	81	-3	3			.988	2	O-38	-0.4
1919	Cin-N	5	12	1	2	0	0	0	3	1	0	.167	.231	.167	21	-1	0			.875	0	/O-5	-0.1
Total	7	263	752	85	188	24	11	3	66	50	66	.250	.299	.319	90	-11	26	**8**		.965	-12	O-201	-3.7

■ FRANK REIBER
Reiber, Frank Bernard "Tubby" b: 9/19/09, Huntington, W.Va. BR/TR, 5'8.5", 169 lbs. Deb: 4/13/33

YEAR	TM/L	G	AB	R	H	2B	3B	HR	RBI	BB	SO	AVG	OBP	SLG	PRO+	BR/A	SB	CS	SBR	FA	FR	G/POS	TPR
1933	Det-A	13	18	3	5	0	1	1	3	2	3	.278	.350	.556	134	1	0	0	0	.929	-2	/C-6	-0.1
1934	Det-A	3	1	0	0	0	0	0	0	0	0	.000	.667	.000	84	0	0	0	0	.000	0	/C-5	0.0
1935	Det-A	8	11	3	3	0	0	0	1	3	3	.273	.429	.273	88	0	0	0	0	1.000	-1	/C-5	0.0
1936	Det-A	20	55	7	15	2	0	1	5	7	7	.273	.333	.364	72	-2	0	1	-1	.982	-4	C-17/O-1	-0.5
Total	4	44	85	13	23	2	1	2	9	12	13	.271	.361	.388	89	-1	0	1	-1	.975	-6	/C-28,O-1	-0.6

■ HERMAN REICH
Reich, Herman Charles b: 11/23/17, Bell, Cal. BR/TL, 6'2", 200 lbs. Deb: 5/3/49

YEAR	TM/L	G	AB	R	H	2B	3B	HR	RBI	BB	SO	AVG	OBP	SLG	PRO+	BR/A	SB	CS	SBR	FA	FR	G/POS	TPR
1949	Was-A	2	2	0	0	0	0	0	0	0	0	.000	.000	.000	-99	-1	0	0	0	.000	0	H	-0.1
	Cle-A	1	2	0	1	0	0	0	0	1	0	.500	.667	.500	215	1	0	0	0	.000	0	/O-1	0.0
	Yr	3	4	0	1	0	0	0	0	1	0	.250	.400	.250	75	-0	0	0	0	.000	0	/O-1	-0.1
	Chi-N	108	386	43	108	18	2	3	34	13	32	.280	.305	.360	80	-12	4			.989	14	1-85,O-16	0.1
Total	1	111	390	43	109	18	2	3	34	14	33	.279	.306	.359	80	-12	4	**0**		.969	14	/1-85,O-17	0.0

■ RICK REICHARDT
Reichardt, Frederic Carl b: 3/16/43, Madison, Wis. BR/TR, 6'3", 215 lbs. Deb: 9/1/64

YEAR	TM/L	G	AB	R	H	2B	3B	HR	RBI	BB	SO	AVG	OBP	SLG	PRO+	BR/A	SB	CS	SBR	FA	FR	G/POS	TPR
1964	LA-A	11	37	0	6	0	0	0	0	0	12	.162	.184	.162	-3	-5	1	0		1.000	0	O-11	-0.6
1965	Cal-A	20	75	8	20	4	0	0	6	5	12	.267	.321	.360	95	-0	4	1	1	.975	1	O-20	0.0
1966	Cal-A	89	319	48	92	5	4	16	44	27	61	.288	.368	.480	145	19	8	4	0	.976	-1	O-87	1.4
1967	Cal-A	146	498	56	132	14	2	17	69	35	90	.265	.322	.404	118	10	5	3	-0	.974	10	*O-138	1.4
1968	Cal-A	151	534	62	136	20	3	21	73	42	118	.255	.330	.421	131	19	8	7	-3	.989	9	*O-148	2.2
1969	Cal-A	137	493	60	125	11	4	13	68	43	100	.254	.324	.371	99	-2	3	6	-3	.981	8	*O-136/1-3	-0.4
1970	Cal-A	9	6	1	1	0	0	0	1	3	0	.167	.444	.167	78	0	0	0	0	1.000	-0	/O-1	0.0
	Was-A	107	277	42	70	14	2	15	46	23	69	.253	.330	.480	127	9	2	4	-2	.985	-8	O-79/3-1	-0.5
	Yr	116	283	43	71	14	2	15	47	26	69	.251	.333	.473	126	9	2	4	-2	.985	-8	O-80/3-1	-0.5
1971	Chi-A	138	496	53	138	14	2	19	62	37	90	.278	.336	.429	112	7	5	10	-5	.981	-7	*O-128/1-9	-1.3
1972	Chi-A	101	291	31	73	14	4	8	43	20	63	.251	.323	.409	114	5	2	3	-1	.981	-10	O-90	-1.1
1973	Chi-A	46	153	15	42	8	1	3	16	8	29	.275	.315	.399	96	-1	2	3	-1	1.000	-2	O-37/D-6	-0.6
	KC-A	41	127	15	28	5	2	3	17	11	28	.220	.283	.362	75	-5	0	1	-1	1.000	-1	D-31/O-7	-0.7
	Yr	87	280	30	70	13	3	6	33	19	57	.250	.300	.382	86	-6	2	4	-2	1.000	-3	O-44,D-37	-1.3
1974	KC-A	1	1	0	1	0	0	0	0	0	0	1.000	1.000	1.000	451	0	0	0	0	.000	0	H	0.0
Total	11	997	3307	391	864	109	24	116	445	263	672	.261	.328	.414	115	56	40	41	-13	.982	-0	O-882/D-37,1-12,3-1	-0.2

■ DICK REICHLE
Reichle, Richard Wendell b: 11/23/1896, Lincoln, Ill. d: 6/13/67, St.Louis, Mo. BL/TR, 6', 185 lbs. Deb: 9/19/22

YEAR	TM/L	G	AB	R	H	2B	3B	HR	RBI	BB	SO	AVG	OBP	SLG	PRO+	BR/A	SB	CS	SBR	FA	FR	G/POS	TPR
1922	Bos-A	6	24	3	6	1	0	0	2	0	2	.250	.280	.292	50	-2	0	0	0	1.000	-0	/O-6	-0.3
1923	Bos-A	122	361	40	93	17	3	1	39	22	34	.258	.315	.330	69	-16	3	6	-3	.976	-7	O-93/1-2	-3.1
Total	2	128	385	43	99	18	3	1	39	22	36	.257	.313	.327	68	-18	3	6	-3	.977	-7	/O-99,1-2	-3.4

■ JESSIE REID
Reid, Jessie Thomas b: 6/1/62, Honolulu, Hawaii BL/TL, 6'1", 200 lbs. Deb: 9/9/87

YEAR	TM/L	G	AB	R	H	2B	3B	HR	RBI	BB	SO	AVG	OBP	SLG	PRO+	BR/A	SB	CS	SBR	FA	FR	G/POS	TPR
1987	SF-N	6	8	1	1	0	0	1	1	1	5	.125	.222	.500	89	-0	0	0	0	1.000	-1	/O-3	-0.1
1988	SF-N	2	2	0	0	0	0	0	0	0	1	.000	.000	.000	-99	-1	0	0	0	.000	0	H	-0.1
Total	2	8	10	1	1	0	0	1	1	1	6	.100	.182	.400	54	-1	0	0	0	1.000	-1	/O-3	-0.2

■ SCOTT REID
Reid, Scott Donald b: 1/7/47, Chicago, Ill. BL/TR, 6'1", 195 lbs. Deb: 9/10/69

YEAR	TM/L	G	AB	R	H	2B	3B	HR	RBI	BB	SO	AVG	OBP	SLG	PRO+	BR/A	SB	CS	SBR	FA	FR	G/POS	TPR
1969	Phi-N	13	19	5	4	0	0	0	0	7	7	.211	.423	.211	85	0	0	1	-1	1.000	0	/O-5	-0.2
1970	Phi-N	25	49	5	6	1	0	0	0	11	20	.122	.283	.143	18	-5	0	0	-1	1.000	3	O-18	-0.3
Total	2	38	68	10	10	1	0	0	1	18	27	.147	.326	.162	37	-5	0	1	-1	1.000	2	/O-23	-0.5

■ BILLY REID
Reid, William Alexander b: 5/17/1857, London, Ont., Can. d: 6/26/40, London, Ont., Can. BL/TR, 6', 170 lbs. Deb: 5/1/1883

YEAR	TM/L	G	AB	R	H	2B	3B	HR	RBI	BB	SO	AVG	OBP	SLG	PRO+	BR/A	SB	CS	SBR	FA	FR	G/POS	TPR
1883	Bal-a	24	97	14	27	3	0	0			4	.278	.307	.309	96	-1				.842	-8	2-23/S-1	-0.7
1884	Pit-a	19	70	11	17	2	0	0			4	.243	.293	.271	84	-1				.724	-12	O-17/3-1,2-1	-0.5
Total	2	43	167	25	44	5	0	0			8	.263	.301	.293	91	-2				.839	-12	/2-24,O-17,3-1,S-1	-1.2

YEAR	TM/L	G	AB	R	H	2B	3B	HR	RBI	BB	SO	AVG	OBP	SLG	PRO+	BR/A	SB	CS	SBR	FA	FR	G/POS	TPR

■ DUKE REILLEY   Reilley, Alexander Aloysius "Midget"   b: 8/25/1884, Chicago, Ill.   d: 3/4/68, Indianapolis, Ind.   BB/TR, 5'4.5", 148 lbs.   Deb: 8/28/09

YEAR	TM/L	G	AB	R	H	2B	3B	HR	RBI	BB	SO	AVG	OBP	SLG	PRO+	BR/A	SB	FA	FR	G/POS	TPR
1909	Cle-A	20	62	10	13	0	0	0	0		4	.210	.258	.210	46	-4	5	.979	2	O-18	-0.3

■ CHARLIE REILLEY   Reilley, Charles E.   b: 1856, Hartford, Conn.   BR/TR, 5'10", 165 lbs.   Deb: 5/1/1879

YEAR	TM/L	G	AB	R	H	2B	3B	HR	RBI	BB	SO	AVG	OBP	SLG	PRO+	BR/A	FA	FR	G/POS	TPR
1879	Tro-N	62	236	17	54	5	1	0	19	1	20	.229	.232	.258	66	-8	.867	-16	C-49,1-11/O-2	-2.2
1880	Cin-N	30	103	8	21	1	0	0	9	0	5	.204	.204	.214	42	-6	.759	-5	O-16,C-13/3-4	-1.1
1881	Det-N	19	70	8	12	2	0	0	3	0	10	.171	.171	.200	16	-7	.889	-4	C-10/O-4,S-3,3-3,1	-0.9
	Wor-N	2	8	2	3	0	0	0	1	0	1	.375	.375	.375	129	0	1.000	-2	/C-2	-0.2
	Yr	21	78	10	15	2	0	0	4	0	11	.192	.192	.218	28	-6	.897	-6	C-12/O-4,S-3,3-3,1	-1.1
1882	Pro-N	3	11	0	2	0	0	0	2	1	2	.182	.250	.182	41	-1	.714	-2	/C-3	-0.3
1884	Bos-U	3	11	1	0	0	0	0	0	0	0	.000	.083	.000	-74	-3	1.000	-1	/O-2,3-1	-0.3
Total	5	119	439	36	92	8	1	0	34	3	38	.210	.215	.232	48	-24	.867	-30	/C-77,O-24,1-12,3S	-5.0

■ ARCH REILLY   Reilly, Archer Edwin   b: 8/17/1891, Alton, Ill.   d: 11/29/63, Columbus, Ohio   BR/TR, 5'10", 163 lbs.   Deb: 6/1/17

YEAR	TM/L	G	AB	R	H	2B	3B	HR	RBI	BB	SO	AVG	OBP	SLG	PRO+	BR/A	FA	FR	G/POS	TPR
1917	Pit-N	1	0	0	0	0	0	0	0	0	0	—	—	—	0	0	1.000	0	/3-1	0.0

■ BARNEY REILLY   Reilly, Bernard Eugene   b: 2/7/1885, Brockton, Mass.   d: 11/15/34, St.Joseph, Mo.   BR/TR, 6'", 175 lbs.   Deb: 7/2/09

YEAR	TM/L	G	AB	R	H	2B	3B	HR	RBI	BB	SO	AVG	OBP	SLG	PRO+	BR/A	SB	FA	FR	G/POS	TPR
1909	Chi-A	12	25	3	5	0	0	0	3		3	.200	.286	.200	56	-1	2	.962	4	2-11/O-1	0.2

■ JOSH REILLY   Reilly, Charles   b: 1868, San Francisco, Cal.   d: 6/13/38, San Francisco, Cal.   Deb: 5/2/1896

YEAR	TM/L	G	AB	R	H	2B	3B	HR	RBI	BB	SO	AVG	OBP	SLG	PRO+	BR/A	SB	FA	FR	G/POS	TPR
1896	Chi-N	9	42	6	9	1	0	0	2	1	1	.214	.233	.238	23	-5	2	.857	-1	/2-8,S-1	-0.4

■ CHARLIE REILLY   Reilly, Charles Thomas "Princeton Charlie" (b: Charles Thomas O'Reilly)   b: 2/15/1867, Princeton, N.J.   d: 12/16/37, Los Angeles, Cal.   BB/TR, 5'11", 190 lbs.   Deb: 10/9/1889

YEAR	TM/L	G	AB	R	H	2B	3B	HR	RBI	BB	SO	AVG	OBP	SLG	PRO+	BR/A	SB	FA	FR	G/POS	TPR
1889	Col-a	6	23	5	11	1	0	3		9		.478	.538	.913	326	7	9	.923	2	/3-6	0.7
1890	Col-a	137	530	75	141	23	3	4	77	35		.266	.319	.343	102	1	43	**.893**	28	*3-137	2.9
1891	Pit-N	114	415	43	91	8	5	3	44	29	58	.219	.277	.284	65	-19	20	.857	2	*3-99,S-11/O-4	-1.1
1892	Phi-N	91	331	42	65	7	3	1	24	18	43	.196	.242	.245	47	-21	13	.905	-3	3-70,O-15/2-4	-0.9
1893	Phi-N	104	416	64	102	16	7	4	56	33	36	.245	.314	.346	76	-16	13	.895	-1	*3-104	-1.2
1894	Phi-N	39	135	21	40	1	2	0	19	16	10	.296	.383	.333	76	-4	9	.874	2	3-28/O-5,2-4,S-1,1	-0.2
1895	Phi-N	49	179	28	48	6	1	0	25	13	12	.268	.335	.313	67	-8	7	.900	-3	S-34,3-11/2-3,O-1	-0.8
1897	Was-N	101	351	64	97	18	3	2	60	34		.276	.359	.362	91	-4	18	.905	18	*3-101	1.4
Total	8	641	2380	342	595	80	24	17	311	180	161	.250	.314	.325	80	-65	132	.890	59	3-556/S-46,O-25,21	0.8

■ HAL REILLY   Reilly, Harold John   b: 4/1/1894, Oshkosh, Wis.   d: 12/24/57, Chicago, Ill.   BR/TR, 6', 180 lbs.   Deb: 6/19/19

YEAR	TM/L	G	AB	R	H	2B	3B	HR	RBI	BB	SO	AVG	OBP	SLG	PRO+	BR/A	FA	FR	G/POS	TPR
1919	Chi-N	1	3	0	0	0	0	0	0	0	0	.000	.000	.000	-99	-0	.000		/O-1	-0.1

■ JOHN REILLY   Reilly, John Good "Long Jong"   b: 10/5/1858, Cincinnati, Ohio   d: 5/31/37, Cincinnati, Ohio   BR/TR, 6'3", 178 lbs.   Deb: 5/18/1880

YEAR	TM/L	G	AB	R	H	2B	3B	HR	RBI	BB	SO	AVG	OBP	SLG	PRO+	BR/A	SB	FA	FR	G/POS	TPR
1880	Cin-N	73	272	21	56	8	4	0	16	3	36	.206	.215	.265	62	-10		.947	-4	*1-72/O-3	-2.0
1883	Cin-a	98	437	103	136	21	14	9	79	9		.311	.325	.485	149	21		.961	6	*1-98/O-1	0.9
1884	Cin-a	105	448	114	152	24	19	**11**	91	5		.339	.366	**.551**	186	39		.971	-2	*1-103/O-3,S-1	2.3
1885	Cin-a	111	482	92	143	18	11	5	60	11		.297	.322	.411	128	13		.963	-5	*1-107/O-7	-0.3
1886	Cin-a	115	441	94	117	12	11	6	79	31		.265	.321	.383	116	7	19	.967	-4	*1-110/O-6	-0.7
1887	Cin-a	134	551	106	170	35	14	10	96	22		.309	.352	.477	127	17	50	.980	-0	*1-127/O-9	0.2
1888	Cin-a	127	527	112	169	28	14	**13**	**103**	17		.321	.363	**.501**	167	36	82	.977	-0	*1-117,O-10	2.2
1889	Cin-a	111	427	84	111	24	13	5	66	34	37	.260	.340	.412	110	4	43	**.984**	-2	*1-109/O-2	-0.4
1890	Cin-N	133	553	114	166	25	**26**	4	86	16	41	.300	.328	.472	133	18	29	.977	-3	*1-132/O-1	0.7
1891	Cin-N	135	546	60	132	20	13	6	64	9	22	.242	.267	.348	78	-18	22	.982	-7	*1-100,O-36	-2.8
Total	10	1142	4684	898	1352	215	139	69	740	157	156	.289	.325	.438	128	127	245	.972	-25	*1-1075/O-78,S-1	0.0

■ JOE REILLY   Reilly, Joseph J.   b: 1861, New York, N.Y.   5'10", 140 lbs.   Deb: 6/8/1885

YEAR	TM/L	G	AB	R	H	2B	3B	HR	RBI	BB	SO	AVG	OBP	SLG	PRO+	BR/A	FA	FR	G/POS	TPR
1885	NY-a	10	40	6	7	3	0	0	3		2	.175	.214	.250	50	-2	.848	1	/2-8,3-2	0.0

■ TOM REILLY   Reilly, Thomas Henry   b: 8/3/1884, St.Louis, Mo.   d: 10/18/18, New Orleans, La.   BR/TR, 5'10",   Deb: 7/27/08

YEAR	TM/L	G	AB	R	H	2B	3B	HR	RBI	BB	SO	AVG	OBP	SLG	PRO+	BR/A	SB	FA	FR	G/POS	TPR
1908	StL-N	29	81	5	14	1	0	1	3		2	.173	.193	.222	34	-6	4	.866	-6	S-29	-1.4
1909	StL-N	5	7	0	2	0	1	0	2		0	.286	.286	.571	176	0	0	1.000	-6	/S-5	0.1
1914	Cle-A	1	1	0	0	0	0	0	0	0	0	.000	.000	.000	-96	-0	0	.000	0	H	0.0
Total	3	35	89	5	16	1	1	1	5		2	.180	.198	.247	44	-6	4	.875	-6	/S-34	-1.3

■ KEVIN REIMER   Reimer, Kevin Michael   b: 6/28/64, Macon, Ga.   BL/TR, 6'2", 215 lbs.   Deb: 9/13/88

YEAR	TM/L	G	AB	R	H	2B	3B	HR	RBI	BB	SO	AVG	OBP	SLG	PRO+	BR/A	SB	CS	SBR	FA	FR	G/POS	TPR
1988	Tex-A	12	25	2	3	0	0	1	2		6	.120	.120	.240	-2	-3	0	0	0	.000	-0	/O-1,D-7	-0.4
1989	Tex-A	3	5	0	0	0	0	0	0	0	1	.000	.000	.000	-98	-1	0	0	0	.000	-0	/D-1	-0.1
1990	Tex-A	64	100	5	26	9	1	2	15	10	22	.260	.333	.430	112	1	0	1	-1	.857	-2	D-21/O-9	-0.2
1991	Tex-A	136	394	46	106	22	0	20	69	33	93	.269	.336	.477	125	12	0	3	-2	.948	-5	O-66,D-56	0.1
1992	Tex-A	148	494	56	132	32	2	16	58	42	103	.267	.337	.437	120	12	2	4	-2	.949	-3	*O-110,D-32	0.5
1993	Mil-A	125	437	53	109	22	1	13	60	30	72	.249	.305	.394	88	-9	5	4	-1	.962	-1	D-83,O-37	-1.4
Total	6	488	1455	162	376	85	4	52	204	115	297	.258	.323	.430	108	12	7	12	-5	.948	-11	O-223,D-200	-1.5

■ MIKE REINBACH   Reinbach, Michael Wayne   b: 8/6/49, San Diego, Cal.   BL/TR, 6'2", 195 lbs.   Deb: 4/7/74

YEAR	TM/L	G	AB	R	H	2B	3B	HR	RBI	BB	SO	AVG	OBP	SLG	PRO+	BR/A	SB	FA	FR	G/POS	TPR
1974	Bal-A	12	20	2	5	1	0	0	2	2	5	.250	.318	.300	81	-0	0	1.000	-1	/O-3,D-3	-0.1

■ WALLY REINECKER   Reinecker, Walter (b: Walter Joseph Smith)   b: 4/21/1890, Pittsburgh, Pa.   d: 4/18/57, Pittsburgh, Pa.   BR/TR, 5'6", 150 lbs.   Deb: 9/17/15

YEAR	TM/L	G	AB	R	H	2B	3B	HR	RBI	BB	SO	AVG	OBP	SLG	PRO+	BR/A	SB	FA	FR	G/POS	TPR
1915	Bal-F	3	8	0	1	0	0	0	0	0	0	.125	.222	.125	-1	-1	0	.571	-2	/3-3	-0.3

■ ART REINHOLZ   Reinholz, Arthur August   b: 1/27/03, Detroit, Mich.   d: 12/29/80, New Port Richey, Fla.   BR/TR, 5'10.5", 175 lbs.   Deb: 9/27/28

YEAR	TM/L	G	AB	R	H	2B	3B	HR	RBI	BB	SO	AVG	OBP	SLG	PRO+	BR/A	SB	CS	SBR	FA	FR	G/POS	TPR
1928	Cle-A	2	3	0	1	0	0	0	0	1	0	.333	.500	.333	122	0	0	0		.833	1	/3-2	0.1

■ CHARLIE REIPSCHLAGER   Reipschlager, Charles W.   BR/TR, 5'6.5", 160 lbs.   Deb: 5/2/1883

YEAR	TM/L	G	AB	R	H	2B	3B	HR	RBI	BB	SO	AVG	OBP	SLG	PRO+	BR/A	SB	FA	FR	G/POS	TPR
1883	NY-a	37	145	8	27	4	2	0		4		.186	.208	.241	42	-9		.936	5	C-29/O-8	-0.3
1884	*NY-a	59	233	21	56	13	2	0		1		.240	.250	.313	85	-4		.925	19	C-51/O-8	1.7
1885	NY-a	72	268	29	65	11	1	0	21	9		.243	.270	.291	84	-4		.879	-8	C-59/O-6,3-6,S-1,2	-0.6
1886	NY-a	65	232	21	49	4	6	0	25	9		.211	.244	.280	67	-9	2	.880	-8	C-57/O-9	-0.8
1887	Cle-a	63	231	20	49	8	3	0	17	11		.212	.251	.273	47	-16	7	.888	3	C-48,1-16	-0.8
Total	5	296	1109	99	246	40	14	0	63	34		.222	.248	.283	66	-43	9	.900	12	C-244/O-31,132S	-0.8

■ BOBBY REIS   Reis, Robert Joseph Thomas   b: 1/2/09, Woodside, N.Y.   d: 5/1/73, St.Paul, Minn.   BR/TR, 6'1", 175 lbs.   Deb: 9/19/31

YEAR	TM/L	G	AB	R	H	2B	3B	HR	RBI	BB	SO	AVG	OBP	SLG	PRO+	BR/A	SB	FA	FR	G/POS	TPR
1931	Bro-N	6	17	3	5	0	0	0	2	2	0	.294	.368	.294	81	-0	0	.933	-1	/3-6	-0.1
1932	Bro-N	1	4	0	1	0	0	0	0	0	0	.250	.250	.250	36	-0	0	.500	1	/3-1	-0.0
1935	Bro-N	52	85	10	21	3	2	0	4	6	13	.247	.297	.329	70	-4	2	.950	2	O-21,P-14/2-4,13	-0.2
1936	Bos-N	37	60	3	13	2	0	0	5	3	6	.217	.254	.250	39	-5	0	1.000	3	P-35/O-2	-0.1
1937	Bos-N	45	86	10	21	5	0	0	6	13	12	.244	.343	.302	84	-2	2	1.000	-4	O-18/P-4,1-4	-0.2
1938	Bos-N	34	49	6	9	0	0	0	4	1	3	.184	.200	.184	7	-6	1	1.000	-4	P-16,O-10/S-3,C2	-0.7
Total	6	175	301	32	70	10	2	0	21	25	35	.233	.291	.279	59	-17	5	1.000	-2	P-69,O-51,312SC	-1.8

■ PETE REISER   Reiser, Harold Patrick   b: 3/17/19, St.Louis, Mo.   d: 10/25/81, Palm Springs, Cal.   BL/TR, 5'11", 185 lbs.   Deb: 7/23/40   C

YEAR	TM/L	G	AB	R	H	2B	3B	HR	RBI	BB	SO	AVG	OBP	SLG	PRO+	BR/A	SB	FA	FR	G/POS	TPR
1940	Bro-N	58	225	34	66	11	4	3	20	15	33	.293	.338	.418	101	-0	2	.960	-4	3-30,O-17/S-5	-0.3
1941	*Bro-N★	137	536	**117**	184	**39**	**17**	14	76	46	71	**.343**	.406	**.558**	163	43	4	.981	12	*O-133	**4.7**
1942	Bro-N★	125	480	89	149	33	5	10	64	48	45	.310	.375	.463	142	25	**20**	.969	-2	*O-125	1.8
1946	Bro-N☆	122	423	75	117	21	5	11	73	55	58	.277	.361	.428	122	12	**34**	.978	7	O-97,3-15	1.6
1947	*Bro-N	110	388	68	120	23	2	5	46	68	41	.309	.415	.418	117	13	14	.988	-5	*O-108	0.2
1948	Bro-N	64	127	17	30	2	1	6	19	29	21	.236	.382	.354	97	1	4	.981	-5	O-30/3-4	-0.6
1949	Bos-N	84	221	32	60	8	3	8	40	33	42	.271	.369	.443	123	7	1	.980	-1	O-63/3-4	0.4
1950	Bos-N	53	78	12	16	1	0	1	10	18	22	.205	.367	.269	75	-2	1	.979	-4	O-24/3-1	-0.4

YEAR	TM/L	G	AB	R	H	2B	3B	HR	RBI	BB	SO	AVG	OBP	SLG	PRO+	BR/A	SB	CS	SBR	FA	FR	G/POS	TPR
1951	Pit-N	74	140	22	38	9	3	2	13	27	20	.271	.389	.421	115	4	4	2	0	.982	-2	O-27/3-5	0.1
1952	Cle-A	34	44	7	6	1	0	3	7	4	16	.136	.208	.364	61	-3	1	1	-0	1.000	-1	O-10	-0.5
Total	10	861	2662	473	786	155	41	58	368	343	369	.295	.380	.450	127	100	87	3		.979	-1	O-634/3-59,S-5	7.0

■ CHARLIE REISING Reising, Charles "Pop" b: 8/28/1861, Lanesville, Ind. d: 7/26/15, Louisville, Ky. Deb: 7/19/1884

YEAR	TM/L	G	AB	R	H	2B	3B	HR	RBI	BB	SO	AVG	OBP	SLG	PRO+	BR/A	SB	CS	SBR	FA	FR	G/POS	TPR
1884	Ind-a	2	8	0	0	0	0	0		1		.000	.111	.000	-62	-1				.400	-1	/O-2	-0.3

■ AL REISS Reiss, Albert Allen b: 1/8/09, Elizabeth, N.J. d: 5/13/89, Red Bank, N.J. BB/TR, 5'10.5", 165 lbs. Deb: 6/22/32

YEAR	TM/L	G	AB	R	H	2B	3B	HR	RBI	BB	SO	AVG	OBP	SLG	PRO+	BR/A	SB	CS	SBR	FA	FR	G/POS	TPR
1932	Phi-A	9	5	0	1	0	0	0	1	1	1	.200	.333	.200	40	-0	0	0	0	1.000	0	/S-6	0.0

■ HEINIE REITZ Reitz, Henry P. b: 6/29/1867, Chicago, Ill. d: 11/10/14, Sacramento, Cal BL/TR, 5'7", 158 lbs. Deb: 4/27/1893

YEAR	TM/L	G	AB	R	H	2B	3B	HR	RBI	BB	SO	AVG	OBP	SLG	PRO+	BR/A	SB	CS	SBR	FA	FR	G/POS	TPR
1893	Bal-N	130	490	90	140	17	13	1	76	65	32	.286	.377	.380	100	1	24			.939	-1	*2-130	0.3
1894	*Bal-N	108	446	86	135	22	**31**	2	105	42	24	.303	.382	.504	105	0	18			**.968**	27	2-97,3-12	2.4
1895	Bal-N	71	245	45	72	15	5	0	29	18	11	.294	.350	.396	90	-4	15			.938	-5	2-48,3-18/S-1	-0.5
1896	*Bal-N	120	464	76	133	15	6	4	106	49	32	.287	.357	.371	91	-6	28			.952	-18	*2-118/S-3	-1.4
1897	*Bal-N	128	477	76	138	15	6	2	84	50		.289	.370	.358	93	-3	23			**.962**	22	*2-128	2.1
1898	Was-N	132	489	62	148	20	2	2	47	32		.303	.357	.364	107	4	11			.959	6	*2-132	1.8
1899	Pit-N	34	130	11	34	4	2	0	15	10		.262	.314	.323	75	-4	3			.975	1	2-34	-0.1
Total	7	723	2741	446	800	108	65	11	462	266	99	.292	.363	.391	97	-13	122			.955	33	2-687/3-30,S-4	4.6

■ KEN REITZ Reitz, Kenneth John b: 6/24/51, San Francisco, Cal BR/TR, 6', 185 lbs. Deb: 9/5/72

YEAR	TM/L	G	AB	R	H	2B	3B	HR	RBI	BB	SO	AVG	OBP	SLG	PRO+	BR/A	SB	CS	SBR	FA	FR	G/POS	TPR
1972	StL-N	21	78	5	28	4	0	0	10	2	4	.359	.375	.410	125	2	0	1	-1	.956	-4	3-20	-0.2
1973	StL-N	147	426	40	100	20	2	6	42	9	25	.235	.257	.333	63	-23	0	1	-1	.974	-6	*3-135/S-1	-3.2
1974	StL-N	154	579	48	157	28	2	7	54	23	63	.271	.301	.363	86	-13	0	0	0	.974	-17	*3-151/S-2,2-1	-3.3
1975	StL-N	161	592	46	159	25	1	5	63	22	54	.269	.300	.340	75	-21	1	1	-0	.946	-21	*3-160	-4.5
1976	SF-N	155	577	40	154	21	1	5	66	24	48	.267	.297	.333	76	-19	5	4	-1	.959	2	*3-155/S-1	-2.0
1977	StL-N	157	587	58	153	36	1	17	79	19	74	.261	.292	.412	88	-12	2	6	-3	**.980**	-7	*3-157	-1.9
1978	StL-N	150	540	41	133	26	2	10	75	23	61	.246	.283	.357	79	-17	1	0	0	**.973**	1	*3-150	-1.9
1979	StL-N	159	605	42	162	41	2	8	73	25	85	.268	.301	.382	84	-14	1	0	0	.972	-13	*3-158	-2.9
1980	StL-N★	151	523	39	141	33	0	8	58	22	44	.270	.303	.379	86	-10	0	1	-1	**.979**	-4	*3-150	-1.9
1981	Chi-N	82	260	10	56	9	1	2	28	15	56	.215	.266	.281	53	-16	0	0	0	**.977**	5	3-81	-1.3
1982	Pit-N	7	10	0	0	0	0	0	0	0	4	.000	.091	.000	-70	-2	0	0	0	1.000	1	/3-4	-0.2
Total	11	1344	4777	366	1243	243	12	68	548	184	518	.260	.293	.359	79	-144	10	14	-5	.970	-58	*3-1321/S-4,2-1	-23.3

■ DESI RELAFORD Relaford, Desmond Lamont b: 9/16/73, Valdosta, Ga. BB/TR, 5'8", 155 lbs. Deb: 8/1/96

YEAR	TM/L	G	AB	R	H	2B	3B	HR	RBI	BB	SO	AVG	OBP	SLG	PRO+	BR/A	SB	CS	SBR	FA	FR	G/POS	TPR
1996	Phi-N	15	40	2	7	2	0	0	1	3	9	.175	.233	.225	21	-1	0	0	0	.933	-1	/S-9,2-4	-0.4

■ BUTCH REMENTER Rementer, Willis J. H. b: 3/14/1878, Philadelphia, Pa. d: 9/23/22, Philadelphia, Pa. TR, Deb: 10/8/04

YEAR	TM/L	G	AB	R	H	2B	3B	HR	RBI	BB	SO	AVG	OBP	SLG	PRO+	BR/A	SB	CS	SBR	FA	FR	G/POS	TPR
1904	Phi-N	1	2	0	0	0	0	0	0	0	0	.000	.000	.000	-99	-0	0			1.000	-0	/C-1	-0.1

■ JACK REMSEN Remsen, John Jay b: 4/1850, Brooklyn, N.Y. BR/TR, 5'11", 189 lbs. Deb: 5/2/1872

YEAR	TM/L	G	AB	R	H	2B	3B	HR	RBI	BB	SO	AVG	OBP	SLG	PRO+	BR/A	SB	CS	SBR	FA	FR	G/POS	TPR
1872	Atl-n	37	164	25	40	4	5	0	13	2	6	.244	.253	.329	66	-10	1	2	-1	.792	2	*O-37	-0.5
1873	Atl-n	50	207	29	61	4	6	1	29	2	2	.295	.301	.386	115	5	1	2	-1	.811	0	*O-50	0.4
1874	Mut-n	64	284	52	65	9	3	2	37	0	5	.229	.229	.303	67	-11	6	0	2	.864	5	*O-63/1-3	-0.2
1875	Har-n	86	358	70	96	10	4	0	34	5	4	.268	.278	.318	102	-1	6	3	0	.887	9	*O-86	0.4
1876	Har-N	69	324	62	89	12	5	1	30	1	15	.275	.277	.352	100	-2				.887	8	*O-69	0.5
1877	StL-N	33	123	14	32	3	4	0	13	4	3	.260	.283	.350	104	1				.906	2	*O-33	0.1
1878	Chi-N	56	224	32	52	11	1	1	19	**17**	33	.232	.286	.304	88	-3				**.944**	6	*O-56	0.0
1879	Chi-N	42	152	14	33	4	2	0	8	2	2	.217	.227	.270	60	-7				.862	-2	O-31,1-11	-1.0
1881	Cle-N	48	172	14	30	4	3	0	13	9	31	.174	.215	.233	43	-11				.873	-1	O-48	-1.2
1884	Phi-N	12	43	9	9	2	0	0	3	6	9	.209	.306	.256	83	-1				.952	0	O-12	-0.1
	Bro-a	81	301	45	67	6	6	3			23	.223	.278	.312	91	-2				.914	4	*O-81	0.0
Total	4 n	237	1013	176	262	27	18	3	113	9	21	.259	.266	.330	88	-16	14	7	0	.845	10	O-236/1-3	0.1
Total	6	341	1339	190	312	42	21	5	86	62	114	.233	.267	.307	84	-24				.900	17	O-330/1-11	-1.7

■ JERRY REMY Remy, Gerald Peter b: 11/8/52, Fall River, Mass. BL/TR, 5'9", 165 lbs. Deb: 4/7/75

YEAR	TM/L	G	AB	R	H	2B	3B	HR	RBI	BB	SO	AVG	OBP	SLG	PRO+	BR/A	SB	CS	SBR	FA	FR	G/POS	TPR
1975	Cal-A	147	569	82	147	17	5	1	46	45	55	.258	.313	.311	82	-13	34	21	-2	.982	10	*2-147	0.2
1976	Cal-A	143	502	64	132	14	3	0	28	38	43	.263	.315	.303	87	-8	35	16	1	.977	15	*2-133/D-5	1.7
1977	Cal-A	154	575	74	145	19	10	4	44	59	59	.252	.324	.341	85	-11	41	17	2	.975	-12	*2-152/3-1	-1.0
1978	Bos-A☆	148	583	87	162	24	6	2	44	40	55	.278	.324	.350	81	-15	30	13	1	.983	2	*2-140/S-1,D-4	-0.1
1979	Bos-A	80	306	49	91	11	2	0	29	26	25	.297	.352	.346	85	-6	14	9	-1	.970	-21	2-76	-2.3
1980	Bos-A	63	230	24	72	7	2	0	9	10	14	.313	.342	.361	88	-4	14	6	1	.977	-3	2-60/O-1	-0.3
1981	Bos-A	88	358	55	110	9	3	0	31	36	30	.307	.371	.338	99	1	9	2	2	.984	-7	2-87	0.0
1982	Bos-A	155	636	89	178	22	3	0	47	55	77	.280	.339	.324	79	-17	16	16	-1	.982	-16	*2-154	-2.6
1983	Bos-A	146	592	73	163	16	5	0	43	40	35	.275	.321	.319	72	-22	11	3	2	.990	-31	*2-144	-4.5
1984	Bos-A	30	104	8	26	1	1	0	8	7	11	.250	.297	.279	58	-6	4	3	-1	.973	-3	2-24	-0.9
Total	10	1154	4455	605	1226	140	38	7	329	356	404	.275	.329	.328	79	-101	208	99	3	.981	-67	*2-1117/D-9,0-1,S3	-9.8

■ RICK RENICK Renick, Warren Richard b: 3/16/44, London, Ohio BR/TR, 6', 190 lbs. Deb: 7/11/68 C

YEAR	TM/L	G	AB	R	H	2B	3B	HR	RBI	BB	SO	AVG	OBP	SLG	PRO+	BR/A	SB	CS	SBR	FA	FR	G/POS	TPR
1968	Min-A	42	97	16	21	5	2	3	13	9	42	.216	.283	.402	101	-0	0	0	0	.946	-0	S-40	0.3
1969	*Min-A	71	139	21	34	3	0	5	17	12	32	.245	.309	.374	88	-2	0	1	-1	.913	-8	3-30,O-10/S-6	-1.1
1970	*Min-A	81	179	20	41	8	0	7	25	22	29	.229	.317	.391	93	-2	0	2	-1	.987	-3	3-30,O-25/S-1	-0.8
1971	Min-A	27	45	4	10	2	0	1	8	5	14	.222	.314	.333	81	-1	0	0	0	.846	-3	/3-7,O-7	-0.5
1972	Min-A	55	93	10	16	2	0	4	8	15	25	.172	.287	.323	77	-2	0	1	-1	1.000	-4	O-21/1-6,3-4,S-1	-0.9
Total	5	276	553	71	122	20	2	20	71	63	142	.221	.304	.373	89	-8	0	4	-2	.940	-18	/3-71,O-63,S-48,1-6	-3.0

■ BILL RENNA Renna, William Benedetto "Big Bill" b: 10/14/24, Hanford, Cal. BR/TR, 6'3", 218 lbs. Deb: 4/14/53

YEAR	TM/L	G	AB	R	H	2B	3B	HR	RBI	BB	SO	AVG	OBP	SLG	PRO+	BR/A	SB	CS	SBR	FA	FR	G/POS	TPR
1953	NY-A	61	121	19	38	6	3	2	13	13	31	.314	.385	.463	133	6	0	1	-1	.983	-6	O-40	-0.2
1954	Phi-A	123	422	52	98	15	4	13	53	41	60	.232	.305	.379	86	-9	1	3	-2	.972	6	*O-115	-1.0
1955	KC-A	100	249	33	53	7	3	7	28	31	42	.213	.305	.349	75	-9	0	3	-2	.992	-6	O-79	-2.1
1956	KC-A	33	48	12	13	0	2	5	10	7	5	.271	.364	.458	101	-0	1	0	0	.950	-6	O-25	-0.6
1958	Bos-A	39	56	15	15	5	0	4	18	6	14	.268	.339	.571	136	3	0	0	0	1.000	-1	O-11	0.1
1959	Bos-A	14	22	2	2	0	0	0	2	9	9	.091	.259	.091	0	-3	0	0	0	1.000	-2	/O-7	-0.5
Total	6	370	918	123	219	36	10	28	119	99	166	.239	.317	.391	91	-15	2	7	-4	.979	-15	O-277	-4.3

■ TONY RENSA Rensa, George Anthony "Pug" b: 9/29/01, Parsons, Pa. d: 1/4/87, Wilkes-Barre, Pa. BR/TR, 5'10", 180 lbs. Deb: 5/30/30

YEAR	TM/L	G	AB	R	H	2B	3B	HR	RBI	BB	SO	AVG	OBP	SLG	PRO+	BR/A	SB	CS	SBR	FA	FR	G/POS	TPR
1930	Det-A	20	37	6	10	2	1	1	3	6	7	.270	.386	.459	111	1	1	0	0	.964	-1	C-18	0.1
	Phi-N	54	172	31	49	11	2	3	31	10	18	.285	.328	.424	75	-7	0	0		.932	-11	C-49	-1.3
1931	Phi-N	19	29	2	3	1	0	0	2	6	2	.103	.257	.138	8	-4	0	0		.958	2	C-17	-0.1
1933	NY-A	8	29	4	9	2	1	0	5	0	2	.310	.333	.448	112	0	0	1	-1	.977	-1	/C-8	-0.1
1937	Chi-A	26	57	10	17	5	1	0	5	8	6	.298	.385	.421	103	0	3	0	1	.975	-1	C-23	0.3
1938	Chi-A	59	165	15	41	8	3	1	19	25	16	.248	.351	.333	71	-7	1	1	0	.982	6	C-57	0.1
1939	Chi-A	14	25	3	5	0	0	0	2	1	2	.200	.231	.200	11	-3	0	0		.972	1	C-13	-0.2
Total	6	200	514	71	134	26	5	5	65	57	64	.261	.338	.372	74	-20	5	2		.965	-4	C-185	-1.2

■ EDGAR RENTERIA Renteria, Edgar Enrique b: 8/7/76, Barranquilla, Colombia BR/TR, 6'1", 172 lbs. Deb: 5/10/96

YEAR	TM/L	G	AB	R	H	2B	3B	HR	RBI	BB	SO	AVG	OBP	SLG	PRO+	BR/A	SB	CS	SBR	FA	FR	G/POS	TPR
1996	Fla-N	106	431	68	133	18	3	5	31	33	68	.309	.361	.399	104	3	16	2	4	.979	12	*S-106	2.7

■ RICH RENTERIA Renteria, Richard Avina b: 12/25/61, Harbor City, Cal. BR/TR, 5'9", 172 lbs. Deb: 9/14/86

YEAR	TM/L	G	AB	R	H	2B	3B	HR	RBI	BB	SO	AVG	OBP	SLG	PRO+	BR/A	SB	CS	SBR	FA	FR	G/POS	TPR
1986	Pit-N	10	12	2	3	1	0	0	1	0	1	.250	.250	.333	58	-1	0	0	0	.600	0	/3-1	-0.1
1987	Sea-A	12	10	2	1	0	0	0	0	1	2	.100	.182	.200	1	-1	1	0	0	.833	1	/2-4,S-1,D-4	0.0
1988	Sea-A	31	88	6	18	9	0	0	6	2	8	.205	.222	.307	45	-7	1	3	-2	.958	4	D-12,S-11/3-5,2-4	-0.3

YEAR	TM/L	G	AB	R	H	2B	3B	HR	RBI	BB	SO	AVG	OBP	SLG	PRO+	BR/A	SB	CS	SBR	FA	FR	G/POS	TPR
1993	Fla-N	103	263	27	67	9	2	2	30	21	31	.255	.315	.327	68	-11	0	2	-1	.989	-4	2-45,3-25/O-1	-1.6
1994	Fla-N	28	49	5	11	0	0	0	4	1	4	.224	.269	.347	57	-3	0	1	-1	.929	-1	3-14/2-6,O-2	-0.4
Total	5	184	422	42	100	20	2	4	41	25	49	.237	.286	.322	61	-23	2	6	-3	.986	1	/2-59,3-45,D-16,SO	-2.4

■ BOB REPASS
Repass, Robert Willis   b: 11/6/17, W.Pittston, Pa.   BR/TR, 6'1", 185 lbs.   Deb: 9/18/39

YEAR	TM/L	G	AB	R	H	2B	3B	HR	RBI	BB	SO	AVG	OBP	SLG	PRO+	BR/A	SB	CS	SBR	FA	FR	G/POS	TPR
1939	StL-N	3	6	0	2	0	0	0	1	0	2	.333	.333	.500	114	0	0			1.000	0	/2-2	0.1
1942	Was-A	81	259	30	62	11	1	2	23	33	30	.239	.328	.313	81	-6	6	1	1	.973	-3	2-33,3-29,S-11	-0.4
Total	2	84	265	30	64	12	1	2	24	33	32	.242	.328	.317	82	-6	6	1		.973	-2	/2-35,3-29,S-11	-0.3

■ ROGER REPOZ
Repoz, Roger Allen   b: 8/3/40, Bellingham, Wash.   BL/TL, 6'3", 195 lbs.   Deb: 9/11/64

YEAR	TM/L	G	AB	R	H	2B	3B	HR	RBI	BB	SO	AVG	OBP	SLG	PRO+	BR/A	SB	CS	SBR	FA	FR	G/POS	TPR
1964	NY-A	11	1	1	0	0	0	0	0	1	1	.000	.500	.000	52	0	0	0	0	1.000	-3	/O-9	-0.3
1965	NY-A	79	218	34	48	7	4	12	28	25	57	.220	.300	.454	112	3	1	1	-0	.993	-2	O-69	-0.2
1966	NY-A	37	43	4	15	4	1	0	9	4	8	.349	.404	.488	161	3	0	0	0	1.000	-10	O-30	-0.8
	KC-A	101	319	40	69	10	3	11	34	44	80	.216	.315	.370	99	0	3	3	-1	.991	-3	O-52,1-45	-1.0
	Yr	138	362	44	84	14	4	11	43	48	88	.232	.325	.384	106	3	3	3	-1	.992	-13	O-82,1-45	-1.8
1967	KC-A	40	87	6	21	6	1	2	8	12	20	.241	.340	.402	122	3	4	2	0	1.000	1	O-31	0.3
	Cal-A	74	176	25	44	9	1	5	20	19	37	.250	.323	.398	116	3	2	2	-1	.959	-3	O-63	-0.3
	Yr	114	263	34	65	15	2	7	28	31	57	.247	.329	.399	118	6	6	4	-1	.972	-1	O-94	0.0
1968	Cal-A	133	375	30	90	8	1	13	54	38	83	.240	.315	.371	111	5	8	7	-2	.987	-5	*O-114	-0.8
1969	Cal-A	103	219	25	36	1	1	8	19	32	52	.164	.271	.288	59	-12	3	3	-2	.985	-5	O-48,1-31	-2.4
1970	Cal-A	137	407	50	97	17	6	18	47	45	90	.238	.319	.442	112	5	4	2	0	.995	-4	*O-110,1-18	-0.6
1971	Cal-A	113	297	39	59	11	1	13	41	60	69	.199	.335	.374	108	4	3	5	-2	1.000	-4	O-97,1-13	-0.8
1972	Cal-A	3	3	0	1	0	0	0	0	0	2	.333	.333	.333	105	0	0	0	0	.000	0	H	0.0
Total	9	831	2145	257	480	73	19	82	260	280	499	.224	.316	.390	106	14	26	25	-7	.989	-39	O-623,1-107	-6.9

■ RIP REPULSKI
Repulski, Eldon John   b: 10/4/27, Sauk Rapids, Minn.   d: 2/10/93, Waite Park, Minn.   BR/TR, 6', 195 lbs.   Deb: 4/14/53

YEAR	TM/L	G	AB	R	H	2B	3B	HR	RBI	BB	SO	AVG	OBP	SLG	PRO+	BR/A	SB	CS	SBR	FA	FR	G/POS	TPR
1953	StL-N	153	567	75	156	25	4	15	66	34	71	.275	.325	.413	91	-8	3	6	-3	.987	-7	*O-153	-2.3
1954	StL-N	152	619	99	175	39	5	19	79	43	75	.283	.333	.454	102	0	8	10	-4	.975	-5	*O-152	-1.5
1955	StL-N	147	512	64	138	28	2	23	73	49	66	.270	.338	.467	111	7	5	7	-3	.974	-5	*O-141	-0.7
1956	StL-N★	112	376	44	104	18	3	11	55	24	46	.277	.332	.428	102	1	2	2	-1	.974	-0	*O-100	-0.5
1957	Phi-N	134	516	65	134	23	4	20	68	19	74	.260	.293	.436	95	-5	2	2	-1	.968	3	*O-130	-0.5
1958	Phi-N	85	238	33	58	9	4	13	40	15	47	.244	.300	.479	103	-0	1	2	-1	.949	2	O-56	-0.5
1959	*LA-N	53	94	11	24	4	0	2	14	13	23	.255	.346	.362	83	-2	0	1	-1	1.000	-5	O-31	-0.9
1960	LA-N	4	5	0	1	0	0	0	0	0	1	.200	.200	.200	9	-1	0	0	0	1.000	-1	/O-2	-0.1
	Bos-A	73	136	14	33	6	1	3	20	10	25	.243	.295	.368	75	-1	0	0	0	1.000	-1	O-33	-0.8
1961	Bos-A	15	25	2	7	1	0	0	1	1	5	.280	.308	.320	66	-1	0	2	-1	1.000	-1	/O-4	-0.3
Total	9	928	3088	407	830	153	23	106	416	207	433	.269	.322	.436	98	-14	25	29	-10	.976	-24	O-802	-8.5

■ LARRY RESSLER
Ressler, Lawrence P.   b: 8/10/1848, France   d: 6/12/18, Reading, Pa.   Deb: 4/26/1875

YEAR	TM/L	G	AB	R	H	2B	3B	HR	RBI	BB	SO	AVG	OBP	SLG	PRO+	BR/A	SB	CS	SBR	FA	FR	G/POS	TPR
1875	Was-n	27	108	17	21	1	0	0	5	0	4	.194	.194	.204	40	-6	4	0	1	.831	6	O-20/2-7	0.1

■ DINO RESTELLI
Restelli, Dino Paul "Dingo"   b: 9/23/24, St.Louis, Mo.   BR/TR, 6'1.5", 191 lbs.   Deb: 6/14/49

YEAR	TM/L	G	AB	R	H	2B	3B	HR	RBI	BB	SO	AVG	OBP	SLG	PRO+	BR/A	SB	CS	SBR	FA	FR	G/POS	TPR
1949	Pit-N	72	232	41	58	11	0	12	40	35	26	.250	.358	.453	113	4	3			.961	5	O-61/1-1	0.6
1951	Pit-N	21	38	1	7	1	0	1	3	2	4	.184	.225	.289	36	-3	0	0	0	.920	-1	O-11	-0.5
Total	2	93	270	42	65	12	0	13	43	37	30	.241	.341	.430	103	1	3	0		.956	4	/O-72,1-1	0.1

■ MERV RETTENMUND
Rettenmund, Mervin Weldon   b: 6/6/43, Flint, Mich.   BR/TR, 5'10", 195 lbs.   Deb: 4/14/68   C

YEAR	TM/L	G	AB	R	H	2B	3B	HR	RBI	BB	SO	AVG	OBP	SLG	PRO+	BR/A	SB	CS	SBR	FA	FR	G/POS	TPR
1968	Bal-A	31	64	10	19	5	0	2	7	18	20	.297	.458	.469	181	8	1	1	-0	1.000	-5	O-23	0.1
1969	*Bal-A	95	190	27	47	10	3	4	25	28	28	.247	.344	.395	105	2	6	1	1	.991	-10	O-78	-1.1
1970	*Bal-A	106	338	60	109	17	2	18	58	38	59	.322	.396	.544	155	25	13	7	-0	.976	-1	O-93	2.0
1971	*Bal-A	141	491	81	156	23	4	11	75	87	60	.318	.424	.448	149	36	15	6	1	.977	-3	*O-134	2.8
1972	Bal-A	102	301	40	70	10	2	6	21	41	37	.233	.325	.339	95	-1	6	4	-1	.989	-6	O-98	-1.3
1973	*Bal-A	95	321	59	84	17	2	9	44	57	38	.262	.380	.411	124	12	11	2	2	.985	3	O-90	1.4
1974	Cin-N	80	208	30	45	6	0	6	28	37	39	.216	.340	.332	90	-2	5	1	1	1.000	-5	O-69	-0.9
1975	*Cin-N	93	188	24	45	6	1	2	19	35	22	.239	.359	.314	86	-2	5	0	2	1.000	-5	O-61/3-1	-0.8
1976	SD-N	86	140	16	32	7	0	2	11	29	23	.229	.361	.321	103	2	4	1	1	.977	2	O-43	0.3
1977	SD-N	107	126	23	36	1	1	4	17	33	28	.286	.438	.444	153	12	1	2	-1	1.000	-4	O-27/3-1	0.6
1978	Cal-A	50	108	16	29	5	1	1	14	30	13	.269	.436	.361	131	7	0	3	-2	.968	-3	O-22,D-18	0.1
1979	*Cal-A	35	76	7	20	2	0	1	10	11	14	.263	.364	.329	91	-1	0	0	0	1.000	-3	D-17/O-9	-0.3
1980	Cal-A	2	4	0	1	0	0	0	0	1	1	.250	.400	.250	84	-0	0	0	0	.000	0	/D-1	0.0
Total	13	1023	2555	393	693	114	16	66	329	445	382	.271	.383	.406	124	97	68	28	4	.985	-41	O-747/D-36,3-2	2.9

■ KEN RETZER
Retzer, Kenneth Leo   b: 4/30/34, Wood River, Ill.   BL/TR, 6', 185 lbs.   Deb: 9/9/61

YEAR	TM/L	G	AB	R	H	2B	3B	HR	RBI	BB	SO	AVG	OBP	SLG	PRO+	BR/A	SB	CS	SBR	FA	FR	G/POS	TPR
1961	Was-A	16	53	7	18	4	0	1	3	4	5	.340	.386	.472	130	2	1	0	0	.988	1	C-16	0.4
1962	Was-A	109	340	36	97	11	2	8	37	26	21	.285	.336	.400	98	-1	2	0	1	.985	-0	C-99	0.3
1963	Was-A	95	265	21	64	10	0	5	31	17	20	.242	.292	.336	76	-9	2	0	1	.981	-11	C-81	-1.7
1964	Was-A	17	32	1	3	0	0	0	1	5	4	.094	.237	.094	-4	-4	0	0	0	.971	4	C-13	0.0
Total	4	237	690	65	182	25	2	14	72	52	50	.264	.318	.367	87	-12	5	0	2	.983	-6	C-209	-1.0

■ DAVE REVERING
Revering, David Alvin   b: 2/12/53, Roseville, Cal.   BL/TR, 6'4", 210 lbs.   Deb: 4/8/78

YEAR	TM/L	G	AB	R	H	2B	3B	HR	RBI	BB	SO	AVG	OBP	SLG	PRO+	BR/A	SB	CS	SBR	FA	FR	G/POS	TPR
1978	Oak-A	152	521	49	141	21	3	16	46	26	55	.271	.305	.415	106	2	0	1	-1	.989	9	*1-138/D-3	0.3
1979	Oak-A	125	472	63	136	25	5	19	77	34	65	.288	.337	.483	125	15	1	4	-2	.986	2	*1-104,D-18	0.7
1980	Oak-A	106	376	48	109	21	5	15	62	32	37	.290	.346	.492	136	17	1	0	0	.989	3	1-95/D-5	1.5
1981	Oak-A	31	87	12	20	1	1	2	10	11	12	.230	.323	.333	94	-2	0	1	-1	.995	-1	1-29/D-2	-0.4
	*NY-A	45	119	8	28	4	1	2	7	11	20	.235	.300	.336	84	-2	0	1	-1	.994	3	1-44	-0.2
	Yr	76	206	20	48	5	2	4	17	22	32	.233	.310	.335	88	-3	0	2	-1	.994	2	1-73/D-2	-0.6
1982	NY-A	14	40	2	6	2	0	0	2	3	4	.150	.209	.200	13	-5	0	0	0	1.000	-1	1-13/D-1	-0.7
	Tor-A	55	135	15	29	6	0	5	18	22	30	.215	.325	.370	83	-3	0	3	-2	1.000	-0	D-49/1-4	-0.7
	Sea-A	29	82	8	17	3	0	1	12	9	17	.207	.286	.378	78	-3	0	0	0	.986	-1	1-27	-0.5
	Yr	98	257	25	52	11	0	7	32	34	51	.202	.296	.346	71	-10	0	3	-2	.992	-3	D-50,1-44	-1.9
Total	5	557	1832	205	486	83	16	62	234	148	240	.265	.321	.430	110	20	2	10	-5	.989	13	1-454/D-78	-0.0

■ HENRY REVILLE
Reville, Henry   b: Baltimore, Md.   Deb: 10/14/1874

YEAR	TM/L	G	AB	R	H	2B	3B	HR	RBI	BB	SO	AVG	OBP	SLG	PRO+	BR/A	SB	CS	SBR	FA	FR	G/POS	TPR
1874	Bal-n	1	4	0	0	0	0	0	0	0	0	.000	.000	.000	-99	-1	0	0	0	1.000	1	/O-1	0.0

■ WILLIAM REXTER
Rexter, William H.   b: Brooklyn, N.Y.   Deb: 9/25/1875

YEAR	TM/L	G	AB	R	H	2B	3B	HR	RBI	BB	SO	AVG	OBP	SLG	PRO+	BR/A	SB	CS	SBR	FA	FR	G/POS	TPR
1875	Atl-n	1	4	0	0	0	0	0	0	0	0	.000	.000	.000	-99	-1	0	0	0	1.000	0	/O-1	-0.1

■ GILBERTO REYES
Reyes, Gilberto Rolando (Polanco)   b: 12/10/63, Santo Domingo, D.R.   BR/TR, 6'2", 203 lbs.   Deb: 6/11/83

YEAR	TM/L	G	AB	R	H	2B	3B	HR	RBI	BB	SO	AVG	OBP	SLG	PRO+	BR/A	SB	CS	SBR	FA	FR	G/POS	TPR
1983	LA-N	19	31	1	5	2	0	0	0	0	5	.161	.188	.226	14	-4	0	0	0	.944	4	C-19	-0.1
1984	LA-N	4	5	0	0	0	0	0	0	0	2	.000	.000	.000	-99	-1	0	0	0	1.000	-0	/C-2	-0.2
1985	LA-N	6	1	0	0	0	0	0	0	1	1	.000	.667	.000	105	0	0	0	0	1.000	-0	/C-6	0.2
1987	LA-N	1	0	0	0	0	0	0	0	0	0	—	—	—	—	—	0	0	0	1.000	0	/C-1	0.0
1988	LA-N	5	9	1	1	0	0	0	0	0	3	.111	.111	.111	-37	-2	0	0	0	1.000	-0	/C-5	-0.1
1989	Mon-N	4	5	0	1	0	0	0	1	0	1	.200	.200	.200	4	-1	0	0	0	1.000	0	/C-4	0.0
1991	Mon-N	83	207	11	45	9	0	0	13	19	51	.217	.286	.261	56	-12	2	4	-2	.975	14	C-80	0.4
Total	7	122	258	13	52	11	0	0	14	20	64	.202	.267	.244	45	-19	2	4	-2	.973	17	C-117	0.2

■ NAP REYES
Reyes, Napoleon Aguilera   b: 11/24/19, Santiago De Cuba, Cuba   d: 9/15/95, Miami, Fla.   BR/TR, 6'1", 205 lbs.   Deb: 5/19/43

YEAR	TM/L	G	AB	R	H	2B	3B	HR	RBI	BB	SO	AVG	OBP	SLG	PRO+	BR/A	SB	CS	SBR	FA	FR	G/POS	TPR
1943	NY-N	40	125	13	32	4	2	0	13	4	12	.256	.290	.320	76	-4	2			.994	-5	1-38/3-1	-1.2
1944	NY-N	116	374	38	108	16	5	8	53	15	24	.289	.325	.422	109	3	2			.990	2	1-63,3-37/O-3	0.3
1945	NY-N	122	431	39	124	15	4	5	44	25	26	.288	.338	.376	97	-2	1			.961	-4	*3-115/1-5	-0.3

YEAR	TM/L	G	AB	R	H	2B	3B	HR	RBI	BB	SO	AVG	OBP	SLG	PRO+	BR/A	SB	CS	SBR	FA	FR	G/POS	TPR
1950	NY-N	1	1	0	0	0	0	0	0	0	0	.000	.000	.000	-99	-0	0			.667	-0	/1-1	-0.1
Total	4	279	931	90	264	35	11	13	110	44	62	.284	.326	.387	99	-3	5			.960	-7	3-153,1-107/O-3	-1.3

■ CARL REYNOLDS

Reynolds, Carl Nettles b: 2/1/03, LaRue, Tex. d: 5/29/78, Houston, Tex. BR/TR, 6', 194 lbs. Deb: 9/1/27

YEAR	TM/L	G	AB	R	H	2B	3B	HR	RBI	BB	SO	AVG	OBP	SLG	PRO+	BR/A	SB	CS	SBR	FA	FR	G/POS	TPR
1927	Chi-A	14	42	5	9	3	0	1	7	5	7	.214	.313	.357	75	-2	1	2	-1	1.000	2	O-13	-0.1
1928	Chi-A	84	291	51	94	21	11	2	36	17	13	.323	.371	.491	126	10	15	3	3	.979	-2	O-74	0.6
1929	Chi-A	131	517	81	164	24	12	11	67	20	37	.317	.348	.474	111	6	19	9	0	.949	-2	*O-130	-0.4
1930	Chi-A	138	563	103	202	25	18	22	104	20	39	.359	.388	.584	148	38	16	4	2	.975	10	*O-132	3.6
1931	Chi-A	118	462	71	134	24	14	6	77	24	26	.290	.333	.442	108	4	17	6	2	.949	-4	*O-109	-0.6
1932	Was-A	102	406	53	124	28	7	9	63	13	19	.305	.332	.475	108	3	8	4	0	.983	5	O-95	0.1
1933	StL-A	135	475	81	136	26	14	8	71	49	25	.286	.357	.451	106	3	5	4	-1	.965	-2	*O-124	-0.5
1934	Bos-A	113	413	61	125	26	9	4	86	27	28	.303	.350	.438	95	-4	5	3	-0	.977	3	*O-100	-0.5
1935	Bos-A	78	244	33	66	13	4	6	35	24	20	.270	.336	.430	91	-4	4	1	1	.975	6	O-64	0.0
1936	Was-A	89	293	41	81	18	2	4	41	21	22	.276	.329	.392	82	-9	8	4	0	.968	-0	O-72	-1.1
1937	Chi-N	7	11	0	3	1	0	0	1	2	2	.273	.385	.364	100	0	0			.800	-0	/O-2	0.0
1938	*Chi-N	125	497	59	150	28	10	3	67	22	32	.302	.335	.416	103	1	9			.983	-3	*O-125	-0.5
1939	Chi-N	88	281	33	69	10	6	4	44	16	38	.246	.290	.367	76	-10	5			.972	2	O-72	-1.1
Total	13	1222	4495	672	1357	247	107	80	699	260	308	.302	.346	.458	107	36	112	40		.970	15	*O-1112	-0.5

■ CHARLIE REYNOLDS

Reynolds, Charles Lawrence b: 5/1/1865, Williamsburg, Ind. d: 7/3/44, Denver, Colo. 5'9", 175 lbs. Deb: 5/8/1889

YEAR	TM/L	G	AB	R	H	2B	3B	HR	RBI	BB	SO	AVG	OBP	SLG	PRO+	BR/A	SB	CS	SBR	FA	FR	G/POS	TPR
1889	KC-a	1	4	1	1	0	0	0	1	0	1	.250	.250	.250	40	-1	0			1.000	-1	/C-1	-0.1
	Bro-a	12	42	5	9	1	1	0	3	1	6	.214	.233	.286	47	-3	2			.892	-1	C-12	-0.1
	Yr	13	46	6	10	1	1	0	4	1	7	.217	.234	.283	46	-3	2			.893	-1	C-13	-0.2

■ DANNY REYNOLDS

Reynolds, Daniel Vance "Squirrel" b: 11/27/19, Stony Point, N.C. BR/TR, 5'11", 158 lbs. Deb: 5/26/45

YEAR	TM/L	G	AB	R	H	2B	3B	HR	RBI	BB	SO	AVG	OBP	SLG	PRO+	BR/A	SB	CS	SBR	FA	FR	G/POS	TPR
1945	Chi-A	29	72	6	12	2	1	0	4	3	8	.167	.200	.222	23	-7	1	2	-1	.947	2	S-14,2-11	-0.5

■ DON REYNOLDS

Reynolds, Donald Edward b: 4/16/53, Arkadelphia, Ark. BR/TR, 5'8", 178 lbs. Deb: 4/7/78 F

YEAR	TM/L	G	AB	R	H	2B	3B	HR	RBI	BB	SO	AVG	OBP	SLG	PRO+	BR/A	SB	CS	SBR	FA	FR	G/POS	TPR
1978	SD-N	57	87	8	22	2	0	0	10	15	14	.253	.363	.276	87	-1	1	0	0	.923	-4	O-25	-0.6
1979	SD-N	30	45	6	10	1	2	0	6	7	6	.222	.327	.333	86	-1	0	1	-1	.950	-1	O-14	-0.3
Total	2	87	132	14	32	3	2	0	16	22	20	.242	.351	.295	87	-2	1	1	-0	.935	-5	/O-39	-0.9

■ CRAIG REYNOLDS

Reynolds, Gordon Craig b: 12/27/52, Houston, Tex. BL/TR, 6'1", 175 lbs. Deb: 8/1/75

YEAR	TM/L	G	AB	R	H	2B	3B	HR	RBI	BB	SO	AVG	OBP	SLG	PRO+	BR/A	SB	CS	SBR	FA	FR	G/POS	TPR
1975	*Pit-N	31	76	8	17	3	0	0	4	3	5	.224	.253	.263	44	-6	0	1	-1	.969	4	S-30	0.0
1976	Pit-N	7	4	1	1	0	0	1	1	0	0	.250	.250	1.000	241	1	0	0	0	.889	2	/S-4,2-1	0.2
1977	Sea-A	135	420	41	104	12	3	4	28	15	23	.248	.279	.319	63	-22	6	6	-2	.955	8	*S-134	-0.2
1978	Sea-A☆	148	548	57	160	16	7	5	44	36	41	.292	.339	.374	101	1	9	6	-1	.960	4	*S-146	2.2
1979	Hou-N★	146	555	63	147	20	9	0	39	21	49	.265	.294	.333	75	-20	12	6	0	.965	-15	*S-143	-2.0
1980	*Hou-N	137	381	34	86	9	6	3	28	20	39	.226	.264	.304	63	-20	2	1	0	.969	12	*S-135	0.4
1981	*Hou-N	87	323	43	84	10	12	4	31	12	31	.260	.287	.402	99	-3	3	3	-1	.973	-5	S-85	0.1
1982	Hou-N	54	118	16	30	2	3	1	7	11	9	.254	.323	.347	95	-1	3	1	0	.958	2	S-35/3-7	-0.2
1983	Hou-N	65	98	10	21	3	0	1	6	6	10	.214	.260	.276	52	-7	0	1	-1	.956	-4	2-26,3-15/S-8,O-1	-1.1
1984	Hou-N	146	527	61	137	15	11	6	60	22	53	.260	.290	.364	89	-10	7	1	2	.965	18	*S-143/3-1	2.3
1985	Hou-N	107	379	43	103	18	8	4	32	12	30	.272	.294	.393	93	-5	4	4	-1	.977	10	*S-102/2-1	1.4
1986	*Hou-N	114	313	32	78	7	3	6	41	12	31	.249	.277	.348	73	-12	5	1	1	.978	-12	S-98/1-5,3-4,O-2,P	-1.7
1987	Hou-N	135	374	35	95	17	3	4	28	30	44	.254	.309	.348	77	-13	5	1	1	.970	-12	*S-129/3-2	-1.4
1988	Hou-N	78	161	20	41	7	0	1	14	8	23	.255	.290	.317	77	-5	3	0	1	.970	-5	S-22,3-19.2-11,1-10	-0.8
1989	Hou-N	101	189	16	38	4	0	2	14	19	18	.201	.254	.254	54	-11	1	0	0	.979	8	2-29,S-26,3/1PO	-0.1
Total	15	1491	4466	480	1142	143	65	42	377	227	406	.256	.293	.345	80	-133	58	32	-2	.966	17	*S-1240/2-68,310P	-0.3

■ HAROLD REYNOLDS

Reynolds, Harold Craig b: 11/26/60, Eugene, Ore. BB/TR, 5'11", 165 lbs. Deb: 9/2/83 F

YEAR	TM/L	G	AB	R	H	2B	3B	HR	RBI	BB	SO	AVG	OBP	SLG	PRO+	BR/A	SB	CS	SBR	FA	FR	G/POS	TPR
1983	Sea-A	20	59	8	12	4	1	0	2	1	9	.203	.230	.305	44	-5	0	2	-1	.975	-1	2-18	-0.6
1984	Sea-A	10	10	3	3	0	0	0	0	0	1	.300	.364	.300	87	-0	1	1	-0	1.000	4	/2-6	0.4
1985	Sea-A	67	104	15	15	3	1	0	6	17	14	.144	.264	.192	27	-10	3	1	0	.960	19	2-61	1.0
1986	Sea-A	126	445	46	99	19	4	1	24	29	42	.222	.275	.290	53	-29	30	12	2	.977	29	*2-126	0.7
1987	Sea-A★	160	530	73	146	31	8	1	35	39	34	.275	.327	.370	80	-15	**60**	20	6	.977	19	*2-160	1.7
1988	Sea-A★	158	598	61	169	26	**11**	4	41	51	51	.283	.341	.383	98	-3	35	29	-7	.977	6	*2-158	0.5
1989	Sea-A	153	613	87	184	24	9	0	43	55	45	.300	.361	.369	103	3	25	18	-3	.980	**27**	*2-151/D-1	3.2
1990	Sea-A	160	642	100	162	36	5	5	55	81	52	.252	.336	.347	91	-6	31	16	-0	.978	15	*2-160	1.3
1991	Sea-A	161	631	95	160	34	6	3	57	72	63	.254	.335	.341	87	-9	28	8	4	.978	-12	*2-159/D-1	0.3
1992	Sea-A	140	458	55	113	23	3	3	33	45	41	.247	.318	.330	81	-11	15	12	-3	.982	-4	*2-134/O-1,D-1	-0.9
1993	Bal-A	145	485	64	122	20	4	4	47	66	47	.252	.346	.334	80	-12	12	11	-3	.986	3	*2-141/D-1	-0.7
1994	Cal-A	74	207	33	48	10	1	0	11	23	18	.232	.312	.290	56	-13	10	7	-1	.996	-13	2-65/D-3	-2.3
Total	12	1374	4782	640	1233	230	53	21	353	480	417	.258	.329	.341	83	-107	250	138	-8	.979	116	*2-1339/D-7,O-1	4.6

■ R. J. REYNOLDS

Reynolds, Robert James b: 4/19/59, Sacramento, Cal. BB/TR, 6', 190 lbs. Deb: 9/1/83

YEAR	TM/L	G	AB	R	H	2B	3B	HR	RBI	BB	SO	AVG	OBP	SLG	PRO+	BR/A	SB	CS	SBR	FA	FR	G/POS	TPR
1983	LA-N	24	55	5	13	0	0	2	11	3	11	.236	.276	.345	72	-2	5	0	2	.931	-2	O-18	-0.3
1984	LA-N	73	240	24	62	12	2	2	24	14	38	.258	.302	.350	84	-6	7	5	-1	.973	-7	O-63	-1.6
1985	LA-N	73	207	22	55	10	4	0	25	13	31	.266	.312	.353	88	-4	6	3	0	.970	-2	O-54	-0.7
	Pit-N	31	130	22	40	5	3	3	17	9	18	.308	.357	.462	129	5	12	2	2	.958	1	O-31	0.7
	Yr	104	337	44	95	15	7	3	42	22	49	.282	.330	.395	104	1	18	5	2	.965	-1	*O-112	0.0
1986	Pit-N	118	402	63	108	30	2	9	48	40	78	.269	.336	.420	105	2	16	9	-1	.955	-15	*O-112	-1.7
1987	Pit-N	117	335	47	87	24	1	7	51	34	80	.260	.328	.400	91	-4	14	1	4	.993	-6	O-99	-1.0
1988	Pit-N	130	323	35	80	14	2	6	51	20	62	.248	.292	.359	87	-6	15	2	5	.974	-6	O-95	-1.2
1989	Pit-N	125	363	45	98	16	2	6	48	34	69	.270	.334	.375	106	3	22	5	4	.990	-1	O-98	0.4
1990	*Pit-N	95	215	25	62	10	1	2	19	23	35	.288	.357	.344	98	-0	12	2	2	.972	-6	O-59	-0.5
Total	8	786	2270	288	605	121	17	35	294	190	419	.267	.325	.381	97	-12	109	29	15	.973	-44	O-629	-5.9

■ RONN REYNOLDS

Reynolds, Ronn Dwayne b: 9/28/58, Wichita, Kan. BR/TR, 6', 200 lbs. Deb: 9/29/82

YEAR	TM/L	G	AB	R	H	2B	3B	HR	RBI	BB	SO	AVG	OBP	SLG	PRO+	BR/A	SB	CS	SBR	FA	FR	G/POS	TPR
1982	NY-N	2	4	0	0	0	0	0	0	0	1	.000	.200	.000	-40	-1	0	0	0	1.000	-1	/C-2	-0.2
1983	NY-N	24	66	4	13	1	0	0	2	8	12	.197	.284	.212	40	-5	0	0	0	.942	-1	C-24	-0.5
1985	NY-N	28	43	4	9	2	0	0	10	0	18	.209	.227	.256	36	-4	0	0	0	.990	6	C-25	0.3
1986	Phi-N	43	126	8	27	4	0	3	10	5	30	.214	.244	.317	52	-8	0	1	-1	.991	4	C-42	-0.5
1987	Hou-N	38	102	5	17	4	0	1	7	3	29	.167	.190	.235	12	-13	0	1	-1	.975	4	C-38	-0.8
1990	SD-N	8	15	1	1	0	0	1	1	0	6	.067	.125	.133	-29	-3	0	0	0	1.000	1	/C-8	-1.2
Total	6	143	356	22	67	12	0	4	21	18	96	.188	.229	.256	32	-34	0	1	-1	.977	10	C-139	-1.9

■ TOMMIE REYNOLDS

Reynolds, Tommie D b: 8/15/41, Arizona, La. BR/TR, 6'2", 190 lbs. Deb: 9/5/63 C

YEAR	TM/L	G	AB	R	H	2B	3B	HR	RBI	BB	SO	AVG	OBP	SLG	PRO+	BR/A	SB	CS	SBR	FA	FR	G/POS	TPR
1963	KC-A	8	19	1	1	0	0	0	1	0	7	.053	.143	.105	-28	-3	0	0	0	.800	-1	/O-5	-0.5
1964	KC-A	31	94	11	19	1	0	2	9	10	22	.202	.292	.277	58	-5	0	0	0	.976	-0	O-25/3-3	-0.7
1965	KC-A	90	270	34	64	11	3	1	22	36	41	.237	.327	.311	83	-5	9	2	2	.982	7	O-83/3-1	-0.4
1967	NY-N	101	136	16	28	1	0	2	9	11	26	.206	.280	.257	56	-8	1	1	0	.971	-13	O-72/3-5,C-1	-2.5
1969	Oak-A	107	315	51	81	10	2	2	20	34	29	.257	.345	.308	87	-4	1	3	-2	.979	6	O-89	-0.5
1970	Cal-A	59	120	11	30	3	1	1	6	10	22	.250	.291	.317	70	-5	0	1	-1	.969	-0	O-32/3-1	-0.7
1971	Cal-A	45	86	4	16	3	0	2	8	6	12	.186	.286	.291	68	-4	0	0	0	.978	-2	O-26/3-1	-0.7
1972	Mil-A	72	130	13	26	5	1	2	13	10	25	.200	.262	.300	68	-5	12	8	-1	.961	-1	O-41/3-3,1-1,C-1	-0.9
Total	8	513	1170	141	265	34	9	12	87	117	166	.226	.307	.296	73	-39	12	8	-1	.973	-4	O-373/3-12,1-1,C-1	-6.5

■ BILL REYNOLDS

Reynolds, William Dee b: 8/14/1884, Eastland, Tex. d: 6/5/24, Carnegie, Okla. BR/TR, 6', 185 lbs. Deb: 9/15/13

YEAR	TM/L	G	AB	R	H	2B	3B	HR	RBI	BB	SO	AVG	OBP	SLG	PRO+	BR/A	SB	CS	SBR	FA	FR	G/POS	TPR
1913	NY-A	5	5	0	0	0	0	0	0	0	1	.000	.000	.000	-99	-1	0			.917	0	/C-5	-0.1
1914	NY-A	4	5	0	2	0	0	0	0	0	3	.400	.400	.400	141	0	0			1.000	0	/C-1	0.1
Total	2	9	10	0	2	0	0	0	0	0	4	.200	.200	.200	19	-1	0			.941	0	/C-6	0.0

YEAR	TM/L	G	AB	R	H	2B	3B	HR	RBI	BB	SO	AVG	OBP	SLG	PRO+	BR/A	SB	CS	SBR	FA	FR	G/POS	TPR

■ BOBBY RHAWN　Rhawn, Robert John "Rocky"　b: 2/13/19, Catawissa, Pa.　d: 6/9/84, Danville, Pa.　BR/TR, 5'8", 180 lbs.　Deb: 9/17/47

1947	NY-N	13	45	7	14	3	0	1	3	8	1	.311	.415	.444	128	2	0			.913	0	/2-8,3-5	0.3
1948	NY-N	36	44	11	12	2	1	1	8	8	6	.273	.385	.432	120	1	3			.872	1	S-14/3-7	0.2
1949	NY-N	14	29	8	5	0	0	0	2	7	2	.172	.333	.172	40	-2	1			.959	4	/2-8	0.2
	Pit-N	3	7	0	1	0	0	0	0	0	0	.143	.143	.143	-23	-1	0			.889	1	/3-2	0.0
	Yr	17	36	8	6	0	0	0	2	7	2	.167	.302	.167	29	-3	1			.959	4	/2-8,3-2	0.2
	Chi-A	24	73	12	15	4	1	0	5	12	8	.205	.318	.288	63	-4	0	1	-1	.959	3	3-19/S-3	-0.2
Total	3	90	198	38	47	9	2	2	18	35	17	.237	.352	.333	84	-4	4	1		.963	8	/3-33,S-17,2-16	0.5

■ CY RHEAM　Rheam, Kenneth Johnston　b: 9/28/1893, Pittsburgh, Pa.　d: 10/23/47, Pittsburgh, Pa.　BR/TR, 6' ", 175 lbs.　Deb: 5/20/14

1914	Pit-F	73	214	15	45	5	3	0	20	9	33	.210	.242	.262	38	-22	6			.976	-5	1-43,3-13,2-11,/O-1	-2.9
1915	Pit-F	34	69	10	12	0	0	1	5	1	7	.174	.186	.217	13	-9	4			.959	0	O-22/1-1	-1.1
Total	2	107	283	25	57	5	3	1	25	10	40	.201	.229	.251	32	-32	10			.976	-5	/1-44,O-23,3-13,2	-4.0

■ BILLY RHIEL　Rhiel, William Joseph　b: 8/16/1900, Youngstown, Ohio　d: 8/16/46, Youngstown, Ohio　BR/TR, 5'11", 175 lbs.　Deb: 4/20/29

1929	Bro-N	76	205	27	57	9	4	4	25	19	25	.278	.339	.420	89	-4	0			.979	1	2-47/3-7,S-2	-0.1
1930	Bos-N	20	47	3	8	4	0	0	4	2	5	.170	.204	.255	11	-7	0			.947	-4	3-13/2-2	-0.9
1932	Det-A	85	250	30	70	13	3	3	38	17	23	.280	.328	.392	82	-7	2	0	1	.956	-5	3-37,1-12/O-8,2-1	-1.0
1933	Det-A	19	17	1	3	0	1	0	1	5	4	.176	.364	.294	75	-0	0	0	0	1.000	0	/O-1	-0.2
Total	4	200	519	61	138	26	8	7	68	43	57	.266	.323	.387	78	-18	2	0		.949	-8	/3-57,2-50,1-12,OS	-2.0

■ DUSTY RHODES　Rhodes, James Lamar　b: 5/13/27, Mathews, Ala.　BL/TR, 6', 180 lbs.　Deb: 7/15/52

1952	NY-N	67	176	34	44	8	1	10	36	23	33	.250	.340	.477	123	5	1	0	0	.917	-4	O-56	0.0
1953	NY-N	76	163	18	38	7	0	11	30	10	28	.233	.277	.479	91	-3	0	1	-1	.965	1	O-47	-0.4
1954	*NY-N	82	164	31	56	7	3	15	50	18	25	.341	.410	.695	181	19	1	0	0	.984	-3	O-37	1.5
1955	NY-N	94	187	22	57	5	2	6	32	27	26	.305	.393	.449	122	7	1	1	0	.986	-4	O-45	0.1
1956	NY-N	111	244	20	53	10	3	8	33	30	41	.217	.303	.381	83	-6	0	0	0	.958	-5	O-68	-1.4
1957	NY-N	92	190	20	39	5	1	4	19	18	34	.205	.278	.305	57	-12	0	0	0	1.000	-6	O-44	-2.0
1959	SF-N	54	48	1	9	2	0	0	7	5	9	.188	.264	.229	34	-5	0	0	0	.000	0	H	-0.5
Total	7	576	1172	146	296	44	10	54	207	131	196	.253	.329	.445	104	5	3	2	-0	.963	-20	O-297	-2.7

■ KARL RHODES　Rhodes, Karl Derrick "Tuffy"　b: 8/21/68, Cincinnati, Ohio　BL/TL, 6', 175 lbs.　Deb: 8/7/90

1990	Hou-N	38	86	12	21	6	1	1	3	13	12	.244	.343	.372	100	0	4	1	1	.955	-1	O-30	-0.1
1991	Hou-N	44	136	7	29	3	1	1	12	14	26	.213	.291	.272	63	-7	2	2	-1	.958	3	O-44	-0.5
1992	Hou-N	5	4	0	0	0	0	0	0	0	0	.000	.000	.000	-99	-1	0	0	0	.000	-1	/O-1	-0.2
1993	Hou-N	5	2	0	0	0	0	0	0	0	0	.000	.000	.000	-99	-1	0	0	0	1.000	0	/O-4	-0.2
	Chi-N	15	52	12	15	2	1	3	7	11	9	.288	.413	.538	155	4	2	0	1	.970	-3	O-14	0.2
	Yr	20	54	12	15	2	1	3	7	11	9	.278	.400	.519	147	4	2	0	1	.971	-4	O-18	0.0
1994	Chi-N	95	269	39	63	10	0	8	19	33	64	.234	.320	.387	84	-6	6	4	-1	.967	-8	O-76	-1.6
1995	Chi-N	13	16	2	2	0	0	0	2	0	4	.125	.125	.125	-34	-3	0	0	0	.889	-2	O-11	-0.5
	Bos-A	10	25	2	2	1	0	0	1	3	4	.080	.179	.120	-20	-4	0	0	0	.947	-1	/O-9	-0.6
Total	6	225	590	74	132	29	3	13	44	74	121	.224	.312	.349	79	-18	14	7	0	.960	-14	O-189	-3.5

■ KEVIN RHOMBERG　Rhomberg, Kevin Jay　b: 11/22/55, Dubuque, Iowa　BR/TR, 6', 175 lbs.　Deb: 9/1/82

1982	Cle-A	16	18	3	6	0	0	1	2	2	4	.333	.400	.500	146	1	0	2	-1	.900	-0	/O-7,3-1,D-4	0.0
1983	Cle-A	12	21	2	10	0	0	0	2	2	4	.476	.522	.476	170	2	1	1	-0	1.000	0	/O-9,D-1	0.0
1984	Cle-A	13	8	0	2	0	0	0	0	0	3	.250	.250	.250	38	-1	0	0	0	1.000	-2	/O-7,1-1,2-1,D-1	-0.2
Total	3	41	47	5	18	0	0	1	4	4	11	.383	.431	.447	140	3	1	3	-2	.963	-4	/O-23,D-6,2-1,13	-0.2

■ HAL RHYNE　Rhyne, Harold J.　b: 3/30/1899, Paso Robles, Cal.　d: 1/7/71, Orangevale, Cal.　BR/TR, 5'8.5", 163 lbs.　Deb: 4/18/26

1926	Pit-N	109	366	46	92	14	3	2	39	35	21	.251	.327	.322	71	-14	1			.967	8	2-66,S-44/3-1	0.0
1927	*Pit-N	62	168	21	46	5	0	0	17	14	9	.274	.330	.304	66	-8	0			.963	-7	2-45,3-10/S-7	-1.2
1929	Bos-A	120	346	41	87	24	5	0	38	25	14	.251	.309	.350	71	-15	4	1	1	.935	-3	*S-113/3-1,O-1	-0.5
1930	Bos-A	107	296	34	60	8	5	0	23	25	19	.203	.269	.264	37	-28	1	4	-2	.944	4	*S-107	-1.5
1931	Bos-A	147	565	75	154	34	3	0	51	57	41	.273	.341	.343	85	-11	3	3	-1	.963	17	*S-147	1.7
1932	Bos-A	71	207	26	47	12	5	0	14	23	14	.227	.310	.333	69	-10	3	2	-0	.966	-2	S-55/3-4,2-1	-0.6
1933	Chi-A	39	83	9	22	1	1	0	10	5	9	.265	.315	.301	67	-4	1	1	-0	.955	5	2-19,3-13/S-2	-0.2
Total	7	655	2031	252	508	98	22	2	192	184	127	.250	.318	.323	69	-91	13	11		.950	23	S-475,2-131/3-29,O	-1.9

■ DEL RICE　Rice, Delbert　b: 10/27/22, Portsmouth, Ohio　d: 1/26/83, Buena Park, Cal.　BR/TR, 6'2", 190 lbs.　Deb: 5/2/45　MC

1945	StL-N	83	253	27	66	17	3	1	28	16	33	.261	.313	.364	86	-5	0			.994	9	C-77	0.7
1946	*StL-N	55	139	10	38	8	1	1	12	8	16	.273	.313	.367	89	-2	0			.977	-0	C-53	0.0
1947	StL-N	97	261	28	57	7	3	12	44	36	40	.218	.315	.406	87	-6	1			.981	4	C-94	0.3
1948	StL-N	100	290	24	57	10	1	4	34	37	46	.197	.298	.279	54	-18	1			.996	8	C-99	-0.4
1949	StL-N	92	284	25	67	16	1	4	29	30	40	.236	.320	.342	74	-10	0			.992	-3	C-92	-0.8
1950	StL-N	130	414	39	101	20	3	9	54	43	65	.244	.323	.372	78	-13	0			.984	6	*C-130	-0.1
1951	StL-N	122	374	34	94	13	1	9	47	34	26	.251	.319	.364	83	-9	0	0	0	.985	2	*C-120	-0.2
1952	StL-N	147	495	43	128	27	2	11	65	33	38	.259	.313	.388	93	-6	0	1	-1	.992	-4	*C-147	-0.4
1953	StL-N†	135	419	32	99	21	1	6	37	48	49	.236	.323	.337	72	-16	0	0	0	.988	-5	*C-135	-1.5
1954	StL-N	56	147	13	37	10	1	2	16	16	21	.252	.325	.374	81	-4	0	1	-1	.985	0	C-52	0.3
1955	StL-N	20	59	6	12	3	0	1	7	7	6	.203	.288	.305	58	-4	0	0	0	.964	-5	C-18	-0.8
	Mil-N	27	71	5	14	0	1	2	7	6	12	.197	.260	.310	53	-5	0	0	0	.981	0	C-22	-0.4
	Yr	47	130	11	26	3	1	3	14	13	18	.200	.273	.308	55	-9	0	0	0	.973	-5	C-40	-1.2
1956	Mil-N	71	188	15	40	9	1	3	17	18	34	.213	.282	.319	65	-10	0	0	0	.983	2	C-65	-0.5
1957	*Mil-N	54	144	15	33	14	1	9	20	17	37	.229	.311	.438	106	1	0	0	0	.992	6	C-48	0.9
1958	Mil-N	43	121	10	27	4	0	2	17	7	30	.223	.271	.306	57	-8	0	0	0	.995	0	C-38	-0.6
1959	Mil-N	13	29	3	6	0	0	1	2	3	6	.207	.258	.310	28	-3	0	0	0	.956	-0	/C-9	-0.3
1960	Chi-N	18	52	2	12	2	0	0	4	2	7	.231	.259	.288	50	-7	0	0	0	.968	-2	C-18	-0.5
	StL-N	1	2	0	0	0	0	0	0	1	0	.000	.333	.000	1	-0	0	0	0	1.000	-0	/C-1	-0.1
	Yr	19	54	2	12	2	0	0	4	3	7	.222	.263	.278	49	-4	0	0	0	.970	-2	C-19	-0.6
	Bal-A	1	1	0	0	0	0	0	0	0	0	.000	.000	.000	-99	-0	0	0	0	1.000	-0	/C-1	0.0
1961	LA-A	44	83	11	20	0	4	1	11	20	19	.241	.388	.434	107	1	0	1	-1	.994	2	C-30	0.3
Total	17	1309	3826	342	908	177	20	79	441	382	522	.237	.312	.356	78	-122	2	3		.987	25	*C-1249	-4.1

■ SAM RICE　Rice, Edgar Charles　b: 2/20/1890, Morocco, Ind.　d: 10/13/74, Rossmoor, Md.　BL/TR, 5'9", 150 lbs.　Deb: 8/7/15　H

1915	Was-A	4	8	0	3	0	0	0	0	0	0	.375	.375	.375	122	0	0			.889	0	/P-4	0.0
1916	Was-A	58	197	26	59	8	3	1	17	15	13	.299	.352	.386	123	5	4			.957	2	O-46/P-5	0.5
1917	Was-A	155	586	77	177	25	7	0	69	50	41	.302	.360	.369	124	16	35			.960	8	*O-155	1.8
1918	Was-A	7	23	3	8	1	0	0	3	2	0	.348	.400	.391	141	1	1			1.000	0	/O-6	0.4
1919	Was-A	141	557	80	179	23	9	3	71	42	26	.321	.376	.411	122	16	26			.962	8	*O-141	1.5
1920	Was-A	153	624	85	211	29	9	3	80	39	23	.338	.381	.428	117	15	63	30	1	.960	21	*O-153	2.5
1921	Was-A	143	561	83	185	39	13	4	79	38	10	.330	.382	.467	121	17	26	12	1	.964	11	*O-141	1.6
1922	Was-A	154	633	91	187	37	13	6	69	48	13	.295	.347	.423	105	3	20	9	1	.951	3	*O-154	0.1
1923	Was-A	148	595	117	188	35	18	3	75	57	12	.316	.381	.450	125	20	20	8	1	.970	8	*O-147	1.9
1924	*Was-A	154	646	106	216	39	14	1	76	46	24	.334	.382	.443	116	14	24	13	-1	.967	4	*O-154	0.6
1925	*Was-A	152	649	111	227	31	13	1	87	37	10	.350	.388	.442	113	12	26	11	0	.968	9	*O-152	1.1
1926	Was-A	152	641	98	216	32	14	3	76	42	20	.337	.380	.445	117	15	24	23	-7	.961	7	*O-152	0.5
1927	Was-A	142	603	98	179	33	14	2	65	36	11	.297	.336	.408	93	-7	19	6	2	.975	-0	*O-139	-1.4
1928	Was-A	148	616	95	202	32	15	2	55	49	15	.328	.379	.438	115	14	16	3	3	.973	-8	*O-147	-0.2
1929	Was-A	150	616	119	199	39	10	1	62	55	9	.323	.382	.424	106	7	16	8	0	.970	7	*O-147	0.3
1930	Was-A	147	593	121	207	35	13	1	73	55	14	.349	.407	.457	118	13	8	-1		.963	4	*O-145	1.0

YEAR	TM/L	G	AB	R	H	2B	3B	HR	RBI	BB	SO	AVG	OBP	SLG	PRO+	BR/A	SB	CS	SBR	FA	FR	G/POS	TPR
1931	Was-A	120	413	81	128	21	8	0	42	35	11	.310	.365	.400	100	1	6	5	-1	.970	1	*O-105	-0.6
1932	Was-A	106	288	58	93	16	7	1	34	32	6	.323	.391	.438	116	7	7	4	-0	.972	-3	O-69	0.0
1933	*Was-A	73	85	19	25	4	3	1	12	2	7	.294	.326	.447	104	0	0	2	-1	1.000	-8	O-39	-0.9
1934	Cle-A	97	335	48	98	19	1	1	33	28	9	.293	.351	.364	83	-8	5	1	1	.963	-7	O-78	-1.6
Total	20	2404	9269	1514	2987	498	184	34	1078	708	275	.322	.374	.427	113	166	351	143		.965	75	*O-2270/P-9	9.1

■ **HAL RICE**   Rice, Harold Housten "Hoot" b: 2/11/24, Morganette, W.Va.   BL/TR, 6'1", 195 lbs. Deb: 4/29/48

YEAR	TM/L	G	AB	R	H	2B	3B	HR	RBI	BB	SO	AVG	OBP	SLG	PRO+	BR/A	SB	CS	SBR	FA	FR	G/POS	TPR
1948	StL-N	8	31	3	10	1	2	0	3	2	4	.323	.364	.484	121	1	0			1.000	-1	/O-8	0.0
1949	StL-N	40	46	3	9	2	1	1	9	3	7	.196	.245	.348	55	-3	0			1.000	-2	O-10	-0.6
1950	StL-N	44	128	12	27	3	1	2	11	10	10	.211	.268	.297	46	-10	0			.972	-1	O-37	-1.3
1951	StL-N	69	236	20	60	12	1	4	38	24	22	.254	.323	.364	84	-5	0	1	-1	.953	-3	O-63	-1.1
1952	StL-N	98	295	37	85	14	5	7	45	16	26	.288	.325	.441	110	3	1	3	-2	.972	-5	O-81	-0.7
1953	StL-N	8	8	0	2	0	0	0	0	0	3	.250	.250	.250	31	-1	0	0	0	.000	0	H	-0.1
	Pit-N	78	286	39	89	16	1	4	42	17	22	.311	.350	.416	99	-0	0	1	-1	.973	14	O-70	1.0
	Yr	86	294	39	91	16	1	4	42	17	25	.310	.347	.412	97	-1	0	1	-1	.973	14	O-70	0.9
1954	Pit-N	28	81	10	14	4	1	1	9	14	24	.173	.295	.284	52	-6	0	2	-1	1.000	3	O-24	-0.5
	Chi-N	51	72	5	11	0	0	0	5	8	15	.153	.237	.153	4	-10	0	0	0	.897	-4	O-24	-1.5
	Yr	79	153	15	25	4	1	1	14	22	39	.163	.269	.222	29	-16	0	2	-1	.966	-2	O-48	-2.0
Total	7	424	1183	129	307	52	12	19	162	94	133	.260	.314	.372	82	-32	1	7		.969	0	O-317	-4.8

■ **HARRY RICE**   Rice, Harry Francis b: 11/22/01, Ware Station, Ill. d: 1/1/71, Portland, Ore.   BL/TR, 5'9", 185 lbs.   Deb: 4/18/23

YEAR	TM/L	G	AB	R	H	2B	3B	HR	RBI	BB	SO	AVG	OBP	SLG	PRO+	BR/A	SB	CS	SBR	FA	FR	G/POS	TPR
1923	StL-A	4	3	0	0	0	0	0	0	0	0	.000	.000	.000	-95	-1	0	0	0	.000	0	H	-0.1
1924	StL-A	54	93	19	26	7	0	0	15	7	5	.280	.350	.355	77	-3	1	3	-2	.917	-0	3-15/2-4,1-2,S-2,O	-0.4
1925	StL-A	103	354	87	127	25	8	11	47	54	15	.359	.450	.568	149	28	8	7	-2	.984	6	O-85/1-3,C-1,2-1,3	2.4
1926	StL-A	148	578	86	181	27	10	9	59	63	40	.313	.384	.441	110	9	10	11	-4	.970	-7	*O-133/3-8,2-4,S-2	0.3
1927	StL-A	137	520	90	149	26	9	7	68	50	21	.287	.351	.412	94	-5	5	4	-1	.938	12	*O-130/3-7	-0.2
1928	Det-A	131	510	87	154	21	12	6	81	44	27	.302	.360	.425	104	3	20	13	-2	.962	1	*O-129/3-2	-0.7
1929	Det-A	130	536	97	163	33	7	6	69	61	23	.304	.379	.425	106	6	6	10	-4	.960	6	*O-127/3-3	-0.1
1930	Det-A	37	128	16	39	6	0	2	24	19	8	.305	.403	.398	102	1	0	3	-2	.944	-0	O-35	-0.3
	NY-A	100	346	62	103	17	5	7	74	31	21	.298	.361	.436	106	3	3	3	-1	.969	8	O-87/1-6,3-1	0.4
	Yr	137	474	78	142	23	5	9	98	50	29	.300	.372	.426	105	4	3	6	-3	.964	7	O-122/1-6,3-1	0.1
1931	Was-A	47	162	32	43	5	6	0	15	12	10	.265	.320	.370	81	-5	2	1	0	.968	-1	O-42	-0.8
1933	Cin-N	143	510	44	133	19	6	0	54	35	24	.261	.316	.322	84	-10	4			**.991**	3	*O-141/3-1	-1.6
Total	10	1034	3740	620	1118	186	63	48	506	376	194	.299	.368	.421	104	25	59	55		.966	39	O-911/3-38,12SC	-1.1

■ **JIM RICE**   Rice, James Edward b: 3/8/53, Anderson, S.C.   BR/TR, 6'2", 205 lbs. Deb: 8/19/74 C

YEAR	TM/L	G	AB	R	H	2B	3B	HR	RBI	BB	SO	AVG	OBP	SLG	PRO+	BR/A	SB	CS	SBR	FA	FR	G/POS	TPR
1974	Bos-A	24	67	6	18	2	1	1	13	4	12	.269	.319	.373	92	-1	0	0	-0	.800	-1	D-16/O-3	-0.2
1975	Bos-A	144	564	92	174	29	4	22	102	36	122	.309	.354	.491	126	17	10	5	0	1.000	-1	O-90,D-54	1.2
1976	Bos-A	153	581	75	164	25	8	25	85	28	123	.282	.320	.482	118	10	8	5	-1	.967	0	O-98,D-54	0.5
1977	Bos-A★	160	644	104	206	29	15	**39**	114	53	120	.320	.376	**.593**	143	36	5	4	-1	.956	1	*D-116,O-44	3.0
1978	Bos-A★	163	677	121	**213**	25	**15**	**46**	**139**	58	126	.315	.373	**.600**	153	**44**	7	5	-1	.989	10	*O-114,D-49	4.8
1979	Bos-A★	158	619	117	201	39	6	39	130	57	97	.325	.385	.596	152	43	9	4	0	.984	2	*O-125,D-33	3.7
1980	Bos-A†	124	504	81	148	22	6	24	86	30	87	.294	.338	.504	121	13	8	3	1	.988	7	*O-109,D-15	1.5
1981	Bos-A	108	451	51	128	18	1	17	62	34	76	.284	.338	.441	116	8	2	2	-1	.988	5	*O-108	0.9
1982	Bos-A	145	573	86	177	24	5	24	97	55	98	.309	.376	.494	129	23	0	1	-1	.969	-1	*O-145	1.8
1983	Bos-A★	155	626	90	191	34	1	**39**	**126**	52	102	.305	.364	.550	137	30	0	2	-1	.984	17	*O-151/D-4	4.1
1984	Bos-A★	159	657	98	184	25	7	28	122	44	102	.280	.326	.467	111	9	4	0	-1	.989	12	*O-157/D-2	1.7
1985	Bos-A★	140	546	85	159	20	3	27	103	51	75	.291	.354	.487	122	16	2	0	1	.964	0	*O-130/D-7	1.2
1986	*Bos-A★	157	618	98	200	39	2	20	110	62	78	.324	.389	.490	137	32	0	1	-0	.977	17	*O-156/D-1	4.2
1987	Bos-A	108	404	66	112	14	0	13	62	45	77	.277	.360	.408	100	1	1	1	-0	.977	4	O-94,D-12	0.1
1988	*Bos-A	135	485	57	128	18	3	15	72	48	89	.264	.334	.406	102	1	1	1	-0	.968	-2	*D-112,O-19	-0.4
1989	Bos-A	56	209	22	49	10	2	3	28	13	40	.234	.283	.344	71	-8	1	0	0	.000	0	D-55	-1.0
Total	16	2089	8225	1249	2452	373	79	382	1451	670	1423	.298	.356	.502	127	275	58	34	-3	.980	71	*O-1543,D-530	27.1

■ **LEN RICE**   Rice, Leonard Oliver b: 9/2/18, Lead, S.Dak. d: 6/13/92, Sonora, Cal.   BR/TR, 6', 175 lbs. Deb: 4/26/44

YEAR	TM/L	G	AB	R	H	2B	3B	HR	RBI	BB	SO	AVG	OBP	SLG	PRO+	BR/A	SB	CS	SBR	FA	FR	G/POS	TPR
1944	Cin-N	10	4	1	0	0	0	0	0	0	0	.000	.000	.000	-99	-1	0			1.000	1	/C-5	0.0
1945	Chi-N	32	99	10	23	3	0	0	7	5	8	.232	.259	.263	49	-7	2			.976	-1	C-29	-0.6
Total	2	42	103	11	23	3	0	0	7	5	8	.223	.259	.252	44	-8	2			.977	0	/C-34	-0.6

■ **BOB RICE**   Rice, Robert Turnbull b: 5/28/1899, Philadelphia, Pa. d: 2/20/86, Elizabethtown, Pa   BR/TR, 5'10", 170 lbs. Deb: 9/1/26

YEAR	TM/L	G	AB	R	H	2B	3B	HR	RBI	BB	SO	AVG	OBP	SLG	PRO+	BR/A	SB	CS	SBR	FA	FR	G/POS	TPR
1926	Phi-N	19	54	3	8	0	1	0	10	3	4	.148	.193	.185	2	-7	0			.864	1	3-15/2-2,S-2	-0.6

■ **LEE RICHARD**   Richard, Lee Edward "Bee Bee" b: 9/18/48, Lafayette, La.   BR/TR, 5'11", 165 lbs. Deb: 4/7/71

YEAR	TM/L	G	AB	R	H	2B	3B	HR	RBI	BB	SO	AVG	OBP	SLG	PRO+	BR/A	SB	CS	SBR	FA	FR	G/POS	TPR
1971	Chi-A	87	260	38	60	7	3	2	17	20	46	.231	.288	.304	66	-12	8	9	-3	.920	-0	S-68,O-16	-0.8
1972	Chi-A	11	29	5	7	0	0	1	0	7	.241	.241	.241	43	-2	1	0	0	1.000	-3	/O-6,S-1	-0.2
1974	Chi-A	32	67	5	11	1	0	0	5	1	8	.164	.222	.179	16	-7	0	0	0	.821	3	3-12/S-6,2-3,0-1,D	-0.4
1975	Chi-A	43	45	11	9	0	1	0	5	4	7	.200	.265	.244	44	-3	2	3	-1	1.000	6	3-12/S-9,2-5,D-5	0.2
1976	StL-N	66	91	12	16	4	2	0	5	4	9	.176	.211	.264	34	-8	1	0	0	.975	12	2-26,S-12/3-1	0.5
Total	5	239	492	71	103	12	6	2	29	33	77	.209	.260	.270	50	-32	12	12	-4	.923	20	/S-96,2-34,3-25,OD	-0.7

■ **GENE RICHARDS**   Richards, Eugene b: 9/29/53, Monticello, S.C.   BL/TL, 6', 175 lbs. Deb: 4/6/77

YEAR	TM/L	G	AB	R	H	2B	3B	HR	RBI	BB	SO	AVG	OBP	SLG	PRO+	BR/A	SB	CS	SBR	FA	FR	G/POS	TPR
1977	SD-N	146	525	79	152	16	11	5	32	60	80	.290	.365	.390	114	11	56	12	10	.963	1	*O-109,1-32	1.6
1978	SD-N	154	555	90	171	26	12	4	45	64	80	.308	.384	.420	135	26	37	17	1	.965	-12	*O-124,1-26	0.9
1979	SD-N	150	545	77	152	17	9	4	41	47	62	.279	.345	.365	100	0	24	8	2	.973	4	*O-132	0.1
1980	SD-N	158	642	91	193	26	8	4	41	61	73	.301	.363	.385	116	14	61	16	9	.979	15	*O-156	3.3
1981	SD-N	104	393	47	113	14	**12**	3	42	53	44	.288	.374	.407	131	17	20	8	1	.975	3	*O-102	1.8
1982	SD-N	132	521	63	149	13	8	3	28	36	52	.286	.335	.359	99	-1	30	20	-3	.977	0	*O-103/1-25	-0.8
1983	SD-N	95	233	37	64	11	3	3	22	17	17	.275	.327	.386	100	0	14	5	1	.980	-1	O-54	-0.2
1984	SF-N	87	135	18	34	4	0	0	4	18	28	.252	.340	.281	79	-3	5	3	-0	.940	-1	O-26	-0.5
Total	8	1026	3549	502	1028	127	63	26	255	356	436	.290	.358	.383	113	63	247	89	21	.972	10	O-806/1-83	6.2

■ **FRED RICHARDS**   Richards, Fred Charles "Fuzzy" b: 11/3/27, Warren, Ohio BL/TL, 6'1.5", 185 lbs. Deb: 9/15/51

YEAR	TM/L	G	AB	R	H	2B	3B	HR	RBI	BB	SO	AVG	OBP	SLG	PRO+	BR/A	SB	CS	SBR	FA	FR	G/POS	TPR
1951	Chi-N	10	27	1	8	0	0	0	0	2	6	.296	.345	.370	91	-0	0	0	0	1.000	1	/1-9	0.1

■ **PAUL RICHARDS**   Richards, Paul Rapier b: 11/21/08, Waxahachie, Tex. d: 5/4/86, Waxahachie, Tex.   BR/TR, 6'1.5", 180 lbs. Deb: 4/17/32 M

YEAR	TM/L	G	AB	R	H	2B	3B	HR	RBI	BB	SO	AVG	OBP	SLG	PRO+	BR/A	SB	CS	SBR	FA	FR	G/POS	TPR
1932	Bro-N	3	8	0	0	0	0	0	0	0	2	.000	.000	.000	-99	-2	0			1.000	4	/C-3	0.1
1933	NY-N	51	87	4	17	3	0	0	10	3	12	.195	.222	.230	30	-8	0			.989	1	C-36	-0.6
1934	NY-N	42	75	10	12	1	0	0	3	13	8	.160	.284	.173	26	-7	0			1.000	2	C-37	-0.4
1935	NY-N	7	4	0	1	0	0	0	0	1	.250	.500	.250	110	0	0			1.000	1	/C-4	0.2
	Phi-A	85	257	31	63	10	1	4	29	24	21	.245	.310	.339	68	-12	0	0	0	.977	-3	C-79	-1.1
1943	Det-A	100	313	32	69	7	5	5	33	38	35	.220	.307	.297	71	-11	1	0	0	**.986**	21	*C-100	1.8
1944	Det-A	95	300	24	71	13	4	0	37	35	30	.237	.318	.310	76	-9	8	3	1	.979	16	C-90	1.3
1945	*Det-A	83	234	26	60	12	1	3	32	19	31	.256	.315	.355	88	-4	4	0	1	**.995**	12	C-83	1.4
1946	Det-A	57	149	13	28	5	2	0	11	23	18	.201	.305	.266	60	-7	2	0		.997	15	C-54	1.2
Total	8	523	1417	140	321	51	15	15	155	157	149	.227	.305	.301	68	-60	15	3		.987	69	C-486	3.9

■ **RICHARDSON**   Richardson b: Boston, Mass. 5'4", 136 lbs. Deb: 7/10/1884

YEAR	TM/L	G	AB	R	H	2B	3B	HR	RBI	BB	SO	AVG	OBP	SLG	PRO+	BR/A	SB	CS	SBR	FA	FR	G/POS	TPR
1884	CP-U	1	4	0	0	0	0	0	0	0	.000	.000	.000	-99	-1				.667	-1	/2-1	-0.2

■ **HARDY RICHARDSON**   Richardson, Abram Harding "Old True Blue"
    b: 4/21/1855, Clarksboro, N.J. d: 1/14/31, Utica, N.Y.   BR/TR, 5'9.5", 170 lbs. Deb: 5/1/1879

YEAR	TM/L	G	AB	R	H	2B	3B	HR	RBI	BB	SO	AVG	OBP	SLG	PRO+	BR/A	SB	CS	SBR	FA	FR	G/POS	TPR
1879	Buf-N	79	336	54	95	18	10	0	37	16	30	.283	.315	.396	130	10				.843	-6	*3-78/C-1	0.6

YEAR	TM/L	G	AB	R	H	2B	3B	HR	RBI	BB	SO	AVG	OBP	SLG	PRO+	BR/A	SB	CS	SBR	FA	FR	G/POS	TPR
1880	Buf-N	83	343	48	89	18	8	0	17	14	37	.259	.289	.359	116	5				.848	-7	*3-81/C-5	0.1
1881	Buf-N	83	344	62	100	18	9	2	53	12	27	.291	.315	.413	129	11				.914	25	*O-79/2-5,S-1,3-1	3.1
1882	Buf-N	83	354	61	96	20	8	2	57	11	33	.271	.293	.390	115	5				.898	16	*2-83	2.1
1883	Buf-N	92	399	73	124	34	7	1	56	22	20	.311	.347	.439	134	16				.903	19	*2-92	3.1
1884	Buf-N	102	439	85	132	27	9	6	60	22	41	.301	.334	.444	118	18				.897	8	2-71,O-24/3-5,1-3	2.3
1885	Buf-N	96	426	90	136	19	11	6	44	20	22	.319	.350	.458	154	24				.905	13	2-50,O-48/S-1,P-1	3.4
1886	Det-N	125	538	125	**189**	27	11	**11**	61	46	27	.351	.402	.504	169	44	42			.899	10	O-80,2-42/P-4,S3	4.8
1887	*Det-N	120	543	131	178	25	18	8	94	31	40	.328	.366	.484	130	20	29			.941	17	2-64,O-59	3.2
1888	Det-N	58	266	60	77	18	2	6	32	17	23	.289	.335	.440	145	13	13			.925	4	2-58	1.9
1889	Bos-N	132	536	122	163	33	10	6	79	48	44	.304	.367	.437	117	10	47			.924	13	2-86,O-46	2.3
1890	Bos-P	130	555	126	181	26	14	13	**146**	52	46	.326	.384	.494	115	16	42			.950	2	*O-124/S-6,1-1	1.1
1891	Bos-a	74	278	45	71	9	4	3	52	40	26	.255	.351	.392	114	5	16			.955	-0	O-60/3-9,S-4,1-3	0.3
1892	Was-N	10	37	2	4	0	0	0	0	5	3	.108	.214	.108	-2	-4	2			.941	-0	/O-7,3-2,2-1	-0.4
	NY-N	64	248	36	53	11	5	2	34	21	26	.214	.278	.323	83	-6	14			.931	-1	2-33,O-17/1-9,S-6	-0.6
	Yr	74	285	38	57	11	5	2	34	26	29	.200	.269	.295	72	-10	16			.933	-1	2-34,O-24/1-9,S3	-1.0
Total	14	1331	5642	1120	1688	303	126	70	822	377	445	.299	.344	.435	130	186	205			.915	113	2-585,O-544,3/S1CP	27.3

■ NOLEN RICHARDSON
Richardson, Clifford Nolen   b: 1/18/03, Chattanooga, Tenn.   d: 9/25/51, Athens, Ga.   BR/TR, 6'1.5", 170 lbs.   Deb: 4/16/29

YEAR	TM/L	G	AB	R	H	2B	3B	HR	RBI	BB	SO	AVG	OBP	SLG	PRO+	BR/A	SB	CS	SBR	FA	FR	G/POS	TPR
1929	Det-A	13	21	2	4	0	0	0	2	2	1	.190	.261	.190	18	-3	1	1	-0	.839	-4	S-13	-0.6
1931	Det-A	38	148	13	40	9	2	0	16	6	3	.270	.299	.358	70	-7	2	1	0	.946	-2	3-38	-0.6
1932	Det-A	69	155	13	34	5	2	0	12	9	13	.219	.262	.277	38	-14	5	2	0	.986	11	3-65/S-4	0.0
1935	NY-A	12	46	3	10	1	1	0	5	3	1	.217	.265	.283	44	-4	0	0	0	.922	-6	S-12	-0.9
1938	Cin-N	35	100	8	29	4	0	0	10	3	4	.290	.311	.330	78	-3	0			.966	-1	S-35	-0.2
1939	Cin-N	1	3	0	0	0	0	0	0	0	0	.000	.000	.000	-99	-1	0			1.000	1	/S-1	0.0
Total	6	168	473	39	117	19	5	0	45	23	22	.247	.282	.309	55	-31	8	4		.969	-2	3-103/S-65	-2.3

■ DANNY RICHARDSON
Richardson, Daniel   b: 1/25/1863, Elmira, N.Y.   d: 9/12/26, New York, N.Y.   BR/TR, 5'8", 165 lbs.   Deb: 5/22/1884   M

YEAR	TM/L	G	AB	R	H	2B	3B	HR	RBI	BB	SO	AVG	OBP	SLG	PRO+	BR/A	SB	CS	SBR	FA	FR	G/POS	TPR
1884	NY-N	74	277	36	70	8	1	1	27	16	17	.253	.294	.300	85	-5				.907	2	O-55/S-19	-0.4
1885	NY-N	49	198	26	52	9	3	0	25	10	14	.263	.298	.338	107	1				.950	-1	O-22,3-21/P-9	0.1
1886	NY-N	68	237	43	55	9	1	1	27	17	21	.232	.283	.291	74	-7	12			.953	-0	O-64/P-5,S-1,3-1,2	-0.9
1887	NY-N	122	450	79	125	19	10	3	62	36	25	.278	.337	.384	105	4	41			.928	15	*2-108,3-14/P-1	1.8
1888	*NY-N	135	561	82	127	16	7	8	61	15	35	.226	.248	.323	82	-12	35			**.942**	9	*2-135	0.2
1889	*NY-N	125	497	88	139	22	8	7	100	46	37	.280	.342	.398	106	3	32			.934	13	*2-125	2.0
1890	NY-P	123	528	102	135	12	9	4	80	37	19	.256	.307	.335	66	-29	37			.900	25	S-68,2-56	0.3
1891	NY-N	123	516	85	139	18	5	4	51	33	27	.269	.313	.347	96	-4	28			.952	**49**	*2-114/S-9	**4.5**
1892	Was-N	142	551	48	132	13	4	3	58	25	45	.240	.274	.294	74	-19	25			.931	**58**	S-93,2-49/3-1,M	4.0
1893	Bro-N	54	206	36	46	6	2	0	27	13	18	.223	.279	.272	49	-15	7			.949	-17	2-46/3-5,S-3	-2.6
1894	Lou-N	116	430	51	109	17	2	1	40	35	31	.253	.317	.309	55	-31	8			.916	3	*S-107,2-10	-1.7
Total	11	1131	4451	676	1129	149	52	32	558	283	289	.254	.301	.332	82	-113	225			.940	156	2-644,S-300,O/3P	7.3

■ JEFF RICHARDSON
Richardson, Jeffrey Scott   b: 8/26/65, Grand Island, Neb.   BR/TR, 6'2", 175 lbs.   Deb: 7/14/89

YEAR	TM/L	G	AB	R	H	2B	3B	HR	RBI	BB	SO	AVG	OBP	SLG	PRO+	BR/A	SB	CS	SBR	FA	FR	G/POS	TPR
1989	Cin-N	53	125	10	21	4	0	2	11	10	23	.168	.235	.248	37	-10	1	0	0	.969	-2	S-39/3-8	-1.0
1991	Pit-N	6	4	0	1	0	0	0	0	0	3	.250	.250	.250	42	-0	0	0	0	.000	-1	/3-3,S-2	-0.1
1993	Bos-A	15	24	3	5	2	0	0	2	1	3	.208	.240	.292	40	-2	0	0	0	1.000	6	/2-8,S-5,3-1,D-2	0.4
Total	3	74	153	13	27	6	0	2	13	11	29	.176	.236	.255	38	-13	1	0	0	.971	3	/S-46,3-12,2-8,D-2	-0.7

■ KEN RICHARDSON
Richardson, Kenneth Franklin   b: 5/2/15, Orleans, Ind.   d: 12/7/87, Woodland Hills, Cal   BR/TR, 5'10.5", 187 lbs.   Deb: 4/14/42

YEAR	TM/L	G	AB	R	H	2B	3B	HR	RBI	BB	SO	AVG	OBP	SLG	PRO+	BR/A	SB	CS	SBR	FA	FR	G/POS	TPR
1942	Phi-A	6	15	1	1	0	0	0	0	2	0	.067	.176	.067	-30	-3	0	0	0	1.000	0	/O-3,1-1,3-1	-0.3
1946	Phi-N	6	20	1	3	1	0	0	2	0	2	.150	.150	.200	3	-3	0	0		.939	-0	/2-6	-0.3
Total	2	12	35	2	4	1	0	0	2	2	2	.114	.162	.143	-14	-5	0	0		.939	-0	/2-6,O-3,3-1,1-1	-0.6

■ BOBBY RICHARDSON
Richardson, Robert Clinton   b: 8/19/35, Sumter, S.C.   BR/TR, 5'9", 170 lbs.   Deb: 8/5/55

YEAR	TM/L	G	AB	R	H	2B	3B	HR	RBI	BB	SO	AVG	OBP	SLG	PRO+	BR/A	SB	CS	SBR	FA	FR	G/POS	TPR
1955	NY-A	11	26	2	4	0	0	0	3	2	0	.154	.214	.154	0	-4	1	1	-0	.864	-5	/2-6,S-4	-0.9
1956	NY-A	5	7	1	1	0	0	0	0	0	0	.143	.143	.143	-25	-1	0	0	0	1.000	2	/2-5	0.1
1957	*NY-A☆	97	305	36	78	11	1	0	19	9	26	.256	.277	.298	58	-18	1	3	-2	.979	5	2-93	-0.8
1958	*NY-A	73	182	18	45	6	2	0	14	8	5	.247	.279	.302	62	-10	1	3	-2	.973	8	2-51,3-13/S-2	0.0
1959	*NY-A☆	134	469	53	141	18	6	2	33	26	20	.301	.337	.377	99	-1	5	5	-2	.970	2	*2-109,S-14,3-12	0.9
1960	*NY-A	150	460	45	116	12	3	1	26	35	19	.252	.305	.298	68	-21	6	6	-2	.973	-4	*2-141,3-11	-1.5
1961	*NY-A	162	662	80	173	17	5	3	49	30	23	.261	.295	.316	67	-32	9	7	-2	.978	-9	*2-161	-2.6
1962	*NY-A★	161	692	99	**209**	38	5	8	59	37	24	.302	.338	.406	103	1	11	9	-2	.982	-3	*2-161	1.3
1963	*NY-A★	151	630	72	167	20	6	3	48	25	22	.265	.295	.330	76	-21	15	1	4	.984	-3	*2-150	0.5
1964	*NY-A★	159	679	90	181	25	4	4	50	28	36	.267	.296	.333	73	-25	11	2	-2	.982	-14	*2-157/S-1	-2.4
1965	NY-A★	160	664	76	164	28	2	6	47	37	39	.247	.288	.322	74	-22	7	5	-1	.981	-3	*2-158	-1.4
1966	NY-A★	149	610	71	153	21	3	7	42	25	28	.251	.281	.330	78	-19	6	3	-2	.980	3	*2-147/3-2	-0.8
Total	12	1412	5386	643	1432	196	37	34	390	262	243	.266	.301	.335	77	-173	73	48	-7	.979	-11	*2-1339/3-38,S-21	-7.6

■ TOM RICHARDSON
Richardson, Thomas Mitchell   b: 8/7/1883, Louisville, Ill.   d: 11/15/39, Onawa, Iowa   BR/TR, 6', 190 lbs.   Deb: 8/2/17

YEAR	TM/L	G	AB	R	H	2B	3B	HR	RBI	BB	SO	AVG	OBP	SLG	PRO+	BR/A	SB	CS	SBR	FA	FR	G/POS	TPR
1917	StL-A	1	1	0	0	0	0	0	0	0	0	.000	.000	.000	-99	-0	0			.000		H	0.0

■ BILL RICHARDSON
Richardson, William Henry   b: 9/24/1878, Salem, Ind.   d: 11/6/49, Sullivan, Ind.   BR/TR, 5'11", 200 lbs.   Deb: 9/20/01

YEAR	TM/L	G	AB	R	H	2B	3B	HR	RBI	BB	SO	AVG	OBP	SLG	PRO+	BR/A	SB	CS	SBR	FA	FR	G/POS	TPR
1901	StL-N	15	52	7	11	2	0	2	7	6		.212	.293	.365	95	-0	1			.981	-1	1-15	-0.2

■ MIKE RICHARDT
Richardt, Michael Anthony   b: 5/24/58, Los Angeles, Cal.   BR/TR, 6', 170 lbs.   Deb: 8/30/80

YEAR	TM/L	G	AB	R	H	2B	3B	HR	RBI	BB	SO	AVG	OBP	SLG	PRO+	BR/A	SB	CS	SBR	FA	FR	G/POS	TPR
1980	Tex-A	22	71	2	16	2	0	0	8	1	7	.225	.236	.254	35	-6	0	0	0	.978	-1	2-20/D-1	-0.6
1982	Tex-A	119	402	34	97	10	0	3	43	23	42	.241	.284	.289	61	-22	9	1	2	.988	4	2-98,D-15/O-6	-1.1
1983	Tex-A	22	83	9	13	2	1	1	7	2	11	.157	.176	.241	14	-10	2	1	0	.992	2	2-20	-0.7
1984	Tex-A	6	9	0	1	0	0	0	0	1	1	.111	.200	.111	-11	-1	0	1	-1	1.000	-1	/2-4	-0.1
	Hou-N	16	15	1	4	1	0	0	2	0	1	.267	.267	.333	73	-1	0	0	0	.000	0	H	-0.1
Total	4	185	580	46	131	15	1	4	60	27	62	.226	.262	.276	50	-40	11	3	2	.988	6	2-142/D-16,O-6	-2.6

■ LANCE RICHBOURG
Richbourg, Lance Clayton   b: 12/18/1897, DeFuniak Springs, Fla.   d: 9/10/75, Crestview, Fla.   BL/TR, 5'10.5", 160 lbs.   Deb: 7/4/21

YEAR	TM/L	G	AB	R	H	2B	3B	HR	RBI	BB	SO	AVG	OBP	SLG	PRO+	BR/A	SB	CS	SBR	FA	FR	G/POS	TPR
1921	Phi-N	10	5	2	1	1	0	0	0	0	3	.200	.200	.400	51	-0	1	1	-0	1.000	2	/2-4	0.1
1924	Was-A	15	32	3	9	2	1	0	1	2	0	.281	.324	.406	90	-1	0	0	0	1.000	1	/O-7	-0.1
1927	Bos-N	115	450	57	139	12	9	2	34	22	30	.309	.342	.389	104	1	24			.953	-4	*O-110	-1.0
1928	Bos-N	148	612	105	206	26	12	2	52	62	39	.337	.399	.428	123	22	11			.972	7	*O-148	1.8
1929	Bos-N	139	557	76	170	24	13	3	56	42	26	.305	.355	.411	93	-6	7			.971	-3	*O-134	-1.0
1930	Bos-N	130	529	81	161	23	8	3	54	19	31	.304	.331	.395	77	-20	13			.971	-3	*O-128	-2.8
1931	Bos-N	97	286	32	82	11	6	2	29	19	14	.287	.331	.388	96	-2	9			.981	-5	O-71	-1.0
1932	Chi-N	44	148	22	38	2	2	1	21	8	4	.257	.295	.318	65	-7	0			.986	-1	O-33	-1.0
Total	8	698	2619	378	806	101	51	13	247	174	147	.308	.352	.400	97	-14	65	1		.970	4	O-631/2-4	-4.9

■ ROB RICHIE
Richie, Robert Eugene   b: 9/5/65, Reno, Nev.   BL/TR, 6'2", 190 lbs.   Deb: 8/19/89

YEAR	TM/L	G	AB	R	H	2B	3B	HR	RBI	BB	SO	AVG	OBP	SLG	PRO+	BR/A	SB	CS	SBR	FA	FR	G/POS	TPR
1989	Det-A	19	49	6	13	4	2	1	10	5	10	.265	.333	.490	132	2	0	1	-1	.917	-1	O-13/D-4	0.0

■ DON RICHMOND
Richmond, Donald Lester   b: 10/27/19, Gillett, Pa.   d: 5/24/81, Elmira, N.Y.   BL/TR, 6'1", 175 lbs.   Deb: 9/16/41

YEAR	TM/L	G	AB	R	H	2B	3B	HR	RBI	BB	SO	AVG	OBP	SLG	PRO+	BR/A	SB	CS	SBR	FA	FR	G/POS	TPR
1941	Phi-A	9	35	3	7	1	1	0	5	0	1	.200	.200	.286	28	-4	0	2	-1	.957	-2	/3-9	-0.7
1946	Phi-A	16	62	3	18	3	0	1	9	0	10	.290	.290	.387	89	-1	1	0	0	.940	-3	3-16	-0.4
1947	Phi-A	19	21	2	4	1	1	0	4	3	3	.190	.292	.333	72	-1	0	0	0	.500	-3	/3-4,2-1	-0.4
1951	StL-N	12	34	3	3	1	0	1	4	3	3	.088	.162	.206	-2	-5	0	1		1.000	5	3-11	-0.1
Total	4	56	152	11	32	6	2	2	22	6	17	.211	.241	.316	51	-11	1	3	-2	.957	-4	/3-40,2-1	-1.6

YEAR	TM/L	G	AB	R	H	2B	3B	HR	RBI	BB	SO	AVG	OBP	SLG	PRO+	BR/A	SB	CS	SBR	FA	FR	G/POS	TPR
■ LEE RICHMOND			Richmond, J Lee		b: 5/5/1857, Sheffield, Ohio			d: 10/1/29, Toledo, Ohio		TL, 5'10", 155 lbs.		Deb: 9/27/1879											
1879	Bos-N	1	6	0	2	0	0	0	1	0	1	.333	.333	.333	118	0				1.000	0	/P-1	0.0
1880	Wor-N	77	309	44	70	8	4	0	34	9	32	.227	.248	.278	72	-10				.827	-13	*P-74,O-20	-0.7
1881	Wor-N	61	252	31	63	5	1	0	28	10	10	.250	.279	.278	71	-8				.937	-1	P-53,O-11	-0.4
1882	Wor-N	55	228	50	64	8	9	2	28	9	11	.281	.308	.421	128	7				.889	2	P-48,O-11	0.0
1883	Pro-N	49	194	41	55	8	6	1	19	15	19	.284	.342	.402	120	5				.714	-10	O-41,P-12	-0.6
1886	Cin-a	8	29	3	8	0	0	0	3	3		.276	.344	.276	92	-0	0			.400	-4	/O-7,P-3	-0.3
Total	6	251	1018	169	262	29	20	3	113	46	73	.257	.289	.334	94	-7	0			.886	-26	P-191/O-90	-2.0
■ JOHN RICHMOND			Richmond, John H.		b: 1854, Pennsylvania		TR, 5'9", 170 lbs.		Deb: 4/22/1875														
1875	Ath-n	29	125	29	25	2	0	0	12	1	4	.200	.206	.216	42	-8	1	0	0	.814	-2	2-17,O-11/C-3	-0.9
1879	Syr-N	62	254	31	54	8	4	1	23	4	24	.213	.225	.287	76	-6				.874	-7	O-35,S-28/C-2	-1.2
1880	Bos-N	32	129	12	32	3	1	0	9	2	18	.248	.260	.287	88	-2				.844	-12	S-31/O-1	-1.1
1881	Bos-N	27	98	13	27	2	2	1	12	6	7	.276	.317	.367	120	2				.969	-0	O-25/S-2	0.2
1882	Cle-N	41	140	12	24	6	2	0	11	11	27	.171	.232	.243	54	-7				.917	3	O-41	-0.4
	Phi-a	18	65	8	12	2	2	0	4	11		.185	.303	.277	87	-1				.892	-1	O-18	-0.1
1883	Col-a	92	385	63	109	7	8	0		25		.283	.327	.343	126	13				**.877**	26	*S-91/O-2	**3.5**
1884	Col-a	105	398	57	100	13	7	3		35		.251	.317	.342	125	13				.866	-9	*S-105	0.4
1885	Pit-a	34	131	14	27	2	0	0	12	8		.206	.262	.252	64	-5				.849	-10	S-23,O-11	-1.3
Total	7	411	1600	210	385	43	28	5	71	102	76	.241	.288	.312	101	8				.866	-10	S-280/O-133/C-2	-0.0
■ AL RICHTER			Richter, Allen Gordon		b: 2/7/27, Norfolk, Va.		BR/TR, 5'11", 165 lbs.		Deb: 9/23/51														
1951	Bos-A	5	11	1	1	0	0	0	0	3	0	.091	.286	.091	5	-1	0	0	0	1.000	2	/S-3	0.1
1953	Bos-A	1	0	0	0	0	0	0	0	0	0	—	—	—	—	0	0	0	0	1.000	1	/S-1	0.1
Total	2	6	11	1	1	0	0	0	0	3	0	.091	.286	.091	5	-1	0	0	0	1.000	3	/S-4	0.1
■ JOHN RICHTER			Richter, John M.		b: 2/8/1873, Louisville, Ky.		d: 10/4/27, Louisville, Ky.		6', 178 lbs.		Deb: 10/6/1898											
1898	Lou-N	3	13	1	2	0	0	0	0	0		.154	.154	.154	-12	-2	0			.929	0	/3-3	-0.1
■ JOE RICKERT			Rickert, Joseph Francis "Diamond Joe"		b: 12/12/1876, London, Ohio		d: 10/15/43, Springfield, Ohio		BR/TR, 5'10.5", 165 lbs.		Deb: 10/12/1898										
1898	Pit-N	2	6	0	1	0	0	0	0	0	0	.167	.167	.167	-5	-1	0			1.000	1	/O-2	0.0
1901	Bos-N	13	60	6	10	1	2	0	1	3		.167	.206	.250	29	-6	1			.974	2	/O-13	-0.4
Total	2	15	66	6	11	1	2	0	1	3		.167	.203	.242	27	-6	1			.979	3	/O-15	-0.4
■ MARV RICKERT			Rickert, Marvin August "Twitch"		b: 1/8/21, Longbranch, Wash.		d: 6/3/78, Oakville, Wash.		BL/TR, 6'2", 195 lbs.		Deb: 9/10/42										
1942	Chi-N	8	26	5	7	0	0	1	1	5		.269	.296	.269	69	-1	0			1.000	1	/O-6	0.0
1946	Chi-N	111	392	44	103	18	3	7	47	28	54	.263	.314	.378	98	-3	3			.972	-6	*O-104	-1.4
1947	Chi-N	71	137	7	20	2	2	0	15	15	17	.146	.230	.190	13	-17	0			.982	-1	O-30/1-7	-2.0
1948	Cin-N	8	6	0	1	0	0	0	0	0	0	.167	.167	.167	-10	-1	0			.000	0	H	-0.1
	*Bos-N	3	13	1	3	0	1	0	2	0	1	.231	.286	.385	81	-0	0			1.000	1	/O-3	0.1
	Yr	11	19	1	4	0	1	0	2	0	1	.211	.250	.316	54	-1	0			1.000	1	/O-3	0.0
1949	Bos-N	100	277	44	81	18	3	6	49	23	38	.292	.347	.444	117	6	1			.981	-0	O-75,1-12	0.2
1950	Pit-N	17	20	0	3	0	0	0	4	0	4	.150	.150	.150	-20	-3	0			.000	-1	/O-3	-0.5
	Chi-A	84	278	38	66	9	2	4	27	21	42	.237	.291	.327	60	-18	0	1	-1	.968	-6	O-78/1-1	-2.6
Total	6	402	1149	139	284	45	9	19	145	88	161	.247	.302	.352	79	-38	4	1		.976	-12	O-299/1-20	-6.3
■ DAVE RICKETTS			Ricketts, David William		b: 7/12/35, Pottstown, Pa.		BB/TR, 6'2", 195 lbs.		Deb: 9/25/63		FC										
1963	StL-N	2	8	0	2	0	0	0	0	0	2	.250	.250	.250	41	-1	0	0	0	1.000	-0	/C-3	-0.1
1965	StL-N	11	29	1	7	0	0	0	1	1	3	.241	.267	.241	40	-2	0	0	0	.977	-2	C-11	-0.4
1967	*StL-N	52	99	11	27	8	0	1	14	4	7	.273	.301	.384	96	-1	0	0	0	1.000	-0	C-21	0.0
1968	*StL-N	20	22	1	3	0	0	0	0	3	0	.136	.136	.136	-18	-3	0	0	0	1.000	-0	/C-1	-0.4
1969	StL-N	30	44	2	12	1	0	0	5	4	5	.273	.333	.295	77	-1	0	0	0	.983	1	/C-8	0.0
1970	Pit-N	14	11	0	2	0	0	0	0	1	3	.182	.250	.182	18	-1	0	0	0	.909	1	/C-7	-0.1
Total	6	130	213	15	53	9	0	1	20	10	23	.249	.283	.305	67	-9	0	0	0	.988	-1	/C-51	-1.0
■ BRANCH RICKEY			Rickey, Wesley Branch "The Mahatma"		b: 12/20/1881, Flat, Ohio		d: 12/9/65, Columbia, Mo.		BL/TR, 5'9", 175 lbs.		Deb: 6/16/05		MH								
1905	StL-A	1	3	0	0	0	0	0	0	0		.000	.000	.000	-99	-1	0			1.000	-0	/C-1	-0.1
1906	StL-A	65	201	22	57	7	3	3	24	16		.284	.345	.393	137	8	4			.954	-8	C-55/O-1	0.7
1907	NY-A	52	137	16	25	1	3	0	15	11		.182	.253	.234	51	-7	4			.846	-5	O-22,C-11/1-9	-1.4
1914	StL-A	2	2	0	0	0	0	0	0	0	1	.000	.000	.000	-99	-0	0			.000	0	HM	-0.1
Total	4	120	343	38	82	8	6	3	39	27	1	.239	.304	.324	97	-0	8			.940	-13	/C-67,O-23,1-9	-0.9
■ CHRIS RICKLEY			Rickley, Christian		b: 10/7/1859, Philadelphia, Pa.		d: 10/25/11, Philadelphia, Pa.		5'8", 160 lbs.		Deb: 6/9/1884										
1884	Phi-U	6	25	5	5	2	0	0		2		.200	.259	.280	68	-2				.757	0	/S-6	-0.1
■ JOHN RICKS			Ricks, John		Deb: 9/21/1891																			
1891	StL-a	5	18	3	3	0	0	0	0	0	2	.167	.167	.167	-4	-3	0			.810	-1	/3-5	-0.3
1894	StL-N	1	1	0	0	0	0	0	0	0	0	.000	.000	.000	-99	-0	0			.250	-1	/3-1	-0.1
Total	2	6	19	3	3	0	0	0	0	0	2	.158	.158	.158	-9	-3	0			.720	-2	/3-6	-0.4
■ FRED RICO			Rico, Alfredo (Cruz)		b: 7/4/44, Jerome, Ariz.		BR/TR, 5'10", 180 lbs.		Deb: 9/1/69												
1969	KC-A	12	26	2	6	1	0	0	2	9	10	.231	.429	.308	108	1	0	1	-1	1.000	4	/O-9,3-1	0.4
■ ART RICO			Rico, Arthur Raymond		b: 7/23/1896, Roxbury, Mass.		d: 1/3/19, Boston, Mass.		BR/TR, 5'9.5", 185 lbs.		Deb: 7/31/16										
1916	Bos-N	4	4	0	0	0	0	0	0	0	0	.000	.000	.000	-99	-1	0			1.000	-0	/C-4	-0.1
1917	Bos-N	13	14	1	4	1	0	0	2	0	2	.286	.286	.357	102	-0	0			.950	-2	C-11/O-2	-0.1
Total	2	17	18	1	4	1	0	0	2	0	2	.222	.222	.278	56	-1	0			.962	-2	/C-15,O-2	-0.2
■ HARRY RICONDA			Riconda, Henry Paul		b: 3/17/1897, New York, N.Y.		d: 11/15/58, Mahopac, N.Y.		BR/TR, 5'10", 175 lbs.		Deb: 4/19/23									
1923	Phi-A	55	175	23	46	11	4	0	12	12	18	.263	.317	.371	80	-6	4	2	0	.911	4	3-47/S-2	0.2
1924	Phi-A	83	281	34	71	16	3	1	21	27	43	.253	.323	.342	71	-13	3	4	-2	.927	3	3-73/S-2	-0.7
1926	Bos-N	4	12	1	2	0	0	0	0	0	2	.167	.286	.167	27	-1	0			.818	-1	/3-4	-0.1
1928	Bro-N	92	281	22	63	15	4	3	35	20	28	.224	.285	.338	63	-16	6			.957	3	2-53,3-21,S-16	-0.9
1929	Pit-N	8	15	3	7	2	0	0	2	0	0	.467	.467	.600	158	1	0			.840	-0	/S-4	0.1
1930	Cin-N	1	1	0	0	0	0	0	0	0	0	.000	.000	.000	-99	-0	0			.000	0	H	0.0
Total	6	243	765	83	189	44	11	4	70	61	91	.247	.309	.349	71	-34	13	6		.922	7	3-145/2-53,S-24	-1.5
■ JOHN RIDDLE			Riddle, John H.		b: 2/1864, Pennsylvania		BR/TR,		Deb: 9/18/1889												
1889	Was-N	11	37	3	8	3	0	0	3	2	8	.216	.256	.297	58	-2	0			.841	1	/C-9,O-2	-0.1
1890	Phi-a	27	85	7	7	0	1	0	2	17		.082	.243	.106	3	-10	4			.914	-2	C-13,O-12/2-2,3-1	-1.0
Total	2	38	122	10	15	3	1	0	5	19	8	.123	.246	.164	20	-12	4			.880	-2	/C-22,O-14,2-2,3-1	-1.1
■ JOHNNY RIDDLE			Riddle, John Ludy "Mutt"		b: 10/3/05, Clinton, S.C.		BR/TR, 5'11", 190 lbs.		Deb: 4/17/30		FC									
1930	Chi-A	25	58	7	14	3	1	0	4	3	6	.241	.290	.328	58	-4	0	0	0	1.000	-3	C-25	-0.4
1937	Was-A	8	26	2	7	0	0	0	3	0	2	.269	.269	.269	46	-2	0	0	0	.971	1	/C-8	-0.1
	Bos-N	2	3	0	0	0	0	0	0	0	0	.000	.250	.000	-29	-1	0	0	0	1.000	1	/C-2	0.0
1938	Bos-N	19	57	6	16	1	0	0	2	4	2	.281	.328	.298	81	-1	0	0	0	.951	4	C-19	0.3
1941	Cin-N	10	10	2	3	0	0	0	0	0	0	.300	.300	.300	69	-0	0	0	0	1.000	1	/C-10	0.1
1944	Cin-N	1	0	0	0	0	0	0	0	0	0	—	—	—	—	0	0	0	0	.000	0	/C-1	0.0
1945	Cin-N	23	45	0	8	0	0	0	2	4	6	.178	.245	.178	19	-5	0	0	0	1.000	4	C-23	-0.1
1948	Pit-N	10	15	1	3	0	0	0	0	1	1	.200	.250	.200	23	-2	0	0	0	1.000	0	C-10	-0.1
Total	7	98	214	18	51	4	1	0	11	13	19	.238	.288	.266	51	-15	0	0	0	.983	7	/C-98	-0.3

YEAR	TM/L	G	AB	R	H	2B	3B	HR	RBI	BB	SO	AVG	OBP	SLG	PRO+	BR/A	SB	CS	SBR	FA	FR	G/POS	TPR

■ HANK RIEBE   Riebe, Harvey Donald   b: 10/10/21, Cleveland, Ohio   BR/TR, 5'9.5", 175 lbs.   Deb: 8/26/42

1942	Det-A	11	35	1	11	2	0	0	2	0	6	.314	.314	.371	85	-1	0	0	0	1.000	-1	C-11	-0.1
1947	Det-A	8	7	0	0	0	0	0	2	0	2	.000	.000	.000	-97	-2	0	0	0	1.000	-0	/C-3	-0.2
1948	Det-A	25	62	0	12	0	0	0	5	3	5	.194	.231	.194	13	-8	0	1	-1	1.000	-2	C-24	-0.7
1949	Det-A	17	33	1	6	2	0	0	2	0	5	.182	.182	.242	12	-4	1	0	0	.960	-2	C-11	-0.5
Total	4	61	137	2	29	4	0	0	11	3	18	.212	.229	.241	26	-15	1	1	-0	.994	-3	/C-49	-1.5

■ NIKCO RIESGO   Riesgo, Damon Nikco   b: 1/11/67, Long Beach, Cal.   BR/TR, 6'2", 185 lbs.   Deb: 4/20/91

1991	Mon-N	4	7	1	1	0	0	0	3	1	1	.143	.400	.143	60	-0	0	0	0	.500	-0	/O-2	0.0

■ JOE RIGGERT   Riggert, Joseph Aloysius   b: 12/11/1886, Janesville, Wis.   d: 12/10/73, Kansas City, Mo.   BR/TR, 5'9.5", 170 lbs.   Deb: 5/12/11

1911	Bos-A	50	146	19	31	4	4	2	13	12		.212	.290	.336	75	-5	5			.929	-4	O-39	-1.1
1914	Bro-N	27	83	6	16	1	3	2	6	4	20	.193	.230	.349	70	-4	2			.972	-1	O-20	-0.5
	StL-N	34	89	9	19	5	2	0	8	5	14	.213	.255	.315	70	-4	4			.961	-3	O-30	-0.9
	Yr	61	172	15	35	6	5	2	14	9	34	.203	.243	.331	70	-7	6			.966	-4	O-50	-1.4
1919	Bos-N	63	240	34	68	8	5	4	17	25	30	.283	.356	.408	135	10	9			.950	2	O-61	0.9
Total	3	174	558	68	134	18	14	8	44	46	64	.240	.305	.366	98	-2	20			.950	-6	O-150	-1.6

■ LEW RIGGS   Riggs, Lewis Sidney   b: 4/22/10, Mebane, N.C.   d: 8/12/75, Durham, N.C.   BL/TR, 6', 175 lbs.   Deb: 4/28/34

1934	StL-N	2	1	0	0	0	0	0	0	0	0	.000	.000	.000	-94	-0	0			.000	0	H	0.0
1935	Cin-N	142	532	73	148	26	8	5	46	43	32	.278	.334	.385	96	-3	8			.928	8	*3-135	1.0
1936	Cin-N★	141	538	69	138	20	12	6	57	38	33	.257	.314	.372	90	-9	5			.968	12	*3-140	0.8
1937	Cin-N	122	384	43	93	17	5	6	45	24	17	.242	.289	.359	79	-13	4			.941	20	*3-100/2-4,S-1	1.0
1938	Cin-N	142	531	53	134	21	13	2	55	40	28	.252	.311	.352	84	-12	3			.947	-1	*3-140	-1.1
1939	Cin-N	22	38	5	6	1	0	0	1	5	4	.158	.256	.184	20	-4	1			.957	-1	3-11	-0.5
1940	*Cin-N	41	72	8	21	7	1	1	9	2	4	.292	.311	.458	109	-0	0			.943	-3	3-11	0.2
1941	*Bro-N	77	197	27	60	13	4	5	36	16	12	.305	.357	.487	131	7	1			.932	-7	3-43/1-1,2-1	0.1
1942	Bro-N	70	180	20	50	5	0	3	22	13	9	.278	.333	.356	100	-0	0			.944	-6	3-46/1-1	-0.6
1946	Bro-N	1	4	0	0	0	0	0	0	0	0	.000	.000	.000	-99	-1	0			1.000	0	/3-1	0.0
Total	10	760	2477	298	650	110	43	28	271	181	140	.262	.317	.375	91	-35	22			.945	27	3-627/2-5,1-2,S-1	0.8

■ TOPPER RIGNEY   Rigney, Emory Elmo   b: 1/7/1897, Groveton, Tex.   d: 6/6/72, San Antonio, Tex.   BR/TR, 5'9", 150 lbs.   Deb: 4/12/22

1922	Det-A	155	536	68	161	17	7	2	63	68	44	.300	.380	.369	99	2	17	8	0	.938	-13	*S-155	0.5
1923	Det-A	129	470	63	148	24	11	1	74	55	35	.315	.389	.419	115	11	7	5	-1	.944	-16	*S-129	0.7
1924	Det-A	147	499	81	144	29	4	4	94	102	39	.289	.410	.407	113	14	11	11	-3	**.967**	10	*S-146	3.4
1925	Det-A	62	146	21	36	5	2	2	18	21	15	.247	.341	.349	77	-5	2	2	-1	.934	-14	S-51/3-4	-1.5
1926	Bos-A	148	525	71	142	32	6	4	53	108	31	.270	.395	.377	105	9	6	8	-3	**.969**	20	*S-146	3.9
1927	Bos-A	8	18	0	2	1	0	0	0	1	2	.111	.158	.167	-16	-3	0	0	0	1.000	-1	/3-4,S-1	-0.4
	Was-A	45	132	20	36	5	4	0	13	22	10	.273	.381	.371	97	0	1	2	-1	.929	-3	S-32/3-6	0.0
	Yr	53	150	20	38	6	4	0	13	23	12	.253	.356	.347	84	-3	1	2	-1	.932	-4	S-33,3-10	-0.4
Total	6	694	2326	324	669	113	39	13	315	377	176	.288	.388	.387	104	28	44	36	-8	.953	-18	S-660/3-14	6.6

■ BILL RIGNEY   Rigney, William Joseph "Specs" or "The Cricket"   b: 1/29/18, Alameda, Cal.   BR/TR, 6'1", 178 lbs.   Deb: 4/16/46   MC

1946	NY-N	110	360	38	85	9	1	3	31	36	29	.236	.307	.292	70	-14	9			.965	3	3-73,S-33	-0.9
1947	NY-N	130	531	84	142	24	3	17	59	51	54	.267	.337	.420	99	-1	7			.974	1	2-72,3-41,S-24	0.5
1948	NY-N★	113	424	72	112	17	3	10	43	47	54	.264	.342	.389	97	-2	4			.967	-1	*2-105/S-7	-0.7
1949	NY-N	122	389	53	108	19	6	6	47	47	38	.278	.356	.404	103	2	3			.928	-17	S-81,2-26,3-14	-0.8
1950	NY-N	56	83	8	15	2	0	0	8	8	13	.181	.253	.205	22	-9	0			.966	6	2-23,3-11	-0.3
1951	*NY-N	44	69	9	16	2	0	4	9	8	7	.232	.321	.435	100	-0	0	1	-1	.953	-3	3-12/2-9	0.5
1952	NY-N	60	90	15	27	5	1	1	14	11	6	.300	.388	.411	121	3	2	3	-1	.889	-1	3-10/2-9,S-4,1-1	0.1
1953	NY-N	19	20	2	5	0	0	0	1	0	5	.250	.250	.250	30	-2	0	0	0	1.000	0	/3-2,2-1	-0.2
Total	8	654	1966	281	510	78	14	41	212	208	206	.259	.334	.376	91	-23	25	4		.971	-13	2-245,3-163,S/1	-1.8

■ CULLEY RIKARD   Rikard, Culley   b: 5/9/14, Oxford, Miss.   BL/TR, 5'11", 183 lbs.   Deb: 9/20/41

1941	Pit-N	6	20	1	4	1	0	0	1	1		.200	.238	.250	38	-2	0			1.000	1	/O-5	-0.1
1942	Pit-N	38	52	6	10	2	1	0	5	7	8	.192	.288	.269	62	-2	0			.958	-4	O-16	-0.7
1947	Pit-N	109	324	57	93	16	4	4	32	50	39	.287	.384	.398	105	4	1			.978	-1	O-79	-0.1
Total	3	153	396	64	107	19	5	4	37	58	48	.270	.365	.374	97	-0	1			.978	-4	O-100	-0.9

■ ERNEST RILES   Riles, Ernest   b: 10/2/60, Cairo, Ga.   BL/TR, 6'1", 180 lbs.   Deb: 5/14/85

1985	Mil-A	116	448	54	128	12	7	5	45	36	54	.286	.342	.377	97	-1	2	2	-1	.957	-19	*S-115/D-1	-0.9
1986	Mil-A	145	524	69	132	24	2	9	47	54	80	.252	.323	.357	82	-12	7	7	-2	.964	-30	*S-142	-3.1
1987	Mil-A	83	276	38	72	11	1	4	38	30	47	.261	.336	.351	80	-7	3	4	-2	.935	-6	3-65,S-21	-1.3
1988	Mil-A	41	127	7	32	6	1	1	9	7	26	.252	.291	.339	75	-4	2	2	-1	.958	1	3-28/S-9,D-5	-0.3
	SF-N	79	187	26	55	7	2	3	28	10	33	.294	.330	.401	114	3	1	2	-1	.975	8	3-30,2-17,S-16	1.2
1989	*SF-N	122	302	43	84	13	2	7	40	28	50	.278	.343	.404	116	6	0	6	-4	.962	-10	3-83,2-18/S-7,O-5	-0.7
1990	SF-N	92	155	22	31	2	1	8	21	26	26	.200	.315	.381	94	-1	0	0	0	.986	-4	S-26,2-24,3-10	-0.4
1991	Oak-A	108	281	30	60	8	4	5	32	31	42	.214	.294	.324	75	-10	3	2	-0	.939	-10	3-69,S-20/2-7,1-5	-1.9
1992	Hou-N	39	61	5	16	1	0	1	4	2	11	.262	.286	.328	77	-2	1	0	0	1.000	-1	/S-6,3-5,1-4,2-2	-0.4
1993	Bos-A	94	143	15	27	8	0	5	20	20	40	.189	.297	.350	69	-7	1	3	-2	1.000	5	2-20,D-15,3-11,/1-1	-0.4
Total	9	919	2504	309	637	92	20	48	284	244	409	.254	.323	.365	89	-36	20	28	-11	.964	-67	S-362,3-301/2D10	-8.2

■ JIM RILEY   Riley, James Joseph   b: 11/10/1886, Buffalo, N.Y.   d: 3/25/49, Buffalo, N.Y.   BR/TR, 6', 165 lbs.   Deb: 8/2/10

1910	Bos-N	1	1	0	0	0	0	0	0	1	1	.000	.500	.000	46	-0	1			.600	-0	/O-1	0.0

■ JIM RILEY   Riley, James Norman   b: 5/25/1895, Bayfield, N.B., Can   d: 5/25/69, Seguin, Tex.   BL/TR, 5'10.5", 185 lbs.   Deb: 7/3/21

1921	StL-A	4	11	0	0	0	0	0	0	1	3	.000	.083	.000	-73	-3	0	0	0	.818	-3	/2-4	-0.6
1923	Was-A	2	3	1	0	0	0	0	0	2	0	.000	.400	.000	12	-0	0	0	0	.882	-1	/1-2	-0.1
Total	2	6	14	1	0	0	0	0	0	3	3	.000	.176	.000	-50	-3	0	0	0	.818	-4	/2-4,1-2	-0.7

■ LEE RILEY   Riley, Leon Francis   b: 8/20/06, Princeton, Neb.   d: 9/13/70, Schenectady, N.Y.   BL/TR, 6'1", 185 lbs.   Deb: 4/19/44

1944	Phi-N	4	12	0	1	0	0	0	0	0	3	.083	.083	.167	-32	-2	0			1.000	-1	/O-3	-0.4

■ BILLY RILEY   Riley, William James "Pigtail Billy"   b: 1855, Cincinnati, Ohio   d: 11/9/1887, Cincinnati, Ohio   BR/TR, 5'10", 160 lbs.   Deb: 5/5/1875

1875	Wes-n	8	33	4	5	1	0	0	1	1	1	.152	.176	.182	23	-3	0			.667	-0	/O-8	-0.2
1879	Cle-N	44	165	14	24	3	0	0	9	2	26	.145	.156	.158	4	-16				.850	4	O-43/1-1,C-1	-1.4

■ FRANK RINGO   Ringo, Frank C.   b: 10/12/1860, Parkville, Mo.   d: 4/12/1889, Kansas City, Mo.   BR , 5'11", 175 lbs.   Deb: 5/1/1883

1883	Phi-N	60	221	24	42	10	1	0	12	6	34	.190	.211	.244	42	-14				.847	-9	C-39,O-11/S-6,32	-1.8
1884	Phi-N	26	91	4	12	2	0	0	6	3	19	.132	.160	.154	-1	-10				.783	-16	C-26	-2.2
	Phi-a	2	6	0	0	0	0	0	0	0	0	.000	.000	.000	-94	-2				.762	1	/C-2	-0.2
1885	Det-N	17	65	12	16	3	0	0	5	0	7	.246	.246	.292	73	-2				.852	2	/C-8,3-8,O-1	0.1
	Pit-a	3	11	0	2	0	0	0	0	0		.182	.182	.182	15	-1				.941	3	/C-3	0.2
1886	Pit-a	15	56	3	12	2	0	0	5	1		.214	.228	.321	72	-2	0			.934	-2	/1-9,C-6	-0.2
	KC-N	16	56	6	13	7	0	0	5	10		.232	.295	.357	92	-1	0			.904	-6	C-13/O-2,3-1	-0.4
Total	4	139	506	49	97	24	3	0	32	15	70	.192	.215	.251	46	-32	0			.844	-24	/C-97,3-14,O1S2	-4.3

■ BOB RINKER   Rinker, Robert John   b: 4/21/21, Audenried, Pa.   BR/TR, 6', 190 lbs.   Deb: 9/6/50

1950	Phi-A	3	3	0	1	0	0	0	0	0	0	.333	.333	.333	72	-0	0	0	0	.000	-0	/C-1	0.0

■ JUAN RIOS   Rios, Juan Onofre Velez (b: Juan Onofre Velez (Rios))   b: 6/14/42, Mayaguez, P.R.   d: 8/28/95, Mayaguez, P.R.   BR/TR, 6'3", 185 lbs.   Deb: 4/9/69

1969	KC-A	87	196	20	44	5	1	5	7	19	.224	.262	.276	50	-13	1	3	-2	.967	-16	2-46,S-32/3-4	-2.8

YEAR	TM/L	G	AB	R	H	2B	3B	HR	RBI	BB	SO	AVG	OBP	SLG	PRO+	BR/A	SB	CS	SBR	FA	FR	G/POS	TPR

■ CAL RIPKEN Ripken, Calvin Edwin Jr. b: 8/24/60, Havre De Grace, Md. BR/TR, 6'4", 215 lbs. Deb: 8/10/81 F

YEAR	TM/L	G	AB	R	H	2B	3B	HR	RBI	BB	SO	AVG	OBP	SLG	PRO+	BR/A	SB	CS	SBR	FA	FR	G/POS	TPR
1981	Bal-A	23	39	1	5	0	0	0	0	1	8	.128	.150	.128	-19	-6	0	0	0	.946	0	S-12/3-6	-0.6
1982	Bal-A	160	598	90	158	32	5	28	93	46	95	.264	.320	.475	115	11	3	3	-1	.972	-7	S-94,3-71	1.0
1983	*Bal-A★	162	663	**121**	**211**	47	2	27	102	58	97	.318	.373	.517	145	39	0	4	-2	.970	16	*S-162	**6.7**
1984	Bal-A★	162	641	103	195	37	7	27	86	71	89	.304	.375	.510	146	39	2	1	0	.971	**39**	*S-162	**9.1**
1985	Bal-A★	161	642	116	181	32	5	26	110	67	68	.282	.351	.469	125	22	2	3	-1	.967	7	*S-161	4.3
1986	Bal-A★	162	627	98	177	35	1	25	81	70	60	.282	.358	.461	123	20	4	2	0	.982	10	*S-162	4.4
1987	Bal-A★	162	624	97	157	28	3	27	98	81	77	.252	.339	.436	106	6	3	5	-2	.973	-4	*S-162	1.3
1988	Bal-A★	161	575	87	152	25	1	23	81	102	69	.264	.372	.431	129	26	2	2	-1	.973	-2	*S-161	3.7
1989	Bal-A★	162	646	80	166	30	0	21	93	57	72	.257	.320	.401	105	3	3	2	-0	.990	4	*S-162	2.0
1990	Bal-A★	161	600	78	150	28	4	21	84	82	66	.250	.345	.415	115	13	3	1	0	**.996**	-29	*S-161	-0.3
1991	Bal-A★	162	650	99	210	46	5	34	114	53	46	.323	.379	.566	164	54	6	1	-1	**.986**	18	*S-162	**8.3**
1992	Bal-A★	162	637	73	160	29	1	14	72	64	50	.251	.326	.366	91	-7	4	3	-1	.984	-13	*S-162	-0.9
1993	Bal-A★	162	641	87	165	26	3	24	90	65	58	.257	.331	.420	96	-4	1	4	-2	.977	-5	*S-162	0.2
1994	Bal-A★	112	444	71	140	19	3	13	75	32	41	.315	.367	.459	106	4	1	0	**.985**	-13	*S-112	0.2
1995	Bal-A★	144	550	71	144	33	2	17	88	52	59	.262	.328	.422	92	-7	0	1	-1	**.989**	-1	*S-144	0.4
1996	*Bal-A★	163	640	94	178	40	1	26	102	59	78	.278	.343	.466	103	2	1	2	-1	.980	1	*S-158/3-6	1.5
Total	16	2381	9217	1366	2549	487	43	353	1369	960	1033	.277	.348	.454	117	214	35	34	-10	.979	21	*S-2299/3-83	41.3

■ BILLY RIPKEN Ripken, William Oliver b: 12/16/64, Havre De Grace, Md. BR/TR, 6'1", 183 lbs. Deb: 7/11/87 F

YEAR	TM/L	G	AB	R	H	2B	3B	HR	RBI	BB	SO	AVG	OBP	SLG	PRO+	BR/A	SB	CS	SBR	FA	FR	G/POS	TPR
1987	Bal-A	58	234	27	72	9	0	2	20	21	23	.308	.363	.372	99	0	4	1	1	.990	-3	2-58	0.0
1988	Bal-A	150	512	52	106	18	1	2	34	33	63	.207	.262	.258	47	-36	8	2	1	.984	2	*2-149/3-2,D-1	-2.7
1989	Bal-A	115	318	31	76	11	2	2	26	22	53	.239	.288	.305	69	-13	1	2	-1	.985	13	*2-114/D-1	0.2
1990	Bal-A	129	406	48	118	28	1	3	38	28	43	.291	.342	.387	107	4	5	2	0	.987	-9	*2-127	-0.2
1991	Bal-A	104	287	24	62	11	1	0	14	15	31	.216	.255	.261	45	-22	0	1	-1	.986	4	*2-103	-1.6
1992	Bal-A	111	330	35	76	15	0	4	36	18	26	.230	.277	.312	63	-17	2	3	-1	**.993**	0	*2-108/D-2	-1.6
1993	Tex-A	50	132	12	25	4	0	0	11	11	19	.189	.272	.220	35	-12	2	0	-1	.992	4	2-34,S-18/3-1	-0.7
1994	Tex-A	32	81	9	25	5	0	0	6	3	11	.309	.333	.370	81	-2	2	0	1	.970	2	3-18,2-12/S-2,1-1	0.0
1995	Cle-A	8	17	4	7	0	0	2	3	0	3	.412	.412	.765	195	2	0	0	0	1.000	0	/2-7,3-1	0.0
1996	Bal-A	57	135	19	31	8	0	2	12	9	18	.230	.283	.333	56	-9	0	0	0	.968	6	2-30,3-25/1-1	-0.3
Total	10	814	2452	261	598	109	5	17	200	160	290	.244	.295	.313	69	-104	22	13	-1	.987	16	2-742/3-47,S-20,D1	-6.9

■ JIMMY RIPPLE Ripple, James Albert b: 10/14/09, Export, Pa. d: 7/16/59, Greensburg, Pa. BL/TR, 5'10", 170 lbs. Deb: 4/20/36

YEAR	TM/L	G	AB	R	H	2B	3B	HR	RBI	BB	SO	AVG	OBP	SLG	PRO+	BR/A	SB	CS	SBR	FA	FR	G/POS	TPR
1936	*NY-N	96	311	42	95	17	2	7	47	28	15	.305	.365	.441	117	7	1			.980	-0	O-76	0.4
1937	*NY-N	121	426	70	135	23	3	5	66	29	20	.317	.362	.420	110	6	3			.980	-9	*O-111	-0.7
1938	NY-N	134	501	68	131	21	3	10	60	49	21	.261	.333	.375	94	-4	2			.976	-3	*O-131	-1.1
1939	NY-N	66	123	10	28	4	0	1	12	8	7	.228	.286	.285	53	-8	0			1.000	-2	O-23	-1.0
	Bro-N	28	106	18	35	8	4	0	22	11	8	.330	.398	.481	131	5	0			1.000	-2	O-28	0.2
	Yr	94	229	28	63	12	4	1	34	19	15	.275	.339	.376	90	-3	0			1.000	-3	O-51	-0.8
1940	Bro-N	7	13	0	3	0	0	0	0	2	1	.231	.333	.231	55	-1	0			1.000	1	/O-3	0.0
	*Cin-N	32	101	15	31	10	0	4	20	13	5	.307	.397	.525	151	7	1			1.000	-5	O-30	0.1
	Yr	39	114	15	34	10	0	4	20	15	6	.298	.389	.491	139	6	1			1.000	-4	O-33	0.1
1941	Cin-N	38	102	10	22	6	1	1	9	9	4	.216	.279	.324	69	-4	0			1.000	-2	O-25	-0.9
1943	Phi-A	32	126	8	30	3	1	0	15	7	7	.238	.284	.278	65	-6	0			1.000	-4	O-31	-1.3
Total	7	554	1809	241	510	92	14	28	251	156	89	.282	.343	.395	101	2	7		0	.984	-27	O-458	-4.3

■ SWEDE RISBERG Risberg, Charles August b: 10/13/1894, San Francisco, Cal d: 10/13/75, Red Bluff, Cal. BR/TR, 6', 175 lbs. Deb: 4/11/17

YEAR	TM/L	G	AB	R	H	2B	3B	HR	RBI	BB	SO	AVG	OBP	SLG	PRO+	BR/A	SB	CS	SBR	FA	FR	G/POS	TPR
1917	*Chi-A	149	474	59	96	20	8	1	45	59	65	.203	.297	.285	76	-13	16			.913	-39	*S-146	-5.1
1918	Chi-A	82	273	36	70	12	3	1	27	23	32	.256	.321	.333	97	-1	5			.944	-8	S-30,3-24,2-12/10	-0.8
1919	Chi-A	119	414	48	106	19	6	2	38	35	38	.256	.317	.345	86	-8	19			.934	-13	S-97,1-22	-1.7
1920	Chi-A	126	458	53	122	21	10	2	65	31	45	.266	.316	.369	81	-14	12	10	-2	.934	-4	*S-124	-0.9
Total	4	476	1619	196	394	72	27	6	175	148	180	.243	.311	.332	83	-36	52	10		.928	-64	S-397/1-29,3-24,2O	-8.5

■ POP RISING Rising, Percival Sumner b: 1/2/1872, Industry, Pa. d: 1/28/38, Rochester, Pa. Deb: 8/10/05

YEAR	TM/L	G	AB	R	H	2B	3B	HR	RBI	BB	SO	AVG	OBP	SLG	PRO+	BR/A	SB	CS	SBR	FA	FR	G/POS	TPR
1905	Bos-A	11	29	2	3	1	1	0	2	2		.103	.161	.207	16	-3	0			1.000	0	/O-6,3-1	-0.3

■ CLAUDE RITCHEY Ritchey, Claude Cassius "Little All Right" b: 10/5/1873, Emlenton, Pa. d: 11/8/51, Emlenton, Pa. BB/TR, 5'6.5", 167 lbs. Deb: 4/22/1897

YEAR	TM/L	G	AB	R	H	2B	3B	HR	RBI	BB	SO	AVG	OBP	SLG	PRO+	BR/A	SB	CS	SBR	FA	FR	G/POS	TPR
1897	Cin-N	101	337	58	95	12	4	0	41	42		.282	.370	.341	83	-8	11			.897	-16	S-70,O-22/2-8	-2.0
1898	Lou-N	151	551	65	140	10	4	5	51	46		.254	.322	.314	84	-11	19			.919	-16	S-80,2-71	-1.8
1899	Lou-N	147	536	65	161	15	7	4	71	49		.300	.370	.377	105	5	21			.938	-6	*2-137,S-11	0.6
1900	*Pit-N	123	476	62	139	17	8	1	67	29		.292	.339	.368	94	-4	18			.952	7	*2-123	0.8
1901	Pit-L	140	540	66	160	20	4	1	74	47		.296	.358	.354	104	4	15			.941	2	*2-139/S-1	1.1
1902	Pit-N	115	405	54	112	13	1	2	55	53		.277	.370	.328	112	8	10			**.966**	6	*2-114/O-1	1.9
1903	*Pit-N	138	506	66	145	28	10	0	59	55		.287	.360	.381	108	6	15			**.961**	19	*2-137	2.8
1904	Pit-N	156	544	79	143	22	12	0	51	59		.263	.338	.347	109	7	12			.958	-2	*2-156/S-2	0.9
1905	Pit-N	153	533	54	136	29	6	0	52	51		.255	.324	.332	93	-4	12			**.961**	-5	*2-153/S-2	-0.8
1906	Pit-N	152	484	46	130	21	5	1	62	68		.269	.369	.339	116	11	6			**.966**	1	*2-151	1.5
1907	Bos-N	144	499	45	127	17	4	2	51	50		.255	.329	.317	103	2	8			**.971**	14	*2-144	1.7
1908	Bos-N	121	421	44	115	10	3	2	36	50		.273	.361	.325	121	12	7			.967	16	*2-120	3.1
1909	Bos-N	30	87	4	15	1	0	0	3	8		.172	.242	.184	31	-7	1			.959	-2	2-25	-0.8
Total	13	1671	5919	708	1618	215	68	18	673	607		.273	.348	.342	101	21	155			.957	19	*2-1478,S-166/O-23	9.0

■ CHARLIE RITTER Ritter, Charles J. Deb: 9/21/1885

YEAR	TM/L	G	AB	R	H	2B	3B	HR	RBI	BB	SO	AVG	OBP	SLG	PRO+	BR/A	SB	CS	SBR	FA	FR	G/POS	TPR
1885	Buf-N	2	6	0	1	0	0	0	0	0	2	.167	.167	.167	8	-1				.813	0	/2-2	0.0

■ FLOYD RITTER Ritter, Floyd Alexander b: 6/1/1870, Dorset, Ohio d: 2/7/43, Stevenson, Wash. BR/TR, 5'8", 155 lbs. Deb: 6/4/1890

YEAR	TM/L	G	AB	R	H	2B	3B	HR	RBI	BB	SO	AVG	OBP	SLG	PRO+	BR/A	SB	CS	SBR	FA	FR	G/POS	TPR
1890	Tol-a	1	3	0	0	0	0	0	0	0		.000	.000	.000	-97	-1	0			.778	0	/C-1	-0.1

■ LEW RITTER Ritter, Lewis Elmer "Old Dog" b: 9/7/1875, Liverpool, Pa. d: 5/27/52, Harrisburg, Pa. BR/TR, 5'9", 150 lbs. Deb: 9/10/02

YEAR	TM/L	G	AB	R	H	2B	3B	HR	RBI	BB	SO	AVG	OBP	SLG	PRO+	BR/A	SB	CS	SBR	FA	FR	G/POS	TPR
1902	Bro-N	16	57	5	12	1	0	0	2	1		.211	.237	.228	43	-4	2			.973	3	C-16	0.1
1903	Bro-N	78	259	26	61	9	6	0	37	19		.236	.290	.317	75	-9	9			.940	-17	C-74/O-2	-1.8
1904	Bro-N	72	214	23	53	4	1	0	19	20		.248	.318	.276	86	-3	17			.966	5	C-57/2-5,3-1	0.9
1905	Bro-N	92	311	32	68	10	5	1	28	15		.219	.255	.293	68	-13	16			.951	-14	C-84/O-4,3-2	-2.0
1906	Bro-N	73	226	22	47	1	3	0	15	16		.208	.263	.239	61	-10	6			.978	-8	C-53/O-9,1-3,3-2	-1.6
1907	Bro-N	93	271	15	55	6	1	0	17	18		.203	.255	.232	57	-14	5			.969	-1	C-89	-0.8
1908	Bro-N	38	99	6	19	1	2	0	7	2		.192	.245	.232	55	-5	0			.961	-3	C-37	-0.5
Total	7	462	1437	129	315	33	17	1	120	96		.219	.271	.268	67	-58	55			.960	-36	C-410/O-15,3-5,21	-5.8

■ WHITEY RITTERSON Ritterson, Edward West b: 4/26/1855, Philadelphia, Pa. d: 7/28/17, Sellersville, Pa. BR/TR, 5'8", Deb: 5/3/1876

YEAR	TM/L	G	AB	R	H	2B	3B	HR	RBI	BB	SO	AVG	OBP	SLG	PRO+	BR/A	SB	CS	SBR	FA	FR	G/POS	TPR
1876	Phi-N	16	52	8	13	3	0	0		0	2	.250	.250	.308	86	-1				.671	-8	C-14/O-4,3-1	-0.7

■ JIM RITZ Ritz, James L. b: 1874, Pittsburgh, Pa. d: 11/10/1896, Pittsburgh, Pa. Deb: 7/20/1894

YEAR	TM/L	G	AB	R	H	2B	3B	HR	RBI	BB	SO	AVG	OBP	SLG	PRO+	BR/A	SB	CS	SBR	FA	FR	G/POS	TPR
1894	Pit-N	1	4	1	0	0	0	0	0	1		.000	.200	.000	-49	-1	1			.750	-0	/3-1	-0.1

■ GERMAN RIVERA Rivera, German (Diaz) b: 7/6/60, Santurce, P.R. BR/TR, 6'2", 195 lbs. Deb: 9/2/83

YEAR	TM/L	G	AB	R	H	2B	3B	HR	RBI	BB	SO	AVG	OBP	SLG	PRO+	BR/A	SB	CS	SBR	FA	FR	G/POS	TPR
1983	LA-N	13	17	1	6	1	0	0	2	2		.353	.421	.412	132	1	0	1	-1	.929	2	/3-8	0.2
1984	LA-N	94	227	20	59	12	2	2	17	21	30	.260	.325	.357	92	-2	0	0	0	.937	16	3-90	1.4
1985	Hou-N	13	36	3	7	2	1	0	2	4	8	.194	.275	.306	64	-2	0	0	0	.941	3	3-11	0.1
Total	3	120	280	24	72	15	3	2	19	27	40	.257	.325	.354	91	-3	0	1	-0	.937	20	3-109	1.7

■ BOMBO RIVERA Rivera, Jesus Manuel (Torres) b: 8/2/52, Ponce, P.R. BR/TR, 5'10", 187 lbs. Deb: 4/17/75

YEAR	TM/L	G	AB	R	H	2B	3B	HR	RBI	BB	SO	AVG	OBP	SLG	PRO+	BR/A	SB	CS	SBR	FA	FR	G/POS	TPR
1975	Mon-N	5	9	1	1	0	0	0	0	2	3	.111	.273	.111	9	-1	0	0	0	.889	-1	/O-5	-0.2

YEAR	TM/L	G	AB	R	H	2B	3B	HR	RBI	BB	SO	AVG	OBP	SLG	PRO+	BR/A	SB	CS	SBR	FA	FR	G/POS	TPR
1976	Mon-N	68	185	22	51	11	4	2	19	13	32	.276	.323	.411	103	0	1	0	0	.950	-0	O-56	-0.1
1978	Min-A	101	251	35	68	8	2	3	23	35	47	.271	.325	.355	101	2	5	3	-0	.982	-9	O-94/D-1	-1.1
1979	Min-A	112	263	37	74	13	5	2	31	17	40	.281	.325	.392	89	-4	5	5	-2	.989	-4	*O-105/D-2	-1.3
1980	Min-A	44	113	13	25	7	0	3	10	4	20	.221	.248	.363	61	-6	0	0	0	.922	-4	O-37/D-1	-1.2
1982	KC-A	5	10	1	1	0	0	0	0	0	2	.100	.100	.100	-45	-2	0	0	0	1.000	-1	/O-3	-0.3
Total	6	335	831	109	220	39	11	10	83	71	144	.265	.324	.374	90	-12	11	8	-2	.970	-19	O-300/D-4	-4.2

■ LUIS RIVERA
Rivera, Luis Antonio (Pedraza)   b: 1/3/64, Cidra, P.R.   BR/TR, 5'9", 170 lbs.   Deb: 8/3/86

YEAR	TM/L	G	AB	R	H	2B	3B	HR	RBI	BB	SO	AVG	OBP	SLG	PRO+	BR/A	SB	CS	SBR	FA	FR	G/POS	TPR
1986	Mon-N	55	166	20	34	11	1	0	13	17	33	.205	.286	.283	58	-9	1	1	-0	.953	-9	S-55	-1.5
1987	Mon-N	18	32	0	5	2	0	0	1	1	8	.156	.182	.219	5	-4	0	0	0	.923	2	S-15	-0.2
1988	Mon-N	123	371	35	83	17	3	4	30	24	69	.224	.273	.318	66	-16	3	4	-2	.962	-6	*S-116	-1.6
1989	Bos-A	93	323	35	83	17	1	5	29	20	60	.257	.302	.362	81	-8	2	3	-1	.958	-3	S-90/2-1,D-1	-0.6
1990	*Bos-A	118	346	38	78	20	0	7	45	25	58	.225	.280	.344	70	-14	4	3	-1	.965	11	*S-112/2-3,3-1	0.4
1991	Bos-A	129	414	64	107	22	3	8	40	35	86	.258	.321	.384	90	-8	4	4	-1	.959	3	*S-129	0.6
1992	Bos-A	102	288	17	62	11	1	0	29	26	56	.215	.287	.260	51	-18	4	3	-1	.966	14	S-93/2-1,3-1,O-1,D	0.1
1993	Bos-A	62	130	13	27	8	1	1	7	11	36	.208	.275	.308	53	-9	1	2	-1	.969	12	2-27,S-27/3-2,D-7	0.4
1994	NY-N	32	43	11	12	2	1	3	5	4	14	.279	.367	.581	144	3	0	1	-1	.971	5	S-11/2-5	0.7
Total	9	732	2113	233	491	110	11	28	199	163	420	.232	.292	.335	71	-83	19	21	-7	.961	29	S-648/2-37,D-10,30	-1.7

■ JIM RIVERA
Rivera, Manuel Joseph "Jungle Jim"   b: 7/22/22, New York, N.Y.   BL/TL, 6', 196 lbs.   Deb: 4/15/52

YEAR	TM/L	G	AB	R	H	2B	3B	HR	RBI	BB	SO	AVG	OBP	SLG	PRO+	BR/A	SB	CS	SBR	FA	FR	G/POS	TPR
1952	StL-A	97	336	45	86	13	6	4	30	29	59	.256	.319	.366	88	-6	8	7	-2	.976	9	O-88	-0.3
	Chi-A	53	201	27	50	7	3	3	18	21	27	.249	.320	.358	88	-4	13	2	3	.988	4	O-53	0.1
	Yr	150	537	72	136	20	9	7	48	50	86	.253	.319	.363	88	-10	21	9	1	.980	12	*O-141	-0.2
1953	Chi-A	156	567	79	147	26	**16**	11	78	53	70	.259	.329	.420	98	-3	22	15	-2	.976	-1	*O-156	-1.2
1954	Chi-A	145	490	62	140	16	8	13	61	49	68	.286	.358	.431	111	7	18	10	-1	.959	-17	*O-143	-1.6
1955	Chi-A	147	454	71	120	24	4	10	52	62	59	.264	.354	.401	100	3	**25**	16	-2	.981	2	*O-143	-0.6
1956	Chi-A	139	491	76	125	23	5	12	66	49	75	.255	.326	.395	88	-9	20	9	1	.976	1	*O-134	-1.4
1957	Chi-A	125	402	51	103	21	6	14	52	40	80	.256	.328	.443	108	4	18	2	4	.974	-7	O-86,1-31	-0.6
1958	Chi-A	116	276	37	62	8	4	9	35	24	49	.225	.289	.380	84	-7	21	3	5	.994	-3	O-99	-1.0
1959	*Chi-A	80	177	18	39	9	4	4	19	11	19	.220	.270	.384	78	-6	5	3	-0	.976	-8	O-69	-1.6
1960	Chi-A	48	17	17	5	0	0	1	3	1	3	.294	.400	.471	136	1	4	0	1	1.000	-6	O-24	-0.4
1961	Chi-A	1	0	0	0	0	0	0	0	0	0	—	—	—	—	0	0	1	1	.000	0	H	-0.1
	KC-A	64	141	20	34	8	0	2	10	24	14	.241	.352	.340	84	-3	6	2	1	.981	-9	O-43	-1.3
	Yr	65	141	20	34	8	0	2	10	24	14	.241	.352	.340	84	-3	6	3	0	.981	-9	O-43	-1.4
Total	10	1171	3552	503	911	155	56	83	422	365	523	.256	.330	.402	96	-25	160	70	6	.977	-36	*O-1038/1-31	-10.0

■ RUBEN RIVERA
Rivera, Ruben (Moreno)   b: 11/14/73, Chorrera, Panama   BR/TR, 6'3", 200 lbs.   Deb: 9/3/95

YEAR	TM/L	G	AB	R	H	2B	3B	HR	RBI	BB	SO	AVG	OBP	SLG	PRO+	BR/A	SB	CS	SBR	FA	FR	G/POS	TPR
1995	NY-A	5	1	0	0	0	0	0	0	0	1	.000	.000	.000	-99	-0	0	0	0	1.000	-1	/O-4	-0.1
1996	*NY-A	46	88	17	25	6	1	2	16	13	26	.284	.384	.443	108	1	6	2	1	1.000	-2	O-45	-0.1
Total	2	51	89	17	25	6	1	2	16	13	27	.281	.385	.438	106	1	6	2	1	1.000	-3	/O-49	-0.2

■ MICKEY RIVERS
Rivers, John Milton   b: 10/31/48, Miami, Fla.   BL/TL, 5'10", 165 lbs.   Deb: 8/4/70

YEAR	TM/L	G	AB	R	H	2B	3B	HR	RBI	BB	SO	AVG	OBP	SLG	PRO+	BR/A	SB	CS	SBR	FA	FR	G/POS	TPR
1970	Cal-A	17	25	6	8	2	0	0	3	3	5	.320	.414	.400	130	1	1	0	0	1.000	0	/O-5	0.1
1971	Cal-A	79	268	31	71	12	2	1	12	19	38	.265	.316	.336	91	-4	13	1	3	.976	-3	O-76	-0.7
1972	Cal-A	58	159	18	34	6	2	0	7	8	26	.214	.256	.277	62	-8	4	3	-1	.981	-1	O-48	-1.3
1973	Cal-A	30	129	26	45	6	4	0	16	8	11	.349	.391	.457	150	3	8	3	1	.909	-4	O-29	0.4
1974	Cal-A	118	466	69	133	19	**11**	3	31	39	47	.285	.342	.393	118	10	30	13	1	.994	10	*O-116	1.7
1975	Cal-A	155	616	70	175	17	**13**	1	53	43	42	.284	.333	.359	103	1	**70**	14	**13**	.977	11	*O-152/D-1	1.9
1976	*NY-A★	137	590	95	184	31	8	8	67	13	51	.312	.330	.432	123	14	43	7	9	.986	9	O-136	2.8
1977	*NY-A	138	565	79	184	18	5	12	69	18	45	.326	.351	.439	115	11	22	14	-2	.982	13	O-136/D-1	1.6
1978	*NY-A	141	559	78	148	25	8	11	48	29	51	.265	.305	.397	98	-3	25	5	5	.980	10	O-138	0.5
1979	NY-A	74	286	37	82	18	5	3	25	13	21	.287	.320	.416	99	-1	3	7	-3	.974	-6	O-69/D-1	-1.3
	Tex-A	58	247	35	74	9	3	6	25	9	18	.300	.327	.433	104	1	7	2	1	.981	3	O-57	0.2
	Yr	132	533	72	156	27	8	9	50	22	39	.293	.323	.424	101	-0	10	9	-2	.978	-3	*O-126/D-1	-1.1
1980	Tex-A	147	630	96	210	32	6	7	60	20	34	.333	.355	.437	119	15	18	7	1	.978	10	*O-141/D-4	2.0
1981	Tex-A	99	399	62	114	21	2	3	26	24	31	.286	.328	.371	107	3	9	5	-0	.996	4	O-97	0.3
1982	Tex-A	19	68	6	16	1	1	1	4	0	7	.235	.235	.324	54	-4	0	0	0	.000	0	D-16	-0.5
1983	Tex-A	96	309	37	88	17	0	1	20	11	21	.285	.312	.350	83	-7	9	4	0	.980	1	D-53,O-23	-0.9
1984	Tex-A	102	313	40	94	13	1	4	33	14	33	.300	.320	.387	91	-4	5	5	-2	1.000	0	D-48,O-30	-0.8
Total	15	1468	5629	785	1660	247	71	61	499	266	471	.295	.329	.397	106	10	267	90	26	.982	57	*O-1253,D-124	6.0

■ JOHNNY RIZZO
Rizzo, John Costa   b: 7/30/12, Houston, Tex.   d: 12/4/77, Houston, Tex.   BR/TR, 6', 190 lbs.   Deb: 4/19/38

YEAR	TM/L	G	AB	R	H	2B	3B	HR	RBI	BB	SO	AVG	OBP	SLG	PRO+	BR/A	SB	CS	SBR	FA	FR	G/POS	TPR
1938	Pit-N	143	555	97	167	31	9	23	111	54	61	.301	.368	.514	139	28	1			.951	-8	*O-140	1.6
1939	Pit-N	94	330	49	86	23	3	6	55	42	27	.261	.349	.403	103	2	0			.974	-0	O-86	-0.2
1940	Pit-N	9	28	1	5	1	0	0	2	5	5	.179	.324	.214	51	-2	0			.818	-2	/O-7	-0.4
	Cin-N	31	110	17	31	6	0	4	17	14	14	.282	.363	.445	121	3	1			.974	5	O-30	0.6
	Phi-N	103	367	53	107	12	2	20	53	37	31	.292	.358	.499	139	19	2			.968	6	O-91/3-7	2.0
	Yr	143	505	71	143	19	2	24	72	56	50	.283	.357	.471	130	20	3			.964	9	*O-128/3-7	2.2
1941	Phi-N	99	235	20	51	9	2	4	24	24	34	.217	.295	.323	77	-7	1			.968	-0	O-62/3-2	-1.1
1942	Bro-N	78	217	31	50	8	0	4	27	24	25	.230	.307	.323	83	-5	2			.977	-2	O-70	-1.0
Total	5	557	1842	268	497	90	16	61	289	200	197	.270	.345	.435	116	38	7			.964	-1	O-486/3-9	1.5

■ PHIL RIZZUTO
Rizzuto, Philip Francis "Scooter" (b: Fiero Francis Rizzuto)   b: 9/25/17, Brooklyn, N.Y.   BR/TR, 5'6", 160 lbs.   Deb: 4/14/41   H

YEAR	TM/L	G	AB	R	H	2B	3B	HR	RBI	BB	SO	AVG	OBP	SLG	PRO+	BR/A	SB	CS	SBR	FA	FR	G/POS	TPR
1941	*NY-A	133	515	65	158	20	9	3	46	27	36	.307	.343	.398	97	-3	14	5	1	.957	16	*S-128	2.2
1942	*NY-A☆	144	553	79	157	24	7	4	68	44	40	.284	.343	.374	104	2	22	6	3	.962	**25**	*S-144	4.0
1946	NY-A	126	471	53	121	17	1	2	38	34	39	.257	.315	.310	74	-16	14	7	0	.961	13	*S-125	0.5
1947	NY-A	153	549	78	150	26	9	2	60	57	31	.273	.350	.364	100	0	11	6	-0	.969	16	*S-151	2.5
1948	NY-A	128	464	65	117	13	2	6	50	60	24	.252	.340	.328	79	-13	6	5	-1	.973	-11	*S-128	-1.8
1949	*NY-A	153	614	110	169	22	7	5	65	72	34	.275	.352	.358	88	-10	18	6	2	**.971**	3	*S-152	0.5
1950	*NY-A★	155	617	125	200	36	7	7	66	92	39	.324	.418	.439	123	25	12	8	-1	**.982**	9	*S-155	**4.1**
1951	*NY-A★	144	540	87	148	21	6	2	43	58	27	.274	.350	.346	92	-5	18	3	4	.968	3	*S-144	1.5
1952	*NY-A★	152	578	89	147	24	10	2	43	67	42	.254	.337	.341	95	-4	17	6	2	.976	19	*S-152	2.8
1953	*NY-A★	134	413	54	112	21	3	2	54	71	39	.271	.383	.351	92	-1	4	7	-3	.963	-3	*S-133	1.1
1954	NY-A	127	307	47	60	11	0	2	15	41	23	.195	.292	.251	51	-20	3	2	-0	.968	-1	*S-126/2-1	-1.3
1955	*NY-A	81	143	19	37	4	1	1	9	22	18	.259	.369	.322	88	-1	7	1	2	.957	-9	S-79/2-1	-0.5
1956	NY-A	31	52	6	12	0	0	0	6	6	6	.231	.310	.231	46	-4	3	0	1	.934	3	S-30	-0.5
Total	13	1661	5816	877	1588	239	62	38	563	651	398	.273	.351	.355	93	-44	149	58	10	.968	86	*S-1647/2-2	15.8

■ MEL ROACH
Roach, Melvin Earl   b: 1/25/33, Richmond, Va.   BR/TR, 6'1", 190 lbs.   Deb: 7/31/53

YEAR	TM/L	G	AB	R	H	2B	3B	HR	RBI	BB	SO	AVG	OBP	SLG	PRO+	BR/A	SB	CS	SBR	FA	FR	G/POS	TPR
1953	Mil-N	5	2	1	0	0	0	0	0	0	0	.000	.000	.000	-99	-1	0	0	0	.000	0	/2-1	-0.1
1954	Mil-N	3	4	0	0	0	0	0	0	0	0	.000	.000	.000	-99	-1	0	0	0	1.000	-0	/1-1	-0.1
1957	Mil-N	7	6	1	1	0	0	0	0	0	2	.167	.167	.167	-11	-1	0	0	0	1.000	0	/2-5	-0.1
1958	Mil-N	44	136	14	42	7	0	3	10	6	15	.309	.338	.426	110	1	0	0	0	.993	-2	2-27/O-7,1-1	0.2
1959	Mil-N	19	31	1	3	0	0	0	3	0	6	.097	.152	.097	-35	-6	0	0	0	.880	1	/2-8,O-4,3-1	-0.4
1960	Mil-N	48	140	12	42	12	0	3	18	6	19	.300	.333	.450	121	0	0	0	0	.975	-2	O-21,2-20/1-1,3-1	-0.5
1961	Mil-N	13	36	3	6	1	0	0	6	2	4	.167	.250	.250	35	-3	0	0	0	1.000	0	/O-9,1-2	-0.6
	Chi-N	23	39	1	5	1	0	1	3	1	9	.128	.150	.179	-1	-6	1	0	0	.981	1	/1-7,2-7	-0.7
	Yr	36	75	4	11	2	0	1	9	3	13	.147	.220	.213	16	-9	1	0	0	1.000	0	/O-9,1-9,2-7	-1.3
1962	Phi-N	65	105	9	20	4	0	0	8	5	19	.190	.227	.229	23	-11	0	0	0	.951	-2	3-26/2-9,1-4,O-3	-1.2
Total	8	227	499	42	119	25	0	7	43	24	75	.238	.278	.331	66	-24	1	0	0	.969	-12	/2-77,O-44,3-28,1	-3.5

YEAR	TM/L	G	AB	R	H	2B	3B	HR	RBI	BB	SO	AVG	OBP	SLG	PRO+	BR/A	SB	CS	SBR	FA	FR	G/POS	TPR

■ MIKE ROACH
Roach, Michael Stephen   b: 12/23/1873, New York, N.Y.   d: 11/12/16, New York, N.Y.   Deb: 8/10/1899

YEAR	TM/L	G	AB	R	H	2B	3B	HR	RBI	BB	SO	AVG	OBP	SLG	PRO+	BR/A	SB	CS	SBR	FA	FR	G/POS	TPR
1899	Was-N	24	78	7	17	1	0	0	7	3		.218	.265	.231	37	-7	3			.964	-5	C-20/1-3	-0.9

■ ROXEY ROACH
Roach, Wilbur Charles   b: 11/28/1882, Anita, Pa.   d: 12/26/47, Bay City, Mich.   BR/TR, 5'11", 160 lbs.   Deb: 5/2/10

YEAR	TM/L	G	AB	R	H	2B	3B	HR	RBI	BB	SO	AVG	OBP	SLG	PRO+	BR/A	SB	CS	SBR	FA	FR	G/POS	TPR
1910	NY-A	70	220	27	47	9	2	0	20	29		.214	.313	.273	79	-5	15			.913	-7	S-58/O-9	-1.1
1911	NY-A	13	40	4	10	2	1	0	2	6		.250	.348	.350	89	-1	0			.891	-1	/S-8,2-5	-0.1
1912	Was-A	2	2	1	1	0	0	0	1	0		.500	.500	2.000	600	1	0			.500	-1	/S-2	0.0
1915	Buf-F	92	346	35	93	20	3	2	31	17	34	.269	.303	.361	85	-13	11			.959	15	S-92	1.0
Total	4	177	608	67	151	31	6	3	54	52	34	.248	.311	.334	85	-17	26			.938	7	S-160/O-9,2-5	-0.2

■ MIKE ROARKE
Roarke, Michael Thomas   b: 11/8/30, West Warwick, R.I.   BR/TR, 6'2", 195 lbs.   Deb: 4/19/61   C

YEAR	TM/L	G	AB	R	H	2B	3B	HR	RBI	BB	SO	AVG	OBP	SLG	PRO+	BR/A	SB	CS	SBR	FA	FR	G/POS	TPR
1961	Det-A	86	229	21	51	6	1	2	22	20	31	.223	.285	.284	51	-16	0	0	0	.988	4	C-85	-0.9
1962	Det-A	56	136	11	29	4	1	4	14	13	17	.213	.287	.346	67	-6	0	0	0	.982	6	C-53	0.1
1963	Det-A	23	44	5	14	0	0	0	1	2	3	.318	.362	.318	89	-0	0	0	0	.986	1	C-16	0.1
1964	Det-A	29	82	4	19	1	0	0	7	10	10	.232	.315	.244	57	-4	0	0	0	.994	3	C-27	0.0
Total	4	194	491	41	113	11	2	6	44	45	61	.230	.297	.297	60	-27	0	0	0	.987	14	C-181	-0.7

■ FRED ROAT
Roat, Frederick R.   b: 11/10/1867, Oregon, Ill.   d: 9/24/13, Oregon, Ill.   TR ,   Deb: 5/10/1890

YEAR	TM/L	G	AB	R	H	2B	3B	HR	RBI	BB	SO	AVG	OBP	SLG	PRO+	BR/A	SB	CS	SBR	FA	FR	G/POS	TPR
1890	Pit-N	57	215	18	48	2	0	2	17	16	22	.223	.286	.260	67	-8	7			.847	2	3-44/1-9,O-4	-0.5
1892	Chi-N	8	31	4	6	0	1	0	2	2	3	.194	.242	.258	51	-2	2			.897	-3	/2-8	-0.5
Total	2	65	246	22	54	2	1	2	19	18	25	.220	.281	.260	65	-10	9			.847	-1	/3-44,1-9,2-8,O-4	-1.0

■ TONY ROBELLO
Robello, Thomas Vardasco   b: 2/9/13, San Leandro, Cal.   d: 12/25/94, Fort Worth, Tex.   BR/TR, 5'10.5", 175 lbs.   Deb: 8/13/33

YEAR	TM/L	G	AB	R	H	2B	3B	HR	RBI	BB	SO	AVG	OBP	SLG	PRO+	BR/A	SB	CS	SBR	FA	FR	G/POS	TPR
1933	Cin-N	14	30	1	7	3	0	0	3	1	5	.233	.258	.333	69	-1				1.000	2	2-11/3-2	0.1
1934	Cin-N	2	2	0	0	0	0	0	0	0	1	.000	.000	.000	-99	-1				.000	0	H	-0.1
Total	2	16	32	1	7	3	0	0	3	1	6	.219	.242	.313	58	-2				1.000	2	/2-11,3-2	0.0

■ SKIPPY ROBERGE
Roberge, Joseph Albert Armand   b: 5/19/17, Lowell, Mass.   d: 6/7/93, Lowell, Mass.   BR/TR, 5'11", 185 lbs.   Deb: 7/18/41

YEAR	TM/L	G	AB	R	H	2B	3B	HR	RBI	BB	SO	AVG	OBP	SLG	PRO+	BR/A	SB	CS	SBR	FA	FR	G/POS	TPR
1941	Bos-N	55	167	12	36	6	0	1	15	9	18	.216	.256	.251	45	-12	1			.978	5	2-46/3-5,S-2	-0.5
1942	Bos-N	74	172	10	37	7	0	1	12	9	19	.215	.258	.273	57	-10	1			.977	8	2-29,3-27/S-6	0.0
1946	Bos-N	48	169	13	39	6	2	2	20	7	12	.231	.270	.325	68	-8	1			.973	2	3-48	-0.5
Total	3	177	508	35	112	19	2	3	47	25	49	.220	.261	.283	57	-30	2			.967	15	/3-80,2-75,S-8	-1.0

■ KEVIN ROBERSON
Roberson, Kevin Lynn   b: 1/29/68, Decatur, Ill.   BB/TR, 6'4", 210 lbs.   Deb: 7/15/93

YEAR	TM/L	G	AB	R	H	2B	3B	HR	RBI	BB	SO	AVG	OBP	SLG	PRO+	BR/A	SB	CS	SBR	FA	FR	G/POS	TPR
1993	Chi-N	62	180	23	34	9	0	9	27	12	48	.189	.251	.372	65	-10	0	1	-1	.963	-6	O-51	-1.8
1994	Chi-N	44	55	8	12	4	0	4	9	2	14	.218	.271	.509	99	-1	0	0	0	.800	-2	/O-9	-0.2
1995	Chi-N	32	38	5	7	1	0	4	6	6	14	.184	.311	.526	118	1	0	1	-1	1.000	-2	O-11	0.0
1996	NY-N	27	36	8	8	1	0	3	9	7	17	.222	.364	.500	134	2	0	0	0	1.000	-2	O-10	0.0
Total	4	165	309	44	61	10	1	20	51	27	93	.197	.277	.430	86	-8	0	2	-1	.955	-12	/O-81	-2.2

■ RED ROBERTS
Roberts, Charles Emory   b: 8/8/18, Carrollton, Ga.   BR/TR, 6', 170 lbs.   Deb: 9/3/43

YEAR	TM/L	G	AB	R	H	2B	3B	HR	RBI	BB	SO	AVG	OBP	SLG	PRO+	BR/A	SB	CS	SBR	FA	FR	G/POS	TPR
1943	Was-A	9	23	1	6	1	0	1	3	4	2	.261	.370	.435	140	1	0	0	0	.778	-5	/S-6,3-1	-0.3

■ SKIPPER ROBERTS
Roberts, Clarence Ashley   b: 1/11/1888, Wardner, Idaho   d: 12/24/63, Long Beach, Cal.   BL/TR, 5'10.5", 175 lbs.   Deb: 6/12/13

YEAR	TM/L	G	AB	R	H	2B	3B	HR	RBI	BB	SO	AVG	OBP	SLG	PRO+	BR/A	SB	CS	SBR	FA	FR	G/POS	TPR
1913	StL-N	26	41	4	6	2	0	0	3	3	13	.146	.205	.195	15	-5	1			.859	-2	C-16	-0.6
1914	Pit-F	33	55	7	12	2	1	0	4	1	11	.218	.246	.291	46	-5	2			.941	-4	C-14	-0.6
	Chi-F	4	3	0	1	0	0	0	1	1	1	.333	.500	.333	138	0	0			.000	0	H	0.0
	Pit-F	19	39	5	10	2	1	1	4	1	8	.256	.293	.436	98	-1	1			.923	-4	/C-9,O-1	-0.4
	Yr	56	97	12	23	4	2	1	9	3	20	.237	.275	.351	70	-6	3			.935	-5	C-23/O-1	-1.0
Total	2	82	138	16	29	6	2	1	12	6	33	.210	.253	.304	54	-11	4			.906	-7	/C-39,O-1	-1.6

■ CURT ROBERTS
Roberts, Curtis Benjamin   b: 8/16/29, Pineland, Tex.   d: 11/14/69, Oakland, Cal.   BR/TR, 5'8", 165 lbs.   Deb: 4/13/54

YEAR	TM/L	G	AB	R	H	2B	3B	HR	RBI	BB	SO	AVG	OBP	SLG	PRO+	BR/A	SB	CS	SBR	FA	FR	G/POS	TPR
1954	Pit-N	134	496	47	115	18	7	1	36	55	49	.232	.311	.302	62	-27	6	3	0	.969	2	*2-131	-1.6
1955	Pit-N	6	17	1	2	1	0	0	0	2	1	.118	.211	.176	4	-2	0	0	0	.913	-1	/2-6	-0.3
1956	Pit-N	31	62	6	11	5	2	0	4	5	12	.177	.239	.323	50	-5	1	0	0	.988	-2	2-27	-0.4
Total	3	171	575	54	128	24	9	1	40	62	62	.223	.300	.301	59	-34	7	3	0	.969	0	2-164	-2.3

■ DAVE ROBERTS
Roberts, David Leonard   b: 6/30/33, Panama City, Pan.   BL/TL, 6', 172 lbs.   Deb: 9/5/62

YEAR	TM/L	G	AB	R	H	2B	3B	HR	RBI	BB	SO	AVG	OBP	SLG	PRO+	BR/A	SB	CS	SBR	FA	FR	G/POS	TPR
1962	Hou-N	16	53	3	13	3	0	1	10	8	8	.245	.355	.358	99	-0	0	0	0	1.000	-1	O-12/1-6	-0.2
1964	Hou-N	61	125	9	23	4	1	1	7	14	28	.184	.271	.256	52	-8	0	0	-1	.983	4	1-34/O-4	-0.6
1966	Pit-N	14	16	3	2	1	0	0	0	0	7	.125	.125	.188	-15	-2	0	0	0	.950	0	/1-2	-0.2
Total	3	91	194	15	38	8	1	2	17	22	43	.196	.284	.278	60	-10	0	0	-1	.983	3	/1-42,O-16	-1.0

■ DAVE ROBERTS
Roberts, David Wayne   b: 2/17/51, Lebanon, Ore.   BR/TR, 6'3", 215 lbs.   Deb: 6/7/72   C

YEAR	TM/L	G	AB	R	H	2B	3B	HR	RBI	BB	SO	AVG	OBP	SLG	PRO+	BR/A	SB	CS	SBR	FA	FR	G/POS	TPR
1972	SD-N	100	418	38	102	17	0	5	33	18	64	.244	.275	.321	74	-16	7	2	1	.931	-6	3-84,2-20/S-3,C-1	-2.3
1973	SD-N	127	479	56	137	20	3	21	64	17	83	.286	.312	.472	124	12	11	2	2	.942	3	*3-111,2-12	1.7
1974	SD-N	113	318	26	53	10	1	5	18	32	69	.167	.247	.252	41	-26	2	0	1	.955	-4	*3-103/S-3,O-1	-3.1
1975	SD-N	33	113	7	32	2	0	2	12	19	19	.283	.367	.354	107	2	3	1	0	.925	3	3-30/2-5	-0.2
1977	SD-N	82	186	15	41	14	1	1	23	11	32	.220	.268	.323	64	-10	2	1	0	.982	-4	C-63/2-2,3-2,S-1	-1.3
1978	SD-N	54	97	7	21	4	1	1	7	12	25	.216	.309	.309	79	-3	0	0	0	.980	-1	C-41/1-8,O-2	-0.4
1979	Tex-A	44	84	12	22	2	1	3	14	7	17	.262	.319	.417	98	-0	1	0	0	.980	2	C-14,O-11/2-8,13D	0.3
1980	Tex-A	101	235	27	56	4	0	10	30	13	38	.238	.281	.383	83	-6	0	1	-1	.930	-21	3-37,S-33,C/O12	-2.6
1981	*Hou-N	27	54	4	13	3	0	1	5	3	6	.241	.281	.352	83	-1	1	0	0	.958	0	1-10/3-7,2-3,C-1	-0.3
1982	Phi-N	28	33	2	6	1	0	0	2	2	8	.182	.229	.212	23	-3	0	1	-1	.818	-1	3-11,C-10/2-7	-0.3
Total	10	709	2017	194	483	77	7	49	208	128	361	.239	.288	.357	83	-53	27	8	3	.939	-35	3-386,C-152/2S10D	-8.4

■ BIP ROBERTS
Roberts, Leon Joseph   b: 10/27/63, Berkeley, Cal.   BB/TR, 5'7", 160 lbs.   Deb: 4/7/86

YEAR	TM/L	G	AB	R	H	2B	3B	HR	RBI	BB	SO	AVG	OBP	SLG	PRO+	BR/A	SB	CS	SBR	FA	FR	G/POS	TPR
1986	SD-N	101	241	34	61	5	2	1	12	14	29	.253	.294	.303	66	-11	14	12	-3	.971	4	2-87	-0.8
1988	SD-N	5	9	1	3	0	0	0	0	1	2	.333	.400	.333	115	0	0	2	-1	.500	-1	/3-2,2-1	-0.2
1989	SD-N	117	329	81	99	15	8	3	25	49	45	.301	.393	.422	133	16	21	11	-0	.976	-8	O-54,3-37,S-14/2-9	0.8
1990	SD-N	149	556	104	172	36	3	9	44	55	65	.309	.378	.433	122	17	46	12	7	.982	-1	O-75,3-56,S-18/2-8	2.4
1991	SD-N	117	424	66	119	13	3	3	32	37	71	.281	.344	.347	92	-4	26	11	1	.978	-7	2-68,O-46	-0.9
1992	Cin-N★	147	532	92	172	34	6	4	45	62	54	.323	.396	.432	131	24	44	16	4	.993	-14	O-79,2-42,3-36	1.4
1993	Cin-N	83	292	46	70	13	0	1	18	38	46	.240	.334	.295	70	-11	26	6	4	.984	-9	2-64,O-11/3-3,S-1	-1.5
1994	SD-N	105	403	52	129	15	5	2	31	39	57	.320	.384	.397	107	6	21	7	2	.976	-15	2-90,O-20	-0.4
1995	SD-N	73	296	40	90	14	0	2	25	17	36	.304	.346	.372	92	-3	20	2	5	.989	4	O-50,2-25/S-7	0.6
1996	KC-A	90	339	39	96	21	2	0	52	25	38	.283	.339	.357	77	-11	12	9	-2	.986	-6	2-63,D-16,O-11	-1.5
Total	10	987	3421	555	1011	166	29	25	284	337	443	.296	.363	.383	103	22	230	88	16	.979	-53	2-457,O-346,3/SD	-0.1

■ LEON ROBERTS
Roberts, Leon Kauffman   b: 1/22/51, Vicksburg, Mich.   BR/TR, 6'3", 200 lbs.   Deb: 9/3/74

YEAR	TM/L	G	AB	R	H	2B	3B	HR	RBI	BB	SO	AVG	OBP	SLG	PRO+	BR/A	SB	CS	SBR	FA	FR	G/POS	TPR
1974	Det-A	17	63	5	17	3	2	0	7	3	10	.270	.303	.381	92	-1	0	2	-1	.926	-3	O-17	-0.6
1975	Det-A	129	447	51	115	17	5	10	38	36	94	.257	.318	.385	94	-4	3	7	-3	.982	8	*O-127/D-1	-0.5
1976	Hou-N	87	235	31	68	11	2	7	33	19	43	.289	.350	.443	136	10	1	0	0	.980	-4	O-60	0.5
1977	Hou-N	19	27	1	2	0	0	0	2	1	9	.074	.107	.074	-55	-6	0	0	0	1.000	-2	/O-9	-0.8
1978	Sea-A	134	472	78	142	21	7	22	92	41	94	.301	.367	.515	146	28	6	3	0	.975	10	*O-128/D-2	3.3
1979	Sea-A	140	450	61	122	24	4	15	54	56	64	.271	.354	.451	114	9	3	4	-1	.983	4	*O-136/D-1	0.7
1980	Sea-A	119	374	48	94	18	3	10	33	43	59	.251	.330	.396	97	-1	3	4	-1	.984	-4	*O-104/D-4	-0.2
1981	Tex-A	72	233	26	65	17	2	4	31	24	38	.279	.351	.421	128	8	3	4	-2	.992	-4	O-71	0.0
1982	Tex-A	31	73	7	17	3	1	1	13	8	21	.233	.282	.315	67	-3	0	0	0	1.000	-5	O-28/D-1	-0.9
	Tor-A	40	105	6	24	4	0	1	5	3	9	.229	.277	.295	52	-7	1	1	0	1.000	-2	D-21,O-16	-1.0
	Yr	71	178	13	41	7	1	2	18	11	30	.230	.279	.303	58	-10	1	1	0	1.000	-7	O-44,D-22	-1.9
1983	KC-A	84	213	24	55	7	0	8	24	17	27	.258	.316	.404	96	-1	1	1	-0	.979	-6	O-76/D-1	-1.0

YEAR	TM/L	G	AB	R	H	2B	3B	HR	RBI	BB	SO	AVG	OBP	SLG	PRO+	BR/A	SB	CS	SBR	FA	FR	G/POS	TPR
1984	KC-A	29	45	4	10	1	1	0	3	4	3	.222	.300	.289	63	-2	0	0	0	1.000	-3	O-16/P-1,D-3	-0.5
Total	11	901	2737	342	731	126	28	78	328	256	428	.267	.335	.419	108	29	26	25	-7	.982	-3	O-788/D-34,P-1	-1.0

■ JIM ROBERTSON
Robertson, Alfred James b: 1/29/28, Chicago, Ill. BR/TR, 5'9", 183 lbs. Deb: 4/15/54

YEAR	TM/L	G	AB	R	H	2B	3B	HR	RBI	BB	SO	AVG	OBP	SLG	PRO+	BR/A	SB	CS	SBR	FA	FR	G/POS	TPR
1954	Phi-A	63	147	9	27	8	0	0	8	23	25	.184	.298	.238	48	-10	0	0	0	.974	-2	C-50	-1.0
1955	KC-A	6	8	1	2	0	0	0	0	1	2	.250	.333	.250	58	-0	0	0	0	1.000	0	/C-4	0.0
Total	2	69	155	10	29	8	0	0	8	24	27	.187	.300	.239	49	-10	0	0	0	.975	-2	/C-54	-1.0

■ ANDRE ROBERTSON
Robertson, Andre Levett b: 10/2/57, Orange, Tex. BR/TR, 5'10", 160 lbs. Deb: 9/3/81

YEAR	TM/L	G	AB	R	H	2B	3B	HR	RBI	BB	SO	AVG	OBP	SLG	PRO+	BR/A	SB	CS	SBR	FA	FR	G/POS	TPR
1981	*NY-A	10	19	1	5	1	0	0	0	3	3	.263	.263	.316	67	-1	1	1	-0	1.000	4	/S-8,2-3	0.3
1982	NY-A	44	118	16	26	5	0	2	9	8	19	.220	.270	.314	61	-6	0	0	0	.966	8	S-27,2-15/3-2	0.4
1983	NY-A	98	322	37	80	16	3	1	22	8	54	.248	.273	.326	67	-15	2	4	-2	.960	22	S-78,2-29	1.2
1984	NY-A	52	140	10	30	5	1	0	6	4	20	.214	.236	.264	40	-12	0	1	-1	.930	11	S-49/2-6	-0.4
1985	NY-A	50	125	16	41	5	0	2	17	6	24	.328	.364	.416	116	3	1	2	-1	.867	-6	3-33,S-14/2-2	-0.4
Total	5	254	724	80	182	32	4	5	54	26	120	.251	.281	.327	69	-31	4	8	-4	.953	38	S-176/2-55,3-35	1.7

■ DARYL ROBERTSON
Robertson, Daryl Berdene b: 1/5/36, Cripple Creek, Colo BR/TR, 6', 184 lbs. Deb: 5/4/62

YEAR	TM/L	G	AB	R	H	2B	3B	HR	RBI	BB	SO	AVG	OBP	SLG	PRO+	BR/A	SB	CS	SBR	FA	FR	G/POS	TPR
1962	Chi-N	9	19	0	2	0	0	0	2	3	10	.105	.190	.105	-18	-3	0	0	0	1.000	-1	/S-6,3-1	-0.4

■ DAVE ROBERTSON
Robertson, Davis Aydelotte b: 9/25/1889, Portsmouth, Va. d: 11/5/70, Virginia Beach, Va. BL/TL, 6', 186 lbs. Deb: 6/5/12

YEAR	TM/L	G	AB	R	H	2B	3B	HR	RBI	BB	SO	AVG	OBP	SLG	PRO+	BR/A	SB	CS	SBR	FA	FR	G/POS	TPR
1912	NY-N	3	2	0	1	0	0	0	1	0	1	.500	.500	.500	169	0	1			1.000	-1	/1-1,O-1	0.0
1914	NY-N	82	256	25	68	12	3	2	32	10	26	.266	.299	.359	99	-2	9			.950	-2	O-71	-0.7
1915	NY-N	141	544	72	160	17	10	3	58	22	52	.294	.326	.379	120	11	22	10	1	.956	-1	*O-138	0.4
1916	*NY-N	150	587	88	180	18	8	12	69	14	56	.307	.326	.426	137	22	21	17	-4	.960	5	*O-144	1.7
1917	*NY-N	142	532	64	138	16	9	12	54	10	47	.259	.276	.391	107	7	17			.942	1	*O-140	-0.7
1919	NY-N	1	0	0	0	0	0	0	0	0	0	—	—	—	—		0	0		.000	0	R	0.0
	Chi-N	27	96	8	20	2	0	1	10	1	10	.208	.224	.260	45	-6	3			.932	-2	O-25	-1.2
	Yr	28	96	8	20	2	0	1	10	1	10	.208	.224	.260	45	-6	3			.932	-2	O-25	-1.2
1920	Chi-N	134	500	68	150	29	11	10	75	40	44	.300	.353	.462	130	18	17	23	-9	.968	-9	*O-134	-0.9
1921	Chi-N	22	36	7	8	3	0	0	14	1	3	.222	.243	.306	44	-3	0	2	-1	1.000	-2	/O-7	-0.7
	Pit-N	60	230	29	74	18	3	6	48	12	16	.322	.361	.504	123	7	4	5	-2	.960	-4	O-58	-0.3
	Yr	82	266	36	82	21	3	6	62	13	19	.308	.345	.477	113	4	4	7	-3	.962	-6	O-65	-1.0
1922	NY-N	42	47	5	13	2	0	1	3	3	7	.277	.320	.383	80	-1	0	0		.909	-2	/O-8	-0.3
Total	9	804	2830	366	812	117	44	47	364	113	262	.287	.318	.409	117	46	94	57		.955	-16	O-726/1-1	-2.7

■ DON ROBERTSON
Robertson, Donald Alexander b: 10/15/30, Harvey, Ill. BL/TL, 5'10", 180 lbs. Deb: 4/13/54

YEAR	TM/L	G	AB	R	H	2B	3B	HR	RBI	BB	SO	AVG	OBP	SLG	PRO+	BR/A	SB	CS	SBR	FA	FR	G/POS	TPR
1954	Chi-N	14	6	2	0	0	0	0	0	0	2	.000	.000	.000	-99	-2	0	0	0	1.000	-2	/O-6	-0.4

■ GENE ROBERTSON
Robertson, Eugene Edward b: 12/25/1898, St.Louis, Mo. d: 10/21/81, Fallon, Nev. BL/TR, 5'7", 152 lbs. Deb: 7/4/19

YEAR	TM/L	G	AB	R	H	2B	3B	HR	RBI	BB	SO	AVG	OBP	SLG	PRO+	BR/A	SB	CS	SBR	FA	FR	G/POS	TPR
1919	StL-A	5	7	1	1	0	0	0	0	1	2	.143	.250	.143	11	-1	0			.750	-2	/S-2	-0.2
1922	StL-A	18	27	2	8	2	1	0	1	1	1	.296	.321	.444	95	-0	1	0	0	.875	1	/3-7,S-6,2-1	0.1
1923	StL-A	78	251	36	62	10	1	0	17	21	7	.247	.310	.295	57	-16	4	2	0	.935	-14	3-74/2-1	-2.4
1924	StL-A	121	439	70	140	25	4	4	52	36	14	.319	.373	.421	99	-1	3	5	-2	.958	-11	*3-111/2-2	-0.5
1925	StL-A	154	582	97	158	26	5	14	76	81	30	.271	.364	.405	90	-8	10	7	-1	.939	-2	*3-154/S-1	-1.1
1926	StL-A	78	247	23	62	12	6	1	19	17	10	.251	.302	.360	69	-12	5	1	1	.924	-5	3-55,S-10/2-3	-1.1
1928	*NY-A	83	251	29	73	9	0	1	36	14	26	.291	.328	.339	78	-8	2	4	-2	.926	-8	3-70/2-3	-1.4
1929	NY-A	90	309	45	92	15	6	0	35	26	9	.298	.358	.385	98	-1	3	3	-1	.966	-11	3-77	-1.0
	Bos-N	8	28	1	8	0	0	0	6	1	0	.286	.310	.286	51	-2	1			.875	-2	/3-6,S-1	-0.3
1930	Bos-N	21	59	7	11	1	0	0	7	5	3	.186	.250	.203	12	-8	0			.949	-2	3-17	-0.9
Total	9	656	2200	311	615	100	23	20	249	205	79	.280	.344	.373	83	-58	29	22		.941	-56	3-571/S-20,2-10	-7.8

■ MIKE ROBERTSON
Robertson, Michael Francis b: 10/9/70, Norwich, Conn. BL/TL, 6', 180 lbs. Deb: 9/6/96

YEAR	TM/L	G	AB	R	H	2B	3B	HR	RBI	BB	SO	AVG	OBP	SLG	PRO+	BR/A	SB	CS	SBR	FA	FR	G/POS	TPR
1996	Chi-A	6	7	0	1	1	0	0	0	0	1	.143	.143	.286	5	-1	0	0	0	1.000	0	/1-2,D-2	-0.1

■ BOB ROBERTSON
Robertson, Robert Eugene b: 10/2/46, Frostburg, Md. BR/TR, 6'1", 210 lbs. Deb: 9/18/67

YEAR	TM/L	G	AB	R	H	2B	3B	HR	RBI	BB	SO	AVG	OBP	SLG	PRO+	BR/A	SB	CS	SBR	FA	FR	G/POS	TPR
1967	Pit-N	9	35	4	6	0	0	2	4	3	12	.171	.237	.343	64	-2	0	0	0	.990	-0	/1-9	-0.3
1969	Pit-N	32	96	7	20	4	1	1	9	8	30	.208	.269	.302	61	-5	1	0	0	.996	1	1-26	-0.6
1970	*Pit-N	117	390	69	112	19	4	27	82	51	98	.287	.372	.564	150	27	4	1	1	.995	3	1-99/3-5,O-3	2.1
1971	*Pit-N	131	469	65	127	18	2	26	72	60	101	.271	.358	.484	137	23	1	2	-1	.993	15	*1-126	2.6
1972	*Pit-N	115	306	25	59	11	0	12	41	41	84	.193	.294	.346	83	-7	1	1	-0	.993	9	1-89,O-23,3-11	-0.4
1973	*Pit-N	119	397	43	95	16	0	14	40	55	77	.239	.333	.385	101	1	0	4	-2	.995	5	*1-107	-0.5
1974	*Pit-N	91	236	25	54	11	0	16	48	33	44	.229	.323	.479	127	7	0	0	0	.991	-1	1-63	0.3
1975	*Pit-N	75	124	17	34	4	0	6	18	23	25	.274	.396	.452	136	7	0	0	0	.996	1	1-27	0.7
1976	Pit-N	61	129	10	28	5	1	2	25	16	23	.217	.303	.318	76	-4	0	1	-1	.996	-0	1-29	-0.7
1978	Sea-A	64	174	17	40	5	2	8	28	24	39	.230	.327	.420	109	2	0	1	-1	1.000	-1	D-29,1-18	-0.1
1979	Tor-A	15	29	1	3	0	0	1	1	3	9	.103	.188	.207	6	-4	0	0	0	1.000	-1	/1-9,D-4	-0.3
Total	11	829	2385	283	578	93	10	115	368	317	546	.242	.334	.434	115	45	7	9	-3	.994	34	1-602/D-33,O-26,3	2.8

■ SHERRY ROBERTSON
Robertson, Sherrard Alexander b: 1/1/19, Montreal, Que., Can. d: 10/23/70, Houghton, S.Dak. BL/TR, 6', 180 lbs. Deb: 9/8/40 C

YEAR	TM/L	G	AB	R	H	2B	3B	HR	RBI	BB	SO	AVG	OBP	SLG	PRO+	BR/A	SB	CS	SBR	FA	FR	G/POS	TPR
1940	Was-A	10	33	4	7	0	1	0	5	6	6	.212	.316	.273	58	-2	0	0	0	.940	1	S-10	0.0
1941	Was-A	1	3	0	0	0	0	0	0	0	3	.000	.000	.000	-99	-1	0	0	0	.750	0	/3-1	-0.1
1943	Was-A	59	120	22	26	4	1	3	14	17	19	.217	.319	.342	97	-0	0	2	-1	.897	-4	3-27/S-1	-0.6
1946	Was-A	74	230	30	46	6	3	6	19	30	42	.200	.292	.330	78	-7	6	2	1	.902	-6	3-38,2-14,S-12,/O-1	-1.1
1947	Was-A	95	266	25	62	9	3	1	23	32	52	.233	.318	.301	74	-9	4	5	-2	.949	-0	O-55,3-10/2-4	-1.4
1948	Was-A	71	187	19	46	11	3	2	22	24	26	.246	.345	.369	90	-3	8	0	2	.939	-1	O-51	-0.4
1949	Was-A	110	374	59	94	17	3	11	42	42	35	.251	.329	.401	95	-5	10	3	1	.947	-8	2-71,3-19,O-13	-0.8
1950	Was-A	71	123	19	32	3	3	2	16	22	18	.260	.372	.382	98	-0	1	1	-0	.952	-9	O-14,2-12/3-1	-0.8
1951	Was-A	62	111	14	21	2	1	1	10	9	22	.189	.256	.252	38	-10	2	1	0	.949	3	O-22	-0.7
1952	Was-A	1	0	0	0	0	0	0	0	0	0						0	0	0	.000	0	R	0.0
	Phi-A	43	60	8	12	3	0	0	5	21	15	.200	.407	.250	81	-0	1	2	-1	.958	-3	/2-8,O-7,3-2	-0.5
	Yr	44	60	8	12	3	0	0	5	21	15	.200	.407	.250	81	-0	1	2	-1	.958	-3	/2-8,O-7,3-2	-0.5
Total	10	597	1507	200	346	55	18	26	151	202	238	.230	.323	.342	83	-37	32	16	0	.946	-27	O-163,2-109/3-98,S	-6.5

■ BILLY JO ROBIDOUX
Robidoux, William Joseph b: 1/13/64, Ware, Mass. BL/TR, 6'1", 200 lbs. Deb: 9/11/85

YEAR	TM/L	G	AB	R	H	2B	3B	HR	RBI	BB	SO	AVG	OBP	SLG	PRO+	BR/A	SB	CS	SBR	FA	FR	G/POS	TPR
1985	Mil-A	18	51	4	9	0	0	3	8	12	16	.176	.333	.392	98	-1	0	0	0	1.000	-1	O-11/1-6,D-1	-0.1
1986	Mil-A	56	181	15	41	8	0	1	21	33	36	.227	.346	.287	72	-6	0	0	0	.986	-2	1-43,D-10	-1.1
1987	Mil-A	23	62	9	12	0	0	1	4	8	17	.194	.286	.194	30	-6	0	1	-1	.983	-0	1-10,D-10	-0.7
1988	Mil-A	33	91	9	23	5	0	0	5	10	14	.253	.313	.308	74	-3	1	1	-0	.983	-1	1-30/D-1	-0.3
1989	Chi-A	16	39	2	5	2	0	0	1	4	9	.128	.209	.179	11	-5	0	0	0	.990	-1	1-15/O-1	-0.6
1990	Bos-A	27	44	3	8	4	0	1	4	6	14	.182	.294	.341	74	-2	0	0	0	.981	-0	1-11/D-4	-0.2
Total	6	173	468	43	98	21	0	5	43	71	106	.209	.315	.286	65	-21	1	2	-1	.986	-6	1-115/D-26,O-12	-3.0

■ AARON ROBINSON
Robinson, Aaron Andrew b: 6/23/15, Lancaster, S.C. d: 3/9/66, Lancaster, S.C. BL/TR, 6'2", 205 lbs. Deb: 5/6/43

YEAR	TM/L	G	AB	R	H	2B	3B	HR	RBI	BB	SO	AVG	OBP	SLG	PRO+	BR/A	SB	CS	SBR	FA	FR	G/POS	TPR
1943	NY-A	1	1	0	0	0	0	0	0	0	0	.000	.000	.000	-99	-0	0	0	0	.000	0	H	0.0
1945	NY-A	50	160	19	45	6	1	8	24	21	23	.281	.368	.481	139	8	0	0	0	1.000	-3	C-45	0.8
1946	NY-A	100	330	32	98	17	2	16	64	48	39	.297	.388	.506	146	21	0	1	-1	.983	-11	C-95	1.5
1947	*NY-A☆	82	252	23	68	11	5	5	36	40	26	.270	.370	.413	119	7	0	1	-1	.997	-0	C-74	1.1
1948	Chi-A	98	326	47	82	14	2	8	39	46	30	.252	.344	.380	96	-2	1	0	0	.989	-5	C-92	-0.1
1949	Det-A	110	331	38	89	12	0	13	56	73	21	.269	.402	.423	118	11	0	2	-2	.986	-1	*C-108	1.4
1950	Det-A	107	283	37	64	9	0	9	37	75	35	.226	.388	.346	86	-3	0	0	0	.993	-1	*C-103	-0.2
1951	Det-A	36	82	3	17	0	0	1	9	17	9	.207	.343	.280	70	-2	0	0	0	1.000	-2	C-35	-0.4
	Bos-A	26	74	9	15	1	1	2	7	10	10	.203	.352	.324	76	-2	0	0	0	.983	-1	C-25	-0.2

YEAR	TM/L	G	AB	R	H	2B	3B	HR	RBI	BB	SO	AVG	OBP	SLG	PRO+	BR/A	SB	CS	SBR	FA	FR	G/POS	TPR
	Yr	62	156	12	32	7	1	2	16	34	19	.205	.347	.301	73	-5	0	0	0	.991	-3	C-60	-0.6
Total	8	610	1839	208	478	74	11	61	272	337	194	.260	.375	.412	112	35	0	6	-4	.990	-26	C-577	3.9

■ VAL ROBINSON
Robinson, Alfred Valentine   Deb: 5/1/1872

YEAR	TM/L	G	AB	R	H	2B	3B	HR	RBI	BB	SO	AVG	OBP	SLG	PRO+	BR/A	SB	CS	SBR	FA	FR	G/POS	TPR
1872	Oly-n	7	30	6	6	0	0	0	4	1	1	.200	.226	.200	34	-2	0	0	0	.750	-0	/O-7	-0.1

■ BROOKS ROBINSON
Robinson, Brooks Calbert   b: 5/18/37, Little Rock, Ark.   BR/TR, 6'1", 190 lbs.   Deb: 9/17/55   CH

YEAR	TM/L	G	AB	R	H	2B	3B	HR	RBI	BB	SO	AVG	OBP	SLG	PRO+	BR/A	SB	CS	SBR	FA	FR	G/POS	TPR
1955	Bal-A	6	22	0	2	0	0	0	1	0	10	.091	.091	.091	-55	-5	0	0	0	.833	-2	/3-6	-0.7
1956	Bal-A	15	44	5	10	4	0	1	1	1	5	.227	.244	.386	70	-2	0	0	0	.944	0	3-14/2-1	-0.2
1957	Bal-A	50	117	13	28	6	1	2	14	7	10	.239	.288	.359	81	-4	1	0	0	.971	4	3-47	0.1
1958	Bal-A	145	463	31	110	16	3	3	32	31	51	.238	.293	.305	68	-21	1	2	-1	.953	10	*3-140,2-16	-1.0
1959	Bal-A	88	313	29	89	15	2	4	24	17	37	.284	.325	.383	96	-2	2	2	-1	.955	7	3-87/2-1	0.4
1960	Bal-A★	152	595	74	175	27	9	14	88	35	49	.294	.333	.440	109	5	2	2	-1	.977	12	*3-152/2-3	1.6
1961	Bal-A★	163	668	89	192	38	7	7	61	47	57	.287	.338	.397	99	-2	1	3	-2	.972	-6	*3-163/2-2,S-1	-0.7
1962	Bal-A★	162	634	77	192	29	9	23	86	42	70	.303	.347	.486	129	23	3	1	0	.979	7	*3-162/S-3,2-2	3.2
1963	Bal-A★	161	589	67	148	26	4	11	67	46	84	.251	.307	.365	91	-8	2	3	-1	.976	9	*3-160/S-1	0.0
1964	Bal-A★	163	612	82	194	35	3	28	**118**	51	64	.317	.373	.521	146	37	1	0	0	.972	-2	*3-163	3.5
1965	Bal-A★	144	559	81	166	25	2	18	80	47	47	.297	.354	.445	123	16	3	0	1	.967	-6	*3-143	0.9
1966	*Bal-A★	157	620	91	167	35	2	23	100	56	36	.269	.333	.444	123	18	2	3	-1	.976	4	*3-157	1.9
1967	Bal-A★	158	610	88	164	25	5	22	77	54	54	.269	.332	.434	126	19	1	3	-2	**.980**	31	*3-158	5.0
1968	Bal-A★	162	608	65	154	36	6	17	75	44	54	.253	.308	.416	118	11	1	1	-0	.970	17	*3-162	3.2
1969	*Bal-A★	156	598	73	140	21	3	23	84	56	55	.234	.303	.395	93	-7	2	1	-0	**.976**	19	*3-156	1.3
1970	Bal-A★	158	608	84	168	31	4	18	94	53	53	.276	.338	.429	109	7	1	1	-0	.966	-1	*3-156	0.4
1971	*Bal-A★	156	589	67	160	21	1	20	92	63	50	.272	.345	.413	115	11	0	0	0	.968	7	*3-156	1.8
1972	Bal-A★	153	556	48	139	23	2	8	64	43	45	.250	.306	.342	90	-7	1	0	0	**.977**	-8	*3-152	-0.3
1973	Bal-A★	155	549	53	141	17	2	9	72	55	50	.257	.328	.344	90	-7	2	0	1	.970	9	*3-154	0.2
1974	*Bal-A★	153	553	46	159	27	0	7	59	56	47	.288	.356	.374	114	11	2	0	1	.967	21	*3-153	3.2
1975	Bal-A	144	482	50	97	15	1	6	53	44	33	.201	.269	.274	57	-28	0	0	0	**.979**	4	*3-143	-2.5
1976	Bal-A	71	218	16	46	8	2	3	11	8	24	.211	.242	.307	64	-11	0	0	0	.969	2	3-71	-1.2
1977	Bal-A	24	47	3	7	2	0	1	4	4	4	.149	.216	.255	30	-5	0	0	0	1.000	2	3-15	-0.3
Total	23	2896	10654	1232	2848	482	68	268	1357	860	990	.267	.325	.401	105	52	28	22	-5	.971	151	*3-2870/2-25,S-5	19.8

■ BRUCE ROBINSON
Robinson, Bruce Philip   b: 4/16/54, LaJolla, Cal.   BL/TR, 6'1", 185 lbs.   Deb: 8/19/78   F

YEAR	TM/L	G	AB	R	H	2B	3B	HR	RBI	BB	SO	AVG	OBP	SLG	PRO+	BR/A	SB	CS	SBR	FA	FR	G/POS	TPR
1978	Oak-A	28	84	5	21	3	1	0	8	3	8	.250	.276	.310	68	-4	0	0	0	.965	7	C-28	0.4
1979	NY-A	6	12	0	2	0	0	0	2	1	0	.167	.231	.167	9	-2	0	0	0	.943	2	/C-6	0.1
1980	NY-A	4	5	0	0	0	0	0	0	0	4	.000	.000	.000	-99	-1	0	0	0	1.000	-0	/C-3	-0.2
Total	3	38	101	5	23	3	1	0	10	4	12	.228	.257	.277	52	-7	0	0	0	.962	9	/C-37	0.3

■ CHARLIE ROBINSON
Robinson, Charles Henry   b: 7/27/1856, Westerly, R.I.   d: 5/18/13,   BL/TR,   Deb: 8/2/1884

YEAR	TM/L	G	AB	R	H	2B	3B	HR	RBI	BB	SO	AVG	OBP	SLG	PRO+	BR/A	SB	CS	SBR	FA	FR	G/POS	TPR
1884	Ind-a	20	80	11	23	2	0	0			3	.287	.313	.313	108	1				.967	-1	C-17/S-3,O-1	0.1
1885	Bro-a	11	40	5	6	2	1	0	4	3		.150	.209	.250	44	-3				.840	-4	C-11	-0.5
Total	2	31	120	16	29	4	1	0	4	6		.242	.278	.292	85	-2				.919	-5	/C-28,S-3,O-1	-0.4

■ RABBIT ROBINSON
Robinson, Clyde   b: 3/5/1882, Wellsburg, W.Va.   d: 4/9/15, Waterbury, Conn.   BR/TR, 5'6", 148 lbs.   Deb: 4/22/03

YEAR	TM/L	G	AB	R	H	2B	3B	HR	RBI	BB	SO	AVG	OBP	SLG	PRO+	BR/A	SB	CS	SBR	FA	FR	G/POS	TPR
1903	Was-A	103	373	41	79	10	8	1	20	33		.212	.279	.290	69	-13	16			.917	2	2-45,O-30,S-24,/3-5	-1.1
1904	Det-A	101	320	30	77	13	6	0	37	29		.241	.314	.319	103	2	14			.925	1	S-30,3-26,O-20,2-19	0.5
1910	Cin-N	2	7	0	0	0	0	0	1	1	0	.000	.125	.000	-66	-1	0			1.000	-1	/3-2	-0.3
Total	3	206	700	71	156	23	14	1	58	63	0	.223	.294	.300	83	-13	30			.940	2	/2-64,S-54,O-50,3	-0.9

■ CRAIG ROBINSON
Robinson, Craig George   b: 8/21/48, Abington, Pa.   BR/TR, 5'10", 165 lbs.   Deb: 9/9/72

YEAR	TM/L	G	AB	R	H	2B	3B	HR	RBI	BB	SO	AVG	OBP	SLG	PRO+	BR/A	SB	CS	SBR	FA	FR	G/POS	TPR
1972	Phi-N	5	15	0	3	1	0	0	1	0	2	.200	.250	.267	46	-4	0	0	0	1.000	2	/S-4	0.2
1973	Phi-N	46	146	11	33	7	0	0	7	0	25	.226	.226	.274	37	-12	1	1	-0	.945	1	S-42/2-4	-0.8
1974	Atl-N	145	452	52	104	4	6	0	29	30	57	.230	.282	.265	52	-29	11	2	2	.956	-17	*S-142	-2.8
1975	Atl-N	10	17	1	1	0	0	0	0	0	5	.059	.059	.059	-65	-4	0	0	0	1.000	1	/S-7	-0.2
	SF-N	29	29	4	2	1	0	0	0	2	6	.069	.129	.103	-34	-5	0	0	0	.941	5	S-12/2-9	-0.0
	Yr	39	46	5	3	1	0	0	0	2	11	.065	.104	.087	-45	-9	0	0	0	.967	6	S-19/2-9	-0.2
1976	SF-N	15	13	4	4	1	0	0	2	3	4	.308	.438	.385	131	1	0	1	-1	.952	4	/2-7,3-2,S-1	0.4
	Atl-N	15	17	4	4	0	0	0	0	2	2	.235	.409	.235	81	-0	0	0	0	.952	2	/2-5,S-2,3-1	0.2
	Yr	30	30	8	8	1	0	0	2	5	6	.267	.421	.300	102	1	0	1	-1	.952	6	2-12/3-3,S-3	0.6
1977	Atl-N	27	29	4	6	1	0	0	1	1	6	.207	.233	.241	25	-3	0	0	0	1.000	4	S-23	0.3
Total	6	292	718	80	157	15	6	0	42	42	107	.219	.265	.256	44	-54	12	4	1	.956	3	S-233/2-25,3-3	-2.7

■ DAVE ROBINSON
Robinson, David Tanner   b: 5/22/46, Minneapolis, Minn.   BB/TL, 6'1", 186 lbs.   Deb: 9/10/70   F

YEAR	TM/L	G	AB	R	H	2B	3B	HR	RBI	BB	SO	AVG	OBP	SLG	PRO+	BR/A	SB	CS	SBR	FA	FR	G/POS	TPR
1970	SD-N	15	38	5	12	2	0	2	6	5	4	.316	.395	.526	151	3	2	0	1	1.000	1	O-13	0.4
1971	SD-N	7	6	0	0	0	0	0	0	1	3	.000	.143	.000	-61	-1	0	0	0	.000	0	H	-0.1
Total	2	22	44	5	12	2	0	2	6	6	7	.273	.360	.455	124	1	2	0	1	1.000	1	/O-13	0.3

■ EARL ROBINSON
Robinson, Earl John   b: 11/3/36, New Orleans, La.   BR/TR, 6'1", 190 lbs.   Deb: 9/10/58

YEAR	TM/L	G	AB	R	H	2B	3B	HR	RBI	BB	SO	AVG	OBP	SLG	PRO+	BR/A	SB	CS	SBR	FA	FR	G/POS	TPR
1958	LA-N	8	15	3	3	0	0	0	1	1	4	.200	.250	.200	20	-2	0	0	0	1.000	1	/3-6	0.0
1961	Bal-A	96	222	37	59	12	3	8	30	31	54	.266	.356	.455	119	6	4	3	-1	.973	-3	O-82	-0.1
1962	Bal-A	29	63	12	18	3	1	1	4	8	10	.286	.366	.413	116	2	0	1	0	1.000	0	O-17	0.2
1964	Bal-A	37	121	11	33	5	1	3	10	7	24	.273	.313	.405	98	-1	1	2	-1	.986	1	O-34	-0.2
Total	4	170	421	63	113	20	5	12	44	47	92	.268	.342	.425	109	5	7	5	-1	.980	-1	O-133/3-6	-0.1

■ FLOYD ROBINSON
Robinson, Floyd Andrew   b: 5/9/36, Prescott, Ark.   BL/TR, 5'9", 175 lbs.   Deb: 8/10/60

YEAR	TM/L	G	AB	R	H	2B	3B	HR	RBI	BB	SO	AVG	OBP	SLG	PRO+	BR/A	SB	CS	SBR	FA	FR	G/POS	TPR
1960	Chi-A	22	46	7	13	0	0	1	11	8		.283	.431	.283	98	1	2	3	-1	.960	-2	O-17	-0.4
1961	Chi-A	132	432	69	134	20	7	11	59	59	32	.310	.389	.465	129	19	7	4	-0	.991	4	*O-106	1.6
1962	Chi-A	156	600	89	187	**45**	10	11	109	72	47	.312	.387	.475	131	27	4	2	0	.973	-10	*O-155	0.8
1963	Chi-A	146	527	71	149	21	6	13	71	62	43	.283	.363	.419	120	15	4	3	-1	.984	-7	*O-137	0.1
1964	Chi-A	141	525	83	158	17	3	11	59	70	41	.301	.388	.408	125	20	9	5	-0	.987	-12	*O-138	0.1
1965	Chi-A	156	577	70	153	15	6	14	66	76	51	.265	.356	.385	117	15	4	1	1	.985	-4	*O-153	0.4
1966	Chi-A	127	342	44	81	11	2	5	35	44	32	.237	.332	.325	96	-1	8	2	1	.962	-14	*O-113	-1.9
1967	Cin-N	55	130	19	31	6	2	1	10	14	14	.238	.313	.338	77	-4	3	1	0	.981	-4	O-39	-1.0
1968	Oak-A	53	81	5	20	5	0	1	14	4	10	.247	.282	.346	94	-0	0	0	0	1.000	-1	O-18	-0.3
	Bos-A	23	24	1	3	0	0	0	2	3	4	.125	.250	.125	15	-2	1	0	0	.833	-3	O-10	-0.6
	Yr	76	105	6	23	5	0	1	16	7	14	.219	.274	.295	74	-3	1	0	0	.963	-4	O-28	-0.9
Total	9	1011	3284	458	929	140	36	67	426	408	282	.283	.367	.409	118	90	42	21	0	.981	-53	O-886	-1.2

■ FRANK ROBINSON
Robinson, Frank   b: 8/31/35, Beaumont, Tex.   BR/TR, 6'1", 195 lbs.   Deb: 4/17/56   MCH

YEAR	TM/L	G	AB	R	H	2B	3B	HR	RBI	BB	SO	AVG	OBP	SLG	PRO+	BR/A	SB	CS	SBR	FA	FR	G/POS	TPR
1956	Cin-N★	152	572	**122**	166	27	6	38	83	64	95	.290	.381	.558	139	32	8	4	0	.976	6	*O-152	3.0
1957	Cin-N★	150	611	97	197	29	5	29	75	44	92	.322	.379	.529	131	27	10	2	2	.989	19	*O-136,1-24	3.8
1958	Cin-N	148	554	90	149	25	6	31	83	62	80	.269	.350	.504	116	12	10	1	2	.991	9	*O-138,3-11	1.7
1959	Cin-N★	146	540	106	168	31	4	36	125	69	93	.311	.397	.583	152	41	18	8	1	.984	-3	*1-125,O-40	2.3
1960	Cin-N	139	464	86	138	33	6	31	83	82	67	.297	.413	**.595**	169	46	13	6	0	.993	7	1-78,O-51/3-1	4.5
1961	*Cin-N★	153	545	117	176	32	7	37	124	71	64	.323	.411	**.611**	164	51	22	3	**5**	.990	10	*O-150/3-1	5.5
1962	Cin-N★	162	609	**134**	208	**51**	2	39	136	76	62	.342	**.424**	**.624**	172	62	18	9	0	.994	9	*O-161	6.0
1963	Cin-N	140	482	79	125	19	3	21	91	81	69	.259	.381	.442	132	23	26	10	2	.984	9	*O-139/1-1	2.9
1964	Cin-N	156	568	103	174	38	6	29	96	79	67	.306	.399	.548	158	45	23	5	4	.986	2	*O-156	4.6
1965	Cin-N★	156	582	109	172	33	5	33	113	70	100	.296	.388	.540	148	38	13	9	-2	.990	2	*O-155	3.3
1966	*Bal-A★	155	576	**122**	182	34	2	**49**	122	87	90	**.316**	**.415**	**.637**	**200**	76	8	5	-1	.985	-4	*O-151/1-3	**6.7**
1967	Bal-A†	129	479	83	149	23	7	30	94	71	84	.311	.408	.576	189	54	2	3	-1	.990	-2	*O-126/1-2	4.8
1968	Bal-A	130	421	69	113	27	1	15	52	73	84	.268	.391	.444	153	30	11	2	2	.962	-8	*O-117/1-3	2.0

YEAR	TM/L	G	AB	R	H	2B	3B	HR	RBI	BB	SO	AVG	OBP	SLG	PRO+	BR/A	SB	CS	SBR	FA	FR	G/POS	TPR
1969	*Bal-A★	148	539	111	166	19	5	32	100	88	62	.308	.417	.540	164	49	9	3	1	.987	-1	*O-134,1-19	4.2
1970	*Bal-A★	132	471	88	144	24	1	25	78	69	70	.306	.402	.520	151	34	2	1	0	.987	6	*O-120/1-7	3.4
1971	*Bal-A★	133	455	82	128	16	2	28	99	72	62	.281	.390	.510	154	34	3	0	1	.973	-4	O-92,1-37	2.4
1972	LA-N	103	342	41	86	6	1	19	59	55	76	.251	.358	.442	129	14	2	3	-1	.967	-1	O-95	0.8
1973	Cal-A★	147	534	85	142	29	0	30	97	82	93	.266	.374	.489	153	38	1	1	-0	.976	-4	*D-127,O-17	3.8
1974	Cal-A★	129	427	75	107	26	2	20	63	75	85	.251	.375	.461	148	28	5	1	1	.000	-1	*D-123/O-1	2.7
	Cle-A	15	50	6	10	1	1	2	5	10	10	.200	.333	.380	106	1	0	1	-1	.958	-1	D-11/1-4	-0.1
	Yr	144	477	81	117	27	3	22	68	85	95	.245	.371	.453	143	29	5	2	0	.848	-1	*D-134/1-4,O-1	2.6
1975	Cle-A	49	118	19	28	5	0	5	9	24	29	.237	.388	.508	152	9	0	0	0	.000	-1	D-42,M	0.8
1976	Cle-A	36	67	5	15	0	0	3	10	11	12	.224	.333	.358	104	1	0	0	0	1.000	-1	D-18/1-2,O-1,M	-0.1
Total	21	2808	10006	1829	2943	528	72	586	1812	1420	1532	.294	.392	.537	154	744	204	77	15	.984	52	*O-2132,D-321,1/3	69.0

■ FRED ROBINSON

Robinson, Frederic Henry b: 7/6/1856, South Acton, Mass. d: 12/18/33, Hudson, Mass. BR/TR, Deb: 4/17/1884 F

YEAR	TM/L	G	AB	R	H	2B	3B	HR	RBI	BB	SO	AVG	OBP	SLG	PRO+	BR/A	SB	CS	SBR	FA	FR	G/POS	TPR
1884	Cin-U	3	13	1	3	0	0	0		0		.231	.231	.231	37	-1				.727	-3	/2-3	-0.4

■ JACKIE ROBINSON

Robinson, Jack Roosevelt b: 1/31/19, Cairo, Ga. d: 10/24/72, Stamford, Conn. BR/TR, 5'11", 204 lbs. Deb: 4/15/47 H

YEAR	TM/L	G	AB	R	H	2B	3B	HR	RBI	BB	SO	AVG	OBP	SLG	PRO+	BR/A	SB	CS	SBR	FA	FR	G/POS	TPR
1947	*Bro-N	151	590	125	175	31	5	12	48	74	36	.297	.383	.427	111	11	29			.989	-3	*1-151	0.2
1948	Bro-N	147	574	108	170	38	8	12	85	57	37	.296	.367	.453	117	13	22			.980	1	*2-116,1-30/3-6	2.0
1949	*Bro-N★	156	593	122	203	38	12	16	124	86	27	.342	.432	.528	150	45	37			.981	-1	*2-156	4.9
1950	Bro-N★	144	518	99	170	39	4	14	81	80	24	.328	.423	.500	139	32	12			.986	11	*2-144	4.7
1951	Bro-N★	153	548	106	185	33	7	19	88	79	27	.338	.429	.527	153	43	25	8	3	.992	17	*2-150	6.8
1952	Bro-N★	149	510	104	157	17	3	19	75	106	40	.308	.440	.465	149	41	24	7	3	.974	4	*2-146	5.6
1953	*Bro-N★	136	484	109	159	34	7	12	95	74	30	.329	.425	.502	137	32	17	4	3	.981	3	O-76,3-44/2-9,1S	3.5
1954	Bro-N★	124	386	62	120	22	4	15	59	63	20	.311	.417	.505	135	22	7	3	0	1.000	-9	O-74,3-50/2-4	1.0
1955	*Bro-N	105	317	51	81	6	2	8	36	61	18	.256	.378	.363	96	1	12	3	2	.966	7	3-84,0-10/1-1,2-1	0.9
1956	*Bro-N	117	357	61	98	15	2	10	43	60	32	.275	.383	.412	106	5	12	5	1	.967	15	3-72,2-22/1-9,0-2	2.2
Total	10	1382	4877	947	1518	273	54	137	734	740	291	.311	.410	.474	131	241	197	30		.983	49	2-748,3-256,1O/S	31.8

■ JACK ROBINSON

Robinson, John W. "Bridgeport" b: 7/15/1880, Portland, Maine d: 7/22/21, Macon, Ga. TR, Deb: 9/6/02

YEAR	TM/L	G	AB	R	H	2B	3B	HR	RBI	BB	SO	AVG	OBP	SLG	PRO+	BR/A	SB	CS	SBR	FA	FR	G/POS	TPR
1902	NY-N	4	9	0	0	0	0	0	0	0	0	.000	.000	.000	-99	-2	0			1.000	1	/C-3	-0.1

■ WILBERT ROBINSON

Robinson, Wilbert "Uncle Robby" b: 6/29/1863, Bolton, Mass. d: 8/8/34, Atlanta, Ga. BR/TR, 5'8.5", 215 lbs. Deb: 4/19/1886 FMCH

YEAR	TM/L	G	AB	R	H	2B	3B	HR	RBI	BB	SO	AVG	OBP	SLG	PRO+	BR/A	SB	CS	SBR	FA	FR	G/POS	TPR
1886	Phi-a	87	342	57	69	11	3	1	30	21		.202	.254	.260	61	-16	33			.893	-10	C-61,1-22/O-5	-1.9
1887	Phi-a	68	264	28	60	6	2	1	24	14		.227	.269	.277	52	-17	15			.901	1	C-67/1-3,O-1	-0.8
1888	Phi-a	66	254	32	62	7	2	1	31	9		.244	.270	.299	83	-5	11			.938	25	C-65/1-1	2.4
1889	Phi-a	69	264	31	61	13	2	0	28	6	34	.231	.251	.295	56	-16	9			.943	4	C-69	-0.5
1890	Phi-a	82	329	32	78	13	4	4	42	16		.237	.279	.337	83	-9	20			.930	4	C-82	-0.9
	Bal-a	14	48	7	13	1	0	0	4	3		.271	.314	.292	75	-2	1			.989	6	C-11/1-3	0.5
	Yr	96	377	39	91	14	4	4	46	19		.241	.283	.332	82	-10	21			.938	-3	C-93/1-3	-0.4
1891	Bal-a	93	334	25	72	8	5	2	46	16	37	.216	.251	.287	54	-22	18			.954	3	C-92/O-1	-0.9
1892	Bal-N	90	330	36	88	14	4	2	57	15	35	.267	.303	.352	95	-3	5			.921	-18	C-87/1-2,O-1	-1.4
1893	Bal-N	95	359	49	120	21	3	3	57	26	22	.334	.382	.435	115	7	17			.942	-8	*C-93/1-1	0.6
1894	*Bal-N	109	414	69	146	21	4	1	98	46	18	.353	.421	.430	101	2	12			.944	-5	*C-109	0.5
1895	*Bal-N	77	282	38	74	19	1	0	48	12	19	.262	.295	.337	61	-17	11			.979	14	C-75	0.3
1896	*Bal-N	67	245	43	85	9	6	2	38	14	13	.347	.385	.457	120	6	9			.948	3	C-67	1.4
1897	*Bal-N	48	181	25	57	9	0	0	23	8		.315	.347	.365	88	-3	0			.965	-2	C-48	0.0
1898	*Bal-N	79	289	29	80	12	2	0	38	16		.277	.317	.332	84	-6	3			.965	-5	C-77	-0.4
1899	*Bal-N	108	356	40	101	15	2	0	47	31		.284	.344	.337	83	-8	5			.949	-18	*C-105	-1.7
1900	StL-N	60	210	26	52	5	1	0	28	11		.248	.291	.281	59	-12	7			.974	-1	C-54	-0.7
1901	Bal-A	68	239	32	72	12	3	0	26	10		.301	.335	.377	93	-3	9			.949	-2	C-67	0.2
1902	Bal-A	91	335	38	98	16	7	1	57	12		.293	.321	.391	93	-4	11			.949	-15	C-87,M	-1.0
Total	17	1371	5075	637	1388	212	51	18	722	286	178	.273	.316	.346	83	-129	196			.941	-36	*C-1316/1-32,O-8	-4.3

■ EDDIE ROBINSON

Robinson, William Edward b: 12/15/20, Paris, Tex. BL/TR, 6'2.5", 210 lbs. Deb: 9/9/42 C

YEAR	TM/L	G	AB	R	H	2B	3B	HR	RBI	BB	SO	AVG	OBP	SLG	PRO+	BR/A	SB	CS	SBR	FA	FR	G/POS	TPR
1942	Cle-A	8	8	1	1	0	0	0	2	1	0	.125	.222	.125	-1	-0	0	0	0	1.000	-0	/1-1	-0.1
1946	Cle-A	8	30	6	12	1	0	3	4	2	4	.400	.438	.733	238	5	0	0	0	.988	-2	/1-8	0.3
1947	Cle-A	95	318	52	78	10	1	14	52	30	18	.245	.314	.415	105	0	1	0	0	.994	-2	1-87	-0.4
1948	*Cle-A	134	493	53	125	18	5	16	83	36	42	.254	.307	.408	91	-9	1	0	0	.995	-1	*1-131	-1.0
1949	Was-A★	143	527	66	155	27	3	18	78	67	30	.294	.381	.459	125	18	3	4	-2	.987	-2	*1-143	1.3
1950	Was-A	36	129	21	30	4	2	1	13	25	4	.233	.365	.318	80	-3	0	0	0	1.000	0	1-36	-0.4
	Chi-A	119	424	62	133	11	2	20	73	60	28	.314	.405	.491	132	21	0	0	0	.987	-7	*1-119	1.1
	Yr	155	553	83	163	15	4	21	86	85	32	.295	.395	.450	120	18	0	0	0	.990	-7	*1-155	0.7
1951	Chi-A★	151	564	85	159	23	5	29	117	77	54	.282	.371	.495	135	27	2	5	-2	.988	-6	*1-147	1.1
1952	Chi-A★	155	594	79	176	33	1	22	104	70	49	.296	.382	.466	134	27	2	0	1	.990	-8	*1-155	1.5
1953	Phi-A★	156	615	64	152	28	4	22	102	63	56	.247	.322	.413	94	-7	1	2	-1	.988	-14	*1-155	-2.8
1954	NY-A	85	142	11	37	9	0	3	27	19	21	.261	.348	.387	105	1	0	0	0	.980	1	1-29	0.0
1955	*NY-A	88	173	25	36	1	0	16	42	36	26	.208	.360	.491	129	7	0	0	0	.995	-2	1-46	0.3
1956	NY-A	26	54	7	12	1	0	5	11	5	3	.222	.323	.519	123	1	0		-1	1.000	-0	1-14	0.0
	KC-A	75	172	13	34	5	1	2	12	26	20	.198	.310	.273	55	-11	0	0	0	.977	-4	1-47	-1.7
	Yr	101	226	20	46	6	1	7	23	31	23	.204	.313	.332	71	-10	0		-1	.983	-4	1-61	-1.7
1957	Det-A	13	9	0	0	0	0	0	0	3	0	.000	.000	.000	-9	-1	0	0	0	1.000	0	/1-1	-0.1
	Cle-A	19	27	1	6	1	0	1	3	0	1	.222	.250	.370	68	-1	0	0	0	1.000	-0	/1-7	-0.1
	Bal-A	4	3	0	0	0	0	0	0	1	1	.000	.250	.000	-28	-1	0	0	0	1.000	0	H	-0.1
	Yr	36	39	1	6	1	0	1	3	4	2	.154	.267	.256	44	-3	0	0	0	1.000	-0	/1-8	-0.3
Total	13	1315	4282	546	1146	172	24	172	723	521	359	.268	.354	.440	113	73	10	12	-4	.990	-45	*1-1126	-1.1

■ YANK ROBINSON

Robinson, William H. b: 9/19/1859, Philadelphia, Pa. d: 8/25/1894, St.Louis, Mo. BR/TR, 5'6.5", 170 lbs. Deb: 8/24/1882

YEAR	TM/L	G	AB	R	H	2B	3B	HR	RBI	BB	SO	AVG	OBP	SLG	PRO+	BR/A	SB	CS	SBR	FA	FR	G/POS	TPR
1882	Det-N	11	39	1	7	1	0	0	2	1	13	.179	.200	.205	30	-3				.800	-4	S-10/O-1,P-1	-0.6
1884	Bal-U	102	415	101	111	24	4	2		37		.267	.327	.359	98	-14				.831	16	3-71,S-14,C-11,P/2	0.7
1885	*StL-a	78	287	63	75	8	8	0	35	29		.261	.344	.345	113	5				.862	-6	O-52,2-19/C-5,31	-0.1
1886	*StL-a	133	481	89	132	26	9	3	71	64		.274	.377	.385	132	19	51			.888	-2	*2-125/3-6,0-1,SP	1.8
1887	*StL-a	125	430	102	131	32	4	1	74	92		.305	.445	.405	125	17	75			.899	-13	*2-117/3-6,0-2,SCP	0.6
1888	*StL-a	134	455	111	105	17	6	3	53	116		.231	.400	.314	117	12	53			.895	-44	*2-102,S-34	-2.4
1889	StL-a	132	452	97	94	17	3	1	70	118	55	.208	.378	.292	81	-10	39			.887	-35	*2-132	-3.3
1890	Pit-P	98	306	59	70	10	3	0	38	101	33	.229	.434	.281	101	12	17			.887	-19	2-98	-0.1
1891	Cin-a	97	342	48	61	9	4	1	37	68	51	.178	.328	.237	57	-19	23			.867	-11	*2-97	-2.2
	StL-a	1	3	0	0	0	0	0	0	0	0	.000	.000	.000	-87	-1	0			.750	-1	/2-1	-0.1
	Yr	98	345	48	61	9	4	1	37	68	51	.177	.325	.235	56	-19	23			.866	-12	2-98	-2.3
1892	Was-N	67	218	26	39	4	3	0	19	58	28	.179	.301	.225	61	-9	11			.852	-4	3-58/S-5,2-4	-1.9
Total	10	978	3428	697	825	148	44	15	399	664	180	.241	.375	.323	101	11	272			.887	-124	2-698,3-143/SOCP1	-6.7

■ BILL ROBINSON

Robinson, William Henry b: 6/26/43, McKeesport, Pa. BR/TR, 6'3", 205 lbs. Deb: 9/20/66 C

YEAR	TM/L	G	AB	R	H	2B	3B	HR	RBI	BB	SO	AVG	OBP	SLG	PRO+	BR/A	SB	CS	SBR	FA	FR	G/POS	TPR
1966	Atl-N	6	11	1	3	1	0	0	1	0	0	.273	.273	.455	96	-0	0	0	0	.800	-1	/O-5	-0.2
1967	NY-A	116	342	31	67	6	1	7	29	28	56	.196	.254	.281	62	-16	2	2	-1	.968	-2	*O-102	-2.6
1968	NY-A	107	342	34	82	16	7	6	40	26	54	.240	.297	.380	107	2	7	6	-2	.985	-5	O-98	-1.3
1969	NY-A	87	222	23	38	11	2	3	21	16	39	.171	.227	.279	42	-18	3	1	0	.963	-3	O-62/1-1	-2.6
1972	Phi-N	82	188	19	45	9	1	8	21	5	30	.239	.259	.426	89	-4	2	4	-1	.982	-8	O-72	-1.1
1973	Phi-N	124	452	62	130	32	1	25	65	27	91	.288	.329	.529	131	16	5	4	-1	.979	-7	*O-113,3-14	0.4
1974	Phi-N	100	280	32	66	14	1	5	29	17	46	.236	.282	.346	72	-11	5	5	-1	.971	-4	O-87	-1.9
1975	*Pit-N	92	200	26	56	12	2	6	33	11	36	.280	.318	.450	112	5	3	5	0	.991	-2	O-57	-0.1
1976	Pit-N	122	393	55	119	22	3	21	64	16	73	.303	.332	.534	142	18	2	4	-2	.993	-12	O-78,3-37/1-3	0.2

YEAR	TM/L	G	AB	R	H	2B	3B	HR	RBI	BB	SO	AVG	OBP	SLG	PRO+	BR/A	SB	CS	SBR	FA	FR	G/POS	TPR
1977	Pit-N	137	507	74	154	32	1	26	104	25	92	.304	.340	.525	125	16	12	6	0	.992	-14	1-86,O-43,3-17	-0.5
1978	Pit-N	136	499	70	123	36	2	14	80	35	105	.246	.302	.411	93	-6	14	11	-2	.988	-4	*O-127,3-29/1-3	-1.8
1979	*Pit-N	148	421	59	111	17	6	24	75	24	81	.264	.305	.504	111	4	13	2	3	.982	-13	*O-125,1-28/3-3	-1.1
1980	Pit-N	100	272	28	78	10	1	12	36	15	45	.287	.324	.463	116	5	1	4	-2	.985	-10	1-49,O-41	-1.2
1981	Pit-N	39	88	8	19	3	0	2	8	5	18	.216	.258	.318	61	-5	1	0	0	1.000	-0	1-23/O-7,3-1	-0.6
1982	Pit-N	31	71	8	17	3	0	4	12	5	19	.239	.289	.451	101	-0	1	1	-1	1.000	-1	O-22	-0.2
	Phi-N	35	69	6	18	6	0	3	19	7	15	.261	.329	.478	121	2	1	1	-0	.960	-1	O-19/1-5	0.0
	Yr	66	140	14	35	9	0	7	31	12	34	.250	.309	.464	111	1	1	2	-1	.984	-1	O-41/1-5	-0.2
1983	Phi-N	10	7	0	1	0	0	0	2	1	4	.143	.250	.143	12	-1	0	0	0	1.000	-1	/1-3,3-2,O-1	-0.2
Total	16	1472	4364	536	1127	229	29	166	641	263	820	.258	.303	.438	104	4	71	49	-8	.979	-84	*O-1059,1-201,3-103	-14.8

■ RAFAEL ROBLES
Robles, Rafael Orlando (Natera) b: 10/20/47, San Pedro De Macoris, D.R. BR/TR, 6', 170 lbs. Deb: 4/8/69

YEAR	TM/L	G	AB	R	H	2B	3B	HR	RBI	BB	SO	AVG	OBP	SLG	PRO+	BR/A	SB	CS	SBR	FA	FR	G/POS	TPR
1969	SD-N	6	20	1	2	0	0	0	0	1	3	.100	.143	.100	-32	-4	1	1	-0	.895	-4	/S-6	-0.8
1970	SD-N	23	89	5	19	1	0	0	3	5	11	.213	.263	.225	33	-8	3	0	1	.968	2	S-23	-0.3
1972	SD-N	18	24	1	4	0	0	0	0	0	3	.167	.167	.167	-5	-3	0	0	0	.952	-2	S-15/3-1	-0.5
Total	3	47	133	7	25	1	0	0	3	6	17	.188	.229	.195	17	-15	4	1	1	.958	-4	/S-44,3-1	-1.6

■ SERGIO ROBLES
Robles, Sergio (Valenzuela) b: 4/16/46, Magdalena, Mexico BR/TR, 6'2", 190 lbs. Deb: 8/27/72

YEAR	TM/L	G	AB	R	H	2B	3B	HR	RBI	BB	SO	AVG	OBP	SLG	PRO+	BR/A	SB	CS	SBR	FA	FR	G/POS	TPR
1972	Bal-A	2	5	0	1	0	0	0	0	0	0	.200	.200	.200	19	-0	0	0	0	1.000	-1	/C-1	-0.2
1973	Bal-A	8	13	0	1	0	0	0	0	0	3	.077	.250	.077	-4	-2	0	0	0	1.000	3	/C-8	0.1
1976	LA-N	6	3	0	0	0	0	0	0	0	0	.000	.000	.000	-99	-1	0	0	0	1.000	1	/C-6	0.0
Total	3	16	21	0	2	0	0	0	0	0	3	.095	.208	.095	-11	-3	0	0	0	1.000	2	/C-15	-0.1

■ TOM ROBSON
Robson, Thomas James b: 1/15/46, Rochester, N.Y. BR/TR, 6'3", 215 lbs. Deb: 9/14/74 C

YEAR	TM/L	G	AB	R	H	2B	3B	HR	RBI	BB	SO	AVG	OBP	SLG	PRO+	BR/A	SB	CS	SBR	FA	FR	G/POS	TPR
1974	Tex-A	6	13	2	3	1	0	0	2	4	3	.231	.412	.308	112	0	0	0	0	1.000	-0	/1-1,D-5	0.0
1975	Tex-A	17	35	3	7	0	0	0	2	1	3	.200	.222	.200	20	-4	0	0	0	1.000	-0	/1-5,D-4	-0.4
Total	2	23	48	5	10	1	0	0	4	5	6	.208	.283	.229	48	-3	0	0	0	1.000	-0	/D-9,1-6	-0.4

■ ADAM ROCAP
Rocap, Adam b: 1854, Philadelphia, Pa. d: 3/29/1892, Philadelphia, Pa. 5'9", 170 lbs. Deb: 5/5/1875

YEAR	TM/L	G	AB	R	H	2B	3B	HR	RBI	BB	SO	AVG	OBP	SLG	PRO+	BR/A	SB	CS	SBR	FA	FR	G/POS	TPR
1875	Ath-n	16	69	13	12	1	0	0	4	1	7	.174	.186	.188	27	-5	3	2	-0	.839	-1	O-12/2-4	-0.6

■ MICKEY ROCCO
Rocco, Michael Dominick b: 3/2/16, St.Paul, Minn. BL/TL, 5'11", 188 lbs. Deb: 6/5/43

YEAR	TM/L	G	AB	R	H	2B	3B	HR	RBI	BB	SO	AVG	OBP	SLG	PRO+	BR/A	SB	CS	SBR	FA	FR	G/POS	TPR
1943	Cle-A	108	405	43	97	14	4	5	46	51	40	.240	.328	.331	99	-0	1	2	-1	**.995**	-5	*1-108	-1.4
1944	Cle-A	155	653	87	174	29	7	13	70	56	51	.266	.325	.392	108	5	4	8	-4	.993	17	*1-155	1.1
1945	Cle-A	143	565	81	149	28	6	10	56	52	40	.264	.326	.388	111	6	0	4	-2	**.992**	4	*1-141	-0.2
1946	Cle-A	34	98	8	24	2	0	2	14	15	15	.245	.345	.327	94	-0	1	1	-0	.996	5	1-27	0.3
Total	4	440	1721	219	444	73	17	30	186	174	146	.258	.327	.372	106	11	6	15	-7	.994	21	1-431	-0.2

■ JACK ROCHE
Roche, John Joseph "Red" b: 11/22/1890, Los Angeles, Cal. d: 3/30/83, Peoria, Ariz. BR/TR, 6'1", 178 lbs. Deb: 5/24/14

YEAR	TM/L	G	AB	R	H	2B	3B	HR	RBI	BB	SO	AVG	OBP	SLG	PRO+	BR/A	SB	CS	SBR	FA	FR	G/POS	TPR
1914	StL-N	12	9	1	6	2	1	0	3	0	1	.667	.700	1.111	441	4	1			.667	-2	/C-9	0.2
1915	StL-N	46	39	2	8	0	1	0	6	4	8	.205	.295	.256	68	-1	1			1.000	0	/C-4	-0.1
1917	StL-N	1	1	0	0	0	0	0	0	0	0	.000	.000	.000	-99	-0	0			.000	-1	/C-1	0.0
Total	3	59	49	3	14	2	2	0	9	4	9	.286	.364	.408	133	2	2			.750	-2	/C-14	0.0

■ BEN ROCHEFORT
Rochefort, Bennett Harold (b: Bennett Harold Rochefort Gilbert) b: 8/15/1896, Camden, N.J. d: 4/2/81, Red Bank, N.J. BL/TR, 6'2", 185 lbs. Deb: 10/3/14

YEAR	TM/L	G	AB	R	H	2B	3B	HR	RBI	BB	SO	AVG	OBP	SLG	PRO+	BR/A	SB	CS	SBR	FA	FR	G/POS	TPR
1914	Phi-A	1	2	0	1	0	0	0	1	0	0	.500	.500	.500	209	0	0			1.000	0	/1-1	0.1

■ LOU ROCHELLI
Rochelli, Louis Joseph b: 1/11/19, Staunton, Ill. d: 10/23/92, Victoria, Tex. BR/TR, 6'1", 175 lbs. Deb: 8/25/44

YEAR	TM/L	G	AB	R	H	2B	3B	HR	RBI	BB	SO	AVG	OBP	SLG	PRO+	BR/A	SB	CS	SBR	FA	FR	G/POS	TPR
1944	Bro-N	5	17	0	3	0	1	0	2	6	3	.176	.263	.294	58	-1	0			.964	-0	/2-5	-0.1

■ LES ROCK
Rock, Lester Henry (b: Lester Henry Schwarzrock) b: 8/19/12, Springfield, Minn. d: 9/9/91, Davis, Cal. BL/TR, 6'2", 184 lbs. Deb: 9/11/36

YEAR	TM/L	G	AB	R	H	2B	3B	HR	RBI	BB	SO	AVG	OBP	SLG	PRO+	BR/A	SB	CS	SBR	FA	FR	G/POS	TPR
1936	Chi-A	2	1	0	0	0	0	0	0	0	0	.000	.000	.000	-97	-0	0	0	0	.000	-0	/1-2	0.0

■ IKE ROCKENFIELD
Rockenfield, Isaac Broc b: 11/3/1876, Omaha, Neb. d: 2/21/27, San Diego, Cal. BR/TR, 5'7", 150 lbs. Deb: 5/5/05

YEAR	TM/L	G	AB	R	H	2B	3B	HR	RBI	BB	SO	AVG	OBP	SLG	PRO+	BR/A	SB	CS	SBR	FA	FR	G/POS	TPR
1905	StL-A	95	322	40	70	12	0	0	16	46		.217	.340	.255	95	-1	11			.926	-8	2-95	-0.6
1906	StL-A	27	89	3	21	4	0	0	8	1		.236	.277	.281	78	-2	0			.956	-5	2-26	-0.8
Total	2	122	411	43	91	16	0	0	24	47		.221	.328	.260	91	-1	11			.933	-14	2-121	-1.4

■ PAT ROCKETT
Rockett, Patrick Edward b: 1/9/55, San Antonio, Tex. BR/TR, 5'11", 170 lbs. Deb: 9/17/76

YEAR	TM/L	G	AB	R	H	2B	3B	HR	RBI	BB	SO	AVG	OBP	SLG	PRO+	BR/A	SB	CS	SBR	FA	FR	G/POS	TPR
1976	Atl-N	4	5	0	1	0	0	0	0	0	1	.200	.200	.200	13	-1	0	0	0	1.000	-1	/S-2	-0.2
1977	Atl-N	93	264	27	67	10	1	0	24	27	32	.254	.330	.303	64	-13	1	2	-1	.940	-11	S-84	-1.6
1978	Atl-N	55	142	6	20	2	0	1	4	13	12	.141	.213	.155	4	-18	1	2	-1	.970	-10	S-51	-2.6
Total	3	152	411	33	88	12	1	1	28	40	45	.214	.289	.251	43	-32	2	4	-2	.949	-21	S-137	-4.4

■ ANDRE RODGERS
Rodgers, Kenneth Andre Ian "Andy" b: 12/2/34, Nassau, Bahamas BR/TR, 6'3", 200 lbs. Deb: 4/16/57

YEAR	TM/L	G	AB	R	H	2B	3B	HR	RBI	BB	SO	AVG	OBP	SLG	PRO+	BR/A	SB	CS	SBR	FA	FR	G/POS	TPR
1957	NY-N	32	86	8	21	2	1	3	9	9	21	.244	.323	.395	92	-1	0	0	0	.950	5	S-20/3-8	0.6
1958	SF-N	22	63	7	13	3	1	2	11	4	14	.206	.254	.381	67	-3	0	0	0	.972	-3	S-18	-0.5
1959	SF-N	71	228	32	57	12	1	6	24	32	50	.250	.345	.390	98	-0	2	1	0	.933	-9	S-66	-0.4
1960	SF-N	81	217	22	53	8	5	2	22	24	44	.244	.328	.355	92	-2	1	1	-0	.953	-4	S-41,3-21/1-6,O-2	-0.4
1961	Chi-N	73	214	27	57	17	0	6	23	25	54	.266	.346	.430	103	1	1	1	-0	.983	1	1-42,S-24/O-2,2-1	-0.1
1962	Chi-N	138	461	40	128	20	8	5	44	44	93	.278	.344	.388	93	-4	5	6	-2	.960	7	*S-133/1-1	1.3
1963	Chi-N	150	516	51	118	17	4	3	33	65	90	.229	.325	.306	79	-12	5	7	-3	.954	-3	*S-150	-0.7
1964	Chi-N	129	448	50	107	17	3	12	46	53	88	.239	.319	.371	90	-5	5	1	1	.965	19	*S-126	2.4
1965	Pit-N	75	178	17	51	12	0	2	25	18	28	.287	.352	.388	108	2	2	1	0	.950	-6	S-33,3-15/1-6,2-1	-0.5
1966	Pit-N	36	49	6	9	1	0	0	4	8	14	.184	.298	.204	43	-4	0	0	-1	.913	-1	/S-5,3-3,O-3,1-2	-0.5
1967	Pit-N	47	61	8	14	3	0	2	8	8	18	.230	.319	.377	98	-0	1	2	-0	1.000	0	/1-9,3-5,S-3,2-2	0.2
Total	11	854	2521	268	628	112	23	45	245	290	507	.249	.331	.365	90	-29	22	20	-5	.956	9	S-619/1-66,3-52,O2	1.8

■ BUCK RODGERS
Rodgers, Robert Leroy b: 8/16/38, Delaware, Ohio BB/TR, 6'2", 195 lbs. Deb: 9/8/61 MC

YEAR	TM/L	G	AB	R	H	2B	3B	HR	RBI	BB	SO	AVG	OBP	SLG	PRO+	BR/A	SB	CS	SBR	FA	FR	G/POS	TPR
1961	LA-A	16	56	8	18	2	0	2	13	1	6	.321	.333	.464	99	-0	0	0	0	.965	-1	C-14	0.0
1962	LA-A	155	565	65	146	34	6	6	61	45	68	.258	.313	.372	86	-12	1	8	-5	.989	1	*C-150	-1.0
1963	LA-A	100	300	24	70	6	0	4	23	29	35	.233	.305	.293	73	-11	2	2	-1	.979	-14	*C-85	-2.4
1964	LA-A	148	514	38	125	18	3	4	54	40	71	.243	.303	.313	80	-15	4	3	-1	.987	14	*C-146	0.5
1965	Cal-A	132	411	33	86	14	3	1	32	35	61	.209	.276	.265	56	-23	4	5	-2	.991	6	*C-128	-1.4
1966	Cal-A	133	454	45	107	20	3	7	48	29	57	.236	.285	.339	81	-12	4	4	-1	.992	-4	*C-133	-1.1
1967	Cal-A	139	429	29	94	13	6	4	41	34	55	.219	.280	.305	76	-13	1	4	-2	.991	-0	*C-134/O-1	-0.7
1968	Cal-A	91	258	13	49	6	0	1	14	16	48	.190	.245	.225	45	-17	2	1	0	.985	0	C-87	-1.4
1969	Cal-A	18	46	4	9	1	0	2	4	5	8	.196	.288	.217	46	-3	0	0	0	1.000	-0	C-18	-0.3
Total	9	932	3033	259	704	114	18	31	288	234	409	.232	.291	.312	74	-107	17	27	-11	.988	3	C-895/O-1	-7.8

■ BILL RODGERS
Rodgers, Wilbur Kincaid "Rawmeat Bill" b: 4/18/1887, Pleasant Ridge, O. d: 12/24/78, Goliad, Tex. BL/TR, 5'9.5", 170 lbs. Deb: 4/15/15

YEAR	TM/L	G	AB	R	H	2B	3B	HR	RBI	BB	SO	AVG	OBP	SLG	PRO+	BR/A	SB	CS	SBR	FA	FR	G/POS	TPR
1915	Cle-A	16	45	8	14	2	0	0	7	8	7	.311	.415	.356	128	2	3	3	-1	.945	-4	2-13	-0.3
	Bos-A	11	6	2	0	0	0	0	0	3	0	.000	.333	.000	-0	-1	0			.900	1	2/-6	0.1
	Yr	27	51	10	14	2	0	0	7	11	9	.275	.403	.314	115	2	3			.938	-3	2-19	-0.2
	Cin-N	72	213	20	51	13	6	0	12	11	29	.239	.299	.338	91	-3	8	5	-1	.947	5	2-56/S-6,3-1,O-1	0.3
1916	Cin-N	3	4	0	0	0	0	0	0	0	0	.000	.000	.000	-99	-0	0	0	0	1.000	-0	/S-1	-0.1
Total	2	102	268	30	65	15	6	0	19	22	40	.243	.316	.328	93	-2	11	8		.945	2	/2-75,S-7,O-1,3-1	-0.1

■ BILL RODGERS
Rodgers, William Sherman b: 12/5/22, Harrisburg, Pa. BL/TL, 6', 162 lbs. Deb: 9/27/44

YEAR	TM/L	G	AB	R	H	2B	3B	HR	RBI	BB	SO	AVG	OBP	SLG	PRO+	BR/A	SB	CS	SBR	FA	FR	G/POS	TPR
1944	Pit-N	2	4	1	1	0	0	0	0	0	0	.250	.250	.250	39	-0	0			.000	-1	/O-1	-0.1
1945	Pit-N	1	1	0	1	0	0	0	0	0	0	1.000	1.000	1.000	440	0	0			.000	0	H	0.0
Total	2	3	5	1	2	0	0	0	0	0	0	.400	.400	.400	120	0	0			—	-1	/O-1	-0.1

YEAR	TM/L	G	AB	R	H	2B	3B	HR	RBI	BB	SO	AVG	OBP	SLG	PRO+	BR/A	SB	CS	SBR	FA	FR	G/POS	TPR
■ ERIC RODIN	Rodin, Eric Chapman b: 2/5/30, Orange, N.J. d: 1/4/91, Somerville, N.J. BR/TR, 6'2", 215 lbs. Deb: 9/7/54																						
1954	NY-N	5	6	0	0	0	0	0	0	0	2	.000	.000	.000	-99	-2	0	0	0	1.000	-1	/O-3	-0.3
■ ALEX RODRIGUEZ	Rodriguez, Alexander Emmanuel b: 7/27/75, New York, N.Y. BR/TR, 6'3", 190 lbs. Deb: 7/8/94																						
1994	Sea-A	17	54	4	11	0	0	0	2	3	20	.204	.246	.204	17	-7	3	0	1	.915	1	S-17	-0.3
1995	*Sea-A	48	142	15	33	6	2	5	19	6	42	.232	.264	.408	71	-7	4	2	0	.953	-2	S-46/D-1	-0.5
1996	Sea-A★	146	601	**141**	215	**54**	1	36	123	59	104	**.358**	.419	.631	161	55	15	4	2	.977	-10	*S-146	**5.4**
Total	3	211	797	160	259	60	3	41	144	68	166	.325	.381	.562	136	42	22	6	3	.968	-11	S-209/D-1	4.6
■ AURELIO RODRIGUEZ	Rodriguez, Aurelio (Ituarte) b: 12/28/47, Cananea, Mexico BR/TR, 5'10", 180 lbs. Deb: 9/1/67																						
1967	Cal-A	29	130	14	31	3	1	1	8	2	21	.238	.250	.300	64	-6	1	0	0	.989	5	3-29	-0.2
1968	Cal-A	76	223	14	54	10	1	1	16	17	36	.242	.299	.309	88	-3	0	2	-1	.921	-7	3-70/2-2	-1.3
1969	Cal-A	159	561	47	130	17	2	7	49	32	88	.232	.276	.307	66	-27	5	3	-0	.954	8	*3-159	-2.0
1970	Cal-A	17	63	6	17	2	0	0	7	3	6	.270	.313	.365	90	-1	0	1	-1	1.000	4	3-17	0.2
	Was-A	142	547	64	135	31	5	19	76	37	81	.247	.303	.426	104	0	15	5	2	.961	13	*3-136/S-7	1.4
	Yr	159	610	70	152	33	7	19	83	40	87	.249	.304	.420	102	-1	15	6	1	.965	17	*3-153/S-7	1.6
1971	Det-A	154	604	68	153	30	7	15	39	27	93	.253	.289	.401	90	-10	4	6	-2	.953	15	*3-153/S-1	0.1
1972	*Det-A	153	601	65	142	23	5	13	56	28	104	.236	.273	.356	83	-14	2	3	-1	.969	24	*3-153/S-2	0.9
1973	Det-A	160	555	46	123	27	3	9	58	31	85	.222	.267	.330	63	-28	3	1	0	.971	10	*3-160/S-1	-1.9
1974	Det-A	159	571	54	127	23	5	5	49	26	70	.222	.258	.306	60	-30	2	1	0	.961	22	*3-159	-1.0
1975	Det-A	151	507	47	124	20	6	13	60	30	63	.245	.287	.385	85	-12	1	1	-0	.953	21	*3-151	0.8
1976	Det-A	128	480	40	115	13	2	8	50	19	61	.240	.270	.325	71	-19	0	4	-2	**.978**	13	*3-128	-0.9
1977	Det-A	96	306	30	67	14	1	10	32	16	36	.219	.258	.369	65	-15	1	1	-0	.972	16	3-95/S-1	-0.1
1978	Det-A	134	385	40	102	25	2	7	43	19	37	.265	.305	.395	93	-5	0	1	-1	**.987**	2	*3-131	-0.5
1979	Det-A	106	343	27	87	18	0	5	36	11	40	.254	.279	.350	66	-17	0	2	-1	.956	5	*3-106/1-1	-1.4
1980	SD-N	89	175	7	35	7	2	2	13	6	26	.200	.227	.297	48	-13	1	1	0	.965	10	3-88/S-2	-0.4
	*NY-A	52	164	14	36	6	1	3	14	7	35	.220	.251	.323	57	-10	0	0	0	.954	-5	3-49/2-6	-1.6
1981	*NY-A	27	52	4	18	2	0	2	8	2	10	.346	.370	.500	151	3	0	0	0	.951	4	3-20/2-3,1-1,D-2	0.7
1982	Chi-A	118	257	24	62	15	1	3	31	11	35	.241	.275	.342	68	-11	0	0	0	.969	19	*3-112/2-3,S-2	0.6
1983	Bal-A	45	67	0	8	0	0	0	2	0	13	.119	.132	.119	-31	-12	0	0	0	.969	6	3-45	-1.1
	*Chi-A	22	20	1	4	1	0	1	1	0	3	.200	.200	.400	58	-1	0	0	0	1.000	4	3-22	0.3
	Yr	67	87	1	12	1	0	1	3	0	16	.138	.148	.184	-9	-13	0	0	0	.978	6	3-67	-0.8
Total	17	2017	6611	612	1570	287	46	124	648	324	943	.237	.276	.351	75	-232	35	31	-8	.964	183	*3-1983/S-16,2D1	-7.4
■ CARLOS RODRIGUEZ	Rodriguez, Carlos (Marquez) b: 11/1/67, Mexico City, Mexico BB/TR, 5'9", 160 lbs. Deb: 6/16/91																						
1991	NY-A	15	37	1	7	0	0	0	2	1	2	.189	.211	.189	11	-4	0	0	0	.957	1	S-11/2-3	-0.3
1994	Bos-A	57	174	15	50	14	1	1	13	11	13	.287	.330	.397	82	-5	1	0	0	.973	2	S-32,2-20/3-4	0.1
1995	Bos-A	13	30	5	10	2	0	0	5	2	2	.333	.394	.400	104	-0	0	0	0	.960	3	/2-7,S-6,3-1	0.4
Total	3	85	241	21	67	16	1	1	20	14	17	.278	.320	.365	75	-9	1	0	0	.972	6	/S-49,2-30,3-5	0.2
■ EDWIN RODRIGUEZ	Rodriguez, Edwin (Morales) b: 8/14/60, Ponce, P.R. BR/TR, 5'11", 175 lbs. Deb: 9/28/82																						
1982	NY-A	3	9	2	3	0	0	0	1	1	1	.333	.400	.333	106	0	0	0	0	.875	1	/2-3	0.1
1983	SD-N	7	12	1	2	1	0	0	0	1	3	.167	.231	.250	34	-1	0	0	0	1.000	-1	/2-5,S-2,3-1	-0.2
1985	SD-N	1	1	0	0	0	0	0	0	0	0	.000	.000	.000	-99	-0	0	0	0	.000	0	/H	0.0
Total	3	11	22	3	5	1	0	0	1	2	4	.227	.292	.273	58	-1	0	0	0	.935	0	/2-8,S-2,3-1	-0.1
■ ELLIE RODRIGUEZ	Rodriguez, Eliseo (Delgado) b: 5/24/46, Fajardo, P.R. BR/TR, 5'11", 185 lbs. Deb: 5/26/68																						
1968	NY-A	9	24	1	5	0	0	0	1	3	3	.208	.296	.208	57	-1	0	0	0	1.000	0	/C-9	0.0
1969	KC-A☆	95	267	27	63	10	0	2	20	31	36	.236	.333	.296	77	-7	3	2	-0	.990	-8	C-90	-1.2
1970	KC-A	80	231	25	52	8	2	1	15	27	35	.225	.317	.290	68	-9	2	1	0	.988	12	*C-75	0.6
1971	Mil-A	115	319	28	67	10	1	1	30	41	51	.210	.315	.257	64	-13	1	1	-0	.992	6	*C-114	-0.4
1972	Mil-A☆	116	355	31	101	14	2	2	35	52	43	.285	.386	.352	123	13	1	4	0	.983	-11	*C-114	0.5
1973	Mil-A	94	290	30	78	8	1	0	30	41	28	.269	.378	.303	96	1	4	3	-1	.986	4	C-75,D-14	0.7
1974	Cal-A	140	395	48	100	20	0	7	36	69	56	.253	.376	.357	119	13	4	5	-2	.992	-10	*C-137/D-1	0.8
1975	Cal-A	90	226	20	53	6	0	3	27	49	37	.235	.384	.301	103	4	2	2	-1	.991	-7	C-90	0.0
1976	LA-N	36	66	10	14	0	0	0	9	19	12	.212	.409	.212	82	0	0	0	0	.986	4	C-33	0.6
Total	9	775	2173	220	533	76	6	16	203	332	291	.245	.359	.308	94	0	17	18	-6	.989	-10	C-737/D-15	1.6
■ HECTOR RODRIGUEZ	Rodriguez, Hector Antonio (Ordenana) b: 6/13/20, Alquizar, Cuba BR/TR, 5'8", 165 lbs. Deb: 4/15/52																						
1952	Chi-A	124	407	55	108	14	1	1	40	47	22	.265	.346	.307	82	-8	7	6	-2	.959	2	*3-113	-1.0
■ HENRY RODRIGUEZ	Rodriguez, Henry Anderson (Lorenzo) b: 11/8/67, Santo Domingo, D.R. BL/TL, 6'1", 180 lbs. Deb: 7/5/92																						
1992	LA-N	53	146	11	32	7	0	3	14	8	30	.219	.260	.329	67	-7	0	0	0	.960	1	O-48/1-1	-0.7
1993	LA-N	76	176	20	39	10	0	8	23	11	39	.222	.267	.415	84	-5	1	0	0	.984	-6	O-48,1-13	-1.2
1994	LA-N	104	306	33	82	14	2	8	49	17	58	.268	.311	.405	91	-5	0	1	-1	.986	0	O-86,1-17	-0.8
1995	LA-N	21	80	6	21	4	1	1	10	5	17	.262	.306	.375	86	-2	0	1	-1	1.000	-1	O-20/1-1	-0.4
	Mon-N	24	58	7	12	0	0	5	6	11	.207	.281	.259	42	-5	0	0	0	1.000	-2	1-10/O-8	-0.8
	Yr	45	138	13	33	4	1	2	15	11	28	.239	.295	.326	65	-7	0	1	-1	.977	-2	O-28,1-11	-1.2
1996	Mon-N★	145	532	81	147	42	1	36	103	37	160	.276	.327	.562	126	17	2	0	1	.947	-9	O-89,1-51	0.1
Total	5	423	1298	158	333	77	4	57	204	84	315	.257	.304	.454	100	-7	3	2	-0	.970	-16	O-299/1-93	-3.8
■ IVAN RODRIGUEZ	Rodriguez, Ivan (Torres) "Pudge" b: 11/27/71, Manati, P.R. BR/TR, 5'9", 165 lbs. Deb: 6/20/91																						
1991	Tex-A	88	280	24	74	16	0	3	27	5	42	.264	.277	.354	75	-10	0	1	-1	.983	14	C-88	0.7
1992	Tex-A	123	420	39	109	16	1	8	37	24	73	.260	.301	.360	87	-8	0	0	0	.983	8	*C-116/D-2	0.7
1993	Tex-A★	137	473	56	129	28	4	10	66	29	70	.273	.320	.412	99	-2	8	7	-2	.991	6	*C-134/D-1	0.9
1994	Tex-A★	99	363	56	108	19	1	16	57	31	42	.298	.364	.488	117	9	6	3	0	.992	-4	C-99	1.0
1995	Tex-A★	130	492	56	149	32	2	12	67	16	48	.303	.330	.449	99	-3	0	2	-1	.990	-2	*C-127/D-1	0.3
1996	*Tex-A★	153	639	116	192	47	3	19	86	38	55	.300	.344	.473	97	-4	5	0	2	.989	10	*C-146/D-6	1.6
Total	6	730	2667	347	761	158	11	68	340	143	330	.285	.327	.429	97	-18	19	13	-2	.988	31	C-710/D-10	5.2
■ JOSE RODRIGUEZ	Rodriguez, Jose "El Hombre Goma" b: 2/23/1894, Havana, Cuba d: 1/21/53, Havana, Cuba BR/TR, 5'8", 150 lbs. Deb: 10/5/16																						
1916	NY-N	1	0	0	0	0	0	0	0	0	—	—	—	—	0	0	0	.000	0	R	0.0
1917	NY-N	7	20	2	4	0	1	0	2	2	1	.200	.273	.300	78	-1	2	1.000	-1	/1-7	-0.2
1918	NY-N	50	125	15	20	0	0	0	15	12	3	.160	.239	.192	33	-10	6	.978	4	2-40/1-8,3-2	-0.4
Total	3	58	145	17	24	0	1	0	17	14	4	.166	.244	.207	39	-10	8	.989	3	/2-40,1-15,3-2	-0.6
■ TONY RODRIGUEZ	Rodriguez, Luis Antonio b: 8/15/70, Rio Piedras, P.R. BR/TR, 5'11", 165 lbs. Deb: 7/6/96																						
1996	Bos-A	27	67	7	16	1	0	1	9	4	8	.239	.292	.299	48	-5	0	0	0	.979	5	S-21/3-5	0.2
■ RUBEN RODRIGUEZ	Rodriguez, Ruben Dario (Martinez) b: 8/4/64, Cabrera, D.R. BR/TR, 6'3", 190 lbs. Deb: 9/17/86																						
1986	Pit-N	2	3	0	0	0	0	0	0	0	0	.000	.000	.000	-98	-1	0	0	0	1.000	0	/C-2	0.0
1988	Pit-N	2	5	1	1	0	0	1	0	0	2	.200	.200	.600	123	0	0	0	0	1.000	0	/C-2	0.0
Total	2	4	8	1	1	0	1	0	0	2	.125	.125	.375	36	-1	0	0	0	1.000	1	/C-4	0.0
■ STEVE RODRIGUEZ	Rodriguez, Steven James b: 11/29/70, Las Vegas, Nev. BR/TR, 5'8", 170 lbs. Deb: 4/30/95																						
1995	Bos-A	6	8	1	1	0	0	0	0	1	1	.125	.222	.125	-6	-1	1	0	0	.667	-2	/S-4,2-1,D-1	-0.2
	Det-A	12	31	4	6	1	0	0	0	5	9	.194	.306	.226	41	-3	1	2	-1	.982	4	2-12/S-1	0.1
	Yr	18	39	5	7	1	0	0	0	6	10	.179	.289	.205	31	-4	2	2	-1	.983	2	2-13/S-5,D-1	-0.1
■ VIC RODRIGUEZ	Rodriguez, Victor Manuel (Rivera) b: 7/14/61, New York, N.Y. BR/TR, 5'11", 173 lbs. Deb: 9/5/84																						
1984	Bal-A	11	17	4	7	3	0	0	2	0	2	.412	.412	.588	177	2	0	0	0	.958	2	/2-7,D-1	0.3

YEAR	TM/L	G	AB	R	H	2B	3B	HR	RBI	BB	SO	AVG	OBP	SLG	PRO+	BR/A	SB	CS	SBR	FA	FR	G/POS	TPR
1989	Min-A	6	11	2	5	2	0	0	0	0	1	.455	.455	.636	191	1	0	0	0	.900	1	/3-5,D-1	0.2
Total	2	17	28	6	12	5	0	0	2	0	3	.429	.429	.607	183	3	0	0	0	.958	3	/2-7,3-5,D-2	0.5

■ GARY ROENICKE
Roenicke, Gary Steven b: 12/5/54, Covina, Cal. BR/TR, 6'3", 205 lbs. Deb: 6/8/76 F

YEAR	TM/L	G	AB	R	H	2B	3B	HR	RBI	BB	SO	AVG	OBP	SLG	PRO+	BR/A	SB	CS	SBR	FA	FR	G/POS	TPR
1976	Mon-N	29	90	9	20	3	1	2	5	4	18	.222	.263	.344	69	-4	0	0	0	.955	-1	O-25	-0.6
1978	Bal-A	27	58	5	15	3	0	3	15	8	3	.259	.358	.466	138	3	0	1	-1	1.000	-3	O-20	-0.1
1979	*Bal-A	133	376	60	98	16	1	25	64	61	74	.261	.381	.508	143	24	1	3	-2	1.000	-13	*O-130/D-2	0.9
1980	Bal-A	118	297	40	71	13	0	10	28	41	49	.239	.343	.384	100	1	2	0	1	1.000	-13	*O-113	-1.5
1981	Bal-A	85	219	31	59	16	3	3	20	23	29	.269	.344	.384	110	3	1	1	-1	.983	-13	O-83	-1.4
1982	Bal-A	137	393	58	106	25	1	21	74	70	73	.270	.392	.499	143	25	6	7	-2	.990	-9	*O-125,1-10	1.1
1983	*Bal-A	115	323	45	84	13	0	19	64	30	35	.260	.331	.477	121	9	2	2	-1	.982	-14	*O-100/1-7,3-2,D-2	-0.8
1984	Bal-A	121	326	36	73	19	1	10	44	58	43	.224	.348	.380	104	3	1	2	-1	.995	-10	*O-117	-1.1
1985	Bal-A	114	225	36	49	9	0	15	43	44	36	.218	.346	.458	121	7	2	2	-1	.993	-8	O-89,D-17	-0.4
1986	NY-A	69	136	11	36	5	0	3	18	27	30	.265	.390	.368	109	3	1	1	-0	1.000	-6	O-37,D-15/3-3,1-2	-0.4
1987	Atl-N	67	151	25	33	8	0	9	28	32	23	.219	.359	.450	107	2	0	0	0	.968	-4	O-44/1-9	-0.3
1988	Atl-N	49	114	11	26	5	0	1	7	8	15	.228	.279	.298	63	-5	0	0	0	1.000	-4	O-35/1-1	-1.1
Total	12	1064	2708	367	670	135	4	121	410	406	428	.247	.354	.434	117	70	16	20	-7	.988	-92	O-918/D-36,1-29,3-5	-5.7

■ RON ROENICKE
Roenicke, Ronald Jon b: 8/19/56, Covina, Cal. BB/TL, 6', 180 lbs. Deb: 9/2/81 F

YEAR	TM/L	G	AB	R	H	2B	3B	HR	RBI	BB	SO	AVG	OBP	SLG	PRO+	BR/A	SB	CS	SBR	FA	FR	G/POS	TPR
1981	LA-N	22	47	6	11	0	0	0	6	8	.234	.321	.234	62	-2	1	1	-0	1.000	-0	O-20	-0.3
1982	LA-N	109	143	18	37	8	0	1	12	21	24	.259	.361	.336	99	1	5	0	2	.984	-19	O-72	-1.9
1983	LA-N	81	145	12	32	4	0	2	12	14	26	.221	.289	.290	61	-8	3	2	-0	.987	-12	O-62	-2.2
	Sea-A	59	198	23	50	12	0	4	23	33	22	.253	.365	.374	100	1	6	2	1	.993	7	O-54/1-8,D-1	0.6
1984	*SD-N	12	20	4	6	1	0	1	2	2	5	.300	.364	.500	141	1	0	0	0	1.000	-2	O-10	-0.2
1985	SF-N	65	133	23	34	9	1	3	13	35	27	.256	.411	.406	136	8	6	2	1	.984	-1	O-35	0.7
1986	Phi-N	102	275	42	68	13	1	5	42	61	52	.247	.384	.356	102	3	2	2	-1	.989	-2	O-83	-0.2
1987	Phi-N	63	78	9	13	3	1	1	4	14	15	.167	.293	.269	49	-6	1	0	0	.964	-6	O-26	-1.2
1988	Cin-N	14	37	4	5	1	0	0	4	5	6	.135	.238	.162	16	-4	0	0	0	1.000	-2	O-14	-0.7
Total	8	527	1076	141	256	51	3	17	113	190	195	.238	.355	.338	92	-5	24	9	2	.989	-37	O-376/1-8,D-1	-5.4

■ OSCAR ROETTGER
Roettger, Oscar Frederick Louis "Okkie" b: 2/19/1900, St.Louis, Mo. d: 7/4/86, St.Louis, Mo. BR/TR, 6', 170 lbs. Deb: 7/7/23 F

YEAR	TM/L	G	AB	R	H	2B	3B	HR	RBI	BB	SO	AVG	OBP	SLG	PRO+	BR/A	SB	CS	SBR	FA	FR	G/POS	TPR
1923	NY-A	5	2	0	0	0	0	0	0	0	0	.000	.000	.000	-98	-1	0	0	0	1.000	0	/P-5	0.0
1924	NY-A	1	0	0	0	0	0	0	0	0	0	—	—	—	—	0	0	0	0	.000	0	/P-1	0.0
1927	Bro-N	5	4	0	0	0	0	0	0	0	1	.000	.333	.000	-4	-0	0	0	0	.000	-1	/O-1	-0.1
1932	Phi-A	26	60	7	14	1	0	0	6	5	4	.233	.292	.250	40	-5	0	0	0	.978	-2	1-15	-0.7
Total	4	37	66	7	14	1	0	0	6	6	5	.212	.288	.227	34	-6	0	0	0	1.000	-2	/1-15,P-6,O-1	-0.8

■ WALLY ROETTGER
Roettger, Walter Henry b: 8/28/02, St.Louis, Mo. d: 9/14/51, Champaign, Ill. BR/TR, 6'1.5", 190 lbs. Deb: 5/1/27 F

YEAR	TM/L	G	AB	R	H	2B	3B	HR	RBI	BB	SO	AVG	OBP	SLG	PRO+	BR/A	SB	CS	SBR	FA	FR	G/POS	TPR
1927	StL-N	5	1	0	0	0	0	0	0	0	1	.000	.500	.000	42	0	0			.500	-1	/O-3	-0.1
1928	StL-N	68	261	27	89	17	4	6	44	10	22	.341	.372	.506	125	9	2			.981	-1	O-66	0.4
1929	StL-N	79	269	27	68	11	3	3	42	13	27	.253	.287	.349	56	-19	0			.993	-4	O-69	-2.5
1930	NY-N	121	420	51	119	15	5	5	51	25	29	.283	.330	.379	72	-19	1			.992	-6	*O-114	-2.9
1931	Cin-N	44	185	25	65	11	4	1	20	7	9	.351	.378	.470	135	8	1			.990	-1	O-44	0.4
	*StL-N	45	151	16	43	12	2	0	17	9	14	.285	.337	.391	92	-2	0			.974	-6	O-42	-1.1
	Yr	89	336	41	108	23	6	1	37	16	23	.321	.360	.435	114	6	1			.983	-7	O-86	-0.7
1932	Cin-N	106	347	26	96	18	3	3	43	23	24	.277	.323	.372	89	-5	0			.991	-9	O-94	-1.2
1933	Cin-N	84	209	13	50	7	1	0	17	8	10	.239	.267	.297	62	-11	0			.977	0	O-55	-1.4
1934	Pit-N	47	106	7	26	5	1	0	11	3	8	.245	.266	.311	53	-7	0			1.000	1	O-23	-0.7
Total	8	599	1949	192	556	96	23	19	245	99	143	.285	.324	.387	85	-46	4			.986	-19	O-510	-9.1

■ ED ROETZ
Roetz, Edward Bernard b: 8/6/05, Philadelphia, Pa. d: 3/16/65, Philadelphia, Pa. BR/TR, 5'10", 160 lbs. Deb: 5/26/29

YEAR	TM/L	G	AB	R	H	2B	3B	HR	RBI	BB	SO	AVG	OBP	SLG	PRO+	BR/A	SB	CS	SBR	FA	FR	G/POS	TPR
1929	StL-A	16	45	7	11	4	1	0	5	4	6	.244	.306	.378	72	-2				.909	-1	/S-8,1-5,2-3,1	-0.2

■ BILLY ROGELL
Rogell, William George b: 11/24/04, Springfield, Ill. BB/TR, 5'10.5", 163 lbs. Deb: 4/14/25

YEAR	TM/L	G	AB	R	H	2B	3B	HR	RBI	BB	SO	AVG	OBP	SLG	PRO+	BR/A	SB	CS	SBR	FA	FR	G/POS	TPR
1925	Bos-A	58	169	12	33	5	1	0	17	11	17	.195	.244	.237	22	-20	0	3	-2	.935	6	2-49/S-6	-1.4
1927	Bos-A	82	207	35	55	14	6	2	28	24	28	.266	.342	.420	99	-1	3	1	0	.966	6	3-53/2-2,O-2	0.7
1928	Bos-A	102	296	33	69	10	4	0	29	22	47	.233	.295	.294	56	-19	2	6	-3	.935	-13	S-67,2-22/O-6,3-3	-2.7
1930	Det-A	54	144	20	24	4	2	0	9	15	23	.167	.250	.222	20	-18	1	2	-1	.938	4	S-33,3-13/O-1	-1.0
1931	Det-A	48	185	21	56	12	3	2	24	24	17	.303	.383	.432	110	3	8	8	-2	.958	11	S-48	1.5
1932	Det-A	144	554	88	150	29	6	6	61	50	38	.271	.332	.394	84	-14	14	6	1	.944	8	*S-139/3-4	0.6
1933	Det-A	155	587	67	173	42	11	0	57	79	34	.295	.381	.404	106	7	6	9	-4	.944	20	*S-155	3.2
1934	*Det-A	154	592	114	175	32	8	3	100	74	36	.296	.374	.392	97	-1	13	3	2	.962	9	*S-154	1.8
1935	*Det-A	150	560	88	154	23	11	6	71	80	29	.275	.367	.387	99	0	3	6	-3	.971	12	*S-150	1.7
1936	Det-A	146	585	85	160	27	5	6	68	73	41	.274	.357	.368	79	-19	14	10	-2	.965	-1	*S-146/3-1	-1.1
1937	Det-A	146	536	85	148	30	7	8	64	83	48	.276	.376	.403	94	-3	5	5	-2	.967	8	*S-146	0.7
1938	Det-A	136	501	76	130	22	8	3	55	86	37	.259	.373	.353	78	-15	9	2	2	.959	6	*S-134	0.4
1939	Det-A	74	174	24	40	6	3	2	23	26	14	.230	.330	.333	65	-9	3	1	0	.931	-2	S-43,3-21/2-2	-0.3
1940	Chi-N	33	59	7	8	0	0	1	3	2	8	.136	.164	.186	-4	-8	1			.900	-5	S-14/3-9,2-3	-1.3
Total	14	1482	5149	755	1375	256	75	42	609	649	416	.267	.351	.370	84	-115	82	62		.956	68	*S-1235,3-104/20	2.8

■ EMMETT ROGERS
Rogers, Emmett b: 1865, Rome, N.Y. BB, 5'10", 165 lbs. Deb: 4/19/1890

YEAR	TM/L	G	AB	R	H	2B	3B	HR	RBI	BB	SO	AVG	OBP	SLG	PRO+	BR/A	SB	CS	SBR	FA	FR	G/POS	TPR
1890	Tol-a	35	110	18	19	3	3	0	7	14		.173	.266	.255	52	-7	2			.924	5	C-34/O-1	0.1

■ FRALEY ROGERS
Rogers, Fraley W. b: 1850, Brooklyn, N.Y. d: 5/10/1881, New York, N.Y. 5'8", 184 lbs. Deb: 4/30/1872

YEAR	TM/L	G	AB	R	H	2B	3B	HR	RBI	BB	SO	AVG	OBP	SLG	PRO+	BR/A	SB	CS	SBR	FA	FR	G/POS	TPR
1872	Bos-n	45	204	39	56	7	1	1	28	1	4	.275	.278	.333	83	-5	2	0	1	.790	-2	*O-41/1-6	-0.3
1873	Bos-n	1	6	1	2	1	0	0	2	0	1	.333	.333	.500	133	0	0	0	0	.813	-1	/1-1	0.0
Total	2 n	46	210	40	58	8	1	1	30	1	5	.276	.280	.338	84	-5	2	0	1	.893	-2	/O-41,1-7	-0.3

■ JIM ROGERS
Rogers, James F. b: 4/9/1872, Hartford, Conn. 5'7.5", 180 lbs. Deb: 4/17/1896 M

YEAR	TM/L	G	AB	R	H	2B	3B	HR	RBI	BB	SO	AVG	OBP	SLG	PRO+	BR/A	SB	CS	SBR	FA	FR	G/POS	TPR
1896	Was-N	38	154	21	43	6	4	1	30	10	9	.279	.323	.390	87	-3	3			.882	-6	3-32/2-6,O-1	-0.7
	Lou-N	72	290	39	75	8	6	0	38	15	14	.259	.297	.328	67	-14	13			.971	-2	1-60,S-12	-1.3
	Yr	110	444	60	118	14	10	1	68	25	23	.266	.306	.349	74	-17	16			.971	-8	1-60,3-32,S-12,/20	-2.0
1897	Lou-N	41	150	22	22	3	2	2	22	22		.147	.260	.233	32	-15	4			.933	-4	2-39/1-3,M	-1.5
Total	2	151	594	82	140	17	12	3	90	47	23	.236	.294	.320	64	-32	20			.970	-12	/1-63,2-45,3-32,SO	-3.5

■ JAY ROGERS
Rogers, Jay Lewis b: 8/3/1888, Sandusky, N.Y. d: 7/1/64, Carlisle, N.Y. BR/TR, 5'11.5", 178 lbs. Deb: 5/22/14

YEAR	TM/L	G	AB	R	H	2B	3B	HR	RBI	BB	SO	AVG	OBP	SLG	PRO+	BR/A	SB	CS	SBR	FA	FR	G/POS	TPR
1914	NY-A	5	8	0	0	0	0	0	0	0	4	.000	.000	.000	-99	-2	0			.923	-0	/C-4	-0.2

■ PACKY ROGERS
Rogers, Stanley Frank (b: Stanley Frank Hazinski) b: 4/26/13, Swoyersville, Pa. BR/TR, 5'8", 175 lbs. Deb: 7/12/38

YEAR	TM/L	G	AB	R	H	2B	3B	HR	RBI	BB	SO	AVG	OBP	SLG	PRO+	BR/A	SB	CS	SBR	FA	FR	G/POS	TPR
1938	Bro-N	23	37	3	7	1	1	0	5	6	7	.189	.302	.270	57	-2	0			1.000	-1	/S-9,3-8,2-3,O-1	-0.2

■ MIKE ROGODZINSKI
Rogodzinski, Michael George b: 2/22/48, Evanston, Ill. BL/TR, 6', 185 lbs. Deb: 5/4/73

YEAR	TM/L	G	AB	R	H	2B	3B	HR	RBI	BB	SO	AVG	OBP	SLG	PRO+	BR/A	SB	CS	SBR	FA	FR	G/POS	TPR
1973	Phi-N	66	80	13	19	2	7	12	19	.237	.337	.350	88	-1	0	0	0	.947	-3	O-16	-0.4
1974	Phi-N	17	15	1	1	0	0	0	1	2	9	.067	.176	.067	-29	-3	0	0	0	.000	-0	/O-1	-0.3
1975	Phi-N	16	19	3	5	1	0	0	1	3	4	.263	.364	.316	86	-0	0	1	-1	.667	-1	/O-2	-0.2
Total	3	99	114	17	25	4	0	2	12	17	24	.219	.321	.307	73	-4	0	1	-1	.909	-4	/O-19	-0.9

■ DAVE ROHDE
Rohde, David Grant b: 5/8/64, Los Altos, Cal. BB/TR, 6'2", 180 lbs. Deb: 4/9/90

YEAR	TM/L	G	AB	R	H	2B	3B	HR	RBI	BB	SO	AVG	OBP	SLG	PRO+	BR/A	SB	CS	SBR	FA	FR	G/POS	TPR
1990	Hou-N	59	98	8	18	4	0	0	5	9	20	.184	.286	.224	44	-7	0	0	0	1.000	-0	2-32/3-4,S-2	-0.7
1991	Hou-N	29	41	3	5	0	0	0	0	5	8	.122	.217	.122	-2	-6	0	0	0	1.000	1	/2-4,3-3,S-3,1-1	-0.5
1992	Cle-A	5	7	0	0	0	0	0	0	2	3	.000	.222	.000	-34	-0	0	0	0	.900	1	/3-5	-0.1
Total	3	93	146	11	23	4	0	0	5	16	31	.158	.263	.185	27	-14	0	0	0	1.000	2	/2-36,3-12,S-5,1-1	-1.3

YEAR	TM/L	G	AB	R	H	2B	3B	HR	RBI	BB	SO	AVG	OBP	SLG	PRO+	BR/A	SB	CS	SBR	FA	FR	G/POS	TPR

■ GEORGE ROHE   Rohe, George Anthony "Whitey"   b: 9/15/1875, Cincinnati, Ohio   d: 6/10/57, Cincinnati, Ohio   BR/TR, 5'9", 165 lbs.   Deb: 5/7/01

YEAR	TM/L	G	AB	R	H	2B	3B	HR	RBI	BB	SO	AVG	OBP	SLG	PRO+	BR/A	SB	CS	SBR	FA	FR	G/POS	TPR
1901	Bal-A	14	36	7	10	2	0	0	4	5		.278	.381	.333	95	-0				.912	-3	/1-8,3-6	-0.2
1905	Chi-A	34	113	14	24	1	0	1	12	12		.212	.310	.248	81	-2	2			.934	-4	2-17,3-17	-0.5
1906	*Chi-A	77	225	14	58	5	1	0	25	16		.258	.316	.289	92	-2	8			.926	2	3-57/2-5,O-1	0.2
1907	Chi-A	144	494	46	105	11	2	2	51	39		.213	.274	.255	71	-15	16			.898	-5	3-76,2-39,S-30	-1.9
Total	4	269	868	81	197	19	3	3	92	72		.227	.294	.266	79	-19	27			.917	-9	3-156/2-61,S-30,10	-2.4

■ DAN ROHN   Rohn, Daniel Jay   b: 1/10/56, Alpena, Mich.   BL/TR, 5'7", 165 lbs.   Deb: 9/2/83

YEAR	TM/L	G	AB	R	H	2B	3B	HR	RBI	BB	SO	AVG	OBP	SLG	PRO+	BR/A	SB	CS	SBR	FA	FR	G/POS	TPR
1983	Chi-N	23	31	3	12	3	2	0	6	2	2	.387	.424	.613	176	3	1	0	0	.923	-0	/2-6,S-1	0.3
1984	Chi-N	25	31	1	4	0	0	1	3	1	6	.129	.156	.226	6	-4	0	0	0	1.000	0	/3-7,2-5,S-5	-0.4
1986	Cle-A	6	10	1	2	0	0	0	2	1	1	.200	.273	.200	32	-1	0	0	0	.900	1	/2-2,3-2,S-1	0.0
Total	3	54	72	5	18	3	2	1	11	4	9	.250	.289	.389	82	-2	1	0	0	.930	1	/2-13,3-9,S-7	-0.1

■ RAY ROHWER   Rohwer, Ray   b: 6/5/1895, Dixon, Cal.   d: 1/24/88, Davis, Cal.   BL/TL, 5'10", 155 lbs.   Deb: 4/13/21

YEAR	TM/L	G	AB	R	H	2B	3B	HR	RBI	BB	SO	AVG	OBP	SLG	PRO+	BR/A	SB	CS	SBR	FA	FR	G/POS	TPR
1921	Pit-N	30	40	6	10	0	0	6	4	8		.250	.318	.425	93	-1	0	1	-1	.842	-1	O-10	-0.3
1922	Pit-N	53	129	19	38	6	3	3	22	10	17	.295	.350	.457	105	1	1	0	0	.938	0	O-30	-0.1
Total	2	83	169	25	48	9	5	3	28	14	25	.284	.342	.450	102	0	1	1	-0	.917	-1	/O-40	-0.4

■ TONY ROIG   Roig, Anton Ambrose   b: 12/23/27, New Orleans, La.   BR/TR, 6'1", 180 lbs.   Deb: 9/13/53

YEAR	TM/L	G	AB	R	H	2B	3B	HR	RBI	BB	SO	AVG	OBP	SLG	PRO+	BR/A	SB	CS	SBR	FA	FR	G/POS	TPR
1953	Was-A	3	8	0	1	0	0	0	0	1		.125	.125	.250	-1	-1	0	0	0	1.000	2	/2-2	0.0
1955	Was-A	29	57	3	13	1	1	0	4	2	15	.228	.254	.281	46	-5	0	0	0	.932	1	S-21/3-8,2-1	-0.3
1956	Was-A	44	119	11	25	5	2	0	7	20	29	.210	.324	.286	62	-6	2	0	1	.973	7	2-27,S-19	0.4
Total	3	76	184	14	39	7	3	0	11	22	45	.212	.296	.283	55	-12	2	0	1	.927	9	/S-40,2-30,3-8	0.1

■ COOKIE ROJAS   Rojas, Octavio Victor (Rivas)   b: 3/6/39, Havana, Cuba   BR/TR, 5'10", 170 lbs.   Deb: 4/10/62   MC

YEAR	TM/L	G	AB	R	H	2B	3B	HR	RBI	BB	SO	AVG	OBP	SLG	PRO+	BR/A	SB	CS	SBR	FA	FR	G/POS	TPR
1962	Cin-N	39	86	9	19	6	0	9	6	9	4	.221	.302	.244	47	-6	1	1	-0	.949	-2	2-30/3-1	-0.6
1963	Phi-N	64	77	18	17	0	1	1	2	3	8	.221	.259	.286	57	-4	4	1	1	.991	16	2-25/O-1	1.5
1964	Phi-N	109	340	58	99	19	5	2	31	22	17	.291	.338	.394	107	3	1	3	-2	.967	-11	O-70,2-20,S-18/C3	-1.1
1965	Phi-N★	142	521	78	158	25	3	3	42	42	33	.303	.359	.380	110	8	5	5	-2	.986	-3	2-84,O-55,S-11/C1	0.9
1966	Phi-N	156	626	77	168	18	1	6	55	35	46	.268	.311	.329	78	-18	4	6	-2	.983	-9	*2-106,O-56/S-2	-2.6
1967	Phi-N	147	528	60	137	21	2	4	45	30	58	.259	.299	.330	79	-14	8	4	0	.977	-4	*2-137/O-9,C-3,SP3	-1.1
1968	Phi-N	152	621	53	144	19	0	9	48	16	55	.232	.251	.306	67	-26	4	8	-4	.987	11	*2-150/C-1	-1.2
1969	Phi-N	110	391	35	89	11	1	4	30	23	28	.228	.272	.292	60	-22	1	6	-3	.980	-3	2-95/O-2	-2.2
1970	StL-N	23	47	2	5	0	0	0	2	3	4	.106	.176	.106	-22	-8	0	0	0	1.000	0	2-10/O-3,S-2	-0.7
	KC-A	98	384	36	100	13	3	2	28	20	29	.260	.297	.326	72	-15	3	7	-3	.982	-1	2-97	-1.1
1971	KC-A★	115	414	56	124	22	6	6	59	39	35	.300	.363	.406	118	10	8	3	1	**.991**	-12	*2-111/S-2,O-1	0.9
1972	KC-A★	137	487	49	127	25	3	0	53	41	35	.261	.319	.331	94	-3	2	8	-4	.986	-2	*2-131/3-6,S-2	-0.2
1973	KC-A★	139	551	78	152	29	3	6	69	37	38	.276	.323	.372	88	-9	18	4	3	.982	9	*2-137	1.1
1974	KC-A☆	144	542	52	147	17	1	6	60	30	43	.271	.313	.339	83	-12	8	4	0	**.987**	-24	*2-141	-3.1
1975	KC-A	120	406	34	103	18	2	2	37	30	24	.254	.305	.323	75	-13	4	5	-2	.980	-15	*2-117/D-1	-2.5
1976	*KC-A	63	132	11	32	6	0	0	16	8	15	.242	.286	.288	68	-5	2	0	1	1.000	-13	2-40/3-6,1-1,D-9	-1.7
1977	*KC-A	64	156	8	39	9	1	0	10	8	17	.250	.287	.321	65	-8	1	3	-2	.944	3	3-31,2-16/D-6	-0.5
Total	16	1822	6309	714	1660	254	25	54	593	396	489	.263	.309	.337	83	-144	74	68	-19	.984	-60	*2-1447,O-197/3SDC1P	-14.2

■ STAN ROJEK   Rojek, Stanley Andrew   b: 4/21/19, N.Tonawanda, N.Y.   BR/TR, 5'10", 170 lbs.   Deb: 9/22/42

YEAR	TM/L	G	AB	R	H	2B	3B	HR	RBI	BB	SO	AVG	OBP	SLG	PRO+	BR/A	SB	CS	SBR	FA	FR	G/POS	TPR
1942	Bro-N	1	0	1	0	0	0	0	0	0		—	—	—		0	0			.000	0	R	0.0
1946	Bro-N	45	47	11	13	2	1	0	2	4	1	.277	.333	.362	96	-0	1			.974	5	S-15/2-6,3-4	0.6
1947	Bro-N	32	80	7	21	0	1	0	7	7	3	.262	.322	.287	61	-4	1			.971	8	S-17/3-9,2-7	0.4
1948	Pit-N	156	641	85	186	27	5	4	51	61	41	.290	.355	.367	94	-4	24			.962	-9	*S-156	-0.4
1949	Pit-N	144	557	72	136	19	2	0	31	50	31	.244	.309	.285	59	-31	4			.966	1	*S-144	-2.0
1950	Pit-N	76	230	28	59	12	1	0	17	18	13	.257	.313	.317	64	-12	2			.967	-15	S-68/2-3	-2.2
1951	Pit-N	8	16	0	3	0	0	0	0	0	0	.188	.188	.188	1	-2	0	0	0	.900	-1	/S-8	-0.3
	StL-N	51	186	21	51	7	3	0	14	10	10	.274	.318	.344	78	-6	0	3	-2	.974	1	S-51	-0.4
	Yr	59	202	21	54	7	3	0	14	10	11	.267	.308	.332	72	-8	0	3	-2	.968	-3	S-59	-0.7
1952	StL-A	9	7	0	1	0	0	0	0	2	0	.143	.333	.143	35	-1	0	0	0	1.000	2	/S-4,2-1	0.1
Total	8	522	1764	225	470	67	13	4	122	152	100	.266	.327	.326	74	-61	32	3		.965	-9	S-463/2-17,3-13	-4.2

■ SCOTT ROLEN   Rolen, Scott Bruce   b: 4/4/75, Evansville, Ind.   BR/TR, 6'4", 210 lbs.   Deb: 8/1/96

YEAR	TM/L	G	AB	R	H	2B	3B	HR	RBI	BB	SO	AVG	OBP	SLG	PRO+	BR/A	SB	CS	SBR	FA	FR	G/POS	TPR
1996	Phi-N	37	130	10	33	7	0	4	18	13	27	.254	.326	.400	88	-2	0	2	-1	.954	-7	3-37	-1.1

■ RED ROLFE   Rolfe, Robert Abial   b: 10/17/08, Penacook, N.H.   d: 7/8/69, Gilford, N.H.   BL/TR, 5'11.5", 170 lbs.   Deb: 6/29/31   MC

YEAR	TM/L	G	AB	R	H	2B	3B	HR	RBI	BB	SO	AVG	OBP	SLG	PRO+	BR/A	SB	CS	SBR	FA	FR	G/POS	TPR
1931	NY-A	1	0	0	0	0	0	0	0	0	0	—	—	—		0	0	0	0	1.000	-0	/S-1	0.0
1934	NY-A	89	279	54	80	13	2	0	18	26	16	.287	.348	.348	86	-6	2	3	-1	.944	4	S-46,3-26	0.0
1935	NY-A	149	639	108	192	33	9	5	67	57	39	.300	.361	.404	103	3	7	3	0	**.964**	-7	*3-136,S-17	0.2
1936	*NY-A	135	568	116	181	39	**15**	10	70	68	38	.319	.392	.493	121	18	3	0	1	**.957**	3	*3-133	2.4
1937	*NY-A★	154	648	143	179	34	10	4	62	90	53	.276	.365	.378	87	-11	4	2	0	.962	5	*3-154	-0.2
1938	*NY-A☆	151	631	132	196	36	8	10	80	74	44	.311	.386	.441	107	8	13	1	3	.959	-7	*3-151	0.6
1939	*NY-A★	152	648	**139**	**213**	**46**	10	14	80	81	41	.329	.404	.495	131	31	7	6	-2	.958	-15	*3-152	1.5
1940	NY-A†	139	588	102	147	26	6	10	53	50	48	.250	.311	.366	78	-20	7	2	-0	.949	-1	*3-138	-1.7
1941	*NY-A	136	561	106	148	22	5	8	42	57	38	.264	.332	.364	85	-12	3	2	-0	.946	-10	*3-134	-1.9
1942	*NY-A	69	265	42	58	8	2	8	25	21	20	.219	.281	.355	80	-8	1	1	-0	.959	5	3-60	-0.3
Total	10	1175	4827	942	1394	257	67	69	497	526	335	.289	.360	.413	100	2	44	20	1	.956	-22	*3-1084/S-64	0.6

■ RAY ROLLING   Rolling, Raymond Copeland   b: 9/8/1886, Martinsburg, Mo.   d: 8/25/66, St.Paul, Minn.   BR/TR, 5'10.5", 160 lbs.   Deb: 9/6/12

YEAR	TM/L	G	AB	R	H	2B	3B	HR	RBI	BB	SO	AVG	OBP	SLG	PRO+	BR/A	SB	CS	SBR	FA	FR	G/POS	TPR
1912	StL-N	5	15	0	3	0	0	0	0	0	5	.200	.200	.200	10	-2	0			.947	0	/2-4	-0.2

■ RED ROLLINGS   Rollings, William Russell   b: 3/21/04, Mobile, Ala.   d: 12/31/64, Mobile, Ala.   BL/TR, 5'11", 167 lbs.   Deb: 4/17/27

YEAR	TM/L	G	AB	R	H	2B	3B	HR	RBI	BB	SO	AVG	OBP	SLG	PRO+	BR/A	SB	CS	SBR	FA	FR	G/POS	TPR
1927	Bos-A	82	184	19	49	4	1	0	9	12	10	.266	.325	.299	64	-9	3	1		.938	-5	3-44,1-10/2-2	-1.2
1928	Bos-A	50	48	7	11	3	1	0	9	6	8	.229	.315	.333	72	-2	0	0	0	1.000	-2	/1-5,2-4,O-4,3-1	-0.4
1930	Bos-N	52	123	10	29	6	0	0	10	9	5	.236	.288	.285	40	-12	2			.973	3	3-28,2-10	-0.7
Total	3	184	355	36	89	13	2	0	28	27	23	.251	.311	.299	57	-23	5	1		.947	-5	/3-73,2-16,1-15,O-4	-2.3

■ RICH ROLLINS   Rollins, Richard John "Red"   b: 4/16/38, Mount Pleasant, Pa.   BR/TR, 5'10", 185 lbs.   Deb: 6/16/61

YEAR	TM/L	G	AB	R	H	2B	3B	HR	RBI	BB	SO	AVG	OBP	SLG	PRO+	BR/A	SB	CS	SBR	FA	FR	G/POS	TPR
1961	Min-A	13	17	3	5	1	0	0	3	2	2	.294	.400	.353	98	0	0	0	0	1.000	1	/2-5,3-4	0.1
1962	Min-A★	159	624	96	186	23	5	16	96	75	61	.298	.379	.428	112	13	3	1	0	.943	-5	*3-159/S-1	1.0
1963	Min-A	136	531	75	163	23	1	16	61	36	59	.307	.360	.444	122	15	2	0	1	.935	-7	*3-132/2-1	1.0
1964	Min-A	148	596	87	161	25	**10**	12	68	53	80	.270	.335	.406	104	3	2	5	-2	.947	-2	*3-146	-0.3
1965	*Min-A	140	469	59	117	22	1	5	32	37	54	.249	.310	.333	79	-12	4	0	1	.958	-4	*3-112,2-16	-1.7
1966	Min-A	90	269	30	66	7	1	10	40	13	34	.245	.290	.390	88	-5	0	2	-1	.953	-6	3-65/2-2,O-1	-1.2
1967	Min-A	109	339	31	83	11	2	6	39	27	58	.245	.306	.342	84	-6	1	1	0	.963	-10	3-97	-1.9
1968	Min-A	93	203	14	49	5	0	6	30	10	34	.241	.287	.355	89	-2	2	0	1	.931	-2	3-56	-0.5
1969	Sea-A	58	187	15	42	9	0	4	21	7	19	.225	.271	.326	68	-9	2	0	1	.948	3	3-47/S-1	-0.5
1970	Mil-A	14	25	3	5	0	0	0	5	3	4	.200	.286	.240	46	-2	0	0	0	1.000	1	/3-7	-0.1
	Cle-A	42	43	6	10	1	0	2	4	3	5	.233	.283	.372	65	-1	0	0	0	.600	-1	/3-5	-0.3
	Yr	56	68	9	15	1	0	2	9	6	9	.221	.284	.324	65	-3	0	0	0	.900	-0	3-12	-0.4
Total	10	1002	3303	419	887	125	20	77	399	266	410	.269	.330	.388	98	-7	17	10	-1	.947	-30	3-830/2-24,S-2,O-1	-4.4

■ BILL ROLLINSON   Rollinson, William (b: William Henry Winslow)   b: 6/10/1856, Fairfield, Maine   d: 9/28/38, Bristow, Va.   Deb: 6/17/1884

YEAR	TM/L	G	AB	R	H	2B	3B	HR	RBI	BB	SO	AVG	OBP	SLG	PRO+	BR/A	SB	CS	SBR	FA	FR	G/POS	TPR
1884	Was-U	1	3	0	0	0	0	0	0	0		.000	.000	.000	-99	-1				.714	0	/C-1	0.0

■ BILL ROMAN   Roman, William Anthony   b: 10/11/38, Detroit, Mich.   BL/TL, 6'4", 190 lbs.   Deb: 9/30/64

YEAR	TM/L	G	AB	R	H	2B	3B	HR	RBI	BB	SO	AVG	OBP	SLG	PRO+	BR/A	SB	CS	SBR	FA	FR	G/POS	TPR
1964	Det-A	3	8	2	3	0	0	1	1	0	2	.375	.375	.750	201	1	0	0		1.000	0	/1-2	0.1

YEAR	TM/L	G	AB	R	H	2B	3B	HR	RBI	BB	SO	AVG	OBP	SLG	PRO+	BR/A	SB	CS	SBR	FA	FR	G/POS	TPR
1965	Det-A	21	27	0	2	0	0	0	0	2	7	.074	.138	.074	-38	-5	0	0	0	1.000	-0	/1-6	-0.6
Total	2	24	35	2	5	0	0	1	1	2	9	.143	.189	.229	17	-4	0	0	0	1.000	-0	/1-8	-0.5

■ JOHNNY ROMANO
Romano, John Anthony "Honey" b: 8/23/34, Hoboken, N.J. BR/TR, 5'11", 205 lbs. Deb: 9/12/58

YEAR	TM/L	G	AB	R	H	2B	3B	HR	RBI	BB	SO	AVG	OBP	SLG	PRO+	BR/A	SB	CS	SBR	FA	FR	G/POS	TPR
1958	Chi-A	4	7	1	2	0	0	0	1	1	0	.286	.375	.286	86	-0	0	0	0	1.000	1	/C-2	0.1
1959	*Chi-A	53	126	20	37	5	1	5	25	23	18	.294	.407	.468	141	8	0	1	-1	.979	1	C-38	1.0
1960	Cle-A	108	316	40	86	12	2	16	52	37	50	.272	.354	.475	126	11	0	0	0	.988	-11	C-99	0.6
1961	Cle-A★	142	509	76	152	29	1	21	80	61	60	.299	.379	.483	132	24	0	0	0	.989	-9	*C-141	2.2
1962	Cle-A★	135	459	71	120	19	3	25	81	73	64	.261	.369	.479	130	20	0	1	-1	.990	-9	*C-130	1.6
1963	Cle-A	89	255	28	55	5	2	10	34	38	49	.216	.322	.369	94	-2	4	3	-1	.993	-11	C-71/O-4	-1.1
1964	Cle-A	106	352	46	85	18	1	19	47	51	83	.241	.349	.460	124	12	2	2	-1	.991	-5	C-96/1-1	1.2
1965	Chi-A	122	356	39	86	11	0	18	48	59	74	.242	.357	.424	129	15	0	2	-1	.992	4	*C-111/O-4,1-2	2.4
1966	Chi-A	122	329	33	76	12	0	15	47	58	72	.231	.348	.404	124	11	0	0	0	.993	3	*C-102	2.2
1967	StL-N	24	58	1	7	1	0	2	3	13	15	.121	.282	.138	24	-5	1	0	0	.983	-1	C-20	-0.5
Total	10	905	2767	355	706	112	10	129	417	414	485	.255	.358	.443	123	93	7	9	-3	.990	-36	C-810/O-8,1-3	9.7

■ TOM ROMANO
Romano, Thomas Michael b: 10/25/58, Syracuse, N.Y. BR/TR, 5'10", 170 lbs. Deb: 9/1/87

YEAR	TM/L	G	AB	R	H	2B	3B	HR	RBI	BB	SO	AVG	OBP	SLG	PRO+	BR/A	SB	CS	SBR	FA	FR	G/POS	TPR
1987	Mon-N	7	3	1	0	0	0	0	0	0	1	.000	.000	.000	-97	-1	0	0	0	.000	-1	/O-3	-0.2

■ ED ROMERO
Romero, Edgardo Ralph (Rivera) b: 12/9/57, Santurce, P.R. BR/TR, 5'11", 175 lbs. Deb: 7/16/77

YEAR	TM/L	G	AB	R	H	2B	3B	HR	RBI	BB	SO	AVG	OBP	SLG	PRO+	BR/A	SB	CS	SBR	FA	FR	G/POS	TPR
1977	Mil-A	10	25	4	7	1	0	0	2	4	3	.280	.379	.320	93	-0	0	0	0	.971	0	S-10	0.1
1980	Mil-A	42	104	20	27	7	0	1	10	9	11	.260	.319	.356	87	-2	2	0	1	.894	-3	S-22,2-15/3-3	0.6
1981	*Mil-A	44	91	6	18	3	0	1	10	4	9	.198	.232	.264	45	-7	0	2	-1	.949	10	S-22,2-18/3-3	0.5
1982	Mil-A	52	144	18	36	8	0	1	7	8	16	.250	.289	.326	73	-5	0	0	0	.975	-1	2-39,S-10/3-2,O-1	-0.5
1983	Mil-A	59	145	17	46	7	0	1	18	8	8	.317	.353	.386	112	2	1	0	0	.962	-10	S-22,O-15/3-5,2D	-0.6
1984	Mil-A	116	357	36	90	12	0	1	31	29	25	.252	.310	.294	71	-13	3	3	-1	.943	2	3-59,S-39,2/10D	-1.0
1985	Mil-A	88	251	24	63	11	1	0	21	26	20	.251	.321	.303	72	-9	1	1	-0	.977	8	S-43,2-31,O-14,/3-1	0.4
1986	*Bos-A	100	233	41	49	11	0	2	23	18	16	.210	.273	.283	51	-16	2	0	1	.959	-8	S-75,3-18/2-4,O-1	-1.7
1987	Bos-A	88	235	23	64	5	0	0	14	18	22	.272	.324	.294	64	-12	0	2	-1	.973	2	2-29,S-24,3-24,/1-8	-0.8
1988	*Bos-A	31	75	8	18	3	0	0	5	3	8	.240	.278	.280	55	-5	0	0	0	1.000	-1	3-15/S-8/2-5,1-1,D	-0.4
1989	Bos-A	46	113	14	24	4	0	0	6	7	7	.212	.264	.248	42	-9	0	2	-1	.983	12	2-22,3-14,S-10	0.4
	Atl-N	7	19	1	5	1	0	1	1	0	0	.263	.263	.474	104	-0	0	0	0	.947	5	/2-4,S-2,3-1	0.5
	Mil-A	15	50	3	10	3	0	0	3	0	10	.200	.200	.260	29	-4	0	0	0	1.000	-0	2-11/3-4,S-1,D-2	-0.4
1990	Det-A	32	70	8	16	3	0	0	4	6	4	.229	.289	.271	57	-4	0	0	0	.982	6	3-27/D-3	0.2
Total	12	730	1912	218	473	79	1	8	155	140	159	.247	.300	.302	67	-83	9	10	-3	.958	30	S-288,2-192,3/01D	-2.7

■ KEVIN ROMINE
Romine, Kevin Andrew b: 5/23/61, Exeter, N.H. BR/TR, 5'11", 185 lbs. Deb: 9/5/85

YEAR	TM/L	G	AB	R	H	2B	3B	HR	RBI	BB	SO	AVG	OBP	SLG	PRO+	BR/A	SB	CS	SBR	FA	FR	G/POS	TPR
1985	Bos-A	24	28	3	6	2	0	0	1	1	4	.214	.241	.286	42	-2	1	0	0	1.000	-5	O-23/D-1	-0.8
1986	Bos-A	35	35	6	9	2	0	0	2	3	9	.257	.316	.314	72	-1	2	0	1	1.000	-6	O-33	-0.7
1987	Bos-A	9	24	5	7	2	0	0	2	2	6	.292	.346	.375	89	-0	0	0	0	1.000	-0	/O-7,D-2	-0.1
1988	*Bos-A	57	78	17	15	2	1	1	6	7	15	.192	.259	.282	49	-5	2	0	1	.957	-13	O-45/D-5	-1.8
1989	Bos-A	92	274	30	75	13	0	1	23	21	53	.274	.330	.332	82	-6	1	1	-0	.982	-2	O-89/D-1	-1.0
1990	Bos-A	70	136	21	37	7	0	2	14	12	27	.272	.336	.368	92	-1	4	0	1	.976	-11	O-64/D-1	-1.2
1991	Bos-A	44	55	7	9	2	0	1	7	3	10	.164	.207	.255	26	-6	1	1	-0	.964	-4	O-23,D-14	-1.1
Total	7	331	630	89	158	30	1	5	55	49	124	.251	.308	.325	73	-22	11	2	2	.980	-41	O-284/D-25	-6.7

■ MARC RONAN
Ronan, Edward Marcus b: 9/19/69, Ozark, Ala. BL/TR, 6'2", 190 lbs. Deb: 9/21/93

YEAR	TM/L	G	AB	R	H	2B	3B	HR	RBI	BB	SO	AVG	OBP	SLG	PRO+	BR/A	SB	CS	SBR	FA	FR	G/POS	TPR
1993	StL-N	6	12	0	1	0	0	0	0	0	5	.083	.083	.083	-56	-3	0	0	0	1.000	2	/C-6	-0.1

■ HENRI RONDEAU
Rondeau, Henri Joseph b: 5/5/1887, Danielson, Conn. d: 5/28/43, Woonsocket, R.I. BR/TR, 5'10.5", 175 lbs. Deb: 4/11/13

YEAR	TM/L	G	AB	R	H	2B	3B	HR	RBI	BB	SO	AVG	OBP	SLG	PRO+	BR/A	SB	CS	SBR	FA	FR	G/POS	TPR
1913	Det-A	35	70	5	13	2	0	0	5	14	16	.186	.321	.214	58	-3	1			1.000	-0	C-16/1-6	-0.4
1915	Was-A	14	40	3	7	0	0	0	4	3		.175	.250	.175	27	-4	1	2	-1	1.000	3	O-11	-0.3
1916	Was-A	50	162	20	36	5	3	1	28	18	18	.222	.311	.309	87	-2	7			.958	3	O-48	-0.2
Total	3	99	272	28	56	7	3	1	37	36	37	.206	.305	.265	71	-9	9	2		.967	4	/O-59,C-16,1-6	-0.9

■ GENE ROOF
Roof, Eugene Lawrence b: 1/13/58, Paducah, Ky. BB/TR, 6'2", 180 lbs. Deb: 9/3/81 F

YEAR	TM/L	G	AB	R	H	2B	3B	HR	RBI	BB	SO	AVG	OBP	SLG	PRO+	BR/A	SB	CS	SBR	FA	FR	G/POS	TPR
1981	StL-N	23	60	11	18	6	0	0	3	12	16	.300	.417	.400	129	3	5	1	1	.950	-2	O-20	0.2
1982	StL-N	11	15	3	4	0	0	0	2	1	4	.267	.313	.267	63	-1	2	0	1	1.000	-1	/O-5	-0.2
1983	StL-N	6	3	1	0	0	0	0	0	0	0	.000	.000	.000	-99	-1	0	0	0	.000	-0	/O-1	-0.1
	Mon-N	8	12	2	2	2	0	0	1	1	3	.167	.231	.333	55	-1	0	0	0	1.000	-1	/O-5	-0.3
	Yr	14	15	3	2	2	0	0	1	1	3	.133	.188	.267	25	-2	0	0	0	1.000	-2	/O-6	-0.3
Total	3	48	90	17	24	8	0	0	6	14	23	.267	.365	.356	102	-1	7	1	2	.958	-5	/O-31	-0.3

■ PHIL ROOF
Roof, Phillip Anthony b: 3/5/41, Paducah, Ky. BR/TR, 6'3", 210 lbs. Deb: 4/29/61 FC

YEAR	TM/L	G	AB	R	H	2B	3B	HR	RBI	BB	SO	AVG	OBP	SLG	PRO+	BR/A	SB	CS	SBR	FA	FR	G/POS	TPR
1961	Mil-N	1	0	0	0	0	0	0	0	0	0	—	—	—	—	—	0	0	0	1.000	-0	/C-1	0.0
1964	Mil-N	1	2	0	0	0	0	0	0	0	1	.000	.000	.000	-99	-1	0	0	0	1.000	1	/C-1	0.1
1965	Cal-A	9	22	1	3	0	0	0	0	0	6	.136	.136	.136	-23	-3	0	0	0	.983	6	C-9	0.2
	Cle-A	43	52	3	9	1	0	0	3	5	13	.173	.259	.192	30	-5	0	0	0	.994	13	C-41	1.0
	Yr	52	74	4	12	1	0	0	3	5	19	.162	.225	.176	15	-8	0	0	0	.992	19	C-50	1.2
1966	KC-A	127	369	33	77	14	3	7	44	37	95	.209	.286	.320	76	-11	2	5	-2	.985	-1	*C-123/1-2	-0.7
1967	KC-A	114	327	23	67	14	5	6	24	23	85	.205	.268	.333	79	-9	4	1	1	.991	-1	*C-113	-0.5
1968	Oak-A	34	64	5	12	0	0	1	2	2	15	.188	.212	.234	37	-5	1	0	0	.968	-1	C-32	-0.5
1969	Oak-A	106	247	19	58	1	2	9	33	35	55	.235	.337	.291	81	-5	1	0	0	.983	-1	*C-106	-0.2
1970	Mil-A	110	321	39	73	7	1	13	37	32	72	.227	.307	.377	87	-6	3	2	-0	.988	8	*C-107/1-1	0.6
1971	Mil-A	41	114	6	22	2	1	1	10	8	28	.193	.252	.254	44	-8	0	1	-1	.975	3	C-39	-0.4
	Min-A	31	87	6	21	4	0	1	6	7	18	.241	.305	.287	67	-4	0	1	-1	.985	8	C-29	0.5
	Yr	72	201	12	43	6	1	2	16	15	46	.214	.275	.269	54	-12	0	2	-1	.980	11	C-68	0.1
1972	Min-A	61	146	16	30	11	1	3	12	6	27	.205	.237	.356	71	-6	0	0	0	.978	-2	C-61	-0.8
1973	Min-A	47	117	10	23	4	1	1	15	3	27	.197	.274	.274	53	-7	0	0	0	.992	6	C-47	0.1
1974	Min-A	44	97	10	19	2	0	2	13	6	24	.196	.257	.268	50	-6	0	0	0	1.000	7	C-44	0.3
1975	Min-A	63	126	18	38	2	0	7	21	9	28	.302	.353	.484	133	5	0	0	0	.989	6	C-63	1.3
1976	Min-A	18	46	1	10	3	0	0	4	2	6	.217	.250	.283	55	-2	0	0	0	.962	-1	C-12/D-1	0.3
	Chi-A	4	9	1	1	0	0	0	0	0	3	.111	.111	.111	-35	-2	0	0	0	1.000	-0	/C-4	-0.2
	Yr	22	55	2	11	3	0	0	4	2	9	.200	.228	.255	40	-4	0	0	0	.967	5	C-16/D-1	0.1
1977	Tor-A	3	5	0	0	0	0	0	0	0	3	.000	.000	.000	-99	-1	0	0	0	1.000	1	/C-3	0.0
Total	15	857	2151	190	463	69	13	43	210	184	504	.215	.284	.319	73	-77	11	10	-3	.986	58	C-835/1-3,D-1	1.1

■ GEORGE ROOKS
Rooks, George Brinton McClellan (b: George Brinton Mc Clellan Ruckser) b: 10/21/1863, Chicago, Ill. d: 3/11/35, Chicago, Ill. BR/TR, 5'11", 170 lbs. Deb: 5/12/1891 F

YEAR	TM/L	G	AB	R	H	2B	3B	HR	RBI	BB	SO	AVG	OBP	SLG	PRO+	BR/A	SB	CS	SBR	FA	FR	G/POS	TPR
1891	Bos-N	5	16	1	2	0	0	0	0	4	1	.125	.300	.125	23	-2	0			1.000	1	/O-5	-0.1

■ ROLANDO ROOMES
Roomes, Rolando Audley b: 2/15/62, Kingston, Jamaica BR/TR, 6'3", 180 lbs. Deb: 4/12/88

YEAR	TM/L	G	AB	R	H	2B	3B	HR	RBI	BB	SO	AVG	OBP	SLG	PRO+	BR/A	SB	CS	SBR	FA	FR	G/POS	TPR
1988	Chi-N	17	16	3	3	0	0	0	0	0	8	.188	.188	.188	8	-2	0	1	-1	.833	-1	/O-5	-0.4
1989	Cin-N	107	315	36	83	18	5	7	34	13	100	.263	.299	.419	100	-1	12	8	-1	.981	-3	*O-100	-0.7
1990	Cin-N	30	61	5	13	0	0	2	7	0	20	.213	.213	.311	41	-5	0	0	0	1.000	-0	O-19	-0.6
	Mon-N	16	14	1	4	1	0	0	1	1	6	.286	.333	.429	112	-0	0	0	0	1.000	-0	/O-6	-0.3
	Yr	46	75	6	17	1	0	2	8	1	26	.227	.237	.333	54	-5	0	2	-1	1.000	-2	O-25	-0.9
Total	3	170	406	45	103	18	6	9	42	14	130	.254	.284	.394	88	-8	12	11	-3	.980	-5	O-130	-2.0

■ FRANK ROONEY
Rooney, Frank (b: Frank Rovny) b: 10/12/1884, Podebrady, Bohemia (Austria-Hungary) d: 4/6/77, Bessemer, Mich. Deb: 4/18/14

YEAR	TM/L	G	AB	R	H	2B	3B	HR	RBI	BB	SO	AVG	OBP	SLG	PRO+	BR/A	SB	CS	SBR	FA	FR	G/POS	TPR
1914	Ind-F	12	35	1	7	0	1	1	8	1	0	.200	.222	.343	47	-3	2			.980	-1	/1-9	-0.5

YEAR	TM/L	G	AB	R	H	2B	3B	HR	RBI	BB	SO	AVG	OBP	SLG	PRO+	BR/A	SB	CS	SBR	FA	FR	G/POS	TPR

■ PAT ROONEY   Rooney, Patrick Eugene   b: 11/28/57, Chicago, Ill.   BR/TR, 6'1", 190 lbs.   Deb: 9/9/81

| 1981 | Mon-N | 4 | 5 | 0 | 0 | 0 | 0 | 0 | 0 | 0 | 3 | .000 | .000 | .000 | -99 | -1 | 0 | 0 | 0 | 1.000 | -1 | /O-2 | -0.2 |

■ JORGE ROQUE   Roque, Jorge (Vargas)   b: 4/28/50, Ponce, P.R.   BR/TR, 5'10", 158 lbs.   Deb: 9/4/70

1970	StL-N	5	1	2	0	0	0	0	0	0	1	.000	.500	.000	45	0	0	0	0	.000	-0	/O-1	0.0
1971	StL-N	3	10	2	3	0	0	0	1	0	3	.300	.300	.300	68	-0	1	0	0	1.000	-0	/O-3	0.0
1972	StL-N	32	67	3	7	2	1	1	5	6	19	.104	.178	.209	10	-8	1	1	-0	.980	-1	O-24	-1.1
1973	Mon-N	25	61	7	9	2	0	1	6	4	17	.148	.212	.230	22	-7	2	2	-1	.878	-3	O-24	-1.1
Total	4	65	139	14	19	4	1	2	12	10	40	.137	.205	.223	20	-15	4	3	-1	.934	-4	/O-52	-2.2

■ LUIS ROSADO   Rosado, Luis (Robles)   b: 12/6/55, Santurce, P.R.   BR/TR, 6', 180 lbs.   Deb: 9/8/77

1977	NY-N	9	24	1	5	1	0	0	3	1	3	.208	.269	.250	42	-2	0	0	0	.980	-0	/1-7,C-1	-0.3
1980	NY-N	2	4	0	0	0	0	0	0	0	1	.000	.000	.000	-99	-1	0	0	0	1.000	-0	/1-1	-0.1
Total	2	11	28	1	5	1	0	0	3	1	4	.179	.233	.214	23	-3	0	0	0	.983	-0	/1-8,C-1	-0.4

■ BUDDY ROSAR   Rosar, Warren Vincent   b: 7/3/14, Buffalo, N.Y.   d: 3/13/94, Rochester, N.Y.   BR/TR, 5'9", 190 lbs.   Deb: 4/29/39

1939	NY-A	43	105	18	29	5	1	0	12	13	10	.276	.356	.343	81	-3	4	0	1	.980	4	C-35	0.4
1940	NY-A	73	228	34	68	11	3	4	37	19	11	.298	.357	.425	106	3	2	7	1	.983	1	C-63	0.8
1941	*NY-A	67	209	25	60	17	2	1	36	22	10	.287	.355	.402	101	0	0	0	0	.996	0	C-60	0.5
1942	*NY-A☆	69	209	18	48	10	0	2	34	17	20	.230	.288	.306	68	-9	1	2	-1	.996	4	C-58	-0.2
1943	Cle-A☆	115	382	53	108	17	1	1	41	33	12	.283	.340	.340	106	2	0	4	-2	.983	7	*C-114	1.5
1944	Cle-A	99	331	29	87	9	3	0	30	34	17	.263	.339	.308	89	-4	1	2	-1	.989	4	C-98	0.5
1945	Phi-A	92	300	23	63	12	1	1	25	20	16	.210	.262	.267	54	-18	2	1	0	.987	-0	C-85	-1.5
1946	Phi-A★	121	424	34	120	22	2	2	47	36	17	.283	.339	.358	96	-3	1	3	-2	**1.000**	7	*C-117	1.0
1947	Phi-A★	102	359	40	93	20	2	1	33	40	13	.259	.335	.334	85	-7	1	3	-2	.996	13	*C-102	1.2
1948	Phi-A★	90	302	30	77	13	0	4	41	39	12	.255	.344	.338	82	-7	0	2	-1	.997	-3	C-90	-0.5
1949	Phi-A	32	95	7	19	2	0	0	6	16	5	.200	.315	.221	45	-7	0	0	0	.992	-2	C-31	-0.8
1950	Bos-A	27	84	13	25	2	0	1	12	7	4	.298	.352	.357	75	-3	0	0	0	.991	-1	C-25	-0.3
1951	Bos-A	58	170	11	39	7	0	1	13	19	14	.229	.307	.288	56	-10	0	0	0	.996	-6	C-56	-0.8
Total	13	988	3198	335	836	147	15	18	367	315	161	.261	.330	.334	84	-67	17	18	-6	.992	33	C-934	1.8

■ JIMMY ROSARIO   Rosario, Angel Ramon (Ferrer)   b: 5/5/45, Bayamon, P.R.   BB/TR, 5'10", 155 lbs.   Deb: 4/8/71

1971	*SF-N	92	192	26	43	6	1	0	13	33	35	.224	.341	.266	75	-5	7	4	-0	1.000	-1	O-67	-0.9
1972	SF-N	7	2	1	0	0	0	0	0	0	0	.000	.000	.000	-99	-1	0	1	-1	.000	-1	/O-1	-0.2
1976	Mil-A	15	37	4	7	0	0	1	5	3	8	.189	.250	.270	53	-2	1	3	-2	1.000	-2	O-12/D-2	-0.7
Total	3	114	231	31	50	6	1	1	18	36	43	.216	.325	.264	70	-8	8	8	-2	1.000	-4	/O-80,D-2	-1.8

■ SANTIAGO ROSARIO   Rosario, Santiago   b: 7/25/39, Guayanilla, P.R.   BL/TL, 5'11", 165 lbs.   Deb: 6/23/65

| 1965 | KC-A | 81 | 85 | 8 | 20 | 3 | 0 | 2 | 8 | 6 | 16 | .235 | .293 | .341 | 81 | -2 | 0 | 0 | 0 | .991 | -1 | 1-31/O-3 | -0.4 |

■ VICTOR ROSARIO   Rosario, Victor Manuel (Rivera)   b: 8/26/66, Hato Mayor Del Rey, D.R.   BR/TR, 5'11", 155 lbs.   Deb: 9/6/90

| 1990 | Atl-N | 9 | 7 | 3 | 1 | 0 | 0 | 0 | 0 | 1 | 2 | .143 | .250 | .143 | 10 | -1 | 0 | 0 | 0 | 1.000 | 1 | /S-3,2-1 | 0.0 |

■ PETE ROSE   Rose, Peter Edward "Charlie Hustle"   b: 4/14/41, Cincinnati, Ohio   BB/TR, 5'11", 200 lbs.   Deb: 4/8/63   M

1963	Cin-N	157	623	101	170	25	9	6	41	55	72	.273	.337	.371	101	1	13	15	-5	.971	-23	*2-157/O-1	-1.3
1964	Cin-N	136	516	64	139	13	2	4	34	36	51	.269	.319	.326	79	-13	4	10	-5	.979	-14	*2-128	-2.3
1965	Cin-N★	162	670	117	**209**	35	11	11	81	69	76	.312	.383	.446	124	23	8	3	1	.975	-18	*2-162	2.1
1966	Cin-N	156	654	97	205	38	5	16	70	37	61	.313	.351	.460	113	11	4	9	-4	.981	-8	*2-140,3-16	1.0
1967	Cin-N★	148	585	86	176	32	8	12	76	56	66	.301	.365	.444	117	13	11	6	-0	.982	-4	*O-123,2-35	0.6
1968	Cin-N†	149	626	94	**210**	42	6	10	49	56	76	**.335**	**.394**	.470	144	38	3	7	-3	.990	7	*O-148/2-3,1-1	3.8
1969	Cin-N★	156	627	**120**	218	33	11	16	82	88	65	**.348**	.432	.512	155	49	7	10	-4	.988	5	*O-156/2-2	4.3
1970	*Cin-N★	159	649	120	**205**	37	9	15	52	73	64	.316	.387	.470	128	26	12	7	-1	**.997**	5	*O-159	2.2
1971	Cin-N★	160	632	86	192	27	4	13	44	68	50	.304	.374	.421	124	24	13	9	-2	.994	4	*O-158	1.9
1972	*Cin-N	154	645	107	**198**	31	11	6	57	73	46	.307	.383	.417	135	31	10	3	1	.994	16	*O-154	4.3
1973	Cin-N★	160	680	115	**230**	36	8	5	64	65	42	**.338**	.401	.437	139	37	10	7	-1	.992	17	*O-159	4.6
1974	Cin-N★	163	652	**110**	185	**45**	7	3	51	106	54	.284	.388	.388	119	21	2	4	-2	**.997**	18	*O-163	3.0
1975	*Cin-N★	162	662	**112**	210	**47**	4	7	74	89	50	.317	.407	.432	130	31	0	1	-1	.963	-36	*3-137,O-35	-0.7
1976	*Cin-N★	162	665	**130**	**215**	**42**	6	10	63	86	54	.323	.406	.450	139	37	9	5	-0	**.969**	-12	*3-159/O-1	2.5
1977	Cin-N★	162	655	95	204	38	7	9	64	66	42	.311	.379	.432	115	16	16	4	2	.958	-24	*3-161	-0.8
1978	Cin-N★	159	655	103	198	**51**	3	7	52	62	30	.302	.365	.421	119	17	13	9	-2	.961	-26	*3-156/O-7,1-2	-1.3
1979	Phi-N★	163	628	90	208	40	5	4	59	95	32	.331	.421	.430	128	29	20	11	-1	.995	-5	*1-159/3-5,2-1	1.4
1980	*Phi-N★	162	655	95	185	**42**	1	1	64	66	33	.282	.354	.354	93	-4	12	8	-1	**.997**	9	*1-162	-0.6
1981	*Phi-N★	107	431	73	**140**	18	5	0	33	46	26	.325	.394	.390	118	12	4	4	-1	.996	9	*1-107	1.4
1982	Phi-N★	162	634	80	172	25	4	3	54	66	32	.271	.347	.338	90	-6	8	8	-2	.995	6	*1-162	-1.3
1983	*Phi-N	151	493	52	121	14	3	0	45	52	28	.245	.320	.286	70	-19	7	7	-2	.990	-2	*1-112,O-35	-3.0
1984	Mon-N	95	278	34	72	6	2	0	23	31	20	.259	.335	.295	82	-6	1	1	0	.988	-3	1-40,O-28	-0.2
	Cin-N	26	96	9	35	9	0	0	11	9	7	.365	.430	.458	143	6	0	0	0	.990	-3	1-23/M	0.2
	Yr	121	374	43	107	15	2	0	34	40	27	.286	.360	.337	99	1	1	1	0	.989	5	1-63,O-28	0.0
1985	Cin-N★	119	405	60	107	12	2	2	46	86	35	.264	.398	.319	98	4	8	1	2	.995	0	*1-110/M	-0.1
1986	Cin-N	72	237	15	52	8	2	0	25	30	31	.219	.317	.270	61	-12	3	0	1	.990	-1	1-61/M	-1.7
Total	24	3562	14053	2165	4256	746	135	160	1314	1566	1143	.303	.377	.409	117	366	198	149	-30	.991	-71	*O-1327,1-939,32	20.0

■ BOBBY ROSE   Rose, Robert Richard   b: 3/15/67, Covina, Cal.   BR/TR, 5'11", 170 lbs.   Deb: 8/12/89

1989	Cal-A	14	38	4	8	1	2	1	3	2	10	.211	.268	.421	93	-1	0	0	0	.920	-1	3-10/2-3	-0.1
1990	Cal-A	7	13	5	5	0	0	1	2	2	1	.385	.467	.615	204	2	0	0	0	1.000	-1	/2-4,3-3	0.1
1991	Cal-A	22	65	5	18	5	1	1	8	3	13	.277	.309	.431	102	-0	0	0	0	1.000	-1	/2-8,O-7,3-4,1-3	-0.1
1992	Cal-A	30	84	10	18	5	0	2	10	8	9	.214	.298	.345	79	-2	1	1	-0	.953	8	2-28/1-2	0.6
Total	4	73	200	24	49	11	3	5	23	15	33	.245	.307	.405	98	-1	1	1	-0	.965	6	/2-43,3-17,O-7,1-5	0.5

■ JOHNNY ROSEBORO   Roseboro, John Junior   b: 5/13/33, Ashland, Ohio   BL/TR, 5'11.5", 190 lbs.   Deb: 6/14/57   C

1957	Bro-N	35	69	6	10	2	0	2	6	10	20	.145	.253	.261	35	-6	0	0	0	.972	3	C-19/1-5	-0.3
1958	LA-N☆	114	384	52	104	11	9	14	43	36	56	.271	.336	.456	104	2	11	8	-2	.987	-16	*C-104/O-5	-1.0
1959	*LA-N	118	397	39	92	14	7	10	38	52	69	.232	.325	.378	81	-11	7	5	-1	.991	6	*C-117	0.2
1960	LA-N	103	287	22	61	15	3	8	42	44	53	.213	.325	.369	84	-6	7	6	-2	.993	3	C-87/1-1,3-1	0.1
1961	LA-N★	128	394	59	99	16	6	18	59	56	62	.251	.350	.459	104	2	6	4	-1	.986	7	*C-125	1.4
1962	LA-N★	128	389	45	97	16	7	5	55	50	60	.249	.345	.380	101	1	12	3	2	.985	-2	*C-128	0.6
1963	*LA-N	135	470	50	111	13	7	9	49	36	50	.236	.295	.351	91	-6	7	6	-2	.992	-10	*C-134	-1.4
1964	LA-N	134	414	42	119	24	1	3	45	44	61	.287	.361	.372	115	9	3	3	-1	.993	1	*C-128	1.6
1965	*LA-N	136	437	42	102	10	0	8	57	34	51	.233	.292	.311	75	-15	1	6	-3	.994	6	*C-131/3-1	-1.5
1966	*LA-N	142	445	47	123	23	2	9	53	44	51	.276	.346	.398	115	9	3	2	-0	.993	6	*C-138	2.4
1967	LA-N	116	334	37	91	18	2	4	24	38	33	.272	.350	.374	117	8	2	4	-2	.984	-11	*C-107	0.0
1968	Min-A	135	380	31	82	12	0	8	39	46	57	.216	.304	.311	82	-7	2	3	-1	.991	-5	*C-117	-0.6
1969	*Min-A★	115	361	33	95	12	0	3	32	39	44	.263	.335	.321	83	-8	5	5	-2	.980	-5	*C-111	-0.4
1970	Was-A	46	86	7	20	0	0	6	18	10	19	.233	.365	.314	94	-0	1	1	-0	1.000	-3	C-30	-0.2
Total	14	1585	4847	512	1206	190	44	104	548	547	677	.249	.329	.371	95	-28	67	56	-14	.989	-22	*C-1476/1-6,O-5,3-2	0.9

■ BOB ROSELLI   Roselli, Robert Edward   b: 12/10/31, San Francisco, Cal.   BR/TR, 5'11", 185 lbs.   Deb: 8/16/55

1955	Mil-N	6	9	1	2	1	0	0	1	1	4	.222	.364	.333	91	-0	0	0	0	.917	0	/C-2	0.0
1956	Mil-N	4	2	1	1	0	0	1	1	0	1	.500	.500	2.000	564	1	0	0	0	1.000	2	/C-3	0.3
1958	Mil-N	1	1	0	0	0	0	0	0	0	0	.000	.000	.000	-99	-0	0	0	0	.000	-0	H	0.0
1961	Chi-A	22	38	2	10	3	0	0	4	0	11	.263	.263	.342	61	-2	0	0	0	1.000	-1	C-10	-0.3

YEAR	TM/L	G	AB	R	H	2B	3B	HR	RBI	BB	SO	AVG	OBP	SLG	PRO+	BR/A	SB	CS	SBR	FA	FR	G/POS	TPR
1962	Chi-A	35	64	4	12	3	1	1	5	11	15	.188	.316	.313	70	-3	1	0	0	.988	-1	C-20	-0.3
Total	5	68	114	8	25	7	1	2	10	12	31	.219	.305	.351	76	-4	1	0	0	.986	-1	/C-35	-0.3

■ DAVE ROSELLO
Rosello, David (Rodriguez)   b: 6/26/50, Mayaguez, P.R.   BR/TR, 5'11", 160 lbs.   Deb: 9/10/72

YEAR	TM/L	G	AB	R	H	2B	3B	HR	RBI	BB	SO	AVG	OBP	SLG	PRO+	BR/A	SB	CS	SBR	FA	FR	G/POS	TPR
1972	Chi-N	5	12	2	3	0	0	1	3	3	2	.250	.400	.500	139	1	0	0	0	.846	1	/S-5	0.2
1973	Chi-N	16	38	4	10	2	0	0	2	2	4	.263	.300	.316	66	-2	2	2	-1	.964	3	2-13/S-1	0.1
1974	Chi-N	62	148	9	30	7	0	0	10	10	28	.203	.253	.250	39	-12	1	1	-0	.972	3	2-49,S-12	-0.7
1975	Chi-N	19	58	7	15	2	0	1	8	9	8	.259	.358	.345	92	-0	0	1	-1	.952	1	S-19	0.2
1976	Chi-N	91	227	27	55	5	1	1	11	41	33	.242	.361	.286	78	-5	1	2	-1	.966	-7	S-86/2-1	-0.4
1977	Chi-N	56	82	18	18	2	1	1	9	12	12	.220	.319	.305	62	-4	0	0	0	.938	-3	3-21,S-10/2-3	-0.7
1979	Cle-A	59	107	20	26	6	1	3	14	15	27	.243	.336	.402	98	-0	1	0	0	.976	-5	2-33,3-14,S-11	-0.3
1980	Cle-A	71	117	16	29	3	0	2	12	9	19	.248	.302	.325	71	-5	0	0	0	.980	3	2-43,3-22/S-3,D-1	0.0
1981	Cle-A	43	84	11	20	4	0	1	7	7	12	.238	.297	.321	79	-2	0	1	-1	.979	3	2-26/3-8,S-4,D-4	0.1
Total	9	422	873	114	206	31	3	10	76	108	145	.236	.321	.313	73	-29	5	7	-3	.975	0	2-168,S-151/3-65,D	-1.5

■ CHIEF ROSEMAN
Roseman, James John   b: 1856, New York, N.Y.   d: 7/4/38, Brooklyn, N.Y.   BR/TR, 5'7", 167 lbs.   Deb: 5/1/1882   M

YEAR	TM/L	G	AB	R	H	2B	3B	HR	RBI	BB	SO	AVG	OBP	SLG	PRO+	BR/A	SB	CS	SBR	FA	FR	G/POS	TPR
1882	Tro-N	82	331	41	78	21	6	1	29	3	41	.236	.243	.344	90	-3				.853	-3	*O-82	-0.6
1883	NY-a	93	398	48	100	13	6	0		11		.251	.271	.314	84	-8				.855	-3	*O-91/1-2	-1.1
1884	*NY-a	107	436	97	130	16	11	4		21		.298	.339	.413	148	23				.885	-2	*O-107	1.7
1885	NY-a	101	410	72	114	13	14	4	46	25		.278	.335	.407	145	22				.865	-7	*O-101/P-1	1.1
1886	NY-a	134	559	90	127	19	10	5	53	24		.227	.269	.324	89	-8	6			.891	-3	*O-134/P-1	-1.2
1887	Phi-a	21	73	16	16	2	1	0	8	10		.219	.352	.274	76	-2	3			.821	-0	O-21	-0.2
	NY-a	60	241	30	55	10	1	1	27	9		.228	.265	.290	57	-14	3			.868	-8	O-59/1-3,P-2	-1.8
	Bro-a	1	3	2	1	0	0	0	1	0		.333	.500	.333	133	0	0			1.000	-3	/O-1	-0.3
	Yr	82	317	48	72	12	2	1	36	19		.227	.290	.287	63	-15	6			.856	-11	O-81/1-3,P-2	-2.3
1890	StL-a	80	302	47	103	26	4	2	58	30		.341	.449	.447	144	16	7			.819	-8	O-58,1-22,M	0.4
	Lou-a	2	8	0	2	0	0	0	0	0		.250	.250	.250	48	-1	0			.864	-1	/1-2	-0.1
	Yr	82	310	47	105	26	2	2	58	30		.339	.444	.442	142	16	7			.819	-9	O-58,1-24	0.3
Total	7	681	2761	443	726	120	49	17	222	133	41	.263	.312	.360	109	27	19			.866	-37	O-654/1-29,P-4	-2.1

■ AL ROSEN
Rosen, Albert Leonard "Flip"   b: 2/29/24, Spartanburg, S.C.   BR/TR, 5'10.5", 180 lbs.   Deb: 9/10/47

YEAR	TM/L	G	AB	R	H	2B	3B	HR	RBI	BB	SO	AVG	OBP	SLG	PRO+	BR/A	SB	CS	SBR	FA	FR	G/POS	TPR
1947	Cle-A	7	9	0	1	0	0	0	0	0	3	.111	.111	.111	-39	-2	0	0	0	.000	1	/3-2,O-1	-0.1
1948	*Cle-A	5	5	0	1	0	0	0	0	0	2	.200	.200	.200	7	-1	0	0	0	1.000	0	/3-2	-0.1
1949	Cle-A	23	44	3	7	2	0	0	5	7	4	.159	.275	.205	28	-5	0	1	-1	1.000	-1	3-10	-0.6
1950	Cle-A	155	554	100	159	23	4	**37**	116	100	72	.287	.405	.543	146	38	5	7	-3	.969	1	*3-154	3.1
1951	Cle-A	154	573	82	152	30	1	24	102	85	71	.265	.362	.447	125	19	7	5	-1	.958	-15	*3-154	0.1
1952	Cle-A★	148	567	101	171	32	5	28	**105**	75	54	.302	.387	.524	162	46	8	6	-1	.958	-20	*3-147/1-4,S-3	2.3
1953	Cle-A★	155	599	**115**	201	27	5	**43**	**145**	85	48	.336	.422	**.613**	181	67	8	7	-2	.964	1	*3-154/1-1,S-1	6.2
1954	*Cle-A★	137	466	76	140	20	2	24	102	85	43	.300	.412	.506	148	33	6	2	1	.959	-14	3-87,1-46/2-1,S-1	1.6
1955	Cle-A★	139	492	61	120	13	1	21	81	92	44	.244	.367	.402	103	4	4	2	0	.963	3	*3-106,1-41	0.4
1956	Cle-A	121	416	64	111	18	2	15	61	58	44	.267	.357	.428	104	2	1	3	-2	.945	-8	*3-116	-0.5
Total	10	1044	3725	603	1063	165	20	192	717	587	385	.285	.386	.495	138	202	39	33	-8	.961	-52	3-932/1-92,S-5,2O	12.4

■ GOODY ROSEN
Rosen, Goodwin George   b: 8/28/12, Toronto, Ont., Can.   d: 4/6/94, Toronto, Ont., Can.   BL/TL, 5'10", 155 lbs.   Deb: 9/14/37

YEAR	TM/L	G	AB	R	H	2B	3B	HR	RBI	BB	SO	AVG	OBP	SLG	PRO+	BR/A	SB	CS	SBR	FA	FR	G/POS	TPR
1937	Bro-N	22	77	10	24	5	1	0	6	6	6	.312	.361	.403	106	1	2			.981	1	O-21	0.1
1938	Bro-N	138	473	75	133	17	11	4	51	65	43	.281	.368	.389	106	5	0			**.989**	13	*O-113	1.5
1939	Bro-N	54	183	22	46	6	4	1	12	23	21	.251	.335	.344	80	-5	4			1.000	-3	O-47	-1.0
1944	Bro-N	89	264	38	69	8	3	0	23	26	27	.261	.330	.314	83	-5	0			.991	12	O-65	0.4
1945	Bro-N†	145	606	126	197	24	11	12	75	50	36	.325	.379	.460	134	26	4			.993	9	*O-141	2.1
1946	Bro-N	3	3	0	1	0	0	0	0	0	1	.333	.333	.333	89	-0	0			.000	-1	/O-1	-0.1
	NY-N	100	310	39	87	11	4	5	30	48	32	.281	.377	.390	117	8	2			.976	4	O-84	0.8
	Yr	103	313	39	88	11	4	5	30	48	33	.281	.377	.390	117	8	2			.976	3	O-85	0.7
Total	6	551	1916	310	557	71	34	22	197	218	166	.291	.364	.398	111	31	12			.989	28	O-472	3.8

■ HARRY ROSENBERG
Rosenberg, Harry   b: 6/22/09, San Francisco, Cal.   BR/TR, 5'9.5", 160 lbs.   Deb: 7/15/30   F

YEAR	TM/L	G	AB	R	H	2B	3B	HR	RBI	BB	SO	AVG	OBP	SLG	PRO+	BR/A	SB	CS	SBR	FA	FR	G/POS	TPR
1930	NY-N	9	5	1	0	0	0	0	0	1	4	.000	.167	.000	-56	-1	0			1.000	-1	/O-3	-0.2

■ LOU ROSENBERG
Rosenberg, Louis   b: 3/5/04, San Francisco, Cal.   d: 9/8/91, Daly City, Cal.   BR/TR, 5'7", 155 lbs.   Deb: 5/22/23   F

YEAR	TM/L	G	AB	R	H	2B	3B	HR	RBI	BB	SO	AVG	OBP	SLG	PRO+	BR/A	SB	CS	SBR	FA	FR	G/POS	TPR
1923	Chi-A	3	4	0	1	0	0	0	0	0	1	.250	.250	.250	32	-0	0	1	-1	1.000	-1	/2-2	-0.2

■ MAX ROSENFELD
Rosenfeld, Max   b: 12/23/02, New York, N.Y.   d: 3/10/69, Miami, Fla.   BR/TR, 5'8", 175 lbs.   Deb: 4/21/31

YEAR	TM/L	G	AB	R	H	2B	3B	HR	RBI	BB	SO	AVG	OBP	SLG	PRO+	BR/A	SB	CS	SBR	FA	FR	G/POS	TPR
1931	Bro-N	9	9	0	2	1	0	0	0	1	1	.222	.300	.333	70	-0	0			1.000	-1	/O-3	-0.1
1932	Bro-N	34	39	8	14	3	0	2	7	0	10	.359	.359	.590	153	3	2			.970	-9	O-30	-0.7
1933	Bro-N	5	9	0	1	0	0	0	0	1	1	.111	.200	.111	-10	-1	0			1.000	0	/O-2	-0.1
Total	3	42	57	8	17	4	0	2	7	2	12	.298	.322	.474	115	1	2			.978	-9	/O-35	-0.9

■ LARRY ROSENTHAL
Rosenthal, Lawrence John   b: 5/21/10, St.Paul, Minn.   d: 3/4/92, Woodbury, Minn.   BL/TL, 6'0.5", 190 lbs.   Deb: 6/20/36

YEAR	TM/L	G	AB	R	H	2B	3B	HR	RBI	BB	SO	AVG	OBP	SLG	PRO+	BR/A	SB	CS	SBR	FA	FR	G/POS	TPR
1936	Chi-A	85	317	71	89	15	8	3	46	59	37	.281	.394	.407	95	-1	2	0	1	.977	6	O-80	0.2
1937	Chi-A	58	97	20	28	5	3	0	9	9	20	.289	.355	.402	90	-1	1	0	0	.980	-3	O-25	-0.4
1938	Chi-A	61	105	14	30	5	1	1	12	12	13	.286	.359	.381	83	-3	0	1	-1	.959	-3	O-22	-0.6
1939	Chi-A	107	324	50	86	21	5	10	51	53	46	.265	.369	.454	106	3	6	4	-1	.990	-3	O-93	-0.3
1940	Chi-A	107	276	46	83	14	5	6	42	64	32	.301	.432	.453	128	15	2	3	-1	.977	-3	O-92	0.6
1941	Chi-A	20	59	9	14	4	0	0	1	12	5	.237	.366	.305	80	-1	0	0	0	.938	-1	O-18	-0.3
	Cle-A	45	75	10	14	3	1	1	8	9	10	.187	.274	.293	53	-5	1	0	0	1.000	-1	O-14/1-1	-0.5
	Yr	65	134	19	28	7	1	1	9	21	15	.209	.316	.299	66	-6	1	0	0	.971	-1	O-32/1-1	-0.8
1944	NY-A	36	101	9	20	3	0	9	19	15	.198	.325	.228	57	-5	1	0	0	.986	3	O-26	-0.8
	Phi-A	32	54	5	11	2	0	1	6	6	9	.204	.271	.296	63	-3	0	0	0	.960	-4	O-19	-0.8
	Yr	68	155	14	31	5	0	1	15	24	24	.200	.307	.252	60	-7	1	0	0	.979	-2	O-45	-1.1
1945	Phi-A	28	75	6	15	3	2	0	5	9	8	.200	.286	.293	68	-3	0	1	-1	1.000	-2	O-21	-0.8
Total	8	579	1483	240	390	75	25	22	189	251	195	.263	.370	.392	96	-5	13	9	-2	.979	-11	O-410/1-1	-3.2

■ SI ROSENTHAL
Rosenthal, Simon   b: 11/13/03, Boston, Mass.   d: 4/7/69, Boston, Mass.   BL/TL, 5'9", 165 lbs.   Deb: 9/8/25

YEAR	TM/L	G	AB	R	H	2B	3B	HR	RBI	BB	SO	AVG	OBP	SLG	PRO+	BR/A	SB	CS	SBR	FA	FR	G/POS	TPR
1925	Bos-A	19	72	6	19	5	2	0	8	7	3	.264	.329	.389	82	-2	1	0	0	.919	0	O-17	-0.3
1926	Bos-A	104	285	34	76	12	3	4	34	19	18	.267	.317	.372	82	-9	4	1	1	.962	-13	O-67	-2.5
Total	2	123	357	40	95	17	5	4	42	26	21	.266	.319	.375	82	-11	5	1	1	.950	-13	/O-84	-2.8

■ BUNNY ROSER
Roser, John William Joseph "Jack"   b: 11/15/01, St.Louis, Mo.   d: 5/6/79, Rocky Hill, Conn.   BL/TL, 5'11", 175 lbs.   Deb: 8/24/22

YEAR	TM/L	G	AB	R	H	2B	3B	HR	RBI	BB	SO	AVG	OBP	SLG	PRO+	BR/A	SB	CS	SBR	FA	FR	G/POS	TPR
1922	Bos-N	32	113	13	27	3	4	1	19	11		.239	.306	.336	69	-5	2	1	0	.915	-2	O-32	-1.0

■ CHET ROSS
Ross, Chester James   b: 4/1/17, Buffalo, N.Y.   d: 2/21/89, Buffalo, N.Y.   BR/TR, 6'1", 195 lbs.   Deb: 9/15/39

YEAR	TM/L	G	AB	R	H	2B	3B	HR	RBI	BB	SO	AVG	OBP	SLG	PRO+	BR/A	SB	CS	SBR	FA	FR	G/POS	TPR
1939	Bos-N	11	31	4	10	1	0	2	10	2	10	.323	.364	.419	118	1	0			1.000	1	/O-8	0.1
1940	Bos-N	149	569	84	160	23	14	17	89	59	127	.281	.352	.460	130	22	4			.962	7	*O-149	2.1
1941	Bos-N	29	50	1	6	1	0	0	4	9	17	.120	.254	.140	14	-6	0			1.000	1	O-12	-0.6
1942	Bos-N	76	220	20	43	7	2	5	19	16	37	.195	.250	.314	66	-10	1			.992	-1	O-57	-1.5
1943	Bos-N	94	285	27	62	12	2	7	32	26	67	.218	.285	.347	84	-7	1			.977	3	O-73	-0.8
1944	Bos-N	54	154	20	35	9	1	2	26	12	23	.227	.287	.403	91	-3	1			1.000	0	O-38	-0.3
Total	6	413	1309	156	316	53	21	34	170	124	281	.241	.309	.392	100	-3	6			.976	11	O-337	-1.0

■ DON ROSS
Ross, Donald Raymond   b: 7/16/14, Pasadena, Cal.   d: 4/4/96, Arcadia, Cal.   BR/TR, 6'1", 185 lbs.   Deb: 4/19/38

YEAR	TM/L	G	AB	R	H	2B	3B	HR	RBI	BB	SO	AVG	OBP	SLG	PRO+	BR/A	SB	CS	SBR	FA	FR	G/POS	TPR
1938	Det-A	77	265	22	69	7	1	5	30	29	11	.260	.333	.306	58	-17	1	0	0	.946	4	3-75	-1.0
1940	Bro-N	10	38	4	11	2	0	1	8	3	3	.289	.341	.421	103	0	1			.879	-0	3-10	0.0
1942	Det-A	87	226	29	62	10	2	3	30	36	16	.274	.379	.376	104	2	2	1	0	.964	-3	O-38,3-20	-0.3

YEAR	TM/L	G	AB	R	H	2B	3B	HR	RBI	BB	SO	AVG	OBP	SLG	PRO+	BR/A	SB	CS	SBR	FA	FR	G/POS	TPR
1943	Det-A	89	247	19	66	13	0	0	18	20	3	.267	.325	.320	82	-5	2	0	1	.985	-8	O-38,S-18/2-7,3-1	-1.4
1944	Det-A	66	167	14	35	5	0	2	15	14	9	.210	.275	.275	54	-10	2	1	0	.958	-1	O-37/S-2,1-1	-1.4
1945	Det-A	8	29	3	11	4	0	0	4	5	1	.379	.471	.517	175	3	2	0	1	.960	-0	/3-8	0.4
	Cle-A	106	363	26	95	15	1	2	43	42	15	.262	.340	.325	97	-1	0	4	-2	.958	-13	*3-106	-1.5
	Yr	114	392	29	106	19	1	2	47	47	16	.270	.350	.339	104	3	2	4	-2	.958	-14	*3-114	-1.1
1946	Cle-A	55	153	12	41	7	0	3	14	17	12	.268	.341	.373	106	1	0	0	0	.944	-12	3-41/O-2	-1.1
Total	7	498	1488	129	390	63	4	12	162	166	70	.262	.338	.334	86	-26	10	6		.946	-33	3-261,0-115/S21	-6.3

■ JOE ROSSI
Rossi, Joseph Anthony b: 3/13/23, Oakland, Cal. BR/TR, 6'1", 205 lbs. Deb: 4/20/52

YEAR	TM/L	G	AB	R	H	2B	3B	HR	RBI	BB	SO	AVG	OBP	SLG	PRO+	BR/A	SB	CS	SBR	FA	FR	G/POS	TPR
1952	Cin-N	55	145	14	32	0	1	1	6	20	20	.221	.319	.255	61	-7	1	0	0	.982	2	C-46	-0.3

■ CLAUDE ROSSMAN
Rossman, Claude R. b: 6/17/1881, Philmont, N.Y. d: 1/16/28, Poughkeepsie, N.Y. BL/TL, 6', 188 lbs. Deb: 9/16/04

YEAR	TM/L	G	AB	R	H	2B	3B	HR	RBI	BB	SO	AVG	OBP	SLG	PRO+	BR/A	SB	CS	SBR	FA	FR	G/POS	TPR
1904	Cle-A	18	62	5	13	5	0	0	6	0		.210	.210	.290	58	-3	0			.933	-4	O-17	-0.9
1906	Cle-A	118	396	49	122	13	2	1	53	17		.308	.338	.359	120	8	11			.984	-8	*1-105/O-1	-0.3
1907	*Det-A	153	571	60	158	21	8	0	69	33		.277	.318	.342	107	3	20			.981	-14	*1-153	-1.6
1908	*Det-A	138	524	45	154	33	13	2	71	27		.294	.330	.418	137	19	8			.981	6	*1-138	2.5
1909	Det-A	82	287	16	75	8	3	0	39	13		.261	.293	.310	87	-5	10			.981	6	1-75	-1.3
	StL-A	2	8	0	1	0	0	0	0	0		.125	.125	.125	-23	-1	0			1.000	-0	/O-2	-0.2
	Yr	84	295	16	76	8	3	0	39	13		.258	.289	.305	84	-6	10			.981	-6	1-75/O-2	-1.5
Total	5	511	1848	175	523	80	26	3	238	90		.283	.318	.359	113	21	49			.982	-26	1-471/O-20	-1.8

■ RICO ROSSY
Rossy, Elam Jose (Ramos) b: 2/16/64, San Juan, P.R. BR/TR, 5'10", 175 lbs. Deb: 9/11/91

YEAR	TM/L	G	AB	R	H	2B	3B	HR	RBI	BB	SO	AVG	OBP	SLG	PRO+	BR/A	SB	CS	SBR	FA	FR	G/POS	TPR
1991	Atl-N	5	1	0	0	0	0	0	0	0	1	.000	.000	.000	-94	-0	0	0	0	.000	0	/S-1	0.0
1992	KC-A	59	149	21	32	8	1	1	12	20	20	.215	.312	.302	71	-5	0	3	-2	.961	5	S-51/3-9,2-3	0.1
1993	KC-A	46	86	10	19	4	0	2	12	9	11	.221	.302	.337	68	-4	0	0	0	.987	1	2-24,3-16,S-11	-0.2
Total	3	110	236	31	51	12	1	3	24	29	32	.216	.307	.314	69	-10	0	3	-2	.966	6	/S-63,2-27,3-25	-0.1

■ FRANK ROTH
Roth, Francis Charles b: 10/11/1878, Chicago, Ill. d: 3/27/55, Burlington, Wis. BR/TR, 5'10", 160 lbs. Deb: 4/18/03 FC

YEAR	TM/L	G	AB	R	H	2B	3B	HR	RBI	BB	SO	AVG	OBP	SLG	PRO+	BR/A	SB	CS	SBR	FA	FR	G/POS	TPR
1903	Phi-N	68	220	27	60	11	4	0	22	9		.273	.304	.359	92	-3	3			.935	-7	C-60/3-1	-0.3
1904	Phi-N	81	229	28	59	8	1	1	20	12		.258	.298	.314	92	-2	8			.958	-11	C-67/1-1,2-1	-0.7
1905	StL-A	35	107	9	25	3	0	0	7	6		.234	.274	.262	74	-3	1			.962	-6	C-29	-0.7
1906	Chi-A	16	51	4	10	1	1	0	7	3		.196	.241	.255	57	-3	1			.990	3	C-15	0.2
1909	Cin-N	56	147	12	35	7	2	0	16	6		.238	.287	.313	87	-3	5			.967	-3	C-54	-0.2
1910	Cin-N	26	29	3	7	2	0	0	3	0	2	.241	.267	.310	71	-1	1			.938	-0	/C-4,O-1	-0.1
Total	6	282	783	83	196	32	8	1	75	36	2	.250	.289	.315	86	-15	19			.956	-24	C-229/O-1,2-1,13	-1.8

■ BRAGGO ROTH
Roth, Robert Frank b: 8/28/1892, Burlington, Wis. d: 9/11/36, Chicago, Ill. BR/TR, 5'7.5", 170 lbs. Deb: 9/1/14 F

YEAR	TM/L	G	AB	R	H	2B	3B	HR	RBI	BB	SO	AVG	OBP	SLG	PRO+	BR/A	SB	CS	SBR	FA	FR	G/POS	TPR
1914	Chi-A	34	126	14	37	4	6	1	10	8	25	.294	.355	.444	142	6	3	3	-1	.924	2	O-34	0.5
1915	Chi-A	70	240	44	60	6	10	3	35	29	50	.250	.338	.396	116	4	12	6	0	.837	-15	3-35,O-30	-1.2
	Cle-A	39	144	23	43	4	7	4	20	22	22	.299	.399	.507	168	12	14	4	2	.878	-6	O-39	0.6
	Yr	109	384	67	103	10	17	7	55	51	72	.268	.361	.438	135	16	26	10	2	.906	-21	O-69,3-35	-0.6
1916	Cle-A	125	409	50	117	19	7	4	72	38	48	.286	.350	.396	117	8	29	14	0	.954	3	*O-112	0.6
1917	Cle-A	145	495	69	141	30	9	1	72	52	73	.285	.355	.388	118	10	51			.957	-0	*O-135	0.3
1918	Cle-A	106	375	53	106	21	12	1	59	53	41	.283	.383	.411	127	13	35			.936	-3	O-106	0.4
1919	Phi-A	48	195	33	63	13	8	5	29	15	21	.323	.377	.549	156	9	11			.975	-5	O-48	0.6
	Bos-A	63	227	32	58	9	4	0	23	24	32	.256	.337	.330	93	-2	9			.943	-4	O-58	-1.0
	Yr	111	422	65	121	22	12	5	52	39	53	.287	.355	.431	124	12	20			.955	-9	*O-106	-0.4
1920	Was-A	138	468	80	136	23	8	9	92	75	57	.291	.395	.432	122	17	24	12	0	.952	-10	*O-128	-0.2
1921	NY-A	43	152	29	43	9	2	2	10	19	20	.283	.370	.408	96	-1	1	2	-1	.923	-3	O-37	-0.7
Total	8	811	2831	427	804	138	73	30	422	335	389	.284	.367	.416	122	81	189	41		.944	-42	O-727/3-35	-0.1

■ BOB ROTHEL
Rothel, Robert Burton b: 9/17/23, Columbia Station, Ohio d: 3/21/84, Huron, Ohio BR/TR, 5'10.5", 170 lbs. Deb: 4/22/45

YEAR	TM/L	G	AB	R	H	2B	3B	HR	RBI	BB	SO	AVG	OBP	SLG	PRO+	BR/A	SB	CS	SBR	FA	FR	G/POS	TPR
1945	Cle-A	4	10	1	2	0	0	0	3	1		.200	.385	.200	75	-0	0	0	0	.875	-1	/3-4	-0.1

■ BOBBY ROTHERMEL
Rothermel, Edward Hill b: 12/18/1870, Fleetwood, Pa. d: 2/11/27, Detroit, Mich. Deb: 6/18/1899

YEAR	TM/L	G	AB	R	H	2B	3B	HR	RBI	BB	SO	AVG	OBP	SLG	PRO+	BR/A	SB	CS	SBR	FA	FR	G/POS	TPR
1899	Bal-N	10	21	1	2	0	0	0	3	1		.095	.136	.095	-34	-4	0			.867	-2	/2-5,3-2,S-1	-0.6

■ JACK ROTHFUSS
Rothfuss, John Albert b: 4/18/1872, Newark, N.J. d: 4/20/47, Basking Ridge, N.J BR/TR, 5'11.5", 195 lbs. Deb: 8/2/1897

YEAR	TM/L	G	AB	R	H	2B	3B	HR	RBI	BB	SO	AVG	OBP	SLG	PRO+	BR/A	SB	CS	SBR	FA	FR	G/POS	TPR
1897	Pit-N	35	115	20	36	3	1	2	18	5		.313	.352	.409	104	1				.984	-1	1-32	0.0

■ CLAUDE ROTHGEB
Rothgeb, Claude James b: 1/1/1880, Milford, Ill. d: 7/6/44, Manitowoc, Wis. BB, 6'0.5", 200 lbs. Deb: 6/17/05

YEAR	TM/L	G	AB	R	H	2B	3B	HR	RBI	BB	SO	AVG	OBP	SLG	PRO+	BR/A	SB	CS	SBR	FA	FR	G/POS	TPR
1905	Was-A	7	16	2	2	0	0	0	0	0		.125	.125	.125	-22	-2	1			.833	-0	/O-4	-0.3

■ JACK ROTHROCK
Rothrock, John Houston b: 3/14/05, Long Beach, Cal. d: 2/2/80, San Bernardino, Cal BB/TR, 5'11.5", 165 lbs. Deb: 7/28/25

YEAR	TM/L	G	AB	R	H	2B	3B	HR	RBI	BB	SO	AVG	OBP	SLG	PRO+	BR/A	SB	CS	SBR	FA	FR	G/POS	TPR
1925	Bos-A	22	55	6	19	3	3	0	7	3	7	.345	.379	.509	124	2	0	0		.893	-4	S-22	0.0
1926	Bos-A	15	17	3	5	1	0	0	2	3	1	.294	.400	.353	101	0	0	0		.692	-2	/S-2	-0.2
1927	Bos-A	117	428	61	111	24	8	1	36	24	46	.259	.302	.360	73	-19	5	5	-2	.953	-9	S-40,2-36,3-20,1-13	-1.1
1928	Bos-A	117	344	52	92	9	4	3	22	33	40	.267	.333	.343	79	-10	12	6	0	.979	-17	O-53,3-17,1S/2PC	-2.9
1929	Bos-A	143	473	70	142	19	7	6	59	43	47	.300	.361	.408	100	-0	23	13	-1	.970	2	*O-128	-0.7
1930	Bos-A	45	65	4	18	3	1	0	4	2	9	.277	.299	.354	67	-3	0	1		.947	1	/O-9,3-1	-0.4
1931	Bos-A	133	475	81	132	32	3	4	42	47	48	.278	.343	.383	96	-3	13	7	-0	.982	-1	O-79,2-23/1-8,3S	-0.8
1932	Bos-A	12	48	3	10	1	0	0	6	5	5	.208	.283	.229	35	-5	3	0	1	.973	2	O-12	-0.2
	Chi-A	39	64	8	12	2	1	0	6	5	9	.188	.246	.250	31	-7	1	0	0	.929	-9	O-19/3-8,1-1	-1.4
	Yr	51	112	11	22	3	1	0	6	10	14	.196	.262	.241	33	-11	4	0	1	.961	-7	O-31/3-8,1-1	-1.6
1934	*StL-N	154	647	106	184	35	3	11	72	49	56	.284	.336	.399	90	-9	10			.975	5	*O-154/2-1	-1.1
1935	StL-N	129	502	76	137	18	5	3	56	57	29	.273	.347	.347	84	-10	7			.980	-5	*O-127	-1.4
1937	Phi-A	88	232	28	62	15	0	0	21	28	15	.267	.346	.332	73	-9	1	0		.992	-6	O-58/2-1	-1.5
Total	11	1014	3350	498	924	162	35	28	327	299	312	.276	.336	.370	85	-73	75	33		.976	-24	O-639/S-78,231CP	-11.6

■ EDD ROUSH
Roush, Edd J b: 5/8/1893, Oakland City, Ind. d: 3/21/88, Bradenton, Fla. BL/TL, 5'11", 170 lbs. Deb: 8/20/13 CH

YEAR	TM/L	G	AB	R	H	2B	3B	HR	RBI	BB	SO	AVG	OBP	SLG	PRO+	BR/A	SB	CS	SBR	FA	FR	G/POS	TPR
1913	Chi-A	9	10	2	1	0	0	0	0	0	2	.100	.100	.100	-42	-2	0			1.000	-0	/O-2	-0.2
1914	Ind-F	74	166	26	54	8	4	1	30	6	20	.325	.353	.440	104	-2	12			.989	2	O-43/1-2	-0.2
1915	New-F	145	551	73	164	20	11	3	60	38	25	.298	.350	.390	115	1	28			.972	4	*O-144	-0.2
1916	NY-N	39	69	4	13	0	1	0	5	1	4	.188	.200	.217	30	-6	4			.952	-1	O-15	-0.9
	Cin-N	69	272	34	78	7	14	0	15	13	19	.287	.336	.415	133	10	15			.971	6	O-69	1.4
	Yr	108	341	38	91	7	15	0	20	14	23	.267	.309	.375	114	4	19			.969	5	O-84	0.5
1917	Cin-N	136	522	82	178	19	14	4	67	27	24	**.341**	.379	.454	162	36	21			.962	2	*O-134	3.4
1918	Cin-N	113	435	61	145	18	10	5	62	22	10	.333	.368	**.455**	153	26	24			.960	8	*O-113	3.0
1919	*Cin-N	133	504	73	162	19	12	4	71	42	19	**.321**	.380	.431	147	29	20			.989	10	*O-133	3.3
1920	Cin-N	149	579	81	196	22	16	4	90	42	22	.339	.386	.453	142	31	36	24	-4	.975	16	*O-139,1-11/2-1	3.4
1921	Cin-N	112	418	68	147	27	12	4	71	31	8	.352	.403	.502	145	27	19	17	-5	.980	-2	*O-108	1.6
1922	Cin-N	49	165	29	58	7	4	1	24	19	5	.352	.428	.461	132	9	5	3	-0	.990	-1	O-43	0.6
1923	Cin-N	138	527	88	185	**41**	18	6	88	46	16	.351	.406	.531	149	36	10	15	-6	.970	-4	*O-137	1.7
1924	Cin-N	121	483	67	168	23	**21**	3	72	22	11	.348	.376	.501	135	22	17	13	-3	.959	-5	*O-119	0.7
1925	Cin-N	134	540	91	183	28	16	8	83	35	14	.339	.383	.494	125	20	22	20	-5	.978	1	*O-134	0.6
1926	Cin-N	144	563	95	182	37	10	7	79	38	17	.323	.366	.462	125	18	8			.955	-12	*O-143/1-1	-0.4
1927	NY-N	140	570	83	173	27	4	7	58	26	15	.304	.335	.402	97	-4	18			.975	-4	*O-138	-1.6
1928	NY-N	46	163	20	41	5	3	2	13	14	8	.252	.311	.356	75	-6	1			.955	-0	O-39	-0.7
1929	NY-N	115	450	76	146	19	7	8	52	45	16	.324	.390	.451	108	6	6			.975	-4	*O-107	-0.5
1931	Cin-N	101	376	46	102	12	5	1	41	17	5	.271	.308	.338	78	-12	2			.981	-4	O-88	-2.2
Total	18	1967	7363	1099	2376	339	182	68	981	484	260	.323	.369	.446	126	240	268	92		.972	23	*O-1848/1-14,2-1	13.1

YEAR	TM/L	G	AB	R	H	2B	3B	HR	RBI	BB	SO	AVG	OBP	SLG	PRO+	BR/A	SB	CS	SBR	FA	FR	G/POS	TPR

■ PHIL ROUTCLIFFE Routcliffe, Philip John "Chicken" b: 10/24/1870, Oswego, N.Y. d: 10/4/18, Oswego, N.Y. BR/TR, 6', 175 lbs. Deb: 4/21/1890

1890	Pit-N	1	4	1	1	0	0	0	1	0	0	.250	.400	.250	102	0	1			1.000	0	/O-1	0.0

■ DAVE ROWAN Rowan, David (b: David Drohan) b: 12/6/1882, Elora, Ont., Canada d: 7/30/55, Toronto, Ont., Can BL/TL, 5'11", 175 lbs. Deb: 5/27/11

1911	StL-A	18	65	7	25	1	1	0	11	4		.385	.420	.431	143	4	0			.945	-2	1-18	0.2

■ WADE ROWDON Rowdon, Wade Lee b: 9/7/60, Riverhead, N.Y. BR/TR, 6'2", 180 lbs. Deb: 9/8/84

1984	Cin-N	4	7	0	2	0	0	0	0	1		.286	.286	.286	58	-0	0	0	0	1.000	1	/S-1,3-1	0.1
1985	Cin-N	5	9	2	2	0	0	0	2	2	1	.222	.364	.222	64	-0	0	0	0	.667	-1	/3-4	-0.2
1986	Cin-N	38	80	9	20	5	1	0	10	9	17	.250	.333	.338	82	-2	2	0	1	.889	-7	/3-7,S-6,O-5,2-3	-0.8
1987	Cin-N	11	31	2	7	1	1	1	4	3	10	.226	.294	.419	83	-1	0	2	-1	.818	-1	/3-9	-0.4
1988	Bal-A	20	30	1	3	0	0	0	0	0	6	.100	.100	.100	-45	-6	1	1	-0	.947	1	/3-8,O-5,D-5	-0.5
Total	5	78	157	14	34	6	2	1	16	14	35	.217	.285	.299	59	-9	3	3	-1	.866	-7	/3-29,O-10,S-7,D2	-1.8

■ DAVE ROWE Rowe, David Elwood b: 10/9/1854, Harrisburg, Pa. d: 12/9/30, Glendale, Cal. BR/TR, 5'9", 180 lbs. Deb: 5/30/1877 FM

1877	Chi-N	2	7	0	2	0	0	0	0	0	3	.286	.286	.286	72	-0				.667	-1	/O-2,P-1	-0.1
1882	Cle-N	24	97	13	25	4	3	1	17	4	9	.258	.287	.392	119	2				.837	-3	O-23/P-1	-0.1
1883	Bal-a	59	256	40	80	11	6	0		2		.313	.318	.402	127	6				.798	-9	O-50/S-7,1-3,P-1	-0.3
1884	StL-U	109	485	95	142	32	11	4		10		.293	.307	.429	117	-5				**.947**	-2	*O-92,S-14/2-2,1P	-0.8
1885	StL-N	16	62	8	10	3	0	0	3	5		.161	.224	.210	44	-4				.906	-2	O-16	-0.5
1886	KC-N	105	429	53	103	24	8	3	57	15	43	.240	.266	.354	82	-11	2			.851	-5	*O-90,S-11/2-4,M	-1.6
1888	KC-a	32	122	14	21	3	4	0	13	6		.172	.217	.262	50	-7	2			.914	2	O-32,M	-0.6
Total	7	347	1458	223	383	77	32	8	90	42	63	.263	.284	.376	99	-19	4			.878	-19	O-305/S-32,2-6,1P	-4.0

■ HARLAND ROWE Rowe, Harland Stimson "Hypie" b: 4/20/1896, Springvale, Me. d: 5/26/69, Springvale, Maine BL/TR, 6'1", 170 lbs. Deb: 6/23/16

1916	Phi-A	17	36	2	5	1	0	0	3	2	8	.139	.184	.167	6	-4	0			.842	-3	/3-8,O-1	-0.7

■ JACK ROWE Rowe, John Charles b: 12/8/1856, Harrisburg, Pa. d: 4/25/11, St.Louis, Mo. BL/TR, 5'8", 170 lbs. Deb: 9/6/1879 FM

1879	Buf-N	8	34	8	12	1	0	0	8	0	1	.353	.353	.382	139	1				.905	2	/C-6,O-2	0.3
1880	Buf-N	79	326	43	82	10	6	1	36	6	17	.252	.265	.328	98	-1				.897	-19	*C-60,O-25/3-3	-2.0
1881	Buf-N	64	246	30	82	11	**11**	1	43	1	12	.333	.336	.480	156	15				.900	-7	C-46/S-7,3-7,O-5	0.9
1882	Buf-N	75	308	43	82	14	5	1	42	12	0	.266	.294	.354	105	1				.950	-13	C-46,S-22/3-7,O-1	-0.9
1883	Buf-N	87	374	65	104	18	7	1	38	15	14	.278	.306	.372	102	1				.899	-17	C-49,O-28,S-18/3-3	-1.2
1884	Buf-N	93	400	85	126	14	14	4	61	23	14	.315	.352	.450	146	20				**.943**	-10	C-65,O-30/S-6	1.3
1885	Buf-N	98	421	62	122	28	8	2	51	13	19	.290	.311	.409	127	11				.834	-14	S-65,C-23,O-12	-0.1
1886	Det-N	111	468	97	142	21	9	6	87	26	27	.303	.340	.425	128	14	12			.880	-13	*S-110/C-3	-0.5
1887	*Det-N	124	537	135	171	30	10	6	96	39	11	.318	.368	.445	121	14	22			.907	-27	*S-124	-1.0
1888	Det-N	105	451	62	125	19	8	2	74	19	28	.277	.311	.368	116	7	10			.861	-9	*S-105	0.1
1889	Pit-N	75	317	57	82	14	3	2	32	12	16	.259	.313	.341	91	-4	5			.896	-10	S-75	-0.8
1890	Buf-P	125	504	77	126	22	7	2	76	48	18	.250	.324	.333	83	-11	10			**.901**	-2	*S-125,M	-0.4
Total	12	1044	4386	764	1256	202	88	28	644	224	177	.286	.323	.392	115	68	59			.882	-147	S-657,C-298,O/3	-4.3

■ SCHOOLBOY ROWE Rowe, Lynwood Thomas b: 1/11/10, Waco, Tex. d: 1/8/61, ElDorado, Ark. BR/TR, 6'4.5", 210 lbs. Deb: 4/15/33 C

1933	Det-A	21	50	6	11	1	0	0	6	1	4	.220	.235	.240	26	-5	0	0	0	1.000	2	P-19	0.0
1934	*Det-A	51	109	15	33	8	1	2	22	6	20	.303	.339	.450	102	-0	0	0	0	**1.000**	-0	P-45	0.0
1935	*Det-A☆	45	109	19	34	3	2	3	28	12	12	.312	.380	.459	120	3	0	0	0	.981	0	P-42	0.0
1936	Det-A★	45	90	16	23	2	1	1	12	13	15	.256	.356	.333	71	-4	0	0	0	.984	2	P-41	0.0
1937	Det-A	10	10	2	2	0	0	0	1	1	4	.200	.273	.200	21	-1	0	0	0	1.000	0	P-10	0.0
1938	Det-A	4	6	1	1	1	0	0	0	0	1	.167	.167	.333	21	-1	0	0	0	.889	1	/P-4	0.0
1939	Det-A	31	61	7	15	0	1	1	12	5	7	.246	.303	.328	57	-4	1	1	-0	.947	0	P-28	0.0
1940	*Det-A	27	67	7	18	6	1	1	18	5	13	.269	.319	.433	85	-2	1	1	-0	**1.000**	-0	P-27	0.0
1941	Det-A	32	55	10	15	0	3	1	12	5	8	.273	.333	.436	93	-1	0	0	0	.927	1	P-27	0.0
1942	Det-A	2	4	0	0	0	0	0	0	0	0	.000	.000	.000	-93	-1	0	0	0	1.000	0	/P-2	0.0
	Bro-N	14	19	2	4	0	0	0	2	1	4	.211	.250	.211	35	-2	0			1.000	0	/P-9	0.0
1943	Phi-N	82	120	14	36	7	0	4	18	15	21	.300	.382	.458	148	7	0			.981	4	P-27	0.0
1946	Phi-N	30	61	4	11	5	0	1	6	3	16	.180	.219	.311	51	-4	0			1.000	-2	P-17	0.0
1947	Phi-N★	43	79	9	22	2	0	2	11	13	18	.278	.380	.380	106	1	0			.974	-1	P-31	0.0
1948	Phi-N	31	52	3	10	0	0	1	4	4	10	.192	.250	.250	36	-5	1			.976	1	P-30	0.0
1949	Phi-N	23	17	1	4	1	0	1	2	4	1	.235	.316	.471	111	0	3			.870	1	P-23	0.0
Total	15	491	909	116	239	36	9	18	153	86	157	.263	.328	.382	87	-17	3	2		.974	2	P-382	0.0

■ BAMA ROWELL Rowell, Carvel William b: 1/13/16, Citronelle, Ala. d: 8/16/93, Citronelle, Ala. BL/TR, 5'11", 185 lbs. Deb: 9/4/39

1939	Bos-N	21	59	5	11	2	2	0	6	1	4	.186	.200	.288	32	-6	0			.853	-2	O-16	-0.9
1940	Bos-N	130	486	46	148	19	8	3	58	18	22	.305	.331	.395	105	2	12			.953	-3	*2-115/O-7	0.6
1941	Bos-N	138	483	49	129	23	6	7	60	39	36	.267	.322	.383	102	0	11			.935	-10	*2-112,O-14/3-2	-0.3
1946	Bos-N	95	293	37	82	12	6	3	31	29	15	.280	.345	.392	108	3	5			.978	-0	O-85	-0.1
1947	Bos-N	113	384	48	106	23	2	5	40	18	14	.276	.310	.385	86	-9	7			.945	-8	*O-100/2-7,3-4	-2.1
1948	Phi-N	77	196	15	47	16	2	1	22	8	14	.240	.270	.357	70	-9	2			.821	-12	3-18,O-17,2-12	-2.1
Total	6	574	1901	200	523	95	26	19	217	113	105	.275	.316	.382	95	-20	37			.945	-35	2-246,O-239/3-24	-4.9

■ ED ROWEN Rowen, W. Edward b: 10/22/1857, Bridgeport, Conn. d: 2/22/1892, Bridgeport, Conn. 5'6", 155 lbs. Deb: 5/1/1882

1882	Bos-N	83	327	36	81	7	4	1	43	19	18	.248	.289	.303	90	-3				.885	-12	O-48,C-34/S-6,3-1	-1.3
1883	Phi-a	49	196	28	43	10	1	0	21	11		.219	.261	.281	69	-7				.855	-2	C-44/O-8,3-1,2-1	-0.6
1884	Phi-a	4	15	4	6	1	0	0	1	1		.400	.471	.467	194	2				.806	-3	/C-4	-0.1
Total	3	136	538	68	130	18	5	1	65	31	18	.242	.284	.299	85	-9				.866	-17	/C-82,O-56,S-6,32	-2.0

■ CHUCK ROWLAND Rowland, Charlie Leland b: 7/23/1899, Warrenton, N.C. d: 1/21/92, Raleigh, N.C. BR/TR, 6'1", 185 lbs. Deb: 5/11/23

1923	Phi-A	5	6	0	0	0	0	0	0	1	2	.000	.000	.000	-99	-2	0	0	0	1.000	0	/C-4	-0.1

■ RICH ROWLAND Rowland, Richard Garnet b: 2/25/64, Cloverdale, Cal. BR/TR, 6'1", 210 lbs. Deb: 9/7/90

1990	Det-A	7	19	3	3	1	0	0	0	2	4	.158	.238	.211	26	-2	0	0	0	.967	-0	/C-5,D-2	-0.2
1991	Det-A	4	4	0	1	0	0	0	1	1	2	.250	.400	.250	83	-0	0	0	0	1.000	0	/C-2,D-1	-0.1
1992	Det-A	6	14	2	3	0	0	0	0	3	3	.214	.353	.214	62	-1	0	0	0	1.000	0	/C-3,1-1,3-1,D-2	-0.1
1993	Det-A	21	46	2	10	3	0	0	4	5	16	.217	.294	.283	56	-3	0	0	0	.988	5	C-17/D-3	0.2
1994	Bos-A	46	118	14	27	3	0	9	20	11	35	.229	.295	.483	92	-2	0	0	0	.972	-1	C-39/1-1,D-4	-0.1
1995	Bos-A	14	29	1	5	0	0	1	1	0	11	.172	.172	.207	-2	-4	0	0	0	.977	2	C-11/D-3	-0.1
Total	6	98	230	22	49	7	0	10	26	22	71	.213	.282	.365	67	-12	0	0	0	.976	5	/C-77,D-15,1-2,3-1	-0.4

■ JIM ROXBURGH Roxburgh, James A. b: 1/17/1858, San Francisco, Cal d: 2/21/34, San Francisco, Cal BR/TR, 5'10", 170 lbs. Deb: 5/30/1884

1884	Bal-a	2	4	1	2	0	0	0		1		.500	.667	.500	275	1				.824	-0	/C-2	0.1
1887	Phi-a	2	8	0	1	0	0	0	0	0		.125	.125	.125	-30	-1	0			.875	-2	/C-2,2-1	-0.1
Total	2	4	12	1	3	0	0	0	0	1		.250	.357	.250	81	-0	0			.840	-2	/C-4,2-1	-0.1

■ STAN ROYER Royer, Stanley Dean b: 8/31/67, Olney, Ill. BR/TR, 6'3", 195 lbs. Deb: 9/11/91

1991	StL-N	9	21	1	6	1	0	0	1	0	4	.286	.318	.333	83	-0	0	0	0	1.000	-2	/3-5	-0.2
1992	StL-N	13	31	6	10	2	0	2	9	1	4	.323	.344	.581	162	2	0	0	0	.900	-0	/3-5,1-4	-0.2
1993	StL-N	24	46	4	14	2	0	1	8	2	14	.304	.333	.413	100	-0	0	1	-0	.857	-1	3-10/1-2	-0.1
1994	StL-N	39	57	3	10	5	0	1	2	0	18	.175	.175	.316	25	-6	0	0	0	.972	-1	1-11/3-5	-0.7
	Bos-A	7	9	0	1	0	0	0	1	0	1	.111	.111	.111	-41	-2	0	0	0	.833	0	/3-3,1-1	-0.2
Total	4	89	164	14	41	10	0	4	21	4	41	.250	.268	.384	74	-7	0	1	-0	.895	-3	/3-28,1-18	-1.0

YEAR	TM/L	G	AB	R	H	2B	3B	HR	RBI	BB	SO	AVG	OBP	SLG	PRO+	BR/A	SB	CS	SBR	FA	FR	G/POS	TPR

■ JERRY ROYSTER   Royster, Jeron Kennis b: 10/18/52, Sacramento, Cal.   BR/TR, 6', 165 lbs.   Deb: 8/14/73   C

YEAR	TM/L	G	AB	R	H	2B	3B	HR	RBI	BB	SO	AVG	OBP	SLG	PRO+	BR/A	SB	CS	SBR	FA	FR	G/POS	TPR
1973	LA-N	10	19	1	4	0	0	0	2	0	5	.211	.211	.211	18	-2	1	0	0	.842	2	/3-6,2-1	0.0
1974	LA-N	6	0	2	0	0	0	0	0	0	0	—	—	—		0	0			1.000	1	/2-1,3-1,O-1	0.1
1975	LA-N	13	36	2	9	2	1	0	1	1	3	.250	.270	.361	77	-1	1	0	0	1.000	-3	/O-7,2-4,3-3,S-1	-0.4
1976	Atl-N	149	533	65	132	13	1	5	45	52	53	.248	.316	.304	72	-19	24	13	-1	.962	17	*3-148/S-2	-0.4
1977	Atl-N	140	445	64	96	10	2	6	28	38	67	.216	.279	.288	47	-33	28	10	2	.953	-29	3-56,S-51,2-38,/O-1	-5.5
1978	Atl-N	140	529	67	137	17	8	2	35	56	49	.259	.333	.333	78	-15	27	17	-2	.974	-13	2-75,S-60/3-1	-1.7
1979	Atl-N	154	601	103	164	25	6	3	51	62	59	.273	.341	.349	83	-13	35	8	6	.948	13	3-80,2-77	1.0
1980	Atl-N	123	392	42	95	17	5	1	20	37	48	.242	.309	.319	73	-14	22	13	-1	.948	-11	2-49,3-48,O-41	-2.6
1981	Atl-N	64	93	13	19	4	1	0	9	7	14	.204	.260	.269	49	-6	7	5	-1	.950	3	3-24,2-13	-0.4
1982	*Atl-N	108	261	43	77	13	2	2	25	22	36	.295	.354	.383	102	1	14	6	1	.943	-2	3-62,O-25,2-16,S-10	-0.1
1983	Atl-N	91	268	32	63	10	3	3	30	28	35	.235	.307	.328	71	-10	11	7	-1	.940	5	3-47,2-26,O-18,S-13	-0.4
1984	Atl-N	81	227	22	47	13	2	1	21	15	41	.207	.259	.295	52	-15	6	4	-1	.973	-6	2-29,3-17,S-16,O-11	-0.9
1985	SD-N	90	249	31	70	13	2	5	31	32	31	.281	.365	.410	118	7	6	5	1	.975	2	2-58,3-29/S-7,O-2	1.0
1986	SD-N	118	257	31	66	12	0	5	26	32	45	.257	.339	.362	95	-1	3	5	-2	.931	-6	3-59,S-24,2-21,/O-7	-0.6
1987	Chi-A	55	154	25	37	11	0	7	23	19	28	.240	.328	.448	101	-0	2	1	0	.969	-8	3-30,O-13/2-5,D-4	-0.8
	NY-A	18	42	1	15	2	0	0	4	4	4	.357	.413	.405	120	1	2	1	0	.909	2	3-13/2-1,S-1,O-1	0.3
	Yr	73	196	26	52	13	0	7	27	23	32	.265	.345	.439	104	1	4	2	0	.954	-5	3-43,O-14/2-6,DS	-0.5
1988	Atl-N	68	102	8	18	3	0	0	1	6	16	.176	.222	.206	22	-10	0	0	0	1.000	-0	O-26,3-10/2-2,S-2	-1.3
Total	16	1428	4208	552	1049	165	33	40	352	411	534	.249	.318	.333	76	-130	189	95	-0	.951	-19	3-634,2-416,SO/D	-12.7

■ WILLIE ROYSTER   Royster, Willie Arthur b: 4/11/54, Clarksville, Va.   BR/TR, 5'11", 180 lbs.   Deb: 9/3/81

YEAR	TM/L	G	AB	R	H	2B	3B	HR	RBI	BB	SO	AVG	OBP	SLG	PRO+	BR/A	SB	CS	SBR	FA	FR	G/POS	TPR
1981	Bal-A	4	4	0	0	0	0	0	0	0	2	.000	.000	.000	-99	-1	0	0	0	1.000	-0	/C-4	-0.1

■ VIC ROZNOVSKY   Roznovsky, Victor Joseph b: 10/19/38, Shiner, Tex.   BL/TR, 6'1", 180 lbs.   Deb: 6/28/64

YEAR	TM/L	G	AB	R	H	2B	3B	HR	RBI	BB	SO	AVG	OBP	SLG	PRO+	BR/A	SB	CS	SBR	FA	FR	G/POS	TPR
1964	Chi-N	35	76	2	15	1	0	0	2	5	18	.197	.247	.211	29	-7	0	1	-1	.976	-6	C-26	-1.3
1965	Chi-N	71	172	9	38	4	1	3	15	16	30	.221	.298	.308	70	-7	1	0	0	.984	2	C-63	-0.5
1966	Bal-A	41	97	4	23	5	0	1	10	9	11	.237	.308	.320	82	-2	0	0	0	.995	-3	C-34	-0.5
1967	Bal-A	45	97	7	20	5	0	0	10	1	20	.206	.214	.258	39	-7	0	0	0	.993	-2	C-23	-0.9
1969	Phi-N	13	13	0	3	0	0	0	1	1	4	.231	.286	.231	47	-1	0	0	0	1.000	0	/C-2	-0.1
Total	5	205	455	22	99	15	1	4	38	32	83	.218	.275	.281	59	-24	1	1	-0	.988	-9	C-148	-2.8

■ AL RUBELING   Rubeling, Albert William b: 5/10/13, Baltimore, Md. d: 1/28/88, Baltimore, Md.   BR/TR, 6', 185 lbs.   Deb: 4/16/40

YEAR	TM/L	G	AB	R	H	2B	3B	HR	RBI	BB	SO	AVG	OBP	SLG	PRO+	BR/A	SB	CS	SBR	FA	FR	G/POS	TPR
1940	Phi-A	108	376	49	92	16	6	4	38	48	58	.245	.330	.351	78	-12	4	5	-2	.933	-7	3-98,2-10	-1.7
1941	Phi-A	6	19	0	5	0	0	0	2	2	1	.263	.333	.263	61	-1	0			.833	-2	/3-6	-0.2
1943	Pit-N	47	168	23	44	8	4	0	9	8	17	.262	.295	.357	85	-4	0			.974	-1	2-44/3-1	-0.2
1944	Pit-N	92	184	22	45	7	2	4	30	19	19	.245	.322	.370	90	-2	4			1.000	-1	O-18,2-17,3-16	-0.3
Total	4	253	747	94	186	31	12	8	79	77	95	.249	.321	.355	82	-19	8	5		.939	-10	3-121/2-71,O-18	-2.4

■ SONNY RUBERTO   Ruberto, John Edward b: 1/2/46, Staten Island, N.Y.   BR/TR, 5'11", 175 lbs.   Deb: 5/25/69   C

YEAR	TM/L	G	AB	R	H	2B	3B	HR	RBI	BB	SO	AVG	OBP	SLG	PRO+	BR/A	SB	CS	SBR	FA	FR	G/POS	TPR
1969	SD-N	19	21	3	3	0	0	0	0	1	7	.143	.182	.143	-8	-3	0	0	0	1.000	4	C-15	0.1
1972	Cin-N	2	3	0	0	0	0	0	0	0	1	.000	.250	.000	-25	-0	0	0	0	1.000	-0	/C-2	-0.1
Total	2	21	24	3	3	0	0	0	0	1	8	.125	.192	.125	-10	-3	0	0	0	1.000	4	/C-17	0.0

■ ART RUBLE   Ruble, William Arthur "Speedy" b: 3/11/03, Knoxville, Tenn. d: 11/1/83, Maryville, Tenn.   BL/TR, 5'10.5", 168 lbs.   Deb: 4/18/27

YEAR	TM/L	G	AB	R	H	2B	3B	HR	RBI	BB	SO	AVG	OBP	SLG	PRO+	BR/A	SB	CS	SBR	FA	FR	G/POS	TPR
1927	Det-A	56	91	16	15	4	2	0	11	14	15	.165	.283	.253	39	-8	2	2	-1	.970	-7	O-43	-1.7
1934	Phi-N	19	54	7	15	4	0	0	8	7	3	.278	.361	.352	81	-1	0			.839	-2	O-14	-0.3
Total	2	75	145	23	30	8	2	0	19	21	18	.207	.311	.290	55	-10	2	2		.929	-9	/O-57	-2.0

■ JOHNNY RUCKER   Rucker, John Joel b: 1/15/17, Crabapple, Ga. d: 8/7/85, Moultrie, Ga.   BL/TR, 6'2", 175 lbs.   Deb: 4/16/40

YEAR	TM/L	G	AB	R	H	2B	3B	HR	RBI	BB	SO	AVG	OBP	SLG	PRO+	BR/A	SB	CS	SBR	FA	FR	G/POS	TPR
1940	NY-N	86	277	38	82	7	5	4	23	7	32	.296	.313	.401	95	-3	4			.954	-3	O-57	-0.9
1941	NY-N	143	622	95	179	38	9	1	42	29	61	.288	.320	.383	95	-6	8			.967	5	*O-142	-0.9
1943	NY-N	132	505	56	138	19	4	2	46	22	44	.273	.304	.339	85	-11	4			.969	3	*O-117	-1.6
1944	NY-N	144	587	79	143	14	8	6	39	24	48	.244	.275	.325	69	-26	8			.985	-6	*O-139	-4.1
1945	NY-N	105	429	58	117	19	11	7	51	20	36	.273	.305	.417	98	-3	7			.978	-1	O-98	-1.0
1946	NY-N	95	197	28	52	8	2	1	13	7	27	.264	.300	.340	81	-5	4			.948	-10	O-54	-1.8
Total	6	705	2617	354	711	105	39	21	214	109	248	.272	.302	.366	87	-54	35			.971	-12	O-607	-10.3

■ JOHN RUDDERHAM   Rudderham, John Edmund b: 8/30/1863, Quincy, Mass. d: 4/3/42, Randolph, Mass.   BR/TR, 5'8", 170 lbs.   Deb: 9/18/1884

YEAR	TM/L	G	AB	R	H	2B	3B	HR	RBI	BB	SO	AVG	OBP	SLG	PRO+	BR/A	SB	CS	SBR	FA	FR	G/POS	TPR
1884	Bos-U	1	4	0	1	0	0	0	0	0	0	.250	.250	.250	53	-0	0			.000	-1	/O-1	-0.1

■ JOE RUDI   Rudi, Joseph Oden b: 9/7/46, Modesto, Cal.   BR/TR, 6'2", 200 lbs.   Deb: 4/11/67   C

YEAR	TM/L	G	AB	R	H	2B	3B	HR	RBI	BB	SO	AVG	OBP	SLG	PRO+	BR/A	SB	CS	SBR	FA	FR	G/POS	TPR
1967	KC-A	19	43	4	8	2	0	0	1	3	7	.186	.239	.233	41	-3	0	0	0	.984	-2	/1-9,O-6	-0.6
1968	Oak-A	68	181	10	32	5	1	1	12	12	32	.177	.236	.232	44	-12	1	1	-0	.987	-3	O-56	-2.2
1969	Oak-A	35	122	10	23	3	1	2	6	5	16	.189	.220	.279	41	-10	1	1	-0	1.000	-2	O-18,1-11	-1.1
1970	Oak-A	106	350	40	108	23	2	11	42	16	61	.309	.342	.480	129	12	3	1	0	.982	-2	O-63,1-28	0.4
1971	*Oak-A	127	513	62	137	23	4	10	52	28	62	.267	.306	.386	97	-4	3	2	-0	.996	7	*O-121/1-5	-0.4
1972	*Oak-A★	147	593	94	181	32	9	19	75	37	62	.305	.348	.486	154	36	3	4	-2	.992	-1	*O-147/3-1	0.3
1973	*Oak-A★	120	437	53	118	25	1	12	66	30	72	.270	.320	.414	111	5	3	3	4	.992	4	*O-117/1-1,D-1	0.3
1974	*Oak-A★	158	593	73	174	39	4	22	99	34	92	.293	.337	.484	143	29	2	3	-1	.984	-7	*O-140,1-27/D-2	1.5
1975	*Oak-A★	126	468	66	130	26	6	21	75	40	56	.278	.339	.494	136	20	2	1	0	.991	-12	1-91,O-44/D-2	0.0
1976	Oak-A	130	500	54	135	32	3	13	94	41	71	.270	.329	.424	124	14	6	1	1	.989	-1	*O-126/1-2,D-2	0.9
1977	Cal-A	64	242	48	64	13	2	13	53	22	48	.264	.336	.496	128	9	1	0	0	1.000	7	O-61/D-3	1.2
1978	Cal-A	133	497	58	127	27	1	17	79	28	82	.256	.298	.416	103	-3	1	0	0	.992	-7	*O-111,D-11,1-10	-0.5
1979	Cal-A	90	330	35	80	11	3	11	61	24	61	.242	.296	.394	87	-7	0	1	0	.989	-6	O-80/1-5,D-3	-0.5
1980	Cal-A	104	372	42	88	17	1	16	53	17	84	.237	.279	.417	90	-7	1	0	0	.991	8	O-90/1-6,D-3	0.1
1981	Bos-A	49	122	14	22	3	0	6	24	8	29	.180	.242	.352	66	-6	0	0	0	1.000	-4	D-21/1-5,O-1	-0.9
1982	Oak-A	71	193	21	41	6	1	5	18	24	35	.212	.303	.332	77	-6	0	1	0	.991	-7	1-49,O-14/D-3	-1.5
Total	16	1547	5556	684	1468	287	39	179	810	369	870	.264	.314	.427	112	69	25	15	-1	.991	3	*O-1195,1-249/D3	-0.0

■ DUTCH RUDOLPH   Rudolph, John Herman b: 7/10/1882, Natrona, Pa. d: 4/17/67, Natrona, Pa.   BL/TL, 5'10", 160 lbs.   Deb: 7/3/03

YEAR	TM/L	G	AB	R	H	2B	3B	HR	RBI	BB	SO	AVG	OBP	SLG	PRO+	BR/A	SB	CS	SBR	FA	FR	G/POS	TPR
1903	Phi-N	1	1	0	0	0	0	0	0	0	0	.000	.000	.000	-99	-0	0			.000	0	H	0.0
1904	Chi-N	2	3	0	1	0	0	0	0	0	0	.333	.333	.333	106	-0	0			1.000	-1	/O-2	-0.1
Total	2	3	4	0	1	0	0	0	0	0	0	.250	.250	.250	52	-0	0			1.000	-1	/O-2	-0.1

■ KEN RUDOLPH   Rudolph, Kenneth Victor b: 12/29/46, Rockford, Ill.   BR/TR, 6'1", 185 lbs.   Deb: 4/20/69

YEAR	TM/L	G	AB	R	H	2B	3B	HR	RBI	BB	SO	AVG	OBP	SLG	PRO+	BR/A	SB	CS	SBR	FA	FR	G/POS	TPR
1969	Chi-N	27	34	7	7	1	0	1	6	6	11	.206	.325	.324	73	-1	0	0	0	.977	0	C-11/O-3	-0.1
1970	Chi-N	20	40	1	4	1	0	0	2	1	12	.100	.122	.125	-30	-7	0	0	0	1.000	1	C-16	-0.5
1971	Chi-N	25	76	5	15	3	0	0	7	6	20	.197	.265	.237	38	-6	0	0	0	1.000	7	C-25	0.2
1972	Chi-N	42	106	10	25	1	1	2	9	6	14	.236	.283	.321	66	-5	1	2	-1	.966	5	C-41	0.1
1973	Chi-N	64	170	12	35	3	2	1	17	7	25	.206	.242	.300	46	-13	1	4	-2	.970	-3	C-64	-1.6
1974	SF-N	57	158	11	41	3	0	0	10	21	15	.259	.350	.278	74	-5	0	1	0	.996	-3	C-56	-0.5
1975	StL-N	44	80	5	16	2	1	0	3	6	10	.200	.229	.262	35	-5	0	0	0	.972	5	C-31	-0.5
1976	StL-N	27	50	1	8	3	0	1	6	2	10	.160	.176	.220	12	-5	0	0	0	.940	2	C-14	-0.4
1977	SF-N	11	15	1	3	0	0	0	3	1	1	.200	.250	.200	22	-2	0	0	0	.946	5	C-11	0.1
	Bal-A	11	14	2	4	1	0	0	2	1	4	.286	.286	.357	79	-0	0	0	0	1.000	5	C-11	0.0
Total	9	328	743	55	158	23	2	6	64	52	121	.213	.268	.273	48	-52	2	6	-3	.980	24	C-280/O-3	-2.3

■ MUDDY RUEL   Ruel, Herold Dominic b: 2/20/1896, St.Louis, Mo. d: 11/13/63, Palo Alto, Cal.   BR/TR, 5'9", 150 lbs.   Deb: 5/29/15   MC

YEAR	TM/L	G	AB	R	H	2B	3B	HR	RBI	BB	SO	AVG	OBP	SLG	PRO+	BR/A	SB	CS	SBR	FA	FR	G/POS	TPR
1915	StL-A	10	14	0	0	0	0	0	1	5	5	.000	.263	.000	-22	-2	0			.958	-1	/C-6	-0.3
1917	NY-A	6	17	1	2	0	0	0	1	2	2	.118	.211	.118	0	-2	1			1.000	-1	/C-6	-0.3

YEAR	TM/L	G	AB	R	H	2B	3B	HR	RBI	BB	SO	AVG	OBP	SLG	PRO+	BR/A	SB	CS	SBR	FA	FR	G/POS	TPR
1918	NY-A	3	6	0	2	0	0	0	0	2	1	.333	.500	.333	148	1	1			1.000	0	/C-2	0.1
1919	NY-A	79	233	18	56	6	0	0	31	34	26	.240	.340	.266	71	-8	4			.975	2	C-79	0.1
1920	NY-A	82	261	30	70	14	1	1	15	15	18	.268	.310	.341	70	-12	4	2	0	.984	0	C-80	-0.6
1921	Bos-A	113	358	41	99	21	1	1	45	41	15	.277	.352	.349	82	-9	2	7	-4	.977	-10	*C-109	-1.6
1922	Bos-A	116	361	34	92	15	1	0	28	41	26	.255	.330	.302	67	-17	4	2	0	.978	-2	*C-112	-1.2
1923	Was-A	136	449	63	142	24	3	0	54	55	21	.316	.394	.383	111	9	4	6	-2	.980	19	*C-133	3.0
1924	*Was-A	149	501	50	142	20	2	0	57	62	20	.283	.370	.331	84	-9	7	11	-5	.980	14	*C-147	0.9
1925	*Was-A	127	393	55	122	9	2	0	54	63	16	.310	.411	.344	95	1	4	5	-2	.982	12	*C-126/1-1	1.6
1926	Was-A	117	368	42	110	22	4	1	53	61	14	.299	.401	.389	109	8	7	6	-2	**.989**	2	*C-117	1.4
1927	Was-A	131	428	61	132	16	5	1	52	63	18	.308	.403	.376	104	6	9	6	-1	.988	-3	*C-128	1.1
1928	Was-A	108	350	31	90	18	2	0	55	44	14	.257	.342	.320	75	-11	12	10	-2	**.989**	7	*C-101/1-2	0.1
1929	Was-A	69	188	16	46	4	2	0	20	31	7	.245	.352	.287	66	-8	0	4	-2	.990	9	C-62	0.3
1930	Was-A	66	198	18	50	3	4	0	26	24	13	.253	.342	.308	66	-9	1	0	0	.986	4	C-60	0.0
1931	Bos-A	33	83	6	25	5	0	0	6	9	6	.301	.370	.361	98	0	0	0	0	.945	1	C-30	0.3
	Det-A	14	50	1	6	1	0	0	3	5	1	.120	.200	.140	-9	-8	0	0	0	.975	3	C-14	-0.4
	Yr	47	133	7	31	6	0	0	9	14	7	.233	.306	.278	56	-8	0	0	0	.958	4	C-44	-0.1
1932	Det-A	51	136	10	32	4	2	0	18	17	6	.235	.320	.294	58	-8	1	0	0	.989	-2	C-49	-0.7
1933	StL-A	36	63	13	12	2	0	0	8	24	4	.190	.414	.222	68	-1	0	0	0	1.000	3	C-28	0.2
1934	Chi-A	22	57	4	12	3	0	0	7	8	5	.211	.308	.263	47	-4	0	0	0	.976	-2	C-21	-0.5
Total	19	1468	4514	494	1242	187	29	4	534	606	238	.275	.365	.332	83	-84	61	59		.982	53	*C-1410/1-3	3.5

■ DUTCH RUETHER

Ruether, Walter Henry   b: 9/13/1893, Alameda, Cal.   d: 5/16/70, Phoenix, Ariz.   BL/TL, 6'1.5", 180 lbs.   Deb: 4/13/17

YEAR	TM/L	G	AB	R	H	2B	3B	HR	RBI	BB	SO	AVG	OBP	SLG	PRO+	BR/A	SB	CS	SBR	FA	FR	G/POS	TPR
1917	Chi-N	31	44	3	12	1	3	0	11	8	11	.273	.385	.432	139	2	0			1.000	1	P-10/1-5	0.1
	Cin-N	19	24	1	5	2	0	0	1	3	6	.208	.296	.292	84	-0	1			.833	-0	/P-7	0.0
	Yr	50	68	4	17	3	3	0	12	11	17	.250	.354	.382	122	2	1			.920	0	P-17/1-5	0.1
1918	Cin-N	2	3	0	0	0	0	0	0	0	2	.000	.000	.000	-99	-1	0			1.000	-0	/P-2	0.0
1919	*Cin-N	42	92	8	24	2	3	0	6	4	18	.261	.292	.348	94	-1	1			.971	-3	P-33	0.0
1920	Cin-N	45	104	3	20	4	0	0	10	5	24	.192	.229	.231	33	-9	0	0	0	.952	0	P-37/1-1	0.0
1921	Cin-N	49	97	12	34	5	2	2	13	4	9	.351	.376	.505	127	3	1	0	0	.966	-1	P-36	0.0
1922	Bro-N	67	125	12	26	6	1	2	20	12	11	.208	.283	.320	56	-9	0	0	0	**1.000**	-0	P-35	0.0
1923	Bro-N	49	117	6	32	1	0	0	10	12	12	.274	.341	.282	68	-5	0	0	0	.968	-2	P-34/1-1	0.0
1924	Bro-N	34	62	5	15	1	1	0	4	5	2	.242	.299	.290	60	-3	0	0	0	.981	-1	P-30	0.0
1925	*Was-A	55	108	18	36	3	2	1	15	10	8	.333	.390	.426	109	2	0	1	-1	.962	-3	P-30/1-1	0.0
1926	Was-A	47	92	6	23	2	0	1	11	6	10	.250	.296	.304	58	-6	0	0	0	.974	-2	P-23	0.0
	*NY-A	13	21	2	2	0	0	0	0	0	1	.095	.136	.095	-39	-4	0	0	0	.875	-1	/P-5	0.0
	Yr	60	113	8	25	2	0	1	11	6	11	.221	.267	.265	40	-10	0	0	0	.957	-3	P-28	0.0
1927	NY-A	35	80	7	21	3	0	0	8	10	15	.262	.330	.338	76	-3	0	0	0	**1.000**	0	P-27	0.0
Total	11	488	969	83	250	30	12	7	111	77	129	.258	.314	.335	76	-33	3	1		.970	-9	P-309/1-8	0.1

■ RUDY RUFER

Rufer, Rudolph Joseph   b: 10/28/26, Ridgewood, N.Y.   BR/TR, 6'0.5", 165 lbs.   Deb: 9/22/49

YEAR	TM/L	G	AB	R	H	2B	3B	HR	RBI	BB	SO	AVG	OBP	SLG	PRO+	BR/A	SB	CS	SBR	FA	FR	G/POS	TPR
1949	NY-N	7	15	1	1	0	0	0	2	2	0	.067	.176	.067	-32	-3	0			.957	-1	/S-7	-0.3
1950	NY-N	15	11	1	1	0	0	0	0	0	1	.091	.091	.091	-52	-2	1			.889	1	/S-8	-0.1
Total	2	22	26	2	2	0	0	0	2	2	1	.077	.143	.077	-40	-5	1			.938	-2	/S-15	-0.4

■ RED RUFFING

Ruffing, Charles Herbert   b: 5/3/04, Granville, Ill.   d: 2/17/86, Mayfield Hts., O.   BR/TR, 6'1.5", 205 lbs.   Deb: 5/31/24   CH

YEAR	TM/L	G	AB	R	H	2B	3B	HR	RBI	BB	SO	AVG	OBP	SLG	PRO+	BR/A	SB	CS	SBR	FA	FR	G/POS	TPR
1924	Bos-A	8	7	0	1	0	1	0	0	0	1	.143	.143	.429	44	-1	0	0	0	1.000	-1	/P-8	0.0
1925	Bos-A	37	79	6	17	4	2	0	11	1	22	.215	.235	.316	39	-8	0	0	0	.983	-1	P-37	0.0
1926	Bos-A	37	51	8	10	1	0	1	5	2	12	.196	.226	.275	31	-5	0	1	-1	.978	-1	P-37	0.0
1927	Bos-A	29	55	5	14	3	1	0	4	0	6	.255	.268	.345	59	-4	0	0	0	.978	0	P-26	0.0
1928	Bos-A	60	121	12	38	13	1	2	19	3	12	.314	.331	.488	115	2	0	0	0	.951	-3	P-42	0.0
1929	Bos-A	60	114	9	35	9	0	2	17	2	13	.307	.325	.439	97	-1	0	0	0	.946	-2	P-35/O-2	-0.1
1930	Bos-A	6	11	2	3	2	0	0	1	0	1	.273	.273	.455	84	-0	0	0	0	.667	-1	P-4	0.0
	NY-A	52	99	15	37	6	2	4	21	7	7	.374	.415	.596	160	9	0	0	0	.938	-2	P-34	0.0
	Yr	58	110	17	40	8	2	4	22	7	8	.364	.402	.582	153	8	0	0	0	.914	-3	P-38	0.0
1931	NY-A	48	109	14	36	8	1	3	12	1	13	.330	.336	.505	125	3	0	0	0	**1.000**	-3	P-37/O-1	0.0
1932	*NY-A	55	124	20	38	6	1	3	19	6	10	.306	.338	.444	106	1	0	0	0	.955	-2	P-35	0.0
1933	NY-A	55	115	10	29	3	1	2	13	7	15	.252	.295	.348	74	-5	0	0	0	.964	-0	P-35	0.0
1934	NY-A★	45	113	11	28	3	0	2	13	3	17	.248	.274	.327	58	-8	0	0	0	.933	-3	P-36	0.0
1935	NY-A	50	109	13	37	10	0	2	18	3	17	.339	.363	.486	125	3	0	0	0	**1.000**	-2	P-30	0.0
1936	*NY-A	53	127	14	37	5	0	5	22	11	12	.291	.348	.449	99	-1	0	0	0	.986	2	P-33	0.0
1937	*NY-A	54	129	11	26	3	1	0	10	13	24	.202	.275	.248	32	-13	0	0	0	.974	-4	P-31	0.0
1938	*NY-A☆	45	107	12	24	4	1	3	17	17	21	.224	.331	.364	74	-4	0	0	0	**1.000**	-2	P-31	0.0
1939	*NY-A★	44	114	12	35	1	0	1	20	7	18	.307	.347	.342	78	-4	1	0	0	.952	-2	P-28	0.0
1940	NY-A★	33	89	8	11	4	0	1	7	3	9	.124	.152	.202	-9	-15	0	0	0	.947	-3	P-30	0.0
1941	*NY-A☆	38	89	10	27	8	1	2	22	4	12	.303	.333	.483	115	1	0	0	0	**1.000**	-3	P-23	0.0
1942	*NY-A☆	30	80	8	20	4	0	1	13	5	13	.250	.302	.338	81	-2	0	0	0	.974	-2	P-24	0.0
1945	NY-A	21	46	4	10	0	1	1	5	0	8	.217	.217	.326	54	-3	0	0	0	.929	-2	P-11	0.0
1946	NY-A	8	25	1	3	1	0	0	1	1	8	.120	.154	.160	-12	-4	0	0	0	1.000	-1	/P-8	0.0
1947	Chi-A	14	24	2	5	0	0	0	3	2	5	.208	.240	.208	26	-2	0	0	0	1.000	-0	/P-9	0.0
Total	22	882	1937	207	521	98	13	36	273	97	266	.269	.306	.389	81	-60	1	1		.968	-35	P-624/O-3	-0.1

■ CHICO RUIZ

Ruiz, Hiraldo (Sablon)   b: 12/5/38, Santo Domingo, Cuba   d: 2/9/72, San Diego, Cal.   BB/TR, 6', 173 lbs.   Deb: 4/13/64

YEAR	TM/L	G	AB	R	H	2B	3B	HR	RBI	BB	SO	AVG	OBP	SLG	PRO+	BR/A	SB	CS	SBR	FA	FR	G/POS	TPR
1964	Cin-N	77	311	33	76	13	2	2	16	7	41	.244	.270	.318	63	-15	11	3	2	.942	-10	3-49,2-30	-2.4
1965	Cin-N	29	18	7	2	1	0	0	1	0	5	.111	.111	.167	-21	-3	1	2	-1	.875	2	/3-4,S-3	-0.2
1966	Cin-N	82	110	13	28	2	1	0	5	5	14	.255	.287	.291	56	-6	1	2	-1	.927	-1	3-27/O-8,S-6	-0.9
1967	Cin-N	105	250	32	55	12	4	0	13	11	35	.220	.259	.300	53	-15	9	4	0	.969	-1	2-56,3-13,S-11,O-5	-1.2
1968	Cin-N	85	139	15	36	2	1	0	9	12	18	.259	.318	.288	78	-3	4	3	-1	.979	4	2-34,1-16/3-5,S-3	0.6
1969	Cin-N	88	196	19	48	4	1	0	13	14	28	.245	.295	.276	58	-11	4	2	0	.949	-7	2-39,S-29/3-7,1O	-1.3
1970	Cal-A	68	107	10	26	3	1	0	12	7	16	.243	.296	.290	64	-5	3	0	1	.985	-0	3-27/2-3,S-3,1-2,C	-0.4
1971	Cal-A	31	19	4	5	0	0	0	2	7	7	.263	.333	.263	76	-1	1	0	0	1.000	2	/3-3,2-2	0.2
Total	8	565	1150	133	276	37	10	2	69	58	164	.240	.281	.295	60	-59	34	16	1	.966	-6	2-164,3-135/S1OC	-5.6

■ CHICO RUIZ

Ruiz, Manuel (Cruz)   b: 11/1/51, Santurce, P.R.   BR/TR, 5'11.5", 170 lbs.   Deb: 7/29/78

YEAR	TM/L	G	AB	R	H	2B	3B	HR	RBI	BB	SO	AVG	OBP	SLG	PRO+	BR/A	SB	CS	SBR	FA	FR	G/POS	TPR
1978	Atl-N	18	46	3	13	3	0	0	2	1	6	.283	.313	.348	76	-1	0	0	0	.984	1	2-14/3-1	0.1
1980	Atl-N	25	26	3	8	2	1	0	2	3	7	.308	.379	.462	129	1	0	1	-1	.875	2	3-16/S-4,2-2	0.2
Total	2	43	72	6	21	5	1	0	4	4	11	.292	.338	.389	95	-0	0	1	-1	.880	3	/3-17,2-16,S-4	0.3

■ JOE RULLO

Rullo, Joseph Vincent   b: 6/16/16, New York, N.Y.   d: 10/28/69, Philadelphia, Pa.   BR/TR, 5'11", 168 lbs.   Deb: 9/22/43

YEAR	TM/L	G	AB	R	H	2B	3B	HR	RBI	BB	SO	AVG	OBP	SLG	PRO+	BR/A	SB	CS	SBR	FA	FR	G/POS	TPR
1943	Phi-A	16	55	2	16	3	0	0	6	8	7	.291	.381	.345	114	1	0	0	0	.963	-1	2-16	0.2
1944	Phi-A	35	96	5	16	0	0	0	5	6	19	.167	.223	.167	12	-11	1	0	0	.954	3	2-33/1-1,O-1	-0.6
Total	2	51	151	7	32	3	0	0	11	14	26	.212	.283	.232	50	-10	1	0	0	.957	2	/2-49,O-1,1-1	-0.4

■ WILLIAM RUMLER

Rumler, William George   b: 3/27/1891, Milford, Neb.   d: 5/26/66, Lincoln, Neb.   BR/TR, 6'1", 190 lbs.   Deb: 5/4/14

YEAR	TM/L	G	AB	R	H	2B	3B	HR	RBI	BB	SO	AVG	OBP	SLG	PRO+	BR/A	SB	CS	SBR	FA	FR	G/POS	TPR
1914	StL-A	34	46	2	8	1	0	0	6	3	12	.174	.240	.196	32	-4	2	2	-1	1.000	-3	C-10/O-6	-0.8
1916	StL-A	27	37	6	12	3	0	0	10	3	7	.324	.375	.405	141	2	0			.971	0	/C-9	0.3
1917	StL-A	78	88	7	23	3	4	1	16	8	9	.261	.323	.420	132	1	2			.938	-0	/O-9	0.3
Total	3	139	171	15	43	7	4	1	32	14	28	.251	.312	.357	107	1	4	2		.986	-3	/C-19,O-15	-0.2

■ PAUL RUNGE

Runge, Paul William   b: 5/21/58, Kingston, N.Y.   BR/TR, 6', 175 lbs.   Deb: 9/25/81

YEAR	TM/L	G	AB	R	H	2B	3B	HR	RBI	BB	SO	AVG	OBP	SLG	PRO+	BR/A	SB	CS	SBR	FA	FR	G/POS	TPR
1981	Atl-N	10	27	2	7	1	0	0	2	4	4	.259	.355	.296	84	-0	0	0	0	.911	-1	S-10	-0.1
1982	Atl-N	4	2	0	0	0	0	0	0	1	0	.000	.000	.000	-96	-1	0	0	0	1.000	0	/H	-0.1

YEAR	TM/L	G	AB	R	H	2B	3B	HR	RBI	BB	SO	AVG	OBP	SLG	PRO+	BR/A	SB	CS	SBR	FA	FR	G/POS	TPR
1983	Atl-N	5	8	0	2	0	0	0	1	1	4	.250	.333	.250	59	-0	0	0	0	1.000	-1	/2-2	-0.1
1984	Atl-N	28	90	5	24	3	1	0	3	10	14	.267	.340	.322	81	-2	5	3	-0	.970	10	2-22/S-7,3-3	0.9
1985	Atl-N	50	87	15	19	3	0	1	5	18	18	.218	.352	.287	76	-2	0	1	-1	.929	8	3-28/S-5,2-2	0.1
1986	Atl-N	7	8	1	2	0	0	0	0	2	4	.250	.400	.250	79	-0	0	0	0	1.000	2	/2-5	0.2
1987	Atl-N	27	47	9	10	1	0	3	8	5	10	.213	.288	.426	82	-1	0	1	-1	.923	1	3-10/S-9,2-2	-0.1
1988	Atl-N	52	76	11	16	5	0	0	7	14	21	.211	.333	.276	73	-2	0	0	0	1.000	-1	3-19/2-7,S-6	-0.4
Total	8	183	345	43	80	13	1	4	26	54	75	.232	.336	.310	77	-9	5	5	-2	.941	13	/3-60,2-40,S-37	0.4

■ **TOM RUNNELLS**   Runnells, Thomas William   b: 4/17/55, Greeley, Colo.   BB/TR, 6′, 175 lbs.   Deb: 8/9/85   MC

YEAR	TM/L	G	AB	R	H	2B	3B	HR	RBI	BB	SO	AVG	OBP	SLG	PRO+	BR/A	SB	CS	SBR	FA	FR	G/POS	TPR
1985	Cin-N	28	35	3	7	1	0	0	0	3	4	.200	.263	.229	37	-3	0	0	0	1.000	1	S-11/2-1	-0.2
1986	Cin-N	12	11	1	1	1	0	0	0	0	2	.091	.091	.182	-26	-2	0	0	0	1.000	1	/2-4,3-3	-0.1
Total	2	40	46	4	8	2	0	0	0	3	6	.174	.224	.217	23	-5	0	0	0	1.000	2	/S-11,2-5,3-3	-0.3

■ **PETE RUNNELS**   Runnels, James Edward (b: James Edward Runnells)   b: 1/28/28, Lufkin, Tex.   d: 5/20/91, Pasadena, Tex.   BL/TR, 6′, 170 lbs.   Deb: 7/1/51   MC

YEAR	TM/L	G	AB	R	H	2B	3B	HR	RBI	BB	SO	AVG	OBP	SLG	PRO+	BR/A	SB	CS	SBR	FA	FR	G/POS	TPR
1951	Was-A	78	273	31	76	12	2	0	25	31	24	.278	.354	.337	89	-3	0	3	-2	.949	-21	S-73	-2.1
1952	Was-A	152	555	70	158	18	3	1	64	72	55	.285	.368	.333	99	-2	0	10	-6	.966	-15	*S-147/2-1	-0.8
1953	Was-A	137	486	64	125	15	5	2	50	64	36	.257	.347	.321	83	-10	3	4	-2	.958	-33	*S-121,2-11	-3.5
1954	Was-A	139	488	75	131	17	15	3	56	78	60	.268	.369	.383	112	10	2	3	-1	.953	-19	*S-107,2-27/O-1	0.0
1955	Was-A	134	503	66	143	16	4	2	49	55	51	.284	.356	.344	94	-3	3	9	-5	.976	-3	*2-132/S-2	-0.3
1956	Was-A	147	578	72	179	29	9	8	76	58	64	.310	.375	.433	113	11	5	5	-2	.995	5	1-81,2-69/S-3	1.0
1957	Was-A	134	473	53	109	18	4	2	35	55	51	.230	.313	.298	69	-20	2	3	-1	.995	2	1-72,3-32,2-23	-2.2
1958	Bos-A	147	568	103	183	32	5	8	59	87	49	.322	.418	.438	127	25	1	2	-1	.985	8	*2-106,1-42	3.3
1959	Bos-A★	147	560	95	176	33	6	6	57	95	48	.314	.415	.427	126	24	6	5	-1	.982	6	*2-101,1-44/S-9	3.3
1960	Bos-A★	143	528	80	169	29	2	2	35	71	51	**.320**	.403	.394	112	12	5	2	0	**.986**	9	*2-129,1-57/3-3	3.2
1961	Bos-A	143	360	49	114	20	3	3	38	46	32	.317	.399	.414	115	9	5	1	1	**.995**	1	*1-113,3-11/2-7,S-1	0.5
1962	Bos-A★	152	562	80	183	33	5	10	60	79	57	**.326**	.411	.456	129	26	3	4	-2	.993	4	*1-151	1.3
1963	Hou-N	124	388	35	98	9	1	2	23	45	42	.253	.335	.296	89	-4	2	0	1	.993	-10	1-70,2-36/3-3	-1.5
1964	Hou-N	22	51	3	10	1	0	1	6	6	14	.196	.305	.216	53	-3	0	0	0	.986	-2	1-14	-0.6
Total	14	1799	6373	876	1854	282	64	49	630	844	627	.291	.376	.378	106	76	37	51	-20	.994	-78	1-644,2-642,S/3O	2.4

■ **JOHN RUSS**   Russ, John   b: 4/1/1858, Cannelton, Ind.   d: 1/18/12, Louisville, Ky.   Deb: 7/4/1882

YEAR	TM/L	G	AB	R	H	2B	3B	HR	RBI	BB	SO	AVG	OBP	SLG	PRO+	BR/A	SB	CS	SBR	FA	FR	G/POS	TPR
1882	Bal-a	1	3	0	1	0	0	0	0	0	0	.333	.333	.333	136	0				.000	-1	/O-1,P-1	0.0

■ **REB RUSSELL**   Russell, Ewell Albert   b: 4/12/1889, Jackson, Miss.   d: 9/30/73, Indianapolis, Ind   BL/TL, 5′11″, 185 lbs.   Deb: 4/18/13

YEAR	TM/L	G	AB	R	H	2B	3B	HR	RBI	BB	SO	AVG	OBP	SLG	PRO+	BR/A	SB	CS	SBR	FA	FR	G/POS	TPR
1913	Chi-A	52	106	9	20	5	3	1	7	1	29	.189	.204	.321	54	-7	0			.952	-5	P-52	0.0
1914	Chi-A	46	64	6	17	1	1	0	7	1	14	.266	.277	.313	78	-2	0			.946	0	P-38	0.0
1915	Chi-A	45	86	11	21	2	3	0	7	4	14	.244	.293	.337	86	-2	1			.971	-4	P-41	0.0
1916	Chi-A	56	91	9	13	0	0	0	6	0	18	.143	.152	.165	-5	-12	1			.974	-2	P-56	0.0
1917	*Chi-A	39	68	5	19	3	3	0	9	2	10	.279	.300	.412	115	1	0			.984	-1	P-35/O-1	0.0
1918	Chi-A	27	50	2	7	3	0	0	3	0	6	.140	.157	.200	8	-6	0			1.000	0	P-19/O-1	0.0
1919	Chi-A	1	0	0	0	0	0	0	0	0	0	—	—	—		0	0			.000	0	/P-1	0.0
1922	Pit-N	60	220	51	81	14	8	12	75	14	18	.368	.423	.668	175	23	4	0		.968	-2	O-60	1.6
1923	Pit-N	94	291	49	84	18	7	9	58	20	21	.289	.341	.491	115	5	3	1	0	.970	-8	O-76	-0.2
Total	9	420	976	142	262	48	25	22	172	42	130	.268	.309	.436	104	0	9	3		.968	-15	P-242,O-138	1.4

■ **RIP RUSSELL**   Russell, Glen David   b: 1/26/15, Los Angeles, Cal.   d: 9/26/76, Los Alamitos, Cal   BR/TR, 6′1″, 180 lbs.   Deb: 5/5/39

YEAR	TM/L	G	AB	R	H	2B	3B	HR	RBI	BB	SO	AVG	OBP	SLG	PRO+	BR/A	SB	CS	SBR	FA	FR	G/POS	TPR
1939	Chi-N	143	542	55	148	24	5	9	79	36	56	.273	.318	.386	87	-11	2			.988	-5	*1-143	-3.1
1940	Chi-N	68	215	15	53	7	2	5	33	8	23	.247	.277	.367	78	-7	1			.982	-6	1-51/3-3	-1.8
1941	Chi-N	6	17	1	5	1	0	0	1	1	5	.294	.333	.353	97	-0	0			.975	0	/1-5	0.0
1942	Chi-N	102	302	32	73	9	0	8	41	17	21	.242	.282	.351	88	-6	0			.974	-12	1-35,2-24,3-10/O-3	-2.0
1946	*Bos-A	80	274	22	57	10	1	6	35	13	30	.208	.247	.318	54	-18	1	1	-0	.942	-1	3-70/2-3	-1.9
1947	Bos-A	26	52	8	8	1	0	1	3	8	7	.154	.267	.231	36	-4	0	0	0	.923	4	3-13	-0.3
Total	6	425	1402	133	344	52	8	29	192	83	142	.245	.289	.356	77	-46	4	1		.984	-22	1-234/3-96,2-27,O-3	-9.1

■ **HARVEY RUSSELL**   Russell, Harvey Holmes   b: 1/10/1887, Marshall, Va.   d: 1/8/80, Alexandria, Va.   BL/TR, 5′9.5″, 163 lbs.   Deb: 4/17/14

YEAR	TM/L	G	AB	R	H	2B	3B	HR	RBI	BB	SO	AVG	OBP	SLG	PRO+	BR/A	SB	CS	SBR	FA	FR	G/POS	TPR
1914	Bal-F	81	168	18	39	3	2	0	13	18	17	.232	.310	.274	58	-12	2			.956	-17	C-47/S-1,O-1	-2.7
1915	Bal-F	53	73	5	19	1	2	0	11	14	5	.260	.407	.329	105	1	1			.989	-4	C-21	-0.2
Total	2	134	241	23	58	4	4	0	24	32	22	.241	.342	.290	73	-11	3			.965	-22	/C-68,O-1,S-1	-2.9

■ **JIM RUSSELL**   Russell, James William   b: 10/1/18, Fayette City, Pa.   d: 11/24/87, Pittsburgh, Pa.   BB/TR, 6′1″, 181 lbs.   Deb: 9/12/42

YEAR	TM/L	G	AB	R	H	2B	3B	HR	RBI	BB	SO	AVG	OBP	SLG	PRO+	BR/A	SB	CS	SBR	FA	FR	G/POS	TPR
1942	Pit-N	5	14	2	1	0	0	0	0	0	4	.071	.133	.071	-38	-2	0			1.000	1	/O-3	-0.2
1943	Pit-N	146	533	79	138	19	11	4	44	77	67	.259	.354	.358	102	3	12			.990	-2	*O-134/1-6	-0.2
1944	Pit-N	152	580	109	181	34	14	8	66	79	63	.312	.399	.460	136	29	6			.986	13	*O-149	3.5
1945	Pit-N	146	510	88	145	24	8	12	77	71	40	.284	.377	.433	120	15	15			.973	3	*O-140	1.1
1946	Pit-N	146	618	68	143	29	6	8	50	67	54	.277	.362	.403	114	10	11			.966	-2	*O-134/1-5	0.1
1947	Pit-N	128	478	68	121	21	8	8	51	63	58	.253	.343	.381	89	-7	7			.980	11	*O-119	-0.2
1948	Bos-N	89	322	44	85	18	1	9	54	46	31	.264	.361	.410	110	5	4			.992	6	O-84	0.6
1949	Bos-N	130	415	57	96	22	1	8	54	64	68	.231	.337	.347	88	-6	3			.975	-9	*O-120	-2.1
1950	Bro-N	77	214	37	49	8	2	10	32	31	36	.229	.329	.425	95	-2	1			.993	4	O-55	0.0
1951	Bro-N	16	13	2	0	0	0	0	0	4	6	.000	.278	.000	-18	-2	0			1.000	-1	/O-4	-0.3
Total	10	1035	3595	554	959	175	51	67	428	503	427	.267	.360	.400	108	44	59	0		.981	27	O-942/1-11	2.3

■ **JOHN RUSSELL**   Russell, John William   b: 1/5/61, Oklahoma City, Okla.   BR/TR, 6′, 200 lbs.   Deb: 6/22/84

YEAR	TM/L	G	AB	R	H	2B	3B	HR	RBI	BB	SO	AVG	OBP	SLG	PRO+	BR/A	SB	CS	SBR	FA	FR	G/POS	TPR
1984	Phi-N	39	99	11	28	8	1	2	11	12	33	.283	.360	.444	123	1	0	1	-1	1.000	-1	O-29/C-2	0.1
1985	Phi-N	81	216	22	47	12	0	9	23	18	72	.218	.278	.398	85	-5	2	0	1	1.000	-6	O-49,1-18	-1.4
1986	Phi-N	93	315	35	76	21	2	13	60	25	103	.241	.303	.444	100	-1	0	1	-1	.976	-5	C-89	-0.1
1987	Phi-N	24	62	5	9	1	0	3	8	3	17	.145	.185	.306	44	-7	0	1	-1	.955	-0	O-10/C-7	-0.7
1988	Phi-N	22	49	5	12	1	0	2	4	3	15	.245	.302	.388	95	-0	0	0	0	.945	3	*C-15	0.3
1989	Atl-N	74	159	14	29	2	0	2	9	8	53	.182	.226	.233	31	-14	0	0	0	.990	-7	C-45,O-14/1-2,3P	-0.5
1990	Tex-A	68	128	16	35	4	0	2	8	11	41	.273	.331	.352	91	-1	1	0	0	.980	2	C-31,D-19/O-6,13	0.1
1991	Tex-A	22	27	3	3	0	0	0	1	1	7	.111	.143	.111	-29	-5	0	0	0	1.000	-0	/O-8,C-5,D-5	-0.5
1992	Tex-A	7	10	1	1	0	0	0	2	1	4	.100	.250	.100	2	-1	0	0	0	1.000	1	/C-4,O-2,D-1	0.0
1993	Tex-A	18	22	1	5	1	0	1	3	2	10	.227	.292	.409	90	-0	0	1	0	1.000	0	C-11/1-3,1-0,1	-0.2
Total	10	448	1087	113	245	50	3	34	129	84	355	.225	.285	.371	79	-32	3	3	-1	.979	-16	C-209,O-119/D13P	-4.5

■ **LLOYD RUSSELL**   Russell, Lloyd Opal   b: 4/10/13, Atoka, Okla.   d: 5/24/68, Waco, Tex.   BR/TR, 5′11″, 166 lbs.   Deb: 4/26/38

YEAR	TM/L	G	AB	R	H	2B	3B	HR	RBI	BB	SO	AVG	OBP	SLG	PRO+	BR/A	SB	CS	SBR	FA	FR	G/POS	TPR
1938	Cle-A	2	0	0	0	0	0	0	0	0	0	—	—	—		0	0	0	0	.000	0	R	0.0

■ **PAUL RUSSELL**   Russell, Paul A.   b: 1870, Reading, Pa.   d: Pottstown, Pa.   Deb: 7/29/1894

YEAR	TM/L	G	AB	R	H	2B	3B	HR	RBI	BB	SO	AVG	OBP	SLG	PRO+	BR/A	SB	CS	SBR	FA	FR	G/POS	TPR
1894	StL-N	3	10	1	1	0	0	0	0	0	2	.100	.100	.100	-52	-2	0			1.000	0	/O-1,3-1,2-1	-0.2

■ **BILL RUSSELL**   Russell, William Ellis   b: 10/21/48, Pittsburg, Kan.   BR/TR, 6′, 175 lbs.   Deb: 4/7/69   MC

YEAR	TM/L	G	AB	R	H	2B	3B	HR	RBI	BB	SO	AVG	OBP	SLG	PRO+	BR/A	SB	CS	SBR	FA	FR	G/POS	TPR
1969	LA-N	98	212	35	48	6	2	5	15	22	45	.226	.302	.344	87	-4	4	1	1	.978	-7	O-86	-1.4
1970	LA-N	81	278	30	72	11	9	0	28	16	28	.259	.306	.363	82	-8	9	1	2	.983	6	O-79/S-1	-0.3
1971	LA-N	91	211	29	48	7	4	2	15	11	39	.227	.266	.327	71	-9	6	3	0	.964	-6	2-41,O-40/S-6	-1.4
1972	LA-N	129	434	47	118	19	5	4	34	34	64	.272	.328	.366	99	-2	15	5	3	.949	15	*S-121/O-6	3.3
1973	LA-N★	162	615	55	163	26	3	4	56	34	63	.265	.305	.337	81	-17	15	7	0	.963	9	*S-162	1.4
1974	*LA-N	160	553	61	149	18	6	5	65	34	53	.269	.338	.351	97	-2	14	5	4	.946	-19	*S-160/O-1	0.1
1975	LA-N	84	252	24	52	9	2	0	14	23	28	.206	.278	.258	52	-17	5	0	2	.963	-21	S-83	-3.0
1976	LA-N★	149	554	53	152	17	3	5	65	21	46	.274	.304	.343	85	-12	15	5	2	.963	-14	*S-149	-0.7
1977	*LA-N	153	634	84	176	28	4	4	51	24	43	.278	.306	.360	78	-20	16	7	1	.963	10	*S-153	†0.8
1978	*LA-N	155	625	72	179	32	4	3	46	30	34	.286	.321	.365	92	-8	10	6	-1	.962	12	*S-155	2.5

YEAR	TM/L	G	AB	R	H	2B	3B	HR	RBI	BB	SO	AVG	OBP	SLG	PRO+	BR/A	SB	CS	SBR	FA	FR	G/POS	TPR
1979	LA-N	153	627	72	170	26	4	7	56	24	43	.271	.299	.359	80	-19	6	9	-4	.957	-26	*S-150	-3.3
1980	LA-N★	130	466	38	123	23	2	3	34	18	44	.264	.296	.341	79	-14	13	2	3	.968	-22	*S-129	-1.9
1981	*LA-N	82	262	20	61	9	2	0	22	19	20	.233	.287	.282	64	-12	2	1	0	.965	10	S-80	0.5
1982	LA-N	153	497	64	136	20	2	3	46	63	30	.274	.360	.340	99	2	10	2	2	.961	-4	*S-150	1.4
1983	*LA-N	131	451	47	111	13	1	1	30	33	31	.246	.303	.286	64	-21	13	9	-2	.964	1	*S-127	-1.0
1984	LA-N	89	262	25	70	12	1	0	19	25	24	.267	.331	.321	85	-5	4	4	-1	.965	-4	S-65,O-18/2-5	-0.6
1985	LA-N	76	169	19	44	6	1	0	13	18	9	.260	.335	.308	83	-3	4	0	1	.919	-7	S-23,O-21/2-8,3-5	-0.7
1986	LA-N	105	216	21	54	11	0	0	15	16	23	.250	.305	.301	73	-8	7	0	2	1.000	-7	O-48,S-32/2-8,3-1	-1.2
Total	18	2181	7318	796	1926	293	57	46	627	483	667	.263	.312	.338	83	-177	167	69	9	.960	-74	*S-1746,O-299/23	-5.5

■ HANK RUSZKOWSKI
Ruszkowski, Henry Alexander b: 11/10/25, Cleveland, Ohio BR/TR, 6', 190 lbs. Deb: 9/26/44

YEAR	TM/L	G	AB	R	H	2B	3B	HR	RBI	BB	SO	AVG	OBP	SLG	PRO+	BR/A	SB	CS	SBR	FA	FR	G/POS	TPR
1944	Cle-A	3	8	1	3	0	0	0	1	0	1	.375	.375	.375	119	0	0	0	0	1.000	-0	/C-2	0.0
1945	Cle-A	14	49	2	10	0	0	0	5	4	9	.204	.264	.204	38	-4	0	0	0	.975	3	C-14	0.0
1947	Cle-A	23	27	5	7	2	0	3	4	2	6	.259	.310	.667	172	2	0	0	0	1.000	-2	C-16	0.1
Total	3	40	84	8	20	2	0	3	10	6	16	.238	.289	.369	91	-2	0	0	0	.981	-1	/C-32	0.1

■ BABE RUTH
Ruth, George Herman "The Bambino" or "The Sultan Of Swat"
b: 2/6/1895, Baltimore, Md. d: 8/16/48, New York, N.Y. BL/TL, 6'2", 215 lbs. Deb: 7/11/14 CH

YEAR	TM/L	G	AB	R	H	2B	3B	HR	RBI	BB	SO	AVG	OBP	SLG	PRO+	BR/A	SB	CS	SBR	FA	FR	G/POS	TPR
1914	Bos-A	5	10	1	2	1	0	0	2	0	4	.200	.200	.300	50	-1	0			1.000	-0	/P-4	0.0
1915	*Bos-A	42	92	16	29	10	1	4	21	9	23	.315	.376	.576	191	9	0			.976	1	P-32	0.0
1916	*Bos-A	67	136	18	37	5	3	3	15	10	23	.272	.322	.419	122	3	0			.973	0	P-44	0.0
1917	Bos-A	52	123	14	40	6	3	2	12	12	18	.325	.385	.472	163	9	0			.984	2	P-41	0.0
1918	*Bos-A	95	317	50	95	26	11	11	66	57	58	.300	.410	.555	194	36	6			.949	3	O-59,P-20,1-13	2.6
1919	Bos-A	130	432	103	139	34	12	29	114	101	58	.322	.456	.657	224	74	7			.996	5	*O-111,P-17/1-5	6.3
1920	NY-A	142	458	158	172	36	9	54	137	148	80	.376	.530	.847	252	107	14	14	-4	.936	-0	*O-141/1-2,P-1	8.6
1921	*NY-A	152	540	177	204	44	16	59	171	144	81	.378	.512	.846	236	115	17	13	-3	.966	4	*O-152/P-2,1-2	9.4
1922	*NY-A	110	406	94	128	24	8	35	99	84	80	.315	.434	.672	181	48	2	5	-2	.964	1	*O-110/1-1	3.7
1923	*NY-A	152	522	151	205	45	13	41	131	170	93	.393	.545	.764	238	116	17	21	-8	.973	16	*O-148/1-4	10.6
1924	*NY-A	153	529	143	200	39	7	46	121	142	81	.378	.513	.739	221	101	9	13	-5	.962	7	*O-152	8.5
1925	NY-A	98	359	61	104	12	2	25	66	59	68	.290	.393	.543	138	20	2	4	-2	.974	9	O-98	1.9
1926	*NY-A	152	495	139	184	30	5	47	146	144	76	.372	.516	.737	228	100	11	9	-2	.979	-1	*O-149/1-2	8.4
1927	*NY-A	151	540	158	192	29	8	60	164	138	89	.356	.487	.772	229	106	7	6	-2	.963	5	*O-151	9.2
1928	*NY-A	154	536	163	173	29	8	54	142	135	87	.323	.461	.709	210	89	4	5	-2	.975	-3	*O-154	7.0
1929	NY-A	135	499	121	172	26	6	46	154	72	60	.345	.430	.697	199	71	5	3	-0	.984	-9	*O-133	5.0
1930	NY-A	145	518	150	186	28	9	49	153	136	61	.359	.493	.732	216	98	10	10	-3	.965	-0	*O-144/P-1	7.3
1931	NY-A	145	534	149	199	31	3	46	163	128	51	.373	.495	.700	223	102	5	4	-1	.972	-12	*O-142/1-1	7.3
1932	*NY-A	133	457	120	156	13	5	41	137	130	62	.341	.489	.661	206	79	2	2	-1	.961	-7	*O-128/1-1	5.8
1933	NY-A★	137	459	97	138	21	3	34	103	114	90	.301	.442	.582	180	57	4	5	-2	.970	-7	*O-132/P-1,1-1	3.8
1934	NY-A★	125	365	78	105	17	4	22	84	103	63	.288	.447	.537	164	40	1	3	-2	.962	-6	*O-111	2.5
1935	Bos-N	28	72	13	13	0	0	6	12	20	24	.181	.359	.431	121	3	0			.952	-4	O-26	0.0
Total	22	2503	8399	2174	2873	506	136	714	2213	2056	1330	.342	.474	.690	209	1382	123	117		.968	5	*O-2241,P-163/1-32	107.7

■ JIM RUTHERFORD
Rutherford, James Hollis b: 9/26/1886, Stillwater, Minn. d: 9/18/56, Cleveland, Ohio BL/TR, 6'1", 180 lbs. Deb: 7/12/10

YEAR	TM/L	G	AB	R	H	2B	3B	HR	RBI	BB	SO	AVG	OBP	SLG	PRO+	BR/A	SB	CS	SBR	FA	FR	G/POS	TPR
1910	Cle-A	1	2	0	1	0	0	0	0	0	0	.500	.500	.500	210	0	0			1.000	-0	/O-1	0.0

■ MICKEY RUTNER
Rutner, Milton b: 3/18/20, Hempstead, N.Y. BR/TR, 5'11", 190 lbs. Deb: 9/11/47

YEAR	TM/L	G	AB	R	H	2B	3B	HR	RBI	BB	SO	AVG	OBP	SLG	PRO+	BR/A	SB	CS	SBR	FA	FR	G/POS	TPR
1947	Phi-A	12	48	4	12	1	0	1	4	3	2	.250	.294	.333	73	-2	0	0	0	.885	-3	3-11	-0.5

■ MARK RYAL
Ryal, Mark Dwayne b: 4/28/60, Henryetta, Okla. BL/TL, 6'1", 185 lbs. Deb: 9/7/82

YEAR	TM/L	G	AB	R	H	2B	3B	HR	RBI	BB	SO	AVG	OBP	SLG	PRO+	BR/A	SB	CS	SBR	FA	FR	G/POS	TPR
1982	KC-A	6	13	0	1	0	0	0	0	1	3	.077	.143	.077	-38	-2	0	0	0	.900	-1	/O-5	-0.3
1985	Chi-A	12	33	4	5	3	0	0	3	3	3	.152	.222	.242	26	-3	0	0	0	1.000	-1	O-12	-0.5
1986	Cal-A	13	32	6	12	0	0	2	5	2	4	.375	.412	.563	164	3	1	0	0	.900	16	/O-6,1-4,D-2	0.2
1987	Cal-A	58	100	7	20	6	0	5	18	3	15	.200	.233	.410	65	-5	0	0	0	.955	-6	O-21/1-4,D-5	-1.1
1989	Phi-N	29	33	2	8	2	0	0	5	1	6	.242	.265	.303	62	-2	0	0	0	1.000	-1	/1-4,O-4	-0.3
1990	Pit-N	9	12	0	1	0	0	0	0	0	3	.083	.083	.083	-56	-3	0	0	0	1.000	-1	/O-4	-0.4
Total	6	127	223	19	47	11	0	7	31	10	34	.211	.245	.354	61	-13	1	0	0	.957	-11	/O-52,1-12,D-7	-2.4

■ CONNIE RYAN
Ryan, Cornelius Joseph b: 2/27/20, New Orleans, La. d: 1/3/96, Metairie, La. BR/TR, 5'11", 175 lbs. Deb: 4/14/42 MC

YEAR	TM/L	G	AB	R	H	2B	3B	HR	RBI	BB	SO	AVG	OBP	SLG	PRO+	BR/A	SB	CS	SBR	FA	FR	G/POS	TPR
1942	NY-N	11	27	4	5	0	0	0	2	4	3	.185	.290	.185	40	-2	1			.944	7	2-11	0.5
1943	Bos-N	132	457	52	97	10	2	1	24	58	56	.212	.301	.249	61	-22	7			.962	-20	*2-100,3-30	-3.8
1944	Bos-N★	88	332	56	98	18	5	4	25	36	44	.295	.364	.416	114	7	13			.974	13	2-80,3-14	2.4
1946	Bos-N	143	502	55	121	28	8	1	48	55	63	.241	.317	.335	84	-11	7			.968	-2	*2-120,3-24	-0.5
1947	Bos-N	150	544	60	144	33	5	5	69	71	60	.265	.351	.371	94	-4	5			.973	-7	*2-150/S-1	-0.4
1948	*Bos-N	51	122	14	26	3	0	0	10	21	16	.213	.333	.238	58	-6	0			.966	4	2-40/3-4	0.0
1949	Bos-N	85	208	28	52	13	1	6	20	21	30	.250	.319	.409	99	-1	1			.973	6	3-25,S-18,2-16/1-3	0.6
1950	Bos-N	20	72	12	14	2	0	3	6	12	9	.194	.326	.347	82	-2	0			1.000	-1	2-20	0.0
	Cin-N	106	367	45	95	18	5	3	43	52	46	.259	.352	.360	87	-5	4			.973	11	*2-103	0.9
	Yr	126	439	57	109	20	5	6	49	64	55	.248	.348	.358	87	-7	4			.978	12	*2-123	0.9
1951	Cin-N	136	473	75	112	17	4	16	53	79	72	.237	.350	.391	97	-0	11	6	-0	.970	-3	*2-121/3-3,1-2,0-1	0.2
1952	Phi-N	154	577	81	139	24	6	12	49	69	72	.241	.327	.366	93	-5	13	5	1	.972	-5	*2-154	-0.1
1953	Phi-N	90	247	47	73	14	6	5	26	30	35	.296	.372	.462	116	6	5	1	1	.958	-5	2-65/1-2	0.5
	Chi-A	17	54	6	12	1	0	0	6	9	12	.222	.333	.241	55	-3	2	0	1	.927	-1	3-16	-0.4
1954	Cin-N	1	0	0	0	0	0	0	0	1	0	—	1.000	—	182	0	0			.000	0	H	0.0
Total	12	1184	3982	535	988	181	42	56	381	518	514	.248	.337	.357	90	-48	69	12		.970	-1	2-980,3-116/S10	0.3

■ CYCLONE RYAN
Ryan, Daniel R. b: 1866, Cappagh White, Ireland d: 1/30/17, Medfield, Mass. TR, 6', 200 lbs. Deb: 8/8/1887

YEAR	TM/L	G	AB	R	H	2B	3B	HR	RBI	BB	SO	AVG	OBP	SLG	PRO+	BR/A	SB	CS	SBR	FA	FR	G/POS	TPR
1887	NY-a	8	32	4	7	1	0	0	3	3	3	.219	.286	.250	59	-2	1			.938	-0	/1-8,P-2	-0.2
1891	Bos-N	1	1	0	0	0	0	0	0	0	0	.000	.000	.000	-89	-0	0			1.000	0	/P-1	0.0
Total	2	9	33	4	7	1	0	0	3	3	3	.212	.278	.242	48	-2	1			1.000	0	/1-8,P-3	-0.2

■ MIKE RYAN
Ryan, J. b: St.Louis, Mo. Deb: 7/25/1895

YEAR	TM/L	G	AB	R	H	2B	3B	HR	RBI	BB	SO	AVG	OBP	SLG	PRO+	BR/A	SB	CS	SBR	FA	FR	G/POS	TPR
1895	StL-N	2	2	0	0	0	0	0	0	0	0	.000	.000	.000	-99	-1	0			.000	-1	/3-2	-0.1

■ JIMMY RYAN
Ryan, James Edward "Pony" b: 2/11/1863, Clinton, Mass. d: 10/26/23, Chicago, Ill. BR/TL, 5'9", 162 lbs. Deb: 10/8/1885

YEAR	TM/L	G	AB	R	H	2B	3B	HR	RBI	BB	SO	AVG	OBP	SLG	PRO+	BR/A	SB	CS	SBR	FA	FR	G/POS	TPR
1885	Chi-N	3	13	2	6	1	0	0	2	1	1	.462	.500	.538	205	1				.737	1	/S-2,O-1	0.2
1886	*Chi-N	84	327	58	100	17	6	4	53	12	28	.306	.330	.431	113	2	10			.828	0	O-70/S-6,3-6,2-5,P	0.1
1887	Chi-N	126	508	117	145	23	10	11	74	53	19	.285	.360	.435	106	1	50			.857	-2	*O-122/P-8,2-3	-0.5
1888	Chi-N	129	549	115	182	33	10	16	64	35	50	.332	.377	.515	170	41	60			.878	4	*O-128/P-8	3.8
1889	Chi-N	135	576	140	177	31	14	17	72	70	62	.307	.388	.498	140	29	45			.926	6	*O-106,S-29	2.9
1890	Chi-P	118	486	99	166	32	5	6	89	60	36	.340	.416	.463	129	20	30			.919	2	*O-118	1.5
1891	Chi-N	118	505	110	140	22	15	9	66	53	38	.277	.355	.434	129	18	27			.905	5	*O-117/S-2,P-2	1.7
1892	Chi-N	128	505	105	148	21	11	10	65	61	41	.293	.375	.438	144	27	27			.921	5	*O-120/S-9	2.5
1893	Chi-N	83	341	82	102	21	7	3	30	59	25	.299	.407	.428	124	14	8			.908	-1	O-73,S-10/P-1	0.7
1894	Chi-N	108	474	132	171	37	7	3	62	50	23	.361	.425	.487	113	10	11			.910	9	*O-108	0.9
1895	Chi-N	108	438	83	139	22	6	4	49	48	22	.317	.392	.445	109	5	18			.937	2	*O-108	-0.1
1896	Chi-N	128	489	83	149	24	10	3	46	46	16	.305	.369	.413	100	1	29			.912	-0	*O-128	-0.9
1897	Chi-N	136	520	103	156	33	5	5	85	50		.300	.369	.458	113	8	27			.945	7	*O-136	0.4
1898	Chi-N	144	572	122	185	32	13	4	79	73		.323	.405	.446	144	34	29			.914	-7	*O-144	1.6
1899	Chi-N	125	525	91	158	20	10	3	68	43		.301	.351	.394	109	6	31			.956	-1	*O-125	-0.4
1900	Chi-N	105	415	66	115	25	6	5	59	29		.277	.329	.393	113	3	19			.913	-11	*O-105	-1.7
1902	Was-A	120	484	92	155	32	6	6	44	43		.320	.384	.448	129	19	10			.949	3	*O-120	1.3

YEAR	TM/L	G	AB	R	H	2B	3B	HR	RBI	BB	SO	AVG	OBP	SLG	PRO+	BR/A	SB	CS	SBR	FA	FR	G/POS	TPR
1903	Was-A	114	437	42	109	25	4	7	46	17		.249	.290	.373	96	-3	9			.970	3	*O-114	-0.7
Total	18	2012	8164	1642	2502	451	157	118	1093	803	361	.306	.374	.444	123	232	418			.918	25	*O-1943/S-58,P23	13.3

■ JACK RYAN   Ryan, John Bernard   b: 11/12/1868, Haverhill, Mass.   d: 8/21/52, Boston, Mass.   BR/TR, 5'10.5", 165 lbs.   Deb: 9/2/1889   C

YEAR	TM/L	G	AB	R	H	2B	3B	HR	RBI	BB	SO	AVG	OBP	SLG	PRO+	BR/A	SB	CS	SBR	FA	FR	G/POS	TPR
1889	Lou-a	21	79	8	14	1	0	0	2	3	17	.177	.207	.190	14	-9	2			.864	-6	C-15/O-4,3-2	-1.2
1890	*Lou-a	93	337	43	73	16	4	0	35	12		.217	.244	.288	58	-19	6			.932	5	C-89/O-3,S-1,1-1	-0.6
1891	Lou-a	75	253	24	57	5	4	2	25	15	40	.225	.271	.300	64	-13	3			.930	-1	C-56,1-11/3-6,O2	-0.8
1894	Bos-N	53	201	39	54	12	7	1	29	13	16	.269	.316	.413	69	-12	3			.911	0	C-51/1-2	-0.5
1895	Bos-N	49	189	22	55	7	0	0	18	6	6	.291	.313	.328	61	-12	3			.951	1	C-43/2-5,O-1	-0.5
1896	Bos-N	8	32	2	3	1	0	0	0	0	1	.094	.094	.125	-40	-7	0			.911	2	/C-8	-0.3
1898	Bro-N	87	301	39	57	11	4	0	24	15		.189	.233	.252	39	-24	5			.960	-3	C-84/3-4,1-1	-1.3
1899	Bal-N	2	4	0	2	1	0	0	1	0		.500	.500	.750	229	1	1			1.000	1	/C-2	0.2
1901	StL-N	83	300	27	59	6	5	0	31	7		.197	.218	.250	37	-24	5			.982	5	C-65/2-9,1-5,O-3	-1.3
1902	StL-N	76	267	23	48	4	4	0	14	4		.180	.195	.225	31	-22	2			.966	-7	C-66/1-4,3-4,2-2,S	-2.4
1903	StL-N	67	227	18	54	5	1	1	10	10		.238	.273	.282	60	-12	2			.971	-9	C-47,1-18/S-2	-1.6
1912	Was-A	1	1	0	0	0	0	0	0	0		.000	.000	.000	-99	-0	0			1.000	0	/3-1	0.0
1913	Was-A	1	1	0	0	0	0	0	0	0	0	.000	.000	.000	-98	-0	0			1.000	0	/C-1	0.0
Total	13	616	2192	245	476	69	29	4	189	85	80	.217	.249	.281	50	-154	32			.947	-6	C-527/1-42,23OS	-10.3

■ BUDDY RYAN   Ryan, John Budd   b: 10/6/1885, Denver, Colo.   d: 7/9/56, Sacramento, Cal.   BL/TR, 5'9.5", 172 lbs.   Deb: 4/11/12

YEAR	TM/L	G	AB	R	H	2B	3B	HR	RBI	BB	SO	AVG	OBP	SLG	PRO+	BR/A	SB	CS	SBR	FA	FR	G/POS	TPR
1912	Cle-A	93	328	53	89	12	9	1	31	30		.271	.343	.372	101	0	12			.963	5	O-90	0.0
1913	Cle-A	73	243	26	72	6	1	0	32	11	13	.296	.332	.329	91	-3	9			.986	-2	O-68/1-1	-0.8
Total	2	166	571	79	161	18	10	1	63	41	13	.282	.339	.354	97	-3	21			.973	3	O-158/1-1	-0.8

■ BLONDY RYAN   Ryan, John Collins   b: 1/4/06, Lynn, Mass.   d: 11/28/59, Swampscott, Mass.   BR/TR, 6'1", 178 lbs.   Deb: 7/13/30

YEAR	TM/L	G	AB	R	H	2B	3B	HR	RBI	BB	SO	AVG	OBP	SLG	PRO+	BR/A	SB	CS	SBR	FA	FR	G/POS	TPR
1930	Chi-A	28	87	9	18	0	4	1	10	6	13	.207	.258	.333	50	-7	2	0	1	.875	-1	3-23/S-2,2-1	-0.6
1933	*NY-N	146	525	47	125	10	5	3	48	15	62	.238	.259	.293	58	-29	0			.950	17	*S-146	-0.6
1934	NY-N	110	385	35	93	19	0	2	41	19	68	.242	.277	.306	57	-23	3			.953	12	3-65,S-30,2-25	-0.6
1935	Phi-N	39	129	13	34	3	0	1	10	7	20	.264	.312	.310	61	-7	1			.912	-3	3-35/2-1,3-1	-0.3
	NY-A	30	105	12	25	1	3	0	11	3	10	.238	.259	.305	48	-8	0	0	0	.908	-4	S-30	-1.1
1937	*NY-N	21	75	10	18	3	1	1	13	6	8	.240	.296	.347	73	-3	0			.941	1	S-19/2-1,3-1	-0.1
1938	NY-N	12	24	1	5	0	0	0	0	1	3	.208	.240	.208	24	-2	0			1.000	-1	/2-5,3-3,S-2	-0.3
Total	6	386	1330	127	318	36	13	8	133	57	184	.239	.271	.304	57	-80	6	0		.936	26	S-264/3-93,2-33	-3.2

■ JACK RYAN   Ryan, John Francis   b: 5/5/05, West Mineral, Kan.   d: 9/2/67, Rochester, Minn.   BR/TR, 6', 185 lbs.   Deb: 6/18/29

YEAR	TM/L	G	AB	R	H	2B	3B	HR	RBI	BB	SO	AVG	OBP	SLG	PRO+	BR/A	SB	CS	SBR	FA	FR	G/POS	TPR
1929	Bos-A	2	3	0	0	0	0	0	0	0		.000	.000	.000	-99	-1	0			1.000	-1	/O-2	-0.2

■ JOHNNY RYAN   Ryan, John Joseph   b: 10/1853, Philadelphia, Pa.   d: 3/22/02, Philadelphia, Pa.   5'7.5", 150 lbs.   Deb: 8/19/1873

YEAR	TM/L	G	AB	R	H	2B	3B	HR	RBI	BB	SO	AVG	OBP	SLG	PRO+	BR/A	SB	CS	SBR	FA	FR	G/POS	TPR
1873	Phi-n	2	8	1	2	0	0	0				.250	.250	.250	47	-1				.800	0	/1-1,O-1	0.0
1874	Bal-n	47	182	29	35	8	1	0	19	5	13	.192	.214	.247	48	-10	3	0	1	.862	13	*O-47/P-1	0.4
1875	NH-n	37	146	17	23	2	2	0	8	3	12	.158	.174	.199	34	-8	10	4	1	.796	-8	0-30,P-10/C-4,S-1	-1.2
1876	Lou-N	64	241	32	61	5	1	1	18	6	23	.253	.271	.295	75	-9				.886	-7	*O-64/P-1	-1.5
1877	Cin-N	6	26	2	4	0	1	0	2	1	5	.154	.185	.231	34	-2				.769	-1	/O-6	-0.3
Total	3 n	86	336	47	60	10	3	0	28	8	25	.179	.198	.226	42	-19	13	4	2	.850	5	/O-78,P-11,C-4,S1	-0.8
Total	2	70	267	34	65	5	2	1	20	7	28	.243	.263	.288	72	-11				.877	-9	/O-70,P-1	-1.8

■ JOHN RYAN   Ryan, John M.   b: Washington, D.C.   Deb: 6/11/1884

YEAR	TM/L	G	AB	R	H	2B	3B	HR	RBI	BB	SO	AVG	OBP	SLG	PRO+	BR/A	SB	CS	SBR	FA	FR	G/POS	TPR
1884	Was-U	7	28	2	4	0	1	0		0	1	.143	.172	.214	17	-4				.667	-1	/O-7,3-1	-0.5
	Wil-U	2	6	0	1	0	0	0		0	1	.167	.286	.167	39	-1				.800	-0	/O-2	-0.1
Yr		9	34	2	5	0	1	0		0	2	.147	.194	.206	22	-4				.706	-1	/O-9,3-1	-0.6

■ MIKE RYAN   Ryan, Michael James   b: 11/25/41, Haverhill, Mass.   BR/TR, 6'2", 205 lbs.   Deb: 10/3/64   C

YEAR	TM/L	G	AB	R	H	2B	3B	HR	RBI	BB	SO	AVG	OBP	SLG	PRO+	BR/A	SB	CS	SBR	FA	FR	G/POS	TPR
1964	Bos-A	1	3	0	1	0	0	0	2	1	0	.333	.500	.333	131	0	0	0	0	1.000	-1	/C-1	0.0
1965	Bos-A	33	107	7	17	0	1	3	9	5	19	.159	.196	.262	27	-10	0	0	0	.981	0	C-33	-0.9
1966	Bos-A	116	369	24	79	15	3	2	32	29	68	.214	.271	.287	55	-21	1	0	0	.992	1	*C-114	-1.4
1967	*Bos-A	79	226	21	45	4	2	2	27	26	42	.199	.285	.261	58	-11	2	0	1	.988	1	C-79	-0.6
1968	Phi-N	96	296	12	53	6	1	1	15	15	59	.179	.219	.216	31	-25	0	3	-2	.991	-4	C-96	-2.8
1969	Phi-N	133	446	41	91	17	2	12	44	30	66	.204	.257	.332	66	-22	1	1	-0	.991	2	*C-132	-1.4
1970	Phi-N	46	134	14	24	8	0	2	11	16	24	.179	.267	.284	49	-10	0	0	0	.992	-12	C-46	-2.1
1971	Phi-N	43	134	9	22	5	1	3	6	10	32	.164	.222	.284	42	-10	0	0	0	1.000	12	C-43	0.3
1972	Phi-N	46	106	6	19	4	0	2	10	10	25	.179	.256	.274	49	-7	0	0	0	.992	6	C-46	0.0
1973	Phi-N	28	69	7	16	2	1	1	5	6	19	.232	.293	.348	75	-3	0	0	0	.992	1	C-27	-0.1
1974	Pit-N	15	30	2	3	0	0	0	0	4	16	.100	.206	.100	-13	-5	0	0	0	1.000	3	C-15	-0.1
Total	11	636	1920	146	370	60	12	28	161	152	370	.193	.253	.280	51	-124	4	4	-1	.991	10	C-632	-9.1

■ TOM RYDER   Ryder, Thomas   BL   Deb: 7/22/1884

YEAR	TM/L	G	AB	R	H	2B	3B	HR	RBI	BB	SO	AVG	OBP	SLG	PRO+	BR/A	SB	CS	SBR	FA	FR	G/POS	TPR
1884	StL-U	8	28	4	7				2			.250	.300	.286	76	-2				.650	-0	/O-8	-0.2

■ GENE RYE   Rye, Eugene Rudolph "Half-Pint" (b: Eugene Rudolph Mercantelli)   b: 11/15/06, Chicago, Ill.   d: 1/21/80, Park Ridge, Ill.   BL/TR, 5'6", 165 lbs.   Deb: 4/22/31

YEAR	TM/L	G	AB	R	H	2B	3B	HR	RBI	BB	SO	AVG	OBP	SLG	PRO+	BR/A	SB	CS	SBR	FA	FR	G/POS	TPR
1931	Bos-A	17	39	3	7	0	0	0	1	2	5	.179	.220	.179	6	-5	0	0	0	.944	-1	O-10	-0.7

■ ALEX SABO   Sabo, Alexander "Giz" (b: Alexander Szabo)   b: 2/14/10, New Brunswick, N.J.   BR/TR, 6', 192 lbs.   Deb: 8/1/36

YEAR	TM/L	G	AB	R	H	2B	3B	HR	RBI	BB	SO	AVG	OBP	SLG	PRO+	BR/A	SB	CS	SBR	FA	FR	G/POS	TPR
1936	Was-A	4	8	1	3	0	0	0	1	0	2	.375	.375	.375	91	-0	0	0	0	.923	1	/C-4	0.1
1937	Was-A	1	0	0	0	0	0	0	0	0	0	—	—	—		-0	0	0	0	1.000	0	/C-1	0.0
Total	2	5	8	1	3	0	0	0	1	0	2	.375	.375	.375	91	-0	0	0	0	.929	1	/C-5	0.1

■ CHRIS SABO   Sabo, Christopher Andrew   b: 1/19/62, Detroit, Mich.   BR/TR, 5'11", 185 lbs.   Deb: 4/4/88

YEAR	TM/L	G	AB	R	H	2B	3B	HR	RBI	BB	SO	AVG	OBP	SLG	PRO+	BR/A	SB	CS	SBR	FA	FR	G/POS	TPR
1988	Cin-N★	137	538	74	146	40	2	11	44	29	52	.271	.316	.414	104	2	46	14	5	**.966**	19	*3-135/S-2	2.7
1989	Cin-N	82	304	40	79	21	1	6	29	25	33	.260	.318	.395	99	-1	14	9	-1	.943	-3	3-76	-0.5
1990	*Cin-N★	148	567	95	153	38	2	25	71	61	58	.270	.345	.476	118	14	25	10	2	**.966**	-6	*3-146	1.1
1991	Cin-N★	153	582	91	175	35	3	26	88	44	79	.301	.356	.505	134	25	19	6	2	.966	-15	*3-151	1.3
1992	Cin-N	96	344	42	84	19	3	12	43	30	54	.244	.307	.442	102	-0	4	5	-2	.961	-1	3-93	-0.3
1993	Cin-N	148	552	86	143	33	2	21	82	43	105	.259	.319	.440	101	-1	6	4	-1	.967	-15	*3-148	-1.6
1994	Bal-A	68	258	41	66	15	3	11	42	20	38	.256	.322	.465	95	-3	1	1	-0	.958	-11	3-37,O-22,D-10	-1.4
1995	Chi-A	20	71	10	18	5	0	1	8	3	12	.254	.303	.366	76	-3	2	0	1	.909	-1	D-15/1-1,3-1	-0.4
	StL-N	5	13	0	2	1	0	0	3	1	2	.154	.214	.231	17	-2	1	0	0	.929	-1	/1-2,3-1	-0.2
1996	Cin-N	54	125	15	32	7	1	3	16	18	27	.256	.354	.400	99	0	2	0	1	.961	6	3-43	0.6
Total	9	911	3354	494	898	214	17	116	426	274	460	.268	.329	.445	109	32	120	49	7	.963	-28	3-831/D-25,O-22,1S	1.3

■ FRANK SACKA   Sacka, Frank   b: 8/30/24, Romulus, Mich.   d: 12/7/94, Dearborn, Mich.   BR/TR, 6', 195 lbs.   Deb: 4/29/51

YEAR	TM/L	G	AB	R	H	2B	3B	HR	RBI	BB	SO	AVG	OBP	SLG	PRO+	BR/A	SB	CS	SBR	FA	FR	G/POS	TPR
1951	Was-A	7	16	1	4	0	0	0	3	3	2	.250	.250	.250	36	-1	0	0	0	.962	2	/C-6	0.0
1953	Was-A	7	18	2	5	0	0	0	3	3	1	.278	.381	.278	82	-0	0	0	0	1.000	2	/C-6	0.2
Total	2	14	34	3	9	0	0	0	6	6	3	.265	.324	.265	62	-2	0	0	0	.982	3	/C-12	0.2

■ MIKE SADEK   Sadek, Michael George   b: 5/30/46, Minneapolis, Minn.   BR/TR, 5'9", 165 lbs.   Deb: 4/13/73

YEAR	TM/L	G	AB	R	H	2B	3B	HR	RBI	BB	SO	AVG	OBP	SLG	PRO+	BR/A	SB	CS	SBR	FA	FR	G/POS	TPR
1973	SF-N	39	66	6	11	1	0	4	11	8		.167	.286	.212	38	-5	1	0	0	.981	7	C-35	0.3
1975	SF-N	42	106	14	25	5	2	0	9	14	14	.236	.325	.321	76	-3	1	0	0	.995	7	C-38	0.5
1976	SF-N	55	93	8	19	2	0	0	7	11	10	.204	.295	.226	48	-6	0	0	0	.985	6	C-51	0.3
1977	SF-N	61	126	12	29	7	0	1	15	12	5	.230	.297	.310	63	-6	2	1	0	.992	10	C-57	0.4
1978	SF-N	40	109	15	26	3	0	2	9	10	11	.239	.303	.321	77	-3	0	0	0	.975	2	C-37	-0.1
1979	SF-N	63	126	14	30	3	0	1	11	15	24	.238	.324	.302	77	-4	1	0	0	.993	1	C-60/O-1	-0.1

YEAR	TM/L	G	AB	R	H	2B	3B	HR	RBI	BB	SO	AVG	OBP	SLG	PRO+	BR/A	SB	CS	SBR	FA	FR	G/POS	TPR
1980	SF-N	64	151	14	38	4	1	1	16	27	18	.252	.365	.311	93	-0	0	0	0	.974	4	C-59	0.6
1981	SF-N	19	36	5	6	3	0	0	3	8	7	.167	.318	.250	64	-1	0	0	0	.979	7	C-19	0.6
Total	8	383	813	88	184	30	4	5	74	108	97	.226	.319	.292	70	-30	6	1	1	.985	45	C-356/O-1	2.5

■ ED SADOWSKI
Sadowski, Edward Roman b: 1/19/31, Pittsburgh, Pa. d: 11/6/93, Garden Grove, Cal. BR/TR, 5'11", 175 lbs. Deb: 4/20/60 F

YEAR	TM/L	G	AB	R	H	2B	3B	HR	RBI	BB	SO	AVG	OBP	SLG	PRO+	BR/A	SB	CS	SBR	FA	FR	G/POS	TPR
1960	Bos-A	38	93	10	20	2	0	3	8	8	13	.215	.284	.333	64	-5	0	0	0	.995	6	C-36	0.2
1961	LA-A	69	164	16	38	13	0	4	12	11	33	.232	.280	.384	68	-8	2	3	-1	.987	8	C-56	0.1
1962	LA-A	27	55	4	11	4	0	1	2	3	14	.200	.228	.327	49	-4	1	0	0	.968	3	C-18	-0.1
1963	LA-A	80	174	24	30	1	1	4	15	17	33	.172	.246	.259	44	-13	2	1	0	.997	20	C-68	0.9
1966	Atl-N	3	9	1	1	0	0	0	1	1	1	.111	.200	.111	-10	-1	0	0	0	1.000	1	/C-3	-0.1
Total	5	217	495	55	100	20	1	12	39	39	94	.202	.262	.319	56	-31	5	4	-1	.991	37	C-181	1.0

■ BOB SADOWSKI
Sadowski, Robert Frank "Sid" b: 1/15/37, St.Louis, Mo. BL/TR, 6', 175 lbs. Deb: 9/16/60

YEAR	TM/L	G	AB	R	H	2B	3B	HR	RBI	BB	SO	AVG	OBP	SLG	PRO+	BR/A	SB	CS	SBR	FA	FR	G/POS	TPR
1960	StL-N	1	1	0	0	0	0	0	0	0	0	.000	.500	.000	47	0	0	0	0	.000	-1	/2-1	-0.1
1961	Phi-N	16	54	4	7	0	0	0	0	4	7	.130	.203	.130	-9	-8	1	0	0	.971	-1	3-14	-0.9
1962	Chi-A	79	130	22	30	3	3	6	24	13	22	.231	.301	.438	97	-1	0	0	0	.955	5	3-16,2-12	0.5
1963	LA-A	88	144	12	36	6	0	1	22	15	34	.250	.321	.313	83	-3	2	1	0	1.000	-3	O-25/3-6,2-4	-0.7
Total	4	184	329	38	73	9	3	7	46	33	63	.222	.295	.331	73	-13	3	1	0	.953	-0	/3-36,O-25,2-17	-1.2

■ OLMEDO SAENZ
Saenz, Olmedo (Sanchez) b: 10/8/70, Chitre Herrera, Pan. BR/TR, 6'2", 185 lbs. Deb: 5/28/94

YEAR	TM/L	G	AB	R	H	2B	3B	HR	RBI	BB	SO	AVG	OBP	SLG	PRO+	BR/A	SB	CS	SBR	FA	FR	G/POS	TPR
1994	Chi-A	5	14	2	2	0	1	0	0	0	5	.143	.143	.286	7	-2	0	0	0	1.000	-0	/3-5	-0.2

■ TOM SAFFELL
Saffell, Thomas Judson b: 7/26/21, Etowah, Tenn. BL/TR, 5'11", 170 lbs. Deb: 7/2/49

YEAR	TM/L	G	AB	R	H	2B	3B	HR	RBI	BB	SO	AVG	OBP	SLG	PRO+	BR/A	SB	CS	SBR	FA	FR	G/POS	TPR
1949	Pit-N	73	205	36	66	7	1	2	25	21	27	.322	.385	.395	107	3	5			.992	-3	O-53	-0.3
1950	Pit-N	67	182	18	37	7	0	2	6	14	34	.203	.264	.275	41	-16	1			.993	6	O-43	-1.1
1951	Pit-N	49	65	11	13	0	0	1	5	5	18	.200	.257	.246	35	-6	1	1	-0	.929	-4	O-17	-1.0
1955	Pit-N	73	113	21	19	1	0	1	3	15	22	.168	.266	.204	27	-12	1	0	0	.964	-7	O-47	-2.0
	KC-A	9	37	5	8	0	0	0	1	4	7	.216	.293	.216	38	-3	1	0	0	.962	-0	/O-9	-0.3
Total	4	271	602	91	143	15	1	6	40	59	108	.238	.307	.296	60	-34	9	1		.980	-8	O-169	-4.7

■ HARRY SAGE
Sage, Harry "Doc" b: 3/16/1864, Rock Island, Ill. d: 5/27/47, Rock Island, Ill. BR/TR, 5'10", 185 lbs. Deb: 4/17/1890

YEAR	TM/L	G	AB	R	H	2B	3B	HR	RBI	BB	SO	AVG	OBP	SLG	PRO+	BR/A	SB	CS	SBR	FA	FR	G/POS	TPR
1890	Tol-a	81	275	40	41	8	4	2	25	29		.149	.235	.229	36	-23	10			.948	8	C-80/O-1	-0.7

■ PONY SAGER
Sager, Samuel B. b: 1847, Marshalltown, Iowa 140 lbs. Deb: 5/6/1871

YEAR	TM/L	G	AB	R	H	2B	3B	HR	RBI	BB	SO	AVG	OBP	SLG	PRO+	BR/A	SB	CS	SBR	FA	FR	G/POS	TPR
1871	Rok-n	8	39	9	11	0	0	0	5	2	2	.282	.317	.282	78	-1	5	1	1	.643	-4	/S-4,O-4	-0.2

■ VIC SAIER
Saier, Victor Sylvester b: 5/4/1891, Lansing, Mich. d: 5/14/67, E.Lansing, Mich. BL/TR, 5'11", 185 lbs. Deb: 5/3/11

YEAR	TM/L	G	AB	R	H	2B	3B	HR	RBI	BB	SO	AVG	OBP	SLG	PRO+	BR/A	SB	CS	SBR	FA	FR	G/POS	TPR
1911	Chi-N	86	259	42	67	15	1	1	37	25	37	.259	.340	.336	89	-3	11			.980	-4	1-73	-0.8
1912	Chi-N	122	451	74	130	25	14	3	61	64	65	.288	.340	.419	107	3	11			.992	-5	*1-120	-0.4
1913	Chi-N	149	519	94	150	15	21	14	92	62	62	.289	.370	.480	141	27	26			.983	-5	*1-149	2.1
1914	Chi-N	153	537	87	129	24	8	18	72	94	61	.240	.357	.415	130	21	19			.986	-11	*1-153	0.8
1915	Chi-N	144	497	74	131	35	11	11	64	64	62	.264	.350	.445	140	23	29	9	3	.985	-5	*1-139	2.0
1916	Chi-N	147	498	60	126	25	3	7	50	79	68	.253	.356	.357	108	7	20	17	-4	.984	-0	*1-147	-0.3
1917	Chi-N	6	21	5	5	1	0	0	2	2	1	.238	.304	.286	75	-1	0			1.000	5	/1-6	0.1
1919	Pit-N	58	166	19	37	3	3	2	17	18	13	.223	.306	.313	83	-3	5			.985	-5	1-51	-1.0
Total	8	865	2948	455	775	143	61	55	395	378	369	.263	.351	.409	119	75	121	26		.986	-33	1-838	2.5

■ EBBA ST.CLAIRE
St.Claire, Edward Joseph b: 8/5/21, Whitehall, N.Y. d: 8/22/82, Whitehall, N.Y. BB/TR, 6'1", 219 lbs. Deb: 4/17/51 F

YEAR	TM/L	G	AB	R	H	2B	3B	HR	RBI	BB	SO	AVG	OBP	SLG	PRO+	BR/A	SB	CS	SBR	FA	FR	G/POS	TPR
1951	Bos-N	72	220	22	62	17	2	1	25	12	24	.282	.322	.391	98	-2	2	0	1	.977	3	C-62	0.4
1952	Bos-N	39	108	5	23	2	4	8	12	8	12	.213	.267	.287	56	-7	0	1	-1	.972	4	C-34	-0.2
1953	Mil-N	33	80	7	16	3	0	2	5	3	9	.200	.229	.313	42	-7	0	0	0	.992	3	C-27	-0.3
1954	NY-N	20	42	5	11	1	0	2	6	12	7	.262	.436	.429	126	2	0	0	0	.975	2	C-16	0.5
Total	4	164	450	39	112	23	2	7	40	35	52	.249	.306	.356	81	-13	2	1	0	.978	12	C-139	0.4

■ LENN SAKATA
Sakata, Lenn Haruki b: 6/8/54, Honolulu, Hawaii BR/TR, 5'9", 160 lbs. Deb: 7/21/77

YEAR	TM/L	G	AB	R	H	2B	3B	HR	RBI	BB	SO	AVG	OBP	SLG	PRO+	BR/A	SB	CS	SBR	FA	FR	G/POS	TPR
1977	Mil-A	53	154	13	25	2	0	2	12	9	22	.162	.209	.214	16	-18	1	3	-2	.985	17	2-53	0.1
1978	Mil-A	30	78	8	15	4	0	3	8	11	11	.192	.267	.244	44	-6	1	0	0	.975	0	2-29	-0.4
1979	Mil-A	4	14	1	7	2	0	1	0	1	0	.500	.500	.643	206	2	0	0	0	1.000	2	/2-4	0.4
1980	Bal-A	43	83	12	16	3	2	1	9	6	10	.193	.247	.313	53	-6	2	1	0	.984	6	2-34/S-4,D-1	0.2
1981	Bal-A	61	150	19	34	4	0	5	15	11	18	.227	.284	.353	83	-4	4	1	0	.963	2	S-42,2-20	0.4
1982	Bal-A	136	343	40	89	18	1	6	31	30	38	.259	.326	.370	91	-4	7	4	-0	.977	-6	2-83,S-56	-0.3
1983	*Bal-A	66	134	23	34	7	0	3	12	16	17	.254	.338	.373	97	-0	8	5	0	.990	4	2-60/C-1,D-1	0.6
1984	Bal-A	81	157	23	30	1	0	3	11	6	15	.191	.221	.255	32	-15	4	1	1	.988	5	2-76/O-1	-0.7
1985	Bal-A	55	97	15	22	3	0	3	6	6	15	.227	.279	.351	73	-4	3	2	-0	.960	-1	2-50/D-1	-0.4
1986	Oak-A	17	34	4	12	2	0	0	5	3	6	.353	.405	.412	133	2	0	1	-1	.984	5	2-16/D-1	0.6
1987	NY-A	19	45	5	12	0	1	2	4	2	4	.267	.313	.444	99	-0	0	1	-1	.929	1	3-12/2-6	0.0
Total	11	565	1289	163	296	46	4	25	109	97	158	.230	.288	.330	71	-52	30	17	-1	.982	36	2-431,S-102/3DOC	0.5

■ MARK SALAS
Salas, Mark Bruce b: 3/8/61, Montebello, Cal. BL/TR, 6', 205 lbs. Deb: 6/19/84

YEAR	TM/L	G	AB	R	H	2B	3B	HR	RBI	BB	SO	AVG	OBP	SLG	PRO+	BR/A	SB	CS	SBR	FA	FR	G/POS	TPR
1984	StL-N	14	20	1	2	1	0	0	0	0	3	.100	.100	.150	-31	-3	0	0	0	1.000	-1	/C-4,O-3	-0.5
1985	Min-A	120	360	51	108	20	5	9	41	18	37	.300	.335	.458	108	3	0	1	-1	.991	2	*C-115/D-3	1.0
1986	Min-A	91	258	28	60	7	4	8	33	18	32	.233	.285	.384	78	-8	3	1	0	.980	-6	C-69/D-8	-1.0
1987	Min-A	22	45	8	17	2	0	3	9	5	6	.378	.440	.622	171	5	0	1	-1	.989	1	C-14	0.5
	NY-A	50	115	13	23	4	0	3	12	10	17	.200	.281	.313	58	-7	0	0	0	1.000	-3	C-41/O-1,D-4	-0.7
	Yr	72	160	21	40	6	0	6	21	15	23	.250	.326	.400	91	-2	0	1	-1	.996	-2	C-55/D-4,O-1	-0.2
1988	Chi-A	75	196	17	49	7	0	3	9	12	17	.250	.303	.332	78	-6	0	0	0	.979	0	C-69/D-1	-0.2
1989	Cle-A	30	77	4	17	4	1	2	7	5	13	.221	.277	.377	81	-2	0	0	0	1.000	-0	D-20/C-5	-0.3
1990	Det-A	74	164	18	38	3	0	9	24	21	28	.232	.323	.415	104	1	0	0	0	.988	-4	C-57/3-1,D-3	-0.1
1991	Det-A	33	57	2	5	1	0	1	7	0	10	.088	.119	.158	-24	-10	0	0	0	1.000	-0	C-11/1-5,D-8	-1.0
Total	8	509	1292	142	319	49	10	38	143	89	163	.247	.302	.389	86	-27	3	3	-1	.987	-11	C-385/D-47,1-5,O3	-2.3

■ ANGEL SALAZAR
Salazar, Argenis Antonio (Yepez) b: 11/4/61, Anaco, Venez. BR/TR, 6', 173 lbs. Deb: 8/10/83

YEAR	TM/L	G	AB	R	H	2B	3B	HR	RBI	BB	SO	AVG	OBP	SLG	PRO+	BR/A	SB	CS	SBR	FA	FR	G/POS	TPR
1983	Mon-N	36	37	5	8	1	1	0	1	1	8	.216	.237	.297	47	-3	0	0	0	.966	2	S-34	0.1
1984	Mon-N	80	174	12	27	4	2	0	12	4	38	.155	.179	.201	7	-22	1	1	-0	.960	-3	S-80	-2.1
1986	KC-A	117	298	24	73	20	2	0	24	7	47	.245	.267	.326	59	-17	1	1	-0	.978	-5	*S-115/2-1	-1.3
1987	KC-A	116	317	24	65	7	0	2	21	6	46	.205	.220	.246	23	-35	4	1	-1	.981	22	*S-116	-0.6
1988	Chi-N	34	60	4	15	1	0	0	1	1	11	.250	.262	.300	58	-3	0	3	-2	.966	7	S-29/2-2,3-1	0.5
Total	5	383	886	69	188	33	6	2	59	19	150	.212	.231	.270	36	-80	6	6	-2	.974	23	S-374/2-3,3-1	-3.4

■ LUIS SALAZAR
Salazar, Luis Ernesto (Garcia) b: 5/19/56, Barcelona, Venez. BR/TR, 5'9", 180 lbs. Deb: 8/15/80

YEAR	TM/L	G	AB	R	H	2B	3B	HR	RBI	BB	SO	AVG	OBP	SLG	PRO+	BR/A	SB	CS	SBR	FA	FR	G/POS	TPR
1980	SD-N	44	169	28	57	4	7	1	25	5	25	.337	.374	.462	140	8	11	2	2	.944	-2	3-42/O-4	0.8
1981	SD-N	109	400	37	121	19	6	3	38	16	72	.303	.331	.403	116	6	11	8	-2	.955	-1	3-94,O-23	0.2
1982	SD-N	145	524	55	127	15	5	8	62	23	80	.242	.277	.336	75	-20	32	9	4	.938	16	*3-129,S-18/O-1	-0.1
1983	SD-N	134	481	52	124	16	2	14	45	17	80	.258	.286	.387	88	-10	24	9	2	.949	10	*3-118,S-19	0.2
1984	*SD-N	93	228	20	55	7	2	6	17	6	38	.241	.261	.329	65	-11	7	1	-0	.970	-5	3-58,O-24/S-4	-0.9
1985	Chi-A	122	327	39	80	18	2	10	45	12	60	.245	.271	.404	79	-10	14	4	2	.968	-19	O-84,3-39/1-6,D-8	-3.0
1986	Chi-A	4	7	1	1	0	0	0	0	0	3	.143	.250	.143	10	-1	0	0	0	.000	0	/D-2	-0.1
1987	SD-N	84	189	13	48	5	0	3	17	10	30	.254	.305	.328	70	-4	3	0	-1	.957	-9	3-38,S-22,O-10,/P1	-1.7
1988	Det-A	130	452	61	122	14	1	12	62	21	70	.270	.307	.385	96	-4	6	3	-1	.992	-10	O-68,S-37,3-31,/21	-1.1
1989	SD-N	95	246	27	66	7	2	8	22	11	44	.268	.302	.411	102	-0	1	3	-2	.968	7	3-72,O-14/S-9,1-2	0.6
	*Chi-N	26	80	7	26	5	0	1	12	4	13	.325	.357	.425	114	1	0	1	-1	.921	-6	3-25/O-2	-0.5
	Yr	121	326	34	92	12	2	9	34	15	57	.282	.316	.414	105	1	1	4	-2	.959	1	3-97,O-16/S-9,1-2	0.1

YEAR	TM/L	G	AB	R	H	2B	3B	HR	RBI	BB	SO	AVG	OBP	SLG	PRO+	BR/A	SB	CS	SBR	FA	FR	G/POS	TPR
1990	Chi-N	115	410	44	104	13	3	12	47	19	59	.254	.293	.388	80	-12	3	1	0	.950	-20	3-91,O-28	-3.3
1991	Chi-N	103	333	34	86	14	1	14	38	15	45	.258	.292	.432	97	-3	0	3	-2	.956	-7	3-86/1-7,O-1	-1.5
1992	Chi-N	98	255	20	53	7	2	5	25	11	34	.208	.241	.310	53	-16	1	1	0	.935	3	3-40,O-34,S-12,/1-5	-1.5
Total	13	1302	4101	438	1070	144	33	94	455	179	653	.261	.294	.381	88	-79	117	51	5	.950	-33	3-863,O-293,S/1D2P	-11.6

■ ED SALES
Sales, Edward A. b: 1861, Harrisburg, Pa. d: 8/10/12, New Haven, Conn. BL/TR. Deb: 7/15/1890

YEAR	TM/L	G	AB	R	H	2B	3B	HR	RBI	BB	SO	AVG	OBP	SLG	PRO+	BR/A	SB	CS	SBR	FA	FR	G/POS	TPR
1890	Pit-N	51	189	19	43	7	3	1	23	16	15	.228	.298	.312	88	-3	3			.871	-14	S-51	-1.2

■ BILL SALKELD
Salkeld, William Franklin b: 3/8/17, Pocatello, Idaho d: 4/22/67, Los Angeles, Cal. BL/TR, 5'10", 190 lbs. Deb: 4/18/45 F

YEAR	TM/L	G	AB	R	H	2B	3B	HR	RBI	BB	SO	AVG	OBP	SLG	PRO+	BR/A	SB	CS	SBR	FA	FR	G/POS	TPR
1945	Pit-N	95	267	45	83	16	1	15	52	50	16	.311	.420	.547	161	23	2			.973	-9	C-86	1.9
1946	Pit-N	69	160	18	47	8	0	3	19	39	16	.294	.432	.400	133	9	2			.972	-1	C-51	1.2
1947	Pit-N	47	61	5	13	2	0	0	8	6	8	.213	.284	.246	41	-5	0			.971	-3	C-15	-0.7
1948	*Bos-N	78	198	26	48	8	1	8	28	42	37	.242	.378	.414	116	6	1			.990	5	C-59	1.5
1949	Bos-N	66	161	17	41	5	0	5	25	44	24	.255	.417	.379	121	8	1			.980	-4	C-63	0.7
1950	Chi-A	1	3	0	0	0	0	0	0	1	0	.000	.250	.000	-33	-1	0	0	0	1.000	-0	/C-1	-0.1
Total	6	356	850	111	232	39	2	31	132	182	101	.273	.402	.433	129	40	6	0		.979	-11	C-275	4.5

■ CHICO SALMON
Salmon, Ruthford Eduardo b: 12/3/40, Colon, Panama BR/TR, 5'10", 170 lbs. Deb: 6/28/64

YEAR	TM/L	G	AB	R	H	2B	3B	HR	RBI	BB	SO	AVG	OBP	SLG	PRO+	BR/A	SB	CS	SBR	FA	FR	G/POS	TPR
1964	Cle-A	86	283	43	87	17	2	4	25	13	37	.307	.342	.424	113	4	10	6	-1	1.000	-8	O-53,2-32,1-13	-0.4
1965	Cle-A	79	120	20	29	8	0	3	12	5	19	.242	.283	.383	87	-2	7	4	-0	.985	-6	1-28,O-17/2-5,3-5	-1.0
1966	Cle-A	126	422	46	108	13	2	7	40	21	41	.256	.291	.346	82	-10	10	1	2	.958	-18	S-61,2-28,1-24,O/3	-2.2
1967	Cle-A	90	203	19	46	13	1	2	19	17	29	.227	.290	.330	82	-5	10	4	1	1.000	1	0-28,1-24,2-24,S/3	-0.2
1968	Cle-A	103	276	24	59	8	1	3	12	12	30	.214	.254	.283	63	-13	7	7	-2	.971	-15	2-45,3-18,S-15,O1	-3.1
1969	*Bal-A	52	91	18	27	5	0	3	12	10	22	.297	.379	.451	130	4	0	0	0	1.000	-5	1-17/2-9,S-9,3-3,O	-0.1
1970	*Bal-A	63	172	19	43	4	0	7	22	8	30	.250	.287	.395	85	-4	2	2	-1	.946	-20	S-33,2-12,3-11,/1-2	-2.2
1971	Bal-A	42	84	11	15	1	0	2	7	3	21	.179	.207	.262	32	-8	0	0	0	1.000	-1	/1-9,2-9,3-6,S-5	-1.1
1972	Bal-A	17	16	2	1	1	0	0	0	0	3	.063	.063	.125	-44	-3	0	0	0	1.000	0	/1-2,3-1	-0.3
Total	9	658	1667	202	415	70	6	31	149	89	233	.249	.291	.354	84	-36	46	24	-1	.959	-75	2-164,S-137,1O/3	-10.6

■ TIM SALMON
Salmon, Timothy James b: 8/24/68, Long Beach, Cal. BR/TR, 6'3", 200 lbs. Deb: 8/21/92

YEAR	TM/L	G	AB	R	H	2B	3B	HR	RBI	BB	SO	AVG	OBP	SLG	PRO+	BR/A	SB	CS	SBR	FA	FR	G/POS	TPR
1992	Cal-A	23	79	8	14	1	0	2	6	11	23	.177	.286	.266	55	-5	1	1	-0	.953	-0	O-21	-0.6
1993	Cal-A	142	515	93	146	35	1	31	95	82	135	.283	.387	.536	141	30	5	6	-2	.980	15	*O-140/D-1	3.8
1994	Cal-A	100	373	67	107	18	2	23	70	54	102	.287	.384	.531	131	17	1	3	-2	.966	8	O-99	2.0
1995	Cal-A	143	537	111	177	34	3	34	105	91	111	.330	.432	.594	165	54	5	5	-2	.988	16	*O-142/D-1	**5.9**
1996	Cal-A	156	581	90	166	27	4	30	98	93	125	.286	.388	.501	125	24	4	2	0	.975	8	*O-153/D-3	2.4
Total	5	564	2085	369	610	115	10	120	374	331	496	.293	.395	.530	138	121	16	17	-5	.977	46	O-555/D-5	13.5

■ JACK SALTZGAVER
Saltzgaver, Otto Hamlin b: 1/23/03, Croton, Iowa d: 2/1/78, Keokuk, Iowa BL/TR, 5'11", 165 lbs. Deb: 4/12/32

YEAR	TM/L	G	AB	R	H	2B	3B	HR	RBI	BB	SO	AVG	OBP	SLG	PRO+	BR/A	SB	CS	SBR	FA	FR	G/POS	TPR
1932	NY-A	20	47	10	6	2	1	0	5	10	10	.128	.281	.213	31	-5	1	1	-0	.958	-3	2-16	-0.7
1934	NY-A	94	350	64	95	8	1	6	36	48	28	.271	.359	.351	90	-4	8	1	2	.953	-16	3-84/1-4	-1.4
1935	NY-A	61	149	17	39	6	0	3	18	23	12	.262	.368	.362	95	-1	0	2	-1	.937	-13	2-25,3-18/1-6	-1.2
1936	NY-A	34	90	14	19	5	0	1	13	13	18	.211	.311	.300	53	-7	0	0	0	.972	-5	3-16/2-6,1-4	-0.9
1937	NY-A	17	11	6	2	0	0	0	0	3	4	.182	.357	.182	40	-1	0	0	0	1.000	0	/1-4	-0.1
1945	Pit-N	52	117	20	38	5	3	0	10	8	8	.325	.368	.419	114	2	0			.963	-4	2-31/3-1	0.0
Total	6	278	764	131	199	26	5	10	82	105	80	.260	.351	.347	85	-15	9	4		.957	-40	3-119/2-78,1-18	-4.3

■ ED SAMCOFF
Samcoff, Edward William b: 9/1/24, Sacramento, Cal. BR/TR, 5'10", 165 lbs. Deb: 4/21/51

YEAR	TM/L	G	AB	R	H	2B	3B	HR	RBI	BB	SO	AVG	OBP	SLG	PRO+	BR/A	SB	CS	SBR	FA	FR	G/POS	TPR
1951	Phi-A	4	11	0	0	0	0	0	0	1	2	.000	.083	.000	-75	-3	0	0	0	1.000	-2	/2-3	-0.4

■ RON SAMFORD
Samford, Ronald Edward b: 2/28/30, Dallas, Tex. BR/TR, 5'11", 156 lbs. Deb: 4/15/54

YEAR	TM/L	G	AB	R	H	2B	3B	HR	RBI	BB	SO	AVG	OBP	SLG	PRO+	BR/A	SB	CS	SBR	FA	FR	G/POS	TPR
1954	NY-N	12	5	2	0	0	0	0	0	0	1	.000	.000	.000	-99	-1	0	1	-1	1.000	1	/2-3	-0.1
1955	Det-A	1	1	0	0	0	0	0	0	0	0	.000	.000	.000	-99	-0	0	0	0	1.000	0	/S-1	0.0
1957	Det-A	54	91	6	20	1	2	0	5	6	15	.220	.276	.275	49	-6	1	0	0	.964	13	S-35,2-11/3-4	0.9
1959	Was-A	91	237	23	53	13	0	5	22	11	29	.224	.264	.342	65	-12	1	0	0	.947	3	S-64,2-23	-0.6
Total	4	158	334	31	73	14	2	5	27	17	46	.219	.263	.317	58	-20	2	1	0	.952	15	S-100/2-37,3-4	0.2

■ BILL SAMPLE
Sample, William Amos b: 4/2/55, Roanoke, Va. BR/TR, 5'9", 175 lbs. Deb: 9/2/78

YEAR	TM/L	G	AB	R	H	2B	3B	HR	RBI	BB	SO	AVG	OBP	SLG	PRO+	BR/A	SB	CS	SBR	FA	FR	G/POS	TPR
1978	Tex-A	8	15	2	7	2	0	0	3	0	3	.467	.467	.600	197	2	0	0	0	.000	-1	/O-2,D-3	0.1
1979	Tex-A	128	325	60	95	21	2	5	35	37	28	.292	.368	.415	112	6	8	6	-1	1.000	-4	*O-103/D-9	-0.2
1980	Tex-A	99	204	29	53	10	0	4	19	18	15	.260	.338	.368	96	-1	8	5	-1	.973	-9	O-72/D-4	-1.3
1981	Tex-A	66	230	36	65	16	0	3	25	17	21	.283	.350	.391	120	6	4	1	1	.993	-1	O-64	0.4
1982	Tex-A	97	360	56	94	14	2	10	29	27	35	.261	.318	.394	99	-1	10	2	2	.981	-2	O-91/D-1	0.0
1983	Tex-A	147	554	80	152	28	3	12	57	44	46	.274	.333	.401	103	2	44	8	8	.988	6	*O-146	1.2
1984	Tex-A	130	489	67	121	20	2	5	33	29	46	.247	.290	.327	68	-21	18	6	2	.986	0	*O-122/D-2	-2.3
1985	NY-A	59	139	18	40	5	0	1	15	9	10	.288	.340	.345	90	-2	2	1	0	.989	-4	O-55	-0.7
1986	Atl-N	92	200	23	57	11	0	6	14	14	26	.285	.341	.430	105	1	1	2	1	.986	-8	O-56/2-1	-0.8
Total	9	826	2516	371	684	127	9	46	230	195	230	.272	.331	.384	100	-7	98	31	11	.987	-19	O-711/D-19,2-1	-3.6

■ AMADO SAMUEL
Samuel, Amado Ruperto b: 12/6/38, San Pedro De Macoris, D.R. BR/TR, 6'1", 170 lbs. Deb: 4/10/62

YEAR	TM/L	G	AB	R	H	2B	3B	HR	RBI	BB	SO	AVG	OBP	SLG	PRO+	BR/A	SB	CS	SBR	FA	FR	G/POS	TPR
1962	Mil-N	76	209	16	43	10	0	3	20	12	54	.206	.249	.297	47	-16	0	2	-1	.958	-4	S-36,2-28/3-3	-1.7
1963	Mil-N	15	17	0	3	1	0	0	0	0	4	.176	.176	.235	18	-2	0	1	-1	.786	2	/S-7,2-4	0.0
1964	NY-N	53	142	7	33	7	0	0	5	4	24	.232	.264	.282	55	-9	0	1	-1	.945	6	S-34,3-17/2-3	-0.2
Total	3	144	368	23	79	18	0	3	25	16	82	.215	.251	.288	49	-26	0	4	-2	.942	4	/S-77,2-35,3-20	-1.9

■ JUAN SAMUEL
Samuel, Juan Milton b: 12/9/60, San Pedro De Macoris, D.R. BR/TR, 5'11", 170 lbs. Deb: 8/24/83

YEAR	TM/L	G	AB	R	H	2B	3B	HR	RBI	BB	SO	AVG	OBP	SLG	PRO+	BR/A	SB	CS	SBR	FA	FR	G/POS	TPR
1983	*Phi-N	18	65	14	18	1	2	2	5	4	16	.277	.329	.446	114	1	3	2	-0	.916	3	2-18	0.5
1984	Phi-N☆	160	701	105	191	36	**19**	15	69	28	168	.272	.307	.442	107	3	72	15	13	.962	-22	*2-160	-0.1
1985	Phi-N	161	663	101	175	31	13	19	74	33	141	.264	.305	.436	102	-0	53	19	5	.983	-2	*2-159	0.8
1986	Phi-N	145	591	90	157	36	12	16	78	26	142	.266	.306	.448	102	-1	42	14	4	.967	-9	*2-143	0.0
1987	Phi-N★	160	655	113	178	37	**15**	28	100	60	162	.272	.338	.502	115	12	35	15	2	.978	-19	*2-160	0.3
1988	Phi-N	157	629	68	153	32	9	12	67	39	151	.243	.300	.380	92	-7	33	10	4	.978	-26	*2-152/O-3,3-1	-2.5
1989	Phi-N	51	199	32	49	3	1	8	20	18	45	.246	.312	.392	100	-0	11	3	2	.993	5	O-50	0.5
	NY-N	86	333	37	76	13	1	3	28	24	75	.228	.300	.300	76	-10	31	9	4	.986	7	O-84	-0.2
	Yr	137	532	69	125	16	2	11	48	42	120	.235	.304	.335	85	-10	42	12	5	.989	11	*O-134	0.3
1990	LA-N	143	492	62	119	24	3	13	52	51	126	.242	.319	.382	95	-4	38	20	-1	.972	-5	*2-108,O-31	-0.9
1991	LA-N★	153	594	74	161	22	6	12	58	49	133	.271	.330	.389	104	2	23	8	2	.978	4	*2-152	1.2
1992	LA-N	47	122	7	32	3	1	0	15	7	22	.262	.308	.303	75	-4	2	2	-1	.974	-2	2-38/O-1	-0.6
	KC-A	29	102	15	29	5	3	0	8	7	27	.284	.336	.392	101	0	6	1	1	.903	-3	O-18,2-10	-0.2
1993	Cin-N	103	261	31	60	10	4	4	26	23	53	.230	.290	.345	72	-11	9	5	-2	.971	3	2-70/1-6,3-4,O-3	-0.7
1994	Det-A	59	136	32	42	9	5	5	21	10	26	.309	.369	.559	134	7	5	2	0	1.000	8	O-27,D-10/2-8,1-2	0.8
1995	Det-A	76	171	28	48	10	0	10	34	24	38	.281	.376	.526	132	8	5	4	1	.983	-1	1-37,D-16/O-9,2-6	0.3
	KC-A	15	34	3	6	0	0	2	5	5	11	.176	.282	.353	63	-2	1	0	0	1.000	0	/O-5,1-1,D-7	-0.3
	Yr	91	205	31	54	10	0	12	39	29	49	.263	.360	.498	121	6	6	4	1	.984	-1	1-38,D-23,O-14/2-6	0.0
1996	Tor-A	69	188	34	48	8	3	8	26	15	65	.255	.320	.457	93	-3	9	1	2	1.000	-9	O-24,D-24,1-17	-1.1
Total	14	1632	5936	846	1542	280	98	157	686	423	1401	.260	.317	.419	101	-8	378	132	34	.972	-75	*2-1184,O-255/1D3	-2.2

■ IKE SAMULS
Samuls, Samuel Earl b: 2/20/1876, Chicago, Ill. d: 1/1/42, Los Angeles, Cal. BR/TR, Deb: 8/3/1895

YEAR	TM/L	G	AB	R	H	2B	3B	HR	RBI	BB	SO	AVG	OBP	SLG	PRO+	BR/A	SB	CS	SBR	FA	FR	G/POS	TPR
1895	StL-N	24	74	5	17	2	0	0	5	5	7	.230	.278	.257	39	-7	5			.750	-3	3-21/S-3	-0.8

■ GUS SANBERG
Sanberg, Gustave E. b: 2/23/1896, Long Island City, N.Y. d: 2/3/30, Los Angeles, Cal. BR/TR, 6'1", 189 lbs. Deb: 5/11/23

YEAR	TM/L	G	AB	R	H	2B	3B	HR	RBI	BB	SO	AVG	OBP	SLG	PRO+	BR/A	SB	CS	SBR	FA	FR	G/POS	TPR
1923	Cin-N	7	17	1	3	1	0	0	1	1	1	.176	.222	.235	21	-2	0	0	0	1.000	-1	/C-5	-0.1

YEAR	TM/L	G	AB	R	H	2B	3B	HR	RBI	BB	SO	AVG	OBP	SLG	PRO+	BR/A	SB	CS	SBR	FA	FR	G/POS	TPR
1924	Cin-N	24	52	1	9	0	0	0	3	2	7	.173	.204	.173	2	-7	0	0	0	1.000	0	C-24	-0.6
Total	2	31	69	2	12	1	0	0	4	3	8	.174	.208	.188	7	-9	0	0	0	1.000	-1	/C-29	-0.9

■ ALEJANDRO SANCHEZ
Sanchez, Alejandro (Pimentel) b: 2/14/59, San Pedro De Macoris, D.R. BR/TR, 6', 185 lbs. Deb: 9/6/82

YEAR	TM/L	G	AB	R	H	2B	3B	HR	RBI	BB	SO	AVG	OBP	SLG	PRO+	BR/A	SB	CS	SBR	FA	FR	G/POS	TPR
1982	Phi-N	7	14	3	4	1	0	2	4	0	4	.286	.286	.786	186	1	0	0	0	1.000	-0	/O-4	0.1
1983	Phi-N	8	7	2	2	0	0	0	2	0	2	.286	.286	.286	59	-0	0	0	0	.500	-1	/O-2	-0.1
1984	SF-N	13	41	3	8	0	1	0	2	0	12	.195	.195	.244	23	-4	2	3	-1	.952	0	O-11	-0.6
1985	Det-A	71	133	19	33	6	2	6	12	0	39	.248	.248	.459	89	-3	2	2	-1	.923	-6	O-31,D-28	-1.0
1986	Min-A	8	16	1	2	0	0	0	1	1	8	.125	.176	.125	-16	-3	0	0	0	.000	-0	/O-1,D-3	-0.3
1987	Oak-A	2	3	0	0	0	0	0	0	0	1	.000	.000	.000	-99	-1	0	0	0	1.000	-0	/O-1,D-1	-0.1
Total	6	109	214	28	49	7	3	8	21	1	66	.229	.233	.402	71	-9	4	5	-2	.929	-7	/O-50,D-32	-2.0

■ CELERINO SANCHEZ
Sanchez, Celerino (Perez) b: 2/3/44, Veracruz, Mexico d: 5/1/92, Leon, Mexico BR/TR, 5'11", 160 lbs. Deb: 6/13/72

YEAR	TM/L	G	AB	R	H	2B	3B	HR	RBI	BB	SO	AVG	OBP	SLG	PRO+	BR/A	SB	CS	SBR	FA	FR	G/POS	TPR
1972	NY-A	71	250	18	62	8	0	1	22	12	30	.248	.293	.304	81	-6	0	0	0	.939	4	3-68	-0.4
1973	NY-A	34	64	12	14	3	0	1	9	2	12	.219	.242	.313	57	-4	1	1	-0	1.000	1	3-11,D-11/S-2,O-2	-0.3
Total	2	105	314	30	76	11	3	1	31	14	42	.242	.283	.306	76	-10	1	1	-0	.943	5	/3-79,D-11,O-2,S-2	-0.7

■ ORLANDO SANCHEZ
Sanchez, Orlando (Marquez) b: 9/7/56, Canovanas, P.R. BL/TR, 6'1", 195 lbs. Deb: 5/6/81

YEAR	TM/L	G	AB	R	H	2B	3B	HR	RBI	BB	SO	AVG	OBP	SLG	PRO+	BR/A	SB	CS	SBR	FA	FR	G/POS	TPR
1981	StL-N	27	49	5	14	2	1	0	6	2	6	.286	.314	.347	90	-1	1	0	0	.926	-2	C-18	-0.2
1982	StL-N	26	37	6	7	0	1	0	3	5	5	.189	.286	.243	49	-2	0	0	0	1.000	-1	C-15	-0.3
1983	StL-N	6	6	0	0	0	0	0	0	0	4	.000	.000	.000	-99	-2	0	0	0	1.000	-0	/C-1	-0.2
1984	KC-A	10	10	0	1	1	0	0	2	0	2	.100	.100	.200	-19	-2	0	0	0	1.000	-0	/C-1	-0.2
	Bal-A	4	8	0	2	0	0	0	1	0	2	.250	.250	.250	40	-1	0	0	0	1.000	-0	/C-4	-0.1
	Yr	14	18	0	3	1	0	0	3	0	4	.167	.167	.222	7	-2	0	0	0	1.000	-0	/C-5	-0.3
Total	4	73	110	11	24	3	2	0	12	7	19	.218	.265	.282	53	-7	1	0	0	.962	-3	/C-39	-1.0

■ REY SANCHEZ
Sanchez, Rey Francisco (Guadalupe) b: 10/5/67, Rio Piedras, P.R. BR/TR, 5'10", 180 lbs. Deb: 9/8/91

YEAR	TM/L	G	AB	R	H	2B	3B	HR	RBI	BB	SO	AVG	OBP	SLG	PRO+	BR/A	SB	CS	SBR	FA	FR	G/POS	TPR
1991	Chi-N	13	23	1	6	0	0	0	2	4	3	.261	.370	.261	77	-0	0	0	0	1.000	2	S-10/2-2	0.2
1992	Chi-N	74	255	24	64	14	3	1	19	10	17	.251	.287	.341	75	-9	2	1	0	.974	14	S-68/2-4	1.1
1993	Chi-N	105	344	35	97	11	2	0	28	15	22	.282	.318	.326	74	-13	1	1	-0	.969	27	S-98	2.1
1994	Chi-N	96	291	26	83	13	1	0	24	20	29	.285	.346	.337	80	-8	2	5	-2	.993	29	2-50,S-30,3-17	2.2
1995	Chi-N	114	428	57	119	22	2	3	27	14	48	.278	.302	.360	75	-16	6	4	-1	.987	4	*2-111/S-4	-0.6
1996	Chi-N	95	289	28	61	9	0	1	12	22	42	.211	.274	.252	40	-25	7	1	2	.977	22	S-92	0.6
Total	6	497	1630	171	430	69	8	5	112	85	161	.264	.307	.325	69	-70	18	12	-2	.973	97	S-302,2-167/3-17	5.6

■ HEINIE SAND
Sand, John Henry b: 7/3/1897, San Francisco, Cal d: 11/3/58, San Francisco, Cal. BR/TR, 5'8", 160 lbs. Deb: 4/17/23

YEAR	TM/L	G	AB	R	H	2B	3B	HR	RBI	BB	SO	AVG	OBP	SLG	PRO+	BR/A	SB	CS	SBR	FA	FR	G/POS	TPR
1923	Phi-N	132	470	85	107	16	5	4	32	82	56	.228	.347	.309	67	-21	7	3	0	.934	-2	*S-120,3-11	-1.0
1924	Phi-N	137	539	79	132	21	6	6	40	52	57	.245	.316	.340	84	-25	5	4	-1	**.959**	2	*S-137	-0.9
1925	Phi-N	148	496	69	138	30	7	3	55	64	65	.278	.364	.385	84	-11	1	1	-0	.928	-6	*S-143	-0.2
1926	Phi-N	149	567	99	154	30	5	4	37	66	56	.272	.350	.363	88	-9	2			.939	-3	*S-149	0.3
1927	Phi-N	141	535	87	160	22	8	1	49	58	59	.299	.369	.376	98	0	5			.949	-15	S-86,3-58	-0.3
1928	Phi-N	141	426	38	90	26	1	0	38	60	47	.211	.310	.277	53	-29	1			.951	-1	*S-137	-1.4
Total	6	848	3033	457	781	145	32	18	251	382	340	.258	.343	.344	77	-94	21	8		.943	-25	S-772/3-69	-3.5

■ RYNE SANDBERG
Sandberg, Ryne Dee b: 9/18/59, Spokane, Wash. BR/TR, 6'2", 180 lbs. Deb: 9/2/81

YEAR	TM/L	G	AB	R	H	2B	3B	HR	RBI	BB	SO	AVG	OBP	SLG	PRO+	BR/A	SB	CS	SBR	FA	FR	G/POS	TPR
1981	Phi-N	13	6	2	1	0	0	0	0	0	1	.167	.167	.167	-5	-1	0	0	0	1.000	4	/S-5,2-1	0.3
1982	Chi-N	156	635	103	172	33	5	7	54	36	90	.271	.314	.372	89	-10	32	12	2	.970	5	*3-133,2-24	-0.5
1983	Chi-N	158	633	94	165	25	4	8	48	51	79	.261	.319	.351	81	-16	37	11	5	.986	41	*2-157/S-1	3.8
1984	*Chi-N★	156	636	**114**	200	36	**19**	19	84	52	101	.314	.369	.520	135	28	32	7	5	**.993**	23	*2-156	**6.4**
1985	Chi-N★	153	609	113	186	31	6	26	83	57	97	.305	.366	.504	127	21	54	11	10	.986	8	*2-153/S-1	4.6
1986	Chi-N★	154	627	68	178	28	5	14	76	46	79	.284	.333	.411	97	-4	34	11	4	**.994**	5	*2-153	1.2
1987	Chi-N★	132	523	81	154	25	2	16	59	59	79	.294	.368	.442	109	8	21	2	5	.985	1	*2-131	2.0
1988	Chi-N★	155	618	77	163	23	8	19	69	54	91	.264	.324	.419	107	5	25	10	2	.987	11	*2-153	2.5
1989	*Chi-N★	157	606	**104**	176	25	5	30	76	59	85	.290	.357	.497	132	24	15	5	2	.992	5	*2-155	3.3
1990	Chi-N★	155	615	**116**	188	30	3	**40**	100	50	84	.306	.359	.559	138	30	25	7	3	.989	7	*2-154	4.3
1991	Chi-N★	158	585	104	170	32	2	26	100	87	89	.291	.384	.485	137	30	22	8	2	**.995**	11	*2-157	4.7
1992	Chi-N★	158	612	100	186	32	8	26	87	68	73	.304	.374	.510	145	35	17	6	2	.990	14	*2-157	5.7
1993	Chi-N★	117	456	67	141	20	5	9	45	37	62	.309	.364	.412	109	6	9	2	2	.988	-4	*2-115	0.7
1994	Chi-N	57	223	36	53	9	5	5	24	23	40	.238	.312	.390	83	-6	2	3	-1	.987	3	2-57	-0.1
1996	Chi-N	150	554	85	135	28	4	25	92	54	116	.244	.319	.444	97	-3	12	8	-1	.991	-11	*2-146	-0.7
Total	15	2029	7938	1264	2268	377	76	270	997	733	1166	.286	.349	.454	115	147	337	103	39	.990	118	*2-1869,3-133/S-7	38.2

■ BEN SANDERS
Sanders, Alexander Bennett b: 2/16/1865, Catharpin, Va. d: 8/29/30, Memphis, Tenn. BR/TR, 6', 210 lbs. Deb: 6/6/1888

YEAR	TM/L	G	AB	R	H	2B	3B	HR	RBI	BB	SO	AVG	OBP	SLG	PRO+	BR/A	SB	CS	SBR	FA	FR	G/POS	TPR
1888	Phi-N	57	236	26	58	11	2	1	25	8	12	.246	.276	.322	86	-4	13			.929	3	P-31,O-25/3-1	-0.3
1889	Phi-N	44	169	21	47	8	2	0	21	6	11	.278	.307	.349	76	-6	4			.879	-3	P-44/O-3	-0.1
1890	Phi-P	52	189	31	59	6	6	0	30	10	10	.312	.347	.407	99	-1	2			.924	1	P-43,O-10	-0.1
1891	Phi-a	40	156	24	39	6	4	1	19	7	12	.250	.291	.359	83	-5	2			.839	-6	O-22,P-19	-0.7
1892	Lou-N	54	198	30	54	12	2	3	18	16	17	.273	.330	.399	131	7	6			.930	-3	P-31,1-15/O-9	0.0
Total	5	247	948	132	257	43	16	5	113	47	62	.271	.310	.366	95	-9	27			.916	-8	P-168/O-69,1-15,3-1	-1.2

■ DEION SANDERS
Sanders, Deion Luwynn b: 8/9/67, Ft.Myers, Fla. BL/TL, 6'1", 195 lbs. Deb: 5/31/89

YEAR	TM/L	G	AB	R	H	2B	3B	HR	RBI	BB	SO	AVG	OBP	SLG	PRO+	BR/A	SB	CS	SBR	FA	FR	G/POS	TPR
1989	NY-A	14	47	7	11	2	0	2	7	3	8	.234	.280	.404	92	-1	1	0	0	.969	-0	O-14	-0.1
1990	NY-A	57	133	24	21	2	2	3	9	13	27	.158	.238	.271	42	-11	8	2	1	.973	-4	O-42/D-4	-1.5
1991	Atl-N	54	110	16	21	1	2	4	13	12	23	.191	.270	.345	68	-5	11	3	2	.952	-5	O-44	-0.9
1992	*Atl-N	97	303	54	92	6	**14**	8	28	18	52	.304	.347	.495	128	10	26	9	2	.983	-1	O-75	1.1
1993	*Atl-N	95	272	42	75	18	6	6	28	16	42	.276	.323	.452	104	1	19	7	2	.986	-0	O-60	0.1
1994	Atl-N	46	191	32	55	10	4	4	21	16	28	.288	.346	.403	93	-2	19	7	2	.980	-2	O-46	-0.3
	Cin-N	46	184	26	51	7	4	0	7	16	35	.277	.342	.359	84	-4	19	9	0	1.000	2	O-45	-0.3
	Yr	92	375	58	106	17	8	4	28	32	63	.283	.344	.381	88	-6	38	16	2	.991	0	O-91	-0.6
1995	Cin-N	33	129	19	31	2	3	1	10	9	18	.240	.300	.326	65	-6	16	3	3	.968	4	O-33	0.0
	SF-N	52	214	29	61	9	5	5	18	18	42	.285	.346	.444	110	3	8	6	-1	.984	1	O-52	0.1
	Yr	85	343	48	92	11	8	6	28	27	60	.268	.329	.399	93	-4	24	9	2	.977	5	O-85	0.1
Total	7	494	1583	249	418	57	36	33	141	121	275	.264	.321	.408	94	-15	127	46	11	.981	-6	O-411/D-4	-1.8

■ JOHN SANDERS
Sanders, John Frank b: 11/20/45, Grand Island, Neb. BR/TR, 6'2", 200 lbs. Deb: 4/13/65

YEAR	TM/L	G	AB	R	H	2B	3B	HR	RBI	BB	SO	AVG	OBP	SLG	PRO+	BR/A	SB	CS	SBR	FA	FR	G/POS	TPR
1965	KC-A	1	0	0	0	0	0	0	0	0	0	—	—	—			0	0	0	.000	0	R	0.0

■ RAY SANDERS
Sanders, Raymond Floyd b: 12/4/16, Bonne Terre, Mo. d: 10/28/83, Washington, Mo. BL/TR, 6'2", 185 lbs. Deb: 4/14/42

YEAR	TM/L	G	AB	R	H	2B	3B	HR	RBI	BB	SO	AVG	OBP	SLG	PRO+	BR/A	SB	CS	SBR	FA	FR	G/POS	TPR
1942	*StL-N	95	282	37	71	17	5	5	39	42	31	.252	.351	.379	106	3	2			.991	-4	1-77	-0.6
1943	*StL-N	144	478	69	134	21	5	11	73	77	33	.280	.381	.414	124	17	1			.995	-7	*1-141	0.2
1944	*StL-N	154	601	87	177	34	9	12	102	71	50	.295	.371	.441	126	21	2			**.994**	-13	*1-152	0.0
1945	StL-N	143	537	85	148	29	3	8	78	83	55	.276	.375	.385	109	9	3			.986	-5	*1-142	-0.5
1946	Bos-N	80	259	43	63	12	0	6	35	50	38	.243	.368	.359	105	3	0			.988	4	1-77	0.3
1948	*Bos-N	5	4	0	1	0	0	0	2	1	0	.250	.400	.250	81	-0	0			.000	0	H	0.0
1949	Bos-N	9	21	0	3	1	0	0	4	4	6	.143	.280	.190	30	-2	0			.984	2	/1-7	0.0
Total	7	630	2182	321	597	114	19	42	329	328	216	.274	.370	.401	115	50	8			.991	-22	1-596	-0.6

■ REGGIE SANDERS
Sanders, Reginald Jerome b: 9/9/49, Birmingham, Ala. BR/TR, 6'2", 205 lbs. Deb: 9/1/74

YEAR	TM/L	G	AB	R	H	2B	3B	HR	RBI	BB	SO	AVG	OBP	SLG	PRO+	BR/A	SB	CS	SBR	FA	FR	G/POS	TPR
1974	Det-A	26	99	12	27	7	0	3	10	5	20	.273	.308	.434	108	1	1	0	0	.987	1	1-25/D-1	0.0

■ REGGIE SANDERS
Sanders, Reginald Laverne b: 12/1/67, Florence, S.C. BR/TR, 6'1", 180 lbs. Deb: 8/22/91

YEAR	TM/L	G	AB	R	H	2B	3B	HR	RBI	BB	SO	AVG	OBP	SLG	PRO+	BR/A	SB	CS	SBR	FA	FR	G/POS	TPR
1991	Cin-N	9	40	6	8	0	0	1	3	0	9	.200	.200	.275	31	-4	1	1	-0	1.000	1	/O-9	-0.4

YEAR	TM/L	G	AB	R	H	2B	3B	HR	RBI	BB	SO	AVG	OBP	SLG	PRO+	BR/A	SB	CS	SBR	FA	FR	G/POS	TPR
1992	Cin-N	116	385	62	104	26	6	12	36	48	98	.270	.357	.462	127	14	16	7	1	.978	5	*O-110	1.9
1993	Cin-N	138	496	90	136	16	4	20	83	51	118	.274	.348	.444	110	7	27	10	2	.975	8	*O-137	1.4
1994	Cin-N	107	400	66	105	20	8	17	62	41	114	.262	.334	.480	110	5	21	9	1	.975	12	*O-104	1.5
1995	*Cin-N★	133	484	91	148	36	6	28	99	69	122	.306	.401	.579	155	39	36	12	4	.983	5	*O-130	4.3
1996	Cin-N	81	287	49	72	17	1	14	33	44	86	.251	.354	.463	114	6	24	8	2	.988	7	O-80	1.3
Total	6	584	2092	364	573	115	25	92	316	253	547	.274	.358	.485	123	67	125	47	9	.979	37	O-570	10.0

■ MIKE SANDLOCK

Sandlock, Michael Joseph b: 10/17/15, Old Greenwich, Conn. BB/TR, 6'1", 185 lbs. Deb: 9/19/42

YEAR	TM/L	G	AB	R	H	2B	3B	HR	RBI	BB	SO	AVG	OBP	SLG	PRO+	BR/A	SB	CS	SBR	FA	FR	G/POS	TPR
1942	Bos-N	2	1	1	1	0	0	0	0	0	0	1.000	1.000	1.000	496	0	0			.000	0	/S-2	0.1
1944	Bos-N	30	30	1	3	0	0	0	2	5	3	.100	.250	.100	1	-4	0			.956	7	3-22/S-7	0.3
1945	Bro-N	80	195	21	55	14	2	2	17	18	19	.282	.346	.405	109	2	2			.991	1	C-47,S-22/2-4,3-2	0.6
1946	Bro-N	19	34	1	5	0	0	0	3	4	4	.147	.216	.147	4	-4	0			.973	6	C-17/3-1	0.3
1953	Pit-N	64	186	10	43	5	0	0	12	12	19	.231	.281	.258	42	-16	0	0	0	.991	16	C-64	0.3
Total	5	195	446	34	107	19	2	2	31	38	45	.240	.304	.305	66	-21	2	0		.989	30	C-128/S-31,3-25,2-4	1.6

■ CHARLIE SANDS

Sands, Charles Duane b: 12/17/47, Newport News, Va. BL/TR, 6'2", 215 lbs. Deb: 6/21/67

YEAR	TM/L	G	AB	R	H	2B	3B	HR	RBI	BB	SO	AVG	OBP	SLG	PRO+	BR/A	SB	CS	SBR	FA	FR	G/POS	TPR
1967	NY-A	1	1	0	0	0	0	0	0	0	1	.000	.000	.000	-99	-0	0	0	0	.000	0	H	0.0
1971	*Pit-N	28	25	4	5	2	0	1	5	7	6	.200	.375	.400	120	1	0	0	0	1.000	0	/C-3	0.1
1972	Pit-N	1	1	0	0	0	0	0	0	0	0	.000	.000	.000	-99	-0	0	0	0	.000	0	H	0.0
1973	Cal-A	17	33	5	9	2	1	0	5	5	10	.273	.368	.485	150	2	0	0	0	.917	-8	C-10	-0.5
1974	Cal-A	43	83	6	16	2	0	4	13	23	17	.193	.374	.361	119	3	0	0	0	1.000	-1	D-21/C-5	0.2
1975	Oak-A	3	2	0	1	0	0	0	0	1	1	.500	.667	.500	239	1	0	0	0	.000	0	/D-1	0.1
Total	6	93	145	15	31	6	1	6	23	36	35	.214	.374	.393	125	6	0	0	0	.955	-8	/D-22,C-18	-0.1

■ TOMMY SANDT

Sandt, Thomas James b: 12/22/50, Brooklyn, N.Y. BR/TR, 5'11", 175 lbs. Deb: 6/29/75 C

YEAR	TM/L	G	AB	R	H	2B	3B	HR	RBI	BB	SO	AVG	OBP	SLG	PRO+	BR/A	SB	CS	SBR	FA	FR	G/POS	TPR
1975	Oak-A	1	0	0	0	0	0	0	0	0	0	—	—	—		—	0	0	0	.000	0	/2-1	0.0
1976	Oak-A	41	67	6	14	1	0	0	3	7	9	.209	.284	.224	52	-4	0	0	0	.966	3	S-29/2-9,3-2	0.1
Total	2	42	67	6	14	1	0	0	3	7	9	.209	.284	.224	52	-4	0	0	0	1.000	3	/S-29,2-10,3-2	0.1

■ JACK SANFORD

Sanford, John Doward b: 6/23/17, Chatham, Va. BR/TR, 6'3", 195 lbs. Deb: 8/24/40

YEAR	TM/L	G	AB	R	H	2B	3B	HR	RBI	BB	SO	AVG	OBP	SLG	PRO+	BR/A	SB	CS	SBR	FA	FR	G/POS	TPR
1940	Was-A	34	122	5	24	4	2	0	10	6	17	.197	.234	.262	30	-13	0	0	0	.993	-2	1-34	-1.7
1941	Was-A	3	5	1	2	0	1	0	0	1	1	.400	.500	.800	251	1	0	0	0	1.000	-0	/1-1	0.1
1946	Was-A	10	26	7	6	0	1	0	1	2	6	.231	.286	.308	70	-1	0	0	0	.971	-2	/1-6	-0.3
Total	3	47	153	13	32	4	4	0	11	9	24	.209	.253	.288	44	-13	0	0	0	.989	-4	/1-41	-1.9

■ MANNY SANGUILLEN

Sanguillen, Manuel De Jesus (Magan) b: 3/21/44, Colon, Panama BR/TR, 6', 193 lbs. Deb: 7/23/67

YEAR	TM/L	G	AB	R	H	2B	3B	HR	RBI	BB	SO	AVG	OBP	SLG	PRO+	BR/A	SB	CS	SBR	FA	FR	G/POS	TPR
1967	Pit-N	30	96	6	26	4	0	0	8	4	12	.271	.300	.313	75	-3	0		-1	.986	-5	C-28	-0.8
1969	Pit-N	129	459	62	139	21	6	5	57	12	48	.303	.325	.407	106	2	8	4	0	.981	4	*C-113	1.3
1970	*Pit-N	128	486	63	158	19	9	7	61	17	45	.325	.348	.444	113	7	2	3	-1	.988	1	*C-125	1.3
1971	*Pit-N☆	138	533	60	170	26	5	7	81	19	32	.319	.346	.426	118	11	6	4	-1	.994	5	*C-135	2.2
1972	*Pit-N★	136	520	55	155	18	8	7	71	21	38	.298	.325	.404	108	4	1	2	-1	.988	-3	*C-127/O-2	0.6
1973	Pit-N	149	589	64	166	26	7	12	65	17	29	.282	.305	.371	99	-3	2	5	-2	.983	4	C-89,O-59	-0.1
1974	Pit-N	151	596	77	171	21	4	7	68	21	27	.287	.317	.371	95	-6	2	2	-1	.985	-6	*C-151	-0.7
1975	*Pit-N☆	133	481	60	158	24	4	9	58	48	31	.328	.393	.451	135	23	5	4	-1	.987	-5	*C-132	2.4
1976	Pit-N	114	389	52	113	16	6	2	36	28	18	.290	.341	.378	103	1	2	4	-2	.978	-7	*C-111	-0.4
1977	Oak-A	152	571	42	157	17	5	6	58	22	35	.275	.304	.354	80	-16	2	5	-2	.985	-8	C-77,D-58/O-9,1-7	-2.7
1978	Pit-N	85	220	15	58	5	1	3	16	9	10	.264	.299	.336	74	-8	2	2	-1	1.000	-2	1-40,C-18	-1.3
1979	*Pit-N	56	74	8	17	5	2	0	4	2	5	.230	.250	.351	59	-4	0	0	0	.947	0	/C-8,1-5	-0.4
1980	*Pit-N	47	48	2	12	3	0	0	2	3	1	.250	.294	.313	68	-2	3	2	-0	.956	-1	/1-5	-0.2
Total	13	1448	5062	566	1500	205	57	65	585	223	331	.296	.329	.398	103	6	35	38	-12	.986	-23	*C-1114/O-70,D-58,1	1.2

■ ED SANICKI

Sanicki, Edward Robert "Butch" b: 7/7/23, Wallington, N.J. BR/TR, 5'9", 175 lbs. Deb: 9/14/49

YEAR	TM/L	G	AB	R	H	2B	3B	HR	RBI	BB	SO	AVG	OBP	SLG	PRO+	BR/A	SB	CS	SBR	FA	FR	G/POS	TPR
1949	Phi-N	7	13	4	3	0	0	3	7	1	4	.231	.286	.923	217	2	0			1.000	-1	/O-6	0.1
1951	Phi-N	13	4	1	2	1	0	0	1	1	1	.500	.600	.750	265	1	1	0	0	1.000	-4	/O-10	-0.3
Total	2	20	17	5	5	1	0	3	8	2	5	.294	.368	.882	231	3	1	0		1.000	-5	/O-16	-0.2

■ BEN SANKEY

Sankey, Benjamin Turner b: 9/2/07, Nauvoo, Ala. BR/TR, 5'10", 155 lbs. Deb: 10/5/29

YEAR	TM/L	G	AB	R	H	2B	3B	HR	RBI	BB	SO	AVG	OBP	SLG	PRO+	BR/A	SB	CS	SBR	FA	FR	G/POS	TPR
1929	Pit-N	2	7	1	1	0	0	0	0	0	1	.143	.143	.143	-28	-1	0			.909	-0	/S-2	-0.1
1930	Pit-N	13	30	6	5	0	0	0	2	3		.167	.219	.167	-5	-5	0			.871	-0	/S-6,2-4	-0.3
1931	Pit-N	57	132	14	30	2	5	0	14	14	10	.227	.301	.318	67	-6	0			.920	-9	S-49/2-2,3-2	-1.1
Total	3	72	169	21	36	2	5	0	14	16	14	.213	.281	.284	49	-13	0			.914	-10	/S-57,2-6,3-2	-1.6

■ ANDRES SANTANA

Santana, Andres Confesor (Belonis) b: 2/5/68, San Pedro De Macoris, D.R. BB/TR, 5'11", 160 lbs. Deb: 9/16/90

YEAR	TM/L	G	AB	R	H	2B	3B	HR	RBI	BB	SO	AVG	OBP	SLG	PRO+	BR/A	SB	CS	SBR	FA	FR	G/POS	TPR
1990	SF-N	6	2	0	0	0	0	0	0	0	0	.000	.000	.000	-99	-1	0	0	0	1.000	1	/S-3	0.0

■ RAFAEL SANTANA

Santana, Rafael Francisco (De La Cruz) b: 1/31/58, LaRomana, D.R. BR/TR, 6'1", 165 lbs. Deb: 4/5/83

YEAR	TM/L	G	AB	R	H	2B	3B	HR	RBI	BB	SO	AVG	OBP	SLG	PRO+	BR/A	SB	CS	SBR	FA	FR	G/POS	TPR
1983	StL-N	30	14	1	3	0	0	0	2	2	2	.214	.353	.214	61	-1	0	1	-1	.857	2	/2-9,S-6,3-4	0.1
1984	NY-N	51	152	14	42	11	1	1	12	9	17	.276	.317	.382	97	-1	0	3	-2	.970	-3	S-50	-0.1
1985	NY-N	154	529	41	136	19	1	1	29	29	54	.257	.296	.302	69	-22	1	0	0	.965	-11	*S-153	-1.9
1986	*NY-N	139	394	38	86	11	0	1	28	36	43	.218	.287	.254	52	-25	0	0	0	.973	17	*S-137/2-1	0.2
1987	NY-N	139	439	41	112	21	2	5	44	29	57	.255	.303	.346	75	-16	1	1	-0	.973	15	*S-138	0.9
1988	NY-A	148	480	50	115	12	1	4	38	33	61	.240	.290	.294	64	-23	1	2	-1	.966	-9	*S-148	-2.1
1990	Cle-A	7	13	3	3	0	0	1	3	0	0	.231	.231	.462	89	-0	0	0	0	1.000	-2	/S-7	-0.2
Total	7	668	2021	188	497	74	5	13	156	138	234	.246	.296	.307	68	-88	3	7	-3	.969	9	S-639/2-10,3-4	-3.1

■ F. P. SANTANGELO

Santangelo, Frank-Paul b: 10/24/67, Livonia, Mich. BB/TR, 5'10", 165 lbs. Deb: 8/2/95

YEAR	TM/L	G	AB	R	H	2B	3B	HR	RBI	BB	SO	AVG	OBP	SLG	PRO+	BR/A	SB	CS	SBR	FA	FR	G/POS	TPR
1995	Mon-N	35	98	11	29	9	1	1	9	12	9	.296	.384	.398	103	1	1	1	-0	.979	-1	O-25/2-5	-0.1
1996	Mon-N	152	393	54	109	20	5	7	56	49	61	.277	.373	.405	103	3	5	2	-0	.983	5	*O-124,3-23/2-5,S-1	0.5
Total	2	187	491	65	138	25	6	8	65	61	70	.281	.375	.405	103	4	6	3	0	.983	3	O-149/3-23,2-10,S-1	0.4

■ BENITO SANTIAGO

Santiago, Benito (Rivera) b: 3/9/65, Ponce, P.R. BR/TR, 6'1", 185 lbs. Deb: 9/14/86

YEAR	TM/L	G	AB	R	H	2B	3B	HR	RBI	BB	SO	AVG	OBP	SLG	PRO+	BR/A	SB	CS	SBR	FA	FR	G/POS	TPR
1986	SD-N	17	62	10	18	2	0	3	6	2	12	.290	.313	.468	115	1	0	1	-1	.946	-6	C-17	-0.5
1987	SD-N	146	546	64	164	33	2	18	79	16	112	.300	.326	.467	111	6	21	12	-1	.976	-7	*C-146	0.8
1988	SD-N	139	492	49	122	22	2	10	46	24	82	.248	.284	.362	86	-10	15	7	-0	.985	-5	*C-136	-0.5
1989	SD-N★	129	462	50	109	16	3	16	62	26	89	.236	.278	.387	88	-9	11	6	-0	.975	-6	*C-127	-0.8
1990	SD-N†	100	344	42	93	8	5	11	53	27	55	.270	.329	.419	103	1	5	5	-2	.980	-5	C-98	0.1
1991	SD-N★	152	580	60	155	22	3	17	87	23	114	.267	.300	.403	93	-7	8	10	-4	.985	-1	*C-151/O-1	-0.2
1992	SD-N★	106	386	37	97	21	0	10	42	21	52	.251	.290	.383	88	-7	2	5	-2	.982	-11	*C-103	-1.6
1993	Fla-N	139	469	49	108	19	6	13	50	37	88	.230	.294	.380	74	-18	10	7	-1	.987	-6	*C-136/O-1	-1.7
1994	Fla-N	101	337	35	92	12	2	11	41	25	57	.273	.325	.424	91	-5	1	1	-0	.991	3	C-97	0.3
1995	*Cin-N	81	266	40	76	20	1	11	44	24	48	.286	.354	.485	119	7	2	1	-0	.996	-2	C-75/1-8	1.3
1996	Phi-N	136	481	71	127	21	2	30	85	49	104	.264	.333	.503	114	8	2	0	1	.987	-7	*C-114,1-14	0.8
Total	11	1246	4425	507	1161	198	26	150	595	274	813	.262	.309	.428	96	-32	77	57	-11	.983	-46	*C-1200/1-22,O-2	-2.0

■ RON SANTO

Santo, Ronald Edward b: 2/25/40, Seattle, Wash. BR/TR, 6', 190 lbs. Deb: 6/26/60

YEAR	TM/L	G	AB	R	H	2B	3B	HR	RBI	BB	SO	AVG	OBP	SLG	PRO+	BR/A	SB	CS	SBR	FA	FR	G/POS	TPR
1960	Chi-N	95	347	44	87	24	2	9	44	31	44	.251	.312	.409	97	-2	0	3	-1	.945	-19	3-94	-2.4
1961	Chi-N	154	578	84	164	32	6	23	83	73	77	.284	.364	.479	120	17	2	3	-1	.937	5	*3-153	2.2
1962	Chi-N	162	604	44	137	20	4	17	83	65	94	.227	.302	.388	74	-22	4	1	1	.955	11	*3-157/S-8	-0.8
1963	Chi-N★	162	630	79	187	29	6	25	99	42	92	.297	.345	.481	128	22	6	4	-1	.951	13	*3-162	3.6
1964	Chi-N☆	161	592	94	185	33	**13**	30	114	**86**	96	.313	**.401**	.564	162	50	3	5	-2	.963	17	*3-161	**6.5**
1965	Chi-N★	164	608	88	173	30	4	33	101	88	109	.285	.379	.510	144	37	3	3	0	.957	19	*3-164	5.4
1966	Chi-N★	155	561	93	175	21	8	30	94	**95**	78	.312	**.417**	.538	161	50	3	5	-2	.956	29	*3-152/S-8	**7.5**

YEAR	TM/L	G	AB	R	H	2B	3B	HR	RBI	BB	SO	AVG	OBP	SLG	PRO+	BR/A	SB	CS	SBR	FA	FR	G/POS	TPR
1967	Chi-N	161	586	107	176	23	4	31	98	**96**	103	.300	.401	.512	153	43	1	5	-3	.957	31	*3-161	**7.3**
1968	Chi-N★	162	577	86	142	17	3	26	98	**96**	106	.246	.357	.421	124	20	3	4	-2	**.971**	17	*3-162	4.0
1969	Chi-N★	160	575	97	166	18	4	29	123	96	97	.289	.392	.485	128	23	1	3	-2	.947	6	*3-160	2.9
1970	Chi-N	154	555	83	148	30	4	26	114	92	108	.267	.372	.476	112	9	2	0	1	.945	13	*3-152/O-1	2.1
1971	Chi-N★	154	555	77	148	22	1	21	88	79	95	.267	.358	.423	105	4	4	0	1	.958	-3	*3-149/O-6	0.2
1972	Chi-N★	133	464	68	140	25	5	17	74	69	75	.302	.397	.487	135	23	1	4	-2	.948	6	*3-129/2-3,S-1,O-1	2.7
1973	Chi-N★	149	536	65	143	29	2	20	77	63	97	.267	.348	.440	109	7	1	2	-1	.950	-12	*3-146	-0.7
1974	Chi-A	117	375	29	83	12	1	5	41	37	72	.221	.295	.299	69	-14	0	2	-1	.970	6	D-47,2-39,3-28,/1S	-1.0
Total	15	2243	8143	1138	2254	365	67	342	1331	1108	1343	.277	.366	.464	123	264	35	41	-14	.954	138	*3-2130/D-47,2SO1	39.5

■ RAFAEL SANTO DOMINGO
Santo Domingo, Rafael (Molina) b: 11/24/55, Orocovis, P.R. BB/TR, 6', 160 lbs. Deb: 9/7/79

YEAR	TM/L	G	AB	R	H	2B	3B	HR	RBI	BB	SO	AVG	OBP	SLG	PRO+	BR/A	SB	CS	SBR	FA	FR	G/POS	TPR
1979	Cin-N	7	6	0	1	0	0	0	0	1	3	.167	.286	.167	26	-1	0	0	0	.000	0	/H	-0.1

■ NELSON SANTOVENIA
Santovenia, Nelson Gil (Mayol) b: 7/27/61, Pinar Del Rio, Cuba BR/TR, 6'3", 215 lbs. Deb: 9/16/87

YEAR	TM/L	G	AB	R	H	2B	3B	HR	RBI	BB	SO	AVG	OBP	SLG	PRO+	BR/A	SB	CS	SBR	FA	FR	G/POS	TPR
1987	Mon-N	2	1	0	0	0	0	0	0	0	0	.000	.000	.000	-97	-0	0	0	0	1.000	-0	/C-1	0.0
1988	Mon-N	92	309	26	73	20	2	8	41	24	77	.236	.294	.392	92	-4	2	3	-1	.983	2	C-86/1-1	0.4
1989	Mon-N	97	304	30	76	14	1	5	31	24	37	.250	.311	.352	88	-5	2	1	0	.981	12	C-89/1-1	1.3
1990	Mon-N	59	163	13	31	3	1	6	28	8	31	.190	.228	.331	54	-11	0	3	-2	.980	2	C-51	-0.9
1991	Mon-N	41	96	7	24	5	0	2	14	2	18	.250	.265	.365	76	-3	0	0	0	.976	-4	C-30/1-7	-0.6
1992	Chi-A	2	3	1	1	0	0	0	2	0	0	.333	.333	1.333	352	1	0	0	0	1.000	0	/C-2	0.1
1993	KC-A	4	8	0	0	0	0	0	0	1	2	.125	.222	.125	-4	-1	0	0	0	1.000	0	/C-4	-0.1
Total	7	297	884	77	206	42	4	22	116	59	165	.233	.286	.354	82	-23	4	7	-3	.981	12	C-263/1-9	0.2

■ EDWARD SANTRY
Santry, Edward b: Chicago, Ill. d: 3/6/1899, Chicago, Ill. Deb: 8/7/1884

YEAR	TM/L	G	AB	R	H	2B	3B	HR	RBI	BB	SO	AVG	OBP	SLG	PRO+	BR/A	SB	CS	SBR	FA	FR	G/POS	TPR
1884	Det-N	6	22	1	4	0	0	0	0	1		.182	.217	.182	29	-2				.821	-0	/S-5,2-1	-0.2

■ JOE SARGENT
Sargent, Joseph Alexander "Horse Belly" b: 9/24/1893, Rochester, N.Y. d: 7/5/50, Rochester, N.Y. BR/TR, 5'10", 165 lbs. Deb: 4/27/21

YEAR	TM/L	G	AB	R	H	2B	3B	HR	RBI	BB	SO	AVG	OBP	SLG	PRO+	BR/A	SB	CS	SBR	FA	FR	G/POS	TPR
1921	Det-A	66	178	21	45	8	5	2	24	24	26	.253	.342	.388	87	-4	2	3	-1	.927	3	2-24,3-23,S-19	0.1

■ BILL SARNI
Sarni, William Florine b: 9/19/27, Los Angeles, Cal. d: 4/15/83, Creve Coeur, Mo. BR/TR, 5'11", 187 lbs. Deb: 5/9/51 C

YEAR	TM/L	G	AB	R	H	2B	3B	HR	RBI	BB	SO	AVG	OBP	SLG	PRO+	BR/A	SB	CS	SBR	FA	FR	G/POS	TPR
1951	StL-N	36	86	7	15	1	0	0	2	9	13	.174	.253	.186	20	-10	1	0	0	.984	0	C-35	-0.8
1952	StL-N	3	5	0	1	0	0	0	0	0	0	.200	.200	.200	11	-1	0	0	0	1.000	2	/C-3	0.2
1954	StL-N	123	380	40	114	18	4	9	70	25	42	.300	.343	.439	101	0	3	3	-1	**.996**	-13	*C-118	-0.8
1955	StL-N	107	325	32	83	15	2	3	34	27	33	.255	.314	.342	74	-12	1	1	-0	.987	-6	C-99	-1.5
1956	StL-N	43	148	12	43	7	2	5	22	8	15	.291	.331	.466	111	2	1	0	0	.992	3	C-41	0.7
	NY-N	78	238	16	55	9	3	5	23	20	31	.231	.293	.357	74	-9	0	1	-1	.993	-6	C-78	-1.3
	Yr	121	386	28	98	16	5	10	45	28	46	.254	.308	.399	88	-7	1	1	-0	.992	-3	*C-119	-0.6
Total	5	390	1182	107	311	50	11	22	151	89	135	.263	.316	.380	84	-29	6	5	-1	.991	-19	C-374	-3.5

■ MACKEY SASSER
Sasser, Mack Daniel b: 8/3/62, Fort Gaines, Ga. BL/TR, 6'1", 210 lbs. Deb: 7/17/87

YEAR	TM/L	G	AB	R	H	2B	3B	HR	RBI	BB	SO	AVG	OBP	SLG	PRO+	BR/A	SB	CS	SBR	FA	FR	G/POS	TPR
1987	SF-N	2	4	0	0	0	0	0	0	0	0	.000	.000	.000	-99	-1	0	0	0	1.000	0	/C-1	-0.1
	Pit-N	12	23	2	5	0	0	0	2	0	2	.217	.217	.217	16	-3	0	0	0	1.000	-1	/C-5	-0.4
	Yr	14	27	2	5	0	0	0	2	0	2	.185	.185	.185	-2	-4	0	0	0	1.000	-1	/C-6	-0.5
1988	*NY-N	60	123	9	35	10	1	1	17	6	9	.285	.314	.407	112	1	0	0	0	.977	9	C-42/3-1,O-1	1.3
1989	NY-N	72	182	17	53	14	2	1	22	7	15	.291	.317	.407	111	2	0	1	-1	.992	-9	C-62/3-1	0.4
1990	NY-N	100	270	31	83	14	0	6	41	15	19	.307	.346	.426	111	4	0	0	0	.975	-9	C-87/1-1	0.0
1991	NY-N	96	228	18	62	14	2	5	35	9	19	.272	.303	.417	101	-1	0	2	-1	.994	-9	C-43,O-21,1-10	-1.0
1992	NY-N	92	141	7	34	6	0	2	19	3	10	.241	.257	.326	65	-7	0	0	0	.989	-11	C-27,1-12/O-9	-1.9
1993	Sea-A	83	188	18	41	10	2	1	21	15	30	.218	.279	.309	57	-12	1	0	0	.946	-3	O-37,D-19/C-4,1-1	-1.5
1994	Sea-A	3	4	0	0	0	0	0	0	0	0	.000	.000	.000	-98	-1	0	0	0	.000	-0	/C-1,O-1	-0.1
1995	Pit-N	14	26	1	4	1	0	0	0	0	0	.154	.154	.192	-9	-4	0	0	0	1.000	-1	C-11	-0.4
Total	9	534	1189	103	317	69	7	16	156	55	104	.267	.301	.377	89	-21	1	3	-2	.983	-24	C-283/O-69,1-24,D3	-3.7

■ TOM SATRIANO
Satriano, Thomas Victor Nicholas b: 8/28/40, Pittsburgh, Pa. BL/TR, 6'1", 190 lbs. Deb: 7/23/61

YEAR	TM/L	G	AB	R	H	2B	3B	HR	RBI	BB	SO	AVG	OBP	SLG	PRO+	BR/A	SB	CS	SBR	FA	FR	G/POS	TPR
1961	LA-A	35	96	15	19	5	1	1	8	12	16	.198	.294	.302	53	-6	2	0	1	.915	-3	3-23,2-10/S-1	-0.5
1962	LA-A	10	19	4	8	2	0	2	6	0	1	.421	.421	.842	238	3	0	0	0	.833	-0	/3-5	0.3
1963	LA-A	23	50	1	9	1	0	0	2	9	10	.180	.305	.200	48	-3	0	0	0	.952	3	3-13/C-2,1-1	0.0
1964	LA-A	108	255	18	51	9	0	1	17	30	37	.200	.284	.247	55	-16	0	2	-1	.917	-2	3-38,1-32,C-25/S2	-2.0
1965	Cal-A	47	79	8	13	2	0	1	4	10	10	.165	.258	.228	40	-6	1	1	-0	1.000	-5	3-15,C-12,2-12/1-3	-0.6
1966	Cal-A	103	226	16	54	5	3	0	24	27	32	.239	.320	.288	78	-6	3	3	-1	.991	-9	C-43,1-36,3-25/2-4	-1.5
1967	Cal-A	90	201	13	45	7	0	4	21	28	25	.224	.319	.318	92	-1	1	0	0	.962	-7	3-38,C-23,2-15/1-5	-0.8
1968	Cal-A	111	297	20	75	9	1	8	35	37	44	.253	.337	.364	117	6	0	0	0	.989	-9	C-85,2-14,3-11,/1-1	0.3
1969	Cal-A	41	108	5	28	2	0	1	16	18	15	.259	.370	.306	95	-1	0	2	-2	1.000	-1	C-36/1-5,2-2	0.0
	Bos-A	47	127	9	24	2	0	0	11	22	12	.189	.318	.205	46	-8	0	0	0	.978	2	C-44	-0.8
	Yr	88	235	14	52	4	0	1	27	40	27	.221	.342	.251	68	-8	0	2	-1	.987	-2	C-80/1-5,2-2	-0.8
1970	Bos-A	59	165	21	39	9	1	3	13	21	23	.236	.326	.358	83	-4	0	0	0	.985	0	C-51	-0.1
Total	10	674	1623	130	365	53	5	21	157	214	225	.225	.317	.303	79	-41	7	8	-3	.987	-26	C-321,3-168/12S	-5.7

■ FRANK SAUCIER
Saucier, Francis Field b: 5/28/26, Leslie, Mo. BL/TR, 6'1", 180 lbs. Deb: 7/21/51

YEAR	TM/L	G	AB	R	H	2B	3B	HR	RBI	BB	SO	AVG	OBP	SLG	PRO+	BR/A	SB	CS	SBR	FA	FR	G/POS	TPR
1951	StL-A	18	14	1	1	1	0	0	0	3	4	.071	.278	.143	16	-2	0	0	0	.714	-1	/O-3	-0.2

■ ED SAUER
Sauer, Edward "Horn" b: 1/3/19, Pittsburgh, Pa. d: 7/1/88, Thousand Oaks, Cal BR/TR, 6'1", 188 lbs. Deb: 9/17/43 F

YEAR	TM/L	G	AB	R	H	2B	3B	HR	RBI	BB	SO	AVG	OBP	SLG	PRO+	BR/A	SB	CS	SBR	FA	FR	G/POS	TPR
1943	Chi-N	14	55	3	15	3	0	0	9	3	6	.273	.322	.327	89	-1	1			1.000	2	O-13	0.1
1944	Chi-N	23	50	3	11	4	0	0	5	2	6	.220	.250	.300	55	-3	0			.960	-0	O-12	-0.4
1945	*Chi-N	49	93	8	24	4	1	2	11	8	23	.258	.317	.387	97	-1	2			1.000	0	O-26	-0.4
1949	StL-N	24	45	5	10	2	1	0	1	3	6	.222	.271	.311	53	-3	0			1.000	0	O-10	-0.5
	Bos-N	79	214	26	57	12	0	3	31	17	34	.266	.323	.364	89	-4	0			.972	-7	O-71	-1.4
	Yr	103	259	31	67	14	1	3	32	20	42	.259	.314	.355	82	-7	0			.974	-9	O-81	-1.9
Total	4	189	457	45	117	25	2	5	57	33	77	.256	.309	.352	83	-11	3			.981	-9	O-132	-2.6

■ HANK SAUER
Sauer, Henry John b: 3/17/17, Pittsburgh, Pa. BR/TR, 6'4", 199 lbs. Deb: 9/9/41 FC

YEAR	TM/L	G	AB	R	H	2B	3B	HR	RBI	BB	SO	AVG	OBP	SLG	PRO+	BR/A	SB	CS	SBR	FA	FR	G/POS	TPR
1941	Cin-N	9	33	4	10	1	0	1	5	1	4	.303	.324	.424	109	0	0			.957	1	/O-8	0.1
1942	Cin-N	7	20	4	5	0	0	2	4	2	2	.250	.318	.550	152	1	0			.976	0	/1-4	0.1
1945	Cin-N	31	116	18	34	1	0	5	20	6	16	.293	.328	.431	112	1	2			.972	1	O-28/1-3	0.1
1948	Cin-N	145	530	78	138	22	1	35	97	60	85	.260	.340	.504	130	20	2			.973	4	*O-132,1-12	1.6
1949	Cin-N	42	152	22	36	6	0	4	16	19	19	.237	.318	.355	79	-4	0			.956	5	O-39/1-1	-0.1
	Chi-N	96	357	59	104	17	1	27	83	37	47	.291	.363	.571	151	24	0			.981	2	*O-96	2.0
	Yr	138	509	81	140	23	1	31	99	55	66	.275	.349	.507	129	19	0			.972	7	*O-135/1-1	1.9
1950	Chi-N★	145	540	85	148	32	2	32	103	60	67	.274	.350	.519	127	19	1			.965	-1	*O-125,1-18	1.2
1951	Chi-N	141	525	77	138	19	4	30	89	45	77	.263	.325	.486	113	7	2	1	0	.981	10	*O-132	1.3
1952	Chi-N★	151	567	89	153	31	3	**37**	**121**	77	92	.270	.361	.531	143	32	1	2	-1	.983	17	*O-151	4.2
1953	Chi-N	108	395	61	104	16	5	19	60	50	56	.263	.349	.473	109	5	0			.970	-2	*O-105	0.4
1954	Chi-N	142	520	98	150	18	1	41	103	70	68	.288	.376	.563	140	30	2	1	0	.963	-2	*O-141	2.2
1955	Chi-N	79	261	29	55	8	1	12	28	26	47	.211	.287	.387	77	-9	0			.984	-1	O-68	-1.4
1956	StL-N	75	151	11	45	4	0	5	24	25	31	.298	.408	.424	124	6	0			1.000	-1	O-37	0.3
1957	NY-N	127	378	46	98	14	1	26	76	49	59	.259	.344	.508	126	13	1	0	0	.992	-12	O-98	-0.4
1958	SF-N	88	236	27	59	6	0	12	46	35	37	.250	.356	.436	111	4	0			.950	-4	O-67	-0.3
1959	SF-N	13	15	1	1	0	0	0	1	0	3	.067	.067	.067	-17	-3	0			.000	-0	/O-1	-0.3
Total	15	1399	4796	709	1278	200	19	288	876	561	714	.266	.347	.496	123	146	11	4		.974	22	*O-1228/1-38	11.0

■ DOUG SAUNDERS
Saunders, Douglas Long b: 12/13/69, Yorba Linda, Cal. BR/TR, 6', 172 lbs. Deb: 6/13/93

YEAR	TM/L	G	AB	R	H	2B	3B	HR	RBI	BB	SO	AVG	OBP	SLG	PRO+	BR/A	SB	CS	SBR	FA	FR	G/POS	TPR
1993	NY-N	28	67	8	14	2	0	0	0	3	4	.209	.243	.239	30	-7	0	0	0	.956	1	2-22/3-4,S-1	-0.5

YEAR	TM/L	G	AB	R	H	2B	3B	HR	RBI	BB	SO	AVG	OBP	SLG	PRO+	BR/A	SB	CS	SBR	FA	FR	G/POS	TPR

■ RUSTY SAUNDERS   Saunders, Russell Collier b: 3/12/06, Trenton, N.J.   d: 11/24/67, Trenton, N.J.   BR/TR, 6'2", 205 lbs.   Deb: 9/24/27

| 1927 | Phi-A | 5 | 15 | 2 | 2 | 1 | 0 | 0 | 2 | 3 | 2 | .133 | .278 | .200 | 24 | -2 | 0 | 0 | 0 | .818 | 0 | /O-4 | -0.2 |

■ AL SAUTERS   Sauters, Al b: Philadelphia, Pa.   Deb: 9/8/1890

| 1890 | Phi-a | 14 | 41 | 1 | 4 | 0 | 0 | 0 | | 0 | 11 | .098 | .288 | .098 | 14 | -4 | | | | .850 | -4 | 3-11/O-2,2-2 | -0.7 |

■ DON SAVAGE   Savage, Donald Anthony b: 3/5/19, Bloomfield, N.J.   d: 12/25/61, Montclair, N.J.   BR/TR, 6', 180 lbs.   Deb: 4/18/44

1944	NY-A	71	239	31	63	7	5	4	24	20	41	.264	.323	.385	98	-1	1	1	-0	.946	-10	3-60	-1.2
1945	NY-A	34	58	5	13	1	0	0	3	3	14	.224	.262	.241	44	-4	1	0	0	.891	1	3-14/O-2	-0.3
Total	2	105	297	36	76	8	5	4	27	23	55	.256	.312	.357	88	-5	2	1	0	.935	-10	/3-74,O-2	-1.5

■ JIMMIE SAVAGE   Savage, James Harold b: 8/29/1883, Southington, Conn.   d: 6/26/40, New Castle, Pa.   BB/TR, 5'5", 150 lbs.   Deb: 9/3/12

1912	Phi-N	2	3	1	0	0	0	0	0	1	0	.000	.250	.000	-27	-1	0			.750	-0	/2-1	-0.1
1914	Pit-F	132	479	81	136	9	9	1	26	67	32	.284	.372	.347	97	-7	17			.963	-9	O-93,3-29,S-11,/2-3	-1.8
1915	Pit-F	14	21	0	3	0	0	0	0	1	0	.143	.182	.143	-8	-3	0			1.000	-1	/O-3,3-1	-0.5
Total	3	148	503	82	139	9	9	1	26	69	32	.276	.364	.336	92	-10	17			.964	-10	/O-96,3-30,S-11,2-4	-2.4

■ TED SAVAGE   Savage, Theodore Edmund (b: Ephesian Savage) b: 2/21/36, Venice, Ill.   BR/TR, 6'1", 185 lbs.   Deb: 4/9/62

1962	Phi-N	127	335	54	89	11	2	7	39	40	66	.266	.347	.373	96	-1	16	5	2	.974	1	*O-109	-0.4
1963	Pit-N	85	149	22	29	2	1	5	14	14	31	.195	.268	.322	69	-6	4	3	-1	.943	-5	O-47	-1.5
1965	StL-N	30	63	7	10	3	0	1	4	6	9	.159	.232	.254	34	-6	1	1	-0	.938	-2	O-20	-0.9
1966	StL-N	16	29	4	5	2	1	0	3	4	7	.172	.273	.310	61	-2	4	0	1	1.000	-1	/O-7	-0.2
1967	StL-N	9	8	1	1	0	0	0	0	1	3	.125	.222	.125	2	-1	0			.000	0	H	-0.1
	Chi-N	96	225	40	49	10	1	5	33	40	54	.218	.348	.338	93	-1	7	6	-2	.979	-5	O-86/3-1	-1.2
	Yr	105	233	41	50	10	1	5	33	41	57	.215	.344	.330	90	-1	7	6	-2	.979	-5	O-86/3-1	-1.3
1968	Chi-N	3	8	0	2	0	0	0	0	0	1	.250	.250	.250	47	-1	0	1	-1	1.000	-1	/O-2	-0.2
	LA-N	61	126	7	26	6	1	2	7	10	20	.206	.270	.317	82	-3	1	2	-1	.985	0	O-39	-0.6
	Yr	64	134	7	28	6	1	2	7	10	21	.209	.269	.313	80	-4	1	3	-2	.986	-1	O-41	-0.7
1969	Cin-N	68	110	20	25	7	0	2	11	20	27	.227	.346	.345	90	-0	3	0	1	.983	-6	O-42/2-1	-0.7
1970	Mil-A	114	276	43	77	10	5	12	50	57	44	.279	.406	.482	143	18	10	6	-1	.953	-10	O-82/1-1	0.4
1971	Mil-A	14	17	2	3	0	0	0	1	5	4	.176	.364	.176	58	-1	1	0	0	1.000	-2	/O-6	-0.3
	KC-A	19	29	2	5	0	0	0	1	3	6	.172	.250	.172	22	-3	2	0	1	1.000	-2	/O-9	-0.5
	Yr	33	46	4	8	0	0	0	2	8	10	.174	.296	.174	36	-4	3	0	1	1.000	-3	O-15	-0.8
Total	9	642	1375	202	321	51	11	34	163	200	272	.233	.335	.361	94	-6	49	24	0	.970	-32	O-449/1-1,2-1,3-1	-6.2

■ BOB SAVERINE   Saverine, Robert Paul "Rabbit" b: 6/2/41, Norwalk, Conn.   BB/TR, 5'9", 165 lbs.   Deb: 9/12/59

1959	Bal-A	1	0	0	0	0	0	0	0	0	0					0	0	0		.000	0	R	0.0
1962	Bal-A	8	21	2	5	2	0	0	3	1	3	.238	.273	.333	66	-1	0	2	-1	1.000	2	/2-7	0.0
1963	Bal-A	115	167	21	39	1	2	1	12	25	44	.234	.333	.281	77	-4	8	3	1	.976	-9	O-59,2-19,S-13	-1.2
1964	Bal-A	46	34	14	5	1	0	0	0	3	6	.147	.216	.176	11	-4	3	1	0	1.000	5	S-15/O-2	0.1
1966	Was-A	120	406	54	102	10	4	5	24	27	62	.251	.301	.333	83	-9	4	3	-1	.972	-19	2-70,3-26,S-11,/O-9	-2.5
1967	Was-A	89	233	22	55	13	0	0	8	17	34	.236	.288	.292	75	-7	8	0	2	.957	-20	2-48,S-10/3-8,O-2	-2.4
Total	6	379	861	114	206	27	6	6	47	73	149	.239	.300	.305	76	-26	23	9	2	.971	-40	2-144/O-72,S-49,3	-6.0

■ CARL SAWATSKI   Sawatski, Carl Ernest "Swats" b: 11/4/27, Shickshinny, Pa.   d: 11/24/91, Little Rock, Ark.   BL/TR, 5'10", 210 lbs.   Deb: 9/29/48

1948	Chi-N	2	2	0	0	0	0	0	0	0	0	.000	.000	.000	-99	-1	0			.000	0	H	-0.1
1950	Chi-N	38	103	4	18	1	0	1	7	11	19	.175	.254	.214	25	-11	0			.983	-1	C-32	-1.1
1953	Chi-N	43	59	5	13	3	0	1	5	7	7	.220	.303	.322	62	-3	0	0	0	.943	-1	C-15	-0.3
1954	Chi-A	43	109	6	20	3	3	1	12	15	20	.183	.282	.294	56	-7	0	0	0	.987	0	C-33	-0.5
1957	*Mil-N	58	105	13	25	4	0	6	17	10	15	.238	.316	.448	110	2	0	0	0	.986	6	C-28	0.8
1958	Mil-N	10	10	1	1	0	0	0	1	2	5	.100	.250	.100	-3	-2	0	0	0	1.000	1	/C-3	-0.1
	Phi-N	60	183	12	42	4	1	5	12	16	42	.230	.302	.344	72	-8	0	0	0	.986	-3	C-53	-0.8
	Yr	70	193	13	43	4	1	5	13	18	47	.223	.299	.332	68	-9	0	0	0	.987	-3	C-56	-0.9
1959	Phi-N	74	198	15	58	10	0	9	43	32	36	.293	.394	.480	129	9	0	0	0	.979	-14	C-69	-0.1
1960	StL-N	78	179	16	41	4	0	6	27	22	24	.229	.313	.352	75	-6	0	0	0	.993	-7	C-67	-1.0
1961	StL-N	86	174	23	52	8	0	10	33	25	17	.299	.387	.517	125	6	0	0	0	.996	-7	C-60/O-1	0.2
1962	StL-N	85	222	26	56	9	1	13	42	36	38	.252	.357	.477	111	2	0	0	0	.997	-1	C-70	0.5
1963	StL-N	56	105	12	25	0	0	6	14	15	28	.238	.333	.410	103	1	2	0	1	.986	-5	C-27	-0.3
Total	11	633	1449	133	351	46	5	58	213	191	251	.242	.333	.401	92	-16	2	0	u	.988	-32	C-457/O-1	-2.8

■ CARL SAWYER   Sawyer, Carl Everett "Huck" b: 10/19/1890, Seattle, Wash.   d: 1/17/57, Los Angeles, Cal.   BR/TR, 5'11", 160 lbs.   Deb: 9/11/15

1915	Was-A	10	32	8	8	1	0	0	3	4	5	.250	.351	.281	88	-0	2			.964	-2	/2-6,S-4	-0.2
1916	Was-A	16	31	3	6	1	0	0	2	4	4	.194	.306	.226	60	-1	3			.963	2	/2-6,S-5,3-1	0.1
Total	2	26	63	11	14	2	0	0	5	8	9	.222	.329	.254	74	-2	5			.964	-1	/2-12,S-9,3-1	-0.1

■ DAVE SAX   Sax, David John b: 9/22/58, Sacramento, Cal.   BR/TR, 6', 185 lbs.   Deb: 9/1/82 F

1982	LA-N	2	2	0	0	0	0	0	0	0	0	.000	.000	.000	-99	-1	0	0	0	1.000	-0	/O-1	-0.1
1983	LA-N	7	8	0	0	0	0	0	1	0	0	.000	.000	.000	-99	-2	0	0	0	.917	0	/C-4	-0.2
1985	Bos-A	22	36	2	11	3	0	0	6	3	3	.306	.359	.389	101	0	0	1	-1	.985	-2	C-16/O-4	-0.2
1986	Bos-A	4	11	1	5	1	0	1	1	0	1	.455	.455	.818	237	2	0	0	0	1.000	-1	/C-2,1-1	0.1
1987	Bos-A	2	3	0	0	0	0	0	0	0	1	.000	.000	.000	-97	-1	0	0	0	1.000	1	/C-2	0.0
Total	5	37	60	3	16	4	0	1	8	3	5	.267	.302	.383	84	-1	0	1	-1	.980	-2	/C-24,O-5,1-1	-0.4

■ OLLIE SAX   Sax, Erik Oliver b: 11/5/04, Branford, Conn.   d: 3/21/82, Newark, N.J.   BR/TR, 5'8", 164 lbs.   Deb: 4/13/28

| 1928 | StL-A | 16 | 17 | 4 | 3 | 0 | 0 | 0 | | 0 | 5 | 3 | .176 | .364 | .176 | 45 | -1 | 0 | 0 | 0 | .955 | 3 | /3-9 | 0.2 |

■ STEVE SAX   Sax, Stephen Louis b: 1/29/60, Sacramento, Cal.   BR/TR, 5'11", 185 lbs.   Deb: 8/18/81 F

1981	*LA-N	31	119	15	33	2	0	2	9	7	14	.277	.317	.345	91	-2	5	7	-3	.975	2	2-29	-0.1
1982	LA-N★	150	638	88	180	23	7	4	47	49	53	.282	.335	.359	97	-3	49	19	3	.977	-9	*2-149	0.0
1983	*LA-N★	155	623	94	175	18	5	5	41	58	73	.281	.343	.350	93	-5	56	30	-1	.961	-30	*2-152	-3.0
1984	LA-N	145	569	70	138	24	4	1	35	47	53	.243	.301	.304	71	-21	34	19	-1	.973	12	*2-141	-0.6
1985	*LA-N	136	488	62	136	8	4	1	42	54	43	.279	.354	.318	92	-3	27	11	2	.969	-9	*2-135/3-1	-0.6
1986	LA-N★	157	633	91	210	43	4	6	56	59	58	.332	.391	.441	139	33	40	17	2	.980	-5	*2-154	3.7
1987	*LA-N	157	610	84	171	22	7	6	46	44	61	.280	.332	.369	88	-11	37	11	5	.982	1	*2-152/3-1,O-1	0.3
1988	*LA-N	160	632	70	175	19	4	5	57	45	51	.277	.326	.343	95	-4	42	12	5	.981	-19	*2-158	-1.2
1989	NY-A★	158	651	88	205	26	3	5	63	52	44	.315	.366	.387	114	13	43	17	3	**.987**	-10	*2-158	1.1
1990	NY-A★	155	615	70	160	24	2	4	42	49	46	.260	.319	.325	80	-16	43	9	8	.987	-13	*2-154	-1.9
1991	NY-A	158	652	85	198	38	2	10	56	41	38	.304	.348	.414	110	8	31	11	3	.990	-7	*2-149/3-5,D-4	0.7
1992	Chi-A	143	567	74	134	26	4	4	47	43	42	.236	.292	.317	72	-22	30	12	2	.972	-28	*2-141/D-1	-4.6
1993	Chi-A	57	119	20	28	5	0	1	8	8	12	.235	.283	.303	59	-7	7	3	0	1.000	-5	O-32,D-21/2-1	-1.2
1994	Oak-A	7	24	2	6	0	1	0	1	0	2	.250	.250	.333	53	-2	0	0	0	1.000	1	/2-6	0.1
Total	14	1769	6940	913	1949	278	47	54	550	556	584	.281	.336	.358	95	-41	444	178	26	.978	-117	*2-1679/O-33,D-26,3	-7.3

■ JIMMY SAY   Say, James I. b: 1862, Baltimore, Md.   d: 6/23/1894, Baltimore, Md.   Deb: 7/22/1882 F

1882	Lou-a	1	4	1	1	0	0	0		0	0	.250	.250	.250	73	-0				.333	-1	/3-1	-0.1
	Phi-a	22	82	12	17	2	0	1		1	1	.207	.217	.268	56	-4				.884	1	S-22	-0.2
	Yr	23	86	13	18	2	0	1		1	1	.209	.218	.267	57	-4				.884	0	S-22/3-1	-0.3
1884	Wil-U	16	59	3	13	1	2	0		1		.220	.233	.305	60	-5				.733	-3	3-16	-0.7
	KC-U	2	8	0	2	0	0	0		0		.250	.250	.250	60	-1				.200	-2	/3-2	-0.3
	Yr	18	67	3	15	1	2	0		1		.224	.239	.299	60	-5				.680	-5	3-18	-1.0

YEAR	TM/L	G	AB	R	H	2B	3B	HR	RBI	BB	SO	AVG	OBP	SLG	PRO+	BR/A	SB	CS	SBR	FA	FR	G/POS	TPR
1887	Cle-a	16	64	9	24	5	3	0	12	1		.375	.385	.547	163	5	0			.714	-4	3-16	0.1
Total	3	57	217	25	57	8	5	1	12	3		.263	.273	.359	90	-5	0			.690	-9	/3-35,S-22	-1.2

■ **LOU SAY**   Say, Louis I.   b: 2/4/1854, Baltimore, Md.   d: 6/5/30, Fallston, Md.   BR/TR, 5'7", 145 lbs.   Deb: 4/14/1873 F

YEAR	TM/L	G	AB	R	H	2B	3B	HR	RBI	BB	SO	AVG	OBP	SLG	PRO+	BR/A	SB	CS	SBR	FA	FR	G/POS	TPR
1873	Mar-n	3	12	1	2	0	0	0	2	0	0	.167	.167	.167	-1	-1	0	0	0	.667	1	/S-2,O-1	0.0
1874	Bal-n	18	66	4	14	3	0	0	5	0	1	.212	.212	.258	50	-3	0	0	0	.786	12	S-18	0.6
1875	Was-n	11	38	4	10	0	0	0	2	0	7	.263	.263	.263	87	-0	0	0	0	.698	-1	/S-8,2-2,O-1	-0.2
1880	Cin-N	48	191	14	38	8	1	0	15	4	31	.199	.215	.251	58	-8				.832	1	S-48	-0.4
1882	Phi-a	49	199	35	45	4	3	1	28	8		.226	.256	.291	75	-6				.867	6	S-49	0.2
1883	Bal-a	74	324	52	83	13	2	1		10		.256	.278	.318	89	-5				.794	7	*S-74	0.4
1884	Bal-U	78	339	65	81	14	2	2		11		.239	.263	.310	66	-25				.795	2	*S-78	-2.0
	KC-U	17	70	6	14	2	0	1		2		.200	.222	.271	56	-6				.860	9	S-16/2-1	0.2
	Yr	95	409	71	95	16	2	3		13		.232	.256	.303	65	-30				.808	10	S-94/2-1	-1.8
Total	3 n	32	116	9	26	3	0	0	9	0	8	.224	.248	.250	57	-5	0	0	0	.750	12	/S-28,2-2,O-2	0.4
Total	4	266	1123	172	261	41	8	5	43	35	31	.232	.256	.297	72	-49				.820	24	S-265/2-1	-1.6

■ **JERRY SCALA**   Scala, Gerard Michael   b: 9/27/24, Bayonne, N.J.   d: 12/14/93, Fallston, Md.   BL/TR, 5'11", 178 lbs.   Deb: 4/22/48

YEAR	TM/L	G	AB	R	H	2B	3B	HR	RBI	BB	SO	AVG	OBP	SLG	PRO+	BR/A	SB	CS	SBR	FA	FR	G/POS	TPR
1948	Chi-A	3	6	1	0	0	0	0	0	0	3	.000	.000	.000	-99	-2				1.000	-0	/O-2	-0.2
1949	Chi-A	37	120	17	30	7	1	1	13	17	19	.250	.348	.350	88	-2	3	3	-1	.988	-3	O-37	-0.8
1950	Chi-A	40	67	8	13	2	1	0	6	10	10	.194	.299	.254	44	-6	0	0	0	1.000	-4	O-23	-1.0
Total	3	80	193	26	43	9	2	1	19	27	32	.223	.321	.306	67	-9	3	3	-1	.993	-7	/O-62	-2.0

■ **SKEETER SCALZI**   Scalzi, Frank John   b: 6/16/13, Lafferty, Ohio   d: 8/25/84, Pittsburgh, Pa.   BR/TR, 5'6", 160 lbs.   Deb: 7/21/39

YEAR	TM/L	G	AB	R	H	2B	3B	HR	RBI	BB	SO	AVG	OBP	SLG	PRO+	BR/A	SB	CS	SBR	FA	FR	G/POS	TPR
1939	NY-N	11	18	3	6	0	0	0	3	2		.333	.429	.333	106	0	1			.875	2	/S-5,3-1	0.3

■ **JOHNNY SCALZI**   Scalzi, John Anthony   b: 3/22/07, Stamford, Conn.   d: 9/27/62, Port Chester, N.Y   BR/TR, 5'7", 170 lbs.   Deb: 6/19/31

YEAR	TM/L	G	AB	R	H	2B	3B	HR	RBI	BB	SO	AVG	OBP	SLG	PRO+	BR/A	SB	CS	SBR	FA	FR	G/POS	TPR
1931	Bos-N	2	1	0	0	0	0	0	0	0	1	.000	.000	.000	-99	-0	0			.000	0	H	0.0

■ **MORT SCANLAN**   Scanlan, Mortimer J.   b: 3/18/1861, Chicago, Ill.   d: 12/29/28, Chicago, Ill.   6'1", 186 lbs.   Deb: 4/21/1890

YEAR	TM/L	G	AB	R	H	2B	3B	HR	RBI	BB	SO	AVG	OBP	SLG	PRO+	BR/A	SB	CS	SBR	FA	FR	G/POS	TPR
1890	NY-N	3	10	0	0	0	0	0	0	2	5	.000	.167	.000	-50	-2	1			1.000	-0	/1-3	-0.2

■ **PATRICK SCANLAN**   Scanlan, Patrick J.   b: 3/25/1861, Nova Scotia, Can.   d: 7/17/13, Springfield, Mass.   Deb: 7/4/1884

YEAR	TM/L	G	AB	R	H	2B	3B	HR	RBI	BB	SO	AVG	OBP	SLG	PRO+	BR/A	SB	CS	SBR	FA	FR	G/POS	TPR
1884	Bos-U	6	24	2	7	1	0	0				.292	.292	.333	90	-1				.800	0	/O-6	-0.1

■ **PAT SCANLON**   Scanlon, James Patrick   b: 9/23/52, Minneapolis, Minn.   BL/TR, 6', 180 lbs.   Deb: 9/27/74

YEAR	TM/L	G	AB	R	H	2B	3B	HR	RBI	BB	SO	AVG	OBP	SLG	PRO+	BR/A	SB	CS	SBR	FA	FR	G/POS	TPR
1974	Mon-N	2	4	1	1	0	0	0	0	0	1	.250	.250	.250	38	-0	0	0	0	1.000	1	/3-1	0.0
1975	Mon-N	60	109	5	20	3	1	2	15	17	25	.183	.294	.284	58	-6	0	1	-1	.957	2	3-28/1-1	-0.5
1976	Mon-N	11	27	2	5	1	0	1	2	2	5	.185	.241	.333	59	-2	0	0	0	.842	-1	/3-7,1-1	-0.3
1977	SD-N	47	79	9	15	3	0	1	11	12	20	.190	.297	.266	58	-5	0	0	0	.957	-5	2-15,3-11/O-1	-0.9
Total	4	120	219	17	41	7	1	4	28	31	51	.187	.288	.283	58	-13	0	1	-1	.938	-3	/3-47,2-15,1-2,O-1	-1.7

■ **RUSS SCARRITT**   Scarritt, Stephen Russell Mallory   b: 1/14/03, Pensacola, Fla.   d: 12/4/94, Pensacola, Fla.   BL/TR, 5'10.5", 165 lbs.   Deb: 4/18/29

YEAR	TM/L	G	AB	R	H	2B	3B	HR	RBI	BB	SO	AVG	OBP	SLG	PRO+	BR/A	SB	CS	SBR	FA	FR	G/POS	TPR
1929	Bos-A	151	540	69	159	26	17	1	71	34	38	.294	.337	.411	94	-6	13	11	-3	.944	1	*O-145	-1.7
1930	Bos-A	113	447	48	129	17	8	2	48	12	49	.289	.332	.376	76	-17	4	7	-3	.967	4	*O-110	-2.1
1931	Bos-A	10	39	2	6	1	0	0	1	2		.154	.195	.179	-1	-6	0			1.000	-1	/O-9	-0.5
1932	Phi-N	11	11	0	2	0	0	0	0	1	2	.182	.250	.182	16	-1	0			1.000	-0	/O-1	-0.1
Total	4	285	1037	119	296	44	25	3	120	49	91	.285	.320	.385	82	-30	17	18		.956	6	O-265	-4.4

■ **LES SCARSELLA**   Scarsella, Leslie George   b: 11/23/13, Santa Cruz, Cal.   d: 12/17/58, San Francisco, Cal   BL/TL, 5'11", 185 lbs.   Deb: 9/15/35

YEAR	TM/L	G	AB	R	H	2B	3B	HR	RBI	BB	SO	AVG	OBP	SLG	PRO+	BR/A	SB	CS	SBR	FA	FR	G/POS	TPR
1935	Cin-N	6	10	4	2	1	0	0	1	4		.200	.385	.300	89	0	1			1.000	1	/1-2	0.0
1936	Cin-N	115	485	63	152	21	9	3	65	14	36	.313	.335	.412	107	3	6			.989	2	*1-115	-0.7
1937	Cin-N	110	329	35	81	11	4	3	34	17	26	.246	.285	.331	70	-14	5			.984	-5	1-65,O-14	-2.7
1939	Cin-N	16	14	0	2	0	0	0	2	0	2	.143	.143	.143	-23	-2	0			.000	0	H	-0.2
1940	Bos-N	18	60	7	18	1	3	0	8	3	5	.300	.344	.417	115	1	2			.986	-1	1-15	-0.1
Total	5	265	898	109	255	34	16	6	109	37	70	.284	.315	.378	92	-13	13			.988	-4	1-197/O-14	-3.7

■ **STEVE SCARSONE**   Scarsone, Steven Wayne   b: 4/11/66, Anaheim, Cal.   BR/TR, 6'2", 170 lbs.   Deb: 5/15/92

YEAR	TM/L	G	AB	R	H	2B	3B	HR	RBI	BB	SO	AVG	OBP	SLG	PRO+	BR/A	SB	CS	SBR	FA	FR	G/POS	TPR
1992	Phi-N	7	13	1	2	0	0	0	1	1	6	.154	.214	.154	6	-2	0	0	0	1.000	-2	/2-3	-0.4
	Bal-A	11	17	2	3	0	0	0	1	1	6	.176	.222	.176	13	-2	0	0	0	.889	-1	/2-5,3-2,S-1	-0.3
1993	SF-N	44	103	16	26	9	0	2	15	4	32	.252	.280	.398	82	-3	0	1	-1	1.000	-5	2-20/3-8,1-6	-0.8
1994	SF-N	52	103	21	28	8	0	2	13	10	20	.272	.336	.408	97	-0	2	2	-1	.990	9	2-22/3-8,1-6,S-1	0.8
1995	SF-N	80	233	33	62	10	3	11	29	18	63	.266	.335	.476	114	4	3	2	-0	.927	-5	3-50,2-13,1-11	-0.2
1996	SF-N	105	283	28	62	12	1	5	29	25	91	.219	.287	.322	63	-16	2	3	-1	.973	-4	2-74,3-14/1-1,S-1	-1.6
Total	5	299	752	101	183	39	4	20	80	59	237	.243	.305	.386	84	-18	5	8	-3	.976	-9	2-137/3-82,1-24,S-3	-2.5

■ **PAUL SCHAAL**   Schaal, Paul   b: 3/3/43, Pittsburgh, Pa.   BR/TR, 5'11", 180 lbs.   Deb: 9/3/64

YEAR	TM/L	G	AB	R	H	2B	3B	HR	RBI	BB	SO	AVG	OBP	SLG	PRO+	BR/A	SB	CS	SBR	FA	FR	G/POS	TPR
1964	LA-A	17	32	3	4	0	0	0	5	5		.125	.176	.125	-16	-5	0	1	-1	1.000	-1	/2-9,3-9	-0.7
1965	Cal-A	155	483	48	108	12	2	9	45	61	88	.224	.312	.313	80	-12	6	3	0	.970	-10	*3-153/2-1	-2.8
1966	Cal-A	138	386	59	94	15	7	6	24	68	56	.244	.364	.365	113	9	6	4	-1	.948	-2	*3-131	0.4
1967	Cal-A	99	272	31	51	9	1	6	20	38	39	.188	.289	.294	76	-8	2	2	-1	.970	-0	3-88/S-2,2,1	-1.2
1968	Cal-A	60	219	22	46	7	1	2	16	29	25	.210	.308	.279	82	-3	4	5	-3	.958	9	3-58	0.3
1969	KC-A	61	205	22	54	6	1	0	13	25	27	.263	.349	.307	84	-3	2	1	0	.897	-19	3-49/2-6,S-6	-2.2
1970	KC-A	124	380	50	102	12	3	5	35	43	39	.268	.344	.355	93	-3	7	4	-0	.938	-16	3-97,S-10/2-6	-2.0
1971	KC-A	161	548	80	150	31	6	11	63	103	51	.274	.391	.412	129	25	7	5	-1	.940	-12	*3-161	1.1
1972	KC-A	127	435	47	99	19	3	6	41	61	59	.228	.325	.326	95	-1	1	3	-2	.947	-16	*3-123/S-1	-2.2
1973	KC-A	121	396	61	114	14	3	8	42	63	45	.288	.392	.399	114	10	5	6	-2	.913	-12	*3-121	-0.5
1974	KC-A	12	34	3	6	2	0	1	4	5	5	.176	.300	.324	75	-1	0	0	0	.949	1	3-12	-0.1
	Cal-A	53	165	10	41	5	0	2	20	18	27	.248	.322	.315	89	-2	2	2	-1	.903	-10	3-51	-1.4
	Yr	65	199	13	47	7	0	3	24	23	32	.236	.318	.317	86	-3	2	2	-1	.914	-9	3-63	-1.5
Total	11	1128	3555	436	869	132	26	57	323	516	466	.244	.344	.344	98	4	43	38	-10	.943	-91	*3-1053/2-23,S-19	-11.4

■ **GERMANY SCHAEFER**   Schaefer, Herman A.   b: 2/4/1877, Chicago, Ill.   d: 5/16/19, Saranac Lake, N.Y.   BR/TR, 5'9", 175 lbs.   Deb: 10/5/01

YEAR	TM/L	G	AB	R	H	2B	3B	HR	RBI	BB	SO	AVG	OBP	SLG	PRO+	BR/A	SB	CS	SBR	FA	FR	G/POS	TPR
1901	Chi-N	2	5	0	3	1	0	0	0	2		.600	.714	.800	352	2	0			1.000	1	/2-1,3-1	0.3
1902	Chi-N	81	291	32	57	2	3	0	14	19		.196	.250	.223	48	-18	12			.864	-9	3-75/1-3,0-2,S-1	-2.8
1905	Det-A	153	554	64	135	17	9	2	47	45		.244	.302	.318	96	-3	19			.955	8	*2-151/S-3	0.7
1906	Det-A	124	446	48	106	14	3	2	42	32		.238	.290	.296	81	-10	31			.948	9	*2-114/S-7	0.0
1907	*Det-A	109	372	45	96	12	1	3	32	30		.258	.313	.315	97	-1	21			.961	-5	2-74,S-18,3-14,/O-1	-0.7
1908	*Det-A	153	584	96	151	20	10	3	52	37		.259	.304	.342	106	2	40			.918	4	S-68,2-58,3-29	0.9
1909	Det-A	87	280	26	70	12	0	0	22	14		.250	.286	.293	79	-7	12			.966	14	2-86/O-1	0.6
	Was-A	37	128	13	31	5	1	1	4	6		.242	.281	.320	94	-1	2			.941	0	2-32/3-1	-0.2
	Yr	124	408	39	101	17	1	1	26	20		.248	.284	.301	84	-8	14			.960	14	*2-118/O-1,3-1	0.4
1910	Was-A	74	229	27	63	6	5	0	14	25		.275	.352	.345	124	7	17			.953	-1	2-35,O-26/3-2	0.5
1911	Was-A	125	440	74	147	14	7	0	45	57		.334	.412	.398	129	19	22			.980	1	*1-108/O-7	1.4
1912	Was-A	60	166	21	41	7	3	0	19	23		.247	.342	.325	90	-2	11			.900	-11	O-19,1-15,2-15/P-1	-1.4
1913	Was-A	54	100	17	32	1	1	0	7	15	12	.320	.419	.350	123	4	6			.926	-2	2-16/1-6,3-2,P-1,O	0.1
1914	Was-A	30	29	6	7	1	0	0	3	3		.241	.313	.276	74	-1	3			1.000	-0	/2-3,O-3	-0.9
1915	New-F	59	154	26	33	5	3	0	8	25	11	.214	.328	.286	78	-6	3			.952	-1	O-17,1-13/3-9,2-2	-0.9
1916	NY-A	1	1	0	0	0	0	0	0	0		.000	.000	.000	-98	-0				.000	0	/O-1	0.0
1918	Cle-A	1	5	2	0	0	0	0	0	0		.000	.000	.000	-91	-1	1			1.000	-0	/2-1	-0.2
Total	15	1150	3784	497	972	117	48	9	308	333	28	.257	.319	.320	96	-15	201	1		.954	5	2-588,1-145,3/SOP	-1.3

YEAR	TM/L	G	AB	R	H	2B	3B	HR	RBI	BB	SO	AVG	OBP	SLG	PRO+	BR/A	SB	CS	SBR	FA	FR	G/POS	TPR

■ JEFF SCHAEFER   Schaefer, Jeffrey Scott   b: 5/31/60, Patchogue, N.Y.   BR/TR, 5'10", 170 lbs.   Deb: 4/7/89

1989	Chi-A	15	10	2	1	0	0	0	0	0	2	.100	.100	.100	-45	-2	1	1	-0	.900	1	/S-5,2-4,3-4,D-1	-0.1
1990	Sea-A	55	107	11	22	3	0	0	6	3	11	.206	.241	.234	33	-10	4	1	1	.933	11	3-26,S-24/2-3	0.4
1991	Sea-A	84	164	19	41	7	1	1	11	5	25	.250	.272	.323	64	-8	3	1	0	.968	2	S-46,3-30,2-11,/D-1	-0.3
1992	Sea-A	65	70	5	8	2	0	1	3	2	10	.114	.139	.186	-10	-10	0	1	-1	.922	14	S-33,3-21/2-7,D-2	0.5
1994	Oak-A	6	8	0	1	0	0	0	0	0	1	.125	.125	.125	-39	-2	0	0	0	.800	-1	/3-3,S-2,1-1	-0.2
Total	5	225	359	37	73	12	1	2	20	10	49	.203	.229	.259	35	-32	8	4	0	.957	28	S-110/3-84,2-25,D1	0.3

■ HARRY SCHAFER   Schafer, Harry C. "Silk Stocking"   b: 8/14/1846, Philadelphia, Pa.   d: 2/28/35, Philadelphia, Pa.   BR/TR, 5'9.5", 143 lbs.   Deb: 5/5/1871

1871	Bos-n	31	149	38	42	7	5	0	28	3	1	.282	.296	.396	94	-2	13	4	2	.684	3	*3-31	0.0
1872	Bos-n	48	225	51	65	10	4	1	37	0	8	.289	.289	.382	99	-2	2	0	1	.795	4	*3-43/O-5,C-2	0.0
1873	Bos-n	60	295	65	79	12	3	2	46	3	1	.268	.275	.349	78	-10	3	4	-2	.732	-15	*3-47,O-13	-2.1
1874	Bos-n	71	327	69	87	10	2	1	45	1	5	.266	.268	.318	83	-8	2	4	-2	.785	6	*3-71/S-1	-0.3
1875	Bos-n	52	222	49	64	9	0	0	17	1	8	.288	.291	.329	111	2	3	2	-0	.795	3	*3-51/O-1	0.4
1876	Bos-N	70	286	47	72	11	0	0	35	4	11	.252	.262	.290	82	-5				.810	3	*3-70	0.0
1877	Bos-N	33	141	20	39	5	2	0	13	0	7	.277	.277	.340	90	-2				.621	-12	O-23/3-9,S-1	-1.3
1878	Bos-N	2	8	0	1	0	0	0	0	0	1	.125	.125	.125	-16	-1				1.000	-1	/O-2	0.0
Total	5 n	262	1218	272	337	48	14	4	173	8	23	.277	.281	.349	91	-20	23	14	-2	.764	0	3-243/O-19,C-2,S-1	-2.0
Total	3	105	435	67	112	16	2	0	48	4	19	.257	.264	.303	83	-8				.810	-9	/3-79,O-25,S-1	-1.5

■ JIMMIE SCHAFFER   Schaffer, Jimmie Ronald   b: 4/5/36, Limeport, Pa.   BR/TR, 5'9", 185 lbs.   Deb: 5/20/61   C

1961	StL-N	68	153	15	39	7	0	1	16	9	29	.255	.301	.320	59	-9	0	0	0	.996	4	C-68	-0.3
1962	StL-N	70	66	7	16	2	1	0	6	6	16	.242	.306	.303	58	-4	1	0	0	.993	7	C-69	0.4
1963	Chi-N	57	142	17	34	7	0	7	19	11	35	.239	.294	.437	102	0	0	0	0	.996	1	C-54	0.3
1964	Chi-N	54	122	9	25	6	1	2	9	17	17	.205	.307	.320	74	-4	2	4	-2	.970	-8	C-43	-1.2
1965	Chi-A	17	31	2	6	3	1	0	1	3	4	.194	.265	.355	79	-1	0	0	0	1.000	3	C-14	0.0
	NY-N	24	37	0	5	3	0	1	0	1	15	.135	.158	.189	-3	-5	0	0	0	.968	-1	C-21	-0.5
1966	Phi-N	8	15	2	2	1	0	1	4	1	7	.133	.188	.400	58	-1	0	0	0	.952	-1	/C-6	-0.1
1967	Phi-N	2	2	1	0	0	0	0	0	1	1	.000	.333	.000	3	-0	0	0	0	1.000	1	/C-1	0.0
1968	Cin-N	4	6	0	1	0	0	0	0	0	1	.167	.167	.167	0	-1	0	0	0	1.000	-1	/C-2	-0.2
Total	8	304	574	53	128	28	3	11	56	49	127	.223	.286	.340	69	-24	3	4	-2	.989	5	C-278	-1.4

■ JOHNNY SCHAIVE   Schaive, John Edward   b: 2/25/34, Springfield, Ill.   BR/TR, 5'8", 175 lbs.   Deb: 9/19/58

1958	Was-A	7	24	1	6	0	0	0	1	1	4	.250	.280	.250	48	-2	0	0	0	1.000	-1	/2-6	-0.2
1959	Was-A	16	59	3	9	2	0	0	2	0	7	.153	.167	.186	-3	-8	0	0	0	.977	4	2-16	-0.3
1960	Was-A	6	12	1	3	1	0	0	0	0	3	.250	.250	.333	57	-1	0	0	0	.917	-2	/2-4	-0.1
1962	Was-A	82	225	20	57	15	1	6	29	6	25	.253	.273	.409	81	-7	0	1	-1	.967	4	3-49/2-6	-0.3
1963	Was-A	3	3	0	0	0	0	0	0	0	1	.000	.000	.000	-99	-1	0	0	0	.000	0	H	-0.1
Total	5	114	323	25	75	18	1	6	32	7	40	.232	.251	.350	61	-18	0	1	-1	.980	7	/3-49,2-32	-1.0

■ ROY SCHALK   Schalk, Le Roy John   b: 11/9/08, Chicago, Ill.   d: 3/11/90, Gainesville, Tex.   BR/TR, 5'10", 168 lbs.   Deb: 9/17/32

1932	NY-A	3	12	3	3	1	0	0	2	2	2	.250	.357	.333	84	-0	0	0	0	.867	-2	/2-3	-0.1
1944	Chi-A	146	587	47	129	14	4	1	44	45	52	.220	.276	.262	55	-34	5	4	-1	.964	-14	*2-142/S-5	-4.4
1945	Chi-A	133	513	50	127	23	1	1	65	32	41	.248	.293	.302	75	-17	3	6	-3	.977	6	*2-133	-0.6
Total	3	282	1112	100	259	38	5	2	109	79	95	.233	.285	.281	64	-52	8	10	-4	.970	-9	2-278/S-5	-5.1

■ RAY SCHALK   Schalk, Raymond William "Cracker"   b: 8/12/1892, Harvey, Ill.   d: 5/19/70, Chicago, Ill.   BR/TR, 5'9", 165 lbs.   Deb: 8/11/12   MCH

1912	Chi-A	23	63	7	18	2	0	0	8	3		.286	.357	.317	96	-0	2			.917	4	C-23	0.6
1913	Chi-A	129	401	38	98	15	5	1	38	27	36	.244	.297	.314	80	-11	14			.980	6	*C-125	-0.1
1914	Chi-A	136	392	30	106	13	2	0	36	38	24	.270	.347	.314	100	1	24	11	1	.974	5	*C-125	2.0
1915	Chi-A	135	413	46	110	14	4	1	54	62	21	.266	.366	.327	104	1	45	18	-6	**.984**	-3	*C-134	0.6
1916	Chi-A	129	410	36	95	12	9	0	41	41	31	.232	.311	.305	84	-8	30	13	1	**.988**	9	*C-124	1.3
1917	*Chi-A	140	424	48	96	12	5	2	51	59	27	.226	.331	.292	88	-4	19			.981	6	*C-139	1.4
1918	Chi-A	108	333	35	73	6	3	0	22	36	22	.219	.301	.255	67	-12	12			.978	-4	*C-106	-0.9
1919	*Chi-A	131	394	57	111	9	3	0	34	51	25	.282	.367	.320	93	-1	11			.981	1	*C-129	1.0
1920	Chi-A	151	485	64	131	25	5	1	61	68	19	.270	.362	.348	89	-6	10	4	1	**.986**	-1	*C-151	0.4
1921	Chi-A	128	416	32	105	24	4	0	47	40	36	.252	.328	.329	69	-19	3	4	-2	**.985**	8	*C-126	-0.6
1922	Chi-A	142	442	57	124	22	3	4	60	67	36	.281	.379	.371	97	0	12	4	1	**.989**	20	*C-142	2.8
1923	Chi-A	123	382	42	87	12	2	1	44	39	28	.228	.306	.277	55	-25	7	4	-0	.983	5	*C-121	-1.3
1924	Chi-A	57	153	15	30	4	2	1	11	21	10	.196	.301	.268	49	-12	5	5	-3	.959	-2	C-56	-0.5
1925	Chi-A	125	343	44	94	18	1	0	52	57	27	.274	.382	.332	87	-4	11	5	0	.983	3	*C-125	0.5
1926	Chi-A	82	226	26	60	9	1	0	32	27	11	.265	.349	.314	77	-7	6	5	1	.977	-6	C-80	-0.8
1927	Chi-A	16	26	2	6	2	0	0	2	2	1	.231	.286	.308	51	-2	0	0	0	1.000	1	C-15,M	0.1
1928	Chi-A	2	1	0	1	0	0	0	1	0	0	1.000	1.000	1.000	433	0	1	0	0	1.000	1	/C-1,M	0.0
1929	NY-N	5	2	0	0	0	0	0	0	0	0	.000	.000	.000	-99	-1	0	0	0	1.000	1	/C-5	0.0
Total	18	1762	5306	579	1345	199	49	11	594	638	355	.253	.340	.316	83	-105	177	69		.981	55	*C-1727	6.5

■ GENE SCHALL   Schall, Eugene David   b: 6/5/70, Abington, Pa.   BR/TR, 6'3", 190 lbs.   Deb: 6/16/95

1995	Phi-N	24	65	2	15	2	0	0	5	6	16	.231	.306	.262	51	-4	0	0	0	.984	-1	1-14/O-4	-0.7
1996	Phi-N	28	66	7	18	5	1	2	10	12	15	.273	.392	.470	123	3	0	0	0	.986	-2	1-19	-0.1
Total	2	52	131	9	33	7	1	2	15	18	31	.252	.351	.366	88	-2	0	0	0	.985	-2	/1-33,O-4	-0.8

■ BIFF SCHALLER   Schaller, Walter   b: 9/23/1889, Chicago, Ill.   d: 10/9/39, Emeryville, Cal.   BL/TR, 5'11", 168 lbs.   Deb: 4/30/11

1911	Det-A	40	60	8	8	0	1	1	7	4		.133	.200	.217	15	-7	1			1.000	-1	O-16/1-1	-0.8
1913	Chi-A	36	96	12	21	3	0	0	4	20	16	.219	.353	.250	78	-2	5			.918	-6	O-32	-1.0
Total	2	76	156	20	29	3	1	1	11	24	16	.186	.298	.237	54	-9	6			.949	-7	/O-48,1-1	-1.8

■ BOBBY SCHANG   Schang, Robert Martin   b: 12/7/1886, Wales Center, N.Y.   d: 8/29/66, Sacramento, Cal.   BR/TR, 5'7", 165 lbs.   Deb: 9/23/14   F

1914	Pit-N	11	35	0	8	1	1	0	4	1	10	.229	.247	.314	64	-2	0			.964	-2	C-10	-0.3
1915	Pit-N	56	125	13	23	6	3	0	4	14	32	.184	.271	.280	68	-5	2	2	-1	.974	-7	C-45	-1.0
	NY-N	12	21	1	3	0	0	0	1	4	5	.143	.280	.143	31	-2	1			.875	-3	/C-6	-0.4
	Yr	68	146	14	26	6	3	0	5	18	37	.178	.273	.260	63	-6	3	2	-0	.960	-9	C-51	-1.4
1927	StL-N	3	5	0	1	0	0	0	0	0	0	.200	.200	.200	7	-1	0			1.000	-0	/C-3	-0.1
Total	3	82	186	14	35	7	4	0	6	18	47	.188	.263	.269	62	-9	3	2		.962	-11	/C-64	-1.8

■ WALLY SCHANG   Schang, Walter Henry   b: 8/22/1889, S.Wales, N.Y.   d: 3/6/65, St.Louis, Mo.   BB/TR, 5'10", 180 lbs.   Deb: 5/9/13   FC

1913	*Phi-A	79	207	32	55	16	3	3	30	34	44	.266	.392	.415	139	12	4			.967	-5	C-72	1.4
1914	*Phi-A	107	307	44	88	11	8	3	45	32	33	.287	.371	.404	138	15	7	7	-2	.956	1	*C-100	2.3
1915	Phi-A	116	359	64	89	9	11	1	44	66	47	.248	.385	.343	122	14	18	3	4	.890	-3	3-43,O-41,C-26	1.9
1916	Phi-A	110	338	41	90	15	8	7	38	38	36	.266	.358	.420	140	16	14			.966	6	O-61,C-36	2.2
1917	Phi-A	118	316	41	90	14	9	3	36	29	24	.285	.362	.415	139	14	6			.956	-10	C-80,3-12/O-6	1.2
1918	*Bos-A	88	225	36	55	7	1	0	20	46	31	.244	.377	.284	101	3	4			.962	-13	C-57,O-16/3-5,S-1	-0.7
1919	Bos-A	113	330	43	101	16	3	5	55	71	42	.306	.436	.373	136	21	15			.972	-4	*C-103	2.7
1920	Bos-A	122	387	58	118	30	7	4	51	64	37	.305	.413	.450	134	20	7	7	-0	.958	-3	C-73,O-40	1.8
1921	*NY-A	134	424	77	134	30	5	6	55	78	35	.316	.428	.453	122	18	7	4	-0	.969	-6	*C-132	1.8
1922	*NY-A	124	408	46	130	21	7	1	53	53	36	.319	.405	.412	111	9	12	6	0	.976	3	*C-119	1.5
1923	*NY-A	84	272	39	75	8	2	2	29	27	17	.276	.360	.342	84	-5	5	2	0	.970	-8	C-81	-0.4
1924	NY-A	114	356	46	104	19	7	5	52	48	43	.292	.382	.427	109	7	2	5	-0	.972	-2	*C-108	0.7
1925	NY-A	73	167	17	40	8	1	2	24	17	19	.240	.310	.335	65	-9	2	1	0	.974	2	C-58	-0.4
1926	StL-A	103	285	36	94	19	5	8	50	32	20	.330	.406	.516	152	13	5	5	-2	.968	-1	C-82/O-3	1.5
1927	StL-A	97	264	40	84	15	2	5	42	41	33	.318	.414	.447	119	9	3	2	0	.976	-9	C-75	0.5

YEAR	TM/L	G	AB	R	H	2B	3B	HR	RBI	BB	SO	AVG	OBP	SLG	PRO+	BR/A	SB	CS	SBR	FA	FR	G/POS	TPR
1928	StL-A	91	245	41	70	10	5	3	39	68	26	.286	.448	.404	121	12	8	2	1	.984	-12	C-82	0.8
1929	StL-A	94	249	43	59	10	5	5	36	74	22	.237	.424	.378	104	6	1	4	-2	**.988**	-6	C-85	0.5
1930	Phi-A	45	92	16	16	4	1	1	9	17	15	.174	.309	.272	47	-7	0	0	0	.973	2	C-36	-0.3
1931	Det-A	30	76	9	14	2	0	0	2	14	11	.184	.311	.211	38	-6	1	0	0	.965	-0	C-30	-0.4
Total	19	1842	5307	769	1506	264	90	59	710	849	573	.284	.393	.401	117	160	121	<u>49</u>		.967	-69	*C-1435,O-167/3S	18.1

■ ART SCHAREIN   Scharein, Arthur Otto "Scoop"   b: 6/30/05, Decatur, Ill.   d: 7/2/69, San Antonio, Tex.   BR/TR, 5'11", 155 lbs.   Deb: 7/6/32   F

YEAR	TM/L	G	AB	R	H	2B	3B	HR	RBI	BB	SO	AVG	OBP	SLG	PRO+	BR/A	SB	CS	SBR	FA	FR	G/POS	TPR
1932	StL-A	81	303	43	92	19	2	0	42	25	10	.304	.363	.380	87	-5	4	8	-4	.965	18	3-77/S-3,2-2	1.4
1933	StL-A	123	471	49	96	13	3	0	26	41	21	.204	.269	.244	35	-44	7	9	-3	.949	14	3-95,S-24/2-7	-2.5
1934	StL-A	1	2	0	1	0	0	0	2	0	0	.500	.500	.500	146	0	0	0	0	.000	0	H	0.0
Total	3	205	776	92	189	32	5	0	70	66	31	.244	.306	.298	56	-49	11	17	-7	.956	32	3-172/S-27,2-9	-1.1

■ GEORGE SCHAREIN   Scharein, George Albert "Tom"   b: 11/21/14, Decatur, Ill.   d: 12/23/81, Decatur, Ill.   BR/TR, 6'1", 174 lbs.   Deb: 4/19/37   F

YEAR	TM/L	G	AB	R	H	2B	3B	HR	RBI	BB	SO	AVG	OBP	SLG	PRO+	BR/A	SB	CS	SBR	FA	FR	G/POS	TPR
1937	Phi-N	146	511	44	123	20	1	0	57	36	47	.241	.293	.284	53	-33	13			.947	9	*S-146	-1.4
1938	Phi-N	117	390	47	93	16	4	1	29	16	33	.238	.268	.308	60	-22	11			.921	-2	S-77,2-39/3-1	-1.7
1939	Phi-N	118	399	35	95	17	1	1	33	13	40	.238	.262	.293	50	-28	4			.958	-9	*S-103	-2.9
1940	Phi-N	7	17	0	5	0	0	0	0	0	3	.294	.294	.294	65	-1	0			.839	-1	/S-7	-0.1
Total	4	388	1317	126	316	53	6	2	119	65	123	.240	.277	.294	54	-84	28			.943	-3	S-347/2-39,3-1	-6.1

■ NICK SCHARF   Scharf, Edward T.   b: 7/1858, Baltimore, Md.   d: 5/12/37, Baltimore, Md.   TR,   Deb: 5/18/1882

YEAR	TM/L	G	AB	R	H	2B	3B	HR	RBI	BB	SO	AVG	OBP	SLG	PRO+	BR/A	SB	CS	SBR	FA	FR	G/POS	TPR
1882	Bal-a	10	39	4	8	1	1	1			0	.205	.205	.359	94	-0				.727	-2	/O-9,3-1	-0.2
1883	Bal-a	3	13	1	2	1	0	0		1		.154	.214	.231	42	-1				.643	-3	/S-3	-0.3
Total	2	13	52	5	10	2	1	1		1		.192	.208	.327	79	-1				.727	-4	/O-9,S-3,3-1	-0.5

■ AL SCHEER   Scheer, Allan G.   b: 10/21/1888, Dayton, Ohio   d: 5/6/59, Logansport, Ind.   BL/TR, 5'9", 165 lbs.   Deb: 8/2/13

YEAR	TM/L	G	AB	R	H	2B	3B	HR	RBI	BB	SO	AVG	OBP	SLG	PRO+	BR/A	SB	CS	SBR	FA	FR	G/POS	TPR
1913	Bro-N	6	22	3	5	0	0	0	0	2	4	.227	.292	.227	48	-1	1			.800	-1	/O-6	-0.3
1914	Ind-F	120	363	63	111	23	6	3	45	49	39	.306	.396	.427	112	-2	5			.926	-5	*O-102/2-4,S-1	-0.7
1915	New-F	155	546	75	146	25	14	2	60	65	38	.267	.353	.375	111	0	31			.971	-2	*O-155	-1.0
Total	3	281	931	141	262	48	20	5	105	116	81	.281	.368	.392	110	1	41			.953	-9	O-263/2-4,S-1	-2.0

■ HEINIE SCHEER   Scheer, Henry   b: 7/31/1900, New York, N.Y.   d: 3/21/76, New Haven, Conn.   BR/TR, 5'8", 146 lbs.   Deb: 4/20/22

YEAR	TM/L	G	AB	R	H	2B	3B	HR	RBI	BB	SO	AVG	OBP	SLG	PRO+	BR/A	SB	CS	SBR	FA	FR	G/POS	TPR
1922	Phi-A	51	135	10	23	3	0	4	12	3	25	.170	.188	.281	21	-16	1	0	0	.976	9	2-30,3-10	-0.6
1923	Phi-A	69	210	26	50	8	1	2	21	17	41	.238	.301	.314	61	-12	3	4	-2	.971	-9	2-61	-2.1
Total	2	120	345	36	73	11	1	6	33	20	66	.212	.259	.301	46	-28	4	4	-1	.973	-0	/2-91,3-10	-2.7

■ FRITZ SCHEEREN   Scheeren, Frederick "Dutch"   b: 9/8/1891, Kokomo, Ind.   d: 6/17/73, Oil City, Pa.   BR/TR, 6', 180 lbs.   Deb: 9/14/14

YEAR	TM/L	G	AB	R	H	2B	3B	HR	RBI	BB	SO	AVG	OBP	SLG	PRO+	BR/A	SB	CS	SBR	FA	FR	G/POS	TPR
1914	Pit-N	11	31	4	9	1	1	1	2	1	6	.290	.313	.452	132	1	1			.824	-3	O-10	-0.3
1915	Pit-N	4	3	0	0	0	0	0	0	0	0	.000	.000	.000	-99	-1	0			.000	-1	/O-1	-0.1
Total	2	15	34	4	9	1	1	1	2	1	6	.265	.286	.412	111	0	1			.824	-4	O-11	-0.4

■ BOB SCHEFFING   Scheffing, Robert Boden   b: 8/11/13, Overland, Mo.   d: 10/26/85, Phoenix, Ariz.   BR/TR, 6'2", 189 lbs.   Deb: 4/27/41   MC

YEAR	TM/L	G	AB	R	H	2B	3B	HR	RBI	BB	SO	AVG	OBP	SLG	PRO+	BR/A	SB	CS	SBR	FA	FR	G/POS	TPR
1941	Chi-N	51	132	9	32	8	0	1	20	5	19	.242	.270	.326	70	-6	2			.966	-6	C-34	-0.7
1942	Chi-N	44	102	7	20	3	0	2	12	7	11	.196	.248	.284	58	-6	2			.986	4	C-32	0.0
1946	Chi-N	63	115	8	32	4	1	0	18	12	18	.278	.346	.330	94	-1	2			1.000	-7	C-40	-0.6
1947	Chi-N	110	363	33	96	11	5	5	50	25	25	.264	.312	.364	82	-10	2			.984	-6	C-97	-1.0
1948	Chi-N	102	293	23	88	18	2	5	45	22	27	.300	.351	.427	114	5	0			.989	-5	C-78	0.6
1949	Chi-N	55	149	12	40	6	1	3	19	9	9	.268	.314	.383	88	-3	0			.977	-3	C-40	-0.4
1950	Chi-N	12	16	0	3	1	0	0	1	0	2	.188	.188	.250	14	-2	0			.917	0	/C-3	-0.2
	Cin-N	21	47	4	13	0	0	2	6	4	2	.277	.333	.404	93	-1	0			1.000	-4	C-11	-0.4
	Yr	33	63	4	16	1	0	2	7	4	4	.254	.299	.365	74	-3	0			.982	-3	C-14	-0.6
1951	Cin-N	47	122	9	31	2	0	2	14	16	9	.254	.345	.320	79	-3	0	0	0	.976	-4	C-41	-0.5
	StL-N	12	18	0	2	0	0	0	2	3	5	.111	.238	.111	-3	-3	0	0	0	1.000	-1	C-11	-0.1
	Yr	59	140	9	33	2	0	2	16	19	14	.236	.331	.293	68	-6	0	0	0	.980	-2	C-52	-0.6
Total	8	517	1357	105	357	53	9	20	187	103	127	.263	.316	.360	86	-28	6	<u>0</u>		.984	-25	C-387	-3.3

■ TED SCHEFFLER   Scheffler, Theodore J.   b: 4/5/1864, New York, N.Y.   d: 2/24/49, Jamaica, N.Y.   BR/TR, 5'10", 160 lbs.   Deb: 8/7/1888

YEAR	TM/L	G	AB	R	H	2B	3B	HR	RBI	BB	SO	AVG	OBP	SLG	PRO+	BR/A	SB	CS	SBR	FA	FR	G/POS	TPR
1888	Det-N	27	94	17	19	1	0	0	4	9	9	.202	.286	.255	74	-2	4			.847	-4	O-27	-0.7
1890	Roc-a	119	445	111	109	12	6	3	34	78		.245	.374	.319	113	13	77			.911	9	*O-119/C-1	1.6
Total	2	146	539	128	128	15	7	3	38	87	<u>9</u>	.237	.360	.308	106	11	81			.899	5	O-146/C-1	0.9

■ FRANK SCHEIBECK   Scheibeck, Frank S.   b: 6/28/1865, Detroit, Mich.   d: 10/22/56, Detroit, Mich.   BR/TR, 5'7", 145 lbs.   Deb: 5/9/1887

YEAR	TM/L	G	AB	R	H	2B	3B	HR	RBI	BB	SO	AVG	OBP	SLG	PRO+	BR/A	SB	CS	SBR	FA	FR	G/POS	TPR
1887	Cle-a	3	9	2	2	0	0	0		2		.222	.364	.222	67	-0				.500	-2	/S-1,3-1,P-1	-0.1
1888	Det-N	1	4	0	0	0	0	0	0	0		.000	.000	.000	-99	-1	0			.500	-1	/S-1	-0.3
1890	Tol-a	134	485	72	117	13	5	1	49	76		.241	.350	.295	88	-5	57			.883	1	*S-134	0.3
1894	Pit-N	28	102	20	36	2	3	1	10	11	9	.353	.416	.461	112	2	7			.891	-8	S-11/O-9,3-3,2-2	-0.4
	Was-N	52	196	49	45	2	4	0	17	45	24	.230	.384	.281	64	-9	11			.876	5	S-52	-0.1
	Yr	80	298	69	81	4	7	1	27	56	33	.272	.394	.342	81	-7	18			.878	-3	S-63/O-9,3-3,2-2	-0.4
1895	Was-N	48	167	17	31	5	2	0	25	17	21	.186	.265	.240	31	-17	5			.888	-2	S-44/3-2,2-2	-1.4
1899	Was-N	27	94	19	27	4	1	0	9	11		.287	.368	.351	99	0	5			.877	-11	S-27	-0.8
1901	Cle-A	93	329	33	70	11	3	0	38	18		.213	.258	.264	47	-24	3			.897	-14	S-92	-2.7
1906	Det-A	3	10	1	1	0	0	0	0	2		.100	.250	.100	11	-1	0			.889	-1	/2-3	-0.2
Total	8	389	1396	213	329	37	18	2	148	182	<u>54</u>	.236	.329	.292	70	-55	88			.884	-33	S-362/O-9,2-7,3P	-5.7

■ RICHIE SCHEINBLUM   Scheinblum, Richard Alan   b: 11/5/42, New York, N.Y.   BB/TR, 6'1", 180 lbs.   Deb: 9/1/65

YEAR	TM/L	G	AB	R	H	2B	3B	HR	RBI	BB	SO	AVG	OBP	SLG	PRO+	BR/A	SB	CS	SBR	FA	FR	G/POS	TPR
1965	Cle-A	4	1	1	0	0	0	0	0	0		.000	.000	.000	-99	-0	0	0	0	.000	0	H	0.0
1967	Cle-A	18	66	8	21	4	2	0	6	5	10	.318	.366	.439	136	3	0	0	-1	.943	-0	O-18	0.1
1968	Cle-A	19	55	3	12	5	0	0	5	5	8	.218	.295	.309	84	-1	0	0	1	1.000	1	O-16	-0.1
1969	Cle-A	102	199	13	37	5	1	1	13	19	30	.186	.267	.236	37	-17	0	2	-3	.974	-1	O-50	-2.3
1971	Was-A	27	49	5	7	3	0	0	4	8	5	.143	.263	.204	36	-4	0	0	0	.933	3	O-13	-0.2
1972	KC-A★	134	450	60	135	21	4	8	66	58	40	.300	.385	.418	139	23	0	1	-1	.965	-3	*O-119	1.7
1973	Cin-N	29	54	5	12	2	0	1	8	10	4	.222	.344	.315	88	-1	0	0	0	.960	-2	O-19	-0.4
	Cal-A	77	229	28	75	10	2	3	21	35	27	.328	.419	.428	150	17	0	0	0	.969	-0	O-54/D-7	1.4
1974	Cal-A	10	26	1	4	0	0	0	2	1	2	.154	.185	.154	-2	-3	0	0	0	.929	-1	/O-8,D-1	-0.5
	KC-A	36	83	7	15	2	0	0	8	12	5	.181	.253	.205	31	-7	0	1	-1	.000	-1	D-17/O-2	-1.0
	Yr	46	109	8	19	2	0	0	4	9	10	.174	.237	.193	24	-10	0	1	-2	.929	-2	D-18,O-10	-1.5
	StL-N	6	6	0	2	0	0	0	0	0	1	.333	.333	.333	88	0	0	0	0	.000	0	H	0.0
Total	8	462	1218	131	320	52	9	13	127	149	135	.263	.346	.352	104	10	0	6	-4	.965	-4	O-299/D-25	-1.3

■ DANNY SCHELL   Schell, Clyde Daniel   b: 12/26/27, Fostoria, Mich.   d: 5/11/72, Mayville, Mich.   BR/TR, 6'1", 195 lbs.   Deb: 4/13/54

YEAR	TM/L	G	AB	R	H	2B	3B	HR	RBI	BB	SO	AVG	OBP	SLG	PRO+	BR/A	SB	CS	SBR	FA	FR	G/POS	TPR
1954	Phi-N	92	272	25	77	14	3	7	33	17	31	.283	.330	.434	97	-2	0	3	-2	.974	1	O-69	-0.6
1955	Phi-N	2	2	0	0	0	0	0	0	0	1	.000	.000	.000	-99	-1	0	0	0	.000	0	H	-0.1
Total	2	94	274	25	77	14	3	7	33	17	32	.281	.328	.431	96	-2	0	3	-2	.974	1	/O-69	-0.7

■ AL SCHELLHASE   Schellhase, Albert Herman "Shelley"   b: 9/13/1864, Evansville, Ind.   d: 1/3/19, Evansville, Ind.   BR/TR, 5'8", 148 lbs.   Deb: 5/7/1890

YEAR	TM/L	G	AB	R	H	2B	3B	HR	RBI	BB	SO	AVG	OBP	SLG	PRO+	BR/A	SB	CS	SBR	FA	FR	G/POS	TPR
1890	Bos-N	9	29	1	4	0	0	0	1		10	.138	.167	.138	-10	-4	0			.778	-1	/O-5,C-2,S-1,3-1	-0.2
1891	Lou-a	7	20	4	3	0	0	0	1	1	2	.150	.190	.150	-2	-3	3			.943	-0	/C-7	-0.4
Total	2	16	49	5	7	0	0	0	2		12	.143	.176	.143	-7	-7	3			.922	-1	/C-9,O-5,3-1,S-1	-0.6

■ FRED SCHEMANSKE   Schemanske, Frederick George "Buck"   b: 4/28/03, Detroit, Mich.   d: 2/18/60, Detroit, Mich.   BR/TR, 6'2", 190 lbs.   Deb: 9/15/23

YEAR	TM/L	G	AB	R	H	2B	3B	HR	RBI	BB	SO	AVG	OBP	SLG	PRO+	BR/A	SB	CS	SBR	FA	FR	G/POS	TPR
1923	Was-A	2	2	0	2	0	0	0	2	1	0	1.000	1.000	1.000	450	1	0	0	0	.000	-0	/P-1	0.0

YEAR	TM/L	G	AB	R	H	2B	3B	HR	RBI	BB	SO	AVG	OBP	SLG	PRO+	BR/A	SB	CS	SBR	FA	FR	G/POS	TPR

■ MIKE SCHEMER Schemer, Michael "Lefty" b: 11/20/17, Baltimore, Md. d: 4/22/83, Miami, Fla. BL/TL, 6', 180 lbs. Deb: 8/8/45

	1945	NY-N	31	108	10	36	3	1	1	10	6	1	.333	.368	.407	114	2		2	.993	4	1-27	0.4
	1946	NY-N	1	1	0	0	0	0	0	0	0	0	.000	.000	.000	-99	-0		0	.000	0	H	0.0
	Total	2	32	109	10	36	3	1	1	10	6	1	.330	.365	.404	112	2		2	.993	4	/1-27	0.4

■ BILL SCHENCK Schenck, William G. b: Brooklyn, N.Y. 5'7", 171 lbs. Deb: 5/29/1882

	1882	Lou-a	60	231	37	60	11	3	0			8	.260	.285	.333	114	4			.814	-7	*3-58/S-2,P-2	-0.1
	1884	Ric-a	42	151	14	31	4	0	3			1	.205	.216	.291	65	-6			.836	-5	S-40/2-2	-1.0
	1885	Bro-a	1	4	0	0	0	0	0	0	0	0	.000	.000	.000	-99	-1			1.000	0	/3-1	-0.1
	Total	3	103	386	51	91	15	3	3	0		9	.236	.255	.313	92	-3			.817	-12	/3-59,S-42,2-2,P-2	-1.2

■ HANK SCHENZ Schenz, Henry Leonard b: 4/11/19, New Richmond, Ohio d: 5/12/88, Cincinnati, Ohio BR/TR, 5'9.5", 175 lbs. Deb: 9/18/46

	1946	Chi-N	6	11	0	2	0	0	0	1	0	0	.182	.182	.182	3	-1	1			1.000	0	/3-5	-0.1
	1947	Chi-N	7	14	2	1	0	0	0	0	2	1	.071	.235	.071	-16	-2	0			.917	0	/3-5	-0.2
	1948	Chi-N	96	337	43	88	17	1	1	14	18	15	.261	.306	.326	74	-12	3			.974	-5	2-78/3-5	-1.4
	1949	Chi-N	7	14	2	6	0	0	0	1	0	0	.429	.467	.429	146	1	2			1.000	1	/3-5	0.2
	1950	Pit-N	58	101	17	23	4	2	1	5	6	7	.228	.271	.337	57	-6	0			.987	1	2-21,3-12/S-4	-0.3
	1951	Pit-N	25	61	5	13	1	0	0	3	0	2	.213	.226	.230	22	-7	0	2	-1	.961	-3	2-19/3-2	-1.0
	*NY-N	8	0	0	0	0	0	0	0	0	0	—	—	—		0	0	0	0	.000	0	R	0.0
	Yr	33	61	6	13	1	0	0	3	0	2	.213	.226	.230	22	-7	0	2	-1	.961	-3	2-19/3-2	-1.0
	Total	6	207	538	70	133	22	3	2	24	27	25	.247	.291	.310	63	-28	6	2		.974	-5	2-118/3-34,S-4	-2.8

■ JOE SCHEPNER Schepner, Joseph Maurice "Gentleman Joe" b: 8/10/1895, Aliquippa, Pa. d: 7/25/59, Mobile, Ala. BR/TR, 5'10", 160 lbs. Deb: 9/11/19

| | 1919 | StL-A | 14 | 48 | 2 | 10 | 4 | 0 | 0 | 6 | 1 | 5 | .208 | .224 | .292 | 43 | -4 | 0 | | | .947 | -1 | 3-13 | -0.5 |

■ BOB SCHERBARTH Scherbarth, Robert Elmer b: 1/18/26, Milwaukee, Wis. BR/TR, 6', 180 lbs. Deb: 4/23/50

| | 1950 | Bos-A | 1 | 0 | 0 | 0 | 0 | 0 | 0 | 0 | 0 | 0 | — | — | — | | 0 | 0 | 0 | 0 | .000 | 0 | /C-1 | 0.0 |

■ HARRY SCHERER Scherer, Harry Deb: 7/24/1889

| | 1889 | Lou-a | 1 | 3 | 0 | 1 | 0 | 0 | 0 | 0 | 0 | 0 | .333 | .333 | .333 | 92 | -0 | 0 | | | .500 | -1 | /O-1 | -0.1 |

■ LOU SCHIAPPACASSE Schiappacasse, Louis Joseph b: 3/29/1881, Ann Arbor, Mich. d: 9/20/10, Ann Arbor, Mich. BR/TR, Deb: 9/7/02

| | 1902 | Det-A | 2 | 5 | 0 | 0 | 0 | 0 | 0 | 1 | 0 | | .000 | .167 | .000 | -50 | -1 | 0 | | | .000 | -1 | /O-2 | -0.2 |

■ MORRIE SCHICK Schick, Maurice Francis b: 4/17/1892, Chicago, Ill. d: 10/25/79, Hazel Crest, Ill. BR/TR, 5'11", 170 lbs. Deb: 4/15/17

| | 1917 | Chi-N | 14 | 34 | 3 | 5 | 0 | 0 | 3 | 3 | 10 | .147 | .216 | .147 | 11 | -3 | 0 | | | .960 | 0 | O-12 | -0.4 |

■ CHUCK SCHILLING Schilling, Charles Thomas b: 10/25/37, Brooklyn, N.Y. BR/TR, 5'11", 170 lbs. Deb: 4/11/61

	1961	Bos-A	158	646	87	167	25	2	5	62	78	77	.259	.340	.327	77	-19	7	6	-2	.991	15	*2-158	1.2
	1962	Bos-A	119	413	48	95	17	1	7	35	29	48	.230	.287	.327	63	-22	1	0	0	.985	13	*2-118	0.4
	1963	Bos-A	146	576	63	135	25	0	8	33	41	72	.234	.291	.319	69	-24	3	2	-0	.985	-14	*2-143	-2.6
	1964	Bos-A	47	163	18	32	6	0	0	7	15	22	.196	.264	.233	38	-13	0	1	-1	.974	0	2-42	-1.2
	1965	Bos-A	71	171	14	41	3	2	3	9	13	17	.240	.293	.333	73	-6	0	1	-1	.976	10	2-41	0.7
	Total	5	541	1969	230	470	76	5	23	146	176	236	.239	.305	.317	68	-84	11	10	-3	.985	24	2-502	-1.5

■ BILL SCHINDLER Schindler, William Gibbons b: 7/10/1896, Perryville, Mo. d: 2/6/79, Perryville, Mo. BR/TR, 5'11", 160 lbs. Deb: 9/3/20

| | 1920 | StL-N | 1 | 2 | 0 | 0 | 0 | 0 | 0 | 0 | 0 | 0 | .000 | .000 | .000 | -99 | -1 | 0 | | | 1.000 | -0 | /C-1 | -0.1 |

■ DUTCH SCHIRICK Schirick, Harry Ernest b: 6/15/1890, Ruby, N.Y. d: 11/12/68, Kingston, N.Y. BR/TR, 5'8", 160 lbs. Deb: 9/17/14

| | 1914 | StL-A | 1 | 0 | 0 | 0 | 0 | 0 | 0 | 0 | 1 | 0 | — | 1.000 | — | 212 | 0 | 2 | | | .000 | 0 | H | 0.1 |

■ LARRY SCHLAFLY Schlafly, Harry Linton b: 9/20/1878, Port Washington, Ohio d: 6/27/19, Canton, Ohio BR/TR, 5'11", 182 lbs. Deb: 9/18/02 M

	1902	Chi-N	10	31	5	10	0	3	0	5	6	.323	.432	.516	198	4	2			1.000	-4	/O-5,2-4,3-2	0.0
	1906	Was-A	123	426	60	105	13	8	2	30	50	.246	.345	.329	117	11	29			.961	15	*2-123	2.9
	1907	Was-A	24	74	10	10	0	1	0	4	22	.135	.354	.176	75	0	7			.928	-9	2-24	-1.1
	1914	Buf-F	51	127	16	33	7	1	2	19	12	22	.260	.338	.378	93	-3	3			.951	2	2-23/1-7,C-1,3OM	-0.2
	Total	4	208	658	91	158	20	12	5	58	90	22	.240	.349	.330	111	11	41			.954	4	2-174/1-7,O-6,3C	1.6

■ ADMIRAL SCHLEI Schlei, George Henry b: 1/12/1878, Cincinnati, Ohio d: 1/24/58, Huntington, W.Va. BR/TR, 5'8.5", 179 lbs. Deb: 4/24/04

	1904	Cin-N	97	291	25	69	8	3	0	32	17	.237	.297	.285	74	-9	7			.977	10	C-88	1.1
	1905	Cin-N	99	314	32	71	8	3	1	36	22	.226	.285	.280	62	-15	9			.962	9	C-89/1-6	1.0
	1906	Cin-N	116	388	44	95	13	8	4	54	29	.245	.304	.351	100	-1	7			.961	9	C-91,1-21	1.8
	1907	Cin-N	84	246	28	67	3	2	0	27	28	.272	.347	.301	99	-1	5			.980	7	C-67/1-3,O-2	1.5
	1908	Cin-N	92	300	31	66	6	4	1	22	22	.220	.278	.277	79	-7	2			.962	-4	C-88	-0.8
	1909	NY-N	92	279	25	68	12	0	0	30	40	.244	.343	.287	94	-0	4			.963	3	C-89	1.2
	1910	NY-N	55	99	10	19	2	1	0	8	14	10	.192	.304	.232	57	-5	4			.986	0	C-49	-0.2
	1911	NY-N	1	1	0	0	0	0	0	0	0	0	.000	.000	.000	-97	-0	0			.000	0	H	0.0
	Total	8	636	1918	195	455	52	21	6	209	172	11	.237	.307	.296	83	-37	38			.968	36	C-561/1-30,O-2	5.6

■ RUDY SCHLESINGER Schlesinger, William Cordes b: 11/5/41, Cincinnati, Ohio BR/TR, 6'2", 175 lbs. Deb: 5/4/65

| | 1965 | Bos-A | 1 | 1 | 0 | 0 | 0 | 0 | 0 | 0 | 0 | 0 | .000 | .000 | .000 | -94 | -0 | 0 | | | .000 | 0 | H | 0.0 |

■ DUTCH SCHLIEBNER Schliebner, Frederick Paul b: 5/19/1891, Charlottenburg, Germany d: 4/15/75, Toledo, Ohio BR/TR, 5'10", 180 lbs. Deb: 4/17/23

	1923	Bro-N	19	76	11	19	4	0	0	4	5	7	.250	.296	.303	60	-4	1	0	0	.981	3	1-19	-0.3
	StL-A	127	444	50	122	19	6	4	52	39	60	.275	.339	.372	82	-12	3	2	-0	.989	1	*1-127	-1.9
	Total	1	146	520	61	141	23	6	4	56	44	67	.271	.333	.362	79	-16	4	2	0	.988	5	1-146	-2.2

■ JAY SCHLUETER Schlueter, Jay D b: 7/31/49, Phoenix, Ariz. BR/TR, 6', 182 lbs. Deb: 6/18/71

| | 1971 | Hou-N | 7 | 3 | 1 | 1 | 0 | 0 | 0 | 0 | 0 | 1 | .333 | .333 | .333 | 92 | -0 | 0 | | | 1.000 | -0 | /O-2 | 0.0 |

■ NORM SCHLUETER Schlueter, Norman John "Duke" b: 9/25/16, Belleville, Ill. BR/TR, 5'10", 175 lbs. Deb: 5/28/38

	1938	Chi-A	35	118	11	27	5	1	0	7	4	15	.229	.254	.288	35	-12	1	0	0	.952	-3	C-34	-1.2
	1939	Chi-A	34	56	5	13	2	1	0	8	1	11	.232	.246	.304	39	-5	2	0	1	.988	1	C-32	-0.3
	1944	Cle-A	49	122	2	15	4	0	0	11	12	22	.123	.201	.156	3	-15	0	2	-1	.985	-8	C-43	-2.4
	Total	3	118	296	18	55	11	2	0	26	17	48	.186	.230	.236	24	-33	3	2		.974	-10	C-109	-3.9

■ RAY SCHMANDT Schmandt, Raymond Henry b: 1/25/1896, St.Louis, Mo. d: 2/2/69, St.Louis, Mo. BR/TR, 6'1", 175 lbs. Deb: 6/24/15

	1915	StL-A	3	4	0	0	0	0	0	0	0	0	.000	.000	.000	-99	-1	0			1.000	-0	/1-1	-0.1
	1918	Bro-N	34	114	11	35	5	4	0	18	7	7	.307	.347	.421	134	4	1			.934	-4	2-34	0.3
	1919	Bro-N	47	127	8	21	0	0	0	10	4	13	.165	.191	.197	16	-13	0			.911	0	2-18,1-12/3-6	-1.3
	1920	*Bro-N	28	63	7	15	2	1	0	7	3	4	.238	.273	.302	63	-3	1	1	0	.995	3	1-20	0.0
	1921	Bro-N	95	350	42	107	8	5	1	43	11	22	.306	.329	.366	81	-10	3	4	2	.989	4	1-92	-1.3
	1922	Bro-N	110	396	54	106	17	3	2	44	21	28	.268	.307	.341	68	-20	6	6	-2	.989	5	*1-110	-2.0
	Total	6	317	1054	122	284	36	13	3	122	46	75	.269	.301	.337	72	-42	11	11		.990	5	1-235/2-52,3-6	-4.4

■ GEORGE SCHMEES Schmees, George Edward "Rocky" b: 9/6/24, Cincinnati, Ohio BL/TL, 6', 190 lbs. Deb: 4/15/52

	1952	StL-A	34	61	9	8	1	1	0	3	9	11	.131	.159	.180	-6	-9	0	0	0	.932	-1	O-19/1-2	-1.0
	Bos-A	42	64	8	13	3	0	0	3	10	11	.203	.311	.250	53	-4	0	1	-1	1.000	-7	O-29/P-2,1-2	-1.4
	Yr	76	125	17	21	4	1	0	6	19	22	.168	.241	.216	29		0	1		.960		O-48/1-4,P-2	-2.4

■ BOSS SCHMIDT Schmidt, Charles b: 9/12/1880, Coal Hill, Ark. d: 11/14/32, Clarksville, Ark. BB/TR, 5'11", 200 lbs. Deb: 4/30/06 F

| | 1906 | Det-A | 68 | 216 | 13 | 47 | 4 | 3 | 0 | 10 | 6 | .218 | .242 | .264 | 57 | -11 | 1 | | | .958 | 7 | C-67 | 0.3 |
| | 1907 | *Det-A | 104 | 349 | 32 | 85 | 6 | 6 | 0 | 23 | 5 | .244 | .269 | .295 | 77 | -10 | 8 | | | .944 | 3 | *C-103 | 0.3 |

YEAR	TM/L	G	AB	R	H	2B	3B	HR	RBI	BB	SO	AVG	OBP	SLG	PRO+	BR/A	SB	CS	SBR	FA	FR	G/POS	TPR
1908	*Det-A	122	419	45	111	14	3	1	38	16		.265	.297	.320	96	-3	5			.951	8	*C-121	1.9
1909	*Det-A	84	253	21	53	8	2	1	28	7		.209	.240	.269	58	-13	7			.955	-6	C-81/O-1	-1.4
1910	Det-A	71	197	22	51	7	7	1	23	2		.259	.277	.381	99	-2	2			.973	-8	C-66	-0.4
1911	Det-A	28	46	4	13	2	1	0	2	0		.283	.298	.370	82	-1	0			1.000	-2	/C-9,O-1	-0.3
Total	6	477	1480	137	360	41	22	3	124	36		.243	.270	.307	79	-39	23			.955	3	C-447/O-2	0.4

■ BUTCH SCHMIDT
Schmidt, Charles John "Butcher Boy"   b: 7/19/1886, Baltimore, Md.   d: 9/4/52, Baltimore, Md.   BL/TL, 6'1.5", 200 lbs.   Deb: 5/11/09

YEAR	TM/L	G	AB	R	H	2B	3B	HR	RBI	BB	SO	AVG	OBP	SLG	PRO+	BR/A	SB	CS	SBR	FA	FR	G/POS	TPR
1909	NY-A	1	2	0	0	0	0	0	0	0		.000	.000	.000	-99	-0	0			.500	F	/P-1	0.0
1913	Bos-N	22	78	6	24	2	1	1	14	2	5	.308	.333	.423	113	1	1			.983	1	1-22	0.1
1914	*Bos-N	147	537	67	153	17	9	1	71	43	55	.285	.350	.356	111	8	14			.990	3	*1-147	0.7
1915	Bos-N	127	458	46	115	26	7	2	60	36	59	.251	.318	.352	107	4	3	10	-5	.987	-4	*1-127	-1.0
Total	4	297	1075	119	292	45	18	4	145	81	119	.272	.335	.358	109	12	18	10		.988	-1	1-296/P-1	-0.2

■ DAVE SCHMIDT
Schmidt, David Frederick   b: 12/22/56, Mesa, Ariz.   BR/TR, 6'1", 190 lbs.   Deb: 4/28/81

YEAR	TM/L	G	AB	R	H	2B	3B	HR	RBI	BB	SO	AVG	OBP	SLG	PRO+	BR/A	SB	CS	SBR	FA	FR	G/POS	TPR
1981	Bos-A	15	42	6	10	1	0	2	3	7	17	.238	.347	.405	109	1	0	0	0	1.000	-4	C-15	-0.3

■ MIKE SCHMIDT
Schmidt, Michael Jack   b: 9/27/49, Dayton, Ohio   BR/TR, 6'2", 203 lbs.   Deb: 9/12/72   H

YEAR	TM/L	G	AB	R	H	2B	3B	HR	RBI	BB	SO	AVG	OBP	SLG	PRO+	BR/A	SB	CS	SBR	FA	FR	G/POS	TPR
1972	Phi-N	13	34	2	7	0	0	1	3	5	15	.206	.325	.294	75	-1	0	0	0	.964	2	3-11/2-1	0.1
1973	Phi-N	132	367	43	72	11	0	18	52	62	136	.196	.326	.373	91	-4	8	2	1	.954	3	*3-125/2-4,1-2,S-2	1.9
1974	Phi-N★	162	568	108	160	28	7	**36**	116	106	138	.282	.398	**.546**	156	43	23	12	-0	.954	26	*3-162	6.9
1975	Phi-N	158	562	93	140	34	3	**38**	95	101	180	.249	.367	.523	139	29	29	12	2	.954	24	*3-151,S-10	5.7
1976	*Phi-N★	160	584	112	153	31	4	**38**	107	100	149	.262	.380	.524	150	39	14	9	-1	.961	25	*3-160	6.4
1977	*Phi-N★	154	544	114	149	27	11	38	101	104	122	.274	.399	.574	151	40	15	8	-0	.964	29	*3-149/S-2,2-1	6.7
1978	*Phi-N	145	513	93	129	27	2	21	78	91	103	.251	.368	.435	122	17	19	6	2	.963	10	*3-139/S-1	2.9
1979	Phi-N★	160	541	109	137	25	4	45	114	**120**	115	.253	.392	.564	153	41	9	5	-0	.954	18	*3-157/S-2	5.8
1980	*Phi-N†	150	548	104	157	25	8	**48**	121	89	119	.286	.388	**.624**	169	50	12	5	1	.946	23	*3-149	7.3
1981	*Phi-N★	102	354	**78**	112	19	2	**31**	91	**73**	71	.316	**.439**	**.644**	195	46	12	4	1	.956	23	*3-101	7.0
1982	Phi-N★	148	514	108	144	26	3	35	87	**107**	131	.280	**.407**	.547	161	45	14	7	0	.950	19	*3-148	6.1
1983	*Phi-N★	154	534	104	136	16	4	**40**	109	**128**	148	.255	.402	.524	156	45	7	8	-3	.959	23	*3-153/S-2	6.4
1984	Phi-N★	151	528	93	146	23	3	36	106	92	116	.277	.388	.536	155	39	5	7	-3	.941	12	*3-145/1-2,S-1	4.8
1985	Phi-N	158	549	89	152	31	5	33	93	87	117	.277	.379	.532	148	36	1	3	-2	.993	1	*1-106,3-54/S-1	3.3
1986	Phi-N★	160	552	97	160	29	1	**37**	119	89	84	.290	.395	**.547**	152	40	1	2	-1	**.980**	-7	*3-124,1-35	2.8
1987	Phi-N★	147	522	88	153	28	0	35	113	83	80	.293	.392	.548	141	32	2	1	0	.971	13	*3-138/1-9,S-3	4.1
1988	Phi-N	108	390	52	97	21	2	12	62	49	42	.249	.342	.405	111	6	3	0	1	.939	3	*3-104/1-3	1.0
1989	Phi-N†	42	148	19	30	7	0	6	28	21	17	.203	.302	.372	91	-2	0	1	-1	.918	-5	3-42	-0.8
Total	18	2404	8352	1506	2234	408	59	548	1595	1507	1883	.267	.384	.527	147	543	174	92	-3	.955	265	*3-2212,1-157/S2	78.4

■ BOB SCHMIDT
Schmidt, Robert Benjamin   b: 4/22/33, St.Louis, Mo.   BR/TR, 6'2", 205 lbs.   Deb: 4/16/58

YEAR	TM/L	G	AB	R	H	2B	3B	HR	RBI	BB	SO	AVG	OBP	SLG	PRO+	BR/A	SB	CS	SBR	FA	FR	G/POS	TPR
1958	SF-N☆	127	393	46	96	20	2	14	54	33	59	.244	.300	.412	90	-6	0	1	-1	.982	-3	*C-123	-0.3
1959	SF-N	71	181	17	44	7	1	5	20	13	24	.243	.297	.376	80	-6	0	2	-1	1.000	-0	C-70	-0.4
1960	SF-N	110	344	31	92	12	1	8	37	26	51	.267	.319	.378	96	-3	0	3	-2	.981	-3	*C-108	-0.2
1961	SF-N	2	6	0	1	0	0	0	1	0	1	.167	.167	.167	-12	-1	0	0	0	1.000	1	/C-2	0.0
	Cin-N	27	70	4	9	0	0	1	4	8	14	.129	.218	.171	5	-10	0	0	0	.993	1	C-27	-0.7
	Yr	29	76	4	10	0	0	1	5	8	15	.132	.214	.171	4	-10	0	0	0	.994	3	C-29	-0.7
1962	Was-A	88	256	28	62	14	0	10	31	14	37	.242	.284	.414	86	-6	0	0	0	.997	-2	C-88	-0.5
1963	Was-A	9	15	3	3	1	0	0	3	3		.200	.333	.267	71	-0	0	0	0	1.000	-1	/C-6	-0.2
1965	NY-A	20	40	4	10	1	0	1	3	3	8	.250	.302	.350	85	-1	0	0	0	.990	2	C-20	0.2
Total	7	454	1305	133	317	55	4	39	150	100	199	.243	.299	.381	84	-33	0	6	-4	.988	-5	C-444	-2.1

■ WALTER SCHMIDT
Schmidt, Walter Joseph   b: 3/20/1887, Coal Hill, Ark.   d: 7/4/73, Modesto, Cal.   BR/TR, 5'9", 159 lbs.   Deb: 4/13/16   F

YEAR	TM/L	G	AB	R	H	2B	3B	HR	RBI	BB	SO	AVG	OBP	SLG	PRO+	BR/A	SB	CS	SBR	FA	FR	G/POS	TPR
1916	Pit-N	64	184	16	35	1	2	2	15	10	13	.190	.236	.250	49	-11	3			.976	0	C-57	-0.8
1917	Pit-N	72	183	9	45	7	0	0	17	11	11	.246	.296	.284	76	-5	4			.978	8	C-61	0.8
1918	Pit-N	105	323	31	77	6	3	0	27	17	19	.238	.281	.276	67	-12	7			.981	16	*C-104	1.3
1919	Pit-N	85	267	23	67	9	2	0	29	23	9	.251	.310	.300	81	-6	5			.982	1	C-85	0.3
1920	Pit-N	94	310	22	86	8	4	0	20	24	15	.277	.337	.329	89	-4	9	3	1	.971	-5	C-92	-0.1
1921	Pit-N	114	393	30	111	9	3	0	38	12	13	.282	.307	.321	65	-20	10	6	-1	**.986**	7	*C-111	-0.7
1922	Pit-N	40	152	21	50	11	1	0	22	1	5	.329	.333	.414	91	-2	1	0	0	.995	-6	C-40	-0.6
1923	Pit-N	97	335	39	83	7	2	0	37	22	12	.248	.300	.281	53	-22	10	5	0	.981	-9	C-96	-2.6
1924	Pit-N	58	177	16	43	3	2	1	20	13	5	.243	.295	.299	59	-10	6	1	1	.986	2	C-57	0.1
1925	StL-N	37	87	12	22	2	1	0	9	4	3	.253	.293	.299	51	-6	1	0	0	.967	6	C-31	0.1
Total	10	766	2411	216	619	63	20	3	234	137	105	.257	.301	.303	68	-99	57	16		.980	20	C-734	-2.7

■ HANK SCHMULBACH
Schmulbach, Henry Alrives   b: 1/17/25, E.St.Louis, Ill.   BL/TR, 5'11", 165 lbs.   Deb: 9/27/43

YEAR	TM/L	G	AB	R	H	2B	3B	HR	RBI	BB	SO	AVG	OBP	SLG	PRO+	BR/A	SB	CS	SBR	FA	FR	G/POS	TPR
1943	StL-A	1	0	1	0	0	0	0	0	0	0	—	—	—	—	0	0	0	0	.000	0	R	0.0

■ DAVE SCHNECK
Schneck, David Lee   b: 6/18/49, Allentown, Pa.   BL/TL, 5'10", 200 lbs.   Deb: 7/14/72

YEAR	TM/L	G	AB	R	H	2B	3B	HR	RBI	BB	SO	AVG	OBP	SLG	PRO+	BR/A	SB	CS	SBR	FA	FR	G/POS	TPR
1972	NY-N	37	123	7	23	3	2	3	10	10	26	.187	.254	.317	63	-6	0	1	-1	.985	-1	O-33	-1.0
1973	NY-N	13	36	2	7	0	1	0	0	4	4	.194	.216	.250	29	-3	0	0	0	1.000	0	O-12	-0.4
1974	NY-N	93	254	23	52	11	1	5	25	16	43	.205	.255	.315	60	-15	4	1	1	.974	0	O-84	-1.7
Total	3	143	413	32	82	14	4	8	35	27	73	.199	.251	.310	58	-24	4	2	0	.979	-0	O-129	-3.1

■ RED SCHOENDIENST
Schoendienst, Albert Fred   b: 2/2/23, Germantown, Ill.   BB/TR, 6', 170 lbs.   Deb: 4/17/45   MCH

YEAR	TM/L	G	AB	R	H	2B	3B	HR	RBI	BB	SO	AVG	OBP	SLG	PRO+	BR/A	SB	CS	SBR	FA	FR	G/POS	TPR
1945	StL-N	137	565	89	157	22	6	1	47	21	17	.278	.305	.343	78	-18	**26**			.983	-0	*O-118,S-10/2-1	-2.1
1946	*StL-N★	142	606	94	170	28	5	0	34	37	27	.281	.322	.343	85	-12	12			**.984**	-1	*2-128,3-12/S-4	-0.4
1947	StL-N	151	659	91	167	25	9	3	48	48	27	.253	.304	.332	66	-32	6			.976	-2	2-142/3-5,O-1	-2.4
1948	StL-N	119	408	64	111	21	4	4	36	28	16	.272	.319	.373	82	-11	1			.980	1	2-96	-0.5
1949	StL-N★	151	640	102	190	25	2	3	54	51	18	.297	.351	.356	86	-11	8			**.987**	24	*2-138,S-14/3-6,O-2	1.9
1950	StL-N	153	642	81	177	**43**	9	7	63	33	32	.276	.313	.403	83	-17	3			.985	8	*2-143,S-10/3-1	-0.2
1951	StL-N	135	553	88	160	32	7	6	54	35	23	.289	.337	.405	98	-3	0	1	-1	.990	16	*2-124/S-8	1.9
1952	StL-N☆	152	620	91	188	40	4	7	67	42	30	.303	.347	.424	113	10	9	6	-1	.977	33	*2-142,3-11/S-3	4.9
1953	StL-N★	146	564	107	193	35	5	15	79	60	23	.342	.405	.502	135	30	3	3	-1	**.983**	25	*2-140	5.8
1954	StL-N★	148	610	98	192	38	8	5	79	54	22	.315	.371	.428	107	7	4	2	0	.980	33	*2-144	4.8
1955	StL-N★	145	553	68	148	21	3	11	51	54	28	.268	.337	.376	89	-8	7	7	-2	**.985**	-15	*2-142	-1.4
1956	StL-N	40	153	22	48	9	0	6	15	13	5	.314	.367	.373	100	0	0	1		.995	-2	2-36	0.1
	NY-N	92	334	39	99	12	3	2	14	28	10	.296	.358	.368	95	-1	3	1		.993	-11	2-85	-0.6
	Yr	132	487	61	147	21	3	8	29	41	15	.302	.358	.370	97	-1	3	2	-3	**.993**	-12	*2-121	-0.5
1957	NY-N	57	254	35	78	8	4	9	33	10	8	.307	.338	.476	116	5	2	1	0	.984	-2	2-57	0.8
	*Mil-N★	93	394	56	122	23	4	6	32	23	7	.310	.349	.434	117	8	2	3	-1	.987	4	2-92/O-2	1.9
	Yr	150	648	91	**200**	31	8	15	65	33	15	.309	.345	.451	117	14	4	4	-1	.986	3	2-149/O-2	2.7
1958	*Mil-N	106	427	47	112	23	1	1	24	31	21	.262	.314	.328	77	-15	3	1	0	**.987**	1	*2-105	-0.7
1959	Mil-N	5	3	0	0	0	0	0	0	0	0	.000	.000	.000	-99	-1	0	0	0	.667	-2	/2-4	-0.1
1960	Mil-N	68	226	21	58	9	1	4	19	17	13	.257	.311	.319	79	-7	0	0	0	.964	-17	2-62	-1.9
1961	StL-N	72	120	9	36	9	1	1	12	12	6	.300	.364	.400	93	-1	1	0	0	.955	-11	2-32	-0.9
1962	StL-N	98	143	21	43	4	0	2	12	9	12	.301	.346	.371	84	-3	0	0	0	.986	-2	2-21/3-4	-0.2
1963	StL-N	6	5	0	0	0	0	0	0	0	1	.000	.000	.000	-91	-1	0	0	0	.000	0	H	-0.1
Total	19	2216	8479	1223	2449	427	78	84	773	606	346	.289	.338	.387	93	-82	89	27		.983	88	*2-1834,O-123/S3	10.6

■ JUMBO SCHOENECK
Schoeneck, Louis N.   b: 3/3/1862, Chicago, Ill.   d: 1/20/30, Chicago, Ill.   BR/TR, 6'3", 223 lbs.   Deb: 4/20/1884

YEAR	TM/L	G	AB	R	H	2B	3B	HR	RBI	BB	SO	AVG	OBP	SLG	PRO+	BR/A	SB	CS	SBR	FA	FR	G/POS	TPR
1884	CP-U	90	366	56	116	22	2	2			8	.317	.326	.404	123	-1				.956	0	*1-90	-1.0
	Bal-U	16	60	5	15	2	0	0			0	.250	.250	.283	56	-5				.962	2	*1-16	-0.5
	Yr	106	426	61	131	24	2	2			8	.308	.320	.387	112	-6				**.957**	2	*1-106	-1.5

YEAR	TM/L	G	AB	R	H	2B	3B	HR	RBI	BB	SO	AVG	OBP	SLG	PRO+	BR/A	SB	CS	SBR	FA	FR	G/POS	TPR
1888	Ind-N	48	169	15	40	4	0	0	20	9	24	.237	.283	.260	73	-5	11			.974	-1	1-48/P-2	-1.0
1889	Ind-N	16	62	3	15	2	2	0	8	3	3	.242	.299	.339	76	-2	1			.978	2	1-16	-0.1
Total	3	170	657	79	186	30	4	2	28	20	27	.283	.308	.350	99	-13	12			.964	3	1-170/P-2	-2.6

■ DICK SCHOFIELD
Schofield, John Richard "Ducky" b: 1/7/35, Springfield, Ill. BB/TR, 5'9", 165 lbs. Deb: 7/3/53 F

YEAR	TM/L	G	AB	R	H	2B	3B	HR	RBI	BB	SO	AVG	OBP	SLG	PRO+	BR/A	SB	CS	SBR	FA	FR	G/POS	TPR
1953	StL-N	33	39	9	7	0	0	2	4	2	11	.179	.220	.333	42	-3	0	0	0	.917	10	S-15	0.6
1954	StL-N	43	7	17	1	0	1	0	1	0	3	.143	.143	.429	42	-1	1	1	-0	1.000	5	S-11	0.1
1955	StL-N	12	4	3	0	0	0	0	0	0	1	.000	.000	.000	-99	-1	0	0	0	1.000	1	/S-3	-0.1
1956	StL-N	16	30	3	3	2	0	0	0	0	6	.100	.100	.167	-30	-5	0	0	0	.923	-1	/S-9	-0.6
1957	StL-N	65	56	10	9	0	0	0	1	7	13	.161	.254	.161	14	-7	1	3	-2	.948	10	S-23	0.2
1958	StL-N	39	108	16	23	4	0	1	8	23	15	.213	.351	.278	67	-4	0	2	-1	.932	-5	S-27	-0.8
	Pit-N	26	27	4	4	0	1	0	2	3	6	.148	.233	.222	22	-3	0	1	-1	1.000	-1	/S-5,3-2	-0.3
	Yr	65	135	20	27	4	1	1	10	26	21	.200	.329	.267	59	-7	0	3	-2	.943	-3	S-32/3-2	-1.1
1959	Pit-N	81	145	21	34	10	1	1	9	16	22	.234	.311	.338	73	-5	1	1	-0	.980	10	2-28/S-8,O-3	0.7
1960	*Pit-N	65	102	9	34	4	1	0	10	16	20	.333	.429	.392	126	5	0	1	-1	.947	8	S-23,2-10/3-1	1.4
1961	Pit-N	60	78	16	15	2	1	0	2	10	19	.192	.284	.244	42	-6	0	1	-1	.923	9	3-11/S-9,2-5,O-3	0.3
1962	Pit-N	54	104	19	30	3	0	2	10	17	22	.288	.388	.375	106	2	0	1	-1	.933	-6	3-20/2-2,S-1	-0.4
1963	Pit-N	138	541	54	133	18	2	3	32	69	83	.246	.334	.303	84	-8	2	4	-2	.966	10	*S-117,2-20/3-1	1.1
1964	Pit-N	121	398	50	98	22	5	3	36	54	60	.246	.346	.349	97	0	1	2	-1	.950	2	*S-111	0.9
1965	Pit-N	31	109	13	25	5	0	0	6	15	19	.229	.323	.275	70	-4	1	0	0	.974	4	S-28	0.3
	SF-N	101	379	39	77	10	1	2	19	33	50	.203	.272	.251	47	-26	4	1	0	.984	-6	S-93	-2.9
	Yr	132	488	52	102	15	1	2	25	48	69	.209	.284	.256	52	-30	3	4	-2	.981	-2	*S-121	-2.6
1966	SF-N	11	16	4	1	0	0	0	0	2	2	.063	.167	.063	-32	-3	0	0	0	1.000	-1	/S-8	-0.1
	NY-A	25	58	5	9	2	0	0	2	4	8	.155	.269	.190	36	-5	0	1	-0	.909	5	S-19	0.2
	LA-N	20	70	10	18	0	0	0	4	8	8	.257	.350	.257	78	-2	1	1	-0	.923	-3	3-19/S-3	-0.5
1967	LA-N	84	232	23	50	10	1	2	15	31	40	.216	.308	.293	79	-6	1	2	-1	.976	-0	S-69/2-4,3-2	-0.1
1968	*StL-N	69	127	14	28	7	1	1	8	13	31	.220	.303	.315	87	-2	1	2	-1	.973	5	S-43,2-23	1.0
1969	Bos-A	94	226	30	58	9	3	2	20	29	44	.257	.351	.350	92	-2	0	2	-1	.981	-2	2-37,S-11/3-9,O-5	0.3
1970	Bos-A	76	139	16	26	1	2	1	14	21	26	.187	.298	.245	48	-9	0	1	-1	.969	-4	2-15,3-15/S-3	-1.4
1971	Mil-A	23	28	2	3	2	0	1	1	2	8	.107	.194	.179	6	-4	0	0	0	1.000	-2	3-12/S-4,2-2	-0.5
	StL-N	34	60	7	13	2	0	1	6	10	9	.217	.347	.300	82	-1	0	0	0	.935	2	S-17,2-13/3-3	0.3
Total	19	1321	3083	394	699	113	20	21	211	390	526	.227	.319	.297	73	-101	12	29	-14	.961	58	S-660,2-159/3-95,O	-0.3

■ DICK SCHOFIELD
Schofield, Richard Craig b: 11/21/62, Springfield, Ill. BR/TR, 5'10", 176 lbs. Deb: 9/8/83 F

YEAR	TM/L	G	AB	R	H	2B	3B	HR	RBI	BB	SO	AVG	OBP	SLG	PRO+	BR/A	SB	CS	SBR	FA	FR	G/POS	TPR
1983	Cal-A	21	54	4	11	2	0	3	4	6	8	.204	.295	.407	92	-1	0	0	0	.929	5	S-21	0.5
1984	Cal-A	140	400	39	77	10	3	4	21	33	79	.192	.264	.262	47	-29	5	2	0	.982	3	*S-140	-1.2
1985	Cal-A	147	438	50	96	19	3	8	41	35	70	.219	.289	.331	70	-18	11	4	1	.963	1	*S-147	-0.3
1986	*Cal-A	139	458	67	114	17	6	13	57	48	55	.249	.327	.397	97	-2	23	5	4	.972	15	*S-137	2.9
1987	Cal-A	134	479	52	120	17	3	9	46	37	63	.251	.307	.355	78	-16	19	3	4	.984	-18	*S-131/2-2,D-1	-1.8
1988	Cal-A	155	527	61	126	11	6	6	34	40	57	.239	.304	.317	76	-16	20	5	3	.983	23	*S-155	2.3
1989	Cal-A	91	302	42	69	11	2	4	26	28	47	.228	.300	.318	76	-10	9	3	1	.983	-8	S-90	-0.9
1990	Cal-A	99	310	41	79	8	1	1	18	52	61	.255	.365	.294	89	-2	3	4	-2	.966	12	S-99	1.6
1991	Cal-A	134	427	44	96	19	3	0	31	50	69	.225	.310	.260	60	-22	8	4	0	.975	12	*S-133	0.0
1992	Cal-A	1	3	0	1	0	0	0	0	0	1	.333	.500	.333	137	0	0	0	0	1.000	-1	/S-1	-0.1
	NY-N	142	420	52	86	18	2	4	36	60	82	.205	.311	.286	71	-14	11	4	1	.988	13	*S-141	1.0
1993	*Tor-A	36	110	11	21	1	2	0	5	16	25	.191	.294	.236	44	-8	3	0	1	.977	5	S-36	-0.2
1994	Tor-A	95	325	38	83	14	1	4	32	34	62	.255	.333	.342	74	-12	7	7	-2	.972	-9	S-95	-1.4
1995	LA-N	9	10	0	1	0	0	0	0	1	3	.100	.182	.100	-25	-2	0	0	0	1.000	3	/S-3,3-1	0.1
	Cal-A	12	20	1	5	0	0	0	2	4	2	.250	.375	.250	67	-1	0	0	0	1.000	1	S-12	0.1
1996	Cal-A	13	16	3	4	0	0	0	2	4	4	.250	.294	.250	40	-1	0	0	0	.889	1	/S-7,2-2,3-1,D-1	0.0
Total	14	1368	4299	505	989	137	32	56	353	446	684	.230	.309	.316	73	-153	120	41	11	.976	56	*S-1348/2-4,3-2,D-2	2.6

■ OTTO SCHOMBERG
Schomberg, Otto H. (b: Otto H. Shambrick) b: 11/14/1864, Milwaukee, Wis. d: 5/3/27, Ottawa, Kan. BL/TL, Deb: 7/7/1886

YEAR	TM/L	G	AB	R	H	2B	3B	HR	RBI	BB	SO	AVG	OBP	SLG	PRO+	BR/A	SB	CS	SBR	FA	FR	G/POS	TPR
1886	Pit-a	72	246	53	67	6	6	1	29	57		.272	.417	.358	144	17	7			.966	-7	1-72	0.1
1887	Ind-N	112	419	91	129	18	16	5	83	56	32	.308	.397	.463	143	27	21			.958	-10	*1-112/O-1	0.4
1888	Ind-N	30	112	11	24	5	1	1	10	10	12	.214	.290	.304	88	-1	6			.857	-5	O-15,1-15	-0.8
Total	3	214	777	155	220	29	23	7	122	123	44	.283	.389	.407	136	43	34			.961	-22	1-199/O-16	-0.3

■ JERRY SCHOONMAKER
Schoonmaker, Jerald Lee b: 12/14/33, Seymour, Mo. BR/TR, 5'11", 190 lbs. Deb: 6/11/55

YEAR	TM/L	G	AB	R	H	2B	3B	HR	RBI	BB	SO	AVG	OBP	SLG	PRO+	BR/A	SB	CS	SBR	FA	FR	G/POS	TPR
1955	Was-A	20	46	5	7	0	1	1	4	5	11	.152	.235	.261	35	-4	1	0	0	.960	-1	O-15	-0.6
1957	Was-A	30	23	5	2	1	0	0	0	2	11	.087	.160	.130	-20	-4	0	0	0	1.000	-3	O-13	-0.7
Total	2	50	69	10	9	1	1	1	4	7	22	.130	.211	.217	16	-8	1	0	0	.975	-4	/O-28	-1.3

■ GENE SCHOTT
Schott, Arthur Eugene b: 7/14/13, Batavia, Ohio d: 11/16/92, Sun City Center, Fla. BR/TR, 6'2", 185 lbs. Deb: 4/16/35

YEAR	TM/L	G	AB	R	H	2B	3B	HR	RBI	BB	SO	AVG	OBP	SLG	PRO+	BR/A	SB	CS	SBR	FA	FR	G/POS	TPR
1935	Cin-N	36	60	6	12	2	0	2	3	3	18	.200	.238	.233	28	-6	0			.965	3	P-33	0.0
1936	Cin-N	39	60	10	18	3	1	1	8	5	18	.300	.354	.433	118	1	0			.947	1	P-31	0.0
1937	Cin-N	50	49	5	7	2	0	0	4	1	14	.143	.160	.184	-7	-7	0			.961	1	P-37	0.0
1938	Cin-N	31	24	3	3	0	0	0	0	1	4	.125	.160	.125	-21	-4	0			1.000	1	P-31	0.0
1939	Phi-N	8	6	3	2	0	1	0	0	0	0	.333	.333	.667	168	1	0			.500	-1	/P-4	0.0
	Bro-N	1	0	0	0	0	0	0	0	0	0	—	—	—		0	0			.000	0	R	0.0
	Yr	9	6	3	2	0	1	0	0	0	0	.333	.333	.667	166	0	0			.500	-1	/P-4	0.0
Total	5	165	199	27	42	7	2	1	14	10	49	.211	.249	.281	45	-15	0			.959	6	P-136	0.0

■ PAUL SCHRAMKA
Schramka, Paul Edward b: 3/22/28, Milwaukee, Wis. BL/TL, 6', 185 lbs. Deb: 4/14/53

YEAR	TM/L	G	AB	R	H	2B	3B	HR	RBI	BB	SO	AVG	OBP	SLG	PRO+	BR/A	SB	CS	SBR	FA	FR	G/POS	TPR
1953	Chi-N	2	0	0	0	0	0	0	0	0	0	—	—	—		0	0	0	0	.000	-0	/O-1	0.0

■ OSSEE SCHRECKENGOST
Schreckengost, Ossee Freeman (a.k.a. Ossee Schreck)
b: 4/11/1875, New Bethlehem, Pa. d: 7/9/14, Philadelphia, Pa. BR/TR, 5'10", 180 lbs. Deb: 9/8/1897

YEAR	TM/L	G	AB	R	H	2B	3B	HR	RBI	BB	SO	AVG	OBP	SLG	PRO+	BR/A	SB	CS	SBR	FA	FR	G/POS	TPR
1897	Lou-N	1	3	0	0	0	0	0	0	0	0	.000	.000	.000	-99	-0	0			1.000	-0	/C-1	-0.1
1898	Cle-N	10	35	5	11	2	3	0	10	0	0	.314	.314	.543	146	2	1			.860	0	/C-9	0.2
1899	StL-N	8	8	0	0	0	0	0	0	0	1	.000	.111	.000	-67	-2	0			1.000	-1	/1-1,O-1	-0.2
	Cle-N	43	150	15	47	8	3	0	10	6		.313	.348	.407	115	3	4			.911	-5	C-39/1-1,S-1,O-1	0.0
	StL-N	66	269	42	77	12	2	2	37	14		.286	.324	.368	88	-5	14			.963	-3	1-41,C-25/2-1	-0.6
	Yr	115	427	57	124	20	5	2	47	21		.290	.328	.375	94	-5	18			.927	-9	C-64,1-43/O-2,S2	-0.8
1901	Bos-A	86	280	37	85	13	5	0	38	19		.304	.356	.386	108	3	6			.926	2	C-72/1-4	1.1
1902	Cle-A	18	74	5	25	0	0	0	9	0		.338	.338	.338	91	-1	2			.975	-1	1-17	-0.2
	Phi-A	79	284	45	92	17	2	2	43	9		.324	.347	.419	107	2	3			.960	22	C-71/1-7,O-1	2.9
	Yr	97	358	50	117	17	2	2	52	9		.327	.345	.402	104	1	5			.960	21	C-71,1-24/O-1	2.7
1903	Phi-A	92	306	26	78	13	4	3	30	11		.255	.285	.353	87	-5	0			.975	18	C-77,1-10	2.1
1904	Phi-A	95	311	23	58	9	1	1	21	5		.186	.199	.232	34	-23	3			.979	5	C-84/1-9	-1.0
1905	*Phi-A	123	420	30	114	19	6	0	45	3		.271	.278	.345	96	-4	9			.984	12	*C-114/1-2	2.1
1906	Phi-A	98	338	29	96	20	1	0	41	10		.284	.305	.358	104	0	5			.971	8	C-89/1-4	1.9
1907	Phi-A	101	356	30	97	16	3	0	38	17		.272	.306	.334	102	-0	4			.985	16	C-99/1-2	2.7
1908	Phi-A	71	207	16	46	7	1	0	16	6		.222	.248	.266	63	-9	1			.978	5	C-65/1-1	0.6
	Chi-A	6	16	1	3	0	0	0	0	1		.188	.235	.188	38	-1	0			.982	4	/C-6	0.4
	Yr	77	223	17	49	7	1	0	16	7		.220	.247	.260	61	-10	1			.978	13	C-71/1-1	1.0
Total	11	895	3057	304	829	136	31	9	338	102		.271	.297	.345	90	-42	52			.970	86	C-751/1-99,O-3,2S	11.9

■ HANK SCHREIBER
Schreiber, Henry Walter b: 7/12/1891, Cleveland, Ohio d: 2/23/68, Indianapolis, Ind. BR/TR, 5'11", 165 lbs. Deb: 4/14/14

YEAR	TM/L	G	AB	R	H	2B	3B	HR	RBI	BB	SO	AVG	OBP	SLG	PRO+	BR/A	SB	CS	SBR	FA	FR	G/POS	TPR
1914	Chi-A	1	2	0	0	0	0	0	0	0	1	.000	.000	.000	-99	-0	0			.000	-1	/O-1	-0.1
1917	Bos-N	2	7	1	2	0	0	0	0	0	1	.286	.286	.286	80	-0	0			1.000	-1	/S-1,3-1	-0.1

YEAR	TM/L	G	AB	R	H	2B	3B	HR	RBI	BB	SO	AVG	OBP	SLG	PRO+	BR/A	SB	CS	SBR	FA	FR	G/POS	TPR
1919	Cin-N	19	58	5	13	4	0	0	4	0	12	.224	.224	.293	56	-3	0			.984	7	3-17/S-2	0.4
1921	NY-N	4	6	2	2	0	0	0	2	1	1	.333	.429	.333	104	0	0	0	0	.500	0	/2-2,S-2,3-1	0.0
1926	Chi-N	10	18	2	1	1	0	0	0	0	1	.056	.056	.111	-55	-4	0			1.000	1	/S-3,3-3,2-1	-0.3
Total	5	36	91	10	18	5	0	0	6	1	16	.198	.207	.253	34	-8	0			.986	6	/3-22,S-8,2-3,O-1	-0.1

■ TED SCHREIBER
Schreiber, Theodore Henry b: 7/11/38, Brooklyn, N.Y. BR/TR, 5'11", 175 lbs. Deb: 4/14/63

YEAR	TM/L	G	AB	R	H	2B	3B	HR	RBI	BB	SO	AVG	OBP	SLG	PRO+	BR/A	SB	CS	SBR	FA	FR	G/POS	TPR
1963	NY-N	39	50	1	8	0	0	0	2	4	14	.160	.236	.160	16	-5	0	1	-1	.977	8	3-17/S-9,2-3	0.2

■ POP SCHRIVER
Schriver, William Frederick b: 7/11/1865, Brooklyn, N.Y. d: 12/27/32, Brooklyn, N.Y. BR/TR, 5'9.5", 172 lbs. Deb: 4/29/1886

YEAR	TM/L	G	AB	R	H	2B	3B	HR	RBI	BB	SO	AVG	OBP	SLG	PRO+	BR/A	SB	CS	SBR	FA	FR	G/POS	TPR
1886	Bro-a	8	21	2	1	0	0	0		2		.048	.130	.048	-43	-3	0			.667	0	/O-5,C-3	-0.3
1888	Phi-N	40	134	15	26	5	2	1	23	7	21	.194	.250	.284	66	-5	2			.870	-3	C-27/S-6,3-6,O-1	-0.6
1889	Phi-N	55	211	24	56	10	0	1	19	16	8	.265	.323	.327	75	-8	5			.920	3	C-48/2-6,3-1	0.0
1890	Phi-N	57	223	37	61	9	6	0	35	22	15	.274	.339	.368	103	0	9			.916	-3	C-34,1-10/3-8,2O	0.1
1891	Chi-N	27	90	15	30	1	4	1	21	10	9	.333	.412	.467	156	7	1			.964	2	C-27/1-2	0.9
1892	Chi-N	92	326	40	73	10	6	1	34	27	25	.224	.297	.301	80	-8	4			.929	-9	C-82,O-10	-1.1
1893	Chi-N	64	229	49	65	8	3	4	34	14	9	.284	.336	.397	96	-2	4			.926	2	C-56/O-5	0.4
1894	Chi-N	96	349	55	96	12	3	3	47	29	21	.275	.341	.352	64	-21	9			.923	-0	*C-88/S-3,3-3,1-2	-1.0
1895	NY-N	24	92	16	29	2	1	1	16	9	10	.315	.382	.391	102	1	3			.898	-3	C-18/1-6	0.0
1897	Cin-N	61	178	29	54	12	4	1	30	19		.303	.374	.433	105	1	3			.959	-4	C-53	0.2
1898	Pit-N	95	315	25	72	15	3	0	32	23		.229	.287	.295	68	-13	0			.957	-5	C-92/1-1	-0.8
1899	Pit-N	91	301	31	85	19	5	1	49	23		.282	.343	.389	101	0	4			.958	5	C-78/1-8	1.0
1900	*Pit-N	37	92	12	27	7	0	1	12	10		.293	.381	.402	115	2	2			.959	-4	C-24/1-1	0.0
1901	StL-N	53	166	17	45	7	3	1	23	12		.271	.335	.367	109	2	2			.971	2	C-24,1-19	0.8
Total	14	800	2727	367	720	117	40	16	375	223	118	.264	.329	.354	88	-48	46			.934	-15	C-654/1-49,O32S	-0.4

■ BOB SCHRODER
Schroder, Robert James b: 12/30/44, Ridgefield, N.J. BL/TR, 6', 175 lbs. Deb: 4/20/65

YEAR	TM/L	G	AB	R	H	2B	3B	HR	RBI	BB	SO	AVG	OBP	SLG	PRO+	BR/A	SB	CS	SBR	FA	FR	G/POS	TPR
1965	SF-N	31	9	4	2	0	0	0	1	1	1	.222	.300	.222	48	-1	0	0	0	1.000	0	/2-4,3-1	0.3
1966	SF-N	10	33	0	8	0	0	0	0	1	1	.242	.242	.242	34	-3	0	0	0	.963	-5	/S-9	-0.8
1967	SF-N	62	135	20	31	4	0	0	7	15	15	.230	.307	.259	64	-6	1	0	0	.993	-10	2-45/3-4	-1.5
1968	SF-N	35	44	5	7	1	1	0	2	7	3	.159	.288	.227	56	-2	0	0	0	.960	-3	2-12/S-4,3-2	-0.6
Total	4	138	221	29	48	5	1	0	12	23	21	.217	.294	.249	58	-11	1	0	0	.989	-15	/2-61,S-13,3-7	-2.6

■ BILL SCHROEDER
Schroeder, Alfred William b: 9/7/58, Baltimore, Md. BR/TR, 6'2", 200 lbs. Deb: 7/13/83

YEAR	TM/L	G	AB	R	H	2B	3B	HR	RBI	BB	SO	AVG	OBP	SLG	PRO+	BR/A	SB	CS	SBR	FA	FR	G/POS	TPR
1983	Mil-A	23	73	7	13	1	0	3	7	3	23	.178	.221	.356	60	-4	0	1	-1	.980	-3	C-23	-0.7
1984	Mil-A	61	210	29	54	6	0	14	25	8	54	.257	.291	.486	115	3	0	1	-1	.987	-5	C-58/1-1,D-3	0.0
1985	Mil-A	53	194	18	47	8	0	8	25	12	61	.242	.293	.407	90	-3	0	1	-1	.987	-7	C-48/1-1,D-4	-0.9
1986	Mil-A	64	217	32	46	14	0	7	19	9	59	.212	.263	.373	69	-10	1	0	0	.995	-4	C-35,1-19,D-10	-1.2
1987	Mil-A	75	250	35	83	12	0	14	42	16	56	.332	.379	.548	138	13	5	2	0	.995	-6	C-67/1-4,D-2	1.1
1988	Mil-A	41	122	9	19	2	0	5	10	6	36	.156	.208	.295	39	-10	0	0	0	1.000	6	C-30,1-10/D-1	-0.4
1989	Cal-A	41	138	16	28	3	0	6	15	3	44	.203	.220	.348	59	-8	0	0	0	.991	10	C-33/1-8	0.3
1990	Cal-A	18	58	7	13	3	0	4	7	1	10	.224	.237	.483	98	-1	0	0	0	1.000	2	C-15/1-3	0.2
Total	8	376	1262	153	303	49	1	61	152	58	343	.240	.282	.426	91	-20	6	5	-4	.992	-8	C-309/1-46,D-20	-1.6

■ RICK SCHU
Schu, Richard Spencer b: 1/26/62, Philadelphia, Pa. BR/TR, 6', 170 lbs. Deb: 9/1/84

YEAR	TM/L	G	AB	R	H	2B	3B	HR	RBI	BB	SO	AVG	OBP	SLG	PRO+	BR/A	SB	CS	SBR	FA	FR	G/POS	TPR
1984	Phi-N	17	29	12	8	2	1	2	5	6	6	.276	.400	.621	180	3	0	0	0	.952	-0	3-15	0.3
1985	Phi-N	112	416	54	105	21	4	7	24	38	78	.252	.318	.373	90	-6	8	6	-1	.933	-10	*3-111	-2.0
1986	Phi-N	92	208	32	57	10	1	8	25	18	44	.274	.338	.447	111	3	2	2	0	.913	1	3-58	0.3
1987	Phi-N	92	196	24	46	6	3	7	23	20	36	.235	.312	.403	85	-4	0	2	-1	.905	-3	3-45,1-28	-0.9
1988	Bal-A	89	270	22	69	9	4	4	20	21	49	.256	.316	.363	92	-3	6	4	-1	.937	-12	3-72/1-4,D-9	-1.6
1989	Bal-A	1	0	0	0	0	0	0	0	0	0	—	—	—	—		0	0	0	1.000	-0	/2-1	—
	Det-A	98	266	25	57	11	0	7	21	24	37	.214	.279	.335	74	-10	1	2	-1	.934	-2	3-83/2-5,1-3,S-3,D	-1.2
	Yr	99	266	25	57	11	0	7	21	24	37	.214	.279	.335	74	-10	1	2	-1	.934	-2	3-83/D-9,2-6,1-3,S	-1.2
1990	Cal-A	61	157	19	42	8	0	6	14	11	25	.268	.315	.433	110	1	1	2	-1	.918	-3	3-38,1-15/O-4,2-1	0.1
1991	Phi-N	17	22	1	2	0	0	0	1	2	6	.091	.130	.091	-37	-4	0	0	0	.667	-1	/3-3,1-1	-0.5
1996	Mon-N	1	4	0	0	0	0	0	0	0	0	.000	.000	.000	-98	-1	0	0	0	.667	-0	/3-1	-0.2
Total	9	580	1568	189	386	67	13	41	134	139	282	.246	.311	.384	91	-20	17	16	-5	.926	-25	3-426/1-51,D2OS	-5.7

■ HEINIE SCHUBLE
Schuble, Henry George b: 11/1/06, Houston, Tex. d: 10/2/90, Baytown, Tex. BR/TR, 5'9", 152 lbs. Deb: 7/8/27

YEAR	TM/L	G	AB	R	H	2B	3B	HR	RBI	BB	SO	AVG	OBP	SLG	PRO+	BR/A	SB	CS	SBR	FA	FR	G/POS	TPR
1927	StL-N	65	218	29	56	6	2	4	28	7	27	.257	.283	.358	69	-10	0			.915	-7	S-65	-1.0
1929	Det-A	92	258	35	60	11	7	2	28	19	23	.233	.288	.353	64	-15	3	2	-0	.886	-10	S-86/3-2	-1.5
1932	Det-A	102	340	58	92	20	6	5	52	24	37	.271	.319	.409	84	-9	14	5	1	.941	8	3-76,S-16	0.6
1933	Det-A	49	96	12	21	4	1	0	6	5	17	.219	.257	.281	42	-8	2	0	1	.951	1	3-23/S-2,2-1	-0.5
1934	Det-A	11	15	2	4	2	0	0	2	1	4	.267	.313	.400	83	-0	0			1.000	0	/S-3,3-2,2-1	0.0
1935	Det-A	11	8	3	2	0	0	0	0	1	0	.250	.333	.250	55	-0	0			.714	1	/3-2,2-1	0.1
1936	StL-N	2	0	0	0	0	0	0	0	0	0	—	—	—	—		0			.000	0	/3-1	0.0
Total	7	332	935	139	235	43	16	11	116	57	108	.251	.296	.367	70	-43	19	7		.906	-6	S-172,3-106/2-3	-2.3

■ WES SCHULMERICH
Schulmerich, Edward Wesley b: 8/21/01, Hillsboro, Ore. d: 6/26/85, Corvallis, Ore. BR/TR, 5'11", 210 lbs. Deb: 5/1/31

YEAR	TM/L	G	AB	R	H	2B	3B	HR	RBI	BB	SO	AVG	OBP	SLG	PRO+	BR/A	SB	CS	SBR	FA	FR	G/POS	TPR
1931	Bos-N	95	327	36	101	17	7	2	43	28	30	.309	.363	.422	115	7	0			.966	-4	O-87	-0.3
1932	Bos-N	119	404	47	105	22	5	11	57	27	61	.260	.314	.421	99	-1	5			.968	3	*O-101	-0.5
1933	Bos-N	29	85	10	21	6	1	1	13	5	10	.247	.289	.376	97	-1	0			.980	-1	O-21	-0.1
	Phi-N	97	365	53	122	19	4	8	59	32	45	.334	.394	.474	130	15	1			.977	-2	*O-97	0.8
	Yr	126	450	63	143	25	5	9	72	37	55	.318	.375	.456	126	15	1			.978	-1	*O-118	0.7
1934	Phi-N	15	52	2	13	1	0	0	1	4	8	.250	.316	.269	51	-3	0			.963	-1	O-13	-0.4
	Cin-N	74	209	21	55	8	3	5	19	22	43	.263	.330	.402	98	-1	1			.976	-2	O-56	-0.5
	Yr	89	261	23	68	9	3	5	20	26	51	.261	.330	.375	88	-4	1			.974	-3	O-69	-0.9
Total	4	429	1442	169	417	73	20	27	192	118	197	.289	.347	.424	109	15	7			.971	-6	O-375	-1.0

■ ART SCHULT
Schult, Arthur William "Dutch" b: 6/20/28, Brooklyn, N.Y. BR/TR, 6'4", 220 lbs. Deb: 5/17/53

YEAR	TM/L	G	AB	R	H	2B	3B	HR	RBI	BB	SO	AVG	OBP	SLG	PRO+	BR/A	SB	CS	SBR	FA	FR	G/POS	TPR
1953	NY-A	7	0	3	0	0	0	0	0	0	0	—	—	—	—		0	0	0	.000	0	R	0.0
1956	Cin-N	5	7	3	3	0	0	0	2	1	1	.429	.500	.429	144	1	0	0	0	.000	-0	/O-1	0.0
1957	Cin-N	21	34	4	9	2	0	0	4	0	2	.265	.286	.324	59	-2	1	0	0	1.000	0	/O-5	-0.2
	Was-A	77	247	30	65	14	0	4	35	14	30	.263	.305	.368	84	-6	0	1	-1	.987	-1	1-35,O-31	-1.1
1959	Chi-N	42	118	17	32	7	0	2	14	7	14	.271	.323	.381	88	-2	0			.985	-4	1-23,O-15	-0.8
1960	Chi-N	12	15	1	2	1	0	0	1	1	3	.133	.188	.200	6	-2	0	0	0	1.000	0	/O-4,1-1	-0.3
Total	5	164	421	58	111	24	0	6	56	23	50	.264	.308	.363	81	-11	1	1	-1	.987	-5	/1-59,O-56	-2.4

■ FRANK SCHULTE
Schulte, Frank M. "Wildfire" b: 9/17/1882, Cohocton, N.Y. d: 10/2/49, Oakland, Cal. BL/TR, 5'11", 170 lbs. Deb: 9/21/04

YEAR	TM/L	G	AB	R	H	2B	3B	HR	RBI	BB	SO	AVG	OBP	SLG	PRO+	BR/A	SB	CS	SBR	FA	FR	G/POS	TPR
1904	Chi-N	20	84	16	24	4	3	2	13	2		.286	.310	.476	141	3	1			.949	0	O-20	0.3
1905	Chi-N	123	493	67	135	15	14	1	47	32		.274	.326	.367	102	0	16			.981	-7	*O-123	-1.3
1906	*Chi-N	146	563	77	158	18	**13**	7	60	31		.281	.324	.396	118	9	25			.975	0	*O-146	0.2
1907	*Chi-N	97	342	44	98	14	7	2	32	22		.287	.339	.386	120	7	7			.973	-3	O-92	0.0
1908	Chi-N	102	386	42	91	20	2	1	43	29		.236	.294	.306	88	-5	15			.994	-6	*O-102	-1.8
1909	Chi-N	140	538	57	142	16	11	4	60	24		.264	.298	.357	101	-2	23			.968	-13	*O-140	-2.4
1910	*Chi-N	151	559	93	168	29	15	**10**	68	39	57	.301	.349	.460	137	22	22			.968	-6	*O-150	0.9
1911	Chi-N	154	577	105	173	30	21	**21**	**107**	76	71	.300	.384	**.534**	**155**	40	**40**			.971	-5	*O-154	2.7
1912	Chi-N	139	553	90	146	27	11	12	64	53	70	.264	.336	.418	106	3	17			.952	-4	*O-139	-0.8
1913	Chi-N	132	497	85	138	28	6	9	68	39	68	.278	.336	.412	113	7	21			.956	-8	*O-130	-0.7
1914	Chi-N	137	465	54	112	22	7	5	61	50	68	.241	.306	.351	95	-3	19			.954	-10	*O-134	-2.1
1915	Chi-N	151	550	66	137	20	6	12	62	49	68	.249	.313	.373	107	4	19	17	-5	.962	4	*O-147	-0.4
1916	Chi-N	72	230	31	68	11	1	5	27	20	35	.296	.352	.417	123	6	9			.951	-3	O-67	0.0

YEAR	TM/L	G	AB	R	H	2B	3B	HR	RBI	BB	SO	AVG	OBP	SLG	PRO+	BR/A	SB	CS	SBR	FA	FR	G/POS	TPR
	Pit-N	55	177	12	45	5	3	0	14	17	19	.254	.323	.316	96	-0	5			.968	-2	O-48	-0.5
	Yr	127	407	43	113	16	4	5	41	37	54	.278	.339	.373	111	6	14			.958	-5	*O-115	-0.5
1917	Pit-N	30	103	11	22	5	1	0	7	10	14	.214	.283	.282	71	-3	5			.963	-0	O-28	-0.6
	Phi-N	64	149	21	32	10	0	1	15	16	22	.215	.299	.302	81	-3	4			.923	-4	O-42	-1.7
	Yr	94	252	32	54	15	1	1	22	26	36	.214	.293	.294	77	-6	9			.943	-10	O-70	-2.3
1918	Was-A	93	267	35	77	14	3	0	44	47	36	.288	.406	.363	135	14	5			.969	1	O-75	1.2
Total	15	1806	6533	906	1766	288	124	92	792	545	<u>515</u>	.270	.332	.395	114	98	233	<u>17</u>		.966	-70	*O-1737	-7.0

■ FRED SCHULTE
Schulte, Fred William "Fritz" (b: Fred William Schult)   b: 1/13/01, Belvidere, Ill.   d: 5/20/83, Belvidere, Ill.   BR/TR, 6'1", 183 lbs.   Deb: 4/15/27

YEAR	TM/L	G	AB	R	H	2B	3B	HR	RBI	BB	SO	AVG	OBP	SLG	PRO+	BR/A	SB	CS	SBR	FA	FR	G/POS	TPR
1927	StL-A	60	189	32	60	16	3	3	34	20	14	.317	.383	.503	124	6	5	3	-0	.916	-3	O-49	0.0
1928	StL-A	146	556	90	159	44	6	7	85	51	60	.286	.347	.424	99	-2	6	5	-1	.973	17	*O-143	0.5
1929	StL-A	121	446	63	137	24	5	3	71	59	44	.307	.389	.404	101	2	8	3	1	**.989**	13	*O-116	0.7
1930	StL-A	113	392	59	109	23	5	5	62	41	44	.278	.348	.401	86	-8	12	8	-1	.966	-2	O-98/1-5	-1.7
1931	StL-A	134	553	100	168	32	7	9	65	56	49	.304	.369	.436	107	6	6	8	-3	.971	6	*O-134	-0.1
1932	StL-A	146	565	106	166	35	6	9	73	71	44	.294	.373	.425	100	1	5	9	-4	.986	0	*O-129/1-5	-1.1
1933	*Was-A	144	550	98	162	30	7	5	87	61	27	.295	.366	.402	104	4	10	12	-4	.980	16	*O-142	0.8
1934	Was-A	136	524	72	156	32	6	3	73	53	34	.298	.363	.399	100	0	3	7	-3	.986	-1	*O-134	-0.8
1935	Was-A	76	226	33	60	6	4	2	23	26	22	.265	.344	.354	83	-5	0	3	-2	.980	-8	O-56	-1.6
1936	Pit-N	74	238	28	62	7	3	1	17	20	20	.261	.320	.328	73	-9	5			.977	-3	O-55	-1.4
1937	Pit-N	29	20	5	2	0	0	0	1	4	4	.100	.280	.100	7	-2	0			.800	-1	/O-4	-0.4
Total	11	1179	4259	686	1241	249	54	47	593	462	361	.291	.362	.408	98	-7	56	<u>58</u>		.976	35	*O-1060/1-10	-5.1

■ HAM SCHULTE
Schulte, Herman Joseph (b: Herman Joseph Schultehenrich)   b: 9/1/12, St.Louis, Mo.   d: 12/21/93, St.Charles, Mo.   BR/TR, 5'8.5", 158 lbs.   Deb: 4/16/40   F

YEAR	TM/L	G	AB	R	H	2B	3B	HR	RBI	BB	SO	AVG	OBP	SLG	PRO+	BR/A	SB	CS	SBR	FA	FR	G/POS	TPR
1940	Phi-N	120	436	44	103	18	2	1	21	32	30	.236	.288	.294	63	-22	3			**.980**	-10	*2-119/S-1	-2.5

■ JOHNNY SCHULTE
Schulte, John Clement   b: 9/8/1896, Fredericktown, Mo.   d: 6/28/78, St.Louis, Mo.   BL/TR, 5'11", 190 lbs.   Deb: 4/18/23   C

YEAR	TM/L	G	AB	R	H	2B	3B	HR	RBI	BB	SO	AVG	OBP	SLG	PRO+	BR/A	SB	CS	SBR	FA	FR	G/POS	TPR
1923	StL-A	7	3	1	0	0	0	0	1	4	0	.000	.571	.000	56	0	0	0	0	1.000	1	/C-1,1-1	0.1
1927	StL-N	64	156	35	45	8	2	9	32	47	19	.288	.456	.538	160	16	1			.956	3	C-59	2.1
1928	Phi-N	65	113	14	28	2	2	4	17	15	12	.248	.336	.407	90	-2	0			.949	-5	C-34	-0.5
1929	Chi-N	31	69	6	18	3	0	0	9	7	11	.261	.329	.304	58	-4	0			.978	0	C-30	-0.2
1932	StL-A	15	24	2	5	2	0	0	3	1	6	.208	.240	.292	35	-2	0			.864	-1	/C-6	-0.2
	Bos-N	10	9	1	2	0	0	1	2	2	1	.222	.364	.556	149	1	0			1.000	1	C-10	0.2
Total	5	192	374	59	98	15	4	14	64	76	49	.262	.388	.436	112	8	1	<u>0</u>		.957	-2	C-140/1-1	1.5

■ JACK SCHULTE
Schulte, John Herman Frank   b: 11/15/1881, Cincinnati, Ohio   d: 8/17/75, Roseville, Mich.   BR/TR, 5'9", 180 lbs.   Deb: 8/19/06

YEAR	TM/L	G	AB	R	H	2B	3B	HR	RBI	BB	SO	AVG	OBP	SLG	PRO+	BR/A	SB	CS	SBR	FA	FR	G/POS	TPR
1906	Bos-N	2	7	0	0	0	0	0	0	0		.000	.000	.000	-99	-2	0			1.000	-1	/S-2	-0.3

■ LEN SCHULTE
Schulte, Leonard Bernard (b: Leonard Bernard Schultehenrich)   b: 12/5/16, St.Charles, Mo.   d: 5/6/86, Orlando, Fla.   BR/TR, 5'10", 160 lbs.   Deb: 9/27/44   F

YEAR	TM/L	G	AB	R	H	2B	3B	HR	RBI	BB	SO	AVG	OBP	SLG	PRO+	BR/A	SB	CS	SBR	FA	FR	G/POS	TPR
1944	StL-A	1	0	0	0	0	0	0	0	0	0	—	1.000	—	188	0	0	0	0	.000	0	H	0.0
1945	StL-A	119	430	37	106	16	1	0	36	24	35	.247	.286	.288	64	-20	0	3	-2	.961	-8	3-71,2-37,S-14	-2.8
1946	StL-A	4	5	1	2	0	0	0	2	0	0	.400	.400	.400	118	0	0	0	0	1.000	1	/2-1,3-1	0.1
Total	3	124	435	38	108	16	1	0	38	25	35	.248	.289	.290	65	-20	0	3	-2	.962	-7	/3-72,2-38,S-14	-2.7

■ HOWIE SCHULTZ
Schultz, Howard Henry "Stretch" or "Steeple"   b: 7/3/22, St.Paul, Minn.   BR/TR, 6'6", 200 lbs.   Deb: 8/16/43

YEAR	TM/L	G	AB	R	H	2B	3B	HR	RBI	BB	SO	AVG	OBP	SLG	PRO+	BR/A	SB	CS	SBR	FA	FR	G/POS	TPR
1943	Bro-N	45	182	20	49	12	0	1	34	6	24	.269	.300	.352	88	-3	3			.986	2	1-45	-0.5
1944	Bro-N	138	526	59	134	32	3	11	83	24	67	.255	.290	.390	92	-8	6			.988	-0	*1-136	-1.6
1945	Bro-N	39	142	18	34	8	2	1	19	10	14	.239	.294	.345	78	-5	2			.984	3	1-38	-0.4
1946	Bro-N	90	249	27	63	14	1	3	27	16	34	.253	.298	.353	84	-6	0			.989	5	1-87	-0.5
1947	Bro-N	2	1	0	0	0	0	0	0	0	0	.000	.000	.000	-96	-0	0			1.000	-0	/1-1	0.0
	Phi-N	114	403	30	90	19	1	6	35	21	70	.223	.264	.320	56	-27	0			.993	-1	*1-114	-3.1
	Yr	116	404	30	90	19	1	6	35	21	70	.223	.263	.319	56	-27	0			.993	-1	*1-115	-3.1
1948	Phi-N	6	13	0	1	0	0	0	1	1	2	.077	.143	.077	-40	-3	0			1.000	0	/1-3	-0.2
	Cin-N	36	72	9	12	0	2	0	9	4	7	.167	.211	.250	25	-8	2			.982	-3	1-26	-1.1
	Yr	42	85	9	13	0	2	0	10	5	9	.153	.200	.224	15	-10	2			.984	-3	1-29	-1.3
Total	6	470	1588	163	383	85	7	24	208	82	218	.241	.281	.349	75	-60	15			.989	6	1-450	-7.4

■ JOHN SCHULTZ
Schultz, John   b: St.Louis, Mo.   Deb: 8/7/1891

YEAR	TM/L	G	AB	R	H	2B	3B	HR	RBI	BB	SO	AVG	OBP	SLG	PRO+	BR/A	SB	CS	SBR	FA	FR	G/POS	TPR
1891	StL-a	1	2	0	0	0	0	0	0	0	0	.000	.000	.000	-87	-0	0			1.000	0	/C-1	0.0

■ JOE SCHULTZ
Schultz, Joseph Charles Jr. "Dode"   b: 8/29/18, Chicago, Ill.   d: 1/10/96, St.Louis, Mo.   BL/TR, 5'11", 184 lbs.   Deb: 9/27/39   FMC

YEAR	TM/L	G	AB	R	H	2B	3B	HR	RBI	BB	SO	AVG	OBP	SLG	PRO+	BR/A	SB	CS	SBR	FA	FR	G/POS	TPR
1939	Pit-N	4	14	3	4	2	0	0	2	2	0	.286	.375	.429	117	0	0			1.000	1	/C-4	0.1
1940	Pit-N	16	36	2	7	0	1	0	4	2	1	.194	.237	.250	35	-3	0			.917	-3	C-13	-0.6
1941	Pit-N	2	2	1	1	0	0	0	0	0	0	.500	.500	.500	183	0	0			.000	0	/C-2	0.0
1943	StL-A	46	92	6	22	5	0	0	8	9	8	.239	.307	.293	74	-3	0	1	-1	.979	-5	C-26	-0.8
1944	StL-A	3	8	1	2	0	0	0	0	0	0	.250	.250	.250	41	-1	0	0	0	.818	-1	/C-3	-0.1
1945	StL-A	41	44	1	13	0	0	0	4	8	1	.295	.340	.341	93	-0	0	0	0	.941	0	C-4	0.0
1946	StL-A	42	57	1	22	4	0	0	14	11	2	.386	.485	.456	156	5	0	0	0	1.000	-5	C-17	0.1
1947	StL-A	43	38	3	7	0	0	1	4	5	4	.184	.262	.263	45	-3	0	0	0	.000	0	H	-0.3
1948	StL-A	43	37	0	7	2	0	0	6	3	5	.189	.302	.189	32	-3	0	0	0	.000	0	H	-0.3
Total	9	240	328	18	85	13	1	1	46	37	21	.259	.334	.314	81	-8	0	1		.964	-12	/C-69	-1.9

■ JOE SCHULTZ
Schultz, Joseph Charles Sr. "Germany"   b: 7/24/1893, Pittsburgh, Pa.   d: 4/13/41, Columbia, S.C.   BR/TR, 5'11.5", 172 lbs.   Deb: 9/28/12   F

YEAR	TM/L	G	AB	R	H	2B	3B	HR	RBI	BB	SO	AVG	OBP	SLG	PRO+	BR/A	SB	CS	SBR	FA	FR	G/POS	TPR
1912	Bos-N	4	12	1	3	1	0	0	4	0	2	.250	.250	.333	58	-1	0			.824	-0	/2-4	-0.1
1913	Bos-N	9	18	2	4	0	0	0	1	2	7	.222	.333	.222	59	-1	0			1.000	0	/O-5,2-1	-0.1
1915	Bro-N	56	120	13	35	3	2	0	4	10	18	.292	.346	.350	109	1	3	4	-2	.894	-4	3-27/S-1	-0.3
	Chi-N	7	8	1	2	0	0	0	0	0	2	.250	.250	.250	51	-0	0			.857	0	/2-2	0.0
	Yr	63	128	14	37	3	2	0	7	10	20	.289	.344	.344	106	1	3	4	-2	.894	-3	3-27/2-2,S-1	-0.3
1916	Pit-N	77	204	18	53	8	2	0	22	7	14	.260	.298	.319	88	-3	6			.840	-15	2-24,3-24/O-6,S-1	-1.9
1919	StL-N	88	229	24	58	9	1	2	21	11	7	.253	.287	.328	90	-3	4			1.000	-7	O-49/2-6,3-1	-1.4
1920	StL-N	99	320	38	84	5	5	0	32	21	11	.262	.308	.309	81	-8	5	4	-1	.945	-4	O-80	-2.0
1921	StL-N	92	275	37	85	20	3	6	45	15	11	.309	.347	.469	116	6	4	3	-1	.977	-2	O-67/3-3,1-2	-0.1
1922	StL-N	112	344	50	108	13	4	2	64	19	16	.314	.350	.392	96	-3	3			.976	2	O-89	-0.6
1923	StL-N	8	7	0	2	0	0	0	1	1	0	.286	.375	.286	78	-0	0			1.000	0	/O-2	0.0
1924	StL-N	12	12	0	2	0	0	0	3	3	0	.167	.333	.167	39	-1	0			1.000	-1	/O-2	-0.2
	Phi-N	88	284	35	80	15	1	5	29	20	18	.282	.329	.394	83	-7	6	2	1	.960	-6	O-76	-1.8
	Yr	100	296	35	82	15	1	5	31	23	18	.277	.329	.385	82	-8	6	2	1	.960	-7	O-78	-2.0
1925	Phi-N	24	64	10	22	6	0	0	4	11	2	.344	.382	.438	100	0	1	1	-0	.923	-2	O-20	-0.3
	Cin-N	33	62	6	20	3	1	0	13	1	1	.323	.354	.403	95	-0	0			.950	-4	O-15/2-1	-0.5
	Yr	57	126	16	42	9	1	0	17	12	3	.333	.368	.421	99	-0	1	1	-0	.932	-6	O-35/2-1	-0.8
Total	11	703	1959	235	558	83	19	15	249	116	102	.285	.327	.370	93	-21	35	<u>16</u>		.966	-42	O-411/3-55,2-38,1S	-9.3

■ JEFF SCHULZ
Schulz, Jeffrey Alan   b: 6/2/61, Evansville, Ind.   BL/TR, 6'1", 190 lbs.   Deb: 9/2/89

YEAR	TM/L	G	AB	R	H	2B	3B	HR	RBI	BB	SO	AVG	OBP	SLG	PRO+	BR/A	SB	CS	SBR	FA	FR	G/POS	TPR
1989	KC-A	7	9	0	2	0	0	0	0	0	0	.222	.222	.222	26	-1	0	0	0	1.000	-0	/O-5	-0.1
1990	KC-A	30	66	5	17	5	1	0	6	6	13	.258	.319	.364	92	-1	0	0	0	.943	-3	O-22/D-1	-0.4
1991	Pit-N	3	3	0	0	0	0	0	0	0	0	.000	.000	.000	-99	-1	0			.000	0	/H	-0.1
Total	3	40	78	5	19	5	1	0	7	6	17	.244	.298	.333	77	-2	0	0	0	.951	-4	/O-27,D-1	-0.6

■ BILL SCHUSTER
Schuster, William Charles "Broadway Bill"   b: 8/4/12, Buffalo, N.Y.   d: 6/28/87, ElMonte, Cal.   BR/TR, 5'9", 164 lbs.   Deb: 9/29/37

YEAR	TM/L	G	AB	R	H	2B	3B	HR	RBI	BB	SO	AVG	OBP	SLG	PRO+	BR/A	SB	CS	SBR	FA	FR	G/POS	TPR
1937	Pit-N	3	6	2	3	1	0	0	1	0	1	.500	.571	.500	193	1	1	0		1.000	1	/S-2	0.2

YEAR	TM/L	G	AB	R	H	2B	3B	HR	RBI	BB	SO	AVG	OBP	SLG	PRO+	BR/A	SB	CS	SBR	FA	FR	G/POS	TPR
1939	Bos-N	2	3	0	0	0	0	0	0	0	1	.000	.000	.000	-99	-1	0			.833	-0	/S-1,3-1	-0.1
1943	Chi-N	13	51	3	15	2	1	0	0	3	2	.294	.333	.373	105	0	0			.977	7	S-13	0.8
1944	Chi-N	60	154	14	34	7	1	1	14	12	16	.221	.277	.299	62	-8	4			.946	-4	S-38/2-6	-1.0
1945	*Chi-N	45	47	8	9	2	1	0	2	7	4	.191	.296	.277	61	-8	2			.949	8	S-22/2-3,3-1	0.7
Total	5	123	261	27	61	11	3	1	17	23	23	.234	.296	.310	72	-10	6			.954	11	/S-76,2-9,3-2	0.6

■ RANDY SCHWARTZ
Schwartz, Douglas Randall b: 2/9/44, Los Angeles, Cal. BL/TL, 6'3", 230 lbs. Deb: 9/8/65

YEAR	TM/L	G	AB	R	H	2B	3B	HR	RBI	BB	SO	AVG	OBP	SLG	PRO+	BR/A	SB	CS	SBR	FA	FR	G/POS	TPR
1965	KC-A	6	7	0	2	0	0	0	1	0	4	.286	.286	.286	64	-0	0	0	0	1.000	1	/1-2	0.0
1966	KC-A	10	11	0	1	0	0	0	1	1	3	.091	.167	.091	-24	-2	0	0	0	1.000	-0	/1-2	-0.2
Total	2	16	18	0	3	0	0	0	2	1	7	.167	.211	.167	10	-2	0	0	0	1.000	1	/1-4	-0.2

■ BILL SCHWARTZ
Schwartz, William August "Pop" or "Scooper Bill" b: 4/3/1864, Jamestown, Ky. d: 12/22/40, Newport, Ky. BR/TR, 6'1", 195 lbs. Deb: 5/3/1883

YEAR	TM/L	G	AB	R	H	2B	3B	HR	RBI	BB	SO	AVG	OBP	SLG	PRO+	BR/A	SB	CS	SBR	FA	FR	G/POS	TPR
1883	Col-a	2	4	0	1	0	0	0				.250	.250	.250	67	-0				.600	-1	/1-1,C-1	-0.1
1884	Cin-U	29	106	14	25	4	0	1			3	.236	.257	.302	64	-8				.837	-4	C-25/O-3,3-1	-0.9
Total	2	31	110	14	26	4	0	1			3	.236	.257	.300	64	-8				.828	-6	/C-26,O-3,3-1,1-1	-1.0

■ BILL SCHWARTZ
Schwartz, William Charles "Blab" b: 4/22/1884, Cleveland, Ohio d: 8/29/61, Nashville, Tenn. BR/TR, 6'2", 185 lbs. Deb: 5/2/04

YEAR	TM/L	G	AB	R	H	2B	3B	HR	RBI	BB	SO	AVG	OBP	SLG	PRO+	BR/A	SB	CS	SBR	FA	FR	G/POS	TPR
1904	Cle-A	24	86	5	13	2	0	0				.151	.151	.174	3	-9	4			.980	-4	1-22/3-1	-1.6

■ BILL SCHWARZ
Schwarz, William De Witt b: 1/30/1891, Birmingham, Ala. d: 6/24/49, Jacksonville, Fla TR, Deb: 8/20/14

YEAR	TM/L	G	AB	R	H	2B	3B	HR	RBI	BB	SO	AVG	OBP	SLG	PRO+	BR/A	SB	CS	SBR	FA	FR	G/POS	TPR
1914	NY-A	1	0	0	0	0	0	0	0	0	0	.000	.000	.000	-99	-0	0			1.000	0	/C-1	0.0

■ AL SCHWEITZER
Schweitzer, Albert Caspar "Cheese" b: 12/23/1882, Cleveland, Ohio d: 1/27/69, Newark, Ohio BR/TR, 5'6", 170 lbs. Deb: 4/30/08

YEAR	TM/L	G	AB	R	H	2B	3B	HR	RBI	BB	SO	AVG	OBP	SLG	PRO+	BR/A	SB	CS	SBR	FA	FR	G/POS	TPR
1908	StL-A	64	182	22	53	4	2	1	14	20		.291	.374	.352	135	8	6			.952	5	O-55	1.2
1909	StL-A	27	76	7	17	2	0	0	2	5		.224	.298	.250	79	-2	3			.933	-3	O-22	-0.6
1910	StL-A	113	379	37	87	11	2	2	37	36		.230	.303	.285	90	-4	26			.937	-4	*O-109	-1.5
1911	StL-A	76	237	31	51	11	4	0	34	43		.215	.338	.295	80	-5	12			.934	-1	O-68	-0.9
Total	4	280	874	97	208	28	8	3	87	104		.238	.327	.299	95	-3	47			.940	-3	O-254	-1.8

■ PI SCHWERT
Schwert, Pius Louis b: 11/22/1892, Angola, N.Y. d: 3/11/41, Washington, D.C. BR/TR, 5'10.5", 160 lbs. Deb: 10/6/14

YEAR	TM/L	G	AB	R	H	2B	3B	HR	RBI	BB	SO	AVG	OBP	SLG	PRO+	BR/A	SB	CS	SBR	FA	FR	G/POS	TPR
1914	NY-A	2	5	0	0	0	0	0	0	2	2	.000	.286	.000	-13	-1	0			.909	1	/C-2	0.0
1915	NY-A	9	18	6	5	3	0	0	6	1	6	.278	.316	.444	128	0	0			.972	0	/C-9	0.1
Total	2	11	23	6	5	3	0	0	6	3	8	.217	.308	.348	97	-0	0			.957	1	/C-11	0.1

■ ART SCHWIND
Schwind, Arthur Edwin b: 11/4/1889, Ft.Wayne, Ind. d: 1/13/68, Sullivan, Ill. BB/TR, 5'8", 150 lbs. Deb: 10/3/12

YEAR	TM/L	G	AB	R	H	2B	3B	HR	RBI	BB	SO	AVG	OBP	SLG	PRO+	BR/A	SB	CS	SBR	FA	FR	G/POS	TPR
1912	Bos-N	1	2	0	1	0	0	0	0	0	0	.500	.500	.500	171	0	0			.000	0	/3-1	0.0

■ JERRY SCHYPINSKI
Schypinski, Gerald Albert b: 9/16/31, Detroit, Mich. BL/TR, 5'10", 170 lbs. Deb: 8/31/55

YEAR	TM/L	G	AB	R	H	2B	3B	HR	RBI	BB	SO	AVG	OBP	SLG	PRO+	BR/A	SB	CS	SBR	FA	FR	G/POS	TPR
1955	KC-A	22	69	7	15	2	0	0	5	1	6	.217	.229	.246	27	-7	0	0	0	.932	-2	S-21/2-2	-0.8

■ MIKE SCIOSCIA
Scioscia, Michael Lorri b: 11/27/58, Upper Darby, Pa. BL/TR, 6'2", 220 lbs. Deb: 4/20/80

YEAR	TM/L	G	AB	R	H	2B	3B	HR	RBI	BB	SO	AVG	OBP	SLG	PRO+	BR/A	SB	CS	SBR	FA	FR	G/POS	TPR
1980	LA-N	54	134	8	34	5	1	1	8	12	9	.254	.315	.328	81	-3	1	0	0	.992	3	C-54	0.2
1981	*LA-N	93	290	27	80	10	0	2	29	36	18	.276	.358	.331	100	1	0	2	-1	.987	-6	C-91	1.0
1982	LA-N	129	365	31	80	11	1	5	38	44	31	.219	.305	.296	70	-14	2	0	1	.986	-7	*C-123	-1.7
1983	LA-N	12	35	3	11	3	0	1	7	5	2	.314	.400	.486	145	2	0	0	0	1.000	-3	*C-11	0.0
1984	LA-N	114	341	29	93	18	0	5	38	52	26	.273	.371	.370	110	6	2	1	0	.985	14	*C-112	2.6
1985	*LA-N	141	429	47	127	26	3	7	53	77	21	.296	.409	.420	136	25	3	3	-1	.986	2	*C-139	3.4
1986	LA-N	122	374	36	94	18	1	5	26	62	23	.251	.362	.345	103	4	3	3	-1	.982	-1	*C-119	1.0
1987	LA-N	142	461	44	122	26	1	6	38	55	23	.265	.344	.364	90	-6	7	4	-0	.989	11	*C-138	1.4
1988	*LA-N	130	408	29	105	18	0	3	35	38	31	.257	.321	.324	88	-6	0	3	-2	.991	8	*C-123	1.0
1989	LA-N★	133	408	40	102	16	0	10	44	52	29	.250	.339	.363	102	2	0	2	-1	.988	18	*C-130	2.7
1990	LA-N★	135	435	46	115	25	0	12	66	55	31	.264	.351	.405	110	7	4	1	0	.989	5	*C-132	2.1
1991	LA-N	119	345	39	91	16	2	8	40	47	32	.264	.357	.391	113	7	4	3	-1	.990	9	*C-115	2.1
1992	LA-N	117	348	19	77	16	3	3	24	32	31	.221	.289	.282	63	-17	3	2	-0	.988	11	*C-108	0.2
Total	13	1441	4373	398	1131	198	12	68	446	567	307	.259	.347	.356	99	9	29	24	-6	.988	67	*C-1395	14.8

■ LOU SCOFFIC
Scoffic, Louis "Weaser" b: 5/20/13, Herrin, Ill. BR/TR, 5'10", 182 lbs. Deb: 4/16/36

YEAR	TM/L	G	AB	R	H	2B	3B	HR	RBI	BB	SO	AVG	OBP	SLG	PRO+	BR/A	SB	CS	SBR	FA	FR	G/POS	TPR
1936	StL-N	4	7	2	3	0	0	0	2	1	2	.429	.500	.429	153	1	0			.875	-0	/O-3	0.0

■ DARYL SCONIERS
Sconiers, Daryl Anthony b: 10/3/58, San Bernardino, Cal. BL/TL, 6'2", 195 lbs. Deb: 9/13/81

YEAR	TM/L	G	AB	R	H	2B	3B	HR	RBI	BB	SO	AVG	OBP	SLG	PRO+	BR/A	SB	CS	SBR	FA	FR	G/POS	TPR
1981	Cal-A	15	52	6	14	1	1	1	7	1	10	.269	.283	.385	91	-1	0	0	0	1.000	1	1-12/D-3	-0.1
1982	Cal-A	12	13	0	2	0	0	0	2	2	1	.154	.267	.154	9	-1	0	0	0	1.000	0	/1-3,D-1	0.0
1983	Cal-A	106	314	49	86	19	3	8	46	17	41	.274	.311	.430	102	0	4	2	0	.986	-5	1-57,D-27/O-1	-0.8
1984	Cal-A	57	160	14	39	4	0	4	17	13	17	.244	.301	.344	78	-5	1	2	-1	.990	-1	1-41/D-1	-0.9
1985	Cal-A	44	98	14	28	6	1	2	12	15	18	.286	.381	.429	122	3	2	1	0	.973	-1	D-20/1-6	0.2
Total	5	234	637	83	169	30	5	15	84	48	87	.265	.317	.399	97	-3	7	5	-1	.989	-6	1-119/D-52,O-1	-1.7

■ SCOTT
Scott Deb: 7/16/1884

YEAR	TM/L	G	AB	R	H	2B	3B	HR	RBI	BB	SO	AVG	OBP	SLG	PRO+	BR/A	SB	CS	SBR	FA	FR	G/POS	TPR
1884	Bal-U	13	53	10	12	1	1	1			2	.226	.255	.340	71	-4				.909	-2	O-13/3-1	-0.5

■ TONY SCOTT
Scott, Anthony b: 9/18/51, Cincinnati, Ohio BB/TR, 6', 175 lbs. Deb: 9/1/73

YEAR	TM/L	G	AB	R	H	2B	3B	HR	RBI	BB	SO	AVG	OBP	SLG	PRO+	BR/A	SB	CS	SBR	FA	FR	G/POS	TPR
1973	Mon-N	11	1	2	0	0	0	0	0	0	1	.000	.000	.000	-97	-0	0	0	0	.000	-2	/O-3	-0.2
1974	Mon-N	19	7	2	2	0	0	0	1	1	3	.286	.375	.286	82	-0	1	1	-0	1.000	-5	O-16	-0.6
1975	Mon-N	92	143	19	26	4	2	0	11	12	38	.182	.259	.238	37	-12	5	6	-2	.962	-9	O-71	-2.6
1977	StL-N	95	292	38	85	16	3	3	41	33	48	.291	.369	.397	107	4	13	10	-2	.996	5	O-89	0.3
1978	StL-N	96	219	28	50	5	2	1	14	14	41	.228	.281	.283	59	-12	5	6	-2	.946	-9	O-77	-2.7
1979	StL-N	153	587	69	152	22	10	6	68	34	92	.259	.305	.361	80	-16	37	17	1	.984	17	*O-151	-0.5
1980	StL-N	143	415	51	104	19	3	0	28	35	68	.251	.310	.311	72	-15	22	10	1	**.997**	1	*O-134	-2.0
1981	StL-N	45	176	21	40	5	2	2	17	5	22	.227	.253	.313	58	-10	10	7	-1	1.000	1	O-44	-1.3
	*Hou-N	55	225	28	66	13	2	2	22	15	32	.293	.338	.396	113	3	8	3	1	.985	1	O-55	0.3
	Yr	100	401	49	106	18	4	4	39	20	54	.264	.301	.359	88	-7	18	10	-1	.992	2	O-99	-1.0
1982	Hou-N	132	460	43	110	16	3	1	29	15	56	.239	.265	.293	61	-26	18	4	3	.982	-3	*O-129	-3.1
1983	Hou-N	80	186	20	42	6	1	2	17	11	39	.226	.269	.301	62	-10	5	4	-1	1.000	-12	O-61	-2.6
1984	Hou-N	25	21	2	4	1	0	0		4	3	.190	.320	.238	63	-1	0	0	0	1.000	-1	/O-6	-0.2
	Mon-N	45	71	8	18	4	0	0	5	7	21	.254	.321	.310	81	-2	1	1	-0	1.000	-2	O-17	-0.4
	Yr	70	92	10	22	5	0	0	5	11	24	.239	.320	.293	78	-3	1	1	-0	1.000	-3	O-23	-0.6
Total	11	991	2803	331	699	111	28	17	253	186	464	.249	.300	.327	75	-97	125	69	-4	.986	-18	O-853	-15.6

■ DONNIE SCOTT
Scott, Donald Malcolm b: 8/16/61, Dunedin, Fla. BB/TR, 5'11", 185 lbs. Deb: 9/30/83

YEAR	TM/L	G	AB	R	H	2B	3B	HR	RBI	BB	SO	AVG	OBP	SLG	PRO+	BR/A	SB	CS	SBR	FA	FR	G/POS	TPR
1983	Tex-A	2	4	0	0	0	0	0	0	0	0	.000	.000	.000	-99	-1	0	0	0	1.000	1	/C-2	0.0
1984	Tex-A	81	235	16	52	9	0	3	20	20	44	.221	.282	.298	59	-13	0	1	-1	.974	4	C-80	-0.6
1985	Sea-A	80	185	18	41	13	0	4	23	15	41	.222	.280	.357	72	-7	1	1	-0	.981	-1	C-74	-1.2
1991	Cin-N	10	19	0	3	0	0	0	0	2	2	.158	.158	.158	-11	-3	0	0	0	1.000	-3	/C-8	-0.6
Total	4	173	443	34	96	22	0	7	43	35	87	.217	.274	.314	60	-24	1	2	-1	.977	-5	C-164	-2.4

■ PETE SCOTT
Scott, Floyd John b: 12/21/1898, Woodland, Cal. d: 5/3/53, Daly City, Cal. BR/TR, 5'11.5", 175 lbs. Deb: 4/13/26

YEAR	TM/L	G	AB	R	H	2B	3B	HR	RBI	BB	SO	AVG	OBP	SLG	PRO+	BR/A	SB	CS	SBR	FA	FR	G/POS	TPR
1926	Chi-N	77	189	34	54	7	3	1	34	22	31	.286	.363	.413	107	2	3			.968	-1	O-59/3-1	-0.2
1927	Chi-N	71	156	28	49	18	1	0	21	19	18	.314	.392	.442	123	5	1			.986	-2	O-36	0.1
1928	Pit-N	60	177	33	55	16	4	5	33	18	14	.311	.378	.497	122	5	1			.979	2	O-42/1-8	0.4
Total	3	208	522	95	158	41	8	6	88	59	63	.303	.377	.450	117	13	5			.976	-1	O-137/1-8,3-1	0.3

■ GARY SCOTT
Scott, Gary Thomas b: 8/22/68, New Rochelle, N.Y. BR/TR, 6', 175 lbs. Deb: 4/9/91

YEAR	TM/L	G	AB	R	H	2B	3B	HR	RBI	BB	SO	AVG	OBP	SLG	PRO+	BR/A	SB	CS	SBR	FA	FR	G/POS	TPR
1991	Chi-N	31	79	8	13	3	0	1	5	13	14	.165	.305	.241	53	-5	0	1	-1	.969	2	3-31	-0.4

YEAR	TM/L	G	AB	R	H	2B	3B	HR	RBI	BB	SO	AVG	OBP	SLG	PRO+	BR/A	SB	CS	SBR	FA	FR	G/POS	TPR
1992	Chi-N	36	96	8	15	2	0	2	11	5	14	.156	.198	.240	23	-10	0	1	-1	.922	-2	3-29/S-2	-1.4
Total	2	67	175	16	28	5	0	3	16	18	28	.160	.250	.240	20		0	2	-1	.946	-0	/3-60,S-2	-1.8

■ GEORGE SCOTT   Scott, George Charles "Boomer"   b: 3/23/44, Greenville, Miss.   BR/TR, 6'2", 215 lbs.   Deb: 4/12/66

YEAR	TM/L	G	AB	R	H	2B	3B	HR	RBI	BB	SO	AVG	OBP	SLG	PRO+	BR/A	SB	CS	SBR	FA	FR	G/POS	TPR
1966	Bos-A★	162	601	73	147	18	7	27	90	65	152	.245	.326	.433	105	4	4	0	1	.991	3	*1-158/3-5	-0.3
1967	*Bos-A	159	565	74	171	21	7	19	82	63	119	.303	.377	.465	136	26	10	8	-2	.987	-5	*1-152/3-2	1.1
1968	Bos-A	124	350	23	60	14	0	3	25	26	88	.171	.239	.237	42	-24	3	5	-2	.987	1	*1-112/3-6	-3.7
1969	Bos-A	152	549	63	139	14	5	16	52	61	74	.253	.332	.384	95	-4	4	3	-1	.954	-6	*3-109,1-53	-1.4
1970	Bos-A	127	480	50	142	24	5	16	63	44	95	.296	.357	.467	117	11	4	11	-5	.934	-8	3-68,1-59	-0.9
1971	Bos-A	146	537	72	141	16	4	24	78	41	102	.263	.321	.441	106	3	0	3	-2	.992	-7	*1-143	-2.1
1972	Mil-A	152	578	71	154	24	4	20	88	52	130	.266	.322	.426	123	15	16	4	2	.992	-5	*1-139,3-23	0.0
1973	Mil-A	158	604	98	185	30	4	24	107	61	94	.306	.372	.488	144	34	9	5	-0	.994	7	*1-157/D-1	2.8
1974	Mil-A	158	604	74	170	36	2	17	82	59	90	.281	.348	.432	124	18	9	9	-3	**.992**	8	*1-148/D-9	1.3
1975	Mil-A★	158	617	86	176	26	4	**36**	**109**	51	97	.285	.343	.515	139	29	6	5	-1	.989	1	*1-144,D-12/3-5	2.1
1976	Mil-A	156	606	73	166	21	5	18	77	53	118	.274	.337	.414	122	15	0	1	-1	.991	-2	*1-155	0.2
1977	Bos-A★	157	584	103	157	26	5	33	95	57	112	.269	.340	.500	112	8	1	1	-0	.985	0	*1-157	-0.1
1978	Bos-A	120	412	51	96	16	4	12	54	44	86	.233	.307	.379	83	-10	1	1	-0	.991	-8	*1-113/D-7	-2.6
1979	Bos-A	45	156	18	35	9	1	4	23	17	22	.224	.301	.372	76	-5	0	0	-0	.986	-2	1-41	-1.0
	KC-A	44	146	19	39	8	2	1	20	12	32	.267	.331	.370	87	-3	1	1	-0	.989	-3	1-41/3-1,D-2	-0.8
	NY-A	16	44	9	14	3	1	1	6	2	7	.318	.348	.500	128	2	1	0	0	1.000	-0	D-15/1-1	0.1
	Yr	105	346	46	88	20	4	6	49	31	61	.254	.319	.387	87	-6	2	1	0	.987	-5	1-83,D-17/3-1	-1.7
Total	14	2034	7433	957	1992	306	60	271	1051	699	1418	.268	.335	.435	113	119	69	57	-14	.990	-25	*1-1773,3-219/D-46	-5.3

■ JIM SCOTT   Scott, James Walter   b: 9/22/1888, Shenandoah, Pa.   d: 5/12/72, S.Pasadena, Fla.   BR/TR, 5'9.5", 165 lbs.   Deb: 4/22/14

YEAR	TM/L	G	AB	R	H	2B	3B	HR	RBI	BB	SO	AVG	OBP	SLG	PRO+	BR/A	SB	CS	SBR	FA	FR	G/POS	TPR
1914	Pit-F	8	24	2	6	1	0	0	1	5	0	.250	.379	.292	85	-1	1			.800	-3	/S-8	-0.3

■ JOHN SCOTT   Scott, John Henry   b: 1/24/52, Jackson, Miss.   BR/TR, 6'2", 165 lbs.   Deb: 9/7/74

YEAR	TM/L	G	AB	R	H	2B	3B	HR	RBI	BB	SO	AVG	OBP	SLG	PRO+	BR/A	SB	CS	SBR	FA	FR	G/POS	TPR
1974	SD-N	14	15	3	1	0	0	0	0	0	4	.067	.067	.067	-65	-3	1	0	0	1.000	-1	/O-8	-0.4
1975	SD-N	25	9	6	0	0	0	0	0	0	2	.000	.000	.000	-99	-2	2	0	1	1.000	-1	/O-1	-0.3
1977	Tor-A	79	233	26	56	9	0	2	15	8	39	.240	.266	.305	54	-15	10	8	-1	.963	-5	O-67/D-2	-2.4
Total	3	118	257	35	57	9	0	2	15	8	45	.222	.245	.280	43	-21	13	8	-1	.965	-6	/O-76,D-2	-3.1

■ LE GRANT SCOTT   Scott, Le Grant Edward   b: 7/25/10, Cleveland, Ohio   d: 11/12/93, Birmingham, Ala.   BL/TL, 5'8.5", 170 lbs.   Deb: 4/19/39

YEAR	TM/L	G	AB	R	H	2B	3B	HR	RBI	BB	SO	AVG	OBP	SLG	PRO+	BR/A	SB	CS	SBR	FA	FR	G/POS	TPR
1939	Phi-N	76	232	31	65	15	1	1	26	22	14	.280	.343	.366	93	-2	5			.959	1	O-55	-0.3

■ EVERETT SCOTT   Scott, Lewis Everett "Deacon"   b: 11/19/1892, Bluffton, Ind.   d: 11/2/60, Fort Wayne, Ind.   BR/TR, 5'8", 148 lbs.   Deb: 4/14/14

YEAR	TM/L	G	AB	R	H	2B	3B	HR	RBI	BB	SO	AVG	OBP	SLG	PRO+	BR/A	SB	CS	SBR	FA	FR	G/POS	TPR
1914	Bos-A	144	539	66	129	15	6	2	37	32	43	.239	.286	.301	76	-17	9	14	-6	.949	-11	*S-143	-2.4
1915	*Bos-A	100	359	25	72	11	0	0	28	17	21	.201	.237	.231	41	-27	4	7	-3	.961	4	*S-100	-2.0
1916	*Bos-A	123	366	37	85	19	2	0	27	23	24	.232	.283	.295	73	-13	8			**.967**	7	*S-121/2-1,3-1	0.0
1917	Bos-A	157	528	40	127	24	7	0	50	20	46	.241	.268	.313	78	-16	12			**.953**	8	*S-157	-0.1
1918	*Bos-A	126	443	40	98	11	5	0	43	12	16	.221	.242	.269	55	-26	11			**.976**	18	*S-126	-0.3
1919	Bos-A	138	507	41	141	19	0	0	38	19	26	.278	.306	.316	79	-15	8			**.976**	7	*S-138	0.0
1920	Bos-A	154	569	41	153	21	12	0	61	21	15	.269	.300	.369	80	-19	4	11	-5	**.973**	17	*S-154	0.6
1921	Bos-A	154	576	65	151	21	9	1	62	27	21	.262	.295	.335	62	-34	5	9	-4	**.972**	**38**	*S-154	1.4
1922	*NY-A	154	557	64	150	23	5	3	45	23	22	.269	.304	.345	67	-27	2	3	-1	**.966**	17	*S-154	0.5
1923	*NY-A	152	533	48	131	16	4	6	60	13	19	.246	.266	.325	54	-37	1	3	-2	**.961**	-11	*S-152	-3.5
1924	NY-A	153	548	56	137	12	6	4	64	21	15	.250	.281	.316	53	-40	3	7	-3	.966	10	*S-153	-1.6
1925	NY-A	22	60	3	13	0	0	0	4	2	2	.217	.242	.217	17	-8	0	1	-1	.988	5	S-18	-0.3
	Was-A	33	103	10	28	6	1	0	18	4	4	.272	.299	.350	65	-6	1	2	-1	.932	3	S-30/3-2	-0.1
	Yr	55	163	13	41	6	1	0	22	6	6	.252	.279	.301	48	-13	1	3	-2	.952	8	S-48/3-2	-0.4
1926	Chi-A	40	143	15	36	10	1	0	13	9	8	.252	.296	.336	67	-7	1	3	-2	.955	5	S-39	0.0
	Cin-N	4	6	1	4	0	0	0	0	0	0	.667	.667	.667	267	1	0			.875	0	/S-4	0.2
Total	13	1654	5837	552	1455	208	58	20	551	243	282	.249	.281	.315	65	-291	69	60		.965	115	*S-1643/3-3,2-1	-7.6

■ MILT SCOTT   Scott, Milton Parker "Mikado Milt"   b: 1/17/1866, Chicago, Ill.   d: 11/3/38, Baltimore, Md.   BR, 5'9", 160 lbs.   Deb: 9/30/1882

YEAR	TM/L	G	AB	R	H	2B	3B	HR	RBI	BB	SO	AVG	OBP	SLG	PRO+	BR/A	SB	CS	SBR	FA	FR	G/POS	TPR
1882	Chi-N	1	5	1	2	0	0	0	0	0	0	.400	.400	.400	151	0				1.000	0	/1-1	0.0
1884	Det-N	110	438	29	108	17	5	3	50	9	62	.247	.262	.329	90	-5				.968	-1	*1-110	-1.7
1885	Det-N	38	148	14	39	7	0	0	12	4	16	.264	.283	.311	92	-2				.967	2	1-38	-0.4
	Pit-a	55	210	15	52	7	1	0	18	5		.248	.272	.290	79	-5				.986	3	1-55	-0.8
1886	Bal-a	137	484	48	92	11	4	2	52	22		.190	.239	.242	52	-26	11			.974	8	*1-137/P-1	-3.0
Total	4	341	1285	107	293	42	10	5	132	40	78	.228	.257	.288	74	-38	11			.973	12	1-341/P-1	-5.9

■ DICK SCOTT   Scott, Richard Edward   b: 7/19/62, Ellsworth, Maine   BR/TR, 6'1", 170 lbs.   Deb: 5/19/89

YEAR	TM/L	G	AB	R	H	2B	3B	HR	RBI	BB	SO	AVG	OBP	SLG	PRO+	BR/A	SB	CS	SBR	FA	FR	G/POS	TPR
1989	Oak-A	3	2	0	0	0	0	0	0	0	0	.000	.000	.000	-99	-1	0	0	0	.000	0	/S-3	-0.1

■ RODNEY SCOTT   Scott, Rodney Darrell   b: 10/16/53, Indianapolis, Ind.   BB/TR, 6', 160 lbs.   Deb: 4/11/75

YEAR	TM/L	G	AB	R	H	2B	3B	HR	RBI	BB	SO	AVG	OBP	SLG	PRO+	BR/A	SB	CS	SBR	FA	FR	G/POS	TPR
1975	KC-A	48	15	13	1	0	0	0	0	1	3	.067	.125	.067	-43	-3	4	2	0	1.000	6	D-22/2-9,S-8,R-0	0.2
1976	Mon-N	7	10	3	4	0	0	0	0	1	1	.400	.455	.400	138	1	2	0	1	1.000	-0	/2-6,S-3	0.1
1977	Oak-A	133	364	56	95	4	4	0	20	43	50	.261	.344	.294	77	-10	33	18	-1	.963	-30	2-71,S-70/3-5,0D	-3.2
1978	Chi-N	78	227	41	64	5	1	0	15	43	41	.282	.403	.313	91	-0	27	10	2	.929	-9	3-59,O-10/2-6,S-6	-0.8
1979	Mon-N	151	562	69	134	12	5	3	42	66	82	.238	.321	.294	69	-22	39	12	5	.980	-15	*2-113,S-39	-2.1
1980	Mon-N	154	567	84	127	13	**13**	0	46	70	75	.224	.310	.293	69	-22	63	13	11	.982	-16	*2-129,S-21	-1.7
1981	*Mon-N	95	336	43	69	9	3	0	26	50	35	.205	.310	.250	60	-16	30	7	5	.983	-15	2-93	-2.2
1982	Mon-N	14	25	2	5	0	0	0	1	3	2	.200	.286	.200	37	-2	5	0	2	.971	-1	2-12	-0.1
	NY-A	10	26	5	5	0	0	0	0	5	2	.192	.310	.192	39	-2	2	0	1	.963	1	/S-6,2-4	0.0
Total	8	690	2132	316	504	43	26	3	150	281	291	.236	.328	.285	71	-77	205	62	24	.979	-81	2-443,S-153/3DO	-9.8

■ JIM SCRANTON   Scranton, James Dean   b: 4/5/60, Torrance, Cal.   BR/TR, 6', 175 lbs.   Deb: 9/5/84

YEAR	TM/L	G	AB	R	H	2B	3B	HR	RBI	BB	SO	AVG	OBP	SLG	PRO+	BR/A	SB	CS	SBR	FA	FR	G/POS	TPR
1984	KC-A	2	2	0	0	0	0	0	0	0	0	.000	.000	.000	-99	-1	0	0	0	1.000	-1	/S-1,3-1	-0.1
1985	KC-A	6	4	1	0	0	0	0	0	0	0	.000	.000	.000	-99	-1	0	0	0	1.000	2	/S-5	0.1
Total	2	8	6	1	0	0	0	0	0	0	0	.000	.000	.000	-99	-1	0	0	0	1.000	2	/S-6,3-1	0.0

■ CHUCK SCRIVENER   Scrivener, Wayne Allison   b: 10/3/47, Alexandria, Va.   BR/TR, 5'9", 170 lbs.   Deb: 9/18/75

YEAR	TM/L	G	AB	R	H	2B	3B	HR	RBI	BB	SO	AVG	OBP	SLG	PRO+	BR/A	SB	CS	SBR	FA	FR	G/POS	TPR
1975	Det-A	4	16	0	4	1	0	0	0	1	1	.250	.250	.313	56	-1	1	0	0	1.000	-2	/3-3,S-2	-0.3
1976	Det-A	80	222	28	49	7	1	2	16	19	34	.221	.282	.288	65	-10	4	4	0	.976	7	2-43,S-37/3-5	0.4
1977	Det-A	61	72	10	6	0	1	0	2	4	9	.083	.143	.083	-35	-13	0	0	0	.981	10	S-50/2-8,3-3	-0.1
Total	3	145	310	38	59	8	2	2	18	24	44	.190	.249	.242	40	-24	5	4	0	.970	15	/S-89,2-51,3-11	-0.0

■ TONY SCRUGGS   Scruggs, Anthony Raymond   b: 3/19/66, Riverside, Cal.   BR/TR, 6'1", 210 lbs.   Deb: 4/8/91

YEAR	TM/L	G	AB	R	H	2B	3B	HR	RBI	BB	SO	AVG	OBP	SLG	PRO+	BR/A	SB	CS	SBR	FA	FR	G/POS	TPR
1991	Tex-A	5	6	1	0	0	0	0	0	0	1	.000	.000	.000	-99	-1	0	0	0	1.000	-1	/O-5	-0.3

■ KEN SEARS   Sears, Kenneth Eugene "Ziggy"   b: 7/6/17, Streator, Ill.   d: 7/17/68, Bridgeport, Tex.   BL/TR, 6'1", 200 lbs.   Deb: 5/2/43

YEAR	TM/L	G	AB	R	H	2B	3B	HR	RBI	BB	SO	AVG	OBP	SLG	PRO+	BR/A	SB	CS	SBR	FA	FR	G/POS	TPR
1943	NY-A	60	187	22	52	7	2	2	22	11	18	.278	.328	.348	97	-1	1	3	-2	.974	1	C-50	0.2
1946	StL-A	7	15	1	5	0	0	0	1	3	0	.333	.444	.333	114	1	0	0	0	1.000	-3	/C-4	-0.2
Total	2	67	202	23	57	7	2	2	23	14	18	.282	.338	.347	99	-0	1	3	-2	.975	-2	/C-54	0.0

■ JIMMY SEBRING   Sebring, James Dennison   b: 3/22/1882, Liberty, Pa.   d: 12/22/09, Williamsport, Pa.   BL/TR, 6', 180 lbs.   Deb: 9/8/02

YEAR	TM/L	G	AB	R	H	2B	3B	HR	RBI	BB	SO	AVG	OBP	SLG	PRO+	BR/A	SB	CS	SBR	FA	FR	G/POS	TPR
1902	Pit-N	19	80	15	26	4	0	2	15	5		.325	.365	.475	153	5	2			.974	4	O-19	0.7
1903	*Pit-N	124	506	71	140	16	13	4	64	32		.277	.325	.383	98	-3	20			.927	7	*O-124	-0.3
1904	Pit-N	80	305	28	82	11	7	0	32	17		.269	.307	.351	100	-1	8			.959	9	O-80	0.3
	Cin-N	56	222	22	50	9	2	0	24	14		.225	.271	.284	65	-9	8			1.000	4	O-56	-1.0
	Yr	136	527	50	132	20	9	0	56	31		.250	.292	.323	85	-10	16			.974	12	*O-136	-0.7

YEAR	TM/L	G	AB	R	H	2B	3B	HR	RBI	BB	SO	AVG	OBP	SLG	PRO+	BR/A	SB	CS	SBR	FA	FR	G/POS	TPR
1905	Cin-N	58	217	31	62	10	5	2	28	14		.286	.329	.406	107	1	11			.885	-6	O-56	-0.8
1909	Bro-N	25	81	11	8	1	1	0	5	11		.099	.207	.136	7	-9	3			.951	-2	O-25	-1.3
	Was-A	1	0	0	0	0	0	0	0	0		—	—	—	—	-0	0	0		.000	-1	/O-1	-0.1
Total	5	363	1411	178	368	51	32	6	168	93		.261	.308	.355	93	-16	52			.945	14	O-361	-2.5

■ FRANK SECORY
Secory, Frank Edward   b: 8/24/12, Mason City, Iowa   d: 4/7/95, Port Huron, Mich.   BR/TR, 6'1", 200 lbs.   Deb: 4/28/40   U

YEAR	TM/L	G	AB	R	H	2B	3B	HR	RBI	BB	SO	AVG	OBP	SLG	PRO+	BR/A	SB	CS	SBR	FA	FR	G/POS	TPR
1940	Det-A	1	1	0	0	0	0	0	0	0	1	.000	.000	.000	-91	-0	0	0	0	.000	0	H	0.0
1942	Cin-N	2	5	1	0	0	0	0	1	3	2	.000	.375	.000	14	-0	0	0	0	.857	0	/O-2	0.0
1944	Chi-N	22	56	10	18	1	0	4	17	6	8	.321	.387	.554	163	5	1			1.000	0	O-17	0.4
1945	*Chi-N	35	57	4	9	1	0	0	6	2	7	.158	.186	.175	1	-8	0			1.000	-1	/O-12	-1.0
1946	Chi-N	33	43	6	10	3	0	3	12	6	6	.233	.327	.512	139	2	0			.833	-3	/O-9	-0.1
Total	5	93	162	21	37	5	0	7	36	17	24	.228	.302	.389	95	-2	1	0		.964	-4	/O-40	-0.7

■ CHARLIE SEE
See, Charles Henry "Chad"   b: 10/13/1896, Pleasantville, N.Y.   d: 7/19/48, Bridgeport, Conn.   BL/TR, 5'10.5", 175 lbs.   Deb: 8/6/19

YEAR	TM/L	G	AB	R	H	2B	3B	HR	RBI	BB	SO	AVG	OBP	SLG	PRO+	BR/A	SB	CS	SBR	FA	FR	G/POS	TPR
1919	Cin-N	8	14	1	4	0	0	0	1	1	0	.286	.333	.286	89	-0	0			.833	-1	/O-4	-0.2
1920	Cin-N	47	82	9	25	4	0	0	15	1	0	.305	.329	.354	97	-0	2	4	-2	1.000	3	O-17/P-1	-0.1
1921	Cin-N	37	106	11	26	5	1	1	7	7	5	.245	.298	.340	72	-4	3	2	-0	.954	-0	O-30	-0.7
Total	3	92	202	21	55	9	1	1	23	9	12	.272	.313	.342	83	-5	5	6		.967	1	/O-51,P-1	-1.0

■ LARRY SEE
See, Ralph Laurence   b: 6/20/60, Norwalk, Cal.   BR/TR, 6'1", 195 lbs.   Deb: 9/3/86

YEAR	TM/L	G	AB	R	H	2B	3B	HR	RBI	BB	SO	AVG	OBP	SLG	PRO+	BR/A	SB	CS	SBR	FA	FR	G/POS	TPR
1986	LA-N	13	20	1	5	2	0	0	2	0	7	.250	.318	.350	90	-0	0	0	0	.979	1	/1-9	0.0
1988	Tex-A	13	23	0	3	0	0	0	0	1	8	.130	.167	.130	-15	-3	0	0	0	1.000	-0	/C-2,1-2/3-1,D-7	-0.4
Total	2	26	43	1	8	2	0	0	2	3	15	.186	.239	.233	32	-4	0	0	0	.967	1	/1-11,D-7,C-2,3-1	-0.4

■ BOB SEEDS
Seeds, Ira Robert "Suitcase Bob"   b: 2/24/07, Ringgold, Tex.   d: 10/28/93, Erick, Okla.   BR/TR, 6', 180 lbs.   Deb: 4/19/30

YEAR	TM/L	G	AB	R	H	2B	3B	HR	RBI	BB	SO	AVG	OBP	SLG	PRO+	BR/A	SB	CS	SBR	FA	FR	G/POS	TPR
1930	Cle-A	85	277	37	79	11	3	3	32	12	22	.285	.315	.379	72	-12	1	3	-2	.953	2	O-70	-1.5
1931	Cle-A	48	134	26	41	4	1	1	10	11	11	.306	.359	.373	88	-2	1	0	0	.966	-2	O-33/1-2	-0.6
1932	Cle-A	2	4	0	0	0	0	0	0	0	0	.000	.000	.000	-94	-1	0	0	0	.000	-0	/O-1	-0.1
	Chi-A	116	434	53	126	18	6	2	45	31	37	.290	.342	.373	91	-6	5	7	-3	.964	-9	*O-112	-2.2
	Yr	118	438	53	126	18	6	2	45	31	37	.288	.339	.370	89	-7	5	7	-3	.964	-9	*O-113	-2.4
1933	Bos-A	82	230	26	56	13	4	0	23	21	20	.243	.310	.335	71	-10	1	3	-2	.985	-5	1-41,O-32	-2.0
1934	Bos-A	8	6	0	1	0	0	0	1	0	1	.167	.167	.167	-13	-1	0	0	0	.000	-0	/O-1	-0.1
	Cle-A	61	186	28	46	8	1	0	18	21	13	.247	.327	.301	62	-10	2	1	0	.977	-4	O-48	-1.5
	Yr	69	192	28	47	8	1	0	19	21	14	.245	.322	.297	59	-11	2	1	0	.977	-4	O-49	-1.6
1936	*NY-A	13	42	12	11	1	0	4	10	5	3	.262	.340	.571	126	1	3	1	0	1.000	1	/O-9,3-3	0.2
1938	NY-N	81	296	35	86	12	3	9	52	20	33	.291	.338	.443	112	4	0			.987	-5	O-76	-0.3
1939	NY-N	63	173	33	46	5	1	5	26	2	31	.266	.352	.393	99	0	1			.975	-8	O-50	-0.9
1940	NY-N	56	155	18	45	5	2	4	16	17	19	.290	.371	.426	118	4	0			.985	-4	O-40	-0.4
Total	9	615	1937	268	537	77	21	28	233	160	190	.277	.336	.382	89	-32	14	15		.970	-35	O-472/1-43,3-3	-9.3

■ PAT SEEREY
Seerey, James Patrick   b: 3/17/23, Wilburton, Okla.   d: 4/28/86, Jennings, Mo.   BR/TR, 5'10", 200 lbs.   Deb: 6/9/43

YEAR	TM/L	G	AB	R	H	2B	3B	HR	RBI	BB	SO	AVG	OBP	SLG	PRO+	BR/A	SB	CS	SBR	FA	FR	G/POS	TPR
1943	Cle-A	26	72	8	16	3	0	1	5	4	19	.222	.263	.306	70	-3	0	0	0	.974	1	O-16	-0.3
1944	Cle-A	101	342	39	80	16	0	15	39	19	99	.234	.276	.412	99	-3	0	2	-1	.986	1	O-86	-0.8
1945	Cle-A	126	414	56	98	22	2	14	56	66	97	.237	.342	.401	120	11	1	2	-1	.975	-15	*O-117	-1.2
1946	Cle-A	117	404	57	91	17	2	26	62	65	101	.225	.334	.470	131	15	2	3	-1	.981	-8	*O-115	0.4
1947	Cle-A	82	216	24	37	4	1	11	29	34	66	.171	.284	.352	78	-7	0	1	-1	.957	-8	O-68	-1.9
1948	Cle-A	10	23	7	6	0	0	1	6	7	8	.261	.433	.391	123	1	0	0	0	1.000	-2	/O-7	-0.1
	Chi-A	95	340	44	78	11	0	18	64	61	94	.229	.347	.421	107	3	0	0	0	.981	-4	O-93	-0.2
	Yr	105	363	51	84	11	0	19	70	68	102	.231	.353	.419	108	4	0	0	0	.982	-2	*O-100	-0.3
1949	Chi-A	4	4	1	0	0	0	0	0	1	4	.000	.429	.000	19	-0	0	0	0	1.000	-1	/O-2	-0.1
Total	7	561	1815	236	406	73	5	86	261	259	485	.224	.321	.412	109	16	3	8	-4	.978	-27	O-504	-4.2

■ EMMETT SEERY
Seery, John Emmett   b: 2/13/1861, Princeville, Ill.   d: 8/7/30, Saranac Lake, N.Y.   BL/TR,   Deb: 4/17/1884

YEAR	TM/L	G	AB	R	H	2B	3B	HR	RBI	BB	SO	AVG	OBP	SLG	PRO+	BR/A	SB	CS	SBR	FA	FR	G/POS	TPR
1884	Bal-U	105	463	113	144	25	7	2	20			.311	.340	.408	114	-7				.828	7	*O-103/C-3,3-2	-0.1
	KC-U	1	4	2	2	1	0	0	1			.500	.600	.750	353	1				.000	-0	/O-1	0.1
	Yr	106	467	115	146	26	7	2	21			.313	.342	.411	116	-6				.828	6	*O-104/C-3,3-2	-0.1
1885	StL-N	59	216	20	35	7	0	1	14	16	37	.162	.220	.208	42	-13				.874	5	O-59/3-1	-0.9
1886	StL-N	126	453	73	108	22	6	2	48	57	82	.238	.324	.327	105	5	24			.883	-5	*O-126/P-2	-0.2
1887	Ind-N	122	465	104	104	18	15	4	28	71	68	.224	.331	.353	93	-2	48			.891	7	*O-122/S-1	0.2
1888	Ind-N	133	500	87	110	20	10	5	50	64	73	.220	.316	.330	104	4	80			.939	1	*O-133/S-1	0.9
1889	Ind-N	127	526	123	165	26	12	8	59	67	59	.314	.401	.454	136	27	19			.909	1	*O-127	2.1
1890	Bro-P	104	394	78	88	12	7	1	60	70	36	.223	.348	.297	69	-17	44			.894	7	*O-104	-1.1
1891	Cin-a	97	372	77	106	15	10	4	36	81	52	.285	.423	.411	128	15	19			.898	3	*O-97	1.3
1892	Lou-N	42	154	18	31	6	1	0	15	29	21	.201	.309	.253	77	-3	6			.961	3	O-42	-0.7
Total	9	916	3547	695	893	152	68	27	300	471	426	.252	.345	.356	104	11	240			.896	36	O-914/3-3,C-3,SP	2.1

■ KEVIN SEFCIK
Sefcik, Kevin John   b: 2/10/71, Tinley Park, Ill.   BR/TR, 5'11", 175 lbs.   Deb: 9/8/95

YEAR	TM/L	G	AB	R	H	2B	3B	HR	RBI	BB	SO	AVG	OBP	SLG	PRO+	BR/A	SB	CS	SBR	FA	FR	G/POS	TPR
1995	Phi-N	5	4	1	0	0	0	0	0	0	2	.000	.000	.000	-99	-1	0	0	0	1.000	0	/3-2	-0.1
1996	Phi-N	44	116	10	33	5	3	0	9	9	16	.284	.346	.379	89	-2	3	0	1	.986	1	S-21,3-20/2-1	0.1
Total	2	49	120	11	33	5	3	0	9	9	18	.275	.336	.367	83	-3	3	0	1	.875	1	/3-22,S-21,2-1	0.0

■ KAL SEGRIST
Segrist, Kal Hill   b: 4/14/31, Greenville, Tex.   BR/TR, 6', 180 lbs.   Deb: 7/16/52

YEAR	TM/L	G	AB	R	H	2B	3B	HR	RBI	BB	SO	AVG	OBP	SLG	PRO+	BR/A	SB	CS	SBR	FA	FR	G/POS	TPR
1952	NY-A	13	23	3	1	0	0	0	1	3	1	.043	.154	.043	-46	-5	0	0	0	.971	0	2-11/3-1	-0.4
1955	Bal-A	7	9	1	3	0	0	0	0	3	0	.333	.455	.333	123	0	0	0	0	1.000	0	/3-3,1-1,2-1	0.1
Total	2	20	32	4	4	0	0	0	1	5	1	.125	.243	.125	-4	-4	0	0	0	.971	0	/2-12,3-4,1-1	-0.3

■ DAVID SEGUI
Segui, David Vincent   b: 7/19/66, Kansas City, Kan.   BB/TL, 6'1", 170 lbs.   Deb: 5/8/90   F

YEAR	TM/L	G	AB	R	H	2B	3B	HR	RBI	BB	SO	AVG	OBP	SLG	PRO+	BR/A	SB	CS	SBR	FA	FR	G/POS	TPR
1990	Bal-A	40	123	14	30	7	0	2	15	11	15	.244	.311	.350	87	-2	0	0	0	.990	-1	1-36/D-4	-0.3
1991	Bal-A	86	212	15	59	7	0	2	22	12	19	.278	.317	.340	85	-4	1	1	-0	.996	1	1-42,O-33/D-4	-0.6
1992	Bal-A	115	189	21	44	9	0	1	17	20	23	.233	.306	.296	68	-8	1	0	0	.998	2	1-95,O-18	-0.8
1993	Bal-A	146	450	54	123	27	0	10	60	58	53	.273	.356	.400	99	-0	2	1	0	.996	4	*1-144/D-1	-0.7
1994	NY-N	92	336	46	81	17	1	10	43	33	43	.241	.311	.387	81	-10	0	0	0	.996	-1	1-78/O-21	-2.0
1995	NY-N	33	73	9	24	3	1	2	11	12	9	.329	.430	.479	144	5	1	3	-2	1.000	-2	O-18/1-7	0.1
	Mon-N	97	383	59	117	22	3	10	57	28	38	.305	.356	.457	109	5	1	4	-2	.997	-0	1-97/O-2	-0.7
	Yr	130	456	68	141	25	4	12	68	40	47	.309	.369	.461	115	10	2	7	-4	.997	-2	*1-104,O-20	-0.6
1996	Mon-N	115	416	69	119	30	1	11	58	60	54	.286	.376	.442	112	8	4	4	-1	.993	6	*1-113	0.2
Total	7	724	2182	287	597	122	6	48	283	234	254	.274	.345	.401	99	-6	10	13	-5	.995	9	1-612/O-92,D-9	-4.8

■ KURT SEIBERT
Seibert, Kurt Elliott   b: 10/16/55, Cheverly, Md.   BB/TR, 6', 165 lbs.   Deb: 9/3/79

YEAR	TM/L	G	AB	R	H	2B	3B	HR	RBI	BB	SO	AVG	OBP	SLG	PRO+	BR/A	SB	CS	SBR	FA	FR	G/POS	TPR
1979	Chi-N	7	5	1	0	0	0	0	0	0	0	.000	.000	.000	-91	-1	0	0	0	1.000	0	/2-1	0.0

■ SOCKS SEIBOLD
Seibold, Harry   b: 4/3/1896, Philadelphia, Pa.   d: 9/21/65, Philadelphia, Pa.   BR/TR, 5'8.5", 162 lbs.   Deb: 9/18/15

YEAR	TM/L	G	AB	R	H	2B	3B	HR	RBI	BB	SO	AVG	OBP	SLG	PRO+	BR/A	SB	CS	SBR	FA	FR	G/POS	TPR
1915	Phi-A	10	26	3	3	1	0	0	2	4	4	.115	.233	.154	16	-3	0			.714	-4	/S-7	-0.7
1916	Phi-A	5	12	0	2	1	0	0	1	0	4	.167	.167	.250	26	-1	0			1.000	2	/P-3,O-1	0.0
1917	Phi-A	36	59	6	13	1	1	0	5	4	8	.220	.281	.271	70	-2	1			.978	2	P-33/O-2	-0.1
1919	Phi-A	15	13	1	2	0	0	0	0	1	2	.154	.154	.154	-13	-2	0			.941	0	P-14	0.0
1929	Bos-N	33	70	6	20	2	0	0	9	6	6	.286	.342	.314	67	-3	0			**1.000**	-1	P-33	0.0
1930	Bos-N	36	90	6	19	1	0	0	5	6	9	.211	.260	.256	29	-11	0			.941	-3	P-36	0.0
1931	Bos-N	33	70	3	9	1	0	0	6	1	5	.129	.141	.129	-28	-13	0			**1.000**	0	P-33	0.0
1932	Bos-N	28	46	2	7	0	0	0	3	2	4	.152	.188	.152	-8	-7	0			1.000	0	P-28	0.0
1933	Bos-N	11	19	0	1	1	0	0	0	1	1	.111	.273	.111	14	-1	0			1.000	0	P-11	0.0
Total	9	207	395	27	76	7	1	1	27	25	43	.192	.242	.223	25	-42	1			.982	-5	P-191/S-7,O-3	-0.8

YEAR	TM/L	G	AB	R	H	2B	3B	HR	RBI	BB	SO	AVG	OBP	SLG	PRO+	BR/A	SB	CS	SBR	FA	FR	G/POS	TPR

■ **RICKY SEILHEIMER**   Seilheimer, Ricky Allen b: 8/30/60, Brenham, Tex.   BL/TR, 5'11", 185 lbs.   Deb: 7/5/80

| 1980 | Chi-A | 21 | 52 | 4 | 11 | 3 | 1 | 1 | 3 | 4 | 15 | .212 | .268 | .365 | 72 | -2 | 1 | 0 | 0 | .946 | -3 | C-21 | -0.4 |

■ **KEVIN SEITZER**   Seitzer, Kevin Lee b: 3/26/62, Springfield, Ill.   BR/TR, 5'11", 180 lbs.   Deb: 9/3/86

1986	KC-A	28	96	16	31	4	1	2	11	19	14	.323	.440	.448	140	6	0	0	0	.987	1	1-22/O-5,3-3	0.6
1987	KC-A★	161	641	105	**207**	33	8	15	83	80	85	.323	.400	.470	126	26	12	7	-1	.947	8	*3-141,1-25/O-3,D-1	2.9
1988	KC-A	149	559	90	170	32	5	5	60	72	64	.304	.389	.406	122	19	10	8	-2	.938	3	*3-147/O-1,D-1	1.9
1989	KC-A	160	597	78	168	17	2	4	48	102	76	.281	.391	.337	107	11	17	8	0	.950	-11	*3-159/S-6,O-3,1-2	0.3
1990	KC-A	158	622	91	171	31	5	6	38	67	66	.275	.347	.370	102	3	7	5	-1	.953	-9	*3-152,2-10	-0.6
1991	KC-A	85	234	28	62	11	3	1	25	29	21	.265	.351	.350	94	-1	4	1	1	.940	0	3-68/D-3	0.0
1992	Mil-A	148	540	74	146	35	1	5	71	57	44	.270	.342	.367	101	1	13	11	-3	**.969**	-13	*3-146/2-2,1-1	-1.5
1993	Oak-A	73	255	24	65	10	2	4	27	27	33	.255	.329	.357	90	-4	4	7	-3	.933	-9	3-46,1-24/O-3,2PDS	-1.7
	Mil-A	47	162	21	47	6	0	7	30	17	15	.290	.361	.457	120	5	3	0	1	.942	-2	3-33/1-7,2-1,O-1,D	0.3
	Yr	120	417	45	112	16	2	11	57	44	48	.269	.341	.396	102	1	7	7	-2	.937	-11	3-79,1-31/D-6,O2PS	-1.4
1994	Mil-A	80	309	44	97	24	2	5	49	30	38	.314	.378	.453	108	4	2	1	0	.924	-4	3-43,1-35/D-4	-0.3
1995	Mil-A★	132	492	56	153	33	3	5	69	64	57	.311	.397	.421	107	7	2	0	1	.968	-6	3-88,1-36,D-14	0.2
1996	Mil-A	132	490	74	155	25	3	12	62	73	68	.316	.409	.453	112	11	6	1	1	.996	0	1-65,D-56,3-12	0.2
	*Cle-A	22	83	11	32	10	0	1	16	14	11	.386	.480	.542	158	8	0	0	0	1.000	2	D-17/1-5	0.8
	Yr	154	573	85	187	35	3	13	78	87	79	.326	.420	.466	118	19	6	1	1	.995	3	D-73,1-70,3-12	1.0
Total	11	1375	5080	712	1504	271	35	72	589	651	592	.296	.380	.406	111	98	80	49	-5	.949	-34	*3-1038,1-222,D/O2SP	3.1

■ **KIP SELBACH**   Selbach, Albert Karl b: 3/24/1872, Columbus, Ohio d: 2/17/56, Columbus, Ohio   BR/TR, 5'7", 190 lbs.   Deb: 4/24/1894

1894	Was-N	97	372	69	114	21	7	7	71	51	20	.306	.390	.511	120	11	21			.915	-9	O-80,S-19	-0.2
1895	Was-N	129	516	115	166	21	**22**	6	55	69	28	.322	.403	.483	129	23	31			.912	16	*O-118/S-6,2-5	2.4
1896	Was-N	127	487	100	148	17	13	5	100	76	28	.304	.405	.423	119	16	49			.946	7	*O-126	1.1
1897	Was-N	124	486	113	152	25	16	5	59	80		.313	.414	.461	131	24	46			.955	13	*O-124	2.4
1898	Was-N	132	515	88	156	28	11	3	60	64		.303	.383	.417	130	21	25			.948	20	*O-131/S-1	2.9
1899	Cin-N	140	521	104	154	27	11	3	87	70		.296	.384	.407	115	12	38			.953	17	*O-140	1.6
1900	NY-N	141	523	98	176	29	12	4	68	72		.337	.425	.461	151	40	36			.951	10	*O-141	3.5
1901	NY-N	125	502	89	145	29	6	1	56	45		.289	.350	.376	115	10	8			.942	-10	*O-125	-0.9
1902	Bal-A	128	503	86	161	27	9	3	60	58		.320	.393	.427	122	16	22			.941	9	*O-127	1.6
1903	Was-A	140	533	68	134	23	12	3	49	41		.251	.305	.356	96	-3	20			.956	-3	*O-140/3-1	-1.5
1904	Was-A	48	178	15	49	8	4	0	14	24		.275	.361	.365	132	7	9			.931	3	O-48	0.8
	Bos-A	98	376	50	97	19	8	0	30	48		.258	.347	.351	114	8	10			.961	1	O-98	0.3
	Yr	146	554	65	146	27	12	0	44	72		.264	.351	.356	120	15	19			.950	4	O-146	1.1
1905	Bos-A	121	418	54	103	16	6	4	47	67		.246	.355	.342	120	12	12			.928	-1	*O-112	0.6
1906	Bos-A	60	228	15	48	9	2	0	23	18		.211	.277	.268	71	-7	7			.966	1	O-58	-1.0
Total	13	1610	6158	1064	1803	299	149	44	779	783	76	.293	.376	.411	121	190	334			.944	74	*O-1568/S-26,2-5,3	13.6

■ **BILL SELBY**   Selby, William Frank b: 6/11/70, Monroeville, Ala.   BL/TR, 5'9", 190 lbs.   Deb: 4/19/96

| 1996 | Bos-A | 40 | 95 | 12 | 26 | 4 | 0 | 3 | 6 | 9 | 11 | .274 | .337 | .411 | 85 | -2 | 1 | 1 | -0 | .980 | -6 | 2-14,3-14/O-6 | -0.8 |

■ **GEORGE SELKIRK**   Selkirk, George Alexander "Twinkletoes"
b: 1/4/08, Huntsville, Ont., Canada d: 1/19/87, Ft.Lauderdale, Fla   BL/TR, 6'1", 182 lbs.   Deb: 8/12/34

1934	NY-A	46	176	23	55	7	5	5	38	15	17	.313	.370	.449	118	4	1	1	-0	.989	-2	O-46	0.1
1935	NY-A	128	491	64	153	29	12	11	94	44	36	.312	.372	.487	128	18	2	7	-4	.975	6	*O-127	1.5
1936	*NY-A★	137	493	93	152	28	9	18	107	94	60	.308	.420	.511	133	28	13	7	-0	.974	3	*O-135	2.2
1937	NY-A	78	256	49	84	13	5	18	68	34	24	.328	.411	.629	157	22	8	2	1	.987	-6	O-69	2.3
1938	NY-A	99	335	58	85	12	5	10	62	68	52	.254	.384	.409	99	1	9	4	0	.973	-3	O-95	-0.4
1939	*NY-A★	128	418	103	128	17	4	21	101	103	49	.306	.452	.517	149	37	12	5	1	**.989**	-4	*O-124	2.6
1940	*NY-A	118	379	68	102	17	5	19	71	84	43	.269	.406	.491	137	23	3	6	-3	.962	-4	*O-111	1.2
1941	*NY-A	70	164	30	36	5	0	6	25	28	30	.220	.340	.360	86	-3	1	0	0	.967	-2	O-47	-0.7
1942	*NY-A	42	78	15	15	3	0	1	10	16	8	.192	.330	.231	60	-3	0	0	0	1.000	-1	O-19	-0.6
Total	9	846	2790	503	810	131	41	108	576	486	319	.290	.400	.483	128	127	49	32	-5	.977	-1	O-773	8.2

■ **RUBE SELLERS**   Sellers, Oliver b: 3/7/1881, Duquesne, Pa. d: 1/14/52, Pittsburgh, Pa.   BR/TR, 5'10", 180 lbs.   Deb: 8/12/10

| 1910 | Bos-N | 12 | 32 | 3 | 5 | 0 | 0 | 0 | 2 | 6 | 5 | .156 | .289 | .156 | 29 | -3 | | | | 1.000 | -2 | /O-9 | -0.6 |

■ **FRANK SELMAN**   Selman, Frank C. (a.k.a. Frank C. Williams 1871-75) b: Baltimore, Md.   Deb: 5/4/1871

1871	Kek-n	14	65	14	15	3	0	1	10	4	0	.231	.275	.323	70	-3	1	0	0	.711	-3	3-14/C-5,S-2	-0.4
1872	Oly-n	9	42	3	10	2	0	0	1	0	1	.238	.238	.286	64	-2	0	2	-1	.788	-3	/C-7,3-2	-0.4
1873	Mar-n	1	3	1	1	0	0	0	0	0	0	.333	.333	.333	129	0	0	0	0	.000	-0	/P-1	0.0
1874	Bal-n	12	54	9	16	3	0	0	3	0	2	.296	.296	.426	130	2	2	0	1	.242	-18	/C-6,S-6,2-2,O-2,3	-1.3
1875	Was-n	1	3	0	1	0	0	0	0	0	0	.333	.333	.333	137	0	0	0	0	1.000	0	/1-1	0.0
Total	5 n	37	167	27	43	8	1	1	16	4	3	.257	.275	.347	88	-2	3	2	-0	.584	-24	/C-18,3-17,SO21P	-2.1

■ **CAREY SELPH**   Selph, Carey Isom b: 12/5/01, Donaldson, Ark. d: 2/24/76, Houston, Tex.   BR/TR, 5'9.5", 175 lbs.   Deb: 5/25/29

1929	StL-N	25	51	8	12	1	1	0	7	6	4	.235	.316	.294	52	-4	1			.981	-5	2-16	-0.7
1932	Chi-A	116	396	50	112	19	8	0	51	31	9	.283	.341	.371	90	-6	7	6	-2	.910	-6	3-71,2-26	-0.7
Total	2	141	447	58	124	20	9	0	58	37	13	.277	.338	.362	85	-10	8	6		.955	-11	/3-71,2-42	-1.4

■ **MIKE SEMBER**   Sember, Michael David b: 2/24/53, Hammond, Ind.   BR/TR, 6', 185 lbs.   Deb: 8/18/77

1977	Chi-N	3	4	0	1	0	0	0	0	0	2	.250	.250	.250	31	-0	0	0	0	1.000	1	/2-1	0.0
1978	Chi-N	9	3	2	1	0	0	0	0	1	1	.333	.500	.333	122	0	0	0	0	.667	1	/3-7,S-1	0.1
Total	2	12	7	2	2	0	0	0	0	1	3	.286	.375	.286	74	0	0	0	0	.667	1	/3-7,S-1,2-1	0.1

■ **ANDY SEMINICK**   Seminick, Andrew Wasil b: 9/12/20, Pierce, W.Va.   BR/TR, 5'11", 187 lbs.   Deb: 9/14/43   C

1943	Phi-N	22	72	9	13	2	0	2	5	7	22	.181	.253	.292	60	-4				.930	1	C-22/O-1	-0.2
1944	Phi-N	22	63	9	14	2	1	2	4	6	17	.222	.300	.286	68	-3	2			.963	1	C-11/O-7	-0.2
1945	Phi-N	80	188	18	45	7	2	6	26	18	38	.239	.313	.394	98	-1	3			.979	-0	C-70/3-4,O-1	0.0
1946	Phi-N	124	406	55	107	15	5	12	52	39	86	.264	.334	.414	115	7	2			.974	-6	*C-118	0.9
1947	Phi-N	111	337	48	85	16	2	13	50	58	69	.252	.370	.427	115	8	4			.978	7	*C-107	2.1
1948	Phi-N	125	391	49	88	11	3	13	44	58	68	.225	.328	.368	90	-5	4			.965	6	*C-124	0.9
1949	Phi-N★	109	334	52	81	11	2	24	68	69	74	.243	.380	.503	138	19	0			.975	7	C-98	3.1
1950	*Phi-N	130	393	55	113	15	3	24	68	68	50	.288	.400	.524	143	26	0			.976	4	*C-124	3.5
1951	Phi-N	101	291	42	66	8	1	11	37	63	67	.227	.370	.375	102	3	1			.979	-3	C-91	0.4
1952	Cin-N	108	336	38	86	16	1	14	50	35	65	.256	.330	.435	111	4	1	3	-2	.973	-4	C-99	0.4
1953	Cin-N	119	387	46	91	12	0	19	64	49	82	.235	.323	.413	90	-6	2	2	-1	.982	-5	C-112	-0.6
1954	Cin-N	86	247	25	58	9	4	7	30	48	39	.235	.364	.389	93	-1	0	1	-1	.989	6	C-82	0.6
1955	Cin-N	6	15	1	2	0	0	0	1	0	3	.133	.133	.133	18	-2	0	0	0	1.000	1	/C-5	0.0
	Phi-N	93	289	32	71	12	1	11	34	32	59	.246	.333	.408	97	-1	3	2	-1	.994	10	C-88	1.1
	Yr	99	304	33	73	12	1	12	35	32	62	.240	.325	.405	93	-3	3	2	-1	**.994**	12	C-93	1.1
1956	Phi-N	60	161	16	32	7	1	7	23	31	38	.199	.332	.360	88	-2	0	0	0	.976	-8	C-54	-0.7
1957	Phi-N	8	11	0	1	0	0	0	0	4	3	.091	.167	.091	-29	-2	0	0	0	1.000	1	/C-8	-0.1
Total	15	1304	3921	495	953	139	26	164	556	582	780	.243	.347	.417	107	40	23	7		.977	15	*C-1213/O-9,3-4	11.3

■ **SONNY SENERCHIA**   Senerchia, Emanuel Robert b: 4/6/31, Newark, N.J.   BR/TR, 6'1", 195 lbs.   Deb: 8/22/52

| 1952 | Pit-N | 29 | 100 | 5 | 22 | 1 | 1 | 4 | 11 | 21 | 14 | .220 | .350 | .360 | 66 | -5 | 0 | 3 | -2 | .953 | -8 | 3-28 | -1.7 |

■ **COUNT SENSENDERFER**   Sensenderfer, John Phillips Jenkins b: 12/28/1847, Philadelphia, Pa. d: 5/3/03, Philadelphia, Pa.   5'9", 170 lbs.   Deb: 5/20/1871

| 1871 | Ath-n | 25 | 127 | 38 | 41 | 5 | 2 | 0 | 23 | 0 | 1 | .323 | .323 | .394 | 106 | 2 | 1 | 5 | 3 | -0 | .814 | -1 | *O-25 | 0.1 |
| 1872 | Ath-n | 1 | 5 | 2 | 2 | 0 | 0 | 0 | 1 | 0 | 0 | .400 | .400 | .400 | 146 | 1 | 0 | 1 | 1 | -1 | .000 | -0 | /O-1 | 0.0 |

YEAR	TM/L	G	AB	R	H	2B	3B	HR	RBI	BB	SO	AVG	OBP	SLG	PRO+	BR/A	SB	CS	SBR	FA	FR	G/POS	TPR
1873	Ath-n	20	86	12	24	1	0	0	8	0	2	.279	.279	.291	65	-4	0	2	-1	.827	0	O-19/1-1	-0.2
1874	Ath-n	5	16	3	3	0	0	0	2	0	0	.188	.188	.188	19	-1	0	0		.625	-1	/O-5	-0.2
Total	4 n	51	234	55	70	6	2	0	34	0	3	.299	.299	.342	85	-5	5	6	-2	.807	-2	/O-50,1-1	-0.4

■ PAUL SENTELL Sentell, Leopold Theodore b: 8/27/1879, New Orleans, La. d: 4/27/23, Cincinnati, Ohio BR/TR, 5'9", 176 lbs. Deb: 4/12/06 U

YEAR	TM/L	G	AB	R	H	2B	3B	HR	RBI	BB	SO	AVG	OBP	SLG	PRO+	BR/A	SB	CS	SBR	FA	FR	G/POS	TPR
1906	Phi-N	63	192	19	44	5	1	1	14	14		.229	.292	.281	79	-5	15			.887	-9	3-33,2-19/O-2,S-1	-1.4
1907	Phi-N	3	3	0	0	0	0	0	0	1		.000	.250	.000	-22	-2	0			1.000	-2	/S-2,O-1	-0.3
Total	2	66	195	19	44	5	1	1	14	15		.226	.291	.277	77	-5	15			1.000	-11	/3-33,2-19,S-3,O-3	-1.7

■ TED SEPKOWSKI Sepkowski, Theodore Walter (b: Theodore Walter Sczepkowski) b: 11/9/23, Baltimore, Md. BL/TR, 5'11", 190 lbs. Deb: 9/9/42

YEAR	TM/L	G	AB	R	H	2B	3B	HR	RBI	BB	SO	AVG	OBP	SLG	PRO+	BR/A	SB	CS	SBR	FA	FR	G/POS	TPR
1942	Cle-A	5	10	0	1	0	0	0	0	0	3	.100	.100	.100	-46	-2	0	0	0	.824	0	/2-2	-0.1
1946	Cle-A	2	8	2	4	1	0	0	1	0	0	.500	.500	.625	228	1	0	0	0	.833	1	/3-2	0.1
1947	Cle-A	10	8	0	1	1	0	0	1	0	0	.125	.222	.250	32	-1	0	0	0	.000	-0	/O-1	-0.1
	NY-A	2	0	1	0	0	0	0	0	0	0	—	—	—	—	0	0	1	-1	.000	0	R	-0.1
	Yr	12	8	1	1	1	0	0	1	0	0	.125	.222	.250	32	-1	0	1	-1	.000	-0	/O-1	-0.2
Total	3	19	26	3	6	2	0	0	1	1	4	.231	.259	.308	61	-1	0	1	-1	.833	-1	/3-2,2-2,O-1	-0.2

■ BILL SERENA Serena, William Robert b: 10/2/24, Alameda, Cal. d: 4/17/96, Hayward, Cal. BR/TR, 5'9.5", 175 lbs. Deb: 9/16/49

YEAR	TM/L	G	AB	R	H	2B	3B	HR	RBI	BB	SO	AVG	OBP	SLG	PRO+	BR/A	SB	CS	SBR	FA	FR	G/POS	TPR
1949	Chi-N	12	37	3	8	1	0	1	7	7	9	.216	.341	.378	95	-0	0			.923	-4	3-11	-0.5
1950	Chi-N	127	435	56	104	20	4	17	61	65	75	.239	.339	.421	100	-5	0	1		.945	-2	*3-125	-0.4
1951	Chi-N	13	39	8	13	3	1	1	4	11	4	.333	.490	.538	173	5	0	2	-1	.941	-4	3-12	-0.5
1952	Chi-N	122	390	49	107	21	5	15	61	39	83	.274	.345	.469	122	11	1	0	0	.971	-1	3-58,2-49	1.1
1953	Chi-N	93	275	30	69	10	5	10	52	41	46	.251	.350	.433	100	0	0	0	0	.983	-15	2-49,3-28	-1.2
1954	Chi-N	41	63	8	10	2	1	4	13	14	18	.159	.321	.381	81	-2	0	0	0	.933	-3	3-12/2-2	-0.5
Total	6	408	1239	154	311	57	16	48	198	177	235	.251	.348	.439	108	14	2	2		.951	-30	3-246,2-100	-1.5

■ PAUL SERNA Serna, Paul David b: 11/16/58, ElCentro, Cal. BR/TR, 5'8", 170 lbs. Deb: 9/1/81

YEAR	TM/L	G	AB	R	H	2B	3B	HR	RBI	BB	SO	AVG	OBP	SLG	PRO+	BR/A	SB	CS	SBR	FA	FR	G/POS	TPR
1981	Sea-A	30	94	11	24	4	0	3	9	3	11	.255	.293	.404	95	-1	2	3	-1	.954	-3	S-23/2-7	-0.2
1982	Sea-A	65	169	15	38	3	0	3	8	4	13	.225	.247	.296	47	-12	0	5	-3	.936	3	S-31,2-18,3-15/D-2	-1.0
Total	2	95	263	26	62	5	0	7	17	7	24	.236	.264	.335	64	-13	2	8	-4	.945	1	/S-54,2-25,3-15/D-2	-1.2

■ SCOTT SERVAIS Servais, Scott Daniel b: 6/4/67, LaCrosse, Wis. BR/TR, 6'2", 195 lbs. Deb: 7/12/91

YEAR	TM/L	G	AB	R	H	2B	3B	HR	RBI	BB	SO	AVG	OBP	SLG	PRO+	BR/A	SB	CS	SBR	FA	FR	G/POS	TPR
1991	Hou-N	16	37	0	6	3	0	0	6	4	8	.162	.244	.243	40	-3	0	0	0	.988	2	C-14	0.0
1992	Hou-N	77	205	12	49	9	0	0	15	11	25	.239	.294	.283	67	-9	0	0	0	.995	-2	C-73	-0.8
1993	Hou-N	85	258	24	63	11	0	11	32	22	45	.244	.316	.415	97	-2	0	0	0	.996	2	C-82	0.4
1994	Hou-N	78	251	27	49	15	1	9	41	10	44	.195	.238	.371	58	-17	0	1	-1	.996	1	C-78	-1.1
1995	Hou-N	28	89	7	20	10	0	1	12	9	15	.225	.303	.371	82	-3	0	1	-1	.977	5	C-28	0.4
	Chi-N	52	175	31	50	12	0	12	35	23	37	.286	.375	.560	145	11	2	1	-1	.981	-2	C-52	1.3
	Yr	80	264	38	70	22	0	13	47	32	52	.265	.351	.496	125	9	2	2	-1	.980	3	C-80	1.7
1996	Chi-N	129	445	42	118	20	0	11	63	30	75	.265	.331	.384	87	-8	0	2	-1	.988	0	*C-128/1-1	0.0
Total	6	465	1460	143	355	80	1	44	204	109	249	.243	.309	.390	87	-30	2	4	-2	.990	6	C-455/1-1	0.2

■ WALTER SESSI Sessi, Walter Anthony "Watsie" b: 7/23/18, Finleyville, Pa. BL/TL, 6'3", 225 lbs. Deb: 9/18/41

YEAR	TM/L	G	AB	R	H	2B	3B	HR	RBI	BB	SO	AVG	OBP	SLG	PRO+	BR/A	SB	CS	SBR	FA	FR	G/POS	TPR
1941	StL-N	5	13	2	0	0	0	0	0	1	2	.000	.071	.000	-74	-3	0			.750	-1	/O-3	-0.4
1946	StL-N	15	14	2	2	0	0	1	2	1	4	.143	.200	.357	54	-1	0			.000	0	H	-0.1
Total	2	20	27	4	2	0	0	1	2	2	6	.074	.138	.185	-9	-4	0			.750	-1	/O-3	-0.5

■ JOHN SEVCIK Sevcik, John Joseph b: 7/11/42, Oak Park, Ill. BR/TR, 6'2", 205 lbs. Deb: 4/24/65

YEAR	TM/L	G	AB	R	H	2B	3B	HR	RBI	BB	SO	AVG	OBP	SLG	PRO+	BR/A	SB	CS	SBR	FA	FR	G/POS	TPR
1965	Min-A	12	16	1	1	1	0	0	1	1	5	.063	.118	.125	-30	-3	0	0	0	1.000	3	C-11	0.0

■ HANK SEVEREID Severeid, Henry Levai b: 6/1/1891, Story City, Iowa d: 12/17/68, San Antonio, Tex. BR/TR, 6', 175 lbs. Deb: 5/15/11

YEAR	TM/L	G	AB	R	H	2B	3B	HR	RBI	BB	SO	AVG	OBP	SLG	PRO+	BR/A	SB	CS	SBR	FA	FR	G/POS	TPR
1911	Cin-N	37	56	5	17	6	1	0	10	3	6	.304	.350	.446	127	2	0			.913	-3	C-22	0.0
1912	Cin-N	50	114	10	27	0	3	0	13	8	11	.237	.287	.289	60	-6	0			.943	-9	C-20/1-7,O-6	-1.4
1913	Cin-N	8	6	0	0	0	0	0	0	1	1	.000	.143	.000	-58	-1	0			1.000	-1	/C-2,O-1	-0.2
1915	StL-A	80	203	12	45	6	1	1	22	16	25	.222	.279	.276	69	-8	2	1	0	.966	-10	C-64	-1.5
1916	StL-A	100	293	23	80	8	2	0	34	26	17	.273	.341	.314	102	1	3			.976	-16	C-89/1-1,3-1	-1.0
1917	StL-A	143	501	45	133	23	4	1	57	28	20	.265	.306	.333	99	-3	6			.966	-19	*C-139/1-1	-1.2
1918	StL-A	51	133	8	34	4	0	0	11	18	4	.256	.357	.286	97	0	4			.946	-5	C-42	-0.2
1919	StL-A	112	351	16	87	12	2	0	36	21	13	.248	.298	.293	65	-16	2			.983	-5	*C-103	-1.3
1920	StL-A	123	422	46	117	14	5	2	49	33	11	.277	.336	.348	79	-13	5	3	-0	.983	3	*C-117	-0.2
1921	StL-A	143	472	66	153	25	7	2	78	42	9	.324	.379	.415	97	-2	7	2	1	.972	-0	*C-126	0.3
1922	StL-A	137	517	49	166	32	7	3	78	28	12	.321	.356	.427	100	-1	4	5	-2	.984	7	*C-133	1.1
1923	StL-A	122	432	50	133	27	6	3	51	31	11	.308	.356	.419	98	-2	3	0	1	.993	10	*C-116	1.3
1924	StL-A	137	432	37	133	23	2	4	48	36	15	.308	.362	.398	90	-7	1	6	-3	.989	-2	*C-130	-0.4
1925	StL-A	34	109	15	40	9	0	1	21	11	2	.367	.425	.477	122	4	2		-1	.993	-0	C-31	0.4
	*Was-A	50	110	11	39	8	1	0	14	13	6	.355	.423	.445	123	4	0	0	0	.986	2	C-35	0.7
	Yr	84	219	26	79	17	1	1	35	24	8	.361	.424	.461	123	9	0	2	-1	.990	1	C-66	1.1
1926	Was-A	22	34	2	7	1	0	0	4	3	2	.206	.270	.235	33	-3	0	0	0	.977	0	C-16	-0.2
	*NY-A	41	127	13	34	8	1	0	13	13	4	.268	.336	.346	79	-4	1	1	-0	.988	-3	C-40	-0.5
	Yr	63	161	15	41	9	1	0	17	16	6	.255	.322	.323	70	-7	1	1	-0	.985	-3	C-56	-0.7
Total	15	1390	4312	408	1245	204	42	17	539	331	169	.289	.342	.367	91	-55	35	19		.978	-56	*C-1225/1-9,O-7,3-1	-4.3

■ RICH SEVERSON Severson, Richard Allen b: 1/18/45, Artesia, Cal. BR/TR, 6', 174 lbs. Deb: 4/10/70

YEAR	TM/L	G	AB	R	H	2B	3B	HR	RBI	BB	SO	AVG	OBP	SLG	PRO+	BR/A	SB	CS	SBR	FA	FR	G/POS	TPR
1970	KC-A	77	240	22	60	11	1	1	22	16	33	.250	.300	.317	70	-10	0	0	0	.962	1	S-50,2-25	-0.2
1971	KC-A	16	30	4	9	0	2	0	3	3	5	.300	.364	.433	126	1	0	0	0	1.000	6	/2-6,S-6,3-1	0.8
Total	2	93	270	26	69	11	3	1	23	19	38	.256	.307	.330	76	-9	0	0	0	.958	7	/S-56,2-31,3-1	0.6

■ ED SEWARD Seward, Edward William (b: Edward William Sourhardt) b: 6/29/1867, Cleveland, Ohio d: 7/30/47, Cleveland, Ohio TR, 5'7", 175 lbs. Deb: 9/30/1885 U

YEAR	TM/L	G	AB	R	H	2B	3B	HR	RBI	BB	SO	AVG	OBP	SLG	PRO+	BR/A	SB	CS	SBR	FA	FR	G/POS	TPR
1885	Pro-N	1	3	0	0	0	0	0		0	2	.000	.000	.000	-99	-1				1.000	1	/P-1	0.0
1887	Phi-a	74	266	31	50	10	0	5	28	16		.188	.239	.282	45	-20	14			.901	-3	P-55,O-21	-0.5
1888	Phi-a	64	225	27	32	3	3	2	14	18		.142	.215	.209	36	-16	12			.887	4	P-57/O-7	-0.1
1889	Phi-a	46	143	22	31	5	3	2	17	22	19	.217	.333	.336	92	-1	6			.885	-4	P-39/O-8,2-1	-0.2
1890	Phi-a	26	72	7	10	4	0	0	2	8		.139	.244	.194	30	-6	3			.811	-2	P-21/O-6	-0.2
1891	Cle-N	7	19	2	4	2	0	1	3	4		.211	.318	.316	81	-0	0			1.000	-2	/O-3,P-3,1-1	-0.2
Total	6	218	728	89	127	24	6	9	62	67	25	.174	.253	.261	52	-44	35			.882	-7	P-176/O-45,1-1,2-1	-1.2

■ GEORGE SEWARD Seward, George E. b: St.Louis, Mo. 5'7.5", 145 lbs. Deb: 5/19/1875

YEAR	TM/L	G	AB	R	H	2B	3B	HR	RBI	BB	SO	AVG	OBP	SLG	PRO+	BR/A	SB	CS	SBR	FA	FR	G/POS	TPR
1875	StL-n	25	96	12	24	0	0	0	8	1	1	.250	.258	.271	92	-0	1	0	0	.817	-2	C-18/O-7,2-2	-0.1
1876	NY-N	1	3	0	0	0	0	0				.000	.000	.000	-99	-1				1.000	-2	/2-1	0.0
1882	StL-a	38	144	23	31	1	1	0		12		.215	.276	.236	71	-4				.776	-0	O-35/C-5	-0.4
Total	2	39	147	23	31	1	1	0		12		.211	.270	.231	68	-5				.776	0	/O-35,C-5,2-1	-0.4

■ LUKE SEWELL Sewell, James Luther b: 1/5/01, Titus, Ala. d: 5/14/87, Akron, Ohio BR/TR, 5'9", 160 lbs. Deb: 6/30/21 FMC

YEAR	TM/L	G	AB	R	H	2B	3B	HR	RBI	BB	SO	AVG	OBP	SLG	PRO+	BR/A	SB	CS	SBR	FA	FR	G/POS	TPR
1921	Cle-A	3	6	0	0	0	0	0	0	0	3	.000	.000	.000	-99	-2	0	0		1.000	1	/C-3	-0.1
1922	Cle-A	41	87	14	23	5	0	0	10	5	6	.264	.312	.322	65	-4	1	1	-0	.963	0	C-39	-0.3
1923	Cle-A	10	10	2	2	0	0	0	1	1	0	.200	.273	.400	76	-0	0			.833	0	/C-7	0.0
1924	Cle-A	63	165	27	48	9	1	0	17	22	12	.291	.387	.358	92	-1	1			.959	5	C-57	0.7
1925	Cle-A	74	220	30	51	10	2	0	18	33	18	.232	.337	.295	61	-12	6	2	1	.971	7	C-66/O-2	-0.2
1926	Cle-A	126	433	41	103	16	4	0	46	35	27	.238	.302	.293	55	-28	9	3	1	.983	2	*C-125	-1.7
1927	Cle-A	128	470	52	138	27	6	0	53	20	23	.294	.328	.377	72	-13	4	4	-6	.963	-2	*C-126	-0.9
1928	Cle-A	122	411	52	111	16	3	3	52	26	27	.270	.320	.375	81	-12	3	4	-2	.972	13	*C-118	0.9
1929	Cle-A	124	406	41	96	16	3	1	39	29	26	.236	.287	.298	49	-31	6	6	-2	.966	4	*C-124	-1.6

YEAR	TM/L	G	AB	R	H	2B	3B	HR	RBI	BB	SO	AVG	OBP	SLG	PRO+	BR/A	SB	CS	SBR	FA	FR	G/POS	TPR
1930	Cle-A	76	292	40	75	21	2	1	43	14	9	.257	.293	.353	61	-18	5	2	0	.974	-2	C-76	-1.1
1931	Cle-A	108	375	45	103	30	4	1	53	36	17	.275	.341	.384	86	-8	1	1	0	.980	-8	*C-104	-0.8
1932	Cle-A	87	300	36	76	20	2	2	52	38	24	.253	.337	.353	74	-11	4	5	-2	.978	4	C-84	-0.4
1933	*Was-A	141	474	65	125	30	4	2	61	48	24	.264	.335	.357	84	-10	7	2	1	.990	-6	*C-141	-0.7
1934	Was-A	72	207	21	49	7	3	2	21	22	10	.237	.313	.329	68	-10	0	1	-1	.994	-1	C-50/O-7,1-6,2-1,3	-0.9
1935	Chi-A	118	421	52	120	19	3	2	67	32	18	.285	.336	.359	78	-14	3	2	-0	.988	6	*C-112	-0.2
1936	Chi-A	128	451	59	113	20	5	5	73	54	16	.251	.332	.350	66	-24	11	2	2	.984	12	*C-126	-0.4
1937	Chi-A☆	122	412	51	111	21	6	1	61	46	18	.269	.343	.357	77	-14	4	5	-2	.985	6	*C-118	-0.3
1938	Chi-A	65	211	23	45	4	1	0	27	20	20	.213	.284	.242	32	-22	0	0	0	.985	7	C-65	-1.1
1939	Cle-A	16	20	1	3	1	0	0	1	3	1	.150	.261	.200	20	-2	0	0	0	.966	-1	C-15/1-1	-0.2
1942	StL-A	6	12	1	1	0	0	0	0	1	5	.083	.154	.083	-32	-2	0	0	0	.944	1	/C-6,M	-0.1
Total	20	1630	5383	653	1393	272	56	20	696	486	307	.259	.323	.341	70	-242	65	44	-7	.978	48	*C-1562/O-9,1-7,32	-9.4

■ JOE SEWELL
Sewell, Joseph Wheeler b: 10/9/1898, Titus, Ala. d: 3/6/90, Mobile, Ala. BL/TR, 5'6.5", 155 lbs. Deb: 9/10/20 FCH

YEAR	TM/L	G	AB	R	H	2B	3B	HR	RBI	BB	SO	AVG	OBP	SLG	PRO+	BR/A	SB	CS	SBR	FA	FR	G/POS	TPR
1920	*Cle-A	22	70	14	23	4	1	0	12	9	4	.329	.412	.414	116	2	1	0	0	.884	3	S-22	0.6
1921	Cle-A	154	572	101	182	36	12	4	93	80	17	.318	.412	.444	117	17	7	6	-2	.944	-3	*S-154	2.5
1922	Cle-A	153	558	80	167	28	7	2	83	73	20	.299	.386	.385	101	3	10	12	-4	.939	12	*S-139,2-12	2.5
1923	Cle-A	153	553	98	195	41	10	3	109	98	12	.353	.456	.479	147	43	9	6	-1	.930	6	*S-151	6.0
1924	Cle-A	153	594	99	188	45	5	4	106	67	13	.316	.388	.429	109	9	3	3	-1	.960	21	*S-153	4.3
1925	Cle-A	155	608	78	204	37	7	1	98	64	4	.336	.402	.424	109	10	7	6	-2	**.967**	16	*S-153/2-3	3.8
1926	Cle-A	154	578	91	187	41	5	4	85	65	6	.324	.399	.433	116	15	17	7	1	.955	3	*S-154	3.3
1927	Cle-A	153	569	83	180	48	5	1	92	51	7	.316	.382	.424	108	7	3	16	-9	**.962**	6	*S-153	1.9
1928	Cle-A	155	588	79	190	40	2	4	70	58	9	.323	.391	.418	111	11	7	1	2	**.963**	27	*S-137,3-19	5.4
1929	Cle-A	152	578	90	182	38	3	7	73	48	4	.315	.372	.427	102	2	6	6	-2	.975	15	*3-152	2.0
1930	Cle-A	109	353	44	102	17	6	0	48	41	3	.289	.374	.371	86	-6	1	4	-2	.950	-0	3-97	-0.2
1931	NY-A	130	484	102	146	22	1	6	64	61	1	.302	.390	.388	111	11	1	1	-0	.952	-2	*3-121/2-1	1.5
1932	*NY-A	125	503	95	137	21	3	11	68	56	3	.272	.349	.392	96	-2	0	2	-1	.974	2	*3-123	0.6
1933	NY-A	135	524	87	143	18	1	2	54	71	4	.273	.361	.323	87	-7	2	2	-1	.964	3	*3-131	0.3
Total	14	1903	7132	1141	2226	436	68	49	1055	842	114	.312	.391	.413	109	116	74	72	-21	.951	107	*S-1216,3-643/2-16	34.5

■ TOMMY SEWELL
Sewell, Thomas Wesley b: 4/16/06, Titus, Ala. d: 7/30/56, Montgomery, Ala. BL/TR, 5'7.5", 155 lbs. Deb: 6/21/27 F

YEAR	TM/L	G	AB	R	H	2B	3B	HR	RBI	BB	SO	AVG	OBP	SLG	PRO+	BR/A	SB	CS	SBR	FA	FR	G/POS	TPR
1927	Chi-N	1	1	0	0	0	0	0	0	0	0	.000	.000	.000	-99	-0			0	.000	0	H	0.0

■ JIMMY SEXTON
Sexton, Jimmy Dale b: 12/15/51, Mobile, Ala. BR/TR, 5'10", 175 lbs. Deb: 9/2/77

YEAR	TM/L	G	AB	R	H	2B	3B	HR	RBI	BB	SO	AVG	OBP	SLG	PRO+	BR/A	SB	CS	SBR	FA	FR	G/POS	TPR
1977	Sea-A	14	37	5	8	1	1	1	3	2	6	.216	.256	.378	71	-1	1	1	-0	.929	3	S-12	0.2
1978	Hou-N	88	141	17	29	3	2	2	6	13	28	.206	.273	.298	64	-7	16	2	4	.981	3	S-58/3-8,2-3	-0.2
1979	Hou-N	52	43	8	9	0	0	0	1	7	7	.209	.320	.209	50	-3	1	3	-2	.943	7	S-11/3-4,2-2	0.3
1981	Oak-A	7	3	3	0	0	0	0	0	0	2	.000	.000	.000	-99	-1	2	0	1	1.000	1	/3-1,D-1	0.1
1982	Oak-A	69	139	19	34	4	0	2	14	9	24	.245	.295	.317	71	-6	16	0	5	.957	-3	S-47/3-8,D-5	-0.1
1983	StL-N	6	9	1	1	1	0	0	0	1	4	.111	.200	.222	17	-1	0	0	0	1.000	1	/S-4,3-2	0.0
Total	6	236	372	53	81	9	3	5	24	32	71	.218	.281	.298	64	-19	36	6	7	.962	5	S-132/3-23,D-6,2-5	0.3

■ TOM SEXTON
Sexton, Thomas William b: 3/14/1865, Rock Island, Ill. d: 2/8/34, Rock Island, Ill. Deb: 9/27/1884

YEAR	TM/L	G	AB	R	H	2B	3B	HR	RBI	BB	SO	AVG	OBP	SLG	PRO+	BR/A	SB	CS	SBR	FA	FR	G/POS	TPR
1884	Mil-U	12	47	9	11	2	0	0		4		.234	.294	.277	136	-1				.853	-1	S-12	-0.2

■ SOCKS SEYBOLD
Seybold, Ralph Orlando b: 11/23/1870, Washingtonville, O d: 12/22/21, Greensburg, Pa. BR/TR, 5'11", 175 lbs. Deb: 8/20/1899

YEAR	TM/L	G	AB	R	H	2B	3B	HR	RBI	BB	SO	AVG	OBP	SLG	PRO+	BR/A	SB	CS	SBR	FA	FR	G/POS	TPR
1899	Cin-N	22	85	13	19	5	1	0	8	6		.224	.283	.306	60	-5	2			.917	1	O-22	-0.5
1901	Phi-A	114	449	74	150	24	14	8	90	40		.334	.397	.503	142	25	15			.954	-5	*O-100,1-14	1.0
1902	Phi-A	137	522	91	165	27	12	**16**	97	43		.316	.375	.506	137	24	6			.963	2	*O-136	1.6
1903	Phi-A	137	522	76	156	**45**	8	8	84	38		.299	.353	.462	137	23	5			.964	2	*O-120,1-18	1.4
1904	Phi-A	143	510	56	149	26	9	3	64	42		.292	.351	.396	129	17	12			.975	-1	*O-129,1-1	1.1
1905	*Phi-A	133	492	64	135	37	4	6	59	42		.274	.341	.402	133	15	5			.983	9	*O-133	2.3
1906	Phi-A	116	411	41	130	23	2	5	59	30		.316	.367	.418	141	19	9			.925	-5	*O-114	0.9
1907	Phi-A	147	564	58	153	29	4	5	92	40		.271	.324	.363	116	10	10			.973	1	*O-147	0.5
1908	Phi-A	48	130	5	28	2	0	0	3	12		.215	.287	.231	64	-5	2			.921	-4	O-34	-1.1
Total	9	997	3685	478	1085	218	54	51	556	293		.294	.353	.424	129	126	66			.961	-3	O-935/1-45	7.2

■ CY SEYMOUR
Seymour, James Bentley b: 12/9/1872, Albany, N.Y. d: 9/20/19, New York, N.Y. BL/TL, 6', 200 lbs. Deb: 4/22/1896

YEAR	TM/L	G	AB	R	H	2B	3B	HR	RBI	BB	SO	AVG	OBP	SLG	PRO+	BR/A	SB	CS	SBR	FA	FR	G/POS	TPR
1896	NY-N	12	32	2	7	0	0	0	0		7	.219	.219	.219	16	-4	0			.857	0	P-11/O-1	-0.1
1897	NY-N	44	137	13	33	5	1	2	14		4	.241	.262	.336	59	-9	3			.850	7	P-38/O-6	-0.2
1898	NY-N	80	297	41	82	5	2	4	23		9	.276	.300	.347	88	-6	8			.887	7	P-45,O-35/2-1	-0.7
1899	NY-N	50	159	25	52	3	2	2	27		4	.327	.344	.409	110	4	3			.839	3	P-32/O-8,1-3,3-1	-0.2
1900	NY-N	23	40	9	12	0	0	0	2		3	.300	.349	.300	84	-1	0			.828	-0	P-13/O-3,1-1	-0.2
1901	Bal-A	134	547	84	166	19	8	1	77		28	.303	.337	.373	93	-6	38			.945	14	*O-133/1-1	-0.2
1902	Bal-A	72	280	38	75	8	8	3	41		18	.268	.317	.386	90	-4	12			.956	1	O-72	-0.8
	Cin-N	62	244	27	83	8	2	2	37		12	.340	.378	.414	132	8	8			.920	4	O-61/P-1,3-1	0.9
1903	Cin-N	135	558	85	191	25	15	7	72		33	.342	.382	.478	130	18	25			.902	5	*O-135	1.4
1904	Cin-N	131	531	71	166	26	13	5	58		29	.313	.352	.439	132	17	11			.951	13	*O-130	2.4
1905	Cin-N	149	581	95	**219**	40	21	8	**121**		51	**.377**	.429	**.559**	175	**51**	21			.947	12	*O-149	5.7
1906	Cin-N	79	307	35	79	7	2	4	38		24	.257	.317	.332	98	-1	9			.968	10	O-79	0.6
	NY-N	72	269	35	86	12	3	4	42		18	.320	.365	.431	145	13	20			.978	2	O-72	0.8
	Yr	151	576	70	165	19	5	8	80		42	.286	.339	.378	120	12	29			.972	8	*O-151	1.4
1907	NY-N	131	473	46	139	25	8	3	75		36	.294	.350	.400	101	13	21			.975	3	*O-126	1.6
1908	NY-N	156	587	60	157	23	2	5	92		30	.267	.306	.339	101	-1	18			.949	11	*O-155	0.5
1909	NY-N	80	280	37	87	12	5	1	30		25	.311	.369	.400	137	12	14			.968	0	O-74	1.0
1910	NY-N	79	287	32	76	9	4	1	40	23	18	.265	.324	.334	92	-3	10			.936	-6	O-76	-1.4
1913	Bos-N	39	73	2	13	2	0	0	10	7	7	.178	.259	.205	33	-6	2			.950	-8	O-18	-0.7
Total	16	1528	5682	737	1723	229	96	52	799	354	32	.303	.347	.405	117	95	222			.945	81	*O-1333,P-140/132	10.4

■ TILLIE SHAFER
Shafer, Arthur Joseph b: 3/22/1889, Los Angeles, Cal. d: 1/10/62, Los Angeles, Cal. BB/TR, 5'10", 165 lbs. Deb: 4/24/09

YEAR	TM/L	G	AB	R	H	2B	3B	HR	RBI	BB	SO	AVG	OBP	SLG	PRO+	BR/A	SB	CS	SBR	FA	FR	G/POS	TPR
1909	NY-N	38	84	11	15	2	1	0	7	14		.179	.296	.226	61	-3	6			.750	-0	3-16,2-13/O-2	-0.4
1910	NY-N	29	21	5	4	1	0	0	1	0	6	.190	.190	.238	25	-2	0			.889	7	/3-8,2-2,S-2	0.3
1912	*NY-N	78	163	48	47	4	1	0	23	30	19	.288	.408	.325	99	2	22			.879	-7	S-31,3-16,2-15	-0.3
1913	*NY-N	138	508	74	146	17	12	5	52	61	55	.287	.369	.398	118	13	32			.923	-9	3-79,2-25,S-16,O-15	0.6
Total	4	283	776	138	212	24	14	5	83	105	80	.273	.366	.360	106	10	60			.903	-12	3-119/2-55,S-49,O	0.2

■ RALPH SHAFER
Shafer, Ralph Newton b: 3/17/1894, Cincinnati, Ohio d: 2/5/50, Akron, Ohio 5'11", Deb: 7/25/14

YEAR	TM/L	G	AB	R	H	2B	3B	HR	RBI	BB	SO	AVG	OBP	SLG	PRO+	BR/A	SB	CS	SBR	FA	FR	G/POS	TPR
1914	Pit-N	1	0	0	0	0	0	0	0	0	0	—	—	—		0			0	.000	0	H	0.0

■ SHAFFER
Shaffer Deb: 9/15/1875

YEAR	TM/L	G	AB	R	H	2B	3B	HR	RBI	BB	SO	AVG	OBP	SLG	PRO+	BR/A	SB	CS	SBR	FA	FR	G/POS	TPR
1875	Atl-n	1	4	0	0	0	0	0	0	0	0	.000	.000	.000	-99	-1	0	0	0	.500	-0	/O-1	-0.1

■ FRANK SHAFFER
Shaffer, Frank Deb: 4/24/1884

YEAR	TM/L	G	AB	R	H	2B	3B	HR	RBI	BB	SO	AVG	OBP	SLG	PRO+	BR/A	SB	CS	SBR	FA	FR	G/POS	TPR
1884	Alt-U	19	74	11	21	2	0	0		3		.284	.312	.311	88	-3				.889	-3	O-17/C-2,3-1	-0.6
	KC-U	44	164	18	28	3	2	0		15		.171	.240	.213	44	-16				.768	-3	O-41/C-2,2-1,S-1,3	-1.7
	Bal-U	3	13	1	1	0	0	0		0		.077	.077	.077	-48	-3				.750	-1	/O-3	-0.3
	Yr	66	251	30	50	5	2	0		18		.199	.253	.235	53	-21				.796	-6	O-61/C-4,3-2,2-1,S	-2.6

■ ORATOR SHAFFER
Shaffer, George b: 1852, Philadelphia, Pa. BL/TR, 5'9", 165 lbs. Deb: 5/23/1874 F

YEAR	TM/L	G	AB	R	H	2B	3B	HR	RBI	BB	SO	AVG	OBP	SLG	PRO+	BR/A	SB	CS	SBR	FA	FR	G/POS	TPR
1874	Har-n	9	35	6	8	0	0	1	3	0	3	.229	.229	.314	69	-1	0	0	0	.710	-2	/O-9	-0.2
	Mut-n	1	5	1	1	0	0	0	0	0	0	.200	.200	.200	28	-0	0	0	0	.000	-0	/O-1	-0.1
	Yr	10	40	7	9	0	0	1	3	0	3	.225	.200	.300	64	-2	0	0	0	.710	-2	O-10	-0.3

YEAR	TM/L	G	AB	R	H	2B	3B	HR	RBI	BB	SO	AVG	OBP	SLG	PRO+	BR/A	SB	CS	SBR	FA	FR	G/POS	TPR
1875	Phi-n	19	70	10	17	2	1	0	6	0	4	.243	.243	.300	84	-1	2	0	1	.769	-2	O-12/3-5,1-2	-0.2
1877	Lou-N	61	260	38	74	9	5	3	34	9	17	.285	.309	.392	101	-2				.835	14	*O-60/1-1	0.8
1878	Ind-N	63	266	48	90	19	6	0	30	13	20	.338	.369	.455	196	28				.842	8	*O-63	2.9
1879	Chi-N	73	316	53	96	13	0	0	35	6	28	.304	.317	.345	111	3				.801	20	*O-72/3-1	1.8
1880	Cle-N	83	338	62	90	14	9	0	21	17	36	.266	.301	.361	126	9				.901	17	*O-83	2.3
1881	Cle-N	85	343	48	88	13	6	1	34	23	20	.257	.303	.338	107	4				.880	2	*O-85	0.4
1882	Cle-N	84	313	37	67	14	2	3	28	27	27	.214	.276	.300	88	-3				.805	-9	*O-84	-1.2
1883	Buf-N	95	401	67	117	11	3	0	41	27	39	.292	.336	.334	103	2				.861	20	*O-95	1.8
1884	StL-U	106	467	130	168	**40**	10	2		30		.360	.398	.501	165	24				.870	4	*O-100/2-7,1-1	1.7
1885	StL-N	69	257	30	50	11	2	0	18	19	31	.195	.250	.253	67	-8				.918	11	O-69	0.1
	Phi-a	2	9	1	2	0	1	0	1	1		.222	.300	.444	125	0				1.000	-1	/O-2	0.0
1886	Phi-a	21	82	15	22	3	3	0	8	8		.268	.333	.378	121	2	3			.815	0	O-21	0.2
1890	Phi-a	100	390	55	110	15	5	1	58	47		.282	.367	.354	115	9	29			**.958**	2	*O-98/1-3	0.6
Total	2 n	29	110	17	26	2	1		9	0	7	.236	.236	.300	76	-3	2	0	1	.737	-4	/O-22,3-5,1-2	-0.5
Total	11	842	3442	584	974	162	52	10	<u>308</u>	227	<u>218</u>	.283	.328	.369	119	66	32			.865	81	O-832/2-7,1-5,3-1	11.4

■ TAYLOR SHAFFER   Shaffer, Taylor b: 7/1870, Philadelphia, Pa.   Deb: 4/17/1890 F

YEAR	TM/L	G	AB	R	H	2B	3B	HR	RBI	BB	SO	AVG	OBP	SLG	PRO+	BR/A	SB	CS	SBR	FA	FR	G/POS	TPR
1890	Phi-a	69	261	28	45	3	4	0	21	28		.172	.258	.215	40	-19	19			.921	4	2-69	-1.0

■ ART SHAMSKY   Shamsky, Arthur Louis b: 10/14/41, St.Louis, Mo. BL/TL, 6'1", 175 lbs. Deb: 4/17/65

YEAR	TM/L	G	AB	R	H	2B	3B	HR	RBI	BB	SO	AVG	OBP	SLG	PRO+	BR/A	SB	CS	SBR	FA	FR	G/POS	TPR
1965	Cin-N	64	96	13	25	4	3	2	10	10	29	.260	.330	.427	104	1	1	0	0	.966	0	O-18/1-1	0.0
1966	Cin-N	96	234	41	54	5	0	21	47	32	45	.231	.323	.521	120	6	0	2	-1	.973	-3	O-74	-0.1
1967	Cin-N	76	147	6	29	3	1	3	13	15	34	.197	.276	.293	56	-8	0	1	-1	.984	-2	O-40	-1.4
1968	NY-N	116	345	30	82	14	4	12	48	21	58	.238	.295	.406	108	3	1	0	0	.993	1	O-82,1-17	-0.2
1969	*NY-N	100	303	42	91	9	3	14	47	36	32	.300	.380	.488	139	16	1	2	-1	.992	-6	O-78/1-9	0.4
1970	NY-N	122	403	48	118	19	2	11	49	49	33	.293	.374	.432	115	9	1	1	-0	1.000	1	O-58,1-56	0.2
1971	NY-N	68	135	13	25	6	2	5	18	21	18	.185	.299	.370	90	-2	1	1	-0	.984	2	O-38/1-1	-0.2
1972	Chi-N	15	16	1	2	0	0	0	1	3	3	.125	.263	.125	12	-2	0	0	0	1.000	0	/1-4	-0.2
	Oak-A	8	7	0	0	0	0	0	0	1	2	.000	.125	.000	-64	-1	0	0	0	.000	0	H	-0.2
Total	8	665	1686	194	426	60	15	68	233	188	254	.253	.333	.427	109	21	5	7	-3	.987	-8	O-388/1-88	-1.7

■ JIM SHANDLEY   Shandley, James H. b: New York d: 11/4/04, Brooklyn, N.Y.   Deb: 5/3/1876

YEAR	TM/L	G	AB	R	H	2B	3B	HR	RBI	BB	SO	AVG	OBP	SLG	PRO+	BR/A	SB	CS	SBR	FA	FR	G/POS	TPR
1876	NY-N	2	8	0	1	0	0	0	0	0	0	.125	.125	.125	-19	-1				.600	-1	/O-2	-0.1

■ WALLY SHANER   Shaner, Walter Dedaker "Skinny" b: 5/24/1900, Lynchburg, Va. d: 11/13/92, Las Vegas, Nev. BR/TR, 6'2", 195 lbs. Deb: 5/4/23

YEAR	TM/L	G	AB	R	H	2B	3B	HR	RBI	BB	SO	AVG	OBP	SLG	PRO+	BR/A	SB	CS	SBR	FA	FR	G/POS	TPR
1923	Cle-A	3	4	1	1	0	0	0	0	1	1	.250	.400	.250	74	-0	0	0	0	1.000	-1	/O-2,3-1	-0.1
1926	Bos-A	69	191	20	54	12	2	0	21	17	13	.283	.348	.366	89	-3	1	0	0	.965	0	O-48	-0.6
1927	Bos-A	122	406	54	111	33	6	3	49	21	35	.273	.311	.406	87	-10	11	4	1	.955	-8	*O-108/1-1	-2.2
1929	Cin-N	13	28	5	9	0	0	1	4	4	5	.321	.406	.429	112	1	1			1.000	-1	/1-8,O-2	-0.1
Total	4	207	629	80	175	45	8	4	74	43	54	.278	.327	.394	89	-12	13	4	<u></u>	.959	-9	O-160/1-9,3-1	-3.0

■ HOWIE SHANKS   Shanks, Howard Samuel "Hank" b: 7/21/1890, Chicago, Ill. d: 7/30/41, Monaca, Pa. BR/TR, 5'11", 170 lbs. Deb: 5/9/12 C

YEAR	TM/L	G	AB	R	H	2B	3B	HR	RBI	BB	SO	AVG	OBP	SLG	PRO+	BR/A	SB	CS	SBR	FA	FR	G/POS	TPR
1912	Was-A	116	399	52	92	14	7	4	48	40		.231	.305	.308	75	-13	21			.962	-2	*O-114	-2.1
1913	Was-A	109	390	38	99	11	5	1	37	15	40	.254	.287	.315	75	-14	24			.978	3	*O-109	-1.6
1914	Was-A	143	500	44	112	22	10	4	64	29	51	.224	.269	.332	78	-16	18	16	-4	.954	-0	*O-139	-3.0
1915	Was-A	141	492	52	123	19	8	0	47	30	42	.250	.297	.321	83	-12	12	14	-5	.982	7	O-80,3-49,2-10	-1.2
1916	Was-A	140	471	51	119	15	7	1	48	41	34	.253	.317	.321	92	-5	23	12	-0	.987	10	O-88,3-31/S-8,1-7	0.2
1917	Was-A	126	430	45	87	15	5	0	28	33	37	.202	.269	.260	62	-20	15			.929	13	S-90,O-26/1-2	-0.5
1918	Was-A	120	436	42	112	19	4	1	56	31	21	.257	.312	.326	94	-4	23			.957	1	O-64,2-48/3-3	-0.4
1919	Was-A	135	491	33	122	8	7	1	54	25	48	.248	.289	.299	66	-23	13			.922	-11	S-94,2-34/O-6	-2.9
1920	Was-A	128	444	56	119	16	7	4	37	29	43	.268	.316	.363	82	-13	11	6	-0	.951	-6	3-63,O-35,1-14,/2S	-1.8
1921	Was-A	154	562	81	170	24	**18**	7	69	57	38	.302	.370	.447	113	10	11	10	-3	**.960**	5	*3-154/2-1	2.2
1922	Was-A	84	272	35	77	10	9	1	32	25	25	.283	.352	.397	100	-0	6	0	2	.920	7	3-54,O-27	-1.1
1923	Bos-A	131	464	38	118	19	5	3	57	19	37	.254	.285	.336	63	-26	6	6	-2	.939	-19	3-83,2-38/O-6,S-1	-3.9
1924	Bos-A	72	193	22	50	16	3	0	25	21	12	.259	.332	.373	81	-6	1	0	0	.972	7	S-41,3-22/O-4,12	0.6
1925	NY-A	66	155	15	40	3	1	1	18	20	15	.258	.343	.310	68	-7	1	0	0	.938	-2	3-26,2-21/O-4	-1.0
Total	14	1665	5699	604	1440	211	96	25	620	415	443	.253	.308	.337	82	-148	185	<u>64</u>		.971	10	O-702,3-485,S2/1	-14.4

■ DOC SHANLEY   Shanley, Harry Root b: 1890, Granbury, Tex. d: 12/13/34, St.Petersburg, Fla BR/TR, 6', 174 lbs. Deb: 9/15/12

YEAR	TM/L	G	AB	R	H	2B	3B	HR	RBI	BB	SO	AVG	OBP	SLG	PRO+	BR/A	SB	CS	SBR	FA	FR	G/POS	TPR
1912	StL-A	5	8	1	0	0	0	0	1		2	.000	.200	.000	-43	-1	0			.833	-2	/S-4	-0.3

■ WARREN SHANNABROOK   Shannabrook, Warren H. b: 11/30/1880, Massillon, Ohio d: 3/10/64, N.Canton, Ohio BR/TR, 6', 170 lbs. Deb: 8/13/06

YEAR	TM/L	G	AB	R	H	2B	3B	HR	RBI	BB	SO	AVG	OBP	SLG	PRO+	BR/A	SB	CS	SBR	FA	FR	G/POS	TPR
1906	Was-A	1	2	0	0	0	0	0	0	0	0	.000	.000	.000	-99	-0	0			1.000	-1	/3-1	-0.1

■ DAN SHANNON   Shannon, Daniel Webster b: 3/23/1865, Bridgeport, Conn. d: 10/25/13, Bridgeport, Conn. 5'9", 175 lbs. Deb: 4/17/1889 M

YEAR	TM/L	G	AB	R	H	2B	3B	HR	RBI	BB	SO	AVG	OBP	SLG	PRO+	BR/A	SB	CS	SBR	FA	FR	G/POS	TPR
1889	Lou-a	121	498	90	128	22	12	4	48	42	52	.257	.315	.373	97	-3	26			.910	7	*2-121,M	0.9
1890	Phi-P	19	75	15	18	5	1	1	16	4	12	.240	.278	.373	72	-4	4			.926	-4	2-19	-0.6
	NY-P	83	324	59	70	7	8	3	44	25	34	.216	.274	.315	53	-25	21			.908	1	2-77/S-6	-1.5
	Yr	102	399	74	88	12	9	4	60	29	46	.221	.275	.326	56	-28	25			.911	-3	2-96/S-6	-2.1
1891	Was-a	19	67	7	9	2	0	0	3	6	9	.134	.205	.164	44	-8	3			.878	1	S-14/2-5,M	-0.6
Total	3	242	964	171	225	36	21	8	111	77	107	.233	.291	.339	73	-39	54			.911	5	2-222/S-20	-1.8

■ FRANK SHANNON   Shannon, John Francis b: 12/3/1873, San Francisco, Cal. d: 2/27/34, Boston, Mass. 5'3", 155 lbs. Deb: 10/1/1892

YEAR	TM/L	G	AB	R	H	2B	3B	HR	RBI	BB	SO	AVG	OBP	SLG	PRO+	BR/A	SB	CS	SBR	FA	FR	G/POS	TPR
1892	Was-N	1	4	0	1	0	0	0	0		2	.250	.250	.250	53	-0				.625	-1	/S-1	-0.1
1896	Lou-N	31	115	14	18	1	1	1	15	13	15	.157	.248	.209	22	-13	3			.830	-13	S-28/3-3	-2.2
Total	2	32	119	14	19	1	1	1	17	13	17	.160	.248	.210	23	-13	3			.820	-14	/S-29,3-3	-2.3

■ JOE SHANNON   Shannon, Joseph Aloysius b: 2/11/1897, Jersey City, N.J. d: 7/28/55, Jersey City, N.J. BR/TR, 5'11", 170 lbs. Deb: 7/7/15 F

YEAR	TM/L	G	AB	R	H	2B	3B	HR	RBI	BB	SO	AVG	OBP	SLG	PRO+	BR/A	SB	CS	SBR	FA	FR	G/POS	TPR
1915	Bos-N	5	10	3	2	0	0	0	1	0	3	.200	.200	.200	22	-1	0			.750	-0	/O-4,2-1	-0.1

■ RED SHANNON   Shannon, Maurice Joseph b: 2/11/1897, Jersey City, N.J. d: 4/12/70, Jersey City, N.J. BB/TR, 5'11", 170 lbs. Deb: 10/7/15 F

YEAR	TM/L	G	AB	R	H	2B	3B	HR	RBI	BB	SO	AVG	OBP	SLG	PRO+	BR/A	SB	CS	SBR	FA	FR	G/POS	TPR
1915	Bos-N	1	3	0	0	0	0	0	0	0	0	.000	.000	.000	-99	-1	0			.857	1	/2-1	0.0
1917	Phi-A	11	35	8	10	0	0	0	7	6	9	.286	.390	.286	108	1	2			.875	-0	S-10	0.1
1918	Phi-A	72	225	23	54	6	5	0	16	42	52	.240	.367	.311	103	3	5			.898	4	S-45,2-26	0.3
1919	Phi-A	39	155	14	42	7	2	0	14	12	28	.271	.331	.342	88	-2	4			.948	-5	2-37	-0.6
	Bos-A	80	290	36	75	11	7	0	17	17	42	.259	.313	.345	90	-5	7			.973	-4	2-79	-0.6
	Yr	119	445	50	117	18	9	0	31	29	70	.263	.320	.344	89	-7	11			.965	-9	*2-116	-1.2
1920	Was-A	63	222	30	64	8	7	0	30	22	32	.288	.352	.387	99	-0	2	5	-2	.919	-19	S-31,2-16,3-15	-1.8
	Phi-A	24	88	4	15	1	1	0	3	4	12	.170	.207	.205	9	-12	1	1	-0	.945	-1	S-24	-1.1
	Yr	87	310	34	79	9	8	0	33	26	44	.255	.313	.335	73	-12	3	6	-3	.931	-21	S-55,2-16,3-15	-2.9
1921	Phi-A	1	1	0	0	0	0	0	0	0	0	.000	.000	.000	-99	-0	0			.000	0	H	0.0
1926	Chi-N	19	51	9	17	5	0	0	6	3	6	.333	.414	.431	126	2	0			.957	-2	S-13	0.1
Total	7	310	1070	124	277	38	22	0	91	109	178	.259	.334	.336	89	-14	21	<u>6</u>		.957	-35	2-159,S-123/3-15	-3.6

■ OWEN SHANNON   Shannon, Owen Dennis Ignatius b: 12/22/1879, Omaha, Neb. d: 4/10/18, Omaha, Neb. BR/TR, Deb: 9/6/03

YEAR	TM/L	G	AB	R	H	2B	3B	HR	RBI	BB	SO	AVG	OBP	SLG	PRO+	BR/A	SB	CS	SBR	FA	FR	G/POS	TPR
1903	StL-A	9	28	1	6	2	0	0	3	1		.214	.241	.286	59	-1	0			.957	-0	/C-8,1-1	-0.1
1907	Was-A	4	7	1	1	0	0	0	0	0		.143	.143	.143	-10	-1	0			1.000	3	/C-4	0.2
Total	2	13	35	2	7	2	0	0	3	1		.200	.222	.257	21	-1	0			.970	2	/C-12,1-1	0.1

■ MIKE SHANNON   Shannon, Thomas Michael "Moonman" b: 7/5/39, St.Louis, Mo. BR/TR, 6'3", 195 lbs. Deb: 9/11/62

YEAR	TM/L	G	AB	R	H	2B	3B	HR	RBI	BB	SO	AVG	OBP	SLG	PRO+	BR/A	SB	CS	SBR	FA	FR	G/POS	TPR
1962	StL-N	10	15	3	2	0	0	0	0	0	3	.133	.188	.133	-11	-2	0	0	0	1.000	-0	/O-7	-0.3
1963	StL-N	32	26	3	8	0	0	1	2	0	6	.308	.333	.423	106	0	0	1	-1	.944	-5	O-26	-0.6

YEAR	TM/L	G	AB	R	H	2B	3B	HR	RBI	BB	SO	AVG	OBP	SLG	PRO+	BR/A	SB	CS	SBR	FA	FR	G/POS	TPR
1964	*StL-N	88	253	30	66	8	2	9	43	19	54	.261	.313	.415	95	-2	4	0	1	.983	-6	O-88	-1.1
1965	StL-N	124	244	32	54	17	3	3	25	28	46	.221	.307	.352	78	-7	2	1	0	.994	-1	*O-101/C-4	-1.1
1966	StL-N	137	459	61	132	20	6	16	64	37	106	.288	.341	.462	120	12	8	4	0	.985	6	*O-129/C-1	1.3
1967	*StL-N	130	482	53	118	18	3	12	77	37	89	.245	.304	.369	93	-5	2	4	-2	.919	-11	*3-122/O-6	-2.1
1968	*StL-N	156	576	62	153	29	2	15	79	37	114	.266	.312	.401	114	9	1	2	-1	.952	-7	*3-156	0.1
1969	StL-N	150	551	51	140	15	5	12	55	49	87	.254	.316	.365	90	-8	1	4	-2	.945	-19	*3-149	-3.0
1970	StL-N	55	174	18	37	9	2	0	22	16	20	.213	.279	.287	51	-12	1	1	0	.919	-13	3-51	-2.5
Total	9	882	2780	313	710	116	23	68	367	224	525	.255	.313	.387	96	-16	19	17	-5	.938	-57	3-478,O-357/C-5	-9.5

■ WALLY SHANNON
Shannon, Walter Charles b: 1/23/33, Cleveland, Ohio d: 2/8/92, Creve Coeur, Mo. BL/TR, 6', 178 lbs. Deb: 7/9/59

YEAR	TM/L	G	AB	R	H	2B	3B	HR	RBI	BB	SO	AVG	OBP	SLG	PRO+	BR/A	SB	CS	SBR	FA	FR	G/POS	TPR
1959	StL-N	47	95	5	27	5	0	0	5	0	12	.284	.292	.337	63	-5	0	0	0	1.000	-11	S-21,2-10	-1.4
1960	StL-N	18	23	2	4	0	0	0	1	3	6	.174	.296	.174	30	-2	0	0	0	1.000	2	2-15/S-1	0.1
Total	2	65	118	7	31	5	0	0	6	3	18	.263	.293	.305	56	-7	0	0	0	.955	-9	/2-25,S-22	-1.3

■ SPIKE SHANNON
Shannon, William Porter b: 2/7/1878, Pittsburgh, Pa. d: 5/16/40, Minneapolis, Minn. BB/TR, 5'11", 180 lbs. Deb: 4/15/04 U

YEAR	TM/L	G	AB	R	H	2B	3B	HR	RBI	BB	SO	AVG	OBP	SLG	PRO+	BR/A	SB	CS	SBR	FA	FR	G/POS	TPR
1904	StL-N	134	500	84	140	10	3	1	26	50		.280	.349	.318	111	9	34			**.978**	9	*O-133	1.0
1905	StL-N	140	544	73	146	16	3	0	41	47		.268	.327	.309	92	-4	27			**.984**	0	*O-140	-1.1
1906	StL-N	80	302	36	78	4	0	0	25	36		.258	.337	.272	94	-1	15			.972	6	O-80	0.1
	NY-N	76	287	42	73	5	1	0	25	34		.254	.342	.279	91	-1	18			.958	-7	O-76	-1.3
	Yr	156	589	78	151	9	1	0	50	70		.256	.339	.275	93	-2	33			.966	-1	*O-156	-1.2
1907	NY-N	155	585	**104**	155	12	5	1	33	82		.265	.363	.308	107	9	33			.977	2	*O-155	0.5
1908	NY-N	77	268	34	60	2	1	1	21	39		.224	.314	.250	77	-6	13			.976	-3	O-74	-1.4
	Pit-N	32	127	10	25	0	2	0	12	9		.197	.250	.228	53	-7	5			.947	1	O-32	-0.8
	Yr	109	395	44	85	2	3	1	33	37		.215	.294	.243	69	-12	18			.964	-2	*O-106	-2.2
Total	5	694	2613	383	677	49	15	3	183	286		.259	.337	.293	96	-1	145			.974	8	O-690	-3.0

■ BILLY SHANTZ
Shantz, Wilmer Ebert b: 7/31/27, Pottstown, Pa. d: 12/13/93, Lauderhill, Fla. BR/TR, 6'1", 160 lbs. Deb: 4/13/54 F

YEAR	TM/L	G	AB	R	H	2B	3B	HR	RBI	BB	SO	AVG	OBP	SLG	PRO+	BR/A	SB	CS	SBR	FA	FR	G/POS	TPR
1954	Phi-A	51	164	13	42	9	3	1	17	17	23	.256	.326	.366	89	-3	0	0	0	.975	-13	C-51	-1.4
1955	KC-A	79	217	18	56	4	1	1	12	11	14	.258	.294	.300	59	-13	0	0	0	.990	-10	C-78	-2.1
1960	NY-A	1	0	0	0	0	0	0	0	0	0	—	—	—	—	—	0	0	0	1.000	0	/C-1	0.0
Total	3	131	381	31	98	13	4	2	29	28	37	.257	.308	.328	72	-15	0	0	0	.984	-23	C-130	-3.5

■ RALPH SHARMAN
Sharman, Ralph Edward "Bally" b: 4/11/1895, Cleveland, Ohio d: 5/24/18, Camp Sheridan, Ala BR/TR, 5'11", 176 lbs. Deb: 9/10/17

YEAR	TM/L	G	AB	R	H	2B	3B	HR	RBI	BB	SO	AVG	OBP	SLG	PRO+	BR/A	SB	CS	SBR	FA	FR	G/POS	TPR
1917	Phi-A	13	37	2	11	2	1	0	2	3	2	.297	.366	.405	137	2	1			.941	-1	O-10	0.0

■ DICK SHARON
Sharon, Richard Louis b: 4/15/50, San Mateo, Cal. BR/TR, 6'2", 195 lbs. Deb: 5/13/73

YEAR	TM/L	G	AB	R	H	2B	3B	HR	RBI	BB	SO	AVG	OBP	SLG	PRO+	BR/A	SB	CS	SBR	FA	FR	G/POS	TPR
1973	Det-A	91	178	20	43	9	0	7	16	10	31	.242	.282	.410	87	-4	2	0	1	.970	-10	O-91	-1.5
1974	Det-A	60	129	12	28	4	0	2	10	14	29	.217	.294	.295	67	-5	4	4	-1	.989	-5	O-56	-1.4
1975	SD-N	91	160	14	31	7	0	4	20	26	35	.194	.306	.313	77	-5	0	2	-1	.948	-7	O-57	-1.6
Total	3	242	467	46	102	20	0	13	46	50	95	.218	.294	.345	79	-14	6	6	-2	.969	-22	O-204	-4.5

■ BILL SHARP
Sharp, William Howard b: 1/18/50, Lima, Ohio BL/TL, 5'10", 178 lbs. Deb: 5/26/73

YEAR	TM/L	G	AB	R	H	2B	3B	HR	RBI	BB	SO	AVG	OBP	SLG	PRO+	BR/A	SB	CS	SBR	FA	FR	G/POS	TPR
1973	Chi-A	77	196	23	54	8	3	4	22	19	28	.276	.349	.408	109	2	2	3	-1	.981	-6	O-70/D-1	0.1
1974	Chi-A	100	320	45	81	13	2	4	24	25	37	.253	.311	.344	86	-6	0	3	-2	.986	-1	O-99	-1.3
1975	Chi-A	18	35	1	7	0	0	0	4	2	3	.200	.243	.200	26	-3	0	0	0	.941	-3	O-14	-0.7
	Mil-A	125	373	37	95	27	3	1	34	19	26	.255	.293	.351	81	-10	0	3	-2	.994	-3	*O-124	-2.0
	Yr	143	408	38	102	27	3	1	38	21	29	.250	.288	.338	76	-14	0	3	-2	.991	-6	*O-138	-2.7
1976	Mil-A	78	180	16	44	4	0	0	11	10	15	.244	.288	.267	64	-8	1	3	-2	.975	0	O-56/D-7	-1.2
Total	4	398	1104	122	281	52	8	9	95	75	109	.255	.306	.341	83	-26	3	12	-6	.985	-5	O-363/D-8	-5.1

■ BUD SHARPE
Sharpe, Bayard Heston b: 8/6/1881, West Chester, Pa. d: 5/31/16, Haddock, Ga. BL/TR, Deb: 4/14/05

YEAR	TM/L	G	AB	R	H	2B	3B	HR	RBI	BB	SO	AVG	OBP	SLG	PRO+	BR/A	SB	CS	SBR	FA	FR	G/POS	TPR
1905	Bos-N	46	170	8	31	3	2	0	11	7		.182	.215	.224	31	-15	0			.904	2	O-42/C-3,1-1	-1.5
1910	Bos-N	115	439	30	105	14	3	0	29	14	31	.239	.264	.285	58	-25	4			.987	7	*1-113	-1.9
	Pit-N	4	16	2	3	0	1	0	1	0	2	.188	.188	.313	43	-1	0			1.000		/1-4	-0.1
	Yr	119	455	32	108	14	4	0	30	14	33	.237	.262	.286	57	-26	4			.987	8	*1-117	-2.0
Total	2	165	625	40	139	17	6	0	41	21	33	.222	.249	.269	50	-41	4			.987	9	1-118/O-42,C-3	-3.5

■ MIKE SHARPERSON
Sharperson, Michael Tyrone b: 10/4/61, Orangeburg, S.C. d: 5/26/96, Las Vegas, Nev. BR/TR, 6'3", 190 lbs. Deb: 4/6/87

YEAR	TM/L	G	AB	R	H	2B	3B	HR	RBI	BB	SO	AVG	OBP	SLG	PRO+	BR/A	SB	CS	SBR	FA	FR	G/POS	TPR
1987	Tor-A	32	96	4	20	4	1	0	9	7	15	.208	.269	.271	43	-8	2	1	0	.971	-5	2-32	-1.1
	LA-N	10	33	7	9	2	0	0	1	4	5	.273	.351	.333	85	-1	1	0	0	1.000	-0	/3-7,2-6	0.1
1988	*LA-N	46	59	8	16	1	0	0	4	1	12	.271	.295	.288	70	-2	0	1	-1	.949	-0	2-20/3-6,S-4	-0.3
1989	LA-N	27	28	2	7	3	0	0	5	4	7	.250	.344	.357	102	0	0	1	-1	1.000	-0	/2-4,1-2,3-2,S-1	0.0
1990	LA-N	129	357	42	106	14	2	3	36	46	39	.297	.379	.373	111	7	15	6	1	.949	9	*3-106,S-15/2-9,1-6	1.4
1991	LA-N	105	216	24	60	11	2	2	20	25	24	.278	.355	.375	108	3	1	3	-2	.981	-5	3-68,S-16,1-10/2-5	-0.3
1992	LA-N★	128	317	48	95	21	0	3	36	47	33	.300	.390	.394	125	12	2	2	-1	.979	1	2-63,3-60/S-2	1.4
1993	LA-N	73	90	13	23	4	0	2	10	5	17	.256	.302	.367	83	-2	2	0	0	.945	1	2-17/3-6,S-3,1-1,0	0.0
1995	Atl-N	7	7	1	1	1	0	0	2	0	2	.143	.143	.286	9	-1	0	0	0	.000	0	/3-1	-0.1
Total	8	557	1203	149	337	61	5	10	123	139	154	.280	.357	.364	103	8	22	14	-2	.952	-0	3-256,2-156/S10	1.1

■ JACK SHARROTT
Sharrott, John Henry b: 8/13/1869, Bangor, Me. d: 12/31/27, Los Angeles, Cal. BR/TR, 5'9", 165 lbs. Deb: 4/22/1890

YEAR	TM/L	G	AB	R	H	2B	3B	HR	RBI	BB	SO	AVG	OBP	SLG	PRO+	BR/A	SB	CS	SBR	FA	FR	G/POS	TPR
1890	NY-N	32	109	16	22	3	2	0	14	0	14	.202	.202	.266	36	-9	3			.932	-2	P-25/O-9	-0.6
1891	NY-N	10	30	5	10	2	0	1	7	1	2	.333	.355	.500	154	2	3			.950	-7	P-10	0.0
1892	NY-N	4	8	1	1	0	0	0	0	0	1	.125	.125	.125	-25	-1	0			.333	-1	/O-3,P-1	-0.2
1893	Phi-N	50	152	25	38	4	3	1	22	8	14	.250	.287	.336	66	-8	4			.824	-8	O-33,P-12	-1.3
Total	4	96	299	47	71	9	5	2	43	9	31	.237	.260	.321	61	-17	15			.927	-10	/P-48,O-45	-2.1

■ SHAG SHAUGHNESSY
Shaughnessy, Francis Joseph b: 4/8/1883, Amboy, Ill. d: 5/15/69, Montreal, Que., Can BR/TR, 6'1.5", 185 lbs. Deb: 4/17/05 C

YEAR	TM/L	G	AB	R	H	2B	3B	HR	RBI	BB	SO	AVG	OBP	SLG	PRO+	BR/A	SB	CS	SBR	FA	FR	G/POS	TPR
1905	Was-A	1	3	0	0	0	0	0	0	0	0	.000	.250	.000	-19	-0	0			.667	-0	/O-1	-0.1
1908	Phi-A	8	29	2	9	0	0	0	1	2		.310	.355	.310	109	0	3			1.000	-1	/O-8	-0.1
Total	2	9	32	2	9	0	0	0	1	2		.281	.343	.281	97	0	3			.938	-1	/O-9	-0.2

■ JON SHAVE
Shave, Jonathan Taylor b: 11/4/67, Waycross, Ga. BR/TR, 6', 185 lbs. Deb: 5/15/93

YEAR	TM/L	G	AB	R	H	2B	3B	HR	RBI	BB	SO	AVG	OBP	SLG	PRO+	BR/A	SB	CS	SBR	FA	FR	G/POS	TPR
1993	Tex-A	17	47	3	15	2	0	0	3	1	5	.319	.319	.362	86	-1	1	3	-2	.917	-2	/S-9,2-8	-0.4

■ AL SHAW
Shaw, Albert Simpson b: 3/1/1881, Toledo, Ill. d: 12/30/74, Danville, Ill. BL/TR, 5'8.5", 165 lbs. Deb: 9/28/07

YEAR	TM/L	G	AB	R	H	2B	3B	HR	RBI	BB	SO	AVG	OBP	SLG	PRO+	BR/A	SB	CS	SBR	FA	FR	G/POS	TPR
1907	StL-N	9	25	2	7	0	0	0	1	3		.280	.379	.280	110	1	1			.947	-1	/O-9	0.0
1908	StL-N	107	367	40	97	13	4	1	19	26		.264	.311	.330	110	3	9			.931	7	O-91/S-4,3-1	0.7
1909	StL-N	114	331	45	82	12	7	2	34	55		.248	.355	.344	125	11	15			.940	-1	O-92	0.7
1914	Bro-F	112	376	81	122	27	7	5	49	44	59	.324	.395	.473	137	14	24			.955	1	*O-102	1.1
1915	KC-F	132	448	67	126	22	10	6	67	46	45	.281	.348	.415	119	4	15			.942	-14	*O-124	-1.8
Total	5	474	1547	235	434	74	28	14	170	173	104	.281	.353	.392	123	33	64			.942	-8	O-418/S-4,3-1	0.7

■ AL SHAW
Shaw, Alfred "Shoddy" b: 10/3/1874, Burslem, England d: 3/25/58, Uhrichsville, Ohio BR/TR, 5'8", 170 lbs. Deb: 6/8/01

YEAR	TM/L	G	AB	R	H	2B	3B	HR	RBI	BB	SO	AVG	OBP	SLG	PRO+	BR/A	SB	CS	SBR	FA	FR	G/POS	TPR
1901	Det-A	55	171	20	46	7	0	1	23	10		.269	.321	.321	76	-6	2			.938	-0	C-42/1-9,3-2,S-1	-0.2
1907	Bos-A	76	198	10	38	7	1	0	7	18		.192	.269	.227	59	-9	4			.971	15	C-73/1-1	1.3
1908	Chi-A	32	49	0	4	1	0	0	2	6		.082	.118	.102	-29	-7	0			.953	2	C-29	-0.4
1909	Bos-N	18	41	1	4	1	0	0	0	1		.098	.213	.098	-3	-5	0			.975	4	C-14	-0.2
Total	4	181	459	31	92	9	3	1	32	35		.200	.267	.240	53	-26	6			.961	20	C-158/1-10,3-2,S-1	0.7

■ BEN SHAW
Shaw, Benjamin Nathaniel b: 6/18/1893, LaCenter, Ky. d: 3/16/59, Cleveland, Ohio BR/TR, 5'11.5", 190 lbs. Deb: 4/11/17

YEAR	TM/L	G	AB	R	H	2B	3B	HR	RBI	BB	SO	AVG	OBP	SLG	PRO+	BR/A	SB	CS	SBR	FA	FR	G/POS	TPR
1917	Pit-N	2	2	0	0	0	0	0	0	0	0	.000	.000	.000	-97	-0	0			1.000	0	H	-0.1

YEAR	TM/L	G	AB	R	H	2B	3B	HR	RBI	BB	SO	AVG	OBP	SLG	PRO+	BR/A	SB	CS	SBR	FA	FR	G/POS	TPR
1918	Pit-N	21	36	5	7	1	0	0	2	2	2	.194	.275	.222	50	-2	0			.981	-2	/1-9,C-5	-0.4
Total	2	23	38	5	7	1	0	0	2	2	2	.184	.262	.211	43	-2	0			.981	-2	/1-9,C-5	-0.5

■ HUNKY SHAW   Shaw, Royal N b: 9/29/1884, Yakima, Wash. d: 7/3/69, Yakima, Wash. BB/TR, 5'8", 165 lbs. Deb: 5/16/08

YEAR	TM/L	G	AB	R	H	2B	3B	HR	RBI	BB	SO	AVG	OBP	SLG	PRO+	BR/A	SB	CS	SBR	FA	FR	G/POS	TPR
1908	Pit-N	1	1	0	0	0	0	0	0	0	0	.000	.000	.000	-99	-0	0			.000	0	H	0.0

■ MARTY SHAY   Shay, Arthur Joseph b: 4/25/1896, Boston, Mass. d: 2/20/51, Worcester, Mass. BR/TR, 5'7.5", 148 lbs. Deb: 9/16/16

YEAR	TM/L	G	AB	R	H	2B	3B	HR	RBI	BB	SO	AVG	OBP	SLG	PRO+	BR/A	SB	CS	SBR	FA	FR	G/POS	TPR
1916	Chi-N	2	7	0	2	0	0	0	0	0	1	.286	.286	.286	68	-0	0			.917	0	/S-2	0.0
1924	Bos-N	19	68	4	16	3	1	0	2	5	5	.235	.297	.309	65	-3	2	1	0	.950	-12	2-19/S-1	-1.5
Total	2	21	75	4	18	3	1	0	2	5	6	.240	.296	.307	66	-4	2	1		.929	-12	/2-19,S-3	-1.5

■ DANNY SHAY   Shay, Daniel C. b: 11/8/1876, Springfield, Ohio d: 12/1/27, Kansas City, Mo. TR, 5'10". Deb: 4/30/01

YEAR	TM/L	G	AB	R	H	2B	3B	HR	RBI	BB	SO	AVG	OBP	SLG	PRO+	BR/A	SB	CS	SBR	FA	FR	G/POS	TPR
1901	Cle-A	19	75	4	17	2	0	0	10	2		.227	.266	.307	61	-4	0			.901	-4	S-19	-0.6
1904	StL-N	99	340	45	87	11	1	1	18	39		.256	.338	.303	103	3	36			.911	-7	S-97/2-2	-0.2
1905	StL-N	78	281	30	67	12	1	0	28	35		.238	.331	.288	88	-3	11			.953	-13	2-39,S-39	-1.6
1907	NY-N	35	79	10	15	1	1	1	6	12		.190	.304	.266	76	-2	5			.931	-7	2-13/S-9,O-2	-1.1
Total	4	231	775	89	186	26	5	2	62	88		.240	.325	.294	90	-6	52			.902	-31	S-164/2-54,O-2	-3.5

■ GERRY SHEA   Shea, Gerald J. b: 7/26/1881, St.Louis, Mo. d: 5/3/64, Berkeley, Mo. TR, 5'7", 160 lbs. Deb: 10/1/05

YEAR	TM/L	G	AB	R	H	2B	3B	HR	RBI	BB	SO	AVG	OBP	SLG	PRO+	BR/A	SB	CS	SBR	FA	FR	G/POS	TPR
1905	StL-N	2	6	0	2	0	0	0	0	0		.333	.333	.333	102	-0	0			.917	1	/C-2	0.1

■ NAP SHEA   Shea, John Edward "Napoleon" b: 5/23/1874, Ware, Mass. d: 7/8/68, Bloomfield Hills, Mich. BR/TR, 5'5", 155 lbs. Deb: 9/11/02

YEAR	TM/L	G	AB	R	H	2B	3B	HR	RBI	BB	SO	AVG	OBP	SLG	PRO+	BR/A	SB	CS	SBR	FA	FR	G/POS	TPR
1902	Phi-N	3	8	1	1	0	0	0	0	1		.125	.300	.125	32	-1	0			1.000	-0	/C-3	-0.1

■ MERV SHEA   Shea, Mervyn David John b: 9/5/1900, San Francisco, Cal. d: 1/27/53, Sacramento, Cal. BR/TR, 5'11", 175 lbs. Deb: 4/23/27 C

YEAR	TM/L	G	AB	R	H	2B	3B	HR	RBI	BB	SO	AVG	OBP	SLG	PRO+	BR/A	SB	CS	SBR	FA	FR	G/POS	TPR
1927	Det-A	34	85	5	15	6	3	0	9	7	15	.176	.239	.318	43	-8	0	0	0	.949	-1	C-31	-0.6
1928	Det-A	39	85	8	20	2	3	0	9	9	11	.235	.316	.329	69	-4	2	2	-1	.951	4	C-30	0.1
1929	Det-A	50	162	23	47	6	0	3	24	19	18	.290	.365	.383	92	-1	2	1	0	.964	-6	C-46	-0.3
1933	Bos-A	16	56	1	8	3	0	0	8	4	7	.143	.200	.196	5	-8	0	0	0	1.000	-0	C-16	-0.8
	StL-A	94	279	26	73	11	1	1	27	43	26	.262	.360	.319	76	-8	2	0	1	.995	9	C-85	0.6
	Yr	110	335	27	81	14	1	1	35	47	33	.242	.335	.299	65	-16	2	0	1	**.996**	7	*C-101	-0.2
1934	Chi-A	62	176	8	28	3	0	0	5	24	19	.159	.260	.176	14	-22	0	1	-1	.972	1	C-60	-1.8
1935	Chi-A	46	122	8	28	2	0	0	13	30	9	.230	.382	.246	64	-5	0	0	0	.990	8	C-43	0.5
1936	Chi-A	14	24	3	3	0	0	0	2	6	5	.125	.300	.125	8	-4	0	0	0	1.000	1	C-14	-0.2
1937	Chi-A	25	71	7	15	1	0	0	5	15	10	.211	.349	.225	48	-5	1	0	0	.966	3	C-25	-0.1
1938	Bro-N	48	120	14	22	5	0	0	12	28	20	.183	.338	.225	56	-6	1			.977	-1	C-47	-0.5
1939	Det-A	4	2	0	0	0	0	0	0	0	1	.000	.000	.000	-93	-0	0			.500	-1	/C-4	-0.1
1944	Phi-N	7	15	2	4	0	0	1	4	4		.267	.421	.467	155	1	0			.952	-0	/C-6	0.1
Total	11	439	1197	105	263	39	7	5	115	189	145	.220	.327	.277	58	-70	8	4		.976	16	C-407	-3.1

■ DANNY SHEAFFER   Sheaffer, Danny Todd b: 8/2/61, Jacksonville, Fla. BR/TR, 6' ", 185 lbs. Deb: 4/9/87

YEAR	TM/L	G	AB	R	H	2B	3B	HR	RBI	BB	SO	AVG	OBP	SLG	PRO+	BR/A	SB	CS	SBR	FA	FR	G/POS	TPR
1987	Bos-A	25	66	5	8	1	0	1	5	0	14	.121	.121	.182	-21	-11	0	0	0	.977	-3	C-25	-1.2
1989	Cle-A	7	16	1	1	0	0	0	0	2	2	.063	.167	.063	-32	-3	0	0	0	.000	0	/3-2,O-1,D-3	-0.3
1993	Col-N	82	216	26	60	9	1	4	32	8	15	.278	.307	.384	72	-9	2	3	-1	.994	-2	C-65/1-7,O-2,3-1	-0.9
1994	Col-N	44	110	11	24	4	0	1	12	10	11	.218	.283	.282	41	-10	0	2	-1	.995	4	C-30/1-2,O-1	-0.5
1995	StL-N	76	208	24	48	10	1	5	30	23	38	.231	.307	.361	76	-7	0	0	0	.993	11	C-67/1-3,3-1	0.7
1996	*StL-N	79	198	10	45	7	1	2	20	9	25	.227	.271	.333	58	-12	3	3	-1	.983	1	C-47,3-17/1-6,O-3	-0.9
Total	6	313	814	77	186	33	5	13	99	52	105	.229	.278	.329	56	-52	5	8	-3	.990	11	C-234/3-21,1-18,OD	-3.1

■ DAVE SHEAN   Shean, David William b: 7/9/1883, Arlington, Mass. d: 5/22/63, Boston, Mass. BR/TR, 5'11", 175 lbs. Deb: 9/10/06

YEAR	TM/L	G	AB	R	H	2B	3B	HR	RBI	BB	SO	AVG	OBP	SLG	PRO+	BR/A	SB	CS	SBR	FA	FR	G/POS	TPR
1906	Phi-A	22	75	7	16	3	2	0	3	5		.213	.280	.307	81	-2	6			.980	-2	2-22	-0.4
1908	Phi-N	14	48	4	7	2	0	0	2	1		.146	.180	.188	17	-5	1			.871	-6	S-14	-1.3
1909	Phi-N	36	112	14	26	2	2	0	4	14		.232	.323	.286	88	-1	3			.982	-2	2-14,1-11/O-3,S-1	-0.4
	Bos-N	75	267	32	66	11	4	1	29	17		.247	.297	.330	90	-4	14			.956	8	2-72	0.3
	Yr	111	379	46	92	13	6	1	33	31		.243	.305	.317	90	-5	17			.960	6	2-86,1-11/O-3,S-1	-0.1
1910	Bos-N	150	543	52	130	12	7	3	36	42	45	.239	.294	.304	71	-21	16			.953	43	*2-148	2.0
1911	Chi-N	54	145	17	28	4	0	0	15	8	15	.193	.240	.221	29	-14	4			.947	1	2-23,S-19/3-1	-1.2
1912	Bos-N	4	10	1	3	0	0	0	0	1	2	.300	.417	.300	96	-0	0			.917	-1	/S-4	-0.1
1917	Cin-N	131	442	36	93	9	5	2	35	22	39	.210	.249	.267	61	-21	10			.961	19	*2-131	0.4
1918	*Bos-A	115	425	58	112	16	3	0	34	40	25	.264	.331	.315	97	-1	11			.967	-9	*2-115	-0.3
1919	Bos-A	29	100	4	14	0	0	0	5	6	7	.140	.189	.140	-7	-14	1			.981	4	2-29	-0.9
Total	9	630	2167	225	495	59	23	6	166	155	133	.228	.284	.285	70	-82	66			.961	55	2-554/S-38,1-11,O3	-1.9

■ RAY SHEARER   Shearer, Ray Solomon b: 9/19/29, Jacobus, Pa. d: 2/21/82, York, Pa. BR/TR, 6', 200 lbs. Deb: 9/18/57

YEAR	TM/L	G	AB	R	H	2B	3B	HR	RBI	BB	SO	AVG	OBP	SLG	PRO+	BR/A	SB	CS	SBR	FA	FR	G/POS	TPR
1957	Mil-N	2	2	1	1	0	0	0	0	1	1	.500	.667	.500	237	1	0	0	0	.000	-0	/O-1	0.0

■ JOHN SHEARON   Shearon, John M. b: 1870, Pittsburg, Pa. d: 2/1/23, Bradford, Pa. Deb: 7/28/1891

YEAR	TM/L	G	AB	R	H	2B	3B	HR	RBI	BB	SO	AVG	OBP	SLG	PRO+	BR/A	SB	CS	SBR	FA	FR	G/POS	TPR
1891	Cle-N	30	124	10	30	1	1	0	13	1	15	.242	.248	.266	48	-9	6			.814	-4	O-25/P-6	-1.1
1896	Cle-N	16	64	6	11	0	1	0	3	4	6	.172	.221	.203	11	-8	3			.818	-4	O-16	-1.2
Total	2	46	188	16	41	1	2	0	16	5	21	.218	.238	.245	34	-17	9			.815	-9	/O-41,P-6	-2.3

■ JIMMY SHECKARD   Sheckard, Samuel James Tilden b: 11/23/1878, Upper Chanceford Twsp., Pa. d: 1/15/47, Lancaster, Pa. BL/TR, 5'9", 175 lbs. Deb: 9/14/1897

YEAR	TM/L	G	AB	R	H	2B	3B	HR	RBI	BB	SO	AVG	OBP	SLG	PRO+	BR/A	SB	CS	SBR	FA	FR	G/POS	TPR
1897	Bro-N	13	49	12	14	3	2	1	14	6		.286	.364	.612	164	4	5			.753	-5	S-11/O-2	0.0
1898	Bro-N	105	408	51	113	17	9	4	64	37		.277	.349	.392	113	6	8			.926	-4	*O-105/3-1	-0.5
1899	Bal-N	147	536	104	158	18	10	3	75	56		.295	.380	.382	104	4	**77**			.943	21	O-146/1-1	1.3
1900	Bro-N	85	273	74	82	19	10	1	39	42		.300	.416	.454	132	13	30			.925	2	O-78	0.9
1901	Bro-N	133	554	116	196	29	**19**	11	104	47		.354	.409	**.534**	168	46	35			.944	7	*O-121,3-12	4.3
1902	Bal-A	4	15	3	4	0	0	0	0	1		.267	.313	.333	76	-0	2			1.000	-1	/O-4	-0.2
	Bro-N	123	486	86	129	20	10	4	37	57		.265	.349	.372	122	13	23			.964	8	*O-123	1.4
1903	Bro-N	139	515	99	171	29	9	**9**	75	75		.332	.423	.476	161	**43**	**67**			.951	23	*O-139	5.5
1904	Bro-N	143	507	70	121	23	6	1	46	56		.239	.317	.314	97	-0	21			.956	7	*O-141/2-2	-0.1
1905	Bro-N	130	480	58	140	20	11	3	41	61		.292	.380	.398	142	27	23			.967	15	*O-129	3.7
1906	*Chi-N	149	549	90	144	27	10	1	45	67		.262	.349	.353	112	9	30			.986	0	*O-149	0.2
1907	*Chi-N	143	484	76	129	23	1	1	36	76		.267	.373	.324	112	10	31			.975	-10	*O-142	-0.7
1908	*Chi-N	115	403	54	93	18	5	2	22	67		.231	.336	.305	101	3	18			.955	-2	*O-115	-0.5
1909	Chi-N	148	525	81	134	29	5	1	43	72		.255	.346	.350	109	7	15			.967	-3	*O-148	1.2
1910	*Chi-N	144	507	82	130	27	6	5	51	83	53	.256	.366	.363	114	11	22			.976	7	*O-143	1.2
1911	Chi-N	156	539	**121**	149	26	11	4	50	**147**	58	.276	**.434**	.388	130	32	32			.963	15	*O-156	3.8
1912	Chi-N	146	523	85	128	22	10	3	47	**122**	81	.245	.392	.342	102	8	15			.962	8	*O-146	0.8
1913	StL-N	52	136	18	27	2	1	0	17	41	25	.199	.388	.228	79	-1	6			.953	-3	O-46	-0.6
	Cin-N	47	116	16	22	1	3	0	7	27	16	.190	.343	.250	71	-3	6			.969	-3	O-38	-0.8
	Yr	99	252	34	49	3	4	0	24	68	41	.194	.368	.238	76	-4	11			.960	-6	O-84	-1.4
Total	17	2122	7605	1296	2084	354	136	56	813	1135	233	.274	.375	.378	120	232	465			.958	82	*O-2071/3-13,S21	19.5

■ JIM SHEEHAN   Sheehan, James Thomas "Big Jim" b: 6/3/13, New Haven, Conn. BR/TR, 6'2", 196 lbs. Deb: 9/26/36

YEAR	TM/L	G	AB	R	H	2B	3B	HR	RBI	BB	SO	AVG	OBP	SLG	PRO+	BR/A	SB	CS	SBR	FA	FR	G/POS	TPR
1936	NY-N	1	4	0	0	0	0	0	0	0	2	.000	.000	.000	-99	-0	0			.833	-0	/C-1	-0.1

■ JACK SHEEHAN   Sheehan, John Thomas b: 4/15/1893, Chicago, Ill. d: 5/29/87, W.Palm Beach, Fla. BB/TR, 5'8.5", 165 lbs. Deb: 9/11/20

YEAR	TM/L	G	AB	R	H	2B	3B	HR	RBI	BB	SO	AVG	OBP	SLG	PRO+	BR/A	SB	CS	SBR	FA	FR	G/POS	TPR
1920	*Bro-N	3	5	0	2	1	0	0	1	0	1	.400	.500	.600	208	1	0	0	0	.875	0	/S-2,3-1	0.1
1921	Bro-N	5	12	2	0	0	0	0	0	1	0	.000	.000	.000	-97	-3	0	0	0	.900	-0	/2-2,S-1,3-1	-0.3
Total	2	8	17	2	2	1	0	0	1	1	1	.118	.167	.176	-7	-3	0	0	0	.909	0	/S-3,2-2,3-2	-0.2

YEAR	TM/L	G	AB	R	H	2B	3B	HR	RBI	BB	SO	AVG	OBP	SLG	PRO+	BR/A	SB	CS	SBR	FA	FR	G/POS	TPR
■ **TOMMY SHEEHAN**					Sheehan, Thomas H. b: 11/6/1877, Sacramento, Cal. d: 5/22/59, Panama City, Pan. BR/TR, 5'8", 160 lbs. Deb: 8/2/00																		
1900	NY-N	1	2	0	0	0	0	0	0	0	0	.000	.000	.000	-99	-1	0			.000	0	/S-1	-0.1
1906	Pit-N	95	315	28	76	6	3	1	34	18		.241	.284	.289	75	-9	13			.947	-5	3-90	-1.3
1907	Pit-N	75	226	23	62	2	3	0	25	23		.274	.341	.310	103	1	10			.941	-1	3-57,S-10	0.3
1908	Bro-N	146	468	45	100	18	2	0	29	53		.214	.302	.261	83	-7	9			.930	-6	*3-145	-0.9
Total	4	317	1011	96	238	26	8	1	88	94		.235	.305	.280	85	-16	32			.938	-12	3-292/S-11	-2.0
■ **BIFF SHEEHAN**					Sheehan, Timothy James b: 2/13/1868, Hartford, Conn. d: 10/21/23, Hartford, Conn. TR, 5'9", 165 lbs. Deb: 7/22/1895																		
1895	StL-N	52	180	24	57	3	6	1	18	20	6	.317	.394	.417	111	3	7			.940	-2	O-41,1-11	-0.1
1896	StL-N	6	19	0	3	0	0	0	1	4	0	.158	.304	.158	25	-2	0			1.000	-1	/O-6	-0.3
Total	2	58	199	24	60	3	6	1	19	24	6	.302	.385	.392	103	2	7			.948	-3	/O-47,1-11	-0.4
■ **EARL SHEELY**					Sheely, Earl Homer "Whitey" b: 2/12/1893, Bushnell, Ill. d: 9/16/52, Seattle, Wash. BR/TR, 6'3.5", 195 lbs. Deb: 4/14/21																		
1921	Chi-A	154	563	68	171	25	6	11	95	57	34	.304	.375	.428	106	5	4	9	-4	.988	5	*1-154	0.2
1922	Chi-A	149	526	72	167	37	4	6	80	60	27	.317	.393	.437	117	14	4	6	-2	.993	2	*1-149	0.7
1923	Chi-A	156	570	74	169	25	3	4	88	79	30	.296	.387	.372	102	4	5	5	-2	.992	-1	*1-156	-0.6
1924	Chi-A	146	535	84	171	34	3	3	103	95	28	.320	.426	.411	120	21	7	4	-0	.991	-10	*1-146	0.2
1925	Chi-A	153	600	93	189	43	3	9	111	68	23	.315	.389	.442	117	16	3	3	-1	.988	-5	*1-153	0.1
1926	Chi-A	145	525	77	157	40	2	6	89	75	13	.299	.394	.417	116	14	3	1	-0	**.995**	-4	*1-144	0.6
1927	Chi-A	45	129	11	27	3	0	2	16	20	5	.209	.320	.279	58	-8	1	3	-2	.982	-4	1-36	-1.5
1929	Pit-N	139	485	63	142	22	4	6	88	75	24	.293	.392	.392	93	-3	6			**.996**	-0	*1-139	-1.6
1931	Bos-N	147	538	30	147	15	2	1	77	34	21	.273	.319	.314	73	-20	0			.992	-3	*1-143	-3.6
Total	9	1234	4471	572	1340	244	27	48	747	563	205	.300	.383	.399	104	45	33	31		.991	-14	*1-1220	-5.5
■ **BUD SHEELY**					Sheely, Hollis Kimball b: 11/26/20, Spokane, Wash. d: 10/17/85, Sacramento, Cal. BL/TR, 6'1", 200 lbs. Deb: 7/26/51 F																		
1951	Chi-A	34	89	2	16	2	0	0	7	6	7	.180	.240	.202	21	-10	0	0	0	.986	3	C-33	-0.5
1952	Chi-A	36	75	1	18	2	0	0	3	12	7	.240	.352	.267	73	-2	0	1	-1	.992	-2	C-31	-0.3
1953	Chi-A	31	46	4	10	1	0	0	2	9	8	.217	.345	.239	58	-2	0	0	0	1.000	1	C-17	-0.1
Total	3	101	210	7	44	5	0	0	12	27	22	.210	.305	.233	49	-14	0	1	-1	.991	2	/C-81	-0.9
■ **CHUCK SHEERIN**					Sheerin, Charles Joseph b: 4/17/09, Brooklyn, N.Y. d: 9/27/86, Valley Stream, N.Y. BR/TR, 5'11.5", 198 lbs. Deb: 4/21/36																		
1936	Phi-N	39	72	4	19	4	0	0	4	7	18	.264	.329	.319	68	-3	0			.942	-3	2-17,3-13/S-5	-0.5
■ **ANDY SHEETS**					Sheets, Andrew Mark b: 11/19/71, Baton Rouge, La. BR/TR, 6'2", 180 lbs. Deb: 4/22/96																		
1996	Sea-A	47	110	18	21	8	0	0	9	10	41	.191	.264	.264	34	-11	2	0	1	.947	8	3-25,2-18/S-7	-0.2
■ **LARRY SHEETS**					Sheets, Larry Kent b: 12/6/59, Staunton, Va. BL/TR, 6'3", 225 lbs. Deb: 9/18/84																		
1984	Bal-A	8	16	3	7	1	0	1	2	1	3	.438	.471	.688	221	3	0	0	0	1.000	0	/O-7	-0.1
1985	Bal-A	113	328	43	86	19	0	17	50	28	52	.262	.324	.442	110	4	0	1	-1	.875	-2	D-93/O-9,1-1	-0.1
1986	Bal-A	112	338	42	92	17	1	18	60	21	56	.272	.319	.488	117	7	0	0	1	.984	-0	D-58,O-32/C-6,13	0.5
1987	Bal-A	135	469	74	148	23	0	31	94	31	67	.316	.362	.563	144	28	1	1	-0	.975	-4	*O-124/1-3,D-7	1.8
1988	Bal-A	136	452	38	104	19	1	10	47	42	72	.230	.304	.343	83	-10	1	6	-3	.974	1	O-76,D-50/1-3	-1.6
1989	Bal-A	102	304	33	74	12	1	7	33	26	58	.243	.309	.359	90	-4	1	1	-0	.000	0	D-88	-0.7
1990	Det-A	131	360	40	94	17	2	10	52	24	42	.261	.311	.403	97	-2	1	3	-2	.981	-7	O-79,D-44	-1.4
1993	Sea-A	11	17	0	2	1	0	0	1	2	1	.118	.250	.176	17	-2	0	0	0	1.000	0	/O-1,D-5	-0.2
Total	8	748	2284	273	607	98	5	94	339	175	351	.266	.323	.437	109	23	6	12	-5	.976	-12	D-345,O-328/1C3	-1.4
■ **GARY SHEFFIELD**					Sheffield, Gary Antonian b: 11/18/68, Tampa, Fla. BR/TR, 5'11", 190 lbs. Deb: 9/3/88																		
1988	Mil-A	24	80	12	19	1	0	4	12	7	7	.237	.299	.400	93	-1	3	1	0	.967	-14	S-24	-0.9
1989	Mil-A	95	368	34	91	18	0	5	32	27	33	.247	.306	.337	82	-9	10	6	-1	.959	-17	S-70,3-21/D-4	-2.2
1990	Mil-A	125	487	67	143	30	1	10	67	44	41	.294	.356	.421	117	11	25	10	2	.934	-4	*3-125	0.9
1991	Mil-A	50	175	25	34	12	2	2	22	19	15	.194	.284	.320	69	-8	5	5	-2	.922	-12	3-43/D-5	-2.1
1992	SD-N★	146	557	87	184	34	3	33	100	48	40	**.330**	.390	.580	168	48	5	6	-2	.961	10	*3-144	5.8
1993	SD-N★	68	258	34	76	12	2	10	36	18	30	.295	.348	.473	115	5	5	1	1	.905	-11	3-67	-0.5
	Fla-N★	72	236	33	69	8	3	10	37	29	34	.292	.384	.479	122	8	12	4	1	.894	-5	3-66	0.5
	Yr	140	494	67	145	20	5	20	73	47	64	.294	.365	.476	119	13	17	5	2	.899	-16	*3-133	0.0
1994	Fla-N	87	322	61	89	16	1	27	78	51	50	.276	.385	.584	144	21	12	6	0	.970	0	O-87	1.9
1995	Fla-N	63	213	46	69	8	0	16	46	55	45	.324	.471	.587	176	27	19	4	3	.942	0	O-61	2.8
1996	Fla-N★	161	519	118	163	33	1	42	120	142	66	.314	**.469**	.624	193	79	16	9	-1	.976	-9	*O-161	6.2
Total	9	891	3215	517	937	172	13	159	550	440	361	.291	.384	.501	139	182	112	52	2	.933	-58	3-466,O-309/S-94,D	12.4
■ **JOHN SHELBY**					Shelby, John T. b: 2/23/58, Lexington, Ky. BB/TR, 6'1", 175 lbs. Deb: 9/15/81																		
1981	Bal-A	7	2	2	0	0	0	0	0	0	1	.000	.000	.000	-99	-1	2	0	1	1.000	-2	/O-4	-0.2
1982	Bal-A	26	35	8	11	3	0	1	2	0	5	.314	.314	.486	116	1	0	1	-1	1.000	-8	O-24	-0.8
1983	*Bal-A	126	325	52	84	15	2	5	27	18	64	.258	.297	.363	82	-8	15	2	3	.981	-14	*O-115/D-1	-2.2
1984	Bal-A	128	383	44	80	12	5	6	30	20	71	.209	.248	.313	55	-24	12	4	1	.993	-10	*O-124	-3.6
1985	Bal-A	69	205	28	58	6	2	7	27	7	44	.283	.307	.434	103	0	5	1	1	.981	0	O-59/2-1,D-3	0.0
1986	Bal-A	135	404	54	92	14	4	11	49	18	75	.228	.264	.364	70	-18	18	6	2	.978	-12	*O-121/D-2	-3.1
1987	Bal-A	21	32	4	6	0	0	1	3	1	13	.188	.212	.281	30	-3	0	1	-1	1.000	-3	O-19/D-1	-0.7
	LA-N	120	476	61	132	26	0	21	69	31	97	.277	.323	.464	108	4	16	6	1	.972	11	*O-117	1.2
1988	*LA-N	140	494	65	130	23	6	10	64	44	128	.263	.323	.395	109	5	16	5	2	.982	0	*O-140	1.0
1989	LA-N	108	345	28	63	11	1	1	12	25	92	.183	.238	.229	35	-29	10	7	-1	.991	0	O-98	-3.5
1990	LA-N	25	24	2	6	1	0	0	2	0	7	.250	.250	.292	50	-2	1	0	0	1.000	-1	O-12	-0.5
	Det-A	78	222	22	55	9	3	4	20	10	51	.248	.280	.369	80	-7	3	5	-2	.973	-1	O-68/D-5	-1.1
1991	Det-A	53	143	19	22	7	3	8	21	3	23	.154	.204	.287	34	-13	0	2	-1	.982	-1	O-47/D-4	-1.6
Total	11	1234	3090	389	739	128	24	70	313	182	671	.239	.282	.364	79	-96	98	40	5	.982	-36	O-948/D-16,2-1	-15.1
■ **BOB SHELDON**					Sheldon, Bob Mitchell b: 11/27/50, Montebello, Cal. BL/TR, 6', 170 lbs. Deb: 4/10/74																		
1974	Mil-A	10	17	4	2	1	0	0	4	2	4	.118	.286	.294	67	-1	0	1	-1	1.000	-1	/2-3,D-4	-0.2
1975	Mil-A	53	181	17	52	3	3	0	14	13	14	.287	.342	.337	92	-2	0	3	-2	.977	-8	2-44/D-6	-1.0
1977	Mil-A	31	64	9	13	4	1	0	3	6	9	.203	.271	.297	55	-4	0	0	0	1.000	1	D-17/2-5	-0.4
Total	3	94	262	30	67	8	5	0	17	23	25	.256	.321	.324	81	-6	0	4	-2	.979	-9	/2-52,D-27	-1.6
■ **HUGH SHELLEY**					Shelley, Hubert Leneirre b: 10/26/10, Rogers, Tex. d: 6/16/78, Beaumont, Tex. BR/TR, 6', 170 lbs. Deb: 6/25/35																		
1935	Det-A	7	8	1	2	0	0	0	1	2	1	.250	.400	.250	74	-0	0	0	0	1.000	-1	/O-5	-0.2
■ **SKEETER SHELTON**					Shelton, Andrew Kemper b: 6/29/1888, Huntington, W.Va. d: 1/9/54, Huntington, W.Va. BR/TR, 5'11", 175 lbs. Deb: 8/25/15																		
1915	NY-A	10	40	1	1	0	0	0	0	2	10	.025	.071	.025	-71	-8	0			1.000	0	O-10	-1.0
■ **BEN SHELTON**					Shelton, Benjamin Davis b: 9/21/69, Chicago, Ill. BR/TL, 6'3", 210 lbs. Deb: 6/16/93																		
1993	Pit-N	15	24	3	6	1	0	2	6	7	3	.250	.333	.542	130	1	0	0	0	.889	-0	/O-6,1-2	0.0
■ **STEVE SHEMO**					Shemo, Stephen Michael b: 4/9/15, Swoyersville, Pa. d: 4/13/92, Eden, N.C. BR/TR, 5'11", 175 lbs. Deb: 4/18/44																		
1944	Bos-N	18	31	3	9	2	0	0	1	3	3	.290	.313	.355	84	-1				.966	3	2-16/3-2	0.3
1945	Bos-N	17	46	4	11	0	0	0	7	3	3	.239	.255	.261	43	-4				.921	-6	2-12/3-3,S-1	-0.9
Total	2	35	77	7	20	2	0	0	8	6	6	.260	.278	.299	60	-4				.948	-3	/2-28,3-5,S-1	-0.6
■ **JACK SHEPARD**					Shepard, Jack Leroy b: 5/13/32, Clovis, Cal. d: 12/31/94, Atherton, Cal. BR/TR, 6'2", 195 lbs. Deb: 6/19/53																		
1953	Pit-N	2	4	0	1	0	0	0	0	0	2	.250	.250	.250	31	-0	0	0	0	.750	-0	/C-2	-0.1
1954	Pit-N	82	227	24	69	8	2	3	22	26	33	.304	.375	.396	103	2	1	0	0	.977	-2	C-67	0.6
1955	Pit-N	94	264	24	63	10	2	2	23	33	25	.239	.323	.314	71	-10	0	0	0	.982	-10	C-77	-1.8

YEAR	TM/L	G	AB	R	H	2B	3B	HR	RBI	BB	SO	AVG	OBP	SLG	PRO+	BR/A	SB	CS	SBR	FA	FR	G/POS	TPR
1956	Pit-N	100	256	24	62	11	2	7	30	25	37	.242	.310	.383	87	-5	1	1	-0	.990	1	C-86/1-2	-0.1
Total	4	278	751	72	195	29	6	12	75	84	97	.260	.334	.362	86	-14	2	1	0	.982	-8	C-232/1-2	-1.4

■ RAY SHEPARDSON Shepardson, Raymond Francis b: 5/3/1897, Little Falls, N.Y. d: 11/8/75, Little Falls, N.Y. BR/TR, 5'11.5", 170 lbs. Deb: 9/19/24

YEAR	TM/L	G	AB	R	H	2B	3B	HR	RBI	BB	SO	AVG	OBP	SLG	PRO+	BR/A	SB	CS	SBR	FA	FR	G/POS	TPR
1924	StL-N	3	6	1	0	0	0	0	0	0	0	.000	.000	.000	-99	-2	0	0	0	1.000	0	/C-3	-0.2

■ RON SHEPHERD Shepherd, Ronald Wayne b: 10/27/60, Longview, Tex. BR/TR, 6'4", 175 lbs. Deb: 9/5/84

YEAR	TM/L	G	AB	R	H	2B	3B	HR	RBI	BB	SO	AVG	OBP	SLG	PRO+	BR/A	SB	CS	SBR	FA	FR	G/POS	TPR
1984	Tor-A	12	4	0	0	0	0	0	0	0	3	.000	.000	.000	-97	-1	0	1	-1	1.000	-1	/O-5,D-4	-0.3
1985	Tor-A	38	35	7	4	2	0	0	1	2	12	.114	.162	.171	-8	-5	3	0	1	1.000	-4	O-16,D-15	-0.9
1986	Tor-A	65	69	16	14	4	0	2	4	3	22	.203	.236	.348	55	-4	0	0	0	1.000	-8	O-32,D-16	-1.3
Total	3	115	108	23	18	6	0	2	5	5	37	.167	.204	.278	29	-11	3	1	0	1.000	-13	/O-53,D-35	-2.5

■ JOHN SHEPPARD Sheppard, John b: Baltimore, Md. Deb: 6/27/1873

YEAR	TM/L	G	AB	R	H	2B	3B	HR	RBI	BB	SO	AVG	OBP	SLG	PRO+	BR/A	SB	CS	SBR	FA	FR	G/POS	TPR
1873	Mar-n	3	11	1	0	0	0	0	0	0	0	.000	.000	.000	-99	-3	0	0	0	.500	-1	/O-2,C-1	-0.3

■ SHERIDAN Sheridan Deb: 10/9/1875

YEAR	TM/L	G	AB	R	H	2B	3B	HR	RBI	BB	SO	AVG	OBP	SLG	PRO+	BR/A	SB	CS	SBR	FA	FR	G/POS	TPR
1875	Atl-n	1	4	0	0	0	0	0	0	0	1	.000	.000	.000	-99	-1	0	0	0	.000	-0	/O-1	-0.1

■ RED SHERIDAN Sheridan, Eugene Anthony b: 11/14/1896, Brooklyn, N.Y. d: 11/25/75, Queens Village, N.Y. BR/TR, 5'10.5", 160 lbs. Deb: 7/3/18

YEAR	TM/L	G	AB	R	H	2B	3B	HR	RBI	BB	SO	AVG	OBP	SLG	PRO+	BR/A	SB	CS	SBR	FA	FR	G/POS	TPR
1918	Bro-N	2	4	0	1	0	0	0	0	1	0	.250	.400	.250	100	0	1	0	0	1.000	-1	/2-2	-0.1
1920	Bro-N	3	2	0	0	0	0	0	0	0	1	.000	.000	.000	-97	-0	0	0	0	1.000	1	/S-3	0.1
Total	2	5	6	0	1	0	0	0	0	1	1	.167	.286	.167	37	-0	1	0	0	1.000	1	/S-3,2-2	0.0

■ NEILL SHERIDAN Sheridan, Neill Rawlins "Wild Horse" b: 11/20/21, Sacramento, Cal. BR/TR, 6'1.5", 195 lbs. Deb: 9/19/48

YEAR	TM/L	G	AB	R	H	2B	3B	HR	RBI	BB	SO	AVG	OBP	SLG	PRO+	BR/A	SB	CS	SBR	FA	FR	G/POS	TPR
1948	Bos-A	2	1	0	0	0	0	0	0	0	0	.000	.000	.000	-95	-0	0	0	0	.000	0	H	0.0

■ PAT SHERIDAN Sheridan, Patrick Arthur b: 12/4/57, Ann Arbor, Mich. BL/TR, 6'3", 175 lbs. Deb: 9/16/81

YEAR	TM/L	G	AB	R	H	2B	3B	HR	RBI	BB	SO	AVG	OBP	SLG	PRO+	BR/A	SB	CS	SBR	FA	FR	G/POS	TPR
1981	KC-A	3	1	0	0	0	0	0	0	0	0	.000	.000	.000	-99	-0	0	0	0	1.000	-1	/O-3	-0.1
1983	KC-A	109	333	43	90	12	2	7	36	20	64	.270	.312	.381	89	-5	12	3	2	.988	-2	*O-100	-0.8
1984	*KC-A	138	481	64	136	24	4	8	53	41	91	.283	.340	.399	103	2	19	6	2	.986	-3	*O-134	-0.3
1985	*KC-A	78	206	18	47	9	2	3	17	23	38	.228	.309	.383	76	-7	11	3	2	.983	-4	O-69/D-1	-1.1
1986	Det-A	98	236	41	56	9	1	6	19	21	57	.237	.302	.360	80	-7	9	2	2	.977	-10	O-90/D-5	-1.7
1987	*Det-A	141	421	57	109	19	3	6	49	44	90	.259	.330	.361	87	-7	18	13	-2	.976	-12	*O-137	-2.4
1988	Det-A	127	347	47	88	9	5	11	47	44	64	.254	.341	.403	112	6	8	6	-1	.981	-6	*O-111/D-3	-0.4
1989	Det-A	50	120	16	29	3	0	3	15	17	21	.242	.336	.342	93	-1	4	0	1	.982	-3	O-35/D-8	-0.4
	*SF-N	70	161	20	33	3	4	3	14	13	45	.205	.264	.329	71	-7	4	1	1	.983	-4	O-66	-1.2
1991	NY-A	62	113	13	23	3	0	4	7	12	21	.204	.286	.332	71	-5	1	1	0	1.000	-3	O-34/D-2	-0.8
Total	9	876	2419	319	611	91	21	51	257	236	501	.253	.321	.371	91	-30	86	35	5	.983	-48	O-779/D-19	-9.2

■ ED SHERLING Sherling, Edward Creech "Shine" b: 7/17/1897, Coalburg, Ala. d: 11/16/65, Enterprise, Cal. BR/TR, 6'1", 185 lbs. Deb: 8/13/24

YEAR	TM/L	G	AB	R	H	2B	3B	HR	RBI	BB	SO	AVG	OBP	SLG	PRO+	BR/A	SB	CS	SBR	FA	FR	G/POS	TPR
1924	Phi-A	4	2	2	1	0	0	0	0	0	0	.500	.500	1.000	278	0	0	0	0	.000	0	H	0.0

■ MONK SHERLOCK Sherlock, John Clinton b: 10/26/04, Buffalo, N.Y. d: 11/26/85, Buffalo, N.Y. BR/TR, 5'10", 175 lbs. Deb: 4/20/30 F

YEAR	TM/L	G	AB	R	H	2B	3B	HR	RBI	BB	SO	AVG	OBP	SLG	PRO+	BR/A	SB	CS	SBR	FA	FR	G/POS	TPR
1930	Phi-N	92	299	51	97	18	2	0	38	27	28	.324	.380	.398	83	-8	0			.990	4	1-70/2-5,O-1	-0.9

■ VINCE SHERLOCK Sherlock, Vincent Thomas "Baldy" b: 3/27/09, Buffalo, N.Y. BR/TR, 6', 180 lbs. Deb: 9/18/35 F

YEAR	TM/L	G	AB	R	H	2B	3B	HR	RBI	BB	SO	AVG	OBP	SLG	PRO+	BR/A	SB	CS	SBR	FA	FR	G/POS	TPR
1935	Bro-N	9	26	4	12	1	0	0	6	1	2	.462	.481	.500	168	3	1			.907	-1	/2-8	0.2

■ DARRELL SHERMAN Sherman, Darrell Edward b: 12/4/67, Los Angeles, Cal. BL/TL, 5'9", 160 lbs. Deb: 4/8/93

YEAR	TM/L	G	AB	R	H	2B	3B	HR	RBI	BB	SO	AVG	OBP	SLG	PRO+	BR/A	SB	CS	SBR	FA	FR	G/POS	TPR
1993	SD-N	37	63	8	14	1	0	0	2	6	8	.222	.319	.238	51	-4	2	1	0	1.000	-3	O-26	-0.8

■ DENNIS SHERRILL Sherrill, Dennis Lee b: 3/3/56, Miami, Fla. BR/TR, 6', 165 lbs. Deb: 9/4/78

YEAR	TM/L	G	AB	R	H	2B	3B	HR	RBI	BB	SO	AVG	OBP	SLG	PRO+	BR/A	SB	CS	SBR	FA	FR	G/POS	TPR
1978	NY-A	2	1	0	0	0	0	0	0	0	1	.000	.000	.000	-99	-0	0	0	0	.000	-0	/3-1,D-1	-0.1
1980	NY-A	3	4	0	1	0	0	0	0	0	1	.250	.250	.250	38	-0	0	0	0	1.000	-0	/S-2,2-1	-0.1
Total	2	5	5	1	1	0	0	0	0	0	2	.200	.200	.200	11	-1	0	0	0	1.000	-1	/S-2,2-1,D-1,3-1	-0.2

■ NORM SHERRY Sherry, Norman Burt b: 7/16/31, New York, N.Y. BR/TR, 5'11", 181 lbs. Deb: 4/12/59 FMC

YEAR	TM/L	G	AB	R	H	2B	3B	HR	RBI	BB	SO	AVG	OBP	SLG	PRO+	BR/A	SB	CS	SBR	FA	FR	G/POS	TPR
1959	LA-N	2	3	0	1	0	0	0	2	0	0	.333	.500	.333	119	0	0	0	0	1.000	-1	/C-2	-0.1
1960	LA-N	47	138	22	39	4	1	8	19	12	29	.283	.353	.500	122	4	0	0	0	.993	-4	C-44	0.2
1961	LA-N	47	121	10	31	2	0	5	21	9	30	.256	.308	.397	78	-4	0	0	0	.993	-4	C-45	0.1
1962	LA-N	35	88	7	16	2	0	3	16	6	17	.182	.242	.307	49	-7	0	0	0	.992	9	C-34	0.3
1963	NY-N	63	147	6	20	1	0	2	11	10	26	.136	.206	.184	13	-16	1	0	0	.980	3	C-61	-1.2
Total	5	194	497	45	107	9	1	18	69	37	102	.215	.280	.346	69	-23	1	0	0	.989	11	C-186	-0.7

■ BARRY SHETRONE Shetrone, Barry Stevan b: 7/6/38, Baltimore, Md. BL/TR, 6'2", 190 lbs. Deb: 7/27/59

YEAR	TM/L	G	AB	R	H	2B	3B	HR	RBI	BB	SO	AVG	OBP	SLG	PRO+	BR/A	SB	CS	SBR	FA	FR	G/POS	TPR
1959	Bal-A	33	79	8	16	1	1	0	5	5	9	.203	.250	.241	36	-7	3	0	1	.947	-4	O-23	-1.2
1960	Bal-A	1	0	1	0	0	0	0	0	0	0	—	—	—	—	—	0	0	0	.000	0	R	0.0
1961	Bal-A	3	7	0	1	0	0	0	0	0	2	.143	.143	.143	-24	-1	0	0	0	1.000	-0	/O-2	-0.2
1962	Bal-A	21	24	3	6	1	0	1	1	0	5	.250	.250	.417	81	-1	0	0	0	1.000	-0	/O-6	-0.1
1963	Was-A	2	2	0	0	0	0	0	0	0	0	.000	.000	.000	-99	-0	0	0	0	.000	0	H	-0.1
Total	5	60	112	12	23	2	1	1	7	5	16	.205	.239	.268	39	-9	3	0	1	.962	-5	/O-31	-1.6

■ JOHN SHETZLINE Shetzline, John Henry b: 1850, Philadelphia, Pa. d: 12/15/1892, Philadelphia, Pa. 5'11.5", 190 lbs. Deb: 5/2/1882

YEAR	TM/L	G	AB	R	H	2B	3B	HR	RBI	BB	SO	AVG	OBP	SLG	PRO+	BR/A	SB	CS	SBR	FA	FR	G/POS	TPR
1882	Bal-a	73	282	23	62	8	3	0		5		.220	.233	.270	75	-7				.800	3	3-52,2-20/O-1,S-1	-0.2

■ JIMMY SHEVLIN Shevlin, James Cornelius b: 7/9/09, Cincinnati, Ohio d: 10/30/74, Ft.Lauderdale, Fla BL/TL, 5'10.5", 155 lbs. Deb: 6/29/30

YEAR	TM/L	G	AB	R	H	2B	3B	HR	RBI	BB	SO	AVG	OBP	SLG	PRO+	BR/A	SB	CS	SBR	FA	FR	G/POS	TPR
1930	Det-A	28	14	4	2	0	0	0	0	3	2	.143	.250	.143	2	-2	0	0	0	1.000	1	1-25	-0.2
1932	Cin-N	7	24	3	5	2	0	0	4	4	0	.208	.345	.292	76	-1	4			.985	-0	/1-7	-0.2
1934	Cin-N	18	39	6	12	2	0	0	6	6	5	.308	.400	.359	107	1	0			1.000	0	/1-10	0.0
Total	3	53	77	13	19	4	0	0	12	12	8	.247	.356	.299	77	-2	4	0		.995	1	/1-42	-0.4

■ PETE SHIELDS Shields, Francis Leroy b: 9/21/1891, Swiftwater, Miss. d: 2/11/61, Jackson, Miss. BR/TR, 6', 175 lbs. Deb: 4/14/15

YEAR	TM/L	G	AB	R	H	2B	3B	HR	RBI	BB	SO	AVG	OBP	SLG	PRO+	BR/A	SB	CS	SBR	FA	FR	G/POS	TPR
1915	Cle-A	23	72	4	15	6	0	0	6	4	14	.208	.250	.292	61	-4	3	3	-1	.974	0	1-23	-0.6

■ TOMMY SHIELDS Shields, Thomas Charles b: 8/14/64, Fairfax, Va. BL/TR, 6', 180 lbs. Deb: 7/25/92

YEAR	TM/L	G	AB	R	H	2B	3B	HR	RBI	BB	SO	AVG	OBP	SLG	PRO+	BR/A	SB	CS	SBR	FA	FR	G/POS	TPR
1992	Bal-A	2	0	0	0	0	0	0	0	0	0	—	—	—	—	—	0	0	0	.000	0	/R	0.0
1993	Chi-N	20	34	4	6	1	0	1	2	0	10	.176	.222	.206	16	-4	0	0	0	1.000	2	/2-7,3-7,1-1,0-1	-0.2
Total	2	22	34	4	6	1	0	1	2	0	10	.176	.222	.206	16	-4	0	0	0	1.000	2	/3-7,2-7,0-1,1-1	-0.2

■ JIM SHILLING Shilling, James Robert b: 5/14/14, Tulsa, Okla. d: 9/12/86, Tulsa, Okla. BR/TR, 5'11", 175 lbs. Deb: 4/21/39

YEAR	TM/L	G	AB	R	H	2B	3B	HR	RBI	BB	SO	AVG	OBP	SLG	PRO+	BR/A	SB	CS	SBR	FA	FR	G/POS	TPR
1939	Cle-A	31	98	8	27	7	2	0	12	7	9	.276	.324	.388	84	-3	1	0	0	.935	4	2-27/S-3	0.2
	Phi-N	11	33	3	10	1	3	0	4	1	4	.303	.324	.515	126	1	0	0	0	.944	-2	/2-5,S-3,3-3,0-1	0.0
Total	1	42	131	11	37	8	5	0	16	8	13	.282	.324	.420	94	-2	1	0	0	.936	2	/2-32,S-6,3-3,0-1	0.2

■ GINGER SHINAULT Shinault, Enoch Erskine b: 9/7/1892, Benton, Ark. d: 12/29/30, Denver, Colo. BR/TR, 5'11", 170 lbs. Deb: 7/4/21

YEAR	TM/L	G	AB	R	H	2B	3B	HR	RBI	BB	SO	AVG	OBP	SLG	PRO+	BR/A	SB	CS	SBR	FA	FR	G/POS	TPR
1921	Cle-A	22	29	5	11	2	0	0	4	6	5	.379	.486	.414	129	2	1			.917	2	C-20	0.4
1922	Cle-A	13	15	1	2	1	0	0	0	2	2	.133	.133	.200	-14	-3	0			.400	-4	C-11	-0.6
Total	2	35	44	6	13	3	0	0	4	6	7	.295	.380	.341	85	-1	1			.868	2	/C-31	-0.2

■ BILLY SHINDLE Shindle, William b: 12/5/1860, Gloucester, N.J. d: 6/3/36, Lakeland, N.J. BR/TR, 5'8.5", 155 lbs. Deb: 10/5/1886

YEAR	TM/L	G	AB	R	H	2B	3B	HR	RBI	BB	SO	AVG	OBP	SLG	PRO+	BR/A	SB	CS	SBR	FA	FR	G/POS	TPR
1886	Det-N	7	26	4	7	0	0	0	4	0	5	.269	.269	.269	62	-1				.900	1	/S-7	0.0
1887	Det-N	22	84	17	24	3	0	0	12	7		.286	.341	.369	94	-1	13			.818	-5	3-21/O-1	-0.4
1888	Bal-a	135	514	61	107	14	8	1	53	20		.208	.249	.272	69	-18	52			**.922**	37	*3-135	1.9
1889	Bal-a	138	567	122	178	24	7	3	64	24	37	.314	.369	.397	116	11	56			.862	20	*3-138	3.0

YEAR	TM/L	G	AB	R	H	2B	3B	HR	RBI	BB	SO	AVG	OBP	SLG	PRO+	BR/A	SB	CS	SBR	FA	FR	G/POS	TPR
1890	Phi-P	132	584	127	189	21	21	10	90	40	30	.324	.371	.483	124	17	51			.856	8	*S-130/3-2	2.6
1891	Phi-N	103	415	68	87	13	1	0	38	33	39	.210	.278	.246	96	-26	17			.874	6	*3-100/S-3	-1.3
1892	Bal-N	143	619	100	156	20	18	3	50	35	34	.252	.301	.357	96	-6	24			.882	36	*3-134/S-9	3.2
1893	Bal-N	125	521	100	156	22	11	1	75	66	17	.261	.353	.351	86	-10	17			.885	8	*3-125	0.0
1894	Bro-N	116	476	94	141	22	9	4	96	29	20	.296	.344	.405	86	-11	19			.897	1	*3-116	-0.8
1895	Bro-N	116	477	91	133	21	2	3	69	47	28	.279	.357	.350	90	-5	17			.897	0	*3-116	-0.2
1896	Bro-N	131	516	75	144	24	9	1	61	24	20	.279	.316	.366	84	-13	24			.912	-12	*3-131	-1.9
1897	Bro-N	134	542	83	154	32	6	4	105	35		.284	.336	.387	96	-4	23			.904	-12	*3-134	-1.1
1898	Bro-N	120	466	50	105	10	3	1	41	10		.225	.249	.266	48	-32	3			.911	7	*3-120	-2.3
Total	13	1422	5807	992	1561	226	97	31	758	388	240	.269	.323	.357	88	-99	318			.892	95	*3-1272,S-149/O-1	2.7

■ RAZOR SHINES
Shines, Anthony Raymond "Ray" b: 7/18/56, Durham, N.C. BB/TR, 6'1", 210 lbs. Deb: 9/9/83

YEAR	TM/L	G	AB	R	H	2B	3B	HR	RBI	BB	SO	AVG	OBP	SLG	PRO+	BR/A	SB	CS	SBR	FA	FR	G/POS	TPR
1983	Mon-N	3	2	0	1	0	0	0	0	0	0	.500	.500	.500	179	0	0	0	0	.000	-0	/O-1	0.0
1984	Mon-N	12	20	0	6	1	0	0	2	0	3	.300	.300	.350	86	-0	0	0	0	1.000	-1	/1-3,3-1	-0.2
1985	Mon-N	47	50	0	6	0	0	0	3	4	9	.120	.185	.120	-14	-8	0	1	-1	.950	0	/1-5,P-1	-0.8
1987	Mon-N	6	9	0	2	0	0	0	0	1	0	.222	.364	.222	58	-0	1	0	0	1.000	-1	/1-2	0.0
Total	4	68	81	0	15	1	0	0	5	5	12	.185	.241	.198	24	-8	1	1	-0	.975	-1	/1-10,P-1,3-1,O-1	-1.0

■ RALPH SHINNERS
Shinners, Ralph Peter b: 10/4/1895, Monches, Wis. d: 7/23/62, Milwaukee, Wis. BR/TR, 6', 180 lbs. Deb: 4/12/22

YEAR	TM/L	G	AB	R	H	2B	3B	HR	RBI	BB	SO	AVG	OBP	SLG	PRO+	BR/A	SB	CS	SBR	FA	FR	G/POS	TPR
1922	NY-N	56	135	16	34	4	2	0	15	5	22	.252	.308	.311	60	-8	3	5	-2	.915	-4	O-37	-1.5
1923	NY-N	33	13	5	2	1	0	0	0	2	1	.154	.267	.231	33	-1	0	0	0	1.000	-1	/O-6	-0.2
1925	StL-N	74	251	39	74	9	2	7	36	12	19	.295	.330	.430	90	-4	8	5	-1	.982	-3	O-66	-1.1
Total	3	163	399	60	110	14	4	7	51	19	42	.276	.320	.383	78	-13	11	10	-3	.959	-8	O-109	-2.8

■ TIM SHINNICK
Shinnick, Timothy James "Dandy" or "Good Eye" b: 11/6/1867, Exeter, N.H. d: 5/18/44, Exeter, N.H. BB/TR, 5'9", 150 lbs. Deb: 4/19/1890

YEAR	TM/L	G	AB	R	H	2B	3B	HR	RBI	BB	SO	AVG	OBP	SLG	PRO+	BR/A	SB	CS	SBR	FA	FR	G/POS	TPR
1890	*Lou-a	133	493	87	126	16	11	1	82	62		.256	.348	.339	105	4	62			.925	-25	*2-130/3-3	-1.1
1891	Lou-a	128	443	79	98	10	11	1	54	54	47	.221	.314	.300	77	-13	36			.915	-21	*2-120/3-7,S-1	-2.5
Total	2	261	936	166	224	26	22	2	136	116	47	.239	.332	.321	91	-9	98			.920	-45	2-250/3-10,S-1	-3.6

■ BILL SHIPKE
Shipke, William Martin "Skipper Bill" or "Muskrat Bill" (b: William Martin Shipkrethaver) b: 11/18/1882, St.Louis, Mo. d: 9/10/40, Omaha, Neb. BR/TR, 5'7", 145 lbs. Deb: 4/23/06

YEAR	TM/L	G	AB	R	H	2B	3B	HR	RBI	BB	SO	AVG	OBP	SLG	PRO+	BR/A	SB	CS	SBR	FA	FR	G/POS	TPR
1906	Cle-A	2	6	0	0	0	0	0	0	0	0	.000	.000	.000	-99	-1	0			.933	2	/2-2	0.0
1907	Was-A	64	189	17	37	3	2	1	9	15		.196	.262	.249	68	-7	6			.944	3	3-63	0.3
1908	Was-A	111	341	40	71	7	8	0	20	38		.208	.297	.276	94	-1	15			.932	-7	*3-110/2-1	-0.5
1909	Was-A	9	16	2	2	1	0	0	0	2		.125	.222	.188	31	-1	0			.905	2	/3-6,S-2	0.1
Total	4	186	552	59	110	11	10	1	29	55		.199	.280	.261	81	-10	21			.935	4	3-179/2-3,S-2	-0.1

■ CRAIG SHIPLEY
Shipley, Craig Barry b: 1/7/63, Parramatta, Australia BR/TR, 6'1", 175 lbs. Deb: 6/22/86

YEAR	TM/L	G	AB	R	H	2B	3B	HR	RBI	BB	SO	AVG	OBP	SLG	PRO+	BR/A	SB	CS	SBR	FA	FR	G/POS	TPR
1986	LA-N	12	27	3	3	0	0	0	4	2	5	.111	.200	.148	-3	-4	0	0	0	.914	-1	S-10/2-1,3-1	-0.4
1987	LA-N	26	35	3	9	1	0	0	0	2	6	.257	.257	.286	45	-3	0	0	0	.949	3	S-18/3-6	0.0
1989	NY-N	4	7	3	1	0	0	0	0	0	1	.143	.143	.143	-19	-1	0	0	0	1.000	-0	/S-3,3-2	-0.1
1991	SD-N	37	91	6	25	3	0	1	6	2	14	.275	.298	.341	77	-3	0	1	-1	.902	-3	S-19,2-14	-0.3
1992	SD-N	52	105	7	26	6	0	0	7	2	21	.248	.262	.305	59	-6	1	1	-0	.986	10	S-23,2-11/3-8	0.5
1993	SD-N	105	230	25	54	9	0	4	22	10	31	.235	.276	.326	59	-13	12	3	2	.964	-8	S-38,3-37,2-12/O-5	-1.7
1994	SD-N	81	240	32	80	14	4	0	30	9	28	.333	.365	.475	120	7	6	6	-2	.936	-8	3-53,S-14,2-13/O1	-0.2
1995	Hou-N	92	232	23	61	8	1	3	24	8	28	.263	.293	.345	73	-10	6	1	1	.982	-2	3-65,S-11/2-4,1-1	-1.0
1996	SD-N	33	92	13	29	5	0	1	7	2	15	.315	.344	.402	101	-0	7	0	2	.985	-2	2-17/S-7,3-4,0-3	0.3
Total	9	442	1059	115	288	47	5	13	102	35	149	.272	.303	.363	79	-33	32	12	2	.964	-8	3-176,S-143/2O1	-2.9

■ ART SHIRES
Shires, Charles Arthur "Art The Great" b: 8/13/07, Italy, Tex. d: 7/13/67, Italy, Tex. BL/TR, 6'1", 195 lbs. Deb: 8/20/28

YEAR	TM/L	G	AB	R	H	2B	3B	HR	RBI	BB	SO	AVG	OBP	SLG	PRO+	BR/A	SB	CS	SBR	FA	FR	G/POS	TPR
1928	Chi-A	33	123	20	42	4	1	1	11	13	10	.341	.409	.431	122	5	0	3	-2	.990	3	1-32	0.3
1929	Chi-A	100	353	41	110	20	7	3	41	32	20	.312	.370	.433	108	4	4	5	-2	.991	0	1-90/2-3	-0.6
1930	Chi-A	37	128	14	33	5	1	0	18	6	6	.258	.291	.336	61	-8	2	0	1	.979	-2	1-33	-1.2
	Was-A	38	84	11	31	5	0	1	19	5	5	.369	.404	.464	119	3	1	3	-2	.982	0	1-21	0.0
	Yr	75	212	25	64	10	1	2	37	11	11	.302	.336	.387	84	-5	3	3	-1	.980	-2	1-54	-1.2
1932	Bos-N	82	298	32	71	11	3	5	30	25	21	.238	.299	.339	74	-11	1			.988	-2	1-80	-2.0
Total	4	290	986	118	287	45	12	11	119	81	62	.291	.347	.395	95	-8	8	11		.988	-1	1-256/2-3	-3.5

■ BART SHIRLEY
Shirley, Barton Arvin b: 1/4/40, Corpus Christi, Tex. BR/TR, 5'10", 183 lbs. Deb: 9/14/64

YEAR	TM/L	G	AB	R	H	2B	3B	HR	RBI	BB	SO	AVG	OBP	SLG	PRO+	BR/A	SB	CS	SBR	FA	FR	G/POS	TPR
1964	LA-N	18	62	6	17	1	1	0	7	4	8	.274	.318	.323	87	-1	0	0	0	.900	1	3-10/S-8	0.0
1966	LA-N	5	2	1	1	0	0	0	0	0	0	.200	.200	.200	13	-1	0	0	0	1.000	1	/S-5	0.1
1967	NY-N	6	12	1	0	0	0	0	0	0	5	.000	.000	.000	-99	-3	0	0	0	.917	0	/2-3	-0.3
1968	LA-N	39	83	6	15	3	0	0	4	10	13	.181	.269	.217	51	-5	0	1	-1	.903	3	S-21,2-18	-0.1
Total	4	75	162	15	33	4	1	0	11	14	28	.204	.267	.241	53	-10	0	1	-1	.936	5	/S-34,2-21,3-10	-0.3

■ MULE SHIRLEY
Shirley, Ernest Raeford b: 5/24/01, Snow Hill, N.C. d: 8/4/55, Goldsboro, N.C. BL/TL, 5'11", 180 lbs. Deb: 5/6/24

YEAR	TM/L	G	AB	R	H	2B	3B	HR	RBI	BB	SO	AVG	OBP	SLG	PRO+	BR/A	SB	CS	SBR	FA	FR	G/POS	TPR
1924	*Was-A	30	77	12	18	2	2	0	16	3	7	.234	.262	.312	49	-6	0	0	0	.984	0	1-25	-0.7
1925	Was-A	14	23	2	3	1	0	0	2	1	7	.130	.167	.174	-14	-4	0	0	0	1.000	0	/1-9	-0.4
Total	2	44	100	14	21	3	2	0	18	4	14	.210	.240	.280	34	-10	0	0	0	.988	0	/1-34	-1.1

■ IVEY SHIVER
Shiver, Ivey Merwin "Chick" b: 1/22/07, Sylvester, Ga. d: 8/31/72, Savannah, Ga. BR/TR, 6'1.5", 190 lbs. Deb: 4/14/31

YEAR	TM/L	G	AB	R	H	2B	3B	HR	RBI	BB	SO	AVG	OBP	SLG	PRO+	BR/A	SB	CS	SBR	FA	FR	G/POS	TPR
1931	Det-A	2	9	2	1	0	0	0	0	0	3	.111	.111	.111	-40	-2	0	0	0	1.000	-1	/O-2	-0.2
1934	Cin-N	19	59	6	12	1	0	0	6	3	15	.203	.242	.322	51	-4	1			1.000	-2	O-15	-0.7
Total	2	21	68	8	13	1	0	0	6	3	18	.191	.225	.294	38	-6	1		0	1.000	-3	/O-17	-0.9

■ GEORGE SHOCH
Shoch, George Quintus b: 1/6/1859, Philadelphia, Pa. d: 9/30/37, Philadelphia, Pa. BR/TR, 5'6", 158 lbs. Deb: 9/10/1886

YEAR	TM/L	G	AB	R	H	2B	3B	HR	RBI	BB	SO	AVG	OBP	SLG	PRO+	BR/A	SB	CS	SBR	FA	FR	G/POS	TPR
1886	Was-N	26	95	11	28	1	2	0	13	2	12	.295	.309	.337	112	1	2			.882	-5	O-25/S-1	-0.4
1887	Was-N	70	264	47	63	9	1	1	18	21	16	.239	.304	.292	70	-10	29			.897	-5	O-63/S-6,2-1	-0.3
1888	Was-N	90	317	46	58	6	3	2	24	25	22	.183	.262	.240	64	-11	23			.900	4	S-52,O-35/2-1,P-1	-0.7
1889	Was-N	30	109	12	26	2	0	0	11	20	5	.239	.385	.257	86	0	9			.905	3	O-29/S-1	0.2
1891	Mil-a	34	127	29	40	7	1	5	16	18	5	.315	.435	.409	118	2	12			.932	3	S-25/3-9	0.6
1892	Bal-N	76	308	42	85	15	3	1	50	24	19	.276	.340	.354	107	2	14			.872	0	S-57,O-12/3-7	0.4
1893	Bro-N	94	327	53	86	17	1	2	54	48	13	.263	.366	.339	92	-2	9			.892	-3	O-46,3-37,S-11/2-3	-0.5
1894	Bro-N	64	239	47	77	6	5	1	37	26	6	.322	.400	.402	101	2	16			.926	-1	O-35,3-14/2-9,S-6	-0.1
1895	Bro-N	61	216	49	56	9	5	0	29	32	6	.259	.368	.366	97	1	7			.952	-6	O-39,2-13/S-6,3-3	-0.6
1896	Bro-N	76	250	36	73	7	4	1	28	33	10	.292	.381	.364	103	3	11			.941	-13	2-62,O-10/3-3,S-1	-0.6
1897	Bro-N	85	284	42	79	9	2	0	38	49		.278	.393	.324	96	2	6			.941	6	2-68,S-13/O-4	0.9
Total	11	706	2536	414	671	89	28	10	323	298	115	.265	.355	.334	94	-10	138			.912	-6	O-298,S-179,2/3P	-1.1

■ COSTEN SHOCKLEY
Shockley, John Costen b: 2/8/42, Georgetown, Del. BL/TL, 6'2", 200 lbs. Deb: 7/17/64

YEAR	TM/L	G	AB	R	H	2B	3B	HR	RBI	BB	SO	AVG	OBP	SLG	PRO+	BR/A	SB	CS	SBR	FA	FR	G/POS	TPR
1964	Phi-N	11	35	4	8	0	0	1	2	2	7	.229	.270	.314	65	-2	0	0	0	.968	-1	/1-9	-0.3
1965	Cal-A	40	107	5	20	2	0	2	17	9	16	.187	.256	.262	49	-7	0	0	0	.996	-1	1-31/O-1	-0.9
Total	2	51	142	9	28	2	0	3	19	11	24	.197	.260	.275	53	-9	0	0	0	.991	-1	/1-40,O-1	-1.2

■ CHARLIE SHOEMAKER
Shoemaker, Charles Landis b: 8/10/39, Los Angeles, Cal. d: 5/31/90, Mount Penn, Pa. BL/TR, 5'10", 155 lbs. Deb: 9/9/61

YEAR	TM/L	G	AB	R	H	2B	3B	HR	RBI	BB	SO	AVG	OBP	SLG	PRO+	BR/A	SB	CS	SBR	FA	FR	G/POS	TPR
1961	KC-A	7	26	5	10	1	0	0	2	3	2	.385	.429	.462	135	1	0			1.000	0	/2-6	0.2
1962	KC-A	5	11	1	2	0	0	0	0	1	6	.182	.182	.182	-2	-2	0			1.000	0	/2-4	0.0
1964	KC-A	16	52	6	11	3	0	0	2	0	9	.212	.212	.327	46	-4	0			.964	-5	2-14	-0.8
Total	3	28	89	12	23	4	0	0	4	4	13	.258	.275	.348	67	-4	0			.981	-3	2-24	-0.6

■ STRICK SHOFNER
Shofner, Frank Strickland b: 7/23/19, Crawford, Tex. BL/TR, 5'10.5", 187 lbs. Deb: 4/19/47

YEAR	TM/L	G	AB	R	H	2B	3B	HR	RBI	BB	SO	AVG	OBP	SLG	PRO+	BR/A	SB	CS	SBR	FA	FR	G/POS	TPR
1947	Bos-A	5	13	1	2	1	0	0	0	0	3	.154	.154	.308	25	-1	0	0	0	1.000	1	/3-4	-0.1

YEAR	TM/L	G	AB	R	H	2B	3B	HR	RBI	BB	SO	AVG	OBP	SLG	PRO+	BR/A	SB	CS	SBR	FA	FR	G/POS	TPR

■ EDDIE SHOKES Shokes, Edward Christopher b: 1/27/20, Charleston, S.C. BL/TL, 6', 170 lbs. Deb: 6/9/41

1941	Cin-N	1	1	0	0	0	0	0	0	0	1	.000	.000	.000	-99	-0	0			.000	0	H	0.0
1946	Cin-N	31	83	3	10	1	0	0	5	18	21	.120	.277	.133	19	-8	1			.996	-1	1-29	-1.2
Total	2	32	84	3	10	1	0	0	5	18	22	.119	.275	.131	18	-9	1			.996	-1	/1-29	-1.2

■ RAY SHOOK Shook, Raymond Curtis b: 11/18/1889, Perry, Ohio d: 9/16/70, South Bend, Ind. BR/TR, 5'7.5", 155 lbs. Deb: 4/16/16

| 1916 | Chi-A | 1 | 0 | 0 | 0 | 0 | 0 | 0 | 0 | 0 | 0 | — | — | — | — | | 0 | 0 | | .000 | 0 | R | 0.0 |

■ RON SHOOP Shoop, Ronald Lee b: 9/19/31, Rural Valley, Pa. BR/TR, 5'11", 180 lbs. Deb: 8/22/59

| 1959 | Det-A | 3 | 7 | 1 | 1 | 0 | 0 | 0 | 1 | 0 | 1 | .143 | .143 | .143 | -20 | -1 | 0 | 0 | 0 | 1.000 | -1 | /C-3 | -0.2 |

■ TOM SHOPAY Shopay, Thomas Michael b: 2/21/45, Bristol, Conn. BL/TR, 5'9.5", 160 lbs. Deb: 9/17/67

1967	NY-A	8	27	2	8	1	0	2	6	1	5	.296	.321	.556	161	2	2	0	1	.917	1	/O-7	0.3
1969	NY-A	28	48	2	4	0	1	0	0	2	10	.083	.120	.125	-33	-9	0	1	-1	1.000	1	O-11	-1.0
1971	*Bal-A	47	74	10	19	2	0	0	5	3	7	.257	.286	.284	62	-4	2	1	0	1.000	-1	O-13	-0.5
1972	Bal-A	49	40	3	9	0	0	0	2	5	12	.225	.311	.225	60	-2	0	0	0	1.000	-0	/O-3	-0.5
1975	Bal-A	40	31	4	5	1	0	0	2	4	7	.161	.257	.194	31	-3	3	0	1	1.000	-3	O-13/C-1,D-3	-0.5
1976	Bal-A	14	20	4	4	0	0	0	1	3	3	.200	.304	.200	53	-1	1	0	0	1.000	-4	O-11/C-1	-0.5
1977	Bal-A	67	69	15	13	3	0	1	4	8	7	.188	.273	.275	53	-4	3	3	-1	1.000	-18	O-52/D-2	-2.5
Total	7	253	309	40	62	7	1	3	20	26	51	.201	.263	.259	50	-21	11	5	0	.993	-24	O-110/D-5,C-2	-4.9

■ DAVE SHORT Short, David Orvis b: 5/11/17, Magnolia, Ark. d: 11/22/83, Shreveport, La. BL/TR, 5'11.5", 162 lbs. Deb: 9/16/40

1940	Chi-A	4	3	1	1	0	0	0	1	2	.333	.500	.333	119	0	0	0	0	.000	0	H	0.0
1941	Chi-A	3	8	0	0	0	0	0	0	2	1	.000	.200	.000	-44	-2	0	0	0	.800	-0	/O-2	-0.2
Total	2	7	11	1	1	0	0	0	0	3	3	.091	.286	.091	3	-1	0	0	0	.800	-0	/O-2	-0.2

■ CHICK SHORTEN Shorten, Charles Henry b: 4/19/1892, Scranton, Pa. d: 10/23/65, Scranton, Pa. BL/TL, 6', 175 lbs. Deb: 9/22/15

1915	Bos-A	6	14	1	3	1	0	0	0	2	.214	.214	.286	51	-1	0			1.000	-1	/O-5	-0.2
1916	*Bos-A	53	112	14	33	2	1	0	11	10	8	.295	.352	.330	105	1	1			1.000	-8	O-33	-0.9
1917	Bos-A	69	168	12	30	4	2	0	16	10	10	.179	.229	.226	39	-12	2			.977	-5	O-43	-2.2
1919	Det-A	95	270	37	85	9	3	0	22	22	13	.315	.366	.370	110	4	5			.973	-6	O-75	-0.8
1920	Det-A	116	364	35	105	9	6	1	40	28	14	.288	.339	.354	86	-7	2	4	-2	.989	-1	O-99	-1.7
1921	Det-A	92	217	33	59	11	3	0	23	20	11	.272	.333	.350	75	-8	2	3	-1	.981	-4	O-51	-1.6
1922	StL-A	55	131	22	36	12	5	2	16	16	8	.275	.354	.489	114	2	0	1	-1	1.000	-2	O-31	-0.3
1924	Cin-N	41	69	7	19	3	0	0	4	2	2	.275	.315	.319	71	-3	0	0	0	1.000	-4	O-15	-0.7
Total	8	527	1345	161	370	51	20	3	134	110	68	.275	.330	.349	87	-25	12	8		.985	-31	O-352	-8.4

■ BURT SHOTTON Shotton, Burton Edwin "Barney" b: 10/18/1884, Brownhelm, Ohio d: 7/29/62, Lake Wales, Fla. BL/TR, 5'11", 175 lbs. Deb: 9/13/09 MC

1909	StL-A	17	61	5	16	1	0	0	5		.262	.328	.295	104	0	3			.915	1	O-17	0.1
1911	StL-A	139	572	84	146	11	8	0	36	51	.255	.317	.302	76	-18	26			.950	7	*O-139	-1.8
1912	StL-A	154	580	87	168	15	8	2	40	86	.290	.390	.353	117	18	35			.941	7	*O-154	1.6
1913	StL-A	147	549	105	163	23	8	1	28	**99**	63	.297	.405	.373	132	27	43			.951	13	*O-146	3.5
1914	StL-A	154	579	82	156	19	9	0	38	64	66	.269	.344	.333	108	6	40	29	-5	.940	2	*O-152	-0.5
1915	StL-A	156	559	93	158	18	11	1	30	118	62	.283	.409	.360	135	31	43	32	-6	.931	-3	*O-154	1.5
1916	StL-A	157	618	97	174	23	6	1	36	**111**	67	.282	.391	.343	127	26	41	28	-5	.950	10	*O-157	2.5
1917	StL-A	118	398	47	89	9	1	1	20	62	47	.224	.330	.259	83	-6	16			.923	-12	*O-107	-2.6
1918	Was-A	126	505	68	132	16	7	0	21	67	28	.261	.349	.321	104	4	25			.942	6	*O-122	0.3
1919	StL-N	85	270	35	77	13	5	1	20	22	25	.285	.341	.381	125	8	16			.927	-5	O-67	-0.1
1920	StL-N	62	180	28	41	5	0	1	12	18	14	.228	.305	.272	69	-7	5	1	1	.959	-1	O-51	-0.9
1921	StL-N	38	48	9	12	1	1	0	7	7	4	.250	.357	.375	96	-0	0	2	-1	.958	-0	O-11	-0.2
1922	StL-N	34	30	5	6	1	0	0	2	4	6	.200	.294	.233	39	-3	0	1	-1	1.000	-1	/O-3	-0.4
1923	StL-N	1	0	0	0	0	0	0	0	0	0	—	—	—	—		0	0	0	.000	0	R	0.0
Total	14	1388	4949	746	1338	154	65	9	290	714	382	.270	.365	.333	110	87	293	93		.942	25	*O-1280	3.0

■ JOHN SHOUPE Shoupe, John F. b: 9/30/1851, Cincinnati, Ohio d: 2/13/20, Cincinnati, Ohio BL/TL, 5'7", 140 lbs. Deb: 5/3/1879

1879	Tro-N	11	44	5	4	0	0	0	1	0	3	.091	.091	.091	-43	-6				.820	-3	S-10/2-1	-0.8
1882	StL-a	2	7	1	0	0	0	0		0		.000	.000	.000	-96	-1				1.000	1	/2-2	-0.2
1884	Was-U	1	4	1	3	0	0	0		0		.750	.750	.750	368	1				.857	2	/O-1	0.2
Total	3	14	55	7	7	0	0	0	1	0	3	.127	.127	.127	-17	-7				.857	-0	/S-10,2-3,O-1	-0.6

■ BRIAN SHOUSE Shouse, Brian Douglas b: 9/26/68, Effingham, Ill. BL/TL, 5'11", 180 lbs. Deb: 7/31/93

| 1993 | Pit-N | 16 | 0 | 0 | 0 | 0 | 0 | 0 | 0 | 0 | 0 | — | — | — | — | | 0 | 0 | 0 | 1.000 | 0 | /P-6 | 0.0 |

■ JOHN SHOVLIN Shovlin, John Joseph "Brode" b: 1/14/1891, Drifton, Pa. d: 2/16/76, Bethesda, Md. BR/TR, 5'7", 163 lbs. Deb: 6/21/11

1911	Pit-N	2	1	1	0	0	0	0	0	0	1	.000	.000	.000	-96	-0	0			.000	0	H	0.0
1919	StL-A	9	35	4	7	0	0	0	1	5	2	.200	.300	.200	41	-3				.936	-2	/2-9	-0.4
1920	StL-A	7	7	2	2	0	0	0	2	0		.286	.286	.286	50	-0	0	0	0	1.000	1	/S-5	0.0
Total	3	18	43	7	9	0	0	0	3	5	3	.209	.292	.209	39	-3	0	0	0	.936	-1	/2-9,S-5	-0.4

■ GEORGE SHUBA Shuba, George Thomas "Shotgun" b: 12/13/24, Youngstown, Ohio BL/TR, 5'11", 180 lbs. Deb: 7/2/48

1948	Bro-N	63	161	21	43	6	0	4	32	34	31	.267	.395	.379	107	3				.936	-10	O-56	-0.9
1949	Bro-N	1	1	0	0	0	0	0	0	0	0	.000	.000	.000	-96	-0	0			.000	0	H	0.0
1950	Bro-N	34	111	15	23	8	2	3	12	13	22	.207	.302	.396	80	-3	2			.984	3	O-27	-0.2
1952	*Bro-N	94	256	40	78	12	1	9	40	38	29	.305	.395	.465	136	13	1	3	-2	.992	-2	O-67	0.7
1953	*Bro-N	74	169	19	43	12	1	5	23	17	20	.254	.326	.426	92	-2	1	2	-1	.984	-5	O-44	-1.0
1954	Bro-N	45	65	3	10	5	0	2	10	7	10	.154	.247	.323	46	-5	0	0	0	.913	-3	O-13	-0.7
1955	*Bro-N	44	51	8	14	2	0	1	8	11	10	.275	.422	.373	110	1	1	0	0	.909	-1	/O-9	-0.1
Total	7	355	814	106	211	45	4	24	125	120	122	.259	.359	.413	104	6	5	5	5	.967	-18	O-216	-2.2

■ FRANK SHUGART Shugart, Frank Harry (b: Frank Harry Shugarts) b: 12/10/1866, Luthersburg, Pa. d: 9/9/44, Clearfield, Pa. BL/TR, 5'8", 170 lbs. Deb: 8/23/1890

1890	Chi-P	29	106	8	20	5	5	0	15	5	13	.189	.232	.330	47	-9	5			.881	-5	S-25/O-5	-1.0
1891	Pit-N	75	320	57	88	19	8	3	33	20	26	.275	.324	.412	117	5	21			.902	9	S-75	1.0
1892	Pit-N	137	554	94	148	19	14	0	62	47	48	.267	.329	.352	106	3	28			.886	9	*S-134/C-2,O-1	1.6
1893	Pit-N	52	210	37	55	7	3	1	32	19	15	.262	.332	.338	80	-6	12			.882	-3	S-51	-0.5
	StL-N	59	246	41	69	10	4	0	28	22	10	.280	.354	.354	88	-4	13			.907	-3	O-28,S-23/3-9	-0.6
	Yr	111	456	78	124	17	7	1	60	41	25	.272	.344	.346	84	-10	25			.868	-3	S-74,O-28/3-9	-1.1
1894	StL-N	133	527	103	154	19	18	7	72	38	37	.292	.350	.436	89	-12	21			.912	-3	*O-122/S-7,3-7	-1.8
1895	Lou-N	113	473	61	125	14	13	4	70	31	25	.264	.315	.374	82	-13	14			.874	-17	*S-88,O-27	-2.3
1897	Phi-N	40	163	20	41	8	2	5	25	8		.252	.287	.417	87	-4	5			.872	-4	S-40	-0.7
1901	Chi-A	107	415	62	104	9	12	2	47	28		.251	.301	.345	81	-11	12			.885	-8	*S-107	-0.9
Total	8	745	3014	483	804	110	79	22	384	218	174	.267	.323	.378	90	-51	131			.883	-30	S-550,O-183/3-16,C	-5.0

■ TERRY SHUMPERT Shumpert, Terrance Darnell b: 8/16/66, Paducah, Ky. BR/TR, 5'11", 190 lbs. Deb: 5/1/90

1990	KC-A	32	91	7	25	6	1	0	8	2	17	.275	.298	.363	85	-2	3	3	-1	.977	2	2-27/D-3	0.0
1991	KC-A	144	369	45	80	16	4	5	34	30	75	.217	.285	.322	67	-17	17	11	-2	.975	3	*2-144	-1.3
1992	KC-A	36	94	6	14	5	1	1	11	3	17	.149	.175	.255	19	-10	2	2	-1	.969	1	2-33/S-1,D-1	-1.0
1993	KC-A	8	10	1	1	0	0	0	2	0	3	.100	.250	.100	-2	-1	1	0	0	1.000	2	/2-8	0.1
1994	KC-A	64	183	28	44	6	2	8	24	13	39	.240	.291	.426	79	-7	18	3	4	.964	-8	2-38,S-24/S-1,D-2	-0.8
1995	Bos-A	21	47	6	11	3	0	0	4	3	13	.234	.294	.298	53	-3	3	1	0	1.000	3	/2-8,3-5,S-3,D-1	0.1
1996	Chi-N	27	31	5	7	1	0	2	6	5	11	.226	.294	.452	92	-0	0	1	-1	.923	-0	3-10/2-4,S-1	-0.1
Total	7	332	825	97	182	37	8	16	86	56	174	.221	.276	.343	66	-41	44	21	1	.974	2	2-262/3-39,D-7,S-6	-3.0

YEAR	TM/L	G	AB	R	H	2B	3B	HR	RBI	BB	SO	AVG	OBP	SLG	PRO+	BR/A	SB	CS	SBR	FA	FR	G/POS	TPR

■ VINCE SHUPE Shupe, Vincent William b: 9/5/21, E.Canton, Ohio d: 4/5/62, Canton, Ohio BL/TL, 5'11", 180 lbs. Deb: 7/7/45

| 1945 | Bos-N | 78 | 283 | 22 | 76 | 8 | 0 | 0 | 15 | 17 | 16 | .269 | .312 | .297 | 69 | -11 | 3 | | | .989 | 1 | 1-77 | -1.5 |

■ ED SICKING Sicking, Edward Joseph b: 3/30/1897, St.Bernard, Ohio d: 8/30/78, Madeira, Ohio BR/TR, 5'9.5", 165 lbs. Deb: 8/26/16

1916	Chi-N	1	1	0	0	0	0	0	0	0	0	.000	.000	.000	-90	-0	0			.000	0	H	0.0
1918	NY-N	46	132	9	33	4	0	0	12	6	11	.250	.283	.280	73	-4	0			.917	-8	3-24,2-18/S-3	-1.3
1919	NY-N	6	15	2	5	0	0	0	3	1	0	.333	.412	.333	127	1	0			.971	3	/S-6	0.4
	Phi-N	61	185	16	40	2	1	0	15	8	17	.216	.253	.238	45	-12	4			.925	5	S-35,2-22	-0.5
	Yr	67	200	18	45	2	1	0	18	9	17	.225	.265	.245	51	-12	4			.933	8	S-41,2-22	-0.1
1920	NY-N	46	134	11	23	3	1	0	9	10	10	.172	.234	.209	28	-12	6	2	1	.915	4	3-28,2-15/S-3	-0.7
	Cin-N	37	123	12	33	3	0	0	17	13	5	.268	.338	.293	83	-2	2	3	-1	.955	1	2-25/S-9,3-2	-0.1
	Yr	83	257	23	56	6	1	0	26	23	15	.218	.285	.249	55	-14	8	5	-1	.952	4	2-40,3-30,S-12	-0.8
1927	Pit-N	6	7	1	1	1	0	0	3	1	0	.143	.250	.286	40	-1	0			1.000	2	/2-5	0.1
Total	5	203	597	51	135	12	2	0	59	39	43	.226	.277	.255	57	-31	14	5		.965	5	/2-85,S-56,3-54	-2.1

■ JOE SIDDALL Siddall, Joseph Todd b: 10/25/67, Windsor, Ont., Can. BL/TR, 6'1", 197 lbs. Deb: 7/28/93

1993	Mon-N	19	20	0	2	1	0	0	1	1	5	.100	.143	.150	-21	-3	0	0	0	1.000	2	C-15/1-1,O-1	-0.1
1995	Mon-N	7	10	4	3	0	0	0	1	3	3	.300	.500	.300	113	1	0	0	0	.882	-3	/C-7	-0.2
1996	Fla-N	18	47	0	7	1	0	0	3	2	8	.149	.184	.170	-6	-7	0	0	0	.977	-1	C-18	-0.7
Total	3	44	77	4	12	2	0	0	5	6	16	.156	.226	.182	10	-10	0	0	0	.972	-2	/C-40,O-1,1-1	-1.0

■ NORM SIEBERN Siebern, Norman Leroy b: 7/26/33, St.Louis, Mo. BL/TR, 6'3", 205 lbs. Deb: 6/15/56

1956	*NY-A	54	162	27	33	1	4	4	21	19	38	.204	.287	.333	66	-9	1	1	-0	.971	0	O-51	-1.1
1958	*NY-A	134	460	79	138	19	5	14	55	66	87	.300	.389	.454	136	24	5	8	-3	.982	5	*O-133	2.0
1959	NY-A	120	380	52	103	17	0	11	53	41	71	.271	.345	.403	108	4	3	1	0	.989	-2	O-93/1-2	-0.2
1960	KC-A	144	520	69	145	31	6	19	69	72	68	.279	.369	.471	125	18	0	0	0	.987	-1	O-75,1-69	0.9
1961	KC-A	153	560	68	166	36	5	18	98	82	91	.296	.387	.475	127	23	2	4	-2	.989	-1	*1-109,O-47	0.9
1962	KC-A★	162	600	114	185	25	6	25	117	110	88	.308	.416	.495	138	35	3	1	0	.994	5	*1-162	2.9
1963	KC-A☆	152	556	80	151	25	3	16	83	79	82	.272	.362	.410	110	9	1	4	-2	.991	4	*1-131,O-16	0.4
1964	Bal-A★	150	478	92	117	24	2	12	56	**106**	87	.245	.384	.379	114	13	2	3	-1	.995	4	*1-149	1.0
1965	Bal-A	106	297	44	76	13	4	8	32	50	49	.256	.365	.407	117	8	1	2	-1	.991	1	1-76	0.4
1966	Cal-A	125	336	29	83	14	1	5	41	63	61	.247	.366	.339	107	6	0	1	-1	.992	1	1-99	0.4
1967	SF-N	46	58	6	9	1	1	0	4	14	13	.155	.319	.207	54	-3	0	0	0	1.000	-0	1-15/O-2	-0.4
	*Bos-A	33	44	2	9	4	0	2	7	6	8	.205	.300	.295	71	-1	0	0	0	.981	1	1-13/O-1	-0.2
1968	Bos-A	27	30	0	2	0	0	0	0	0	5	.067	.067	.067	-56	-5	0	0	0	1.000	-1	/1-2,O-2	-0.7
Total	12	1406	4481	662	1217	206	38	132	636	708	748	.272	.372	.423	117	122	18	25	-10	.992	17	1-827,O-420	5.9

■ DICK SIEBERT Siebert, Richard Walther b: 2/19/12, Fall River, Mass. d: 12/9/78, Minneapolis, Minn. BL/TL, 6', 170 lbs. Deb: 9/7/32 F

1932	Bro-N	6	7	1	2	0	0	0	2	2	.286	.444	.286	104	0	1.000	-0	/1-2	0.0
1936	Bro-N	2	2	0	0	0	0	0	0	0	0	.000	.000	.000	-99	-0	0			1.000	0	/O-1	0.0
1937	StL-N	22	38	3	7	2	0	0	2	4	8	.184	.279	.237	41	-3	1			.979	-1	/1-7	-0.4
1938	StL-N	1	1	0	1	0	0	0	0	0	0	1.000	1.000	1.000	427	0	0			.000	0	H	0.0
	Phi-A	48	194	24	55	8	3	0	28	10	9	.284	.329	.356	73	-8	2	3	-1	1.000	5	1-46	-0.9
1939	Phi-A	101	402	58	118	28	3	6	47	21	22	.294	.329	.423	93	-6	4	1	1	.991	5	1-99	-1.0
1940	Phi-A	154	595	69	170	31	6	5	77	33	34	.286	.325	.383	85	-14	8	6	-1	.985	8	*1-154	-2.1
1941	Phi-A	123	467	63	156	28	8	5	79	37	22	.334	.385	.460	126	17	1	3	-2	.990	6	*1-123	1.2
1942	Phi-A	153	612	57	159	25	7	2	74	24	17	.260	.291	.333	76	-21	4	5	-2	.989	-2	*1-152	-3.6
1943	Phi-A★	146	558	50	140	26	7	1	72	33	21	.251	.295	.328	83	-14	6	7	-2	.990	4	*1-145	-2.2
1944	Phi-A	132	468	52	143	27	6	1	52	62	17	.306	.387	.423	133	21	2	0	1	.993	-4	1-74,O-58	1.2
1945	Phi-A	147	573	62	153	29	1	7	51	50	33	.267	.328	.358	99	-1	2	7	-4	.991	10	*1-147	-0.5
Total	11	1035	3917	439	1104	204	40	32	482	276	185	.282	.332	.379	96	-29	30	32		.990	31	1-949/O-59	-8.3

■ FRED SIEFKE Siefke, Frederick Edwin b: 3/27/1870, New York, N.Y. d: 4/18/1893, New York, N.Y. 5'11", 168 lbs. Deb: 5/2/1890

| 1890 | Bro-a | 16 | 58 | 1 | 8 | 2 | 0 | 0 | 3 | 5 | | .138 | .206 | .172 | 12 | -6 | 2 | | | .811 | 0 | 3-16 | -0.5 |

■ JOHN SIEGEL Siegel, John b: York, Pa. Deb: 6/9/1884

| 1884 | Phi-U | 8 | 31 | 4 | 7 | 2 | 0 | 0 | | 1 | | .226 | .250 | .290 | 68 | -2 | | | | .533 | -5 | /3-8 | -0.6 |

■ JOHNNY SIEGLE Siegle, John Herbert b: 7/8/1874, Urbana, Ohio d: 2/12/68, Urbana, Ohio BR/TR, 5'10", 165 lbs. Deb: 9/15/05

1905	Cin-N	17	56	9	17	1	2	1	8	7		.304	.391	.446	135	2	0			.960	-1	O-16	0.0
1906	Cin-N	22	68	4	8	2	2	0	7	3		.118	.178	.206	19	-7	0			.959	0	O-21	-0.8
Total	2	39	124	13	25	3	4	1	15	10		.202	.277	.315	75	-4	0			.959	-1	/O-37	-0.8

■ OSCAR SIEMER Siemer, Oscar Sylvester "Cotton" b: 8/14/01, St.Louis, Mo. d: 12/5/59, St.Louis, Mo. BR/TR, 5'9", 162 lbs. Deb: 5/20/25

1925	Bos-N	16	46	5	14	0	1	1	6	1	0	.304	.319	.413	94	-1	0	0	0	.900	-2	C-16	-0.2
1926	Bos-N	31	73	3	15	1	0	0	5	2	7	.205	.227	.219	22	-8	0	0	0	.920	-2	C-30	-0.9
Total	2	47	119	8	29	1	1	1	11	3	7	.244	.262	.294	51	-9	0	0	0	.913	-4	/C-46	-1.1

■ RUBEN SIERRA Sierra, Ruben Angel (Garcia) b: 10/6/65, Rio Piedras, P.R. BB/TR, 6'1", 175 lbs. Deb: 6/1/86

1986	Tex-A	113	382	50	101	13	10	16	55	22	65	.264	.306	.476	106	2	7	8	-3	.972	-10	*O-107/D-3	-1.4
1987	Tex-A	158	643	97	169	35	4	30	109	39	114	.263	.307	.470	102	-0	16	11	-2	.963	5	*O-157	-0.2
1988	Tex-A	156	615	77	156	32	2	23	91	44	91	.254	.305	.424	99	-2	18	4	3	.979	6	*O-153/D-1	0.2
1989	Tex-A★	162	634	101	194	35	**14**	29	**119**	43	82	.306	.352	**.543**	146	36	8	2	1	.973	6	*O-162	3.9
1990	Tex-A	159	608	70	170	37	2	16	96	49	86	.280	.334	.426	111	8	9	0	3	.967	5	*O-151/D-7	0.7
1991	Tex-A★	161	661	110	203	44	5	25	116	56	91	.307	.361	.502	139	33	16	4	2	.979	5	*O-161	3.6
1992	Tex-A★	124	500	66	139	30	6	14	70	31	59	.278	.320	.446	117	9	12	4	1	.970	-0	*O-119/D-4	0.8
	*Oak-A	27	101	17	28	4	1	3	17	14	9	.277	.365	.426	128	4	2	0	1	1.000	1	O-25/D-2	0.5
	Yr	151	601	83	167	34	7	17	87	45	68	.278	.328	.443	119	13	14	4	2	.976	1	O-144/D-6	1.3
1993	Oak-A	158	630	77	147	23	5	22	101	52	97	.233	.292	.390	87	-14	25	5	5	.977	7	*O-133,D-25	-0.7
1994	Oak-A★	110	426	71	114	21	1	23	92	23	64	.268	.305	.484	108	2	8	5	-1	.948	-4	O-98,D-10	-0.5
1995	Oak-A	70	264	40	70	17	0	12	42	24	42	.265	.326	.466	109	2	4	4	-1	.957	-5	O-62/D-7	-0.5
	*NY-A	56	215	33	56	15	0	7	44	22	34	.260	.329	.428	96	-2	1	0	0	.950	1	D-46,O-10	-0.4
	Yr	126	479	73	126	32	0	19	86	46	76	.263	.328	.449	103	1	5	4	-1	.956	-5	O-72,D-53	-0.9
1996	NY-A	96	360	39	93	17	1	11	52	40	58	.258	.333	.403	83	-9	1	3	-2	.984	2	D-61,O-33	-1.3
	Det-A	46	158	22	35	9	1	1	20	20	25	.222	.309	.310	58	-10	3	1	0	.914	1	O-23,D-20	-1.0
	Yr	142	518	61	128	26	2	12	72	60	83	.247	.325	.375	76	-19	4	4	-1	.950	4	D-81,O-56	-2.3
Total	11	1596	6197	870	1675	332	52	232	1024	479	917	.270	.323	.453	109	58	130	51	8	.970	16	*O-1394,D-186	3.7

■ ROY SIEVERS Sievers, Roy Edward "Squirrel" b: 11/18/26, St.Louis, Mo. BR/TR, 6'1", 195 lbs. Deb: 4/21/49 C

1949	StL-A	140	471	84	144	28	1	16	91	70	75	.306	.398	.471	124	16	1	5	-3	.973	6	*O-125/3-7	1.3
1950	StL-A	113	370	46	88	20	4	10	57	34	42	.238	.305	.395	75	-16	1	3	-2	.983	6	O-78,3-21	-1.4
1951	StL-A	31	89	10	20	2	1	1	11	9	21	.225	.303	.303	62	-5	0	0	0	.985	-2	O-25	-0.7
1952	StL-A	11	30	3	6	0	0	0	5	1	4	.200	.226	.300	44	-2	0	0	0	.968	-1	/1-7	-0.4
1953	StL-A	92	285	37	77	15	0	8	35	32	47	.270	.344	.407	100	-0	0	1	-1	.992	-6	1-76	-1.0
1954	Was-A	145	514	75	119	26	6	24	102	80	77	.232	.337	.446	120	12	2	1	1	.971	9	*O-133/1-8	1.5
1955	Was-A	144	509	74	138	20	8	25	106	73	66	.271	.367	.489	136	24	1	1	-0	.988	-1	*O-129,1-17/3-2	1.6
1956	Was-A★	152	550	92	139	27	2	29	95	100	88	.253	.373	.467	121	17	0	0	0	.987	-2	O-78,1-76	1.0
1957	Was-A☆	152	572	99	172	23	5	**42**	**114**	76	55	.301	.389	.579	163	49	1	1	-0	.985	4	O-130,1-21	4.4
1958	Was-A	148	550	85	162	18	1	39	108	53	63	.295	.361	.544	148	34	1	1	-0	.991	6	O-114,1-33	3.1
1959	Was-A★	115	385	55	93	19	0	21	49	53	62	.242	.336	.455	116	9	1	1	-0	.989	5	1-93,O-13	0.5
1960	Chi-A	127	444	87	131	22	0	28	93	74	69	.295	.399	.534	152	33	1	1	-0	.993	-7	*1-114/O-6	1.7

YEAR	TM/L	G	AB	R	H	2B	3B	HR	RBI	BB	SO	AVG	OBP	SLG	PRO+	BR/A	SB	CS	SBR	FA	FR	G/POS	TPR
1961	Chi-A★	141	492	76	145	26	6	27	92	61	62	.295	.379	.537	144	30	1	0	0	.993	0	*1-132	1.9
1962	Phi-N	144	477	61	125	19	5	21	80	56	80	.262	.348	.455	117	11	2	1	0	.991	-1	*1-130/O-7	0.4
1963	Phi-N	138	450	46	108	19	2	19	82	43	72	.240	.313	.418	110	5	0	2	-1	.989	-1	*1-126	-0.2
1964	Phi-N	49	120	7	22	3	1	4	16	13	20	.183	.269	.325	67	-5	0	0	0	.992	-1	1-33	-0.8
	Was-A	33	58	5	10	1	0	0	11	9	14	.172	.284	.397	87	1	0	0	0	1.000	1	1-15	0.0
1965	Was-A	12	21	3	4	1	0	0	0	4	3	.190	.320	.238	62	-1	0	0	0	1.000	-1	/1-7	-0.2
Total	17	1887	6387	945	1703	292	42	318	1147	841	920	.267	.357	.475	124	210	14	19	-7	.991	19	1-888,O-838/3-30	12.7

■ FRANK SIFFELL
Siffell, Frank b: 1860, Germany d: 10/26/09, Philadelphia, Pa. Deb: 6/14/1884

YEAR	TM/L	G	AB	R	H	2B	3B	HR	RBI	BB	SO	AVG	OBP	SLG	PRO+	BR/A	SB	CS	SBR	FA	FR	G/POS	TPR
1884	Phi-a	7	17	3	3	1	0	0	3		0	.176	.222	.235	46	-1				.875	-3	/C-7	-0.3
1885	Phi-a	3	10	0	1	0	0	0	0		0	.100	.100	.100	-35	-2				.750	-3	/C-2,O-1	-0.4
Total	2	10	27	3	4	1	0	0	3		0	.148	.179	.185	16	-3				.841	-6	/C-9,O-1	-0.7

■ FRANK SIGAFOOS
Sigafoos, Francis Leonard b: 3/21/04, Easton, Pa. d: 4/12/68, Indianapolis, Ind. BR/TR, 5'9", 170 lbs. Deb: 9/3/26

YEAR	TM/L	G	AB	R	H	2B	3B	HR	RBI	BB	SO	AVG	OBP	SLG	PRO+	BR/A	SB	CS	SBR	FA	FR	G/POS	TPR
1926	Phi-A	13	43	4	11	0	0	0	2	0	3	.256	.256	.256	32	-4	0	0	0	.915	-3	S-12	-0.6
1929	Det-A	14	23	3	4	1	0	0	2	5	4	.174	.321	.217	41	-2	0	2	-1	.909	-2	/3-6,S-5	-0.4
	Chi-A	7	3	1	1	0	0	0	1	2	1	.333	.600	.333	148	1	0	0	0	1.000	1	/2-6	0.2
	Yr	21	26	4	5	1	0	0	3	7	5	.192	.364	.231	56	-1	0	2	-1	.909	-1	/3-6,2-6,S-5	-0.2
1931	Cin-N	21	65	6	11	2	0	0	8	0	6	.169	.182	.200	3	-9	0		2	.881	-3	3-15/S-2	-1.1
Total	3	55	134	14	27	3	0	0	13	7	14	.201	.246	.224	25	-15	0		2	.887	-7	/3-21,S-19,2-6	-1.9

■ PADDY SIGLIN
Siglin, Wesley Peter b: 9/24/1891, Aurelia, Iowa d: 8/5/56, Oakland, Cal. BR/TR, 5'10", 160 lbs. Deb: 9/12/14

YEAR	TM/L	G	AB	R	H	2B	3B	HR	RBI	BB	SO	AVG	OBP	SLG	PRO+	BR/A	SB	CS	SBR	FA	FR	G/POS	TPR
1914	Pit-N	14	39	4	6	0	0	0	2	4	6	.154	.233	.154	16	-4	1			.911	-6	2-11	-1.1
1915	Pit-N	6	7	1	2	0	0	0	0	1	2	.286	.375	.286	103	0	1			.800	-0	/2-1	0.0
1916	Pit-N	3	4	0	1	0	0	0	0	2		.250	.250	.250	53	-0	0			.857	0	/2-3	0.0
Total	3	23	50	5	9	0	0	0	2	5	10	.180	.255	.180	32	-4	2			.895	-5	/2-15	-1.1

■ TRIPP SIGMAN
Sigman, Wesley Triplett b: 1/17/1899, Mooresville, N.C. d: 3/8/71, Augusta, Ga. BL/TR, 6', 180 lbs. Deb: 9/18/29

YEAR	TM/L	G	AB	R	H	2B	3B	HR	RBI	BB	SO	AVG	OBP	SLG	PRO+	BR/A	SB	CS	SBR	FA	FR	G/POS	TPR
1929	Phi-N	10	29	8	15	1	0	2	9	3	1	.517	.563	.759	210	5	0			.944	-2	O-10	0.2
1930	Phi-N	52	100	15	27	4	1	4	6	6	9	.270	.324	.450	79	-4	1			.932	-1	O-19	-0.6
Total	2	62	129	23	42	5	1	6	15	9	10	.326	.379	.519	108	1	1			.935	-3	/O-29	-0.4

■ EDDIE SILBER
Silber, Edward James b: 6/6/14, Philadelphia, Pa. d: 10/26/76, Dunedin, Fla. BR/TR, 5'11", 170 lbs. Deb: 9/3/37

YEAR	TM/L	G	AB	R	H	2B	3B	HR	RBI	BB	SO	AVG	OBP	SLG	PRO+	BR/A	SB	CS	SBR	FA	FR	G/POS	TPR
1937	StL-A	22	83	10	26	2	0	0	4	5	13	.313	.352	.337	74	-3	0	2	-1	.871	-7	O-21	-1.1
1939	StL-A	1	1	0	0	0	0	0	0	0	0	.000	.000	.000	-98	-0	0	0	0	.000	0	H	0.0
Total	2	23	84	10	26	2	0	0	4	5	14	.310	.348	.333	72	-3	0	2	-1	.871	-7	/O-21	-1.1

■ ED SILCH
Silch, Edward "Baldy" b: 2/22/1865, St.Louis, Mo. d: 1/15/1895, St.Louis, Mo. TR, 6'2", 180 lbs. Deb: 4/29/1888

YEAR	TM/L	G	AB	R	H	2B	3B	HR	RBI	BB	SO	AVG	OBP	SLG	PRO+	BR/A	SB	CS	SBR	FA	FR	G/POS	TPR
1888	Bro-a	14	48	5	13	4	0	0	3		4	.271	.327	.354	118	1	4			.870	-2	O-14	-0.1

■ DANNY SILVA
Silva, Daniel James b: 10/5/1896, Everett, Mass. d: 4/4/74, Hyannis, Mass. BR/TR, 6', 170 lbs. Deb: 8/11/19

YEAR	TM/L	G	AB	R	H	2B	3B	HR	RBI	BB	SO	AVG	OBP	SLG	PRO+	BR/A	SB	CS	SBR	FA	FR	G/POS	TPR
1919	Was-A	1	4	0	1	0	0	0	0	0	0	.250	.250	.250	41	-0	0			1.000	1	/3-1	0.0

■ AL SILVERA
Silvera, Aaron Albert b: 8/26/35, San Diego, Cal. BR/TR, 6', 180 lbs. Deb: 6/12/55

YEAR	TM/L	G	AB	R	H	2B	3B	HR	RBI	BB	SO	AVG	OBP	SLG	PRO+	BR/A	SB	CS	SBR	FA	FR	G/POS	TPR
1955	Cin-N	13	7	3	1	0	0	0	2	0	1	.143	.143	.143	-23	-1	0	0	0	.000	-0	/O-1	-0.2
1956	Cin-N	1	0	0	0	0	0	0	0	0	0	—	—	—	—	-0	0	0	0	.000	-0	R	0.0
Total	2	14	7	3	1	0	0	0	2	0	1	.143	.143	.143	-23	-1	0	0	0	—	-0	/O-1	-0.2

■ CHARLIE SILVERA
Silvera, Charles Anthony Ryan "Swede" b: 10/13/24, San Francisco, Cal BR/TR, 5'10", 175 lbs. Deb: 9/29/48 C

YEAR	TM/L	G	AB	R	H	2B	3B	HR	RBI	BB	SO	AVG	OBP	SLG	PRO+	BR/A	SB	CS	SBR	FA	FR	G/POS	TPR
1948	NY-A	4	14	1	8	0	0	0		0	1	.571	.571	.714	243	3	0	0	0	1.000	0	/C-4	0.3
1949	*NY-A	58	130	8	41	2	0	0	13	18	5	.315	.403	.331	95	0	2	1	0	.985	4	C-51	0.6
1950	NY-A	18	25	2	4	0	0	0	1	1	2	.160	.192	.160	-9	-4	0	0	0	.959	3	C-15	-0.1
1951	NY-A	18	51	5	14	3	0	1	7	5	3	.275	.339	.392	101	-0	0	0	0	1.000	0	C-18	0.1
1952	NY-A	20	55	4	18	3	0	0	11	5	2	.327	.383	.382	121	2	0	3	-2	1.000	1	C-18	-0.2
1953	NY-A	42	82	11	23	3	1	0	12	9	5	.280	.352	.341	91	-1	0	1	-1	.992	6	C-39/3-1	0.6
1954	NY-A	20	37	1	10	1	0	0	4	3	2	.270	.341	.297	79	-1	0	1	-1	.962	5	C-18	0.4
1955	NY-A	14	26	1	5	0	0	0	1	6	4	.192	.344	.192	48	-2	0	0	0	1.000	3	C-11	0.2
1956	NY-A	7	9	0	2	0	0	0	0	2	3	.222	.364	.222	60	-0	0	0	0	.909	-1	/C-7	-0.1
1957	Chi-N	26	53	1	11	0	0	0	2	4	5	.208	.263	.264	43	-4	0	0	0	.982	3	C-26	-0.1
Total	10	227	482	34	136	15	2	1	52	53	32	.282	.356	.328	86	-8	2	6	-3	.985	21	C-209/3-1	1.7

■ LUIS SILVERIO
Silverio, Luis Pascual (Delmonte) b: 10/23/56, Villa Gonzalez, D.R. BR/TR, 5'11", 165 lbs. Deb: 9/9/78

YEAR	TM/L	G	AB	R	H	2B	3B	HR	RBI	BB	SO	AVG	OBP	SLG	PRO+	BR/A	SB	CS	SBR	FA	FR	G/POS	TPR
1978	KC-A	8	11	7	6	2	1	0	3	1	1	.545	.615	.909	315	3	1	1	-0	.833	-2	/O-6,D-2	0.1

■ TOM SILVERIO
Silverio, Tomas Roberto (Veloz) b: 10/14/45, Santiago, D.R. BL/TL, 5'10", 170 lbs. Deb: 4/30/70

YEAR	TM/L	G	AB	R	H	2B	3B	HR	RBI	BB	SO	AVG	OBP	SLG	PRO+	BR/A	SB	CS	SBR	FA	FR	G/POS	TPR
1970	Cal-A	15	15	1	0	0	0	0	0	2	4	.000	.118	.000	-67	-3	0	1	-1	1.000	-2	/O-5,1-1	-0.7
1971	Cal-A	3	3	0	1	0	0	0	0	0	0	.333	.333	.333	96	-0	0	0	0	.000	-1	/O-1	-0.1
1972	Cal-A	13	12	1	2	0	0	0	0	0	5	.167	.167	.167	-1	-1	0	0	0	1.000	-1	/O-4	-0.3
Total	3	31	30	2	3	0	0	0	0	2	9	.100	.156	.100	-27	-5	0	1	-1	1.000	-4	/O-10,1-1	-1.1

■ DAVE SILVESTRI
Silvestri, David Joseph b: 9/29/67, St.Louis, Mo. BR/TR, 6', 180 lbs. Deb: 4/27/92

YEAR	TM/L	G	AB	R	H	2B	3B	HR	RBI	BB	SO	AVG	OBP	SLG	PRO+	BR/A	SB	CS	SBR	FA	FR	G/POS	TPR
1992	NY-A	7	13	3	4		0	1	0		3	.308	.308	.615	154	1	0	0	0	.889	1	/S-6	0.2
1993	NY-A	7	21	4	6	1	0	1	4	5	3	.286	.423	.476	146	2	0	0	0	.955	2	/S-4,3-3	0.3
1994	NY-A	12	18	4	2	0	1	0	2	4	9	.111	.273	.389	71	-1	0	1	-1	1.000	1	/2-9,3-2,S-1	-0.1
1995	NY-A	17	21	4	2	0	0	1	4	4	9	.095	.269	.238	34	-2	0	0	0	1.000	2	/2-7,1-4,S-1,D-4	0.0
	Mon-N	39	72	12	19	6	0	2	7	9	27	.264	.346	.431	100	-0	3	1	0	1.000	-3	/S-9,3-8,1-4,2-3,O	-0.2
1996	Mon-N	86	162	16	33	4	0	1	17	34	41	.204	.342	.247	57	-9	2	1	0	.913	-8	/3-47,S-10/O-2,12	-1.0
Total	5	168	307	42	66	11	3	6	35	56	92	.215	.338	.329	76	-10	4	2	0	.910	-0	/3-60,S-31,2-10D	-0.8

■ KEN SILVESTRI
Silvestri, Kenneth Joseph "Hawk" b: 5/3/16, Chicago, Ill. d: 3/31/92, Tallahassee, Fla. BB/TR, 6'1", 200 lbs. Deb: 4/18/39 MC

YEAR	TM/L	G	AB	R	H	2B	3B	HR	RBI	BB	SO	AVG	OBP	SLG	PRO+	BR/A	SB	CS	SBR	FA	FR	G/POS	TPR
1939	Chi-A	22	75	6	13	3	0	2	5	6	13	.173	.244	.293	36	-8	0	1	-1	.947	-0	C-20	-0.7
1940	Chi-A	28	24	5	6	2	0	2	10	4	7	.250	.357	.583	138	1	0	0	0	1.000	-0	/C-1	0.1
1941	NY-A	17	40	6	10	5	0	1	4	7	6	.250	.362	.450	115	1	0	0	0	1.000	0	C-13	0.2
1946	NY-A	15	21	4	6	1	0	0	1	3	7	.286	.375	.333	98	0	0	0	0	.977	2	C-12	0.3
1947	NY-A	3	10	0	2	0	0	0	0	2	2	.000	.333	.000	51	-0	0	0	0	1.000	0	/C-3	-0.2
1949	Phi-N	4	4	1	0	0	0	0	0	2	1	.000	.333	.000	-3	-0	0	0	0	1.000	0	/C-1,2-1,S-1	0.0
1950	*Phi-N	11	20	2	5	0	0	0	1	3	3	.250	.400	.350	101	0	0	0	0	1.000	-1	/C-9	-0.1
1951	Phi-N	2	9	2	2	1	0	0	4	1	2	.222	.417	.222	78	-0	0	0	0	1.000	-3	/C-3,2-1	-0.3
Total	8	102	203	26	44	11	1	5	25	31	41	.217	.326	.355	78	-6	0	1		.974	-3	/C-62,2-2,S-1	-0.7

■ AL SIMMONS
Simmons, Aloysius Harry "Bucketfoot Al" (b: Aloys Szymanski)
b: 5/22/02, Milwaukee, Wis. d: 5/26/56, Milwaukee, Wis. BR/TR, 5'11", 190 lbs. Deb: 4/15/24 CH

YEAR	TM/L	G	AB	R	H	2B	3B	HR	RBI	BB	SO	AVG	OBP	SLG	PRO+	BR/A	SB	CS	SBR	FA	FR	G/POS	TPR
1924	Phi-A	152	594	69	183	31	9	8	102	30	60	.308	.343	.431	98	-4	16	15	-4	.976	7	*O-152	-1.1
1925	Phi-A	153	654	122	**253**	43	12	24	129	35	41	.387	.419	.599	146	42	7	14	-6	.966	5	*O-153	2.8
1926	Phi-A	147	583	90	199	53	10	19	109	48	49	.341	.392	.564	139	31	11	3	2	.975	-4	*O-147	1.7
1927	Phi-A	106	406	86	159	36	11	15	108	31	30	.392	.436	.645	168	39	10	2	2	.985	3	*O-105	3.4
1928	Phi-A	119	464	78	163	33	9	15	107	31	30	.351	.396	.558	144	28	1	4	-2	.988	2	*O-114	1.9
1929	*Phi-A	143	581	114	212	41	9	34	**157**	31	38	.365	.398	.642	158	46	4	2	0	.989	17	*O-142	4.9
1930	*Phi-A	138	554	**152**	211	41	16	36	165	39	34	.381	.423	.708	173	58	9	2	2	**.990**	6	*O-136	4.9
1931	*Phi-A	128	513	105	200	37	13	22	128	47	45	**.390**	.444	.641	172	52	3	3	-1	.987	8	*O-128	4.6
1932	*Phi-A	154	670	144	**216**	28	9	35	151	47	76	.322	.368	.548	129	26	4	5	-5	.980	-5	*O-154	1.0
1933	Chi-A★	146	605	85	200	29	10	14	119	39	49	.331	.373	.481	130	24	5	1	1	.990	14	*O-145	3.0
1934	Chi-A★	138	558	102	192	36	7	18	104	53	58	.344	.403	.530	135	28	3	2	-0	.987	5	*O-138	2.5

YEAR	TM/L	G	AB	R	H	2B	3B	HR	RBI	BB	SO	AVG	OBP	SLG	PRO+	BR/A	SB	CS	SBR	FA	FR	G/POS	TPR
1935	Chi-A★	128	525	68	140	22	7	16	79	33	43	.267	.313	.427	87	-12	4	6	-2	.981	1	*O-126	-1.8
1936	Det-A	143	568	96	186	38	6	13	112	49	35	.327	.383	.484	112	10	6	4	-1	.986	-4	*O-138/1-1	0.0
1937	Was-A	103	419	60	117	21	10	8	84	27	35	.279	.329	.434	95	-5	3	2	-0	.984	5	*O-102	-0.4
1938	Was-A	125	470	79	142	23	6	21	95	38	40	.302	.357	.511	123	14	2	1	0	.983	-8	*O-117	0.2
1939	Bos-N	93	330	39	93	17	5	7	43	22	40	.282	.331	.427	110	3	0			.982	1	O-82	0.0
	*Cin-N	9	21	0	3	0	0	0	1	2	3	.143	.217	.143	-1	-3	0			.938	1	/O-5	-0.2
	Yr	102	351	39	96	17	5	7	44	24	43	.274	.324	.410	103	-0	0			.978	1	O-87	-0.2
1940	Phi-A	37	81	7	25	4	0	1	19	4	8	.309	.341	.395	92	-1	0	0	0	.963	1	O-18	0.0
1941	Phi-A	9	24	1	3	1	0	0	1	1	2	.125	.160	.167	-14	-4	0	0	0	1.000	1	/O-5	-0.4
1943	Bos-A	40	133	9	27	5	0	1	12	8	21	.203	.248	.263	49	-9	0	1	-1	.986	-2	O-33	-1.4
1944	Phi-A	4	6	1	3	0	0	0	2	0	0	.500	.500	.500	189	1	0	0	0	1.000	-0	/O-2	0.0
Total	20	2215	8759	1507	2927	539	149	307	1827	615	737	.334	.380	.535	132	361	88	64		.982	53	*O-2142/1-1	25.6

■ **HACK SIMMONS**   Simmons, George Washington   b: 1/29/1885, Brooklyn, N.Y.   d: 4/26/42, Arverne, N.Y.   BR/TR, 5'8", 179 lbs.   Deb: 4/15/10

YEAR	TM/L	G	AB	R	H	2B	3B	HR	RBI	BB	SO	AVG	OBP	SLG	PRO+	BR/A	SB	CS	SBR	FA	FR	G/POS	TPR
1910	Det-A	42	110	12	25	3	1	0	9	10		.227	.303	.273	75	-3	1			.984	-0	1-22/3-7,O-2	-0.3
1912	NY-A	110	401	45	96	17	2	0	41	33		.239	.308	.292	68	-17	19			.946	-21	2-88,1-13/S-4	-4.0
1914	Bal-F	114	352	50	95	16	5	1	38	32	26	.270	.341	.352	86	-11	7			.894	-8	O-73,2-26/1-4,S3	-2.4
1915	Bal-F	39	88	8	18	7	1	1	14	10	9	.205	.293	.341	76	-4	1			1.000	-3	2-13,O-13	-0.9
Total	4	305	951	115	234	43	9	2	102	85	35	.246	.318	.317	76	-36	28			.953	-32	2-127/O-88,1-39,3S	-7.6

■ **JOHN SIMMONS**   Simmons, John Earl   b: 7/7/24, Birmingham, Ala.   BR/TR, 6'1.5", 192 lbs.   Deb: 4/22/49

YEAR	TM/L	G	AB	R	H	2B	3B	HR	RBI	BB	SO	AVG	OBP	SLG	PRO+	BR/A	SB	CS	SBR	FA	FR	G/POS	TPR
1949	Was-A	62	93	12	20	0	0	0	5	11	6	.215	.298	.215	38	-8	0	0	0	1.000	-5	O-26	-1.4

■ **JOE SIMMONS**   Simmons, Joseph S.   b: 6/13/1845, New York, N.Y.   5'9", 166 lbs.   Deb: 5/8/1871   M

YEAR	TM/L	G	AB	R	H	2B	3B	HR	RBI	BB	SO	AVG	OBP	SLG	PRO+	BR/A	SB	CS	SBR	FA	FR	G/POS	TPR
1871	Chi-n	27	129	29	28	6	1	0	17	1	0	.217	.223	.279	39	-12	4	1	1	.894	-1	*O-25/1-2	-0.7
1872	Cle-n	18	90	11	23	5	1	0	9	1	2	.256	.264	.333	87	-1	1	0	0	.938	0	1-15/O-3	0.0
1875	Wes-n	13	53	5	9	1	0	0	4	0	2	.170	.170	.189	23	-4	1	2	-1	.733	-1	O-10/1-3,M	-0.5
Total	3 n	58	272	45	60	12	2	0	30	2	4	.221	.226	.279	51	-17	6	3	0	.855	-1	/O-38,1-20	-1.2

■ **NELSON SIMMONS**   Simmons, Nelson Bernard   b: 6/27/63, Washington, D.C.   BB/TR, 6'1", 185 lbs.   Deb: 9/4/84

YEAR	TM/L	G	AB	R	H	2B	3B	HR	RBI	BB	SO	AVG	OBP	SLG	PRO+	BR/A	SB	CS	SBR	FA	FR	G/POS	TPR
1984	Det-A	9	30	4	13	2	0	0	3	2	5	.433	.469	.500	169	3	1	0	0	1.000	-1	/O-5,D-4	0.2
1985	Det-A	75	251	31	60	11	0	10	33	26	41	.239	.310	.402	94	-2	1	0	0	.945	-1	O-38,D-31	-0.5
1987	Bal-A	16	49	3	13	1	1	1	4	3	8	.265	.308	.388	85	-1	0	1	-1	1.000	-1	O-13/D-1	-0.1
Total	3	100	330	38	86	14	1	11	40	31	54	.261	.324	.409	99	-1	2	1	0	.963	-1	/O-56,D-36	-0.4

■ **TED SIMMONS**   Simmons, Ted Lyle   b: 8/9/49, Highland Park, Mich.   BB/TR, 6', 200 lbs.   Deb: 9/21/68

YEAR	TM/L	G	AB	R	H	2B	3B	HR	RBI	BB	SO	AVG	OBP	SLG	PRO+	BR/A	SB	CS	SBR	FA	FR	G/POS	TPR
1968	StL-N	2	3	0	1	0	0	0	0	1	1	.333	.500	.333	156	0	0	0	0	1.000	-1	/C-2	0.0
1969	StL-N	5	14	0	3	0	1	0	3	1	1	.214	.267	.357	73	-1	0	0	0	.957	-1	/C-4	-0.2
1970	StL-N	82	284	29	69	8	2	3	24	37	37	.243	.334	.317	74	-10	2	2	-1	.990	-3	C-79	-0.9
1971	StL-N	133	510	64	155	32	4	7	77	36	50	.304	.353	.424	115	10	1	3	-2	.989	-13	*C-130	0.0
1972	StL-N☆	152	594	70	180	36	6	16	96	29	57	.303	.338	.465	127	19	1	3	-2	.991	-6	*C-135,1-15	3.0
1973	StL-N★	161	619	62	192	36	2	13	91	61	47	.310	.374	.438	124	21	2	2	-1	.987	10	*C-153/1-6,O-2	3.7
1974	StL-N☆	152	599	66	163	33	6	20	103	47	35	.272	.331	.447	117	11	0	3	-2	.986	-4	*C-141,1-12	1.3
1975	StL-N	157	581	80	193	32	3	18	100	63	35	.332	.398	.491	141	32	1	3	-2	.983	-6	*C-154/1-2,O-2	3.2
1976	StL-N	150	546	60	159	35	3	5	75	73	35	.291	.375	.394	117	14	0	7	-4	.993	-9	*C-113,1-30/O-7,3-2	0.2
1977	StL-N★	150	516	82	164	25	3	21	95	79	37	.318	.410	.500	145	35	2	6	-3	.987	-14	*C-143/O-1	2.2
1978	StL-N★	152	516	71	148	40	5	22	80	77	39	.287	.383	.512	150	35	1	1	-0	.988	-6	*C-134,O-23	3.3
1979	StL-N†	123	448	68	127	22	0	26	87	61	34	.283	.374	.507	137	23	0	1	-1	.985	-5	*C-122	2.2
1980	StL-N	145	495	84	150	33	2	21	98	59	45	.303	.379	.505	140	27	1	0	0	.985	-9	*C-129/O-5	2.4
1981	*Mil-A	100	380	45	82	13	3	14	61	23	32	.216	.266	.376	88	-8	0	1	-1	.975	-9	C-75,D-22/1-4	-1.6
1982	*Mil-A	137	539	73	145	29	2	23	97	32	40	.269	.312	.451	114	8	0	0	0	.995	-1	*C-121,D-15	1.1
1983	Mil-A★	153	600	76	185	39	3	13	108	41	51	.308	.355	.448	129	22	4	2	0	.975	-4	C-86,D-66	2.0
1984	Mil-A	132	497	44	110	24		4	52	30	40	.221	.270	.300	60	-28	3	0	1	.995	-1	D-77,1-37,3-14	-3.3
1985	Mil-A	143	528	60	144	28	2	12	76	57	32	.273	.345	.402	104	4	1	1	-0	.992	-3	D-99,1-28,C-15/3-2	-0.3
1986	Atl-N	76	127	14	32	5	0	4	25	12	14	.252	.321	.386	89	-2	1	0	0	.964	-3	1-14,C-10/3-9	-0.5
1987	Atl-N	73	177	20	49	8	0	4	30	21	23	.277	.354	.390	92	-2	1	1	-0	.984	-1	1-28,C-15/3-2	-0.4
1988	Atl-N	78	107	6	21	6	0	2	11	15	9	.196	.295	.308	70	-4	0	1	-0	.993	-1	1-19,C-10	-0.6
Total	21	2456	8680	1074	2472	483	47	248	1389	855	694	.285	.352	.437	118	208	21	33	-14	.987	-79	*C-1771,D-279,1/O3	16.8

■ **MIKE SIMMS**   Simms, Michael Howard   b: 1/12/67, Orange, Cal.   BR/TR, 6'4", 185 lbs.   Deb: 9/5/90

YEAR	TM/L	G	AB	R	H	2B	3B	HR	RBI	BB	SO	AVG	OBP	SLG	PRO+	BR/A	SB	CS	SBR	FA	FR	G/POS	TPR
1990	Hou-N	12	13	3	4	1	0	1	2	0	4	.308	.308	.615	152	1	0	0	0	1.000	-0	/1-6	0.1
1991	Hou-N	49	123	18	25		0	3	16	18	38	.203	.305	.317	80	-3	1	0	0	.889	-5	O-41	-0.9
1992	Hou-N	15	24	1	6	1	0	1	3	2	9	.250	.333	.417	116	0	0	0	0	1.000	-1	/O-9,1-1	-0.1
1994	Hou-N	6	12	1	1	1	0	0	0	0	5	.083	.083	.167	-39	-2	1	0	0	.857	-0	/O-3	-0.2
1995	Hou-N	50	121	14	31	4	0	9	24	13	28	.256	.343	.512	131	5	1	2	-1	.995	-1	1-25,O-12	0.1
1996	Hou-N	49	68	6	12	2	1	1	8	4	16	.176	.233	.279	38	-6	1	0	0	1.000	-1	O-12/1-5	-0.7
Total	6	181	361	43	79	14	1	15	53	37	100	.219	.300	.388	91	-6	4	2	0	.932	-8	/O-77,1-37	-1.7

■ **HANK SIMON**   Simon, Henry Joseph   b: 8/25/1862, Hawkinsville, N.Y.   d: 1/1/25, Albany, N.Y.   BR/TR,   Deb: 10/7/1887

YEAR	TM/L	G	AB	R	H	2B	3B	HR	RBI	BB	SO	AVG	OBP	SLG	PRO+	BR/A	SB	CS	SBR	FA	FR	G/POS	TPR
1887	Cle-a	3	10	1	1	0	0	0	0	0		.100	.100	.100	-45	-2	0			1.000	-1	/O-3	-0.2
1890	Bro-a	89	373	66	96	17	11	0	38	34		.257	.323	.362	105	2	23			.951	6	O-89	0.4
	Syr-a	38	156	33	47	5	3	2	23	17		.301	.370	.410	145	9	12			.941	-3	O-38	0.4
	Yr	127	529	99	143	22	14	2	61	51		.270	.337	.376	116	10	35			.948	3	*O-127	0.8
Total	2	130	539	100	144	22	14	2	61	51		.267	.333	.371	113	9	35			.949	3	O-130	0.6

■ **MIKE SIMON**   Simon, Michael Edward   b: 4/13/1883, Hayden, Ind.   d: 6/10/63, Los Angeles, Cal.   BR/TR, 5'11", 188 lbs.   Deb: 6/27/09

YEAR	TM/L	G	AB	R	H	2B	3B	HR	RBI	BB	SO	AVG	OBP	SLG	PRO+	BR/A	SB	CS	SBR	FA	FR	G/POS	TPR
1909	Pit-N	12	18	2	3	0	0	0	2	1		.167	.211	.167	16	-2	0			.917	0	/C-9	-0.1
1910	Pit-N	22	50	3	10	0	1	0	5	1	2	.200	.216	.240	31	-4	1			1.000	-4	C-14	-0.8
1911	Pit-N	71	215	19	49	4	3	0	22	10	14	.228	.275	.274	52	-14	1			.968	-1	C-68	-0.8
1912	Pit-N	42	113	10	34	2	1	0	11	5	9	.301	.331	.336	84	-3	1			.991	3	C-40	0.4
1913	Pit-N	92	255	23	63	6	2	1	17	10	15	.247	.281	.298	68	-11	3			.975	19	C-92	1.5
1914	StL-F	93	276	21	57	11	2	0	21	18	21	.207	.263	.261	41	-27	2			.984	12	C-78	-0.9
1915	Bro-F	47	142	7	25	5	1	0	12	9	12	.176	.225	.225	27	-16	1			.992	-0	C-45	-1.4
Total	7	379	1069	85	241	28	10	1	90	54	73	.225	.269	.273	51	-77	9			.979	30	C-346	-2.1

■ **SYL SIMON**   Simon, Sylvester Adam "Sammy"   b: 12/14/1897, Evansville, Ind.   d: 2/28/73, Chandler, Ind.   BR/TR, 5'10.5", 170 lbs.   Deb: 10/1/23

YEAR	TM/L	G	AB	R	H	2B	3B	HR	RBI	BB	SO	AVG	OBP	SLG	PRO+	BR/A	SB	CS	SBR	FA	FR	G/POS	TPR
1923	StL-A	1	1	0	0	0	0	0	0	0	0	.000	.000	.000	-95	-0	0	0	0	.000	0	H	0.0
1924	StL-A	23	32	5	8	1	1	0	6	3	5	.250	.314	.344	66	-2	0	0	0	.889	0	/3-6,S-5	-0.1
Total	2	24	33	5	8	1	1	0	6	3	5	.242	.306	.333	61	-2	0	0	0	.889	-0	/3-6,S-5	-0.1

■ **MEL SIMONS**   Simons, Melbern Ellis "Butch"   b: 7/1/1900, Carlyle, Ill.   d: 11/10/74, Paducah, Ky.   BL/TR, 5'10", 175 lbs.   Deb: 4/14/31

YEAR	TM/L	G	AB	R	H	2B	3B	HR	RBI	BB	SO	AVG	OBP	SLG	PRO+	BR/A	SB	CS	SBR	FA	FR	G/POS	TPR
1931	Chi-A	68	189	24	52	9	0	0	12	12	17	.275	.318	.323	73	-7	1	1	-0	.950	-9	O-59	-1.8
1932	Chi-A	7	5	0	0	0	0	0	0	0	1	.000	.000	.000	-99	-2	0	0	0	1.000	-0	/O-6	-0.4
Total	2	75	194	24	52	9	0	0	12	12	18	.268	.311	.314	69	-9	1	1	-0	.951	-12	/O-65	-2.2

■ **HARRY SIMPSON**   Simpson, Harry Leon "Suitcase" or "Goody"   b: 12/3/25, Atlanta, Ga.   d: 4/3/79, Akron, Ohio   BL/TR, 6'1", 180 lbs.   Deb: 4/21/51

YEAR	TM/L	G	AB	R	H	2B	3B	HR	RBI	BB	SO	AVG	OBP	SLG	PRO+	BR/A	SB	CS	SBR	FA	FR	G/POS	TPR
1951	Cle-A	122	332	51	76	7	0	7	24	45	48	.229	.325	.313	77	-10	6	4	-1	.971	-4	O-68,1-50	-1.8
1952	Cle-A	146	545	66	145	21	10	10	65	56	82	.266	.337	.390	111	6	5	3	-0	.988	-4	*O-127,1-28	-0.9
1953	Cle-A	82	242	25	55	3	1	7	22	18	27	.227	.284	.335	68	-11	0	0	0	.968	-6	O-69/1-2	-2.0
1955	Cle-A	3	1	0	0	0	0	0	0	0	0	.000	.667	.000	88	0	0	0	0	.000	0	H	0.0
	KC-A	112	396	42	119	16	7	5	52	36	61	.301	.359	.414	106	3	3	5	-2	.978	1	*O-100/1-3	-0.2
	Yr	115	397	43	119	16	7	5	52	36	61	.300	.361	.413	106	3	3	5	-2	.978	1	*O-100/1-3	-0.2

YEAR	TM/L	G	AB	R	H	2B	3B	HR	RBI	BB	SO	AVG	OBP	SLG	PRO+	BR/A	SB	CS	SBR	FA	FR	G/POS	TPR
1956	KC-A★	141	543	76	159	22	11	21	105	47	82	.293	.350	.490	119	13	2	3	-1	.965	-15	*O-111,1-32	-1.1
1957	KC-A	50	179	24	53	9	6	6	24	12	28	.296	.340	.514	128	6	0	1	-1	.996	1	1-27,O-21	0.3
	*NY-A	75	224	27	56	7	3	7	39	19	36	.250	.309	.402	94	-2	1	0	0	.952	-2	O-42,1-21	-0.8
	Yr	125	403	51	109	16	9	13	63	31	64	.270	.323	.452	110	4	1	1	-0	.957	-2	O-63,1-48	-0.5
1958	NY-A	24	51	1	11	2	1	0	6	6	12	.216	.310	.294	70	-2	0	0	0	1.000	-3	O-15	-0.5
	KC-A	78	212	21	56	7	1	7	27	26	33	.264	.345	.406	104	1	0	2	-1	.990	-3	1-43,O-11	-0.6
	Yr	102	263	22	67	9	2	7	33	32	45	.255	.338	.384	98	-0	0	2	-1	.990	-5	1-43,O-26	-1.1
1959	KC-A	8	14	1	4	0	0	1	2	2	1	.286	.412	.500	146	1	0	0	0	1.000	0	/1-4	0.1
	Chi-A	38	75	5	14	5	1	2	13	4	14	.187	.228	.360	59	-5	0	0	0	.947	-2	O-12/1-1	-0.7
	Yr	46	89	6	18	5	1	3	15	6	18	.202	.260	.382	75	-3	0	0	0	.947	-2	O-12/1-5	-0.6
	Pit-N	9	15	3	4	2	0	0	2	0	2	.267	.267	.400	75	-1	0	0	0	1.000	-0	/O-3	-0.1
Total	8	888	2829	343	752	101	41	73	381	271	429	.266	.332	.408	102	-1	17	18	-6	.974	-37	O-579,1-211	-7.8

■ JOE SIMPSON
Simpson, Joe Allen   b: 12/31/51, Purcell, Okla.   BL/TL, 6'3", 175 lbs.   Deb: 9/2/75

YEAR	TM/L	G	AB	R	H	2B	3B	HR	RBI	BB	SO	AVG	OBP	SLG	PRO+	BR/A	SB	CS	SBR	FA	FR	G/POS	TPR
1975	LA-N	9	6	3	2	0	0	0	0	0	2	.333	.333	.333	89	-0	0	0	0	1.000	-2	/O-6	-0.2
1976	LA-N	23	30	2	4	1	0	0	0	1	6	.133	.161	.167	-7	-4	0	1	-1	1.000	-4	O-20	-1.0
1977	LA-N	29	23	2	4	0	0	0	1	2	6	.174	.240	.174	13	-3	1	1	-0	.957	-6	O-28/1-1	-1.0
1978	LA-N	10	5	1	2	0	0	0	1	0	2	.400	.400	.400	125	0	0	0	0	1.000	-3	O-10	-0.3
1979	Sea-A	120	265	29	75	11	0	2	27	11	21	.283	.314	.347	77	-9	6	3	0	.966	-5	*O-105/D-3	-1.6
1980	Sea-A	129	365	42	91	15	3	3	34	28	43	.249	.305	.332	74	-13	17	4	3	.977	-8	*O-119/1-3	-2.3
1981	Sea-A	91	288	32	64	11	3	2	30	15	41	.222	.263	.302	60	-15	12	3	2	.978	-0	O-88	-1.7
1982	Sea-A	105	296	39	76	14	4	2	23	22	48	.257	.313	.351	80	-8	8	14	-6	.984	-7	O-97	-2.3
1983	KC-A	91	119	16	20	2	2	0	8	11	21	.168	.250	.218	30	-11	1	1	-0	.995	-1	1-54,O-38/P-2,D-1	-1.3
Total	9	607	1397	166	338	54	12	9	124	90	190	.242	.291	.317	67	-63	45	27	-3	.978	-35	O-511/1-58,D-4,P-2	-11.7

■ MARTY SIMPSON
Simpson, Martin   b: Baltimore, Md.   Deb: 5/14/1873

YEAR	TM/L	G	AB	R	H	2B	3B	HR	RBI	BB	SO	AVG	OBP	SLG	PRO+	BR/A	SB	CS	SBR	FA	FR	G/POS	TPR
1873	Mar-n	4	15	4	2	0	0	0	2	0	0	.133	.133	.133	-27	-2	0	0	0	.792	0	/2-3,C-1	-0.1

■ DICK SIMPSON
Simpson, Richard Charles   b: 7/28/43, Washington, D.C.   BR/TR, 6'4", 176 lbs.   Deb: 9/21/62

YEAR	TM/L	G	AB	R	H	2B	3B	HR	RBI	BB	SO	AVG	OBP	SLG	PRO+	BR/A	SB	CS	SBR	FA	FR	G/POS	TPR
1962	LA-A	6	8	1	2	1	0	0	1	2	3	.250	.400	.375	114	0	0	0	0	1.000	-1	/O-4	0.0
1964	LA-A	21	50	11	7	1	0	2	4	8	15	.140	.259	.280	55	-3	2	2	-1	1.000	-2	/O-16	-0.7
1965	Cal-A	8	27	2	6	1	0	0	3	2	8	.222	.276	.259	54	-2	1	0	0	.875	-1	/O-8	-0.3
1966	Cin-N	92	84	26	20	2	0	4	14	10	32	.238	.333	.405	96	-0	0	1	-1	.921	-18	O-64	-2.1
1967	Cin-N	44	54	8	14	3	0	1	6	7	11	.259	.344	.370	94	-0	0	1	-1	.973	-6	O-26	-0.3
1968	StL-N	26	56	11	13	0	0	3	8	8	21	.232	.328	.393	117	1	0	1	-1	1.000	-3	O-22	-0.4
	Hou-N	59	177	25	33	7	2	3	11	20	61	.186	.284	.299	77	-5	4	4	-1	.970	-6	O-49	-1.7
	Yr	85	233	36	46	7	2	6	19	28	82	.197	.294	.322	86	-4	4	5	-2	.979	-9	O-71	-2.1
1969	NY-A	6	11	2	3	0	0	0	4	3	6	.273	.429	.455	153	1	0	0	0	1.000	-1	/O-5	0.0
	Sea-A	26	51	8	9	2	0	2	5	4	17	.176	.236	.333	59	-3	3	1	0	1.000	-3	O-17	-0.7
	Yr	32	62	10	12	4	0	2	9	7	23	.194	.275	.355	77	-2	3	1	0	1.000	-4	O-22	-0.7
Total	7	288	518	94	107	19	2	15	56	64	174	.207	.301	.338	84	-11	10	10	-3	.967	-35	O-211	-6.2

■ DUKE SIMS
Sims, Duane B   b: 6/5/41, Salt Lake City, Ut.   BL/TR, 6'2", 205 lbs.   Deb: 9/22/64

YEAR	TM/L	G	AB	R	H	2B	3B	HR	RBI	BB	SO	AVG	OBP	SLG	PRO+	BR/A	SB	CS	SBR	FA	FR	G/POS	TPR
1964	Cle-A	2	6	0	0	0	0	0	0	0	2	.000	.000	.000	-99	-2	0	0	0	1.000	-1	/C-1	-0.1
1965	Cle-A	48	118	9	21	0	0	3	15	15	33	.178	.271	.331	69	-5	0	0	0	.980	-2	C-40	-0.5
1966	Cle-A	52	133	12	35	2	2	6	19	11	31	.263	.338	.444	122	4	0	1	-1	.975	-5	C-48	0.1
1967	Cle-A	88	272	25	55	8	2	12	37	30	64	.202	.295	.379	97	-1	3	3	-1	.989	-3	C-85	0.0
1968	Cle-A	122	361	48	90	21	0	11	44	62	68	.249	.367	.399	134	17	1	3	-2	.983	-1	C-84,1-31/O-4	2.0
1969	Cle-A	114	326	40	77	8	0	18	45	66	80	.236	.374	.426	120	10	1	2	-1	.991	-4	*C-102/O-3,1-1	1.2
1970	Cle-A	110	345	46	91	12	0	23	56	46	59	.264	.360	.499	128	13	0	4	-2	.993	-2	C-39,O-36,1-29	0.8
1971	LA-N	90	230	23	63	7	2	6	25	30	39	.274	.360	.400	122	7	0	1	-1	.992	0	C-74	1.0
1972	LA-N	51	151	7	29	7	0	2	11	17	23	.192	.278	.278	60	-8	0	0	0	.989	-1	C-48	-0.8
	*Det-A	38	98	11	31	4	0	4	19	19	18	.316	.432	.480	166	9	0	0	0	.994	-3	C-25/O-4	0.8
1973	Det-A	80	252	31	61	10	0	8	30	30	36	.242	.327	.377	92	-3	1	2	-1	.979	-2	C-68/O-6	0.1
	NY-A	4	9	3	3	0	0	1	1	3	1	.333	.500	.667	234	2	0	0	0	1.000	1	/C-1,D-2	0.2
	Yr	84	261	34	64	10	0	9	31	33	37	.245	.334	.387	97	-1	1	2	-1	.979	-2	C-69/O-6,D-2	0.3
1974	NY-A	5	15	1	2	1	0	0	2	1	5	.133	.188	.200	12	-2	0	0	0	1.000	-0	/C-1,D-3	-0.2
	Tex-A	39	106	7	22	0	0	3	6	8	24	.208	.282	.292	67	-4	0	0	0	.970	-3	C-30/O-1,D-2	-0.7
	Yr	44	121	8	24	1	0	3	8	9	29	.198	.271	.281	60	-6	0	0	0	.971	-3	C-31/D-5,O-1	-0.7
Total	11	843	2422	263	580	80	6	100	310	338	483	.239	.341	.401	111	38	6	16	-8	.986	-20	C-646/1-61,O-54,D-7	3.9

■ GREG SIMS
Sims, Gregory Emmett   b: 6/28/46, San Francisco, Cal   BB/TR, 6', 190 lbs.   Deb: 4/15/66

YEAR	TM/L	G	AB	R	H	2B	3B	HR	RBI	BB	SO	AVG	OBP	SLG	PRO+	BR/A	SB	CS	SBR	FA	FR	G/POS	TPR
1966	Hou-N	7	6	1	1	0	0	0	0	1	3	.167	.286	.167	32	-1	0	0	0	.500	-0	/O-1	-0.1

■ MATT SINATRO
Sinatro, Matthew Stephen   b: 3/22/60, Hartford, Conn.   BR/TR, 5'9", 175 lbs.   Deb: 9/22/81

YEAR	TM/L	G	AB	R	H	2B	3B	HR	RBI	BB	SO	AVG	OBP	SLG	PRO+	BR/A	SB	CS	SBR	FA	FR	G/POS	TPR
1981	Atl-N	12	32	4	9	1	1	0	4	5	4	.281	.378	.375	111	1	1	0	0	1.000	4	C-12	0.6
1982	Atl-N	37	81	10	11	2	0	1	4	4	9	.136	.176	.198	4	-10	0	1	-1	1.000	4	C-35	-0.7
1983	Atl-N	7	12	0	2	0	0	0	2	2	1	.167	.286	.167	26	-1	0	0	0	.967	2	/C-7	0.0
1984	Atl-N	2	4	0	0	0	0	0	0	0	0	.000	.000	.000	-93	-1	0	0	0	1.000	-0	/C-2	-0.2
1987	Oak-A	6	3	0	0	0	0	0	0	0	1	.000	.000	.000	-99	-1	0	0	0	1.000	-0	/C-6	-0.1
1988	Oak-A	10	9	1	3	2	0	0	5	0	1	.333	.333	.556	149	1	0	0	0	1.000	-0	/C-9	0.3
1989	Det-A	13	25	2	3	0	0	0	1	1	3	.120	.185	.120	-13	-4	0	0	0	1.000	0	C-13	-0.3
1990	Sea-A	30	50	2	15	1	0	0	4	4	10	.300	.352	.320	88	-1	1	0	0	.992	7	C-28	0.7
1991	Sea-A	5	8	1	2	0	0	0	0	1	0	.250	.333	.250	64	-0	0	0	0	1.000	1	/C-5	0.1
1992	Sea-A	18	28	0	3	0	0	0	0	0	5	.107	.107	.107	-40	-5	0	0	0	1.000	0	C-18	-0.5
Total	10	140	252	20	48	6	1	2	21	17	35	.190	.244	.234	34	-22	2	1	0	.996	19	C-135	-0.1

■ HOSEA SINER
Siner, Hosea John   b: 3/20/1885, Shelburn, Ind.   d: 6/10/48, Sullivan, Ind.   BR/TR, 5'10.5", 185 lbs.   Deb: 7/28/09

YEAR	TM/L	G	AB	R	H	2B	3B	HR	RBI	BB	SO	AVG	OBP	SLG	PRO+	BR/A	SB	CS	SBR	FA	FR	G/POS	TPR
1909	Bos-N	10	23	1	3	0	0	0	1	2		.130	.200	.130	3	-1	3			.909	-1	/3-5,2-1,S-1	-0.4

■ DUANE SINGLETON
Singleton, Duane Earl   b: 8/6/72, Staten Island, N.Y.   BL/TR, 6'1", 170 lbs.   Deb: 8/4/94

YEAR	TM/L	G	AB	R	H	2B	3B	HR	RBI	BB	SO	AVG	OBP	SLG	PRO+	BR/A	SB	CS	SBR	FA	FR	G/POS	TPR
1994	Mil-A	2	0	0	0	0	0	0	0	0	—	—	—	—	—	—	0	0	0	1.000	-1	/O-2	-0.1
1995	Mil-A	13	31	0	2	0	0	0	1	1	10	.065	.094	.065	-55	-7	1	0	0	1.000	-1	O-11	-0.7
1996	Det-A	18	56	5	9	1	0	0	3	4	15	.161	.230	.179	5	-8	0	2	-1	1.000	0	O-15	-0.9
Total	3	33	87	5	11	1	0	0	5	5	25	.126	.183	.138	-16	-15	1	2	-1	1.000	-2	/O-28	-1.7

■ KEN SINGLETON
Singleton, Kenneth Wayne   b: 6/10/47, New York, N.Y.   BB/TR, 6'4", 213 lbs.   Deb: 6/24/70

YEAR	TM/L	G	AB	R	H	2B	3B	HR	RBI	BB	SO	AVG	OBP	SLG	PRO+	BR/A	SB	CS	SBR	FA	FR	G/POS	TPR
1970	NY-N	69	198	22	52	8	0	5	26	30	48	.263	.362	.379	99	0	1	1	-0	.968	-0	O-51	-0.3
1971	NY-N	115	298	34	73	5	0	13	46	61	64	.245	.377	.393	120	10	0	1	-1	.974	-5	O-96	0.0
1972	Mon-N	142	507	77	139	23	2	14	50	70	99	.274	.364	.410	118	13	5	10	-5	.972	-0	*O-137	0.2
1973	Mon-N	162	560	100	169	26	2	23	103	123	91	.302	.429	.479	146	41	2	8	-4	.983	3	*O-161	3.3
1974	Mon-N	148	511	68	141	20	4	9	74	93	84	.276	.387	.376	108	9	5	2	0	.955	-9	*O-143	-0.6
1975	Bal-A	155	586	88	176	37	4	15	55	118	82	.300	.418	.454	156	49	3	5	-2	.990	-6	*O-155	3.5
1976	Bal-A	154	544	62	151	25	2	13	70	79	76	.278	.369	.403	134	25	0	3	-1	.983	-3	*O-134,D-19	1.6
1977	Bal-A★	152	536	90	176	24	0	24	99	107	101	.328	.442	.507	168	57	0	1	-1	.986	1	*O-150/D-1	4.9
1978	Bal-A	149	502	67	147	21	2	20	81	98	94	.293	.410	.462	154	40	0	0	0	.976	-13	*O-140/D-5	2.2
1979	*Bal-A★	159	570	93	168	29	1	35	111	109	118	.295	.409	.533	158	49	3	1	0	.981	-6	*O-143,D-16	3.6
1980	Bal-A	156	583	85	177	28	3	24	104	92	94	.304	.399	.485	143	37	0	3	-1	.981	-10	*O-151/D-5	1.9
1981	Bal-A★	103	363	48	101	16	1	13	49	57	53	.278	.382	.435	135	18	0	0	0	1.000	-3	O-72,D-30	1.2
1982	Bal-A	156	561	71	141	27	2	14	77	86	93	.251	.353	.381	102	4	0	1	-0	1.000	0	*D-148/O-5	-0.3
1983	*Bal-A	151	507	52	140	21	3	18	84	99	83	.276	.395	.436	131	25	0	2	-1	.000	0	*D-150	1.9

YEAR	TM/L	G	AB	R	H	2B	3B	HR	RBI	BB	SO	AVG	OBP	SLG	PRO+	BR/A	SB	CS	SBR	FA	FR	G/POS	TPR
1984	Bal-A	111	363	28	78	7	1	6	36	37	60	.215	.287	.289	61	-19	0	0	0	.000	0	*D-103	-2.2
Total	15	2082	7189	985	2029	317	25	246	1065	1263	1246	.282	.391	.436	132	359	21	36	-15	.980	-52	*O-1538,D-477	20.9

■ FRED SINGTON
Sington, Frederic William b: 2/24/10, Birmingham, Ala.   BR/TR, 6'2", 215 lbs.   Deb: 9/23/34

YEAR	TM/L	G	AB	R	H	2B	3B	HR	RBI	BB	SO	AVG	OBP	SLG	PRO+	BR/A	SB	CS	SBR	FA	FR	G/POS	TPR
1934	Was-A	9	35	2	10	2	0	0	6	4	3	.286	.359	.343	85	-1	0	1	-1	.933	-1	/O-9	-0.2
1935	Was-A	20	22	1	4	0	0	0	3	5	1	.182	.333	.182	38	-2	0	0	0	.889	0	/O-4	-0.2
1936	Was-A	25	94	13	30	8	0	1	28	15	9	.319	.413	.436	116	3	0	0	0	.946	-1	O-25	0.1
1937	Was-A	78	228	27	54	15	4	3	36	37	33	.237	.348	.377	87	-4	1	1	-0	.961	-3	O-64	-0.9
1938	Bro-N	17	53	10	19	6	1	2	5	13	5	.358	.493	.623	200	8	1			1.000	-2	O-17	0.6
1939	Bro-N	32	84	13	23	5	0	1	7	15	15	.274	.384	.369	100	1	0			.978	-1	O-22	-0.1
Total	6	181	516	66	140	36	5	7	85	89	66	.271	.382	.401	104	5	2	2		.961	-7	O-141	-0.7

■ DICK SIPEK
Sipek, Richard Francis b: 1/16/23, Chicago, Ill.   BL/TR, 5'9", 170 lbs.   Deb: 4/28/45

YEAR	TM/L	G	AB	R	H	2B	3B	HR	RBI	BB	SO	AVG	OBP	SLG	PRO+	BR/A	SB	CS	SBR	FA	FR	G/POS	TPR
1945	Cin-N	82	156	14	38	6	2	0	13	9	15	.244	.302	.308	71	-6	0			.972	-0	O-31	-0.8

■ JOHN SIPIN
Sipin, John White b: 8/29/46, Watsonville, Cal.   BR/TR, 6'1.5", 175 lbs.   Deb: 5/24/69

YEAR	TM/L	G	AB	R	H	2B	3B	HR	RBI	BB	SO	AVG	OBP	SLG	PRO+	BR/A	SB	CS	SBR	FA	FR	G/POS	TPR
1969	SD-N	68	229	22	51	12	2	2	9	8	44	.223	.252	.319	61	-13	2	0	1	.976	-2	2-60	-1.0

■ GEORGE SISLER
Sisler, George Harold "Georgeous George"
b: 3/24/1893, Manchester, Ohio   d: 3/26/73, Richmond Heights, Mo.   BL/TL, 5'11", 170 lbs.   Deb: 6/28/15   FMCH

YEAR	TM/L	G	AB	R	H	2B	3B	HR	RBI	BB	SO	AVG	OBP	SLG	PRO+	BR/A	SB	CS	SBR	FA	FR	G/POS	TPR
1915	StL-A	81	274	28	78	10	2	3	29	7	27	.285	.307	.369	106	0	10	9	-2	.989	-3	1-36,O-29,P-15	-0.8
1916	StL-A	151	580	83	177	21	11	4	76	40	37	.305	.355	.400	133	21	34	26	-5	.985	-2	*1-141/P-3,O-3,3-2	0.8
1917	StL-A	135	539	60	190	30	9	2	52	30	19	.353	.390	.453	163	38	37			.985	-4	*1-133/2-2	4.0
1918	StL-A	114	452	69	154	21	9	2	41	40	17	.341	.400	.440	159	31	45			.990	9	*1-114/P-2	3.8
1919	StL-A	132	511	96	180	31	15	10	83	27	20	.352	.390	.530	153	33	28			.991	13	*1-131	4.3
1920	StL-A	154	631	137	257	49	18	19	122	46	19	.407	.449	.632	179	68	42	17	2	.990	15	*1-154/P-1	7.8
1921	StL-A	138	582	125	216	38	18	12	104	34	27	.371	.411	.560	137	31	35	11	4	.993	-2	*1-138	3.6
1922	StL-A	142	586	134	246	42	18	8	105	49	14	.420	.467	.594	169	59	51	19	4	.988	12	*1-141	6.6
1924	StL-A	151	636	94	194	27	10	9	74	31	29	.305	.340	.421	90	-12	19	17	-5	.984	1	*1-151,M	-2.3
1925	StL-A	150	649	100	224	21	15	12	105	27	24	.345	.371	.479	109	6	11	12	-4	.983	11	*1-150/P-1,M	0.4
1926	StL-A	150	613	78	178	21	12	7	71	30	30	.290	.327	.398	84	-16	12	8	-1	.987	-4	*1-149/P-1,M	-3.0
1927	StL-A	149	614	87	201	32	8	5	97	24	15	.327	.357	.430	100	-1	27	7	4	.984	-11	*1-149	0.3
1928	Was-A	20	49	1	12	1	0	0	2	1	2	.245	.260	.265	39	-4	0	-1	-1	1.000	-2	/1-5,O-5	-0.8
	Bos-N	118	491	71	167	26	4	4	68	30	15	.340	.380	.434	119	13	11			.988	7	*1-118/P-1	0.9
1929	Bos-N	154	629	67	205	40	8	2	79	33	17	.326	.363	.424	98	-2	6			.982	3	*1-154	-1.3
1930	Bos-N	116	431	54	133	15	7	3	67	23	15	.309	.346	.397	82	-12	7			.987	5	*1-107	-1.6
Total	15	2055	8267	1284	2812	425	164	102	1175	472	327	.340	.379	.468	124	254	375	127		.987	88	*1-1971/O-37,P23	22.7

■ DICK SISLER
Sisler, Richard Allan b: 11/2/20, St.Louis, Mo.   BL/TR, 6'2", 205 lbs.   Deb: 4/16/46   FMC

YEAR	TM/L	G	AB	R	H	2B	3B	HR	RBI	BB	SO	AVG	OBP	SLG	PRO+	BR/A	SB	CS	SBR	FA	FR	G/POS	TPR
1946	*StL-N	83	235	17	61	11	2	3	42	14	28	.260	.307	.362	86	-5	0			.988	-2	1-37,O-29	-1.1
1947	StL-N	46	74	4	15	2	1	0	9	3	8	.203	.234	.257	29	-8	0			.976	1	1-10/O-5	-0.8
1948	Phi-N	121	446	60	122	21	3	11	56	47	46	.274	.344	.408	105	3	1			.983	-4	*1-120	-0.2
1949	Phi-N	121	412	42	119	19	6	7	50	25	38	.289	.333	.415	102	0	0			.987	-9	*1-96	-0.9
1950	*Phi-N★	141	523	79	155	29	4	13	83	64	50	.296	.373	.442	115	12	1			.987	2	*O-137	0.8
1951	Phi-N	125	428	46	123	20	5	8	52	40	39	.287	.351	.414	107	4	1	0	0	.968	0	*O-111	0.1
1952	Cin-N	11	27	3	5	1	1	0	4	3	5	.185	.267	.296	56	-2	0	0	0	1.000	-1	/O-7	-0.3
	StL-N	119	418	48	109	14	5	13	60	29	35	.261	.312	.411	99	-2	3	3	-1	.985	2	*1-114	-0.5
	Yr	130	445	51	114	15	6	13	64	32	40	.256	.309	.404	96	-3	3	3	-1	.985	1	*1-114/O-7	-0.8
1953	StL-N	32	43	3	11	1	1	0	4	1	4	.256	.273	.326	55	-3	0	0	0	1.000	1	1-10	-0.2
Total	8	799	2606	302	720	118	28	55	360	226	253	.276	.336	.406	101	-0	6	3		.985	-10	1-387,O-289	-3.1

■ SIBBY SISTI
Sisti, Sebastian Daniel b: 7/26/20, Buffalo, N.Y.   BR/TR, 5'11", 175 lbs.   Deb: 7/21/39   C

YEAR	TM/L	G	AB	R	H	2B	3B	HR	RBI	BB	SO	AVG	OBP	SLG	PRO+	BR/A	SB	CS	SBR	FA	FR	G/POS	TPR
1939	Bos-N	63	215	19	49	7	1	1	11	12	38	.228	.269	.284	52	-15	4			.994	0	2-34,3-17,S-10	-1.2
1940	Bos-N	123	459	73	115	19	5	6	34	36	64	.251	.311	.353	87	-9	4			.936	-2	*3-102,2-16	-0.8
1941	Bos-N	140	541	72	140	24	3	1	45	38	76	.259	.309	.320	81	-15	7			.916	-8	*3-137/2-2,S-2	-2.0
1942	Bos-N	129	407	50	86	11	4	4	35	45	55	.211	.296	.287	73	-14	5			.970	-4	*2-124/O-1	-1.1
1946	Bos-N	1	0	0	0					0	0	—	—	—			0			.000	0	/3-1	0.0
1947	Bos-N	56	153	22	43	8	0	2	15	20	17	.281	.371	.373	100	1	2			.947	-9	S-51/2-1	-0.6
1948	*Bos-N	83	221	30	54	6	2	0	21	31	34	.244	.340	.290	73	-7	0			.972	-5	2-44,S-26	-0.9
1949	Bos-N	101	268	39	69	12	0	5	22	34	42	.257	.343	.358	93	-2	1			.989	-13	O-48,2-21,S-18,/3-1	-1.5
1950	Bos-N	69	105	21	18	3	1	2	11	16	19	.171	.287	.276	52	-7	1			.931	0	S-23,2-19,3-13,/10	-0.6
1951	Bos-N	114	362	46	101	20	2	2	38	32	50	.279	.341	.362	96	-2	4	5	-2	.944	-23	S-55,2-52/3-6,10	-2.2
1952	Bos-N	90	245	19	52	10	1	4	24	14	43	.212	.255	.310	58	-15	2	0	1	.966	-12	2-33,O-23,S-18,/3-9	-2.5
1953	Mil-N	38	23	8	5	1	0	0	4	5	2	.217	.357	.261	69	-1	0	0	0	1.000	4	2-13/S-6,3-4	0.3
1954	Mil-N	9	0	2	0					0	0	—	—	—			0			.000	0	R	0.0
Total	13	1016	2999	401	732	121	19	27	260	283	440	.244	.313	.324	79	-85	30	5		.973	-72	2-359,3-290,S/O1	-13.1

■ ED SIXSMITH
Sixsmith, Edward b: 2/26/1863, Philadelphia, Pa.   d: 12/12/26, Philadelphia, Pa.   BR/TR,   Deb: 9/11/1884

YEAR	TM/L	G	AB	R	H	2B	3B	HR	RBI	BB	SO	AVG	OBP	SLG	PRO+	BR/A	SB	CS	SBR	FA	FR	G/POS	TPR
1884	Phi-N	1	2	0	0	0	0	0		0	0	.000	.000	.000	-99	-0				1.000	-1	/C-1	-0.1

■ TED SIZEMORE
Sizemore, Theodore Crawford b: 4/15/45, Gadsden, Ala.   BR/TR, 5'10", 165 lbs.   Deb: 4/7/69

YEAR	TM/L	G	AB	R	H	2B	3B	HR	RBI	BB	SO	AVG	OBP	SLG	PRO+	BR/A	SB	CS	SBR	FA	FR	G/POS	TPR
1969	LA-N	159	590	69	160	20	5	4	46	45	40	.271	.328	.342	95	-5	5	5	-2	.979	-6	*2-118,S-46/O-1	0.3
1970	LA-N	96	340	40	104	10	1	4	34	34	19	.306	.369	.350	98	-1	0	5	1	.984	-7	2-86/O-9,S-2	0.1
1971	StL-N	135	478	53	126	14	5	3	42	42	26	.264	.324	.333	83	-10	4	6	-2	.976	-3	2-93,S-39,O-15,/3-1	-0.4
1972	StL-N	120	439	53	116	17	4	2	38	37	36	.264	.327	.335	90	-6	8	3	1	.976	0	*2-111	0.2
1973	StL-N	142	521	69	147	22	1	1	54	68	34	.282	.367	.334	96	-0	6	4	-1	.981	9	2-139/3-3	1.8
1974	StL-N	129	504	68	126	17	0	2	47	70	37	.250	.341	.296	80	-11	4	3	-0	.980	13	2-128/S-1,O-1	0.9
1975	StL-N	153	562	56	135	23	1	3	49	45	37	.240	.299	.301	64	-27	1	5	-3	.972	-25	2-153	-4.9
1976	LA-N	84	266	18	64	9	1	0	18	15	22	.241	.281	.278	60	-14	2	3	-1	.986	-3	2-71/3-3,C-2	-1.0
1977	*Phi-N	152	519	64	146	20	3	4	47	52	40	.281	.348	.355	85	-9	8	11	-4	.986	9	2-152	0.6
1978	*Phi-N	108	351	38	77	12	0	0	25	25	29	.219	.273	.254	48	-24	8	1	2	.978	4	*2-107	-1.1
1979	Chi-N	98	330	36	82	17	0	2	24	32	25	.248	.321	.318	68	-14	3	3	-1	.973	15	2-96	0.8
	Bos-A	26	88	12	23	7	0	1	6	4	9	.261	.301	.375	77	-3	1	0	0	.993	9	2-26/C-2	0.7
1980	Bos-A	9	23	1	5	1	0	0	0	0	3	.217	.217	.261	29	-2	0	0	0	.927	3	/2-8	-0.0
Total	12	1411	5011	577	1311	188	21	23	430	469	350	.262	.327	.321	80	-125	59	46	-10	.979	25	*2-1288/S-88,O3C	-1.8

■ FRANK SKAFF
Skaff, Francis Michael b: 9/30/13, LaCrosse, Wis.   d: 4/12/88, Towson, Md.   BR/TR, 5'10", 185 lbs.   Deb: 9/11/35   MC

YEAR	TM/L	G	AB	R	H	2B	3B	HR	RBI	BB	SO	AVG	OBP	SLG	PRO+	BR/A	SB	CS	SBR	FA	FR	G/POS	TPR
1935	Bro-N	6	11	4	6	1	1	0	3	0	2	.545	.545	.818	267	2	0			.857	-0	/3-3	0.2
1943	Phi-A	32	64	8	18	2	1	1	8	6	11	.281	.343	.391	115	1	0	0	0	.976	1	1-18/3-3,S-1	0.2
Total	2	38	75	12	24	3	2	1	11	6	13	.320	.370	.453	138	4	0			.900	1	/1-18,3-6,S-1	0.4

■ DAVE SKAGGS
Skaggs, David Lindsey b: 6/12/51, Santa Monica, Cal.   BR/TR, 6'2", 200 lbs.   Deb: 4/17/77

YEAR	TM/L	G	AB	R	H	2B	3B	HR	RBI	BB	SO	AVG	OBP	SLG	PRO+	BR/A	SB	CS	SBR	FA	FR	G/POS	TPR
1977	Bal-A	80	216	22	62	9	1	1	24	20	34	.287	.347	.352	97	-0	0	0	0	.995	-1	C-80	0.1
1978	Bal-A	36	86	6	13	1	1	0	2	9	14	.151	.232	.186	20	-9	0	0	0	.988	5	C-35	-0.5
1979	*Bal-A	63	137	9	34	8	0	1	14	13	14	.248	.313	.328	76	-4	0	0	0	.984	2	C-63	0.0
1980	Bal-A	2	5	0	1	0	0	0	0	0	0	.200	.200	.200	10	-1	0	0	0	1.000	1	/C-2	-0.0
	Cal-A	24	66	7	13	1	0	0	9	9	13	.197	.293	.242	50	-4	0	0	0	.968	-10	C-24	-1.4
	Yr	26	71	7	14	1	0	0	9	9	13	.197	.287	.239	47	-5	0	0	0	.971	-9	C-26	-1.4
Total	4	205	510	44	123	18	2	2	49	51	76	.241	.310	.302	72	-19	0	0	0	.988	-3	C-204	-1.8

■ BUD SKETCHLEY
Sketchley, Harry Clement b: 3/30/19, Virden, Man., Can.   d: 12/19/79, Los Angeles, Cal.   BL/TL, 5'10", 180 lbs.   Deb: 4/14/42

YEAR	TM/L	G	AB	R	H	2B	3B	HR	RBI	BB	SO	AVG	OBP	SLG	PRO+	BR/A	SB	CS	SBR	FA	FR	G/POS	TPR
1942	Chi-A	13	36	1	7	1	0	0	3	7	4	.194	.326	.222	57	-2	0	1	-1	.952	-1	O-12	-0.4

YEAR	TM/L	G	AB	R	H	2B	3B	HR	RBI	BB	SO	AVG	OBP	SLG	PRO+	BR/A	SB	CS	SBR	FA	FR	G/POS	TPR

■ ROE SKIDMORE Skidmore, Robert Roe b: 10/30/45, Decatur, Ill. BR/TR, 6'3", 188 lbs. Deb: 9/17/70

| 1970 | Chi-N | 1 | 1 | 0 | 1 | 0 | 0 | 0 | 0 | 0 | 0 | 1.000 | 1.000 | 1.000 | 390 | 0 | 0 | 0 | 0 | .000 | 0 | H | 0.0 |

■ BILL SKIFF Skiff, William Franklin b: 10/16/1895, New Rochelle, N.Y. d: 12/25/76, Bronxville, N.Y. BR/TR, 5'10", 170 lbs. Deb: 5/17/21

1921	Pit-N	16	45	7	13	2	0	0	11	0	4	.289	.289	.333	63	-2	1	1	-0	.982	-2	C-13	-0.4
1926	NY-A	6	11	0	1	0	0	0	0	0	1	.091	.091	.091	-53	-2	0	0	-0	1.000	-1	/C-6	-0.3
Total	2	22	56	7	14	2	0	0	11	0	5	.250	.250	.286	40	-5	1	1	-0	.984	-3	/C-19	-0.7

■ ALEXANDER SKINNER Skinner, Alexander b: 8/14/1856, Chicago, Ill. d: 3/5/01, Washington, Mass. Deb: 7/12/1884

1884	Bal-U	1	3	0	1	0	0	0	0	0	0	.333	.333	.333	93	-0				1.000	0	/O-1	0.0
	CP-U	1	3	1	1	0	0	0	0	0	0	.333	.333	.333	103	-0				.000	-0	/O-1	0.0
	Yr	2	6	1	2	0	0	0	0	0	0	.333	.333	.333	98	-0				1.000	-0	/O-2	0.0

■ CAMP SKINNER Skinner, Elisha Harrison b: 6/25/1897, Douglasville, Ga. d: 8/4/44, Douglasville, Ga. BL/TR, 5'11", 165 lbs. Deb: 5/2/22

1922	NY-A	27	33	1	6	0	0	0	0	0	4	.182	.206	.182	2	-5	1	0	0	1.000	-0	/O-4	-0.5
1923	Bos-A	7	13	1	3	2	0	0	1	0	0	.231	.231	.385	60	-1	0	0	0	.000	-1	/O-2	-0.2
Total	2	34	46	2	9	2	0	0	3	0	4	.196	.213	.239	18	-6	1	0	0	1.000	-2	/O-6	-0.7

■ JOEL SKINNER Skinner, Joel Patrick b: 2/21/61, LaJolla, Cal. BR/TR, 6'4", 204 lbs. Deb: 6/12/83 F

1983	Chi-A	6	11	2	3	0	0	0	1	0	1	.273	.273	.273	49	-1	0	0	0	.960	2	/C-6	0.2
1984	Chi-A	43	80	4	17	2	0	0	3	7	19	.213	.276	.237	42	-6	0	0	0	.989	10	C-43	0.6
1985	Chi-A	22	44	9	15	4	1	1	5	5	13	.341	.408	.545	153	3	0	0	0	.971	4	C-21	0.8
1986	Chi-A	60	149	17	30	5	1	4	20	9	43	.201	.252	.329	55	-10	1	0	0	.988	-7	C-60	-1.3
	NY-A	54	166	6	43	4	0	1	17	7	40	.259	.289	.301	62	-9	0	4	-2	.981	6	C-54	-0.3
	Yr	114	315	23	73	9	1	5	37	16	83	.232	.271	.314	58	-18	1	4	-2	.984	-1	*C-114	-1.6
1987	NY-A	64	139	9	19	4	0	3	14	8	46	.137	.189	.230	11	-18	0	0	0	.984	-3	C-64	-1.7
1988	NY-A	88	251	23	57	15	0	4	23	14	72	.227	.268	.335	68	-11	0	0	0	.990	-7	C-85/O-2,1-1	-1.1
1989	Cle-A	79	178	10	41	10	0	1	13	9	42	.230	.271	.303	61	-9	1	1	-0	.990	-4	C-79	-1.1
1990	Cle-A	49	139	16	35	4	1	2	16	7	44	.252	.288	.338	75	-5	0	0	0	.996	0	C-49	-0.2
1991	Cle-A	99	284	23	69	14	0	1	24	14	67	.243	.281	.303	61	-15	0	2	-1	.991	1	C-99	-1.0
Total	9	564	1441	119	329	62	3	17	136	80	387	.228	.271	.311	60	-81	3	7	-3	.988	3	C-560/O-2,1-1	-5.3

■ BOB SKINNER Skinner, Robert Ralph b: 10/3/31, LaJolla, Cal. BL/TR, 6'4", 190 lbs. Deb: 4/13/54 FMC

1954	Pit-N	132	470	67	117	15	5	8	46	47	59	.249	.317	.370	80	-15	4	0	1	.986	-3	*1-118/O-2	-2.2
1956	Pit-N	113	233	29	47	8	3	5	29	26	50	.202	.285	.326	65	-12	1	1	-0	.977	-9	O-36,1-23/3-1	-2.5
1957	Pit-N	126	387	58	118	12	6	13	49	38	50	.305	.390	.468	127	15	10	4	1	.963	3	O-93/1-9,3-1	1.3
1958	Pit-N★	144	529	93	170	33	9	13	70	58	55	.321	.390	.491	135	27	12	4	1	.977	9	*O-141	3.0
1959	Pit-N	143	547	78	153	18	4	13	61	67	65	.280	.358	.399	102	3	10	7	-1	.964	6	*O-142/1-1	0.1
1960	*Pit-N★	145	571	83	156	33	6	15	86	59	86	.273	.342	.431	109	7	11	8	-2	.981	7	*O-141	0.6
1961	Pit-N	119	381	61	102	20	3	3	42	51	49	.268	.360	.360	91	-3	3	5	-2	.973	-1	O-97	-0.8
1962	Pit-N	144	510	87	154	29	7	20	75	76	89	.302	.397	.504	140	30	10	4	1	.960	1	*O-139	2.3
1963	Pit-N	34	122	18	33	5	5	0	8	13	22	.270	.341	.393	110	2	4	1	1	.983	2	O-32	-0.2
	Cin-N	72	194	25	49	10	2	3	17	21	42	.253	.332	.371	99	0	1	2	-1	1.000	2	O-51	-0.2
	Yr	106	316	43	82	15	7	3	25	34	64	.259	.335	.380	103	2	5	3	-0	.993	3	O-83	0.0
1964	Cin-N	25	59	6	13	3	0	3	5	4	12	.220	.270	.424	89	-1	0	0	0	.913	1	O-12	-0.1
	*StL-N	55	118	10	32	5	0	1	16	11	20	.271	.333	.339	83	-2	0	0	0	.938	-1	O-31	-0.5
	Yr	80	177	16	45	8	0	4	21	15	32	.254	.313	.367	85	-3	0	0	0	.930	-0	O-43	-0.6
1965	StL-N	80	152	25	47	5	4	5	26	12	30	.309	.360	.493	126	5	1	0	0	.935	-4	O-33	-0.5
1966	StL-N	49	45	2	7	1	0	1	5	2	17	.156	.208	.244	25	-5	0	0	0	.000	0	H	-0.5
Total	12	1381	4318	642	1198	197	58	103	531	485	646	.277	.353	.421	108	52	67	36	-2	.969	14	O-950,1-151/3-2	0.7

■ LOU SKIZAS Skizas, Louis Peter "The Nervous Greek" b: 6/2/32, Chicago, Ill. BR/TR, 5'11", 175 lbs. Deb: 4/19/56

1956	NY-A	6	6	0	1	0	0	0	1	0	2	.167	.167	.167	-12	-1	0	0	0	.000	0	H	-0.1
	KC-A	83	297	39	94	11	3	11	39	15	17	.316	.349	.485	118	6	3	1	0	.975	5	O-74	0.8
	Yr	89	303	39	95	11	3	11	40	15	19	.314	.346	.479	116	5	3	1	0	.975	5	O-74	0.7
1957	KC-A	119	376	34	92	14	1	18	44	27	15	.245	.299	.431	95	-4	5	2	0	.976	-9	O-76,3-32	-1.6
1958	Det-A	23	33	4	8	2	0	1	2	5	1	.242	.342	.394	95	-0	0	0	0	.750	-3	/O-5,3-4	-0.3
1959	Chi-A	8	13	3	1	0	0	0	0	3	2	.077	.250	.077	-6	-2	0	0	0	1.000	-0	/O-6	-0.2
Total	4	239	725	80	196	27	4	30	86	50	37	.270	.319	.443	102	-1	8	3	1	.973	-7	O-161/3-36	-1.4

■ BILL SKOWRON Skowron, William Joseph "Moose" b: 12/18/30, Chicago, Ill. BR/TR, 5'11", 195 lbs. Deb: 4/13/54

1954	NY-A	87	215	37	73	12	9	7	41	19	18	.340	.396	.577	170	19	2	1	0	.986	-1	1-61/3-5,2-2	1.7
1955	*NY-A	108	288	46	92	17	3	12	61	21	32	.319	.372	.524	141	15	1	1	-0	.989	-3	1-74/3-3	0.8
1956	*NY-A	134	464	78	143	21	6	23	90	50	60	.308	.383	.528	143	27	4	4	-1	.993	-3	*1-120/3-2	2.1
1957	*NY-A★	122	457	54	139	15	5	17	88	31	60	.304	.351	.470	125	14	3	2	0	.992	6	*1-115	1.3
1958	*NY-A★	126	465	61	127	22	3	14	73	28	69	.273	.320	.424	107	3	1	1	-0	**.993**	-2	*1-118/3-2	-0.8
1959	NY-A★	74	282	39	84	13	5	15	59	20	47	.298	.351	.539	145	16	1	0	0	.991	0	1-72	1.2
1960	*NY-A	146	538	63	166	34	3	26	91	38	95	.309	.356	.528	144	30	2	3	-1	.991	9	*1-142	2.6
1961	*NY-A☆	150	561	76	150	23	4	28	89	35	108	.267	.320	.472	115	8	0	1	-1	.991	-1	*1-149	-0.5
1962	*NY-A	140	478	63	129	16	6	23	80	36	99	.270	.328	.472	116	9	1	1	-1	.991	-5	*1-135	-0.5
1963	*LA-N	89	237	19	48	8	0	4	19	13	49	.203	.253	.287	59	-13	0	1	-0	.991	-1	1-66/3-1	-1.9
1964	Was-A	73	262	28	71	10	0	13	41	11	56	.271	.308	.458	110	3	0	1	-0	.994	-2	1-66	-0.2
	Chi-A	73	273	19	80	11	3	4	38	19	36	.293	.341	.399	108	3	0	0	0	.998	-1	1-70	-0.1
	Yr	146	535	47	151	21	3	17	79	30	92	.282	.325	.428	109	5	0	1	-0	.996	-3	*1-136	-0.3
1965	Chi-A†	146	559	63	153	24	3	18	78	32	77	.274	.319	.424	116	9	1	3	-2	.994	-6	*1-145	-0.5
1966	Chi-A	120	337	27	84	15	2	6	29	26	45	.249	.309	.359	98	-2	1	1	-0	.991	1	1-98	-0.7
1967	Chi-A	8	8	0	0	0	0	0	0	0	4	.000	.000	.000	-99	-2	0	0	0	.000	0	H	-0.2
	Cal-A	62	123	8	27	2	1	5	10	4	18	.220	.267	.276	63	-6	0	0	0	.988	-1	1-32	-0.9
	Yr	70	131	8	27	2	1	5	10	4	22	.206	.252	.290	53	-8	0	0	0	.988	-1	1-32	-1.1
Total	14	1658	5547	681	1566	243	53	211	888	383	870	.282	.335	.459	121	134	16	18	-6	.992	-3	*1-1463/3-13,2-2	3.4

■ BOB SKUBE Skube, Robert Jacob b: 10/8/57, Northridge, Cal. BL/TL, 6', 180 lbs. Deb: 9/17/82

1982	Mil-A	4	3	0	2	0	0	0	0	0	0	.667	.667	.667	285	1	0	0	0	.000	-1	/O-1,D-1	0.0
1983	Mil-A	12	25	2	5	1	1	0	9	4	7	.200	.310	.320	80	-1	0	0	0	1.000	-0	/O-8,1-1,D-2	-0.1
Total	2	16	28	2	7	1	1	0	9	4	7	.250	.344	.321	95	-0	0	0	0	1.000	-1	/O-9,D-3,1-1	-0.1

■ GORDON SLADE Slade, Gordon Leigh "Oskie" b: 10/9/04, Salt Lake City, Utah d: 1/2/74, Long Beach, Cal. BR/TR, 5'10.5", 160 lbs. Deb: 4/21/30

1930	Bro-N	25	37	8	8	2	0	1	2	3	5	.216	.275	.351	51	-3	0			.938	10	S-21	0.7
1931	Bro-N	85	272	27	65	13	2	1	29	23	28	.239	.310	.313	68	-12	3			.947	11	S-82/3-2	0.7
1932	Bro-N	79	250	23	60	15	1	1	23	11	26	.240	.280	.320	62	-13	3			.943	11	S-55,3-23	0.2
1933	StL-N	39	62	6	7	1	0	0	3	6	7	.113	.191	.129	-7	-8	1			.941	3	S-31/2-1	-0.5
1934	Cin-N	138	555	61	158	19	8	4	52	25	34	.285	.320	.369	86	-11	6			.952	2	S-97,2-39	-0.1
1935	Cin-N	71	196	22	55	10	0	1	14	16	16	.281	.341	.347	88	-3	0			.927	-12	S-30,2-19/O-8,3-7	-1.2
Total	6	437	1372	147	353	60	11	8	123	84	116	.257	.307	.335	73	-51	12			.945	25	S-316/2-59,3-32,O-8	-0.2

■ ART SLADEN Sladen, Arthur b: 10/28/1860, Dracut, Mass. d: 2/28/14, Dracut, Mass. Deb: 4/22/1884

| 1884 | Bos-U | 2 | 7 | 0 | 0 | 0 | 0 | 0 | 0 | 0 | | .000 | .000 | .000 | -99 | -2 | | | | 1.000 | -1 | /O-2 | -0.2 |

■ JIMMY SLAGLE Slagle, James Franklin "Rabbit" or "Shorty" b: 7/11/1873, Worthville, Pa. d: 5/10/56, Chicago, Ill. BL/TR, 5'7", 144 lbs. Deb: 4/17/1899

| 1899 | Was-N | 147 | 599 | 92 | 163 | 15 | 8 | 0 | 41 | 55 | | .272 | .338 | .324 | 83 | -13 | 22 | | | .953 | 20 | *O-146 | -0.3 |
| 1900 | Phi-N | 141 | 574 | 115 | 165 | 16 | 9 | 0 | 45 | 60 | | .287 | .358 | .347 | 96 | -2 | 34 | | | .922 | 1 | *O-141 | -1.1 |

YEAR	TM/L	G	AB	R	H	2B	3B	HR	RBI	BB	SO	AVG	OBP	SLG	PRO+	BR/A	SB	CS	SBR	FA	FR	G/POS	TPR
1901	Phi-N	48	183	20	37	6	2	1	20	16		.202	.277	.273	59	-10	5			.930	6	O-48	-0.7
	Bos-N	66	255	35	69	7	0	0	7	34		.271	.359	.298	84	-4	14			.935	-2	O-66	-1.1
	Yr	114	438	55	106	13	2	1	27	50		.242	.325	.288	74	-13	19			.932	4	*O-114	-1.8
1902	Chi-N	115	454	64	143	11	4	0	28	53		.315	.387	.357	133	20	40			.965	7	*O-113	2.1
1903	Chi-N	139	543	104	162	20	6	0	44	81		.298	.393	.357	118	17	33			.936	2	*O-139	1.0
1904	Chi-N	120	481	73	125	12	10	1	31	41		.260	.322	.333	102	1	28			.921	-3	*O-120	-0.9
1905	Chi-N	155	568	96	153	19	4	0	37	97		.269	.379	.317	104	8	27			.962	3	*O-155	0.4
1906	Chi-N	127	498	71	119	8	6	0	33	63		.239	.324	.279	83	-8	25			.976	2	*O-127	-1.3
1907	*Chi-N	136	489	71	126	6	6	0	32	76		.258	.359	.294	99	3	28			.962	-10	*O-136	-1.5
1908	Chi-N	104	352	38	78	4	1	0	26	43		.222	.306	.239	71	-10	17			.976	-6	*O-101	-2.3
Total	10	1298	4996	779	1340	124	56	2	344	619		.268	.352	.317	97	3	273			.950	22	O-1292	-5.7

■ JACK SLATTERY
Slattery, John Terrence   b: 1/6/1878, S.Boston, Mass.   d: 7/17/49, Boston, Mass.   BR/TR, 6'2", 191 lbs.   Deb: 9/28/01   MC

YEAR	TM/L	G	AB	R	H	2B	3B	HR	RBI	BB	SO	AVG	OBP	SLG	PRO+	BR/A	SB	CS	SBR	FA	FR	G/POS	TPR
1901	Bos-A	1	3	1	1	0	0	0	1	1		.333	.500	.333	137	0	0			1.000	0	/C-1	0.0
1903	Cle-A	4	11	1	0	0	0	0	0	0		.000	.000	.000	-99	-3	0			.885	-1	/1-2	-0.4
	Chi-A	63	211	8	46	3	2	0	20	2		.218	.233	.251	47	-14	2			.974	-8	C-56/1-5	-1.7
	Yr	67	222	9	46	3	2	0	20	2		.207	.221	.239	40	-16	2			.974	-9	C-56/1-7	-2.1
1906	StL-N	3	7	0	2	0	0	0	0	1		.286	.375	.286	111	0	0			1.000	-1	/C-2	0.0
1909	Was-A	32	56	4	12	2	0	0	6	2		.214	.254	.250	62	-2	1			.953	-1	1-11/C-6	-0.3
Total	4	103	288	14	61	5	2	0	27	6		.212	.236	.243	47	-18	3			.974	-10	/C-65,1-18	-2.4

■ MIKE SLATTERY
Slattery, Michael J.   b: 11/26/1866, Boston, Mass.   d: 10/16/04, Boston, Mass.   BL/TL, 6'2", 210 lbs.   Deb: 4/17/1884

YEAR	TM/L	G	AB	R	H	2B	3B	HR	RBI	BB	SO	AVG	OBP	SLG	PRO+	BR/A	SB	CS	SBR	FA	FR	G/POS	TPR
1884	Bos-U	106	413	60	86	6	2	0		4		.208	.216	.232	36	-44				.802	6	*O-96,1-11	-3.6
1888	*NY-N	103	391	50	96	12	6	1	35	13	28	.246	.272	.315	87	-6	26			.919	1	*O-103	-0.8
1889	*NY-N	12	48	7	14	0	1	0	12	4	3	.292	.346	.396	107	0	2			.852	1	O-12	-0.1
1890	NY-P	97	411	80	126	20	11	5	67	27	25	.307	.352	.445	103	-2	18			.905	-14	*O-97	-1.5
1891	Cin-N	41	158	24	33	3	2	1	16	10	10	.209	.256	.272	53	-10	1			.941	0	O-41	-1.0
	Was-a	15	60	8	17	1	0	0	5	4	5	.283	.358	.300	93	-0	6			.862	-2	O-15	-0.2
Total	5	374	1481	229	372	44	21	8	135	62	71	.251	.284	.325	77	-61	53			.883	-11	O-364/1-11	-7.1

■ DON SLAUGHT
Slaught, Donald Martin   b: 9/11/58, Long Beach, Cal.   BR/TR, 6'1", 190 lbs.   Deb: 7/6/82

YEAR	TM/L	G	AB	R	H	2B	3B	HR	RBI	BB	SO	AVG	OBP	SLG	PRO+	BR/A	SB	CS	SBR	FA	FR	G/POS	TPR
1982	KC-A	43	115	14	32	6	0	3	8	9	12	.278	.331	.409	102	0	0	0	0	.994	-2	C-43	0.4
1983	KC-A	83	276	21	86	13	4	0	28	11	27	.312	.338	.388	99	-1	3	1	0	.964	-7	C-79/D-1	-0.4
1984	*KC-A	124	409	48	108	27	4	4	42	20	55	.264	.302	.379	86	-8	0	0	0	.982	-10	*C-123/D-1	-1.2
1985	Tex-A	102	343	34	96	17	4	8	35	20	41	.280	.331	.423	103	1	5	4	-1	.990	-11	*C-102	-0.6
1986	Tex-A	95	314	39	83	17	1	13	46	16	59	.264	.310	.449	101	-0	3	2	-0	.993	-6	C-91/D-2	-0.1
1987	Tex-A	95	237	25	53	15	2	8	16	24	51	.224	.298	.405	84	-6	0	3	-2	.985	-0	C-85/D-5	-0.4
1988	NY-A	97	322	33	91	25	1	9	43	24	54	.283	.338	.450	120	11	1	0	0	.979	-12	C-94/D-1	0.3
1989	NY-A	117	350	34	88	21	3	5	38	30	57	.251	.319	.371	95	-2	1	1	-0	.991	-5	*C-105/D-3	-0.2
1990	*Pit-N	84	230	27	69	18	3	4	29	27	27	.300	.381	.457	134	11	0	1	-1	.979	-3	C-78	1.2
1991	*Pit-N	77	220	19	65	17	1	1	29	21	32	.295	.365	.395	116	5	1	0	0	.987	-5	C-69/3-1	0.4
1992	*Pit-N	87	255	26	88	17	3	4	37	17	23	.345	.391	.482	147	16	2	2	-1	.988	-2	C-79	1.7
1993	Pit-N	116	377	34	113	19	2	10	55	29	56	.300	.359	.440	113	7	2	1	0	.993	-10	*C-105	0.3
1994	Pit-N	76	240	21	69	7	0	2	21	34	31	.287	.383	.342	90	-2	0	0	0	.994	-1	C-74	0.2
1995	Pit-N	35	112	13	34	6	0	0	13	9	8	.304	.361	.357	88	-2	0	0	0	.996	2	C-33	0.3
1996	Cal-A	62	207	23	67	9	0	6	32	13	20	.324	.369	.454	109	3	0	0	0	.992	-8	C-59/D-1	-0.1
	Chi-A	14	36	2	9	1	0	0	4	2	2	.250	.289	.278	47	-3	0	0	0	.986	1	C-12/D-1	-0.1
	Yr	76	243	25	76	10	0	6	36	15	22	.313	.358	.428	100	0	0	0	0	.991	-7	C-71/D-2	-0.2
Total	15	1307	4043	413	1151	235	28	77	476	306	555	.285	.341	.414	105	27	18	15	-4	.987	-78	*C-1231/D-15,3-1	1.7

■ ENOS SLAUGHTER
Slaughter, Enos Bradsher "Country"   b: 4/27/16, Roxboro, N.C.   BL/TR, 5'9", 192 lbs.   Deb: 4/19/38   H

YEAR	TM/L	G	AB	R	H	2B	3B	HR	RBI	BB	SO	AVG	OBP	SLG	PRO+	BR/A	SB	CS	SBR	FA	FR	G/POS	TPR
1938	StL-N	112	395	59	109	20	10	8	58	32	38	.276	.330	.438	104	1	1			.970	-2	O-92	-0.4
1939	StL-N	149	604	95	193	**52**	5	12	86	44	53	.320	.371	.482	120	16	2			.968	**16**	*O-149	2.6
1940	StL-N	140	516	96	158	25	13	17	73	50	35	.306	.370	.504	131	21	8			.989	5	*O-132	1.8
1941	StL-N★	113	425	71	132	22	9	13	76	53	28	.311	.390	.496	139	22	4			.947	-8	*O-108	0.7
1942	*StL-N★	152	591	100	**188**	31	**17**	13	98	88	30	.318	.412	.494	153	41	9			.987	4	*O-151	3.9
1946	*StL-N★	156	609	100	183	30	8	18	**130**	69	41	.300	.374	.465	131	24	9			.981	6	*O-156	2.4
1947	StL-N★	147	551	100	162	31	13	10	86	59	27	.294	.366	.452	111	9	4			.982	9	*O-142	1.0
1948	StL-N★	146	549	91	176	27	11	11	90	81	29	.321	.409	.470	130	25	4			.971	6	*O-146	2.2
1949	StL-N★	151	568	92	191	34	**13**	13	96	79	37	.336	.418	.511	141	35	3			.983	1	*O-150	2.8
1950	StL-N★	148	556	82	161	26	7	10	101	66	33	.290	.367	.415	100	1	3			.978	-1	*O-145	-0.6
1951	StL-N★	123	409	48	115	17	8	4	64	67	25	.281	.386	.391	109	8	7	2	1	.995	-0	*O-106	0.5
1952	StL-N★	140	510	73	153	17	12	11	101	70	25	.300	.386	.445	130	22	6	1	1	.989	2	*O-137	0.2
1953	StL-N★	143	492	64	143	34	6	6	89	80	28	.291	.395	.433	116	14	4	4	-1	**.996**	-6	*O-137	0.2
1954	NY-A	69	125	19	31	4	2	1	19	28	8	.248	.386	.336	102	2	0	2	-1	.974	-6	O-30	-0.7
1955	NY-A	10	9	1	1	0	0	0	1	1	1	.111	.200	.111	-15	-1	0	0	0	.000	0	H	-0.1
	KC-A	108	267	49	86	12	4	5	34	40	17	.322	.414	.453	132	13	2	3	-1	.985	-4	O-77	0.5
	Yr	118	276	50	87	12	4	5	35	41	18	.315	.408	.442	127	12	2	3	-1	.985	-4	O-77	0.4
1956	KC-A	91	223	37	62	14	3	2	23	29	20	.278	.364	.395	100	0	1	0	0	.981	-3	O-56	-0.5
	*NY-A	24	83	15	24	4	2	0	4	5	6	.289	.330	.386	91	-1	1	1	-0	1.000	-2	O-20	-0.4
	Yr	115	306	52	86	18	5	2	27	34	26	.281	.355	.392	97	-1	2	1	0	.985	-5	O-76	-0.9
1957	*NY-A	96	209	24	53	7	1	5	34	40	19	.254	.373	.368	105	3	0	2	-1	1.000	0	O-64	-0.5
1958	*NY-A	77	138	21	42	4	1	4	19	21	16	.304	.396	.435	133	7	2	0	1	.957	-3	O-35	0.1
1959	NY-A	74	99	10	17	2	0	6	21	13	19	.172	.268	.374	77	-4	1	0	0	.946	-5	O-26	-0.9
	Mil-N	11	18	0	3	0	0	0	3	3	3	.167	.286	.167	27	-2	0	0	0	1.000	-1	/O-5	-0.3
Total	19	2380	7946	1247	2383	413	148	169	1304	1018	538	.300	.382	.453	122	256	71	15		.980	-0	*O-2064	16.3

■ SCOTTIE SLAYBACK
Slayback, Elbert   b: 10/5/01, Paducah, Ky.   d: 11/30/79, Cincinnati, Ohio   BR/TR, 5'8", 165 lbs.   Deb: 9/26/26

YEAR	TM/L	G	AB	R	H	2B	3B	HR	RBI	BB	SO	AVG	OBP	SLG	PRO+	BR/A	SB	CS	SBR	FA	FR	G/POS	TPR
1926	NY-N	2	8	0	0	0	0	0	0	0	0	.000	.000	.000	-99	-2	0			.889	-1	/2-2	-0.4

■ BRUCE SLOAN
Sloan, Bruce Adams "Fatso"   b: 10/4/14, McAlester, Okla.   d: 9/24/73, Oklahoma City, Okla.   BL/TL, 5'9", 195 lbs.   Deb: 4/29/44

YEAR	TM/L	G	AB	R	H	2B	3B	HR	RBI	BB	SO	AVG	OBP	SLG	PRO+	BR/A	SB	CS	SBR	FA	FR	G/POS	TPR
1944	NY-N	59	104	7	28	4	1	1	9	13	8	.269	.350	.356	99	0	0			.935	-4	O-21	-0.5

■ TOD SLOAN
Sloan, Yale Yeastman   b: 12/24/1890, Madisonville, Tenn.   d: 9/12/56, Akron, Ohio   BL/TR, 6', 175 lbs.   Deb: 9/22/13

YEAR	TM/L	G	AB	R	H	2B	3B	HR	RBI	BB	SO	AVG	OBP	SLG	PRO+	BR/A	SB	CS	SBR	FA	FR	G/POS	TPR
1913	StL-A	7	26	2	7	1	0	0	2	1	9	.269	.321	.308	87	-0	1			.950	2	/O-7	0.1
1917	StL-A	109	313	32	72	6	2	2	25	28	34	.230	.307	.281	83	-6	8			.963	-3	O-77	-1.5
1919	StL-A	27	63	9	15	1	3	0	6	12	3	.238	.364	.349	99	0	0			.933	1	O-20	-0.1
Total	3	143	402	43	94	8	5	2	33	41	46	.234	.319	.294	86	-6	9			.957	-1	O-104	-1.5

■ RON SLOCUM
Slocum, Ronald Reece   b: 7/2/45, Modesto, Cal.   BR/TR, 6'2", 185 lbs.   Deb: 9/8/69

YEAR	TM/L	G	AB	R	H	2B	3B	HR	RBI	BB	SO	AVG	OBP	SLG	PRO+	BR/A	SB	CS	SBR	FA	FR	G/POS	TPR
1969	SD-N	13	24	6	7	0	1	1	0	0	5	.292	.292	.458	112	0	0	0	0	.938	-1	/2-4,3-4,S-1	-0.1
1970	SD-N	60	71	8	10	2	2	1	11	8	24	.141	.237	.268	37	-7	0	1	-1	.978	13	C-19,S-17,3-11,2-9	0.6
1971	SD-N	7	18	1	0	0	0	0	0	0	8	.000	.053	.000	-90	-5	0	0	0	.905	1	/3-6	-0.3
Total	3	80	113	15	17	2	3	2	16	8	37	.150	.220	.265	33	-11	0	1	-1	.887	13	/3-21,C-19,S-18,2	0.2

■ CRAIG SMAJSTRLA
Smajstrla, Craig Lee   b: 6/19/62, Houston, Tex.   BB/TR, 5'9", 165 lbs.   Deb: 9/6/88

YEAR	TM/L	G	AB	R	H	2B	3B	HR	RBI	BB	SO	AVG	OBP	SLG	PRO+	BR/A	SB	CS	SBR	FA	FR	G/POS	TPR
1988	Hou-N	8	3	0	0	0	0	0	0	0	1	.000	.000	.000	-99	-1	0	0	0	1.000	0	/2-2	-0.1

■ CHARLIE SMALL
Small, Charles Albert   b: 10/24/05, Auburn, Me.   d: 1/14/53, Auburn, Me.   BL/TL, 5'11", 180 lbs.   Deb: 7/7/30

YEAR	TM/L	G	AB	R	H	2B	3B	HR	RBI	BB	SO	AVG	OBP	SLG	PRO+	BR/A	SB	CS	SBR	FA	FR	G/POS	TPR
1930	Bos-A	25	18	1	3	1	0	0	0	2	5	.167	.250	.222	22	-2	1	0	0	1.000	-0	/O-1	-0.2

YEAR	TM/L	G	AB	R	H	2B	3B	HR	RBI	BB	SO	AVG	OBP	SLG	PRO+	BR/A	SB	CS	SBR	FA	FR	G/POS	TPR

■ HANK SMALL   Small, George Henry   b: 7/31/53, Atlanta, Ga.   BR/TR, 6'3", 205 lbs.   Deb: 9/27/78

1978	Atl-N	1	4	0	0	0	0	0	0	0	0	.000	.000	.000	-90	-1	0	0	0	1.000	0	/1-1	-0.1

■ JIM SMALL   Small, James Arthur   b: 3/8/37, Portland, Ore.   BL/TL, 6'1.5", 180 lbs.   Deb: 6/22/55

1955	Det-A	12	4	2	0	0	0	0	0	1	1	.000	.200	.000	-44	-1	0	0	0	1.000	-1	/O-4	-0.1
1956	Det-A	58	91	13	29	4	2	0	10	6	10	.319	.361	.407	102	0	0	0	0	.940	-3	O-26	-0.3
1957	Det-A	36	42	7	9	2	0	0	0	2	11	.214	.250	.262	39	-4	0	2	-1	1.000	-3	O-14	-0.8
1958	KC-A	2	4	0	0	0	0	0	0	1	0	.000	.200	.000	-39	-1	0	0	0	1.000	-1	/O-1	-0.1
Total	4	108	141	22	38	6	2	0	10	10	22	.270	.318	.340	75	-5	0	2	-1	.957	-6	/O-45	-1.3

■ ROY SMALLEY   Smalley, Roy Frederick Jr.   b: 10/25/52, Los Angeles, Cal.   BB/TR, 6'1", 185 lbs.   Deb: 4/30/75   F

1975	Tex-A	78	250	22	57	8	0	3	33	30	42	.228	.311	.296	73	-8	4	0	1	.941	-6	S-59,2-19/C-1	0.3
1976	Tex-A	41	129	15	29	2	0	1	8	29	27	.225	.367	.264	85	-1	2	0	1	.963	-6	2-38/S-5	-0.3
	Min-A	103	384	46	104	16	3	2	36	47	79	.271	.353	.344	103	3	0	4	-2	.967	5	*S-103	1.9
	Yr	144	513	61	133	18	3	3	44	76	106	.259	.357	.324	98	2	2	4	-2	.966	-1	*S-108,2-38	1.6
1977	Min-A	150	584	93	135	21	5	6	56	74	89	.231	.319	.315	75	-19	5	5	-2	.958	19	*S-150	1.5
1978	Min-A	158	586	80	160	31	3	19	77	85	70	.273	.366	.433	122	18	2	8	-4	.970	18	*S-157	**5.3**
1979	Min-A★	162	621	94	168	28	3	24	95	80	80	.271	.357	.441	110	9	2	3	-1	.968	**33**	*S-161/1-1	**5.6**
1980	Min-A	133	486	64	135	24	1	12	63	65	63	.278	.365	.405	103	3	3	3	-1	.975	21	*S-125/1-3,D-3	3.7
1981	Min-A	56	167	24	44	7	1	7	22	31	24	.263	.379	.443	128	7	0	0	0	.946	-17	S-37,D-15/1-1	-0.8
1982	Min-A	4	13	2	2	1	0	0	0	3	4	.154	.313	.231	51	-1	0	0	0	1.000	1	/S-4	0.0
	NY-A	142	486	55	125	24	2	20	67	68	100	.257	.348	.418	111	8	0	1	-1	.977	-19	S-89,3-53/2-1,D-4	-0.4
	Yr	146	499	57	127	15	2	20	67	71	104	.255	.347	.413	109	7	0	1	-1	.979	-18	S-93,3-53/D-4,2-1	-0.4
1983	NY-A	130	451	70	124	24	1	18	62	58	68	.275	.360	.452	127	17	3	3	-1	.959	-16	S-91,3-26,1-22	0.7
1984	NY-A	67	209	17	50	8	1	7	26	15	35	.239	.290	.388	89	-4	2	1	-0	.905	-9	3-35,S-13/1-5,D-5	-0.4
	Chi-A	47	135	15	23	4	0	4	13	22	30	.170	.287	.289	57	-8	1	1	-0	.947	-8	3-38/S-3,1-1,D-2	-1.6
	Yr	114	344	32	73	12	1	11	39	37	65	.212	.289	.349	76	-12	3	2	-0	.923	-17	3-73,S-16/D-7,1-6	-2.0
1985	Min-A	129	388	57	100	20	0	12	45	60	65	.258	.359	.402	102	2	0	2	-1	.987	-15	D-56,S-49,3-14,/1-1	-1.1
1986	Min-A	143	459	59	113	20	4	20	57	68	80	.246	.343	.438	108	6	1	3	-2	.963	-4	*D-114,S-19/3-8	-0.1
1987	*Min-A	110	309	32	85	16	1	8	34	36	52	.275	.353	.411	98	-0	2	0	1	.850	-3	D-73,3-14/S-4	-0.5
Total	13	1653	5657	745	1454	244	25	163	694	771	908	.257	.348	.395	103	32	27	34	-12	.966	14	*S-1069,D-272,3/21C	13.8

■ ROY SMALLEY   Smalley, Roy Frederick Sr.   b: 6/9/26, Springfield, Mo.   BR/TR, 6'3", 190 lbs.   Deb: 4/20/48   F

1948	Chi-N	124	361	25	78	11	4	4	36	23	76	.216	.265	.302	55	-23	0			.941	9	*S-124	-0.8
1949	Chi-N	135	477	57	117	21	10	8	35	36	77	.245	.304	.382	85	-12	2			.947	14	*S-132	1.2
1950	Chi-N	154	557	58	128	21	9	21	85	49	114	.230	.297	.413	85	-14	2			.945	21	*S-154	1.9
1951	Chi-N	79	238	24	55	7	4	3	31	25	53	.231	.304	.395	85	-6	0	0	0	.953	-13	S-74	-1.3
1952	Chi-N	87	261	36	58	14	1	5	30	29	58	.222	.305	.341	78	-8	0	0	0	.952	-11	S-82	-1.4
1953	Chi-N	82	253	20	63	9	0	6	25	28	57	.249	.329	.356	77	-8	0	0	0	.932	-6	S-77	-0.9
1954	Mil-N	25	36	5	8	1	0	0	7	4	9	.222	.317	.306	67	-2	0	0	0	.950	4	/S-9,2-7,1-2	0.3
1955	Phi-N	92	260	33	51	11	1	7	39	39	58	.196	.306	.327	69	-11	0	0	0	.974	-16	S-87/2-1,3-1	-2.0
1956	Phi-N	65	168	14	38	9	3	0	16	23	29	.226	.323	.315	74	-6	0	0	0	.949	-1	S-60	-0.3
1957	Phi-N	28	31	5	5	0	1	1	1	1	9	.161	.212	.323	42	-3	0	0	0	.941	1	S-20	-0.1
1958	Phi-N	1	2	0	0	0	0	0	0	0	1	.000	.000	.000	-99	-1	0	0	0	.714	0	/S-1	0.0
Total	11	872	2644	277	601	103	33	61	305	257	541	.227	.300	.360	77	-93	4	0		.947	3	S-820/2-8,1-2,3-1	-3.4

■ WILL SMALLEY   Smalley, William Darwin "Deacon"   b: 6/27/1871, Oakland, Cal.   d: 10/11/1891, Bay City, Mich.   BR/TR,   Deb: 4/19/1890

1890	Cle-N	136	502	62	107	11	1	0	42	60	44	.213	.303	.239	60	-23	10			.895	17	*3-136	-0.2
1891	Was-a	11	38	5	6	0	1	0	3	5	2	.158	.256	.211	35	-3	0			.762	-2	/3-9,2-2	-0.4
Total	2	147	540	67	113	11	2	0	45	65	46	.209	.300	.237	58	-27	10			.887	15	3-145/2-2	-0.6

■ JOE SMAZA   Smaza, Joseph Paul   b: 7/7/23, Detroit, Mich.   d: 5/30/79, Royal Oak, Mich.   BL/TL, 5'11", 175 lbs.   Deb: 9/18/46

1946	Chi-A	2	5	2	1	0	0	0	0	0	0	.200	.200	.200	12	-1	0	0	0	.000	-1	/O-1	-0.1

■ BILL SMILEY   Smiley, William B.   b: 1856, Baltimore, Md.   d: 7/11/1884, Baltimore, Md.   Deb: 10/13/1874

1874	Bal-n	2	7	0	0	0	0	0	0	0	0	.000	.000	.000	-99	-1	0	0	0	.786	1	/3-2	-0.1
1882	StL-a	59	240	30	51	4	2	0		6		.213	.232	.246	59	-10				.885	-7	*2-57/O-2	-1.5
	Bal-a	16	61	3	9	0	0	0		0		.148	.148	.148	-0	-6				.843	2	2-16/S-2	-0.4
	Yr	75	301	33	60	4	2	0		6		.199	.215	.226	48	-16				.874	-5	2-73/O-2,S-2	-1.9

■ EDGAR SMITH   Smith, Albert Edgar   b: 10/15/1860, North Haven, Conn.   TR, 6', 200 lbs.   Deb: 6/20/1883

1883	Bos-N	30	115	10	25	5	3	0	16	5	11	.217	.250	.313	68	-4				.905	-0	O-30/C-1	-0.4

■ ALECK SMITH   Smith, Alexander Benjamin "Broadway Aleck"   b: 1871, New York, N.Y.   d: 7/9/19, New York, N.Y.   TR,   Deb: 4/23/1897

1897	Bro-N	66	237	36	71	13	1	1	39	4		.300	.317	.376	87	-5	12			.903	-6	C-43,O-18/1-6	-0.7
1898	Bro-N	52	199	25	52	6	5	0	23	3		.261	.276	.342	77	-7	7			.909	-10	O-26,C-20/3-2,21	-1.6
1899	Bro-N	17	61	6	11	0	1	0	6	2		.180	.206	.213	15	-7	0			.917	-3	C-17	-0.8
	Bal-N	41	120	17	46	6	4	0	25	4		.383	.417	.500	144	7	7			.951	-4	C-36/O-2,1-1	0.5
	Yr	58	181	23	57	6	5	0	31	6		.315	.347	.403	101	-0	7			.939	-7	C-53/O-2,1-1	-0.3
1900	Bro-N	7	25	2	6	0	0	0	3	1		.240	.269	.240	39	-2	2			.875	-2	/3-6,C-1	-0.4
1901	NY-N	26	78	5	11	0	0	0	6	0		.141	.141	.141	-19	-12	2			.962	-2	C-24	-1.1
1902	Bal-N	41	145	10	34	1	0	0	21	8		.234	.275	.255	45	-11	0			.947	-6	C-27/1-7,O-4,2-3,3	-1.3
1903	Bos-N	11	33	4	10	1	0	0	4	3		.303	.303	.333	86	-1	0			.932	0	C-10	0.0
1904	Chi-N	10	29	2	6	1	0	0	1	3		.207	.281	.241	62	-1	1			.778	-2	/O-6,C-1,3-1	-0.3
1906	NY-N	16	28	0	5	0	0	0	0	0		.179	.207	.179	20	-3	1			1.000	-1	/C-8,1-3,O-1	-0.3
Total	9	287	955	107	252	30	11	1	130	26		.264	.288	.321	69	-41	37			.933	-35	C-187/O-57,1-18,32	-6.0

■ AL SMITH   Smith, Alphonse Eugene "Fuzzy"   b: 2/7/28, Kirkwood, Mo.   BR/TR, 6'1", 191 lbs.   Deb: 7/10/53

1953	Cle-A	47	150	28	36	9	3	0	14	20	25	.240	.341	.360	92	-1	2	0	1	.920	-3	O-39/3-2	-0.6
1954	*Cle-A	131	481	101	135	29	6	11	50	88	65	.281	.399	.435	126	20	2	9	-5	.984	-3	*O-109,3-21/S-4	0.8
1955	Cle-A★	154	607	**123**	186	27	4	22	77	93	77	.306	.411	.473	132	30	11	6	-0	.977	-17	*O-120,3-45/S-5,2-1	0.7
1956	Cle-A	141	526	87	144	26	5	16	71	84	72	.274	.382	.433	112	11	6	3	0	.981	-7	*O-122,3-28/2-1	-0.2
1957	Cle-A	135	507	78	125	23	5	11	49	79	70	.247	.353	.377	100	2	12	6	0	.913	-16	3-84,O-58	-1.6
1958	Chi-A	139	480	61	121	23	5	12	58	48	77	.252	.336	.396	100	-0	3	3	-1	.970	-1	*O-138/3-1	-1.0
1959	*Chi-A	129	472	65	112	16	4	17	55	46	74	.237	.312	.396	94	-5	7	5	-1	.980	10	*O-128/3-1	-0.2
1960	Chi-A★	142	536	80	169	31	3	12	72	50	65	.315	.377	.451	124	18	8	3	1	.966	-5	*O-141	0.7
1961	Chi-A	147	532	88	148	29	4	28	93	56	67	.278	.352	.506	128	20	4	4	-1	.948	-11	3-80,O-71	0.5
1962	Chi-A	142	511	62	149	23	8	16	82	57	60	.292	.366	.462	122	16	3	3	-1	.935	-23	*3-105,O-39	-0.8
1963	Bal-A	120	368	45	100	17	1	10	39	32	74	.272	.335	.405	110	5	9	0	3	.971	-4	O-97	-0.1
1964	Cle-A	61	136	15	22	1	4	9	8	32		.162	.214	.272	34	-7	0	1	-1	1.000	-1	O-48/3-1	-1.9
	Bos-A	29	51	10	11	4	0	7	13	10		.216	.385	.412	116	2	0	0	0	.917	-2	3-10/O-8	0.0
	Yr	90	187	25	33	5	1	16	21	42		.176	.267	.310	59	-10	1	1	-1	.987	-4	O-56,3-11	-1.9
Total	12	1517	5357	843	1458	258	46	164	676	674	768	.272	.360	.429	113	105	67	43	-6	.974	-84	*O-1118,3-378/S-9,2	-3.7

■ TONY SMITH   Smith, Anthony   b: 5/14/1884, Chicago, Ill.   d: 2/27/64, Galveston, Tex.   BR/TR, 5'9", 150 lbs.   Deb: 8/12/07

1907	Was-A	51	139	12	26	1	1	0	8	18		.187	.285	.209	63	-5	3			.920	-9	S-51	-1.5
1910	Bro-N	106	321	31	58	10	1	1	16	69	53	.181	.329	.227	65	-11	9			.941	12	*S-101/3-6	0.6
1911	Bro-N	13	40	3	6	1	0	0	2	8	7	.150	.292	.175	33	-3	1			.870	0	S-10/2-3	-0.3
Total	3	170	500	46	90	12	2	1	26	95	<u>60</u>	.180	.314	.218	62	-19	13			.931	3	S-162/3-6,2-3	-1.2

YEAR	TM/L	G	AB	R	H	2B	3B	HR	RBI	BB	SO	AVG	OBP	SLG	PRO+	BR/A	SB	CS	SBR	FA	FR	G/POS	TPR

■ KLONDIKE SMITH
Smith, Armstrong Frederick   b: 1/4/1887, London, England   d: 11/15/59, Springfield, Mass.   BL/TL, 5'9", 160 lbs.   Deb: 9/28/12

| 1912 | NY-A | 7 | 27 | 0 | 5 | 1 | 0 | 0 | 0 | 0 | 0 | .185 | .185 | .222 | 15 | -3 | 1 | | | 1.000 | -1 | /O-7 | -0.5 |

■ BILLY SMITH
Smith, Billy Edward   b: 7/14/53, Jonesboro, La.   BB/TR, 6'2.5", 185 lbs.   Deb: 4/13/75

1975	Cal-A	59	143	10	29	5	1	0	14	12	27	.203	.265	.252	50	-10	1	3	-2	.932	-9	S-50/1-6,3-2,D-4	-1.6
1976	Cal-A	13	8	0	3	0	0	0	0	0	2	.375	.375	.375	128	0	0	0	0	.625	-1	S-10/D-1	0.0
1977	Bal-A	109	367	44	79	12	2	5	29	33	71	.215	.282	.300	62	-19	3	2	-0	.991	4	*2-104/S-5,1-2,3-1	-0.8
1978	Bal-A	85	250	29	65	12	2	5	30	27	40	.260	.335	.384	108	3	3	0	1	.986	-1	2-83/S-2	0.8
1979	*Bal-A	68	189	18	47	9	4	6	33	15	33	.249	.311	.434	102	-0	1	0	0	.980	-8	2-63/S-5	-0.4
1981	SF-N	36	61	6	11	0	0	1	5	9	16	.180	.286	.230	48	-4	0	0	0	.971	-0	S-21/2-5,3-3	-0.3
Total	6	370	1018	107	234	38	9	17	111	96	189	.230	.299	.335	79	-30	8	5	-1	.987	-15	2-255/S-93,1-8,3D	-2.3

■ BOBBY GENE SMITH
Smith, Bobby Gene   b: 5/28/34, Hood River, Ore.   BR/TR, 5'11", 185 lbs.   Deb: 4/16/57

1957	StL-N	93	185	24	39	7	1	3	18	13	35	.211	.263	.308	52	-13	1	1	-0	.973	-8	O-79	-2.5
1958	StL-N	28	88	8	25	3	0	2	5	2	18	.284	.308	.386	79	-3	1	0	0	1.000	-1	O-27	-0.5
1959	StL-N	43	60	11	13	1	1	1	7	1	9	.217	.230	.317	41	-5	0	0	0	.971	-4	O-32	-1.0
1960	Phi-N	98	217	24	62	5	2	4	27	10	28	.286	.317	.382	90	-3	2	3	-1	1.000	1	O-70/3-1	-0.6
1961	Phi-N	79	174	16	44	7	0	2	18	15	32	.253	.316	.328	72	-7	0	1	-1	.971	6	O-47	-0.4
1962	NY-N	8	22	1	3	0	1	0	2	3	2	.136	.240	.227	26	-2	0	1	-1	1.000	-1	/O-6	-0.4
	Chi-N	13	29	3	5	0	1	0	2	2	6	.172	.226	.276	33	-3	0	1	-1	1.000	-1	/O-7	-0.5
	StL-N	91	130	13	30	9	0	0	12	7	14	.231	.270	.300	48	-10	1	1	-0	1.000	-14	O-80	-2.6
	Yr	112	181	17	38	9	1	0	16	12	22	.210	.259	.287	43	-15	1	3	-2	1.000	-15	O-93	-3.5
1965	Cal-A	23	57	1	13	3	0	0	5	2	10	.228	.267	.281	57	-3	0	1	-1	1.000	-0	O-15	-0.5
Total	7	476	962	101	234	35	5	13	96	55	154	.243	.286	.331	64	-48	5	9	-4	.986	-22	O-363/3-1	-9.0

■ BRICK SMITH
Smith, Brick Dudley   b: 5/2/59, Charlotte, N.C.   BR/TR, 6'4", 225 lbs.   Deb: 9/13/87

1987	Sea-A	5	8	1	1	0	0	0	0	0	4	.125	.300	.125	18	-1	0	0	0	.963	0	/1-3,D-1	-0.1
1988	Sea-A	4	10	1	1	0	0	0	1	0	1	.100	.100	.100	-42	-2	0	0	0	1.000	1	/1-4	-0.1
Total	2	9	18	2	2	0	0	0	1	2	5	.111	.200	.111	-12	-3	0	0	0	.983	1	/1-7,D-1	-0.2

■ BERNIE SMITH
Smith, Calvin Bernard   b: 9/4/41, Ponchatoula, La.   BR/TR, 5'9", 164 lbs.   Deb: 7/31/70

1970	Mil-A	44	76	8	21	3	1	1	6	11	12	.276	.382	.382	110	2	1	3	-2	.979	-7	O-39	-0.8
1971	Mil-A	15	36	1	5	1	0	1	3	0	5	.139	.162	.250	15	-4	0	0	0	.923	-3	O-12	-0.8
Total	2	59	112	9	26	4	1	2	9	11	17	.232	.317	.339	83	-3	1	3	-2	.967	-9	/O-51	-1.6

■ REGGIE SMITH
Smith, Carl Reginald   b: 4/2/45, Shreveport, La.   BB/TR, 6', 195 lbs.   Deb: 9/18/66   C

1966	Bos-A	6	26	1	4	1	0	0	0	0	5	.154	.154	.192	-1	-3	0	0	0	.944	1	/O-6	-0.3
1967	*Bos-A	158	565	78	139	24	6	15	61	57	95	.246	.316	.389	99	-1	16	6	1	.983	17	*O-144/2-6	1.2
1968	Bos-A	155	558	78	148	37	5	15	69	64	77	.265	.345	.430	125	17	22	18	-4	.985	10	*O-155	1.7
1969	Bos-A★	143	543	87	168	29	7	25	93	54	67	.309	.373	.527	142	29	7	13	-6	.959	6	*O-139	2.2
1970	Bos-A	147	580	109	176	32	7	22	74	51	60	.303	.364	.497	126	20	10	7	-1	.977	16	*O-145	2.7
1971	Bos-A	159	618	85	175	33	2	30	96	63	82	.283	.354	.489	128	21	11	3	2	.966	16	*O-159	3.2
1972	Bos-A★	131	467	75	126	25	4	21	74	68	63	.270	.367	.475	142	25	15	4	2	.981	5	*O-129	2.9
1973	Bos-A	115	423	79	128	23	2	21	69	68	49	.303	.400	.515	148	28	3	2	-0	.983	7	*O-104/1-1,D-8	2.9
1974	StL-N★	143	517	79	160	26	9	23	100	71	70	.309	.394	.528	158	39	4	3	-1	.976	6	*O-132/1-1	4.0
1975	StL-N★	135	477	67	144	26	3	19	76	63	59	.302	.387	.488	137	24	9	7	-2	.963	-5	O-69,1-66/3-1	1.1
1976	StL-N	47	170	20	37	7	1	8	23	14	28	.218	.281	.412	94	-2	1	2	-1	.986	7	1-17,O-16,3-13	0.2
	LA-N	65	225	35	63	8	4	10	26	18	42	.280	.336	.484	133	9	2	0	1	.985	3	O-58/3-1	1.0
	Yr	112	395	55	100	15	5	18	49	32	70	.253	.312	.453	116	6	3	2	-0	.989	10	O-74,1-17,3-14	1.2
1977	*LA-N★	148	488	104	150	27	4	32	87	104	76	.307	**.432**	.576	**168**	51	7	5	-1	.980	-7	*O-140	3.7
1978	*LA-N★	128	447	82	132	27	2	29	93	70	90	.295	.392	.559	**164**	38	12	5	1	.950	-4	*O-126	3.1
1979	LA-N	68	234	41	64	13	1	10	32	31	50	.274	.363	.466	126	9	6	5	-1	.988	6	O-62	1.3
1980	LA-N★	92	311	47	100	13	0	15	55	41	63	.322	.402	.508	155	24	5	6	-2	.994	6	O-84	2.6
1981	*LA-N	41	35	5	7	1	0	1	8	7	8	.200	.333	.314	88	-0	0	0	0	1.000	0	/1-2	0.0
1982	SF-N	106	349	51	99	11	0	18	56	46	46	.284	.367	.470	133	15	7	0	2	.982	2	1-99	1.5
Total	17	1987	7033	1123	2020	363	57	314	1092	890	1030	.287	.370	.489	136	342	137	86	-11	.976	93	*O-1668,1-186/3D2	35.0

■ CHARLIE SMITH
Smith, Charles J.   b: 12/11/1840, Brooklyn, N.Y.   d: 11/15/1897, Great Neck, N.Y.   5'10.5", 150 lbs.   Deb: 5/18/1871

| 1871 | Mut-n | 14 | 72 | 15 | 19 | 2 | 1 | 0 | 5 | 1 | 1 | .264 | .274 | .319 | 77 | -1 | 6 | 0 | 2 | .688 | -1 | 3-12/2-3 | -0.1 |

■ POP SMITH
Smith, Charles Marvin   b: 10/12/1856, Digby, N.S., Canada   d: 4/18/27, Boston, Mass.   BR/TR, 5'11", 170 lbs.   Deb: 5/1/1880   U

1880	Cin-N	83	334	35	69	10	9	0	27	6	36	.207	.221	.290	72	-9				.855	-11	*2-83	-1.6
1881	Cle-N	10	34	1	4	0	0	0	3	0	8	.118	.118	.118	-27	-5				.838	-2	3-10	-0.6
	Buf-N	3	11	3	0	0	0	0	1	3	5	.000	.214	.000	-27	-1				.840	-1	/2-3	-0.2
	Wor-N	11	41	1	3	0	0	0	2	3	5	.073	.136	.073	-31	-6				.955	2	/O-8,2-3	-0.4
	Yr	24	86	5	7	0	0	0	6	6	18	.081	.141	.081	-28	-12				.838	-1	3-10/O-8,2-6	-1.2
1882	Phi-a	20	65	10	6	0	0	0	2	12		.092	.234	.092	12	-6				.732	2	3-11/S-4,O-3,2-2	-0.3
	Lou-a	3	11	1	2	0	0	0	0			.182	.182	.182	24	-1				.778	-0	/S-3	-0.1
	Yr	23	76	11	8	0	0	0	2	12		.105	.227	.105	14	-7				.732	2	3-11/S-7,O-3,2-2	-0.4
1883	Col-a	97	405	82	106	14	**17**	4		22		.262	.300	.410	137	18				.889	18	*2-73,3-24/P-3	3.1
1884	Col-a	108	445	78	106	18	10	6		20		.238	.289	.364	122	12				.905	29	*2-108	3.9
1885	Pit-a	106	453	85	113	11	13	0	35	25		.249	.293	.331	98	-1				.922	33	*2-106	3.2
1886	Pit-a	126	483	75	105	20	9	2	57	42		.217	.288	.308	87	-7	38			**.895**	21	*S-98,2-28/C-1	1.4
1887	Pit-N	122	456	69	98	12	7	2	54	30	48	.215	.283	.285	62	-22	30			.914	-6	*2-89,S-33	-2.2
1888	Pit-N	131	481	61	99	15	2	4	52	22	78	.206	.248	.270	71	-15	37			.901	-2	S-75,2-56	-1.3
1889	Pit-N	72	258	26	54	10	2	5	27	24	38	.209	.292	.322	79	-7	12			.897	-0	S-58/2-9,3-3,0-3	-0.3
	Bos-N	59	208	21	54	13	4	0	32	23	30	.260	.345	.361	92	-3	11			.890	-0	S-59	0.1
	Yr	131	466	47	108	23	6	5	59	47	68	.232	.315	.339	85	-9	23			.894	-0	*S-117/2-9,3-3,0-3	-0.2
1890	Bos-N	134	463	82	106	16	12	1	53	80	81	.229	.353	.322	90	-5	39			.918	-20	*2-134/S-1	-1.5
1891	Was-a	37	90	13	16	2	2	0	13	13	16	.178	.295	.244	57	-5	2			.919	7	2-19/S-5,3-4	0.3
Total	12	1112	4238	643	941	141	87	24	358	325	345	.222	.287	.313	86	-64	169			.903	70	2-713,S-336/3OPC	3.5

■ CHARLEY SMITH
Smith, Charles William   b: 9/15/37, Charleston, S.C.   d: 11/29/94, Reno, Nev.   BR/TR, 6', 177 lbs.   Deb: 9/8/60

1960	LA-N	18	60	2	10	1	1	0	5	1	15	.167	.180	.217	8	-8	0	0	0	.953	0	3-18	-0.8
1961	LA-N	9	24	4	6	1	0	2	3	1	6	.250	.280	.542	103	-0	0	0	0	1.000	-0	/3-4,S-3	0.0
	Phi-N	112	411	43	102	13	4	9	47	23	76	.248	.296	.365	75	-15	3	4	-2	.924	-3	3-94,S-14	-1.7
	Yr	121	435	47	108	14	4	11	50	24	82	.248	.295	.375	77	-15	3	4	-2	.926	-3	3-98,S-17	-1.7
1962	Chi-A	65	145	11	30	4	0	2	17	9	32	.207	.258	.276	44	-12	0	1	-1	.944	2	3-54	-1.0
1963	Chi-A	4	7	0	2	0	0	1	3	0	1	.286	.286	.571	136	-0	0	0	0	1.000	0	/S-1	0.2
1964	Chi-A	2	7	1	1	0	0	0	1	0	1	.143	.250	.429	87	-0	0	0	0	1.000	3	/3-2	0.3
	NY-N	127	444	43	106	12	0	20	58	19	101	.239	.275	.402	90	-7	2	2	-1	.917	-12	3-85,S-36,O-13	-2.1
1965	NY-N	135	499	49	122	20	3	16	62	17	123	.244	.275	.393	89	-9	2	1	0	.957	10	*3-131/S-6,2-1	-0.1
1966	StL-N	116	391	34	104	13	4	10	43	22	81	.266	.305	.396	93	-4	0	1	-1	.964	-1	*3-107/S-1	-0.9
1967	NY-A	135	425	38	95	15	3	9	38	32	110	.224	.279	.336	84	-9	0	2	-1	.947	11	*3-115	-0.1
1968	NY-A	46	70	2	16	4	1	1	7	5	18	.229	.280	.357	95	-1	0	0	0	.961	4	3-13	0.3
1969	Chi-N	2	2	0	0	0	0	0	0	0	0	.000	.000	.000	-89	-0	0	0	0	.000	0	H	-0.1
Total	10	771	2484	228	594	83	18	69	281	130	565	.239	.281	.370	82	-65	7	12	-5	.945	16	3-623/S-61,O-13,2-1	-6.1

■ CHRIS SMITH
Smith, Christopher William   b: 7/18/57, Torrance, Cal.   BB/TR, 6', 185 lbs.   Deb: 5/14/81

| 1981 | Mon-N | 7 | 7 | 0 | 0 | 0 | 0 | 0 | 0 | 0 | 2 | .000 | .000 | .000 | -99 | -2 | 0 | 0 | 0 | 1.000 | 0 | /2-1 | -0.2 |
| 1982 | Mon-N | 2 | 5 | 0 | 0 | 0 | 0 | 0 | 0 | 0 | 1 | .000 | .000 | .000 | -98 | -1 | 0 | 0 | 0 | .000 | 0 | /H | -0.1 |

YEAR	TM/L	G	AB	R	H	2B	3B	HR	RBI	BB	SO	AVG	OBP	SLG	PRO+	BR/A	SB	CS	SBR	FA	FR	G/POS	TPR
1983	SF-N	22	67	13	22	6	1	1	11	7	12	.328	.408	.493	153	5	0	0	0	.976	-2	1-15/O-4,3-1	0.2
Total	3	31	76	13	22	6	1	1	11	7	15	.289	.365	.434	124	3	0	0	0	.976	-2	/1-15,O-4,3-1,2-1	-0.1

■ EARL SMITH   Smith, Earl Calvin b: 3/14/28, Sunnyside, Wash. BR/TR, 6′, 185 lbs. Deb: 4/14/55

YEAR	TM/L	G	AB	R	H	2B	3B	HR	RBI	BB	SO	AVG	OBP	SLG	PRO+	BR/A	SB	CS	SBR	FA	FR	G/POS	TPR
1955	Pit-N	5	16	1	1	0	0	0	0	0	4	.063	.286	.063	-1	-2	0	0	0	1.000	-0	/O-5	-0.3

■ EARL SMITH   Smith, Earl Leonard "Sheriff" b: 1/20/1891, Oak Hill, Ohio   d: 3/14/43, Portsmouth, Ohio BB/TR, 5′11″, 170 lbs. Deb: 9/12/16

YEAR	TM/L	G	AB	R	H	2B	3B	HR	RBI	BB	SO	AVG	OBP	SLG	PRO+	BR/A	SB	CS	SBR	FA	FR	G/POS	TPR
1916	Chi-N	14	27	2	7	0	1	0	4	2	5	.259	.310	.370	98	-0				.800	-3	/O-7	-0.3
1917	StL-A	52	199	31	56	7	7	0	10	15	21	.281	.332	.387	124	5	5			.977	5	O-51	0.8
1918	StL-A	89	286	28	77	10	5	0	32	13	16	.269	.303	.339	97	-3	13			.952	1	O-81	-0.6
1919	StL-A	88	252	21	63	12	5	1	36	18	27	.250	.300	.349	80	-7	1			.971	10	O-68	-0.2
1920	StL-A	103	353	45	108	21	8	3	55	13	18	.306	.336	.436	100	-1	11	4	1	.916	-5	3-70,O-15	-0.3
1921	StL-A	25	78	7	26	4	2	2	14	3	4	.333	.366	.513	115	1	0	0	0	.878	3	3-13/O-4	-0.3
	Was-A	59	180	20	39	5	2	2	12	10	19	.217	.266	.300	46	-15	1	0	0	.949	4	O-43/3-1	-1.3
	Yr	84	258	27	65	9	4	4	26	13	23	.252	.296	.364	69	-13	1	0	0	.944	0	O-47,3-14	-1.4
1922	Was-A	65	205	22	53	12	2	1	23	8	17	.259	.293	.351	71	-10	4	4	-1	.917	1	O-49/3-2	-1.3
Total	7	495	1580	176	429	72	32	9	186	82	127	.272	.311	.375	90	-30	36	8		.952	10	O-318/3-86	-3.3

■ EARL SMITH   Smith, Earl Sutton "Oil" b: 2/14/1897, Hot Springs, Ark.   d: 6/8/63, Little Rock, Ark. BL/TR, 5′10.5″, 180 lbs. Deb: 4/24/19

YEAR	TM/L	G	AB	R	H	2B	3B	HR	RBI	BB	SO	AVG	OBP	SLG	PRO+	BR/A	SB	CS	SBR	FA	FR	G/POS	TPR
1919	NY-N	21	36	5	9	0	8	3	3			.250	.308	.361	102	0	1			.973	-3	C-14/2-1	-0.2
1920	NY-N	91	262	20	77	7	1	3	30	18	16	.294	.344	.340	98	-0	5	2	0	.976	-5	C-82	0.0
1921	*NY-N	89	229	35	77	8	4	10	51	27	8	.336	.409	.537	148	16	4	3	-1	.965	-10	C-78	0.9
1922	*NY-N	90	234	29	65	11	4	9	39	37	12	.278	.383	.474	119	7	1	1	-0	.978	-2	C-75	0.8
1923	NY-N	24	34	2	7	1	1	1	4	4	1	.206	.289	.382	77	-1	0	0	0	.975	2	C-12	0.1
	Bos-N	72	191	22	55	15	1	3	19	22	10	.288	.364	.424	112	3	0	1	-1	.975	-4	C-54	0.2
	Yr	96	225	24	62	16	2	4	23	26	11	.276	.353	.418	106	2	0	1	-1	.975	-2	C-66	0.3
1924	Bos-N	33	59	1	16	3	0	0	8	6	3	.271	.338	.322	81	-1	0	1	-1	.946	-1	C-13	-0.2
	Pit-N	39	111	12	41	10	1	4	21	13	4	.369	.435	.586	168	11	2	0	1	.974	0	C-35	1.3
	Yr	72	170	13	57	13	1	4	29	19	7	.335	.402	.494	140	10	2	1	0	.967	-1	C-48	1.1
1925	*Pit-N	109	329	34	103	22	3	6	64	31	13	.313	.374	.471	107	3	4	1	1	.968	11	C-96	1.9
1926	Pit-N	105	292	29	101	17	2	2	46	28	7	.346	.407	.438	121	9	1			.964	4	C-98	1.9
1927	*Pit-N	66	189	16	51	3	1	5	25	21	11	.270	.346	.376	87	-3	0			.986	-4	C-61	-0.4
1928	Pit-N	32	85	8	21	6	0	2	11	11	7	.247	.333	.388	85	-2	0			.967	-4	C-28	-0.4
	*StL-N	24	58	3	13	2	0	0	7	5	4	.224	.286	.259	42	-5	0			1.000	-1	C-18	-0.4
	Yr	56	143	11	34	8	0	2	18	16	11	.238	.314	.336	68	-7	0			.980	-5	C-46	-0.7
1929	StL-N	57	145	9	50	8	0	1	22	18	6	.345	.417	.434	107	3	0			.962	-5	C-50	0.1
1930	StL-N	8	10	0	0	0	0	0	3	1	1	.000	.231	.000	-36	-2	0			.913	1	/C-6	-0.1
Total	12	860	2264	225	686	115	19	46	355	247	106	.303	.374	.432	111	37	18	9		.971	-20	C-720/2-1	5.6

■ EDGAR SMITH   Smith, Edgar Eugene b: 6/12/1862, Providence, R.I.   d: 11/3/1892, Providence, R.I. BR/TR, 5′10″, 160 lbs. Deb: 5/25/1883

YEAR	TM/L	G	AB	R	H	2B	3B	HR	RBI	BB	SO	AVG	OBP	SLG	PRO+	BR/A	SB	CS	SBR	FA	FR	G/POS	TPR
1883	Pro-N	2	9	1	2	1	0	0	1	0	2	.222	.222	.333	64	-0				1.000	-0	/1-2,O-2	-0.1
	Phi-N	1	4	1	3	0	0	0	1	0	0	.750	.750	.750	393	1				.000	-1	/P-1,O-1	0.0
	Yr	3	13	3	5	1	0	0	2	0	2	.385	.385	.462	158	1				1.000	-1	/O-3,1-2,P-1	-0.1
1884	Was-a	14	57	5	5	0	1	0		1		.088	.103	.123	-30	-8				.794	5	O-12/P-3	-0.2
1885	Pro-N	1	4	0	1	0	0	0	0	0	0	.250	.250	.250	65	-0				.750	-0	/P-1	0.0
1890	Cle-N	8	24	2	7	0	0	0	4	4	1	.292	.393	.375	126	1	0			.900	1	/P-6,O-2	0.0
Total	4	26	98	10	18	1	1	0	6	5	3	.184	.223	.235	47	-6	0			.821	5	/O-17,P-11,1-2	-0.3

■ MAYO SMITH   Smith, Edward Mayo b: 1/17/15, New London, Mo.   d: 11/24/77, Boynton Beach, Fla BL/TR, 6′, 183 lbs. Deb: 6/24/45 M

YEAR	TM/L	G	AB	R	H	2B	3B	HR	RBI	BB	SO	AVG	OBP	SLG	PRO+	BR/A	SB	CS	SBR	FA	FR	G/POS	TPR
1945	Phi-A	73	203	18	43	5	0	0	11	36	13	.212	.333	.236	67	-7	0	1	-1	.976	-8	O-65	-2.0

■ ELMER SMITH   Smith, Elmer Ellsworth b: 3/23/1868, Pittsburgh, Pa.   d: 11/3/45, Pittsburgh, Pa. BL/TL, 5′11″, 178 lbs. Deb: 9/10/1886

YEAR	TM/L	G	AB	R	H	2B	3B	HR	RBI	BB	SO	AVG	OBP	SLG	PRO+	BR/A	SB	CS	SBR	FA	FR	G/POS	TPR
1886	Cin-a	9	28	6	8	1	1	0	2	9		.286	.459	.393	163	3	0			.600	-2	P-9/O-1	0.0
1887	Cin-a	52	186	26	47	10	6	0	23	11		.253	.298	.371	84	-5	5			.851	-6	P-52/O-2	-0.1
1888	Cin-a	40	129	15	29	4	1	0	9	20		.225	.329	.271	88	-1	2			.838	-6	P-40/O-2	-0.1
1889	Cin-a	29	83	12	23	3	1	2	17	7	18	.277	.348	.410	112	1	1			.821	-4	P-29	0.0
1892	Pit-N	138	511	86	140	16	14	4	63	82	43	.274	.375	.384	129	20	22			.885	-5	*O-124,P-17	0.8
1893	Pit-N	128	518	121	179	26	23	7	103	77	23	.346	.435	.525	158	44	26			.921	3	*O-128	3.3
1894	Pit-N	125	489	128	174	33	19	6	72	65	12	.356	.436	.538	135	29	33			.933	4	*O-125/P-1	1.9
1895	Pit-N	124	480	88	145	14	12	1	81	55	25	.302	.381	.387	104	5	34			.896	-3	*O-123	-0.6
1896	Pit-N	122	484	121	175	21	14	6	94	74	18	.362	.454	.500	158	45	33			.946	9	*O-122	3.6
1897	Pit-N	123	467	99	145	19	17	6	54	70		.310	.408	.463	135	26	25			.904	3	*O-123	1.6
1898	Cin-N	123	486	79	166	21	10	1	66	69		.342	.425	.432	136	25	20			.949	4	*O-123/P-1	1.8
1899	Cin-N	87	339	65	101	13	6	1	24	47		.298	.385	.381	108	5	10			.922	-1	O-87	-0.2
1900	Cin-N	29	111	14	31	4	4	1	18	18		.279	.389	.414	125	4	5			.930	0	O-27	-0.1
	NY-N	85	312	47	81	9	7	2	34	24		.260	.317	.353	89	-5	14			.953	-8	O-83	-1.8
	Yr	114	423	61	112	13	11	3	52	42		.265	.337	.369	99	-1	19			.944	-8	*O-110	-1.6
1901	Pit-N	4	4	0	0	0	0	0	0	2		.000	.333	.000	1	-0	0			1.000	-0	/O-1	-0.1
	Bos-N	16	57	5	10	2	1	0	3	6		.175	.254	.246	41	-4	2			.833	-3	/O-15	-0.8
	Yr	20	61	5	10	2	1	0	3	8		.164	.261	.230	40	-5	2			.846	-3	/O-16	-0.9
Total	14	1234	4684	912	1454	196	136	37	663	636	139	.310	.398	.434	126	191	232			.921	-17	*O-1086,P-149	9.5

■ ELMER SMITH   Smith, Elmer John b: 9/21/1892, Sandusky, Ohio   d: 8/3/84, Columbia, Ky. BL/TR, 5′10″, 165 lbs. Deb: 9/20/14

YEAR	TM/L	G	AB	R	H	2B	3B	HR	RBI	BB	SO	AVG	OBP	SLG	PRO+	BR/A	SB	CS	SBR	FA	FR	G/POS	TPR
1914	Cle-A	13	53	5	17	3	0	0	8	2	11	.321	.345	.377	113	1	1	1	-0	1.000	1	O-13	0.1
1915	Cle-A	144	476	37	118	23	12	3	67	36	75	.248	.301	.366	97	-4	10	11	-4	.923	0	*O-123	-1.4
1916	Cle-A	79	213	25	59	15	3	3	40	18	35	.277	.336	.418	119	4	3			.966	-2	O-57	0.0
	Was-A	45	168	12	36	10	3	2	27	18	28	.214	.298	.345	94	-2	4			.988	1	O-45	-0.3
	Yr	124	381	37	95	25	6	5	67	36	63	.249	.319	.386	108	2	7			.976	-1	*O-102	-0.3
1917	Was-A	35	117	8	26	4	3	1	17	5	14	.222	.260	.308	74	-4	1			.901	-0	O-29	-0.7
	Cle-A	64	161	21	42	5	1	3	22	13	18	.261	.316	.360	99	-1	6			.986	-1	O-40	-0.4
	Yr	99	278	29	68	9	4	3	39	18	32	.245	.293	.338	89	-5	7			.943	-1	O-69	-1.1
1919	Cle-A	114	395	60	110	24	6	9	54	41	30	.278	.354	.438	115	7	15			.957	-6	*O-111	-0.7
1920	*Cle-A	129	456	82	144	37	10	12	103	53	35	.316	.391	.520	135	22	5	4	-1	.970	-8	*O-129	0.5
1921	Cle-A	129	431	98	125	28	9	16	85	56	46	.290	.374	.508	121	13	2	1	-1	.971	-8	*O-127	-0.4
1922	Bos-N	73	231	43	66	13	6	6	32	25	21	.286	.358	.472	116	5	0	3	-2	.947	2	O-58	0.1
	*NY-A	21	27	1	5	0	0	1	5	3	5	.185	.267	.296	46	-2	0	0	-0	.933	-2	O-11	-0.3
	Yr	94	258	44	71	13	6	7	37	28	26	.275	.348	.453	108	3	0	3	-2	.945	1	O-69	-0.3
1923	NY-A	70	183	30	56	6	2	5	35	21	21	.306	.377	.475	121	5	3	1	0	.948	-2	O-47	-1.0
1925	Cin-N	96	284	47	77	13	7	8	46	28	20	.271	.339	.451	102	0	6	5	-1	.967	-5	O-80	-1.0
Total	10	1012	3195	469	881	181	62	70	541	319	359	.276	.344	.437	112	44	54	27		.957	-29	O-870	-4.5

■ MIKE SMITH   Smith, Elwood Hope b: 11/16/04, Norfolk, Va.   d: 5/31/81, Chesapeake, Va. BL/TR, 5′11.5″, 170 lbs. Deb: 9/4/26

YEAR	TM/L	G	AB	R	H	2B	3B	HR	RBI	BB	SO	AVG	OBP	SLG	PRO+	BR/A	SB	CS	SBR	FA	FR	G/POS	TPR
1926	NY-N	4	7	0	1	0	0	0	0	0	2	.143	.143	.143	-23	-1	0			1.000	0	/O-1	-0.1

■ CARR SMITH   Smith, Emanuel Carr b: 4/8/01, Kernersville, N.C.   d: 4/14/89, Miami, Fla. BR/TR, 6′1″, 175 lbs. Deb: 9/23/23

YEAR	TM/L	G	AB	R	H	2B	3B	HR	RBI	BB	SO	AVG	OBP	SLG	PRO+	BR/A	SB	CS	SBR	FA	FR	G/POS	TPR
1923	Was-A	5	9	0	1	0	0	0	0	0	0	.111	.111	.222	-14	-2	0	0	0	1.000	-1	/O-4	-0.3
1924	Was-A	5	10	1	2	1	0	0	1	0	3	.200	.200	.200	3	-1	0	0	0	1.000	-1	/O-4	-0.3
Total	2	10	19	1	3	1	0	0	1	0	3	.158	.158	.211	-5	-3	0	0	0	1.000	-3	/O-8	-0.6

■ ERNIE SMITH   Smith, Ernest Henry "Kansas City Kid" b: 10/11/1899, Totowa, N.J.   d: 4/6/73, Brooklyn, N.Y. BR/TR, 5′8″, 155 lbs. Deb: 4/17/30

YEAR	TM/L	G	AB	R	H	2B	3B	HR	RBI	BB	SO	AVG	OBP	SLG	PRO+	BR/A	SB	CS	SBR	FA	FR	G/POS	TPR
1930	Chi-A	24	79	5	19	3	0	0	3	5	6	.241	.286	.278	45	-7	2	0	1	.920	0	S-21	-0.3

YEAR	TM/L	G	AB	R	H	2B	3B	HR	RBI	BB	SO	AVG	OBP	SLG	PRO+	BR/A	SB	CS	SBR	FA	FR	G/POS	TPR

■ FRANK SMITH   Smith, Frank L. b: 11/24/1857, Canada d: 10/11/28, Canandaigua, N.Y.   Deb: 8/6/1884

| 1884 | Pit-a | 10 | 36 | 3 | 9 | 0 | 1 | 0 | | 0 | | .250 | .250 | .306 | 79 | -1 | | | | .930 | -3 | /C-7,O-3 | -0.3 |

■ FRED SMITH   Smith, Fred Vincent b: 7/29/1886, Cleveland, Ohio d: 5/28/61, Cleveland, Ohio   BR/TR, 5'11.5", 185 lbs.   Deb: 4/17/13   F

1913	Bos-N	92	285	35	65	9	3	0	27	29	55	.228	.302	.281	65	-12	7			.920	-14	3-59,2-14,S-11,/O-4	-2.7
1914	Buf-F	145	473	48	104	12	10	2	45	49	78	.220	.297	.300	62	-33	24			.930	-0	*3-127,S-19/1-1	-2.8
1915	Buf-F	35	114	8	27	2	4	0	11	13	15	.237	.320	.325	80	-5	2			.920	3	S-32/3-1	0.1
	Bro-F	110	385	41	95	16	6	5	58	25	49	.247	.298	.358	85	-15	21			.920	1	S-94,3-15	-0.6
	Yr	145	499	49	122	18	10	5	69	38	64	.244	.303	.351	84	-19	23			.920	5	*S-126,3-16	-0.5
1917	StL-N	56	165	11	30	0	2	1	17	17	22	.182	.262	.224	51	-9	4			.950	7	3-51/2-2,S-1	-0.2
Total	4	438	1422	143	321	39	25	8	158	133	219	.226	.299	.305	69	-73	58			.932	-3	3-253,S-157/201	-6.2

■ GEORGE SMITH   Smith, George Cornelius b: 7/7/37, St.Petersburg, Fla. d: 6/15/87, St.Petersburg, Fla.   BR/TR, 5'10", 170 lbs.   Deb: 8/4/63

1963	Det-A	52	171	16	37	8	2	0	17	18	34	.216	.298	.287	63	-8	4	0	1	.982	11	2-52	0.9
1964	Det-A	5	7	1	2	0	0	0	0	1	1	.286	.375	.286	86	-0	0	0		1.000	1	/2-3	0.1
1965	Det-A	32	53	6	5	0	0	1	3	3	18	.094	.143	.151	-16	-8	0	0	0	.984	1	2-22/S-3,3-3	-0.5
1966	Bos-A	128	403	41	86	19	4	8	37	37	86	.213	.284	.340	71	-15	4	0	1	.969	16	*2-109,S-19	1.1
Total	4	217	634	64	130	27	6	9	57	59	142	.205	.278	.309	62	-31	9	0	3	.974	30	2-186/S-22,3-3	1.6

■ HEINIE SMITH   Smith, George Henry b: 10/24/1871, Pittsburgh, Pa. d: 6/25/39, Buffalo, N.Y.   BR/TR, 5'9.5", 160 lbs.   Deb: 9/8/1897   M

1897	Lou-N	21	76	7	20	3	0	1	7	3		.263	.300	.342	72	-3	1			.928	-3	2-21	-0.4
1898	Lou-N	35	121	14	23	4	0	0	13	6		.190	.246	.223	35	-10	6			.910	-6	2-33	-1.3
1899	Pit-N	15	53	9	15	3	1	0	12	5		.283	.345	.377	98	-0	2			.851	3	2-15/S-1	-0.2
1901	NY-N	9	29	5	6	2	1	1	4	1		.207	.233	.448	99	-0	1			.969	-1	/2-7,P-2	-0.1
1902	NY-N	138	511	46	129	19	2	0	33	17		.252	.278	.297	78	-14	32			.953	4	*2-138,M	-0.6
1903	Det-A	93	336	36	75	11	3	1	22	19		.223	.271	.283	68	-13	12			.928	-2	2-93	-1.2
Total	6	311	1126	117	268	42	7	3	91	51		.238	.276	.296	71	-41	54			.934	-11	2-307/P-2,S-1	-3.8

■ GERMANY SMITH   Smith, George J. b: 4/21/1863, Pittsburgh, Pa. d: 12/1/27, Altoona, Pa.   BR/TR, 6', 175 lbs.   Deb: 4/17/1884

1884	Alt-U	25	108	9	34	8	1	0		1		.315	.321	.407	118	-1				.871	6	S-25/P-1	0.5
	Cle-N	72	291	31	74	14	4	4	26	2	45	.254	.259	.371	93	-3				.879	9	2-42,S-30	0.7
1885	Bro-a	108	419	63	108	17	11	4	62	10		.258	.275	.379	105	1				.884	**40**	*S-108	3.7
1886	Bro-a	105	426	66	105	17	6	2	45	19		.246	.279	.329	89	-7	22			.860	13	*S-105/O-1,C-1	0.6
1887	Bro-a	103	435	79	128	19	16	4	72	13		.294	.316	.439	108	2	26			**.886**	**32**	*S-101/3-2	2.8
1888	Bro-a	103	402	47	86	10	7	3	61	22		.214	.255	.296	76	-11	27			.844	6	*S-103/2-1	-0.3
1889	*Bro-a	121	446	89	103	23	5	3	53	40	42	.231	.296	.314	73	-16	35			.899	-4	*S-120/O-1	-1.1
1890	*Bro-N	129	481	76	92	6	5	4	47	42	23	.191	.260	.231	43	-35	24			.904	4	*S-129	-2.1
1891	Cin-N	138	512	50	103	11	5	3	53	38	32	.201	.258	.260	50	-33	16			.909	11	*S-138	-1.2
1892	Cin-N	139	506	58	121	13	8	6	83	42	52	.239	.297	.336	93	-6	19			.920	25	*S-139	2.3
1893	Cin-N	130	500	63	118	18	4	4	56	38	20	.236	.293	.320	61	-30	14			**.934**	20	*S-130	-0.4
1894	Cin-N	127	482	73	127	33	5	3	76	41	28	.263	.324	.371	65	-30	15			.911	20	*S-127	-0.3
1895	Cin-N	127	503	75	151	23	6	4	74	34	24	.300	.345	.394	87	-12	13			.923	2	*S-127	-1.6
1896	Cin-N	120	456	65	131	21	9	3	71	28	22	.287	.330	.393	84	-13	22			.926	-10	*S-120	-1.6
1897	Bro-N	112	428	47	86	17	3	0	29	14		.201	.233	.255	30	-44	1			.908	-11	*S-112	-4.6
1898	StL-N	51	157	16	25	2	1	0	9	24		.159	.275	.204	37	-12	1			.904	-5	S-51	-1.5
Total	15	1710	6552	907	1592	251	94	47	797	408	288	.243	.289	.332	74	-249	235			.902	157	*S-1665/2-43,3OCP	-2.8

■ JUD SMITH   Smith, Grant Judson b: 1/13/1869, Green Oak, Mich. d: 12/7/47, Los Angeles, Cal.   BR/TR,   Deb: 5/21/1893

1893	Cin-N	17	43	7	10	1	0	1	5	9	5	.233	.365	.326	82	-1	1			.750	-2	/O-9,3-6,S-1	-0.3
	StL-N	4	13	1	1	0	0	0	0	1	2	.077	.200	.077	-25	-2	0			.889	1	/3-4	-0.1
	Yr	21	56	8	11	1	0	1	5	10	7	.196	.328	.268	58	-3	1			.844	-1	3-10/O-9,S-1	-0.4
1896	Pit-N	10	35	6	12	2	1	0	4	2	2	.343	.395	.457	129	1	3			.909	2	3-10	0.3
1898	Was-N	66	234	33	71	7	5	3	28	22		.303	.378	.415	127	8	11			.903	-10	3-47,S-10/1-7,2-1	0.0
1901	Pit-N	6	21	1	3	1	0	0	3			.143	.250	.190	28	-2	0			.947	0	/3-6	-0.2
Total	4	103	346	48	97	11	6	4	37	37	9	.280	.363	.382	109	5	15			.900	-9	/3-73,S-11,O-9,12	-0.3

■ GREG SMITH   Smith, Gregory Alan b: 4/5/67, Baltimore, Md.   BB/TR, 5'11", 170 lbs.   Deb: 9/2/89

1989	Chi-N	4	5	1	2	1	0	0	1	0	1	.400	.500	.400	149	0	0	0	0	.778	0	/2-2	0.1
1990	Chi-N	18	44	4	9	2	1	0	5	2	5	.205	.239	.295	43	-3	1	0	0	1.000	4	/2-7,S-7	0.1
1991	LA-N	5	3	1	0	0	0	0	0	0	2	.000	.000	.000	-99	-1	0	0	0	.944	0	/2-1	0.0
Total	3	27	52	6	11	2	1	0	7	2	7	.212	.255	.288	47	-4	1	0	0	.944	4	/2-10,S-7	0.1

■ HAL SMITH   Smith, Harold Raymond "Cura" b: 6/1/31, Barling, Ark.   BR/TR, 5'11", 189 lbs.   Deb: 5/2/56   C

1956	StL-N	75	227	27	64	12	0	4	23	15	22	.282	.326	.401	94	-2	1	0	0	.982	-2	C-66	-0.1
1957	StL-N☆	100	333	25	93	12	3	2	37	18	18	.279	.316	.351	78	-10	2	2	-1	.990	-1	C-97	-0.8
1958	StL-N	77	220	13	50	4	1	1	24	14	14	.227	.274	.268	42	-18	0	0	0	.989	-1	C-71	-1.6
1959	StL-N★	142	452	50	122	15	3	13	50	15	28	.270	.295	.403	78	-14	2	6	-3	.989	5	*C-141	-0.6
1960	StL-N	127	337	20	77	16	0	2	28	29	33	.228	.292	.294	56	-20	1	0	0	.990	18	*C-124	0.5
1961	StL-N	45	125	6	31	6	1	0	10	11	12	.248	.314	.296	57	-7	0	0	0	.993	17	C-45	1.2
1965	Pit-N	4	3	0	0	0	0	0	0	0	1	.000	.000	.000	-99	-1	0	0	0	1.000	2	/C-4	0.1
Total	7	570	1697	126	437	63	8	23	172	102	128	.258	.301	.345	69	-73	6	8	-3	.989	38	C-548	-1.3

■ HAL SMITH   Smith, Harold Wayne b: 12/7/30, W.Frankfort, Ill.   BR/TR, 6', 195 lbs.   Deb: 4/11/55

1955	Bal-A	135	424	41	115	23	4	4	52	30	21	.271	.322	.373	93	-6	1	3	-2	.986	-3	*C-125	-0.6
1956	Bal-A	77	229	16	60	14	0	3	18	17	22	.262	.316	.362	85	-6	1	0	0	.994	3	C-71	0.0
	KC-A	37	142	15	39	9	2	2	24	3	12	.275	.290	.408	82	-4	1	1	-0	.986	1	C-37	-0.2
	Yr	114	371	31	99	23	2	5	42	20	34	.267	.306	.380	85	-10	2	1	-0	.991	5	*C-108	-0.2
1957	KC-A	107	360	41	109	26	6	13	41	14	44	.303	.331	.483	118	7	2	2	-1	.983	-1	*C-103	0.9
1958	KC-A	99	315	32	86	19	2	5	46	25	47	.273	.330	.394	97	-2	0	0	0	.949	-1	3-43,C-31,1-14	-0.1
1959	KC-A	108	292	36	84	12	0	5	31	34	39	.288	.368	.380	104	3	0	3	-2	.953	7	3-77,C-22	0.9
1960	*Pit-N	77	258	37	76	18	5	11	45	22	48	.295	.355	.508	132	11	1	1	-0	.985	-6	C-71	0.9
1961	Pit-N	67	193	12	43	10	3	2	26	11	38	.223	.268	.321	55	-13	0	0	0	.990	-1	C-65	-1.0
1962	Hou-N	109	345	32	81	14	0	12	35	24	55	.235	.288	.380	84	-9	0	0	0	.986	2	C-92/3-6,1-2	-0.4
1963	Hou-N	31	58	1	14	2	0	0	2	4	15	.241	.290	.276	68	-2	0	0	0	.985	-3	C-11	-0.5
1964	Cin-N	32	66	6	8	1	0	0	3	2	21	.121	.206	.136	14	-7	1	0	0	.983	-1	C-20	-1.0
Total	10	879	2682	269	715	148	10	58	323	196	361	.267	.320	.394	94	-29	7	10	-4	.986	-3	C-648,3-126/1-16	-1.1

■ HARRY SMITH   Smith, Harry Thomas b: 10/31/1874, Yorkshire, England d: 2/17/33, Salem, N.J.   BR/TR,   Deb: 7/11/01   M

1901	Phi-A	11	34	3	11	1	0	0	0	3		.324	.378	.353	99	0	1			.969	-3	/C-9,O-1	-0.2
1902	Pit-N	50	185	14	35	4	0	0	12	4		.189	.211	.222	32	-15	4			.972	-2	C-50	-1.2
1903	*Pit-N	61	212	15	37	3	2	0	19	12		.175	.222	.208	22	-22	2			.974	-4	C-60/O-1	-1.9
1904	Pit-N	47	141	17	35	3	1	0	18	16		.248	.346	.284	92	-0	5			.964	-4	C-44/O-3	0.1
1905	Pit-N	1	3	0	0	0	0	0	0	1		.000	.000	.000	-98	-1	1			1.000	0	/C-1	-0.1
1906	Pit-N	1	1	0	0	0	0	0	0	0		.000	.000	.000	-96	-1	0			.800	1	/C-1	-0.1
1907	Pit-N	18	38	4	10	1	0	0	1	4		.263	.364	.289	103	0	0			.939	-3	C-18	-0.1
1908	Bos-N	41	130	13	32	2	2	1	16	7		.246	.295	.315	96	-1	2			.975	0	C-38	0.3
1909	Bos-N	43	113	9	19	4	0	1	7	6		.168	.203	.221	30	-9	3			.972	2	C-31,M	-0.5
1910	Bos-N	70	147	8	35	4	0	1	15	5	14	.238	.263	.286	57	-8	5			.949	3	C-38	-0.2
Total	10	343	1004	83	214	22	7	2	89	55	14	.213	.262	.255	54	-56	23			.967	-9	C-290/O-5	-3.8

YEAR	TM/L	G	AB	R	H	2B	3B	HR	RBI	BB	SO	AVG	OBP	SLG	PRO+	BR/A	SB	CS	SBR	FA	FR	G/POS	TPR

■ HARRY SMITH Smith, Harry W. b: 2/5/1856, N.Vernon, Ind. d: 6/4/1898, Queensville, Ind. BR/TR, 6', 175 lbs. Deb: 5/8/1877

YEAR	TM/L	G	AB	R	H	2B	3B	HR	RBI	BB	SO	AVG	OBP	SLG	PRO+	BR/A	SB	CS	SBR	FA	FR	G/POS	TPR
1877	Chi-N	24	94	7	19	1	0	0	3	4	6	.202	.235	.213	37	-7				.853	-7	2-14,O-10	-1.3
	Cin-N	10	36	4	9	2	1	0	3	1	5	.250	.270	.361	109	0				.879	1	/C-8,2-3,O-3	0.1
	Yr	34	130	11	28	3	1	0	6	5	11	.215	.244	.254	54	-7				.837	-7	2-17,O-13/C-8	-1.2
1889	Lou-a	1	2	0	1	0	0	0	1	0	1	.500	.500	.500	189	0	0			.000	-2	/O-1,C-1	-0.1
Total	2	35	132	11	29	3	1	0	7	5	12	.220	.248	.258	56	-6	0			.720	-8	/2-17,O-14,C-9	-1.3

■ HARVEY SMITH Smith, Harvey Fetterhoff b: 7/24/1871, Union Deposit, Pa d: 11/12/62, Harrisburg, Pa. BL/TR, 5'8", 160 lbs. Deb: 8/19/1896

YEAR	TM/L	G	AB	R	H	2B	3B	HR	RBI	BB	SO	AVG	OBP	SLG	PRO+	BR/A	SB	CS	SBR	FA	FR	G/POS	TPR
1896	Was-N	36	131	21	36	7	2	0	17	12	7	.275	.345	.359	86	-3	9			.861	3	3-36	0.1

■ HAPPY SMITH Smith, Henry Joseph b: 7/14/1883, Coquille, Ore. d: 2/26/61, San Jose, Cal. BL/TR, 6', 185 lbs. Deb: 4/15/10

YEAR	TM/L	G	AB	R	H	2B	3B	HR	RBI	BB	SO	AVG	OBP	SLG	PRO+	BR/A	SB	CS	SBR	FA	FR	G/POS	TPR
1910	Bro-N	35	76	6	18	2	0	0	5	4	14	.237	.275	.263	59	-4	4			.974	2	O-16	-0.3

■ JACK SMITH Smith, Jack b: 6/23/1895, Chicago, Ill. d: 5/2/72, Westchester, Ill. BL/TL, 5'8", 165 lbs. Deb: 9/30/15

YEAR	TM/L	G	AB	R	H	2B	3B	HR	RBI	BB	SO	AVG	OBP	SLG	PRO+	BR/A	SB	CS	SBR	FA	FR	G/POS	TPR
1915	StL-N	4	16	2	3	0	0	0	0	1	5	.188	.235	.313	65	-1	0			1.000	-1	/O-4	-0.2
1916	StL-N	130	357	43	87	6	5	6	34	20	50	.244	.291	.339	94	-3	24	16	-2	.949	-11	*O-120	-2.5
1917	StL-N	137	462	64	137	16	11	3	34	38	65	.297	.351	.398	133	18	25			.961	-10	*O-128	0.2
1918	StL-N	42	166	24	35	2	1	0	4	7	21	.211	.260	.235	53	-9	5			.941	1	O-42	-1.3
1919	StL-N	119	408	47	91	16	3	0	15	26	29	.223	.271	.277	69	-16	30			.960	-0	*O-111	-2.6
1920	StL-N	91	313	53	104	22	5	1	28	25	23	.332	.385	.444	143	17	14	9	-1	.963	-10	O-83	0.1
1921	StL-N	116	411	86	135	22	9	7	33	21	24	.328	.361	.477	122	12	11	6	-0	.955	-6	*O-103	-0.2
1922	StL-N	143	510	117	158	23	12	8	46	50	30	.310	.375	.449	117	13	18	7	1	.951	-8	*O-136	-0.3
1923	StL-N	124	407	98	126	16	6	5	41	27	20	.310	.356	.415	105	3	32	11	3	.974	4	O-109	0.3
1924	StL-N	124	459	91	130	18	6	2	33	33	27	.283	.333	.362	88	-8	24	16	-2	.968	10	*O-114	-0.8
1925	StL-N	80	243	53	61	11	4	0	31	19	13	.251	.308	.379	73	-10	20	2	5	.958	-3	O-64	-1.2
1926	StL-N	1	1	0	0	0	0	0	0	0	1	.000	.000	.000	-96	-0	0			.000	0	H	0.0
	Bos-N	96	322	46	100	15	2	1	25	28	12	.311	.369	.388	114	7	11			.973	2	O-83	0.3
	Yr	97	323	46	100	15	2	1	25	28	13	.310	.368	.387	113	6	11			.973	2	O-83	0.3
1927	Bos-N	84	183	27	58	6	4	1	24	16	12	.317	.375	.410	119	5	8			.950	-0	O-48	-1.0
1928	Bos-N	96	254	30	71	9	2	1	32	21	14	.280	.335	.343	82	-7	6			.988	1	O-65	-1.0
1929	Bos-N	19	20	2	5	0	0	0	2	2	2	.250	.318	.250	45	-2	0			.833	-3	/O-9	-0.5
Total	15	1406	4532	783	1301	182	71	40	382	334	348	.287	.339	.385	103	18	228	67		.961	-36	*O-1219	-9.5

■ STUB SMITH Smith, James A. b: 11/26/1876, Elmwood, Ill. BL/TR, 5'6", 145 lbs. Deb: 9/10/1898

YEAR	TM/L	G	AB	R	H	2B	3B	HR	RBI	BB	SO	AVG	OBP	SLG	PRO+	BR/A	SB	CS	SBR	FA	FR	G/POS	TPR
1898	Bos-N	3	10	1	1	0	0	0	0	0	0	.100	.100	.100	-41	-2	0			.933	1	/S-3	-0.1

■ RED SMITH Smith, James Carlisle b: 4/6/1890, Greenville, S.C. d: 10/11/66, Atlanta, Ga. BR/TR, 5'11", 165 lbs. Deb: 9/5/11

YEAR	TM/L	G	AB	R	H	2B	3B	HR	RBI	BB	SO	AVG	OBP	SLG	PRO+	BR/A	SB	CS	SBR	FA	FR	G/POS	TPR
1911	Bro-N	28	111	10	29	6	1	0	19	5	13	.261	.299	.333	80	-3	5			.900	-2	3-28	-0.5
1912	Bro-N	128	486	75	139	28	6	4	57	54	51	.286	.362	.393	111	8	22			.938	5	*3-125	1.3
1913	Bro-N	151	540	70	160	**40**	10	6	76	45	67	.296	.358	.441	124	16	22			.933	-1	*3-151	1.7
1914	Bro-N	90	330	39	81	10	8	4	48	30	26	.245	.310	.361	97	-2	11			.937	12	3-90	1.4
	Bos-N	60	207	30	65	17	1	3	37	28	24	.314	.401	.449	153	14	4			.937	10	3-60	2.8
	Yr	150	537	69	146	27	9	7	85	58	50	.272	.346	.395	119	12	15			.937	23	*3-150	4.2
1915	Bos-N	157	549	66	145	34	4	5	65	67	49	.264	.345	.352	116	12	10	5	0	.947	-6	*3-157	1.4
1916	Bos-N	150	509	48	132	16	10	3	60	53	55	.259	.333	.348	114	9	13			.928	-4	*3-150	1.1
1917	Bos-N	147	505	60	149	31	6	2	62	53	61	.295	.369	.392	142	26	16			.925	-21	*3-147	0.9
1918	Bos-N	119	429	55	128	20	3	2	65	45	47	.298	.373	.373	133	18	8			.922	4	*3-119	2.7
1919	Bos-N	87	241	24	59	6	0	1	25	40	22	.245	.359	.282	98	-2	6			.981	-0	O-48,3-23	-0.0
Total	9	1117	3907	477	1087	208	49	27	514	420	415	.278	.353	.377	120	100	117	5		.932	-2	*3-1050/O-48	12.8

■ HARRY SMITH Smith, James Harry b: 5/15/1890, Baltimore, Md. d: 4/1/22, Charlotte, N.C. BR/TR, 5'10", 180 lbs. Deb: 9/21/14

YEAR	TM/L	G	AB	R	H	2B	3B	HR	RBI	BB	SO	AVG	OBP	SLG	PRO+	BR/A	SB	CS	SBR	FA	FR	G/POS	TPR
1914	NY-N	5	7	0	3	0	0	0	2	3	1	.429	.600	.429	215	1	1			1.000	2	/C-4	0.3
1915	NY-N	21	32	1	4	0	1	0	3	6	12	.125	.263	.188	40	-2	0	1	-1	.967	-3	C-18	-0.5
	Bro-F	28	65	5	13	0	0	1	4	7	16	.200	.278	.246	48	-5	2			.967	-5	C-19/O-1	-1.0
1917	Cin-N	8	17	0	2	0	0	0	1	2	7	.118	.211	.118	2	-2	0			.978	4	/C-7	0.3
1918	Cin-N	13	27	4	5	1	2	0	4	3	6	.185	.267	.370	95	-0	1			1.000	-0	/C-6,O-1	-0.2
Total	4	75	148	10	27	1	3	1	14	21	42	.182	.284	.250	59	-8	4	1		.975	-4	/C-54,O-2	-1.1

■ JIMMY SMITH Smith, James Lawrence "Greenfield Jimmy" b: 5/15/1895, Pittsburgh, Pa. d: 1/1/74, Pittsburgh, Pa. BB/TR, 5'9", 152 lbs. Deb: 9/26/14

YEAR	TM/L	G	AB	R	H	2B	3B	HR	RBI	BB	SO	AVG	OBP	SLG	PRO+	BR/A	SB	CS	SBR	FA	FR	G/POS	TPR
1914	Chi-F	3	6	1	3	1	0	0	0	0	0	.500	.500	.667	229	1	0			1.000	1	/S-3	0.2
1915	Chi-F	95	318	32	69	11	4	4	30	14	65	.217	.250	.314	62	-23	4			.904	-14	S-92/2-1	-3.3
	Bal-F	33	108	9	19	1	1	1	11	11	23	.176	.258	.231	37	-11	3			.883	-4	S-33	-1.3
	Yr	128	426	41	88	12	5	5	41	25	88	.207	.252	.293	55	-34	7			.898	-18	*S-125/2-1	-4.6
1916	Pit-N	36	96	4	18	1	1	0	5	6	22	.188	.257	.219	46	-6	0			.929	1	S-27/3-6	-0.4
1917	NY-N	36	96	12	22	5	1	0	9	9	18	.229	.295	.302	86	-2	6			.971	-2	2-29/S-7	-0.3
1918	Bos-N	34	102	8	23	3	4	1	14	3	13	.225	.255	.363	91	-2	1			1.000	-1	2-10/S-9,O-6,3-5	-0.2
1919	*Cin-N	28	40	9	11	1	3	1	10	4	8	.275	.341	.525	163	3	1			1.000	-2	/3-6,S-5,2-4,O-4	0.2
1921	Phi-N	67	247	31	57	8	1	4	22	11	28	.231	.266	.320	50	-18	2	8	-4	.971	8	2-66	-1.3
1922	Phi-N	38	114	13	25	1	0	1	6	5	9	.219	.258	.254	30	-12	1	3	-2	.952	-3	S-23,2-13/3-1	-1.4
Total	8	370	1127	119	247	32	15	12	108	63	186	.219	.265	.306	60	-69	18	11		.910	-16	S-199,2-123/3-18,O	-7.8

■ JIM SMITH Smith, James Lorne b: 9/8/54, Santa Monica, Cal. BR/TR, 6'3", 185 lbs. Deb: 4/12/82

YEAR	TM/L	G	AB	R	H	2B	3B	HR	RBI	BB	SO	AVG	OBP	SLG	PRO+	BR/A	SB	CS	SBR	FA	FR	G/POS	TPR
1982	Pit-N	42	42	5	10	2	1	0	4	5	7	.238	.319	.333	80	-1	0	1	-1	.929	8	S-29/2-3,3-1	0.8

■ JOHN SMITH Smith, John b: Baltimore, Md. Deb: 4/14/1873

YEAR	TM/L	G	AB	R	H	2B	3B	HR	RBI	BB	SO	AVG	OBP	SLG	PRO+	BR/A	SB	CS	SBR	FA	FR	G/POS	TPR
1873	Mar-n	5	19	2	2	0	0	0	1	0	1	.105	.105	.105	-49	-3	0	0	0	.773	-2	/S-3,O-2	-0.3
1874	Bal-n	6	21	1	4	1	0	0	1	0	1	.190	.190	.238	37	-1	0	0	0	.731	-10	/S-6	-1.0
1875	NH-n	1	3	0	0	0	0	0	0	1	0	.000	.250	.000	-6	-0	0	0	0	.500	-1	/S-1	-0.1
Total	3 n	12	43	3	6	1	0	0	2	1	2	.140	.159	.163	1	-5	0	0	0	.722	-12	/S-10,O-2	-1.4

■ DWIGHT SMITH Smith, John Dwight b: 11/8/63, Tallahassee, Fla. BL/TR, 5'11", 175 lbs. Deb: 5/1/89

YEAR	TM/L	G	AB	R	H	2B	3B	HR	RBI	BB	SO	AVG	OBP	SLG	PRO+	BR/A	SB	CS	SBR	FA	FR	G/POS	TPR
1989	*Chi-N	109	343	52	111	19	6	9	52	31	51	.324	.383	.493	138	17	9	4	0	.975	1	*O-102	1.7
1990	Chi-N	117	290	34	76	15	6	6	27	28	46	.262	.331	.376	88	-5	11	6	-0	.986	-4	O-81	-1.1
1991	Chi-N	90	167	16	38	7	2	3	21	11	32	.228	.279	.347	72	-6	3	3	-1	.962	-3	O-42	-1.1
1992	Chi-N	109	217	28	60	10	3	3	24	13	40	.276	.320	.392	98	-1	9	8	-2	.979	-10	O-63	-1.5
1993	Chi-N	111	310	51	93	17	5	11	35	25	51	.300	.358	.494	127	11	8	6	-1	.955	-8	O-89	0.1
1994	Cal-A	45	122	19	32	5	1	5	18	7	20	.262	.302	.443	88	-3	2	3	-1	.912	-2	O-31/D-2	-0.6
	Bal-A	28	74	12	23	2	1	3	12	5	17	.311	.363	.446	111	1	0	1	-1	.939	-4	O-22/D-3	-0.4
	Yr	73	196	31	55	7	2	8	30	12	37	.281	.325	.459	97	-1	2	4	-2	.922	-6	O-53/D-5	-1.0
1995	*Atl-N	103	131	16	33	8	2	3	21	13	35	.252	.329	.412	91	-2	0	3	-2	.923	-4	O-25	-0.8
1996	Atl-N	101	153	16	31	5	0	3	16	17	42	.203	.287	.294	51	-11	1	3	-2	.962	-0	O-29	-1.3
Total	8	813	1807	244	497	88	20	46	226	150	334	.275	.335	.422	101	2	42	37	-10	.964	-34	O-484/D-5	-5.0

■ JOHN SMITH Smith, John J. b: 1858, New York, N.Y. 5'11", 210 lbs. Deb: 5/1/1882

YEAR	TM/L	G	AB	R	H	2B	3B	HR	RBI	BB	SO	AVG	OBP	SLG	PRO+	BR/A	SB	CS	SBR	FA	FR	G/POS	TPR
1882	Tro-N	35	149	27	36	4	3	0	14	3	24	.242	.257	.309	84	-2				.960	-0	1-35	-0.6
	Wor-N	19	70	10	17	3	2	0	5	1	10	.243	.293	.343	101	0				.939	1	1-19	-0.1
	Yr	54	219	37	53	7	5	0	19	4	34	.242	.269	.320	90	-2				.952	1	1-54	-0.7

■ JACK SMITH Smith, John Joseph (b: John Joseph Coffey) b: 8/8/1893, Oswayo, Pa. d: 12/4/62, New York, N.Y. BR/TR, 5'9", Deb: 5/18/12

YEAR	TM/L	G	AB	R	H	2B	3B	HR	RBI	BB	SO	AVG	OBP	SLG	PRO+	BR/A	SB	CS	SBR	FA	FR	G/POS	TPR
1912	Det-A	1	0	0	0	0	0	0	0	0	0	—	—	—	—	0				1.000	1	/3-1	0.1

YEAR	TM/L	G	AB	R	H	2B	3B	HR	RBI	BB	SO	AVG	OBP	SLG	PRO+	BR/A	SB	CS	SBR	FA	FR	G/POS	TPR

■ JOHN SMITH
Smith, John Marshall   b: 9/27/06, Washington, D.C.   d: 5/9/82, Silver Spring, Md.   BB/TR, 6'1", 180 lbs.   Deb: 9/17/31

YEAR	TM/L	G	AB	R	H	2B	3B	HR	RBI	BB	SO	AVG	OBP	SLG	PRO+	BR/A	SB	CS	SBR	FA	FR	G/POS	TPR
1931	Bos-A	4	15	2	2	0	0	0	1	2	1	.133	.235	.133	-1	-2	1	0	0	1.000	-1	/1-4	-0.3

■ KEITH SMITH
Smith, Keith Lavarne   b: 5/3/53, Palmetto, Fla.   BR/TR, 5'9", 178 lbs.   Deb: 8/2/77

YEAR	TM/L	G	AB	R	H	2B	3B	HR	RBI	BB	SO	AVG	OBP	SLG	PRO+	BR/A	SB	CS	SBR	FA	FR	G/POS	TPR
1977	Tex-A	23	67	13	16	4	0	2	6	4	7	.239	.301	.388	85	-1	2	0	1	.975	-1	O-22	-0.2
1979	StL-N	6	13	1	3	0	0	0	0	0	1	.231	.231	.231	26	-1	0	1	-1	1.000	2	/O-5	-0.2
1980	StL-N	24	31	3	4	1	0	0	2	2	2	.129	.182	.161	-3	-4	0	0	0	1.000	-1	/O-7	-0.6
Total	3	53	111	17	23	5	0	2	8	6	10	.207	.261	.306	54	-7	2	1	0	.985	0	/O-34	-0.8

■ KEN SMITH
Smith, Kenneth Earl   b: 2/12/58, Youngstown, Ohio   BL/TR, 6'1", 195 lbs.   Deb: 9/22/81

YEAR	TM/L	G	AB	R	H	2B	3B	HR	RBI	BB	SO	AVG	OBP	SLG	PRO+	BR/A	SB	CS	SBR	FA	FR	G/POS	TPR
1981	Atl-N	5	3	0	1	1	0	0	0	1	1	.333	.333	.667	174	0	0	0	0	1.000	0	/1-4	0.1
1982	Atl-N	48	41	6	12	1	0	0	3	6	13	.293	.383	.317	94	-0	0	0	0	1.000	-1	/1-6,O-3	-0.2
1983	Atl-N	30	12	2	2	0	0	1	2	1	5	.167	.231	.417	71	-1	1	0	0	1.000	2	1-13	0.2
Total	3	83	56	8	15	2	0	1	5	7	19	.268	.349	.357	93	-0	1	0	1	1.000	1	/1-23,O-3	0.1

■ L. SMITH
Smith, L.   Deb: 9/7/1882

YEAR	TM/L	G	AB	R	H	2B	3B	HR	RBI	BB	SO	AVG	OBP	SLG	PRO+	BR/A	SB	CS	SBR	FA	FR	G/POS	TPR
1882	Bal-a	1	3	0	0	0	0	0		0		.000	.000	.000	-99	-1				1.000	-0	/O-1	-0.1

■ PADDY SMITH
Smith, Lawrence Patrick   b: 5/16/1894, Pelham, N.Y.   d: 12/2/90, New Rochelle, N.Y.   BL/TR, 6', 195 lbs.   Deb: 7/6/20

YEAR	TM/L	G	AB	R	H	2B	3B	HR	RBI	BB	SO	AVG	OBP	SLG	PRO+	BR/A	SB	CS	SBR	FA	FR	G/POS	TPR
1920	Bos-A	2	2	0	0	0	0	0	0	0	1	.000	.000	.000	-99	-1	0			.000	0	/C-1	-0.1

■ BULL SMITH
Smith, Lewis Oscar   b: 8/20/1880, Plum, W.Va.   d: 5/1/28, Charleston, W.Va.   BR/TR, 6', 180 lbs.   Deb: 8/30/04

YEAR	TM/L	G	AB	R	H	2B	3B	HR	RBI	BB	SO	AVG	OBP	SLG	PRO+	BR/A	SB	CS	SBR	FA	FR	G/POS	TPR
1904	Pit-N	13	42	2	6	0	1	0	0	1		.143	.163	.190	9	-5	0			.857	-0	O-13	-0.6
1906	Chi-N	1	1	0	0	0	0	0	0	0		.000	.000	.000	-95	-0	0			.000	0	H	0.0
1911	Was-A	1	0	0	0	0	0	0	0	0		—	—	—	—	0	0			.000	0	R	0.0
Total	3	15	43	2	6	0	1	0	0	1		.140	.159	.186	6	-5	0			.857	-0	/O-13	-0.6

■ LEO SMITH
Smith, Lionel H.   b: 5/13/1859, Brooklyn, N.Y.   d: 8/30/35, Brooklyn, N.Y.   5'6", 142 lbs.   Deb: 8/28/1890

YEAR	TM/L	G	AB	R	H	2B	3B	HR	RBI	BB	SO	AVG	OBP	SLG	PRO+	BR/A	SB	CS	SBR	FA	FR	G/POS	TPR
1890	Roc-a	35	112	11	21	1	3	0	11	14		.188	.283	.250	62	-5	1			.948	8	S-35	0.5

■ LONNIE SMITH
Smith, Lonnie   b: 12/22/55, Chicago, Ill.   BR/TR, 5'9", 170 lbs.   Deb: 9/2/78

YEAR	TM/L	G	AB	R	H	2B	3B	HR	RBI	BB	SO	AVG	OBP	SLG	PRO+	BR/A	SB	CS	SBR	FA	FR	G/POS	TPR
1978	Phi-N	17	4	6	0	0	0	0	0	4	3	.000	.500	.000	50	0	4	0	1	1.000	-3	O-11	-0.2
1979	Phi-N	17	30	4	5	2	0	0	0	3	1	.167	.194	.233	15	-4	2	1	0	1.000	-1	O-11	-0.5
1980	*Phi-N	100	298	69	101	14	4	3	20	26	48	.339	.399	.443	128	12	33	13	2	.969	-9	O-82	0.2
1981	*Phi-N	62	176	40	57	14	3	2	11	18	14	.324	.402	.472	141	10	21	10	0	.971	2	O-51	1.1
1982	*StL-N★	156	592	120	182	35	8	8	69	64	74	.307	.383	.434	127	23	68	26	5	.970	-1	*O-149	2.3
1983	StL-N	130	492	83	158	31	5	8	45	41	55	.321	.384	.453	131	21	43	18	2	.941	3	*O-126	2.3
1984	StL-N	145	504	77	126	20	4	6	49	70	90	.250	.352	.341	98	1	50	13	7	.948	-3	*O-140	0.1
1985	StL-N	28	96	15	25	2	2	0	7	15	20	.260	.377	.323	98	1	12	6	0	1.000	-1	O-28	-0.2
	*KC-A	120	448	77	115	23	4	6	41	41	69	.257	.325	.366	88	-7	40	7	8	.958	-3	*O-119	-0.6
1986	KC-A	134	508	80	146	25	7	8	44	46	78	.287	.358	.411	107	6	26	9	2	.965	4	*O-118,D-10	0.7
1987	KC-A	48	167	26	42	7	1	3	8	24	31	.251	.359	.359	89	-2	9	4	0	.915	-2	O-32,D-15	-0.4
1988	Atl-N	43	114	14	27	3	0	3	9	10	25	.237	.298	.342	79	-3	4	2	0	.968	-1	O-35	-0.6
1989	Atl-N	134	482	89	152	34	4	21	79	76	95	.315	.420	.533	166	44	25	12	0	.993	9	*O-132	5.2
1990	Atl-N	135	466	72	142	27	9	9	42	58	69	.305	.389	.459	125	17	10	10	-3	.956	5	*O-122	1.7
1991	*Atl-N	122	353	58	97	19	1	7	44	50	64	.275	.379	.394	111	7	9	5	-0	.965	-8	O-99	-0.3
1992	*Atl-N	84	158	23	39	8	2	6	33	17	37	.247	.331	.437	109	2	4	0	1	.954	0	O-35	0.3
1993	Pit-N	94	199	35	57	5	4	6	24	43	42	.286	.425	.442	133	12	9	4	0	.981	-4	O-60	0.7
	Bal-A	9	24	8	5	1	0	2	3	8	10	.208	.406	.500	136	1	0	0	0	1.000	0	/O-4,D-5	0.2
1994	Bal-A	35	59	13	12	3	0	2	11	18		.203	.338	.254	53	-4	1	0	0	1.000	0	D-30/O-2	-0.1
Total	17	1613	5170	909	1488	273	58	98	533	623	849	.288	.374	.420	117	138	370	140	27	.964	-12	*O-1356/D-60	11.5

■ MARK SMITH
Smith, Mark Edward   b: 5/7/70, Pasadena, Cal.   BR/TR, 6'3", 205 lbs.   Deb: 5/14/94

YEAR	TM/L	G	AB	R	H	2B	3B	HR	RBI	BB	SO	AVG	OBP	SLG	PRO+	BR/A	SB	CS	SBR	FA	FR	G/POS	TPR
1994	Bal-A	3	7	0	1	0	0	0	0	0	2	.143	.143	.143	-25	-1	0	0	0	1.000	0	/O-3	-0.1
1995	Bal-A	37	104	11	24	5	0	3	15	12	22	.231	.316	.365	76	-4	3	0	1	1.000	2	O-32/D-3	-0.2
1996	Bal-A	27	78	9	19	2	0	4	10	3	20	.244	.298	.423	80	-3	0	2	-1	.980	2	O-20/D-6	-0.2
Total	3	67	189	20	44	7	0	7	27	15	44	.233	.303	.381	74	-8	3	2	-0	.992	4	/O-55,D-9	-0.5

■ RED SMITH
Smith, Marvin Harold   b: 7/17/1900, Ashley, Ill.   d: 2/19/61, Los Angeles, Cal.   BL/TR, 5'7", 165 lbs.   Deb: 4/14/25

YEAR	TM/L	G	AB	R	H	2B	3B	HR	RBI	BB	SO	AVG	OBP	SLG	PRO+	BR/A	SB	CS	SBR	FA	FR	G/POS	TPR
1925	Phi-A	20	14	1	4	0	0	1	2	5		.286	.375	.286	65	-1	0	0	0	.864	1	S-16/3-2	0.1

■ MILT SMITH
Smith, Milton   b: 3/27/29, Columbus, Ga.   BR/TR, 5'10", 165 lbs.   Deb: 7/21/55

YEAR	TM/L	G	AB	R	H	2B	3B	HR	RBI	BB	SO	AVG	OBP	SLG	PRO+	BR/A	SB	CS	SBR	FA	FR	G/POS	TPR
1955	Cin-N	36	102	15	20	3	1	3	8	13	24	.196	.293	.333	62	-6	2	2	-1	.915	-2	3-28/2-5	-0.8

■ NATE SMITH
Smith, Nathaniel Beverly   b: 4/26/35, Chicago, Ill.   BR/TR, 5'11", 170 lbs.   Deb: 9/19/62

YEAR	TM/L	G	AB	R	H	2B	3B	HR	RBI	BB	SO	AVG	OBP	SLG	PRO+	BR/A	SB	CS	SBR	FA	FR	G/POS	TPR
1962	Bal-A	5	9	3	2	1	0	0	0	1	4	.222	.364	.333	95	0	0	0	0	1.000	1	/C-3	0.1

■ OLLIE SMITH
Smith, Oliver H.   b: 1868, Mt.Vernon, Ohio   BL/TL,   Deb: 7/11/1894

YEAR	TM/L	G	AB	R	H	2B	3B	HR	RBI	BB	SO	AVG	OBP	SLG	PRO+	BR/A	SB	CS	SBR	FA	FR	G/POS	TPR
1894	Lou-N	38	134	26	40	6	1	3	20	20		.299	.427	.425	114	5	13			.883	-2	O-38	0.0

■ OZZIE SMITH
Smith, Osborne Earl   b: 12/26/54, Mobile, Ala.   BB/TR, 5'11", 150 lbs.   Deb: 4/7/78

YEAR	TM/L	G	AB	R	H	2B	3B	HR	RBI	BB	SO	AVG	OBP	SLG	PRO+	BR/A	SB	CS	SBR	FA	FR	G/POS	TPR
1978	SD-N	159	590	69	152	17	6	1	46	47	43	.258	.312	.312	81	-15	40	12	5	.970	26	*S-159	3.6
1979	SD-N	156	587	77	124	18	6	0	27	37	37	.211	.260	.262	46	-45	28	7	4	.976	21	*S-155	-0.3
1980	SD-N	158	609	67	140	18	5	0	35	71	49	.230	.315	.276	70	-23	57	15	8	.974	41	*S-158	4.7
1981	SD-N★	110	450	53	100	11	2	0	21	41	37	.222	.294	.256	62	-22	22	12	-1	.976	26	*S-110	1.5
1982	*StL-N★	140	488	58	121	24	1	2	43	68	32	.248	.342	.314	84	-8	25	5	5	.984	33	*S-139	4.4
1983	StL-N★	159	552	69	134	30	6	3	50	64	36	.243	.323	.335	82	-12	34	7	6	.975	18	*S-158	2.7
1984	StL-N★	124	412	53	106	20	5	1	44	56	17	.257	.349	.337	96	-0	35	7	6	.982	26	*S-124	4.5
1985	*StL-N★	158	537	70	148	22	3	6	54	65	27	.276	.356	.361	102	3	31	8	5	.983	16	*S-158	4.0
1986	StL-N★	153	514	67	144	19	4	0	54	79	27	.280	.378	.333	99	3	31	7	5	.978	-9	*S-144	1.3
1987	*StL-N★	158	600	104	182	40	4	0	75	89	36	.303	.394	.383	105	8	43	9	8	.987	19	*S-158	4.7
1988	StL-N★	153	575	80	155	27	1	3	51	74	43	.270	.354	.336	98	1	57	9	12	.972	23	*S-150	5.1
1989	StL-N★	155	593	82	162	30	8	2	50	55	37	.273	.337	.361	96	-2	29	7	5	.976	9	*S-153	2.2
1990	StL-N★	143	512	61	130	21	1	1	50	61	33	.254	.336	.305	77	-14	32	6	6	.980	-13	*S-140	-1.0
1991	StL-N★	150	550	96	157	30	3	3	50	83	36	.285	.380	.367	110	11	35	9	5	.987	-21	*S-150	0.6
1992	StL-N★	132	518	73	153	20	2	0	31	59	34	.295	.367	.342	105	6	43	9	8	.985	8	*S-132	3.3
1993	StL-N	141	545	75	157	22	6	1	53	43	18	.288	.341	.356	89	-8	21	8	2	.974	18	*S-134	2.2
1994	StL-N★	98	381	51	100	18	3	3	30	38	26	.262	.329	.349	79	-12	6	3	0	.982	-2	S-96	-0.5
1995	StL-N†	44	156	16	31	5	1	0	11	17	12	.199	.286	.244	44	-13	4	3	-1	.964	1	S-41	-0.8
1996	*StL-N★	82	227	36	64	10	2	2	18	25	9	.282	.358	.370	92	-2	7	5	-1	.969	5	S-52	0.8
Total	19	2573	9396	1257	2460	402	69	28	793	1072	589	.262	.339	.328	87	-145	580	148	85	.978	243	*S-2511	43.0

■ KEITH SMITH
Smith, Patrick Keith   b: 10/20/61, Los Angeles, Cal.   BB/TR, 6'1", 175 lbs.   Deb: 4/12/84

YEAR	TM/L	G	AB	R	H	2B	3B	HR	RBI	BB	SO	AVG	OBP	SLG	PRO+	BR/A	SB	CS	SBR	FA	FR	G/POS	TPR
1984	NY-A	2	4	0	0	0	0	0	0	0	2	.000	.200	.000	-41	-1	0	0	0	.923	2	/S-2	0.2
1985	NY-A	4	0	1	0	0	0	0	0	0		—	—	—	—	0	0	0	0	1.000	0	/S-3	0.0
Total	2	6	4	1	0	0	0	0	0	0	2	.000	.200	.000	-41	-1	0	0	0	.929	3	/S-5	0.2

■ PAUL SMITH
Smith, Paul Leslie   b: 3/19/31, New Castle, Pa.   BL/TL, 5'8", 165 lbs.   Deb: 4/14/53

YEAR	TM/L	G	AB	R	H	2B	3B	HR	RBI	BB	SO	AVG	OBP	SLG	PRO+	BR/A	SB	CS	SBR	FA	FR	G/POS	TPR
1953	Pit-N	118	389	41	110	12	7	4	44	24	23	.283	.329	.380	85	-9	3	0	1	.985	-2	1-74,O-19	-1.3
1957	Pit-N	81	150	12	38	4	0	3	11	12	17	.253	.313	.340	78	-5	0	2	-1	1.000	-3	O-33/1-1	-1.1
1958	Pit-N	6	3	0	1	0	0	0	0	0	0	.333	.667	.333	180	0	0	0	0	.000	0	H	0.1
	Chi-N	18	20	1	3	0	0	0	1	3	4	.150	.261	.150	13	-2	0	0	0	.941	0	/1-4	-0.3

YEAR	TM/L	G	AB	R	H	2B	3B	HR	RBI	BB	SO	AVG	OBP	SLG	PRO+	BR/A	SB	CS	SBR	FA	FR	G/POS	TPR
	Yr	24	23	1	4	0	0	0	1	6	4	.174	.345	.174	44	-2	3	0	0	.941	0	/1-4	-0.2
Total	3	223	562	54	152	16	7	7	56	42	44	.270	.326	.361	81	-15	3	2	-0	.984	-5	/1-79,O-52	-2.6

◼ PAUL SMITH
Smith, Paul Stoner b: 5/7/1888, Mt.Zion, Ill. d: 7/3/58, Decatur, Ill. BL/TR, 6'1", 190 lbs. Deb: 9/19/16

YEAR	TM/L	G	AB	R	H	2B	3B	HR	RBI	BB	SO	AVG	OBP	SLG	PRO+	BR/A	SB	CS	SBR	FA	FR	G/POS	TPR
1916	Cin-N	10	44	5	10	0	1	0	1	1	8	.227	.244	.273	60	-2	3			1.000	-1	O-10	-0.4

◼ RAY SMITH
Smith, Raymond Edward b: 9/18/55, Glendale, Cal. BR/TR, 6'1", 185 lbs. Deb: 4/9/81

YEAR	TM/L	G	AB	R	H	2B	3B	HR	RBI	BB	SO	AVG	OBP	SLG	PRO+	BR/A	SB	CS	SBR	FA	FR	G/POS	TPR
1981	Min-A	15	40	4	8	1	0	1	1	0	3	.200	.200	.300	40	-3	0	0	0	1.000	1	C-15	-0.1
1982	Min-A	9	23	1	5	0	1	0	1	1	3	.217	.250	.304	50	-2	0	0	0	1.000	0	/C-9	0.0
1983	Min-A	59	152	11	34	5	0	0	8	10	12	.224	.276	.257	46	-11	1	0	0	.984	11	C-59	0.2
Total	3	83	215	16	47	6	1	1	10	11	18	.219	.260	.270	45	-16	1	0	0	.988	14	/C-83	0.1

◼ DICK SMITH
Smith, Richard Arthur b: 5/17/39, Lebanon, Ore. BR/TR, 6'2", 205 lbs. Deb: 7/20/63

YEAR	TM/L	G	AB	R	H	2B	3B	HR	RBI	BB	SO	AVG	OBP	SLG	PRO+	BR/A	SB	CS	SBR	FA	FR	G/POS	TPR
1963	NY-N	20	42	4	10	0	1	0	3	5	10	.238	.319	.286	74	-1	3	2	-0	1.000	-2	O-10/1-2	-0.4
1964	NY-N	46	94	14	21	6	1	0	3	1	29	.223	.247	.309	57	-6	6	2	1	.987	-3	1-18,O-13	-1.0
1965	LA-N	10	6	0	0	0	0	0	0	0	3	.000	.000	.000	-99	-2	0	0	0	1.000	-3	/O-9	-0.6
Total	3	76	142	18	31	6	2	0	7	6	42	.218	.260	.289	56	-8	9	4	0	1.000	-8	/O-32,1-20	-2.0

◼ DICK SMITH
Smith, Richard Harrison b: 7/21/27, Blandburg, Pa. BR/TR, 5'8", 160 lbs. Deb: 9/14/51

YEAR	TM/L	G	AB	R	H	2B	3B	HR	RBI	BB	SO	AVG	OBP	SLG	PRO+	BR/A	SB	CS	SBR	FA	FR	G/POS	TPR
1951	Pit-N	12	46	2	8	0	0	0	4	8	8	.174	.296	.174	29	-4	0	2	-1	.936	2	3-12	-0.3
1952	Pit-N	29	66	8	7	1	0	0	5	9	3	.106	.213	.121	-5	-9	0	0	0	.958	5	3-16/2-4,S-4	-0.5
1953	Pit-N	13	43	4	7	0	1	0	2	6	6	.163	.265	.209	26	-5	0	1	-1	.961	5	S-13	0.1
1954	Pit-N	12	31	2	3	1	1	0	0	6	5	.097	.243	.194	16	-4	0	0	0	.933	2	/3-9	-0.2
1955	Pit-N	4	0	1	0	0	0	0	0	1	0	—	1.000	—	198	-0	0	0	0	.000	0	/S-1	0.0
Total	5	70	186	17	25	2	2	0	11	30	22	.134	.255	.167	15	-22	0	3	-2	.944	14	/3-37,S-18,2-4	-0.9

◼ DICK SMITH
Smith, Richard Kelly b: 8/25/44, Lincolnton, N.C. BR/TR, 6'5", 200 lbs. Deb: 8/20/69

YEAR	TM/L	G	AB	R	H	2B	3B	HR	RBI	BB	SO	AVG	OBP	SLG	PRO+	BR/A	SB	CS	SBR	FA	FR	G/POS	TPR
1969	Was-A	21	28	2	3	0	0	0		4	7	.107	.242	.107	1	-4	0	0	0	.909	-2	/O-9	-0.6

◼ RED SMITH
Smith, Richard Paul b: 5/18/04, Brokaw, Wis. d: 3/8/78, Toledo, Ohio BR/TR, 5'10", 185 lbs. Deb: 5/31/27 C

YEAR	TM/L	G	AB	R	H	2B	3B	HR	RBI	BB	SO	AVG	OBP	SLG	PRO+	BR/A	SB	CS	SBR	FA	FR	G/POS	TPR
1927	NY-N	1	0	0	0	0	0	0	0	0	0	—	—	—	—		0	0	0	1.000	-0	/C-1	0.0

◼ BOB SMITH
Smith, Robert Eldridge b: 4/22/1895, Rogersville, Tenn. d: 7/19/87, Waycross, Ga. BR/TR, 5'10", 175 lbs. Deb: 4/19/23

YEAR	TM/L	G	AB	R	H	2B	3B	HR	RBI	BB	SO	AVG	OBP	SLG	PRO+	BR/A	SB	CS	SBR	FA	FR	G/POS	TPR
1923	Bos-N	115	375	30	94	16	3	0	40	17	35	.251	.285	.309	59	-23	4	9	-4	.944	14	*S-101/2-8	-0.3
1924	Bos-N	106	347	32	79	12	3	2	38	15	26	.228	.260	.297	51	-25	5	2	0	.958	8	S-80,3-23	-0.6
1925	Bos-N	58	174	17	49	9	4	0	23	5	6	.282	.302	.379	80	-6	2	2	-1	.906	3	S-21,2-15,P-13/O-1	0.0
1926	Bos-N	40	84	10	25	6	2	0	13	2	4	.298	.314	.417	105	-0	0			.972	2	P-33	0.0
1927	Bos-N	54	109	10	27	3	1	1	10	2	4	.248	.261	.321	60	-7	0			.966	2	P-41	0.0
1928	Bos-N	39	92	11	23	2	0	1	8	1	6	.250	.258	.304	49	-7	2			.965	3	P-38	0.0
1929	Bos-N	39	99	12	17	4	2	1	8	2	8	.172	.188	.283	16	-14	1			.986	4	P-34/S-5	0.2
1930	Bos-N	39	81	7	19	2	0	0	4	0	5	.235	.235	.259	20	-10	0			.984	2	P-38	0.0
1931	Chi-N	36	87	7	19	2	0	0	4	5	2	.218	.261	.241	35	-8	0			**1.000**	1	P-36	0.0
1932	*Chi-N	36	42	5	10	4	1	0	4	2	0	.238	.238	.381	64	-2	1			1.000	3	P-34/2-2	0.2
1933	Cin-N	23	25	2	5	1	0	0	1	1	2	.200	.231	.240	35	-2	1			.882	0	P-16/S-1	0.0
	Bos-N	14	20	1	4	0	1	0	2	0	1	.200	.200	.300	45	-2	0			1.000	1	P-14	0.0
	Yr	37	45	3	9	1	1	0	3	1	3	.200	.217	.267	39	-4	1			.946	0	P-30/S-1	0.0
1934	Bos-N	42	36	5	9	0	0	1	1	0	1	.250	.250	.278	44	-3	0			1.000	1	P-39	0.0
1935	Bos-N	47	63	3	17	0	0	0	4	1	5	.270	.281	.270	53	-4	0			.980	-1	P-46	0.0
1936	Bos-N	35	45	1	10	2	0	0	4	0	4	.222	.222	.267	33	-4	0			1.000	1	P-35	0.0
1937	Bos-N	19	10	1	2	0	0	0	0	1	1	.200	.273	.200	33	-1	0			1.000	-1	P-18	0.0
Total	15	742	1689	154	409	64	17	5	166	52	110	.242	.265	.309	53	-117	16	13		.981	42	P-435,S-208/23O	-0.5

◼ JOE SMITH
Smith, Salvatore (b: Salvatore Persico) b: 12/29/1893, New York, N.Y. d: 1/12/74, Yonkers, N.Y. BR/TR, 5'7", 170 lbs. Deb: 7/7/13

YEAR	TM/L	G	AB	R	H	2B	3B	HR	RBI	BB	SO	AVG	OBP	SLG	PRO+	BR/A	SB	CS	SBR	FA	FR	G/POS	TPR
1913	NY-A	14	32	1	5	0	0	0	2	1	14	.156	.182	.156	-1	-4	1			.952	0	C-14	-0.3

◼ SKYROCKET SMITH
Smith, Samuel J. b: 3/19/1868, St.Louis, Mo. d: 4/26/16, St.Louis, Mo. BR, 6'2", 170 lbs. Deb: 4/18/1888

YEAR	TM/L	G	AB	R	H	2B	3B	HR	RBI	BB	SO	AVG	OBP	SLG	PRO+	BR/A	SB	CS	SBR	FA	FR	G/POS	TPR
1888	Lou-a	58	206	27	49	9	4	1	31	24		.238	.349	.335	122	7	5			.970	-0	1-58	0.1

◼ SYD SMITH
Smith, Sydney E. b: 8/31/1883, Smithville, S.C. d: 6/5/61, Orangeburg, S.C. BR/TR, 5'10", 190 lbs. Deb: 4/14/08

YEAR	TM/L	G	AB	R	H	2B	3B	HR	RBI	BB	SO	AVG	OBP	SLG	PRO+	BR/A	SB	CS	SBR	FA	FR	G/POS	TPR
1908	Phi-A	46	128	8	26	8	0	1	10	4		.203	.233	.289	65	-5	0			.975	-0	C-31/1-6,O-1	-0.3
	StL-A	27	76	6	14	4	0	0	5	4		.184	.225	.237	50	-4	2			.977	8	C-24	0.7
	Yr	73	204	14	40	12	0	1	15	8		.196	.230	.270	60	-9	2			.976	8	C-55/1-6,O-1	0.4
1910	Cle-A	9	27	1	9	1	0	0	3	2		.333	.400	.370	140	1	0			.958	0	/C-9	0.2
1911	Cle-A	58	154	8	46	8	1	1	21	11		.299	.353	.383	104	1	0			.979	9	C-48/1-1,3-1	1.3
1914	Pit-N	5	11	1	3	0	0	0	0	1		.273	.273	.273	65	-1	0			1.000	-0	/C-3	0.0
1915	Pit-N	1	1	0	0	0	0	0	0	0		.000	.000	.000	-99	-0	0			.000	0	H	0.0
Total	5	146	397	24	98	21	1	2	40	22	1	.247	.291	.320	83	-8	2			.977	16	C-115/1-7,3-1,O-1	1.9

◼ TOM SMITH
Smith, Thomas N. b: 1851, Guelph, Ontario, Canada d: 3/28/1889, Detroit, Mich. Deb: 9/15/1875

YEAR	TM/L	G	AB	R	H	2B	3B	HR	RBI	BB	SO	AVG	OBP	SLG	PRO+	BR/A	SB	CS	SBR	FA	FR	G/POS	TPR
1875	Atl-n	3	13	0	1	0	0	0	1	0		.077	.077	.077	-53	-2	0	0	0	.783	0	/2-3	-0.1

◼ TOMMY SMITH
Smith, Tommy Alexander b: 8/1/48, Albemarle, N.C. BL/TR, 6'3", 215 lbs. Deb: 9/6/73

YEAR	TM/L	G	AB	R	H	2B	3B	HR	RBI	BB	SO	AVG	OBP	SLG	PRO+	BR/A	SB	CS	SBR	FA	FR	G/POS	TPR
1973	Cle-A	14	41	6	10	2	0	2	3	1	2	.244	.262	.439	93	-1	1	0	0	1.000	-1	O-13	-0.2
1974	Cle-A	23	31	4	3	1	0	0	0	2	7	.097	.176	.129	-11	-4	0	0	0	.938	-2	O-17/D-1	-0.7
1975	Cle-A	8	8	0	1	0	0	0	2	0	1	.125	.125	.125	-29	-1	0	0	0	1.000	-0	/O-3,D-3	-0.2
1976	Cle-A	55	164	17	42	3	1	2	12	8	8	.256	.291	.323	80	-4	0	0	2	.979	-0	O-50/D-2	-0.4
1977	Sea-A	21	27	1	7	1	1	0	4	0	6	.259	.259	.370	70	-1	0	1	-1	1.000	-0	O-14	-0.2
Total	5	121	271	28	63	7	2	4	21	11	24	.232	.265	.317	68	-12	1	1		.977	-5	/O-97,D-6	-1.9

◼ VINNIE SMITH
Smith, Vincent Ambrose b: 12/7/15, Richmond, Va. d: 12/14/79, Virginia Beach, Va BR/TR, 6'1", 176 lbs. Deb: 9/10/41 U

YEAR	TM/L	G	AB	R	H	2B	3B	HR	RBI	BB	SO	AVG	OBP	SLG	PRO+	BR/A	SB	CS	SBR	FA	FR	G/POS	TPR
1941	Pit-N	9	33	3	10	1	0	0	1	1	5	.303	.324	.333	86	-1	0			.941	-2	/C-9	-0.2
1946	Pit-N	7	21	2	4	0	0	0	4	1	5	.190	.227	.190	19	-2	0			.967	1	/C-7	-0.1
Total	2	16	54	5	14	1	0	0	5	2	10	.259	.286	.278	59	-3	0			.953	-1	/C-16	-0.3

◼ WALLY SMITH
Smith, Wallace H. b: 3/13/1889, Philadelphia, Pa. d: 6/10/30, Florence, Ariz. BR/TR, 5'11.5", 180 lbs. Deb: 4/17/11

YEAR	TM/L	G	AB	R	H	2B	3B	HR	RBI	BB	SO	AVG	OBP	SLG	PRO+	BR/A	SB	CS	SBR	FA	FR	G/POS	TPR
1911	StL-N	81	194	23	42	5	2	1	19	21	33	.216	.303	.330	79	-6	5			.936	2	3-26,S-25/2-8,O-1	-0.2
1912	StL-N	75	219	22	56	5	5	0	26	29	27	.256	.351	.324	87	-3	4			.949	-1	3-32,S-22/1-6	-0.2
1914	Was-A	45	97	11	19	4	1	0	8	3	12	.196	.235	.258	46	-7	3	4	-2	.955	-4	2-12/1-7,S-7,3-5,O	-1.3
Total	3	201	510	56	117	15	11	2	53	53	72	.229	.312	.314	77	-15	12	4		.947	-3	/3-63,S-54,2-20,1O	-1.7

◼ WIB SMITH
Smith, Wilbur Floyd b: 8/30/1886, Evart, Mich. d: 11/18/59, Fargo, N.D. BL/TR, 5'10.5", 165 lbs. Deb: 5/31/09

YEAR	TM/L	G	AB	R	H	2B	3B	HR	RBI	BB	SO	AVG	OBP	SLG	PRO+	BR/A	SB	CS	SBR	FA	FR	G/POS	TPR
1909	StL-A	17	42	3	8	0	0	0	2	0		.190	.190	.190	22	-4	0			.836	-9	C-13/1-1	-1.4

◼ RED SMITH
Smith, Willard Jehu b: 4/11/1892, Logansport, Ind. d: 7/17/72, Noblesville, Ind. BR/TR, 5'8", 165 lbs. Deb: 9/17/17

YEAR	TM/L	G	AB	R	H	2B	3B	HR	RBI	BB	SO	AVG	OBP	SLG	PRO+	BR/A	SB	CS	SBR	FA	FR	G/POS	TPR
1917	Pit-N	11	21	1	3	0	0	0	2	3	4	.143	.250	.190	35	-2	1			1.000	2	/C-6	0.0
1918	Pit-N	15	24	1	4	1	0	0	3	3	2	.167	.259	.208	42	-2	0			.939	-1	C-10	-0.2
Total	2	26	45	2	7	1	0	0	5	6	4	.156	.255	.200	38	-3	1			.969	1	/C-16	-0.2

◼ BILL SMITH
Smith, William E. b: Cleveland, Ohio d: 8/9/1886, Toronto, Ont., Can. 5'11", 178 lbs. Deb: 9/17/1884

YEAR	TM/L	G	AB	R	H	2B	3B	HR	RBI	BB	SO	AVG	OBP	SLG	PRO+	BR/A	SB	CS	SBR	FA	FR	G/POS	TPR
1884	Cle-N	1	3	0	0	0	0	0	0	0	2	.000	.000	.000	-97	-1				.000	-0	/O-1	-0.1

◼ BILL SMITH
Smith, William J. b: Baltimore, Md. d: 8/9/1886, Deb: 4/14/1873 M

YEAR	TM/L	G	AB	R	H	2B	3B	HR	RBI	BB	SO	AVG	OBP	SLG	PRO+	BR/A	SB	CS	SBR	FA	FR	G/POS	TPR
1873	Mar-n	6	23	2	4	0	0	0	1	0	1	.174	.174	.174	5	-2	0	0	0	.500	-3	/O-3,C-2,2-1,M	-0.4

YEAR	TM/L	G	AB	R	H	2B	3B	HR	RBI	BB	SO	AVG	OBP	SLG	PRO+	BR/A	SB	CS	SBR	FA	FR	G/POS	TPR

■ WILLIE SMITH   Smith, Willie   b: 2/11/39, Anniston, Ala.   BL/TL, 6′, 190 lbs.   Deb: 6/18/63

1963	Det-A	17	8	2	1	0	0	0	0	0	1	.125	.125	.125	-29	-1	0	0	0	1.000	0	P-11	0.0
1964	LA-A	118	359	46	108	14	6	11	51	8	39	.301	.320	.465	128	11	7	5	-1	.977	-6	O-87,P-15	-0.1
1965	Cal-A	136	459	52	120	14	9	14	57	32	60	.261	.311	.423	109	4	9	8	-2	.980	-0	*O-123/1-2	-0.4
1966	Cal-A	90	195	18	36	3	2	1	20	12	37	.185	.243	.236	39	-15	1	0	0	.974	-3	O-52	-2.2
1967	Cle-A	21	32	0	7	2	0	0	2	1	10	.219	.242	.281	54	-2	0	2	-1	.800	-1	O-4,1-3	-0.5
1968	Cle-A	33	42	1	6	2	0	0	3	3	14	.143	.217	.190	25	-4	0	0	0	1.000	-0	/1-7,P-2,O-1	-0.5
	Chi-N	55	142	13	39	8	2	5	25	12	33	.275	.335	.465	129	5	0	0	0	1.000	-0	O-38/1-4,P-1	-0.1
1969	Chi-N	103	195	21	48	9	1	9	25	25	49	.246	.332	.441	102	0	0	0	0	.929	-7	O-33,1-24	-1.0
1970	Chi-N	87	167	15	36	9	1	5	24	11	32	.216	.268	.371	62	-10	2	1	0	.994	-5	1-43/O-1	-1.8
1971	Cin-N	31	55	3	9	2	0	1	4	3	9	.164	.207	.255	31	-5	0	0	0	1.000	1	1-10	-0.5
Total	9	691	1654	171	410	63	21	46	211	107	284	.248	.297	.395	94	-18	20	16	-4	.975	-24	O-339/1-93,P-29	-7.1

■ HOMER SMOOT   Smoot, Homer Vernon "Doc"   b: 3/23/1878, Galestown, Md.   d: 3/25/28, Salisbury, Md.   BL/TR, 5′10″, 180 lbs.   Deb: 4/17/02

1902	StL-N	129	518	58	161	19	4	3	48	23		.311	.350	.380	130	17	20			.931	-1	*O-129	0.9
1903	StL-N	129	500	67	148	22	8	4	49	32		.296	.342	.396	114	8	17			.942	-7	*O-129	-0.7
1904	StL-N	137	520	58	146	23	6	3	66	37		.281	.331	.365	120	12	23			.966	2	*O-137	0.6
1905	StL-N	139	534	73	166	21	16	4	58	33		.311	.359	.433	140	24	21			.975	1	*O-138	1.9
1906	StL-N	86	343	41	85	9	10	0	31	11		.248	.289	.332	98	-2	3			.953	2	O-86	-0.6
	Cin-N	60	220	11	57	8	1	1	17	13		.259	.315	.318	93	-2	0			.944	1	O-59	-0.4
	Yr	146	563	52	142	17	11	1	48	24		.252	.300	.327	96	-4	3			.950	2	*O-145	-1.0
Total	5	680	2635	308	763	102	45	15	269	149		.290	.336	.380	120	57	84			.953	-2	O-678	1.7

■ HENRY SMOYER   Smoyer, Henry Neitz "Hennie" (b: Henry Neitz Smowery)   b: 4/24/1890, Fredericksburg, Pa.   d: 2/28/58, DuBois, Pa.   BR/TR, 5′6″,   Deb: 8/14/12

1912	StL-A	6	14	1	3	0	0	0	0	2		.214	.313	.214	53	-1	0			1.000	-0	/S-4,3-2	-0.1

■ FRANK SMYKAL   Smykal, Frank John (b: Frank John Smejkal)   b: 10/13/1889, Chicago, Ill.   d: 8/11/50, Chicago, Ill.   BR/TR, 5′7″, 150 lbs.   Deb: 8/30/16

1916	Pit-N	6	10	1	3	0	0	0	2	3	1	.300	.500	.300	147	1	1			.842	-1	/S-5,3-1	0.1

■ CLANCY SMYRES   Smyres, Clarence Melvin   b: 5/24/22, Culver City, Cal.   BB/TR, 5′11.5″, 175 lbs.   Deb: 4/18/44

1944	Bro-N	5	2	1	0	0	0	0	0	0	0	.000	.000	.000	-99	-1	0			.000	0	H	-0.1

■ RED SMYTH   Smyth, James Daniel   b: 1/30/1893, Holly Springs, Miss.   d: 4/14/58, Inglewood, Cal.   BL/TR, 5′9″, 152 lbs.   Deb: 8/11/15

1915	Bro-N	19	22	3	3	0	0	0	3	4	2	.136	.269	.182	37	-2	1	2	-1	1.000	-1	/O-9	-0.4
1916	Bro-N	2	5	0	0	0	0	0	0	0	3	.000	.000	.000	-97	-1	0			1.000	-0	/2-2	-0.2
1917	Bro-N	29	24	5	3	0	0	0	1	4	6	.125	.250	.125	16	-2	0			.667	-1	/3-4,O-2	-0.3
	StL-N	38	72	5	15	0	2	0	4	4	9	.208	.269	.264	66	-3	3			.889	-5	O-23	-1.0
	Yr	67	96	10	18	0	2	0	5	8	15	.188	.264	.229	52	-5	3			.871	-6	O-25/3-4	-1.3
1918	StL-N	40	113	19	24	1	0	0	4	16	11	.212	.315	.257	78	-2	3			.956	-0	O-25,2-11	-0.4
Total	4	128	236	32	45	2	4	0	12	28	31	.191	.285	.233	60	-10	7	2		.934	-7	/O-59,2-13,3-4	-2.3

■ JOHN SNEED   Sneed, Jonathon L.   b: Columbus, Ohio   d: 1/4/1899, Memphis, Tenn.   5′8″, 160 lbs.   Deb: 5/1/1884

1884	Ind-a	27	102	14	22	4	0	1		6		.216	.259	.284	79	-2				.817	-0	O-27	-0.3
1890	Tol-a	9	30	3	6	0	0	0	4	8		.200	.368	.200	66	-1	5			.889	2	/O-9	0.1
	Col-a	128	484	114	141	13	15	2	65	63		.291	.383	.393	138	26	39			.883	-8	*O-126/S-2	1.2
	Yr	137	514	117	147	13	15	2	69	71		.286	.382	.381	133	25	44			.883	-5	*O-135/S-2	1.3
1891	Col-a	99	366	66	94	9	6	1	61	55	29	.257	.364	.322	103	4	24			.894	-4	*O-99	-0.3
Total	3	263	982	197	263	26	21	4	130	132	29	.268	.364	.349	117	27	68			.879	-10	O-261/S-2	0.7

■ CHARLIE SNELL   Snell, Charles Anthony (b: Charles Anthony Schnell)
b: 11/29/1893, Hampstead, Md.   d: 4/4/88, Reading, Pa.   BR/TR, 5′11″, 160 lbs.   Deb: 7/19/12

1912	StL-A	8	19	0	4	1	0	0	0	3		.211	.348	.263	78	-0	0			.941	2	/C-8	0.2

■ WALLY SNELL   Snell, Walter Henry "Doc"   b: 5/19/1889, W.Bridgewater, Mass.   d: 7/23/80, Providence, R.I.   BR/TR, 5′10″, 170 lbs.   Deb: 8/1/13

1913	Bos-A	5	8	1	3	0	0	0		0	1	.375	.375	.375	117	0	1			1.000	0	/C-1	0.1

■ DUKE SNIDER   Snider, Edwin Donald "The Silver Fox"   b: 9/19/26, Los Angeles, Cal.   BL/TR, 6′, 190 lbs.   Deb: 4/17/47   CH

1947	Bro-N	40	83	6	20	3	1	0	5	3	24	.241	.276	.301	51	-6	2			.980	-2	O-25	-0.9
1948	Bro-N	53	160	22	39	6	6	5	21	12	27	.244	.297	.450	96	-2	4			.989	-3	O-47	-0.7
1949	*Bro-N	146	552	100	161	28	7	23	92	56	92	.292	.361	.493	122	16	12			.984	4	*O-145	1.2
1950	Bro-N★	152	620	109	**199**	31	10	31	107	58	79	.321	.379	.553	139	33	16			.983	9	*O-151	3.4
1951	Bro-N★	150	606	96	168	26	6	29	101	62	97	.277	.344	.483	118	14	14	10	-2	.987	5	*O-150	0.9
1952	*Bro-N☆	144	534	80	162	25	7	21	92	55	77	.303	.368	.494	136	25	7	4	-0	.992	1	*O-141	2.1
1953	*Bro-N★	153	590	**132**	198	38	4	42	126	82	90	.336	.419	**.627**	165	56	16	7	1	.987	-3	*O-151	4.6
1954	*Bro-N★	149	584	**120**	199	39	10	40	130	84	96	.341	.427	.647	170	60	6	6	-2	.981	-5	*O-148	4.6
1955	*Bro-N★	148	538	**126**	166	34	6	42	**136**	104	87	.309	.421	.628	169	55	9	7	-2	.989	1	*O-146	4.7
1956	*Bro-N★	151	542	112	158	33	2	**43**	101	**99**	101	.292	**.402**	.598	152	41	3	3	-1	.984	-0	*O-150	3.2
1957	Bro-N	139	508	91	139	25	7	40	92	77	104	.274	.370	.587	139	27	4	3	-2	.990	-6	*O-136	1.1
1958	LA-N	106	327	45	102	12	3	15	58	32	49	.312	.375	.505	126	12	2	2	-1	.987	-13	O-92	-0.6
1959	*LA-N	126	370	59	114	11	2	23	88	58	71	.308	.402	.535	137	20	1	5	-3	.975	-17	O-107	-0.4
1960	LA-N	101	235	38	57	13	5	14	36	46	54	.243	.369	.519	131	11	0	1	-1	.965	-12	O-75	-0.4
1961	LA-N	85	233	35	69	8	3	16	56	29	43	.296	.376	.562	133	11	1	1	-0	.975	-2	O-66	0.6
1962	LA-N	80	158	28	44	11	3	5	30	36	32	.278	.418	.481	150	13	2	0	1	.967	-1	O-39	0.6
1963	NY-N★	129	354	44	86	8	3	14	45	56	74	.243	.348	.401	113	7	0	1	-1	.986	-10	*O-106	-0.8
1964	SF-N	91	167	16	35	7	0	4	17	22	40	.210	.302	.323	74	-5	0	0	0	.979	-5	O-43	-1.3
Total	18	2143	7161	1259	2116	358	85	407	1333	971	1237	.295	.381	.540	138	388	99	50		.985	-62	*O-1918	22.3

■ VAN SNIDER   Snider, Van Voorhees   b: 8/11/63, Birmingham, Ala.   BL/TR, 6′3″, 185 lbs.   Deb: 9/2/88

1988	Cin-N	11	28	4	6	0	1	0	6	0	13	.214	.214	.357	59	-2	0	1	-1	1.000	-1	/O-8	-0.3
1989	Cin-N	8	7	1	1	0	0	0	0	0	5	.143	.143	.143	-17	-1	0	0	0	1.000	-2	/O-6	-0.3
Total	2	19	35	5	7	0	1	0	6	0	18	.200	.200	.314	44	-3	0	1	-1	1.000	-2	/O-14	-0.6

■ ROXY SNIPES   Snipes, Wyatt Eure "Rock"   b: 10/28/1896, Marion, S.C.   d: 5/1/41, Fayetteville, N.C.   BL/TR, 6′, 185 lbs.   Deb: 7/15/23

1923	Chi-A	1	1	0	0	0	0	0	0	0	0	.000	.000	.000	-99	-0	0			.000	0	H	0.0

■ CHAPPIE SNODGRASS   Snodgrass, Amzie Beal   b: 3/18/1870, Springfield, Ohio   d: 9/9/51, New York, N.Y.   BR/TR, 5′10″, 165 lbs.   Deb: 5/15/01

1901	Bal-A	3	10	0	1	0	0	0	1	0		.100	.100	.100	-43	-2	0			.500	-1	/O-2	-0.3

■ FRED SNODGRASS   Snodgrass, Frederick Carlisle "Snow"   b: 10/19/1887, Ventura, Cal.   d: 4/5/74, Ventura, Cal.   BR/TR, 5′11.5″, 175 lbs.   Deb: 6/4/08

1908	NY-N	6	4	1	1	0	0	0		0		.250	.250	.250	57	-0	1			1.000	1	/C-3	0.1
1909	NY-N	28	70	10	21	5	0	1	6	7		.300	.387	.414	146	4	10			.921	-1	O-20/C-2,1-1	0.3
1910	NY-N	123	396	69	127	22	8	2	44	71	52	.321	.440	.432	154	32	33			.970	-8	*O-101/1-9,C-1,1-1	2.0
1911	*NY-N	151	534	83	157	27	10	1	77	72	59	.294	.393	.388	115	13	51			.973	9	*O-149/1-1,3-1	1.4
1912	*NY-N	146	535	91	144	24	9	3	69	70	65	.269	.362	.364	96	-1	43			.948	-3	*O-116,1-27/2-1	-1.1
1913	*NY-N	141	457	65	133	21	6	3	49	53	44	.291	.373	.383	115	11	27			.968	5	*O-133/1-3,2-1	1.1
1914	NY-N	113	392	54	103	20	4	0	44	39	43	.263	.336	.334	103	2	25			.977	5	O-96,1-14/2-1,3-1	0.2
1915	NY-N	80	252	36	49	9	0	0	20	35	33	.194	.307	.210	68	-8	11	12	-4	.935	4	O-75	-1.3
	Bos-N	23	79	10	22	2	0	0	9	7	9	.278	.352	.304	104	1	0	4	-2	.938	-2	O-18/1-5	-0.5
	Yr	103	331	46	71	11	0	0	29	42	42	.215	.318	.248	76	-7	11	16	-6	.935	2	O-93/1-5	-1.8
1916	Bos-N	112	382	33	95	13	5	1	32	34	54	.249	.318	.317	100	0	14			.983	13	*O-110	0.9
Total	9	923	3101	453	852	143	42	11	351	386	359	.275	.367	.359	110	53	215	16		.965	24	O-818/1-60,C-6,23	3.1

YEAR	TM/L	G	AB	R	H	2B	3B	HR	RBI	BB	SO	AVG	OBP	SLG	PRO+	BR/A	SB	CS	SBR	FA	FR	G/POS	TPR

■ CHRIS SNOPEK Snopek, Christopher Charles b: 9/20/70, Cynthiana, Ky. BR/TR, 6'1", 185 lbs. Deb: 7/31/95

1995	Chi-A	22	68	12	22	4	0	1	7	9	12	.324	.403	.426	121	2	1	0	0	1.000	-0	3-17/S-6	0.3
1996	Chi-A	46	104	18	27	6	1	6	18	6	16	.260	.306	.510	107	0	0	1	-1	.939	4	3-27,S-12/D-3	0.4
Total	2	68	172	30	49	10	1	7	25	15	28	.285	.346	.477	113	3	1	1	-0	.959	4	/3-44,S-18,D-3	0.7

■ CHARLIE SNOW Snow, Charles M. b: 8/3/1849, Lowell, Mass. Deb: 10/1/1874

| 1874 | Atl-n | 1 | 1 | 0 | 1 | 0 | 0 | 0 | 0 | 0 | 0 | 1.000 | 1.000 | 1.000 | 615 | 1 | 0 | 0 | 0 | .000 | -1 | /C-1 | 0.0 |

■ J. T. SNOW Snow, Jack Thomas b: 2/26/68, Long Beach, Cal. BB/TL, 6'2", 200 lbs. Deb: 9/20/92

1992	NY-A	7	14	1	2	1	0	0	2	5	5	.143	.368	.214	67	-0	0	0	0	1.000	-0	/1-6,D-1	-0.1
1993	Cal-A	129	419	60	101	18	2	16	57	55	88	.241	.332	.408	95	-3	3	0	1	.995	-2	*1-129	-1.5
1994	Cal-A	61	223	22	49	4	0	8	30	19	48	.220	.290	.345	62	-13	0	1	-1	.996	-1	1-61	-1.9
1995	Cal-A	143	544	80	157	22	1	24	102	52	91	.289	.354	.465	112	9	2	1	0	.997	-17	*1-143	-2.1
1996	Cal-A	155	575	69	148	20	1	17	67	56	96	.257	.329	.384	81	-17	1	6	-3	.993	1	*1-154	-3.1
Total	5	495	1775	232	457	65	4	65	258	187	328	.257	.333	.408	91	-24	6	8	-3	.995	-19	1-493/D-1	-8.7

■ BERNIE SNYDER Snyder, Bernard Austin b: 8/25/13, Philadelphia, Pa. BR/TR, 6', 165 lbs. Deb: 9/15/35

| 1935 | Phi-A | 10 | 32 | 5 | 11 | 1 | 0 | 0 | 3 | 1 | 2 | .344 | .364 | .375 | 92 | -0 | 0 | 0 | 0 | .880 | -3 | /2-5,S-4 | -0.2 |

■ CHARLES SNYDER Snyder, Charles b: Camden, N.J. d: 3/3/01, Philadelphia, Pa. BR/TR, Deb: 9/19/1890

| 1890 | Phi-a | 9 | 33 | 5 | 9 | 1 | 0 | 0 | 4 | 2 | | .273 | .314 | .303 | 84 | -1 | 0 | | | .583 | -3 | /O-5,C-5 | -0.4 |

■ POP SNYDER Snyder, Charles N. b: 10/6/1854, Washington, D.C. d: 10/29/24, Washington, D.C. BR/TR, 5'11.5", 184 lbs. Deb: 6/16/1873 MU

1873	Was-n	28	108	16	21	2	0	0	4	3	3	.194	.216	.213	29	-9	0	1	-1	.848	-1	C-28/O-3	-0.7
1874	Bal-n	39	151	24	33	4	0	1	17	1	2	.219	.224	.265	56	-7	0	0	0	.789	-3	C-39	-0.5
1875	Phi-n	66	263	38	64	8	2	1	25	4	4	.243	.255	.300	89	-3	3	8	-4	.825	4	*C-66/1-1	-0.1
1876	Lou-N	56	224	21	44	4	1	1	9	2	7	.196	.204	.237	39	-16				.833	11	*C-55/O-4	-0.3
1877	Lou-N	61	248	23	64	7	2	2	28	3	14	.258	.267	.327	73	-10				.910	15	*C-61/O-1,S-1	0.7
1878	Bos-N	60	226	21	48	5	0	0	14	1	19	.212	.216	.235	44	-14				.912	5	*C-58/O-2	-0.7
1879	Bos-N	81	329	42	78	16	3	2	35	5	31	.237	.249	.325	85	-6				.925	24	*C-80/O-2	1.9
1881	Bos-N	62	219	14	50	8	0	0	16	3	23	.228	.239	.265	61	-9				.897	3	*C-60/O-1,S-1,2-1	-0.4
1882	Cin-a	72	309	49	90	12	2	1	50	9		.291	.311	.353	117	4				.916	19	*C-70/1-2,O-1,M	2.3
1883	Cin-a	58	250	38	64	14	6	0	34	8		.256	.279	.360	99	-1				.919	14	C-57/S-2,M	1.4
1884	Cin-a	67	268	32	69	9	9	0	39	7		.257	.276	.358	101	-1				.922	27	C-65/1-2,O-1,M	2.9
1885	Cin-a	39	152	13	36	4	3	1	19	6		.237	.270	.322	85	-3				.880	3	C-38/1-1	0.3
1886	Cin-a	60	220	33	41	8	3	0	28	13		.186	.242	.250	52	-13	11			.874	-5	C-41,1-19/O-1	-1.3
1887	Cle-a	74	282	33	72	12	6	0	27	9		.255	.281	.340	75	-10	5			.905	19	C-63/1-13	1.1
1888	Cle-a	64	237	22	51	7	3	0	14	6		.215	.238	.270	64	-10	9			.901	8	C-58/1-4,O-3	0.3
1889	Cle-N	22	83	5	16	3	0	0	12	2	12	.193	.221	.229	26	-8	4			.907	2	C-22	-0.4
1890	Cle-P	13	48	5	9	1	0	0	12	1	9	.188	.220	.208	16	-6	1			.958	3	C-13	-0.1
1891	Was-a	8	27	4	5	0	1	0	2	0	3	.185	.241	.296	45	-2	0			1.000	1	/1-4,C-3,O-1,M	-0.2
Total	3 n	133	522	78	118	14	2	2	46	8	9	.226	.238	.272	66	-19	3	9	-5	.819	3	C-133/O-3,1-1	-1.3
Total	15	797	3122	355	737	110	39	7	339	75	118	.236	.256	.303	73	-104	30			.904	148	C-744/1-45,O-17,S2	7.5

■ REDLEG SNYDER Snyder, Emanuel Sebastian (b: Emanuel Sebastian Schneider) b: 12/12/1854, Camden, N.J. d: 11/24/32, Camden, N.J. BR/TR, 5'10", 175 lbs. Deb: 4/25/1876

1876	Cin-N	55	205	10	31	3	1	0	12	1	19	.151	.155	.176	12	-17				.825	5	*O-55	-1.2
1884	Wil-U	17	52	4	10	0	0	0		1		.192	.208	.192	21	-6				.976	1	1-16/O-1	-0.7
Total	2	72	257	14	41	3	1	0	12	2	19	.160	.166	.179	14	-24				.825	6	/O-56,1-16	-1.9

■ COONEY SNYDER Snyder, Frank C. b: Toronto, Ontario, Canada d: 3/9/17, Toronto, Ont., Can. 6'3", 180 lbs. Deb: 5/19/1898

| 1898 | Lou-N | 17 | 61 | 4 | 10 | 0 | 0 | 0 | 6 | 3 | | .164 | .215 | .164 | 9 | -7 | 0 | | | .935 | -6 | C-17 | -1.1 |

■ FRANK SNYDER Snyder, Frank Elton "Pancho" b: 5/27/1893, San Antonio, Tex. d: 1/5/62, San Antonio, Tex. BR/TR, 6'2", 185 lbs. Deb: 8/25/12 C

1912	StL-N	11	18	2	2	0	0	0	0	2	7	.111	.200	.111	-14	-3	1			.919	0	C-11	-0.2
1913	StL-N	7	21	1	4	0	0	0	2	0	4	.190	.190	.286	35	-2	0			.956	7	/C-7	0.0
1914	StL-N	100	326	19	75	15	4	1	25	13	28	.230	.262	.310	71	-13	1			.979	5	C-98	0.0
1915	StL-N	144	473	41	141	22	7	2	55	39	49	.298	.353	.387	124	13	3	6	-3	.983	7	*C-142	3.1
1916	StL-N	132	406	23	105	12	4	0	39	18	31	.259	.290	.308	84	-8	7			.973	9	C-72,1-46/S-1	0.5
1917	StL-N	115	313	18	74	9	2	1	33	27	43	.236	.301	.288	83	-6	4			.975	0	C-94/2-1	0.2
1918	StL-N	39	112	5	28	7	1	0	10	6	13	.250	.288	.330	92	-1	4			.959	2	C-27/1-3	0.3
1919	StL-N	50	154	7	28	4	2	0	14	5	13	.182	.213	.234	36	-12	2			.983	5	C-48/1-1	-0.4
	NY-N	32	92	7	21	6	0	0	11	8	9	.228	.297	.293	79	-2	1			.983	-4	C-31	-0.5
	Yr	82	246	14	49	10	2	0	25	13	22	.199	.245	.256	53	-14	3			.983	1	C-79/1-1	-0.9
1920	NY-N	87	264	26	66	13	4	3	27	17	18	.250	.295	.364	89	-4	2	2	-1	.978	1	C-84	0.2
1921	*NY-N	108	309	36	99	13	2	8	45	27	24	.320	.382	.453	120	9	3	4	-2	.985	5	*C-101	1.7
1922	*NY-N	104	318	34	109	21	5	5	51	23	25	.343	.387	.487	123	11	1	5	-3	.990	-3	*C-97	0.9
1923	*NY-N	120	402	37	103	13	6	5	63	24	29	.256	.298	.356	73	-17	5	3	-0	.990	3	*C-112	-0.9
1924	*NY-N	118	354	37	107	18	3	6	53	30	43	.302	.357	.412	109	4	3	0	1	.987	-16	*C-110	-0.4
1925	NY-N	107	325	21	78	9	1	11	50	20	49	.240	.286	.375	70	-16	0	0	0	.985	2	C-96	-0.8
1926	NY-N	55	148	10	32	3	2	5	16	13	19	.216	.280	.365	73	-6	0			.981	0	C-55	-0.8
1927	StL-N	63	194	7	50	9	2	3	30	9	18	.258	.291	.299	56	-12	0			.981	0	C-62	-0.8
Total	16	1392	4229	331	1122	170	44	47	525	281	416	.265	.313	.386	90	-65	37	20		.981	16	*C-1247/1-50,2-1,S	2.6

■ JERRY SNYDER Snyder, Gerald George b: 7/21/29, Jenks, Okla. BR/TR, 6', 170 lbs. Deb: 5/8/52

1952	Was-A	36	57	5	9	2	0	2	5	8		.158	.226	.193	18	-6	1	0	0	.965	7	2-19/S-4	0.2
1953	Was-A	29	62	10	21	4	0	2	5	8		.339	.388	.403	117	2	1	1	-0	.988	7	S-17/2-4	0.9
1954	Was-A	64	154	17	36	3	1	0	17	15	18	.234	.302	.266	60	-8	3	0	1	.978	9	S-48/2-3	0.5
1955	Was-A	46	107	7	24	5	0	0	6	6	16	.224	.265	.271	47	-8	1	1	-0	.977	1	2-22,S-20	-0.5
1956	Was-A	43	148	14	40	3	1	2	14	10	9	.270	.321	.345	76	-5	1	0	0	.968	-5	S-35/2-7	-0.6
1957	Was-A	42	93	6	14	1	0	1	4	4	9	.151	.186	.194	4	-12	0	1	-1	.966	1	S-15,2-13/3-1	-1.1
1958	Was-A	6	9	1	1	0	0	0	1	1	1	.111	.200	.111	-12	-1	0	0	0	1.000	-1	/2-2,S-1	-0.2
Total	7	266	630	60	145	18	2	3	47	46	59	.230	.284	.279	54	-41	7	3	0	.971	20	S-140/2-70,3-1	-0.8

■ JIM SNYDER Snyder, James C. A. b: 9/15/1847, Brooklyn, N.Y. d: 12/1/22, Rockaway Beach, N.Y 5'7", 130 lbs. Deb: 5/7/1872

| 1872 | Eck-n | 26 | 107 | 16 | 28 | 2 | 2 | 0 | 11 | 0 | 1 | .262 | .262 | .318 | 91 | 0 | 0 | 0 | 0 | .763 | 4 | S-25/C-1,O-1 | 0.3 |

■ CORY SNYDER Snyder, James Cory b: 11/11/62, Inglewood, Cal. BR/TR, 6'3", 185 lbs. Deb: 6/13/86

1986	Cle-A	103	416	58	113	21	1	24	69	16	123	.272	.299	.500	115	6	2	3	-1	.987	-7	O-74,S-34,3-11,/D-1	-0.2
1987	Cle-A	157	577	74	136	24	2	33	82	31	166	.236	.276	.456	89	-12	5	1	1	.971	2	*O-139,S-18	-1.2
1988	Cle-A	142	511	71	139	24	3	26	75	42	101	.272	.329	.483	121	13	5	1	1	.985	14	*O-141/D-1	2.3
1989	Cle-A	132	489	49	105	17	0	18	59	23	134	.215	.253	.360	70	-21	6	5	-1	.997	19	*O-125/S-7,D-2	-0.7
1990	Cle-A	123	438	46	102	27	3	14	55	21	118	.233	.271	.404	87	-10	1	4	-2	.975	2	*O-120/S-5	-1.3
1991	Chi-A	50	117	10	22	4	0	3	11	6	41	.188	.228	.299	46	-9	1	0	0	.981	-2	O-29,1-18	-1.2
	Tor-A	21	49	4	7	0	1	0	6	3	19	.143	.192	.184	4	-6	0	0	0	1.000	-1	O-14/1-4,3-3,D-3	-0.9
	Yr	71	166	14	29	4	1	3	17	9	60	.175	.217	.265	33	-15	1	0	0	.985	-5	O-43,1-22/3-3,D-3	-2.1
1992	SF-N	124	390	48	105	22	2	14	57	23	96	.269	.313	.444	119	7	4	4	-1	.992	-5	O-70,1-27,3-14,/2S	-0.1
1993	LA-N	143	516	61	137	33	1	11	56	47	147	.266	.332	.407	100	-1	3	2	0	.979	-8	*O-115,3-23,1-12,/S	-1.0
1994	LA-N	73	153	18	36	6	0	6	18	14	47	.235	.304	.392	85	-4	1	0	0	.967	-8	O-50/1-9,3-6,S-4,2	-1.2
Total	9	1068	3656	439	902	178	13	149	488	226	992	.247	.293	.425	95	-36	28	19	-3	.983	3	O-877/S-73,132D	-5.5

YEAR	TM/L	G	AB	R	H	2B	3B	HR	RBI	BB	SO	AVG	OBP	SLG	PRO+	BR/A	SB	CS	SBR	FA	FR	G/POS	TPR

■ JIM SNYDER Snyder, James Robert b: 8/15/32, Dearborn, Mich. BR/TR, 6'1", 185 lbs. Deb: 9/15/61 MC

1961	Min-A	3	5	0	0	0	0	0	0	0	1	.000	.000	.000	-95	-1	0	0	0	1.000	0	/2-3	-0.1
1962	Min-A	12	10	1	1	0	0	0	1	0	0	.100	.100	.100	-44	-2	0	1	-1	.941	-6	/2-5,1-1	-0.8
1964	Min-A	26	71	3	11	2	0	1	9	4	11	.155	.211	.225	21	-8	0	0	0	.990	-4	2-25	-1.0
Total	3	41	86	4	12	2	0	1	10	4	12	.140	.187	.198	6	-11	0	1	-1	.984	-10	/2-33,1-1	-1.9

■ JACK SNYDER Snyder, John William b: 10/6/1886, Lincoln, Pa. d: 12/13/81, Brownsville, Pa. BR/TR, 5'9", 168 lbs. Deb: 6/13/14

1914	Buf-F	1	0	0	0	0	0	0	0	1	0	—	1.000	—	183	0	0	0		.000	0	/C-1	0.0
1917	Bro-N	7	11	1	3	0	0	0	1	0	2	.273	.273	.273	66	-0	0	0		1.000	0	/C-5	0.0
Total	2	8	11	1	3	0	0	0	1	1	2	.273	.333	.273	84	-0	0	0		1.000	0	/C-6	0.0

■ JOSH SNYDER Snyder, Joshua M. b: 3/1844, Brooklyn, N.Y. d: 4/21/1881, Brooklyn, N.Y. Deb: 5/18/1872

| 1872 | Eck-n | 9 | 37 | 2 | 6 | 2 | 0 | 0 | 1 | 1 | 1 | .162 | .184 | .216 | 27 | -3 | 0 | 0 | 0 | .778 | 2 | /O-9 | 0.0 |

■ RUSS SNYDER Snyder, Russell Henry b: 6/22/34, Oak, Neb. BL/TR, 6'1", 190 lbs. Deb: 4/18/59

1959	KC-A	73	243	41	76	13	2	3	21	19	29	.313	.367	.420	113	5	6	2	1	.986	3	O-64	0.5
1960	KC-A	125	304	45	79	10	5	4	26	20	28	.260	.308	.365	81	-9	7	3	0	.986	-10	O-91	-2.2
1961	Bal-A	115	312	46	91	13	5	1	13	20	32	.292	.334	.375	92	-4	5	3	-0	.966	-16	*O-108	-2.5
1962	Bal-A	139	416	47	127	19	4	9	40	17	46	.305	.336	.435	113	6	7	4	-0	.974	-3	*O-121	-0.4
1963	Bal-A	148	429	51	110	21	2	7	36	40	48	.256	.323	.364	95	-3	18	5	2	.988	-18	*O-130	-2.5
1964	Bal-A	56	93	11	27	3	0	1	7	11	22	.290	.365	.355	102	1	0	2	-1	.971	-9	O-40	-1.1
1965	Bal-A	132	345	49	93	11	2	1	29	27	38	.270	.324	.322	83	-7	3	4	-2	1.000	-7	*O-106	-2.2
1966	*Bal-A	117	373	66	114	21	5	3	41	38	37	.306	.370	.413	127	13	2	1	0	.986	-13	*O-104	-0.5
1967	Bal-A	108	275	40	65	8	2	4	23	32	48	.236	.318	.324	91	-3	5	2	0	.985	-1	O-69	-0.8
1968	Chi-A	38	82	2	11	2	0	1	5	4	16	.134	.174	.195	12	-9	0	0	0	1.000	-5	O-22	-1.8
	Cle-A	68	217	30	61	8	2	2	23	25	21	.281	.355	.364	120	6	1	1	-0	.991	4	O-54/1-1	0.7
	Yr	106	299	32	72	10	2	3	28	29	37	.241	.308	.318	90	-3	1	1	-0	.992	-1	O-76/1-1	-1.1
1969	Cle-A	122	266	26	66	10	0	2	24	25	33	.248	.313	.308	72	-10	3	2	-0	.961	-4	O-84	-1.8
1970	Mil-A	124	276	34	64	11	0	4	31	16	40	.232	.274	.315	62	-15	1	3	-2	.966	-16	*O-106	-3.7
Total	12	1365	3631	488	984	150	29	42	319	294	438	.271	.327	.363	94	-28	58	32	-2	.981	-96	*O-1099/1-1	-18.3

■ CHIEF SOCKALEXIS Sockalexis, Louis M. b: 10/24/1871, Old Town, Maine d: 12/24/13, Burlington, Maine BL/TR, 5'11", 185 lbs. Deb: 4/22/1897

1897	Cle-N	66	278	43	94	9	8	3	42	18		.338	.385	.460	116	5	16			.888	1	O-66	0.1
1898	Cle-N	21	67	11	15	2	0	0	10	1		.224	.246	.254	44	-5	0			.964	2	O-16	-0.4
1899	Cle-N	7	22	0	6	1	0	0	3	1		.273	.304	.318	76	-1	0			.818	1	/O-5	0.0
Total	3	94	367	54	115	12	8	3	55	20		.313	.355	.414	103	-0	16			.896	4	/O-87	-0.3

■ BILL SODD Sodd, William b: 9/18/14, Ft.Worth, Tex. BR/TR, 6'2", 210 lbs. Deb: 9/27/37

| 1937 | Cle-A | 1 | 1 | 0 | 0 | 0 | 0 | 0 | 0 | 0 | 0 | .000 | .000 | .000 | -99 | -0 | 0 | 0 | | .000 | 0 | H | 0.0 |

■ ERIC SODERHOLM Soderholm, Eric Thane b: 9/24/48, Cortland, N.Y. BR/TR, 5'11", 187 lbs. Deb: 9/3/71

1971	Min-A	21	64	9	10	4	0	1	4	10	17	.156	.299	.266	59	-1	0	1	-1	.942	3	3-20	-0.1
1972	Min-A	93	287	28	54	10	0	13	39	19	48	.188	.246	.359	75	-10	3	3	-1	.942	2	3-79	-1.1
1973	Min-A	35	111	22	33	7	2	1	9	21	16	.297	.414	.423	131	6	1	2	-1	.921	0	3-33/S-1	0.5
1974	Min-A	141	464	63	128	18	3	10	51	48	68	.276	.350	.392	110	6	7	3	0	.956	-4	*3-130/S-1	0.2
1975	Min-A	117	419	62	120	17	2	11	58	53	66	.286	.367	.415	119	11	3	5	-2	.969	12	*3-113/D-3	2.1
1977	Chi-A	130	460	77	129	20	3	25	67	47	47	.280	.352	.500	129	18	2	4	-2	**.978**	0	*3-126/D-3	1.5
1978	Chi-A	143	457	57	118	17	1	20	67	39	44	.258	.322	.431	109	4	2	2	-1	.964	0	*3-128,D-11/2-1	0.2
1979	Chi-A	56	210	31	53	8	2	6	34	19	19	.252	.314	.395	90	-3	0	1	-1	.986	15	3-56	1.0
	Tex-A	63	147	15	40	6	0	4	19	12	9	.272	.331	.395	96	-1	0	0	0	.944	0	3-37,D-14/1-2	-0.1
	Yr	119	357	46	93	14	2	10	53	31	28	.261	.321	.395	93	-4	0	1	-1	.975	15	3-93,D-14/1-2	0.9
1980	*NY-A	95	275	38	79	13	1	11	35	27	25	.287	.353	.462	123	9	0	0	0	.952	-1	D-51,3-37	0.5
Total	9	894	2894	402	764	120	14	102	383	295	359	.264	.337	.421	110	37	18	21	-7	.962	27	3-759/D-82,1-2,S2	4.7

■ RICK SOFIELD Sofield, Richard Michael b: 12/16/56, Cheyenne, Wyo. BL/TR, 6'1", 195 lbs. Deb: 4/6/79

1979	Min-A	35	93	8	28	5	0	0	12	12	27	.301	.381	.355	96	-0	2	3	-1	.954	-3	O-35	-0.5
1980	Min-A	131	417	52	103	18	4	9	49	24	92	.247	.291	.374	75	-15	4	5	-2	.979	-5	*O-126/D-2	-2.6
1981	Min-A	41	102	9	18	2	0	0	5	8	22	.176	.236	.196	24	-10	3	2	-0	.983	-1	O-34	-1.2
Total	3	207	612	69	149	25	4	9	66	44	141	.243	.296	.342	71	-25	9	10	-3	.975	-8	O-195/D-2	-4.3

■ LUIS SOJO Sojo, Luis Beltran (Sojo) b: 1/3/66, Caracas, Venez. BR/TR, 5'11", 170 lbs. Deb: 7/14/90

1990	Tor-A	33	80	14	18	3	0	1	9	5	5	.225	.271	.300	58	-4	1	1	-0	.969	-3	2-15/S-5,0-5,3-4,D	-0.8
1991	Cal-A	113	364	38	94	14	1	3	20	14	26	.258	.295	.327	72	-14	4	2	0	.981	20	*2-107/S-2,3-1,OD	0.8
1992	Cal-A	106	368	37	100	12	3	7	43	14	24	.272	.300	.378	88	-7	7	11	-5	.985	2	2-96/3-9,S-5	-0.7
1993	Tor-A	19	47	5	8	2	0	0	6	4	2	.170	.235	.213	21	-5	0	0	0	1.000	1	/2-8,S-8,3-3	-0.6
1994	Sea-A	63	213	32	59	9	2	6	22	8	25	.277	.309	.423	85	-5	2	1	0	.973	18	2-40,S-24/3-1,D-2	1.4
1995	*Sea-A	102	339	50	98	18	2	7	39	23	19	.289	.336	.416	93	-4	4	2	0	.983	-14	S-80,2-19/O-6	-0.9
1996	Sea-A	77	247	20	52	8	1	1	16	10	13	.211	.244	.263	28	-27	2	2	-1	.940	3	3-33,2-27,S-19	-1.4
	*NY-A	18	40	3	11	2	0	0	5	1	4	.275	.293	.325	55	-3	0	0	0	1.000	3	2-14/S-4,3-1	0.1
	Yr	95	287	23	63	10	1	1	21	11	17	.220	.251	.272	32	-30	2	2	-1	.986	13	2-41,3-34,S-23	-1.3
Total	7	531	1698	199	440	68	9	25	160	79	118	.259	.296	.354	72	-69	20	19	-5	.980	34	2-326/S-147/3OD	-2.1

■ TONY SOLAITA Solaita, Tolia b: 1/15/47, Nuuuli, Amer.Samoa d: 2/10/90, Tafuna, Amer.Samoa BL/TL, 6', 215 lbs. Deb: 9/16/68

1968	NY-A	1	1	0	0	0	0	0	0	0	0	.000	.000	.000	-99	-0	0	0	0	1.000	-0	/1-1	0.0
1974	KC-A	96	239	31	64	12	0	7	30	35	70	.268	.364	.406	115	5	0	3	-2	.991	3	1-65,D-14/O-1	0.3
1975	KC-A	93	231	35	60	11	0	16	44	39	79	.260	.371	.515	145	14	0	1	-1	.994	3	D-37,1-35	1.4
1976	KC-A	31	68	4	16	4	0	0	9	6	17	.235	.297	.294	73	-2	0	0	0	.974	0	D-14/1-5	-0.3
	Cal-A	63	215	25	58	9	0	9	33	34	44	.270	.369	.437	145	13	1	1	0	.998	8	1-54/D-7	1.7
	Yr	94	283	29	74	13	0	9	42	40	61	.261	.353	.403	120	10	1	1	0	.996	8	1-59,D-21	1.4
1977	Cal-A	116	324	40	78	15	0	14	53	56	77	.241	.353	.417	113	7	1	3	-2	.990	1	1-91/D-6	0.2
1978	Cal-A	60	94	10	21	3	0	1	14	16	25	.223	.336	.287	80	-2	0	0	0	1.000	1	D-18,1-11	-0.2
1979	Mon-N	29	42	5	12	4	0	1	7	11	16	.286	.434	.452	143	3	0	0	0	.989	0	1-13	0.3
	Tor-A	36	102	14	27	8	1	2	13	17	16	.265	.370	.422	112	2	1	0	0	1.000	0	D-26/1-6	0.1
Total	7	525	1316	164	336	66	1	50	203	214	345	.255	.361	.421	120	39	2	8	-4	.993	17	1-281,D-122/O-1	3.5

■ MOSE SOLOMON Solomon, Mose Hirsch "The Rabbi Of Swat" b: 12/8/1900, New York, N.Y. d: 6/25/66, Miami, Fla. BL/TL, 5'9.5", 180 lbs. Deb: 9/30/23

| 1923 | NY-N | 2 | 8 | 0 | 3 | 1 | 0 | 0 | 1 | 0 | 1 | .375 | .375 | .500 | 131 | 0 | 0 | 0 | 0 | .833 | -0 | /O-2 | 0.0 |

■ MOOSE SOLTERS Solters, Julius Joseph (b: Julius Joseph Soltesz) b: 3/22/06, Pittsburgh, Pa. d: 9/28/75, Pittsburgh, Pa. BR/TR, 6', 190 lbs. Deb: 4/17/34

1934	Bos-A	101	365	61	109	25	4	7	58	18	50	.299	.333	.447	93	-5	9	4	0	.933	2	O-89	-0.6
1935	Bos-A	24	79	15	19	6	1	0	8	2	7	.241	.268	.342	53	-6	1	0	0	.966	3	O-21	-0.4
	StL-A	127	552	79	182	39	6	18	104	34	35	.330	.369	.520	122	15	10	1	2	.989	16	*O-127	2.7
	Yr	151	631	94	201	45	7	18	112	36	42	.319	.356	.498	113	9	11	2	2	.985	19	*O-148	2.3
1936	StL-A	152	628	100	183	45	7	17	134	41	48	.291	.336	.467	93	-10	3	0	1	.956	-3	*O-147	-0.3
1937	Cle-A	152	589	90	190	42	11	20	109	42	56	.323	.372	.533	125	19	6	9	-4	.953	2	*O-149	1.2
1938	Cle-A	67	199	30	40	6	3	2	22	13	28	.201	.250	.291	36	-21	4	1	0	.969	1	O-46	-1.8
1939	Cle-A	41	102	19	28	7	2	2	19	9	15	.275	.333	.441	100	-0	2	1	0	.915	-3	O-25	-0.4
	StL-A	40	131	14	27	6	0	1	14	10	20	.206	.262	.267	35	-13	1	0	0	.935	0	O-30	-1.2
	Yr	81	233	33	55	13	2	3	33	19	35	.236	.294	.343	63	-14	3	1	0	.927	-3	O-55	-1.6
1940	Chi-A	116	428	65	132	28	3	12	80	27	54	.308	.351	.472	110	5	3	3	-1	.971	5	*O-107	0.4
1941	Chi-A	76	251	24	65	9	4	4	43	18	31	.259	.311	.375	82	-7	3	2	-0	.966	1	O-63	-1.0

YEAR	TM/L	G	AB	R	H	2B	3B	HR	RBI	BB	SO	AVG	OBP	SLG	PRO+	BR/A	SB	CS	SBR	FA	FR	G/POS	TPR
1943	Chi-A	42	97	6	15	0	0	1	8	7	5	.155	.212	.186	17	-10	0	1	-1	.941	-3	O-21	-1.7
Total 9		938	3421	503	990	213	42	83	599	221	377	.289	.334	.449	96	-32	42	23	-1	.960	36	O-825	-3.1

■ JOCK SOMERLOTT Somerlott, John Wesley b: 10/26/1882, Flint, Ind. d: 4/21/65, Butler, Ind. BR/TR, 6', 160 lbs. Deb: 9/19/10

YEAR	TM/L	G	AB	R	H	2B	3B	HR	RBI	BB	SO	AVG	OBP	SLG	PRO+	BR/A	SB	CS	SBR	FA	FR	G/POS	TPR
1910	Was-A	16	63	6	14	0	0	0	2	3		.222	.258	.222	53	-3	2			.994	0	1-16	-0.4
1911	Was-A	13	40	2	7	0	0	0	2	0		.175	.195	.175	4	-5	2			.992	2	1-12	-0.4
Total 2		29	103	8	21	0	0	0	4	3		.204	.234	.204	32	-9	4			.993	2	/1-28	-0.8

■ ED SOMERVILLE Somerville, Edward G. b: 3/1/1853, Philadelphia, Pa. d: 10/1/1877, London, Ont., Canada BR/TR, Deb: 4/30/1875

YEAR	TM/L	G	AB	R	H	2B	3B	HR	RBI	BB	SO	AVG	OBP	SLG	PRO+	BR/A	SB	CS	SBR	FA	FR	G/POS	TPR
1875	Cen-n	14	57	6	13	3	0	0	6	1	3	.228	.241	.281	88	-0	1	0	0	.771	-6	2-14/S-1	-0.5
	NH-n	33	136	14	29	5	0	0	7	1	3	.213	.219	.250	72	-3	1	2	-1	.802	13	2-29/3-2,1-1,S-1	0.7
	Yr	47	193	20	42	8	0	0	13	2	6	.218	.226	.259	77	-3	2	2	-1	.794	7	2-43/S-2,3-2,1-1	0.2
1876	Lou-N	64	256	29	48	5	1	0	14	1	6	.188	.191	.215	30	-21				.870	30	*2-64	0.7

■ JOE SOMMER Sommer, Joseph John b: 11/20/1858, Covington, Ky. d: 1/16/38, Cincinnati, Ohio BR/TR, Deb: 7/8/1880

YEAR	TM/L	G	AB	R	H	2B	3B	HR	RBI	BB	SO	AVG	OBP	SLG	PRO+	BR/A	SB	CS	SBR	FA	FR	G/POS	TPR
1880	Cin-N	24	88	10	16	1	0	0	6	0	2	.182	.182	.193	28	-6				.913	-1	O-22/S-1,3-1,C-1	-0.7
1882	Cin-a	80	354	82	102	12	6	1	29	24		.288	.333	.364	128	10				**.925**	4	*O-80	1.2
1883	Cin-a	97	413	79	115	5	7	3	52	20		.278	.312	.359	106	2				.854	-1	*O-94/3-3,P-1	0.0
1884	Bal-a	107	479	96	129	11	10	4		8		.269	.293	.359	107	2				.841	6	*3-97/O-9,2-1	0.8
1885	Bal-a	110	471	84	118	23	6	1	44	24		.251	.291	.331	98	-1				.921	12	*O-107/S-2,3-2,P1	0.7
1886	Bal-a	139	560	79	117	18	4	1	52	24		.209	.245	.261	60	-26	31			.900	13	*O-95,2-32,3/SP	-1.2
1887	Bal-a	131	463	88	123	11	5	0	65	63		.266	.358	.311	93	0	29			.902	0	*O-110,2-13,3/SP	-0.1
1888	Bal-a	79	297	31	65	10	0	0	35	18		.219	.266	.253	68	-10	13			.871	-4	O-44,S-34/2-2,1-1	-1.3
1889	Bal-a	106	386	51	85	13	2	1	36	42	49	.220	.298	.272	62	-19	18			.929	9	*O-105/S-1	-1.1
1890	Cle-N	9	35	4	8	1	0	0	0	2		.229	.270	.257	55	-2	0			.789	-2	/O-9,P-1	-0.4
	Bal-a	38	129	13	33	4	2	0	23	13		.256	.324	.318	85	-3	10			.892	1	O-38	-0.3
Total 10		920	3675	617	911	109	42	11	342	238	53	.248	.297	.309	88	-54	101			.901	38	O-713,3-124/2SP1C	-2.4

■ PETE SOMMERS Sommers, Joseph Andrews b: 10/26/1866, Cleveland, Ohio d: 7/22/08, Cleveland, Ohio BR/TR, 5'11.5", 181 lbs. Deb: 4/27/1887

YEAR	TM/L	G	AB	R	H	2B	3B	HR	RBI	BB	SO	AVG	OBP	SLG	PRO+	BR/A	SB	CS	SBR	FA	FR	G/POS	TPR
1887	NY-a	33	116	9	21	3	0	1	12	7		.181	.234	.232	32	-11	6			.830	-8	C-31/O-1,1-1	-1.3
1888	Bos-N	4	13	1	3	1	0	0	0	3		.231	.231	.308	69	-0				.880	4	/C-4	-0.1
1889	Chi-N	12	45	5	10	5	0	0	8	2	8	.222	.271	.333	65	-2	0			.836	-5	C-11/O-1	-0.6
	Ind-N	23	84	12	21	2	2	2	14	1	16	.250	.267	.393	82	-3	2			.905	-2	C-21/O-2	-0.3
	Yr	35	129	17	31	7	2	2	22	3	24	.240	.269	.372	76	-5	2			.882	-7	C-32/O-3	-0.9
1890	NY-N	17	47	4	5	1	1	0	1	4	13	.106	.192	.170	6	-6	0			.837	1	C-11/1-5,O-2	-0.4
	Cle-N	9	34	4	7	1	1	0	1	2	3	.206	.250	.294	60	-2	0			.906	1	/C-8,O-1	-0.1
	Yr	26	81	8	12	2	2	0	2	6	16	.148	.216	.222	28	-8	0			.865	1	C-19/1-5,O-3	-0.5
Total 4		98	339	35	67	13	4	3	36	16	43	.198	.242	.286	50	-24	8			.860	-15	/C-86,O-7,1-6	-2.8

■ BILL SOMMERS Sommers, William Dunn b: 2/17/23, Brooklyn, N.Y. BR/TR, 6', 180 lbs. Deb: 4/25/50

YEAR	TM/L	G	AB	R	H	2B	3B	HR	RBI	BB	SO	AVG	OBP	SLG	PRO+	BR/A	SB	CS	SBR	FA	FR	G/POS	TPR
1950	StL-A	65	137	24	35	5	1	0	14	25	14	.255	.370	.307	72	-5	0	1	-1	.917	-9	3-37,2-21	-1.4

■ BILL SORRELL Sorrell, William b: 10/14/40, Morehead, Ky. BL/TR, 6', 190 lbs. Deb: 9/2/65

YEAR	TM/L	G	AB	R	H	2B	3B	HR	RBI	BB	SO	AVG	OBP	SLG	PRO+	BR/A	SB	CS	SBR	FA	FR	G/POS	TPR
1965	Phi-N	10	13	2	5	0	0	1	2	2	1	.385	.467	.615	206	2	0	0	0	.000	0	/3-1	0.2
1967	SF-N	18	17	1	3	1	0	0	1	3	2	.176	.300	.235	56	-1	0	0	0	1.000	-2	/O-5	-0.3
1970	KC-A	57	135	12	36	2	0	4	14	10	13	.267	.317	.370	89	-2	1	0	0	.873	-6	3-29/O-4,1-3	-0.9
Total 3		85	165	15	44	3	0	5	17	15	16	.267	.328	.376	95	-1	1	0	0	.873	-8	/3-30,O-9,1-3	-1.0

■ CHICK SORRELLS Sorrells, Raymond Edwin b: 7/31/1896, Stringtown, Okla. d: 7/20/83, Terrell, Tex. BR/TR, 5'9", 155 lbs. Deb: 9/18/22

YEAR	TM/L	G	AB	R	H	2B	3B	HR	RBI	BB	SO	AVG	OBP	SLG	PRO+	BR/A	SB	CS	SBR	FA	FR	G/POS	TPR
1922	Cle-A	2	1	0	0	0	0	0	0	0	0	.000	.000	.000	-99	-0	0	0	0	1.000	1	/S-1	0.1

■ PAUL SORRENTO Sorrento, Paul Anthony b: 11/17/65, Somerville, Mass. BL/TR, 6'2", 195 lbs. Deb: 9/8/89

YEAR	TM/L	G	AB	R	H	2B	3B	HR	RBI	BB	SO	AVG	OBP	SLG	PRO+	BR/A	SB	CS	SBR	FA	FR	G/POS	TPR
1989	Min-A	14	21	2	5	0	0	1	5	4		.238	.385	.238	74	-0	1			1.000	-0	/1-5,D-5	-0.1
1990	Min-A	41	121	11	25	4	1	5	13	12	31	.207	.284	.380	79	-4	1	1	-0	.992	-1	D-23,1-15	-0.7
1991	*Min-A	26	47	6	12	2	0	4	13	4	11	.255	.314	.553	129	2	0	0	0	1.000	1	1-13/D-2	0.2
1992	Cle-A	140	458	52	123	24	1	18	60	51	89	.269	.343	.443	121	12	0	3	-2	.993	-1	*1-121,D-11	0.1
1993	Cle-A	148	463	75	119	26	1	18	65	58	121	.257	.342	.434	108	5	3	1	0	.995	-0	*1-144/O-3,D-1	-0.5
1994	Cle-A	95	322	43	90	14	0	14	62	34	68	.280	.348	.453	104	2	0	1	-1	.995	1	1-86/D-8	-0.5
1995	*Cle-A	104	323	50	76	14	0	25	79	51	71	.235	.340	.511	116	7	1	1	-1	.992	-2	1-91,D-11	-0.5
1996	Sea-A	143	471	67	136	32	1	23	93	57	103	.289	.374	.507	120	15	0	2	-1	.990	-2	*1-138	-0.1
Total 8		711	2226	306	586	116	4	107	386	272	498	.263	.346	.463	112	37	5	9	-4	.993	-5	1-613/D-61,O-3	-2.1

■ SAMMY SOSA Sosa, Samuel Peralta b: 11/12/68, San Pedro De Macoris, D.R. BR/TR, 6', 165 lbs. Deb: 6/16/89

YEAR	TM/L	G	AB	R	H	2B	3B	HR	RBI	BB	SO	AVG	OBP	SLG	PRO+	BR/A	SB	CS	SBR	FA	FR	G/POS	TPR
1989	Tex-A	25	84	8	20	3	0	1	3	0	20	.238	.238	.310	52	-5	0	2	-1	.944	-2	O-19	-0.9
	Chi-A	33	99	19	27	5	0	3	10	11	27	.273	.357	.414	120	3	7	3	0	.969	-5	O-33/D-6	-0.2
	Yr	58	183	27	47	8	0	4	13	11	47	.257	.306	.366	89	-3	7	5	-1	.960	-7	O-52/D-6	-1.1
1990	Chi-A	153	532	72	124	26	10	15	70	33	150	.233	.285	.404	93	-7	32	16	0	.962	9	*O-152	-0.2
1991	Chi-A	116	316	39	64	10	1	10	33	14	98	.203	.241	.335	59	-19	13	6	0	.973	-3	*O-111/D-2	-2.3
1992	Chi-N	67	262	41	68	7	2	8	25	19	63	.260	.319	.393	98	-1	15	7	0	.961	-3	O-67	-0.6
1993	Chi-N	159	598	92	156	25	5	33	93	38	135	.261	.309	.485	111	6	36	11	4	.976	5	*O-158	0.7
1994	Chi-N	105	426	59	128	17	6	25	70	25	92	.300	.342	.545	128	16	22	13	-1	.973	5	*O-105	1.7
1995	Chi-N★	144	564	89	151	17	3	36	119	58	134	.268	.341	.500	121	15	34	7	6	.962	14	*O-143	3.1
1996	Chi-N	124	498	84	136	21	2	40	100	34	134	.273	.326	.564	128	17	18	5	2	.964	12	*O-124	2.7
Total 8		926	3379	503	874	131	29	171	523	232	853	.259	.312	.466	108	24	177	70	11	.967	28	O-912/D-8	4.0

■ DENNY SOTHERN Sothern, Dennis Elwood b: 1/20/04, Washington, D.C. d: 12/7/77, Durham, N.C. BR/TR, 5'11", 175 lbs. Deb: 9/10/26

YEAR	TM/L	G	AB	R	H	2B	3B	HR	RBI	BB	SO	AVG	OBP	SLG	PRO+	BR/A	SB	CS	SBR	FA	FR	G/POS	TPR
1926	Phi-N	14	53	5	13	1	0	3	10	4	10	.245	.310	.434	94	-1	0			.975	2	O-13	0.0
1928	Phi-N	141	579	92	165	27	5	5	38	34	53	.285	.327	.375	80	-17	17			.964	8	*O-136	-1.8
1929	Phi-N	76	294	52	90	21	3	5	27	16	24	.306	.346	.449	90	-5	13			.967	3	O-71	-0.6
1930	Phi-N	90	347	66	97	26	1	5	36	22	37	.280	.326	.403	70	-17	6			.967	8	O-84	-1.3
	Pit-N	17	51	4	9	4	0	1	4	3	4	.176	.222	.314	28	-6	2			.971	-1	O-13	-0.7
	Yr	107	398	70	106	30	1	6	40	25	41	.266	.313	.392	65	-23	8			.967	8	O-97	-2.0
1931	Bro-N	19	31	10	5	1	0	0	0	4	8	.161	.257	.194	23	-3	0			.958	-1	O-10	-0.5
Total 5		357	1355	219	379	80	9	19	115	83	136	.280	.325	.394	77	-50	38			.966	20	O-327	-4.9

■ STEVE SOUCHOCK Souchock, Stephen "Bud" b: 3/3/19, Yatesboro, Pa. BR/TR, 6'2.5", 203 lbs. Deb: 5/25/46

YEAR	TM/L	G	AB	R	H	2B	3B	HR	RBI	BB	SO	AVG	OBP	SLG	PRO+	BR/A	SB	CS	SBR	FA	FR	G/POS	TPR
1946	NY-A	47	86	15	26	3	3	2	11	0	13	.302	.362	.477	131	3	0	3	-2	.964	-2	1-20	-0.1
1948	NY-A	44	118	11	24	3	1	3	11	7	13	.203	.248	.322	51	-9	3	0	1	.988	-2	1-32	-1.0
1949	Chi-A	84	252	29	59	13	5	7	37	25	38	.234	.303	.409	90	-6	3	0	1	.951	2	O-39,1-30	-0.6
1951	Det-A	91	188	33	46	10	3	11	28	18	27	.245	.314	.505	118	3	2	0	-1	.941	-6	O-59/3-3,1-1,2-1	-0.6
1952	Det-A	92	265	40	66	16	4	13	45	21	28	.249	.304	.487	117	4	1	0	0	.964	1	O-56,3-13/1-9	0.2
1953	Det-A	89	278	29	84	13	3	11	46	8	35	.302	.326	.489	119	5	5	1	1	.962	-1	O-80/1-1	0.2
1954	Det-A	25	39	6	7	1	0	1	8	2	10	.179	.220	.462	84	-1	1	1	-0	1.000	-1	/O-9,3-2	-0.3
1955	Det-A	1	1	0	1	0	0	0	0	0	0	1.000	1.000	1.000	449	0	0	0	0	.000	0	H	0.0
Total 8		473	1227	163	313	58	20	50	186	88	164	.255	.307	.457	106	1	15	9	-1	.957	-10	O-243/1-93,3-18,2-1	-2.2

■ CLYDE SOUTHWICK Southwick, Clyde Aubra b: 11/3/1886, Maxwell, Iowa d: 10/14/61, Freeport, Ill. BL/TR, 6', 180 lbs. Deb: 8/22/11

YEAR	TM/L	G	AB	R	H	2B	3B	HR	RBI	BB	SO	AVG	OBP	SLG	PRO+	BR/A	SB	CS	SBR	FA	FR	G/POS	TPR
1911	StL-A	4	12	3	3	0	0	0	0	3		.250	.308	.250	58	-1				.938	-1	/C-4	-0.1

■ BILL SOUTHWORTH Southworth, William Frederick b: 11/10/45, Madison, Wis. BR/TR, 6'2", 205 lbs. Deb: 10/2/64

YEAR	TM/L	G	AB	R	H	2B	3B	HR	RBI	BB	SO	AVG	OBP	SLG	PRO+	BR/A	SB	CS	SBR	FA	FR	G/POS	TPR
1964	Mil-N	3	7	2	2	1	0	0	2	0		.286	.444	.714	219	1	0	0	0	1.000	-1	/3-2	0.0

YEAR	TM/L	G	AB	R	H	2B	3B	HR	RBI	BB	SO	AVG	OBP	SLG	PRO+	BR/A	SB	CS	SBR	FA	FR	G/POS	TPR

■ BILLY SOUTHWORTH   Southworth, William Harrison   b: 3/9/1893, Harvard, Neb.   d: 11/15/69, Columbus, Ohio   BL/TR, 5'9", 170 lbs.   Deb: 8/4/13   MC

1913	Cle-A	1	0	0	0	0	0	0	0	0	0	—	—	—	—	0	0			.000	0	/O-1	0.0
1915	Cle-A	60	177	25	39	2	5	0	8	36	12	.220	.352	.288	90	-1	2	4	-2	.942	1	O-44	-0.4
1918	Pit-N	64	246	37	84	5	7	2	43	26	9	.341	.409	.443	154	17	19			.980	9	O-64	2.4
1919	Pit-N	121	453	56	127	14	14	4	61	32	22	.280	.329	.400	114	7	23			.968	5	*O-121	0.4
1920	Pit-N	146	546	64	155	17	13	2	53	52	20	.284	.348	.374	104	4	23	25	-8	**.991**	10	*O-142	-0.5
1921	Bos-N	141	569	86	175	25	15	7	79	36	13	.308	.351	.441	115	11	22	20	-5	.975	9	*O-141	0.4
1922	Bos-N	43	158	27	51	4	4	4	18	18	1	.323	.392	.475	128	7	4	1	1	.955	5	O-41	0.9
1923	Bos-N	153	611	95	195	29	16	6	78	61	23	.319	.383	.448	124	21	14	16	-5	.943	6	*O-151/2-2	1.1
1924	*NY-N	94	281	40	72	13	0	3	36	32	16	.256	.332	.335	81	-7	1	6	-3	.935	-3	O-75	-1.7
1925	NY-N	123	473	79	138	19	5	6	44	51	11	.292	.363	.391	97	-1	6	13	-6	.964	-8	O-119	-2.2
1926	NY-N	36	116	23	38	6	1	5	30	7	1	.328	.366	.526	139	6	1			.970	-2	O-29	0.2
	*StL-N	99	391	76	124	22	6	11	69	26	9	.317	.364	.488	123	11	13			.971	-3	O-99	0.2
	Yr	135	507	99	162	28	7	16	99	33	10	.320	.365	.497	127	17	14			.971	-5	O-128	0.4
1927	StL-N	92	306	52	92	15	5	2	39	23	7	.301	.350	.402	98	-1	10			.970	-7	O-83	-1.3
1929	StL-N	19	32	1	6	0	0	0	3	2	4	.188	.235	.250	20	-4	0			1.000	-0	/O-5,M	-0.4
Total	13	1192	4359	661	1296	173	91	52	561	402	148	.297	.359	.415	111	69	138	85		.965	23	*O-1115/2-2	-0.9

■ JOHN SOWDERS   Sowders, John   b: 12/10/1866, Louisville, Ky.   d: 7/29/39, Indianapolis, Ind   BR/TL, 6',   Deb: 6/28/1887   F

1887	Ind-N	1	2	0	0	0	0	0	0	0	1	.000	.000	.000	-99	-1	0			1.000	-1	/O-1,P-1	0.0
1889	KC-a	28	87	11	19	3	0	0	6	4	20	.218	.269	.253	46	-6	1			.842	-3	P-25/O-3	-0.1
1890	Bro-P	40	132	14	25	3	0	1	20	10	12	.189	.246	.235	27	-14	0			.921	-2	P-39/O-3	-0.1
Total	3	69	221	25	44	6	0	1	26	14	33	.199	.253	.240	33	-21	1			.884	-6	/P-65,O-7	-0.2

■ LEN SOWDERS   Sowders, Leonard   b: 6/29/1861, Louisville, Ky.   d: 11/19/1888, Indianapolis, Ind.   5'11.5", 172 lbs.   Deb: 9/10/1886   F

1886	Bal-a	23	76	10	20	3	1	0	14	12		.263	.364	.329	121	2	6			.889	-1	O-23/1-1	0.1

■ AL SPALDING   Spalding, Albert Goodwill   b: 9/2/1850, Byron, Ill.   d: 9/9/15, San Diego, Cal.   BR/TR, 6'1", 170 lbs.   Deb: 5/5/1871   MH

1871	Bos-n	31	144	43	39	10	1	1	31	8	1	.271	.309	.375	93	-2	2	0	1	.776	-3	*P-31/O-9	-0.2
1872	Bos-n	48	237	60	84	11	5	0	47	3	1	.354	.363	.443	139	9	3	0	1	**.902**	5	*P-48/O-7	-0.2
1873	Bos-n	60	322	83	106	18	2	1	60	3	1	.329	.335	.407	110	1	1	0	0	.855	5	*P-60,O-13	-0.3
1874	Bos-n	71	362	80	119	13	1	0	54	3	0	.329	.334	.370	119	6	2	1	0	**.854**	5	*P-71/O-6	-0.1
1875	Bos-n	74	343	68	107	15	3	0	56	3	3	.312	.318	.373	134	10	2	2	-1	.906	-1	*P-72,O-18/1-4	-0.3
1876	Chi-N	66	292	54	91	14	2	0	44	6	3	.312	.326	.373	118	3				.951	5	*P-61,O-10/1-3,SM	-0.2
1877	Chi-N	60	254	29	65	7	6	0	35	3	16	.256	.265	.331	77	-8				.959	6	*1-45,2-13/P-4,3M	-0.2
1878	Chi-N	1	4	0	2	0	0	0	0	0	0	.500	.500	.500	215	-0				.429	-2	/2-1	-0.2
Total	5 n	284	1408	334	455	67	12	2	248	20	6	.323	.333	.392	121	24	10	3	1	.868	13	P-282/O-53,1-4	-1.1
Total	3	127	550	83	158	21	8	0	79	9	19	.287	.299	.355	99	-4				.948	5	/P-65,1-48,203S	-0.5

■ DICK SPALDING   Spalding, Charles Harry   b: 10/13/1893, Philadelphia, Pa.   d: 2/3/50, Philadelphia, Pa.   BL/TL, 5'11", 185 lbs.   Deb: 4/18/27   C

1927	Phi-N	115	442	68	131	16	3	0	25	38	40	.296	.352	.346	86	-7	5			**.992**	3	*O-113	-1.1
1928	Was-A	16	23	1	8	0	0	0	0	0	4	.348	.348	.348	84	-1	0	2	-1	1.000	-3	O-11	-0.5
Total	2	131	465	69	139	16	3	0	25	38	44	.299	.352	.346	86	-8	5	2		.993	-0	*O-124	-1.6

■ AL SPANGLER   Spangler, Albert Donald   b: 7/8/33, Philadelphia, Pa.   BL/TL, 6', 175 lbs.   Deb: 9/16/59   C

1959	Mil-N	6	12	3	5	0	0	0	0	1	1	.417	.462	.583	192	2	1	0	0	1.000	-1	/O-4	0.1
1960	Mil-N	101	105	26	28	5	2	0	6	14	17	.267	.358	.352	103	1	6	2	1	.989	-14	O-92	-1.4
1961	Mil-N	68	97	23	26	2	0	0	6	28	9	.268	.432	.289	102	2	4	2	0	1.000	-7	O-44	-0.6
1962	Hou-N	129	418	51	119	10	9	5	35	70	46	.285	.391	.388	119	14	7	6	-2	.960	-0	*O-121	0.5
1963	Hou-N	120	430	52	121	25	4	4	27	50	38	.281	.358	.386	122	13	5	8	-3	.987	3	*O-113	0.6
1964	Hou-N	135	449	51	110	18	5	4	38	41	43	.245	.314	.334	88	-7	7	8	-3	.964	-5	*O-127	-2.3
1965	Hou-N	38	112	18	24	1	1	1	7	14	8	.214	.302	.268	66	-5	1	0	-0	.956	-1	O-33	-0.8
	Cal-A	51	96	17	25	1	0	1	8	9		.260	.317	.271	70	-4	4	0	1	.973	-4	O-24	-0.5
1966	Cal-A	6	9	2	6	0	0	0	0	2	2	.667	.727	.667	312	3	0	0	0	1.000	-1	/O-3	0.2
1967	Chi-N	62	130	18	33	7	0	0	13	23	17	.254	.366	.308	91	-1	2	2	-1	.986	-3	O-41	-0.6
1968	Chi-N	88	177	21	48	9	3	2	18	20	24	.271	.348	.390	114	3	0	1	-1	.973	-5	O-48	-0.5
1969	Chi-N	82	213	23	45	8	1	4	23	21	16	.211	.285	.315	60	-11	0	0	-0	.950	-7	O-58	-2.4
1970	Chi-N	21	14	2	2	1	0	1	1	3	3	.143	.294	.429	81	-0	0	0	0	1.000	-1	/O-6	-0.2
1971	Chi-N	5	5	0	2	0	0	0	0	0	0	.400	.400	.400	111	0	0	0	0			H	0.0
Total	13	912	2267	307	594	87	26	21	175	295	234	.262	.350	.351	100	10	37	32	-8	.973	-45	O-714	-8.2

■ BOB SPEAKE   Speake, Robert Charles "Spook"   b: 8/22/30, Springfield, Mo.   BL/TL, 6'1", 178 lbs.   Deb: 4/16/55

1955	Chi-N	95	261	36	57	9	5	12	43	28	71	.218	.301	.429	91	-4	3	4	-2	.959	-3	O-55/1-8	-1.2
1957	Chi-N	129	418	65	97	14	5	16	50	38	68	.232	.301	.404	89	-8	5	6	-2	.974	6	O-60,1-39	-1.0
1958	SF-N	66	71	9	15	3	0	3	10	13	15	.211	.333	.380	90	-1	0	1	-1	.938	0	O-10	-0.1
1959	SF-N	15	11	0	1	0	0	0	1	1	4	.091	.167	.091	-30	-2	0	0	0	.000	0	H	-0.2
Total	4	305	761	110	170	26	10	31	104	80	158	.223	.302	.406	88	-14	8	11	-4	.966	3	O-125/1-47	-2.5

■ TRIS SPEAKER   Speaker, Tristram E "The Grey Eagle"   b: 4/4/1888, Hubbard, Tex.   d: 12/8/58, Lake Whitney, Tex.   BL/TL, 5'11.5", 193 lbs.   Deb: 9/14/07   MH

1907	Bos-A	7	19	0	3	0	0	0	1			.158	.200	.158	14	-2	0			1.000	1	/O-4	-0.1
1908	Bos-A	31	116	12	26	2	2	0	9	4		.224	.262	.276	73	-4	3			1.000	5	O-31	0.0
1909	Bos-A	143	544	73	168	26	13	7	77	38		.309	.362	.443	151	30	35			.973	**23**	*O-142	5.2
1910	Bos-A	141	538	92	183	20	14	7	65	52		.340	.404	.468	169	42	35			.957	15	*O-140	5.5
1911	Bos-A	141	500	88	167	34	13	8	70	59		.334	.418	.502	158	39	25			.956	6	*O-138	3.7
1912	*Bos-A	153	580	136	222	**53**	12	**10**	90	82		.383	**.464**	.567	185	65	52			.958	22	*O-153	**7.7**
1913	Bos-A	141	520	94	189	35	22	3	71	65	22	.363	.441	.533	180	53	46			.942	24	*O-139	7.3
1914	Bos-A	158	571	101	**193**	**46**	18	4	90	77	25	.338	.423	.503	178	55	42	29	-5	.968	28	*O-156/P-1,1-1	7.6
1915	*Bos-A	150	547	108	176	25	12	0	69	81	14	.322	.416	.411	152	38	29	25	-6	.976	13	*O-150	4.0
1916	Cle-A	151	546	102	**211**	41	8	2	79	82	20	**.386**	**.470**	.502	181	57	35	27	-6	.975	9	*O-151	**5.7**
1917	Cle-A	142	523	90	184	42	11	2	60	67	14	.352	.432	.486	168	43	30			.980	8	*O-142	4.7
1918	Cle-A	127	471	73	150	**33**	11	0	61	64	9	.318	.403	.435	140	23	27			.973	11	*O-127	3.0
1919	Cle-A	134	494	83	146	38	12	2	63	73	12	.296	.395	.433	125	15	18			.983	19	*O-134,M	2.9
1920	*Cle-A	150	552	137	214	**50**	11	8	107	97	13	.388	.483	.562	171	61	10	13	-5	.977	10	*O-148,M	5.2
1921	Cle-A	132	506	107	183	**52**	14	3	75	68	13	.362	.439	.538	146	37	2	4	-2	**.984**	10	*O-128,M	3.3
1922	Cle-A	131	426	85	161	**48**	8	11	71	77	11	.378	**.474**	.606	178	52	8	3	1	**.983**	8	*O-109,M	5.0
1923	Cle-A	150	574	133	218	**59**	11	17	130	93	15	.380	.469	.610	163	71	8	8	3	.968	10	*O-150,M	6.4
1924	Cle-A	135	486	94	167	36	9	9	65	72	13	.344	.432	.510	141	31	5	7	-3	.963	5	*O-128,M	2.3
1925	Cle-A	117	429	79	167	35	5	12	87	70	12	.389	**.479**	.578	166	46	5	2	1	.967	10	*O-109,M	**4.5**
1926	Cle-A	150	539	96	164	52	8	7	86	94	15	.304	.408	.469	127	23	6	1	1	.981	10	*O-149,M	2.4
1927	Was-A	141	523	71	171	43	6	2	73	55	8	.327	.395	.444	119	15	9	8	-2	.967	-2	*O-120,1-17	0.6
1928	Phi-A	64	191	28	51	22	2	3	30	10	5	.267	.310	.450	95	-2	5	7	-3	.975	1	O-50	-0.0
Total	22	2789	10195	1882	3514	792	222	117	1529	1381	**220**	.345	.428	.500	156	793	432	129		.970	248	*O-2698/1-18,P-1	86.5

■ HORACE SPEED   Speed, Horace Arthur   b: 10/4/51, Los Angeles, Cal.   BR/TR, 6'1", 180 lbs.   Deb: 4/10/75

1975	SF-N	17	15	2	2	0	0	0	1	1	8	.133	.235	.200	21	-2	0	0	0	.900	-2	/O-9	-0.4
1978	Cle-A	70	106	13	24	4	1	0	4	14	31	.226	.322	.283	72	-3	2	4	-2	.977	-12	O-61/D-3	-1.9
1979	Cle-A	26	14	6	2	1	0	0	1	5	7	.143	.368	.143	44	-1	2	0	0	.875	-5	O-16/D-4	-0.5
Total	3	113	135	21	28	5	1	0	6	20	46	.207	.318	.259	63	-6	4	5	-4	.956	-19	/O-86,D-7	-2.8

■ TIM SPEHR   Spehr, Timothy Joseph   b: 7/2/66, Excelsior Springs, Mo.   BR/TR, 6'2", 205 lbs.   Deb: 7/18/91

1991	KC-A	37	74	7	14	5	0	3	14	9	18	.189	.286	.378	82	-2	1	0	0	.986	12	C-37	1.1

YEAR	TM/L	G	AB	R	H	2B	3B	HR	RBI	BB	SO	AVG	OBP	SLG	PRO+	BR/A	SB	CS	SBR	FA	FR	G/POS	TPR
1993	Mon-N	53	87	14	20	6	0	2	10	6	20	.230	.287	.368	71	-4	2	0	1	.954	9	C-49	0.7
1994	Mon-N	52	36	8	9	3	1	0	5	4	11	.250	.325	.389	84	-1	2	0	1	1.000	10	C-46/O-2	1.0
1995	Mon-N	41	35	4	9	5	0	1	3	6	7	.257	.366	.486	118	1	0	0	0	.990	8	C-38	0.9
1996	Mon-N	63	44	4	4	1	0	1	3	3	15	.091	.167	.182	-8	-7	1	0	0	.985	8	C-58/O-1	0.2
Total	5	246	276	37	56	20	1	7	35	28	71	.203	.283	.359	69	-13	6	0	2	.980	46	C-228/O-3	3.9

■ CHRIS SPEIER
Speier, Chris Edward b: 6/28/50, Alameda, Cal. BR/TR, 6'1", 182 lbs. Deb: 4/7/71

YEAR	TM/L	G	AB	R	H	2B	3B	HR	RBI	BB	SO	AVG	OBP	SLG	PRO+	BR/A	SB	CS	SBR	FA	FR	G/POS	TPR
1971	*SF-N	157	601	74	141	17	6	8	46	56	90	.235	.307	.323	80	-16	4	7	-3	.958	-12	*S-156	-1.1
1972	SF-N★	150	562	74	151	25	2	15	71	82	92	.269	.365	.400	116	14	9	4	0	.974	-5	*S-150	3.3
1973	SF-N★	153	542	58	135	17	4	11	71	66	69	.249	.333	.356	87	-8	4	5	-2	.956	-10	*S-150/2-1	0.0
1974	SF-N☆	141	501	55	125	19	5	9	53	62	64	.250	.337	.361	91	-5	3	2	-0	.969	3	*S-135/2-4	1.6
1975	SF-N	141	487	60	132	30	5	10	69	70	50	.271	.364	.415	111	8	4	5	-2	**.982**	1	*S-136/3-1	2.3
1976	SF-N	145	495	51	112	18	4	3	40	60	52	.226	.315	.297	72	-17	2	2	-1	.974	-1	S-135/2-7,3-5,1-1	-0.2
1977	SF-N	6	17	1	3	1	0	0	0	0	3	.176	.176	.235	9	-2	0	0	0	.920	2	/S-5	0.0
	Mon-N	139	531	58	125	30	6	5	38	67	78	.235	.322	.343	81	-14	1	2	-1	.970	-12	*S-138	-1.1
	Yr	145	548	59	128	31	6	5	38	67	81	.234	.318	.339	79	-16	1	2	-1	.968	-10	*S-143	-1.1
1978	Mon-N	150	501	47	126	18	3	5	51	60	75	.251	.333	.329	87	-8	1	0	0	.975	1	*S-148	1.3
1979	Mon-N	113	344	31	78	13	1	7	26	43	45	.227	.318	.331	78	-10	0	0	0	.970	4	S-112	0.6
1980	Mon-N	128	388	35	103	14	4	1	32	52	38	.265	.352	.330	91	-3	0	3	-2	.965	-0	S-127/3-1	0.9
1981	*Mon-N	96	307	33	69	10	2	2	25	38	29	.225	.310	.290	70	-11	1	2	-1	.964	-11	S-96	-1.4
1982	Mon-N	156	530	41	136	26	4	7	60	47	67	.257	.318	.360	88	-9	1	6	-3	.982	-21	*S-155	-1.9
1983	Mon-N	88	261	31	67	12	2	2	22	29	37	.257	.336	.341	88	-2	2	1	0	.962	-11	S-74,3-12/2-2	-0.8
1984	Mon-N	25	40	1	6	0	0	0	1	1	8	.150	.171	.150	-10	-6	0	0	0	.960	-2	S-13/3-4	-0.7
	StL-N	38	118	9	21	7	1	3	8	9	19	.178	.242	.331	61	-7	0	0	0	.983	10	S-34/3-2	0.6
	Yr	63	158	10	27	7	1	3	9	10	27	.171	.225	.285	44	-12	0	0	0	.980	8	S-47/3-6	-0.1
	Min-A	12	33	2	7	0	0	0	1	3	7	.212	.278	.212	36	-3	0	0	0	.977	-3	S-12	-0.5
1985	Chi-N	106	218	16	53	11	0	4	24	17	34	.243	.298	.349	72	-8	1	3	-2	.964	2	S-58,3-31,2-13	-0.4
1986	Chi-N	95	155	21	44	8	0	6	23	15	32	.284	.351	.452	111	2	2	2	-1	.984	9	3-53,S-23/2-7	1.2
1987	*SF-N	111	317	39	79	13	0	11	39	42	51	.249	.343	.394	99	-0	4	7	-3	.989	2	2-55,3-44,S-22	0.1
1988	SF-N	82	171	26	37	9	1	3	18	23	39	.216	.313	.333	89	-2	3	3	-1	.985	3	2-45,3-22,S-12	0.2
1989	SF-N	28	37	7	9	4	0	0	2	5	9	.243	.333	.351	99	-0	0	0	0	1.000	-2	/3-9,S-9,2-4,1-1	-0.2
Total	19	2260	7156	770	1759	302	50	112	720	847	988	.246	.329	.349	88	-107	42	54	-20	.970	-52	*S-1900,3-184,2/1	3.8

■ BOB SPENCE
Spence, John Robert b: 2/10/46, San Diego, Cal. BL/TR, 6'4", 215 lbs. Deb: 9/5/69

YEAR	TM/L	G	AB	R	H	2B	3B	HR	RBI	BB	SO	AVG	OBP	SLG	PRO+	BR/A	SB	CS	SBR	FA	FR	G/POS	TPR
1969	Chi-A	12	26	0	4	1	0	0	3	0	9	.154	.154	.192	-4	-4	0	0	0	1.000	-0	/1-6	-0.5
1970	Chi-A	46	130	11	29	4	1	4	15	11	32	.223	.289	.362	75	-5	0	0	0	.994	3	1-37	-0.5
1971	Chi-A	14	27	2	4	0	0	0	1	5	6	.148	.281	.148	24	-3	0	0	0	.986	-1	/1-7	-0.4
Total	3	72	183	13	37	5	1	4	19	16	47	.202	.270	.306	57	-11	0	0	0	.993	2	/1-50	-1.4

■ STAN SPENCE
Spence, Stanley Orville b: 3/20/15, S.Portsmouth, Ky. d: 1/9/83, Kinston, N.C. BL/TL, 5'10.5", 180 lbs. Deb: 6/8/40

YEAR	TM/L	G	AB	R	H	2B	3B	HR	RBI	BB	SO	AVG	OBP	SLG	PRO+	BR/A	SB	CS	SBR	FA	FR	G/POS	TPR
1940	Bos-A	51	68	5	19	2	1	2	13	4	9	.279	.319	.426	88	-1	0	1	-1	1.000	-4	O-15	-0.6
1941	Bos-A	86	203	22	47	10	3	2	28	18	14	.232	.304	.340	68	-10	1	0	0	1.000	-1	O-52/1-1	-1.3
1942	Was-A☆	149	629	94	203	27	**15**	4	79	62	16	.323	.384	.432	131	26	5	2	0	.973	-3	*O-149	1.6
1943	Was-A	149	570	72	152	23	10	12	88	84	39	.267	.366	.405	130	23	8	1	2	.983	3	*O-148	2.1
1944	Was-A★	153	592	83	187	31	8	18	100	69	28	.316	.391	.486	157	43	3	7	-3	.989	19	*O-150/1-3	5.2
1946	Was-A★	152	578	83	169	50	10	16	87	62	31	.292	.365	.497	148	34	1	7	-4	.982	8	*O-150	3.3
1947	Was-A★	147	506	62	141	22	6	16	73	81	41	.279	.378	.441	131	22	2	2	-1	.984	8	*O-142	2.2
1948	Bos-A	114	391	71	92	17	4	12	61	82	33	.235	.368	.391	97	-1	0	2	-1	.977	-1	O-92/1-14	-0.7
1949	Bos-A	7	20	3	3	1	0	1	0	6	1	.150	.346	.200	43	-1	0	0	0	1.000	1	/O-5	-0.1
	StL-A	104	314	46	77	13	3	13	45	52	36	.245	.356	.430	103	1	1	1	-0	.995	3	O-87/1-1	-0.1
	Yr	111	334	49	80	14	3	13	46	58	37	.240	.355	.416	99	-1	1	1	-0	.996	4	O-92/1-1	-0.2
Total	9	1112	3871	541	1090	196	60	95	575	520	248	.282	.369	.437	126	135	21	23	-8	.984	34	O-990/1-19	11.6

■ SPENCER
Spencer Deb: 6/3/1872

YEAR	TM/L	G	AB	R	H	2B	3B	HR	RBI	BB	SO	AVG	OBP	SLG	PRO+	BR/A	SB	CS	SBR	FA	FR	G/POS	TPR
1872	Nat-n	1	4	1	0	0	0	0	0	0	0	.000	.000	.000	-86	-1	0	0	0	.429	-1	/S-1	-0.1

■ CHET SPENCER
Spencer, Chester Arthur b: 3/4/1883, S.Webster, Ohio d: 11/10/38, Portsmouth, Ohio BL/TR, 6', 180 lbs. Deb: 8/22/06

YEAR	TM/L	G	AB	R	H	2B	3B	HR	RBI	BB	SO	AVG	OBP	SLG	PRO+	BR/A	SB	CS	SBR	FA	FR	G/POS	TPR
1906	Bos-N	8	27	1	4	1	0	0	0			.148	.148	.185	4	-3	0			.875	-1	/O-8	-0.5

■ DARYL SPENCER
Spencer, Daryl Dean "Big Dee" b: 7/13/29, Wichita, Kan. BR/TR, 6'2", 190 lbs. Deb: 9/17/52

YEAR	TM/L	G	AB	R	H	2B	3B	HR	RBI	BB	SO	AVG	OBP	SLG	PRO+	BR/A	SB	CS	SBR	FA	FR	G/POS	TPR
1952	NY-N	7	17	0	5	0	1	0	3	1	4	.294	.333	.412	105	0	0	0	0	1.000	1	/S-3,3-3	0.2
1953	NY-N	118	408	55	85	18	5	20	56	42	74	.208	.287	.424	81	-13	0	1	-1	.927	-10	S-53,3-36,2-32	-1.8
1956	NY-N	146	489	46	108	13	2	14	42	35	65	.221	.277	.342	66	-24	1	3	-2	.974	-2	2-70,S-66,3-12	-1.8
1957	NY-N	148	534	65	133	31	2	11	50	50	50	.249	.315	.376	85	-11	3	1	0	.950	14	*S-110,2-36/3-6	1.6
1958	SF-N	148	539	71	138	20	5	17	74	73	60	.256	.348	.406	101	2	1	0	0	.955	-1	*S-134,2-17	1.4
1959	SF-N	152	555	59	147	20	1	12	62	58	67	.265	.334	.369	89	-8	5	0	2	.970	-4	*2-151/S-4	0.1
1960	StL-N	148	507	70	131	20	3	16	58	81	74	.258	.366	.404	102	3	1	1	-0	.946	-24	*S-138,2-16	-1.0
1961	StL-N	37	130	19	33	4	0	4	21	23	17	.254	.366	.377	89	-2	1	0	0	.956	-1	S-37	0.1
	LA-N	60	189	27	46	7	0	8	27	20	35	.243	.329	.407	86	-4	0	1	-1	.964	1	3-57/S-3	0.1
	Yr	97	319	46	79	11	0	12	48	43	52	.248	.344	.395	88	-5	1	1	-0	.964	0	3-57,S-40	0.2
1962	LA-N	77	157	24	37	5	1	2	12	32	31	.236	.365	.318	91	-1	0	0	0	.925	7	3-57,S-10	0.7
1963	LA-N	7	9	0	1	0	0	0	0	3	2	.111	.333	.111	37	-1	0	0	0	1.000	-0	/3-3	-0.1
	Cin-N	50	155	21	37	7	0	1	23	31	37	.239	.369	.303	93	0	0	0	0	.979	3	3-48	0.3
	Yr	57	164	21	38	7	0	1	23	34	39	.232	.367	.293	91	-0	0	0	0	.979	2	3-51	0.2
Total	10	1098	3689	457	901	145	20	105	428	449	516	.244	.329	.380	88	-59	13	7	-0	.953	-13	S-558,2-322,3-222	-0.2

■ TUBBY SPENCER
Spencer, Edward Russell b: 1/26/1884, Oil City, Pa. d: 2/1/45, San Francisco, Cal. BR/TR, 5'10", 215 lbs. Deb: 7/23/05

YEAR	TM/L	G	AB	R	H	2B	3B	HR	RBI	BB	SO	AVG	OBP	SLG	PRO+	BR/A	SB	CS	SBR	FA	FR	G/POS	TPR
1905	StL-A	35	115	6	27	1	2	0	11	7		.235	.285	.278	83	-2	2			.962	-6	C-34	-0.5
1906	StL-A	58	188	15	33	6	1	0	17	7		.176	.205	.218	34	-15	4			.935	-5	C-54	-1.6
1907	StL-A	71	230	27	61	11	1	1	25	7		.265	.299	.335	102	-0	1			.957	-2	C-63	0.4
1908	StL-A	91	286	19	60	6	1	0	28	17		.210	.254	.238	60	-13	1			.983	-1	C-88	-0.6
1909	Bos-A	28	74	6	12	1	0	0	9	6		.162	.225	.176	26	-6	2			.992	-4	C-26	-0.9
1911	Phi-N	11	32	2	5	1	0	1	3	7		.156	.229	.281	42	-3	0			.925	-1	C-11	-0.3
1916	Det-A	19	54	2	20	1	1	0	10	6	6	.370	.443	.481	172	5	2			.988	-7	C-19	0.0
1917	Det-A	70	192	13	46	8	3	0	22	15	15	.240	.313	.313	95	-1	0			.978	-2	C-62	0.1
1918	Det-A	66	155	11	34	8	1	0	8	19	18	.219	.313	.284	83	-3	1			.966	-12	C-48/1-1	-1.3
Total	9	449	1326	106	298	43	10	3	133	87	46	.225	.281	.279	76	-37	13			.966	-40	C-405/1-1	-4.7

■ TOM SPENCER
Spencer, Hubert Thomas b: 2/28/51, Gallipolis, Ohio BR/TR, 6', 170 lbs. Deb: 7/17/78 C

YEAR	TM/L	G	AB	R	H	2B	3B	HR	RBI	BB	SO	AVG	OBP	SLG	PRO+	BR/A	SB	CS	SBR	FA	FR	G/POS	TPR
1978	Chi-A	29	65	3	12	1	0	0	4	2	9	.185	.209	.200	15	-7	0	1	-1	1.000	-1	O-27/D-2	-1.0

■ JIM SPENCER
Spencer, James Lloyd b: 7/30/47, Hanover, Pa. BL/TL, 6'2", 195 lbs. Deb: 9/7/68 F

YEAR	TM/L	G	AB	R	H	2B	3B	HR	RBI	BB	SO	AVG	OBP	SLG	PRO+	BR/A	SB	CS	SBR	FA	FR	G/POS	TPR
1968	Cal-A	19	68	2	13	1	0	0	5	3	10	.191	.236	.206	36	-5	0	0	0	.994	3	1-19	-0.4
1969	Cal-A	113	386	39	98	14	3	10	31	26	53	.254	.304	.383	96	-4	1	0	0	.991	-1	*1-107	-1.4
1970	Cal-A	146	511	61	140	20	4	12	68	28	61	.274	.312	.399	98	-3	0	2	-1	**.995**	-1	*1-142	-1.8
1971	Cal-A	148	510	50	121	21	2	18	59	48	63	.237	.307	.392	104	1	0	1	-0	**.996**	2	*1-145	-1.2
1972	Cal-A	82	212	13	47	9	1	1	14	12	25	.222	.263	.259	59	-11	0	1	-0	.990	-1	1-35,O-24	-2.0
1973	Cal-A	29	87	10	21	4	2	2	11	9	9	.241	.320	.402	111	1	0	0	0	1.000	-2	1-26/D-2	-0.3
	Tex-A★	102	352	35	94	12	3	4	43	34	41	.267	.333	.352	97	-0	3	2	-1	.999	5	1-99/D-1	-0.5
	Yr	131	439	45	115	16	5	6	54	43	50	.262	.331	.362	100	-0	3	3	-2	.999	3	*1-125/D-3	-0.8
1974	Tex-A	118	352	36	98	11	4	7	44	22	27	.278	.326	.392	109	3	1	2	-1	.998	1	1-60,D-54	-0.1

YEAR	TM/L	G	AB	R	H	2B	3B	HR	RBI	BB	SO	AVG	OBP	SLG	PRO+	BR/A	SB	CS	SBR	FA	FR	G/POS	TPR
1975	Tex-A	132	403	50	107	18	1	11	47	35	43	.266	.327	.397	105	2	0	1	-1	.995	5	1-99,D-25	0.1
1976	Chi-A	150	518	53	131	13	2	14	70	49	52	.253	.319	.367	100	-0	6	4	-1	**.998**	8	*1-143/D-2	-0.3
1977	Chi-A	128	470	56	116	16	1	18	69	36	50	.247	.310	.400	90	-7	1	2	-1	.991	2	*1-125	-1.3
1978	*NY-A	71	150	12	34	9	1	7	24	15	32	.227	.297	.440	107	1	0	1	-1	1.000	1	D-35,1-15	-0.1
1979	NY-A	106	295	60	85	15	3	23	53	38	25	.288	.369	.593	158	23	0	2	-1	.992	-0	D-71,1-26	1.7
1980	*NY-A	97	259	38	61	9	0	13	43	30	44	.236	.317	.421	102	0	1	0	0	.990	2	1-75,D-15	-0.2
1981	NY-A	25	63	6	9	2	0	2	4	9	7	.143	.250	.270	50	-4	0	0	0	1.000	2	1-25	-0.3
	*Oak-A	54	171	14	35	6	0	2	9	10	20	.205	.249	.275	53	-11	1	0	0	.997	2	1-48	-1.1
	Yr	79	234	20	44	8	0	4	13	19	27	.188	.249	.274	52	-15	1	0	0	.998	5	1-73	-1.4
1982	Oak-A	33	101	6	17	3	1	2	5	3	20	.168	.192	.277	28	-10	0	0	0	.992	2	1-32	-1.0
Total	15	1553	4908	541	1227	179	27	146	599	407	582	.250	.316	.387	98	-26	11	19	-8	.995	30	*1-1221,D-205/O-24	-10.2

■ BEN SPENCER
Spencer, Lloyd Benjamin   b: 5/15/1890, Patapsco, Md.   d: 9/1/70, Finksburg, Md.   BL/TL, 5'8", 160 lbs.   Deb: 9/8/13   F

| 1913 | Was-A | 8 | 21 | 2 | 6 | 1 | 1 | 0 | 2 | 2 | 4 | .286 | .348 | .429 | 124 | 1 | 0 | | | .917 | -1 | /O-8 | -0.1 |

■ ROY SPENCER
Spencer, Roy Hampton   b: 2/22/1900, Scranton, N.C.   d: 2/8/73, Port Charlotte, Fla   BR/TR, 5'10", 168 lbs.   Deb: 4/19/25

1925	Pit-N	14	28	1	6	1	0	0	2	1	3	.214	.241	.250	24	-3	1	0	0	.905	-2	C-11	-0.4
1926	Pit-N	28	43	5	17	3	0	0	4	1	0	.395	.409	.465	128	2	0			.970	-1	C-12	0.2
1927	*Pit-N	38	92	9	26	3	1	0	13	3	3	.283	.305	.337	67	-4	0			.974	2	C-34	-0.1
1929	Was-A	50	116	18	18	4	0	1	9	8	15	.155	.222	.216	13	-15	0	0	0	.967	-2	C-41	-1.3
1930	Was-A	93	321	32	82	11	4	0	36	18	27	.255	.303	.315	57	-21	3	0	1	.989	5	C-93	-0.7
1931	Was-A	145	483	48	133	16	3	1	60	35	21	.275	.327	.327	72	-19	0	0	0	.985	7	*C-145	-0.2
1932	Was-A	102	317	28	78	9	0	1	41	24	17	.246	.301	.284	53	-22	0	1	-1	.978	-10	C-98	-2.5
1933	Cle-A	75	227	26	46	7	0	0	23	23	17	.203	.282	.242	38	-20	0			.990	5	C-72	-1.0
1934	Cle-A	5	7	0	1	1	0	0	2	0	1	.143	.143	.286	8	-1	0	0	0	1.000	1	/C-4	0.0
1936	NY-N	19	18	3	5	1	0	0	3	2	3	.278	.350	.333	86	-0	0			1.000	1	C-14	0.1
1937	Bro-N	51	117	5	24	2	2	0	8	7	8	.205	.256	.256	39	-10	0			1.000	9	C-45	0.1
1938	Bro-N	16	45	2	12	1	1	0	6	5	6	.267	.340	.333	84	-1	0			.968	-0	C-16	-0.1
Total	12	636	1814	177	448	57	13	3	203	128	130	.247	.301	.298	56	-115	4	1		.984	16	C-585	-5.9

■ VERN SPENCER
Spencer, Vernon Murray   b: 2/4/1894, Wixom, Mich.   d: 6/3/71, Wixom, Mich.   BL/TR, 5'7", 165 lbs.   Deb: 7/4/20

| 1920 | NY-N | 45 | 140 | 15 | 28 | 2 | 3 | 0 | 19 | 11 | 17 | .200 | .258 | .257 | 49 | -9 | 4 | 3 | -1 | .932 | -1 | O-40 | -1.4 |

■ PAUL SPERAW
Speraw, Paul Bachman "Polly" or "Birdie"   b: 10/5/1893, Annville, Pa.   d: 2/22/62, Cedar Rapids, Iowa   BR/TR, 5'8.5", 145 lbs.   Deb: 9/15/20

| 1920 | StL-A | 1 | 2 | 0 | 0 | 0 | 0 | 0 | 0 | 0 | 0 | .000 | .000 | .000 | -97 | -1 | 0 | 0 | 0 | 1.000 | 0 | /3-1 | 0.0 |

■ ED SPERBER
Sperber, Edwin George   b: 1/21/1895, Cincinnati, Ohio   d: 1/5/76, Cincinnati, Ohio   BL/TL, 5'11", 175 lbs.   Deb: 4/16/24

1924	Bos-N	24	59	8	17	2	0	1	12	10	9	.288	.400	.373	113	2	3	1	0	.897	-3	O-17	-0.2
1925	Bos-N	2	2	0	0	0	0	0	0	0	0	.000	.000	.000	-99	-1	0	0	0	.000	0	H	-0.1
Total	2	26	61	8	17	2	0	1	12	10	9	.279	.389	.361	106	1	3	1	0	.897	-3	/O-17	-0.3

■ ROB SPERRING
Sperring, Robert Walter   b: 10/10/49, San Francisco, Cal.   BR/TR, 6'1", 185 lbs.   Deb: 8/11/74

1974	Chi-N	42	107	9	22	3	0	1	5	9	28	.206	.267	.262	46	-8	1	2	-1	.952	5	2-35/S-8	-0.2
1975	Chi-N	65	144	25	30	4	1	1	9	16	31	.208	.292	.271	54	-9	0	2	-1	.946	12	3-22,2-17,S-16,/O-8	0.3
1976	Chi-N	43	93	8	24	3	0	0	7	9	25	.258	.324	.290	69	-4	0	2	-1	.955	-3	3-20,S-15/2-4,O-3	-1.3
1977	Hou-N	58	129	6	24	3	0	1	9	12	23	.186	.255	.233	35	-12	0	0	0	.940	-2	S-22,2-20,3-11	-1.2
Total	4	208	473	48	100	13	1	3	30	46	107	.211	.283	.262	51	-32	1	6	-3	.964	6	/2-76,S-61,3-53,O	-2.4

■ STAN SPERRY
Sperry, Stanley Kenneth   b: 2/19/14, Evansville, Wis.   d: 9/27/62, Evansville, Wis.   BL/TR, 5'10.5", 164 lbs.   Deb: 7/28/36

1936	Phi-N	20	37	2	5	3	0	0	4	3	5	.135	.200	.216	11	-5	0			.900	-4	2-15	-0.8
1938	Phi-A	60	253	28	69	6	3	0	27	15	9	.273	.313	.320	61	-15	1	2	-1	.959	-8	2-60	-1.9
Total	2	80	290	30	74	9	3	0	31	18	14	.255	.299	.307	54	-20	1	2		.951	-12	/2-75	-2.7

■ BILL SPIERS
Spiers, William James   b: 6/5/66, Orangeburg, S.C.   BL/TR, 6'2", 190 lbs.   Deb: 4/7/89

1989	Mil-A	114	345	44	88	9	3	4	33	21	63	.255	.300	.333	79	-10	10	2	2	.962	14	S-89,3-12/2-4,1D	1.2
1990	Mil-A	112	363	44	88	15	3	2	36	16	45	.242	.276	.317	66	-17	11	6	-0	.976	-7	*S-111	-1.6
1991	Mil-A	133	414	71	117	13	6	8	54	34	55	.283	.340	.401	107	4	14	8	-1	.970	-11	*S-128/O-1,D-2	0.1
1992	Mil-A	12	16	2	5	2	0	0	2	1	4	.313	.353	.438	123	0	1	1	-0	1.000	1	/S-5,2-4,3-1,D-1	-0.2
1993	Mil-A	113	340	43	81	8	4	2	36	29	51	.238	.306	.303	65	-16	9	8	-2	.971	-24	*2-104/O-7,S-4,D-1	-3.9
1994	Mil-A	73	214	27	54	10	1	0	17	19	42	.252	.316	.308	59	-13	7	1	2	.947	-6	3-35,S-35/O-2,1D	-1.2
1995	NY-N	63	72	5	15	2	1	0	11	12	15	.208	.321	.264	58	-4	0	1	-1	.794	3	3-11/2-6	-0.1
1996	Hou-N	122	218	27	55	10	1	6	26	20	34	.252	.321	.390	95	-2	7	0	2	.959	4	3-77/2-7,1-4,S-4,O	0.4
Total	8	742	1982	263	503	69	19	22	215	152	309	.254	.310	.341	79	-58	59	27	2	.970	-27	S-376,3-136,2/OD1	-5.3

■ HARRY SPIES
Spies, Henry   b: 6/12/1866, New Orleans, La.   d: 7/8/42, Los Angeles, Cal.   BR/TR, 5'11.5", 170 lbs.   Deb: 4/20/1895

1895	Cin-N	14	50	2	11	0	1	0	5	3	2	.220	.264	.260	34	-5	0			.867	2	C-12/1-2	-0.2
	Lou-N	72	276	42	74	14	7	2	35	11	19	.268	.313	.391	86	-7	4			.981	-3	1-47,C-26/S-1	-0.5
	Yr	86	326	44	85	14	8	2	40	14	21	.261	.305	.371	78	-12	4			.979	-1	1-49,C-38/S-1	-0.7

■ ED SPIEZIO
Spiezio, Edward Wayne   b: 10/31/41, Joliet, Ill.   BR/TR, 5'11", 180 lbs.   Deb: 7/23/64   F

1964	StL-N	12	12	0	4	0	0	0	0	0	1	.333	.333	.333	81	-0	0	0	0	.000	0	H	0.0
1965	StL-N	10	18	0	3	0	0	0	5	1	4	.167	.250	.167	18	-2	0	0	0	1.000	0	/3-3	-0.2
1966	StL-N	26	73	4	16	5	1	2	10	5	11	.219	.269	.397	82	-2	1	0	0	.885	-4	3-19	-0.6
1967	*StL-N	55	105	9	22	2	0	3	10	7	18	.210	.265	.314	66	-5	2	1	0	.962	-0	3-19/O-7	-0.6
1968	*StL-N	29	51	1	8	0	0	0	2	5	6	.157	.232	.157	19	-5	1	1	0	1.000	0	O-11/3-2	-0.6
1969	SD-N	121	355	29	83	9	0	13	43	38	64	.234	.315	.369	95	-3	1	2	-1	.939	1	3-98/O-1	-0.3
1970	SD-N	110	316	45	90	18	1	12	42	43	42	.285	.377	.462	129	13	4	0	1	.953	2	3-93	1.5
1971	SD-N	97	308	16	71	10	1	7	36	22	50	.231	.290	.338	83	-8	6	5	-1	.962	1	3-91/O-1	-1.0
1972	SD-N	20	29	2	4	0	0	0	4	1	6	.138	.167	.207	6	-4	0	0	0	1.000	-2	/3-5	-0.6
	Chi-A	74	277	20	66	10	1	2	23	12	43	.238	.277	.303	71	-10	0	0	-1	.952	7	3-74	-0.5
Total	9	554	1544	126	367	54	4	39	177	134	245	.238	.306	.355	88	-25	16	10	-1	.949	4	3-404/O-20	-2.9

■ SCOTT SPIEZIO
Spiezio, Scott Edward   b: 9/21/72, Joliet, Ill.   BB/TR, 6'2", 205 lbs.   Deb: 9/14/96   F

| 1996 | Oak-A | 9 | 29 | 6 | 9 | 2 | 0 | 2 | 8 | 4 | 4 | .310 | .394 | .586 | 149 | 2 | 0 | 1 | 0 | .833 | -1 | /3-5,D-4 | 0.0 |

■ CHARLIE SPIKES
Spikes, Leslie Charles   b: 1/23/51, Bogalusa, La.   BR/TR, 6'3", 220 lbs.   Deb: 9/1/72

1972	NY-A	14	34	2	5	1	0	0	1	1	13	.147	.171	.176	4	-4	0	1	-1	1.000	0	/O-9	-0.6
1973	Cle-A	140	506	68	120	12	3	23	73	45	103	.237	.306	.409	98	-3	5	3	-0	.964	5	*O-111,D-26	-0.4
1974	Cle-A	155	568	63	154	23	1	22	80	34	100	.271	.320	.431	116	9	10	7	-1	.968	0	*O-154	0.2
1975	Cle-A	111	345	41	79	13	3	11	33	30	51	.229	.291	.380	84	-6	7	6	-2	.974	1	*O-103/D-2	-1.1
1976	Cle-A	101	334	34	79	11	5	3	31	23	50	.237	.296	.326	83	-7	5	6	-2	.985	5	O-98/D-2	-1.3
1977	Cle-A	32	95	13	22	2	0	3	11	11	17	.232	.324	.347	86	-2	0	2	-1	.972	-3	O-27/D-2	-0.7
1978	Det-A	10	28	1	7	1	0	0	2	6	4	.250	.344	.286	77	-1	0	0	0	.909	-1	/O-9	-0.3
1979	Atl-N	66	93	12	26	8	0	3	21	5	30	.280	.316	.462	102	-0	0	3	-0	.842	-3	O-15	-0.4
1980	Atl-N	41	36	6	10	1	0	0	3	0	20	.278	.350	.306	82	-1	0	1	0	1.000	-2	/O-7	-0.3
Total	9	670	2039	240	502	72	12	65	256	154	388	.246	.306	.389	96	-14	27	25	-7	.969	2	O-533/D-32	-4.9

■ HARRY SPILMAN
Spilman, William Harry   b: 7/18/54, Albany, Ga.   BL/TR, 6'1", 190 lbs.   Deb: 9/11/78

1978	Cin-N	4	4	1	1	0	0	0	0	0	0	.250	.250	.250	40	-0	0	0	0	.000	0	H	0.0
1979	*Cin-N	43	56	7	12	3	0	0	5	7	5	.214	.323	.268	63	-3	0	0	0	1.000	-0	1-12/3-4	-0.3
1980	Cin-N	65	101	14	27	3	0	4	19	9	19	.267	.333	.426	110	1	0	0	0	.986	0	1-18/O-2,C-1,3-1	0.0
1981	Cin-N	23	24	4	4	1	0	0	3	3	7	.167	.259	.208	33	-2	0	0	0	1.000	0	/3-3,1-2	-0.2

YEAR	TM/L	G	AB	R	H	2B	3B	HR	RBI	BB	SO	AVG	OBP	SLG	PRO+	BR/A	SB	CS	SBR	FA	FR	G/POS	TPR
	*Hou-N	28	34	5	10	0	0	0	1	2	3	.294	.333	.294	83	-1	0	1	-1	1.000	-0	1-13	-0.2
	Yr	51	58	9	14	1	0	0	4	5	10	.241	.302	.259	61	-3	0	1	-1	.984	-0	1-15/3-3	-0.4
1982	Hou-N	38	61	7	17	2	0	3	11	5	10	.279	.333	.459	129	2	0	0	0	.989	-1	1-11	0.1
1983	Hou-N	42	78	7	13	3	0	1	9	5	12	.167	.217	.244	29	-8	0	0	0	1.000	-2	1-19/C-6	-1.1
1984	Hou-N	32	72	14	19	2	0	2	15	12	10	.264	.369	.375	118	2	0	0	0	.978	-3	1-18/C-8	-0.2
1985	Hou-N	44	66	3	9	1	0	1	4	3	7	.136	.174	.197	4	-9	0	0	0	1.000	-1	1-19/C-2	-1.1
1986	Det-A	24	49	6	12	2	0	3	8	3	8	.245	.288	.469	102	-0	0	0	0	1.000	0	D-11/3-2,C-1,1-1	0.0
	SF-N	58	94	12	27	7	0	2	22	12	13	.287	.368	.426	124	3	0	0	0	.994	0	1-19/3-5,C-1,2-1,O	0.2
1987	*SF-N	83	90	5	24	5	0	1	14	9	20	.267	.333	.356	87	-2	1	1	-0	.875	-2	3-10/1-9,C-1	-0.5
1988	SF-N	40	40	4	7	1	1	1	3	4	6	.175	.250	.325	67	-2	0	0	0	1.000	1	/1-6,C-2,O-1	-0.2
	Hou-N	7	5	0	0	0	0	0	0	0	3	.000	.000	.000	-99	-1	0	0	0	1.000	0	/1-1	-0.1
	Yr	47	45	4	7	1	1	1	3	4	9	.156	.224	.289	48	-3	0	0	0	1.000	1	1-7,C-2,O-1	-0.3
1989	Hou-N	32	36	7	10	3	0	0	3	7	2	.278	.395	.361	122	1	0	0	0	1.000	0	/1-9,C-1	0.1
Total	12	563	810	96	192	34	1	18	117	81	126	.237	.309	.348	85	-17	1	2	-1	.991	-8	1-157/3-25,CDO2	-3.5

■ HAL SPINDEL
Spindel, Harold Stewart b: 5/27/13, Chandler, Okla. BR/TR, 6', 185 lbs. Deb: 4/23/39

YEAR	TM/L	G	AB	R	H	2B	3B	HR	RBI	BB	SO	AVG	OBP	SLG	PRO+	BR/A	SB	CS	SBR	FA	FR	G/POS	TPR
1939	StL-A	48	119	13	32	3	1	0	11	8	7	.269	.315	.311	59	-7	0	2	-1	.993	-0	C-32	-0.6
1945	Phi-N	36	87	7	20	3	0	0	8	6	7	.230	.280	.264	53	-6	0			.964	-0	C-31	-0.4
1946	Phi-N	1	3	0	1	0	0	0	1	0	0	.333	.333	.333	92	-0	0			1.000	-0	/C-1	0.0
Total	3	85	209	20	53	6	1	0	20	14	14	.254	.300	.292	57	-13	0	2		.980	0	/C-64	-1.0

■ ANDY SPOGNARDI
Spognardi, Andrea Ettore b: 10/18/08, Boston, Mass. BR/TR, 5'9.5", 160 lbs. Deb: 9/2/32

YEAR	TM/L	G	AB	R	H	2B	3B	HR	RBI	BB	SO	AVG	OBP	SLG	PRO+	BR/A	SB	CS	SBR	FA	FR	G/POS	TPR
1932	Bos-A	17	34	9	10	1	0	0	1	6	6	.294	.400	.324	92	-0	0	0	0	.979	3	/2-9,S-3,3-2	0.3

■ AL SPOHRER
Spohrer, Alfred Ray b: 12/3/02, Philadelphia, Pa. d: 7/17/72, Plymouth, N.H. BR/TR, 5'10.5", 175 lbs. Deb: 4/13/28

YEAR	TM/L	G	AB	R	H	2B	3B	HR	RBI	BB	SO	AVG	OBP	SLG	PRO+	BR/A	SB	CS	SBR	FA	FR	G/POS	TPR
1928	NY-N	2	2	0	0	0	0	0	0	0	0	.000	.000	.000	-99	-1	0			1.000	0	/C-2	-0.1
	Bos-N	51	124	15	27	3	0	0	9	5	11	.218	.254	.242	32	-12	1			.976	-5	C-48	-1.5
	Yr	53	126	15	27	3	0	0	9	5	11	.214	.250	.238	30	-13	1			.977	-5	C-50	-1.6
1929	Bos-N	114	342	42	93	21	8	2	48	26	35	.272	.327	.398	82	-11	3			.954	-10	*C-109	-1.0
1930	Bos-N	112	356	44	113	22	8	2	37	22	24	.317	.361	.441	96	-3	3			.957	-18	*C-108	-1.0
1931	Bos-N	114	350	23	84	17	5	0	27	22	27	.240	.285	.317	64	-18	2			.982	-0	*C-111	-1.1
1932	Bos-N	104	335	31	90	12	2	0	33	15	26	.269	.300	.316	69	-15	2			.991	-0	*C-100	0.1
1933	Bos-N	67	184	11	46	6	1	1	12	11	13	.250	.292	.310	78	-6	3			.972	-6	C-65	-0.9
1934	Bos-N	100	265	25	59	15	0	0	17	14	18	.223	.262	.279	49	-20	1			.977	0	C-98	-1.5
1935	Bos-N	92	260	22	63	7	1	0	16	9	12	.242	.273	.288	55	-17	0			.958	-10	C-90	-2.3
Total	8	756	2218	213	575	103	25	6	199	124	166	.259	.301	.336	70	-101	13			.972	-39	C-731	-9.3

■ JIM SPOTTS
Spotts, James Russell b: 4/10/09, Honey Brook, Pa. d: 6/15/64, Medford, N.J. BR/TR, 5'10.5", 175 lbs. Deb: 4/23/30

YEAR	TM/L	G	AB	R	H	2B	3B	HR	RBI	BB	SO	AVG	OBP	SLG	PRO+	BR/A	SB	CS	SBR	FA	FR	G/POS	TPR
1930	Phi-N	3	2	1	0	0	0	0	0	0	1	.000	.000	.000	-93	-1	0			1.000	0	/C-2	0.0

■ CHARLIE SPRAGUE
Sprague, Charles Wellington b: 10/10/1864, Cleveland, Ohio d: 12/31/12, Des Moines, Iowa BL/TL, 5'11", 150 lbs. Deb: 9/17/1887

YEAR	TM/L	G	AB	R	H	2B	3B	HR	RBI	BB	SO	AVG	OBP	SLG	PRO+	BR/A	SB	CS	SBR	FA	FR	G/POS	TPR
1887	Chi-N	3	13	0	2	0	0	0	0	0	2	.154	.154	.154	-13	-2	0			.667	-0	/P-3,O-1	-0.1
1889	Cle-N	2	7	2	1	0	0	0	1	1	0	.143	.250	.143	11	-1	1			.857	1	/P-2	0.0
1890	Tol-a	55	199	25	47	5	6	1	19	16		.236	.303	.337	86	-4	10			.892	-6	O-40,P-19	-0.7
Total	3	60	219	27	50	5	6	1	19	17	2	.228	.293	.320	77	-7	11			.892	-6	/O-41,P-24	-0.8

■ ED SPRAGUE
Sprague, Edward Nelson Jr. b: 7/25/67, Castro Valley, Cal. BR/TR, 6'2", 215 lbs. Deb: 5/8/91 F

YEAR	TM/L	G	AB	R	H	2B	3B	HR	RBI	BB	SO	AVG	OBP	SLG	PRO+	BR/A	SB	CS	SBR	FA	FR	G/POS	TPR
1991	Tor-A	61	160	17	44	7	0	4	20	19	43	.275	.363	.394	105	2	0	3	-2	.870	-1	3-35,1-22/C-2,D-2	-0.2
1992	*Tor-A	22	47	6	11	2	0	1	7	3	7	.234	.280	.340	70	-2	0	0	0	.985	1	C-15/1-4,3-1,D-2	-0.1
1993	*Tor-A	150	546	50	142	31	1	12	73	32	85	.260	.313	.386	86	-11	1	0	0	.955	-9	*3-150	-1.9
1994	Tor-A	109	405	38	97	19	1	11	44	23	95	.240	.298	.373	71	-18	1	0	0	.946	-12	*3-107/1-3	-2.8
1995	Tor-A	144	521	77	127	27	2	18	74	58	96	.244	.337	.407	93	-5	0	0	0	.958	-1	*3-139/1-7,D-2	-0.6
1996	Tor-A	159	591	88	146	35	2	36	101	60	146	.247	.329	.496	104	1	0	0	0	.956	-15	*3-148,D-10	-1.3
Total	6	645	2270	276	567	121	6	82	319	195	472	.250	.323	.417	91	-33	2	3	-1	.949	-37	3-580/1-36,C-17,D	-6.9

■ HARRY SPRATT
Spratt, Henry Lee b: 7/10/1887, Broadford, Va. d: 7/3/69, Washington, D.C. BL/TR, 5'8.5", 175 lbs. Deb: 4/13/11

YEAR	TM/L	G	AB	R	H	2B	3B	HR	RBI	BB	SO	AVG	OBP	SLG	PRO+	BR/A	SB	CS	SBR	FA	FR	G/POS	TPR
1911	Bos-N	62	154	22	37	4	4	2	13	13	25	.240	.299	.357	77	-5	1			.892	-8	S-26/2-5,3-4,O-4	-1.2
1912	Bos-N	27	89	6	23	3	2	3	15	7	11	.258	.313	.438	102	-0	2			.842	-13	S-23	-1.2
Total	2	89	243	28	60	7	6	5	28	20	36	.247	.304	.387	86	-6	3			.871	-22	/S-49,2-5,O-4,3-4	-2.4

■ GEORGE SPRIGGS
Spriggs, George Herman b: 5/22/41, Jewell, Md. BL/TR, 5'11", 175 lbs. Deb: 9/15/65

YEAR	TM/L	G	AB	R	H	2B	3B	HR	RBI	BB	SO	AVG	OBP	SLG	PRO+	BR/A	SB	CS	SBR	FA	FR	G/POS	TPR
1965	Pit-N	9	2	5	1	0	0	0	0	0	0	.500	.500	.500	182	0	2	0		.000	-0	/O-1	0.0
1966	Pit-N	9	7	0	1	0	0	0	0	0	3	.143	.143	.143	-20	-1	0	0	0	.000	0	H	-0.1
1967	Pit-N	38	57	14	10	1	1	0	5	6	20	.175	.254	.228	39	-4	3	0	1	1.000	-2	O-13	-0.6
1969	KC-A	23	29	4	4	2	1	0	3	0	8	.138	.242	.276	44	-2	0	0	0	1.000	-1	O-6	-0.4
1970	KC-A	51	130	12	27	2	3	1	7	14	32	.208	.285	.292	59	-7	4	3	-1	.953	1	O-36	-0.9
Total	5	130	225	35	43	5	5	1	12	23	63	.191	.269	.271	51	-15	9	3	1	.965	-3	/O-56	-2.0

■ STEVE SPRINGER
Springer, Steven Michael b: 2/11/61, Long Beach, Cal. BR/TR, 6', 190 lbs. Deb: 5/22/90

YEAR	TM/L	G	AB	R	H	2B	3B	HR	RBI	BB	SO	AVG	OBP	SLG	PRO+	BR/A	SB	CS	SBR	FA	FR	G/POS	TPR
1990	Cle-A	4	12	1	2	0	0	0	1	0	6	.167	.167	.167	-7	-2	0	0	0	1.000	-1	/3-3,D-1	-0.2
1992	NY-N	4	5	0	2	1	0	0	0	1	1	.400	.400	.600	182	0	0	0	0	1.000	-0	/2-1,3-1	-0.0
Total	2	8	17	1	4	1	0	0	1	1	7	.235	.235	.294	48	-1	0	0	0	1.000	-1	/3-4,2-1,D-1	-0.2

■ JOE SPRINZ
Sprinz, Joseph Conrad "Mule" b: 8/3/02, St.Louis, Mo. d: 1/11/94, Fremont, Cal. BR/TR, 5'11", 185 lbs. Deb: 7/16/30

YEAR	TM/L	G	AB	R	H	2B	3B	HR	RBI	BB	SO	AVG	OBP	SLG	PRO+	BR/A	SB	CS	SBR	FA	FR	G/POS	TPR
1930	Cle-A	17	45	5	8	1	0	0	2	4	4	.178	.245	.200	14	-6	0	0	0	1.000	6	C-17	0.1
1931	Cle-A	1	3	0	0	0	0	0	0	0	0	.000	.000	.000	-95	-1	0	0	0	1.000	-0	/C-1	-0.1
1933	StL-N	3	5	1	1	0	0	0	0	2	1	.200	.333	.200	53	-0	0	0	0	1.000	2	/C-3	0.2
Total	3	21	53	6	9	1	0	0	2	5	5	.170	.241	.189	12	-7	0	0	0	1.000	8	/C-21	0.2

■ FREDDY SPURGEON
Spurgeon, Fred b: 10/9/1900, Wabash, Ind. d: 11/5/70, Kalamazoo, Mich. BR/TR, 5'11.5", 160 lbs. Deb: 9/19/24

YEAR	TM/L	G	AB	R	H	2B	3B	HR	RBI	BB	SO	AVG	OBP	SLG	PRO+	BR/A	SB	CS	SBR	FA	FR	G/POS	TPR
1924	Cle-A	3	7	0	1	1	0	0	0	0	0	.143	.250	.286	37	-1	0	0	0	.882	1	/2-3	-0.0
1925	Cle-A	107	376	50	108	9	3	0	32	15	21	.287	.315	.327	62	-22	8	5	-1	.927	-4	3-56,2-46/S-3	-2.0
1926	Cle-A	149	614	101	181	31	3	0	49	27	36	.295	.327	.355	77	-21	7	2	1	.962	-8	*2-149	-2.3
1927	Cle-A	57	179	30	45	6	1	1	19	18	14	.251	.323	.313	65	-9	8	1	2	.938	-8	2-52	-1.3
Total	4	316	1176	181	335	47	7	1	100	60	71	.285	.322	.339	70	-53	23	8	2	.958	-19	2-250/3-56,S-3	-5.6

■ ED SPURNEY
Spurney, Edward Frederick b: 1/19/1872, Cleveland, Ohio d: 10/12/32, Cleveland, Ohio Deb: 6/26/1891

YEAR	TM/L	G	AB	R	H	2B	3B	HR	RBI	BB	SO	AVG	OBP	SLG	PRO+	BR/A	SB	CS	SBR	FA	FR	G/POS	TPR
1891	Pit-N	3	7	2	2	1	0	0	2	1	0	.286	.444	.429	158	1	0			.889	-1	/S-3	0.0

■ MIKE SQUIRES
Squires, Michael Lynn b: 3/5/52, Kalamazoo, Mich. BL/TL, 5'11", 185 lbs. Deb: 9/1/75 C

YEAR	TM/L	G	AB	R	H	2B	3B	HR	RBI	BB	SO	AVG	OBP	SLG	PRO+	BR/A	SB	CS	SBR	FA	FR	G/POS	TPR
1975	Chi-A	20	65	5	15	0	0	0	4	8	5	.231	.315	.231	55	-3	3	0	1	.988	0	1-20	-0.4
1977	Chi-A	3	3	0	0	0	0	0	0	0	0	.000	.000	.000	-99	-1	0			1.000	0	/1-1	0.0
1978	Chi-A	46	150	25	42	9	2	0	19	16	21	.280	.349	.367	101	0	4	4	-1	.997	-2	1-45	-0.6
1979	Chi-A	122	295	44	78	10	1	2	22	19	22	.264	.320	.325	74	-10	15	5	2	.995	4	*1-110/O-1	-0.9
1980	Chi-A	131	343	38	97	11	3	2	33	33	24	.283	.347	.350	92	-3	8	9	-3	.995	4	*1-114/C-2	-0.7
1981	Chi-A	92	294	35	78	9	0	0	25	22	17	.265	.316	.296	79	-8	7	2	1	.992	2	1-88/O-1	-0.9
1982	Chi-A	116	195	33	52	9	3	1	21	14	13	.267	.316	.359	85	-4	3	3	1	.995	7	*1-109	-0.1
1983	*Chi-A	143	153	21	34	4	1	1	11	22	11	.222	.328	.281	67	-6	3	5	1	.996	6	*1-124/3-1,D-5	-0.4
1984	Chi-A	104	82	9	15	1	0	0	6	6	7	.183	.239	.195	21	-9	2	2	1	1.000	4	1-77,3-13/O-3,P-1	-0.6
1985	Chi-A	2	0	1	0	0	0	0	0	0	0					0	0	0	0	.000	0	/R	0.0
Total	10	779	1580	211	411	53	10	6	141	143	108	.260	.323	.318	78	-43	45	28	-3	.995	25	1-688/3-14,D-5,OCP	-4.6

YEAR	TM/L	G	AB	R	H	2B	3B	HR	RBI	BB	SO	AVG	OBP	SLG	PRO+	BR/A	SB	CS	SBR	FA	FR	G/POS	TPR

■ MARV STAEHLE Staehle, Marvin Gustave b: 3/13/42, Oak Park, Ill. BL/TR, 5'10", 172 lbs. Deb: 9/15/64

1964	Chi-A	6	5	0	2	0	0	0	2	0	0	.400	.400	.400	127	0	1	0	0	.000	0	H	0.0
1965	Chi-A	7	7	0	3	0	0	0	2	0	0	.429	.429	.429	154	0	0	0	0	.000	0	H	0.0
1966	Chi-A	8	15	2	2	0	0	0	0	4	2	.133	.316	.133	37	-1	1	0	0	1.000	1	/2-6	0.0
1967	Chi-A	32	54	1	6	1	0	0	1	4	8	.111	.172	.130	-10	-7	1	1	-0	1.000	1	2-17/S-5	-0.7
1969	Mon-N	6	17	4	7	2	0	1	1	2	4	.412	.474	.706	226	3	0	0	0	.944	-1	/2-4	0.3
1970	Mon-N	104	321	41	70	9	1	0	26	39	21	.218	.309	.252	52	-21	1	3	-2	.963	-13	2-91/S-1	-2.9
1971	Atl-N	22	36	5	4	0	0	0	1	5	4	.111	.238	.111	2	-5	0	0	0	1.000	4	/2-7,3-1	0.0
Total	7	185	455	53	94	12	1	1	33	54	35	.207	.296	.244	50	-30	4	4	-1	.971	-8	2-125/S-6,3-1	-3.3

■ HEINIE STAFFORD Stafford, Henry Alexander b: 11/1/1891, Orleans, Vt. d: 1/29/72, Lake Worth, Fla. BR/TR, 5'7", 160 lbs. Deb: 10/5/16

| 1916 | NY-N | 1 | 1 | 0 | 0 | 0 | 0 | 0 | 0 | 0 | 0 | .000 | .000 | .000 | -99 | -0 | 0 | | | .000 | 0 | H | 0.0 |

■ GENERAL STAFFORD Stafford, James Joseph "Jamsey" b: 7/9/1868, Webster, Mass. d: 9/18/23, Worcester, Mass. BR/TR, 5'8", 165 lbs. Deb: 8/27/1890 F

1890	Buf-P	15	49	11	7	1	0	0	3	7	8	.143	.250	.163	13	-6	2			.893	-2	P-12/O-4	-0.2
1893	NY-N	67	281	58	79	7	4	5	27	25	31	.281	.344	.388	94	-3	19			.901	-7	O-67	-1.1
1894	NY-N	14	46	10	10	1	1	0	4	10	7	.217	.368	.283	59	-3	2			.750	-3	/3-6,O-5,2-1,1-1	-0.5
1895	NY-N	123	463	79	129	12	5	3	73	40	32	.279	.344	.346	80	-13	42			.911	-9	*2-109,O-12/3-2	-1.4
1896	NY-N	59	230	28	66	9	1	0	40	13	18	.287	.333	.335	79	-7	15			.897	-5	O-53/S-6	-1.3
1897	NY-N	7	23	0	2	0	0	0	3	3		.087	.192	.087	-26	-4	0			1.000	-3	/O-5,S-2	-0.7
	Lou-N	111	432	68	120	16	5	7	53	31		.278	.330	.387	92	-6	14			.887	-12	*S-103/O-7,3-1	-1.4
	Yr	118	455	68	122	16	5	7	56	34		.268	.323	.371	86	-10	14			.882	-16	*S-105,O-12/3-1	-2.1
1898	Lou-N	49	181	26	54	3	0	1	25	19		.298	.368	.331	103	-1	7			.901	-8	2-28,O-22/3-1	-0.6
	Bos-N	37	123	21	32	2	0	1	8	4		.260	.289	.301	66	-6	3			.909	-4	O-35/1-1	-1.1
	Yr	86	304	47	86	5	0	2	33	23		.283	.337	.319	87	-5	10			.924	-12	O-57,2-28/3-1,1-1	-1.7
1899	Bos-N	55	182	29	55	4	2	1	40	7		.302	.328	.396	89	-4	9			.956	-9	O-41,2-5,S-5	-1.4
	Was-N	31	118	11	29	5	1	1	14	5		.246	.276	.331	67	-6	4			.951	-5	2-17,S-13/3-2	-0.9
	Yr	86	300	40	84	9	3	4	54	12		.280	.308	.370	81	-9	13			.956	-14	O-41,2-22,S-18/3-2	-2.3
Total	8	568	2128	341	583	60	19	21	290	164	96	.274	.331	.350	82	-56	117			.911	-67	O-251,2-160/S,3P1	-10.6

■ BOB STAFFORD Stafford, Robert M. b: 6/26/1872, Oak Ridge, N.C. d: 8/20/16, Moores Springs, N.C. Deb: 10/12/1890

| 1890 | Phi-a | 1 | 2 | 0 | 0 | 0 | 0 | 0 | 0 | 0 | | .000 | .000 | .000 | -99 | -0 | 0 | | | 1.000 | 1 | /O-1 | 0.0 |

■ STEVE STAGGS Staggs, Stephen Robert b: 5/6/51, Anchorage, Alaska BR/TR, 5'9", 150 lbs. Deb: 7/1/77

1977	Tor-A	72	290	37	75	11	4	2	28	36	38	.259	.340	.359	90	-3	5	9	-4	.965	-14	2-72	-1.6
1978	Oak-A	47	78	10	19	2	2	0	0	19	17	.244	.392	.321	108	2	2	3	-1	.976	-3	2-40/S-2,3-2,D-2	0.0
Total	2	119	368	47	94	13	6	2	28	55	55	.255	.352	.351	94	-2	7	12	-5	.968	-17	2-112/D-2,3-2,S-2	-1.6

■ CHICK STAHL Stahl, Charles Sylvester b: 1/10/1873, Avilla, Ind. d: 3/28/07, W.Baden, Ind. BL/TL, 5'10", 160 lbs. Deb: 4/19/1897 M

1897	*Bos-N	114	469	112	166	30	13	4	97	38		.354	.406	.499	130	19	18			.928	-3	*O-111	0.6
1898	Bos-N	125	467	72	144	21	8	3	52	46		.308	.375	.407	118	10	6			.968	-2	*O-125	0.0
1899	Bos-N	148	576	122	202	23	19	7	52	72		.351	.426	.493	139	30	33			.969	6	*O-148/P-1	2.2
1900	Bos-N	136	553	88	163	23	16	5	82	34		.295	.336	.421	96	-7	27			.968	9	*O-135	-0.7
1901	Bos-A	131	515	105	156	20	16	6	72	54		.303	.377	.439	128	20	29			.957	-1	*O-131	0.9
1902	Bos-A	127	508	92	164	22	11	2	58	37		.323	.375	.421	117	12	24			.953	-5	*O-125	-0.1
1903	*Bos-A	77	299	60	82	12	6	2	44	28		.274	.338	.375	108	3	10			.961	-2	O-74	-0.4
1904	Bos-A	157	587	83	170	27	**19**	3	67	64		.290	.366	.416	139	27	11			.961	-14	*O-157	0.4
1905	Bos-A	134	500	61	129	17	4	0	47	50		.258	.332	.308	102	-3	18			.977	-6	*O-134	-1.1
1906	Bos-A	155	595	63	170	24	6	4	51	47		.286	.346	.366	123	16	13			.961	10	*O-155,M	2.0
Total	10	1304	5069	858	1546	219	118	36	622	470		.305	.369	.416	121	133	189			.961	-8	*O-1295/P-1	3.8

■ JAKE STAHL Stahl, Garland b: 4/13/1879, Elkhart, Ind. d: 9/18/22, Monrovia, Cal. BR/TR, 6'2", 195 lbs. Deb: 4/20/03 M

1903	Bos-A	40	92	14	22	3	5	2	8	4		.239	.286	.446	111	1	1			.956	-2	C-28/O-1	0.1
1904	Was-A	142	520	54	136	29	12	3	50	21		.262	.309	.381	119	10	25			.978	6	*1-119,O-23	1.3
1905	Was-A	141	501	66	125	22	12	5	66	28		.250	.311	.371	121	11	41			.986	-2	*1-140,M	0.9
1906	Was-A	137	482	38	107	9	8	0	51	21		.222	.266	.274	73	-16	30			.983	-2	*1-136,M	-2.4
1908	NY-A	75	274	34	70	18	5	2	42	11		.255	.304	.380	120	5	17			.933	4	O-68/1-6	0.7
	Bos-A	78	262	29	64	9	11	0	23	20		.244	.333	.363	123	7	13			.984	-1	1-78	0.4
	Yr	153	536	63	134	27	16	2	65	31		.250	.319	.371	122	12	30			.984	2	1-84,O-68	1.1
1909	Bos-A	127	435	62	128	19	12	6	60	43		.294	.377	.434	153	27	16			.986	-11	*1-126	1.6
1910	Bos-A	144	531	68	144	19	16	**10**	77	42		.271	.334	.424	134	19	22			.985	-7	*1-142	1.3
1912	*Bos-A	95	326	40	98	21	6	3	60	31		.301	.372	.429	123	9	13			.980	-2	1-92,M	0.6
1913	Bos-A	2	2	0	0	0	0	0	0	0		.000	.000	.000	-98	-0	0			.000	0	HM	-0.1
Total	9	981	3425	405	894	149	87	31	437	221	1	.261	.323	.382	120	73	178			.983	-14	1-839/O-92,C-28	4.4

■ LARRY STAHL Stahl, Larry Floyd b: 6/29/41, Belleville, Ill. BL/TL, 6'1", 185 lbs. Deb: 9/11/64

1964	KC-A	15	46	7	12	1	0	3	6	1	10	.261	.277	.478	102	-0	0	0	0	.955	1	O-10	0.0
1965	KC-A	28	81	9	16	2	1	4	14	5	16	.198	.253	.395	82	-2	1	0	0	1.000	1	O-21	-0.2
1966	KC-A	119	312	37	78	11	5	5	34	17	63	.250	.291	.365	90	-5	5	3	-0	.980	-4	O-94	-1.3
1967	NY-N	71	155	9	37	5	0	1	18	8	25	.239	.285	.290	66	-7	2	2	-1	.969	3	O-43	-0.7
1968	NY-N	53	183	15	43	7	2	3	10	21	34	.235	.314	.344	97	-0	3	0	1	.983	1	O-47/1-9	-0.2
1969	SD-N	95	162	10	32	6	2	3	10	17	31	.198	.278	.315	68	-7	3	3	-1	.981	0	O-37,1-13	-0.9
1970	SD-N	52	66	5	12	2	0	0	2	14	14	.182	.206	.212	13	-8	2	2	-1	1.000	-3	O-20	-1.3
1971	SD-N	114	308	27	78	13	4	8	36	26	59	.253	.311	.399	107	2	4	3	-0	.987	6	O-75/1-7	0.3
1972	SD-N	107	297	31	67	9	3	7	20	31	62	.226	.299	.347	89	-5	1	3	-2	.986	-1	O-76/1-1	-1.1
1973	*Cin-N	76	111	17	25	2	2	1	12	14	34	.225	.317	.333	85	-2	1	0	0	1.000	-6	O-29/1-2	-0.9
Total		730	1721	167	400	58	19	36	163	142	357	.232	.293	.351	86	-35	22	16	-3	.983	-1	O-452/1-32	-6.3

■ SCOTT STAHOVIAK Stahoviak, Scott Edmund b: 3/6/70, Waukegan, Ill. BL/TR, 6'5", 210 lbs. Deb: 9/10/93

1993	Min-A	20	57	1	11	4	0	1	3	2	15	.193	.233	.263	33	-5	0	2	-1	.922	3	3-19	-0.4
1995	Min-A	94	263	28	70	19	3	3	23	30	61	.266	.344	.373	86	-5	5	1	-1	.998	7	1-69,3-22/D-1	-0.2
1996	Min-A	130	405	72	115	30	3	13	61	59	114	.284	.378	.469	110	7	3	3	-1	.994	10	*1-114/D-9	0.6
Total	3	244	725	101	196	53	3	16	85	92	197	.270	.355	.418	96	-3	8	6	-3	.996	20	1-183/3-41,D-10	0.2

■ ROY STAIGER Staiger, Roy Joseph b: 1/6/50, Tulsa, Okla. BR/TR, 6', 195 lbs. Deb: 9/12/75

1975	NY-N	13	19	2	3	1	0	0	0	0	4	.158	.158	.211	2	-3	0	0	0	1.000	4	3-13	-0.1
1976	NY-N	95	304	23	67	8	1	2	26	25	35	.220	.282	.273	62	-16	3	3	-1	.967	19	3-93/S-1	0.2
1977	NY-N	40	123	16	31	9	0	1	11	4	20	.252	.276	.374	76	-5	1	0	0	.934	3	3-36/S-1	0.1
1979	NY-A	4	11	1	3	1	0	0	1	1	0	.273	.333	.364	90	-0	0	0	0	1.000	0	/3-4	0.0
Total	4	152	457	42	104	19	1	4	38	30	59	.228	.277	.300	64	-23	4	3	-1	.960	26	3-146/S-2	0.2

■ TUCK STAINBACK Stainback, George Tucker b: 8/4/11, Los Angeles, Cal. d: 11/29/92, Camarillo, Cal. BR/TR, 5'11.5", 175 lbs. Deb: 4/17/34

1934	Chi-N	104	359	47	110	14	3	2	46	8	42	.306	.327	.379	90	-5	7			.955	-6	O-96/3-1	-1.5
1935	Chi-N	47	94	16	24	4	0	3	11	0	13	.255	.271	.394	76	-4	1			.932	-5	O-28	-0.9
1936	Chi-N	44	75	13	13	3	0	1	5	6	14	.173	.235	.253	31	-7	1			1.000	-4	O-26	-1.2
1937	Chi-N	72	160	18	37	9	0	1	14	7	16	.231	.268	.287	49	-11	3			.981	-2	O-49	-1.4
1938	StL-N	6	10	2	0	0	0	0	0	0	3	.000	.000	.000	-95	-3	0			1.000	1	/O-2	-0.2
	Phi-N	30	81	9	21	5	0	1	9	3	5	.259	.294	.333	74	-3	1			.980	-1	O-25	-0.6
	Bro-N	35	104	15	34	6	3	0	20	2	4	.327	.346	.442	113	1	1			.982	-1	O-23	0.0
	Yr	71	195	26	55	9	3	1	31	5	10	.282	.307	.374	86	-4	2			.982	-3	O-50	-0.8
1939	Bro-N	68	201	22	54	7	0	3	19	4	23	.269	.290	.348	68	-9	0			.938	-5	O-55	-1.6

YEAR	TM/L	G	AB	R	H	2B	3B	HR	RBI	BB	SO	AVG	OBP	SLG	PRO+	BR/A	SB	CS	SBR	FA	FR	G/POS	TPR
1940	Det-A	15	40	4	9	2	0	0	1	1	9	.225	.262	.275	36	-4	0	0	0	.968	4	/O-9	-0.1
1941	Det-A	94	200	19	49	8	1	2	10	3	21	.245	.260	.325	49	-15	6	3	0	.948	-15	O-80	-3.2
1942	*NY-A	15	10	0	2	0	0	0	0	0	0	.200	.200	.200	13	-1	0	0	0	1.000	-0	/O-3	-0.1
1943	*NY-A	71	231	31	60	11	2	0	10	7	16	.260	.285	.325	77	-7	3	3	-1	.993	-1	O-60	-1.3
1944	NY-A	30	78	13	17	3	0	0	5	3	7	.218	.247	.256	42	-6	1	0	0	.957	-3	O-24	-1.0
1945	NY-A	95	327	40	84	12	2	5	32	13	20	.257	.289	.352	82	-9	0	4	-2	.968	9	O-83	-0.7
1946	Phi-A	91	291	35	71	10	2	0	20	7	20	.244	.264	.292	56	-18	3	2	-0	.963	3	O-66	-2.0
Total	13	817	2261	284	585	90	14	17	204	64	213	.259	.284	.333	68	-101	27	12		.965	-29	O-629/3-1	-15.8

■ MATT STAIRS
Stairs, Matthew Wade b: 2/27/68, St.John, N.B., Canada   BL/TR, 5'9", 175 lbs.   Deb: 5/29/92

YEAR	TM/L	G	AB	R	H	2B	3B	HR	RBI	BB	SO	AVG	OBP	SLG	PRO+	BR/A	SB	CS	SBR	FA	FR	G/POS	TPR
1992	Mon-N	13	30	2	5	2	0	0	5	7	7	.167	.324	.233	61	-1	0	0	0	.933	-1	O-10	-0.3
1993	Mon-N	6	8	1	3	1	0	0	2	0	1	.375	.375	.500	126	0	0	0	0	1.000	-0	/O-1	0.0
1995	*Bos-A	39	88	8	23	7	1	1	17	4	14	.261	.301	.398	77	-3	0	1	-1	.913	-4	O-23/D-2	-0.8
1996	Oak-A	61	137	21	38	5	1	10	23	19	23	.277	.369	.547	133	7	1	1	-0	.985	0	O-44/1-1,D-5	0.5
Total	4	119	263	32	69	15	2	11	47	30	45	.262	.342	.460	106	3	1	2	-1	.962	-5	/O-78,D-7,1-1	-0.6

■ GALE STALEY
Staley, George Gaylord b: 5/2/1899, DePere, Wis. d: 4/19/89, Walnut Creek, Cal.   BL/TR, 5'8.5", 167 lbs.   Deb: 9/16/25

YEAR	TM/L	G	AB	R	H	2B	3B	HR	RBI	BB	SO	AVG	OBP	SLG	PRO+	BR/A	SB	CS	SBR	FA	FR	G/POS	TPR
1925	Chi-N	7	26	2	11	2	0	0	3	2	1	.423	.464	.500	144	2	0	1	-1	.979	4	/2-7	0.5

■ VIRGIL STALLCUP
Stallcup, Thomas Virgil "Red" b: 1/3/22, Ravensford, N.C. d: 5/2/89, Greenville, S.C.   BR/TR, 6'3", 185 lbs.   Deb: 4/18/47

YEAR	TM/L	G	AB	R	H	2B	3B	HR	RBI	BB	SO	AVG	OBP	SLG	PRO+	BR/A	SB	CS	SBR	FA	FR	G/POS	TPR
1947	Cin-N	8	1	1	0	0	0	0	0	0	0	.000	.000	.000	-99	-0	0			.000	0	/S-1	0.0
1948	Cin-N	149	539	40	123	30	4	3	65	18	52	.228	.253	.315	55	-36	2			.956	-0	*S-148	-2.8
1949	Cin-N	141	575	49	146	28	5	3	45	9	44	.254	.268	.336	60	-33	1			.962	-10	*S-141	-3.3
1950	Cin-N	136	483	44	121	23	2	8	54	17	39	.251	.276	.356	65	-26	4			**.973**	-5	*S-136	-2.1
1951	Cin-N	121	428	33	103	17	2	8	49	6	40	.241	.251	.346	58	-26	2	4	-2	**.969**	-8	*S-117	-2.8
1952	Cin-N	2	1	0	0	0	0	0	0	0	0	.000	.000	.000	-99	-0	0			.000	0	/S-1	0.0
	StL-N	29	31	4	4	1	0	0	1	1	5	.129	.156	.161	-12	-5	0			1.000	2	S-12	-0.3
	Yr	31	32	4	4	1	0	0	1	1	5	.125	.152	.156	-15	-5	0			1.000	2	S-13	-0.3
1953	StL-N	1	1	0	0	0	0	0	0	0	0	.000	.000	.000	-99	-0	0			.000	0	H	0.0
Total	7	587	2059	171	497	99	13	22	214	51	181	.241	.260	.334	58	-127	9	4		.965	-21	S-556	-11.3

■ GEORGE STALLER
Staller, George Walborn "Stopper" b: 4/1/16, Rutherford Heights, Pa. d: 7/3/92, Harrisburg, Pa.   BL/TL, 5'11", 190 lbs.   Deb: 9/14/43 C

YEAR	TM/L	G	AB	R	H	2B	3B	HR	RBI	BB	SO	AVG	OBP	SLG	PRO+	BR/A	SB	CS	SBR	FA	FR	G/POS	TPR
1943	Phi-A	21	85	14	23	1	3	3	12	5	6	.271	.326	.459	129	3	1	0	0	.977	-1	O-20	0.1

■ GEORGE STALLINGS
Stallings, George Tweedy "Gentleman George" b: 11/17/1867, Augusta, Ga. d: 5/13/29, Haddock, Ga.   BR/TR, 6'1", 187 lbs.   Deb: 5/22/1890 M

YEAR	TM/L	G	AB	R	H	2B	3B	HR	RBI	BB	SO	AVG	OBP	SLG	PRO+	BR/A	SB	CS	SBR	FA	FR	G/POS	TPR
1890	Bro-N	4	11	1	0	0	0	0	0	0	3	.000	.154	.000	-54	-2	0			.933	-1	/C-4	-0.3
1897	Phi-N	2	9	1	2	1	0	0	0	0	0	.222	.222	.333	47	-1	0			1.000	1	/O-1,1-1,M	0.0
1898	Phi-N	1	0	1	0	0	0	0	0	0	0	—	—	—	—	0	0			.000	0	/HM	0.0
Total	3	7	20	3	2	1	0	0	0	0	3	.100	.182	.150	-7	-3	0			.933	-1	/C-4,1-1,O-1	-0.3

■ OSCAR STANAGE
Stanage, Oscar Harland b: 3/17/1883, Tulare, Cal. d: 11/11/64, Detroit, Mich.   BR/TR, 5'11", 190 lbs.   Deb: 5/19/06 C

YEAR	TM/L	G	AB	R	H	2B	3B	HR	RBI	BB	SO	AVG	OBP	SLG	PRO+	BR/A	SB	CS	SBR	FA	FR	G/POS	TPR
1906	Cin-N	1	1	0	0	0	0	0	0	0	0	.000	.000	.000	-96	-0	0			1.000	-0	/C-1	0.0
1909	*Det-A	77	252	17	66	8	6	0	21	11		.262	.266	.341	98	-1	2			.964	-8	C-77	-0.3
1910	Det-A	88	275	24	57	7	4	2	25	20		.207	.266	.284	68	-11	1			.952	-4	C-84	-0.7
1911	Det-A	141	503	45	133	13	7	3	51	20		.264	.297	.336	73	-20	3			.952	-13	*C-141	-1.8
1912	Det-A	121	394	35	103	9	4	0	41	34		.261	.305	.305	83	-8	3			.950	-28	*C-120	-2.5
1913	Det-A	80	241	19	54	13	2	0	21	21	35	.224	.292	.295	73	-9	5			.960	-6	C-77	-1.1
1914	Det-A	122	400	16	77	8	2	0	25	24	58	.192	.242	.233	41	-29	2	1	0	.960	-6	C-122	-2.7
1915	Det-A	100	300	27	67	9	2	1	31	20	41	.223	.274	.277	62	-15	5	1	1	.964	-9	*C-100	-1.7
1916	Det-A	94	291	16	69	17	3	0	30	17	48	.237	.286	.316	78	-9	3			.969	-3	C-94	-1.2
1917	Det-A	99	297	19	61	14	1	0	30	20	35	.205	.262	.259	59	-15	3			.977	-4	C-95	-1.3
1918	Det-A	54	186	9	47	4	0	1	14	11	18	.253	.294	.290	80	-5	2			.980	-2	C-47/1-5,S-1	-1.1
1919	Det-A	38	120	9	29	4	1	0	15	7	12	.242	.295	.317	73	-4	1			.974	1	C-36/1-1	-0.1
1920	Det-A	78	238	12	55	17	0	0	17	14	21	.231	.277	.303	55	-16	0			.958	-10	C-77	-2.0
1925	Det-A	3	5	0	1	0	0	0	0	0	0	.200	.200	.200	2	-1	0			1.000	-1	/C-3	-0.2
Total	14	1096	3503	248	819	123	34	8	321	219	268	.234	.284	.295	69	-142	30	2		.961	-107	*C-1074/1-6,S-1	-16.7

■ JERRY STANDAERT
Standaert, Jerome John b: 11/2/01, Chicago, Ill. d: 8/4/64, Chicago, Ill.   BR/TR, 5'10", 168 lbs.   Deb: 4/16/25

YEAR	TM/L	G	AB	R	H	2B	3B	HR	RBI	BB	SO	AVG	OBP	SLG	PRO+	BR/A	SB	CS	SBR	FA	FR	G/POS	TPR
1925	Bro-N	1	1	0	0	0	0	0	0	0	1	.000	.000	.000	-99	-0	0	0	0	.000	0	H	0.0
1926	Bro-N	66	113	13	39	8	2	0	14	5	7	.345	.378	.478	124	4	0			.918	-11	2-21,3-14/S-6	-0.6
1929	Bos-A	19	18	1	3	2	0	0	4	3	2	.167	.286	.278	47	-1	0			.958	-0	1-10	-0.2
Total	3	86	132	14	42	10	2	0	18	8	10	.318	.362	.424	111	2	0			.918	-11	/2-21,3-14,1-10,S-6	-0.8

■ PETE STANICEK
Stanicek, Peter Louis b: 4/18/63, Harvey, Ill.   BB/TR, 5'11", 175 lbs.   Deb: 9/1/87 F

YEAR	TM/L	G	AB	R	H	2B	3B	HR	RBI	BB	SO	AVG	OBP	SLG	PRO+	BR/A	SB	CS	SBR	FA	FR	G/POS	TPR
1987	Bal-A	30	113	9	31	3	0	0	9	8	19	.274	.333	.301	72	-4	8	1	2	.975	-6	2-19,D-10/3-2	-0.7
1988	Bal-A	83	261	29	60	7	1	4	17	28	45	.230	.314	.310	78	-7	12	6	0	.985	-5	O-65,2-16/D-1	-1.3
Total	2	113	374	38	91	10	1	4	26	36	64	.243	.320	.307	76	-11	20	7	2	.967	-10	/O-65,2-35,D-11,3-2	-2.0

■ STEVE STANICEK
Stanicek, Stephen Blair b: 6/19/61, Lake Forest, Ill.   BR/TR, 6', 190 lbs.   Deb: 9/16/87 F

YEAR	TM/L	G	AB	R	H	2B	3B	HR	RBI	BB	SO	AVG	OBP	SLG	PRO+	BR/A	SB	CS	SBR	FA	FR	G/POS	TPR
1987	Mil-A	4	7	2	2	0	0	0	0	0	2	.286	.286	.286	51	-0	0	0	0	.000	0	/D-1	0.0
1989	Phi-N	9	9	0	1	0	0	0	1	0	3	.111	.111	.111	-36	-2	0	0	0	.000	0	H	-0.2
Total	2	13	16	2	3	0	0	0	1	0	5	.188	.188	.188	0	-2	0	0	0		0	/D-1	-0.2

■ TOM STANKARD
Stankard, Thomas Francis b: 3/20/1882, Waltham, Mass. d: 6/13/58, Waltham, Mass.   BR/TR, 6', 190 lbs.   Deb: 7/2/04

YEAR	TM/L	G	AB	R	H	2B	3B	HR	RBI	BB	SO	AVG	OBP	SLG	PRO+	BR/A	SB	CS	SBR	FA	FR	G/POS	TPR
1904	Pit-N	2	2	0	0	0	0	0	0	0	0	.000	.000	.000	-97	-0	0			.000	-1	/S-1,3-1	-0.1

■ ANDY STANKIEWICZ
Stankiewicz, Andrew Neal b: 8/10/64, Inglewood, Cal.   BR/TR, 5'9", 165 lbs.   Deb: 4/11/92

YEAR	TM/L	G	AB	R	H	2B	3B	HR	RBI	BB	SO	AVG	OBP	SLG	PRO+	BR/A	SB	CS	SBR	FA	FR	G/POS	TPR
1992	NY-A	116	400	52	107	22	2	2	25	38	42	.268	.339	.348	93	-3	9	5	-0	.973	6	S-81,2-34/D-1	0.9
1993	NY-A	16	9	5	0	0	0	0	0	1	1	.000	.100	.000	-73	-2	0	0	0	1.000	6	/2-6,3-4,S-1,D-1	0.4
1994	Hou-N	37	54	10	14	3	0	1	5	12	12	.259	.403	.370	109	1	1	1	-0	1.000	5	S-17/2-6,3-1	0.2
1995	Hou-N	43	52	6	6	1	0	0	7	12	19	.115	.281	.135	15	-6	4	2	0	.985	12	S-14/2-6,3-3	0.6
1996	Mon-N	64	77	12	22	5	1	0	9	6	12	.286	.360	.372	92	-1	1	0	0	.969	1	2-19,S-13/3-1	0.2
Total	5	276	592	85	149	31	3	3	46	69	86	.252	.339	.329	85	-11	15	8	-0	.976	25	S-126/2-71,3-9,D-2	2.3

■ EDDIE STANKY
Stanky, Edward Raymond "The Brat" or "Muggsy" b: 9/3/16, Philadelphia, Pa.   BR/TR, 5'8", 170 lbs.   Deb: 4/21/43 MC

YEAR	TM/L	G	AB	R	H	2B	3B	HR	RBI	BB	SO	AVG	OBP	SLG	PRO+	BR/A	SB	CS	SBR	FA	FR	G/POS	TPR
1943	Chi-N	142	510	92	125	15	1	2	47	92	42	.245	.363	.278	88	-3	4			.966	12	*2-131,S-12/3-2	1.8
1944	Chi-N	13	25	4	6	0	0	0	0	2	2	.240	.296	.320	74	-1	1			.875	2	/2-3,S-3,3-3	0.1
	Bro-N	89	261	32	72	9	2	0	16	44	13	.276	.382	.326	102	3	3			.961	-18	2-58,S-35/3-1	-1.0
	Yr	102	286	36	78	9	2	0	16	46	15	.273	.375	.325	100	2	4			.958	-16	2-61,S-38/3-4	-0.9
1945	Bro-N	153	555	**128**	143	29	5	1	39	**148**	42	.258	.417	.333	111	18	6			.962	9	*2-153/S-1	3.6
1946	Bro-N	144	483	98	132	24	7	0	36	**137**	56	.273	**.436**	.326	124	25	8			.977	-5	*2-141	3.1
1947	*Bro-N★	146	559	97	141	24	5	3	53	103	39	.252	.373	.329	85	-8	3			**.985**	7	*2-146	0.8
1948	*Bos-N†	67	247	49	79	14	2	1	29	61	13	.320	.455	.417	140	18	5			.981	5	2-66	2.6
1949	Bos-N	138	506	90	144	24	5	1	42	113	38	.285	.417	.358	116	19	3			.979	-9	*2-135	1.6
1950	NY-N☆	152	527	115	158	25	5	8	51	**144**	50	.300	**.460**	.412	131	35	9			.976	2	*2-151	4.1
1951	*NY-N	145	515	88	127	17	2	14	43	127	63	.247	.401	.369	108	12	8	5	-1	.977	-1	*2-140	1.7
1952	StL-N	53	83	13	19	4	0	0	7	19	9	.229	.373	.277	83	-1	0	0	0	1.000	-0	2-20,M	-0.1
1953	StL-N	17	30	5	8	1	0	0	1	6	4	.267	.405	.267	80	-0	0			1.000	1	/2-8,M	0.1
Total	11	1259	4301	811	1154	185	35	29	364	996	374	.268	.410	.348	109	116	48	5		.975	4	*2-1152/S-51,3-6	18.4

YEAR	TM/L	G	AB	R	H	2B	3B	HR	RBI	BB	SO	AVG	OBP	SLG	PRO+	BR/A	SB	CS	SBR	FA	FR	G/POS	TPR

■ FRED STANLEY
Stanley, Frederick Blair   b: 8/13/47, Farnhamville, Iowa   BR/TR, 5'10", 167 lbs.   Deb: 9/11/69   C

YEAR	TM/L	G	AB	R	H	2B	3B	HR	RBI	BB	SO	AVG	OBP	SLG	PRO+	BR/A	SB	CS	SBR	FA	FR	G/POS	TPR
1969	Sea-A	17	43	2	12	2	1	0	4	3	8	.279	.326	.372	96	-0	1	0	0	.962	-4	S-15/2-1	-0.3
1970	Mil-A	6	0	1	0	0	0	0	0	0	0	—	—	—	—	—	0	0	0	1.000	1	/2-2	0.1
1971	Cle-A	60	129	14	29	4	0	2	12	27	25	.225	.363	.302	83	-2	1	0	0	.971	7	S-55/2-3	1.1
1972	Cle-A	6	12	1	2	1	0	0	0	2	3	.167	.286	.250	58	-1	0	0	0	.917	-3	/S-5,2-1	-0.4
	SD-N	39	85	15	17	2	0	0	2	12	19	.200	.306	.224	57	-4	1	0	0	.989	3	2-21,S-17/3-4	0.1
1973	NY-A	26	66	6	14	0	1	1	5	7	16	.212	.288	.288	65	-3	0	0	0	.981	3	S-21/2-3	0.3
1974	NY-A	33	38	2	7	0	0	0	3	3	2	.184	.244	.184	25	-4	1	2	-1	.973	12	S-19,2-15	0.9
1975	NY-A	117	252	34	56	5	1	0	15	21	27	.222	.285	.250	53	-15	3	1	0	.977	4	S-83,2-33/3-1	-0.4
1976	*NY-A	110	260	32	62	2	2	1	20	34	29	.238	.329	.273	78	-6	0	0	0	.983	-24	*S-110/2-3	-1.9
1977	*NY-A	48	46	6	12	0	0	1	7	8	6	.261	.370	.326	93	-0	1	1	0	.958	3	S-42/3-3,2-2	0.4
1978	*NY-A	81	160	14	35	7	0	1	9	25	31	.219	.324	.281	73	-5	0	0	0	.959	-5	S-71,2-11/3-4	-0.3
1979	NY-A	57	100	9	20	1	0	2	14	5	17	.200	.238	.270	38	-9	0	1	-1	.978	6	S-31,3-16/2-8,1O	0.5
1980	NY-A	49	86	13	18	3	0	0	5	5	5	.209	.269	.244	42	-7	0	0	0	.923	7	S-19,2-17,3-12	0.2
1981	*Oak-A	66	145	15	28	4	0	0	7	15	24	.193	.269	.221	44	-10	2	0	1	.986	-17	S-62/2-6	-2.2
1982	Oak-A	101	228	33	44	7	0	2	17	29	32	.193	.287	.250	51	-15	0	1	-1	.963	-20	S-98/2-2	-2.8
Total	14	816	1650	197	356	38	5	10	120	196	243	.216	.302	.263	62	-80	11	6	-0	.971	-19	S-648,2-128/3O1	-4.7

■ JIM STANLEY
Stanley, James F.   b: 1889,   BB/TR, 5'6", 148 lbs.   Deb: 4/19/14

YEAR	TM/L	G	AB	R	H	2B	3B	HR	RBI	BB	SO	AVG	OBP	SLG	PRO+	BR/A	SB	CS	SBR	FA	FR	G/POS	TPR
1914	Chi-F	54	98	13	19	3	0	0	4	19	14	.194	.347	.224	61	-6	2			.878	-10	S-40/3-3,2-1,0-1	-1.5

■ JOE STANLEY
Stanley, Joseph   b: New Jersey   Deb: 4/24/1884

YEAR	TM/L	G	AB	R	H	2B	3B	HR	RBI	BB	SO	AVG	OBP	SLG	PRO+	BR/A	SB	CS	SBR	FA	FR	G/POS	TPR
1884	Bal-U	6	21	3	5	1	0	0		0	0	.238	.238	.286	53	-2				.444	-2	/O-6	-0.4

■ JOE STANLEY
Stanley, Joseph Bernard   b: 4/2/1881, Washington, D.C.   d: 9/13/67, Detroit, Mich.   BB/TR, 5'9.5", 150 lbs.   Deb: 9/11/1897   F

YEAR	TM/L	G	AB	R	H	2B	3B	HR	RBI	BB	SO	AVG	OBP	SLG	PRO+	BR/A	SB	CS	SBR	FA	FR	G/POS	TPR
1897	Was-N	1	1	0	0	0	0	0	0	0	0	.000	.000	.000	-99	-0	0			.000	-0	/P-1	-0.1
1902	Was-A	3	12	2	4	0	0	0	1	0	0	.333	.333	.333	85	-0	0			.833	-1	/O-3	-0.1
1903	Bos-N	86	308	40	77	12	5	1	47	18		.250	.306	.331	85	-6	10			.902	3	O-77/P-1,S-1	-0.7
1904	Bos-N	3	8	0	0	0	0	0	0	0		.000	.000	.000	-99	-2	0			.800	1	/O-3	-0.2
1905	Was-A	28	92	13	24	2	1	1	17	7		.261	.313	.337	111	1	4			.944	0	O-27	0.0
1906	Was-A	73	221	18	36	0	4	0	9	20		.163	.236	.199	38	-15	6			.934	-5	O-63/P-1	-2.6
1909	Chi-N	22	52	4	7	1	0	0	2	6		.135	.224	.154	17	-5	0			.947	-4	O-16	-1.1
Total	7	216	694	77	148	15	10	2	76	51		.213	.275	.272	66	-28	20			.918	-6	O-189/P-3,S-1	-4.7

■ MICKEY STANLEY
Stanley, Mitchell Jack   b: 7/20/42, Grand Rapids, Mich   BR/TR, 6'1", 195 lbs.   Deb: 9/13/64

YEAR	TM/L	G	AB	R	H	2B	3B	HR	RBI	BB	SO	AVG	OBP	SLG	PRO+	BR/A	SB	CS	SBR	FA	FR	G/POS	TPR
1964	Det-A	4	11	3	3	0	0	0	1	0	1	.273	.273	.273	52	-1	0	0	0	1.000	-1	/O-4	-0.2
1965	Det-A	30	117	14	28	6	0	3	13	3	12	.239	.258	.368	75	-4	1	0	0	.986	3	O-29	-0.3
1966	Det-A	92	235	28	68	15	4	3	19	17	20	.289	.337	.426	115	-7	2	1	0	1.000	6	O-82	0.4
1967	Det-A	145	333	38	70	7	3	7	24	29	46	.210	.273	.312	71	-12	9	2	2	.982	-8	*O-129/1-8	-2.6
1968	*Det-A	153	583	88	151	16	6	11	60	42	57	.259	.313	.364	102	-4	1	4	-3	1.000	3	*O-130,1-15/S-9,2-1	-0.4
1969	Det-A	149	592	73	139	28	1	16	70	52	56	.235	.299	.367	82	-15	8	4	0	.985	-19	*O-101,S-59/1-4	-3.6
1970	Det-A	142	568	83	143	21	11	13	47	45	56	.252	.307	.396	92	-8	10	1	2	1.000	6	*O-132/1-9	-0.7
1971	Det-A	139	401	43	117	14	5	7	41	24	44	.292	.332	.404	103	1	1	3	-2	.988	6	*O-139	0.1
1972	*Det-A	142	435	45	102	16	6	14	55	29	49	.234	.282	.395	97	-3	1	0	0	.994	6	*O-139	-0.3
1973	Det-A	157	602	81	147	23	5	17	57	48	65	.244	.300	.384	86	-13	0	4	-3	.993	13	*O-157	0.1
1974	Det-A	99	394	40	87	13	2	8	34	26	63	.221	.271	.325	68	-17	5	3	-0	.992	6	O-91,1-12/2-1	-1.7
1975	Det-A	52	164	26	42	7	3	3	19	15	27	.256	.322	.390	96	-1	1	1	-0	.983	-1	O-28,1-14/3-7,D-1	-0.5
1976	Det-A	84	214	34	55	17	1	4	29	14	19	.257	.303	.402	101	-0	2	0	1	.969	-2	O-38,1-17,3/S2D	-0.4
1977	Det-A	75	222	30	51	9	1	8	23	18	30	.230	.287	.387	78	-7	0	0	0	.972	-6	O-57/1-3,S-3,D-2	-1.5
1978	Det-A	53	151	15	40	9	0	3	8	9	19	.265	.306	.384	90	-2	0	1	-0	.960	-6	O-34,1-12	-1.1
Total	15	1516	5022	641	1243	201	48	117	500	371	564	.248	.300	.377	89	-77	44	23	-1	.991	2	*O-1290/1-94,S3D2	-13.8

■ MIKE STANLEY
Stanley, Robert Michael   b: 6/25/63, Ft.Lauderdale, Fla   BR/TR, 6'1", 185 lbs.   Deb: 6/24/86

YEAR	TM/L	G	AB	R	H	2B	3B	HR	RBI	BB	SO	AVG	OBP	SLG	PRO+	BR/A	SB	CS	SBR	FA	FR	G/POS	TPR
1986	Tex-A	15	30	4	10	3	0	1	1	3	3	.333	.394	.533	146	2	1	0	0	.857	1	/3-7,C-4,0-1,D-3	0.1
1987	Tex-A	78	216	34	59	8	1	6	37	31	48	.273	.367	.403	104	2	3	0	1	.980	-11	C-61,1-12/0-1,D-5	-0.5
1988	Tex-A	94	249	21	57	8	0	3	27	37	62	.229	.329	.297	75	-7	0	0	0	.991	-3	C-64,D-18/1-6,3-2	-0.7
1989	Tex-A	67	122	9	30	3	1	1	11	12	29	.246	.324	.311	78	-3	1	0	0	.978	-4	C-25,D-21/1-7,3-3	-0.7
1990	Tex-A	103	189	21	47	8	1	2	19	30	25	.249	.352	.333	92	-1	1	0	0	.985	-3	C-63,D-14/3-8,1-6	-0.2
1991	Tex-A	95	181	25	45	13	1	3	25	34	44	.249	.373	.381	111	4	0	0	0	.980	-10	C-58,1-12/3-6,OD	-0.4
1992	NY-A	68	173	24	43	7	0	8	27	33	45	.249	.372	.428	124	7	0	0	0	.980	5	C-55/1-4,D-6	1.4
1993	NY-A	130	423	70	129	17	1	26	84	57	85	.305	.394	.534	152	31	1	1	-0	.996	-9	*C-122/D-2	2.8
1994	NY-A	82	290	54	87	20	0	17	57	39	56	.300	.387	.545	142	18	0	0	0	.993	-0	C-72/1-7,D-4	2.0
1995	*NY-A★	118	399	63	107	29	1	18	83	57	106	.268	.367	.481	120	12	1	1	-0	.993	-4	*C-107,D-10	1.4
1996	Bos-A	121	397	73	107	20	1	24	69	69	62	.270	.384	.506	119	12	2	0	1	.985	-27	*C-105,D-10	-0.7
Total	11	971	2669	398	721	136	7	109	440	402	569	.270	.370	.449	118	76	10	2	2	.988	-66	C-736/D-99,1-54,3O	4.5

■ JACK STANSBURY
Stansbury, John James   b: 12/6/1885, Phillipsburg, N.J.   d: 12/26/70, Easton, Pa.   BR/TR, 5'9", 165 lbs.   Deb: 6/30/18

YEAR	TM/L	G	AB	R	H	2B	3B	HR	RBI	BB	SO	AVG	OBP	SLG	PRO+	BR/A	SB	CS	SBR	FA	FR	G/POS	TPR
1918	Bos-A	20	47	3	6	1	0	0	2	6	3	.128	.241	.149	18	-5	0			.980	2	3-18/O-2	-0.2

■ BUCK STANTON
Stanton, George Washington   b: 6/19/06, Stantonsburg, N.C   d: 1/1/92, San Antonio, Tex.   BL/TL, 5'10", 150 lbs.   Deb: 9/5/31

YEAR	TM/L	G	AB	R	H	2B	3B	HR	RBI	BB	SO	AVG	OBP	SLG	PRO+	BR/A	SB	CS	SBR	FA	FR	G/POS	TPR
1931	StL-A	13	15	3	3	2	0	0		0	6	.200	.200	.333	37	-1	0	0	0	.750	-0	/O-1	-0.1

■ HARRY STANTON
Stanton, Harry Andrew   b: St.Louis, Mo.   TR ,   Deb: 10/14/00

YEAR	TM/L	G	AB	R	H	2B	3B	HR	RBI	BB	SO	AVG	OBP	SLG	PRO+	BR/A	SB	CS	SBR	FA	FR	G/POS	TPR
1900	StL-N	1	0	0	0					0	0	—	—	—	—	—	0	0		.000	-0	/C-1	0.0

■ LEROY STANTON
Stanton, Leroy Bobby   b: 4/10/46, Latta, S.C.   BR/TR, 6'1", 195 lbs.   Deb: 9/10/70

YEAR	TM/L	G	AB	R	H	2B	3B	HR	RBI	BB	SO	AVG	OBP	SLG	PRO+	BR/A	SB	CS	SBR	FA	FR	G/POS	TPR
1970	NY-N	4	4	0	1	0	1	0	0	0	1	.250	.250	.750	157	0	0	0	0	1.000	-0	/O-1	0.0
1971	NY-N	5	21	2	4	0	0	0	2	2	4	.190	.261	.238	43	-2	0	0	0	1.000	-0	/O-5	-0.2
1972	Cal-A	127	402	44	101	15	3	12	39	22	100	.251	.297	.393	110	3	2	3	-1	.983	2	*O-124	-0.2
1973	Cal-A	119	306	41	72	9	2	8	34	27	88	.235	.301	.356	92	-4	3	3	-1	.965	-7	*O-107	-1.6
1974	Cal-A	118	415	48	111	21	2	11	62	33	107	.267	.329	.407	117	8	10	8	-2	.975	4	*O-114	0.6
1975	Cal-A	137	440	67	115	20	3	14	82	52	85	.261	.347	.416	124	14	18	6	2	.961	-2	*O-131/D-1	1.3
1976	Cal-A	93	231	12	44	13	1	2	25	24	57	.190	.270	.281	66	-10	2	6	-3	.985	-15	O-79/D-4	-3.3
1977	Sea-A	133	454	56	125	24	1	27	90	42	115	.275	.343	.511	131	18	0	1	-0	.953	2	O-91,D-33	1.7
1978	Sea-A	93	302	24	55	11	0	3	24	34	80	.182	.267	.248	46	-21	1	0	0	1.000	-0	D-59,O-30	-2.5
Total	9	829	2575	294	628	114	13	77	358	236	636	.244	.313	.388	103	6	36	27	-5	.972	-9	O-682/D-97	-4.2

■ TOM STANTON
Stanton, Thomas Patrick   b: 10/25/1874, St.Louis, Mo.   d: 1/17/57, St.Louis, Mo.   BB/TR, 5'10", 175 lbs.   Deb: 4/19/04

YEAR	TM/L	G	AB	R	H	2B	3B	HR	RBI	BB	SO	AVG	OBP	SLG	PRO+	BR/A	SB	CS	SBR	FA	FR	G/POS	TPR
1904	Chi-N	1	3	0	0	0	0	0	0	0		.000	.000	.000	-99	-1	0			1.000	-0	/C-1	-0.1

■ JOE STAPLES
Staples, Joseph F.   b: Buffalo, N.Y.   Deb: 9/19/1885

YEAR	TM/L	G	AB	R	H	2B	3B	HR	RBI	BB	SO	AVG	OBP	SLG	PRO+	BR/A	SB	CS	SBR	FA	FR	G/POS	TPR
1885	Buf-N	7	22	0	1	0	0	0	0	0	9	.045	.045	.045	-68	-4				.545	-3	/O-6,2-1	-0.7

■ DAVE STAPLETON
Stapleton, David Leslie   b: 1/16/54, Fairhope, Ala.   BR/TR, 6'1", 178 lbs.   Deb: 5/30/80

YEAR	TM/L	G	AB	R	H	2B	3B	HR	RBI	BB	SO	AVG	OBP	SLG	PRO+	BR/A	SB	CS	SBR	FA	FR	G/POS	TPR
1980	Bos-A	106	449	61	144	33	5	7	45	13	32	.321	.341	.463	112	6	3	2	-0	.979	10	2-94/1-8,O-6,3-2,D	2.1
1981	Bos-A	93	355	45	101	17	1	10	42	21	22	.285	.326	.423	108	3	0	4	-2	.948	-7	S-33,3-25,2-23,1/D	-0.4
1982	Bos-A	150	538	66	142	28	1	14	65	31	40	.264	.308	.398	87	-10	2	4	-2	.991	2	*1-106,S-27/23OD	-1.3
1983	Bos-A	151	542	54	134	31	1	10	66	40	44	.247	.301	.363	76	-18	1	1	-0	.993	-2	*1-145/2-5	-2.9
1984	Bos-A	13	39	4	9	2	0	0	1	3	3	.231	.286	.282	53	-2	0	0	0	1.000	0	1-10/D-1	-0.2
1985	Bos-A	30	66	4	15	6	0	0	2	4	11	.227	.271	.318	58	-4	0	0	0	1.000	-0	2-14/1-8,D-5	-0.2
1986	*Bos-A	39	39	4	5	3	0	0	3	2	8	.128	.171	.154	-11	-6	0	0	0	1.000	3	1-29/2-6,3-2	-0.4
Total	7	582	2028	238	550	118	8	41	224	114	162	.271	.312	.398	90	-31	6	11	-5	.993	7	1-318,2-151/S3DO	-3.3

YEAR	TM/L	G	AB	R	H	2B	3B	HR	RBI	BB	SO	AVG	OBP	SLG	PRO+	BR/A	SB	CS	SBR	FA	FR	G/POS	TPR

■ WILLIE STARGELL
Stargell, Wilver Dornel b: 3/6/40, Earlsboro, Okla. BL/TL, 6'2.5", 225 lbs. Deb: 9/16/62 CH

YEAR	TM/L	G	AB	R	H	2B	3B	HR	RBI	BB	SO	AVG	OBP	SLG	PRO+	BR/A	SB	CS	SBR	FA	FR	G/POS	TPR
1962	Pit-N	10	31	1	9	3	1	0	4	3	10	.290	.353	.452	114	1	0	1	-1	.929	-0	/O-9	-0.1
1963	Pit-N	108	304	34	74	11	6	11	47	19	85	.243	.292	.428	104	1	0	2	-1	.953	-8	O-65,1-16	-1.3
1964	Pit-N★	117	421	53	115	19	7	21	78	17	92	.273	.305	.501	123	11	1	1	-0	.900	-7	O-59,1-50	-0.2
1965	Pit-N★	144	533	68	145	25	8	27	107	39	127	.272	.330	.501	130	19	1	1	-0	.965	0	*O-137/1-7	1.3
1966	Pit-N★	140	485	84	153	30	0	33	102	48	109	.315	.381	.581	164	41	2	3	-1	.945	-4	*O-127,1-15	3.0
1967	Pit-N	134	462	54	125	18	6	20	73	67	103	.271	.367	.465	136	23	1	0	0	.938	-2	O-98,1-37	1.5
1968	Pit-N	128	435	57	103	15	1	24	67	47	105	.237	.320	.441	129	14	5	0	2	.945	-3	*O-113,1-13	0.7
1969	Pit-N	145	522	89	160	31	6	29	92	61	120	.307	.381	.556	164	44	1	0	0	.970	-2	*O-116,1-23	3.4
1970	*Pit-N	136	474	70	125	18	3	31	85	44	119	.264	.333	.511	125	14	0	1	-1	.976	7	*O-125/1-1	1.5
1971	*Pit-N★	141	511	104	151	26	0	**48**	125	83	154	.295	.401	.628	188	**59**	0	0	0	.984	3	*O-138	**5.8**
1972	*Pit-N	138	495	75	145	28	2	33	112	65	129	.293	.377	.558	166	42	1	1	-0	.984	-13	*1-101,O-32	2.0
1973	*Pit-N★	148	522	106	156	**43**	3	**44**	**119**	80	129	.299	.395	**.646**	189	61	0	0	0	.975	-7	*O-142	**6.3**
1974	*Pit-N	140	508	90	153	37	4	25	96	87	106	.301	.409	.537	169	49	0	2	-1	.967	0	*O-135/1-1	4.5
1975	*Pit-N	124	461	71	136	32	2	22	90	58	109	.295	.377	.516	147	29	0	0	0	.992	-10	*1-122	1.1
1976	Pit-N	117	428	54	110	20	3	20	65	50	101	.257	.342	.458	124	13	2	0	1	.988	-10	*1-111	-0.5
1977	Pit-N	63	186	29	51	12	0	13	35	31	55	.274	.386	.548	144	12	0	1	-1	.986	-1	1-55	0.7
1978	Pit-N★	122	390	60	115	18	2	28	97	50	93	.295	.385	.567	156	29	3	2	-0	.994	-2	*1-112	2.2
1979	*Pit-N	126	424	60	119	19	0	32	82	47	105	.281	.357	.552	138	21	0	1	-1	**.997**	-6	*1-113	0.8
1980	Pit-N	67	202	28	53	10	1	11	38	26	52	.262	.352	.485	129	8	0	0	0	.992	0	1-54	0.5
1981	Pit-N	38	60	2	17	4	0	0	9	5	9	.283	.338	.350	93	-1	0	0	0	1.000	-2	/1-9	-0.4
1982	Pit-N	74	73	6	17	4	0	3	17	10	24	.233	.325	.411	102	0	0	0	0	1.000	0	/1-8	0.0
Total	21	2360	7927	1195	2232	423	55	475	1540	937	1936	.282	.363	.529	147	488	17	16	-5	.961	-51	*O-1296,1-848	32.8

■ MATT STARK
Stark, Matthew Scott b: 1/21/65, Whittier, Cal. BR/TR, 6'4", 225 lbs. Deb: 4/8/87

YEAR	TM/L	G	AB	R	H	2B	3B	HR	RBI	BB	SO	AVG	OBP	SLG	PRO+	BR/A	SB	CS	SBR	FA	FR	G/POS	TPR
1987	Tor-A	5	12	0	1	0	0	0	0	0	0	.083	.083	.083	-55	-3	0	0	0	1.000	1	/C-5	-0.2
1990	Chi-A	8	16	0	4	1	0	0	3	1	6	.250	.294	.313	71	-1	0	0	0	.000	0	/D-6	-0.1
Total	2	13	28	0	5	1	0	0	3	1	6	.179	.207	.214	15	-3	0	0	0	1.000	1	/D-6,C-5	-0.3

■ DOLLY STARK
Stark, Monroe Randolph b: 1/19/1885, Ripley, Miss. d: 12/1/24, Memphis, Tenn. BR/TR, 5'9", 160 lbs. Deb: 9/12/09

YEAR	TM/L	G	AB	R	H	2B	3B	HR	RBI	BB	SO	AVG	OBP	SLG	PRO+	BR/A	SB	CS	SBR	FA	FR	G/POS	TPR
1909	Cle-A	19	60	4	12	0	0	0	1	6		.200	.273	.200	48	-3	4			.875	-10	S-19	-1.5
1910	Bro-N	30	103	7	17	3	0	0	8	7	19	.165	.225	.194	23	-10	2			.893	-1	S-30	-1.1
1911	Bro-N	70	193	25	57	4	1	0	19	20	24	.295	.370	.326	100	1	6			.910	-3	S-34,2-18/3-3	-0.1
1912	Bro-N	8	22	2	4	0	0	0	2	1	3	.182	.217	.182	10	-3	2			.892	0	/S-7	-0.2
Total	4	127	378	38	90	7	1	0	30	34	46	.238	.308	.262	66	-15	14			.896	-14	/S-90,2-18,3-3	-2.9

■ GEORGE STARNAGLE
Starnagle, George Henry (b: George Henry Steuernagel)
b: 10/6/1873, Belleville, Ill. d: 2/15/46, Belleville, Ill. BR/TR, 5'11", 175 lbs. Deb: 9/14/02

YEAR	TM/L	G	AB	R	H	2B	3B	HR	RBI	BB	SO	AVG	OBP	SLG	PRO+	BR/A	SB	CS	SBR	FA	FR	G/POS	TPR
1902	Cle-A	1	3	0	0	0	0	0	0	0		.000	.000	.000	-99	-1	0			.667	-1	/C-1	-0.1

■ CHARLIE STARR
Starr, Charles Watkin b: 8/30/1878, Pike Co., Ohio d: 10/18/37, Pasadena, Cal. TR, 5'10.5", 165 lbs. Deb: 4/29/05

YEAR	TM/L	G	AB	R	H	2B	3B	HR	RBI	BB	SO	AVG	OBP	SLG	PRO+	BR/A	SB	CS	SBR	FA	FR	G/POS	TPR
1905	StL-A	26	97	9	20	0	0	0	6	7		.206	.260	.206	51	-5	0			.938	-4	2-18/3-6	-1.0
1908	Pit-N	20	59	8	11	2	0	0	8	13		.186	.342	.220	80	-0	6			.926	-5	2-12/S-5,3-2	-0.7
1909	Bos-N	61	216	16	48	2	3	0	6	31		.222	.333	.259	80	-4	7			.931	-9	2-54/S-6,3-3	-1.5
	Phi-N	3	3	0	0	0	0	0	0	0		.000	.000	.000	-99	-1	0			.000	0	H	-0.1
	Yr	64	219	16	48	2	3	0	6	31		.219	.329	.256	78	-4	7			.931	-9	2-54/S-6,3-3	-1.6
Total	3	110	375	33	79	4	3	0	20	51		.211	.315	.237	72	-10	13			.931	-18	/2-84,S-11,3-11	-3.3

■ CHICK STARR
Starr, William b: 2/26/11, Brooklyn, N.Y. d: 8/12/91, LaJolla, Cal. BR/TR, 6'1", 175 lbs. Deb: 8/23/35

YEAR	TM/L	G	AB	R	H	2B	3B	HR	RBI	BB	SO	AVG	OBP	SLG	PRO+	BR/A	SB	CS	SBR	FA	FR	G/POS	TPR
1935	Was-A	12	24	1	5	0	0	0	1	0	1	.208	.208	.208	8	-3	0	0	0	.971	2	C-12	-0.1
1936	Was-A	1	0	0	0	0	0	0	0	0	0	—	—	—	—	0	0	0	0	.000	0	/C-1	0.0
Total	2	13	24	1	5	0	0	0	1	0	1	.208	.208	.208	8	-3	0	0	0	.971	2	/C-13	-0.1

■ JOE START
Start, Joseph "Old Reliable" or "Rocks" b: 10/14/1842, New York, N.Y. d: 3/27/27, Providence, R.I. BL/TL, 5'9", 165 lbs. Deb: 5/18/1871 M

YEAR	TM/L	G	AB	R	H	2B	3B	HR	RBI	BB	SO	AVG	OBP	SLG	PRO+	BR/A	SB	CS	SBR	FA	FR	G/POS	TPR
1871	Mut-n	33	161	35	58	5	1	1	34	3	0	.360	.372	.422	140	10	4	2	0	.921	-2	*1-33	0.6
1872	Mut-n	55	282	62	76	4	0	0	50	0	0	.270	.270	.284	75	-6	3	3	-1	**.955**	2	*1-55	-0.2
1873	Mut-n	53	251	42	67	8	3	1	28	4	0	.267	.278	.335	82	-5	1	0	0	.943	5	*1-53/O-2,M	0.2
1874	Mut-n	63	306	67	96	13	3	2	45	4	0	.314	.323	.395	125	7	5	0	2	**.961**	4	*1-63/O-2	1.0
1875	Mut-n	69	314	58	90	10	5	4	30	3	0	.287	.293	.389	128	7	1	4	-2	.948	2	*1-69	0.6
1876	NY-N	56	264	40	73	6	0	0	21	1	2	.277	.279	.299	107	3				**.964**	3	*1-56	0.4
1877	Har-N	60	271	55	90	3	6	1	21	6	2	.332	.347	.399	150	16				**.964**	-2	*1-60	1.2
1878	Chi-N	61	285	58	**100**	12	5	1	27	2	3	.351	.355	.439	150	14				.957	-7	*1-61	0.9
1879	Pro-N	66	317	70	101	11	5	2	37	7	4	.319	.333	.404	144	15				**.973**	0	*1-65/O-1	1.2
1880	Pro-N	82	345	53	96	14	6	0	27	13	20	.278	.304	.354	126	10				.971	-3	*1-82	-0.1
1881	Pro-N	79	348	56	114	12	6	0	29	9	7	.328	.349	.397	135	13				.963	-4	*1-79	0.2
1882	Pro-N	82	356	58	117	8	10	0	48	11	7	.329	.349	.407	142	16				.974	2	*1-82	0.8
1883	Pro-N	87	370	63	105	16	7	1	57	22	16	.284	.324	.373	108	4				.957	-1	*1-87	-0.5
1884	*Pro-N	93	381	80	105	10	5	2	32	35	25	.276	.337	.344	117	9				**.980**	1	*1-93	-0.1
1885	Pro-N	101	374	47	103	11	4	0	41	39	10	.275	.344	.326	122	11				.972	1	*1-101	0.0
1886	Was-N	31	122	10	27	4	1	0	17	5	13	.221	.252	.270	63	-5	4			.973	-2	1-31	-1.0
Total	5 n	273	1314	264	387	40	12	8	187	14	0	.295	.302	.361	108	13	14	9	-1	.948	11	1-273/O-4	2.2
Total	11	798	3433	590	1031	107	55	7	357	150	109	.300	.330	.370	127	104	4			.968	-7	1-797/O-1	3.0

■ DAVE STATON
Staton, David Alan b: 4/12/68, Seattle, Wash. BR/TR, 6'5", 215 lbs. Deb: 9/8/93

YEAR	TM/L	G	AB	R	H	2B	3B	HR	RBI	BB	SO	AVG	OBP	SLG	PRO+	BR/A	SB	CS	SBR	FA	FR	G/POS	TPR
1993	SD-N	17	42	7	11	3	0	5	9	3	12	.262	.326	.690	161	3	0	0	0	1.000	3	1-12	0.5
1994	SD-N	29	66	6	12	2	0	4	6	10	18	.182	.289	.394	78	-2	0	0	0	1.000	4	1-20	0.0
Total	2	46	108	13	23	5	0	9	15	13	30	.213	.303	.509	110	1	0	0	0	1.000	7	/1-32	0.5

■ JOE STATON
Staton, Joseph b: 3/8/48, Seattle, Wash. BL/TL, 6'3", 175 lbs. Deb: 9/5/72

YEAR	TM/L	G	AB	R	H	2B	3B	HR	RBI	BB	SO	AVG	OBP	SLG	PRO+	BR/A	SB	CS	SBR	FA	FR	G/POS	TPR
1972	Det-A	6	2	1	0	0	0	0	0	0	1	.000	.000	.000	-97	-0	0	1	-1	1.000	0	/1-2	-0.1
1973	Det-A	9	17	2	4	0	0	0	3	0	3	.235	.235	.235	31	-2	1	0	0	.969	2	/1-5	0.0
Total	2	15	19	3	4	0	0	0	3	0	4	.211	.211	.211	18	-2	1	1	-0	.973	2	/1-7	-0.1

■ JIGGER STATZ
Statz, Arnold John b: 10/20/1897, Waukegan, Ill. d: 3/16/88, Corona Del Mar, Cal. BR/TR, 5'7.5", 150 lbs. Deb: 7/30/19

YEAR	TM/L	G	AB	R	H	2B	3B	HR	RBI	BB	SO	AVG	OBP	SLG	PRO+	BR/A	SB	CS	SBR	FA	FR	G/POS	TPR
1919	NY-N	21	60	7	18	2	1	0	6	3	8	.300	.333	.367	112	1	2			.977	1	O-18/2-5	-0.1
1920	NY-N	16	30	0	4	0	1	0	5	2	9	.133	.188	.200	11	-3	0	1	-1	.944	-3	O-12	-0.8
	Bos-A	2	3	0	0	0	0	0	0	0	0	.000	.000	.000	-99	-1	0	0	0	1.000	-1	/O-2	-0.2
1922	Chi-N	110	462	77	137	19	5	1	34	41	31	.297	.355	.366	85	-10	16	13	-3	.959	9	*O-110	-1.1
1923	Chi-N	154	655	110	209	33	8	10	70	56	42	.319	.375	.440	114	14	29	23	-5	.975	18	O-154	1.5
1924	Chi-N	135	549	69	152	22	5	3	49	37	50	.277	.325	.352	80	-15	13	9	-2	.961	15	*O-131/2-1	-1.1
1925	Chi-N	38	148	21	38	6	3	2	14	11	16	.257	.317	.378	76	-6	4	0	1	.943	2	O-37	-0.5
1927	Bro-N	130	507	64	139	24	7	1	21	26	43	.274	.310	.355	77	-17	10			.990	15	*O-122/2-1	-0.9
1928	Bro-N	77	171	28	40	8	1	0	16	18	12	.234	.311	.292	59	-10	3			.965	-6	O-52/2-1	-1.8
Total	8	683	2585	376	737	114	31	17	215	194	211	.285	.337	.334	88	-47	77	46		.969	48	O-638/2-8	-5.0

■ RUSTY STAUB
Staub, Daniel Joseph b: 4/1/44, New Orleans, La. BL/TR, 6'2", 200 lbs. Deb: 4/9/63 C

YEAR	TM/L	G	AB	R	H	2B	3B	HR	RBI	BB	SO	AVG	OBP	SLG	PRO+	BR/A	SB	CS	SBR	FA	FR	G/POS	TPR
1963	Hou-N	150	513	43	115	17	4	6	45	59	58	.224	.310	.308	84	-10	0	0	0	.989	-1	*1-109,O-49	-1.9
1964	Hou-N	89	292	26	63	10	2	8	35	21	31	.216	.275	.346	78	-9	1	1	-0	.992	-1	1-49,O-38	-1.5
1965	Hou-N	131	410	43	105	20	1	14	63	52	57	.256	.337	.412	120	11	3	0	1	.951	4	O-112/1-1	1.1
1966	Hou-N	153	554	60	155	28	3	13	81	58	61	.280	.349	.412	119	14	2	1	0	.962	9	*O-148/1-1	1.7
1967	Hou-N★	149	546	71	182	**44**	1	10	74	60	47	.333	.402	.473	155	40	0	4	-2	.962	7	*O-144	3.9

YEAR	TM/L	G	AB	R	H	2B	3B	HR	RBI	BB	SO	AVG	OBP	SLG	PRO+	BR/A	SB	CS	SBR	FA	FR	G/POS	TPR
1968	Hou-N★	161	591	54	172	37	1	6	72	73	57	.291	.376	.387	132	26	2	0	1	.992	-1	*1-147,O-15	1.5
1969	Mon-N☆	158	549	89	166	26	5	29	79	110	61	.302	.427	.526	165	52	3	4	-2	.966	7	*O-156	5.0
1970	Mon-N★	160	569	98	156	23	7	30	94	112	93	.274	.396	.497	138	33	12	11	-3	.985	11	*O-160	3.3
1971	Mon-N☆	162	599	94	186	34	6	19	97	74	42	.311	.394	.482	147	38	9	5	-0	.945	5	*O-162	3.6
1972	NY-N	66	239	32	70	11	0	9	38	31	13	.293	.379	.452	139	13	0	1	-1	.982	0	O-65	1.0
1973	*NY-N	152	585	77	163	36	1	15	76	74	52	.279	.363	.421	118	15	1	1	-0	.978	11	*O-152	1.9
1974	NY-N	151	561	65	145	22	2	19	78	77	39	.258	.351	.406	113	10	2	1	0	.983	9	*O-147	1.3
1975	NY-N	155	574	93	162	30	4	19	105	77	55	.282	.376	.448	134	27	2	0	1	.986	8	*O-153	3.0
1976	Det-A★	161	589	73	176	28	3	15	96	83	49	.299	.392	.433	136	29	3	1	0	.970	-6	*O-126,D-36	1.8
1977	Det-A	158	623	84	173	34	3	22	101	59	47	.278	.341	.448	107	6	1	1	-0	.000	0	*D-156	0.1
1978	Det-A	162	642	75	175	30	1	24	121	76	35	.273	.352	.435	117	15	3	1	0	.000	0	*D-162	1.0
1979	Det-A	68	246	32	58	12	1	9	40	32	18	.236	.336	.402	95	-2	1	0	0	.000	0	D-66	-0.3
	Mon-N	38	86	9	23	3	0	3	14	14	10	.267	.370	.407	113	2	0	0	0	.994	-2	1-22/O-1	-0.2
1980	Tex-A	109	340	42	102	23	2	9	55	39	18	.300	.375	.459	131	15	1	1	-0	.977	-2	D-57,1-30,O-14	0.8
1981	NY-N	70	161	9	51	9	0	5	21	22	12	.317	.402	.466	148	11	1	0	0	.989	-2	1-41	0.7
1982	NY-N	112	219	11	53	9	0	3	27	24	10	.242	.317	.324	80	-5	0	0	0	.959	2	O-27,1-18	-0.5
1983	NY-N	104	115	5	34	6	0	3	28	14	10	.296	.377	.426	123	4	0	0	0	.976	-1	/1-5,O-5	0.3
1984	NY-N	78	72	2	19	4	0	1	18	4	9	.264	.303	.361	87	-1	0	0	0	1.000	-0	/1-3	-0.2
1985	NY-N	54	45	2	12	3	0	1	4	4	5	.267	.400	.400	128	2	0	0	0	1.000	-0	/O-1	0.2
Total	23	2951	9720	1189	2716	499	47	292	1466	1255	888	.279	.366	.431	125	334	47	33	-6	.969	55	*O-1675,D-477,1-426	27.6

■ ECKY STEARNS

Stearns, Daniel Eckford b: 10/17/1861, Buffalo, N.Y. d: 6/28/44, Glendale, Cal. BL/TR, 6'1", 185 lbs. Deb: 8/17/1880

YEAR	TM/L	G	AB	R	H	2B	3B	HR	RBI	BB	SO	AVG	OBP	SLG	PRO+	BR/A	SB	CS	SBR	FA	FR	G/POS	TPR
1880	Buf-N	28	104	8	19	6	1	0	13	3	23	.183	.206	.260	55	-5				.774	-9	O-20/C-8,3-5,S-1	-1.4
1881	Det-N	3	11	1	1	1	0	0	0	0	2	.091	.091	.182	-16	-1				.714	-1	/S-3	-0.2
1882	Cin-a	49	214	28	55	10	2	0	35	6		.257	.277	.322	96	-1				.931	-2	1-35,O-12/2-2,S-1	-0.5
1883	Bal-a	93	382	54	94	10	9	1		**34**		.246	.308	.327	101	1				.947	3	*1-92/O-1	-0.5
1884	Bal-a	100	396	61	94	12	3	3		28		.237	.298	.306	94	-3				.949	-1	*1-100/2-1	-1.0
1885	Bal-a	67	253	40	47	3	8	1	29	38		.186	.306	.273	85	-2				.973	1	1-63/O-3,C-2	-0.8
	Buf-N	30	105	7	21	6	1	0	9	8	23	.200	.257	.276	70	-3				.821	-7	S-19,1-12/C-2	-1.1
1889	KC-a	139	560	96	160	24	12	3	87	56	69	.286	.351	.387	104	1	67			.967	-0	*1-135/3-4	-0.7
Total	7	509	2025	295	491	72	36	8	173	173	117	.242	.303	.325	94	-14	67			.956	-10	1-437/O-36,SC32	-6.4

■ JOHN STEARNS

Stearns, John Hardin b: 8/21/51, Denver, Col. BR/TR, 6', 185 lbs. Deb: 9/22/74 C

YEAR	TM/L	G	AB	R	H	2B	3B	HR	RBI	BB	SO	AVG	OBP	SLG	PRO+	BR/A	SB	CS	SBR	FA	FR	G/POS	TPR
1974	Phi-N	1	2	0	1	0	0	0	0	1	0	.500	.500	.500	173	0	0	0	0	1.000	-1	/C-1	0.0
1975	NY-N	59	169	25	32	5	1	3	10	17	15	.189	.271	.284	57	-10	4	1	1	.994	6	C-54	-0.1
1976	NY-N	32	103	13	27	6	0	2	10	16	11	.262	.367	.379	119	3	1	2	-1	.987	3	C-30	0.7
1977	NY-N★	139	431	52	108	25	1	12	55	77	76	.251	.373	.397	112	10	9	8	-2	.982	4	*C-127/1-6	1.5
1978	NY-N	143	477	65	126	24	1	15	73	70	57	.264	.368	.413	122	16	25	13	-0	.985	-3	*C-141/3-1	1.7
1979	NY-N☆	155	538	58	131	29	2	9	66	52	57	.243	.315	.355	86	-11	15	15	-5	.983	5	*C-121,1-16,3-11/O	-0.8
1980	NY-N★	91	319	42	91	25	1	0	45	33	24	.285	.354	.370	105	3	7	3	0	.985	5	C-74,1-16/3-1	0.4
1981	NY-N	80	273	25	74	12	1	1	24	24	17	.271	.330	.333	90	-3	12	2	2	.983	-2	C-66/1-9,3-4	-0.2
1982	NY-N★	98	352	46	103	25	3	4	28	30	35	.293	.352	.415	114	7	17	7	1	.987	-7	C-81,3-12	0.4
1983	NY-N	4	0	0	0	0	0	0	0	0	0	—	—	—		0	0	0		.000	0	/R	0.0
1984	NY-N	8	17	6	3	1	0	0	1	4	2	.176	.333	.235	63	-1	1	0	0	1.000	-1	/C-4,1-2	-0.1
Total	11	810	2681	334	696	152	10	46	312	323	294	.260	.345	.375	102	13	91	51	-3	.985	10	C-699/1-49,3-29,O-6	4.1

■ JOHN STEDRONSKY

Stedronsky, John b: Troy, N.Y. Deb: 9/25/1879

YEAR	TM/L	G	AB	R	H	2B	3B	HR	RBI	BB	SO	AVG	OBP	SLG	PRO+	BR/A	SB	CS	SBR	FA	FR	G/POS	TPR
1879	Chi-N	4	12	0	1	0	0	0		0	3	.083	.083	.083	-42	-2				.789	1	/3-4	0.0

■ FARMER STEELMAN

Steelman, Morris James b: 6/29/1875, Millville, N.J. d: 9/16/44, Merchantville, N.J. TR, Deb: 9/15/1899

YEAR	TM/L	G	AB	R	H	2B	3B	HR	RBI	BB	SO	AVG	OBP	SLG	PRO+	BR/A	SB	CS	SBR	FA	FR	G/POS	TPR
1899	Lou-N	4	15	2	1	0	1	0	2		2	.067	.176	.200	3	-2	0			.929	-2	/C-4	-0.3
1900	Bro-N	1	4	0	0	0	0	0	0		0	.000	.000	.000	-94	-1	0			1.000	0	/C-1	-0.1
1901	Bro-N	1	3	0	1	0	0	0	0		0	.333	.333	.333	91	-0	0			.875	1	/C-1	0.1
	Phi-A	27	88	5	23	2	0	0	7		10	.261	.350	.284	74	-3	4			1.000	2	C-14,O-12	0.0
1902	Phi-A	10	32	1	6	1	0	0	6		2	.188	.235	.219	25	-3	2			1.000	1	/C-5,O-5	-0.2
Total	4	43	142	8	31	3	1	0	15		14	.218	.297	.254	52	-9	6			.985	1	/C-25,O-17	-0.5

■ JIM STEELS

Steels, James Earl b: 5/30/61, Jackson, Miss. BL/TL, 5'10", 185 lbs. Deb: 4/6/87

YEAR	TM/L	G	AB	R	H	2B	3B	HR	RBI	BB	SO	AVG	OBP	SLG	PRO+	BR/A	SB	CS	SBR	FA	FR	G/POS	TPR
1987	SD-N	62	68	9	13	1	0	0	6	11	14	.191	.304	.235	47	-5	3	2	-0	.960	-6	O-28	-1.2
1988	Tex-A	36	53	4	10	1	0	0	5	0	15	.189	.189	.208	11	-6	2	0	1	1.000	-5	O-17/1-7,D-7	-1.1
1989	SF-N	13	12	0	1	0	0	0	0	2	4	.083	.214	.083	-12	-2	0	0	0	1.000	0	/1-3,O-1	-0.2
Total	3	111	133	13	24	2	1	0	11	13	33	.180	.253	.211	28	-13	5	2	0	.973	-11	O-46,1-10,D-7	-2.5

■ GENE STEERE

Steere, Frederick Eugene b: 8/16/1872, S.Scituate, R.I. d: 3/13/42, San Francisco, Cal Deb: 8/29/1894

YEAR	TM/L	G	AB	R	H	2B	3B	HR	RBI	BB	SO	AVG	OBP	SLG	PRO+	BR/A	SB	CS	SBR	FA	FR	G/POS	TPR
1894	Pit-N	10	39	3	8	0	0	0	3	2		.205	.244	.205	9	-6	2			.896	-2	S-10	-0.6

■ JOHN STEFERO

Stefero, John Robert b: 9/22/59, Sumter, S.C. BL/TR, 5'8", 185 lbs. Deb: 6/24/83

YEAR	TM/L	G	AB	R	H	2B	3B	HR	RBI	BB	SO	AVG	OBP	SLG	PRO+	BR/A	SB	CS	SBR	FA	FR	G/POS	TPR
1983	Bal-A	9	11	2	5	1	0	0	4	3	2	.455	.571	.545	213	2	0	0	0	.920	0	/C-9	0.2
1986	Bal-A	52	120	14	28	3	0	2	13	16	25	.233	.324	.300	72	-4	0	1	-1	.984	-2	C-50/2-1	-0.4
1987	Mon-N	18	56	4	11	0	0	1	3	3	17	.196	.237	.250	28	-6	0	0	0	.981	-0	C-17	-0.5
Total	3	79	187	20	44	3	0	3	20	22	44	.235	.316	.299	67	-8	0	1	-1	.979	-2	/C-76,2-1	-0.7

■ DAVE STEGMAN

Stegman, David William b: 1/30/54, Inglewood, Cal. BR/TR, 5'11", 190 lbs. Deb: 9/4/78

YEAR	TM/L	G	AB	R	H	2B	3B	HR	RBI	BB	SO	AVG	OBP	SLG	PRO+	BR/A	SB	CS	SBR	FA	FR	G/POS	TPR
1978	Det-A	8	14	3	4	2	0	1	3	1	2	.286	.333	.643	164	1	0	0	0	1.000	-2	/O-7	-0.1
1979	Det-A	12	31	6	6	0	0	3	5	2	3	.194	.242	.484	88	-1	1	1	-0	1.000	1	/O-12	0.0
1980	Det-A	65	130	12	23	5	0	2	9	14	23	.177	.257	.262	41	-10	1	1	-0	.988	-13	O-57/D-2	-2.6
1982	NY-A	2	0	0	0	0	0	0	0	0	0	—	—	—		0	0	0	0	.000	0	/D-1	0.0
1983	Chi-A	30	53	5	9	2	0	0	4	10	9	.170	.302	.208	42	-4	0	1	-1	1.000	-7	O-29	-1.2
1984	Chi-A	55	92	13	24	1	2	2	11	4	18	.261	.306	.380	85	-2	3	0	1	.985	-9	O-46/D-3	-1.1
Total	6	172	320	39	66	10	2	8	32	31	55	.206	.280	.325	64	-16	5	3	-0	.991	-31	O-151/D-6	-5.1

■ JUSTIN STEIN

Stein, Justin Marion "Ott" b: 8/9/11, St.Louis, Mo. d: 5/1/92, Creve Coeur, Mo. BR/TR, 5'11", 180 lbs. Deb: 5/28/38

YEAR	TM/L	G	AB	R	H	2B	3B	HR	RBI	BB	SO	AVG	OBP	SLG	PRO+	BR/A	SB	CS	SBR	FA	FR	G/POS	TPR
1938	Phi-N	11	39	6	10	0	1	0	2	2	4	.256	.293	.308	67	-2	0			.880	0	/3-7,2-3	-0.2
	Cin-N	11	18	3	6	1	0	0	1	0		.333	.333	.389	101	-0	0			.857	1	/S-7,2-2	0.1
Yr	22	57	9	16	1	1	0	3	2	5	.281	.305	.333	78	-2	0			.857	1	/3-7,S-7,2-5	-0.1

■ BILL STEIN

Stein, William Allen b: 1/21/47, Battle Creek, Mich. BR/TR, 5'10", 170 lbs. Deb: 9/6/72

YEAR	TM/L	G	AB	R	H	2B	3B	HR	RBI	BB	SO	AVG	OBP	SLG	PRO+	BR/A	SB	CS	SBR	FA	FR	G/POS	TPR
1972	StL-N	14	35	2	11	1	0	0	3	0	7	.314	.314	.543	141	2	1	0	0	1.000	-3	/3-4,O-4	-0.2
1973	StL-N	32	55	4	12	2	0	0	2	7	18	.218	.306	.255	57	-3	0	0	0	1.000	-2	O-10/1-2,3-1	-0.5
1974	Chi-A	13	43	5	12	1	0	0	5	7	8	.279	.380	.302	96	0	0	0	0	.871	-3	3-11/D-2	-0.2
1975	Chi-A	76	226	23	61	7	1	3	21	18	32	.270	.327	.350	90	-3	2	2	-1	.974	3	2-28,3-24,D-18/O-1	0.1
1976	Chi-A	117	392	32	105	15	2	4	36	22	67	.268	.310	.347	92	-5	4	3	-0	.960	-11	2-58,3-58/1-1,SOD	-1.3
1977	Sea-A	151	556	53	144	26	5	13	67	29	79	.259	.302	.394	89	-10	3	4	-2	.964	-11	*3-147/S-2,D-3	-2.4
1978	Sea-A	114	403	41	105	24	4	4	37	37	56	.261	.323	.370	95	-3	1	0	0	.929	-6	*3-111/D-1	-1.0
1979	Sea-A	88	250	28	62	9	2	2	17	19	28	.248	.301	.384	82	-7	1	2	-0	.959	11	3-67,2-17/S-3	0.3
1980	Sea-A	67	198	16	53	7	1	5	27	16	25	.268	.326	.379	92	-2	1	1	-0	.972	5	3-34,2-14/1-8,D-5	0.3
1981	Tex-A	53	115	21	38	6	0	2	22	7	15	.330	.369	.435	138	5	1	2	-1	1.000	1	1-20/O-8,3-7,2-3,S	0.4
1982	Tex-A	85	184	14	44	8	0	1	16	12	23	.239	.293	.299	66	-8	0	0	0	.952	2	3-34,3-28/S-6,10D	-0.5
1983	Tex-A	78	232	21	72	15	1	2	33	8	31	.310	.333	.409	105	1	2	3	-1	.975	-2	2-32,1-23,3-10/D-6	-0.3
1984	Tex-A	27	43	3	12	1	0	0	3	5	9	.279	.354	.302	81	-1	0	0	0	.967	-3	2-11/1-3,3-4	-0.3
1985	Tex-A	44	79	5	20	3	1	1	12	1	15	.253	.272	.354	69	-3	0	0	0	.952	5	3-11/1-8,2-3,0-3,D	-0.3
Total	14	959	2811	268	751	122	18	44	311	186	413	.267	.316	.370	91	-37	16	16	-5	.950	-13	3-516,2-200/1DOS	-5.6

YEAR	TM/L	G	AB	R	H	2B	3B	HR	RBI	BB	SO	AVG	OBP	SLG	PRO+	BR/A	SB	CS	SBR	FA	FR	G/POS	TPR

■ TERRY STEINBACH
Steinbach, Terry Lee b: 3/2/62, New Ulm, Minn. BR/TR, 6'1", 195 lbs. Deb: 9/12/86

YEAR	TM/L	G	AB	R	H	2B	3B	HR	RBI	BB	SO	AVG	OBP	SLG	PRO+	BR/A	SB	CS	SBR	FA	FR	G/POS	TPR
1986	Oak-A	6	15	3	5	0	0	2	4	1	0	.333	.375	.733	208	2	0	0	0	.962	-0	/C-5	0.2
1987	Oak-A	122	391	66	111	16	3	16	56	32	66	.284	.352	.463	122	12	1	2	-1	.986	-12	*C-107,3-10/1-1,D-8	0.6
1988	*Oak-A★	104	351	42	93	19	1	9	51	33	47	.265	.338	.402	110	5	3	0	1	.983	5	C-84/3-9,1-8,O-1,D	1.6
1989	*Oak-A★	130	454	37	124	13	1	7	42	30	66	.273	.321	.352	93	-5	1	2	-1	.985	-7	*C-103,O-14,1/3D	-0.7
1990	Oak-A	114	379	32	95	15	2	9	57	19	66	.251	.294	.372	89	-7	0	1	-1	.988	-4	C-83,D-25/1-3	-0.7
1991	Oak-A	129	456	50	125	31	1	6	67	22	70	.274	.318	.386	99	-2	2	2	-1	.980	-24	*C-117/1-9,D-2	-2.0
1992	*Oak-A	128	438	48	122	20	1	12	53	45	58	.279	.347	.411	118	10	2	3	-1	.985	-4	*C-124/1-5,D-2	1.2
1993	Oak-A★	104	389	47	111	19	1	10	43	25	65	.285	.333	.416	107	3	3	3	-1	.989	-22	C-86,1-15/D-6	-1.6
1994	Oak-A	103	369	51	105	21	2	11	57	26	62	.285	.332	.442	106	2	2	1	-0	**.998**	-2	C-93/1-6,D-6	0.5
1995	Oak-A	114	406	43	113	26	1	15	65	25	74	.278	.325	.458	107	2	1	3	-2	.993	-2	*C-111/1-2	0.6
1996	Oak-A	145	514	79	140	25	1	35	100	49	115	.272	.343	.529	121	14	0	1	-1	.991	-10	*C-137/1-1,D-4	1.1
Total	11	1199	4162	498	1144	205	14	132	595	307	689	.275	.331	.426	108	37	15	18	-6	.988	-83	*C-1050/D-64,13O	0.8

■ HANK STEINBACHER
Steinbacher, Henry John b: 3/22/13, Sacramento, Cal. d: 4/3/77, Sacramento, Cal. BL/TR, 5'11", 180 lbs. Deb: 4/21/37

YEAR	TM/L	G	AB	R	H	2B	3B	HR	RBI	BB	SO	AVG	OBP	SLG	PRO+	BR/A	SB	CS	SBR	FA	FR	G/POS	TPR
1937	Chi-A	26	73	13	19	4	1	1	9	4	7	.260	.299	.384	71	-4	2	0	1	.960	-2	O-15	-0.5
1938	Chi-A	106	399	59	132	23	8	4	61	41	19	.331	.393	.459	110	7	1	3	-2	.963	-4	O-101	-0.2
1939	Chi-A	71	111	16	19	2	1	1	15	21	8	.171	.303	.234	38	-10	0	0	0	1.000	-2	O-22	-1.2
Total	3	203	583	88	170	29	10	6	85	66	34	.292	.364	.407	92	-7	3	3	-1	.968	-8	O-138	-1.9

■ GENE STEINBRENNER
Steinbrenner, Eugene Gass b: 11/17/1892, Pittsburgh, Pa. d: 4/25/70, Pittsburgh, Pa. BR/TR, 5'8.5", 155 lbs. Deb: 4/25/12

YEAR	TM/L	G	AB	R	H	2B	3B	HR	RBI	BB	SO	AVG	OBP	SLG	PRO+	BR/A	SB	CS	SBR	FA	FR	G/POS	TPR
1912	Phi-N	3	9	0	2	1	0	0	1	0	3	.222	.222	.333	48	-1	0			.900	-1	/2-3	-0.1

■ BILL STEINECKE
Steinecke, William Robert b: 2/7/07, Cincinnati, Ohio d: 7/20/86, St.Augustine, Fla BR/TR, 5'8.5", 175 lbs. Deb: 9/16/31

YEAR	TM/L	G	AB	R	H	2B	3B	HR	RBI	BB	SO	AVG	OBP	SLG	PRO+	BR/A	SB	CS	SBR	FA	FR	G/POS	TPR
1931	Pit-N	4	4	0	0	0	0	0	0	0	0	.000	.000	.000	-99	-1	0	0	0	.000	0	/C-1	-0.1

■ BEN STEINER
Steiner, Benjamin Saunders b: 7/28/21, Alexandria, Va. d: 10/27/88, Venice, Fla. BL/TR, 5'11", 165 lbs. Deb: 4/17/45

YEAR	TM/L	G	AB	R	H	2B	3B	HR	RBI	BB	SO	AVG	OBP	SLG	PRO+	BR/A	SB	CS	SBR	FA	FR	G/POS	TPR
1945	Bos-A	78	304	39	78	8	3	3	20	31	29	.257	.327	.332	89	-4	10	6	-1	.967	-4	2-77	-0.4
1946	Bos-A	3	4	1	1	0	0	0	0	0	0	.250	.250	.250	38	-0	0	0	0	.750	0	/3-1	0.0
1947	Det-A	1	0	1	0	0	0	0	0	0	0	—	—	—	—	0	0	0	0	.000	0	R	0.0
Total	3	82	308	41	79	8	3	3	20	31	29	.256	.326	.331	89	-4	10	6	-1	.967	-4	/2-77,3-1	-0.4

■ RED STEINER
Steiner, James Harry b: 1/7/15, Los Angeles, Cal. BL/TR, 6', 185 lbs. Deb: 5/11/45

YEAR	TM/L	G	AB	R	H	2B	3B	HR	RBI	BB	SO	AVG	OBP	SLG	PRO+	BR/A	SB	CS	SBR	FA	FR	G/POS	TPR
1945	Cle-A	12	20	0	3	0	0	0	0	1	4	.150	.190	.150	-1	-3	0	0	0	1.000	1	/C-4	-0.2
	Bos-A	26	59	6	12	1	0	0	4	14	2	.203	.356	.220	67	-2	0	0	0	.986	-5	C-24	-0.6
	Yr	38	79	6	15	1	0	0	4	15	6	.190	.319	.203	52	-4	0	0	0	.989	-4	C-28	-0.8

■ HARRY STEINFELDT
Steinfeldt, Harry M. b: 9/29/1877, St.Louis, Mo. d: 8/17/14, Bellevue, Ky. BR/TR, 5'9.5", 180 lbs. Deb: 4/22/1898

YEAR	TM/L	G	AB	R	H	2B	3B	HR	RBI	BB	SO	AVG	OBP	SLG	PRO+	BR/A	SB	CS	SBR	FA	FR	G/POS	TPR
1898	Cin-N	88	308	47	91	18	6	0	43	27		.295	.354	.393	107	2	9			.917	-1	2-31,O-29,3-22/S1	0.1
1899	Cin-N	107	386	62	94	16	8	0	43	40		.244	.324	.326	77	-12	19			.885	-6	3-59,2-40/S-8,O-2	-1.4
1900	Cin-N	134	510	57	125	29	7	2	66	27		.245	.292	.341	76	-18	14			.922	36	3-67,2-64/O-2,S-2	1.9
1901	Cin-N	105	382	40	95	18	7	6	47	28		.249	.303	.380	104	1	12			.886	10	3-55,2-50	1.3
1902	Cin-N	129	479	53	133	20	7	1	49	24		.278	.316	.355	98	-3	12			.912	22	*3-129/O-1	2.1
1903	Cin-N	118	439	71	137	32	12	6	83	47		.312	.386	.481	132	16	6			.937	7	*3-104,S-14	2.4
1904	Cin-N	99	349	35	85	11	6	1	52	29		.244	.313	.318	87	-5	16			.887	-7	3-98	-1.0
1905	Cin-N	114	384	49	104	16	9	1	39	30		.271	.329	.367	97	-3	15			.919	14	*3-103/1-1,2-1,O-1	1.6
1906	*Chi-N	151	539	81	**176**	27	10	3	**83**	47		.327	.395	.430	149	31	29			**.954**	-17	*3-150/2-1	2.0
1907	*Chi-N	152	542	52	144	25	5	1	70	37		.266	.323	.336	100	-0	12			**.967**	-5	*3-151	-0.1
1908	*Chi-N	150	539	63	130	20	6	1	62	36		.241	.294	.306	88	-8	12			.940	-12	*3-150	-1.6
1909	Chi-N	151	528	73	133	27	6	2	59	57		.252	.331	.337	105	3	22			.940	2	*3-151	1.1
1910	*Chi-N	129	448	70	113	21	1	2	58	36	29	.252	.323	.317	88	-7	10			**.946**	0	*3-128	-0.4
1911	Bos-N	19	63	5	16	4	0	1	8	6	3	.254	.338	.365	89	-1	1			.810	-5	3-19	-0.6
Total	14	1646	5896	758	1576	284	90	27	762	471	32	.267	.330	.360	101	0	194			.926	38	*3-1386,2-187/OS1	7.4

■ BILL STELLBAUER
Stellbauer, William Jennings b: 3/20/1894, Bremond, Tex. d: 2/16/74, New Braunfels, Tex BR/TR, 5'10", 175 lbs. Deb: 4/12/16

YEAR	TM/L	G	AB	R	H	2B	3B	HR	RBI	BB	SO	AVG	OBP	SLG	PRO+	BR/A	SB	CS	SBR	FA	FR	G/POS	TPR
1916	Phi-A	25	48	2	13	2	1	0	5	6	7	.271	.352	.354	118	1	2			.857	-4	O-14	-0.3

■ RICK STELMASZEK
Stelmaszek, Richard Francis b: 10/8/48, Chicago, Ill. BL/TR, 6'1", 195 lbs. Deb: 6/25/71 C

YEAR	TM/L	G	AB	R	H	2B	3B	HR	RBI	BB	SO	AVG	OBP	SLG	PRO+	BR/A	SB	CS	SBR	FA	FR	G/POS	TPR
1971	Was-A	6	6	0	0	0	0	0	0	0	3	.000	.000	.000	-99	-2	0	0	0	1.000	-1	/C-3	-0.3
1973	Tex-A	7	9	0	1	0	0	0	0	0	2	.111	.200	.111	-11	-1	0	0	0	1.000	-0	/C-7	-0.1
	Cal-A	22	26	2	4	1	0	0	3	6	7	.154	.313	.192	49	-2	0	0	0	1.000	-2	C-22	-0.3
	Yr	29	35	2	5	1	0	0	3	6	9	.143	.286	.171	34	-3	0	0	0	1.000	-2	C-29	-0.4
1974	Chi-N	25	44	2	10	2	0	1	7	10	6	.227	.370	.341	96	-0	0	0	0	.983	-6	C-16	-0.5
Total	3	60	88	4	15	3	0	1	10	17	18	.170	.305	.239	55	-5	0	0	0	.993	-9	/C-48	-1.2

■ FRED STEM
Stem, Frederick Boothe b: 9/22/1885, Oxford, N.C. d: 9/5/64, Darlington, S.C. BL/TR, 6'2", 160 lbs. Deb: 9/15/08

YEAR	TM/L	G	AB	R	H	2B	3B	HR	RBI	BB	SO	AVG	OBP	SLG	PRO+	BR/A	SB	CS	SBR	FA	FR	G/POS	TPR
1908	Bos-N	20	72	9	20	0	1	0	3	2		.278	.297	.306	94	-1	1			.995	-1	1-19	-0.2
1909	Bos-N	73	245	13	51	2	3	0	11	12		.208	.254	.241	51	-14	5			.989	10	1-68	-0.5
Total	2	93	317	22	71	2	4	0	14	14		.224	.263	.256	60	-15	6			.990	10	/1-87	-0.7

■ CASEY STENGEL
Stengel, Charles Dillon "The Old Professor" b: 7/30/1890, Kansas City, Mo. d: 9/29/75, Glendale, Cal. BL/TL, 5'11", 175 lbs. Deb: 9/17/12 MCH

YEAR	TM/L	G	AB	R	H	2B	3B	HR	RBI	BB	SO	AVG	OBP	SLG	PRO+	BR/A	SB	CS	SBR	FA	FR	G/POS	TPR
1912	Bro-N	17	57	9	18	1	0	1	13	15	9	.316	.466	.386	140	5	5			.902	-2	O-17	0.2
1913	Bro-N	124	438	60	119	16	8	7	43	56	58	.272	.356	.393	110	7	19			.960	2	*O-119	0.3
1914	Bro-N	126	412	55	130	13	10	4	60	56	55	.316	**.404**	.425	143	24	19			.964	-8	*O-121	1.1
1915	Bro-N	132	459	52	109	20	12	3	50	34	46	.237	.294	.353	94	-4	5	10	-5	.959	-4	*O-129	-1.6
1916	*Bro-N	127	462	66	129	27	8	8	53	33	51	.279	.329	.424	127	9	11			.965	3	*O-121	1.1
1917	Bro-N	150	549	69	141	23	12	6	73	60	62	.257	.335	.375	115	10	18			.969	13	*O-150	1.6
1918	Pit-N	39	122	18	30	4	1	1	12	16	14	.246	.343	.320	99	0	11			.973	-2	O-37	-0.5
1919	Pit-N	89	321	38	94	10	10	4	43	35	35	.293	.364	.424	131	13	12			.957	-4	O-87	1.0
1920	Phi-N	129	445	53	130	25	6	9	50	38	35	.292	.356	.436	121	12	7	13	-6	.954	-3	*O-118	-0.5
1921	Phi-N	24	59	7	18	3	1	0	4	6	7	.305	.369	.390	94	-0	1	1	-0	.969	2	/O-15	0.1
	NY-N	18	22	4	5	1	0	0	2	1	5	.227	.261	.273	41	-2	0	1	-1	.875	-3	/O-8	-0.6
	Yr	42	81	11	23	4	1	0	6	7	12	.284	.341	.358	81	-2	1	2	-1	.950	-2	O-23	-0.5
1922	*NY-N	84	250	48	92	8	10	7	48	21	17	.368	.436	.564	155	21	4	2	0	.969	-4	O-77	1.1
1923	*NY-N	75	218	39	74	11	5	5	43	20	18	.339	.400	.505	139	17	6	2	1	.983	-7	O-57	0.3
1924	Bos-N	131	461	57	129	20	6	5	39	45	39	.280	.348	.382	100	0	13	13	-4	.978	-7	*O-126	-1.9
1925	Bos-N	12	13	0	1	0	0	0	2	1	2	.077	.143	.077	-46	-3	0	1	-1	1.000	0	/O-1	-0.4
Total	14	1277	4288	575	1219	182	89	60	535	437	453	.284	.356	.410	119	107	131	43		.964	-9	*O-1183	1.9

■ MIKE STENHOUSE
Stenhouse, Michael Steven b: 5/29/58, Pueblo, Colo. BL/TR, 6'1", 195 lbs. Deb: 10/3/82 F

YEAR	TM/L	G	AB	R	H	2B	3B	HR	RBI	BB	SO	AVG	OBP	SLG	PRO+	BR/A	SB	CS	SBR	FA	FR	G/POS	TPR
1982	Mon-N	1	0	0	0	0	0	0	0	0	0	.000	.000	.000	-98	-0	0	0	0	.000	0	/H	0.0
1983	Mon-N	24	40	2	5	1	0	0	2	4	10	.125	.205	.150	-0	-5	0	0	0	1.000	-3	/O-9,1-5	-0.9
1984	Mon-N	80	175	14	32	8	0	4	16	26	32	.183	.292	.297	69	-7	0	0	0	.986	-3	O-48,1-14	-1.2
1985	Min-A	81	179	23	40	5	0	5	21	29	18	.223	.332	.335	79	-5	1	0	0	.929	-3	D-27,O-16/1-8	-0.6
1986	Bos-A	21	21	1	2	1	0	0	1	12	5	.095	.424	.143	63	-0	0	0	0	1.000	-0	/O-4,1-3	-0.1
Total	5	207	416	40	79	15	0	9	40	71	66	.190	.309	.291	67	-18	1	0	0	.973	-5	/O-77,1-30,D-27	-2.8

■ RENNIE STENNETT
Stennett, Renaldo Antonio (Porte) b: 4/5/51, Colon, Panama BR/TR, 5'11", 175 lbs. Deb: 7/10/71

YEAR	TM/L	G	AB	R	H	2B	3B	HR	RBI	BB	SO	AVG	OBP	SLG	PRO+	BR/A	SB	CS	SBR	FA	FR	G/POS	TPR
1971	Pit-N	50	153	24	54	5	4	1	15	7	9	.353	.381	.458	137	7	1	1	-0	.954	2	2-36	1.2
1972	*Pit-N	109	370	43	106	14	5	3	30	9	43	.286	.307	.376	95	-4	4	3	-1	.977	6	2-49,O-41/S-6	0.4
1973	Pit-N	128	466	45	113	13	3	10	55	16	63	.242	.268	.358	74	-18	2	3	-1	.981	-0	2-84,S-43/O-5	-1.0

YEAR	TM/L	G	AB	R	H	2B	3B	HR	RBI	BB	SO	AVG	OBP	SLG	PRO+	BR/A	SB	CS	SBR	FA	FR	G/POS	TPR
1974	*Pit-N	157	673	84	196	29	3	7	56	32	51	.291	.325	.374	99	-3	8	9	-3	.980	13	*2-154/O-2	1.5
1975	*Pit-N	148	616	89	176	25	7	7	62	33	42	.286	.326	.383	97	-4	5	4	-1	.979	13	*2-144	1.6
1976	Pit-N	157	654	59	168	31	9	2	60	19	32	.257	.279	.341	75	-23	18	6	2	.981	17	*2-157/S-4	0.6
1977	Pit-N	116	453	53	152	20	4	5	51	29	24	.336	.378	.430	113	9	28	18	-2	.982	-7	*2-113	0.8
1978	Pit-N	106	333	30	81	9	2	3	35	13	22	.243	.276	.309	60	-18	2	1	0	.971	-12	2-80/3-6	-2.5
1979	*Pit-N	108	319	31	76	13	2	0	24	24	25	.238	.292	.292	57	-19	1	4	-2	.974	6	*2-102	-0.9
1980	SF-N	120	397	34	97	13	2	2	37	22	31	.244	.287	.302	66	-18	4	4	-1	.973	-13	*2-111	-2.8
1981	SF-N	38	87	8	20	0	0	1	7	3	6	.230	.264	.264	51	-6	2	1	0	1.000	-2	2-19	-0.7
Total	11	1237	4521	500	1239	177	41	41	432	207	348	.274	.308	.359	85	-96	75	54	-10	.978	23	*2-1049/S-53,O-48,3	-1.8

■ JAKE STENZEL

Stenzel, Jacob Charles (b: Jacob Charles Stelzle)
b: 6/24/1867, Cincinnati, Ohio   d: 1/6/19, Cincinnati, Ohio   BR/TR, 5'10", 168 lbs.   Deb: 6/16/1890

YEAR	TM/L	G	AB	R	H	2B	3B	HR	RBI	BB	SO	AVG	OBP	SLG	PRO+	BR/A	SB	CS	SBR	FA	FR	G/POS	TPR
1890	Chi-N	11	41	3	11	1	0	0	3	1	0	.268	.286	.293	66	-2				.857	-4	/O-6,C-6	-0.4
1892	Pit-N	3	9	0	0	0	0	0	0	1	3	.000	.100	.000	-69	-2	1			1.000	0	/O-2,C-1	-0.1
1893	Pit-N	60	224	57	81	13	4	6	37	24	17	.362	.423	.509	150	16	16			.905	-9	O-45,C-12/S-1,2-1	0.4
1894	Pit-N	131	522	148	185	39	20	13	121	75	13	.354	.441	.580	146	40	61			.925	-1	*O-131	2.2
1895	Pit-N	129	514	114	192	38	13	7	97	57	25	.374	.447	.539	162	50	53			.912	-5	*O-129	2.8
1896	Pit-N	114	479	104	173	26	14	2	82	32	13	.361	.410	.486	141	28	57			.922	-3	*O-114/1-1	1.3
1897	*Bal-N	131	536	113	189	43	7	4	116	36		.353	.404	.481	135	25	69			.932	-11	*O-131	0.4
1898	Bal-N	35	138	33	35	5	2	0	22	12		.254	.340	.319	87	-2	4			.926	-2	O-35	-0.6
	StL-N	108	404	64	114	15	11	1	33	41		.282	.367	.381	112	7	21			.943	0	*O-108	-0.1
	Yr	143	542	97	149	20	13	1	55	53		.275	.360	.365	106	5	25			.940	-2	O-143	-0.7
1899	StL-N	35	128	21	35	9	0	1	19	16		.273	.367	.367	99	-2	8			.949	-1	O-33	-0.3
	Cin-N	9	29	5	9	1	0	0	3	4		.310	.412	.345	106	1	2			1.000	-1	/O-7	-0.1
	Yr	44	157	26	44	10	0	1	22	20		.280	.376	.363	101	1	10			.957	-2	O-40	-0.4
Total	9	766	3024	662	1024	190	71	32	533	299	71	.339	.408	.480	135	161	292			.927	-36	O-741/C-19,1-1,2S	5.5

■ RAY STEPHENS

Stephens, Carl Ray   b: 9/22/62, Houston, Tex.   BR/TR, 6', 190 lbs.   Deb: 9/20/90

YEAR	TM/L	G	AB	R	H	2B	3B	HR	RBI	BB	SO	AVG	OBP	SLG	PRO+	BR/A	SB	CS	SBR	FA	FR	G/POS	TPR
1990	StL-N	5	15	2	2	1	0	1	1	0	3	.133	.133	.400	41	-1	0	0	0	1.000	2	/C-5	0.1
1991	StL-N	6	7	0	2	0	0	0	0	1	3	.286	.375	.286	88	-0	0	0	0	1.000	1	/C-6	0.1
1992	Tex-A	8	13	0	2	0	0	0	0	1	5	.154	.154	.154	-14	-2	0	0	0	1.000	-0	/C-6,D-1	-0.2
Total	3	19	35	2	6	1	0	1	1	1	11	.171	.194	.286	32	-3	0	0	0	1.000	3	/C-17,D-1	0.0

■ GENE STEPHENS

Stephens, Glen Eugene   b: 1/20/33, Gravette, Ark.   BL/TR, 6'3.5", 175 lbs.   Deb: 4/16/52

YEAR	TM/L	G	AB	R	H	2B	3B	HR	RBI	BB	SO	AVG	OBP	SLG	PRO+	BR/A	SB	CS	SBR	FA	FR	G/POS	TPR
1952	Bos-A	21	53	10	12	5	0	0	5	3	8	.226	.268	.321	59	-3	4	2	0	.962	0	O-13	-0.4
1953	Bos-A	78	221	30	45	6	2	3	18	29	56	.204	.302	.290	57	-13	3	3	-1	.966	-7	O-72	-2.3
1955	Bos-A	109	157	25	46	9	4	3	18	20	34	.293	.380	.459	114	-3	3	0	0	.947	-11	O-75	-0.9
1956	Bos-A	104	63	22	17	2	0	1	7	12	12	.270	.387	.349	85	-1	0	1	-1	.983	-17	O-71	-1.8
1957	Bos-A	120	173	25	46	6	4	3	26	26	20	.266	.362	.399	102	1	0	2	-1	.987	-19	O-90	-2.2
1958	Bos-A	134	270	38	59	10	1	9	25	22	46	.219	.280	.363	71	-11	1	2	-1	.975	-4	*O-110	-3.3
1959	Bos-A	92	270	34	75	13	1	3	39	29	33	.278	.356	.367	95	-1	5	2	0	.981	-5	O-85	-0.3
1960	Bos-A	35	109	9	25	4	0	2	11	14	22	.229	.317	.321	71	-4	5	1	1	.951	-1	O-31	-0.6
	Bal-A	84	193	38	46	11	0	5	11	25	25	.238	.329	.373	91	-2	4	2	0	.992	-10	O-77	-1.6
	Yr	119	302	47	71	15	0	7	22	39	47	.235	.325	.354	83	-7	9	3	1	.979	-11	*O-108	-2.2
1961	Bal-A	32	58	4	11	2	0	2	14	7		.190	.347	.224	58	-3	1	1	-0	1.000	-6	O-30	-1.0
	KC-A	62	183	22	38	6	1	4	26	16	27	.208	.279	.317	58	-11	3	2	-0	.968	1	O-54	-1.3
	Yr	94	241	26	49	8	1	4	28	30	34	.203	.297	.295	59	-14	4	3	-1	.975	-5	O-84	-2.3
1962	KC-A	5	4	0	0	0	0	0	0	1	0	.000	.200	.000	-39	-1	0	0	0	.000	0	H	-0.1
1963	Chi-A	6	18	5	7	0	0	1	2	1	3	.389	.421	.556	174	2	0	0	0	.909	1	/O-5	0.3
1964	Chi-A	82	116	21	33	4	2	3	17	21	28	.234	.341	.355	97	-0	1	2	-1	.969	-5	O-59	-0.9
Total	12	964	1913	283	460	78	15	37	207	233	322	.240	.327	.355	82	-45	27	20	-4	.973	-87	O-772	-16.4

■ JIM STEPHENS

Stephens, James Walter "Little Nemo"   b: 12/10/1883, Salineville, Ohio   d: 1/2/65, Oxford, Ala.   BR/TR, 5'6.5", 157 lbs.   Deb: 4/11/07

YEAR	TM/L	G	AB	R	H	2B	3B	HR	RBI	BB	SO	AVG	OBP	SLG	PRO+	BR/A	SB	CS	SBR	FA	FR	G/POS	TPR
1907	StL-A	58	173	15	35	6	3	0	11	15		.202	.270	.272	73	-4	5			.967	-4	C-56	-0.5
1908	StL-A	47	150	14	30	4	1	0	6	9		.200	.255	.240	61	-6	0			.960	-0	C-45	-0.3
1909	StL-A	79	223	18	49	5	0	3	18	13		.220	.278	.283	83	-5	5			.980	3	C-72	0.5
1910	StL-A	99	289	24	62	3	7	0	23	16		.215	.261	.273	72	-10	2			.971	-2	C-96	0.1
1911	StL-A	70	212	11	49	5	5	0	17	17		.231	.300	.302	71	-8	1			.949	-2	C-66	-0.4
1912	StL-A	75	205	13	51	7	5	0	22	7		.249	.274	.332	76	-8	3			.954	4	C-66	0.2
Total	6	428	1252	95	276	30	21	3	97	77		.220	.273	.285	73	-42	14			.965	3	C-401	-0.4

■ VERN STEPHENS

Stephens, Vernon Decatur "Junior" or "Buster"   b: 10/23/20, McAlister, N.Mex.   d: 11/3/68, Long Beach, Cal.   BR/TR, 5'10", 185 lbs.   Deb: 9/13/41

YEAR	TM/L	G	AB	R	H	2B	3B	HR	RBI	BB	SO	AVG	OBP	SLG	PRO+	BR/A	SB	CS	SBR	FA	FR	G/POS	TPR
1941	StL-A	3	2	0	1	0	0	0	0	0	0	.500	.500	.500	160	0	0	0	0	.500	-0	/S-1	0.0
1942	StL-A	145	575	84	169	26	6	14	92	41	53	.294	.341	.433	115	9	1	3	-2	.944	-10	*S-144	0.7
1943	StL-A★	137	512	75	148	27	3	22	91	54	73	.289	.357	.482	142	25	3	2	-0	.943	-25	*S-123,O-11	0.8
1944	*StL-A★	145	559	91	164	32	1	20	109	62	54	.293	.365	.462	128	19	2	2	-1	.954	-4	*S-143	2.7
1945	StL-A†	149	571	90	165	27	3	24	89	55	70	.289	.352	.473	132	21	2	1	0	.961	-17	*S-144/3-4	1.7
1946	StL-A★	115	450	67	138	19	4	14	64	35	49	.307	.357	.460	121	11	0	1	-1	.950	0	*S-112	1.8
1947	StL-A	150	562	74	157	18	4	15	83	70	61	.279	.359	.406	110	8	8	4	0	.970	12	*S-149	2.9
1948	Bos-A★	155	635	114	171	25	8	29	137	77	56	.269	.350	.471	112	7	1	0	0	.971	10	*S-155	2.6
1949	Bos-A★	155	610	113	177	31	2	39	159	101	73	.290	.391	.539	135	28	2	2	-1	.966	4	*S-155	4.1
1950	Bos-A☆	149	628	125	185	34	6	30	144	65	43	.295	.361	.511	120	10	6	1	0	.981	-0	*S-146	1.6
1951	Bos-A	109	377	62	113	21	2	17	78	38	33	.300	.364	.501	120	9	1	2	-1	.978	14	3-89/S-2	2.1
1952	Bos-A	92	295	35	75	13	2	7	44	39	41	.254	.343	.383	95	-2	2	2	-1	.957	-4	S-53,3-29	0.5
1953	Chi-A	44	129	14	24	6	0	1	14	13	18	.186	.261	.256	39	-11	2	0	0	.990	-3	3-38/S-3	-0.2
	StL-A	46	165	16	53	8	0	4	17	18	24	.321	.388	.442	121	5	0	0	0	.954	-2	3-46	0.2
	Yr	90	294	30	77	14	0	5	31	31	42	.262	.332	.361	85	-6	2	0	0	.968	-5	3-84/S-3	-1.2
1954	Bal-A	101	365	31	104	17	1	8	46	17	36	.285	.317	.403	104	-1	0	3	-2	.966	-6	3-96	-1.1
1955	Bal-A	3	6	0	1	0	0	0	0	0	0	.167	.286	.167	26	-1	0	0	0	1.000	-0	/3-2	-0.1
	Chi-A	22	56	10	14	3	0	3	7	7	11	.250	.333	.464	110	1	0	0	0	1.000	4	3-18	0.5
	Yr	25	62	10	15	3	0	3	7	7	11	.242	.329	.435	102	0	0	0	0	1.000	4	3-20	0.5
Total	15	1720	6497	1001	1859	307	42	247	1174	692	685	.286	.355	.460	118	137	25	22	-6	.960	-20	*S-1330,3-322/O-11	19.6

■ RIGGS STEPHENSON

Stephenson, Jackson Riggs "Old Hoss"   b: 1/5/1898, Akron, Ala.   d: 11/15/85, Tuscaloosa, Ala.   BR/TR, 5'10", 185 lbs.   Deb: 4/13/21

YEAR	TM/L	G	AB	R	H	2B	3B	HR	RBI	BB	SO	AVG	OBP	SLG	PRO+	BR/A	SB	CS	SBR	FA	FR	G/POS	TPR
1921	Cle-A	65	206	45	68	17	2	2	34	23	15	.330	.408	.461	119	7	4	1	1	.942	-1	2-54/3-2	0.7
1922	Cle-A	86	233	47	79	24	5	2	32	27	18	.339	.421	.511	141	15	3	0	1	.952	-6	3-34,2-25/O-3	1.2
1923	Cle-A	91	301	48	96	20	6	5	65	15	25	.319	.357	.475	118	16	5	5	-2	.970	11	2-66/O-3,3-2	1.6
1924	Cle-A	71	240	33	89	20	0	4	44	27	10	.371	.439	.504	141	15	1	2	-1	.961	-13	2-58/O-7	0.1
1925	Cle-A	19	54	8	16	3	1	1	9	7	2	.296	.387	.444	110	1	1	1	-0	.946	1	O-16	0.1
1926	Chi-N	82	281	40	95	18	3	3	44	31	16	.338	.404	.456	129	12	2			.950	-4	O-74	0.4
1927	Chi-N	152	579	101	199	46	9	7	82	65	28	.344	.415	.491	142	36	8			.975	4	*O-146/3-6	3.0
1928	Chi-N	137	512	75	166	36	9	8	90	68	29	.324	.407	.477	132	25	4			.982	0	*O-135	1.6
1929	*Chi-N	136	495	91	179	36	6	17	110	67	21	.362	.445	.562	147	39	10			.984	-0	*O-130	2.7
1930	Chi-N	109	341	56	125	21	1	5	68	32	20	.367	.421	.478	116	10	2			.958	-5	O-80	0.2
1931	Chi-N	80	263	34	84	14	4	1	52	37	14	.319	.405	.414	119	9	1			.985	-2	O-66	0.2
1932	*Chi-N	147	583	86	189	49	4	4	85	54	27	.324	.383	.443	123	20	3			.984	-5	*O-147	0.5
1933	Chi-N	97	346	45	114	17	4	4	51	34	16	.329	.397	.436	138	18	5			.985	-2	O-91	1.2
1934	Chi-N	38	74	5	16	7	1	0	7	8	5	.216	.293	.216	39	-6	0			1.000	1	O-15	-0.5
Total	14	1310	4508	714	1515	321	63	63	773	494	247	.336	.407	.473	130	206	53	9		.978	-21	O-913,2-203/3-44	12.8

YEAR	TM/L	G	AB	R	H	2B	3B	HR	RBI	BB	SO	AVG	OBP	SLG	PRO+	BR/A	SB	CS	SBR	FA	FR	G/POS	TPR

■ JOHN STEPHENSON   Stephenson, John Herman b: 4/13/41, S.Portsmouth, Ky. BL/TR, 5'11", 180 lbs. Deb: 4/14/64

YEAR	TM/L	G	AB	R	H	2B	3B	HR	RBI	BB	SO	AVG	OBP	SLG	PRO+	BR/A	SB	CS	SBR	FA	FR	G/POS	TPR
1964	NY-N	37	57	2	9	0	0	1	2	4	18	.158	.226	.211	24	-6	0	0	0	.800	-4	3-14/O-8	-1.1
1965	NY-N	62	121	9	26	5	0	4	15	8	19	.215	.264	.355	75	-4	0	1	-1	.981	-9	C-47/O-2	-1.3
1966	NY-N	63	143	17	28	1	1	1	11	8	28	.196	.248	.238	37	-12	0	0	0	.973	-1	C-52/O-1	-1.2
1967	Chi-N	18	49	3	11	3	1	0	5	1	6	.224	.255	.327	62	-2	0	0	0	1.000	1	C-13	-0.1
1968	Chi-N	2	2	0	0	0	0	0	0	0	0	.000	.000	.000	-94	-0	0	0	0	.000	0	H	-0.1
1969	SF-N	22	27	2	6	2	0	0	3	0	4	.222	.222	.296	45	-2	0	0	0	.941	-3	/C-9,3-1	-0.5
1970	SF-N	23	43	3	3	1	0	0	6	2	7	.070	.111	.093	-45	-9	0	0	0	1.000	0	/C-9,O-1	-0.6
1971	Cal-A	98	279	24	61	17	0	3	25	22	21	.219	.283	.312	74	-10	0	0	0	.992	-9	C-88	-1.7
1972	Cal-A	66	146	14	40	3	1	2	17	11	8	.274	.342	.349	112	2	0	0	0	.993	-7	C-56	-0.4
1973	Cal-A	60	122	9	30	5	0	1	9	7	7	.246	.292	.311	76	-4	0	0	0	.980	-8	C-56	-1.1
Total	10	451	989	83	214	37	3	12	93	63	118	.216	.272	.296	64	-48	0	1	-1	.986	-38	C-330/3-15,O-12	-8.1

■ JOE STEPHENSON   Stephenson, Joseph Chester b: 6/30/21, Detroit, Mich. BR/TR, 6'2", 185 lbs. Deb: 9/19/43 F

YEAR	TM/L	G	AB	R	H	2B	3B	HR	RBI	BB	SO	AVG	OBP	SLG	PRO+	BR/A	SB	CS	SBR	FA	FR	G/POS	TPR
1943	NY-N	9	24	4	6	1	0	0	1	0	5	.250	.250	.292	56	-1	0			.973	2	/C-6	0.1
1944	Chi-N	4	8	1	1	0	0	0	0	1	3	.125	.222	.125	-1	-1	1			1.000	1	/C-3	0.0
1947	Chi-A	16	35	3	5	0	0	0	3	1	7	.143	.211	.143	-1	-5	0	0	0	.959	0	C-13	-0.4
Total	3	29	67	8	12	1	0	0	4	2	15	.179	.225	.194	19	-7	1	0		.970	3	/C-22	-0.3

■ PHIL STEPHENSON   Stephenson, Phillip Raymond b: 9/19/60, Guthrie, Okla. BL/TL, 6'1", 195 lbs. Deb: 4/5/89

YEAR	TM/L	G	AB	R	H	2B	3B	HR	RBI	BB	SO	AVG	OBP	SLG	PRO+	BR/A	SB	CS	SBR	FA	FR	G/POS	TPR
1989	Chi-N	17	21	0	3	0	0	0	2	3	3	.143	.217	.143	5	-3	1	0	0	1.000	-1	/O-3	-0.3
	SD-N	10	17	4	6	0	0	2	2	3	2	.353	.450	.706	225	3	0	0	0	.977	1	/1-8	0.3
	Yr	27	38	4	9	0	0	2	2	5	5	.237	.326	.395	100	0	1	0	0	.977	-0	/1-8,O-3	0.0
1990	SD-N	103	182	26	38	9	1	4	19	30	43	.209	.321	.335	80	-5	2	1	0	.997	3	1-60	-0.5
1991	SD-N	11	7	0	2	0	0	0	2	3		.286	.444	.286	106	0	0	0	0	.000	0	/H	0.0
1992	SD-N	53	71	5	11	2	1	0	8	10	11	.155	.259	.211	34	-6	0	0	0	1.000	-3	O-15/1-7	-1.0
Total	4	194	298	35	60	11	2	6	29	47	62	.201	.310	.312	73	-10	3	1	0	.993	-1	/1-75,O-18	-1.5

■ DUMMY STEPHENSON   Stephenson, Reuben Crandol b: 9/22/1869, Petersburg, N.J. d: 12/1/24, Trenton, N.J. BR/TR, 5'11.5", 180 lbs. Deb: 9/9/1892

YEAR	TM/L	G	AB	R	H	2B	3B	HR	RBI	BB	SO	AVG	OBP	SLG	PRO+	BR/A	SB	CS	SBR	FA	FR	G/POS	TPR
1892	Phi-N	8	37	4	10	3	0	0	5	0	2	.270	.289	.351	94	-0	0			.800	-2	/O-8	-0.2

■ BOB STEPHENSON   Stephenson, Robert Lloyd b: 8/11/28, Blair, Okla. BR/TR, 6', 165 lbs. Deb: 4/14/55

YEAR	TM/L	G	AB	R	H	2B	3B	HR	RBI	BB	SO	AVG	OBP	SLG	PRO+	BR/A	SB	CS	SBR	FA	FR	G/POS	TPR
1955	StL-N	67	111	19	27	3	0	0	6	5	18	.243	.276	.270	46	-9	2	1	0	.938	-1	S-48/2-7,3-1	-0.7

■ WALTER STEPHENSON   Stephenson, Walter McQueen "Tarzan" b: 3/27/11, Saluda, N.C. d: 7/4/93, Shreveport, La. BR/TR, 6', 180 lbs. Deb: 4/29/35

YEAR	TM/L	G	AB	R	H	2B	3B	HR	RBI	BB	SO	AVG	OBP	SLG	PRO+	BR/A	SB	CS	SBR	FA	FR	G/POS	TPR
1935	*Chi-N	16	26	2	10	1	1	0	2	1	5	.385	.407	.500	142	1	0			1.000	2	/C-6	0.3
1936	Chi-N	6	12	0	1	0	0	0	1	0	5	.083	.083	.083	-54	-3	0			1.000	1	/C-4	-0.3
1937	Phi-N	10	23	1	6	0	0	0	3	2	3	.261	.320	.261	55	-1	0			.967	0	/C-7	-0.1
Total	3	32	61	3	17	1	1	0	6	3	13	.279	.313	.328	70	-2	0			.971	2	/C-17	-0.1

■ DUTCH STERRETT   Sterrett, Charles Hurlbut b: 10/1/1889, Milroy, Pa. d: 12/9/65, Baltimore, Md. BR/TR, 5'11.5", 165 lbs. Deb: 6/20/12

YEAR	TM/L	G	AB	R	H	2B	3B	HR	RBI	BB	SO	AVG	OBP	SLG	PRO+	BR/A	SB	CS	SBR	FA	FR	G/POS	TPR
1912	NY-A	66	230	30	61	4	7	1	32	11		.265	.310	.357	85	-5	8			.972	-7	O-37,1-17,C-10,2-1	-1.3
1913	NY-A	21	35	0	6	0	0	0	3	1	5	.171	.216	.171	14	-4	1			1.000	-1	/1-6,C-1	-0.5
Total	2	87	265	30	67	4	7	1	35	12	5	.253	.298	.332	77	-9	9			.986	-8	/O-37,1-23,C-11,2-1	-1.8

■ CHUCK STEVENS   Stevens, Charles Augustus b: 7/10/18, Van Houten, N.Mex BB/TR, 6'1", 180 lbs. Deb: 9/16/41

YEAR	TM/L	G	AB	R	H	2B	3B	HR	RBI	BB	SO	AVG	OBP	SLG	PRO+	BR/A	SB	CS	SBR	FA	FR	G/POS	TPR
1941	StL-A	4	13	2	2	0	0	0	2	0	1	.154	.154	.154	-18	-2	0	0	0	.966	-1	/1-4	-0.3
1946	StL-A	122	432	53	107	17	4	3	27	47	62	.248	.324	.326	78	-12	4	6	-2	.995	3	*1-120	-1.9
1948	StL-A	85	287	34	75	12	4	1	26	41	26	.261	.354	.341	83	-6	2	2	-1	.991	1	1-85	-0.7
Total	3	211	732	89	184	29	8	4	55	88	89	.251	.333	.329	79	-20	6	8	-3	.993	3	1-209	-2.9

■ LEE STEVENS   Stevens, De Wain Lee b: 7/10/67, Kansas City, Mo. BL/TL, 6'4", 205 lbs. Deb: 7/16/90

YEAR	TM/L	G	AB	R	H	2B	3B	HR	RBI	BB	SO	AVG	OBP	SLG	PRO+	BR/A	SB	CS	SBR	FA	FR	G/POS	TPR
1990	Cal-A	67	248	28	53	10	0	7	32	22	75	.214	.278	.339	73	-9	1	1	-0	.994	-4	1-67	-1.9
1991	Cal-A	18	58	8	17	7	0	0	9	6	12	.293	.359	.414	113	1	1	2	-1	.989	-1	1-11/O-9	-0.1
1992	Cal-A	106	312	25	69	19	0	7	37	29	64	.221	.289	.349	78	-10	1	4	-2	.995	-4	1-91/D-2	-2.2
1996	Tex-A	27	78	6	18	2	3	3	12	6	22	.231	.294	.449	79	-3	0	0	0	.994	0	1-18/O-5	-0.4
Total	4	218	696	67	157	38	3	17	90	63	173	.226	.292	.362	79	-21	3	7	-3	.994	-8	1-187/O-14,D-2	-4.6

■ ED STEVENS   Stevens, Edward Lee "Big Ed" b: 1/12/25, Galveston, Tex. BL/TL, 6'1", 190 lbs. Deb: 8/9/45 C

YEAR	TM/L	G	AB	R	H	2B	3B	HR	RBI	BB	SO	AVG	OBP	SLG	PRO+	BR/A	SB	CS	SBR	FA	FR	G/POS	TPR
1945	Bro-N	55	201	29	55	14	3	4	29	32	20	.274	.376	.433	125	7	0			.987	-4	1-55	0.4
1946	Bro-N	103	310	34	75	13	7	10	60	27	44	.242	.300	.426	104	0	2			.986	-4	1-99	-0.9
1947	Bro-N	5	13	0	2	1	0	0	1	5		.154	.214	.231	18	-2	0			.971	1	/1-4	-0.1
1948	Pit-N	128	429	47	109	19	6	10	69	35	53	.254	.313	.396	89	-8	4			.996	5	*1-117	-0.3
1949	Pit-N	67	221	22	58	10	1	4	32	22	24	.262	.332	.371	86	-4	1			.995	10	1-58	0.5
1950	Pit-N	17	46	2	9	2	0	0	3	4	5	.196	.260	.239	31	-5	0			1.000	1	1-12	-0.4
Total	6	375	1220	134	308	59	17	28	193	121	151	.252	.322	.398	95	-10	7			.992	13	1-345	-0.8

■ R C STEVENS   Stevens, R C b: 7/22/34, Moultrie, Ga. BL/TR, 6'5", 219 lbs. Deb: 4/15/58

YEAR	TM/L	G	AB	R	H	2B	3B	HR	RBI	BB	SO	AVG	OBP	SLG	PRO+	BR/A	SB	CS	SBR	FA	FR	G/POS	TPR
1958	Pit-N	59	90	16	24	3	1	7	18	5	25	.267	.320	.556	129	3	0	0	0	.991	3	1-52	0.4
1959	Pit-N	3	7	2	2	0	0	1	1	0	0	.286	.286	.714	157	0	0	0	0	1.000	0	/1-1	0.0
1960	Pit-N	9	3	1	0	0	0	0	0	0	1	.000	.000	.000	-99	-1	0	0	0	1.000	1	/1-7	0.0
1961	Was-A	33	62	2	8	1	0	0	2	7	15	.129	.217	.145	-1	-9	1	0	0	1.000	4	1-25	-0.6
Total	4	104	162	21	34	4	1	8	21	12	41	.210	.273	.395	77	-6	1	0	0	.995	7	/1-85	-0.2

■ ROBERT STEVENS   Stevens, Robert Deb: 5/4/1875

YEAR	TM/L	G	AB	R	H	2B	3B	HR	RBI	BB	SO	AVG	OBP	SLG	PRO+	BR/A	SB	CS	SBR	FA	FR	G/POS	TPR
1875	Was-n	1	4	0	1	0	0	0	0	0	0	.250	.250	.250	77	-0	0	0	0	.000	-1	/O-1	-0.1

■ BOBBY STEVENS   Stevens, Robert Jordan b: 4/17/07, Chevy Chase, Md. BL/TR, 5'8", 149 lbs. Deb: 7/3/31

YEAR	TM/L	G	AB	R	H	2B	3B	HR	RBI	BB	SO	AVG	OBP	SLG	PRO+	BR/A	SB	CS	SBR	FA	FR	G/POS	TPR
1931	Phi-N	12	35	3	12	0	0	0	4	2	2	.343	.410	.343	97	-0	0			.870	-5	S-10	-0.4

■ TODD STEVERSON   Steverson, Todd Anthony b: 11/15/71, Los Angeles, Cal. BR/TR, 6'2", 195 lbs. Deb: 4/28/95

YEAR	TM/L	G	AB	R	H	2B	3B	HR	RBI	BB	SO	AVG	OBP	SLG	PRO+	BR/A	SB	CS	SBR	FA	FR	G/POS	TPR
1995	Det-A	30	42	11	11	1	0	0	2	6	10	.262	.354	.405	97	-0	2	0	1	1.000	-6	O-27/D-1	-0.6
1996	SD-N	1	1	0	0	0	0	0	0	0	1	.000	.000	.000	-99	-0	0	0	0	.000	0	/H	0.0
Total	2	31	43	11	11	1	0	0	2	6	11	.256	.347	.395	93	-0	2	0	1	1.000	-6	O-27/D-1	-0.6

■ ACE STEWART   Stewart, Asa b: 2/14/1869, Terre Haute, Ind. d: 4/17/12, Terre Haute, Ind. BR/TR, 5'10", 176 lbs. Deb: 4/18/1895

YEAR	TM/L	G	AB	R	H	2B	3B	HR	RBI	BB	SO	AVG	OBP	SLG	PRO+	BR/A	SB	CS	SBR	FA	FR	G/POS	TPR
1895	Chi-N	97	365	52	88	8	10	8	76	39	40	.241	.314	.384	75	-16	14			.911	-8	*2-97	-1.6

■ TUFFY STEWART   Stewart, Charles Eugene b: 7/31/1883, Chicago, Ill. d: 11/18/34, Chicago, Ill. BL/TL, 5'10", 167 lbs. Deb: 8/8/13

YEAR	TM/L	G	AB	R	H	2B	3B	HR	RBI	BB	SO	AVG	OBP	SLG	PRO+	BR/A	SB	CS	SBR	FA	FR	G/POS	TPR
1913	Chi-N	9	8	1	1	1	0	0	2	2	5	.125	.300	.250	58	-0	1			1.000	0	/O-1	0.0
1914	Chi-N	2	1	0	0	0	0	0	0	0	0	.000	.000	.000	-99	-0	0			.000	0	H	0.0
Total	2	11	9	1	1	1	0	0	2	2	5	.111	.273	.222	43	-1	1			1.000	0	/O-1	0.0

■ BUD STEWART   Stewart, Edward Perry b: 6/15/16, Sacramento, Cal. BL/TR, 5'11", 170 lbs. Deb: 4/19/41

YEAR	TM/L	G	AB	R	H	2B	3B	HR	RBI	BB	SO	AVG	OBP	SLG	PRO+	BR/A	SB	CS	SBR	FA	FR	G/POS	TPR
1941	Pit-N	73	172	27	46	4	0	0	10	12	17	.267	.315	.308	76	-5	3			.962	-2	O-41	-0.9
1942	Pit-N	82	183	21	40	8	4	0	20	22	16	.219	.302	.306	76	-5	2			1.000	-4	O-34,3-10/2-6	-1.1
1948	NY-A	6	5	1	1	1	0	0	0	0	0	.200	.200	.400	58	-0	0	0	0	.000	0	/H	-0.1
	Was-A	118	401	56	112	17	13	7	69	49	27	.279	.361	.439	115	8	8	9	-3	.975	-4	*O-114	-0.5
	Yr	124	406	57	113	18	13	7	69	49	27	.278	.359	.438	115	7	8	9	-3	.975	-4	*O-114	-0.5
1949	Was-A	118	388	58	110	23	4	8	43	49	37	.284	.368	.425	112	6	6	4	-1	.982	-7	*O-105	-0.6
1950	Was-A	118	378	46	101	15	6	4	35	46	33	.267	.348	.370	88	-7	5	4	-1	.991	-3	*O-100	-1.4
1951	Chi-A	95	217	40	60	13	5	6	40	29	9	.276	.367	.465	127	8	1	6	-3	.983	-7	O-63	-0.4
1952	Chi-A	92	225	23	60	10	0	5	30	28	17	.267	.350	.378	104	1	3	0	1	.982	-4	O-60	-0.5

YEAR	TM/L	G	AB	R	H	2B	3B	HR	RBI	BB	SO	AVG	OBP	SLG	PRO+	BR/A	SB	CS	SBR	FA	FR	G/POS	TPR
1953	Chi-A	53	59	16	16	2	0	2	13	14	3	.271	.411	.407	118	2	1	0	0	1.000	-4	O-16	-0.2
1954	Chi-A	18	13	0	1	0	0	0	0	3	2	.077	.250	.077	-7	-2	0	0	0	1.000	-0	/O-2	-0.2
Total	9	773	2041	288	547	96	32	32	260	252	157	.268	.351	.393	102	5	29	23		.982	-35	O-535/3-10,2-6	-5.8

■ GLEN STEWART Stewart, Glen Weldon "Gabby" b: 9/29/12, Tullahoma, Tenn. BR/TR, 6′, 175 lbs. Deb: 6/26/40

YEAR	TM/L	G	AB	R	H	2B	3B	HR	RBI	BB	SO	AVG	OBP	SLG	PRO+	BR/A	SB	CS	SBR	FA	FR	G/POS	TPR
1940	NY-N	15	29	1	4	1	0	0	1	1	2	.138	.167	.172	-6	-4	0			.875	1	/3-6,S-5	-0.3
1943	Phi-N	110	336	23	71	10	1	2	24	32	41	.211	.284	.265	61	-17	1			.947	-9	S-77,2-18/1-8,C-1	-1.9
1944	Phi-N	118	377	32	83	11	5	0	29	28	40	.220	.274	.276	57	-22	0			.963	5	3-83,S-32/2-1	-1.5
Total	3	243	742	56	158	22	6	2	53	61	83	.213	.275	.267	56	-42	1			.953	-4	S-114/3-89,2-19,1C	-3.9

■ JIMMY STEWART Stewart, James Franklin b: 6/11/39, Opelika, Ala. BB/TR, 6′, 165 lbs. Deb: 9/3/63

YEAR	TM/L	G	AB	R	H	2B	3B	HR	RBI	BB	SO	AVG	OBP	SLG	PRO+	BR/A	SB	CS	SBR	FA	FR	G/POS	TPR
1963	Chi-N	13	37	1	11	2	0	0	1	1	7	.297	.316	.351	87	-1	1	1	-0	.973	1	/S-9,2-1	0.0
1964	Chi-N	132	415	59	105	17	0	3	33	49	61	.253	.335	.316	81	-9	10	8	-2	.981	-7	2-61,S-45/O-4,3-1	-1.0
1965	Chi-N	116	282	26	63	9	4	0	19	30	53	.223	.303	.284	65	-12	13	3	2	.955	-11	O-55,S-48	-2.3
1966	Chi-N	57	90	4	16	4	1	0	4	7	12	.178	.253	.244	38	-7	1	1	-0	1.000	-1	O-15/2-4,S,2,3-2	-1.0
1967	Chi-N	6	6	1	1	0	0	0	1	0	0	.167	.167	.167	-4	-1	0	0	0	.000	0	H	-0.1
	Chi-A	24	18	5	3	0	0	0	1	1	6	.167	.211	.167	13	-2	1	0	0	1.000	-0	/O-6,2-5,S-2	-0.2
1969	Cin-N	119	221	26	56	3	4	4	24	19	33	.253	.310	.357	83	-5	4	2	0	.973	-9	O-66,2-18/3-6,S-1	-1.6
1970	*Cin-N	101	105	15	28	3	1	1	8	8	13	.267	.325	.343	79	-3	5	3	-0	1.000	-11	O-48,2-18/3-9,C1	-1.4
1971	Cin-N	80	82	7	19	2	2	0	9	9	12	.232	.308	.305	76	-3	3	1	0	1.000	-10	O-19/3-9,2-6	-1.3
1972	Hou-N	68	96	14	21	5	2	0	5	9	9	.219	.265	.313	65	-5	0	1	-1	1.000	-5	O-11/1-9,2-8,3-2	-1.2
1973	Hou-N	61	68	6	13	0	0	0	3	9	12	.191	.295	.191	37	-5	0	0	0	1.000	-1	/3-8,O-3,2-1	-1.3
Total	10	777	1420	164	336	45	14	8	112	139	218	.237	.308	.305	71	-53	38	20	-1	.969	-53	O-227,2-122,S/31C	-10.7

■ STUFFY STEWART Stewart, John Franklin b: 1/31/1894, Jasper, Fla. d: 12/30/80, Lake City, Fla. BR/TR, 5′9.5″, 160 lbs. Deb: 9/3/16

YEAR	TM/L	G	AB	R	H	2B	3B	HR	RBI	BB	SO	AVG	OBP	SLG	PRO+	BR/A	SB	CS	SBR	FA	FR	G/POS	TPR
1916	StL-N	9	17	0	3	0	0	0	0	0	3	.176	.176	.176	9	-2	0			.833	-2	/2-8	-0.4
1917	StL-N	13	9	4	0	0	0	0	0	0	4	.000	.000	.000	-99	-2	0			1.000	-3	/O-7,2-2	-0.5
1922	Pit-N	3	13	3	2	0	0	0	0	0	1	.154	.154	.154	-20	-2	0			.875	-1	/2-3	-0.3
1923	Bro-N	4	11	3	4	1	0	1	1	1	0	.364	.417	.727	202	2	0			.786	-1	/2-3	0.0
1925	Was-A	7	17	3	6	1	0	0	3	1	2	.353	.389	.412	105	0	1			.929	1	/3-5,2-1	0.1
1926	Was-A	62	63	27	17	6	1	0	9	6	6	.270	.333	.397	92	-1	8	4	0	.975	2	2-25/3-1	0.6
1927	Was-A	56	129	24	31	6	2	0	4	8	15	.240	.285	.318	57	-8	12	2	2	.939	1	2-37/3-2	-0.4
1929	Was-A	22	6	10	0	0	0	0	1	0	1	.000	.143	.000	-60	-1	0			1.000	2	/2-3	0.0
Total	8	176	265	74	63	14	3	1	18	17	32	.238	.284	.325	61	-15	21	7		.932	4	/2-82,3-8,O-7	-0.9

■ MARK STEWART Stewart, Mark "Big Slick" b: 10/11/1889, Whitlock, Tenn. d: 1/17/32, Memphis, Tenn. BL/TR, 6′1″, 180 lbs. Deb: 10/4/13

YEAR	TM/L	G	AB	R	H	2B	3B	HR	RBI	BB	SO	AVG	OBP	SLG	PRO+	BR/A	SB	CS	SBR	FA	FR	G/POS	TPR
1913	Cin-N	1	1	0	0	0	0	0	0	0	0	.000	.000	.000	-99	-0	0			.000	0	/C-1	0.0

■ SHANNON STEWART Stewart, Shannon Harold b: 2/25/74, Cincinnati, Ohio BR/TR, 6′, 175 lbs. Deb: 9/2/95

YEAR	TM/L	G	AB	R	H	2B	3B	HR	RBI	BB	SO	AVG	OBP	SLG	PRO+	BR/A	SB	CS	SBR	FA	FR	G/POS	TPR
1995	Tor-A	12	38	2	8	0	0	0	1	5	5	.211	.318	.211	41	-3	2	0	1	.955	-1	O-12	-0.4
1996	Tor-A	7	17	2	3	1	0	0	2	1	4	.176	.222	.235	16	-2	1	0	0	.800	-2	/O-6	-0.4
Total	2	19	55	4	11	1	0	0	3	6	9	.200	.290	.218	34	-5	3	0	1	.926	-4	/O-18	-0.8

■ NEB STEWART Stewart, Walter Nesbitt b: 5/21/18, S.Charleston, Ohio d: 6/8/90, London, Ohio BR/TR, 6′1″, 195 lbs. Deb: 9/8/40

YEAR	TM/L	G	AB	R	H	2B	3B	HR	RBI	BB	SO	AVG	OBP	SLG	PRO+	BR/A	SB	CS	SBR	FA	FR	G/POS	TPR
1940	Phi-N	10	31	3	4	0	0	0	1	1	5	.129	.156	.129	-21	-5	0			.944	0	/O-9	-0.5

■ BILL STEWART Stewart, William Wayne b: 4/15/28, Bay City, Mich. BR/TR, 5′11″, 200 lbs. Deb: 4/17/55

YEAR	TM/L	G	AB	R	H	2B	3B	HR	RBI	BB	SO	AVG	OBP	SLG	PRO+	BR/A	SB	CS	SBR	FA	FR	G/POS	TPR
1955	KC-A	11	18	2	2	1	0	0	1	6		.111	.158	.167	-13	-3	0	0	0	1.000	-0	/O-6	-0.3

■ ROYLE STILLMAN Stillman, Royle Eldon b: 1/2/51, Santa Monica, Cal. BL/TL, 5′11″, 180 lbs. Deb: 6/22/75

YEAR	TM/L	G	AB	R	H	2B	3B	HR	RBI	BB	SO	AVG	OBP	SLG	PRO+	BR/A	SB	CS	SBR	FA	FR	G/POS	TPR
1975	Bal-A	13	14	1	6	0	0	0	1	1	3	.429	.467	.429	165	1	0	0	0	1.000	-0	/O-2	0.1
1976	Bal-A	20	22	0	2	0	0	0	1	3	4	.091	.200	.091	-14	-3	0	0	0	1.000	-0	/1-2,D-5	-0.3
1977	Chi-A	56	119	18	25	7	1	3	13	17	21	.210	.309	.361	82	-3	2	1	0	.977	-3	O-26,D-13/1-1	-0.7
Total	3	89	155	19	33	7	1	3	15	21	28	.213	.307	.329	77	-5	2	1	0	.978	-3	/O-28,D-18,1-3	-0.9

■ KURT STILLWELL Stillwell, Kurt Andrew b: 6/4/65, Glendale, Cal. BB/TR, 5′11″, 175 lbs. Deb: 4/13/86 F

YEAR	TM/L	G	AB	R	H	2B	3B	HR	RBI	BB	SO	AVG	OBP	SLG	PRO+	BR/A	SB	CS	SBR	FA	FR	G/POS	TPR
1986	Cin-N	104	279	31	64	6	1	0	26	30	47	.229	.309	.258	56	-16	6	2	1	.951	-2	S-80	-1.2
1987	Cin-N	131	395	54	102	20	7	4	33	32	50	.258	.317	.375	79	-12	4	6	-2	.914	-21	S-51,2-37,3-20	-3.1
1988	KC-A★	128	459	63	115	28	5	10	53	47	76	.251	.324	.399	100	0	6	5	-1	.976	-18	*S-124	-0.8
1989	KC-A	130	463	52	121	20	7	7	54	42	64	.261	.327	.380	99	-1	9	6	-1	.970	-32	*S-130	-2.4
1990	KC-A	144	506	60	126	35	4	3	51	39	60	.249	.308	.352	85	-10	0	2	-1	.957	-20	*S-141	-2.1
1991	KC-A	122	385	44	102	17	1	6	51	33	56	.265	.325	.361	89	-6	3	4	-2	.959	-25	*S-118	-2.4
1992	SD-N	114	379	35	86	15	3	2	24	26	58	.227	.278	.298	62	-19	4	1	1	.970	-14	*2-111	-3.3
1993	SD-N	57	121	9	26	4	0	1	11	11	22	.215	.286	.273	49	-9	4	3	-1	.921	-8	S-30/3-3	-1.2
	Cal-A	22	61	2	16	2	0	2	3	4	11	.262	.308	.361	76	-2	2	0	1	.952	-4	2-18/S-7	-0.5
1996	Tex-A	46	77	12	21	4	0	1	4	10	11	.273	.364	.364	79	-2	0	0	0	.964	-9	2-21/S-9,3-6,1-1,D	-0.9
Total	9	998	3125	362	779	151	30	34	310	274	455	.249	.313	.349	82	-76	38	29	-6	.958	-151	S-690,2-187/3D1	-17.9

■ RON STILLWELL Stillwell, Ronald Roy b: 12/3/39, Los Angeles, Cal. BR/TR, 5′11″, 165 lbs. Deb: 7/3/61 F

YEAR	TM/L	G	AB	R	H	2B	3B	HR	RBI	BB	SO	AVG	OBP	SLG	PRO+	BR/A	SB	CS	SBR	FA	FR	G/POS	TPR
1961	Was-A	8	16	3	2	1	0	0	1	1	4	.125	.176	.188	-3	-2	0	0	0	.929	-1	/S-5	-0.3
1962	Was-A	6	22	5	6	0	0	0	2	3	2	.273	.333	.273	66	-1	0	0	0	1.000	-2	/2-6,S-1	-0.3
Total	2	14	38	8	8	1	0	0	3	4	6	.211	.268	.237	37	-3	0	0	0	.929	-3	/2-6,S-6	-0.6

■ CRAIG STIMAC Stimac, Craig Steven b: 11/18/54, Oak Park, Ill. BR/TR, 6′2″, 185 lbs. Deb: 8/12/80

YEAR	TM/L	G	AB	R	H	2B	3B	HR	RBI	BB	SO	AVG	OBP	SLG	PRO+	BR/A	SB	CS	SBR	FA	FR	G/POS	TPR
1980	SD-N	20	50	5	11	2	0	0	7	1	6	.220	.235	.260	40	-4	0	0	0	.982	4	C-11/3-2	0.0
1981	SD-N	9	9	0	1	0	0	0	0	0	3	.111	.111	.111	-40	-2	0	0	0	.000	0	/H	-0.2
Total	2	29	59	5	12	2	0	0	7	1	9	.203	.217	.237	29	-4	0	0	0	.982	4	/C-11,3-2	-0.2

■ KELLY STINNETT Stinnett, Kelly Lee b: 2/14/70, Lawton, Okla. BR/TR, 5′11″, 195 lbs. Deb: 4/5/94

YEAR	TM/L	G	AB	R	H	2B	3B	HR	RBI	BB	SO	AVG	OBP	SLG	PRO+	BR/A	SB	CS	SBR	FA	FR	G/POS	TPR
1994	NY-N	47	150	20	38	6	2	2	14	11	28	.253	.325	.360	79	-4	2	0	1	.979	-5	C-44	-0.6
1995	NY-N	77	196	23	43	8	1	4	18	29	65	.219	.338	.332	80	-5	2	0	1	.983	1	C-67	0.1
1996	Mil-A	14	26	1	2	0	0	0	0	2	11	.077	.172	.077	-32	-5	0	0	0	.960	1	C-14/D-1	-0.3
Total	3	138	372	44	83	14	3	6	32	42	104	.223	.322	.325	71	-15	4	0	1	.980	-2	C-125/D-1	-0.8

■ BOB STINSON Stinson, Gorrell Robert b: 10/11/45, Elkin, N.C. BB/TR, 5′11.5″, 185 lbs. Deb: 9/23/69

YEAR	TM/L	G	AB	R	H	2B	3B	HR	RBI	BB	SO	AVG	OBP	SLG	PRO+	BR/A	SB	CS	SBR	FA	FR	G/POS	TPR
1969	LA-N	4	8	1	3	0	0	0	2	0	2	.375	.375	.375	119	0	0	1	-1	.952	1	/C-4	0.0
1970	LA-N	4	3	1	0	0	0	0	0	0	1	.000	.000	.000	-99	-1	0	0	0	1.000	-0	/C-3	-0.1
1971	StL-N	17	19	3	4	1	0	0	1	0	7	.211	.250	.263	44	-1	0	0	0	.971	2	/C-6,O-3	0.1
1972	Hou-N	27	35	3	6	1	0	0	2	1	6	.171	.216	.200	19	-2	0	0	0	.964	-4	C-12/O-3	-0.9
1973	Mon-N	48	111	12	29	6	1	3	12	17	15	.261	.374	.414	114	3	0	1	-1	.979	-3	C-35/3-1	-0.0
1974	Mon-N	38	87	4	15	2	0	1	6	15	16	.172	.294	.230	45	-6	1	0	0	.979	1	C-29	-0.9
1975	KC-A	63	147	18	39	9	1	1	9	18	29	.265	.349	.361	98	0	1	0	0	.993	7	C-59/1-1,2-1,O-1,D	1.0
1976	*KC-A	79	209	26	55	7	1	2	25	25	29	.263	.345	.335	99	0	3	0	0	.979	-6	C-79	-0.4
1977	Sea-A	105	297	27	80	11	1	8	32	37	50	.269	.362	.394	107	4	0	3	-2	.984	-7	C-99/D-1	-0.2
1978	Sea-A	124	364	46	94	14	3	11	55	45	42	.258	.349	.404	112	6	2	1	0	.987	-18	*C-123/D-1	-0.9
1979	Sea-A	95	247	19	60	8	0	6	28	33	38	.243	.342	.348	85	-4	1	2	-1	.978	-7	C-91	-0.9
1980	Sea-A	48	107	6	23	2	0	1	8	15	19	.215	.282	.262	50	-7	0	3	-2	.979	-9	C-45	-0.9
Total	12	652	1634	166	408	61	7	33	180	201	254	.250	.340	.356	93	-10	8	10	-6	.984	-44	C-585/O-7,D-3,213	-4.3

■ GAT STIRES Stires, Garrett b: 10/13/1849, Hunterdon Co., N.J. d: 6/13/33, Byron, Ill. BL/TR, 5′8″, 180 lbs. Deb: 5/6/1871

YEAR	TM/L	G	AB	R	H	2B	3B	HR	RBI	BB	SO	AVG	OBP	SLG	PRO+	BR/A	SB	CS	SBR	FA	FR	G/POS	TPR
1871	Rok-n	25	110	23	30	4	6	2	24	7	5	.273	.316	.473	129	5	3	0	1	.837	1	*O-25	0.5

YEAR	TM/L	G	AB	R	H	2B	3B	HR	RBI	BB	SO	AVG	OBP	SLG	PRO+	BR/A	SB	CS	SBR	FA	FR	G/POS	TPR

■ SNUFFY STIRNWEISS Stirnweiss, George Henry b: 10/26/18, New York, N.Y. d: 9/15/58, Newark Bay, N.J. BR/TR, 5'8.5", 175 lbs. Deb: 4/22/43

1943	*NY-A	83	274	34	60	8	4	1	25	47	37	.219	.333	.288	82	-5	11	9	-2	.938	-6	S-68/2-4	-0.9
1944	NY-A	154	643	**125**	**205**	35	**16**	8	43	73	87	.319	.389	.460	137	32	**55**	11	**10**	**.982**	19	*2-154	7.1
1945	NY-A†	152	632	**107**	**195**	32	**22**	10	64	78	62	**.309**	.385	**.476**	143	34	33	17	-0	.970	26	*2-152	**7.2**
1946	NY-A★	129	487	75	122	19	7	0	37	66	58	.251	.340	.318	83	-9	18	6	**2**	.991	-6	3-79,2-46/S-4	-0.9
1947	*NY-A	148	571	102	146	18	5	5	41	89	47	.256	.358	.342	96	-1	5	3	-0	.983	-11	*2-148	-0.1
1948	NY-A	141	515	90	130	20	7	3	32	86	62	.252	.360	.336	87	-8	5	4	-1	**.993**	-11	*2-141	-1.1
1949	*NY-A	70	157	29	41	8	2	0	11	29	20	.261	.360	.338	90	-1	3	2	-0	.974	4	2-51/3-4	0.4
1950	NY-A	7	2	0	0	0	0	0	0	0	0	.000	.000	.000	-99	-1	0	0	0	1.000	1	/2-4	0.0
	StL-A	93	326	32	71	16	2	1	24	51	49	.218	.324	.288	56	-21	3	3	-1	.975	-24	2-62,3-31/S-5	-4.2
	Yr	100	328	32	71	16	2	1	24	51	49	.216	.322	.287	55	-22	3	3	-1	.975	-23	2-66,3-31/S-5	-4.2
1951	Cle-A	50	88	10	19	1	0	1	4	22	25	.216	.373	.261	78	-2	1	0	0	.992	7	2-25/3-2	0.7
1952	Cle-A	1	0	0	0	0	0	0	0	0	0	—	—	—	—	0	0	0	0	.000	0	/3-1	0.0
Total	10	1028	3695	604	989	157	68	29	281	541	447	.268	.362	.371	102	19	134	55	7	.980	-1	2-787,3-117/S-77	8.2

■ JACK STIVETTS Stivetts, John Elmer "Happy Jack" b: 3/31/1868, Ashland, Pa. d: 4/18/30, Ashland, Pa. BR/TR, 6'2", 185 lbs. Deb: 6/26/1889

1889	StL-a	27	79	12	18	2	2	0	7	3	13	.228	.265	.304	55	-5	0			.896	-1	P-26/O-1	-0.1
1890	StL-a	67	226	36	65	15	6	7	43	16		.288	.337	.500	128	4	2			.894	4	P-54,O-10/1-3	0.1
1891	StL-a	85	302	45	92	10	2	7	54	10	32	.305	.331	.421	100	-4	4			.898	3	P-64,O-24	-0.2
1892	*Bos-N	71	240	40	71	14	2	3	36	27	28	.296	.369	.408	124	6	8			.904	-0	P-54,O-18/1-1	0.0
1893	Bos-N	50	172	32	51	5	6	3	25	12	14	.297	.342	.448	101	-1	0			.955	-4	P-38/O-8,3-3	-0.1
1894	Bos-N	68	244	55	80	12	7	8	64	16	21	.328	.369	.533	107	0	3			.943	-4	P-45,O-16/1-4	-0.1
1895	Bos-N	46	158	20	30	6	4	0	24	6	18	.190	.228	.278	26	-19	1			.961	-1	P-38/1-5,O-2	-0.3
1896	Bos-N	67	221	42	76	9	6	3	49	12	10	.344	.380	.480	119	5	4			.946	-6	P-42,O-12/1-5,3-1	-0.2
1897	*Bos-N	61	199	41	73	9	9	2	37	15		.367	.417	.533	141	11	2			.926	-3	O-29,P-18/2-2,1-2	0.1
1898	Bos-N	41	111	16	28	1	1	2	16	10		.252	.314	.333	81	-3	1			.909	-5	O-14,1-10/S-4,2P	-0.8
1899	Cle-N	18	39	8	8	1	1	0	2	6		.205	.326	.282	73	-1	0			1.000	1	/O-7,P-7,S-1,3-1	-0.2
Total	11	601	1991	347	592	84	46	35	357	133	136	.297	.344	.438	104	-7	31			.924	-17	P-388,O-141/1S32	-1.9

■ MILT STOCK Stock, Milton Joseph b: 7/11/1893, Chicago, Ill. d: 7/16/77, Fairhope, Ala. BR/TR, 5'8", 154 lbs. Deb: 9/29/13 C

1913	NY-N	7	17	2	3	1	0	0	1	2	1	.176	.263	.235	43	-1	2			.838	2	/S-7	0.1
1914	NY-N	115	365	52	96	17	1	3	41	34	21	.263	.333	.340	103	2	11			.939	15	*3-113/S-1	2.2
1915	*Phi-N	69	227	37	59	7	3	1	15	22	26	.260	.325	.330	98	-0	6	2	1	.971	2	3-55/S-4	0.5
1916	Phi-N	132	509	61	143	25	6	1	43	27	33	.281	.320	.360	105	2	21	26	-9	.955	-6	*3-117,S-15	-1.0
1917	Phi-N	150	564	76	149	27	6	3	53	51	34	.264	.326	.349	103	2	25			.942	-9	*3-133,S-19	-0.4
1918	Phi-N	123	481	62	132	14	1	1	42	35	22	.274	.325	.314	89	-6	20			.946	-5	*3-123	-0.9
1919	StL-N	135	492	56	151	16	4	0	52	49	21	.307	.371	.356	127	17	17			.966	17	2-77,3-58	4.3
1920	StL-N	155	639	85	204	28	6	0	76	40	27	.319	.360	.382	117	14	15	17	-6	.939	-8	3-155	0.9
1921	StL-N	149	587	85	180	27	4	3	84	48	26	.307	.360	.388	100	1	11	3	2	.940	-22	*3-149	-0.9
1922	StL-N	151	581	85	177	33	9	5	79	42	29	.305	.352	.418	103	1	7	12	-5	.950	-9	*3-149/S-1	-0.1
1923	StL-N	151	603	63	174	33	2	2	96	40	21	.289	.334	.363	86	-13	9	6	-1	.955	-14	*3-150/2-1	-1.4
1924	Bro-N	142	561	66	136	14	4	2	52	26	32	.242	.277	.292	54	-36	3	8	-4	.931	-23	*3-142	-5.2
1925	Bro-N	146	616	98	202	28	9	1	62	38	28	.328	.368	.408	101	1	8	1	2	.978	5	*2-141/3-5	0.6
1926	Bro-N	3	8	0	0	0	0	0	0	1	0	.000	.111	.000	-69	-2	0			.923	-1	/2-3	-0.2
Total	14	1628	6249	839	1806	270	58	22	696	455	321	.289	.339	.361	98	-17	155	75		.945	-59	*3-1349,2-222/S-47	-1.5

■ KEVIN STOCKER Stocker, Kevin Douglas b: 2/13/70, Spokane, Wash. BB/TR, 6'1", 175 lbs. Deb: 7/7/93

1993	*Phi-N	70	259	46	84	12	3	2	31	30	43	.324	.411	.417	124	11	5	0	2	.958	-5	S-70	1.7
1994	Phi-N	82	271	38	74	11	2	2	28	44	41	.273	.388	.351	92	-1	2	2	-1	.959	-2	S-82	0.4
1995	Phi-N	125	412	42	90	14	3	1	32	43	75	.218	.306	.274	54	-26	6	1	1	.969	8	*S-125	-0.6
1996	Phi-N	119	394	46	100	22	6	5	41	43	89	.254	.339	.378	87	-7	6	4	-1	.975	5	*S-119	0.8
Total	4	396	1336	172	348	59	14	10	132	160	248	.260	.353	.348	85	-24	19	7	2	.967	10	S-396	2.3

■ LEN STOCKWELL Stockwell, Leonard Clark b: 8/25/1859, Cordova, Ill. d: 1/28/05, Niles, Cal. BR/TR, 5'11", 165 lbs. Deb: 5/17/1879

1879	Cle-N	2	6	0	0	0	0	0	0	0	2	.000	.000	.000	-99	-1				1.000	1	/O-2	0.0
1884	Lou-a	2	9	0	1	0	0	0	0	0	0	.111	.111	.111	-29	-1				.667	-1	/O-2,C-1	-0.2
1890	Cle-N	2	7	2	2	1	0	0	0	0		.286	.286	.429	110	0	0			1.000	0	/O-1,1-1	0.0
Total	3	6	22	2	3	1	0	0	0	0	5	.136	.136	.182	-1	-2	0			.900	1	/O-5,1-1,C-1	-0.2

■ STODDARD Stoddard Deb: 9/25/1875

| 1875 | Atl-n | 2 | 9 | 1 | 1 | 1 | 0 | 0 | 0 | 0 | 1 | .111 | .111 | .222 | 15 | -1 | 0 | 0 | 0 | .800 | -0 | /O-2 | -0.1 |

■ AL STOKES Stokes, Albert John (b: Albert John Stocek) b: 1/1/1900, Chicago, Ill. d: 12/19/86, Grantham, N.H. BR/TR, 5'9", 175 lbs. Deb: 5/10/25

1925	Bos-A	17	52	7	11	0	1	0	1	4	8	.212	.268	.250	32	-5	0	0	0	.969	3	C-17	-0.2
1926	Bos-A	30	86	7	14	3	3	0	6	8	28	.163	.234	.267	32	-9	0	0	0	.931	-4	C-29	-1.1
Total	2	47	138	14	25	3	4	0	7	12	36	.181	.247	.261	32	-15	0	0	0	.946	-1	/C-46	-1.3

■ GENE STONE Stone, Eugene Daniel b: 1/16/44, Burbank, Cal. BL/TL, 5'11", 190 lbs. Deb: 5/13/69

| 1969 | Phi-N | 18 | 28 | 4 | 6 | 0 | 1 | 0 | 4 | 9 | | .214 | .313 | .286 | 70 | -1 | 0 | 0 | 0 | 1.000 | -1 | /1-5 | -0.2 |

■ GEORGE STONE Stone, George Robert b: 9/3/1877, Lost Nation, Iowa d: 1/3/45, Clinton, Iowa BL/TL, 5'9", 175 lbs. Deb: 4/20/03

1903	Bos-A	2	2	0	0	0	0	0	0	0	0	.000	.000	.000	-95	-0	0			.000	0	H	0.0
1905	StL-A	154	632	76	**187**	25	13	7	52	44		.296	.347	.410	147	32	26			.954	2	*O-154	2.9
1906	StL-A	154	581	91	208	25	20	6	71	52		**.358**	**.417**	**.501**	195	63	35			.968	-1	*O-154	5.9
1907	StL-A	155	596	77	191	13	11	4	59	59		.320	.387	.399	151	36	23			.970	-3	*O-155	2.9
1908	StL-A	148	588	89	165	21	8	5	31	55		.281	.345	.369	131	21	20			.947	-0	*O-148	1.6
1909	StL-A	83	310	33	89	5	4	1	15	24		.287	.340	.339	123	8	8			.928	-3	O-81	0.7
1910	StL-A	152	562	60	144	17	12	0	40	48		.256	.315	.329	108	5	20			.972	-2	*O-145	-0.5
Total	7	848	3271	426	984	106	68	23	268	282		.301	.360	.396	145	164	132			.958	-3	O-837	13.5

■ RON STONE Stone, Harry Ronald b: 9/9/42, Corning, Cal. BL/TL, 6'2", 195 lbs. Deb: 4/13/66

1966	KC-A	26	22	2	6	1	0	0	0	2	2	.273	.273	.318	71	-1	1	1	-0	1.000	-1	/O-4,1-3	-0.3
1969	Phi-N	103	222	22	53	7	1	1	24	29	28	.239	.335	.293	79	-5	3	1	0	.978	-3	O-69	-1.2
1970	Phi-N	123	321	30	84	12	5	3	39	38	45	.262	.342	.358	90	-4	5	6	-2	.968	-3	O-99/1-6	-1.4
1971	Phi-N	95	185	16	42	8	1	3	25	25	36	.227	.319	.314	80	-4	2	2	-1	.964	-4	O-51/1-3	-1.2
1972	Phi-N	41	54	3	9	0	1	0	3	9	11	.167	.286	.204	40	-4	0	0	0	1.000	1	O-15	-0.4
Total	5	388	804	73	194	28	8	6	89	101	122	.241	.329	.318	81	-18	11	10	-3	.973	-11	O-238/1-12	-4.5

■ JEFF STONE Stone, Jeffrey Glen b: 12/26/60, Kennett, Mo. BL/TR, 6', 175 lbs. Deb: 9/9/83

1983	Phi-N	9	4	2	3	0	2	0	3	0	1	.750	.750	1.750	580	2	4	0	1	.000	-0	/O-1	0.3
1984	Phi-N	51	185	27	67	4	6	1	15	9	26	.362	.398	.465	139	10	27	5	5	.916	-2	O-46	1.1
1985	Phi-N	88	264	36	70	4	3	1	11	15	50	.265	.307	.337	78	-8	15	5	2	.966	-6	O-69	-1.5
1986	Phi-N	82	249	32	69	6	4	6	19	20	52	.277	.341	.406	101	0	19	6	2	.982	2	O-58	0.3
1987	Phi-N	66	125	19	32	7	1	1	16	8	38	.256	.316	.352	74	-5	3	1	1	1.000	-1	O-25	-0.6
1988	Bal-A	26	61	4	10	1	0	0	1	4	11	.164	.215	.180	12	-7	4	1	1	.963	-2	O-21/D-1	-0.9
1989	Tex-A	22	36	5	6	1	2	0	5	3	5	.167	.250	.306	55	-2	0	1	0			D-15/O-3	-0.4
	Bos-A	18	15	3	3	0	0	0	1	1	2	.200	.250	.200	27	-1	1	0	0	1.000	-3	O-11/D-3	-0.5
	Yr	40	51	8	9	1	2	0	6	4	7	.176	.250	.275	46	-4	1	1	0	1.000	-5	D-18,O-14	-0.9
1990	Bos-A	10	2	1	1	0	0	0	0	1	0	.500	.500	.500	173	-0	0	1	-1	.000	-0	/D-2	-0.2
Total	8	372	941	129	261	23	18	11	72	60	186	.277	.328	.375	75	-10	55	20	11	.963	-14	O-234/D-21	-2.2

YEAR	TM/L	G	AB	R	H	2B	3B	HR	RBI	BB	SO	AVG	OBP	SLG	PRO+	BR/A	SB	CS	SBR	FA	FR	G/POS	TPR

■ JOHN STONE   Stone, John Thomas "Rocky"   b: 10/10/05, Lynchburg, Tenn.   d: 11/30/55, Shelbyville, Tenn.   BL/TR, 6'1", 178 lbs.   Deb: 8/31/28

1928	Det-A	26	113	20	40	10	3	2	21	5	8	.354	.387	.549	141	6	1	0	0	.962	-1	O-26	0.3
1929	Det-A	51	150	23	39	11	2	2	15	11	13	.260	.311	.400	81	-5	1	1	0	.986	-1	O-36	-0.8
1930	Det-A	127	425	60	132	29	11	3	56	32	49	.311	.360	.452	102	1	6	9	-4	.966	0	*O-109	-0.9
1931	Det-A	147	584	86	191	28	11	10	76	56	48	.327	.388	.464	119	16	13	13	-4	.959	4	*O-147	0.6
1932	Det-A	145	582	106	173	35	12	17	108	58	64	.297	.361	.486	113	10	2	1	0	.961	3	*O-142	0.3
1933	Det-A	148	574	86	161	33	11	11	80	54	37	.280	.344	.434	103	1	1	4	-2	.970	1	*O-141	-0.7
1934	Was-A	113	419	77	132	28	7	7	67	52	26	.315	.395	.465	126	17	1	2	-1	.966	7	*O-112	1.7
1935	Was-A	125	455	78	143	27	18	1	78	39	29	.314	.372	.459	118	11	4	5	-2	.955	5	*O-114	0.5
1936	Was-A	123	437	95	149	22	11	15	90	60	26	.341	.421	.545	145	31	8	0	2	.967	7	*O-114	3.1
1937	Was-A	139	542	84	179	33	15	6	88	66	36	.330	.401	.480	127	23	6	4	-1	.984	7	*O-137	2.2
1938	Was-A	56	213	24	52	12	4	3	28	30	16	.244	.337	.380	85	-5	2	1	0	.974	-2	O-53	-0.8
Total	11	1200	4494	739	1391	268	105	77	707	463	352	.310	.376	.467	116	106	45	40	-10	.967	24	*O-1131	5.5

■ TIGE STONE   Stone, William Arthur   b: 9/18/01, Macon, Ga.   d: 1/1/60, Jacksonville, Fla.   BR/TR, 5'8", 145 lbs.   Deb: 8/23/23

| 1923 | StL-N | 5 | 1 | 0 | 1 | 0 | 0 | 0 | 0 | 2 | 0 | 1.000 | 1.000 | 1.000 | 438 | 1 | 0 | 0 | 0 | .000 | -2 | /O-4,P-1 | -0.2 |

■ JOHN STONEHAM   Stoneham, John Andrew   b: 11/8/08, Wood River, Ill.   BL/TR, 5'9.5", 168 lbs.   Deb: 9/18/33

| 1933 | Chi-A | 10 | 25 | 4 | 3 | 0 | 0 | 1 | 3 | 2 | 2 | .120 | .185 | .240 | 12 | -3 | 0 | 0 | 0 | 1.000 | -2 | /O-9 | -0.5 |

■ HOWIE STORIE   Storie, Howard Edward "Sponge"   b: 5/15/11, Pittsfield, Mass.   d: 7/27/68, Pittsfield, Mass.   BR/TR, 5'10", 175 lbs.   Deb: 9/7/31

1931	Bos-A	6	17	2	2	0	0	0	0	3	2	.118	.250	.118	-1	-2	0	0	0	1.000	0	/C-6	-0.2
1932	Bos-A	6	8	0	3	0	0	0	0	0	0	.375	.375	.375	98	-0	0	0	0	1.000	0	/C-5	0.0
Total	2	12	25	2	5	0	0	0	0	3	2	.200	.286	.200	31	-2	0	0	0	1.000	1	/C-11	-0.2

■ ALAN STORKE   Storke, Alan Marshall   b: 9/27/1884, Auburn, N.Y.   d: 3/18/10, Newton, Mass.   BR/TR, 6'1",   Deb: 9/24/06

1906	Pit-N	5	12	1	3	1	0	0	1	1		.250	.308	.333	96	-0	1			1.000	0	/3-2,S-1	
1907	Pit-N	112	357	24	92	6	6	1	39	16		.258	.295	.317	90	-5	6			.925	-13	3-67,1-23/2-7,S-5	-1.8
1908	Pit-N	64	202	20	51	5	3	1	12	9		.252	.284	.322	93	-2	4			.988	-6	1-49/3-6,2-1	-1.0
1909	Pit-N	37	118	12	30	5	2	0	12	7		.254	.302	.331	89	-2	1			.994	-0	1-18,3-14	-0.2
	StL-N	48	174	11	49	5	0	0	10	12		.282	.328	.310	105	1	5			.958	-1	S-44/2-4,1-1	-0.2
	Yr	85	292	23	79	10	2	0	22	19		.271	.317	.318	97	-1	6			.958	-2	S-44,1-19,3-14/2-4	-0.2
Total	4	266	863	68	225	22	11	2	74	45		.261	.300	.319	94	-8	17			.990	-20	/1-91,3-89,S-50,2	-3.0

■ LIN STORTI   Storti, Lindo Ivan   b: 12/5/06, Santa Monica, Cal.   d: 7/24/82, Ontario, Cal.   BB/TR, 5'11", 165 lbs.   Deb: 9/18/30

1930	StL-A	7	28	6	9	1	1	0	2	6		.321	.367	.429	98	-0	0	0	0	.975	1	/2-6	0.1
1931	StL-A	86	273	32	60	15	4	3	26	15	50	.220	.263	.337	55	-19	0	2	-1	.926	9	3-67/2-7	-0.7
1932	StL-A	53	193	19	50	11	2	3	26	5	20	.259	.278	.383	66	-10	1	0	0	.956	-4	3-51	-1.0
1933	StL-A	70	210	26	41	7	4	3	21	25	31	.195	.281	.310	53	-15	2	2	-1	.934	-2	3-32,2-24	-1.4
Total	4	216	704	83	160	34	11	9	75	47	107	.227	.277	.345	59	-44	3	4	-2	.936	4	3-150/2-37	-3.0

■ TOM STOUCH   Stouch, Thomas Carl   b: 12/2/1870, Perrysville, Ohio   d: 10/7/56, Lancaster, Pa.   BR/TR, 6'2", 165 lbs.   Deb: 7/7/1898

| 1898 | Lou-N | 4 | 16 | 4 | 5 | 1 | 0 | 0 | 6 | 1 | | .313 | .353 | .375 | 110 | 0 | 0 | | | .850 | -2 | /2-4 | -0.2 |

■ GEORGE STOVALL   Stovall, George Thomas "Firebrand"   b: 11/23/1878, Leeds, Mo.   d: 11/5/51, Burlington, Iowa   BR/TR, 6'2", 180 lbs.   Deb: 7/4/04   FM

1904	Cle-A	52	181	18	54	10	1	1	31	2		.298	.317	.381	121	4	3			.978	-2	1-38/2-9,0-3,3-1	0.1
1905	Cle-A	112	423	41	115	31	1	1	47	13		.272	.295	.357	105	1	13			.973	-5	1-60,2-46/O-4	-0.7
1906	Cle-A	116	443	54	121	19	5	0	37	8		.273	.288	.339	97	-3	15			.985	-5	1-55,3-30,2-19	-1.0
1907	Cle-A	124	466	38	110	17	6	1	36	18		.236	.267	.305	82	-11	13			.983	-4	*1-122/3-2	-2.0
1908	Cle-A	138	534	71	156	29	6	2	45	17		.292	.316	.380	126	13	14			**.990**	3	*1-132/O-5,S-1	1.5
1909	Cle-A	145	565	60	139	17	10	0	49	6		.246	.259	.322	80	-15	25			**.988**	10	*1-145	-0.8
1910	Cle-A	142	521	49	136	19	4	0	52	14		.261	.284	.313	86	-10	16			**.988**	7	*1-132/2-2	-0.4
1911	Cle-A	126	458	48	124	17	7	0	79	21		.271	.306	.338	79	-14	11			**.986**	7	*1-118/2-2,M	-0.8
1912	StL-A	116	398	35	101	17	5	0	45	14		.254	.286	.322	76	-14	11			.983	5	1-94,M	-1.0
1913	StL-A	89	303	34	87	14	3	1	24	7	23	.287	.305	.363	98	-3	7			.988	8	1-76,M	0.4
1914	KC-F	124	450	51	128	20	5	7	75	23	35	.284	.323	.398	100	-9	6			.989	-1	*1-116/3-1,M	-0.8
1915	KC-F	130	480	48	111	21	3	0	44	29	36	.231	.283	.287	63	-32	8			.987	5	*1-129,M	-3.3
Total	12	1414	5222	547	1382	231	56	15	564	172	94	.265	.292	.339	91	-93	142			.986	32	*1-1217/2-78,3OS	-8.8

■ HARRY STOVEY   Stovey, Harry Duffield (b: Harry Duffield Stowe)   b: 12/20/1856, Philadelphia, Pa.   d: 9/20/37, New Bedford, Mass   BR/TR, 5'11.5", 175 lbs.   Deb: 5/1/1880   M

1880	Wor-N	83	355	76	94	21	**14**	6	28	12	46	.265	.289	.454	136	11				.860	-5	O-46,1-37/P-2	0.2
1881	Wor-N	75	341	57	92	25	7	2	30	12	23	.270	.295	.402	111	3				.955	-5	*1-57,O-18,M	-0.7
1882	Wor-N	84	360	90	104	13	10	5	26	22	34	.289	.330	.422	136	14				.956	4	1-43,O-41	-0.2
1883	Phi-a	94	421	**110**	128	**31**	6	**14**	66	27		.304	.346	**.506**	158	25				**.965**	0	*1-93/O-3,P-1	1.4
1884	Phi-a	104	448	**124**	146	22	**23**	10	83	26		.326	.368	.545	182	38				.960	-1	*1-104	2.3
1885	Phi-a	112	486	**130**	153	27	9	**13**	75	39		.315	.371	.488	160	31				.967	4	*1-82,O-30,M	2.2
1886	Phi-a	123	489	115	144	28	11	7	59	64		.294	.377	.440	154	31	**68**			.870	3	O-63,1-62/P-1	2.2
1887	Phi-a	124	497	125	142	31	12	4	77	56		.286	.366	.421	119	13	74			.902	5	O-80,1-46	1.5
1888	Phi-a	130	530	127	152	25	**20**	9	65	62		.287	.365	.460	165	**39**	87			.943	4	*O-118,1-13	3.5
1889	Phi-a	137	556	**152**	171	38	13	**19**	119	77	68	.308	.393	**.525**	162	45	63			.897	18	*O-137/1-1	**4.9**
1890	Bos-P	118	481	142	144	25	11	12	84	81	38	.299	.406	.472	126	17	**97**			.921	2	*O-117/1-1	1.2
1891	Bos-N	134	544	118	152	31	**20**	**16**	95	79	69	.279	.373	**.498**	137	21	57			.910	9	*O-134/1-1	2.2
1892	Bos-N	38	146	21	24	8	1	0	12	14	19	.164	.252	.233	43	-11	20			.901	0	O-38	-1.1
	Bal-N	74	283	58	77	14	11	4	55	40	32	.272	.364	.442	140	13	20			.913	3	O-64,1-10	0.6
	Yr	112	429	79	101	22	12	4	67	54	51	.235	.326	.371	106	2	40			.908	-3	*O-102,1-10	-0.5
1893	Bal-N	8	26	4	4	2	0	0	5	8	3	.154	.353	.231	55	-1	1			.864	0	/O-7	-0.1
	Bro-N	48	175	43	44	6	6	1	29	44	11	.251	.402	.371	111	9	22			.901	-3	O-48	0.0
	Yr	56	201	47	48	8	6	1	34	52	14	.239	.395	.353	103	4	23			.895	-2	O-55	-0.1
Total	14	1486	6138	1492	1771	347	174	122	908	663	343	.289	.361	.461	142	294	509			.896	40	O-944,1-550/P-4	21.5

■ RAY STOVIAK   Stoviak, Raymond Thomas   b: 6/6/15, Scottdale, Pa.   BL/TL, 6'1", 195 lbs.   Deb: 6/5/38

| 1938 | Phi-N | 10 | 10 | 1 | 0 | 0 | 0 | 0 | 0 | 0 | 3 | .000 | .000 | .000 | -99 | -3 | 0 | | | 1.000 | -1 | /O-4 | -0.4 |

■ JOE STRAIN   Strain, Joseph Allan   b: 4/30/54, Denver, Colo.   BR/TR, 5'10", 169 lbs.   Deb: 6/28/79

1979	SF-N	67	257	27	62	8	1	1	12	13	21	.241	.286	.292	62	-14	8	4	0	.982	-1	2-67/3-1	-1.1
1980	SF-N	77	189	26	54	6	0	0	16	10	10	.286	.322	.317	81	-5	1	2	-1	.989	-11	2-42/3-6,S-1	-1.5
1981	Chi-N	25	74	7	14	1	0	0	1	5	7	.189	.250	.203	28	-7	0	0	0	.975	7	2-20	0.2
Total	3	169	520	60	130	15	1	1	29	28	38	.250	.293	.288	64	-25	9	6	-1	.983	-5	2-129/3-7,S-1	-2.4

■ PAUL STRAND   Strand, Paul Edward   b: 12/19/1893, Carbonado, Wash.   d: 7/2/74, Salt Lake City, Utah   BL/TL, 6'0.5", 190 lbs.   Deb: 5/15/13

1913	Bos-N	7	6	0	1	0	0	0	0	0	0	.167	.167	.167	-5	-1	0			.875	-1	/P-7	0.0
1914	Bos-N	18	24	2	8	2	0	0	3	0	2	.333	.333	.417	123	1	0			.813	-0	P-16	0.0
1915	Bos-N	24	22	3	2	0	0	0	2	0	4	.091	.091	.091	-47	-4	0			.750	-1	/P-6,O-5	-0.2
1924	Phi-A	47	167	15	38	9	4	0	13	4	9	.228	.254	.329	49	-13	3	3	3	.988	-6	O-44	-2.2
Total	4	96	219	20	49	11	4	0	18	4	15	.224	.244	.311	47	-18	3			.989	-7	/O-49,P-29	-2.4

■ LARRY STRANDS   Strands, John Lawrence   b: 12/5/1885, Chicago, Ill.   d: 1/19/57, Forest Park, Ill.   BR/TR, 5'10.5", 165 lbs.   Deb: 4/25/15

| 1915 | New-F | 35 | 75 | 7 | 14 | 3 | 1 | 1 | 11 | 6 | 11 | .187 | .247 | .293 | 55 | -6 | 1 | | | .852 | -7 | 3-12/2-9,O-2 | -1.3 |

YEAR	TM/L	G	AB	R	H	2B	3B	HR	RBI	BB	SO	AVG	OBP	SLG	PRO+	BR/A	SB	CS	SBR	FA	FR	G/POS	TPR

■ SAMMY STRANG
Strang, Samuel Nicklin "The Dixie Thrush" (b: Samuel Strang Nicklin)
b: 12/16/1876, Chattanooga, Tenn.   d: 3/13/32, Chattanooga, Tenn.   BB/TR, 5'8", 160 lbs.   Deb: 7/10/1896

YEAR	TM/L	G	AB	R	H	2B	3B	HR	RBI	BB	SO	AVG	OBP	SLG	PRO+	BR/A	SB	CS	SBR	FA	FR	G/POS	TPR
1896	Lou-N	14	46	6	12	0	0	0	7	6	6	.261	.346	.261	64	-2	4			.803	-8	S-14	-0.8
1900	Chi-N	27	102	15	29	3	0	0	9	8	8	.284	.348	.314	86	-1	1			.887	-11	3-16/S-9,2-2	-1.1
1901	NY-N	135	493	55	139	14	6	1	34	59		.282	.364	.341	109	9	40			.877	2	3-91,2-37/O-5,S-4	1.2
1902	Chi-A	137	536	108	158	18	5	3	46	76		.295	.387	.364	114	14	38			.890	5	*3-137	1.9
	Chi-N	3	11	1	4	0	0	0	0	0		.364	.364	.364	128	0	1			1.000	-1	/2-2,3-2	0.0
1903	Bro-N	135	508	101	138	21	5	0	38	75		.272	.376	.333	106	8	46			.914	-7	*3-124/O-8,2-3	0.0
1904	Bro-N	77	271	28	52	11	0	1	9	45		.192	.316	.244	75	-6	16			.910	-32	2-63,3-12/S-1	-3.9
1905	*NY-N	111	294	51	76	9	4	3	29	58		.259	.389	.347	117	10	23			.915	-17	2-47,O-38/S-9,13	-0.9
1906	NY-N	113	313	50	100	16	4	4	49	54		.319	.423	.435	164	25	21			.944	3	2-57,O-39/S-4,31	3.0
1907	NY-N	123	306	56	77	20	4	0	30	60		.252	.388	.382	137	16	21			.947	-1	O-70,2-13/3-7,1S	1.4
1908	NY-N	28	53	8	5	0	0	0	2	23		.094	.385	.094	52	-1	5			.863	-3	2-14/O-5,S-3	-0.5
Total	10	903	2933	479	790	112	28	16	253	464	6	.269	.377	.343	113	72	216			.891	-70	3-393,2-238,O/S1	0.5

■ ALAN STRANGE
Strange, Alan Cochrane "Inky"   b: 11/7/06, Philadelphia, Pa.   d: 6/27/94, Seattle, Wash.   BR/TR, 5'9", 162 lbs.   Deb: 4/17/34

YEAR	TM/L	G	AB	R	H	2B	3B	HR	RBI	BB	SO	AVG	OBP	SLG	PRO+	BR/A	SB	CS	SBR	FA	FR	G/POS	TPR
1934	StL-A	127	430	39	100	17	2	1	45	48	28	.233	.310	.288	51	-31	3	1	0	.955	4	*S-125	-1.9
1935	StL-A	49	147	8	34	6	1	0	17	17	7	.231	.311	.286	53	-10	0	0	0	.960	5	S-49	-0.6
	Was-A	20	54	3	10	2	1	0	5	4	1	.185	.241	.259	30	-6	0	0	0	.974	3	S-16	-0.2
	Yr	69	201	11	44	8	2	0	22	21	8	.219	.293	.279	47	-16	0	0	0	.963	5	S-65	-0.8
1940	StL-A	54	167	26	31	8	3	0	6	22	12	.186	.284	.269	43	-14	2	1	0	.962	3	S-35/2-4	-0.7
1941	StL-A	45	112	14	26	4	0	0	11	15	5	.232	.323	.268	56	-7	1	0	0	.973	2	S-32/1-2,3-1	-0.3
1942	StL-A	19	37	3	10	2	0	0	5	3	1	.270	.325	.324	82	-1	0	1	-1	.935	5	3-10/S-3,2-1	0.3
Total	5	314	947	93	211	39	7	1	89	109	54	.223	.304	.282	50	-69	6	3	0	.959	18	S-260/3-11,2-5,1-2	-3.4

■ DOUG STRANGE
Strange, Joseph Douglas   b: 4/13/64, Greenville, S.C.   BB/TR, 6'2", 170 lbs.   Deb: 7/13/89

YEAR	TM/L	G	AB	R	H	2B	3B	HR	RBI	BB	SO	AVG	OBP	SLG	PRO+	BR/A	SB	CS	SBR	FA	FR	G/POS	TPR
1989	Det-A	64	196	16	42	4	1	1	14	17	36	.214	.280	.260	54	-12	3	3	-1	.878	1	3-54/2-9,S-9,D-1	-1.1
1991	Chi-N	3	9	0	4	1	0	0	1	0	1	.444	.500	.556	188	1	0	0	0	.800	-1	/3-3	0.0
1992	Chi-N	52	94	7	15	1	0	1	5	10	15	.160	.240	.202	26	-9	1	0	0	.900	-0	3-33,2-12	-1.0
1993	Tex-A	145	484	58	124	29	0	7	60	43	69	.256	.321	.360	86	-10	6	4	-1	.980	-9	*2-135/3-9,S-1	-1.5
1994	Tex-A	73	226	26	48	12	1	5	26	15	38	.212	.270	.341	56	-15	1	3	-2	.970	7	2-53,3-13/O-3	-0.7
1995	*Sea-A	74	155	19	42	9	2	2	21	10	25	.271	.323	.394	85	-4	0	3	-2	.948	5	3-41/2-5,O-4,D-1	0.1
1996	Sea-A	88	183	19	43	7	1	3	23	14	31	.235	.293	.333	58	-12	1	0	0	.961	-7	3-39,O-11,D-10/12	-1.8
Total	7	499	1347	145	318	63	5	19	150	109	215	.236	.299	.333	69	-60	13	13	-4	.978	-4	2-217,3-192/ODS1	-6.0

■ ASA STRATTON
Stratton, Asa Evans   b: 2/10/1853, Grafton, Mass.   d: 8/14/25, Fitchburg, Mass.   Deb: 6/17/1881

YEAR	TM/L	G	AB	R	H	2B	3B	HR	RBI	BB	SO	AVG	OBP	SLG	PRO+	BR/A	SB	CS	SBR	FA	FR	G/POS	TPR
1881	Wor-N	1	4	0	1	0	0	0	0	2		.250	.250	.250	55	-0				.333	-1	/S-1	-0.2

■ SCOTT STRATTON
Stratton, C. Scott   b: 10/2/1869, Campbellsburg, Ky.   d: 3/8/39, Louisville, Ky.   BL/TR, 6', 180 lbs.   Deb: 4/21/1888

YEAR	TM/L	G	AB	R	H	2B	3B	HR	RBI	BB	SO	AVG	OBP	SLG	PRO+	BR/A	SB	CS	SBR	FA	FR	G/POS	TPR
1888	Lou-a	67	249	35	64	8	1	1	29	12		.257	.310	.309	101	0	10			.821	-5	O-38,P-33	-0.5
1889	Lou-a	62	229	30	66	7	5	4	34	13	36	.288	.332	.415	114	3	10			.915	5	O-29,P-19,1-17	0.3
1890	*Lou-a	55	189	29	61	3	5	0	24	16		.323	.385	.392	132	8	8			.977	5	P-50/O-5	0.0
1891	Pit-N	2	8	1	1	0	0	0	0	0	3	.125	.125	.125	-28	-1	0			.900	1	/P-2	0.0
	Lou-a	34	115	9	27	2	0	0	8	11	13	.235	.307	.252	61	-6	8			.939	2	P-20/1-8,O-6	-0.3
1892	Lou-N	63	219	22	56	2	9	0	23	17	21	.256	.318	.347	110	2	9			.915	1	P-42,O-17/1-6	-0.1
1893	Lou-N	60	217	34	49	8	5	0	16	25	15	.226	.309	.309	70	-9	6			.975	0	P-37,O-24/1-1	-0.4
1894	Lou-N	13	37	9	12	1	2	0	4	2	2	.324	.390	.459	112	1	1			.929	2	/P-7,O-5	0.1
	Chi-N	23	96	29	36	5	4	3	23	6	1	.375	.417	.604	136	5	3			.933	-1	P-15/O-5,1-2	0.0
	Yr	36	133	38	48	6	6	3	27	10	3	.361	.410	.564	131	6	4			.932	1	P-22/O-10/1-2	0.1
1895	Chi-N	10	24	3	7	1	1	0	2	4		.292	.393	.417	102	0	1			.833	-1	/P-5,O-4	-0.1
Total	8	389	1383	201	379	37	32	8	163	108	93	.274	.335	.364	103	4	56			.938	15	P-230,O-133/1-34	-1.0

■ JOE STRAUB
Straub, Joseph   b: 1/19/1858, Germany   d: 2/13/29, Pueblo, Colo.   BR/TR, 5'10", 160 lbs.   Deb: 6/24/1880

YEAR	TM/L	G	AB	R	H	2B	3B	HR	RBI	BB	SO	AVG	OBP	SLG	PRO+	BR/A	SB	CS	SBR	FA	FR	G/POS	TPR
1880	Tro-N	3	12	1	3	0	0	0	3	1	3	.250	.308	.250	87	-0				.815	0	/C-3	0.0
1882	Phi-a	8	32	2	6	2	0	0	1	1		.188	.212	.250	50	-2				.830	-1	/C-7,O-1	-0.2
1883	Col-a	27	100	4	13	0	0	0		4		.130	.163	.130	-5	-11				.860	-3	C-14,1-12/O-1	-1.3
Total	3	38	144	7	22	2	0	0	4	6	3	.153	.187	.167	17	-13				.843	-4	/C-24,1-12,O-2	-1.5

■ JOE STRAUSS
Strauss, Joseph "Dutch" or "The Socker" (b: Joseph Strasser)
b: 11/16/1858, Cincinnati, Ohio   d: 6/24/06, Cincinnati, Ohio   BR/TR,   Deb: 7/27/1884

YEAR	TM/L	G	AB	R	H	2B	3B	HR	RBI	BB	SO	AVG	OBP	SLG	PRO+	BR/A	SB	CS	SBR	FA	FR	G/POS	TPR
1884	KC-U	16	60	4	12	3	0	0		1		.200	.213	.250	46	-6				.833	-1	O-10/C-3,2-2,3-1	-0.6
1885	Lou-a	2	6	0	1	0	0	0		0		.167	.167	.167	6	-1				.000	-2	/O-1,C-1	0.0
1886	Lou-a	74	297	36	64	5	6	1	31	8		.215	.239	.283	60	-15	25			.857	4	O-73/P-2,C-1	-1.1
	Bro-a	9	36	6	9	1	1	0	5	1		.250	.270	.333	88	-1	4			1.000	5	O-7,C-2	0.0
	Yr	83	333	42	73	6	7	1	36	9		.219	.242	.288	63	-16	29			.866	5	O-80/C-3,P-2	-1.1
Total	3	101	399	46	86	9	7	1	36	10		.216	.237	.281	59	-22	29			.861	2	/O-91,C-7,P-2,23	-1.9

■ DARRYL STRAWBERRY
Strawberry, Darryl Eugene   b: 3/12/62, Los Angeles, Cal.   BL/TL, 6'6", 190 lbs.   Deb: 5/6/83

YEAR	TM/L	G	AB	R	H	2B	3B	HR	RBI	BB	SO	AVG	OBP	SLG	PRO+	BR/A	SB	CS	SBR	FA	FR	G/POS	TPR
1983	NY-N	122	420	63	108	15	7	26	74	47	128	.257	.338	.512	134	17	19	6	2	.984	6	*O-117	2.3
1984	NY-N★	147	522	75	131	27	4	26	97	75	131	.251	.345	.467	128	19	27	8	3	.980	4	*O-146	2.3
1985	NY-N★	111	393	78	109	15	4	29	79	73	96	.277	.392	.557	167	36	26	11	1	.991	-4	*O-110	3.0
1986	*NY-N★	136	475	76	123	27	5	27	93	72	141	.259	.363	.507	142	27	28	12	1	.975	2	*O-131	2.7
1987	NY-N★	154	532	108	151	32	5	39	104	97	122	.284	.401	.583	165	51	36	12	4	.972	1	*O-151	5.0
1988	*NY-N★	153	543	101	146	27	3	**39**	101	85	127	.269	.371	**.545**	**168**	47	29	14	0	.971	7	*O-150	**5.2**
1989	NY-N†	134	476	69	107	26	1	29	77	61	105	.225	.314	.466	126	15	11	4	1	.972	9	*O-131	2.2
1990	NY-N★	152	542	92	150	18	1	37	108	70	110	.277	.361	.518	140	29	15	8	-0	.989	6	*O-149	3.2
1991	LA-N†	139	505	86	134	22	4	28	99	75	125	.265	.364	.491	141	28	10	8	-2	.978	-2	*O-136	2.1
1992	LA-N	43	156	20	37	8	0	5	25	19	34	.237	.324	.385	101	2	3	1	0	.986	-1	O-42	-0.1
1993	LA-N	32	100	12	14	2	0	5	12	16	19	.140	.271	.310	59	-6	1	0	0	.905	-4	O-29	-1.1
1994	SF-N	29	92	13	22	3	1	4	17	19	22	.239	.369	.424	111	2	0	3	-2	.969	-2	O-27	0.1
1995	*NY-A	32	87	15	24	4	1	3	13	10	22	.276	.364	.448	111	1	0	0	0	.909	1	D-15,O-11	0.1
1996	*NY-A	63	202	35	53	13	0	11	36	31	55	.262	.360	.490	111	3	6	5	-1	1.000	-5	O-34,D-26	0.1
Total	14	1447	5045	843	1309	239	36	308	935	750	1237	.259	.359	.504	140	270	211	92	8	.977	23	*O-1364/D-41	26.6

■ GABBY STREET
Street, Charles Evard "Old Sarge"   b: 9/30/1882, Huntsville, Ala.   d: 2/6/51, Joplin, Mo.   BR/TR, 5'11", 180 lbs.   Deb: 9/13/04   MC

YEAR	TM/L	G	AB	R	H	2B	3B	HR	RBI	BB	SO	AVG	OBP	SLG	PRO+	BR/A	SB	CS	SBR	FA	FR	G/POS	TPR
1904	Cin-N	11	33	1	4	1	0	0		0		.121	.147	.152	-7	-4	2			.973	4	C-11	0.1
1905	Cin-N	2	2	0	0	0	0	0	0	0	2	.000	.500	.000	48	0	0			1.000	1	/C-1	0.1
	Bos-N	3	12	0	2	0	0	0	0	0		.167	.167	.167	-1	-1	0			.778	-2	/C-3	-0.4
	Cin-N	29	91	8	23	5	1	0	8	6		.253	.306	.330	81	-2	1			.975	3	C-26	0.4
	Yr	34	105	8	25	5	1	0	8	6		.238	.289	.305	73	-4	2			.957	2	C-30	0.1
1908	Was-A	131	394	31	81	12	7	1	32	40		.206	.289	.279	92	-3	5			.973	-1	*C-128	0.9
1909	Was-A	137	407	25	86	12	1	0	29	26		.211	.262	.246	63	-17	4			.981	11	*C-137	0.7
1910	Was-A	89	257	13	52	9	1	0	16	23		.202	.273	.237	63	-11	1			**.978**	9	C-86	0.7
1911	Was-A	72	216	16	48	7	0	0	14	14		.222	.279	.264	53	-14	4			.973	7	C-71	0.1
1912	NY-A	29	88	4	16	1	0	0	6	7		.182	.258	.216	34	-8	1			.958	-2	C-29	-0.5
1931	StL-N	1	2	0	0	0	0	0		0		.000	.000	.000	-96	-0				1.000	0	/C-1,M	0.0
Total	8	504	1501	98	312	44	11	2	105	119	0	.208	.273	.256	66	-60	17			.974	32	C-493	2.0

■ WALT STREULI
Streuli, Walter Herbert   b: 9/26/35, Memphis, Tenn.   BR/TR, 6'2", 195 lbs.   Deb: 9/25/54

YEAR	TM/L	G	AB	R	H	2B	3B	HR	RBI	BB	SO	AVG	OBP	SLG	PRO+	BR/A	SB	CS	SBR	FA	FR	G/POS	TPR
1954	Det-A	1	0	0	0	0	0	0	0	0	0	—	1.000	—	195	0	0	0	0	1.000	-0	/C-1	0.0
1955	Det-A	2	4	1	1	0	0	0	1	0	0	.250	.250	.500	100	-0	0	0	0	1.000	0	/C-2	0.0

YEAR	TM/L	G	AB	R	H	2B	3B	HR	RBI	BB	SO	AVG	OBP	SLG	PRO+	BR/A	SB	CS	SBR	FA	FR	G/POS	TPR
1956	Det-A	3	8	0	2	1	0	0	1	1	2	.250	.333	.375	87	-0	0	0	0	.933	0	/C-3	0.0
Total	3	6	12	1	3	2	0	0	2	2	2	.250	.357	.417	106	0	0	0	0	.957	0	/C-6	0.0

■ JOHN STRICK
Strick, John Quincy Adams   Deb: 5/18/1882

YEAR	TM/L	G	AB	R	H	2B	3B	HR	RBI	BB	SO	AVG	OBP	SLG	PRO+	BR/A	SB	CS	SBR	FA	FR	G/POS	TPR
1882	Lou-a	32	110	17	18	6	1	0		9		.164	.227	.236	60	-4				.898	-0	C-21/O-6,2-6,S-1,1	-0.3

■ CUB STRICKER
Stricker, John A. (b: John A. Streaker)   b: 2/15/1860, Philadelphia, Pa.   d: 11/19/37, Philadelphia, Pa.   BR/TR, 5'3", 138 lbs.   Deb: 5/2/1882 M

YEAR	TM/L	G	AB	R	H	2B	3B	HR	RBI	BB	SO	AVG	OBP	SLG	PRO+	BR/A	SB	CS	SBR	FA	FR	G/POS	TPR
1882	Phi-a	72	272	34	59	6	1	0	18	15		.217	.258	.246	63	-12				.904	23	*2-72/P-2,O-1	1.2
1883	Phi-a	89	330	67	90	8	0	1	40	19		.273	.312	.306	93	-4				.837	-20	*2-88/C-2	-2.0
1884	Phi-a	107	399	59	92	16	11	1		19		.231	.267	.333	89	-6				.870	-34	*2-107/O-1,C-1,P-1	-3.5
1885	Phi-a	106	398	71	93	9	3	1	41	21		.234	.284	.279	74	-12				.879	-13	*2-106	-2.0
1887	Cle-a	131	534	122	141	19	4	2	53	53		.264	.334	.326	87	-8	86			.912	10	*2-126/S-6,P-3	0.5
1888	Cle-a	127	493	80	115	13	6	1	33	50		.233	.294	.290	96	-0	60			.929	23	*2-122/O-6,P-2	2.5
1889	Cle-N	136	566	83	142	10	4	1	47	58	18	.251	.323	.288	73	-19	32			.932	7	*2-135/S-1	-0.4
1890	Cle-P	127	544	93	133	19	8	2	65	54	16	.244	.318	.320	77	-17	24			.905	5	*2-109,S-20	-0.3
1891	Bos-a	139	514	96	111	15	4	0	46	63	34	.216	.309	.261	64	-23	54			.942	24	*2-139	0.7
1892	StL-N	28	98	12	20	1	0	0	11	10	7	.204	.297	.214	58	-4	5			.939	-4	2-27/S-1,M	-0.8
	Bal-N	75	269	45	71	5	5	3	37	32	18	.264	.344	.353	108	3	13			.918	3	2-75	0.6
	Yr	103	367	57	91	6	5	3	48	42	25	.248	.332	.316	96	-1	18			.923	-2	*2-102/S-1	-0.2
1893	Was-N	59	218	28	39	7	1	0	20	20	12	.179	.248	.220	25	-24	4			.903	7	2-39,O-12/S-4,3-4	-1.4
Total	11	1196	4635	790	1106	128	47	12	411	414	105	.239	.306	.294	78	-125	278			.907	30	*2-1145/S-32,OP3C	-4.9

■ GEORGE STRICKLAND
Strickland, George Bevan "Bo"   b: 1/10/26, New Orleans, La.   BR/TR, 6'1", 180 lbs.   Deb: 5/7/50 MC

YEAR	TM/L	G	AB	R	H	2B	3B	HR	RBI	BB	SO	AVG	OBP	SLG	PRO+	BR/A	SB	CS	SBR	FA	FR	G/POS	TPR
1950	Pit-N	23	27	0	3	0	0	0	2	3	8	.111	.226	.111	-8	-4	0			.978	3	S-19/3-1	-0.1
1951	Pit-N	138	454	59	98	12	7	9	47	65	83	.216	.318	.333	73	-17	4	2	0	.943	12	*S-125,2-13	0.5
1952	Pit-N	76	232	17	41	6	2	5	22	21	45	.177	.248	.284	46	-17	4	2	0	.953	15	2-45,S-28/1-1,3-1	0.2
	Cle-A	31	88	8	19	4	0	1	8	14	15	.216	.324	.295	78	-2	0	0	0	.964	10	S-30/2-1	0.9
1953	Cle-A	123	419	43	119	17	4	5	47	51	52	.284	.362	.379	103	3	0	0	0	.974	16	*S-122/1-1	2.7
1954	*Cle-A	112	361	42	77	12	3	6	37	55	62	.213	.319	.313	72	-13	2	1	0	.961	-12	*S-112	-1.6
1955	Cle-A	130	388	34	81	9	5	2	34	49	60	.209	.302	.273	54	-25	1	0	0	.976	8	*S-128	-0.6
1956	Cle-A	85	171	22	36	1	2	3	17	22	27	.211	.301	.292	56	-11	0	1	-1	.986	16	2-28,S-28,3-26	0.8
1957	Cle-A	89	201	21	47	8	2	1	19	26	29	.234	.325	.308	75	-7	0	3	-2	.980	15	2-48,S-23,3-19	1.1
1959	Cle-A	132	441	55	105	15	2	3	48	51	64	.238	.317	.302	74	-15	1	1	-0	.971	-9	3-80,S-50/2-4	-2.0
1960	Cle-A	32	42	4	7	0	0	1	3	4	8	.167	.255	.238	35	-4	0	0	0	.962	1	S-14,3-12/2-2	-0.3
Total	10	971	2824	305	633	84	27	36	284	361	453	.224	.314	.311	70	-112	12	10		.963	74	S-679,2-141,3/1	1.6

■ GEORGE STRIEF
Strief, George Andrew   b: 10/16/1856, Cincinnati, Ohio   d: 4/1/46, Cleveland, Ohio   BR/TR, 5'7", 172 lbs.   Deb: 5/1/1879 U

YEAR	TM/L	G	AB	R	H	2B	3B	HR	RBI	BB	SO	AVG	OBP	SLG	PRO+	BR/A	SB	CS	SBR	FA	FR	G/POS	TPR
1879	Cle-N	71	264	24	46	7	1	0	15	10	23	.174	.204	.208	37	-17				.918	-9	O-55,2-16	-2.6
1882	Pit-a	79	297	45	58	9	6	2		13		.195	.229	.286	76	-7				.917	0	*2-78/S-1	-0.4
1883	StL-a	82	302	22	68	9	0	1	22	12		.225	.255	.265	64	-13				.899	6	*2-67,O-15	-0.5
1884	StL-a	48	184	22	37	5	2	2		13		.201	.254	.283	72	-6				.848	-3	O-44/2-3,1-1	-0.9
	KC-U	15	56	5	6	5	0	0		4		.107	.167	.196	11	-8				.900	8	2-15	0.1
	CP-U	15	53	6	11	5	0	0		3		.208	.250	.302	67	-4				.905	-2	2-15	-0.5
	Yr	30	109	11	17	10	0	0		7		.156	.207	.248	40	-11				.902	7	2-30	-0.4
	Cle-N	8	29	2	7	2	0	0	0	0	5	.241	.241	.310	70	-1				1.000	-0	/O-6,3-2	-0.1
1885	Phi-a	44	175	19	48	8	5	0	27	9		.274	.310	.377	110	1				.828	-2	3-19,S-10/O-8,2-7	-0.1
Total	5	362	1360	145	281	50	14	5	64	64	28	.207	.242	.275	67	-53				.899	-1	2-201,O-128/3S1	-5.0

■ LOU STRINGER
Stringer, Louis Bernard   b: 5/13/17, Grand Rapids, Mich   BR/TR, 5'11", 173 lbs.   Deb: 4/15/41

YEAR	TM/L	G	AB	R	H	2B	3B	HR	RBI	BB	SO	AVG	OBP	SLG	PRO+	BR/A	SB	CS	SBR	FA	FR	G/POS	TPR
1941	Chi-N	145	512	59	126	31	4	5	53	59	86	.246	.324	.352	94	-4	3			.960	20	*2-137/S-7	2.6
1942	Chi-N	121	406	45	96	10	5	9	41	31	55	.236	.292	.352	92	-6	3			.955	2	*2-113/3-1	0.3
1946	Chi-N	80	209	26	51	3	1	3	19	26	34	.244	.328	.311	83	-4	0			.956	-5	2-62/S-1,3-1	-0.5
1948	Bos-A	4	11	1	1	0	0	1	1	0	3	.091	.091	.364	17	-1	0	0	0	.947	2	/2-2	0.1
1949	Bos-A	35	41	10	11	4	0	1	6	5	10	.268	.348	.439	100	-0	0	0	0	.978	3	/2-9	0.3
1950	Bos-A	24	17	7	5	1	0	0	2	0	2	.294	.294	.353	59	-1	1	0	0	.778	3	/3-3,2-1,S-1	0.2
Total	6	409	1196	148	290	49	10	19	122	121	192	.242	.313	.348	90	-17	7	0		.958	25	2-324/S-9,3-5	3.0

■ JOE STRIPP
Stripp, Joseph Valentine "Jersey Joe"   b: 2/3/03, Harrison, N.J.   d: 6/10/89, Orlando, Fla.   BR/TR, 5'11.5", 175 lbs.   Deb: 7/2/28

YEAR	TM/L	G	AB	R	H	2B	3B	HR	RBI	BB	SO	AVG	OBP	SLG	PRO+	BR/A	SB	CS	SBR	FA	FR	G/POS	TPR
1928	Cin-N	42	139	18	40	7	3	1	17	8	8	.288	.340	.403	95	-1	0			.931	-7	O-21,3-17/S-1	-0.8
1929	Cin-N	64	187	24	40	3	2	3	20	24	15	.214	.313	.299	55	-13	2			.960	8	3-55/2-2	-0.2
1930	Cin-N	130	464	74	142	37	6	3	64	51	37	.306	.367	.431	100	1	15			.996	0	1-75,3-48	-0.4
1931	Cin-N	105	426	71	138	26	2	3	42	21	31	.324	.359	.415	114	8	5			.957	4	3-96/1-9	1.6
1932	Bro-N	138	534	94	162	36	9	6	64	36	30	.303	.350	.438	113	9	14			.954	16	3-93,1-43	2.7
1933	Bro-N	141	537	69	149	20	7	1	51	26	23	.277	.312	.346	92	-7	5			.967	5	*3-140	0.7
1934	Bro-N	104	384	50	121	19	6	1	40	22	20	.315	.354	.404	108	4	2			.941	-6	3-96/1-7,S-1	0.1
1935	Bro-N	109	373	44	114	13	5	3	43	22	15	.306	.344	.391	99	-0	2			.962	7	3-88,1-15/O-1	0.8
1936	Bro-N	110	439	51	139	31	1	1	60	22	12	.317	.351	.399	100	0	2			.968	8	*3-106	1.1
1937	Bro-N	90	300	37	73	10	2	1	26	20	18	.243	.291	.300	60	-17	1			.971	-6	3-66,1-14/S-3	-2.3
1938	StL-N	54	199	24	57	7	0	0	18	18	10	.286	.349	.322	81	-5	0			.977	-8	3-51	-1.2
	Bos-N	59	229	19	63	10	0	1	19	10	7	.275	.305	.332	84	-6	2			.966	1	3-58	-0.4
	Yr	113	428	43	120	17	0	1	37	28	17	.280	.326	.327	82	-10	2			.971	-7	*3-109	-1.6
Total	11	1146	4211	575	1238	219	43	24	464	280	226	.294	.340	.384	96	-27	50			.961	21	3-914,1-163/OS2	1.7

■ ALLIE STROBEL
Strobel, Albert Irving   b: 6/11/1884, Boston, Mass.   d: 2/10/55, Hollywood, Fla.   BR/TR, 6', 160 lbs.   Deb: 8/29/05

YEAR	TM/L	G	AB	R	H	2B	3B	HR	RBI	BB	SO	AVG	OBP	SLG	PRO+	BR/A	SB	CS	SBR	FA	FR	G/POS	TPR
1905	Bos-N	5	19	1	2	0	0	0	2	0		.105	.105	.105	-38	-3	0			1.000	-0	/3-4,O-1	-0.4
1906	Bos-N	100	317	28	64	10	3	1	24	29		.202	.273	.262	69	-12	2			.946	-6	2-93/S-6,O-1	-1.8
Total	2	105	336	29	66	10	3	1	26	29		.196	.264	.253	63	-15	2			1.000	-6	/2-93,S-6,3-4,O-2	-2.2

■ JIM STRONER
Stroner, James Melvin   b: 5/29/01, Chicago, Ill.   d: 12/6/75, Tarboro, N.C.   BR/TR, 5'10", 175 lbs.   Deb: 5/1/29

YEAR	TM/L	G	AB	R	H	2B	3B	HR	RBI	BB	SO	AVG	OBP	SLG	PRO+	BR/A	SB	CS	SBR	FA	FR	G/POS	TPR
1929	Pit-N	6	8	0	3	1	0	0	0	1	0	.375	.444	.500	130	0	0			.571	-0	/3-2	0.0

■ ED STROUD
Stroud, Edwin Marvin   b: 10/31/39, Lapine, Ala.   BL/TR, 5'11", 180 lbs.   Deb: 9/11/66

YEAR	TM/L	G	AB	R	H	2B	3B	HR	RBI	BB	SO	AVG	OBP	SLG	PRO+	BR/A	SB	CS	SBR	FA	FR	G/POS	TPR
1966	Chi-A	12	36	3	6	2	0	0	1	2	8	.167	.231	.222	33	-3	3	0	1	1.000	-0	O-11	-0.3
1967	Chi-A	20	27	6	8	0	1	0	3	1	5	.296	.345	.370	116	0	7	2	1	1.000	-1	O-12	0.0
	Was-A	87	204	36	41	5	3	1	10	25	29	.201	.291	.270	69	-7	8	6	-1	.983	-13	O-79	-2.7
	Yr	107	231	42	49	5	4	1	13	26	34	.212	.297	.281	75	-7	15	8	-0	.985	-14	O-91	-2.7
1968	Was-A	105	306	41	73	10	10	4	23	20	50	.239	.285	.376	102	-0	9	3	1	.979	-4	O-84	-0.9
1969	Was-A	123	206	35	52	5	6	4	29	30	33	.252	.353	.393	114	4	12	12	2	.982	-11	O-85	-0.8
1970	Was-A	129	433	69	115	11	5	5	32	40	49	.266	.332	.349	92	-5	29	8	4	.993	2	*O-118	-0.4
1971	Chi-A	53	141	19	25	3	4	2	11	20	20	.177	.237	.248	36	-12	4	5	-2	1.000	-11	O-44	-2.9
Total	6	529	1353	209	320	37	28	14	100	129	224	.237	.307	.336	87	-22	72	36		.988	-38	O-433	-8.0

■ STEVE STROUGHTER
Stroughter, Stephen Lewis   b: 3/15/52, Visalia, Cal.   BL/TR, 6'2", 190 lbs.   Deb: 4/7/82

YEAR	TM/L	G	AB	R	H	2B	3B	HR	RBI	BB	SO	AVG	OBP	SLG	PRO+	BR/A	SB	CS	SBR	FA	FR	G/POS	TPR
1982	Sea-A	26	47	4	8	1	0	1	3		9	.170	.235	.255	34	-0	0	0	0	1.000	1	/O-3,D-9	-0.3

■ AMOS STRUNK
Strunk, Amos Aaron   b: 1/22/1889, Philadelphia, Pa.   d: 7/22/79, Llanerch, Pa.   BL/TL, 5'11.5", 175 lbs.   Deb: 9/24/08

YEAR	TM/L	G	AB	R	H	2B	3B	HR	RBI	BB	SO	AVG	OBP	SLG	PRO+	BR/A	SB	CS	SBR	FA	FR	G/POS	TPR
1908	Phi-A	12	34	4	8	1	0	0	0	4		.235	.316	.265	83	-1	0			.903	1	O-11	0.0
1909	Phi-A	11	35	1	4	0	0	0	2			.114	.139	.114	-20	-5	2			1.000	-1	/O-9	-0.7
1910	*Phi-A	16	48	9	16	0	1	0	2	3		.333	.373	.375	135	2	4			1.000	-0	O-14	0.0
1911	*Phi-A	74	215	42	55	7	1		21	35		.256	.363	.321	93	-1	13			.958	1	O-62/1-2	-0.2
1912	Phi-A	122	412	58	119	13	12	3	63	47	29	.289	.366	.400	123	13	29			.990	11	*O-116	1.8
1913	*Phi-A	94	292	30	89	11	12	0	46	29	23	.305	.368	.425	135	12	14			.962	-2	O-81	0.8

YEAR	TM/L	G	AB	R	H	2B	3B	HR	RBI	BB	SO	AVG	OBP	SLG	PRO+	BR/A	SB	CS	SBR	FA	FR	G/POS	TPR
1914	*Phi-A	122	404	58	111	15	3	2	45	57	38	.275	.364	.342	117	10	25	22	-6	**.987**	9	*O-120	0.8
1915	Phi-A	132	485	76	144	28	16	1	45	56	45	.297	.371	.427	144	25	17	19	-6	.980	12	*O-111,1-19	2.6
1916	Phi-A	150	544	71	172	30	9	3	49	66	59	.316	.393	.421	152	35	21	23	-8	.978	2	*O-143/1-7	2.3
1917	Phi-A	148	540	83	152	26	7	1	45	68	37	.281	.363	.361	123	16	16			**.986**	-2	*O-146	0.6
1918	*Bos-A	114	413	50	106	18	9	0	35	36	13	.257	.316	.344	101	-1	20			**.988**	-5	*O-113	-1.3
1919	Bos-A	48	184	27	50	11	3	0	17	13	13	.272	.323	.364	98	-1	3			.968	-1	O-48	-0.6
	Phi-A	60	194	15	41	6	4	0	13	23	15	.211	.298	.284	63	-9	3			.981	1	O-52	-1.3
	Yr	108	378	42	91	17	7	0	30	36	28	.241	.310	.323	79	-11	6			.974	-1	*O-100	-1.9
1920	Phi-A	58	202	23	60	9	3	0	20	21	9	.297	.363	.371	94	-1	0	6	-4	.990	-4	O-54	-1.3
	Chi-A	53	188	33	45	8	1	1	16	28	15	.239	.338	.309	72	-7	1	0	0	.981	-1	O-49	-1.0
	Yr	111	390	56	105	17	4	1	36	49	24	.269	.351	.341	83	-8	1	6	-3	.985	-5	*O-103	-2.3
1921	Chi-A	121	401	68	133	19	10	3	69	38	27	.332	.391	.451	116	10	7	10	-4	.970	-8	*O-111	-0.9
1922	Chi-A	92	311	36	90	11	4	0	33	33	28	.289	.358	.350	85	-6	9	6	-1	.989	2	O-74/1-7	-1.0
1923	Chi-A	54	54	7	17	0	0	0	8	8	5	.315	.403	.315	92	-0	1	0	0	1.000	-0	/O-5,1-2	0.0
1924	Chi-A	1	1	0	0	0	0	0	0	0	0	.000	.000	.000	-99	-0	0	0	0	.000	0	H	0.0
	Phi-A	30	42	5	6	0	0	0	1	7	4	.143	.265	.143	7	-6	0	0	0	1.000	-3	/O-8	-0.8
	Yr	31	43	5	6	0	0	0	1	7	4	.140	.260	.140	5	-6	0	0	0	1.000	-3	/O-8	-0.8
Total	17	1512	4999	696	1418	213	96	15	530	573	331	.284	.359	.374	112	86	185	86		.980	13	*O-1327/1-37	0.0

■ AL STRUVE Struve, Albert b: St.Louis, Mo. Deb: 6/22/1884

YEAR	TM/L	G	AB	R	H	2B	3B	HR	RBI	BB	SO	AVG	OBP	SLG	PRO+	BR/A	SB	CS	SBR	FA	FR	G/POS	TPR
1884	StL-a	2	7	2	2	0	0	0		0	0	.286	.286	.286	84	-0				.000	1	/O-1,C-1	0.1

■ LUKE STUART Stuart, Luther Lane b: 5/23/1892, Alamance Co., N.C. d: 6/15/47, Winston-Salem, N.C. BR/TR, 5'8", 165 lbs. Deb: 7/28/21

YEAR	TM/L	G	AB	R	H	2B	3B	HR	RBI	BB	SO	AVG	OBP	SLG	PRO+	BR/A	SB	CS	SBR	FA	FR	G/POS	TPR
1921	StL-A	3	3	2	1	0	0	1	2	0	1	.333	.333	1.333	291	1	0	0	0	1.000	-1	/2-3	0.0

■ DICK STUART Stuart, Richard Lee "Dr. Strangeglove" b: 11/7/32, San Francisco, Cal. BR/TR, 6'4", 212 lbs. Deb: 7/10/58

YEAR	TM/L	G	AB	R	H	2B	3B	HR	RBI	BB	SO	AVG	OBP	SLG	PRO+	BR/A	SB	CS	SBR	FA	FR	G/POS	TPR
1958	Pit-N	67	254	38	68	12	5	16	48	11	75	.268	.311	.543	124	7	0	0	0	.973	0	1-64	0.3
1959	Pit-N	118	397	64	118	15	2	27	78	42	86	.297	.367	.549	141	22	1	1	0	.976	1	*1-105/O-1	1.6
1960	*Pit-N	122	438	48	114	17	5	23	83	39	107	.260	.321	.479	115	8	0	0	0	.986	-1	*1-108	-0.3
1961	Pit-N★	138	532	83	160	28	8	35	117	34	121	.301	.347	.581	140	28	0	3	-2	.983	-2	*1-132/O-1	1.3
1962	Pit-N	114	394	52	90	11	4	16	64	32	94	.228	.290	.398	83	-11	0	1	-1	.982	-7	*1-101	-1.7
1963	Bos-A	157	612	81	160	25	4	42	**118**	44	144	.261	.312	.521	125	18	0	0	0	.979	8	*1-155	2.0
1964	Bos-A	156	603	73	168	27	1	33	114	37	130	.279	.323	.491	117	12	0	0	0	.981	1	*1-155	0.7
1965	Phi-N	149	538	53	126	19	1	28	95	39	136	.234	.290	.429	101	-1	1	0	0	.986	3	*1-143/3-1	-0.5
1966	NY-N	31	87	7	19	0	0	4	13	9	26	.218	.292	.356	81	-2	0	1	-1	.974	-1	1-23	-0.6
	*LA-N	38	91	4	24	1	0	3	9	11	17	.264	.356	.374	112	2	0	1	-1	.991	3	1-25	0.3
	Yr	69	178	11	43	1	0	7	22	20	43	.242	.325	.365	97	-1	0	2	-2	.982	2	1-48	-0.3
1969	Cal-A	22	51	3	8	2	0	1	4	3	21	.157	.204	.255	29	-5	0	0	0	.991	-1	1-13	-0.8
Total	10	1112	3997	506	1055	157	30	228	743	301	957	.264	.319	.489	117	77	2	7	-4	.982	13	*1-1024/O-2,3-1	2.3

■ BILL STUART Stuart, William Alexander "Chauncey" b: 8/28/1873, Boalsburg, Pa. d: 10/14/28, Fort Worth, Tex. 5'11", 170 lbs. Deb: 8/15/1895

YEAR	TM/L	G	AB	R	H	2B	3B	HR	RBI	BB	SO	AVG	OBP	SLG	PRO+	BR/A	SB	CS	SBR	FA	FR	G/POS	TPR
1895	Pit-N	19	77	5	19	3	0	0	10	2	6	.247	.275	.286	47	-6	2			.913	-1	S-17/2-2	-0.5
1899	NY-N	1	3	0	0	0	0	0	0	0	0	.000	.000	.000	-99	-1	0			1.000	-0	/2-1	-0.1
Total	2	20	80	5	19	3	0	0	10	2	6	.237	.265	.275	42	-7	2			.909	-1	/S-17,2-3	-0.6

■ FRANKLIN STUBBS Stubbs, Franklin Lee b: 10/21/60, Richlands, N.C. BL/TL, 6'2", 215 lbs. Deb: 4/28/84

YEAR	TM/L	G	AB	R	H	2B	3B	HR	RBI	BB	SO	AVG	OBP	SLG	PRO+	BR/A	SB	CS	SBR	FA	FR	G/POS	TPR
1984	LA-N	87	217	22	42	2	3	8	17	24	63	.194	.274	.341	73	-8	2	2	-1	.993	-1	1-51,O-20	-1.3
1985	LA-N	10	9	0	2	0	0	0	2	0	3	.222	.222	.222	25	-1	0	0	0	1.000	-0	/1-4	-0.1
1986	LA-N	132	420	55	95	11	1	23	58	37	107	.226	.292	.421	101	-2	7	1	2	.969	-4	*O-124,1-13	-0.9
1987	LA-N	129	386	48	90	16	3	16	52	31	85	.233	.292	.415	87	-9	8	1	2	**.994**	7	*1-111,O-18	-0.8
1988	*LA-N	115	242	30	54	13	0	8	34	23	61	.223	.293	.376	94	-2	11	3	2	.978	2	1-84,O-13	-0.4
1989	LA-N	69	103	11	30	6	0	4	15	16	27	.291	.387	.466	145	6	3	2	-0	.948	1	O-28/1-7	0.7
1990	Hou-N	146	448	59	117	23	2	23	71	48	114	.261	.335	.475	124	13	19	6	2	.991	-9	1-72,O-71	-1.1
1991	Mil-A	103	362	48	77	16	2	11	38	35	71	.213	.286	.359	79	-11	13	4	2	.991	-0	1-92/O-4,D-4	-1.1
1992	Mil-A	92	288	37	66	11	1	9	42	27	68	.229	.297	.368	87	-5	11	8	-2	.987	6	1-68,D-16/O-1	-0.7
1995	Det-A	62	116	13	29	11	0	2	19	19	27	.250	.360	.397	97	-0	0	1	-1	.972	-7	1-20,O-20/D-3	-0.9
Total	10	945	2591	323	602	109	12	104	348	260	626	.232	.305	.404	97	-19	74	28	5	.989	-19	1-522,O-299/D-23	-5.5

■ MOOSE STUBING Stubing, Lawrence George b: 3/31/38, Bronx, N.Y. BL/TL, 6'3", 220 lbs. Deb: 4/14/67 MC

YEAR	TM/L	G	AB	R	H	2B	3B	HR	RBI	BB	SO	AVG	OBP	SLG	PRO+	BR/A	SB	CS	SBR	FA	FR	G/POS	TPR
1967	Cal-A	5	5	0	0	0	0	0	0	0	4	.000	.000	.000	-99	-1	0	0	0	.000	0	H	-0.1

■ SEEM STUDLEY Studley, Seymour L. "Warhorse" b: Washington, D.C. d: 1874, Washington, D.C. Deb: 4/20/1872

YEAR	TM/L	G	AB	R	H	2B	3B	HR	RBI	BB	SO	AVG	OBP	SLG	PRO+	BR/A	SB	CS	SBR	FA	FR	G/POS	TPR
1872	Nat-n	5	21	3	2	0	0	0	2	0	1	.095	.095	.095	-35	-4	0	0	0	.571	-1	/O-5	-0.3

■ GEORGE STUMPF Stumpf, George Frederick b: 12/15/10, New Orleans, La. d: 3/6/93, Metairie, La. BL/TL, 5'8", 155 lbs. Deb: 9/19/31

YEAR	TM/L	G	AB	R	H	2B	3B	HR	RBI	BB	SO	AVG	OBP	SLG	PRO+	BR/A	SB	CS	SBR	FA	FR	G/POS	TPR
1931	Bos-A	7	28	2	7	1	1	0	4	1	2	.250	.276	.357	69	-1	0	0	0	1.000	-7	/O-7	-0.3
1932	Bos-A	79	169	18	34	2	2	1	18	18	21	.201	.278	.254	40	-15	1	1	-0	.952	-7	O-51	-2.3
1933	Bos-A	22	41	8	14	3	0	0	5	4	2	.341	.400	.415	117	1	4	0	1	1.000	-3	O-15	-0.1
1936	Chi-A	10	22	3	6	1	0	0	5	2	1	.273	.333	.318	59	-1	0	0	0	1.000	1	/O-4	-0.1
Total	4	118	260	31	61	7	3	1	32	25	26	.235	.302	.296	57	-17	5	1	1	.969	-11	/O-77	-2.8

■ BILL STUMPF Stumpf, William Frederick b: 3/21/1892, Baltimore, Md. d: 2/14/66, Crownsville, Md. BR/TR, 6'0.5", 175 lbs. Deb: 5/11/12

YEAR	TM/L	G	AB	R	H	2B	3B	HR	RBI	BB	SO	AVG	OBP	SLG	PRO+	BR/A	SB	CS	SBR	FA	FR	G/POS	TPR
1912	NY-A	42	129	8	31	1	0	0	10	6		.240	.279	.240	46	-9	5			.892	-6	S-26/2-8,3-5,1-1,0	-1.3
1913	NY-A	12	29	5	6	1	0	0	1	3	3	.207	.281	.241	53	-2	0			.818	-3	/S-6,2-4,O-1	-0.5
Total	2	54	158	13	37	1	0	0	11	9	3	.234	.280	.241	47	-11	5			.877	-9	/S-32,2-12,3-5,O1	-1.8

■ GUY STURDY Sturdy, Guy R. b: 8/7/1899, Sherman, Tex. d: 5/4/65, Marshall, Tex. BL/TL, 6'0.5", 180 lbs. Deb: 9/30/27

YEAR	TM/L	G	AB	R	H	2B	3B	HR	RBI	BB	SO	AVG	OBP	SLG	PRO+	BR/A	SB	CS	SBR	FA	FR	G/POS	TPR
1927	StL-A	5	21	5	9	1	0	0	5	1	0	.429	.455	.476	137	1	2	0	1	.974	-1	/1-5	0.1
1928	StL-A	54	45	3	10	1	0	1	8	8	4	.222	.340	.311	70	-2	1	0	0	1.000	-0	/1-1	-0.2
Total	2	59	66	8	19	2	0	1	13	9	4	.288	.373	.364	91	-1	3	0	1	.975	-1	/1-6	-0.1

■ BOBBY STURGEON Sturgeon, Robert Howard b: 8/6/19, Clinton, Ind. BR/TR, 6', 175 lbs. Deb: 4/16/40

YEAR	TM/L	G	AB	R	H	2B	3B	HR	RBI	BB	SO	AVG	OBP	SLG	PRO+	BR/A	SB	CS	SBR	FA	FR	G/POS	TPR
1940	Chi-N	7	21	1	4	1	0	0	2	0	1	.190	.190	.238	18	-2	0			.848	2	/S-7	0.0
1941	Chi-N	129	433	45	106	15	3	0	25	9	30	.245	.260	.293	58	-25	2			.956	-4	*S-126/2-1,3-1	-2.1
1942	Chi-N	63	162	8	40	7	1	0	7	4	13	.247	.269	.302	70	-7	2			.988	21	2-32,S-29/3-2	1.7
1946	Chi-N	100	294	26	87	12	1	2	21	10	18	.296	.319	.361	94	-3	0			.934	-13	S-72,2-21	-1.3
1947	Chi-N	87	232	16	59	10	5	0	21	7	12	.254	.276	.341	66	-12	0			.975	13	S-45,2-30/3-5	0.4
1948	Bos-N	34	78	10	17	3	1	0	4	4	5	.218	.256	.282	46	-6	3			.938	-3	2-18/S-4,3-4	-0.9
Total	6	420	1220	106	313	48	12	2	80	34	79	.257	.277	.318	68	-56	7			.951	14	S-283,2-102/3-12	-2.2

■ DEAN STURGIS Sturgis, Dean Donnell b: 12/1/1892, Beloit, Kan. d: 6/4/50, Uniontown, Pa. BR/TR, 6'1", 180 lbs. Deb: 5/1/14

YEAR	TM/L	G	AB	R	H	2B	3B	HR	RBI	BB	SO	AVG	OBP	SLG	PRO+	BR/A	SB	CS	SBR	FA	FR	G/POS	TPR
1914	Phi-A	4	4	1	1	0	0	0	0	0	2	.250	.400	.250	100	-1				1.000	0	/C-1	0.0

■ JOHNNY STURM Sturm, John Peter Joseph b: 1/23/16, St.Louis, Mo. BL/TL, 6'1", 185 lbs. Deb: 4/14/41

YEAR	TM/L	G	AB	R	H	2B	3B	HR	RBI	BB	SO	AVG	OBP	SLG	PRO+	BR/A	SB	CS	SBR	FA	FR	G/POS	TPR
1941	*NY-A	124	524	58	125	17	3	3	36	37	50	.239	.293	.300	58	-32	3	5	-2	.990	-2	*1-124	-4.5

■ GEORGE STUTZ Stutz, George "Kid" or "Satan" b: 2/12/1893, Philadelphia, Pa. d: 12/29/30, Philadelphia, Pa. BL/TR, 5'5", 150 lbs. Deb: 8/17/26

YEAR	TM/L	G	AB	R	H	2B	3B	HR	RBI	BB	SO	AVG	OBP	SLG	PRO+	BR/A	SB	CS	SBR	FA	FR	G/POS	TPR
1926	Phi-N	6	9	0	0	0	0	0	0	0	2	.000	.000	.000	-95	-2	0			.938	1	/S-5	-0.1

■ LENA STYLES Styles, William Graves b: 11/27/1899, Gurley, Ala. d: 3/14/56, Hunstville, Ala. BR/TR, 6'1", 185 lbs. Deb: 9/10/19

YEAR	TM/L	G	AB	R	H	2B	3B	HR	RBI	BB	SO	AVG	OBP	SLG	PRO+	BR/A	SB	CS	SBR	FA	FR	G/POS	TPR
1919	Phi-A	8	22	0	6	1	0	0	5	1	6	.273	.304	.318	74	-1	0			.974	0	/C-8	0.0
1920	Phi-A	24	50	5	13	3	1	0	8	6	7	.260	.339	.360	84	-1	1	0	0	.966	2	/C-9,1-7	0.1
1921	Phi-A	4	5	0	1	0	0	0	0	0	2	.200	.200	.200	2	-1	0	0	0	.333	-1	/C-2	-0.2

YEAR	TM/L	G	AB	R	H	2B	3B	HR	RBI	BB	SO	AVG	OBP	SLG	PRO+	BR/A	SB	CS	SBR	FA	FR	G/POS	TPR
1930	Cin-N	7	12	2	3	0	1	0	1	1	2	.250	.357	.417	91	-0	0			.875	0	/C-5,1-1	0.0
1931	Cin-N	34	87	7	21	3	0	0	5	8	7	.241	.313	.276	63	-4	0			.949	-7	C-31	-0.9
Total	5	77	176	14	44	7	2	0	16	16	24	.250	.320	.313	71	-7	1	0		.929	-6	/C-55,1-8	-1.0

■ CHRIS STYNES Stynes, Christopher Desmond b: 1/19/73, Queens, N.Y. BR/TR, 5'9", 170 lbs. Deb: 5/19/95

YEAR	TM/L	G	AB	R	H	2B	3B	HR	RBI	BB	SO	AVG	OBP	SLG	PRO+	BR/A	SB	CS	SBR	FA	FR	G/POS	TPR
1995	KC-A	22	35	7	6	1	0	0	2	4	3	.171	.256	.200	20	-4	0	0	0	.982	6	2-17/D-2	0.2
1996	KC-A	36	92	8	27	6	0	0	6	2	5	.293	.293	.359	70	-4	5	2	0	.939	-2	O-19/2-5,3-2,D-3	-0.6
Total	2	58	127	15	33	7	0	0	8	6	8	.260	.293	.315	56	-8	5	2	0	.986	4	/2-22,O-19,D-5,3-2	-0.4

■ NEIL STYNES Stynes, Cornelius William b: 12/10/1868, Arlington, Mass. d: 3/26/44, Somerville, Mass. BR/TR, 6', 165 lbs. Deb: 9/8/1890

YEAR	TM/L	G	AB	R	H	2B	3B	HR	RBI	BB	SO	AVG	OBP	SLG	PRO+	BR/A	SB	FA	FR	G/POS	TPR
1890	Cle-P	2	8	0	0	0	0	0	0	0	0	.000	.000	.000	-99	-2	0	.846	-0	/C-2	-0.2

■ KEN SUAREZ Suarez, Kenneth Raymond b: 4/12/43, Tampa, Fla. BR/TR, 5'9", 175 lbs. Deb: 4/14/66

YEAR	TM/L	G	AB	R	H	2B	3B	HR	RBI	BB	SO	AVG	OBP	SLG	PRO+	BR/A	SB	CS	SBR	FA	FR	G/POS	TPR
1966	KC-A	35	69	5	10	0	1	0	2	15	26	.145	.298	.174	41	-5	2	0	1	.954	5	C-34	0.3
1967	KC-A	39	63	7	15	5	0	2	9	16	21	.238	.392	.413	143	4	1	0	0	.979	7	C-36	1.3
1968	Cle-A	17	10	1	1	0	0	0	1	0	3	.100	.182	.100	-13	-1	0	0	0	1.000	1	C-12/2-1,3-1,0-1	0.0
1969	Cle-A	36	85	7	25	5	0	1	9	15	12	.294	.400	.388	117	3	1	0	0	.991	6	C-36	1.0
1971	Cle-A	50	123	10	25	7	0	1	9	18	15	.203	.315	.285	65	-5	0	1	-1	.993	9	C-48	0.4
1972	Tex-A	25	33	2	5	1	0	0	4	1	4	.152	.176	.182	7	-4	0	0	0	.965	1	C-17	-0.3
1973	Tex-A	93	278	25	69	11	0	1	27	33	16	.248	.339	.299	84	-5	1	2	-1	.989	3	C-90	0.1
Total	7	295	661	57	150	29	1	5	60	99	97	.227	.334	.297	81	-13	5	3	-0	.984	31	C-273/O-1,3-1,2-1	2.8

■ LUIS SUAREZ Suarez, Luis Abelardo b: 8/24/16, Alto Songo, Cuba d: 6/5/91, Havana, Cuba BR/TR, 5'11", 170 lbs. Deb: 5/28/44

YEAR	TM/L	G	AB	R	H	2B	3B	HR	RBI	BB	SO	AVG	OBP	SLG	PRO+	BR/A	SB	CS	SBR	FA	FR	G/POS	TPR
1944	Was-A	1	2	0	0	0	0	0	0	0	0	.000	.000	.000	-99	-1	0	0	0	1.000	0	/3-1	1.0

■ TONY SUCK Suck, Anthony (b: Charles Anthony Zuck) b: 6/11/1858, Chicago, Ill. d: 1/29/1895, Chicago, Ill. 5'9", 164 lbs. Deb: 8/9/1883

YEAR	TM/L	G	AB	R	H	2B	3B	HR	RBI	BB	SO	AVG	OBP	SLG	PRO+	BR/A	FA	FR	G/POS	TPR
1883	Buf-N	2	7	1	0	0	0	0	0	0	4	.000	.125	.000	-56	-1	.000	-2	/O-1,C-1	-0.3
1884	CP-U	53	188	18	28	2	0	0			13	.149	.204	.160	12	-26	.904	-5	C-28,S-15,O-12,/3-1	-2.5
	Bal-U	3	10	2	3	0	0	0			0	.300	.300	.300	75	-1	.882	2	/C-3	0.1
	Yr	56	198	20	31	2	0	0			13	.157	.209	.167	15	-26	.901	-3	C-31,S-15,O-12,/3-1	-2.4
Total	2	58	205	21	31	2	0	0	0	14	4	.151	.205	.161	12	-27	.894	-5	/C-32,S-15,O-13,3-1	-2.7

■ BILL SUDAKIS Sudakis, William Paul "Suds" b: 3/27/46, Joliet, Ill. BB/TR, 6'1", 190 lbs. Deb: 9/3/68

YEAR	TM/L	G	AB	R	H	2B	3B	HR	RBI	BB	SO	AVG	OBP	SLG	PRO+	BR/A	SB	CS	SBR	FA	FR	G/POS	TPR
1968	LA-N	24	87	11	24	4	2	3	12	15	14	.276	.382	.471	168	7	1	0	0	.953	4	3-24	1.3
1969	LA-N	132	462	50	108	17	5	14	53	40	94	.234	.296	.383	96	-5	3	2	-0	.946	11	*3-121	0.7
1970	LA-N	94	269	37	71	11	0	14	44	35	46	.264	.355	.461	122	8	0	0	-1	.983	-6	C-38,3-37/O-3,1-1	0.5
1971	LA-N	41	83	10	16	3	0	3	7	12	21	.193	.302	.337	86	-2	0	1	-1	1.000	1	C-19/3-3,1-1,0-1	-0.1
1972	NY-N	18	49	3	7	0	0	1	6	4	14	.143	.236	.204	27	-5	0	0	0	.967	1	/1-7,C-5	-0.5
1973	Tex-A	82	235	32	60	11	0	15	43	23	53	.255	.322	.494	132	9	0	1	-1	.962	-4	3-29,1-24/C-9,OD	0.3
1974	NY-A	89	259	26	60	8	0	7	39	25	48	.232	.302	.344	87	-5	0	0	0	.990	-1	D-39,1-33/3-3,C-1	-0.6
1975	Cal-A	30	58	4	7	2	0	1	6	12	15	.121	.282	.207	43	-4	1	1	-0	.941	-1	D-13/C-5,1-2	-0.2
	Cle-A	20	46	4	9	0	0	1	3	4	7	.196	.260	.261	48	-3	0	1	-0	1.000	-1	1-12/C-6	-0.5
	Yr	50	104	8	16	2	0	2	9	16	22	.154	.273	.231	45	-7	1	2	-1	1.000	-2	1-14,D-13,C-11	-1.1
Total	8	530	1548	177	362	56	7	59	214	172	313	.234	.313	.393	102	-9	2	6	-2	.942	6	3-217/C-83,1-80,DO	0.5

■ PETE SUDER Suder, Peter "Pecky" b: 4/16/16, Aliquippa, Pa. BR/TR, 6', 175 lbs. Deb: 4/15/41

YEAR	TM/L	G	AB	R	H	2B	3B	HR	RBI	BB	SO	AVG	OBP	SLG	PRO+	BR/A	SB	CS	SBR	FA	FR	G/POS	TPR
1941	Phi-A	139	531	45	130	20	9	4	52	19	47	.245	.271	.339	62	-31	1	3	-2	.957	-7	*3-136/S-3	-3.6
1942	Phi-A	128	476	46	122	20	4	4	54	24	39	.256	.293	.340	78	-15	4	4	-1	.954	3	S-69,3-34,2-31	-0.8
1943	Phi-A	131	475	30	105	14	5	3	41	14	40	.221	.243	.291	56	-28	1	1	-0	.971	-8	2-95,3-32/S-5	-3.3
1946	Phi-A	128	455	38	128	20	3	2	50	18	37	.281	.309	.352	85	-10	1	1	-1	.959	1	S-67,3-33,2-12/1O	-0.5
1947	Phi-A	145	528	45	127	28	4	5	60	35	44	.241	.290	.337	73	-21	0	3	-2	**.986**	-17	*2-140/S-3,3-2	-3.1
1948	Phi-A	148	519	64	125	23	5	7	60	60	60	.241	.321	.345	77	-18	1	3	-2	.988	-1	*2-148	-1.2
1949	Phi-A	118	445	44	119	24	6	10	75	22	35	.267	.306	.416	93	-8	0	4	-3	.975	7	2-89,3-36/S-2	0.2
1950	Phi-A	77	248	34	61	10	0	8	35	23	31	.246	.310	.383	78	-9	2	5	-1	.979	1	2-47,3-11,S-10/1-4	-0.7
1951	Phi-A	123	440	46	108	18	1	1	42	30	42	.245	.295	.298	59	-25	5	5	-2	**.987**	10	*2-103,S-18/3-3	-1.1
1952	Phi-A	74	228	22	55	7	2	1	20	16	17	.241	.291	.303	61	-12	1	1	-0	.991	3	2-43,S-17,3-16	-1.2
1953	Phi-A	115	454	44	130	11	3	4	35	17	35	.286	.312	.350	76	-16	3	3	-1	.974	4	3-72,2-38/S-7	-1.2
1954	Phi-A	69	205	8	41	11	1	0	16	7	16	.200	.226	.263	34	-19	0	0	0	.961	9	2-35,3-20/S-2	-1.0
1955	KC-A	26	81	3	17	4	1	0	1	2	13	.210	.229	.284	37	-7	0	1	-1	.990	-3	2-24	-1.0
Total	13	1421	5085	469	1268	210	44	49	541	288	456	.249	.291	.337	71	-220	19	28	-11	.982	2	2-805,3-395,S/10	-18.0

■ WILLIAM SUERO Suero, Williams (Urban) b: 11/7/66, Santo Domingo, D.R. d: 11/30/95, Santo Domingo, D.R. BR/TR, 5'9", 175 lbs. Deb: 4/9/92

YEAR	TM/L	G	AB	R	H	2B	3B	HR	RBI	BB	SO	AVG	OBP	SLG	PRO+	BR/A	SB	CS	SBR	FA	FR	G/POS	TPR
1992	Mil-A	18	16	4	3	1	0	0	0	2	1	.188	.316	.250	62	-1	1	1	-0	.971	4	2-15/S-1,D-2	0.3
1993	Mil-A	15	14	0	4	0	0	0	0	1	3	.286	.333	.286	69	-1	0	1	-1	.944	3	/2-8,3-1	0.2
Total	2	33	30	4	7	1	0	0	0	3	4	.233	.324	.267	65	-1	1	2	-1	.962	7	/2-23,D-2,3-1,S-1	0.5

■ JOE SUGDEN Sugden, Joseph b: 7/31/1870, Philadelphia, Pa. d: 6/28/59, Philadelphia, Pa. BB/TR, 5'10", 180 lbs. Deb: 7/20/1893 C

YEAR	TM/L	G	AB	R	H	2B	3B	HR	RBI	BB	SO	AVG	OBP	SLG	PRO+	BR/A	SB	FA	FR	G/POS	TPR
1893	Pit-N	27	92	20	24	4	3	0	12	10	11	.261	.340	.370	90	-1	1	.956	-0	C-27	0.0
1894	Pit-N	39	139	23	46	13	2	2	23	14	2	.331	.404	.496	117	4	3	.910	-5	C-31/3-4,S-3,0-1	0.1
1895	Pit-N	49	155	28	48	4	1	1	17	16	12	.310	.385	.368	100	1	4	.903	3	C-49	0.7
1896	Pit-N	80	301	42	89	5	7	0	36	19	9	.296	.348	.359	90	-4	5	.952	1	C-70/1-7,O-4	0.4
1897	Pit-N	84	288	31	64	6	4	0	38	18		.222	.275	.271	46	-22	9	.941	-4	C-81/1-3	-1.5
1898	StL-N	89	289	29	73	7	1	0	34	23		.253	.314	.284	70	-11	5	.937	0	C-60,O-15/1-8	-0.5
1899	Cle-N	76	250	19	69	5	1	0	14	11		.276	.307	.304	73	-9	2	.935	-0	C-66/O-4,1-3,3-1	-0.4
1901	Chi-A	48	153	21	42	7	1	0	19	13		.275	.339	.333	89	-2	4	.970	4	C-42/1-5	0.6
1902	StL-A	68	200	25	50	7	2	0	15	20		.250	.330	.305	78	-5	2	.956	-2	C-61/1-4,P-1	-0.1
1903	StL-A	79	241	18	51	4	0	0	22	25		.212	.288	.228	58	-11	4	.983	6	C-66/1-8	0.2
1904	StL-A	105	348	25	93	6	3	0	30	28		.267	.311	.302	107	4	6	**.989**	-1	C-79/1-28	1.3
1905	StL-A	90	266	21	46	4	0	0	23	23		.173	.247	.188	41	-17	3	.983	19	C-76/1-9	1.0
1912	Det-A	1	4	1	1	0	0	0	0	0		.250	.250	.250	44	-0	0	.941	0	/1-1	0.0
Total	13	835	2726	303	696	72	25	3	283	220	34	.255	.319	.303	78	-75	48	.957	22	C-708/1-76,O3SP	1.8

■ GUS SUHR Suhr, August Richard b: 1/3/06, San Francisco, Cal. BL/TR, 6', 180 lbs. Deb: 4/15/30

YEAR	TM/L	G	AB	R	H	2B	3B	HR	RBI	BB	SO	AVG	OBP	SLG	PRO+	BR/A	SB	FA	FR	G/POS	TPR
1930	Pit-N	151	542	93	155	26	14	17	107	80	56	.286	.380	.480	106	5	11	.992	-7	*1-151	-1.5
1931	Pit-N	87	270	26	57	13	4	4	32	38	25	.211	.308	.333	73	-10	4	.993	0	1-76	-1.6
1932	Pit-N	154	581	78	153	31	16	5	81	63	39	.263	.337	.398	99	-1	7	.988	-10	*1-154	-2.3
1933	Pit-N	154	566	72	151	31	11	10	75	72	52	.267	.350	.413	117	14	2	.991	-4	*1-154	-0.5
1934	Pit-N	151	573	67	162	36	13	13	103	66	52	.283	.360	.459	115	12	4	.994	-5	*1-151	-0.6
1935	Pit-N	153	529	68	144	33	12	10	81	70	54	.272	.357	.437	109	7	6	.989	-7	*1-149/O-2	-1.5
1936	Pit-N☆	156	583	111	182	33	12	11	118	95	34	.312	.410	.467	133	30	8	**.993**	-4	*1-156	1.1
1937	Pit-N	151	575	69	160	28	14	9	97	83	42	.278	.369	.402	109	9	2	.993	-4	*1-151	-1.2
1938	Pit-N	145	530	82	156	35	14	3	64	87	37	.294	.394	.430	126	21	4	.993	-8	*1-145	-0.4
1939	Pit-N	63	204	23	59	10	2	1	31	25	23	.289	.367	.373	101	1	4	.993	-4	1-52	-0.9
	Phi-N	60	198	21	63	12	2	3	24	34	14	.318	.421	.444	137	12	1	.995	1	1-60	0.7
	Yr	123	402	44	122	22	4	4	55	59	37	.303	.394	.408	118	13	5	.994	-4	*1-112	-0.2
1940	Phi-N	10	25	4	4	0	0	0	2	5	5	.160	.300	.400	95	-0	0	.967	-2	/1-7	0.0
Total	11	1435	5176	714	1446	288	114	84	818	718	433	.279	.368	.428	112	101	53	.992	-53	*1-1406/O-2	-8.9

■ CLYDE SUKEFORTH Sukeforth, Clyde Leroy "Sukey" b: 11/30/01, Washington, Me. BL/TR, 5'10", 155 lbs. Deb: 5/23/26 MC

YEAR	TM/L	G	AB	R	H	2B	3B	HR	RBI	BB	SO	AVG	OBP	SLG	PRO+	BR/A	SB	FA	FR	G/POS	TPR
1926	Cin-N	1	1	0	0	0	0	0	0	0	1	.000	.000	.000	-99	-0	0	.000	0	H	0.0
1927	Cin-N	38	58	12	11	2	0	0	2	7	2	.190	.277	.224	37	-5	2	.970	1	C-24	-0.3
1928	Cin-N	33	53	5	7	2	1	0	3	3	5	.132	.179	.208	1	-8	0	.966	2	C-26	-0.6

YEAR	TM/L	G	AB	R	H	2B	3B	HR	RBI	BB	SO	AVG	OBP	SLG	PRO+	BR/A	SB	CS	SBR	FA	FR	G/POS	TPR
1929	Cin-N	84	237	31	84	16	2	1	33	17	6	.354	.398	.451	115	6	8			.981	-8	C-76	0.4
1930	Cin-N	94	296	30	84	9	3	1	19	17	12	.284	.325	.345	65	-17	1			.976	-3	C-82	-1.1
1931	Cin-N	112	351	22	90	15	4	0	25	38	13	.256	.334	.322	82	-8	0			.965	-8	*C-106	-0.8
1932	Bro-N	59	111	14	26	4	4	0	12	6	10	.234	.280	.342	68	-5	1			.991	-3	C-36	-0.7
1933	Bro-N	20	36	1	2	0	0	0	0	2	1	.056	.105	.056	-55	-7	0			.983	3	C-18	-0.4
1934	Bro-N	27	43	5	7	1	0	0	1	1	6	.163	.182	.186	-1	-6	0			1.000	-1	C-18	-0.6
1945	Bro-N	18	51	2	15	1	0	0	4	1	4	.294	.345	.314	85	-1	0			.947	-3	C-13	-0.3
Total	10	486	1237	122	326	50	14	2	96	95	57	.264	.319	.331	71	-51	12			.974	-20	C-399	-4.4

■ GUY SULARZ   Sularz, Guy Patrick b: 11/7/55, Minneapolis, Minn. BR/TR, 5'11", 165 lbs. Deb: 9/2/80

YEAR	TM/L	G	AB	R	H	2B	3B	HR	RBI	BB	SO	AVG	OBP	SLG	PRO+	BR/A	SB	CS	SBR	FA	FR	G/POS	TPR
1980	SF-N	25	65	3	16	1	1	0	3	9	6	.246	.338	.292	79	-2	1	0	0	.975	12	2-21/3-5	1.2
1981	SF-N	10	20	0	4	0	0	0	2	2	4	.200	.304	.200	46	-1	0	1	-1	1.000	4	/2-6,3-1	0.3
1982	SF-N	63	101	15	23	3	0	1	7	9	11	.228	.291	.287	62	-5	3	0	1	.961	10	S-37,3-14/2-9	0.9
1983	SF-N	10	20	3	2	0	0	0	0	3	2	.100	.217	.100	-10	-3	0	0	0	.917	3	/S-6,3-4	0.3
Total	4	108	206	21	45	4	1	1	12	23	23	.218	.300	.262	59	-11	4	1	1	.954	29	/S-43,2-36,3-24	2.4

■ ERNIE SULIK   Sulik, Ernest Richard "Dave" b: 7/7/10, San Francisco, Cal. d: 5/31/63, Oakland, Cal. BL/TL, 5'10", 178 lbs. Deb: 4/15/36

YEAR	TM/L	G	AB	R	H	2B	3B	HR	RBI	BB	SO	AVG	OBP	SLG	PRO+	BR/A	SB	CS	SBR	FA	FR	G/POS	TPR
1936	Phi-N	122	404	69	116	14	4	6	36	40	22	.287	.353	.386	90	-6	4			.971	-6	*O-105	-1.5

■ SULLIVAN   Sullivan b: Bristol, R.I. Deb: 5/14/1875

YEAR	TM/L	G	AB	R	H	2B	3B	HR	RBI	BB	SO	AVG	OBP	SLG	PRO+	BR/A	SB	CS	SBR	FA	FR	G/POS	TPR
1875	NH-n	2	8	3	3	0	0	0	2	0	1	.375	.375	.375	185	1	1	0	0	1.000	-1	/O-2	0.0

■ ANDY SULLIVAN   Sullivan, Andrew R. b: 8/30/1884, Southborough, Mass d: 2/14/20, Framingham, Mass. TR, Deb: 9/13/04

YEAR	TM/L	G	AB	R	H	2B	3B	HR	RBI	BB	SO	AVG	OBP	SLG	PRO+	BR/A	SB	CS	SBR	FA	FR	G/POS	TPR
1904	Bos-N	1	1	0	0	0	0	0	0	0	1	.000	.500	.000						1.000	-0	/S-1	0.0

■ JACKIE SULLIVAN   Sullivan, Carl Mancel b: 2/22/18, Princeton, Tex. d: 10/15/92, Dallas, Tex. BR/TR, 5'11", 172 lbs. Deb: 7/6/44

YEAR	TM/L	G	AB	R	H	2B	3B	HR	RBI	BB	SO	AVG	OBP	SLG	PRO+	BR/A	SB	CS	SBR	FA	FR	G/POS	TPR
1944	Det-A	1	1	0	0	0	0	0	0	0	0				-95	-0				1.000	-0	/2-1	

■ DAN SULLIVAN   Sullivan, Daniel C. "Link" b: 5/9/1857, Providence, R.I. d: 10/26/1893, Providence, R.I. TR, 5'11", 194 lbs. Deb: 5/2/1882

YEAR	TM/L	G	AB	R	H	2B	3B	HR	RBI	BB	SO	AVG	OBP	SLG	PRO+	BR/A	SB	CS	SBR	FA	FR	G/POS	TPR
1882	Lou-a	67	286	44	78	8	2	0			9	.273	.295	.315	112	4				.878	7	*C-54,3-10/O-4,S-1	1.2
1883	Lou-a	37	147	8	31	5	2	0			3	.211	.227	.272	65	-5				.897	-7	C-32/O-2,3-2,S-1	-0.9
1884	Lou-a	63	247	27	59	8	6	0	26		9	.239	.268	.320	95	-1				.930	-15	C-63/O-1	-0.9
1885	Lou-a	13	44	3	8	1	0	0	4		2	.182	.234	.205	40	-3				.948	-3	C-13	-0.4
	StL-a	17	60	4	7	2	0	0	3		6	.117	.197	.150	10	-6				.956	1	C-13/1-4	-0.4
	Yr	30	104	7	15	3	0	0	7		8	.144	.212	.173	22	-9				.952	-2	C-26/1-4	-0.8
1886	Pit-a	1	4	0	0	0	0	0	0	0	0	.000	.000	.000	-99	-1	0			.600	-1	/C-1	-0.2
Total	5	198	788	86	183	24	10	0	33		29	.232	.261	.288	84	-12				.908	-18	C-176/3-12,O-7,1S	-1.6

■ DENNY SULLIVAN   Sullivan, Dennis J. b: 6/26/1858, Boston, Mass. d: 12/31/25, Boston, Mass. TR, 5'9", 170 lbs. Deb: 8/25/1879

YEAR	TM/L	G	AB	R	H	2B	3B	HR	RBI	BB	SO	AVG	OBP	SLG	PRO+	BR/A	SB	CS	SBR	FA	FR	G/POS	TPR
1879	Pro-N	5	19	5	5	2	0	0	2	1	1	.263	.300	.368	121	0				.429	-4	/3-4,O-1	-0.3
1880	Bos-N	1	4	1	1	0	0	0	1	0	1	.250	.250	.250	72	-0				.857	-1	/C-1	-0.1
Total	2	6	23	6	6	2	0	0	3	1	2	.261	.292	.348	113	0				.429	-4	/3-4,C-1,O-1	-0.4

■ DENNY SULLIVAN   Sullivan, Dennis William b: 9/28/1882, Hillsboro, Wis. d: 6/2/56, W.Los Angeles, Cal BL/TR, 5'10", Deb: 4/22/05

YEAR	TM/L	G	AB	R	H	2B	3B	HR	RBI	BB	SO	AVG	OBP	SLG	PRO+	BR/A	SB	CS	SBR	FA	FR	G/POS	TPR
1905	Was-A	3	11	0	0	0	0	0	0	0	1	.000	.083	.000	-76	-2	0			1.000	-1	/O-3	-0.3
1907	Bos-A	144	551	73	135	18	0	1	26		44	.245	.315	.283	92	-4	16			.975	1	*O-143	-0.9
1908	Bos-A	101	355	33	85	7	8	0	25		14	.239	.276	.304	86	-6	14			.981	6	O-97	-0.3
	Cle-A	4	6	0	0	0	0	0	0	0	0	.000	.000	.000	-99	-1	0			1.000	-0	/O-2	-0.2
	Yr	105	361	33	85	7	8	0	25		14	.235	.272	.299	83	-7	14			.982	7	O-99	-0.5
1909	Cle-A	3	2	0	1	0	0	0	0	0	0	.500	.500	.500	207	-1	0			.000	-1	/O-2	-0.1
Total	4	255	925	106	221	25	8	1	51		59	.239	.296	.286	87	-13	30			.978	7	O-247	-1.8

■ HAYWOOD SULLIVAN   Sullivan, Haywood Cooper b: 12/15/30, Donalsonville, Ga. BR/TR, 6'4", 215 lbs. Deb: 9/20/55 FM

YEAR	TM/L	G	AB	R	H	2B	3B	HR	RBI	BB	SO	AVG	OBP	SLG	PRO+	BR/A	SB	CS	SBR	FA	FR	G/POS	TPR
1955	Bos-A	2	6	1	0	0	0	0	0	0	0	.000	.000	.000	-92	-2	0	0	0	1.000	1	/C-1	-0.1
1957	Bos-A	2	1	0	0	0	0	0	0	0	1	.000	.000	.000	-95	-0	0	0	0	1.000	-0	/C-1	0.0
1959	Bos-A	4	2	0	0	0	0	0	0	1	1	.000	.333	.000	-0	-0	0	0	0	1.000	1	/C-2	0.0
1960	Bos-A	52	124	9	20	1	0	3	10	16	24	.161	.257	.242	35	-11	0	0	0	.992	6	C-50	-0.4
1961	KC-A	117	331	42	80	16	2	6	40	46	45	.242	.334	.356	83	-7	1	0	0	.984	-6	C-88,1-16/O-5	-0.9
1962	KC-A	95	274	33	68	7	2	4	29	31	54	.248	.327	.332	74	-9	1	0	0	.980	-9	C-94/1-1	-1.5
1963	KC-A	40	113	9	24	6	1	0	8	15	15	.212	.305	.283	62	-5	0	0	0	.992	8	C-37	0.4
Total	7	312	851	94	192	30	5	13	87	109	140	.226	.314	.318	69	-36	2	0	1	.985	-5	C-274/1-17,O-5	-2.5

■ JOHN SULLIVAN   Sullivan, John Eugene b: 2/16/1873, Illinois d: 6/5/24, St.Paul, Minn. BR/TR, 5'10", 170 lbs. Deb: 4/19/05

YEAR	TM/L	G	AB	R	H	2B	3B	HR	RBI	BB	SO	AVG	OBP	SLG	PRO+	BR/A	SB	CS	SBR	FA	FR	G/POS	TPR
1905	Det-A	13	32	4	5	0	0	0	0	4	4	.156	.250	.156	29	-2	0			.964	4	C-12	0.3
1908	Pit-N	1	1	0	0	0	0	0	0	0	0	.000	.000	.000	-99	-0	0			1.000	0	/C-1	0.0
Total	2	14	33	4	5	0	0	0	0	4	4	.152	.243	.152	26	-3	0			.965	4	/C-13	0.3

■ CHUB SULLIVAN   Sullivan, John Frank b: 1/12/1856, Boston, Mass. d: 9/12/1881, Boston, Mass. BR/TR, 6', 164 lbs. Deb: 9/24/1877

YEAR	TM/L	G	AB	R	H	2B	3B	HR	RBI	BB	SO	AVG	OBP	SLG	PRO+	BR/A	SB	CS	SBR	FA	FR	G/POS	TPR
1877	Cin-N	8	32	4	8	0	0	0	4	1	0	.250	.273	.250	74	-1				.944	-1	/1-8	-0.1
1878	Cin-N	61	244	29	63	4	2	0	20	2	9	.258	.264	.291	91	-2				**.975**	5	*1-61	0.1
1880	Wor-N	43	166	22	43	6	3	0		4	6	.259	.276	.331	97	-1				.983	3	1-43	-0.2
Total	3	112	442	55	114	10	5	0	24	7	15	.258	.269	.303	92	-4				.976	7	1-112	-0.2

■ JOHN SULLIVAN   Sullivan, John Lawrence b: 3/21/1890, Williamsport, Pa. d: 4/1/66, Milton, Pa. BR/TR, 5'11", 180 lbs. Deb: 4/18/20

YEAR	TM/L	G	AB	R	H	2B	3B	HR	RBI	BB	SO	AVG	OBP	SLG	PRO+	BR/A	SB	CS	SBR	FA	FR	G/POS	TPR
1920	Bos-N	81	250	36	74	14	4	1	28	29	29	.296	.374	.396	126	9	3	2	-0	.977	-2	O-66/1-6	0.3
1921	Bos-N	5	5	0	0	0	0	0	0	0	0	.000	.000	.000	-99	-1	0	0	0	.000	0	H	-0.1
	Chi-N	76	240	28	79	14	4	4	41	19	26	.329	.381	.471	124	8	3	5	-2	.962	-7	O-66	-0.5
	Yr	81	245	28	79	14	4	4	41	19	26	.322	.374	.461	120	7	3	5	-2	.962	-6	O-66	-0.6
Total	2	162	495	64	153	28	8	5	69	48	55	.309	.374	.428	123	16	6	7	-2	.969	-9	O-132/1-6	-0.3

■ JOHN SULLIVAN   Sullivan, John Paul b: 11/2/20, Chicago, Ill. BR/TR, 5'10", 170 lbs. Deb: 6/7/42 C

YEAR	TM/L	G	AB	R	H	2B	3B	HR	RBI	BB	SO	AVG	OBP	SLG	PRO+	BR/A	SB	CS	SBR	FA	FR	G/POS	TPR
1942	Was-A	94	357	38	84	16	1	0	42	25	30	.235	.285	.286	61	-19	2	0	1	.936	-11	S-92	-2.4
1943	Was-A	134	456	49	95	12	2	1	55	57	59	.208	.298	.250	63	-20	6	2	1	.946	11	*S-133	0.1
1944	Was-A	138	471	49	118	12	1	0	30	52	43	.251	.325	.280	77	-13	3	3	-1	.934	-14	*S-138	-1.7
1947	Was-A	49	133	13	34	0	1	0	5	22	14	.256	.361	.271	79	-3	2	2	0	.963	8	S-40/2-1	0.6
1948	Was-A	85	173	25	36	4	1	0	12	22	25	.208	.297	.243	46	-13	2	2	-1	.951	2	S-57/2-4	-0.8
1949	StL-A	105	243	29	55	8	3	0	18	38	35	.226	.331	.284	61	-13	5	2	0	.942	-9	S-71,3-23/2-6	-1.8
Total	6	605	1833	203	422	52	9	1	162	216	206	.230	.312	.270	66	-80	18	11	-1	.942	-13	S-531/3-23,2-11	-6.0

■ JOHN SULLIVAN   Sullivan, John Peter b: 1/3/41, Somerville, N.J. BL/TR, 6', 195 lbs. Deb: 9/20/63

YEAR	TM/L	G	AB	R	H	2B	3B	HR	RBI	BB	SO	AVG	OBP	SLG	PRO+	BR/A	SB	CS	SBR	FA	FR	G/POS	TPR
1963	Det-A	3	5	0	0	0	0	0	0	2	1	.000	.286	.000	-11	-1	0	0	0	1.000	0	/C-2	0.0
1964	Det-A	2	3	0	0	0	0	0	0	0	1	.000	.000	.000	-99	-1	0	0	0	1.000	0	/C-2	-0.1
1965	Det-A	34	86	5	23	0	0	0	11	9	13	.267	.344	.337	93	-0	0	0	0	.994	1	C-29	0.2
1967	NY-N	65	147	4	32	5	0	0	6	6	26	.218	.248	.252	44	-11	0	0	0	.991	-11	C-57	-2.3
1968	Phi-N	12	18	0	4	0	0	0	1	2	4	.222	.300	.222	59	-1	0	0	0	.967	-0	/C-8	-0.1
Total	5	116	259	9	59	5	0	0	18	19	45	.228	.283	.270	59	-13	0	0	2	.991	-10	/C-98	-2.3

■ JOE SULLIVAN   Sullivan, Joseph Daniel b: 1/6/1870, Charlestown, Mass. d: 11/2/1897, Charlestown, Mass. 5'10", 178 lbs. Deb: 4/27/1893

YEAR	TM/L	G	AB	R	H	2B	3B	HR	RBI	BB	SO	AVG	OBP	SLG	PRO+	BR/A	SB	CS	SBR	FA	FR	G/POS	TPR
1893	Was-N	128	508	72	134	16	13	2	64	36	24	.264	.322	.358	83	-14	7			.860	-29	*S-128	-3.0
1894	Was-N	17	60	7	15	0	0	0	5	6	2	.250	.357	.300	62	-3	3			.900	-3	/2-8,S-6,3-1,O-1	-0.4
	Phi-N	75	304	63	107	10	8	3	63	23	10	.352	.407	.467	113	7	10			.887	-16	S-75	-0.4
	Yr	92	364	70	122	10	8	3	68	29	12	.335	.398	.440	105	4	13			.884	-19	S-81/2-8,3-1,O-1	-0.8
1895	Phi-N	94	373	75	126	7	3	2	50	24	20	.338	.395	.389	102	2	15			.879	-16	*S-89/O-6	-0.9

YEAR	TM/L	G	AB	R	H	2B	3B	HR	RBI	BB	SO	AVG	OBP	SLG	PRO+	BR/A	SB	CS	SBR	FA	FR	G/POS	TPR
1896	Phi-N	48	191	45	48	5	3	2	24	18	12	.251	.347	.340	83	-4	9			.962	-4	O-45/S-2,3-2	-1.0
	StL-N	51	212	25	62	4	2	2	21	9	12	.292	.351	.358	91	-3	5			.955	-6	O-45/2-7	-1.0
	Yr	99	403	70	110	9	5	4	45	27	24	.273	.349	.350	87	-7	14			.959	-10	O-90/2-7,S-2,3-2	-2.0
Total	4	413	1648	287	492	45	29	11	227	116	80	.299	.362	.381	93	-14	49			.872	-73	S-300/O-97,2-15,3-3	-6.7

■ MARC SULLIVAN
Sullivan, Marc Cooper   b: 7/25/58, Quincy, Mass.   BR/TR, 6'4", 205 lbs.   Deb: 10/1/82   F

YEAR	TM/L	G	AB	R	H	2B	3B	HR	RBI	BB	SO	AVG	OBP	SLG	PRO+	BR/A	SB	CS	SBR	FA	FR	G/POS	TPR
1982	Bos-A	2	6	0	2	0	0	0	0	0	2	.333	.333	.333	79	-0	0	0	0	1.000	1	/C-2	0.1
1984	Bos-A	2	6	1	3	0	0	0	1	1	0	.500	.571	.500	191	0	0	0	0	.950	1	/C-2	0.2
1985	Bos-A	32	69	10	12	2	0	2	3	6	15	.174	.240	.290	43	-6	0	0	0	.993	4	C-32	-0.1
1986	Bos-A	41	119	15	23	4	0	1	14	7	32	.193	.262	.252	40	-10	0	0	0	.986	-5	C-41	-1.2
1987	Bos-A	60	160	11	27	5	0	2	10	4	43	.169	.199	.237	15	-20	0	0	0	.994	0	C-60	-1.6
Total	5	137	360	37	67	11	0	5	28	18	92	.186	.237	.258	33	-34	0	0	0	.990	1	C-137	-2.6

■ MARTY SULLIVAN
Sullivan, Martin C.   b: 10/20/1862, Lowell, Mass.   d: 1/6/1894, Lowell, Mass.   BR/TR,   Deb: 4/30/1887

YEAR	TM/L	G	AB	R	H	2B	3B	HR	RBI	BB	SO	AVG	OBP	SLG	PRO+	BR/A	SB	CS	SBR	FA	FR	G/POS	TPR
1887	Chi-N	115	472	98	134	13	16	7	77	36	53	.284	.340	.424	98	-5	35			.847	-7	*O-115/P-1	-1.2
1888	Chi-N	75	314	40	74	12	6	7	39	15	32	.236	.273	.379	99	-2	9			.927	3	O-75	-0.1
1889	Ind-N	69	256	45	73	11	3	4	35	50	31	.285	.404	.398	122	10	15			.910	-5	O-64/1-5	0.2
1890	Bos-N	121	505	82	144	19	7	6	61	56	48	.285	.357	.386	108	3	33			.951	4	*O-120/3-1	0.3
1891	Bos-N	17	67	15	15	1	0	2	7	5	3	.224	.288	.328	71	-3	7			.926	-2	O-17	-0.5
	Cle-N	1	4	0	1	0	0	0	0	0	1	.250	.250	.250	44	-0	0			.000	-0	O-1	-0.1
	Yr	18	71	15	16	1	0	2	8	5	4	.225	.286	.324	69	-3	7			.926	-3	O-18	-0.6
Total	5	398	1618	280	441	56	32	26	220	162	168	.273	.341	.395	104	3	99			.909	-8	O-392/1-5,3-1,P-1	-1.4

■ MIKE SULLIVAN
Sullivan, Michael Joseph   b: 6/10/1860, Webster, Mass.   d: 6/16/29, Webster, Mass.   BR/TR, 5'8.5", 165 lbs.   Deb: 4/26/1888

YEAR	TM/L	G	AB	R	H	2B	3B	HR	RBI	BB	SO	AVG	OBP	SLG	PRO+	BR/A	SB	CS	SBR	FA	FR	G/POS	TPR
1888	Phi-a	28	112	20	31	5	6	1	19	3		.277	.296	.455	140	4	10			.742	-6	O-18,3-10	-0.2

■ PAT SULLIVAN
Sullivan, Patrick J.   b: 12/22/1862, Milwaukee, Wis.   TR, 5'11", 165 lbs.   Deb: 8/30/1884

YEAR	TM/L	G	AB	R	H	2B	3B	HR	RBI	BB	SO	AVG	OBP	SLG	PRO+	BR/A	SB	CS	SBR	FA	FR	G/POS	TPR
1884	KC-U	31	114	15	22	3	1	0		4		.193	.220	.237	44	-11				.767	1	3-21/O-9,C-1,P-1	-0.9

■ RUSS SULLIVAN
Sullivan, Russell Guy   b: 2/19/23, Fredericksburg, Va   BL/TR, 6', 196 lbs.   Deb: 9/8/51

YEAR	TM/L	G	AB	R	H	2B	3B	HR	RBI	BB	SO	AVG	OBP	SLG	PRO+	BR/A	SB	CS	SBR	FA	FR	G/POS	TPR
1951	Det-A	7	26	2	5	1	0	1	2	1	2	.192	.250	.346	60	-2	0	0	0	.938	0	/O-7	-0.2
1952	Det-A	15	52	7	17	2	1	3	5	3	5	.327	.375	.577	161	4	1	0	0	.826	-2	O-14	0.2
1953	Det-A	23	72	7	18	5	1	1	6	13	5	.250	.379	.389	109	1	0	0	0	.958	3	O-20	0.4
Total	3	45	150	16	40	8	2	5	12	18	11	.267	.357	.447	118	4	1	0	0	.920	1	/O-41	0.4

■ SUTER SULLIVAN
Sullivan, Suter G.   b: 10/14/1872, Baltimore, Md.   d: 4/19/25, Baltimore, Md.   6', 170 lbs.   Deb: 7/24/1898

YEAR	TM/L	G	AB	R	H	2B	3B	HR	RBI	BB	SO	AVG	OBP	SLG	PRO+	BR/A	SB	CS	SBR	FA	FR	G/POS	TPR
1898	StL-N	42	144	10	32	3	0	0	12	13		.222	.300	.243	55	-8	1			.875	-13	S-23,O-10/2-6,1P	-1.9
1899	Cle-N	127	473	37	116	16	3	0	55	25		.245	.297	.292	67	-22	16			.938	5	*3-101,O-20/S-3,12	-1.6
Total	2	169	617	47	148	19	3	0	67	38		.240	.298	.280	64	-30	17			.889	-8	3-101/O-30,S21P	-3.5

■ TOM SULLIVAN
Sullivan, Thomas Brandon   b: 12/19/06, Nome, Alaska   d: 8/16/44, Seattle, Wash.   BR/TR, 6', 190 lbs.   Deb: 6/14/25

YEAR	TM/L	G	AB	R	H	2B	3B	HR	RBI	BB	SO	AVG	OBP	SLG	PRO+	BR/A	SB	CS	SBR	FA	FR	G/POS	TPR
1925	Cin-N	1	1	0	0	0	0	0	0	0	0	.000	.000	.000	-99	-0	0	0	0	1.000	-0	/C-1	0.0

■ SLEEPER SULLIVAN
Sullivan, Thomas Jefferson "Old Iron Hands"   b: St.Louis, Mo.   d: 9/25/1899, Camden, N.J.   BR/TR, 175 lbs.   Deb: 5/3/1881

YEAR	TM/L	G	AB	R	H	2B	3B	HR	RBI	BB	SO	AVG	OBP	SLG	PRO+	BR/A	SB	CS	SBR	FA	FR	G/POS	TPR
1881	Buf-N	35	121	13	23	4	0	0	15	1	21	.190	.197	.223	32	-9				.853	-12	C-31/O-5	-2.0
1882	StL-a	51	188	24	34	3	3	0			3	.181	.194	.229	40	-12				.840	-18	C-51	-2.7
1883	StL-a	8	27	2	6	1	0	0				.222	.222	.296	62	-1				.939	5	C-6,O-2	0.3
1884	StL-U	2	9	0	1	0	0	0				.111	.111	.111	-31	-2				.000	-1	/O-1,C-1,P-1	-0.2
Total	4	96	345	39	64	7	4	0	15	4	21	.186	.195	.229	37	-24				.852	-27	/C-89,O-8,P-1	-4.6

■ TED SULLIVAN
Sullivan, Timothy Paul   b: 1851, County Clare, Ireland   d: 7/5/29, Washington, D.C.   Deb: 9/9/1884   MU

YEAR	TM/L	G	AB	R	H	2B	3B	HR	RBI	BB	SO	AVG	OBP	SLG	PRO+	BR/A	SB	CS	SBR	FA	FR	G/POS	TPR
1884	KC-U	3	9	0	3	0	0	0		1		.333	.400	.333	143	0				1.000	-2	/O-2,S-1,M	-0.1

■ BILL SULLIVAN
Sullivan, William   b: 7/4/1853, Holyoke, Mass.   d: 11/13/1884, Holyoke, Mass.   Deb: 8/9/1878

YEAR	TM/L	G	AB	R	H	2B	3B	HR	RBI	BB	SO	AVG	OBP	SLG	PRO+	BR/A	SB	CS	SBR	FA	FR	G/POS	TPR
1878	Chi-N	2	6	1	1	0	0	0	0	0	0	.167	.167	.167	9	-1				1.000	-1	/O-2	-0.1

■ BILLY SULLIVAN
Sullivan, William Joseph Jr.   b: 10/23/10, Chicago, Ill.   d: 1/4/94, Sarasota, Fla.   BL/TR, 6', 170 lbs.   Deb: 6/9/31   F

YEAR	TM/L	G	AB	R	H	2B	3B	HR	RBI	BB	SO	AVG	OBP	SLG	PRO+	BR/A	SB	CS	SBR	FA	FR	G/POS	TPR
1931	Chi-A	92	363	48	100	16	5	2	33	20	14	.275	.315	.364	83	-10	4	4	-1	.912	-9	3-83/O-2,1-1	-1.4
1932	Chi-A	93	307	31	97	16	1	1	45	20	9	.316	.358	.384	99	-1	1	3	-2	.990	-3	1-52,3-17/C-5,0-3	-0.8
1933	Chi-A	54	125	9	24	0	0	0	13	10	5	.192	.252	.208	24	-14	0	0	0	.982	-3	1-22/C-8	-1.7
1935	Cin-N	85	241	29	64	9	4	2	36	19	16	.266	.324	.361	87	-4	4			.992	2	1-40,3-15/2-6	-0.5
1936	Cle-A	93	319	39	112	32	6	2	48	16	9	.351	.382	.508	117	7	5	2	0	.968	-3	C-72/3-5,1,3-0-1	0.8
1937	Cle-A	72	168	26	48	12	3	3	22	17	7	.286	.355	.446	100	-0	1	4	-2	.949	-6	C-38/1-5,3-1	-0.6
1938	StL-A	111	375	35	104	16	1	7	49	20	10	.277	.316	.381	74	-16	8	5	-1	.990	-1	C-99/1-6	-1.2
1939	StL-A	118	332	53	96	17	5	5	50	34	18	.289	.362	.416	96	-2	3	3	-1	.954	4	O-59,C-19/1-4	0.0
1940	*Det-A	78	220	36	68	14	4	3	41	31	11	.309	.399	.450	109	4	2	0	1	.976	1	C-57/3-6	0.9
1941	Det-A	85	234	29	66	15	1	3	29	35	11	.282	.375	.393	94	-1	0	3	-2	.976	5	C-63	0.7
1942	Bro-N	43	101	11	27	2	1	1	14	12	6	.267	.345	.337	98	0	1			.962	-0	C-41	0.2
1947	Pit-N	38	55	1	14	3	0	0	8	6	3	.255	.328	.309	68	-2	1			1.000	0	C-12	-0.1
Total	12	962	2840	347	820	152	32	29	388	240	119	.289	.346	.395	91	-40	30	24		.972	-11	C-414,1-133,3/02	-3.7

■ BILLY SULLIVAN
Sullivan, William Joseph Sr.   b: 2/1/1875, Oakland, Wis.   d: 1/28/65, Newberg, Ore.   BR/TR, 5'9", 155 lbs.   Deb: 9/13/1899   FM

YEAR	TM/L	G	AB	R	H	2B	3B	HR	RBI	BB	SO	AVG	OBP	SLG	PRO+	BR/A	SB	CS	SBR	FA	FR	G/POS	TPR
1899	Bos-N	22	74	10	20	2	0	2	12	1		.270	.308	.378	80	-2	2			.952	5	C-22	0.4
1900	Bos-N	72	238	36	65	6	0	8	41	9		.273	.302	.399	83	-7	4			.974	0	C-66/S-1,2-1	-0.1
1901	Chi-A	98	367	54	90	15	6	4	56	10		.245	.271	.351	74	-14	12			.967	-1	C-97/3-1	-0.5
1902	Chi-A	76	263	36	64	12	3	1	26	6		.243	.268	.323	66	-13	11			.967	-3	C-70/1-2,O-2	-0.8
1903	Chi-A	32	111	10	21	4	0	1	7	5		.189	.224	.252	45	-8	3			.988	-2	C-31	-0.7
1904	Chi-A	108	371	29	85	18	4	1	44	12		.229	.255	.307	81	-9	11			.964	2	*C-107	0.5
1905	Chi-A	98	323	25	65	10	3	2	26	13		.201	.239	.269	64	-14	14			.974	-4	C-92/1-2,3-1	-1.0
1906	*Chi-A	118	387	37	83	18	4	2	33	22		.214	.262	.297	77	-11	10			.974	-4	*C-118	-0.4
1907	Chi-A	112	329	30	59	8	4	0	36	21		.179	.235	.228	49	-19	6			.983	-1	*C-108/2-1	-1.2
1908	Chi-A	137	430	40	82	8	4	0	29	22		.191	.235	.228	51	-23	15			.985	-20	*C-137	-3.6
1909	Chi-A	97	265	11	43	9	0	0	16	17		.162	.216	.174	28	-21	9			.983	5	C-97,M	-1.0
1910	Chi-A	45	142	10	26	6	1	0	6	7		.183	.227	.225	43	-10	0			.976	12	C-45	0.8
1911	Chi-A	89	256	26	55	9	3	0	31	16		.215	.266	.273	52	-17	1			.986	1	C-89	-0.7
1912	Chi-A	41	91	9	19	2	1	0	15	9		.209	.287	.253	57	-5	0			.975	-1	C-41	-0.1
1914	Chi-A	1	1	0	0	0	0	0	0	0		—	—	—	—	-0	0			1.000	-0	/C-1	0.0
1916	Det-A	1	1	0	0	0	0	0	0	0		—	—	—	—	-0	0			.000	0	/C-1	0.0
Total	16	1147	3647	363	777	119	33	21	378	170	0	.213	.254	.281	63	-172	98			.979	-8	*C-1122/1-4,032S	-8.4

■ HOMER SUMMA
Summa, Homer Wayne   b: 11/3/1898, Gentry, Mo.   d: 1/29/66, Los Angeles, Cal.   BL/TR, 5'10.5", 170 lbs.   Deb: 9/13/20

YEAR	TM/L	G	AB	R	H	2B	3B	HR	RBI	BB	SO	AVG	OBP	SLG	PRO+	BR/A	SB	CS	SBR	FA	FR	G/POS	TPR
1920	Pit-N	10	22	1	7	1	0	0	1	0	0	.318	.400	.455	141	1	1	0	0	.950	2	/O-6	0.2
1922	Cle-A	12	46	9	16	3	3	1	6	1	1	.348	.400	.609	159	4	1	2	-1	1.000	0	O-12	0.2
1923	Cle-A	137	525	92	172	27	6	3	69	33	20	.328	.374	.419	109	6	9	13	-5	.951	-13	*O-136	-1.9
1924	Cle-A	111	390	55	113	21	6	2	38	11	16	.290	.311	.390	79	-14	4	2	-0	.941	-6	O-95	-2.4
1925	Cle-A	75	224	28	74	10	4	0	25	13	6	.330	.375	.384	92	-2	3	2	-0	.966	-9	O-54/3-2	-1.3
1926	Cle-A	154	581	74	179	31	6	4	79	47	19	.308	.368	.403	100	0	15	8	-0	.975	-7	*O-154	-0.5
1927	Cle-A	145	574	73	164	41	7	4	74	32	18	.286	.331	.402	89	-11	6	5	-1	.955	-8	*O-145	-2.8
1928	Cle-A	134	504	60	143	26	3	3	57	20	15	.284	.319	.365	78	-16	4	2	-0	.971	-4	*O-132	-2.9
1929	*Phi-A	37	81	12	22	6	0	0	10	2	1	.272	.298	.321	57	-5	1	1	-0	.980	-5	O-24	-1.1
1930	Phi-A	25	54	10	15	2	1	1	5	4	1	.278	.339	.407	85	-1	0			.938	0	O-15	-0.2
Total	10	840	3001	414	905	166	34	18	361	166	88	.302	.346	.398	92	-38	44	35	-8	.961	-36	O-773/3-2	-12.5

YEAR	TM/L	G	AB	R	H	2B	3B	HR	RBI	BB	SO	AVG	OBP	SLG	PRO+	BR/A	SB	CS	SBR	FA	FR	G/POS	TPR

■ CHAMP SUMMERS
Summers, John Junior b: 6/15/46, Bremerton, Wash. BL/TR, 6'2", 205 lbs. Deb: 5/4/74 C

YEAR	TM/L	G	AB	R	H	2B	3B	HR	RBI	BB	SO	AVG	OBP	SLG	PRO+	BR/A	SB	CS	SBR	FA	FR	G/POS	TPR
1974	Oak-A	20	24	2	3	1	0	0	3	1	5	.125	.160	.167	-6	-3	0	0	0	1.000	-4	O-12/D-2	-0.8
1975	Chi-N	76	91	14	21	5	1	1	16	10	13	.231	.314	.341	78	-3	0	0	0	.889	-4	O-18	-0.8
1976	Chi-N	83	126	11	26	2	0	3	13	13	31	.206	.286	.294	59	-7	1	0	0	.964	-5	O-26,1-10/C-1	-1.4
1977	Cin-N	59	76	11	13	4	0	3	6	6	16	.171	.241	.342	53	-5	0	0	0	1.000	-1	O-16/3-1	-0.6
1978	Cin-N	13	35	4	9	2	0	1	3	7	4	.257	.381	.400	118	0	1	2	1	.933	-2	O-12	-0.2
1979	Cin-N	27	60	10	12	2	1	1	11	13	15	.200	.351	.317	83	-1	0	1	-1	.941	-2	O-13/1-6	-0.4
	Det-A	90	246	47	77	12	1	20	51	40	33	.313	.415	.614	168	24	7	6	-2	.989	-10	O-69,D-10/1-4	1.0
1980	Det-A	120	347	61	103	19	1	17	60	52	52	.297	.396	.504	142	21	4	3	-1	.953	-8	D-64,O-47/1-1	0.9
1981	Det-A	64	165	16	42	8	0	3	21	19	35	.255	.342	.382	98	0	1	1	-0	.964	-2	D-37,O-18	-0.4
1982	SF-N	70	125	15	31	5	0	4	19	16	17	.248	.347	.384	105	1	0	1	-1	.913	-3	O-31/1-3	-0.4
1983	SF-N	29	22	3	3	0	0	0	3	7	8	.136	.345	.136	39	-1	0	0	0	1.000	0	/O-1	-0.1
1984	*SD-N	47	54	5	10	3	0	1	12	4	15	.185	.254	.296	54	-3	0	0	0	1.000	-1	/1-8	-0.5
Total	11	698	1371	199	350	63	4	54	218	188	244	.255	.353	.425	111	24	15	13	-3	.959	-41	O-263,D-113/13C	-3.7

■ KID SUMMERS
Summers, William b: Toronto, Ont., Canada d: 10/16/1895, Toronto, Ont., Can. TR, Deb: 8/5/1893

YEAR	TM/L	G	AB	R	H	2B	3B	HR	RBI	BB	SO	AVG	OBP	SLG	PRO+	BR/A	SB	CS	SBR	FA	FR	G/POS	TPR
1893	StL-N	2	1	1	0	0	0	0	0	0	0	.000	.500	.000	37	0	0			.500	-0	/O-1,C-1	0.0

■ CARL SUMNER
Sumner, Carl Ringdahl "Lefty" b: 9/28/08, Cambridge, Mass. BL/TL, 5'8", 170 lbs. Deb: 7/28/28

YEAR	TM/L	G	AB	R	H	2B	3B	HR	RBI	BB	SO	AVG	OBP	SLG	PRO+	BR/A	SB	CS	SBR	FA	FR	G/POS	TPR
1928	Bos-A	16	29	6	8	1	1	0	3	5	6	.276	.382	.379	103	0	0	0	0	.923	-3	O-10	-0.3

■ ART SUNDAY
Sunday, Arthur (b: August Wacher) b: 1/21/1862, Springfield, Ohio BL/TL, 5'9", 193 lbs. Deb: 5/5/1890

YEAR	TM/L	G	AB	R	H	2B	3B	HR	RBI	BB	SO	AVG	OBP	SLG	PRO+	BR/A	SB	CS	SBR	FA	FR	G/POS	TPR
1890	Bro-P	24	83	26	22	5	1	0	11	7	7	.265	.419	.349	100	1	0			.909	-5	O-24	-0.4

■ BILLY SUNDAY
Sunday, William Ashley "Parson" or "The Evangelist" b: 11/19/1862, Ames, Iowa d: 11/6/35, Chicago, Ill. BR/TR, 5'10", 160 lbs. Deb: 5/22/1883

YEAR	TM/L	G	AB	R	H	2B	3B	HR	RBI	BB	SO	AVG	OBP	SLG	PRO+	BR/A	SB	CS	SBR	FA	FR	G/POS	TPR
1883	Chi-N	14	54	6	13	4	0	0	5	1	18	.241	.255	.315	68	-2				.647	-5	O-14	-0.6
1884	Chi-N	43	176	25	39	4	1	4	28	4	36	.222	.239	.324	70	-7				.663	-9	O-43	-1.5
1885	*Chi-N	46	172	36	44	3	3	2	20	12	33	.256	.304	.343	95	-2				.825	-9	O-46	-1.1
1886	Chi-N	28	103	16	25	2	2	0	6	7	26	.243	.291	.301	70	-4	10			.914	-5	O-28	-0.5
1887	Chi-N	50	199	41	58	6	6	3	32	21	20	.291	.362	.427	105	0	34			.766	-8	O-50	-0.7
1888	Pit-N	120	505	69	119	14	3	0	15	12	36	.236	.256	.275	75	-14	71			.939	17	*O-120	-0.1
1889	Pit-N	81	321.	62	77	10	6	2	25	27	33	.240	.307	.327	85	-6	47			.946	6	O-81	0.0
1890	Pit-N	86	358	58	92	9	2	1	33	32	20	.257	.327	.302	94	-1	56			.883	11	O-86/P-1	0.6
	Phi-N	31	119	26	31	3	1	0	6	18	7	.261	.367	.303	93	-0	28			.950	3	O-31	0.2
	Yr	117	477	84	123	12	3	1	39	50	27	.258	.337	.302	94	-1	84			.900	15	*O-117/P-1	0.8
Total	8	499	2007	339	498	55	24	12	170	134	229	.248	.300	.317	86	-37	246			.883	9	O-499/P-1	-3.7

■ JIM SUNDBERG
Sundberg, James Howard b: 5/18/51, Galesburg, Ill. BR/TR, 6', 195 lbs. Deb: 4/4/74

YEAR	TM/L	G	AB	R	H	2B	3B	HR	RBI	BB	SO	AVG	OBP	SLG	PRO+	BR/A	SB	CS	SBR	FA	FR	G/POS	TPR
1974	Tex-A☆	132	368	45	91	13	3	3	36	62	61	.247	.356	.323	99	2	2	4	-2	.990	6	*C-132	1.2
1975	Tex-A	155	472	45	94	9	0	6	36	51	77	.199	.283	.256	54	-28	3	1	0	.981	5	*C-155	-1.6
1976	Tex-A	140	448	33	102	24	2	3	34	37	61	.228	.287	.310	73	-15	0	0	0	.991	17	*C-140	0.6
1977	Tex-A	149	453	61	132	20	3	6	65	53	77	.291	.368	.389	105	5	2	3	-1	.994	23	*C-149	3.0
1978	Tex-A★	149	518	54	144	23	6	6	58	64	70	.278	.361	.380	108	7	2	5	-2	.997	16	*C-148/D-1	2.5
1979	Tex-A	150	495	50	136	23	4	5	64	51	51	.275	.348	.368	94	-3	3	3	-1	.995	9	*C-150	1.1
1980	Tex-A	151	505	59	138	24	1	10	63	64	67	.273	.356	.384	106	6	2	2	-1	.993	6	*C-151	1.6
1981	Tex-A	102	339	42	94	17	2	3	28	50	48	.277	.372	.366	120	10	2	5	-2	.996	-3	C-98/O-2	0.9
1982	Tex-A	139	470	37	118	22	5	10	47	49	57	.251	.323	.383	98	-2	2	6	-3	.991	-2	*C-132/O-1	-0.2
1983	Tex-A	131	378	30	76	14	0	2	28	35	64	.201	.272	.254	47	-27	0	4	-2	.993	5	*C-131	-1.9
1984	Mil-A★	110	348	43	91	19	4	7	43	38	63	.261	.334	.399	106	3	1	1	-0	.995	7	*C-109	1.4
1985	*KC-A	115	367	38	90	12	4	10	35	33	67	.245	.309	.381	88	-6	0	2	-1	.992	1	*C-112	-0.1
1986	KC-A	140	429	41	91	9	1	12	42	57	91	.212	.305	.322	69	-18	1	1	-0	.995	-1	*C-134	-1.1
1987	Chi-N	61	139	9	28	2	0	4	15	19	40	.201	.306	.302	60	-8	0	0	0	.994	9	C-57	0.3
1988	Chi-N	24	54	8	13	1	0	2	9	8	15	.241	.339	.370	99	0	0	0	0	1.000	4	C-20	0.0
	Tex-A	38	91	13	26	4	0	4	15	5	17	.286	.323	.462	114	1	0	0	0	1.000	5	C-36	0.3
1989	Tex-A	76	147	13	29	7	1	2	8	23	37	.197	.306	.299	70	-5	0	0	0	.992	1	C-73/D-1	-0.1
Total	16	1962	6021	621	1493	243	36	95	624	699	963	.248	.328	.348	89	-78	20	37	-16	.993	96	*C-1927/O-3,D-2	7.9

■ B.J. SURHOFF
Surhoff, William James b: 8/4/64, Bronx, N.Y. BL/TR, 6'1", 190 lbs. Deb: 4/8/87 F

YEAR	TM/L	G	AB	R	H	2B	3B	HR	RBI	BB	SO	AVG	OBP	SLG	PRO+	BR/A	SB	CS	SBR	FA	FR	G/POS	TPR
1987	Mil-A	115	395	50	118	22	4	7	68	36	30	.299	.357	.423	103	2	11	10	-3	.984	6	C-98,3-10/1-1,D-7	1.1
1988	Mil-A	139	493	47	121	21	0	5	38	31	49	.245	.294	.318	71	-19	21	6	3	.990	-8	*C-106,3-31/1-2,SO	-1.7
1989	Mil-A	126	436	42	108	17	4	5	55	25	29	.248	.293	.339	79	-13	14	12	-3	.985	-9	*C-106,D-12/3-6	-1.6
1990	Mil-A	135	474	55	131	21	4	6	59	41	37	.276	.335	.376	99	-0	18	7	1	.985	-6	*C-125,3-11	0.3
1991	Mil-A	143	505	57	146	19	4	5	68	26	33	.289	.324	.372	94	-4	5	8	-3	.995	-4	*C-127/3-5,O-2,2D	-0.4
1992	Mil-A	139	480	63	121	19	1	4	62	46	41	.252	.320	.321	82	-11	14	8	-1	.990	-6	*C-109,1-17/O-7,3D	-0.1
1993	Mil-A	148	552	66	151	38	3	7	79	36	47	.274	.320	.391	92	-7	12	9	-2	.949	-7	*3-121,O-24/1-8,CD	-1.6
1994	Mil-A	40	134	20	35	11	2	5	22	16	14	.261	.340	.485	105	1	0	1	-1	.923	-4	3-18,C-12/1-8,OD	-0.4
1995	Mil-A	117	415	72	133	26	3	13	73	37	43	.320	.382	.492	118	11	7	3	0	.993	-5	O-60,1-55,C-18/3-D3	0.9
1996	*Bal-A	143	537	74	157	27	6	21	82	47	79	.292	.353	.482	110	7	0	1	-1	.948	-8	*3-106,O-27,D-10/1	-0.3
Total	10	1245	4421	546	1221	221	30	78	606	341	402	.276	.331	.393	95	-35	102	65	-8	.988	-26	C-704,3-311,O/1D2S	-3.8

■ GEORGE SUSCE
Susce, George Cyril Methodius "Good Kid" b: 8/13/08, Pittsburgh, Pa. d: 2/25/86, Sarasota, Fla. BR/TR, 5'11.5", 200 lbs. Deb: 4/23/29 FC

YEAR	TM/L	G	AB	R	H	2B	3B	HR	RBI	BB	SO	AVG	OBP	SLG	PRO+	BR/A	SB	CS	SBR	FA	FR	G/POS	TPR
1929	Phi-N	17	17	5	5	3	0	1	1	1	2	.294	.368	.647	137	1	0			.900	-2	C-11	-0.1
1932	Det-A	2	0	0	0	0	0	0	0	0	0					0	0			1.000	-0	/C-2	0.0
1939	Pit-N	31	75	8	17	3	1	1	4	12	5	.227	.333	.333	81	-2	0			.984	2	C-31	0.2
1940	StL-A	61	113	6	24	4	0	0	13	9	9	.212	.282	.248	38	-10	1	0	0	.984	6	C-61	-0.1
1941	Cle-A	1	0	0	0	0	0	0	0	0	0					0	0			1.000	-0	/C-1	0.0
1942	Cle-A	2	1	1	1	0	0	0	0	0	0	1.000	1.000	1.000	492	1	0	0	0	1.000	-0	/C-2	0.1
1943	Cle-A	3	1	0	0	0	0	0	0	0	0	.000	.000	.000	-99	-0	0	0	0	1.000	1	/C-3	0.0
1944	Cle-A	29	61	3	14	0	0	0	4	2	5	.230	.254	.246	45	-4	0	0	0	.948	1	C-29	-0.2
Total	8	146	268	23	61	11	1	2	22	25	21	.228	.301	.299	60	-15	1	0		.974	8	C-140	-0.1

■ PETE SUSKO
Susko, Peter Jonathan b: 7/2/04, Laura, Ohio d: 5/22/78, Jacksonville, Fla. BL/TL, 5'11", 172 lbs. Deb: 8/1/34

YEAR	TM/L	G	AB	R	H	2B	3B	HR	RBI	BB	SO	AVG	OBP	SLG	PRO+	BR/A	SB	CS	SBR	FA	FR	G/POS	TPR
1934	Was-A	58	224	25	64	5	3	2	25	18	10	.286	.342	.362	85	-5	3	4	-2	.988	3	1-58	-0.9

■ BUTCH SUTCLIFFE
Sutcliffe, Charles Inigo b: 7/22/15, Fall River, Mass. d: 3/2/94, Fall River, Mass. BR/TR, 5'8.5", 165 lbs. Deb: 8/28/38

YEAR	TM/L	G	AB	R	H	2B	3B	HR	RBI	BB	SO	AVG	OBP	SLG	PRO+	BR/A	SB	CS	SBR	FA	FR	G/POS	TPR
1938	Bos-N	4	4	1	1	0	0	0	2	1	0	.250	.500	.250	124	0	0			.800	0	/C-3	0.1

■ SY SUTCLIFFE
Sutcliffe, Elmer Ellsworth b: 4/15/1862, Wheaton, Ill. d: 2/13/1893, Wheaton, Ill. BL/TL, 6'2", 170 lbs. Deb: 10/2/1884

YEAR	TM/L	G	AB	R	H	2B	3B	HR	RBI	BB	SO	AVG	OBP	SLG	PRO+	BR/A	SB	CS	SBR	FA	FR	G/POS	TPR
1884	Chi-N	4	15	4	3	0	0	0	0	0	0	.200	.294	.267	72	-0				.976	2	/C-4	0.2
1885	Chi-N	11	43	5	8	1	1	0	4	2	5	.186	.222	.256	47	-3				.838	-5	C-11/O-1	-0.6
	StL-N	16	49	2	6	1	0	0	6	5	10	.122	.204	.143	15	-4				.881	-2	C-14/O-2	-0.5
	Yr	27	92	7	14	2	1	0	8	7	15	.152	.212	.196	32	-7				.862	-7	C-25/O-3	-1.1
1888	Det-N	49	191	17	49	5	3	0	23	5	14	.257	.276	.314	88	-3	6			.901	7	S-24,C-14/1-5,02	0.6
1889	Cle-N	46	161	17	40	3	2	1	21	14	6	.248	.309	.311	75	-5				.892	9	C-37/1-8,O-1	0.6
1890	Cle-P	99	386	62	127	14	8	2	60	33	16	.329	.382	.422	125	14	10			.883	-4	C-84,O-15/S-4,3-2	1.3
1891	Was-a	53	201	29	71	8	3	2	33	17	17	.353	.409	.453	153	14	8			.918	-4	O-35,C-22/S-3,3-1	0.9
1892	Bal-N	66	276	41	77	10	7	1	27	14	15	.279	.316	.377	107	1	12			.958	-7	1-66	0.9
Total	7	344	1322	177	381	43	24	6	174	92	87	.288	.336	.371	107	13	41			.887	-5	C-186/1-79,OS32	1.6

■ GARY SUTHERLAND
Sutherland, Gary Lynn b: 9/27/44, Glendale, Cal. BR/TR, 6', 185 lbs. Deb: 9/17/66 F

YEAR	TM/L	G	AB	R	H	2B	3B	HR	RBI	BB	SO	AVG	OBP	SLG	PRO+	BR/A	SB	CS	SBR	FA	FR	G/POS	TPR
1966	Phi-N	3	3	0	0	0	0	0	0	0	0	.000	.000	.000	-99	-1	0	0	0	1.000	1	/S-1	0.0

YEAR	TM/L	G	AB	R	H	2B	3B	HR	RBI	BB	SO	AVG	OBP	SLG	PRO+	BR/A	SB	CS	SBR	FA	FR	G/POS	TPR
1967	Phi-N	103	231	23	57	12	1	1	19	17	22	.247	.298	.320	76	-7	0	3	-2	.928	-16	S-66,O-25	-2.3
1968	Phi-N	67	138	16	38	7	0	0	16	8	15	.275	.315	.326	93	-1	0	0	0	.968	-3	2-17,S-10,3-10,/O-7	-0.3
1969	Mon-N	141	544	63	130	26	1	3	35	37	31	.239	.290	.307	67	-24	5	7	-3	.971	10	*2-139,S-15/O-1	-0.5
1970	Mon-N	116	359	37	74	10	0	3	26	31	22	.206	.273	.259	43	-29	2	2	-1	.975	3	2-97,S-15/3-1	-1.8
1971	Mon-N	111	304	25	78	7	2	4	26	18	12	.257	.302	.332	79	-8	3	4	-2	.963	-1	2-56,S-46/O-4,3-2	-0.3
1972	Hou-N	5	8	0	1	0	0	0	1	0	0	.125	.125	.125	-29	-1	0	0	0	.000	-1	/2-1,3-1	-0.2
1973	Hou-N	16	54	8	14	5	0	0	3	3	5	.259	.298	.352	80	-2	0	0	0	.971	-4	2-14/S-1	-0.5
1974	Det-A	149	619	60	157	20	1	5	49	26	37	.254	.284	.313	69	-25	1	3	-2	.976	-23	*2-147,S-10/3-4	-4.4
1975	Det-A	129	503	51	130	12	3	6	39	45	41	.258	.323	.330	81	-12	0	2	-1	.968	-7	2-128	-1.4
1976	Det-A	42	117	10	24	5	2	0	6	7	12	.205	.250	.282	53	-7	0	1	-1	.984	1	2-42	-0.4
	Mil-A	59	115	9	25	2	0	1	9	8	7	.217	.274	.261	58	-6	0	2	-1	.955	-0	2-45/1-2,D-8	-0.6
	Yr	101	232	19	49	7	2	1	15	15	19	.211	.262	.272	56	-13	0	3	-2	.970	1	2-87/D-8,1-2	-1.0
1977	SD-N	80	103	5	25	3	0	1	11	7	15	.243	.291	.301	66	-5	0	0	0	.943	-4	2-30,3-21/1-4	-0.8
1978	StL-N	10	6	1	1	0	0	0	0	0	0	.167	.167	.167	-7	-1	0	0	0	1.000	1	/2-1	0.0
Total	13	1031	3104	308	754	109	10	24	239	207	219	.243	.292	.308	69	-129	11	24	-11	.971	-42	2-717,S-164/3OD1	-13.5

■ LEO SUTHERLAND
Sutherland, Leonardo (Cantin)   b: 4/6/58, Santiago De Cuba, Cuba   BL/TL, 5'10", 165 lbs.   Deb: 8/11/80

YEAR	TM/L	G	AB	R	H	2B	3B	HR	RBI	BB	SO	AVG	OBP	SLG	PRO+	BR/A	SB	CS	SBR	FA	FR	G/POS	TPR
1980	Chi-A	34	89	9	23	3	0	0	5	1	11	.258	.267	.292	53	-6	4	1	0	.943	-1	O-23	-0.7
1981	Chi-A	11	12	6	2	0	0	0	0	3	1	.167	.333	.167	49	-1	2	1	0	1.000	-3	/O-7	-0.4
Total	2	45	101	15	25	3	0	0	5	4	12	.248	.276	.277	53	-6	6	2	0	.949	-4	/O-30	-1.1

■ GLENN SUTKO
Sutko, Glenn Edward   b: 5/9/68, Atlanta, Ga.   BR/TR, 6'3", 225 lbs.   Deb: 10/3/90

YEAR	TM/L	G	AB	R	H	2B	3B	HR	RBI	BB	SO	AVG	OBP	SLG	PRO+	BR/A	SB	CS	SBR	FA	FR	G/POS	TPR
1990	Cin-N	1	1	0	0	0	0	0	0	0	1	.000	.000	.000	-96	-0	0	0	0	1.000	0	/C-1	0.0
1991	Cin-N	10	10	0	1	0	0	0	1	2	6	.100	.250	.100	2	-1	0	0	0	.875	0	/C-9	-0.1
Total	2	11	11	0	1	0	0	0	1	2	7	.091	.231	.091	-6	-2	0	0	0	.889	0	/C-10	-0.1

■ EZRA SUTTON
Sutton, Ezra Ballou   b: 9/17/1850, Palmyra, N.Y.   d: 6/20/07, Braintree, Mass.   BR/TR, 5'8.5", 153 lbs.   Deb: 5/4/1871

YEAR	TM/L	G	AB	R	H	2B	3B	HR	RBI	BB	SO	AVG	OBP	SLG	PRO+	BR/A	SB	CS	SBR	FA	FR	G/POS	TPR
1871	Cle-n	29	128	35	45	3	7	3	23	1	0	.352	.357	.555	166	11	3	1	0	.795	-1	*3-29/O-2,C-1	0.5
1872	Cle-n	22	107	30	30	6	1	0	11	1	1	.280	.287	.355	102	1	1	0	0	.718	-5	3-22	-0.4
1873	Ath-n	51	242	51	81	7	6	0	33	2	2	.335	.340	.413	114	2	1	3	-2	.806	1	*3-43/S-8,2-2	0.0
1874	Ath-n	55	243	54	71	10	3	0	28	0	2	.292	.292	.358	99	-2	6	4	-1	.827	-1	3-36,S-20	-0.4
1875	Ath-n	75	358	83	116	11	7	1	59	1	3	.324	.326	.402	136	9	13	10	-2	.803	14	*3-73/P-2,1-2,SO	1.8
1876	Phi-N	54	236	45	70	7	1	3	31	3	2	.297	.305	.419	141	10				.915	-4	1-29,2-15/3-8,0-4	0.5
1877	Bos-N	58	253	43	74	10	6	0	39	4	10	.292	.304	.379	110	2				.882	9	S-36,3-22	-0.4
1878	Bos-N	60	239	31	54	9	3	1	29	2	14	.226	.232	.301	69	-9				.888	-1	*3-59/S-1	-0.7
1879	Bos-N	84	339	54	84	13	4	0	34	2	18	.248	.252	.310	82	-7				.884	-12	S-51,3-33	-1.4
1880	Bos-N	76	288	41	72	9	2	0	25	7	7	.250	.268	.295	94	-2				.896	4	S-39,3-37	0.6
1881	Bos-N	83	333	43	97	12	4	0	31	13	6	.291	.318	.351	116	6				.877	-3	*3-81/S-2	0.4
1882	Bos-N	81	319	44	80	8	1	2	38	24	25	.251	.303	.301	94	-1				.856	-5	*3-77/S-4	-0.3
1883	Bos-N	94	414	101	134	28	15	3	73	17	12	.324	.350	.486	147	22				.866	-1	*3-93/O-1,S-1	1.8
1884	Bos-N	110	468	102	**162**	28	7	3	61	29	22	.346	.384	.455	164	34				**.908**	-4	*3-110	2.7
1885	Bos-N	110	457	78	143	23	8	4	47	17	25	.313	.338	.425	151	24				.875	-0	3-91,S-16/2-2,1-1	2.4
1886	Bos-N	116	499	83	138	21	6	3	48	26	21	.277	.312	.361	108	5	18			.859	-5	O-43,S-28,3-28,2-18	0.0
1887	Bos-N	77	326	58	99	14	9	3	46	13	6	.304	.342	.429	113	5	17			.875	15	S-37,O-18,2-13,3-11	1.7
1888	Bos-N	28	110	16	24	3	1	1	6	7	3	.218	.277	.291	80	-2	10			.859	-5	3-27/S-1	-0.7
Total	5 n	232	1078	253	343	37	24	4	153	5	8	.318	.321	.408	122	21	24	18	-4	.796	7	3-203/S-29,01P2C	1.5
Total	13	1031	4281	739	1231	190	73	21	518	164	174	.288	.315	.381	118	88	45			.871	-30	3-677,S-216/O21	6.6

■ DALE SVEUM
Sveum, Dale Curtis   b: 11/23/63, Richmond, Cal.   BB/TR, 6'2", 185 lbs.   Deb: 5/12/86

YEAR	TM/L	G	AB	R	H	2B	3B	HR	RBI	BB	SO	AVG	OBP	SLG	PRO+	BR/A	SB	CS	SBR	FA	FR	G/POS	TPR
1986	Mil-A	91	317	35	78	13	2	7	35	32	63	.246	.317	.366	83	-8	4	3	-1	.865	-8	3-65,2-13,S-13	-1.6
1987	Mil-A	153	535	86	135	27	3	25	95	40	133	.252	.306	.454	95	-5	2	6	-3	.965	-12	*S-142,2-13	-0.8
1988	Mil-A	129	467	41	113	14	4	9	51	21	122	.242	.276	.347	73	-18	1	0	0	.955	-6	*S-127/2-1,D-1	-1.3
1990	Mil-A	48	117	15	23	7	0	1	12	12	30	.197	.282	.282	59	-6	0	1	-1	.918	-6	3-22,2-16/1-5,S-5	-1.3
1991	Mil-A	90	266	33	64	19	1	4	43	32	78	.241	.324	.365	93	-2	2	4	-2	.968	-7	S-51,3-38/2-2,D-3	-0.8
1992	Phi-N	54	135	13	24	4	0	2	16	16	39	.178	.265	.252	47	-9	0	0	0	.948	2	S-34/3-5,1-4	-0.6
	Chi-A	40	114	15	25	9	0	2	12	12	29	.219	.294	.351	81	-3	1	1	-0	.944	-10	S-37/1-2,3-2	-1.1
1993	Oak-A	30	79	12	14	2	1	2	6	16	21	.177	.316	.304	72	-3	0	0	0	.976	-4	1-14/3-7,2-4,SOD	-0.8
1994	Sea-A	10	27	3	5	0	0	1	2	4	10	.185	.241	.296	37	-3	0	0	0	.909	1	/3-3,D-4	-0.2
1996	Pit-N	12	34	9	12	5	0	1	5	3	3	.353	.450	.588	166	3	0	0	0	.913	-1	3-10	0.3
Total	9	657	2091	262	493	100	11	54	277	189	531	.236	.301	.372	82	-54	10	15	-6	.958	-52	S-410,3-152/21DO	-8.2

■ HARRY SWACINA
Swacina, Harry Joseph "Swats"   b: 8/22/1881, St.Louis, Mo.   d: 6/21/44, Birmingham, Ala.   BR/TR, 6'2", 190 lbs.   Deb: 9/13/07

YEAR	TM/L	G	AB	R	H	2B	3B	HR	RBI	BB	SO	AVG	OBP	SLG	PRO+	BR/A	SB	CS	SBR	FA	FR	G/POS	TPR
1907	Pit-N	26	95	9	19	1	1	0	10	4		.200	.240	.232	47	-6	1			.996	-1	1-26	-0.9
1908	Pit-N	53	176	7	38	6	1	0	13	5		.216	.238	.261	59	-8	4			.983	-5	1-50	-1.7
1914	Bal-F	158	617	70	173	26	8	0	90	14	23	.280	.297	.348	73	-33	15			.985	10	*1-158	-2.9
1915	Bal-F	85	301	24	74	13	1	1	38	9	11	.246	.268	.306	59	-21	9			.986	6	1-75/2-1	-1.9
Total	4	322	1189	110	304	46	11	1	151	32	<u>34</u>	.256	.276	.315	66	-69	29			.986	10	1-309/2-1	-7.4

■ ANDY SWAN
Swan, Andrew J.   Deb: 7/23/1884

YEAR	TM/L	G	AB	R	H	2B	3B	HR	RBI	BB	SO	AVG	OBP	SLG	PRO+	BR/A	SB	CS	SBR	FA	FR	G/POS	TPR
1884	Was-a	5	21	3	3	1	0	0		0	0	.143	.143	.190	9	-2				.824	-3	/1-3,3-1	-0.5
	Ric-a	3	10	2	5	0	0	0		0	0	.500	.500	.500	230	1				1.000	0	/1-3	0.1
	Yr	8	31	5	8	1	0	0		0	0	.258	.258	.290	85	-0				.902	-3	/1-6,3-2	-0.4

■ MARTY SWANDELL
Swandell, John Martin (b: Martin Schwendel)   b: 1845, Brooklyn, N.Y.   d: 10/25/06, Brooklyn, N.Y.   TL, 5'10.5", 146 lbs.   Deb: 5/7/1872   U

YEAR	TM/L	G	AB	R	H	2B	3B	HR	RBI	BB	SO	AVG	OBP	SLG	PRO+	BR/A	SB	CS	SBR	FA	FR	G/POS	TPR
1872	Eck-n	14	55	7	11	0	0	0	4	2	1	.200	.228	.200	38	-3	0	0	0	.625	-2	/3-8,O-4,1-1,2-1	-0.4
1873	Res-n	2	9	1	1	0	0	0	1	0	0	.111	.111	.111	-37	-1	0	0	0	.909	-0	/1-2	-0.1
Total	2 n	16	64	8	12	0	0	0	5	2	1	.188	.212	.188	27	-4	0	0	0	.944	-3	/3-8,O-4,1-3,2-1	-0.5

■ PINKY SWANDER
Swander, Edward O.   b: 7/4/1880, Portsmouth, Ohio   d: 10/24/44, Springfield, Mass.   BL/TL, 5'9", 180 lbs.   Deb: 9/18/03

YEAR	TM/L	G	AB	R	H	2B	3B	HR	RBI	BB	SO	AVG	OBP	SLG	PRO+	BR/A	SB	CS	SBR	FA	FR	G/POS	TPR
1903	StL-A	14	51	9	14	2	2	0	6	10		.275	.413	.392	146	4	0			.833	-2	O-14	0.1
1904	StL-A	1	1	0	0	0	0	0	0	0		.000	.000	.000	-99	-0	0			.000	0	H	0.0
Total	2	15	52	9	14	2	2	0	6	10		.269	.406	.385	142	4	0			.833	-2	/O-14	0.1

■ EVAR SWANSON
Swanson, Ernest Evar   b: 10/15/02, DeKalb, Ill.   d: 7/17/73, Galesburg, Ill.   BR/TR, 5'9", 170 lbs.   Deb: 4/18/29

YEAR	TM/L	G	AB	R	H	2B	3B	HR	RBI	BB	SO	AVG	OBP	SLG	PRO+	BR/A	SB	CS	SBR	FA	FR	G/POS	TPR
1929	Cin-N	148	574	100	172	35	12	4	43	41	47	.300	.353	.423	96	-5	33			.970	-3	*O-142	-1.6
1930	Cin-N	95	301	43	93	15	3	4	22	11	17	.309	.335	.399	81	-10	4			.963	0	O-71	-1.3
1932	Chi-A	14	52	9	16	3	1	0	8	8	3	.308	.400	.404	116	2	3	1	0	.960	-2	O-14	-0.1
1933	Chi-A	144	539	102	165	25	7	1	63	93	35	.306	.411	.384	117	18	19	11	-1	.973	-5	*O-139	0.4
1934	Chi-A	117	426	71	127	9	5	0	34	59	31	.298	.385	.343	86	-6	10	3	1	.980	-3	*O-105	-1.2
Total	5	518	1892	325	573	87	28	7	170	212	133	.303	.376	.390	98	-1	69	<u>15</u>		.971	-14	O-471	-3.8

■ KARL SWANSON
Swanson, Karl Edward   b: 12/17/03, N.Henderson, Ill.   BL/TR, 5'10", 155 lbs.   Deb: 8/12/28

YEAR	TM/L	G	AB	R	H	2B	3B	HR	RBI	BB	SO	AVG	OBP	SLG	PRO+	BR/A	SB	CS	SBR	FA	FR	G/POS	TPR
1928	Chi-A	22	64	2	9	1	0	0	6	4	7	.141	.191	.156	-8	-10	3	0	1	.943	1	2-21	-0.7
1929	Chi-A	2	1	0	0	0	0	0	0	0	0	.000	.000	.000	-99	-0	0	0	0	.000	0	H	0.0
Total	2	24	65	2	9	1	0	0	6	4	7	.138	.188	.154	-9	-10	3	0	1	.943	1	/2-21	-0.7

■ STAN SWANSON
Swanson, Stanley Lawrence   b: 5/19/44, Yuba City, Cal.   BR/TR, 5'11", 168 lbs.   Deb: 6/23/71

YEAR	TM/L	G	AB	R	H	2B	3B	HR	RBI	BB	SO	AVG	OBP	SLG	PRO+	BR/A	SB	CS	SBR	FA	FR	G/POS	TPR
1971	Mon-N	49	106	14	26	3	0	2	11	10	13	.245	.310	.330	81	-3	1	3	-2	1.000	-6	O-38	-1.2

■ BILL SWANSON
Swanson, William Andrew   b: 10/12/1888, New York, N.Y.   d: 10/14/54, New York, N.Y.   BB/TR, 5'6", 156 lbs.   Deb: 9/2/14

YEAR	TM/L	G	AB	R	H	2B	3B	HR	RBI	BB	SO	AVG	OBP	SLG	PRO+	BR/A	SB	CS	SBR	FA	FR	G/POS	TPR
1914	Bos-A	11	20	0	4	2	0	0	3	4	.200	.304	.300	82	-0	0	1	-1	.875	-3	/2-6,3-3,S-1	-0.5

YEAR	TM/L	G	AB	R	H	2B	3B	HR	RBI	BB	SO	AVG	OBP	SLG	PRO+	BR/A	SB	CS	SBR	FA	FR	G/POS	TPR

■ ED SWARTWOOD
Swartwood, Cyrus Edward b: 1/12/1859, Rockford, Ill. d: 5/15/24, Pittsburgh, Pa. BL/TR, 5'11", 198 lbs. Deb: 8/11/1881 U

YEAR	TM/L	G	AB	R	H	2B	3B	HR	RBI	BB	SO	AVG	OBP	SLG	PRO+	BR/A	SB	CS	SBR	FA	FR	G/POS	TPR
1881	Buf-N	1	3	0	1	0	0	0		1	0	.333	.500	.333	170	0				.500	-1	/O-1	0.0
1882	Pit-a	76	325	86	107	18	11	4		21		.329	.370	.489	197	33				.788	-8	*O-73/1-4	2.2
1883	Pit-a	94	412	86	147	24	8	3		25		.357	.394	.476	187	40				.936	2	1-60,O-37/C-3	3.1
1884	Pit-a	102	399	74	115	19	6	0		33		.288	.365	.366	137	18				.804	-3	*O-79,1-22/3-1,P-1	0.9
1885	Bro-a	99	399	80	106	8	9	0	49	36		.266	.334	.331	110	6				.851	-10	*O-95/1-4,S-1,C-1	-0.7
1886	Bro-a	122	471	95	132	13	10	3	58	70		.280	.377	.369	133	20	37			.884	7	*O-122/C-1	2.2
1887	Bro-a	91	363	72	92	14	8	1	54	46		.253	.342	.344	91	-4	29			.835	2	O-91	-0.3
1890	Tol-a	126	462	106	151	23	11	3	64	80		.327	.444	.444	157	37	53			.925	8	*O-126/P-1	3.5
1892	Pit-N	13	42	8	10	1	0	0	4	13	11	.238	.418	.262	106	1	1			.933	4	O-13	0.4
Total	9	724	2876	607	861	120	63	14	229	325	11	.299	.379	.400	142	152	120			.856	0	O-637/1-90,C-5,PS3	11.3

■ CHARLIE SWEASY
Sweasy, Charles James (b: Charles James Swasey) b: 11/2/1847, Newark, N.J. d: 3/30/08, Newark, N.J. BR/TR, 5'9", 172 lbs. Deb: 5/19/1871 M

YEAR	TM/L	G	AB	R	H	2B	3B	HR	RBI	BB	SO	AVG	OBP	SLG	PRO+	BR/A	SB	CS	SBR	FA	FR	G/POS	TPR
1871	Oly-n	5	19	5	4	1	0	0	4	1	0	.211	.250	.263	50	-1	0	0	0	.788	-1	/2-5	-0.1
1872	Cle-n	12	57	8	16	0	0	0	6	2	1	.281	.305	.281	86	-0	1	0	0	.833	3	2-11/O-1	0.1
1873	Bos-n	1	4	0	1	0	0	0	0	0	0	.250	.250	.250	45	-0				.714	-1	/2-1	-0.1
1874	Bal-n	8	33	2	8	0	0	0	4	2	0	.242	.286	.242	72	-1	0	0	0	.646	-6	2-8,O-1	-0.5
	Atl-n	10	44	4	5	1	0	0	3	0	0	.114	.114	.136	-23	-5	0	0	0	.879	5	2-10	-0.1
	Yr	18	77	6	13	1	0	0	7	2	0	.169	.190	.182	21	-6	0	0	0	.781	-4	2-18/O-1	-0.6
1875	RS-n	19	76	7	13	1	0	0	4	3	1	.171	.203	.184	39	-4	2	4	-2	.828	-5	2-19,M	-0.9
1876	Cin-N	56	225	18	46	5	2	0	10	2	5	.204	.211	.244	60	-8				.864	2	*2-55/O-1	-0.5
1878	Pro-N	55	212	23	37	3	0	0	8	7	23	.175	.201	.189	29	-16				.846	-9	*2-55	-1.9
Total	5 n	55	233	26	47	3	0	0	21	8	2	.202	.228	.215	47	-12	3	4	-2	.808	-3	/2-54,O-2	-1.6
Total	2	111	437	41	83	8	2	0	18	9	28	.190	.206	.217	44	-24				.855	-6	2-110/O-1	-2.4

■ BUCK SWEENEY
Sweeney, Charles Francis b: 4/15/1890, Pittsburgh, Pa. d: 3/13/55, Pittsburgh, Pa. Deb: 9/28/14

YEAR	TM/L	G	AB	R	H	2B	3B	HR	RBI	BB	SO	AVG	OBP	SLG	PRO+	BR/A	SB	CS	SBR	FA	FR	G/POS	TPR
1914	Phi-A	1	1	0	0	0	0	0	0	0	1	.000	.000	.000	-99	-0				1.000	-0	/O-1	-0.1

■ CHARLIE SWEENEY
Sweeney, Charles J. b: 4/13/1863, San Francisco, Cal d: 4/4/02, San Francisco, Cal. BR/TR, 5'10.5", 181 lbs. Deb: 5/11/1882

YEAR	TM/L	G	AB	R	H	2B	3B	HR	RBI	BB	SO	AVG	OBP	SLG	PRO+	BR/A	SB	CS	SBR	FA	FR	G/POS	TPR
1882	Pro-N	1	4	0	0	0	0	0		0	1	.000	.000	.000	-99	-1				.500	0	/O-1	-0.1
1883	Pro-N	22	87	9	19	3	0	0	15	2	10	.218	.236	.253	47	-5				.863	3	P-20/O-7	0.0
1884	Pro-N	41	168	24	50	9	0	1	19	11	17	.298	.341	.369	126	5				.940	-2	P-27,O-17/1-1	-0.2
	StL-U	45	171	31	54	14	2	1		10		.316	.354	.439	134	2				.943	4	P-33,O-13/1-1	-0.1
1885	StL-N	71	267	27	55	7	1	0	24	12	33	.206	.240	.240	59	-11				.827	-3	O-39,P-35	-1.0
1886	StL-N	17	64	4	16	2	0	0	7	3	10	.250	.284	.281	77	-2	0			.929	-1	P-11/O-4,S-2	-0.1
1887	Cle-a	36	133	22	30	4	4	0	19	21		.226	.331	.316	83	-2	11			.936	-4	1-20,O-10/P-3,S3	-0.7
Total	6	233	894	117	224	39	7	2	84	59	71	.251	.297	.317	90	-14	11			.909	-3	P-129/O-91,1-22,S3	-2.2

■ DAN SWEENEY
Sweeney, Daniel J. b: 1/28/1868, Philadelphia, Pa. d: 7/13/13, Louisville, Ky. 5'5", 160 lbs. Deb: 4/18/1895

YEAR	TM/L	G	AB	R	H	2B	3B	HR	RBI	BB	SO	AVG	OBP	SLG	PRO+	BR/A	SB	CS	SBR	FA	FR	G/POS	TPR
1895	Lou-N	22	90	18	24	5	0	1	16	17	2	.267	.389	.356	99	1	2			.794	-4	O-22	-0.4

■ JEFF SWEENEY
Sweeney, Edward Francis "Ed" b: 7/19/1888, Chicago, Ill. d: 7/4/47, Chicago, Ill. BR/TR, 6'1", 200 lbs. Deb: 5/16/08

YEAR	TM/L	G	AB	R	H	2B	3B	HR	RBI	BB	SO	AVG	OBP	SLG	PRO+	BR/A	SB	CS	SBR	FA	FR	G/POS	TPR
1908	NY-A	32	82	4	12	2	0	0	2	5		.146	.195	.171	19	-7	0			.955	-0	C-25/1-1,O-1	-0.6
1909	NY-A	67	176	19	47	3	0	0	21	16		.267	.328	.284	93	-1	3			.947	3	C-62/1-3	0.8
1910	NY-A	78	215	25	43	4	4	0	13	17		.200	.271	.256	62	-10	12			.974	5	C-77	0.2
1911	NY-A	83	229	17	53	6	5	0	18	14		.231	.299	.301	63	-12	8			.964	-3	C-83	-0.7
1912	NY-A	110	351	37	94	12	1	0	30	27		.268	.325	.308	77	-11	6			.955	-1	*C-108	-0.1
1913	NY-A	117	351	35	93	10	2	2	40	37	41	.265	.348	.322	96	-1	11			.964	9	*C-112/1-1,O-1	1.9
1914	NY-A	87	258	25	55	8	1	1	22	35	30	.213	.316	.264	75	-7	19	6	2	.980	2	C-78	0.4
1915	NY-A	53	137	12	26	2	0	0	5	25	12	.190	.319	.204	57	-6	3	3	-1	.975	-6	C-53	-0.9
1919	Pit-N	17	42	0	4	1	0	0	0	5	6	.095	.191	.119	-5	-5	1			.944	-3	C-15	-0.8
Total	9	644	1841	174	427	48	13	3	151	181	89	.232	.310	.277	73	-59	63	9		.964	6	C-613/1-5,O-2	0.2

■ HANK SWEENEY
Sweeney, Henry Leon b: 12/28/15, Franklin, Tenn. d: 5/6/80, Columbia, Tenn. BL/TL, 6', 185 lbs. Deb: 10/1/44

YEAR	TM/L	G	AB	R	H	2B	3B	HR	RBI	BB	SO	AVG	OBP	SLG	PRO+	BR/A	SB	CS	SBR	FA	FR	G/POS	TPR
1944	Pit-N	1	2	0	0	0	0	0	0	0	1	.000	.000	.000	-96	-1	0			1.000	0	/1-1	0.0

■ JERRY SWEENEY
Sweeney, Jeremiah H. b: 1860, Boston, Mass. d: 8/25/1891, Boston, Mass. 5'9.5", 157 lbs. Deb: 8/22/1884

YEAR	TM/L	G	AB	R	H	2B	3B	HR	RBI	BB	SO	AVG	OBP	SLG	PRO+	BR/A	SB	CS	SBR	FA	FR	G/POS	TPR
1884	KC-U	31	129	16	34	3	0	0		4		.264	.286	.287	85	-6				.958	3	1-31	-0.7

■ ROONEY SWEENEY
Sweeney, John J. b: 1860, New York, N.Y. 5'8", 155 lbs. Deb: 7/25/1883

YEAR	TM/L	G	AB	R	H	2B	3B	HR	RBI	BB	SO	AVG	OBP	SLG	PRO+	BR/A	SB	CS	SBR	FA	FR	G/POS	TPR
1883	Bal-a	25	101	13	21	5	2	0		4		.208	.238	.297	69	-4				.878	-1	C-23/O-3	-0.3
1884	Bal-U	48	186	37	42	7	1	0		15		.226	.284	.274	63	-14				.917	-8	C-33,O-16/3-1	-1.7
1885	StL-N	3	11	1	1	0	0	0		0		.091	.091	.091	-44	-2				.750	-0	/O-2,C-1	-0.2
Total	3	76	298	51	64	12	3	0	0	19	4	.215	.262	.275	62	-19				.905	-9	/C-57,O-21,3-1	-2.2

■ MARK SWEENEY
Sweeney, Mark Patrick b: 10/26/69, Framingham, Mass. BL/TL, 6'1", 195 lbs. Deb: 8/4/95

YEAR	TM/L	G	AB	R	H	2B	3B	HR	RBI	BB	SO	AVG	OBP	SLG	PRO+	BR/A	SB	CS	SBR	FA	FR	G/POS	TPR
1995	StL-N	37	77	5	21	2	0	2	13	10	15	.273	.356	.377	94	-0	1	1	-0	.994	-1	1-19/O-1	-0.3
1996	*StL-N	98	170	32	45	9	0	3	22	33	29	.265	.387	.371	101	2	3	0	1	.984	-5	O-43,1-15	-0.4
Total	2	135	247	37	66	11	0	5	35	43	44	.267	.378	.372	99	1	4	1	1	.968	-6	O-44,1-34	-0.7

■ MIKE SWEENEY
Sweeney, Michael John b: 7/22/73, Orange, Cal. BR/TR, 6'1", 195 lbs. Deb: 9/14/95

YEAR	TM/L	G	AB	R	H	2B	3B	HR	RBI	BB	SO	AVG	OBP	SLG	PRO+	BR/A	SB	CS	SBR	FA	FR	G/POS	TPR
1995	KC-A	4	4	1	1	0	0	0	0	0	0	.250	.250	.250	30	-0	0	0	0	.875	-0	/C-4	-0.1
1996	KC-A	50	165	23	46	10	0	4	24	18	21	.278	.364	.412	98	-0	1	2	-1	.994	-0	C-26,D-22	-0.1
Total	2	54	169	24	47	10	0	4	24	18	21	.278	.361	.408	97	-0	1	2	-1	.989	-0	/C-30,D-22	-0.2

■ PETE SWEENEY
Sweeney, Peter Jay b: 12/31/1863, California d: 8/22/01, San Francisco, Cal BR/TR, Deb: 9/28/1888

YEAR	TM/L	G	AB	R	H	2B	3B	HR	RBI	BB	SO	AVG	OBP	SLG	PRO+	BR/A	SB	CS	SBR	FA	FR	G/POS	TPR
1888	Was-N	11	44	3	8	0	1	0	5	0	4	.182	.182	.227	32	-3				.784	-0	/3-8,O-3	-0.4
1889	Was-N	49	193	13	44	7	3	1	23	11	26	.228	.284	.311	70	-8	8			.802	-10	3-47/2-1,O-1	-1.5
	StL-a	9	38	8	14	2	0	0	8	1	5	.368	.415	.421	122	-1				.780	-1	/3-8,O-1	-0.2
1890	StL-a	49	190	23	34	3	2	0	10	17		.179	.271	.216	38	-16	8			.880	-3	2-23,3-21/1-3,O-2	-1.7
	Lou-a	2	7	1	1	0	0	0	1	1		.143	.250	.286	59	-0	1			.889	-1	/S-2	-0.2
	Phi-a	14	49	5	8	1	1	0	0	7		.163	.281	.224	50	-3	0			.915	-6	2-9,O-4,3-2	-0.2
	Yr	65	246	29	43	5	3	0	11	25		.175	.272	.220	41	-19	9			.889	-12	2-32,3-23/O-6,1S	-2.6
Total	3	134	521	53	109	14	7	1	47	37	35	.209	.280	.269	57	-30	19			.799	-24	/3-86,2-33,O-11,1S	-4.5

■ BILL SWEENEY
Sweeney, William John b: 3/6/1886, Covington, Ky. d: 5/26/48, Cambridge, Mass. BR/TR, 5'11", 175 lbs. Deb: 6/14/07

YEAR	TM/L	G	AB	R	H	2B	3B	HR	RBI	BB	SO	AVG	OBP	SLG	PRO+	BR/A	SB	CS	SBR	FA	FR	G/POS	TPR
1907	Chi-N	3	10	1	1	0	0	0		1	1	.100	.182	.100	-11	-1	1			.571	-4	/S-3	-0.7
	Bos-N	58	191	24	50	2	0	0	18	15		.262	.316	.272	85	-3	8			.871	3	3-23,S-15,O-11/21	-0.3
	Yr	61	201	25	51	2	0	0	19	16		.254	.309	.264	79	-4	9			.871	-4	3-23,S-18,O-11/21	-1.0
1908	Bos-N	127	418	44	102	18	3	0	40	45		.244	.317	.294	97	-0	17			.930	12	*3-123/S-3,2-1	1.8
1909	Bos-N	138	493	44	120	19	3	1	36	37		.243	.296	.300	81	-11	25			.903	8	*3-112,S-26	0.1
1910	Bos-N	150	499	43	133	22	4	5	46	61	28	.267	.349	.357	101	1	25			.903	-1	*S-110,3-21,1-17	0.5
1911	Bos-N	137	523	92	164	33	6	3	63	77	26	.314	.404	.417	120	15	33			.944	11	*2-136	2.4
1912	Bos-N	153	593	84	204	31	13	1	100	68	34	.344	.416	.445	133	29	27			.959	27	*2-153	5.0
1913	Bos-N	139	502	65	129	17	6	0	47	66	50	.257	.347	.315	88	-6	18			.939	-7	*2-137	-0.7
1914	Chi-N	45	145	16	40	14	5	1	38	53	15	.276	.298	.276	71	-15	18			.954	15	*2-134	0.7
Total	8	1039	3692	442	1004	153	40	11	389	423	153	.272	.349	.344	100	8	172			.949	69	2-566,3-279,S/10	7.9

■ BILL SWEENEY
Sweeney, William Joseph b: 12/29/04, Cleveland, Ohio d: 4/18/57, San Diego, Cal. BR/TR, 5'11", 180 lbs. Deb: 4/13/28

YEAR	TM/L	G	AB	R	H	2B	3B	HR	RBI	BB	SO	AVG	OBP	SLG	PRO+	BR/A	SB	CS	SBR	FA	FR	G/POS	TPR
1928	Det-A	89	309	47	78	15	5	0	19	15	28	.252	.287	.333	62	-18	12	9	-2	.993	4	1-75/O-3	-2.1
1930	Bos-A	88	243	32	75	15	0	4	30	9	15	.309	.333	.412	91	-4	5	3	-0	.997	-1	1-56/3-1	-0.9

YEAR	TM/L	G	AB	R	H	2B	3B	HR	RBI	BB	SO	AVG	OBP	SLG	PRO+	BR/A	SB	CS	SBR	FA	FR	G/POS	TPR
1931	Bos-A	131	498	48	147	30	3	1	58	20	30	.295	.322	.373	87	-10	5	12	-6	**.993**	10	*1-124	-1.6
Total	3	308	1050	127	300	58	8	5	107	44	73	.286	.314	.370	80	-32	22	24	-8	.994	13	1-255/O-3,3-1	-4.6

■ RICK SWEET
Sweet, Ricky Joe   b: 9/7/52, Longview, Wash.   BB/TR, 6'1", 200 lbs.   Deb: 4/8/78   C

YEAR	TM/L	G	AB	R	H	2B	3B	HR	RBI	BB	SO	AVG	OBP	SLG	PRO+	BR/A	SB	CS	SBR	FA	FR	G/POS	TPR
1978	SD-N	88	226	15	50	8	0	1	11	27	22	.221	.307	.270	68	-9	1	4	-2	.984	3	C-76	-0.8
1982	NY-N	3	3	0	1	0	0	0	0	0	1	.333	.333	.333	88	-0	0	0	0	.000	0	/H	0.0
	Sea-A	88	258	29	66	6	1	4	24	20	24	.256	.314	.333	76	-8	3	0	1	.993	-6	C-83	-1.1
1983	Sea-A	93	249	18	55	9	0	1	22	13	26	.221	.260	.269	44	-19	2	2	-1	.987	-3	C-85	-1.9
Total	3	272	736	62	172	23	1	6	57	60	73	.234	.294	.292	63	-37	6	6	-2	.988	-7	C-244	-3.8

■ HAM SWEIGERT
Sweigert, Hampton   Deb: 10/12/1890

YEAR	TM/L	G	AB	R	H	2B	3B	HR	RBI	BB	SO	AVG	OBP	SLG	PRO+	BR/A	SB	CS	SBR	FA	FR	G/POS	TPR
1890	Phi-a	1	1	0	0	0	0	0	0	0	1	.000	.500	.000	49	0	1			.000	-0	/O-1	0.0

■ AUGIE SWENTOR
Swentor, August William   b: 11/21/1899, Seymour, Conn.   d: 11/10/69, Waterbury, Conn.   BR/TR, 6', 185 lbs.   Deb: 9/12/22

YEAR	TM/L	G	AB	R	H	2B	3B	HR	RBI	BB	SO	AVG	OBP	SLG	PRO+	BR/A	SB	CS	SBR	FA	FR	G/POS	TPR
1922	Chi-A	1	1	0	0	0	0	0	0	0	1	.000	.000	.000	-99	-0	0	0	0	.000	0	H	0.0

■ STEVE SWETONIC
Swetonic, Stephen Albert   b: 8/13/03, Mt.Pleasant, Pa.   d: 4/22/74, Canonsburg, Pa.   BR/TR, 5'11", 185 lbs.   Deb: 4/17/29

YEAR	TM/L	G	AB	R	H	2B	3B	HR	RBI	BB	SO	AVG	OBP	SLG	PRO+	BR/A	SB	CS	SBR	FA	FR	G/POS	TPR
1929	Pit-N	42	48	11	13	3	1	0	2	2	6	.271	.314	.375	68	-2	0			.960	2	P-41	0.0
1930	Pit-N	23	36	2	4	2	0	0	2	1	5	.111	.135	.167	-27	-8	0			1.000	-1	P-23	0.0
1931	Pit-N	14	7	0	1	0	0	0	0	1	3	.143	.250	.143	8	-1	0			1.000	-0	P-14	0.0
1932	Pit-N	24	54	1	5	1	0	0	2	2	7	.093	.125	.111	-37	-10	0			**1.000**	-1	P-24	0.0
1933	Pit-N	31	55	3	11	0	2	0	4	1	7	.200	.214	.273	38	-4	0			.950	-1	P-31	0.0
1935	Pit-N	1	0	1	0	0	0	0	0	0	0	—	—	—		0	0			.000	0	R	0.0
Total	6	135	200	18	34	6	3	0	10	7	28	.170	.202	.230	13	-26	0			.973	-2	P-133	0.0

■ POP SWETT
Swett, William E.   b: 4/16/1870, San Francisco, Cal   d: 11/22/34, San Francisco, Cal   6', 175 lbs.   Deb: 5/3/1890

YEAR	TM/L	G	AB	R	H	2B	3B	HR	RBI	BB	SO	AVG	OBP	SLG	PRO+	BR/A	SB	CS	SBR	FA	FR	G/POS	TPR
1890	Bos-P	37	94	16	18	4	3	1		12	14	.191	.321	.330	69	-4	4			.820	-8	C-34/O-3	-0.8

■ BOB SWIFT
Swift, Robert Virgil   b: 3/6/15, Salina, Kan.   d: 10/17/66, Detroit, Mich.   BR/TR, 5'11.5", 180 lbs.   Deb: 4/16/40   MC

YEAR	TM/L	G	AB	R	H	2B	3B	HR	RBI	BB	SO	AVG	OBP	SLG	PRO+	BR/A	SB	CS	SBR	FA	FR	G/POS	TPR
1940	StL-A	130	398	37	97	20	1	0	39	28	39	.244	.295	.299	53	-27	1	0	0	.980	-20	*C-128	-3.6
1941	StL-A	63	170	13	44	7	0	0	21	22	11	.259	.344	.300	69	-7	2	1	0	.985	-4	C-58	-0.6
1942	StL-A	29	76	3	15	4	0	1	8	3	5	.197	.228	.289	44	-6	0	2	-1	1.000	-1	C-28	-0.7
	Phi-A	60	192	9	44	3	0	0	15	13	17	.229	.278	.245	48	-13	1	2	-1	.970	2	C-60	-0.8
	Yr	89	268	12	59	7	0	1	23	16	22	.220	.264	.257	47	-19	1	4	-2	.977	1	C-88	-1.5
1943	Phi-A	77	224	16	43	5	1	1	11	35	16	.192	.301	.237	58	-11	0	0	0	.976	-3	C-77	-0.9
1944	Det-A	80	247	15	63	11	1	1	19	27	16	.255	.331	.320	82	-5	2	0	0	.982	1	C-76	0.1
1945	*Det-A	95	279	19	65	5	0	0	24	26	14	.233	.298	.251	56	-15	1	0	0	.988	0	C-94	-0.9
1946	Det-A	42	107	13	25	2	0	2	10	14	7	.234	.322	.308	72	-4	0	0	0	.980	-4	C-42	-0.7
1947	Det-A	97	279	23	70	11	0	1	21	33	16	.251	.330	.301	74	-9	2	2	-1	.989	-0	C-97	-0.4
1948	Det-A	113	292	23	65	6	0	4	33	51	29	.223	.338	.284	65	-14	1	0	0	.991	6	*C-112	-0.1
1949	Det-A	74	189	16	45	6	0	2	18	26	20	.238	.330	.302	68	-9	0	0	0	.989	1	C-69	-0.5
1950	Det-A	67	132	14	30	4	0	2	9	25	6	.227	.350	.303	66	-6	0	0	0	.995	8	C-66	0.3
1951	Det-A	44	104	8	20	5	0	0	5	12	10	.192	.276	.192	28	-10	0	0	0	.982	2	C-43	-0.7
1952	Det-A	28	58	3	8	1	0	0	4	7	7	.138	.242	.155	12	-7	0	0	0	.977	6	C-28	0.0
1953	Det-A	2	3	0	1	1	0	0	1	2	1	.333	.600	.667	245	1	0	0	0	1.000	1	/C-2	0.2
Total	14	1001	2750	212	635	86	3	14	238	324	233	.231	.313	.280	61	-141	10	6	-4	.985	-5	C-980	-9.3

■ JOSH SWINDELL
Swindell, Joshua Ernest   b: 7/5/1883, Rose Hill, Kan.   d: 3/19/69, Fruita, Colo.   BR/TR, 6', 180 lbs.   Deb: 9/16/11

YEAR	TM/L	G	AB	R	H	2B	3B	HR	RBI	BB	SO	AVG	OBP	SLG	PRO+	BR/A	SB	CS	SBR	FA	FR	G/POS	TPR
1911	Cle-A	4	4	0	1	0	0	0	0	0	0	.250	.250	.250	39	-0	0			.800	-0	/P-4	0.0
1913	Cle-A	1	0	0	0	0	0	0	0	0	0	—	—	—		0	0			.000	0	R	0.0
Total	2	5	4	0	1	0	0	0	0	0	0	.250	.250	.250	39	-0	0			.800	-0	/P-4	0.0

■ CHARLIE SWINDELLS
Swindells, Charles Jay "Swin"   b: 10/26/1878, Rockford, Ill.   d: 7/22/40, Portland, Ore.   BR/TR, 5'11.5", 180 lbs.   Deb: 9/7/04

YEAR	TM/L	G	AB	R	H	2B	3B	HR	RBI	BB	SO	AVG	OBP	SLG	PRO+	BR/A	SB	CS	SBR	FA	FR	G/POS	TPR
1904	StL-N	3	8	0	1	0	0	0	0	0	0	.125	.125	.125	-24	-1	0			1.000	-0	/C-3	-0.1

■ STEVE SWISHER
Swisher, Steven Eugene   b: 8/9/51, Parkersburg, W.Va.   BR/TR, 6'2", 205 lbs.   Deb: 6/14/74

YEAR	TM/L	G	AB	R	H	2B	3B	HR	RBI	BB	SO	AVG	OBP	SLG	PRO+	BR/A	SB	CS	SBR	FA	FR	G/POS	TPR
1974	Chi-N	90	280	21	60	5	0	5	27	37	63	.214	.310	.286	65	-12	0	3	-2	.987	-1	C-90	-1.2
1975	Chi-N	93	254	20	54	16	2	1	22	30	57	.213	.306	.303	66	-11	0	1	0	.979	-8	C-93	-1.6
1976	Chi-N☆	109	377	25	89	13	3	5	42	20	82	.236	.278	.326	65	-18	2	1	0	.983	-3	*C-107	-1.9
1977	Chi-N	74	205	21	39	7	0	5	15	9	47	.190	.231	.298	37	-19	0	0	0	.976	-3	C-72	-2.0
1978	StL-N	45	115	11	32	5	1	1	10	8	14	.278	.331	.365	96	-1	1	0	0	.991	6	C-42	0.7
1979	StL-N	38	73	4	11	1	1	1	3	6	17	.151	.215	.233	22	-8	0	0	0	.974	-1	C-33	-0.6
1980	StL-N	18	24	2	6	1	0	0	2	1	7	.250	.280	.292	58	-1	0	0	0	.957	0	/C-8	-0.1
1981	SD-N	16	28	2	4	0	0	0	3	2	11	.143	.200	.143	-2	-4	0	0	0	.971	-0	C-10	-0.4
1982	SD-N	26	58	2	10	1	0	2	3	5	24	.172	.238	.293	50	-4	0	0	0	.981	-1	C-26	-0.2
Total	9	509	1414	108	305	49	7	20	124	118	322	.216	.281	.303	59	-78	4	4	-2	.982	-5	C-481	-7.3

■ RON SWOBODA
Swoboda, Ronald Alan "Rocky"   b: 6/30/44, Baltimore, Md.   BR/TR, 6'2", 205 lbs.   Deb: 4/12/65

YEAR	TM/L	G	AB	R	H	2B	3B	HR	RBI	BB	SO	AVG	OBP	SLG	PRO+	BR/A	SB	CS	SBR	FA	FR	G/POS	TPR
1965	NY-N	135	399	52	91	15	3	19	50	33	102	.228	.292	.424	102	-0	2	3	-1	.947	1	*O-112	-1.4
1966	NY-N	112	342	34	76	9	4	8	50	31	76	.222	.296	.342	79	-10	3	4	0	.987	0	O-97	-1.4
1967	NY-N	134	449	47	126	17	3	13	53	41	96	.281	.342	.419	119	11	3	1	0	.957	3	*O-108,1-20	0.8
1968	NY-N	132	450	46	109	14	6	11	59	52	113	.242	.326	.373	109	6	8	1	2	.975	4	*O-125	0.6
1969	*NY-N	109	327	38	77	10	2	9	52	43	90	.235	.328	.361	91	-3	1	0	0	.988	0	O-97	-0.9
1970	NY-N	115	245	29	57	8	2	9	40	40	72	.233	.343	.392	96	-1	2	4	-2	.984	-12	*O-100	-1.8
1971	Mon-N	39	75	7	19	4	3	0	6	11	16	.253	.364	.387	112	-2	0	0	0	.977	-3	O-26	-0.3
	NY-A	54	138	17	36	2	1	2	20	27	35	.261	.393	.333	114	4	0	0	0	.965	-3	O-47	-0.1
1972	NY-A	63	113	9	28	8	0	1	12	17	29	.248	.346	.345	110	-4	5	0	0	.983	-5	O-35/1-2	-0.5
1973	NY-A	35	43	6	5	0	0	1	2	4	18	.116	.191	.186	7	-5	0	0	0	1.000	-4	O-20/D-4	-0.3
Total	9	928	2581	285	624	87	24	73	344	299	647	.242	.325	.379	101	4	20	14	-4	.972	-18	O-767/1-22,D-4	-5.1

■ LOU SYLVESTER
Sylvester, Louis J.   b: 2/14/1855, Springfield, Ill.   BR/TR, 5'3", 165 lbs.   Deb: 4/18/1884

YEAR	TM/L	G	AB	R	H	2B	3B	HR	RBI	BB	SO	AVG	OBP	SLG	PRO+	BR/A	SB	CS	SBR	FA	FR	G/POS	TPR
1884	Cin-U	82	333	67	89	13	8	2		18		.267	.305	.372	97	-12				.792	0	*O-81/P-6,S-2	-1.0
1886	Lou-a	45	154	41	35	5	3	0	17	29		.227	.350	.299	98	0	3			.913	-0	O-45	-0.1
	Cin-a	17	55	10	10	0	0	3	8	7		.182	.286	.345	94	-0	2			.909	1	O-17	0.0
	Yr	62	209	51	45	5	3	3	25	36		.215	.333	.311	97	-0	5			.912	1	O-62	-0.1
1887	StL-a	29	112	20	25	3	1		18	13		.223	.310	.339	73	-5	13			.923	2	O-29/2-1	-0.3
Total	3	173	654	138	159	22	14	6	43	67		.243	.315	.347	93	-17	18			.854	0	O-172/P-6,S-2,2-1	-1.4

■ JOE SZEKELY
Szekely, Joseph   b: 2/2/25, Cleveland, Ohio   BR/TR, 5'11", 180 lbs.   Deb: 9/13/53

YEAR	TM/L	G	AB	R	H	2B	3B	HR	RBI	BB	SO	AVG	OBP	SLG	PRO+	BR/A	SB	CS	SBR	FA	FR	G/POS	TPR
1953	Cin-N	5	13	1	1	0	0	0	0	0	6	.077	.077	.077	-59	-3	0	0	0	1.000	1	/O-3	-0.2

■ KEN SZOTKIEWICZ
Szotkiewicz, Kenneth John   b: 2/25/47, Wilmington, Del.   BL/TR, 6', 165 lbs.   Deb: 4/7/70

YEAR	TM/L	G	AB	R	H	2B	3B	HR	RBI	BB	SO	AVG	OBP	SLG	PRO+	BR/A	SB	CS	SBR	FA	FR	G/POS	TPR
1970	Det-A	47	84	9	9	1	0	3	9	12	29	.107	.219	.226	23	-9	0	0	0	.971	9	S-44	0.4

■ JERRY TABB
Tabb, Jerry Lynn   b: 3/17/52, Altus, Okla.   BL/TR, 6'2", 195 lbs.   Deb: 9/8/76

YEAR	TM/L	G	AB	R	H	2B	3B	HR	RBI	BB	SO	AVG	OBP	SLG	PRO+	BR/A	SB	CS	SBR	FA	FR	G/POS	TPR
1976	Chi-N	11	24	2	7	1	0	0	3	2	7	.292	.370	.292	82	-0	0	0	0	1.000	-1	/1-6	-0.1
1977	Oak-A	51	144	8	32	9	0	6	19	10	26	.222	.273	.368	74	-6	0	1	0	.993	-2	1-36/D-5	-1.0
1978	Oak-A	12	9	0	1	0	0	0	1	2	5	.111	.273	.111	12	-1	0	0	0	1.000	-0	/1-2,D-2	-0.1
Total	3	74	177	10	40	10	0	6	20	15	33	.226	.286	.345	72	-7	0	1	0	.994	-3	/1-44,D-7	-1.2

■ PAT TABLER
Tabler, Patrick Sean   b: 2/2/58, Hamilton, Ohio   BR/TR, 6'2", 200 lbs.   Deb: 8/21/81

YEAR	TM/L	G	AB	R	H	2B	3B	HR	RBI	BB	SO	AVG	OBP	SLG	PRO+	BR/A	SB	CS	SBR	FA	FR	G/POS	TPR
1981	Chi-N	35	101	11	19	3	1	0	3	13	26	.188	.281	.267	54	-6	0	1	-1	.982	1	2-35	-0.4
1982	Chi-N	25	85	9	20	4	2	1	7	6	20	.235	.293	.365	81	-2	0	0	0	.949	-5	3-25	-0.8

YEAR	TM/L	G	AB	R	H	2B	3B	HR	RBI	BB	SO	AVG	OBP	SLG	PRO+	BR/A	SB	CS	SBR	FA	FR	G/POS	TPR
1983	Cle-A	124	430	56	125	23	5	6	65	56	63	.291	.374	.409	111	8	2	4	-2	.948	-3	O-88,3-25/2-2,D-6	0.0
1984	Cle-A	144	473	56	137	21	3	10	68	47	62	.290	.358	.410	110	7	3	1	0	.998	-13	1-67,O-43,3-36,/2D	-1.1
1985	Cle-A	117	404	47	111	18	3	5	59	27	55	.275	.323	.371	90	-5	0	6	-4	.983	1	1-92,D-18/3-4,2-1	-1.4
1986	Cle-A	130	473	61	154	29	2	6	48	29	75	.326	.368	.433	119	13	3	1	0	.990	1	*1-107,D-18	0.6
1987	Cle-A★	151	553	66	170	34	3	11	86	51	84	.307	.372	.439	113	12	5	2	0	.984	5	1-82,D-66	0.9
1988	Cle-A	41	143	16	32	5	1	1	17	23	27	.224	.335	.294	76	-4	1	0	0	1.000	-1	D-29,1-10	-0.6
	KC-A	89	301	37	93	17	2	1	49	23	41	.309	.362	.389	109	4	2	3	-1	.986	-2	D-40,O-37/1-7,3-1	-0.1
	Yr	130	444	53	125	22	3	2	66	46	68	.282	.353	.358	98	0	3	3	-1	.986	-2	D-69,O-37,1-17/3-1	-1.1
1989	KC-A	123	390	36	101	11	1	2	42	37	42	.259	.326	.308	80	-9	0	0	0	.970	-2	O-55,D-39,1-20/23	-1.1
1990	KC-A	75	195	12	53	14	0	1	19	20	21	.272	.343	.359	98	-0	0	2	-1	.986	-0	O-42,D-15/3-6,1-5	-0.3
	NY-N	17	43	6	12	1	1	1	10	3	8	.279	.340	.419	108	0	0	0	0	1.000	1	O-10	-0.0
1991	*Tor-A	82	185	20	40	5	1	1	21	29	21	.216	.326	.270	64	-8	0	0	0	.985	-1	D-57,1-20/O-1	-1.2
1992	*Tor-A	49	135	11	34	5	0	0	16	11	14	.252	.308	.289	65	-6	0	0	0	1.000	-1	1-34/O-8,3-1,D-2	-1.0
Total	12	1202	3911	454	1101	190	25	47	512	375	559	.282	.348	.379	99	3	16	20	-7	.988	-14	1-444,D-291,O/32	-6.4

■ GREG TABOR
Tabor, Gregory Steven b: 5/21/61, Castro Valley, Cal. BR/TR, 6'", 165 lbs. Deb: 9/10/87

YEAR	TM/L	G	AB	R	H	2B	3B	HR	RBI	BB	SO	AVG	OBP	SLG	PRO+	BR/A	SB	CS	SBR	FA	FR	G/POS	TPR
1987	Tex-A	9	9	4	1	0	0	0	1	0	4	.111	.111	.222	-15	-1	0	0	0	.938	4	/2-4,D-1	0.2

■ JIM TABOR
Tabor, James Reubin "Rawhide" b: 11/5/16, New Hope, Ala. d: 8/22/53, Sacramento, Cal. BR/TR, 6'2", 175 lbs. Deb: 8/2/38

YEAR	TM/L	G	AB	R	H	2B	3B	HR	RBI	BB	SO	AVG	OBP	SLG	PRO+	BR/A	SB	CS	SBR	FA	FR	G/POS	TPR
1938	Bos-A	19	57	8	18	3	2	1	8	1	6	.316	.328	.491	98	-1	0	1	-1	.889	1	3-11/S-2	0.0
1939	Bos-A	149	577	76	167	33	8	14	95	40	54	.289	.337	.447	95	-6	16	10	-1	.923	7	*3-148	0.1
1940	Bos-A	120	459	73	131	28	6	21	81	42	58	.285	.345	.510	114	8	14	10	-2	.926	5	*3-120	1.3
1941	Bos-A	126	498	65	139	29	3	16	101	36	48	.279	.328	.446	100	2	17	9	-0	.930	2	*3-125	0.3
1942	Bos-A	139	508	56	128	18	2	12	75	37	47	.252	.303	.366	85	-12	6	13	-6	.924	-9	*3-138	-2.5
1943	Bos-A	137	537	57	130	26	3	13	85	43	54	.242	.299	.374	95	-5	7	7	-2	.938	-8	*3-133/O-2	-1.5
1944	Bos-A	116	438	58	125	25	3	13	72	31	38	.285	.334	.445	123	11	4	4	-1	.950	3	*3-114	1.5
1946	Phi-N	124	463	53	124	15	2	10	50	36	51	.268	.322	.374	100	-1	3			.954	-3	*3-124	-0.3
1947	Phi-N	75	251	27	59	14	0	4	31	20	21	.235	.297	.339	71	-11	2			.916	-17	3-67	-2.8
Total	9	1005	3788	473	1021	191	29	104	598	286	377	.270	.322	.418	99	-20	69	54		.933	-19	3-980/O-2,S-2	-3.9

■ JEFF TACKETT
Tackett, Jeffrey Wilson b: 12/1/65, Fresno, Cal. BR/TR, 6'2", 200 lbs. Deb: 9/11/91

YEAR	TM/L	G	AB	R	H	2B	3B	HR	RBI	BB	SO	AVG	OBP	SLG	PRO+	BR/A	SB	CS	SBR	FA	FR	G/POS	TPR
1991	Bal-A	6	8	1	1	0	0	0	2	2		.125	.300	.125	23	-1	0	0	0	1.000		/C-6	0.0
1992	Bal-A	65	179	21	43	8	1	5	24	17	28	.240	.313	.380	91	-1	0	0	0	.997	6	C-64/3-1	0.7
1993	Bal-A	39	87	8	15	3	0	0	9	13	28	.172	.280	.207	32	-8	0	0	0	.989	5	C-38/P-1	-0.2
1994	Bal-A	26	53	5	12	3	1	2	9	5	13	.226	.317	.434	87	-1	0	0	0	.980	5	C-26	0.1
Total	4	136	327	35	71	14	2	7	42	37	71	.217	.304	.336	72	-12	0	0	0	.992	13	C-134/P-1,3-1	0.6

■ DOUG TAITT
Taitt, Douglas John "Poco" b: 8/3/02, Bay City, Mich. d: 12/12/70, Portland, Ore. BL/TR, 6', 176 lbs. Deb: 4/10/28

YEAR	TM/L	G	AB	R	H	2B	3B	HR	RBI	BB	SO	AVG	OBP	SLG	PRO+	BR/A	SB	CS	SBR	FA	FR	G/POS	TPR
1928	Bos-A	143	482	51	144	28	14	3	61	36	32	.299	.350	.434	107	4	13	6	0	.975	5	*O-139/P-1	0.0
1929	Bos-A	26	65	6	18	4	0	0	6	8	5	.277	.365	.338	84	-1	0	1	-1	.955	-0	O-21	-0.3
	Chi-A	47	124	11	21	7	0	0	12	8	13	.169	.220	.226	15	-16	0	0	0	.966	0	O-30	-1.7
	Yr	73	189	17	39	11	0	0	18	16	18	.206	.272	.265	39	-17	0	1	-1	.961	0	O-51	-2.0
1931	Phi-N	38	151	13	34	4	2	1	15	4	14	.225	.245	.298	42	-12	0	0		.990	5	O-38	-1.0
1932	Phi-N	4	2	0	0	0	0	0	1	2	0	.000	.500	.000	43	0	0			.000	0	H	0.0
Total	4	258	824	81	217	43	16	4	95	58	64	.263	.314	.369	79	-26	13	7		.975	10	O-228/P-1	-3.0

■ BOB TALBOT
Talbot, Robert Dale b: 6/6/27, Visalia, Cal. BR/TR, 6', 170 lbs. Deb: 9/16/53

YEAR	TM/L	G	AB	R	H	2B	3B	HR	RBI	BB	SO	AVG	OBP	SLG	PRO+	BR/A	SB	CS	SBR	FA	FR	G/POS	TPR
1953	Chi-N	8	30	5	10	0	1	0	0	0	4	.333	.333	.400	88	-1	1	0	0	1.000	3	/O-7	0.2
1954	Chi-N	114	403	45	97	15	4	1	19	16	25	.241	.275	.305	50	-29	3	6	-3	.985	-6	*O-111	-4.3
Total	2	122	433	50	107	15	5	1	19	16	29	.247	.279	.312	53	-30	4	6	-2	.986	-4	O-118	-4.1

■ TIM TALTON
Talton, Marion Lee b: 1/14/39, Pikeville, N.C. BL/TR, 6'3", 200 lbs. Deb: 7/8/66

YEAR	TM/L	G	AB	R	H	2B	3B	HR	RBI	BB	SO	AVG	OBP	SLG	PRO+	BR/A	SB	CS	SBR	FA	FR	G/POS	TPR
1966	KC-A	37	53	8	18	3	1	2	6	1	5	.340	.364	.547	163	4	0	1	-1	1.000	-1	C-14/1-9	0.3
1967	KC-A	46	59	7	15	3	1	0	5	7	13	.254	.333	.339	102	0	0	0	0	.971	-5	C-22/1-1	-0.4
Total	2	83	112	15	33	6	2	2	11	8	18	.295	.347	.438	131	4	0	1	-1	.980	-6	/C-36,1-10	-0.1

■ JOHN TAMARGO
Tamargo, John Felix b: 11/7/51, Tampa, Fla. BB/TR, 5'10", 180 lbs. Deb: 9/3/76

YEAR	TM/L	G	AB	R	H	2B	3B	HR	RBI	BB	SO	AVG	OBP	SLG	PRO+	BR/A	SB	CS	SBR	FA	FR	G/POS	TPR
1976	StL-N	10	10	2	3	0	0	0	1	3	0	.300	.462	.300	118	1	0	0	0	1.000	-1	/C-1	0.0
1977	StL-N	4	4	0	0	0	0	0	0	0	0	.000	.000	.000	-99	-1	0	0	0	1.000	-0	/C-1	-0.1
1978	StL-N	6	6	0	0	0	0	0	0	0	0	.000	.000	.000	-99	-2	0	0	0	.000	0	/C-1	-0.2
	SF-N	36	92	6	22	4	1	1	8	18	7	.239	.364	.337	101	1	1	1	-0	.965	-2	C-31	-0.1
	Yr	42	98	6	22	4	1	1	8	18	9	.224	.345	.316	89	-1	1	1	-0	.965	-2	C-32	-0.3
1979	SF-N	30	60	7	12	3	0	2	6	4	8	.200	.250	.350	66	-3	0	0	0	.985	-6	C-17	-0.9
	Mon-N	12	21	0	8	2	0	0	5	3	3	.381	.458	.476	157	2	0	0	0	1.000	-1	/C-4	0.1
	Yr	42	81	7	20	5	0	2	11	7	11	.247	.307	.383	92	-1	0	0	0	.989	-7	C-21	-0.8
1980	Mon-N	37	51	4	14	3	0	1	13	6	5	.275	.351	.392	107	1	0	0	0	.975	-2	/C-12	-0.1
Total	5	135	244	19	59	12	1	4	33	34	27	.242	.335	.348	92	1	1	1	-0	.974	-12	/C-67	-1.3

■ LEO TANKERSLEY
Tankersley, Lawrence William b: 6/8/01, Terrell, Tex. d: 9/18/80, Dallas, Tex. BR/TR, 6', 176 lbs. Deb: 7/2/25

YEAR	TM/L	G	AB	R	H	2B	3B	HR	RBI	BB	SO	AVG	OBP	SLG	PRO+	BR/A	SB	CS	SBR	FA	FR	G/POS	TPR
1925	Chi-A	1	3	0	0	0	0	0	0	0	0	.000	.000	.000	-99	-1	0	0	0	1.000	-1	/C-1	-0.2

■ JESSE TANNEHILL
Tannehill, Jesse Niles "Powder" b: 7/14/1874, Dayton, Ky. d: 9/22/56, Dayton, Ky. BB/TL, 5'8", 150 lbs. Deb: 6/17/1894 FC

YEAR	TM/L	G	AB	R	H	2B	3B	HR	RBI	BB	SO	AVG	OBP	SLG	PRO+	BR/A	SB	CS	SBR	FA	FR	G/POS	TPR
1894	Cin-N	5	11	0	0	0	0	0	1	1	2	.000	.083	.000	-76	-3	0			.600	-1	/P-5	0.0
1897	Pit-N	56	184	22	49	8	2	0	22	18		.266	.338	.332	80	-5	4			.900	7	O-33,P-21	-0.1
1898	Pit-N	60	152	25	44	9	3	1	17	7		.289	.321	.408	111	1	4			.956	4	P-43/O-7	0.0
1899	Pit-N	47	132	17	34	5	3	0	10	8		.258	.310	.341	79	-4	2			.954	3	P-40/O-1	-0.1
1900	Pit-N	34	110	19	37	7	0	0	17	5		.336	.365	.400	110	1	2			.924	1	P-29/O-4	0.0
1901	Pit-N	42	135	19	33	3	3	1	12	6		.244	.277	.333	74	-5	0			.917	-2	P-32,O-10	-0.1
1902	Pit-N	44	148	27	43	6	1	1	17	12		.291	.348	.365	116	3	1			.969	-3	P-26,O-16	-0.2
1903	NY-A	40	111	18	26	6	2	1	13	8		.234	.292	.351	87	-2	1			.969	2	P-32/O-5	-0.1
1904	Bos-A	45	122	14	24	2	6	0	6	9		.197	.252	.311	73	-4	1			.991	2	P-33/O-2	-0.1
1905	Bos-A	37	93	11	21	2	0	1	12	16		.226	.339	.280	96	0	1			.946	2	P-37	0.0
1906	Bos-A	31	79	12	22	2	2	0	4	6		.278	.329	.354	114	1	1			.948	-1	P-27	0.0
1907	Bos-A	21	51	2	10	3	1	0	6	2		.196	.241	.294	71	-2	0			.981	0	P-18	0.0
1908	Bos-A	1	2	0	1	0	0	0	0	0		.500	.500	.500	219	0	0			1.000	0	/P-1	0.0
	Was-A	26	43	1	11	1	0	0	3	2		.256	.289	.279	92	-0	0			.897	1	P-10	0.0
	Yr	27	45	1	12	1	0	0	3	2		.267	.298	.289	99	-0	0			.907	2	P-11	0.0
1909	Was-A	16	36	2	6	1	0	0	0	5		.167	.286	.194	55	-2	0			1.000	-0	/O-9,P-3	-0.3
1911	Cin-N	1	1	0	0	0	0	0	0	0	1	.000	.000	.000	-99	-0	0			1.000	-0	/P-1	0.0
Total	15	506	1410	189	361	55	23	5	141	105	3	.256	.311	.338	90	-20	19			.953	16	P-358/O-87	-1.1

■ LEE TANNEHILL
Tannehill, Lee Ford b: 10/26/1880, Dayton, Ky. d: 2/16/38, Live Oak, Fla. BR/TR, 5'11", 170 lbs. Deb: 4/22/03 F

YEAR	TM/L	G	AB	R	H	2B	3B	HR	RBI	BB	SO	AVG	OBP	SLG	PRO+	BR/A	SB	CS	SBR	FA	FR	G/POS	TPR
1903	Chi-A	138	503	48	113	14	3	2	50	25		.225	.263	.276	65	-22	10			.908	-5	*S-138	-2.1
1904	Chi-A	153	547	50	125	31	5	0	61	20		.229	.260	.303	81	-13	14			.947	28	*3-153	2.2
1905	Chi-A	142	480	38	96	17	2	0	39	45		.200	.274	.244	67	-17	8			.931	28	*3-142	1.8
1906	*Chi-A	116	378	26	69	8	3	0	33	31		.183	.254	.220	50	-21	7			.951	39	3-99,S-17	2.4
1907	Chi-A	33	108	9	26	2	0	0	11	8		.241	.293	.259	79	-2	3			.912	-1	3-31/S-2	0.4
1908	Chi-A	141	482	44	104	15	0	0	35	25		.216	.257	.259	69	-17	6			.935	18	*3-136/S-5	0.7
1909	Chi-A	155	531	39	118	21	5	0	47	31		.222	.269	.281	77	-15	12			.941	7	*3-91,S-64	-0.1
1910	Chi-A	67	230	17	51	10	1	1	21	11		.222	.263	.278	73	-8	3			.947	3	S-38,1-23/3-6	-0.4
1911	Chi-A	141	516	60	131	17	6	0	49	32		.254	.300	.310	73	-20	0			.957	43	*S-102,2-27/3-7,1-5	2.8

YEAR	TM/L	G	AB	R	H	2B	3B	HR	RBI	BB	SO	AVG	OBP	SLG	PRO+	BR/A	SB	CS	SBR	FA	FR	G/POS	TPR
1912	Chi-A	4	3	0	0	0	0	0	1	0		.000	.400	.000	18	-0	0			.667	-1	/3-3,S-1	-0.1
Total	10	1090	3778	331	833	135	27	3	346	229		.220	.269	.273	70	-134	63			.938	165	3-668,S-367/1-28,2	7.2

■ CHUCK TANNER Tanner, Charles William b: 7/4/29, New Castle, Pa. BL/TL, 6', 185 lbs. Deb: 4/12/55 FM

YEAR	TM/L	G	AB	R	H	2B	3B	HR	RBI	BB	SO	AVG	OBP	SLG	PRO+	BR/A	SB	CS	SBR	FA	FR	G/POS	TPR
1955	Mil-N	97	243	27	60	9	3	6	27	27	32	.247	.322	.383	91	-3	0	0	0	.981	-4	O-62	-1.0
1956	Mil-N	60	63	6	15	2	0	1	4	10	10	.238	.342	.317	84	-1	0	0	0	.800	-3	/O-8	-0.4
1957	Mil-N	22	69	5	17	3	0	2	6	5	4	.246	.297	.377	86	-2	0	0	0	1.000	-0	O-18	-0.3
	Chi-N	95	318	42	91	16	2	7	42	23	20	.286	.338	.415	103	1	0	2	-1	.988	-1	O-82	-0.6
	Yr	117	387	47	108	19	2	9	48	28	24	.279	.331	.408	100	-0	0	2	-1	.990	-1	*O-100	-0.9
1958	Chi-N	73	103	10	27	6	0	4	17	9	10	.262	.321	.437	100	-0	1	0	0	.955	-2	O-15	-0.3
1959	Cle-A	14	48	6	12	2	0	1	5	2	9	.250	.280	.354	76	-2	0	0	0	1.000	-1	O-10	-0.3
1960	Cle-A	21	25	2	7	1	0	0	4	4	6	.280	.379	.320	94	-0	1	0	0	1.000	-1	/O-4	-0.0
1961	LA-A	7	8	0	1	0	0	0	0	2	2	.125	.300	.125	16	-1	0	0	0	.000	-0	/O-1	-0.1
1962	LA-A	7	8	0	1	0	0	0	0	0	0	.125	.125	.125	-34	-1	0	0	0	.000	-1	/O-2	-0.2
Total	8	396	885	98	231	39	5	21	105	82	93	.261	.325	.388	93	-10	2	2	-1	.983	-13	O-202	-3.2

■ WALTER TAPPAN Tappan, Walter Van Dorn "Tap" b: 10/8/1890, Carlinville, Ill. d: 12/19/67, Lynwood, Cal. BR/TR, 5'8", 158 lbs. Deb: 4/16/14

YEAR	TM/L	G	AB	R	H	2B	3B	HR	RBI	BB	SO	AVG	OBP	SLG	PRO+	BR/A	SB	CS	SBR	FA	FR	G/POS	TPR
1914	KC-F	18	39	1	8	1	0	1	3	1	0	.205	.225	.308	46	-4	1			.875	-3	/S-8,3-6,2-1	-0.7

■ EL TAPPE Tappe, Elvin Walter b: 5/21/27, Quincy, Ill. BR/TR, 5'11", 180 lbs. Deb: 4/24/54 MC

YEAR	TM/L	G	AB	R	H	2B	3B	HR	RBI	BB	SO	AVG	OBP	SLG	PRO+	BR/A	SB	CS	SBR	FA	FR	G/POS	TPR
1954	Chi-N	46	119	5	22	3	0	0	4	10	9	.185	.248	.210	21	-14	0	0	0	.986	6	C-46	-0.6
1955	Chi-N	2	0	0	0	0	0	0	0	0	0	—	—	—		0	0	0	0	1.000	1	/C-2	0.1
1956	Chi-N	3	1	0	0	0	0	0	0	1	0	.000	.500	.000	51	0	0	0	0	1.000	0	/C-3	0.0
1958	Chi-N	17	28	2	6	0	0	0	4	3	1	.214	.290	.214	37	-2	0	0	0	.962	-1	C-16	-0.3
1960	Chi-N	51	103	11	24	7	0	0	3	11	12	.233	.313	.301	70	-4	0	1	-1	.992	9	C-49	0.6
1962	Chi-N	26	53	3	11	0	0	0	6	4	3	.208	.288	.208	34	-5	0	0	0	1.000	4	C-26,M	0.0
Total	6	145	304	21	63	10	0	0	17	29	25	.207	.283	.240	41	-25	0	1	-1	.989	19	C-142	-0.2

■ TED TAPPE Tappe, Theodore Nash b: 2/2/31, Seattle, Wash. BL/TR, 6'3", 185 lbs. Deb: 9/14/50

YEAR	TM/L	G	AB	R	H	2B	3B	HR	RBI	BB	SO	AVG	OBP	SLG	PRO+	BR/A	SB	CS	SBR	FA	FR	G/POS	TPR
1950	Cin-N	7	5	1	1	0	0	1	1	1	1	.200	.333	.800	187	1	0	0	0	.000	0	H	0.1
1951	Cin-N	4	3	0	1	0	0	0	0	0	0	.333	.333	.333	79	-0	0	0	0	.000	0	H	0.0
1955	Chi-N	23	50	12	13	2	0	4	10	11	11	.260	.413	.540	151	4	0	0	0	1.000	-2	O-15	0.1
Total	3	34	58	13	15	2	0	5	11	12	12	.259	.403	.552	151	5	0	0	0	1.000	-2	/O-15	0.2

■ TONY TARASCO Tarasco, Anthony Giacinto b: 12/9/70, New York, N.Y. BL/TR, 6', 185 lbs. Deb: 4/30/93

YEAR	TM/L	G	AB	R	H	2B	3B	HR	RBI	BB	SO	AVG	OBP	SLG	PRO+	BR/A	SB	CS	SBR	FA	FR	G/POS	TPR
1993	*Atl-N	24	35	6	8	2	0	0	2	0	5	.229	.250	.286	43	-3	0	1	-1	1.000	-3	O-12	-0.6
1994	Atl-N	87	132	16	36	6	0	5	19	9	17	.273	.319	.432	91	-2	5	0	2	1.000	-8	O-45	-0.8
1995	Mon-N	126	438	64	109	18	4	14	40	51	78	.249	.330	.404	89	-7	24	3	5	.979	6	*O-116	0.1
1996	*Bal-A	31	84	14	20	3	0	1	9	7	15	.238	.297	.310	54	-6	5	3	-0	1.000	-3	O-23/D-6	-0.5
Total	4	268	689	100	173	29	4	20	70	67	115	.251	.320	.392	83	-17	34	7	6	.986	-3	O-196/D-6	-1.8

■ ARLIE TARBERT Tarbert, Wilbur Arlington b: 9/10/04, Cleveland, Ohio d: 11/27/46, Cleveland, Ohio BR/TR, 6', 160 lbs. Deb: 6/18/27

YEAR	TM/L	G	AB	R	H	2B	3B	HR	RBI	BB	SO	AVG	OBP	SLG	PRO+	BR/A	SB	CS	SBR	FA	FR	G/POS	TPR
1927	Bos-A	33	69	5	13	1	0	0	5	3	12	.188	.253	.203	20	-8	0	0	0	.944	-4	O-27	-1.3
1928	Bos-A	6	17	1	3	1	0	0	2	1	1	.176	.222	.235	21	-2	1	0	0	.900	-0	/O-6	-0.2
Total	2	39	86	6	16	2	0	0	7	4	13	.186	.247	.209	20	-10	1	0	0	.935	-5	/O-33	-1.5

■ DANNY TARTABULL Tartabull, Danilo (Mora) b: 10/30/62, San Juan, P.R. BR/TR, 6'1", 205 lbs. Deb: 9/7/84 F

YEAR	TM/L	G	AB	R	H	2B	3B	HR	RBI	BB	SO	AVG	OBP	SLG	PRO+	BR/A	SB	CS	SBR	FA	FR	G/POS	TPR
1984	Sea-A	10	20	3	6	1	0	2	7	2	3	.300	.391	.650	185	2	0	0	0	.931	2	/S-8,2-1	0.4
1985	Sea-A	19	61	8	20	7	1	1	7	8	14	.328	.406	.525	152	4	1	0	0	.940	-3	S-16/3-4	0.3
1986	Sea-A	137	511	76	138	25	6	25	96	61	157	.270	.349	.489	124	17	4	8	-4	.953	1	*O-101,2-31/3-1,D-3	1.2
1987	KC-A	158	582	95	180	27	3	34	101	79	136	.309	.393	.541	141	35	9	4	0	.976	-6	*O-149/D-6	2.2
1988	KC-A	146	507	80	139	38	3	26	102	76	119	.274	.373	.515	145	31	8	5	-1	.963	-4	*O-130/D-13	2.2
1989	KC-A	133	441	54	118	22	0	18	62	69	123	.268	.370	.440	128	18	4	2	0	.982	-5	O-71,D-55	0.8
1990	KC-A	88	313	41	84	19	0	15	60	36	93	.268	.344	.473	128	11	1	1	-0	.965	-4	O-52,D-32	0.5
1991	KC-A★	132	484	78	153	35	3	31	100	65	121	.316	.400	.593	170	46	6	3	0	.965	-10	*O-124/D-6	3.2
1992	NY-A	123	421	72	112	19	0	25	85	103	115	.266	.410	.489	152	33	2	2	-1	.980	1	O-69,D-53	3.1
1993	NY-A	138	513	87	128	33	2	31	102	92	156	.250	.366	.503	135	26	0	0	0	.978	-1	D-88,O-50	1.9
1994	NY-A	104	399	68	102	24	1	19	67	66	111	.256	.362	.464	115	10	1	1	-0	1.000	-0	D-78,O-26	0.2
1995	NY-A	59	192	25	43	12	0	6	28	33	54	.224	.341	.380	88	-3	0	1	-0	1.000	-0	D-39,O-18	-0.6
	Oak-A	24	88	9	23	4	0	2	7	10	28	.261	.337	.375	90	-1	0	1	-0	1.000	-0	D-22/O-1	-0.4
	Yr	83	280	34	66	16	0	8	35	43	82	.236	.340	.379	89	-4	0	2	-0	1.000	-0	D-61,O-19	-1.0
1996	Chi-A	132	472	58	120	23	3	27	101	64	128	.254	.343	.487	113	8	1	2	-1	.973	3	*O-122,D-10	0.6
Total	13	1403	5004	754	1366	289	22	262	925	764	1358	.273	.371	.497	133	237	37	30	-7	.971	-31	O-913,D-405/2S3	15.6

■ JOSE TARTABULL Tartabull, Jose Milages (Guzman) b: 11/27/38, Cienfuegos, Cuba BL/TL, 5'11", 165 lbs. Deb: 4/10/62 F

YEAR	TM/L	G	AB	R	H	2B	3B	HR	RBI	BB	SO	AVG	OBP	SLG	PRO+	BR/A	SB	CS	SBR	FA	FR	G/POS	TPR
1962	KC-A	107	310	49	86	6	5	0	22	20	19	.277	.323	.329	73	-12	19	5	3	.974	4	O-85	-1.0
1963	KC-A	79	242	27	58	8	5	1	19	17	17	.240	.290	.326	68	-10	16	1	4	.986	-3	O-71	-1.3
1964	KC-A	104	100	9	20	2	0	0	3	5	12	.200	.238	.220	28	-10	4	0	1	.978	-12	O-59	-2.2
1965	KC-A	68	218	28	68	11	4	1	19	18	20	.312	.364	.413	122	6	11	5	0	.986	7	O-54	1.1
1966	KC-A	37	127	13	30	2	3	0	4	11	13	.236	.297	.299	74	-4	8	1	2	1.000	0	O-32	-0.4
	Bos-A	68	195	28	54	7	4	0	11	6	11	.277	.299	.354	79	-6	11	3	2	.989	-2	O-47	-0.9
	Yr	105	322	41	84	9	7	0	15	17	24	.261	.298	.332	77	-10	19	4	3	.994	-2	O-79	-1.3
1967	*Bos-A	115	247	36	55	1	2	0	10	23	26	.223	.289	.243	54	-13	6	6	-2	.989	-12	O-83	-3.4
1968	Bos-A	72	139	24	39	6	0	0	6	6	5	.281	.310	.324	87	-2	2	3	-1	.984	-4	O-43	-1.0
1969	Oak-A	75	266	28	71	11	1	0	11	9	24	.267	.291	.316	73	-10	3	4	-2	.993	1	O-63	-1.5
1970	Oak-A	24	13	5	3	2	0	0	2	0	2	.231	.231	.385	69	-1	1	0	0	1.000	1	/O-6	-0.2
Total	9	749	1857	247	484	56	24	2	107	115	136	.261	.304	.320	74	-61	81	28	8	.986	-24	O-543	-10.8

■ LA SCHELLE TARVER Tarver, La Schelle b: 1/30/59, Modesto, Cal. BL/TL, 5'11", 165 lbs. Deb: 7/12/86

YEAR	TM/L	G	AB	R	H	2B	3B	HR	RBI	BB	SO	AVG	OBP	SLG	PRO+	BR/A	SB	CS	SBR	FA	FR	G/POS	TPR
1986	Bos-A	13	25	3	3	0	0	0	1	1	4	.120	.154	.120	-24	-4	0	1	-1	1.000	-1	/O-9	-0.6

■ WILLIE TASBY Tasby, Willie b: 1/8/33, Shreveport, La. BR/TR, 5'11", 175 lbs. Deb: 9/9/58

YEAR	TM/L	G	AB	R	H	2B	3B	HR	RBI	BB	SO	AVG	OBP	SLG	PRO+	BR/A	SB	CS	SBR	FA	FR	G/POS	TPR
1958	Bal-A	18	50	6	10	3	0	1	1	7	15	.200	.310	.320	78	-1	1	1	-0	1.000	-4	O-16	-0.7
1959	Bal-A	142	505	69	126	16	5	13	48	34	80	.250	.305	.378	88	-9	3	5	-2	.968	3	*O-137	-1.5
1960	Bal-A	39	85	9	18	2	1	0	3	9	12	.212	.295	.259	52	-6	1	0	0	.980	-8	O-36	-1.4
	Bos-A	105	385	68	108	17	1	7	37	51	54	.281	.372	.384	101	2	3	1	0	.979	3	*O-102	0.0
	Yr	144	470	77	126	19	2	7	40	60	66	.268	.358	.362	93	-3	4	1	-0	.979	-5	*O-138	-1.5
1961	Was-A	141	494	54	124	13	2	17	63	58	94	.251	.332	.389	93	-5	4	10	-5	.985	-2	*O-139	-1.5
1962	Was-A	11	34	4	7	0	0	2	6	2	6	.206	.250	.206	24	-4	0	0	0	1.000	-4	/O-10	-0.6
	Cle-A	75	199	25	48	7	0	4	17	25	41	.241	.326	.337	81	-5	0	2	-0	1.000	-12	O-66/3-1	-2.2
	Yr	86	233	29	55	7	0	6	17	27	47	.236	.315	.318	73	-9	0	2	-0	.992	-14	O-76/3-1	-2.8
1963	Cle-A	52	116	11	26	3	1	1	5	16	25	.224	.318	.371	93	-1	0	2	-0	.992	-3	O-37/2-1	-0.4
Total	6	583	1868	246	467	61	10	46	174	201	327	.250	.328	.367	89	-28	12	20	-8	.980	-22	O-543/2-1,3-1	-8.7

■ POP TATE Tate, Edward Christopher "Dimples" b: 12/22/1860, Richmond, Va. d: 6/25/32, Richmond, Va. BR/TL, 5'10", 178 lbs. Deb: 9/26/1885

YEAR	TM/L	G	AB	R	H	2B	3B	HR	RBI	BB	SO	AVG	OBP	SLG	PRO+	BR/A	SB	CS	SBR	FA	FR	G/POS	TPR
1885	Bos-N	4	13	1	2	0	0	0	2	1	3	.154	.214	.154	21	-0				.865	1	/C-4	0.0
1886	Bos-N	31	106	13	24	7	0	0	3	7	17	.226	.274	.274	70	-4	0			.885	-3	C-31	-0.3
1887	Bos-N	60	231	34	60	5	3	0	27	10		.260	.296	.307	68	-10	7			.924	13	C-53/O-8	-0.1
1888	Bos-N	41	148	18	34	7	1	1	16	9		.230	.278	.311	86	-2	3			.854	-3	C-41/O-1	-0.1
1889	Bal-a	72	253	28	46	6	3	1	27	13	37	.182	.236	.241	35	-22	4			.938	-5	C-62/1-10	-1.7
1890	Bal-a	19	71	7	13	1	0	0	6	4		.183	.284	.225	48	-5	3			.923	-2	C-11/1-8	-0.5
Total	6	227	822	101	179	22	9	2	71	41	73	.218	.269	.274	58	-43	17			.905	3	C-202/1-18,O-9	-1.9

YEAR	TM/L	G	AB	R	H	2B	3B	HR	RBI	BB	SO	AVG	OBP	SLG	PRO+	BR/A	SB	CS	SBR	FA	FR	G/POS	TPR

■ BENNIE TATE
Tate, Henry Bennett b: 12/3/01, Whitwell, Tenn. d: 10/27/73, W.Frankfort, Ill. BL/TR, 5'8", 165 lbs. Deb: 4/29/24

YEAR	TM/L	G	AB	R	H	2B	3B	HR	RBI	BB	SO	AVG	OBP	SLG	PRO+	BR/A	SB	CS	SBR	FA	FR	G/POS	TPR
1924	*Was-A	21	43	2	13	2	0	0	7	1	2	.302	.318	.349	74	-2	0	0	0	.841	-3	C-14	-0.4
1925	Was-A	16	27	0	13	3	0	0	7	2	2	.481	.517	.593	185	4	0	0	0	.955	2	C-14	0.5
1926	Was-A	59	142	17	38	5	2	1	13	15	1	.268	.338	.352	82	-4	0	0	0	.960	-5	C-45	-0.6
1927	Was-A	61	131	12	41	5	1	1	24	8	4	.313	.361	.389	95	-1	0	3	-2	.977	4	C-39	0.4
1928	Was-A	57	122	10	30	6	0	0	15	10	4	.246	.303	.295	58	-7	0	4	-2	.985	2	C-30	-0.5
1929	Was-A	81	265	26	78	12	3	0	30	16	8	.294	.335	.362	79	-8	2	5	-2	.971	-2	C-74	-0.6
1930	Was-A	14	20	1	5	0	0	0	2	0	1	.250	.250	.250	27	-2	0	0	0	.933	-1	/C-9	-0.2
	Chi-A	72	230	26	73	11	2	0	27	18	10	.317	.367	.383	94	-2	2	1	0	.981	-10	C-70	-0.5
	Yr	86	250	27	78	11	2	0	29	18	11	.312	.358	.372	88	-4	2	1	0	.978	-11	C-79	-0.7
1931	Chi-A	89	273	27	73	12	3	0	22	26	10	.267	.331	.333	80	-8	1	1	-0	.987	7	C-85	0.4
1932	Chi-A	4	10	1	1	0	0	0	0	1	0	.100	.182	.100	-27	-2	0	0	0	1.000	0	/C-4	-0.1
	Bos-A	81	273	21	67	12	5	2	26	20	6	.245	.297	.348	68	-13	0	1	-1	.974	-5	C-76	-1.4
	Yr	85	283	22	68	12	5	2	26	21	6	.240	.293	.339	65	-15	0	1	-1	.975	-5	C-80	-1.5
1934	Chi-N	11	24	1	3	0	0	0	0	1	3	.125	.160	.125	-23	-4	0			1.000	-3	/C-8	-0.7
Total	10	566	1560	144	435	68	16	4	173	118	51	.279	.330	.351	78	-50	5	15		.974	-14	C-468	-3.7

■ HUGHIE TATE
Tate, Hugh Henry b: 5/19/1880, Everett, Pa. d: 8/7/56, Greenville, Pa. BR/TR, 5'11", 190 lbs. Deb: 9/21/05

YEAR	TM/L	G	AB	R	H	2B	3B	HR	RBI	BB	SO	AVG	OBP	SLG	PRO+	BR/A	SB	CS	SBR	FA	FR	G/POS	TPR
1905	Was-A	4	13	1	4	0	1	0	2	0		.308	.308	.462	149	1	1			1.000	0	/O-3	0.1

■ LEE TATE
Tate, Lee Willie "Skeeter" b: 3/18/32, Black Rock, Ark. BR/TR, 5'10", 165 lbs. Deb: 9/12/58

YEAR	TM/L	G	AB	R	H	2B	3B	HR	RBI	BB	SO	AVG	OBP	SLG	PRO+	BR/A	SB	CS	SBR	FA	FR	G/POS	TPR
1958	StL-N	10	35	4	7	2	0	1	4	3		.200	.282	.257	42	-3	0	0	0	.950	-4	/S-9	-0.6
1959	StL-N	41	50	5	7	1	1	1	4	5	7	.140	.232	.260	29	-5	0	0	0	.927	1	S-39/2-,3-2	-0.3
Total	2	51	85	9	14	3	1	2	5	9	10	.165	.253	.259	34	-8	0	0	0	.934	-4	/S-48,3-2,2-2	-0.9

■ JIM TATUM
Tatum, James Ray b: 10/9/67, Grossmont, Cal. BR/TR, 6'2", 200 lbs. Deb: 9/18/92

YEAR	TM/L	G	AB	R	H	2B	3B	HR	RBI	BB	SO	AVG	OBP	SLG	PRO+	BR/A	SB	CS	SBR	FA	FR	G/POS	TPR
1992	Mil-A	5	8	0	1	0	0	0	1	2		.125	.222	.125	-0	-1	0	0	0	1.000	-0	/3-5	-0.1
1993	Col-N	92	98	7	20	5	0	1	12	5	27	.204	.250	.286	37	-9	0	0	0	.978	-2	1-12/3-6,O-3	-1.1
1995	Col-N	34	34	4	8	1	1	0	4	1	7	.235	.257	.324	40	-3	0	0	0	1.000	-1	/O-2,C-1	-0.4
1996	Bos-A	2	8	1	1	0	0	0	0	0	2	.125	.125	.125	-35	-2	0	0	0	1.000	-0	/3-2	-0.2
	SD-N	5	3	0	0	0	0	0	0	0	1	.000	.000	.000	-99	-1	0	0	0	.000	0	/3-1	-0.1
Total	4	138	151	12	30	6	1	1	16	7	39	.199	.239	.272	30	-16	0	0	0	.944	-3	/3-14,1-12,O-5,C-1	-1.9

■ JARVIS TATUM
Tatum, Jarvis b: 10/11/46, Fresno, Cal. BR/TR, 6', 185 lbs. Deb: 9/7/68

YEAR	TM/L	G	AB	R	H	2B	3B	HR	RBI	BB	SO	AVG	OBP	SLG	PRO+	BR/A	SB	CS	SBR	FA	FR	G/POS	TPR
1968	Cal-A	17	51	7	9	1	0	0	2	0	9	.176	.176	.196	13	-5	0	0	0	1.000	-0	O-11	-0.7
1969	Cal-A	10	22	2	7	0	0	0	0	0	6	.318	.318	.318	83	-1	0	1	-1	.857	1	/O-5	-0.2
1970	Cal-A	75	181	28	43	7	0	0	6	17	35	.238	.303	.276	63	-9	1	0	0	.982	-5	O-58	-1.7
Total	3	102	254	37	59	8	0	0	8	17	50	.232	.280	.264	56	-15	1	1	-0	.979	-6	/O-74	-2.6

■ TOMMY TATUM
Tatum, V T b: 7/16/19, Decatur, Tex. d: 11/7/89, Oklahoma City, Okla BR/TR, 6', 185 lbs. Deb: 8/1/41

YEAR	TM/L	G	AB	R	H	2B	3B	HR	RBI	BB	SO	AVG	OBP	SLG	PRO+	BR/A	SB	CS	SBR	FA	FR	G/POS	TPR
1941	Bro-N	8	12	1	2	1	0	0	1	1	3	.167	.231	.250	34	-1	0			1.000	-1	/O-3	-0.2
1947	Bro-N	4	6	0	0	0	0	0	0	0	1	.000	.000	.000	-96	-2	0			1.000	-1	/O-4	-0.3
	Cin-N	69	176	19	48	5	2	1	16	16	16	.273	.333	.341	80	-5	7			1.000	4	O-49/2-1	-0.3
	Yr	73	182	19	48	5	2	1	16	16	17	.264	.323	.330	74	-7	7			1.000	3	O-52/2-1	-0.6
Total	2	81	194	20	50	6	2	1	17	17	20	.258	.318	.325	72	-8	7			1.000	2	/O-56,2-1	-0.8

■ EDDIE TAUBENSEE
Taubensee, Edward Kenneth b: 10/31/68, Beeville, Tex. BL/TR, 6'3", 205 lbs. Deb: 5/18/91

YEAR	TM/L	G	AB	R	H	2B	3B	HR	RBI	BB	SO	AVG	OBP	SLG	PRO+	BR/A	SB	CS	SBR	FA	FR	G/POS	TPR
1991	Cle-A	26	66	5	16	2	1	0	8	5	16	.242	.296	.303	66	-3	0	0	0	.979	-7	C-25	-0.9
1992	Hou-N	104	297	23	66	15	0	5	28	31	78	.222	.300	.323	80	-8	2	1	0	.992	4	*C-103	0.1
1993	Hou-N	94	288	26	72	11	1	9	42	21	44	.250	.301	.389	86	-6	1	0	0	.992	4	C-90	0.3
1994	Hou-N	5	10	0	1	0	0	0	0	0	3	.100	.100	.100	-50	-2	0	0	0	1.000	1	/C-5	-0.1
	Cin-N	61	177	29	52	8	2	8	21	15	21	.294	.349	.497	118	4	2	0	1	.990	-1	C-61	0.7
	Yr	66	187	29	53	8	2	8	21	15	31	.283	.337	.476	110	2	2	0	1	.990	-0	C-66	0.6
1995	*Cin-N	80	218	32	62	14	2	9	44	22	52	.284	.355	.491	121	6	2	2	-1	.983	-9	C-65/1-3	0.0
1996	Cin-N	108	327	46	95	20	0	12	48	26	64	.291	.343	.462	111	4	3	4	-2	.981	-11	C-94	-0.2
Total	6	478	1383	161	364	70	6	43	191	120	285	.263	.324	.416	99	-4	10	7	-3	.988	-19	C-443/1-3	-0.1

■ FRED TAUBY
Tauby, Fred Joseph (b: Fred Joseph Taubensee) b: 3/27/06, Canton, Ohio d: 11/23/55, Concordia, Cal. BR/TR, 5'9.5", 168 lbs. Deb: 9/1/35

YEAR	TM/L	G	AB	R	H	2B	3B	HR	RBI	BB	SO	AVG	OBP	SLG	PRO+	BR/A	SB	CS	SBR	FA	FR	G/POS	TPR
1935	Chi-A	13	32	5	4	1	0	0	2	2	3	.125	.176	.156	-13	-5	0	0	0	1.000	0	/O-7	-0.4
1937	Phi-N	11	20	2	0	0	0	0	3	0	5	.000	.000	.000	-93	-5	1			1.000	-2	/O-7	-0.7
Total	2	24	52	7	4	1	0	0	5	2	8	.077	.111	.096	-43	-11	1	0	0	1.000	-0	/O-14	-1.1

■ DON TAUSSIG
Taussig, Donald Franklin b: 2/19/32, New York, N.Y. BR/TR, 6', 180 lbs. Deb: 4/23/58

YEAR	TM/L	G	AB	R	H	2B	3B	HR	RBI	BB	SO	AVG	OBP	SLG	PRO+	BR/A	SB	CS	SBR	FA	FR	G/POS	TPR
1958	SF-N	39	50	10	10	0	4	3	8			.200	.245	.260	35	-5	0	0	0	1.000	-9	O-36	-1.4
1961	StL-N	98	188	27	54	14	5	2	25	16	34	.287	.343	.447	98	-1	2	2	-1	.992	-9	O-87	-1.3
1962	Hou-N	16	25	1	5	0	0	1	1	2	11	.200	.259	.320	59	-2	0	0	0	1.000	1	/O-4	-0.1
Total	3	153	263	38	69	14	5	3	30	21	53	.262	.317	.399	84	-7	2	2	-1	.994	-17	O-127	-2.8

■ JESUS TAVAREZ
Tavarez, Jesus Rafael (Alcantaras) b: 3/26/71, Santo Domingo, D.R. BB/TR, 6', 170 lbs. Deb: 5/23/94

YEAR	TM/L	G	AB	R	H	2B	3B	HR	RBI	BB	SO	AVG	OBP	SLG	PRO+	BR/A	SB	CS	SBR	FA	FR	G/POS	TPR
1994	Fla-N	17	39	4	7	0	0	0	4	1	5	.179	.200	.179	-0	-6	1	1	-0	1.000	2	O-11	-0.4
1995	Fla-N	63	190	31	55	6	2	2	13	16	27	.289	.348	.374	90	-2	7	5	-1	1.000	-10	O-61	-1.4
1996	Fla-N	98	114	14	25	3	0	0	6	7	18	.219	.264	.246	37	-10	5	1	1	1.000	-15	O-65	-2.4
Total	3	178	343	49	87	9	2	2	23	24	50	.254	.304	.309	63	-18	13	7	-0	1.000	-23	O-137	-4.2

■ JACKIE TAVENER
Tavener, John Adam "Rabbit" b: 12/27/1897, Celina, Ohio d: 9/14/69, Fort Worth, Tex. BL/TR, 5'5", 138 lbs. Deb: 9/24/21

YEAR	TM/L	G	AB	R	H	2B	3B	HR	RBI	BB	SO	AVG	OBP	SLG	PRO+	BR/A	SB	CS	SBR	FA	FR	G/POS	TPR
1921	Det-A	2	4	0	0	0	0	0	0	0	0	.000	.000	.000	-99	-1	0	0	0	1.000	1	/S-2	0.0
1925	Det-A	134	453	45	111	11	11	6	47	39	60	.245	.309	.318	60	-28	5	4	-1	.963	7	*S-134	-0.8
1926	Det-A	156	532	65	141	22	14	1	58	52	53	.265	.332	.365	80	-16	8	7	-2	.952	9	*S-156	0.8
1927	Det-A	116	419	60	115	22	9	5	59	36	38	.274	.333	.406	90	-7	19	8	1	.948	4	*S-114	0.9
1928	Det-A	132	473	59	123	24	15	5	52	33	51	.260	.314	.406	86	-11	13	8	-1	.944	14	*S-131	1.7
1929	Cle-A	92	250	25	53	9	4	2	27	26	28	.212	.289	.304	51	-19	1	4	-3	.945	23	S-89	1.1
Total	6	632	2131	254	543	88	53	13	243	186	231	.255	.318	.364	75	-82	46	31	-5	.951	58	S-626	3.7

■ ALEX TAVERAS
Taveras, Alejandro Antonio (Betances) b: 10/9/55, Santiago, D.R. BR/TR, 5'10", 155 lbs. Deb: 9/9/76

YEAR	TM/L	G	AB	R	H	2B	3B	HR	RBI	BB	SO	AVG	OBP	SLG	PRO+	BR/A	SB	CS	SBR	FA	FR	G/POS	TPR
1976	Hou-N	14	46	3	10	0	0	0	2	1		.217	.250	.217	37	-4	1	2	-1	.923	1	/2-7,S-7	-0.3
1982	LA-N	11	3	1	1	0	0	0	2	0	1	.333	.333	.667	178	0	0	0	0	1.000	4	/2-4,3-4,S-2	0.4
1983	LA-N	10	4	0	0	0	0	0	0	0	2	.000	.000	.000	-99	-1	0	0	0	.000	2	/S-3,2-2,3-1	0.1
Total	3	35	53	4	11	0	0	0	4	2	3	.208	.236	.226	34	-5	1	2	-1	.938	7	/2-13,S-12,3-5	0.2

■ FRANK TAVERAS
Taveras, Franklin Crisostomo (Fabian) b: 12/24/49, Las Matas De Santa Cruz, D.R. BR/TR, Deb: 9/10/1874

YEAR	TM/L	G	AB	R	H	2B	3B	HR	RBI	BB	SO	AVG	OBP	SLG	PRO+	BR/A	SB	CS	SBR	FA	FR	G/POS	TPR
1971	Pit-N	1	0	0	0	0	0	0	—	—	—				0	0	0	0	0	.000	0	R	0.0
1972	Pit-N	4	3	0	0	0	0	0	0	1		.000	.250	.000	-24	-0	0	0	0	1.000	0	/S-4	-0.1
1974	*Pit-N	126	333	33	82	4	2	0	26	25	41	.246	.303	.270	63	-16	13	4	2	.941	-17	*S-124	-1.9
1975	*Pit-N	134	378	44	80	9	4	0	23	37	42	.212	.285	.257	52	-24	17	6	2	.953	-15	*S-132	-2.5
1976	Pit-N	144	519	76	134	8	6	0	24	44	79	.258	.320	.297	75	-16	58	11	11	.952	-5	*S-141	0.8
1977	Pit-N	147	544	72	137	20	10	1	29	38	71	.252	.308	.331	69	-23	70	18	10	.962	-22	*S-146	-2.0
1978	Pit-N	157	654	81	182	31	9	0	38	29	60	.278	.314	.353	82	-16	46	25	-1	.946	-29	*S-157	-2.8
1979	Pit-N	11	45	4	11	3	0	0	1	2	8	.244	.234	.311	48	-3	2	1	0	.935	-4	S-11	-0.7
	NY-N	153	635	89	167	26	9	1	33	33	66	.263	.301	.337	77	-21	42	19	1	.966	-21	*S-153	-2.5
	Yr	164	680	93	178	29	9	1	34	33	74	.262	.298	.335	75	-25	44	20	1	.964	-25	*S-164	-3.2
1980	NY-N	141	562	65	157	27	0	0	25	23	64	.279	.309	.327	80	-16	32	18	-1	.959	-39	*S-140	-4.3
1981	NY-N	84	283	30	65	11	3	0	11	12	36	.230	.266	.290	58	-16	16	4	2	.931	-22	S-79	-3.0

YEAR	TM/L	G	AB	R	H	2B	3B	HR	RBI	BB	SO	AVG	OBP	SLG	PRO+	BR/A	SB	CS	SBR	FA	FR	G/POS	TPR
1982	Mon-N	48	87	9	14	5	1	0	4	7	6	.161	.223	.241	29	-8	4	0	1	.947	-1	S-26,2-19	-0.7
Total	11	1150	4043	503	1029	144	44	2	214	249	474	.255	.302	.313	71	-159	300	106	26	.953	-175	*S-1113/2-19	-19.7

■ TONY TAYLOR
Taylor, Antonio Nemesio (Sanchez)   b: 12/19/35, Central Alara, Cuba   BR/TR, 5'9", 179 lbs.   Deb: 4/15/58   C

YEAR	TM/L	G	AB	R	H	2B	3B	HR	RBI	BB	SO	AVG	OBP	SLG	PRO+	BR/A	SB	CS	SBR	FA	FR	G/POS	TPR
1958	Chi-N	140	497	63	117	15	3	6	27	40	93	.235	.301	.314	64	-25	21	6	3	.968	9	*2-137/3-1	-0.4
1959	Chi-N	150	624	96	175	30	8	8	38	45	86	.280	.335	.393	94	-5	23	9	2	.970	10	*2-149/S-2	1.7
1960	Chi-N	19	76	14	20	3	3	1	9	8	12	.263	.341	.421	108	1	2	0	1	.977	-2	2-19	0.1
	Phi-N★	127	505	66	145	22	4	4	35	33	86	.287	.333	.370	92	-5	24	11	1	.968	-6	*2-123/3-4	0.2
	Yr	146	581	80	165	25	7	5	44	41	98	.284	.334	.377	94	-4	26	11	1	.969	-8	*2-142/3-4	0.3
1961	Phi-N	106	400	47	100	17	3	2	26	29	59	.250	.304	.322	67	-19	11	5	0	.980	0	2-91/3-3	-0.8
1962	Phi-N	152	625	87	162	21	5	7	43	68	82	.259	.337	.342	85	-12	20	9	1	.972	-15	*2-150/S-2	-1.1
1963	Phi-N	157	640	102	180	20	10	5	49	42	99	.281	.332	.367	102	2	23	9	2	**.986**	-9	*2-149,3-13	1.0
1964	Phi-N	154	570	62	143	13	6	4	46	46	74	.251	.321	.316	81	-13	13	7	-0	.977	-21	*2-150	-2.3
1965	Phi-N	106	323	41	74	14	3	3	27	22	58	.229	.303	.319	77	-10	5	4	-1	.988	-2	2-86/3-5	-0.6
1966	Phi-N	125	434	47	105	14	8	5	40	31	56	.242	.294	.346	77	-14	8	4	0	.988	4	2-68,3-52	-0.6
1967	Phi-N	132	462	55	110	16	6	2	34	42	74	.238	.308	.312	77	-13	10	9	-2	.991	-8	1-58,3-44,2-42,/S-3	-2.7
1968	Phi-N	145	547	59	137	20	2	3	38	39	60	.250	.304	.311	85	-10	22	5	4	.966	16	*3-138/2-5,1-1	1.2
1969	Phi-N	138	557	68	146	24	5	3	30	42	62	.262	.318	.339	87	-10	19	10	-0	.967	-2	3-71,2-57,1-10	-0.9
1970	Phi-N	124	439	74	132	26	9	9	55	50	67	.301	.376	.462	127	17	9	11	-4	.966	-1	2-59,3-38,O-18,/S-1	1.6
1971	Phi-N	36	107	9	25	2	1	1	5	9	10	.234	.293	.299	68	-4	2	2	-1	1.000	5	2-14,3-11/1-2	0.0
	Det-A	55	181	27	52	10	2	3	19	12	11	.287	.335	.414	107	1	5	1	1	.995	1	2-51/3-3	0.7
1972	*Det-A	78	228	33	69	12	4	1	20	14	34	.303	.344	.404	119	5	5	1	1	.966	-8	2-67/3-8,1-1	0.1
1973	Det-A	84	275	35	63	9	3	5	24	17	29	.229	.276	.338	68	-12	9	5	-0	.987	-14	2-72/1-6,3-4,O-1,D	-2.3
1974	Phi-N	62	64	5	21	4	0	2	13	6	6	.328	.394	.484	139	3	0	0	0	1.000	-1	/1-7,3-5,2-4	0.2
1975	Phi-N	79	103	13	25	5	1	1	17	17	18	.243	.355	.340	90	-1	3	3	-1	.913	1	3-16/1-4,2-3	-0.1
1976	Phi-N	26	23	2	6	1	0	0	3	1	7	.261	.320	.304	76	-1	0	0	0	.000	-0	/2-2,3-1	-0.1
Total	19	2195	7680	1005	2007	298	86	75	598	613	1083	.261	.322	.352	88	-123	234	111	4	.976	-41	*2-1498,3-417/1OSD	-5.1

■ BEN TAYLOR
Taylor, Benjamin Eugene   b: 9/30/27, Metropolis, Ill.   BL/TL, 6', 175 lbs.   Deb: 7/29/51

YEAR	TM/L	G	AB	R	H	2B	3B	HR	RBI	BB	SO	AVG	OBP	SLG	PRO+	BR/A	SB	CS	SBR	FA	FR	G/POS	TPR
1951	StL-A	33	93	14	24	2	1	3	6	9	22	.258	.304	.398	95	-1	1	1	-0	.972	-2	1-25	-0.4
1952	Det-A	7	18	0	3	0	0	0	0	0	5	.167	.167	.167	-7	-3	0	0	0	1.000	-0	/1-4	-0.3
1955	Mil-N	12	10	2	1	0	0	0	0	2	4	.100	.250	.100	-3	-1	0	0	0	1.000	-0	/1-1	-0.2
Total	3	52	121	16	28	2	1	3	6	11	31	.231	.306	.339	73	-5	1	1	-0	.976	-2	/1-30	-0.9

■ CHINK TAYLOR
Taylor, C L   b: 2/9/1898, Burnet, Tex.   d: 7/7/80, Temple, Tex.   BR/TR, 5'9", 160 lbs.   Deb: 4/18/25

YEAR	TM/L	G	AB	R	H	2B	3B	HR	RBI	BB	SO	AVG	OBP	SLG	PRO+	BR/A	SB	CS	SBR	FA	FR	G/POS	TPR
1925	Chi-N	8	6	2	0	0	0	0	0	0	0	.000	.000	.000	-99	-2	0	0	0	.000	-1	/O-2	-0.2

■ CARL TAYLOR
Taylor, Carl Means   b: 1/20/44, Sarasota, Fla.   BR/TR, 6'2", 207 lbs.   Deb: 4/11/68

YEAR	TM/L	G	AB	R	H	2B	3B	HR	RBI	BB	SO	AVG	OBP	SLG	PRO+	BR/A	SB	CS	SBR	FA	FR	G/POS	TPR
1968	Pit-N	44	71	5	15	1	0	0	7	10	10	.211	.309	.225	63	-3	1	0	0	.979	-6	C-29/O-2	-0.8
1969	Pit-N	104	221	30	77	10	1	4	33	31	36	.348	.435	.457	153	17	0	1	-1	.914	-1	O-36,1-24	1.3
1970	StL-N	104	245	39	61	12	2	6	45	41	30	.249	.359	.388	98	0	5	2	0	.986	-4	O-46,1-15/3-1	-0.6
1971	Pit-N	7	12	1	2	0	1	0	2	0	5	.167	.167	.333	39	-1	0	0	0	1.000	0	/O-1	-0.1
	KC-A	20	39	3	7	0	0	0	3	5	13	.179	.273	.179	30	-3	0	1	-1	.964	1	O-12	-0.4
1972	KC-A	63	113	17	30	2	1	0	11	17	16	.265	.366	.301	101	1	4	1	1	.982	-5	C-21/O-7,1-6,3-5	-0.4
1973	KC-A	69	145	18	33	6	1	0	16	32	20	.228	.367	.283	79	-3	2	2	-1	.980	2	C-63/1-2,D-1	0.0
Total	6	411	846	113	225	31	6	10	115	136	130	.266	.371	.352	103	9	12	7	-1	.980	-14	C-113,O-104/13D	-1.0

■ DANNY TAYLOR
Taylor, Daniel Turney   b: 12/23/1900, Lash, Pa.   d: 10/11/72, Latrobe, Pa.   BR/TR, 5'10", 190 lbs.   Deb: 6/30/26

YEAR	TM/L	G	AB	R	H	2B	3B	HR	RBI	BB	SO	AVG	OBP	SLG	PRO+	BR/A	SB	CS	SBR	FA	FR	G/POS	TPR
1926	Was-A	21	50	10	15	0	1	1	5	5	7	.300	.364	.400	102	0	1	2	-1	1.000	-1	O-12	-0.3
1929	Chi-N	2	3	0	0	0	0	0	0	1	1	.000	.250	.000	-32	-1	0			1.000	-0	/O-1	-0.1
1930	Chi-N	74	219	43	62	14	3	2	37	27	34	.283	.364	.402	84	-5	6			.971	-1	O-52	-0.9
1931	Chi-N	88	270	48	81	13	6	5	41	31	46	.300	.372	.448	117	7	4			.989	4	O-67	0.6
1932	Chi-N	6	22	3	5	2	0	0	3	3	1	.227	.320	.318	73	-1	1			.900	-0	/O-6	-0.1
	Bro-N	105	395	84	128	22	7	11	48	33	41	.324	.378	.499	136	20	13			.989	4	O-96	1.7
	Yr	111	417	87	133	24	7	11	51	36	42	.319	.374	.489	133	19	14			.983	4	*O-102	1.6
1933	Bro-N	103	358	75	102	21	9	9	40	47	45	.285	.366	.469	144	21	11			.977	2	*O-91	1.8
1934	Bro-N	120	405	62	121	24	6	7	57	63	47	.299	.396	.440	130	19	12			.975	-8	*O-108	0.7
1935	Bro-N	112	352	51	102	19	5	7	59	46	32	.290	.372	.432	118	10	6			.970	-6	O-99	0.0
1936	Bro-N	43	116	12	34	6	0	2	15	11	14	.293	.359	.397	102	1	2			.981	-3	O-31	-0.3
Total	9	674	2190	388	650	121	37	44	305	267	268	.297	.374	.446	121	71	56	2		.979	-10	O-563	3.1

■ DWIGHT TAYLOR
Taylor, Dwight Bernard   b: 3/24/60, Los Angeles, Cal.   BL/TL, 5'9", 166 lbs.   Deb: 4/14/86

YEAR	TM/L	G	AB	R	H	2B	3B	HR	RBI	BB	SO	AVG	OBP	SLG	PRO+	BR/A	SB	CS	SBR	FA	FR	G/POS	TPR
1986	KC-A	4	2	1	0	0	0	0	0	0	0	.000	.000	.000	-98	-1	0	0	0	.000	-1	/O-1,D-2	-0.1

■ ED TAYLOR
Taylor, Edward James   b: 11/17/01, Chicago, Ill.   d: 1/30/92, Chula Vista, Cal.   BR/TR, 5'6.5", 160 lbs.   Deb: 4/14/26

YEAR	TM/L	G	AB	R	H	2B	3B	HR	RBI	BB	SO	AVG	OBP	SLG	PRO+	BR/A	SB	CS	SBR	FA	FR	G/POS	TPR
1926	Bos-N	92	272	37	73	8	2	0	33	38	26	.268	.368	.313	93	-1	4			.945	-1	3-62,S-33	0.4

■ LIVE OAK TAYLOR
Taylor, Edward S.   Deb: 8/21/1877

YEAR	TM/L	G	AB	R	H	2B	3B	HR	RBI	BB	SO	AVG	OBP	SLG	PRO+	BR/A	SB	CS	SBR	FA	FR	G/POS	TPR
1877	Har-N	2	8	0	3	0	0	0	0	0	2	.375	.375	.375	153	0				1.000	-1	/O-2	0.0
1884	Pit-a	41	152	22	32	4	1	0		6		.211	.255	.250	64	-6				.798	-1	O-41	-0.7
Total	2	43	160	22	35	4	1	0	0	6	2	.219	.260	.256	68	-5				.802	-1	/O-43	-0.7

■ FRED TAYLOR
Taylor, Frederick Rankin   b: 12/3/24, Zanesville, Ohio   BL/TR, 6'3", 201 lbs.   Deb: 9/12/50

YEAR	TM/L	G	AB	R	H	2B	3B	HR	RBI	BB	SO	AVG	OBP	SLG	PRO+	BR/A	SB	CS	SBR	FA	FR	G/POS	TPR
1950	Was-A	6	16	1	2	1	0	0	1	2	.125	.176	.125	-23	-3	0	0	0	.968	0	/1-3	-0.3
1951	Was-A	6	12	1	2	1	0	0	0	0	4	.167	.167	.250	12	-2	0	0	0	.962	-0	/1-4	-0.2
1952	Was-A	10	19	3	5	1	0	0	4	4	4	.263	.364	.316	93	-0	0	0	0	1.000	1	/1-5	0.1
Total	3	22	47	5	9	2	0	0	4	4	8	.191	.255	.234	33	-5	0	0	0	.979	1	/1-10	-0.4

■ HARRY TAYLOR
Taylor, Harry Leonard   b: 4/4/1866, Halsey Valley, N.Y.   d: 7/12/55, Buffalo, N.Y.   BL, 6'2", 160 lbs.   Deb: 4/18/1890

YEAR	TM/L	G	AB	R	H	2B	3B	HR	RBI	BB	SO	AVG	OBP	SLG	PRO+	BR/A	SB	CS	SBR	FA	FR	G/POS	TPR
1890	*Lou-a	134	553	115	169	7	7	0	53	68		.306	.383	.344	117	14	45			.982	5	*1-118,S-12/2-4,C-1	1.2
1891	Lou-a	93	356	81	105	7	4	2	37	55	33	.295	.397	.354	116	10	15			.979	3	1-92/3-1,2-1,C-1	0.7
1892	Lou-N	125	493	66	128	7	1	0	34	58	23	.260	.342	.278	96	1	24			.923	-8	O-73,1-34,2-14,/3S	-1.0
1893	Bal-N	88	360	50	102	9	1	1	54	32	11	.283	.347	.322	77	-12	24			.976	-3	*1-88	-1.4
Total	4	440	1762	312	504	30	13	3	178	213	67	.286	.367	.323	102	14	108			.979	-2	1-332/O-73,2S3C	-0.5

■ HARRY TAYLOR
Taylor, Harry Warren   b: 12/26/07, McKeesport, Pa.   d: 4/27/69, Toledo, Ohio   BL/TL, 6'1.5", 185 lbs.   Deb: 4/14/32

YEAR	TM/L	G	AB	R	H	2B	3B	HR	RBI	BB	SO	AVG	OBP	SLG	PRO+	BR/A	SB	CS	SBR	FA	FR	G/POS	TPR
1932	Chi-N	10	8	1	1	0	0	0	1	.125	.222	.125	-4	-1	0			1.000	-0	/1-1	-0.1

■ SANDY TAYLOR
Taylor, James B.   5'10.5", 175 lbs.   Deb: 8/11/1879

YEAR	TM/L	G	AB	R	H	2B	3B	HR	RBI	BB	SO	AVG	OBP	SLG	PRO+	BR/A	SB	CS	SBR	FA	FR	G/POS	TPR
1879	Tro-N	24	97	10	21	0	8	1	8	1	8	.216	.224	.258	63	-4				.765	-3	O-24	-0.8

■ ZACK TAYLOR
Taylor, James Wren   b: 7/27/1898, Yulee, Fla.   d: 9/19/74, Orlando, Fla.   BR/TR, 5'11.5", 180 lbs.   Deb: 6/15/20   MC

YEAR	TM/L	G	AB	R	H	2B	3B	HR	RBI	BB	SO	AVG	OBP	SLG	PRO+	BR/A	SB	CS	SBR	FA	FR	G/POS	TPR
1920	Bro-N	9	13	3	5	0	0	0	5	0	2	.385	.385	.538	158	1	0	1	-1	.882	-1	/C-9	-0.1
1921	Bro-N	30	102	6	20	0	0	0	8	1	8	.196	.212	.235	17	-12	2	0	1	.965	0	C-30	-1.0
1922	Bro-N	7	14	0	3	0	0	0	2	1	1	.214	.267	.214	26	-2	0	0	0	.950	0	/C-6	-0.2
1923	Bro-N	96	337	29	97	11	6	6	46	9	13	.288	.312	.356	78	-11	2	5	-2	.967	14	C-84	0.4
1924	Bro-N	99	345	36	100	9	4	1	39	14	14	.290	.344	.348	81	-9	0	1	-1	**.988**	-8	C-93	-1.2
1925	Bro-N	109	352	33	109	16	4	3	44	17	19	.310	.343	.403	92	-4	0	0	0	.959	-5	C-96	-0.8
1926	Bos-N	125	432	36	110	22	3	0	42	28	27	.255	.303	.319	74	-17	1			.985	2	*C-123	-0.7
1927	Bos-N	30	96	8	23	2	1	1	14	8	5	.240	.298	.313	69	-4	0			.988	12	C-27	0.9
	NY-N	83	258	18	60	7	3	0	21	17	20	.233	.283	.283	52	-17	2			.972	-4	C-81	-1.6
	Yr	113	354	26	83	9	4	1	35	25	25	.234	.287	.291	56	-22	2			.978	8	*C-108	-0.7

YEAR	TM/L	G	AB	R	H	2B	3B	HR	RBI	BB	SO	AVG	OBP	SLG	PRO+	BR/A	SB	CS	SBR	FA	FR	G/POS	TPR
1928	Bos-N	125	399	36	100	15	1	2	30	33	29	.251	.313	.308	66	-20	2			.985	-12	*C-124	-2.1
1929	Bos-N	34	101	8	25	7	0	0	10	7	9	.248	.303	.317	56	-7	0			.965	6	C-31	-0.2
	*Chi-N	64	215	29	59	16	3	1	31	19	18	.274	.336	.391	79	-7	0			.979	-1	C-64	0.0
	Yr	98	316	37	84	23	3	1	41	26	27	.266	.326	.367	72	-14	0			.974	5	C-95	0.0
1930	Chi-N	32	95	12	22	2	1	1	11	2	12	.232	.255	.305	34	-10	0			1.000	-1	C-28	-0.8
1931	Chi-N	8	4	0	1	0	0	0	0	2	1	.250	.500	.250	106	0	0			1.000	1	/C-5	0.1
1932	Chi-N	21	30	2	6	1	0	0	3	1	4	.200	.226	.233	24	-3	0			1.000	3	C-14	0.0
1933	Chi-N	16	11	0	0	0	0	0	0	0	1	.000	.000	.000	-99	-3	0			1.000	-0	C-12	-0.3
1934	NY-A	4	7	0	1	0	0	0	0	0	0	.143	.143	.143	-28	-1	0	0	0	1.000	-0	/C-3	-0.2
1935	Bro-N	26	54	2	7	3	0	0	5	2	8	.130	.155	.185	-3	-8	0			.970	0	C-26	-0.7
Total	16	918	2865	258	748	113	28	9	311	161	192	.261	.304	.329	68	-135	9	7		.977	1	C-856	-8.3

■ **JOE TAYLOR**   Taylor, Joe Cephus   b: 3/2/26, Chapman, Ala.   BR/TR, 6'1", 185 lbs.   Deb: 8/26/54

YEAR	TM/L	G	AB	R	H	2B	3B	HR	RBI	BB	SO	AVG	OBP	SLG	PRO+	BR/A	SB	CS	SBR	FA	FR	G/POS	TPR
1954	Phi-A	18	58	5	13	1	1	2	8	2	9	.224	.250	.328	57	-4	0	1	-1	.943	-0	O-16	-0.6
1957	Cin-N	33	107	14	28	7	0	4	9	6	24	.262	.301	.439	89	-2	0	1	-1	.971	4	O-27	0.0
1958	StL-N	18	23	2	7	3	0	1	3	2	4	.304	.360	.565	135	1	0	0	0	1.000	-0	/O-5	0.1
	Bal-A	36	77	11	21	4	0	2	9	7	19	.273	.333	.403	107	1	0	0	0	.972	-2	O-21	-0.2
1959	Bal-A	14	32	2	5	1	0	1	2	11	5	.156	.372	.281	84	-0	0	0	0	1.000	-3	O-12	-0.3
Total	4	119	297	34	74	16	1	9	31	28	61	.249	.314	.401	92	-4	0	2	-2	.969	-1	/O-81	-1.0

■ **LEO TAYLOR**   Taylor, Leo Thomas "Chink"   b: 5/13/01, Walla Walla, Wash.   d: 5/20/82, Seattle, Wash.   BR/TR, 5'10.5", 150 lbs.   Deb: 5/3/23

YEAR	TM/L	G	AB	R	H	2B	3B	HR	RBI	BB	SO	AVG	OBP	SLG	PRO+	BR/A	SB	CS	SBR	FA	FR	G/POS	TPR
1923	Chi-A	1	0	0	0	0	0	0	0	0	0	—	—	—	—	0	0	0	0	.000	0	R	0.0

■ **HAWK TAYLOR**   Taylor, Robert Dale   b: 4/3/39, Metropolis, Ill.   BR/TR, 6'2", 190 lbs.   Deb: 6/9/57

YEAR	TM/L	G	AB	R	H	2B	3B	HR	RBI	BB	SO	AVG	OBP	SLG	PRO+	BR/A	SB	CS	SBR	FA	FR	G/POS	TPR
1957	Mil-N	7	1	2	0	0	0	0	0	0	0	.000	.000	.000	-99	-0	0	0	0	.000	0	/C-1	0.0
1958	Mil-N	4	8	1	1	1	0	0	0	0	3	.125	.125	.250	-4	-1	0	0	0	1.000	-0	/O-4	-0.2
1961	Mil-N	20	26	1	5	0	0	1	3	1	11	.192	.276	.308	58	-2	0	1	-1	1.000	-0	/O-5,C-1	-0.2
1962	Mil-N	20	47	3	12	0	0	0	2	2	10	.255	.286	.255	48	-3	0	1	-1	.960	1	O-11	-0.3
1963	Mil-N	16	29	1	2	0	0	0	0	1	12	.069	.100	.069	-51	-6	0	0	0	1.000	-0	/O-8	-0.7
1964	NY-N	92	225	20	54	8	0	4	23	8	33	.240	.272	.329	70	-9	0	0	0	.981	5	C-45,O-16	-0.8
1965	NY-N	25	46	5	7	4	0	1	4	10	1	.152	.170	.413	61	-3	0	0	0	.962	-2	C-15/1-1	-0.5
1966	NY-N	53	109	5	19	2	0	3	12	3	19	.174	.204	.275	32	-10	0	1	-1	1.000	-4	C-29,1-13	-1.5
1967	NY-N	13	37	3	9	3	0	0	4	2	8	.243	.282	.324	74	-1	0	0	0	.955	5	C-12	0.4
	Cal-A	23	52	5	16	3	0	1	3	4	8	.308	.357	.423	135	2	0	0	0	1.000	2	C-19	0.5
1969	KC-A	64	89	7	24	5	0	3	21	6	19	.270	.316	.427	105	0	0	0	0	.909	-4	O-18/C-6	-0.4
1970	KC-A	57	55	3	9	3	0	0	6	6	16	.164	.238	.236	33	-5	0	0	0	1.000	-0	/C-3,1-1	-0.3
Total	11	394	724	56	158	25	0	16	82	36	146	.218	.259	.319	62	-38	0	3	-2	.984	-1	C-131/O-62,1-15	-4.2

■ **BOB TAYLOR**   Taylor, Robert Lee   b: 3/20/44, Leland, Miss.   BL/TR, 5'9", 170 lbs.   Deb: 4/9/70

YEAR	TM/L	G	AB	R	H	2B	3B	HR	RBI	BB	SO	AVG	OBP	SLG	PRO+	BR/A	SB	CS	SBR	FA	FR	G/POS	TPR
1970	SF-N	63	84	12	16	2	0	2	10	12	13	.190	.320	.262	58	-5	0	0	0	1.000	-3	O-26/C-1	-0.9

■ **SAMMY TAYLOR**   Taylor, Samuel Douglas   b: 2/27/33, Woodruff, S.C.   BL/TR, 6'2", 185 lbs.   Deb: 4/27/58

YEAR	TM/L	G	AB	R	H	2B	3B	HR	RBI	BB	SO	AVG	OBP	SLG	PRO+	BR/A	SB	CS	SBR	FA	FR	G/POS	TPR
1958	Chi-N	96	301	30	78	12	2	6	36	27	46	.259	.320	.372	84	-7	2	1	0	.988	-11	C-87	-1.3
1959	Chi-N	110	353	41	95	13	2	13	43	35	47	.269	.338	.428	103	1	0	0	0	.982	-15	*C-109	-0.8
1960	Chi-N	74	150	14	31	9	0	3	17	6	18	.207	.242	.327	55	-10	0	1	-1	.978	-9	C-43	-1.8
1961	Chi-N	89	235	26	56	8	2	8	23	23	39	.238	.317	.391	86	-5	0	0	0	.989	-8	C-75	-1.0
1962	Chi-N	7	15	0	2	1	0	0	1	3	3	.133	.278	.200	30	-1	0	0	0	1.000	-1	/C-6	-0.3
	NY-N	68	158	12	35	4	2	3	20	23	17	.222	.328	.329	76	-5	0	0	0	.991	-9	C-50	-1.2
	Yr	75	173	12	37	5	2	3	21	26	20	.214	.323	.318	72	-6	0	0	0	.992	-10	C-56	-1.5
1963	NY-N	22	35	3	9	1	0	1	6	5	7	.257	.350	.314	91	-0	0	0	0	1.000	0	C-13	0.0
	Cin-N	3	6	0	0	0	0	0	0	0	2	.000	.000	.000	-97	-1	0	0	0	.833	-1	/C-2	-0.3
	Yr	25	41	3	9	1	0	1	6	5	9	.220	.304	.268	65	-2	0	0	0	.984	-1	C-15	-0.3
	Cle-A	4	10	1	3	0	0	0	1	0	4	.300	.300	.300	69	-0	0	0	0	1.000	-1	/C-2	-0.1
Total	6	473	1263	127	309	47	9	33	147	122	181	.245	.315	.375	84	-29	3	2	0	.986	-55	C-387	-6.8

■ **TOMMY TAYLOR**   Taylor, Thomas Livingstone Carlton   b: 9/17/1892, Mexia, Tex.   d: 4/5/56, Greenville, Miss.   BR/TR, 5'8.5", 160 lbs.   Deb: 7/9/24

YEAR	TM/L	G	AB	R	H	2B	3B	HR	RBI	BB	SO	AVG	OBP	SLG	PRO+	BR/A	SB	CS	SBR	FA	FR	G/POS	TPR
1924	*Was-A	26	73	11	19	3	1	0	10	2	8	.260	.289	.329	61	-4	2	0	1	.923	-5	3-16/2-2,O-1	-0.8

■ **BILLY TAYLOR**   Taylor, William H.   b: 12/1870, Butler, Ky.   d: 9/12/05, Cincinnati, Ohio   5'10", 160 lbs.   Deb: 9/19/1898

YEAR	TM/L	G	AB	R	H	2B	3B	HR	RBI	BB	SO	AVG	OBP	SLG	PRO+	BR/A	SB	CS	SBR	FA	FR	G/POS	TPR
1898	Lou-N	9	24	2	6	1	0	0	2	1		.250	.308	.292	73	-1	1			.909	-1	/3-7,2-1	-0.2

■ **BILLY TAYLOR**   Taylor, William Henry "Bollicky Bill"   b: 1855, Washington, D.C.   d: 5/14/1900, Jacksonville, Fla.   BR/TR, 5'11.5", 204 lbs.   Deb: 5/21/1881

YEAR	TM/L	G	AB	R	H	2B	3B	HR	RBI	BB	SO	AVG	OBP	SLG	PRO+	BR/A	SB	CS	SBR	FA	FR	G/POS	TPR
1881	Wor-N	6	28	3	3	1	0	0	2	0	2	.107	.107	.143	-21	-4				.882	1	/O-5,P-1	-0.2
	Det-N	1	4	0	2	2	0	0	1	0	0	.500	.500	1.000	346	1				.750	-0	/3-1	0.1
	Cle-N	24	103	6	25	1	0	0	12	0	8	.243	.243	.252	59	-5				.859	-1	O-23/P-1,3-1	-0.6
	Yr	31	135	9	30	4	0	0	15	0	10	.222	.222	.252	50	-7				.864	-0	O-28/P-2,3-2	-0.7
1882	Pit-a	70	299	40	84	16	13	3		7		.281	.297	.452	157	17				.862	-11	C-27,1-23,3-14,/OP	0.5
1883	Pit-a	83	369	43	96	13	7	2		9		.260	.278	.350	106	3				.747	-15	O-37,C-33,P-19,/1-9	-0.9
1884	StL-U	43	186	44	68	23	1	3		7		.366	.389	.548	175	11				.872	1	P-33,1-10/O-4	0.4
	Phi-a	30	111	8	28	6	2	0		2		.252	.272	.342	93	-1				.784	2	P-30	0.0
1885	Phi-a	6	21	0	4	0	0	0	2	0		.190	.190	.190	19	-2				.556	-1	/P-6	0.0
1886	Bal-a	10	39	4	12	8	1	0	8	1		.308	.329	.359	117	1	1			.800	-1	/P-8,1-1,C-1	0.0
1887	Phi-a	1	4	0	1	0	0	0	1	0		.250	.250	.250	40	-0				1.000	-0	/P-1	0.0
Total	7	274	1164	148	323	62	24	8	26	26	10	.277	.294	.393	121	21	1			.820	-26	P-100/O-77,C-61,13	-0.7

■ **BILL TAYLOR**   Taylor, William Michael   b: 12/30/29, Alhambra, Cal.   BL/TR, 6'3", 212 lbs.   Deb: 4/14/54

YEAR	TM/L	G	AB	R	H	2B	3B	HR	RBI	BB	SO	AVG	OBP	SLG	PRO+	BR/A	SB	CS	SBR	FA	FR	G/POS	TPR
1954	NY-N	55	65	4	12	1	0	2	10	3	15	.185	.243	.292	38	-6	0	0	0	1.000	-3	/O-9	-0.9
1955	NY-N	65	64	9	17	4	0	4	12	1	16	.266	.277	.516	104	0	0	0	0	.000	-1	/O-2	-0.1
1956	NY-N	1	4	0	1	1	0	0	0	0	1	.250	.250	.500	96	0	0	0	0	1.000	-0	/O-1	0.0
1957	NY-N	11	9	0	0	0	0	0	0	1	2	.000	.100	.000	-70	-2	0	0	0	.000	0	H	-0.2
	Det-A	9	23	4	8	2	0	1	3	0	3	.348	.348	.565	142	1	0	0	0	1.000	-1	/O-5	0.0
1958	Det-A	8	8	0	3	0	0	0	1	0	2	.375	.375	.375	100	-0	0	0	0	1.000	-0	/O-1	0.0
Total	5	149	173	17	41	8	0	7	26	5	39	.237	.267	.405	74	-7	0	0	0	1.000	-5	/O-18	-1.2

■ **ZACHARY TAYLOR**   Taylor, Zachary H.   De

YEAR	TM/L	G	AB	R	H	2B	3B	HR	RBI	BB	SO	AVG	OBP	SLG	PRO+	BR/A	SB	CS	SBR	FA	FR	G/POS	TPR
1874	Bal-n	13	48	3	12	0	0	0	3	0	1	.250	.250	.250	61	-2	0	0	0	.914	-1	1-13	-0.2

■ **BIRDIE TEBBETTS**   Tebbetts, George Robert   b: 11/10/12, Burlington, Vt.   BR/TR, 5'11.5", 170 lbs.   Deb: 9/16/36   M

YEAR	TM/L	G	AB	R	H	2B	3B	HR	RBI	BB	SO	AVG	OBP	SLG	PRO+	BR/A	SB	CS	SBR	FA	FR	G/POS	TPR
1936	Det-A	10	33	7	10	2	1	4	5	3		.303	.395	.545	129	1	0	0	0	.982	2	C-10	0.4
1937	Det-A	50	162	15	31	4	3	2	16	10	13	.191	.238	.290	32	-18	0	0	0	.963	-4	C-48	-1.8
1938	Det-A	53	143	16	42	6	2	1	25	12	13	.294	.348	.385	79	-5	1	2	-1	.985	-5	C-53	-0.7
1939	Det-A	106	341	37	89	22	2	4	53	25	20	.261	.315	.372	70	-16	0	1	0	.970	15	*C-100	-0.8
1940	*Det-A	111	379	46	112	24	4	4	46	35	14	.296	.357	.412	90	-6	4	5	-2	.975	18	*C-107	1.8
1941	Det-A☆	110	359	28	102	19	4	2	47	38	29	.284	.354	.376	85	-8	1	2	-1	.977	7	C-98	0.6
1942	Det-A★	99	308	24	76	11	0	1	27	39	17	.247	.335	.292	71	-11	4	0	1	.977	7	C-97	0.5
1946	Det-A	87	280	20	68	11	2	1	34	28	23	.243	.312	.307	69	-11	1	3	-2	.982	-1	C-87	-1.0
1947	Det-A	20	53	1	5	1	0	0	3	2	3	.094	.143	.113	-27	-9	0	1	-1	1.000	8	C-20	-0.1
	Bos-A	90	291	22	87	10	1	1	28	21	10	.299	.346	.344	86	-5	2	4	-2	.974	-3	C-89	-0.4
	Yr	110	344	23	92	11	1	1	30	24	13	.267	.315	.308	73	-14	2	5	-2	.980	5	*C-109	-0.5
1948	Bos-A★	128	446	54	125	26	2	5	68	62	32	.280	.371	.381	95	-2	5	2	0	.981	-9	*C-126	-0.2
1949	Bos-A★	122	403	42	109	14	0	5	48	62	22	.270	.369	.342	83	-9	8	1	2	.980	-6	*C-118	-0.5
1950	Bos-A	79	268	33	83	10	1	8	45	29	26	.310	.377	.444	100	-0	1	1	-0	.988	-6	C-74	-0.3

YEAR	TM/L	G	AB	R	H	2B	3B	HR	RBI	BB	SO	AVG	OBP	SLG	PRO+	BR/A	SB	CS	SBR	FA	FR	G/POS	TPR
1951	Cle-A	55	137	8	36	6	0	2	18	8	7	.263	.308	.350	82	-4	0	0	0	.977	-1	C-44	-0.3
1952	Cle-A	42	101	4	25	4	0	1	8	12	9	.248	.339	.317	89	-1	0	1	-1	.986	-4	C-37	-0.4
Total	14	1162	3704	357	1000	169	22	38	469	389	261	.270	.341	.358	81	-103	29	23	-5	.978	19	*C-1108	-2.1

■ PUSSY TEBEAU   Tebeau, Charles Alston b: 2/22/1870, Worcester, Mass. d: 3/25/50, Pittsfield, Mass. BR/TR, 5'10", 175 lbs. Deb: 7/22/1895

YEAR	TM/L	G	AB	R	H	2B	3B	HR	RBI	BB	SO	AVG	OBP	SLG	PRO+	BR/A	SB	CS	SBR	FA	FR	G/POS	TPR
1895	Cle-N	2	6	3	3	0	0	0	1	2	1	.500	.625	.500	182	1	1			1.000	1	/O-2	0.1

■ GEORGE TEBEAU   Tebeau, George E. "White Wings" b: 12/26/1861, St.Louis, Mo. d: 2/4/23, Denver, Colo. BR/TR, 5'9", 175 lbs. Deb: 4/16/1887 F

YEAR	TM/L	G	AB	R	H	2B	3B	HR	RBI	BB	SO	AVG	OBP	SLG	PRO+	BR/A	SB	CS	SBR	FA	FR	G/POS	TPR
1887	Cin-a	85	318	57	94	12	5	4	33	31		.296	.364	.403	111	4	37			.887	4	O-84/P-1	0.5
1888	Cin-a	121	411	72	94	12	12	3	51	61		.229	.338	.338	111	6	37			.911	4	*O-121	0.6
1889	Cin-a	135	496	110	125	21	11	7	70	69	62	.252	.350	.381	105	3	61			.887	-5	*O-94/P-1	-0.5
1890	Tol-a	94	381	71	102	16	10	1	36	51		.268	.359	.370	112	6	55			.951	3	*O-94/P-1	0.4
1894	Was-N	61	222	41	50	10	6	0	28	37	20	.225	.341	.324	63	-13	17			.857	-9	O-61	-2.0
	Cle-N	40	150	32	47	9	4	0	25	25	18	.313	.411	.427	99	0	9			.928	-5	O-27,1-12/3-1	-0.5
	Yr	101	372	73	97	19	10	0	53	62	38	.261	.369	.366	78	-12	26			.880	-14	O-88,1-12/3-1	-2.5
1895	Cle-N	91	337	57	110	16	6	0	68	50	28	.326	.415	.409	107	5	12			.873	-9	O-49,1-42	-0.5
Total	6	627	2315	440	622	96	54	15	311	324	128	.269	.364	.376	103	11	228			.900	-19	O-570/1-55,P-2,3-1	-2.0

■ PATSY TEBEAU   Tebeau, Oliver Wendell b: 12/5/1864, St.Louis, Mo. d: 5/15/18, St.Louis, Mo. BR/TR, 5'8", 163 lbs. Deb: 9/20/1887 FM

YEAR	TM/L	G	AB	R	H	2B	3B	HR	RBI	BB	SO	AVG	OBP	SLG	PRO+	BR/A	SB	CS	SBR	FA	FR	G/POS	TPR
1887	Chi-N	20	68	8	11	3	0	0	10	4	4	.162	.208	.206	14	-8	8			.855	-3	3-20	-1.0
1889	Cle-N	136	521	72	147	20	6	8	76	37	41	.282	.332	.390	103	1	26			.897	0	*3-136	0.5
1890	Cle-P	110	450	86	134	26	6	5	74	34	20	.298	.351	.416	114	8	14			**.872**	13	3-110,M	2.0
1891	Cle-N	61	249	38	65	8	3	1	41	16	13	.261	.313	.329	84	-6	12			.884	6	3-61/O-1,M	0.3
1892	*Cle-N	86	340	47	83	13	3	2	49	23	34	.244	.307	.318	86	-7	6			.911	-2	3-74/2-5,1-4,S-3,M	-0.5
1893	Cle-N	116	486	90	160	32	8	2	102	32	11	.329	.375	.440	110	4	19			.980	6	1-57,3-56/2-3,M	0.8
1894	Cle-N	125	523	82	158	23	7	3	89	35	35	.302	.347	.390	75	-23	30			.977	-5	*1-115,2-10/3-2,SM	-2.1
1895	*Cle-N	63	264	50	84	13	2	2	52	16	18	.318	.362	.405	92	-4	8			.992	6	1-49/2-9,3-6,M	0.3
1896	*Cle-N	132	543	56	146	22	6	2	94	21	22	.269	.300	.343	65	-29	20			.985	7	*1-122/3-7,2-5,SPM	-1.8
1897	Cle-N	109	412	62	110	15	9	0	59	30		.267	.323	.347	73	-17	11			**.994**	0	1-92,2-18/3-2,SM	-1.4
1898	Cle-N	131	477	53	123	11	4	1	63	53		.258	.301	.304	86	-7	5			.984	3	1-91,2-34/S-7,3M	1.3
1899	StL-N	77	281	27	69	10	3	1	26	18		.246	.303	.313	67	-13	5			.980	-3	1-65,S-11/3-1,2M	-1.3
1900	StL-N	1	4	0	0	0	0	0	0	0		.000	.000	.000	-99	-1	0			.700	-1	/S-1,M	-0.1
Total	13	1167	4618	671	1290	196	57	27	735	319	198	.279	.332	.364	86	-101	164			.984	28	1-595,3-478/2SPO	-4.5

■ DICK TEED   Teed, Richard Leroy b: 3/8/26, Springfield, Mass. BB/TR, 5'11", 180 lbs. Deb: 7/24/53

YEAR	TM/L	G	AB	R	H	2B	3B	HR	RBI	BB	SO	AVG	OBP	SLG	PRO+	BR/A	SB	CS	SBR	FA	FR	G/POS	TPR
1953	Bro-N	1	1	0	0	0	0	0	0	0	1	.000	.000	.000	-98	-0	0	0	0	.000	0	H	0.0

■ WILFREDO TEJADA   Tejada, Wilfredo Aristides (Andujar) b: 11/12/62, Santo Domingo, D.R. BR/TR, 6', 175 lbs. Deb: 9/9/86

YEAR	TM/L	G	AB	R	H	2B	3B	HR	RBI	BB	SO	AVG	OBP	SLG	PRO+	BR/A	SB	CS	SBR	FA	FR	G/POS	TPR
1986	Mon-N	10	25	1	6	1	0	0	2	2	8	.240	.296	.280	60	-1	0	0	0	1.000	-1	C-10	-0.1
1988	Mon-N	8	15	1	4	2	0	0	2	0	4	.267	.267	.400	85	-0	0	0	0	1.000	3	/C-7	0.3
Total	2	18	40	2	10	3	0	0	4	2	12	.250	.286	.325	70	-1	0	0	0	1.000	2	/C-17	0.2

■ JOHNNY TEMPLE   Temple, John Ellis b: 8/8/27, Lexington, N.C. d: 1/9/94, Anderson, S.C. BR/TR, 5'11", 175 lbs. Deb: 4/15/52 C

YEAR	TM/L	G	AB	R	H	2B	3B	HR	RBI	BB	SO	AVG	OBP	SLG	PRO+	BR/A	SB	CS	SBR	FA	FR	G/POS	TPR
1952	Cin-N	30	97	8	19	3	0	1	5	5	1	.196	.235	.258	37	-8	2	1	0	.984	-1	2-22	-0.8
1953	Cin-N	63	110	14	29	4	0	1	9	7	12	.264	.314	.327	67	-5	0	4	0	.964	10	2-44	0.6
1954	Cin-N	146	505	60	155	14	8	0	44	62	24	.307	.385	.366	94	-1	21	7	2	.973	-10	*2-144	0.0
1955	Cin-N	150	588	94	165	20	3	0	50	80	32	.281	.368	.325	81	-13	19	4	3	.971	-3	*2-149/S-1	-0.1
1956	Cin-N★	154	632	88	180	18	3	2	41	58	40	.285	.346	.332	78	-17	14	4	2	.981	-7	*2-154/O-1	-1.0
1957	Cin-N★	145	557	85	158	24	4	0	37	94	34	.284	.391	.341	92	-2	19	5	3	.974	-21	*2-145	-0.8
1958	Cin-N	141	542	82	166	31	6	3	47	91	41	.306	.406	.402	109	11	15	8	-0	.979	-19	*2-141/1-1	0.2
1959	Cin-N★	149	598	102	186	35	6	8	67	72	40	.311	.387	.430	114	14	14	3	2	.974	-26	*2-149	0.2
1960	Cle-A	98	381	50	102	13	1	2	19	32	20	.268	.326	.323	79	-11	11	5	0	.974	-30	2-77,3-17	-3.4
1961	Cle-A★	129	518	73	143	22	3	3	30	61	36	.276	.352	.347	90	-6	9	4	-0	.969	-30	2-129	-2.2
1962	Bal-A	78	270	28	71	8	1	1	17	36	22	.263	.352	.311	85	-4	7	4	-0	.981	-19	2-71	-1.6
	Hou-N	31	95	14	25	4	0	0	2	7	11	.263	.314	.305	72	-4	1	0	0	.941	2	2-26/3-1	-0.9
1963	Hou-N	100	322	22	85	12	1	1	17	41	24	.264	.347	.317	99	1	7	2	1	.970	-20	2-61,3-29	-1.4
1964	Cin-N	6	3	0	0	0	0	0	0	2	1	.000	.400	.000	23	-0	0	0	0	.000	0	H	0.0
Total	13	1420	5218	720	1484	208	36	22	395	648	338	.284	.365	.351	91	-46	140	48	13	.974	-183	*2-1312/3-47,1OS	-11.2

■ GARRY TEMPLETON   Templeton, Garry Lewis b: 3/24/56, Lockney, Tex. BB/TR, 5'11", 190 lbs. Deb: 8/9/76

YEAR	TM/L	G	AB	R	H	2B	3B	HR	RBI	BB	SO	AVG	OBP	SLG	PRO+	BR/A	SB	CS	SBR	FA	FR	G/POS	TPR
1976	StL-N	53	213	32	62	8	2	1	17	7	33	.291	.317	.362	91	-3	11	7	-1	.922	1	S-53	0.4
1977	StL-N★	153	621	94	200	19	18	8	79	15	70	.322	.339	.449	111	8	28	24	-6	.958	-3	*S-151	1.6
1978	StL-N	155	647	82	181	31	13	2	47	22	87	.280	.304	.377	91	-10	34	11	4	.953	23	*S-155	3.8
1979	StL-N†	154	672	105	211	32	19	9	62	18	91	.314	.333	.458	113	9	26	10	2	.960	18	*S-150	4.7
1980	StL-N	118	504	83	161	19	9	4	43	18	43	.319	.343	.417	108	4	31	15	0	.959	28	*S-115	4.7
1981	StL-N	80	333	47	96	16	8	1	33	14	51	.288	.317	.393	98	-2	8	12	-5	.960	5	S-76	0.7
1982	SD-N	141	563	76	139	25	8	6	64	26	82	.247	.281	.352	80	-17	27	16	-2	.961	-24	*S-136	-3.2
1983	SD-N	126	460	39	121	20	2	3	40	21	57	.263	.295	.335	77	-15	16	6	1	.960	-14	*S-123	-1.7
1984	*SD-N	148	493	40	127	19	3	2	35	39	81	.258	.313	.320	79	-14	8	7	-0	.960	-23	*S-146	-2.4
1985	SD-N★	148	546	63	154	30	2	6	55	41	88	.282	.333	.377	100	-0	16	6	1	.968	-7	*S-148	0.9
1986	SD-N	147	510	42	126	21	2	2	44	35	86	.247	.297	.308	68	-22	10	5	0	.966	-28	*S-144	-3.9
1987	SD-N	148	510	42	113	13	5	5	48	42	92	.222	.282	.296	55	-33	14	3	2	.972	9	*S-146	-1.0
1988	SD-N	110	362	35	90	15	7	3	36	20	50	.249	.286	.354	85	-8	8	2	1	.968	15	*S-105/3-2	1.7
1989	SD-N	142	506	43	129	26	3	6	40	23	80	.255	.287	.354	82	-13	1	4	-3	.970	13	*S-140	1.0
1990	SD-N	144	505	45	125	25	3	9	59	24	95	.248	.282	.354	75	-19	1	4	-3	.957	-3	*S-135	-1.9
1991	SD-N	32	57	5	11	1	1	1	6	1	9	.193	.207	.298	39	-5	0	1	-1	.950	-3	3-15/S-1	-0.8
	NY-N	80	219	20	50	9	1	2	20	9	29	.228	.259	.306	59	-12	3	1	0	.963	5	S-40,1-25/3-2,O-2	-0.6
	Yr	112	276	25	61	10	2	3	26	10	38	.221	.248	.304	54	-17	3	2	-1	.963	2	S-41,1-25,3-17/O-2	-1.4
Total	16	2079	7721	893	2096	329	106	70	728	375	1092	.271	.306	.369	87	-150	242	129		.961	7	*S-1964/1-25,3-19,O	4.0

■ GENE TENACE   Tenace, Fury Gene (b: Fiore Gino Tennaci) b: 10/10/46, Russellton, Pa. BR/TR, 6', 190 lbs. Deb: 5/29/69 MC

YEAR	TM/L	G	AB	R	H	2B	3B	HR	RBI	BB	SO	AVG	OBP	SLG	PRO+	BR/A	SB	CS	SBR	FA	FR	G/POS	TPR
1969	Oak-A	16	38	1	6	1	0	1	2	1	15	.158	.200	.237	23	-4	0	0	0	1.000	-0	C-13	-0.4
1970	Oak-A	38	105	19	32	6	0	7	20	23	30	.305	.430	.562	178	12	0	2	-1	.990	4	C-30	1.6
1971	*Oak-A	65	179	26	49	7	0	7	25	29	34	.274	.381	.430	132	8	2	1	0	.994	-6	C-52/O-1	0.4
1972	*Oak-A	82	227	22	51	5	3	5	32	24	42	.225	.307	.339	97	-1	0	0	0	.979	-8	C-49/O-9,1-7,2-2,3	-0.9
1973	*Oak-A	160	510	83	132	18	2	24	84	101	94	.259	.391	.443	142	32	2	2	-1	.989	-11	*1-134,C-33/2-1,D-3	1.2
1974	*Oak-A	158	484	71	102	17	1	26	73	110	105	.211	.370	.411	133	25	2	9	-5	.995	0	*1-106,C-79/2-3	0.9
1975	*Oak-A★	158	498	83	127	17	0	29	87	106	127	.255	.398	.464	146	35	2	1	1	.984	-16	*C-125,1-68/D-1	2.2
1976	Oak-A	128	417	64	104	19	1	22	66	81	91	.249	.376	.458	150	28	5	4	-1	.995	-20	1-70,C-65/D-2	0.5
1977	SD-N	147	437	66	102	24	4	15	61	125	119	.233	.417	.410	137	31	5	5	-3	.980	-7	C-99,1-36,3-14	2.5
1978	SD-N	142	401	60	90	18	4	16	61	101	98	.224	.394	.409	135	24	2	4	-3	.993	-3	1-80,C-71/3-1	1.8
1979	SD-N	151	463	61	122	16	4	20	67	105	106	.263	.407	.445	141	31	4	4	-3	**.998**	-3	C-94,1-72	2.5
1980	SD-N	133	316	46	70	11	1	17	50	92	63	.222	.403	.424	139	21	4	4	-3	.979	-7	*C-104,1-19	1.7
1981	StL-N	58	129	26	30	7	0	5	22	38	26	.233	.421	.403	131	8	0	0	0	.994	-6	C-38/1-7	0.6
1982	*StL-N	66	124	18	32	7	0	7	18	36	31	.258	.439	.500	160	12	1	0	-0	.994	1	C-37/1-7	1.5
1983	Pit-N	4	17	1	3	0	0	0	2	6	12	.177	.346	.258	68	-2	0	0	0	.989	-7	1-19/C-3,0-1	0.0
Total	15	1555	4390	653	1060	179	20	201	674	984	998	.241	.391	.429	137	261	36	42	-14	.986	-92	C-892,1-625/3OD2	15.3

■ JOHN TENER   Tener, John Kinley b: 7/25/1863, County Tyrone, Ireland d: 5/19/46, Pittsburgh, Pa. BR/TR, 6'4", 180 lbs. Deb: 6/8/1885

YEAR	TM/L	G	AB	R	H	2B	3B	HR	RBI	BB	SO	AVG	OBP	SLG	PRO+	BR/A	SB	CS	SBR	FA	FR	G/POS	TPR
1885	Bal-a	1	4	0	0	0	0	0	0	0		.000	.000	.000	-99	-1				.000	-1	/O-1	-0.2
1888	Chi-N	12	46	4	9	1	0	0	1	1	15	.196	.229	.217	40	-3	1			.892	0	P-12/O-1	0.0

YEAR TM/L	G	AB	R	H	2B	3B	HR	RBI	BB	SO	AVG	OBP	SLG	PRO+	BR/A	SB	CS	SBR	FA	FR	G/POS	TPR
1889 Chi-N	42	150	18	41	4	2	1	19	7	22	.273	.306	.347	78	-5	2			.929	3	P-35/O-6,1-2	-0.1
1890 Pit-P	18	63	7	12	0	0	2	5	7	10	.190	.301	.286	62	-3	1			.966	2	P-14/O-2,3-2	-0.2
Total 4	73	263	29	62	5	2	3	25	15	47	.236	.287	.304	66	-12	4			.933	4	/P-61,O-10,3-2,1-2	-0.5

■ TOM TENNANT
Tennant, Thomas Francis b: 7/3/1882, Monroe, Wis. d: 2/15/55, San Carlos, Cal. BL/TL, 5'11", 165 lbs. Deb: 4/18/12

YEAR TM/L	G	AB	R	H	2B	3B	HR	RBI	BB	SO	AVG	OBP	SLG	PRO+	BR/A	SB	CS	SBR	FA	FR	G/POS	TPR
1912 StL-A	2	2	1	0	0	0	0	0	0	0	.000	.000	.000	-99	-1	0			.000	0	H	-0.1

■ FRED TENNEY
Tenney, Fred Clay b: 7/9/1859, Marlborough, N.H. d: 6/15/19, Fall River, Mass. Deb: 4/28/1884

YEAR TM/L	G	AB	R	H	2B	3B	HR	RBI	BB	SO	AVG	OBP	SLG	PRO+	BR/A	SB	CS	SBR	FA	FR	G/POS	TPR
1884 Was-U	32	119	17	28	3	1	0	6			.235	.272	.277	69	-8				.867	-1	O-27/1-6	-0.8
Bos-U	4	17	1	2	0	0	0	0			.118	.118	.118	-29	-3				.750	-1	/P-4	0.0
Wil-U	1	3	0	0	0	0	0	0			.000	.000	.000	-97	-1				1.000		/P-1	0.0
Yr	37	139	18	30	3	1	0	6			.216	.248	.252	53	-12				.867	-1	O-27/1-6,P-5	-0.8

■ FRED TENNEY
Tenney, Frederick b: 11/26/1871, Georgetown, Mass. d: 7/3/52, Boston, Mass. BL/TL, 5'9", 155 lbs. Deb: 6/16/1894 M

YEAR TM/L	G	AB	R	H	2B	3B	HR	RBI	BB	SO	AVG	OBP	SLG	PRO+	BR/A	SB	CS	SBR	FA	FR	G/POS	TPR
1894 Bos-N	27	86	23	34	7	1	2	21	12	9	.395	.469	.570	139	5	6			.893	-4	C-20/O-6,1-1	0.5
1895 Bos-N	49	173	35	47	9	1	1	21	24	5	.272	.360	.353	78	-6	6			.885	-4	O-28,C-21	-0.8
1896 Bos-N	88	348	64	117	14	3	2	49	36	12	.336	.400	.411	108	4	18			.957	1	O-60,C-27	0.3
1897 *Bos-N	132	566	125	180	24	3	1	85	49		.318	.376	.376	93	-6	34			.988	5	*1-128/O-4	-0.4
1898 Bos-N	117	488	106	160	25	5	0	62	33		.328	.370	.400	114	8	23			.980	5	*1-117/C-1	1.1
1899 Bos-N	150	603	115	209	19	17	1	67	63		.347	.411	.439	122	17	28			.978	10	*1-150	2.5
1900 Bos-N	112	437	77	122	13	5	1	56	39		.279	.346	.339	80	-13	17			.981	9	*1-111	-0.4
1901 Bos-N	115	451	66	127	13	1	1	22	37		.282	.340	.322	85	-9	15			.976	7	*1-113/C-2	-0.3
1902 Bos-N	134	489	88	154	18	3	2	30	73		.315	.409	.376	141	28	21			**.985**	13	*1-134	3.9
1903 Bos-N	122	447	79	140	22	3	3	41	70		.313	.415	.396	137	26	21			.974	8	*1-122	3.1
1904 Bos-N	147	533	76	144	17	9	1	37	57		.270	.351	.341	118	13	17			.986	8	*1-144/O-4	1.9
1905 Bos-N	149	549	84	158	18	3	0	28	67		.288	.368	.332	111	11	17			.982	22	*1-148/P-1,M	2.9
1906 Bos-N	143	544	61	154	12	8	1	28	58		.283	.357	.340	121	15	17			.983	10	*1-143,M	2.2
1907 Bos-N	150	554	83	151	18	8	0	26	82		.273	.371	.334	121	17	15			.989	9	*1-149,M	2.5
1908 NY-N	156	583	**101**	149	20	1	2	49	72		.256	.344	.304	102	4	17			.990	10	*1-156	1.4
1909 NY-N	101	375	43	88	8	2	3	30	52		.235	.333	.291	92	-2	8			.986	8	1-98	0.6
1911 Bos-N	102	369	52	97	13	4	1	36	50	17	.263	.352	.328	84	-7	5			.985	2	1-96/O-2,M	-0.5
Total 17	1994	7595	1278	2231	270	77	22	688	874	43	.294	.371	.358	109	107	285			.983	124	*1-1810,O-104/CP	20.9

■ FRANK TEPEDINO
Tepedino, Frank Ronald b: 11/23/47, Brooklyn, N.Y. BL/TL, 5'11", 192 lbs. Deb: 5/12/67

YEAR TM/L	G	AB	R	H	2B	3B	HR	RBI	BB	SO	AVG	OBP	SLG	PRO+	BR/A	SB	CS	SBR	FA	FR	G/POS	TPR
1967 NY-A	9	5	0	2	0	0	0	0	1	1	.400	.500	.400	175	1	0	0	0	1.000	0	/1-1	0.1
1969 NY-A	13	39	6	9	0	0	0	4	4	4	.231	.302	.231	53	-2	1	0	0	.950	-1	O-13	-0.4
1970 NY-A	16	19	2	6	2	0	0	2	1	2	.316	.350	.421	118	0	0	1	-1	1.000	-1	/1-1,O-1	-0.1
1971 NY-A	6	6	0	0	0	0	0	0	0	0	.000	.000	.000	-99	-2	0	0	0	1.000	-0	/O-1	-0.2
Mil-A	53	106	11	21	1	0	2	7	4	17	.198	.234	.264	41	-8	2	2	-1	.986	3	1-28	-0.8
Yr	59	112	11	21	1	0	2	7	4	17	.188	.222	.250	34	-10	2	2	-1	.986	3	1-28/O-1	-1.0
1972 NY-A	8	8	0	0	0	0	0	0	0	1	.000	.000	.000	-99	-2	0	0	0	.000	0	H	-0.2
1973 Atl-N	74	148	20	45	5	0	4	29	13	21	.304	.360	.419	107	1	0	0	0	.992	2	1-58	0.1
1974 Atl-N	78	169	11	39	5	1	0	16	9	13	.231	.274	.272	51	-11	1	2	-1	.988	1	1-46	-1.4
1975 Atl-N	8	7	0	0	0	0	0	0	1	2	.000	.125	.000	-61	-2	0	0	0	.000	0	H	-0.2
Total 8	265	507	50	122	13	1	6	58	33	61	.241	.290	.306	65	-24	4	5	-3	.989	4	1-134/O-15	-3.1

■ JOE TEPSIC
Tepsic, Joseph John b: 9/18/23, Slovan, Pa. BR/TR, 5'9", 170 lbs. Deb: 7/12/46

YEAR TM/L	G	AB	R	H	2B	3B	HR	RBI	BB	SO	AVG	OBP	SLG	PRO+	BR/A	SB	CS	SBR	FA	FR	G/POS	TPR
1946 Bro-N	15	5	2	0	0	0	0	0	1	1	.000	.167	.000	-50	-1	0			1.000	-0	/O-1	-0.1

■ JERRY TERRELL
Terrell, Jerry Wayne b: 7/13/46, Waseca, Minn. BR/TR, 6', 170 lbs. Deb: 4/14/73

YEAR TM/L	G	AB	R	H	2B	3B	HR	RBI	BB	SO	AVG	OBP	SLG	PRO+	BR/A	SB	CS	SBR	FA	FR	G/POS	TPR
1973 Min-A	124	438	43	116	15	2	0	32	21	56	.265	.300	.315	71	-17	13	7	-0	.962	-14	S-81,3-30,2-14/OD	-2.2
1974 Min-A	116	229	43	56	4	6	0	19	11	27	.245	.279	.314	68	-10	3	2	-0	.960	**23**	S-34,2-26,3D/O1	1.7
1975 Min-A	108	385	48	110	16	2	1	36	19	27	.286	.324	.345	88	-6	4	4	-1	.947	-3	S-41,2-39,13/OD	-0.6
1976 Min-A	89	171	29	42	3	1	0	8	9	15	.246	.287	.275	64	-8	11	2	2	.988	5	2-31,3-26,S-16,D/O	0.3
1977 Min-A	93	214	32	48	6	0	1	20	11	21	.224	.265	.266	46	-16	10	4	1	.953	5	3-59,2-14/S-7,10D	-1.0
1978 KC-A	73	133	14	27	1	0	0	8	4	13	.203	.226	.211	23	-13	8	4	0	1.000	6	2-31,3-25,S-11,/1-5	-0.6
1979 KC-A	31	40	5	12	3	0	1	2	1	1	.300	.317	.450	102	-0	1	0	0	.963	3	3-19/2-7,P-1,S-1,D	0.3
1980 KC-A	23	16	4	1	0	0	0	0	0	1	.063	.063	.063	-65	-4	0	0	0	1.000	2	/O-7,1-3,2-3,P-1,D	-0.2
Total 8	657	1626	218	412	48	11	4	125	76	160	.253	.289	.304	66	-73	50	23	1	.961	28	3-192,S-191,2/D1OP	-2.3

■ TOM TERRELL
Terrell, John Thomas b: 6/19/1867, Louisville, Ky. d: 7/9/1893, Louisville, Ky. Deb: 10/5/1886

YEAR TM/L	G	AB	R	H	2B	3B	HR	RBI	BB	SO	AVG	OBP	SLG	PRO+	BR/A	SB	CS	SBR	FA	FR	G/POS	TPR
1886 Lou-a	1	4	1	1	0	0	0	0	0	0	.250	.250	.250	54	-2				.000	-2	/O-1,C-1	-0.2

■ TERRY
Terry b: Attleboro, Pa. Deb: 4/26/1875

YEAR TM/L	G	AB	R	H	2B	3B	HR	RBI	BB	SO	AVG	OBP	SLG	PRO+	BR/A	SB	CS	SBR	FA	FR	G/POS	TPR
1875 Was-n	6	22	0	4	0	1	0	2	0	1	.182	.182	.273	58	-1	0	0	0	.810	-3	/1-4,O-3	-0.3

■ ADONIS TERRY
Terry, William H b: 8/7/1864, Westfield, Mass. d: 2/24/15, Milwaukee, Wis. BR/TR, 5'11.5", 168 lbs. Deb: 5/1/1884 U

YEAR TM/L	G	AB	R	H	2B	3B	HR	RBI	BB	SO	AVG	OBP	SLG	PRO+	BR/A	SB	CS	SBR	FA	FR	G/POS	TPR
1884 Bro-a	67	236	15	55	10	3	0		8		.233	.258	.301	81	-5				.764	-1	P-56,O-13	0.1
1885 Bro-a	71	264	23	45	1	3	1	20	10		.170	.201	.208	29	-21				.883	2	O-47,P-25/3-1	-1.3
1886 Bro-a	75	299	34	71	8	9	2	39	10		.237	.265	.344	89	-5	17			.934	4	P-34,O-32,S-13	-0.4
1887 Bro-a	86	352	56	103	6	10	3	65	16		.293	.323	.392	98	-2	27			.895	3	O-49,P-40/S-2	-0.4
1888 Bro-a	30	115	13	29	6	0	0	8	5		.252	.283	.304	89	-2	7			.909	1	P-23/O-7,1-2	0.0
1889 *Bro-a	49	160	29	48	6	6	2	26	14	14	.300	.356	.450	129	5	8			.963	5	P-41,1-10	0.0
1890 *Bro-N	99	363	63	101	17	9	4	59	40	34	.278	.356	.408	122	10	32			.930	-1	O-54,P-46/1-1	0.2
1891 Bro-N	30	91	10	19	7	1	0	6	9	26	.209	.301	.308	78	-2				.957	-2	P-25/O-5	-0.1
1892 Bal-N	1	4	0	0	0	0	0	0	0	0	.000	.000	.000	-97	-1	0			1.000		/P-1	0.0
Pit-N	31	100	10	16	0	4	2	11	10	11	.160	.236	.300	62	-5	2			.938	-0	P-30/O-1	-0.1
Yr	32	104	10	16	0	4	2	11	10	12	.154	.228	.288	56	-6	2			.940	-0	P-31/O-1	-0.1
1893 Pit-N	26	71	9	18	4	3	0	11	3	12	.254	.293	.394	84	-2	1			.920	-2	P-26	-0.1
1894 Pit-N	1	0	0	0	0	0	0	0	0	0	—	—	—	—	0	0			.000	0	/P-1	0.0
Chi-N	30	95	19	33	4	2	0	17	11	12	.347	.415	.432	99	-0	3			.875	-2	P-23/O-7,1-2	-0.1
Yr	31	95	19	33	4	2	0	17	11	12	.347	.415	.432	99	-0	3			.875	-2	P-24/O-7,1-2	-0.1
1895 Chi-N	40	137	18	30	3	2	1	10	2	17	.219	.236	.292	33	-14	1			.895	2	P-38/O-1,S-1	-0.1
1896 Chi-N	30	99	14	26	4	2	0	15	8	12	.263	.324	.343	73	-4	4			.968	-2	P-30	0.0
1897 Chi-N	1	3	0	0	0	0	0	0	0	0	.000	.000	.000	-96	-1				.750	-1	/P-1	0.0
Total 14	667	2389	314	594	76	54	15	287	146	139	.249	.295	.344	85	-50	106			.903	10	P-440,O-216/S13	-2.2

■ BILL TERRY
Terry, William Harold "Memphis Bill" b: 10/30/1898, Atlanta, Ga. d: 1/9/89, Jacksonville, Fla. BL/TL, 6'1", 200 lbs. Deb: 9/24/23 MH

YEAR TM/L	G	AB	R	H	2B	3B	HR	RBI	BB	SO	AVG	OBP	SLG	PRO+	BR/A	SB	CS	SBR	FA	FR	G/POS	TPR
1923 NY-N	3	7	1	1	0	0	0	0	2	2	.143	.333	.143	30	-1	0	0	0	1.000	0	/1-2	-0.1
1924 *NY-N	77	163	26	39	7	2	5	24	17	18	.239	.311	.399	91	-2	1		-0	.988	-2	1-35	-0.6
1925 NY-N	133	489	75	156	31	6	11	70	42	52	.319	.374	.474	120	14	4	5	-2	.990	-4	*1-126	0.8
1926 NY-N	98	225	26	65	12	5	5	43	22	17	.289	.352	.453	117	5	3			.979	4	1-38,O-14	0.5
1927 NY-N	150	580	101	189	32	13	20	121	46	53	.326	.377	.529	141	31	5			.993	5	*1-150	2.6
1928 NY-N	149	568	100	185	36	11	17	101	64	36	.326	.394	.518	136	29	7			.993	-2	*1-149	1.4
1929 NY-N	150	607	103	226	39	5	14	117	48	35	.372	.418	.522	132	31	10			.994	7	*1-149/O-1	2.0
1930 NY-N	154	633	139	**254**	39	15	23	129	57	33	**.401**	.452	.619	159	61	8			.990	13	*1-154	5.0
1931 NY-N	153	611	**121**	213	43	**20**	9	112	47	36	.349	.397	.529	150	**42**	8			.990	9	*1-153	3.6
1932 NY-N	154	643	124	225	42	11	28	117	32	23	.350	.382	.580	158	49	4			.991	14	*1-154,M	4.9
1933 *NY-N★	123	475	68	153	20	5	6	58	40	23	.322	.375	.423	129	19	3			.992	1	*1-117,M	0.9
1934 NY-N★	153	602	109	213	30	6	8	83	60	47	.354	.414	.463	138	34	0			**.994**	6	*1-153,M	2.6
1935 NY-N★	145	596	91	203	32	8	6	64	41	55	.341	.383	.451	126	22	7			**.996**	6	*1-143,M	1.2

YEAR	TM/L	G	AB	R	H	2B	3B	HR	RBI	BB	SO	AVG	OBP	SLG	PRO+	BR/A	SB	CS	SBR	FA	FR	G/POS	TPR
1936	*NY-N	79	229	36	71	10	5	2	39	19	19	.310	.363	.424	112	4	0			.996	3	1-56,M	0.1
Total	14	1721	6428	1120	2193	373	112	154	1078	537	449	.341	.393	.506	137	338	56	6		.992	67	*1-1579/O-15	24.9

■ ZEB TERRY   Terry, Zebulon Alexander b: 6/17/1891, Denison, Tex. d: 3/14/88, Los Angeles, Cal. BR/TR, 5'8", 129 lbs. Deb: 4/12/16

YEAR	TM/L	G	AB	R	H	2B	3B	HR	RBI	BB	SO	AVG	OBP	SLG	PRO+	BR/A	SB	CS	SBR	FA	FR	G/POS	TPR
1916	Chi-A	94	269	20	51	8	4	0	17	33	36	.190	.292	.249	62	-12	4			.935	-10	S-93	-1.9
1917	Chi-A	2	1	0	0	0	0	0	0	2	0	.000	.667	.000	102	0	0			1.000	-1	/S-1	0.0
1918	Bos-N	28	105	17	32	2	2	0	8	8	14	.305	.360	.362	125	3	1			.977	8	S-27	1.4
1919	Pit-N	129	472	46	107	12	6	0	27	31	26	.227	.280	.278	65	-19	12			.960	-31	*S-127	-4.8
1920	Chi-N	133	496	56	139	26	9	0	52	44	22	.280	.341	.369	102	2	12	16	-6	.962	14	S-70,2-63	1.9
1921	Chi-N	123	488	59	134	18	1	2	45	27	19	.275	.318	.328	71	-20	1	13	-8	.972	5	*2-122	-1.2
1922	Chi-N	131	496	56	142	24	2	0	67	34	16	.286	.335	.343	74	-19	2	11	-6	.964	9	*2-125/S-4,3-3	-1.2
Total	7	640	2327	254	605	90	24	2	216	179	133	.260	.318	.322	78	-64	32	40		.956	-5	S-322,2-310/3-3	-6.5

■ WAYNE TERWILLIGER   Terwilliger, Willard Wayne "Twig" b: 6/27/25, Clare, Mich. BR/TR, 5'11", 170 lbs. Deb: 8/6/49 C

YEAR	TM/L	G	AB	R	H	2B	3B	HR	RBI	BB	SO	AVG	OBP	SLG	PRO+	BR/A	SB	CS	SBR	FA	FR	G/POS	TPR
1949	Chi-N	36	112	11	25	2	1	2	10	16	22	.223	.326	.313	74	-4	0			.978	2	2-34	0.2
1950	Chi-N	133	480	63	116	22	3	10	32	43	63	.242	.311	.363	77	-16	13			.967	-9	*2-126/1-1,3-1,0-1	-1.9
1951	Chi-N	50	192	26	41	6	0	1	10	29	21	.214	.317	.245	52	-12	3	1	0	.969	-4	2-49	-1.3
	Bro-N	37	50	11	14	1	0	0	4	8	7	.280	.390	.300	87	-0	1	0	0	.949	6	2-24/3-1	0.7
	Yr	87	242	37	55	7	0	1	14	37	28	.227	.332	.256	59	-12	4	1	1	.964	3	2-73/3-1	-0.6
1953	Was-A	134	464	62	117	24	4	4	46	64	65	.252	.343	.347	89	-6	7	4	-0	.982	5	*2-133	0.6
1954	Was-A	106	337	42	70	10	1	3	24	32	40	.208	.282	.270	55	-21	3	3	-1	.972	13	2-90,3-10/S-3	-0.4
1955	NY-N	80	257	29	66	16	1	1	18	36	42	.257	.350	.339	84	-5	2	4	-2	.985	26	2-78/S-1,3-1	2.4
1956	NY-N	14	18	0	4	1	0	0	0	0	5	.222	.222	.278	34	-2	0	0		.958	2	/2-6	0.1
1959	KC-A	74	180	27	48	11	0	2	18	19	31	.267	.337	.361	90	-2	2	2	-1	.972	20	2-63/S-2,3-1	2.0
1960	KC-A	2	1	0	0	0	0	0	0	0	0	.000	.000	.000	-99	-0	0	0		1.000	0	/2-2	0.0
Total	9	666	2091	271	501	93	10	22	162	247	296	.240	.323	.325	76	-69	31	14		.974	64	2-605/3-14,S-6,01	2.4

■ AL TESCH   Tesch, Albert John "Tiny" b: 1/27/1891, Jersey City, N.J. d: 8/3/47, Jersey City, N.J. BB/TR, 5'10", 155 lbs. Deb: 8/21/15

YEAR	TM/L	G	AB	R	H	2B	3B	HR	RBI	BB	SO	AVG	OBP	SLG	PRO+	BR/A	SB	CS	SBR	FA	FR	G/POS	TPR
1915	Bro-F	8	7	2	2	1	0	0	2	0	0	.286	.286	.429	100	-0	0			.867	3	/2-3	0.3

■ NICK TESTA   Testa, Nicholas b: 6/29/28, New York, N.Y. BR/TR, 5'8", 180 lbs. Deb: 4/23/58 C

YEAR	TM/L	G	AB	R	H	2B	3B	HR	RBI	BB	SO	AVG	OBP	SLG	PRO+	BR/A	SB	CS	SBR	FA	FR	G/POS	TPR
1958	SF-N	1	0	0	0	0	0	0	0	0	0	—	—	—		0	0	0		.000	-1	/C-1	0.0

■ DICK TETTELBACH   Tettelbach, Richard Morley "Tut" b: 6/26/29, New Haven, Conn. d: 1/26/95, E.Harwich, Mass. BR/TR, 6', 195 lbs. Deb: 9/25/55

YEAR	TM/L	G	AB	R	H	2B	3B	HR	RBI	BB	SO	AVG	OBP	SLG	PRO+	BR/A	SB	CS	SBR	FA	FR	G/POS	TPR
1955	NY-A	2	5	0	0	0	0	0	0	0	0	.000	.000	.000	-99	-1	0	0	0	1.000	0	/O-2	-0.2
1956	Was-A	18	64	10	10	1	2	1	9	14	15	.156	.308	.281	56	-4	0	1	-1	1.000	0	O-18	-0.4
1957	Was-A	9	11	2	2	0	0	0	1	4	2	.182	.400	.182	65	-0	0	0	0	.900	2	/O-3	-0.1
Total	3	29	80	12	12	1	2	1	10	18	17	.150	.306	.250	49	-6	0	1	-1	.980	2	/O-23	-0.7

■ MICKEY TETTLETON   Tettleton, Mickey Lee b: 9/16/60, Oklahoma City, Okla. BB/TR, 6'2", 200 lbs. Deb: 6/30/84

YEAR	TM/L	G	AB	R	H	2B	3B	HR	RBI	BB	SO	AVG	OBP	SLG	PRO+	BR/A	SB	CS	SBR	FA	FR	G/POS	TPR
1984	Oak-A	33	76	10	20	2	1	1	5	11	21	.263	.356	.355	105	1	0	0	0	.992	0	C-32	0.2
1985	Oak-A	78	211	23	53	12	0	3	15	28	59	.251	.344	.351	98	0	2	2	-1	.989	-1	C-76/D-1	0.2
1986	Oak-A	90	211	26	43	9	0	10	35	39	51	.204	.331	.389	103	1	7	1	2	.984	-2	C-89	0.5
1987	Oak-A	82	211	19	41	3	0	8	26	30	65	.194	.295	.322	68	-10	1	1	-0	.987	4	C-80/1-1,D-1	-0.2
1988	Bal-A	86	283	31	74	11	1	11	37	28	70	.261	.332	.424	113	5	0	1	-1	.992	-10	C-80	0.1
1989	Bal-A★	117	411	72	106	21	2	26	65	73	117	.258	.371	.509	150	28	3	2	0	.994	-7	C-75,D-43	2.4
1990	Bal-A	135	444	68	99	21	2	15	51	106	160	.223	.378	.381	117	14	2	4	-2	.991	-13	C-90,D-40/1-5,O-1	0.4
1991	Det-A	154	501	85	132	17	2	31	89	101	131	.263	.389	.491	140	30	3	3	-1	.990	-15	*C-125,D-24/O-3,1-1	2.0
1992	Det-A	157	525	82	125	25	0	32	83	122	137	.238	.383	.469	137	29	0	6	-4	.996	-18	*C-113,D-40/1-3,O-2	1.2
1993	Det-A	152	522	79	128	25	4	32	110	109	139	.245	.376	.492	132	25	3	7	-3	.992	-17	1-59,C-56,O-55/D-4	0.3
1994	Det-A★	107	339	57	84	18	2	17	51	97	98	.248	.422	.463	127	18	0	1	-1	.992	-15	C-53,1-24,D-22,O-18	0.3
1995	Tex-A	134	429	76	102	19	1	32	78	107	110	.238	.384	.510	131	12	0	0	0	.972	-3	0-63,D-58/1-9,C-3	1.2
1996	*Tex-A	143	491	78	121	26	1	24	83	95	137	.246	.372	.450	100	0	2	1	0	.977	-2	*D-115,1-23	-1.1
Total	13	1468	4654	706	1128	209	16	242	728	946	1295	.242	.374	.450	122	165	23	29	-11	.991	-100	C-872,D-348,O1	7.5

■ TIM TEUFEL   Teufel, Timothy Shawn b: 7/7/58, Greenwich, Conn. BR/TR, 6', 175 lbs. Deb: 9/3/83

YEAR	TM/L	G	AB	R	H	2B	3B	HR	RBI	BB	SO	AVG	OBP	SLG	PRO+	BR/A	SB	CS	SBR	FA	FR	G/POS	TPR
1983	Min-A	21	78	11	24	7	1	3	6	2	8	.308	.325	.538	128	3	0	0	0	.990	-1	2-18/S-1,D-1	0.2
1984	Min-A	157	568	76	149	30	3	14	61	76	73	.262	.351	.400	103	3	1	3	-2	.984	-12	*2-157	-0.4
1985	Min-A	138	434	58	113	24	3	10	50	48	70	.260	.338	.399	95	-2	4	2	0	.980	-33	*2-137/D-1	-3.1
1986	*NY-N	93	279	35	69	20	1	4	31	32	42	.247	.327	.369	94	-2	1	3	-1	.971	-18	2-84/1-3,3-1	-1.9
1987	NY-N	97	299	55	92	29	0	14	61	44	53	.308	.390	.545	155	24	3	2	-0	.972	-11	2-92/1-1	1.6
1988	*NY-N	90	273	35	64	20	4	4	31	29	41	.234	.310	.352	94	-2	0	1	-1	.981	12	2-84/1-3	1.2
1989	NY-N	83	219	27	56	11	0	2	15	32	50	.256	.353	.333	102	1	1	3	-2	.960	-1	2-40,1-33	-0.2
1990	NY-N	80	175	28	43	11	0	10	24	15	33	.246	.305	.480	113	2	0	0	0	.991	-4	1-24,2-24,3-10	-0.3
1991	NY-N	20	34	2	4	0	0	1	2	2	8	.118	.167	.206	4	-4	1	1	-0	1.000	0	/1-6,3-5,2-1	-0.5
	SD-N	97	307	39	70	16	0	11	42	49	69	.228	.336	.388	100	1	8	2	1	.987	-14	2-65,3-48	-1.2
	Yr	117	341	41	74	16	0	12	44	51	77	.217	.321	.370	91	-3	9	3	1	.987	-14	2-66,3-53/1-6	-1.7
1992	SD-N	101	246	23	55	10	0	6	25	31	45	.224	.313	.337	83	-5	2	1	0	.987	-3	2-52,3-26/1-5	-0.8
1993	SD-N	96	200	26	50	11	2	7	31	27	39	.250	.339	.430	102	1	2	1	0	.990	-8	2-52/3-9,1-8	-0.1
Total	11	1073	3112	415	789	185	12	86	379	387	531	.254	.339	.404	100	19	23	19	-5	.984	-88	2-806/3-99,1-83,DS	-5.5

■ GEORGE TEXTOR   Textor, George Bernhardt b: 12/27/1888, Newport, Ky. d: 3/10/54, Massillon, Ohio BB/TR, 5'10.5", 174 lbs. Deb: 4/19/14

YEAR	TM/L	G	AB	R	H	2B	3B	HR	RBI	BB	SO	AVG	OBP	SLG	PRO+	BR/A	SB	CS	SBR	FA	FR	G/POS	TPR
1914	Ind-F	22	57	2	10	0	0	0	4	2	9	.175	.230	.175	10	-8	0			.955	2	C-21	-0.5
1915	New-F	3	6	1	2	0	0	0	0	0	0	.333	.333	.333	93	-0	0			1.000	-1	/C-3	-0.1
Total	2	25	63	3	12	0	0	0	4	2	9	.190	.239	.190	17	-8	0			.957	1	/C-24	-0.6

■ MOE THACKER   Thacker, Morris Benton b: 5/21/34, Louisville, Ky. BR/TR, 6'3", 210 lbs. Deb: 4/20/58

YEAR	TM/L	G	AB	R	H	2B	3B	HR	RBI	BB	SO	AVG	OBP	SLG	PRO+	BR/A	SB	CS	SBR	FA	FR	G/POS	TPR
1958	Chi-N	11	24	4	6	1	0	2	3	1	7	.250	.280	.542	113	0	0	0	0	.952	4	/C-9	0.1
1960	Chi-N	54	90	5	14	1	0	0	6	14	20	.156	.269	.167	23	-9	1	1	-0	.980	5	C-50	-0.3
1961	Chi-N	25	35	3	6	0	0	0	2	11	11	.171	.383	.171	53	-1	0	0	0	.973	-1	C-25	-0.2
1962	Chi-N	65	107	8	20	5	0	0	9	14	40	.187	.287	.234	40	-9	0	1	-1	.996	13	C-65	0.5
1963	StL-N	3	4	0	0	0	0	0	0	0	3	.000	.000	.000	-91	-1	0	0	0	1.000	1	/C-3	0.0
Total	5	158	260	20	46	7	0	2	20	40	81	.177	.291	.227	41	-20	1	3	-1	.984	18	C-152	0.1

■ AL THAKE   Thake, Albert b: 9/21/1849, Wymondham, England d: 9/1/1872, Brooklyn, N.Y. 6', Deb: 6/13/1872

YEAR	TM/L	G	AB	R	H	2B	3B	HR	RBI	BB	SO	AVG	OBP	SLG	PRO+	BR/A	SB	CS	SBR	FA	FR	G/POS	TPR
1872	Atl-n	18	78	14	23	2	2	0	15	0	2	.295	.295	.372	89	-3	2	0	1	.808	-1	O-18/2-1	-0.2

■ RON THEOBALD   Theobald, Ronald Merrill b: 7/28/43, Oakland, Cal. BR/TR, 5'8", 165 lbs. Deb: 4/12/71

YEAR	TM/L	G	AB	R	H	2B	3B	HR	RBI	BB	SO	AVG	OBP	SLG	PRO+	BR/A	SB	CS	SBR	FA	FR	G/POS	TPR
1971	Mil-A	126	388	50	107	12	2	1	23	38	39	.276	.345	.325	92	-3	11	8	-2	.973	1	*2-111/S-1,3-1	0.6
1972	Mil-A	125	391	45	86	11	0	1	19	68	38	.220	.343	.256	81	-5	0	7	-4	.988	-13	*2-113	-1.9
Total	2	251	779	95	193	23	2	2	42	106	77	.248	.344	.290	87	-9	11	15	-6	.980	-12	2-224/3-1,S-1	-1.3

■ GEORGE THEODORE   Theodore, George Basil b: 11/13/47, Salt Lake City, Ut. BR/TR, 6'4", 190 lbs. Deb: 4/14/73

YEAR	TM/L	G	AB	R	H	2B	3B	HR	RBI	BB	SO	AVG	OBP	SLG	PRO+	BR/A	SB	CS	SBR	FA	FR	G/POS	TPR
1973	*NY-N	45	116	14	30	4	0	1	15	10	13	.259	.323	.319	80	-3	1	0	0	.984	4	O-33/1-4	-0.2
1974	NY-N	60	76	7	12	1	0	1	1	8	14	.158	.247	.211	29	-7	0	0	0	.990	-5	1-14,O-12	-1.4
Total	2	105	192	21	42	5	0	2	16	18	27	.219	.292	.276	60	-10	1	0	0	.958	-3	/O-45,1-18	-1.6

■ TOMMY THEVENOW   Thevenow, Thomas Joseph b: 9/6/03, Madison, Ind. d: 7/29/57, Madison, Ind. BR/TR, 5'10", 155 lbs. Deb: 9/4/24

YEAR	TM/L	G	AB	R	H	2B	3B	HR	RBI	BB	SO	AVG	OBP	SLG	PRO+	BR/A	SB	CS	SBR	FA	FR	G/POS	TPR
1924	StL-N	23	89	4	18	4	1	0	7	1	6	.202	.211	.270	28	-9	1	3	-2	.951	8	S-23	0.0
1925	StL-N	50	175	17	47	7	2	0	17	7	12	.269	.301	.331	60	-11	3	0		.950	3	S-50	-0.2
1926	*StL-N	156	563	64	144	15	5	2	63	27	26	.256	.291	.311	60	-32	8			.956	18	*S-156	0.3
1927	StL-N	59	191	23	37	6	1	0	4	14	8	.194	.249	.236	29	-19	2			.945	7	S-59	-0.6

YEAR	TM/L	G	AB	R	H	2B	3B	HR	RBI	BB	SO	AVG	OBP	SLG	PRO+	BR/A	SB	CS	SBR	FA	FR	G/POS	TPR
1928	*StL-N	69	171	11	35	8	3	0	13	20	12	.205	.288	.287	50	-13	0			.931	-4	S-64/3-3,1-1	-1.1
1929	Phi-N	90	317	30	72	11	0	0	35	25	25	.227	.288	.262	35	-32	3			.953	3	S-90	-1.7
1930	Phi-N	156	573	57	164	21	1	0	78	23	26	.286	.316	.326	52	-44	1			.941	-2	*S-156	-2.6
1931	Pit-N	120	404	35	86	12	1	0	38	28	22	.213	.266	.248	39	-34	0			.964	9	*S-120	-1.4
1932	Pit-N	59	194	12	46	3	3	0	26	7	12	.237	.264	.284	48	-14	0			.918	-1	S-29,3-22	-1.1
1933	Pit-N	73	253	20	79	5	1	0	34	3	5	.312	.320	.340	89	-4	2			.975	-13	2-61/S-3,3-1	-1.4
1934	Pit-N	122	446	37	121	16	2	0	54	20	20	.271	.306	.316	65	-21	0			.969	-18	2-75,3-44/S-1	-3.3
1935	Pit-N	110	408	38	97	9	9	0	47	12	23	.238	.261	.304	50	-29	1			.951	4	3-82,S-13/2-8	-2.0
1936	Cin-N	106	321	25	75	7	2	0	36	15	23	.234	.268	.268	48	-24	2			.945	-9	S-68,2-33,3-12	-2.7
1937	Bos-N	21	34	5	4	0	1	0	2	4	2	.118	.211	.176	7	-4	0			.969	1	S-12/3-6,2-2	-0.3
1938	Pit-N	15	25	2	5	0	0	0	2	4	2	.200	.333	.200	49	-1	0			1.000	3	/2-9,S-4,3-1	0.2
Total	15	1229	4164	380	1030	124	32	2	456	210	222	.247	.285	.294	52	-292	23	3		.950	9	S-848,2-188,3/1	-17.9

■ HENRY THIELMAN
Thielman, Henry Joseph b: 10/3/1880, St.Cloud, Minn. d: 9/2/42, New York, N.Y. BR/TR, 5'11", 175 lbs. Deb: 4/17/02 F

YEAR	TM/L	G	AB	R	H	2B	3B	HR	RBI	BB	SO	AVG	OBP	SLG	PRO+	BR/A	SB	CS	SBR	FA	FR	G/POS	TPR
1902	NY-N	6	9	0	1	0	0	0	0	2		.111	.273	.111	19	-1	0			.800	1	/P-2,O-3	-0.1
	Cin-N	28	91	6	12	0	2	0	4	5		.132	.177	.176	8	-10	0			.910	-2	P-25/O-3	-0.2
	Yr	34	100	6	13	0	2	0	4	7		.130	.187	.170	9	-11	1			.903	-1	P-27/O-6	-0.3
1903	Bro-N	9	23	3	5	1	0	1	2	5		.217	.357	.391	117	1	0			.750	-0	/O-5,P-4	-0.1
Total	2	43	123	9	18	1	2	1	6	12		.146	.222	.211	30	-10	1			.918	-1	/P-31,O-11	-0.4

■ ANDRES THOMAS
Thomas, Andres Perez (b: Andres Perez (Thomas) b: 11/10/63, Boca Chica, D.R. BR/TR, 6'1", 185 lbs. Deb: 9/3/85

YEAR	TM/L	G	AB	R	H	2B	3B	HR	RBI	BB	SO	AVG	OBP	SLG	PRO+	BR/A	SB	CS	SBR	FA	FR	G/POS	TPR
1985	Atl-N	15	18	6	5	0	0	0	2	0	2	.278	.278	.278	53	-1	0	0	0	.920	3	S-10	0.2
1986	Atl-N	102	323	26	81	17	2	6	32	8	49	.251	.269	.372	71	-14	4	6	-2	.958	26	S-97	1.8
1987	Atl-N	82	324	29	75	11	0	5	39	14	50	.231	.268	.312	50	-23	6	5	-1	.953	9	S-81	-0.8
1988	Atl-N	153	606	54	153	22	2	13	68	14	95	.252	.271	.360	76	-20	7	3	-0	.959	-8	*S-150	-1.7
1989	Atl-N	141	554	41	118	18	0	13	57	12	62	.213	.230	.316	53	-35	3	3	-1	.956	6	*S-138	-2.0
1990	Atl-N	84	278	26	61	8	0	5	30	11	43	.219	.249	.302	48	-20	2	1	0	.967	3	S-72/3-5	-1.2
Total	6	577	2103	182	493	76	4	42	228	59	301	.234	.256	.334	61	-113	22	18	-4	.958	38	S-548/3-5	-3.7

■ PINCH THOMAS
Thomas, Chester David b: 1/24/1888, Camp Point, Ill. d: 12/24/53, Modesto, Cal. BL/TR, 5'9.5", 173 lbs. Deb: 4/24/12

YEAR	TM/L	G	AB	R	H	2B	3B	HR	RBI	BB	SO	AVG	OBP	SLG	PRO+	BR/A	SB	CS	SBR	FA	FR	G/POS	TPR
1912	Bos-A	13	30	0	6	0	0	0	5	2		.200	.250	.200	28	-3	1			.966	2	/C-8	0.0
1913	Bos-A	38	91	6	26	1	2	1	15	2	11	.286	.309	.374	97	-1	1			.983	1	C-31	0.3
1914	Bos-A	66	130	9	25	1	0	0	5	18	17	.192	.291	.200	48	-8	1			.966	-2	C-64/1-1	-0.6
1915	*Bos-A	86	203	21	48	4	4	0	21	13	20	.236	.286	.296	76	-7	3	2	-0	.969	4	C-82	0.3
1916	*Bos-A	99	216	21	57	10	1	1	21	33	13	.264	.364	.333	109	4	4			.981	-8	C-90	0.2
1917	Bos-A	83	202	24	48	7	0	0	24	27	9	.238	.333	.272	86	-2	2			**.986**	3	C-77	0.7
1918	Cle-A	32	73	2	18	0	1	0	5	6	6	.247	.304	.274	68	-3	0			.948	1	C-24	-0.1
1919	Cle-A	34	46	2	5	0	0	0	2	4	3	.109	.180	.109	-17	-7	0			.980	-2	C-21	-0.8
1920	*Cle-A	9	9	2	3	1	0	0	3	0	1	.333	.500	.444	147	1	0	0	0	1.000	-7	/C-7	0.2
1921	Cle-A	21	35	1	9	3	0	0	4	10	2	.257	.422	.343	96	0	0	0	0	.882	-6	C-19	-0.5
Total	10	481	1035	88	245	27	8	2	102	118	82	.237	.318	.284	78	-25	12	2		.973	-5	C-423/1-1	-0.3

■ DAN THOMAS
Thomas, Danny Lee b: 5/9/51, Birmingham, Ala. d: 6/12/80, Mobile, Ala. BR/TR, 6'2", 190 lbs. Deb: 9/2/76

YEAR	TM/L	G	AB	R	H	2B	3B	HR	RBI	BB	SO	AVG	OBP	SLG	PRO+	BR/A	SB	CS	SBR	FA	FR	G/POS	TPR
1976	Mil-A	32	105	13	29	5	1	4	15	14	28	.276	.372	.457	145	6	1	2	-1	.955	-0	O-32	0.4
1977	Mil-A	22	70	11	19	3	2	2	11	8	11	.271	.354	.457	119	2	0	2	-1	1.000	1	/O-9,D-9	0.1
Total	2	54	175	24	48	8	3	6	26	22	39	.274	.365	.457	134	8	1	4	-2	.966	0	/O-41,D-9	0.5

■ DERREL THOMAS
Thomas, Derrel Osbon b: 1/14/51, Los Angeles, Cal. BB/TR, 6', 160 lbs. Deb: 9/14/71

YEAR	TM/L	G	AB	R	H	2B	3B	HR	RBI	BB	SO	AVG	OBP	SLG	PRO+	BR/A	SB	CS	SBR	FA	FR	G/POS	TPR
1971	Hou-N	5	5	0	0	0	0	0	0	0	2	.000	.000	.000	-99	-1	0	1	-1	1.000	1	/2-1	-0.1
1972	SD-N	130	500	48	115	15	5	5	36	41	73	.230	.291	.310	76	-17	9	9	-3	.967	-18	2-83,S-49/O-3	-2.8
1973	SD-N	113	404	34	96	7	1	0	22	34	52	.238	.300	.260	61	-21	15	5	2	.914	-14	S-74,2-47	-2.3
1974	SD-N	141	523	48	129	24	6	3	41	51	58	.247	.315	.333	85	-11	7	8	-3	.976	6	*2-104,3-22,O-20,/S	-0.4
1975	SF-N	144	540	99	149	21	9	6	48	57	56	.276	.348	.381	98	-1	28	13	1	.974	-7	*2-141/O-1	0.0
1976	SF-N	81	272	38	63	5	4	2	19	29	26	.232	.315	.301	73	-9	10	11	-4	.964	2	2-69/O-2,S-1,3-1	-0.7
1977	SF-N	148	506	75	135	13	10	8	44	46	70	.267	.330	.379	90	-7	15	13	-1	.991	10	O-78,2-27,S-26,/31	0.0
1978	SD-N	128	352	36	80	10	2	3	26	35	37	.227	.300	.293	73	-13	11	6	-0	.991	-4	O-77,2-40,3-26,1-14	-1.1
1979	LA-N	141	406	47	104	15	4	5	44	41	49	.256	.332	.350	87	-6	18	5	2	.996	9	*O-119,3-18/2-5,S1	-0.6
1980	LA-N	117	297	32	79	18	3	1	22	26	48	.266	.327	.357	93	-3	7	9	-3	.987	-1	O-52,S-49,2-18/C3	-0.4
1981	*LA-N	80	218	25	54	4	0	4	24	25	23	.248	.325	.321	87	-3	7	2	1	.986	-10	2-30,S-26,O-18,3-10	-1.0
1982	LA-N	66	98	13	26	2	1	0	2	10	12	.265	.333	.306	82	-2	2	3	-1	1.000	-7	O-28,2-18,3-14,/S-6	-1.0
1983	*LA-N	118	192	38	48	6	2	2	8	27	36	.250	.348	.375	101	1	9	3	1	.990	-12	O-82,S-13/2-9,3-7	-1.1
1984	Mon-N	108	243	26	62	12	2	0	20	20	33	.255	.312	.321	82	-6	0	4	-2	.963	-38	S-62,O-48,2-15,/31	-4.4
	Cal-A	14	29	3	4	0	1	0	2	3	4	.138	.219	.207	19	-3	0	0	0	.889	-5	/O-7,S-4,3-3	-0.9
1985	Phi-N	63	92	16	19	2	0	4	12	11	14	.207	.291	.359	79	-3	2	0	1	.906	-1	S-21/O-7,C-1,2-1,3	-0.9
Total	15	1597	4677	585	1163	154	54	43	370	456	593	.249	.319	.332	83	-105	140	92	-13	.970	-94	2-608,O-542,S3/1C	-17.6

■ FRANK THOMAS
Thomas, Frank Edward "The Big Hurt" b: 5/27/68, Columbus, Ga. BR/TR, 6'5", 240 lbs. Deb: 8/2/90

YEAR	TM/L	G	AB	R	H	2B	3B	HR	RBI	BB	SO	AVG	OBP	SLG	PRO+	BR/A	SB	CS	SBR	FA	FR	G/POS	TPR
1990	Chi-A	60	191	39	63	11	3	7	31	44	54	.330	.460	.529	180	23	0	1	-1	.989	-5	1-51/D-8	1.4
1991	Chi-A	158	559	104	178	31	2	32	109	**138**	112	.318	**.454**	.553	**181**	**69**	1	2	-1	.996	-4	*D-101,1-56	5.5
1992	Chi-A	160	573	108	185	**46**	2	24	115	**122**	88	.323	**.446**	.536	176	**64**	6	3	0	.992	-10	*1-158/D-2	4.3
1993	*Chi-A★	153	549	106	174	36	0	41	128	112	54	.317	.434	.607	180	66	4	2	0	.989	-9	*1-150/D-4	4.3
1994	Chi-A★	113	399	**106**	141	34	1	38	101	**109**	61	.353	**.494**	**.729**	**214**	**74**	2	3	-1	.991	-8	1-99,D-13	5.0
1995	Chi-A★	145	493	102	152	27	0	40	111	**136**	74	.308	.463	.606	184	69	3	2	-0	.991	-13	1-90,D-54	4.0
1996	Chi-A†	141	527	110	184	26	0	40	134	109	70	.349	.465	.626	182	72	1	1	-0	.992	-4	*1-139	4.8
Total	7	930	3291	675	1077	211	8	222	729	770	513	.327	.458	.599	185	437	17	14	-3	.991	-52	1-743,D-182	29.3

■ FRANK THOMAS
Thomas, Frank Joseph b: 6/11/29, Pittsburgh, Pa. BR/TR, 6'3", 205 lbs. Deb: 8/17/51

YEAR	TM/L	G	AB	R	H	2B	3B	HR	RBI	BB	SO	AVG	OBP	SLG	PRO+	BR/A	SB	CS	SBR	FA	FR	G/POS	TPR
1951	Pit-N	39	148	21	39	9	2	2	16	9	15	.264	.306	.392	84	-4	0	2	-1	1.000	1	O-37	-0.5
1952	Pit-N	6	21	1	2	0	0	0	0	1	1	.095	.136	.095	-34	-4	0	0	0	1.000	0	/O-5	-0.5
1953	Pit-N	128	455	68	116	22	1	30	102	50	93	.255	.331	.505	115	8	1	2	-1	.976	10	*O-118	1.2
1954	Pit-N★	153	577	81	172	32	7	23	94	51	74	.298	.365	.497	124	19	3	2	-0	.989	12	*O-153	2.4
1955	Pit-N★	142	510	72	125	16	2	25	72	60	76	.245	.327	.431	101	-0	2	0	1	.984	-0	*O-139	-0.6
1956	Pit-N	157	588	69	166	24	3	25	80	36	61	.282	.329	.461	112	8	0	5	-3	.942	-8	*3-111,O-56/2-4	-0.3
1957	Pit-N	151	594	72	172	30	1	23	89	44	66	.290	.342	.460	116	12	0	4	-2	.977	5	1-71,O-59,3-31	0.5
1958	Pit-N★	149	562	89	158	26	4	35	109	42	79	.281	.339	.528	129	21	0	1	-1	.926	-32	*3-139/O-8,1-2	-1.1
1959	Cin-N	108	374	41	84	18	2	12	47	27	56	.225	.282	.380	72	-16	0	0	0	.927	-13	3-64,O-33,1-14	-3.3
1960	Chi-N	135	479	54	114	12	1	21	64	28	74	.238	.280	.399	84	-12	1	0	0	.983	-10	1-50,O-49,3-33	-2.8
1961	Chi-N	15	50	7	13	2	0	3	8	1	8	.260	.288	.420	84	-1	0	0	0	1.000	-0	O-10/1-6	-0.3
	Mil-N	124	423	58	120	13	3	25	67	29	70	.284	.338	.506	128	15	2	4	-2	.954	-8	*O-109,1-11	0.7
	Yr	139	473	65	133	15	3	27	73	31	78	.281	.333	.497	123	14	2	4	-2	.956	-8	*O-119,1-17	0.4
1962	NY-N	156	571	69	152	23	3	34	94	48	95	.266	.332	.496	117	12	2	1	0	.962	8	*O-126,1-11,3-10	1.1
1963	NY-N	126	420	34	109	9	1	15	60	33	48	.260	.318	.393	102	1	0	0	0	.988	5	O-96,1-15/3-1	0.4
1964	NY-N	60	197	19	50	6	1	3	19	10	29	.254	.297	.340	81	-5	1	1	-0	1.000	4	O-31,1-19/3-2	-0.4
	Phi-N	39	143	20	42	11	0	7	26	5	12	.294	.318	.517	132	5	0	1	-0	.976	1	1-36	0.4
	Yr	99	340	39	92	17	1	10	45	15	41	.271	.305	.415	103	0	1	2	-0	.982	5	1-55,O-31/3-2	0.0
1965	Phi-N	35	77	7	20	4	0	3	7	4	10	.260	.296	.351	83	-2	0	3	-1	1.000	-3	O-12,1-11/3-1	-0.6
	Hou-N	23	58	7	10	2	0	1	3	4	11	.172	.213	.362	63	-3	0	0	0	.984	-2	1-16/3-2,O-1	-0.3
	Mil-N	15	33	3	7	3	0	0	1	2	11	.212	.257	.303	57	-2	0	0	0	.979	-1	/1-6,O-3	-0.3
	Yr	73	168	17	37	9	0	4	17	9	36	.220	.260	.345	71	-7	0	3	-1	.985	-6	1-33,O-16/3-3	-1.5
1966	Chi-N	5	5	0	0	0	0	0	0	0	1	.000	.000	.000	-99	-1	0	0	0	.000	0	H	-0.1
Total	16	1766	6285	792	1671	262	31	286	962	484	894	.266	.323	.454	108	52	15	22	-9	.978	-31	*O-1045,3-394,1/2	-5.1

YEAR	TM/L	G	AB	R	H	2B	3B	HR	RBI	BB	SO	AVG	OBP	SLG	PRO+	BR/A	SB	CS	SBR	FA	FR	G/POS	TPR
■ FRED THOMAS						Thomas, Frederick Harvey "Tommy"			b: 12/19/1892, Milwaukee, Wis.			d: 1/15/86, Rice Lake, Wis.			BR/TR, 5'10", 160 lbs.		Deb: 4/22/18						
1918	*Bos-A	44	144	19	37	2	1	1	11	15	20	.257	.331	.306	94	-1	4			.968	5	3-41/S-1	0.6
1919	Phi-A	124	453	42	96	11	10	2	23	43	52	.212	.283	.294	61	-24	12			.945	-5	*3-124	-2.5
1920	Phi-A	76	255	27	59	6	3	1	11	26	17	.231	.307	.290	58	-15	8	4	0	.960	1	3-61,S-12	-1.0
	Was-A	3	7	0	1	0	0	0	0	0	1	.143	.143	.143	-25	-1	0	1	-1	1.000	2	/3-2	-0.1
	Yr	79	262	27	60	6	3	1	11	26	18	.229	.303	.286	56	-16	8	5	-1	.962	3	3-63,S-12	-1.0
Total	3	247	859	88	193	19	14	4	45	84	90	.225	.297	.293	65	-41	24	5		.954	3	3-228/S-13	-2.9
■ GEORGE THOMAS						Thomas, George Edward			b: 11/29/37, Minneapolis, Minn.			BR/TR, 6'3.5", 190 lbs.			Deb: 9/11/57		C					
1957	Det-A	1	1	0	0	0	0	0	0	0	1	.000	.000	.000	-97	-0	0	0	0	.000	-0	/3-1	-0.1
1958	Det-A	1	0	0	0	0	0	0	0	0	0	—	—	—	—	0	0	0	0	.000	-0	/O-1	0.0
1961	Det-A	17	6	2	0	0	0	0	0	0	4	.000	.000	.000	-97	-2	0	0	0	.000	-0	/O-2,S-1	-0.1
	LA-A	79	282	39	79	12	1	13	59	21	66	.280	.337	.468	101	-0	3	6	-3	.986	-11	O-45,3-38	-1.6
	Yr	96	288	41	79	12	1	13	59	21	70	.274	.330	.458	99	-1	3	6	-3	.986	-10	O-47,3-38/S-1	-1.7
1962	LA-A	56	181	13	43	10	2	4	12	11	37	.238	.320	.381	91	-2	0	0	0	.957	1	O-51	-0.4
1963	LA-A	53	167	14	35	7	1	4	15	9	32	.210	.254	.335	68	-8	0	0	0	.941	-2	O-39,3-10/1-4	-1.2
	Det-A	49	109	13	26	4	1	1	11	11	22	.239	.314	.321	76	-3	2	1	0	1.000	-1	O-40/2-1	-0.7
	Yr	102	276	27	61	11	2	5	26	20	54	.221	.279	.330	71	-11	2	1	0	.974	-4	O-79,3-10/1-4,2-1	-1.9
1964	Det-A	105	308	39	88	15	2	12	44	18	53	.286	.331	.464	117	6	4	1	1	.988	-2	O-90/3-1	0.1
1965	Det-A	79	169	19	36	5	1	3	10	12	39	.213	.273	.308	64	-8	2	3	-1	.948	-3	O-59/2-1	-1.5
1966	Bos-A	69	173	25	41	4	0	5	20	23	38	.237	.333	.347	87	-2	1	0	0	1.000	0	O-48/3-6,C-2,1-2	-0.4
1967	*Bos-A	65	89	10	19	2	0	1	6	3	13	.213	.255	.270	51	-5	0	1	-1	.973	-8	O-43/1-3,C-1	-1.7
1968	Bos-A	12	10	3	2	0	0	1	1	3	3	.200	.273	.500	122	0	1	0	0	1.000	-2	/O-9	-0.1
1969	Bos-A	29	51	9	18	3	1	0	8	3	11	.353	.400	.451	131	2	0	0	0	1.000	-4	O-12,1-10/C-1,3-1	0.0
1970	Bos-A	38	99	13	34	8	0	2	13	11	12	.343	.420	.485	139	6	0	0	0	.972	-5	O-26/3-6	0.0
1971	Bos-A	9	13	0	1	0	0	0	1	1	4	.077	.143	.077	-34	-2	0	0	0	1.000	-4	/O-5	-0.4
	Min-A	23	30	4	8	1	0	0	2	4	3	.267	.353	.300	84	-0	0	0	0	1.000	-4	O-11/1-1,3-1	-0.5
	Yr	32	43	4	9	1	0	0	3	5	7	.209	.292	.233	48	-2	0	0	0	1.000	-8	O-16/1-1,3-1	-0.9
Total	13	685	1688	203	430	71	9	46	202	133	343	.255	.318	.389	92	-20	13	12	-3	.976	-42	O-481/3-64,1C2S	-8.8
■ HERB THOMAS						Thomas, Herbert Mark		b: 5/26/02, Sampson City, Fla.			d: 12/4/91, Starke, Fla.			BR/TR, 5'4.5", 157 lbs.			Deb: 8/28/24					
1924	Bos-N	32	127	12	28	4	1	1	8	9	8	.220	.288	.291	58	-8	5	2	0	.983	8	O-32	-0.1
1925	Bos-N	5	17	2	4	0	1	0	1	0	1	.235	.350	.353	88	-0	0	1	-1	.963	-1	/2-5	-0.2
1927	Bos-N	24	74	11	17	6	1	0	6	3	9	.230	.269	.338	67	-4	2			.972	-11	2-17/S-2	-1.4
	NY-N	13	17	2	3	1	0	1	1	1	1	.176	.263	.353	64	-1	0			.900	1	/O-3,S-1	-0.1
	Yr	37	91	13	20	7	2	0	7	4	10	.220	.268	.341	65	-5	2			.972	-11	2-17/S-3,O-3	-1.5
Total	3	74	235	27	52	11	4	1	15	15	18	.221	.285	.315	63	-13	7	3		.976	-4	/O-35,2-22,S-3	-1.8
■ IRA THOMAS						Thomas, Ira Felix		b: 1/22/1881, Ballston Spa, N.Y.			d: 10/11/58, Philadelphia, Pa.			BR/TR, 6'2", 200 lbs.			Deb: 5/18/06		C			
1906	NY-A	44	115	12	23	1	2	0	15	8		.200	.258	.243	52	-6	2			.938	-5	C-42	-0.8
1907	NY-A	80	208	20	40	5	4	1	24	10		.192	.240	.269	58	-10	5			.953	8	C-61/1-2	0.3
1908	*Det-A	40	101	6	31	1	0	0	8	5		.307	.346	.317	111	1	0			.972	-5	C-29	-0.2
1909	Phi-A	84	256	22	57	9	3	0	31	18		.223	.282	.281	79	-6	4			**.985**	12	C-84	1.5
1910	*Phi-A	60	180	14	50	8	2	1	19	6		.278	.301	.361	108	1	2			.967	8	C-60	1.5
1911	*Phi-A	103	297	33	81	14	3	0	39	23		.273	.341	.340	92	-3	4			.974	6	*C-103	1.2
1912	Phi-A	48	139	14	30	4	1	2	13	8		.216	.268	.295	63	-7	3			.971	-1	C-48	-0.4
1913	Phi-A	22	53	3	15	4	1	0	6	4	8	.283	.333	.396	116	1	0			.983	3	C-21	0.5
1914	Phi-A	2	3	0	0	0	0	0	0	0	0	.000	.000	.000	-99	-1	0			1.000	0	/C-1	0.0
1915	Phi-A	1	0	0	0	0	0	0	0	0	0	—	—	—	—	0	0			1.000	0	/C-1	0.0
Total	10	484	1352	124	327	46	17	3	155	82	8	.242	.296	.308	82	-30	20			.970	26	C-450/1-2	3.6
■ GORMAN THOMAS						Thomas, James Gorman		b: 12/12/50, Charleston, S.C.			BR/TR, 6'2", 210 lbs.			Deb: 4/6/73							
1973	Mil-A	59	155	16	29	7	1	2	11	14	61	.187	.254	.284	53	-10	5	5	-2	.957	-4	O-50/3-1,D-3	-1.7
1974	Mil-A	17	46	10	12	4	0	2	11	8	15	.261	.370	.478	143	3	4	0	1	1.000	-1	O-13/D-2	0.3
1975	Mil-A	121	240	34	43	12	2	10	28	31	84	.179	.273	.371	80	-7	4	2	0	.961	-13	*O-113/D-6	-2.4
1976	Mil-A	99	227	27	45	9	2	8	36	31	67	.198	.297	.361	94	-2	2	3	-1	.986	-5	O-94/3-1,D-1	-1.2
1978	Mil-A	137	452	70	111	24	1	32	86	73	133	.246	.353	.515	141	24	3	4	-2	.983	-4	*O-137	1.4
1979	Mil-A	156	557	97	136	29	0	45	123	98	175	.244	.359	.539	138	30	1	5	-3	.991	5	*O-152/D-4	2.3
1980	Mil-A	162	628	78	150	26	3	38	105	58	170	.239	.305	.471	113	8	8	5	-1	.985	3	*O-160/D-2	0.5
1981	*Mil-A★	103	363	54	94	22	0	21	65	50	85	.259	.352	.493	149	22	4	5	-2	.979	3	O-97/D-6	2.1
1982	*Mil-A	158	567	96	139	29	1	**39**	112	84	143	.245	.347	.506	139	30	3	10	-2	.991	10	*O-157	3.2
1983	Mil-A	46	164	21	30	6	1	5	18	23	50	.183	.287	.323	73	-6	2	1	0	.992	-0	O-46	-0.8
	Cle-A	106	371	51	82	17	0	17	51	57	98	.221	.326	.404	96	-2	8	3	1	.982	12	*O-106	0.7
	Yr	152	535	72	112	23	1	22	69	80	148	.209	.314	.379	90	-7	10	4	1	.985	11	*O-152	-0.1
1984	Sea-A	35	108	6	17	3	0	1	13	28	27	.157	.336	.213	56	-5	0	3	-2	1.000	-3	O-34/D-1	-1.1
1985	Sea-A	135	484	76	104	16	1	32	87	84	126	.215	.332	.450	111	8	3	2	-0	.000	0	*D-133	0.5
1986	Sea-A	57	170	24	33	4	0	10	26	27	55	.194	.308	.394	89	-3	2	1	-1			D-52	-0.5
	Mil-A	44	145	21	26	4	1	6	10	31	50	.179	.324	.345	80	-4	2	2	-1	.980	-1	D-36/1-6	-0.6
	Yr	101	315	45	59	8	1	16	36	58	105	.187	.316	.371	85	-6	3	4	-2	.980	-1	D-88/1-6	-1.1
Total	13	1435	4677	681	1051	212	13	268	782	697	1339	.225	.328	.448	114	86	50	49	-14	.984	1	*O-1159,D-246/1-6,3	2.7
■ LEE THOMAS						Thomas, James Leroy		b: 2/5/36, Peoria, Ill.			BL/TR, 6'2", 198 lbs.			Deb: 4/22/61		C					
1961	NY-A	2	2	0	1	0	0	0	0	0	0	.500	.500	.500	177	0	0	0	0	.000	0	H	0.0
	LA-A	130	450	77	128	11	5	24	70	47	74	.284	.355	.491	111	6	0	5	-3	.966	-3	O-86,1-34	-0.7
	Yr	132	452	77	129	11	5	24	70	47	74	.285	.355	.491	111	6	0	5	-3	.966	-3	O-86,1-34	-0.7
1962	LA-A★	160	583	88	169	21	2	26	104	55	74	.290	.357	.467	124	19	6	1	1	.982	-10	1-90,O-74	0.0
1963	LA-A	149	528	52	116	12	6	9	55	53	82	.220	.302	.316	78	-15	6	0	2	.996	3	*1-104,O-43	-1.8
1964	LA-A	47	172	14	47	8	1	2	24	18	22	.273	.342	.366	108	2	1	0	0	.949	-1	O-47/1-1	-0.1
	Bos-A	107	401	44	103	19	2	13	42	34	29	.257	.321	.411	97	-2	2	1	0	.995	3	*O-107/1-1	-0.4
	Yr	154	573	58	150	27	3	15	66	52	51	.262	.328	.398	100	0	3	1	0	.981	2	*O-154/1-2	-0.5
1965	Bos-A	151	521	74	141	27	4	22	75	72	42	.271	.362	.464	126	18	6	2	1	.984	5	*1-127,O-20	1.7
1966	Atl-N	39	126	11	25	1	1	6	15	10	15	.198	.263	.365	71	-5	1	0	-0	.987	-1	1-36	-0.6
	Chi-N	75	149	15	36	4	0	1	9	14	15	.242	.319	.289	70	-6	0	0	0	.992	-1	1-20,O-17	-0.9
	Yr	114	275	26	61	5	1	7	24	24	30	.222	.294	.324	71	-11	1	1	-0	.989	1	1-56,O-17	-1.5
1967	Chi-N	77	191	16	42	4	1	2	23	15	22	.220	.287	.283	61	-9	0	0	0	.969	-4	O-43,1-10	-1.7
1968	Hou-N	90	201	14	39	4	0	1	14	12	22	.194	.250	.229	61	-13	2	1	0	.973	-1	O-48/1-2	-1.9
Total	8	1027	3324	405	847	111	22	106	428	332	397	.255	.328	.397	99	-6	25	11	1	.975	-7	O-485,1-425	-6.4
■ BUD THOMAS						Thomas, John Tillman		b: 3/10/29, Sedalia, Mo.			BR/TR, 6', 180 lbs.			Deb: 9/2/51							
1951	StL-A	14	20	3	7	0	0	1	0	1	3	.350	.350	.500	124	1	2	0	1	1.000	1	S-14	0.3
■ KITE THOMAS						Thomas, Keith Marshall		b: 4/27/23, Kansas City, Kan.			d: 1/7/95, Rocky Mount, N.C.			BR/TR, 6'1.5", 195 lbs.			Deb: 4/19/52					
1952	Phi-A	75	116	24	29	6	1	6	18	20	27	.250	.365	.474	124	4	0	1	-1	.957	-3	O-29	-0.1
1953	Phi-A	24	49	1	6	0	0	0	2	3	6	.122	.173	.122	-18	-8	0	0	0	1.000	-0	O-15	-0.9
	Was-A	38	58	10	17	3	2	1	12	11	7	.293	.414	.466	141	4	0	0	0	1.000	-2	O-8,C-1	0.2
	Yr	62	107	11	23	3	2	1	14	14	13	.215	.311	.308	68	-5	0	0	0	1.000	-2	O-23/C-1	-0.7
Total	2	137	223	35	52	9	3	7	32	34	40	.233	.340	.395	98	-1	0	1	-1	.978	-5	/O-52,C-1	-0.8
■ LEO THOMAS						Thomas, Leo Raymond "Tommy"		b: 7/26/23, Turlock, Cal.			BR/TR, 5'11.5", 178 lbs.			Deb: 4/29/50						
1950	StL-A	35	121	19	24	6	0	1	9	20	14	.198	.312	.273	49	-9	0	1	-1	.964	-4	3-35	-1.3
1952	StL-A	41	124	12	29	5	1	0	12	9	11	.234	.336	.290	73	-4	2	0	1	.934	4	3-37/S-3,2-1	0.0

YEAR	TM/L	G	AB	R	H	2B	3B	HR	RBI	BB	SO	AVG	OBP	SLG	PRO+	BR/A	SB	CS	SBR	FA	FR	G/POS	TPR
	Chi-A	19	24	1	4	0	0	0	6	6	4	.167	.333	.167	42	-2	0	0	0	.952	1	/3-9	-0.1
	Yr	60	148	13	33	5	1	0	18	23	11	.223	.335	.270	68	-5	2	0	1	.936	4	3-46/S-3,2-1	-0.1
Total	2	95	269	32	57	11	1	1	27	43	25	.212	.325	.271	59	-15	2	1	0	.948	5	/3-81,S-3,2-1	-1.4

■ RAY THOMAS

Thomas, Raymond Joseph b: 7/9/10, Dover, N.H. d: 12/6/93, Wilson, N.C. BR/TR, 5'10.5", 175 lbs. Deb: 7/21/38

YEAR	TM/L	G	AB	R	H	2B	3B	HR	RBI	BB	SO	AVG	OBP	SLG	PRO+	BR/A	SB	CS	SBR	FA	FR	G/POS	TPR
1938	Bro-N	1	3	1	1	0	0	0	0	0	0	.333	.333	.333	82	-0	0			1.000	0	/C-1	0.0

■ RED THOMAS

Thomas, Robert William b: 4/25/1898, Hargrove, Ala. d: 3/29/62, Fremont, Ohio BR/TR, 5'11", 165 lbs. Deb: 9/13/21

YEAR	TM/L	G	AB	R	H	2B	3B	HR	RBI	BB	SO	AVG	OBP	SLG	PRO+	BR/A	SB	CS	SBR	FA	FR	G/POS	TPR
1921	Chi-N	8	30	5	8	3	0	1	5	4	5	.267	.371	.467	120	1	0	1	-1	.962	1	/O-8	0.1

■ ROY THOMAS

Thomas, Roy Allen b: 3/24/1874, Norristown, Pa. d: 11/20/59, Norristown, Pa. BL/TR, 5'11", 150 lbs. Deb: 4/14/1899 FC

YEAR	TM/L	G	AB	R	H	2B	3B	HR	RBI	BB	SO	AVG	OBP	SLG	PRO+	BR/A	SB	CS	SBR	FA	FR	G/POS	TPR
1899	Phi-N	150	547	137	178	12	4	0	47	115		.325	.457	.362	130	35	42			.952	4	*O-135,1-14	2.6
1900	Phi-N	140	531	132	168	4	3	0	33	115		.316	.451	.335	119	26	37			.958	-2	*O-139/P-1	1.2
1901	Phi-N	129	479	102	148	5	2	1	28	100		.309	.437	.334	123	22	27			.967	-2	*O-129	1.0
1902	Phi-N	138	500	89	143	4	7	0	24	107		.286	.414	.322	127	24	17			.974	5	*O-138	2.2
1903	Phi-N	130	477	88	156	11	2	1	27	107		.327	.453	.365	139	34	17			.963	14	*O-130	3.8
1904	Phi-N	139	496	92	144	6	6	3	29	102		.290	.416	.345	141	32	28			.974	15	*O-139	4.0
1905	Phi-N	147	562	118	178	11	6	0	31	93		.317	.417	.358	137	32	23			.983	19	*O-147	4.5
1906	Phi-N	142	493	81	125	10	7	0	16	107		.254	.393	.302	117	17	22			.986	10	*O-142	2.2
1907	Phi-N	121	419	70	102	15	3	1	23	83		.243	.374	.301	113	11	11			.980	5	*O-121	1.3
1908	Phi-N	6	24	2	4	0	0	0	0	2		.167	.231	.167	26	-2	0			1.000	-1	/O-6	-0.3
	Pit-N	102	386	52	99	11	10	1	24	49		.256	.348	.345	121	11	11			.975	5	*O-101	1.3
	Yr	108	410	54	103	11	10	1	24	51		.251	.341	.334	116	9	11			.976	4	*O-107	1.0
1909	Bos-N	82	281	36	74	9	1	0	11	47		.263	.369	.302	104	3	5			.976	-2	O-76	-0.1
1910	Phi-N	23	71	7	13	0	2	0	4	7	5	.183	.266	.239	46	-5	4			.952	-2	O-20	-0.8
1911	Phi-N	21	30	5	5	2	0	0	2	8	6	.167	.342	.233	61	-1	0			1.000	1	O-11	-0.1
Total	13	1470	5296	1011	1537	100	53	7	299	1042	11	.290	.413	.333	124	240	244			.972	71	*O-1434/1-14,P-1	22.8

■ VALMY THOMAS

Thomas, Valmy b: 10/21/28, Santurce, P.R. BR/TR, 5'9", 165 lbs. Deb: 4/16/57

YEAR	TM/L	G	AB	R	H	2B	3B	HR	RBI	BB	SO	AVG	OBP	SLG	PRO+	BR/A	SB	CS	SBR	FA	FR	G/POS	TPR
1957	NY-N	88	241	30	60	10	3	6	31	16	29	.249	.298	.390	83	-6	0	0	0	.991	2	C-88	-0.1
1958	SF-N	63	143	14	37	5	0	3	16	13	24	.259	.325	.357	82	-4	1	0	0	.992	2	C-61	0.1
1959	Phi-N	66	140	5	28	2	0	1	7	9	19	.200	.253	.236	31	-14	1	0	0	.980	15	C-65/3-1	0.4
1960	Bal-A	8	16	0	1	0	0	0	0	1	0	.063	.118	.063	-51	-3	0	1	-1	1.000	1	/C-8	-0.3
1961	Cle-A	27	86	7	18	3	0	2	6	6	7	.209	.261	.314	54	-6	0	0	0	.988	9	C-27	0.4
Total	5	252	626	56	144	20	3	12	60	45	79	.230	.285	.329	64	-33	2	1	0	.988	29	C-249/3-1	0.5

■ BILL THOMAS

Thomas, William Miskey b: 12/8/1877, Norristown, Pa. d: 1/14/50, Evansburg, Pa. BR/TR, 5'10", 190 lbs. Deb: 5/1/02 F

YEAR	TM/L	G	AB	R	H	2B	3B	HR	RBI	BB	SO	AVG	OBP	SLG	PRO+	BR/A	SB	CS	SBR	FA	FR	G/POS	TPR
1902	Phi-N	6	17	1	2	0	0	0	0	1		.118	.167	.118	-12	-2	0			.500	-1	/O-3,1-1,2-1	-0.4

■ WALT THOMAS

Thomas, William Walter "Tommy" b: 4/28/1884, Foot Of Ten, Pa. d: 6/6/50, Altoona, Pa. BR/TR, 5'8", Deb: 9/18/08

YEAR	TM/L	G	AB	R	H	2B	3B	HR	RBI	BB	SO	AVG	OBP	SLG	PRO+	BR/A	SB	CS	SBR	FA	FR	G/POS	TPR
1908	Bos-N	5	13	2	2	0	0	0	1	3		.154	.313	.154	51	-1	2			.864	-1	/S-5	-0.2

■ ART THOMASON

Thomason, Arthur Wilson b: 2/12/1889, Liberty, Mo. d: 5/2/44, Kansas City, Mo. BL/TL, 5'8", 150 lbs. Deb: 8/10/10

YEAR	TM/L	G	AB	R	H	2B	3B	HR	RBI	BB	SO	AVG	OBP	SLG	PRO+	BR/A	SB	CS	SBR	FA	FR	G/POS	TPR
1910	Cle-A	20	70	4	12	0	1	0	2	5		.171	.227	.200	33	-5	3			.944	2	O-20	-0.5

■ GARY THOMASSON

Thomasson, Gary Leah b: 7/29/51, San Diego, Cal. BL/TL, 6'1", 180 lbs. Deb: 9/5/72

YEAR	TM/L	G	AB	R	H	2B	3B	HR	RBI	BB	SO	AVG	OBP	SLG	PRO+	BR/A	SB	CS	SBR	FA	FR	G/POS	TPR
1972	SF-N	10	27	5	9	1	1	0	1	1	7	.333	.357	.444	125	1	0	0	0	1.000	-2	/1-7,O-2	-0.1
1973	SF-N	112	235	35	67	10	4	4	30	22	43	.285	.346	.413	105	1	2	0	1	.992	-3	1-47,O-43	-0.4
1974	SF-N	120	315	41	77	14	3	2	29	38	56	.244	.326	.327	79	-8	7	1	2	.981	1	O-76,1-15	-1.0
1975	SF-N	114	326	44	74	12	3	7	32	37	48	.227	.308	.347	78	-10	9	3	1	.978	1	O-74,1-17	-0.5
1976	SF-N	103	328	45	85	20	5	8	38	30	45	.259	.323	.424	107	2	8	3	1	.959	-7	O-54,1-39	-0.9
1977	SF-N	145	446	63	114	24	6	17	71	75	102	.256	.364	.451	118	12	16	4	2	.959	-5	*O-113,1-31	-0.5
1978	Oak-A	47	154	17	31	4	1	5	16	15	44	.201	.272	.338	74	-6	4	1	1	.969	2	O-44/1-5	-0.5
	*NY-A	55	116	20	32	4	1	3	20	13	22	.276	.349	.405	114	2	0	2	-1	.972	4	O-50/D-1	0.0
	Yr	102	270	37	63	8	2	8	36	28	66	.233	.305	.367	92	-3	4	3	-1	.971	2	O-94/1-5,D-1	-0.5
1979	LA-N	115	315	39	78	11	1	14	45	43	70	.248	.340	.422	108	4	4	2	0	.980	-12	*O-100/1-1	-1.2
1980	LA-N	80	111	6	24	3	0	1	12	17	26	.216	.326	.270	69	-4	0	0	0	.974	-6	O-31/1-1	-1.2
Total	9	901	2373	315	591	103	25	61	294	291	463	.249	.332	.391	98	-5	50	16	5	.970	-24	O-587,1-163/D-1	-5.3

■ JIM THOME

Thome, James Howard b: 8/27/70, Peoria, Ill. BL/TR, 6'3", 190 lbs. Deb: 9/4/91

YEAR	TM/L	G	AB	R	H	2B	3B	HR	RBI	BB	SO	AVG	OBP	SLG	PRO+	BR/A	SB	CS	SBR	FA	FR	G/POS	TPR
1991	Cle-A	27	98	7	25	4	2	1	9	5	16	.255	.298	.367	82	-2	1	1	-0	.900	1	3-27	-0.2
1992	Cle-A	40	117	8	24	3	1	2	12	10	34	.205	.279	.299	63	-6	2	0	1	.882	-6	3-40	-1.2
1993	Cle-A	47	154	28	41	11	0	7	22	29	36	.266	.396	.474	133	8	2	1	0	.950	-2	3-47	0.6
1994	Cle-A	98	321	58	86	20	1	20	52	46	84	.268	.360	.523	124	11	3	3	-1	.940	-1	3-94	0.9
1995	*Cle-A	137	452	92	142	29	3	25	73	97	113	.314	.440	.558	155	41	4	3	-1	.948	-14	*3-134/D-1	2.5
1996	*Cle-A	151	505	122	157	28	5	38	116	123	141	.311	.451	.612	165	56	2	2	-1	.953	-6	*3-150/D-1	4.4
Total	6	500	1647	315	475	95	12	93	284	310	424	.288	.407	.530	141	107	14	10	-2	.940	-27	3-492/D-2	7.0

■ ANDREW THOMPSON

Thompson, Andrew M. b: 1845, Illinois Deb: 4/26/1875 M

YEAR	TM/L	G	AB	R	H	2B	3B	HR	RBI	BB	SO	AVG	OBP	SLG	PRO+	BR/A	SB	CS	SBR	FA	FR	G/POS	TPR
1875	Was-n	11	41	3	4	0	1	0	1	0	0	.098	.098	.146	-17	-4	0	0	0	.624	-7	C-11/O-1	-1.0

■ BOBBY THOMPSON

Thompson, Bobby La Rue b: 11/3/53, Charlotte, N.C. BB/TR, 5'11", 175 lbs. Deb: 4/16/78

YEAR	TM/L	G	AB	R	H	2B	3B	HR	RBI	BB	SO	AVG	OBP	SLG	PRO+	BR/A	SB	CS	SBR	FA	FR	G/POS	TPR
1978	Tex-A	64	120	23	27	3	3	2	12	9	26	.225	.290	.350	79	-3	7	2	1	.982	-5	O-52/D-3	-0.9

■ TIM THOMPSON

Thompson, Charles Lemoine b: 3/1/24, Coalport, Pa. BL/TR, 5'11", 190 lbs. Deb: 4/28/54 C

YEAR	TM/L	G	AB	R	H	2B	3B	HR	RBI	BB	SO	AVG	OBP	SLG	PRO+	BR/A	SB	CS	SBR	FA	FR	G/POS	TPR
1954	Bro-N	10	13	2	2	1	0	0	1	1	1	.154	.214	.231	15	-2	0	0	0	.909	-1	/C-2,O-1	-0.2
1956	KC-A	92	268	21	73	13	2	1	27	17	23	.272	.321	.347	76	-9	2	4	-2	.981	2	C-68	-0.6
1957	KC-A	81	230	25	47	10	0	9	19	18	26	.204	.262	.339	62	-13	0	0	0	.993	-3	C-62	-1.3
1958	Det-A	4	6	1	1	0	0	0	0	3	2	.167	.444	.167	70	-0	0	0	0	1.000	-1	/C-4	-0.1
Total	4	187	517	49	123	24	2	8	47	39	52	.238	.294	.338	68	-24	2	4	-2	.986	-3	C-136/O-1	-2.2

■ DANNY THOMPSON

Thompson, Danny Leon b: 2/1/47, Wichita, Kan. d: 12/10/76, Rochester, Minn. BR/TR, 6', 183 lbs. Deb: 6/25/70

YEAR	TM/L	G	AB	R	H	2B	3B	HR	RBI	BB	SO	AVG	OBP	SLG	PRO+	BR/A	SB	CS	SBR	FA	FR	G/POS	TPR
1970	*Min-A	96	302	25	66	9	0	0	22	7	39	.219	.236	.248	33	-27	0	0	0	.986	-12	2-81,3-37/S-6	-3.5
1971	Min-A	48	57	10	15	2	0	0	7	7	12	.263	.344	.298	81	-1	0	0	0	.897	1	3-17/2-3,S-1	0.0
1972	Min-A	144	573	54	158	22	6	4	48	34	57	.276	.319	.356	96	-3	3	4	-2	.957	-9	*S-144	0.8
1973	Min-A	99	347	29	78	13	2	1	36	16	41	.225	.263	.282	52	-22	1	1	-0	.950	7	S-95/3-1,D-1	-0.4
1974	Min-A	97	264	25	66	6	1	4	25	22	29	.250	.313	.326	81	-6	1	1	-0	.963	-21	S-88/3-5,D-1	-1.8
1975	Min-A	112	355	25	96	11	2	5	37	18	30	.270	.306	.355	85	-8	0	3	-2	.941	-17	*S-100/3-7,2-1,D-3	-1.7
1976	Min-A	34	122	9	29	4	0	0	6	3	8	.234	.258	.266	53	-7	1	1	-0	.988	-1	S-34	-0.4
	Tex-A	64	196	12	42	3	0	1	13	13	19	.214	.267	.245	49	-12	2	0	-0	.976	-7	3-39,2-14,S-10/D-1	-2.0
	Yr	98	320	21	71	7	0	1	19	16	27	.222	.263	.253	51	-20	3	3	-1	.981	-9	S-44,3-39,2-14,/D-1	-2.5
Total	7	694	2218	189	550	70	11	15	194	120	235	.248	.289	.310	70	-88	8	11	-4	.956	-60	S-478,3-106/2-99,D	-9.1

■ DON THOMPSON

Thompson, Donald Newlin b: 12/28/23, Swepsonville, N.C. BL/TL, 6', 185 lbs. Deb: 4/24/49

YEAR	TM/L	G	AB	R	H	2B	3B	HR	RBI	BB	SO	AVG	OBP	SLG	PRO+	BR/A	SB	CS	SBR	FA	FR	G/POS	TPR
1949	Bos-N	7	11	0	2	0	0	0	0	0	0	.182	.182	.182	-2	-2	0			.800	-0	/O-2	-0.2
1951	Bro-N	80	118	25	27	0	0	0	6	12	12	.229	.305	.254	51	-8	2	8	-4	.987	-11	O-61	-2.5
1953	*Bro-N	96	153	25	37	5	0	1	12	14	13	.242	.310	.294	57	-9	2	3	-1	.989	-14	O-81	-2.6
1954	Bro-N	34	25	2	1	0	0	0	1	5	5	.040	.226	.040	-25	-5	0	1	-1	1.000	-0	O-29	-1.4
Total	4	217	307	52	67	8	0	2	19	31	32	.218	.296	.254	46	-23	4	11		.984	-35	O-173	-6.7

■ FRANK THOMPSON

Thompson, Frank Deb: 9/11/1875

YEAR	TM/L	G	AB	R	H	2B	3B	HR	RBI	BB	SO	AVG	OBP	SLG	PRO+	BR/A	SB	CS	SBR	FA	FR	G/POS	TPR
1875	Atl-n	1	5	1	2	0	0	0	1	0	0	.400	.400	.400	205	1	0	0	0	.000	-1	/O-1	0.0

YEAR	TM/L	G	AB	R	H	2B	3B	HR	RBI	BB	SO	AVG	OBP	SLG	PRO+	BR/A	SB	CS	SBR	FA	FR	G/POS	TPR

■ FRANK THOMPSON
Thompson, Frank E b: 7/2/1895, Springfield, Mo. d: 6/27/40, Jasper Co., Mo. BR/TR, 5'8", 155 lbs. Deb: 5/6/20

| 1920 | StL-A | 22 | 53 | 7 | 9 | 0 | 0 | 0 | 5 | 13 | 10 | .170 | .343 | .170 | 38 | -4 | 1 | 1 | -0 | .878 | -4 | 3-14/2-2 | -0.8 |

■ HANK THOMPSON
Thompson, Henry Curtis b: 12/8/25, Oklahoma City, Okla d: 9/30/69, Fresno, Cal. BL/TR, 5'9", 174 lbs. Deb: 7/17/47

1947	StL-A	27	78	10	20	1	1	0	5	10	7	.256	.341	.295	76	-2	1	0		.957	1	2-19	0.0
1949	NY-N	75	275	51	77	10	4	9	34	42	30	.280	.377	.444	120	8	5			.961	-8	2-69/3-1	0.4
1950	NY-N	148	512	82	148	17	6	20	91	83	60	.289	.391	.463	123	19	8			.944	5	*3-138,O-10	2.1
1951	*NY-N	87	264	37	62	8	4	8	33	43	23	.235	.342	.386	95	-1	1	2	-1	.925	-14	3-71	-1.8
1952	NY-N	128	423	67	110	13	9	17	67	50	38	.260	.344	.454	119	10	4	4	-1	.979	9	O-72,3-46/2-4	1.4
1953	NY-N	114	388	80	117	15	8	24	74	60	39	.302	.400	.567	146	27	6	5	-1	.956	-3	*3-101/O-9,2-1	1.9
1954	*NY-N	136	448	76	118	18	1	26	86	90	58	.263	.392	.482	126	19	3	0	-1	.945	-4	*3-130/2-2,O-1	1.3
1955	NY-N	135	432	65	106	13	1	17	63	84	55	.245	.373	.398	105	5	2	2	-1	.943	2	*3-124/2-7,S-1	0.7
1956	NY-N	83	183	24	43	9	0	8	29	31	26	.235	.349	.415	105	2	2	1	0	.908	0	3-44,O-10/S-1	0.2
Total	9	933	3003	492	801	104	34	129	482	493	337	.267	.374	.453	118	87	33	15		.941	-13	3-655,O-102,2/S	6.2

■ HOMER THOMPSON
Thompson, Homer Thomas b: 6/1/1891, Spring City, Tenn. d: 9/12/57, Atlanta, Ga. BR/TR, 5'9", 160 lbs. Deb: 10/5/12

| 1912 | NY-A | 1 | 0 | 0 | 0 | 0 | 0 | 0 | 0 | 0 | 0 | — | — | — | | | | | | .500 | -1 | /C-1 | 0.0 |

■ SHAG THOMPSON
Thompson, James Alfred b: 4/29/1893, Haw River, N.C. d: 1/7/90, Black Mountain, N.C BL/TR, 5'8.5", 165 lbs. Deb: 6/8/14

1914	Phi-A	16	29	3	5	0	1	0	2	7	8	.172	.351	.241	82	-0	1			.941	1	/O-8	0.1
1915	Phi-A	17	33	5	11	2	0	0	2	4	6	.333	.405	.394	144	2	0	1	-1	1.000	0	/O-7	0.1
1916	Phi-A	15	17	4	0	0	0	0	0	7	6	.000	.292	.000	-12	-2	1			1.000	0	/O-8	-0.3
Total	3	48	79	12	16	2	1	0	4	18	20	.203	.357	.253	87	-0	2	1		.978	1	/O-23	-0.1

■ JASON THOMPSON
Thompson, Jason Dolph b: 7/6/54, Hollywood, Cal. BL/TL, 6'3", 210 lbs. Deb: 4/23/76

1976	Det-A	123	412	45	90	12	1	17	54	68	72	.218	.331	.376	103	2	2	4	-2	.994	2	*1-117	-0.7
1977	Det-A☆	158	585	87	158	24	5	31	105	73	91	.270	.352	.487	120	15	0	1	-1	.991	-7	*1-158	-0.2
1978	Det-A★	153	589	79	169	25	3	26	96	74	96	.287	.367	.472	130	24	0	0	0	.993	-5	*1-151	1.0
1979	Det-A	145	492	58	121	16	1	20	79	70	90	.246	.341	.404	97	-2	2	0	0	.994	1	*1-140/D-2	-0.9
1980	Det-A	36	126	10	27	5	0	4	20	13	26	.214	.293	.349	73	-5	0	1	-1	1.000	4	1-36	-0.4
	Cal-A	102	312	59	99	14	0	17	70	70	60	.317	.442	.526	168	33	2	0	1	1.000	-3	1-47,D-45	2.6
	Yr	138	438	69	126	19	0	21	90	83	86	.288	.402	.475	141	28	2	1	0	1.000	1	1-83,D-45	2.2
1981	Pit-N	86	223	36	54	13	0	15	42	59	49	.242	.401	.502	150	17	0	0	0	.989	-1	1-78	1.3
1982	Pit-N★	156	550	87	156	32	0	31	101	101	107	.284	.397	.511	148	37	1	0	0	.993	-1	*1-155	2.9
1983	Pit-N	152	517	70	134	20	1	18	76	99	128	.259	.379	.406	115	14	1	0	0	.993	-6	*1-151	-0.1
1984	Pit-N	154	543	61	138	22	0	17	74	87	73	.254	.359	.389	110	9	0	0	0	.990	-10	*1-152	-1.1
1985	Pit-N	123	402	42	97	17	1	12	61	64	84	.241	.372	.378	111	9	0	0	0	.992	2	*1-114	0.5
1986	Mon-N	30	51	6	10	4	0	0	4	18	12	.196	.406	.275	92	1	0	1	-1	.962	-3	1-15	-0.4
Total	11	1418	4802	640	1253	204	12	208	782	816	862	.261	.369	.438	121	155	8	7	-2	.992	-28	*1-1314/D-47	4.5

■ JASON THOMPSON
Thompson, Jason Michael b: 6/13/71, Orlando, Fla. BL/TL, 6'4", 200 lbs. Deb: 6/9/96

| 1996 | SD-N | 13 | 49 | 4 | 11 | 4 | 0 | 2 | 6 | 1 | 14 | .224 | .240 | .429 | 76 | -2 | 0 | 0 | 0 | .964 | 1 | 1-13 | -0.2 |

■ TUG THOMPSON
Thompson, John P. b: London, Ontario, Canada BL/TR, 5'8", 160 lbs. d: 8/31/1882

1882	Cin-a	1	5	0	1	0	0	0		0		.200	.200	.200	33	-0				.000	-1	/O-1	-0.1
1884	Ind-a	24	97	10	20	3	0	0		2		.206	.222	.237	51	-5				.429	-11	O-12,C-12	-1.4
Total	2	25	102	10	21	3	0	0		2		.206	.221	.235	50	-5				.409	-11	/O-13,C-12	-1.5

■ FRESCO THOMPSON
Thompson, Lafayette Fresco "Tommy" b: 6/6/02, Centreville, Ala. d: 11/20/68, Fullerton, Cal. BR/TR, 5'8", 150 lbs. Deb: 9/5/25

1925	Pit-N	14	37	4	9	2	1	0	8	4	1	.243	.317	.351	66	-2	1	0		.977	-2	2-12	-0.4
1926	NY-N	2	8	1	5	0	0	0	1	2	0	.625	.700	.625	262	2	1			1.000	-1	/2-2	0.1
1927	Phi-N	153	597	78	181	32	14	1	70	34	36	.303	.343	.409	99	-1	19			.963	-5	*2-153	-0.1
1928	Phi-N	152	634	99	182	34	11	3	50	42	27	.287	.332	.390	85	-14	19			.966	9	*2-152	-0.1
1929	Phi-N	148	623	115	202	41	3	4	53	75	34	.324	.398	.419	96	-1	16			.965	12	*2-148	1.5
1930	Phi-N	122	478	77	135	34	4	4	46	35	29	.282	.331	.395	70	-24	7			.955	1	*2-112	-1.5
1931	Bro-N	74	181	26	48	6	1	1	21	23	16	.265	.351	.326	84	-3	5			.946	-3	2-43,S-10/3-5	-0.4
1932	Bro-N	3	1	0	0	0	0	0	0	0	0	.000	.000	.000	-99	-0	0			.000	0	H	0.0
1934	NY-N	1	1	0	0	0	0	0	0	0	0	.000	.000	.000	-99	-0	0			.000	0	H	0.0
Total	9	669	2560	400	762	149	34	13	249	215	143	.298	.353	.398	88	-45	69	1		.962	10	2-622/S-10,3-5	-0.9

■ MILT THOMPSON
Thompson, Milton Bernard b: 1/5/59, Washington, D.C. BL/TR, 5'11", 170 lbs. Deb: 9/4/84

1984	Atl-N	25	99	16	30	1	0	2	4	11	11	.303	.373	.374	103	1	14	2	3	.956	3	O-25	0.6
1985	Atl-N	73	182	17	55	7	4	0	6	7	36	.302	.339	.363	91	-2	9	4	0	.964	-5	O-49	-0.9
1986	Phi-N	96	299	38	75	7	1	6	23	26	62	.251	.313	.341	78	-9	19	4	3	.991	-6	O-89	-0.5
1987	Phi-N	150	527	86	159	26	9	7	43	42	87	.302	.353	.425	102	-2	46	10	8	.989	9	*O-146	1.3
1988	Phi-N	122	378	53	109	16	2	2	33	39	59	.288	.356	.357	103	3	17	9	0	.983	5	*O-112	0.4
1989	StL-N	155	545	60	158	28	8	4	68	39	91	.290	.342	.393	106	4	27	8	3	.978	2	*O-147	0.7
1990	StL-N	135	418	42	91	14	7	6	30	39	60	.218	.292	.328	70	-17	25	5	5	.971	-4	*O-116	-2.0
1991	StL-N	115	326	55	100	16	5	6	34	32	53	.307	.369	.442	126	11	16	9	-1	.991	9	O-91	1.9
1992	StL-N	109	208	31	61	9	1	4	17	16	39	.293	.350	.404	116	4	18	6	2	.974	-3	O-45	0.2
1993	*Phi-N	129	340	42	89	14	2	4	44	40	57	.262	.343	.350	87	-5	9	2	1	.994	-3	*O-106	-1.0
1994	Phi-N	87	220	29	60	7	0	3	30	23	28	.273	.350	.345	80	-6	7	2	1	1.000	-6	O-79	-1.2
	Hou-N	9	21	5	6	0	0	0	3	1	2	.286	.318	.429	97	-0	2	0	0	1.000	-0	/O-6	0.0
	Yr	96	241	34	66	7	0	3	33	24	30	.274	.347	.353	82	-6	9	2	1	1.000	-6	O-85	-1.2
1995	Hou-N	92	132	14	29	9	0	2	19	14	21	.220	.299	.333	71	-6	4	0	0	.979	-3	O-34	-0.9
1996	LA-N	48	51	2	6	1	0	0	1	6	10	.118	.211	.137	-6	-8	1	1	0	1.000	-3	O-1	-1.1
	Col-N	14	15	1	1	0	0	0	2	1	3	.067	.125	.133	-25	-3	0	0	0	1.000	0	/O-1	-0.3
	Yr	62	66	3	7	1	0	0	3	7	13	.106	.192	.136	-12	-11	1	1	0	1.000	-3	O-18	-1.4
Total	13	1359	3761	491	1029	156	37	47	357	336	635	.274	.337	.372	94	-31	214	66	25	.984	4	*O-1063	-2.8

■ ROBBY THOMPSON
Thompson, Robert Randall b: 5/10/62, W.Palm Beach, Fla. BR/TR, 5'11", 170 lbs. Deb: 4/8/86

1986	SF-N	149	549	73	149	27	3	7	47	42	112	.271	.329	.370	97	-3	12	15	-5	.976	1	*2-149/S-1	-0.2
1987	*SF-N	132	420	62	110	26	5	10	44	40	91	.262	.338	.419	104	2	16	11	-2	.972	6	*2-126	1.2
1988	SF-N†	138	477	66	126	24	6	7	48	40	111	.264	.326	.384	108	4	14	5	1	.978	-9	*2-134	0.2
1989	*SF-N	148	547	91	132	26	11	13	50	51	133	.241	.321	.400	108	5	12	2	2	.989	5	*2-148	1.8
1990	SF-N	144	498	67	122	22	3	15	56	34	96	.245	.301	.392	92	-7	14	4	2	.989	28	*2-142	2.6
1991	SF-N	144	492	74	129	24	5	19	48	63	95	.262	.353	.447	128	18	14	7	0	.985	10	*2-144	3.2
1992	SF-N	128	443	54	115	25	1	14	49	43	75	.260	.336	.415	118	10	5	4	1	.978	20	*2-120	3.1
1993	SF-N†	128	494	85	154	30	2	19	65	45	97	.312	.377	.496	136	25	10	4	1	.988	11	*2-128	3.9
1994	SF-N	35	129	13	27	8	2	2	7	15	32	.209	.292	.349	69	-6	3	1	0	.989	4	2-35	0.0
1995	SF-N	95	336	51	75	15	0	8	23	42	76	.223	.317	.339	75	-12	1	2	-1	.993	-16	2-91	-2.3
1996	SF-N	63	227	35	48	11	1	5	21	24	69	.211	.301	.335	70	-10	2	1	-1	.976	-10	2-62	-1.6
Total	11	1304	4612	671	1187	238	39	119	458	439	987	.257	.331	.403	105	27	103	62	-6	.983	50	*2-1279/S-1	11.9

■ TOMMY THOMPSON
Thompson, Rupert Lockhart b: 5/19/10, Elkhart, Ill. d: 5/24/71, Auburn, Cal. BL/TR, 5'9.5", 155 lbs. Deb: 9/3/33

1933	Bos-N	24	97	6	18	1	0	0	6	4	6	.186	.218	.196	21	-10	0			1.000	0	O-24	-1.0
1934	Bos-N	105	343	40	91	12	3	0	37	13	19	.265	.300	.318	71	-15	2			.964	10	O-82	-0.8
1935	Bos-N	112	297	34	81	7	1	4	30	36	17	.273	.353	.343	96	-1	2			.965	1	O-85	-0.2
1936	Bos-N	106	266	37	76	9	4	4	36	31	12	.286	.362	.365	103	2	3			1.000	0	O-39,1-25	-0.2
1938	Chi-A	19	18	2	2	0	0	0	3	1	3	.111	.158	.111	-31	-4	0			1.000	-0	/1-1	-0.3
1939	Chi-A	1	0	0	0	0	0	0	0	1	0	—	—	—		-0	0	0	0	.000	0	H	0.0

YEAR	TM/L	G	AB	R	H	2B	3B	HR	RBI	BB	SO	AVG	OBP	SLG	PRO+	BR/A	SB	CS	SBR	FA	FR	G/POS	TPR
	StL-A	30	86	23	26	5	0	1	7	23	7	.302	.455	.395	117	4	0	0	0	.977	-0	O-23	0.3
	Yr	31	86	23	26	5	0	1	8	23	7	.302	.455	.395	117	4	0	0	0	.977	-0	O-23	0.3
Total	6	397	1107	142	294	34	4	9	119	108	63	.266	.335	.328	84	-23	7	0		.975	13	O-253/1-26	-2.2

■ RYAN THOMPSON   Thompson, Ryan Orlando   b: 11/4/67, Chestertown, Md.   BR/TR, 6'3", 200 lbs.   Deb: 9/1/92

YEAR	TM/L	G	AB	R	H	2B	3B	HR	RBI	BB	SO	AVG	OBP	SLG	PRO+	BR/A	SB	CS	SBR	FA	FR	G/POS	TPR
1992	NY-N	30	108	15	24	7	1	3	10	8	24	.222	.276	.389	88	-2	2	2	-1	.988	0	O-29	-0.3
1993	NY-N	80	288	34	72	19	2	11	26	19	81	.250	.304	.444	98	-2	2	7	-4	.987	10	O-76	0.3
1994	NY-N	98	334	39	75	14	1	18	59	26	94	.225	.304	.434	90	-6	1	1	-0	.989	8	O-98	0.0
1995	NY-N	75	267	39	67	13	0	7	31	19	77	.251	.310	.378	83	-7	3	1	0	.985	8	O-74	0.0
1996	Cle-A	8	22	2	7	0	0	1	5	1	6	.318	.348	.455	101	-0	0	0	0	1.000	0	/O-8	-0.3
Total	5	291	1019	129	245	53	4	40	131	75	282	.240	.303	.418	91	-17	8	11	-4	.988	24	O-285	-0.3

■ SAM THOMPSON   Thompson, Samuel Luther "Big Sam"   b: 3/5/1860, Danville, Ind.   d: 11/7/22, Detroit, Mich.   BL/TL, 6'2", 207 lbs.   Deb: 7/2/1885   H

YEAR	TM/L	G	AB	R	H	2B	3B	HR	RBI	BB	SO	AVG	OBP	SLG	PRO+	BR/A	SB	CS	SBR	FA	FR	G/POS	TPR
1885	Det-N	63	254	58	77	11	9	7	44	16	22	.303	.344	.500	170	19				.885	7	O-62/3-1	2.2
1886	Det-N	122	503	101	156	18	13	8	89	35	31	.310	.355	.445	138	22	13			.945	10	*O-122	2.6
1887	*Det-N	127	545	118	203	29	23	11	166	32	19	.372	.416	.571	166	47	22			.909	7	*O-127	4.3
1888	Det-N	56	238	51	67	10	8	6	40	23	10	.282	.352	.466	159	16	5			.882	-7	O-56	0.7
1889	Phi-N	128	533	103	158	36	4	20	111	36	22	.296	.348	.492	123	11	24			.901	-7	*O-128	0.1
1890	Phi-N	132	549	116	172	41	9	4	102	42	29	.313	.371	.443	133	21	25			.939	2	*O-132	1.7
1891	Phi-N	133	554	108	163	23	10	7	90	52	20	.294	.363	.410	122	15	29			.937	19	*O-133	2.6
1892	Phi-N	153	609	109	186	28	11	9	104	59	19	.305	.377	.432	145	33	28			.937	4	*O-153	2.8
1893	Phi-N	131	600	130	222	37	13	11	126	50	17	.370	.424	.530	153	44	18			.931	-11	*O-131/1-1	2.2
1894	Phi-N	99	437	108	178	29	27	13	141	40	13	.407	.458	.686	177	53	24			.977	-4	*O-99	3.2
1895	Phi-N	119	538	131	211	45	21	18	165	31	11	.392	.430	.654	177	56	27			.943	12	*O-118	4.7
1896	Phi-N	119	517	103	154	28	7	12	100	28	13	.298	.341	.449	109	4	12			.974	18	*O-119	1.0
1897	Phi-N	3	13	2	3	0	1	0	3	1		.231	.286	.385	78	-0				.833	0	/O-3	-0.1
1898	Phi-N	14	63	14	22	5	3	1	15	4		.349	.388	.571	182	6	2			1.000	2	O-14	0.7
1906	Det-A	8	31	4	7	0	1	0	3	1		.226	.250	.290	67	-1	0			1.000	-0	/O-8	-0.2
Total	15	1407	5984	1256	1979	340	160	127	1299	450	226	.331	.384	.505	146	344	229			.935	53	*O-1405/1-1,3-1	28.5

■ SCOT THOMPSON   Thompson, Vernon Scot   b: 12/7/55, Grove City, Pa.   BL/TL, 6'3", 195 lbs.   Deb: 9/3/78

YEAR	TM/L	G	AB	R	H	2B	3B	HR	RBI	BB	SO	AVG	OBP	SLG	PRO+	BR/A	SB	CS	SBR	FA	FR	G/POS	TPR
1978	Chi-N	19	36	7	15	3	0	0	2	2	4	.417	.447	.500	147	2	0	0	0	1.000	-2	/O-5,1-2	0.0
1979	Chi-N	128	346	36	100	13	5	2	29	17	37	.289	.324	.373	82	-9	4	3	-1	.971	-9	*O-100	-2.3
1980	Chi-N	102	226	26	48	10	1	2	13	28	31	.212	.302	.292	62	-11	6	6	-2	.963	-6	O-66,1-12	-2.2
1981	Chi-N	57	115	8	19	5	0	0	8	7	8	.165	.213	.209	19	-12	2	0	1	.980	-5	O-30/1-3	-1.9
1982	Chi-N	49	74	11	27	5	1	0	7	5	4	.365	.405	.459	138	4	0	1	-1	1.000	4	O-23/1-4	0.2
1983	Chi-N	53	88	4	17	3	1	0	10	3	14	.193	.220	.250	28	-9	0	0	0	1.000	-5	O-29/1-1	-1.5
1984	SF-N	120	245	30	75	7	1	1	31	30	26	.306	.382	.355	112	5	5	5	-0	.998	-1	1-87/O-6	0.0
1985	SF-N	64	111	8	23	5	0	0	6	2	10	.207	.221	.252	34	-10	0	0	0	.995	2	1-24	-1.0
	Mon-N	34	32	2	9	1	0	0	4	3	7	.281	.343	.313	90	-0	0	0	0	1.000	-0	/1-3,O-3	-0.1
	Yr	98	143	10	32	6	0	0	10	5	17	.224	.250	.266	47	-10	0	0	0	.995	2	1-27/O-3	-1.1
Total	8	626	1273	132	333	52	9	5	110	97	141	.262	.315	.328	76	-40	17	13	-3	.973	-27	O-262,1-136	-8.8

■ BOBBY THOMSON   Thomson, Robert Brown "The Staten Island Scot"   b: 10/25/23, Glasgow, Scotland   BR/TR, 6'2", 185 lbs.   Deb: 9/9/46

YEAR	TM/L	G	AB	R	H	2B	3B	HR	RBI	BB	SO	AVG	OBP	SLG	PRO+	BR/A	SB	CS	SBR	FA	FR	G/POS	TPR
1946	NY-N	18	54	8	17	4	1	2	9	4	5	.315	.362	.537	152	3	0			.935	3	3-16	0.4
1947	NY-N	138	545	105	154	26	5	29	85	40	78	.283	.336	.508	121	13	1			.980	9	*O-127/2-9	1.5
1948	NY-N★	138	471	75	117	20	2	16	63	30	77	.248	.296	.401	87	-11	2			.970	6	*O-125	-1.1
1949	NY-N★	156	641	99	198	35	9	27	109	44	45	.309	.355	.518	132	26	10			.982	20	*O-156	3.6
1950	NY-N	149	563	79	142	22	7	25	85	55	45	.252	.324	.449	101	-1	3			.978	10	*O-149	0.3
1951	*NY-N★	148	518	89	152	27	8	32	101	73	57	.293	.385	.562	150	36	5	5	-2	.966	-11	O-77,3-69	2.0
1952	NY-N★	153	608	89	164	29	14	24	108	52	74	.270	.331	.482	122	16	5	2	0	.940	-7	3-91,O-63	0.5
1953	NY-N	154	608	80	175	22	6	26	106	43	57	.288	.338	.472	106	4	4	2	0	.983	0	*O-154	0.1
1954	Mil-N	43	99	7	23	3	0	2	15	12	29	.232	.315	.323	71	-4	0	0	0	.980	1	O-26	-0.5
1955	Mil-N	101	343	40	88	13	3	12	56	34	52	.257	.324	.414	99	-1	2	1	0	.969	0	O-91	-0.5
1956	Mil-N	142	451	59	106	10	4	20	74	43	75	.235	.304	.408	95	-5	2	4	-2	.974	-4	O-136/3-3	-1.7
1957	Mil-N	41	148	15	35	5	3	4	23	8	27	.236	.285	.392	86	-4	2	1	0	.988	-1	O-38	-0.7
	NY-N	81	215	24	52	7	4	8	38	19	39	.242	.303	.423	93	-3	1	2	-1	.992	-4	O-71/3-1	-1.1
	Yr	122	363	39	87	12	7	12	61	27	66	.240	.296	.410	90	-6	3	3	-1	.990	-5	O-109/3-1	-1.8
1958	Chi-N	152	547	67	155	27	5	21	82	56	76	.283	.354	.466	117	13	4			.989	4	*O-148/3-4	0.8
1959	Chi-N	122	374	55	97	15	2	11	52	35	50	.259	.326	.398	93	-4	1	0	0	.987	-7	O-116	-1.6
1960	Bos-A	40	114	12	30	3	1	5	20	11	18	.263	.328	.439	102	0	0	1	-1	.971	-5	O-27/1-1	-0.3
	Bal-A	3	6	0	0	0	0	0	0	1	3	.000	.000	.000	-99	-2	0	0	0	.000	-1	/O-2	-0.3
	Yr	43	120	12	30	3	1	5	20	11	18	.250	.328	.417	93	-2	0	1	-1	.971	-5	O-29/1-1	-0.3
Total	15	1779	6305	903	1705	267	74	264	1026	559	804	.270	.333	.462	111	77	38	20		.980	20	*O-1506,3-184/2-9,1	1.7

■ DICKIE THON   Thon, Richard William   b: 6/20/58, South Bend, Ind.   BR/TR, 5'11", 175 lbs.   Deb: 5/22/79

YEAR	TM/L	G	AB	R	H	2B	3B	HR	RBI	BB	SO	AVG	OBP	SLG	PRO+	BR/A	SB	CS	SBR	FA	FR	G/POS	TPR
1979	*Cal-A	35	56	6	19	3	0	0	8	5	10	.339	.393	.393	117	2	0	0	0	.923	3	2-24/S-8,3-1,D-1	0.5
1980	Cal-A	80	267	32	68	12	2	0	15	10	28	.255	.284	.315	65	-13	7	5	-1	.928	-12	S-22,2-21,D-15,3/1	-2.3
1981	*Hou-N	49	95	13	26	6	0	0	3	9	13	.274	.337	.337	96	-0	6	1	1	.950	-5	2-28,S-13/3-5	-0.3
1982	Hou-N	136	496	73	137	31	10	3	36	37	48	.276	.328	.397	110	5	37	8	6	.975	5	*S-119/3-8,2-1	2.9
1983	Hou-N★	154	619	81	177	28	9	20	79	54	73	.286	.341	.457	128	21	34	16	1	.966	21	*S-154	5.9
1984	Hou-N	5	17	3	6	0	1	0	1	0	4	.353	.389	.471	151	1	0	1	-1	1.000	-0	/S-5	0.1
1985	Hou-N	84	251	26	63	6	1	6	29	18	50	.251	.301	.355	85	-5	8	3	1	.967	7	S-79	0.9
1986	*Hou-N	106	278	24	69	13	1	3	21	29	49	.248	.319	.335	83	-6	6	5	-1	.972	-2	*S-104	-0.3
1987	Hou-N	32	66	6	14	1	0	1	3	16	17	.212	.366	.273	75	-2	0	1	-1	.925	-8	S-31	-0.7
1988	SD-N	95	258	36	68	12	2	1	18	33	49	.264	.349	.337	100	1	19	4	3	.954	-20	S-70/2-3,1-1	-1.1
1989	Phi-N	136	435	45	118	18	4	15	60	33	81	.271	.321	.434	115	7	6	3	0	.972	16	*S-129	3.4
1990	Phi-N	149	552	54	141	20	4	8	48	37	77	.255	.306	.350	80	-15	12	5	1	.969	4	*S-148	0.0
1991	Phi-N	146	539	44	136	18	4	9	44	25	84	.252	.285	.351	79	-16	11	5	0	.969	-8	*S-146	-1.4
1992	Tex-A	95	275	30	68	15	3	4	37	20	40	.247	.298	.367	89	-5	12	2	2	.958	0	S-87	0.3
1993	Mil-A	85	245	23	66	10	1	1	33	22	39	.269	.330	.331	79	-7	6	5	-1	.966	-11	S-28,3-25,2-22,D-14	-1.7
Total	15	1387	4449	496	1176	193	42	71	435	348	658	.264	.319	.374	95	-33	167	63	12	.965	-13	*S-1143/2-98,3D1	6.2

■ JACK THONEY   Thoney, John "Bullet Jack" (b: John Thoeny)   b: 12/8/1879, Ft.Thomas, Ky.   d: 10/24/48, Covington, Ky.   BR/TR, 5'10", 175 lbs.   Deb: 4/26/02

YEAR	TM/L	G	AB	R	H	2B	3B	HR	RBI	BB	SO	AVG	OBP	SLG	PRO+	BR/A	SB	CS	SBR	FA	FR	G/POS	TPR
1902	Cle-A	28	105	14	30	7	1	0	11	9		.286	.342	.371	102	0	4			.891	-15	2-14,S-11/O-2	-1.3
	Bal-A	3	11	1	0	0	0	0	0	1		.000	.083	.000	-72	-3	1			.778	2	/3-3	-0.4
	Yr	31	116	15	30	7	1	0	11	10		.259	.317	.336	84	-2	5			.891	-17	2-14,S-11/3-3,0-2	-1.7
1903	Cle-A	32	122	10	25	3	0	1	9	2		.205	.218	.254	42	-9	7			.889	1	O-24/2-5,3-2	-0.9
1904	Was-A	17	70	6	21	3	0	0	6	1		.300	.310	.343	108	0	2			.860	2	O-17	0.1
	NY-A	36	128	17	24	4	2	0	12	8		.188	.241	.250	53	-7	9			.826	1	3-26,O-10	-0.7
	Yr	53	198	23	45	7	2	0	18	9		.227	.264	.283	71	-7	11			.886	3	O-27,3-26	-0.6
1908	Bos-A	109	416	58	106	5	9	2	30	13		.255	.282	.325	94	-4	16			.948	8	*O-101	0.0
1909	Bos-A	13	40	1	5	1	0	0	3	2		.125	.167	.150	0	-5	2			.960	-0	O-10	-0.4
1911	Bos-A	26	20	5	5	0	0	0	2	0		.250	.250	.250	40	-2	1			.000	0	H	-0.2
Total	6	264	912	112	216	23	12	3	73	36		.237	.269	.298	75	-27	42			.929	-4	O-164/3-31,2-19,S	-3.8

■ ANDY THORNTON   Thornton, Andre   b: 8/13/49, Tuskegee, Ala.   BR/TR, 6'2", 205 lbs.   Deb: 7/28/73

YEAR	TM/L	G	AB	R	H	2B	3B	HR	RBI	BB	SO	AVG	OBP	SLG	PRO+	BR/A	SB	CS	SBR	FA	FR	G/POS	TPR
1973	Chi-N	17	35	3	7	3	0	0	3	6		.200	.333	.286	68	-1	0	0	0	.989	2	/1-9	0.0
1974	Chi-N	107	303	41	79	16	4	10	46	48	50	.261	.369	.439	120	9	2	1	0	.992	8	1-90/3-1	1.2
1975	Chi-N	120	372	70	109	21	4	18	60	88	63	.293	.433	.516	156	32	3	2	0	.988	3	*1-113/3-2	2.8
1976	Chi-N	27	85	8	17	6	0	2	14	20	14	.200	.364	.341	93	-0	2	0	1	.987	1	1-25	0.0

YEAR	TM/L	G	AB	R	H	2B	3B	HR	RBI	BB	SO	AVG	OBP	SLG	PRO+	BR/A	SB	CS	SBR	FA	FR	G/POS	TPR
	Mon-N	69	183	20	35	5	2	9	24	28	32	.191	.308	.388	93	-2	2	1	0	.994	-0	1-43,O-11	-0.6
	Yr	96	268	28	52	11	2	11	38	48	46	.194	.327	.373	93	-2	4	1	1	.991	1	1-68,O-11	-0.6
1977	Cle-A	131	433	77	114	20	5	28	70	70	82	.263	.379	.527	149	30	3	4	-2	.995	-3	*1-117/D-9	1.9
1978	Cle-A	145	508	97	133	22	4	33	105	93	72	.262	.382	.516	152	37	4	7	-3	.995	5	*1-145	3.0
1979	Cle-A	143	515	89	120	31	1	26	93	90	93	.233	.351	.449	114	11	5	4	-3	.994	-3	*1-130,D-13	-0.1
1981	Cle-A	69	226	22	54	12	0	6	30	23	37	.239	.309	.372	97	-1	3	1	0	.986	-1	D-53,1-11	-0.4
1982	Cle-A★	161	589	90	161	26	1	32	116	109	81	.273	.389	.484	139	34	6	7	-2	1.000	0	*D-152/1-8	2.5
1983	Cle-A	141	508	78	143	27	1	17	77	87	72	.281	.389	.439	123	18	4	2	0	.991	2	*D-114,1-27	1.4
1984	Cle-A★	155	587	91	159	26	0	33	99	91	79	.271	.371	.484	132	27	5	5	-1	.979	0	*D-144,1-11	2.1
1985	Cle-A	124	461	49	109	13	0	22	88	47	75	.236	.337	.408	94	-4	3	2	-0	.000	0	*D-122	-0.7
1986	Cle-A	120	401	49	92	14	0	17	66	65	67	.229	.338	.392	100	1	4	1	1	.000	0	*D-110	-0.1
1987	Cle-A	36	85	8	10	2	0	0	5	10	25	.118	.211	.141	-4	-13	1	0	0	.000	0	D-21	-1.3
Total	14	1565	5291	792	1342	244	22	253	895	876	851	.254	.364	.452	129	177	48	37	-8	.992	14	D-738,1-729/O-11,3	11.7

■ JOHN THORNTON
Thornton, John b: 1870, Washington, D.C. 5'10.5", 175 lbs. Deb: 8/14/1889

YEAR	TM/L	G	AB	R	H	2B	3B	HR	RBI	BB	SO	AVG	OBP	SLG	PRO+	BR/A	SB	CS	SBR	FA	FR	G/POS	TPR
1889	Was-N	1	4	0	0	0	0	0	1	0	1	.000	.000	.000	-99	-1	0			1.000	-0	/P-1	0.0
1891	Phi-N	39	123	7	17	3	0	0	6	2	10	.138	.152	.163	-8	-17	1			.881	-0	P-37/O-3	-0.2
1892	Phi-N	5	13	1	5	0	0	0	2	0	0	.385	.385	.385	133	0	0			.857	-1	/P-3,O-2	-0.1
	StL-N	1	3	0	0	0	0	0	0	0	2	.000	.000	.000	-99	-1	0			.000	-1	/O-1	-0.1
	Yr	6	16	1	5	0	0	0	2	0	2	.313	.313	.313	90	-0	0			.500	-1	/P-3,O-3	-0.2
Total	3	46	143	8	22	3	0	0	9	2	13	.154	.166	.175	-1	-18	1			.881	-1	/P-41,O-6	-0.4

■ LOU THORNTON
Thornton, Louis b: 4/26/63, Montgomery, Ala. BL/TL, 6'2", 185 lbs. Deb: 4/8/85

YEAR	TM/L	G	AB	R	H	2B	3B	HR	RBI	BB	SO	AVG	OBP	SLG	PRO+	BR/A	SB	CS	SBR	FA	FR	G/POS	TPR
1985	*Tor-A	56	72	18	17	1	1	1	8	2	24	.236	.267	.319	58	-4	1	0	0	.957	-7	O-35,D-16	-1.1
1987	Tor-A	12	2	5	1	0	0	0	0	0	0	.500	.667	.500	212	0	0	1	-1	.000	-2	/O-4,D-6	-0.2
1988	Tor-A	11	2	1	0	0	0	0	0	0	0	.000	.000	.000	-99	0	0	0		1.000	-4	/O-10/D-1	-0.5
1989	NY-N	13	13	5	4	1	0	0	1	0	1	.308	.308	.385	102	-0	2	0	1	1.000	-1	/O-6	-0.0
1990	NY-N	3	0	0	0	0	0	0	0	0	0	—	—	—	—	—	0	0	0	1.000	-1	/O-2	-0.1
Total	5	95	89	29	22	2	1	1	9	3	25	.247	.280	.326	65	-4	3	1	0	.965	-13	/O-57,D-23	-1.9

■ OTIS THORNTON
Thornton, Otis Benjamin b: 6/30/45, Docena, Ala. BR/TR, 6'1", 186 lbs. Deb: 7/6/73

YEAR	TM/L	G	AB	R	H	2B	3B	HR	RBI	BB	SO	AVG	OBP	SLG	PRO+	BR/A	SB	CS	SBR	FA	FR	G/POS	TPR
1973	Hou-N	2	3	0	0	0	0	0	1	0	2	.000	.000	.000	-99	-1	0			1.000	0	/C-2	-0.1

■ WALTER THORNTON
Thornton, Walter Miller b: 2/18/1875, Lewiston, Maine d: 7/14/60, Los Angeles, Cal. BL/TL, 6'1", 180 lbs. Deb: 7/1/1895

YEAR	TM/L	G	AB	R	H	2B	3B	HR	RBI	BB	SO	AVG	OBP	SLG	PRO+	BR/A	SB	CS	SBR	FA	FR	G/POS	TPR
1895	Chi-N	8	22	4	7	1	0	1	7	3	1	.318	.400	.500	123	1	0			.900	-1	/P-7,1-1	0.0
1896	Chi-N	9	22	6	8	0	1	0	1	5	2	.364	.481	.455	142	2	2			.800	-1	/P-5,O-3	0.0
1897	Chi-N	75	265	39	85	9	6	0	55	30		.321	.402	.400	108	4	13			.781	-11	O-59,P-16	-1.0
1898	Chi-N	62	210	34	62	5	2	0	14	22		.295	.362	.338	101	1	8			.877	-3	O-34,P-28	-0.3
Total	4	154	519	83	162	15	9	1	77	60	3	.312	.390	.382	108	7	23			.821	-15	/O-96,P-56,1-1	-1.3

■ BOB THORPE
Thorpe, Benjamin Robert b: 11/19/26, Caryville, Fla. BR/TR, 6'1.5", 190 lbs. Deb: 4/19/51

YEAR	TM/L	G	AB	R	H	2B	3B	HR	RBI	BB	SO	AVG	OBP	SLG	PRO+	BR/A	SB	CS	SBR	FA	FR	G/POS	TPR
1951	Bos-N	2	2	1	1	0	0	0	0	0	0	.500	.500	1.500	448	1	0	0	0	.000	0	H	0.1
1952	Bos-N	81	292	20	76	8	2	3	26	5	42	.260	.275	.332	70	-13	3	1	0	.972	-0	O-72	-1.6
1953	Mil-N	27	37	1	6	1	0	0	5	1	6	.162	.184	.189	-3	-6	0	1	-1	1.000	-5	O-18	-1.1
Total	3	110	331	22	83	9	3	3	32	6	48	.251	.266	.323	64	-17	3	2	-0	.975	-5	/O-90	-2.6

■ JIM THORPE
Thorpe, James Francis b: 5/28/1887, Prague, Okla. d: 3/28/53, Long Beach, Cal. BR/TR, 6'1", 185 lbs. Deb: 4/14/13

YEAR	TM/L	G	AB	R	H	2B	3B	HR	RBI	BB	SO	AVG	OBP	SLG	PRO+	BR/A	SB	CS	SBR	FA	FR	G/POS	TPR
1913	NY-N	19	35	6	5	0	0	0	2	1	9	.143	.167	.229	12	-4	2			.944	-1	/O-9	-0.5
1914	NY-N	30	31	5	6	1	0	0	2	0	4	.194	.194	.226	25	-3	1			.750	-2	/O-4	-0.5
1915	NY-N	17	52	8	12	3	1	0	1	2	16	.231	.259	.327	82	-1	4	2	0	.933	-2	/O-15	-0.5
1917	Cin-N	77	251	29	62	2	8	4	36	6	35	.247	.267	.367	98	-2	11			.962	2	O-69	-0.5
	*NY-N	26	57	12	11	3	2	0	4	8	10	.193	.303	.316	93	-0	1			.939	-3	/O-18	-0.5
	Yr	103	308	41	73	5	10	4	40	14	45	.237	.275	.357	97	-2	12			.958	-1	O-87	-1.0
1918	NY-N	58	113	15	28	4	4	1	11	4	18	.248	.286	.381	105	0	3			.983	-12	O-44	-1.5
1919	NY-N	2	3	0	1	0	0	0	0	0	0	.333	.333	.333	102	-0	0			1.000	-1	/O-2	-0.1
	Bos-N	60	156	16	51	7	3	1	25	6	30	.327	.360	.429	143	7	7			.926	-7	O-38/1-2	-0.2
	Yr	62	159	16	52	7	3	1	26	6	30	.327	.359	.428	142	7	7			.928	-7	O-40/1-2	-0.3
Total	6	289	698	91	176	20	18	7	82	27	122	.252	.286	.362	99	-3	29	2		.951	-25	O-199/1-2	-4.3

■ BUCK THRASHER
Thrasher, Frank Edward b: 8/6/1889, Watkinsville, Ga. d: 6/12/38, Cleveland, Ohio BL/TR, 5'11", 182 lbs. Deb: 9/27/16

YEAR	TM/L	G	AB	R	H	2B	3B	HR	RBI	BB	SO	AVG	OBP	SLG	PRO+	BR/A	SB	CS	SBR	FA	FR	G/POS	TPR
1916	Phi-A	7	29	4	9	2	1	0	4	2	1	.310	.355	.448	148	1	0			1.000	-1	/O-7	0.0
1917	Phi-A	23	77	5	18	2	1	0	2	3	12	.234	.272	.286	71	-3	0			.938	-3	O-22	-0.8
Total	2	30	106	9	27	4	2	0	6	5	13	.255	.295	.330	92	-1	0			.951	-4	/O-29	-0.8

■ MARV THRONEBERRY
Throneberry, Marvin Eugene "Marvelous Marv"
b: 9/2/33, Collierville, Tenn. d: 6/23/94, Fisherville, Tenn. BL/TL, 6', 197 lbs. Deb: 9/25/55 F

YEAR	TM/L	G	AB	R	H	2B	3B	HR	RBI	BB	SO	AVG	OBP	SLG	PRO+	BR/A	SB	CS	SBR	FA	FR	G/POS	TPR
1955	NY-A	1	2	1	2	1	0	0	0	0	0	1.000	1.000	1.500	574	1	0	0	0	1.000	0	/1-1	0.2
1958	*NY-A	60	150	30	34	5	2	7	19	19	40	.227	.318	.427	107	1	1	1	-0	.991	-1	1-40/O-5	-0.3
1959	NY-A	80	192	27	46	5	0	8	22	18	51	.240	.305	.391	93	-2	0	0	0	.989	-1	1-54,O-13	-0.6
1960	KC-A	104	236	29	59	9	2	11	41	23	60	.250	.317	.445	103	0	0	0	0	.991	1	1-71	-0.4
1961	KC-A	40	130	17	31	2	1	6	24	19	30	.238	.336	.408	96	-2	0	0	0	.996	1	1-30,O-10	-0.2
	Bal-A	56	96	9	20	3	0	5	11	12	20	.208	.296	.396	86	-2	0	0	0	.923	-3	O-15,1-11	-0.6
	Yr	96	226	26	51	5	1	11	35	31	50	.226	.319	.403	93	-3	0	0	0	.991	-2	1-41,O-25	-0.8
1962	Bal-A	9	9	1	0	0	0	0	0	4	6	.000	.308	.000	-9	-1	0	0	0	1.000	-0	/O-2	-0.2
	NY-N	116	357	29	87	11	3	16	49	34	83	.244	.309	.426	94	-4	1	3	-2	.981	4	1-97	-0.8
1963	NY-N	14	14	0	2	1	0	0	1	1	5	.143	.200	.214	19	-1	0	0	0	1.000	-0	/1-3	-0.2
Total	7	480	1186	143	281	37	8	53	170	130	295	.237	.313	.416	94	-10	3	4	-2	.987	1	1-307/O-45	-3.1

■ FAYE THRONEBERRY
Throneberry, Maynard Faye b: 6/22/31, Fisherville, Tenn. BL/TR, 6', 190 lbs. Deb: 4/15/52 F

YEAR	TM/L	G	AB	R	H	2B	3B	HR	RBI	BB	SO	AVG	OBP	SLG	PRO+	BR/A	SB	CS	SBR	FA	FR	G/POS	TPR
1952	Bos-A	98	310	38	80	11	3	5	23	33	67	.258	.331	.361	86	-6	16	7	1	.955	-0	O-86	-0.9
1955	Bos-A	60	144	20	37	7	3	6	27	14	31	.257	.327	.472	104	-0	0	0	0	.960	1	O-34	-0.1
1956	Bos-A	24	50	6	11	2	0	1	3	3	16	.220	.264	.320	48	-4	0	0	0	.909	-2	O-13	-0.6
1957	Bos-A	1	1	0	0	0	0	0	0	0	1	.000	.000	.000	-95	-0	0	0	0	.000	0	H	0.0
	Was-A	68	195	21	36	8	2	2	12	17	37	.185	.254	.277	45	-15	0	0	-1	.983	-6	O-58	-2.6
	Yr	69	196	21	36	8	2	2	12	17	38	.184	.252	.276	45	-15	0	0	-1	.983	-6	O-58	-2.6
1958	Was-A	44	87	12	16	1	1	4	7	4	28	.184	.245	.356	64	-5	0	1	-1	1.000	-3	O-26	-1.0
1959	Was-A	117	327	36	82	11	2	10	42	33	61	.251	.325	.388	95	-2	6	4	-1	.953	-2	O-86	-0.9
1960	Was-A	85	157	18	39	7	1	1	23	18	33	.248	.330	.325	78	-4	4	1	-0	.947	-3	O-34	-1.0
1961	LA-A	24	31	1	6	0	0	0	5	10	19	.194	.306	.226	40	-3	0	0	0	1.000	-0	/O-5	-0.2
Total	8	521	1302	152	307	48	12	29	137	127	284	.236	.309	.358	79	-39	23	14	-2	.962	-15	O-342	-7.2

■ GARY THURMAN
Thurman, Gary Montez b: 11/12/64, Indianapolis, Ind. BR/TR, 5'10", 175 lbs. Deb: 8/30/87

YEAR	TM/L	G	AB	R	H	2B	3B	HR	RBI	BB	SO	AVG	OBP	SLG	PRO+	BR/A	SB	CS	SBR	FA	FR	G/POS	TPR
1987	KC-A	27	81	12	24	2	0	0	5	8	20	.296	.360	.321	81	-2	7	2	1	.971	4	O-27	0.3
1988	KC-A	35	66	6	11	1	0	0	2	4	20	.167	.214	.182	12	-8	5	1	1	.949	-7	O-32/D-1	-1.5
1989	KC-A	72	87	24	17	2	1	0	5	15	26	.195	.314	.241	59	-4	16	0	5	.949	-17	O-60/D-4	-1.8
1990	KC-A	23	60	5	14	3	0	0	3	2	12	.233	.258	.283	52	-4	1	1	-0	1.000	-2	O-21	-0.7
1991	KC-A	80	184	24	51	9	2	0	13	11	42	.277	.321	.359	87	-3	15	5	2	.970	-5	O-72	-0.7
1992	KC-A	88	200	25	49	6	3	0	20	9	34	.245	.281	.305	62	-10	9	6	-1	.986	2	O-67/D-9	-1.0
1993	Det-A	75	89	22	19	2	2	0	13	10	34	.213	.300	.281	58	-5	5	2	2	.950	-12	O-53/D-9	-1.5
1995	Sea-A	13	25	3	8	2	0	0	3	1	3	.320	.346	.400	93	-0	5	2	1	1.000	-1	/O-9	-0.1
Total	8	413	792	121	193	27	6	2	64	61	187	.244	.299	.301	65	-37	65	17	9	.971	-37	O-341/D-23	-7.0

YEAR	TM/L	G	AB	R	H	2B	3B	HR	RBI	BB	SO	AVG	OBP	SLG	PRO+	BR/A	SB	CS	SBR	FA	FR	G/POS	TPR

■ BOB THURMAN
Thurman, Robert Burns b: 5/14/17, Wichita, Kan. BL/TL, 6'1", 205 lbs. Deb: 4/14/55

YEAR	TM/L	G	AB	R	H	2B	3B	HR	RBI	BB	SO	AVG	OBP	SLG	PRO+	BR/A	SB	CS	SBR	FA	FR	G/POS	TPR
1955	Cin-N	82	152	19	33	2	3	7	22	17	26	.217	.296	.408	80	-5	0	2	-1	.949	-4	O-36	-1.1
1956	Cin-N	80	139	25	41	5	2	8	22	10	14	.295	.342	.532	123	4	0	0	0	.953	-3	O-29	0.0
1957	Cin-N	74	190	38	47	4	2	16	40	15	33	.247	.306	.542	114	3	0	0	0	.987	-0	O-44	0.0
1958	Cin-N	94	178	23	41	7	4	4	20	20	38	.230	.322	.382	81	-5	1	2	-1	.976	2	O-41	-0.6
1959	Cin-N	4	4	1	1	0	0	0	2	0	1	.250	.250	.250	33	-0	0	0	0	.000	0	H	0.0
Total	5	334	663	106	163	18	11	35	106	62	112	.246	.315	.465	99	-3	1	4	-2	.970	-5	O-150	-1.7

■ EDDIE TIEMEYER
Tiemeyer, Edward Carl b: 5/9/1885, Cincinnati, Ohio d: 9/27/46, Cincinnati, Ohio BR/TR, 5'11.5", 185 lbs. Deb: 8/19/06

YEAR	TM/L	G	AB	R	H	2B	3B	HR	RBI	BB	SO	AVG	OBP	SLG	PRO+	BR/A	SB	CS	SBR	FA	FR	G/POS	TPR
1906	Cin-N	5	11	3	2	0	0	0	0	0	1	.182	.250	.182	33	-1	0			1.000	0	/3-3,P-1	0.0
1907	Cin-N	1	0	1	0	0	0	0	0	0	0	—	1.000	—	206	0	0			.000	0	H	0.0
1909	NY-A	3	8	1	3	1	0	0	0	0	1	.375	.444	.500	197	1	0			.962	-1	/1-3	0.0
Total	3	9	19	5	5	1	0	0	0	0	3	.263	.364	.316	110	0	0			.962	-1	/1-3,3-3,P-1	0.0

■ MIKE TIERNAN
Tiernan, Michael Joseph "Silent Mike" b: 1/21/1867, Trenton, N.J. d: 11/9/18, New York, N.Y. BL/TL, 5'11", 165 lbs. Deb: 4/30/1887

YEAR	TM/L	G	AB	R	H	2B	3B	HR	RBI	BB	SO	AVG	OBP	SLG	PRO+	BR/A	SB	CS	SBR	FA	FR	G/POS	TPR
1887	NY-N	103	407	82	117	13	12	10	62	32	31	.287	.344	.452	125	14	28			.865	-9	*O-103/P-5	0.3
1888	*NY-N	113	443	75	130	16	8	9	52	42	42	.293	.364	.427	153	28	52			.960	-9	*O-113	2.3
1889	*NY-N	122	499	147	167	23	14	10	73	96	32	.335	.447	.497	163	47	33			.896	-3	*O-122	3.5
1890	NY-N	133	553	132	168	25	21	13	59	68	53	.304	.385	.495	156	38	56			.896	-15	*O-133	1.6
1891	NY-N	134	542	111	166	30	12	16	73	69	32	.306	.388	.494	163	43	53			.901	-9	*O-134	2.7
1892	NY-N	116	450	79	129	16	10	5	66	57	46	.287	.369	.400	135	20	20			.899	-3	*O-116	1.0
1893	NY-N	125	511	114	158	19	12	14	102	72	24	.309	.399	.476	131	23	26			.927	-9	*O-125	0.6
1894	*NY-N	112	424	84	117	19	13	5	77	54	21	.276	.359	.417	87	-9	28			.922	-11	*O-111	-2.1
1895	NY-N	120	476	127	165	23	21	7	70	66	19	.347	.427	.527	149	36	36			.946	-5	*O-119	1.7
1896	NY-N	133	521	132	192	24	16	7	89	77	18	.369	.452	.516	159	48	35			.970	-2	*O-133	2.9
1897	NY-N	127	528	123	174	29	10	5	72	61		.330	.400	.451	128	22	40			.931	-11	*O-127	0.2
1898	NY-N	103	415	90	116	15	11	5	49	43		.280	.357	.405	122	12	19			.973	-12	*O-103	-0.7
1899	NY-N	35	137	17	35	4	2	0	7	10		.255	.306	.314	73	-5	2			.938	-4	O-35	-1.1
Total	13	1476	5906	1313	1834	256	162	106	851	747	318	.311	.392	.463	138	314	428			.924	-92	*O-1474/P-5	12.9

■ COTTON TIERNEY
Tierney, James Arthur b: 2/10/1894, Kansas City, Kan. d: 4/18/53, Kansas City, Mo. BR/TR, 5'8", 175 lbs. Deb: 9/23/20

YEAR	TM/L	G	AB	R	H	2B	3B	HR	RBI	BB	SO	AVG	OBP	SLG	PRO+	BR/A	SB	CS	SBR	FA	FR	G/POS	TPR
1920	Pit-N	12	46	4	11	5	0	0	8	3	4	.239	.286	.348	79	-1	1	1	-0	.964	-2	2-10/S-2	-0.3
1921	Pit-N	117	442	49	132	22	8	3	52	24	31	.299	.338	.405	93	-5	4	6	-2	.965	-27	2-72,3-32/O-4,S-3	-3.0
1922	Pit-N	122	441	58	152	26	14	7	86	22	40	.345	.378	.515	127	16	7	8	-3	.964	-37	*2-105/O-2,S-1,3-1	-2.0
1923	Pit-N	29	120	22	35	5	2	2	23	2	10	.292	.309	.417	88	-3	2	1	0	.941	-3	2-29	-0.5
	Phi-N	121	480	68	152	31	1	11	65	24	42	.317	.352	.454	100	-2	3	4	-2	.975	18	*2-115/O-7,3-2	1.5
	Yr	150	600	90	187	36	3	13	88	26	52	.312	.343	.447	97	-4	5	5	-2	.968	15	*2-144/O-7,3-2	1.0
1924	Bos-N	136	505	38	131	16	1	6	58	22	37	.259	.296	.331	71	-22	11	8	-2	.964	-1	2-115,3-22	-2.1
1925	Bro-N	93	265	27	68	14	4	2	39	12	23	.257	.294	.362	68	-13	0	3	-2	.963	-1	3-61/1-1,2-1	-1.1
Total	6	630	2299	266	681	119	30	31	331	109	187	.296	.332	.415	93	-29	28	31	-10	.966	-53	2-447,3-118/OS1	-7.5

■ BILL TIERNEY
Tierney, William J. b: 5/14/1858, Boston, Mass. d: 9/21/1898, Boston, Mass. Deb: 5/2/1882

YEAR	TM/L	G	AB	R	H	2B	3B	HR	RBI	BB	SO	AVG	OBP	SLG	PRO+	BR/A	SB	CS	SBR	FA	FR	G/POS	TPR
1882	Cin-a	1	5	1	0	0	0	0		0		.000	.000	.000	-95	-1				.917	0	/1-1	-0.1
1884	Bal-U	1	3	0	1	0	0	0		0	1	.333	.500	.333	142	0				1.000	-0	/O-1	0.0
Total	2	2	8	1	1	0	0	0		0		.125	.222	.125	13	-1				1.000	0	/O-1,1-1	-0.1

■ JOHN TILLEY
Tilley, John C. b: New York, N.Y. BR, 5'7", 154 lbs. Deb: 8/23/1882

YEAR	TM/L	G	AB	R	H	2B	3B	HR	RBI	BB	SO	AVG	OBP	SLG	PRO+	BR/A	SB	CS	SBR	FA	FR	G/POS	TPR
1882	Cle-N	15	56	2	5	1	1	0	4	2	11	.089	.121	.143	-16	-7				.857	2	O-15	-0.5
1884	Tol-a	17	56	5	10	2	0	0		4		.179	.246	.214	50	-3				.632	-4	O-17	-0.7
	StP-U	9	26	2	4	1	0	0		3		.154	.241	.192	61	-3				.938	0	/O-9	-0.3
Total	2	41	138	9	19	4	1	0	4	9	11	.138	.196	.181	23	-13				.818	-2	/O-41	-1.5

■ BOB TILLMAN
Tillman, John Robert b: 3/24/37, Nashville, Tenn. BR/TR, 6'4", 205 lbs. Deb: 4/15/62

YEAR	TM/L	G	AB	R	H	2B	3B	HR	RBI	BB	SO	AVG	OBP	SLG	PRO+	BR/A	SB	CS	SBR	FA	FR	G/POS	TPR
1962	Bos-A	81	249	28	57	6	4	14	38	19	65	.229	.286	.454	93	-4	0	0	0	.983	-4	C-66	-0.5
1963	Bos-A	96	307	24	69	10	2	8	32	34	64	.225	.304	.349	80	-8	0	0	0	.992	1	C-95	-0.4
1964	Bos-A	131	425	43	118	18	1	17	61	49	74	.278	.352	.445	114	9	0	0	0	.989	-8	*C-131	0.7
1965	Bos-A	111	368	20	79	10	6	6	35	40	69	.215	.292	.307	66	-16	0	0	0	.988	-7	*C-106	-1.8
1966	Bos-A	78	204	12	47	8	0	3	24	22	35	.230	.305	.314	71	-7	0	0	0	.990	-3	C-72	-0.7
1967	Bos-A	30	64	4	12	1	0	1	4	3	18	.188	.224	.250	37	-5	0	0	0	.977	2	C-26	-0.3
	NY-A	22	63	5	16	1	0	2	9	7	17	.254	.329	.365	109	1	0	0	0	.970	0	C-15	0.2
	Yr	52	127	9	28	2	0	3	13	10	35	.220	.277	.307	70	-5	0	0	0	.974	2	C-41	-0.1
1968	Atl-N	86	236	16	52	4	0	5	20	16	55	.220	.278	.301	74	-8	1	0	0	.990	-1	C-75	-0.4
1969	*Atl-N	69	190	18	37	5	0	12	29	18	47	.195	.264	.411	86	-4	0	0	0	.988	-10	C-69	-1.2
1970	Atl-N	71	223	19	53	5	0	11	30	20	66	.238	.300	.408	83	-6	0	0	0	.988	-2	C-70	-0.5
Total	9	775	2329	189	540	68	10	79	282	228	510	.232	.302	.371	85	-49	1	0	0	.988	-31	C-725	-4.9

■ RUSTY TILLMAN
Tillman, Kerry Jerome b: 8/29/60, Jacksonville, Fla. BR/TR, 6', 185 lbs. Deb: 6/6/82

YEAR	TM/L	G	AB	R	H	2B	3B	HR	RBI	BB	SO	AVG	OBP	SLG	PRO+	BR/A	SB	CS	SBR	FA	FR	G/POS	TPR
1982	NY-N	12	13	4	2	1	0	0	0	0	4	.154	.154	.231	6	-2	1	0	0	1.000	-1	/O-3	-0.2
1986	Oak-A	22	39	6	10	1	0	1	6	3	11	.256	.310	.359	88	-1	2	0	1	.952	-3	O-17	-0.4
1988	SF-N	4	4	1	1	0	0	1	3	2	1	.250	.500	1.000	335	1	0	0	0	1.000	-0	/O-1	0.1
Total	3	38	56	11	13	2	0	2	9	5	16	.232	.295	.375	88	-1	3	0	1	.958	-4	/O-21	-0.5

■ OZZIE TIMMONS
Timmons, Osborne Llewellyn b: 9/18/70, Tampa, Fla. BR/TR, 6'2", 205 lbs. Deb: 4/26/95

YEAR	TM/L	G	AB	R	H	2B	3B	HR	RBI	BB	SO	AVG	OBP	SLG	PRO+	BR/A	SB	CS	SBR	FA	FR	G/POS	TPR
1995	Chi-N	77	171	30	45	10	1	8	28	13	32	.263	.315	.474	107	1	3	0	1	.970	-6	O-55	-0.5
1996	Chi-N	65	140	18	28	4	0	7	16	15	30	.200	.282	.379	71	-6	1	0	0	1.000	-3	O-47	-1.0
Total	2	142	311	48	73	14	1	15	44	28	62	.235	.300	.431	90	-5	4	0	1	.985	-9	O-102	-1.5

■ BEN TINCUP
Tincup, Austin Ben b: 12/14/1890, Adair, Okla. d: 7/5/80, Claremore, Okla. BL/TR, 6'1", 180 lbs. Deb: 5/22/14 C

YEAR	TM/L	G	AB	R	H	2B	3B	HR	RBI	BB	SO	AVG	OBP	SLG	PRO+	BR/A	SB	CS	SBR	FA	FR	G/POS	TPR
1914	Phi-N	31	53	3	9	1	1	0	1	0	18	.170	.170	.226	16	-6	0			.926	1	P-28	0.0
1915	Phi-N	11	9	1	0	0	0	0	1	0	3	.000	.000	.000	-99	-2	0			1.000	0	P-10	0.0
1916	Phi-N	1	1	0	0	0	0	0	0	0	0	.000	.000	.000	-97	-0	0			.000	0	H	0.0
1918	Phi-N	11	8	0	1	1	0	0	0	0	4	.125	.125	.250	13	-1	0			.800	1	/P-8,O-1	0.0
1928	Chi-N	2	3	0	0	0	0	0	0	0	0	.000	.000	.000	-99	-1	0			1.000	0	/P-2	0.0
Total	5	56	74	4	10	2	1	0	2	0	25	.135	.135	.189	-4	-10	0			.917	2	/P-48,O-1	0.0

■ RON TINGLEY
Tingley, Ronald Irvin b: 5/27/59, Presque Isle, Maine BR/TR, 6'2", 180 lbs. Deb: 9/25/82

YEAR	TM/L	G	AB	R	H	2B	3B	HR	RBI	BB	SO	AVG	OBP	SLG	PRO+	BR/A	SB	CS	SBR	FA	FR	G/POS	TPR
1982	SD-N	8	20	0	2	0	0	0	0	0	7	.100	.100	.100	-46	-4	0	0	0	.957	3	/C-8	-0.1
1988	Cle-A	9	24	1	4	0	0	0	2	2	8	.167	.231	.292	44	-2	0	0	0	1.000	3	/C-9	0.2
1989	Cal-A	4	3	0	1	0	0	0	0	1	0	.333	.500	.333	142	0	0	0	0	.889	0	/C-4	0.1
1990	Cal-A	5	4	0	0	0	0	0	0	1	2	.000	.200	.000	-25	-0	0	0	0	1.000	1	/C-5	0.0
1991	Cal-A	45	115	11	23	7	0	1	13	8	34	.200	.258	.287	51	-8	1	1	-0	.988	10	C-45	0.4
1992	Cal-A	71	127	15	25	2	1	3	8	13	35	.197	.282	.299	62	-6	0	1	-1	.987	11	C-69	0.7
1993	Cal-A	58	90	7	18	7	0	0	12	9	22	.200	.280	.278	49	-6	1	2	-1	.995	9	C-58	0.4
1994	Fla-N	19	52	4	9	3	1	1	2	5	18	.173	.246	.327	46	-4	0	0	0	.990	2	C-18	-0.1
	Chi-A	5	5	0	0	0	0	0	0	0	1	.000	.000	.000	-99	-1	0	0	0	1.000	-1	/C-5	0.0
1995	Det-A	54	124	14	28	8	4	18	15	38	.226	.309	.403	84	-3	0	1	-0	.991	-5	C-53/1-1	-0.5
Total	9	278	563	52	110	27	6	3	55	54	165	.195	.271	.307	56	-35	2	5	-2	.989	37	C-274/1-1	1.1

■ JOE TINKER
Tinker, Joseph Bert b: 7/27/1880, Muscotah, Kan. d: 7/27/48, Orlando, Fla. BR/TR, 5'9", 175 lbs. Deb: 4/17/02 MH

YEAR	TM/L	G	AB	R	H	2B	3B	HR	RBI	BB	SO	AVG	OBP	SLG	PRO+	BR/A	SB	CS	SBR	FA	FR	G/POS	TPR
1902	Chi-N	131	494	55	129	19	5	2	54	26		.261	.298	.332	97	-3	27			.906	4	*S-124/3-8	0.9
1903	Chi-N	124	460	67	134	21	7	2	70	37		.291	.345	.380	110	5	27			.906	0	*S-107,3-19	1.0

YEAR	TM/L	G	AB	R	H	2B	3B	HR	RBI	BB	SO	AVG	OBP	SLG	PRO+	BR/A	SB	CS	SBR	FA	FR	G/POS	TPR
1904	Chi-N	141	488	55	108	12	13	3	41	29		.221	.268	.318	80	-12	41			.925	19	*S-140/O-1	1.1
1905	Chi-N	149	547	70	135	18	8	2	66	34		.247	.292	.320	79	-15	31			.940	17	*S-149	0.5
1906	*Chi-N	148	523	75	122	18	4	1	64	43		.233	.293	.289	77	-14	30			**.944**	4	*S-147/3-1	-0.6
1907	*Chi-N	117	402	36	89	11	3	1	36	25		.221	.269	.271	65	-17	20			.939	16	*S-113	0.2
1908	*Chi-N	157	548	67	146	22	14	6	68	32		.266	.307	.391	117	8	30			**.958**	30	*S-157	4.8
1909	Chi-N	143	516	56	132	26	11	4	57	17		.256	.280	.372	100	-4	23			**.940**	20	*S-143	2.1
1910	*Chi-N	134	473	48	136	25	9	3	69	24	35	.288	.322	.397	110	3	20			.942	16	*S-132	2.5
1911	Chi-N	144	536	61	149	24	12	4	69	39	31	.278	.327	.390	100	-2	30			**.937**	23	*S-143	3.1
1912	Chi-N	142	550	80	155	24	7	0	75	38	21	.282	.331	.351	87	-11	25			.943	25	*S-142	2.6
1913	Cin-N	110	382	47	121	20	13	1	57	20	26	.317	.352	.445	127	12	10			.968	17	*S-101/3-9,M	**3.9**
1914	Chi-F	126	438	50	112	21	7	2	46	38	30	.256	.317	.349	86	-16	19			.947	19	*S-125,M	1.3
1915	Chi-F	31	67	7	18	2	1	0	9	13	5	.269	.387	.328	109	0	3			.914	-2	S-16/2-5,3-4,M	-0.1
1916	Chi-N	7	10	0	1	0	0	0	1	1	1	.100	.182	.100	-11	-1	0			.909	-0	/S-4,3-2,M	-0.2
Total	15	1804	6434	774	1687	263	114	31	782	416	149	.262	.308	.353	95	-66	336			.938	208	*S-1743/3-43,2-5,O	23.1

■ LEE TINSLEY

Tinsley, Lee Owen   b: 3/4/69, Shelbyville, Ky.   BB/TR, 5'10", 185 lbs.   Deb: 4/6/93

YEAR	TM/L	G	AB	R	H	2B	3B	HR	RBI	BB	SO	AVG	OBP	SLG	PRO+	BR/A	SB	CS	SBR	FA	FR	G/POS	TPR
1993	Sea-A	11	19	2	3	1	0	1	2	2	9	.158	.238	.368	60	-1	0	0	0	.900	-1	/O-6,D-2	-0.2
1994	Bos-A	78	144	27	32	4	0	2	14	19	36	.222	.317	.292	56	-9	13	0	4	.991	-5	O-60,D-10	-1.1
1995	*Bos-A	100	341	61	97	17	1	7	41	39	74	.284	.360	.402	95	-2	18	8	1	.979	0	O-97	-0.4
1996	Phi-N	31	52	1	7	0	0	0	2	4	22	.135	.196	.135	-10	-8	2	4	-2	.960	-4	O-22	-1.5
	Bos-A	92	192	28	47	6	1	3	14	13	56	.245	.300	.333	58	-12	6	8	-3	.993	-6	O-83	-2.1
Total	4	312	748	119	186	28	2	13	73	77	197	.249	.322	.344	70	-33	39	20	0	.983	-17	O-268/D-12	-5.3

■ JIM TIPPER

Tipper, James   b: 6/18/1849, Middletown, Conn.   d: 4/21/1895, New Haven, Conn.   5'5.5", 148 lbs.   Deb: 4/26/1872 ·

YEAR	TM/L	G	AB	R	H	2B	3B	HR	RBI	BB	SO	AVG	OBP	SLG	PRO+	BR/A	SB	CS	SBR	FA	FR	G/POS	TPR
1872	Man-n	24	112	23	31	5	1	0	15	0	0	.277	.277	.339	94	-0				.778	-1	O-19/3-5	0.0
1874	Har-n	45	197	36	60	8	0	0	20	1	7	.305	.308	.345	104	-0	0	1	-1	.812	-1	*O-45	0.0
1875	NH-n	41	159	10	25	1	0	0	4	1	6	.157	.162	.164	16	-12	1	0	0	.790	-3	O-41	-1.3
Total	3 n	110	468	69	116	14	1	0	39	2	13	.248	.251	.282	76	-12	1	1	-1	.799	-5	O-105/3-5	-1.3

■ ERIC TIPTON

Tipton, Eric Gordon "Dukie" or "Blue Devil"   b: 4/20/15, Petersburg, Va.   BR/TR, 5'11", 190 lbs.   Deb: 6/9/39

YEAR	TM/L	G	AB	R	H	2B	3B	HR	RBI	BB	SO	AVG	OBP	SLG	PRO+	BR/A	SB	CS	SBR	FA	FR	G/POS	TPR
1939	Phi-A	47	104	12	24	4	2	1	14	13	7	.231	.316	.337	68	-5	0	0	1	.942	-5	O-34	-1.0
1940	Phi-A	2	8	2	1	0	1	0	0	1	1	.125	.222	.375	53	-1	0	0	0	1.000	-0	/O-1	-0.1
1941	Phi-A	1	4	0	2	0	0	0	0	0	0	.500	.500	.500	169	0	0	0	0	1.000	-0	/O-1	0.0
1942	Cin-N	63	207	22	46	5	5	4	18	25	14	.222	.309	.353	94	-2	1			.977	-1	O-58	-0.6
1943	Cin-N	140	493	82	142	26	7	9	49	85	36	.288	.395	.424	138	27	1			.984	-1	*O-139	2.0
1944	Cin-N	140	479	62	144	28	3	3	36	59	32	.301	.380	.390	121	15	5			.983	3	*O-139	1.1
1945	Cin-N	108	331	32	80	17	1	1	34	40	37	.242	.327	.344	89	-5	11			.970	-1	O-83	-1.0
Total	7	501	1626	212	439	80	19	22	151	223	127	.270	.360	.383	112	30	20	0		.977	-6	O-456	0.4

■ JOE TIPTON

Tipton, Joe Hicks   b: 2/18/22, McCaysville, Ga.   d: 3/1/94, Birmingham, Ala.   BR/TR, 5'11", 185 lbs.   Deb: 5/2/48

YEAR	TM/L	G	AB	R	H	2B	3B	HR	RBI	BB	SO	AVG	OBP	SLG	PRO+	BR/A	SB	CS	SBR	FA	FR	G/POS	TPR
1948	*Cle-A	47	90	11	26	3	0	1	13	4	10	.289	.333	.356	85	-2	0	0		.971	0	C-40	0.0
1949	Chi-A	67	191	20	39	5	3	3	19	27	17	.204	.306	.309	65	-10	1	1	-0	.992	2	C-53	-0.5
1950	Phi-A	64	184	15	49	5	1	6	20	19	16	.266	.335	.402	90	-3	0	0		.987	-4	C-59	-0.5
1951	Phi-A	72	213	23	51	9	0	3	20	51	25	.239	.389	.324	92	0	1	0	-0	.969	2	C-72	0.5
1952	Phi-A	23	68	6	13	4	0	3	8	16	10	.191	.337	.382	94	-0	0	0		.990	-2	C-23	-0.2
	Cle-A	43	105	15	26	2	0	6	22	21	21	.248	.383	.438	137	6	1	0		.971	-8	C-35	-0.1
	Yr	66	173	21	39	6	0	9	30	36	31	.225	.365	.416	119	5	1	0		.979	-11	C-58	-0.3
1953	Cle-A	47	109	17	25	2	0	6	13	19	13	.229	.359	.413	111	2	0	0		1.000	-7	C-46	-0.4
1954	Was-A	54	157	9	35	6	1	1	10	30	30	.223	.354	.293	83	-2	0	1	-1	.992	3	C-52	0.3
Total	7	417	1117	116	264	36	5	29	125	186	142	.236	.351	.355	91	-11	3	3	-1	.984	-14	C-380	-0.9

■ TOM TISCHINSKI

Tischinski, Thomas Arthur   b: 7/12/44, Kansas City, Mo.   BR/TR, 5'10", 190 lbs.   Deb: 4/11/69

YEAR	TM/L	G	AB	R	H	2B	3B	HR	RBI	BB	SO	AVG	OBP	SLG	PRO+	BR/A	SB	CS	SBR	FA	FR	G/POS	TPR
1969	Min-A	37	47	2	9	0	0	0	2	8	8	.191	.309	.191	42	-3	0	0	0	1.000	0	C-32	-0.3
1970	Min-A	24	46	6	9	0	0	1	2	9	6	.196	.327	.261	63	-2	0	0	0	.990	1	C-22	-0.0
1971	Min-A	21	23	0	3	2	0	0	2	1	4	.130	.200	.217	18	-3	0	0	0	.982	3	C-21	0.1
Total	3	82	116	8	21	2	0	1	6	18	18	.181	.296	.224	46	-8	0	0	0	.992	4	/C-75	-0.2

■ JOHN TITUS

Titus, John Franklin "Silent John"   b: 2/21/1876, St.Clair, Pa.   d: 1/8/43, St.Clair, Pa.   BL/TL, 5'9", 156 lbs.   Deb: 6/8/03

YEAR	TM/L	G	AB	R	H	2B	3B	HR	RBI	BB	SO	AVG	OBP	SLG	PRO+	BR/A	SB	CS	SBR	FA	FR	G/POS	TPR
1903	Phi-N	72	280	38	80	15	6	2	34	19		.286	.340	.404	115	5	5			.952	3	O-72	0.3
1904	Phi-N	146	504	60	148	25	5	4	55	46		.294	.362	.387	136	22	15			.952	8	*O-140	2.3
1905	Phi-N	147	548	99	169	36	14	2	89	69		.308	.397	.436	154	39	11			.962	9	*O-147	4.1
1906	Phi-N	145	484	65	129	22	5	1	57	78		.267	.378	.339	124	17	12			.974	-5	*O-142	2.0
1907	Phi-N	145	523	72	144	23	12	3	63	47		.275	.345	.382	130	18	9			.928	-5	*O-142	0.9
1908	Phi-N	149	539	75	154	24	5	2	48	53		.286	.365	.360	127	18	27			.963	-3	*O-149	1.1
1909	Phi-N	151	540	69	146	22	6	3	46	66		.270	.367	.350	121	16	23			.971	1	*O-149	1.7
1910	Phi-N	143	535	91	129	26	5	3	35	93	44	.241	.358	.325	96	0	20			.976	1	*O-142	-0.6
1911	Phi-N	76	236	35	67	14	1	8	26	32	16	.284	.372	.453	129	9	3			.979	-1	O-60	0.5
1912	Phi-N	45	157	43	43	9	5	3	22	33	14	.274	.403	.452	125	6	6			.917	-7	O-42	-0.3
	Bos-N	96	345	56	112	23	6	2	48	49	20	.325	.422	.443	134	19	5			.965	-5	O-96	0.9
	Yr	141	502	99	155	32	11	5	70	82	34	.309	.416	.446	131	25	11			.952	-12	*O-138	0.6
1913	Bos-N	87	269	33	80	14	2	5	38	35	22	.297	.392	.420	129	12	4			.919	-7	O-75	0.2
Total	11	1402	4960	738	1401	253	72	38	561	620	116	.282	.373	.385	127	181	140			.959	7	*O-1356	13.1

■ JIM TOBIN

Tobin, James Anthony "Abba Dabba"   b: 12/27/12, Oakland, Cal.   d: 5/19/69, Oakland, Cal.   BR/TR, 6', 185 lbs.   Deb: 4/30/37   F

YEAR	TM/L	G	AB	R	H	2B	3B	HR	RBI	BB	SO	AVG	OBP	SLG	PRO+	BR/A	SB	CS	SBR	FA	FR	G/POS	TPR
1937	Pit-N	21	34	7	15	4	0	0	6	4	3	.441	.500	.559	187	4	0			.938	-2	P-20	0.0
1938	Pit-N	56	103	8	25	6	1	0	11	9	12	.243	.310	.320	73	-4	0			**1.000**	-2	P-40	0.0
1939	Pit-N	43	74	9	18	3	1	2	11	2	12	.243	.263	.392	75	-3	0			1.000	-1	P-25	0.0
1940	Bos-N	20	43	5	12	3	0	0	3	1	10	.279	.295	.349	82	-1	0			.957	-1	P-15	0.0
1941	Bos-N	43	103	6	19	5	0	0	9	10	31	.184	.257	.233	40	-8	1			.966	4	P-33	0.0
1942	Bos-N	47	114	14	28	4	0	6	15	16	23	.246	.344	.421	126	4	0			.947	6	P-37	0.0
1943	Bos-N	46	107	8	30	4	0	2	6	16	28	.280	.319	.374	101	-0	0			.927	-2	P-33/1-1	0.0
1944	Bos-N★	62	116	13	22	5	1	2	18	16	28	.190	.288	.302	63	-6	0			.972	7	P-43	0.0
1945	Bos-N	41	77	9	11	3	0	0	3	12	15	.143	.290	.299	64	-4	0			**1.000**	2	P-27	0.0
	*Det-A	17	25	2	3	0	0	2	5	1	5	.120	.154	.360	44	-2	0	0	0	.950	1	P-14	0.0
Total	9	396	796	81	183	35	3	17	102	80	162	.230	.303	.345	82	-20	1	0		.965	17	P-287/1-1	0.0

■ JOHNNY TOBIN

Tobin, John Martin "Tip"   b: 9/15/06, Jamaica Plain, Mass.   d: 8/6/83, Rhinebeck, N.Y.   BR/TR, 6'3", 187 lbs.   Deb: 9/22/32

YEAR	TM/L	G	AB	R	H	2B	3B	HR	RBI	BB	SO	AVG	OBP	SLG	PRO+	BR/A	SB	CS	SBR	FA	FR	G/POS	TPR
1932	NY-N	1	1	0	0	0	0	0	0	0	0	.000	.000	.000	-99	-0	0	0	0	.000	0	H	0.0

■ JOHNNY TOBIN

Tobin, John Patrick "Jackie"   b: 1/8/21, Oakland, Cal.   d: 1/18/82, Oakland, Cal.   BL/TR, 6', 165 lbs.   Deb: 4/20/45   F

YEAR	TM/L	G	AB	R	H	2B	3B	HR	RBI	BB	SO	AVG	OBP	SLG	PRO+	BR/A	SB	CS	SBR	FA	FR	G/POS	TPR
1945	Bos-A	84	278	25	70	6	2	0	21	26	24	.252	.320	.288	75	-8	2	6	-3	.951	9	3-72/2-5,O-1	0.0

■ JACK TOBIN

Tobin, John Thomas   b: 5/4/1892, St.Louis, Mo.   d: 12/10/69, St.Louis, Mo.   BL/TL, 5'8", 142 lbs.   Deb: 4/16/14   C

YEAR	TM/L	G	AB	R	H	2B	3B	HR	RBI	BB	SO	AVG	OBP	SLG	PRO+	BR/A	SB	CS	SBR	FA	FR	G/POS	TPR
1914	StL-F	139	529	81	143	24	10	3	35	51	53	.270	.340	.393	94	-12	20			.952	5	*O-132	-1.4
1915	StL-F	158	625	92	**184**	26	13	6	51	68	42	.294	.366	.406	111	2	31			.965	3	*O-158	-0.3
1916	StL-A	77	150	16	32	4	1	0	10	12	13	.213	.272	.253	61	-7	7			.842	-9	O-41	-2.0
1918	StL-A	122	480	59	133	19	5	0	36	48	26	.277	.349	.338	111	7	13			.971	-1	*O-122	-0.1
1919	StL-A	127	486	54	159	22	7	6	57	36	24	.327	.376	.438	125	15	8			.963	-2	*O-123	0.9
1920	StL-A	147	593	94	202	34	10	4	62	39	23	.341	.383	.452	117	14	21	13	-2	.960	5	*O-147	0.6
1921	StL-A	150	671	132	236	31	**18**	8	59	45	22	.352	.395	.487	117	16	7	12	-5	.956	8	*O-150	0.8
1922	StL-A	146	625	122	207	34	8	13	66	56	22	.331	.388	.474	119	17	7	9	-3	.940	-8	*O-145	-0.4
1923	StL-A	151	637	91	202	32	15	13	73	42	13	.317	.363	.476	113	10	8	7	-2	.969	-8	*O-151	-1.0

YEAR	TM/L	G	AB	R	H	2B	3B	HR	RBI	BB	SO	AVG	OBP	SLG	PRO+	BR/A	SB	CS	SBR	FA	FR	G/POS	TPR
1924	StL-A	136	569	87	170	30	8	2	48	50	12	.299	.357	.390	87	-11	6	10	-4	.957	2	*O-132	-2.1
1925	StL-A	77	193	25	58	11	0	2	27	9	5	.301	.335	.389	79	-6	8	2	-1	1.000	-5	O-39/1-3	-1.2
1926	Was-A	27	33	5	7	0	1	0	3	0	0	.212	.212	.273	26	-4	0	0	0	1.000	-2	/O-7	-0.5
	Bos-A	51	209	26	57	9	0	1	14	16	3	.273	.324	.330	73	-8	6	5	-1	.966	-3	O-51	-1.6
	Yr	78	242	31	64	9	1	1	17	16	3	.264	.310	.322	67	-12	6	5	-1	.970	-5	O-58	-2.1
1927	Bos-A	111	374	52	116	18	3	2	40	36	9	.310	.371	.390	100	0	5	4	-1	.947	-5	O-93	-1.1
Total	13	1619	6174	936	1906	294	99	64	581	508	267	.309	.364	.420	106	33	147	62		.957	-14	*O-1491/1-3	-9.4

■ BILL TOBIN
Tobin, William F. b: 10/10/1854, Hartford, Conn. d: 10/10/12, Hartford, Conn. BL, Deb: 7/21/1880

YEAR	TM/L	G	AB	R	H	2B	3B	HR	RBI	BB	SO	AVG	OBP	SLG	PRO+	BR/A	SB	CS	SBR	FA	FR	G/POS	TPR
1880	Wor-N	5	16	1	2	0	0	0	3	0	5	.125	.125	.125	-14	-2				1.000	-0	/1-5	-0.2
	Tro-N	33	136	14	22	1	1	0	8	4	20	.162	.186	.184	24	-11				.950	-1	1-33	-1.4
	Yr	38	152	15	24	1	1	0	11	4	25	.158	.179	.178	20	-12				.958	-1	1-38	-1.6

■ AL TODD
Todd, Alfred Chester b: 1/7/02, Troy, N.Y. d: 3/8/85, Elmira, N.Y. BR/TR, 6'1", 198 lbs. Deb: 4/25/32

YEAR	TM/L	G	AB	R	H	2B	3B	HR	RBI	BB	SO	AVG	OBP	SLG	PRO+	BR/A	SB	CS	SBR	FA	FR	G/POS	TPR
1932	Phi-N	33	70	8	16	5	0	0	9	1	9	.229	.260	.300	45	-5	1			.899	-4	C-25	-0.9
1933	Phi-N	73	136	13	28	4	0	0	10	4	18	.206	.239	.235	32	-12	1			.983	5	C-34/O-2	-0.6
1934	Phi-N	91	302	33	96	22	2	4	41	10	39	.318	.344	.444	96	-2	3			.976	-2	C-82	-0.1
1935	Phi-N	107	328	40	95	18	3	3	42	19	35	.290	.334	.390	85	-7	3			.968	-12	C-87	-1.4
1936	Pit-N	76	267	28	73	10	5	2	28	11	24	.273	.307	.371	80	-8	4			.976	1	C-70	-0.3
1937	Pit-N	133	514	51	158	18	10	8	86	16	36	.307	.330	.428	104	1	2			.972	-2	*C-128	0.7
1938	Pit-N	133	491	52	130	19	7	7	75	18	31	.265	.296	.375	83	-13	2			.985	10	*C-132	0.4
1939	Bro-N	86	245	28	68	10	0	5	32	13	16	.278	.317	.380	83	-6	1			.985	8	C-73	0.5
1940	Chi-N	104	381	31	97	13	2	6	42	11	29	.255	.283	.346	74	-14	1			.984	-6	*C-104	-1.2
1941	Chi-N	6	6	1	1	0	0	0	0	0	1	.167	.167	.167	-6	-1	0			.000	0	H	-0.1
1943	Chi-N	21	45	1	6	0	0	0	1	1	5	.133	.152	.133	-17	-7	0			.986	4	C-17	-0.3
Total	11	863	2785	286	768	119	29	35	366	104	243	.276	.307	.377	82	-74	18			.977	1	C-752/O-2	-3.3

■ PHIL TODT
Todt, Philip Julius "Hook" b: 8/9/01, St.Louis, Mo. d: 11/15/73, St.Louis, Mo. BL/TL, 6', 175 lbs. Deb: 4/25/24

YEAR	TM/L	G	AB	R	H	2B	3B	HR	RBI	BB	SO	AVG	OBP	SLG	PRO+	BR/A	SB	CS	SBR	FA	FR	G/POS	TPR
1924	Bos-A	52	103	17	27	8	2	1	14	6	9	.262	.309	.408	84	-3	0	1	-1	.983	-3	1-18/O-4	-0.7
1925	Bos-A	141	544	62	151	29	13	11	75	44	29	.278	.343	.439	97	-4	3	2	-0	.991	3	*1-140	-0.9
1926	Bos-A	154	599	56	153	19	12	7	69	40	38	.255	.306	.362	76	-23	3	2	-0	.988	10	*1-154	-2.2
1927	Bos-A	140	516	55	122	22	6	6	52	28	23	.236	.280	.337	61	-32	6	2	1	.991	9	*1-139	-3.0
1928	Bos-A	144	539	61	136	31	8	12	73	26	47	.252	.290	.406	83	-16	6	5	-1	.997	3	*1-144	-2.6
1929	Bos-A	153	534	49	140	38	10	4	64	31	28	.262	.305	.393	80	-17	6	7	-2	.991	-3	*1-153	-3.0
1930	Bos-A	111	383	49	103	22	5	11	62	24	33	.269	.312	.439	92	-7	4	1	1	.993	3	*1-104	-1.2
1931	*Phi-A	62	197	23	48	14	2	5	44	8	22	.244	.273	.411	73	-9	1	1	-0	.995	-4	1-52	-1.7
Total	8	957	3415	372	880	183	58	57	453	207	229	.258	.305	.395	81	-111	29	21	-4	.992	24	1-904/O-4	-15.3

■ BOBBY TOLAN
Tolan, Robert b: 11/19/45, Los Angeles, Cal. BL/TL, 5'11", 170 lbs. Deb: 9/3/65 C

YEAR	TM/L	G	AB	R	H	2B	3B	HR	RBI	BB	SO	AVG	OBP	SLG	PRO+	BR/A	SB	CS	SBR	FA	FR	G/POS	TPR
1965	StL-N	17	69	8	13	2	0	0	6	0	4	.188	.200	.217	16	-8	2	1	0	.970	-1	O-17	-1.0
1966	StL-N	43	93	10	16	5	1	1	6	6	15	.172	.238	.280	43	-7	1	2	-1	.952	-1	O-26/1-1	-1.1
1967	*StL-N	110	265	35	67	7	3	6	32	19	43	.253	.313	.370	96	-2	12	7	-1	.992	-9	O-80,1-13	-1.6
1968	*StL-N	92	278	28	64	12	1	5	17	13	42	.230	.272	.335	82	-7	9	5	-0	.967	-2	O-67/1-9	-1.4
1969	Cin-N	152	637	104	194	25	10	21	93	27	92	.305	.348	.474	122	17	26	12	1	.974	11	*O-150	2.0
1970	*Cin-N	152	589	112	186	34	6	16	80	62	94	.316	.388	.475	130	25	57	20	5	.978	8	*O-150	3.0
1972	*Cin-N	149	604	88	171	28	5	8	82	44	88	.283	.338	.386	112	9	42	15	4	.990	13	*O-149	1.9
1973	Cin-N	129	457	42	94	14	2	9	51	27	68	.206	.253	.304	57	-28	15	10	-2	.966	-4	*O-120	-4.1
1974	SD-N	95	357	45	95	16	1	4	40	20	41	.266	.321	.384	101	-1	9	3	-3	.971	-2	O-88	-1.0
1975	SD-N	147	506	58	129	19	4	5	43	28	45	.255	.307	.338	84	-12	11	13	-5	.971	-2	*O-120,1-27	-2.6
1976	*Phi-N	110	272	32	71	7	0	5	35	7	39	.261	.290	.342	76	-9	10	5	0	.992	-12	1-50,O-35	-2.6
1977	Phi-N	15	16	1	2	0	0	0	1	1	4	.125	.176	.125	-17	-3	0	0	0	.944	1	/1-5	-0.3
	Pit-N	49	74	7	15	4	0	2	9	4	10	.203	.244	.338	53	-5	1	1	-1	1.000	-0	1-20/O-2	-0.6
	Yr	64	90	8	17	4	0	2	10	5	14	.189	.232	.300	40	-8	1	1	-0	.992	-0	1-25/O-2	-0.9
1979	SD-N	22	21	2	4	0	1	0	2	0	2	.190	.190	.286	30	-2	0	0	0	1.000	-0	/1-5,O-1	-0.2
Total	13	1282	4238	572	1121	173	34	86	497	258	587	.265	.317	.382	96	-32	193	100	-2	.976	-1	*O-1005,1-130	-9.6

■ JOSE TOLENTINO
Tolentino, Jose (Franco) b: 6/3/61, Mexico City, Mexico BL/TL, 6'1", 195 lbs. Deb: 7/28/91

YEAR	TM/L	G	AB	R	H	2B	3B	HR	RBI	BB	SO	AVG	OBP	SLG	PRO+	BR/A	SB	CS	SBR	FA	FR	G/POS	TPR
1991	Hou-N	44	54	6	14	4	0	1	6	4	9	.259	.310	.389	101	-0	0	0	0	.982	1	1-10/O-1	0.1

■ WAYNE TOLLESON
Tolleson, Jimmy Wayne b: 11/22/55, Spartanburg, S.C. BB/TR, 5'9", 160 lbs. Deb: 9/1/81

YEAR	TM/L	G	AB	R	H	2B	3B	HR	RBI	BB	SO	AVG	OBP	SLG	PRO+	BR/A	SB	CS	SBR	FA	FR	G/POS	TPR
1981	Tex-A	14	24	6	4	0	0	0	1	1	5	.167	.200	.167	7	-3	2	0	1	1.000	-0	/3-6,S-2	-0.3
1982	Tex-A	38	70	6	8	1	0	0	2	5	14	.114	.173	.129	-16	-11	1	1	-0	.958	5	S-26/3-4,2-1	-0.5
1983	Tex-A	134	470	64	122	13	2	3	20	40	68	.260	.320	.315	77	-14	33	10	4	.972	-10	*2-112,S-26/D-1	-1.3
1984	Tex-A	118	338	35	72	9	2	0	9	27	47	.213	.277	.251	46	-24	22	4	4	.979	-7	*2-109/S-7,3-5,0D	-2.3
1985	Tex-A	123	323	45	101	9	5	1	18	21	46	.313	.355	.381	100	1	21	12	-1	.972	-4	S-81,2-29,3-12/D-6	0.3
1986	Chi-A	81	260	39	65	7	3	3	29	38	43	.250	.346	.335	84	-5	13	6	0	.955	-10	3-65,S-18/O-2,D-2	-1.5
	NY-A	60	215	22	61	9	2	0	14	14	33	.284	.333	.344	86	-4	4	4	-1	.981	6	S-56/3-7,2-3	0.6
	Yr	141	475	61	126	16	5	3	43	52	76	.265	.340	.339	85	-9	17	10	-1	.981	-4	S-74,3-72/2-3,0D	-0.9
1987	NY-A	121	349	48	77	4	0	1	22	43	72	.221	.306	.241	48	-25	5	3	-0	.970	-3	*S-119/3-3	-1.7
1988	NY-A	21	59	8	15	2	0	0	5	8	12	.254	.348	.288	79	-1	1	0	0	.981	1	2-12,3-10/S-1	0.5
1989	NY-A	80	140	16	23	5	2	1	9	16	23	.164	.255	.250	43	-10	1	0	0	.912	10	3-28,S-28,2-13,D-10	0.1
1990	NY-A	73	74	12	11	1	1	0	4	6	21	.149	.213	.189	13	-9	1	0	0	.983	15	S-45,2-13/3-3,D-5	0.8
Total	10	863	2322	301	559	60	17	9	133	219	384	.241	.308	.293	66	-106	108	41	8	.974	7	S-409,2-292,3/DO	-5.3

■ TIM TOLMAN
Tolman, Timothy Lee b: 4/20/56, Santa Monica, Cal. BR/TR, 6', 195 lbs. Deb: 9/9/81

YEAR	TM/L	G	AB	R	H	2B	3B	HR	RBI	BB	SO	AVG	OBP	SLG	PRO+	BR/A	SB	CS	SBR	FA	FR	G/POS	TPR
1981	Hou-N	4	8	0	1	0	0	0	0	0	2	.125	.125	.125	-30	-1	0	0	0	1.000	-1	/O-3	-0.3
1982	Hou-N	15	26	4	5	2	0	1	3	4	3	.192	.300	.385	98	-0	0	0	0	1.000	-0	/O-5,1-1	-0.1
1983	Hou-N	43	56	4	11	4	0	2	10	6	9	.196	.274	.375	83	-2	0	1	-1	1.000	-2	/1-7,O-3	-0.4
1984	Hou-N	14	17	2	3	1	0	0	0	3	8	.176	.176	.235	16	-2	0	0	0	1.000	-1	/O-3,1-1	-0.3
1985	Hou-N	31	43	4	6	1	0	1	2	8	10	.140	.178	.302	33	-4	0	1	-1	1.000	-1	/O-9,1-6	-0.6
1986	Det-A	16	34	4	6	1	0	0	2	6	4	.176	.300	.206	41	-3	1	1	-0	1.000	-1	/O-4,1-3,D-9	-0.4
1987	Det-A	9	12	3	1	1	0	0	7	2	2	.083	.450	.167	77	-0	0	0	0	1.000	-0	/O-7,D-2	-0.1
Total	7	132	196	21	33	10	0	5	24	24	31	.168	.266	.296	58	-11	1	3	-2	1.000	-6	/O-34,1-18,D-11	-2.2

■ CHICK TOLSON
Tolson, Charles Julius "Toby" b: 11/6/1898, Washington, D.C. d: 4/16/65, Washington, D.C. BR/TR, 6', 185 lbs. Deb: 7/3/25

YEAR	TM/L	G	AB	R	H	2B	3B	HR	RBI	BB	SO	AVG	OBP	SLG	PRO+	BR/A	SB	CS	SBR	FA	FR	G/POS	TPR
1925	Cle-A	3	12	0	3	0	0	0	2	1	1	.250	.357	.250	56	-0	0	0		1.000	-0	/1-3	-0.1
1926	Chi-N	57	80	4	25	6	1	1	8	5	8	.313	.353	.450	113	0	0			.991	0	1-13	0.1
1927	Chi-N	39	54	6	16	4	0	2	17	4	9	.296	.345	.481	119	1	0			1.000	0	/1-8	0.1
1929	*Chi-N	32	109	13	28	5	0	1	19	9	16	.257	.325	.330	63	-6	0			.978	-2	1-31	-1.0
1930	Chi-N	13	20	0	6	1	0	0	1	7	5	.300	.462	.350	99	0	0			.979	1	/1-5	0.0
Total	5	144	275	23	78	16	1	4	45	26	39	.284	.350	.393	90	-4	0	0		.985	-1	/1-60	-0.9

■ ANDY TOMBERLIN
Tomberlin, Andy Lee b: 11/7/66, Monroe, N.C. BL/TL, 5'11", 160 lbs. Deb: 8/12/93

YEAR	TM/L	G	AB	R	H	2B	3B	HR	RBI	BB	SO	AVG	OBP	SLG	PRO+	BR/A	SB	CS	SBR	FA	FR	G/POS	TPR
1993	Pit-N	27	42	4	12	0	1	1	5	2	14	.286	.333	.405	97	-0	0	0	0	1.000	-0	/O-7	-0.1
1994	Bos-A	18	36	1	7	0	1	1	6	2	12	.194	.310	.333	63	-2	1	0	0	1.000	-0	O-11/P-1,D-5	-0.2
1995	Oak-A	46	85	15	18	0	0	6	15	7	25	.212	.256	.353	60	-5	4	1	1	.979	-9	O-42/D-2	-1.3
1996	NY-N	63	66	12	17	4	0	1	10	9	24	.258	.355	.455	120	2	0	0	0	1.000	-4	O-17/1-1	-0.2
Total	4	154	229	32	54	4	2	9	26	22	75	.236	.308	.389	84	-6	5	1	1	.988	-13	/O-77,D-7,1-1,P-1	-1.8

■ GEORGE TOMER
Tomer, George Clarence b: 11/26/1895, Perry, Iowa d: 12/15/84, Perry, Iowa BL/TR, 6', 180 lbs. Deb: 9/17/13

YEAR	TM/L	G	AB	R	H	2B	3B	HR	RBI	BB	SO	AVG	OBP	SLG	PRO+	BR/A	SB	CS	SBR	FA	FR	G/POS	TPR
1913	StL-A	1	1	0	0	0	0	0	0	0	1	.000	.000	.000	-99	-0	0			.000	0	H		0.0

YEAR	TM/L	G	AB	R	H	2B	3B	HR	RBI	BB	SO	AVG	OBP	SLG	PRO+	BR/A	SB	CS	SBR	FA	FR	G/POS	TPR

■ PHIL TOMNEY   Tomney, Philip Howard "Buster"   b: 7/17/1863, Reading, Pa.   d: 3/18/1892, Reading, Pa.   BR/TR, 5'7", 155 lbs.   Deb: 9/7/1888

YEAR	TM/L	G	AB	R	H	2B	3B	HR	RBI	BB	SO	AVG	OBP	SLG	PRO+	BR/A	SB	CS	SBR	FA	FR	G/POS	TPR
1888	Lou-a	34	120	15	18	3	0	0	4	7		.150	.197	.175	20	-11	11			.882	6	S-34	-0.3
1889	Lou-a	112	376	61	80	8	5	4	38	46	47	.213	.304	.293	71	-13	26			.857	27	*S-112	1.7
1890	*Lou-a	108	386	72	107	21	7	1	58	43		.277	.357	.376	119	9	27			.902	18	*S-108	2.9
Total	3	254	882	148	205	32	12	5	100	96	47	.232	.313	.313	86	-15	64			.878	50	S-254	4.3

■ TONY TONNEMAN   Tonneman, Charles Richard   b: 9/10/1881, Chicago, Ill.   d: 8/7/51, Prescott, Ariz.   BR/TR, 5'10.5", 175 lbs.   Deb: 9/19/11

YEAR	TM/L	G	AB	R	H	2B	3B	HR	RBI	BB	SO	AVG	OBP	SLG	PRO+	BR/A	SB	CS	SBR	FA	FR	G/POS	TPR
1911	Bos-A	2	5	0	1	0	0	0	3	1		.200	.333	.400	105	0	0			.900	1	/C-2	0.1

■ BERT TOOLEY   Tooley, Albert R.   b: 8/30/1886, Howell, Mich.   d: 8/17/76, Marshall, Mich.   BR/TR, 5'10", 155 lbs.   Deb: 4/12/11

YEAR	TM/L	G	AB	R	H	2B	3B	HR	RBI	BB	SO	AVG	OBP	SLG	PRO+	BR/A	SB	CS	SBR	FA	FR	G/POS	TPR
1911	Bro-N	119	433	55	89	11	3	1	29	53	63	.206	.295	.252	56	-25	18			.925	-8	*S-114	-2.6
1912	Bro-N	77	265	34	62	6	5	2	37	19	21	.234	.285	.317	67	-13	12			.885	-15	S-76	-2.1
Total	2	196	698	89	151	17	8	3	66	72	84	.216	.291	.277	60	-37	30			.909	-24	S-190	-4.7

■ SPECS TOPORCER   Toporcer, George   b: 2/9/1899, New York, N.Y.   d: 5/17/89, Huntington Station, N.Y.   BL/TR, 5'10.5", 165 lbs.   Deb: 4/13/21

YEAR	TM/L	G	AB	R	H	2B	3B	HR	RBI	BB	SO	AVG	OBP	SLG	PRO+	BR/A	SB	CS	SBR	FA	FR	G/POS	TPR
1921	StL-N	22	53	4	14	1	0	0	2	3	4	.264	.304	.283	57	-3	0			.938	0	2-12/S-2	-0.2
1922	StL-N	116	352	56	114	25	3	3	36	24	18	.324	.370	.455	117	8	2	1	0	.939	-23	S-91/3-6,2-1,0-1	-0.5
1923	StL-N	97	303	45	77	11	3	3	35	41	14	.254	.349	.340	84	-6	4	3	-1	.945	-13	2-52,S-33/1-1,3-1	-1.5
1924	StL-N	70	198	30	62	10	3	1	24	11	14	.313	.362	.409	108	2	2	3	-1	.974	-16	3-33,S-25/2-3	-1.0
1925	StL-N	83	268	38	76	13	4	2	26	36	15	.284	.373	.384	92	-2	7	2	1	.960	-3	S-66/2-7	0.3
1926	*StL-N	64	88	13	22	3	2	0	9	8	9	.250	.327	.330	74	-3	1			.983	-9	2-27/S-5,3-1	-0.4
1927	StL-N	86	290	37	72	13	4	0	19	27	16	.248	.314	.321	68	-13	5			.980	-11	3-54,S-27/2-2,1-1	-1.9
1928	StL-N	8	14	0	0	0	0	0	0	0	3	.000	.000	.000	-98	-4	0			1.000	0	/1-1,2-1	-0.4
Total	8	546	1566	223	437	76	22	9	151	150	93	.279	.347	.373	90	-20	22	9		.946	-74	S-249,2-105/310	-6.4

■ JEFF TORBORG   Torborg, Jeffrey Allen   b: 11/26/41, Plainfield, N.J.   BR/TR, 6'0.5", 195 lbs.   Deb: 5/10/64   MC

YEAR	TM/L	G	AB	R	H	2B	3B	HR	RBI	BB	SO	AVG	OBP	SLG	PRO+	BR/A	SB	CS	SBR	FA	FR	G/POS	TPR
1964	LA-N	28	43	4	10	1	1	0	4	3	8	.233	.298	.302	75	-1	0	0	0	.977	-2	C-27	-0.3
1965	LA-N	56	150	8	36	5	1	3	13	10	26	.240	.292	.347	85	-3	0	0	0	.991	4	C-53	0.3
1966	LA-N	46	120	4	27	3	0	1	13	10	23	.225	.285	.275	61	-6	0	0	0	.986	6	C-45	0.2
1967	LA-N	76	196	11	42	4	1	2	12	13	31	.214	.267	.276	60	-10	1	3	-2	.989	12	C-75	0.3
1968	LA-N	37	93	2	15	2	0	0	4	6	10	.161	.212	.183	21	-9	0	0	0	.991	4	C-37	0.3
1969	LA-N	51	124	7	23	4	0	0	7	9	17	.185	.241	.218	31	-12	1	0	0	.996	11	C-50	0.1
1970	LA-N	64	134	11	31	8	0	1	17	14	15	.231	.304	.313	69	-6	1	1	-0	.983	10	C-63	0.5
1971	Cal-A	55	123	6	25	5	0	0	5	3	6	.203	.222	.244	34	-11	0	0	0	.987	5	C-49	-0.6
1972	Cal-A	59	153	5	32	3	0	1	8	14	21	.209	.280	.229	56	-8	0	0	0	.998	16	C-58	1.1
1973	Cal-A	102	255	20	56	7	0	1	18	21	32	.220	.279	.259	57	-15	0	2	-1	.991	8	*C-102	-0.4
Total	10	574	1391	78	297	42	3	8	101	103	189	.214	.270	.265	56	-82	3	6	-3	.990	79	C-559	1.5

■ EARL TORGESON   Torgeson, Clifford Earl "The Earl Of Snohomish"   b: 1/1/24, Snohomish, Wash.   d: 11/8/90, Everett, Wash.   BL/TL, 6'3", 180 lbs.   Deb: 4/15/47   C

YEAR	TM/L	G	AB	R	H	2B	3B	HR	RBI	BB	SO	AVG	OBP	SLG	PRO+	BR/A	SB	CS	SBR	FA	FR	G/POS	TPR
1947	Bos-N	128	399	73	112	20	6	16	78	82	59	.281	.403	.481	137	24	11			.984	-1	*1-117	1.9
1948	*Bos-N	134	438	70	111	23	5	10	67	81	54	.253	.372	.397	110	9	19			.993	1	*1-129	0.9
1949	Bos-N	25	100	17	26	5	1	4	19	13	4	.260	.345	.450	118	2	4			.988	-3	1-25	-0.1
1950	Bos-N	156	576	**120**	167	30	3	23	87	119	69	.290	.412	.472	141	39	15			.986	-0	*1-156	3.4
1951	Bos-N	155	581	99	153	21	4	24	92	102	70	.263	.375	.437	127	24	20	11	-1	.988	-1	*1-155	1.5
1952	Bos-N	122	382	49	88	17	0	5	34	81	38	.230	.366	.314	94	0	11	7	-1	.989	-1	*1-105/O-5	-0.6
1953	Phi-N	111	379	58	104	25	8	11	64	53	57	.274	.366	.470	117	10	7	1	2	.987	-3	*1-105	0.4
1954	Phi-N	135	490	63	133	22	6	5	54	75	52	.271	.368	.371	93	-3	7	1	2	.990	-10	*1-133	-1.8
1955	Phi-N	47	150	29	40	5	1	4	17	32	20	.267	.396	.360	104	2	2	3	-1	.995	-4	1-43	-0.3
	Det-A	89	300	58	85	10	1	9	50	61	29	.283	.404	.413	123	12	9	0	3	.992	-0	1-83	1.0
1956	Det-A	117	318	61	84	9	3	12	42	78	47	.264	.409	.425	120	12	6	4	-1	.992	-7	1-83	0.0
1957	Det-A	30	50	5	12	2	1	1	5	12	10	.240	.387	.380	108	1	0	0	0	1.000	0	1-17	0.0
	Chi-A	86	251	53	74	11	2	7	46	49	44	.295	.410	.438	131	13	7	3	0	.998	-5	1-70/O-1	0.4
	Yr	116	301	58	86	13	3	8	51	61	54	.286	.404	.429	127	14	7	3	0	.999	-5	1-87/O-1	0.4
1958	Chi-A	96	188	37	50	8	0	10	30	62	46	.266	.415	.468	146	14	7	2	1	.978	-2	1-73	1.0
1959	*Chi-A	127	277	40	61	5	3	9	45	62	55	.220	.363	.357	100	2	7	6	-2	.983	-6	*1-103	-1.1
1960	Chi-A	68	57	12	15	2	0	4	9	21	8	.263	.462	.404	137	5	1	0	0	.983	0	1-10	0.5
1961	Chi-A	20	15	1	1	0	0	0	1	3	5	.067	.222	.067	-19	-3	0	0	0	1.000	0	/1-1	-0.3
	NY-A	22	18	2	2	0	0	0	0	8	3	.111	.385	.111	42	-1	0	1	-1	.969	-0	/1-8	-0.2
	Yr	42	33	4	3	0	0	0	1	11	8	.091	.318	.091	16	-4	0	1	-1	.970	-0	/1-9	-0.5
Total	15	1668	4969	848	1318	215	46	149	740	980	653	.265	.387	.417	118	162	133	39		.989	-39	*1-1416/O-6	6.6

■ RED TORPHY   Torphy, Walter Anthony   b: 11/6/1891, Fall River, Mass.   d: 2/11/80, Fall River, Mass.   BR/TR, 5'11", 169 lbs.   Deb: 9/25/20

YEAR	TM/L	G	AB	R	H	2B	3B	HR	RBI	BB	SO	AVG	OBP	SLG	PRO+	BR/A	SB	CS	SBR	FA	FR	G/POS	TPR
1920	Bos-N	3	15	1	3	2	0	0	2	0	1	.200	.200	.333	54	-1	0	0	0	.969	-1	/1-3	-0.2

■ FRANK TORRE   Torre, Frank Joseph   b: 12/30/31, Brooklyn, N.Y.   BL/TL, 6'3", 205 lbs.   Deb: 4/20/56   F

YEAR	TM/L	G	AB	R	H	2B	3B	HR	RBI	BB	SO	AVG	OBP	SLG	PRO+	BR/A	SB	CS	SBR	FA	FR	G/POS	TPR
1956	Mil-N	111	159	17	41	6	0	0	16	11	4	.258	.306	.296	67	-7	1	0	0	.993	6	1-89	-0.4
1957	*Mil-N	129	364	46	99	19	5	5	40	29	19	.272	.341	.393	104	2	0	0	0	**.996**	4	*1-117	-0.3
1958	*Mil-N	138	372	41	115	22	5	6	55	42	14	.309	.390	.444	131	17	2	0	1	**.994**	6	*1-122	1.8
1959	Mil-N	115	263	23	60	15	1	1	33	35	12	.228	.326	.304	75	-9	0	0	0	.994	-0	1-87	-1.4
1960	Mil-N	21	44	2	9	1	0	0	5	3	2	.205	.255	.227	36	-4	0	0	0	1.000	-1	1-17	-0.6
1962	Phi-N	108	168	13	52	8	2	0	20	24	6	.310	.408	.381	117	5	1	1	0	.980	3	1-76	0.6
1963	Phi-N	92	112	8	28	7	2	1	10	11	7	.250	.333	.375	105	1	0	0	0	.989	5	1-56	0.5
Total	7	714	1482	150	404	78	15	13	179	155	64	.273	.352	.372	101	5	4	1	1	.993	19	1-564	0.2

■ JOE TORRE   Torre, Joseph Paul   b: 7/18/40, Brooklyn, N.Y.   BR/TR, 6'2", 212 lbs.   Deb: 9/25/60   FM

YEAR	TM/L	G	AB	R	H	2B	3B	HR	RBI	BB	SO	AVG	OBP	SLG	PRO+	BR/A	SB	CS	SBR	FA	FR	G/POS	TPR
1960	Mil-N	2	2	0	1	0	0	0	0	0	0	.500	.500	.500	189	0	0	0	0	.000	0	H	0.0
1961	Mil-N	113	406	40	113	21	4	10	42	28	60	.278	.331	.424	105	2	3	5	-2	.982	-8	*C-112	-0.3
1962	Mil-N	80	220	23	62	8	1	5	26	24	24	.282	.358	.395	105	2	1	0	0	.986	9	C-63	1.0
1963	Mil-N☆	142	501	57	147	19	4	14	71	42	79	.293	.354	.431	126	17	1	5	-3	.994	-7	*C-105,1-37/O-2	1.0
1964	Mil-N★	154	601	87	193	36	5	20	109	36	67	.321	.366	.498	140	31	2	4	-2	**.995**	-8	*C-96,1-70	2.4
1965	Mil-N★	148	523	68	152	21	1	27	80	61	79	.291	.373	.489	140	28	0	1	0	.991	-6	*C-100,1-49	2.6
1966	Atl-N★	148	546	83	172	20	3	36	101	60	61	.315	.385	.560	150	41	0	4	-2	.984	-3	*C-114,1-36	4.2
1967	Atl-N★	135	477	67	132	18	1	20	68	49	75	.277	.348	.444	127	16	2	2	-1	.991	-5	*C-114,1-23	1.7
1968	Atl-N	115	424	45	115	11	2	10	55	34	72	.271	.333	.377	112	7	1	0	0	**.996**	-11	C-92,1-29	0.1
1969	StL-N	159	602	72	174	29	6	18	101	66	85	.289	.364	.447	126	21	0	0	0	.996	-3	*1-144,C-17	2.3
1970	StL-N★	161	624	89	203	27	9	21	100	70	91	.325	.399	.498	136	33	2	3	-1	.987	-8	C-90,3-73/1-1	2.8
1971	StL-N★	161	634	97	**230**	34	8	24	**137**	63	70	**.363**	.424	.555	169	57	4	1	1	.951	-17	*3-161	4.1
1972	StL-N★	149	544	71	157	26	6	11	81	54	64	.289	.361	.419	123	17	3	0	1	.963	-15	*3-117,1-27	-0.1
1973	StL-N★	141	519	67	149	17	2	13	69	65	79	.287	.377	.403	116	14	2	1	0	.993	-12	*1-114,3-58	-0.6
1974	StL-N	147	529	59	149	28	1	11	70	69	88	.282	.373	.401	117	14	1	2	-1	.992	9	*1-139,3-18	0.8
1975	NY-N	114	361	33	89	16	3	6	35	35	55	.247	.317	.357	91	-5	0	0	0	.993	-8	3-83,1-24	-0.7
1976	NY-N	114	310	36	95	10	3	5	31	21	35	.306	.360	.406	124	9	0	0	0	.989	7	1-78/3-4	0.6
1977	NY-N	26	51	2	9	2	0	1	9	3	11	.176	.208	.294	34	-1	0	0	0	.988	-1	1-16/3-1,M	-0.7
Total	18	2209	7874	996	2342	344	59	252	1185	779	1094	.297	.367	.452	129	299	23	29	-11	.990	-93	C-903,1-787,3/O	19.6

■ GIL TORRES   Torres, Don Gilberto (Nunez)   b: 8/23/15, Regla, Cuba   d: 1/10/83, Regla, Cuba   BR/TR, 6', 155 lbs.   Deb: 4/25/40   F

YEAR	TM/L	G	AB	R	H	2B	3B	HR	RBI	BB	SO	AVG	OBP	SLG	PRO+	BR/A	SB	CS	SBR	FA	FR	G/POS	TPR
1940	Was-A	2	0	0	0	0	0	0	—	—	0	—	—	—		0	0	0	0	1.000	0	/P-2	0.0
1944	Was-A	134	524	42	140	20	6	0	58	21	24	.267	.297	.328	82	-14	10	7	-1	.952	9	*3-123,2-10/1-4	-0.5
1945	Was-A	147	562	39	133	12	5	0	48	21	29	.237	.264	.276	62	-30	7	4	-0	.953	-21	*S-145/3-2	-4.3
1946	Was-A	63	185	18	47	8	0	0	13	11	12	.254	.296	.297	70	-8	3	2	-0	.939	2	S-31,3-18/2-7,P-3	0.4
Total	4	346	1271	99	320	40	11	0	119	53	65	.252	.282	.301	72	-51	20	13	-2	.951	-11	S-176,3-143/2P1	-5.2

YEAR	TM/L	G	AB	R	H	2B	3B	HR	RBI	BB	SO	AVG	OBP	SLG	PRO+	BR/A	SB	CS	SBR	FA	FR	G/POS	TPR

■ FELIX TORRES Torres, Felix (Sanchez) b: 5/1/32, Ponce, P.R. BR/TR, 5'11", 165 lbs. Deb: 4/10/62

1962	LA-A	127	451	44	117	19	4	11	74	28	73	.259	.308	.392	90	-7	0	0	0	.938	-3	*3-123	-1.0
1963	LA-A	138	463	40	121	32	1	4	51	30	73	.261	.310	.361	93	-5	1	0	0	.939	-4	*3-122/1-2	-1.0
1964	LA-A	100	277	25	64	10	0	12	28	13	56	.231	.268	.397	91	-5	1	3	-2	.970	-0	3-72/1-3	-0.8
Total	3	365	1191	109	302	61	5	27	153	71	202	.254	.300	.381	91	-18	2	3	-1	.945	-8	3-317/1-5	-2.8

■ HECTOR TORRES Torres, Hector Epitacio (Marroquin) b: 9/16/45, Monterrey, Mexico BR/TR, 6', 175 lbs. Deb: 4/10/68 C

1968	Hou-N	128	466	44	104	11	1	1	24	18	64	.223	.252	.258	54	-26	2	3	-1	.958	-4	*S-127/2-1	-2.2
1969	Hou-N	34	69	5	11	1	0	1	8	2	12	.159	.183	.217	12	-8	0	0	0	.944	0	S-22	-0.7
1970	Hou-N	31	65	6	16	1	2	0	5	6	8	.246	.310	.323	73	-3	0	0	0	.947	1	S-22/2-6	0.0
1971	Chi-N	31	58	4	13	3	0	0	2	4	10	.224	.274	.276	49	-4	0	0	0	.962	1	S-18/2-4	-0.2
1972	Mon-N	83	181	14	28	4	1	2	7	13	26	.155	.215	.221	24	-18	0	2	-1	.965	14	2-60,S-16/0-2,P3	-0.2
1973	Mon-N	38	66	3	6	1	0	0	2	7	13	.091	.189	.106	-16	-10	0	1	-1	.952	7	S-22,2-13	-0.2
1975	SD-N	112	352	31	91	12	0	5	26	22	32	.259	.302	.335	82	-10	2	1	0	.971	11	S-75,3-42,2-16	0.8
1976	SD-N	74	215	8	42	6	0	4	15	16	31	.195	.254	.279	56	-13	2	1	0	.949	-16	S-63/3-4,2-3	-2.5
1977	Tor-N	91	266	33	64	7	3	5	26	16	33	.241	.286	.346	70	-11	1	1	0	.980	-2	S-68,2-23/3-2	-0.6
Total	9	622	1738	148	375	46	7	18	115	104	229	.216	.262	.281	55	-103	7	11	-5	.962	11	S-433,2-126/30P	-5.8

■ RICARDO TORRES Torres, Ricardo J. (Martinez) b: 4/16/1891, Regla, Cuba d: 4/17/60, Regla, Cuba BR/TR, 5'11", 160 lbs. Deb: 5/18/20 F

1920	Was-A	16	30	8	10	1	0	0	3	1	4	.333	.355	.367	94	-1	0	0	0	1.000	-1	/1-7,C-5	-0.1
1921	Was-A	2	3	1	1	0	0	0	0	1	1	.333	.500	.333	122	0	0	0	0	.750	-1	/C-2	-0.1
1922	Was-A	4	4	0	0	0	0	0	0	1	1	.000	.000	.000	-99	-1	0	0	0	1.000	1	/C-3	0.0
Total	3	22	37	9	11	1	0	0	3	3	6	.297	.333	.324	76	-1	0	0	0	.955	-1	/C-10,1-7	-0.2

■ RUSTY TORRES Torres, Rosendo (Hernandez) b: 9/30/48, Aguadilla, P.R. BB/TR, 5'10", 180 lbs. Deb: 9/20/71

1971	NY-A	9	26	5	10	3	0	2	3	0	8	.385	.385	.731	223	4	0	1	-1	1.000	0	/O-5	0.3
1972	NY-A	80	199	15	42	7	3	3	13	18	44	.211	.280	.291	73	-7	0	4	-2	.978	-6	O-62	-2.1
1973	Cle-A	122	312	31	64	8	1	7	28	50	62	.205	.321	.304	76	-9	6	5	-1	.976	-5	*O-114	-2.0
1974	Cle-A	108	150	19	28	2	0	3	12	13	24	.187	.252	.260	48	-10	2	1	0	.959	-19	O-94/D-1	-3.3
1976	Cal-A	120	264	37	54	16	3	6	27	36	39	.205	.300	.356	98	-1	4	4	-1	.990	-11	*O-105/3-1,D-6	-1.7
1977	Cal-A	58	77	9	12	1	1	3	10	10	18	.156	.253	.312	55	-5	0	1	-1	.984	12	O-54	-1.9
1978	Chi-A	16	44	7	14	3	0	3	6	6	7	.318	.400	.591	174	4	0	1	-1	.964	-2	O-14	0.1
1979	Chi-A	90	170	26	43	5	0	8	24	23	37	.253	.349	.424	107	2	6	3	-1	.976	-13	O-85	-1.3
1980	KC-A	51	72	10	12	0	0	0	3	8	7	.167	.250	.167	16	-8	1	3	-2	.973	-4	O-40/D-1	-1.4
Total	9	654	1314	159	279	45	5	35	126	164	246	.212	.303	.334	82	-30	13	20	-8	.977	-73	O-573/D-8,3-1	-13.3

■ KELVIN TORVE Torve, Kelvin Curtis b: 1/10/60, Rapid City, S.Dak. BL/TR, 6'3", 205 lbs. Deb: 6/25/88

1988	Min-A	12	16	1	3	0	0	1	2	1	2	.188	.235	.375	66	-1	0	1	-1	1.000	0	/1-4,D-1	-0.1
1990	NY-N	20	38	0	11	4	0	0	2	4	9	.289	.386	.395	116	1	0	0	0	1.000	-2	/1-9,O-1	-0.2
1991	NY-N	10	8	0	0	0	0	0	0	0	1	.000	.000	.000	-99	-2	0	0	0	1.000	1	/1-1	-0.1
Total	3	42	62	1	14	4	0	1	4	5	12	.226	.304	.339	78	-2	0	1	-1	1.000	-2	/1-14,O-1,D-1	-0.4

■ CESAR TOVAR Tovar, Cesar Leonardo "Pepito" (b: Cesar Leonard Perez (Tovar)) b: 7/3/40, Caracas, Venez. d: 7/14/94, Caracas, Venez. BR/TR, 5'9", 155 lbs. Deb: 4/12/65

1965	Min-A	18	25	3	5	1	0	0	2	2	3	.200	.259	.240	41	-2	2	0	1	.800	1	/2-4,3-2,0-2,S-1	-0.1
1966	Min-A	134	465	57	121	19	5	2	41	44	50	.260	.329	.335	86	-7	16	6	1	.978	-8	2-76,S-31,O-24	-0.8
1967	Min-A	164	649	98	173	32	7	6	47	46	51	.267	.328	.365	97	-2	19	11	-1	.994	-4	O-74,3-70,2-36,/S-9	-1.1
1968	Min-A	157	613	89	167	31	6	6	47	34	41	.272	.328	.372	106	5	35	13	3	.966	-2	O-78,3-75,S2/PC1	0.6
1969	*Min-A	158	535	99	154	25	5	11	52	37	37	.288	.344	.415	109	6	45	12	6	.983	9	*O-113,2-41,3-20	1.9
1970	*Min-A	161	650	120	195	36	13	10	54	52	47	.300	.356	.442	118	15	30	15	0	.977	0	*O-151/2-8,3-4	0.8
1971	Min-A	157	657	94	204	29	3	1	45	36	39	.311	.357	.368	103	3	18	14	-3	.986	4	*O-154/3-7,2-2	-0.4
1972	Min-A	141	548	86	145	20	6	2	31	39	39	.265	.329	.334	93	-4	21	10	0	.983	7	*O-139	-0.4
1973	Phi-N	97	328	49	88	18	4	1	21	29	35	.268	.337	.357	90	-4	6	4	-1	.928	-15	3-46,O-24,2-22	-2.1
1974	Tex-A	138	562	78	164	24	6	4	58	47	33	.292	.356	.377	114	11	13	9	-2	.980	-1	*O-135/D-3	0.3
1975	Tex-A	102	427	53	110	16	0	3	28	27	33	.258	.306	.316	77	-13	16	11	-2	.919	-3	D-66,O-31/2-1	-2.2
	*Oak-A	19	26	5	6	1	0	0	3	3	3	.231	.310	.269	66	-1	4	0	1	1.000	-0	/2-4,3-3,S-1,D-7	0.0
	Yr	121	453	58	116	17	0	3	31	30	28	.256	.307	.313	76	-14	20	11	-1	.919	-3	D-73,O-31/2-5,3S	-2.2
1976	Oak-A	29	45	1	8	0	0	0	4	4	4	.178	.275	.178	36	-3	1	2	-1	.958	-5	O-20/D-4	-1.0
	NY-A	13	39	2	6	1	0	0	2	4	3	.154	.250	.179	27	-3	0	1	-1	1.000	1	D-10/2-3	-0.4
	Yr	42	84	3	14	1	0	0	6	8	7	.167	.263	.179	32	-7	1	3	-2	.958	-4	O-20,D-14/2-3	-1.4
Total	12	1488	5569	834	1546	253	55	46	435	413	410	.278	.337	.368	99	-0	226	108	3	.980	-18	O-945,3-227,2/DS1CP	-4.9

■ BABE TOWNE Towne, Jay King b: 3/12/1880, Coon Rapids, Iowa d: 10/29/38, Des Moines, Iowa BR/TR, 5'10", 180 lbs. Deb: 8/1/06

| 1906 | *Chi-A | 14 | 36 | 3 | 10 | 0 | 0 | 0 | 6 | 7 | | .278 | .395 | .278 | 115 | 1 | 0 | | | .923 | -4 | C-13 | -0.2 |

■ GEORGE TOWNSEND Townsend, George Hodgson "Sleepy" b: 6/4/1867, Hartsdale, N.Y. d: 3/15/30, New Haven, Conn. BR/TR, 5'7.5", 180 lbs. Deb: 6/25/1887

1887	Phi-a	31	109	12	21	3	0	0	14	3		.193	.214	.220	21	-12	8			.865	-7	C-28/O-3	-1.3
1888	Phi-a	42	161	13	25	6	0	0	12	4		.155	.181	.193	20	-14	2			.912	-2	C-42	-1.1
1890	Bal-a	18	67	6	16	4	1	0	9	4		.239	.282	.328	76	-2	3			.930	2	C-18	0.1
1891	Bal-a	61	204	29	39	5	4	0	18	20	21	.191	.263	.255	52	-13	3			.909	-11	C-58/O-3	-1.6
Total	4	152	541	60	101	18	5	0	53	31	21	.187	.239	.238	40	-41	16			.905	-17	C-146/O-6	-3.9

■ JIM TOY Toy, James Madison b: 2/20/1858, Beaver Falls, Pa. d: 3/13/19, Beaver Falls, Pa. 5'6", 160 lbs. Deb: 4/20/1887

1887	Cle-a	109	423	56	94	20	5	1	56	17		.222	.256	.300	56	-25	8			.975	3	1-82,O-11,C-10,/3S	-2.5
1890	Bro-a	44	160	11	29	3	0	1	7	11		.181	.238	.200	30	-14	2			.867	-1	C-44	-0.9
Total	2	153	583	67	123	23	5	1	63	28		.211	.251	.273	50	-39	10			.859	3	/1-82,C-54,O-11,3S	-3.4

■ JIM TRABER Traber, James Joseph b: 12/26/61, Columbus, Ohio BL/TL, 6', 194 lbs. Deb: 9/21/84

1984	Bal-A	10	21	3	5	0	0	0	2	2	4	.238	.304	.238	54	-1	0	0	0	.000	0	/D-9	-0.1
1986	Bal-A	65	212	28	54	7	0	13	44	18	31	.255	.328	.472	116	4	0	0	0	.988	1	1-29,D-21/O-8	0.3
1988	Bal-A	103	352	25	78	6	0	10	45	19	42	.222	.260	.324	65	-17	1	2	-1	.990	8	1-57,D-30,O-11	-1.6
1989	Bal-A	86	234	14	49	8	0	4	26	19	41	.209	.269	.295	61	-12	4	3	-1	.998	5	1-69/D-5	-1.3
Total	4	264	819	70	186	21	0	27	117	58	118	.227	.283	.352	77	-26	5	5	-2	.993	15	1-155/D-65,O-19	-2.7

■ DICK TRACEWSKI Tracewski, Richard Joseph b: 2/3/35, Eynon, Pa. BR/TR, 5'11", 167 lbs. Deb: 4/12/62 MC

1962	LA-N	15	2	3	0	0	0	0	0	2	0	.000	.500	.000	50	1	0	0	0	1.000	2	/S-4	0.2
1963	*LA-N	104	217	23	49	2	1	1	10	19	39	.226	.288	.258	63	-10	2	3	-1	.957	19	S-81,2-23	1.3
1964	LA-N	106	304	31	75	13	4	1	26	31	61	.247	.316	.326	88	-5	3	3	-1	.970	-2	2-56,3-30,S-19	-0.1
1965	*LA-N	78	186	17	40	6	1	0	20	25	30	.215	.315	.263	69	-7	2	6	-3	.950	8	3-53,2-14/S-7	-0.2
1966	Det-A	81	124	15	24	4	1	0	7	10	32	.194	.254	.218	36	-10	1	1	0	.947	11	2-70/S-3	0.2
1967	Det-A	74	107	19	30	4	2	1	9	8	22	.280	.330	.383	107	1	1	1	0	.965	9	S-44,2-12,3-10	1.3
1968	*Det-A	90	212	30	33	3	1	4	15	24	51	.156	.242	.236	44	-14	0	1	0	.982	-5	S-51,3-16,2-14	-1.6
1969	Det-A	66	79	10	11	1	2	0	4	15	20	.139	.277	.165	25	-8	1	1	0	.957	16	S-41,2-13/3-6	1.2
Total	8	614	1231	148	262	31	9	8	91	134	253	.213	.291	.272	65	-53	15	14	-4	.958	60	S-250,2-202,3-115	2.4

■ JIM TRACY Tracy, James Edwin b: 12/31/55, Hamilton, Ohio BL/TR, 6', 185 lbs. Deb: 7/20/80

1980	Chi-N	42	122	12	31	3	3	3	9	13	37	.254	.326	.402	95	-1	2	2	-1	.950	-7	O-31/1-1	-1.0
1981	Chi-N	45	63	6	15	2	1	0	5	12	14	.238	.360	.302	85	-1	1	0	0	1.000	1	O-11	-0.2
Total	2	87	185	18	46	5	4	3	14	25	51	.249	.338	.368	92	-2	3	2	-0	.964	-8	/O-42,1-1	-1.2

■ JOHN TRAFFLEY Traffley, John M. b: 1862, Chicago, Ill. d: 5/15/1900, Baltimore, Md. 5'9", 180 lbs. Deb: 6/15/1889 F

| 1889 | Lou-a | 1 | 2 | 0 | 1 | 0 | 0 | 0 | 0 | 1 | | .500 | .500 | .500 | 189 | 0 | 1 | 0 | | .000 | -1 | /O-1 | 0.0 |

YEAR	TM/L	G	AB	R	H	2B	3B	HR	RBI	BB	SO	AVG	OBP	SLG	PRO+	BR/A	SB	CS	SBR	FA	FR	G/POS	TPR

■ BILL TRAFFLEY   Traffley, William Franklin   b: 12/21/1859, Staten Island, N.Y   d: 6/23/08, Des Moines, Iowa   BR/TR, 5'11.5", 185 lbs.   Deb: 7/27/1878   F

1878	Chi-N	2	9	1	1	0	0	0	0	1	0	.111	.111	.111	-25	-1				1.000	-1	/C-2	-0.2
1883	Cin-a	30	105	17	21	5	0	0	8	4		.200	.229	.248	51	-6				.851	2	C-29/S-2	-0.2
1884	Bal-a	53	210	25	37	4	6	0		3		.176	.192	.252	42	-13				.926	-8	C-47/O-6,1-1	-1.6
1885	Bal-a	69	254	27	39	4	5	1	20	17		.154	.215	.220	38	-17				**.943**	2	C-61,O-10/2-3	-0.9
1886	Bal-a	25	85	15	18	0	1	0	7	10		.212	.295	.235	68	-3	8			.952	-3	C-25	-0.2
Total	5	179	663	85	116	13	12	1	<u>36</u>	34	<u>1</u>	.175	.220	.235	45	-40	8			.927	-8	C-164/O-16,2-3,S1	-3.1

■ WALT TRAGESSER   Tragesser, Walter Joseph   b: 6/14/1887, Lafayette, Ind.   d: 12/14/70, Lafayette, Ind.   BR/TR, 6', 175 lbs.   Deb: 7/30/13

1913	Bos-N	2	0	0	0	0	0	0	0	0		—	—	—	—		0			1.000	-0	/C-2	0.0
1915	Bos-N	7	7	1	0	0	0	0	0	0	2	.000	.000	.000	-99	-2	0			.944	1	/C-7	-0.1
1916	Bos-N	41	54	3	11	1	0	0	4	5	10	.204	.283	.222	59	-2	0			.971	4	C-29	0.3
1917	Bos-N	98	297	23	66	10	2	0	25	15	36	.222	.264	.269	68	-12	5			.971	-2	C-94	-0.7
1918	Bos-N	7	1	0	0	0	0	0	0	0	0	.000	.000	.000	-99	-0	0			.833	1	/C-7	0.0
1919	Bos-N	20	40	3	7	2	0	0	3	2	10	.175	.233	.225	39	-3	1			.959	-0	C-14	-0.3
	Phi-N	35	114	7	27	7	0	0	8	9	31	.237	.298	.298	74	-3	4			.953	4	C-34	0.4
	Yr	55	154	10	34	9	0	0	11	11	41	.221	.281	.279	67	-6	5			.954	4	C-48	0.1
1920	Phi-N	62	176	17	37	11	1	6	26	4	36	.210	.236	.386	73	-7	4	0	1	.944	-13	C-52	-1.6
Total	7	272	689	54	148	31	3	6	66	35	125	.215	.260	.295	67	-29	14	<u>0</u>		.961	-6	C-239	-2.0

■ RED TRAMBACK   Tramback, Stephen Joseph   b: 11/1/15, Iselin, Pa.   d: 12/28/79, Buffalo, N.Y.   BL/TL, 6', 175 lbs.   Deb: 9/15/40

1940	NY-N	2	4	0	1	0	0	0	0	1	1	.250	.400	.250	82	-0	1			.667	-0	/O-1	0.0

■ ALAN TRAMMELL   Trammell, Alan Stuart   b: 2/21/58, Garden Grove, Cal.   BR/TR, 6', 175 lbs.   Deb: 9/9/77

1977	Det-A	19	43	6	8	0	0	0	0	4	12	.186	.255	.186	21	-5	0	0	0	.961	-7	S-19	-1.0
1978	Det-A	139	448	49	120	14	6	2	34	45	56	.268	.337	.339	88	-6	3	1	0	.979	6	*S-139	1.7
1979	Det-A	142	460	68	127	11	4	6	50	43	55	.276	.338	.357	85	-9	17	14	-3	.961	-14	*S-142	-1.1
1980	Det-A	146	560	107	168	21	5	9	65	69	63	.300	.380	.404	112	11	12	12	-4	.980	-27	*S-144	-0.2
1981	Det-A	105	392	52	101	15	3	2	31	49	31	.258	.345	.327	91	-3	10	3	1	.983	6	*S-105	1.5
1982	Det-A	157	489	66	126	34	3	9	57	52	47	.258	.329	.395	97	-2	19	8	1	.978	-8	*S-157	0.6
1983	Det-A	142	505	83	161	31	2	14	66	57	64	.319	.388	.471	139	28	30	10	3	.979	-18	*S-140	2.6
1984	*Det-A†	139	555	85	174	34	5	14	69	60	63	.314	.383	.468	135	27	19	13	-2	.980	-12	*S-114,D-22	2.4
1985	Det-A	149	605	79	156	21	7	13	57	50	71	.258	.317	.380	90	-8	14	5	1	.977	-16	*S-149	-0.8
1986	Det-A	151	574	107	159	33	7	21	75	59	57	.277	.350	.469	121	16	25	12	0	.969	6	*S-149/D-2	3.5
1987	*Det-A★	151	597	109	205	34	3	28	105	60	47	.343	.406	.551	157	49	21	2	5	.971	-10	*S-149	5.4
1988	Det-A†	128	466	73	145	24	1	15	69	46	46	.311	.373	.464	140	25	7	4	-0	.980	-7	*S-125	2.8
1989	Det-A	121	449	54	109	20	3	5	43	45	45	.243	.317	.334	86	-8	10	2	-2	.985	12	*S-117/D-2	1.6
1990	Det-A★	146	559	71	170	37	1	14	89	68	55	.304	.381	.449	130	24	12	10	-2	.979	1	*S-142/D-3	3.3
1991	Det-A	101	375	57	93	20	0	9	55	37	39	.248	.320	.373	90	-5	11	2	2	.979	4	S-92/D-6	0.8
1992	Det-A	29	102	11	28	7	1	1	11	15	4	.275	.373	.392	114	2	2	2	-1	.977	-1	S-27/D-1	0.3
1993	Det-A	112	401	72	132	25	3	12	60	38	38	.329	.390	.496	137	21	12	8	1	.989	-13	S-63,3-35/O-8,D-6	1.1
1994	Det-A	76	292	38	78	17	1	8	28	16	35	.267	.307	.414	84	-8	3	0	1	.968	-4	S-63,D-11	-0.6
1995	Det-A	74	223	28	60	12	0	2	23	27	19	.269	.348	.350	83	-5	3	1	0	.980	-6	S-60/D-6	-0.5
1996	Det-A	66	193	16	45	2	0	1	16	10	27	.233	.271	.259	35	-19	6	0	2	.976	-4	S-43,2-11/3-8,O-1	-1.6
Total	20	2293	8288	1231	2365	412	55	185	1003	850	874	.285	.354	.415	110	126	236	109	5	.977	-111	*S-2139/D-59,320	21.8

■ CECIL TRAVIS   Travis, Cecil Howell   b: 8/8/13, Riverdale, Ga.   BL/TR, 6'1.5", 185 lbs.   Deb: 5/16/33

1933	Was-A	18	43	7	13	1	0	0	2	2	5	.302	.348	.326	80	-1	0	0	0	.974	4	3-15	0.3
1934	Was-A	109	392	48	125	22	4	1	53	24	37	.319	.361	.403	101	0	1	5	-3	.937	3	3-99	0.4
1935	Was-A	138	534	85	170	27	8	0	61	41	28	.318	.371	.399	104	4	4	2	0	.963	21	*3-114,O-16	2.7
1936	Was-A	138	517	77	164	34	10	2	92	39	21	.317	.366	.433	102	1	4	4	-1	.938	-13	S-71,O-53/2-4,3-2	-0.9
1937	Was-A	135	526	72	181	27	7	0	66	39	34	.344	.395	.439	115	13	3	2	-0	.965	-11	*S-129	1.0
1938	Was-A☆	146	567	96	190	30	5	5	67	58	22	.335	.401	.432	117	16	6	5	-1	.950	3	*S-143	2.6
1939	Was-A	130	476	55	139	20	9	5	63	34	25	.292	.342	.403	97	-3	0	3	-2	.958	-4	*S-118	0.1
1940	Was-A★	136	528	60	170	37	11	2	76	48	23	.322	.381	.445	121	16	0	1	-1	.934	16	*3-113,S-23	3.3
1941	Was-A★	152	608	106	**218**	39	19	7	101	52	25	.359	.410	.520	152	44	2	2	-1	.964	2	*S-136,3-16	5.3
1945	Was-A	15	54	4	13	2	1	0	10	4	5	.241	.293	.315	83	-1	0	1	0	.920	3	S-14	-0.1
1946	Was-A	137	465	45	117	22	3	1	56	45	47	.252	.323	.318	85	-10	2	4	-0	.959	-19	S-75,3-56	-2.7
1947	Was-A	74	204	10	44	4	1	1	10	18	27	.216	.273	.260	50	-14	1	3	-2	.932	-2	3-39,S-15	-1.8
Total	12	1328	4914	665	1544	265	78	27	657	402	291	.314	.370	.416	109	64	23	32	-12	.955	5	S-710,3-468/O-69,2	10.2

■ BRIAN TRAXLER   Traxler, Brian Lee   b: 9/26/67, Waukegan, Ill.   BL/TL, 5'10", 200 lbs.   Deb: 4/24/90

1990	LA-N	9	11	0	1	1	0	0	0	1	2	.091	.091	.182	-28	-2	0	0	0	1.000	1	/1-3	-0.2

■ JIM TRAY   Tray, James   b: 2/14/1860, Jackson, Mich.   d: 7/28/05, Jackson, Mich.   5'11", 180 lbs.   Deb: 9/6/1884

1884	Ind-a	6	21	2	6	0	0	0		2		.286	.348	.286	112	0				.857	-2	/C-4,1-2	-0.1

■ PIE TRAYNOR   Traynor, Harold Joseph   b: 11/11/1899, Framingham, Mass.   d: 3/16/72, Pittsburgh, Pa.   BR/TR, 6', 170 lbs.   Deb: 9/15/20   MH

1920	Pit-N	17	52	6	11	3	1	0	3	3	6	.212	.268	.308	63	-3	1	3	-2	.860	-6	S-17	-0.9
1921	Pit-N	7	19	0	5	0	0	0	2	1	2	.263	.300	.263	49	-1	0	0	0	.917	1	/3-3,S-1	0.0
1922	Pit-N	142	571	89	161	17	12	4	81	27	28	.282	.319	.375	77	-20	17	3	3	.945	-6	*3-124,S-18	-1.0
1923	Pit-N	153	616	108	208	19	**19**	12	101	34	19	.338	.377	.489	124	20	28	13	1	.950	8	*3-152/S-1	4.0
1924	Pit-N	142	545	86	160	26	13	5	82	37	26	.294	.340	.417	100	-1	24	18	-4	.968	9	*3-141	1.5
1925	*Pit-N	150	591	114	189	39	14	6	106	52	19	.320	.377	.464	106	5	15	9	-1	**.957**	23	*3-150/S-1	3.5
1926	Pit-N	152	574	83	182	25	17	3	92	38	14	.317	.361	.436	108	5	8			.952	-7	*3-148/S-3	2.1
1927	*Pit-N	149	573	93	196	32	9	5	106	22	11	.342	.370	.455	112	8	11			.962	13	*3-143/S-9	2.8
1928	Pit-N	144	569	91	192	38	12	3	124	28	10	.337	.370	.462	112	9	12			.946	4	*3-144	2.0
1929	Pit-N	130	540	94	192	27	12	4	108	30	7	.356	.393	.472	111	9	13			.951	-1	*3-130	1.2
1930	Pit-N	130	497	90	182	22	11	9	119	48	19	.366	.423	.509	124	24	7			.941	5	*3-130	2.9
1931	Pit-N	155	615	81	183	37	15	2	103	54	28	.298	.354	.416	107	6	6			.925	-9	*3-155	0.7
1932	Pit-N	135	513	74	169	27	10	2	68	32	20	.329	.373	.433	118	13	3			.936	-3	*3-127	1.9
1933	Pit-N★	154	624	85	190	27	6	1	82	35	24	.304	.342	.372	104	3	5			.946	-1	*3-154	1.3
1934	Pit-N★	119	444	62	137	22	10	1	61	21	27	.309	.341	.410	98	-2	3			.954	-10	*3-110,M	-0.7
1935	Pit-N	57	204	24	57	10	3	1	36	10	17	.279	.323	.373	84	-5	2			.888	-3	3-49/1-1,M	-0.6
1937	Pit-N	5	3	2	0	0	0	0	1	0	0	.167	.167	.167	-9	-2	0			1.000	1	/3-3,M	0.0
Total	17	1941	7559	1183	2416	371	164	58	1273	472	278	.320	.362	.435	107	68	158	<u>46</u>		.947	31	*3-1863/S-50,1-1	20.7

■ FRED TREACEY   Treacey, Frederick S.   b: 1847, Brooklyn, N.Y.   5'9.5", 145 lbs.   Deb: 5/16/1871   F

1871	Chi-n	25	124	39	42	7	5	**4**	33	2	9	.339	.349	.573	144	5	13	5	1	**.918**	7	*O-25	0.9
1872	Ath-n	47	236	53	65	7	3	2	29	5	10	.275	.290	.356	97	-1	7	5	-1	.814	-2	*O-47	-0.1
1873	Phi-n	51	243	49	62	7	2	1	32	5	6	.255	.270	.313	70	-10	5		-1	.771	5	*O-51	-0.4
1874	Chi-n	35	148	18	28	5	0	0	12	0	6	.189	.200	.223	35	-10	4	4	-1	.790	7	O-35	-0.3
1875	Cen-n	11	46	9	12	3	0	0		2	1	.261	.292	.326	124	1	1	0	0	.848	1	O-11	0.3
	Phi-n	43	179	23	38	3	0	0	15	1	3	.212	.217	.263	63	-7	6	3	-1	.858	2	O-43	-0.1
	Yr	54	225	32	50	6	0	0	17	3	3	.222	.232	.276	75	-6	7	3	-1	.856	4	O-54	-0.1
1876	NY-N	57	256	47	54	5	1	0	18	1	5	.211	.214	.238	58	-10			-2	.844	12	*O-57	0.1
Total	5 n	212	976	191	247	32	13	7	123	17	30	.253	.265	.334	84	-21	33	20	-2	.826	20	O-212	0.0

■ PETE TREACEY   Treacey, Peter   b: 1852, Brooklyn, N.Y.   Deb: 8/5/1876   F

1876	NY-N	2	5	1	0	1	0	0	0	0	1	.000	.167	.000	-46	-1				.750	-1	/S-2	-0.2

YEAR	TM/L	G	AB	R	H	2B	3B	HR	RBI	BB	SO	AVG	OBP	SLG	PRO+	BR/A	SB	CS	SBR	FA	FR	G/POS	TPR

■ RAY TREADAWAY
Treadaway, Edgar Raymond b: 10/31/07, Ragland, Ala. d: 10/12/35, Chattanooga, Tenn. BL/TR, 5'7", 150 lbs. Deb: 9/17/30

1930	Was-A	6	19	1	4	2	0	0	1	0	3	.211	.211	.316	31	-2	0	0	0	.833	-1	/3-4	-0.3

■ GEORGE TREADAWAY
Treadaway, George B. BL , 6', 185 lbs. Deb: 4/27/1893

1893	Bal-N	115	458	78	119	16	17	1	67	58	50	.260	.348	.376	91	-7	24			.901	9	*O-115	-0.3
1894	Bro-N	123	479	124	157	27	26	4	102	72	43	.328	.418	.518	134	28	27			.892	1	*O-122/1-1	1.6
1895	Bro-N	86	339	54	87	14	3	7	54	33	22	.257	.326	.378	88	-6	9			.886	-9	O-86	-1.8
1896	Lou-N	2	7	0	1	0	0	0	1	1	0	.143	.250	.143	5	-1	0			.500	-1	/O-1,1-1	-0.2
Total	4	326	1283	256	364	57	46	12	224	164	115	.284	.368	.428	106	14	60			.891	-0	O-324/1-2	-0.7

■ JEFF TREADAWAY
Treadaway, Hugh Jeffery b: 1/22/63, Columbus, Ga. BL/TR, 5'10", 170 lbs. Deb: 9/4/87

1987	Cin-N	23	84	9	28	4	0	2	4	2	6	.333	.356	.452	108	1	1	0	0	.958	-7	2-21	-0.5
1988	Cin-N	103	301	30	76	19	4	2	23	27	30	.252	.320	.362	92	-3	2	0	1	.984	3	2-97/3-2	0.4
1989	Atl-N	134	473	58	131	18	3	8	40	30	38	.277	.320	.378	96	-3	3	2	0	.981	3	*2-123/3-6	0.5
1990	Atl-N	128	474	56	134	20	2	11	59	25	42	.283	.323	.403	93	-5	3	4	-2	.976	10	*2-122	0.6
1991	*Atl-N	106	306	41	98	17	2	3	32	23	19	.320	.372	.418	115	6	2	2	-1	.960	-8	2-93	0.0
1992	*Atl-N	61	126	5	28	6	1	0	5	9	16	.222	.274	.286	55	-7	1	2	-1	.993	1	2-45/3-1	-0.8
1993	Cle-A	97	221	25	67	14	1	2	27	14	21	.303	.350	.403	102	1	1	1	-0	.933	1	3-42,2-19/D-4	0.2
1994	LA-N	52	67	14	20	3	0	0	5	5	8	.299	.356	.343	89	-1	1	1	-0	.950	-1	2-24/3-3	-0.1
1995	LA-N	17	17	2	2	0	1	0	3	0	2	.118	.118	.235	-11	-3	0	0	0	.000	-1	/3-2,2-1	-0.3
	Mon-N	41	50	4	12	2	0	0	10	5	2	.240	.309	.280	55	-3	0	1	-1	1.000	-2	2-11/3-1	-0.5
	Yr	58	67	6	14	2	1	0	13	5	4	.209	.264	.269	41	-6	0	1	-1	1.000	-2	2-12/3-3	-0.8
Total	9	762	2119	244	596	103	14	28	208	140	184	.281	.329	.383	94	-17	14	13	-4	.975	-1	2-556/3-57,D-4	-0.5

■ RED TREADAWAY
Treadaway, Thadford Leon b: 4/28/20, Athalone, N.C. d: 5/26/94, Atlanta, Ga. BL/TR, 5'10", 175 lbs. Deb: 7/25/44

1944	NY-N	50	170	23	51	5	2	0	5	13	11	.300	.350	.353	98	-0	2			.957	1	O-38	-0.1
1945	NY-N	88	224	31	54	4	2	4	23	20	13	.241	.303	.330	75	-8	3			.940	-9	O-60	-2.0
Total	2	138	394	54	105	9	4	4	28	33	24	.266	.323	.340	85	-8	5			.948	-8	/O-98	-2.1

■ FRANK TRECHOCK
Trechock, Frank Adam b: 12/24/15, Windber, Pa. d: 1/16/89, Minneapolis, Minn. BR/TR, 5'10", 175 lbs. Deb: 9/19/37

1937	Was-A	1	4	0	2	0	0	0	1	0	0	.500	.500	.500	160	0	0	0	0	.750	0	/S-1	0.1

■ NICK TREMARK
Tremark, Nicholas Joseph b: 10/15/12, Yonkers, N.Y. BL/TL, 5'5", 150 lbs. Deb: 8/9/34

1934	Bro-N	17	28	3	7	1	0	0	6	2	2	.250	.300	.286	61	-2	0			1.000	-1	/O-9	-0.3
1935	Bro-N	10	13	1	3	1	0	0	3	1	1	.231	.286	.308	61	-1	0			1.000	-1	/O-4	-0.1
1936	Bro-N	8	32	6	8	2	0	0	1	3	2	.250	.333	.313	74	-1	0			1.000	1	/O-8	0.0
Total	3	35	73	10	18	4	0	0	10	6	5	.247	.313	.301	67	-3	0			1.000	-0	/O-21	-0.4

■ CHRIS TREMIE
Tremie, Christopher James b: 10/17/69, Houston, Tex. BR/TR, 6', 200 lbs. Deb: 7/1/95

1995	Chi-A	10	24	0	4	0	0	0	0	1	2	.167	.200	.167	-3	-4	0	0	0	.976	-1	/C-9,D-1	-0.4

■ OVERTON TREMPER
Tremper, Carlton Overton b: 3/22/06, Brooklyn, N.Y. d: 1/9/96, Clearwater, Fla. BR/TR, 5'10", 163 lbs. Deb: 6/16/27

1927	Bro-N	26	60	4	14	0	0	0	4	0	2	.233	.246	.233	29	-6	0			1.000	-4	O-18	-1.1
1928	Bro-N	10	31	1	6	2	1	0	1	0	1	.194	.194	.323	33	-3	0			1.000	-0	O-9	-0.4
Total	2	36	91	5	20	2	1	0	5	0	3	.220	.228	.264	30	-9	0			1.000	-4	/O-27	-1.5

■ GEORGE TRENWITH
Trenwith, George b: Ireland d: 2/1/1890, Philadelphia, Pa. Deb: 4/30/1875

1875	Cen-n	10	45	5	8	2	0	0	4	1	2	.178	.196	.222	49	-2	0	0	0	.583	-6	3-10	-0.7
	NH-n	6	25	1	6	2	0	0	3	0	1	.240	.240	.320	106	0	0	0	0	.692	-2	/3-6	-0.1
	Yr	16	70	6	14	4	0	0	7	1	3	.200	.211	.257	69	-2	0	0	0	.629	-8	3-16	-0.8

■ MIKE TRESH
Tresh, Michael b: 2/23/14, Hazleton, Pa. d: 10/4/66, Detroit, Mich. BR/TR, 5'11", 170 lbs. Deb: 9/4/38 F

1938	Chi-A	10	29	3	7	0	0	0	2	8	4	.241	.405	.310	80	-1	0			.978	2	C-10	0.1
1939	Chi-A	119	352	49	91	5	2	0	38	64	30	.259	.377	.284	70	-13	3	2	-0	.985	2	*C-119	-0.5
1940	Chi-A	135	480	62	135	15	5	1	64	49	40	.281	.349	.340	78	-14	3	10	-5	.983	7	*C-135	-0.1
1941	Chi-A	115	390	38	98	10	1	0	33	38	27	.251	.319	.282	61	-21	1	0	0	.981	10	*C-115	-0.1
1942	Chi-A	72	233	21	54	8	1	0	15	28	24	.232	.314	.275	68	-9	2	0	1	.977	-6	C-72	-0.9
1943	Chi-A	86	279	20	60	3	0	0	20	37	20	.215	.307	.226	57	-14	2	1	0	.982	-1	C-85	-0.9
1944	Chi-A	93	312	22	81	8	1	0	25	37	15	.260	.342	.292	83	-5	0	3	-2	.981	-3	C-93	-0.5
1945	Chi-A†	150	458	50	114	12	4	0	47	65	37	.249	.342	.275	82	-8	6	3	0	.984	-2	*C-150	-0.1
1946	Chi-A	80	217	28	47	5	2	0	21	36	24	.217	.336	.258	70	-5	2	1	0	.995	14	C-79	1.0
1947	Chi-A	90	274	19	66	6	2	0	20	26	26	.241	.311	.277	67	-12	2	0	1	.975	-7	C-89	-1.3
1948	Chi-A	39	108	10	27	1	0	1	11	9	9	.250	.308	.287	61	-6	0	0	0	.983	-1	C-34	-0.5
1949	Cle-A	38	37	4	8	0	0	0	1	5	7	.216	.310	.216	41	-3	0	0	0	1.000	6	C-38	0.3
Total	12	1027	3169	326	788	75	14	2	297	402	263	.249	.335	.283	71	-113	19	21	-7	.983	22	*C-1019	-3.5

■ TOM TRESH
Tresh, Thomas Michael b: 9/20/37, Detroit, Mich. BB/TR, 6', 191 lbs. Deb: 9/3/61 F

1961	NY-A	9	8	1	2	0	0	0	0	0	1	.250	.250	.250	36	-1	0	0	0	1.000	3	/S-3	0.2
1962	*NY-A★	157	622	94	178	26	5	20	93	67	74	.286	.359	.441	119	17	4	8	-4	.970	-11	*S-111,O-43	1.0
1963	*NY-A★	145	520	91	140	28	5	25	71	83	79	.269	.374	.487	140	29	3	3	-1	.981	2	*O-144	2.4
1964	*NY-A	153	533	75	131	25	5	16	73	73	110	.246	.344	.402	105	5	13	0	4	.996	-14	*O-146	-1.3
1965	NY-A	156	602	94	168	29	6	26	74	59	92	.279	.348	.477	133	25	5	2	0	.970	-21	*O-154	-0.3
1966	NY-A	151	537	76	125	12	4	27	68	86	89	.233	.345	.421	123	18	5	4	-1	.985	28	O-84,3-64	4.1
1967	NY-A	130	448	45	98	23	3	14	53	50	86	.219	.303	.377	104	2	1	0	0	.972	4	*O-118	-0.1
1968	NY-A	152	507	60	99	18	3	11	52	76	97	.195	.305	.308	89	-5	10	5	0	.951	9	*S-119,O-27	1.7
1969	NY-A	45	143	16	26	5	2	1	9	17	23	.182	.269	.266	52	-9	2	1	0	.980	1	S-41	-0.5
	Det-A	94	331	46	74	13	1	13	37	39	47	.224	.309	.387	90	-5	2	1	-1	.965	-18	S-77,O-11/3-1	-1.7
	Yr	139	474	59	100	18	3	14	46	56	70	.211	.297	.350	79	-14	4	3	-1	.971	-18	*S-118,O-11/3-1	-2.2
Total	9	1192	4251	595	1041	179	34	153	530	550	698	.245	.337	.411	113	75	45	25	-2	.979	-19	O-727,S-351/3-65	5.5

■ ALEX TREVINO
Trevino, Alejandro (Castro) b: 8/26/57, Monterrey, Mex. BR/TR, 5'11", 170 lbs. Deb: 9/11/78 F

1978	NY-N	6	12	3	3	0	0	0	2	1	1	.250	.308	.250	60	-1	0	0	0	1.000	0	/C-5,3-1	-0.1
1979	NY-N	79	207	24	56	11	1	0	20	20	27	.271	.338	.333	87	-3	2	2	-1	.976	10	C-36,3-27/2-8	0.7
1980	NY-N	106	355	26	91	11	2	0	37	13	41	.256	.285	.299	65	-17	0	3	-2	.977	-5	C-86,3-14/2-1	-2.2
1981	NY-N	56	149	17	39	2	0	0	10	13	19	.262	.325	.275	73	-5	3	0	1	.963	2	C-45/2-4,O-2,3-1	-0.2
1982	Cin-N	120	355	24	89	10	3	1	33	34	34	.251	.321	.304	74	-11	3	1	0	.979	4	*C-116/3-2	-0.3
1983	Cin-N	74	167	14	36	8	1	1	13	17	20	.216	.288	.293	59	-9	0	0	0	.987	11	C-63/3-4,2-1	0.4
1984	Cin-N	6	6	0	1	0	0	0	0	0	2	.167	.167	.167	-6	-1	0	0	0	1.000	-0	/C-4	-0.1
	Atl-N	79	266	36	65	16	0	3	28	16	27	.244	.290	.338	71	-10	5	2	0	.989	7	C-79	0.0
	Yr	85	272	36	66	16	0	3	28	16	29	.243	.287	.335	69	-11	5	2	0	.989	6	C-83	-0.1
1985	SF-N	57	157	17	34	10	1	6	19	20	24	.217	.305	.408	103	2	0	0	0	.978	-5	C-55/3-1	0.2
1986	LA-N	89	202	31	53	13	0	4	26	27	35	.262	.352	.386	111	3	1	1	-1	.969	-4	C-63/1-1	0.3
1987	LA-N	72	144	16	32	7	1	3	16	6	28	.222	.273	.347	65	-8	1	0	0	.987	-3	C-45/O-2,3-1	-0.8
1988	Hou-N	78	193	19	48	17	0	2	13	24	29	.249	.341	.368	108	2	1	0	0	.977	-3	C-74/O-1	-0.2
1989	Hou-N	59	131	15	38	7	1	2	16	7	18	.290	.331	.405	113	2	0	0	0	.989	0	C-32/1-2,3-2	0.0
1990	Hou-N	42	69	3	13	3	0	1	5	6	11	.188	.273	.275	53	-4	0	1	-1	.992	6	C-30/1-1	-0.0
	NY-N	9	10	0	3	1	0	0	3	1	0	.300	.364	.400	110	0	0	0	0	.929	0	/C-7	0.1
	Cin-N	7	7	0	3	0	0	1	3	0	2	.429	.500	.571	186	1	0	0	0	1.000	1	/C-2	0.2
	Yr	58	86	3	19	4	0	2	11	7	13	.221	.302	.314	71	-3	0	1	-1	.982	7	C-39/1-1	0.3
Total	13	939	2430	245	604	117	10	23	244	205	317	.249	.312	.333	81	-61	19	11	-2	.979	16	C-742/3-53,2-14,O,1	-1.6

YEAR	TM/L	G	AB	R	H	2B	3B	HR	RBI	BB	SO	AVG	OBP	SLG	PRO+	BR/A	SB	CS	SBR	FA	FR	G/POS	TPR

■ BOBBY TREVINO   Trevino, Carlos (Castro) b: 8/15/43, Monterrey, Mexico   BR/TR, 6'2", 185 lbs.   Deb: 5/22/68   F

| 1968 | Cal-A | 17 | 40 | 1 | 9 | 1 | 0 | 0 | 1 | 2 | 9 | .225 | .262 | .250 | 58 | -2 | 0 | 1 | -1 | .962 | -0 | O-11 | -0.4 |

■ GUS TRIANDOS   Triandos, Gus b: 7/30/30, San Francisco, Cal   BR/TR, 6'3", 215 lbs.   Deb: 8/13/53

1953	NY-A	18	51	5	8	2	0	1	6	3	9	.157	.204	.255	24	-6	0	0	0	.991	0	1-12/C-5	-0.6
1954	NY-A	2	1	0	0	0	0	0	0	0	1	.000	.000	.000	-99	-0	0	0	0	.000	0	/C-1	0.0
1955	Bal-A	140	481	47	133	17	3	12	65	40	55	.277	.335	.399	104	1	0	0	0	.989	0	*1-103,C-36/3-1	-0.4
1956	Bal-A	131	452	47	126	18	1	21	88	44	73	.279	.351	.462	122	12	0	0	0	.989	10	C-89,1-52	2.2
1957	Bal-A☆	129	418	44	106	21	1	19	72	38	73	.254	.320	.445	114	6	0	0	0	.992	-2	*C-120	0.9
1958	Bal-A★	137	474	59	116	10	0	30	79	60	65	.245	.331	.456	120	12	0	0	0	.987	1	*C-132	2.2
1959	Bal-A★	126	393	43	85	7	1	25	73	65	56	.216	.332	.430	110	5	0	0	0	.981	7	*C-125	1.4
1960	Bal-A	109	364	36	98	18	0	12	54	41	62	.269	.345	.418	107	3	0	0	0	.989	-7	*C-105	0.2
1961	Bal-A	115	397	35	97	21	0	17	63	44	60	.244	.321	.426	101	-0	0	0	0	.989	4	*C-114	0.9
1962	Bal-A	66	207	20	33	7	0	6	23	29	43	.159	.263	.280	49	-15	0	0	0	.985	-2	C-63	-1.5
1963	Det-A	106	327	28	78	13	0	14	41	32	67	.239	.318	.407	98	-1	0	0	0	**.998**	-6	C-90	-0.3
1964	Phi-N	73	188	17	47	9	0	8	33	26	41	.250	.344	.426	117	5	0	0	0	.985	-2	C-64/1-1	1.0
1965	Phi-N	30	82	3	14	2	0	1	4	9	17	.171	.253	.195	29	-8	0	0	0	.975	-5	C-28	-1.3
	Hou-N	24	72	5	13	2	0	2	7	5	14	.181	.244	.292	54	-5	0	0	0	.970	-2	C-20	-0.6
	Yr	54	154	8	27	4	0	2	11	14	31	.175	.249	.240	40	-12	0	0	0	.973	-7	C-48	-1.9
Total	13	1206	3907	389	954	147	6	167	608	440	636	.244	.324	.413	103	10	1	0	0	.987	-4	C-992,1-168/3-1	4.1

■ MANNY TRILLO   Trillo, Jesus Manuel Marcano (b: Jesus Manuel Marcano (Trillo))   b: 12/25/50, Caripito, Ven.   BR/TR, 6'1", 164 lbs.   Deb: 6/28/73

1973	Oak-A	17	12	0	3	2	0	0	3	0	4	.250	.250	.417	90	-0	0	0	0	.941	5	2-16	0.5
1974	*Oak-A	21	33	3	5	0	0	0	2	2	8	.152	.222	.152	10	-4	0	0	0	.949	6	2-21	0.2
1975	Chi-N	154	545	55	135	12	2	7	70	45	78	.248	.309	.316	70	-21	1	7	-4	.967	16	*2-153/S-1	-0.1
1976	Chi-N	158	582	42	139	24	3	4	59	53	70	.239	.306	.311	69	-23	17	6	2	.981	18	*2-156/S-1	0.7
1977	Chi-N★	152	504	51	141	18	5	7	57	44	58	.280	.344	.377	84	-11	3	5	-2	.970	30	*2-149	2.7
1978	Chi-N	152	552	53	144	17	5	4	55	50	67	.261	.325	.332	75	-18	0	7	-4	.978	**29**	*2-149	1.8
1979	Phi-N	118	431	49	112	22	1	6	42	20	59	.260	.299	.357	76	-15	4	7	-3	.985	2	*2-118	-0.4
1980	*Phi-N	141	531	68	155	25	9	4	43	32	46	.292	.336	.412	102	1	8	3	1	.987	19	*2-140	3.1
1981	*Phi-N★	94	349	37	100	14	3	6	36	26	37	.287	.341	.395	104	2	10	4	1	**.994**	11	2-94	2.0
1982	Phi-N	149	549	52	149	24	1	0	39	33	53	.271	.316	.319	76	-17	8	10	-4	**.994**	4	*2-149	-0.8
1983	Cle-A★	88	320	33	87	13	1	1	29	21	46	.272	.317	.328	75	-11	1	3	-2	.989	3	2-87	-0.5
	Mon-N	31	121	16	32	8	0	2	16	10	18	.264	.331	.380	97	-0	0	0	0	.979	-6	2-31	-0.5
1984	SF-N	98	401	45	102	21	1	4	36	25	55	.254	.303	.342	84	-9	0	0	0	.988	-8	2-96/3-4	-1.5
1985	SF-N	125	451	36	101	16	2	3	25	40	65	.224	.289	.288	65	-21	0	0	0	.981	4	2-120/3-1	-1.4
1986	Chi-N	81	152	22	45	10	0	1	19	16	21	.296	.363	.382	98	-0	0	2	-1	.949	-0	3-53,1-11/2-6	-0.2
1987	Chi-N	108	214	27	63	8	0	8	26	25	37	.294	.368	.444	110	3	0	3	-2	.994	-4	1-47,3-35,2-10/S-6	-0.6
1988	Chi-N	76	164	15	41	5	0	1	14	8	32	.250	.285	.299	65	-7	2	0	1	.994	-8	1-24,3-17,2-13,S-7	-0.7
1989	Cin-N	17	39	3	8	0	0	0	1	2	5	.205	.262	.205	34	-3	0	0	0	1.000	-4	2-10/1-3,S-1	-0.3
Total	17	1780	5950	598	1562	239	33	61	571	452	742	.263	.318	.345	80	-155	56	57	-17	.981	129	*2-1518,3-110/1S	3.5

■ COAKER TRIPLETT   Triplett, Herman Coaker b: 12/18/11, Boone, N.C.   d: 1/30/92, Boone, N.C.   BR/TR, 5'11", 185 lbs.   Deb: 4/19/38

1938	Chi-N	12	36	4	9	2	1	0	2	1	5	.250	.250	.361	65	-2	0			1.000	-1	/O-9	-0.3
1941	StL-N	76	185	29	53	6	3	3	21	18	27	.286	.350	.400	104	1	0			.965	-3	O-46	-0.4
1942	StL-N	64	154	18	42	7	4	1	23	17	15	.273	.345	.390	107	1	1			.966	-3	O-46	-0.4
1943	StL-N	9	25	1	2	0	0	1	4	1	6	.080	.115	.200	-9	-4	0			1.000	-0	/O-6	-0.4
	Phi-N	105	360	45	98	16	4	14	52	28	28	.272	.325	.456	129	11	2			.970	2	O-90	0.8
	Yr	114	385	46	100	16	4	15	56	29	34	.260	.312	.439	120	7	2			.972	1	O-96	0.4
1944	Phi-N	84	184	15	43	5	1	1	25	19	10	.234	.305	.288	70	-7	1			.989	-1	O-44	-1.0
1945	Phi-N	120	363	36	87	11	1	7	46	40	27	.240	.315	.333	83	-9	6			.945	-3	O-92	-1.7
Total	6	470	1307	148	334	47	14	27	173	123	114	.256	.320	.375	97	-8	10			.965	-9	O-333	-3.4

■ HAL TROSKY   Trosky, Harold Arthur Sr. (b: Harold Arthur Troyavesky Sr.)   b: 11/11/12, Norway, Iowa   d: 6/18/79, Cedar Rapids, Ia.   BL/TR, 6'2", 207 lbs.   Deb: 9/11/33   F

1933	Cle-A	11	44	6	13	1	2	1	8	2	12	.295	.340	.477	110	0	0	0	0	.990	-1	1-11	-0.1
1934	Cle-A	154	625	117	206	45	9	35	142	58	49	.330	.388	.598	149	42	2	1	-1	.986	0	*1-154	2.5
1935	Cle-A	154	632	84	171	33	7	26	113	46	60	.271	.321	.468	100	-4	1	2	-1	.993	-1	*1-153	-1.9
1936	Cle-A	151	629	124	216	45	9	42	**162**	36	58	.343	.382	.644	148	41	6	5	-1	.985	1	*1-151/2-1	2.3
1937	Cle-A	153	601	104	179	36	9	32	128	65	60	.298	.367	.547	127	21	3	1	1	.993	-2	*1-152	0.2
1938	Cle-A	150	554	106	185	40	4	19	110	67	40	.334	.407	.542	138	32	5	1	1	.993	4	*1-148	1.8
1939	Cle-A	122	448	89	150	31	4	25	104	52	28	.335	.405	.589	157	37	2	3	-1	.992	11	*1-118	3.1
1940	Cle-A	140	522	85	154	39	4	25	93	79	45	.295	.392	.529	140	31	1	7	-5	.991	-7	*1-139	1.0
1941	Cle-A	89	310	43	91	17	0	11	51	44	21	.294	.383	.455	127	12	1	2	-1	.989	-3	1-85	0.3
1944	Chi-A	135	497	55	120	32	2	10	70	62	30	.241	.327	.374	101	1	3	2	-0	.993	-9	*1-130	-1.7
1946	Chi-A	88	299	22	76	12	3	2	31	34	37	.254	.330	.334	89	-4	4	3	-1	.991	-8	1-80	-1.8
Total	11	1347	5161	835	1561	331	58	228	1012	545	440	.302	.371	.522	130	210	28	23	-5	.991	-12	*1-1321/2-1	5.7

■ MIKE TROST   Trost, Michael J. b: 1866, Philadelphia, Pa.   d: 3/24/01, Philadelphia, Pa.   TR , 6'0.5", 180 lbs.   Deb: 8/21/1890

1890	StL-a	17	51	10	13	2	0	1	7	6		.255	.345	.353	93	-1	4			.890	1	C-13/O-4	0.0
1895	Lou-N	3	12	1	1	0	0	0	1	0	1	.083	.083	.083	-61	-3	1			1.000	-1	/1-3	-0.3
Total	2	20	63	11	14	2	0	1	8	6	1	.222	.300	.302	66	-4	5			.890	0	/C-13,O-4,1-3	-0.3

■ SAM TROTT   Trott, Samuel W. b: 3/1859, Maryland   d: 6/5/25, Catonsville, Md.   BL/TL, 5'9", 190 lbs.   Deb: 5/29/1880   M

1880	Bos-N	39	125	14	26	4	1	0	9			.208	.227	.256	65	-4				.893	6	C-36/O-4	0.2
1881	Det-N	6	25	3	5	2	1	0	2	1	3	.200	.231	.360	80	-1				.868	-2	/C-6	-0.3
1882	Det-N	32	129	11	31	7	1	0	12	0	13	.240	.240	.310	75	-4				.890	7	C-23/S-3,2-3,103	0.3
1883	Det-N	75	295	27	72	14	1	0	29	10	23	.244	.269	.298	76	-8				.882	-17	2-42,C-34/O-6,1-1	-2.0
1884	Bal-a	71	284	36	73	17	9	3			4	.257	.272	.412	116	4				.931	16	C-60/2-6,O-5	2.3
1885	Bal-a	21	88	12	24	2	1	0	12	5		.273	.312	.341	108	1				.882	-5	C-17/O-4,2-2,S-1	-0.2
1887	Bal-a	85	300	44	77	16	3	0	37	27		.257	.322	.330	87	-4	8			.915	5	C-69,2-11/O-3,1S	0.6
1888	Bal-a	31	120	18	30	11	4	0	22	4		.250	.280	.454	145	5	1			.908	-4	C-27/O-3,2-1,1-1	0.3
Total	8	360	1354	166	338	73	22	3	123	54	44	.250	.280	.343	93	-11	9			.906	6	C-272/2-65,O1S3	1.2

■ QUINCY TROUPPE   Trouppe, Quincy Thomas b: 12/25/12, Dublin, Ga.   d: 8/12/93, Creve Coeur, Mo.   BB/TR, 6'2.5", 225 lbs.   Deb: 4/30/52

| 1952 | Cle-A | 6 | 10 | 1 | 1 | 0 | 0 | 0 | 1 | 3 | | .100 | .182 | .100 | -22 | -2 | 0 | 0 | 0 | 1.000 | 2 | /C-6 | 0.1 |

■ DASHER TROY   Troy, John Joseph b: 5/8/1856, New York, N.Y.   d: 3/30/38, Ozone Park, N.Y.   BR/TR, 5'5", 154 lbs.   Deb: 8/23/1881

1881	Det-N	11	44	2	15	0	0	0	4	3	8	.341	.383	.409	143	2				.792	-4	/3-7,2-4	-0.1
1882	Det-N	40	152	22	37	7	2	0	14	5	10	.243	.268	.316	86	-2				.847	-19	2-31,S-11	-1.9
	Pro-N	4	17	1	4	0	0	0	1	0	1	.235	.235	.235	52	-1				.750	-1	/S-4	-0.2
	Yr	44	169	23	41	7	2	0	15	5	11	.243	.264	.308	83	-3				.847	-21	2-31,S-15	-2.1
1883	NY-N	85	316	37	68	7	4	0	20	9	33	.215	.237	.297	54	-17				.879	-14	*2-73,S-12	-2.6
1884	*NY-a	107	421	80	111	22	10	2		19		.264	.300	.378	123	11				.879	-21	*2-107	-0.6
1885	NY-a	45	177	24	39	3	3	2	12	5		.220	.258	.305	84	-3				.866	-13	2-42/O-2,S-1	-1.3
Total	5	292	1127	166	274	42	20	4	51	41	52	.243	.274	.327	92	-10				.873	-72	2-257/S-28,3-7,O-2	-6.8

■ FRED TRUAX   Truax, Frederick W. b: 1868   d: 12/18/1899, Omaha, Neb.   Deb: 8/18/1890

| 1890 | Pit-N | 1 | 3 | 0 | 1 | 0 | 0 | 0 | 1 | 1 | 1 | .333 | .500 | .333 | 163 | 0 | 1 | 0 | | 1.000 | 0 | /O-1 | 0.0 |

YEAR	TM/L	G	AB	R	H	2B	3B	HR	RBI	BB	SO	AVG	OBP	SLG	PRO+	BR/A	SB	CS	SBR	FA	FR	G/POS	TPR

■ HARRY TRUBY — Truby, Harry Garvin "Bird Eye" b: 5/12/1870, Ironton, Ohio d: 3/21/53, Ironton, Ohio TR , 5'11", 185 lbs. Deb: 8/21/1895 U

1895	Chi-N	33	119	17	40	3	0	0	16	10	7	.336	.402	.361	92	-1	7			.950	0	2-33	0.1
1896	Chi-N	29	109	13	28	2	2	0	31	6	5	.257	.314	.367	76	-4	4			.935	1	2-28	-0.2
	Pit-N	8	32	1	5	0	0	0	3	2	4	.156	.206	.156	-4	-5	1			.949	-4	/2-8	-0.7
	Yr	37	141	14	33	2	2	0	34	8	9	.234	.287	.319	59	-9	5			.938	-3	2-36	-0.9
Total	2	70	260	31	73	5	2	0	50	18	16	.281	.342	.338	75	-10	12			.944	-3	/2-69	-0.8

■ FRANK TRUESDALE — Truesdale, Frank Day b: 3/31/1884, St.Louis, Mo. d: 8/27/43, Albuquerque, N.Mex. BB/TR, 5'8", 145 lbs. Deb: 4/27/10

1910	StL-A	123	415	39	91	7	2	1	25	48		.219	.303	.253	79	-9	29			.914	-5	*2-122	-1.7
1911	StL-A	1	0	1	0	0	0	0	0	0		—	—	—	—	0	0			.000	0	R	0.0
1914	NY-A	77	217	22	46	4	0	0	13	39	35	.212	.340	.230	72	-5	11	11	-3	.947	-2	2-67/3-4	-1.2
1918	Bos-A	15	36	6	10	1	0	0	2	4	5	.278	.350	.306	100	0	1			.913	-1	2-10	0.0
Total	4	216	668	68	147	12	2	1	40	91	40	.220	.318	.249	78	-14	41	11		.924	-7	2-199/3-4	-2.9

■ ED TRUMBULL — Trumbull, Edward J. (b: Edward J. Trembly) b: 11/3/1860, Chicopee, Mass. d: 1/14/37, Kingston, Pa. Deb: 5/10/1884

| 1884 | Was-a | 25 | 86 | 5 | 10 | 2 | 0 | 0 | | 2 | | .116 | .136 | .140 | -11 | -10 | | | | .828 | -0 | O-15,P-10 | -0.5 |

■ GREG TUBBS — Tubbs, Gregory Alan b: 8/31/62, Smithville, Tenn. BR/TR, 5'9", 185 lbs. Deb: 8/1/93

| 1993 | Cin-N | 35 | 59 | 10 | 11 | 0 | 0 | 1 | 2 | 14 | 10 | .186 | .351 | .237 | 61 | -3 | 3 | 1 | 0 | .975 | -4 | O-21 | -0.6 |

■ EDDIE TUCKER — Tucker, Eddie Jack "Scooter" b: 11/18/66, Greenville, Miss. BR/TR, 6'2", 205 lbs. Deb: 6/14/92

1992	Hou-N	20	50	4	6	1	0	0	3	3	13	.120	.200	.140	-2	-7	1	1	-0	.976	-6	C-19	-1.3
1993	Hou-N	9	26	1	5	1	0	0	3	2	3	.192	.250	.231	31	-3	0	0	0	1.000	2	/C-8	0.0
1995	Hou-N	5	7	1	2	0	0	1	1	0	0	.286	.286	.714	164	1	0	0	0	1.000	-0	/C-3	0.0
	Cle-A	17	20	2	0	0	0	0	0	5	4	.000	.231	.000	-33	-4	0	0	0	.982	1	C-17	-0.2
Total	3	51	103	9	13	2	0	1	7	10	20	.126	.224	.175	11	-13	1	1	-0	.986	-3	/C-47	-1.5

■ MICHAEL TUCKER — Tucker, Michael Anthony b: 6/25/71, S.Boston, Va. BL/TR, 6'2", 185 lbs. Deb: 4/26/95

1995	KC-A	62	177	23	46	10	4	4	17	18	51	.260	.332	.384	84	-4	2	3	-1	.986	1	O-36,D-22	-0.7
1996	KC-A	108	339	55	88	18	4	12	53	40	69	.260	.350	.442	101	1	10	4	1	.989	-2	O-98/1-9,D-5	-0.4
Total	2	170	516	78	134	28	4	16	70	58	120	.260	.344	.422	95	-3	12	7	-1	.989	-2	O-134/D-27,1-9	-1.1

■ OLLIE TUCKER — Tucker, Oliver Dinwiddie b: 1/27/02, Radiant, Va. d: 7/13/40, Radiant, Va. BL/TR, 5'11", 180 lbs. Deb: 4/17/27

1927	Was-A	20	24	1	5	2	0	0	4	2		.208	.321	.292	61	-1	0			1.000	-0	/O-5	-0.2
1928	Cle-A	14	47	5	6	0	1	0	6	9	5	.128	.255	.191	19	-6	0	2	-1	1.000	-0	O-14	-0.8
Total	2	34	71	6	11	2	1	0	10	11	5	.155	.277	.225	33	-7	0	2	-1	1.000	-1	/O-19	-1.0

■ TOMMY TUCKER — Tucker, Thomas Joseph "Foghorn" b: 10/28/1863, Holyoke, Mass. d: 10/22/35, Montague, Mass. BB/TR, 5'11", 165 lbs. Deb: 4/16/1887

1887	Bal-a	136	524	114	144	15	9	6	84	29		.275	.347	.372	107	7	85			.976	4	*1-136	-0.3
1888	Bal-a	136	520	74	149	17	12	6	61	16		.287	.330	.400	137	21	43			.975	4	*1-129/O-7,P-1	1.1
1889	Bal-a	134	527	103	196	22	11	5	99	42	26	.372	.450	.484	163	46	63			.964	-1	*1-123,O-12	3.0
1890	Bos-N	132	539	104	159	17	8	1	62	56	22	.295	.387	.362	110	7	43			.979	-2	*1-132	-0.1
1891	Bos-N	140	548	103	148	16	5	2	69	37	30	.270	.349	.328	87	-10	26			.976	-3	*1-140/P-1	-1.9
1892	*Bos-N	149	542	85	153	15	7	1	62	45	35	.282	.365	.341	104	3	22			.972	-12	*1-149	-1.5
1893	Bos-N	121	486	83	138	13	2	1	91	27	31	.284	.347	.362	82	-15	8			.980	-11	*1-121	-2.4
1894	Bos-N	123	500	112	165	24	6	3	100	53	21	.330	.412	.420	94	-5	18			.985	2	*1-123/O-1	-0.2
1895	Bos-N	125	462	87	115	19	6	3	73	61	29	.249	.360	.335	74	-18	15			.978	5	*1-125	-0.8
1896	Bos-N	122	474	74	144	27	5	2	72	30	29	.304	.363	.395	94	-5	6			.985	3	*1-122	0.0
1897	Bos-N	4	14	0	3	2	0	0	4	2		.214	.313	.357	72	-1	0			.957	1	/1-4	0.0
	Was-N	93	352	52	119	18	5	5	61	27		.338	.403	.460	128	14	18			.984	-3	*1-93	1.0
	Yr	97	366	52	122	20	5	5	65	29		.333	.399	.456	126	14	18			.982	-2	1-97	1.0
1898	Bro-N	73	283	35	79	9	4	1	34	12		.279	.325	.350	94	-3	1			.991	7	1-73	0.4
	StL-N	72	252	18	60	7	2	0	20	18		.238	.319	.282	71	-9	1			.973	-0	1-72	-0.9
	Yr	145	535	53	139	16	6	1	54	30		.260	.322	.318	83	-12	2			.982	7	*1-145	-0.5
1899	Cle-N	127	456	40	110	19	3	0	40	24		.241	.297	.296	68	-20	3			.977	-1	*1-127	-1.9
Total	13	1687	6479	1084	1882	240	85	42	932	479	223	.290	.364	.373	101	12	352			.978	-8	*1-1669/O-20,P-2	-4.5

■ THURMAN TUCKER — Tucker, Thurman Lowell "Joe E." b: 9/26/17, Gordon, Tex. d: 5/7/93, Oklahoma City, Okla. BL/TR, 5'11", 170 lbs. Deb: 4/14/42

1942	Chi-A	7	24	2	3	0	1	0	1	0	4	.125	.125	.208	-7	-7	0			.900	-1	/O-5	-0.5
1943	Chi-A	139	528	81	124	15	6	3	39	79	72	.235	.336	.303	87	-6	29	17	-2	.988	15	*O-132	0.0
1944	Chi-A★	124	446	59	128	15	6	2	46	57	40	.287	.368	.361	110	7	13	12	-3	.991	18	*O-120	1.6
1946	Chi-A	121	438	62	126	20	3	1	36	54	45	.288	.367	.354	106	5	9	10	-3	.990	-2	*O-110	-0.9
1947	Chi-A	89	254	28	60	9	4	1	17	38	25	.236	.336	.315	85	-5	10	4	1	.978	-1	O-65	-0.9
1948	*Cle-A	83	242	52	63	13	2	1	19	31	17	.260	.347	.343	86	-5	11	2	2	1.000	-1	O-66	-0.6
1949	Cle-A	80	197	28	48	5	2	0	14	18	19	.244	.307	.289	59	-12	1	0	0	.984	2	O-42	-1.1
1950	Cle-A	57	101	13	18	2	0	1	7	14	14	.178	.284	.228	34	-10	4	2	0	.968	-5	O-34	-1.5
1951	Cle-A	1	1	0	0	0	0	0	0	0	0	.000	.000	.000	-99	-0	0			.000	0	H	0.0
Total	9	701	2231	325	570	79	24	9	179	291	237	.255	.342	.325	89	-28	77	47	-5	.988	29	O-574	-3.2

■ BRIAN TURANG — Turang, Brian Craig b: 6/14/67, Long Beach, Cal. BR/TR, 5'10", 170 lbs. Deb: 8/13/93

1993	Sea-A	40	140	22	35	11	1	0	7	17	20	.250	.340	.343	83	-3	6	2	1	.986	-2	O-38/3-2,2-1,D-1	-0.5
1994	Sea-A	38	112	9	21	5	1	1	8	24	25	.188	.242	.277	33	-11	3	1	0	.978	-4	O-30/2-5,D-4	-1.5
Total	2	78	252	31	56	16	2	1	15	24	45	.222	.297	.313	60	-14	9	3	1	.983	-6	/O-68,2-6,D-5,3-2	-2.0

■ JERRY TURBIDY — Turbidy, Jeremiah b: 7/4/1852, Dudley, Mass. d: 9/5/20, Webster, Mass. 5'8", 165 lbs. Deb: 7/27/1884

| 1884 | KC-U | 13 | 49 | 5 | 11 | 4 | 0 | 0 | | | 3 | .224 | .269 | .306 | 85 | -2 | | | | .830 | 6 | S-13 | 0.3 |

■ EDDIE TURCHIN — Turchin, Edward Lawrence "Smiley" b: 2/10/17, New York, N.Y. d: 2/8/82, Brookhaven, N.Y. BR/TR, 5'10", 165 lbs. Deb: 5/9/43

| 1943 | Cle-A | 11 | 13 | 4 | 3 | 0 | 0 | 0 | 1 | 3 | 1 | .231 | .375 | .231 | 84 | -0 | 0 | 0 | 0 | 1.000 | 0 | /3-4,S-2 | 0.2 |

■ PETE TURGEON — Turgeon, Eugene Joseph b: 1/3/1897, Minneapolis, Minn. d: 1/24/77, Wichita Falls, Tex BR/TR, 5'6", 145 lbs. Deb: 9/20/23

| 1923 | Chi-N | 3 | 6 | 1 | 1 | 0 | 0 | 0 | 0 | 0 | 0 | .167 | .167 | .167 | -12 | -1 | 0 | 0 | 0 | .875 | 0 | /S-2 | -0.1 |

■ CHRIS TURNER — Turner, Christopher Wan b: 3/23/69, Bowling Green, Ky. BR/TR, 6'2", 190 lbs. Deb: 8/27/93

1993	Cal-A	25	75	9	21	5	0	1	13	9	16	.280	.365	.387	99	0	1	1	-0	.992	-4	C-25	-0.2
1994	Cal-A	58	149	23	36	7	1	1	12	10	29	.242	.294	.322	58	-9	3	0	1	.997	4	C-57	-0.2
1995	Cal-A	5	10	1	1	0	0	0	1	0	3	.100	.100	.100	-48	-2	0	0	0	1.000	-0	/C-4,D-1	-0.1
1996	Cal-A	4	3	0	1	0	0	0	1	0	0	.333	.500	.333	119	0	0	0	0	1.000	-0	/C-3,O-1	0.0
Total	4	92	237	33	59	12	1	2	27	20	48	.249	.313	.333	68	-11	4	1	1	.996	-0	/C-89,O-1,D-1	-0.5

■ EARL TURNER — Turner, Earl Edwin b: 5/6/23, Pittsfield, Mass. BR/TR, 5'9", 170 lbs. Deb: 9/25/48

1948	Pit-N	2	1	0	0	0	0	0	0	0	0	.000	.000	.000	-98	-0	0			.000	0	/C-1	0.0
1950	Pit-N	40	74	10	18	0	0	3	5	4	13	.243	.282	.365	66	-4	1			.974	2	C-34	-0.1
Total	2	42	75	10	18	0	0	3	5	4	13	.240	.278	.360	64	-4	1			.974	2	/C-35	-0.1

■ TUCK TURNER — Turner, George A. b: 2/13/1873, W.New Brighton, N.Y. d: 7/16/45, Staten Island, N.Y. BB/TL, 5'6.5", 155 lbs. Deb: 8/18/1893

1893	Phi-N	36	155	32	50	4	3	1	13	9	19	.323	.364	.426	105	1	7			.933	-2	O-36	-0.2
1894	Phi-N	80	339	91	141	21	9	1	82	23	13	.416	.456	.540	143	24	11			.916	-9	O-78/P-1	0.8
1895	Phi-N	59	210	51	81	8	6	2	43	25	11	.386	.453	.510	147	16	14			.847	-8	O-55	0.3
1896	Phi-N	13	32	12	7	1	2	0	1	7	7	.219	.375	.281	75	-1	6			.905	2	O-8	0.0
	StL-N	51	203	30	50	7	8	1	27	14	21	.246	.298	.374	80	-7	6			.961	-5	O-51	-1.4
	Yr	64	235	42	57	8	8	1	27	22	26	.243	.310	.362	79	-8	12			.948	-4	O-59	-1.4

YEAR	TM/L	G	AB	R	H	2B	3B	HR	RBI	BB	SO	AVG	OBP	SLG	PRO+	BR/A	SB	CS	SBR	FA	FR	G/POS	TPR
1897	StL-N	103	416	58	121	17	12	2	41	35		.291	.350	.404	101	-0	8			.945	-7	*O-102	-1.3
1898	StL-N	35	141	20	28	8	0	0	7	14		.199	.280	.255	52	-9	1			.929	-3	O-34	-1.3
Total	6	377	1496	294	478	67	38	7	213	128	69	.320	.377	.429	111	24	53			.920	-32	O-364/P-1	-3.1

■ JERRY TURNER
Turner, John Webber   b: 1/17/54, Texarkana, Ark.   BL/TL, 5'9", 180 lbs.   Deb: 9/2/74

YEAR	TM/L	G	AB	R	H	2B	3B	HR	RBI	BB	SO	AVG	OBP	SLG	PRO+	BR/A	SB	CS	SBR	FA	FR	G/POS	TPR
1974	SD-N	17	48	4	14	1	0	0	2	3	5	.292	.333	.313	85	-1	2	1	0	1.000	-1	O-13	-0.3
1975	SD-N	11	22	1	6	0	0	0	0	2	1	.273	.333	.273	74	-1	0	0	0	.909	-2	/O-4	-0.1
1976	SD-N	105	281	41	75	16	5	5	37	32	38	.267	.342	.413	123	8	12	6	0	.960	-2	O-74	0.3
1977	SD-N	118	289	43	71	16	1	10	48	31	43	.246	.319	.412	105	1	12	4	1	.947	3	O-69	0.3
1978	SD-N	106	225	28	63	9	1	8	37	21	32	.280	.349	.436	128	8	6	4	-1	.970	-7	O-58	-0.2
1979	SD-N	138	448	55	111	23	2	9	61	34	58	.248	.304	.368	88	-9	4	2	0	.958	-1	*O-115	-1.5
1980	SD-N	85	153	22	44	5	0	3	18	10	18	.288	.339	.379	106	1	8	3	1	1.000	-4	O-34	-0.4
1981	SD-N	33	31	5	7	0	0	2	6	4	3	.226	.314	.419	115	0	0	1	-1	.833	-1	/O-4	-0.1
	Chi-A	10	12	1	2	0	0	0	2	1	2	.167	.231	.167	16	-1	0	0	0	1.000	0	/O-1	-0.1
1982	Det-A	85	210	21	52	3	0	8	27	20	37	.248	.313	.376	88	-4	1	3	-2	.909	-4	D-50,O-13	-1.1
1983	SD-N	25	23	1	3	0	0	0	1	0	8	.130	.167	.130	-17	-4	0	0	0	.000	0	/O-1	-0.4
Total	10	733	1742	222	448	73	9	45	238	159	245	.257	.322	.387	101	-1	45	24	-1	.959	-18	O-386/D-50	-3.6

■ SHANE TURNER
Turner, Shane Lee   b: 1/8/63, Los Angeles, Cal.   BL/TR, 5'10", 180 lbs.   Deb: 8/19/88

YEAR	TM/L	G	AB	R	H	2B	3B	HR	RBI	BB	SO	AVG	OBP	SLG	PRO+	BR/A	SB	CS	SBR	FA	FR	G/POS	TPR
1988	Phi-N	18	35	1	6	0	0	0	1	5	9	.171	.275	.171	30	-3	0	0	0	.941	-2	/3-8,S-5	-0.6
1991	Bal-A	4	1	0	0	0	0	0	0	0	0	.000	.000	.000	-99	-0	0	0	0	1.000	0	/2-1,D-1	0.0
1992	Sea-A	34	74	8	20	5	0	0	5	9	15	.270	.349	.338	93	-1	2	1	0	.881	-5	3-18,O-15	-0.6
Total	3	56	110	9	26	5	0	0	6	14	24	.236	.323	.282	71	-4	2	1	0	.898	-7	/3-26,O-15,S-5,D2	-1.2

■ TERRY TURNER
Turner, Terrence Lamont "Cotton Top"   b: 2/28/1881, Sandy Lake, Pa.   d: 7/18/60, Cleveland, Ohio   BR/TR, 5'8", 149 lbs.   Deb: 8/25/01   C

YEAR	TM/L	G	AB	R	H	2B	3B	HR	RBI	BB	SO	AVG	OBP	SLG	PRO+	BR/A	SB	CS	SBR	FA	FR	G/POS	TPR
1901	Pit-N	2	7	0	3	0	0	0	1	0		.429	.429	.429	145	0	0			.833	1	/3-2	0.2
1904	Cle-A	111	404	41	95	9	6	1	45	11		.235	.255	.295	74	-13	5			.940	3	*S-111	-0.7
1905	Cle-A	155	586	49	155	16	14	6	72	14		.265	.289	.360	104	0	17			.946	-26	*S-155	-2.5
1906	Cle-A	147	584	85	170	27	7	2	62	35		.291	.338	.372	124	15	27			**.960**	23	*S-147	4.6
1907	Cle-A	140	524	57	127	20	7	0	46	19		.242	.272	.307	84	-11	27			**.950**	-4	*S-139	-1.3
1908	Cle-A	60	201	21	48	11	1	0	19	15		.239	.298	.303	95	-1	18			.952	-4	O-36,S-17	-0.7
1909	Cle-A	53	208	25	52	7	4	0	16	14		.250	.304	.322	94	-2	14			.969	10	2-26,S-26	1.0
1910	Cle-A	150	574	71	132	14	6	0	33	53		.230	.301	.275	79	-13	31			.973	2	S-94,3-46/2-9	-0.9
1911	Cle-A	117	417	59	105	16	9	0	28	34		.252	.310	.333	78	-13	29			.970	2	3-94,2-14,S-10	-0.9
1912	Cle-A	103	370	54	114	14	4	0	33	31		.308	.363	.368	106	3	19			**.951**	-2	*3-103	0.1
1913	Cle-A	120	388	60	96	13	4	0	44	55	35	.247	.348	.302	88	-4	13			.954	16	3-71,2-25,S-21	1.5
1914	Cle-A	121	428	43	105	14	9	1	33	44	36	.245	.319	.327	91	-5	17	13	-3	**.963**	21	*3-104,2-17	1.8
1915	Cle-A	75	262	35	66	14	1	0	14	29	13	.252	.329	.313	90	-3	12	11	-3	.965	-9	2-51,3-20	-1.4
1916	Cle-A	124	428	52	112	15	3	0	38	40	29	.262	.325	.311	86	-7	15			.963	5	3-77,2-42	-0.2
1917	Cle-A	69	180	16	37	7	0	0	15	14	19	.206	.263	.244	51	-11	4			.980	-1	3-40,2-23/S-1	-1.3
1918	Cle-A	74	233	24	58	7	2	0	23	22	15	.249	.316	.296	77	-6	6			.969	-4	3-46,2-26/S-1	-1.1
1919	Phi-A	38	127	7	24	3	0	0	6	5	9	.189	.220	.213	21	-13	2			.946	1	S-19,2-17/3-1	-1.1
Total	17	1659	5921	699	1499	207	77	8	528	435	156	.253	.308	.318	89	-83	256	24		.952	34	S-741,3-604,2/O	-2.0

■ TOM TURNER
Turner, Thomas Richard   b: 9/8/16, Custer Co., Okla.   d: 5/14/86, Kennewick, Wash.   BR/TR, 6'2", 195 lbs.   Deb: 4/25/40

YEAR	TM/L	G	AB	R	H	2B	3B	HR	RBI	BB	SO	AVG	OBP	SLG	PRO+	BR/A	SB	CS	SBR	FA	FR	G/POS	TPR
1940	Chi-A	37	96	11	20	1	2	0	6	3	12	.208	.240	.260	29	-10	1	0	0	.969	2	C-29	-0.6
1941	Chi-A	38	126	7	30	5	0	0	8	9	15	.238	.289	.278	51	-9	2	0	1	.979	5	C-35	0.0
1942	Chi-A	56	182	18	44	9	1	3	21	19	15	.242	.313	.352	89	-3	0	1	-1	.971	-1	C-54	0.0
1943	Chi-A	51	154	16	37	7	1	2	11	13	21	.240	.299	.338	86	-3	0	0	0	.978	4	C-49	0.5
1944	Chi-A	36	113	9	26	6	0	2	13	5	16	.230	.263	.336	71	-5	0	1	-1	.958	-2	C-36	-0.6
	*StL-A	15	25	2	8	1	0	0	4	2	5	.320	.370	.360	103	0	0	0	0	.969	-1	C-11	0.0
	Yr	51	138	11	34	7	0	2	17	7	21	.246	.283	.341	77	-5	0	1	-1	.960	-3	C-47	-0.6
Total	5	233	696	63	165	29	4	7	63	51	84	.237	.290	.320	70	-29	4	2	0	.972	7	C-214	-0.7

■ BILL TUTTLE
Tuttle, William Robert   b: 7/4/29, Elwood, Ill.   BR/TR, 6', 190 lbs.   Deb: 9/10/52

YEAR	TM/L	G	AB	R	H	2B	3B	HR	RBI	BB	SO	AVG	OBP	SLG	PRO+	BR/A	SB	CS	SBR	FA	FR	G/POS	TPR
1952	Det-A	7	25	2	6	0	0	0	2	0	1	.240	.240	.240	34	-2	0	0	0	1.000	1	/O-6	-0.2
1954	Det-A	147	530	64	141	20	11	7	58	62	60	.266	.345	.385	102	1	5	8	-3	.985	4	*O-145	-0.5
1955	Det-A	154	603	102	168	23	4	14	78	76	54	.279	.360	.400	107	6	6	3	0	.985	15	*O-154	1.4
1956	Det-A	140	546	61	138	22	4	9	65	38	48	.253	.303	.357	73	-22	5	4	-1	.976	10	*O-137	-2.0
1957	Det-A	133	451	49	113	12	4	5	47	44	41	.251	.319	.328	75	-15	2	4	-1	.982	6	*O-128	-1.8
1958	KC-A	148	511	77	118	14	9	11	51	74	49	.231	.329	.358	88	-9	7	9	-3	.988	1	*O-145	-1.4
1959	KC-A	126	463	74	139	19	6	7	43	48	38	.300	.371	.413	113	9	10	6	-1	.984	12	*O-121	-0.4
1960	KC-A	151	559	75	143	21	3	8	40	66	52	.256	.337	.347	85	-11	5	3	-1	.988	17	*O-148	-0.4
1961	KC-A	25	84	15	22	2	0	3	8	9	9	.262	.333	.333	77	-3	0	0	0	.951	-1	O-25	-0.5
	Min-A	113	370	38	91	12	3	5	38	43	41	.246	.324	.335	73	-14	1	3	-2	.943	-13	3-85,O-64/2-2	-3.0
	Yr	138	454	53	113	14	5	5	46	52	50	.249	.326	.335	73	-16	1	3	-2	.970	-14	O-89,3-85/2-2	-3.5
1962	Min-A	110	123	21	26	4	1	1	13	19	14	.211	.322	.285	62	-0	6	1	0	.973	-31	*O-104	-3.9
1963	Min-A	16	3	0	0	0	0	0	0	0	0	.000	.250	.000	-22	-0	0	0	0	1.000	0	O-14	-0.5
Total	11	1270	4268	578	1105	149	47	67	443	480	416	.259	.336	.363	88	-65	38	44	-15	.983	14	*O-1191/3-85,2-2	-12.1

■ GUY TUTWILER
Tutwiler, Guy Isbell "King Tut"   b: 7/17/1889, Coalburg, Ala.   d: 8/15/30, Birmingham, Ala.   BL/TR, 6', 175 lbs.   Deb: 8/29/11

YEAR	TM/L	G	AB	R	H	2B	3B	HR	RBI	BB	SO	AVG	OBP	SLG	PRO+	BR/A	SB	CS	SBR	FA	FR	G/POS	TPR
1911	Det-A	13	32	3	6	2	0	0	1	2		.188	.235	.250	34	-3	0			.778	-4	/2-6,O-3	-0.7
1913	Det-A	14	47	4	10	0	1	0	7	4	12	.213	.275	.255	56	-3	2			.987	1	1-14	-0.2
Total	2	27	79	7	16	2	1	0	10	6	12	.203	.259	.253	47	-6	2			.987	-2	/1-14,2-6,O-3	-0.9

■ ART TWINEHAM
Twineham, Arthur W. "Old Hoss"   b: 11/26/1866, Galesburg, Ill.   BL/TL, 6'1.5", 190 lbs.   Deb: 9/11/1893

YEAR	TM/L	G	AB	R	H	2B	3B	HR	RBI	BB	SO	AVG	OBP	SLG	PRO+	BR/A	SB	CS	SBR	FA	FR	G/POS	TPR
1893	StL-N	14	48	8	15	2	0	0	11	1		.313	.340	.354	84	-1	2			.928	2	C-14	0.2
1894	StL-N	38	127	22	40	4	1	1	16	9	11	.315	.387	.386	87	-2	2			.939	4	C-38	0.4
Total	2	52	175	30	55	6	1	1	27	10	13	.314	.375	.377	86	-3	2			.936	7	/C-52	0.6

■ LARRY TWITCHELL
Twitchell, Lawrence Grant   b: 2/18/1864, Cleveland, Ohio   d: 8/23/30, Cleveland, Ohio   BR/TR, 6', 185 lbs.   Deb: 4/30/1886

YEAR	TM/L	G	AB	R	H	2B	3B	HR	RBI	BB	SO	AVG	OBP	SLG	PRO+	BR/A	SB	CS	SBR	FA	FR	G/POS	TPR
1886	Det-N	4	16	0	1	0	0	0	0	0	2	.063	.063	.063	-60	-3	0			1.000	0	/P-4,O-2	-0.1
1887	*Det-N	65	264	44	88	14	6	0	51	8	19	.333	.358	.432	115	4	12			.871	-6	O-53,P-15	-0.2
1888	Det-N	131	524	71	128	19	4	5	67	28	45	.244	.286	.324	95	-3	14			.885	-9	*O-131/P-2	-1.6
1889	Cle-N	134	549	73	151	16	11	4	95	29	37	.275	.315	.366	92	-7	17			.916	-10	*O-134/P-1	-1.8
1890	Cle-P	56	233	33	52	6	3	2	36	17	17	.223	.279	.300	60	-14	4			.821	-9	O-56	-2.0
	Buf-P	44	172	24	38	3	1	2	17	23	12	.221	.316	.285	67	-7	4			.918	-1	O-32,P-13/1-3	-0.7
	Yr	100	405	57	90	9	4	4	53	40	29	.222	.295	.294	63	-21	8			.857	-10	O-88,P-13/1-3	-2.7
1891	Col-a	57	224	32	62	9	4	0	35	20	8	.277	.341	.379	113	3	10			.887	-10	O-56/P-6	-0.7
1892	Was-N	51	192	20	42	9	4	0	20	11	31	.219	.275	.318	82	-5	8			.897	-5	O-48/S-3,3-1	-1.1
1893	Lou-N	45	187	37	58	11	3	2	31	17	20	.310	.377	.433	125	7	7			.874	-2	O-45	0.2
1894	Lou-N	52	210	31	56	16	3	2	32	15	20	.267	.316	.400	77	-9	8			.908	6	O-51/P-1	-0.5
Total	9	639	2571	362	676	103	40	19	384	168	231	.263	.313	.356	91	-34	84			.890	-45	O-608/P-42,S-3,13	-8.5

■ BABE TWOMBLY
Twombly, Clarence Edward   b: 1/18/1896, Jamaica Plain, Mass.   d: 11/23/74, San Clemente, Cal.   BL/TR, 5'10", 165 lbs.   Deb: 4/14/20   F

YEAR	TM/L	G	AB	R	H	2B	3B	HR	RBI	BB	SO	AVG	OBP	SLG	PRO+	BR/A	SB	CS	SBR	FA	FR	G/POS	TPR
1920	Chi-N	78	183	25	43	1	1	0	14	17	20	.235	.303	.284	68	-7	5	9	-4	.970	0	O-45/2-2	-1.5
1921	Chi-N	87	175	22	66	8	1	0	18	11	10	.377	.414	.451	129	8	4	6	-2	.968	0	O-45	0.3
Total	2	165	358	47	109	9	2	0	32	28	30	.304	.357	.366	98	0	9	15	-6	.969	0	/O-90,2-2	-1.2

■ GEORGE TWOMBLY
Twombly, George Frederick "Silent George"   b: 6/4/1892, Boston, Mass.   d: 2/17/75, Lexington, Mass.   BR/TR, 5'9", 165 lbs.   Deb: 7/9/14   F

YEAR	TM/L	G	AB	R	H	2B	3B	HR	RBI	BB	SO	AVG	OBP	SLG	PRO+	BR/A	SB	CS	SBR	FA	FR	G/POS	TPR
1914	Cin-N	68	240	22	56	0	5	0	19	14	27	.233	.284	.275	64	-11	12			.968	1	O-68	-1.4
1915	Cin-N	46	66	5	13	0	1	0	5	8	8	.197	.293	.227	57	-3	5	3	-0	1.000	-4	O-24	-0.9

YEAR	TM/L	G	AB	R	H	2B	3B	HR	RBI	BB	SO	AVG	OBP	SLG	PRO+	BR/A	SB	CS	SBR	FA	FR	G/POS	TPR
1916	Cin-N	3	5	0	0	0	0	0	0	1	1	.000	.167	.000	-48	-1	0			1.000	-0	/O-1	-0.1
1917	Bos-N	32	102	8	19	1	1	0	9	18	5	.186	.314	.216	68	-3	4			.943	-5	O-29/1-1	-1.1
1919	Was-A	1	4	0	0	0	0	0	0	0	0	.000	.000	.000	-99	-1	0			.000	-1	/O-1	-0.2
Total	5	150	417	35	88	1	7	0	33	41	41	.211	.289	.247	62	-18	21	3		.967	-9	O-123/1-1	-3.7

■ JIM TYACK
Tyack, James Frederick b: 1/9/11, Florence, Mont. d: 1/3/95, Bakersfield, Cal. BL/TR, 6'2", 195 lbs. Deb: 4/20/43

YEAR	TM/L	G	AB	R	H	2B	3B	HR	RBI	BB	SO	AVG	OBP	SLG	PRO+	BR/A	SB	CS	SBR	FA	FR	G/POS	TPR
1943	Phi-A	54	155	11	40	8	1	0	23	14	9	.258	.320	.323	88	-2	1	1	-0	.977	1	O-38	-0.4

■ FRED TYLER
Tyler, Frederick Franklin "Clancy" b: 12/16/1891, Derry, N.H. d: 10/14/45, E.Derry, N.H. BR/TR, 5'10.5", 180 lbs. Deb: 4/14/14 F

YEAR	TM/L	G	AB	R	H	2B	3B	HR	RBI	BB	SO	AVG	OBP	SLG	PRO+	BR/A	SB	CS	SBR	FA	FR	G/POS	TPR
1914	Bos-N	6	19	2	2	0	0	0	1	2	2	.105	.150	.105	-24	-3	0			1.000	-1	/C-6	-0.3

■ JOHNNIE TYLER
Tyler, John Anthony "Ty Ty" or "Katz" (b: John Tylka) b: 7/30/06, Mt.Pleasant, Pa. d: 7/11/72, Mt.Pleasant, Pa. BB/TR, 6', 175 lbs. Deb: 9/16/34

YEAR	TM/L	G	AB	R	H	2B	3B	HR	RBI	BB	SO	AVG	OBP	SLG	PRO+	BR/A	SB	CS	SBR	FA	FR	G/POS	TPR
1934	Bos-N	3	6	0	1	0	0	0	1	0	3	.167	.167	.167	-11	-1	0			1.000	1	/O-1	0.0
1935	Bos-N	13	47	7	16	2	1	2	11	4	3	.340	.404	.553	168	4	0			.893	-0	O-11	0.4
Total	2	16	53	7	17	2	1	2	12	4	6	.321	.379	.509	148	3	0			.906	1	O-12	0.4

■ EARL TYREE
Tyree, Earl Carlton "Ty" b: 3/4/1890, Huntsville, Ill. d: 5/17/54, Rushville, Ill. BR/TR, 5'8", 160 lbs. Deb: 10/5/14

YEAR	TM/L	G	AB	R	H	2B	3B	HR	RBI	BB	SO	AVG	OBP	SLG	PRO+	BR/A	SB	CS	SBR	FA	FR	G/POS	TPR
1914	Chi-N	1	4	0	0	0	0	0	0	0	0	.000	.000	.000	-99	-1	0			1.000	-1	/C-1	-0.2

■ JIM TYRONE
Tyrone, James Vernon b: 1/29/49, Alice, Tex. BR/TR, 6'1", 185 lbs. Deb: 8/27/72 F

YEAR	TM/L	G	AB	R	H	2B	3B	HR	RBI	BB	SO	AVG	OBP	SLG	PRO+	BR/A	SB	CS	SBR	FA	FR	G/POS	TPR
1972	Chi-N	13	8	1	0	0	0	0	0	0	3	.000	.000	.000	-90	-2	1	0	0	1.000	0	/O-4	-0.1
1974	Chi-N	57	81	19	15	0	1	3	3	6	8	.185	.241	.321	54	-5	1	1	-0	.962	-8	O-32/3-1	-1.5
1975	Chi-N	11	22	0	5	0	1	0	3	1	4	.227	.261	.318	58	-1	1	1	0	1.000	-1	/O-8	-0.3
1977	Oak-A	96	294	32	72	11	1	5	26	25	62	.245	.304	.340	76	-10	3	1	0	.950	1	O-81/1-1,S-1,D-4	-1.1
Total	4	177	405	52	92	11	3	8	32	32	77	.227	.284	.328	67	-18	6	3	0	.955	-7	O-125/D-4,S-1,13	-3.0

■ WAYNE TYRONE
Tyrone, Oscar Wayne b: 8/1/50, Alice, Tex. BR/TR, 6'1", 185 lbs. Deb: 7/15/76 F

YEAR	TM/L	G	AB	R	H	2B	3B	HR	RBI	BB	SO	AVG	OBP	SLG	PRO+	BR/A	SB	CS	SBR	FA	FR	G/POS	TPR
1976	Chi-N	30	57	3	13	1	0	1	5	3	0	.228	.267	.298	55	-3	0			1.000	-3	/O-7,1-5,3-5	-0.7

■ TY TYSON
Tyson, Albert Thomas b: 6/1/1892, Wilkes-Barre, Pa. d: 8/16/53, Buffalo, N.Y. BR/TR, 5'11", 169 lbs. Deb: 4/13/26

YEAR	TM/L	G	AB	R	H	2B	3B	HR	RBI	BB	SO	AVG	OBP	SLG	PRO+	BR/A	SB	CS	SBR	FA	FR	G/POS	TPR
1926	NY-N	97	335	40	98	16	1	3	35	15	28	.293	.329	.373	90	-5	6			.980	3	O-92	-0.8
1927	NY-N	43	159	24	42	7	2	1	17	10	19	.264	.308	.352	76	-5	5			.929	-3	O-41	-1.1
1928	Bro-N	59	210	25	57	11	1	1	21	10	14	.271	.317	.348	75	-8	3			.965	0	O-55	-1.1
Total	3	199	704	89	197	34	4	5	73	35	61	.280	.320	.361	82	-19	14			.966	0	O-188	-3.0

■ TURKEY TYSON
Tyson, Cecil Washington "Slim" b: 12/6/14, Elm City, N.C. BL/TR, 6'5.5", 225 lbs. Deb: 4/23/44

YEAR	TM/L	G	AB	R	H	2B	3B	HR	RBI	BB	SO	AVG	OBP	SLG	PRO+	BR/A	SB	CS	SBR	FA	FR	G/POS	TPR
1944	Phi-N	1	1	0	0	0	0	0	0	0	0	.000	.000	.000	-99	-0	0			.000	0	H	0.0

■ MIKE TYSON
Tyson, Michael Ray b: 1/13/50, Rocky Mount, N.C. BR/TR, 5'9", 170 lbs. Deb: 9/5/72

YEAR	TM/L	G	AB	R	H	2B	3B	HR	RBI	BB	SO	AVG	OBP	SLG	PRO+	BR/A	SB	CS	SBR	FA	FR	G/POS	TPR
1972	StL-N	13	37	1	7	1	0	0	0	1	9	.189	.211	.216	22	-4	0	1	-1	.981	4	2-11/S-2	0.0
1973	StL-N	144	469	48	114	15	4	1	33	23	66	.243	.281	.299	61	-25	2	5	-2	.944	-19	*S-128,2-16	-3.0
1974	StL-N	151	422	35	94	14	5	1	37	26	70	.223	.266	.287	55	-26	4	2	0	.955	15	*S-143,2-12	0.6
1975	StL-N	122	368	45	98	16	3	2	37	24	39	.266	.316	.342	80	-10	5	2	0	.971	-12	S-95,2-24/3-5	-1.3
1976	StL-N	76	245	26	70	12	9	3	28	16	34	.286	.340	.445	117	5	3	1	0	.971	8	2-74	1.8
1977	StL-N	138	418	42	103	15	2	7	57	30	48	.246	.300	.342	73	-16	3	4	-2	.979	22	*2-135	-1.1
1978	StL-N	125	377	26	88	16	0	3	26	24	41	.233	.279	.300	63	-19	2	0	1	.977	0	*2-124	-1.1
1979	StL-N	75	190	18	42	8	2	5	20	13	28	.221	.275	.363	72	-8	2	1	0	.975	8	2-71	0.4
1980	Chi-N	123	341	34	81	19	3	2	23	15	61	.238	.274	.337	65	-16	1	2	-1	.968	9	*2-117	-0.1
1981	Chi-N	50	92	6	17	2	0	2	8	7	15	.185	.250	.272	46	-7	1	0	0	.940	-3	2-36/S-1	-0.5
Total	10	1017	2959	281	714	118	28	27	269	175	411	.241	.287	.327	69	-126	23	18	-4	.973	36	2-620,S-369/3-5	-1.9

■ BOB UECKER
Uecker, Robert George b: 1/26/35, Milwaukee, Wis. BR/TR, 6'1", 190 lbs. Deb: 4/13/62

YEAR	TM/L	G	AB	R	H	2B	3B	HR	RBI	BB	SO	AVG	OBP	SLG	PRO+	BR/A	SB	CS	SBR	FA	FR	G/POS	TPR
1962	Mil-N	33	64	5	16	2	0	1	8	7	15	.250	.324	.328	78	-2	0	0	0	.982	4	C-24	0.3
1963	Mil-N	13	16	3	4	2	0	0	2	0	5	.250	.333	.375	105	0	0	0	0	.958	1	/C-6	0.1
1964	StL-N	40	106	8	21	1	0	1	6	17	24	.198	.315	.236	53	-6	0	1	-1	.987	5	C-40	-0.1
1965	StL-N	53	145	17	33	7	0	2	10	24	27	.228	.345	.317	80	-3	0	1	-1	.985	-1	C-49	-0.3
1966	Phi-N	78	207	15	43	6	0	1	30	22	36	.208	.284	.338	72	-8	0	1	0	.985	1	C-76	-0.3
1967	Phi-N	18	35	3	6	2	0	0	7	5	9	.171	.275	.229	45	-2	0	0	0	.973	0	C-17	-0.2
	Atl-N	62	158	14	23	2	0	3	13	19	51	.146	.237	.215	31	-14	0	1	-1	.972	5	C-59	-0.8
	Yr	80	193	17	29	4	0	3	20	24	60	.150	.244	.218	33	-16	0	1	-1	.972	5	C-76	-1.0
Total	6	297	731	65	146	22	0	14	74	96	167	.200	.295	.287	63	-35	0	5	-2	.981	14	C-271	-1.3

■ FRENCHY UHALT
Uhalt, Bernard Bartholomew b: 4/27/10, Bakersfield, Cal. BL/TR, 5'10", 180 lbs. Deb: 4/17/34

YEAR	TM/L	G	AB	R	H	2B	3B	HR	RBI	BB	SO	AVG	OBP	SLG	PRO+	BR/A	SB	CS	SBR	FA	FR	G/POS	TPR
1934	Chi-A	57	165	28	40	5	1	0	16	29	12	.242	.359	.285	66	-7	6	5	-1	.935	-1	O-40	-1.0

■ TED UHLAENDER
Uhlaender, Theodore Otto b: 10/21/40, Chicago Heights, Ill. BL/TR, 6'2", 190 lbs. Deb: 9/4/65

YEAR	TM/L	G	AB	R	H	2B	3B	HR	RBI	BB	SO	AVG	OBP	SLG	PRO+	BR/A	SB	CS	SBR	FA	FR	G/POS	TPR
1965	Min-A	13	22	1	4	0	0	0	1	0	2	.182	.182	.182	3	-1	0	0	0	1.000	1	/O-4	-0.2
1966	Min-A	105	367	39	83	12	2	2	22	27	33	.226	.281	.286	60	-19	10	2	2	.985	12	*O-100	-1.0
1967	Min-A	133	415	41	107	19	7	6	49	13	45	.258	.285	.381	88	-7	4	4	-1	.996	7	*O-118	-0.7
1968	Min-A	140	488	52	138	21	5	7	52	28	46	.283	.330	.389	110	5	16	7	1	.986	-2	*O-129	-0.3
1969	*Min-A	152	554	93	151	18	6	8	62	44	52	.273	.331	.356	90	-7	15	9	-1	.997	-6	*O-150	-2.2
1970	Cle-A	141	473	56	127	21	2	11	46	39	44	.268	.326	.391	92	-5	3	6	-3	.991	-14	*O-134	-3.0
1971	Cle-A	141	500	52	144	20	3	2	47	38	44	.288	.338	.352	88	-7	3	6	-3	.992	1	*O-131	-1.7
1972	*Cin-N	73	113	9	18	3	0	0	6	13	11	.159	.246	.186	26	-11	0	1	-1	.976	-2	O-27	-1.6
Total	8	898	2932	343	772	114	21	36	285	202	277	.263	.313	.353	86	-54	52	35	-5	.991	-3	O-793	-10.7

■ GEORGE UHLE
Uhle, George Ernest "The Bull" b: 9/18/1898, Cleveland, Ohio d: 2/26/85, Lakewood, Ohio BR/TR, 6', 190 lbs. Deb: 4/30/19 C

YEAR	TM/L	G	AB	R	H	2B	3B	HR	RBI	BB	SO	AVG	OBP	SLG	PRO+	BR/A	SB	CS	SBR	FA	FR	G/POS	TPR
1919	Cle-A	26	43	7	13	2	1	0	6	1	5	.302	.318	.395	94	-1	0			.915	0	P-26	0.0
1920	*Cle-A	27	32	4	11	0	0	0	2	2	0	.344	.382	.344	91	-0	1	0	0	1.000	0	P-27	0.0
1921	Cle-A	48	94	21	23	2	3	1	18	6	9	.245	.290	.362	64	-5	0	0	0	.938	-3	P-41	0.0
1922	Cle-A	56	109	21	29	8	2	0	14	13	6	.266	.350	.376	88	-2	1	2	-1	.932	-3	P-50	0.0
1923	Cle-A	58	144	23	52	10	3	0	22	7	10	.361	.391	.472	127	5	2	1	0	.982	0	P-54	0.0
1924	Cle-A	59	107	10	33	6	1	1	19	4	8	.308	.339	.411	92	-2	0	1	-1	1.000	1	P-28	0.0
1925	Cle-A	55	101	10	29	3	1	3	17	7	7	.287	.339	.376	81	-3	0	0	0	.943	-3	P-29	0.0
1926	Cle-A	50	132	16	30	3	0	1	11	10	12	.227	.287	.273	46	-10	2	0	0	.933	-0	P-39	0.0
1927	Cle-A	43	79	4	21	7	1	0	14	5	12	.266	.310	.380	78	-3	0	1	-1	.974	-1	P-25	0.0
1928	Cle-A	55	98	9	28	3	2	1	17	8	4	.286	.340	.388	90	-2	0	0	0	.972	3	P-31	0.0
1929	Det-A	40	108	18	37	1	1	0	13	6	6	.343	.377	.370	93	-1	0	0	0	.929	-3	P-32	0.0
1930	Det-A	59	117	15	36	4	2	2	21	9	8	.308	.352	.427	95	-1	0	0	0	.975	-3	P-33	0.0
1931	Det-A	53	90	8	22	3	0	1	6	8	6	.244	.306	.378	76	-3	0	1	-1	1.000	-1	P-29	0.0
1932	Det-A	38	55	2	10	3	1	0	4	6	5	.182	.262	.273	37	-5	0	0	0	1.000	-1	P-33	0.0
1933	Det-A	1	0	0	0	0	0	0	0	0	0	—	—	—	—					.000	0	/P-1	0.0
	NY-N	8	5	1	0	0	0	0	0	0	1	.000	.000	.000	-50	-1	0			1.000	0	/P-6	0.0
	NY-A	12	20	1	8	1	0	0	1	4	2	.400	.500	.450	163	2	0			1.000	-1	/P-12	0.0
1934	NY-A	10	5	1	3	1	0	0	1	0	0	.600	.600	1.000	329	2	0			1.000	-0	/P-10	0.0
1936	Cle-A	24	21	1	8	1	0	0	3	4	5	.381	.435	.571	145	2	0			1.000	-1	/P-7	0.0
Total	17	722	1360	172	393	60	21	9	187	98	112	.289	.339	.384	86	-29	6	8		.960	-15	P-513	0.0

■ MAURY UHLER
Uhler, Maurice William b: 12/14/1886, Pikesville, Md. d: 5/4/18, Baltimore, Md. BR/TR, 5'11", 165 lbs. Deb: 4/14/14

YEAR	TM/L	G	AB	R	H	2B	3B	HR	RBI	BB	SO	AVG	OBP	SLG	PRO+	BR/A	SB	CS	SBR	FA	FR	G/POS	TPR
1914	Cin-N	46	56	12	12	2	0	0	3	5	11	.214	.279	.250	56	-3	4			.932	-8	O-36	-1.3

YEAR	TM/L	G	AB	R	H	2B	3B	HR	RBI	BB	SO	AVG	OBP	SLG	PRO+	BR/A	SB	CS	SBR	FA	FR	G/POS	TPR

■ CHARLIE UHLIR   Uhlir, Charles Karel   b: 7/30/12, Chicago, Ill.   d: 7/9/84, Spirit Lake, Iowa   BL/TL, 5'7.5", 150 lbs.   Deb: 8/3/34

YEAR	TM/L	G	AB	R	H	2B	3B	HR	RBI	BB	SO	AVG	OBP	SLG	PRO+	BR/A	SB	CS	SBR	FA	FR	G/POS	TPR
1934	Chi-A	14	27	3	4	0	0	0	3	2	6	.148	.207	.148	-7	-4	0	0	0	1.000	-1	/O-6	-0.5

■ MIKE ULISNEY   Ulisney, Michael Edward "Slugs"   b: 9/28/17, Greenwald, Pa.   BR/TR, 5'9", 165 lbs.   Deb: 5/5/45

YEAR	TM/L	G	AB	R	H	2B	3B	HR	RBI	BB	SO	AVG	OBP	SLG	PRO+	BR/A	SB	CS	SBR	FA	FR	G/POS	TPR
1945	Bos-N	11	18	4	7	1	0	1	4	1	0	.389	.421	.611	184	2	0			.714	-2	/C-4	0.0

■ SCOTT ULLGER   Ullger, Scott Matthew   b: 6/10/56, New York, N.Y.   BR/TR, 6'2", 186 lbs.   Deb: 4/17/83

YEAR	TM/L	G	AB	R	H	2B	3B	HR	RBI	BB	SO	AVG	OBP	SLG	PRO+	BR/A	SB	CS	SBR	FA	FR	G/POS	TPR
1983	Min-A	35	79	8	15	4	0	0	5	5	21	.190	.247	.241	34	-7	0	2	-1	.990	-2	1-30/3-3,D-1	-1.1

■ GEORGE ULRICH   Ulrich, George T.   b: 6/5/1869, Philadelphia, Pa.   Deb: 5/1/1892

YEAR	TM/L	G	AB	R	H	2B	3B	HR	RBI	BB	SO	AVG	OBP	SLG	PRO+	BR/A	SB	CS	SBR	FA	FR	G/POS	TPR
1892	Was-N	6	24	1	7	1	0	0	0	0	4	.292	.292	.333	92	-0	2			.889	-1	/3-3,S-2,C-2	-0.1
1893	Cin-N	1	3	0	0	0	0	0	0	0	0	.000	.250	.000	-31	-1	1			1.000	-0	/O-1	0.0
1896	NY-N	14	45	4	8	1	0	0	1	1	1	.178	.229	.200	14	-6	0			.920	-1	O-11/3-3	-0.5
Total	3	21	72	5	15	2	0	0	1	1	5	.208	.250	.236	35	-7	3			.923	-1	/O-12,3-6,C-2,S-2	-0.7

■ TOM UMPHLETT   Umphlett, Thomas Mullen   b: 5/12/30, Scotland Neck, N.C   BR/TR, 6'2", 180 lbs.   Deb: 4/16/53

YEAR	TM/L	G	AB	R	H	2B	3B	HR	RBI	BB	SO	AVG	OBP	SLG	PRO+	BR/A	SB	CS	SBR	FA	FR	G/POS	TPR
1953	Bos-A	137	495	53	140	27	5	3	59	34	30	.283	.331	.376	86	-10	4	2	0	.983	6	*O-136	-0.9
1954	Was-A	114	342	21	75	8	3	1	33	17	42	.219	.256	.269	46	-26	1	2	-1	.989	0	*O-101	-3.2
1955	Was-A	110	323	34	70	10	0	2	19	24	35	.217	.271	.266	47	-25	2	1	0	.988	4	*O-103	-2.5
Total	3	361	1160	108	285	45	8	6	111	75	107	.246	.293	.314	65	-61	7	5	-1	.986	10	O-340	-6.6

■ BOB UNGLAUB   Unglaub, Robert Alexander   b: 7/31/1881, Baltimore, Md.   d: 11/29/16, Baltimore, Md.   BR/TR, 5'11", 178 lbs.   Deb: 4/15/04   M

YEAR	TM/L	G	AB	R	H	2B	3B	HR	RBI	BB	SO	AVG	OBP	SLG	PRO+	BR/A	SB	CS	SBR	FA	FR	G/POS	TPR
1904	NY-A	6	19	2	4	0	0	0	2	0		.211	.211	.211	32	-1	0			.786	-1	/3-4,S-1	-0.3
	Bos-A	9	13	1	2	1	0	0	2	1		.154	.214	.231	39	-1	0			.625	-2	/2-3,3-2,S-1	-0.3
	Yr	15	32	3	6	1	0	0	4	1		.188	.212	.219	35	-2	0			.842	-3	/3-6,2-3,S-2	-0.6
1905	Bos-A	43	121	18	27	5	1	0	11	6		.223	.260	.281	71	-4	2			.928	1	3-21/2-7,1-2	-0.3
1907	Bos-A	139	544	49	138	17	13	1	62	23		.254	.284	.338	99	-3	14			.986	-1	*1-139,M	-0.9
1908	Bos-A	72	266	23	70	11	3	1	25	7		.263	.287	.338	100	-1	6			.980	2	1-72	-0.1
	Was-A	72	276	23	85	10	5	0	29	8		.308	.327	.380	142	11	8			.928	11	3-39,2-27/1-4	2.5
	Yr	144	542	46	155	21	8	1	54	15		.286	.308	.360	120	9	14			.981	12	1-76,3-39,2-27	2.4
1909	Was-A	130	480	43	127	14	9	3	41	22		.265	.301	.350	111	4	15			.992	1	1-57,O-42,2-25,/3-4	0.3
1910	Was-A	124	431	29	101	9	4	0	44	21		.234	.270	.274	74	-14	21			.985	6	*1-124	-1.0
Total	6	595	2150	188	554	67	35	5	216	88		.258	.288	.328	99	-10	66			.986	15	1-398/3-70,2-62,OS	-0.1

■ TIM UNROE   Unroe, Timothy Brian   b: 10/7/70, Round Lake Beach, Ill.   BR/TR, 6'3", 200 lbs.   Deb: 5/30/95

YEAR	TM/L	G	AB	R	H	2B	3B	HR	RBI	BB	SO	AVG	OBP	SLG	PRO+	BR/A	SB	CS	SBR	FA	FR	G/POS	TPR
1995	Mil-A	2	4	0	1	0	0	0	0	0	0	.250	.250	.250	29	-0	0	0	0	1.000	-0	/1-2	-0.1
1996	Mil-A	14	16	5	3	0	0	0	0	4	5	.188	.300	.188	39	-1	0	1	-1	.976	1	1-11/3-3,O-1,D-1	-0.1
Total	2	16	20	5	4	0	0	0	0	4	5	.200	.333	.200	38	-2	0	1	-1	.981	1	/1-13,3-3,D-1,O-1	-0.2

■ AL UNSER   Unser, Albert Bernard   b: 10/12/12, Morrisonville, Ill.   d: 7/7/95, Decatur, Ill.   BR/TR, 6'1", 175 lbs.   Deb: 9/14/42   F

YEAR	TM/L	G	AB	R	H	2B	3B	HR	RBI	BB	SO	AVG	OBP	SLG	PRO+	BR/A	SB	CS	SBR	FA	FR	G/POS	TPR
1942	Det-A	4	8	2	3	0	0	0	0	0	2	.375	.375	.375	103	0	0	0		1.000	1	/C-4	0.1
1943	Det-A	38	101	14	25	5	0	0	4	15	15	.248	.350	.297	84	-2	0	1	-1	.982	-3	C-37	-0.3
1944	Det-A	11	25	2	3	0	1	1	5	3	2	.120	.214	.320	49	-2	0	0		.864	-4	/2-5,C-1	-0.6
1945	Cin-N	67	204	23	54	10	3	3	21	14	24	.265	.318	.387	98	-1	0	0		.956	5	C-61	0.2
Total	4	120	338	41	85	15	4	4	30	32	43	.251	.322	.355	90	-5	0	1		.967	-7	C-103/2-5	-0.6

■ DEL UNSER   Unser, Delbert Bernard   b: 12/9/44, Decatur, Ill.   BL/TL, 6'1", 180 lbs.   Deb: 4/10/68   FC

YEAR	TM/L	G	AB	R	H	2B	3B	HR	RBI	BB	SO	AVG	OBP	SLG	PRO+	BR/A	SB	CS	SBR	FA	FR	G/POS	TPR
1968	Was-A	156	635	66	146	13	7	1	30	46	66	.230	.284	.277	73	-21	11	6	-0	.988	19	*O-156/1-1	-1.2
1969	Was-A	153	581	69	166	19	**8**	7	57	58	54	.286	.351	.382	111	8	8	10	-4	.972	6	*O-149	0.2
1970	Was-A	119	322	37	83	5	3	0	30	30	29	.258	.321	.326	83	-7	1	1	-0	.984	-3	*O-103	-1.6
1971	Was-A	153	581	63	148	19	6	9	41	59	68	.255	.326	.355	98	-2	11	6	-0	.981	3	*O-151	-0.7
1972	Cle-A	132	383	29	91	12	0	1	17	28	44	.238	.291	.277	67	-15	5	9	-4	.989	-1	*O-119	-2.5
1973	Phi-N	136	440	64	127	20	4	11	52	47	55	.289	.359	.427	114	9	5	8	-3	.988	17	*O-132	1.7
1974	Phi-N	142	454	72	120	18	5	11	61	50	62	.264	.339	.399	101	1	6	4	-1	.981	6	*O-135	0.0
1975	NY-N	147	531	65	156	18	2	10	53	42	76	.294	.340	.392	107	4	3	4	-2	.987	12	*O-144	1.1
1976	NY-N	77	276	28	63	13	2	5	25	18	44	.228	.278	.344	80	-8	4	4	-1	.995	4	O-77	-0.9
	Mon-N	69	220	29	50	6	2	7	15	11	44	.227	.264	.368	75	-8	3	3	-1	.963	-6	O-65	-1.9
	Yr	146	496	57	113	19	4	12	40	29	84	.228	.272	.355	78	-16	7	7	-2	.990	-3	*O-142	-2.8
1977	Mon-N	113	289	33	79	14	1	12	40	33	41	.273	.348	.453	116	6	2	5	-2	.976	-7	O-72,1-27	-0.6
1978	Mon-N	130	179	16	35	5	0	2	15	24	29	.196	.294	.257	56	-10	2	0	-1	.994	1	1-64,O-33	-1.1
1979	Phi-N	95	141	26	42	8	0	6	29	14	33	.298	.361	.482	124	5	0	1	-1	.978	-4	O-30,1-22	-0.1
1980	*Phi-N	96	110	15	29	6	4	0	10	10	21	.264	.325	.391	99	-1	0	0	-0	1.000	3	1-31,O-23	0.0
1981	Phi-N	62	59	5	9	0	0	0	6	13	9	.153	.306	.203	45	-4	0	0	-0	1.000	-1	1-18,O-16	-0.7
1982	Phi-N	19	14	0	0	0	0	0	0	3	2	.000	.176	.000	-46	-3	0	0	-0	1.000	-1	/1-5,O-2	-0.4
Total	15	1799	5215	617	1344	179	42	87	481	481	675	.258	.321	.358	93	-47	64	60	-17	.984	48	*O-1407,1-168	-8.7

■ JOHN UPHAM   Upham, John Leslie   b: 12/29/41, Windsor, Ont., Can.   BL/TL, 6', 180 lbs.   Deb: 4/16/67

YEAR	TM/L	G	AB	R	H	2B	3B	HR	RBI	BB	SO	AVG	OBP	SLG	PRO+	BR/A	SB	CS	SBR	FA	FR	G/POS	TPR
1967	Chi-N	8	3	1	2	0	0	0	0	0	0	.667	.667	.667	270	1	0	0	0	.000	-1	/P-5	-0.1
1968	Chi-N	13	10	0	2	0	0	0	0	0	3	.200	.200	.200	19	-1	0	0	0	1.000	-1	/P-2,O-2	-0.1
Total	2	21	13	1	4	0	0	0	0	0	3	.308	.308	.308	78	-0	0	0	0	1.000	-1	/P-7,O-2	-0.1

■ DIXIE UPRIGHT   Upright, R T   b: 5/30/26, Kannapolis, N.C.   d: 11/13/86, Concord, N.C.   BL/TL, 6', 175 lbs.   Deb: 4/18/53

YEAR	TM/L	G	AB	R	H	2B	3B	HR	RBI	BB	SO	AVG	OBP	SLG	PRO+	BR/A	SB	CS	SBR	FA	FR	G/POS	TPR
1953	StL-A	9	8	3	2	0	0	1	1	1	3	.250	.333	.625	151	0	0	0	0	.000	0	H	0.0

■ WILLIE UPSHAW   Upshaw, Willie Clay   b: 4/27/57, Blanco, Tex.   BL/TL, 6', 185 lbs.   Deb: 4/9/78   C

YEAR	TM/L	G	AB	R	H	2B	3B	HR	RBI	BB	SO	AVG	OBP	SLG	PRO+	BR/A	SB	CS	SBR	FA	FR	G/POS	TPR
1978	Tor-A	95	224	26	53	8	2	1	17	21	35	.237	.302	.304	69	-9	4	6	-2	.943	-6	O-52,D-18,1-10	-2.1
1980	Tor-A	34	61	10	13	3	1	1	5	6	14	.213	.284	.344	68	-3	0	1	0	.983	1	1-14,D-12/O-1	-0.2
1981	Tor-A	61	111	15	19	3	1	4	10	11	16	.171	.252	.324	61	-6	2	1	0	1.000	-2	D-15,1-14,O-14	-0.9
1982	Tor-A	160	580	77	155	25	7	21	75	52	91	.267	.329	.443	100	-1	8	8	-2	.989	-1	*1-155/D-5	-1.3
1983	Tor-A	160	579	99	177	26	7	27	104	61	98	.306	.377	.515	134	27	10	7	-1	.985	3	*1-159/D-1	1.9
1984	Tor-A	152	569	79	158	31	9	19	84	55	86	.278	.347	.464	118	13	10	4	-1	.990	-3	*1-151/D-1	0.1
1985	*Tor-A	148	501	79	138	31	5	15	65	48	71	.275	.344	.447	112	8	8	8	-2	.992	1	*1-147/D-1	-0.1
1986	Tor-A	155	573	85	144	28	6	9	60	78	87	.251	.343	.368	91	-5	23	5	4	.992	5	*1-154/D-1	-0.8
1987	Tor-A	150	512	68	125	22	4	15	58	58	78	.244	.325	.391	87	-10	10	11	-2	.993	12	*1-146	-1.1
1988	Cle-A	149	493	58	121	22	3	11	50	62	66	.245	.332	.369	94	-3	12	9	-2	.991	-1	*1-144	-1.6
Total	10	1264	4203	596	1103	199	45	123	528	452	642	.262	.337	.419	102	11	88	59	-9	.990	11	*1-1094/O-67,D-54	-6.1

■ TOM UPTON   Upton, Thomas Herbert "Muscles"   b: 12/29/26, Esther, Mo.   BR/TR, 6', 160 lbs.   Deb: 4/19/50   F

YEAR	TM/L	G	AB	R	H	2B	3B	HR	RBI	BB	SO	AVG	OBP	SLG	PRO+	BR/A	SB	CS	SBR	FA	FR	G/POS	TPR
1950	StL-A	124	389	50	92	5	6	2	30	52	45	.237	.328	.296	58	-24	7	2	1	.946	-10	*S-115/2-2,3-1	-2.3
1951	StL-A	52	131	9	26	4	3	0	12	12	22	.198	.271	.275	46	-10	1	1	0	.949	-4	S-47	-1.2
1952	Was-A	5	5	1	0	0	0	0	0	1	0	.000	.167	.000	-53	-1	0	0	0	1.000	0	/S-3	0.1
Total	3	181	525	60	118	9	9	2	42	65	67	.225	.313	.288	55	-35	8	3	1	.948	-13	S-165/2-2,3-1	-3.4

■ LUKE URBAN   Urban, Louis John   b: 3/22/1898, Fall River, Mass.   d: 12/7/80, Somerset, Mass.   BR/TR, 5'8", 168 lbs.   Deb: 7/19/27

YEAR	TM/L	G	AB	R	H	2B	3B	HR	RBI	BB	SO	AVG	OBP	SLG	PRO+	BR/A	SB	CS	SBR	FA	FR	G/POS	TPR
1927	Bos-N	35	111	11	32	6	0	0	10	3		.288	.313	.333	79	-4	1			.947	-8	C-34	-0.9
1928	Bos-N	15	17	0	3	0	0	0	0	2	1	.176	.222	.176	6	-2	0			1.000	1	C-10	-0.1
Total	2	50	128	11	35	6	0	0	10	5		.273	.301	.313	69	-6	1			.955	-7	/C-44	-1.0

■ BILLY URBANSKI   Urbanski, William Michael   b: 6/5/03, Linoleumville, N.Y   d: 7/12/73, Perth Amboy, N.J.   BR/TR, 5'8", 165 lbs.   Deb: 7/4/31

YEAR	TM/L	G	AB	R	H	2B	3B	HR	RBI	BB	SO	AVG	OBP	SLG	PRO+	BR/A	SB	CS	SBR	FA	FR	G/POS	TPR
1931	Bos-N	82	303	22	72	13	4	0	10	32		.238	.274	.307	58	-18	11			.961	11	3-68,S-19	-0.2
1932	Bos-N	136	563	80	153	25	8	6	46	28	60	.272	.307	.387	89	-10	8			.946	1	*S-136	0.3
1933	Bos-N	144	566	65	142	21	4	0	35	33	48	.251	.298	.302	78	-17	4			.953	-4	*S-143	-1.1

YEAR	TM/L	G	AB	R	H	2B	3B	HR	RBI	BB	SO	AVG	OBP	SLG	PRO+	BR/A	SB	CS	SBR	FA	FR	G/POS	TPR
1934	Bos-N	146	605	104	177	30	6	7	53	56	37	.293	.357	.397	110	9	4			.961	-10	*S-146	0.7
1935	Bos-N	132	514	53	118	17	0	4	30	40	32	.230	.286	.286	59	-30	3			.939	-27	*S-129	-5.0
1936	Bos-N	122	494	55	129	17	5	0	26	31	42	.261	.310	.316	74	-18	2			.937	-18	S-80,3-38	-3.0
1937	Bos-N	1	1	0	0	0	0	0	0	0	0	.000	.000	.000	-99	-0	0			.000	0	H	
Total	7	763	3046	379	791	123	27	19	207	198	252	.260	.309	.337	81	-85	24			.949	-47	S-653,3-106	-8.3

■ JOSE URIBE

Uribe, Jose Altagracia (Played Under Real Name Of Jose Altagracia Gonzalez (Uribe) In 1984) b: 1/21/59, San Cristobal, D.R. BR/TR, 5'10", 165 lbs. Deb: 9/13/84

YEAR	TM/L	G	AB	R	H	2B	3B	HR	RBI	BB	SO	AVG	OBP	SLG	PRO+	BR/A	SB	CS	SBR	FA	FR	G/POS	TPR
1984	StL-N	8	19	4	4	0	0	0	3	0	2	.211	.211	.211	19	-2	1	0	0	.955	0	/S-5,2-1	-0.1
1985	SF-N	147	476	46	113	20	4	3	26	30	57	.237	.285	.315	71	-19	8	2	1	.961	-2	*S-145/2-1	-0.7
1986	SF-N	157	453	46	101	15	1	3	43	61	76	.223	.315	.280	69	-18	22	11	0	.977	12	*S-156	0.8
1987	*SF-N	95	309	44	90	16	5	5	30	24	35	.291	.344	.424	107	3	12	2	2	.971	11	S-95	2.3
1988	SF-N	141	493	47	124	10	7	3	35	36	69	.252	.302	.318	82	-12	14	10	-2	.970	-3	*S-140	-0.6
1989	*SF-N	151	453	34	100	12	6	3	30	34	74	.221	.275	.280	61	-23	6	6	-2	.973	8	*S-150	-0.6
1990	SF-N	138	415	35	103	8	6	1	24	29	49	.248	.297	.304	68	-18	5	9	-4	.965	16	*S-134	0.3
1991	SF-N	90	231	23	51	8	4	1	12	20	33	.221	.283	.303	67	-10	3	4	-2	.966	9	S-87	-0.1
1992	SF-N	66	162	24	39	9	1	2	13	14	25	.241	.301	.346	88	-3	2	2	-1	.971	9	S-62	0.9
1993	Hou-N	45	53	4	13	1	0	0	3	8	5	.245	.355	.264	71	-2	1	0	0	.944	6	S-41	0.6
Total	10	1038	3064	307	738	99	34	19	219	256	425	.241	.300	.314	75	-105	74	46	-5	.969	62	*S-1015/2-2	2.8

■ LON URY

Ury, Louis Newton "Old Sleep" b: 1877, Ft.Scott, Kan. d: 3/4/18, Kansas City, Mo. TR, 6', Deb: 9/9/03

YEAR	TM/L	G	AB	R	H	2B	3B	HR	RBI	BB	SO	AVG	OBP	SLG	PRO+	BR/A	SB	CS	SBR	FA	FR	G/POS	TPR
1903	StL-N	2	7	1	1	0	0	0	1	0	0	.143	.143	.143	-19	-2	0			1.000	0	/1-2	-0.1

■ BOB USHER

Usher, Robert Royce b: 3/1/25, San Diego, Cal. BR/TR, 6'1.5", 180 lbs. Deb: 4/16/46

YEAR	TM/L	G	AB	R	H	2B	3B	HR	RBI	BB	SO	AVG	OBP	SLG	PRO+	BR/A	SB	CS	SBR	FA	FR	G/POS	TPR
1946	Cin-N	92	152	16	31	5	1	1	14	13	27	.204	.271	.270	56	-9	2			.982	-12	O-80/3-1	-2.5
1947	Cin-N	9	22	2	4	0	0	1	1	2	2	.182	.250	.318	50	-2	0			1.000	0	/O-8	-0.2
1950	Cin-N	106	321	51	83	17	0	6	35	27	38	.259	.316	.368	79	-10	3			.985	-5	O-93	-1.8
1951	Cin-N	114	303	27	63	12	2	5	25	19	36	.208	.257	.310	51	-21	4	5	-2	.974	-3	O-98	-3.0
1952	Chi-N	1	0	0	0	0	0	0	0	1	0	—	1.000	—	197	0	0	0	0	.000	0	H	0.0
1957	Cle-A	10	8	1	1	0	0	0		1	3	.125	.222	.125	-3	-1	0	0	0	1.000	-2	/O-4,3-1	-0.3
	Was-A	96	295	36	77	7	1	5	27	27	30	.261	.327	.342	84	-6				.979	3	O-95	-0.8
	Yr	106	303	37	78	7	1	5	27	28	33	.257	.324	.337	82	-7				.979	2	O-99/3-1	-1.1
Total	6	428	1101	133	259	41	4	18	102	90	136	.235	.295	.329	69	-49	9	5		.980	-19	O-378/3-2	-8.6

■ DUTCH USSAT

Ussat, William August b: 4/11/04, Dayton, Ohio d: 5/29/59, Dayton, Ohio BR/TR, 6'1", 170 lbs. Deb: 9/13/25

YEAR	TM/L	G	AB	R	H	2B	3B	HR	RBI	BB	SO	AVG	OBP	SLG	PRO+	BR/A	SB	CS	SBR	FA	FR	G/POS	TPR
1925	Cle-A	1	1	0	0	0	0	0	0	0	0	.000	.000	.000	-99	-0	0	0	0	1.000	0	/2-1	0.0
1927	Cle-A	4	16	4	3	0	1	0	2	0	1	.188	.278	.313	53	-1	0	0	0	1.000	-1	/3-4	-0.2
Total	2	5	17	4	3	0	1	0	2	0	1	.176	.263	.294	44	-1	0	0	0	1.000	-1	/3-4,2-1	-0.2

■ TEX VACHE

Vache, Ernest Lewis b: 11/17/1894, Santa Monica, Cal. d: 6/11/53, Los Angeles, Cal. BR/TR, 6'1", 200 lbs. Deb: 4/16/25

YEAR	TM/L	G	AB	R	H	2B	3B	HR	RBI	BB	SO	AVG	OBP	SLG	PRO+	BR/A	SB	CS	SBR	FA	FR	G/POS	TPR
1925	Bos-A	110	252	41	79	15	1	3	48	21	33	.313	.382	.464	114	5	2	2	-1	.908	-12	O-53	-1.0

■ GENE VADEBONCOEUR

Vadeboncoeur, Onesime Eugene b: 7/15/1858, Louisville, Que., Can. d: 10/16/35, Haverhill, Mass. BR/TR, 5'6", 150 lbs. Deb: 7/11/1884

YEAR	TM/L	G	AB	R	H	2B	3B	HR	RBI	BB	SO	AVG	OBP	SLG	PRO+	BR/A	SB	CS	SBR	FA	FR	G/POS	TPR
1884	Phi-N	4	14	1	3	0	0	0	3	1	2	.214	.267	.214	56	-1				.846	-1	/C-4	-0.1

■ HARRY VAHRENHORST

Vahrenhorst, Harry Henry "Van" b: 2/13/1885, St.Louis, Mo. d: 10/10/43, St.Louis, Mo. BR/TR, 6'1", 175 lbs. Deb: 9/21/04

YEAR	TM/L	G	AB	R	H	2B	3B	HR	RBI	BB	SO	AVG	OBP	SLG	PRO+	BR/A	SB	CS	SBR	FA	FR	G/POS	TPR
1904	StL-A	1	1	0	0	0	0	0	0	0	0	.000	.000	.000	-99	-0	0			.000	0	H	0.0

■ MIKE VAIL

Vail, Michael Lewis b: 11/10/51, San Francisco, Cal. BR/TR, 6', 185 lbs. Deb: 8/18/75

YEAR	TM/L	G	AB	R	H	2B	3B	HR	RBI	BB	SO	AVG	OBP	SLG	PRO+	BR/A	SB	CS	SBR	FA	FR	G/POS	TPR
1975	NY-N	38	162	17	49	8	1	3	17	9	37	.302	.339	.420	115	3	0	0	0	.971	11	O-36	1.3
1976	NY-N	53	143	8	31	5	1	0	9	6	19	.217	.248	.266	49	-10	0	1	-1	.941	-1	O-35	-1.4
1977	NY-N	108	279	29	73	12	1	8	35	19	58	.262	.310	.398	94	-3	0	7	-4	.965	2	O-85	-0.8
1978	Cle-A	14	34	2	8	2	1	0	2	1	9	.235	.257	.353	71	-1	1	1	0	1.000	0	/O-9,D-1	-0.2
	Chi-N	74	180	15	60	6	2	4	33	3	24	.333	.344	.456	109	2	0	1	-1	.981	-9	O-45/3-1	-1.0
1979	Chi-N	87	179	28	60	8	2	7	35	14	27	.335	.393	.520	131	7	0	2	-1	.964	-4	O-39/3-2	0.1
1980	Chi-N	114	312	30	93	17	2	6	47	14	77	.298	.330	.423	101	0	2	5	-2	.963	-4	O-77	-0.9
1981	Cin-N	31	31	1	5	0	0	0	3	0	9	.161	.161	.161	-8	-4	0	0	0	1.000	-1	/O-3	-0.5
1982	Cin-N	78	189	19	48	10	1	4	29	6	33	.254	.277	.381	81	-5	0	0	0	.988	-1	O-52	-0.6
1983	SF-N	18	26	1	4	1	0	0	3	0	7	.154	.185	.192	5	-3	0	0	0	1.000	-1	/1-4,O-2	-0.5
	Mon-N	34	53	5	15	2	0	2	4	8	10	.283	.387	.434	128	2	0	1	0	.958	1	O-15/1-1,3-1	0.3
	Yr	52	79	6	19	3	0	2	7	8	17	.241	.326	.354	90	-1	0	1	0	.960	0	O-17/1-5,3-1	-0.2
1984	LA-N	16	16	1	1	0	0	0	2	1	7	.063	.118	.063	-49	-3	0	0	0	1.000	-0	/O-1	-0.4
Total	10	665	1604	146	447	71	11	34	219	81	317	.279	.315	.400	95	-17	3	17	-9	.968	-5	O-399/1-5,3-4,D-1	-4.6

■ PEDRO VALDES

Valdes, Pedro Jose (Manzo) b: 6/29/73, Fajardo, P.R. BL/TL, 6'1", 180 lbs. Deb: 5/15/96

YEAR	TM/L	G	AB	R	H	2B	3B	HR	RBI	BB	SO	AVG	OBP	SLG	PRO+	BR/A	SB	CS	SBR	FA	FR	G/POS	TPR
1996	Chi-N	9	8	2	1	1	0	0	1	0	5	.125	.222	.250	24	-1	0	0	0	1.000	-1	/O-2	-0.1

■ ROY VALDES

Valdes, Rogelio Lazaro (Rojas) b: 2/20/20, Havana, Cuba BR/TR, 5'11", 185 lbs. Deb: 5/3/44

YEAR	TM/L	G	AB	R	H	2B	3B	HR	RBI	BB	SO	AVG	OBP	SLG	PRO+	BR/A	SB	CS	SBR	FA	FR	G/POS	TPR
1944	Was-A	1	0	0	0	0	0	0	0	0	0	.000	.000	.000	-99	-0	0	0	0	.000	0	H	0.0

■ SANDY VALDESPINO

Valdespino, Hilario (Borroto) b: 1/14/39, San Jose De Las Lajas, Cuba BL/TL, 5'8", 170 lbs. Deb: 4/12/65

YEAR	TM/L	G	AB	R	H	2B	3B	HR	RBI	BB	SO	AVG	OBP	SLG	PRO+	BR/A	SB	CS	SBR	FA	FR	G/POS	TPR
1965	*Min-A	108	245	38	64	8	2	1	22	20	28	.261	.322	.322	80	-6	7	4	-0	.990	0	O-57	-0.9
1966	Min-A	52	108	11	19	1	1	1	3	4	24	.176	.212	.259	33	-9	2	2	-1	1.000	-1	O-23	-1.3
1967	Min-A	99	91	9	16	2	0	1	3	5	22	.165	.206	.216	23	-9	3	1	0	.977	-11	O-65	-2.4
1968	Atl-N	36	86	8	20	1	0	1	4	10	20	.233	.320	.279	81	-2	0	0	0	.976	1	O-20	-0.2
1969	Hou-N	41	119	11	29	4	0	0	12	15	19	.244	.328	.277	73	-4	2	2	-1	.976	1	O-29	-0.5
	Sea-A	20	38	3	8	1	0	0	5	5	7	.211	.250	.237	37	-3	0	0	0	.889	2	/O-7	-0.2
1970	Mil-A	8	9	0	0	0	0	0	0	0	4	.000	.000	.000	-99	-2	0	0	0	.000	0	/O-1	-0.3
1971	KC-A	18	63	10	20	6	0	2	15	2	5	.317	.338	.508	138	3	0	0	0	.950	-2	O-15	0.0
Total	7	382	765	96	176	23	3	7	67	57	129	.230	.288	.295	66	-33	14	10	-2	.974	-10	O-217	-5.8

■ JULIO VALDEZ

Valdez, Julio Julian (b: Julio Julian Castillo (Valdez) b: 6/3/56, San Cristobal, D.R. BB/TR, 6'2", 160 lbs. Deb: 9/2/80

YEAR	TM/L	G	AB	R	H	2B	3B	HR	RBI	BB	SO	AVG	OBP	SLG	PRO+	BR/A	SB	CS	SBR	FA	FR	G/POS	TPR
1980	Bos-A	8	19	4	5	1	0	0	4	0	5	.263	.300	.474	103	-0	2	0	1	.935	7	/S-8	0.8
1981	Bos-A	17	23	1	5	0	0	0	0	0	3	.217	.217	.217	24	-2	1	0	-1	.955	3	/S-17	0.1
1982	Bos-A	28	20	5	5	1	0	0	1	0	7	.250	.250	.300	48	-1	1	0	0	.976	7	S-22/D-3	0.6
1983	Bos-A	12	25	3	3	0	0	0	1	1	3	.120	.185	.120	-13	-4	0	0	0	.939	-1	/2-9,S-2,D-1	-0.5
Total	4	65	87	11	18	2	0	0	8	1	18	.207	.233	.264	36	-8	3	1	0	.955	16	/S-49,2-9,D-4	1.0

■ JOSE VALDIVIELSO

Valdivielso, Jose (Lopez) (b: Jose Martinez De Valdivielso (Lopez)) b: 5/22/34, Matanzas, Cuba BR/TR, 6'1", 175 lbs. Deb: 6/21/55

YEAR	TM/L	G	AB	R	H	2B	3B	HR	RBI	BB	SO	AVG	OBP	SLG	PRO+	BR/A	SB	CS	SBR	FA	FR	G/POS	TPR
1955	Was-A	94	294	32	65	12	6	2	28	20	38	.221	.280	.316	63	-16	1	2	-1	.956	9	S-94	0.0
1956	Was-A	90	246	18	58	8	2	4	29	29	36	.236	.319	.333	72	-10	3	1	0	.947	16	S-90	1.3
1959	Was-A	24	14	1	4	0	0	0	1	0	3	.286	.333	.286	72	-0	1	0	0	1.000	5	S-21	0.5
1960	Was-A	117	268	23	57	1	1	2	19	20	36	.213	.277	.246	43	-21	0	0	0	.954	9	*S-115/3-1	-0.7
1961	Min-A	76	149	15	29	5	0	1	8	9	19	.195	.236	.248	28	-15	1	1	-0	.971	-2	S-43,2-15,3-14	-1.4
Total	5	401	971	89	213	26	9	9	85	79	132	.219	.284	.290	55	-63	6	6	-2	.955	37	S-363/2-15,3-15	-0.3

■ JOHN VALENTIN

Valentin, John William b: 2/18/67, Mineola, N.Y. BR/TR, 6', 170 lbs. Deb: 7/27/92

YEAR	TM/L	G	AB	R	H	2B	3B	HR	RBI	BB	SO	AVG	OBP	SLG	PRO+	BR/A	SB	CS	SBR	FA	FR	G/POS	TPR
1992	Bos-A	58	185	21	51	13	0	5	25	20	17	.276	.353	.427	110	3	1	0	0	.963	5	S-58	1.1
1993	Bos-A	144	468	50	130	40	3	11	66	49	77	.278	.349	.447	106	3	3	4	-2	.971	5	*S-144	1.7
1994	Bos-A	84	301	53	95	26	2	9	49	42	38	.316	.405	.505	127	13	3	5	1	.979	1	S-83/D-1	2.0
1995	*Bos-A	135	520	108	155	37	2	27	102	81	67	.298	.403	.533	136	29	20	5	3	.973	6	*S-135	4.7

YEAR	TM/L	G	AB	R	H	2B	3B	HR	RBI	BB	SO	AVG	OBP	SLG	PRO+	BR/A	SB	CS	SBR	FA	FR	G/POS	TPR
1996	Bos-A	131	527	84	156	29	3	13	59	63	258	.296	.379	.436	102	3	9	10	-3	.971	6	*S-118,3-12/D-1	1.5
Total	5	552	2001	316	587	145	10	65	301	255	258	.293	.380	.473	116	50	36	20	-1	.972	22	S-538/3-12,D-2	11.0

■ JOSE VALENTIN
Valentin, Jose Antonio b: 10/12/69, Manati, P.R. BB/TR, 5'10", 175 lbs. Deb: 9/17/92

YEAR	TM/L	G	AB	R	H	2B	3B	HR	RBI	BB	SO	AVG	OBP	SLG	PRO+	BR/A	SB	CS	SBR	FA	FR	G/POS	TPR
1992	Mil-A	4	3	1	0	0	0	0	0	0	0	.000	.000	.000	-99	-1	0	0	0	.667	-1	/2-1,S-1	-0.2
1993	Mil-A	19	53	10	13	1	2	1	7	7	16	.245	.344	.396	100	0	1	0	0	.922	-0	S-19	0.1
1994	Mil-A	97	285	47	68	19	0	11	46	38	75	.239	.332	.421	89	-5	12	3	2	.954	**28**	S-83,2-18/3-1	2.9
1995	Mil-A	112	338	62	74	23	3	11	49	37	83	.219	.296	.402	75	-13	16	8	0	.971	20	*S-104/3-1,D-4	1.4
1996	Mil-A	154	552	90	143	33	7	24	95	66	145	.259	.325	.438	97	-4	17	4	3	.950	-3	*S-151	0.9
Total	5	386	1231	210	298	76	12	47	198	148	319	.242	.325	.438	89	-23	46	15	5	.956	43	S-358/2-19,D-4,3-2	5.1

■ ELLIS VALENTINE
Valentine, Ellis Clarence b: 7/30/54, Helena, Ark. BR/TR, 6'4", 207 lbs. Deb: 9/3/75

YEAR	TM/L	G	AB	R	H	2B	3B	HR	RBI	BB	SO	AVG	OBP	SLG	PRO+	BR/A	SB	CS	SBR	FA	FR	G/POS	TPR
1975	Mon-N	12	33	2	12	4	0	1	3	2	4	.364	.400	.576	161	3	0	0	0	.867	-1	O-11	0.1
1976	Mon-N	94	305	36	85	15	2	7	39	30	51	.279	.343	.410	108	3	14	1	4	.972	0	O-88	0.4
1977	Mon-N★	127	508	63	149	28	2	25	76	30	58	.293	.333	.504	124	15	13	5	1	.972	1	*O-126	1.1
1978	Mon-N	151	570	75	165	35	4	25	76	35	88	.289	.333	.489	129	19	13	8	-1	.970	14	*O-146	2.7
1979	Mon-N	146	548	73	151	29	3	21	82	22	74	.276	.305	.454	105	1	11	9	-2	.983	1	*O-144	-0.6
1980	Mon-N	86	311	40	98	22	2	13	67	25	44	.315	.372	.524	147	19	5	5	-2	.970	1	O-83	1.6
1981	Mon-N	22	76	8	16	3	0	3	15	6	11	.211	.268	.368	78	-2	0	1	-1	1.000	-0	O-21	-0.4
	NY-N	48	169	15	35	8	1	5	21	5	38	.207	.230	.355	65	-9	0	3	-2	.957	3	O-47	-1.0
	Yr	70	245	23	51	11	1	8	36	11	49	.208	.242	.359	69	-11	0	4	-2	.969	3	O-68	-1.4
1982	NY-N	111	337	33	97	14	1	8	48	5	38	.288	.300	.407	97	-3	1	3	-2	.983	-1	O-98	-0.6
1983	Cal-A	86	271	30	65	10	2	13	43	18	48	.240	.287	.435	97	-2	2	1	0	.963	-7	O-85	-1.2
1985	Tex-A	11	38	5	8	1	0	2	4	2	8	.211	.250	.395	72	-2	0	1	-1	1.000	-1	/O-7,D-4	-0.4
Total	10	894	3166	380	881	169	15	123	474	180	462	.278	.319	.458	113	42	59	37	-5	.972	10	O-856/D-4	1.7

■ FRED VALENTINE
Valentine, Fred Lee "Squeaky" b: 1/19/35, Clarksdale, Miss. BB/TR, 6'1", 190 lbs. Deb: 9/7/59

YEAR	TM/L	G	AB	R	H	2B	3B	HR	RBI	BB	SO	AVG	OBP	SLG	PRO+	BR/A	SB	CS	SBR	FA	FR	G/POS	TPR
1959	Bal-A	12	19	0	6	0	0	0	1	3	6	.316	.409	.316	104	0	0	1	-1	.889	-2	/O-8	-0.2
1963	Bal-A	26	41	5	11	1	0	0	1	8	5	.268	.388	.293	98	0	0	0	0	1.000	-1	O-10	-0.2
1964	Was-A	102	212	20	48	5	0	4	20	21	44	.226	.305	.307	71	-8	4	2	0	.978	-4	O-57	-1.5
1965	Was-A	12	29	6	7	0	0	0	1	4	5	.241	.353	.241	73	-1	3	0	1	1.000	-0	O-11	0.0
1966	Was-A	146	508	77	140	29	7	16	59	51	63	.276	.353	.455	132	21	22	10	1	.980	-4	*O-138/1-2	1.2
1967	Was-A	151	457	52	107	16	1	11	44	56	76	.234	.331	.346	104	4	17	3	3	.989	-6	*O-136	-0.6
1968	Was-A	37	101	11	24	2	0	3	7	6	11	.238	.294	.347	96	-1	1	0	0	1.000	-1	O-27	-0.3
	Bal-A	47	91	9	17	3	2	1	5	7	20	.187	.253	.330	75	-3	0	0	0	.972	-1	O-26	-0.9
	Yr	84	192	20	41	5	2	4	12	13	31	.214	.274	.339	86	-4	1	0	0	.986	-3	O-53	-0.9
Total	7	533	1458	180	360	56	10	36	138	156	228	.247	.331	.373	106	13	47	16	5	.983	-20	O-413/1-2	-2.2

■ BOB VALENTINE
Valentine, Robert Deb: 5/20/1876

YEAR	TM/L	G	AB	R	H	2B	3B	HR	RBI	BB	SO	AVG	OBP	SLG	PRO+	BR/A	SB	CS	SBR	FA	FR	G/POS	TPR
1876	NY-N	1	3	0	0	0	0	0	0	0	0	.000	.000	.000	-99	-1				.400	-0	/C-1	-0.1

■ BOBBY VALENTINE
Valentine, Robert John b: 5/13/50, Stamford, Conn. BR/TR, 5'10", 189 lbs. Deb: 9/2/69 MC

YEAR	TM/L	G	AB	R	H	2B	3B	HR	RBI	BB	SO	AVG	OBP	SLG	PRO+	BR/A	SB	CS	SBR	FA	FR	G/POS	TPR
1969	LA-N	5	0	3	0	0	0	0	0	0	0	—	—	—	—	0	0	0	0	.000	0	R	0.0
1971	LA-N	101	281	32	70	10	2	1	25	15	20	.249	.292	.310	75	-10	5	3	-0	.961	-1	S-37,3-23,2-21,O-11	-0.7
1972	LA-N	119	391	42	107	11	2	3	32	27	33	.274	.324	.335	90	-5	5	5	-2	.976	0	2-49,3-39,O-16,S-10	-0.4
1973	Cal-A	32	126	12	38	5	2	1	13	5	9	.302	.338	.397	112	1	6	1	1	.948	0	S-25/O-8	0.6
1974	Cal-A	117	371	39	97	10	3	3	39	25	25	.261	.313	.329	90	-5	8	5	-1	.950	-8	O-62,S-36,3-15,/2D	-1.3
1975	Cal-A	26	57	5	16	2	0	0	5	4	3	.281	.339	.316	92	-0	0	2	-1	.958	-2	D-13/1-3,3-2,O-2	-0.4
	SD-N	7	15	1	2	0	0	1	1	4	0	.133	.316	.333	86	-0	1	0	0	1.000	-1	/O-4	-0.1
1976	SD-N	15	49	3	18	4	0	0	4	6	2	.367	.436	.449	165	4	1	0	0	1.000	-1	O-10/1-4	0.4
1977	SD-N	44	67	5	12	3	0	1	10	7	10	.179	.257	.269	46	-5	0	0	0	.962	-2	S-10,3-10/1-1	-0.6
	NY-N	42	83	8	11	1	0	1	3	6	9	.133	.191	.181	-12	0	0	0	1.000	-1	1-15,S-14/3-4	-1.2
	Yr	86	150	13	23	4	0	2	13	13	19	.153	.221	.220	20	-17	0	0	0	.969	-2	S-24,1-16,3-14	-1.8
1978	NY-N	69	160	17	43	7	0	1	18	19	18	.269	.350	.331	95	-1	1	1	-0	.977	-9	2-45/3-9	-0.8
1979	Sea-A	62	98	9	27	7	0	0	7	22	5	.276	.408	.337	102	2	1	0	0	.971	-6	S-29,O-15/2-4,3CD	-0.5
Total	10	639	1698	176	441	59	9	12	157	140	134	.260	.319	.326	86	-31	27	20	-4	.957	-27	S-161,O-128,23/1DC	-5.0

■ BENNY VALENZUELA
Valenzuela, Benjamin Beltran "Papelero" b: 6/2/33, Los Mochis, Mexico BR/TR, 5'10", 175 lbs. Deb: 4/27/58

YEAR	TM/L	G	AB	R	H	2B	3B	HR	RBI	BB	SO	AVG	OBP	SLG	PRO+	BR/A	SB	CS	SBR	FA	FR	G/POS	TPR
1958	StL-N	10	14	0	3	1	0	0	3	1	0	.214	.267	.286	45	0	0	0	0	.875	0	/3-3	-0.1

■ DAVE VALLE
Valle, David b: 10/30/60, Bayside, N.Y. BR/TR, 6'2", 200 lbs. Deb: 9/7/84

YEAR	TM/L	G	AB	R	H	2B	3B	HR	RBI	BB	SO	AVG	OBP	SLG	PRO+	BR/A	SB	CS	SBR	FA	FR	G/POS	TPR
1984	Sea-A	13	27	4	8	1	0	1	4	1	5	.296	.321	.444	111	0	0	0	0	1.000	2	C-13	0.3
1985	Sea-A	31	70	2	11	1	0	0	4	1	17	.157	.181	.171	-3	-10	0	0	0	.976	-1	C-31	-1.0
1986	Sea-A	22	53	10	18	3	0	5	15	7	7	.340	.417	.679	191	7	0	0	0	.982	-4	C-12/1-4	0.3
1987	Sea-A	95	324	40	83	16	3	12	53	15	46	.256	.295	.435	86	-7	2	0	-1	.989	1	C-75,D-14/1-2,O-1	-0.1
1988	Sea-A	93	290	29	67	15	2	10	50	18	32	.231	.297	.400	89	-5	0	0	-1	.989	6	C-84/1-1,D-3	0.7
1989	Sea-A	94	316	32	75	10	3	7	34	29	32	.237	.313	.354	85	-6	0	0	-0	.993	-3	C-93	-0.3
1990	Sea-A	107	308	37	66	15	0	7	33	45	48	.214	.328	.331	84	-6	1	2	-1	**.997**	-0	*C-104/1-1	-0.1
1991	Sea-A	132	324	38	63	8	1	8	32	34	49	.194	.289	.299	63	-16	0	1	-0	.992	9	*C-129/1-2	-0.2
1992	Sea-A	124	367	39	88	16	1	9	30	27	58	.240	.306	.362	86	-7	0	0	-0	.990	-3	*C-122	-0.4
1993	Sea-A	135	423	48	109	19	0	13	63	48	56	.258	.357	.395	100	1	1	0	0	.995	9	*C-135	1.7
1994	Bos-A	30	76	6	12	2	1	1	5	2	18	.158	.256	.250	30	-8	1	0	-0	.982	-1	C-28/1-2	-0.7
	Mil-A	16	36	8	14	6	0	1	5	9	4	.389	.522	.639	189	5	0	1	0	1.000	-1	C-12/D-2	0.5
	Yr	46	112	14	26	8	1	2	10	18	22	.232	.348	.375	83	-3	1	1	-0	.986	-1	C-40/1-2,D-2	-0.2
1995	Tex-A	36	75	7	18	3	0	3	5	9	18	.240	.305	.280	52	-3	1	0	0	.993	7	C-29/1-7	0.3
1996	Tex-A	42	86	14	26	6	1	3	17	9	17	.302	.368	.500	109	1	0	0	0	.994	8	C-35/1-5,D-1	1.0
Total	13	970	2775	314	658	121	12	77	350	258	413	.237	.316	.373	86	-55	5	7	-3	.992	29	C-902/1-24,D-20,O-1	2.0

■ HECTOR VALLE
Valle, Hector Jose b: 10/27/40, Vega Baja, P.R. BR/TR, 5'9", 180 lbs. Deb: 6/6/65

YEAR	TM/L	G	AB	R	H	2B	3B	HR	RBI	BB	SO	AVG	OBP	SLG	PRO+	BR/A	SB	CS	SBR	FA	FR	G/POS	TPR
1965	LA-N	9	13	1	4	0	0	0	2	2	3	.308	.400	.308	110	0	0	0	0	1.000	-0	/C-6	0.0

■ ELMER VALO
Valo, Elmer William b: 3/5/21, Ribnik, Czech. BL/TR, 5'11", 190 lbs. Deb: 9/22/40 C

YEAR	TM/L	G	AB	R	H	2B	3B	HR	RBI	BB	SO	AVG	OBP	SLG	PRO+	BR/A	SB	CS	SBR	FA	FR	G/POS	TPR
1940	Phi-A	6	23	6	8	0	0	0	3	0	0	.348	.423	.348	104		2	0	1	1.000	1	/O-6	0.1
1941	Phi-A	15	50	13	21	0	1	2	6	4	2	.420	.463	.580	179	6	0	0	0	1.000	-1	O-10	0.4
1942	Phi-A	133	459	64	115	13	10	2	40	70	21	.251	.355	.336	95	-1	13	8	-1	.964	1	*O-122	-0.8
1943	Phi-A	77	249	31	55	6	2	3	18	35	13	.221	.319	.297	81	-5	2	6	-3	.986	-1	O-63	-1.3
1946	Phi-A	108	348	59	107	21	6	1	31	60	18	.307	.411	.411	131	17	9	8	-2	.974	1	O-90	1.2
1947	Phi-A	112	370	60	111	12	6	5	36	64	21	.300	.406	.405	123	14	11	3	2	.973	-1	*O-104	1.0
1948	Phi-A	113	383	72	117	17	4	3	46	81	13	.305	.432	.394	120	16	10	6	-1	.983	-1	*O-109	0.9
1949	Phi-A	150	547	86	155	27	6	5	85	119	32	.283	.413	.404	121	21	14	11	-2	.981	10	*O-150	2.1
1950	Phi-A	129	446	62	125	16	5	10	46	82	22	.280	.400	.406	109	9	12	7	-1	.982	4	*O-117	0.6
1951	Phi-A	123	444	75	134	27	8	7	55	75	20	.302	.412	.446	129	21	11	6	-3	.981	-0	*O-116	1.6
1952	Phi-A	129	388	69	109	24	8	1	37	101	16	.281	.432	.407	126	19	12	11	-3	.962	-3	*O-121	1.0
1953	Phi-A	50	85	15	19	3	0	0	9	22	7	.224	.383	.259	73	-2	0	1	-1	1.000	-1	O-25	-0.4
1954	Phi-A	95	224	28	48	11	6	1	36	50	16	.214	.360	.330	90	-1	0	1	-1	.965	2	O-62	-0.3
1955	KC-A	112	283	50	103	17	4	3	37	52	18	.364	.463	.484	153	24	5	3	-0	.987	2	O-72	2.2
1956	KC-A	9	9	1	2	0	0	0	1	2	1	.222	.300	.222	40	-1	0	0	0	.000	-0	/O-1	-0.1
	Phi-N	98	291	40	84	13	5	3	34	60	22	.289	.419	.406	118	9	7	3	-1	.966	-0	O-87	-0.5
1957	Bro-N	81	161	14	44	10	1	4	26	25	16	.273	.374	.422	104	1	5	3	-0	1.000	-4	O-36	-0.5
1958	LA-N	65	101	9	25	2	1	1	14	12	11	.248	.327	.317	69	-4	0	0	0	1.000	-6	O-26	-1.2
1959	Cle-A	34	24	3	7	0	0	0	5	7	0	.292	.452	.292	113	1	0	0	0	1.000	-1	/O-2	0.1

YEAR	TM/L	G	AB	R	H	2B	3B	HR	RBI	BB	SO	AVG	OBP	SLG	PRO+	BR/A	SB	CS	SBR	FA	FR	G/POS	TPR
1960	NY-A	8	5	1	0	0	0	0	0	2	1	.000	.286	.000	-17	-1	0	0	0	.000	-1	/O-2	-0.2
	Was-A	76	64	6	18	3	0	0	16	17	4	.281	.439	.328	112	2	0	0	0	1.000	-1	/O-6	0.2
	Yr	84	69	7	18	3	0	0	16	19	5	.261	.427	.304	103	2	0	0	0	1.000	-1	/O-8	0.0
1961	Min-A	33	32	0	5	2	0	0	4	3	3	.156	.250	.219	25	-3	0	0	0	1.000	-0	/O-1	-0.3
	Phi-N	50	43	4	8	2	0	1	8	8	6	.186	.327	.302	69	-2	0	0	0	.000	-0	/O-1	-0.2
Total	20	1806	5029	768	1420	228	73	58	601	942	284	.282	.399	.391	114	142	110	79	-14	.977	1	*O-1329	6.5

■ DEACON Van BUREN
Van Buren, Edward Eugene b: 12/14/1870, LaSalle Co., Ill. d: 6/29/57, Portland, Ore. BL/TR, 5'10", 175 lbs. Deb: 4/21/04

YEAR	TM/L	G	AB	R	H	2B	3B	HR	RBI	BB	SO	AVG	OBP	SLG	PRO+	BR/A	SB	CS	SBR	FA	FR	G/POS	TPR
1904	Bro-N	1	1	0	1	0	0	0	0	0		1.000	1.000	1.000	531	0	0			.000	0	H	0.0
	Phi-N	12	43	2	10	2	0	0	3	3		.233	.283	.279	76	-1	2			.962	1	O-12	-0.1
	Yr	13	44	2	11	2	0	0	3	3		.250	.298	.295	86	-1	2			.962	1	O-12	-0.1

■ TY Van BURKLEO
Van Burkleo, Tyler Lee b: 10/7/63, Oakland, Cal. BL/TL, 6'5", 225 lbs. Deb: 7/28/93

YEAR	TM/L	G	AB	R	H	2B	3B	HR	RBI	BB	SO	AVG	OBP	SLG	PRO+	BR/A	SB	CS	SBR	FA	FR	G/POS	TPR
1993	Cal-A	12	33	2	5	3	0	1	1	6	9	.152	.282	.333	63	-2	1	0	0	1.000	-2	1-12	-0.4
1994	Col-N	2	5	0	0	0	0	0	0	0	1	.000	.000	.000	-86	-1	0	0	0	1.000	0	/1-2	-0.1
Total	2	14	38	2	5	3	0	1	1	6	10	.132	.250	.289	42	-3	1	0	0	1.000	-1	/1-14	-0.5

■ AL Van CAMP
Van Camp, Albert Joseph b: 9/7/03, Moline, Ill. d: 2/2/81, Davenport, Iowa BR/TR, 5'11.5", 175 lbs. Deb: 9/11/28

YEAR	TM/L	G	AB	R	H	2B	3B	HR	RBI	BB	SO	AVG	OBP	SLG	PRO+	BR/A	SB	CS	SBR	FA	FR	G/POS	TPR
1928	Cle-A	5	17	0	4	1	0	0	0	0		.235	.235	.294	38	-2	1	0		.980	-1	/1-5	-0.2
1931	Bos-A	101	324	34	89	15	4	0	33	20	24	.275	.319	.346	79	-10	3	2	-0	.973	-5	O-59,1-25	-2.0
1932	Bos-A	34	103	10	23	4	2	0	6	4	17	.223	.252	.301	44	-9	0	0	0	.985	1	1-25	-1.0
Total	3	140	444	44	116	20	6	0	41	24	42	.261	.301	.333	69	-21	4	2	0	.991	-5	/O-59,1-55	-3.2

■ CARL VANDAGRIFT
Vandagrift, Carl William b: 4/22/1883, Cantrall, Ill. d: 10/9/20, Fort Wayne, Ind. BR/TR, 5'8", 155 lbs. Deb: 5/19/14

YEAR	TM/L	G	AB	R	H	2B	3B	HR	RBI	BB	SO	AVG	OBP	SLG	PRO+	BR/A	SB	CS	SBR	FA	FR	G/POS	TPR
1914	Ind-F	43	136	25	34	4	0	0	9	9	15	.250	.301	.279	53	-11	7			.925	-6	2-28,3-12/S-5	-1.8

■ JOHN VANDER WAL
Vander Wal, John Henry b: 4/29/66, Grand Rapids, Mich. BL/TL, 6'1", 180 lbs. Deb: 9/6/91

YEAR	TM/L	G	AB	R	H	2B	3B	HR	RBI	BB	SO	AVG	OBP	SLG	PRO+	BR/A	SB	CS	SBR	FA	FR	G/POS	TPR
1991	Mon-N	21	61	4	13	4	1	1	8	1	18	.213	.226	.361	63	-3	0	0	0	1.000	-1	O-17	-0.5
1992	Mon-N	105	213	21	51	8	2	4	20	24	36	.239	.316	.352	90	-3	3	0	1	.981	0	O-57/1-7	-0.3
1993	Mon-N	106	215	34	50	7	4	5	30	27	30	.233	.321	.372	81	-6	6	3	0	.988	-12	1-42,O-38	-2.1
1994	Col-N	91	110	12	27	3	1	5	15	16	31	.245	.341	.427	85	-3	2	1	0	1.000	-2	1-14/O-7	-0.6
1995	*Col-N	105	101	15	35	8	1	5	21	16	23	.347	.436	.594	131	4	1	1	0	.957	-1	1-10,O-10	0.2
1996	Col-N	104	151	20	38	6	2	5	31	19	38	.252	.339	.417	76	-6	2	2	-1	1.000	-3	O-26,1-10	-1.1
Total	6	532	851	106	214	36	11	25	125	103	176	.251	.334	.408	89	-16	14	7	0	.986	-19	O-155/1-83	-4.4

■ FRED Van DUSEN
Van Dusen, Frederick William b: 7/31/37, Jackson Heights, N.Y. BL/TL, 6'3", 180 lbs. Deb: 9/11/55

YEAR	TM/L	G	AB	R	H	2B	3B	HR	RBI	BB	SO	AVG	OBP	SLG	PRO+	BR/A	SB	CS	SBR	FA	FR	G/POS	TPR
1955	Phi-N	1	0	0	0	0	0	0	0	0	0	—	1.000	—	199	0	0	0	0	.000	0	H	0.0

■ BILL Van DYKE
Van Dyke, William Jennings b: 12/15/1863, Paris, Ill. d: 5/5/33, ElPaso, Tex. BR/TR, 5'8", 170 lbs. Deb: 4/17/1890

YEAR	TM/L	G	AB	R	H	2B	3B	HR	RBI	BB	SO	AVG	OBP	SLG	PRO+	BR/A	SB	CS	SBR	FA	FR	G/POS	TPR
1890	Tol-a	129	502	74	129	14	11	2	54	25		.257	.296	.341	85	-12	73			.924	-7	*O-110,3-18/2-2,C-1	-1.9
1892	StL-N	4	16	2	2	1	0	0	1	0	1	.125	.125	.125	-26	-2	0			.875	-1	/O-4	-0.3
1893	Bos-N	3	12	2	3	0	0	0	1	0	1	.250	.250	.333	50	-1	1			1.000	-1	/O-3	-0.1
Total	3	136	530	78	134	15	11	2	56	25	2	.253	.290	.334	81	-14	74			.924	-8	O-117/3-18,2-2,C-1	-2.3

■ DAVE Van GORDER
Van Gorder, David Thomas b: 3/27/57, Los Angeles, Cal. BR/TR, 6'2", 205 lbs. Deb: 6/15/82

YEAR	TM/L	G	AB	R	H	2B	3B	HR	RBI	BB	SO	AVG	OBP	SLG	PRO+	BR/A	SB	CS	SBR	FA	FR	G/POS	TPR
1982	Cin-N	51	137	4	25	3	1	0	7	14	19	.182	.263	.219	35	-12	1	0	0	.986	-2	C-51	-1.2
1984	Cin-N	38	101	10	23	2	0	0	6	12	17	.228	.310	.248	56	-6	0	0	0	1.000	2	C-36/1-1	-0.3
1985	Cin-N	73	151	12	36	7	0	2	24	9	19	.238	.286	.325	67	-7	0	0	0	.989	-3	C-70	-0.8
1986	Cin-N	9	10	0	0	0	0	0	0	1	2	.000	.091	.000	-70	-2	0	0	0	1.000	1	/C-7	-0.2
1987	Bal-A	12	21	4	5	0	0	1	1	3	6	.238	.333	.381	91	-0	0	0	0	.978	1	C-12	0.1
Total	5	183	420	30	89	12	1	3	38	39	63	.212	.282	.267	52	-26	1	0	0	.990	-2	C-176/1-1	-2.4

■ GEORGE Van HALTREN
Van Haltren, George Edward Martin "Rip"
b: 3/30/1866, St.Louis, Mo. d: 9/29/45, Oakland, Cal. BL/TL, 5'11", 170 lbs. Deb: 6/27/1887 M

YEAR	TM/L	G	AB	R	H	2B	3B	HR	RBI	BB	SO	AVG	OBP	SLG	PRO+	BR/A	SB	CS	SBR	FA	FR	G/POS	TPR
1887	Chi-N	45	172	30	35	4	0	3	17	15	15	.203	.271	.279	47	-13	12			.927	-3	O-27,P-20	-0.9
1888	Chi-N	81	318	46	90	14	4	4	34	22	34	.283	.329	.437	133	11	21			.872	-2	O-57,P-30	0.1
1889	Chi-N	134	543	126	168	20	10	9	81	82	41	.309	.405	.433	128	21	28			.898	-3	*O-130/S-3,2-1	1.3
1890	Bro-P	92	376	84	126	8	9	5	54	41	23	.335	.405	.444	119	10	35			.896	5	O-67,P-28/S-3	0.5
1891	Bal-a	139	566	136	180	14	15	9	83	71	46	.318	.398	.443	139	29	75			.882	-12	O-81,S-59/P-6,2-2	1.5
1892	Bal-N	135	556	105	168	20	12	7	57	70	34	.302	.382	.419	139	26	49			.850	-7	*O-129/P-4,3-3,1SM	1.9
	Pit-N	13	55	10	11	2	0	0	5	6	0	.200	.279	.309	77	-2	6			.905	-2	O-13	-0.4
	Yr	148	611	115	179	22	14	7	62	76	34	.293	.373	.409	133	25	55			.854	-2	*O-142/P-4,3-3,1S	1.5
1893	Pit-N	124	529	129	179	14	13	6	79	75	25	.338	.422	.423	127	24	37			.869	-6	*O-111,S-12/2-2	1.0
1894	*NY-N	137	519	109	172	22	4	7	104	55	22	.331	.400	.430	101	2	43			.914	-7	*O-137	-0.7
1895	NY-N	131	521	113	177	23	19	8	103	57	29	.340	.408	.503	137	29	32			.914	-3	*O-131/P-1	1.3
1896	NY-N	133	562	136	197	18	**21**	5	74	55	36	.351	.410	.484	139	32	39			.952	4	*O-133/P-2	2.1
1897	NY-N	129	564	117	186	22	9	2	64	40		.330	.375	.417	112	10	50			.937	9	*O-129	0.8
1898	NY-N	156	654	129	204	28	16	2	68	59		.312	.372	.413	129	24	36			.917	-2	*O-156	1.0
1899	NY-N	151	604	117	182	21	3	2	58	74		.301	.378	.356	106	8	31			.932	3	*O-151	0.1
1900	NY-N	141	571	114	180	30	7	1	51	50		.315	.371	.398	118	14	**45**			.939	10	*O-141/P-1	1.2
1901	NY-N	135	543	82	182	23	6	1	47	51		.335	.396	.405	138	28	24			.941	4	*O-135/P-1	2.1
1902	NY-N	24	88	14	23	1	2	0	7	17		.261	.381	.318	117	3	6			.925	2	O-24	0.3
1903	NY-N	84	280	42	72	6	1	0	28	28		.257	.327	.286	72	-9	14			.959	-6	O-75	-1.9
Total	17	1984	8021	1639	2532	285	161	69	1014	868	<u>305</u>	.316	.385	.417	121	245	583			.915	-6	*O-1827/P-93,S231	11.1

■ JOHN VANN
Vann, John Silas b: 6/7/1893, Fairland, Okla. d: 6/10/58, Shreveport, La. BR/TR, Deb: 6/11/13

YEAR	TM/L	G	AB	R	H	2B	3B	HR	RBI	BB	SO	AVG	OBP	SLG	PRO+	BR/A	SB	CS	SBR	FA	FR	G/POS	TPR
1913	StL-N	1	0	0	0	0	0	0	0	0	1	.000	.000	.000	-99	-0	0			.000	0	H	0.0

■ JAY Van NOY
Van Noy, Jay Lowell b: 11/4/28, Garland, Utah BL/TR, 6'1", 200 lbs. Deb: 6/18/51

YEAR	TM/L	G	AB	R	H	2B	3B	HR	RBI	BB	SO	AVG	OBP	SLG	PRO+	BR/A	SB	CS	SBR	FA	FR	G/POS	TPR
1951	StL-N	6	7	1	0	0	0	0	0	1	6	.000	.125	.000	-63	-2	0	0	0	1.000	-0	/O-1	-0.2

■ MAURICE Van ROBAYS
Van Robays, Maurice Rene "Bomber" b: 11/15/14, Detroit, Mich. d: 3/1/65, Detroit, Mich. BR/TR, 6'0.5", 190 lbs. Deb: 9/7/39

YEAR	TM/L	G	AB	R	H	2B	3B	HR	RBI	BB	SO	AVG	OBP	SLG	PRO+	BR/A	SB	CS	SBR	FA	FR	G/POS	TPR
1939	Pit-N	27	105	13	33	9	2	2	16	6	10	.314	.351	.457	89	2	0			.919	-4	O-25/3-1	-0.2
1940	Pit-N	145	572	82	156	27	7	11	116	33	58	.273	.316	.402	98	-3	2			.963	-4	*O-143/1-1	-1.5
1941	Pit-N	129	457	62	129	23	5	4	78	41	29	.282	.343	.381	104	2	0			.974	7	*O-121	0.2
1942	Pit-N	100	328	29	76	13	5	1	46	30	24	.232	.298	.311	76	-10	0			.986	5	O-84	-1.0
1943	Pit-N	69	236	32	68	17	7	1	35	18	19	.288	.344	.432	119	5	0			.940	-3	O-60	-0.1
1946	Pit-N	59	146	14	31	5	1	1	12	11	15	.212	.272	.308	63	-7	0			.955	-5	O-37/1-2	-1.5
Total	6	529	1844	232	493	94	27	20	303	139	155	.267	.321	.380	97	-11	2			.966	-5	O-470/1-3,3-1	-4.1

■ ANDY Van SLYKE
Van Slyke, Andrew James b: 12/21/60, Utica, N.Y. BL/TR, 6'2", 192 lbs. Deb: 6/17/83

YEAR	TM/L	G	AB	R	H	2B	3B	HR	RBI	BB	SO	AVG	OBP	SLG	PRO+	BR/A	SB	CS	SBR	FA	FR	G/POS	TPR
1983	StL-N	101	309	51	81	15	5	8	38	46	64	.262	.360	.421	115	7	21	7	2	.974	-10	O-69,3-30/1-9	-0.3
1984	StL-N	137	361	45	88	16	4	7	50	63	71	.244	.356	.368	107	5	28	5	5	1.000	-12	O-81,3-32,1-30	-0.5
1985	*StL-N	146	424	61	110	25	6	13	55	47	54	.259	.336	.439	116	9	34	6	7	.996	-2	*O-142/1-2	1.0
1986	Cin-N	137	418	48	113	23	7	13	61	47	85	.270	.345	.452	119	10	21	8	6	.969	3	*O-110,1-38	1.1
1987	Pit-N	157	564	93	165	36	11	21	82	56	122	.293	.361	.507	126	20	34	8	5	.988	10	*O-150/1-1	3.0
1988	Pit-N★	154	587	101	169	23	**15**	25	100	57	126	.288	.352	.506	146	33	30	4	4	.991	17	*O-152	5.1
1989	Pit-N	130	476	64	113	18	9	9	53	47	100	.237	.310	.370	97	-2	16	4	2	.989	14	*O-123/1-2	1.1
1990	Pit-N	136	493	67	140	26	6	17	77	66	89	.284	.367	.465	133	23	14	4	2	.976	3	*O-133	2.5
1991	*Pit-N	138	491	87	130	24	7	17	83	71	85	.265	.362	.446	128	19	10	3	1	.996	1	*O-135	1.9
1992	*Pit-N★	154	614	103	**199**	45	12	14	89	58	99	.324	.386	.505	152	41	12	3	2	.989	11	*O-154	5.4
1993	Pit-N†	83	323	42	100	13	4	8	50	24	40	.310	.361	.449	116	7	11	2	2	.995	3	O-78	1.0

YEAR	TM/L	G	AB	R	H	2B	3B	HR	RBI	BB	SO	AVG	OBP	SLG	PRO+	BR/A	SB	CS	SBR	FA	FR	G/POS	TPR
1994	Pit-N	105	374	41	92	18	3	6	30	52	72	.246	.341	.358	82	-9	7	0	2	.992	6	O-99	-0.4
1995	Bal-A	17	63	6	10	1	0	3	8	5	15	.159	.221	.317	37	-6	0	0	0	.978	2	O-17	-0.4
	Phi-N	63	214	26	52	10	2	3	16	28	41	.243	.336	.350	81	-5	7	0	2	.984	3	O-56	-0.2
Total 13		1658	5711	835	1562	293	91	164	792	667	1063	.274	.352	.443	120	151	245	59	38	.988	48	*O-1499/1-82,3-62	20.3

■ IKE Van ZANDT Van Zandt, Charles Isaac b: 1877, Brooklyn, N.Y. d: 9/14/08, Nashua, N.H. BL/ Deb: 8/5/01

YEAR	TM/L	G	AB	R	H	2B	3B	HR	RBI	BB	SO	AVG	OBP	SLG	PRO+	BR/A	SB	CS	SBR	FA	FR	G/POS	TPR
1901	NY-N	3	6	1	1	0	0	0	0	0	0	.167	.167	.167	-3	-1	0			.333	-2	/P-2,O-1	-0.1
1904	Chi-N	3	11	0	0	0	0	0	0	0	0	.000	.000	.000	-99	-3	0			1.000		/O-3	-0.3
1905	StL-A	94	322	31	75	15	1	1	20		7	.233	.252	.295	77	-10	7			.874	-13	O-75/P-1,1-1	-2.9
Total 3		100	339	32	76	15	1	1	20		7	.224	.242	.283	69	-13	7			.868	-14	/O-79,P-3,1-1	-3.3

■ DICK Van ZANT Van Zant, Richard "Foghorn Dick" b: 11/1864, Indiana d: 8/6/12, Wayne Co., Ind. Deb: 10/4/1888

YEAR	TM/L	G	AB	R	H	2B	3B	HR	RBI	BB	SO	AVG	OBP	SLG	PRO+	BR/A	SB	CS	SBR	FA	FR	G/POS	TPR
1888	Cle-a	10	31	1	8	1	0	0	1		1	.258	.303	.290	93	-0	1			.784	0	3-10	0.0

■ EDDIE VARGAS Vargas, Hediberto (Rodriguez) b: 2/23/59, Guanica, P.R. BR/TR, 6'4", 205 lbs. Deb: 9/8/82

YEAR	TM/L	G	AB	R	H	2B	3B	HR	RBI	BB	SO	AVG	OBP	SLG	PRO+	BR/A	SB	CS	SBR	FA	FR	G/POS	TPR
1982	Pit-N	8	8	1	3	1	0	0	3	0	2	.375	.375	.500	139	0	0	0	0	1.000	0	/1-5	0.0
1984	Pit-N	18	31	3	7	2	0	0	2	3	5	.226	.294	.290	65	-1	0	0	0	.982	-0	1-13	-0.2
Total 2		26	39	4	10	3	0	0	5	3	7	.256	.310	.333	80	-1	0	0	0	.986	-0	/1-18	-0.2

■ BUCK VARNER Varner, Glen Gann b: 8/17/30, Hixson, Tenn. BL/TR, 5'10", 170 lbs. Deb: 9/19/52

YEAR	TM/L	G	AB	R	H	2B	3B	HR	RBI	BB	SO	AVG	OBP	SLG	PRO+	BR/A	SB	CS	SBR	FA	FR	G/POS	TPR
1952	Was-A	2	4	0	0	0	0	0	0	0	1	.000	.200	.000	-43	-1	0	0	0	1.000	0	/O-1	-0.1

■ PETE VARNEY Varney, Richard Fred b: 4/10/49, Roxbury, Mass. BR/TR, 6'3", 235 lbs. Deb: 8/26/73

YEAR	TM/L	G	AB	R	H	2B	3B	HR	RBI	BB	SO	AVG	OBP	SLG	PRO+	BR/A	SB	CS	SBR	FA	FR	G/POS	TPR
1973	Chi-A	5	4	0	0	0	0	0	0	0	1	.000	.200	.000	-38	-1	0	0	0	1.000	0	/C-5	0.0
1974	Chi-A	9	28	1	7	0	0	0	2	1	8	.250	.276	.250	51	-2	0	0	0	.981	1	/C-9	0.0
1975	Chi-A	36	107	12	29	5	1	2	8	6	28	.271	.316	.393	98	-1	2	0	1	.988	-1	C-34/D-2	0.0
1976	Chi-A	14	41	5	10	2	0	3	5	2	9	.244	.279	.512	128	1	0	0	0	.988	1	C-14	0.3
	Atl-N	5	10	0	1	0	0	0	0	1	2	.100	.100	.100	-41	-2	0	0	0	1.000	-1	/C-5	-0.2
Total 4		69	190	18	47	7	1	5	15	10	47	.247	.289	.374	86	-4	2	0	1	.988	1	/C-67,D-2	0.1

■ GARY VARSHO Varsho, Gary Andrew b: 6/20/61, Marshfield, Wis. BL/TR, 5'11", 190 lbs. Deb: 7/6/88

YEAR	TM/L	G	AB	R	H	2B	3B	HR	RBI	BB	SO	AVG	OBP	SLG	PRO+	BR/A	SB	CS	SBR	FA	FR	G/POS	TPR
1988	Chi-N	46	73	6	20	3	0	0	1	1	6	.274	.284	.315	69	-3	5	0	2	.906	-2	O-18	-0.4
1989	Chi-N	61	87	10	16	4	2	0	6	4	13	.184	.220	.276	38	-7	3	0	1	.929	-3	O-21	-1.0
1990	Chi-N	46	48	10	12	4	0	0	1	1	6	.250	.265	.333	59	-3	2	0	1	1.000	-0	/O-3	0.0
1991	*Pit-N	99	187	23	51	11	2	4	23	19	34	.273	.346	.417	115	4	9	2	2	.989	-4	O-54/1-3	0.0
1992	*Pit-N	103	162	22	36	6	3	4	22	10	32	.222	.267	.370	80	-3	1	0	0	.984	-5	O-44	-1.1
1993	Cin-N	77	95	8	22	2	0	2	11	9	19	.232	.305	.358	77	-3	1	0	0	1.000	-6	O-22	-0.5
1994	Pit-N	67	82	15	21	6	3	0	5	4	19	.256	.307	.402	82	-2	0	1	1	.926	-10	O-36/1-1	-1.3
1995	Phi-N	72	103	7	26	1	1	0	11	7	17	.252	.313	.282	58	-6	2	0	1	.939	-4	O-25	-0.9
Total 8		571	837	101	204	41	11	10	84	55	146	.244	.296	.355	78	-25	27	5	8	.963	-30	O-223/1-4	-5.5

■ JIM VATCHER Vatcher, James Ernest b: 5/27/66, Santa Monica, Cal. BR/TR, 5'10", 165 lbs. Deb: 5/30/90

YEAR	TM/L	G	AB	R	H	2B	3B	HR	RBI	BB	SO	AVG	OBP	SLG	PRO+	BR/A	SB	CS	SBR	FA	FR	G/POS	TPR
1990	Phi-N	36	46	5	12	1	0	1	4	4	6	.261	.320	.348	84	-1	0	0	0	1.000	-6	O-24	-0.8
	Atl-N	21	27	2	7	1	1	0	3	1	9	.259	.286	.370	75	-1	0	0	0	1.000	-1	/O-6	-0.2
	Yr	57	73	7	19	2	1	1	7	5	15	.260	.308	.356	80	-1	0	0	0	1.000	-6	O-30	-1.0
1991	SD-N	17	20	3	4	0	0	0	2	2	6	.200	.333	.200	52	-1	0	0	0	.900	-2	O-11	-0.3
1992	SD-N	13	16	1	4	1	0	0	2	3	6	.250	.368	.313	93	-0	0	0	0	1.000	-2	O-13	-0.2
Total 3		87	109	11	27	3	1	1	11	12	27	.248	.322	.321	77	-3	1	0	0	.980	-11	/O-54	-1.5

■ GLENN VAUGHAN Vaughan, Glenn Edward "Sparky" b: 2/15/44, Compton, Cal. BB/TR, 5'11", 170 lbs. Deb: 9/20/63

YEAR	TM/L	G	AB	R	H	2B	3B	HR	RBI	BB	SO	AVG	OBP	SLG	PRO+	BR/A	SB	CS	SBR	FA	FR	G/POS	TPR
1963	Hou-N	9	30	1	5	0	0	0	0	2	5	.167	.219	.167	14	-3	1	0	0	.914	-3	/S-9,3-1	-0.7

■ ARKY VAUGHAN Vaughan, Joseph Floyd b: 3/9/12, Clifty, Ark. d: 8/30/52, Eagleville, Cal. BL/TR, 5'10.5", 175 lbs. Deb: 4/17/32 H

YEAR	TM/L	G	AB	R	H	2B	3B	HR	RBI	BB	SO	AVG	OBP	SLG	PRO+	BR/A	SB	CS	SBR	FA	FR	G/POS	TPR
1932	Pit-N	129	497	71	158	15	10	4	61	39	26	.318	.375	.412	113	11	10			.934	-20	*S-128	0.1
1933	Pit-N	152	573	85	180	29	19	9	97	64	23	.314	.388	.478	146	35	3			.945	-9	*S-152	3.8
1934	Pit-N★	149	558	115	186	41	11	12	94	94	38	.333	.431	.511	148	41	10			.952	3	*S-149	5.1
1935	Pit-N★	137	499	108	192	34	10	19	99	97	18	.385	.491	.607	187	67	4			.950	-11	*S-137	6.1
1936	Pit-N☆	156	568	122	190	30	11	9	78	118	21	.335	.453	.474	146	44	6			.945	-11	*S-156	4.1
1937	Pit-N★	126	469	71	151	17	17	5	72	54	22	.322	.394	.463	132	22	7			.956	0	*S-108,O-12	2.8
1938	Pit-N☆	148	541	88	174	35	5	7	68	104	21	.322	.433	.444	140	36	14			.961	18	*S-147	6.4
1939	Pit-N★	152	595	94	182	30	11	6	62	70	20	.306	.385	.424	119	18	12			.962	3	*S-152	3.9
1940	Pit-N★	156	594	113	178	40	15	7	95	88	25	.300	.393	.453	134	30	12			.942	8	*S-155/3-2	5.1
1941	Pit-N★	106	374	69	118	20	7	6	38	50	13	.316	.399	.455	141	21	8			.958	-12	S-97/3-3	1.7
1942	Bro-N★	128	495	82	137	18	4	2	49	51	17	.277	.348	.341	100	1	8			.959	-10	*3-119/S-5,2-1	-0.8
1943	Bro-N	149	610	112	186	39	6	5	66	60	13	.305	.370	.413	126	20	20			.965	-24	S-99,3-55	0.4
1947	*Bro-N	64	126	24	41	5	2	2	25	27	11	.325	.444	.444	132	7	4			1.000	1	O-22,3-10	0.7
1948	Bro-N	65	123	19	30	3	0	3	22	22	8	.244	.354	.341	86	-2	0			1.000	1	*O-26/3-8	-0.2
Total 14		1817	6622	1173	2103	356	128	96	926	937	276	.318	.406	.453	136	352	118			.951	-59	*S-1485,3-197/O2	39.2

■ FRED VAUGHN Vaughn, Frederick Thomas "Muscles" b: 10/18/18, Coalinga, Cal. d: 3/2/64, Near Lake Wales, Fla. BR/TR, 5'10", 185 lbs. Deb: 8/20/44

YEAR	TM/L	G	AB	R	H	2B	3B	HR	RBI	BB	SO	AVG	OBP	SLG	PRO+	BR/A	SB	CS	SBR	FA	FR	G/POS	TPR
1944	Was-A	30	109	10	28	2	1	1	21	9	24	.257	.319	.321	87	-2	2	2	-1	.942	-2	2-26/3-3	-0.3
1945	Was-A	80	268	28	63	7	4	1	25	23	48	.235	.298	.302	81	-7	0	3	-2	.946	-5	2-76/S-1	-1.0
Total 2		110	377	38	91	9	5	2	46	32	72	.241	.304	.308	83	-9	2	5	-2	.945	-6	2-102/3-3,S-1	-1.3

■ GREG VAUGHN Vaughn, Gregory Lamont b: 7/3/65, Sacramento, Cal. BR/TR, 6', 195 lbs. Deb: 8/10/89

YEAR	TM/L	G	AB	R	H	2B	3B	HR	RBI	BB	SO	AVG	OBP	SLG	PRO+	BR/A	SB	CS	SBR	FA	FR	G/POS	TPR
1989	Mil-A	38	113	18	30	3	0	5	23	13	23	.265	.341	.425	116	2	4	1	3	.943	3	O-24,D-13	-0.1
1990	Mil-A	120	382	51	84	26	2	17	61	33	91	.220	.284	.432	98	-3	7	4	-0	.967	-1	*O-106/D-8	-0.6
1991	Mil-A	145	542	81	132	24	5	27	98	62	125	.244	.322	.456	116	10	2	2	-1	.994	13	O-135/D-10	1.8
1992	Mil-A	141	501	77	114	18	2	23	78	60	123	.228	.316	.409	104	-2	15	15	-5	.990	-3	O-131/D-7	-0.2
1993	Mil-A	154	569	97	152	28	2	30	97	89	118	.267	.371	.482	129	24	10	7	-0	.986	4	O-94,D-58	2.1
1994	Mil-A	95	370	59	94	24	1	19	55	51	93	.254	.346	.478	105	2	9	5	-0	.982	-0	O-81,D-14	-0.1
1995	Mil-A	108	392	67	88	19	1	17	59	55	89	.224	.340	.408	83	-10	10	4	1	1.000	0	*D-104	-1.6
1996	Mil-A☆	102	375	78	105	19	0	31	95	58	99	.280	.382	.571	129	16	5	2	0	.980	-2	*O-100/D-1	1.1
	*SD-N	43	141	20	29	3	1	10	22	24	31	.206	.329	.454	109	2	4	1	-3	.974	3	O-39	0.4
Total 8		946	3385	548	828	161	14	179	588	445	792	.245	.336	.459	111	45	66	41	-5	.983	17	O-710,D-215	2.8

■ FARMER VAUGHN Vaughn, Harry Francis b: 3/1/1864, Ruraldale, Ohio d: 2/21/14, Cincinnati, Ohio BR/TR, 6'3", 177 lbs. Deb: 10/7/1886

YEAR	TM/L	G	AB	R	H	2B	3B	HR	RBI	BB	SO	AVG	OBP	SLG	PRO+	BR/A	SB	CS	SBR	FA	FR	G/POS	TPR
1886	Cin-a	1	3	0	0	0	0	0	0	0	0	.000	.250	.000	-19	-0	0			.917	1	/C-1	0.0
1888	Lou-a	51	189	15	37	4	2	1	21	4		.196	.216	.254	52	-10	4			.863	-2	O-28,C-25	-1.0
1889	Lou-a	90	360	39	86	11	5	3	45	7	41	.239	.253	.322	65	-18	13			.900	3	C-54,O-20,1-18/3-3	-1.0
1890	NY-P	44	166	27	44	7	0	1	22	10	9	.265	.307	.325	63	-10	6			.877	-12	C-30/O-12/3-1,2-1	-1.6
1891	Cin-a	51	175	21	45	7	1	1	14	14	15	.257	.316	.326	77	-6	7			.923	7	C-44/O-6,1-2,3-2,P	0.3
	Mil-a	25	99	13	33	7	0	0	9	4	5	.333	.359	.404	98	-2	1			.924	2	C-64/O-7,1-6,3-2,P	0.2
	Yr	76	274	34	78	14	1	1	23	18	20	.285	.331	.354	85	-8	8			.923	9	C-108/O-13,1-8,3-4,P2	0.5
1892	Cin-N	91	346	45	88	10	5	2	50	16	13	.254	.295	.329	90	-5	10			.929	-13	C-67/1-14,O-11,3-6	-1.3
1893	Cin-N	121	483	68	135	17	12	6	108	35	17	.280	.332	.371	85	-12	16			.969	1	C-80,O-23,1-21	-0.5
1894	Cin-N	72	284	50	88	15	5	8	64	12	11	.310	.338	.482	92	-6	7			.918	-1	C-43,1-27/O-8,S-3	-0.5
1895	Cin-N	92	334	60	102	23	5	1	48	17	10	.305	.339	.413	90	-7	15			.934	11	C-77,1-15/3-1,2-1	0.9
1896	Cin-N	114	433	71	127	20	2	6	66	16	21	.293	.320	.395	82	-14	7			.984	3	1-57,C-57	-0.3
1897	Cin-N	54	199	21	58	13	5	0	30	11	11	.291	.329	.407	80	-1	7			.986	-0	1-39,C-33	-0.5
1898	Cin-N	78	275	35	84	12	4	2	46	11	5	.305	.339	.389	101	-1	4			.979	-3	1-39,C-33	0.0

YEAR	TM/L	G	AB	R	H	2B	3B	HR	RBI	BB	SO	AVG	OBP	SLG	PRO+	BR/A	SB	CS	SBR	FA	FR	G/POS	TPR
1899	Cin-N	31	108	9	19	1	0	0	2	3		.176	.198	.185	5	-14	2			.982	3	1-21/C-7,O-1	-0.9
Total	13	915	3454	474	946	147	53	21	525	151	128	.274	.307	.365	80	-112	92			.926	-0	C-553,1-253,O/3S2P	-5.9

■ MO VAUGHN
Vaughn, Maurice Samuel b: 12/15/67, Norwalk, Conn. BL/TR, 6'1", 225 lbs. Deb: 6/27/91

YEAR	TM/L	G	AB	R	H	2B	3B	HR	RBI	BB	SO	AVG	OBP	SLG	PRO+	BR/A	SB	CS	SBR	FA	FR	G/POS	TPR
1991	Bos-A	74	219	21	57	12	0	4	32	26	43	.260	.344	.370	93	-2	2	1	0	.985	-2	1-49,D-16	-0.7
1992	Bos-A	113	355	42	83	16	2	13	57	47	67	.234	.328	.400	97	-2	3	3	-1	.982	-2	1-85,D-20	-1.1
1993	Bos-A	152	539	86	160	34	1	29	101	79	130	.297	.395	.525	136	28	4	3	-1	.987	-9	*1-131,D-19	0.7
1994	Bos-A	111	394	65	122	25	1	26	82	57	112	.310	.410	.576	144	26	4	4	-1	.989	-5	*1-106/D-1	0.9
1995	*Bos-A★	140	550	98	165	28	3	39	126	68	150	.300	.391	.575	142	34	11	4	1	.992	-3	*1-138/D-2	1.7
1996	Bos-A★	161	635	118	207	29	1	44	143	95	154	.326	.425	.583	146	47	2	0	1	.988	-10	*1-146,D-15	2.0
Total	6	751	2692	430	794	144	8	155	541	372	656	.295	.391	.527	133	132	26	15	-1	.988	-30	1-655/D-73	3.5

■ BOBBY VAUGHN
Vaughn, Robert b: 6/4/1885, Stamford, N.Y. d: 4/11/65, Seattle, Wash. BR/TR, 5'9", 150 lbs. Deb: 6/12/09

YEAR	TM/L	G	AB	R	H	2B	3B	HR	RBI	BB	SO	AVG	OBP	SLG	PRO+	BR/A	SB	CS	SBR	FA	FR	G/POS	TPR
1909	NY-A	5	14	1	2	0	0	0	0	1		.143	.200	.143	8	-1	1			.882	-3	/2-4,S-1	-0.5
1915	StL-F	144	521	69	146	19	9	0	32	58	38	.280	.356	.351	94	-10	24			.953	-8	*2-127,S-12/3-8	-1.7
Total	2	149	535	70	148	19	9	0	32	59	38	.277	.352	.346	92	-11	25			.951	-11	2-131/S-13,3-8	-2.2

■ BOBBY VEACH
Veach, Robert Hayes b: 6/29/1888, Island, Ky. d: 8/7/45, Detroit, Mich. BL/TR, 5'11", 160 lbs. Deb: 8/6/12

YEAR	TM/L	G	AB	R	H	2B	3B	HR	RBI	BB	SO	AVG	OBP	SLG	PRO+	BR/A	SB	CS	SBR	FA	FR	G/POS	TPR
1912	Det-A	23	79	8	27	5	1	0	15	5		.342	.388	.430	138	4	2			.927	2	O-22	0.5
1913	Det-A	137	491	54	132	22	10	0	64	53	31	.269	.341	.354	107	4	22			.917	-5	*O-135	-0.7
1914	Det-A	149	531	56	146	19	14	1	72	50	29	.275	.341	.369	110	6	20	20	-6	.965	3	*O-145	-0.4
1915	Det-A	152	569	81	178	40	10	3	112	68	43	.313	.390	.434	140	27	16	19	-7	.975	3	*O-152	1.6
1916	Det-A	150	566	92	173	33	15	3	91	52	41	.306	.367	.433	135	23	24	15	-2	.967	4	*O-150	1.9
1917	Det-A	154	571	79	182	31	12	8	103	61	44	.319	.393	.457	160	40	21			.956	5	*O-154	4.0
1918	Det-A	127	499	59	139	21	13	3	78	35	23	.279	.331	.391	123	11	21			.977	3	*O-127/P-1	0.8
1919	Det-A	139	538	87	191	45	17	3	101	33	33	.355	.390	.519	160	40	19			.967	11	*O-138	4.3
1920	Det-A	154	612	92	188	39	15	11	113	36	22	.307	.353	.474	121	15	11	7	-1	.967	15	*O-154	1.6
1921	Det-A	150	612	110	207	43	13	16	128	48	31	.338	.387	.529	133	28	14	10	-2	.974	15	*O-149	2.8
1922	Det-A	155	618	96	202	34	13	9	126	42	27	.327	.371	.468	123	20	9	1	-2	.982	8	*O-154	1.8
1923	Det-A	114	293	45	94	13	2	2	39	29	21	.321	.388	.406	111	5	10	3	1	.943	-14	O-85	-1.2
1924	Bos-A	142	519	77	153	35	9	5	99	47	18	.295	.359	.426	102	0	5	5	-2	.956	-1	*O-130	-1.1
1925	Bos-A	1	5	0	1	0	0	0	0	2	1	.200	.333	.200	38	-0	0	0	0	1.000	0	/O-1	0.0
	NY-A	56	116	13	41	10	2	0	15	8	0	.353	.400	.474	123	4	1	4	-2	.957	-7	O-33	-0.6
	*Was-A	18	37	4	9	3	0	0	8	3	3	.243	.300	.324	60	-2	0	0	0	.923	-3	O-11	-0.5
	Yr	75	158	17	51	13	2	0	25	12	4	.323	.374	.449	106	1	1	4	-2	.952	-10	O-45	-1.1
Total	14	1821	6656	953	2063	393	147	64	1166	571	367	.310	.370	.442	127	225	195	84		.964	38	*O-1740/P-1	14.8

■ PEEK-A-BOO VEACH
Veach, William Walter b: 6/15/1862, Indianapolis, Ind d: 11/12/37, Indianapolis, Ind. Deb: 8/24/1884

YEAR	TM/L	G	AB	R	H	2B	3B	HR	RBI	BB	SO	AVG	OBP	SLG	PRO+	BR/A	SB	CS	SBR	FA	FR	G/POS	TPR
1884	KC-U	27	82	9	11	1	0	1		9		.134	.220	.183	27	-10				.833	-1	O-14,P-12/2-1,1-1	-0.6
1887	Lou-a	1	3	0	0	0	0	0		1		.000	.250	.000	-26	-0	0			.750	-0	/P-1	0.0
1890	Cle-N	64	238	24	56	10	5	0	32	33	28	.235	.336	.319	93	-1	9			.971	6	1-64	0.1
	Pit-N	8	30	6	9	1	1	2	5	8	3	.300	.447	.600	231	5				.968	0	/1-8	0.5
	Yr	72	268	30	65	11	6	2	37	41	31	.243	.349	.351	107	4	9			.971	7	1-72	0.6
Total	3	100	353	39	76	12	6	3	37	51	31	.215	.319	.309	90	-6	9			.971	6	/1-73,O-14,P-13,2-1	0.0

■ COOT VEAL
Veal, Orville Inman b: 7/9/32, Sandersville, Ga. BR/TR, 6'1", 165 lbs. Deb: 7/30/58

YEAR	TM/L	G	AB	R	H	2B	3B	HR	RBI	BB	SO	AVG	OBP	SLG	PRO+	BR/A	SB	CS	SBR	FA	FR	G/POS	TPR
1958	Det-A	58	207	29	53	2	0	0	16	14	21	.256	.306	.324	69	-9	1	1	-0	.981	-8	S-58	-1.3
1959	Det-A	77	89	12	18	1	0	0	15	6	7	.202	.276	.247	42	-7	0	0	0	.962	10	S-72	0.5
1960	Det-A	27	64	8	19	5	1	0	8	11	7	.297	.400	.406	115	2	0	0	0	.988	-2	S-22/3-3,2-1	0.1
1961	Was-A	69	218	21	44	10	0	0	8	19	29	.202	.275	.248	41	-18	1	8	-5	.974	0	S-63	-1.7
1962	Pit-N	1	1	0	0	0	0	0	0	0	0	.000	.000	.000	-99	-0	0	0	0	.000	0	H	0.0
1963	Det-A	15	32	5	7	0	0	0	4	4	4	.219	.306	.219	48	-2	0	0	0	.980	4	S-12	0.2
Total	6	247	611	75	141	26	3	1	51	56	69	.231	.301	.288	59	-34	2	9	-5	.976	4	S-227/3-3,2-1	-2.2

■ JESUS VEGA
Vega, Jesus Anthony (Morales) b: 10/14/55, Bayamon, P.R. BR/TR, 6'1", 176 lbs. Deb: 9/5/79

YEAR	TM/L	G	AB	R	H	2B	3B	HR	RBI	BB	SO	AVG	OBP	SLG	PRO+	BR/A	SB	CS	SBR	FA	FR	G/POS	TPR
1979	Min-A	4	7	0	0	0	0	0	0	0	0	.000	.000	.000	-96	-1	0	0	0	.000	0	/D-3	-0.2
1980	Min-A	12	30	3	5	0	0	0	4	3	7	.167	.242	.167	13	-4	1	0	0	1.000	0	/1-2,D-9	-0.3
1982	Min-A	71	199	23	53	6	0	5	29	8	19	.266	.295	.372	80	-6	6	1	1	.974	-1	D-39,1-18/O-1	-0.8
Total	3	87	236	26	58	6	0	5	33	11	26	.246	.279	.335	65	-11	7	1	1	.975	-1	/D-51,1-20,O-1	-1.3

■ RANDY VELARDE
Velarde, Randy Lee b: 11/24/62, Midland, Tex. BR/TR, 6', 185 lbs. Deb: 8/20/87

YEAR	TM/L	G	AB	R	H	2B	3B	HR	RBI	BB	SO	AVG	OBP	SLG	PRO+	BR/A	SB	CS	SBR	FA	FR	G/POS	TPR
1987	NY-A	8	22	1	4	1	0	0	0	0	6	.182	.182	.182	-3	-3	0	0	0	.933	0	/S-8	-0.3
1988	NY-A	48	115	18	20	6	0	5	12	8	24	.174	.240	.357	65	-6	1	1	-0	.967	8	2-24,S-14,3-11	0.4
1989	NY-A	33	100	12	34	4	2	2	11	7	14	.340	.389	.480	145	6	0	3	-2	.954	2	3-27/S-9	0.6
1990	NY-A	95	229	21	48	6	2	5	19	20	53	.210	.276	.319	66	-11	0	3	-2	.945	9	3-74,S-15/O-5,2D	-0.2
1991	NY-A	80	184	19	45	11	1	1	15	18	43	.245	.322	.332	81	-1	3	1	0	.935	7	3-50,S-31/O-2	0.4
1992	NY-A	121	412	57	112	24	1	7	46	38	78	.272	.336	.386	103	1	7	2	1	.974	-8	S-75,3-26,O-23/2-3	-0.1
1993	NY-A	85	226	28	68	13	2	7	24	18	39	.301	.363	.469	126	8	2	2	-1	.932	-1	O-50,S-26,3-16/D-1	0.7
1994	NY-A	77	280	47	78	16	1	9	34	22	61	.279	.340	.439	103	1	4	2	0	.944	5	S-49,3-27/O-7,2-5	0.5
1995	*NY-A	111	367	60	102	19	1	7	46	55	64	.278	.378	.392	102	5	5	1	1	.976	-15	2-62,S-28,O-20,3-19	-1.5
1996	Cal-A	136	530	82	151	27	3	14	54	70	118	.285	.374	.426	104	5	7	7	-2	.982	-26	*2-114,3-28/S-7	-1.5
Total	10	794	2465	345	662	126	13	57	262	256	500	.269	.344	.400	99	-1	29	22	-5	.934	-22	3-278,S-262,2O/D	0.0

■ GUILLERMO VELASQUEZ
Velasquez, Guillermo (Burgara) b: 4/23/68, Mexicali, Mexico BL/TR, 6'3", 220 lbs. Deb: 9/14/92

YEAR	TM/L	G	AB	R	H	2B	3B	HR	RBI	BB	SO	AVG	OBP	SLG	PRO+	BR/A	SB	CS	SBR	FA	FR	G/POS	TPR
1992	SD-N	15	23	1	7	0	0	1	5	1	7	.304	.333	.435	114	0	0	0	0	.933	-2	/1-3,O-2	-0.1
1993	SD-N	79	143	7	30	2	0	3	20	13	35	.210	.276	.287	50	-10	0	0	0	.984	-1	1-38/O-6	-1.4
Total	2	94	166	8	37	2	0	4	25	14	42	.223	.283	.307	58	-10	0	0	0	.981	-2	/1-41,O-8	-1.5

■ FREDDIE VELAZQUEZ
Velazquez, Federico Antonio (Velasquez) b: 12/6/37, Santo Domingo, D.R. BR/TR, 6'1", 185 lbs. Deb: 4/20/69

YEAR	TM/L	G	AB	R	H	2B	3B	HR	RBI	BB	SO	AVG	OBP	SLG	PRO+	BR/A	SB	CS	SBR	FA	FR	G/POS	TPR
1969	Sea-A	6	16	1	2	2	0	0	2	1	3	.125	.176	.250	18	-2	0	0	0	1.000	-1	/C-5	-0.2
1973	Atl-N	15	23	2	8	1	0	0	3	1	3	.348	.375	.391	105	0	0	0	0	.975	2	C-11	0.2
Total	2	21	39	3	10	3	0	0	5	2	6	.256	.293	.333	71	-2	0	0	0	.985	1	/C-16	0.0

■ OTTO VELEZ
Velez, Otoniel (Franceschi) b: 11/29/50, Ponce, P.R. BR/TR, 6', 195 lbs. Deb: 9/4/73

YEAR	TM/L	G	AB	R	H	2B	3B	HR	RBI	BB	SO	AVG	OBP	SLG	PRO+	BR/A	SB	CS	SBR	FA	FR	G/POS	TPR
1973	NY-A	23	77	9	15	4	0	2	9	15	24	.195	.326	.325	87	-1	0	1	-1	.959	1	O-23	-0.2
1974	NY-A	27	67	9	14	1	1	2	10	15	24	.209	.354	.343	103	1	0	0	0	.986	-4	1-21/O-3,3-2	-0.4
1975	NY-A	6	8	0	2	0	0	0	1	2	0	.250	.400	.250	89	0	0	0	0	1.000	0	/1-1,D-1	0.0
1976	*NY-A	49	94	11	25	6	0	2	10	23	26	.266	.410	.394	137	6	0	0	0	.979	-3	O-24/1-8,3-1,D-5	0.2
1977	Tor-A	120	360	50	92	19	3	16	62	65	87	.256	.371	.458	123	13	4	2	0	.973	0	O-79,D-28	0.5
1978	Tor-A	91	248	29	66	14	2	9	38	45	61	.266	.383	.448	130	11	1	3	-2	.982	7	O-74/1-1,D-9	1.4
1979	Tor-A	99	274	45	79	21	0	15	48	46	45	.288	.396	.529	145	18	0	1	-1	.971	-5	O-73/1-6,D-9	0.9
1980	Tor-A	104	357	54	96	12	3	20	62	54	86	.269	.368	.487	126	13	0	0	0	.975	0	D-97/1-3	1.0
1981	Tor-A	80	240	32	51	9	2	11	28	55	60	.213	.366	.404	114	4	0	3	-2	1.000	0	D-74/1-1	0.1
1982	Tor-A	28	52	4	10	1	0	1	6	5	13	.192	.354	.269	68	-2	1	0	0	.000	0	D-24	-0.3
1983	Cle-A	10	25	1	2	0	0	0	0	1	8	.080	.179	.080	-25	-4	0	0	0	.000	0	/D-8	-0.1
Total	11	637	1802	244	452	87	11	78	272	336	414	.251	.372	.441	122	61	6	10	-4	.973	6	O-276,D-255/1-41,3	3.1

■ PAT VELTMAN
Veltman, Arthur Patrick b: 3/24/06, Mobile, Ala. d: 10/1/80, San Antonio, Tex. BR/TR, 6', 175 lbs. Deb: 4/17/26

YEAR	TM/L	G	AB	R	H	2B	3B	HR	RBI	BB	SO	AVG	OBP	SLG	PRO+	BR/A	SB	CS	SBR	FA	FR	G/POS	TPR
1926	Chi-A	5	4	1	1	0	0	0	0	1	1	.250	.400	.250	75	-0	0	0	0	1.000	-0	/S-1	0.0
1928	NY-N	1	3	1	1	0	0	0	1	0	0	.333	.500	.333	282	1	0	0	0	1.000	0	/O-1	0.1
1929	NY-N	2	1	0	1	0	0	0	0	0	0	1.000	1.000	1.000	81	0	0	0	0	1.000	-0	/C-1	0.0
1931	Bos-N	1	1	0	0	0	0	0	0	0	0	.000	.000	.000	-99	-0	0	0	0	.000	0	H	0.0

YEAR	TM/L	G	AB	R	H	2B	3B	HR	RBI	BB	SO	AVG	OBP	SLG	PRO+	BR/A	SB	CS	SBR	FA	FR	G/POS	TPR
1932	NY-N	2	1	0	0	0	0	0	0	0	1	.000	.000	.000	-99	-0	0			.000	0	H	0.0
1934	Pit-N	12	28	1	3	0	0	0	2	0	1	.107	.107	.107	-41	-6	0			1.000	-2	C-11	-0.7
Total	6	23	38	4	5	0	1	0	2	4	3	.132	.214	.184	7	-5	0	0		1.000	-2	/C-12,O-1,S-1	-0.6

■ MAX VENABLE
Venable, William McKinley b: 6/6/57, Phoenix, Ariz.   BL/TR, 5'10", 185 lbs.   Deb: 4/8/79

YEAR	TM/L	G	AB	R	H	2B	3B	HR	RBI	BB	SO	AVG	OBP	SLG	PRO+	BR/A	SB	CS	SBR	FA	FR	G/POS	TPR
1979	SF-N	55	85	12	14	1	1	0	3	10	18	.165	.260	.200	29	-8	3	3	-1	.914	-5	O-25	-1.5
1980	SF-N	64	138	13	37	5	0	0	10	15	22	.268	.340	.304	83	-3	8	2	1	1.000	-5	O-40	-0.9
1981	SF-N	18	32	2	6	0	2	0	1	4	3	.188	.278	.313	68	-1	3	1	0	1.000	0	/O-5	-0.1
1982	SF-N	71	125	17	28	2	1	1	7	7	16	.224	.265	.280	53	-8	9	3	1	.986	-4	O-53	-1.2
1983	SF-N	94	228	28	50	7	4	6	27	22	34	.219	.296	.364	85	-5	15	2	3	.993	3	O-66	-0.1
1984	Mon-N	38	71	7	17	2	0	2	7	3	7	.239	.280	.352	80	-2	1	0		1.000	-4	O-27	-0.7
1985	Cin-N	77	135	21	39	12	3	0	10	6	17	.289	.319	.422	101	-0	11	3	2	1.000	0	O-39	-0.1
1986	Cin-N	108	147	17	31	7	1	2	15	17	24	.211	.293	.313	64	-7	7	2	1	.969	-10	O-57	-1.8
1987	Cin-N	7	7	2	1	0	0	0	2	0	0	.143	.143	.143	-23	-1	0	0		1.000	-1	/O-4	-0.2
1989	Cal-A	20	53	7	19	4	0	4	1	16	.358	.550	.434	128	1	0	0		1.000	-3	O-13	-0.1
1990	Cal-A	93	189	26	49	9	3	4	21	24	31	.259	.343	.402	110	3	5	1	1	.975	-12	O-77/D-1	-1.0
1991	Cal-A	82	187	24	46	8	2	3	21	11	30	.246	.295	.358	80	-5	2	1	0	.967	-11	O-65/D-3	-1.8
Total	12	727	1397	176	337	57	17	18	128	120	218	.241	.304	.345	81	-37	64	18	8	.982	-54	O-471/D-4	-9.5

■ ROBIN VENTURA
Ventura, Robin Mark b: 7/14/67, Santa Maria, Cal.   BL/TR, 6'1", 185 lbs.   Deb: 9/12/89

YEAR	TM/L	G	AB	R	H	2B	3B	HR	RBI	BB	SO	AVG	OBP	SLG	PRO+	BR/A	SB	CS	SBR	FA	FR	G/POS	TPR
1989	Chi-A	16	45	5	8	3	0	0	7	8	6	.178	.315	.244	61	-2	0	0	0	.962	2	3-16	0.0
1990	Chi-A	150	493	48	123	17	1	5	54	55	53	.249	.326	.318	83	-10	1	4	-2	.939	-0	*3-147/1-1	-1.2
1991	Chi-A	157	606	92	172	25	1	23	100	80	67	.284	.371	.442	127	24	2	4	-2	.959	1	*3-151,1-31	2.3
1992	Chi-A★	157	592	85	167	38	1	16	93	93	71	.282	.380	.431	128	25	2	4	-2	.957	24	*3-157/1-2	4.6
1993	*Chi-A	157	554	85	145	27	1	22	94	105	82	.262	.382	.433	121	20	1	6	-3	.965	-5	*3-155/1-4	1.2
1994	Chi-A	109	401	57	113	15	1	18	78	61	69	.282	.379	.459	117	11	3	1	0	.935	-3	*3-108/1-3,S-1	0.7
1995	Chi-A	135	492	79	145	22	0	26	93	75	98	.295	.389	.498	135	26	4	3	-1	.948	-3	*3-121,1-18/D-1	2.0
1996	Chi-A	158	586	96	168	31	2	34	105	78	81	.287	.372	.520	129	26	1	3	-2	.974	-0	*3-150,1-14	2.1
Total	8	1039	3769	547	1041	178	7	144	624	555	527	.276	.371	.442	120	119	14	25	-11	.955	14	3-1005/1-73,D-1,S	11.7

■ VINCE VENTURA
Ventura, Vincent b: 4/18/17, New York, N.Y.   BR/TR, 6'1.5", 190 lbs.   Deb: 5/8/45

YEAR	TM/L	G	AB	R	H	2B	3B	HR	RBI	BB	SO	AVG	OBP	SLG	PRO+	BR/A	SB	CS	SBR	FA	FR	G/POS	TPR
1945	Was-A	18	58	4	12	0	0	0	2	4	4	.207	.258	.207	39	-5	0	0	0	.886	-1	O-15	-0.7

■ QUILVIO VERAS
Veras, Quilvio Alberto (Perez) b: 4/3/71, Santo Domingo, D.R.   BB/TR, 5'9", 170 lbs.   Deb: 4/25/95

YEAR	TM/L	G	AB	R	H	2B	3B	HR	RBI	BB	SO	AVG	OBP	SLG	PRO+	BR/A	SB	CS	SBR	FA	FR	G/POS	TPR
1995	Fla-N	124	440	86	115	20	7	5	32	80	68	.261	.386	.373	101	4	**56**	21	4	.986	7	*2-122/O-2	2.2
1996	Fla-N	73	253	40	64	8	1	4	14	51	42	.253	.382	.340	96	1	8	8	-2	.986	6	2-67	0.9
Total	2	197	693	126	179	28	8	9	46	131	110	.258	.384	.361	99	5	64	29	2	.986	13	2-189/O-2	3.1

■ EMIL VERBAN
Verban, Emil Matthew "Dutch" or "Antelope" b: 8/27/15, Lincoln, Ill.   d: 6/8/89, Quincy, Ill.   BR/TR, 5'11", 165 lbs.   Deb: 4/18/44

YEAR	TM/L	G	AB	R	H	2B	3B	HR	RBI	BB	SO	AVG	OBP	SLG	PRO+	BR/A	SB	CS	SBR	FA	FR	G/POS	TPR
1944	*StL-N	146	498	51	128	14	2	0	43	19	14	.257	.287	.293	62	-25	0			.968	-6	*2-146	-2.4
1945	StL-N†	155	597	59	166	22	8	0	72	19	15	.278	.304	.342	77	-19	4			**.978**	-19	*2-155	-2.9
1946	StL-N	1	1	0	0	0	0	0	0	0	0	.000	.000	.000	-96	-0	0			.000	0	H	0.0
	Phi-N★	138	473	44	130	17	5	0	34	21	18	.275	.306	.332	83	-12	5			.963	-3	*2-138	-0.6
	Yr	139	474	44	130	17	5	0	34	21	18	.274	.305	.331	83	-12	5			.963	-3	*2-138	-0.6
1947	Phi-N★	155	540	50	154	14	0	0	42	23	8	.285	.316	.341	77	-18	5			.982	17	*2-155	0.9
1948	Phi-N	55	169	14	39	5	1	0	11	11	5	.231	.282	.272	51	-11	0			.975	-4	2-54	-1.3
	Chi-N	56	248	37	73	15	1	0	16	4	7	.294	.308	.375	88	-5	4			.964	6	2-56	0.4
	Yr	111	417	51	112	20	2	0	27	15	12	.269	.297	.333	72	-17	4			.969	2	*2-110	-0.9
1949	Chi-N	98	343	38	99	11	1	0	22	8	2	.289	.309	.327	72	-14	3			.965	3	2-88	-0.7
1950	Chi-N	45	37	7	4	1	0	0	1	3	5	.108	.175	.135	-17	-6	0			.966	6	/2-8,S-3,3-1,O-1	-0.1
	Bos-N	4	5	1	0	0	0	0	0	0	0	.000	.000	.000	-99	-1	0			.833	1	/2-2	0.0
	Yr	49	42	8	4	1	0	0	1	3	5	.095	.156	.119	-27	-8	0			.927	7	2-10/S-3,3-1,O-1	-0.1
Total	7	853	2911	301	793	99	26	1	241	108	74	.272	.301	.325	73	-113	21			.971	2	2-802/S-3,O-1,3-1	-6.7

■ GENE VERBLE
Verble, Gene Kermit "Satchel" b: 6/29/28, Concord, N.C.   BR/TR, 5'10", 163 lbs.   Deb: 4/17/51

YEAR	TM/L	G	AB	R	H	2B	3B	HR	RBI	BB	SO	AVG	OBP	SLG	PRO+	BR/A	SB	CS	SBR	FA	FR	G/POS	TPR
1951	Was-A	68	177	16	36	3	2	0	15	18	10	.203	.277	.243	42	-14	1	1	-0	.978	-2	S-28,2-19/3-1	-1.3
1953	Was-A	13	21	4	4	0	0	0	2	2	1	.190	.261	.190	24	-2	0	0	0	1.000	2	/S-8	0.0
Total	2	81	198	20	40	3	2	0	17	20	11	.202	.275	.237	40	-16	1	1	-0	.981	1	/S-36,2-19,3-1	-1.3

■ FRANK VERDI
Verdi, Frank Michael b: 6/2/26, Brooklyn, N.Y.   BR/TR, 5'10.5", 170 lbs.   Deb: 5/10/53

YEAR	TM/L	G	AB	R	H	2B	3B	HR	RBI	BB	SO	AVG	OBP	SLG	PRO+	BR/A	SB	CS	SBR	FA	FR	G/POS	TPR
1953	NY-A	1	0	0	0	0	0	0	0	0	0	—	—	—			0	0	0	.000	0	/S-1	0.0

■ JOHNNY VERGEZ
Vergez, John Louis b: 7/9/06, Oakland, Cal.   d: 7/15/91, Davis, Cal.   BR/TR, 5'8", 165 lbs.   Deb: 4/14/31

YEAR	TM/L	G	AB	R	H	2B	3B	HR	RBI	BB	SO	AVG	OBP	SLG	PRO+	BR/A	SB	CS	SBR	FA	FR	G/POS	TPR
1931	NY-N	152	565	67	157	24	2	13	81	29	65	.278	.320	.396	94	-6	11			.932	-3	*3-152	0.0
1932	NY-N	118	376	42	98	21	3	6	43	25	36	.261	.310	.380	86	-8	1			.935	5	*3-111/S-1	0.5
1933	NY-N	123	458	57	124	21	6	16	72	39	66	.271	.332	.448	123	13	1			.928	-14	*3-123	0.7
1934	NY-N	108	320	31	64	18	4	7	27	28	55	.200	.269	.328	60	-19	1			.943	10	*3-104	-0.5
1935	Phi-N	148	546	56	136	27	4	9	63	46	67	.249	.312	.363	73	-21	8			**.953**	-7	*3-148/S-2	-2.2
1936	Phi-N	15	40	4	11	2	0	1	5	3	11	.275	.326	.400	86	-1	0			.964	0	3-12	-0.2
	StL-N	8	18	1	3	1	0	0	1	3	3	.167	.211	.222	17	-2	0			.929	0	/3-8	-0.2
	Yr	23	58	5	14	3	0	1	6	6	14	.241	.290	.345	66	-3	0			.952	0	3-20	-0.2
Total	6	672	2323	258	593	114	16	52	292	171	303	.255	.311	.385	87	-44	22			.939	-8	3-658/S-3	-1.7

■ MICKEY VERNON
Vernon, James Barton b: 4/22/18, Marcus Hook, Pa.   BL/TL, 6'2", 180 lbs.   Deb: 7/8/39   MC

YEAR	TM/L	G	AB	R	H	2B	3B	HR	RBI	BB	SO	AVG	OBP	SLG	PRO+	BR/A	SB	CS	SBR	FA	FR	G/POS	TPR
1939	Was-A	76	276	23	71	15	4	1	30	24	28	.257	.317	.351	76	-10	1	1	-0	.985	-3	1-75	-2.0
1940	Was-A	5	19	0	3	0	0	0	0	0	0	.158	.158	.158	-19	-3	0	0	0	1.000	-0	/1-4	-0.4
1941	Was-A	138	531	73	159	27	11	9	93	43	51	.299	.352	.443	114	9	9	3	1	.992	-6	*1-132	-0.6
1942	Was-A	151	621	76	168	34	6	9	86	59	63	.271	.337	.388	104	3	25	6	4	.982	-8	*1-151	-1.1
1943	Was-A	145	553	89	148	29	6	7	70	67	55	.268	.357	.387	122	16	24	8	2	.990	-11	*1-143	0.0
1946	Was-A★	148	587	88	207	51	8	8	85	49	64	.353	.403	.508	163	47	14	10	-2	.990	-1	*1-147	3.6
1947	Was-A	154	600	77	159	29	12	7	85	49	42	.265	.320	.388	99	-3	12	12	-4	.987	-4	*1-154	-1.7
1948	Was-A★	150	558	78	135	27	7	3	48	54	43	.242	.310	.332	73	-23	15	11	-2	.989	5	*1-150	-2.1
1949	Cle-A	153	584	72	170	27	4	18	83	58	51	.291	.357	.443	113	9	7	4	-2	.991	19	*1-153	2.4
1950	Cle-A	28	90	8	17	0	0	0	10	12	10	.189	.284	.189	24	-10	2	0	1	.996	1	1-25	-0.8
	Was-A	90	327	47	100	17	3	9	65	50	29	.306	.404	.459	127	14	6	1	0	.990	1	1-85	1.3
	Yr	118	417	55	117	17	3	9	75	62	39	.281	.379	.400	104	4	8	1	2	**.991**	2	*1-110	0.5
1951	Was-A	141	546	69	160	30	7	9	87	53	45	.293	.358	.423	112	9	7	6	-2	**.994**	-4	*1-137	-0.3
1952	Was-A	154	569	71	143	33	9	10	80	89	66	.251	.353	.394	111	9	7	7	-2	**.993**	1	*1-153	0.2
1953	Was-A★	152	608	101	205	43	11	15	115	63	57	.337	.403	.518	151	43	4	4	-2	.992	-3	*1-152	3.1
1954	Was-A	151	597	90	173	33	14	20	97	61	61	.290	.360	.492	140	29	4	4	-2	.992	-9	*1-148	1.1
1955	Was-A★	150	538	74	162	23	8	14	85	74	50	.301	.389	.452	133	25	0	1	-0	.994	-8	*1-144	0.6
1956	Bos-A★	119	403	67	125	28	4	15	84	57	40	.310	.405	.511	125	15	1	0	0	.989	-3	*1-108	0.5
1957	Bos-A	102	270	36	65	18	1	7	38	41	35	.241	.351	.393	97	-0	0	0	0	.992	4	1-70	0.4
1958	Cle-A★	119	355	49	104	22	3	8	55	44	56	.293	.374	.439	126	13	0	1	0	.987	-2	1-96	0.4
1959	Mil-N	74	91	8	20	4	0	3	14	7	20	.220	.283	.363	77	-3	0	0	0	.983	1	1-10/O-4	-0.3
1960	Pit-N	9	8	0	1	0	0	0	1	1	0	.125	.222	.125	-2	-1	0	0	0	.000	0	H	-0.1
Total	20	2409	8731	1196	2495	490	120	172	1311	955	869	.286	.359	.428	116	186	137	90	-13	.990	-32	*1-2237/O-4	3.7

■ ZOILO VERSALLES
Versalles, Zoilo Casanova (Rodriguez) "Zorro"
b: 12/18/39, Veldado, Cuba   d: 6/9/95, Bloomington, Minn.   BR/TR, 5'10", 150 lbs.   Deb: 8/1/59

YEAR	TM/L	G	AB	R	H	2B	3B	HR	RBI	BB	SO	AVG	OBP	SLG	PRO+	BR/A	SB	CS	SBR	FA	FR	G/POS	TPR
1959	Was-A	29	59	4	9	0	0	1	1	4	15	.153	.219	.203	17	-7	1	0	0	.943	3	S-29	-0.2
1960	Was-A	15	45	2	6	2	2	0	4	2	5	.133	.170	.267	16	-5	0	0	0	.935	-1	S-15	-0.6

YEAR	TM/L	G	AB	R	H	2B	3B	HR	RBI	BB	SO	AVG	OBP	SLG	PRO+	BR/A	SB	CS	SBR	FA	FR	G/POS	TPR
1961	Min-A	129	510	65	143	25	5	7	53	25	61	.280	.315	.390	83	-13	16	9	-1	.952	-2	*S-129	-0.5
1962	Min-A	160	568	69	137	18	3	17	67	37	71	.241	.290	.373	74	-22	5	5	-2	.970	32	*S-160	2.3
1963	Min-A★	159	621	74	162	31	13	0	54	33	66	.261	.303	.401	94	-6	7	4	-0	.961	-2	*S-159	0.3
1964	Min-A	160	659	94	171	33	10	20	64	42	88	.259	.312	.431	103	2	14	4	2	.957	-17	*S-160	-0.2
1965	*Min-A★	160	666	**126**	182	45	12	19	77	41	122	.273	.322	.462	115	11	27	5	5	.950	2	*S-160	3.1
1966	Min-A	137	543	73	135	20	6	7	36	40	85	.249	.308	.346	82	-12	10	12	-4	.942	-17	*S-135	-2.2
1967	Min-A	160	581	63	116	16	7	6	50	33	113	.200	.250	.282	53	-34	5	3	-0	.958	2	*S-159	-1.9
1968	LA-N	122	403	29	79	16	3	2	24	26	84	.196	.245	.266	57	-22	6	4	-1	.954	8	*S-119	-0.3
1969	Cle-A	72	217	21	49	11	1	1	13	21	47	.226	.300	.300	66	-10	3	1	0	.975	-11	2-46,3-30/S-3	-1.8
	Was-A	31	75	9	20	2	1	0	6	3	13	.267	.304	.320	79	-2	1	0	0	.935	-1	S-13/2-6,3-5	-0.2
	Yr	103	292	30	69	13	2	1	19	24	60	.236	.301	.305	69	-12	4	1	1	.978	-12	2-52,3-35,S-16	-2.0
1971	Atl-N	66	194	21	37	11	0	5	22	11	40	.191	.234	.325	53	-12	2	1	0	.902	-14	3-30,S-24/2-1	-2.6
Total	12	1400	5141	650	1246	230	63	95	471	318	810	.242	.292	.367	82	-133	97	48	0	.956	-20	*S-1265/3-65,2-53	-4.8

■ TOM VERYZER

Veryzer, Thomas Martin   b: 2/11/53, Port Jefferson, N.Y   BR/TR, 6'1", 185 lbs.   Deb: 8/14/73

YEAR	TM/L	G	AB	R	H	2B	3B	HR	RBI	BB	SO	AVG	OBP	SLG	PRO+	BR/A	SB	CS	SBR	FA	FR	G/POS	TPR
1973	Det-A	18	20	1	6	0	1	0	2	2	4	.300	.364	.400	108	0	0	0	0	.857	-5	S-18	-0.4
1974	Det-A	22	55	4	13	2	0	2	9	5	8	.236	.300	.382	92	-1	1	0	0	.927	-10	S-20	-0.9
1975	Det-A	128	404	37	102	13	1	5	48	23	76	.252	.301	.327	74	-14	2	6	-3	.960	-4	*S-128	-0.8
1976	Det-A	97	354	31	83	8	2	1	25	21	44	.234	.289	.277	64	-16	1	4	-2	.966	-1	S-97	-0.8
1977	Det-A	125	350	31	69	12	1	2	28	16	44	.197	.232	.254	31	-33	0	1	-1	.969	10	*S-124	-1.1
1978	Cle-A	130	421	48	114	18	4	1	32	13	46	.271	.301	.340	81	-11	1	2	-1	.963	-4	*S-129	-0.1
1979	Cle-A	149	449	41	99	9	3	0	34	34	54	.220	.281	.254	45	-34	2	5	-2	.974	4	*S-148	-1.6
1980	Cle-A	109	358	28	97	12	0	2	28	10	25	.271	.306	.321	72	-14	0	0	0	.971	-1	*S-108	-0.5
1981	Cle-A	75	221	13	54	4	0	0	14	10	19	.244	.280	.262	58	-12	1	0	0	.970	-7	S-75	-1.1
1982	NY-N	40	54	6	18	2	0	0	4	3	4	.333	.368	.370	108	1	1	0	0	.962	-1	2-26,S-16	0.1
1983	Chi-N	59	88	5	18	3	0	1	3	3	13	.205	.231	.273	37	-8	0	0	0	.978	7	S-28,3-17	0.1
1984	*Chi-N	44	74	5	14	1	0	0	4	3	11	.189	.259	.203	29	-7	0	0	0	.966	-2	S-36/3-5,2-4	-0.7
Total	12	996	2848	250	687	84	12	14	231	143	329	.241	.285	.294	61	-148	9	23	-11	.966	-14	S-927/2-30,3-22	-7.8

■ ERNIE VICK

Vick, Henry Arthur   b: 7/2/1900, Toledo, Ohio   d: 7/16/80, Ann Arbor, Mich.   BR/TR, 5'9.5", 185 lbs.   Deb: 6/29/22

YEAR	TM/L	G	AB	R	H	2B	3B	HR	RBI	BB	SO	AVG	OBP	SLG	PRO+	BR/A	SB	CS	SBR	FA	FR	G/POS	TPR
1922	StL-N	3	6	1	2	2	0	0	0	0	0	.333	.333	.667	159	0	0	0	0	.875	-0	/C-3	0.0
1924	StL-N	16	23	2	8	1	0	0	3	3	3	.348	.423	.391	159	1	0	0	0	.974	3	C-16	0.4
1925	StL-N	14	32	3	6	2	1	0	3	3	1	.188	.257	.313	44	-3	0	0	0	.929	-1	/C-9	-0.2
1926	StL-N	24	51	6	10	2	0	0	4	3	4	.196	.241	.235	27	-5	0	0		.944	-1	C-23	-0.5
Total	4	57	112	12	26	7	1	0	7	9	8	.232	.289	.313	58	-7	0	0		.944	-1	/C-51	-0.3

■ SAMMY VICK

Vick, Samuel Bruce   b: 4/12/1895, Batesville, Miss.   d: 8/17/86, Memphis, Tenn.   BR/TR, 5'10.5", 163 lbs.   Deb: 9/20/17

YEAR	TM/L	G	AB	R	H	2B	3B	HR	RBI	BB	SO	AVG	OBP	SLG	PRO+	BR/A	SB	CS	SBR	FA	FR	G/POS	TPR
1917	NY-A	10	36	4	10	3	0	0	2	1	6	.278	.297	.361	100	-0	2			.882	-1	O-10	-0.2
1918	NY-A	2	3	1	2	0	0	0	1	0	0	.667	.667	.667	296	1	0			.000	-1	/O-1	0.0
1919	NY-A	106	407	59	101	15	9	2	27	35	55	.248	.308	.344	82	-10	9			.952	-4	*O-100	-2.3
1920	NY-A	51	118	21	26	7	1	0	11	14	20	.220	.313	.297	60	-7	1	1	-0	.949	-4	O-33	-1.3
1921	Bos-A	44	77	5	20	3	1	0	9	1	10	.260	.269	.325	52	-6	0	1	-1	1.000	-1	O-14	-0.8
Total	5	213	641	90	159	28	11	2	50	51	91	.248	.305	.335	76	-22	12	2		.951	-11	O-158	-4.6

■ GEORGE VICO

Vico, George Steve "Sam"   b: 8/9/23, San Fernando, Cal.   d: 1/13/94, Redondo Beach, Cal.   BL/TR, 6'4", 200 lbs.   Deb: 4/20/48

YEAR	TM/L	G	AB	R	H	2B	3B	HR	RBI	BB	SO	AVG	OBP	SLG	PRO+	BR/A	SB	CS	SBR	FA	FR	G/POS	TPR
1948	Det-A	144	521	50	139	23	9	8	58	39	39	.267	.326	.392	88	-11	2	2	-1	.988	-3	*1-142	-1.5
1949	Det-A	67	142	15	27	5	2	4	18	21	17	.190	.311	.338	72	-6	0	0	0	.985	2	1-53	-0.4
Total	2	211	663	65	166	28	11	12	76	60	56	.250	.323	.380	85	-17	2	2	-1	.987	-1	1-195	-1.9

■ JOSE VIDAL

Vidal, Jose (Nicolas) "Papito"   b: 4/3/40, Batey Lechugas, D.R.   BR/TR, 6', 190 lbs.   Deb: 9/5/66

YEAR	TM/L	G	AB	R	H	2B	3B	HR	RBI	BB	SO	AVG	OBP	SLG	PRO+	BR/A	SB	CS	SBR	FA	FR	G/POS	TPR
1966	Cle-A	17	32	4	6	1	1	0	3	5	11	.188	.297	.281	67	-1	0	1	-1	1.000	-1	O-11	-0.3
1967	Cle-A	16	34	4	4	0	0	0	0	7	12	.118	.268	.118	17	-3	0	1	-0	1.000	-1	O-10	-0.6
1968	Cle-A	37	54	5	9	0	0	2	5	2	15	.167	.196	.278	43	-4	3	0	1	1.000	-5	O-26/1-1	-1.0
1969	Sea-A	18	26	7	5	0	1	1	2	4	8	.192	.323	.385	99	-0	1	1	-0	.917	-0	O-6	-0.1
Total	4	88	146	20	24	1	2	3	10	18	46	.164	.261	.260	53	-8	4	3	-1	.985	-7	/O-53,1-1	-2.0

■ HECTOR VILLANUEVA

Villanueva, Hector (Balasquide)   b: 10/2/64, Rio Piedras, P.R.   BR/TR, 6'1", 220 lbs.   Deb: 6/1/90

YEAR	TM/L	G	AB	R	H	2B	3B	HR	RBI	BB	SO	AVG	OBP	SLG	PRO+	BR/A	SB	CS	SBR	FA	FR	G/POS	TPR
1990	Chi-N	52	114	14	31	4	1	7	18	4	27	.272	.308	.509	112	1	1	0	0	.991	-4	C-23,1-14	-0.2
1991	Chi-N	71	192	23	53	6	1	13	32	21	30	.276	.347	.542	140	9	0	0	0	.979	-9	C-55/1-6	0.4
1992	Chi-N	51	112	9	17	6	0	2	13	11	24	.152	.228	.259	37	-9	0	0	0	.978	-2	C-28/1-6	-0.2
1993	StL-N	17	55	7	8	1	0	3	9	4	17	.145	.203	.327	40	-5	0	0	0	1.000	-1	C-17	-0.5
Total	4	191	473	53	109	21	2	25	72	40	98	.230	.293	.442	98	-4	1	0	0	.984	-7	C-123/1-26	-0.5

■ FERNANDO VINA

Vina, Fernando   b: 4/16/69, Sacramento, Cal.   BL/TR, 5'9", 170 lbs.   Deb: 4/10/93

YEAR	TM/L	G	AB	R	H	2B	3B	HR	RBI	BB	SO	AVG	OBP	SLG	PRO+	BR/A	SB	CS	SBR	FA	FR	G/POS	TPR
1993	Sea-A	24	45	5	10	0	0	0	2	4	3	.222	.327	.267	61	-2	6	0	2	1.000	6	2-16/S-4,D-2	0.6
1994	NY-N	79	124	20	31	6	0	0	6	12	11	.250	.372	.298	78	-3	3	1	0	.979	-2	2-13,3-12/S-9,0-6	0.0
1995	Mil-A	113	288	46	74	7	7	3	29	22	28	.257	.329	.361	75	-10	6	3	0	.983	10	2-99/S-6,3-2	0.5
1996	Mil-A	140	554	94	157	19	10	7	46	38	35	.283	.344	.392	81	-16	16	7	1	.979	8	*2-137	0.2
Total	4	356	1011	165	272	34	17	10	83	76	77	.269	.343	.366	78	-31	31	11	3	.981	26	2-265/S-19,3-14,0D	1.3

■ CHARLIE VINSON

Vinson, Charles Anthony "Chuck"   b: 1/5/44, Washington, D.C.   BL/TL, 6'3", 207 lbs.   Deb: 9/19/66

YEAR	TM/L	G	AB	R	H	2B	3B	HR	RBI	BB	SO	AVG	OBP	SLG	PRO+	BR/A	SB	CS	SBR	FA	FR	G/POS	TPR
1966	Cal-A	13	22	3	4	2	0	1	6	5	9	.182	.357	.409	123	1	0	0	0	1.000	-1	1-11	0.0

■ RUBE VINSON

Vinson, Ernest Augustus   b: 3/20/1879, Dover, Del.   d: 10/12/51, Chester, Pa.   5'9", 168 lbs.   Deb: 9/27/04

YEAR	TM/L	G	AB	R	H	2B	3B	HR	RBI	BB	SO	AVG	OBP	SLG	PRO+	BR/A	SB	CS	SBR	FA	FR	G/POS	TPR
1904	Cle-A	15	49	12	15	1	0	0	2		10	.306	.433	.327	143	3	2			1.000	3	O-15	0.6
1905	Cle-A	39	134	12	26	3	1	0	9		7	.194	.245	.231	51	-7	4			.930	-3	O-36	-1.4
1906	Chi-A	10	24	2	6	0	0	0	3		2	.250	.308	.250	77	-1	1			.600	-3	/O-7	-0.4
Total	3	64	207	26	47	4	1	0	14		19	.227	.301	.256	77	-5	7			.919	-3	/O-58	-1.2

■ JIM VIOX

Viox, James Harry   b: 12/30/1890, Lockland, Ohio   d: 1/6/69, Erlanger, Ky.   BR/TR, 5'7", 150 lbs.   Deb: 5/9/12

YEAR	TM/L	G	AB	R	H	2B	3B	HR	RBI	BB	SO	AVG	OBP	SLG	PRO+	BR/A	SB	CS	SBR	FA	FR	G/POS	TPR
1912	Pit-N	33	70	8	13	2	3	1	7	3	9	.186	.219	.343	53	-5	2			.957	-4	3-10/S-8,0-3,2-1	-0.9
1913	Pit-N	137	492	86	156	32	8	2	65	64	28	.317	.399	.427	142	29	14			.959	-43	*2-124,S-10	-1.6
1914	Pit-N	143	506	52	134	18	5	1	57	63	33	.265	.351	.326	106	6	9			.939	-25	*2-138/S-2,O-2	-2.2
1915	Pit-N	150	503	56	129	17	8	2	45	75	31	.256	.357	.334	111	10	12	8	-1	.954	-23	*2-134,3-13/O-2	-1.4
1916	Pit-N	43	132	12	33	7	0	1	17	17	11	.250	.340	.326	104	3	2			.937	-16	2-25,3-11	-1.6
Total	5	506	1703	214	465	76	24	7	191	222	112	.273	.361	.358	116	41	39	8		.949	-111	2-422/3-34,S-20,0-7	-7.7

■ BILL VIRDON

Virdon, William Charles   b: 6/9/31, Hazel Park, Mich.   BL/TR, 6', 175 lbs.   Deb: 4/12/55   MC

YEAR	TM/L	G	AB	R	H	2B	3B	HR	RBI	BB	SO	AVG	OBP	SLG	PRO+	BR/A	SB	CS	SBR	FA	FR	G/POS	TPR
1955	StL-N	144	534	58	150	18	6	17	68	36	64	.281	.327	.433	100	-1	2	4	-2	.966	-6	*O-142	-1.0
1956	StL-N	24	71	10	15	2	0	2	9	5	8	.211	.273	.324	60	-4	0		-1	.982	-1	O-24	-0.7
	Pit-N	133	509	67	170	21	10	8	37	33	63	.334	.376	.462	126	19	6	6	-2	.989	4	*O-130	1.4
	Yr	157	580	77	185	23	10	10	46	38	71	.319	.361	.445	118	14	6	7	-2	.988	3	*O-154	0.7
1957	Pit-N	144	561	59	141	28	11	8	50	33	69	.251	.293	.383	82	-15	3	3	-1	.986	12	*O-141	-1.3
1958	Pit-N	144	604	75	161	24	11	9	46	52	70	.267	.326	.387	90	-9	5	3	0	.993	11	*O-143	-0.6
1959	Pit-N	144	519	67	132	24	2	8	41	55	65	.254	.329	.355	83	-12	7	4	-0	.979	**24**	*O-144	0.4
1960	*Pit-N	120	409	60	108	16	9	8	40	40	44	.264	.330	.406	99	-0	2	6	-2	.985	3	*O-109	0.3
1961	Pit-N	146	599	81	156	22	8	9	58	49	45	.260	.316	.369	81	-16	5	8	-3	.985	11	*O-145	-1.7
1962	Pit-N	156	663	82	164	27	**10**	6	47	36	55	.247	.289	.377	69	-30	5	13	-6	.976	5	*O-156	-4.0
1963	Pit-N	142	554	59	149	22	8	8	53	43	55	.269	.322	.374	99	-1	1	2	-1	.988	6	*O-142	-0.4
1964	Pit-N	145	473	59	115	11	3	3	27	30	44	.243	.288	.298	66	-21	1	5	-4	.976	-7	*O-134	-3.9
1965	Pit-N	135	481	58	134	22	5	4	24	30	49	.279	.322	.370	94	-4	4	3	-1	.970	-2	*O-128	-1.3

YEAR	TM/L	G	AB	R	H	2B	3B	HR	RBI	BB	SO	AVG	OBP	SLG	PRO+	BR/A	SB	CS	SBR	FA	FR	G/POS	TPR
1968	Pit-N	6	3	1	1	0	0	1	2	0	2	.333	.333	1.333	388	1	0	0	0	1.000	-1	/O-4	-0.1
Total	12	1583	5980	735	1596	237	81	91	502	442	647	.267	.318	.379	89	-95	47	54	-18	.982	69	*O-1542	-12.9

■ OZZIE VIRGIL
Virgil, Osvaldo Jose Jr.   b: 12/7/56, Mayaguez, P.R.   BR/TR, 6'1", 205 lbs.   Deb: 10/5/80   F

YEAR	TM/L	G	AB	R	H	2B	3B	HR	RBI	BB	SO	AVG	OBP	SLG	PRO+	BR/A	SB	CS	SBR	FA	FR	G/POS	TPR
1980	Phi-N	1	5	1	1	0	0	0	0	0	1	.200	.200	.400	60	-0	0	0	0	1.000	-1	/C-1	-0.1
1981	Phi-N	6	6	0	0	0	0	0	0	0	2	.000	.000	.000	-96	-2	0	0	0	1.000	-1	/C-1	-0.2
1982	Phi-N	49	101	11	24	6	0	3	8	10	26	.238	.306	.386	91	-1	0	1	-1	.964	4	C-35	0.3
1983	*Phi-N	55	140	11	30	7	0	6	23	8	34	.214	.272	.393	83	-4	0	2	-1	.966	-5	C-51	-0.8
1984	Phi-N	141	456	61	119	21	2	18	68	45	91	.261	.334	.434	113	7	1	1	-0	.992	-3	*C-137	1.0
1985	Phi-N★	131	426	47	105	16	3	19	55	49	85	.246	.331	.432	109	5	0	0	0	**.994**	-4	*C-120	0.7
1986	Atl-N	114	359	45	80	9	0	15	48	63	73	.223	.345	.373	93	-2	1	0	0	.984	14	*C-111	2.0
1987	Atl-N★	123	429	57	106	13	1	27	72	47	81	.247	.331	.471	104	2	0	1	-1	.989	-2	*C-122	0.8
1988	Atl-N	107	320	23	82	10	0	9	31	22	54	.256	.314	.372	92	-3	2	0	1	.990	-11	C-96	-0.8
1989	Tor-A	9	11	2	2	1	0	1	2	4	3	.182	.400	.545	167	1	0	0	0	1.000	-0	/C-1,D-6	0.1
1990	Tor-A	3	5	0	0	0	0	0	0	0	3	.000	.000	.000	-98	-1	0	0	0	1.000	-0	/C-2,D-1	-0.1
Total	11	739	2258	258	549	84	6	98	307	248	453	.243	.326	.416	101	1	4	5	-2	.987	-8	C-677/D-7	2.9

■ OZZIE VIRGIL
Virgil, Osvaldo Jose Sr. (Pichardo)   b: 5/17/33, Montecristi, D.R.   BR/TR, 6', 175 lbs.   Deb: 9/23/56   FC

YEAR	TM/L	G	AB	R	H	2B	3B	HR	RBI	BB	SO	AVG	OBP	SLG	PRO+	BR/A	SB	CS	SBR	FA	FR	G/POS	TPR
1956	NY-N	3	12	2	5	1	0	0	1	0	2	.417	.417	.667	186	1	0	0		.800	-2	/3-3	0.0
1957	NY-N	96	226	26	53	0	2	4	24	14	27	.235	.279	.305	57	-14	2	3	-1	.926	9	3-62,O-24/S-1	-0.6
1958	Det-A	49	193	19	47	10	2	3	19	8	20	.244	.274	.363	69	-9	1	0	0	.981	3	3-49	-0.5
1960	Det-A	62	132	16	30	4	2	3	13	4	14	.227	.250	.356	60	-8	1	1	-0	.974	4	3-42/2-8,S-5,C-1	0.1
1961	Det-A	20	30	1	4	0	0	1	1	1	5	.133	.161	.233	4	-4	0	0	0	.938	-1	/3-9,C-3,2-1,S-1	-0.5
	KC-A	11	21	1	3	0	0	0	0	0	3	.143	.143	.143	-23	-4	0	0	0	.818	0	/3-4,C-3	-0.3
	Yr	31	51	2	7	0	0	1	1	1	8	.137	.154	.196	-7	-8	0	0	0	.889	-1	3-13/C-6,2-1,S-1	-0.8
1962	Bal-A	1	0	0	0	0	0	0	0	1	0	—	1.000	—	209	0	0	0	0	.000	0	H	0.0
1965	Pit-N	39	49	3	13	2	0	1	5	2	10	.265	.294	.367	85	-1	0	0	0	1.000	2	C-15/3-7,2-5	0.1
1966	SF-N	42	89	7	19	2	0	2	9	4	12	.213	.247	.303	51	-6	0	1	-0	.984	-1	3-13,3-13/1-5,2O	-0.6
1969	SF-N	1	1	0	0	0	0	0	0	0	0	.000	.000	.000	-99	-0	0	0	0	.000	0	H	0.0
Total	9	324	753	75	174	19	7	14	73	34	91	.231	.264	.331	59	-43	5	5	-1	.951	19	3-189/C-35,O2S1	-2.3

■ JAKE VIRTUE
Virtue, Jacob Kitchline "Guesses"   b: 3/2/1865, Philadelphia, Pa.   d: 2/3/43, Camden, N.J.   BB/TL, 5'9.5", 165 lbs.   Deb: 7/21/1890

YEAR	TM/L	G	AB	R	H	2B	3B	HR	RBI	BB	SO	AVG	OBP	SLG	PRO+	BR/A	SB	CS	SBR	FA	FR	G/POS	TPR
1890	Cle-N	62	223	39	68	6	5	2	25	49	15	.305	.432	.404	147	16	9			.982	0	1-62	1.2
1891	Cle-N	139	517	82	135	19	14	2	72	75	40	.261	.363	.364	107	6	15			.972	-10	*1-139	-1.0
1892	*Cle-N	147	557	98	157	15	20	2	89	84	68	.282	.380	.391	128	20	14			.984	-4	*1-147	0.8
1893	Cle-N	97	378	87	100	16	10	1	60	54	14	.265	.358	.368	88	-7	11			.975	1	1-73,O-13/S-5,3P	-0.7
1894	Cle-N	29	89	15	23	4	1	0	10	13	3	.258	.359	.326	64	-5	1			.885	-2	O-21/2-3,1-2,P-1	-0.6
Total	5	474	1764	321	483	60	50	7	256	275	140	.274	.376	.376	111	30	50			.978	-15	1-423/O-34,3-5,S2P	-0.3

■ JOE VISNER
Visner, Joseph Paul (b: Joseph Paul Vezina)   b: 9/27/1859, Minneapolis, Minn.   d: 6/17/45, Fosston, Minn.   BL/TR, 5'11", 180 lbs.   Deb: 7/4/1885

YEAR	TM/L	G	AB	R	H	2B	3B	HR	RBI	BB	SO	AVG	OBP	SLG	PRO+	BR/A	SB	CS	SBR	FA	FR	G/POS	TPR
1885	Bal-a	4	13	2	3	0	0	0	2	2		.231	.333	.231	82	-0				.750	-1	/O-4	-0.1
1889	*Bro-a	80	295	56	76	12	10	8	68	36	36	.258	.346	.447	125	9	13			.871	-16	C-53,O-29	-0.2
1890	Pit-P	127	521	110	139	15	**22**	3	71	76	44	.267	.369	.397	114	13	18			.893	-6	*O-127	0.2
1891	Was-a	18	68	13	19	2	3	1	7	8	7	.279	.355	.441	134	3	2			.806	-2	O-17/C-1,3-1	-0.3
	StL-a	6	27	2	4	0	0	0	1	0	3	.148	.148	.222	5	-4	0			1.000	0	/O-6	-0.0
	Yr	24	95	15	23	2	3	1	8	8	10	.242	.301	.379	94	-1	2			.846	-2	O-23/C-1,3-1	-0.3
Total	4	235	924	183	241	29	36	12	149	122	90	.261	.354	.409	115	21	33			.892	-25	O-183/C-54,3-1	-0.4

■ JOE VITELLI
Vitelli, Antonio Joseph   b: 4/12/08, McKees Rocks, Pa.   d: 2/7/67, Pittsburgh, Pa.   BR/TR, 6'1", 195 lbs.   Deb: 5/30/44

YEAR	TM/L	G	AB	R	H	2B	3B	HR	RBI	BB	SO	AVG	OBP	SLG	PRO+	BR/A	SB	CS	SBR	FA	FR	G/POS	TPR
1944	Pit-N	4	3	0	0	0	0	0	0	0	0	.000	.000	.000	-96	-1	0			.750	0	/P-4	0.0
1945	Pit-N	1	0	1	0	0	0	0	0	0	0	—	—	—			0			.000	0	R	0.0
Total	2	5	3	1	0	0	0	0	0	0	0	.000	.000	.000	-96	-1	0			.750	0	/P-4	0.0

■ JOE VITIELLO
Vitiello, Joseph David   b: 4/11/70, Cambridge, Mass.   BR/TR, 6'2", 215 lbs.   Deb: 4/29/95

YEAR	TM/L	G	AB	R	H	2B	3B	HR	RBI	BB	SO	AVG	OBP	SLG	PRO+	BR/A	SB	CS	SBR	FA	FR	G/POS	TPR
1995	KC-A	53	130	13	33	4	0	7	21	8	25	.254	.317	.446	95	-1	0	0	0	.982	-0	D-38/1-8	-0.5
1996	KC-A	85	257	29	62	15	1	8	40	38	69	.241	.346	.401	90	-3	2	0	1	1.000	0	D-70/1-9,O-1	-0.7
Total	2	138	387	42	95	19	1	15	61	46	94	.245	.336	.416	92	-5	2	0	1	.990	-0	D-108/1-17,O-1	-1.2

■ OSSIE VITT
Vitt, Oscar Joseph   b: 1/4/1890, San Francisco, Cal.   d: 1/31/63, Oakland, Cal.   BR/TR, 5'10", 150 lbs.   Deb: 4/11/12   M

YEAR	TM/L	G	AB	R	H	2B	3B	HR	RBI	BB	SO	AVG	OBP	SLG	PRO+	BR/A	SB	CS	SBR	FA	FR	G/POS	TPR
1912	Det-A	76	273	39	67	4	4	0	19	18		.245	.297	.293	70	-11	17			.929	0	O-28,3-24,2-15	-1.2
1913	Det-A	99	359	45	86	11	3	2	33	31	18	.240	.304	.304	79	-10	5			.960	5	2-78,3-17/O-2	-0.6
1914	Det-A	66	195	35	49	7	0	0	8	31	6	.251	.354	.287	90	-1	10	8	-2	.964	2	2-36,3-16/O-2,S-1	-0.1
1915	Det-A	152	560	116	140	18	13	1	48	80	22	.250	.348	.334	99	-0	26	18	-3	**.964**	14	*3-151/2-2	1.9
1916	Det-A	153	597	88	135	17	12	0	42	75	28	.226	.314	.295	80	-14	18			**.964**	28	*3-151/S-2	2.1
1917	Det-A	140	512	65	130	13	6	0	47	56	15	.254	.329	.303	93	-3	18			.940	-17	*3-140	-2.0
1918	Det-A	81	267	29	64	5	2	0	17	32	6	.240	.321	.277	83	-5	9			.953	-4	3-66/2-9,O-3	0.1
1919	Bos-A	133	469	64	114	10	4	0	40	44	11	.243	.309	.277	69	-18	9			**.970**	14	*3-133	0.1
1920	Bos-A	87	296	50	65	10	4	1	28	43	10	.220	.321	.291	66	-14	5	4	-1	.986	-6	3-64,2-21	-1.7
1921	Bos-A	78	232	29	44	11	0	1	13	45	13	.190	.321	.246	48	-17	1	2	-1	.962	-2	3-71/O-3,1-2	-1.6
Total	10	1065	3760	464	894	106	48	4	295	455	131	.238	.322	.295	80	-93	114	32		.960	40	3-833,2-161/OS1	-3.0

■ JOSE VIZCAINO
Vizcaino, Jose Luis (Pimental)   b: 3/26/68, San Cristobal, D.R.   BB/TR, 6'1", 150 lbs.   Deb: 9/10/89

YEAR	TM/L	G	AB	R	H	2B	3B	HR	RBI	BB	SO	AVG	OBP	SLG	PRO+	BR/A	SB	CS	SBR	FA	FR	G/POS	TPR
1989	LA-N	7	10	2	2	0	0	0	0	0	3	.200	.200	.200	15	-1	0	0	0	.882	2	/S-5	0.1
1990	LA-N	37	51	3	14	1	1	0	2	4	8	.275	.327	.333	85	-1	1	1	-0	.956	5	S-11/2-6	0.2
1991	Chi-N	93	145	7	38	5	0	0	10	5	18	.262	.287	.297	61	-7	2	1	-0	.947	7	S-57,S-33/2-9	0.1
1992	Chi-N	86	285	25	64	10	4	1	17	14	35	.225	.261	.298	57	-16	3	0	1	.969	8	S-81,3-44,2-34	0.6
1993	Chi-N	151	551	74	158	19	4	4	54	46	71	.287	.345	.358	90	-7	12	9	-2	.968	3	S-83,3-44,2-34	0.6
1994	NY-N	103	410	47	105	13	3	3	33	33	62	.256	.315	.324	68	-19	1	11	-6	.970	-12	*S-102	-2.8
1995	NY-N	135	509	66	146	21	5	3	56	35	76	.287	.334	.365	87	-9	8	3	1	**.984**	10	*S-134/2-1	1.3
1996	NY-N	96	363	47	110	12	6	1	32	29	58	.303	.358	.377	101	1	9	5	-0	.986	2	2-93	0.7
	*Cle-A	48	179	23	51	5	2	3	17	7	24	.285	.312	.335	64	-10	6	2	1	.981	2	2-45/S-4,D-1	-0.4
Total	8	756	2503	294	688	86	25	12	217	172	353	.275	.324	.344	79	-70	42	32	-7	.973	23	S-420,2-193,3/D	-1.3

■ OMAR VIZQUEL
Vizquel, Omar Enrique (Gonzalez)   b: 4/24/67, Caracas, Venez.   BB/TR, 5'9", 155 lbs.   Deb: 4/3/89

YEAR	TM/L	G	AB	R	H	2B	3B	HR	RBI	BB	SO	AVG	OBP	SLG	PRO+	BR/A	SB	CS	SBR	FA	FR	G/POS	TPR
1989	Sea-A	143	387	45	85	7	3	1	20	28	40	.220	.274	.261	50	-25	1	4	-2	.971	11	*S-143	-0.7
1990	Sea-A	81	255	19	63	3	2	2	18	18	22	.247	.297	.298	66	-11	4	1	1	.980	-3	S-81	-0.7
1991	Sea-A	142	426	42	98	16	4	1	41	45	37	.230	.304	.293	66	-19	7	2	1	.980	24	*S-138/2-1	1.5
1992	Sea-A	136	483	49	142	20	4	0	21	32	38	.294	.340	.352	94	-4	15	13	-3	**.989**	0	*S-136	0.3
1993	Sea-A	158	560	68	143	14	2	2	31	50	71	.255	.319	.331	67	-25	12	14	-5	.980	**23**	*S-155/D-2	0.5
1994	Cle-A	69	286	39	78	10	1	1	33	23	23	.273	.327	.325	69	-13	13	4	2	.981	-4	S-69	-0.5
1995	*Cle-A	136	542	87	144	28	6	6	56	59	59	.266	.339	.351	79	-16	29	11	4	.986	-3	*S-136	1.6
1996	*Cle-A	151	542	98	161	36	1	9	64	56	42	.297	.367	.417	98	-1	35	9	5	.971	-1	*S-150	1.6
Total	8	1016	3481	447	914	134	17	22	284	311	332	.263	.325	.330	75	-114	116	58	0	.979	50	*S-1008/D-2,2-1	1.6

■ OTTO VOGEL
Vogel, Otto Henry   b: 10/26/1899, Mendota, Ill.   d: 7/19/69, Iowa City, Iowa   BR/TR, 6', 195 lbs.   Deb: 6/5/23

YEAR	TM/L	G	AB	R	H	2B	3B	HR	RBI	BB	SO	AVG	OBP	SLG	PRO+	BR/A	SB	CS	SBR	FA	FR	G/POS	TPR
1923	Chi-N	41	81	10	17	1	1	0	6	7	11	.210	.297	.272	51	-6	2	3	-1	.929	-2	O-24/3-1	-1.0
1924	Chi-N	70	172	28	46	11	0	1	24	10	26	.267	.319	.372	84	-4	4	4	-1	.956	1	O-53/3-2	-0.7
Total	2	111	253	38	63	11	3	2	30	17	37	.249	.312	.340	73	-10	6	7	-2	.948	5	/O-77,3-3	-1.7

■ JACK VOIGT
Voigt, John David   b: 5/17/66, Sarasota, Fla.   BR/TR, 6'1", 175 lbs.   Deb: 8/3/92

YEAR	TM/L	G	AB	R	H	2B	3B	HR	RBI	BB	SO	AVG	OBP	SLG	PRO+	BR/A	SB	CS	SBR	FA	FR	G/POS	TPR
1992	Bal-A	1	0	0	0	0	0	0	0	0	0					0	0	0	0	.000	0	/R	0.0
1993	Bal-A	64	152	32	45	11	1	6	23	25	33	.296	.395	.500	133	8	1	0	0	.987	-1	O-43/1-5,3-3,D-9	0.5

YEAR	TM/L	G	AB	R	H	2B	3B	HR	RBI	BB	SO	AVG	OBP	SLG	PRO+	BR/A	SB	CS	SBR	FA	FR	G/POS	TPR
1994	Bal-A	59	141	15	34	5	0	3	20	18	25	.241	.331	.340	70	-6	0	0	0	.989	-4	O-54/1-6,D-2	-1.0
1995	Bal-A	3	1	1	1	0	0	0	0	0	0	1.000	1.000	1.000	416	0	0	0	0	1.000	0	/1-1,D-1	0.1
	Tex-A	33	62	8	10	3	0	2	8	10	14	.161	.278	.306	51	-5	0	0	0	1.000	-2	O-25/1-5,D-2	-0.7
	Yr	36	63	9	11	3	0	2	8	10	14	.175	.288	.317	56	-4	0	0	0	1.000	-2	O-25/1-6,D-3	-0.6
1996	Tex-A	5	9	1	1	0	0	0	0	0	2	.111	.111	.111	-41	-2	0	0	0	1.000	0	/O-3,3-1	-0.2
Total	5	165	365	57	91	19	1	11	51	53	74	.249	.346	.397	91	-5	1	0	0	.991	-7	O-125/1-17,D-14,3-4	-1.3

■ CLYDE VOLLMER
Vollmer, Clyde Frederick b: 9/24/21, Cincinnati, Ohio BR/TR, 6'1", 190 lbs. Deb: 5/31/42

YEAR	TM/L	G	AB	R	H	2B	3B	HR	RBI	BB	SO	AVG	OBP	SLG	PRO+	BR/A	SB	CS	SBR	FA	FR	G/POS	TPR
1942	Cin-N	12	43	2	4	0	0	1	4	1	5	.093	.114	.163	-20	-7	0			1.000	1	O-11	-0.6
1946	Cin-N	9	22	1	4	0	0	0	1	1	3	.182	.217	.182	14	-2	2			1.000	-3	/O-7	-0.6
1947	Cin-N	78	155	19	34	10	0	1	13	9	18	.219	.267	.303	51	-11	0			.984	-7	O-66	-2.0
1948	Cin-N	7	9	0	1	0	0	0	0	0	1	.111	.200	.111	-14	-1	0			.000	-1	/O-2	-0.2
	Was-A	1	5	1	2	0	0	0	0	0	1	.400	.400	.400	116	0	0			1.000	0	/O-1	0.0
1949	Was-A	129	443	58	112	17	1	14	59	53	62	.253	.335	.391	94	-6	1	2	-1	.982	4	*O-114	-0.7
1950	Was-A	6	14	4	4	0	0	0	1	2	3	.286	.375	.286	75	-0	1	0	0	1.000	0	/O-3	0.0
	Bos-A	57	169	35	48	10	0	7	37	21	35	.284	.363	.467	102	-0	1	0	0	.954	-2	O-39	-0.3
	Yr	63	183	39	52	10	0	7	38	23	38	.284	.364	.454	100	-0	2	0	1	.957	-1	O-42	-0.3
1951	Bos-A	115	386	66	97	9	2	22	85	55	66	.251	.346	.456	105	2	0	0	0	.986	0	*O-106	-0.2
1952	Bos-A	90	250	35	66	12	4	11	50	39	47	.264	.370	.476	124	8	2	2	-1	1.000	-1	O-70	0.4
1953	Bos-A	1	0	0	0	0	0	0	0	0	0	—	1.000	—	180	0	0	0	0	.000	0	H	0.2
	Was-A	118	408	54	106	15	3	11	74	48	59	.260	.342	.392	100	0	0	2	-1	.979	7	*O-106	0.2
	Yr	119	408	54	106	15	3	11	74	49	59	.260	.343	.392	101	0	0	2	-1	.979	7	*O-106	0.2
1954	Was-A	62	117	8	30	4	0	2	15	12	28	.256	.331	.342	89	-2	0	0	0	1.000	-3	O-26	-0.6
Total	10	685	2021	283	508	77	10	69	339	243	328	.251	.335	.402	95	-19	7	6		.984	-3	O-551	-4.6

■ FRITZ Von KOLNITZ
Von Kolnitz, Alfred Holmes b: 5/20/1893, Charleston, S.C. d: 3/18/48, Mount Pleasant, S.C. BR/TR, 5'10.5", 175 lbs. Deb: 4/18/14

YEAR	TM/L	G	AB	R	H	2B	3B	HR	RBI	BB	SO	AVG	OBP	SLG	PRO+	BR/A	SB	CS	SBR	FA	FR	G/POS	TPR
1914	Cin-N	41	104	8	23	2	0	0	6	6	16	.221	.270	.240	51	-6	4			.914	-4	3-20,O-11/C-2,1-1	-1.1
1915	Cin-N	50	78	6	15	4	1	0	6	7	11	.192	.259	.269	59	-4	1	3	-2	.933	-6	3-18/S-6,1-3,C-2,0	-1.2
1916	Chi-A	24	44	1	10	3	0	0	7	2	6	.227	.261	.295	66	-2	0			.909	-5	3-13	-0.7
Total	3	115	226	15	48	9	1	0	19	15	33	.212	.264	.261	56	-12	5	3		.918	-15	/3-51,O-12,S-6,1C	-3.0

■ JOE VOSMIK
Vosmik, Joseph Franklin b: 4/4/10, Cleveland, Ohio d: 1/27/62, Cleveland, Ohio BR/TR, 6', 185 lbs. Deb: 9/13/30

YEAR	TM/L	G	AB	R	H	2B	3B	HR	RBI	BB	SO	AVG	OBP	SLG	PRO+	BR/A	SB	CS	SBR	FA	FR	G/POS	TPR
1930	Cle-A	9	26	1	6	2	0	0	4	1	1	.231	.259	.308	42	-2	0	0	0	.933	1	/O-5	-0.2
1931	Cle-A	149	591	80	189	36	14	7	117	38	30	.320	.363	.464	110	7	7	7	-2	.970	6	*O-147	0.1
1932	Cle-A	153	621	106	194	39	12	10	97	58	42	.312	.376	.462	109	8	2	3	-1	**.989**	24	*O-153	1.9
1933	Cle-A	119	438	53	115	20	10	4	56	42	13	.263	.331	.381	84	-10	0	2	-1	.985	6	*O-113	-1.1
1934	Cle-A	104	405	71	138	33	2	6	78	35	10	.341	.393	.477	122	13	1	1	0	.976	-2	*O-104	0.6
1935	Cle-A★	152	620	93	**216**	**47**	**20**	10	110	59	30	.348	.408	.537	140	36	2	1	0	.986	1	*O-150	2.9
1936	Cle-A	138	506	76	145	29	7	7	94	79	21	.287	.383	.413	96	-2	5	1	1	.978	-1	*O-136	-0.6
1937	StL-A	144	594	81	193	47	9	4	93	49	38	.325	.377	.455	108	7	2	3	-1	.972	8	*O-143	0.8
1938	Bos-A	146	621	121	**201**	37	6	9	86	59	26	.324	.384	.446	103	3	0	3	-2	.978	3	*O-146	-0.1
1939	Bos-A	145	554	93	153	29	6	7	84	66	33	.276	.356	.388	87	-10	4	3	-1	.974	-4	*O-144	-1.9
1940	Bro-N	116	404	45	114	14	6	1	42	22	21	.282	.321	.354	81	-10	0			.976	0	O-99	-1.5
1941	Bro-N	25	56	0	11	0	0	0	4	4	4	.196	.250	.196	26	-5	0			1.000	-5	O-18	-1.2
1944	Was-A	14	36	2	7	2	0	0	9	2	3	.194	.237	.250	41	-3	0			1.000	-2	O-12	-0.2
Total	13	1414	5472	818	1682	335	92	65	874	514	272	.307	.369	.438	104	29	23	24		.979	34	*O-1370	-0.9

■ ALEX VOSS
Voss, Alexander b: 5/16/1858, Roswell, Ga. d: 8/31/06, Cincinnati, Ohio BR/TR, 6'1", 180 lbs. Deb: 4/17/1884

YEAR	TM/L	G	AB	R	H	2B	3B	HR	RBI	BB	SO	AVG	OBP	SLG	PRO+	BR/A	SB	CS	SBR	FA	FR	G/POS	TPR
1884	Was-U	63	245	33	47	9	0	0			5	.192	.208	.229	33	-27				.848	4	P-27,3-16,1-15,O/S	-1.6
	KC-U	14	45	1	4	0	0	0			0	.089	.089	.089	-53	-10				.867	1	/O-8,P-7	-0.4
	Yr	77	290	34	51	9	0	0			5	.176	.190	.207	21	-36				.859	5	P-34,O-21,3-16,1/S	-2.0

■ BILL VOSS
Voss, William Edward b: 10/31/43, Glendale, Cal. BL/TL, 6'2", 160 lbs. Deb: 9/14/65

YEAR	TM/L	G	AB	R	H	2B	3B	HR	RBI	BB	SO	AVG	OBP	SLG	PRO+	BR/A	SB	CS	SBR	FA	FR	G/POS	TPR
1965	Chi-A	11	33	4	6	0	1	1	3	3	5	.182	.250	.333	68	-1	0	0	0	1.000	-1	O-10	-0.4
1966	Chi-A	2	2	0	0	0	0	0	0	0	2	.000	.000	.000	-99	-1	0	0	0	1.000	-0	/O-1	-0.1
1967	Chi-A	13	22	4	2	0	0	0	0	0	1	.091	.091	.091	-48	-4	1	1	-0	1.000	-2	O-11	-0.7
1968	Chi-A	61	167	14	26	2	1	2	15	16	34	.156	.238	.216	38	-12	5	3	-0	.963	-4	O-55	-2.2
1969	Cal-A	133	349	33	91	11	4	2	40	35	40	.261	.328	.332	90	-5	5	3	-0	.995	-1	*O-111/1-2	-0.9
1970	Cal-A	80	181	21	44	4	3	3	30	23	18	.243	.335	.348	92	-2	2	1	0	.979	2	O-55	-0.2
1971	Mil-A	97	275	31	69	4	0	10	30	24	45	.251	.313	.375	95	-2	1	1	0	.987	-4	O-79	-1.1
1972	Mil-A	27	36	1	3	1	0	0	1	6	4	.083	.195	.111	-7	-5	0	1	-1	.929	-3	O-11	-0.9
	Oak-A	40	97	10	22	5	1	2	5	8	16	.227	.299	.330	92	-1	0	0	0	1.000	-1	O-34	-0.4
	Yr	67	133	11	25	6	1	2	6	14	20	.188	.270	.271	64	-6	0	1	-1	.987	-4	O-45	-1.3
	StL-N	11	15	1	4	2	0	0	3	2	2	.267	.353	.400	115	0	0	0	0	1.000	-0	/O-2	0.0
Total	8	475	1177	119	267	29	10	19	127	117	167	.227	.300	.317	78	-33	15	11	-2	.986	-11	O-369/1-2	-6.9

■ PHIL VOYLES
Voyles, Philip Vance b: 5/12/1900, Murphy, N.C. d: 11/3/72, Marlborough, Mass. BL/TR, 5'11.5", 175 lbs. Deb: 9/4/29

YEAR	TM/L	G	AB	R	H	2B	3B	HR	RBI	BB	SO	AVG	OBP	SLG	PRO+	BR/A	SB	CS	SBR	FA	FR	G/POS	TPR
1929	Bos-N	20	68	9	16	1	0	0	14	6	8	.235	.297	.294	49	-1	5			.922	-2	O-20	-0.8

■ GEORGE VUKOVICH
Vukovich, George Stephen b: 6/24/56, Chicago, Ill. BL/TR, 6', 198 lbs. Deb: 4/13/80

YEAR	TM/L	G	AB	R	H	2B	3B	HR	RBI	BB	SO	AVG	OBP	SLG	PRO+	BR/A	SB	CS	SBR	FA	FR	G/POS	TPR
1980	*Phi-N	78	58	6	13	1	1	0	8	6	9	.224	.297	.276	58	-3	0	0	0	.933	-9	O-28	-1.3
1981	*Phi-N	20	26	5	10	0	0	1	4	1	0	.385	.407	.500	150	2	1	0	0	1.000	-2	/O-9	0.0
1982	Phi-N	123	335	41	91	18	2	6	42	32	47	.272	.335	.391	100	0	2	9	-5	.977	-6	*O-102	-1.3
1983	Cle-A	124	312	31	77	13	2	3	44	24	37	.247	.305	.330	72	-12	3	4	-2	.986	-13	*O-122	-2.9
1984	Cle-A	134	437	38	133	22	5	9	60	34	61	.304	.356	.439	117	10	1	4	-2	.994	14	*O-130	1.8
1985	Cle-A	149	434	43	106	22	0	8	45	30	75	.244	.295	.350	76	-14	2	2	-1	.988	-7	*O-137	-2.6
Total	6	628	1602	164	430	76	10	27	203	127	229	.268	.324	.379	92	-18	9	19	-9	.987	-22	O-528	-6.3

■ JOHN VUKOVICH
Vukovich, John Christopher b: 7/31/47, Sacramento, Cal. BR/TR, 6'1", 190 lbs. Deb: 9/11/70 MC

YEAR	TM/L	G	AB	R	H	2B	3B	HR	RBI	BB	SO	AVG	OBP	SLG	PRO+	BR/A	SB	CS	SBR	FA	FR	G/POS	TPR
1970	Phi-N	3	8	1	1	0	0	0	0	0	0	.125	.222	.125	-5	-1	0	0	0	.778	1	/S-2,3-1	0.0
1971	Phi-N	74	217	11	36	5	0	0	14	12	34	.166	.213	.189	15	-24	2	1	0	.956	10	3-74	-1.6
1973	Mil-A	55	128	10	16	3	0	2	9	9	40	.125	.182	.195	7	-16	0	2	-1	.948	-4	3-40,1-13/S-1	-2.2
1974	Mil-A	38	80	5	15	1	0	3	11	1	16	.188	.198	.313	45	-6	2	1	0	.945	-2	S-12,3-12,2-11/1-4	-0.2
1975	Cin-N	31	38	4	8	2	0	0	5	5	5	.211	.286	.289	59	-2	0	1	0	.925	7	3-31	0.5
1976	Phi-N	4	8	1	2	0	0	0	2	0	2	.125	.125	.500	14	-0	1	0	0	1.000	-0	/3-4,1-1	-0.1
1977	Phi-N	2	2	0	0	0	0	0	0	0	2	.000	.000	.000	-96	-1	0	0	0	.000	0	H	-0.1
1979	Phi-N	10	15	0	3	0	0	0	1	0	3	.200	.200	.267	25	-1	0	0	0	1.000	-0	2/3-7,2-3	0.0
1980	Phi-N	49	62	4	10	1	0	0	5	2	9	.161	.200	.210	14	-7	0	1	-1	.958	9	3-34/2-9,S-5,1-1	0.0
1981	Phi-N	11	1	0	0	0	0	0	0	0	1	.000	.000	.000	-96	-0	0	0	0	.800	7	/3-9,1-1,2-1	0.0
Total	10	277	559	37	90	14	1	6	44	29	109	.161	.205	.222	20	-59	4	5	-2	.951	18	3-212/2-24,1-20,S	-4.5

■ FRANK WADDEY
Waddey, Frank Orum b: 8/21/05, Memphis, Tenn. d: 10/21/90, Knoxville, Tenn. BL/TL, 5'10.5", 185 lbs. Deb: 4/16/31

YEAR	TM/L	G	AB	R	H	2B	3B	HR	RBI	BB	SO	AVG	OBP	SLG	PRO+	BR/A	SB	CS	SBR	FA	FR	G/POS	TPR
1931	StL-A	14	22	3	6	1	0	0	2	3	3	.273	.333	.318	70	-1	0			1.000	-3	/O-7	-0.4

■ HAM WADE
Wade, Abraham Lincoln b: 12/20/1880, Spring City, Pa. d: 7/21/68, Riverside, N.J. BR/TR, 5'8", 155 lbs. Deb: 9/9/07

YEAR	TM/L	G	AB	R	H	2B	3B	HR	RBI	BB	SO	AVG	OBP	SLG	PRO+	BR/A	SB	CS	SBR	FA	FR	G/POS	TPR
1907	NY-N	1	0	0	0	0	0	0	0	0	0	—	—	—	208	0	0			1.000	0	/O-1	0.0

■ GALE WADE
Wade, Galeard Lee b: 1/20/29, Hollister, Mo. BL/TR, 6'1.5", 185 lbs. Deb: 4/11/55

YEAR	TM/L	G	AB	R	H	2B	3B	HR	RBI	BB	SO	AVG	OBP	SLG	PRO+	BR/A	SB	CS	SBR	FA	FR	G/POS	TPR
1955	Chi-N	9	33	5	6	1	0	1	1	4	3	.182	.270	.303	52	-2	0	0	0	.867	-2	/O-9	-0.5
1956	Chi-N	10	12	0	0	0	0	0	1	1	0	.000	.077	.000	-78	-3	0	0	0	.875	-0	/O-3	-0.4
Total	2	19	45	5	6	1	0	1	2	5	3	.133	.220	.222	18	-5	0	0	0	.870	-2	/O-12	-0.9

YEAR	TM/L	G	AB	R	H	2B	3B	HR	RBI	BB	SO	AVG	OBP	SLG	PRO+	BR/A	SB	CS	SBR	FA	FR	G/POS	TPR

■ RIP WADE
Wade, Richard Frank   b: 1/12/1898, Duluth, Minn.   d: 6/16/57, Sandstone, Minn.   BL/TR, 5'11", 174 lbs.   Deb: 4/19/23

| | 1923 Was-A | 33 | 69 | 8 | 16 | 2 | 2 | 1 | 14 | 5 | 10 | .232 | .284 | .406 | 84 | -2 | 0 | 0 | 0 | .967 | -2 | O-19 | -0.5 |

■ WOODY WAGENHORST
Wagenhorst, Ellwood Otto   b: 6/3/1863, Kutztown, Pa.   d: 2/12/46, Washington, D.C.   5'11", 165 lbs.   Deb: 6/25/1888

| 1888 Phi-N | 2 | 8 | 0 | 1 | 0 | 0 | 0 | 0 | 0 | 1 | .125 | .125 | .125 | -19 | -1 | 0 | | | .800 | -1 | /3-2 | -0.2 |

■ BUTTS WAGNER
Wagner, Albert   b: 9/17/1871, Chartiers, Pa.   d: 11/26/28, Pittsburgh, Pa.   BR/TR, 5'10", 170 lbs.   Deb: 4/27/1898   F

1898 Was-N	63	223	20	50	11	2	1	31	14		.224	.279	.305	67	-10	4			.833	-11	3-39,O-10/S-8,2-5	-1.9
Bro-N	11	38	2	9	1	1	0	3	2		.237	.275	.316	69	-2	0			.813	-3	3-11	-0.4
Yr	74	261	22	59	12	3	1	34	16		.226	.279	.307	68	-12	4			.828	-14	3-50,O-10/S-8,2-5	-2.3

■ HEINIE WAGNER
Wagner, Charles F.   b: 9/23/1880, New York, N.Y.   d: 3/20/43, New Rochelle, N.Y.   BR/TR, 5'9", 183 lbs.   Deb: 7/1/02   MC

1902 NY-N	17	56	4	12	4	0	0	2	0		.214	.214	.232	38	-4	3			.862	-3	S-17	-0.6
1906 Bos-A	9	32	1	9	0	0	0	4	1		.281	.303	.281	83	-1	2			.943	1	/2-9	0.1
1907 Bos-A	111	385	29	82	10	4	2	21	31		.213	.275	.275	76	-10	20			.931	2	*S-109/2-1,3-1	-0.5
1908 Bos-A	153	526	62	130	11	5	1	46	27		.247	.288	.293	86	-8	20			.939	32	*S-153	3.0
1909 Bos-A	124	430	53	110	16	7	1	49	35		.256	.316	.333	103	1	18			.933	14	*S-123/2-1	2.0
1910 Bos-A	142	491	61	134	26	7	1	52	44		.273	.335	.360	115	8	26			.927	-12	*S-140	0.2
1911 Bos-A	80	261	34	67	13	8	1	38	29		.257	.340	.379	101	0	15			.946	-4	2-40,S-32	-0.2
1912 *Bos-A	144	504	75	138	25	6	2	68	62		.274	.358	.359	100	1	21			.922	-13	*S-144	0.0
1913 Bos-A	110	365	43	83	14	8	2	34	40	29	.227	.316	.326	86	-7	9			.938	4	*S-105/2-4	0.7
1915 Bos-A	84	267	38	64	11	2	0	29	37	34	.240	.339	.296	93	-1	8	4	0	.927	-16	2-79/3-1,O-1	-1.7
1916 Bos-A	6	8	2	4	1	0	0	0	0	0	.500	.636	.625	278	2	2			1.000	2	/3-4,2-1,S-1	0.5
1918 Bos-A	3	8	0	1	0	0	0	0	3	0	.125	.222	.125	5	-0	0			.900	-1	/2-2,3-1	-0.1
Total 12	983	3333	402	834	128	47	10	343	310	63	.250	.319	.326	95	-19	144	4		.928	8	S-824,2-137/3-7,O-1	3.4

■ HAL WAGNER
Wagner, Harold Edward   b: 7/2/15, E.Riverton, N.J.   d: 8/7/79, Riverside, N.J.   BL/TR, 6', 165 lbs.   Deb: 10/3/37

1937 Phi-A	1	0	0	0				0	0					0	0	0	0	0	1.000	0	/C-1	0.0
1938 Phi-A	33	88	10	20	2	1	0	8	8	9	.227	.299	.273	45	-7	0	0	0	.972	-1	/C-30	-0.7
1939 Phi-A	5	8	0	1	0	0	0	0	0	3	.125	.125	.125	-37	-2	0	0	0	1.000	-2	/C-5	-0.1
1940 Phi-A	34	75	9	19	5	1	0	10	11	6	.253	.356	.347	85	-1	0	0	0	.964	3	C-28	0.3
1941 Phi-A	46	131	18	29	8	2	1	15	19	9	.221	.320	.336	75	-5	1	0	0	.976	2	C-42	0.1
1942 Phi-A☆	104	288	26	68	17	1	1	30	24	29	.236	.304	.313	74	-10	0	0	0	.986	-2	C-94	-0.6
1943 Phi-A	111	289	22	69	17	1	1	26	36	17	.239	.327	.315	89	-4	3	3	-1	.980	-1	C-99	-0.7
1944 Phi-A	5	4	0	1	0	0	0	0	0	0	.250	.250	.250	44	-0	0	0	0	1.000	0	/C-1	0.0
Bos-A	66	223	21	74	13	4	1	38	29	14	.332	.418	.439	147	15	3	0	0	.970	4	C-64	1.9
Yr	71	227	21	75	13	4	1	38	29	14	.330	.415	.436	145	15	3	0	0	.971	4	C-65	1.9
1946 *Bos-A★	117	370	39	85	12	2	6	52	69	32	.230	.354	.322	85	-5	3	1	0	.983	-7	*C-116	-0.6
1947 Bos-A	21	65	5	15	3	0	0	6	9	5	.231	.324	.277	63	-3	0	0	0	.978	-1	C-21	-0.3
Det-A	71	191	19	55	10	4	0	33	28	16	.288	.382	.419	119	5	0	1	0	.990	-4	C-71	0.5
Yr	92	256	24	70	13	4	0	39	37	21	.273	.367	.383	105	-2	0	1	0	.987	-5	C-92	-0.2
1948 Det-A	54	109	10	22	3	0	0	10	10	11	.202	.326	.229	48	-8	1	0	0	.989	-4	C-52	-0.8
Phi-N	3	4	0	0	0	0	0	0	0	0	.000	.000	.000	-99	-1	0			1.000	1	/C-1	0.0
1949 Phi-N	1	1	0	0	0	0	0	0	0	0	.000	.000	.000	-99	-1	0			.750	-1	/C-1	-0.2
Total 12	672	1849	179	458	90	12	15	228	253	152	.248	.343	.334	87	-27	10	6		.981	-21	C-626	-1.1

■ HONUS WAGNER
Wagner, John Peter "The Flying Dutchman"   b: 2/24/1874, Chartiers, Pa.   d: 12/6/55, Carnegie, Pa.   BR/TR, 5'11", 200 lbs.   Deb: 7/19/1897   FMCH

1897 Lou-N	61	237	37	80	17	4	2	39	15		.338	.379	.468	127	9	19			.908	3	O-52/2-9	0.7
1898 Lou-N	151	588	80	176	29	3	10	105	31		.299	.341	.410	117	10	27			.972	-4	1-75,3-65,2-10	0.7
1899 Lou-N	147	571	98	192	43	13	7	113	40		.336	.391	.494	142	31	37			.928	1	3-75,O-61/2-7,1-4	2.6
1900 *Pit-N	135	527	107	201	45	22	4	100	41		**.381**	.434	.573	175	52	38			.965	-8	*O-118/3-9,2-7,1P	3.3
1901 Pit-N	140	549	101	194	37	11	6	**126**	53		.353	.417	.494	159	41	**49**			.918	10	S-61,O-54,3-24/2-1	5.1
1902 Pit-N	136	534	**105**	176	30	16	3	91	43		.330	.394	**.463**	159	36	42			1.000	8	O-61,S-44,1-32/P2	4.4
1903 *Pit-N	129	512	97	182	30	**19**	5	101	44		**.355**	.414	.518	160	39	46			.933	25	*S-111,O-12/1-6	6.3
1904 Pit-N	132	490	97	171	**44**	14	4	75	59		**.349**	**.423**	**.520**	186	50	53			.929	20	*S-145/O-2	4.8
1905 Pit-N	147	548	114	199	32	14	6	101	54		.363	.427	.505	173	49	57			.935	20	*S-137/O-2,3-1	7.3
1906 Pit-N	142	516	**103**	175	**38**	9	2	71	58		**.339**	.416	.459	166	40	53			.941	24	*S-138/1-4	7.3
1907 Pit-N	142	515	98	180	**38**	14	6	82	46		**.350**	.408	**.513**	186	49	**61**			.938	4	*S-151	6.3
1908 Pit-N	151	568	100	**201**	**39**	19	10	**109**	54		**.354**	**.415**	**.542**	205	65	53			.943	-7	*S-138/1-4	7.0
1909 *Pit-N	137	495	92	168	**39**	10	5	**100**	66		**.339**	**.420**	.489	168	39	35			.940	6	*S-136/O-1	5.2
1910 Pit-N	150	556	90	**178**	34	8	4	81	59	47	.320	.390	.432	132	22	24			.935	3	*S-138,1-11/2-2	3.2
1911 Pit-N	130	473	87	158	23	16	9	89	67	34	**.334**	.423	.507	154	35	20			.932	4	*S-101,1-28/O-1	4.5
1912 Pit-N	145	558	91	181	35	20	7	**102**	59	38	.324	.395	.496	145	34	26			**.962**	23	*S-143	6.6
1913 Pit-N	114	413	51	124	18	4	3	56	26	40	.300	.349	.385	114	7	21			**.962**	13	*S-105	3.1
1914 Pit-N	150	552	60	139	15	9	1	50	51	51	.252	.317	.317	93	-5	23			**.950**	7	*S-132,3-17/1-1	1.4
1915 Pit-N	156	566	68	155	32	17	6	78	39	64	.274	.325	.422	127	16	22	15	-2	**.948**	-5	*S-131/2-12,1-10	2.0
1916 Pit-N	123	432	45	124	15	9	1	39	34	36	.287	.350	.370	120	11	11			.942	-15	1-47,3-18/2-2,SM	0.1
1917 Pit-N	74	230	15	61	7	1	0	24	24	17	.265	.337	.304	94	-1	5			.985	0	1-50,S-12/3-2	-0.7
Total 21	2792	10430	1736	3415	640	252	101	1732	963	327	.327	.391	.466	150	631	722	15		.940	101	*S-1887,O-372,13/2P	81.2

■ JOE WAGNER
Wagner, Joseph Bernard   b: 4/24/1889, New York, N.Y.   d: 11/15/48, Bronx, N.Y.   BR/TR, 5'11", 165 lbs.   Deb: 4/25/15

| 1915 Cin-N | 75 | 197 | 17 | 35 | 5 | 2 | 0 | 13 | 8 | 35 | .178 | .210 | .223 | 31 | -17 | 4 | 6 | -2 | .961 | 6 | 2-46,S-12/3-2 | -1.4 |

■ LEON WAGNER
Wagner, Leon Lamar   b: 5/13/34, Chattanooga, Tenn.   BL/TR, 6'1", 195 lbs.   Deb: 6/22/58

1958 SF-N	74	221	31	70	9	0	13	35	18	34	.317	.371	.534	139	12	1	0		.949	-0	O-57	0.9
1959 SF-N	87	129	20	29	4	3	5	22	25	24	.225	.363	.419	110	2	0	0		.941	-2	O-28	-0.0
1960 StL-N	39	98	12	21	2	0	4	11	17	17	.214	.336	.357	83	-2	0	1	-1	.963	1	O-32	-0.4
1961 LA-A	133	453	74	127	19	2	28	79	48	65	.280	.353	.517	116	9	5	1	-1	.971	-2	*O-116	0.5
1962 LA-A★	160	612	96	164	21	5	37	107	50	87	.268	.328	.500	123	17	7	5	-1	.972	-7	*O-156	1.3
1963 LA-A★	149	550	73	160	11	4	26	90	49	73	.291	.356	.456	134	24	5	7	-3	.960	-4	*O-141	1.3
1964 Cle-A	163	641	94	162	19	2	31	100	56	121	.253	.319	.434	108	6	14	2	3	.959	-1	*O-163	0.0
1965 Cle-A	144	517	91	152	18	1	28	79	60	52	.294	.371	.495	143	29	12	2	2	.957	-9	*O-134	1.7
1966 Cle-A	150	549	70	153	20	0	23	66	46	69	.279	.336	.441	121	14	5	2	0	.990	-8	*O-139	0.0
1967 Cle-A	135	433	56	105	15	1	15	54	37	76	.242	.320	.386	107	4	3	3	-1	.980	-7	*O-117	-1.1
1968 Cle-A	38	49	5	9	0	0	0	0	6	12	.184	.273	.265	65	-2	0	0	0	.500	-3	O-10	-0.7
Chi-A	69	162	14	46	8	0	1	18	21	31	.284	.366	.352	117	4	2	1	0	.941	-8	O-46	-0.7
Yr	107	211	19	55	12	0	1	24	27	37	.261	.345	.332	106	2	2	1	0	.895	-11	/O-1	-1.4
1969 SF-N	11	6	0	2	0	0	0	0	4	2	.333	.467	.333	130	1	0	0	0	1.000	0	/O-1	0.1
Total 12	1352	4426	636	1202	150	15	211	669	435	652	.272	.343	.455	121	117	54	24		.964	-44	*O-1140	1.6

■ MARK WAGNER
Wagner, Mark Duane   b: 3/4/54, Conneaut, Ohio   BR/TR, 6'1", 175 lbs.   Deb: 8/20/76

1976 Det-A	39	115	9	30	7	0	0	6	18	.261	.298	.330	81	-3	0	2	-1	.947	10	S-39	1.0
1977 Det-A	22	48	4	7	1	0	0	3	4	12	.146	.226	.250	28	-5	0	1	0	.923	-1	S-21/2-1	-0.5
1978 Det-A	39	109	10	26	3	0	0	8	9	11	.239	.272	.284	55	-6	0	2	-1	.964	-6	S-35/2-4	-0.9
1979 Det-A	75	146	16	40	4	0	0	13	16	25	.274	.346	.315	77	-4	3	2	-0	.974	8	S-41,2-29/3-2,D-1	0.7
1980 Det-A	45	72	5	17	1	0	0	2	7	10	.236	.304	.250	52	-4	0	1	-1	.935	2	S-28/3-9,2-6	-0.1
1981 Tex-A	50	85	15	22	4	1	0	14	8	11	.259	.323	.365	103	0	1	2	-1	.964	-0	S-43/2-4,3-2	0.5
1982 Tex-A	60	179	14	43	4	1	0	8	11	25	.240	.280	.274	56	-11	2	1	-0	.955	-5	S-60	-0.5
1983 Tex-A	2	2	0	0	0	0	0	0	0	0	.000	.000	.000	-99	-1	0	0	0	1.000	1	/S-2	0.1
1984 Oak-A	82	87	8	20	3	0	0	12	10	5	.230	.287	.310	70	-4	0	0	1	.951	12	S-57,3-15/2-8,PD	1.0
Total 9	414	843	81	205	20	3	0	71	61	130	.243	.297	.299	66	-38	8	7	-2	.953	26	S-326/2-52,3-28,DP	1.3

YEAR	TM/L	G	AB	R	H	2B	3B	HR	RBI	BB	SO	AVG	OBP	SLG	PRO+	BR/A	SB	CS	SBR	FA	FR	G/POS	TPR

■ BILL WAGNER Wagner, William Joseph b: 1/2/1894, Jesup, Iowa d: 1/11/51, Waterloo, Iowa BR/TR, 6', 187 lbs. Deb: 7/16/14

1914	Pit-N	3	1	0	0	0	0	0	0	0	0	.000	.000	.000	-99	-0	0			1.000	0	/C-3	0.0
1915	Pit-N	5	5	0	0	0	0	0	0	1	2	.000	.167	.000	-48	-1	0			1.000	2	/C-3	0.1
1916	Pit-N	19	38	2	9	0	2	0	2	5	8	.237	.326	.342	104	0	0			.936	2	C-15	0.3
1917	Pit-N	53	151	15	31	7	2	0	9	11	22	.205	.264	.278	64	-6	1			.958	-4	C-37,1-12	-0.9
1918	Bos-N	13	47	2	10	0	0	1	7	4	5	.213	.275	.277	71	-2	0			.917	-5	C-13	-0.6
Total	5	93	242	19	50	7	4	1	18	21	37	.207	.273	.281	69	-9	1			.947	-5	/C-71,1-12	-1.1

■ KERMIT WAHL Wahl, Kermit Emerson b: 11/18/22, Columbia, S.Dak. d: 9/16/87, Tucson, Ariz. BR/TR, 5'11", 170 lbs. Deb: 6/23/44

1944	Cin-N	4	1	0	0	0	0	0	0	0	0	.000	.000	.000	-99	-0	0			.000	0	/3-1	0.0
1945	Cin-N	71	194	18	39	8	2	0	10	23	22	.201	.286	.263	54	-12	2			.948	5	2-32,S-31/3-7	-0.3
1947	Cin-N	39	81	8	14	0	0	1	4	6	12	.173	.239	.210	20	-9	0			.964	6	3-20/S-9,2-2	-0.3
1950	Phi-A	89	280	26	72	12	3	2	27	30	30	.257	.331	.343	74	-11	1	1	-0	.946	11	3-61,S-18/2-2	0.0
1951	Phi-A	20	59	4	11	2	0	0	6	9	5	.186	.294	.220	40	-5	0	0	0	.967	2	3-18	-0.3
	StL-A	8	27	2	9	1	1	0	3	0	3	.333	.333	.444	106	0	0	0	0	.950	1	/3-6	0.0
	Yr	28	86	6	20	3	1	0	9	9	8	.233	.305	.291	60	-5	0	0	0	.962	3	3-24	-0.3
Total	5	231	642	58	145	23	6	3	50	68	72	.226	.302	.294	60	-37	3	1		.949	25	3-113/S-58,2-36	-0.9

■ EDDIE WAITKUS Waitkus, Edward Stephen b: 9/4/19, Cambridge, Mass. d: 9/15/72, Jamaica Plain, Mass. BL/TL, 6'1", 175 lbs. Deb: 4/15/41

1941	Chi-N	12	28	1	5	1	0	0	0	0	3	.179	.207	.179	10	-3	0			.949	-1	/1-9	-0.5
1946	Chi-N	113	441	50	134	24	5	4	55	23	14	.304	.340	.408	114	6	3			.996	4	*1-106	0.4
1947	Chi-N	130	514	60	150	28	6	2	35	32	17	.292	.336	.381	94	-5	3			.994	8	*1-126	-0.2
1948	Chi-N★	139	562	87	166	27	10	7	44	43	19	.295	.348	.416	110	7	11			.992	7	*1-116,O-20	1.1
1949	Phi-N†	54	209	41	64	16	3	1	28	33	12	.306	.403	.426	126	9	3			.994	1	1-54	0.9
1950	*Phi-N	154	641	102	182	32	5	2	44	55	29	.284	.341	.359	86	-12	3			.993	-1	*1-154	-1.8
1951	Phi-N	145	610	65	157	27	4	1	46	53	22	.257	.317	.320	73	-23	0	3	-2	.992	-2	*1-144	-3.4
1952	Phi-N	146	499	51	144	29	4	2	49	64	23	.289	.371	.375	108	7	2	2	-1	.991	-2	*1-146	0.0
1953	Phi-N	81	247	24	72	9	2	1	16	13	23	.291	.330	.356	79	-7	1	1	-0	.989	-1	1-59	-1.1
1954	Bal-A	95	311	35	88	17	4	2	33	28	25	.283	.344	.383	107	2	0	1	-1	1.000	1	1-78	-0.2
1955	Bal-A	38	85	2	22	1	1	0	9	11	10	.259	.344	.294	78	-2	2	0	1	.974	-2	1-26	-0.5
	Phi-N	33	107	10	30	5	0	2	14	17	7	.280	.379	.383	105	1	0	1	0	.996	0	1-31	-0.7
Total	11	1140	4254	528	1214	215	44	24	373	372	204	.285	.344	.374	96	-21	28	8		.993	10	*1-1049/O-20	-5.4

■ CHARLIE WAITT Waitt, Charles C. b: 10/14/1853, Hallowell, Me. BR, d: 10/21/12, San Francisco, Cal. 5'11", 165 lbs. Deb: 5/25/1875

1875	StL-n	30	113	14	23	10	0	0	12	0	1	.204	.217	.292	83	-1	3	2	-1	.787	-3	O-28/1-4	-0.4
1877	Chi-N	10	41	2	4	0	0	0	2	0	3	.098	.098	.098	-34	-6				.793	2	O-10	-0.4
1882	Bal-a	72	250	19	39	4	0	0		0	13	.156	.198	.172	28	-17				.874	0	*O-72	-1.6
1883	Phi-N	1	3	0	1	0	0	0	0	0	1	.333	.333	.333	114	0				.333	-1	/O-1	-0.1
Total	3	83	294	21	44	4	0	0	2	0	4	.150	.186	.163	18	-24				.855	1	/O-83	-2.1

■ DON WAKAMATSU Wakamatsu, Wilbur Donald b: 2/22/63, Hood River, Ore. BR/TR, 6'2", 200 lbs. Deb: 5/22/91

1991	Chi-A	18	31	2	7	0	0	0	6	1	5	.226	.250	.226	33	-1	0			1.000	-0	C-18	-0.3

■ HOWARD WAKEFIELD Wakefield, Howard John b: 4/2/1884, Bucyrus, Ohio d: 4/16/41, Chicago, Ill. BR/TR, 6'1", 205 lbs. Deb: 9/18/05 F

1905	Cle-A	10	26	3	4	0	0	0		1		.154	.185	.154	8	-3	0			.926	-3	/C-8	-0.5
1906	Was-A	77	211	17	59	9	2	1	21	7		.280	.303	.355	111	2	6			.946	-15	C-60	-0.8
1907	Cle-A	26	37	4	5	2	0	0	4	2		.135	.200	.189	24	-3	0			.930	-1	C-11	-0.3
Total	3	113	274	24	68	11	2	1	25	10		.248	.277	.314	89	-4	6			.943	-18	/C-79	-1.6

■ DICK WAKEFIELD Wakefield, Richard Cummings b: 5/6/21, Chicago, Ill. d: 8/26/85, Redford, Mich. BL/TR, 6'4", 210 lbs. Deb: 6/26/41 F

1941	Det-A	7	7	0	1	0	0	0	0	0	1	.143	.143	.143	-22	-1	0	0	0	1.000	0	/O-1	-0.1
1943	Det-A★	155	633	91	**200**	**38**	8	7	79	62	60	.316	.377	.434	127	21	4	5	-2	.959	-6	*O-155	0.6
1944	Det-A	78	276	53	98	15	5	12	53	55	29	.355	.464	.576	186	33	2	2	-1	.963	-4	O-78	2.5
1946	Det-A	111	396	64	106	11	5	12	59	59	55	.268	.364	.412	110	6	3	5	-2	.964	0	*O-104	-0.1
1947	Det-A	112	368	59	104	15	5	8	51	80	44	.283	.412	.416	127	17	1	4	-2	.950	-2	*O-101	0.7
1948	Det-A	110	322	50	89	20	5	11	53	70	55	.276	.406	.472	129	15	0	1	-1	.948	0	O-86	1.0
1949	Det-A	59	126	17	26	3	1	6	19	32	24	.206	.367	.389	100	0	0	0	0	1.000	2	O-32	0.0
1950	NY-A	3	2	1	1	0	0	0	1	1	1	.500	.667	.500	208	0	0	0	0	.000	0	H	0.0
1952	NY-N	3	2	0	0	0	0	0	0	1	1	.000	.333	.000	-0	-0	0	0	0	.000	0	H	0.0
Total	9	638	2132	334	625	102	29	56	315	360	270	.293	.396	.447	130	92	10	17	-7	.959	-11	O-557	4.6

■ MATT WALBECK Walbeck, Matthew Lovick b: 10/2/69, Sacramento, Cal. BB/TR, 5'11", 195 lbs. Deb: 4/7/93

1993	Chi-N	11	30	2	6	2	0	1	6	1	6	.200	.226	.367	56	-2	0	0		1.000	-0	C-11	-0.2
1994	Min-A	97	338	31	69	12	0	5	35	17	37	.204	.246	.284	36	-32	1	1	-0	.993	-7	C-95/D-1	-3.1
1995	Min-A	115	393	40	101	18	1	1	44	25	71	.257	.303	.316	61	-22	3	1	0	.991	-15	*C-113	-2.8
1996	Min-A	63	215	25	48	10	0	2	24	9	34	.223	.254	.298	38	-20	3	1	0	.994	-6	C-61	-2.0
Total	4	286	976	98	224	42	1	9	109	52	148	.230	.271	.302	47	-77	7	3	0	.992	-28	C-280/D-1	-8.1

■ ED WALCZAK Walczak, Edwin Joseph "Husky" b: 9/21/18, Arctic, R.I. BR/TR, 5'11", 180 lbs. Deb: 9/3/45

1945	Phi-N	20	57	6	12	3	0	0	8	8	5	.211	.286	.263	55	-3	0			.966	1	2-17/S-2	-0.2

■ FRED WALDEN Walden, Thomas Fred b: 6/25/1890, Fayette, Mo. d: 9/27/55, Jefferson Barracks, Mo. BR/TR, Deb: 6/3/12

1912	StL-A	1	0	0	0	0	0	0	0	0	0	—	—	—		0	0			.000	-1	/C-1	-0.1

■ IRV WALDRON Waldron, Irving J. b: 1/21/1876, Hillside, N.Y. d: 7/22/44, Worcester, Mass. BR/TR, Deb: 4/25/01

1901	Mil-A	62	266	48	79	8	6	0	29	16		.297	.342	.372	103	1	12			.883	-2	O-62	-0.5
	Was-A	79	332	54	107	14	3	0	23	22		.322	.368	.383	110	5	8			.955	-5	O-78	-0.5
	Yr	141	598	102	186	22	9	0	52	38		.311	.356	.378	107	6	20			.923	-7	*O-140	-1.0

■ JIM WALEWANDER Walewander, James b: 5/2/62, Chicago, Ill. BB/TR, 5'10", 160 lbs. Deb: 5/31/87

1987	Det-A	53	54	24	13	3	1	1	4	7	6	.241	.328	.389	93	-0	2	1		1.000	15	2-24,3-17/S-3,D-8	1.4
1988	Det-A	88	175	23	37	5	0	0	6	12	26	.211	.262	.240	43	-13	11	4	1	.977	14	2-61/S-8,3-3,D-9	0.4
1990	NY-A	9	5	1	1	0	0	0	1	0	0	.200	.200	.400	64	-0	1	1	-0	1.000	1	/2-2,3-2,S-1,D-2	0.1
1993	Cal-A	12	8	2	1	1	0	0	3	5	1	.125	.462	.125	64	-0	1	1	-0	1.000	6	/S-6,2-2,D-3	0.5
Total	4	162	242	50	52	9	1	1	14	24	33	.215	.286	.273	57	-14	15	7	0	.982	37	/2-89,D-22,3-22,S	2.4

■ RUBE WALKER Walker, Albert Bluford b: 5/16/26, Lenoir, N.C. d: 12/12/92, Morganton, N.C. BL/TR, 6'1", 185 lbs. Deb: 4/20/48 C

1948	Chi-N	79	171	17	47	8	0	5	26	24	17	.275	.371	.409	115	4	0			.980	-3	C-44	0.4
1949	Chi-N	56	172	11	42	4	1	3	22	9	18	.244	.282	.331	66	-9	0			.964	-5	C-43	-1.1
1950	Chi-N	74	213	19	49	7	1	6	16	18	34	.230	.290	.357	70	-10	0			.975	1	C-62	-0.6
1951	Chi-N	37	107	12	25	5	0	3	12	5	13	.234	.311	.327	71	-4	0	0	0	.969	-4	C-31	-0.7
	Bro-N	36	74	6	18	4	0	2	9	6	14	.243	.300	.378	80	-2	0	0	0	.972	-5	C-23	-0.6
	Yr	73	181	15	43	9	0	5	21	11	27	.238	.307	.348	74	-7	0	0	0	.970	-9	C-54	-1.3
1952	Bro-N	46	139	9	36	8	0	3	19	8	17	.259	.304	.338	77	-4	0	0	0	.987	5	C-40	0.3
1953	Bro-N	43	95	5	23	6	0	3	9	8	17	.242	.301	.400	79	-3	0	0	0	.978	1	C-28	-0.1
1954	Bro-N	50	155	12	28	6	1	5	23	24	17	.181	.294	.323	59	-10	0	0	0	.996	1	C-47	-0.6
1955	Bro-N	48	103	6	26	5	0	3	15	15	11	.252	.347	.359	86	-2	0	0	0	.987	2	C-35	0.1
1956	*Bro-N	54	146	5	31	4	1	3	20	17	18	.212	.248	.329	65	-10	0	0	0	.986	-3	C-43	-1.1
1957	Bro-N	60	166	10	30	8	0	2	23	15	23	.181	.249	.265	35	-15	0	0	0	.992	-6	C-50	-1.9
1958	LA-N	25	44	3	5	0	0	0	3	5	10	.114	.204	.114	14	-6	0	0	0	.985	-2	C-20	-0.7
Total	11	608	1585	114	360	69	3	35	192	150	213	.227	.296	.341	68	-71	3	1		.982	-15	C-466	-6.6

YEAR	TM/L	G	AB	R	H	2B	3B	HR	RBI	BB	SO	AVG	OBP	SLG	PRO+	BR/A	SB	CS	SBR	FA	FR	G/POS	TPR

■ TONY WALKER   Walker, Anthony Bruce   b: 7/1/59, San Diego, Cal.   BR/TR, 6'2", 205 lbs.   Deb: 4/8/86

| 1986 | Hou-N | 84 | 90 | 19 | 20 | 7 | 0 | 2 | 10 | 11 | 15 | .222 | .307 | .367 | 87 | -2 | 11 | 3 | 2 | .986 | -14 | O-68 | -1.5 |

■ FRANK WALKER   Walker, Charles Franklin   b: 9/22/1894, Enoree, S.C.   d: 9/16/74, Bristol, Tenn.   BR/TR, 5'11", 165 lbs.   Deb: 9/6/17

1917	Det-A	2	2	0	0	0	0	0	0	0	1	.000	.000	.000	-99	-0	0			.000	0	H	-0.1
1918	Det-A	55	167	10	33	10	3	1	20	7	29	.198	.234	.311	67	-8	3			.922	-2	O-45	-1.4
1920	Phi-A	24	91	10	21	2	2	0	10	5	14	.231	.286	.297	54	-6	0	2	-1	.983	-1	O-24	-1.0
1921	Phi-A	19	66	6	15	3	0	1	6	8	11	.227	.311	.318	60	-4	1	0	-0	.961	1	O-19	-0.4
1925	NY-N	39	81	12	18	1	0	1	5	9	11	.222	.308	.272	51	-6	1	1	-0	.960	-4	O-21	-0.8
Total	5	139	407	38	87	16	5	3	41	29	66	.214	.273	.300	58	-24	5	3		.949	-4	O-109	-3.7

■ TILLY WALKER   Walker, Clarence William   b: 9/4/1887, Telford, Tenn.   d: 9/20/59, Unicoi, Tenn   BR/TR, 5'11", 165 lbs.   Deb: 4/12/11

1911	Was-A	95	356	44	99	6	4	2	39	15		.278	.311	.334	82	-10	12			.917	-1	O-94	-1.6
1912	Was-A	39	110	22	30	2	1	0	9	8		.273	.333	.309	83	-2	11			.837	-3	O-34/2-1	-0.6
1913	StL-A	23	85	7	25	4	1	0	11	2	9	.294	.310	.365	100	-0	5			.911	-0	O-23	-0.2
1914	StL-A	151	517	67	154	24	16	6	78	51	72	.298	.365	.441	148	28	29	17	-2	.972	16	*O-145	3.9
1915	StL-A	144	510	53	137	20	7	5	49	36	77	.269	.323	.365	110	4	20	17	-4	.940	15	*O-139	0.8
1916	*Bos-A	128	467	68	124	29	11	3	46	23	45	.266	.303	.394	109	2	14			.959	-4	*O-128	-0.9
1917	Bos-A	106	337	41	83	18	7	2	37	25	38	.246	.300	.359	102	-1	6			.972	6	O-96	0.0
1918	Phi-A	114	414	56	122	20	0	11	48	41	44	.295	.360	.423	135	16	8			.953	-5	*O-109	1.6
1919	Phi-A	125	456	47	133	30	6	10	64	26	41	.292	.330	.450	116	7	8			.933	-4	*O-115	-0.4
1920	Phi-A	149	585	79	157	23	7	17	82	41	59	.268	.321	.419	94	-8	8	3	1	.940	6	*O-149	-1.2
1921	Phi-A	142	556	89	169	32	5	23	101	73	41	.304	.389	.504	125	21	3	5	-2	.955	-2	*O-142	1.6
1922	Phi-A	153	565	111	160	31	4	37	99	61	67	.283	.357	.549	130	21	4	3	-1	.956	-2	*O-148	0.8
1923	Phi-A	52	109	12	30	5	2	2	16	14	11	.275	.368	.413	104	1	2	1	-1	1.000	-2	O-26	-0.3
Total	13	1421	5067	696	1423	244	71	118	679	416	504	.281	.339	.427	115	80	129	47		.949	41	*O-1348/2-1	3.5

■ CHICO WALKER   Walker, Cleotha   b: 11/25/57, Jackson, Miss.   BB/TR, 5'9", 179 lbs.   Deb: 9/2/80

1980	Bos-A	19	57	3	12	0	0	1	5	6	10	.211	.297	.263	52	-4	3	2	-0	.958	1	2-11/D-7	-0.3
1981	Bos-A	6	17	3	6	0	0	0	2	1	2	.353	.389	.353	108	0	0	2	-1	1.000	-2	/2-5	-0.3
1983	Bos-A	4	5	2	2	0	2	0	1	0	0	.400	.400	1.200	299	1	0	0	0	1.000	0	/O-3	0.1
1984	Bos-A	3	2	0	0	0	0	0	1	0	1	.000	.000	.000	-96	-1	0	0	0	1.000	0	/2-1	-0.1
1985	Chi-N	21	12	3	1	0	0	0	0	0	5	.083	.083	.083	-48	-2	1	0	0	1.000	-2	/O-6,2-2	-0.4
1986	Chi-N	28	101	21	28	3	2	1	7	10	20	.277	.342	.376	91	-1	15	4	2	.956	-5	O-26	-0.5
1987	Chi-N	47	105	15	21	4	0	0	7	12	23	.200	.282	.238	38	-9	11	4	1	.974	-5	O-33/3-2	-1.4
1988	Cal-A	33	78	8	12	1	0	0	2	6	15	.154	.214	.167	8	-9	2	1	0	.933	-2	O-17/2-7,3-2	-1.2
1991	Chi-N	124	374	51	96	10	1	6	34	33	57	.257	.317	.337	80	-9	13	5	1	.929	-23	/O-57,O-53/2-6	-3.4
1992	Chi-N	19	26	2	3	0	0	0	2	3	4	.115	.207	.115	-6	-4	1	0	0	1.000	-7	/O-6,2-2,-3-2	-0.4
	NY-N	107	227	24	70	12	1	4	36	24	46	.308	.375	.423	127	8	14	1	4	.971	-7	3-36,2-16,O-15	0.5
	Yr	126	253	26	73	12	1	4	38	27	50	.289	.357	.391	113	5	15	1	4	.960	-7	3-38,O-21,2-18	0.1
1993	NY-N	115	213	18	48	7	1	5	19	14	29	.225	.273	.338	63	-11	7	0	2	.976	-4	2-24,3-23,O-15	-1.3
Total	11	526	1217	150	299	37	7	17	116	109	212	.246	.308	.329	75	-41	67	19	9	.968	-49	O-174,3-122/2-74,D	-8.7

■ DUANE WALKER   Walker, Duane Allen   b: 3/13/57, Pasadena, Tex.   BL/TL, 6', 185 lbs.   Deb: 5/25/82

1982	Cin-N	86	239	26	52	10	5	5	22	27	58	.218	.302	.322	73	-8	9	3	1	.992	0	O-69	-0.9
1983	Cin-N	109	225	14	53	12	1	2	29	20	43	.236	.298	.324	70	-9	6	3	0	.956	0	O-60	-1.1
1984	Cin-N	83	195	35	57	10	3	10	28	33	35	.292	.395	.528	150	14	3	3	0	.950	-5	O-68	0.8
1985	Cin-N	37	48	5	8	2	1	2	6	6	18	.167	.259	.375	72	-2	1	0	0	.882	-1	O-10	-0.3
	Tex-A	53	132	14	23	2	0	5	11	15	29	.174	.264	.303	54	-8	2	1	0	1.000	1	O-32,D-10	-0.8
1988	StL-N	24	22	1	4	1	0	0	3	2	7	.182	.250	.227	38	-2	0	0	0	.000	-2	/O-4,1-1	-0.4
Total	5	392	861	95	197	37	5	24	99	103	190	.229	.313	.367	86	-16	25	10	2	.967	-6	O-243/D-10,1-1	-2.7

■ ERNIE WALKER   Walker, Ernest Robert   b: 9/17/1890, Blossburg, Ala.   d: 4/1/65, Pell City, Ala.   BL/TR, 6', 165 lbs.   Deb: 4/13/13   F

1913	StL-A	7	14	0	3	0	0	0	2	0	5	.214	.214	.214	26	-1	0			1.000	-0	/O-2	-0.2
1914	StL-A	74	131	19	39	5	3	1	14	13	26	.298	.366	.405	137	6	6	4	-1	.960	-6	O-38	-0.3
1915	StL-A	50	109	15	23	4	2	0	9	23	32	.211	.348	.284	93	0	5	8	-3	.881	-6	/O-33	-1.1
Total	3	131	254	34	65	9	5	1	25	36	63	.256	.351	.343	112	4	11	12		.928	-12	/O-73	-1.6

■ DIXIE WALKER   Walker, Fred "The People's Cherce"   b: 9/24/10, Villa Rica, Ga.   d: 5/17/82, Birmingham, Ala.   BL/TR, 6'1", 175 lbs.   Deb: 4/28/31   FC

1931	NY-A	2	10	1	3	2	0	1	0	4		.300	.300	.500	113	0	0			1.000	0	/O-2	0.0
1933	NY-A	98	328	68	90	15	7	15	51	26	28	.274	.330	.500	125	9	2	2	-1	.962	5	O-77	0.9
1934	NY-A	17	17	2	2	0	0	0	0	1	3	.118	.167	.118	-27	-3	0	0	0	1.000	-0	/O-1	-0.3
1935	NY-A	8	13	1	2	1	0	0	1	0	1	.154	.154	.231	-2	-2	0	0	0	.750	-1	/O-2	-0.2
1936	NY-A	6	20	3	7	0	2	1	5	1	3	.350	.381	.700	167	2	1	1	-0	1.000	-1	/O-5	0.0
	Chi-A	26	70	12	19	2	0	0	11	14	6	.271	.400	.300	73	-2	1	0	0	1.000	1	O-17	-0.2
	Yr	32	90	15	26	2	2	1	16	15	9	.289	.396	.389	92	-1	2	1	0	1.000	0	O-22	-0.2
1937	Chi-A	154	593	105	179	28	16	9	95	78	26	.302	.383	.449	109	9	1	2	-1	.952	-10	*O-154	-0.6
1938	Det-A	127	454	84	140	27	6	6	43	65	32	.308	.396	.434	122	8	5	4	-1	.979	-9	*O-114	-1.0
1939	Det-A	43	154	30	47	4	5	4	19	15	8	.305	.367	.474	106	1	4	1	1	.970	4	O-37	0.4
	Bro-N	61	225	27	63	6	4	2	38	20	10	.280	.339	.369	87	-4	1			.968	2	O-59	-0.4
1940	Bro-N	143	556	75	171	37	8	6	66	42	21	.308	.357	.435	111	8	3			.973	2	*O-136	0.3
1941	*Bro-N	148	531	88	165	32	8	9	71	70	18	.311	.391	.452	131	23	4			.976	11	*O-146	2.7
1942	Bro-N	118	393	57	114	28	1	6	54	47	15	.290	.367	.412	126	13	1			.986	11	*O-110	0.7
1943	Bro-N★	140	540	83	163	32	6	9	71	49	24	.302	.363	.411	123	16	3			.969	3	*O-136	1.2
1944	Bro-N★	147	535	77	191	37	8	13	91	72	27	.357	.434	.529	173	53	6			.962	-3	*O-140	4.4
1945	Bro-N†	154	607	102	182	42	9	8	124	75	16	.300	.381	.438	128	24	5			.992	12	*O-153	2.8
1946	Bro-N★	150	576	80	184	29	9	9	116	67	28	.319	.391	.448	136	28	14			.969	-8	*O-149	1.4
1947	*Bro-N★	148	529	77	162	31	3	9	94	97	26	.306	.415	.427	119	19	6			.964	-8	*O-147	0.3
1948	Pit-N	129	408	39	129	19	3	2	54	52	18	.316	.393	.392	111	8	1			.977	-12	*O-112	-1.0
1949	Pit-N	88	181	26	51	4	1	1	18	26	18	.282	.372	.331	88	-2	0			.984	-1	*O-39/1-3	-0.2
Total	18	1905	6740	1037	2064	376	96	105	1023	817	325	.306	.383	.437	121	202	59	10		.972	-16	*O-1736/1-3	10.6

■ GEE WALKER   Walker, Gerald Holmes   b: 3/19/08, Gulfport, Miss.   d: 3/20/81, Whitfield, Miss.   BR/TR, 5'11", 188 lbs.   Deb: 4/14/31   FC

1931	Det-A	59	189	20	56	17	2	1	28	14	21	.296	.345	.423	98	-1	10	7	-1	.953	-3	O-44	-0.8
1932	Det-A	127	480	71	155	32	6	8	78	13	38	.323	.345	.456	104	1	30	6	5	.949	4	*O-116	0.3
1933	Det-A	127	483	68	135	29	7	9	64	15	49	.280	.304	.424	89	-10	26	9	2	.942	-1	*O-113	-1.3
1934	*Det-A	98	347	54	104	19	2	6	39	19	20	.300	.340	.418	94	-4	20	9	1	.947	2	O-80	-0.4
1935	*Det-A	98	362	52	109	22	6	7	53	15	21	.301	.329	.453	104	0	6	4	-0	.954	-5	O-85	-0.6
1936	Det-A	134	550	105	194	55	5	12	93	23	30	.353	.387	.536	125	19	17	8	0	.948	5	*O-125	1.7
1937	Det-A†	151	635	105	213	42	4	18	113	41	74	.335	.380	.499	117	15	23	7	3	.956	-6	*O-151	0.6
1938	Chi-A	120	442	69	135	23	6	16	87	38	32	.305	.360	.493	109	5	9	4	-0	.958	-5	*O-107	-0.4
1939	Chi-A	149	598	95	174	30	11	13	111	28	43	.291	.330	.443	94	-8	17	6	2	.967	-4	*O-147	-0.2
1940	Was-A	140	595	87	175	29	7	13	96	24	58	.294	.325	.432	101	-2	21	4	4	.967	-8	*O-140	-0.7
1941	Cle-A	121	445	56	126	26	11	6	48	18	46	.283	.313	.431	100	-3	12	6	0	.982	8	*O-105	-0.2
1942	Cin-N	119	422	40	97	20	2	5	50	31	44	.230	.290	.322	79	-12	11			.973	4	*O-110	-1.4
1943	Cin-N	114	429	48	105	23	2	5	54	12	38	.245	.270	.329	74	-16	6			.980	-5	*O-106	-2.9
1944	Cin-N	121	546	56	153	21	3	5	62	23	48	.280	.318	.366	96	-4	7			.967	-4	*O-117	-1.8
1945	Cin-N	106	316	28	80	11	2	2	21	16	39	.253	.289	.320	71	-13	8			.962	-7	O-67/3-3	-2.4
Total	15	1784	6771	954	1991	399	76	124	997	330	600	.294	.331	.430	99	-32	223	70		.961	-7	*O-1613/3-3	-10.5

■ GREG WALKER
Walker, Gregory Lee b: 10/6/59, Douglas, Ga. BL/TR, 6'3", 210 lbs. Deb: 9/18/82

YEAR	TM/L	G	AB	R	H	2B	3B	HR	RBI	BB	SO	AVG	OBP	SLG	PRO+	BR/A	SB	CS	SBR	FA	FR	G/POS	TPR
1982	Chi-A	11	17	3	7	2	1	2	7	2	3	.412	.474	1.000	292	4	0	0	0	.000	0	/D-4	0.4
1983	*Chi-A	118	307	32	83	16	3	10	55	28	57	.270	.335	.440	107	3	2	1	0	.985	-7	1-59,D-21	-0.8
1984	Chi-A	136	442	62	130	29	2	24	75	35	66	.294	.349	.532	134	19	8	5	-1	.995	-5	*1-101,D-21	0.7
1985	Chi-A	163	601	77	155	38	4	24	92	44	100	.258	.311	.454	102	0	5	2	0	.994	-3	*1-151/D-7	-1.1
1986	Chi-A	78	282	37	78	10	6	13	51	29	44	.277	.348	.493	122	8	1	2	-1	.993	-1	1-77/D-1	0.1
1987	Chi-A	157	566	85	145	33	2	27	94	75	112	.256	.348	.465	110	9	2	1	0	.994	-14	*1-154/D-3	-1.6
1988	Chi-A	99	377	45	93	22	1	8	42	29	77	.247	.306	.374	90	-6	0	1	-1	.993	-14	1-98	-2.9
1989	Chi-A	77	233	25	49	14	0	5	26	23	50	.210	.290	.335	77	-7	0	0	0	.987	-6	1-48,D-23	-1.7
1990	Chi-A	2	5	0	1	0	0	0	0	0	2	.200	.200	.200	12	-1	0	0	0	1.000	0	/1-1,D-1	0.0
	Bal-A	14	34	2	5	0	0	0	2	3	9	.147	.237	.147	10	-4	1	0	0	.000	0	D-11	-0.4
	Yr	16	39	2	6	0	0	0	2	3	11	.154	.233	.154	10	-5	1	0	0	1.000	0	D-12/1-1	-0.4
Total	9	855	2864	368	746	164	19	113	444	268	520	.260	.328	.449	108	26	19	12	-2	.993	-49	1-689/D-92	-7.3

■ HARRY WALKER
Walker, Harry William "Harry The Hat" b: 10/22/16, Pascagoula, Miss. BL/TR, 6'2", 190 lbs. Deb: 9/25/40 FMC

YEAR	TM/L	G	AB	R	H	2B	3B	HR	RBI	BB	SO	AVG	OBP	SLG	PRO+	BR/A	SB	CS	SBR	FA	FR	G/POS	TPR
1940	StL-N	7	27	2	5	2	0	0	6	0	2	.185	.185	.259	20	-3	0			1.000	2	/O-7	-0.1
1941	StL-N	7	15	3	4	1	0	0	1	2	1	.267	.353	.333	88	-0	0			.875	-1	/O-5	-0.2
1942	*StL-N	74	191	38	60	12	2	0	16	11	14	.314	.355	.398	112	2	2			.968	-1	O-56/2-2	-0.1
1943	*StL-N★	148	564	86	166	28	6	2	53	40	24	.294	.341	.376	102	1	5			.965	-5	*O-144/2-1	-1.3
1946	*StL-N	112	346	53	82	14	6	3	27	30	29	.237	.300	.338	77	-11	12			.974	5	O-92/1-8	-1.1
1947	StL-N	10	25	2	5	1	0	0	0	4	2	.200	.310	.240	46	-2	0			.938	-2	O-10	-0.4
	Phi-N★	130	488	79	181	28	16	1	41	59	37	.371	.443	.500	156	41	13			.966	14	*O-127/1-4	4.6
	Yr	140	513	81	186	29	16	1	41	63	39	.363	.436	.487	150	39	13			.964	12	*O-137/1-4	4.2
1948	Phi-N	112	332	34	97	11	2	2	23	33	30	.292	.358	.355	95	-1	4			.981	-1	O-81/1-4,3-1	-0.4
1949	Chi-N	42	159	20	42	6	3	1	14	11	6	.264	.312	.358	81	-4	2			.947	-3	O-39	-1.0
	Cin-N	86	314	53	100	15	2	1	23	34	17	.318	.385	.389	107	4	4			.963	-2	O-77/1-1	0.2
	Yr	128	473	73	142	21	5	2	37	45	23	.300	.361	.378	99	-0	6			.959	-2	*O-116/1-1	-0.8
1950	StL-N	60	150	17	31	5	0	0	7	18	12	.207	.292	.240	40	-13	0			.969	-1	O-46/1-2	-1.5
1951	StL-N	8	26	6	8	1	0	0	2	2	1	.308	.357	.346	90	-0	0	0	0	1.000	-0	/O-6,1-1	-0.2
1955	StL-N	11	14	2	5	2	0	0	1	1	0	.357	.400	.500	137	1	0	0	0	1.000	1	/O-1,M	0.2
Total	11	807	2651	385	786	126	37	10	214	245	175	.296	.358	.383	103	15	42	0		.968	10	O-691/1-20,2-3,3-1	-1.3

■ HUB WALKER
Walker, Harvey Willos b: 8/17/06, Gulfport, Miss. d: 11/26/82, San Jose, Cal. BL/TR, 5'10.5", 175 lbs. Deb: 4/15/31 F

YEAR	TM/L	G	AB	R	H	2B	3B	HR	RBI	BB	SO	AVG	OBP	SLG	PRO+	BR/A	SB	CS	SBR	FA	FR	G/POS	TPR
1931	Det-A	90	252	72	72	13	1	0	16	23	25	.286	.355	.345	82	-6	10	1	2	.961	-0	O-66	-0.7
1935	Det-A	9	25	4	4	3	0	0	1	3	4	.160	.250	.280	38	-2	0	0	0	1.000	-0	/O-7	-0.3
1936	Cin-N	92	258	49	71	18	1	4	23	35	32	.275	.366	.399	113	5	8			.970	-4	O-73/C-1,1-1	-0.1
1937	Cin-N	78	221	33	55	9	4	1	19	34	24	.249	.349	.339	92	-1	7			.993	4	O-58/2-3	0.0
1945	*Det-A	28	23	4	3	0	0	0	1	9	4	.130	.375	.130	46	-1	1	0	0	1.000	-0	/O-7	-0.3
Total	5	297	779	117	205	43	6	5	60	104	89	.263	.354	.353	92	-5	26	1		.975	-4	O-211/2-3,1-1,C-1	-1.4

■ JOHNNY WALKER
Walker, John Miles b: 12/11/1896, Toulon, Ill. d: 8/19/76, Hollywood, Fla. BR/TR, 6', 175 lbs. Deb: 9/19/19

YEAR	TM/L	G	AB	R	H	2B	3B	HR	RBI	BB	SO	AVG	OBP	SLG	PRO+	BR/A	SB	CS	SBR	FA	FR	G/POS	TPR
1919	Phi-A	3	9	0	0	0	0	0	0	0	2	.000	.000	.000	-99	-2	0			.941	-0	/C-3	-0.2
1920	Phi-A	9	22	0	5	1	0	0	5	0	1	.227	.227	.273	32	-2	0	0	0	.960	-1	/C-6	-0.2
1921	Phi-A	113	423	41	109	14	5	2	46	9	29	.258	.278	.329	54	-30	5	0	2	.989	-6	1-99/C-7	-3.5
Total	3	125	454	41	114	15	5	2	51	9	32	.251	.270	.319	50	-35	5	0		.968	-7	/1-99,C-16	-3.9

■ SPEED WALKER
Walker, Joseph Richard b: 1/23/1898, Munhall, Pa. d: 6/20/59, W.Mifflin, Pa. BR/TR, 6', 170 lbs. Deb: 9/15/23

YEAR	TM/L	G	AB	R	H	2B	3B	HR	RBI	BB	SO	AVG	OBP	SLG	PRO+	BR/A	SB	CS	SBR	FA	FR	G/POS	TPR
1923	StL-N	2	7	1	2	0	0	0	0	0	0	.286	.286	.286	52	-0	0	0	0	1.000	-0	/1-2	-0.1

■ LARRY WALKER
Walker, Larry Kenneth Robert b: 12/1/66, Maple Ridge, B.C., Canada BL/TR, 6'2", 185 lbs. Deb: 8/16/89

YEAR	TM/L	G	AB	R	H	2B	3B	HR	RBI	BB	SO	AVG	OBP	SLG	PRO+	BR/A	SB	CS	SBR	FA	FR	G/POS	TPR
1989	Mon-N	20	47	4	8	0	0	0	4	5	13	.170	.264	.170	26	-4	1	1	-0	1.000	0	O-15	-0.5
1990	Mon-N	133	419	59	101	18	3	19	51	49	112	.241	.328	.434	112	6	21	7	2	.985	9	*O-124	1.5
1991	Mon-N	137	487	59	141	30	2	16	64	42	102	.290	.352	.458	128	17	14	9	-1	.991	9	*O-102,1-39	2.1
1992	Mon-N★	143	528	85	159	31	4	23	93	41	97	.301	.358	.506	143	28	18	6	2	.993	14	*O-139	4.4
1993	Mon-N	138	490	85	130	24	5	22	86	80	76	.265	.375	.469	119	15	29	7	5	.979	10	*O-132/1-4	2.6
1994	Mon-N	103	395	76	127	44	2	19	86	47	74	.322	.399	.587	151	30	15	5	2	.973	4	O-68,1-35	2.9
1995	*Col-N	131	494	96	151	31	5	36	101	49	72	.306	.381	.607	121	11	16	3	3	.988	1	*O-129	1.1
1996	Col-N	83	272	58	75	18	4	18	58	20	58	.276	.342	.570	106	-1	18	2	4	.994	-3	O-83	-0.2
Total	8	888	3132	522	892	196	25	153	543	333	604	.285	.363	.510	125	102	132	40	16	.987	43	O-792/1-78	13.9

■ FLEET WALKER
Walker, Moses Fleetwood b: 10/7/1856, Mt.Pleasant, Ohio d: 5/11/24, Cleveland, Ohio BR/TR, 159 lbs. Deb: 5/1/1884 F

YEAR	TM/L	G	AB	R	H	2B	3B	HR	RBI	BB	SO	AVG	OBP	SLG	PRO+	BR/A	SB	CS	SBR	FA	FR	G/POS	TPR
1884	Tol-a	42	152	23	40	2	3	0		8		.263	.325	.316	106	1				.887	-6	C-41/O-1	-0.1

■ OSCAR WALKER
Walker, Oscar b: 3/18/1854, Brooklyn, N.Y. d: 5/20/1889, Brooklyn, N.Y. BL/TL, 5'10", 166 lbs. Deb: 9/17/1875

YEAR	TM/L	G	AB	R	H	2B	3B	HR	RBI	BB	SO	AVG	OBP	SLG	PRO+	BR/A	SB	CS	SBR	FA	FR	G/POS	TPR
1875	Atl-n	1	2	0	0	0	0	0	0	1	0	.000	.333	.000	30	-0	0	0	0	.400	-0	/1-1,O-1	0.0
1879	Buf-N	72	287	35	79	15	6	1	35	8	38	.275	.295	.380	118	5				.946	3	*1-72	0.5
1880	Buf-N	34	126	12	29	4	2	1	15	6	18	.230	.265	.317	95	-1				.917	-2	1-24,O-11	-0.4
1882	StL-a	76	318	48	76	15	7	7		10		.239	.262	.396	115	4				.846	8	*O-75/2-1,1-1	1.0
1884	Bro-a	95	382	59	103	12	8	2		9		.270	.292	.359	110	4				.868	-0	O-59,1-36	-0.1
1885	Bal-a	4	13	1	0	0	0	0	0	0		.000	.000	.000	-99	-3				.667	-1	/O-4	-0.4
Total	5	281	1126	155	287	46	23	11	51	33	56	.255	.278	.366	109	9				.850	8	O-149,1-133/2-1	0.6

■ TODD WALKER
Walker, Todd Arthur b: 5/25/73, Bakersfield, Cal. BL/TR, 6', 180 lbs. Deb: 8/30/96

YEAR	TM/L	G	AB	R	H	2B	3B	HR	RBI	BB	SO	AVG	OBP	SLG	PRO+	BR/A	SB	CS	SBR	FA	FR	G/POS	TPR
1996	Min-A	25	82	8	21	6	0	0	6	4	13	.256	.291	.329	55	-6	2	0	1	.956	-0	3-20/2-4,D-1	-0.5

■ WALT WALKER
Walker, Walter S. b: 3/12/1860, Berlin, Mich. d: 2/28/22, Pontiac, Mich. TR, 5'10.5", 162 lbs. Deb: 5/8/1884

YEAR	TM/L	G	AB	R	H	2B	3B	HR	RBI	BB	SO	AVG	OBP	SLG	PRO+	BR/A	SB	CS	SBR	FA	FR	G/POS	TPR
1884	Det-N	1	4	1	1	0	0	0	0	0	0	.250	.250	.250	61	-0				.750	-1	C-1	-0.1

■ WELDAY WALKER
Walker, Welday Wilberforce b: 6/1859, Steubenville, Ohio d: 11/23/37, Steubenville, Ohio Deb: 7/15/1884 F

YEAR	TM/L	G	AB	R	H	2B	3B	HR	RBI	BB	SO	AVG	OBP	SLG	PRO+	BR/A	SB	CS	SBR	FA	FR	G/POS	TPR
1884	Tol-a	5	18	1	4	1	0	0		2		.222	.222	.278	60	-1				.667	-1	/O-5	-0.2

■ CURT WALKER
Walker, William Curtis b: 7/3/1896, Beeville, Tex. d: 12/9/55, Beeville, Tex. BL/TR, 5'9.5", 170 lbs. Deb: 9/17/19

YEAR	TM/L	G	AB	R	H	2B	3B	HR	RBI	BB	SO	AVG	OBP	SLG	PRO+	BR/A	SB	CS	SBR	FA	FR	G/POS	TPR
1919	NY-A	1	1	0	0	0	0	0	0	0	0	.000	.000	.000	-99	-0	0			.000	0	H	0.0
1920	NY-N	8	14	0	1	0	0	0	0	0	3	.071	.133	.071	-41	-3	0	0	0	1.000	-0	/O-4	-0.4
1921	NY-N	64	192	30	55	13	5	3	35	15	8	.286	.338	.453	107	2	4	3	-1	.978	1	O-58	-0.2
	Phi-N	21	77	11	26	2	1	0	8	5	5	.338	.378	.390	96	-0	0	2	-1	.970	-5	O-21	-0.8
	Yr	85	269	41	81	15	6	3	43	20	13	.301	.349	.435	104	1	4	5	-2	.976	-4	*O-79	-1.0
1922	Phi-N	148	581	102	196	36	11	12	89	56	46	.337	.399	.499	119	16	11	4		.955	6	*O-147	1.1
1923	Phi-N	140	527	66	148	26	5	6	66	45	31	.281	.337	.378	79	-16	12	12	-4	.947	5	*O-137/1-1	-2.3
1924	Phi-N	24	71	11	21	6	1	1	8	7	4	.296	.359	.451	103	-0	0	1	-1	.900	-4	O-20	-0.5
	Cin-N	109	397	55	119	21	10	4	46	44	15	.300	.371	.433	117	10	7	5	-1	.978	0	O-109	-0.3
	Yr	133	468	66	140	27	11	5	54	51	19	.299	.369	.436	114	10	7	6	-2	.969	-4	*O-129	-0.3
1925	Cin-N	145	509	86	162	22	16	6	71	57	31	.318	.387	.460	118	15	14	11	-2	**.983**	2	*O-141	0.5
1926	Cin-N	155	571	83	175	24	20	6	78	60	31	.306	.372	.450	124	19	3			.961	4	*O-152	1.2
1927	Cin-N	146	527	60	154	16	10	6	80	47	19	.292	.350	.395	102	2	5			.957	3	*O-141	-0.5
1928	Cin-N	123	427	64	119	15	6	3	73	49	14	.279	.354	.412	101	1	19			.955	4	*O-122	-0.3
1929	Cin-N	141	492	76	154	28	15	7	83	85	17	.313	.416	.474	126	23	17			.969	-6	*O-138	0.7
1930	Cin-N	134	472	54	145	26	11	8	51	46	30	.307	.391	.460	110	9	4			.965	-6	*O-120	-0.5
Total	12	1359	4858	718	1475	235	117	64	688	535	254	.304	.374	.440	110	77	96	38		.963	2	*O-1310/1-1	-1.8

■ HOWARD WALL
Wall, Howard Deb: 9/13/1873

YEAR	TM/L	G	AB	R	H	2B	3B	HR	RBI	BB	SO	AVG	OBP	SLG	PRO+	BR/A	SB	CS	SBR	FA	FR	G/POS	TPR
1873	Was-n	1	4	1	1	0	0	0	0	0	0	.250	.250	.250	51	-0	0	0	0	.000	0	/S-1	0.0

YEAR	TM/L	G	AB	R	H	2B	3B	HR	RBI	BB	SO	AVG	OBP	SLG	PRO+	BR/A	SB	CS	SBR	FA	FR	G/POS	TPR

■ JOE WALL   Wall, Joseph Francis "Gummy"   b: 7/24/1873, Brooklyn, N.Y.   d: 7/17/36, Brooklyn, N.Y.   BL/TL,   Deb: 9/22/01

YEAR	TM/L	G	AB	R	H	2B	3B	HR	RBI	BB	SO	AVG	OBP	SLG	PRO+	BR/A	SB	CS	SBR	FA	FR	G/POS	TPR
1901	NY-N	4	8	0	4	0	0	0	1	0		.500	.500	.500	198	1	0			1.000	-3	/C-2,O-1	-0.1
1902	NY-N	6	14	2	5	2	0	0	0	2		.357	.438	.500	191	2	0			1.000	-0	/C-3	0.1
	Bro-N	5	18	0	3	0	0	0	0	3		.167	.318	.167	50	-1	0			.893	-3	/C-5	-0.4
	Yr	11	32	2	8	2	0	0	0	5		.250	.368	.313	110	1	0			.893	-3	/C-5,O-3	-0.3
Total	2	15	40	2	12	2	0	0	1	5		.300	.391	.350	127	2	0			.903	-6	/C-7,O-4	-0.4

■ JACK WALLACE   Wallace, Clarence Eugene   b: 8/6/1890, Winnfield, La.   d: 10/15/60, Winnfield, La.   BR/TR, 5'10.5", 175 lbs.   Deb: 9/27/15

| 1915 | Chi-N | 2 | 7 | 1 | 2 | 0 | 0 | 0 | 1 | 0 | 2 | .286 | .375 | .286 | 101 | 0 | 0 | | | 1.000 | 2 | /C-2 | 0.2 |

■ DON WALLACE   Wallace, Donald Allen   b: 8/25/40, Sapulpa, Okla.   BL/TR, 5'8", 165 lbs.   Deb: 4/12/67

| 1967 | Cal-A | 23 | 6 | 2 | 0 | 0 | 0 | 0 | 3 | 2 | | .000 | .333 | .000 | 6 | -1 | 0 | 1 | -1 | 1.000 | 2 | /2-4,1-1,3-1 | 0.1 |

■ DOC WALLACE   Wallace, Frederick Renshaw "Jesse"   b: 9/30/1893, Church Hill, Md.   d: 12/31/64, Haverford, Pa.   BR/TR, 5'6.5", 135 lbs.   Deb: 5/2/19

| 1919 | Phi-N | 2 | 4 | 0 | 1 | 0 | 0 | 0 | 0 | 0 | 1 | .250 | .250 | .250 | 47 | -0 | 0 | | | .875 | 0 | /S-2 | 0.0 |

■ JIM WALLACE   Wallace, James L.   b: 11/14/1881, Boston, Mass.   d: 5/16/53, Revere, Mass.   BL/TL, 5'9", 150 lbs.   Deb: 8/24/05

| 1905 | Pit-N | 7 | 29 | 3 | 6 | 1 | 0 | 0 | 3 | 3 | | .207 | .281 | .241 | 55 | -2 | 2 | | | .929 | 1 | /O-7 | -0.1 |

■ BOBBY WALLACE   Wallace, Rhoderick John   b: 11/4/1873, Pittsburgh, Pa.   d: 11/3/60, Torrance, Cal.   BR/TR, 5'8", 170 lbs.   Deb: 9/15/1894   MUCH

YEAR	TM/L	G	AB	R	H	2B	3B	HR	RBI	BB	SO	AVG	OBP	SLG	PRO+	BR/A	SB	CS	SBR	FA	FR	G/POS	TPR
1894	Cle-N	4	13	0	2	1	0	0	1	0	1	.154	.154	.231	-8	-2	0			1.000	1	/P-4	0.0
1895	Cle-N	30	98	16	21	2	3	0	10	6	17	.214	.274	.296	44	-9	0			.910	3	P-30	0.0
1896	*Cle-N	45	149	19	35	6	3	1	17	11	21	.235	.287	.336	60	-9	2			.950	-2	O-23,P-22/1-1	-0.8
1897	Cle-N	130	516	99	173	33	21	4	112	48		.335	.394	.504	129	19	14			.928	3	*3-130/O-1	2.2
1898	Cle-N	154	593	81	160	25	13	3	99	63		.270	.344	.371	106	5	7			.936	17	*3-141,2-13	2.3
1899	StL-N	151	577	91	170	28	14	12	108	54		.295	.357	.454	119	13	17			.919	39	*S-100,3-52	5.3
1900	StL-N	126	485	70	130	25	9	4	70	40		.268	.328	.381	96	-4	7			.934	3	*S-126/3-1	0.8
1901	StL-N	134	550	69	178	34	15	2	91	20		.324	.351	.451	138	24	15			.929	**30**	*S-134	**6.2**
1902	StL-A	133	494	71	141	32	9	1	63	45		.285	.350	.393	107	5	18			.948	11	*S-131/P-1,O-1	2.2
1903	StL-A	135	511	63	136	21	7	1	54	28		.266	.309	.341	97	-2	18			.924	18	*S-135	2.3
1904	StL-A	139	541	57	149	29	4	2	69	42		.275	.330	.355	124	15	20			**.947**	8	*S-139	3.0
1905	StL-A	156	587	67	159	25	9	1	59	45		.271	.324	.349	120	12	13			.935	20	*S-156	3.9
1906	StL-A	139	476	64	123	21	7	2	67	58		.258	.344	.345	121	13	24			.949	3	*S-138	2.2
1907	StL-A	147	538	56	138	20	7	0	70	54		.257	.328	.320	107	5	16			.941	7	*S-147	1.8
1908	StL-A	137	487	59	123	24	4	1	60	52		.253	.327	.324	111	7	5			**.951**	18	*S-137	3.1
1909	StL-A	116	403	36	96	12	2	0	35	38		.238	.310	.278	92	-3	7			.946	11	S-87,3-29	1.2
1910	StL-A	138	508	47	131	19	7	0	37	49		.258	.324	.323	110	6	12			.948	22	S-99,3-39	3.6
1911	StL-A	125	410	35	95	12	2	0	31	46		.232	.312	.271	66	-18	8			.943	2	*S-124/2-1,M	-0.8
1912	StL-A	100	323	39	78	14	5	0	31	43		.241	.332	.316	89	-4	3			.942	8	S-87,3-10/2-2,M	1.2
1913	StL-A	55	147	11	31	5	0	0	21	14	16	.211	.293	.245	59	-7	1			.931	-5	S-39/3-7	-1.0
1914	StL-A	26	73	3	16	2	1	0	5	5	13	.219	.269	.274	66	-3	1	1	-0	.889	-11	S-19/3-2	-1.5
1915	StL-A	9	13	1	3	0	1	0	4	5	0	.231	.444	.385	154	1	0	1	-1	.848	1	/S-9	0.2
1916	StL-A	14	18	0	5	0	0	0	1	2	1	.278	.350	.278	93	-0	0			.958	1	/3-9,S-5	0.6
1917	StL-N	8	10	0	1	0	0	0	2	0	1	.100	.100	.100	-40	-2	0			1.000	-1	/3-5,S-2	-0.3
1918	StL-N	32	98	3	15	1	0	0	4	9	9	.153	.202	.163	12	-10	1			.959	2	2-17,S-12/3-1	-0.8
Total	25	2383	8618	1057	2309	391	143	34	1121	774	79	.268	.332	.358	106	53	201	2		.938	211	*S-1826,3-426/P201	36.9

■ TIM WALLACH   Wallach, Timothy Charles   b: 9/14/57, Huntington Park, Cal.   BR/TR, 6'3", 200 lbs.   Deb: 9/6/80

YEAR	TM/L	G	AB	R	H	2B	3B	HR	RBI	BB	SO	AVG	OBP	SLG	PRO+	BR/A	SB	CS	SBR	FA	FR	G/POS	TPR
1980	Mon-N	5	11	1	2	0	0	2	1	2	5	.182	.250	.455	93	-0	0	0	0	1.000	-1	/O-3,1-1	-0.2
1981	*Mon-N	71	212	19	50	9	1	4	13	15	37	.236	.299	.344	81	-5	0	1	-1	1.000	-4	O-35,1-16,3-15	-1.3
1982	Mon-N	158	596	89	160	31	3	28	97	36	81	.268	.314	.471	115	9	6	4	-1	.948	-6	*3-156/O-2,1-1	-0.1
1983	Mon-N	156	581	54	156	33	3	19	70	55	97	.269	.338	.434	113	9	0	3	-2	.956	-7	*3-156	-0.2
1984	Mon-N★	160	582	55	143	25	4	18	72	50	101	.246	.313	.395	102	0	3	7	-3	.959	16	*3-160/S-1	1.1
1985	Mon-N★	155	569	70	148	36	3	22	81	38	79	.260	.312	.450	117	10	9	9	-3	.967	37	*3-154	4.3
1986	Mon-N	134	480	50	112	22	1	18	71	44	72	.233	.311	.396	94	-5	8	6	-1	.958	15	*3-132	0.8
1987	Mon-N★	153	593	89	177	42	4	26	123	37	98	.298	.347	.514	121	16	9	5	-0	.952	-0	*3-150/P-1	1.3
1988	Mon-N	159	592	52	152	32	5	12	69	38	88	.257	.305	.389	93	-6	2	6	-3	.962	12	*3-153/2-1	0.2
1989	Mon-N★	154	573	76	159	42	0	13	77	58	81	.277	.345	.419	116	12	3	7	-3	.958	6	*3-153/P-1	1.7
1990	Mon-N	161	626	69	185	37	5	21	98	42	80	.296	.343	.471	126	20	6	9	-4	.954	4	*3-161	2.2
1991	Mon-N	151	577	60	130	22	1	13	73	50	100	.225	.294	.334	77	-18	2	4	-1	**.968**	6	*3-149	-1.3
1992	Mon-N	150	537	53	120	29	1	9	59	50	81	.223	.299	.331	79	-15	2	2	-1	.964	18	3-85,1-71	-0.2
1993	LA-N	133	477	42	106	19	1	12	62	32	70	.222	.275	.342	68	-23	0	0	-1	.958	0	*3-130/1-1	-2.4
1994	LA-N	113	414	68	116	21	1	23	78	46	80	.280	.358	.502	130	17	0	2	-1	.959	-10	*3-113	0.6
1995	*LA-N	97	327	24	87	22	2	9	38	27	69	.266	.330	.428	107	2	0	0	0	.976	-11	3-96/1-1	-0.8
1996	Cal-A	57	190	23	45	7	0	8	20	18	47	.237	.304	.400	78	-7	1	0	0	.941	3	3-46/1-3,D-8	-0.4
	*LA-N	45	162	14	37	3	1	4	22	12	32	.228	.286	.333	68	-8	0	1	-1	.971	-7	3-45	-1.6
Total	17	2212	8099	908	2085	432	36	260	1125	649	1307	.257	.319	.416	103	10	51	66	-24	.959	71	*3-2054/1-94,ODP2S	3.7

■ JACK WALLAESA   Wallaesa, John   b: 8/31/19, Easton, Pa.   d: 12/27/86, Easton, Pa.   BB/TR, 6'3", 191 lbs.   Deb: 9/22/40

1940	Phi-A	6	20	3	3	0	0	0	2	0	2	.150	.150	.150	-22	-4	0	0	0	.903	1	/S-6	-0.2
1942	Phi-A	36	117	13	30	4	1	2	13	8	26	.256	.315	.359	90	-2	0	1	-1	.920	-7	S-36	-0.8
1946	Phi-A	63	194	16	38	4	2	5	11	14	47	.196	.250	.314	57	-12	0	0	0	.916	-16	S-59	-2.6
1947	Chi-A	81	205	25	40	9	1	7	32	23	51	.195	.279	.351	78	-7	2	2	-1	.968	13	S-27,O-22/3-1	0.6
1948	Chi-A	33	48	2	9	0	0	1	3	1	12	.188	.204	.250	21	-6	1	0	0	1.000	-0	/S-5,O-1	-0.1
Total	5	219	584	56	120	17	4	15	61	46	138	.205	.267	.325	65	-30	3	3	-1	.933	-10	S-133/O-23,3-1	-3.5

■ NORM WALLEN   Wallen, Norman Edward (b: Norman Edward Walentoski)   b: 2/13/17, Milwaukee, Wis.   BR/TR, 5'11.5", 175 lbs.   Deb: 4/20/45

| 1945 | Bos-N | 4 | 15 | 1 | 2 | 0 | 1 | 0 | 1 | 1 | 1 | .133 | .188 | .267 | 25 | -2 | 0 | | | .800 | -2 | /3-4 | -0.3 |

■ TY WALLER   Waller, Elliott Tyrone   b: 3/14/57, Fresno, Cal.   BR/TR, 6', 180 lbs.   Deb: 9/6/80   C

1980	StL-N	5	12	3	1	0	0	0	0	1	5	.083	.154	.083	-31	-2	0	0	0	1.000	-2	/3-5	-0.5
1981	Chi-N	30	71	10	19	2	1	3	13	4	18	.268	.307	.451	108	0	2	0	0	.978	-2	3-22/2-3,O-3	-0.2
1982	Chi-N	17	21	4	5	0	0	0	1	2	4	.238	.304	.238	52	-1	0	0	0	1.000	-2	/O-7,3-1	-0.3
1987	Hou-N	11	6	1	1	0	0	0	0	0	3	.167	.167	.333	30	-1	0	0	0	1.000	-1	/O-3	-0.1
Total	4	63	110	18	26	3	1	3	14	7	31	.236	.282	.364	78	-4	2	0	0	.961	-6	/3-28,O-13,2-3	-1.1

■ DENNY WALLING   Walling, Dennis Martin   b: 4/17/54, Neptune, N.J.   BL/TR, 6'1", 185 lbs.   Deb: 9/7/75   C

YEAR	TM/L	G	AB	R	H	2B	3B	HR	RBI	BB	SO	AVG	OBP	SLG	PRO+	BR/A	SB	CS	SBR	FA	FR	G/POS	TPR
1975	Oak-A	6	8	0	1	0	0	0	2	0	4	.125	.125	.250	7	-1	0	0	0	1.000	-1	/O-3	-0.2
1976	Oak-A	3	11	1	3	0	0	0	0	0	0	.273	.273	.273	63	-1	0	0	0	.889	-3	/O-3	-0.1
1977	Hou-N	6	21	1	6	0	0	0	6	2	4	.286	.348	.381	105	0	0	1	-1	1.000	-3	/O-5	0.0
1978	Hou-N	120	247	30	62	11	3	3	36	30	24	.251	.335	.356	101	0	9	2	0	.980	1	O-78	0.1
1979	Hou-N	82	147	21	48	8	4	3	31	17	21	.327	.396	.497	151	10	3	0	0	.985	-3	O-42	0.6
1980	*Hou-N	100	284	30	85	8	5	3	29	35	26	.299	.376	.387	123	9	4	9	-7	1.000	-6	1-63,O-19	-0.2
1981	*Hou-N	65	158	23	37	0	0	5	23	28	14	.234	.349	.367	109	2	1	0	1	.990	-5	1-27,O-27	-0.4
1982	Hou-N	85	146	22	30	4	1	4	14	23	19	.205	.314	.267	69	-6	4	2	0	1.000	-4	O-32,1-20	-1.1
1983	Hou-N	100	135	24	40	5	3	3	15	16	16	.296	.364	.444	132	6	4	2	0	.992	-3	1-42,3-13,O-13	0.0
1984	Hou-N	87	249	37	70	11	5	3	31	16	28	.281	.327	.402	112	3	3	5	-1	.956	-1	3-52,1-16/O-6	0.2
1985	Hou-N	119	345	44	93	20	1	7	45	25	26	.270	.319	.394	101	-0	5	5	0	.938	-2	3-51,1-46,O-13	-0.5
1986	*Hou-N	130	382	54	119	23	1	13	58	36	31	.312	.367	.479	136	18	1	0	0	.960	-2	*3-102,O-11/1-4	1.8
1987	Hou-N	110	325	45	92	21	4	5	33	39	25	.283	.360	.418	112	5	5	1	0	.970	-3	3-79,1-16/O-7	-0.1
1988	Hou-N	65	176	19	43	10	2	1	20	15	18	.244	.304	.341	88	-3	1	0	0	.950	9	3-51/1-3,O-1	0.6

YEAR	TM/L	G	AB	R	H	2B	3B	HR	RBI	BB	SO	AVG	OBP	SLG	PRO+	BR/A	SB	CS	SBR	FA	FR	G/POS	TPR
	StL-N	19	58	3	13	3	0	0	1	2	7	.224	.250	.276	50	-4	1	0	0	1.000	-2	O-11/3-5,1-1	-0.7
	Yr	84	234	22	56	13	2	1	21	17	25	.239	.291	.325	79	-7	2	0	1	.941	6	3-56,O-12/1-4	-0.1
1989	StL-N	69	79	9	24	7	0	1	11	14	12	.304	.409	.430	136	4	0	0	0	.969	-2	1-20/3-9,O-6	0.2
1990	StL-N	78	127	7	28	5	0	1	19	8	15	.220	.267	.283	51	-8	0	0	0	1.000	0	1-15,3-11/O-8	-0.9
1991	Tex-A	24	44	1	4	1	0	0	2	3	8	.091	.184	.114	-16	-7	0	0	0	.950	-3	3-14/O-5	-1.0
1992	Hou-N	3	3	1	1	0	0	0	0	0	0	.333	.333	.333	94	-0	0	0	0	.000	0	/H	0.0
Total	18	1271	2945	372	799	142	30	49	380	308	316	.271	.341	.390	107	29	44	18	2	.947	-25	3-387,O-290,1-273	-1.7

■ JOE WALLIS   Wallis, Harold Joseph b: 1/9/52, E.St.Louis, Ill. BB/TR, 5'10", 195 lbs. Deb: 9/2/75

YEAR	TM/L	G	AB	R	H	2B	3B	HR	RBI	BB	SO	AVG	OBP	SLG	PRO+	BR/A	SB	CS	SBR	FA	FR	G/POS	TPR
1975	Chi-N	16	56	9	16	2	2	1	4	5	14	.286	.344	.446	113	1	2	0	1	1.000	-0	O-15	0.1
1976	Chi-N	121	338	51	86	11	5	5	21	33	62	.254	.323	.361	86	-6	3	9	-5	.976	2	O-90	-1.3
1977	Chi-N	56	80	14	20	3	0	2	8	16	25	.250	.375	.363	89	-1	0	1	-1	.974	-8	O-35	-1.0
1978	Chi-N	28	55	7	17	2	1	1	6	5	13	.309	.367	.436	110	1	0	2	-1	1.000	-6	O-25	-0.5
	Oak-A	85	279	28	66	16	1	6	26	26	42	.237	.302	.366	91	-4	1	4	-2	.980	3	O-80/D-1	-0.7
1979	Oak-A	23	78	6	11	2	0	1	3	10	18	.141	.247	.205	25	-8	1	0	0	1.000	-1	O-23	-1.0
Total	5	329	886	115	216	36	9	16	68	95	174	.244	.318	.359	86	-17	7	16	-8	.982	-9	O-268/D-1	-4.4

■ LEE WALLS   Walls, Ray Lee b: 1/6/33, San Diego, Cal. d: 10/11/93, Los Angeles, Cal. BR/TR, 6'3", 205 lbs. Deb: 4/21/52 C

YEAR	TM/L	G	AB	R	H	2B	3B	HR	RBI	BB	SO	AVG	OBP	SLG	PRO+	BR/A	SB	CS	SBR	FA	FR	G/POS	TPR
1952	Pit-N	32	80	6	15	0	1	2	5	8	22	.188	.261	.287	51	-5	0	0		1.000	0	O-19	-0.6
1956	Pit-N	143	474	72	130	20	11	11	54	50	83	.274	.346	.432	110	7	3	5	-2	.967	6	*O-133/3-1	0.4
1957	Pit-N	8	22	3	4	1	0	0	0	2	5	.182	.250	.227	30	-2	1	0	0	1.000	1	/O-7	-0.2
	Chi-N	117	366	42	88	10	5	6	33	27	67	.240	.294	.344	72	-15	5	3	-0	.984	-5	O-94/3-1	-2.6
	Yr	125	388	45	92	11	5	6	33	29	72	.237	.292	.338	70	-17	6	3	0	.985	-4	*O-101/3-1	-2.8
1958	Chi-N★	136	513	80	156	19	3	24	72	47	62	.304	.371	.493	128	21	4	4	-1	.992	5	*O-132	1.8
1959	Chi-N	120	354	43	91	18	3	8	33	42	73	.257	.344	.393	97	-1	0	2	-1	.967	-8	*O-119	-1.5
1960	Cin-N	29	84	12	23	3	2	1	7	17	20	.274	.396	.393	115	2	2	0	1	.960	1	O-24/1-2	0.2
	Phi-N	65	181	19	36	6	1	3	19	14	32	.199	.256	.292	50	-13	3	2	-0	.947	-9	3-34,O-13/1-7	-2.4
	Yr	94	265	31	59	9	3	4	26	31	52	.223	.304	.325	72	-10	5	2	0	.958	-8	O-37,3-34/1-9	-2.2
1961	Phi-N	91	261	32	73	6	4	8	30	19	48	.280	.329	.425	99	-1	2	2	-1	.987	-6	1-28,3-26,O-17	-1.0
1962	LA-N	60	109	9	29	3	1	0	17	10	21	.266	.328	.312	77	-3	1	0	0	.929	-4	O-17,1-11/3-4	-0.8
1963	LA-N	64	86	12	20	1	0	3	11	7	25	.233	.290	.349	89	-1	0	2		1.000	-2	O-18/1-5,3-2	-0.4
1964	LA-N	37	28	1	5	1	0	0	3	2	12	.179	.233	.214	29	-3	0	0	0	1.000	-2	/O-6,C-1	-0.5
Total	10	902	2558	331	670	88	31	66	284	245	470	.262	.330	.398	96	-14	21	18	-5	.977	-23	O-599/3-68,1-53,C-1	-7.6

■ AUSTIN WALSH   Walsh, Austin Edward b: 9/1/1891, Cambridge, Mass. d: 1/26/55, Glendale, Cal. BL/TL, 5'11", 175 lbs. Deb: 4/19/14

YEAR	TM/L	G	AB	R	H	2B	3B	HR	RBI	BB	SO	AVG	OBP	SLG	PRO+	BR/A	SB	CS	SBR	FA	FR	G/POS	TPR
1914	Chi-F	57	121	14	29	6	1	1	10	4	25	.240	.264	.331	65	-9	0			1.000	-3	O-30	-1.3

■ JIMMY WALSH   Walsh, James Charles b: 9/22/1885, Kallila, Ireland d: 7/3/62, Syracuse, N.Y. BL/TR, 5'10.5", 170 lbs. Deb: 8/26/12

YEAR	TM/L	G	AB	R	H	2B	3B	HR	RBI	BB	SO	AVG	OBP	SLG	PRO+	BR/A	SB	CS	SBR	FA	FR	G/POS	TPR
1912	Phi-A	31	107	11	27	8	2	0	15	12		.252	.328	.364	101	0	7			.947	0	O-30	-0.1
1913	Phi-A	97	303	56	77	16	5	0	27	38	40	.254	.341	.340	102	1	15			.961	1	O-90	-0.2
1914	NY-A	43	136	13	26	1	3	1	11	29	21	.191	.338	.265	80	-2	6	9	-4	.977	-1	O-41	-0.9
	*Phi-A	68	216	35	51	11	6	3	36	30	27	.236	.340	.384	123	6	6	12	-5	.966	-0	O-56/1-3,3-3,S-1	-0.2
	Yr	111	352	48	77	12	9	4	47	59	48	.219	.337	.338	106	4	12	21	-9	.971	-1	O-97/1-3,3-3,S-1	-1.1
1915	Phi-A	117	417	48	86	15	6	1	20	57	64	.206	.306	.278	78	-11	22	12	-1	.976	7	*O-109/3-2,1-1	-1.0
1916	Phi-A	114	390	42	91	13	6	1	27	54	36	.233	.330	.305	95	-1	27	14	-0	.939	-3	*O-113/1-1	-0.9
	*Bos-A	14	17	5	3	1	0	0	2	4	2	.176	.333	.235	71	-0	3	2	-0	1.000	-3	/O-6,3-2	-0.4
	Yr	128	407	47	94	14	6	1	29	58	38	.231	.330	.302	94	-2	30	16	-1	.940	-3	*O-119/3-2,1-1	-1.3
1917	Bos-A	57	185	25	49	6	3	0	12	25	14	.265	.352	.330	109	3	6			.982	5	O-47	0.0
Total	6	541	1771	235	410	71	31	6	150	249	204	.232	.330	.317	96	-4	92	49		.964	5	O-492/3-7,1-5,S-1	-3.7

■ JOHN WALSH   Walsh, John Gabriel b: 3/25/1879, Wilkes-Barre, Pa. d: 4/25/47, Jamaica, N.Y. BR/TR, 5'8.5", 162 lbs. Deb: 6/22/03

YEAR	TM/L	G	AB	R	H	2B	3B	HR	RBI	BB	SO	AVG	OBP	SLG	PRO+	BR/A	SB	CS	SBR	FA	FR	G/POS	TPR
1903	Phi-N	1	3	0	0	0	0	0	0	0		.000	.000	.000	-99	-1	0			1.000	-0	/3-1	-0.1

■ JOE WALSH   Walsh, Joseph Francis b: 10/14/1886, Minersville, Pa. d: 1/6/67, Buffalo, N.Y. BR/TR, 6'2", 170 lbs. Deb: 10/8/10

YEAR	TM/L	G	AB	R	H	2B	3B	HR	RBI	BB	SO	AVG	OBP	SLG	PRO+	BR/A	SB	CS	SBR	FA	FR	G/POS	TPR
1910	NY-A	1	4	0	2	1	0	0	2	0		.500	.500	.750	275	-1	0			1.000	-1	/C-1	0.0
1911	NY-A	4	9	2	2	1	0	0	0	0		.222	.222	.333	51	-1	0			1.000	-3	/C-4	-0.3
Total	2	5	13	2	4	2	0	0	2	0		.308	.308	.462	114	0	0			1.000	-4	/C-5	-0.3

■ JOE WALSH   Walsh, Joseph Patrick "Tweet" b: 3/13/17, Roxbury, Mass. BR/TR, 5'10", 155 lbs. Deb: 7/1/38

YEAR	TM/L	G	AB	R	H	2B	3B	HR	RBI	BB	SO	AVG	OBP	SLG	PRO+	BR/A	SB	CS	SBR	FA	FR	G/POS	TPR
1938	Bos-N	4	8	0	0	0	0	0	0	0	2	.000	.000	.000	-99	-2	0			.900	-2	/S-4	-0.4

■ JOE WALSH   Walsh, Joseph R. "Reddy" b: 11/5/1864, Chicago, Ill. d: 8/8/11, Omaha, Neb. BL/TR, Deb: 9/3/1891

YEAR	TM/L	G	AB	R	H	2B	3B	HR	RBI	BB	SO	AVG	OBP	SLG	PRO+	BR/A	SB	CS	SBR	FA	FR	G/POS	TPR
1891	Bal-a	26	100	14	21	0	1	1	10	6	18	.210	.255	.260	47	-7	4			.865	6	S-13,2-13	0.0

■ DEE WALSH   Walsh, Leo Thomas b: 3/28/1890, St.Louis, Mo. d: 7/14/71, St.Louis, Mo. BB/TR, 5'9.5", 165 lbs. Deb: 4/10/13

YEAR	TM/L	G	AB	R	H	2B	3B	HR	RBI	BB	SO	AVG	OBP	SLG	PRO+	BR/A	SB	CS	SBR	FA	FR	G/POS	TPR
1913	StL-A	23	53	8	9	0	1	0	5	6	11	.170	.302	.208	51	-3	3			.933	2	S-22/3-1	0.1
1914	StL-A	7	23	1	2	0	0	0	1	2	4	.087	.160	.087	-27	-4	1	1	-0	.919	-0	/S-7	-0.4
1915	StL-A	59	150	13	33	5	0	0	6	14	25	.220	.308	.253	71	-5	6	6	-2	.951	1	O-45/3-2,P-1,2-1,S	-0.8
Total	3	89	226	22	44	5	1	0	12	22	40	.195	.292	.226	56	-11	10	7		.924	3	/O-45,S-30,3-3,2P	-1.1

■ JIMMY WALSH   Walsh, Michael Timothy "Runt" b: 3/25/1886, Lima, Ohio d: 1/21/47, Baltimore, Md. BR/TR, 5'9", 174 lbs. Deb: 4/25/10

YEAR	TM/L	G	AB	R	H	2B	3B	HR	RBI	BB	SO	AVG	OBP	SLG	PRO+	BR/A	SB	CS	SBR	FA	FR	G/POS	TPR
1910	Phi-N	88	242	28	60	8	3	3	25	38		.248	.323	.343	91	-3	5			.947	-2	2-26,O-26/S-9,3-5	-0.6
1911	Phi-N	94	289	29	78	20	3	1	31	21	30	.270	.324	.370	93	-4	5			.962	-6	O-48,2-14/S-9,3CP1	-1.1
1912	Phi-N	51	150	16	40	6	3	2	19	8	20	.267	.304	.387	83	-4	3			.944	0	2-31,3-12/C-5	-0.4
1913	Phi-N	26	30	3	10	4	0	0	5	1	5	.333	.355	.467	128	1	1			1.000	-0	/2-6,S-3,3-1,O-1	0.0
1914	Bal-F	120	428	54	132	25	4	10	65	22	56	.308	.345	.456	113	0	18			.932	3	*3-113/2-1,S-1,O-1	0.7
1915	Bal-F	106	401	43	121	20	1	9	60	21	44	.302	.340	.424	111	-1	12			.936	-9	*3-106	-0.6
	StL-F	17	31	5	6	1	0	0	1	3	4	.194	.306	.226	48	-2	1			.913	-1	/3-9	-0.3
	Yr	123	432	48	127	21	1	9	61	24	48	.294	.337	.410	106	-4	13			.934	-10	*3-115	-0.9
Total	6	502	1571	178	447	84	14	25	212	101	197	.285	.332	.404	102	-13	45			.925	-14	3-253/2-78,OSC1P	-2.3

■ TOM WALSH   Walsh, Thomas Joseph b: 2/28/1885, Davenport, Iowa d: 3/16/63, Naples, Fla. BR/TR, 5'11", 170 lbs. Deb: 8/15/06

YEAR	TM/L	G	AB	R	H	2B	3B	HR	RBI	BB	SO	AVG	OBP	SLG	PRO+	BR/A	SB	CS	SBR	FA	FR	G/POS	TPR
1906	Chi-N	2	1	0	0	0	0	0	0	0		.000	.000	.000	-95	-0	0			1.000	0	/C-2	0.0

■ WALT WALSH   Walsh, Walter William b: 4/30/1897, Newark, N.J. d: 1/15/66, Avon By The Sea, N.J. BR/TR, 5'11", 170 lbs. Deb: 5/4/20

YEAR	TM/L	G	AB	R	H	2B	3B	HR	RBI	BB	SO	AVG	OBP	SLG	PRO+	BR/A	SB	CS	SBR	FA	FR	G/POS	TPR
1920	Phi-N	2	0	0	0	0	0	0	0	0						0	0	0	0	0		R	0.0

■ ROXY WALTERS   Walters, Alfred John b: 11/5/1892, San Francisco, Cal. d: 6/3/56, Alameda, Cal. BR/TR, 5'8.5", 160 lbs. Deb: 9/16/15

YEAR	TM/L	G	AB	R	H	2B	3B	HR	RBI	BB	SO	AVG	OBP	SLG	PRO+	BR/A	SB	CS	SBR	FA	FR	G/POS	TPR
1915	NY-A	2	3	0	1	0	0	0	0	0	0	.333	.333	.333	100	-0	0			1.000	2	/C-2	0.2
1916	NY-A	66	203	13	54	9	3	0	23	14	42	.266	.320	.340	96	-1	2			.974	17	C-65	2.2
1917	NY-A	61	171	16	45	2	0	0	14	9	22	.263	.304	.275	76	-5	2			.968	11	C-57	1.1
1918	NY-A	64	191	18	38	5	1	0	12	9	18	.199	.239	.236	42	-14	3			.953	-5	C-50/O-9	-1.8
1919	Bos-A	48	135	7	26	2	0	0	9	7	15	.193	.259	.207	33	-12	1			.982	5	C-47	-0.4
1920	Bos-A	88	258	25	51	11	1	0	28	30	21	.198	.303	.248	49	-18	2	2	-1	.980	8	C-85/1-2	-0.5
1921	Bos-A	54	169	17	34	2	1	0	14	10	11	.201	.254	.237	27	-19	3	0	1	.990	15	C-54	-0.2
1922	Bos-A	38	98	4	19	2	0	0	6	6	8	.194	.240	.214	19	-12	0	0	0	.967	6	C-36	-0.4
1923	Bos-A	40	104	9	26	4	0	0	5	2	16	.250	.264	.288	45	-8	0	1	-1	.974	7	C-36/2-1	-0.2
1924	Cle-A	32	74	10	19	2	0	0	5	6	6	.257	.345	.284	63	-4	0	1	-1	.979	6	C-25/2-7	0.2
1925	Cle-A	5	20	1	4	0	0	0	1	0	2	.200	.200	.200	2	-3	0	0	0	1.000	-0	/C-5	-0.3
Total	11	498	1426	119	317	41	6	0	116	97	151	.222	.281	.259	51	-96	13	5		.975	70	C-462/O-9,2-8,1-2	0.1

YEAR	TM/L	G	AB	R	H	2B	3B	HR	RBI	BB	SO	AVG	OBP	SLG	PRO+	BR/A	SB	CS	SBR	FA	FR	G/POS	TPR

■ DAN WALTERS Walters, Daniel Gene b: 8/15/66, Brunswick, Maine BR/TR, 6'4", 225 lbs. Deb: 6/1/92

1992	SD-N	57	179	14	45	11	1	4	22	10	28	.251	.298	.391	92	-2	1	0	0	.992	7	C-55	0.8
1993	SD-N	27	94	6	19	3	0	1	10	7	13	.202	.257	.266	40	-8	0	0	0	.970	-3	C-26	-1.0
Total	2	84	273	20	64	14	1	5	32	17	41	.234	.284	.348	73	-10	1	0	0	.985	4	/C-81	-0.2

■ FRED WALTERS Walters, Fred James "Whale" b: 9/4/12, Laurel, Miss. d: 2/1/80, Laurel, Miss. BR/TR, 6'1", 210 lbs. Deb: 4/17/45

| 1945 | Bos-A | 40 | 93 | 2 | 16 | 2 | 0 | 0 | 5 | 10 | 9 | .172 | .252 | .194 | 29 | -8 | 1 | 1 | -0 | .993 | 6 | C-38 | -0.1 |

■ KEN WALTERS Walters, Kenneth Rogers b: 11/11/33, Fresno, Cal. BR/TR, 6'1", 180 lbs. Deb: 4/12/60

1960	Phi-N	124	426	42	102	10	6	8	37	16	50	.239	.269	.319	60	-24	4	3	-1	.988	6	*O-119	-2.5
1961	Phi-N	86	180	23	41	8	2	2	14	5	25	.228	.253	.328	53	-12	2	2	-1	.975	-6	O-56/1-5,3-1	-2.1
1963	Cin-N	49	75	6	14	2	0	1	7	4	14	.187	.237	.253	40	-6	0	2	-1	.889	-5	O-21/1-1	-1.3
Total	3	259	681	71	157	20	8	11	58	25	89	.231	.261	.314	56	-42	6	7	-2	.979	-5	O-196/1-6,3-1	-5.9

■ BUCKY WALTERS Walters, William Henry b: 4/19/09, Philadelphia, Pa. d: 4/20/91, Abington, Pa. BR/TR, 6'1", 180 lbs. Deb: 9/18/31 MC

1931	Bos-N	9	38	2	8	2	0	0	0	0	3	.211	.211	.263	28	-4	0			.947	0	/3-6,2-3	-0.3
1932	Bos-N	22	75	8	14	3	1	0	4	2	14	.187	.208	.253	24	-8	0			.910	2	3-22	-0.5
1933	Bos-A	52	195	27	50	8	3	4	28	19	24	.256	.326	.390	90	-3	1	1	-0	.940	1	3-43/2-7	0.1
1934	Bos-A	23	88	10	19	4	4	4	18	3	12	.216	.242	.489	79	-4	0	0	0	.906	6	3-23	0.3
	Phi-N	83	300	36	78	20	3	4	38	19	54	.260	.308	.387	75	-11	1			.950	-7	3-80/2-3,P-2	-1.4
1935	Phi-N	49	96	14	24	2	1	0	6	9	12	.250	.314	.292	58	-6	0			1.000	1	P-24,3-5,2-2,3-1	-0.2
1936	Phi-N	64	121	12	29	10	1	1	16	7	15	.240	.281	.364	66	-6	0			.974	9	P-40/3-1,3-1	0.0
1937	Phi-N★	56	137	15	38	6	0	1	16	5	16	.277	.303	.343	69	-6	1			.988	5	P-37/3-3	-0.1
1938	Phi-N	15	35	6	10	2	0	1	3	1	5	.286	.306	.429	103	-0	1			.955	0	P-12	0.0
	Cin-N	36	64	10	9	1	0	0	5	7	18	.141	.236	.156	10	-8	0			.981	2	P-27	0.0
	Yr	51	99	16	19	3	0	1	8	8	23	.192	.259	.253	42	-8	1			.973	3	P-39	0.0
1939	*Cin-N☆	40	120	16	39	8	1	1	16	5	12	.325	.357	.433	111	2	1			.979	4	P-39	0.0
1940	*Cin-N★	37	117	11	24	3	0	1	18	4	14	.205	.231	.256	34	-11	2			.945	-1	P-36	0.0
1941	Cin-N★	39	106	6	20	6	0	0	9	7	13	.189	.239	.245	36	-9	0			.977	2	P-37	0.0
1942	Cin-N	40	99	13	24	6	1	2	13	3	13	.242	.265	.384	89	-2	0			.961	1	P-34/O-1	-0.1
1943	Cin-N	37	90	11	24	7	1	1	12	6	15	.267	.313	.400	107	0	1			.971	1	P-34	0.0
1944	Cin-N★	37	107	9	30	4	0	0	13	8	18	.280	.330	.318	86	-2	0			1.000	1	P-34	0.0
1945	Cin-N	24	61	11	14	3	0	3	8	3	14	.230	.266	.426	93	-1	2			.975	-0	P-22	0.0
1946	Cin-N	24	55	6	7	2	0	0	5	4	12	.127	.186	.164	-0	-7	2			.940	2	P-22	0.0
1947	Cin-N	20	45	3	12	2	0	0	4	2	13	.267	.298	.311	62	-2	0			.962	-1	P-20	0.0
1948	Cin-N	7	15	1	4	0	0	0	2	0	2	.267	.267	.267	46	-1	0			1.000	1	/P-7,M	0.0
1950	Bos-N	1	2	0	0	0	0	0	0	0	0	.000	.000	.000	-99	-1	0			1.000	0	/P-1	0.0
Total	19	715	1966	227	477	99	16	23	234	114	303	.243	.286	.344	69	-90	12	1		.974	28	P-428,3-184/2-16,O	-2.2

■ DANNY WALTON Walton, Daniel James "Mickey" b: 7/14/47, Los Angeles, Cal. BR/TR, 6', 200 lbs. Deb: 4/20/68

1968	Hou-N	2	2	0	0	0	0	0	0	0	1	.000	.000	.000	-99	-0	0	0	0	.000	0	H	-0.1
1969	Sea-A	23	92	12	20	1	2	3	10	5	26	.217	.280	.370	82	-3	2	0	1	.976	-1	O-23	-0.4
1970	Mil-A	117	397	32	102	20	1	17	66	51	126	.257	.350	.441	116	9	2	3	-1	.965	-6	*O-114	-0.4
1971	Mil-A	30	69	5	14	3	0	2	9	7	22	.203	.286	.333	76	-2	0	0	0	.923	-4	O-19/3-1	-0.7
	NY-A	5	14	1	2	0	0	1	2	0	7	.143	.143	.357	40	-1	0	0	0	1.000	-1	/O-4	-0.2
	Yr	35	83	6	16	3	0	3	11	7	29	.193	.264	.337	71	-3	0	0	0	.933	-5	O-23/3-1	-0.9
1973	Min-A	37	96	13	17	1	1	4	8	17	28	.177	.301	.333	75	-3	0	0	0	1.000	-3	O-18,D-11/3-1	-0.7
1975	Min-A	42	63	4	11	2	0	1	8	4	18	.175	.224	.254	34	-6	0	0	0	.962	-1	/1-7,C-2,D-6	-0.7
1976	LA-N	18	15	0	2	0	0	0	2	1	2	.133	.188	.133	-8	-2	0	0	0	.000	0	H	-0.3
1977	Hou-N	13	21	0	4	0	0	0	1	0	5	.190	.190	.190	3	-3	0	0	0	.956	0	/1-5	-0.3
1980	Tex-A	10	10	2	2	0	0	0	1	3	5	.200	.385	.200	67	-0	0	0	0	1.000	0	/D-1	0.0
Total	9	297	779	69	174	27	4	28	107	88	240	.223	.310	.376	90	-12	4	3	-1	.966	-15	O-178/D-18,1-12,C3	-3.8

■ JEROME WALTON Walton, Jerome O'Terrell b: 7/8/65, Newnan, Ga. BR/TR, 6'1", 175 lbs. Deb: 4/4/89

1989	*Chi-N	116	475	64	139	23	3	5	46	27	77	.293	.339	.385	99	-1	24	7	3	.990	4	*O-115	0.3
1990	Chi-N	101	392	63	103	16	2	2	21	50	70	.263	.352	.329	82	-8	14	7	0	.977	3	O-98	-0.8
1991	Chi-N	123	270	42	59	13	1	5	17	19	55	.219	.277	.330	67	-12	7	3	0	.983	-10	*O-101	-2.5
1992	Chi-N	30	55	7	7	0	1	0	1	9	13	.127	.273	.164	26	-5	1	2	-1	.944	-3	O-24	-1.0
1993	Cal-A	5	2	2	0	0	0	0	0	0	2	.000	.000	.000	-2	-0	1	0	0	1.000	0	/O-1,D-4	-0.0
1994	Cin-N	46	68	10	21	4	0	1	9	4	12	.309	.347	.412	98	-0	1	3	-2	1.000	6	O-26/1-7	-0.8
1995	*Cin-N	102	162	32	47	12	1	8	22	17	25	.290	.372	.525	134	8	10	7	1	.982	-15	O-89/1-3	-1.0
1996	Atl-N	37	47	9	16	5	0	1	4	5	10	.340	.404	.511	132	2	0	0	0	1.000	-3	O-28	-0.1
Total	8	560	1471	229	392	73	8	22	120	132	264	.266	.335	.372	91	-16	58	29	1	.983	-31	O-482/1-10,D-4	-5.9

■ REGGIE WALTON Walton, Reginald Sherard b: 10/24/52, Kansas City, Mo. BR/TR, 6'3", 205 lbs. Deb: 6/13/80

1980	Sea-A	31	83	8	23	6	0	2	9	3	10	.277	.310	.422	98	-1	2	2	-1	.929	-2	O-17,D-11	-0.4
1981	Sea-A	12	6	1	0	0	0	0	0	1	2	.000	.143	.000	-54	-1	0	0	0	.000	-2	/O-4,D-1	-0.3
1982	Pit-N	13	15	1	3	1	0	0	0	1	1	.200	.294	.267	56	-1	0	0	0	1.000	-1	/O-2	-0.2
Total	3	56	104	10	26	7	0	2	9	5	13	.250	.297	.375	83	-3	2	2	-1	.929	-5	/O-23,D-12	-0.9

■ BILL WAMBSGANSS Wambsganss, William Adolph b: 3/19/1894, Cleveland, Ohio d: 12/8/85, Lakewood, Ohio BR/TR, 5'11", 175 lbs. Deb: 8/4/14

1914	Cle-A	43	143	12	31	6	2	0	12	8	24	.217	.277	.287	67	-6	2	7	-4	.921	-1	S-36/2-4	-0.9
1915	Cle-A	121	375	30	73	4	4	0	21	36	50	.195	.272	.227	48	-23	8	9	-3	.938	7	2-78,3-35	-1.6
1916	Cle-A	136	475	57	117	14	4	0	45	41	40	.246	.313	.293	77	-13	13			.925	-8	*S-106,2-24/3-5	-1.8
1917	Cle-A	141	499	52	127	17	6	0	43	37	42	.255	.315	.313	85	-9	16			.951	15	*2-137/1-3	1.4
1918	Cle-A	87	315	34	93	15	2	0	40	21	21	.295	.345	.356	102	0	16			.952	-2	2-87	0.4
1919	Cle-A	139	526	60	146	17	6	0	60	32	24	.278	.323	.344	82	-13	18			.963	11	*2-139	0.5
1920	*Cle-A	153	565	83	138	16	11	0	55	54	26	.244	.316	.317	66	-28	9	18	-8	.960	8	*2-153	-2.1
1921	Cle-A	107	410	80	117	28	5	2	47	44	27	.285	.359	.393	90	-6	13	7	-0	.963	-18	*2-103/3-2	-2.0
1922	Cle-A	142	538	89	141	22	6	0	47	60	26	.262	.341	.325	74	-19	17	10	-1	.961	-9	*2-125,S-16	-2.4
1923	Cle-A	101	345	59	100	20	4	1	59	43	15	.290	.373	.380	99	0	10	9	-2	.963	5	2-88/3-4	0.4
1924	Bos-A	156	632	93	174	41	5	0	49	54	33	.275	.336	.356	79	-21	14	8	-1	.963	14	*2-156	-0.5
1925	Bos-A	111	360	50	83	12	4	1	41	52	21	.231	.329	.294	59	-22	3	5	-2	.957	4	*2-103/1-6	-1.7
1926	Phi-A	54	54	11	19	3	0	0	1	8	8	.352	.444	.407	116	2	1	1	-0	.923	0	S-17/2-8	0.2
Total	13	1491	5237	710	1359	215	59	7	520	490	357	.259	.328	.327	78	-157	140	74		.958	26	*2-1205,S-175/31	-10.2

■ LLOYD WANER Waner, Lloyd James "Little Poison" b: 3/16/06, Harrah, Okla. d: 7/22/82, Oklahoma City, Okla. BL/TR, 5'9", 150 lbs. Deb: 4/12/27 FH

1927	*Pit-N	150	629	**133**	223	17	6	2	27	37	23	.355	.396	.410	108	9	14			.976	-1	*O-150/2-1	-0.2
1928	Pit-N	152	659	121	221	22	14	5	61	40	13	.335	.377	.434	107	7	8			.980	7	*O-152	0.3
1929	Pit-N	151	662	134	234	28	**20**	5	74	37	20	.353	.395	.479	113	13	6			.987	16	*O-151	1.7
1930	Pit-N	68	260	32	94	8	3	1	36	5	5	.362	.376	.427	93	-2	3			.983	2	O-65	-0.5
1931	Pit-N	154	681	90	**214**	25	13	4	57	39	16	.314	.352	.407	104	4	7			.979	**18**	*O-153/2-1	1.2
1932	Pit-N	134	565	90	188	27	12	2	38	31	11	.333	.367	.430	116	12	0			.986	12	*O-131	1.6
1933	Pit-N	121	500	59	138	14	5	0	26	22	8	.276	.307	.324	80	-13	3			.982	1	*O-114	-1.9
1934	Pit-N	140	611	95	173	27	6	1	48	38	12	.283	.326	.352	80	-17	2			.979	12	*O-139	-1.1
1935	Pit-N	122	537	83	166	22	14	3	46	22	10	.309	.336	.402	95	-5	1			.989	6	*O-121	-0.3
1936	Pit-N	106	414	67	133	18	3	0	31	31	5	.321	.369	.399	104	3	1			.992	6	O-92	0.2
1937	Pit-N	129	537	80	177	23	4	1	45	34	12	.330	.370	.393	107	6	3			.988	5	*O-123	0.8
1938	Pit-N☆	147	619	79	194	25	7	5	57	28	11	.313	.343	.401	103	2	5			.986	2	*O-144	-0.1
1939	Pit-N	112	379	49	108	15	3	0	24	17	13	.285	.321	.340	79	-11	0			.992	6	O-92/3-1	-0.8
1940	Pit-N	72	166	30	43	3	0	0	3	5	5	.259	.285	.277	56	-10	2			.989	0	O-42	-1.3

YEAR	TM/L	G	AB	R	H	2B	3B	HR	RBI	BB	SO	AVG	OBP	SLG	PRO+	BR/A	SB	CS	SBR	FA	FR	G/POS	TPR
1941	Pit-N	3	4	2	1	0	0	0	1	2	0	.250	.500	.250	116	0	0			1.000	0	/O-1	0.1
	Bos-N	19	51	7	21	1	0	0	4	2	0	.412	.434	.431	151	3	1			.969	-1	O-15	0.2
	Cin-N	55	164	17	42	4	1	0	6	8	0	.256	.291	.293	64	-8	0			.986	-3	O-44	-1.4
	Yr	77	219	26	64	5	1	0	11	12	0	.292	.329	.324	85	-4	1			.981	-4	O-60	-1.1
1942	Phi-N	101	287	23	75	7	3	0	10	16	6	.261	.300	.307	82	-7	1			.967	-1	O-75	-1.2
1944	Bro-N	15	14	3	4	0	0	0	1	3	0	.286	.412	.286	101	0	0			1.000	-2	/O-4	-0.2
	Pit-N	19	14	2	5	0	0	0	2	2	0	.357	.438	.357	120	1	0			1.000	-2	/O-7	-0.2
	Yr	34	28	5	9	0	0	0	3	5	0	.321	.424	.321	110	1	0			1.000	-4	O-11	-0.4
1945	Pit-N	23	19	5	5	0	0	0	1	1	3	.263	.300	.263	55	-1	0			1.000	-0	/O-3	-0.1
Total	18	1993	7772	1201	2459	281	118	27	598	420	173	.316	.353	.393	99	-13	67			.983	76	*O-1818/2-2,3-1	-3.4

■ PAUL WANER   Waner, Paul Glee "Big Poison" b: 4/16/03, Harrah, Okla. d: 8/29/65, Sarasota, Fla. BL/TL, 5'8.5", 153 lbs. Deb: 4/13/26 FCH

YEAR	TM/L	G	AB	R	H	2B	3B	HR	RBI	BB	SO	AVG	OBP	SLG	PRO+	BR/A	SB	CS	SBR	FA	FR	G/POS	TPR
1926	Pit-N	144	536	101	180	35	22	8	79	66	19	.336	.413	.528	144	34	11			.976	8	*O-139	3.1
1927	*Pit-N	155	623	114	237	42	18	9	131	60	14	.380	.437	.549	152	46	5			.980	8	*O-143,1-14	4.2
1928	Pit-N	152	602	142	223	50	19	6	86	77	16	.370	.446	.547	152	48	6			.975	5	*O-131,1-24	4.0
1929	Pit-N	151	596	131	200	43	15	15	100	89	24	.336	.424	.534	133	32	15			.986	2	*O-143/1-7	2.1
1930	Pit-N	145	589	117	217	32	18	8	77	57	18	.368	.428	.525	128	29	18			.959	-3	*O-143	1.4
1931	Pit-N	150	559	88	180	35	10	6	70	73	21	.322	.404	.453	131	27	6			.976	15	*O-138,1-10	3.1
1932	Pit-N	154	630	107	215	62	10	8	82	56	24	.341	.397	.510	144	39	13			.974	3	*O-154	3.2
1933	Pit-N★	154	618	101	191	38	16	7	70	60	20	.309	.372	.456	136	29	3			.981	5	*O-154	2.7
1934	Pit-N★	146	599	122	217	32	16	14	90	68	24	.362	.429	.539	154	47	8			.985	7	*O-145	4.6
1935	Pit-N★	139	549	98	176	29	12	11	78	61	22	.321	.392	.477	128	23	2			.983	3	*O-136	2.0
1936	Pit-N	148	585	107	218	53	9	5	94	74	29	.373	.446	.520	156	48	7			.960	9	*O-145	4.9
1937	Pit-N★	154	619	94	219	30	9	2	74	63	34	.354	.413	.441	132	30	4			.970	1	*O-150/1-3	2.5
1938	Pit-N	148	625	77	175	31	6	6	69	47	28	.280	.331	.378	94	-5	2			.977	2	*O-147	-1.3
1939	Pit-N	125	461	62	151	30	6	3	45	35	18	.328	.375	.438	120	13	0			.978	2	O-106	1.1
1940	Pit-N	89	238	32	69	16	1	1	32	23	14	.290	.352	.378	102	1	0			.985	-5	O-45/1-8	-0.7
1941	Bro-N	11	35	5	6	0	0	0	4	8	0	.171	.326	.171	41	-2	0			.923	-2	/O-9	-0.5
	Bos-N	95	294	40	82	10	2	2	46	47	14	.279	.378	.347	110	6	1			.965	-4	O-77/1-7	-0.3
	Yr	106	329	45	88	10	2	2	50	55	14	.267	.372	.328	102	3	1			.961	-6	O-86/1-7	-0.8
1942	Bos-N	114	333	43	86	17	1	1	39	62	20	.258	.376	.324	108	6	2			.969	-8	O-94	-0.7
1943	Bro-N	82	225	29	70	16	0	1	26	35	9	.311	.406	.396	132	11	0			.960	-1	O-57	0.7
1944	Bro-N	83	136	16	39	4	1	0	16	27	7	.287	.405	.331	111	4	0			.983	-2	O-32	0.0
	NY-A	9	7	1	1	0	0	0	1	2	1	.143	.333	.143	37	-0	1	0	0	.000	0	H	0.0
1945	NY-A	1	0	0	0	0	0	0	0	1	0	—	1.000	—	191	0	0	0	0	.000	0	H	0.0
Total	20	2549	9459	1627	3152	605	191	113	1309	1091	376	.333	.404	.473	133	464	104	0		.975	40	*O-2288/1-73	36.1

■ JACK WANNER   Wanner, Clarence Curtis "Johnny" b: 11/29/1885, Geneseo, Ill. d: 5/28/19, Geneseo, Ill. BR/TR, 5'11.5", 190 lbs. Deb: 9/28/09

YEAR	TM/L	G	AB	R	H	2B	3B	HR	RBI	BB	SO	AVG	OBP	SLG	PRO+	BR/A	SB	CS	SBR	FA	FR	G/POS	TPR
1909	NY-A	3	8	0	1	0	0	0	0	2		.125	.300	.125	35	-0	1			.600	-2	/S-2	-0.3

■ PEE-WEE WANNINGER   Wanninger, Paul Louis b: 12/12/02, Birmingham, Ala. d: 3/7/81, N.Augusta, S.C. BL/TR, 5'7", 150 lbs. Deb: 4/22/25

YEAR	TM/L	G	AB	R	H	2B	3B	HR	RBI	BB	SO	AVG	OBP	SLG	PRO+	BR/A	SB	CS	SBR	FA	FR	G/POS	TPR
1925	NY-A	117	403	35	95	13	6	1	22	11	34	.236	.256	.305	43	-36	3	5	-2	.944	-6	*S-111/3-3,2-1	-3.1
1927	Bos-A	18	60	4	12	0	1	0	6	2		.200	.284	.200	28	-6	2	4	-2	.890	-1	S-15	-0.8
	Cin-N	28	93	14	23	2	2	0	3	10	9	.247	.293	.312	64	-5	0			.953	6	S-28	0.4
Total	2	163	556	53	130	15	8	1	31	23	43	.234	.266	.295	45	-47	5	9		.941	-1	S-154/3-3,2-1	-3.5

■ AARON WARD   Ward, Aaron Lee b: 8/28/1896, Booneville, Ark. d: 1/30/61, New Orleans, La. BR/TR, 5'10.5", 160 lbs. Deb: 8/14/17

YEAR	TM/L	G	AB	R	H	2B	3B	HR	RBI	BB	SO	AVG	OBP	SLG	PRO+	BR/A	SB	CS	SBR	FA	FR	G/POS	TPR
1917	NY-A	8	26	0	3				1	1	5	.115	.148	.115	-19	-4	0			.926	-2	/S-7	-0.7
1918	NY-A	20	32	2	4	1	0	0	1	2	7	.125	.176	.156	0	-4	1			.941	4	S-12/O-4,2-3	0.0
1919	NY-A	27	34	5	7	2	0	0	2	5	6	.206	.308	.265	61	-2	0			1.000	2	/1-5,3-3,S-2,2-1	0.0
1920	NY-A	127	496	62	127	18	7	11	54	33	84	.256	.304	.387	79	-17	7	5	-1	.965	22	*3-114,S-12	1.1
1921	*NY-A	153	556	77	170	30	10	5	75	42	68	.306	.363	.423	98	-2	6	8	-3	.961	19	*2-124,3-33	1.8
1922	*NY-A	154	558	69	149	19	5	7	68	45	64	.267	.328	.357	77	-19	6	4	-1	.974	3	*2-152/3-2	-1.3
1923	*NY-A	152	567	79	161	26	11	10	82	56	65	.284	.351	.422	101	-0	8	8	-2	.980	13	*2-152	1.2
1924	NY-A	120	400	42	101	13	10	8	66	40	45	.253	.324	.395	85	-11	1	4	-2	.973	8	*2-120/S-1	-0.4
1925	NY-A	125	439	41	108	22	3	4	38	49	49	.246	.326	.337	70	-20	1	4	-2	.966	-11	*2-113,3-10	-2.9
1926	NY-A	22	31	5	10	2	0	0	3	2	6	.323	.364	.387	97	-0	0	0	0	1.000	-4	/2-4,3-1	-0.4
1927	Chi-A	145	463	75	125	25	8	5	56	63	56	.270	.360	.391	97	-1	6	5	-1	.963	-19	*2-139/3-6	-1.6
1928	Cle-A	6	9	0	1	0	0	0	0	2	2	.111	.200	.111	-16	-2	0	0	0	.818	2	/3-3,S-2,2-1	0.1
Total	12	1059	3611	457	966	158	54	50	446	339	457	.268	.335	.383	85	-81	36	38		.970	35	2-809,3-172/S10	-3.1

■ CHUCK WARD   Ward, Charles William b: 7/30/1894, St.Louis, Mo. d: 4/4/69, Indian Rocks, Fla. BR/TR, 5'11.5", 170 lbs. Deb: 4/11/17

YEAR	TM/L	G	AB	R	H	2B	3B	HR	RBI	BB	SO	AVG	OBP	SLG	PRO+	BR/A	SB	CS	SBR	FA	FR	G/POS	TPR
1917	Pit-N	125	423	25	100	12	3	0	43	32	43	.236	.302	.279	76	-11	5			.912	-27	*S-112/2-8,3-5	-3.7
1918	Bro-N	2	6	0	2	0	0	0	3	0	0	.333	.333	.333	104	0	0			1.000	-1	/3-2	-0.1
1919	Bro-N	45	150	7	35	1	2	0	8	7	11	.233	.277	.267	62	-7	0			.920	-6	3-45	-1.2
1920	Bro-N	19	71	7	11	1	0	0	4	3	3	.155	.200	.169	6	-8	1	0	0	.928	-9	S-19	-1.7
1921	Bro-N	12	28	1	2	1	0	0	4	2		.071	.188	.107	-19	-5	0	0	0	.937	4	S-12	0.0
1922	Bro-N	33	91	12	25	5	1	0	14	5	8	.275	.320	.352	74	-4	1	1	-0	.934	-3	S-31/3-2	-0.4
Total	6	236	769	52	175	20	6	0	72	51	67	.228	.286	.269	63	-35	7	1		.919	-41	S-174/3-54,2-8	-7.1

■ CHRIS WARD   Ward, Chris Gilbert b: 5/18/49, Oakland, Cal. BL/TL, 6', 180 lbs. Deb: 9/10/72

YEAR	TM/L	G	AB	R	H	2B	3B	HR	RBI	BB	SO	AVG	OBP	SLG	PRO+	BR/A	SB	CS	SBR	FA	FR	G/POS	TPR
1972	Chi-N	1	1	0	0	0	0	0	0	0	0	.000	.000	.000	-90	-0	0	0	0	.000	0	H	0.0
1974	Chi-N	92	137	8	28	4	0	1	15	18	13	.204	.297	.255	53	-8	0	2	-1	.977	1	O-22/1-6	-0.9
Total	2	93	138	8	28	4	0	1	15	18	13	.203	.295	.254	52	-8	0	2	-1	.977	1	/O-22,1-6	-0.9

■ PIGGY WARD   Ward, Frank Gray b: 4/16/1867, Chambersburg, Pa. d: 10/24/12, Altoona, Pa. BB/TR, 5'9.5", 196 lbs. Deb: 6/12/1883

YEAR	TM/L	G	AB	R	H	2B	3B	HR	RBI	BB	SO	AVG	OBP	SLG	PRO+	BR/A	SB	CS	SBR	FA	FR	G/POS	TPR
1883	Phi-N	1	5	0	0	0	0	0	0	0	2	.000	.000	.000	-99	-1				1.000	-1	/3-1	-0.2
1889	Phi-N	7	25	0	4	1	0	0	4	0	7	.160	.160	.200	0	-3	1			.848	-2	/2-6,O-1	-0.5
1891	Pit-N	6	18	3	6	0	0	0	2	3	3	.333	.455	.333	134	1	3			.833	-1	/O-5	0.0
1892	Bal-N	56	186	28	54	6	5	1	33	31	18	.290	.403	.392	137	10	10			.892	1	O-43/2-7,S-5,C-1	0.9
1893	Bal-N	11	49	11	12	1	3	0	5	5	2	.245	.327	.388	88	-1	4			.846	-1	/O-9,1-2	-0.2
	Cin-N	42	150	44	42	4	1	0	10	37	10	.280	.440	.320	101	3	27			.827	-2	O-40/1-1	-0.1
	Yr	53	199	55	54	5	4	0	15	42	12	.271	.415	.337	99	2	31			.832	-3	O-49/1-3	-0.3
1894	Was-N	98	347	86	105	11	7	0	36	80	31	.303	.447	.370	103	9	41			.900	-23	2-79,O-12/S-3,3-1	-0.9
Total	6	221	780	172	223	23	16	1	90	156	73	.286	.419	.360	106	17	86			.852	-29	O-110/2-92,S-8,13C	-1.0

■ GARY WARD   Ward, Gary Lamell b: 12/6/53, Los Angeles, Cal. BR/TR, 6'2", 202 lbs. Deb: 9/3/79

YEAR	TM/L	G	AB	R	H	2B	3B	HR	RBI	BB	SO	AVG	OBP	SLG	PRO+	BR/A	SB	CS	SBR	FA	FR	G/POS	TPR
1979	Min-A	10	14	2	4	0	0	1	3	3	3	.286	.412	.286	89	-0	0	1	-1	1.000	-1	/O-5,D-3	-0.1
1980	Min-A	13	41	11	19	6	2	1	10	3	6	.463	.500	.780	228	7	0	0	0	1.000	-2	O-12	0.4
1981	Min-A	85	295	42	78	7	6	3	29	28	48	.264	.328	.359	92	-3	5	2	0	.975	6	O-80/D-2	0.0
1982	Min-A	152	570	85	165	33	7	28	91	37	105	.289	.334	.519	127	19	13	1	3	.989	13	*O-150/D-2	3.0
1983	Min-A★	157	623	76	173	34	5	19	88	44	98	.278	.328	.440	105	4	8	1	2	.978	26	*O-152/D-2	2.6
1984	Tex-A	155	602	97	171	21	7	21	79	55	95	.284	.344	.447	113	10	7	5	-1	.987	12	*O-148/D-5	1.7
1985	Tex-A★	154	593	77	170	28	7	15	70	39	97	.287	.332	.433	106	4	26	7	4	.969	3	*O-153/D-1	0.5
1986	Tex-A	105	380	54	120	15	2	5	51	31	72	.316	.373	.405	109	6	12	8	-1	.996	13	O-104/D-1	1.4
1987	NY-A	146	529	65	131	22	1	16	78	33	101	.248	.294	.384	78	-17	9	1	2	.985	-4	O-94,D-36,1-15	-2.3
1988	NY-A	91	231	26	52	8	0	4	24	24	41	.225	.304	.312	73	-8	0	1	-1	.992	-4	O-54,1-11/3-2,D-9	-1.5
1989	NY-A	8	17	3	5	1	0	0	1	3	5	.294	.400	.353	115	1	0	0	0	1.000	-1	/O-6,D-1	-0.1
	Det-A	105	273	24	69	10	2	9	29	21	54	.251	.304	.400	99	-0	1	3	-2	.990	0	O-51,1-26,D-26	-0.6
	Yr	113	292	27	74	11	2	9	30	24	59	.253	.310	.397	100	-1	1	3	-2	.991	-1	O-57,D-27,1-26	-0.7

YEAR	TM/L	G	AB	R	H	2B	3B	HR	RBI	BB	SO	AVG	OBP	SLG	PRO+	BR/A	SB	CS	SBR	FA	FR	G/POS	TPR
1990	Det-A	106	309	32	79	11	2	9	46	30	50	.256	.324	.392	98	-1	2	0	1	.988	-4	O-85,D-13/1-2	-0.7
Total	12	1287	4479	594	1236	196	41	130	597	351	775	.276	.330	.425	104	20	83	30	7	.984	55	*O-1094,D-101/13	4.3

■ JIM WARD
Ward, James H. H. b: 3/2/1855, Boston, Mass. d: 6/4/1886, Boston, Mass. Deb: 8/3/1876

YEAR	TM/L	G	AB	R	H	2B	3B	HR	RBI	BB	SO	AVG	OBP	SLG	PRO+	BR/A	SB	CS	SBR	FA	FR	G/POS	TPR
1876	Phi-N	1	4	1	2	0	0	0	1	0	1	.500	.500	.500	236	1				.750	-0	/C-1	0.0

■ RUBE WARD
Ward, John Andrew b: 2/6/1879, New Lexington, Ohio d: 1/17/45, Akron, Ohio Deb: 4/28/02

YEAR	TM/L	G	AB	R	H	2B	3B	HR	RBI	BB	SO	AVG	OBP	SLG	PRO+	BR/A	SB	CS	SBR	FA	FR	G/POS	TPR
1902	Bro-N	13	31	4	9	1	0	0	2	2		.290	.333	.323	102	0	0			.850	-1	O-11	-0.2

■ JOHN WARD
Ward, John E. b: Washington, D.C. Deb: 5/23/1884

YEAR	TM/L	G	AB	R	H	2B	3B	HR	RBI	BB	SO	AVG	OBP	SLG	PRO+	BR/A	SB	CS	SBR	FA	FR	G/POS	TPR
1884	Was-U	1	4	0	1	0	0	0				.250	.250	.250	54	-0				.000	-1	/O-1	-0.1

■ JAY WARD
Ward, John Francis b: 9/9/38, Brookfield, Mo. BR/TR, 6'1", 185 lbs. Deb: 5/6/63 C

YEAR	TM/L	G	AB	R	H	2B	3B	HR	RBI	BB	SO	AVG	OBP	SLG	PRO+	BR/A	SB	CS	SBR	FA	FR	G/POS	TPR
1963	Min-A	9	15	0	1	1	0	0	2	1	5	.067	.125	.133	-27	-3	0	0	0	1.000	-1	/3-4,O-1	-0.3
1964	Min-A	12	31	4	7	2	0	0	2	6	13	.226	.351	.290	80	-1	0	0	0	.977	0	/2-9,O-3	-0.3
1970	Cin-N	6	3	0	0	0	0	0	0	2	1	.000	.400	.000	17	-0	0	0	0	1.000	-0	/3-2,1-1,2-1	0.0
Total	3	27	49	4	8	3	0	0	4	9	19	.163	.293	.224	46	-3	0	0	0	.977	-1	/2-10,3-6,O-4,1-1	-0.3

■ JOHN WARD
Ward, John Montgomery b: 3/3/1860, Bellefonte, Pa. d: 3/4/25, Augusta, Ga. BL/TR, 5'9", 165 lbs. Deb: 7/15/1878 MH

YEAR	TM/L	G	AB	R	H	2B	3B	HR	RBI	BB	SO	AVG	OBP	SLG	PRO+	BR/A	SB	CS	SBR	FA	FR	G/POS	TPR
1878	Pro-N	37	138	14	27	5	4	1	15	2	13	.196	.207	.312	69	-5				.866	2	P-37	0.0
1879	Pro-N	83	364	71	104	9	4	2	41	7	14	.286	.299	.349	115	6				.938	3	*P-70,3-16/O-8	0.1
1880	Pro-N	86	356	53	81	12	2	0	27	6	16	.228	.240	.272	76	-9				.983	14	*P-70,3-25/O-2,M	0.7
1881	Pro-N	85	357	56	87	18	6	0	53	5	10	.244	.254	.328	83	-7				.887	6	O-40,P-39,S-13	-0.3
1882	Pro-N	83	355	58	87	10	3	1	39	13	22	.245	.272	.299	83	-7				.824	10	O-50,P-33/S-4	0.1
1883	NY-N	88	380	76	97	18	7	7	54	8	25	.255	.271	.395	100	-0				.859	19	O-56,P-34/3-5,S2	1.3
1884	NY-N	113	482	98	122	11	8	2	51	28	47	.253	.294	.322	91	-5				.847	6	O-59,2-47/P-9,M	0.2
1885	NY-N	111	446	72	101	8	9	0	37	17	39	.226	.255	.285	75	-12				.904	6	*S-111	-0.4
1886	NY-N	122	491	82	134	17	5	2	81	19	46	.273	.300	.340	93	-5	36			.870	-3	*S-122	-0.6
1887	NY-N	129	545	114	184	16	5	1	53	29	12	.338	.375	.391	119	15	111			.919	30	*S-129	3.9
1888	*NY-N	122	510	70	128	14	5	2	49	9	13	.251	.265	.310	84	-10	38			.857	-3	*S-122	-1.0
1889	*NY-N	114	479	87	143	13	4	1	67	27	7	.299	.339	.349	92	-5	62			.890	6	*S-108/2-7	0.6
1890	Bro-P	128	561	134	188	15	12	4	60	51	22	.335	.393	.426	112	8	63			.878	21	*S-128,M	2.9
1891	Bro-N	105	441	85	122	13	5	0	39	36	10	.277	.335	.329	94	-3	57			.878	-0	S-87,2-18,M	0.3
1892	Bro-N	148	614	109	163	13	3	1	47	82	19	.265	.355	.301	103	6	88			.920	3	*2-148,M	1.1
1893	NY-N	135	588	129	193	27	9	2	77	47	5	.328	.379	.415	111	8	46			.918	7	*2-134,M	1.5
1894	*NY-N	136	540	100	143	12	5	0	77	34	6	.265	.310	.306	49	-45	39			.924	5	*2-136,M	-2.6
Total	17	1825	7647	1408	2104	231	96	26	867	420	326	.275	.314	.341	93	-69	540			.885	133	S-826,2-491,PO/3	7.8

■ JOE WARD
Ward, Joseph A. b: 9/2/1884, Philadelphia, Pa. d: 8/11/34, Philadelphia, Pa. TR, Deb: 4/24/06

YEAR	TM/L	G	AB	R	H	2B	3B	HR	RBI	BB	SO	AVG	OBP	SLG	PRO+	BR/A	SB	CS	SBR	FA	FR	G/POS	TPR
1906	Phi-N	35	129	12	38	8	6	0	11	5		.295	.321	.450	140	5	2			.929	-6	3-27/2-3,S-1	-0.9
1909	NY-A	9	28	3	5	0	0	0	0	1		.179	.233	.179	30	-2	2			.846	-5	/2-7,1-1	-0.9
	Phi-N	74	184	21	49	8	2	0	23	9		.266	.304	.332	96	-1	7			.944	-10	2-48/S-8,1-5,O-2	-1.3
1910	Phi-N	48	124	11	18	2	1	0	13	3	11	.145	.178	.177	4	-15	1			.975	2	1-32/S-1,3-1	-1.5
Total	3	166	465	47	110	18	9	0	47	18	11	.237	.271	.314	78	-14	12			.929	-20	/2-58,1-38,3-28,SO	-3.7

■ HAP WARD
Ward, Joseph Nichols b: 11/15/1885, Leesburg, N.J. d: 9/13/79, Elmer, N.J. Deb: 5/18/12

YEAR	TM/L	G	AB	R	H	2B	3B	HR	RBI	BB	SO	AVG	OBP	SLG	PRO+	BR/A	SB	CS	SBR	FA	FR	G/POS	TPR
1912	Det-A	1	2	0	0	0	0	0	0	0	0	.000	.000	.000	-99	-1	0			1.000	0	/O-1	0.0

■ KEVIN WARD
Ward, Kevin Michael b: 9/28/61, Lansdale, Pa. BR/TR, 6'1", 195 lbs. Deb: 5/10/91

YEAR	TM/L	G	AB	R	H	2B	3B	HR	RBI	BB	SO	AVG	OBP	SLG	PRO+	BR/A	SB	CS	SBR	FA	FR	G/POS	TPR
1991	SD-N	44	107	13	26	7	2	2	8	9	27	.243	.308	.402	95	-1	1	4	-2	.982	-2	O-33	-0.6
1992	SD-N	81	147	12	29	5	0	3	12	14	38	.197	.276	.293	60	-8	2	3	-1	.946	-6	O-51	-1.7
Total	2	125	254	25	55	12	2	5	20	23	65	.217	.289	.339	75	-9	3	7	-3	.961	-9	/O-84	-2.3

■ PETE WARD
Ward, Peter Thomas b: 7/26/39, Montreal, Que., Can BL/TR, 6'1", 200 lbs. Deb: 9/21/62 C

YEAR	TM/L	G	AB	R	H	2B	3B	HR	RBI	BB	SO	AVG	OBP	SLG	PRO+	BR/A	SB	CS	SBR	FA	FR	G/POS	TPR
1962	Bal-A	8	21	1	3	2	0	0	2	4	5	.143	.280	.238	44	-2	0	0	0	1.000	-0	/O-6	-0.2
1963	Chi-A	157	600	80	177	34	6	22	84	52	77	.295	.356	.482	135	27	7	6	-2	.923	-5	*3-154/2-1,S-1	2.1
1964	Chi-A	144	539	61	152	28	3	23	94	56	76	.282	.352	.473	131	22	1	1	-0	.958	13	*3-138	3.4
1965	Chi-A	138	507	62	125	25	3	10	57	56	83	.247	.329	.367	104	2	2	4	-2	.952	9	*3-134/2-1	0.7
1966	Chi-A	84	251	22	55	7	1	3	24	24	49	.219	.295	.291	74	-1	3	1	0	.989	-2	O-59,3-16/1-5	-1.4
1967	Chi-A	146	467	49	109	16	2	18	62	61	109	.233	.336	.392	119	12	3	2	-0	.991	-17	O-89,1-39,3-22	-1.3
1968	Chi-A	125	399	43	86	10	0	15	50	76	85	.216	.355	.366	117	11	4	3	-1	.946	-9	3-77,1-31,O-22	-0.1
1969	Chi-A	105	199	22	49	7	0	6	32	33	38	.246	.362	.372	101	1	0	0	0	.994	-2	1-25,3-21/O-9	-0.3
1970	NY-A	66	77	5	20	2	1	1	18	9	17	.260	.337	.377	102	0	0	0	0	1.000	-1	1-13	-0.1
Total	9	973	3060	345	776	136	17	98	427	371	539	.254	.342	.405	116	65	20	17	-4	.945	-14	3-562,O-185,1/2S	2.8

■ PRESTON WARD
Ward, Preston Meyer b: 7/24/27, Columbia, Mo. BL/TR, 6'3", 198 lbs. Deb: 4/20/48

YEAR	TM/L	G	AB	R	H	2B	3B	HR	RBI	BB	SO	AVG	OBP	SLG	PRO+	BR/A	SB	CS	SBR	FA	FR	G/POS	TPR
1948	Bro-N	42	146	9	38	9	2	1	15	23		.260	.329	.370	86	-3	0			.990	-2	1-38	-0.5
1950	Chi-N	80	285	31	72	11	2	6	33	27	42	.253	.317	.368	81	-8	3			.995	10	1-76	-0.4
1953	Chi-N	33	100	10	23	5	0	4	12	18	21	.230	.347	.400	92	-1	3	1	0	.961	-7	O-27/1-7	-0.8
	Pit-N	88	281	35	59	7	1	8	27	44	39	.210	.319	.327	69	-12	1	3	-2	.991	4	1-78	-1.2
	Yr	121	381	45	82	12	1	12	39	62	60	.215	.327	.346	76	-13	4	4	-1	.991	-3	1-85,O-27	-2.0
1954	Pit-N	117	360	37	97	16	2	7	48	39	61	.269	.341	.383	90	-5	0	0	0	.984	5	1-48,O-42,3-11	-0.4
1955	Pit-N	84	179	16	38	4	5	2	25	22	28	.212	.299	.380	80	-6	0	0	0	.998	2	1-48/O-1	-0.6
1956	Pit-N	16	30	3	10	0	1	1	11	6	4	.333	.444	.500	157	2	0	0	0	1.000	-5	/3-5,O-5	-0.2
	Cle-A	87	150	18	38	10	0	6	21	16	20	.253	.325	.440	98	-1	0	0	0	.988	-1	1-60,O-17	-0.1
1957	Cle-A	10	11	2	2	1	0	0	0	2	2	.182	.182	.273	23	-1	0	0	0	1.000	-0	/1-1	-0.1
1958	Cle-A	48	148	22	50	3	1	4	21	10	27	.338	.384	.453	133	6	0	1	-1	.957	-3	3-24,1-21	0.2
	KC-A	81	268	28	68	10	1	6	24	27	36	.254	.322	.366	87	-5	0	-1	-1	.989	-7	1-39,3-34/O-2	-1.5
	Yr	129	416	50	118	13	2	10	45	37	63	.284	.344	.397	103	2	0	0	-1	.992	-10	1-60,3-58/O-2	-1.3
1959	KC-A	58	109	8	27	4	1	2	19	7	12	.248	.293	.358	76	-4	0	0	0	.982	-3	1-22/O-1	-0.8
Total	9	744	2067	219	522	83	15	50	262	231	315	.253	.328	.380	88	-36	7	6		.992	-3	1-438/O-95,3-74	-6.0

■ TURNER WARD
Ward, Turner Max b: 4/11/65, Orlando, Fla. BB/TR, 6'2", 200 lbs. Deb: 9/10/90

YEAR	TM/L	G	AB	R	H	2B	3B	HR	RBI	BB	SO	AVG	OBP	SLG	PRO+	BR/A	SB	CS	SBR	FA	FR	G/POS	TPR
1990	Cle-A	14	46	10	16	2	1	1	10	3	8	.348	.388	.500	147	3	3	0	1	.957	0	O-13/D-1	0.4
1991	Cle-A	40	100	11	23	7	0	0	5	10	16	.230	.300	.300	66	-4	0	0	0	1.000	-3	O-38	-0.7
	Tor-A	8	13	1	4	0	0	0	2	1	2	.308	.357	.308	83	-0	0	0	0	1.000	-1	O-6	-0.2
	Yr	48	113	12	27	7	0	0	7	11	18	.239	.306	.301	68	-5	0	0	0	1.000	-3	O-44	-0.9
1992	Tor-A	18	29	7	10	3	0	1	3	4	4	.345	.424	.552	164	3	0	1	-1	1.000	-1	O-12	0.1
1993	Tor-A	72	167	20	32	4	4	3	28	23	26	.192	.293	.311	62	-9	3	3	-1	.990	-7	O-65/1-1	-1.7
1994	Mil-A	102	367	55	85	15	2	9	45	52	68	.232	.332	.357	74	-14	6	2	1	.985	3	O-99/3-1	-1.2
1995	Mil-A	44	129	19	34	3	1	4	16	14	21	.264	.340	.395	86	-3	6	1	1	.989	-2	O-40/D-1	-0.4
1996	Mil-A	43	67	7	12	2	1	2	10	13	17	.179	.313	.328	59	-4	3	0	1	1.000	-4	O-32/D-1	-0.7
Total	7	341	918	130	216	36	7	21	119	120	162	.235	.327	.358	78	-29	21	7	2	.989	-14	O-305/D-3,3-1,1-1	-4.4

■ BUZZY WARES
Wares, Clyde Ellsworth b: 3/23/1886, Vandalia, Mich. d: 5/26/64, South Bend, Ind. BR/TR, 5'10", 150 lbs. Deb: 9/15/13 C

YEAR	TM/L	G	AB	R	H	2B	3B	HR	RBI	BB	SO	AVG	OBP	SLG	PRO+	BR/A	SB	CS	SBR	FA	FR	G/POS	TPR
1913	StL-A	11	35	5	10	2	0	0	1	1	3	.286	.306	.343	92	-1	2			.973	-4	/2-9	-0.5
1914	StL-A	81	215	20	45	10	1	0	23	28	35	.209	.300	.265	73	-7	10	10	-3	.903	-2	S-68/2-8	-0.7
Total	2	92	250	25	55	12	1	0	24	29	38	.220	.301	.276	76	-7	12	10		.973	-6	/S-68,2-17	-1.2

■ FRED WARNER
Warner, Frederick John Rodney b: 1855, Philadelphia, Pa. d: 2/13/1886, Philadelphia, Pa. 5'7", 155 lbs. Deb: 4/30/1875

YEAR	TM/L	G	AB	R	H	2B	3B	HR	RBI	BB	SO	AVG	OBP	SLG	PRO+	BR/A	SB	CS	SBR	FA	FR	G/POS	TPR
1875	Cen-n	14	57	11	14	4	0	0	2	1	2	.246	.259	.316	107	1	0	0	0	.784	-0	O-14	0.1
1876	Phi-N	1	3	0	0	0	0	0	0	0	0	.000	.000	.000	-99	-1	0	0	0	.600	-0	/O-1	-0.1

YEAR	TM/L	G	AB	R	H	2B	3B	HR	RBI	BB	SO	AVG	OBP	SLG	PRO+	BR/A	SB	CS	SBR	FA	FR	G/POS	TPR
1878	Ind-N	43	165	19	41	4	0	0	10	2	15	.248	.257	.273	86	-2				.907	-3	*S-41/O-2	-0.3
1879	Cle-N	76	316	32	77	11	4	0	22	2	20	.244	.248	.304	82	-6				.827	0	3-54,O-21/1-1	-0.5
1883	Phi-N	39	141	13	32	6	1	0	13	5	21	.227	.253	.284	69	-5				.775	-9	3-38/O-1	-1.2
1884	Bro-a	84	352	40	78	4	0	1		17		.222	.259	.241	64	-13				.824	-6	*3-84	-1.7
Total	5	243	977	104	228	25	5	1	45	26	56	.233	.254	.272	73	-27				.815	-18	3-176/S-41,O-25,1-1	-3.8

■ HOOKS WARNER
Warner, Hoke Hayden b: 5/22/1894, Del Rio, Tex. d: 2/19/47, San Francisco, Cal BL/TR, 5'10.5", 170 lbs. Deb: 8/21/16

YEAR	TM/L	G	AB	R	H	2B	3B	HR	RBI	BB	SO	AVG	OBP	SLG	PRO+	BR/A	SB	CS	SBR	FA	FR	G/POS	TPR
1916	Pit-N	44	168	12	40	1	1	2	14	6	19	.238	.264	.292	70	-6	6			.899	-11	3-42/2-1	-1.9
1917	Pit-N	3	5	0	1	0	0	0	0	0	1	.200	.200	.200	22	-0	0			1.000	1	/3-1	0.1
1919	Pit-N	6	8	0	1	0	0	0	2	3	1	.125	.364	.125	48	-0	0			.818	1	/3-3	0.0
1921	Chi-N	14	38	4	8	1	0	0	3	2	1	.211	.268	.237	35	-3	1	1	-0	.957	-1	3-10	-0.4
Total	4	67	219	16	50	2	1	2	19	11	22	.228	.268	.274	61	-10	7	1		.906	-10	/3-56,2-1	-2.2

■ JOHN WARNER
Warner, John Joseph b: 8/15/1872, New York, N.Y. d: 12/21/43, Far Rockaway, N.Y. BL/TR, 5'11", 165 lbs. Deb: 4/23/1895

YEAR	TM/L	G	AB	R	H	2B	3B	HR	RBI	BB	SO	AVG	OBP	SLG	PRO+	BR/A	SB	CS	SBR	FA	FR	G/POS	TPR
1895	Bos-N	3	7	2	1	0	0	0	1	1	0	.143	.333	.143	24	-1	0			.917	1	/C-3	0.0
	Lou-N	67	232	20	62	4	2	1	20	11	16	.267	.320	.315	68	-11	10			.931	-10	C-64/1-3,2-1	-1.2
	Yr	70	239	22	63	4	2	1	21	12	16	.264	.320	.310	67	-11	10			.930	-10	C-67/1-3,2-1	-1.2
1896	Lou-N	33	110	9	25	1	1	0	10	10	10	.227	.303	.255	50	-8	3			.939	9	C-32/1-1	0.4
	NY-N	19	54	9	14	1	0	0	3	3	7	.259	.310	.278	57	-3	1			.922	-1	C-19	-0.2
	Yr	52	164	18	39	2	1	0	13	13	17	.238	.306	.262	52	-11	4			.934	9	C-51/1-1	0.2
1897	NY-N	110	397	50	109	6	3	2	51	26		.275	.344	.320	78	-11	8			.952	16	*C-110	1.4
1898	NY-N	110	373	40	96	14	5	0	42	22		.257	.316	.322	86	-7	9			.968	15	*C-109/O-1	1.7
1899	NY-N	88	293	38	78	8	1	0	19	15		.266	.315	.300	72	-11	15			.952	12	C-82/1-3	0.7
1900	NY-N	34	108	15	27	4	0	0	13	8		.250	.319	.287	71	-4	1			.948	3	C-31	0.1
1901	NY-N	87	291	19	70	6	1	0	20	3		.241	.268	.268	58	-16	3			.967	-3	C-84	-1.1
1902	Bos-A	65	222	19	52	5	7	0	12	13		.234	.286	.320	66	-11	0			.979	4	C-64	0.0
1903	NY-N	89	285	38	81	8	5	0	34	7		.284	.322	.347	87	-5	5			**.986**	12	C-85	1.4
1904	NY-N	86	287	29	57	5	1	1	15	14		.199	.253	.233	48	-17	7			**.982**	2	C-86	-0.7
1905	StL-N	41	137	9	35	2	2	1	12	6		.255	.301	.321	88	-2	2			.958	3	C-41	0.5
	Det-A	36	119	12	24	7	0	1	7	8		.202	.252	.269	65	-5	2			.974	1	C-36	0.0
1906	Det-A	50	153	15	37	4	2	0	10	12		.242	.326	.294	92	-1	4			.978	9	C-49	1.3
	Was-A	32	103	5	21	4	1	1	9	2		.204	.226	.291	65	-5	3			.968	9	C-32	0.8
	Yr	82	256	20	58	8	3	1	19	14		.227	.288	.293	82	-5	7			.974	18	C-81	2.1
1907	Was-A	72	207	11	53	5	0	0	17	12		.256	.306	.280	95	-1	3			.971	-8	C-64	-0.5
1908	Was-A	51	116	8	28	2	1	0	8	8		.241	.313	.276	100	0	7			.982	1	C-41/1-1	-0.1
Total	14	1073	3494	348	870	81	35	6	303	181	33	.249	.303	.297	74	-118	83			.966	73	*C-1032/1-8,O-1,2-1	5.1

■ JACKIE WARNER
Warner, John Joseph b: 8/1/43, Monrovia, Cal. BR/TR, 6', 180 lbs. Deb: 4/12/66

YEAR	TM/L	G	AB	R	H	2B	3B	HR	RBI	BB	SO	AVG	OBP	SLG	PRO+	BR/A	SB	CS	SBR	FA	FR	G/POS	TPR
1966	Cal-A	45	123	22	26	4	1	7	16	9	55	.211	.265	.431	99	-1	0	0	0	.984	-2	O-37	-0.4

■ JACK WARNER
Warner, John Ralph b: 8/29/03, Evansville, Ind. d: 3/13/86, Mt.Vernon, Ill. BR/TR, 5'9.5", 165 lbs. Deb: 9/24/25

YEAR	TM/L	G	AB	R	H	2B	3B	HR	RBI	BB	SO	AVG	OBP	SLG	PRO+	BR/A	SB	CS	SBR	FA	FR	G/POS	TPR
1925	Det-A	10	39	7	13	0	0	0	2	3	6	.333	.381	.333	84	-1	0	0	0	1.000	-2	3-10	-0.2
1926	Det-A	100	311	41	78	8	6	0	34	38	24	.251	.342	.315	71	-12	8	4	0	.956	-4	3-95/S-3	-1.0
1927	Det-A	139	559	78	149	22	9	1	45	47	45	.267	.330	.343	74	-21	14	4	2	.947	-5	*3-138	-1.7
1928	Det-A	75	206	33	44	4	4	0	13	16	15	.214	.274	.272	43	-17	4	4	-1	.944	6	3-52/S-7	-0.9
1929	Bro-N	17	62	3	17	2	0	0	4	7	6	.274	.348	.306	65	-3	3			.945	-2	S-17	-0.3
1930	Bro-N	21	25	4	8	1	0	0	0	2	7	.320	.370	.360	79	-1	1			1.000	2	/3-8	0.1
1931	Bro-N	9	4	2	2	0	0	0	0	1	1	.500	.600	.500	200	1	0			1.000	2	/S-2,3-1	0.3
1933	Phi-N	107	340	31	76	15	1	0	22	28	33	.224	.285	.274	53	-20	1			.973	5	2-71,3-30/S-1	-1.2
Total	8	478	1546	199	387	52	20	1	120	142	137	.250	.319	.312	65	-75	31	12		.950	0	3-334/2-71,S-30	-4.9

■ HAL WARNOCK
Warnock, Harold Charles b: 1/6/12, New York, N.Y. BL/TR, 6'2", 180 lbs. Deb: 9/2/35

YEAR	TM/L	G	AB	R	H	2B	3B	HR	RBI	BB	SO	AVG	OBP	SLG	PRO+	BR/A	SB	CS	SBR	FA	FR	G/POS	TPR
1935	StL-A	6	7	1	2	2	0	0	0	0	3	.286	.286	.571	112	0	0	0	0	1.000	-1	/O-2	-0.1

■ BENNIE WARREN
Warren, Bennie Louis b: 3/2/12, Elk City, Okla. d: 5/11/94, Oklahoma City, Okla. BR/TR, 6'1", 184 lbs. Deb: 9/13/39

YEAR	TM/L	G	AB	R	H	2B	3B	HR	RBI	BB	SO	AVG	OBP	SLG	PRO+	BR/A	SB	CS	SBR	FA	FR	G/POS	TPR
1939	Phi-N	18	56	4	13	0	0	1	7	7	7	.232	.317	.286	65	-3	0			.958	-4	C-17	-0.5
1940	Phi-N	106	289	33	71	6	1	12	34	40	46	.246	.339	.398	107	3	1			.975	-4	C-97/1-1	0.6
1941	Phi-N	121	345	34	74	13	2	9	35	44	66	.214	.309	.342	86	-6	0			.973	-4	*C-110	-0.2
1942	Phi-N	90	225	19	47	6	3	7	20	24	36	.209	.288	.356	92	-3	0			.972	-2	C-78/1-1	0.1
1946	NY-N	39	69	7	11	1	1	4	8	14	21	.159	.301	.377	91	-1	0			.965	1	/C-30	0.2
1947	NY-N	3	5	0	1	0	0	0	0	2	0	.200	.200	.200	6	-1	0			1.000	-1	/C-3	-0.1
Total	6	377	989	97	217	26	7	33	104	129	177	.219	.313	.360	92	-11	1			.972	-13	C-335/1-2	0.1

■ BILL WARREN
Warren, William Hackney "Hack" b: 2/11/1883, Missouri d: 1/28/60, Whiteville, Tenn. BR/TR, 5'8", 165 lbs. Deb: 4/30/14

YEAR	TM/L	G	AB	R	H	2B	3B	HR	RBI	BB	SO	AVG	OBP	SLG	PRO+	BR/A	SB	CS	SBR	FA	FR	G/POS	TPR
1914	Ind-F	26	50	5	12	2	0	0	5	5	7	.240	.309	.280	55	-4	2			.931	-5	C-23	-0.8
1915	New-F	5	3	0	1	0	0	0	1	0	0	.333	.333	.333	93	-0	0			1.000	-0	/C-1,1-1	0.0
Total	2	31	53	5	13	2	0	0	6	5	7	.245	.310	.283	57	-4	2			.932	-5	/C-24,1-1	-0.8

■ RABBIT WARSTLER
Warstler, Harold Burton b: 9/13/03, N.Canton, Ohio d: 5/31/64, N.Canton, Ohio BR/TR, 5'7.5", 150 lbs. Deb: 7/24/30

YEAR	TM/L	G	AB	R	H	2B	3B	HR	RBI	BB	SO	AVG	OBP	SLG	PRO+	BR/A	SB	CS	SBR	FA	FR	G/POS	TPR
1930	Bos-A	54	162	16	30	2	3	1	13	20	21	.185	.275	.253	36	-16	0	2	-1	.947	-3	S-54	-1.3
1931	Bos-A	66	181	20	44	5	3	0	10	15	27	.243	.304	.304	65	-9	2	3	-1	.933	1	2-42,S-19/3-1	-0.5
1932	Bos-A	115	388	26	82	15	5	0	34	22	43	.211	.259	.276	40	-35	9	6	-1	.939	**28**	*S-107	0.1
1933	Bos-A	92	322	44	70	13	1	1	17	42	36	.217	.308	.273	55	-20	2	4	-2	.951	1	S-87	-1.4
1934	Phi-A	117	419	56	99	19	3	1	36	51	30	.236	.321	.303	64	-22	9	3	1	.969	16	*2-107/S-2	0.1
1935	Phi-A	138	496	62	124	20	7	3	59	56	53	.250	.326	.337	72	-20	4			.959	2	*2-136/3-2	-0.7
1936	Phi-A	66	236	27	59	8	6	1	24	36	16	.250	.354	.347	75	-9	2			.973	11	2-66	0.6
	Bos-N	74	304	27	64	6	0	0	17	22	33	.211	.266	.230	37	-27	2			.948	13	S-74	-0.9
1937	Bos-N	149	555	57	124	20	3	0	36	51	62	.223	.291	.276	60	-31	4			.942	-11	*S-149	-3.1
1938	Bos-N	142	467	37	108	10	4	0	40	48	38	.231	.303	.270	65	-22	3			.937	-7	*S-135/2-7	-1.9
1939	Bos-N	114	342	34	83	11	3	0	24	24	31	.243	.292	.292	62	-19	2			.953	-1	S-49,2-43,3-21	-1.1
1940	Bos-N	33	57	6	12	0	0	0	4	10	5	.211	.328	.211	54	-3	0			.974	-1	2-24/3-2,S-1	-0.3
	Chi-N	45	159	19	36	4	1	0	18	8	19	.226	.263	.283	52	-11	1			.939	-1	S-28,2-17	-0.9
	Yr	78	216	25	48	4	1	0	22	18	24	.222	.282	.264	53	-14	1			.960	-2	2-41,S-29/3-2	-1.2
Total	11	1205	4088	431	935	133	36	11	332	405	414	.229	.300	.287	59	-243	42	22		.942	49	S-705,2-442/3-26	-11.3

■ CARL WARWICK
Warwick, Carl Wayne b: 2/27/37, Dallas, Tex. BR/TL, 5'10", 170 lbs. Deb: 4/11/61

YEAR	TM/L	G	AB	R	H	2B	3B	HR	RBI	BB	SO	AVG	OBP	SLG	PRO+	BR/A	SB	CS	SBR	FA	FR	G/POS	TPR
1961	LA-N	19	11	2	1	0	0	0	0	0	2	.091	.231	.091	-9	-2	0	0	0	1.000	-4	O-12	-0.6
	StL-N	55	152	27	38	6	2	4	16	18	33	.250	.329	.395	83	-4	3	0	1	.970	-5	O-48	-1.1
	Yr	74	163	29	39	6	2	4	17	20	36	.239	.320	.374	77	-5	3	0	1	.970	-10	O-60	-1.7
1962	StL-N	13	23	4	8	0	1	0	4	2	2	.348	.400	.478	123	1	1	2	0	1.000	-1	O-10	0.0
	Hou-N	130	477	63	124	17	1	16	60	38	77	.260	.319	.400	98	-3	2	3	1	.986	1	*O-128	-1.1
	Yr	143	500	67	132	17	1	16	64	40	79	.264	.319	.404	98	-3	3	5	1	.986	-0	*O-138	-1.1
1963	Hou-N	150	528	49	134	19	5	7	47	49	70	.254	.320	.348	98	-1	3	3	4	.988	-2	*O-141/1-2	-1.3
1964	*StL-N	88	158	14	41	7	1	3	15	11	30	.259	.308	.373	83	-3	2	0	1	.933	-6	O-49	-1.1
1965	StL-N	50	77	3	12	2	1	0	6	4	18	.156	.198	.208	13	-3	0	0	0	.960	-3	O-21/1-4	-0.4
	Bal-N	9	14	3	0	0	0	0	0	3	2	.000	.176	.000	-44	-3	0	0	0	1.000	-1	/O-3	-0.4
1966	Chi-N	16	22	3	5	0	0	0	3	2	7	.227	.227	.227	27	-2				.980	-24	O-10	-0.4
Total	6	530	1462	168	363	51	10	30	149	127	241	.248	.309	.360	87	-26	13	6	0	.980	-24	O-422/1-6	-7.3

■ BILL WARWICK
Warwick, Firmin Newton b: 11/26/1897, Philadelphia, Pa. d: 12/19/84, San Antonio, Tex. BR/TR, 6'0.5", 180 lbs. Deb: 7/18/21

YEAR	TM/L	G	AB	R	H	2B	3B	HR	RBI	BB	SO	AVG	OBP	SLG	PRO+	BR/A	SB	CS	SBR	FA	FR	G/POS	TPR
1921	Pit-N	1	1	0	0	0	0	0	0	0	0	.000	.000	.000	-97	-0	0	1		.500	-0	/C-1	0.0
1925	StL-N	13	41	8	12	1	2	1	6	5	5	.293	.370	.488	114	1	0	1	-1	1.000	-4	C-13	-0.3

YEAR	TM/L	G	AB	R	H	2B	3B	HR	RBI	BB	SO	AVG	OBP	SLG	PRO+	BR/A	SB	CS	SBR	FA	FR	G/POS	TPR
1926	StL-N	9	14	0	5	0	0	0	2	0	2	.357	.357	.357	89	-0	0	0		.923	2	/C-9	0.2
Total	3	23	56	8	17	1	2	1	8	5	7	.304	.361	.446	105	0	0	1		.954	-2	/C-23	-0.1

■ JIMMY WASDELL
Wasdell, James Charles   b: 5/15/14, Cleveland, Ohio   d: 8/6/83, New Port Richey, Fla.   BL/TL, 5'11", 185 lbs.   Deb: 9/3/37

YEAR	TM/L	G	AB	R	H	2B	3B	HR	RBI	BB	SO	AVG	OBP	SLG	PRO+	BR/A	SB	CS	SBR	FA	FR	G/POS	TPR
1937	Was-A	32	110	13	28	4	4	2	12	7	13	.255	.299	.418	82	-4	0	1	-1	.995	-0	1-21/O-7	-0.7
1938	Was-A	53	140	19	33	2	1	2	16	12	12	.236	.296	.307	55	-10	5	2	0	.996	-1	1-26/O-6	-1.3
1939	Was-A	29	109	12	33	5	1	0	13	9	16	.303	.361	.367	94	-1	3	1	0	.964	-2	1-28	-0.6
1940	Was-A	10	35	3	3	1	0	0	0	2	7	.086	.135	.114	-37	-7	0	0	0	1.000	-1	/1-8	-0.9
	Bro-N	77	230	35	64	14	4	3	37	18	24	.278	.334	.413	99	-1	4			.947	-2	O-42,1-17	-1.1
1941	*Bro-N	94	265	39	79	14	3	4	48	16	15	.298	.345	.419	110	3	2			.956	-6	O-54,1-15	-0.8
1942	Pit-N	122	409	44	106	11	2	3	38	47	22	.259	.337	.318	90	-4	1			.957	-3	O-97/1-7	-1.4
1943	Pit-N	4	2	0	1	0	0	0	1	2	0	.500	.750	.500	256	1	0			.000	0	H	0.1
	Phi-N	141	522	54	136	19	6	4	67	46	22	.261	.323	.343	96	-3	6			.988	-8	1-82,O-56	-2.0
	Yr	145	524	54	137	19	6	4	68	48	22	.261	.326	.344	97	-2	6			.988	-8	1-82,O-56	-1.9
1944	Phi-N	133	451	47	125	20	3	3	40	45	17	.277	.344	.355	100	1	0			.980	-9	*O-121/1-4	-1.5
1945	Phi-N	134	500	65	150	19	8	7	60	32	11	.300	.346	.412	113	7	7			.967	-2	O-65,1-63	-0.2
1946	Phi-N	26	51	7	13	0	2	1	5	3	2	.255	.309	.392	101	-0	0			.923	-2	O-11/1-2	-0.3
	Cle-A	32	41	1	11	0	0	0	4	4	4	.268	.333	.268	74	-1	1	0	0	.939	-2	/1-4,O-3	-0.3
1947	Cle-A	1	1	0	0	0	0	0	0	0	0	.000	.000	.000	-99	-0	0	0	0	.000	0	H	0.0
Total	11	888	2866	339	782	109	34	29	341	243	165	.273	.332	.365	96	-20	29	4		.966	-45	O-462,1-277	-11.0

■ LINK WASEM
Wasem, Lincoln William   b: 1/30/11, Birmingham, Ohio   d: 3/6/79, S.Laguna, Cal.   BR/TR, 5'9.5", 180 lbs.   Deb: 5/5/37

YEAR	TM/L	G	AB	R	H	2B	3B	HR	RBI	BB	SO	AVG	OBP	SLG	PRO+	BR/A	SB	CS	SBR	FA	FR	G/POS	TPR
1937	Bos-N	2	1	0	0	0	0	0	0	0	0	.000	.000	.000	-99	-0	0			1.000	0	/C-2	0.0

■ LIBE WASHBURN
Washburn, Libeus   b: 6/16/1874, Lyme, N.H.   d: 3/22/40, Malone, N.Y.   BB/TL, 5'10", 180 lbs.   Deb: 5/30/02

YEAR	TM/L	G	AB	R	H	2B	3B	HR	RBI	BB	SO	AVG	OBP	SLG	PRO+	BR/A	SB	CS	SBR	FA	FR	G/POS	TPR
1902	NY-N	6	9	1	4	0	0	0		0	2	.444	.615	.444	229	2	1			1.000	-1	/O-3	0.1
1903	Phi-N	8	18	1	3	0	0	0		1	1	.167	.211	.167	8	-2	0			1.000	-1	/P-4,O-2	-0.1
Total	2	14	27	2	7	0	0	0		1	3	.259	.375	.259	89	-0	1			1.000	-1	/O-5,P-4	0.0

■ CLAUDELL WASHINGTON
Washington, Claudell   b: 8/31/54, Los Angeles, Cal.   BL/TL, 6', 190 lbs.   Deb: 7/5/74

YEAR	TM/L	G	AB	R	H	2B	3B	HR	RBI	BB	SO	AVG	OBP	SLG	PRO+	BR/A	SB	CS	SBR	FA	FR	G/POS	TPR
1974	*Oak-A	73	221	16	63	10	5	0	19	13	44	.285	.328	.376	109	2	6	8	-3	.985	-1	D-38,O-32	-0.5
1975	*Oak-A★	148	590	86	182	24	7	10	77	32	80	.308	.344	.424	120	14	40	15	3	.963	-3	*O-148	0.8
1976	Oak-A	134	490	65	126	20	6	5	53	30	90	.257	.304	.353	96	-4	37	20	-1	.978	-1	*O-126/D-4	-1.3
1977	Tex-A	129	521	63	148	31	2	12	68	25	112	.284	.321	.420	99	-2	21	8	2	.978	-1	*O-127/D-1	-0.7
1978	Tex-A	12	42	1	7	0	0	0	2	1	12	.167	.186	.167	-0	-6	0	1	-1	.917	-1	/O-7,D-4	-0.8
	Chi-A	86	314	33	83	16	5	6	31	12	57	.264	.294	.404	94	-4	5	5		.959	-2	O-82/D-1	-1.1
	Yr	98	356	34	90	16	5	6	33	13	69	.253	.281	.376	83	-9	5	6		.957	-3	O-89/D-5	-1.9
1979	Chi-A	131	471	79	132	33	5	13	66	28	93	.280	.325	.454	108	4	19	11	-1	.974	4	*O-122/D-3	0.1
1980	Chi-A	32	90	15	26	4	2	1	12	5	19	.289	.333	.411	103	0	4	2	0	.933	-2	O-23/D-2	-0.2
	NY-N	79	284	38	78	16	4	10	42	20	63	.275	.325	.465	121	7	17	5	2	.978	2	O-70	0.8
1981	Atl-N	85	320	37	93	22	3	5	37	15	47	.291	.330	.425	110	3	12	6	0	.993	2	O-79	0.2
1982	*Atl-N	150	563	94	150	24	6	16	80	50	107	.266	.333	.416	104	3	33	10	4	.950	-4	*O-139	-0.2
1983	Atl-N	134	496	75	138	24	8	9	44	35	103	.278	.326	.413	96	-3	31	9	4	.974	-1	*O-128	-0.1
1984	Atl-N★	120	416	62	119	21	2	17	61	59	77	.286	.376	.469	127	16	21	9	1	.967	-5	*O-107	0.8
1985	Atl-N	122	398	62	110	14	6	15	43	40	66	.276	.344	.455	115	7	14	4	2	.962	-14	O-99	-0.8
1986	Atl-N	40	137	17	37	11	0	5	14	14	26	.270	.338	.460	112	2	4	7	-3	.957	-5	O-38	-0.8
	NY-A	54	135	19	32	5	0	6	16	7	33	.237	.285	.407	87	-3	6	1	1	.985	-6	O-39	-0.8
1987	NY-A	102	312	42	87	17	0	9	44	27	54	.279	.336	.420	100	-0	10	1	2	.988	2	O-72,D-13	0.0
1988	NY-A	126	455	62	140	22	3	11	64	24	74	.308	.345	.442	120	11	15	6	1	.984	2	*O-117	1.0
1989	Cal-A	110	418	53	114	18	4	13	42	27	84	.273	.320	.428	111	5	13	5	1	.975	-3	*O-100/D-7	0.1
1990	Cal-A	12	34	3	6	1	0	1	3	2	8	.176	.222	.294	44	-3	1	0	0	1.000	1	/O-9	-0.2
	NY-A	33	80	4	13	1	0	1	9	4	17	.162	.193	.200	7	-10	3	1	0	1.000	1	O-21/D-2	-1.0
	Yr	45	114	7	19	2	1	1	9	4	25	.167	.195	.228	18	-13	4	1	1	1.000	2	O-30/D-2	-1.2
Total	17	1912	6787	926	1884	334	69	164	824	468	1266	.278	.328	.420	106	40	312	134	13	.973	-37	*O-1685/D-75	-4.7

■ HERB WASHINGTON
Washington, Herbert Lee   b: 11/16/51, Belzoni, Miss.   BR/TR, 6', 170 lbs.   Deb: 4/4/74

YEAR	TM/L	G	AB	R	H	2B	3B	HR	RBI	BB	SO	AVG	OBP	SLG	PRO+	BR/A	SB	CS	SBR	FA	FR	G/POS	TPR
1974	*Oak-A	92	0	29	0	0	0	0	0	0	0	—	—	—	—	0	29	16	-1	.000	0	R	-0.3
1975	Oak-A	13	0	4	0	0	0	0	0	0	0	—	—	—	—	0	2	1	0	.000	0	R	0.0
Total	2	105	0	33	0	0	0	0	0	0	0	—	—	—	—	0	31	17	-1			-0,-0	-0.3

■ LA RUE WASHINGTON
Washington, La Rue   b: 9/7/53, Long Beach, Cal.   BR/TR, 6', 170 lbs.   Deb: 9/7/78

YEAR	TM/L	G	AB	R	H	2B	3B	HR	RBI	BB	SO	AVG	OBP	SLG	PRO+	BR/A	SB	CS	SBR	FA	FR	G/POS	TPR
1978	Tex-A	3	3	0	0	0	0	0	0	0	1	.000	.000	.000	-99	-1	0	0	0	1.000	2	/2-2,D-1	0.1
1979	Tex-A	25	18	5	5	0	0	0	2	4	0	.278	.409	.278	90	-1	2	1	0	1.000	-3	O-13/3-1,D-1	-0.3
Total	2	28	21	5	5	0	0	0	2	4	1	.238	.360	.238	67	-1	2	1	0	1.000	-1	/O-13,D-2,2-2,3-1	-0.2

■ RON WASHINGTON
Washington, Ronald   b: 4/29/52, New Orleans, La.   BR/TR, 5'11", 163 lbs.   Deb: 9/10/77   C

YEAR	TM/L	G	AB	R	H	2B	3B	HR	RBI	BB	SO	AVG	OBP	SLG	PRO+	BR/A	SB	CS	SBR	FA	FR	G/POS	TPR
1977	LA-N	10	19	4	7	0	0	0	1	0	2	.368	.400	.368	108	0	1	1	-0	.857	-2	S-10	-0.1
1981	Min-A	28	84	8	19	3	1	0	5	4	14	.226	.270	.286	56	-5	4	1	1	.951	6	S-26/O-2	0.4
1982	Min-A	119	451	48	122	17	6	5	39	14	79	.271	.294	.368	78	-14	3	3	-1	.972	-44	S-91,2-37/3-1	-5.1
1983	Min-A	99	317	28	78	7	3	4	26	22	50	.246	.297	.325	69	-13	10	5	0	.962	-17	S-81,2-14/3-1,D-1	-2.2
1984	Min-A	88	197	25	58	11	5	3	23	4	31	.294	.312	.447	102	0	1	1	0	.978	-16	S-71/2-9,3-2,D-4	-1.2
1985	Min-A	70	135	24	37	6	4	1	14	8	15	.274	.315	.400	89	-2	5	1	1	.951	-4	S-31,2-24/3-7,1D	-0.2
1986	Min-A	48	74	15	19	3	0	4	11	3	21	.257	.286	.459	96	-1	1	2	-1	.917	-5	2-16,D-15/S-7,3-3	-0.2
1987	Bal-A	26	79	7	16	3	1	1	6	1	6	.203	.213	.304	36	-7	0	1	0	1.000	-2	3-20/2-3,O-2,S-1,D	-0.6
1988	Cle-A	69	223	30	57	14	2	2	21	9	35	.256	.300	.363	82	-5	3	3	-1	.933	-14	S-54/3-8,2-7,D-1	-1.6
1989	Hou-N	7	7	1	1	1	0	0	0	0	4	.143	.143	.286	20	-1	0	0	0	.000	-0	/2-1,3-1	-0.1
Total	10	564	1586	190	414	65	22	20	146	65	266	.261	.294	.368	79	-49	28	18	-2	.958	-88	S-372,2-111/3DO1	-11.0

■ GEORGE WASHINGTON
Washington, Sloan Vernon "Vern"   b: 6/4/07, Linden, Tex.   d: 2/17/85, Linden, Tex.   BL/TR, 5'11.5", 190 lbs.   Deb: 4/17/35

YEAR	TM/L	G	AB	R	H	2B	3B	HR	RBI	BB	SO	AVG	OBP	SLG	PRO+	BR/A	SB	CS	SBR	FA	FR	G/POS	TPR
1935	Chi-A	108	339	40	96	22	3	8	47	10	18	.283	.310	.437	89	-7	1	0	0	.974	0	O-79	-0.9
1936	Chi-A	20	49	6	8	2	0	1	5	1	4	.163	.180	.265	8	-7	0	0	0	.938	-2	O-12	-0.8
Total	2	128	388	46	104	24	3	9	52	11	22	.268	.294	.415	78	-15	1	0	0	.970	-2	/O-91	-1.7

■ U L WASHINGTON
Washington, U L   b: 10/27/53, Stringtown, Okla.   BB/TR, 5'11", 175 lbs.   Deb: 9/6/77

YEAR	TM/L	G	AB	R	H	2B	3B	HR	RBI	BB	SO	AVG	OBP	SLG	PRO+	BR/A	SB	CS	SBR	FA	FR	G/POS	TPR
1977	KC-A	10	20	0	4	1	1	0	1	5	4	.200	.360	.350	94	-0	1	0	0	.872	0	/S-9	0.1
1978	KC-A	69	129	10	34	2	1	0	9	10	20	.264	.317	.295	71	-5	12	6	0	.927	-11	S-49,2-19/D-1	-1.2
1979	KC-A	101	268	32	68	12	5	2	25	20	44	.254	.306	.358	77	-9	10	7	-1	.970	3	S-50,2-46/3-1,D-3	-1.2
1980	*KC-A	153	549	79	150	16	11	6	53	53	78	.273	.337	.375	94	-4	20	7	2	.957	-26	*S-152	-1.1
1981	*KC-A	98	339	40	77	19	1	2	29	41	43	.227	.311	.307	79	-8	10	10	-3	.973	-21	S-98	-2.4
1982	KC-A	119	437	64	125	19	3	10	60	38	48	.286	.343	.412	106	4	23	7	3	.961	-11	*S-117/D-1	0.7
1983	KC-A	144	547	76	129	19	6	5	41	48	78	.236	.299	.320	70	-22	40	7	8	.947	-10	*S-140/D-1	-1.0
1984	*KC-A	63	170	18	38	6	0	1	10	14	31	.224	.283	.276	55	-10	4	6	-2	.961	0	S-61	-0.7
1985	Mon-N	68	193	24	48	9	4	1	17	15	33	.249	.303	.352	88	-4	3	0	0	.978	-14	2-43/S-9,3-3	-1.2
1986	Pit-N	72	135	14	27	0	4	0	10	15	27	.200	.280	.259	49	-9	6	0	2	.947	-8	S-51/2-3	-1.2
1987	Pit-N	10	10	1	3	0	0	0	0	3	4	.300	.417	.300	93	0	0	0	0	.833	-0	S-1,3-1	0.0
Total	11	907	2797	358	703	103	36	27	255	261	409	.251	.315	.343	82	-67	132	53		.956	-93	S-737,2-111/D-6,3-5	-8.0

■ MARK WASINGER
Wasinger, Mark Thomas   b: 8/4/61, Monterey, Cal.   BR/TR, 6', 165 lbs.   Deb: 5/27/86

YEAR	TM/L	G	AB	R	H	2B	3B	HR	RBI	BB	SO	AVG	OBP	SLG	PRO+	BR/A	SB	CS	SBR	FA	FR	G/POS	TPR
1986	SD-N	3	8	0	0	0	0	0	1	0	2	.000	.000	.000	-99	-2	0	0	1	.500	-1	/3-3,2-1	-0.4
1987	SF-N	44	80	16	22	3	0	1	3	8	14	.275	.341	.350	88	-1	2	0	1	.973	3	3-21,2-10/S-2	0.2
1988	SF-N	3	2	1	0	0	0	0	0	0	0	.000	.000	.000	-99	-1	0	0	0	.000	0	/3-1	-0.1
Total	3	50	90	17	22	3	0	1	4	8	16	.244	.306	.311	68	-4	2	0	1	.907	2	/3-25,2-11,S-2	-0.3

YEAR	TM/L	G	AB	R	H	2B	3B	HR	RBI	BB	SO	AVG	OBP	SLG	PRO+	BR/A	SB	CS	SBR	FA	FR	G/POS	TPR

■ FRED WATERMAN   Waterman, Frederick A.   b: 12/1845, New York, N.Y.   d: 12/16/1899, Cincinnati, Ohio   5'7.5", 148 lbs.   Deb: 5/5/1871

1871	Oly-n	32	158	46	50	7	4	0	17	10	0	.316	.357	.411	127	7	11	3	2	.695	2	*3-28/C-6	0.5
1872	Oly-n	9	45	13	17	1	2	0	6	0	0	.378	.378	.489	173	4	0	0	0	.843	3	/3-7,C-2,M	0.4
1873	Was-n	15	80	20	28	1	1	0	12	1	1	.350	.358	.387	125	3	0	0	0	.617	-6	/S-9,O-4,3-2	-0.3
1875	Chi-n	5	20	2	6	0	0	0	3	0	2	.300	.300	.300	108	0	0	1	0	.545	-3	/3-5	-0.3
Total	4 n	61	303	81	101	9	7	0	38	11	3	.333	.357	.409	132	13	11	4	1	.713	-4	/3-42,S-9,C-8,O-4	0.3

■ JOHN WATHAN   Wathan, John David   b: 10/4/49, Cedar Rapids, Iowa   BR/TR, 6'2", 205 lbs.   Deb: 5/26/76   MC

1976	*KC-A	27	42	5	12	1	0	0	5	2	5	.286	.333	.310	88	-1	0	2	-1	.984	-1	C-23/1-3	-0.2
1977	*KC-A	55	119	18	39	5	3	2	21	5	8	.328	.355	.471	122	3	2	0	1	.993	-2	C-35/1-5,D-2	-0.2
1978	*KC-A	67	190	19	57	10	1	2	28	3	12	.300	.325	.395	99	-1	2	1	0	1.000	1	1-47,C-21	-0.2
1979	KC-A	90	199	26	41	7	3	2	28	7	24	.206	.233	.302	42	-16	2	1	0	.993	-2	1-49,C-23,D-11/O-3	-2.0
1980	*KC-A	126	453	57	138	14	7	6	58	50	42	.305	.377	.406	114	10	17	3	3	.982	-11	C-77,O-35,1-12	0.4
1981	*KC-A	89	301	24	76	9	3	1	19	19	23	.252	.301	.312	78	-9	11	6	-0	.979	-11	C-73,O-16/1-1	-1.8
1982	KC-A	121	448	79	121	11	3	3	51	48	46	.270	.343	.328	85	-7	36	9	5	.980	-17	*C-120/1-3	-1.5
1983	KC-A	128	437	49	107	18	3	2	32	27	56	.245	.290	.314	66	-20	28	7	4	.985	-4	C-92,1-37/O-9	-1.8
1984	*KC-A	97	171	17	31	7	1	2	10	21	34	.181	.271	.269	50	-12	6	6	-2	.975	5	C-59,1-33/O-1,D-4	-0.7
1985	*KC-A	60	145	11	34	8	1	1	9	17	15	.234	.319	.324	76	-4	1	1	-0	.986	12	C-49/1-6,D-2	0.9
Total	10	860	2505	305	656	90	25	21	261	199	265	.262	.320	.343	83	-56	105	36	10	.982	-31	C-572,1-196/O-64,D	-6.7

■ DAVE WATKINS   Watkins, David Roger   b: 3/15/44, Owensboro, Ky.   BR/TR, 5'10", 185 lbs.   Deb: 4/9/69

| 1969 | Phi-N | 69 | 148 | 17 | 26 | 2 | 1 | 4 | 12 | 22 | 53 | .176 | .291 | .284 | 63 | -7 | 2 | 3 | -1 | .981 | -5 | C-54/O-5,3-1 | -1.2 |

■ GEORGE WATKINS   Watkins, George Archibald   b: 6/4/1900, Freestone Co., Tex   d: 6/1/70, Houston, Tex.   BL/TR, 6', 175 lbs.   Deb: 4/15/30

1930	*StL-N	119	391	85	146	32	7	17	87	24	49	.373	.415	.621	141	25	5			.956	-6	O-89,1-13/2-1	1.1
1931	*StL-N	131	503	93	145	30	13	13	51	31	66	.288	.336	.477	112	7	15			.958	-6	*O-129	-0.7
1932	StL-N	127	458	67	143	35	3	9	63	45	46	.312	.384	.461	122	15	18			.949	3	*O-120	1.0
1933	StL-N	138	525	66	146	24	5	5	62	39	62	.278	.342	.371	98	-0	11			.953	1	*O-135	-0.7
1934	NY-N	105	296	38	73	18	3	6	33	24	34	.247	.316	.389	90	-5	2			.944	-10	O-81	-1.7
1935	Phi-N	150	600	80	162	25	5	17	76	40	78	.270	.320	.413	87	-12	3			.958	-5	*O-148	-1.2
1936	Phi-N	19	70	7	17	4	0	2	5	5	13	.243	.293	.386	74	-3	2			.889	-3	O-17	-0.6
	Bro-N	105	364	54	93	24	6	4	43	38	34	.255	.334	.387	93	-4	5			.969	-4	*O-98	-1.1
	Yr	124	434	61	110	28	6	6	48	43	47	.253	.328	.387	90	-6	7			.959	-7	*O-115	-1.7
Total	7	894	3207	490	925	192	42	73	420	246	382	.288	.347	.443	105	24	61			.954	-20	O-817/1-13,2-1	-3.9

■ ED WATKINS   Watkins, James Edward   b: 6/21/1877, Philadelphia, Pa.   d: 3/29/33, Kelvin, Ariz.   Deb: 9/6/02

| 1902 | Phi-N | 1 | 3 | 0 | 0 | 0 | 0 | 0 | 0 | 0 | 1 | .000 | .250 | .000 | -22 | -0 | 0 | | | 1.000 | -0 | /O-1 | -0.1 |

■ BILL WATKINS   Watkins, William Henry   b: 5/5/1858, Brantford, Ont., Can   d: 6/9/37, Port Huron, Mich.   5'10", 156 lbs.   Deb: 8/1/1884   M

| 1884 | Ind-a | 34 | 127 | 16 | 26 | 4 | 0 | 0 | | 5 | | .205 | .241 | .236 | 58 | -6 | | | | .845 | -6 | 3-23/2-9,S-2,M | -1.0 |

■ NEAL WATLINGTON   Watlington, Julius Neal   b: 12/25/22, Yanceyville, N.C.   BL/TR, 6', 195 lbs.   Deb: 7/10/53

| 1953 | Phi-A | 21 | 44 | 4 | 7 | 1 | 0 | 0 | 3 | 3 | 8 | .159 | .213 | .182 | 7 | -6 | 0 | 1 | -1 | .978 | 0 | /C-9 | -0.6 |

■ ART WATSON   Watson, Arthur Stanhope "Watty"   b: 1/11/1884, Jeffersonville, Ind.   d: 5/9/50, Buffalo, N.Y.   BL/TR, 5'10", 175 lbs.   Deb: 5/19/14

1914	Bro-F	22	46	7	13	4	1	1	3	1	6	.283	.298	.478	140	-0	0			.977	2	C-18	0.3
1915	Bro-F	9	19	4	5	0	3	0	1	3	4	.263	.364	.579	164	1	0			.957	-3	/C-7	-0.1
	Buf-F	22	30	6	14	1	0	1	13	0	4	.467	.467	.600	195	3	0			.778	-4	C-6,O-1	-0.1
	Yr	31	49	10	19	1	3	1	14	3	8	.388	.423	.592	182	4	0			.878	-7	C-13/O-1	-0.2
Total	2	53	95	17	32	5	4	2	17	4	14	.337	.364	.537	147	4	0			.946	-5	/C-31,O-1	0.1

■ JOHNNY WATSON   Watson, John Thomas   b: 1/16/08, Tazewell, Va.   d: 4/29/65, Huntington, W.Va.   BL/TR, 6', 175 lbs.   Deb: 9/26/30

| 1930 | Det-A | 4 | 12 | 1 | 3 | 2 | 0 | 0 | 3 | 1 | 2 | .250 | .308 | .417 | 80 | -0 | 0 | 0 | 0 | .933 | -1 | /S-4 | -0.1 |

■ BOB WATSON   Watson, Robert Jose "Bull"   b: 4/10/46, Los Angeles, Cal.   BR/TR, 6'2", 205 lbs.   Deb: 9/9/66   C

1966	Hou-N	1	1	0	0	0	0	0	0	0	0	.000	.000	.000	-99	-0	0	0	0	.000	0	H	0.0
1967	Hou-N	6	14	1	3	0	0	1	2	0	3	.214	.214	.429	82	-0	0	0	0	.958	0	/1-3	-0.1
1968	Hou-N	45	140	13	32	7	0	2	8	13	32	.229	.299	.321	88	-2	1	0	0	.885	-5	O-40	-1.0
1969	Hou-N	20	40	3	11	3	0	0	3	6	9	.275	.396	.350	113	1	0	0	0	1.000	0	/O-6,1-5,C-1	0.0
1970	Hou-N	97	327	48	89	19	2	11	46	24	59	.272	.330	.443	110	3	1	1	-0	.992	-8	1-83/C-6,O-1	-1.2
1971	Hou-N	129	468	49	135	17	3	9	67	41	56	.288	.348	.395	113	8	2	3	-2	.985	-10	O-87,1-45	-1.3
1972	Hou-N	147	548	74	171	27	4	16	86	53	83	.312	.381	.464	142	30	1	6	-2	.978	-6	*O-143/1-2	1.8
1973	Hou-N★	158	573	97	179	24	3	16	94	85	73	.312	.405	.449	137	31	3	4	-2	.969	-4	*O-142,1-26/C-3	2.2
1974	Hou-N	150	524	69	156	19	4	11	67	60	61	.298	.373	.412	125	18	3	4	-2	.981	-10	*O-140,1-35	0.1
1975	Hou-N★	132	485	67	157	27	1	18	85	40	50	.324	.379	.495	152	32	3	5	-2	.993	-2	*1-118/O-9	2.1
1976	Hou-N	157	585	76	183	31	3	16	102	62	64	.313	.381	.458	151	38	5	3	-1	.990	-2	*1-155	2.6
1977	Hou-N	151	554	77	160	38	6	22	110	57	69	.289	.362	.498	141	30	5	0	2	.994	12	*1-146	3.5
1978	Hou-N	139	461	51	133	25	4	14	79	51	57	.289	.364	.451	137	22	3	1	0	.992	10	*1-128	2.6
1979	Hou-N	49	163	15	39	4	3	0	18	16	23	.239	.307	.319	75	-6	0	0	0	.993	3	1-44	-0.6
	Bos-A	84	312	48	105	19	4	13	53	29	33	.337	.402	.548	145	20	3	2	-1	.988	2	1-58,D-26	1.7
1980	*NY-A	130	469	62	144	25	4	13	68	48	56	.307	.373	.456	128	18	2	1	0	.990	-2	*1-104,D-21	1.0
1981	*NY-A	59	156	15	33	3	0	1	12	24	17	.212	.317	.385	103	1	0	0	0	.997	-1	1-50/D-6	-0.3
1982	NY-A	9	17	3	4	3	0	0	3	0	0	.235	.350	.412	110	0	0	0	0	1.000	-1	/1-6,D-1	-0.1
	Atl-N	57	114	16	28	3	1	5	22	14	20	.246	.328	.421	104	1	0	0	0	1.000	-1	1-27/O-2	-0.5
1983	Atl-N	65	149	14	46	9	0	6	37	18	23	.309	.383	.490	131	6	0	2	-1	.984	-3	1-34	-0.4
1984	Atl-N	49	85	4	18	4	0	2	12	9	12	.212	.287	.329	68	-4	0	0	0	.983	1	1-19	-0.4
Total	19	1832	6185	802	1826	307	41	184	989	653	796	.295	.367	.447	130	247	27	28	-9	.991	-27	*1-1088,O-570/DC	12.1

■ ALLIE WATT   Watt, Albert Bailey   b: 12/12/1899, Philadelphia, Pa.   d: 3/15/68, Norfolk, Va.   BR/TR, 5'8", 154 lbs.   Deb: 10/3/20   F

| 1920 | Was-A | 1 | 1 | 0 | 1 | 1 | 0 | 0 | 1 | 0 | 0 | 1.000 | 1.000 | 2.000 | 700 | 1 | 0 | 0 | 0 | 1.000 | 0 | /2-1 | 0.1 |

■ JOHNNY WATWOOD   Watwood, John Clifford "Lefty"   b: 8/17/05, Alexander City, Ala.   d: 3/1/80, Goodwater, Ala.   BL/TL, 6'1", 186 lbs.   Deb: 4/16/29

1929	Chi-A	85	278	33	84	12	6	2	28	22	21	.302	.351	.410	98	-1	6	3	0	.942	-2	O-77	-0.7
1930	Chi-A	133	427	75	129	25	6	2	51	52	35	.302	.382	.393	100	2	5	7	-3	.989	3	1-62,O-52	-0.7
1931	Chi-A	128	367	51	104	16	6	1	47	56	30	.283	.380	.368	103	4	9	3	1	.944	-3	*O-102/1-4	0.2
1932	Chi-A	13	49	5	15	2	0	0	1	3		.306	.333	.347	82	-1	0	0	0	.960	-2	O-13	-0.4
	Bos-A	95	266	26	66	11	0	0	30	20	11	.248	.301	.289	55	-17	7	4	-0	.945	-1	O-46,1-18	-2.2
	Yr	108	315	31	81	13	0	0	30	21	14	.257	.306	.298	59	-19	7	4	-0	.948	-4	O-59,1-18	-2.6
1933	Bos-A	13	30	2	4	0	0	0	2	3		.133	.212	.133	-7	-5	0	0	0	.950	-1	/O-9	-0.5
1939	Phi-N	2	6	0	1	0	0	0	0	0	0	.167	.167	.167	-11	-1	0	0	0	.933	-1	/1-2	-0.2
Total	6	469	1423	192	403	66	16	5	158	154	103	.283	.356	.363	89	-19	27	17		.948	-0	O-299/1-86	-4.5

■ BOB WAY   Way, Robert Clinton   b: 4/2/06, Emlenton, Pa.   d: 6/20/74, Pittsburgh, Pa.   BR/TR, 5'10.5", 168 lbs.   Deb: 4/12/27

| 1927 | Chi-A | 5 | 3 | 1 | 1 | 0 | 0 | 0 | 1 | 0 | 0 | .333 | .333 | .333 | 75 | -0 | 0 | 0 | 0 | 1.000 | 0 | /2-1 | 0.0 |

■ ROY WEATHERLY   Weatherly, Cyril Roy "Stormy"   b: 2/25/15, Warren, Tex.   d: 1/19/91, Woodville, Tex.   BL/TR, 5'6.5", 170 lbs.   Deb: 6/27/36

1936	Cle-A	84	349	64	117	26	5	16	29	16	29	.335	.368	.519	115	6	3	8	-4	.973	-6	O-84	0.3
1937	Cle-A	53	134	19	27	4	0	5	13	6	14	.201	.246	.343	47	-12	3	0	1	.964	-3	O-38/3-1	-1.5
1938	Cle-A	83	210	30	55	14	3	2	18	14	14	.262	.308	.386	74	-9	8	5	-1	.975	-1	O-55	-1.1
1939	Cle-A	95	323	43	100	16	6	1	32	19	23	.310	.348	.406	95	-3	5	3	0	.961	-8	O-76	-1.1
1940	Cle-A	135	578	90	175	35	11	12	59	27	26	.303	.335	.464	108	4	9	5	-2	.969	6	*O-135	0.1
1941	Cle-A	102	363	59	105	21	5	3	37	32	20	.289	.350	.399	103	1	2	5	-2	.968	-8	O-88	-1.4

YEAR	TM/L	G	AB	R	H	2B	3B	HR	RBI	BB	SO	AVG	OBP	SLG	PRO+	BR/A	SB	CS	SBR	FA	FR	G/POS	TPR
1942	Cle-A	128	473	61	122	23	7	5	39	35	25	.258	.310	.368	96	-5	8	13	-5	.991	2	*O-117	-1.4
1943	*NY-A	77	280	37	74	8	3	7	28	18	9	.264	.311	.389	104	0	4	7	-3	.983	-2	O-68	-0.9
1946	NY-A	2	2	0	1	0	0	0	0	0	0	.500	.500	.500	178	0	0	0	0	.000	0	H	0.0
1950	NY-N	52	69	10	18	3	3	0	11	13	10	.261	.378	.391	102	1	0	0		1.000	-1	O-15	-0.1
Total	10	811	2781	415	794	152	44	43	290	180	170	.286	.331	.418	99	-16	42	49		.975	-10	O-676/3-1	-7.1

■ ART WEAVER
Weaver, Arthur Coggshall "Six O'Clock" b: 4/7/1879, Wichita, Kan. d: 3/23/17, Denver, Colo. TR, 6'1", 160 lbs. Deb: 9/14/02

YEAR	TM/L	G	AB	R	H	2B	3B	HR	RBI	BB	SO	AVG	OBP	SLG	PRO+	BR/A	SB	CS	SBR	FA	FR	G/POS	TPR
1902	StL-N	11	33	2	6	0	1	0	3	1		.182	.206	.242	40	-2				.983	2	C-11	0.0
1903	StL-N	16	49	4	12	0	0	0	5	4		.245	.302	.245	58	-3	1			.969	3	C-16	0.2
	Pit-N	16	48	8	11	0	1	0	3	2		.229	.260	.271	50	-3	0			.978	-1	C-11/1-5	-0.3
	Yr	32	97	12	23	0	1	0	8	6		.237	.282	.258	54	-6	1			.972	1	C-27/1-5	-0.1
1905	StL-A	28	92	5	11	2	1	0	3	1		.120	.129	.163	-8	-11	0			.962	5	C-28	-0.4
1908	Chi-A	15	35	1	7	1	0	0	1	1		.200	.222	.229	47	-2	0			.953	-5	C-15	-0.7
Total	4	86	257	20	47	5	2	0	15	9		.183	.211	.218	31	-22	1			.967	4	/C-81,1-5	-1.2

■ BUCK WEAVER
Weaver, George Daniel b: 8/18/1890, Pottstown, Pa. d: 1/31/56, Chicago, Ill. BB/TR, 5'11", 170 lbs. Deb: 4/11/12

YEAR	TM/L	G	AB	R	H	2B	3B	HR	RBI	BB	SO	AVG	OBP	SLG	PRO+	BR/A	SB	CS	SBR	FA	FR	G/POS	TPR
1912	Chi-A	147	523	55	117	21	8	1	43	9		.224	.245	.300	58	-31	12			.915	-6	*S-147	-2.5
1913	Chi-A	151	533	51	145	17	8	4	52	15	60	.272	.302	.356	94	-7	20			.929	34	*S-151	4.2
1914	Chi-A	136	541	64	133	20	9	2	28	20	40	.246	.279	.327	83	-14	14	20	-8	.928	5	*S-134	-0.6
1915	Chi-A	148	563	83	151	18	11	3	49	32	58	.268	.316	.355	98	-4	24	20	-5	.939	1	*S-148	0.4
1916	Chi-A	151	582	78	132	27	6	3	38	30	48	.227	.280	.309	76	-19	22	13	-1	.941	7	3-85,S-66	-0.8
1917	*Chi-A	118	447	64	127	16	5	3	32	27	29	.284	.332	.362	110	4	19			.949	9	*3-107,S-10	1.7
1918	Chi-A	112	420	37	126	12	5	0	29	11	24	.300	.323	.362	103	-1	20			.941	-0	S-98,3-11/2-1	0.4
1919	*Chi-A	140	571	89	169	33	9	3	75	11	21	.296	.315	.401	100	-3	22			.963	0	3-97,S-43	0.4
1920	Chi-A	151	629	102	208	34	8	2	74	28	23	.331	.365	.420	107	6	19	17	-5	.933	-10	*3-127,S-25	-0.1
Total	9	1254	4809	623	1308	198	69	21	420	183	303	.272	.307	.355	92	-68	172	70		.935	39	S-822,3-427/2-1	3.1

■ JIM WEAVER
Weaver, James Francis b: 10/10/59, Kingston, N.Y. BL/TL, 6'3", 190 lbs. Deb: 4/10/85

YEAR	TM/L	G	AB	R	H	2B	3B	HR	RBI	BB	SO	AVG	OBP	SLG	PRO+	BR/A	SB	CS	SBR	FA	FR	G/POS	TPR
1985	Det-A	12	7	2	1	1	0	0	0	1	4	.143	.250	.286	47	-1	0	1	-1	1.000	-2	/O-4,D-4	-0.3
1987	Sea-A	7	4	2	0	0	0	0	0	0	3	.000	.333	.000	-1	-1	1	1	-0	1.000	-1	/O-4	-0.1
1989	SF-N	12	20	2	4	3	0	0	2	0	7	.200	.200	.350	56	-1	1	0	0	1.000	0	/O-8	-0.3
Total	3	31	31	6	5	4	0	0	2	1	14	.161	.235	.290	47	-2	2	2	-1	1.000	-4	/O-16,D-4	-0.7

■ FARMER WEAVER
Weaver, William B. b: 3/23/1865, Parkersburg, W.Va. d: 1/23/43, Akron, Ohio BL , Deb: 9/16/1888

YEAR	TM/L	G	AB	R	H	2B	3B	HR	RBI	BB	SO	AVG	OBP	SLG	PRO+	BR/A	SB	CS	SBR	FA	FR	G/POS	TPR
1888	Lou-a	26	112	12	28	1	1	0	8	3		.250	.276	.277	79	-3	12			.878	-2	O-26	-0.5
1889	Lou-a	124	499	62	145	17	6	0	60	40	22	.291	.352	.349	102	2	21			.918	-1	*O-123/C-2,3-1,2-1	-0.1
1890	*Lou-a	130	557	101	161	27	9	3	67	29		.289	.333	.386	115	8	45			.933	-1	*O-127/S-2,3-1	0.2
1891	Lou-a	135	565	76	160	25	7	1	55	33	23	.283	.335	.358	99	-2	30			.956	17	*O-132/C-4	0.9
1892	Lou-N	138	551	58	140	15	4	0	57	40	17	.254	.315	.296	92	-4	30			.902	-11	*O-122,C-15/1-1	-1.8
1893	Lou-N	106	439	79	128	17	7	2	49	27	21	.292	.348	.376	100	-0	17			.913	-1	O-85,C-21	-0.3
1894	Lou-N	64	244	19	54	5	2	3	24	7	11	.221	.249	.295	33	-27	3			.958	-0	0-35,C-17,1-10/2-1	-2.2
	Pit-N	30	115	16	40	7	2	0	24	6	1	.348	.405	.443	105	1	4			.943	-10	C-14,S-12/3-5,O-1	-0.5
	Yr	94	359	35	94	12	4	3	48	13	12	.262	.301	.343	58	-25	7			.947	-10	O-36,C-31,S1/32	-2.7
Total	7	753	3082	423	856	114	38	9	344	185	86	.278	.330	.348	95	-25	162			.927	-9	O-651/C-73,S132	-4.3

■ SKEETER WEBB
Webb, James Laverne b: 11/4/09, Meridian, Miss. d: 7/8/86, Meridian, Miss. BR/TR, 5'9.5", 150 lbs. Deb: 7/20/32

YEAR	TM/L	G	AB	R	H	2B	3B	HR	RBI	BB	SO	AVG	OBP	SLG	PRO+	BR/A	SB	CS	SBR	FA	FR	G/POS	TPR
1932	StL-N	1	0	0	0	0	0	0	0	0	0	—	—	—	—	0	0			.000	0	/S-1	0.0
1938	Cle-A	20	58	11	16	2	0	0	2	8	7	.276	.364	.310	72	-2	1	0	0	.964	-2	S-13/3-3,2-2	-0.3
1939	Cle-A	81	269	28	71	14	1	2	26	15	24	.264	.305	.346	68	-13	1	1	-0	.932	-9	S-81	-1.4
1940	Chi-A	84	334	33	79	11	2	1	29	30	33	.237	.299	.290	53	-23	3	6	-3	.969	-10	2-74/S-7,3-1	-2.8
1941	Chi-A	29	84	7	16	2	0	0	6	3	9	.190	.227	.214	18	-10	0	0	0	.940	6	2-18/S-5,3-3	-0.3
1942	Chi-A	32	94	5	16	2	1	0	4	4	13	.170	.204	.213	18	-10	1	2	-1	.961	2	2-29	-0.9
1943	Chi-A	58	213	15	50	5	2	0	22	6	19	.235	.256	.277	56	-12	5	4	-1	.953	-3	2-54	-1.4
1944	Chi-A	139	513	44	108	19	6	0	30	20	39	.211	.242	.271	47	-37	7	3	0	.944	-5	*S-135/2-5	-3.2
1945	*Det-A	118	407	43	81	12	2	0	21	30	35	.199	.254	.238	41	-31	8	7	-2	.957	-3	*S-104,2-11	-0.2
1946	Det-A	64	169	12	37	1	1	0	17	9	18	.219	.258	.237	37	-14	2	2	-1	.972	15	2-50/S-8	0.3
1947	Det-A	50	79	13	16	3	0	0	6	7	9	.203	.267	.241	41	-6	3	0	1	.992	12	2-30/S-6	0.8
1948	Phi-A	23	54	5	8	2	0	0	3	0	9	.148	.148	.185	-12	-9	0	0	0	1.000	1	/2-9,S-8	-0.5
Total	12	699	2274	216	498	73	15	3	166	132	215	.219	.263	.268	46	-168	33	26		.946	32	S-368,2-282/3-7	-9.9

■ EARL WEBB
Webb, William Earl b: 9/17/1897, Bon Air, Tenn. d: 5/23/65, Jamestown, Tenn. BL/TR, 6'1", 185 lbs. Deb: 8/13/25

YEAR	TM/L	G	AB	R	H	2B	3B	HR	RBI	BB	SO	AVG	OBP	SLG	PRO+	BR/A	SB	CS	SBR	FA	FR	G/POS	TPR
1925	NY-N	4	3	0	0	0	0	0	0	1	1	.000	.250	.000	-31	-1	0	0	0	.000	0	H	-0.1
1927	Chi-N	102	332	58	100	18	4	14	52	48	31	.301	.391	.506	138	18	3			.959	2	O-86	1.4
1928	Chi-N	62	140	22	35	7	3	3	23	14	17	.250	.318	.407	90	-3	0			.986	2	O-31	-0.3
1930	Bos-A	127	449	61	145	30	6	16	66	44	56	.323	.385	.523	133	22	2	1	0	.959	-5	*O-116	0.7
1931	Bos-A	151	589	96	196	67	3	14	103	70	51	.333	.404	.528	151	43	2	2	-1	.948	-3	*O-151	2.8
1932	Bos-A	52	192	23	54	9	1	5	27	25	15	.281	.364	.417	105	2	0	0	0	.964	-3	O-50/1-2	-0.4
	Det-A	88	338	49	97	19	8	3	51	39	18	.287	.361	.417	97	-1	1	1	-0	.955	0	O-85	-0.6
	Yr	140	530	72	151	28	9	8	78	64	33	.285	.362	.417	100	1	1	1	-0	.958	-2	*O-135/1-2	-1.0
1933	Det-A	6	11	1	3	0	0	0	3	0	0	.273	.429	.273	87	0	0	0	0	1.000	-1	/O-2	-0.1
	Chi-A	58	107	16	31	5	0	1	8	16	13	.290	.382	.364	103	1	0	0	0	1.000	-4	O-16,1-10	-0.4
	Yr	64	118	17	34	5	0	1	11	19	13	.288	.387	.356	101	1	0	0	0	1.000	-5	O-18,1-10	-0.5
Total	7	650	2161	326	661	155	25	56	333	260	202	.306	.381	.478	125	82	8			.958	-11	O-537/1-12	3.0

■ BILL WEBB
Webb, William Joseph b: 6/25/1895, Chicago, Ill. d: 1/12/43, Chicago, Ill. BR/TR, 5'10", 161 lbs. Deb: 9/17/17 C

YEAR	TM/L	G	AB	R	H	2B	3B	HR	RBI	BB	SO	AVG	OBP	SLG	PRO+	BR/A	SB	CS	SBR	FA	FR	G/POS	TPR
1917	Pit-N	5	15	1	3	0	0	0	0	2	3	.200	.294	.200	51	-1	0			1.000	1	/2-4,S-1	0.0

■ HARRY WEBER
Weber, Harry b: Indianapolis, Ind. Deb: 7/22/1884

YEAR	TM/L	G	AB	R	H	2B	3B	HR	RBI	BB	SO	AVG	OBP	SLG	PRO+	BR/A	SB	CS	SBR	FA	FR	G/POS	TPR
1884	Ind-a	3	8	0	0	0	0	0		0		.000	.111	.000	-62	-1				.794	1	/C-3	0.0

■ JOE WEBER
Weber, Joseph Edward b: 2/15/1862, Hamilton, Ont., Canada d: 12/15/21, Hamilton, Ont., Canada Deb: 5/30/1884

YEAR	TM/L	G	AB	R	H	2B	3B	HR	RBI	BB	SO	AVG	OBP	SLG	PRO+	BR/A	SB	CS	SBR	FA	FR	G/POS	TPR
1884	Det-N	2	8	0	0	0	0	0		0	2	.000	.000	.000	-99	-2				.750	0	/O-2	-0.2

■ LENNY WEBSTER
Webster, Leonard Irell b: 2/10/65, New Orleans, La. BR/TR, 5'9", 185 lbs. Deb: 9/1/89

YEAR	TM/L	G	AB	R	H	2B	3B	HR	RBI	BB	SO	AVG	OBP	SLG	PRO+	BR/A	SB	CS	SBR	FA	FR	G/POS	TPR
1989	Min-A	14	20	3	6	2	0	0	1	3	2	.300	.391	.400	116	1	0	0	0	1.000	-2	C-14	-0.1
1990	Min-A	2	6	1	2	1	0	0	0	1	1	.333	.429	.500	149	0	0	0	0	1.000	-1	/C-2	0.0
1991	Min-A	18	34	7	10	1	0	3	8	6	10	.294	.400	.588	162	3	0	0	0	.986	4	C-17	0.7
1992	Min-A	53	118	10	33	10	1	1	13	9	11	.280	.331	.407	102	0	0	2	-1	.995	-1	C-49/D-1	0.2
1993	Min-A	49	106	14	21	2	0	1	8	11	8	.198	.274	.245	40	-9	1	0	0	1.000	3	C-45/D-1	-0.4
1994	Mon-N	57	143	13	39	10	0	5	23	16	24	.273	.370	.448	111	3	0	0	0	.996	-1	C-46	0.4
1995	Phi-N	49	150	18	40	9	0	4	14	16	27	.267	.337	.407	94	-1	0	1		.990	1	C-43	0.2
1996	Mon-N	78	174	18	40	10	0	2	17	25	21	.230	.333	.322	72	-6	1	1	0	.998	10	C-63	0.7
Total	8	320	751	84	191	45	1	16	84	87	104	.254	.338	.381	90	-10	1	2	-1	.995	16	C-279/D-2	1.7

■ MITCH WEBSTER
Webster, Mitchell Dean b: 5/16/59, Larned, Kan. BB/TL, 6', 185 lbs. Deb: 9/2/83

YEAR	TM/L	G	AB	R	H	2B	3B	HR	RBI	BB	SO	AVG	OBP	SLG	PRO+	BR/A	SB	CS	SBR	FA	FR	G/POS	TPR
1983	Tor-A	11	11	2	2	0	0	0	0	1	0	.182	.250	.182	20	-1	0	0	0	1.000	-3	/O-7,D-2	-0.4
1984	Tor-A	26	22	9	5	2	0	0	4	1	7	.227	.261	.409	79	-1	4	1		.875	-3	O-10/1-1,D-9	-0.3
1985	Tor-A	4	1	0	0	0	0	0	0	0	0	.000	.000	.000	-98	-0	0	1		1.000	-1	/O-2,D-2	-0.2
	Mon-N	74	212	32	58	8	2	11	30	20	33	.274	.336	.486	135	9	15	4		.993	-5	O-64	0.1
1986	Mon-N	151	576	89	167	31	13	8	49	57	78	.290	.358	.431	117	14	36	15		.977	-4	*O-146	1.5
1987	Mon-N	156	588	101	165	30	9	15	63	70	95	.281	.363	.435	107	7	33	15	2	.982	1	*O-153	0.6
1988	Mon-N	81	259	33	66	5	2	2	13	36	37	.255	.357	.313	90	-2	12	10	-2	.994	-3	O-71	-1.0

YEAR	TM/L	G	AB	R	H	2B	3B	HR	RBI	BB	SO	AVG	OBP	SLG	PRO+	BR/A	SB	CS	SBR	FA	FR	G/POS	TPR
	Chi-N	70	264	36	70	11	6	4	26	19	50	.265	.322	.398	101	0	10	4	1	.971	2	O-65	0.1
	Yr	151	523	69	136	16	8	6	39	55	87	.260	.340	.356	95	-2	22	14	-2	.982	-1	*O-136	-0.9
1989	*Chi-N	98	272	40	70	12	4	3	19	30	55	.257	.333	.364	92	-2	14	2	3	.965	-1	O-74	-0.3
1990	Cle-A	128	437	58	110	20	6	12	55	20	61	.252	.289	.407	93	-6	22	6	3	.991	9	*O-118/1-3,D-3	0.4
1991	Cle-A	13	32	2	4	0	0	0	0	3	9	.125	.200	.125	-8	-5	2	2	-1	1.000	-1	O-10	-0.6
	Pit-N	36	97	9	17	3	4	1	9	9	31	.175	.245	.320	59	-6	0	0	0	.963	-2	O-29	-0.8
	LA-N	58	74	12	21	5	1	1	10	9	21	.284	.361	.419	122	2	0	1	-1	1.000	-8	O-36/1-1	-0.8
	Yr	94	171	21	38	8	5	2	19	18	52	.222	.296	.363	86	-3	0	1	-1	.978	-10	O-65/1-1	-1.6
1992	LA-N	135	262	33	70	12	5	6	35	27	49	.267	.340	.420	116	5	11	5	0	.977	-12	O-90	-0.9
1993	LA-N	88	172	26	42	6	2	2	14	11	24	.244	.297	.337	74	-7	4	6	-2	.950	-9	O-56	-1.9
1994	LA-N	82	84	16	23	4	0	4	12	8	13	.274	.344	.464	116	2	1	2	-1	1.000	-12	O-48	-1.1
1995	*LA-N	54	56	6	10	1	1	1	3	4	14	.179	.246	.286	44	-5	0	0	0	1.000	-7	O-25	-1.2
Total	13	1265	3419	504	900	150	55	70	342	325	578	.263	.332	.401	101	5	160	73	4	.980	-50	*O-1004/D-16,1-5	-6.8

■ RAY WEBSTER   Webster, Ramon Alberto b: 8/31/42, Colon, Panama BL/TL, 6', 185 lbs. Deb: 4/11/67

YEAR	TM/L	G	AB	R	H	2B	3B	HR	RBI	BB	SO	AVG	OBP	SLG	PRO+	BR/A	SB	CS	SBR	FA	FR	G/POS	TPR
1967	KC-A	122	360	41	92	15	4	11	51	32	44	.256	.320	.411	118	7	5	3	-0	.989	-3	1-83,O-15	-0.1
1968	Oak-A	66	196	17	42	11	1	3	23	12	24	.214	.260	.327	81	-5	3	0	1	.988	-1	1-55	-1.1
1969	Oak-A	64	77	5	20	0	1	1	13	12	8	.260	.367	.325	99	0	0	0	0	1.000	1	1-13	0.1
1970	SD-N	95	116	12	30	3	0	2	11	11	12	.259	.323	.336	80	-3	1	1	-0	.981	-1	1-15/O-1	-0.6
1971	SD-N	10	8	0	1	0	0	0	0	2	1	.125	.300	.125	26	-1	0	0	0	.000	0	H	-0.1
	Oak-A	7	5	0	0	0	0	0	0	0	2	.000	.000	.000	-99	-1	0	0	0	1.000	0	/1-1	-0.1
	Chi-N	16	16	1	5	2	0	0	0	1	3	.313	.353	.438	107	0	0	0	0	1.000	0	/1-1	0.0
Total	5	380	778	76	190	31	6	17	98	70	94	.244	.309	.365	99	-3	9	4	0	.989	-4	1-168/O-16	-1.9

■ RAY WEBSTER   Webster, Raymond George b: 11/15/37, Grass Valley, Cal. BR/TR, 6', 175 lbs. Deb: 4/17/59

YEAR	TM/L	G	AB	R	H	2B	3B	HR	RBI	BB	SO	AVG	OBP	SLG	PRO+	BR/A	SB	CS	SBR	FA	FR	G/POS	TPR
1959	Cle-A	40	74	10	15	2	1	2	10	5	7	.203	.253	.338	63	-4	1	0	0	.929	0	2-24/3-4	-0.3
1960	Bos-A	7	3	1	0	0	0	0	1	1	0	.000	.250	.000	-25	-1	0	0	0	1.000	1	/2-1	0.0
Total	2	47	77	11	15	2	1	2	11	6	7	.195	.253	.325	59	-5	1	0	0	.931	1	/2-25,3-4	-0.3

■ PETE WECKBECKER   Weckbecker, Peter b: 8/30/1864, Butler, Pa. d: 5/16/35, Hampton, Va. 5'7", 150 lbs. Deb: 10/5/1889

YEAR	TM/L	G	AB	R	H	2B	3B	HR	RBI	BB	SO	AVG	OBP	SLG	PRO+	BR/A	SB	CS	SBR	FA	FR	G/POS	TPR
1889	Ind-N	1	1	0	0	0	0	0	2	0	0	.000	.000	.000	-98	-0	0			1.000	0	/C-1	0.0
1890	*Lou-a	32	101	17	24	1	0	0	11	8		.238	.300	.248	63	-4	7			.941	1	C-32	-0.1
Total	2	33	102	17	24	1	0	0	13	8	0	.235	.297	.245	61	-5	7			.941	1	/C-33	-0.1

■ ERIC WEDGE   Wedge, Eric Michael b: 1/27/68, Fort Wayne, Ind. BR/TR, 6'3", 215 lbs. Deb: 10/5/91

YEAR	TM/L	G	AB	R	H	2B	3B	HR	RBI	BB	SO	AVG	OBP	SLG	PRO+	BR/A	SB	CS	SBR	FA	FR	G/POS	TPR
1991	Bos-A	1	1	0	1	0	0	0	0	0	0	1.000	1.000	1.000	434	0	0	0	0	.000	0	/D-1	0.0
1992	Bos-A	27	68	11	17	2	0	5	11	13	18	.250	.370	.500	133	3	0	0	0	1.000	-0	D-20/C-5	0.2
1993	Col-N	9	11	2	2	0	0	0	1	0	4	.182	.182	.182	-2	-2	0	0	0	1.000	1	/C-1	-0.1
1994	Bos-A	2	6	0	0	0	0	0	0	1	3	.000	.143	.000	-56	-1	0	0	0	1.000	0	/D-2	-0.1
Total	4	39	86	13	20	2	0	5	12	14	25	.233	.340	.430	104	1	0	0	0	1.000	0	/D-23,C-6	0.0

■ BERT WEEDEN   Weeden, Charles Albert b: 12/21/1882, Northwood, N.H. d: 1/7/39, Northwood, N.H. BL/TL, 6', 200 lbs. Deb: 6/4/11

YEAR	TM/L	G	AB	R	H	2B	3B	HR	RBI	BB	SO	AVG	OBP	SLG	PRO+	BR/A	SB	CS	SBR	FA	FR	G/POS	TPR
1911	Bos-N	1	1	0	0	0	0	0	0	0	0	.000	.000	.000	-93	-0	0			.000	0	H	0.0

■ JOHNNY WEEKLY   Weekly, Johnny b: 6/14/37, Waterproof, La. d: 11/24/74, Walnut Creek, Cal. BR/TR, 6' ", 200 lbs. Deb: 4/13/62

YEAR	TM/L	G	AB	R	H	2B	3B	HR	RBI	BB	SO	AVG	OBP	SLG	PRO+	BR/A	SB	CS	SBR	FA	FR	G/POS	TPR
1962	Hou-N	13	26	3	5	1	0	2	2	7	4	.192	.364	.462	129	1	0	0	0	1.000	-1	/O-7	0.0
1963	Hou-N	34	80	4	18	3	0	3	14	7	14	.225	.295	.375	98	-0	0	0	0	1.000	1	O-23	-0.1
1964	Hou-N	6	15	0	2	0	0	0	3	1	3	.133	.188	.133	-8	-2	0	0	0	1.000	1	/O-5	-0.2
Total	3	53	121	7	25	4	0	5	19	15	21	.207	.299	.364	92	-1	0	0	0	1.000	1	/O-35	-0.3

■ JOHN WEHNER   Wehner, John Paul b: 6/29/67, Pittsburgh, Pa. BR/TR, 6'3", 204 lbs. Deb: 7/17/91

YEAR	TM/L	G	AB	R	H	2B	3B	HR	RBI	BB	SO	AVG	OBP	SLG	PRO+	BR/A	SB	CS	SBR	FA	FR	G/POS	TPR
1991	Pit-N	37	106	15	36	7	0	0	7	7	17	.340	.381	.406	123	3	3	0	1	.936	7	3-36	1.2
1992	*Pit-N	55	123	11	22	6	0	0	4	12	22	.179	.252	.228	37	-10	3	0	1	.961	5	3-34,1-13/2-5	-0.6
1993	Pit-N	29	35	3	5	0	0	0	0	6	10	.143	.268	.143	14	-4	0	0	0	1.000	-1	O-13/2-3,3-3	-0.5
1994	Pit-N	2	4	1	1	1	0	0	3	0	1	.250	.250	.500	88	-0	0	0	0	1.000	0	/3-1	0.0
1995	Pit-N	52	107	13	33	0	3	0	5	10	17	.308	.368	.364	92	-1	3	1	0	1.000	-4	O-23,3-19/C-1,S-1	-0.5
1996	Pit-N	86	139	19	36	9	1	2	13	8	22	.259	.299	.381	76	-5	10	6	-1	.971	3	O-29,3-24,2-12/C-1	-0.8
Total	6	261	514	62	133	23	4	2	32	43	89	.259	.316	.331	76	-17	10	6	-1	.963	7	3-117/O-65,21CS	-1.2

■ RALPH WEIGEL   Weigel, Ralph Richard "Wig" b: 10/2/21, Coldwater, Ohio d: 4/15/92, Memphis, Tenn. BR/TR, 6'1", 180 lbs. Deb: 9/18/46

YEAR	TM/L	G	AB	R	H	2B	3B	HR	RBI	BB	SO	AVG	OBP	SLG	PRO+	BR/A	SB	CS	SBR	FA	FR	G/POS	TPR
1946	Cle-A	6	12	0	2	0	0	0	0	0	2	.167	.167	.167	-7	-2	1	0	0	/C-6			-0.3
1948	Chi-A	66	163	8	38	7	3	0	26	13	18	.233	.294	.313	64	-9	1	2	-1	.969	-7	C-39/O-2	-1.4
1949	Was-A	34	60	4	14	2	0	0	4	8	6	.233	.324	.267	58	-3	0	1	-1	.985	1	C-21	-0.3
Total	3	106	235	12	54	9	3	0	30	21	26	.230	.296	.294	59	-14	2	3	-1	.976	-8	/C-66,O-2	-2.0

■ PODGE WEIHE   Weihe, John Garibaldi b: 11/13/1862, Cincinnati, Ohio d: 4/15/14, Cincinnati, Ohio BR/TR, 5'11", 175 lbs. Deb: 8/6/1883

YEAR	TM/L	G	AB	R	H	2B	3B	HR	RBI	BB	SO	AVG	OBP	SLG	PRO+	BR/A	SB	CS	SBR	FA	FR	G/POS	TPR
1883	Cin-a	1	4	1	1	0	0	0		0		.250	.250	.250	58	-0				1.000	0	/O-1	0.0
1884	Ind-a	63	256	29	65	13	2	4		9		.254	.279	.367	112	3				.860	-0	O-58/2-4,1-3	0.2
Total	2	64	260	30	66	13	2	4		9		.254	.279	.365	111	2				.864	0	/O-59,2-4,1-3	0.2

■ DICK WEIK   Weik, Richard Henry "Legs" b: 11/17/27, Waterloo, Iowa d: 4/21/91, Harvey, Ill. BR/TR, 6'3.5", 184 lbs. Deb: 9/8/48

YEAR	TM/L	G	AB	R	H	2B	3B	HR	RBI	BB	SO	AVG	OBP	SLG	PRO+	BR/A	SB	CS	SBR	FA	FR	G/POS	TPR
1948	Was-A	3	4	1	3	0	1	0	0	0	0	.750	.750	1.250	439	2	0	0	0	1.000	-0	/P-3	0.0
1949	Was-A	28	28	3	5	0	0	0	2	1	8	.179	.207	.179	2	-4	0	0	0	.964	1	P-27	0.0
1950	Was-A	14	13	0	2	0	0	0	0	0	3	.154	.154	.154	-22	-4	0	0	0	1.000	-1	P-14	0.0
	Cle-A	11	5	0	1	1	0	0	0	0	4	.200	.200	.400	52	-0	0	0	0	1.000	0	P-11	0.0
	Yr	25	18	0	3	1	0	0	0	0	7	.167	.167	.222	-1	-3	0	0	0	1.000	-1	P-25	0.0
1953	Cle-A	1	0	1	0	0	0	0	0	0	0	—	—	—	—	0	0	0	0	.000	0	R	0.0
	Det-A	12	2	1	1	1	0	0	0	0	1	.500	.500	1.000	300	1	0	0	0	1.000	0	P-12	0.0
	Yr	13	2	2	1	1	0	0	0	0	1	.500	.500	1.000	301	1	0	0	0	1.000	0	P-12	0.0
1954	Det-A	9	1	0	0	0	0	0	0	0	0	.000	.000	.000	-99	-0	0	0	0	.500	-1	/P-9	0.0
Total	5	78	53	6	12	2	1	0	3	1	16	.226	.241	.302	43	-5	0	0	0	.958	-1	/P-76	0.0

■ ELMER WEINGARTNER   Weingartner, Elmer William "Dutch" b: 8/13/18, Cleveland, Ohio BR/TR, 5'11", 178 lbs. Deb: 4/19/45

YEAR	TM/L	G	AB	R	H	2B	3B	HR	RBI	BB	SO	AVG	OBP	SLG	PRO+	BR/A	SB	CS	SBR	FA	FR	G/POS	TPR
1945	Cle-A	20	39	5	9	1	0	0	4	1	11	.231	.302	.256	66	-2	0	0	0	.871	-3	S-20	-0.4

■ PHIL WEINTRAUB   Weintraub, Philip "Mickey" b: 10/12/07, Chicago, Ill. d: 6/21/87, Palm Springs, Cal BL/TL, 6'1", 195 lbs. Deb: 9/5/33

YEAR	TM/L	G	AB	R	H	2B	3B	HR	RBI	BB	SO	AVG	OBP	SLG	PRO+	BR/A	SB	CS	SBR	FA	FR	G/POS	TPR
1933	NY-N	8	15	3	3	0	0	0	2	3	2	.200	.333	.400	110	0	0			.667	-3	/O-6	-0.3
1934	NY-N	31	74	13	26	2	0	0	15	15	10	.351	.461	.378	130	4	0			.944	-4	O-20	0.0
1935	NY-N	64	112	18	27	3	3	1	6	17	13	.241	.341	.348	87	-2	0			.975	-1	1-19/O-7	-0.6
1937	Cin-N	49	177	27	48	10	4	3	20	19	25	.271	.345	.424	113	3	1			.976	-2	O-47	-0.1
	NY-N	6	9	3	3	2	0	0	1	1	1	.333	.400	.556	155	1	0			1.000	-0	/O-1	0.0
	Yr	55	186	30	51	12	4	3	21	20	26	.274	.348	.430	115	4	1			.976	-3	O-48	-0.1
1938	Phi-N	100	351	51	109	23	2	4	45	64	43	.311	.422	.422	137	21	1			.988	2	1-98	1.2
1944	NY-N	104	361	55	114	18	9	13	77	59	59	.316	.412	.524	162	31	0			.992	3	1-99	2.9
1945	NY-N	82	283	45	77	9	1	10	42	54	29	.272	.389	.417	122	10	2			.993	3	1-77	0.8
Total	7	444	1382	215	407	67	19	32	207	232	182	.295	.398	.440	133	69	4			.990	-4	1-293/O-81	3.9

■ AL WEIS   Weis, Albert John b: 4/2/38, Franklin Square, N.Y BB/TR, 6', 170 lbs. Deb: 9/15/62

YEAR	TM/L	G	AB	R	H	2B	3B	HR	RBI	BB	SO	AVG	OBP	SLG	PRO+	BR/A	SB	CS	SBR	FA	FR	G/POS	TPR
1962	Chi-A	7	12	2	1	0	0	0	0	3	3	.083	.267	.083	-1	-2	1	0	0	.882	-1	/S-4,2-1,3-1	-0.2
1963	Chi-A	99	210	41	57	9	0	0	18	18	37	.271	.335	.314	85	-4	15	1	4	.990	14	2-48,S-27/3-1	1.9
1964	Chi-A	133	328	36	81	4	4	2	23	28	41	.247	.300	.302	70	-13	22	7	2	.966	12	*2-116/S-9,O-2	0.9
1965	Chi-A	103	135	29	40	4	3	1	12	12	22	.296	.362	.393	122	4	4	1	1	.975	25	2-74/S-7,3-2,O-2	3.4

YEAR	TM/L	G	AB	R	H	2B	3B	HR	RBI	BB	SO	AVG	OBP	SLG	PRO+	BR/A	SB	CS	SBR	FA	FR	G/POS	TPR
1966	Chi-A	129	187	20	29	4	1	0	9	17	50	.155	.233	.187	24	-18	3	5	-2	.987	**37**	2-96,S-18	2.2
1967	Chi-A	50	53	9	13	2	0	0	4	1	7	.245	.273	.283	67	-2	3	3	-1	.986	11	2-32,S-13	1.0
1968	NY-N	90	274	15	47	6	0	1	14	21	63	.172	.236	.204	33	-22	3	1	0	.958	7	S-59,2-29/3-2	-1.0
1969	*NY-N	103	247	20	53	9	2	2	23	15	51	.215	.260	.291	53	-16	3	3	-1	.960	13	S-52,2-43/3-1	0.3
1970	NY-N	75	121	20	25	7	1	1	11	7	21	.207	.256	.306	50	-9	1	1	0	.952	2	2-44,S-15	-0.4
1971	NY-N	11	11	3	0	0	0	0	0	1	2	4	.000	.154	.000	-54	-2	0	0	0	1.000	1	/2-5,3-2	-0.2
Total	10	800	1578	195	346	45	11	7	115	117	299	.219	.279	.275	59	-84	55	22	3	.975	121	2-488,S-204/3-9,O-4	7.9

■ BUTCH WEIS
Weis, Arthur John   b: 3/2/01, St.Louis, Mo.   BL/TL, 5'11", 180 lbs.   Deb: 4/15/22

YEAR	TM/L	G	AB	R	H	2B	3B	HR	RBI	BB	SO	AVG	OBP	SLG	PRO+	BR/A	SB	CS	SBR	FA	FR	G/POS	TPR
1922	Chi-N	2	2	2	1	0	0	0	0	0	0	.500	.500	.500	156	0	0	0	0	.000	0	H	0.0
1923	Chi-N	22	26	2	6	1	0	0	2	5	8	.231	.355	.269	67	-1	0	1	-1	1.000	-1	/O-6	-0.3
1924	Chi-N	37	133	19	37	8	1	0	23	15	14	.278	.356	.353	90	-1	4	5	-2	.978	6	O-36	0.0
1925	Chi-N	67	180	16	48	5	3	2	25	23	22	.267	.350	.361	81	-5	2	4	-2	.964	-5	O-47	-1.3
Total	4	128	341	39	92	14	4	2	50	43	44	.270	.353	.352	84	-7	6	10	-4	.973	0	/O-89	-1.6

■ BUD WEISER
Weiser, Harry Budson   b: 1/8/1891, Shamokin, Pa.   d: 7/31/61, Shamokin, Pa.   BR/TR, 5'11", 165 lbs.   Deb: 4/29/15

YEAR	TM/L	G	AB	R	H	2B	3B	HR	RBI	BB	SO	AVG	OBP	SLG	PRO+	BR/A	SB	CS	SBR	FA	FR	G/POS	TPR
1915	Phi-N	37	64	6	9	0	0	0	8	7	12	.141	.236	.172	24	-6	2	2	-1	.897	-5	O-20	-1.4
1916	Phi-N	4	10	1	3	1	0	0	1	0	3	.300	.300	.400	110	-0	0	0		1.000	-1	/O-4	-0.1
Total	2	41	74	7	12	1	0	0	9	7	15	.162	.244	.203	36	-6	2	2		.912	-6	/O-24	-1.5

■ GARY WEISS
Weiss, Gary Lee   b: 12/27/55, Brenham, Tex.   BB/TR, 5'10", 170 lbs.   Deb: 9/13/80

YEAR	TM/L	G	AB	R	H	2B	3B	HR	RBI	BB	SO	AVG	OBP	SLG	PRO+	BR/A	SB	CS	SBR	FA	FR	G/POS	TPR
1980	LA-N	8	0	2	0	0	0	0	0	0	0	—	—	—			0	0	0	.000	0	/R	0.0
1981	LA-N	14	19	2	2	0	0	0	1	1	4	.105	.150	.105	-28	-3	0	0	0	.920	-1	S-13	-0.4
Total	2	22	19	4	2	0	0	0	1	1	4	.105	.150	.105	-28	-3	0	0	0	.920	-1	/S-13	-0.4

■ JOE WEISS
Weiss, Joseph Harold   b: 1/27/1894, Chicago, Ill.   d: 7/7/67, Cedar Rapids, Iowa   BR/TR, 6', 165 lbs.   Deb: 8/29/15

YEAR	TM/L	G	AB	R	H	2B	3B	HR	RBI	BB	SO	AVG	OBP	SLG	PRO+	BR/A	SB	CS	SBR	FA	FR	G/POS	TPR
1915	Chi-F	29	85	6	19	1	2	0	11	3	24	.224	.250	.282	53	-7	0			.992	-1	1-29	-1.0

■ WALT WEISS
Weiss, Walter William   b: 11/28/63, Tuxedo, N.Y.   BB/TR, 6', 175 lbs.   Deb: 7/12/87

YEAR	TM/L	G	AB	R	H	2B	3B	HR	RBI	BB	SO	AVG	OBP	SLG	PRO+	BR/A	SB	CS	SBR	FA	FR	G/POS	TPR
1987	Oak-A	16	26	3	12	4	0	0	1	2		.462	.500	.615	208	4	1	2	-1	.974	5	S-11/D-2	0.8
1988	*Oak-A	147	452	44	113	17	3	3	39	35	56	.250	.317	.321	82	-10	4	4	-1	.979	10	*S-147	1.0
1989	*Oak-A	84	236	30	55	11	0	3	21	21	39	.233	.298	.318	76	-7	6	1	1	.953	-14	S-84	-1.5
1990	*Oak-A	138	445	50	118	17	1	2	35	46	53	.265	.339	.321	89	-5	9	3	1	.979	-26	*S-137	-2.0
1991	Oak-A	40	133	15	30	6	1	0	13	12	14	.226	.290	.286	63	-7	6	0	2	.970	-10	S-40	-1.2
1992	*Oak-A	103	316	36	67	5	2	0	21	43	39	.212	.308	.241	59	-16	6	3	0	.956	-1	*S-103	-2.4
1993	Fla-N	158	500	50	133	14	2	1	39	79	73	.266	.369	.308	79	-11	7	3	0	.977	-18	*S-153	-1.7
1994	Col-N	110	423	58	106	11	4	1	32	56	58	.251	.338	.303	59	-25	12	7	1	.973	-3	*S-110	-1.2
1995	*Col-N	137	427	65	111	17	3	1	25	98	57	.260	.404	.321	73	-17	15	3	3	.974	12	*S-136	1.0
1996	Col-N	155	517	89	146	20	2	8	48	58	78	.282	.385	.375	79	-18	10	2	2	.957	-7	*S-155	-1.0
Total	10	1088	3475	440	891	122	18	19	274	472	469	.256	.350	.318	76	-112	76	28	6	.970	-60	*S-1076/D-2	-8.2

■ JOHNNY WELAJ
Welaj, John Ludwig   b: 5/27/14, Moss Creek, Pa.   BR/TR, 6', 164 lbs.   Deb: 5/2/39

YEAR	TM/L	G	AB	R	H	2B	3B	HR	RBI	BB	SO	AVG	OBP	SLG	PRO+	BR/A	SB	CS	SBR	FA	FR	G/POS	TPR
1939	Was-A	63	201	23	55	11	2	1	33	13	20	.274	.318	.363	80	-7	13	2	3	.975	-4	O-55	-0.9
1940	Was-A	88	215	31	55	9	0	3	21	19	20	.256	.322	.340	77	-7	8	7	-2	.978	-1	O-53	-1.2
1941	Was-A	49	96	16	20	4	0	0	5	6	16	.208	.255	.250	36	-9	3	1	0	.979	-0	O-19	-1.0
1943	Phi-A	93	281	45	68	16	1	0	15	15	17	.242	.280	.306	72	-11	12	5	1	.960	0	O-72	-1.5
Total	4	293	793	115	198	40	3	4	74	53	73	.250	.298	.323	71	-34	36	15	2	.970	-5	O-199	-4.6

■ CURT WELCH
Welch, Curtis Benton   b: 2/11/1862, E.Liverpool, Ohio   d: 8/29/1896, E.Liverpool, Ohio   BR/TR, 5'10", 175 lbs.   Deb: 5/1/1884

YEAR	TM/L	G	AB	R	H	2B	3B	HR	RBI	BB	SO	AVG	OBP	SLG	PRO+	BR/A	SB	CS	SBR	FA	FR	G/POS	TPR
1884	Tol-a	109	425	61	95	24	5	0		10		.224	.248	.304	76	-12				.888	16	*O-107/2-2,C-2,1-1	0.2
1885	*StL-a	112	432	84	117	18	8	3	69	23		.271	.318	.370	112	5				**.946**	14	*O-112	1.4
1886	*StL-a	138	563	114	158	31	13	2	95	29		.281	.332	.393	121	11	59			**.952**	14	*O-138/2-2	1.9
1887	*StL-a	131	544	98	151	32	7	3	108	25		.278	.322	.379	86	-15	89			.941	19	*O-123/2-8,1-1	0.2
1888	Phi-a	136	549	125	155	22	8	1	61	33		.282	.355	.357	129	20	95			.952	4	*O-135/2-3	1.9
1889	Phi-a	125	516	134	140	**39**	6	0	39	67	30	.271	.375	.370	114	13	66			.923	8	*O-125	1.5
1890	Phi-a	103	396	100	106	21	4	2	40	49		.268	.392	.356	123	16	64			.919	14	*O-103/P-1	2.2
	Bal-a	19	68	16	9	4	0	0	5	9		.132	.253	.191	30	-6	8			.974	2	O-17/1-2	-0.4
	Yr	122	464	116	115	25	4	2	45	58		.248	.372	.332	109	9	72			.926	16	*O-120/1-2,P-1	1.8
1891	Bal-a	132	514	122	138	22	10	3	55	77	42	.268	.400	.368	119	17	50			.946	19	*O-113,2-21/S-2	2.8
1892	Bal-N	63	237	42	56	1	3	1	22	36	9	.236	.363	.278	92	-0	14			.905	-4	O-63	-0.6
	Cin-N	25	94	14	19	0	2	1	7	7	8	.202	.299	.277	75	-3	7			.925	-0	O-25	-0.4
	Yr	88	331	56	75	1	5	2	29	43	17	.227	.345	.278	88	-3	21			.911	-4	O-88	-1.0
1893	Lou-N	14	47	5	8	1	0	0	2	16	4	.170	.400	.191	64	-1	1			.912	-0	O-14	-0.1
Total	10	1107	4385	915	1152	215	66	16	503	381	93	.263	.345	.353	107	45	453			.933	107	*O-1075/2-36,1SCP	10.6

■ FRANK WELCH
Welch, Frank Tiguer "Bugger"   b: 8/10/1897, Birmingham, Ala.   d: 7/25/57, Birmingham, Ala.   BR/TR, 5'9", 175 lbs.   Deb: 9/9/19

YEAR	TM/L	G	AB	R	H	2B	3B	HR	RBI	BB	SO	AVG	OBP	SLG	PRO+	BR/A	SB	CS	SBR	FA	FR	G/POS	TPR
1919	Phi-A	15	54	5	9	1	2	1	7	1	10	.167	.262	.333	66	-3	0			.909	0	O-15	-0.4
1920	Phi-A	100	360	43	93	17	5	4	40	26	41	.258	.312	.367	78	-12	2	9	-5	.937	-6	O-97	-2.9
1921	Phi-A	115	403	48	115	18	6	7	45	34	43	.285	.347	.412	92	-5	6	0	2	.943	3	*O-104	-0.8
1922	Phi-A	114	375	43	97	17	3	11	49	40	40	.259	.335	.408	90	-6	3	4	-2	.949	-0	*O-104	-1.5
1923	Phi-A	125	421	56	125	19	9	4	55	48	40	.297	.374	.413	106	4	1	4	-2	.967	2	*O-117	-0.2
1924	Phi-A	94	293	47	85	13	2	5	31	35	27	.290	.372	.399	98	-1	2	3	-1	.985	1	O-74	-0.5
1925	Phi-A	85	202	40	56	5	4	4	41	29	14	.277	.373	.401	90	-3	2	1	0	.968	-3	O-57	-0.8
1926	Phi-A	75	174	26	49	8	1	4	23	26	9	.282	.381	.408	100	0	2	5	-2	.975	-5	O-49	-1.0
1927	Bos-A	15	28	2	5	2	0	0	4	5	1	.179	.303	.250	46	-2	0	2	-1	1.000	2	/O-6	-0.2
Total	9	738	2310	310	634	100	31	41	295	250	225	.274	.350	.398	92	-27	18	28		.955	-5	O-623	-8.3

■ HERB WELCH
Welch, Herbert M. "Dutch"   b: 10/19/1898, Roellen, Tenn.   d: 4/13/67, Memphis, Tenn.   BL/TR, 5'6", 154 lbs.   Deb: 9/15/25

YEAR	TM/L	G	AB	R	H	2B	3B	HR	RBI	BB	SO	AVG	OBP	SLG	PRO+	BR/A	SB	CS	SBR	FA	FR	G/POS	TPR
1925	Bos-A	13	38	2	11	0	1	0	2	6		.289	.289	.342	60	-2	0	0	0	.893	5	S-13	0.4

■ TUB WELCH
Welch, James T.   b: 7/3/1866, St.Louis, Mo.   TR, 5'11", 230 lbs.   Deb: 6/12/1890

YEAR	TM/L	G	AB	R	H	2B	3B	HR	RBI	BB	SO	AVG	OBP	SLG	PRO+	BR/A	SB	CS	SBR	FA	FR	G/POS	TPR
1890	Tol-a	35	108	15	31	3	1	0	14	8		.287	.358	.361	109	1	7			.930	0	C-25,1-10	0.2
1895	Lou-N	47	153	18	37	4	1	1	8	13	7	.242	.310	.301	62	-8	2			.888	-1	C-28,1-20	-0.5
Total	2	82	261	33	68	7	2	2	22	21	7	.261	.330	.326	80	-7	9			.911	-1	/C-53,1-30	-0.3

■ MILT WELCH
Welch, Milton Edward   b: 7/26/24, Farmersville, Ill   BR/TR, 5'10", 175 lbs.   Deb: 6/5/45

YEAR	TM/L	G	AB	R	H	2B	3B	HR	RBI	BB	SO	AVG	OBP	SLG	PRO+	BR/A	SB	CS	SBR	FA	FR	G/POS	TPR
1945	Det-A	1	2	0	0	0	0	0	0	0	1	.000	.000	.000	-94	-0	0	0	0	1.000	1	/C-1	0.0

■ HARRY WELCHONCE
Welchonce, Harry Monroe "Welch"   b: 11/20/1883, North Point, Pa.   d: 2/26/77, Arcadia, Cal.   BL/TR, 6', 170 lbs.   Deb: 4/17/11

YEAR	TM/L	G	AB	R	H	2B	3B	HR	RBI	BB	SO	AVG	OBP	SLG	PRO+	BR/A	SB	CS	SBR	FA	FR	G/POS	TPR
1911	Phi-N	26	66	9	14	4	0	0	6	7	8	.212	.288	.273	56	-4	0			.929	-3	O-17	-0.8

■ MIKE WELDAY
Welday, Lyndon Earl   b: 12/19/1879, Conway, Iowa   d: 5/28/42, Leavenworth, Kan.   BL/TL,   Deb: 4/21/07

YEAR	TM/L	G	AB	R	H	2B	3B	HR	RBI	BB	SO	AVG	OBP	SLG	PRO+	BR/A	SB	CS	SBR	FA	FR	G/POS	TPR
1907	Chi-A	24	35	2	8	1	1	0	0	6		.229	.341	.314	113	1	0			.938	-3	O-15	-0.2
1909	Chi-A	29	74	3	14	0	0	0	5	4		.189	.231	.189	34	-5	2			.886	1	O-20	-0.6
Total	2	53	109	5	22	1	1	0	5	10		.202	.269	.229	60	-5	2			.900	-2	/O-35	-0.8

■ OLLIE WELF
Welf, Oliver Henry   b: 1/17/1889, Cleveland, Ohio   d: 6/15/67, Cleveland, Ohio   BR/TL, 5'9", 160 lbs.   Deb: 8/30/16

YEAR	TM/L	G	AB	R	H	2B	3B	HR	RBI	BB	SO	AVG	OBP	SLG	PRO+	BR/A	SB	CS	SBR	FA	FR	G/POS	TPR
1916	Cle-A	1	0	0	0	0	0	0	0	0		—	—	—			0	0		.000	0	R	0.0

■ BRAD WELLMAN
Wellman, Brad Eugene   b: 8/17/59, Lodi, Cal.   BR/TR, 6', 170 lbs.   Deb: 9/4/82

YEAR	TM/L	G	AB	R	H	2B	3B	HR	RBI	BB	SO	AVG	OBP	SLG	PRO+	BR/A	SB	CS	SBR	FA	FR	G/POS	TPR
1982	SF-N	6	4	1	1	0	0	0	0	0	1	.250	.250	.250	40	-0	0	0	0	1.000	0	/2-2	0.0
1983	SF-N	82	182	15	39	3	0	1	16	22	39	.214	.299	.247	55	-11	5	3	-0	.965	2	2-74/S-2	-0.7
1984	SF-N	93	265	23	60	9	1	2	25	19	41	.226	.278	.291	62	-14	10	5	0	.977	16	2-54,S-34/3-9	0.7

YEAR	TM/L	G	AB	R	H	2B	3B	HR	RBI	BB	SO	AVG	OBP	SLG	PRO+	BR/A	SB	CS	SBR	FA	FR	G/POS	TPR
1985	SF-N	71	174	16	41	11	1	0	16	4	33	.236	.269	.310	65	-9	5	2	0	.983	-2	2-36,3-25/S-3	-1.1
1986	SF-N	12	13	0	2	0	0	0	1	1	2	.154	.214	.154	3	-2	0	0	0	1.000	-0	/S-8,2-1,3-1	-0.2
1987	LA-N	3	4	1	1	0	0	0	1	0	1	.250	.250	.250	34	-0	0	0	0	1.000	1	/2-1,S-1,3-1	0.0
1988	KC-A	71	107	11	29	3	0	1	6	6	23	.271	.322	.327	81	-3	1	2	-1	.972	15	2-46,S-15/3-4,D-3	1.3
1989	KC-A	103	178	30	41	4	0	2	12	7	36	.230	.263	.287	55	-11	5	3	0	.995	19	2-64,S-34/3-3,D-1	1.1
Total	8	441	927	97	214	30	2	6	77	59	176	.231	.282	.287	61	-48	26	15	-1	.978	50	2-278/S-97,3-43,D-4	1.1

■ BOB WELLMAN
Wellman, Robert Joseph b: 7/15/25, Norwood, Ohio d: 12/20/94, Villa Hills, Ky. BR/TR, 6'4", 210 lbs. Deb: 9/23/48

YEAR	TM/L	G	AB	R	H	2B	3B	HR	RBI	BB	SO	AVG	OBP	SLG	PRO+	BR/A	SB	CS	SBR	FA	FR	G/POS	TPR
1948	Phi-A	4	10	1	2	0	1	0	0	3	2	.200	.385	.400	109	0	0	0	0	1.000	0	/1-2,O-1	0.0
1950	Phi-A	11	15	1	5	0	0	1	1	0	3	.333	.333	.533	121	0	0	0	0	1.000	0	/O-2	0.0
Total	2	15	25	2	7	0	1	1	1	3	5	.280	.357	.480	117	1	0	0	0	.889	0	/O-3,1-2	0.0

■ GREG WELLS
Wells, Gregory De Wayne b: 4/25/54, McIntosh, Ala. BR/TR, 6'5", 218 lbs. Deb: 8/10/81

YEAR	TM/L	G	AB	R	H	2B	3B	HR	RBI	BB	SO	AVG	OBP	SLG	PRO+	BR/A	SB	CS	SBR	FA	FR	G/POS	TPR
1981	Tor-A	32	73	7	18	5	0	0	5	5	12	.247	.295	.315	71	-3	0	2	-1	.994	-0	1-22/D-3	-0.5
1982	Min-A	15	54	5	11	1	2	0	3	1	8	.204	.263	.296	39	-5	0	0	0	.962	-2	1-10/D-5	-0.7
Total	2	47	127	12	29	6	2	0	8	6	20	.228	.263	.307	58	-7	0	2	-1	.983	-2	/1-32,D-8	-1.2

■ JAKE WELLS
Wells, Jacob b: 8/9/1863, Memphis, Tenn. d: 3/16/27, Hendersonville, N.C. BR/TR, 5'11", 167 lbs. Deb: 8/10/1888

YEAR	TM/L	G	AB	R	H	2B	3B	HR	RBI	BB	SO	AVG	OBP	SLG	PRO+	BR/A	SB	CS	SBR	FA	FR	G/POS	TPR
1888	Det-N	16	57	5	9	1	0	0	2		0	.158	.158	.175	6	-6	0			.917	5	C-16	0.0
1890	StL-a	30	105	17	25	3	0	0		12	10	.238	.333	.267	67	-5	1			.941	2	C-28/O-3	-0.1
Total	2	46	162	22	34	4	0	0		14	10	5	.210	.277	.235	50	-11	1			.932	6	/C-44,O-3	-0.1

■ LEO WELLS
Wells, Leo Donald b: 7/18/17, Kansas City, Kan. BR/TR, 5'9", 170 lbs. Deb: 4/16/42

YEAR	TM/L	G	AB	R	H	2B	3B	HR	RBI	BB	SO	AVG	OBP	SLG	PRO+	BR/A	SB	CS	SBR	FA	FR	G/POS	TPR
1942	Chi-A	35	62	8	12	2	0	1	4	4	5	.194	.242	.274	46	-5	1	0	0	1.000	11	S-12/3-6	0.7
1946	Chi-A	45	127	11	24	4	1	1	11	12	34	.189	.259	.260	47	-9	3	4	-2	.942	8	3-38/S-2	-0.3
Total	2	80	189	19	36	6	1	2	15	16	39	.190	.254	.265	47	-14	4	4	-1	.938	19	/3-44,S-14	0.4

■ JIMMY WELSH
Welsh, James Daniel b: 10/9/02, Denver, Colo. d: 10/30/70, Oakland, Cal. BL/TR, 6'1", 174 lbs. Deb: 4/14/25

YEAR	TM/L	G	AB	R	H	2B	3B	HR	RBI	BB	SO	AVG	OBP	SLG	PRO+	BR/A	SB	CS	SBR	FA	FR	G/POS	TPR
1925	Bos-N	122	484	69	151	25	8	7	63	20	24	.312	.350	.440	110	5	7	4	-0	.960	6	*O-116/2-3	0.4
1926	Bos-N	134	490	69	136	18	11	3	57	19	28	.278	.333	.378	100	-1	6			.965	10	*O-129	0.0
1927	Bos-N	131	497	72	143	26	7	9	54	23	27	.288	.330	.423	109	4	11			.969	13	*O-129/1-1	0.9
1928	NY-N	124	476	77	146	22	5	9	54	29	30	.307	.357	.431	104	3	4			.981	-0	*O-117	-0.5
1929	NY-N	38	129	25	32	7	0	2	8	9	3	.248	.331	.349	69	-6	3			.940	-6	O-35	-1.4
	Bos-N	53	186	24	54	8	7	2	16	13	9	.290	.350	.441	98	-1	1			.979	9	O-51	0.4
	Yr	91	315	49	86	15	7	4	24	22	12	.273	.342	.403	86	-7	4			.970	2	O-86	-1.0
1930	Bos-N	113	422	51	116	21	9	3	36	29	23	.275	.327	.389	75	-18	5			.980	11	*O-110	-1.3
Total	6	715	2684	387	778	127	47	35	288	156	144	.290	.340	.411	98	-14	37	4		.971	42	O-687/2-3,1-1	-1.5

■ LEW WENDELL
Wendell, Lewis Charles b: 3/22/1892, New York, N.Y. d: 7/11/53, Brooklyn, N.Y. BR/TR, 5'11", 178 lbs. Deb: 6/10/15

YEAR	TM/L	G	AB	R	H	2B	3B	HR	RBI	BB	SO	AVG	OBP	SLG	PRO+	BR/A	SB	CS	SBR	FA	FR	G/POS	TPR
1915	NY-N	20	36	0	8	1	1	0	5	2	7	.222	.263	.306	76	-1	0			.920	-5	C-18	-0.6
1916	NY-N	2	2	0	0	0	0	0	0	0	2	.000	.000	.000	-99	-0	0			.000	0	H	-0.1
1924	Phi-N	21	32	3	8	1	0	0	2	3	5	.250	.314	.281	54	-2	0	0	0	1.000	-1	C-17	-0.3
1925	Phi-N	18	26	0	2	0	0	0	3	1	3	.077	.111	.077	-47	-6	0	0	0	.909	-1	/C-9	-0.6
1926	Phi-N	1	4	0	0	0	0	0	0	0	0	.000	.000	.000	-95	-1	0	0	0	.333	-1	/C-1	-0.2
Total	5	62	100	3	18	2	1	0	10	6	17	.180	.226	.220	23	-10	0	0	0	.925	-8	/C-45	-1.8

■ JACK WENTZ
Wentz, John George (b: John George Wernz) b: 3/4/1863, Louisville, Ky. d: 9/14/07, Louisville, Ky. BR/TR, 5'10.5", 175 lbs. Deb: 4/15/1891

YEAR	TM/L	G	AB	R	H	2B	3B	HR	RBI	BB	SO	AVG	OBP	SLG	PRO+	BR/A	SB	CS	SBR	FA	FR	G/POS	TPR
1891	Lou-a	1	4	0	1	0	0	0	0	0	0	.250	.250	.250	44	-0	0			.667	-1	/2-1	-0.1

■ STAN WENTZEL
Wentzel, Stanley Aaron b: 1/13/17, Lorane, Pa. d: 11/28/91, St.Lawrence, Pa. BR/TR, 6'1", 200 lbs. Deb: 9/23/45

YEAR	TM/L	G	AB	R	H	2B	3B	HR	RBI	BB	SO	AVG	OBP	SLG	PRO+	BR/A	SB	CS	SBR	FA	FR	G/POS	TPR
1945	Bos-N	4	19	3	4	0	1	0	6	0	3	.211	.211	.316	45	-1	1			1.000	-1	/O-4	-0.3

■ JULIE WERA
Wera, Julian Valentine b: 2/9/02, Winona, Minn. d: 12/12/75, Rochester, Minn. BR/TR, 5'8", 164 lbs. Deb: 4/14/27

YEAR	TM/L	G	AB	R	H	2B	3B	HR	RBI	BB	SO	AVG	OBP	SLG	PRO+	BR/A	SB	CS	SBR	FA	FR	G/POS	TPR
1927	NY-A	38	42	7	10	3	0	1	8	1	5	.238	.273	.381	70	-2	0	0	0	1.000	3	3-19	0.1
1929	NY-A	5	12	1	5	0	0	0	2	1	1	.417	.462	.417	137	1	0	0	0	1.000	-1	/3-4	0.0
Total	2	43	54	8	15	3	0	1	10	2	6	.278	.316	.389	85	-1	0	0	0	1.000	2	/3-23	0.1

■ BILLY WERBER
Werber, William Murray b: 6/20/08, Berwyn, Md. BR/TR, 5'10", 170 lbs. Deb: 6/25/30

YEAR	TM/L	G	AB	R	H	2B	3B	HR	RBI	BB	SO	AVG	OBP	SLG	PRO+	BR/A	SB	CS	SBR	FA	FR	G/POS	TPR
1930	NY-A	4	14	5	4	0	0	0	2	3	1	.286	.412	.286	84	-0	0	0	0	.955	1	/S-3,3-1	0.1
1933	NY-A	3	2	0	0	0	0	0	0	0	0	.000	.000	.000	-99	-1	0	0	0	.000	0	/3-1	-0.1
	Bos-A	108	425	64	110	30	6	3	39	33	39	.259	.312	.379	83	-11	15	5	2	.910	-17	S-71,3-38/2-2	-1.8
	Yr	111	427	64	110	30	6	3	39	33	39	.258	.311	.377	82	-12	15	5	2	.910	-17	S-71,3-39/2-2	-1.9
1934	Bos-A	152	623	129	200	41	10	11	67	77	37	.321	.397	.472	115	14	40	15	3	.941	20	*3-130,S-22	4.1
1935	Bos-A	124	462	84	118	30	3	14	61	69	41	.255	.357	.424	95	-8	29	7	5	.942	17	*3-123	2.1
1936	Bos-A	145	535	89	147	29	6	10	67	89	37	.275	.382	.407	90	-8	23	13	-1	.935	-12	*3-101,O-45/2-1	-1.7
1937	Phi-A	128	493	85	144	31	4	7	70	74	35	.292	.386	.414	103	-1	35	13	3	.958	-0	*3-125/O-3	1.0
1938	Phi-A	134	499	92	129	22	7	11	69	93	40	.259	.377	.397	96	-1	19	15	-3	.935	0	*3-134	-0.2
1939	*Cin-N	147	599	115	173	35	5	5	57	91	46	.289	.388	.389	109	11	15			.933	13	*3-143	2.5
1940	*Cin-N	143	584	105	162	35	5	12	48	68	40	.277	.361	.416	113	11	16			.962	3	*3-143	1.7
1941	Cin-N	109	418	56	100	9	2	4	46	53	24	.239	.328	.299	77	-11	14			.959	13	*3-107	0.4
1942	NY-N	98	370	51	76	9	2	1	13	51	22	.205	.308	.249	64	-15	9			.927	10	3-93	-0.4
Total	11	1295	5024	875	1363	271	50	78	539	701	363	.271	.364	.392	97	-10	215	68		.944	49	*3-1143/S-96,O-48,2	7.7

■ PERRY WERDEN
Werden, Percival Wheritt b: 7/21/1865, St.Louis, Mo. d: 1/9/34, Minneapolis, Minn. BR/TR, 6'2", 220 lbs. Deb: 4/24/1884

YEAR	TM/L	G	AB	R	H	2B	3B	HR	RBI	BB	SO	AVG	OBP	SLG	PRO+	BR/A	SB	CS	SBR	FA	FR	G/POS	TPR
1884	StL-U	18	76	7	18	2	0	0		0		.237	.256	.263	56	-6				.893	-1	P-16/O-6	-0.2
1888	Was-N	3	10	0	3	0	0	0	2	1	4	.300	.364	.300	120	0	0			.857	0	/O-3	0.0
1890	Tol-a	128	498	113	147	22	20	6	72	78		.295	.404	.456	149	32	59			.972	6	*1-124/O-5	2.7
1891	Bal-a	139	552	102	160	20	18	6	104	52	59	.290	.363	.424	124	15	46			.980	1	*1-139	0.7
1892	StL-N	149	598	73	154	22	6	8	84	59	52	.258	.328	.355	112	9	20			.982	12	*1-149	1.2
1893	StL-N	125	500	73	138	22	29	4	94	49	25	.276	.349	.442	109	4	11			.968	3	*1-124/O-1	0.3
1897	Lou-N	131	506	76	153	21	14	5	83	40		.302	.366	.429	113	9	14			.984	18	*1-131	2.4
Total	7	693	2740	444	773	109	87	26	439	281	140	.282	.359	.414	119	63	150			.978	38	1-667/P-16,O-15	7.1

■ JOHNNY WERHAS
Werhas, John Charles "Peaches" b: 2/7/38, Highland Park, Mich. BR/TR, 6'2", 200 lbs. Deb: 4/14/64

YEAR	TM/L	G	AB	R	H	2B	3B	HR	RBI	BB	SO	AVG	OBP	SLG	PRO+	BR/A	SB	CS	SBR	FA	FR	G/POS	TPR
1964	LA-N	29	83	6	16	2	1	0	8	13	12	.193	.302	.241	59	-4	0	0	0	.952	4	3-28	-0.1
1965	LA-N	3	4	1	0	0	0	0	0	1	0	.000	.250	.000	-24	-0	0	0	0	1.000	-0	/1-1	-0.1
1967	LA-N	7	7	0	1	0	0	0	0	0	3	.143	.143	.143	-20	-1	0	0	0	.000	0	H	-0.1
	Cal-A	49	75	8	12	1	1	2	6	10	22	.160	.267	.280	64	-3	0	0	0	.963	1	3-30/1-4,O-1	-0.3
Total	3	89	168	15	29	3	2	2	14	24	39	.173	.280	.250	57	-9	0	0	0	.956	4	/3-58,1-5,O-1	-0.6

■ DON WERNER
Werner, Donald Paul b: 3/8/53, Appleton, Wis. BR/TR, 6'1", 185 lbs. Deb: 9/2/75

YEAR	TM/L	G	AB	R	H	2B	3B	HR	RBI	BB	SO	AVG	OBP	SLG	PRO+	BR/A	SB	CS	SBR	FA	FR	G/POS	TPR
1975	Cin-N	7	8	0	1	0	0	0	0	1	1	.125	.222	.125	-2	-1	0	0	0	.923	0	/C-7	-0.1
1976	Cin-N	3	4	0	2	1	0	0	1	0	1	.500	.600	.750	275	1	0	0	0	1.000	1	/C-3	0.2
1977	Cin-N	10	23	3	4	0	0	2	4	2	9	.174	.240	.435	75	-1	0	1	-1	1.000	1	C-10	-0.0
1978	Cin-N	50	113	7	17	2	1	0	11	14	30	.150	.250	.186	23	-11	1	0	0	.987	5	C-49	-0.6
1980	Cin-N	24	64	2	11	2	0	0	5	7	10	.172	.264	.203	32	-6	1	0	0	.962	1	C-24	-0.4
1981	Tex-A	2	8	1	2	1	0	0	2	0	2	.250	.250	.500	47	-1	0	0	0	1.000	-0	/D-2	-0.0
1982	Tex-A	22	59	4	12	1	0	0	2	3	7	.203	.242	.237	34	-5	0	0	0	.980	1	C-22	-0.4
Total	7	118	279	17	49	7	1	2	24	27	53	.176	.256	.229	36	-24	2	1	-1	.979	9	C-115/D-2	-1.4

■ JOE WERRICK
Werrick, Joseph Abraham b: 10/25/1861, St.Paul, Minn. d: 5/10/43, St.Peter, Minn. BR/TR, 5'9", 151 lbs. Deb: 9/27/1884

YEAR	TM/L	G	AB	R	H	2B	3B	HR	RBI	BB	SO	AVG	OBP	SLG	PRO+	BR/A	SB	CS	SBR	FA	FR	G/POS	TPR
1884	StP-U	9	27	3	2	1	0	0	0		1	.074	.107	.074	-81	-8	0			.756	-0	/S-9	-0.8

YEAR	TM/L	G	AB	R	H	2B	3B	HR	RBI	BB	SO	AVG	OBP	SLG	PRO+	BR/A	SB	CS	SBR	FA	FR	G/POS	TPR
1886	Lou-a	136	561	75	140	20	14	3	62	33		.250	.294	.351	96	-6	19			.853	-1	*3-136	-0.3
1887	Lou-a	136	533	90	152	21	13	7	99	38		.285	.336	.413	106	2	49			.831	-0	*3-136	0.4
1888	Lou-a	111	413	49	89	12	7	0	51	30		.215	.274	.278	79	-9	15			.811	-13	3-89,S-11/2-8,O-3	-1.8
Total	4	392	1534	217	383	53	34	10	212	102		.250	.300	.348	94	-21	83			.834	-14	3-361/S-20,2-8,O-3	-2.5

■ DON WERT
Wert, Donald Ralph b: 7/29/38, Strasburg, Pa. BR/TR, 5'9", 165 lbs. Deb: 5/11/63

YEAR	TM/L	G	AB	R	H	2B	3B	HR	RBI	BB	SO	AVG	OBP	SLG	PRO+	BR/A	SB	CS	SBR	FA	FR	G/POS	TPR
1963	Det-A	78	251	31	65	6	2	7	25	24	51	.259	.329	.382	95	-1	3	3	-1	.957	3	3-47,2-21/S-8	0.4
1964	Det-A	148	525	63	135	18	5	9	55	50	74	.257	.329	.362	91	-6	3	4	-2	.965	0	*3-142/S-4	-0.9
1965	Det-A	162	609	81	159	22	2	12	54	73	71	.261	.343	.363	100	1	5	6	-2	.976	5	*3-161/S-3,2-1	0.0
1966	Det-A	150	559	56	150	20	2	11	70	64	69	.268	.346	.370	103	4	6	3	0	.972	-18	*3-150	-1.9
1967	Det-A	142	534	60	137	23	2	6	40	44	59	.257	.321	.341	93	-4	1	1	0	.978	-5	*3-140/S-1	-1.1
1968	*Det-A★	150	536	44	107	15	1	12	37	37	79	.200	.258	.299	66	-22	0	3	-2	.966	-6	*3-150/S-2	-3.5
1969	Det-A	132	423	46	95	11	1	14	50	49	60	.225	.307	.355	81	-11	3	1	0	.966	-0	*3-129	-1.1
1970	Det-A	128	363	34	79	13	0	6	33	44	56	.218	.309	.303	69	-15	1	3	-2	.953	-2	*3-117/2-2	-2.0
1971	Was-A	20	40	2	2	1	0	0	2	4	10	.050	.156	.075	-35	-7	0	0	0	1.000	-4	/S-7,3-7,2-1	-1.1
Total	9	1110	3840	417	929	129	15	77	366	389	529	.242	.317	.343	87	-61	22	24	-8	.968	-27	*3-1043/S-25,2-25	-11.2

■ DENNIS WERTH
Werth, Dennis Dean b: 12/29/52, Lincoln, Ill. BR/TR, 6'1", 200 lbs. Deb: 9/17/79

YEAR	TM/L	G	AB	R	H	2B	3B	HR	RBI	BB	SO	AVG	OBP	SLG	PRO+	BR/A	SB	CS	SBR	FA	FR	G/POS	TPR
1979	NY-A	3	4	1	1	0	0	0	0	0	0	.250	.250	.250	36	-0	0	0	0	1.000	0	/1-1	0.0
1980	NY-A	39	65	15	20	3	0	3	12	12	19	.308	.416	.492	150	5	0	1	-1	1.000	-2	1-12/O-8,C-1,3-1,D	0.2
1981	NY-A	34	55	7	6	1	0	0	1	12	12	.109	.269	.127	18	-5	1	0	0	1.000	0	1-19/O-8,C-3,D-4	-0.6
1982	KC-A	41	15	5	2	0	0	0	2	4	2	.133	.316	.133	29	-1	0	0	0	.990	2	1-35/C-2	0.1
Total	4	117	139	28	29	4	0	3	15	28	33	.209	.341	.302	82	-2	1	1	0	.996	0	/1-67,O-16,D-12,C3	-0.3

■ DEL WERTZ
Wertz, Dwight Lyman Moody b: 10/11/1888, Canton, Ohio d: 5/26/58, Sarasota, Fla. BR/TR, 5'10", 160 lbs. Deb: 5/23/14

YEAR	TM/L	G	AB	R	H	2B	3B	HR	RBI	BB	SO	AVG	OBP	SLG	PRO+	BR/A	SB	CS	SBR	FA	FR	G/POS	TPR
1914	Buf-F	3	0	1	0	0	0	0	0	0	0	—	—	—	—	0	0			1.000	0	/S-1	0.0

■ VIC WERTZ
Wertz, Victor Woodrow b: 2/9/25, York, Pa. d: 7/7/83, Detroit, Mich. BL/TR, 6', 186 lbs. Deb: 4/15/47

YEAR	TM/L	G	AB	R	H	2B	3B	HR	RBI	BB	SO	AVG	OBP	SLG	PRO+	BR/A	SB	CS	SBR	FA	FR	G/POS	TPR
1947	Det-A	102	333	60	96	22	4	6	44	47	66	.288	.376	.432	121	10	2	0	1	.965	-2	O-83	0.4
1948	Det-A	119	391	49	97	19	9	7	67	48	70	.248	.335	.396	92	-6	0	0	0	.954	1	O-98	-1.0
1949	Det-A★	155	608	96	185	26	6	20	133	80	61	.304	.385	.465	124	20	2	3	-1	.981	4	*O-155	1.3
1950	Det-A	149	559	99	172	37	4	27	123	91	55	.308	.408	.533	135	29	0	1	-1	.967	-8	*O-145	1.3
1951	Det-A★	138	501	86	143	24	4	27	94	78	61	.285	.383	.511	139	27	0	3	-2	.989	3	*O-131	2.3
1952	Det-A☆	85	285	46	70	15	3	17	51	46	44	.246	.352	.498	134	12	1	0	0	.986	2	O-79	1.2
	StL-A	37	130	22	45	5	0	6	19	23	20	.346	.444	.523	164	12	1	0	0	.955	-3	O-36	0.8
	Yr	122	415	68	115	20	3	23	70	69	64	.277	.381	.506	143	24	1	0	0			*O-115	2.0
1953	StL-A	128	440	61	118	18	6	19	70	72	54	.268	.376	.466	124	15	1	4	-2	.974	7	*O-121	1.6
1954	Bal-A	29	94	5	19	1	0	1	13	11	17	.202	.286	.245	50	-6	0	0	0	.963	2	O-27	-0.6
	*Cle-A	94	295	33	81	14	2	14	48	34	40	.275	.350	.478	123	8	0	2	-1	.989	1	1-83/O-5	0.5
	Yr	123	389	38	100	15	2	15	61	45	57	.257	.334	.422	106	2	0	2	-1	.989	4	1-83,O-32	-0.1
1955	Cle-A	74	257	30	65	11	2	14	55	32	33	.253	.338	.475	112	3	1	1	0	.984	-3	1-63/O-9	-0.4
1956	Cle-A	136	481	65	127	22	0	32	106	75	87	.264	.359	.509	127	18	0	0	0	.991	1	*1-133	1.0
1957	Cle-A★	144	515	84	145	21	0	28	105	78	88	.282	.378	.485	136	26	2	3	-1	.988	-2	*1-139	1.5
1958	Cle-A	25	43	5	12	1	0	3	12	5	7	.279	.354	.512	139	2	0	0	0	.980	0	/1-8	0.2
1959	Bos-A	94	247	38	68	13	0	7	49	22	32	.275	.339	.413	101	0	0	0	0	.992	2	1-64	-0.2
1960	Bos-A	131	443	45	125	22	0	19	103	37	54	.282	.339	.460	110	5	0	2	-1	.987	3	*1-117	-0.1
1961	Bos-A	99	317	33	83	16	2	11	60	38	43	.262	.345	.429	103	1	0	0	0	.991	3	1-86	-0.2
	Det-A	8	6	0	1	0	0	0	1	0	1	.167	.167	.167	-10	-1	0	0	0	.000	0	H	-0.1
	Yr	107	323	33	84	16	2	11	61	38	44	.260	.342	.424	101	0	0	0	0	.991	3	1-86	-0.3
1962	Det-A	74	105	7	34	2	0	5	18	5	13	.324	.360	.486	121	3	0	0	0	.988	1	1-16	0.2
1963	Det-A	6	5	0	0	0	0	0	0	0	1	.000	.000	.000	-97	-1	0	0	0	.000	0	H	-0.1
	Min-A	35	44	3	6	0	0	3	7	6	5	.136	.240	.341	59	-3	0	0	0	1.000	1	/1-6	-0.2
	Yr	41	49	3	6	0	0	3	7	6	6	.122	.218	.306	44	-4	0	0	0	1.000	1	/1-6	-0.3
Total	17	1862	6099	867	1692	289	42	266	1178	828	842	.277	.366	.469	121	177	9	19	-9	.973	12	O-889,1-715	9.4

■ JIM WESSINGER
Wessinger, James Michael b: 9/25/55, Utica, N.Y. BR/TR, 5'10", 165 lbs. Deb: 8/4/79

YEAR	TM/L	G	AB	R	H	2B	3B	HR	RBI	BB	SO	AVG	OBP	SLG	PRO+	BR/A	SB	CS	SBR	FA	FR	G/POS	TPR
1979	Atl-N	10	7	2	0	0	0	0	0	0	4	.000	.125	.000	-59	-2	0	0	0	.833	1	/2-2	-0.1

■ MAX WEST
West, Max Edward b: 11/28/16, Dexter, Mo. BL/TR, 6'1.5", 182 lbs. Deb: 4/19/38

YEAR	TM/L	G	AB	R	H	2B	3B	HR	RBI	BB	SO	AVG	OBP	SLG	PRO+	BR/A	SB	CS	SBR	FA	FR	G/POS	TPR
1938	Bos-N	123	418	47	98	16	5	10	63	38	38	.234	.300	.368	92	-6	5			.986	-9	*O-109/1-7	-1.9
1939	Bos-N	130	449	67	128	26	6	19	82	51	55	.285	.364	.497	139	23	1			.974	-7	*O-124	1.2
1940	Bos-N★	139	524	72	137	27	5	7	72	65	54	.261	.344	.372	103	3	2			.975	1	*O-102,1-36	-0.5
1941	Bos-N	138	484	63	134	28	4	12	68	72	68	.277	.373	.426	130	20	5			.981	6	*O-132	1.9
1942	Bos-N	134	452	54	115	22	0	16	56	68	59	.254	.354	.409	126	15	4			.991	-1	1-85,O-50	0.7
1946	Bos-N	1	0	0	0	0	0	0	0	0	1	.000	.000	.000	-99	-0	0			1.000	-0	/1-1	0.0
	Cin-N	72	202	16	43	13	0	5	18	32	36	.213	.323	.351	95	-1	1			.952	-1	O-58	-0.5
	Yr	73	203	16	43	13	0	5	18	32	37	.212	.322	.350	94	-2	1			.952	-4	O-58/1-1	-0.5
1948	Pit-N	87	146	19	26	4	0	8	21	27	29	.178	.330	.370	82	-4	1			.991	-4	1-32,O-16	-0.8
Total	7	824	2676	338	681	136	20	77	380	353	340	.254	.344	.407	114	50	19			.975	-15	O-591,1-161	0.1

■ BUCK WEST
West, Milton Douglas b: 8/29/1860, Spring Mill, Ohio d: 1/13/29, Mansfield, Ohio BL/TR, 5'10", 200 lbs. Deb: 8/24/1884

YEAR	TM/L	G	AB	R	H	2B	3B	HR	RBI	BB	SO	AVG	OBP	SLG	PRO+	BR/A	SB	CS	SBR	FA	FR	G/POS	TPR
1884	Cin-a	33	131	20	32	2	8	1	15	2		.244	.256	.405	107	-4	4			.825	-6	O-33	-0.5
1890	Cle-N	37	151	20	37	6	1	2	29	7	11	.245	.283	.338	82	-4	4			.831	-1	O-37	-0.6
Total	2	70	282	40	69	8	9	3	44	9	11	.245	.271	.369	94	-4	4			.828	-7	/O-70	-1.1

■ DICK WEST
West, Richard Thomas b: 11/24/15, Louisville, Ky. d: 3/13/96, Fort Wayne, Ind. BR/TR, 6'2", 180 lbs. Deb: 9/28/38

YEAR	TM/L	G	AB	R	H	2B	3B	HR	RBI	BB	SO	AVG	OBP	SLG	PRO+	BR/A	SB	CS	SBR	FA	FR	G/POS	TPR
1938	Cin-N	1	1	0	0	0	0	0	0	0	0	.000	.000	.000	-99	-0	0			.000	0	H	0.0
1939	Cin-N	8	19	1	4	0	0	0	4	1	4	.211	.250	.211	25	-2	0			1.000	-1	/O-5,C-1	-0.3
1940	Cin-N	7	28	4	11	2	0	1	6	0	2	.393	.393	.571	161	2	1			1.000	-3	/C-7	0.0
1941	Cin-N	67	172	15	37	5	2	1	17	6	23	.215	.246	.285	49	-12	4			.970	-3	C-64	-1.2
1942	Cin-N	33	79	9	14	3	0	1	8	5	13	.177	.226	.253	40	-6	1			.989	3	C-17/O-6	-0.3
1943	Cin-N	3	0	1	0	0	0	0	0	0	0	—	—	—		0	0			.000	0	R	0.0
Total	6	119	299	30	66	10	2	3	35	12	42	.221	.253	.298	55	-18	6			.977	-4	/C-89,O-11	-1.8

■ SAM WEST
West, Samuel Filmore b: 10/5/04, Longview, Tex. d: 11/23/85, Lubbock, Tex. BL/TL, 5'11", 165 lbs. Deb: 4/17/27 C

YEAR	TM/L	G	AB	R	H	2B	3B	HR	RBI	BB	SO	AVG	OBP	SLG	PRO+	BR/A	SB	CS	SBR	FA	FR	G/POS	TPR
1927	Was-A	38	67	9	16	4	1	0	6	8	8	.239	.320	.328	69	-3	1	0	0	.939	-1	O-18	-0.5
1928	Was-A	125	378	59	114	30	7	3	40	20	23	.302	.338	.442	104	1	5	6	-2	.996	-10	*O-116	-1.7
1929	Was-A	142	510	60	136	16	8	3	75	45	41	.267	.326	.347	73	-20	9	8	-2	.978	15	*O-139	-1.6
1930	Was-A	120	411	75	135	22	10	6	67	37	34	.328	.385	.474	116	10	5	5	-2	.972	3	*O-118	0.4
1931	Was-A	132	526	77	175	43	13	3	91	30	37	.333	.369	.481	121	14	6	8	-3	.990	21	*O-127	2.2
1932	Was-A	146	554	88	159	27	12	6	83	48	57	.287	.345	.412	96	-4	4	5	-2	.979	19	*O-143	0.5
1933	StL-A★	133	517	93	155	25	12	11	48	59	49	.300	.373	.458	112	8	10	6	-3	.988	8	*O-127	0.8
1934	StL-A★	122	482	90	157	22	10	9	55	62	55	.326	.403	.469	115	11	3	6	-2	.988	0	*O-120	-0.1
1935	StL-A☆	138	527	93	158	37	4	10	70	75	46	.300	.388	.442	109	8	1	6	-3	.989	17	*O-135	1.5
1936	StL-A	152	533	78	148	26	4	7	70	70	70	.278	.386	.381	87	-8	2	0	0	.983	9	*O-148	-0.3
1937	StL-A	122	457	68	150	37	4	7	58	46	28	.328	.390	.473	115	11	1	7	-2	.988	12	*O-105	1.7
1938	StL-A	44	165	17	51	8	2	1	27	14	9	.309	.363	.400	91	-2	0	0	0	.971	-5	O-41	-0.6
	Was-A	92	344	51	104	19	5	6	47	33	21	.302	.363	.430	105	2	1	1	0	.983	-0	O-85	-0.3
	Yr	136	509	68	155	27	7	6	74	47	30	.305	.363	.420	100	0	1	0	0	.979	-6	*O-126	-0.9
1939	Was-A	115	390	52	110	20	3	8	52	67	29	.282	.387	.397	109	7	1	0	0	.992	3	O-89,1-17	0.5
1940	Was-A	57	99	7	25	6	1	0	18	16	13	.253	.357	.364	93	-1	0	2	-1	.990	-1	1-12/O-9	-0.4

YEAR	TM/L	G	AB	R	H	2B	3B	HR	RBI	BB	SO	AVG	OBP	SLG	PRO+	BR/A	SB	CS	SBR	FA	FR	G/POS	TPR
1941	Was-A	26	37	3	10	0	0	0	6	11	2	.270	.438	.270	95	1	1	0	0	1.000	-0	/O-8	0.0
1942	Chi-A	49	151	14	35	5	0	0	25	31	18	.232	.363	.265	80	-2	2	0	1	.983	-3	O-45	-0.7
Total	16	1753	6148	934	1838	347	101	75	838	696	540	.299	.371	.425	103	34	53	56	-18	.983	93	*O-1573/1-29	2.4

■ MAX WEST   West, Walter Maxwell b: 7/14/04, Sunset, Tex.   d: 4/25/71, Houston, Tex.   BR/TR, 5'11", 165 lbs.   Deb: 9/18/28

YEAR	TM/L	G	AB	R	H	2B	3B	HR	RBI	BB	SO	AVG	OBP	SLG	PRO+	BR/A	SB	CS	SBR	FA	FR	G/POS	TPR
1928	Bro-N	7	21	4	6	1	1	0	1	4	1	.286	.400	.429	118	1	0			.882	1	/O-6	0.2
1929	Bro-N	5	8	1	2	1	0	0	1	1	0	.250	.333	.375	77	-0	0			1.000	-1	/O-2	-0.1
Total	2	12	29	5	8	2	1	0	2	5	1	.276	.382	.414	107	0	0			.895	1	/O-8	0.1

■ BILLY WEST   West, William Nelson b: 8/21/1840, Philadelphia, Pa.   Deb: 5/22/1874

YEAR	TM/L	G	AB	R	H	2B	3B	HR	RBI	BB	SO	AVG	OBP	SLG	PRO+	BR/A	SB	CS	SBR	FA	FR	G/POS	TPR
1874	Atl-n	9	35	4	8	0	0	0	2	1	2	.229	.250	.257	71	-1	0	0	0	.663	-1	/2-9,S-1	-0.2
1876	NY-N	1	4	0	0	0	0	0	0	0	0	.000	.000	.000	-99	-1				1.000	-1	/2-1	-0.1

■ OSCAR WESTERBERG   Westerberg, Oscar William b: 7/8/1882, Alameda, Cal.   d: 4/17/09, Alameda, Cal.   BB/TR,   Deb: 9/5/07

YEAR	TM/L	G	AB	R	H	2B	3B	HR	RBI	BB	SO	AVG	OBP	SLG	PRO+	BR/A	SB	CS	SBR	FA	FR	G/POS	TPR
1907	Bos-N	2	6	0	2	0	0	0	1	1		.333	.429	.333	139	0	0			1.000	-1	/S-2	0.0

■ JIM WESTLAKE   Westlake, James Patrick b: 7/3/30, Sacramento, Cal.   BL/TL, 6'1", 190 lbs.   Deb: 4/16/55 F

YEAR	TM/L	G	AB	R	H	2B	3B	HR	RBI	BB	SO	AVG	OBP	SLG	PRO+	BR/A	SB	CS	SBR	FA	FR	G/POS	TPR
1955	Phi-N	1	1	0	0	0	0	0	0	0	0	.000	.000	.000	0	0	0	0	0	.000	0	H	0.0

■ WALLY WESTLAKE   Westlake, Waldon Thomas b: 11/8/20, Gridley, Cal.   BR/TR, 6', 186 lbs.   Deb: 4/15/47 F

YEAR	TM/L	G	AB	R	H	2B	3B	HR	RBI	BB	SO	AVG	OBP	SLG	PRO+	BR/A	SB	CS	SBR	FA	FR	G/POS	TPR
1947	Pit-N	112	407	59	111	17	4	17	69	27	63	.273	.324	.459	103	-0	5			.988	4	*O-109	-0.2
1948	Pit-N	132	428	78	122	10	6	17	65	46	40	.285	.360	.456	117	10	2			.976	-0	*O-125	0.3
1949	Pit-N	147	525	77	148	24	8	23	104	45	69	.282	.345	.490	118	12	6			.982	5	*O-143	1.0
1950	Pit-N	139	477	69	136	15	6	24	95	48	78	.285	.359	.493	118	11	1			**.991**	4	*O-123	1.0
1951	Pit-N	50	181	28	51	4	0	16	45	9	26	.282	.323	.569	131	7	0	1	-1	.908	3	3-34,O-11	1.0
	StL-N★	73	267	36	68	8	5	6	39	24	42	.255	.325	.390	91	-4	1	2	-1	.982	2	O-68	-0.5
	Yr	123	448	64	119	12	5	22	84	33	68	.266	.324	.462	107	3	1	3	-2	.984	7	O-79,3-34	0.5
1952	StL-N	21	74	7	16	3	0	0	10	8	11	.216	.293	.257	53	-5	1	1	-0	1.000	6	O-15	0.1
	Cin-N	59	183	29	37	4	0	3	14	31	29	.202	.324	.273	67	-7	0	2	-1	.992	-2	O-56	-1.2
	Yr	80	257	36	53	7	0	3	24	39	40	.206	.315	.268	63	-12	1	3	-2	.995	5	O-71	-1.1
	Cle-A	29	69	11	16	4	1	1	9	8	16	.232	.312	.362	93	-1	0	0		1.000	-3	O-28	-0.5
1953	Cle-A	82	218	42	72	7	1	9	46	35	29	.330	.427	.495	153	17	2	1	0	.963	-11	O-72	-0.6
1954	*Cle-A	85	240	36	63	9	2	11	42	26	37	.262	.340	.454	114	4	0	1	-1	.964	-7	O-70	-0.1
1955	Cle-A	16	20	2	5	1	0	1	3	5	9	.250	.348	.300	73	-1	0	0		1.000	-0	/O-7	-0.1
	Bal-A	8	24	0	3	1	0	0	6	2	1	.125	.300	.167	30	-2	0	1	-1	1.000	-1	/O-7	-0.4
	Yr	24	44	2	8	2	0	1	9	7	10	.182	.321	.227	49	-3	0	1	-1	1.000	-2	O-14	-0.5
1956	Phi-N	5	4	0	0	0	0	0	0	0	3	.000	.000	.000	-41	-1	0	0		.000	0	H	-0.1
Total	10	958	3117	474	848	107	33	127	539	317	453	.272	.346	.450	111	41	19	7		.983	1	O-834/3-34	2.4

■ AL WESTON   Weston, Alfred John b: 12/11/05, Lynn, Mass.   BR/TR, 6', 195 lbs.   Deb: 7/7/29

YEAR	TM/L	G	AB	R	H	2B	3B	HR	RBI	BB	SO	AVG	OBP	SLG	PRO+	BR/A	SB	CS	SBR	FA	FR	G/POS	TPR
1929	Bos-N	3	3	0	0	0	0	0	0	0	0	.000	.000	.000	-99	-1	0			.000	0	H	-0.1

■ WES WESTRUM   Westrum, Wesley Noreen b: 11/28/22, Clearbrook, Minn.   BR/TR, 5'11", 185 lbs.   Deb: 9/17/47 MC

YEAR	TM/L	G	AB	R	H	2B	3B	HR	RBI	BB	SO	AVG	OBP	SLG	PRO+	BR/A	SB	CS	SBR	FA	FR	G/POS	TPR
1947	NY-N	6	12	1	5	1	0	0	1	0	0	.417	.417	.500	142	0	0			1.000	0	/C-2	0.1
1948	NY-N	66	125	14	20	3	1	4	16	20	36	.160	.276	.296	54	-8	3			.981	8	C-63	0.3
1949	NY-N	64	169	23	41	4	1	7	28	37	39	.243	.385	.402	111	4	1			.980	-0	C-62	0.7
1950	NY-N	140	437	68	103	13	3	23	71	92	73	.236	.371	.437	111	9	2			**.999**	10	*C-139	2.5
1951	*NY-N	124	361	59	79	12	1	20	70	104	93	.219	.400	.418	119	14	1	0	0	.987	8	*C-122	2.8
1952	NY-N☆	114	322	47	71	11	0	14	43	76	68	.220	.374	.385	110	7	1	2	-1	.978	-4	*C-112	0.8
1953	NY-N☆	107	290	40	65	5	0	12	30	56	73	.224	.352	.366	86	-5	2	0	1	.982	4	*C-106/3-1	0.4
1954	*NY-N	98	246	25	46	3	1	8	27	45	60	.187	.310	.305	63	-13	0	1	-1	.985	12	C-98	0.3
1955	NY-N	69	137	11	29	1	0	4	18	24	18	.212	.333	.307	71	-5	0	1	-1	.987	10	C-68	0.6
1956	NY-N	68	132	10	29	5	2	3	8	25	28	.220	.348	.356	91	-1	0	0	0	.982	13	C-67	1.4
1957	NY-N	63	91	4	15	2	0	2	10	24	26	.165	.255	.209	27	-9	0	1	-1	.966	2	C-63	-0.7
Total	11	919	2322	302	503	59	8	96	315	489	514	.217	.357	.373	95	-6	10	5		.985	64	C-902/3-1	9.2

■ JEFF WETHERBY   Wetherby, Jeffrey Barrett b: 10/18/63, Granada Hills, Cal.   BL/TL, 6'2", 195 lbs.   Deb: 6/7/89

YEAR	TM/L	G	AB	R	H	2B	3B	HR	RBI	BB	SO	AVG	OBP	SLG	PRO+	BR/A	SB	CS	SBR	FA	FR	G/POS	TPR
1989	Atl-N	52	48	5	10	2	1	1	4	7	4	6	.208	.269	.354	75	-2	1	0	0	1.000	-2	/O-9	-0.4

■ DUTCH WETZEL   Wetzel, Franklin Burton b: 7/7/1893, Columbus, Ind.   d: 3/5/42, Hollywood, Cal.   BR/TR, 5'9.5", 177 lbs.   Deb: 9/15/20

YEAR	TM/L	G	AB	R	H	2B	3B	HR	RBI	BB	SO	AVG	OBP	SLG	PRO+	BR/A	SB	CS	SBR	FA	FR	G/POS	TPR
1920	StL-A	7	21	5	9	1	1	0	4	5	1	.429	.520	.571	183	2	0	1	-1	.875	0	/O-6	0.2
1921	StL-A	61	119	16	25	2	0	2	10	9	20	.210	.271	.277	38	-11	0	0	0	.981	-2	O-27	-1.4
Total	2	68	140	21	34	3	1	2	15	13	21	.243	.312	.321	59	-8	0	1	-1	.957	-2	/O-33	-1.2

■ BILL WHALEY   Whaley, William Carl b: 2/10/1899, Indianapolis, Ind.   d: 3/3/43, Indianapolis, Ind.   BR/TR, 5'11", 178 lbs.   Deb: 4/18/23

YEAR	TM/L	G	AB	R	H	2B	3B	HR	RBI	BB	SO	AVG	OBP	SLG	PRO+	BR/A	SB	CS	SBR	FA	FR	G/POS	TPR
1923	StL-A	23	50	5	12	2	1	0	1	4	2	.240	.309	.320	62	-3	0	0	0	1.000	-0	O-13	-0.4

■ BERT WHALING   Whaling, Albert James b: 6/22/1888, Los Angeles, Cal.   d: 1/21/65, Sawtelle, Cal.   BR/TR, 6', 185 lbs.   Deb: 4/22/13

YEAR	TM/L	G	AB	R	H	2B	3B	HR	RBI	BB	SO	AVG	OBP	SLG	PRO+	BR/A	SB	CS	SBR	FA	FR	G/POS	TPR
1913	Bos-N	79	211	22	51	8	2	0	25	10	32	.242	.283	.299	65	-10	3			**.990**	1	C-77	-0.4
1914	Bos-N	60	172	18	36	7	0	0	12	21	28	.209	.303	.250	65	-7	2			.981	12	C-59	1.0
1915	Bos-N	72	190	10	42	6	2	0	13	8	38	.221	.264	.274	66	-8	0	1	-1	.986	1	C-69	-0.3
Total	3	211	573	50	129	21	4	0	50	39	98	.225	.283	.276	65	-25	5	1		.986	14	C-205	0.3

■ MACK WHEAT   Wheat, McKinley Davis b: 6/9/1893, Polo, Mo.   d: 8/14/79, Los Banos, Cal.   BR/TR, 5'11.5", 167 lbs.   Deb: 4/14/15 F

YEAR	TM/L	G	AB	R	H	2B	3B	HR	RBI	BB	SO	AVG	OBP	SLG	PRO+	BR/A	SB	CS	SBR	FA	FR	G/POS	TPR
1915	Bro-N	8	14	0	1	0	0	0	0	0	5	.071	.071	.071	-56	-3	0			.957	-0	/C-8	-0.3
1916	Bro-N	2	2	0	0	0	0	0	0	0	1	.000	.000	.000	-97	-0	0			1.000	0	/C-2	0.0
1917	Bro-N	29	60	2	8	1	0	0	0	1	12	.133	.161	.150	-4	-7	1			.968	1	C-18/O-7	-0.7
1918	Bro-N	57	157	11	34	7	1	0	3	8	24	.217	.255	.293	67	-6	2			.966	-1	C-38/O-7	-0.6
1919	Bro-N	41	112	5	23	3	0	0	2	8	22	.205	.246	.232	43	-8	1			.944	-4	C-38	-0.9
1920	Phi-N	78	230	15	52	10	3	3	20	8	35	.226	.261	.335	67	-10	3	1	0	.961	9	C-74	0.4
1921	Phi-N	10	27	1	5	2	1	0	4	0	3	.185	.241	.333	47	-2	0	0	0	.980	5	/C-9	0.3
Total	7	225	602	34	123	23	5	4	35	19	102	.204	.241	.279	52	-37	7	1		.961	9	C-187/O-16	-1.8

■ ZACK WHEAT   Wheat, Zachary Davis "Buck" b: 5/23/1888, Hamilton, Mo.   d: 3/11/72, Sedalia, Mo.   BL/TR, 5'10", 170 lbs.   Deb: 9/11/09 FH

YEAR	TM/L	G	AB	R	H	2B	3B	HR	RBI	BB	SO	AVG	OBP	SLG	PRO+	BR/A	SB	CS	SBR	FA	FR	G/POS	TPR
1909	Bro-N	26	102	15	31	7	3	0	4	6		.304	.343	.431	145	5	1			.952	2	O-26	0.6
1910	Bro-N	156	606	78	172	36	15	2	55	47	80	.284	.341	.403	120	13	16			.962	6	*O-156	1.2
1911	Bro-N	140	534	55	153	26	13	5	76	29	58	.287	.332	.412	112	6	21			.955	-3	*O-136	-0.4
1912	Bro-N	123	453	70	138	28	7	8	65	39	40	.305	.362	.450	128	16	16			.968	3	*O-120	1.2
1913	Bro-N	138	535	64	161	28	10	7	58	25	45	.301	.335	.430	114	8	19			.978	9	*O-135	1.1
1914	Bro-N	145	533	66	170	26	9	9	89	47	50	.319	.374	.452	143	27	20			.962	18	*O-144	4.1
1915	Bro-N	146	528	64	136	15	12	5	66	52	42	.258	.330	.360	107	5	21	14	-2	.953	10	*O-144	0.6
1916	*Bro-N	149	568	76	177	32	13	9	73	43	49	.312	.366	**.461**	149	32	19			.975	9	*O-149	3.7
1917	Bro-N	109	362	38	113	15	11	1	41	20	18	.312	.352	.423	133	13	5			.979	5	O-98	1.7
1918	Bro-N	105	409	39	137	15	3	0	51	16	17	**.335**	.369	.386	131	14	9			.979	4	*O-105	1.4
1919	Bro-N	137	536	70	159	23	11	5	62	33	27	.297	.344	.409	123	14	15			.971	-1	*O-137	0.4
1920	*Bro-N	148	583	89	191	26	13	9	73	48	21	.328	.385	.463	138	29	8	10	-4	.971	-4	*O-148	1.1
1921	Bro-N	148	568	91	182	31	10	14	85	44	19	.320	.372	.484	121	16	11	8	-2	.965	-4	*O-148	-0.1
1922	Bro-N	152	600	92	201	29	12	16	112	45	22	.335	.388	.503	129	25	9	6	-1	**.991**	2	*O-152	1.5
1923	Bro-N	98	349	63	131	13	5	8	65	23	12	.375	.424	.510	148	20	7			.908	-11	O-87	0.8
1924	Bro-N	141	566	92	212	41	8	14	97	49	18	.375	.428	.549	165	52	3			.965	5	*O-139	4.5
1925	Bro-N	150	616	125	221	42	14	14	103	40	22	.359	.403	.541	143	38	2			.962	0	*O-149	2.7
1926	Bro-N	111	411	68	119	31	5	5	35	21	14	.290	.326	.411	99	-2	4			.955	2	*O-102	-0.8

YEAR	TM/L	G	AB	R	H	2B	3B	HR	RBI	BB	SO	AVG	OBP	SLG	PRO+	BR/A	SB	CS	SBR	FA	FR	G/POS	TPR
1927	Phi-A	88	247	34	80	12	1	1	38	18	5	.324	.379	.393	95	-1	2	3	-1	.983	-3	O-62	-0.8
Total	19	2410	9106	1289	2884	476	172	132	1248	650	559	.317	.367	.450	129	335	205	49		.966	50	*O-2337	24.3

■ **WOODY WHEATON**   Wheaton, Elwood Pierce   b: 10/3/14, Philadelphia, Pa.   d: 12/11/95, Lancaster, Pa.   BL/TL, 5'8.5", 160 lbs.   Deb: 9/28/43

YEAR	TM/L	G	AB	R	H	2B	3B	HR	RBI	BB	SO	AVG	OBP	SLG	PRO+	BR/A	SB	CS	SBR	FA	FR	G/POS	TPR
1943	Phi-A	7	30	2	6	2	0	0	3	2		.200	.294	.267	65	-1	0	0	0	1.000	1	/O-7	-0.1
1944	Phi-A	30	59	1	11	2	0	0	5	5	8	.186	.250	.220	35	-5	1	2	-1	1.000	2	P-11/O-8	-0.2
Total	2	37	89	3	17	4	0	0	7	8	5	.191	.265	.236	45	-6	1	2	-1	.981	3	/O-15,P-11	-0.3

■ **DON WHEELER**   Wheeler, Donald Wesley "Scott"   b: 9/29/22, Minneapolis, Minn   BR/TR, 5'10", 175 lbs.   Deb: 4/23/49

YEAR	TM/L	G	AB	R	H	2B	3B	HR	RBI	BB	SO	AVG	OBP	SLG	PRO+	BR/A	SB	CS	SBR	FA	FR	G/POS	TPR
1949	Chi-A	67	192	17	46	9	2	1	22	27	19	.240	.333	.323	76	-6	2	0	1	.976	3	C-58	0.0

■ **ED WHEELER**   Wheeler, Edward   b: 6/15/1878, Sherman, Mich.   d: 8/15/60, Ft.Worth, Tex.   BB/TR, 5'10", 160 lbs.   Deb: 5/10/02

YEAR	TM/L	G	AB	R	H	2B	3B	HR	RBI	BB	SO	AVG	OBP	SLG	PRO+	BR/A	SB	CS	SBR	FA	FR	G/POS	TPR
1902	Bro-N	30	96	4	12	0	0	0	5	3		.125	.152	.125	-15	-13	1			.863	-3	3-11,2-10/S-5	-1.6

■ **ED WHEELER**   Wheeler, Edward Raymond   b: 5/24/15, Los Angeles, Cal.   d: 8/4/83, Centralia, Wash.   BR/TR, 5'9", 160 lbs.   Deb: 4/19/45

YEAR	TM/L	G	AB	R	H	2B	3B	HR	RBI	BB	SO	AVG	OBP	SLG	PRO+	BR/A	SB	CS	SBR	FA	FR	G/POS	TPR
1945	Cle-A	46	72	12	14	2	0	0	1	8	13	.194	.275	.222	47	-5	1	1	-0	.912	-6	3-14,S-11/2-3	-1.1

■ **GEORGE WHEELER**   Wheeler, George Harrison "Heavy"   b: 11/10/1881, Shelburn, Ind.   d: 6/14/18, Clinton, Ind.   BL/TR, 5'9.5", 180 lbs.   Deb: 7/27/10

YEAR	TM/L	G	AB	R	H	2B	3B	HR	RBI	BB	SO	AVG	OBP	SLG	PRO+	BR/A	SB	CS	SBR	FA	FR	G/POS	TPR
1910	Cin-N	3	3	0	0	0	0	0	0	0	2	.000	.000	.000	-99	-1	0			.000	0	H	-0.1

■ **HARRY WHEELER**   Wheeler, Harry Eugene   b: 3/3/1858, Versailles, Ind.   d: 10/9/1900, Cincinnati, Ohio   BR/TR, 5'11", 165 lbs.   Deb: 6/19/1878   M

YEAR	TM/L	G	AB	R	H	2B	3B	HR	RBI	BB	SO	AVG	OBP	SLG	PRO+	BR/A	SB	CS	SBR	FA	FR	G/POS	TPR
1878	Pro-N	7	27	7	4	0	0	0	1	2	15	.148	.207	.148	18	-2				.875	-2	/P-7	0.0
1879	Cin-N	1	3	0	0	0	0	0	0	0	2	.000	.000	.000	-99	-1				1.000	0	/O-1,P-1	-0.1
1880	Cle-N	1	4	0	1	0	0	0	0	0	2	.250	.250	.250	72	-0				1.000	-0	/O-1	0.0
	Cin-N	17	65	1	6	2	0	0	2	0	15	.092	.092	.123	-28	-8				.750	1	O-17	-0.8
	Yr	18	69	1	7	2	0	0	2	0	15	.101	.101	.130	-22	-8				.759	1	O-18	-0.8
1882	Cin-a	76	344	59	86	11	11	1	29		7	.250	.265	.355	102	-1				.808	-5	*O-64,1-12/P-4	-0.7
1883	Col-a	82	371	42	84	6	7	0	6			.226	.239	.280	72	-10				.803	-2	*O-82/2-1,P-1	-1.2
1884	StL-a	5	19	0	5	2	0	0	1			.263	.300	.368	113	0				.600	-1	/O-5	-0.1
	KC-U	14	62	11	16	1	0	0	3			.258	.292	.274	83	-3				.769	0	O-13/P-1,M	-0.3
	CP-U	37	158	29	36	5	3	1	4			.228	.247	.316	70	-11				.774	-5	O-37	-1.4
	Bal-U	17	69	3	18	2	0	0				.261	.261	.290	60	-5				.815	-1	O-17	-0.1
	Yr	68	289	43	70	8	3	1	7			.242	.260	.301	70	-19				.781	-5	O-67/P-1	-2.3
Total	6	257	1122	152	256	29	21	2	32	23	32	.228	.244	.297	74	-41				.791	-14	O-237/P-14,1-12,2-1	-5.2

■ **DICK WHEELER**   Wheeler, Richard (b: Richard Wheeler Maynard)   b: 1/14/1898, Keene, N.H.   d: 2/12/62, Lexington, Mass.   BR/TR, 5'11", 185 lbs.   Deb: 6/17/18

YEAR	TM/L	G	AB	R	H	2B	3B	HR	RBI	BB	SO	AVG	OBP	SLG	PRO+	BR/A	SB	CS	SBR	FA	FR	G/POS	TPR
1918	StL-N	3	6	0	0	0	0	0	0	0	3	.000	.000	.000	-99	-1	0			.000	-1	/O-2	-0.3

■ **BOBBY WHEELOCK**   Wheelock, Warren H.   b: 8/6/1864, Charlestown, Mass.   d: 3/13/28, Boston, Mass.   BR/TR, 5'8", 160 lbs.   Deb: 5/19/1887

YEAR	TM/L	G	AB	R	H	2B	3B	HR	RBI	BB	SO	AVG	OBP	SLG	PRO+	BR/A	SB	CS	SBR	FA	FR	G/POS	TPR
1887	Bos-N	48	166	32	42	4	2	2	15	15	15	.253	.315	.337	81	-4	20			.878	-7	O-28,S-20/2-4	-0.9
1890	Col-a	52	190	24	45	6	1	1	16	25		.237	.326	.295	89	-2	34			.885	-1	S-52	0.0
1891	Col-a	136	498	82	114	15	1	0	39	78	55	.229	.336	.285	76	-12	52			.899	19	*S-136	1.3
Total	3	236	854	138	201	25	4	3	70	118	70	.235	.330	.285	80	-18	106			.894	11	S-208/O-28,2-4	0.4

■ **JIMMY WHELAN**   Whelan, James Francis   b: 5/11/1890, Kansas City, Mo.   d: 11/29/29, Dayton, Ohio   BR/TR, 5'8.5", 165 lbs.   Deb: 4/24/13

YEAR	TM/L	G	AB	R	H	2B	3B	HR	RBI	BB	SO	AVG	OBP	SLG	PRO+	BR/A	SB	CS	SBR	FA	FR	G/POS	TPR
1913	StL-N	1	1	0	0	0	0	0	0	0	0	.000	.000	.000	-99	-1	0			.000	0	H	0.0

■ **TOM WHELAN**   Whelan, Thomas Joseph   b: 1/3/1894, Lynn, Mass.   d: 6/26/57, Boston, Mass.   BR/TR, 5'11", 175 lbs.   Deb: 8/13/20

YEAR	TM/L	G	AB	R	H	2B	3B	HR	RBI	BB	SO	AVG	OBP	SLG	PRO+	BR/A	SB	CS	SBR	FA	FR	G/POS	TPR
1920	Bos-N	1	1	0	0	0	0	0	0	0	1	.000	.500	.000	54	0	0	0	0	1.000	0	/1-1	0.0

■ **PETE WHISENANT**   Whisenant, Thomas Peter   b: 12/14/29, Asheville, N.C.   d: 3/22/96, Port Charlotte, Fla.   BR/TR, 6'2", 200 lbs.   Deb: 4/16/52   C

YEAR	TM/L	G	AB	R	H	2B	3B	HR	RBI	BB	SO	AVG	OBP	SLG	PRO+	BR/A	SB	CS	SBR	FA	FR	G/POS	TPR
1952	Bos-N	24	52	3	10	2	0	0	7	4	13	.192	.250	.231	35	-5	1	1	-0	.973	2	O-14	-0.3
1955	StL-N	58	115	10	22	5	1	2	9	5	29	.191	.225	.304	39	-10	2	0	1	.964	1	O-40	-1.2
1956	Chi-N	103	314	37	75	16	3	11	46	24	53	.239	.295	.414	89	-5	8	2	1	.992	6	O-93	-0.3
1957	Cin-N	67	90	18	19	3	2	5	11	5	24	.211	.253	.456	80	-3	0	1	-1	.982	-9	O-43	-1.4
1958	Cin-N	85	203	33	48	9	2	11	40	18	37	.236	.299	.463	93	-3	3	0	1	1.000	-1	O-66/2-1	-0.6
1959	Cin-N	36	71	13	17	2	0	5	11	9	18	.239	.316	.479	105	0	0	0	0	.966	-2	O-21	-0.3
1960	Cin-N	1	1	0	0	0	0	0	0	0	0	.000	.000	.000	-98	-0	0	0	0	.000	0	H	0.0
	Cle-A	7	6	0	1	0	0	0	0	0	2	.167	.167	.167	-10	-1	0	0	0	1.000	0	/O-2	-0.1
	Was-A	58	115	19	26	9	0	3	9	19	14	.226	.336	.383	95	-1	2	1	0	1.000	-9	O-47	-1.2
	Yr	65	121	19	27	9	0	3	9	19	16	.223	.329	.372	90	-2	2	1	0	1.000	-10	O-49	-1.4
1961	Min-A	10	6	1	0	0	0	0	0	1	2	.000	.143	.000	-55	-1	0	0	0	1.000	-0	O-5	-0.3
	Cin-N	26	15	6	3	0	0	0	1	2	4	.200	.294	.200	34	-1	1	0	0	1.000	-4	O-12/C,1,3-1	-0.5
Total	8	475	988	140	221	46	8	37	134	86	196	.224	.287	.399	80	-30	17	5	2	.988	-20	O-343/3-1,C,1,2-1	-6.3

■ **LARRY WHISENTON**   Whisenton, Larry   b: 7/3/56, St.Louis, Mo.   BL/TL, 6'1", 190 lbs.   Deb: 9/17/77

YEAR	TM/L	G	AB	R	H	2B	3B	HR	RBI	BB	SO	AVG	OBP	SLG	PRO+	BR/A	SB	CS	SBR	FA	FR	G/POS	TPR
1977	Atl-N	4	4	1	1	0	0	0	1	0	3	.250	.250	.250	31	-0	0	0	0	.000	0	H	-0.1
1978	Atl-N	6	16	1	3	1	0	0	2	3		.188	.235	.250	32	-1	0	0	0	1.000	0	/O-4	-0.2
1979	Atl-N	13	37	3	9	2	1	0	1	3	3	.243	.300	.351	72	-1	0	0	0	1.000	3	O-13	0.1
1981	Atl-N	9	5	1	1	0	0	0	2	1		.200	.429	.200	81	0	0	0	0	.000	-1	/O-2	-0.1
1982	*Atl-N	84	143	21	34	7	2	4	17	23	33	.238	.343	.399	103	1	2	2	-1	.964	-2	O-34	-0.3
Total	5	116	205	27	48	10	3	4	21	29	42	.234	.329	.371	90	-2	3	2	-0	.968	-1	/O-53	-0.6

■ **LEW WHISTLER**   Whistler, Lewis W. (b: Lewis Wissler)   b: 3/10/1868, St.Louis, Mo.   d: 12/30/59, St.Louis, Mo.   TR, 5'10.5", 178 lbs.   Deb: 8/7/1890

YEAR	TM/L	G	AB	R	H	2B	3B	HR	RBI	BB	SO	AVG	OBP	SLG	PRO+	BR/A	SB	CS	SBR	FA	FR	G/POS	TPR
1890	NY-N	45	170	27	49	9	7	2	29	20	37	.288	.366	.459	140	8	8			.982	-2	1-45	0.4
1891	NY-N	72	265	39	65	8	7	3	38	24	45	.245	.315	.362	101	0	4			.852	-16	S-33,O-22/1-7,23	-1.3
1892	Bal-N	52	209	32	47	6	6	2	21	18	22	.225	.296	.340	90	-3	12			.973	-1	1-51/O-1	-0.7
	Lou-N	80	285	42	67	4	7	5	34	30	45	.235	.312	.351	109	3	14			.978	-2	1-72,2-10	-0.2
	Yr	132	494	74	114	10	13	7	55	48	67	.231	.305	.346	101	-0	26			.976	-3	*1-123,2-10/O-1	-0.9
1893	Lou-N	13	47	5	10	1	1	0	9	5	5	.213	.302	.277	59	-3	1			.946	-0	1-13	-0.3
	StL-N	10	38	5	9	1	0	0	2	3	2	.237	.293	.263	48	-3	0			.923	-1	/O-9,1-1	-0.4
	Yr	23	85	10	19	2	1	0	11	8	7	.224	.298	.271	54	-6	1			.949	-2	1-14/O-9	-0.7
Total	4	272	1014	150	247	29	28	12	133	100	156	.244	.318	.363	103	3	39			.976	-22	1-189/S-33,O-32,23	-2.5

■ **LOU WHITAKER**   Whitaker, Louis Rodman   b: 5/12/57, Brooklyn, N.Y.   BL/TR, 5'11", 160 lbs.   Deb: 9/9/77

YEAR	TM/L	G	AB	R	H	2B	3B	HR	RBI	BB	SO	AVG	OBP	SLG	PRO+	BR/A	SB	CS	SBR	FA	FR	G/POS	TPR
1977	Det-A	11	32	5	8	1	0	0	2	4	6	.250	.333	.281	66	-1	2	2	-1	1.000	-3	/2-9	-0.5
1978	Det-A	139	484	71	138	12	7	3	58	61	65	.285	.366	.357	101	3	7	7	-2	.978	12	*2-136/D-2	2.3
1979	Det-A	127	423	75	121	14	8	3	42	78	66	.286	.398	.378	107	8	20	10	0	.986	-3	*2-126	1.7
1980	Det-A	145	477	68	111	19	1	1	45	73	79	.233	.335	.283	69	-18	8	4	0	.985	-3	*2-143	-1.2
1981	Det-A	109	335	48	88	14	4	5	36	40	42	.263	.343	.373	103	2	5	3	-0	.985	-1	*2-108	1.4
1982	Det-A	152	560	76	160	22	8	15	65	48	58	.286	.343	.434	111	8	11	3	2	**.988**	12	*2-149/D-1	3.0
1983	Det-A★	161	643	94	206	40	6	12	72	67	70	.320	.385	.457	134	31	17	10	-1	.983	-13	*2-160	2.4
1984	*Det-A★	143	558	90	161	25	1	13	56	62	63	.289	.360	.407	112	10	6	5	-1	.979	-11	*2-142	0.3
1985	Det-A★	152	609	102	170	29	8	21	73	80	56	.279	.365	.456	124	21	6	4	-1	.985	-16	*2-150	1.0
1986	Det-A★	144	584	95	157	26	6	20	73	63	70	.269	.340	.437	110	8	13	6	-1	.984	-1	*2-141	1.1
1987	*Det-A†	149	604	110	160	38	6	16	59	71	108	.265	.343	.427	107	7	13	5	1	.976	-14	*2-148	0.0
1988	Det-A	115	403	54	111	18	2	12	55	66	61	.275	.377	.419	128	17	2	0	1	.984	-23	*2-110	-0.1
1989	Det-A	148	509	77	128	21	1	28	85	89	59	.251	.366	.462	135	25	6	3	0	.985	-3	*2-146/D-2	2.9
1990	Det-A	132	472	75	112	22	2	18	60	74	71	.237	.338	.461	107	5	8	2	1	.991	12	*2-130/D-1	2.1
1991	Det-A	138	470	94	131	26	2	23	78	90	45	.279	.391	.489	142	29	4	2	1	**.994**	-11	*2-135/D-3	2.1
1992	Det-A	130	453	77	126	26	0	19	71	81	46	.278	.389	.461	137	24	6	4	-1	.984	-15	*2-119,D-10	1.2
1993	Det-A	119	383	72	111	32	1	9	67	78	46	.290	.415	.449	133	22	3	3	1	.981	14	*2-110	3.6

YEAR	TM/L	G	AB	R	H	2B	3B	HR	RBI	BB	SO	AVG	OBP	SLG	PRO+	BR/A	SB	CS	SBR	FA	FR	G/POS	TPR
1994	Det-A	92	322	67	97	21	2	12	43	41	47	.301	.382	.491	122	11	2	0	1	.970	-3	2-83/D-5	1.2
1995	Det-A	84	249	36	73	14	0	14	44	31	41	.293	.376	.518	130	11	4	0	1	.985	-11	2-63/D-8	0.5
Total	19	2390	8570	1386	2369	420	65	244	1084	1197	1099	.276	.366	.426	117	223	143	75	-2	.984	-69	*2-2308/D-32	25.0

■ STEVE WHITAKER Whitaker, Stephen Edward b: 5/7/43, Tacoma, Wash. BL/TR, 6'1", 187 lbs. Deb: 8/23/66

YEAR	TM/L	G	AB	R	H	2B	3B	HR	RBI	BB	SO	AVG	OBP	SLG	PRO+	BR/A	SB	CS	SBR	FA	FR	G/POS	TPR
1966	NY-A	31	114	15	28	3	2	7	15	9	24	.246	.306	.491	130	4	0	0	0	.955	-0	O-31	0.3
1967	NY-A	122	441	37	107	12	3	11	50	23	89	.243	.285	.358	92	-6	2	5	-2	.982	6	*O-114	-0.9
1968	NY-A	28	60	3	7	2	0	0	3	8	18	.117	.221	.150	14	-6	0	1	-1	.917	-1	O-14	-1.0
1969	Sea-A	69	116	15	29	1	0	6	13	12	29	.250	.326	.440	114	2	2	0	1	.962	-2	O-39	-0.1
1970	SF-N	16	27	3	3	1	0	0	4	2	14	.111	.172	.148	-13	-4	0	0	0	.857	-2	/O-9	-0.7
Total	5	266	758	73	174	20	6	24	85	54	174	.230	.285	.367	92	-10	4	6	-2	.967	0	O-207	-2.4

■ FUZZ WHITE White, Albert Eugene b: 6/27/18, Springfield, Mo. BL/TR, 6', 175 lbs. Deb: 9/17/40

YEAR	TM/L	G	AB	R	H	2B	3B	HR	RBI	BB	SO	AVG	OBP	SLG	PRO+	BR/A	SB	CS	SBR	FA	FR	G/POS	TPR
1940	StL-A	2	2	0	0	0	0	0	0	0	0	.000	.000	.000	-98	-1	0	0	0	.000	0	H	-0.1
1947	NY-N	7	13	3	3	0	0	0	0	0	0	.231	.231	.231	23	-1	0	0		1.000	0	/O-5	-0.2
Total	2	9	15	3	3	0	0	0	0	0	0	.200	.200	.200	6	-2	0	0		1.000	0	/O-5	-0.3

■ C. B. WHITE White, C. B. b: Wakeman, Ohio Deb: 6/1/1883

YEAR	TM/L	G	AB	R	H	2B	3B	HR	RBI	BB	SO	AVG	OBP	SLG	PRO+	BR/A	SB	CS	SBR	FA	FR	G/POS	TPR
1883	Phi-N	1	1	0	0	0	0	0	0	0	0	.000	.000	.000	-99	-0				.667	0	/S-1,3-1	0.0

■ CHARLIE WHITE White, Charles b: 8/12/28, Kinston, N.C. BL/TR, 5'11", 192 lbs. Deb: 4/18/54

YEAR	TM/L	G	AB	R	H	2B	3B	HR	RBI	BB	SO	AVG	OBP	SLG	PRO+	BR/A	SB	CS	SBR	FA	FR	G/POS	TPR
1954	Mil-N	50	93	14	22	4	0	1	8	9	8	.237	.304	.312	65	-5	0	0	0	.981	-2	C-28	-0.6
1955	Mil-N	12	30	3	7	1	0	0	4	5	7	.233	.361	.267	74	-1	0	0	0	1.000	-2	C-10	-0.2
Total	2	62	123	17	29	5	0	1	12	14	15	.236	.319	.301	67	-6	0	0	0	.986	-4	/C-38	-0.8

■ DERRICK WHITE White, Derrick Ramon b: 10/12/69, San Rafael, Cal. BR/TR, 6'1", 220 lbs. Deb: 7/22/93

YEAR	TM/L	G	AB	R	H	2B	3B	HR	RBI	BB	SO	AVG	OBP	SLG	PRO+	BR/A	SB	CS	SBR	FA	FR	G/POS	TPR
1993	Mon-N	17	49	6	11	3	0	2	4	2	12	.224	.269	.408	75	-2	2	0	1	.993	-0	1-17	-0.3
1995	Det-A	39	48	3	9	2	0	0	2	0	7	.188	.188	.229	8	-6	1	0	0	.981	-1	1-16,D-11/O-9	-0.8
Total	2	56	97	9	20	5	0	2	6	2	19	.206	.230	.320	42	-8	3	0	1	.990	-2	/1-33,D-11,O-9	-1.1

■ DEVON WHITE White, Devon Markes b: 12/29/62, Kingston, Jamaica BB/TR, 6'2", 180 lbs. Deb: 9/2/85

YEAR	TM/L	G	AB	R	H	2B	3B	HR	RBI	BB	SO	AVG	OBP	SLG	PRO+	BR/A	SB	CS	SBR	FA	FR	G/POS	TPR
1985	Cal-A	21	7	1	1	0	0	0	0	1	3	.143	.333	.143	37	-1	3	1	0	1.000	-5	O-16	-0.5
1986	*Cal-A	29	51	8	12	1	1	1	3	6	8	.235	.316	.353	83	-1	6	0	2	.961	-3	O-28	-0.3
1987	Cal-A	159	639	103	168	33	5	24	87	39	135	.263	.307	.443	99	-3	32	11	3	.980	14	*O-159	0.8
1988	Cal-A	122	455	76	118	22	2	11	51	23	84	.259	.298	.389	93	-5	17	8	0	.976	15	*O-116	0.7
1989	Cal-A★	156	636	86	156	18	13	12	56	31	129	.245	.283	.371	84	-15	44	16	4	.989	15	*O-154/D-1	-0.1
1990	Cal-A	125	443	57	96	17	3	11	44	44	116	.217	.292	.343	79	-13	21	6	3	.972	8	*O-122	-0.5
1991	*Tor-A	156	642	110	181	40	10	17	60	55	135	.282	.345	.455	115	12	33	10	4	.998	17	*O-156	2.9
1992	*Tor-A	153	641	98	159	26	7	17	60	47	133	.248	.304	.390	89	-10	37	4	9	.985	15	*O-152/D-1	1.0
1993	*Tor-A★	146	598	116	163	42	6	15	52	57	127	.273	.343	.438	108	6	34	4	8	.993	13	*O-145	2.3
1994	Tor-A	100	403	67	109	24	6	13	49	21	80	.270	.315	.457	95	-4	11	3	2	.978	8	O-98	0.3
1995	Tor-A	101	427	61	121	23	5	10	53	29	97	.283	.336	.431	99	-2	11	2	2	.989	8	O-99	0.6
1996	Fla-N	146	552	77	151	37	6	17	84	38	99	.274	.320	.455	108	5	22	6	3	.987	2	*O-139	0.6
Total	12	1414	5494	866	1435	283	64	148	599	391	1146	.261	.316	.417	98	-31	271	71	39	.985	108	*O-1384/D-2	7.8

■ DON WHITE White, Donald William b: 1/8/19, Everett, Wash. d: 6/15/87, Carlsbad, Cal. BR/TR, 6'1", 195 lbs. Deb: 4/19/48

YEAR	TM/L	G	AB	R	H	2B	3B	HR	RBI	BB	SO	AVG	OBP	SLG	PRO+	BR/A	SB	CS	SBR	FA	FR	G/POS	TPR
1948	Phi-A	86	253	29	62	14	2	4	28	19	16	.245	.303	.328	68	-12	0	1	-1	.957	-4	O-54,3-17	-1.9
1949	Phi-A	57	169	12	36	6	0	0	10	14	12	.213	.279	.249	40	-15	2	0	1	.989	-2	O-48/3-4	-1.8
Total	2	143	422	41	98	20	2	1	38	33	28	.232	.291	.296	57	-27	2	1	0	.971	-6	O-102/3-21	-3.7

■ ED WHITE White, Edward Perry b: 4/6/26, Anniston, Ala. d: 9/28/82, Lakeland, Fla. BR/TR, 6'2", 200 lbs. Deb: 9/16/55

YEAR	TM/L	G	AB	R	H	2B	3B	HR	RBI	BB	SO	AVG	OBP	SLG	PRO+	BR/A	SB	CS	SBR	FA	FR	G/POS	TPR
1955	Chi-A	3	4	0	2	0	0	0	0	0	1	.500	.600	.500	193	0	0	0	0	1.000	-0	/O-2	0.0

■ ELDER WHITE White, Elder Lafayette b: 12/23/34, Colerain, N.C. BR/TR, 5'11", 165 lbs. Deb: 4/10/62

YEAR	TM/L	G	AB	R	H	2B	3B	HR	RBI	BB	SO	AVG	OBP	SLG	PRO+	BR/A	SB	CS	SBR	FA	FR	G/POS	TPR
1962	Chi-N	23	53	4	8	2	0	0	1	8	11	.151	.274	.189	26	-5	3	0	1	.986	0	S-15/3-1	-0.3

■ ELMER WHITE White, Elmer b: 5/23/1850, Caton, N.Y. d: 3/17/1872, Caton, N.Y. Deb: 5/4/1871

YEAR	TM/L	G	AB	R	H	2B	3B	HR	RBI	BB	SO	AVG	OBP	SLG	PRO+	BR/A	SB	CS	SBR	FA	FR	G/POS	TPR
1871	Cle-n	15	70	13	18	2	0	0	9	1	6	.257	.268	.286	63	-3	0	1	-1	.783	-1	O-15/C-3	-0.2

■ FRANK WHITE White, Frank b: 9/4/50, Greenville, Miss. BR/TR, 5'11", 170 lbs. Deb: 6/12/73 C

YEAR	TM/L	G	AB	R	H	2B	3B	HR	RBI	BB	SO	AVG	OBP	SLG	PRO+	BR/A	SB	CS	SBR	FA	FR	G/POS	TPR
1973	KC-A	51	139	20	31	6	1	0	5	8	23	.223	.265	.281	50	-9	3	1	0	.937	7	S-37,2-11	0.2
1974	KC-A	99	204	19	45	6	3	1	18	5	33	.221	.239	.294	50	-13	3	4	-2	.962	25	2-50,S-29,3-16/D-3	1.4
1975	KC-A	111	304	43	76	10	2	7	36	20	39	.250	.298	.365	84	-7	11	3	2	.987	15	2-67,S-42/3-4,CD	1.6
1976	*KC-A	152	446	39	102	17	6	2	46	19	42	.229	.265	.307	67	-19	20	11	-1	.973	21	*2-130,S-37	1.2
1977	*KC-A	152	474	59	116	21	5	5	50	25	67	.245	.285	.342	70	-20	23	5	4	.989	-3	*2-152/S-4	-0.9
1978	*KC-A★	143	461	66	127	24	6	7	50	26	59	.275	.318	.399	98	-2	13	10	2	.978	-17	*2-140	-1.1
1979	*KC-A★	127	467	73	124	26	4	10	48	25	54	.266	.304	.403	87	-9	28	8	4	.982	-23	*2-125	-2.0
1980	*KC-A	154	560	70	148	23	4	7	60	19	69	.264	.291	.357	76	-19	19	6	2	.988	-7	*2-153	-1.5
1981	*KC-A★	94	364	35	91	17	1	9	38	19	50	.250	.287	.376	91	-5	4	2	0	.988	-16	2-93	-1.7
1982	*KC-A★	145	524	71	156	45	6	11	56	16	65	.298	.321	.469	114	8	10	7	-1	.978	-15	*2-144	0.0
1983	KC-A	146	549	52	143	35	6	11	77	20	51	.260	.286	.406	88	-11	13	5	1	.990	9	*2-145	0.6
1984	*KC-A	129	479	58	130	22	5	17	56	27	72	.271	.313	.445	106	3	5	5	-2	.985	13	*2-129	1.9
1985	*KC-A	149	563	62	140	25	1	22	69	28	86	.249	.285	.414	88	-11	10	4	1	.980	14	*2-149	1.0
1986	KC-A★	151	566	76	154	37	3	22	84	43	88	.272	.326	.465	110	6	4	4	-1	.987	-0	*2-151/S-1,3-1	1.1
1987	KC-A	154	563	67	138	32	2	17	78	51	86	.245	.310	.400	84	-13	1	3	-2	.987	8	*2-152/D-1	0.0
1988	KC-A	150	537	48	126	25	1	8	58	21	67	.235	.269	.330	66	-25	7	3	0	.994	7	*2-148/D-3	-1.2
1989	KC-A	135	418	34	107	22	1	2	36	30	52	.256	.309	.328	80	-11	3	2	-0	.985	-2	*2-132/O-1	-0.1
1990	KC-A	82	241	20	52	14	1	2	21	10	32	.216	.256	.307	58	-14	1	0	0	.978	1	2-79/O-1	-1.2
Total	18	2324	7859	912	2006	407	58	160	886	412	1035	.255	.295	.383	85	-173	178	83	4	.984	45	*2-2150,S-150/3DOC	-0.7

■ DOC WHITE White, Guy Harris b: 4/9/1879, Washington, D.C. d: 2/19/69, Silver Spring, Md. BL/TL, 6'1", 150 lbs. Deb: 4/22/01

YEAR	TM/L	G	AB	R	H	2B	3B	HR	RBI	BB	SO	AVG	OBP	SLG	PRO+	BR/A	SB	CS	SBR	FA	FR	G/POS	TPR
1901	Phi-N	31	98	15	27	3	1	1	10	2		.276	.297	.357	87	-2	1			.951	2	P-31/O-1	0.0
1902	Phi-N	61	179	17	47	3	1	1	15	11		.263	.305	.307	89	-2	5			.931	-2	P-36,O-19	-0.6
1903	Chi-A	38	99	10	20	3	0	0	5	19		.202	.331	.232	74	-2	1			.969	3	P-37/O-1	0.0
1904	Chi-A	33	76	7	12	2	0	0	2	10		.158	.184	.184	42	-5	3			.951	1	P-30/O-2	-0.1
1905	Chi-A	37	90	7	15	2	0	0	7	4		.167	.202	.233	40	-6	3			.961	2	P-36/O-1	0.0
1906	*Chi-A	29	65	11	12	1	1	0	3	13		.185	.321	.231	75	-1	2			.922	2	P-28/O-1	0.0
1907	Chi-A	48	90	12	20	1	0	0	2	12		.222	.314	.233	77	-2	2			.986	2	P-46/O-2,2-1	-0.1
1908	Chi-A	51	109	12	25	1	0	0	10	12		.229	.306	.239	79	-2	4			.986	6	P-41/O-3	-0.1
1909	Chi-A	72	192	24	45	1	5	0	7	33		.234	.347	.292	106	3	7			.926	-4	O-40,P-24	-0.3
1910	Chi-A	56	126	14	25	1	2	0	8	14		.198	.279	.238	65	-5	2			.972	1	P-33,O-14	-0.3
1911	Chi-A	39	78	12	20	1	0	0	6	7		.256	.318	.295	74	-3	1			.919	-1	P-34/1-2,O-1	-0.3
1912	Chi-A	32	56	5	7	1	1	0	0	7		.125	.222	.179	15	-6	0			1.000	-1	P-32	-0.1
1913	Chi-A								0	7		.120	.214	.120	-2	-3	0			.959	2	P-19/1-1	-0.1
Total	13	547	1283	147	278	22	13	2	75	147	1	.217	.298	.259	74	-36	32			.960	15	P-427/O-85,1-3,2-1	-1.4

■ DEACON WHITE White, James Laurie b: 12/7/1847, Caton, N.Y. d: 7/7/39, Aurora, Ill. BL/TR, 5'11", 175 lbs. Deb: 5/4/1871 FM

YEAR	TM/L	G	AB	R	H	2B	3B	HR	RBI	BB	SO	AVG	OBP	SLG	PRO+	BR/A	SB	CS	SBR	FA	FR	G/POS	TPR
1871	Cle-n	29	146	40	47	6	5	1	21	4	1	.322	.340	.452	132	7	2	5	-1	.821	-5	*C-29/S-2,2-1,30	0.0
1872	Cle-n	22	109	21	37	2	2	0	22	4	1	.339	.363	.394	140	6	0	0	0	.882	1	C-14/2-7,O-5,M	0.3
1873	Bos-n	60	310	79	121	15	6	0	66	3	0	.390	.390	.477	144	14	6	2	1	.845	2	*C-56/O-9	1.1
1874	Bos-n	70	353	75	106	15	2	1	52	4	0	.300	.308	.380	113	3	1	1	-0	.837	-0	*C-58,O-21/1-1	0.3
1875	Bos-n	80	371	76	136	23	3	1	60	3	2	.367	.372	.453	178	27	2	3	-1	.880	15	*C-75,O-14/1-1	3.6

YEAR	TM/L	G	AB	R	H	2B	3B	HR	RBI	BB	SO	AVG	OBP	SLG	PRO+	BR/A	SB	CS	SBR	FA	FR	G/POS	TPR
1876	Chi-N	66	303	66	104	18	1	1	**60**	7	3	.343	.358	.419	141	11				.844	7	*C-63/O-3,1-3,3P	1.7
1877	Bos-N	59	266	51	**103**	14	**11**	2	49	8	3	**.387**	**.405**	**.545**	**190**	**26**				.963	1	1-35,O-19/C-7	2.3
1878	Cin-N	61	258	41	81	4	1	0	29	10	5	.314	.340	.337	136	11				.909	-4	*C-48,O-16/3-1	0.7
1879	Cin-N	78	333	55	110	16	6	1	52	6	9	.330	.342	.423	159	21				.901	2	*C-59,O-21/1-2,M	2.2
1880	Cin-N	35	141	21	42	4	2	0	9	7	7	.298	.340	.355	137	6				.738	-3	O-33/1-3,2-1	0.1
1881	Buf-N	78	319	58	99	24	4	0	53	9	8	.310	.329	.411	133	12				.943	-9	1-26,2-25,O-17,/3C	0.2
1882	Buf-N	83	337	51	95	17	0	1	33	15	16	.282	.313	.341	108	3				.837	-10	*3-63,C-20	-0.4
1883	Buf-N	94	391	62	114	14	5	0	47	23	18	.292	.331	.353	106	3				.797	-10	*3-77,C-22	-0.6
1884	Buf-N	110	452	82	147	16	11	5	74	32	13	.325	.370	.442	149	25				.825	-7	*3-108/C-3	1.7
1885	Buf-N	98	404	54	118	6	6	0	57	12	11	.292	.313	.337	106	2				.888	1	*3-98	0.4
1886	Det-N	124	491	65	142	19	5	1	76	31	35	.289	.331	.354	106	3	9			.847	-9	*3-124	-0.2
1887	*Det-N	111	449	71	136	20	11	3	75	26	15	.303	.353	.416	109	5	20			.848	-3	*3-106/O-3,1-2	0.6
1888	Det-N	125	527	75	157	22	5	4	71	21	24	.298	.336	.381	128	16	12			.857	-3	*3-125	1.5
1889	Pit-N	55	225	35	57	10	1	0	26	16	18	.253	.314	.307	82	-5	2			.872	-10	3-52/1-3	-1.2
1890	Buf-P	122	439	62	114	13	4	0	47	67	30	.260	.381	.308	93	2	3			.905	19	3-64,1-57/S-1,P-1	1.6
Total 5 n		261	1289	291	447	51	23	5	221	15	6	.347	.354	.434	143	56	11	8	-2	.854	12	C-232/O-50,2-8,1S3	5.4
Total 15		1299	5335	849	1619	217	73	18	756	292	215	.303	.344	.382	123	138	46			.853	-33	3-826,C-226,10/2PS	10.6

■ JERRY WHITE
White, Jerome Cardell b: 8/23/52, Shirley, Mass. BB/TR, 5'11", 165 lbs. Deb: 9/16/74

YEAR	TM/L	G	AB	R	H	2B	3B	HR	RBI	BB	SO	AVG	OBP	SLG	PRO+	BR/A	SB	CS	SBR	FA	FR	G/POS	TPR
1974	Mon-N	9	10	0	4	1	1	0	2	0	0	.400	.400	.700	193	1	3	0	1	1.000	-2	/O-7	0.0
1975	Mon-N	39	97	14	29	4	1	2	7	10	7	.299	.364	.423	113	2	5	2	0	.976	2	O-30	0.3
1976	Mon-N	114	278	32	68	11	1	2	21	27	31	.245	.316	.313	76	-8	15	7	0	.982	-10	O-92	-2.2
1977	Mon-N	16	21	4	4	0	0	0	1	1	3	.190	.227	.190	14	-3	1	0	0	1.000	-1	/O-8	-0.4
1978	Mon-N	18	10	2	2	0	0	0	0	1	3	.200	.273	.200	34	-1	1	0	0	1.000	-1	/O-3	-0.2
	Chi-N	59	136	22	37	6	0	1	10	23	16	.272	.377	.338	90	-1	4	3	-1	.981	-3	O-54	-0.6
	Yr	77	146	24	39	6	0	1	10	24	19	.267	.371	.329	89	-1	5	3	-0	.981	-4	O-57	-0.8
1979	Mon-N	88	138	30	41	7	1	3	18	21	23	.297	.394	.428	125	6	8	4	0	.983	-8	O-43	-0.3
1980	Mon-N	110	214	22	56	9	3	7	23	30	37	.262	.355	.430	118	5	8	7	-2	.946	-12	O-84	-1.0
1981	*Mon-N	59	119	11	26	5	1	3	11	13	17	.218	.295	.353	82	-3	5	2	0	.952	-5	O-39	-0.9
1982	Mon-N	69	115	13	28	6	1	2	13	8	26	.243	.304	.365	85	-2	3	3	-1	1.000	-4	O-30	-0.8
1983	Mon-N	40	34	4	5	1	0	0	0	12	8	.147	.383	.176	60	-1	4	0	1	1.000	-3	O-13	-0.3
1986	StL-N	25	24	1	3	0	0	1	3	2	3	.125	.192	.250	21	-3	0	0	0	1.000	-1	/O-6	-0.4
Total 11		646	1196	155	303	50	9	21	109	148	174	.253	.339	.363	94	-8	57	28	0	.974	-48	O-409	-6.8

■ JACK WHITE
White, John Peter b: 8/31/05, New York, N.Y. d: 6/19/71, Flushing, N.Y. BB/TR, 5'7.5", 150 lbs. Deb: 6/22/27

YEAR	TM/L	G	AB	R	H	2B	3B	HR	RBI	BB	SO	AVG	OBP	SLG	PRO+	BR/A	SB	CS	SBR	FA	FR	G/POS	TPR
1927	Cin-N	5	4	1	0	0	0	0	0	0	0	.000	.000	.000	-99	-1	0			1.000	0	/2-3,S-2	-0.1
1928	Cin-N	1	3	0	0	0	0	0	0	0	1	.000	.000	.000	-99	-1	0			.833	-1	/2-1	-0.1
Total 2		6	7	1	0	0	0	0	0	0	1	.000	.000	.000	-99	-2	0			.929	-0	/2-4,S-2	-0.2

■ JACK WHITE
White, John Wallace b: 1/19/1878, Traders Point, Ind. d: 9/30/63, Indianapolis, Ind BR/TR, 5'6", Deb: 6/26/04

YEAR	TM/L	G	AB	R	H	2B	3B	HR	RBI	BB	SO	AVG	OBP	SLG	PRO+	BR/A	SB	CS	SBR	FA	FR	G/POS	TPR
1904	Bos-N	1	5	1	0	0	0	0	0	0	0	.000	.000	.000	-99	-1	0			1.000	1	/O-1	-0.1

■ JO-JO WHITE
White, Joyner Clifford b: 6/1/09, Red Oak, Ga. d: 10/9/86, Tacoma, Wash. BL/TR, 5'11", 165 lbs. Deb: 4/15/32 FMC

YEAR	TM/L	G	AB	R	H	2B	3B	HR	RBI	BB	SO	AVG	OBP	SLG	PRO+	BR/A	SB	CS	SBR	FA	FR	G/POS	TPR
1932	Det-A	80	208	25	54	6	3	2	21	22	19	.260	.330	.346	73	-8	6	8	-3	.962	-0	O-48	-1.3
1933	Det-A	91	234	43	59	9	5	2	34	27	26	.252	.337	.359	83	-6	5	5	-2	.977	-0	O-54	-0.9
1934	*Det-A	115	384	97	120	18	5	0	44	69	39	.313	.419	.385	108	9	28	6	5	.959	-0	*O-100	0.8
1935	*Det-A	114	412	82	99	13	12	0	32	68	42	.240	.348	.345	83	-10	19	10	-0	.962	-2	O-98	-1.4
1936	Det-A	58	51	11	14	3	0	0	6	9	10	.275	.383	.333	78	-1	2	0	-1	.938	-7	O-18	-0.4
1937	Det-A	94	305	50	75	5	7	0	21	50	40	.246	.354	.308	67	-14	12	7	-1	.973	-3	O-82	-1.9
1938	Det-A	78	206	40	54	6	1	0	15	30	15	.262	.359	.301	63	-11	3	4	-2	.967	-0	O-55	-1.2
1943	Phi-A	139	500	69	124	17	7	1	30	61	51	.248	.335	.316	91	-4	12	4	1	.966	-4	*O-133	-1.5
1944	Phi-A	85	267	30	59	4	2	1	21	40	27	.221	.329	.262	71	-8	5	4	-1	.949	-1	O-74/S-1	-1.5
	Cin-N	24	85	9	20	2	0	0	5	10	7	.235	.316	.259	65	-4	0			1.000	-0	O-23	-0.4
Total 9		878	2652	456	678	83	42	8	229	386	276	.256	.353	.328	82	-57	92	48		.965	-16	O-685/S-1	-10.0

■ MIKE WHITE
White, Joyner Michael b: 12/18/38, Detroit, Mich. BR/TR, 5'8", 160 lbs. Deb: 9/21/63 F

YEAR	TM/L	G	AB	R	H	2B	3B	HR	RBI	BB	SO	AVG	OBP	SLG	PRO+	BR/A	SB	CS	SBR	FA	FR	G/POS	TPR
1963	Hou-N	3	7	0	2	0	0	0	0	0	0	.286	.286	.286	69	-0	0	0	0	1.000	1	/2-2	0.1
1964	Hou-N	89	280	30	76	11	3	0	27	20	47	.271	.320	.332	89	-4	1	1	-0	.978	2	O-72,2-10/3-3	-0.5
1965	Hou-N	8	9	0	0	0	0	0	0	1	2	.000	.100	.000	-74	-2	0	0	0	1.000	-0	/3-1	-0.3
Total 3		100	296	30	78	11	3	0	27	21	49	.264	.312	.321	84	-7	1	1	-0	.985	-4	/O-72,2-12,3-4	-0.7

■ MYRON WHITE
White, Myron Alan b: 8/1/57, Long Beach, Cal. BL/TL, 5'11", 180 lbs. Deb: 9/4/78

YEAR	TM/L	G	AB	R	H	2B	3B	HR	RBI	BB	SO	AVG	OBP	SLG	PRO+	BR/A	SB	CS	SBR	FA	FR	G/POS	TPR
1978	LA-N	7	4	1	2	0	0	0	0	0	0	.500	.500	.500	181	0	0	1	-1	1.000	-1	/O-4	-0.2

■ RONDELL WHITE
White, Rondell Bernard b: 2/23/72, Milledgeville, Ga. BR/TR, 6'1", 205 lbs. Deb: 9/1/93

YEAR	TM/L	G	AB	R	H	2B	3B	HR	RBI	BB	SO	AVG	OBP	SLG	PRO+	BR/A	SB	CS	SBR	FA	FR	G/POS	TPR
1993	Mon-N	23	73	9	19	3	1	2	15	7	16	.260	.325	.411	91	-1	1	2	-1	1.000	-3	O-21	-0.6
1994	Mon-N	40	97	16	27	10	1	2	13	9	18	.278	.358	.464	111	2	1	1	-0	.946	-3	O-29	-0.2
1995	Mon-N	130	474	87	140	33	4	13	57	41	87	.295	.359	.464	111	8	25	5	5	.986	6	*O-119	1.4
1996	Mon-N	88	334	35	98	19	4	6	41	22	53	.293	.341	.428	99	-1	14	6	1	.990	5	O-86	0.4
Total 4		281	978	147	284	65	10	23	126	79	174	.290	.350	.448	105	7	41	14	4	.985	5	O-255	1.0

■ ROY WHITE
White, Roy Hilton b: 12/27/43, Los Angeles, Cal. BB/TR, 5'10", 172 lbs. Deb: 9/7/65 C

YEAR	TM/L	G	AB	R	H	2B	3B	HR	RBI	BB	SO	AVG	OBP	SLG	PRO+	BR/A	SB	CS	SBR	FA	FR	G/POS	TPR
1965	NY-A	14	42	7	14	2	0	0	3	4	7	.333	.404	.381	125	2	2	1	0	1.000	-	O-10/2-1	0.1
1966	NY-A	115	316	39	71	13	2	7	20	37	43	.225	.308	.345	91	-4	14	7	0	.957	0	O-82/2-2	-0.7
1967	NY-A	70	214	22	48	8	0	2	18	19	25	.224	.291	.290	75	-7	10	4	1	.968	-6	O-36,3-17	-1.6
1968	NY-A	159	577	89	154	20	7	17	62	73	50	.267	.352	.414	136	25	20	11	-1	.997	10	*O-154	2.9
1969	NY-A★	130	448	55	130	30	5	7	74	81	51	.290	.400	.426	136	25	18	10	-1	.989	11	*O-126	2.9
1970	NY-A☆	162	609	109	180	30	6	22	94	95	66	.296	.391	.473	144	38	24	10	1	.994	7	*O-161	3.9
1971	NY-A	147	524	86	153	22	7	19	84	86	66	.292	.399	.469	154	40	14	7	0	**1.000**	10	*O-145	4.5
1972	NY-A	155	556	76	150	29	6	10	54	**99**	59	.270	.385	.376	131	26	23	7	3	.994	9	*O-155	3.4
1973	NY-A	162	639	88	157	22	3	18	60	78	81	.246	.330	.374	101	1	16	9	-1	.977	4	*O-162	-0.3
1974	NY-A	136	473	68	130	19	8	7	43	67	44	.275	.367	.393	121	15	15	6	1	.993	-3	O-67,D-53	1.5
1975	NY-A	148	556	81	161	32	5	12	59	72	50	.290	.373	.430	129	22	16	15	-4	.984	11	O-135/1-7,D-2	2.3
1976	*NY-A	156	626	**104**	179	29	3	14	65	83	52	.286	.370	.409	129	24	31	13	2	.987	6	O-156	2.6
1977	*NY-A	143	519	72	139	25	2	14	52	75	58	.268	.360	.405	109	8	18	11	-1	.981	10	*O-135/D-4	1.1
1978	*NY-A	103	346	44	93	13	3	8	43	42	35	.269	.351	.393	112	6	10	4	-1	.992	-4	*O-74,D-23	-0.1
1979	NY-A	81	205	24	44	6	0	3	27	23	21	.215	.294	.288	59	-12	2	1	-2	1.000	0	D-29,O-27	-1.4
Total 15		1881	6650	964	1803	300	51	160	758	934	708	.271	.363	.404	122	211	233	117	-0	.988	71	*O-1625,D-111/312	21.1

■ SAMMY WHITE
White, Samuel Charles b: 7/7/28, Wenatchee, Wash. d: 8/5/91, Princeville, Hawaii BR/TR, 6'3", 195 lbs. Deb: 9/26/51

YEAR	TM/L	G	AB	R	H	2B	3B	HR	RBI	BB	SO	AVG	OBP	SLG	PRO+	BR/A	SB	CS	SBR	FA	FR	G/POS	TPR
1951	Bos-A	4	11	0	2	0	0	0	0	0	3	.182	.182	.182	-1	-2	0	0	0	1.000	1	/C-4	-0.1
1952	Bos-A	115	381	35	107	20	2	10	49	16	43	.281	.310	.423	95	-4	2	3	-1	.983	-2	*C-110	-0.2
1953	Bos-A☆	136	476	59	130	34	2	13	66	29	48	.273	.318	.435	96	-4	3	2	-0	.986	9	*C-131	1.0
1954	Bos-A	137	493	46	139	25	2	14	75	21	50	.282	.311	.426	90	-8	3	3	-2	.979	13	*C-133	0.9
1955	Bos-A	143	544	65	142	30	4	11	64	44	58	.261	.324	.392	84	-13	2	1	-1	.984	-0	*C-143	-0.9
1956	Bos-A	111	392	28	96	15	4	5	44	35	40	.245	.307	.332	61	-23	1	4	-1	.984	7	*C-114	-1.0
1957	Bos-A	111	340	24	73	10	1	5	31	25	38	.215	.268	.276	46	-25	0	1	1	.985	-4	*C-111	-2.7
1958	Bos-A	102	328	25	85	15	3	6	35	21	37	.259	.306	.378	81	-9	1	2	0	.988	-2	*C-102	-0.6
1959	Bos-A	119	377	36	107	13	4	1	42	23	39	.284	.327	.347	81	-9	4	0	0	.990	-0	*C-119	-0.3
1961	Mil-N	21	63	1	14	1	0	1	6	2	11	.222	.246	.262	43	-5	0	0	0	.974	4	C-20	0.0

YEAR	TM/L	G	AB	R	H	2B	3B	HR	RBI	BB	SO	AVG	OBP	SLG	PRO+	BR/A	SB	CS	SBR	FA	FR	G/POS	TPR
1962	Phi-N	41	97	7	21	4	0	2	12	2	16	.216	.240	.320	50	-7	0	0	0	.975	5	C-40	-0.1
Total	11	1043	3502	324	916	167	20	66	421	218	381	.262	.307	.377	79	-109	14	15	-5	.984	30	*C-1027	-4.0

■ SAM WHITE   White, Samuel Lambeth b: 8/23/1892, Greater Preston, Yorkshire, England d: 11/11/29, Philadelphia, Pa. BL/TR, 6', 185 lbs. Deb: 9/8/19

YEAR	TM/L	G	AB	R	H	2B	3B	HR	RBI	BB	SO	AVG	OBP	SLG	PRO+	BR/A	SB	CS	SBR	FA	FR	G/POS	TPR
1919	Bos-N	1	1	0	0	0	0	0	0	0	0	.000	.000	.000	-99	-0	0			1.000	2	/C-1	0.1

■ BARNEY WHITE   White, William Barney "Bear" b: 6/25/23, Paris, Tex. BR/TR, 5'11", 186 lbs. Deb: 6/5/45

YEAR	TM/L	G	AB	R	H	2B	3B	HR	RBI	BB	SO	AVG	OBP	SLG	PRO+	BR/A	SB	CS	SBR	FA	FR	G/POS	TPR
1945	Bro-N	4	2	0	0	0	0	0	0	1	1	.000	.500	.000	46	0	0			1.000	0	/S-1,3-1	0.0

■ BILL WHITE   White, William De Kova b: 1/28/34, Lakewood, Fla. BL/TL, 6', 195 lbs. Deb: 5/7/56

YEAR	TM/L	G	AB	R	H	2B	3B	HR	RBI	BB	SO	AVG	OBP	SLG	PRO+	BR/A	SB	CS	SBR	FA	FR	G/POS	TPR
1956	NY-N	138	508	63	130	23	7	22	59	47	72	.256	.324	.459	108	5	15	8	-0	.989	2	*1-138/O-2	-0.3
1958	SF-N	26	29	5	7	1	0	1	4	7	5	.241	.389	.379	107	1	1	0	0	1.000	1	/1-3,O-2	0.0
1959	StL-N☆	138	517	77	156	33	9	12	72	34	61	.302	.347	.470	108	5	15	10	-2	.962	-2	O-92,1-71	-0.6
1960	StL-N★	144	554	81	157	27	10	16	79	42	83	.283	.336	.455	105	3	12	6	0	.990	-6	*1-123,O-29	-1.4
1961	StL-N★	153	591	89	169	28	11	20	90	64	84	.286	.357	.472	107	6	8	11	-4	.989	-2	*1-151	-1.4
1962	StL-N	159	614	93	199	31	3	20	102	58	69	.324	.388	.482	120	18	9	7	-2	.993	1	*1-146,O-27	0.8
1963	StL-N	162	658	106	200	26	9	27	109	59	100	.304	.361	.491	131	25	10	9	-2	.991	-2	*1-162	1.5
1964	*StL-N★	160	631	92	191	37	4	21	102	52	103	.303	.357	.474	121	17	7	6	-2	.996	-1	*1-160	0.8
1965	StL-N	148	543	82	157	26	3	24	73	63	86	.289	.367	.481	125	18	3	3	-1	.992	6	*1-144	1.6
1966	Phi-N	159	577	85	159	23	6	22	103	68	109	.276	.355	.451	122	18	16	6	1	.994	7	*1-158	1.6
1967	Phi-N	110	308	29	77	6	2	8	33	52	61	.250	.358	.360	107	5	6	1	1	.993	1	1-95	0.1
1968	Phi-N	127	385	34	92	16	2	9	40	39	79	.239	.312	.361	102	1	0	1	-1	.994	4	1-111	-0.4
1969	StL-N	49	57	7	12	1	0	0	4	11	15	.211	.338	.228	61	-2	1	0	0	1.000	1	1-15	-0.2
Total	13	1673	5972	843	1706	278	65	202	870	596	927	.286	.353	.455	115	120	103	68	-10	.992	8	*1-1477,O-152	2.1

■ BILL WHITE   White, William Dighton b: 5/1/1860, Bridgeport, Ohio d: 12/29/24, Bellaire, Ohio TR , Deb: 5/3/1884

YEAR	TM/L	G	AB	R	H	2B	3B	HR	RBI	BB	SO	AVG	OBP	SLG	PRO+	BR/A	SB	CS	SBR	FA	FR	G/POS	TPR
1884	Pit-a	74	291	25	66	7	10	0		13		.227	.262	.320	87	-4				.807	-11	S-60,3-10/O-4	-1.4
1886	Lou-a	135	557	96	143	17	10	1	66	37		.257	.304	.329	93	-7	14			.871	17	*S-135/P-1	1.0
1887	Lou-a	132	512	85	129	7	9	2	79	47		.252	.315	.313	74	-18	41			.869	22	*S-132	0.4
1888	Lou-a	49	198	35	55	6	5	1	30	7		.278	.313	.374	122	4	15			.816	-3	S-38,3-11	0.3
	*StL-a	76	275	31	48	2	3	2	30	21		.175	.238	.225	44	-18	6			.892	-3	S-74/2-2	-1.8
	Yr	125	473	66	103	8	8	3	60	28		.218	.269	.288	74	-15	21			.864	-6	*S-112,3-11/2-2	-1.5
Total	4	466	1833	272	441	39	37	6	205	125		.241	.292	.312	82	-43	76			.860	22	S-439/3-21,O-4,2P	-1.5

■ BILL WHITE   White, William Edward b: Milner, Ga. Deb: 6/21/1879

YEAR	TM/L	G	AB	R	H	2B	3B	HR	RBI	BB	SO	AVG	OBP	SLG	PRO+	BR/A	SB	CS	SBR	FA	FR	G/POS	TPR
1879	Pro-N	1	4	1	1	0	0	0				.250	.250	.250	67	-0				1.000	0	/1-1	0.0

■ WARREN WHITE   White, William Warren (a.k.a. William Warren) 5'10.5", 170 lbs. Deb: 6/17/1871 M

YEAR	TM/L	G	AB	R	H	2B	3B	HR	RBI	BB	SO	AVG	OBP	SLG	PRO+	BR/A	SB	CS	SBR	FA	FR	G/POS	TPR
1871	Oly-n	1	4	0	0	0	0	0	0	0	0	.000	.000	.000	-99	-1	0	0	0	1.000	-1	/2-1	-0.1
1872	Nat-n	10	45	7	13	0	0	0	4	0	0	.289	.289	.289	67	-3	0	0	0	.861	8	/3-9,S-1,M	0.3
1873	Was-n	39	160	29	43	3	4	0	21	0	1	.269	.269	.338	82	-3	1	1	-0	.717	5	*3-37/S-3	-0.3
1874	Bal-n	45	212	21	57	1	0	0	18	1	2	.269	.272	.274	76	-5	0	0	0	.765	25	*3-45/C-2,M	1.5
1875	Chi-n	69	287	37	71	9	0	0	23	0	3	.247	.247	.279	82	-5	5	10	-5	.813	7	*3-59/S-5,O-5,2-2	-0.3
1884	Was-U	4	18	2	1	0	0	0		0		.056	.056	.056	-68	-4				.692	-1	/3-2,S-1,2-1	-0.5
Total	5 n	164	708	94	184	13	4	0	66	1	6	.260	.261	.290	78	-17	7	11	-5	.773	43	3-150/S-9,O-5,2C	1.4

■ ED WHITED   Whited, Edward Morris b: 2/9/64, Bristol, Pa. BR/TR, 6'3", 195 lbs. Deb: 7/5/89

YEAR	TM/L	G	AB	R	H	2B	3B	HR	RBI	BB	SO	AVG	OBP	SLG	PRO+	BR/A	SB	CS	SBR	FA	FR	G/POS	TPR
1989	Atl-N	36	74	5	12	4	0	1	4	6	15	.162	.225	.243	33	-6	1	0	0	.914	-0	3-29/1-3	-0.7

■ BURGESS WHITEHEAD   Whitehead, Burgess Urquhart "Whitey" b: 6/29/10, Tarboro, N.C. d: 11/25/93, Windsor, N.C. BR/TR, 5'10.5", 160 lbs. Deb: 4/30/33

YEAR	TM/L	G	AB	R	H	2B	3B	HR	RBI	BB	SO	AVG	OBP	SLG	PRO+	BR/A	SB	CS	SBR	FA	FR	G/POS	TPR
1933	StL-N	12	7	2	2	0	0	0	1	0	1	.286	.286	.286	60	-0	0			1.000	0	/S-9,2-3	0.0
1934	*StL-N	100	332	55	92	13	5	1	24	12	19	.277	.310	.355	73	-13	5			.962	-1	2-48,S-29,3-28	-0.9
1935	StL-N★	107	338	45	89	10	2	0	33	11	14	.263	.289	.305	57	-20	5			.980	5	2-80/3-8,S-6	-1.0
1936	*NY-N	154	632	99	176	31	3	4	47	29	32	.278	.317	.356	82	-16	14			.969	29	*2-153	2.3
1937	*NY-N★	152	574	64	164	15	6	5	52	28	20	.286	.323	.359	84	-13	7			.974	26	*2-152	2.3
1939	NY-N	95	335	31	80	6	3	2	24	24	19	.239	.299	.293	59	-19	1			.970	21	2-91/S-4,3-1	0.7
1940	NY-N	133	568	68	160	9	6	4	36	26	17	.282	.319	.340	81	-15	9			.947	13	3-74,2-57/S-4	0.3
1941	NY-N	116	403	41	92	15	4	1	23	14	10	.228	.258	.293	54	-25	7			.970	-0	*2-104/3-1	-1.9
1946	Pit-N	55	127	10	28	1	2	0	5	2	6	.220	.261	.260	47	-9	3			.963	-6	2-30/3-4,S-1	-1.4
Total	9	924	3316	415	883	100	31	17	245	150	138	.266	.304	.331	72	-130	51			.972	86	2-718,3-116/S-53	0.4

■ MILT WHITEHEAD   Whitehead, Milton P. b: 1862, Canada d: 8/15/01, Highland, Cal. BB , Deb: 4/20/1884

YEAR	TM/L	G	AB	R	H	2B	3B	HR	RBI	BB	SO	AVG	OBP	SLG	PRO+	BR/A	SB	CS	SBR	FA	FR	G/POS	TPR
1884	StL-U	99	393	61	83	15	1	1		8		.211	.227	.262	46	-37				.803	-11	*S-94/O-2,P-1,23	-4.2
	KC-U	5	22	2	3	0	0	0		0		.136	.136	.136	-20	-4				.857	-1	/2-3,C-1,S-1,3-1	-0.4
	Yr	104	415	63	86	15	1	1		8		.207	.222	.255	43	-41				.804	-12	S-95/2-4,O-2,3PC	-4.6

■ GIL WHITEHOUSE   Whitehouse, Gilbert Arthur b: 10/15/1893, Somerville, Mass. d: 2/14/26, Brewer, Me. BB/TR, 5'10", 170 lbs. Deb: 6/20/12

YEAR	TM/L	G	AB	R	H	2B	3B	HR	RBI	BB	SO	AVG	OBP	SLG	PRO+	BR/A	SB	CS	SBR	FA	FR	G/POS	TPR
1912	Bos-N	2	3	0	0	0	0	0		0	3	.000	.000	.000	-98	-1	0			.667	-1	/C-2	-0.2
1915	New-F	35	120	16	27	6	2	0	9	6	16	.225	.268	.308	66	-8	3			.949	-1	O-28/P-1,C-1	-1.1
Total	2	37	123	16	27	6	2	0	9	6	19	.220	.262	.301	61	-9	3			.846	-2	/O-28,C-3,P-1	-1.3

■ GURDON WHITELEY   Whiteley, Gurdon W. b: 10/5/1859, Ashaway, R.I. d: 11/24/24, Cranston, R.I. 5'11", 190 lbs. Deb: 8/7/1884

YEAR	TM/L	G	AB	R	H	2B	3B	HR	RBI	BB	SO	AVG	OBP	SLG	PRO+	BR/A	SB	CS	SBR	FA	FR	G/POS	TPR
1884	Cle-N	8	34	4	5	0	0	0	1	8		.147	.171	.147	1	-4				.800	1	/O-8	-0.3
1885	Bos-N	33	135	14	25	2	2	1	7	1	25	.185	.191	.252	44	-8				.781	-2	O-32/C-1	-1.0
Total	2	41	169	18	30	2	2	1	7	2	33	.178	.187	.231	34	-12				.785	-1	/O-40,C-1	-1.3

■ GEORGE WHITEMAN   Whiteman, George "Lucky" b: 12/23/1882, Peoria, Ill. d: 2/10/47, Houston, Tex. BR/TR, 5'7", 160 lbs. Deb: 9/13/07

YEAR	TM/L	G	AB	R	H	2B	3B	HR	RBI	BB	SO	AVG	OBP	SLG	PRO+	BR/A	SB	CS	SBR	FA	FR	G/POS	TPR
1907	Bos-A	4	12	0	2	0	0	0	1	0		.167	.167	.167	6	-1	0			1.000	1	/O-2	-0.2
1913	NY-A	11	32	8	11	3	1	0	2	7	2	.344	.462	.500	181	4	2			.938	1	O-11	0.5
1918	*Bos-A	71	214	24	57	11	0	1	28	20	9	.266	.335	.346	107	2	9			.935	-11	O-69	-1.5
Total	3	86	258	32	70	17	1	1	31	27	11	.271	.345	.357	113	4	11			.936	-11	/O-82	-1.2

■ MARK WHITEN   Whiten, Mark Anthony b: 11/25/66, Pensacola, Fla. BB/TR, 6'3", 210 lbs. Deb: 7/12/90

YEAR	TM/L	G	AB	R	H	2B	3B	HR	RBI	BB	SO	AVG	OBP	SLG	PRO+	BR/A	SB	CS	SBR	FA	FR	G/POS	TPR
1990	Tor-A	33	88	12	24	1	1	2	7	7	14	.273	.326	.375	94	-1	2	0	1	1.000	2	O-30/D-2	0.1
1991	Tor-A	46	149	12	33	4	2	2	19	11	35	.221	.280	.329	65	-7	0	1	-1	1.000	1	O-42	-0.6
	Cle-A	70	258	34	66	14	4	7	26	19	50	.256	.312	.422	100	-0	4	2	0	.962	11	O-67/D-3	0.9
	Yr	116	407	46	99	18	6	9	45	30	85	.243	.300	.388	87	-8	4	3	-1	.975	14	*O-109/D-3	0.3
1992	Cle-A	148	508	73	129	19	4	9	43	72	102	.254	.349	.360	101	2	16	12	-2	.980	13	*O-144/D-2	1.0
1993	StL-N	152	562	81	142	13	4	25	99	58	110	.253	.325	.423	100	-0	15	8	-0	.971	1	*O-148	-0.3
1994	StL-N	92	334	57	98	18	2	14	53	37	75	.293	.366	.485	122	10	10	5	0	.964	15	O-90	2.3
1995	Bos-A	32	108	13	20	3	0	1	10	8	21	.185	.241	.241	25	-12	1	0	1	1.000	2	O-31/D-1	-1.0
	Phi-N	60	210	38	57	10	1	11	37	31	63	.269	.365	.481	120	6	7	0	2	.965	2	O-55	0.8
1996	Phi-N	60	182	33	43	8	0	7	21	33	62	.236	.356	.396	96	-1	13	3	2	.945	3	O-51	0.3
	Atl-N	36	90	12	23	5	1	3	17	16	25	.256	.368	.433	105	1	2	5	-2	.933	-2	O-29	-0.5
	Yr	96	272	45	66	13	1	10	38	49	87	.243	.360	.408	98	0	15	8	-0	.942	1	O-80	-0.2
	Sea-A	40	140	31	42	7	0	12	33	21	40	.300	.399	.607	150	11	2	1	0	.969	4	O-39	1.3
Total	7	769	2631	396	677	102	20	93	365	313	599	.257	.339	.417	102	9	72	37	-1	.971	53	O-726/D-8	4.3

■ FRED WHITFIELD   Whitfield, Fred Dwight b: 1/7/38, Vandiver, Ala. BL/TL, 6'1", 190 lbs. Deb: 5/27/62

YEAR	TM/L	G	AB	R	H	2B	3B	HR	RBI	BB	SO	AVG	OBP	SLG	PRO+	BR/A	SB	CS	SBR	FA	FR	G/POS	TPR
1962	StL-N	73	158	20	42	7	1	8	34	7	21	.266	.301	.475	95	-2	1	0	0	.987	1	1-38	-0.2
1963	Cle-A	109	346	44	87	17	3	21	54	24	61	.251	.307	.500	123	9	0	1	-1	.987	-3	1-92	0.1
1964	Cle-A	101	293	29	79	13	1	10	29	12	58	.270	.303	.423	100	-1	0	5	-3	.992	-2	1-79	-0.9

YEAR	TM/L	G	AB	R	H	2B	3B	HR	RBI	BB	SO	AVG	OBP	SLG	PRO+	BR/A	SB	CS	SBR	FA	FR	G/POS	TPR
1965	Cle-A	132	468	49	137	23	1	26	90	16	42	.293	.319	.513	131	16	2	2	-1	.993	4	*1-122	1.4
1966	Cle-A	137	502	59	121	15	2	27	78	27	76	.241	.285	.440	105	1	1	2	-1	.991	-4	*1-132	-1.3
1967	Cle-A	100	257	24	56	10	0	9	31	25	45	.218	.290	.362	91	-3	3	3	-1	.993	4	1-66	-0.5
1968	Cin-N	87	171	15	44	8	0	6	32	9	29	.257	.302	.409	105	1	0	3	-2	.981	-1	1-41	-0.5
1969	Cin-N	74	74	2	11	0	0	1	8	18	27	.149	.315	.189	42	-5	0	0	0	.985	1	1-14	-0.5
1970	Mon-N	4	15	0	1	0	0	0	0	1	3	.067	.125	.067	-47	-3	0	0	0	.976	2	/1-4	-0.2
Total	9	817	2284	242	578	93	8	108	356	139	371	.253	.301	.443	107	14	7	16	-8	.990	3	1-588	-2.6

■ TERRY WHITFIELD
Whitfield, Terry Bertland b: 1/12/53, Blythe, Cal. BL/TR, 6'1", 197 lbs. Deb: 9/29/74

YEAR	TM/L	G	AB	R	H	2B	3B	HR	RBI	BB	SO	AVG	OBP	SLG	PRO+	BR/A	SB	CS	SBR	FA	FR	G/POS	TPR
1974	NY-A	2	5	0	1	0	0	0	0	0	1	.200	.200	.200	16	-1	0	0	0	.000	-1	/O-1	-0.1
1975	NY-A	28	81	9	22	1	1	0	7	1	17	.272	.280	.309	67	-4	1	0	0	.978	0	O-25/D-1	-0.4
1976	NY-A	1	0	0	0	0	0	0	0	0	0	—	—	—	—	0	0	0	0	.000	-1	/O-1	-0.1
1977	SF-N	114	326	41	93	21	3	7	36	20	46	.285	.334	.433	103	1	2	3	-1	.972	-3	O-84	-0.6
1978	SF-N	149	488	70	141	20	2	10	32	33	69	.289	.337	.400	109	5	5	11	-5	.988	0	*O-140	-0.6
1979	SF-N	133	394	52	113	20	4	5	44	36	47	.287	.353	.396	111	6	5	4	-1	.957	2	*O-106	0.3
1980	SF-N	118	321	38	95	16	2	4	26	20	44	.296	.339	.396	107	3	4	2	0	.987	-0	O-95	-0.1
1984	LA-N	87	180	15	44	8	0	4	18	17	35	.244	.313	.356	88	-3	1	4	-2	.988	-5	O-58	-1.1
1985	*LA-N	79	104	8	27	7	0	3	16	6	27	.260	.300	.413	101	-0	0	0	0	.926	-5	O-28	-0.6
1986	LA-N	19	14	0	1	0	0	0	0	0	5	.071	.316	.071	14	-1	0	0	0	1.000	-0	/O-1	-0.2
Total	10	730	1913	233	537	93	12	33	179	138	288	.281	.332	.394	103	6	18	24	-9	.976	-12	O-539/D-1	-3.5

■ ED WHITING
Whiting, Edward C. (a.k.a. Harry Zieber) b: 1860, Philadelphia, Pa. BL/TR, 188 lbs. Deb: 5/2/1882

YEAR	TM/L	G	AB	R	H	2B	3B	HR	RBI	BB	SO	AVG	OBP	SLG	PRO+	BR/A	SB	CS	SBR	FA	FR	G/POS	TPR
1882	Bal-a	74	308	43	80	14	5	0		7			.260	.276	.338	115	5				.834	-7	*C-72/1-3,O-2	0.0
1883	Lou-a	58	240	35	70	16	4	2		9			.292	.317	.417	145	12				.884	-8	C-50/O-6,2-2,3-1,1	0.6
1884	Lou-a	42	157	16	35	7	3	0	18	9			.223	.274	.306	93	-1				.891	-4	C-40/O-2,1-2	0.1
1886	Was-N	6	21	0	0	0	0	0	0	1	12		.000	.045	.000	-90	-5	0			.919	-3	/C-6	-0.6
Total	4	180	726	94	185	37	12	2	18	26	12	.255	.282	.347	114	12	0			.866	-20	C-168/O-10,1-6,23	0.1

■ DICK WHITMAN
Whitman, Dick Corwin b: 11/9/20, Woodburn, Ore. BL/TR, 5'11", 170 lbs. Deb: 4/16/46

YEAR	TM/L	G	AB	R	H	2B	3B	HR	RBI	BB	SO	AVG	OBP	SLG	PRO+	BR/A	SB	CS	SBR	FA	FR	G/POS	TPR
1946	Bro-N	104	265	39	69	15	3	2	31	22	19	.260	.317	.362	92	-3	5			1.000	-2	O-85	-0.9
1947	Bro-N	4	10	1	4	0	0	0	2	1	0	.400	.455	.400	124	0	0			1.000	0	/O-3	0.0
1948	Bro-N	60	165	24	48	13	0	0	20	14	12	.291	.346	.370	91	-1	2			.990	-1	O-48	-0.5
1949	*Bro-N	23	49	8	9	2	0	0	2	4	4	.184	.245	.224	26	-5	0			.952	-1	O-11	-0.7
1950	*Phi-N	75	132	21	33	7	0	0	12	10	10	.250	.317	.303	65	-6	1			.983	-4	O-32	-1.1
1951	Phi-N	19	17	0	2	0	0	0	0	0	1	.118	.118	.118	-37	-3	0	0	0	.000	-3	/O-6	-0.6
Total	6	285	638	93	165	37	3	2	67	51	46	.259	.316	.335	78	-20	10			.992	-11	O-185	-3.8

■ FRANK WHITMAN
Whitman, Walter Franklin "Hooker" b: 8/15/24, Marengo, Ind. d: 2/6/94, Maryville, Ill. BR/TR, 6'2", 175 lbs. Deb: 6/30/46

YEAR	TM/L	G	AB	R	H	2B	3B	HR	RBI	BB	SO	AVG	OBP	SLG	PRO+	BR/A	SB	CS	SBR	FA	FR	G/POS	TPR
1946	Chi-A	17	16	7	1	0	0	0	1	2	6	.063	.211	.063	-22	-3	0	1	-1	1.000	4	/S-6,1-1,2-1	0.1
1948	Chi-A	3	6	0	0	0	0	0	0	0	3	.000	.000	.000	-99	-2	0	0	0	.500	-1	/S-1	-0.3
Total	2	20	22	7	1	0	0	0	1	2	9	.045	.160	.045	-43	-4	0	1	-1	.885	3	/S-7,2-1,1-1	-0.2

■ DAN WHITMER
Whitmer, Daniel Charles b: 11/23/55, Redlands, Cal. BR/TR, 6'3", 195 lbs. Deb: 7/20/80 C

YEAR	TM/L	G	AB	R	H	2B	3B	HR	RBI	BB	SO	AVG	OBP	SLG	PRO+	BR/A	SB	CS	SBR	FA	FR	G/POS	TPR
1980	Cal-A	48	87	8	21	3	0	0	7	4	21	.241	.275	.276	53	-6	1	0	0	1.000	4	C-48	0.0
1981	Tor-A	7	9	0	1	1	0	0	0	1	2	.111	.200	.222	20	-1	0	0	0	1.000	1	/C-7	0.0
Total	2	55	96	8	22	4	0	0	7	5	23	.229	.267	.271	49	-7	1	0	0	1.000	5	/C-55	0.0

■ DARRELL WHITMORE
Whitmore, Darrell Lamont b: 11/18/68, Front Royal, Va. BL/TR, 6'1", 210 lbs. Deb: 6/25/93

YEAR	TM/L	G	AB	R	H	2B	3B	HR	RBI	BB	SO	AVG	OBP	SLG	PRO+	BR/A	SB	CS	SBR	FA	FR	G/POS	TPR
1993	Fla-N	76	250	24	51	8	2	4	19	10	72	.204	.249	.300	44	-20	4	2	0	.979	2	O-69	-2.0
1994	Fla-N	9	22	1	5	1	0	0		3	5	.227	.320	.273	55	-1	0	1	-1	1.000	1	O-6	-0.1
1995	Fla-N	27	58	6	11	2	0	1	2	5	15	.190	.254	.276	40	-5	0	0	0	.960	-3	O-16	-0.8
Total	3	112	330	31	67	11	2	5	21	18	92	.203	.255	.294	44	-27	4	3	-1	.978	-0	/O-91	-2.9

■ PINKY WHITNEY
Whitney, Arthur Carter b: 1/2/05, San Antonio, Tex. d: 9/1/87, Center, Tex. BR/TR, 5'10", 165 lbs. Deb: 4/11/28

YEAR	TM/L	G	AB	R	H	2B	3B	HR	RBI	BB	SO	AVG	OBP	SLG	PRO+	BR/A	SB	CS	SBR	FA	FR	G/POS	TPR
1928	Phi-N	151	585	73	176	35	4	10	103	36	30	.301	.342	.426	96	-4	3			.955	3	*3-149	0.7
1929	Phi-N	154	612	89	200	43	14	8	115	61	35	.327	.390	.482	108	7	7			.967	**21**	*3-154	3.1
1930	Phi-N	149	606	87	207	41	5	8	117	40	41	.342	.383	.465	97	-3	3			.965	20	*3-148	2.3
1931	Phi-N	130	501	64	144	36	5	9	74	30	38	.287	.331	.433	96	-4	6			.948	-6	*3-128	-0.2
1932	Phi-N	154	624	93	186	33	11	13	124	35	66	.298	.335	.449	97	-4	6			**.960**	5	*3-151/2-5	1.2
1933	Phi-N	31	121	12	32	4	2	3	19	8	9	.264	.310	.372	83	-3	1			.963	-4	3-30	-0.6
	Bos-N	100	382	42	94	17	2	8	49	25	23	.246	.296	.364	95	-4	2			.971	1	3-85,2-18	0.4
	Yr	131	503	54	126	21	4	11	68	33	31	.250	.299	.366	92	-6	3			.969	-4	*3-115,2-18	-0.2
1934	Bos-N	146	563	58	146	26	2	12	79	25	54	.259	.294	.377	85	-14	7			.968	3	*3-111,2-36/S-2	-0.5
1935	Bos-N	126	458	41	125	23	4	4	60	24	36	.273	.312	.367	89	-8	2			.958	4	3-74,2-49	0.4
1936	Bos-N	10	40	1	7	0	0	0	5	2	4	.175	.233	.175	12	-5	0			.971	-3	3-10	-0.3
	Phi-N★	114	411	44	121	17	3	6	59	37	35	.294	.354	.394	92	-4	10			.955	10	*3-111/2-1	0.9
	Yr	124	451	45	128	17	3	6	64	39	37	.284	.343	.375	86	-9	2			.956	11	*3-121/2-1	0.5
1937	Phi-N	138	487	56	166	19	4	8	79	43	44	.341	.395	.446	118	13	6			**.982**	3	*3-130	1.9
1938	Phi-N	102	300	27	83	9	1	2	38	27	22	.277	.336	.343	90	-4	0			.934	-2	3-75/1-4,2-2	-0.5
1939	Phi-N	34	75	9	14	0	1	0	6	7	4	.187	.256	.253	38	-7	0			.991	1	1-12/2-8,3-2	-0.2
Total	12	1539	5765	696	1701	303	56	93	927	400	438	.295	.343	.415	96	-43	45			.961	62	*3-1358,2-119/1S	8.1

■ ART WHITNEY
Whitney, Arthur Wilson b: 1/16/1858, Brockton, Mass. d: 8/15/43, Lowell, Mass. BR/TR, 5'8", 155 lbs. Deb: 5/1/1880 F

YEAR	TM/L	G	AB	R	H	2B	3B	HR	RBI	BB	SO	AVG	OBP	SLG	PRO+	BR/A	SB	CS	SBR	FA	FR	G/POS	TPR
1880	Wor-N	76	302	38	67	13	5	1	36	9	15	.222	.244	.308	79	-7				.860	-1	*3-76	-0.6
1881	Det-N	58	214	23	39	7	5	0	9	7	15	.182	.208	.262	45	-13				.849	7	*3-58	-0.5
1882	Pro-N	11	40	2	3	0	0	0	2	2	11	.075	.119	.075	-36	-6				.784	-2	S-11	-0.7
	Det-N	31	115	10	21	0	0	0	4	1	12	.183	.190	.183	20	-10				.854	1	3-22/S-8,P-3	-0.6
	Yr	42	155	12	24	0	0	0	5	3	23	.155	.171	.155	5	-16				.854	-1	3-22,S-19/P-3	-1.3
1884	Pit-a	23	94	10	28	4	0	0				.298	.305	.340	109	1				.916	4	3-21/O-1,S-1	0.4
1885	Pit-a	90	373	53	87	10	4	0	28	16		.233	.267	.282	74	-11				**.918**	-14	*S-75/3-8,2-4,O-3	-2.1
1886	Pit-a	136	511	70	122	13	4	0	55	51		.239	.315	.280	87	-6	15			**.906**	11	*3-95,S-42/P-1	0.7
1887	Pit-N	119	431	57	112	11	4	0	51	55	18	.260	.346	.304	87	-4	10			**.924**	-4	*3-119	-0.5
1888	*NY-N	90	328	28	72	1	4	1	28	8	21	.220	.240	.256	59	-15	7			.887	7	3-90	-0.7
1889	*NY-N	129	473	71	103	12	2	1	59	56	39	.218	.303	.258	57	-26	19			.882	0	*3-129/P-1	-1.8
1890	NY-P	119	442	71	97	12	3	0	45	64	19	.219	.322	.260	52	-31	8			.865	-12	3-88,S-31	-3.1
1891	Cin-a	93	347	42	69	6	1	3	33	31	20	.199	.270	.248	44	-27	8			.903	-5	3-93	-2.4
	StL-a	3	11	0	0	0	0	0	0	0	2	.000	.083	.000	-66	-2	0			.867	2	/3-3	-0.1
	Yr	96	358	42	69	6	1	3	33	32	22	.193	.265	.240	41	-29	8			**.902**	-3	3-96	-2.5
Total	11	978	3681	475	820	89	32	6	349	302	173	.223	.285	.269	64	-158	67			.888	-6	3-802,S-168/P-5,2O	-12.0

■ FRANK WHITNEY
Whitney, Frank Thomas "Jumbo" b: 2/18/1856, Brockton, Mass. d: 10/30/43, Baltimore, Md. BR/TR, 5'7.5", 152 lbs. Deb: 5/17/1876 F

YEAR	TM/L	G	AB	R	H	2B	3B	HR	RBI	BB	SO	AVG	OBP	SLG	PRO+	BR/A	SB	CS	SBR	FA	FR	G/POS	TPR
1876	Bos-N	34	139	27	33	7	1	0	15	1	3	.237	.243	.302	79	-3				.818	3	O-34/2-1	-0.1

■ JIM WHITNEY
Whitney, James Evans "Grasshopper Jim" b: 11/10/1857, Conklin, N.Y. d: 5/21/1891, Binghamton, N.Y. BL/TR, 6'2", 172 lbs. Deb: 5/2/1881

YEAR	TM/L	G	AB	R	H	2B	3B	HR	RBI	BB	SO	AVG	OBP	SLG	PRO+	BR/A	SB	CS	SBR	FA	FR	G/POS	TPR
1881	Bos-N	75	282	37	72	17	3	0	32	19	18	.255	.302	.337	106	3				.808	-9	*P-66,O-15/1-2	-0.5
1882	Bos-N	61	251	49	81	18	7	5	48	24	13	.323	.382	.510	183	24				.886	-3	P-49/O-9,1-6	0.3
1883	Bos-N	96	409	78	115	27	10	5	57	25	29	.281	.323	.433	124	11				.921	-4	P-62/O-40/1-2	0.0
1884	Bos-N	66	270	41	70	17	5	3	40	16	38	.259	.301	.393	117	5				1.000	-1	P-38/O-15,1-15/3-1	-0.4
1885	Bos-N	72	290	59	68	13	4	0	36	17	24	.234	.277	.290	86	-4				.901	5	P-51,O-17/1-5	-0.3
1886	KC-N	67	247	25	59	13	3	2	23	29	39	.239	.319	.340	94	-2	5			.927	6	P-46,O-22/3-1	-0.1
1887	Was-N	54	201	29	53	9	6	2	22	18	24	.264	.324	.398	105	2	10			.905	2	P-47/O-7	-0.2
1888	Was-N	42	141	13	24	0	0	1	17	7	20	.170	.209	.191	30	-11	3			.882	-2	P-39/O-3,1-1	-0.2

YEAR	TM/L	G	AB	R	H	2B	3B	HR	RBI	BB	SO	AVG	OBP	SLG	PRO+	BR/A	SB	CS	SBR	FA	FR	G/POS	TPR
1889	Ind-N	10	32	6	12	4	1	0	4	5	6	.375	.474	.563	185	4	2			1.000	-1	/P-9,O-1	0.0
1890	Phi-a	7	21	3	5	0	0	0		1	1	.238	.273	.238	52	-1	0			.900	-1	/P-6,O-1	0.0
Total	10	550	2144	316	559	113	39	18	280	161	211	.261	.313	.375	112	30	20			.900	-9	P-413,O-130/1-31,3	-1.8

■ ERNIE WHITT Whitt, Leo Ernest b: 6/13/52, Detroit, Mich. BL/TR, 6'2", 200 lbs. Deb: 9/12/76

YEAR	TM/L	G	AB	R	H	2B	3B	HR	RBI	BB	SO	AVG	OBP	SLG	PRO+	BR/A	SB	CS	SBR	FA	FR	G/POS	TPR
1976	Bos-A	8	18	4	4	2	0	1	3	2	2	.222	.300	.500	117	0	0	0	0	1.000	-1	/C-8	0.0
1977	Tor-A	23	41	4	7	3	0	0	6	2	12	.171	.209	.244	23	-4	0	0	0	1.000	1	C-14	-0.3
1978	Tor-A	2	4	0	0	0	0	0	0	1	1	.000	.200	.000	-38	-1	0	0	0	1.000	0	/C-1	
1980	Tor-A	106	295	23	70	12	2	6	34	22	30	.237	.290	.353	72	-12	1	3	-2	.986	6	*C-105	-0.4
1981	Tor-A	74	195	16	46	9	0	1	16	20	30	.236	.307	.297	70	-7	5	2	0	.991	9	C-72	0.5
1982	Tor-A	105	284	28	74	14	2	11	42	26	34	.261	.323	.440	98	-1	3	1	0	.982	1	C-98/D-1	0.3
1983	Tor-A	123	344	53	88	15	2	17	56	50	55	.256	.350	.459	114	7	1	1	-0	.992	6	*C-119	1.7
1984	Tor-A	124	315	35	75	12	1	15	46	43	49	.238	.331	.425	104	2	0	3	-2	.994	12	*C-118	1.7
1985	*Tor-A★	139	412	55	101	21	2	19	64	47	59	.245	.324	.444	105	2	3	6	-3	.988	6	*C-134	1.1
1986	Tor-A	131	395	48	106	19	2	16	56	35	39	.268	.328	.448	106	3	0	1	-1	.991	-4	*C-129	0.6
1987	Tor-A	135	446	57	120	24	1	19	75	44	50	.269	.336	.455	105	3	0	1	-1	.994	6	*C-131	1.6
1988	Tor-A	127	398	63	100	11	2	16	70	61	38	.251	.352	.410	112	8	4	2	0	.994	-6	*C-123	1.1
1989	*Tor-A	129	385	42	101	24	1	11	53	52	53	.262	.350	.416	117	9	5	4	-1	.992	-2	*C-115/D-8	1.3
1990	Atl-N	67	180	14	31	8	0	2	10	23	27	.172	.266	.250	40	-14	0	2	-1	.991	2	C-59	-1.1
1991	Bal-N	35	62	5	15	2	0	0	3	8	12	.242	.329	.274	71	-2	0	0	0	1.000	-1	C-20/D-2	-0.2
Total	15	1328	3774	447	938	176	15	134	534	436	491	.249	.327	.410	98	-9	22	26	-9	.991	36	*C-1246/D-11	7.9

■ POSSUM WHITTED Whitted, George Bostic b: 2/4/1890, Durham, N.C. d: 10/16/62, Wilmington, N.C. BR/TR, 5'8.5", 168 lbs. Deb: 9/16/12

YEAR	TM/L	G	AB	R	H	2B	3B	HR	RBI	BB	SO	AVG	OBP	SLG	PRO+	BR/A	SB	CS	SBR	FA	FR	G/POS	TPR
1912	StL-N	12	46	7	12	3	0	0	7	3	5	.261	.306	.326	75	-2	1			.857	-3	3-12	-0.5
1913	StL-N	123	404	44	89	10	5	0	38	31	44	.220	.282	.270	59	-21	9			.989	5	O-41,S-38,3-22,/21	-1.5
1914	StL-N	20	31	3	4	1	0	0	1	0	3	.129	.129	.161	-14	-4	1			.889	-3	/3-5,O-3,2-1	-0.8
	*Bos-N	66	218	36	57	11	4	2	31	18	18	.261	.326	.376	109	2	10			.967	4	O-38,2-15/1-4,3S	0.5
	Yr	86	249	39	61	12	4	2	32	18	21	.245	.304	.349	95	-2	11			.957	1	O-41,2-16/3-9,1S	-0.3
1915	*Phi-N	128	448	46	126	17	3	1	43	29	47	.281	.328	.339	101	0	24	15	-2	.978	4	*O-119/1-7	-0.4
1916	Phi-N	147	526	68	148	20	12	6	68	19	46	.281	.309	.399	113	6	29	17	-2	.964	5	*O-136,1-16	0.2
1917	Phi-N	149	553	69	155	24	9	3	70	30	56	.280	.317	.373	107	3	10			.977	4	*O-141,1-10/3-7,2-1	0.0
1918	Phi-N	24	86	7	21	4	0	0	3	4	10	.244	.278	.291	69	-3	5			.982	2	O-22/1-1	-0.2
1919	Phi-N	78	289	32	72	14	1	3	32	14	20	.249	.284	.336	80	-7	5			.955	0	O-47,2-26/1-2	-1.0
	Pit-N	35	131	15	51	7	7	0	21	6	4	.389	.420	.550	183	13	7			.988	3	1-33/3-2,O-1	1.5
	Yr	113	420	47	123	21	8	3	53	20	24	.293	.327	.402	112	5	12			.955	3	O-48,1-35,2-26,/3-2	0.5
1920	Pit-N	134	494	53	129	11	12	1	74	35	36	.261	.314	.338	85	-10	11	11	-3	.961	-3	*3-125,1-10/O-1	-1.1
1921	Pit-N	108	403	60	114	23	7	7	63	26	21	.283	.328	.427	96	-3	5	10	-5	.988	9	*O-102/1-7	-0.6
1922	Bro-N	1	1	0	0	0	0	0	0	0	0	.000	.000	.000	-99	-0	0			.000	0	H	0.0
Total	11	1025	3630	440	978	145	60	23	451	215	310	.269	.313	.361	95	-27	116	53		.975	27	O-651,3-177/12S	-3.9

■ FLOYD WICKER Wicker, Floyd Euliss b: 9/12/43, Burlington, N.C. BL/TR, 6'2", 175 lbs. Deb: 6/23/68

YEAR	TM/L	G	AB	R	H	2B	3B	HR	RBI	BB	SO	AVG	OBP	SLG	PRO+	BR/A	SB	CS	SBR	FA	FR	G/POS	TPR
1968	StL-N	5	4	2	2	0	0	0	0	0	0	.500	.500	.500	204	0	0	0	0	.000	0	H	0.1
1969	Mon-N	41	39	2	4	0	0	0	2	0	20	.103	.146	.103	-29	-7	0	0	0	1.000	-2	O-11	-1.0
1970	Mil-A	15	41	3	8	1	0	1	3	1	8	.195	.214	.293	38	-4	0	0	0	1.000	-1	O-12	-0.5
1971	Mil-A	11	8	0	1	0	0	0	0	2	0	.125	.300	.125	24	-1	0	0	0	.000	0	H	-0.1
	SF-N	9	21	3	3	0	0	0	1	2	5	.143	.250	.143	14	-2	0	0	0	1.000	1	/O-7	-0.2
Total	4	81	113	10	18	1	0	1	6	7	33	.159	.215	.195	15	-13	0	0	0	1.000	-3	/O-30	-1.7

■ AL WICKLAND Wickland, Albert b: 1/27/1888, Chicago, Ill. d: 3/14/80, Port Washington, Wis. BL/TL, 5'7", 155 lbs. Deb: 8/21/13

YEAR	TM/L	G	AB	R	H	2B	3B	HR	RBI	BB	SO	AVG	OBP	SLG	PRO+	BR/A	SB	CS	SBR	FA	FR	G/POS	TPR
1913	Cin-N	26	79	7	17	5	5	0	8	6	19	.215	.279	.405	94	0	3			.983	1	O-24	-0.2
1914	Chi-F	157	536	74	148	31	10	6	68	**81**	58	.276	.375	.405	119	7	17			.962	-1	*O-157	-0.1
1915	Chi-F	30	86	11	21	2	2	1	5	13	11	.244	.343	.349	101	-1	3			.946	-2	O-24	-0.4
	Pit-F	110	389	63	117	12	8	1	30	52	47	.301	.386	.380	117	5	23			.968	4	*O-109	0.4
	Yr	140	475	74	138	14	10	2	35	65	58	.291	.378	.375	114	4	26			.966	2	*O-133	0.0
1918	Bos-N	95	332	55	87	7	13	4	32	53	39	.262	.367	.398	139	17	12			.975	3	O-95	1.6
1919	NY-A	26	46	2	7	1	0	0	1	2	8	.152	.188	.174	2	-6	0			1.000	-4	O-15	-1.1
Total	5	444	1468	212	397	58	38	12	144	207	184	.270	.364	.386	117	22	58			.968	-1	O-424	0.2

■ CHRIS WIDGER Widger, Christopher Jon b: 5/21/71, Wilmington, Del. BR/TR, 6'3", 195 lbs. Deb: 6/23/95

YEAR	TM/L	G	AB	R	H	2B	3B	HR	RBI	BB	SO	AVG	OBP	SLG	PRO+	BR/A	SB	CS	SBR	FA	FR	G/POS	TPR
1995	*Sea-A	23	45	2	9	0	0	1	2	3	11	.200	.250	.267	34	-4	0	0	0	1.000	-4	C-19/O-3,D-1	-0.8
1996	Sea-A	8	11	1	2	0	0	0	0	0	5	.182	.250	.182	12	-1	0	0	0	.905	-0	/C-7	-0.2
Total	2	31	56	3	11	0	0	1	2	3	16	.196	.250	.250	30	-6	0	0	0	.976	-5	/C-26,O-3,D-1	-1.0

■ TOM WIEDENBAUER Wiedenbauer, Thomas John b: 11/5/58, Menomonie, Wis. BR/TR, 6'1", 180 lbs. Deb: 9/14/79

YEAR	TM/L	G	AB	R	H	2B	3B	HR	RBI	BB	SO	AVG	OBP	SLG	PRO+	BR/A	SB	CS	SBR	FA	FR	G/POS	TPR
1979	Hou-N	4	6	0	4	1	0	0	2	0	2	.667	.667	.833	326	2	0	0	0	1.000	-1	/O-3	0.1

■ STUMP WIEDMAN Wiedman, George E. b: 2/17/1861, Rochester, N.Y. d: 3/2/05, New York, N.Y. BR/TR, 5'7.5", 165 lbs. Deb: 8/26/1880 U

YEAR	TM/L	G	AB	R	H	2B	3B	HR	RBI	BB	SO	AVG	OBP	SLG	PRO+	BR/A	SB	CS	SBR	FA	FR	G/POS	TPR
1880	Buf-N	23	78	8	8	1	0	0	3	2	11	.103	.125	.115	-18	-9				.893	-3	P-17,O-13	-0.5
1881	Det-N	13	47	8	12	1	0	0	5	2	2	.255	.286	.277	75	-1				**1.000**	-2	P-13	0.0
1882	Det-N	50	193	20	42	7	1	0	20	2	19	.218	.226	.264	57	-9				.906	0	P-46/O-6,S-1	0.0
1883	Det-N	79	313	34	58	6	1	1	24	4	38	.185	.196	.220	27	-26				.909	4	P-52,O-35/2-4	-1.2
1884	Det-N	81	300	24	49	6	0	0	26	13	41	.163	.198	.183	22	-26				.846	-3	O-53,P-26/S-1,2-1	-1.9
1885	Det-N	44	153	7	24	2	1	1	14	8	32	.157	.199	.203	30	-12				.869	-5	P-38/O-7,2-1	-0.3
1886	KC-N	51	179	13	30	2	0	0	7	5	46	.168	.190	.179	12	-19	3			.936	5	P-51/O-3	-0.1
1887	Det-N	21	82	12	17	2	0	0	11	3	3	.207	.235	.232	29	-8	6			.837	-1	P-21/O-2	-0.1
	NY-a	14	46	5	7	1	1	0	1	4		.152	.222	.217	23	-5	2			.882	2	P-12/O-3	0.0
	NY-N	1	3	0	1	0	0	0	0	0		.333	.333	.333	90	-0				.500	-0	/P-1	0.0
1888	NY-N	2	7	1	0	0	0	0	0	2	1	.000	.222	.000	-24	-1	0			.714	-0	/P-2	0.0
Total	9	379	1401	132	248	28	4	2	112	45	193	.177	.203	.207	28	-115	11			.885	-10	P-279,O-122/2-6,S-2	-4.1

■ TOM WIEGHAUS Wieghaus, Thomas Robert b: 2/1/57, Chicago Heights, Ill BR/TR, 6', 195 lbs. Deb: 10/4/81

YEAR	TM/L	G	AB	R	H	2B	3B	HR	RBI	BB	SO	AVG	OBP	SLG	PRO+	BR/A	SB	CS	SBR	FA	FR	G/POS	TPR
1981	Mon-N	1	1	0	0	0	0	0	0	0	0	.000	.000	.000	-99	-0	0	0	0	1.000	1	/C-1	0.1
1983	Mon-N	1	0	0	0	0	0	0	0	0	0	—	—	—	-99	-0	0	0	0	1.000	-0	/C-1	0.0
1984	Hou-N	6	10	0	0	0	0	0	1	1	3	.000	.091	.000	-78	-2	0	0	0	1.000	2	/C-6	0.0
Total	3	8	11	0	0	0	0	0	1	1	3	.000	.083	.000	-80	-2	0	0	0	1.000	3	/C-8	0.1

■ WHITEY WIETELMANN Wietelmann, William Frederick b: 3/15/19, Zanesville, Ohio BB/TR, 6', 170 lbs. Deb: 9/6/39 C

YEAR	TM/L	G	AB	R	H	2B	3B	HR	RBI	BB	SO	AVG	OBP	SLG	PRO+	BR/A	SB	CS	SBR	FA	FR	G/POS	TPR
1939	Bos-N	23	69	2	14	4	0	0	5	2	9	.203	.225	.217	21	-8	1			.953	2	S-22/2-1	-0.5
1940	Bos-N	35	41	3	8	1	0	0	1	5	5	.195	.283	.220	43	-3	0			.962	3	2-15/3-9,S-3	0.0
1941	Bos-N	16	33	1	3	0	0	0	0	1	2	.091	.118	.091	-43	-6	0			1.000	3	2-10/S-5,3-2	-0.3
1942	Bos-N	13	34	4	7	2	0	0	4	6	5	.206	.289	.265	64	-1	0			.941	-1	S-11/2-1	-0.1
1943	Bos-N	153	534	33	115	14	1	0	39	46	40	.215	.281	.245	53	-31	9			.957	20	*S-153	0.0
1944	Bos-N	125	417	46	100	18	1	2	32	33	25	.240	.300	.302	67	-18	0			.954	-6	*S-103,2-23/3-1	-1.6
1945	Bos-N	123	428	53	116	15	3	4	33	39	27	.271	.335	.348	89	-6	4			.972	3	2-87,S-39/3-2,P-1	0.4
1946	Bos-N	44	78	7	16	0	0	0	5	14	8	.205	.326	.205	52	-4	0			.915	-6	S-16/3-8,2-4,P-3	-0.9
1947	Pit-N	48	128	21	30	4	1	1	19	15	9	.234	.300	.305	59	-7	0			.885	-13	S-22,2-14/3-6,1-1	-1.9
Total	9	580	1762	170	409	55	6	7	122	156	131	.232	.298	.282	63	-85	14			.952	3	S-374,2-155/3P1	-4.9

■ ALAN WIGGINS Wiggins, Alan Anthony b: 2/17/58, Los Angeles, Cal. d: 1/6/91, Los Angeles, Cal. BB/TR, 6'2", 160 lbs. Deb: 9/4/81

YEAR	TM/L	G	AB	R	H	2B	3B	HR	RBI	BB	SO	AVG	OBP	SLG	PRO+	BR/A	SB	CS	SBR	FA	FR	G/POS	TPR
1981	SD-N	15	14	4	5	0	0	0	0	1	0	.357	.400	.357	125	0	2	0	1	.750	-1	/O-4	0.0
1982	SD-N	72	254	40	65	3	3	1	15	13	19	.256	.295	.303	71	-10	33	6	6	.967	1	O-68/2-1	-0.5
1983	SD-N	144	503	83	139	20	2	0	22	65	43	.276	.360	.324	94	-2	66	13	12	.992	-1	*O-105,1-45	0.4

YEAR	TM/L	G	AB	R	H	2B	3B	HR	RBI	BB	SO	AVG	OBP	SLG	PRO+	BR/A	SB	CS	SBR	FA	FR	G/POS	TPR
1984	*SD-N	158	596	106	154	19	7	3	34	75	57	.258	.344	.329	90	-6	70	21	8	.962	-29	*2-157	-2.2
1985	SD-N	10	37	3	2	1	0	0	0	2	4	.054	.103	.081	-49	-7	0	1	-1	1.000	-3	/2-9	-1.2
	Bal-A	76	298	43	85	11	4	0	21	29	16	.285	.353	.349	96	-1	30	13	1	.960	-24	2-76	-2.1
1986	Bal-A	71	239	30	60	3	1	0	11	22	20	.251	.314	.272	62	-12	21	7	2	.978	-19	2-66/D-1	-2.6
1987	Bal-A	85	306	37	71	4	2	1	15	28	34	.232	.299	.268	53	-20	20	7	2	.983	-0	D-44,2-33/O-5	-1.7
Total	7	631	2247	346	581	61	19	5	118	235	193	.259	.331	.309	80	-57	242	68	32	.967	-76	2-342,O-182/D-45,1	-9.9

■ **DEL WILBER**   Wilber, Delbert Quentin "Babe"   b: 2/24/19, Lincoln Park, Mich   BR/TR, 6'3", 200 lbs.   Deb: 4/21/46   MC

YEAR	TM/L	G	AB	R	H	2B	3B	HR	RBI	BB	SO	AVG	OBP	SLG	PRO+	BR/A	SB	CS	SBR	FA	FR	G/POS	TPR
1946	StL-N	4	4	0	0	0	0	0	0	1	0	.000	.200	.000	-39	-1	0			1.000	1	/C-4	0.0
1947	StL-N	51	99	7	23	8	1	0	12	5	13	.232	.269	.333	57	-6	0			.983	1	C-34	-0.4
1948	StL-N	27	58	5	11	2	0	0	10	4	9	.190	.242	.224	25	-6	0			.949	-3	C-26	-0.8
1949	StL-N	2	4	0	1	0	0	0	0	0	0	.250	.250	.250	33	-0	0			1.000	0	/C-2	0.0
1951	Phi-N	84	245	30	68	7	3	8	34	17	26	.278	.324	.429	102	0	0	1	-1	.978	4	C-73	0.6
1952	Phi-N	2	2	0	0	0	0	0	0	0	1	.000	.000	.000	-99	-1	0	0	0	.000	-0	H	-0.1
	Bos-A	47	135	7	36	10	1	3	23	7	20	.267	.308	.422	94	-2	1	0	0	.995	1	C-39	0.1
1953	Bos-A	58	112	16	27	6	1	7	29	6	21	.241	.286	.500	103	-0	0	0	0	.980	-3	C-28/1-2	-0.2
1954	Bos-A	24	61	2	8	2	1	1	7	4	6	.131	.185	.246	15	-7	0	0	0	.950	-5	C-18	-1.3
Total	8	299	720	67	174	35	7	19	115	44	96	.242	.287	.389	79	-23	1	1		.978	-4	C-224/1-2	-2.1

■ **CLAUDE WILBORN**   Wilborn, Claude Edward   b: 9/1/12, Woodsdale, N.C.   d: 11/13/92, Roxboro, N.C.   BL/TR, 6'1", 180 lbs.   Deb: 9/8/40

YEAR	TM/L	G	AB	R	H	2B	3B	HR	RBI	BB	SO	AVG	OBP	SLG	PRO+	BR/A	SB	CS	SBR	FA	FR	G/POS	TPR
1940	Bos-N	5	7	0	0	0	0	0	0	0	1	.000	.000	.000	-99	-2				.500	-1	/O-3	-0.4

■ **TED WILBORN**   Wilborn, Thaddeaus Iglehart   b: 12/16/58, Waco, Tex.   BB/TR, 6', 165 lbs.   Deb: 4/5/79

YEAR	TM/L	G	AB	R	H	2B	3B	HR	RBI	BB	SO	AVG	OBP	SLG	PRO+	BR/A	SB	CS	SBR	FA	FR	G/POS	TPR
1979	Tor-A	22	12	3	0	0	0	0	0	1	7	.000	.077	.000	-76	-3	0	1	-1	.875	-2	/O-7,D-4	-0.5
1980	NY-A	8	8	2	2	0	0	0	1	0	1	.250	.250	.250	38	-1	0	0	0	1.000	1	/O-3	-0.0
Total	2	30	20	5	2	0	0	0	1	1	8	.100	.143	.100	-33	-4	0	1	-1	.933	-1	/O-10,D-4	-0.5

■ **WILEY**   Wiley   Deb: 6/23/1884

YEAR	TM/L	G	AB	R	H	2B	3B	HR	RBI	BB	SO	AVG	OBP	SLG	PRO+	BR/A	SB	CS	SBR	FA	FR	G/POS	TPR
1884	Was-U	1	4	0	0	0	0	0	0	0	0	.000	.000	.000	-99	-1				.333	-1	/3-1	-0.2

■ **ROB WILFONG**   Wilfong, Robert Donald   b: 9/1/53, Pasadena, Cal.   BL/TR, 6'1", 185 lbs.   Deb: 4/10/77

YEAR	TM/L	G	AB	R	H	2B	3B	HR	RBI	BB	SO	AVG	OBP	SLG	PRO+	BR/A	SB	CS	SBR	FA	FR	G/POS	TPR
1977	Min-A	73	171	22	42	1	1	1	13	17	26	.246	.321	.281	67	-7	10	4	1	.959	4	2-66/D-1	0.0
1978	Min-A	92	199	23	53	8	0	1	11	19	27	.266	.336	.322	84	-4	8	4	0	.986	6	2-80/D-5	0.7
1979	Min-A	140	419	71	131	22	6	9	59	29	54	.313	.360	.458	115	8	11	4	1	.979	21	*2-133/O-3	3.6
1980	Min-A	131	416	55	103	16	5	8	45	34	61	.248	.309	.368	79	-12	10	6	-1	.995	-4	*2-120/O-6	-1.1
1981	Min-A	93	305	32	75	11	3	3	19	29	43	.246	.311	.331	80	-8	2	4	-1	.980	4	2-93	-0.1
1982	Min-A	25	81	7	13	1	0	0	5	7	13	.160	.236	.173	14	-9	2	0	0	.980	-0	2-22	-1.0
	*Cal-A	55	102	17	25	4	2	1	11	7	17	.245	.294	.353	77	-3	4	0	1	.982	9	2-28/3-5,O-3,S-2,D	0.7
	Yr	80	183	24	38	5	2	1	16	14	30	.208	.268	.273	49	-13	4	2	0	.981	9	2-50/3-5,O-3,S-2,D	-0.3
1983	Cal-A	65	177	17	45	7	1	2	17	10	25	.254	.294	.339	74	-6	0	2	-1	.995	12	2-39,3-13/S-6,D-1	0.6
1984	Cal-A	108	307	31	76	13	2	6	33	20	53	.248	.298	.362	82	-8	3	2	-0	.975	9	2-97/S-4,D-1	-0.2
1985	Cal-A	83	217	16	41	3	0	4	13	16	32	.189	.245	.258	38	-19	4	1	1	.986	21	2-69/D-2	0.5
1986	*Cal-A	92	288	25	63	11	3	3	33	16	34	.219	.265	.309	56	-18	1	4	-2	.982	9	2-90	-0.8
1987	SF-N	2	8	2	1	1	0	0	2	1	2	.125	.222	.500	89	-0	1	0	0	.833	-2	/2-2	-0.2
Total	11	959	2690	318	668	97	23	39	261	205	387	.248	.305	.345	77	-86	54	33	-4	.982	80	2-839/3-18,S-12,OD	2.7

■ **SPIDER WILHELM**   Wilhelm, Charles Ernest   b: 5/23/29, Baltimore, Md.   d: 10/20/92, Venice, Fla.   BR/TR, 5'9", 170 lbs.   Deb: 9/6/53

YEAR	TM/L	G	AB	R	H	2B	3B	HR	RBI	BB	SO	AVG	OBP	SLG	PRO+	BR/A	SB	CS	SBR	FA	FR	G/POS	TPR
1953	Phi-A	7	7	1	2	1	0	0	0	0	3	.286	.286	.429	87	-0	0	0	0	.875	-0	/S-6	0.0

■ **JIM WILHELM**   Wilhelm, James Webster   b: 9/20/52, San Rafael, Cal.   BR/TR, 6'3", 190 lbs.   Deb: 9/4/78

YEAR	TM/L	G	AB	R	H	2B	3B	HR	RBI	BB	SO	AVG	OBP	SLG	PRO+	BR/A	SB	CS	SBR	FA	FR	G/POS	TPR
1978	SD-N	10	19	2	7	2	0	0	4	0	2	.368	.400	.474	155	1	1	0	0	1.000	-3	O-10	-0.1
1979	SD-N	39	103	8	25	4	3	0	8	2	12	.243	.257	.340	65	-5	1	1	-0	.985	0	O-30	-0.6
Total	2	49	122	10	32	6	3	0	12	2	14	.262	.280	.361	79	-4	2	1	0	.987	-2	/O-40	-0.7

■ **JOE WILHOIT**   Wilhoit, Joseph William   b: 12/20/1885, Hiawatha, Kan.   d: 9/25/30, Santa Barbara, Cal.   BL/TR, 6'2", 175 lbs.   Deb: 4/12/16

YEAR	TM/L	G	AB	R	H	2B	3B	HR	RBI	BB	SO	AVG	OBP	SLG	PRO+	BR/A	SB	CS	SBR	FA	FR	G/POS	TPR
1916	Bos-N	116	383	44	88	13	4	2	38	27	45	.230	.282	.300	82	-8	18			.979	2	*O-108	-1.4
1917	Bos-N	54	186	20	51	5	0	1	10	17	15	.274	.335	.317	107	2	5			.928	-3	O-52	-0.4
	Pit-N	9	10	0	2	0	0	0	0	1	1	.200	.273	.200	44	-1	0			1.000	-0	/O-3,1-1	-0.1
	*NY-N	34	50	9	17	2	2	0	8	8	5	.340	.431	.460	179	5	0			1.000	-2	O-11	0.3
	Yr	97	246	29	70	7	2	1	18	26	21	.285	.353	.341	118	6	5			.941	-5	O-66/1-1	-0.2
1918	NY-N	64	135	13	37	3	3	0	15	17	14	.274	.355	.341	115	3	4			.975	-8	O-55	-0.7
1919	Bos-A	6	18	7	6	0	0	0	2	5	2	.333	.478	.333	138	1	1			1.000	-1	/O-5	0.0
Total	4	283	782	93	201	23	9	3	73	75	82	.257	.323	.321	101	2	28			.969	-11	O-234/1-1	-2.3

■ **DENNEY WILIE**   Wilie, Dennis Ernest   b: 9/22/1890, Mt.Calm, Tex.   d: 6/20/66, Hayward, Cal.   BL/TL, 5'8", 155 lbs.   Deb: 7/27/11

YEAR	TM/L	G	AB	R	H	2B	3B	HR	RBI	BB	SO	AVG	OBP	SLG	PRO+	BR/A	SB	CS	SBR	FA	FR	G/POS	TPR
1911	StL-N	28	51	10	12	3	1	0	3	8	11	.235	.361	.333	97	0	3			1.000	-3	O-15	-0.3
1912	StL-N	30	48	2	11	0	1	0	6	7	9	.229	.351	.271	73	-1	0			.917	-3	O-16	-0.5
1915	Cle-A	45	131	14	33	4	1	2	10	26	18	.252	.384	.344	115	4	2	6	-3	.910	-2	O-35	-0.4
Total	3	103	230	26	56	7	3	2	19	41	38	.243	.372	.326	102	2	5	6		.925	-8	/O-66	-1.2

■ **HARRY WILKE**   Wilke, Henry Joseph   b: 12/14/1900, Cincinnati, Ohio   d: 6/21/91, Hamilton, Ohio   BR/TR, 5'10.5", 171 lbs.   Deb: 5/12/27

YEAR	TM/L	G	AB	R	H	2B	3B	HR	RBI	BB	SO	AVG	OBP	SLG	PRO+	BR/A	SB	CS	SBR	FA	FR	G/POS	TPR
1927	Chi-N	3	9	0	0	0	0	0	0	0	1	.000	.000	.000	-99	-1	0			1.000	0	/3-3	-0.2

■ **CURTIS WILKERSON**   Wilkerson, Curtis Vernon   b: 4/26/61, Petersburg, Va.   BB/TR, 5'9", 158 lbs.   Deb: 9/10/83

YEAR	TM/L	G	AB	R	H	2B	3B	HR	RBI	BB	SO	AVG	OBP	SLG	PRO+	BR/A	SB	CS	SBR	FA	FR	G/POS	TPR
1983	Tex-A	16	35	7	6	1	2	0	1	2	5	.171	.216	.229	23	-4	3	0	1	1.000	2	/S-9,2-2,3-2	0.0
1984	Tex-A	153	484	47	120	12	0	1	26	22	72	.248	.283	.279	55	-29	12	10	-2	.944	-28	*S-116,2-47	-4.9
1985	Tex-A	129	360	35	88	11	6	0	22	22	63	.244	.295	.308	65	-17	14	7	0	.957	3	*S-110,2-19/D-2	-0.4
1986	Tex-A	110	236	27	56	10	3	0	15	11	42	.237	.274	.305	56	-14	9	7	-2	.968	5	2-60,S-56/D-2	0.3
1987	Tex-A	85	138	28	37	5	3	2	14	6	16	.268	.308	.391	84	-3	6	3	0	.946	11	S-33,2-28,3-18/D-4	0.9
1988	Tex-A	117	338	41	99	12	5	0	28	26	43	.293	.347	.358	95	-2	9	4	0	.970	10	2-87,S-24,3-11/D-1	1.3
1989	*Chi-N	77	160	19	39	4	2	1	10	9	33	.244	.280	.313	64	-7	4	2	0	.881	-8	3-26,2-15/S-7,O-1	-2.1
1990	Chi-N	77	186	21	41	5	1	0	16	7	36	.220	.249	.258	37	-16	2	5	-1	.888	-4	3-52,2-14/S-1,O-1	-2.1
1991	*Pit-N	85	191	20	36	9	1	2	18	15	40	.188	.246	.277	48	-13	2	1	0	.992	3	2-30,S-15,3-14	-0.9
1992	KC-A	111	296	27	74	10	1	2	29	18	47	.250	.295	.311	68	-13	18	7	1	.968	-4	S-69,2-39/3-5,D-1	-1.1
1993	KC-A	12	28	2	4	0	0	0	0	1	6	.143	.172	.143	-13	-4	2	0	1	1.000	-1	2-10/S-4	-0.4
Total	11	972	2452	272	600	78	23	8	179	138	403	.245	.288	.305	63	-123	81	43	-2	.957	11	S-444,2-351,3/DO	-7.6

■ **RICK WILKINS**   Wilkins, Richard David   b: 6/4/67, Jacksonville, Fla.   BL/TR, 6'2", 210 lbs.   Deb: 6/6/91

YEAR	TM/L	G	AB	R	H	2B	3B	HR	RBI	BB	SO	AVG	OBP	SLG	PRO+	BR/A	SB	CS	SBR	FA	FR	G/POS	TPR
1991	Chi-N	86	203	21	45	9	0	6	22	19	56	.222	.307	.355	82	-5	3	3	-1	.993	9	C-82	0.7
1992	Chi-N	83	244	20	66	9	1	8	22	28	53	.270	.346	.414	111	4	0	2	-1	.993	10	C-73	1.8
1993	Chi-N	136	446	78	135	23	1	30	73	50	99	.303	.377	.561	149	30	2	1	0	.996	5	*C-133	4.2
1994	Chi-N	100	313	44	71	25	2	7	39	40	86	.227	.318	.387	84	-8	4	3	-1	.993	-5	C-95/1-2	-0.7
1995	Chi-N	50	162	24	31	2	0	6	14	36	51	.191	.342	.315	76	-5	0	0	0	.988	-6	C-49/1-2	-0.7
	Hou-N	15	40	6	10	1	0	1	5	10	10	.250	.400	.350	107	1	0	0	0	1.000	0	C-13	0.1
	Yr	65	202	30	41	3	0	7	19	46	61	.203	.353	.322	82	-4	0	0	0	.990	-7	C-62/1-2	-0.6
1996	Hou-N	84	254	34	54	8	2	6	23	46	81	.213	.336	.331	84	-5	0	1	-0	.990	-7	C-82	-0.7
	SF-N	52	157	19	46	10	0	8	36	21	40	.293	.376	.510	137	8	0	0	0	.991	-7	C-42/1-7	0.2
	Yr	136	411	53	100	18	2	14	59	67	121	.243	.351	.399	105	4	0	1	-3	.990	-15	*C-124/1-7	-0.5
Total	6	606	1819	246	458	87	6	72	234	250	476	.252	.346	.425	108	21	9	12	-6	.993	-2	C-569/1-11	4.9

■ **BOBBY WILKINS**   Wilkins, Robert Linwood   b: 8/11/22, Denton, N.C.   BR/TR, 5'9", 165 lbs.   Deb: 4/18/44

YEAR	TM/L	G	AB	R	H	2B	3B	HR	RBI	BB	SO	AVG	OBP	SLG	PRO+	BR/A	SB	CS	SBR	FA	FR	G/POS	TPR
1944	Phi-A	24	25	7	6	0	0	0	3	1	4	.240	.296	.240	55	-1	0	0	0	.943	5	/S-9	0.4

YEAR	TM/L	G	AB	R	H	2B	3B	HR	RBI	BB	SO	AVG	OBP	SLG	PRO+	BR/A	SB	CS	SBR	FA	FR	G/POS	TPR
1945	Phi-A	62	154	22	40	6	0	0	4	10	17	.260	.305	.299	76	-5	2	4	-2	.923	0	S-40/O-4	-0.4
Total	2	86	179	29	46	6	0	0	7	11	21	.257	.304	.291	73	-6	2	4	-2	.926	5	/S-49,O-4	0.0

■ ED WILKINSON
Wilkinson, Edward Henry b: 6/20/1890, Jacksonville, Ore d: 4/9/18, Tucson, Ariz. BR/TR, 6', 170 lbs. Deb: 7/4/11

YEAR	TM/L	G	AB	R	H	2B	3B	HR	RBI	BB	SO	AVG	OBP	SLG	PRO+	BR/A	SB	CS	SBR	FA	FR	G/POS	TPR
1911	NY-A	10	13	2	3	0	0	1	0			.231	.231	.231	27	-1	0			.800	-1	/O-3,2-1	-0.2

■ BOB WILL
Will, Robert Lee "Butch" b: 7/15/31, Berwyn, Ill. BL/TL, 5'10.5", 175 lbs. Deb: 4/16/57

YEAR	TM/L	G	AB	R	H	2B	3B	HR	RBI	BB	SO	AVG	OBP	SLG	PRO+	BR/A	SB	CS	SBR	FA	FR	G/POS	TPR
1957	Chi-N	70	112	13	25	3	0	1	10	5	21	.223	.256	.277	44	-9	1	0	0	.963	-5	O-30	-1.5
1958	Chi-N	6	4	1	1	0	0	0	0	2	0	.250	.500	.250	108	0	0	0	0	.000	0	/O-1	0.0
1960	Chi-N	138	475	58	121	20	9	6	53	47	54	.255	.323	.373	91	-6	1	5	-3	.992	2	*O-121	-1.3
1961	Chi-N	86	113	9	29	9	0	0	8	15	19	.257	.344	.336	80	-3	0	1	-1	1.000	-6	O-30/1-1	-1.0
1962	Chi-N	87	92	6	22	3	0	2	15	13	22	.239	.333	.337	78	-3	0	0	0	1.000	-1	/O-9	-0.4
1963	Chi-N	23	23	0	4	0	0	0	1	1	3	.174	.208	.174	11	-3	0	0	0	1.000	-0	/1-1	-0.3
Total	6	410	819	87	202	35	9	9	87	83	119	.247	.317	.344	80	-22	2	6	-3	.988	-10	O-191/1-2	-4.5

■ JERRY WILLARD
Willard, Gerald Duane b: 3/14/60, Oxnard, Cal. BL/TR, 6'2", 195 lbs. Deb: 4/11/84

YEAR	TM/L	G	AB	R	H	2B	3B	HR	RBI	BB	SO	AVG	OBP	SLG	PRO+	BR/A	SB	CS	SBR	FA	FR	G/POS	TPR
1984	Cle-A	87	246	21	55	8	1	10	37	26	55	.224	.298	.386	86	-5	1	0	0	.981	-1	C-76/D-1	-0.2
1985	Cle-A	104	300	39	81	13	0	7	36	28	59	.270	.334	.383	97	-1	0	0	0	.990	-0	C-96/D-1	0.4
1986	Oak-A	75	161	17	43	7	0	4	26	22	28	.267	.362	.385	112	3	0	1	-1	.994	-11	C-71/D-1	-0.5
1987	Oak-A	7	6	1	1	0	0	0	0	2	1	.167	.375	.167	55	-0	0	0	0	1.000	-0	/1-1,3-1,D-3	-0.1
1990	Chi-A	3	3	0	0	0	0	0	0	0	2	.000	.000	.000	-99	-1	0	0	0	.000	0	/C-1	-0.1
1991	*Atl-N	17	14	1	3	0	0	1	4	2	5	.214	.313	.429	100	-0	0	0	0	1.000	-0	/C-1	0.0
1992	Atl-N	26	23	2	8	1	0	2	7	1	3	.348	.375	.652	175	2	0	0	0	1.000	0	/C-1	0.3
	Mon-N	21	25	0	3	0	0	0	1	1	7	.120	.154	.120	-22	-4	0	0	0	.952	0	/1-5	-0.4
	Yr	47	48	2	11	1	0	2	8	2	10	.229	.260	.375	76	-2	0	0	0	.952	-5	/1-5,C-1	-0.1
1994	Sea-A	6	5	1	1	0	0	1	3	1	1	.200	.333	.800	177	1	0	0	0	.000	-0	/C-1,D-1	0.0
Total	8	346	783	82	195	29	1	25	114	83	161	.249	.323	.384	95	1	1	1	-1	.988	-11	C-247/D-7,1-6,3-1	-0.6

■ RIP WILLIAMS
Williams, Alva Mitchel "Buff" b: 1/31/1882, Carthage, Ill. d: 7/23/33, Keokuk, Iowa BR/TR, 5'11.5", 187 lbs. Deb: 4/12/11

YEAR	TM/L	G	AB	R	H	2B	3B	HR	RBI	BB	SO	AVG	OBP	SLG	PRO+	BR/A	SB	CS	SBR	FA	FR	G/POS	TPR
1911	Bos-A	95	284	36	68	8	5	0	31	24		.239	.314	.303	73	-10	9			.975	1	1-57,C-38	-0.6
1912	Was-A	61	157	14	50	11	4	0	22	7		.318	.352	.439	125	4	2			.978	4	C-48	1.2
1913	Was-A	66	106	9	30	6	2	1	12	9	16	.283	.339	.406	115	2	3			.985	-4	C-18/1-9,O-5	-0.1
1914	Was-A	81	169	17	47	6	4	1	22	13	19	.278	.341	.379	112	2	2	2	-1	.975	-5	C-44/1-8,O-1	0.8
1915	Was-A	91	197	14	48	8	4	0	31	18	20	.244	.320	.325	91	-2	4	3	-1	.967	8	C-40,1-15/3-1	-0.9
1916	Was-A	76	202	16	54	10	2	0	20	15	19	.267	.324	.337	100	-0	5			.982	-9	1-34,C-23/3-1	-0.9
1918	Cle-A	28	71	5	17	2	2	0	7	9	6	.239	.325	.324	87	-1	2			.980	-2	1-21/C-1	-0.4
Total	7	498	1186	111	314	51	23	2	145	95	80	.265	.328	.352	97	-6	27	5		.977	-6	C-212,1-144/O-6,3-2	-0.0

■ ART WILLIAMS
Williams, Arthur Franklin b: 8/26/1877, Somerville, Mass. d: 5/16/41, Arlington, Va. TR , Deb: 5/7/02

YEAR	TM/L	G	AB	R	H	2B	3B	HR	RBI	BB	SO	AVG	OBP	SLG	PRO+	BR/A	SB	CS	SBR	FA	FR	G/POS	TPR
1902	Chi-N	47	160	17	37	3	0	0	14	15		.231	.309	.250	75	-4	9			.917	-3	O-24,1-19	-0.9

■ GUS WILLIAMS
Williams, August Joseph "Gloomy Gus" b: 5/7/1888, Omaha, Neb. d: 4/16/64, Sterling, Ill. BL/TL, 6', 185 lbs. Deb: 4/12/11 F

YEAR	TM/L	G	AB	R	H	2B	3B	HR	RBI	BB	SO	AVG	OBP	SLG	PRO+	BR/A	SB	CS	SBR	FA	FR	G/POS	TPR
1911	StL-A	9	26	1	7	3	0	0	4	0		.269	.296	.385	93	-0	0			.867	-1	/O-7	-0.2
1912	StL-A	64	216	32	63	13	7	2	32	27		.292	.370	.444	138	10	18			.930	-2	O-62	0.9
1913	StL-A	148	538	72	147	21	16	5	53	57	87	.273	.346	.400	121	13	31			.951	4	*O-143	1.1
1914	StL-A	144	499	51	126	19	6	4	47	36	120	.253	.308	.339	98	-3	35	20	-2	.933	2	*O-142	-0.9
1915	StL-A	45	119	15	24	2	2	1	11	6	16	.202	.246	.277	59	-7	11	1	3	.949	-5	O-35	-1.1
Total	5	410	1398	171	367	58	31	12	147	126	223	.263	.327	.374	110	14	95	21		.939	2	O-389	-0.2

■ BERNIE WILLIAMS
Williams, Bernabe (Figueroa) b: 9/13/68, San Juan, P.R. BB/TR, 6'2", 180 lbs. Deb: 7/7/91

YEAR	TM/L	G	AB	R	H	2B	3B	HR	RBI	BB	SO	AVG	OBP	SLG	PRO+	BR/A	SB	CS	SBR	FA	FR	G/POS	TPR
1991	NY-A	85	320	43	76	19	4	3	34	48	57	.237	.339	.350	91	-3	10	5	0	.979	6	O-85	0.0
1992	NY-A	62	261	39	73	14	2	5	26	29	36	.280	.354	.406	113	5	7	6	-2	.995	8	O-62	1.1
1993	NY-A	139	567	67	152	31	4	12	68	53	106	.268	.335	.400	100	-0	9	9	-3	.989	5	*O-139	-0.1
1994	NY-A	108	408	80	118	29	1	12	57	61	54	.289	.386	.453	120	14	16	9	-1	.990	5	*O-107	1.4
1995	*NY-A	144	563	93	173	29	9	18	82	75	98	.307	.393	.487	129	25	8	6	-1	.982	16	*O-144	3.3
1996	*NY-A	143	551	108	168	26	7	29	102	82	72	.305	.395	.535	130	26	17	4	3	.986	9	*O-140/D-2	3.0
Total	6	681	2670	430	760	148	27	79	369	348	423	.285	.370	.449	116	66	67	39	-3	.986	49	O-677/D-2	8.7

■ BERNIE WILLIAMS
Williams, Bernard b: 10/8/48, Alameda, Cal. BR/TR, 6'1", 175 lbs. Deb: 9/7/70

YEAR	TM/L	G	AB	R	H	2B	3B	HR	RBI	BB	SO	AVG	OBP	SLG	PRO+	BR/A	SB	CS	SBR	FA	FR	G/POS	TPR
1970	SF-N	7	16	2	5	2	0	0	1	2	1	.313	.389	.438	122	1	1	1	-0	1.000	1	/O-6	0.1
1971	SF-N	35	73	8	13	1	0	1	5	12	24	.178	.294	.233	52	-4	1	1	-0	.933	-5	O-27	-1.1
1972	SF-N	46	68	12	13	3	1	3	9	7	22	.191	.267	.397	85	-2	0	0	0	1.000	2	O-15	-0.1
1974	SD-N	14	15	1	2	0	0	0	0	0	6	.133	.133	.133	-26	-2	0	0	0	1.000	-1	/O-3	-0.4
Total	4	102	172	23	33	6	1	4	15	21	53	.192	.280	.308	66	-8	2	2	-1	.974	-3	/O-51	-1.5

■ BILLY WILLIAMS
Williams, Billy Leo b: 6/15/38, Whistler, Ala. BL/TR, 6'1", 175 lbs. Deb: 8/6/59 CH

YEAR	TM/L	G	AB	R	H	2B	3B	HR	RBI	BB	SO	AVG	OBP	SLG	PRO+	BR/A	SB	CS	SBR	FA	FR	G/POS	TPR
1959	Chi-N	18	33	0	5	1	0	2	7	1	7	.152	.176	.212	3	-5	0	0	0	1.000	-0	O-10	-0.5
1960	Chi-N	12	47	4	13	0	2	2	7	5	12	.277	.346	.489	127	2	0	0	0	.962	0	O-12	0.1
1961	Chi-N	146	529	75	147	20	7	25	86	45	70	.278	.340	.484	114	10	6	6	-2	.954	-2	*O-135	0.2
1962	Chi-N★	159	618	94	184	22	8	22	91	70	72	.298	.373	.466	119	17	9	9	-3	.967	16	*O-159	2.0
1963	Chi-N	161	612	87	175	36	9	25	95	68	78	.286	.359	.497	136	29	7	6	-2	.987	16	*O-160	3.7
1964	Chi-N★	162	645	100	201	39	2	33	98	59	84	.312	.371	.532	145	38	10	7	-1	.950	1	*O-162	3.0
1965	Chi-N★	164	645	115	203	39	6	34	108	65	76	.315	.380	.552	155	46	10	6	1	.968	-3	*O-164	4.3
1966	Chi-N	162	648	100	179	23	5	29	91	69	61	.276	.350	.461	122	19	6	3	0	.976	-8	*O-162	2.0
1967	Chi-N	162	634	92	176	21	12	28	84	68	67	.278	.349	.481	129	24	6	3	0	.989	-3	*O-162	1.3
1968	Chi-N★	163	642	91	185	30	8	30	98	48	53	.288	.340	.500	140	29	4	1	1	.967	-11	*O-163	1.1
1969	Chi-N	163	642	103	188	33	10	21	95	59	70	.293	.356	.474	116	12	3	2	-0	.957	2	*O-160	0.5
1970	Chi-N	161	636	137	205	34	4	42	129	72	65	.322	.393	.586	142	35	7	1	2	.989	8	*O-154	3.6
1971	Chi-N	157	594	86	179	27	5	28	93	77	44	.301	.384	.505	131	24	7	5	-1	.977	7	*O-154	2.4
1972	Chi-N★	150	574	95	191	34	6	37	122	62	59	**.333**	.403	**.606**	166	48	3	1	0	.984	-5	*O-144/1-5	4.1
1973	Chi-N★	156	576	72	166	22	2	20	86	76	72	.288	.372	.438	115	13	4	3	-1	.985	12	*O-138,1-19	1.7
1974	Chi-N	117	404	55	113	22	0	16	68	67	44	.280	.383	.453	128	16	4	5	-2	.986	2	1-65,O-43	1.1
1975	*Oak-A	155	520	68	127	20	1	23	81	76	61	.244	.343	.419	117	10	0	0	0	.971	-0	*D-145/1-7	0.8
1976	Oak-A	120	351	36	74	12	0	11	41	56	48	.211	.323	.339	98	-1	1	0	0	.000	-0	*D-106/O-1	-0.3
Total	18	2488	9350	1410	2711	434	88	426	1475	1045	1046	.290	.364	.492	131	371	90	49	-2	.973	52	*O-2088,D-251/1-96	31.1

■ DALLAS WILLIAMS
Williams, Dallas McKinley b: 2/28/58, Brooklyn, N.Y. BL/TL, 5'11", 165 lbs. Deb: 9/19/81

YEAR	TM/L	G	AB	R	H	2B	3B	HR	RBI	BB	SO	AVG	OBP	SLG	PRO+	BR/A	SB	CS	SBR	FA	FR	G/POS	TPR
1981	Bal-A	2	2	0	1	0	0	0	0	0	0	.500	.500	.500	189	0	0	0	0	1.000	-0	/O-1	0.0
1983	Cin-N	18	36	2	2	0	0	0	1	3	6	.056	.128	.056	-46	-7	0	0	0	1.000	-1	O-12	-0.9
Total	2	20	38	2	3	0	0	0	1	3	6	.079	.146	.079	-35	-7	0	0	0	1.000	-1	/O-13	-0.9

■ DANA WILLIAMS
Williams, Dana Lamont b: 3/20/63, Weirton, W.Va. BR/TR, 5'10", 170 lbs. Deb: 6/21/89

YEAR	TM/L	G	AB	R	H	2B	3B	HR	RBI	BB	SO	AVG	OBP	SLG	PRO+	BR/A	SB	CS	SBR	FA	FR	G/POS	TPR
1989	Bos-A	8	5	1	1	1	0	0	0	0	1	.200	.333	.400	100	0	0	0	0	1.000	0	/O-1,D-2	0.0

■ DAVEY WILLIAMS
Williams, David Carlous b: 11/2/27, Dallas, Tex. BR/TR, 5'10", 160 lbs. Deb: 9/16/49 C

YEAR	TM/L	G	AB	R	H	2B	3B	HR	RBI	BB	SO	AVG	OBP	SLG	PRO+	BR/A	SB	CS	SBR	FA	FR	G/POS	TPR
1949	NY-N	13	50	7	12	1	1	1	4			.240	.333	.360	86	-1	0			.953	-10	2-13	-1.1
1951	*NY-N	30	64	17	17	1	0	2	8	5	8	.266	.319	.375	85	-1	1	1	-0	1.000	2	2-22	0.1
1952	NY-N	138	540	70	137	26	3	13	55	48	63	.254	.324	.385	95	-4	2	3	-1	.973	-15	*2-138	-1.4
1953	NY-N★	112	340	51	101	11	2	3	34	44	19	.297	.382	.368	95	-1	2	5	-2	.982	0	2-95	0.2
1954	*NY-N	142	544	65	121	18	3	9	46	43	33	.222	.285	.316	56	-35	1	1	-0	**.982**	-7	*2-142	-3.3
1955	NY-N	82	247	25	62	4	1	3	16	17	17	.251	.305	.323	67	-12	0	2	-1	.968	-8	2-71	-1.6
Total	6	517	1785	235	450	61	10	32	163	164	144	.252	.321	.351	79	-54	6	12		.978	-38	2-481	-7.1

YEAR	TM/L	G	AB	R	H	2B	3B	HR	RBI	BB	SO	AVG	OBP	SLG	PRO+	BR/A	SB	CS	SBR	FA	FR	G/POS	TPR

■ KEITH WILLIAMS   Williams, David Keith b: 4/21/72, Bedford, Pa.   BR/TR, 6', 190 lbs.   Deb: 6/7/96

| 1996 | SF-N | 9 | 20 | 0 | 5 | 0 | 0 | 0 | 0 | 0 | 6 | .250 | .250 | .250 | 34 | -2 | 0 | 0 | 0 | 1.000 | 0 | /O-4 | -0.2 |

■ DEWEY WILLIAMS   Williams, Dewey Edgar "Dee" b: 2/5/16, Durham, N.C.   BR/TR, 6', 160 lbs.   Deb: 6/28/44

1944	Chi-N	79	262	23	63	7	2	0	27	23	18	.240	.302	.282	65	-12	2			.981	4	C-77	-0.3
1945	*Chi-N	59	100	16	28	2	0	2	5	13	13	.280	.363	.400	114	-2	0			.978	1	C-54	0.6
1946	Chi-N	4	5	0	1	0	0	0	0	0	2	.200	.200	.200	14	-1	0			1.000	0	/C-2	0.0
1947	Chi-N	3	2	0	0	0	0	0	0	0	1	.000	.000	.000	-99	-1	0			.000	0	/C-1	-0.1
1948	Cin-N	48	95	9	16	2	0	1	5	10	18	.168	.248	.221	29	-10	0			.961	-3	C-47	-1.1
Total	5	193	464	48	108	11	4	3	37	46	52	.233	.302	.293	67	-20	2			.976	3	C-181	-0.9

■ EARL WILLIAMS   Williams, Earl Baxter b: 1/27/03, Cumberland Gap, Tenn.   d: 3/10/58, Knoxville, Tenn.   BR/TR, 6'0.5", 185 lbs.   Deb: 5/27/28

| 1928 | Bos-N | 3 | 2 | 0 | 0 | 0 | 0 | 0 | 0 | 0 | 1 | .000 | .000 | .000 | -99 | -1 | 0 | | | 1.000 | 0 | /C-1 | -0.1 |

■ EARL WILLIAMS   Williams, Earl Craig b: 7/14/48, Newark, N.J.   BR/TR, 6'3", 220 lbs.   Deb: 9/13/70

1970	Atl-N	10	19	4	7	4	0	0	5	3	4	.368	.455	.579	165	2	0	0	0	1.000	1	/1-4,3-3	0.3
1971	Atl-N	145	497	64	129	14	1	33	87	42	80	.260	.326	.491	121	12	0	1	-1	.981	-8	C-72,3-42,1-31	0.4
1972	Atl-N	151	565	72	146	24	2	28	87	62	118	.258	.338	.457	113	9	0	0	0	.980	-19	*C-116,3-21,1-20	-0.7
1973	*Bal-A	132	459	58	109	18	1	22	83	66	107	.237	.337	.425	114	9	0	2	-1	.987	-9	C-95,1-42/D-2	0.0
1974	*Bal-A	118	413	47	105	16	0	14	52	40	79	.254	.330	.395	111	6	0	2	-1	.983	-14	C-75,1-47/D-1	-0.9
1975	Atl-N	111	383	42	92	13	0	11	50	34	63	.240	.307	.360	82	-10	0	0	0	.989	-5	1-90,C-11	-2.1
1976	Atl-N	61	184	18	39	3	0	9	26	19	33	.212	.289	.375	82	-5	0	0	0	.995	-9	C-38,1-17	-1.4
	Mon-N	61	190	17	45	10	2	8	29	14	32	.237	.289	.437	100	-1	0	0	0	.981	4	1-47,C-13	0.3
	Yr	122	374	35	84	13	2	17	55	33	65	.225	.289	.406	91	-6	0	0	0	.986	-2	1-64,C-51	-1.1
1977	Oak-A	100	348	39	84	13	0	13	38	18	58	.241	.288	.391	84	-8	2	0	1	.989	-4	D-45,C-36,1-29	-1.3
Total	8	889	3058	361	756	115	6	138	457	298	574	.247	.321	.424	105	14	2	5	-2	.984	-60	C-456,1-327/3-66,D	-5.4

■ EDDIE WILLIAMS   Williams, Edward Laquan b: 11/1/64, Shreveport, La.   BR/TR, 6', 175 lbs.   Deb: 4/18/86

1986	Cle-A	5	7	2	1	0	0	0	1	0	3	.143	.143	.143	-22	-1	0	0	0	.000	-2	/O-4	-0.3
1987	Cle-A	22	64	9	11	4	0	1	4	9	19	.172	.284	.281	50	-5	0	0	0	.982	2	3-22	-0.3
1988	Cle-A	10	21	3	4	0	0	0	0	1	9	.190	.227	.190	18	-2	0	0	0	1.000	3	3-10	0.0
1989	Chi-A	66	201	25	55	8	0	3	10	18	31	.274	.345	.358	101	1	1	2	-1	.909	1	3-65	0.1
1990	SD-N	14	42	5	12	3	0	3	4	5	6	.286	.362	.571	151	3	0	1	-1	.897	-1	3-13	0.1
1994	SD-N	49	175	32	58	11	1	11	42	15	26	.331	.394	.594	158	14	0	1	-1	.988	-1	1-46/3-1	0.7
1995	SD-N	97	296	35	77	11	1	12	47	23	47	.260	.322	.426	99	-1	0	0	0	.989	-1	1-81	-0.9
1996	Det-A	77	215	22	43	5	0	6	26	18	50	.200	.268	.307	45	-18	0	2	-1	1.000	-0	D-52/1-7,3-3,0-2	-2.2
Total	8	340	1021	133	261	42	2	36	135	88	185	.256	.324	.406	94	-10	1	6	-3	.989	-1	1-134,3-114/D-52,O	-2.8

■ DIB WILLIAMS   Williams, Edwin Dibrell b: 1/19/10, Greenbrier, Ark.   d: 4/2/92, Searcy, Ark.   BR/TR, 5'11.5", 175 lbs.   Deb: 4/27/30

1930	Phi-A	67	191	24	50	10	3	3	23	15	19	.262	.322	.393	77	-7	2	1	0	.951	4	2-39,S-19/3-1	0.0
1931	*Phi-A	86	294	41	79	12	2	6	40	19	21	.269	.313	.384	78	-10	2	0	1	.931	7	S-72,2-10/O-1	0.5
1932	Phi-A	62	215	30	54	10	1	4	24	22	23	.251	.329	.363	76	-8	0	1	-1	.952	7	2-53/S-3	0.1
1933	Phi-A	115	408	52	118	20	5	11	73	32	35	.289	.342	.444	106	2	1	0	0	.921	-9	S-84,2-29/1-2	0.0
1934	Phi-A	66	205	25	56	10	1	2	17	21	18	.273	.341	.361	84	-5	0	1	-1	.956	-0	2-53/S-2	-0.2
1935	Phi-A	4	10	0	1	0	0	0	0	0	1	.100	.100	.100	-49	-2	0	0	0	1.000	-2	/2-2	-0.4
	Bos-A	75	251	26	63	12	4	3	25	24	23	.251	.319	.335	65	-13	2	0	1	.952	-5	3-30,2-29,S-15,/1-1	-1.4
	Yr	79	261	26	64	12	4	3	25	24	24	.245	.311	.326	61	-15	2	0	1	.973	-7	2-31,3-30,S-15,/1-1	-1.8
Total	6	475	1574	198	421	74	12	29	201	133	140	.267	.327	.385	82	-43	7	3	0	.955	1	2-215,S-195/31O	-1.4

■ DENNY WILLIAMS   Williams, Evon Daniel b: 12/13/1899, Portland, Ore.   d: 3/23/29, San Clemente, Cal.   BL/TR, 5'8.5", 150 lbs.   Deb: 4/15/21

1921	Cin-N	10	7	0	0	0	0	0	0	0	0	.000	.000	.000	-99	-2	0	1	-1	1.000	0	/O-1	-0.3
1924	Bos-A	25	85	17	31	3	0	0	4	10	5	.365	.438	.400	117	3	3	3	-1	.972	-2	O-19	-0.1
1925	Bos-A	69	218	28	50	1	3	0	13	17	11	.229	.285	.261	39	-20	2	6	-3	.953	-2	O-52	-2.7
1928	Bos-A	16	18	1	4	0	0	0	1	1	3	.222	.263	.222	29	-2	0	0	0	1.000	-2	/O-6	-0.4
Total	4	120	328	46	85	4	3	0	18	28	19	.259	.319	.290	56	-21	5	10	-5	.959	-7	/O-78	-3.5

■ CY WILLIAMS   Williams, Fred b: 12/21/1887, Wadena, Ind.   d: 4/23/74, Eagle River, Wis.   BL/TL, 6'2", 180 lbs.   Deb: 7/18/12

1912	Chi-N	28	62	3	15	1	1	0	1	6	14	.242	.309	.290	65	-3	2			1.000	-2	O-22	-0.6
1913	Chi-N	49	156	17	35	3	3	4	32	5	24	.224	.262	.359	76	-6	5			.976	-5	O-44	-1.3
1914	Chi-N	55	94	12	19	7	0	5	13	13	13	.202	.312	.266	73	-3	2			.941	-3	O-27	-0.7
1915	Chi-N	151	518	59	133	22	6	13	64	26	49	.257	.305	.398	112	5	15	10	-2	.968	4	*O-149	0.1
1916	Chi-N	118	405	55	113	19	9	**12**	66	51	64	.279	.372	.459	140	19	6			.989	-4	*O-116	1.1
1917	Chi-N	138	468	53	113	22	4	5	42	38	78	.241	.308	.338	91	-5	8			.960	12	*O-136	0.0
1918	Phi-N	94	351	49	97	14	1	6	39	27	30	.276	.337	.373	109	4	10			.968	0	O-91	-0.1
1919	Phi-N	109	435	54	121	21	1	9	39	30	43	.278	.335	.393	111	5	9			.970	4	*O-108	0.2
1920	Phi-N	148	590	88	192	36	10	**15**	72	32	45	.325	.364	.497	139	28	18	12	-2	.972	10	*O-147	2.6
1921	Phi-N	146	562	67	180	28	6	18	75	30	32	.320	.357	.488	112	9	5	15	-8	.979	16	*O-146	0.6
1922	Phi-N	151	584	98	180	30	6	26	92	74	49	.308	.392	.514	120	17	11	14	-5	.973	2	*O-150	0.3
1923	Phi-N	136	535	98	157	22	3	**41**	114	59	57	.293	.371	.576	131	21	11	10	-3	.981	-3	*O-135	0.6
1924	Phi-N	148	558	101	183	31	11	24	93	67	49	.328	.403	.552	137	28	7	12	-5	.962	-3	*O-145	1.1
1925	Phi-N	107	314	78	104	11	5	13	60	53	34	.331	.435	.522	132	17	4	9	-4	.989	-5	O-96	0.2
1926	Phi-N	107	336	63	116	13	4	18	53	38	35	.345	.418	**.568**	155	26	2			.963	-8	O-93	1.2
1927	Phi-N	131	492	86	135	18	2	**30**	98	61	57	.274	.365	.502	128	19	0			.970	1	*O-130	1.2
1928	Phi-N	99	238	31	61	9	0	12	37	54	34	.256	.400	.445	117	8	0			1.000	-2	O-69	0.1
1929	Phi-N	66	65	11	19	2	0	5	21	22	9	.292	.471	.554	144	5	0			.966	-0	O-11	0.4
1930	Phi-N	21	17	1	8	2	0	1	4	5	2	.471	.571	.588	169	2	0			1.000	-1	/O-3	0.1
Total	19	2002	6780	1024	1981	306	74	251	1005	690	721	.292	.365	.470	123	197	115	82		.973	16	*O-1818	7.1

■ PAPA WILLIAMS   Williams, Fred b: 7/17/13, Meridian, Miss.   d: 11/2/93, Meridian, Miss.   BR/TR, 6'1", 200 lbs.   Deb: 4/19/45

| 1945 | Cle-A | 16 | 19 | 0 | 4 | 0 | 0 | 0 | 1 | 2 | 1 | .211 | .250 | .211 | 36 | -2 | 0 | 0 | 0 | 1.000 | 0 | /1-3 | -0.1 |

■ GEORGE WILLIAMS   Williams, George b: 10/23/39, Detroit, Mich.   BR/TR, 5'11", 165 lbs.   Deb: 7/16/61

1961	Phi-N	17	36	4	9	0	0	0	4	4	4	.250	.325	.250	56	-2	0	0	0	.967	2	2-15	0.1
1962	Hou-N	5	8	1	3	1	0	0	2	0	1	.375	.375	.500	143	0	0	0	0	1.000	0	/2-3	0.1
1964	KC-A	37	91	10	19	6	0	0	2	6	12	.209	.265	.275	49	-6	0	0	0	.970	-3	2-20/S-2,3-2,O-2	-0.8
Total	3	59	135	15	31	7	0	0	5	10	17	.230	.288	.281	56	-8	0	0	0	.970	-1	/2-38,O-2,3-2,S-2	-0.6

■ GEORGE WILLIAMS   Williams, George Erik b: 4/22/69, LaCrosse, Wis.   BB/TR, 5'10", 190 lbs.   Deb: 7/14/95

1995	Oak-A	29	79	13	23	5	1	3	14	11	21	.291	.391	.494	136	4	0	0	0	.956	-3	C-13,D-10	0.1
1996	Oak-A	56	132	17	20	5	0	3	10	28	32	.152	.313	.258	48	-10	0	0	0	.982	-3	C-43,D-11	-1.1
Total	2	85	211	30	43	10	1	6	24	39	53	.204	.341	.346	80	-6	0	0	0	.975	-7	/C-56,D-21	-1.0

■ GERALD WILLIAMS   Williams, Gerald Floyd b: 8/10/66, New Orleans, La.   BR/TR, 6'2", 190 lbs.   Deb: 9/15/92

1992	NY-A	15	27	7	8	2	0	3	6	0	3	.296	.296	.704	174	2	2	0	1	.913	-1	O-12	0.2
1993	NY-A	42	67	11	10	2	0	1	6	4	14	.149	.186	.269	21	-8	2	0	1	.956	-8	O-37/D-1	-1.6
1994	NY-A	57	86	19	25	8	0	4	13	4	17	.291	.322	.523	118	2	1	3	-2	.957	-11	O-43/D-2	-1.0
1995	*NY-A	100	182	33	45	18	2	6	28	22	34	.247	.332	.467	106	1	4	6	-2	.993	-6	O-92/D-2	-0.6
1996	NY-A	99	233	37	63	15	4	5	30	15	39	.270	.325	.433	88	-5	7	8	-3	.978	-11	O-92/D-2	-1.8
	Mil-A	26	92	6	19	4	0	1	4	4	18	.207	.247	.293	25	-11	3	1	1	.987	4	O-26	-0.6
	Yr	125	325	43	82	19	4	6	34	19	57	.252	.304	.382	70	-15	10	9	-2	.981	-7	*O-118/D-2	-2.4
Total	5	339	687	113	170	49	9	18	87	46	125	.247	.302	.424	84	-18	19	14	-3	.977	-32	O-302/D-7	-5.4

YEAR	TM/L	G	AB	R	H	2B	3B	HR	RBI	BB	SO	AVG	OBP	SLG	PRO+	BR/A	SB	CS	SBR	FA	FR	G/POS	TPR

■ HARRY WILLIAMS   Williams, Harry Peter   b: 6/23/1890, Omaha, Neb.   d: 12/21/63, Huntington Park, Cal.   BR/TR, 6'1.5", 200 lbs.   Deb: 8/7/13   F

1913	NY-A	27	82	18	21	3	1	1	12	15	10	.256	.378	.354	114	2	6			.981	-2	1-27	0.0
1914	NY-A	59	178	9	29	5	2	1	17	26	26	.163	.287	.230	56	-9	3	6	-3	.976	-5	1-58	-2.1
Total	2	86	260	27	50	8	3	2	29	41	36	.192	.316	.269	75	-7	9	6		.977	-7	/1-85	-2.1

■ JIM WILLIAMS   Williams, James Alfred   b: 4/29/47, Zachary, La.   BR/TR, 6'2", 190 lbs.   Deb: 9/8/69

1969	SD-N	13	25	4	7	1	0	0	2	3	11	.280	.357	.320	95	-0	0	0	0	.900	-0	/O-6	-0.1
1970	SD-N	11	14	4	4	0	0	0	0	1	3	.286	.333	.286	70	-1	1	0	0	1.000	-1	/O-6	-0.1
Total	2	24	39	8	11	1	0	0	2	4	14	.282	.349	.308	86	-1	1	0	0	.938	-2	/O-12	-0.2

■ JIMY WILLIAMS   Williams, James Francis   b: 10/4/43, Santa Maria, Cal.   BR/TR, 5'10", 170 lbs.   Deb: 4/26/66   MC

1966	StL-N	13	11	1	3	0	0	0	1	1	5	.273	.333	.273	71	-0	0	0	0	1.000	-2	/S-7,2-3	-0.2
1967	StL-N	1	2	0	0	0	0	0	0	0	1	.000	.000	.000	-99	-1	0	0	0	1.000	1	/S-1	0.0
Total	2	14	13	1	3	0	0	0	1	1	6	.231	.286	.231	46	-1	0	0	0	1.000	-1	/S-8,2-3	-0.2

■ JIMMY WILLIAMS   Williams, James Thomas   b: 12/20/1876, St.Louis, Mo.   d: 1/16/65, St.Petersburg, Fla   BR/TR, 5'9", 175 lbs.   Deb: 4/15/1899

1899	Pit-N	152	617	126	219	28	**27**	9	116	60		.355	.417	.532	160	50	26			.902	7	*3-152	5.2
1900	*Pit-N	106	416	73	110	15	11	5	68	32		.264	.323	.389	95	-4	18			.889	6	*3-103/S-4	0.3
1901	Bal-A	130	501	113	159	26	**21**	7	96	56		.317	.388	.495	138	25	21			.935	-2	*2-130	2.5
1902	Bal-A	125	498	83	156	27	**21**	8	83	36		.313	.361	.500	131	19	14			.945	4	*2-104,3-19/1-1	2.5
1903	NY-A	132	502	60	134	30	12	3	82	39		.267	.326	.392	108	5	9			**.957**	16	*2-132	2.6
1904	NY-A	146	559	62	147	31	7	2	74	38		.263	.314	.354	106	4	14			.951	17	*2-146	2.7
1905	NY-A	129	470	54	107	8	6	2	62	50		.228	.306	.343	95	-3	14			**.964**	6	*2-129	0.4
1906	NY-A	139	501	62	139	25	7	3	77	44		.277	.342	.373	112	7	8			.958	11	*2-139	2.0
1907	NY-A	139	504	53	136	17	11	2	63	35		.270	.319	.359	107	3	14			.966	-3	*2-139	-0.1
1908	StL-A	148	539	63	127	20	7	4	53	55		.236	.310	.321	104	3	7			.963	5	*2-148	0.8
1909	StL-A	110	374	32	73	3	6	0	22	29		.195	.257	.235	60	-17	6			.962	-6	*2-109	-2.9
Total	11	1456	5481	781	1507	242	138	49	796	474		.275	.337	.396	114	90	151			.955	61	*2-1176,3-274/S-4,1	16.0

■ KEN WILLIAMS   Williams, Kenneth Roy   b: 6/28/1890, Grants Pass, Ore.   d: 1/22/59, Grants Pass, Ore.   BL/TR, 6', 170 lbs.   Deb: 7/14/15

1915	Cin-N	71	219	22	53	10	4	0	16	15	20	.242	.296	.324	86	-4	4	3	-1	.948	2	O-62	-0.6
1916	Cin-N	10	27	1	3	0	0	0	1	2	5	.111	.172	.111	-12	-4	1			.955	1	O-10	-0.3
1918	StL-A	2	1	0	0	0	0	0	1	1	0	.000	.500	.000	53	0	0			.000	0	H	0.0
1919	StL-A	65	227	32	68	10	5	6	35	26	25	.300	.367	.467	133	10	7			.937	4	O-63	1.0
1920	StL-A	141	521	90	160	34	13	10	72	41	26	.307	.362	.480	118	12	18	8	1	.961	8	O-138	1.0
1921	StL-A	146	547	115	190	31	7	24	117	74	42	.347	.429	.561	142	35	20	17	-4	.932	7	O-145	2.5
1922	StL-A	153	585	128	194	34	11	**39**	**155**	74	31	.332	.413	.627	162	51	37	20	-1	.970	7	O-153	4.4
1923	StL-A	147	555	106	198	37	12	29	91	79	32	.357	.439	.623	168	54	18	17	-5	.967	12	O-145	4.8
1924	StL-A	114	398	78	129	21	4	18	84	69	17	.324	.425	.533	137	23	20	11	-1	.968	6	O-109	1.9
1925	StL-A	102	411	83	136	31	5	25	105	37	14	.331	.390	**.613**	144	24	10	5	0	.955	5	O-102	2.0
1926	StL-A	108	347	55	97	15	7	17	74	39	23	.280	.354	.510	118	7	5	4	-1	.948	1	O-92/2-1	0.1
1927	StL-A	131	423	70	136	23	6	17	74	57	30	.322	.403	.525	135	21	9	7	-2	.965	-0	O-113	1.8
1928	Bos-A	133	462	59	140	25	1	8	67	37	15	.303	.361	.413	104	2	4	9	-3	.971	-3	O-127	-1.3
1929	Bos-A	74	139	21	48	14	2	3	21	15	7	.345	.409	.540	146	9	1	5	-3	.963	-5	O-39/1-2	0.0
Total	14	1397	4862	860	1552	285	77	196	913	566	287	.319	.393	.530	136	241	154	106		.958	49	*O-1298/1-2,2-1	17.3

■ KENNY WILLIAMS   Williams, Kenneth Royal   b: 4/6/64, Berkeley, Cal.   BR/TR, 6'2", 187 lbs.   Deb: 9/2/86

1986	Chi-A	15	31	2	4	0	0	1	1	1	11	.129	.182	.226	10	-4	1	1	-0	1.000	0	O-10/D-1	-0.4
1987	Chi-A	116	391	48	110	18	2	11	50	10	83	.281	.315	.422	91	-6	21	10	0	.981	6	*O-115	-0.3
1988	Chi-A	73	220	18	35	4	2	8	28	10	64	.159	.223	.305	46	-16	6	5	-1	.959	-4	O-38,3-32/D-3	-2.3
1989	Det-A	94	258	29	53	5	1	6	23	18	63	.205	.270	.302	63	-13	9	4	0	.979	4	O-87/1-1,D-1	-1.1
1990	Det-A	57	83	10	11	2	0	0	5	3	24	.133	.172	.157	-7	-12	2	1	-1	1.000	-3	O-47/D-6	-1.7
	Tor-A	49	72	13	14	6	1	0	8	7	18	.194	.275	.306	61	-4	7	2	1	1.000	-7	O-30/D-9	-1.0
	Yr	106	155	23	25	8	1	0	13	10	42	.161	.222	.226	25	-16	9	4	0	1.000	-10	O-77,D-15	-2.7
1991	Tor-A	13	29	5	6	2	0	1	3	4	5	.207	.324	.379	90	-0	1	0	0	1.000	0	/O-9,D-2	0.0
	Mon-N	34	70	11	19	5	2	0	1	3	22	.271	.311	.400	100	-0	2	1	0	.957	1	O-24	0.0
Total	6	451	1154	136	252	42	8	27	119	56	290	.218	.271	.339	66	-55	49	25	-0	.981	-3	O-360/3-32,D-22,1-1	-6.8

■ MARK WILLIAMS   Williams, Mark Westley   b: 7/28/53, Elmira, N.Y.   BL/TL, 6', 180 lbs.   Deb: 5/20/77

1977	Oak-A	3	2	0	0	0	0	0	1	0	0	.000	.333	.000	0	-0	0	0	0	1.000	-0	/O-1	0.0

■ MATT WILLIAMS   Williams, Matthew Derrick   b: 11/28/65, Bishop, Cal.   BR/TR, 6'2", 205 lbs.   Deb: 4/11/87

1987	SF-N	84	245	28	46	9	2	8	21	16	68	.188	.240	.339	54	-17	4	3	-1	.975	20	S-70,3-17	0.7
1988	SF-N	52	156	17	32	6	1	8	19	8	41	.205	.253	.410	91	-3	0	1	-1	.967	10	3-43,S-14	0.7
1989	*SF-N	84	292	31	59	18	1	18	50	14	72	.202	.244	.455	98	-3	1	2	-1	.961	6	3-73,S-30	0.4
1990	SF-N★	159	617	87	171	27	2	33	**122**	33	138	.277	.321	.488	124	17	7	4	-0	.959	4	*3-159	2.2
1991	SF-N	157	589	72	158	24	5	34	98	33	128	.268	.314	.499	129	19	5	5	-2	.964	9	*3-155/S-4	2.8
1992	SF-N	146	529	58	120	13	5	20	66	39	109	.227	.287	.384	94	-7	7	7	-2	.945	7	*3-144	-0.2
1993	SF-N	145	579	105	170	33	4	38	110	27	80	.294	.330	.561	137	27	1	3	-2	.970	3	*3-144	2.8
1994	SF-N★	112	445	74	119	16	3	**43**	96	33	87	.267	.321	.607	141	23	1	0	-1	.963	9	*3-110	3.2
1995	SF-N†	76	283	53	95	17	1	23	65	30	58	.336	.403	.647	177	30	2	0	1	.958	6	3-74	3.5
1996	SF-N†	105	404	69	122	16	1	22	85	39	91	.302	.372	.510	135	20	1	2	-1	.951	3	3-92,1-13/S-1	1.9
Total	10	1120	4139	594	1092	179	25	247	732	272	872	.264	.315	.498	123	106	29	27	-8	.959	77	*3-1011,S-119/1-13	18.0

■ OTTO WILLIAMS   Williams, Otto George   b: 11/2/1877, Newark, N.J.   d: 3/19/37, Omaha, Neb.   BR/TR, 5'8", 165 lbs.   Deb: 10/5/02   C

1902	StL-N	2	5	0	2	0	0	0	2	1		.400	.500	.400	185	1	1			.813	-2	/S-2	0.2
1903	StL-N	53	187	10	38	4	2	0	9	9		.203	.240	.246	40	-15	6			.885	-5	S-52/2-1	-1.7
	Chi-N	38	130	14	29	5	0	0	13	4		.223	.246	.262	46	-9	8			.937	5	S-26/2-7,1-3,3-1	-0.3
	Yr	91	317	24	67	9	2	0	22	13		.211	.242	.252	42	-24	14			.904	0	S-78/2-8,1-3,3-1	-2.0
1904	Chi-N	57	185	21	37	4	1	0	8	13		.200	.256	.232	51	-10	9			.973	-0	O-21,1-11,S-10/23	-1.2
1906	Was-A	20	51	3	7	0	0	0	2	2		.137	.185	.137	1	-6	0			.897	-4	/S-8,2-6,1-2,3-1	-0.6
Total	4	170	558	48	113	13	3	0	34	29		.203	.244	.237	43	-40	24			.905	1	/S-98,O-21,2-20,13	-3.6

■ REGGIE WILLIAMS   Williams, Reginald Bernard   b: 5/5/66, Laurens, S.C.   BB/TR, 6'1", 180 lbs.   Deb: 9/8/92

1992	Cal-A	14	26	5	6	1	1	0	2	1	10	.231	.259	.346	68	-1	0	2	-1	1.000	-1	O-12/D-2	-0.4
1995	LA-N	15	11	2	1	0	0	0	1	2	3	.091	.231	.091	-12	-2	0	0	0	1.000	-4	O-14	-0.6
Total	2	29	37	7	7	1	1	0	3	3	13	.189	.250	.270	44	-3	0	2	-1	1.000	-5	/O-26,D-2	-1.0

■ REGGIE WILLIAMS   Williams, Reginald Dewayne   b: 8/29/60, Memphis, Tenn.   BR/TR, 5'11", 185 lbs.   Deb: 9/2/85

1985	LA-N	22	9	4	3	0	0	0	0	0	4	.333	.333	.333	90	-0	1	0	0	.900	-3	O-15	-0.3
1986	LA-N	128	303	35	84	14	2	4	32	23	57	.277	.326	.376	102	-6	9	3	-1	.984	-16	*O-124	-1.9
1987	LA-N	39	36	6	4	0	0	0	4	5	9	.111	.220	.111	-9	-6	1	1	-0	.913	-8	O-30	-1.4
1988	Cle-A	11	31	7	7	2	0	0	3	0	6	.226	.226	.387	66	-1	0	0	0	1.000	-2	O-11	-0.4
Total	4	200	379	52	98	16	2	5	39	28	76	.259	.304	.351	97	-7	11	4	1	.974	-29	O-180	-3.9

■ DICK WILLIAMS   Williams, Richard Hirschfeld   b: 5/7/29, St.Louis, Mo.   BR/TR, 6', 190 lbs.   Deb: 6/10/51   MC

1951	Bro-N	23	60	5	12	4	1	0	5	4	10	.200	.250	.333	54	-4	0	0	0	1.000	-2	O-15	-0.6
1952	Bro-N	36	68	13	21	4	1	0	11	2	10	.309	.329	.397	99	-0	0	0	0	1.000	-2	O-25/1-1,3-1	-0.2
1953	*Bro-N	30	55	4	12	2	0	5	2	1	7	.218	.237	.564	62	-3	0	0	0	.923	-3	O-24	-1.1
1954	Bro-N	16	34	5	5	0	0	0	1	3	7	.147	.194	.235	11	-5	0	0	0	1.000	-4	O-14	-0.9
1956	Bro-N	7	7	0	2	0	0	0	0	0	1	.286	.286	.286	50	-0	0	0	0	1.000	0	H	0.0

YEAR	TM/L	G	AB	R	H	2B	3B	HR	RBI	BB	SO	AVG	OBP	SLG	PRO+	BR/A	SB	CS	SBR	FA	FR	G/POS	TPR
	Bal-A	87	353	45	101	18	4	11	37	30	40	.286	.342	.453	117	7	5	5	-2	.990	-3	O-81,1-10,2-10,/3-4	-0.2
1957	Bal-A	47	167	16	39	10	2	1	17	14	21	.234	.293	.335	76	-6	0	1	-1	1.000	0	O-26,3-15,1-12	-0.8
	Cle-A	67	205	33	58	7	0	6	17	12	19	.283	.326	.405	99	-1	3	4	-2	.973	-3	O-37,3-19	-0.7
	Yr	114	372	49	97	17	2	7	34	26	40	.261	.311	.374	89	-7	3	5	-2	.984	-2	O-63,3-34,1-12	-1.5
1958	Bal-A	128	409	36	113	17	0	4	32	37	47	.276	.339	.347	94	-3	6	4	-6	1.000	-9	O-70,3-45,1-26,/2-7	-2.0
1959	KC-A	130	488	72	130	33	1	16	75	28	60	.266	.313	.436	102	-0	4	1	1	.957	-8	3-80,1-32,O-23,/2-3	-1.1
1960	KC-A	127	420	47	121	31	0	12	65	39	68	.288	.350	.448	113	7	0	0	0	.951	5	3-57,1-34,O-25	0.9
1961	Bal-A	103	310	37	64	15	2	8	24	20	38	.206	.255	.345	61	-19	0	4	-2	.968	-10	O-75,1-20/3-2	-3.6
1962	Bal-A	82	178	20	44	7	1	5	18	14	21	.247	.306	.315	72	-7	0	0	0	1.000	5	O-29,1-21/3-4	-1.2
1963	Bos-A	79	136	15	35	8	0	2	12	15	25	.257	.331	.360	91	-1	0	0	0	.976	-6	3-17,1-11/O-7	-0.9
1964	Bos-A	61	69	10	11	2	0	0	5	11	7	.159	.247	.406	74	-3	0	0	0	1.000	5	1-21,3-13/O-5	-0.2
Total	13	1023	2959	358	768	157	12	70	331	227	392	.260	.315	.392	92	-38	12	21	-9	.989	-46	O-456,3-257,1/2	-12.2

■ RINALDO WILLIAMS
Williams, Rinaldo Lewis b: 12/18/1893, Santa Cruz, Cal. d: 4/24/66, Cottonwood, Ariz. BL/TR, Deb: 10/8/14

YEAR	TM/L	G	AB	R	H	2B	3B	HR	RBI	BB	SO	AVG	OBP	SLG	PRO+	BR/A	SB	CS	SBR	FA	FR	G/POS	TPR
1914	Bro-F	4	15	1	4	2	0	0	1	0	0	.267	.267	.400	81	-1	0			.923	-0	/3-4	-0.1

■ BOB WILLIAMS
Williams, Robert Elias b: 4/27/1884, Monday, Ohio d: 8/6/62, Nelsonville, Ohio BR/TR, 6', 190 lbs. Deb: 7/3/11

YEAR	TM/L	G	AB	R	H	2B	3B	HR	RBI	BB	SO	AVG	OBP	SLG	PRO+	BR/A	SB	CS	SBR	FA	FR	G/POS	TPR
1911	NY-A	20	47	3	9	2	0	0	8	5		.191	.269	.234	38	-4	1			.942	-1	C-20	-0.3
1912	NY-A	20	44	7	6	1	0	0	3	9		.136	.283	.159	26	-4	0			.930	-2	C-20	-0.5
1913	NY-A	6	19	0	3	0	0	0	0	1	3	.158	.200	.158	5	-2	0			.971	0	/C-6	-0.2
Total	3	46	110	10	18	3	0	0	11	15	3	.164	.264	.191	28	-10	1			.941	-3	/C-46	-1.0

■ TED WILLIAMS
Williams, Theodore Samuel "The Kid", "The Thumper" or "The Splendid Splinter" b: 8/30/18, San Diego, Cal. BL/TR, 6'3", 205 lbs. Deb: 4/20/39 MH

YEAR	TM/L	G	AB	R	H	2B	3B	HR	RBI	BB	SO	AVG	OBP	SLG	PRO+	BR/A	SB	CS	SBR	FA	FR	G/POS	TPR
1939	Bos-A	149	565	131	185	44	11	31	145	107	64	.327	.436	.609	158	51	2	1	0	.945	2	*O-149	4.3
1940	Bos-A★	144	561	134	193	43	14	23	113	96	54	.344	.442	.594	159	52	4	4	-1	.960	1	*O-143/P-1	4.0
1941	Bos-A★	143	456	135	185	33	3	37	120	145	27	.406	.551	.735	232	98	2	4	-2	.961	-5	*O-133	7.9
1942	Bos-A★	150	522	141	186	34	5	36	137	145	51	.356	.499	.648	214	87	3	2	-0	.988	3	*O-150	8.1
1946	*Bos-A★	150	514	142	176	37	8	38	123	156	44	.342	.497	.667	211	85	0	0	0	.971	-0	*O-150	7.9
1947	Bos-A★	156	528	125	181	40	9	32	114	162	47	.343	.499	.634	199	79	0	1	-1	.975	1	*O-156	7.2
1948	Bos-A★	137	509	124	188	44	3	25	127	126	41	.369	.497	.615	185	68	4	0	1	.983	0	*O-134	5.8
1949	Bos-A★	155	566	150	194	39	3	43	159	162	48	.343	.490	.650	187	77	1	1	-0	.983	3	*O-155	6.7
1950	Bos-A★	89	334	82	106	24	1	28	97	82	21	.317	.452	.647	163	32	3	0	1	.956	-4	O-86	2.4
1951	Bos-A★	148	531	109	169	28	4	30	126	144	45	.318	.464	.556	159	49	1	1	-0	.988	3	*O-147	4.5
1952	Bos-A	6	10	2	4	0	1	1	3	2	2	.400	.500	.900	264	2	0	0	0	1.000	-0	/O-2	0.2
1953	Bos-A†	37	91	17	37	6	0	13	34	19	10	.407	.509	.901	261	20	0	1	1	.970	-4	O-26	1.5
1954	Bos-A★	117	386	93	133	23	1	29	89	136	32	.345	.516	.635	193	58	0	0	0	.982	-3	*O-115	5.0
1955	Bos-A★	98	320	77	114	21	3	28	83	91	24	.356	.501	.703	203	50	2	1	0	.989	-1	O-93	4.4
1956	Bos-A★	136	400	71	138	28	2	24	82	102	39	.345	.479	.605	164	41	0	0	0	.973	-4	*O-110	3.0
1957	Bos-A★	132	420	96	163	28	1	38	87	119	43	.388	.528	.731	227	82	0	1	-1	.995	-3	*O-125	7.1
1958	Bos-A★	129	411	81	135	23	2	26	85	98	49	.328	.462	.584	174	46	1	0	0	.957	-12	*O-114	2.9
1959	Bos-A	103	272	32	69	15	0	10	43	52	27	.254	.377	.419	113	6	0	0	0	.970	-8	O-76	-0.5
1960	Bos-A★	113	310	56	98	15	0	29	72	75	41	.316	.454	.645	187	40	1	1	0	.993	-2	O-87	3.3
Total	19	2292	7706	1798	2654	525	71	521	1839	2019	709	.344	.483	.634	186	1024	24	17	-3	.974	-34	*O-2151/P-1	85.7

■ WALT WILLIAMS
Williams, Walter Allen "No-Neck" b: 12/19/43, Brownwood, Tex. BR/TR, 5'6", 185 lbs. Deb: 4/21/64 C

YEAR	TM/L	G	AB	R	H	2B	3B	HR	RBI	BB	SO	AVG	OBP	SLG	PRO+	BR/A	SB	CS	SBR	FA	FR	G/POS	TPR
1964	Hou-N	10	9	1	0	0	0	0	0	0	2	.000	.000	.000	-99	-2	1	0	0	1.000	-1	/O-5	-0.3
1967	Chi-A	104	275	35	66	16	3	3	15	17	20	.240	.289	.353	92	-3	3	2	-0	.983	-2	O-73	-1.0
1968	Chi-A	63	133	6	32	6	0	1	8	4	17	.241	.273	.308	75	-4	0	1	-1	1.000	-2	O-34	-1.0
1969	Chi-A	135	471	59	143	22	1	3	32	26	33	.304	.344	.374	96	-3	6	2	1	.985	-2	*O-111	-0.6
1970	Chi-A	110	315	43	79	18	1	3	15	19	30	.251	.298	.343	73	-12	3	3	-1	.949	2	O-79	-1.5
1971	Chi-A	114	361	43	106	17	3	8	35	24	27	.294	.346	.424	114	6	5	5	-2	1.000	-0	O-90/3-1	-0.2
1972	Chi-A	77	221	22	55	7	1	2	11	13	20	.249	.291	.317	79	-6	6	1	1	.990	1	O-57/3-1	-0.7
1973	Cle-A	104	350	43	101	15	1	8	38	14	29	.289	.318	.406	101	-1	9	4	0	.970	5	O-61,D-26	0.1
1974	NY-A	43	53	5	6	0	0	0	3	1	10	.113	.130	.113	-30	-9	2	1	0	.955	-6	O-24/D-3	-1.6
1975	NY-A	82	185	27	52	5	1	5	16	8	23	.281	.321	.400	105	1	0	1	-1	.982	-3	O-31,D-17/2-6	-0.5
Total	10	842	2373	284	640	106	11	33	173	126	211	.270	.311	.365	91	-33	34	19	-1	.981	-6	O-565/D-46,2-6,3-2	-7.3

■ WASH WILLIAMS
Williams, Washington J. b: Philadelphia, Pa. d: 1/1890, Philadelphia, Pa. 5'11", 180 lbs. Deb: 8/5/1884

YEAR	TM/L	G	AB	R	H	2B	3B	HR	RBI	BB	SO	AVG	OBP	SLG	PRO+	BR/A	SB	CS	SBR	FA	FR	G/POS	TPR
1884	Ric-a	2	8	0	2	0	0	0	0	0	0	.250	.250	.250	64	-0				.500	-1	/O-2	-0.1
1885	Chi-N	1	4	0	1	0	0	0	0	0	0	.250	.250	.250	54	-0				.500	-0	/O-1,P-1	-0.1
Total	2	3	12	0	3	0	0	0	0	0	0	.250	.250	.250	61	-1				.500	-1	/O-3,P-1	-0.2

■ BILLY WILLIAMS
Williams, William b: 6/13/33, Newberry, S.C. BL/TR, 6'3", 195 lbs. Deb: 8/15/69

YEAR	TM/L	G	AB	R	H	2B	3B	HR	RBI	BB	SO	AVG	OBP	SLG	PRO+	BR/A	SB	CS	SBR	FA	FR	G/POS	TPR
1969	Sea-A	4	10	1	0	0	0	0	0	1	4	.000	.167	.000	-51	-2	0	0	0	1.000	1	/O-3	-0.2

■ WOODY WILLIAMS
Williams, Woodrow Wilson b: 8/21/12, Pamplin, Va. d: 2/24/95, Appomattox, Va. BR/TR, 5'11", 175 lbs. Deb: 9/5/38

YEAR	TM/L	G	AB	R	H	2B	3B	HR	RBI	BB	SO	AVG	OBP	SLG	PRO+	BR/A	SB	CS	SBR	FA	FR	G/POS	TPR
1938	Bro-N	20	51	6	17	1	1	0	6	4	1	.333	.382	.392	111	1	1			.931	-7	S-18/3-1	-0.5
1943	Cin-N	30	69	8	26	2	1	0	11	1	3	.377	.386	.435	139	3	0			.986	1	2-12/3-7,S-5	0.5
1944	Cin-N	155	653	73	157	23	3	1	35	44	24	.240	.290	.289	66	-30	7			.971	15	*2-155	-0.6
1945	Cin-N	133	482	46	114	14	0	0	27	39	24	.237	.296	.266	58	-27	6			.969	-2	*2-133	-2.9
Total	4	338	1255	133	314	40	5	1	79	88	52	.250	.301	.292	69	-52	14			.971	-1	2-300/S-23,3-8	-3.5

■ NED WILLIAMSON
Williamson, Edward Nagle b: 10/24/1857, Philadelphia, Pa. d: 3/3/1894, Willow Springs, Ark BR/TR, 5'11", 210 lbs. Deb: 5/1/1878

YEAR	TM/L	G	AB	R	H	2B	3B	HR	RBI	BB	SO	AVG	OBP	SLG	PRO+	BR/A	SB	CS	SBR	FA	FR	G/POS	TPR
1878	Ind-N	63	250	31	58	10	2	1	19	5	15	.232	.247	.300	91	-2				.867	-4	*3-63	-0.3
1879	Chi-N	80	320	66	94	20	13	1	36	24	31	.294	.343	.447	149	16				.871	17	*3-70/1-6,C-4	3.2
1880	Chi-N	75	311	65	78	20	2	0	31	15	26	.251	.285	.328	101	-0				.893	12	*3-63,C-11/2-3	1.4
1881	Chi-N	82	343	56	92	12	6	1	48	19	19	.268	.307	.347	100	-0				.909	22	*3-76/2-4,P-3,SC	2.2
1882	Chi-N	83	348	66	98	27	4	3	60	27	21	.282	.333	.408	130	11				.881	16	*3-83/P-1	2.6
1883	Chi-N	98	402	83	111	49	5	2	59	22	48	.276	.314	.438	118	8				.807	18	*3-97/C-3,P-1	2.1
1884	Chi-N	107	417	84	116	18	8	27	84	46	56	.278	.344	.554	164	28				.861	24	*3-99,C-10/P-2	4.7
1885	*Chi-N	113	407	87	97	16	5	3	65	75	60	.238	.357	.324	106	2				.892	12	*3-113/P-2,C-1	1.5
1886	*Chi-N	121	430	69	93	17	8	6	58	80	71	.216	.339	.335	92	-6	13			.869	-2	*S-121/C-4,P-2	-0.6
1887	Chi-N	127	439	77	117	20	14	9	73	73	57	.267	.377	.437	111	5	45			.890	-31	*S-127/P-1	-2.1
1888	Chi-N	132	452	75	113	9	14	8	73	65	71	.250	.352	.385	126	14	25			.884	-12	*S-132	0.5
1889	Chi-N	47	173	16	41	3	1	1	30	23	22	.237	.340	.283	71	-6	2			.844	-24	S-47	-2.4
1890	Chi-P	73	261	34	51	7	3	2	26	36	35	.195	.311	.268	53	-17	3			.809	-20	3-52,S-21	-2.8
Total	13	1201	4553	809	1159	228	85	64	667	506	532	.255	.332	.384	112	54	88			.866	28	3-716,S-450/CP21	10.0

■ HOWIE WILLIAMSON
Williamson, Nathaniel Howard b: 12/23/04, Little Rock, Ark. d: 8/15/69, Texarkana, Ark. BL/TL, 6', 170 lbs. Deb: 7/7/28

YEAR	TM/L	G	AB	R	H	2B	3B	HR	RBI	BB	SO	AVG	OBP	SLG	PRO+	BR/A	SB	CS	SBR	FA	FR	G/POS	TPR
1928	StL-N	10	9	0	2	0	0	0	0	1	4	.222	.300	.222	38	-1	0			.000	0	H	-0.1

■ JULIUS WILLIGROD
Willigrod, Julius b: Iowa d: 11/27/06, San Francisco, Cal BL, Deb: 7/15/1882

YEAR	TM/L	G	AB	R	H	2B	3B	HR	RBI	BB	SO	AVG	OBP	SLG	PRO+	BR/A	SB	CS	SBR	FA	FR	G/POS	TPR
1882	Det-N	1	3	0	1	0	0	0	0	0	0	.333	.333	.333	115	0				1.000	-1	/S-1	0.0
	Cle-N	9	36	5	5	1	1	0	2	3	7	.139	.205	.222	38	-2				.813	-3	/O-9	-0.5
	Yr	10	39	5	6	1	1	0	2	3	7	.154	.214	.231	44	-2				.813	-3	/O-9,S-1	-0.5

■ HUGH WILLINGHAM
Willingham, Thomas Hugh b: 5/30/06, Dalhart, Tex. d: 6/15/88, ElReno, Okla. BR/TR, 6', 180 lbs. Deb: 9/13/30

YEAR	TM/L	G	AB	R	H	2B	3B	HR	RBI	BB	SO	AVG	OBP	SLG	PRO+	BR/A	SB	CS	SBR	FA	FR	G/POS	TPR
1930	Chi-A	3	4	2	1	0	0	0	0	1	0	.250	.500	.250	100	-0				1.000	-0	/2-1	0.0
1931	Phi-N	23	35	5	9	2	1	1	3	2	1	.257	.297	.457	93	-1	0			.875	0	/S-8,3-2,O-1	0.0
1932	Phi-N	4	2	0	0	0	0	0	0	0	0	.000	.000	.000	-89	-1				.000	0	H	-0.1

YEAR	TM/L	G	AB	R	H	2B	3B	HR	RBI	BB	SO	AVG	OBP	SLG	PRO+	BR/A	SB	CS	SBR	FA	FR	G/POS	TPR
1933	Phi-N	1	1	0	0	0	0	0	0	0	0	.000	.000	.000	-89	-0	0			.000	0	H	0.0
Total	4	31	42	7	10	2	1	1	3	4	10	.238	.304	.405	82	-1	0	0	0	.875	-0	/S-8,3-2,0-1,2-1	-0.1

■ WILLS Wills Deb: 5/14/1884

YEAR	TM/L	G	AB	R	H	2B	3B	HR	RBI	BB	SO	AVG	OBP	SLG	PRO+	BR/A	SB	CS	SBR	FA	FR	G/POS	TPR
1884	Was-a	4	15	1	2	2	0	0		0		.133	.133	.267	31	-1				.889	2	/O-4	0.1
	KC-U	5	21	2	3	1	0	0		0		.143	.143	.190	0	-3				1.000	1	/O-5	-0.3
Total	1	9	36	3	5	3	0	0		0		.139	.139	.222	13	-4				.938	2	/O-9	-0.2

■ DAVE WILLS Wills, Davis Bowles b: 1/26/1877, Charlottesville, Va. d: 10/12/59, Washington, D.C. BL/TL, Deb: 6/8/1899

YEAR	TM/L	G	AB	R	H	2B	3B	HR	RBI	BB	SO	AVG	OBP	SLG	PRO+	BR/A	SB	CS	SBR	FA	FR	G/POS	TPR
1899	Lou-N	24	94	15	21	3	1	0	12	2		.223	.240	.277	41	-8	1			.957	-3	1-24	-1.0

■ BUMP WILLS Wills, Elliott Taylor b: 7/27/52, Washington, D.C. BB/TR, 5'9", 177 lbs. Deb: 4/7/77 F

YEAR	TM/L	G	AB	R	H	2B	3B	HR	RBI	BB	SO	AVG	OBP	SLG	PRO+	BR/A	SB	CS	SBR	FA	FR	G/POS	TPR
1977	Tex-A	152	541	87	155	28	6	9	62	65	96	.287	.363	.410	109	8	28	12	1	.982	3	*2-150/S-1,1,D-1	2.3
1978	Tex-A	157	539	78	135	17	4	9	57	49	91	.250	.333	.347	91	-5	52	14	7	.981	21	*2-156	3.5
1979	Tex-A	146	543	90	148	21	3	5	46	53	58	.273	.326	.350	88	-5	35	11	4	.976	8	*2-146	1.3
1980	Tex-A	146	578	102	152	31	5	5	58	51	71	.263	.326	.360	90	-7	34	9	5	.984	19	*2-144	2.5
1981	Tex-A	102	410	51	103	13	2	2	41	32	49	.251	.307	.307	82	-10	12	9	-2	.983	9	*2-101/D-1	0.4
1982	Chi-N	128	419	64	114	18	4	6	38	40	76	.272	.351	.377	101	2	35	10	5	.963	-18	*2-103	-0.7
Total	6	831	3030	472	807	128	24	36	302	310	441	.266	.338	.360	94	-20	196	65	20	.979	41	2-800/D-2,S-2,1-1	9.3

■ MAURY WILLS Wills, Maurice Morning b: 10/2/32, Washington, D.C. BB/TR, 5'11", 170 lbs. Deb: 6/6/59 FM

YEAR	TM/L	G	AB	R	H	2B	3B	HR	RBI	BB	SO	AVG	OBP	SLG	PRO+	BR/A	SB	CS	SBR	FA	FR	G/POS	TPR
1959	*LA-N	83	242	27	63	5	2	0	7	13	27	.260	.298	.298	55	-15	7	3	0	.966	2	S-82	-0.7
1960	LA-N	148	516	75	152	15	2	0	27	35	47	.295	.343	.331	80	-13	**50**	12	**8**	.945	21	*S-145	2.7
1961	LA-N★	148	613	105	173	12	10	1	31	59	50	.282	.346	.339	76	-19	**35**	15	2	.959	12	*S-148	0.6
1962	LA-N★	165	695	130	208	13	**10**	6	48	51	57	.299	.349	.373	100	0	**104**	13	**23**	.956	-5	*S-165	3.3
1963	*LA-N☆	134	527	83	159	19	3	0	34	44	48	.302	.357	.349	112	8	**40**	19	1	.959	-5	*S-109,3-33	1.3
1964	LA-N	158	630	81	173	15	5	2	34	41	73	.275	.319	.324	88	-11	**53**	17	**6**	.963	-8	*S-149/3-6	-0.2
1965	*LA-N★	158	650	92	186	14	7	0	33	40	64	.286	.331	.329	93	-6	**94**	31	10	.970	21	*S-155	3.7
1966	*LA-N★	143	594	60	162	14	2	1	39	34	60	.273	.314	.308	80	-16	38	24	-3	.967	9	*S-139/3-4	0.3
1967	Pit-N	149	616	92	186	12	9	3	45	31	44	.302	.336	.365	100	0	29	13	3	.948	3	*3-144/S-2	1.2
1968	Pit-N	153	627	76	174	12	6	0	31	45	57	.278	.327	.316	95	-3	52	21	3	.957	-9	*3-141,S-10	-0.9
1969	Mon-N	47	189	23	42	3	0	0	8	20	21	.222	.297	.238	51	-12	15	6	1	.950	-3	S-46/2-1	-0.9
	LA-N	104	434	57	129	7	8	4	39	39	40	.297	.357	.378	114	8	25	15	-1	.969	7	S-104	2.6
	Yr	151	623	80	171	10	8	4	47	59	61	.274	.338	.335	94	-5	40	21	-1	.963	4	*S-150/2-1	1.7
1970	LA-N	132	522	77	141	19	3	0	34	50	34	.270	.334	.318	79	-15	28	13	1	.959	-19	*S-126/3-4	-1.9
1971	LA-N	149	601	73	169	14	3	3	44	40	44	.281	.326	.329	92	-7	15	8	-0	.978	1	*S-144/3-4	1.3
1972	LA-N	71	132	16	17	3	1	0	4	10	18	.129	.190	.167	2	-17	1	1	-0	.984	-4	S-31,3-26	-1.9
Total	14	1942	7588	1067	2134	177	71	20	458	552	684	.281	.331	.331	88	-118	586	208	51	.963	30	*S-1555,3-362/2-1	10.5

■ KID WILLSON Willson, Frank Hoxie b: 11/3/1895, Bloomington, Neb. d: 4/17/64, Union Gap, Wash. BL/TL, 6'1", 190 lbs. Deb: 7/2/18

YEAR	TM/L	G	AB	R	H	2B	3B	HR	RBI	BB	SO	AVG	OBP	SLG	PRO+	BR/A	SB	CS	SBR	FA	FR	G/POS	TPR
1918	Chi-A	4	1	2	0	0	0	0	0	1	1	.000	.500	.000	50	0	0			.000	0	H	0.0
1927	Chi-A	7	10	1	1	0	0	0	1	0	2	.100	.100	.100	-49	-2	0	0	0	1.000	0	/O-2	-0.2
Total	2	11	11	3	1	0	0	0	1	1	3	.091	.167	.091	-31	-2	0	0	0	1.000	0	/O-2	-0.2

■ WALT WILMOT Wilmot, Walter Robert b: 10/18/1863, Plover, Wis. d: 2/1/29, Chicago, Ill. BB/TR, Deb: 4/20/1888

YEAR	TM/L	G	AB	R	H	2B	3B	HR	RBI	BB	SO	AVG	OBP	SLG	PRO+	BR/A	SB	CS	SBR	FA	FR	G/POS	TPR
1888	Was-N	119	473	61	106	16	9	4	43	23	55	.224	.263	.321	91	-5	46			.872	11	*O-119	0.3
1889	Was-N	108	432	88	125	19	**19**	9	57	51	32	.289	.367	.484	146	26	40			.927	15	*O-108	3.2
1890	Chi-N	139	571	114	159	15	13	**13**	99	64	44	.278	.353	.419	120	12	76			.938	13	*O-139	1.8
1891	Chi-N	121	498	102	137	14	10	11	71	55	21	.275	.353	.410	122	13	42			.922	-5	*O-121	0.4
1892	Chi-N	92	380	47	82	8	7	2	35	40	20	.216	.297	.287	76	-11	31			.903	2	O-92	-1.2
1893	Chi-N	94	392	69	118	14	14	3	61	40	8	.301	.367	.431	114	7	39			.873	-0	*O-93	0.1
1894	Chi-N	133	597	134	197	45	12	5	130	35	23	.330	.368	.471	96	-8	74			.872	-7	*O-133	-1.8
1895	Chi-N	108	466	86	132	16	6	8	72	30	19	.283	.327	.395	80	-16	28			.914	4	*O-108	-1.7
1897	NY-N	11	34	8	9	2	0	1	4	2		.265	.306	.412	91	-1	1			.938	0	/O-9	-0.1
1898	NY-N	35	138	16	33	4	2	0	22	9		.239	.286	.341	82	-4	4			.886	-5	O-34	-1.1
Total	10	960	3981	725	1098	152	92	58	594	349	222	.276	.337	.404	105	14	381			.903	28	O-956	-0.1

■ ARCHIE WILSON Wilson, Archie Clifton b: 11/25/23, Los Angeles, Cal. BR/TR, 5'11", 175 lbs. Deb: 9/18/51

YEAR	TM/L	G	AB	R	H	2B	3B	HR	RBI	BB	SO	AVG	OBP	SLG	PRO+	BR/A	SB	CS	SBR	FA	FR	G/POS	TPR
1951	NY-A	4	4	0	0	0	0	0	0	0	0	.000	.000	.000	-44	-1	0	0	0	1.000	-0	/O-2	-0.1
1952	NY-A	3	2	0	1	0	0	0	1	0	0	.500	.500	.500	190	1	0	0		.000	0	H	0.0
	Was-A	26	96	8	20	2	3	0	14	5	11	.208	.255	.292	54	-6	0	0	0	.971	1	O-24	-0.7
	Bos-A	18	38	1	10	3	0	0	2	2	3	.263	.300	.342	73	-1	0	0		.944	-2	O-13	-0.4
	Yr	47	136	9	31	5	3	0	17	7	14	.228	.271	.309	61	-8	0	0	0	.966	-1	O-37	-1.1
Total	2	51	140	9	31	5	3	0	17	7	14	.221	.268	.300	58	-8	0	0	0	.967	-1	/O-39	-1.2

■ ART WILSON Wilson, Arthur Earl "Dutch" b: 12/11/1885, Macon, Ill. d: 6/12/60, Chicago, Ill. BR/TR, 5'8", 170 lbs. Deb: 9/29/08

YEAR	TM/L	G	AB	R	H	2B	3B	HR	RBI	BB	SO	AVG	OBP	SLG	PRO+	BR/A	SB	CS	SBR	FA	FR	G/POS	TPR
1908	NY-N	1	0	0	0	0	0	0	0	0		—	—	—	—	0	0			.000	0	R	0.0
1909	NY-N	19	42	4	10	2	1	0	5	4		.238	.304	.333	96	-0	0			.985	-4	C-19	-0.4
1910	NY-N	26	52	10	14	4	1	0	5	9	6	.269	.387	.385	125	2	2			.975	-1	C-25/1-1	0.3
1911	*NY-N	66	109	17	33	9	1	1	19	12	12	.303	.411	.431	132	5	6			.963	-6	C-64	0.3
1912	*NY-N	65	121	17	35	6	0	3	19	13	14	.289	.358	.413	107	1	2			.960	1	C-61	0.5
1913	*NY-N	54	79	5	15	1	0	0	8	11	11	.190	.289	.215	45	-5	1			.965	6	C-49	0.3
1914	Chi-F	137	440	78	128	31	8	10	64	70	80	.291	.394	.466	142	20	13			.974	14	*C-132	**4.6**
1915	Chi-F	96	269	44	82	11	2	7	31	65	38	.305	.442	.439	157	21	8			.980	-8	C-87	2.0
1916	Pit-N	53	128	11	33	5	2	1	12	13	22	.258	.331	.352	109	2	4			.981	-9	C-39	-0.5
	Chi-N	36	114	5	22	3	1	0	5	6	14	.193	.233	.237	40	-8	1			.953	-4	C-34	-1.1
	Yr	89	242	16	55	8	3	1	17	19	41	.227	.286	.298	76	-7	5			.967	-13	C-73	-1.6
1917	Chi-N	81	211	17	45	9	2	2	25	32	36	.213	.322	.303	86	-3	6			.968	7	C-75	1.2
1918	Bos-N	89	280	15	69	8	2	0	19	24	31	.246	.310	.289	87	-4	5			.977	-10	C-85	-0.8
1919	Bos-N	71	191	14	49	8	1	0	16	25	19	.257	.346	.309	102	1	2			.977	-2	C-64/1-1	0.5
1920	Bos-N	16	19	0	1	0	0	0	0	1	1	.053	.143	.053	-44	-4	0	0	0	1.000	-2	/3-6,C-2	-0.5
1921	Cle-A	2	1	1	0	0	0	0	0	0		.000	.000	.000	-99	-0	0	0	0	1.000	0	/C-2	0.0
Total	14	812	2056	237	536	96	22	24	226	292	289	.261	.357	.364	110	28	50	0		.972	-18	C-738/3-6,1-2	6.4

■ ARTIE WILSON Wilson, Arthur Lee b: 10/28/20, Springfield, Ala. BL/TR, 5'10", 162 lbs. Deb: 4/18/51

YEAR	TM/L	G	AB	R	H	2B	3B	HR	RBI	BB	SO	AVG	OBP	SLG	PRO+	BR/A	SB	CS	SBR	FA	FR	G/POS	TPR
1951	NY-N	19	22	2	4	0	0	0	1	2	1	.182	.250	.182	18	-2	2	0	1	1.000	3	/2-3,S-3,1-1	0.1

■ CHARLIE WILSON Wilson, Charles Woodrow "Swamp Baby" b: 1/13/05, Clinton, S.C. d: 12/19/70, Rochester, N.Y. BB/TR, 5'10.5", 178 lbs. Deb: 4/14/31

YEAR	TM/L	G	AB	R	H	2B	3B	HR	RBI	BB	SO	AVG	OBP	SLG	PRO+	BR/A	SB	CS	SBR	FA	FR	G/POS	TPR
1931	Bos-N	16	58	7	11	4	0	1	11	3	5	.190	.230	.310	45	-5	0			.917	-2	3-14	-0.6
1932	StL-N	24	96	7	19	3	3	1	2	3	8	.198	.222	.323	43	-8	0			.935	-7	S-24	-1.2
1933	StL-N	1	1	0	0	0	0	0	0	0		.000	.000	.000	-95	-0	0					/S-1	-0.1
1935	StL-N	16	31	1	10	0	0	0	3	3	2	.323	.364	.323	83	-1	0			.933	-1	/3-8	-0.1
Total	4	57	186	15	40	7	3	2	14	8	16	.215	.247	.317	50	-13	0			.935	-10	/S-25,3-22	-1.9

■ CRAIG WILSON Wilson, Craig b: 11/28/64, Annapolis, Md. BR/TR, 5'11", 175 lbs. Deb: 9/6/89

YEAR	TM/L	G	AB	R	H	2B	3B	HR	RBI	BB	SO	AVG	OBP	SLG	PRO+	BR/A	SB	CS	SBR	FA	FR	G/POS	TPR
1989	StL-N	6	4	1	1	0	0	0	1	1	2	.250	.400	.250	87	-0	0	0		.500	-0	/3-2	0.0
1990	StL-N	55	121	13	30	2	0	0	7	8	14	.248	.295	.264	55	-7	0	2	-1	.971	-0	3-13,O-13/2-9,1-1	-0.9
1991	StL-N	60	82	5	14	2	0	0	13	6	10	.171	.229	.207	20	-5	0	0	0	.905	-1	3-12/O-5,1-4,2-3	-1.1
1992	StL-N	61	106	6	33	1	0	0	13	10	16	.311	.371	.368	113	2	1	2	-1	.970	-3	3-18,2-11/O-3	-0.4
1993	KC-A	21	49	6	13	1	0	1	3	7	6	.265	.357	.347	85	-1	1	1	-0	1.000	-3	3-15/2-1,O-1	-0.4
Total	5	203	362	31	91	11	0	1	37	32	50	.251	.312	.290	68	-15	2	5	-2	.957	-8	/3-60,2-24,0-22,1-5	-2.6

YEAR	TM/L	G	AB	R	H	2B	3B	HR	RBI	BB	SO	AVG	OBP	SLG	PRO+	BR/A	SB	CS	SBR	FA	FR	G/POS	TPR

■ DAN WILSON
Wilson, Daniel Allen b: 3/25/69, Arlington Heights, Ill. BR/TR, 6'3", 190 lbs. Deb: 9/7/92

YEAR	TM/L	G	AB	R	H	2B	3B	HR	RBI	BB	SO	AVG	OBP	SLG	PRO+	BR/A	SB	CS	SBR	FA	FR	G/POS	TPR
1992	Cin-N	12	25	2	9	1	0	0	3	3	8	.360	.429	.400	132	1	0	0	0	1.000	0	/C-9	0.2
1993	Cin-N	36	76	6	17	3	0	0	8	9	16	.224	.306	.263	54	-5	0	0	0	.994	-0	C-35	-0.4
1994	Sea-A	91	282	24	61	14	2	3	27	10	57	.216	.246	.312	42	-25	1	2	-1	.986	6	C-91	-1.4
1995	*Sea-A	119	399	40	111	22	3	9	51	33	63	.278	.336	.416	94	-4	2	1	0	.995	12	*C-119	1.5
1996	Sea-A★	138	491	51	140	24	0	18	83	32	88	.285	.333	.444	94	-5	1	2	-1	.996	-2	*C-135	0.1
Total	5	396	1273	123	338	64	5	30	172	87	232	.266	.316	.394	81	-38	4	5	-2	.993	15	C-389	-0.0

■ DESI WILSON
Wilson, Desi Bernard b: 5/9/69, Glen Cove, N.Y. BL/TL, 6'7", 230 lbs. Deb: 8/7/96

YEAR	TM/L	G	AB	R	H	2B	3B	HR	RBI	BB	SO	AVG	OBP	SLG	PRO+	BR/A	SB	CS	SBR	FA	FR	G/POS	TPR
1996	SF-N	41	118	10	32	2	0	2	12	12	27	.271	.338	.339	83	-3	0	2	-1	.984	-1	1-33	-0.8

■ EDDIE WILSON
Wilson, Edward Francis b: 9/7/09, Hamden, Conn. d: 4/11/79, Hamden, Conn. BL/TL, 5'11", 165 lbs. Deb: 6/21/36

YEAR	TM/L	G	AB	R	H	2B	3B	HR	RBI	BB	SO	AVG	OBP	SLG	PRO+	BR/A	SB	CS	SBR	FA	FR	G/POS	TPR
1936	Bro-N	52	173	28	60	8	1	3	25	14	25	.347	.402	.457	129	7	3			.926	-5	O-47	0.0
1937	Bro-N	36	54	11	12	4	1	1	8	17	14	.222	.408	.389	116	3	1			.966	-3	O-21	-0.2
Total	2	88	227	39	72	12	2	4	33	31	39	.317	.404	.441	126	10	4			.936	-9	/O-68	-0.2

■ FRANK WILSON
Wilson, Francis Edward "Squash" b: 4/20/01, Malden, Mass. d: 11/25/74, Leicester, Mass. BR/TR, 6', 185 lbs. Deb: 6/20/24

YEAR	TM/L	G	AB	R	H	2B	3B	HR	RBI	BB	SO	AVG	OBP	SLG	PRO+	BR/A	SB	CS	SBR	FA	FR	G/POS	TPR
1924	Bos-N	61	215	20	51	7	0	1	15	23	22	.237	.311	.284	63	-11	3	4	-2	.973	3	O-55	-1.3
1925	Bos-N	12	31	3	13	1	1	0	4	1	1	.419	.486	.516	171	4	2	1	0	1.000	1	O-10	0.3
1926	Bos-N	87	236	22	56	11	3	0	23	20	21	.237	.300	.309	70	-10	3			.934	1	O-56	-1.3
1928	Cle-A	2	1	0	0	0	0	0	0	0	0	.000	.500	.000	41	-0	0	0	0	.000	0	H	0.0
	StL-A	6	5	1	0	0	0	0	0	0	0	.000	.000	.000	-97	-1	0	0	0	.000	-0	/O-1	-0.2
	Yr	8	6	1	0	0	0	0	0	0	1	.000	.143	.000	-58	-1	0	0	0	.000	-0	/O-1	-0.2
Total	4	168	488	46	120	19	4	1	38	48	44	.246	.315	.307	72	-19	8	5		.958	4	O-122	-2.5

■ TUG WILSON
Wilson, George Archer b: 1860, Brooklyn, N.Y. d: 11/28/14, New York, N.Y. 5'8", 175 lbs. Deb: 5/9/1884

YEAR	TM/L	G	AB	R	H	2B	3B	HR	RBI	BB	SO	AVG	OBP	SLG	PRO+	BR/A	SB	CS	SBR	FA	FR	G/POS	TPR
1884	Bro-a	24	82	13	19	4	0	0		5		.232	.276	.280	81	-2				.826	-3	O-12,C-10/1-3,2-1	-0.4

■ SQUANTO WILSON
Wilson, George Francis b: 3/29/1889, Old Town, Me. d: 3/26/67, Winthrop, Maine BB/TR, 5'9.5", 170 lbs. Deb: 10/2/11

YEAR	TM/L	G	AB	R	H	2B	3B	HR	RBI	BB	SO	AVG	OBP	SLG	PRO+	BR/A	SB	CS	SBR	FA	FR	G/POS	TPR
1911	Det-A	5	16	2	3	0	0	0	0	2		.188	.278	.188	29	-1	0			.900	-1	/C-5	-0.2
1914	Bos-A	1	0	0	0	0	0	0	0	0	0	—	—	—		-0	0			.000	0	/1-1	0.0
Total	2	6	16	2	3	0	0	0	0	2	0	.188	.278	.188	29	-1	0			.900	-1	/C-5,1-1	-0.2

■ ICEHOUSE WILSON
Wilson, George Peacock b: 9/14/12, Maricopa, Cal. d: 10/13/73, Moraga, Cal. BR/TR, 6', 186 lbs. Deb: 5/31/34

YEAR	TM/L	G	AB	R	H	2B	3B	HR	RBI	BB	SO	AVG	OBP	SLG	PRO+	BR/A	SB	CS	SBR	FA	FR	G/POS	TPR
1934	Det-A	1	1	0	0	0	0	0	0	0	0	.000	.000	.000	-99	-0	0	0	0	.000	0	H	0.0

■ GEORGE WILSON
Wilson, George Washington "Teddy" b: 8/30/25, Cherryville, N.C. d: 10/29/74, Gastonia, N.C. BL/TR, 6'1.5", 185 lbs. Deb: 4/15/52

YEAR	TM/L	G	AB	R	H	2B	3B	HR	RBI	BB	SO	AVG	OBP	SLG	PRO+	BR/A	SB	CS	SBR	FA	FR	G/POS	TPR
1952	Chi-A	8	9	0	1	0	0	0	1	1	2	.111	.200	.111	-12	-1	0	0	0	1.000	0	/O-1	-0.1
	NY-N	62	112	9	27	7	0	2	16	3	14	.241	.261	.357	69	-5	0	0	0	.923	-3	O-21/1-2	-0.9
1953	NY-N	11	8	0	1	0	0	0	0	2	2	.125	.364	.125	34	-1	0	0	0	.000	0	H	-0.1
1956	NY-N	53	68	5	9	1	0	1	2	5	14	.132	.192	.191	3	-9	0	0	0	1.000	0	/O-8	-1.0
	*NY-A	11	12	1	2	0	0	0	0	3	0	.167	.333	.167	37	-1	0	0	0	.750	-2	/O-6	-0.3
Total	3	145	209	15	40	8	0	3	19	14	32	.191	.246	.273	41	-17	0	0	0	.932	-5	/O-36,1-2	-2.4

■ GLENN WILSON
Wilson, Glenn Dwight b: 12/22/58, Baytown, Tex. BR/TR, 6'1", 190 lbs. Deb: 4/15/82

YEAR	TM/L	G	AB	R	H	2B	3B	HR	RBI	BB	SO	AVG	OBP	SLG	PRO+	BR/A	SB	CS	SBR	FA	FR	G/POS	TPR
1982	Det-A	84	322	39	94	15	1	12	34	15	51	.292	.323	.457	111	4	2	3	-1	.987	7	O-80/D-4	0.8
1983	Det-A	144	503	55	135	25	6	11	65	25	79	.268	.307	.408	97	-3	1	1	-0	.988	-7	*O-143	-1.5
1984	Phi-N	132	341	28	82	21	3	6	31	17	56	.240	.279	.372	80	-10	7	1	-0	.968	-12	*O-109/3-4	-2.4
1985	Phi-N★	161	608	73	167	39	5	14	102	35	117	.275	.314	.424	102	-0	7	4	-0	.968	20	*O-158	1.6
1986	Phi-N	155	584	70	158	30	4	15	84	42	91	.271	.324	.413	98	-2	5	1	1	.989	21	*O-154	1.5
1987	Phi-N	154	569	55	150	21	2	14	54	38	82	.264	.311	.381	80	-17	3	6	-3	.968	15	*O-154/P-1	-0.9
1988	Sea-A	78	284	28	71	10	1	3	17	15	52	.250	.288	.324	68	-12	1	1	-0	.980	1	O-75/D-2	-1.5
	Pit-N	37	126	11	34	8	0	2	15	3	18	.270	.292	.381	93	-2	0	0	0	.985	-1	O-35	-0.4
1989	Pit-N	100	330	42	93	20	4	9	49	32	39	.282	.347	.448	130	12	1	4	-2	.977	1	O-85,1-10	0.9
	Hou-N	28	102	8	22	6	0	2	15	5	14	.216	.252	.333	68	-5	0	1	-1	.966	5	O-25	-0.1
	Yr	128	432	50	115	26	4	11	64	37	53	.266	.326	.421	116	8	1	5	-3	.974	6	*O-110,1-10	0.8
1990	Hou-N	118	368	42	90	14	0	10	55	26	64	.245	.296	.364	83	-9	0	3	-2	.975	7	*O-108/1-1	-0.6
1993	Pit-N	10	14	2	2	0	0	0	0	0	2	.143	.143	.143	-23	-2	0	0	0	.875	-2	/O-5	-0.2
Total	10	1201	4151	451	1098	209	26	98	521	253	672	.265	.309	.398	93	-46	27	25	-7	.977	57	*O-1131/1-11,D3P	-2.8

■ GRADY WILSON
Wilson, Grady Herbert b: 11/23/22, Columbus, Ga. BR/TR, 6'0.5", 170 lbs. Deb: 5/15/48

YEAR	TM/L	G	AB	R	H	2B	3B	HR	RBI	BB	SO	AVG	OBP	SLG	PRO+	BR/A	SB	CS	SBR	FA	FR	G/POS	TPR
1948	Pit-N	12	10	1	1	1	0	0	1	0	3	.100	.100	.200	-20	-2	0			.846	1	/S-7	-0.1

■ HENRY WILSON
Wilson, Henry C. b: 4/8/1877, Baltimore, Md. Deb: 10/12/1898

YEAR	TM/L	G	AB	R	H	2B	3B	HR	RBI	BB	SO	AVG	OBP	SLG	PRO+	BR/A	SB	CS	SBR	FA	FR	G/POS	TPR
1898	Bal-N	1	2	0	0	0	0	0		0	1	.000	.333	.000	-2	-0	0			1.000	0	/C-1	0.0

■ JIMMIE WILSON
Wilson, James "Ace" b: 7/23/1900, Philadelphia, Pa. d: 5/31/47, Bradenton, Fla. BR/TR, 6'1.5", 200 lbs. Deb: 4/17/23 MC

YEAR	TM/L	G	AB	R	H	2B	3B	HR	RBI	BB	SO	AVG	OBP	SLG	PRO+	BR/A	SB	CS	SBR	FA	FR	G/POS	TPR
1923	Phi-N	85	252	27	66	9	0	1	25	4	17	.262	.276	.310	49	-19	4	2	0	.960	-3	C-69/O-2	-1.9
1924	Phi-N	95	280	32	78	16	3	6	39	17	12	.279	.322	.421	87	-6	5	4	-1	.968	5	C-82/1-2,O-1	0.3
1925	Phi-N	108	335	42	110	19	3	3	54	32	25	.328	.390	.430	100	1	5	3	-0	.982	-9	C-89/O-1	-0.3
1926	Phi-N	90	279	40	85	10	2	4	32	25	20	.305	.362	.398	99	-0	3			.950	0	C-79	0.5
1927	Phi-N	128	443	50	122	15	2	2	45	34	15	.275	.330	.332	77	-14	13			.975	-19	*C-124	-2.4
1928	Phi-N	21	70	11	21	4	1	0	13	9	8	.300	.380	.386	97	-0	3			.990	2	C-20	0.3
	*StL-N	120	411	45	106	26	2	2	50	45	24	.258	.333	.345	76	-14	9			.983	1	*C-120	-0.3
	Yr	141	481	56	127	30	3	2	63	54	32	.264	.340	.351	79	-14	12			.985	2	*C-140	0.0
1929	StL-N	120	394	59	128	27	8	4	71	43	19	.325	.394	.464	111	7	4			.972	5	*C-119	2.0
1930	*StL-N	107	362	54	115	25	7	1	58	28	17	.318	.368	.434	90	-6	8			.987	10	C-99	1.2
1931	*StL-N	115	383	45	105	20	2	0	51	28	15	.274	.332	.337	77	-12	5			.985	11	*C-110	0.6
1932	StL-N	92	274	36	68	16	2	2	28	15	18	.248	.290	.343	67	-13	9			.982	2	C-75/1-3,2-1	-0.7
1933	StL-N★	113	369	34	94	17	0	1	45	23	33	.255	.300	.309	71	-14	8			.982	2	*C-107	-0.6
1934	Phi-N	90	277	25	81	11	0	3	35	14	10	.292	.326	.365	75	-10	1			.987	2	C-77/1-1,2-1,M	-0.4
1935	Phi-N★	93	290	38	81	20	0	1	37	19	19	.279	.326	.359	76	-10	1			.982	8	C-78/2-1,M	0.2
1936	Phi-N	85	230	25	64	12	0	1	27	12	21	.278	.314	.343	70	-10	5			.960	-6	C-63/1-1,M	-1.3
1937	Phi-N	39	87	15	24	3	0	1	8	6	4	.276	.323	.345	75	-3	1			.978	-1	C-22/1-2,M	-0.4
1938	Phi-N	3	2	0	0	0	0	0	0	0	0	.000	.000	.000	-99	-1	0			1.000	0	/C-1,M	0.0
1939	Cin-N	4	3	0	1	0	0	0		0	0	.333	.333	.333	79	-0	0			.000	-0	/C-1	0.0
1940	*Cin-N	16	37	2	9	2	0	0	3	2	1	.243	.282	.297	59	-2	1			.982	3	C-16	0.2
Total	18	1525	4778	580	1358	252	32	32	621	356	280	.284	.336	.370	82	-123	86	9		.977	11	*C-1351/1-9,O-4,2-3	-3.0

■ GARY WILSON
Wilson, James Garrett b: 1/12/1877, Baltimore, Md. d: 5/1/69, Randallstown, Md. BR/TR, 5'7", 168 lbs. Deb: 9/27/02

YEAR	TM/L	G	AB	R	H	2B	3B	HR	RBI	BB	SO	AVG	OBP	SLG	PRO+	BR/A	SB	CS	SBR	FA	FR	G/POS	TPR
1902	Bos-A	2	8	0	1	0	0	0	1	0		.125	.125	.125	-30	-1	0			.800	0	/2-2	-0.1

■ JIM WILSON
Wilson, James George b: 12/29/60, Corvallis, Ore. BR/TR, 6'3", 230 lbs. Deb: 9/13/85

YEAR	TM/L	G	AB	R	H	2B	3B	HR	RBI	BB	SO	AVG	OBP	SLG	PRO+	BR/A	SB	CS	SBR	FA	FR	G/POS	TPR
1985	Cle-A	4	14	2	5	0	0	0	4	0	3	.357	.400	.357	110	0	0	0	0	1.000	-1	/1-2,D-2	-0.1
1989	Sea-A	5	8	0	0	0	0	0	0	1	3	.000	.000	.000	-97	-2	0	0	0	.000	-0	/D-5	-0.2
Total	2	9	22	2	5	0	0	0	4	1	6	.227	.261	.227	36	-2	0	0	0	1.000	-1	/D-7,1-2	-0.3

■ CHIEF WILSON
Wilson, John Owen b: 8/21/1883, Austin, Tex. d: 2/22/54, Bertram, Tex. BL/TR, 6'2", 185 lbs. Deb: 4/15/08

YEAR	TM/L	G	AB	R	H	2B	3B	HR	RBI	BB	SO	AVG	OBP	SLG	PRO+	BR/A	SB	CS	SBR	FA	FR	G/POS	TPR
1908	Pit-N	144	529	47	120	8	7	3	43	22		.227	.260	.285	74	-16	12			.955	1	*O-144	-2.5
1909	*Pit-N	154	569	64	155	22	12	4	59	19		.272	.303	.374	102	-2	17			.957	6	O-154	-0.2
1910	Pit-N	146	536	59	148	14	13	6	50	21	68	.276	.312	.373	94	-0	8			.972	3	O-146	-1.1
1911	Pit-N	148	544	72	163	34	12	12	**107**	41	55	.300	.353	.472	125	15	10			.977	7	O-146	1.5

YEAR	TM/L	G	AB	R	H	2B	3B	HR	RBI	BB	SO	AVG	OBP	SLG	PRO+	BR/A	SB	CS	SBR	FA	FR	G/POS	TPR
1912	Pit-N	152	583	80	175	19	36	11	95	35	67	.300	.342	.513	134	22	16			.961	1	*O-152	1.6
1913	Pit-N	155	580	71	154	12	14	10	73	32	62	.266	.307	.386	102	-1	9			.969	6	*O-155	-0.3
1914	StL-N	154	580	64	150	27	12	9	73	32	66	.259	.302	.393	107	2	14			.983	17	*O-154	1.3
1915	StL-N	107	348	33	96	13	6	3	39	19	43	.276	.321	.374	110	3	8	15	-7	.984	12	*O-105	0.5
1916	StL-N	120	355	30	85	8	2	3	32	20	46	.239	.289	.299	81	-8	4			.955	-11	*O-113	-2.7
Total	9	1280	4624	520	1246	157	114	59	571	241	407	.269	.311	.391	105	9	98	15		.968	42	*O-1269	-1.9

■ LES WILSON
Wilson, Lester Wilbur "Tug" b: 7/17/1885, St.Louis, Mich. d: 4/4/69, Edmonds, Wash. BL/TR, 5'11", 170 lbs. Deb: 7/15/11

YEAR	TM/L	G	AB	R	H	2B	3B	HR	RBI	BB	SO	AVG	OBP	SLG	PRO+	BR/A	SB	CS	SBR	FA	FR	G/POS	TPR
1911	Bos-A	5	7	0	0	0	0	0	0	0	2	.000	.222	.000	-36	-1	0			1.000	-1	/O-3	-0.2

■ HACK WILSON
Wilson, Lewis Robert b: 4/26/1900, Ellwood City, Pa. d: 11/23/48, Baltimore, Md. BR/TR, 5'6", 190 lbs. Deb: 9/29/23 H

YEAR	TM/L	G	AB	R	H	2B	3B	HR	RBI	BB	SO	AVG	OBP	SLG	PRO+	BR/A	SB	CS	SBR	FA	FR	G/POS	TPR
1923	NY-N	3	10	0	2	0	0	0	0	0	1	.200	.200	.200	6	-1	0	0	0	.857	-1	/O-3	-0.2
1924	*NY-N	107	383	62	113	19	12	10	57	44	46	.295	.369	.486	131	16	4	3	-1	.967	-7	*O-103	0.2
1925	NY-N	62	180	28	43	7	4	6	30	21	33	.239	.322	.422	92	-3	5	2	0	.975	-11	O-50	-1.5
1926	Chi-N	142	529	97	170	36	8	21	109	69	61	.321	.406	.539	150	38	10			.973	2	*O-140	3.0
1927	Chi-N	146	551	119	175	30	12	30	129	71	70	.318	.401	.579	160	45	13			.967	-1	*O-146	3.5
1928	Chi-N	145	520	89	163	32	9	31	120	77	94	.313	.404	.588	159	44	4			.960	-10	*O-143	2.3
1929	*Chi-N	150	574	135	198	30	5	39	159	78	83	.345	.425	.618	155	49	3			.970	-3	*O-150	3.2
1930	Chi-N	155	585	146	208	35	6	56	190	105	84	.356	.454	.723	177	74	3			.951	-7	*O-155	4.8
1931	Chi-N	112	395	66	103	22	4	13	61	63	69	.261	.362	.435	112	7	1			.978	-5	*O-103	-0.5
1932	Bro-N	135	481	77	143	37	5	23	123	51	85	.297	.366	.538	142	28	2			.955	-9	*O-125	1.1
1933	Bro-N	117	360	41	96	13	2	9	54	52	50	.267	.359	.389	119	10	7			.963	-7	O-90/2-5	-0.1
1934	Bro-N	67	172	24	45	5	0	6	27	40	33	.262	.401	.395	120	7	0			.974	-3	O-43	0.2
	Phi-N	7	20	0	2	0	0	0	3	3	4	.100	.217	.100	-11	-3	0			1.000	-1	/O-6	-0.4
	Yr	74	192	24	47	5	0	6	30	43	37	.245	.383	.365	105	3	0			.977	-4	O-49	-0.2
Total	12	1348	4760	884	1461	266	67	244	1062	674	713	.307	.395	.545	145	311	52	5		.965	-62	*O-1257/2-5	15.6

■ TACK WILSON
Wilson, Michael b: 5/16/55, Shreveport, La. BR/TR, 5'10", 185 lbs. Deb: 4/9/83

YEAR	TM/L	G	AB	R	H	2B	3B	HR	RBI	BB	SO	AVG	OBP	SLG	PRO+	BR/A	SB	CS	SBR	FA	FR	G/POS	TPR
1983	Min-A	5	4	4	1	1	0	0	0	1	0	.250	.250	.500	97	-0	0	0	0	1.000	-0	/O-1,D-2	0.0
1987	Cal-A	7	2	5	1	0	0	0	0	1	0	.500	.667	.500	224	-0	0	0	0	1.000	-1	/O-4,D-2	-0.1
Total	2	12	6	9	2	1	0	0	1	1	0	.333	.429	.500	150	-0	0	0	0	1.000	-2	/O-5,D-4	-0.1

■ NIGEL WILSON
Wilson, Nigel Edward b: 1/12/70, Oshawa, Ont., Can. BL/TL, 6'1", 185 lbs. Deb: 9/8/93

YEAR	TM/L	G	AB	R	H	2B	3B	HR	RBI	BB	SO	AVG	OBP	SLG	PRO+	BR/A	SB	CS	SBR	FA	FR	G/POS	TPR
1993	Fla-N	7	16	0	0	0	0	0	0	0	11	.000	.000	.000	-95	-4	0	0	0	1.000	-0	/O-3	-0.5
1995	Cin-N	5	7	0	0	0	0	0	0	0	4	.000	.000	.000	-99	-2	0	0	0	1.000	-0	/O-2	-0.2
1996	*Cle-N	10	12	2	3	0	0	2	5	1	6	.250	.308	.750	156	1	0	0	0	.000	-0	/O-1,D-3	0.0
Total	3	22	35	2	3	0	0	2	5	1	21	.086	.111	.257	-7	-5	0	0	0	1.000	-1	/O-6,D-3	-0.7

■ PARKE WILSON
Wilson, Parke Asel b: 10/26/1867, Keithsburg, Ill. d: 12/20/34, Hermosa Beach, Cal BR/TR, 5'11", 166 lbs. Deb: 7/19/1893

YEAR	TM/L	G	AB	R	H	2B	3B	HR	RBI	BB	SO	AVG	OBP	SLG	PRO+	BR/A	SB	CS	SBR	FA	FR	G/POS	TPR
1893	NY-N	31	114	16	28	4	1	2	21	7	9	.246	.289	.351	70	-6	5			.969	-7	C-31	-0.8
1894	NY-N	49	175	35	58	5	5	1	32	14	5	.331	.387	.434	99	-0	8			.841	-9	C-34,1-15	-1.0
1895	NY-N	67	238	32	56	9	0	0	30	14	16	.235	.281	.273	44	-20	11			.938	3	C-53,1-11/3-3	-1.0
1896	NY-N	75	253	33	60	2	0	0	23	13	14	.237	.277	.245	39	-22	9			.936	-4	C-71/1-2	-1.5
1897	NY-N	46	154	29	46	9	3	0	22	15		.299	.365	.396	104	1	5			.929	-2	C-30,1-10/O-4,2-1	0.2
1898	NY-N	1	4	0	0	0	0	0	0	0	0	.000	.000	.000	-99	-1	0			1.000	-0	/O-1	-0.1
1899	NY-N	97	328	49	88	8	6	0	42	43		.268	.360	.329	93	-1	16			.925	-8	C-31,1-29,S-19,3/O	-0.5
Total	7	366	1266	194	336	37	15	3	170	106	44	.265	.327	.325	73	-49	54			.926	-27	C-250/1-67,S3O2	-4.2

■ BOB WILSON
Wilson, Robert b: 2/22/25, Dallas, Tex. d: 4/23/85, Dallas, Tex. BR/TR, 5'11", 197 lbs. Deb: 5/17/58

YEAR	TM/L	G	AB	R	H	2B	3B	HR	RBI	BB	SO	AVG	OBP	SLG	PRO+	BR/A	SB	CS	SBR	FA	FR	G/POS	TPR
1958	LA-N	3	5	0	1	0	0	0	0	0	2	.200	.200	.200	6	-1	0	0	0	1.000	-0	/O-1	-0.1

■ RED WILSON
Wilson, Robert James b: 3/7/29, Milwaukee, Wis. BR/TR, 6', 200 lbs. Deb: 9/22/51

YEAR	TM/L	G	AB	R	H	2B	3B	HR	RBI	BB	SO	AVG	OBP	SLG	PRO+	BR/A	SB	CS	SBR	FA	FR	G/POS	TPR
1951	Chi-A	4	11	1	3	1	0	0	0	0	2	.273	.333	.364	90	-0	0	0	0	1.000	-1	/C-4	-0.1
1952	Chi-A	2	3	0	0	0	0	0	0	0	1	.000	.000	.000	-99	-1	0	0	0	1.000	1	/C-2	0.0
1953	Chi-A	71	164	21	41	6	1	0	26	12	12	.250	.353	.299	75	-5	2	3	-1	.981	10	C-63	0.6
1954	Chi-A	8	20	2	4	0	0	1	1	1	2	.200	.238	.350	58	-1	0	0	0	1.000	4	C-8	0.3
	Det-A	54	170	22	48	11	1	2	22	27	12	.282	.381	.394	115	4	3	1	0	.996	2	C-53	0.9
	Yr	62	190	24	52	11	1	3	23	28	14	.274	.367	.389	108	3	3	1	0	.997	6	C-61	1.2
1955	Det-A	78	241	26	53	9	0	2	17	26	23	.220	.296	.282	57	-14	1	2	-1	.984	-6	C-72	-1.9
1956	Det-A	78	228	32	66	12	6	7	38	42	18	.289	.400	.452	124	9	2	1	0	.991	3	C-78	1.5
1957	Det-A	60	180	21	43	8	1	3	15	25	19	.239	.341	.344	86	-3	2	3	-1	1.000	1	C-60	-0.1
1958	Det-A	103	298	31	89	13	1	5	29	35	30	.299	.376	.379	101	2	10	0	3	.992	7	*C-101	1.8
1959	Det-A	67	228	28	60	17	0	4	35	10	23	.263	.300	.408	88	-4	2	2	-1	.988	2	C-64	0.0
1960	Det-A	45	134	17	29	4	0	1	14	16	14	.216	.300	.269	54	-8	3	0	1	.980	-0	C-45	-0.5
	Cle-A	32	88	5	19	3	0	1	10	6	7	.216	.274	.284	53	-6	0	0	0	.989	7	C-30	0.3
	Yr	77	222	22	48	7	0	2	24	22	21	.216	.290	.275	53	-14	3	0	1	.984	7	C-75	-0.2
Total	10	602	1765	206	455	84	8	24	189	215	163	.258	.341	.355	87	-28	25	12	0	.990	31	C-580	2.8

■ MIKE WILSON
Wilson, Samuel Marshall b: 12/2/1896, Edge Hill, Pa. d: 5/16/78, Boynton Beach, Fla BR/TR, 5'10.5", 160 lbs. Deb: 6/4/21

YEAR	TM/L	G	AB	R	H	2B	3B	HR	RBI	BB	SO	AVG	OBP	SLG	PRO+	BR/A	SB	CS	SBR	FA	FR	G/POS	TPR
1921	Pit-N	5	4	0	0	0	0	0	0	0	0	.000	.000	.000	-97	-1	0	0	0	.833	0	/C-5	-0.1

■ NEIL WILSON
Wilson, Samuel O'Neil b: 6/14/35, Lexington, Tenn. BL/TR, 6'1", 175 lbs. Deb: 4/17/60

YEAR	TM/L	G	AB	R	H	2B	3B	HR	RBI	BB	SO	AVG	OBP	SLG	PRO+	BR/A	SB	CS	SBR	FA	FR	G/POS	TPR
1960	SF-N	6	10	0	0	0	0	0	0	1	2	.000	.091	.000	-77	-2	0	0	0	.958	0	/C-6	-0.2

■ TOM WILSON
Wilson, Thomas G. "Slats" b: 6/3/1890, Fleming, Kan. d: 3/7/53, San Pedro, Cal. BB/TR, 6'1.5", 160 lbs. Deb: 9/8/14

YEAR	TM/L	G	AB	R	H	2B	3B	HR	RBI	BB	SO	AVG	OBP	SLG	PRO+	BR/A	SB	CS	SBR	FA	FR	G/POS	TPR
1914	Was-A	1	1	0	0	0	0	0	0	0	0	.000	.000	.000	-96	-0	0			.000	0	/C-1	0.0

■ BILL WILSON
Wilson, William Donald b: 11/6/28, Central City, Neb. BR/TR, 6'2", 200 lbs. Deb: 9/24/50

YEAR	TM/L	G	AB	R	H	2B	3B	HR	RBI	BB	SO	AVG	OBP	SLG	PRO+	BR/A	SB	CS	SBR	FA	FR	G/POS	TPR
1950	Chi-A	3	6	0	0	0	0	0	0	0	2	.000	.250	.000	-33	-1	0	0	0	1.000	-1	/O-2	-0.2
1953	Chi-A	9	17	1	1	0	0	0	0	1	7	.059	.111	.059	-51	-4	0	0	0	1.000	-0	/O-3	-0.4
1954	Chi-A	20	35	4	6	1	0	2	5	7	5	.171	.310	.371	83	-1	0	1	-1	.943	-2	O-19	-0.4
	Phi-A	94	323	43	77	10	1	15	33	39	59	.238	.335	.415	104	1	1	2	-1	.989	8	O-91	0.5
	Yr	114	358	47	83	11	1	17	38	46	64	.232	.333	.411	102	0	1	3	-2	.984	6	O-110	0.1
1955	KC-A	98	273	39	61	12	0	15	38	24	63	.223	.289	.432	91	-5	1	1	-0	.969	-3	O-82/P-1	-1.2
Total	4	224	654	87	145	23	1	32	77	72	136	.222	.308	.407	92	-10	2	4	-2	.979	3	O-197/P-1	-1.7

■ BILL WILSON
Wilson, William G. b: 10/28/1867, Hannibal, Mo. d: 5/9/24, St.Paul, Minn. TR, Deb: 4/30/1890

YEAR	TM/L	G	AB	R	H	2B	3B	HR	RBI	BB	SO	AVG	OBP	SLG	PRO+	BR/A	SB	CS	SBR	FA	FR	G/POS	TPR
1890	Pit-N	83	304	30	65	11	3	0	21	22	50	.214	.271	.270	65	-13	5			.874	2	C-38,O-25,1-18/S-1	-0.8
1897	Lou-N	105	381	43	81	12	4	1	41	18		.213	.273	.273	41	-33	9			.940	-1	C-103/3-1	-1.9
1898	Lou-N	29	102	5	17	1	2	0	13	5		.167	.213	.245	32	-9	3			.895	-4	C-28/1-1	-1.0
Total	3	217	787	78	163	24	9	2	75	45	50	.207	.257	.268	49	-56	17			.912	-3	C-169/O-25,1-19,3S	-3.7

■ MOOKIE WILSON
Wilson, William Hayward b: 2/9/56, Bamberg, S.C. BB/TR, 5'10", 170 lbs. Deb: 9/2/80

YEAR	TM/L	G	AB	R	H	2B	3B	HR	RBI	BB	SO	AVG	OBP	SLG	PRO+	BR/A	SB	CS	SBR	FA	FR	G/POS	TPR
1980	NY-N	27	105	16	26	5	3	0	4	12	19	.248	.325	.352	91	-1	7	7	-2	.973	2	O-26	-0.3
1981	NY-N	92	328	49	89	8	8	3	14	20	59	.271	.317	.372	96	-2	24	12	0	.983	6	O-80	0.1
1982	NY-N	159	639	90	178	25	9	5	55	32	102	.279	.315	.369	91	-8	58	16	8	.988	17	*O-156	1.3
1983	NY-N	152	638	91	176	25	6	7	51	18	103	.276	.300	.367	85	-15	54	16	7	.984	13	*O-148	0.0
1984	NY-N	154	587	88	162	28	10	10	54	26	90	.276	.309	.409	102	-1	46	9	8	.990	17	*O-146	2.1
1985	NY-N	93	337	56	93	16	6	6	26	28	52	.276	.332	.424	113	5	24	9	2	.964	2	O-83	0.7
1986	*NY-N	123	381	61	110	17	5	9	45	32	72	.289	.345	.430	116	8	25	7	6	.979	-6	*O-114	0.2
1987	NY-N	124	385	58	115	19	7	9	34	35	85	.299	.360	.455	120	11	21	6	3	.963	-8	*O-109	0.3
1988	*NY-N	112	378	61	112	17	5	8	41	27	63	.296	.346	.431	128	13	15	4	2	.976	-7	*O-104	0.6

YEAR	TM/L	G	AB	R	H	2B	3B	HR	RBI	BB	SO	AVG	OBP	SLG	PRO+	BR/A	SB	CS	SBR	FA	FR	G/POS	TPR
1989	NY-N	80	249	22	51	10	1	3	18	10	47	.205	.238	.289	53	-16	7	4	-0	.975	-3	O-71	-2.2
	*Tor-A	54	238	32	71	9	1	2	17	3	37	.298	.313	.370	93	-3	12	1	3	.991	-3	O-54	-0.5
1990	Tor-A	147	588	81	156	36	4	3	51	31	102	.265	.302	.355	82	-15	23	4	5	.992	8	*O-141/D-6	-0.6
1991	*Tor-A	86	241	26	58	12	4	2	28	8	35	.241	.280	.349	70	-10	11	3	2	.973	-1	O-41,D-34	-1.2
Total	12	1403	5094	731	1397	227	71	67	438	282	866	.274	.315	.386	96	-35	327	98	39	.982	38	*O-1273/D-40	0.5

■ WILLIE WILSON
Wilson, Willie James b: 7/9/55, Montgomery, Ala. BB/TR, 6'3", 195 lbs. Deb: 9/4/76

YEAR	TM/L	G	AB	R	H	2B	3B	HR	RBI	BB	SO	AVG	OBP	SLG	PRO+	BR/A	SB	CS	SBR	FA	FR	G/POS	TPR
1976	KC-A	12	6	0	1	0	0	0	0	0	2	.167	.167	.167	-2	-1	2	1	0	.875	-2	/O-6	-0.2
1977	KC-A	13	34	10	11	2	0	0	1	1	8	.324	.343	.382	97	-0	6	3	0	.960	0	/O-9,D-2	0.0
1978	*KC-A	127	198	43	43	8	2	0	16	16	33	.217	.282	.278	57	-11	46	12	7	.978	-14	*O-112/D-6	-2.1
1979	KC-A	154	588	113	185	18	13	6	49	28	92	.315	.353	.420	106	4	**83**	12	**18**	.985	15	*O-152/D-2	2.9
1980	*KC-A	161	**705**	**133**	**230**	28	**15**	3	49	28	81	.326	.357	.421	112	11	79	10	**18**	.988	22	*O-159	4.3
1981	KC-A	102	439	54	133	10	7	1	32	18	42	.303	.336	.364	103	1	34	8	5	.987	22	*O-101	2.6
1982	KC-A★	136	585	87	194	19	**15**	3	46	26	81	**.332**	.366	.431	118	14	37	11	5	.987	15	*O-135	2.9
1983	KC-A★	137	576	90	159	22	8	2	33	33	75	.276	.316	.352	84	-13	59	8	13	.975	1	*O-136	-0.3
1984	*KC-A	128	541	81	163	24	9	2	44	39	56	.301	.352	.390	104	3	47	5	**11**	.990	10	*O-128	2.1
1985	*KC-A	141	605	87	168	25	**21**	4	43	29	94	.278	.316	.408	96	-4	43	11	6	.995	3	*O-140	0.0
1986	KC-A	156	631	77	170	20	7	9	44	31	97	.269	.313	.366	82	-16	34	8	5	.993	5	*O-155	-1.0
1987	KC-A	146	610	97	170	18	15	4	30	32	88	.279	.321	.377	82	-16	59	11	**11**	**.997**	-3	*O-143/D-2	-0.6
1988	KC-A	147	591	81	155	17	**11**	1	37	22	106	.262	.291	.333	74	-21	35	7	6	.989	-0	*O-142	-2.0
1989	KC-A	112	383	58	97	17	7	3	43	27	78	.253	.304	.358	86	-7	24	6	4	.977	-3	*O-108/D-1	-1.0
1990	KC-A	115	307	49	89	13	3	2	42	30	57	.290	.357	.371	106	3	24	6	4	1.000	-6	*O-106/D-1	-0.1
1991	Oak-A	113	294	38	70	14	4	0	28	18	43	.238	.291	.313	71	-12	20	5	3	.983	-8	O-87/D-9	-1.4
1992	*Oak-A	132	396	38	107	15	5	0	37	35	65	.270	.331	.333	91	-4	28	8	4	.981	7	*O-120/D-5	0.4
1993	Chi-N	105	221	29	57	11	3	1	11	11	40	.258	.302	.348	75	-8	7	2	1	.991	-18	O-82	-2.7
1994	Chi-N	17	21	4	5	0	2	0	1	0	6	.238	.273	.429	80	-1	1	0	0	1.000	-5	O-10	-0.4
Total	19	2154	7731	1169	2207	281	147	41	585	425	1144	.285	.328	.376	93	-77	668	134	120	.987	53	*O-2031/D-28	3.4

■ ED WINCENIAK
Winceniak, Edward Joseph b: 4/16/29, Chicago, Ill. BR/TR, 5'9", 165 lbs. Deb: 4/25/56

YEAR	TM/L	G	AB	R	H	2B	3B	HR	RBI	BB	SO	AVG	OBP	SLG	PRO+	BR/A	SB	CS	SBR	FA	FR	G/POS	TPR
1956	Chi-N	15	17	1	2	0	0	0	0	1	3	.118	.167	.118	-22	-3	0	0	0	.889	-0	/3-4,2-1	-0.3
1957	Chi-N	17	50	5	12	3	0	1	8	2	9	.240	.269	.360	68	-2	0	0	0	1.000	-5	/S-5,3-4,2-3	-0.5
Total	2	32	67	6	14	3	0	1	8	3	12	.209	.243	.299	45	-5	0	0	0	.955	-3	/3-8,S-5,2-4	-0.8

■ GORDIE WINDHORN
Windhorn, Gordon Ray b: 12/19/33, Watseka, Ill. BR/TR, 6'1", 185 lbs. Deb: 9/10/59

YEAR	TM/L	G	AB	R	H	2B	3B	HR	RBI	BB	SO	AVG	OBP	SLG	PRO+	BR/A	SB	CS	SBR	FA	FR	G/POS	TPR
1959	NY-A	7	11	0	0	0	0	0	0	0	3	.000	.000	.000	-99	-3	0	0	0	1.000	-1	/O-4	-0.4
1961	LA-N	34	33	10	8	2	1	2	6	4	3	.242	.324	.545	115	1	0	1	-1	.944	-2	O-17	-0.3
1962	KC-A	14	19	1	3	1	0	0	1	0	3	.158	.158	.211	-2	-3	0	0	0	1.000	-2	O-7	-0.4
	LA-A	40	45	9	8	6	0	0	1	7	10	.178	.288	.311	63	-2	1	0	-0	1.000	-7	O-27	-1.0
	Yr	54	64	10	11	7	0	0	2	7	13	.172	.254	.281	44	-5	1	1	-0	1.000	-9	O-34	-1.4
Total	3	95	108	20	19	9	1	2	8	11	19	.176	.252	.333	55	-7	1	2	-1	.981	-12	/O-55	-2.1

■ BILL WINDLE
Windle, Willis Brewer b: 12/13/04, Galena, Kan. d: 12/8/81, Corpus Christi, Tex BL/TL, 5'11.5", 170 lbs. Deb: 9/27/28

YEAR	TM/L	G	AB	R	H	2B	3B	HR	RBI	BB	SO	AVG	OBP	SLG	PRO+	BR/A	SB	CS	SBR	FA	FR	G/POS	TPR
1928	Pit-N	1	1	1	1	1	0	0	1	0	0	1.000	1.000	2.000	641	1	0			1.000	0	/1-1	0.1
1929	Pit-N	2	1	0	0	0	0	0	0	0	1	.000	.000	.000	-98	-0	0			1.000	-0	/1-2	0.0
Total	2	3	2	1	1	1	0	0	1	0	1	.500	.500	1.000	264	0	0			1.000	-0	/1-3	0.1

■ ROBBIE WINE
Wine, Robert Paul Jr. b: 7/13/62, Norristown, Pa. BR/TR, 6'2", 190 lbs. Deb: 9/2/86 F

YEAR	TM/L	G	AB	R	H	2B	3B	HR	RBI	BB	SO	AVG	OBP	SLG	PRO+	BR/A	SB	CS	SBR	FA	FR	G/POS	TPR
1986	Hou-N	9	12	2	3	1	0	0	1	4		.250	.308	.333	79	-0	0	0	0	1.000	3	/C-8	0.3
1987	Hou-N	14	29	1	3	1	0	0	1	10	.103	.133	.138	-29	-5	0	0	0	.979	-1	C-12	-0.6
Total	2	23	41	3	6	2	0	0	2	14	.146	.186	.195	2	-6	0	0	0	.988	2	/C-20	-0.3

■ BOBBY WINE
Wine, Robert Paul Sr. b: 9/17/38, New York, N.Y. BR/TR, 6'1", 187 lbs. Deb: 9/20/60 FMC

YEAR	TM/L	G	AB	R	H	2B	3B	HR	RBI	BB	SO	AVG	OBP	SLG	PRO+	BR/A	SB	CS	SBR	FA	FR	G/POS	TPR
1960	Phi-N	4	14	1	2	0	0	0	0	0	2	.143	.143	.143	-22	-2	0	0	0	1.000	0	/S-4	-0.2
1962	Phi-N	112	311	30	76	15	0	4	25	11	49	.244	.270	.331	62	-17	2	0	1	.979	7	S-89,3-20	-0.3
1963	Phi-N	142	418	29	90	14	3	6	44	14	83	.215	.242	.306	58	-23	1	3	-2	.971	15	*S-132/3-8	-0.2
1964	Phi-N	126	283	28	60	8	3	4	34	25	37	.212	.276	.304	64	-13	1	0	0	.965	7	*S-108,3-16	0.0
1965	Phi-N	139	394	31	90	8	1	5	33	31	69	.228	.285	.292	64	-19	0	0	0	.967	22	*S-135/1-4	1.2
1966	Phi-N	46	89	2	21	5	0	0	5	6	13	.236	.292	.292	63	-4	0	1	-1	.974	12	S-40/O-2	0.9
1967	Phi-N	135	363	27	69	12	5	2	28	29	77	.190	.250	.267	48	-25	3	2	-0	**.980**	29	*S-134/1-2	1.6
1968	Phi-N	27	71	5	12	3	0	2	9	6	17	.169	.234	.296	58	-4	0	0	0	.972	3	S-25/3-1	0.2
1969	Mon-N	121	303	23	74	8	1	3	25	24	65	.232	.288	.300	43	-28	0	0	0	.949	17	*S-118/1-1,3-1	0.1
1970	Mon-N	159	501	40	116	21	3	3	51	39	94	.232	.288	.303	59	-29	0	1	-0	.976	20	*S-159	0.4
1971	Mon-N	119	340	25	68	9	0	1	16	25	46	.200	.255	.235	39	-27	0	0	0	.982	2	*S-119	-1.2
1972	Mon-N	34	18	2	4	1	0	0	0	0	2	.222	.222	.278	41	-1	0	0	0	1.000	5	3-21/S-4,2-1	0.4
Total	12	1164	3172	249	682	104	16	30	268	214	538	.215	.265	.286	54	-194	7	7	-4	.972	137	*S-1067/3-67,102	3.2

■ RALPH WINEGARNER
Winegarner, Ralph Lee b: 10/29/09, Benton, Kan. d: 4/14/88, Wichita, Kan. BR/TR, 6', 182 lbs. Deb: 9/20/30 C

YEAR	TM/L	G	AB	R	H	2B	3B	HR	RBI	BB	SO	AVG	OBP	SLG	PRO+	BR/A	SB	CS	SBR	FA	FR	G/POS	TPR
1930	Cle-A	5	22	5	10	1	0	0	2	1	7	.455	.478	.500	143	2	0	0	0	.857	1	/3-5	0.2
1932	Cle-A	7	7	1	1	0	0	0	0	0	5	.143	.143	.143	-24	-1	0	0	0	.750	-0	/P-5	0.0
1934	Cle-A	32	51	9	10	2	0	1	5	3	11	.196	.241	.294	37	-5	0	0	0	1.000	1	P-22/O-1	0.0
1935	Cle-A	65	84	11	26	4	1	3	17	9	12	.310	.376	.488	120	2	1	1	-0	.944	-2	P-25/O-4,3-3,1-1	0.2
1936	Cle-A	18	16	0	2	0	0	0	2	1	6	.125	.176	.125	-24	-3	0	0	0	1.000	-0	/P-9	0.2
1949	StL-A	9	5	2	2	0	0	1	2	1	2	.400	.500	1.000	280	1	0	0	0	1.000	-0	/P-9	0.0
Total	6	136	185	28	51	7	1	5	28	15	43	.276	.330	.405	86	-4	1	1	-0	.952	2	/P-70,3-8,O-5,1-1	0.4

■ DAVE WINFIELD
Winfield, David Mark b: 10/3/51, St.Paul, Minn. BR/TR, 6'6", 220 lbs. Deb: 6/19/73

YEAR	TM/L	G	AB	R	H	2B	3B	HR	RBI	BB	SO	AVG	OBP	SLG	PRO+	BR/A	SB	CS	SBR	FA	FR	G/POS	TPR
1973	SD-N	56	141	9	39	4	1	3	12	12	19	.277	.333	.383	107	1	0	0	0	.956	-1	O-36/1-1	-0.2
1974	SD-N	145	498	57	132	18	4	20	75	40	96	.265	.321	.438	116	8	9	7	-2	.960	7	*O-131	0.8
1975	SD-N	143	509	74	136	20	2	15	76	69	82	.267	.358	.403	118	13	23	4	5	.972	10	*O-138	2.2
1976	SD-N	137	492	81	139	26	4	13	69	65	78	.283	.370	.431	138	24	26	7	4	.982	12	*O-134	3.6
1977	SD-N★	157	615	104	169	29	7	25	92	58	75	.275	.337	.467	126	19	16	7	1	.972	20	*O-156	3.4
1978	SD-N	158	587	88	181	30	5	24	97	55	81	.308	.370	.499	153	39	21	9	1	.979	-19	*O-154/1-2	1.5
1979	SD-N★	159	597	97	184	27	10	34	**118**	85	71	.308	.396	.558	**167**	55	15	9	-1	.986	11	*O-157	**5.9**
1980	SD-N★	162	558	89	154	25	6	20	87	79	83	.276	.368	.450	135	27	23	7	3	.987	-4	*O-159	2.0
1981	*NY-A★	105	388	52	114	25	1	13	68	43	41	.294	.366	.464	140	20	11	3	3	.985	-0	*O-102/D-1	1.4
1982	NY-A★	140	539	84	151	24	8	37	106	45	64	.280	.336	.560	143	29	5	3	-0	.974	12	*O-135/D-4	3.7
1983	NY-A★	152	598	99	169	26	8	32	116	58	77	.283	.348	.513	139	30	15	6	1	.978	-11	*O-151	1.5
1984	NY-A★	141	567	106	193	34	4	19	100	53	71	.340	.397	.515	156	43	6	4	-1	.994	2	*O-140	4.0
1985	NY-A★	155	633	105	174	34	6	26	114	52	96	.275	.330	.471	119	15	19	7	2	.991	12	*O-152/D-2	2.2
1986	NY-A	154	565	90	148	31	5	24	104	77	106	.262	.352	.462	121	17	6	5	-1	.984	5	*O-145/3-2,D-6	1.5
1987	NY-A★	156	575	83	158	22	1	27	97	76	96	.275	.359	.457	116	14	5	6	-2	.989	-4	*O-145/D-8	0.7
1988	NY-A★	149	559	96	180	37	2	25	107	69	88	.322	.398	.530	159	44	9	4	0	.989	-3	*O-141/D-4	3.7
1990	NY-A	20	61	7	13	3	0	2	6	4	13	.213	.273	.361	75	-2	0	0	0	1.000	-3	O-12/D-7	-0.5
	Cal-A	112	414	63	114	18	2	19	72	48	68	.275	.352	.466	130	16	0	0	0	.989	-8	*O-108/D-3	0.7
	Yr	132	475	70	127	21	2	21	78	52	81	.267	.342	.453	122	14	0	0	0	.989	-8	*O-120,D-10	0.2
1991	Cal-A	150	568	75	149	27	4	28	86	56	109	.262	.330	.472	119	13	7	2	1	.990	-1	*O-115,D-34	0.9
1992	*Tor-A	156	583	92	169	33	3	26	108	82	89	.290	.378	.491	136	28	2	3	-1	1.000	0	*D-130,O-26	2.3
1993	Min-A	143	547	72	148	27	2	21	76	45	106	.271	.326	.442	104	2	2	3	-1	1.000	0	*D-105,O-31/1-5	-0.4
1994	Min-A	77	294	35	74	15	3	10	43	31	51	.252	.323	.425	91	-5	2	1	0	1.000	0	D-76/O-1	-0.8
1995	Cle-A	46	115	11	22	5	0	2	4	14	26	.191	.285	.287	49	-0	1	0	0	.000	0	D-39	-1.1
Total	22	2973	11003	1669	3110	540	88	465	1833	1216	1686	.283	.355	.475	130	440	223	96	9	.982	34	*O-2469,D-419/1-8,3	38.5

YEAR	TM/L	G	AB	R	H	2B	3B	HR	RBI	BB	SO	AVG	OBP	SLG	PRO+	BR/A	SB	CS	SBR	FA	FR	G/POS	TPR

■ AL WINGO Wingo, Absalom Holbrook "Red" b: 5/6/1898, Norcross, Ga. d: 10/9/64, Detroit, Mich. BL/TR, 5'11", 180 lbs. Deb: 9/9/19 F

1919	Phi-A	15	59	9	18	1	3	0	2	4	12	.305	.349	.424	115	1	0			.815	-3	O-15	-0.3
1924	Det-A	78	150	21	43	12	2	1	26	21	13	.287	.374	.413	105	1	2	5	-2	.925	-8	O-43	-1.1
1925	Det-A	130	440	104	163	34	10	5	68	69	31	.370	.456	.527	151	37	14	13	-4	.971	8	*O-122	3.1
1926	Det-A	108	298	45	84	19	0	1	45	52	32	.282	.389	.356	94	-1	4	2	0	.923	4	O-74/3-2	-0.2
1927	Det-A	75	137	15	32	8	2	0	20	25	14	.234	.352	.321	74	-5	1	0		.891	4	O-34	-0.9
1928	Det-A	87	242	30	69	13	2	2	30	40	17	.285	.389	.380	101	2	2	2	-1	.968	-3	O-71	-0.6
Total	6	493	1326	224	409	87	19	9	191	211	119	.308	.404	.423	114	36	23	22		.944	-6	O-359/3-2	-0.0

■ ED WINGO Wingo, Edmond Armand (b: Edmond Armand La Riviere)
b: 10/8/1895, St.Anne De Bellevue, Que., Canada d: 12/5/64, Lachine, Que., Can. BR/TR, 5'6", 145 lbs. Deb: 10/2/20

| 1920 | Phi-A | 1 | 4 | 0 | 1 | 0 | 0 | 0 | 1 | 0 | 0 | .250 | .250 | .250 | 32 | -0 | 0 | 0 | 0 | 1.000 | 1 | /C-1 | 0.0 |

■ IVEY WINGO Wingo, Ivey Brown b: 7/8/1890, Gainesville, Ga. d: 3/1/41, Waycross, Ga. BL/TR, 5'10", 160 lbs. Deb: 4/20/11 FMC

1911	StL-N	25	57	4	12	2	0	0	3	3	7	.211	.250	.246	40	-5	0			.916	0	C-18	-0.3
1912	StL-N	100	310	38	82	18	8	2	44	23	45	.265	.317	.394	96	-3	8			.957	4	C-92	0.9
1913	StL-N	112	307	25	78	5	8	2	35	17	41	.254	.295	.342	83	-8	18			.945	-4	C-98/1-5,O-1	-0.4
1914	StL-N	80	237	24	71	8	5	4	26	18	17	.300	.352	.426	132	9	15			.958	-3	C-70/O-4	1.2
1915	Cin-N	119	339	26	75	11	6	3	29	13	33	.221	.250	.316	69	-14	10	11	-4	.966	3	C-98/O-1	-0.8
1916	Cin-N	119	347	30	85	8	11	2	40	25	27	.245	.298	.349	100	-0	4			.958	7	*C-107,M	1.6
1917	Cin-N	121	399	37	106	16	11	2	39	25	13	.266	.311	.376	115	6	9			.967	-5	*C-120	1.2
1918	Cin-N	100	323	35	82	15	6	0	31	19	18	.254	.297	.337	95	-3	6			.973	-6	C-93/O-5	-0.1
1919	*Cin-N	76	245	30	67	12	6	0	27	23	19	.273	.336	.371	115	5	4			.969	3	C-75	1.6
1920	Cin-N	108	364	32	96	11	5	2	38	19	13	.264	.300	.338	84	-8	6	4	-1	.958	-10	*C-107/2-2	-1.2
1921	Cin-N	97	295	20	79	7	6	3	38	21	14	.268	.319	.363	84	-7	3	2	-0	.959	5	C-92/O-1	0.3
1922	Cin-N	80	260	24	74	13	3	3	45	23	11	.285	.343	.392	91	-4	1	4	-2	.964	4	C-78	0.2
1923	Cin-N	61	171	10	45	9	2	1	24	9	11	.263	.304	.357	75	-6	1	1	-0	.969	3	C-65/1-1	-0.1
1924	Cin-N	66	192	21	55	5	4	1	23	14	8	.286	.338	.370	91	-2	1	1	-0	.989	5	C-55	0.5
1925	Cin-N	55	146	6	30	7	0	0	12	11	8	.205	.261	.253	33	-15	1	2	-1	.965	-3	C-55	-0.9
1926	Cin-N	7	10	0	2	0	0	0	1	1	0	.200	.333	.200	48	-1	0			1.000	-0	/C-7	-0.1
1929	Cin-N	1	1	0	0	0	0	0	0	0	0	.000	.000	.000	-99	-0	0			.000	0	/C-1	-0.0
Total	17	1327	4003	362	1039	147	81	25	455	264	285	.260	.307	.355	91	-56	87	25		.962	11	*C-1233/O-12,1-6,2	3.6

■ GEORGE WINKELMAN Winkelman, George Edward b: 2/18/1865, Washington, D.C. d: 5/19/60, Washington, D.C. BL/TL, Deb: 8/4/1883

1883	Lou-a	4	13	2	0	0	0	0	0	0		.000	.071	.000	-81	-3	0			.625	0	/O-4	-0.2
1886	Was-N	1	5	0	1	0	0	0	0	0	1	.200	.200	.200	23	-0	0			.000	-1	/O-1,P-1	0.0
Total	2	5	18	2	1	0	0	0	0	0	1	.056	.105	.056	-51	-3	0			.625	-0	/O-5,P-1	-0.2

■ HERM WINNINGHAM Winningham, Herman Son b: 12/1/61, Orangeburg, S.C. BL/TR, 5'11", 185 lbs. Deb: 9/1/84

1984	NY-N	14	27	5	11	1	0	0	5	1	7	.407	.429	.519	167	2	2	1	0	1.000	-4	O-10	-0.2
1985	Mon-N	125	312	30	74	6	5	3	21	28	72	.237	.300	.317	77	-10	20	9	1	.983	-4	*O-116	-1.7
1986	Mon-N	90	185	23	40	6	3	4	11	18	51	.216	.286	.346	74	-7	12	7	-1	.980	-7	O-66/S-1	-1.7
1987	Mon-N	137	347	34	83	20	3	4	41	34	68	.239	.307	.349	71	-14	29	10	3	.975	-8	*O-131	-2.2
1988	Mon-N	47	90	10	21	2	1	0	6	12	18	.233	.324	.278	71	-3	4	5	-2	.982	-3	O-30	-0.9
	Cin-N	53	113	6	26	1	3	0	15	5	27	.230	.263	.292	57	-6	8	3	1	1.000	-3	O-42	-1.1
	Yr	100	203	16	47	3	4	0	21	17	45	.232	.291	.286	63	-9	12	8	-1	.992	-7	O-85	-2.0
1989	Cin-N	115	251	40	63	11	3	3	13	24	50	.251	.316	.355	88	-4	14	5	1	.980	-7	O-64	-1.1
1990	*Cin-N	84	160	20	41	8	3	1	17	14	31	.256	.316	.425	98	-1	6	4	-1	1.000	-9	O-64	-1.2
1991	Cin-N	98	169	17	38	6	1	1	4	11	40	.225	.272	.290	56	-10	4	4	-1	.953	-8	O-66	-2.1
1992	Bos-A	105	234	27	55	8	1	1	14	10	53	.235	.266	.291	52	-15	6	5	-1	.975	-4	O-67/D-6,S-1	-2.2
Total	9	868	1888	212	452	69	26	19	147	157	417	.239	.298	.334	74	-67	105	53	-0	.980	-58	O-677/D-6,S-1	-14.4

■ TOM WINSETT Winsett, John Thomas "Long Tom" b: 11/24/09, McKenzie, Tenn. d: 7/20/87, Memphis, Tenn. BL/TR, 6'2", 190 lbs. Deb: 4/20/30

1930	Bos-A	1	1	0	0	0	0	0	0	1		.000	.000	.000	-99	-0	0	0	0	.000	0	H	0.0
1931	Bos-A	64	76	6	15	1	0	1	7	4	21	.197	.247	.250	33	-8	0	0	0	1.000	-0	/O-8	-0.8
1933	Bos-A	6	12	1	1	0	0	0	1	0	6	.083	.154	.083	-36	-2	0	0	0	1.000	-2	/O-4	-0.4
1935	StL-N	7	12	2	6	1	0	0	2	2	3	.500	.571	.583	203	2	0	0	0	.000	-1	/O-2	0.1
1936	Bro-N	22	85	13	20	0	1	1	18	11	14	.235	.330	.353	83	-2	0	0	0	1.000	1	O-21	-0.1
1937	Bro-N	118	350	32	83	15	5	5	42	45	64	.237	.329	.351	84	-7	3			.960	1	*O-101/P-1	-0.9
1938	Bro-N	12	30	6	9	1	0	1	7	6	4	.300	.417	.433	131	2	0			.882	-2	O-9	0.0
Total	7	230	566	60	134	25	5	8	76	69	113	.237	.325	.341	79	-16	3	0		.963	-2	O-145/P-1	-2.1

■ MATT WINTERS Winters, Matthew Littleton b: 3/18/60, Buffalo, N.Y. BL/TR, 6'3", 215 lbs. Deb: 5/30/89

| 1989 | KC-A | 42 | 107 | 14 | 25 | 6 | 0 | 2 | 9 | 14 | 23 | .234 | .322 | .346 | 89 | -1 | 0 | 0 | 0 | .939 | -4 | O-31/D-3 | -0.6 |

■ KETTLE WIRTS Wirts, Elwood Vernon b: 10/31/1897, Consumne, Cal. d: 7/12/68, Sacramento, Cal. BR/TR, 5'11", 170 lbs. Deb: 7/20/21

1921	Chi-N	7	11	0	2	0	0	0	1	0	3	.182	.182	.182	-3	-2	0	0	0	1.000	1	/C-5	-0.1
1922	Chi-N	31	58	7	10	2	0	1	6	12	15	.172	.314	.259	48	-4	0	0	0	.968	-5	C-27	-0.8
1923	Chi-N	5	5	2	1	0	0	0	1	2	0	.200	.429	.200	71	-0	0	0	0	1.000	1	/C-3	0.1
1924	Chi-A	6	12	0	1	0	0	0	0	2	2	.083	.214	.083	-22	-2	1	0	0	1.000	1	/C-5	-0.1
Total	4	49	86	9	14	2	0	2	8	16	20	.163	.294	.221	35	-8	1	0	0	.981	-3	/C-40	-0.9

■ HUGHIE WISE Wise, Hugh Edward b: 3/9/06, Campbellsville, Ky. d: 7/21/87, Plantation, Fla. BB/TR, 6', 178 lbs. Deb: 9/26/30

| 1930 | Det-A | 2 | 6 | 0 | 2 | 0 | 0 | 0 | 0 | 0 | 0 | .333 | .333 | .333 | 68 | -0 | 0 | 0 | 0 | 1.000 | 1 | /C-2 | 0.1 |

■ CASEY WISE Wise, Kendall Cole b: 9/8/32, Lafayette, Ind. BB/TR, 6', 170 lbs. Deb: 4/16/57

1957	Chi-N	43	106	12	19	3	1	0	7	11	14	.179	.256	.226	32	-10	0	0	0	.940	3	2-31/S-5	-0.5
1958	*Mil-N	31	71	8	14	1	0	0	4	4	8	.197	.240	.211	23	-8	1	1	-0	1.000	3	2-10/S-7,3-1	-0.7
1959	Mil-N	22	76	11	13	2	0	1	5	10	5	.171	.267	.237	39	-7	0	0	0	.989	-4	2-20/S-5	-1.3
1960	Det-A	30	68	6	10	0	2	2	5	4	9	.147	.194	.294	29	-7	1	0	0	.983	-4	2-17,S-10/3-1	-0.3
Total	4	126	321	37	56	6	3	3	17	29	36	.174	.243	.240	31	-32	2	1	0	.968	-2	/2-78,S-27,3-2	-2.8

■ NICK WISE Wise, Nicholas Joseph b: 6/15/1866, Boston, Mass. d: 1/15/23, Boston, Mass. BR/TR, 5'11", 194 lbs. Deb: 6/20/1888

| 1888 | Bos-N | 1 | 3 | 0 | 0 | 0 | 0 | 0 | 0 | 0 | | .000 | .000 | .000 | -98 | -0 | 0 | | | .000 | -0 | /O-1,C-1 | -0.1 |

■ SAM WISE Wise, Samuel Washington "Modoc" b: 8/18/1857, Akron, Ohio d: 1/22/10, Akron, Ohio BL/TR, 5'10.5", 170 lbs. Deb: 7/30/1881

1881	Det-N	1	4	0	2	0	0	0	0	2		.500	.500	.500	207	0				.571	-0	/3-1	0.0
1882	Bos-N	78	298	44	66	11	4	4	34	5	45	.221	.234	.326	105	-7				.852	-13	*S-72/3-6	-1.5
1883	Bos-N	96	406	73	110	25	7	4	58	13	74	.271	.294	.397	105	2				.823	-2	*S-96	0.1
1884	Bos-N	114	426	60	91	15	9	4	41	25	104	.214	.257	.319	81	-9				.884	8	*S-107/2-7	-0.2
1885	Bos-N	107	424	71	120	20	10	4	46	25	61	.283	.323	.406	139	18				.858	13	*S-79,2-22/O-6	3.1
1886	Bos-N	96	387	71	112	19	12	4	72	33	61	.289	.345	.432	140	19	31			.956	-24	1-57,2-20,S-18/O-1	-1.0
1887	Bos-N	113	467	103	156	27	17	9	92	36	44	.334	.390	.522	151	32	43			.869	-6	S-72,O-27,2-16	2.2
1888	Bos-N	105	417	66	100	19	12	4	40	34	66	.240	.306	.372	113	6	33			.888	10	S-89/3-6,1-5,O-4,2	1.7
1889	Was-N	121	472	79	118	15	8	4	62	61	62	.250	.341	.341	97	-0	24			.916	-23	2-72,S-26,3-13,O-10	-1.6
1890	Buf-P	119	505	95	148	29	11	6	102	46	45	.293	.359	.430	120	14	14			.906	5	*2-119	2.1
1891	Bal-a	103	388	70	96	14	5	1	48	62	52	.247	.364	.317	94	-1	33			.888	-13	*2-99/S-4	-0.8
1893	Was-N	122	521	102	162	27	17	5	77	49	27	.311	.375	.457	124	16	20			.924	14	*2-91,3-31	2.7
Total	12	1175	4715	834	1281	221	112	49	672	389	643	.272	.332	.397	115	90	203			.859	-33	S-563,2-448/3,1,O	6.8

■ PHIL WISNER Wisner, Philip N. b: 7/1869, Washington, D.C. d: 7/5/36, Washington, D.C. TR Deb: 8/30/1895

| 1895 | Was-N | 1 | 0 | 0 | 0 | 0 | 0 | 0 | 0 | 0 | 0 | — | — | — | | | 0 | | | .250 | -1 | /S-1 | 0.0 |

YEAR	TM/L	G	AB	R	H	2B	3B	HR	RBI	BB	SO	AVG	OBP	SLG	PRO+	BR/A	SB	CS	SBR	FA	FR	G/POS	TPR

■ DAVE WISSMAN   Wissman, David Alvin   b: 2/17/41, Greenfield, Mass.   BL/TR, 6'2", 178 lbs.   Deb: 9/15/64

| 1964 | Pit-N | 16 | 27 | 2 | 4 | 0 | 0 | 0 | 1 | 9 | | .148 | .179 | .148 | -7 | -4 | 0 | 0 | 0 | 1.000 | -1 | O-10 | -0.6 |

■ TEX WISTERZIL   Wisterzil, George John   b: 3/7/1891, Detroit, Mich.   d: 6/27/64, San Antonio, Tex.   BR/TR, 5'9.5", 150 lbs.   Deb: 4/14/14

1914	Bro-F	149	534	54	137	18	10	0	66	34	47	.257	.314	.328	76	-27	17			.956	16	*3-149	-0.6
1915	Bro-F	36	106	13	33	3	3	0	21	21	7	.311	.438	.396	137	5	8			.949	3	3-31	1.0
	Chi-F	7	20	3	4	1	0	0	3	2		.200	.304	.250	60	-1	0			.955	0	/3-6	-0.1
	StL-F	8	24	1	5	1	0	0	4	2	2	.208	.296	.250	52	-2	2			.939	2	/3-8	0.1
	Chi-F	42	144	12	36	3	1	0	14	5	10	.250	.280	.285	63	-10	2			.968	3	3-42	0.0
	Yr	93	294	29	78	8	4	0	39	31	21	.265	.345	.320	90	-7	12			.958	8	3-87	1.0
Total	2	242	828	83	215	26	14	0	105	65	68	.260	.326	.325	81	-34	29			.957	29	3-236	0.4

■ MICKEY WITEK   Witek, Nicholas Joseph   b: 12/19/15, Luzerne, Pa.   d: 8/24/90, Kingston, Pa.   BR/TR, 5'10", 170 lbs.   Deb: 4/16/40

1940	NY-N	119	433	34	111	7	0	3	31	24	17	.256	.295	.293	62	-22	2			.958	19	S-89,2-32	0.7
1941	NY-N	26	94	11	34	5	0	1	16	4	2	.362	.388	.447	132	4	0			.933	2	2-23	0.7
1942	NY-N	148	553	72	144	19	6	5	48	36	20	.260	.306	.344	89	-9	2			.978	-1	*2-147	0.0
1943	NY-N	153	622	68	195	17	6	6	55	41	23	.314	.356	.370	109	7	1			.967	16	*2-153	3.3
1946	NY-N	82	284	32	75	13	2	4	29	28	10	.264	.330	.366	97	-1	1			.962	-12	2-42,3-35	-1.1
1947	NY-N	51	160	22	35	4	1	3	17	15	12	.219	.286	.313	58	-10	1			.983	11	2-40/3-3	0.4
1949	NY-A	1	1	0	1	0	0	0	0	0	0	1.000	1.000	1.000	430	0	0	0	0	.000	0	H	0.0
Total	7	580	2147	239	595	65	9	22	196	148	84	.277	.324	.347	90	-30	7	0		.969	34	2-437/S-89,3-38	4.0

■ FRANK WITHROW   Withrow, Frank Blaine "Kid"   b: 6/14/1891, Greenwood, Mo.   d: 9/5/66, Omaha, Neb.   BR/TR, 5'11.5", 187 lbs.   Deb: 4/15/20

1920	Phi-N	48	132	8	24	4	1	0	12	8	26	.182	.239	.227	33	-11	0	0	0	.973	-1	C-48	-0.5
1922	Phi-N	10	21	3	7	2	0	0	3	3	5	.333	.417	.429	108	0	0	0	0	.909	0	/C-8	0.2
Total	2	58	153	11	31	6	1	0	15	11	31	.203	.265	.255	45	-11	0	0	0	.965	1	/C-56	-0.3

■ CORKY WITHROW   Withrow, Raymond Wallace   b: 11/28/37, High Coal, W.Va.   BR/TR, 6'3.5", 197 lbs.   Deb: 9/6/63

| 1963 | StL-N | 6 | 9 | 0 | 0 | 0 | 0 | 0 | 1 | 0 | 2 | .000 | .000 | .000 | -91 | -2 | 0 | 0 | 0 | 1.000 | -0 | /O-2 | -0.3 |

■ RON WITMEYER   Witmeyer, Ronald Herman   b: 6/28/67, West Islip, N.Y.   BL/TL, 6'3", 215 lbs.   Deb: 8/25/91

| 1991 | Oak-A | 11 | 19 | 0 | 1 | 0 | 0 | 0 | 0 | 0 | 5 | .053 | .053 | .053 | -75 | -4 | 0 | 0 | 0 | 1.000 | 0 | /1-8 | -0.5 |

■ WHITEY WITT   Witt, Lawton Walter (b: Ladislaw Waldemar Wittkowski)   b: 9/28/1895, Orange, Mass.   d: 7/14/88, Salem Co., N.J.   BL/TR, 5'7", 150 lbs.   Deb: 4/12/16

1916	Phi-A	143	563	64	138	16	15	2	36	55	71	.245	.315	.337	101	-1	19			.902	-1	*S-142	0.6
1917	Phi-A	128	452	62	114	13	4	0	28	45	45	.252	.346	.299	98	1	12			.935	5	*S-111/O-7,3-6	1.2
1919	Phi-A	122	460	56	123	15	6	0	33	46	26	.267	.334	.326	85	-9	11			.972	-3	O-59,2-56/3-2	-1.3
1920	Phi-A	65	218	29	70	11	3	1	25	27	16	.321	.396	.413	113	5	2	3	-1	.960	-3	O-50,2-10/S-2	-0.8
1921	Phi-A	154	629	100	198	31	11	4	45	77	52	.315	.390	.418	106	7	16	15	-4	.959	-2	*O-154	-1.0
1922	*NY-A	140	528	98	157	11	6	4	40	89	29	.297	.400	.364	98	3	5	8	-3	.976	-5	*O-139	-1.5
1923	*NY-A	146	596	113	187	18	10	6	56	67	42	.314	.386	.408	107	8	2	7	-4	.979	4	*O-144	-0.3
1924	NY-A	147	600	88	178	26	5	1	36	45	20	.297	.346	.362	83	-15	9	7	-2	.976	-1	*O-144	-2.6
1925	NY-A	31	40	9	8	2	1	0	6	2		.200	.304	.300	55	-3	1	1	-0	1.000	-1	O-10	-0.4
1926	Bro-N	63	85	13	22	1	1	0	3	12	6	.259	.351	.294	76	-2	1			.920	-2	O-22	-0.5
Total	10	1139	4171	632	1195	144	62	18	302	489	309	.287	.362	.364	97	-6	78	41		.971	-16	O-729,S-255/2-66,3	-6.6

■ JERRY WITTE   Witte, Jerome Charles   b: 7/30/15, St.Louis, Mo.   BR/TR, 6'1", 190 lbs.   Deb: 9/10/46

1946	StL-A	18	73	7	14	2	0	2	4	0	18	.192	.192	.301	35	-7	0	0	0	.967	-2	1-18	-1.1
1947	StL-A	34	99	4	14	2	1	2	12	11	22	.141	.227	.242	30	-10	0	0	0	.983	-1	1-27	-1.3
Total	2	52	172	11	28	4	1	4	16	11	40	.163	.213	.267	32	-16	0	0	0	.977	-4	/1-45	-2.4

■ JOHN WOCKENFUSS   Wockenfuss, Johnny Bilton   b: 2/27/49, Welch, W.Va.   BR/TR, 6', 190 lbs.   Deb: 8/11/74

1974	Det-A	13	29	1	4	1	0	0	2	3	2	.138	.219	.172	13	-3	0	0		.932	-1	C-13	-0.4
1975	Det-A	35	118	15	27	6	3	4	13	10	15	.229	.289	.432	97	-1	0	0		.982	-4	C-34	0.4
1976	Det-A	60	144	18	32	7	2	3	10	17	14	.222	.309	.361	92	-1	0	3	-2	.941	-7	C-59	-1.0
1977	Det-A	53	164	26	45	8	1	9	25	14	18	.274	.331	.500	117	3	0	0		.985	-7	C-37/O-9,D-3	-0.2
1978	Det-A	71	187	23	53	5	0	7	22	21	14	.283	.359	.422	116	4	0	1	-1	.978	-8	O-60/D-2	-0.6
1979	Det-A	87	231	27	61	9	1	15	46	18	40	.264	.323	.506	116	4	2	2	-1	.996	5	1-31,C-20,D-18,/O-6	0.2
1980	Det-A	126	372	56	102	13	2	16	65	60	64	.274	.391	.449	126	16	1	4	-2	.983	-6	1-52,C-28,C-25,O-23	1.1
1981	Det-A	70	172	20	37	4	0	9	25	28	22	.215	.325	.395	103	1	0	0		.984	-3	D-39,1-25/C-5,0-1	-0.5
1982	Det-A	70	193	28	58	9	0	8	32	29	21	.301	.392	.472	135	10	0	0		.981	-3	C-24,1-17,D-17,O/3	0.6
1983	Det-A	92	245	32	66	8	1	9	44	31	37	.269	.351	.420	114	5	1	-0		1.000	4	D-39,C-29,1-13,/3O	0.8
1984	Phi-N	86	180	20	52	3	1	6	24	30	24	.289	.390	.417	125	7	1	0	0	.996	-1	1-39,C-21/3-2	0.2
1985	Phi-N	32	37	1	6	0	0	0	2	8	7	.162	.311	.162	35	-3	0	0	0	1.000	-1	/1-7,C-2	-0.5
Total	12	795	2072	267	543	73	11	86	310	277	278	.262	.351	.432	114	42	5	11	-5	.972	-27	C-269,1-184,DO/3	-0.1

■ ANDY WOEHR   Woehr, Andrew Emil   b: 2/4/1896, Fort Wayne, Ind.   d: 7/24/90, Fort Wayne, Ind.   BR/TR, 5'11", 165 lbs.   Deb: 9/15/23

1923	Phi-N	13	41	3	14	2	0	0	3	1	1	.341	.357	.390	87	-1	0	0	0	.975	3	3-13	0.3
1924	Phi-N	50	152	11	33	4	5	0	17	5	8	.217	.252	.309	44	-12	2	2	-1	.920	-5	3-44/2-1	-1.5
Total	2	63	193	14	47	6	5	0	20	6	9	.244	.274	.326	53	-13	2	2	-1	.935	-2	/3-57,2-1	-1.2

■ JOE WOERLIN   Woerlin, Joseph   b: 10/9/1864, France   d: 6/22/19, St.Louis, Mo.   Deb: 7/21/1895

| 1895 | Was-N | 1 | 3 | 1 | 1 | 0 | 0 | 0 | 0 | 0 | 0 | .333 | .333 | .333 | 73 | -0 | 0 | | | 1.000 | -1 | /S-1 | 0.0 |

■ JIM WOHLFORD   Wohlford, James Eugene   b: 2/28/51, Visalia, Cal.   BR/TR, 5'11", 175 lbs.   Deb: 9/1/72

1972	KC-A	15	25	3	6	1	0	0	2	6	2	.240	.321	.280	80	-1	0	0	0	.950	-2	/2-8	-0.3
1973	KC-A	45	109	21	29	1	3	2	10	11	12	.266	.333	.385	95	-1	0	0		1.000	3	D-19,O-13	0.1
1974	KC-A	143	501	55	136	16	7	2	44	39	74	.271	.328	.343	88	-7	16	13	-3	.982	1	*O-138/D-1	-1.6
1975	KC-A	116	353	45	90	10	5	0	34	34	37	.255	.322	.312	78	-10	12	7	-1	.953	-6	*O-102/D-4	-2.0
1976	*KC-A	107	293	47	73	10	2	0	24	29	24	.249	.319	.307	83	-6	22	16	-3	.975	-1	O-93/2-1,D-3	-1.3
1977	Mil-A	129	391	41	97	16	3	2	36	21	49	.248	.288	.320	65	-19	17	16	-5	.981	-2	*O-125/2-1,D-1	-2.9
1978	Mil-A	46	118	16	35	7	2	1	19	6	10	.297	.331	.415	108	1	3	2	-0	.982	-5	O-35/D-4	-0.5
1979	Mil-A	63	175	19	46	13	1	1	17	8	28	.263	.295	.366	77	-6	6	2	-1	.969	-2	O-55/D-5	-0.9
1980	SF-N	91	193	17	54	6	4	1	24	13	23	.280	.329	.368	96	-1	1	4	-2	.989	-2	O-49/3-1	-0.7
1981	SF-N	50	68	4	11	3	0	1	3	9	7	.162	.258	.250	30	-3	0	0	0	1.000	-3	O-10	-1.0
1982	SF-N	97	250	37	64	12	1	2	25	30	36	.256	.336	.336	97	-0	3	1	-0	.992	-2	O-72	-0.6
1983	Mon-N	83	141	7	39	8	0	1	14	5	14	.277	.301	.355	82	-4	0	3	-1	.988	-11	O-61	-1.6
1984	Mon-N	95	213	20	64	13	2	5	29	14	27	.300	.344	.451	127	7	0	0		.989	-2	O-59/3-2	0.4
1985	Mon-N	70	125	7	24	5	1	0	15	16	18	.192	.284	.272	60	-7	0	2	-1	1.000	-5	O-43	-1.4
1986	Mon-N	70	94	10	25	4	2	1	11	9	15	.266	.330	.383	97	-0	0	1	-0	1.000	-5	O-22/3-6	-0.5
Total	15	1220	3049	349	793	125	33	21	305	241	376	.260	.316	.343	85	-62	89	68	-14	.980	-41	O-877/D-37,2-10,3-9	-14.8

■ JOHN WOJCIK   Wojcik, John Joseph   b: 4/6/42, Olean, N.Y.   BL/TR, 6' ", 175 lbs.   Deb: 9/9/62

1962	KC-A	16	43	8	13	0	0	0	9	13	4	.302	.474	.395	131	3	3	0		1.000	-1	O-12	0.2
1963	KC-A	19	59	7	11	0	0	0	2	5	5	.186	.284	.186	33	-5	2	0		1.000	0	O-17	-0.5
1964	KC-A	6	22	1	3	0	0	0	0	1	0	.136	.208	.136	-2	-3	0	0	0	1.000	-0	/O-6	-0.4
Total	3	41	124	16	27	0	0	0	11	19	9	.218	.345	.250	64	-5	5	0	0	1.000	-1	/O-35	-0.7

■ RAY WOLF   Wolf, Raymond Bernard "Grandpa"   b: 7/15/04, Chicago, Ill.   d: 10/6/79, Fort Worth, Tex.   BR/TR, 5'11", 175 lbs.   Deb: 7/27/27

| 1927 | Cin-N | 1 | 1 | 0 | 0 | 0 | 0 | 0 | 0 | 0 | 0 | .000 | .000 | .000 | -99 | -0 | 0 | | | 1.000 | -0 | /1-1 | 0.0 |

YEAR	TM/L	G	AB	R	H	2B	3B	HR	RBI	BB	SO	AVG	OBP	SLG	PRO+	BR/A	SB	CS	SBR	FA	FR	G/POS	TPR

■ JIMMY WOLF
Wolf, William Van Winkle "Chicken" b: 5/12/1862, Louisville, Ky. d: 5/16/03, Louisville, Ky. BR/TR, 5'9", 190 lbs. Deb: 5/2/1882 M

YEAR	TM/L	G	AB	R	H	2B	3B	HR	RBI	BB	SO	AVG	OBP	SLG	PRO+	BR/A	SB	CS	SBR	FA	FR	G/POS	TPR
1882	Lou-a	78	318	46	95	11	8	0		9		.299	.318	.384	144	14				.902	-2	*O-70/S-9,1-1,P-1	1.1
1883	Lou-a	98	389	59	102	17	9	1		5		.262	.272	.360	110	4				.890	17	*O-78,C-20/S-5,2-1	1.9
1884	Lou-a	110	486	79	146	24	11	3	73	4		.300	.310	.414	140	20				.884	0	*O-101,C-11/S-1,31	1.7
1885	Lou-a	112	483	79	141	23	17	1	52	11		.292	.309	.416	128	13				.917	-0	*O-111/C-2,3-1,P-1	0.9
1886	Lou-a	130	545	93	148	17	12	3	61	27		.272	.310	.363	105	-0	23			.934	9	*O-122/1-8,C-3,2P	0.5
1887	Lou-a	137	569	103	160	27	13	2	102	34		.281	.331	.385	97	-4	45			.940	8	*O-128,1-11	0.5
1888	Lou-a	128	538	80	154	28	11	0	67	25		.286	.320	.379	126	15	41			.886	7	O-85,S-39/3-4,C1	1.8
1889	Lou-a	130	546	72	159	20	9	3	57	29	34	.291	.333	.377	104	2	18			.946	-1	O-88,1-16,2S/3M	-0.1
1890	*Lou-a	134	543	100	**197**	29	11	4	98	43		**.363**	.421	.479	169	46	46			.939	-2	*O-123,3-12	3.6
1891	Lou-a	138	537	67	136	17	8	1	82	42	36	.253	.317	.320	83	-12	13			.918	5	*O-133/1-5,3-1	-1.0
1892	StL-N	3	14	1	2	0	0	0	1	0	1	.143	.143	.143	-14	-2	0			1.000	-1	/O-3	-0.3
Total	11	1198	4968	779	1440	213	109	18	593	229	71	.290	.327	.387	118	97	186			.918	41	*O-1042/S-64,1C32P	10.2

■ HARRY WOLFE
Wolfe, Harold "Whitey" b: 11/24/1890, Massachusetts d: 7/28/71, Fort Wayne, Ind. BR/TR, 5'8", 160 lbs. Deb: 4/15/17

YEAR	TM/L	G	AB	R	H	2B	3B	HR	RBI	BB	SO	AVG	OBP	SLG	PRO+	BR/A	SB	CS	SBR	FA	FR	G/POS	TPR
1917	Chi-N	9	5	1	2	0	0	0	1	1	1	.400	.500	.400	164	0	0			1.000	0	/O-2,S-1	0.0
	Pit-N	3	5	0	0	0	0	0	0	1	4	.000	.167	.000	-45	-1	0			.875	1	/2-1,S-1	0.0
	Yr	12	10	1	2	0	0	0	1	2	5	.200	.333	.200	61	-0	0			1.000	1	/O-2,S-2,2-1	0.1

■ LARRY WOLFE
Wolfe, Laurence Marcy b: 3/2/53, Melbourne, Fla. BR/TR, 5'11", 170 lbs. Deb: 9/16/77

YEAR	TM/L	G	AB	R	H	2B	3B	HR	RBI	BB	SO	AVG	OBP	SLG	PRO+	BR/A	SB	CS	SBR	FA	FR	G/POS	TPR
1977	Min-A	8	25	3	6	1	0	1	1	0		.240	.269	.280	51	-2	0	0	0	1.000	0	/3-8	-0.2
1978	Min-A	88	235	25	55	10	1	3	25	36	27	.234	.336	.323	85	-4	0	1	-1	.953	6	3-81/S-7	0.8
1979	Bos-A	47	78	12	19	4	0	3	15	17	21	.244	.385	.410	109	1	0	0	0	.963	6	2-27/3-9,S-2,C1D	0.8
1980	Bos-A	18	23	3	3	0	0	0	4	0	5	.130	.130	.304	15	-3	0	0	0	1.000	1	3-14/D-4	-0.2
Total	4	161	361	43	83	16	1	7	50	54	53	.230	.332	.338	84	-7	0	1	-1	.957	13	3-112/2-27,S-9,D1C	0.5

■ POLLY WOLFE
Wolfe, Roy Chamberlain b: 9/1/1888, Knoxville, Ill. d: 11/21/38, Morris, Ill. BL/TR, 5'10", 170 lbs. Deb: 9/22/12

YEAR	TM/L	G	AB	R	H	2B	3B	HR	RBI	BB	SO	AVG	OBP	SLG	PRO+	BR/A	SB	CS	SBR	FA	FR	G/POS	TPR
1912	Chi-A	1	1	0	0	0	0	0	0	0	0	.000	.000	.000	-99	-0	0			.000	0	H	0.0
1914	Chi-A	8	28	0	6	0	0	0		3	6	.214	.290	.214	53	-2	1	1	-0	.875	-1	/O-7	-0.4
Total	2	9	29	0	6	0	0	0		3	6	.207	.281	.207	47	-2	1	1		.875	-1	/O-7	-0.4

■ ABE WOLSTENHOLME
Wolstenholme, Abraham Lincoln b: 3/4/1861, Philadelphia, Pa. d: 3/4/16, Philadelphia, Pa. Deb: 6/4/1883

YEAR	TM/L	G	AB	R	H	2B	3B	HR	RBI	BB	SO	AVG	OBP	SLG	PRO+	BR/A	SB	CS	SBR	FA	FR	G/POS	TPR
1883	Phi-N	3	11	0	1	1	0	0	0	0	0	.091	.091	.182	-22	-3				.727	-3	/C-2,O-1	-0.4

■ HARRY WOLTER
Wolter, Harry Meigs b: 7/11/1884, Monterey, Cal. d: 7/7/70, Palo Alto, Cal. BL/TL, 5'10", 175 lbs. Deb: 5/14/07

YEAR	TM/L	G	AB	R	H	2B	3B	HR	RBI	BB	SO	AVG	OBP	SLG	PRO+	BR/A	SB	CS	SBR	FA	FR	G/POS	TPR
1907	Cin-N	4	15	1	2	0	0	0	1	0		.133	.133	.133	-16	-2	0			1.000	-0	/O-4	-0.3
	Pit-N	1	1	0	0	0	0	0	0	0		.000	.000	.000	-99	-0	0			.000	-0	/P-1	0.0
	StL-N	16	47	4	16	0	0	0	6	3		.340	.380	.340	130	3	2			.962	3	O-12/P-3	0.5
	Yr	21	63	5	18	0	0	0	7	3		.286	.318	.286	91	-1	1			.969	3	O-16/P-4	0.2
1909	Bos-A	54	121	14	29	2	4	2	10	9		.240	.292	.372	107	1	2			.978	-1	1-17,P-11/O-9	0.0
1910	NY-A	135	479	84	128	15	9	4	42	66		.267	.364	.361	120	13	39			.940	-3	*O-129/1-2	0.4
1911	NY-A	122	434	78	132	17	15	4	36	62		.304	.396	.440	125	15	28			.951	4	*O-113/1-2	1.3
1912	NY-A	12	32	8	11	2	1	0	1	10		.344	.512	.469	171	4	5			.923	-1	/O-9	0.2
1913	NY-A	127	425	53	108	18	6	2	43	80	50	.254	.377	.339	109	9	13			.946	-7	*O-121	-0.5
1917	Chi-N	117	353	44	88	15	7	0	28	38	40	.249	.324	.331	94	-2	7			.942	-4	O-97/1-1	-1.2
Total	7	588	1907	286	514	69	42	12	167	268	90	.270	.365	.369	114	39	95			.941	-10	O-494/1-22,P-15	0.4

■ HARRY WOLVERTON
Wolverton, Harry Sterling "Fighting Harry"
b: 12/6/1873, Mt.Vernon, Ohio d: 2/4/37, Oakland, Cal. BL/TR, 5'11", 205 lbs. Deb: 9/25/1898 M

YEAR	TM/L	G	AB	R	H	2B	3B	HR	RBI	BB	SO	AVG	OBP	SLG	PRO+	BR/A	SB	CS	SBR	FA	FR	G/POS	TPR
1898	Chi-N	13	49	4	16	1	0	0	2	1		.327	.353	.347	101	0	1			.848	3	3-13	0.3
1899	Chi-N	99	389	50	111	14	11	1	49	30		.285	.350	.386	105	-6	2	14		.860	-6	3-98/S-1	-0.2
1900	Chi-N	3	11	2	2	0	0	0	0	2		.182	.308	.182	38	-1	1			.875	-2	/3-3	-0.2
	Phi-N	101	383	42	108	10	8	3	58	20		.282	.323	.373	92	-5	4			.881	-9	*3-101	-1.3
	Yr	104	394	44	110	10	8	3	58	22		.279	.322	.368	91	-6	5			.881	-11	*3-104	-1.5
1901	Phi-N	93	379	42	117	15	4	0	43	22		.309	.356	.369	108	4	13			**.921**	3	3-93	0.8
1902	Was-A	59	249	35	62	8	3	1	23	13		.249	.292	.317	68	-11	3			.904	3	3-59	-0.7
	Phi-N	34	136	12	40	8	3	2	16	9		.294	.347	.346	114	2	3			.931	9	3-34	1.2
1903	Phi-N	123	494	72	152	13	12	0	53	18		.308	.342	.383	110	5	10			**.941**	1	*3-123	0.7
1904	Phi-N	102	398	43	106	15	5	0	49	26		.266	.321	.329	105	2	4			.925	1	*3-102	0.7
1905	Bos-N	122	463	38	104	15	7	0	55	23		.225	.276	.300	73	-16	10			.934	4	*3-122	-0.8
1912	NY-A	34	50	6	15	1	1	0	4	2		.300	.340	.360	94	-0	1			.821	-1	/3-8,M	-0.1
Total	9	783	3001	346	833	95	53	7	352	166		.278	.326	.352	96	-17	83			.909	6	3-756/S-1	0.4

■ TONY WOMACK
Womack, Anthony Darrell b: 9/25/69, Chatham, Va. BL/TR, 5'9", 160 lbs. Deb: 9/10/93

YEAR	TM/L	G	AB	R	H	2B	3B	HR	RBI	BB	SO	AVG	OBP	SLG	PRO+	BR/A	SB	CS	SBR	FA	FR	G/POS	TPR
1993	Pit-N	15	24	5	2	0	0	0	0	3	3	.083	.185	.083	-25	-4	2	0	1	.971	5	/S-6	0.2
1994	Pit-N	5	12	4	4	0	0	0	1	2	3	.333	.429	.333	101	0	0	0	0	.750	-3	/2-3,S-2	-0.3
1996	Pit-N	17	30	11	10	3	1	0	5	6	1	.333	.459	.500	148	3	2	0	1	1.000	-4	/O-6,2-4	-0.1
Total	3	37	66	20	16	3	1	0	6	8	7	.242	.359	.318	80	-2	4	0	1	.973	-2	/S-8,2-7,O-6	-0.2

■ SID WOMACK
Womack, Sidney Kirk "Tex" b: 10/2/1896, Greensburg, La. d: 8/28/58, Jackson, Miss. BR/TR, 5'10.5", 185 lbs. Deb: 8/15/26

YEAR	TM/L	G	AB	R	H	2B	3B	HR	RBI	BB	SO	AVG	OBP	SLG	PRO+	BR/A	SB	CS	SBR	FA	FR	G/POS	TPR
1926	Bos-N	1	3	0	0	0	0	0	0	0	0	.000	.000	.000	-99	-1	0			1.000	0	/C-1	-0.1

■ WOOD
Wood Deb: 9/30/1874

YEAR	TM/L	G	AB	R	H	2B	3B	HR	RBI	BB	SO	AVG	OBP	SLG	PRO+	BR/A	SB	CS	SBR	FA	FR	G/POS	TPR
1874	Bal-n	1	5	0	0	0	0	0	0	0	1	.000	.000	.000	-99	-1	0	0	0	.000	-2	/2-1	-0.3

■ DOC WOOD
Wood, Charles Spencer b: 2/28/1900, Batesville, Miss. d: 11/3/74, New Orleans, La. BR/TR, 5'10", 150 lbs. Deb: 7/21/23

YEAR	TM/L	G	AB	R	H	2B	3B	HR	RBI	BB	SO	AVG	OBP	SLG	PRO+	BR/A	SB	CS	SBR	FA	FR	G/POS	TPR
1923	Phi-A	3	3	0	1	0	0	0	0	0	0	.333	.333	.333	75	-0	0	0	0	.833	1	/S-3	0.1

■ TED WOOD
Wood, Edward Robert b: 1/4/67, Mansfield, Ohio BL/TL, 6'2", 178 lbs. Deb: 9/4/91

YEAR	TM/L	G	AB	R	H	2B	3B	HR	RBI	BB	SO	AVG	OBP	SLG	PRO+	BR/A	SB	CS	SBR	FA	FR	G/POS	TPR
1991	SF-N	10	25	0	3	0	0	0	1	2	11	.120	.185	.120	-13	-4	0	0	0	.909	-1	/O-8	-0.6
1992	SF-N	24	58	5	12	2	0	1	3	6	15	.207	.292	.293	70	-2	0	0	0	.972	1	O-16	-0.2
1993	Mon-N	13	26	4	5	1	0	0	3	3	3	.192	.276	.231	36	-2	0	0	0	1.000	-0	/O-8	-0.3
Total	3	47	109	9	20	3	0	1	7	11	29	.183	.264	.239	42	-8	0	0	0	.968	-1	/O-32	-1.1

■ FRED WOOD
Wood, Fred S. b: 1863, Hamilton, Ont., Canada d: 8/23/33, New York, N.Y. 5'5", 150 lbs. Deb: 5/14/1884 F

YEAR	TM/L	G	AB	R	H	2B	3B	HR	RBI	BB	SO	AVG	OBP	SLG	PRO+	BR/A	SB	CS	SBR	FA	FR	G/POS	TPR
1884	Det-N	12	42	4	2	0	0	0	1	3	18	.048	.111	.048	-51	-7				.889	-1	/C-7,O-6,S-1	-0.7
1885	Buf-N	1	4	0	1	0	0	0	0	0		.250	.250	.250	60	-0				.833	-0	/C-1	0.0
Total	2	13	46	4	3	0	0	0	1	3	18	.065	.122	.065	-41	-7				.883	-1	/C-8,O-6,S-1	-0.7

■ GEORGE WOOD
Wood, George A. "Dandy" b: 11/9/1858, Boston, Mass. d: 4/4/24, Harrisburg, Pa. BL/TR, 5'10.5", 175 lbs. Deb: 5/1/1880 MU

YEAR	TM/L	G	AB	R	H	2B	3B	HR	RBI	BB	SO	AVG	OBP	SLG	PRO+	BR/A	SB	CS	SBR	FA	FR	G/POS	TPR
1880	Wor-N	81	327	37	80	16	5	0	28	10	37	.245	.267	.324	91	-4				.887	-7	*O-80/3-2,1-1	-1.3
1881	Det-N	80	337	54	100	18	9	2	19	32		.297	.334	.421	131	11				.862	9	*O-80	0.7
1882	Det-N	84	375	69	101	12	12	**7**	29	14	30	.269	.296	.421	127	11				.884	2	*O-84	1.2
1883	Det-N	99	441	81	133	26	11	5	47	25		.302	.339	.444	142	23				.876	9	*O-99/P-1	2.6
1884	Det-N	114	473	79	119	16	10	8	29	39	75	.252	.309	.378	122	13				.896	3	*O-114/3-1	1.3
1885	Det-N	82	362	62	105	19	8	5	28	13	19	.290	.315	.428	138	14				.885	0	O-70,3-12/S-1,P-1	1.2
1886	Phi-N	106	450	81	123	18	15	4	50	23	75	.273	.349	.407	115	7	9			.904	-5	*O-97/S-6,3-3	0.0
1887	Phi-N	113	491	118	142	22	19	14	66	40	51	.289	.350	.497	125	14	19			.873	-10	*O-104/S-3,3-3,2-3	-0.3
1888	Phi-N	106	433	67	99	19	6	6	51	39	44	.229	.303	.342	100	0	20			.905	4	*O-104/3-2,P-2	-0.3
1889	Phi-N	97	422	77	106	21	4	5	53	53	33	.251	.336	.355	86	-9	17			.915	-4	*O-104/S-6,P-1	-1.3
	Bal-a	3	10	1	2	0	0	0	1	0		.200	.200	.200	14	-1	1			1.000	-0	/O-3	-0.1
1890	Phi-P	132	539	115	156	20	14	9	102	51	35	.289	.360	.429	108	4	20			.895	14	*O-132/3-1	1.1

YEAR	TM/L	G	AB	R	H	2B	3B	HR	RBI	BB	SO	AVG	OBP	SLG	PRO+	BR/A	SB	CS	SBR	FA	FR	G/POS	TPR
1891	Phi-a	132	528	105	163	18	14	3	61	72	52	.309	.399	.413	128	20	22			.939	7	*O-122/3-6,S-5,M	2.1
1892	Bal-N	21	76	9	17	1	1	0	10	10	8	.224	.330	.263	78	-2	1			.911	2	O-21	0.0
	Cin-N	30	107	10	21	2	4	0	14	10	17	.196	.271	.290	71	-4	4			.863	2	O-30	-0.6
	Yr	51	183	19	38	3	5	0	24	20	25	.208	.296	.279	74	-6	5			.885	1	O-51	-0.6
Total	13	1280	5371	965	1467	228	132	68	601	418	547	.273	.329	.403		116	98		113	.895	10	*O-1232/3-30,SP21	6.9

■ HARRY WOOD
Wood, Harold Austin b:2/10/1881, Waterville, Maine. d:5/18/55, Bethesda, Md. BL/TR, 5'10", 155 lbs. Deb:4/19/03

YEAR	TM/L	G	AB	R	H	2B	3B	HR	RBI	BB	SO	AVG	OBP	SLG	PRO+	BR/A	SB	CS	SBR	FA	FR	G/POS	TPR
1903	Cin-N	2	3	0	0	0	0	0	0	0	1	.000	.250	.000	-24	-0	0			.000	-1	/O-2	-0.1

■ JAKE WOOD
Wood, Jacob b:6/22/37, Elizabeth, N.J. BR/TR, 6'1", 170 lbs. Deb:4/11/61

YEAR	TM/L	G	AB	R	H	2B	3B	HR	RBI	BB	SO	AVG	OBP	SLG	PRO+	BR/A	SB	CS	SBR	FA	FR	G/POS	TPR
1961	Det-A	162	663	96	171	17	14	11	69	58	141	.258	.321	.376	83	-16	30	9	4	.969	-27	*2-162	-2.1
1962	Det-A	111	367	60	83	10	5	8	30	33	59	.226	.292	.346	68	-17	24	3	5	.950	-31	2-90	-3.3
1963	Det-A	85	351	50	95	11	2	11	27	24	61	.271	.330	.407	102	1	18	5	2	.958	-11	2-81/3-1	0.0
1964	Det-A	64	125	11	29	2	2	1	7	4	24	.232	.256	.304	54	-8	0	0	0	.989	-1	1-11,2-10/3-6,O-1	-1.0
1965	Det-A	58	104	12	30	3	0	2	7	10	19	.288	.357	.375	107	1	3	3	-1	.977	-2	2-20/1-1,S-1,3-1	0.0
1966	Det-A	98	230	39	58	9	3	2	27	28	48	.252	.336	.343	94	-1	4	3	-1	.968	-13	2-52/3-4,1-2	-1.2
1967	Det-A	14	20	2	1	1	0	0	0	1	7	.050	.095	.100	-41	-3	0	0	0	1.000	-0	/1-2,2-2	-0.4
	Cin-N	16	17	1	2	0	0	0	1	1	3	.118	.167	.118	-15	-3	0	0	0	1.000	-0	/O-2	-0.3
Total	7	608	1877	279	469	53	26	35	168	159	362	.250	.313	.362	82	-46	79	23	10	.963	-85	2-417/1-16,3-12,OS	-8.3

■ JIMMY WOOD
Wood, James Leon b:12/1/1844, Brooklyn, N.Y. d:11/30/1886, TR, 5'8.5", 150 lbs. Deb:5/8/1871 M

YEAR	TM/L	G	AB	R	H	2B	3B	HR	RBI	BB	SO	AVG	OBP	SLG	PRO+	BR/A	SB	CS	SBR	FA	FR	G/POS	TPR
1871	Chi-n	28	135	45	51	10	6	3	29	11	3	.378	.425	.563	163	9	18	2	4	.887	9	*2-28,M	1.3
1872	Tro-n	25	113	40	38	11	4	2	27	2	1	.336	.348	.558	172	9	1	0	0	.886	-0	2-25,M	0.5
	Eck-n	7	30	10	6	1	1	0	4	1	1	.200	.294	.300	98	1	1	0	0	.840	-1	/2-7,M	0.0
	Yr	32	143	50	44	12	5	2	27	6	2	.308	.336	.503	158	10	4	0	1	.875	-1	2-32	0.5
1873	Phi-n	42	209	67	67	11	1	0	27	8	1	.321	.346	.383	112	3	8	3	1	.850	4	*2-42,M	0.2
Total	3 n	102	487	162	162	33	12	3	83	25	6	.333	.365	.468	140	21	30	5	6	.868	12	2-102	2.0

■ JOE WOOD
Wood, Joe "Smokey Joe" (b: Howard Ellsworth Wood) b:10/25/1889, Kansas City, Mo. d:7/27/85, West Haven, Conn BR/TR, 5'11", 180 lbs. Deb:8/24/08 F

YEAR	TM/L	G	AB	R	H	2B	3B	HR	RBI	BB	SO	AVG	OBP	SLG	PRO+	BR/A	SB	CS	SBR	FA	FR	G/POS	TPR
1908	Bos-A	6	7	1	0	0	0	0	0	0	0	.000	.000	.000	-97	-1	0			.889	-1	/P-6	0.0
1909	Bos-A	24	55	4	9	0	1	0	3	0	0	.164	.207	.200	28	-5	0			.971	-4	P-24	0.0
1910	Bos-A	35	69	9	18	2	1	1	5	5	0	.261	.311	.362	108	0	0			.975	2	P-35	0.0
1911	Bos-A	44	88	15	23	4	2	1	11	10	0	.261	.343	.420	114	1	1			.947	2	P-44	0.0
1912	*Bos-A	43	124	16	36	13	1	1	13	11	0	.290	.348	.435	118	2	0			.974	8	P-43	0.0
1913	Bos-A	24	56	10	15	5	0	0	6	4	7	.268	.317	.357	95	-1	1			.955	4	P-23	0.0
1914	Bos-A	21	43	2	6	1	1	0	3	3	14	.140	.213	.163	13	-5	1			1.000	1	P-18	0.0
1915	Bos-A	29	54	6	14	1	1	1	7	5	10	.259	.322	.370	111	0	1	1	-0	.982	1	P-25	0.0
1917	Cle-A	10	6	1	0	0	0	0	0	0	3	.000	.000	.000	-93	-1	0			1.000	0	/P-5	0.0
1918	Cle-A	119	422	41	125	22	4	5	66	36	38	.296	.356	.403	118	8	8			.962	0	O-95,2-19/1-4	0.5
1919	Cle-A	72	192	30	49	10	6	0	27	32	21	.255	.367	.370	101	1	3			.932	-8	O-64/P-1	-1.1
1920	*Cle-A	61	137	25	37	11	2	1	30	25	16	.270	.390	.401	107	2	1	1	-0	.987	-6	O-55/P-1	-0.7
1921	Cle-A	66	194	32	71	16	5	4	60	25	17	.366	.438	.562	151	15	2	0	1	.973	-13	O-64	-0.1
1922	Cle-A	142	505	74	150	33	8	8	92	50	63	.297	.367	.442	109	7	5	1	1	.960	-2	*O-141	0.0
Total	14	696	1952	266	553	118	33	23	325	208	189	.283	.357	.411	110	25	23	3		.962	-11	O-419,P-225/2-19,1	-1.4

■ JOE WOOD
Wood, Joseph Perry "J.P." or "Little Joe" b:10/3/19, Houston, Tex. d:3/25/85, Houston, Tex. BR/TR, 5'9.5", 160 lbs. Deb:5/2/43

YEAR	TM/L	G	AB	R	H	2B	3B	HR	RBI	BB	SO	AVG	OBP	SLG	PRO+	BR/A	SB	CS	SBR	FA	FR	G/POS	TPR
1943	Det-A	60	164	22	53	4	4	1	17	6	13	.323	.347	.415	114	2	2	2	-1	.896	-16	2-22,3-18	-1.4

■ KEN WOOD
Wood, Kenneth Lanier b:7/1/24, Lincolnton, N.C. BR/TR, 6', 200 lbs. Deb:4/28/48

YEAR	TM/L	G	AB	R	H	2B	3B	HR	RBI	BB	SO	AVG	OBP	SLG	PRO+	BR/A	SB	CS	SBR	FA	FR	G/POS	TPR
1948	StL-A	10	24	2	2	0	1	0	2	1	4	.083	.120	.167	-24	-4	0	0	0	1.000	1	/O-5	-0.4
1949	StL-A	7	6	0	0	0	0	0	0	1	2	.000	.143	.000	-58	-1	0	0	0	.000	-1	/O-3	-0.3
1950	StL-A	128	369	42	83	24	0	13	62	38	58	.225	.299	.396	74	-17	0	0	-2	.952	-2	O-94	-2.3
1951	StL-A	109	333	40	79	19	0	15	44	27	49	.237	.296	.429	92	-6	1	2	-1	.959	-4	*O-100	-1.4
1952	Bos-A	15	20	0	2	0	0	0	0	3	4	.100	.217	.100	-9	-3	0	0	-1	.889	-4	O-13	-0.7
	Was-A	61	210	26	50	8	6	6	32	30	21	.238	.333	.419	112	3	0	0	-1	.954	8	O-56	0.9
	Yr	76	230	26	52	8	6	6	32	33	25	.226	.323	.391	99	-1	0	1	-1	.951	5	O-69	0.2
1953	Was-A	12	33	0	7	1	0	0	3	2	3	.212	.257	.242	36	-3	0	0	0	1.000	1	/O-7	-0.3
Total	6	342	995	110	223	52	7	34	143	102	141	.224	.298	.393	81	-31	1	7	-4	.956	-1	O-278	-4.5

■ BOB WOOD
Wood, Robert Lynn b:7/28/1865, Thorn Hill, Ohio d:5/22/43, Churchill, Ohio BR/TR, 5'8.5", 153 lbs. Deb:5/2/1898

YEAR	TM/L	G	AB	R	H	2B	3B	HR	RBI	BB	SO	AVG	OBP	SLG	PRO+	BR/A	SB	CS	SBR	FA	FR	G/POS	TPR
1898	Cin-N	39	109	14	30	6	0	0	16	9		.275	.331	.330	84	-2	1			.943	1	C-29/O-1,1-1	0.1
1899	Cin-N	62	194	34	61	11	0	0	24	25		.314	.406	.443	131	9	3			.937	-10	C-53/O-2,3-2,1-1	0.3
1900	Cin-N	45	139	17	37	8	1	0	22	10		.266	.320	.338	84	-3	3			.967	-6	C-18,3-15/O-1	-0.7
1901	Cle-A	98	346	45	101	23	3	1	49	12		.292	.327	.384	101	-0	6			.952	-1	C-84/3-4,O-3,12S	0.7
1902	Cle-A	81	258	23	76	18	2	0	40	27		.295	.375	.380	114	6	1			.941	-7	C-52,1-16/O-2,23	0.4
1904	Det-A	49	175	15	43	6	2	1	17	5		.246	.271	.320	89	-3	1			.974	10	C-47	1.3
1905	Det-A	8	24	1	2	1	0	0	0	1		.083	.120	.125	-22	-3	0			.886	-0	/C-7	-0.3
Total	7	382	1245	149	350	73	15	2	168	89		.281	.339	.369	102	3	15			.951	-14	C-290/3-22,102S	1.8

■ ROY WOOD
Wood, Roy Winton "Woody" b:8/29/1892, Monticello, Ark. d:4/6/74, Fayetteville, Ark. BR/TR, 6', 175 lbs. Deb:6/16/13

YEAR	TM/L	G	AB	R	H	2B	3B	HR	RBI	BB	SO	AVG	OBP	SLG	PRO+	BR/A	SB	CS	SBR	FA	FR	G/POS	TPR
1913	Pit-N	14	35	4	10	4	0	0	2	1	8	.286	.306	.400	105	-0	1			.895	1	/O-8,1-1	0.1
1914	Cle-A	72	220	24	52	6	3	1	15	13	26	.236	.300	.305	79	-6	6	9	-4	.946	-1	O-40,1-20	-1.4
1915	Cle-A	33	78	5	15	2	1	0	3	2	13	.192	.232	.244	41	-6	1	2	-1	.990	-1	1-21/O-2	-0.9
Total	3	119	333	33	77	12	4	1	20	16	47	.231	.285	.300	73	-12	9	11		.936	-1	/O-50,1-42	-2.2

■ LARRY WOODALL
Woodall, Charles Lawrence b:7/26/1894, Staunton, Va. d:5/16/63, Cambridge, Mass. BR/TR, 5'9", 165 lbs. Deb:5/20/20 C

YEAR	TM/L	G	AB	R	H	2B	3B	HR	RBI	BB	SO	AVG	OBP	SLG	PRO+	BR/A	SB	CS	SBR	FA	FR	G/POS	TPR
1920	Det-A	18	49	4	12	1	0	0	5	2	6	.245	.275	.265	45	-4	0	0	0	.988	2	C-15	-0.1
1921	Det-A	46	80	10	29	4	1	0	14	6	7	.363	.407	.438	117	2	1	0	0	.966	-7	C-25	-0.4
1922	Det-A	50	125	19	43	2	2	0	18	6	8	.344	.388	.392	107	2	2	1	-1	.977	-10	C-40	-0.7
1923	Det-A	71	148	20	41	12	2	1	19	12	9	.277	.371	.405	106	2	2	1	0	.983	-5	C-60	-0.1
1924	Det-A	67	165	23	51	9	2	0	25	21	5	.309	.387	.388	102	1	0	0	0	.986	0	C-62	0.4
1925	Det-A	75	171	20	35	4	1	0	13	24	8	.205	.303	.240	39	-15	0	0	0	.967	-7	C-75	-1.8
1926	Det-A	67	146	18	34	5	0	0	15	15	2	.233	.304	.267	49	-11	0	0	0	.979	-4	C-59	-1.1
1927	Det-A	88	246	28	69	8	6	0	39	37	9	.280	.375	.362	90	-2	9	1	2	.997	4	C-86	0.8
1928	Det-A	65	186	19	39	7	1	0	13	24	10	.210	.300	.258	47	-14	0	0	0	.992	4	C-62	-0.4
1929	Det-A	1	0	0	0	0	0	0	0	0	0	.000	.000	.000	-99	-0	0	0	0	.000	0	H	0.0
Total	10	548	1317	161	353	52	15	1	161	159	67	.268	.347	.333	77	-40	16	4	2	.984	-22	C-484	-3.4

■ DARRELL WOODARD
Woodard, Darrell Lee b:12/10/56, Wilmar, Ark. BR/TR, 5'11", 160 lbs. Deb:8/6/78

YEAR	TM/L	G	AB	R	H	2B	3B	HR	RBI	BB	SO	AVG	OBP	SLG	PRO+	BR/A	SB	CS	SBR	FA	FR	G/POS	TPR
1978	Oak-A	33	9	10	0	0	0	0	0	0	0	.000	.100	.000	-73	-2	3	4	-2	.964	9	2-14/3-1,D-1	0.5

■ MIKE WOODARD
Woodard, Michael Cary b:3/2/60, Melrose Park, Ill. BL/TR, 5'9", 155 lbs. Deb:9/11/85

YEAR	TM/L	G	AB	R	H	2B	3B	HR	RBI	BB	SO	AVG	OBP	SLG	PRO+	BR/A	SB	CS	SBR	FA	FR	G/POS	TPR
1985	SF-N	24	82	12	20	1	0	0	4	7	7	.244	.287	.256	56	-5	6	1	1	.990	-5	2-23	-0.9
1986	SF-N	48	79	14	20	2	1	0	5	10	9	.253	.337	.342	92	-1	7	2	1	.986	-2	2-23/S-2,3-2	-0.1
1987	SF-N	10	19	0	4	1	0	0	5	1	0	.211	.211	.263	26	-2	1	0	0	1.000	2	/2-8	0.0
1988	Chi-A	18	45	3	6	0	0	0	4	1	5	.133	.170	.178	-2	-6	0	1	0	.975	4	2-14/D-2	0.0
Total	4	100	225	29	50	4	2	1	19	16	18	.222	.277	.271	55	-14	14	4	2	.985	-1	/2-68,D-2,3-2,S-2	-1.2

■ RED WOODHEAD
Woodhead, James b:7/9/1851, Chelsea, Mass. d:9/7/1881, Boston, Mass. 5'6", 160 lbs. Deb:4/15/1873

YEAR	TM/L	G	AB	R	H	2B	3B	HR	RBI	BB	SO	AVG	OBP	SLG	PRO+	BR/A	SB	CS	SBR	FA	FR	G/POS	TPR
1873	Mar-n	1	5	1	0	0	0	0	0	0	0	.000	.000	.000	-99	-1	0	0	0	.900	-1	/S-1	0.0
1879	Syr-N	34	131	4	21	1	0	0	8	0	23	.160	.160	.168	9	-12	0	0	0	.792	-7	3-34	-1.7

YEAR	TM/L	G	AB	R	H	2B	3B	HR	RBI	BB	SO	AVG	OBP	SLG	PRO+	BR/A	SB	CS	SBR	FA	FR	G/POS	TPR

■ GENE WOODLING
Woodling, Eugene Richard b: 8/16/22, Akron, Ohio BL/TR, 5'9.5", 195 lbs. Deb: 9/23/43 C

YEAR	TM/L	G	AB	R	H	2B	3B	HR	RBI	BB	SO	AVG	OBP	SLG	PRO+	BR/A	SB	CS	SBR	FA	FR	G/POS	TPR
1943	Cle-A	8	25	5	8	1	1	1	5	1	5	.320	.346	.600	186	2	0	0	0	1.000	-1	/O-6	0.2
1946	Cle-A	61	133	8	25	1	4	0	9	16	13	.188	.280	.256	54	-8	1	2	-1	1.000	-3	O-37	-1.4
1947	Pit-N	22	79	7	21	2	0	0	10	7	5	.266	.326	.342	75	-3	0			.968	1	O-21	-0.2
1949	*NY-A	112	296	60	80	13	7	5	44	52	21	.270	.381	.412	110	5	2	2	-1	.982	-10	/O-98	-1.0
1950	*NY-A	122	449	81	127	20	10	6	60	70	31	.283	.381	.412	106	5	5	3	-0	.993	10	*O-118	1.0
1951	*NY-A	120	420	65	118	15	8	15	71	62	37	.281	.373	.462	130	17	0	4	-2	.993	4	*O-118	1.1
1952	*NY-A	122	408	58	126	19	6	12	63	59	31	.309	.397	.473	151	28	1	4	-2	.996	6	*O-119	2.8
1953	*NY-A	125	395	64	121	26	4	10	58	82	29	.306	.429	.468	147	30	2	7	-4	.996	4	*O-119	2.6
1954	NY-A	97	304	33	76	12	5	3	40	53	35	.250	.361	.352	99	1	3	4	-2	.983	-1	O-89	-0.5
1955	Bal-A	47	145	22	32	8	2	3	18	24	18	.221	.335	.352	91	-2	1	1	-0	1.000	-8	O-44	-1.2
	Cle-A	79	259	33	72	15	1	5	35	36	15	.278	.372	.402	104	2	2	4	-2	.993	-3	O-70	-0.5
	Yr	126	404	55	104	21	3	8	53	60	33	.257	.359	.384	100	1	3	5	-2	.995	-11	*O-114	-1.7
1956	Cle-A	100	317	56	83	17	0	8	38	69	29	.262	.398	.391	107	6	2	6	-3	.981	-0	O-85	-0.2
1957	Cle-A	133	430	74	138	25	2	19	78	64	35	.321	.412	.521	155	34	0	5	-3	.992	11	*O-113	3.5
1958	Bal-A	133	413	57	114	16	1	15	65	66	49	.276	.378	.429	128	18	4	2	0	.974	-10	*O-116	0.1
1959	Bal-A★	140	440	63	132	22	2	14	77	78	35	.300	.405	.455	139	26	1	1	-0	.981	-13	*O-124	0.8
1960	Bal-A	140	435	57	123	18	3	11	62	84	40	.283	.403	.414	123	18	3	0	1	.995	-3	*O-124	1.0
1961	Was-A	110	342	39	107	16	4	10	57	50	24	.313	.404	.471	135	18	1	0		.988	-3	O-90	1.1
1962	Was-A	44	107	19	30	4	0	5	16	24	5	.280	.421	.458	138	7	1	0	0	.953	-4	O-30	0.1
	NY-N	81	190	18	52	8	1	5	24	24	22	.274	.358	.405	103	1	0	0	0	.986	-4	O-48	-0.5
Total	17	1796	5587	830	1585	257	63	147	830	921	479	.284	.388	.431	123	206	29	45		.989	-29	*O-1566	8.8

■ SAM WOODRUFF
Woodruff, Orville Francis b: 12/27/1876, Chilo, Ohio d: 7/22/37, Cincinnati, Ohio BR/TR, 5'9", 160 lbs. Deb: 4/14/04

YEAR	TM/L	G	AB	R	H	2B	3B	HR	RBI	BB	SO	AVG	OBP	SLG	PRO+	BR/A	SB	CS	SBR	FA	FR	G/POS	TPR
1904	Cin-N	87	306	20	58	14	3	0	20	19		.190	.244	.255	50	-19	9			.932	-4	3-61,2-17/S-8,O-1	-2.1
1910	Cin-N	21	61	6	9	1	0	0	2	7	8	.148	.235	.164	18	-6	2			.933	-1	3-17/2-4	-0.7
Total	2	108	367	26	67	15	3	0	22	26	8	.183	.242	.240	45	-25	11			.932	-5	/3-78,2-21,S-8,O-1	-2.8

■ PETE WOODRUFF
Woodruff, Peter Frank b: 6/1873, New York BR/TR, Deb: 9/19/1899

YEAR	TM/L	G	AB	R	H	2B	3B	HR	RBI	BB	SO	AVG	OBP	SLG	PRO+	BR/A	SB	CS	SBR	FA	FR	G/POS	TPR
1899	NY-N	20	61	11	15	1	1	2	7	9		.246	.343	.393	105	0	3			1.000	-1	O-19/1-1	-0.2

■ AL WOODS
Woods, Alvis b: 8/8/53, Oakland, Cal. BL/TL, 6'3", 195 lbs. Deb: 4/7/77

YEAR	TM/L	G	AB	R	H	2B	3B	HR	RBI	BB	SO	AVG	OBP	SLG	PRO+	BR/A	SB	CS	SBR	FA	FR	G/POS	TPR
1977	Tor-A	122	440	58	125	17	4	6	35	36	38	.284	.338	.382	94	-3	8	7	-2	.969	-2	*O-115/D-4	-1.2
1978	Tor-A	62	220	19	53	12	3	3	25	11	23	.241	.280	.364	78	-7	1	2	-1	.978	3	O-60	-0.7
1979	Tor-A	132	436	57	121	24	4	5	36	40	28	.278	.340	.385	94	-3	6	4	-1	.991	6	O-88,D-13	-0.5
1980	Tor-A	109	373	54	112	18	2	15	47	37	35	.300	.365	.480	124	12	4	4	-1	.973	9	O-77/D-2	1.3
1981	Tor-A	85	288	20	71	15	0	1	21	19	31	.247	.293	.309	69	-11	3	4	-2	.973	3	O-64,D-10	-1.8
1982	Tor-A	85	201	20	47	11	1	3	24	21	20	.234	.306	.343	71	-8	1	3	-2	.970	-7	O-7	0.2
1986	Min-A	23	28	5	9	1	0	2	8	3	5	.321	.387	.571	153	2	0	0	0	.000	0	/D-7	-4.1
Total	7	618	1986	233	538	98	14	35	196	167	180	.271	.328	.387	93	-19	23	24	-8	.974	6	O-531/D-38	

■ GARY WOODS
Woods, Gary Lee b: 7/20/54, Santa Barbara, Cal BR/TR, 6'2", 190 lbs. Deb: 9/14/76

YEAR	TM/L	G	AB	R	H	2B	3B	HR	RBI	BB	SO	AVG	OBP	SLG	PRO+	BR/A	SB	CS	SBR	FA	FR	G/POS	TPR
1976	Oak-A	6	8	0	1	0	0	0	0	0	3	.125	.125	.125	-28	-1	0	0	0	1.000	-1	/O-4,D-1	-0.2
1977	Tor-A	60	227	21	49	9	1	0	17	7	38	.216	.246	.264	38	-19	5	4	-1	.994	3	O-60	-2.0
1978	Tor-A	8	19	1	3	1	0	0	1	0	5	.158	.200	.211	15	-2	1	0	0	1.000	-0	O-6	-0.2
1980	*Hou-N	19	53	9	20	5	0	2	15	2	9	.377	.400	.585	186	6	1	0	0	1.000	-2	O-40	0.4
1981	*Hou-N	54	110	10	23	4	1	0	12	11	22	.209	.281	.264	58	-6	2	1	0	.984	-3	*O-103	-1.0
1982	Chi-N	117	245	28	66	15	1	4	30	21	48	.269	.327	.388	97	-1	3	3	-1	1.000	-14	O-73/2-1	-1.9
1983	Chi-N	93	190	25	46	9	0	3	22	15	27	.242	.298	.353	76	-6	5	3	-0	.971	-11	O-62/2-3	-2.0
1984	*Chi-N	87	98	13	23	4	1	3	10	15	21	.235	.336	.388	94	-1	2	1	0	1.000	-13	O-56	-1.5
1985	Chi-N	81	82	11	20	3	0	4	14	18	14	.244	.354	.280	72	-3	0	1	-1	1.000	-13	O-56	-1.8
Total	9	525	1032	117	251	50	4	13	110	86	187	.243	.303	.337	76	-34	19	13	-2	.992	-54	O-418/2-4,D-1	-10.2

■ JIM WOODS
Woods, James Jerome "Woody" b: 9/17/39, Chicago, Ill. BR/TR, 6', 175 lbs. Deb: 9/27/57

YEAR	TM/L	G	AB	R	H	2B	3B	HR	RBI	BB	SO	AVG	OBP	SLG	PRO+	BR/A	SB	CS	SBR	FA	FR	G/POS	TPR
1957	Chi-N	2	0	1	0	0	0	0	0	0	0	—	—	—		0	0	0	0	.000	0	R	0.0
1960	Phi-N	11	34	4	6	0	0	1	3	3	13	.176	.243	.265	39	-3	0	0	0	.939	2	3-11	-0.1
1961	Phi-N	23	48	6	11	3	0	2	9	4	15	.229	.302	.417	89	-1	0	0	0	.968	-1	3-15	-0.1
Total	3	36	82	11	17	3	0	3	12	7	28	.207	.278	.354	69	-4	0	0	0	.953	1	/3-26	-0.2

■ RON WOODS
Woods, Ronald Lawrence b: 2/1/43, Hamilton, Ohio BR/TR, 5'10", 173 lbs. Deb: 4/22/69

YEAR	TM/L	G	AB	R	H	2B	3B	HR	RBI	BB	SO	AVG	OBP	SLG	PRO+	BR/A	SB	CS	SBR	FA	FR	G/POS	TPR
1969	Det-A	17	15	3	4	0	0	2	3	3	3	.267	.353	.467	122	0	0	0	0	1.000	-2	/O-7	-0.2
	NY-A	72	171	18	30	5	2	1	7	22	29	.175	.273	.246	48	-12	2	0	1	1.000	-3	O-67	-1.8
	Yr	89	186	21	34	5	2	3	10	24	32	.183	.280	.263	54	-11	2	0	1	.974	-6	O-74	-2.0
1970	NY-A	95	225	30	51	5	3	8	27	33	35	.227	.326	.382	100	-0	4	2	0	.929	-1	O-78	-1.0
1971	NY-A	25	32	4	8	1	0	1	2	4	2	.250	.333	.375	107	0	0	0	0	.989	-1	O-9	-0.1
	Mon-N	51	138	26	41	7	3	1	17	19	18	.297	.382	.413	125	5	2	2	-1	.991	-1	O-45	0.1
1972	Mon-N	97	221	21	57	5	1	10	31	22	33	.258	.325	.425	110	2	3	3	-1	.977	-9	*O-114	-1.3
1973	Mon-N	135	318	45	73	8	3	11	56	34	34	.230	.345	.311	80	-7	12	6	0	.987	-12	O-73	-2.0
1974	Mon-N	90	127	15	26	0	0	1	12	17	17	.205	.303	.228	48	-8	6	5	-1	.984	-12	O-61	-2.4
Total	6	582	1247	162	290	34	12	26	130	175	171	.233	.328	.342	87	-19	27	18	-2	.984	-45	O-454	-8.7

■ TRACY WOODSON
Woodson, Tracy Michael b: 10/5/62, Richmond, Va. BR/TR, 6'3", 215 lbs. Deb: 4/7/87

YEAR	TM/L	G	AB	R	H	2B	3B	HR	RBI	BB	SO	AVG	OBP	SLG	PRO+	BR/A	SB	CS	SBR	FA	FR	G/POS	TPR
1987	LA-N	53	136	14	31	8	1	1	11	9	21	.228	.286	.324	63	-7	1	1	-0	.958	-1	3-45/1-7	-1.0
1988	*LA-N	65	173	15	43	4	1	3	15	7	32	.249	.282	.335	79	-5	2	0	-1	.938	-5	3-41,1-25	-1.3
1989	LA-N	4	6	0	0	0	0	0	0	0	1	.000	.000	.000	-99	-2	0	0	0	1.000	0	/3-1	-0.2
1992	StL-N	31	114	9	35	8	0	1	22	3	10	.307	.331	.404	110	1	0	0	0	.945	-6	3-26/1-3	-0.6
1993	StL-N	62	77	4	16	2	0	2	14	1	14	.208	.218	.234	21	-9	2	2	-0	.909	2	3-28,1-11	-0.7
Total	5	215	506	42	125	22	2	7	50	20	78	.247	.281	.328	70	-22	5	3	-1	.943	-10	3-141/1-46	-3.8

■ WOODY WOODWARD
Woodward, William Frederick b: 9/23/42, Miami, Fla. BR/TR, 6'2", 185 lbs. Deb: 9/9/63

YEAR	TM/L	G	AB	R	H	2B	3B	HR	RBI	BB	SO	AVG	OBP	SLG	PRO+	BR/A	SB	CS	SBR	FA	FR	G/POS	TPR
1963	Mil-N	10	2	1	0	0	0	0	0	0	0	.000	.000	.000	-99	-1	0	0	0	1.000	3	/S-5	0.2
1964	Mil-N	77	115	18	24	7	1	0	11	6	28	.209	.260	.243	43	-9	0	1	-1	.958	13	2-40,S-18/3-7,1-1	0.6
1965	Mil-N	112	265	17	55	7	4	0	11	10	50	.208	.236	.264	41	-21	2	2	-1	.977	11	*S-107/2-8	-0.6
1966	Atl-N	144	455	46	120	23	0	4	43	37	54	.264	.325	.327	81	-11	3	2	-1	.973	-6	2-79,S-73	-0.7
1967	Atl-N	136	429	30	97	15	2	0	25	37	51	.226	.289	.270	62	-21	0	6	-4	.982	9	*2-120,S-16	-0.7
1968	Atl-N	12	24	2	4	2	0	0	1	1	6	.167	.200	.208	23	-2	0	0	0	.973	-3	/S-6,3-2,2-1	-0.5
	Cin-N	56	119	13	29	2	0	0	10	7	23	.244	.297	.261	64	-5	0	0	0	.968	1	S-41/2-9,1-1	-0.3
	Yr	68	143	15	33	4	0	0	11	8	29	.231	.281	.252	58	-7	2	0	1	.966	-2	S-93/2-2	0.0
1969	Cin-N	97	241	36	63	12	0	0	15	24	40	.261	.333	.311	77	-7	3	2	-0	.973	2	S-77,3-20,2-10/1-2	-0.8
1970	*Cin-N	100	264	23	59	8	1	0	14	20	24	.223	.283	.288	53	-17	1	2	-1	.987	5	S-85,3-63/2-9	-0.6
1971	Cin-N	136	273	22	66	6	1	0	17	28	22	.242	.310	.282	70	-10	4	3	-1	.974	23	S-521,2-278/3-92,1	-2.9
Total	9	880	2187	208	517	79	14	1	148	169	301	.236	.295	.287	64	-103	14	15	-5				

■ JUNIOR WOOTEN
Wooten, Earl Hazwell b: 1/16/24, Pelzer, S.C. BR/TL, 5'11", 160 lbs. Deb: 9/16/47

YEAR	TM/L	G	AB	R	H	2B	3B	HR	RBI	BB	SO	AVG	OBP	SLG	PRO+	BR/A	SB	CS	SBR	FA	FR	G/POS	TPR
1947	Was-A	6	24	0	2	0	0	0	0	0	4	.083	.083	.083	-55	-5	1	0	0	.905	-1	/O-6	-0.6
1948	Was-A	88	258	34	66	8	3	1	23	24	21	.256	.324	.322	74	-10	2	1	0	.979	1	O-73/1-6,P-1	-1.2
Total	2	94	282	34	68	8	3	1	23	24	25	.241	.305	.301	64	-15	3	1	0	.972	1	/O-79,1-6,P-1	-1.8

■ FAVEL WORDSWORTH
Wordsworth, Favel Perry b: 12/22/1850, New York, N.Y. d: 8/12/1888, New York, N.Y. Deb: 4/28/1873

YEAR	TM/L	G	AB	R	H	2B	3B	HR	RBI	BB	SO	AVG	OBP	SLG	PRO+	BR/A	SB	CS	SBR	FA	FR	G/POS	TPR
1873	Res-n	12	42	5	10	3	0	0	3	2	1	.238	.273	.262	58	-2	0	0	0	.643	-3	S-11/O-1	-0.4

YEAR	TM/L	G	AB	R	H	2B	3B	HR	RBI	BB	SO	AVG	OBP	SLG	PRO+	BR/A	SB	CS	SBR	FA	FR	G/POS	TPR

■ CHUCK WORKMAN   Workman, Charles Thomas   b: 1/6/15, Leeton, Mo.   d: 1/3/53, Kansas City, Mo.   BL/TR, 6′, 175 lbs.   Deb: 9/18/38

YEAR	TM/L	G	AB	R	H	2B	3B	HR	RBI	BB	SO	AVG	OBP	SLG	PRO+	BR/A	SB	CS	SBR	FA	FR	G/POS	TPR
1938	Cle-A	2	5	1	2	0	0	0	0	0	0	.400	.400	.400	103	0	0	0	0	.500	-0	/O-1	0.0
1941	Cle-A	9	4	2	0	0	0	0	0	1	1	.000	.200	.000	-45	-1	0	0	0	.000	H		-0.1
1943	Bos-N	153	615	71	153	17	1	10	67	53	72	.249	.311	.328	86	-11	12			.988	6	*O-149/1-3,3-1	-1.5
1944	Bos-N	140	418	46	87	18	3	11	53	42	41	.208	.287	.344	74	-15	1			.983	-3	*O-103,3-19	-2.3
1945	Bos-N	139	514	77	141	16	2	25	87	51	58	.274	.347	.459	122	14	9			.910	-17	*3-107,O-24	-0.1
1946	Bos-N	25	48	5	8	2	0	2	7	3	11	.167	.231	.333	58	-3	0			.920	-1	O-12	-0.5
	Pit-N	58	145	11	32	4	1	2	16	11	19	.221	.280	.303	64	-7	2			1.000	6	O-40/3-1	-0.3
	Yr	83	193	16	40	6	1	4	23	14	30	.207	.268	.311	63	-10	2			.986	5	O-52/3-1	-0.8
Total	6	526	1749	213	423	57	7	50	230	161	202	.242	.311	.368	91	-24	24	0		.985	-8	O-329,3-128/1-3	-4.8

■ HANK WORKMAN   Workman, Henry Kilgariff   b: 2/5/26, Los Angeles, Cal.   BL/TR, 6′1″, 185 lbs.   Deb: 9/4/50

YEAR	TM/L	G	AB	R	H	2B	3B	HR	RBI	BB	SO	AVG	OBP	SLG	PRO+	BR/A	SB	CS	SBR	FA	FR	G/POS	TPR
1950	NY-A	2	5	1	1	0	0	0	0	0	1	.200	.200	.200	3	-1	0	0	0	1.000	-0	/1-1	-0.1

■ HERB WORTH   Worth, Herbert   b: 5/2/1847, Brooklyn, N.Y.   d: 4/27/14, Brooklyn, N.Y.   Deb: 7/29/1872

YEAR	TM/L	G	AB	R	H	2B	3B	HR	RBI	BB	SO	AVG	OBP	SLG	PRO+	BR/A	SB	CS	SBR	FA	FR	G/POS	TPR
1872	Atl-n	1	5	1	1	0	0	0	0	0	0	.200	.200	.400	68	-0				1.000	0	/O-1	0.0

■ CRAIG WORTHINGTON   Worthington, Craig Richard   b: 4/17/65, Los Angeles, Cal.   BR/TR, 6′, 200 lbs.   Deb: 4/26/88

YEAR	TM/L	G	AB	R	H	2B	3B	HR	RBI	BB	SO	AVG	OBP	SLG	PRO+	BR/A	SB	CS	SBR	FA	FR	G/POS	TPR
1988	Bal-A	26	81	5	15	2	0	2	4	9	24	.185	.267	.284	56	-5	1	0	0	.961	1	3-26	-0.4
1989	Bal-A	145	497	57	123	23	0	15	70	61	114	.247	.335	.384	105	4	1	2	-1	.951	-10	*3-145	-0.6
1990	Bal-A	133	425	46	96	17	0	8	44	63	96	.226	.330	.322	86	-7	1	2	-1	.945	-12	*3-131/D-2	-1.9
1991	Bal-A	31	102	11	23	8	0	4	12	12	14	.225	.313	.373	93	-1	0	1	-1	.975	-3	3-30	-0.4
1992	Cle-A	9	24	0	4	0	0	0	2	2	4	.167	.231	.167	13	-3	0	1	-1	.857	1	/3-9	-0.2
1995	Cin-N	10	18	1	5	1	0	1	2	2	1	.278	.350	.500	122	1	0	0	0	1.000	0	/1-4,3-2	0.0
	Tex-A	26	68	4	15	4	0	1	6	7	8	.221	.293	.368	69	-3	0	0	0	.980	-0	3-26	-0.3
1996	Tex-A	13	19	2	3	0	0	1	4	6	3	.158	.360	.316	68	-1	0	0	0	.917	1	/3-7,1-6	0.0
Total	7	393	1234	126	284	50	0	33	144	162	264	.230	.323	.351	90	-15	3	6	-3	.950	-21	3-376/1-10,D-2	-3.8

■ RED WORTHINGTON   Worthington, Robert Lee   b: 4/24/06, Alhambra, Cal.   d: 12/8/63, Sepulveda, Cal.   BR/TR, 5′11″, 170 lbs.   Deb: 4/14/31

YEAR	TM/L	G	AB	R	H	2B	3B	HR	RBI	BB	SO	AVG	OBP	SLG	PRO+	BR/A	SB	CS	SBR	FA	FR	G/POS	TPR
1931	Bos-N	128	491	47	143	25	10	4	44	26	38	.291	.328	.407	100	-1	1			**.988**	-3	*O-124	-1.3
1932	Bos-N	105	435	62	132	35	8	8	61	15	24	.303	.330	.476	118	9	1			.987	-1	*O-104	0.1
1933	Bos-N	17	45	3	7	4	0	0	0	1	3	.156	.174	.244	20	-5	0			.900	-1	O-10	-0.7
1934	Bos-N	41	65	6	16	5	0	0	6	6	5	.246	.319	.323	78	-2	0			.920	-1	O-11	-0.3
	StL-N	1	1	0	0	0	0	0	0	0	0	.000	.000	.000	-94	-0	0			.000	0	H	
	Yr	42	66	6	16	5	0	0	6	6	6	.242	.315	.318	75	-2	0			.920	-1	O-11	-0.3
Total	4	292	1037	118	298	69	18	12	111	48	71	.287	.321	.423	103	1	2			.981	-7	O-249	-2.2

■ CHUCK WORTMAN   Wortman, William Lewis   b: 1/5/1892, Baltimore, Md.   d: 8/19/77, Las Vegas, Nev.   BR/TR, 5′7″, 150 lbs.   Deb: 7/20/16

YEAR	TM/L	G	AB	R	H	2B	3B	HR	RBI	BB	SO	AVG	OBP	SLG	PRO+	BR/A	SB	CS	SBR	FA	FR	G/POS	TPR
1916	Chi-N	69	234	17	47	4	2	2	16	18	22	.201	.258	.261	54	-13	4			.908	-21	S-69	-3.5
1917	Chi-N	75	190	24	33	4	1	0	9	18	23	.174	.245	.205	36	-14	6			.918	-8	S-65/2-1,3-1	-2.2
1918	*Chi-N	17	17	4	2	0	0	1	3	1	2	.118	.167	.294	39	-1	3			.864	2	/2-8,S-4	0.1
Total	3	161	441	45	82	8	3	3	28	37	47	.186	.249	.238	46	-28	13			.913	-27	S-138/2-9,3-1	-5.6

■ RON WOTUS   Wotus, Ronald Allan   b: 3/3/61, Colchester, Conn.   BR/TR, 6′1″, 164 lbs.   Deb: 9/3/83

YEAR	TM/L	G	AB	R	H	2B	3B	HR	RBI	BB	SO	AVG	OBP	SLG	PRO+	BR/A	SB	CS	SBR	FA	FR	G/POS	TPR
1983	Pit-N	5	3	0	0	0	0	0	0	0	1	.000	.000	.000	-98	-1	0	0	0	1.000	1	/S-2,2-1	0.0
1984	Pit-N	27	55	4	12	6	0	0	2	6	8	.218	.295	.327	75	-2	0	0	0	.976	9	S-17/2-7	0.9
Total	2	32	58	4	12	6	0	0	2	6	9	.207	.281	.310	66	-3	0	0	0	.976	10	/S-19,2-8	0.9

■ JIMMY WOULFE   Woulfe, James Joseph   b: 11/25/1859, New Orleans, La.   d: 12/20/24, New Orleans, La.   TR, 5′11″,   Deb: 5/16/1884

YEAR	TM/L	G	AB	R	H	2B	3B	HR	RBI	BB	SO	AVG	OBP	SLG	PRO+	BR/A	SB	CS	SBR	FA	FR	G/POS	TPR
1884	Cin-a	8	34	3	5	0	1	0	2	1		.147	.171	.206	22	-3				.625	-3	/O-7,3-1	-0.6
	Pit-a	15	53	7	6	1	0	0	1	0		.113	.113	.132	-20	-7				.893	1	O-15	-0.6
	Yr	23	87	10	11	1	1	0	3	1		.126	.136	.161	-3	-10				.795	-2	O-22/3-1	-1.2

■ AL WRIGHT   Wright, Albert Edgar "A-1"   b: 11/11/12, San Francisco, Cal   BR/TR, 6′1.5″, 170 lbs.   Deb: 4/25/33

YEAR	TM/L	G	AB	R	H	2B	3B	HR	RBI	BB	SO	AVG	OBP	SLG	PRO+	BR/A	SB	CS	SBR	FA	FR	G/POS	TPR
1933	Bos-N	4	1	0	1	0	0	0	0	0	0	1.000	1.000	1.000	515	1	0			.500	-0	/2-3	0.0

■ AB WRIGHT   Wright, Albert Owen   b: 11/16/05, Terlton, Okla.   BR/TR, 6′1.5″, 190 lbs.   Deb: 4/20/35

YEAR	TM/L	G	AB	R	H	2B	3B	HR	RBI	BB	SO	AVG	OBP	SLG	PRO+	BR/A	SB	CS	SBR	FA	FR	G/POS	TPR
1935	Cle-A	67	160	17	38	11	1	2	18	10	17	.237	.291	.356	68	-9	2	1	0	.984	-8	O-47	-1.7
1944	Bos-N	71	195	20	50	9	0	7	35	18	31	.256	.326	.410	102	0	0			.968	-4	O-47	-0.6
Total	2	138	355	37	88	20	1	9	53	28	48	.248	.310	.386	85	-9	2	1		.974	-11	/O-94	-2.3

■ CY WRIGHT   Wright, Ceylon   b: 8/16/1893, Minneapolis, Minn.   d: 11/7/47, Hines, Ill.   BL/TR, 5′9″, 150 lbs.   Deb: 6/30/16

YEAR	TM/L	G	AB	R	H	2B	3B	HR	RBI	BB	SO	AVG	OBP	SLG	PRO+	BR/A	SB	CS	SBR	FA	FR	G/POS	TPR
1916	Chi-A	8	18	0	0	0	0	0	1	7		.000	.053	.000	-83	-4	0			.844	-1	/S-8	-0.5

■ GLENN WRIGHT   Wright, Forest Glenn "Buckshot"   b: 2/6/01, Archie, Mo.   d: 4/6/84, Olathe, Kan.   BR/TR, 5′11″, 170 lbs.   Deb: 4/15/24

YEAR	TM/L	G	AB	R	H	2B	3B	HR	RBI	BB	SO	AVG	OBP	SLG	PRO+	BR/A	SB	CS	SBR	FA	FR	G/POS	TPR
1924	Pit-N	153	616	80	177	28	18	7	111	27	52	.287	.318	.425	96	-5	14	6		.946	11	*S-153	2.3
1925	*Pit-N	153	614	97	189	32	10	18	121	31	32	.308	.341	.480	100	-2	3	7	-3	.939	0	*S-153/3-1	1.1
1926	Pit-N	119	458	73	141	15	15	8	77	19	26	.308	.335	.459	106	2	6			.927	-13	*S-116	0.2
1927	*Pit-N	143	570	78	160	26	4	9	105	39	46	.281	.328	.388	85	-13	4			.942	-17	*S-143	-1.1
1928	Pit-N	108	407	63	126	20	8	8	66	21	53	.310	.343	.457	103	1	3			.927	-24	*S-101/1-1,O-1	-1.1
1929	Bro-N	24	25	4	5	0	0	1	6	3	6	.200	.286	.320	51	-2	0			.667	-3	/S-3	-0.4
1930	Bro-N	135	532	83	171	28	12	22	126	32	70	.321	.360	.543	116	11	2			.964	-2	*S-134	2.2
1931	Bro-N	77	268	36	76	9	4	9	32	14	35	.284	.324	.448	106	1	1			.942	6	S-75	1.4
1932	Bro-N	127	446	50	122	31	5	11	60	12	57	.274	.293	.439	96	-4	4			.939	8	*S-122/1-2	1.3
1933	Bro-N	71	192	19	49	13	0	1	18	11	24	.255	.299	.339	85	-4	1			.936	-4	S-51/1-9,3-2	-0.6
1935	Chi-A	9	25	1	3	1	0	0	1	0	6	.120	.120	.160	-27	-5	0	0	0	.943	-0	/2-7	-0.4
Total	11	1119	4153	584	1219	203	76	94	723	209	407	.294	.328	.447	99	-19	38	13		.941	-37	*S-1051/1-12,230	4.5

■ GEORGE WRIGHT   Wright, George   b: 1/28/1847, Yonkers, N.Y.   d: 8/21/37, Boston, Mass.   BR/TR, 5′9.5″, 150 lbs.   Deb: 5/5/1871   FMH

YEAR	TM/L	G	AB	R	H	2B	3B	HR	RBI	BB	SO	AVG	OBP	SLG	PRO+	BR/A	SB	CS	SBR	FA	FR	G/POS	TPR
1871	Bos-n	16	80	33	33	7	5	0	11	6	1	.412	.453	.625	200	10	9	1	2	.816	-5	S-15/1-1	1.1
1872	Bos-n	48	255	87	86	16	6	2	32	3	1	.337	.345	.471	141	10	14	4	2	.838	22	*S-48	2.3
1873	Bos-n	59	325	99	126	19	8	3	50	2	8	.388	.402	.523	160	20	3	5	-2	**.808**	15	*S-59	2.2
1874	Bos-n	60	313	76	103	10	**15**	2	44	5	6	.329	.340	.476	150	15	2	0	1	.821	5	*S-60/3-1	1.4
1875	Bos-n	79	408	106	136	20	7	2	61	2	6	.333	.337	.431	159	22	13	6	0	.861	4	*S-79/P-2	2.0
1876	Bos-N	70	335	72	100	18	6	1	34	6		.299	.315	.397	134	11				.888	13	*S-68/2-2,P-1	2.1
1877	Bos-N	61	290	58	80	15	1	0	35	9	15	.276	.298	.334	95	-2				.878	9	*2-58/S-3	0.8
1878	Bos-N	59	267	35	60	5	1	0	12	6	22	.225	.242	.251	58	-13				**.947**	11	*S-59	0.1
1879	Pro-N	85	388	79	107	15	10	1	42	13	20	.276	.299	.374	122	9				.924	21	*S-85,M	3.2
1880	Bos-N	1	4	2	1	0	0	0	0	0	0	.250	.250	.250	72	-0				1.000	-0	/S-1	0.0
1881	Bos-N	7	25	4	5	0	0	0	3	0	1	.200	.286	.200	58	-1				.963	-7	/S-7	-0.3
1882	Pro-N	46	185	14	30	1	2	0	9	4	36	.162	.180	.189	19	-16				.873	-7	S-46	-2.0
Total	5 n	262	1381	401	484	72	41	9	198	24	16	.350	.362	.482	156	78	41	16	3	.831	50	S-261/P-2,3-1,1-1	9.0
Total		329	1494	264	383	54	20	2	132	43	103	.256	.277	.323	93	-11				.911	42	S-269/2-60,P-1	3.9

■ GEORGE WRIGHT   Wright, George De Witt   b: 12/22/58, Oklahoma City, Okla   BB/TR, 5′11″, 180 lbs.   Deb: 4/10/82

YEAR	TM/L	G	AB	R	H	2B	3B	HR	RBI	BB	SO	AVG	OBP	SLG	PRO+	BR/A	SB	CS	SBR	FA	FR	G/POS	TPR
1982	Tex-A	150	557	69	147	20	5	11	50	30	78	.264	.305	.377	91	-8	3	7	-3	.981	11	*O-149	-0.5
1983	Tex-A	162	634	79	175	28	6	18	80	41	82	.276	.322	.424	106	3	8	7	-2	.985	10	*O-161	0.7
1984	Tex-A	101	383	40	93	19	4	9	48	15	54	.243	.275	.384	78	-13	0	2	-1	.983	-3	*O-80,D-18	-2.0
1985	Tex-A	109	363	21	69	13	0	2	18	25	49	.190	.242	.242	33	-33	4	7	-3	.991	-1	*O-102/D-4	-4.1
1986	Tex-A	49	106	10	23	8	2	0	4	7	23	.217	.252	.321	53	-7	3	5	-2	.969	-5	O-42	-1.5
	Mon-N	56	117	12	22	5	2	0	5	1	28	.188	.264	.265	47	-9	1	4	-1	1.000	-2	O-32	-1.3
Total	5	627	2160	231	529	88	18	42	208	126	314	.245	.289	.361	-66	-66	19	29	-12	.984	10	O-566/D-22	-8.7

YEAR	TM/L	G	AB	R	H	2B	3B	HR	RBI	BB	SO	AVG	OBP	SLG	PRO+	BR/A	SB	CS	SBR	FA	FR	G/POS	TPR

■ JOE WRIGHT   Wright, Joseph S.   b: 1873, Pittsburgh, Pa.   BL/TL, 5'8", 175 lbs.   Deb: 7/14/1895

1895	Lou-N	60	228	30	63	10	4	1	30	12	28	.276	.315	.368	81	-7	7			.963	-2	O-60	-1.1
1896	Lou-N	2	7	0	2	0	0	0	0	0	1	.286	.286	.286	53	-0	0			1.000	-0	/O-2	-0.1
	Pit-N	15	52	5	16	2	1	0	6	1	2	.308	.321	.385	89	-1	1			.958	-2	O-12/3-1	-0.3
	Yr	17	59	5	18	2	1	0	6	1	3	.305	.317	.373	85	-1	1			.962	-2	O-14/3-1	-0.4
Total	2	77	287	35	81	12	5	1	36	13	31	.282	.316	.369	82	-8	8			.963	-5	/O-74,3-1	-1.5

■ PAT WRIGHT   Wright, Patrick Francis   b: 7/5/1865, Pottsville, Pa.   d: 5/29/43, Springfield, Ill.   BB/TR, 6'2", 190 lbs.   Deb: 7/11/1890

| 1890 | Chi-N | 1 | 2 | 0 | 0 | 0 | 0 | 0 | 0 | 1 | 0 | .000 | .333 | .000 | -1 | -0 | 0 | | | 1.000 | 0 | /2-1 | 0.0 |

■ SAM WRIGHT   Wright, Samuel   b: 11/25/1848, New York, N.Y.   d: 5/6/28, Boston, Mass.   BR/TR, 5'7.5", 146 lbs.   Deb: 4/21/1875   F

1875	NH-n	33	127	10	24	4	0	0	5	1		.189	.195	.220	51	-5	1	0	0	.807	12	S-33	0.5
1876	Bos-N	2	8	0	1	0	0	0	0	0	0	.125	.125	.125	-16	-1				.778	-0	/S-2	-0.1
1880	Cin-N	9	34	0	3	0	0	0	0	0	5	.088	.088	.088	-40	-5				.889	-2	/S-9	-0.6
1881	Bos-N	1	4	0	1	0	0	0	0	0	0	.250	.250	.250	60	-0				.667	-1	/S-1	-0.1
Total	3	12	46	0	5	0	0	0	0	0	5	.109	.109	.109	-27	-6	1	0	0	.843	-3	/S-12	-0.8

■ TAFFY WRIGHT   Wright, Taft Shedron   b: 8/10/11, Tabor City, N.C.   d: 10/22/81, Orlando, Fla.   BL/TR, 5'10", 180 lbs.   Deb: 4/18/38

1938	Was-A	100	263	37	92	18	10	2	36	13	17	.350	.389	.517	134	13	1	2	-1	.982	-4	O-60	0.5
1939	Was-A	129	499	77	154	29	11	3	93	18	39	.309	.359	.435	110	6	1	2	-1	.950	-3	*O-123	-0.2
1940	Chi-A	147	581	79	196	31	9	5	88	43	25	.337	.385	.448	114	12	4	7	-3	.963	-4	*O-144	-0.2
1941	Chi-A	136	513	71	165	35	5	10	97	60	27	.322	.399	.468	130	23	5	4	-1	.973	-2	*O-134	1.1
1942	Chi-A	85	300	43	100	13	5	0	47	48	9	.333	.432	.410	141	19	1	8	-5	.968	-1	O-81	1.0
1946	Chi-A	115	422	46	116	19	4	7	52	42	17	.275	.342	.389	108	4	10	3	1	.991	-3	*O-107	-0.3
1947	Chi-A	124	401	48	130	13	0	4	54	48	17	.324	.398	.387	123	14	8	6	-1	.971	-4	*O-100	0.4
1948	Chi-A	134	455	50	127	15	6	4	61	38	18	.279	.341	.365	91	-7	2	1	0	.987	1	*O-114	-1.2
1949	Phi-A	59	149	14	35	2	5	2	25	16	6	.235	.321	.356	82	-4	0	0	0	.970	-0	O-35	-0.6
Total	9	1029	3583	465	1115	175	55	38	553	346	155	.311	.376	.423	116	80	32	33	-10	.972	-21	O-898	0.5

■ TOM WRIGHT   Wright, Thomas Everette   b: 9/22/23, Shelby, N.C.   BL/TR, 5'11.5", 180 lbs.   Deb: 9/15/48

1948	Bos-A	3	2	1	1	0	1	0	0	0	0	.500	.500	1.500	400	1	0	0	0	.000	0	H	0.1
1949	Bos-A	5	4	1	1	1	0	0	1	1	1	.250	.400	.500	128	0	0	0	0	.000	0	H	0.0
1950	Bos-A	54	107	17	34	7	0	0	20	6	18	.318	.360	.383	82	-3	0	0	0	.953	-2	O-24	-0.6
1951	Bos-A	28	63	8	14	1	1	1	9	11	8	.222	.347	.317	73	-2	0	0	0	.950	-4	O-18	-0.6
1952	StL-A	29	66	6	16	0	0	1	6	12	20	.242	.359	.288	79	-1	1	1	-0	.976	1	O-18	-0.2
	Chi-A	60	132	15	34	10	2	1	21	16	16	.258	.348	.386	102	1	0	0	0	.969	-2	O-34	-0.2
	Yr	89	198	21	50	10	2	2	27	28	36	.253	.348	.354	94	-1	2	1	-0	.971	-1	O-52	-0.4
1953	Chi-A	77	132	14	33	5	3	2	25	12	21	.250	.322	.379	86	-3	0	0	0	.978	-5	O-33	-0.9
1954	Was-A	76	171	13	42	4	4	1	17	18	38	.246	.325	.333	85	-4	0	0	0	1.000	0	O-43	-0.7
1955	Was-A	7	7	0	0	0	0	0	0	0	1	.000	.000	.000	-99	-2	0	0	0	.000	0	H	-0.2
1956	Was-A	2	1	0	0	0	0	0	0	0	0	.000	.000	.000	-99	-0	0	0	0	.000	0	H	0.0
Total	9	341	685	75	175	28	11	6	99	76	123	.255	.336	.355	85	-14	2	1	0	.977	-13	O-170	-3.3

■ DICK WRIGHT   Wright, Willard James   b: 5/5/1890, Worcester, N.Y.   d: 1/24/52, Bethlehem, Pa.   BR/TR, 5'10", 170 lbs.   Deb: 6/30/15

| 1915 | Bro-F | 4 | 5 | 0 | 0 | 0 | 0 | 0 | 0 | 0 | 0 | .000 | .000 | .000 | -99 | -1 | | | | .833 | -1 | /C-3 | -0.2 |

■ HARRY WRIGHT   Wright, William Henry   b: 1/10/1835, Sheffield, England   d: 10/3/1895, Atlantic City, N.J.   BR/TR, 5'9.5", 157 lbs.   Deb: 5/5/1871   FMH

1871	Bos-n	31	147	42	44	5	2	0	26	13	2	.299	.356	.361	103	1	7	1	2	.855	-0	*O-30/P-9,S-1,M	0.2
1872	Bos-n	48	208	39	52	5	1	0	23	9	2	.250	.281	.284	70	-8	0	0	0	.866	-4	*O-48/P-7,M	-0.7
1873	Bos-n	58	266	57	67	10	4	2	35	10	3	.252	.279	.342	77	-10	1	1	-0	.837	-4	*O-58/P-13,M	-0.8
1874	Bos-n	40	184	44	58	4	2	2	27	4	2	.315	.330	.391	123	4	1	0	0	.827	-2	*O-40/P-6,M	0.2
1875	Bos-n	1	4	1	1	0	0	0	0	0	1	.250	.250	.250	72	-0	0	0	0	1.000	-0	/O-1,M	0.0
1876	Bos-N	1	3	0	0	0	0	0	0	0	0	.000	.000	.000	-98	-1				.000	-0	/O-1,M	-0.1
1877	Bos-N	1	4	0	0	0	0	0	0	0	0	.000	.000	.000	-97	-1				.667	1	/O-1,M	0.0
Total	5 n	178	809	183	222	24	9	4	111	36	10	.274	.305	.341	90	-13	9	2	2	.846	-11	O-177/P-35,S-1	-1.1
Total	2	2	7	0	0	0	0	0	0	0	0	.000	.000	.000	-97	-1				.667	1	/O-2	-0.1

■ BILL WRIGHT   Wright, William Hiram   Deb: 9/16/1887

| 1887 | Was-N | 1 | 3 | 0 | 2 | 0 | 0 | 0 | 0 | 0 | 0 | .667 | .667 | .667 | 286 | 1 | 0 | | | .778 | -0 | /C-1 | 0.0 |

■ RASTY WRIGHT   Wright, William Smith   b: 1/31/1863, Birmingham, Mich.   d: 10/14/22, Duluth, Minn.   BL, 6'1", 185 lbs.   Deb: 4/17/1890

1890	Syr-a	88	348	82	106	10	6	0	27	69		.305	.428	.368	150	29	30			.907	4	O-88	2.5
	Cle-N	13	45	7	5	1	0	0	2	12	4	.111	.298	.133	27	-4	3			.917	-1	O-13	-0.4
Total	1	101	393	89	111	11	6	0	29	81	4	.282	.412	.341	135	25	33			.908	3	O-101	2.1

■ RUSS WRIGHTSTONE   Wrightstone, Russell Guy   b: 3/18/1893, Bowmansdale, Pa.   d: 2/25/69, Harrisburg, Pa.   BL/TR, 5'10.5", 176 lbs.   Deb: 4/19/20

1920	Phi-N	76	206	23	54	6	3	1	17	10	25	.262	.303	.345	82	-5	3	2	-0	.934	6	3-56/S-2,2-1	0.3
1921	Phi-N	109	372	59	110	13	4	9	51	18	20	.296	.332	.425	92	-5	4	4	-1	.922	4	3-54,O-37/2-4	-0.1
1922	Phi-N	99	331	56	101	18	6	5	33	28	17	.305	.365	.441	98	-2	4	5	-2	.973	13	3-40,S-35/1-2	1.4
1923	Phi-N	119	392	59	107	21	7	7	57	21	19	.273	.315	.416	82	-12	5	2	0	.942	-4	3-72,S-21/2-9	-0.7
1924	Phi-N	118	388	55	119	24	4	7	58	27	15	.307	.363	.443	102	1	5	4	-1	.944	-8	3-97/2-9,S-5,0-1	-0.1
1925	Phi-N	92	286	48	99	18	5	14	61	19	18	.346	.389	.591	135	14	0	3	-2	.937	-19	O-45,S-12,3-11,2/1	-0.8
1926	Phi-N	112	368	55	113	23	1	7	57	27	11	.307	.356	.432	106	3	5			.977	-0	1-53,3-37,2-13,/O-5	0.2
1927	Phi-N	141	533	62	163	24	5	6	75	48	20	.306	.365	.403	104	4	9			.989	1	*1-136/2-1,3-1	-0.4
1928	Phi-N	33	91	12	19	5	1	1	11	14	5	.209	.321	.319	65	-4	0			.936	-4	O-26/1-4	-1.0
	NY-N	30	25	3	4	0	1	1	5	3	2	.160	.280	.280	38	-2	0			1.000	-0	/1-2	-0.2
	Yr	63	116	10	23	5	2	2	16	17	7	.198	.306	.310	60	-7	0			.936	-4	O-26/1-6	-1.2
Total	9	929	2992	427	889	152	34	60	425	215	152	.297	.349	.431	99	-9	35	20		.942	-12	3-368,1-203,O/S2	-1.4

■ ZEKE WRIGLEY   Wrigley, George Watson   b: 1/18/1874, Philadelphia, Pa.   d: 9/28/52, Philadelphia, Pa.   5'8.5", 150 lbs.   Deb: 8/31/1896

1896	Was-N	5	9	1	1	0	0	0	2	1	1	.111	.200	.111	-17	-2	0			.909	3	/2-3,S-1	0.1
1897	Was-N	104	388	65	110	14	8	3	64	21		.284	.320	.384	86	-9	5			.885	-2	O-36,S-33,3-30,/2-9	-1.0
1898	Was-N	111	400	50	98	9	10	2	39	20		.245	.283	.333	76	-14	10			.895	11	S-97,2-11/O-3,3-1	0.2
1899	NY-N	4	15	1	3	0	0	0	1	1		.200	.250	.200	25	-2	1			.818	-1	/3-5	-0.3
	Bro-N	15	49	4	10	2	0	0	11	3		.204	.250	.327	56	-3	2			.870	-4	S-14/3-1	-0.5
	Yr	19	64	5	13	2	0	0	12	4		.203	.250	.297	49	-5	3			.870	-5	S-14/3-6	-0.8
Total	4	239	861	121	222	25	20	5	117	46	1	.258	.296	.351	78	-29	18			.892	7	S-145/O-39,3-37,2	-1.5

■ RICK WRONA   Wrona, Richard James   b: 12/10/63, Tulsa, Okla.   BR/TR, 6'1", 185 lbs.   Deb: 9/3/88

1988	Chi-N	4	6	0	0	0	0	0	0	0	1	.000	.000	.000	-96	-1	0	0	0	1.000	1	/C-2	0.0
1989	*Chi-N	38	92	11	26	2	1	2	14	2	21	.283	.305	.391	91	-1	0	0	0	.983	2	C-37	0.2
1990	Chi-N	16	29	3	5	0	0	0	2	0	11	.172	.226	.172	10	-3	1	0	0	.970	3	C-16	0.0
1992	Cin-N	11	23	0	4	0	0	0	0	1	6	.174	.174	.174	-1	-3	0	0	0	.965	3	C-10/1-1	-0.2
1993	Chi-A	4	8	0	1	0	0	0	1	0	1	.125	.125	.125	-33	-1	0	0	0	1.000	-1	/C-4	-0.2
1994	Mil-A	6	10	2	5	4	0	0	3	1	1	.500	.545	1.200	319	3	0	0	0	.923	-1	/C-5,1-1	0.2
Total	6	79	168	16	41	6	1	4	20	4	41	.244	.270	.345	66	-6	1	0	0	.976	8	/C-74,1-2	0.2

■ YATS WUESTLING   Wuestling, George   b: 10/18/03, St.Louis, Mo.   d: 4/26/70, St.Louis, Mo.   BR/TR, 5'11", 167 lbs.   Deb: 6/15/29

1929	Det-A	54	130	13	30	4	1	0	16	9	24	.200	.250	.240	27	-16	1	3	-2	.943	-2	S-52/2-1,3-1	-1.4
1930	Det-A	4	9	0	0	0	0	0	0	1	2	.000	.182	.000	-48	-2	0	0	0	.842	1	/S-4	-0.1
	NY-A	25	58	5	11	3	1	0	3	8	14	.190	.242	.224	20	-7	0	1	-1	.918	4	S-21/3-3	-0.2

YEAR	TM/L	G	AB	R	H	2B	3B	HR	RBI	BB	SO	AVG	OBP	SLG	PRO+	BR/A	SB	CS	SBR	FA	FR	G/POS	TPR
	Yr	29	67	5	11	0	1	0	3	6	17	.164	.233	.194	10	-9	0	1	-1	.904	5	S-25/3-3	-0.3
Total	2	83	217	18	41	4	2	0	19	15	41	.189	.245	.226	21	-26	1	4	-2	.931	2	/S-77,3-4,2-1	-1.7

■ JOE WYATT Wyatt, Loral John b: 4/6/1900, Petersburg, Ind. d: 12/5/70, Oblong, Ill. BR/TR, 6'1", 175 lbs. Deb: 9/11/24

YEAR	TM/L	G	AB	R	H	2B	3B	HR	RBI	BB	SO	AVG	OBP	SLG	PRO+	BR/A	SB	CS	SBR	FA	FR	G/POS	TPR
1924	Cle-A	4	12	1	2	0	0	0	1	2	1	.167	.286	.167	18	-1	0	0	0	.833	-1	/O-4	-0.3

■ REN WYLIE Wylie, James Renwick b: 12/14/1861, Elizabeth, Pa. d: 8/17/51, Wilkinsburg, Pa. BR/TR, 5'11", 155 lbs. Deb: 8/11/1882

YEAR	TM/L	G	AB	R	H	2B	3B	HR	RBI	BB	SO	AVG	OBP	SLG	PRO+	BR/A	SB	CS	SBR	FA	FR	G/POS	TPR
1882	Pit-a	1	3	0	0	0	0	0		0		.000	.000	.000	-99	-1				1.000	0	/O-1	0.0

■ FRANK WYMAN Wyman, Frank H. b: 5/10/1862, Haverhill, Mass. d: 2/4/16, Everett, Mass. Deb: 6/10/1884

YEAR	TM/L	G	AB	R	H	2B	3B	HR	RBI	BB	SO	AVG	OBP	SLG	PRO+	BR/A	SB	CS	SBR	FA	FR	G/POS	TPR
1884	KC-U	30	124	16	27	4	0	0			3	.218	.236	.250	55	-11				.743	5	O-25/P-3,1,3-3	-0.5
	CP-U	2	8	1	3	0	0	0			0	.375	.375	.375	129	0				.846	-0	/1-2	-0.1
	Yr	32	132	17	30	4	0	0			3	.227	.244	.258	60	-10				.743	4	O-25/1-5,P-3,3-3	-0.6

■ BUTCH WYNEGAR Wynegar, Harold Delano b: 3/14/56, York, Pa. BB/TR, 6', 194 lbs. Deb: 4/9/76

YEAR	TM/L	G	AB	R	H	2B	3B	HR	RBI	BB	SO	AVG	OBP	SLG	PRO+	BR/A	SB	CS	SBR	FA	FR	G/POS	TPR
1976	Min-A★	149	534	58	139	21	2	10	69	79	63	.260	.358	.363	109	9	0	0	0	.978	-10	*C-137,D-15	0.3
1977	Min-A★	144	532	76	139	22	3	10	79	68	61	.261	.347	.370	97	-1	2	3	-1	.993	-11	*C-142/3-1	-0.9
1978	Min-A	135	454	36	104	22	1	4	45	47	42	.229	.310	.308	73	-15	1	0	0	.988	-3	*C-131/3-1	-1.5
1979	Min-A	149	504	74	136	20	0	7	57	74	36	.270	.366	.351	91	-4	2	2	-1	.992	-4	*C-146/D-2	-0.3
1980	Min-A	146	486	61	124	18	3	5	57	63	36	.255	.343	.335	81	-11	3	1	0	.988	4	*C-142/D-1	-0.2
1981	Min-A	47	150	11	37	5	0	0	10	17	9	.247	.327	.280	72	-5	0	1	-1	.995	-1	C-37/D-9	-0.5
1982	Min-A	24	86	9	18	4	0	1	8	10	12	.209	.292	.291	59	-5	0	0	0	.986	-2	C-24	-0.5
	NY-A	63	191	27	56	8	1	3	20	40	21	.293	.418	.393	126	9	0	1	-1	.993	-1	C-62	1.1
	Yr	87	277	36	74	12	1	4	28	50	33	.267	.381	.361	106	4	0	1	-1	.991	-2	C-86	0.6
1983	NY-A	94	301	40	89	18	2	6	42	52	29	.296	.401	.429	133	16	1	1	-0	.985	-13	*C-93	0.7
1984	NY-A	129	442	48	118	13	1	6	45	65	35	.267	.361	.342	99	2	1	4	-2	.993	-4	*C-126	0.3
1985	NY-A	102	309	27	69	15	0	5	32	64	43	.223	.357	.320	89	-2	0	0	-0	.990	2	C-96	0.4
1986	NY-A	61	194	19	40	4	1	7	29	30	21	.206	.313	.345	80	-5	0	0	0	.994	2	C-57	-0.3
1987	Cal-A	31	92	4	19	2	0	0	5	9	13	.207	.277	.228	37	-8	0	0	0	.994	3	C-28/D-1	-0.4
1988	Cal-A	27	55	8	14	4	1	1	8	8	7	.255	.349	.418	117	1	0	0	0	.981	-0	C-26	0.2
Total	13	1301	4330	498	1102	176	15	65	506	626	428	.255	.351	.347	93	-19	10	13	-5	.989	-43	*C-1247/D-28,3-2	-1.6

■ EARLY WYNN Wynn, Early "Gus" b: 1/6/20, Hartford, Ala. BB/TR, 6', 200 lbs. Deb: 9/13/39 CH

YEAR	TM/L	G	AB	R	H	2B	3B	HR	RBI	BB	SO	AVG	OBP	SLG	PRO+	BR/A	SB	CS	SBR	FA	FR	G/POS	TPR
1939	Was-A	3	6	0	1	0	0	0	1	1	1	.167	.286	.167	20	-1	0	0	0	1.000	-1	/P-3	0.0
1941	Was-A	5	15	1	2	1	0	0	0	0	5	.133	.133	.200	-14	-2	0	0	0	.917	0	/P-5	0.0
1942	Was-A	30	69	4	15	2	0	0	7	3	13	.217	.250	.246	40	-6	0	0	0	.953	-1	P-30	0.0
1943	Was-A	38	98	6	29	3	1	0	11	1	11	.296	.303	.378	102	-0	0	0	0	.947	-2	P-37	0.0
1944	Was-A	43	92	4	19	2	0	1	6	3	21	.207	.232	.261	42	-7	0	0	0	.972	-2	P-33	0.0
1946	Was-A	25	47	4	15	2	0	0	5	5	7	.319	.385	.426	134	0	0	0	0	.962	-0	P-17	0.0
1947	Was-A☆	54	120	6	33	6	0	2	13	1	19	.275	.281	.375	84	-3	0	0	0	.980	-1	P-33	0.0
1948	Was-A	73	106	9	23	3	1	0	16	14	22	.217	.308	.264	55	-7	0	0	0	.950	-1	P-33	0.0
1949	Cle-A	35	70	3	10	1	0	1	7	4	10	.143	.189	.200	3	-10	0	0	0	**1.000**	1	P-26	0.0
1950	Cle-A	39	77	12	18	5	1	2	10	10	12	.234	.322	.403	87	-2	0	0	0	.932	1	P-32	0.0
1951	Cle-A	41	108	8	20	8	1	1	13	7	9	.185	.235	.306	48	-9	0	0	0	.982	-1	P-37	0.0
1952	Cle-A	44	99	5	22	2	0	0	9	6	15	.222	.287	.242	52	-6	0	0	0	.943	-1	P-42	0.0
1953	Cle-A	37	91	11	25	2	0	3	10	7	17	.275	.327	.396	97	-1	0	0	0	**1.000**	-1	P-36	0.0
1954	*Cle-A	40	93	10	17	3	0	0	4	7	13	.183	.240	.215	25	-10	0	0	0	.957	-3	P-40	0.0
1955	Cle-A★	34	84	8	15	3	0	1	7	6	17	.179	.233	.250	29	-9	0	0	0	.944	-3	P-32	0.0
1956	Cle-A★	38	101	5	23	5	0	1	15	7	22	.228	.278	.307	53	-7	0	0	0	.955	-3	P-38	0.0
1957	Cle-A★	40	86	4	10	0	0	0	4	11	23	.116	.216	.116	-7	-13	0	0	0	**1.000**	1	P-40	0.0
1958	Chi-A★	40	75	7	15	1	0	0	11	10	25	.200	.294	.213	43	-6	0	0	0	**1.000**	-2	P-40	0.0
1959	*Chi-A★	37	90	11	22	7	0	2	8	9	18	.244	.320	.389	95	-1	0	0	0	.957	-1	P-37	0.0
1960	Chi-A★	36	75	8	15	2	1	1	7	14	17	.200	.333	.293	72	-3	0	0	0	.972	-2	P-36	0.0
1961	Chi-A	17	37	4	6	0	0	0	2	3	11	.162	.225	.162	5	-5	0	0	0	1.000	-2	P-17	0.0
1962	Chi-A	27	54	5	7	1	0	0	2	7	17	.130	.230	.148	4	-7	0	0	0	**1.000**	-2	P-27	0.0
1963	Cle-A	20	11	1	3	0	0	0	0	0	5	.273	.385	.273	89	-0	0	0	0	1.000	-0	P-20	0.0
Total	23	796	1704	136	365	59	5	17	173	141	330	.214	.275	.285	54	-111	1	0	0	.967	-25	P-691	0.0

■ JIM WYNN Wynn, James Sherman b: 3/12/42, Hamilton, Ohio BR/TR, 5'9", 170 lbs. Deb: 7/10/63

YEAR	TM/L	G	AB	R	H	2B	3B	HR	RBI	BB	SO	AVG	OBP	SLG	PRO+	BR/A	SB	CS	SBR	FA	FR	G/POS	TPR
1963	Hou-N	70	250	31	61	10	5	4	27	30	53	.244	.325	.372	107	2	4	2	0	.963	-2	O-53,S-21/3-2	-0.2
1964	Hou-N	67	219	19	49	7	0	5	18	24	58	.224	.303	.324	81	-5	5	5	-2	.958	5	O-64	-0.5
1965	Hou-N	157	564	90	155	30	7	22	73	84	126	.275	.374	.470	146	36	43	4	**11**	.978	20	*O-155	6.1
1966	Hou-N	105	418	62	107	21	1	18	62	41	81	.256	.324	.440	118	9	13	10	-2	.978	11	*O-104	1.3
1967	Hou-N★	158	594	102	148	29	3	37	107	74	137	.249	.334	.495	139	29	16	4	2	.968	9	*O-157	3.4
1968	Hou-N	156	542	85	146	23	5	26	67	90	131	.269	.378	.474	158	40	11	17	-7	.988	15	*O-153	4.5
1969	Hou-N	149	495	113	133	17	1	33	87	**148**	142	.269	.440	.507	168	53	23	7	3	.985	11	*O-149	6.0
1970	Hou-N	157	554	82	156	32	2	27	88	106	96	.282	.398	.493	143	36	24	5	4	.987	10	*O-151	4.2
1971	Hou-N	123	404	38	82	16	0	7	45	56	63	.203	.303	.295	72	-14	10	5	0	.988	2	*O-116	-2.0
1972	Hou-N	145	542	117	148	29	3	24	90	103	99	.273	.391	.470	147	36	17	7	1	.983	6	*O-144	3.9
1973	Hou-N	139	481	90	106	14	5	20	55	91	102	.220	.349	.395	106	6	14	11	-2	.986	3	*O-133	0.0
1974	*LA-N★	150	535	104	145	17	4	32	108	108	104	.271	.393	.497	154	41	18	15	-4	.992	11	*O-148	4.3
1975	LA-N★	130	412	80	102	16	0	18	58	110	77	.248	.407	.417	135	25	7	3	0	.983	-1	*O-120	2.0
1976	Atl-N	148	449	75	93	19	1	17	66	**127**	111	.207	.382	.367	107	9	16	6	1	.971	11	*O-138	1.6
1977	NY-A	30	77	7	11	2	1	1	3	15	16	.143	.292	.234	43	-6	1	0	0	1.000	2	D-15/O-8	-0.5
	Mil-A	36	117	10	23	3	1	0	10	17	31	.197	.299	.239	49	-8	3	1	0	.967	-2	O-17,D-15	-0.9
	Yr	66	194	17	34	5	2	1	13	32	47	.175	.292	.237	46	-14	4	1	0	.981	1	D-30,O-25	-1.4
Total	15	1920	6653	1105	1665	285	39	291	964	1224	1427	.250	.369	.436	129	289	225	101	7	.981	110	*O-1810/D-30,S-21,3	33.2

■ MARVELL WYNNE Wynne, Marvell b: 12/17/59, Chicago, Ill. BL/TL, 5'11", 185 lbs. Deb: 6/15/83

YEAR	TM/L	G	AB	R	H	2B	3B	HR	RBI	BB	SO	AVG	OBP	SLG	PRO+	BR/A	SB	CS	SBR	FA	FR	G/POS	TPR
1983	Pit-N	103	366	66	89	16	2	7	26	38	52	.243	.319	.355	85	-7	12	10	-2	.983	-0	*O-102	-1.4
1984	Pit-N	154	653	77	174	24	11	0	39	42	81	.266	.311	.337	82	-16	24	19	-4	.990	5	*O-154	-2.1
1985	Pit-N	103	337	21	69	6	3	2	18	18	48	.205	.247	.258	42	-26	10	5	-0	.987	6	O-99	-2.5
1986	SD-N	137	288	34	76	19	2	7	37	15	45	.264	.303	.417	98	-2	11	11	-3	.986	-11	*O-125	-1.9
1987	SD-N	98	188	17	47	8	2	4	24	20	37	.250	.322	.346	80	-5	11	6	-0	.981	-10	O-71	-1.7
1988	SD-N	128	333	37	88	13	4	11	42	31	62	.264	.327	.426	117	7	3	4	-2	.987	-11	*O-113	-1.0
1989	SD-N	105	294	19	74	11	1	6	35	12	41	.252	.283	.357	82	-8	3	3	-1	.971	-7	O-96	-1.7
	*Chi-N	20	48	8	9	2	1	1	4	1	7	.188	.220	.333	52	-3	2	0	1	.944	-2	O-13	-0.6
	Yr	125	342	27	83	13	2	7	39	13	48	.243	.275	.354	77	-11	5	1	0	.968	-9	*O-109	-2.3
1990	Chi-N	92	186	21	38	8	2	4	19	14	25	.204	.264	.333	59	-11	3	2	-0	.991	-9	O-66	-2.2
Total	8	940	2693	300	664	107	28	40	244	191	398	.247	.298	.352	81	-72	80	58	-11	.985	-41	O-839	-15.1

■ JOHNNY WYROSTEK Wyrostek, John Barney b: 7/12/19, Fairmont City, Ill. d: 12/12/86, St.Louis, Mo. BL/TR, 6'2", 180 lbs. Deb: 9/10/42

YEAR	TM/L	G	AB	R	H	2B	3B	HR	RBI	BB	SO	AVG	OBP	SLG	PRO+	BR/A	SB	CS	SBR	FA	FR	G/POS	TPR
1942	Pit-N	9	35	0	4	0	1	0	3	3	2	.114	.184	.171	4	-4	0			1.000	1	/O-8	-0.4
1943	Pit-N	51	79	7	12	3	0	0	1	3	15	.152	.183	.190	7	-9	0			.919	-5	O-20/3-2,1-1,2-1	-1.6
1946	Phi-N	145	545	73	153	30	4	6	45	70	42	.281	.366	.383	116	12	7			.981	17	*O-142	2.4
1947	Phi-N	128	454	68	124	24	7	5	51	61	45	.273	.364	.390	104	4	7			.971	-0	*O-126	-0.2
1948	Cin-N	136	512	74	140	24	9	17	76	52	63	.273	.344	.455	119	12	7			.977	4	*O-130	0.8
1949	Cin-N	134	474	54	118	20	4	9	46	58	63	.249	.333	.365	86	-9	7			.971	-1	*O-129	-1.4
1950	Cin-N★	131	509	70	145	34	5	8	76	52	38	.285	.357	.418	103	2	1			.980	2	*O-129/1-4	-0.5
1951	Cin-N★	142	537	52	167	31	3	8	61	54	54	.311	.376	.391	105	9	1			.970	-7	*O-139	-0.7
1952	Cin-N	30	106	12	25	1	3	1	10	18	7	.236	.347	.330	89	-1	2			1.000	2	O-29/1-1	-0.1

YEAR	TM/L	G	AB	R	H	2B	3B	HR	RBI	BB	SO	AVG	OBP	SLG	PRO+	BR/A	SB	CS	SBR	FA	FR	G/POS	TPR
	Phi-N	98	321	45	88	16	3	1	37	44	26	.274	.363	.352	100	2	1	7	-4	.972	8	O-88	0.2
	Yr	128	427	57	113	17	6	2	47	62	33	.265	.359	.347	97	0	2	9	-5	.980	10	*O-117/1-1	0.1
1953	Phi-N	125	409	42	111	14	2	6	47	38	43	.271	.339	.359	83	-10	0	3	-2	.962	2	*O-110	-1.3
1954	Phi-N	92	259	28	62	12	4	3	28	29	39	.239	.318	.351	74	-10	0	0	0	.990	-5	O-55,1-22	-1.7
Total	11	1221	4240	525	1149	209	45	58	481	482	437	.271	.349	.383	98	-5	33	13		.975	16	*O-1105/1-28,3-2,2	-4.5

■ HENRY YAIK
Yaik, Henry b: 3/1/1864, Detroit, Mich. d: 9/21/35, Detroit, Mich. 5'11", 185 lbs. Deb: 10/3/1888

YEAR	TM/L	G	AB	R	H	2B	3B	HR	RBI	BB	SO	AVG	OBP	SLG	PRO+	BR/A	SB	CS	SBR	FA	FR	G/POS	TPR
1888	Pit-N	2	6	0	2	0	0	0	1	0	0	.333	.429	.333	158	0	0			.625	2	/O-1,C-1	0.2

■ AD YALE
Yale, William M. b: 4/17/1870, Bristol, Conn. d: 4/27/48, Bridgeport, Conn. Deb: 9/18/05

YEAR	TM/L	G	AB	R	H	2B	3B	HR	RBI	BB	SO	AVG	OBP	SLG	PRO+	BR/A	SB	CS	SBR	FA	FR	G/POS	TPR
1905	Bro-N	4	13	1	1	0	0	0	0	1	0	.077	.143	.077	-37	-2	0			1.000	-0	/1-4	-0.3

■ HUGH YANCY
Yancy, Hugh b: 10/16/49, Sarasota, Fla. BR/TR, 5'11", 170 lbs. Deb: 7/5/72

YEAR	TM/L	G	AB	R	H	2B	3B	HR	RBI	BB	SO	AVG	OBP	SLG	PRO+	BR/A	SB	CS	SBR	FA	FR	G/POS	TPR
1972	Chi-A	3	9	0	1	1	0	0	0	0	0	.111	.111	.111	-33	-1	0	1	-1	1.000	0	/3-3	-0.2
1974	Chi-A	1	0	0	0	0	0	0	0	0	0	—	—	—	—	-0	0	0	0	.000	0	/D-1	0.0
1976	Chi-A	3	10	0	1	0	0	0	0	0	3	.100	.100	.200	-14	-1	0	0	0	1.000	-1	/2-3	-0.2
Total	3	7	19	0	2	1	0	0	0	0	3	.105	.105	.158	-23	-3	0	1	-1	1.000	-0	/2-3,3-3,D-1	-0.4

■ GEORGE YANKOWSKI
Yankowski, George Edward b: 11/19/22, Cambridge, Mass. BR/TR, 6', 180 lbs. Deb: 8/17/42

YEAR	TM/L	G	AB	R	H	2B	3B	HR	RBI	BB	SO	AVG	OBP	SLG	PRO+	BR/A	SB	CS	SBR	FA	FR	G/POS	TPR
1942	Phi-A	6	13	0	2	1	0	0	2	0	2	.154	.154	.231	7	-2	0	0	0	1.000	0	/C-6	-0.1
1949	Phi-A	12	18	0	3	1	0	0	2	0	2	.167	.167	.222	3	-3	0	0	0	1.000	1	/C-6	-0.1
Total	2	18	31	0	5	2	0	0	4	0	4	.161	.161	.226	5	-4	0	0	0	1.000	1	/C-12	-0.2

■ GEORGE YANTZ
Yantz, George Webb b: 7/27/1886, Louisville, Ky. d: 2/26/67, Louisville, Ky. BR/TR, 5'6.5", 168 lbs. Deb: 9/30/12

YEAR	TM/L	G	AB	R	H	2B	3B	HR	RBI	BB	SO	AVG	OBP	SLG	PRO+	BR/A	SB	CS	SBR	FA	FR	G/POS	TPR
1912	Chi-N	1	1	0	1	0	0	0	0	0	0	1.000	1.000	1.000	449	0	0			.000	0	/C-1	0.0

■ YAM YARYAN
Yaryan, Clarence Everett b: 11/5/1892, Knowlton, Iowa d: 11/16/64, Birmingham, Ala. BR/TR, 5'10.5", 180 lbs. Deb: 4/23/21

YEAR	TM/L	G	AB	R	H	2B	3B	HR	RBI	BB	SO	AVG	OBP	SLG	PRO+	BR/A	SB	CS	SBR	FA	FR	G/POS	TPR
1921	Chi-A	45	102	11	31	8	2	0	15	9	16	.304	.366	.422	102	0	0	0	0	.933	-6	C-34	-0.4
1922	Chi-A	36	71	9	14	2	0	2	9	6	10	.197	.269	.310	51	-5	1	0	0	.966	-1	C-26	-0.5
Total	2	81	173	20	45	10	2	2	24	15	26	.260	.326	.376	81	-5	1	0	0	.948	-8	/C-60	-0.9

■ CARL YASTRZEMSKI
Yastrzemski, Carl Michael "Yaz" b: 8/22/39, Southampton, N.Y. BL/TR, 5'11", 182 lbs. Deb: 4/11/61 H

YEAR	TM/L	G	AB	R	H	2B	3B	HR	RBI	BB	SO	AVG	OBP	SLG	PRO+	BR/A	SB	CS	SBR	FA	FR	G/POS	TPR
1961	Bos-A	148	583	71	155	31	6	11	80	50	96	.266	.327	.396	90	-9	6	5	-1	.963	1	*O-147	-1.8
1962	Bos-A	160	646	99	191	43	6	19	94	66	82	.296	.364	.469	118	17	7	4	-0	.969	16	*O-160	2.2
1963	Bos-A★	151	570	91	183	40	3	14	68	95	72	.321	.419	.475	145	38	8	5	-1	.980	13	*O-151	4.4
1964	Bos-A	151	567	77	164	29	9	15	67	75	90	.289	.374	.451	122	19	6	5	-1	.973	28	*O-148/3-2	3.9
1965	Bos-A†	133	494	78	154	45	3	20	72	70	58	.312	.398	.536	154	36	7	6	-2	.987	6	*O-130	3.6
1966	Bos-A☆	160	594	81	165	39	2	16	80	84	60	.278	.368	.431	117	14	8	9	-3	.985	17	*O-158	2.2
1967	*Bos-A★	161	579	112	189	31	4	44	121	91	69	.326	.421	.622	189	65	10	8	-2	.978	13	*O-161	7.3
1968	Bos-A★	157	539	90	162	32	2	23	74	119	90	.301	.429	.495	168	50	13	6	0	.991	17	*O-155/1-3	6.6
1969	Bos-A★	162	603	96	154	28	2	40	111	101	91	.255	.363	.507	134	27	15	7	-0	.985	10	*O-143,1-22	2.9
1970	Bos-A★	161	566	125	186	29	0	40	102	128	66	.329	.453	.592	174	62	23	13	-1	.990	2	1-94,O-69	5.2
1971	Bos-A★	148	508	75	129	21	2	15	70	106	60	.254	.363	.392	112	12	8	7	-2	.993	14	*O-146	1.8
1972	Bos-A	125	455	70	120	18	2	12	68	67	44	.264	.363	.391	118	12	5	4	-1	.974	8	O-83,1-42	1.4
1973	Bos-A†	152	540	82	160	25	4	19	95	105	58	.296	.411	.463	138	30	9	7	-2	.994	-5	*1-107,3-31,O-14	1.5
1974	Bos-A★	148	515	93	155	25	2	15	79	104	48	.301	.421	.445	139	31	12	7	-1	.997	-7	1-84,O-63/D-4	1.5
1975	*Bos-A★	149	543	91	146	30	1	14	60	87	67	.269	.372	.405	110	9	8	4	0	.996	-1	*1-140/O-8,D-2	-0.1
1976	Bos-A	155	546	71	146	23	2	21	102	80	67	.267	.362	.432	118	12	5	6	-2	.998	-8	1-94,O-51,D-10	-0.7
1977	Bos-A	150	558	99	165	27	3	28	102	73	40	.296	.378	.505	124	18	11	1	3	1.000	14	*O-140/1-7,D-6	2.8
1978	Bos-A†	144	523	70	145	21	2	17	81	76	44	.277	.372	.423	111	9	4	5	-2	.986	6	O-71,1-50,D-27	0.6
1979	Bos-A★	147	518	69	140	28	1	21	87	62	46	.270	.351	.450	108	6	3	3	-1	.996	6	D-56,1-51,O-36	0.4
1980	Bos-A	105	364	49	100	21	1	15	50	44	38	.275	.353	.462	115	8	0	2	-1	1.000	-3	D-49,O-39,1-16	0.0
1981	Bos-A	91	338	36	83	14	1	7	53	49	28	.246	.341	.355	95	-1	0	1	-0	.992	3	D-48,1-39	-0.3
1982	Bos-A	131	459	53	126	22	1	16	72	59	50	.275	.360	.431	110	7	0	1	-1	1.000	-6	*D-102,1-14/O-2	0.2
1983	Bos-A★	119	380	38	101	24	0	10	56	54	29	.266	.360	.408	103	3	0	0	0	1.000	-1	*D-107/1-2,O-1	0.2
Total	23	3308	11988	1816	3419	646	59	452	1844	1845	1393	.285	.382	.462	128	474	168	116	-19	.981	149	*O-2076,1-765,D/3	45.5

■ AL YATES
Yates, Albert Arthur b: 5/26/45, Jersey City, N.J. BR/TR, 6'2", 210 lbs. Deb: 5/13/71

YEAR	TM/L	G	AB	R	H	2B	3B	HR	RBI	BB	SO	AVG	OBP	SLG	PRO+	BR/A	SB	CS	SBR	FA	FR	G/POS	TPR
1971	Mil-A	24	47	5	13	2	0	1	4	3	7	.277	.320	.383	100	-0	1	0	0	1.000	1	O-12	0.0

■ BERT YEABSLEY
Yeabsley, Robert Watkins b: 12/17/1893, Philadelphia, Pa. d: 2/8/61, Philadelphia, Pa. BR/TR, 5'9.5", 175 lbs. Deb: 5/28/19

YEAR	TM/L	G	AB	R	H	2B	3B	HR	RBI	BB	SO	AVG	OBP	SLG	PRO+	BR/A	SB	CS	SBR	FA	FR	G/POS	TPR
1919	Phi-N	3	0	0	0	0	0	0	0	1	0	—	1.000	—	200	0	0			.000	0	H	0.0

■ GEORGE YEAGER
Yeager, George J. "Doc" b: 6/5/1874, Cincinnati, Ohio d: 7/5/40, Cincinnati, Ohio BR/TR, 5'10", 190 lbs. Deb: 9/25/1896

YEAR	TM/L	G	AB	R	H	2B	3B	HR	RBI	BB	SO	AVG	OBP	SLG	PRO+	BR/A	SB	CS	SBR	FA	FR	G/POS	TPR
1896	Bos-N	2	5	1	1	0	0	0	0	0	1	.200	.200	.200	5	-1	0			1.000	-0	/1-2	-0.1
1897	*Bos-N	30	95	20	23	2	3	2	15	7		.242	.294	.389	75	-4	2			.970	1	C-13,O-10/2-4,3-1	-0.2
1898	Bos-N	68	221	37	59	13	1	3	24	16		.267	.328	.376	96	-2	1			.951	-3	C-37,1-17/O-9,S-2	-0.2
1899	Bos-N	3	8	1	1	0	0	0	0	1		.125	.222	.125	-3	-1	0			1.000	0	/O-2,C-1	-0.1
1901	Cle-A	39	139	13	31	5	0	0	14	4		.223	.250	.259	43	-11	2			.964	3	C-25/1-5,0-3,2-2	-0.5
	Pit-N	26	91	9	24	2	1	0	10	4		.264	.302	.308	75	-3	1			.971	-2	C-20/3-4,1-1	-0.3
1902	NY-N	38	108	6	22	2	1	0	9	11		.204	.277	.241	60	-5	1			.946	-1	C-27/1-3,O-1	-0.3
	Bal-A	11	38	3	7	1	0	0	0	2		.184	.225	.211	20	-4	0			.930	1	C-11	-0.1
Total	6	217	705	90	168	25	6	5	73	45	1	.238	.290	.312	69	-30	7			.953	-1	C-134/1-28,O23S	-1.8

■ JOE YEAGER
Yeager, Joseph F. "Little Joe" b: 8/28/1875, Philadelphia, Pa. d: 7/2/37, Detroit, Mich. BR/TR, 5'10", 160 lbs. Deb: 4/22/1898

YEAR	TM/L	G	AB	R	H	2B	3B	HR	RBI	BB	SO	AVG	OBP	SLG	PRO+	BR/A	SB	CS	SBR	FA	FR	G/POS	TPR
1898	Bro-N	43	134	12	23	5	1	0	15	7		.172	.218	.224	27	-13	1			.908	6	P-36/O-4,S-2,2-1	-0.1
1899	Bro-N	23	47	12	9	0	0	0	4	6		.191	.234	.234	55	-3	0			.914	3	S-11,P-10/O-1,3-1	0.1
1900	Bro-N	3	9	0	3	0	0	0	0	0		.333	.333	.333	79	-0	0			1.000	-1	/P-2,3-1	0.0
1901	Det-A	41	125	18	37	7	1	2	17	4		.296	.343	.416	105	1	3			.919	5	P-26,S-12/2-1	0.3
1902	Det-A	50	161	17	39	6	5	1	23	5		.242	.282	.360	76	-6	0			.957	-1	P-19,O-13,2-12/S3	-0.8
1903	Det-A	109	402	36	103	15	6	0	43	18		.256	.303	.323	91	-4	9			.921	-9	*3-107/P-1,S-1	-1.2
1905	NY-A	115	401	54	107	16	7	0	42	25		.267	.330	.342	102	1	8			.923	0	3-91,S-21	0.5
1906	NY-A	57	123	20	37	6	1	0	12	13		.301	.347	.366	129	5	3			.905	-1	S-22,2-13/3-3	0.5
1907	StL-A	123	436	32	104	21	7	1	44	31		.239	.294	.326	98	-2	11			.938	7	3-91,2-17,S-10	1.0
1908	StL-A	10	15	2	5	1	0	0	1	1		.333	.474	.400	183	2	2			1.000	0	/2-4,S-1	0.2
Total	10	574	1853	204	467	77	29	4	201	110		.252	.312	.331	92	-20	37			.927	10	3-295/P-94,S-83,2O	0.5

■ STEVE YEAGER
Yeager, Stephen Wayne b: 11/24/48, Huntington, W.Va. BR/TR, 6', 190 lbs. Deb: 8/2/72

YEAR	TM/L	G	AB	R	H	2B	3B	HR	RBI	BB	SO	AVG	OBP	SLG	PRO+	BR/A	SB	CS	SBR	FA	FR	G/POS	TPR
1972	LA-N	35	106	18	29	0	1	4	16	16	26	.274	.374	.406	124	4	0	0	0	.984	9	C-35	1.4
1973	LA-N	54	134	18	34	5	2	4	20	15	33	.254	.342	.336	93	-1	1	0	0	.981	5	C-50	0.6
1974	*LA-N	94	316	41	84	16	1	12	41	32	77	.266	.337	.437	120	7	2	2	-1	.992	13	*C-93	2.4
1975	LA-N	135	452	34	103	16	1	12	54	40	75	.228	.302	.347	83	-11	2	5	-2	.992	12	*C-135	0.4
1976	LA-N	117	359	42	77	11	3	6	35	30	84	.214	.288	.354	83	-9	3	1	0	.985	9	*C-115	0.4
1977	*LA-N	125	387	53	99	21	2	16	55	43	84	.256	.336	.444	108	4	3	3	-2	.977	12	*C-123	1.8
1978	*LA-N	94	228	19	44	7	0	4	23	36	41	.193	.303	.276	63	-11	0	0	0	.988	11	*C-91	0.3
1979	LA-N	105	310	33	67	9	2	13	41	29	68	.216	.283	.384	81	-9	0	0	0	.984	11	*C-103	0.6
1980	LA-N	96	227	20	48	8	0	6	20	20	54	.211	.275	.273	55	-14	2	3	-1	.984	-4	C-95	-0.9
1981	LA-N	42	86	5	18	1	0	2	16	11	14	.209	.261	.337	71	-4	0	0	0	.994	-5	C-40	-0.2
1982	LA-N	82	196	13	48	5	2	2	18	13	28	.245	.295	.321	74	-7	0	0	-0	.990	7	C-76	0.2
1983	*LA-N	113	335	31	68	8	3	15	41	29	67	.203	.256	.379	74	-13	1	1	-0	.985	-6	*C-112	-1.5
1984	LA-N	74	197	16	45	4	0	4	29	20	38	.228	.300	.310	72	-7	0	0	0	.994	-6	C-65	-1.2
1985	*LA-N	53	121	4	25	4	1	0	9	7	24	.207	.250	.256	43	-9	0	1	-0	.992	9	C-48	0.0

YEAR	TM/L	G	AB	R	H	2B	3B	HR	RBI	BB	SO	AVG	OBP	SLG	PRO+	BR/A	SB	CS	SBR	FA	FR	G/POS	TPR
1986	Sea-A	50	130	10	27	2	0	2	12	12	23	.208	.275	.269	48	-9	0	0	0	1.000	-0	C-49	-0.7
Total	15	1269	3584	357	816	118	16	102	410	342	726	.228	.300	.355	83	-88	14	18	-7	.987	90	*C-1230	3.6

■ BILL YEATMAN
Yeatman, William Suter   b: 3/1839, Alexandria, Va.   d: 4/20/01, York, Pa.   Deb: 4/20/1872

YEAR	TM/L	G	AB	R	H	2B	3B	HR	RBI	BB	SO	AVG	OBP	SLG	PRO+	BR/A	SB	CS	SBR	FA	FR	G/POS	TPR
1872	Nat-n	1	4	0	0	0	0	0	0	0	1	.000	.000	.000	-86	-1	0	0	0	.000	-0	/O-1	-0.1

■ ERIC YELDING
Yelding, Eric Girard   b: 2/22/65, Montrose, Ala.   BR/TR, 5'11", 170 lbs.   Deb: 4/9/89

YEAR	TM/L	G	AB	R	H	2B	3B	HR	RBI	BB	SO	AVG	OBP	SLG	PRO+	BR/A	SB	CS	SBR	FA	FR	G/POS	TPR
1989	Hou-N	70	90	19	21	2	0	0	9	7	19	.233	.296	.256	61	-4	11	5	0	1.000	6	S-15,2-13/O-8	0.3
1990	Hou-N	142	511	69	130	9	5	1	28	39	87	.254	.307	.297	69	-21	64	25	4	.971	-6	O-94,S-40,2-10/3-3	-2.2
1991	Hou-N	78	276	19	67	11	1	1	20	13	46	.243	.277	.301	66	-13	11	9	-2	.939	-14	S-72/O-4	-2.5
1992	Hou-N	9	8	1	2	0	0	0	0	0	3	.250	.250	.250	44	-1	0	0	0	.000	-1	/S-2,O-2	-0.2
1993	Chi-N	69	108	14	22	5	1	1	10	11	22	.204	.277	.296	54	-7	3	2	-0	.984	12	2-32/3-7,S-1,O-1	0.6
Total	5	368	993	122	242	27	7	3	67	70	177	.244	.294	.294	66	-46	89	41	2	.948	-3	S-130,O-109/2-55,3	-4.0

■ ARCHIE YELLE
Yelle, Archie Joseph   b: 6/11/1892, Saginaw, Mich.   d: 5/2/83, Woodland, Cal.   BR/TR, 5'10.5", 170 lbs.   Deb: 5/12/17

YEAR	TM/L	G	AB	R	H	2B	3B	HR	RBI	BB	SO	AVG	OBP	SLG	PRO+	BR/A	SB	CS	SBR	FA	FR	G/POS	TPR
1917	Det-A	25	51	4	7	1	0	0	0	5	4	.137	.214	.157	13	-5	2			.975	-1	C-24	-0.6
1918	Det-A	56	144	7	25	3	0	0	7	9	15	.174	.227	.194	28	-13	0			.948	7	C-52	-0.2
1919	Det-A	6	4	1	0	0	0	0	0	1	0	.000	.200	.000	-42	-1	0			.833	-1	/C-6	-0.1
Total	3	87	199	12	32	4	0	0	7	15	19	.161	.223	.181	23	-19	2			.952	5	/C-82	-0.9

■ STEVE YERKES
Yerkes, Stephen Douglas   b: 5/15/1888, Hatboro, Pa.   d: 1/31/71, Lansdale, Pa.   BR/TR, 5'9", 165 lbs.   Deb: 9/29/09

YEAR	TM/L	G	AB	R	H	2B	3B	HR	RBI	BB	SO	AVG	OBP	SLG	PRO+	BR/A	SB	CS	SBR	FA	FR	G/POS	TPR
1909	Bos-A	5	7	0	2	0	0	0	0	0		.286	.286	.286	79	-0	0			1.000	-1	/S-2	-0.1
1911	Bos-A	142	502	70	140	24	3	1	57	52		.279	.354	.345	96	-2	14			.927	-20	*S-116,2-14,3-11	-1.4
1912	*Bos-A	131	523	73	132	22	6	0	42	41		.252	.312	.317	76	-17	4			.943	-15	*2-131	-3.5
1913	Bos-A	137	483	67	129	29	6	1	48	50	32	.267	.338	.358	101	1	11			.957	-19	2-129	-2.2
1914	Bos-A	92	293	23	64	17	2	1	23	14	23	.218	.259	.300	68	-13	5	6	-2	.972	4	2-91	-1.3
	Pit-F	39	142	18	48	9	5	1	25	11	13	.338	.386	.493	139	5	2			.974	8	S-39	1.6
1915	Pit-F	121	434	44	125	17	8	1	49	30	27	.288	.337	.371	100	-7	17			.967	-3	*2-114/S-8	-0.9
1916	Chi-N	44	137	12	36	6	2	1	10	9	7	.263	.308	.358	94	-1	1			.919	1	2-41	0.1
Total	7	711	2521	307	676	124	32	6	254	207	**102**	.268	.328	.350	93	-33	54	6		.956	-45	2-520,S-165/3-11	-7.7

■ TOM YEWCIC
Yewcic, Thomas J. "Kibby"   b: 5/9/32, Conemaugh, Pa.   BR/TR, 5'11", 180 lbs.   Deb: 6/27/57

YEAR	TM/L	G	AB	R	H	2B	3B	HR	RBI	BB	SO	AVG	OBP	SLG	PRO+	BR/A	SB	CS	SBR	FA	FR	G/POS	TPR
1957	Det-A	1	1	0	0	0	0	0	0	0	0	.000	.000	.000	-97	-0	0	0	0	.833	1	/C-1	0.0

■ ED YEWELL
Yewell, Edwin Leonard   b: 8/22/1862, Washington, D.C.   d: 9/15/40, Washington, D.C.   Deb: 5/12/1884

YEAR	TM/L	G	AB	R	H	2B	3B	HR	RBI	BB	SO	AVG	OBP	SLG	PRO+	BR/A	SB	CS	SBR	FA	FR	G/POS	TPR
1884	Was-a	27	93	14	23	3	1	0		1		.247	.263	.301	95	-0				.885	-3	2-11/O-8,3-7,S-2	-0.2
	Was-U	1	4	0	0	0	0	0		0		.000	.000	.000	-99	-1				.571	-0	/3-1	-0.1
Total	1	28	97	14	23	3	1	0		1		.237	.253	.289	85	-2				.773	-3	/2-11,3-8,O-8,S-2	-0.3

■ JOE YINGLING
Yingling, Joseph Granville   b: 7/23/1866, Westminster, Md.   d: 10/24/46, Manchester, Md.   BR/TL, 5'7.5", 145 lbs.   Deb: 5/28/1886

YEAR	TM/L	G	AB	R	H	2B	3B	HR	RBI	BB	SO	AVG	OBP	SLG	PRO+	BR/A	SB	CS	SBR	FA	FR	G/POS	TPR
1886	Was-N	1	2	0	0	0	0	0	0	0	0	.000	.000	.000	-99	-1	0			.500	0	/P-1	0.0
1894	Phi-N	1	4	0	1	0	0	0	0	0	1	.250	.250	.250	21	-1	0			1.000	0	/S-1	-0.1
Total	2	6	0	1	0	0	0	0	0	2	.167	.167	.167	-14	-1	0			1.000	-1	/S-1,P-1	-0.1

■ BILL YOHE
Yohe, William Clyde   b: 9/2/1878, Mt.Elere, Ill.   d: 12/24/38, Bremerton, Wash.   TR, 5'8", 180 lbs.   Deb: 8/30/09

YEAR	TM/L	G	AB	R	H	2B	3B	HR	RBI	BB	SO	AVG	OBP	SLG	PRO+	BR/A	SB	CS	SBR	FA	FR	G/POS	TPR
1909	Was-a	21	72	6	15	2	0	0	4	3		.208	.240	.236	53	-4	2			.921	3	3-19	-0.1

■ TONY YORK
York, Anthony Batton   b: 11/27/12, Irene, Tex.   d: 4/18/70, Hillsboro, Tex.   BR/TR, 5'10", 165 lbs.   Deb: 4/18/44

YEAR	TM/L	G	AB	R	H	2B	3B	HR	RBI	BB	SO	AVG	OBP	SLG	PRO+	BR/A	SB	CS	SBR	FA	FR	G/POS	TPR
1944	Chi-N	28	85	4	20	1	0	0	7	4	11	.235	.270	.247	46	-6	0			.940	10	S-15,3-12	0.5

■ RUDY YORK
York, Preston Rudolph   b: 8/17/13, Ragland, Ala.   d: 2/5/70, Rome, Ga.   BR/TR, 6'1", 209 lbs.   Deb: 8/22/34   MC

YEAR	TM/L	G	AB	R	H	2B	3B	HR	RBI	BB	SO	AVG	OBP	SLG	PRO+	BR/A	SB	CS	SBR	FA	FR	G/POS	TPR
1934	Det-A	3	6	0	1	0	0	0	0	2	3	.167	.286	.167	19	-1	0			1.000	-0	/C-2	-0.1
1937	Det-A	104	375	72	115	18	3	35	103	41	52	.307	.375	.651	150	25	3	2	-0	.960	-19	C-54,3-41/1-2	0.9
1938	Det-A★	135	463	85	138	27	2	33	127	92	74	.298	.417	.579	139	28	1	2	-1	.990	-17	*C-116,O-14/1-1	2.8
1939	*Det-A	102	329	66	101	16	1	20	68	41	50	.307	.387	.544	126	12	5	0	2	.985	-8	C-67,1-19	0.7
1940	*Det-A	155	588	105	186	46	6	33	134	89	88	.316	.410	.583	141	35	3	2	-0	.990	5	*1-155	2.3
1941	Det-A★	155	590	91	153	29	3	27	111	92	88	.259	.360	.456	104	-1	3	3	-0	.986	-1	*1-155	-1.0
1942	Det-A★	153	577	81	150	26	4	21	90	73	71	.260	.343	.428	107	5	3	3	-1	.988	15	*1-152	1.0
1943	Det-A★	155	571	90	155	22	11	**34**	**118**	84	88	.271	.366	**.527**	148	33	5	5	-2	.990	18	*1-155	4.3
1944	Det-A☆	151	583	77	161	27	7	18	98	68	73	.276	.353	.439	119	14	5	3	-0	.989	5	*1-151	1.1
1945	*Det-A	155	595	71	157	25	5	18	87	60	85	.264	.331	.413	109	5	6	6	-2	.988	-2	*1-155	-1.0
1946	*Bos-A★	154	579	78	160	30	6	17	119	86	93	.276	.371	.437	118	15	3	2	-0	.994	6	*1-154	1.2
1947	Bos-A	48	184	16	39	7	0	6	27	22	32	.212	.296	.348	73	-7	1	0	-0	.995	1	1-48	-0.8
	Chi-A☆	102	400	40	97	18	4	15	64	36	55	.243	.305	.420	104	-0	1	0	0	.995	-1	*1-102	-0.5
	Yr	150	584	56	136	25	4	21	91	58	87	.233	.302	.397	94	-8	1	0	-0	**.995**	0	*1-150	-1.3
1948	Phi-A	31	51	4	8	0	0	0	6	7	15	.157	.259	.157	12	-6	0	0	0	.988	-1	1-14	-0.7
Total	13	1603	5891	876	1621	291	52	277	1152	792	867	.275	.362	.483	121	160	38	26	-4	.990	16	*1-1263,C-239/3O	10.2

■ TOM YORK
York, Thomas Jefferson   b: 7/13/1851, Brooklyn, N.Y.   d: 2/17/36, New York, N.Y.   BL, 5'9", 165 lbs.   Deb: 5/9/1871   MU

YEAR	TM/L	G	AB	R	H	2B	3B	HR	RBI	BB	SO	AVG	OBP	SLG	PRO+	BR/A	SB	CS	SBR	FA	FR	G/POS	TPR
1871	Tro-n	29	145	36	37	5	7	2	23	9	1	.255	.299	.428	104	0	2	2	-1	.855	3	*O-29	0.3
1872	Bal-n	51	248	66	66	10	4	1	41	4	1	.266	.278	.351	88	-5	2	1	0	.916	11	*O-51	0.6
1873	Bal-n	57	277	70	84	10	4	2	49	3	3	.303	.311	.412	113	4	3	1	0	**.872**	11	*O-57	1.2
1874	Phi-n	50	224	36	56	4	7	0	37	5	4	.250	.266	.330	87	-4	1	0	0	.861	8	*O-50	0.5
1875	Har-n	86	375	68	111	14	7	0	37	3	6	.296	.302	.371	126	8	7	3	0	.868	4	*O-86	1.1
1876	Har-N	67	263	47	68	12	7	1	39	10	4	.259	.286	.369	108	1				.899	2	*O-67	0.2
1877	Har-N	56	237	43	67	16	7	1	37	3	11	.283	.292	.422	137	10				.865	0	*O-56	0.7
1878	Pro-N	62	269	56	83	19	**10**	1	26	8	19	.309	.329	.465	159	16				.873	4	*O-62,M	1.6
1879	Pro-N	81	342	69	106	25	5	1	50	19	28	.310	.346	.421	154	20				.898	-4	*O-81	1.0
1880	Pro-N	53	203	21	43	9	2	0	18	8	29	.212	.242	.276	77	-4				.934	-3	O-53	-0.8
1881	Pro-N	85	316	57	96	23	5	2	47	29	26	.304	.362	.427	150	19				.859	-2	*O-85,M	1.4
1882	Pro-N	81	321	48	86	23	7	1	40	19	14	.268	.309	.393	123	8				.873	-3	*O-81	0.5
1883	Cle-N	100	381	56	99	29	5	2	46	**37**	55	.260	.325	.378	114	8				.864	0	*O-100	0.6
1884	Bal-a	83	314	64	70	14	7	1	34			.223	.325	.322	105	3				.843	-5	*O-83	-0.3
1885	Bal-a	22	87	6	23	4	2	0	12	8		.264	.326	.356	117	2				.938	1	O-22	0.2
Total	5 n	273	1269	276	354	43	32	5	187	24	15	.279	.292	.375	106	4	15	7	0	.875	37	O-273	3.7
Total	10	690	2733	467	741	174	57	10	**315**	**175**	**186**	.271	.317	.387	126	83				.878	-8	O-690	5.1

■ NED YOST
Yost, Edgar Frederick   b: 8/19/55, Eureka, Cal.   BR/TR, 6'1", 190 lbs.   Deb: 4/12/80   C

YEAR	TM/L	G	AB	R	H	2B	3B	HR	RBI	BB	SO	AVG	OBP	SLG	PRO+	BR/A	SB	CS	SBR	FA	FR	G/POS	TPR
1980	Mil-A	15	31	0	5	0	0	0	0	0	9	.161	.161	.161	-12	-5	0	0	0	1.000	2	C-15	-0.2
1981	Mil-A	18	27	4	6	0	0	0	3	3	6	.222	.300	.556	150	1	0	0	0	.956	2	C-16	0.4
1982	*Mil-A	40	98	13	27	6	3	1	8	7	20	.276	.324	.429	111	1	3	1	0	.977	-2	C-39/D-1	0.1
1983	Mil-A	61	196	21	44	5	1	6	28	5	36	.224	.244	.352	67	-10	3	0	1	.971	-6	C-61	-1.3
1984	Tex-A	80	242	15	44	4	0	6	25	6	47	.182	.202	.273	29	-23	1	1	-2	.995	-5	C-78	-2.5
1985	Mon-N	5	11	1	2	0	0	0	0	0	3	.182	.182	.182	2	-1	0	0	0	.962	1	/C-5	-0.1
Total	6	219	605	54	128	15	4	16	64	21	117	.212	.238	.329	56	-37	7	2	-1	.982	-8	C-214/D-1	-3.8

■ EDDIE YOST
Yost, Edward Frederick Joseph "The Walking Man"   b: 10/13/26, Brooklyn, N.Y.   BR/TR, 5'10", 170 lbs.   Deb: 8/16/44   MC

YEAR	TM/L	G	AB	R	H	2B	3B	HR	RBI	BB	SO	AVG	OBP	SLG	PRO+	BR/A	SB	CS	SBR	FA	FR	G/POS	TPR
1944	Was-A	7	14	4	2	0	0	0	0	4	5	.143	.200	.143	-1	-2	0	0	0	.917	-1	/3-3,S-2	-0.2
1946	Was-A	8	25	1	2	1	0	0	1	5	5	.080	.233	.120	1	-3	2	1	0	1.000	1	/3-7	-0.3
1947	Was-A	115	428	52	102	17	3	0	14	45	57	.238	.314	.292	71	-16	3	5	-2	.958	-9	*3-114	-2.8
1948	Was-A	145	555	74	138	32	11	2	50	82	51	.249	.349	.357	91	-7	4	3	-1	.966	-13	*3-145	-2.1
1949	Was-A	124	435	57	110	19	7	9	45	91	41	.253	.383	.391	107	7	3	3	-1	.954	-2	*3-122	0.1

YEAR	TM/L	G	AB	R	H	2B	3B	HR	RBI	BB	SO	AVG	OBP	SLG	PRO+	BR/A	SB	CS	SBR	FA	FR	G/POS	TPR
1950	Was-A	155	573	114	169	26	2	11	58	141	63	.295	.440	.405	123	30	6	6	-2	.945	-2	*3-155	2.2
1951	Was-A	154	568	109	161	36	4	12	65	126	55	.283	.423	.424	132	32	6	4	-1	.954	-27	*3-152/O-3	0.3
1952	Was-A☆	157	587	92	137	32	3	12	49	129	73	.233	.378	.359	110	13	4	3	-1	.962	-35	*3-157	-2.7
1953	Was-A	152	577	107	157	30	7	9	45	123	59	.272	.403	.395	119	21	7	4	-0	.965	-13	*3-152	0.5
1954	Was-A	155	539	101	138	26	4	11	47	131	71	.256	.406	.380	123	24	7	3	0	.968	3	*3-155	2.5
1955	Was-A	122	375	64	91	17	5	7	48	95	54	.243	.410	.371	117	15	4	3	-1	.943	-6	*3-107	0.8
1956	Was-A	152	515	94	119	17	2	11	53	151	82	.231	.412	.336	100	9	8	5	-1	.963	-11	*3-135/O-8	2.0
1957	Was-A	110	414	47	104	13	5	9	38	73	49	.251	.370	.372	104	5	1	11	-6	.952	-11	*3-107	-1.0
1958	Was-A	134	406	55	91	16	0	8	37	81	43	.224	.365	.323	93	-0	3	6	-3	**.964**	-15	*3-114/O-4,1-2	-1.8
1959	Det-A	148	521	**115**	145	19	0	21	61	135	77	.278	**.437**	.436	133	32	9	2	2	**.962**	-11	*3-146/2-1	2.3
1960	Det-A	143	497	78	129	23	2	14	47	125	69	.260	**.416**	.398	118	19	5	4	-1	.933	-27	*3-142	-1.0
1961	LA-A	76	213	29	43	4	0	3	15	50	48	.202	.358	.263	62	-10	2	1	-1	.964	-10	3-67	-2.0
1962	LA-A	52	104	22	25	9	1	0	10	30	21	.240	.415	.346	111	3	0	2	-1	.950	-3	3-28/1-7	0.0
Total	18	2109	7346	1215	1863	337	56	139	683	1614	920	.254	.395	.371	109	172	72	66	-18	.957	-169	*3-2008/O-15,1S2	-3.2

■ **ELMER YOTER**   Yoter, Elmer Elsworth b: 6/26/1900, Plainfield, Pa. d: 7/26/66, Camp Hill, Pa. BR/TR, 5'7", 155 lbs. Deb: 9/9/21

YEAR	TM/L	G	AB	R	H	2B	3B	HR	RBI	BB	SO	AVG	OBP	SLG	PRO+	BR/A	SB	CS	SBR	FA	FR	G/POS	TPR
1921	Phi-A	3	3	0	0	0	0	0	0	0	0	.000	.000	.000	-99	-1				.000	0	H	-0.1
1924	Cle-A	19	66	3	18	1	1	0	7	5	8	.273	.324	.318	65	-3	0	0	0	.905	-2	3-19	-0.4
1927	Chi-N	13	27	2	6	1	1	0	5	4	4	.222	.323	.333	76	-1	0			.947	-0	3-11	-0.1
1928	Chi-N	1	0	0	0	0	0	0	0	0	0	—	—	—	—		0			.000	0	/3-1	0.0
Total	4	36	96	5	24	2	2	0	12	9	12	.250	.314	.313	63	-5	0	0		.915	-2	/3-31	-0.6

■ **DEL YOUNG**   Young, Delmer Edward b: 5/11/12, Cleveland, Ohio d: 12/8/79, San Francisco, Cal. BB/TR, 5'11", 168 lbs. Deb: 4/19/37 F

YEAR	TM/L	G	AB	R	H	2B	3B	HR	RBI	BB	SO	AVG	OBP	SLG	PRO+	BR/A	SB	CS	SBR	FA	FR	G/POS	TPR
1937	Phi-N	109	360	36	70	9	2	0	24	18	55	.194	.235	.231	25	-37	6			.950	10	*2-108	-2.1
1938	Phi-N	108	340	27	78	13	2	0	31	20	35	.229	.276	.279	55	-21	0			.933	-2	S-87,2-17	-1.6
1939	Phi-N	77	217	22	57	9	2	3	20	8	24	.263	.289	.364	77	-8	1			.946	-18	S-55,2-17	-2.1
1940	Phi-N	15	33	2	8	0	1	0	1	2	1	.242	.286	.303	65	-2	0			.962	-0	/S-6,2-5	-0.1
Total	4	309	950	87	213	31	7	3	76	48	115	.224	.264	.281	48	-68	7			.938	-10	S-148,2-147	-5.9

■ **DEL YOUNG**   Young, Delmer John b: 10/24/1885, Macon, Mo. d: 12/17/59, Cleveland, Ohio BL/TR, 5'11", 195 lbs. Deb: 9/24/09 F

YEAR	TM/L	G	AB	R	H	2B	3B	HR	RBI	BB	SO	AVG	OBP	SLG	PRO+	BR/A	SB	CS	SBR	FA	FR	G/POS	TPR
1909	Cin-N	2	7	0	2	0	0	0	1	1		.286	.375	.286	106	-0	0			1.000	0	/O-2	0.0
1914	Buf-F	80	174	17	48	5	5	4	22	3	13	.276	.288	.431	92	-6	0			.944	-6	O-41	-1.4
1915	Buf-F	12	15	0	2	0	0	0	0	1	0	.133	.188	.133	-9	-2	1			.667	-1	/O-3	-0.4
Total	3	94	196	17	52	5	5	4	23	5	13	.265	.284	.403	85	-8	1			.933	-7	/O-46	-1.8

■ **DMITRI YOUNG**   Young, Dmitri Dell b: 10/11/73, Vicksburg, Miss. BB/TR, 6'2", 215 lbs. Deb: 8/29/96

YEAR	TM/L	G	AB	R	H	2B	3B	HR	RBI	BB	SO	AVG	OBP	SLG	PRO+	BR/A	SB	CS	SBR	FA	FR	G/POS	TPR
1996	StL-N	16	29	3	7	0	0	2	4	5	5	.241	.353	.241	60	-1	0	1	-1	.976	-2	1-10	-0.4

■ **DON YOUNG**   Young, Donald Wayne b: 10/18/45, Houston, Tex. BR/TR, 6'2", 185 lbs. Deb: 9/9/65

YEAR	TM/L	G	AB	R	H	2B	3B	HR	RBI	BB	SO	AVG	OBP	SLG	PRO+	BR/A	SB	CS	SBR	FA	FR	G/POS	TPR
1965	Chi-N	11	35	1	2	0	0	0	2	0	11	.057	.057	.143	-45	-7	0	0	0	.933	-2	O-11	-1.0
1969	Chi-N	101	272	36	65	12	3	6	27	38	74	.239	.343	.371	89	-4	1	5	-3	.975	-4	*O-100	-1.6
Total	2	112	307	37	67	12	3	6	29	38	85	.218	.314	.345	76	-10	1	5	-3	.972	-6	O-111	-2.6

■ **ERIC YOUNG**   Young, Eric Orlando b: 5/18/67, New Brunswick, N.J. BR/TR, 5'9", 180 lbs. Deb: 7/30/92

YEAR	TM/L	G	AB	R	H	2B	3B	HR	RBI	BB	SO	AVG	OBP	SLG	PRO+	BR/A	SB	CS	SBR	FA	FR	G/POS	TPR
1992	LA-N	49	132	9	34	1	0	1	11	8	9	.258	.300	.288	68	-5	6	1	1	.957	10	2-43	0.7
1993	Col-N	144	490	82	132	16	8	3	42	63	41	.269	.357	.353	78	-15	42	19	1	.962	-10	2-79,O-52	-2.2
1994	Col-N	90	228	37	62	13	1	7	30	38	17	.272	.381	.430	95	-1	18	7	1	.981	0	O-60/2-1	0.0
1995	*Col-N	120	366	68	116	21	**9**	6	36	49	29	.317	.405	.473	101	-1	35	12	3	.973	-6	2-77,O-19	0.1
1996	Col-N★	141	568	113	184	23	4	8	74	47	31	.324	.396	.421	90	-11	**53**	19	5	.985	**28**	*2-139	2.9
Total	5	544	1784	309	528	74	22	25	193	205	127	.296	.379	.404	89	-33	154	58	11	.974	23	2-339,O-131	1.5

■ **ERNIE YOUNG**   Young, Ernest Wesley b: 7/8/69, Chicago, Ill. BR/TR, 6'1", 190 lbs. Deb: 5/17/94

YEAR	TM/L	G	AB	R	H	2B	3B	HR	RBI	BB	SO	AVG	OBP	SLG	PRO+	BR/A	SB	CS	SBR	FA	FR	G/POS	TPR
1994	Oak-A	11	30	2	2	1	0	0	3	1	8	.067	.097	.100	-54	-7	0	0	0	.958	0	O-10/D-1	-0.6
1995	Oak-A	26	50	9	10	3	0	2	5	8	12	.200	.310	.380	83	-1	0	0	0	.946	-3	O-24	-0.5
1996	Oak-A	141	462	72	112	19	4	19	64	52	118	.242	.328	.424	92	-6	7	5	-1	.997	-1	*O-140	-1.1
Total	3	178	542	83	124	23	4	21	72	61	138	.229	.315	.402	84	-15	7	5	-1	.991	-4	O-174/D-1	-2.2

■ **GEORGE YOUNG**   Young, George Joseph b: 4/1/1890, Brooklyn, N.Y. d: 3/13/50, Brightwaters, N.Y. BL/TR, 6', 185 lbs. Deb: 8/10/13

YEAR	TM/L	G	AB	R	H	2B	3B	HR	RBI	BB	SO	AVG	OBP	SLG	PRO+	BR/A	SB	CS	SBR	FA	FR	G/POS	TPR
1913	Cle-A	2	2	0	0	0	0	0	0	0	0	.000	.000	.000	-97	-0	0			.000	0	H	-0.1

■ **GERALD YOUNG**   Young, Gerald Anthony b: 10/22/64, Tela, Honduras BB/TR, 6'2", 185 lbs. Deb: 7/8/87

YEAR	TM/L	G	AB	R	H	2B	3B	HR	RBI	BB	SO	AVG	OBP	SLG	PRO+	BR/A	SB	CS	SBR	FA	FR	G/POS	TPR
1987	Hou-N	71	274	44	88	9	2	1	15	26	27	.321	.382	.380	107	4	26	9	2	.980	5	O-67	0.8
1988	Hou-N	149	576	79	148	21	9	0	37	66	66	.257	.336	.325	94	-3	65	27	3	.992	13	*O-145	0.9
1989	Hou-N	146	533	71	124	17	3	0	38	74	60	.233	.328	.276	77	-13	34	25	-5	**.998**	26	*O-143	0.5
1990	Hou-N	57	154	15	27	4	1	0	4	20	23	.175	.270	.234	41	-12	6	3	0	.990	-2	O-50	-1.5
1991	Hou-N	108	142	26	31	3	1	1	11	24	17	.218	.331	.275	77	-4	16	5	2	1.000	-14	O-84	-1.8
1992	Hou-N	74	76	14	14	1	1	0	4	10	11	.184	.279	.224	46	-5	6	2	1	.964	-15	O-57	-2.2
1993	Col-N	19	19	5	1	0	0	0	1	4	1	.053	.217	.053	-20	-3	0	1	-1	.882	-3	O-11	-0.7
1994	StL-N	16	41	5	13	3	2	0	3	3	8	.317	.364	.488	122	1	2	1	0	1.000	-1	O-11	0.0
Total	8	640	1815	259	446	58	19	3	113	227	213	.246	.332	.304	82	-36	155	73	3	.990	9	O-568	-4.0

■ **HERMAN YOUNG**   Young, Herman John b: 4/14/1886, Boston, Mass. d: 12/13/66, Ipswich, Mass. BR/TR, 5'8", 155 lbs. Deb: 6/11/11

YEAR	TM/L	G	AB	R	H	2B	3B	HR	RBI	BB	SO	AVG	OBP	SLG	PRO+	BR/A	SB	CS	SBR	FA	FR	G/POS	TPR
1911	Bos-N	9	25	2	6	0	0	0	0	3		.240	.269	.240	40	-1	0			.905	4	/3-5,S-3	0.2

■ **JOHN YOUNG**   Young, John Thomas b: 2/9/49, Los Angeles, Cal. BL/TL, 6'3", 210 lbs. Deb: 9/9/71

YEAR	TM/L	G	AB	R	H	2B	3B	HR	RBI	BB	SO	AVG	OBP	SLG	PRO+	BR/A	SB	CS	SBR	FA	FR	G/POS	TPR
1971	Det-A	2	4	1	2	1	0	0	1	0	0	.500	.500	.750	241	1	0	0	0	1.000	-0	/1-1	0.0

■ **KEVIN YOUNG**   Young, Kevin Stacey b: 6/16/69, Alpena, Mich. BR/TR, 6'3", 210 lbs. Deb: 7/12/92

YEAR	TM/L	G	AB	R	H	2B	3B	HR	RBI	BB	SO	AVG	OBP	SLG	PRO+	BR/A	SB	CS	SBR	FA	FR	G/POS	TPR
1992	Pit-N	10	7	2	4	0	0	0	4	2	2	.571	.667	.571	256	2	1	0	0	.750	-1	/3-7,1-1	0.1
1993	Pit-N	141	449	38	106	24	3	6	47	36	82	.236	.306	.343	73	-17	2	2	-1	**.998**	7	*1-135/3-6	-2.1
1994	Pit-N	59	122	15	25	7	2	1	11	8	34	.205	.260	.320	49	-9	0	2	-1	1.000	6	1-37,3-17/O-1	-1.1
1995	Pit-N	56	181	13	42	9	0	6	22	9	53	.232	.272	.381	69	-9	1	3	-2	.919	6	3-48/1-6	-0.4
1996	KC-A	55	132	20	32	6	0	8	23	11	32	.242	.307	.470	93	-2	3	3	-1	1.000	-1	1-27,O-17/3-7,D-3	-0.8
Total	5	321	891	88	209	46	5	21	107	65	201	.235	.295	.368	74	-35	7	10	-4	.998	10	1-206/3-85,O-18,D-3	-4.3

■ **PEP YOUNG**   Young, Lemuel Floyd b: 8/29/07, Jamestown, N.C. d: 1/14/62, Jamestown, N.C. BR/TR, 5'9", 162 lbs. Deb: 4/25/33

YEAR	TM/L	G	AB	R	H	2B	3B	HR	RBI	BB	SO	AVG	OBP	SLG	PRO+	BR/A	SB	CS	SBR	FA	FR	G/POS	TPR
1933	Pit-N	25	20	3	6	1	1	0	5	0	5	.300	.300	.450	112	0	0			1.000	0	/2-1,S-1	0.1
1934	Pit-N	19	17	3	4	0	0	0	2	0	4	.235	.235	.235	26	-2	0			1.000	2	/2-2,S-2	0.1
1935	Pit-N	128	494	60	131	25	10	7	82	21	59	.265	.298	.399	83	-13	2			.952	-12	*2-107/3-6,O-6,S-4	-1.6
1936	Pit-N	125	475	47	118	23	10	6	77	29	45	.248	.293	.377	77	-16	3			.966	-24	*2-123	-3.1
1937	Pit-N	113	408	43	106	20	3	9	54	26	63	.260	.308	.390	88	-8	4			.942	18	S-45,3-39,2-30	1.6
1938	Pit-N	149	562	58	156	36	5	4	79	40	64	.278	.329	.381	94	-5	7			.973	**32**	*2-149	3.5
1939	Pit-N	84	293	34	81	14	3	3	29	23	29	.276	.333	.375	92	-4	1			.967	3	2-84	0.4
1940	Pit-N	54	136	19	34	8	2	2	20	12	23	.250	.320	.382	94	-1	1			.909	-5	S-7,3-5	-0.4
1941	Cin-N	4	12	2	2	0	0	0	0	1		.167	.231	.167	13	-1	0			.923	1	/3-3	-0.1
	StL-N	2	2	0	0	0	0	0	0	0		.000	.000	.000	-94	-1	0			.000	0	H	-0.1
	Yr	6	14	2	2	0	0	0	0	1		.143	.200	.143	-2	-2	0			.923	1	/3-3	-0.2
1945	StL-N	36	47	5	7	1	0	1	4	1	8	.149	.167	.234	10	-6	0			.978	1	S-11/3-9,2-3	-0.5
Total	10	730	2466	274	645	128	34	32	347	152	312	.262	.308	.380	85	-56	18			.964	17	2-532/S-70,3-62,O-6	-0.1

■ **MIKE YOUNG**   Young, Michael Darren b: 3/20/60, Oakland, Cal. BB/TR, 6'2", 195 lbs. Deb: 9/14/82

YEAR	TM/L	G	AB	R	H	2B	3B	HR	RBI	BB	SO	AVG	OBP	SLG	PRO+	BR/A	SB	CS	SBR	FA	FR	G/POS	TPR
1982	Bal-A	6	2	2	0	0	0	0	0	0	1	.000	.000	.000	-99	-1	0	0	0	1.000	-0	/O-1,D-2	-0.1

YEAR	TM/L	G	AB	R	H	2B	3B	HR	RBI	BB	SO	AVG	OBP	SLG	PRO+	BR/A	SB	CS	SBR	FA	FR	G/POS	TPR
1983	Bal-A	25	36	5	6	2	1	0	2	2	8	.167	.231	.278	40	-3	1	0	0	.929	-4	O-22/D-3	-0.7
1984	Bal-A	123	401	59	101	17	2	17	52	58	110	.252	.356	.431	119	12	6	2	1	.982	-9	*O-115/D-1	-0.1
1985	Bal-A	139	450	72	123	22	1	28	81	48	104	.273	.349	.513	136	21	1	5	-3	.975	2	O-90,D-37	1.5
1986	Bal-A	117	369	43	93	15	1	9	42	49	90	.252	.344	.371	96	-1	3	1	0	.962	2	O-69,D-38	-0.1
1987	Bal-A	110	363	46	87	10	1	16	39	46	91	.240	.328	.405	96	-2	0	0	-1	.975	-3	O-60,D-47	-0.9
1988	Phi-N	75	146	13	33	14	0	1	14	26	43	.226	.347	.342	96	0	0	0	0	.938	-2	O-42	-0.3
	Mil-A	8	14	2	0	0	0	0	0	2	5	.000	.176	.000	-46	-3	0	0	0	.000	-1	/O-2,D-5	-0.4
1989	Cle-A	32	59	2	11	0	0	1	5	6	13	.186	.273	.237	44	-4	1	2	-1	1.000	-0	D-15/O-1	-0.6
Total	8	635	1840	244	454	80	6	72	235	237	465	.247	.339	.414	107	20	22	17	-4	.969	-18	O-402,D-148	-1.7

■ BABE YOUNG
Young, Norman Robert b: 7/1/15, Astoria, N.Y. d: 12/25/83, Everett, Mass. BL/TL, 6'2.5", 185 lbs. Deb: 9/26/36

YEAR	TM/L	G	AB	R	H	2B	3B	HR	RBI	BB	SO	AVG	OBP	SLG	PRO+	BR/A	SB	CS	SBR	FA	FR	G/POS	TPR
1936	NY-N	1	1	0	0	0	0	0	0	0	0	.000	.000	.000	-99	-0	0			.000	0	H	0.0
1939	NY-N	22	75	8	23	4	0	3	14	5	6	.307	.373	.480	127	3	0			.982	-2	1-22	-0.1
1940	NY-N	149	556	75	159	27	4	17	101	69	28	.286	.367	.441	121	16	4			.992	-2	*1-147	0.0
1941	NY-N	152	574	90	152	28	5	25	104	66	39	.265	.346	.462	124	17	1			.986	-4	*1-150	0.0
1942	NY-N	101	287	37	80	17	1	11	59	34	22	.279	.365	.460	140	14	1			.972	-4	O-54,1-18	0.7
1946	NY-N	104	291	30	81	11	0	7	33	30	21	.278	.346	.388	107	3	3			.988	-2	1-49,O-24	0.3
1947	NY-N	14	14	0	1	1	0	0	0	0	1	.071	.071	.143	-44	-3	0			.000	0	H	-0.9
	Cin-N	95	364	55	103	21	3	14	79	35	26	.283	.349	.473	117	8	0			.990	-2	1-93	-0.3
	Yr	109	378	55	104	22	3	14	79	35	27	.275	.340	.460	111	5	0			.990	-2	1-93	0.3
1948	Cin-N	49	130	11	30	7	2	1	12	19	12	.231	.329	.338	84	-3	0			.993	0	1-31/O-1	-0.3
	StL-N	41	111	14	27	5	2	1	13	16	6	.243	.339	.351	82	-3	0			.996	-4	1-35	-0.7
	Yr	90	241	25	57	12	4	2	25	35	18	.237	.333	.344	83	-5	0			.995	-4	1-66/O-1	-1.0
Total	8	728	2403	320	656	121	17	79	415	274	161	.273	.352	.436	117	52	9			.989	-25	1-545/O-79	-1.1

■ RALPH YOUNG
Young, Ralph Stuart b: 9/19/1889, Philadelphia, Pa. d: 1/24/65, Philadelphia, Pa. BB/TR, 5'5", 165 lbs. Deb: 4/10/13

YEAR	TM/L	G	AB	R	H	2B	3B	HR	RBI	BB	SO	AVG	OBP	SLG	PRO+	BR/A	SB	CS	SBR	FA	FR	G/POS	TPR
1913	NY-A	7	15	2	1	0	0	0	0	3	3	.067	.222	.067	-15	-2	2			.857	1	/S-7	0.0
1915	Det-A	123	378	44	92	6	5	0	31	53	31	.243	.339	.286	83	-7	12	11	-3	.950	8	*2-119	-0.1
1916	Det-A	153	528	60	139	16	6	1	45	62	43	.263	.342	.322	96	-2	20	20	-6	.966	8	*2-146/S-6,3-1	-0.4
1917	Det-A	141	503	64	116	18	2	1	35	61	35	.231	.317	.280	83	-9	8			.958	8	*2-141	0.7
1918	Det-A	91	298	31	56	7	1	0	21	54	17	.188	.313	.218	63	-11	15			.939	-12	2-91	-1.9
1919	Det-A	125	456	63	96	13	5	1	25	53	32	.211	.294	.268	60	-24	8			.970	17	*2-120/S-5	-0.1
1920	Det-A	150	594	84	173	21	6	0	33	85	30	.291	.382	.347	96	1	8	13	-5	.969	-11	*2-150	-1.0
1921	Det-A	107	401	70	120	8	3	0	29	69	23	.299	.406	.334	91	-1	11	9	-2	.947	-23	*2-106	-2.2
1922	Phi-A	125	470	62	105	19	2	1	35	55	21	.223	.309	.279	53	-32	8	6	-1	.960	-15	*2-120	-2.2
Total	9	1022	3643	480	898	108	30	4	254	495	235	.247	.339	.296	79	-86	92	59		.959	-28	2-993/S-18,3-1	-9.4

■ DICK YOUNG
Young, Richard Ennis b: 6/3/28, Seattle, Wash. BL/TR, 5'11", 175 lbs. Deb: 9/11/51

YEAR	TM/L	G	AB	R	H	2B	3B	HR	RBI	BB	SO	AVG	OBP	SLG	PRO+	BR/A	SB	CS	SBR	FA	FR	G/POS	TPR
1951	Phi-N	15	68	7	16	5	0	0	2	3	6	.235	.268	.309	55	-4	0	1	-1	.922	-9	2-15	-1.4
1952	Phi-N	5	9	3	2	1	0	0	0	1	3	.222	.300	.333	76	-0	1	0	0	.900	-0	/2-2	-0.0
Total	2	20	77	10	18	6	0	0	2	4	9	.234	.272	.312	58	-5	1	1	-0	.919	-9	2-17	-1.4

■ BOBBY YOUNG
Young, Robert George b: 1/22/25, Granite, Md. d: 1/28/85, Baltimore, Md. BL/TR, 6'1", 175 lbs. Deb: 7/28/48

YEAR	TM/L	G	AB	R	H	2B	3B	HR	RBI	BB	SO	AVG	OBP	SLG	PRO+	BR/A	SB	CS	SBR	FA	FR	G/POS	TPR
1948	StL-N	3	1	0	0	0	0	0	0	0	1	.000	.000	.000	-95	-0	0			1.000	0	/3-1	0.0
1951	StL-A	147	611	75	159	13	9	1	31	44	51	.260	.310	.316	67	-28	8	7	-2	.980	1	*2-147	-2.2
1952	StL-A	149	575	59	142	15	9	4	39	56	48	.247	.314	.325	76	-19	3	3	-1	.984	-9	*2-149	-2.2
1953	StL-A	148	537	48	137	22	2	4	25	41	40	.255	.309	.326	70	-22	2	1	0	.977	-17	*2-148	-3.1
1954	Bal-A	130	432	43	106	13	6	4	24	54	42	.245	.331	.331	88	-7	4	4	-1	.976	-14	*2-127	-1.5
1955	Bal-A	59	186	15	37	3	0	1	8	11	23	.199	.244	.231	30	-19	1	4	-2	.985	-14	*2-58	-1.5
	Cle-A	18	45	7	14	1	1	0	6	1	2	.311	.326	.378	86	-1	0	0	-0	.983	7	2-11/3-1	0.6
	Yr	77	231	12	51	4	1	1	14	12	25	.221	.259	.260	42	-19	1	4	-2	.985	-9	2-69/3-1	-0.9
1956	Cle-A	1	0	0	0	0	0	0	0	0	0	—	—	—	0					.000	0	R	-0.9
1958	Phi-N	32	60	7	14	1	1	1	4	4	7	.233	.246	.333	52	-4	0	0	-0	.968	-2	2-21	-0.6
Total	8	687	2447	244	609	68	28	15	137	208	212	.249	.308	.318	71	-100	18	19		.980	-32	2-661/3-2	-10.5

■ RUSS YOUNG
Young, Russell Charles b: 9/15/02, Bryan, Ohio d: 5/13/84, Roseville, Cal. BB/TR, 6', 175 lbs. Deb: 4/16/31

YEAR	TM/L	G	AB	R	H	2B	3B	HR	RBI	BB	SO	AVG	OBP	SLG	PRO+	BR/A	SB	CS	SBR	FA	FR	G/POS	TPR
1931	StL-A	16	34	2	4	0	0	1	2	2	4	.118	.167	.206	-3	-5	0	0	0	1.000	2	C-16	-0.2

■ JOEL YOUNGBLOOD
Youngblood, Joel Randolph b: 8/28/51, Houston, Tex. BR/TR, 6', 180 lbs. Deb: 4/13/76 C

YEAR	TM/L	G	AB	R	H	2B	3B	HR	RBI	BB	SO	AVG	OBP	SLG	PRO+	BR/A	SB	CS	SBR	FA	FR	G/POS	TPR
1976	Cin-N	55	57	8	11	1	1	0	1	2	8	.193	.233	.246	35	-5	1	0	0	.938	-1	/O-9,3-6,C-1,2-1	-0.6
1977	StL-N	25	27	1	5	2	0	0	1	3	5	.185	.267	.259	43	-2	0	2	-1	1.000	-3	O-11/3-6	-0.7
	NY-N	70	182	16	46	11	1	0	11	13	40	.253	.303	.324	72	-7	1	0	-2	.954	2	2-33,O-22,3-10	-0.6
	Yr	95	209	17	51	13	1	0	12	16	45	.244	.298	.316	67	-10	1	2	-3			2-33,O-22,3-10	-0.6
1978	NY-N	113	266	40	67	12	8	7	30	16	39	.252	.297	.436	106	1	4	0	1	.989	2	O-33,2-33,3-16	-1.3
1979	NY-N	158	590	90	162	37	5	16	60	60	84	.275	.349	.436	117	13	18	13	-2	.985	4	*O-147,2-13,3-12	0.4
1980	NY-N	146	514	58	142	26	2	8	69	52	69	.276	.345	.381	105	4	14	11	-2	.984	15	*O-121,3-21/2-6	1.0
1981	NY-N★	43	143	16	50	10	2	4	25	12	19	.350	.408	.532	167	4	2	5	-2	.962	2	O-41	1.2
1982	NY-N	80	202	21	52	12	0	3	21	8	37	.257	.302	.361	85	-4	2	0	-0	.969	-6	O-63/2-8,S-1,3-1	-1.7
	Mon-N	40	90	16	18	2	0	0	8	9	21	.200	.294	.222	45	-6	2	1	0	1.000	-3	O-35	-1.0
	Yr	120	292	37	70	14	0	3	29	17	58	.240	.300	.318	73	-10	4	1	-0	.979	-12	O-98/2-8,S-1,3-1	-2.7
1983	SF-N	124	373	59	109	20	3	17	53	33	59	.292	.358	.499	139	19	7	4	-0	.948	-30	2-64,3-28,O-22	-1.1
1984	SF-N	134	469	50	119	17	1	10	51	48	86	.254	.328	.358	96	-2	6	6	-2	.887	-26	*3-117,O-11/2-5	-3.4
1985	SF-N	95	230	24	62	12	0	5	28	18	34	.255	.325	.402	105	1	3	2	-0	.955	0	O-56/3-1	-0.1
1986	SF-N	97	184	20	47	12	0	5	24	18	34	.255	.313	.402	105	1	1	0	-1	1.000	-3	O-45/1-7,3-5,2-4,S	-0.7
1987	SF-N	69	91	8	23	5	0	3	11	5	13	.253	.296	.385	83	-2	1	1	-0	1.000	-0	O-22/3-2	-0.6
1988	SF-N	83	123	12	31	5	0	2	16	10	17	.252	.313	.285	76	-4	1	1	-0	.980	-3	O-45	-0.6
1989	Cin-N	76	118	13	25	5	0	3	13	13	21	.212	.301	.331	78	-3	0	1	-1	.970	-10	O-45	-1.7
Total	14	1408	3659	453	969	180	23	80	422	332	589	.265	.332	.392	103	15	60	55	-15	.981	-78	O-745,3-218,2/1SC	-10.1

■ HENRY YOUNGMAN
Youngman, Henry b: 1865, Indiana, Pa. d: 1/24/36, Pittsburgh, Pa. TR, Deb: 4/19/1890

YEAR	TM/L	G	AB	R	H	2B	3B	HR	RBI	BB	SO	AVG	OBP	SLG	PRO+	BR/A	SB	CS	SBR	FA	FR	G/POS	TPR
1890	Pit-N	13	47	6	6	1	1	0	4	6	9	.128	.226	.191	25	-4	1			.750	-2	/3-7,2-6	-0.5

■ ROSS YOUNGS
Youngs, Ross Middlebrook "Pep" (b: Royce Middlebrook Youngs)
b: 4/10/1897, Shiner, Tex. d: 10/22/27, San Antonio, Tex. BL/TR, 5'8", 162 lbs. Deb: 9/25/17 H

YEAR	TM/L	G	AB	R	H	2B	3B	HR	RBI	BB	SO	AVG	OBP	SLG	PRO+	BR/A	SB	CS	SBR	FA	FR	G/POS	TPR
1917	NY-N	7	26	5	9	2	3	0	1	1	5	.346	.370	.654	218	3	1			1.000	1	/O-7	0.4
1918	NY-N	121	474	70	143	16	8	1	25	44	46	.302	.368	.376	129	18	10			.950	-6	*O-120/2-7	0.5
1919	NY-N	130	489	73	152	**31**	7	2	43	51	47	.311	.384	.415	142	26	24			.942	2	*O-130	2.1
1920	NY-N	153	581	92	204	27	14	6	78	75	55	.351	.427	.477	161	48	18	18	-5	.935	-4	*O-153	3.6
1921	*NY-N	141	504	90	165	24	16	3	102	71	47	.327	.411	.456	129	24	21	17	-4	.978	-4	*O-137	0.6
1922	*NY-N	149	559	105	185	34	10	7	86	55	50	.331	.398	.456	121	24	17	9	-0	.942	-4	*O-147	1.1
1923	*NY-N	152	596	**121**	200	33	12	3	87	73	36	.336	.412	.446	128	27	13	19	-8	.959	1	*O-152	1.0
1924	*NY-N	133	526	112	187	33	12	10	74	77	31	.356	.441	.521	161	49	11	9	-2	.955	-1	*O-132/2-2	3.6
1925	NY-N	130	500	82	132	24	6	6	53	66	51	.264	.354	.372	89	-7	17	11	-3	.952	-6	*O-127/2-3	-2.1
1926	NY-N	95	372	62	114	12	5	3	43	37	19	.306	.372	.398	109	5	21			.974	-2	O-94	1.0
Total	10	1211	4627	812	1491	236	93	42	592	550	390	.322	.399	.441	131	212	153	83		.953	-4	*O-1199/2-12	10.8

■ EDDIE YOUNT
Yount, Floyd Edwin b: 12/19/16, Newton, N.C. d: 10/26/73, Newton, N.C. BR/TR, 6'1", 185 lbs. Deb: 9/9/37

YEAR	TM/L	G	AB	R	H	2B	3B	HR	RBI	BB	SO	AVG	OBP	SLG	PRO+	BR/A	SB	CS	SBR	FA	FR	G/POS	TPR
1937	Phi-A	4	7	1	2	0	0	0	1	0	1	.286	.286	.286	45	-1	0	0		1.000	0	/O-2	-0.1
1939	Pit-N	2	2	0	0	0	0	0	0	1	2	.000	.000	.000	-99	-1	0	0	0	.000	-0	H	-0.1
Total	2	6	9	1	2	0	0	0	1	1	3	.222	.222	.222	14	-1	0	0		1.000	-0	/O-2	-0.2

YEAR	TM/L	G	AB	R	H	2B	3B	HR	RBI	BB	SO	AVG	OBP	SLG	PRO+	BR/A	SB	CS	SBR	FA	FR	G/POS	TPR

■ ROBIN YOUNT
Yount, Robin R b: 9/16/55, Danville, Ill. BR/TR, 6′, 170 lbs. Deb: 4/5/74 F

YEAR	TM/L	G	AB	R	H	2B	3B	HR	RBI	BB	SO	AVG	OBP	SLG	PRO+	BR/A	SB	CS	SBR	FA	FR	G/POS	TPR
1974	Mil-A	107	344	48	86	14	5	3	26	12	46	.250	.277	.346	79	-10	7	7	-2	.962	-11	*S-107	-1.1
1975	Mil-A	147	558	67	149	28	2	8	52	33	69	.267	.309	.367	90	-8	12	4	1	.939	-23	*S-145	-1.5
1976	Mil-A	161	638	59	161	19	3	2	54	38	69	.252	.294	.301	76	-20	16	11	-2	.963	-5	*S-161/O-1	-0.7
1977	Mil-A	154	605	66	174	34	4	4	49	41	80	.288	.335	.377	94	-5	16	7	1	.964	-9	*S-153	0.4
1978	Mil-A	127	502	66	147	23	9	9	71	24	43	.293	.326	.428	110	5	16	5	2	.959	22	*S-125	4.5
1979	Mil-A	149	577	72	154	26	5	8	51	35	52	.267	.310	.371	83	-15	11	8	-2	.969	5	*S-149	0.6
1980	Mil-A★	143	611	121	179	49	10	23	87	26	67	.293	.323	.519	131	22	20	5	3	.961	0	S-93/D-3	4.0
1981	*Mil-A	96	377	50	103	15	5	10	49	22	37	.273	.317	.419	116	6	4	1	1	.985	28	S-93/D-3	4.5
1982	*Mil-A★	156	635	129	210	46	12	29	114	54	63	.331	.384	.578	171	59	14	3	2	.969	-4	*S-154/D-1	7.0
1983	Mil-A★	149	578	102	178	42	10	17	80	72	58	.308	.387	.503	155	44	12	5	1	.973	-5	*S-139/D-8	5.2
1984	Mil-A	160	624	105	186	27	7	16	80	67	67	.298	.367	.441	127	24	14	4	2	.971	15	*S-120,D-39	5.0
1985	Mil-A	122	466	76	129	26	3	15	68	49	56	.277	.348	.442	115	10	10	4	1	.970	4	*O-108,D-12/1-2	1.0
1986	Mil-A	140	522	82	163	31	7	9	46	62	73	.312	.389	.450	124	19	14	5	1	.997	12	*O-131/1-3,D-6	2.6
1987	Mil-A	158	635	99	198	25	9	21	103	76	94	.312	.386	.479	124	23	19	9	0	.987	6	*O-150/D-8	2.5
1988	Mil-A	162	621	92	190	38	11	13	91	63	63	.306	.373	.465	132	27	22	4	4	.996	15	*O-158/D-4	4.1
1989	Mil-A	160	614	101	195	38	9	21	103	63	71	.318	.384	.511	153	42	19	3	4	.981	4	*O-143,D-17	4.6
1990	Mil-A	158	587	98	145	17	5	17	77	78	89	.247	.337	.380	102	3	15	8	-0	.991	6	*O-117/D-13	0.0
1991	Mil-A	130	503	66	131	20	4	10	77	54	79	.260	.337	.376	99	0	6	4	-1	.994	4	*O-139/D-11	0.2
1992	Mil-A	150	557	71	147	40	3	8	77	53	81	.264	.331	.390	103	3	15	6	1	.995	4	*O-114/1-7,D-6	-0.3
1993	Mil-A	127	454	62	117	25	3	8	51	44	93	.258	.330	.379	91	-5	9	2	2	.997	4	*O-114/1-7,D-6	-0.3
Total	20	2856	11008	1632	3142	583	126	251	1406	966	1350	.285	.346	.430	115	223	271	105	18	.964	71	*S-1479;O-1218,D/1	43.1

■ JEFF YURAK
Yurak, Jeffrey Lynn b: 2/26/54, Pasadena, Cal. BB/TR, 6′3″, 195 lbs. Deb: 9/15/78

YEAR	TM/L	G	AB	R	H	2B	3B	HR	RBI	BB	SO	AVG	OBP	SLG	PRO+	BR/A	SB	CS	SBR	FA	FR	G/POS	TPR
1978	Mil-A	5	5	0	0	0	0	0	0	1	0	.000	.167	.000	-49	-1	0	0	0	1.000	0	/O-1	-0.1

■ SAL YVARS
Yvars, Salvador Anthony b: 2/20/24, New York, N.Y. BR/TR, 5′10″, 187 lbs. Deb: 9/27/47

YEAR	TM/L	G	AB	R	H	2B	3B	HR	RBI	BB	SO	AVG	OBP	SLG	PRO+	BR/A	SB	CS	SBR	FA	FR	G/POS	TPR
1947	NY-N	1	5	0	1	0	0	0	0	0	2	.200	.200	.200	6	-1	0			1.000	-0	/C-1	-0.1
1948	NY-N	15	38	4	8	1	0	1	6	3	1	.211	.286	.316	62	-2	0			1.000	3	/C-15	0.1
1949	NY-N	3	8	0	0	0	0	0	0	1	1	.000	.111	.000	-68	-2	0			.963	2	/C-9	0.0
1950	NY-N	9	14	0	2	0	0	0	0	1	2	.143	.200	.143	-8	-2	0			.942	-3	C-23	0.0
1951	*NY-N	25	41	9	13	2	0	2	3	5	7	.317	.417	.512	147	3	0	0	0	.988	7	C-59	0.4
1952	NY-N	66	151	15	37	3	0	4	18	10	16	.245	.296	.344	77	-5	0	0	0	1.000	6	C-20	0.0
1953	NY-N	23	47	1	13	0	0	0	6	4	6	.277	.370	.277	71	-2	0			1.000	1	C-26	-0.1
	StL-N	30	57	4	14	2	0	1	6	4	6	.246	.306	.333	67	-3	0	1	-1	.989	2	C-46	-0.1
	Yr	53	104	5	27	2	0	1	7	11	7	.260	.336	.308	69	-4	0	1	-1	.994	3	C-21	-0.2
1954	StL-N	38	57	8	14	4	0	2	8	6	5	.246	.328	.421	93	-1	1	0	0	1.000	-2	C-21	-0.2
Total	8	210	418	41	102	12	0	10	42	37	41	.244	.315	.344	76	-14	1	1		.987	10	C-176	0.0

■ ELMER ZACHER
Zacher, Elmer Henry "Silver" b: 9/17/1883, Buffalo, N.Y. d: 12/20/44, Buffalo, N.Y. BR/TR, 5′9″, 190 lbs. Deb: 4/30/10

YEAR	TM/L	G	AB	R	H	2B	3B	HR	RBI	BB	SO	AVG	OBP	SLG	PRO+	BR/A	SB	CS	SBR	FA	FR	G/POS	TPR
1910	NY-N	1	0	0	0	0	0	0	0	0	0					0	0			1.000	-0	/O-1	0.0
	StL-N	47	132	7	28	5	1	0	10	10	19	.212	.278	.265	61	-7	3			.966	3	O-36/2-1	-0.6
	Yr	48	132	7	28	5	1	0	10	10	19	.212	.278	.265	61	-7	3			.966	2	O-37/2-1	-0.6

■ FRED ZAHNER
Zahner, Frederick Joseph b: 6/5/1870, Louisville, Ky. d: 7/24/1900, Louisville, Ky. Deb: 7/23/1894

YEAR	TM/L	G	AB	R	H	2B	3B	HR	RBI	BB	SO	AVG	OBP	SLG	PRO+	BR/A	SB	CS	SBR	FA	FR	G/POS	TPR
1894	Lou-N	13	45	7	9	0	1	0	3	3	5	.200	.250	.244	21	-6	2			.778	-5	C-10/O-2,1-1	-0.8
1895	Lou-N	21	49	7	11	1	1	0	6	6	4	.224	.321	.286	61	-3	0			.824	-6	C-21	-0.6
Total	2	34	94	14	20	1	2	0	9	9	9	.213	.288	.266	42	-8	2			.805	-11	/C-31,O-2,1-1	-1.4

■ FRANKIE ZAK
Zak, Frank Thomas b: 2/22/22, Passaic, N.J. d: 2/6/72, Passaic, N.J. BR/TR, 5′10″, 150 lbs. Deb: 4/21/44

YEAR	TM/L	G	AB	R	H	2B	3B	HR	RBI	BB	SO	AVG	OBP	SLG	PRO+	BR/A	SB	CS	SBR	FA	FR	G/POS	TPR
1944	Pit-N☆	87	160	33	48	3	1	0	11	22	18	.300	.385	.331	99	1	6			.948	6	S-67	1.0
1945	Pit-N	15	28	2	4	2	0	0	3	3	5	.143	.226	.214	22	-3	0			.971	1	S-10/2-1	-0.2
1946	Pit-N	21	20	8	4	0	0	0	0	1	0	.200	.238	.200	24	-2	0			.929	9	S-10	0.7
Total	3	123	208	43	56	5	1	0	14	26	23	.269	.350	.303	82	-4	6			.948	15	/S-87,2-1	1.5

■ JACK ZALUSKY
Zalusky, John Francis b: 6/22/1879, Minneapolis, Minn d: 8/11/35, Minneapolis, Minn. BR/TR, 5′11.5″, 172 lbs. Deb: 9/4/03

YEAR	TM/L	G	AB	R	H	2B	3B	HR	RBI	BB	SO	AVG	OBP	SLG	PRO+	BR/A	SB	CS	SBR	FA	FR	G/POS	TPR
1903	NY-A	7	16	2	5	0	0	0	1	1		.313	.353	.313	95	-0	0			1.000	-1	/C-6,1-1	-0.1

■ EDUARDO ZAMBRANO
Zambrano, Eduardo Jose (Guerra) b: 2/1/66, Maracaibo, Venez. BR/TR, 6′2″, 175 lbs. Deb: 9/19/93

YEAR	TM/L	G	AB	R	H	2B	3B	HR	RBI	BB	SO	AVG	OBP	SLG	PRO+	BR/A	SB	CS	SBR	FA	FR	G/POS	TPR
1993	Chi-N	8	17	1	5	0	0	0	2	1	3	.294	.333	.294	71	-1	0	0	0	1.000	-2	/O-4,1-2	-0.3
1994	Chi-N	67	116	17	30	7	0	6	18	16	29	.259	.353	.474	115	3	2	1	0	.944	-4	O-27/1-9,3-4	-0.2
Total	2	75	133	18	35	7	0	6	20	17	32	.263	.351	.451	109	2	2	1	0	.946	-6	/O-31,1-11,3-4	-0.5

■ JOE ZAPUSTAS
Zapustas, Joseph John b: 7/25/07, Boston, Mass. BR/TR, 6′1″, 185 lbs. Deb: 9/28/33

YEAR	TM/L	G	AB	R	H	2B	3B	HR	RBI	BB	SO	AVG	OBP	SLG	PRO+	BR/A	SB	CS	SBR	FA	FR	G/POS	TPR
1933	Phi-A	2	5	0	1	0	0	0	0	0	0	.200	.200	.200	6	-1	0	0	0	1.000	-1	/O-2	-0.1

■ JOSE ZARDON
Zardon, Jose Antonio (Sanchez) "Guineo" b: 5/20/23, Havana, Cuba BR/TR, 6′, 150 lbs. Deb: 4/18/45

YEAR	TM/L	G	AB	R	H	2B	3B	HR	RBI	BB	SO	AVG	OBP	SLG	PRO+	BR/A	SB	CS	SBR	FA	FR	G/POS	TPR
1945	Was-A	54	131	13	38	5	3	0	13	7	11	.290	.326	.374	112	1	3	1	0	.972	-1	O-43	-0.1

■ AL ZARILLA
Zarilla, Allen Lee "Zeke" b: 5/1/19, Los Angeles, Cal. d: 9/4/96, Honolulu, Hawaii BL/TR, 5′11″, 180 lbs. Deb: 6/30/43 C

YEAR	TM/L	G	AB	R	H	2B	3B	HR	RBI	BB	SO	AVG	OBP	SLG	PRO+	BR/A	SB	CS	SBR	FA	FR	G/POS	TPR
1943	StL-A	70	228	27	58	7	1	2	17	17	20	.254	.309	.320	82	-5	1	1	-0	.962	-2	O-60	-1.1
1944	*StL-A	100	288	43	86	13	6	6	45	29	33	.299	.375	.448	127	10	1	1	-0	.977	-2	O-79	0.4
1946	StL-A	125	371	46	96	14	9	4	43	27	37	.259	.311	.377	87	-7	3	5	-2	.973	3	*O-107	-1.1
1947	StL-A	127	380	34	85	15	6	3	38	40	45	.224	.303	.318	71	-15	3	6	-3	.986	-10	*O-110	-3.5
1948	StL-A★	144	529	77	174	39	3	12	74	48	42	.329	.389	.482	128	19	11	6	-0	.962	-9	*O-136	0.3
1949	StL-A	15	56	10	14	1	0	1	6	8	2	.250	.354	.321	76	-2	0	1	-0	1.000	-5	*O-15	-0.8
	Bos-A	124	474	68	133	32	4	9	71	48	51	.281	.352	.422	97	-5	4	4	-1	.984	-2	*O-122	-1.2
	Yr	139	530	78	147	33	4	10	77	56	53	.277	.352	.411	95	-5	5	5	-2	.985	-7	*O-137	-2.0
1950	Bos-A	130	471	92	153	32	10	9	74	76	47	.325	.423	.493	122	17	2	3	-1	.976	-4	*O-128	0.6
1951	Chi-A	120	382	56	98	21	2	10	60	60	57	.257	.363	.401	109	5	2	4	-2	.983	-12	*O-117	-1.2
1952	Chi-A	39	99	14	23	4	1	2	14	7	15	.232	.333	.354	90	-1	1	0	0	.974	-6	O-32	-0.8
	StL-A	48	130	20	31	6	0	1	9	27	15	.238	.373	.308	88	-1	1	0	0	.976	-1	O-35	-0.2
	Bos-A	21	60	9	11	0	1	2	7	7	8	.183	.269	.317	58	-4	0	1	-0	.941	-1	O-19	-0.5
	Yr	108	289	43	65	10	2	5	24	48	29	.225	.339	.325	83	-6	5	1	-1	.968	-7	O-86	-1.5
1953	Bos-A	57	67	11	13	2	0	0	4	14	13	.194	.333	.224	50	-4	0	1	-1	.947	-5	O-18	-1.0
Total	10	1120	3535	507	975	186	43	61	456	415	382	.276	.357	.405	102	10	33	33	-10	.974	-53	O-978	-10.1

■ NORM ZAUCHIN
Zauchin, Norbert Henry b: 11/17/29, Royal Oak, Mich. BR/TR, 6′4.5″, 220 lbs. Deb: 9/23/51

YEAR	TM/L	G	AB	R	H	2B	3B	HR	RBI	BB	SO	AVG	OBP	SLG	PRO+	BR/A	SB	CS	SBR	FA	FR	G/POS	TPR
1951	Bos-A	5	12	0	2	1	0	0	1	0	6	.167	.167	.250	11	-2	0	1	-0	.957	-0	/1-4	-0.2
1955	Bos-A	130	477	65	114	10	0	27	93	69	105	.239	.339	.430	97	-3	3	0	1	.995	1	*1-126	-0.8
1956	Bos-A	44	84	12	18	2	0	2	11	14	22	.214	.333	.310	63	-0	0	0	0	.990	-1	1-31	-0.6
1957	Bos-A	52	91	11	24	3	0	4	14	9	13	.264	.343	.396	96	-0	0	0	0	.972	0	1-36	-0.2
1958	Was-A	96	303	35	69	8	2	15	37	38	68	.228	.316	.416	101	0	2	0	0	.995	-0	1-91	-0.4
1959	Was-A	19	71	11	15	4	0	2	4	7	14	.211	.291	.394	87	-1	0	0	0	.995	-0	1-19	-0.5
Total	6	346	1038	134	242	28	2	50	159	137	226	.233	.327	.408	93	-11	5	1	1	.993	-0	1-307	-2.7

■ GREG ZAUN
Zaun, Gregory Owen b: 4/14/71, Glendale, Cal. BB/TR, 5′10″, 170 lbs. Deb: 6/24/95

YEAR	TM/L	G	AB	R	H	2B	3B	HR	RBI	BB	SO	AVG	OBP	SLG	PRO+	BR/A	SB	CS	SBR	FA	FR	G/POS	TPR
1995	Bal-A	40	104	18	27	5	0	3	14	16	14	.260	.358	.394	94	-1	1	1	-0	.987	4	C-39/D-1	0.5
1996	Bal-A	50	108	16	25	8	1	1	13	11	15	.231	.314	.352	69	-5	0	0	0	.987	-0	C-49	-0.2
	Fla-N	10	31	4	9	1	0	1	2	3	5	.290	.353	.419	107	0	1	0	0	1.000	0	C-10	0.2
Total	2	100	243	38	61	14	1	5	29	30	34	.251	.338	.379	84	-5	2	1	-0	.989	5	/C-98,D-1	0.5

YEAR	TM/L	G	AB	R	H	2B	3B	HR	RBI	BB	SO	AVG	OBP	SLG	PRO+	BR/A	SB	CS	SBR	FA	FR	G/POS	TPR
■ ZAY	Zay Deb: 10/7/1886																						
1886	Bal-a	1	1	0	0	0	0	0	0	0	0	.000	.000	.000	-99	-0	0			.000	-0	/O-1,P-1	0.0
■ JOE ZDEB	Zdeb, Joseph Edmund b: 6/27/53, Compton, Ill. BR/TR, 5'11", 185 lbs. Deb: 4/7/77																						
1977	*KC-A	105	195	26	58	5	2	2	23	16	23	.297	.351	.374	97	-1	6	5	-1	.970	-18	O-93/3-1,D-4	-2.2
1978	KC-A	60	127	18	32	2	3	0	11	7	18	.252	.291	.315	69	-5	3	0	1	.957	-9	O-52/2-1,3-1,D-1	-1.6
1979	KC-A	15	23	3	4	1	1	0	0	2	4	.174	.240	.304	45	-2	1	0	0	1.000	-1	/O-9	-0.3
Total	3	180	345	47	94	8	6	2	34	25	45	.272	.322	.348	83	-8	10	5	0	.967	-29	O-154/D-5,3-2,2-1	-4.1
■ DAVE ZEARFOSS	Zearfoss, David William Tilden b: 1/1/1868, Schenectady, N.Y. d: 9/12/45, Wilmington, Del. TR , 5'9", Deb: 4/17/1896																						
1896	NY-N	19	60	5	13	1	1	0	6	5	5	.217	.288	.267	48	-4	2			.893	-4	C-19	-0.5
1897	NY-N	5	10	1	3	0	0	0	0	*	0	.300	.300	.500	112	0	0			.880	2	/C-5	0.2
1898	NY-N	1	1	0	1	0	0	0	0	0	0	1.000	1.000	1.000	489	0	0			1.000	1	/C-1	0.1
1904	StL-N	27	80	7	17	0	2	0	9	10		.213	.300	.237	70	-2	0			.966	-2	C-25	-0.2
1905	StL-N	20	51	2	8	0	1	0	2	4		.157	.218	.196	24	-5	0			.966	-0	C-19	-0.4
Total	5	72	202	15	42	3	3	0	17	19	5	.208	.279	.252	56	-11	2			.943	-3	/C-69	-0.8
■ GEORGE ZEBER	Zeber, George William b: 8/29/50, Ellwood City, Pa. BB/TR, 5'11", 170 lbs. Deb: 5/7/77																						
1977	*NY-A	25	65	8	21	3	0	3	10	9	11	.323	.405	.508	149	5	0	0	0	.961	1	2-21/S-2,3-2,D-1	0.7
1978	NY-A	3	6	0	0	0	0	0	0	0	0	.000	.000	.000	-99	-2	0	0	0	.750	-1	/2-1	-0.3
Total	2	28	71	8	21	3	0	3	10	9	11	.296	.375	.465	129	3	0	0	0	.953	-0	/2-22,3-2,S-2,D-1	0.4
■ ROLLIE ZEIDER	Zeider, Rollie Hubert "Bunions" b: 11/16/1883, Auburn, Ind. d: 9/12/67, Garrett, Ind. BR/TR, 5'10", 162 lbs. Deb: 4/14/10																						
1910	Chi-A	136	498	57	108	9	2	0	31	62		.217	.305	.243	75	-12	49			.931	-2	2-87,S-45/3-4	-1.6
1911	Chi-A	73	217	39	55	3	0	2	21	29		.253	.347	.295	82	-4	28			.997	-5	1-29,S-17,3-10/2-9	-0.8
1912	Chi-A	130	420	57	103	12	10	1	42	50		.245	.330	.329	91	-4	47			.979	6	1-66,3-56/S-1	0.1
1913	Chi-A	16	20	4	7	0	0	0	2	4	1	.350	.458	.350	139	1	3			1.000	1	/3-6,1-3,2-1	0.4
	NY-A	50	159	15	37	2	0	0	12	25	9	.233	.341	.245	72	-4	3			.901	-14	S-24,2-19/1-4,3-2	-1.8
	Yr	66	179	19	44	2	0	0	14	29	10	.246	.354	.257	79	-3	6			.901	-11	S-24,2-20/3-8,1-7	-1.4
1914	Chi-F	119	452	60	124	13	2	1	36	44	28	.274	.344	.319	86	-15	35			.936	-0	*3-117/S-1	-1.2
1915	Chi-F	129	494	65	112	22	5	0	34	43	24	.227	.297	.279	66	-30	16			.941	1	2-83,3-30,S-21	-2.8
1916	Chi-N	98	345	29	81	11	2	1	22	26	26	.235	.294	.287	71	-11	9			.928	-8	3-55,2-33/O-7,S1	-2.0
1917	Chi-N	108	354	36	86	14	2	0	27	28	30	.243	.302	.294	77	-9	17			.901	-21	S-48,3-26,2-24/10	-3.0
1918	*Chi-N	82	251	31	56	13	2	0	26	23	20	.223	.288	.251	63	-10	16			.956	-11	2-79/1-1,3-1	-1.9
Total	9	941	3210	393	769	89	22	5	253	334	138	.240	.315	.286	77	-99	223			.945	-52	2-335,3-307,S1/O	-14.6
■ TODD ZEILE	Zeile, Todd Edward b: 9/9/65, Van Nuys, Cal. BR/TR, 6'1", 190 lbs. Deb: 8/18/89																						
1989	StL-N	28	82	7	21	3	1	1	8	9	14	.256	.330	.354	92	-1	0	0	0	.971	-2	C-23	-0.1
1990	StL-N	144	495	62	121	25	3	15	57	67	77	.244	.337	.398	101	1	2	4	-2	.988	-11	*C-105,3-24,1-11,/O	-0.6
1991	StL-N	155	565	76	158	36	3	11	81	62	94	.280	.356	.412	115	12	17	11	-2	.943	-7	*3-154	0.4
1992	StL-N	126	439	51	113	18	4	7	48	68	70	.257	.357	.364	108	6	7	10	-4	.960	-7	*3-124	-0.5
1993	StL-N	157	571	82	158	36	1	17	103	70	76	.277	.356	.433	112	10	5	4	-1	.923	-5	*3-153	0.5
1994	StL-N	113	415	62	111	25	1	19	75	52	56	.267	.353	.470	114	9	1	3	-2	.960	7	*3-112	1.0
1995	StL-N	34	127	16	37	6	0	5	22	18	23	.291	.384	.457	121	4	1	0	0	.980	1	1-34	0.2
	Chi-N	79	299	34	68	16	0	9	30	16	53	.227	.274	.371	69	-14	0	0	0	.939	-10	3-75/O-2,1-1	-2.5
	Yr	113	426	50	105	22	0	14	52	34	76	.246	.308	.397	85	-10	1	0	0	.939	-9	3-75,1-35/O-2	-2.3
1996	Phi-N	134	500	61	134	24	0	20	80	67	88	.268	.356	.436	105	4	1	1	-0	.962	-14	*3-106,1-28	-1.3
	*Bal-A	29	117	17	28	8	0	5	19	15	16	.239	.326	.436	91	-2	0	0	0	.963	2	3-29	0.1
Total	8	999	3610	468	949	197	13	109	523	444	567	.263	.346	.415	105	30	34	33	-10	.945	-49	3-777,C-128/1-74,O	-2.8
■ BART ZELLER	Zeller, Barton Wallace b: 7/22/41, Chicago Heights, Ill. BR/TR, 6'1", 185 lbs. Deb: 5/21/70 C																						
1970	StL-N	1	0	0	0	0	0	0	0	0	0	—	—	—	—		0	0	0	1.000	-0	/C-1	0.0
■ GUS ZERNIAL	Zernial, Gus Edward "Ozark Ike" b: 6/27/23, Beaumont, Tex. BR/TR, 6'2.5", 210 lbs. Deb: 4/19/49																						
1949	Chi-A	73	198	29	63	17	2	5	38	15	26	.318	.366	.500	132	8	0	1	-1	1.000	-5	O-46	0.0
1950	Chi-A	143	543	75	152	16	4	29	93	38	110	.280	.330	.484	110	3	0	2	-1	.969	2	*O-137	-0.2
1951	Chi-A	4	19	2	2	0	0	0	4	2	2	.105	.190	.105	-19	-3	0	0	0	.933	1	/O-4	-0.2
	Phi-A	139	552	90	151	30	5	33	125	61	99	.274	.350	.525	132	21	2	2	-1	.974	10	*O-138	2.4
	Yr	143	571	92	153	30	5	**33**	**129**	63	101	.268	.345	.511	127	18	2	2	-1	.972	11	*O-142	2.2
1952	Phi-A	145	549	76	144	15	1	29	100	70	87	.262	.347	.452	114	9	5	1	1	.972	-1	*O-141	0.4
1953	Phi-A★	147	556	85	158	21	3	42	108	57	79	.284	.355	.559	138	27	4	0	1	.972	13	*O-141	3.5
1954	Phi-A	97	336	42	84	8	2	14	62	30	60	.250	.319	.411	98	-2	0	1	-0	.953	-1	O-90/1-2	-0.7
1955	KC-A	120	413	62	105	9	3	30	84	30	90	.254	.317	.508	116	6	1	0	0	.964	8	*O-103	0.9
1956	KC-A	109	272	36	61	12	0	16	44	33	66	.224	.317	.445	99	-2	2	0	1	.984	2	O-69	-0.3
1957	KC-A	131	437	56	103	20	1	27	69	34	84	.236	.292	.471	104	-0	1	1	-0	.952	0	*O-113/1-1	-0.8
1958	Det-A	66	124	8	40	7	1	5	23	6	25	.323	.354	.516	127	4	0	0	0	.939	-2	O-24	0.1
1959	Det-A	60	132	11	30	7	0	7	26	7	27	.227	.266	.417	80	-4	0	0	0	.972	-3	1-32/O-1	-0.9
Total	11	1434	4131	572	1093	159	22	237	776	383	755	.265	.331	.486	115	66	15	7	0	.968	24	*O-1007/1-35	4.2
■ CHARLIE ZIEGLER	Ziegler, Charles W. b: 1/13/1875, Canton, Ohio d: 4/18/04, Canton, Ohio Deb: 9/23/1899																						
1899	Cle-N	2	8	2	2	0	0	0	0	0		.250	.250	.250	40	-1	0			.750	-1	/S-1,2-1	-0.2
1900	Phi-N	3	11	0	3	0	0	0	1	0		.273	.273	.273	51	-1	0			.889	-1	/3-3	-0.2
Total	2	5	19	2	5	0	0	0	1	0		.263	.263	.263	47	-1	0			.889	-2	/3-3,2-1,S-1	-0.4
■ BENNY ZIENTARA	Zientara, Benedict Joseph b: 2/14/20, Chicago, Ill. d: 4/16/85, Lake Elsinore, Cal. BR/TR, 5'9", 165 lbs. Deb: 9/11/41																						
1941	Cin-N	9	21	3	6	0	0	0	2	1	3	.286	.318	.286	71	-1	0			.914	1	/2-6	0.1
1946	Cin-N	78	280	26	81	10	2	0	16	14	11	.289	.323	.339	91	-4	3			.970	24	2-39,3-36	2.4
1947	Cin-N	117	418	60	108	18	1	0	24	23	23	.258	.297	.321	64	-22	2			.976	-17	*2-100,3-13	-3.2
1948	Cin-N	74	187	17	35	1	2	0	7	12	11	.187	.236	.214	23	-20	0			.990	12	2-60/3-3,S-2	-0.5
Total	4	278	906	106	230	29	5	2	49	50	48	.254	.293	.304	64	-46	5			.976	20	2-205/3-52,S-2	-1.2
■ BILL ZIES	Zies, William BL , Deb: 8/9/1891																						
1891	StL-a	2	3	0	1	0	0	0	0	0	0	.333	.333	.333	79	-0	0			1.000	0	/C-2	0.0
■ CHIEF ZIMMER	Zimmer, Charles Louis b: 11/23/1860, Marietta, Ohio d: 8/22/49, Cleveland, Ohio BR/TR, 6', 190 lbs. Deb: 7/18/1884 MU																						
1884	Det-N	8	29	0	2	1	0	0	0	1	14	.069	.100	.103	-38	-4				.830	-1	/C-6,O-2	-0.5
1886	NY-a	6	19	1	3	0	0	0	1	1		.158	.238	.158	26	-2	0			.893	3	/C-6	0.2
1887	Cle-a	14	52	9	12	5	0	0	4	4		.231	.298	.327	76	-2	1			.923	-4	C-12/1-2	-0.4
1888	Cle-a	65	212	27	51	11	4	0	22	18		.241	.312	.330	109	3	15			.917	7	C-59/O-3,1-3,S-1	1.3
1889	Cle-N	84	259	47	67	9	9	1	21	44	35	.259	.368	.375	110	5	14			.931	7	C-81/1-3	1.6
1890	Cle-N	125	444	54	95	16	6	2	57	46	54	.214	.303	.291	75	-14	15			.937	12	*C-125	0.9
1891	Cle-N	116	440	55	112	21	4	6	69	33	49	.255	.312	.341	87	-9	15			.936	18	C-116/3-1	1.8
1892	*Cle-N	111	413	63	108	29	13	1	64	32	47	.262	.325	.402	115	6	18			.938	11	*C-111	2.3
1893	Cle-N	57	227	27	70	13	7	2	41	16	15	.308	.357	.454	108	1	4			.968	5	C-56/3-1	1.1
1894	Cle-N	90	341	55	97	20	5	4	65	17	31	.284	.328	.408	74	-17	14			**.963**	10	*C-89	0.2
1895	Cle-N	88	315	60	107	21	2	5	56	33	30	.340	.417	.467	121	10	14			.975	9	*C-84/1-3	2.1
1896	*Cle-N	91	336	46	93	18	3	3	46	31	48	.277	.354	.375	87	-7	4			**.972**	9	*C-91/3-1	1.0
1897	Cle-N	80	294	50	93	22	3	0	40	25		.316	.378	.412	103	1	8			.976	7	C-80	1.4
1898	Cle-N	20	63	5	15	2	1	0	2	6		.238	.304	.270	66	-3	2			.970	-4	C-19	0.3
1899	Cle-N	20	73	9	25	2	1	0	14	5		.342	.407	.479	154	5	1			.957	-1	C-20	0.5
	Lou-N	75	262	43	78	11	3	6	29	22		.298	.370	.385	107	3	9			.985	1	C-62,1-11	0.9

YEAR	TM/L	G	AB	R	H	2B	3B	HR	RBI	BB	SO	AVG	OBP	SLG	PRO+	BR/A	SB	CS	SBR	FA	FR	G/POS	TPR
	Yr	95	335	52	103	13	4	4	43	27		.307	.378	.406	117	8	10			**.978**	0	C-82,1-11	1.4
1900	*Pit-N	82	271	27	80	7	10	0	35	17		.295	.361	.395	108	3	4			.961	5	C-78/1-2	1.4
1901	Pit-N	69	236	17	52	7	3	0	21	20		.220	.292	.275	63	-11	6			.975	-7	C-68	-1.0
1902	Pit-N	42	142	13	38	4	2	0	17	11		.268	.338	.324	101	0	4			.969	-1	C-41/1-1	0.4
1903	Phi-N	37	118	9	26	3	1	0	19	9		.220	.292	.288	68	-5	3			.968	4	C-35,M	0.3
Total	19	1280	4546	617	1224	222	76	26	625	390	323	.269	.339	.369	95	-35	151			.952	102	*C-1239/1-25,O3S	15.8

■ DON ZIMMER Zimmer, Donald William b: 1/17/31, Cincinnati, Ohio BR/TR, 5'9", 177 lbs. Deb: 7/2/54 MC

YEAR	TM/L	G	AB	R	H	2B	3B	HR	RBI	BB	SO	AVG	OBP	SLG	PRO+	BR/A	SB	CS	SBR	FA	FR	G/POS	TPR
1954	Bro-N	24	33	3	6	0	1	0	0	3	8	.182	.270	.242	34	-3	2	0	1	.939	3	S-13	0.1
1955	*Bro-N	88	280	38	67	10	1	15	50	19	66	.239	.292	.443	89	-5	5	3	-0	.976	9	2-62,S-21/3-8	0.9
1956	Bro-N	17	20	4	6	1	0	0	2	0	7	.300	.333	.350	78	-1	0	1	-1	.944	2	/S-8,3-3,2-1	0.1
1957	Bro-N	84	269	23	59	9	1	6	19	16	63	.219	.263	.327	52	-18	1	3	-2	.957	9	3-39,S-37/2-5	-0.6
1958	LA-N	127	455	52	119	15	2	17	60	28	92	.262	.306	.415	86	-10	14	2	3	.965	**33**	*S-114,3-12/2-1,O-1	3.5
1959	*LA-N	97	249	21	41	7	1	4	28	37	56	.165	.275	.249	38	-22	3	1	0	.972	2	S-88/3-5,2-1	-1.3
1960	Chi-N	132	368	37	95	16	7	6	35	27	56	.258	.309	.389	90	-5	8	6	-1	.980	6	2-75,3-45/S-5,O-2	0.6
1961	Chi-N★	128	477	57	120	25	4	13	40	25	70	.252	.292	.403	81	-14	5	1	1	.973	0	*2-116/3-5,O-1	-0.1
1962	NY-N	14	52	3	4	1	0	0	1	3	10	.077	.127	.096	-38	-10	0	1	-1	.961	5	3-14	-0.7
	Cin-N	63	192	16	48	11	2	2	16	14	30	.250	.304	.359	75	-7	1	2	-1	.949	-1	3-43,2-17/S-1	-0.7
	Yr	77	244	19	52	12	2	2	17	17	40	.213	.267	.303	51	-17	1	3	-2	.952	4	3-57,2-17/S-1	-1.3
1963	LA-N	22	23	4	5	1	0	1	2	3	10	.217	.308	.391	107	0	0	0	0	.933	2	3-10/2-1,S-1	0.2
	Was-A	83	298	37	74	12	1	13	44	18	57	.248	.296	.426	100	-1	3	2	-0	.935	3	3-78/2-2	0.2
1964	Was-A	121	341	38	84	16	2	12	38	27	94	.246	.302	.411	96	-2	1	3	-2	.955	-13	3-87/O-4,C-2,2-1	-1.9
1965	Was-A	95	226	20	45	6	0	2	17	26	59	.199	.287	.252	56	-13	2	0	1	.966	-7	C-33,3-26,2-12	-1.9
Total	12	1095	3283	353	773	130	22	91	352	246	678	.235	.291	.372	76	-112	45	25	-2	.941	53	3-375,2-294,S/CO	-1.5

■ EDDIE ZIMMERMAN Zimmerman, Edward Desmond b: 1/4/1883, Oceanic, N.J. d: 5/6/45, Emmaus, Pa. BR/TR, 5'9", 160 lbs. Deb: 9/29/06

YEAR	TM/L	G	AB	R	H	2B	3B	HR	RBI	BB	SO	AVG	OBP	SLG	PRO+	BR/A	SB	CS	SBR	FA	FR	G/POS	TPR
1906	StL-N	5	14	0	3	0	0	0	1	0		.214	.214	.214	35	-1	0			.929	-0	/3-5	-0.1
1911	Bro-N	122	417	31	77	10	7	3	36	34	37	.185	.249	.264	46	-32	9			**.961**	3	*3-122	-2.7
Total	2	127	431	31	80	10	7	3	37	34	37	.186	.248	.262	45	-33	9			.960	3	3-127	-2.8

■ JERRY ZIMMERMAN Zimmerman, Gerald Robert b: 9/21/34, Omaha, Neb. BR/TR, 6'2", 185 lbs. Deb: 4/14/61 C

YEAR	TM/L	G	AB	R	H	2B	3B	HR	RBI	BB	SO	AVG	OBP	SLG	PRO+	BR/A	SB	CS	SBR	FA	FR	G/POS	TPR
1961	*Cin-N	76	204	8	42	5	0	0	10	11	21	.206	.253	.230	29	-15	1	1	-0	.975	3	C-76	-1.5
1962	Min-A	34	62	8	17	4	0	0	7	3	5	.274	.318	.339	74	-2	0	0	0	.992	2	C-34	0.1
1963	Min-A	39	56	3	13	1	0	0	3	2	8	.232	.259	.250	43	-4	0	0	0	1.000	6	C-39	0.2
1964	Min-A	63	120	6	24	3	0	0	12	10	15	.200	.278	.225	42	-9	0	0	0	.993	6	C-63	-0.2
1965	*Min-A	83	154	8	33	1	1	1	11	12	23	.214	.275	.253	49	-10	0	0	0	**.997**	12	C-82	0.5
1966	Min-A	60	119	11	30	4	1	1	15	11	23	.252	.341	.328	88	-1	0	0	0	.996	9	C-59	1.0
1967	Min-A	104	234	13	39	3	0	1	12	22	49	.167	.244	.192	28	-20	0	1	-1	.992	15	*C-104	-0.2
1968	Min-A	24	45	3	5	1	0	0	1	5	10	.111	.184	.133	-3	-5	0	0	0	.991	5	C-24	0.1
Total	8	483	994	60	203	22	2	3	72	78	154	.204	.270	.239	43	-73	1	2	-1	.991	58	C-481	0.0

■ HEINIE ZIMMERMAN Zimmerman, Henry b: 2/9/1887, New York, N.Y. d: 3/14/69, New York, N.Y. BR/TR, 5'11.5", 176 lbs. Deb: 9/8/07

YEAR	TM/L	G	AB	R	H	2B	3B	HR	RBI	BB	SO	AVG	OBP	SLG	PRO+	BR/A	SB	CS	SBR	FA	FR	G/POS	TPR
1907	*Chi-N	5	9	0	2	1	0	0	1	0		.222	.222	.333	70	-0	1			.789	1	/2-4,S-1,O-1	0.1
1908	Chi-N	46	113	17	33	4	1	0	9	1		.292	.298	.345	101	-0	2			.923	-10	2-20/O-8,S-1,3-1	-1.2
1909	Chi-N	65	183	23	50	9	2	0	21	3		.273	.285	.344	93	-3	7			.945	-7	2-31,S-12/3-4	-1.1
1910	*Chi-N	99	335	35	95	16	6	3	38	20	36	.284	.326	.394	111	3	7			.948	-10	2-32,S-26,3-23/O1	-0.7
1911	Chi-N	143	535	80	164	22	17	9	85	25	50	.307	.343	.462	124	14	23			.946	-1	*2-108,3-20,1-11	1.1
1912	Chi-N	145	557	95	**207**	41	14	**14**	99	38	60	**.372**	.418	**.571**	**169**	**50**	23			.916	2	*3-121,1-22	5.1
1913	Chi-N	127	447	69	140	28	12	9	95	41	40	.313	.379	.490	147	26	18			.912	3	*3-125	3.4
1914	Chi-N	146	564	75	167	36	12	4	87	20	46	.296	.326	.424	123	12	17			.897	-21	*3-118,S-15,2-12	-0.4
1915	Chi-N	139	520	65	138	28	11	3	62	21	33	.265	.300	.379	105	1	19	13	-2	.943	-9	*2-100,3-36/S-4	1.9
1916	Chi-N	107	398	54	116	25	5	6	64	16	33	.291	.324	.425	116	6	15	12	-2	.932	7	3-85,2-14/S-4	1.9
	NY-N	40	151	22	41	4	0	0	19	7	10	.272	.304	.298	90	-2	9	8	-2	.943	-3	3-40/2-1	-0.5
	Yr	147	549	76	157	29	5	6	**83**	23	43	.286	.318	.390	110	5	24	20	-5	.935	4	*3-125,2-15/S-4	1.4
1917	*NY-N	150	585	61	174	22	9	5	**102**	16	43	.297	.317	.391	121	11	13			.947	13	*3-149/2-5	3.0
1918	NY-N	121	463	43	126	19	10	1	56	13	23	.272	.294	.363	102	-1	14			.955	-4	*3-100,1-19	-0.5
1919	NY-N	123	444	56	113	20	6	4	58	21	30	.255	.296	.354	96	-3	8			.940	-1	*3-123	-0.5
Total	13	1456	5304	695	1566	275	105	58	796	242	404	.295	.331	.419	121	114	175	33		.928	-38	3-945,2-327/S1O	9.5

■ ROY ZIMMERMAN Zimmerman, Roy Franklin b: 9/13/16, Pine Grove, Pa. d: 11/22/91, Pine Grove, Pa. BL/TL, 6'2", 187 lbs. Deb: 9/2/45

YEAR	TM/L	G	AB	R	H	2B	3B	HR	RBI	BB	SO	AVG	OBP	SLG	PRO+	BR/A	SB	CS	SBR	FA	FR	G/POS	TPR
1945	NY-N	27	98	14	27	1	0	5	16	5	16	.276	.330	.439	111	1	1			.988	-2	1-25/O-1	-0.3

■ BILL ZIMMERMAN Zimmerman, William H. b: 1/20/1889, Kengen, Germany d: 10/4/52, Newark, N.J. BR/TR, 5'8.5", 172 lbs. Deb: 4/14/15

YEAR	TM/L	G	AB	R	H	2B	3B	HR	RBI	BB	SO	AVG	OBP	SLG	PRO+	BR/A	SB	CS	SBR	FA	FR	G/POS	TPR
1915	Bro-N	22	57	3	16	2	0	0	7	4	8	.281	.328	.316	93	-0	1			.864	-4	O-18	-0.6

■ FRANK ZINN Zinn, Frank b: 12/21/1865, Phoenixville, Pa. d: 5/12/36, Manayunk, Pa. 5'8", 150 lbs. Deb: 4/18/1888

YEAR	TM/L	G	AB	R	H	2B	3B	HR	RBI	BB	SO	AVG	OBP	SLG	PRO+	BR/A	SB	CS	SBR	FA	FR	G/POS	TPR
1888	Phi-a	2	7	0	0	0	0	0	0	1		.000	.125	.000	-59	-1	0			.938	-1	/C-2	-0.1

■ GUY ZINN Zinn, Guy b: 2/13/1887, Hallbrook, W.Va. d: 10/6/49, Clarksburg, W.Va. BL/TR, 5'10.5", 170 lbs. Deb: 9/11/11

YEAR	TM/L	G	AB	R	H	2B	3B	HR	RBI	BB	SO	AVG	OBP	SLG	PRO+	BR/A	SB	CS	SBR	FA	FR	G/POS	TPR
1911	NY-A	9	27	5	4	0	2	0	1	4		.148	.281	.296	57	-2	0			.923	-0	/O-8	-0.2
1912	NY-A	106	401	56	105	15	10	6	55	50		.262	.345	.394	105	2	17			.893	-12	*O-106	-1.5
1913	Bos-N	36	138	15	41	8	2	1	15	4	23	.297	.322	.406	105	0	3			.948	4	O-35	0.3
1914	Bal-F	61	225	30	63	10	6	3	25	16	26	.280	.336	.418	101	-3	6			.935	-5	O-57	-1.1
1915	Bal-F	102	312	30	84	18	3	5	43	35	28	.269	.343	.394	104	-3	2			.949	-5	O-88	-1.2
Total	5	314	1103	136	297	51	23	15	139	109	77	.269	.338	.398	103	-6	28			.927	-17	O-294	-3.7

■ BUD ZIPFEL Zipfel, Marion Sylvester b: 11/18/38, Belleville, Ill. BL/TR, 6'3", 200 lbs. Deb: 7/26/61

YEAR	TM/L	G	AB	R	H	2B	3B	HR	RBI	BB	SO	AVG	OBP	SLG	PRO+	BR/A	SB	CS	SBR	FA	FR	G/POS	TPR
1961	Was-A	50	170	17	34	7	5	4	18	15	49	.200	.265	.371	69	-8	1	1	-0	.983	-4	1-44	-1.7
1962	Was-A	68	184	21	44	4	1	6	21	17	43	.239	.307	.370	82	-5	1	2	-1	.976	-2	1-26,O-23	-1.1
Total	2	118	354	38	78	11	6	10	39	32	92	.220	.287	.370	76	-13	2	3	-1	.981	-7	/1-70,O-23	-2.8

■ RICHIE ZISK Zisk, Richard Walter b: 2/6/49, Brooklyn, N.Y. BR/TR, 6'1", 208 lbs. Deb: 9/8/71

YEAR	TM/L	G	AB	R	H	2B	3B	HR	RBI	BB	SO	AVG	OBP	SLG	PRO+	BR/A	SB	CS	SBR	FA	FR	G/POS	TPR
1971	Pit-N	7	15	2	3	1	0	0	0	3	7	.200	.368	.467	136	1	0	0	0	1.000	-1	/O-6	0.0
1972	Pit-N	17	37	4	7	3	0	0	4	7	10	.189	.318	.270	70	-1	0	0	0	.938	-2	O-12	-0.4
1973	Pit-N	103	333	44	108	23	7	10	54	21	63	.324	.364	.526	148	20	0	0	0	.987	-2	O-84	1.9
1974	*Pit-N	149	536	75	168	30	3	17	100	65	91	.313	.388	.476	146	33	1	1	-0	.985	9	*O-141	3.6
1975	*Pit-N	147	504	69	146	27	3	20	75	68	109	.290	.376	.474	136	25	0	1	-1	.975	1	*O-140	2.0
1976	Pit-N	155	581	91	168	35	2	21	89	52	96	.289	.348	.465	135	20	1	0	0	.987	6	*O-152	2.4
1977	Chi-A★	141	531	78	154	17	6	30	101	55	98	.290	.360	.514	135	25	0	4	-2	.982	6	*O-109,D-28	2.3
1978	Tex-A★	140	511	68	134	19	1	22	85	58	76	.262	.341	.432	116	11	3	3	-1	.988	-2	O-90,D-49	0.2
1979	Tex-A	144	503	69	132	21	5	18	64	57	75	.262	.338	.416	103	2	1	1	-0	.972	-4	O-134/D-3	-0.8
1980	Tex-A	135	448	48	130	17	2	19	77	39	72	.290	.347	.460	123	9	0	2	-2	.980	-3	D-86,O-37	0.5
1981	Sea-A	94	357	42	111	16	1	16	43	28	63	.311	.366	.485	138	17	0	2	-1	.000		D-93	1.3
1982	Sea-A	131	503	61	147	28	1	21	62	49	89	.292	.356	.477	133	14	2	1	0	.000		*D-130	1.1
1983	Sea-A	90	285	30	69	12	0	12	36	30	61	.242	.314	.411	94	-3	0	0	0	.000		D-84	-0.6
Total	13	1453	5144	681	1477	245	26	207	792	533	910	.287	.355	.466	126	176	8	15	-9	.981	14	O-905,D-473	13.5

■ BILLY ZITZMANN Zitzmann, William Arthur b: 11/19/1895, Long Island City, N.Y. d: 5/29/85, Passaic, N.J. BR/TR, 5'10.5", 175 lbs. Deb: 4/17/19

YEAR	TM/L	G	AB	R	H	2B	3B	HR	RBI	BB	SO	AVG	OBP	SLG	PRO+	BR/A	SB	CS	SBR	FA	FR	G/POS	TPR
1919	Pit-N	11	26	5	5	1	0	0	2	6		.192	.192	.231	26	-2	2			.917	-3	/O-8	-0.5
	Cin-N	2	1	0	0	0	0	0	0	0	0	.000	.000	.000	-99	-0	0			.000	-1	/O-1	-0.1
	Yr	13	27	5	5	1	0	0	2	6		.185	.185	.222	22	-3	2			.917	-2	/O-9	-0.6
1925	Cin-N	104	301	53	76	13	3	0	21	35	22	.252	.342	.316	71	-12	11	11	-3	.959	-14	O-89/S-1	-3.3

YEAR	TM/L	G	AB	R	H	2B	3B	HR	RBI	BB	SO	AVG	OBP	SLG	PRO+	BR/A	SB	CS	SBR	FA	FR	G/POS	TPR
1926	Cin-N	53	94	21	23	2	1	0	3	6	7	.245	.304	.287	61	-5	3			.965	-3	O-31	-1.0
1927	Cin-N	88	232	47	66	10	4	0	24	20	18	.284	.352	.362	94	-1	9			.958	-9	O-60/S-8,3-3	-1.3
1928	Cin-N	101	266	53	79	9	3	3	33	13	22	.297	.337	.387	90	-4	13			.958	-6	O-78/3-1	-1.5
1929	Cin-N	47	84	18	19	3	0	0	6	9	10	.226	.309	.262	45	-7	4			.940	-3	O-22/1-5	-1.0
Total	6	406	1004	197	268	38	11	3	89	83	85	.267	.333	.336	77	-32	42	11		.956	-37	O-289/S-9,1-5,3-4	-8.7

■ EDDIE ZOSKY
Zosky, Edward James b: 2/10/68, Whittier, Cal. BR/TR, 6', 175 lbs. Deb: 9/2/91

YEAR	TM/L	G	AB	R	H	2B	3B	HR	RBI	BB	SO	AVG	OBP	SLG	PRO+	BR/A	SB	CS	SBR	FA	FR	G/POS	TPR
1991	Tor-A	18	27	2	4	1	1	0	2	0	8	.148	.148	.259	10	-3	0	0	0	1.000	1	S-18	-0.1
1992	Tor-A	8	7	1	2	1	0	1	2	0	2	.286	.286	.571	129	0	0	0	0	.923	1	/S-8	0.1
1995	Fla-N	6	5	0	1	0	0	0	1	0	0	.200	.200	.200	6	-1	0	0	0	.667	-0	/S-4,2-1	-0.1
Total	3	32	39	3	7	1	2	0	3	0	10	.179	.179	.308	31	-4	0	0	0	.963	2	/S-30,2-1	-0.1

■ JON ZUBER
Zuber, Jon Edward b: 12/10/69, Encino, Cal. BL/TL, 6', 190 lbs. Deb: 4/19/96

YEAR	TM/L	G	AB	R	H	2B	3B	HR	RBI	BB	SO	AVG	OBP	SLG	PRO+	BR/A	SB	CS	SBR	FA	FR	G/POS	TPR
1996	Phi-N	30	91	7	23	4	1	0	10	6	11	.253	.299	.330	64	-5	1	0		.987	-2	1-22	-0.8

■ BOB ZUPCIC
Zupcic, Robert b: 8/18/66, Pittsburgh, Pa. BR/TR, 6'4", 220 lbs. Deb: 9/7/91

YEAR	TM/L	G	AB	R	H	2B	3B	HR	RBI	BB	SO	AVG	OBP	SLG	PRO+	BR/A	SB	CS	SBR	FA	FR	G/POS	TPR
1991	Bos-A	18	25	3	4	1	0	0	3	1	6	.160	.192	.280	28	-3	0	0	0	.875	-5	O-16	-0.7
1992	Bos-A	124	392	46	108	19	1	3	43	25	60	.276	.325	.352	84	-8	2	2	-1	.977	-2	*O-114/D-5	-1.3
1993	Bos-A	141	286	40	69	24	2	2	26	27	54	.241	.311	.360	75	-10	5	2	0	.979	-19	*O-122/D-5	-3.0
1994	Bos-A	4	4	0	0	0	0	0	0	0	1	.000	.000	.000	-96	-1	0	0	0	1.000	0	/O-2,D-1	-0.2
	Chi-A	32	88	10	18	4	1	1	8	4	16	.205	.239	.307	40	-7	0	1	-1	1.000	-1	O-28/3-2,1-1	-0.9
	Yr	36	92	10	18	4	1	1	8	4	17	.196	.229	.293	34	-9	0	1	-1	1.000	-1	O-30/3-2,D-1,1-1	-1.1
Total	4	319	795	99	199	47	4	8	80	57	137	.250	.305	.346	73	-30	7	5	-1	.977	-27	O-282/D-11,3-2,1-1	-6.1

■ FRANK ZUPO
Zupo, Frank Joseph "Noodles" b: 8/29/39, San Francisco, Cal BL/TR, 5'11", 182 lbs. Deb: 7/1/57

YEAR	TM/L	G	AB	R	H	2B	3B	HR	RBI	BB	SO	AVG	OBP	SLG	PRO+	BR/A	SB	CS	SBR	FA	FR	G/POS	TPR
1957	Bal-A	10	12	2	1	0	0	0	0	1	4	.083	.154	.083	-36	-2	0	0	0	.913	0	/C-8	-0.2
1958	Bal-A	1	2	0	0	0	0	0	0	0	1	.000	.000	.000	-99	-1	0	0	0	1.000	0	/C-1	0.0
1961	Bal-A	5	4	1	2	1	0	0	0	1	1	.500	.600	.750	268	1	0	0	0	1.000	1	/C-4	0.1
Total	3	16	18	3	3	1	0	0	0	2	6	.167	.250	.222	31	-2	0	0	0	.941	1	/C-13	-0.1

■ PAUL ZUVELLA
Zuvella, Paul b: 10/31/58, San Mateo, Cal. BR/TR, 6', 178 lbs. Deb: 9/4/82 C

YEAR	TM/L	G	AB	R	H	2B	3B	HR	RBI	BB	SO	AVG	OBP	SLG	PRO+	BR/A	SB	CS	SBR	FA	FR	G/POS	TPR
1982	Atl-N	2	1	0	0	0	0	0	0	0	0	.000	.000	.000	-96	-0	0	0	0	.800	1	/S-1	0.1
1983	Atl-N	3	5	0	0	0	0	0	0	2	1	.000	.375	.000	11	-0	0	0	0	.750	-2	/S-2	-0.2
1984	Atl-N	11	25	2	5	1	0	0	1	2	3	.200	.259	.240	38	-2	0	0	0	1.000	1	/2-6,S-6	-0.1
1985	Atl-N	81	190	16	48	8	1	0	4	16	14	.253	.311	.305	69	-8	2	0	0	.986	9	2-42,S-33/3-5	0.5
1986	NY-A	21	48	2	4	0	0	0	0	2	6	.083	.170	.104	-24	-8	0	0	0	.966	4	S-21	-0.3
1987	NY-A	14	34	2	6	0	0	0	3	0	3	.176	.176	.176	-6	-5	0	0	0	1.000	-1	/2-7,S-6,3-1	-0.6
1988	Cle-A	51	130	9	30	5	1	0	7	8	13	.231	.275	.285	56	-5	0	0	0	.959	-3	S-49	-0.8
1989	Cle-A	24	58	10	16	2	0	2	6	1	11	.276	.300	.414	98	-1	0	0	0	.963	-3	S-15/3-5,D-3	-0.3
1991	KC-A	2	0	0	0	0	0	0	0	0	0	—	—	—	—	0	0	0	0	.000	0	/3-2	0.0
Total	9	209	491	41	109	17	2	2	20	34	50	.222	.275	.277	52	-32	2	0	0	.959	5	S-133/2-55,3-13,D-3	-1.7

■ DUTCH ZWILLING
Zwilling, Edward Harrison b: 11/2/1888, St.Louis, Mo. d: 3/27/78, LaCrescenta, Cal. BL/TL, 5'6.5", 160 lbs. Deb: 8/14/10 C

YEAR	TM/L	G	AB	R	H	2B	3B	HR	RBI	BB	SO	AVG	OBP	SLG	PRO+	BR/A	SB	CS	SBR	FA	FR	G/POS	TPR
1910	Chi-A	27	87	7	16	5	0	0	5	11		.184	.283	.241	67	-3	1			.940	-2	O-27	-0.7
1914	Chi-F	154	592	91	185	38	6	**16**	95	46	68	.313	.363	.485	138	18	21			.962	2	*O-154	1.4
1915	Chi-F	150	548	65	157	32	7	13	**94**	67	65	.286	.366	.442	135	16	24			.979	8	*O-148/1-3	1.8
1916	Chi-N	35	53	4	6	1	0	1	8	4	6	.113	.175	.189	11	-6	0			1.000	0	O-10	-0.9
Total	4	366	1280	167	364	76	15	30	202	128	139	.284	.351	.438	127	26	46			.969	6	O-339/1-3	1.6

The Pitcher Register

The Pitcher Register consists of the central pitching statistics of every man who has pitched in major league play since 1871, *without exception*. Pitcher batting is expressed in Batting Runs in the Pitcher Batting column, and in the newly added columns for base hits and batting average. Pitcher defense is expressed in Fielding Runs in the Pitcher Defense column.

The pitchers are listed alphabetically by surname and, when more than one pitcher bears the name, alphabetically by *given* name—not by "use name," by which we mean the name he may have had applied to him during his playing career. This is the standard method of alphabetizing used in other biographical reference works, and in the case of baseball it makes it easier to find a lesser-known player with a common surname like Smith or Johnson. This method also jibes with that employed in the Team Roster and Annual Record where, for example, Charles "Old Hoss" Radbourn is shown not as the puzzling O. Radbourn or H. Radbourn, as some reference books have it, but as C. Radbourn. On the whole, we have been conservative in ascribing nicknames, doing so only when the player was in fact known by that name during his playing days.

Each person in the Pitcher Register can be found by finding the Pitcher Register list in the Contents and selecting the title whose names alphabetically surround the surname of pitcher you desire. Pitcher batting and pitcher defense, because the win-denominated numbers they produce are so small, are not sorted for single-season leaders (although the all-time leaders in these categories, single season and lifetime, will be found in the separate section called "All-Time Leaders"). Symbols denoting All Star Game selection and/or play appear to the right of the team/league column. An additional finding aid is an asterisk alongside the team for which a player appeared in postseason competition, thus making for easy cross-reference to the earlier sections on postseason play.

The record of a man who pitched in more than one season is given in one line for each season, plus a career total line. If he pitched for more than one team in a given year, his totals for each team are given on separate lines; and if the teams for which he pitched in his "traded year" are in the same league, then his full record is stated in both separate and combined fashion. (In the odd case of a man playing for three or more clubs in one year, with some of these clubs being in the same league, the combined total line will reflect only his play in that one league.) A man who pitched in only one year has no additional career total line since it would be identical to his seasonal listing.

In *Total Baseball 1*, fractional innings were calculated for teams in the Annual Record but were rounded off to the nearest whole inning for individuals, in accordance with baseball scoring practice.

Pitching records for the National Association are included in the Pitcher Register because the editors, like most baseball historians, regard it as a major league, inasmuch as it was the only professional league of its day and supplied the National League of 1876 with most of its personnel. Unless Major League Baseball reverses the position it adopted in 1969 and restores the NA to official major league status, we will continue the practice of carrying separate totals for the National Association rather than integrating them into the career marks of those pitchers whose major league tenures began before 1876 and concluded in that year or after it.

Gaps remain elsewhere in the official record of baseball and in the ongoing process of sabermetric reconstruction. The reader will note occasional blank elements in biographical lines; these are not typographical lapses but signs that the information does not exist or has not yet been found. However, unlike the case of batting records, there are no incomplete statistical columns for pitchers. Where official statistics did not exist or the raw data have not survived, as with batters facing pitchers before 1908 in the American League and before 1903 in the National, we have constructed figures from the available raw data. For example, to obtain a pitcher's BFP—Batters Facing Pitchers—for calculating Opponents' On Base Percentage or Batting Average, we have subtracted league base hits from league at-bats, divided by league innings pitched, multiplied by the pitcher's innings and added his hits and walks allowed and hit-by-pitch, if available.

For a key to the team and league abbreviations used in the Pitcher Register go to the last page of the book. For a guide to the other procedures and abbreviations employed in the Pitcher Register, review the comments on the prodigiously extended pitching record on the next page.

Looking at the biographical line for any pitcher, we see first his use name in full capitals, then his given name and nickname (and any other name he may have used or been born with, such as the matronymic of a Latin American player). His date and place of birth follow "b" and his date and place of death follow "d"; years through 1900 are expressed fully, in four digits, and years after 1900 are expressed in only their last two digits. Then come his manner of batting and throwing, abbreviated for a left-handed batter who throws right as BL/TR (a switch-hitter would be shown as BB for "bats both" and a switch thrower as TB for "throws both"). Next, and for most pitchers last, is the pitcher's debut date.

Some pitchers continue in major league baseball after their pitching days are through, as managers, coaches, or even umpires. A pitcher whose biographical line concludes with an M can also be located in the Manager

Roster; one whose line bears a C will be listed in the Coach Roster; and one with a U occupies a place in the Umpire Roster. (In the last case we have placed a U on the biographical line only for those pitchers who umpired in at least six games in a year, for in the nineteenth century—and especially in the years of the National Association—there were literally hundreds of players who were pressed into service as umpires for a game or two; it would be misleading to accord such pitchers the same code we give to Bob Emslie or Bill Dinneen.) The select few who have been enshrined in the Baseball Hall of Fame are noted with an H. They are also listed in the Hall of Fame Roster found toward the end of "Awards and Honors." An F in this line denotes family connection—father-son-grandfather-grandson or brother.

YEAR	TM/L	W	L	PCT	G	GS	CG	SH	SV	IP	H	HR	BB	SO	RAT	ERA	ERA+	OAV	OOB	BH	AVG	PB	PR	/A	PD	TPI
● RIP VAN WINKLE																										

Van Winkle, Rip "Half Moon" (Also Played in 1874 as Geoffrey Crayon)
b: 4/30/1820, Plattekill, N.Y.   d: 12/12/80, Hudson, N.Y.   BL/TL, 5'5", 145 lbs.   Deb: 5/7/1874 MUCHF ♦

YEAR	TM/L	W	L	PCT	G	GS	CG	SH	SV	IP	H	HR	BB	SO	RAT	ERA	ERA+	OAV	OOB	BH	AVG	PB	PR	/A	PD	TPI
1874	Bos-n	27	30	.474	57	57	56	1	0	498	502	5	18	20	9.4	3.90	104	.258	.270	40	.167	-3	5	3	-1	-0.1
1875	Wes-n	29	22	.569	52	51	50	2	1	450	491	4	25	16	10.3	4.02	106	.260	.272	50	.200	1	7	7	0	0.5
1883	Bal-a	5	18	.217	27	23	19	0	1	196	207	7	76	77	10.0	3.44	101	.274	.340	18	.180	-0	-3	1	0	-0.1
1884	Was-U	0	1	.000	1	1	1	0	0	8	10	0	2	3	13.5	4.50	110	.309	.349	0	.000	1	-0	-0	0	0.0
	KC-U	5	2	.714	8	6	5	0	0	52	66	0	9	14	13.0	4.33	104	.312	.340	9	.250	2	3	1	0	0.1
	Yr	5	3	.625	7	7	6	0	0	60	76	0	11	17	13.0	4.35	104	.311	.341	9	.225	2	3	1	0	0.1
1890	Cin-P	0	0	—	1	1	1	0	0	0	5	2	2	0	∞	∞	-97	1.000	1.000	1	.250	0	-2	-2	0	-0.2
1907	NY-N	16	13	.552	35	34	18	0	2	251	224	19	78	170	10.8	2.76	126	.236	.293	30	.250	1	17	20	2	2.2
1908	NY-N	16	12	.571	36	35	14	1	5	278	224	15	48	205	8.8	2.20	130	.215	.250	25	.200	1	24	20	-3	2.2
1909	NY-N	25	7	.781	36	35	18	0	5	273	202	24	82	208	9.4	2.21	164	.201	.261	20	.147	-1	42	43	1	4.2
1910	NY-N	18	12	.600	37	36	19	0	2	291	230	21	83	283	9.4	2.81	135	.211	.267	38	.277	4	40	32	1	3.6
1911	NY-N	20	10	.667	36	35	21	0	4	286	210	18	61	289	8.6	1.76	188	.202	.246	40	.296	4	54	49	-1	5.5
1912	NY-N	21	12	.636	35	35	13	0	3	262	215	23	77	249	10.0	2.92	116	.219	.275	34	.281	3	18	14	1	1.7
1913	NY-N	19	10	.655	36	36	18	0	3	290	219	24	64	251	8.8	2.08	184	.202	.247	31	.263	3	51	56	2	5.9
1914	Ind-F	11	11	.500	32	32	12	0	5	236	199	19	75	201	10.4	3.20	126	.226	.287	22	.227	-1	11	22	1	2.2
1915	NY-N	22	9	.710	36	36	15	0	5	280	217	11	88	243	9.8	2.38	155	.211	.274	33	.311	3	39	41	1	4.2
1936	NY-N☆	7	3	.700	13	13	5	0	3	96	79	7	28	72	10.0	3.00	140	.218	.274	11	.196	1	10	13	3	1.5
	Bos-A	5	7	.417	16	16	1	0	0	104	114	8	29	72	12.4	3.81	112	.271	.318	20	.189	0	4	5	-2	0.7
1967	*Bos-A★	0	1	.000	1	1	0	0	0	⅓	5	2	1	1	180.0	108.00	1200	.833	.857	0	.000	0	-2	-2	0	-0.2
Total	2 n	56	52	.519	109	108	106	3	1	948	993	9	43	36	9.8	3.96	105	.259	.271	90	.184	-2	12	7	7	0.4
Total	14	190	128	.597	384	375	180	1	38	2903	2486	199	803	2338	10.2	2.76	134	.226	.285	294	.224	23	304	313	6	33.6

A black diamond appears at the end of the biographical line for pitchers who also appear in the Player Register by virtue of their having played in 100 or more games at another position, including pinch hitter, or having played more than half of their total major league games at another position, or having played more games at a position other than pitcher in at least one year.

The explanations for the statistical column heads follow; for more technical information about formulas and calculations, see the Glossary. The vertical rules in the column-header line separate the stats into six logical groupings: year, team, league; wins and losses; game-related counting stats; inning-related counting stats; basic calculated averages; pitcher batting; sabermetric figures of more complex calculation; and run-denominated Linear Weights stats for pitching, fielding, and Total Pitcher Index.

Note that the TPI (Total Pitcher Index) in this edition differs from those in earlier volumes, because for players who were both batters and pitchers, the method of allocating Wins between TPI and TPR (Total Player Rating) was improved. Previously, if a pitcher pitched in over half his games, all his batting was included with his pitcher rating (TPI); if he pitched in less than half his games, his Batting Wins were thrown over to his batter rating (TPR), with his TPI including only his Pitching Wins and Pitcher Defense. The new method prorates batting proportionally with the number of games pitched. In addition, fielding ratings at nonpitching positions for players who pitched in over half their games, previously omitted, are now part of the Total Baseball Ranking. In any case, the TPR values of batter-pitchers should remain about the same. Thus in 1918, Babe Ruth now has a batter rating of 2.6 Wins and a pitcher rating of 2.9 (total 5.5). Prior to the fourth edition his marks used to be 4.1 and 1.0, respectively, or 5.1 overall, with none of his batting counted in with his pitching record even though he pitched 20 of 95 games. The large jump in his pitcher rating is because now his pitcher batting is compared against average batting for pitchers.

Also—and this is a key difference—the formula for Total Pitcher Index has been revised to employ the Relief Ranking formula (see Glossary) for all pitchers, not just relievers. The principal effect will be to calculate Pitcher Wins for relievers instead of Adjusted Pitcher Runs, as was formerly the case. The TPI will still be the sum of pitching, batting, fielding, and baserunning runs, but the Pitcher Runs will be expressed as Ranking Runs rather than Adjusted Pitching Runs. Check the Glossary for the specifics, but the net effect will be to raise the TPIs of relief closers and, to a lesser extent, starters who average a high number of innings per start, and to lower somewhat the TPIs of mopup relievers (few saves, few decisions) and starters with many no-decision games.

Taken out from the Pitcher Register of earlier editions are the following statistics: Hits Per Game and Bases on Balls Per Game (still available in the Annual Record and Leaders sections, and now stated in combined fashion as Ratio); Strikeouts Per Game (still available in the Annual Record and Leaders sections and, in any event, fairly evident from a glance at the SO and IP columns); Park Factor for pitchers (still available from the Annual Record); Clutch Pitching Index, newly developed for Total Baseball but which we have judged to be of lesser interest and value than the more established sabermetric measures (still, it is present in the Annual Record and Leaders sections); and Wins Above Team, a stat that has so many cautions associated with it that we judged it to be of little value when applied to all pitchers.

Finally, we have made an upward adjustment to overall league performance in the Federal League of 1914-15 and the Union Association of 1884 (thus lowering individual ratings), because while both leagues are regarded as major leagues, there can be no doubt that their caliber of play was not equivalent to that in the rival leagues of those years. Suffice it to say here that league earned run averages were reduced by 20 percent for the UA and 10 percent for the FL. A full explanantion of the adjustment procedure may be found in the Glossary, under "League Performance."

YEAR Year in which a man pitched (When a space in the column is blank, this indicates that the man pitched for two or more clubs in the last year stated in the column; if those clubs were in the same league, then the man will also have a combined total line, beginning with the abbreviation "Yr" placed in the TM/L column.)

* Denotes postseason play, World Series or League Championship Series.

Yr Year's totals for pitching with two or more clubs in same league (see comments for YEAR)

★ Named to All Star Game, played

☆ Named to All Star Game, did not play

† Named to All Star Game, replaced because of injury

TM/L Team and League (see comments for YEAR)

W Wins

L Losses

PCT Win Percentage (Wins divided by decisions)

G Games pitched

GS Games Started

CG Complete Games

SH Shutouts (Complete-game shutouts only)

SV Saves (Employing definition in force at the time, and 1969 definition for years prior to 1969)

IP Innings Pitched (Fractional innings included, as discussed above)

H Hits allowed

HR Home Runs allowed

BB Bases on Balls allowed

SO Strikeouts

RAT Ratio (Hits allowed plus walks allowed per nine innings)

ERA Earned Run Average (In a handful of cases, a pitcher will have faced one or more batters for his full season's work yet failed to retire any of them [thus having an innings-pitched figure of zero]; if any of the men he put on base came around to score earned runs, these runs produced an infinite ERA, expressed in the pitcher's record as ∞. (see Van Winkle's 1890 season)

ERA⁺ Adjusted Earned Run Average normalized to league average and adjusted for home-park factor. (See comments for /A.)

OAV Opponents' Batting Average

OOB Opponents' On Base Percentage

BH Base Hits (as a batter)

AVG Batting Average

PB Pitcher Batting (Expressed in Batting Runs. Pitcher Batting is park-adjusted and weighted, for those who played primarily at other positions, by the ratio of games pitched to games played. For more technical data about Runs Per Win and Batting Run formulas, see Glossary.)

PR Pitching Runs (Linear Weights measure of runs saved *beyond* what a league-average pitcher might have saved, defined as zero. New to this edition, the formula used to calculate Relief Ranking is now employed for all pitchers; this creates small differences for starters but large differences for relievers, especially closers [see Glossary for further detail]. Occasionally the curious figure of – 0 will appear in this column, or in the columns of other Linear Weights measures of batting, fielding, and the TPI. This "negative zero" figure signifies a run contribution that falls below the league average, but to so small a degree that it cannot be said to have cost the team a run.

/A Adjusted (This signifies that the stat to the immediate left, in this instance Pitching Runs, is here normalized to league average and adjusted for home-park factor. A mark of 100 is a league-average performance, and superior marks exceed 100. An innovation for this edition is to use three-year averages for pitching park factors. If a team moved, or the park changed dramatically, then two-year averages are employed; if the park was used for only one year, then of course only that run-scoring data is used.)

PD Pitcher Defense (Expressed in Fielding Runs. See comment above on PB and see Glossary.)

TPI Total Pitcher Index (The sum, expressed in wins beyond league average, of a pitcher's Pitching Runs, [now expressed as Ranking Runs—see Glossary] Batting Runs—in the AL since 1973—and Fielding Runs, all divided by the Runs Per Win factor for that year—which is generally around 10, historically in the 9–11 range; see Glossary.)

Total For players whose careers include play in the National Association as well as other major leagues, two totals are given, as described above and as illustrated in Rip Van Winkle's record, where the record of his years in the National Association is shown alongside the notation "Total 2 n," where *2* stands for the number of years totaled and *n* stands for National Association. For players whose careers began in 1876 or later, the lifetime record is shown alongside the notation "Total x," where *x* stands for the number of post-1875 years totaled.

YEAR TM/L	W	L	PCT	G	GS	CG	SH	SV	IP	H	HR	BB	SO	RAT	ERA	ERA+	OAV	OOB	BH	AVG	PB	PR	/A	PD	TPI

● DON AASE
Aase, Donald William b: 9/8/54, Orange, Cal. BR/TR, 6'3", 210 lbs. Deb: 7/26/77

YEAR TM/L	W	L	PCT	G	GS	CG	SH	SV	IP	H	HR	BB	SO	RAT	ERA	ERA+	OAV	OOB	BH	AVG	PB	PR	/A	PD	TPI
1977 Bos-A	6	2	.750	13	13	4	2	0	92¹	85	6	19	49	10.2	3.12	144	.244	.285	0	—	0	10	14	-0	1.0
1978 Cal-A	11	8	.579	29	29	6	1	0	178²	185	14	80	93	13.4	4.03	90	.270	.348	0	—	0	-5	-8	-0	-0.7
1979 *Cal-A	9	10	.474	37	28	7	1	2	185¹	200	19	77	96	13.5	4.81	85	.277	.347	0	—	0	-12	-15	-2	-1.4
1980 Cal-A	8	13	.381	40	21	5	1	2	175	193	13	66	74	13.4	4.06	97	.287	.351	0	—	0	-1	-3	-1	-0.3
1981 Cal-A	4	4	.500	39	0	0	0	11	65¹	56	4	24	38	11.0	2.34	156	.234	.304	0	—	0	10	9	-0	1.5
1982 Cal-A	3	3	.500	24	0	0	0	4	52	45	5	23	40	11.8	3.46	117	.243	.327	0	—	0	4	3	-0	0.4
1984 Cal-A	4	1	.800	23	0	0	0	8	39	30	1	19	28	11.3	1.62	246	.221	.316	0	—	0	10	10	-0	1.7
1985 Bal-A	10	6	.625	54	0	0	0	14	88	83	6	35	67	12.2	3.78	106	.258	.332	0	—	0	4	2	-0	0.5
1986 Bal-A★	6	7	.462	66	0	0	0	34	81²	71	6	28	67	10.9	2.98	139	.234	.298	0	—	0	11	11	-0	2.4
1987 Bal-A	1	0	1.000	7	0	0	0	2	8	8	1	4	3	13.5	2.25	195	.276	.364	0	—	0	2	2	-0	0.5
1988 Bal-N	0	0	—	35	0	0	0	2	46²	40	4	37	28	14.9	4.05	96	.240	.377	0	—	0	-0	-1	-0	0.0
1989 NY-N	1	5	.167	49	0	0	0	2	59¹	56	5	26	34	12.6	3.94	83	.245	.324	0	—	0	-3	-4	-1	-0.5
1990 LA-N	3	1	.750	32	0	0	0	3	38	33	5	19	24	12.3	4.97	74	.232	.323	0	.000	-1	-5	-6	-1	-0.7
Total 13	66	60	.524	448	91	22	5	82	1109¹	1085	89	457	641	12.6	3.80	103	.259	.333	0	.000	-1	23	15	-5	4.4

● BERT ABBEY
Abbey, Bert Wood b: 11/29/1869, Essex, Vt. d: 6/11/62, Essex Junction, Vt. BR/TR, 5'11", 175 lbs. Deb: 6/14/1892

YEAR TM/L	W	L	PCT	G	GS	CG	SH	SV	IP	H	HR	BB	SO	RAT	ERA	ERA+	OAV	OOB	BH	AVG	PB	PR	/A	PD	TPI
1892 Was-N	5	18	.217	27	22	19	0	1	195²	207	7	76	77	13.3	3.45	94	.261	.330	9	.120	-3	-4	-4	2	-0.5
1893 Chi-N	2	4	.333	7	7	5	0	0	56	74	1	20	6	15.8	5.46	85	.308	.371	6	.231	-0	-5	-5	0	-0.4
1894 Chi-N	2	7	.222	11	11	10	0	0	92	119	3	37	24	15.6	5.18	108	.310	.375	5	.128	-5	1	4	-1	-0.2
1895 Chi-N	0	1	.000	1	1	1	0	0	8	10	1	2	3	14.6	4.50	113	.303	.361	1	.333	1	0	1	0	0.1
Bro-N	5	2	.714	8	6	5	0	0	52	66	0	9	14	13.5	4.33	102	.304	.341	5	.263	1	3	0	1	0.2
Yr	5	3	.625	9	7	6	0	0	60	76	1	11	17	13.5	4.35	103	.303	.340	6	.273	1	3	1	1	0.3
1896 Bro-N	8	8	.500	25	18	12	0	0	164¹	210	7	48	37	14.6	5.15	80	.308	.361	12	.190	-0	-14	-19	-2	-1.5
Total 5	22	40	.355	79	65	52	0	1	568	686	18	192	161	14.3	4.52	92	.292	.352	38	.169	-8	-19	-23	0	-2.3

● CHARLIE ABBEY
Abbey, Charles S. b: 10/14/1866, Falls City, Neb. d: 4/27/26, San Francisco, Cal. BL, 5'8.5", 169 lbs. Deb: 8/16/1893 ♦

YEAR TM/L	W	L	PCT	G	GS	CG	SH	SV	IP	H	HR	BB	SO	RAT	ERA	ERA+	OAV	OOB	BH	AVG	PB	PR	/A	PD	TPI
1896 Was-N	0	0	—	1	0	0	0	0	2	4	0	0	1	27.0	4.50	98	.500	.500	79	.262	0	-0	-0	-0	0.0

● JIM ABBOTT
Abbott, James Anthony b: 9/19/67, Flint, Mich. BL/TL, 6'3", 200 lbs. Deb: 4/8/89

YEAR TM/L	W	L	PCT	G	GS	CG	SH	SV	IP	H	HR	BB	SO	RAT	ERA	ERA+	OAV	OOB	BH	AVG	PB	PR	/A	PD	TPI
1989 Cal-A	12	12	.500	29	29	4	2	0	181¹	190	13	74	115	13.3	3.92	97	.274	.347	0	—	0	-1	-2	-1	-0.2
1990 Cal-A	10	14	.417	33	33	4	1	0	211²	246	16	72	105	13.7	4.51	85	.295	.355	0	—	0	-14	-16	1	-1.5
1991 Cal-A	18	11	.621	34	34	5	1	0	243	222	14	73	158	11.1	2.89	142	.244	.304	0	—	0	33	33	3	4.1
1992 Cal-A	7	15	.318	29	29	7	0	0	211	208	12	68	130	11.9	2.77	144	.263	.325	0	—	0	27	28	2	3.0
1993 NY-A	11	14	.440	32	32	4	1	0	214	221	22	73	95	12.5	4.37	95	.271	.334	0	—	0	-1	-5	1	-0.1
1994 NY-A	9	8	.529	24	24	2	0	0	160¹	167	24	64	90	13.1	4.55	101	.273	.344	0	—	0	5	0	0	0.3
1995 Chi-A	6	4	.600	17	17	3	0	0	112¹	116	10	35	45	12.2	3.36	132	.269	.325	0	—	0	17	14	-0	1.0
Cal-A	5	4	.556	13	13	1	1	0	84²	93	4	29	41	13.1	4.15	113	.280	.340	0	—	0	5	5	1	0.5
Yr	11	8	.579	30	30	4	1	0	197	209	14	64	86	12.5	3.70	123	.273	.330	0	—	0	22	19	0	1.5
1996 Cal-A	2	18	.100	27	23	1	0	0	142	171	14	78	58	16.0	7.48	65	.306	.395	0	—	0	-39	-41	1	-4.2
Total 8	80	100	.444	238	234	31	6	0	1560¹	1634	138	566	837	12.9	4.11	102	.273	.339	0	—	0	31	17	7	2.9

● KYLE ABBOTT
Abbott, Lawrence Kyle b: 2/18/68, Newburyport, Mass. BL/TL, 6'4", 200 lbs. Deb: 9/10/91

YEAR TM/L	W	L	PCT	G	GS	CG	SH	SV	IP	H	HR	BB	SO	RAT	ERA	ERA+	OAV	OOB	BH	AVG	PB	PR	/A	PD	TPI
1991 Cal-A	1	2	.333	5	5	0	0	0	19²	22	2	13	12	16.5	4.58	90	.301	.414	0	—	0	-1	-1	0	-0.1
1992 Phi-N	1	14	.067	31	19	0	0	0	133¹	147	20	45	88	13.0	5.13	68	.283	.341	2	.069	-1	-24	-24	-1	-2.8
1995 Phi-N	2	0	1.000	18	0	0	0	0	28¹	28	5	16	21	14.0	3.81	111	.267	.364	1	.500	0	1	0	1	0.1
1996 Cal-A	0	1	.000	3	0	0	0	0	4	10	1	5	3	33.8	20.25	24	.500	.600	0	—	0	-7	-7	0	-1.1
Total 4	4	17	.190	57	22	0	0	0	185¹	207	26	79	124	14.0	5.20	75	.288	.360	3	.097	-1	-31	-31	-1	-3.9

● DAN ABBOTT
Abbott, Leander Franklin "Big Dan" b: 3/16/1862, Portage, Ohio d: 2/13/30, Ottawa Lake, Mich. BR/TR, 5'11", 190 lbs. Deb: 4/19/1890

YEAR TM/L	W	L	PCT	G	GS	CG	SH	SV	IP	H	HR	BB	SO	RAT	ERA	ERA+	OAV	OOB	BH	AVG	PB	PR	/A	PD	TPI
1890 Tol-a	0	2	.000	3	1	1	0	1	13	19	0	8	3	19.4	6.23	63	.328	.418	1	.143	0	-3	-3	1	-0.4

● PAUL ABBOTT
Abbott, Paul David b: 9/15/67, Van Nuys, Cal. BR/TR, 6'3", 185 lbs. Deb: 8/21/90

YEAR TM/L	W	L	PCT	G	GS	CG	SH	SV	IP	H	HR	BB	SO	RAT	ERA	ERA+	OAV	OOB	BH	AVG	PB	PR	/A	PD	TPI
1990 Min-A	0	5	.000	7	7	0	0	0	34²	37	0	28	25	17.1	5.97	70	.282	.412	0	—	0	-8	-7	-1	-1.1
1991 Min-A	3	1	.750	15	3	0	0	0	47¹	38	5	36	43	14.1	4.75	90	.232	.370	0	—	0	-3	-3	-0	-0.5
1992 Min-A	0	0	—	6	0	0	0	0	11	12	1	5	13	14.7	3.27	124	.279	.367	0	—	0	1	1	1	-0.1
1993 Cle-A	0	1	.000	5	5	0	0	0	18¹	19	5	11	7	14.7	6.38	68	.260	.357	0	—	0	-4	-4	0	-0.2
Total 4	3	7	.300	33	15	0	0	0	111¹	106	11	80	88	15.2	5.25	80	.258	.381	0	—	0	-15	-13	-0	-1.9

● GLENN ABBOTT
Abbott, William Glenn b: 2/16/51, Little Rock, Ark. BR/TR, 6'6", 200 lbs. Deb: 7/29/73

YEAR TM/L	W	L	PCT	G	GS	CG	SH	SV	IP	H	HR	BB	SO	RAT	ERA	ERA+	OAV	OOB	BH	AVG	PB	PR	/A	PD	TPI
1973 Oak-A	1	0	1.000	5	3	1	0	0	18²	16	3	7	6	11.1	3.86	92	.225	.295	0	—	0	-0	-1	-0	0.0
1974 Oak-A	5	7	.417	19	17	3	0	0	96	89	4	34	38	11.8	3.00	111	.247	.317	0	—	0	7	3	-0	0.4
1975 *Oak-A	5	5	.500	30	15	3	1	0	114¹	109	12	50	51	12.7	4.25	85	.253	.333	0	—	0	-6	-8	-1	-0.5
1976 Oak-A	2	4	.333	19	10	0	0	0	62¹	87	6	16	27	15.0	5.49	61	.333	.374	0	—	0	-14	-15	0	-1.1
1977 Sea-A	12	13	.480	36	34	7	0	0	204¹	212	32	56	100	12.3	4.45	92	.270	.328	0	—	0	-9	-8	-0	-0.9
1978 Sea-A	7	15	.318	29	28	8	1	0	155¹	191	22	44	67	13.7	5.27	72	.303	.350	0	—	0	-26	-25	-3	-3.1
1979 Sea-A	4	10	.286	23	19	3	0	0	116²	138	19	38	25	13.8	5.17	84	.301	.358	0	—	0	-12	-11	-1	-1.2
1980 Sea-A	12	12	.500	31	31	7	2	0	215	228	27	49	78	11.7	4.10	101	.272	.315	0	—	0	-2	1	2	0.3
1981 Sea-A	4	9	.308	22	20	1	0	0	130¹	127	14	28	35	10.7	3.94	98	.258	.298	0	—	0	-4	-1	-1	-0.4
1983 Sea-A	5	3	.625	14	14	2	0	0	82¹	103	9	15	38	13.3	4.59	93	.311	.349	0	—	0	-5	-3	-1	-0.5
Det-A	2	1	.667	7	7	1	1	0	46²	43	5	7	11	9.6	1.93	203	.244	.273	0	—	0	11	10	-1	0.7
Yr	7	4	.636	21	21	3	1	0	129	146	14	22	49	11.7	3.63	114	.285	.314	0	—	0	6	7	-1	0.3
1984 Det-A	3	4	.429	7	7	1	0	0	44	62	3	14	8	14.7	5.93	66	.326	.360	0	—	0	-9	-10	-1	-1.3
Total 11	62	83	.428	248	206	37	5	0	1286	1405	162	352	484	12.5	4.39	89	.280	.331	0	—	0	-69	-67	-7	-7.6

● AL ABER
Aber, Albert Julius "Lefty" b: 7/31/27, Cleveland, Ohio d: 5/20/93, Garfield Heights, Ohio BL/TL, 6'2", 195 lbs. Deb: 9/15/50

YEAR TM/L	W	L	PCT	G	GS	CG	SH	SV	IP	H	HR	BB	SO	RAT	ERA	ERA+	OAV	OOB	BH	AVG	PB	PR	/A	PD	TPI
1950 Cle-A	1	0	1.000	1	1	0	0	0	9	5	1	4	4	9.0	2.00	217	.167	.265	0	.000	0	3	2	-0	0.2
1953 Cle-A	1	1	.500	6	0	0	0	0	6	6	0	9	4	22.5	7.50	60	.240	.441	0	—	1	-2	-2	0	-0.6
Det-A	4	3	.571	17	10	2	0	0	66²	63	3	41	34	14.0	4.45	91	.260	.367	3	.130	-1	-3	-3	1	-0.3
Yr	5	4	.556	23	10	2	0	0	72²	69	3	50	38	14.7	4.71	86	.258	.375	3	.130	-1	-6	-5	1	-0.9
1954 Det-A	5	11	.313	32	18	4	0	3	124²	121	8	40	54	11.8	3.97	93	.257	.320	5	.128	-1	-3	-4	1	-0.6
1955 Det-A	6	3	.667	39	1	0	0	3	80	86	9	28	37	12.8	3.37	114	.257	.334	1	.059	-2	5	4	1	0.3
1956 Det-A	4	4	.500	42	0	0	0	7	63	65	6	25	21	13.1	3.43	120	.270	.343	1	.300	1	5	5	1	0.7
1957 Det-A	3	3	.500	28	0	0	0	1	37	46	4	15	15	14.1	6.81	57	.315	.367	1	.125	-0	-12	-12	1	-1.8
KC-A	0	0	—	3	0	0	0	0	3	6	0	1	0	24.0	12.00	33	.400	.471	1	1.000	0	-3	-3	0	0.1
Yr	3	3	.500	31	0	0	0	1	40	52	4	16	15	14.6	7.20	54	.317	.367	2	.222	-0	-15	-15	1	-1.7
Total 6	24	25	.490	168	30	7	0	14	389¹	398	29	160	169	13.0	4.18	93	.269	.342	14	.140	-3	-11	-13	3	-2.0

● BILL ABERNATHIE
Abernathie, William Edward b: 1/30/29, Torrance, Cal. BR/TR, 5'10", 190 lbs. Deb: 9/27/52

YEAR TM/L	W	L	PCT	G	GS	CG	SH	SV	IP	H	HR	BB	SO	RAT	ERA	ERA+	OAV	OOB	BH	AVG	PB	PR	/A	PD	TPI
1952 Cle-A	0	0	—	1	0	0	0	0	2	4	1	1	0	22.5	13.50	25	.444	.500	0	.000	-0	-2	-2	-0	-0.2

● TED ABERNATHY
Abernathy, Talmadge Lafayette b: 10/30/21, Bynum, N.C. BR/TL, 6'2", 210 lbs. Deb: 9/19/42

YEAR TM/L	W	L	PCT	G	GS	CG	SH	SV	IP	H	HR	BB	SO	RAT	ERA	ERA+	OAV	OOB	BH	AVG	PB	PR	/A	PD	TPI
1942 Phi-A	0	0	—	1	0	0	0	0	2²	2	0	3	1	16.9	10.13	37	.222	.417	0	—	0	-2	-2	-0	-0.3
1943 Phi-A	0	3	.000	5	2	0	0	0	14²	24	3	13	10	22.7	12.89	26	.353	.457	1	.250	0	-16	-15	0	-2.3
1944 Phi-A	0	0	—	1	0	0	0	0	3	5	0	2	1	18.0	3.00	116	.417	.462	0	.000	0	0	0	-0	0.0
Total 3	0	3	.000	7	2	1	0	0	20¹	31	0	17	12	21.2	11.07	50	.348	.453	1	.200	0	-17	-17	0	-2.3

● TED ABERNATHY
Abernathy, Theodore Wade b: 3/6/33, Stanley, N.C. BR/TR, 6'4", 215 lbs. Deb: 4/13/55

YEAR TM/L	W	L	PCT	G	GS	CG	SH	SV	IP	H	HR	BB	SO	RAT	ERA	ERA+	OAV	OOB	BH	AVG	PB	PR	/A	PD	TPI
1955 Was-A	5	9	.357	40	14	3	2	0	119¹	136	6	67	79	15.8	5.96	64	.294	.392	4	.154	-1	-26	-28	1	-2.9
1956 Was-A	1	3	.250	5	4	2	0	0	30¹	35	2	10	18	13.6	4.15	104	.292	.351	2	.182	-0	0	1	2	0.2
1957 Was-A	2	10	.167	26	16	2	0	0	85	100	9	65	50	17.9	6.78	57	.314	.437	4	.167	0	-28	-27	1	-3.2

YEAR	TM/L	W	L	PCT	G	GS	CG	SH	SV	IP	H	HR	BB	SO	RAT	ERA	ERA+	OAV	OOB	BH	AVG	PB	PR	/A	PD	TPI
1960	Was-A	0	0	—	2	0	0	0	0	3	4	0	4	1	24.0	12.00	32	.308	.471	1	1.000	0	-3	-3	0	0.1
1963	Cle-A	7	2	.778	43	0	0	0	12	59⅓	54	3	29	47	12.6	2.88	126	.251	.340	2	.400	1	5	5	2	1.3
1964	Cle-A	2	6	.250	53	0	0	0	11	72⅔	66	5	46	57	14.1	4.33	83	.247	.362	0	.000	-1	-6	-6	3	-0.6
1965	Chi-N	4	6	.400	**84**	0	0	0	**31**	136⅓	113	7	56	104	11.5	2.57	143	.227	.311	3	.167	0	15	17	4	2.6
1966	Chi-N	1	3	.250	20	0	0	0	4	27⅔	26	4	17	18	14.6	6.18	60	.255	.372	0	.000	-0	-8	-8	2	-1.2
	Atl-N	4	4	.500	38	0	0	0	4	65⅓	58	5	36	42	12.9	3.86	94	.247	.347	2	.250	1	-2	-2	1	-0.1
	Yr	5	7	.417	58	0	0	0	8	93	84	9	53	60	13.3	4.55	80	.248	.349	2	.167	0	-10	-9	2	-1.3
1967	Cin-N	6	3	.667	70	0	0	0	28	106⅓	63	1	41	88	9.2	1.27	295	.170	.261	1	.059	-1	**25**	**29**	2	**4.5**
1968	Cin-N	10	7	.588	**78**	0	0	0	13	134⅔	111	9	55	64	11.4	2.47	128	.228	.312	0	.000	0	8	10	3	1.9
1969	Chi-N	4	3	.571	56	0	0	0	3	85⅓	75	8	42	55	12.4	3.16	127	.234	.325	2	.250	0	4	8	2	1.0
1970	Chi-N				11	0	0	0	1	9	9	2	2	9	15.0	2.00	225	.281	.395	0	—	-0	2	3	0	0.1
	StL-N	1	0	1.000	11	0	0	0	1	18⅓	15	1	5	8	14.7	2.95	140	.246	.395	0	.000	-0	2	2	1	0.2
	Yr	1	0	1.000	22	0	0	0	2	27⅓	24	0	7	10	14.5	2.63	161	.255	.386	0	.000	-0	4	5	1	0.3
	KC-A	9	3	.750					12	55⅔	41	3	38	49	12.9	2.59	144	.209	.340	3	.214	-1	7	7	0	1.8
1971	KC-A	4	6	.400	63	0	0	0	23	81	60	3	50	55	12.9	2.56	134	.210	.339	1	.077	-1	8	8	2	1.3
1972	KC-A	3	4	.429	45	0	0	0	5	58⅓	44	3	28	28	10.2	1.70	179	.210	.284	0	.000	-1	9	9	1	1.3
Total 14		63	69	.477	681	34	7	2	148	1147⅔	1010	70	592	765	12.9	3.46	106	.241	.341	25	.138	-4	12	26	27	8.6

● **WOODY ABERNATHY**   Abernathy, Virgil Woodrow   b: 2/1/15, Forest City, N.C.   d: 12/5/94, Louisville, Ky.   BL/TL, 6', 170 lbs.   Deb: 7/28/46

YEAR	TM/L	W	L	PCT	G	GS	CG	SH	SV	IP	H	HR	BB	SO	RAT	ERA	ERA+	OAV	OOB	BH	AVG	PB	PR	/A	PD	TPI
1946	NY-N	1	1	.500	15	1	0	0	1	40	32	5	10	6	9.4	3.37	102	.232	.284		.000	-1	0	0	-1	-0.2
1947	NY-N	0	0	—	1	0	0	0	0	2	4	0	1	0	22.5	9.00	45	.400	.455	0	.000	0	-1	-1	-0	0.0
Total 2		1	1	.500	16	1	0	0	1	42	36	5	11	6	10.1	3.64	95	.243	.296	0	.000	-1	-1	-1	-1	-0.2

● **HARRY ABLES**   Ables, Harry Terrell "Hans"   b: 10/4/1884, Terrell, Tex.   d: 2/8/51, San Antonio, Tex.   BR/TL, 6'2.5", 200 lbs.   Deb: 9/4/05

YEAR	TM/L	W	L	PCT	G	GS	CG	SH	SV	IP	H	HR	BB	SO	RAT	ERA	ERA+	OAV	OOB	BH	AVG	PB	PR	/A	PD	TPI
1905	StL-A	1	3	.000	6	3	1	0	0	30⅔	37	0	13	11	14.7	3.82	67	.301	.368	0	.000	-1	-4	-4	-1	-0.6
1909	Cle-A	1	1	.500	5	3	3	0	0	29⅔	26	1	10	24	11.2	2.12	122	.226	.294	0	.000	-1	1	1	-1	-0.2
1911	NY-A	0	1	.000	3	2	0	0	0	11	16	0	7	6	18.8	9.82	37	.333	.418	0	.000	-1	-8	-8	-0	-0.6
Total 3		1	5	.167	14	8	4	0	0	71⅓	79	1	30	41	13.9	4.04	67	.276	.347	0	.000	-4	-11	-11	-2	-1.4

● **GEORGE ABRAMS**   Abrams, George Allen   b: 11/9/1899, Seattle, Wash.   d: 12/5/86, Clearwater, Fla.   BR/TR, 5'9", 170 lbs.   Deb: 4/19/23

YEAR	TM/L	W	L	PCT	G	GS	CG	SH	SV	IP	H	HR	BB	SO	RAT	ERA	ERA+	OAV	OOB	BH	AVG	PB	PR	/A	PD	TPI
1923	Cin-N	0	0	—	3	0	0	0	0	4⅔	10	0	3	2	27.0	9.64	40	.500	.583	1	1.000	0	-3	-3	-0	0.0

● **JOHNNY ABREGO**   Abrego, Johnny Ray   b: 7/4/62, Corpus Christi, Tex   BR/TR, 6', 185 lbs.   Deb: 9/4/85

YEAR	TM/L	W	L	PCT	G	GS	CG	SH	SV	IP	H	HR	BB	SO	RAT	ERA	ERA+	OAV	OOB	BH	AVG	PB	PR	/A	PD	TPI
1985	Chi-N	1	1	.500	6	5	0	0	0	24	32	3	12	13	16.5	6.38	63	.352	.427	0	.000	-1	-7	-6	0	-0.5

● **JUAN ACEVEDO**   Acevedo, Juan Carlos   b: 5/5/70, Juarez, Mexico   BR/TR, 6'2", 195 lbs.   Deb: 4/30/95

YEAR	TM/L	W	L	PCT	G	GS	CG	SH	SV	IP	H	HR	BB	SO	RAT	ERA	ERA+	OAV	OOB	BH	AVG	PB	PR	/A	PD	TPI
1995	Col-N	4	6	.400	17	11	0	0	0	65⅔	82	15	20	40	14.8	6.44	84	.317	.379	1	.056	-2	-17	-8	-1	-1.2

● **JIM ACKER**   Acker, James Justin   b: 9/24/58, Freer, Tex.   BR/TR, 6'2", 212 lbs.   Deb: 4/7/83

YEAR	TM/L	W	L	PCT	G	GS	CG	SH	SV	IP	H	HR	BB	SO	RAT	ERA	ERA+	OAV	OOB	BH	AVG	PB	PR	/A	PD	TPI
1983	Tor-A	5	1	.833	38	5	0	0	1	97⅔	103	7	38	44	13.7	4.33	99	.273	.352	0	—	0	-3	-2	1	-0.1
1984	Tor-A	3	5	.375	32	3	0	0	1	72	79	3	25	33	13.8	4.38	94	.286	.358	0	—	0	-3	-2	-0	-0.5
1985	*Tor-A	7	2	.778	61	0	0	0	10	86⅓	86	7	43	42	13.8	3.23	130	.268	.360	0	—	0	9	9	1	1.2
1986	Tor-A	2	4	.333	23	5	0	0	0	60	63	6	22	32	13.1	4.35	97	.281	.351	0	—	0	-1	-1	0	0.0
	Atl-N	3	8	.273	21	14	0	0	0	95	100	7	26	37	12.0	3.79	105	.274	.324	3	.107	-1	-1	2	1	0.2
1987	Atl-N	4	9	.308	68	0	0	0	14	114⅔	109	11	51	68	12.9	4.16	104	.253	.338	3	.214	-0	-1	2	1	0.5
1988	Atl-N	0	4	.000	21	1	0	0	0	42	45	6	14	25	12.9	4.71	78	.280	.341	2	.400	1	-6	-5	0	-0.3
1989	Atl-N	0	6	.000	59	0	0	0	0	97⅔	84	5	20	68	9.7	2.67	137	.237	.280	1	.143	-0	9	11	1	0.7
	*Tor-A	2	1	.667	14	0	0	0	0	28⅓	24	1	12	24	11.8	1.59	237	.235	.322	0	—	0	7	7	1	0.9
1990	Tor-A	4	4	.500	59	0	0	0	1	91⅔	103	9	30	54	13.4	3.83	103	.281	.341	0	—	0	1	1	1	0.2
1991	*Tor-A	3	5	.375	54	4	0	0	1	88⅓	77	16	36	44	11.7	5.20	81	.238	.318	0	—	0	-11	-10	-0	-0.8
1992	Sea-A	0	0	—	17	0	0	0	0	30⅔	45	4	12	11	16.7	5.28	75	.338	.393	0	—	0	-5	-4	-0	0.0
Total 10		33	49	.402	467	32	0	0	30	904⅓	918	82	329	482	12.7	3.97	102	.267	.337	9	.167		-5	10	8	2.0

● **TOM ACKER**   Acker, Thomas James   b: 3/7/30, Paterson, N.J.   BR/TR, 6'4", 215 lbs.   Deb: 4/20/56

YEAR	TM/L	W	L	PCT	G	GS	CG	SH	SV	IP	H	HR	BB	SO	RAT	ERA	ERA+	OAV	OOB	BH	AVG	PB	PR	/A	PD	TPI
1956	Cin-N	4	3	.571	29	7	1	1	1	83⅔	60	7	29	54	9.8	2.37	168	.201	.277	1	.053	-1	13	15	1	1.2
1957	Cin-N	10	5	.667	49	6	1	0	4	108⅔	122	16	41	67	14.2	4.97	83	.293	.368	1	.053	-1	-13	-10	-0	-1.5
1958	Cin-N	4	3	.571	38	10	3	0	1	124⅔	126	10	43	90	12.4	4.55	91	.266	.331	2	.067	-1	-8	-6	-2	-0.6
1959	Cin-N	1	2	.333	37	0	0	0	1	63⅓	57	10	37	45	13.9	4.12	98	.246	.359	1	.111	-0	-1	-0	-1	-0.2
Total 4		19	13	.594	153	23	5	1	8	380⅓	365	43	150	256	12.6	4.12	99	.257	.335	5	.065	-3	-10	-1	-2	-1.1

● **FRITZ ACKLEY**   Ackley, Florian Frederick   b: 4/10/37, Hayward, Wis.   BL/TR, 6'1.5", 202 lbs.   Deb: 9/21/63

YEAR	TM/L	W	L	PCT	G	GS	CG	SH	SV	IP	H	HR	BB	SO	RAT	ERA	ERA+	OAV	OOB	BH	AVG	PB	PR	/A	PD	TPI
1963	Chi-A	1	0	1.000	2	2	0	0	0	13	7	2	7	11	9.7	2.08	169	.167	.286	1	.200	0	2	2	0	0.2
1964	Chi-A	0	0	—	3	2	0	0	0	6⅓	10	2	4	6	19.9	8.53	41	.345	.424	1	1.000	1	-3	-4	0	0.1
Total 2		1	0	1.000	5	4	0	0	0	19⅓	17	4	11	17	13.0	4.19	83	.239	.341	2	.333	1	-1	-2	1	0.3

● **CY ACOSTA**   Acosta, Cecilio (Miranda)   b: 11/22/46, Sabino, Mexico   BR/TR, 5'10", 165 lbs.   Deb: 6/4/72

YEAR	TM/L	W	L	PCT	G	GS	CG	SH	SV	IP	H	HR	BB	SO	RAT	ERA	ERA+	OAV	OOB	BH	AVG	PB	PR	/A	PD	TPI
1972	Chi-A	3	0	1.000	26	0	0	0	5	34⅔	25	2	17	28	10.9	1.56	201	.210	.309	0	.000	-0	6	6	-1	0.7
1973	Chi-A	10	6	.625	48	0	0	0	18	97	66	3	39	60	10.4	2.23	178	.193	.289	0	.000	-0	17	19	-1	3.6
1974	Chi-A	0	3	.000	27	0	0	0	3	45⅔	43	3	18	19	13.0	3.74	100	.256	.346	0	.000	-0	-1	-0	0	0.0
1975	Phi-N	0	0	—	6	0	0	0	1	8⅔	9	2	3	2	12.5	6.23	60	.273	.333	0	—	0	-3	-2	-0	-0.1
Total 4		13	9	.591	107	0	0	0	27	186	143	15	77	109	11.2	2.66	140	.216	.309	0	.000	0	20	22	-2	4.2

● **ED ACOSTA**   Acosta, Eduardo Elixbet   b: 3/9/44, Boquete, Panama   BB/TR, 6'5", 215 lbs.   Deb: 9/7/70

YEAR	TM/L	W	L	PCT	G	GS	CG	SH	SV	IP	H	HR	BB	SO	RAT	ERA	ERA+	OAV	OOB	BH	AVG	PB	PR	/A	PD	TPI
1970	Pit-N	0	0	—	3	0	0	0	0	2⅔	5	1	2	1	27.0	13.50	29	.417	.533	0	—	0	-3	-3	-0	-0.2
1971	SD-N	3	5	.375	8	6	3	1	0	46	43	4	7	16	9.8	2.74	120	.246	.275	0	.000	-2	4	3	-1	0.1
1972	SD-N	3	6	.333	46	2	0	0	0	89	105	7	30	53	14.0	4.45	74	.302	.362	1	.083	-0	-10	-11	-1	-1.2
Total 3		6	9	.400	57	8	3	1	0	137⅔	153	12	39	70	12.8	4.05	81	.286	.339	1	.034	-2	-9	-11	-1	-1.3

● **JOSE ACOSTA**   Acosta, Jose "Acostica"   b: 3/4/1891, Havana, Cuba   d: 11/16/77, Havana, Cuba   BR/TR, 5'6", 134 lbs.   Deb: 7/28/20   F

YEAR	TM/L	W	L	PCT	G	GS	CG	SH	SV	IP	H	HR	BB	SO	RAT	ERA	ERA+	OAV	OOB	BH	AVG	PB	PR	/A	PD	TPI
1920	Was-A	5	4	.556	17	5	4	1	1	82⅔	92	1	26	9	12.8	4.03	93	.290	.344	6	.240	1	-2	-3	-1	-0.4
1921	Was-A	5	4	.556	33	7	2	0	3	115⅔	148	4	36	30	14.3	4.36	94	.317	.366	2	.067	-2	-1	-3	-1	-0.5
1922	Chi-A	0	2	.000	5	1	0	0	0	15	25	4	6	6	18.6	8.40	48	.417	.470	1	.200	0	-7	-7	-0	-0.8
Total 3		10	10	.500	55	13	6	1	4	213⅓	265	9	68	45	14.0	4.51	88	.314	.365	9	.150	-1	-10	-13	-4	-1.7

● **MARK ACRE**   Acre, Mark Robert   b: 9/16/68, Concord, Cal.   BR/TR, 6'8", 235 lbs.   Deb: 5/13/94

YEAR	TM/L	W	L	PCT	G	GS	CG	SH	SV	IP	H	HR	BB	SO	RAT	ERA	ERA+	OAV	OOB	BH	AVG	PB	PR	/A	PD	TPI
1994	Oak-A	5	1	.833	34	0	0	0	0	34⅓	24	4	23	21	12.6	3.41	130	.202	.336	0	—	0	5	4	-1	1.0
1995	Oak-A	1	2	.333	43	0	0	0	0	52	52	7	28	47	14.2	5.71	78	.256	.352	0	—	0	-6	-7	-1	-0.4
1996	Oak-A	1	3	.250	22	0	0	0	2	25	38	4	9	18	17.6	6.12	79	.339	.398	0	—	0	-3	-4	-0	-0.3
Total 3		7	6	.538	99	0	0	0	2	111⅓	114	16	60	86	14.5	5.09	88	.263	.359	0	—	0	-4	-7	-1	0.3

● **ACE ADAMS**   Adams, Ace Townsend   b: 3/2/12, Willows, Cal.   BR/TR, 5'10.5", 182 lbs.   Deb: 4/15/41

YEAR	TM/L	W	L	PCT	G	GS	CG	SH	SV	IP	H	HR	BB	SO	RAT	ERA	ERA+	OAV	OOB	BH	AVG	PB	PR	/A	PD	TPI
1941	NY-N	4	1	.800	38	0	0	0	1	71	84	3	35	18	15.2	4.82	77	.304	.385	1	.083	-1	-9	-9	-1	-0.8
1942	NY-N	7	4	.636	**61**	0	0	0	11	88	69	1	31	33	10.2	1.84	183	.223	.293	1	.100	-1	**14**	**15**	0	2.3
1943	NY-N☆	11	7	.611	**70**	3	1	0	9	140⅓	121	5	55	46	11.4	2.82	122	.236	.311	4	.125	-1	9	10	-1	1.1
1944	NY-N	8	11	.421	**65**	4	1	0	13	137⅔	149	8	58	32	13.8	4.25	86	.279	.354	3	.103	-2	-10	-9	-2	-1.6
1945	NY-N	11	9	.550	65	6	0	0	**15**	113	109	7	44	39	12.3	3.42	114	.252	.324	3	.188	0	5	6	1	1.3
1946	NY-N	0	1	.000	3	0	0	0	0	3	1	0	1	3	33.8	16.88	20	.500	.526	0	—	0	-4	-4	-0	-1.1
Total 6		41	33	.554	302	7	2	0	49	552⅔	541	26	224	171	12.6	3.47	104	.260	.334	12	.121	-4	5	9	-3	1.2

● **BABE ADAMS**   Adams, Charles Benjamin   b: 5/18/1882, Tipton, Ind.   d: 7/27/68, Silver Spring, Md   BL/TR, 5'11.5", 185 lbs.   Deb: 4/18/06

YEAR	TM/L	W	L	PCT	G	GS	CG	SH	SV	IP	H	HR	BB	SO	RAT	ERA	ERA+	OAV	OOB	BH	AVG	PB	PR	/A	PD	TPI
1906	StL-N	0	1	.000	1	1	0	0	0	4	9	0	2	0	24.8	13.50	19	.474	.524	0	.000	-0	-5	-5	-0	-0.8
1907	Pit-N	0	2	.000	4	3	1	0	0	22	40	1	3	11	18.8	6.95	35	.408	.442	2	.286	0	-11	-11	0	-0.8

YEAR TM/L	W	L	PCT	G	GS	CG	SH	SV	IP	H	HR	BB	SO	RAT	ERA	ERA+	OAV	OOB	BH	AVG	PB	PR	/A	PD	TPI
1909 *Pit-N	12	3	.800	25	12	7	3	2	130	88	0	23	65	7.9	1.11	246	.196	.240	2	.051	-3	22	23	-1	2.5
1910 Pit-N	18	9	.667	34	30	16	3	0	245	217	4	60	101	10.4	2.24	138	.240	.291	16	.193	1	22	23	-5	2.0
1911 Pit-N	22	12	.647	40	37	24	6	0	293¹	253	5	42	133	**9.3**	2.33	147	.237	**.271**	26	.252	4	35	36	-3	3.5
1912 Pit-N	11	8	.579	28	20	11	2	0	170¹	169	4	35	63	10.9	2.91	112	.262	.303	12	.226	4	10	7	-2	0.8
1913 Pit-N	21	10	.677	43	37	24	4	0	313²	271	8	49	144	9.2	2.15	140	.235	.267	33	.289	9	37	30	-1	3.7
1914 Pit-N	13	16	.448	40	35	19	3	1	283	253	5	39	91	9.5	2.51	105	.244	**.276**	16	.165	1	9	4	-2	0.3
1915 Pit-N	14	14	.500	40	30	17	2	2	245	229	6	34	62	9.7	2.87	95	.252	.280	12	.141	0	-3	-4	-0	-0.7
1916 Pit-N	2	9	.182	16	10	4	1	0	72¹	91	2	12	22	13.2	5.72	47	.320	.355	6	.273	-2	-25	-24	-0	-3.2
1918 Pit-N	1	1	.500	3	3	2	0	0	22²	15	0	4	6	7.5	1.19	241	.197	.237	3	.333	1	4	4	-1	0.5
1919 Pit-N	17	10	.630	34	29	23	6	1	263¹	213	1	23	92	**8.2**	1.98	152	.220	**.241**	17	.185	-0	27	30	-4	2.7
1920 Pit-N	17	13	.567	35	33	19	**8**	2	263	240	6	18	84	**8.9**	2.16	149	.244	**.259**	29	.146	-5	29	31	-2	2.8
1921 Pit-N	14	5	.737	25	20	11	2	0	160	155	4	18	55	**9.7**	2.64	**145**	.251	**.272**	16	.254	3	20	21	-2	2.5
1922 Pit-N	8	11	.421	27	19	12	4	0	171¹	191	1	15	39	11.0	3.57	114	.287	.307	16	.286	4	10	10	1	1.4
1923 Pit-N	13	7	.650	26	22	11	0	1	158²	196	8	25	38	12.6	4.42	114	.309	.336	15	.273	5	-7	-7	-2	-0.7
1924 Pit-N	3	1	.750	9	3	2	0	0	39²	31	1	3	5	7.7	1.13	338	.209	.225	2	.182	-0	12	12	-1	1.0
1925 *Pit-N	6	5	.545	33	10	3	0	3	101¹	129	7	17	18	13.2	5.42	82	.306	.338	7	.226	0	-13	-11	-2	-1.2
1926 Pit-N	2	3	.400	19	0	0	0	0	36²	51	5	8	7	14.5	6.14	64	.347	.381	2	.222	-0	-9	-9	-1	-1.3
Total 19	194	140	.581	482	354	206	44	15	2995¹	2841	68	430	1036	10.0	2.76	118	.253	.284	216	.212	24	161	161	-32	15.0

● **RED ADAMS**   Adams, Charles Dwight b: 10/7/21, Parlier, Cal. BR/TR, 6', 185 lbs. Deb: 5/5/46 C

YEAR TM/L	W	L	PCT	G	GS	CG	SH	SV	IP	H	HR	BB	SO	RAT	ERA	ERA+	OAV	OOB	BH	AVG	PB	PR	/A	PD	TPI
1946 Chi-N	0	1	.000	8	0	0	0	0	12	18	1	7	8	18.8	8.25	40	.353	.431	0	.000	-0	-6	-7	1	-0.5

● **DAN ADAMS**   Adams, Daniel Leslie "Rube" b: 6/19/1887, St.Louis, Mo. d: 10/6/64, St.Louis, Mo. BR/TR, 5'11.5", 165 lbs. Deb: 5/22/14

YEAR TM/L	W	L	PCT	G	GS	CG	SH	SV	IP	H	HR	BB	SO	RAT	ERA	ERA+	OAV	OOB	BH	AVG	PB	PR	/A	PD	TPI
1914 KC-F	4	9	.308	36	14	6	0	3	136	141	3	52	38	13.2	3.51	79	.273	.347	7	.152	-2	-9	-11	-1	-1.3
1915 KC-F	0	2	.000	11	2	0	0	0	35	41	2	13	16	14.1	4.63	57	.301	.367	1	.111	-1	-7	-8	0	-0.5
Total 2	4	11	.267	47	16	6	0	3	171	182	5	65	54	13.4	3.74	74	.279	.351	8	.145	-2	-17	-19	-1	-1.8

● **WILLIE ADAMS**   Adams, James Irvin b: 9/27/1890, Clearfield, Pa. d: 6/18/37, Albany, N.Y. BR/TR, 6'4", 180 lbs. Deb: 6/30/12

YEAR TM/L	W	L	PCT	G	GS	CG	SH	SV	IP	H	HR	BB	SO	RAT	ERA	ERA+	OAV	OOB	BH	AVG	PB	PR	/A	PD	TPI
1912 StL-A	2	3	.400	13	5	0	0	0	46¹	50	0	19	16	13.8	3.88	85	.284	.360	0	.000	-2	-3	-3	-1	-0.6
1913 StL-A	0	0	—	4	0	0	0	0	9	12	1	4	5	19.0	10.00	29	.286	.388	0	.000	-0	-7	-7	-0	0.0
1914 Pit-F	1	1	.500	15	2	1	0	2	55¹	70	4	22	14	15.1	3.74	77	.326	.391	1	.067	-1	-5	-5	-1	-0.5
1918 Phi-A	5	12	.294	32	14	7	0	0	169	164	2	97	39	14.5	4.42	66	.272	.383	8	.140	-3	-31	-28	1	-2.9
1919 Phi-A	0	0	—	1	0	0	0	0	4²	7	1	2	0	19.3	3.86	89	.389	.476	0	.000	-0	-0	-0	-0	0.0
Total 5	8	16	.333	65	21	8	0	2	284¹	303	8	144	74	14.8	4.37	69	.287	.383	9	.102	-6	-46	-43	-2	-4.0

● **JOE ADAMS**   Adams, Joseph Edward b: 10/28/1877, Cowden, Ill. d: 10/8/52, Montgomery City, Mo BR/TR, 6', 190 lbs. Deb: 4/26/02

YEAR TM/L	W	L	PCT	G	GS	CG	SH	SV	IP	H	HR	BB	SO	RAT	ERA	ERA+	OAV	OOB	BH	AVG	PB	PR	/A	PD	TPI
1902 StL-N	0	0	—	1	0	0	0	0	4	9	0	2	0	27.0	9.00	30	.450	.522	0	.000	-0	-3	-3	1	-0.4

● **KARL ADAMS**   Adams, Karl Tutwiler "Rebel" b: 8/11/1891, Columbus, Ga. d: 9/17/67, Everett, Wash. BR/TR, 6'2", 170 lbs. Deb: 4/19/14

YEAR TM/L	W	L	PCT	G	GS	CG	SH	SV	IP	H	HR	BB	SO	RAT	ERA	ERA+	OAV	OOB	BH	AVG	PB	PR	/A	PD	TPI
1914 Cin-N	0	0	—	4	0	0	0	0	8	14	1	6	5	21.4	9.00	33	.424	.500	1	.500	0	-6	-5	0	0.1
1915 Chi-N	1	9	.100	26	12	3	0	0	107	105	5	43	57	12.6	4.71	59	.267	.342	0	.000	-4	-23	-23	0	-2.4
Total 2	1	9	.100	30	12	3	0	0	115	119	5	48	62	13.2	5.01	56	.279	.355	1	.031	-4	-29	-28	0	-2.3

● **RICK ADAMS**   Adams, Reuben Alexander b: 12/23/1878, Paris, Tex. d: 3/10/55, Paris, Tex. BL/TL, 6', 165 lbs. Deb: 7/13/05

YEAR TM/L	W	L	PCT	G	GS	CG	SH	SV	IP	H	HR	BB	SO	RAT	ERA	ERA+	OAV	OOB	BH	AVG	PB	PR	/A	PD	TPI
1905 Was-A	2	5	.286	11	6	3	1	0	62²	63	1	24	25	13.6	3.59	74	.264	.351	4	.174	0	-7	-7	0	-0.6

● **BOB ADAMS**   Adams, Robert Andrew b: 1/20/07, Birmingham, Ala. d: 3/6/70, Jacksonville, Fla. BR/TR, 6'0.5", 165 lbs. Deb: 9/27/31

YEAR TM/L	W	L	PCT	G	GS	CG	SH	SV	IP	H	HR	BB	SO	RAT	ERA	ERA+	OAV	OOB	BH	AVG	PB	PR	/A	PD	TPI
1931 Phi-N	0	1	.000	1	1	0	0	0	6	14	1	0	3	22.5	9.00	47	.424	.441	0	.000	-0	-3	-3	-0	-0.4
1932 Phi-N	0	0	—	4	0	0	0	0	6	7	0	2	2	13.5	1.50	294	.318	.375	0	—	0	2	2	0	0.0
Total 2	0	1	.000	5	1	0	0	0	12	21	0	3	5	18.0	5.25	82	.382	.414	0	—	0	-2	-1	-0	-0.4

● **BOB ADAMS**   Adams, Robert Burdette b: 7/24/01, Holyoke, Mass. BR/TR, 5'11", 168 lbs. Deb: 9/22/25

YEAR TM/L	W	L	PCT	G	GS	CG	SH	SV	IP	H	HR	BB	SO	RAT	ERA	ERA+	OAV	OOB	BH	AVG	PB	PR	/A	PD	TPI
1925 Bos-A	0	0	—	2	0	0	0	0	5²	10	1	3	1	20.6	7.94	57	.417	.481	1	.333	-0	-2	-2	1	0.1

● **TERRY ADAMS**   Adams, Terry Wayne b: 3/6/73, Mobile, Ala. BR/TR, 6'3", 205 lbs. Deb: 8/10/95

YEAR TM/L	W	L	PCT	G	GS	CG	SH	SV	IP	H	HR	BB	SO	RAT	ERA	ERA+	OAV	OOB	BH	AVG	PB	PR	/A	PD	TPI
1995 Chi-N	1	1	.500	18	0	0	0	1	18	22	0	10	15	16.0	6.50	63	.289	.372	0	—	-0	-5	-5	-0	-0.5
1996 Chi-N	3	6	.333	69	0	0	0	5	101	84	6	49	78	11.9	2.94	145	.231	.324	0	.000	-0	14	15	-0	1.2
Total 2	4	7	.364	87	0	0	0	5	119	106	6	59	93	12.6	3.48	122	.241	.333	0	.000	-0	10	10	-0	0.7

● **WILLIE ADAMS**   Adams, William Edward b: 10/8/72, Gallup, N.Mex. BR/TR, 6'7", 215 lbs. Deb: 6/11/96

YEAR TM/L	W	L	PCT	G	GS	CG	SH	SV	IP	H	HR	BB	SO	RAT	ERA	ERA+	OAV	OOB	BH	AVG	PB	PR	/A	PD	TPI
1996 Oak-A	3	4	.429	12	12	1	1	0	76¹	76	11	23	68	12.3	4.01	120	.257	.321	0	—	0	8	7	-1	0.7

● **JOEL ADAMSON**   Adamson, Joel Lee b: 7/2/71, Lakewood, Cal. BL/TL, 6'4", 185 lbs. Deb: 4/10/96

YEAR TM/L	W	L	PCT	G	GS	CG	SH	SV	IP	H	HR	BB	SO	RAT	ERA	ERA+	OAV	OOB	BH	AVG	PB	PR	/A	PD	TPI
1996 Fla-N	0	0	—	9	0	0	0	0	11	18	1	7	7	21.3	7.36	55	.400	.491	0	—	0	-4	-4	0	-0.4

● **MIKE ADAMSON**   Adamson, John Michael b: 9/13/47, San Diego, Cal. BR/TR, 6'2", 185 lbs. Deb: 7/1/67

YEAR TM/L	W	L	PCT	G	GS	CG	SH	SV	IP	H	HR	BB	SO	RAT	ERA	ERA+	OAV	OOB	BH	AVG	PB	PR	/A	PD	TPI
1967 Bal-A	0	1	.000	3	2	0	0	0	9²	9	1	12	8	19.6	8.38	38	.257	.447	1	.500	1	-6	-6	-0	-0.5
1968 Bal-A	0	2	.000	2	2	0	0	0	7²	9	2	4	4	15.3	9.39	31	.281	.361	1	.333	0	-5	-6	-0	-1.1
1969 Bal-A	0	1	.000	6	0	0	0	0	8	10	0	6	2	18.0	4.50	79	.357	.471	0	.000	-0	-1	-1	1	-0.1
Total 3	0	4	.000	11	4	0	0	0	25¹	28	3	22	14	17.8	7.46	43	.295	.427	2	.333	1	-12	-12	-0	-1.7

● **GRADY ADKINS**   Adkins, Grady Emmett "Butcher Boy" b: 6/29/1897, Jacksonville, Ark d: 3/31/66, Little Rock, Ark. BR/TR, 5'11", 175 lbs. Deb: 4/13/28

YEAR TM/L	W	L	PCT	G	GS	CG	SH	SV	IP	H	HR	BB	SO	RAT	ERA	ERA+	OAV	OOB	BH	AVG	PB	PR	/A	PD	TPI
1928 Chi-A	10	16	.385	36	27	14	0	1	224²	235	12	89	54	13.2	3.73	109	.278	.351	10	.143	-3	8	8	-1	0.4
1929 Chi-A	2	11	.154	31	15	5	0	0	138¹	168	12	67	24	15.4	5.33	80	.303	.379	11	.239	2	-17	-16	2	-0.8
Total 2	12	27	.308	67	42	19	0	1	363	403	24	156	78	14.0	4.34	95	.288	.363	21	.181	-1	-9	-8	1	-0.4

● **DEWEY ADKINS**   Adkins, John Dewey b: 5/11/18, Norcatur, Kan. BR/TR, 6'2", 195 lbs. Deb: 9/19/42

YEAR TM/L	W	L	PCT	G	GS	CG	SH	SV	IP	H	HR	BB	SO	RAT	ERA	ERA+	OAV	OOB	BH	AVG	PB	PR	/A	PD	TPI
1942 Was-A	0	0	—	1	1	0	0	0	6¹	7	0	6	3	18.5	9.95	37	.259	.394	1	.500	0	-4	-4	-0	0.0
1943 Was-A	0	0	—	7	0	0	0	0	10¹	9	0	5	1	12.2	2.61	123	.241	.341	0	—	0	1	1	-1	-0.1
1949 Chi-N	2	4	.333	30	5	1	0	0	82¹	98	10	39	43	15.0	5.68	71	.298	.372	4	.200	1	-15	-15	-0	-0.7
Total 3	2	4	.333	38	6	1	0	0	99	114	10	50	47	14.9	5.64	70	.291	.371	5	.227	1	-19	-19	-0	-0.8

● **DOC ADKINS**   Adkins, Merle Theron b: 8/5/1872, Troy, Wis. d: 2/21/34, Durham, N.C. BR/TR, 5'10.5", 220 lbs. Deb: 6/24/02

YEAR TM/L	W	L	PCT	G	GS	CG	SH	SV	IP	H	HR	BB	SO	RAT	ERA	ERA+	OAV	OOB	BH	AVG	PB	PR	/A	PD	TPI
1902 Bos-A	1	1	.500	4	2	1	0	0	20	30	2	7	3	16.6	4.05	88	.345	.394	2	.222	-0	-1	-1	0	-0.1
1903 NY-A	0	0	—	2	1	0	0	1	7	10	0	5	0	20.6	7.71	40	.333	.444	0	.000	-0	-4	-4	-1	-0.2
Total 2	1	1	.500	6	3	1	0	1	27	40	2	12	3	17.7	5.00	69	.342	.408	2	.167	-1	-5	-5	-0	-0.3

● **STEVE ADKINS**   Adkins, Steven Thomas b: 10/26/64, Chicago, Ill. BR/TL, 6'6", 210 lbs. Deb: 9/12/90

YEAR TM/L	W	L	PCT	G	GS	CG	SH	SV	IP	H	HR	BB	SO	RAT	ERA	ERA+	OAV	OOB	BH	AVG	PB	PR	/A	PD	TPI
1990 NY-A	1	2	.333	5	5	0	0	0	24	19	4	29	14	18.0	6.38	62	.226	.425	0	—	0	-7	-6	-0	-0.7

● **JUAN AGOSTO**   Agosto, Juan Roberto (Gonzalez) b: 2/23/58, Rio Piedras, P.R. BL/TL, 6'2", 190 lbs. Deb: 9/7/81

YEAR TM/L	W	L	PCT	G	GS	CG	SH	SV	IP	H	HR	BB	SO	RAT	ERA	ERA+	OAV	OOB	BH	AVG	PB	PR	/A	PD	TPI
1981 Chi-A	0	0	—	2	0	0	0	0	5²	5	1	2	3	9.5	4.76	75	.238	.273	0	—	0	-1	-1	0	0.1
1982 Chi-A	0	0	—	1	0	0	0	0	2	7	0	0	1	31.5	18.00	22	.538	.538	0	—	0	-3	-3	0	0.0
1983 *Chi-A	2	2	.500	39	0	0	0	7	41²	41	2	11	29	11.4	4.10	102	.283	.338	0	—	0	-0	-0	0	0.0
1984 Chi-A	2	1	.667	49	0	0	0	7	55¹	54	2	34	26	14.8	3.09	135	.270	.384	0	—	0	6	7	2	0.4
1985 Chi-A	4	3	.571	54	0	0	0	1	60¹	45	3	39	39	10.6	3.58	121	.210	.296	0	—	0	4	5	2	0.7
1986 Chi-A	0	2	.000	9	0	0	0	0	4²	6	0	4	3	19.3	7.71	56	.300	.417	0	—	0	-2	-2	-0	-0.7
Min-A	1	2	.333	17	1	0	0	0	20¹	43	1	14	9	26.1	8.85	49	.443	.522	0	—	0	-11	-10	0	-1.4
Yr	1	4	.200	26	1	0	0	0	25	49	1	18	12	24.8	8.64	50	.419	.504	0	—	0	-12	-12	0	-2.1
1987 Hou-N	1	1	.500	27	0	0	0	2	27¹	26	1	10	6	11.9	2.63	149	.248	.313	0	.000	-0	4	4	1	0.4
1988 Hou-N	10	2	.833	75	0	0	0	4	91²	76	6	30	33	10.2	2.26	147	.226	.291	0	.000	-0	12	11	4	1.9
1989 Hou-N	4	5	.444	71	0	0	0	4	83	81	3	32	46	12.5	2.93	116	.256	.329	1	.200	-0	-0	-0	1	0.6
1990 Hou-N	9	8	.529	**82**	0	0	0	4	92¹	91	4	39	50	13.4	4.29	87	.261	.347	0	.000	-0	-5	-6	2	-0.9

YEAR	TM/L	W	L	PCT	G	GS	CG	SH	SV	IP	H	HR	BB	SO	RAT	ERA	ERA+	OAV	OOB	BH	AVG	PB	PR	/A	PD	TPI
1991	StL-N	5	3	.625	72	0	0	0	2	86	92	4	39	34	14.5	4.81	77	.291	.383	1	.333	1	-11	-10	1	-0.8
1992	StL-N	2	4	.333	22	0	0	0	0	31²	39	2	9	13	14.5	6.25	54	.312	.372	0	.000	-0	-10	-10	1	-1.7
	Sea-A	0	0	—	17	1	0	0	0	18¹	27	0	3	12	14.7	5.89	67	.346	.370	0	—	0	-4	-4	0	0.0
1993	Hou-N	0	0	—	6	0	0	0	0	6	8	1	0	3	12.0	6.00	65	.308	.308	0	—	0	-1	-1	-0	0.0
Total 13		40	33	.548	543	2	0	0	29	626¹	639	30	248	307	13.2	4.01	94	.272	.349	2	.100	-1	-16	-17	14	-1.4

● RICK AGUILERA
Aguilera, Richard Warren b: 12/31/61, San Gabriel, Cal.   BR/TR, 6'5", 200 lbs.   Deb: 6/12/85

YEAR	TM/L	W	L	PCT	G	GS	CG	SH	SV	IP	H	HR	BB	SO	RAT	ERA	ERA+	OAV	OOB	BH	AVG	PB	PR	/A	PD	TPI
1985	NY-N	10	7	.588	21	19	2	0	0	122¹	118	8	37	74	11.6	3.24	107	.258	.317	10	.278	3	5	3	-0	0.7
1986	*NY-N	10	7	.588	28	20	2	0	0	141²	145	15	36	104	11.9	3.88	91	.263	.316	8	.157	2	-2	-5	2	-0.2
1987	NY-N	11	3	.786	18	17	1	0	0	115	124	12	33	77	12.5	3.60	105	.276	.330	9	.225	3	6	2	2	0.8
1988	*NY-N	0	4	.000	11	3	0	0	0	24²	29	2	10	16	14.6	6.93	46	.296	.367	1	.250	-0	-10	-10	0	-1.4
1989	NY-N	6	6	.500	36	0	0	0	7	69¹	59	3	21	80	10.6	2.34	140	.231	.295	0	.000	-0	9	7	-0	1.3
	Min-A	3	5	.375	11	11	3	0	0	75²	71	5	17	50	10.6	3.21	129	.245	.289	0	—	0	8	6	1	0.8
1990	Min-A	5	3	.625	56	0	0	0	32	65¹	55	5	19	61	10.7	2.76	151	.224	.291	0	—	0	8	10	-1	1.9
1991	*Min-A★	4	5	.444	63	0	0	0	42	69	44	3	30	61	9.8	2.35	182	.183	.277	0	—	0	13	15	0	3.3
1992	Min-A★	2	6	.250	64	0	0	0	41	66²	60	7	17	52	10.5	2.84	143	.238	.289	0	—	0	8	9	-1	1.8
1993	Min-A★	4	3	.571	65	0	0	0	34	72¹	60	9	14	59	9.3	3.11	140	.223	.264	0	—	0	10	10	1	1.7
1994	Min-A	1	4	.200	44	0	0	0	23	44²	57	7	10	46	13.5	3.63	134	.306	.342	0	—	0	6	6	-0	1.3
1995	Min-A	1	1	.500	22	0	0	0	12	25	20	2	4	29	9.7	2.52	189	.222	.278	0	—	0	7	8	-0	1.7
	*Bos-A	2	2	.500	30	0	0	0	20	30¹	26	4	7	23	9.8	2.67	182	.228	.273	0	—	0	6	7	-0	1.7
	Yr	3	3	.500	52	0	0	0	32	55¹	46	6	11	52	9.6	2.60	185	.222	.268	0	—	0	13	14	0	2.7
1996	Min-A	8	6	.571	19	19	2	0	0	111¹	124	20	17	82	12.4	5.42	95	.276	.321	0	—	0	-5	-3	-1	-0.6
Total 12		67	62	.519	488	89	10	0	211	1033¹	992	102	284	822	11.3	3.48	116	.251	.306	28	.203	8	67	64	3	14.1

● HANK AGUIRRE
Aguirre, Henry John b: 1/31/31, Azusa, Cal. d: 9/5/94, Bloomfield Hills, Mich.   BR/TL, 6'4", 205 lbs.   Deb: 9/10/55 C

YEAR	TM/L	W	L	PCT	G	GS	CG	SH	SV	IP	H	HR	BB	SO	RAT	ERA	ERA+	OAV	OOB	BH	AVG	PB	PR	/A	PD	TPI
1955	Cle-A	2	0	1.000	4	1	1	1	0	12²	6	0	12	6	12.8	1.42	281	.143	.333	0	.000	-1	4	4	-0	0.4
1956	Cle-A	3	5	.375	16	9	2	1	1	65¹	63	7	27	31	12.5	3.72	113	.253	.329	2	.111	-1	3	4	-1	0.2
1957	Cle-A	1	1	.500	10	1	0	0	0	20¹	26	0	13	9	17.3	5.75	65	.317	.411	0	.000	-1	-4	-5	-0	-0.5
1958	Det-A	3	4	.429	44	3	0	0	5	69²	67	5	27	38	12.3	3.75	108	.255	.326	3	.214	—	0	2	1	0.3
1959	Det-A	0	0	—	3	0	0	0	0	2²	4	0	3	3	23.6	3.38	120	.364	.500	0	—	0	0	0	0	0.0
1960	Det-A	5	3	.625	37	6	1	0	10	94²	75	7	30	80	10.3	2.85	139	.217	.286	1	.036	-3	11	12	-2	0.7
1961	Det-A	4	4	.500	45	0	0	0	8	55¹	44	5	38	32	13.7	3.25	126	.224	.356	0	.000	-1	5	5	-1	0.7
1962	Det-A★	16	8	.667	42	22	11	2	3	216	162	14	65	156	9.7	2.21	184	.205	.269	2	.027	-8	42	45	-3	3.7
1963	Det-A	14	15	.483	38	33	14	3	0	225²	222	25	68	134	11.9	3.67	102	.256	.316	10	.132	-1	-3	-3	0	-0.3
1964	Det-A	5	10	.333	32	27	3	0	1	161²	134	15	59	88	11.2	3.79	97	.223	.301	3	.057	-4	-3	-2	-1	-0.9
1965	Det-A	14	10	.583	32	32	10	2	0	208	185	24	60	141	11.0	3.59	97	.236	.298	6	.086	-2	-3	-3	-1	-0.7
1966	Det-A	3	9	.250	30	14	2	0	0	103²	104	14	26	50	11.5	3.82	91	.260	.310	3	.120	-1	-4	-4	-2	-0.6
1967	Det-A	0	1	.000	31	1	0	0	0	41¹	34	2	17	33	11.1	2.40	136	.219	.297	1	.500	—	10	9	-1	0.8
1968	LA-N	1	2	.333	25	0	0	0	3	39¹	32	0	13	25	11.0	0.69	403	.227	.306	0	.000	-0	10	9	1	0.8
1969	Chi-N	1	0	1.000	41	0	0	0	0	45	45	2	12	34	11.8	2.60	155	.269	.326	2	.400	1	5	7	1	0.3
1970	Chi-N	3	0	1.000	17	0	0	0	0	14	13	3	9	11	14.8	4.50	100	.250	.371	0	.000	-0	-1	-0	-1	-0.1
Total 16		75	72	.510	447	149	44	9	33	1375²	1216	123	479	856	11.4	3.24	116	.236	.307	33	.085	-21	67	79	-16	4.2

● PAT AHEARNE
Ahearne, Patrick Howard b: 12/10/69, San Francisco, Cal.   BR/TR, 6'3", 195 lbs.   Deb: 6/14/95

YEAR	TM/L	W	L	PCT	G	GS	CG	SH	SV	IP	H	HR	BB	SO	RAT	ERA	ERA+	OAV	OOB	BH	AVG	PB	PR	/A	PD	TPI
1995	Det-A	0	2	.000	4	3	0	0	0	10	20	2	5	4	22.5	11.70	41	.400	.455	0	—	0	-8	-8	0	-1.1

● EDDIE AINSMITH
Ainsmith, Edward Wilbur "Dorf" b: 2/4/1892, Cambridge, Mass. d: 9/6/81, Ft.Lauderdale, Fla   BR/TR, 5'11", 180 lbs.   Deb: 8/9/10 ♦

YEAR	TM/L	W	L	PCT	G	GS	CG	SH	SV	IP	H	HR	BB	SO	RAT	ERA	ERA+	OAV	OOB	BH	AVG	PB	PR	/A	PD	TPI
1913	Was-A	0	0	—	1	0	0	0	0	0¹	2	0	0	0	54.0	54.00	5	.667	.667	49	.214	0	-2	-2	0	0.0

● RALEIGH AITCHISON
Aitchison, Raleigh Leonidas b: 12/5/1887, Tyndall, S.D. d: 9/26/58, Columbus, Kan.   BR/TL, 5'11.5", 175 lbs.   Deb: 4/19/11

YEAR	TM/L	W	L	PCT	G	GS	CG	SH	SV	IP	H	HR	BB	SO	RAT	ERA	ERA+	OAV	OOB	BH	AVG	PB	PR	/A	PD	TPI
1911	Bro-N	0	1	.000	1	0	0	0	0	1¹	1	0	0	1	13.5	0.00	—	.200	.333	0	—	0	1	0	-0	0.4
1914	Bro-N	12	7	.632	26	17	8	3	0	172¹	156	4	60	87	11.4	2.66	107	.244	.312	10	.196	1	2	4	-3	0.2
1915	Bro-N	0	4	.000	7	5	2	0	0	32²	36	3	6	14	12.1	4.96	56	.267	.308	0	.000	-0	-8	-8	0	-0.9
Total 3		12	12	.500	34	22	10	3	0	206¹	193	7	67	101	11.6	3.01	95	.247	.311	10	.169	1	-5	-4	-3	-0.3

● JACK AKER
Aker, Jackie Delane b: 7/13/40, Tulare, Cal.   BR/TR, 6'2", 190 lbs.   Deb: 5/3/64 C

YEAR	TM/L	W	L	PCT	G	GS	CG	SH	SV	IP	H	HR	BB	SO	RAT	ERA	ERA+	OAV	OOB	BH	AVG	PB	PR	/A	PD	TPI
1964	KC-A	0	1	.000	9	0	0	0	0	16¹	17	6	10	7	18.2	8.82	43	.266	.412	0	.000	-0	-9	-9	1	-0.5
1965	KC-A	4	3	.571	34	0	0	0	3	51¹	45	3	18	26	11.6	3.16	111	.242	.319	0	.000	-1	2	2	1	0.3
1966	KC-A	8	4	.667	66	0	0	0	32	113	81	7	26	68	8.9	1.99	171	.201	.258	2	.095	-1	18	18	3	3.2
1967	KC-A	3	6	.273	57	0	0	0	12	88	87	9	26	65	12.5	4.30	74	.264	.334	1	.125	-0	-10	-11	2	-1.5
1968	Oak-A	4	4	.500	54	0	0	0	11	74²	72	6	33	44	13.4	4.10	69	.258	.349	1	.143	-0	-9	-11	0	-1.5
1969	Sea-A	0	2	.000	15	0	0	0	0	16²	25	4	13	7	21.1	7.56	48	.357	.464	0	.000	-0	-7	-7	1	-1.0
	NY-A	8	4	.667	38	0	0	0	11	65²	51	4	22	40	10.6	2.06	169	.217	.295	1	.111	-0	11	10	2	2.4
	Yr	8	6	.571	53	0	0	0	14	82¹	76	8	35	47	12.6	3.17	111	.248	.333	1	.100	-0	4	3	2	1.4
1970	NY-A	2	2	.667	41	0	0	0	16	70	57	3	20	36	10.4	2.06	171	.226	.293	1	.063	-1	13	11	-0	1.3
1971	NY-A	4	4	.500	41	0	0	0	4	55²	48	3	26	24	12.0	2.59	125	.238	.325	0	.000	-0	5	4	1	0.7
1972	NY-A	0	0	—	6	0	0	0	0	6	6	1	3	3	13.5	3.00	98	.238	.360	0	—	0	-0	-0	0	0.1
	Chi-N	6	6	.500	48	0	0	0	17	67	65	4	23	36	12.5	2.96	129	.259	.333	0	.000	-0	4	6	2	1.7
1973	Chi-N	4	5	.444	47	0	0	0	12	63²	76	8	23	25	14.3	4.10	96	.308	.371	0	.000	-1	-3	-1	2	-0.1
1974	Atl-N	0	1	.000	17	0	0	0	0	16²	17	3	7	14	14.0	3.78	100	.298	.394	0	—	0	-0	-0	0	0.0
	NY-A	2	1	.667	24	0	0	0	2	41¹	33	4	14	18	10.7	3.48	102	.213	.287	1	.500	1	0	-1	0	0.0
	Yr	2	2	.500	41	0	0	0	2	58	50	7	23	25	11.6	3.57	102	.234	.314	1	.333	1	0	-0	-1	0.0
Total 11		47	45	.511	495	0	0	0	123	746	679	64	274	404	12.0	3.28	105	.247	.324	7	.076	-5	14	13	13	5.1

● DARREL AKERFELDS
Akerfelds, Darrel Wayne b: 6/12/62, Denver, Colo.   BR/TR, 6'2", 210 lbs.   Deb: 8/1/86

YEAR	TM/L	W	L	PCT	G	GS	CG	SH	SV	IP	H	HR	BB	SO	RAT	ERA	ERA+	OAV	OOB	BH	AVG	PB	PR	/A	PD	TPI
1986	Oak-A	0	0	—	2	0	0	0	0	5¹	7	2	3	5	16.9	6.75	57	.304	.385	0	—	0	-2	-2	0	0.0
1987	Cle-A	2	6	.250	16	13	1	0	0	74²	84	18	38	42	15.5	6.75	67	.284	.378	0	—	0	-19	-18	-0	-1.7
1989	Tex-A	0	1	.000	6	0	0	0	0	11	11	1	5	9	13.1	3.27	121	.250	.327	0	—	0	1	1	0	0.1
1990	Phi-N	5	2	.714	71	0	0	0	0	93	65	10	54	42	11.8	3.77	101	.201	.320	1	.167	-0	-9	-9	1	-0.5
1991	Phi-N	2	1	.667	30	0	0	0	0	49²	49	5	27	31	14.3	5.26	70	.257	.357	0	.000	-0	-9	-9	1	-0.5
Total 5		9	10	.474	125	13	1	0	3	233²	216	36	127	129	13.7	5.08	79	.246	.350	1	.111	-0	-28	-28	0	-2.1

● JERRY AKERS
Akers, Albert Earl b: 11/1/1887, Shelbyville, Ind. d: 5/15/79, Bay Pines, Fla.   BR/TR, 5'11", 175 lbs.   Deb: 5/4/12

YEAR	TM/L	W	L	PCT	G	GS	CG	SH	SV	IP	H	HR	BB	SO	RAT	ERA	ERA+	OAV	OOB	BH	AVG	PB	PR	/A	PD	TPI
1912	Was-A	1	1	.500	5	1	0	0	0	20¹	24	1	15	11	18.1	4.87	68	.300	.423	2	.333	0	-4	-3	-1	-0.4

● GIBSON ALBA
Alba, Gibson Alberto (Rosado) b: 1/18/60, Santiago, D.R.   BL/TL, 6'2", 160 lbs.   Deb: 5/3/88

YEAR	TM/L	W	L	PCT	G	GS	CG	SH	SV	IP	H	HR	BB	SO	RAT	ERA	ERA+	OAV	OOB	BH	AVG	PB	PR	/A	PD	TPI
1988	StL-N	0	0	—	3	0	0	0	0	3¹	1	0	2	3	8.1	2.70	129	.091	.231	0	—	0	-0	-0	-0	0.0

● JOE ALBANESE
Albanese, Joseph Peter b: 6/26/33, New York, N.Y.   BR/TR, 6'3", 215 lbs.   Deb: 7/18/58

YEAR	TM/L	W	L	PCT	G	GS	CG	SH	SV	IP	H	HR	BB	SO	RAT	ERA	ERA+	OAV	OOB	BH	AVG	PB	PR	/A	PD	TPI
1958	Was-A	0	0	—	6	0	0	0	0	6	8	1	2	3	15.0	4.50	85	.348	.400	0	—	0	-0	-0	-0	0.0

● JOSE ALBERRO
Alberro, Jose Edgardo b: 6/29/69, San Juan, P.R.   BR/TR, 6'2", 190 lbs.   Deb: 4/27/95

YEAR	TM/L	W	L	PCT	G	GS	CG	SH	SV	IP	H	HR	BB	SO	RAT	ERA	ERA+	OAV	OOB	BH	AVG	PB	PR	/A	PD	TPI
1995	Tex-A	0	0	—	12	0	0	0	0	20²	26	2	12	10	17.0	7.40	65	.299	.390	0	—	0	-6	-6	0	-0.4
1996	Tex-A	0	1	.000	5	1	0	0	0	9¹	14	1	7	2	20.3	5.79	92	.368	.467	0	—	0	-1	-0	-0	-0.4
Total 2		0	1	.000	17	1	0	0	0	30	40	3	19	12	18.0	6.90	72	.320	.414	0	—	0	-7	-6	0	-0.4

● CY ALBERTS
Alberts, Frederick Joseph b: 1/14/1882, Grand Rapids, Mich d: 8/27/17, Fort Wayne, Ind.   BR/TR, 6', 230 lbs.   Deb: 9/17/10

YEAR	TM/L	W	L	PCT	G	GS	CG	SH	SV	IP	H	HR	BB	SO	RAT	ERA	ERA+	OAV	OOB	BH	AVG	PB	PR	/A	PD	TPI
1910	StL-N	1	2	.333	4	3	2	0	0	27²	35	1	20	10	17.9	6.18	48	.330	.437	0	.000	-0	-10	-10	-1	-1.0

● ED ALBOSTA
Albosta, Edward John "Rube" b: 10/27/18, Saginaw, Mich.   BR/TR, 6'1", 175 lbs.   Deb: 9/3/41

YEAR	TM/L	W	L	PCT	G	GS	CG	SH	SV	IP	H	HR	BB	SO	RAT	ERA	ERA+	OAV	OOB	BH	AVG	PB	PR	/A	PD	TPI
1941	Bro-N	0	2	.000	2	2	0	0	0	13	11	1	8	5	13.2	6.23	59	.239	.352	0	.000	-1	-4	-4	0	-0.5

YEAR	TM/L	W	L	PCT	G	GS	CG	SH	SV	IP	H	HR	BB	SO	RAT	ERA	ERA+	OAV	OOB	BH	AVG	PB	PR	/A	PD	TPI
1946	Pit-N	0	6	.000	17	6	0	0	0	39²	41	3	35	19	17.5	6.13	58	.266	.405	1	.125	-0	-12	-11	0	-1.6
Total	2	0	8	.000	19	8	0	0	0	52²	52	4	43	24	16.4	6.15	58	.260	.393	1	.083	-1	-16	-15	0	-2.1

● ED ALBRECHT
Albrecht, Edward Arthur b: 2/28/29, Affton, Mo. d: 12/29/79, Cahokia, Ill. BR/TR, 5'10.5", 165 lbs. Deb: 10/2/49

YEAR	TM/L	W	L	PCT	G	GS	CG	SH	SV	IP	H	HR	BB	SO	RAT	ERA	ERA+	OAV	OOB	BH	AVG	PB	PR	/A	PD	TPI
1949	StL-A	1	0	1.000	1	1	1	0	0	5	1	0	4	1	9.0	5.40	84	.063	.250	0	.000	-0	-1	-0	0	-0.1
1950	StL-A	0	1	.000	2	1	0	0	0	6²	6	0	7	1	17.6	5.40	92	.250	.419	0	.000	-0	-1	-0	0	-0.1
Total	2	1	1	.500	3	2	1	0	0	11²	7	0	11	2	13.9	5.40	88	.175	.353	0	.000	-0	-1	-1	-0	-0.2

● VIC ALBURY
Albury, Victor b: 5/12/47, Key West, Fla. BL/TL, 6', 190 lbs. Deb: 8/7/73

YEAR	TM/L	W	L	PCT	G	GS	CG	SH	SV	IP	H	HR	BB	SO	RAT	ERA	ERA+	OAV	OOB	BH	AVG	PB	PR	/A	PD	TPI
1973	Min-A	1	0	1.000	14	0	0	0	0	23¹	13	-1	19	13	12.3	2.70	147	.169	.333	0	—	0	3	3	-1	0.0
1974	Min-A	8	9	.471	32	22	4	1	0	164	159	19	80	85	13.4	4.12	91	.259	.350	0	—	0	-9	-7	-1	-0.8
1975	Min-A	6	7	.462	32	15	2	0	1	135	115	16	97	72	14.4	4.53	84	.237	.388	0	.000	0	-11	-11	1	-0.9
1976	Min-A	3	1	.750	23	0	0	0	0	50¹	51	0	24	23	13.8	3.58	100	.271	.360	0	—	0	-0	-0	-0	-0.1
Total	4	18	17	.514	101	37	6	1	1	372²	338	36	220	193	13.8	4.11	91	.247	.357	0	.000	0	-18	-14	-1	-1.8

● SANTO ALCALA
Alcala, Santo (b: Santo Anibal (Alcala)) b: 12/23/52, San Pedro De Macoris, D.R. BR/TR, 6'5", 195 lbs. Deb: 4/10/76

YEAR	TM/L	W	L	PCT	G	GS	CG	SH	SV	IP	H	HR	BB	SO	RAT	ERA	ERA+	OAV	OOB	BH	AVG	PB	PR	/A	PD	TPI
1976	Cin-N	11	4	.733	30	21	3	1	0	132	131	12	67	67	13.7	4.70	74	.261	.352	6	.140	-0	-18	-18	-1	-2.0
1977	Cin-N	1	1	.500	7	2	0	0	0	15²	22	1	7	9	17.2	5.74	68	.349	.423	0	.000	-0	-3	-3	0	-0.4
	Mon-N	2	6	.250	31	10	0	0	2	101²	104	12	47	64	13.5	4.69	81	.263	.344	2	.080	-1	-9	-10	-1	-1.0
	Yr	3	7	.300	38	12	0	0	2	117¹	126	13	54	73	14.0	4.83	79	.273	.352	2	.071	-1	-12	-13	-1	-1.4
Total	2	14	11	.560	68	33	3	1	2	249¹	257	25	121	140	13.8	4.76	77	.267	.352	8	.113	-2	-30	-31	-2	-3.4

● DALE ALDERSON
Alderson, Dale Leonard b: 3/9/18, Belden, Neb. d: 2/12/82, Garden Grove, Cal. BR/TR, 5'10", 190 lbs. Deb: 9/18/43

YEAR	TM/L	W	L	PCT	G	GS	CG	SH	SV	IP	H	HR	BB	SO	RAT	ERA	ERA+	OAV	OOB	BH	AVG	PB	PR	/A	PD	TPI
1943	Chi-N	0	1	.000	4	2	0	0	0	14	21	2	3	4	15.4	6.43	52	.356	.387	0	.000	-0	-5	-5	0	-0.3
1944	Chi-N	0	0	—	12	1	0	0	0	21²	31	2	9	7	16.6	6.65	53	.344	.404	0	.000	-1	-7	-7	1	-0.3
Total	2	0	1	.000	16	3	0	0	0	35²	52	4	12	11	16.1	6.56	53	.349	.398	0	.000	-1	-12	-12	1	-0.3

● SCOTT ALDRED
Aldred, Scott Phillip b: 6/12/68, Flint, Mich. BL/TL, 6'4", 195 lbs. Deb: 9/9/90

YEAR	TM/L	W	L	PCT	G	GS	CG	SH	SV	IP	H	HR	BB	SO	RAT	ERA	ERA+	OAV	OOB	BH	AVG	PB	PR	/A	PD	TPI
1990	Det-A	1	2	.333	4	3	0	0	0	14¹	13	0	10	7	15.1	3.77	105	.265	.400	0	—	0	0	0	-0	0.0
1991	Det-A	2	4	.333	11	11	1	0	0	57¹	58	9	30	35	13.8	5.18	80	.266	.355	0	—	0	-7	-7	0	-0.6
1992	Det-A	3	8	.273	16	13	0	0	0	65	80	12	33	34	16.1	6.78	58	.307	.391	0	—	0	-21	-20	1	-2.8
1993	Col-N	0	0	—	5	0	0	0	0	6²	10	1	9	5	27.0	10.80	44	.357	.526	0	—	0	-5	-4	0	0.0
	Mon-N	1	0	1.000	3	0	0	0	0	5¹	9	1	4	1	16.9	6.75	62	.375	.400	0	—	0	-2	-2	0	-0.2
	Yr	1	0	1.000	8	0	0	0	0	12	19	2	13	6	21.8	9.00	50	.358	.460	0	—	0	-7	-6	0	-0.2
1996	Det-A	0	4	.000	11	8	0	0	0	43¹	49	9	26	36	18.5	9.35	54	.328	.420	0	—	0	-21	-21	-1	-1.5
	Min-A	6	5	.545	25	17	0	0	0	122	134	20	42	75	13.2	5.09	101	.281	.343	0	—	0	-1	1	-1	-0.2
	Yr	6	9	.400	36	25	0	0	0	165¹	194	29	68	111	14.4	6.21	82	.292	.360	0	—	0	-22	-20	-2	-1.7
Total	5	13	23	.361	75	52	1	0	0	314	364	52	151	196	15.1	6.13	75	.294	.375	0	—	0	-56	-53	-1	-5.3

● MIKE ALDRETE
Aldrete, Michael Peter b: 1/29/61, Carmel, Cal. BL/TL, 5'11", 185 lbs. Deb: 5/28/86 ◆

YEAR	TM/L	W	L	PCT	G	GS	CG	SH	SV	IP	H	HR	BB	SO	RAT	ERA	ERA+	OAV	OOB	BH	AVG	PB	PR	/A	PD	TPI
1996	*NY-A	0	0	—	1	0	0	0	0	1	1	0	0	0	9.0	0.00	—	.333	.333	17	.250	1	1	1	0	0.0

● JAY ALDRICH
Aldrich, Jay Robert b: 4/14/61, Alexandria, La. BR/TR, 6'3", 210 lbs. Deb: 6/5/87

YEAR	TM/L	W	L	PCT	G	GS	CG	SH	SV	IP	H	HR	BB	SO	RAT	ERA	ERA+	OAV	OOB	BH	AVG	PB	PR	/A	PD	TPI
1987	Mil-A	3	1	.750	31	0	0	0	0	58¹	71	8	13	22	13.3	4.94	93	.306	.348	0	—	0	-3	-2	-1	-0.4
1989	Mil-A	1	0	1.000	16	0	0	0	1	26	24	3	13	12	13.2	3.81	101	.253	.349	0	—	0	0	0	0	0.1
	Atl-N	1	2	.333	8	0	0	0	0	12¹	7	2	6	7	9.5	2.19	167	.167	.271	0	.000	0	2	2	0	0.4
1990	Bal-A	1	2	.333	7	0	0	0	1	12	17	1	7	5	18.0	8.25	46	.327	.407	0	—	0	-6	-6	0	-1.3
Total	3	6	5	.545	62	0	0	0	2	108²	119	12	39	46	13.3	4.72	89	.283	.348	0	.000	-0	-7	-6	-1	-1.2

● VIC ALDRIDGE
Aldridge, Victor Eddington b: 10/25/1893, Indian Springs, Ind. d: 4/17/73, Terre Haute, Ind. BR/TR, 5'9.5", 175 lbs. Deb: 4/15/17

YEAR	TM/L	W	L	PCT	G	GS	CG	SH	SV	IP	H	HR	BB	SO	RAT	ERA	ERA+	OAV	OOB	BH	AVG	PB	PR	/A	PD	TPI
1917	Chi-N	6	6	.500	30	6	1	1	2	106²	100	1	37	44	11.7	3.12	93	.252	.319	4	.138	-2	-5	-3	3	-0.2
1918	Chi-N	0	1	.000	3	0	0	0	0	12¹	11	0	6	10	12.4	1.46	191	.275	.370	1	.333	0	2	2	-0	0.2
1922	Chi-N	16	15	.516	36	34	20	2	0	258¹	287	14	56	66	12.4	3.52	119	.286	.332	26	.260	3	17	20	1	2.5
1923	Chi-N	16	9	.640	30	30	15	2	0	217	209	17	67	64	11.5	3.48	115	.251	.307	19	.268	3	12	15	-1	1.5
1924	Chi-N	15	12	.556	32	32	20	0	0	244¹	261	10	80	74	12.8	3.50	112	.279	.341	15	.176	1	13	11	-0	0.7
1925	*Pit-N	15	7	.682	30	26	14	1	0	213¹	218	15	74	88	12.5	3.63	123	.269	.334	20	.233	-1	15	20	-3	1.3
1926	Pit-N	10	13	.435	30	26	12	1	1	190	204	7	73	61	13.3	4.07	97	.279	.348	16	.225	-1	-5	-3	-2	-0.6
1927	*Pit-N	15	10	.600	35	34	17	1	1	239¹	248	16	74	86	12.3	4.25	97	.270	.328	21	.219	-0	-9	-4	-3	-0.7
1928	NY-N	4	7	.364	22	17	3	0	2	119¹	133	7	45	33	13.7	4.83	81	.285	.352	11	.275	2	-11	-12	-1	-0.9
Total	9	97	80	.548	248	205	102	8	6	1600²	1671	87	512	526	12.5	3.76	107	.273	.333	133	.229	2	26	44	-3	3.8

● DOYLE ALEXANDER
Alexander, Doyle Lafayette b: 9/4/50, Cordova, Ala. BR/TR, 6'3", 205 lbs. Deb: 6/26/71

YEAR	TM/L	W	L	PCT	G	GS	CG	SH	SV	IP	H	HR	BB	SO	RAT	ERA	ERA+	OAV	OOB	BH	AVG	PB	PR	/A	PD	TPI
1971	LA-N	6	6	.500	17	12	4	0	0	92¹	105	6	18	30	12.1	3.80	85	.282	.317	9	.273	3	-3	-6	-1	-0.5
1972	Bal-A	6	8	.429	35	9	2	2	2	106¹	78	5	30	49	9.2	2.45	125	.203	.262	2	.080	-1	7	7	2	1.1
1973	*Bal-A	12	8	.600	29	26	10	0	0	174²	169	19	52	63	11.7	3.86	97	.258	.319	0	—	0	-1	-3	1	-0.1
1974	Bal-A	6	9	.400	30	12	2	0	0	114¹	127	7	43	40	13.7	4.01	86	.290	.359	0	—	0	-5	-7	3	-0.5
1975	Bal-A	8	8	.500	32	11	3	1	1	133¹	127	7	47	46	11.8	3.04	116	.251	.316	0	—	0	11	7	2	1.0
1976	Bal-A	3	4	.429	11	6	2	1	0	64¹	58	3	24	17	11.5	3.50	94	.247	.317	0	—	0	0	-2	1	0.2
	*NY-A	10	5	.667	19	19	5	2	0	136²	114	9	39	41	10.3	3.29	104	.229	.289	0	—	0	3	2	-2	0.0
	Yr	13	9	.591	30	25	7	3	0	201	172	12	63	58	10.7	3.36	100	.234	.297	0	—	0	4	0	-1	0.2
1977	Tex-A	17	11	.607	34	34	12	1	0	237	221	24	82	82	11.6	3.65	112	.246	.311	0	—	0	11	11	1	1.4
1978	Tex-A	9	10	.474	31	28	7	1	0	191	198	18	71	81	12.7	3.86	97	.270	.336	0	—	0	-2	-3	2	-0.1
1979	Tex-A	5	7	.417	23	18	0	0	0	113¹	114	11	69	50	14.6	4.45	93	.268	.371	0	—	0	-3	-4	2	-0.1
1980	Atl-N	14	11	.560	35	35	7	1	0	231²	227	20	74	114	11.8	4.20	89	.256	.316	15	.181	0	-15	-12	3	-0.8
1981	SF-N	11	7	.611	24	24	1	1	0	152¹	156	11	44	77	11.9	2.89	118	.263	.316	9	.176	1	10	9	-2	1.0
1982	NY-A	1	7	.125	16	11	0	0	0	66²	81	14	26	32	12.8	6.08	66	.298	.332	0	—	0	-15	-15	-0	-1.5
1983	NY-A	0	2	.000	8	5	0	0	0	28¹	31	6	7	12	12.1	6.35	61	.277	.319	0	—	0	-7	-8	-0	-0.3
	Tor-A	7	6	.538	17	15	5	0	0	116²	126	14	26	46	11.8	3.93	109	.279	.319	0	—	0	4	5	-1	0.2
	Yr	7	8	.467	25	20	5	0	0	145	157	20	33	63	11.9	4.41	96	.278	.319	0	—	0	-6	-3	-0	-0.1
1984	Tor-A	17	6	.739	36	35	11	2	0	261²	238	21	59	139	10.3	3.13	131	.242	.287	0	—	0	25	28	-0	2.2
1985	*Tor-A	17	10	.630	36	36	6	1	0	260²	268	28	67	142	11.8	3.45	122	.266	.315	0	—	0	20	22	0	2.1
1986	Tor-A	5	4	.556	17	17	3	0	0	111	120	18	20	65	11.7	4.46	95	.273	.310	0	—	0	-3	-3	-1	-0.3
	Atl-N	6	6	.500	17	17	2	0	0	117¹	135	9	27	74	11.7	3.84	104	.287	.312	8	.211	1	-2	-1	1	0.2
1987	Atl-N	5	10	.333	16	16	3	0	0	117²	115	21	27	64	11.0	4.13	105	.257	.302	1	.029	-3	-1	-3	-2	-0.1
	*Det-A☆	9	0	1.000	11	11	3	2	0	88¹	63	9	26	44	9.1	1.53	276	.201	.263	0	—	0	29	26	0	3.0
1988	Det-A	14	11	.560	34	34	5	1	0	229	260	30	46	126	12.2	4.32	90	.282	.320	0	—	0	-9	-13	-3	-1.5
1989	Det-A	6	18	.250	33	33	5	1	0	223	245	28	76	95	13.0	4.44	90	.280	.341	0	—	0	-14	-15	0	-1.4
Total	19	194	174	.527	561	464	98	18	3	3367²	3376	324	978	1528	11.8	3.76	102	.261	.316	44	.166	1	38	32	7	5.2

● GERALD ALEXANDER
Alexander, Gerald Paul b: 3/26/68, Baton Rouge, La. BR/TR, 5'11", 190 lbs. Deb: 9/9/90

YEAR	TM/L	W	L	PCT	G	GS	CG	SH	SV	IP	H	HR	BB	SO	RAT	ERA	ERA+	OAV	OOB	BH	AVG	PB	PR	/A	PD	TPI
1990	Tex-A	0	0	—	3	2	0	0	0	7	14	5	0	8	25.7	7.71	51	.438	.526	0	—	0	-3	-3	0	0.0
1991	Tex-A	5	3	.625	30	9	0	0	0	89¹	93	11	48	50	14.5	5.24	77	.272	.366	0	—	0	-11	-12	0	-0.9
1992	Tex-A	1	0	1.000	3	0	0	0	0	1²	5	1	4	1	32.4	27.00	14	.500	.545	0	—	0	-4	-4	0	-1.7
Total	3	6	3	.667	36	11	0	0	0	98	112	12	54	59	15.6	5.79	69	.292	.385	0	—	0	-19	-19	0	-2.6

● PETE ALEXANDER
Alexander, Grover Cleveland b: 2/26/1887, Elba, Neb. d: 11/4/50, St.Paul, Neb. BR/TR, 6'1", 185 lbs. Deb: 4/15/11 H

YEAR	TM/L	W	L	PCT	G	GS	CG	SH	SV	IP	H	HR	BB	SO	RAT	ERA	ERA+	OAV	OOB	BH	AVG	PB	PR	/A	PD	TPI
1911	Phi-N	28	13	.683	48	37	31	7	3	367	285	5	129	227	10.3	2.57	134	.219	.293	24	.174	-2	34	35	1	3.6
1912	Phi-N	19	17	.528	46	34	25	3	3	310¹	289	11	105	195	11.4	2.81	129	.251	.317	21	.186	-2	21	28	1	3.1
1913	Phi-N	22	8	.733	47	36	23	9	2	306¹	288	9	75	159	10.8	2.79	120	.254	.302	13	.126	-4	14	19	2	1.4
1914	Phi-N	27	15	.643	46	39	32	6	1	355	327	6	76	214	10.5	2.38	123	.244	.290	32	.234	1	16	22	4	3.3
1915	*Phi-N	31	10	.756	49	42	36	12	3	376	253	6	64	241	7.8	1.22	225	.191	.234	22	.169	0	64	64	7	8.6
1916	Phi-N	33	12	.733	48	45	38	16	3	389	323	6	50	167	8.9	1.55	171	.230	.262	33	.239	8	46	48	1	7.3

YEAR	TM/L	W	L	PCT	G	GS	CG	SH	SV	IP	H	HR	BB	SO	RAT	ERA	ERA+	OAV	OOB	BH	AVG	PB	PR	/A	PD	TPI
1917	Phi-N	**30**	13	.698	45	44	**34**	**8**	0	**388**	336	4	56	**200**	9.2	**1.83**	153	.234	.266	30	.216	4	**38**	**42**	2	**5.9**
1918	Chi-N	2	1	.667	3	3	3	0	0	26	19	0	3	15	8.0	1.73	161	.207	.240	1	.100	-1	3	3	0	0.3
1919	Chi-N	16	11	.593	30	27	20	**9**	1	235	180	3	38	121	8.3	**1.72**	167	**.211**	.245	12	.171	1	31	30	5	**4.4**
1920	Chi-N	**27**	14	.659	46	40	**33**	7	5	363¹	335	8	69	173	10.0	**1.91**	168	.248	.285	27	.305	4	**50**	**52**	2	**7.1**
1921	Chi-N	15	13	.536	31	30	21	3	1	252	286	10	33	77	11.4	3.39	113	.296	.320	29	.305	0	6	11	-2	1.8
1922	Chi-N	16	13	.552	33	31	20	1	1	245²	283	8	34	48	11.7	3.63	116	.295	.321	15	.176	-2	13	16	3	1.7
1923	Chi-N	22	12	.647	39	36	26	3	2	305	308	17	30	72	**10.0**	3.19	126	.259	**.277**	24	.216	0	28	28	4	3.2
1924	Chi-N	12	5	.706	21	20	12	0	0	169¹	183	9	25	33	11.1	3.03	129	.272	.299	15	.231	1	16	16	2	1.7
1925	Chi-N	15	11	.577	32	30	20	1	0	236	270	14	29	63	11.5	3.39	127	.288	.312	19	.241	3	23	24	-2	2.3
1926	Chi-N	3	3	.500	7	7	4	0	0	52	55	0	7	12	10.7	3.46	125	.270	.294	7	.467	3	2	1	0	0.6
	*StL-N	9	7	.563	23	16	11	2	2	148¹	136	8	24	35	9.8	2.91	134	.242	.276	6	.120	-4	15	16	-0	1.3
	Yr	12	10	.545	30	23	15	2	2	200¹	191	8	31	47	10.1	3.05	127	.250	**.281**	13	.200	-1	17	19	1	1.9
1927	StL-N	21	10	.677	37	30	22	2	3	268	261	11	38	48	10.1	2.52	157	.258	**.286**	23	.245	3	**42**	**43**	1	**5.2**
1928	*StL-N	16	9	.640	34	31	18	1	2	243²	262	15	37	59	11.1	3.36	119	.277	.306	25	.291	6	17	17	-1	1.0
1929	StL-N	9	8	.529	22	19	8	0	0	132	149	10	23	33	11.8	3.89	120	.285	.317	2	.049	-4	12	11	2	1.0
1930	Phi-N	0	3	.000	9	3	0	0	0	21²	40	1	6	6	19.1	9.14	60	.396	.430	0	.000	-0	-10	-9	-1	-1.0
Total	20	373	208	.642	696	600	437	90	32	5190	4868	164	951	2198	10.2	2.56	135	.250	.288	378	.209	24	484	522	31	64.9

● MANNY ALEXANDER

Alexander, Manuel De Jesus (b: Manuel De Jesus (Alexander))
b: 3/20/71, San Pedro De Macoris, D.R.   BR/TR, 5'10", 150 lbs.   Deb: 9/18/92 ♦

YEAR	TM/L	W	L	PCT	G	GS	CG	SH	SV	IP	H	HR	BB	SO	RAT	ERA	ERA+	OAV	OOB	BH	AVG	PB	PR	/A	PD	TPI
1996	*Bal-A	0	0	—	1	0	0	0	0	0²	1	1	4	0	67.5	67.50	7	.500	.833	7	.103	0	-5	-5	0	0.0

● BOB ALEXANDER

Alexander, Robert Somerville   b: 8/7/22, Vancouver, B.C., Can   d: 4/7/93, Oceanside, Cal.   BR/TR, 6'2.5", 205 lbs.   Deb: 4/11/55

YEAR	TM/L	W	L	PCT	G	GS	CG	SH	SV	IP	H	HR	BB	SO	RAT	ERA	ERA+	OAV	OOB	BH	AVG	PB	PR	/A	PD	TPI
1955	Bal-A	1	0	1.000	4	0	0	0	0	8	10	0	2	1	24.8	13.50	28	.444	.524	0	—	0	-4	-4	-0	-0.9
1957	Cle-A	0	1	.000	5	0	0	0	0	7	10	0	5	1	20.6	9.00	41	.357	.471	0	.000	-0	-4	-4	-0	-0.6
Total	2	1	1	.500	9	0	0	0	0	11	18	0	7	2	22.1	10.64	35	.391	.491	0	.000	-0	-8	-8	-1	-1.5

● BRIAN ALLARD

Allard, Brian Marshall   b: 1/3/58, Spring Valley, Ill.   BR/TR, 6'1", 175 lbs.   Deb: 8/8/79

YEAR	TM/L	W	L	PCT	G	GS	CG	SH	SV	IP	H	HR	BB	SO	RAT	ERA	ERA+	OAV	OOB	BH	AVG	PB	PR	/A	PD	TPI
1979	Tex-A	1	3	.250	7	4	2	0	0	33¹	36	4	13	14	13.2	4.32	96	.283	.350	0	—	0	-0	-1	0	-0.1
1980	Tex-A	0	1	.000	5	2	0	0	0	14¹	13	0	10	10	15.1	5.65	69	.236	.364	0	—	0	-3	-3	-0	-0.1
1981	Sea-A	3	2	.600	7	7	1	0	0	48	48	5	8	20	10.5	3.75	103	.265	.296	0	—	0	-0	1	0	-0.1
Total	3	4	6	.400	19	13	3	0	0	95²	97	9	31	44	12.1	4.23	94	.267	.327	0	—	0	-3	-3	-1	-0.2

● FRANK ALLEN

Allen, Frank Leon   b: 8/26/1889, Newbern, Ala.   d: 7/30/33, Gainesville, Ala.   BR/TL, 5'9", 175 lbs.   Deb: 4/24/12

YEAR	TM/L	W	L	PCT	G	GS	CG	SH	SV	IP	H	HR	BB	SO	RAT	ERA	ERA+	OAV	OOB	BH	AVG	PB	PR	/A	PD	TPI
1912	Bro-N	3	9	.250	20	15	5	1	0	109	119	1	57	58	14.6	3.63	92	.285	.373	6	.167	2	-3	-3	0	-0.1
1913	Bro-N	4	18	.182	34	25	11	0	2	174²	144	6	81	82	12.1	2.83	116	.231	.329	7	.137	-1	7	9	-3	0.7
1914	Bro-N	8	14	.364	36	21	10	1	0	171¹	165	6	57	68	11.8	3.10	92	.265	.330	6	.128	0	-6	-5	-1	-0.7
	Pit-F	1	0	1.000	1	1	0	0	0	7	9	0	3		11.6	5.14	56	.321	.321	1	.500	1	-2	-2	-0	-0.1
1915	Pit-F	23	13	.639	41	37	24	6	0	283¹	230	9	100	127	10.8	2.51	108	.227	.304	7	.079	-6	7	6	-1	0.7
1916	Bos-N	8	2	.800	19	14	7	2	1	113	102	1	31	63	10.9	2.07	120	.244	.302	7	.206	3	7	5	-1	0.7
1917	Bos-N	3	11	.214	29	14	2	1	0	112	124	3	47	56	14.2	3.94	65	.297	.376	5	.172	-2	-15	-17	-2	-2.1
Total	6	50	67	.427	180	127	60	10	3	970¹	893	26	373	457	12.1	2.93	98	.252	.330	39	.135	1	-5	-7	-1	-1.5

● JOHN ALLEN

Allen, John Marshall   b: 10/27/1890, Berkeley Springs, W.Va.   d: 9/24/67, Hagerstown, Md.   BR/TR, 6'1", 170 lbs.   Deb: 6/2/14

YEAR	TM/L	W	L	PCT	G	GS	CG	SH	SV	IP	H	HR	BB	SO	RAT	ERA	ERA+	OAV	OOB	BH	AVG	PB	PR	/A	PD	TPI
1914	Bal-F	0	0	—	1	0	0	0	0	2	2	0	2	2	22.5	18.00	17	.286	.500	0	—	0	-3	-3	0	0.0

● JOHNNY ALLEN

Allen, John Thomas   b: 9/30/05, Lenoir, N.C.   d: 3/29/59, St.Petersburg, Fla   BR/TR, 6', 180 lbs.   Deb: 4/19/32

YEAR	TM/L	W	L	PCT	G	GS	CG	SH	SV	IP	H	HR	BB	SO	RAT	ERA	ERA+	OAV	OOB	BH	AVG	PB	PR	/A	PD	TPI
1932	*NY-A	17	4	**.810**	33	21	13	3	4	192	162	10	76	109	11.4	3.70	110	.228	.306	9	.123	-2	17	8	-1	0.5
1933	NY-A	15	7	.682	25	24	10	1	1	184²	171	9	87	119	12.8	4.39	89	.242	.328	13	.181	0	-2	-10	-1	-1.1
1934	NY-A	5	2	.714	13	10	4	0	0	71²	62	3	32	54	12.1	2.89	141	.227	.313	5	.192	1	13	9	0	0.9
1935	NY-A	13	6	.684	23	23	12	2	0	167	149	11	58	113	11.4	3.61	112	**.238**	.307	15	.224	1	16	8	1	1.0
1936	Cle-A	20	10	.667	36	31	19	4	1	243	234	5	97	165	12.3	3.44	146	.256	.328	14	.161	-3	43	43	2	4.5
1937	Cle-A	15	1	**.938**	24	20	14	0	0	173	157	6	67	87	11.5	2.55	181	.244	.313	6	.090	-7	40	40	1	2.7
1938	Cle-A★	14	8	.636	30	27	13	0	0	200	189	15	81	112	12.3	4.18	111	.246	.321	20	.253	4	13	10	2	1.5
1939	Cle-A	9	7	.563	28	26	9	2	0	175	199	9	56	79	13.3	4.58	96	.291	.347	16	.225	1	-1	-3	-3	0.1
1940	Cle-A	9	8	.529	32	17	5	3	5	138²	126	3	48	62	11.5	3.44	123	.243	.311	10	.208	0	15	12	-0	1.4
1941	StL-A	2	5	.286	20	9	2	0	1	67	89	4	29	27	16.1	6.58	65	.319	.387	3	.136	0	-18	-17	-0	-1.6
	*Bro-N	3	0	1.000	11	4	1	0	0	57¹	38	6	12	21	7.8	2.51	146	.188	.234	1	.050	-2	7	7	-0	0.1
1942	Bro-N	10	6	.625	27	15	5	1	0	118	106	11	39	50	11.2	3.20	102	.238	.302	7	.179	-0	1	1	0	0.1
1943	Bro-N	5	1	.833	17	1	0	0	1	38	42	3	25	15	16.3	4.26	79	.280	.390	3	.429	2	-4	-4	0	-0.4
	NY-N	1	3	.250	15	0	0	0	0	41	37	4	14	24	11.2	3.07	112	.245	.309	0	.000	-0	-2	-1	0	0.1
	Yr	6	4	.600	32	1	0	0	1	79	79	7	39	39	13.4	3.65	93	.261	.345	3	.143	-0	-2	-4	-1	-0.8
1944	NY-N	4	7	.364	18	13	2	1	0	84	88	7	24	33	12.2	4.07	90	.260	.313	2	.083	-2	-4	-4	-1	-0.8
Total	13	142	75	.654	352	241	109	17	18	1950¹	1849	104	738	1070	11.9	3.75	113	.249	.321	124	.173	-8	138	102	6	8.9

● LLOYD ALLEN

Allen, Lloyd Cecil   b: 5/8/50, Merced, Cal.   BR/TR, 6'1", 185 lbs.   Deb: 9/1/69

YEAR	TM/L	W	L	PCT	G	GS	CG	SH	SV	IP	H	HR	BB	SO	RAT	ERA	ERA+	OAV	OOB	BH	AVG	PB	PR	/A	PD	TPI
1969	Cal-A	0	1	.000	4	1	0	0	0	10	5	1	10	5	13.5	5.40	65	.147	.341	1	.500	1	-2	-2	1	-0.1
1970	Cal-A	1	1	.500	8	2	0	0	0	24	23	0	11	12	13.1	2.63	138	.261	.350	0	.000	-0	3	3	-0	0.3
1971	Cal-A	4	6	.400	54	1	0	0	15	94	75	4	40	72	11.0	2.49	130	.221	.303	5	.294	2	10	8	0	1.4
1972	Cal-A	3	7	.300	42	6	0	0	5	85¹	76	7	55	53	14.1	3.48	84	.240	.357	2	.118	-1	-4	-5	-1	-0.9
1973	Cal-A	0	0	—	5	0	0	0	0	8²	15	1	5	4	20.8	10.38	34	.417	.488	0	—	0	-6	-7	-0	-0.2
	Tex-A	0	6	.000	23	1	0	0	0	41	58	3	39	25	22.4	9.22	40	.326	.459	0	—	0	-25	-25	-1	-3.2
	Yr	0	6	.000	28	1	0	0	0	49²	73	4	44	29	22.4	9.42	39	.338	.460	0	—	0	-31	-32	-1	-3.4
1974	Tex-A	0	1	.000	14	0	0	0	0	22	24	2	18	18	17.6	6.55	54	.276	.406	0	—	0	-7	-7	-1	-0.4
	Chi-A	0	1	.000	7	0	0	0	0	7	7	0	12	3	25.7	10.29	36	.259	.500	0	—	0	-5	-5	-0	-1.1
	Yr	0	2	.000	20	0	0	0	0	29	31	2	30	21	19.2	7.45	48	.265	.419	0	—	0	-12	-12	-1	-1.3
1975	Chi-A	0	2	.000	3	2	0	0	0	5¹	8	2	6	2	23.6	11.81	33	.348	.483	0	—	0	-5	-5	0	-1.3
Total	7	8	25	.242	159	19	0	0	22	297¹	291	19	196	194	15.1	4.69	70	.258	.373	8	.200	0	-41	-46	-4	-5.3

● MYRON ALLEN

Allen, Myron Smith "Zeke"   b: 3/22/1854, Kingston, N.Y.   d: 3/8/24, Kingston, N.Y.   BR/TR, 5'8", 150 lbs.   Deb: 7/19/1883 ♦

YEAR	TM/L	W	L	PCT	G	GS	CG	SH	SV	IP	H	HR	BB	SO	RAT	ERA	ERA+	OAV	OOB	BH	AVG	PB	PR	/A	PD	TPI
1883	NY-N	0	1	.000	1	1	1	0	0	9²	8	0	3	1	12.4	1.13	275	.276	.344			-1	2	2	-0	0.1
1887	Cle-a	1	0	1.000	2	0	0	0	0	9²	9	0	3	1	12.1	0.93	466	.243	.317	128	.276	0	4	4	-0	0.3
1888	KC-a	0	2	.000	2	2	2	0	0	18	17	0	1	2	10.0	2.50	137	.239	.270	29	.213	-1	2	1	0	0.3
Total	3	1	3	.250	5	3	3	0	0	35²	34	0	7	3	11.1	1.77	205	.248	.299	157	.259	-1	7	7	0	0.7

● NEIL ALLEN

Allen, Neil Patrick   b: 1/24/58, Kansas City, Kan.   BR/TR, 6'2", 190 lbs.   Deb: 4/15/79

YEAR	TM/L	W	L	PCT	G	GS	CG	SH	SV	IP	H	HR	BB	SO	RAT	ERA	ERA+	OAV	OOB	BH	AVG	PB	PR	/A	PD	TPI
1979	NY-N	6	10	.375	50	5	0	0	8	99	100	4	47	65	13.4	3.55	103	.268	.350	0	.000	-2	2	1	0	0.0
1980	NY-N	7	10	.412	59	0	0	0	22	97¹	87	7	40	79	11.7	3.70	96	.244	.320	2	.143	-0	-1	-2	-1	-0.4
1981	NY-N	7	6	.538	43	0	0	0	18	66²	64	6	24	50	12.2	2.97	117	.259	.349	1	.200	1	4	4	1	1.1
1982	NY-N	3	7	.300	50	0	0	0	19	64²	65	5	30	59	13.4	3.06	119	.266	.349	1	.167	1	4	4	0	0.9
1983	NY-N	2	7	.222	21	4	1	1	2	54	57	4	32	32	15.5	4.50	81	.278	.386	0	.000	-0	-5	-5	-1	-1.0
	StL-N	10	6	.625	25	18	4	2	0	121²	122	6	48	74	12.6	3.70	98	.265	.335	5	.128	-2	-1	-1	-0	-0.2
	Yr	12	13	.480	46	22	5	3	2	175²	179	12	84	106	13.5	3.94	92	.265	.351	5	.102	-2	-6	-6	-1	-1.2
1984	StL-N	9	6	.600	57	1	0	0	3	119	105	9	44	66	11.6	3.55	98	.239	.315	0	—	0	-1	-1	0	0.1
1985	StL-N	1	4	.200	23	1	0	0	2	29	32	3	17	16	15.5	5.59	63	.283	.382	0	.000	-0	-6	-7	-0	-1.2
	NY-A	1	0	1.000	17	0	0	0	0	29¹	16	2	13	16	12.0	2.76	145	.234	.315	0	—	0	4	4	0	0.3
1986	Chi-A	7	2	.778	22	17	2	0	0	113	101	8	38	57	11.2	3.82	113	.244	.311	0	—	0	4	4	0	0.3
1987	Chi-A	0	7	.000	15	10	0	0	0	49²	74	6	26	26	18.5	7.07	65	.365	.442	0	—	0	-14	-14	-1	-1.6
	NY-A	0	1	.000	8	1	0	0	0	24²	23	2	10	16	13.1	3.65	120	.242	.314	0	—	0	2	2	0	0.1
	Yr	0	8	.000	23	11	0	0	0	74¹	97	8	36	42	16.1	5.93	76	.321	.393	0	—	0	-12	-12	-1	-1.5
1988	NY-A	5	3	.625	41	0	0	0	2	117¹	121	14	37	61	12.3	3.84	103	.268	.326	0	—	0	2	2	-2	-0.1

YEAR	TM/L	W	L	PCT	G	GS	CG	SH	SV	IP	H	HR	BB	SO	RAT	ERA	ERA+	OAV	OOB	BH	AVG	PB	PR	/A	PD	TPI
1989	Cle-A	0	1	.000	3	0	0	0	0	3	8	1	0	0	24.0	15.00	26	.500	.500	0	—	0	-4	-4	0	-1.0
Total	11	58	70	.453	434	59	7	6	75	988¹	985	73	417	611	12.8	3.88	97	.264	.339	15	.130	-1	-9	-11	-3	-2.9

● **BOB ALLEN** Allen, Robert Earl "Thin Man" b: 7/2/14, Smithville, Tenn. BR/TR, 6'1", 165 lbs. Deb: 9/19/37

YEAR	TM/L	W	L	PCT	G	GS	CG	SH	SV	IP	H	HR	BB	SO	RAT	ERA	ERA+	OAV	OOB	BH	AVG	PB	PR	/A	PD	TPI
1937	Phi-N	0	1	.000	3	1	0	0	0	12	18	2	8	8	19.5	6.75	64	.321	.406	1	.333	0	-4	-3	-1	-0.3

● **BOB ALLEN** Allen, Robert Gray b: 10/23/37, Tatum, Tex. BL/TL, 6'2", 185 lbs. Deb: 4/14/61

YEAR	TM/L	W	L	PCT	G	GS	CG	SH	SV	IP	H	HR	BB	SO	RAT	ERA	ERA+	OAV	OOB	BH	AVG	PB	PR	/A	PD	TPI
1961	Cle-A	3	2	.600	48	0	0	0	3	81²	96	7	40	42	15.1	3.75	105	.294	.373	2	.167	-0	3	2	-0	0.1
1962	Cle-A	1	1	.500	30	0	0	0	4	30²	29	5	25	23	15.8	5.87	66	.250	.383	0	.000	-1	-6	-7	0	-0.6
1963	Cle-A	1	2	.333	43	0	0	0	2	56	58	5	29	51	14.1	4.66	78	.266	.355	1	.200	-0	-6	-6	0	-0.4
1966	Cle-A	2	2	.500	36	0	0	0	5	51¹	56	2	13	33	12.4	4.21	82	.273	.323	1	.111	-0	-4	-4	1	-0.4
1967	Cle-A	0	5	.000	47	0	0	0	5	54¹	49	4	25	50	12.4	2.98	110	.243	.329	0	—	0	2	2	1	0.3
Total	5	7	12	.368	204	0	0	0	19	274	288	23	132	199	14.0	4.11	89	.270	.353	4	.129	-1	-13	-14	2	-1.0

● **DANA ALLISON** Allison, Dana Eric b: 8/14/66, Front Royal, Va. BR/TL, 6'3", 215 lbs. Deb: 4/9/91

YEAR	TM/L	W	L	PCT	G	GS	CG	SH	SV	IP	H	HR	BB	SO	RAT	ERA	ERA+	OAV	OOB	BH	AVG	PB	PR	/A	PD	TPI
1991	Oak-A	1	1	.500	11	0	0	0	0	11	16	0	5	4	17.2	7.36	52	.381	.447	0	—	0	-4	-4	0	-0.6

● **DOUG ALLISON** Allison, Douglas L. b: 7/1845, Philadelphia, Pa. d: 12/19/16, Washington, D.C. BR/TR, 5'10.5", 160 lbs. Deb: 5/5/1871 F♦

YEAR	TM/L	W	L	PCT	G	GS	CG	SH	SV	IP	H	HR	BB	SO	RAT	ERA	ERA+	OAV	OOB	BH	AVG	PB	PR	/A	PD	TPI
1878	Pro-N	0	0	—	1	0	0	0	0	5	11	0	1	0	21.6	1.80	123	.440	.462	22	.289	—				

● **MACK ALLISON** Allison, Mack Pendleton b: 1/23/1887, Owensboro, Ky. d: 3/13/64, Mount Vernon, Mo. BR/TR, 6'1", 185 lbs. Deb: 9/13/11

YEAR	TM/L	W	L	PCT	G	GS	CG	SH	SV	IP	H	HR	BB	SO	RAT	ERA	ERA+	OAV	OOB	BH	AVG	PB	PR	/A	PD	TPI
1911	StL-A	2	1	.667	3	3	3	0	0	26¹	24	1	14	6	10.6	2.05	165	.253	.304	2	.200	-0	4	4	-1	0.3
1912	StL-A	6	17	.261	31	20	11	1	1	169	171	4	49	43	12.0	3.62	92	.269	.327	7	.135	-3	-6	-6	-1	-1.1
1913	StL-A	1	3	.250	11	4	3	0	0	51¹	52	0	13	12	11.9	2.28	129	.287	.345	0	.000	-2	4	4	-2	-0.1
Total	3	9	21	.300	45	27	17	1	1	246²	247	4	67	57	11.9	3.17	102	.271	.328	9	.118	-6	2	2	-4	-0.9

● **LUIS ALOMA** Aloma, Luis (Barba) "Witto" b: 7/23/23, Havana, Cuba BR/TR, 6'2", 195 lbs. Deb: 4/19/50

YEAR	TM/L	W	L	PCT	G	GS	CG	SH	SV	IP	H	HR	BB	SO	RAT	ERA	ERA+	OAV	OOB	BH	AVG	PB	PR	/A	PD	TPI
1950	Chi-A	7	2	.778	42	0	0	0	4	87²	77	6	53	49	13.4	3.80	118	.234	.342	1	.067	-2	8	7	-0	0.4
1951	Chi-A	6	0	1.000	25	1	1	1	3	69¹	52	3	24	25	10.1	1.82	222	.215	.291	7	.350	2	18	17	-2	1.5
1952	Chi-A	3	1	.750	25	0	0	0	2	60	42	5	11	18	12.1	4.27	85	.278	.331	0	.000	-1	-3	-3	-0	-0.5
1953	Chi-A	2	0	1.000	24	0	0	0	2	38¹	41	7	23	23	15.0	4.70	86	.283	.381	0	.000	-1	-3	-3	-0	-0.2
Total	4	18	3	.857	116	1	1	1	15	255¹	212	21	111	115	12.5	3.44	120	.245	.333	8	.167	-2	20	18	-2	1.2

● **MATTY ALOU** Alou, Mateo Rojas (b: Mateo Rojas (Alou)) b: 12/22/38, Haina, D.R. BL/TL, 5'9", 160 lbs. Deb: 9/26/60 F♦

YEAR	TM/L	W	L	PCT	G	GS	CG	SH	SV	IP	H	HR	BB	SO	RAT	ERA	ERA+	OAV	OOB	BH	AVG	PB	PR	/A	PD	TPI
1965	SF-N	0	0	—	1	0	0	0	0	1	0	0	0	0	0.0	0.00	—	.000	.000	75	.231	0	1	1	-0	0.6

● **GARVIN ALSTON** Alston, Garvin James b: 12/8/71, Mt.Vernon, N.Y. BR/TR, 6'2", 185 lbs. Deb: 6/6/96

YEAR	TM/L	W	L	PCT	G	GS	CG	SH	SV	IP	H	HR	BB	SO	RAT	ERA	ERA+	OAV	OOB	BH	AVG	PB	PR	/A	PD	TPI
1996	Col-N	1	0	1.000	6	0	0	0	0	6	9	1	3	5	19.5	9.00	60	.375	.464	0	—	-0	-3	-2	0	-0.3

● **PORFI ALTAMIRANO** Altamirano, Porfirio (Ramirez) b: 5/17/52, Darillo, Nic. BR/TR, 6', 175 lbs. Deb: 5/9/82

YEAR	TM/L	W	L	PCT	G	GS	CG	SH	SV	IP	H	HR	BB	SO	RAT	ERA	ERA+	OAV	OOB	BH	AVG	PB	PR	/A	PD	TPI
1982	Phi-N	5	1	.833	29	0	0	0	2	39	41	2	14	26	12.9	4.15	88	.281	.348	1	.250	0	-2	-2	0	-0.3
1983	Phi-N	2	3	.400	31	0	0	0	0	41¹	38	9	15	24	12.0	3.70	96	.255	.331	0	.000	-0	-0	-1	0	-0.1
1984	Chi-N	0	0	—	5	0	0	0	0	11¹	8	2	1	7	7.1	4.76	82	.195	.214	0	.000	-0	-1	-1	0	0.0
Total	3	7	4	.636	65	0	0	0	2	91²	87	13	30	57	11.8	4.03	91	.259	.325	1	.125	-0	-4	-4	1	-0.4

● **ERNIE ALTEN** Alten, Ernest Matthias "Lefty" b: 12/1/1894, Avon, Ohio d: 9/9/81, Napa, Cal. BR/TL, 6', 175 lbs. Deb: 4/17/20

YEAR	TM/L	W	L	PCT	G	GS	CG	SH	SV	IP	H	HR	BB	SO	RAT	ERA	ERA+	OAV	OOB	BH	AVG	PB	PR	/A	PD	TPI
1920	Det-A	0	1	.000	14	1	0	0	0	23	40	2	9	4	19.6	9.00	41	.392	.446	0	.000	-1	-13	-13	0	-0.5

● **NICK ALTROCK** Altrock, Nicholas b: 9/15/1876, Cincinnati, Ohio d: 1/20/65, Washington, D.C. BB/TL, 5'10", 197 lbs. Deb: 7/14/1898 C♦

YEAR	TM/L	W	L	PCT	G	GS	CG	SH	SV	IP	H	HR	BB	SO	RAT	ERA	ERA+	OAV	OOB	BH	AVG	PB	PR	/A	PD	TPI
1898	Lou-N	3	3	.500	11	7	6	0	0	70	89	2	21	13	14.5	4.50	79	.307	.360	7	.241	0	-7	-7	2	-0.3
1902	Bos-A	2	0	1.000	3	2	1	0	0	18	19	0	7	5	13.5	2.00	179	.271	.346	0	.000	-1	3	3	1	0.3
1903	Bos-A	0	1	.000	1	1	1	0	0	8	13	0	4	4	19.1	9.00	34	.361	.425	2	.667	1	-5	-5	1	-0.3
	Chi-A	4	3	.571	12	8	6	1	0	71	59	3	19	19	10.3	2.15	130	.226	.286	9	.300	2	6	5	3	1.1
	Yr	4	4	.500	13	9	7	1	0	79	72	3	23	22	11.2	2.85	99	.242	.303	11	.333	4	1	-0	4	0.8
1904	Chi-A	19	14	.576	38	36	31	6	1	307	274	2	48	87	9.5	2.96	83	.240	.272	22	.198	4	-12	-17	4	-1.3
1905	Chi-A	23	12	.657	38	34	31	3	0	315²	274	3	63	97	9.7	1.88	131	.236	.276	14	.125	-3	27	21	8	2.8
1906	*Chi-A	20	13	.606	38	30	25	4	0	287²	269	0	42	99	9.8	2.06	123	.250	.281	16	.160	-1	20	15	4	2.1
1907	Chi-A	7	13	.350	30	21	15	1	2	213²	210	3	31	61	10.2	2.57	93	.259	.288	13	.181	1	-1	-4	5	0.2
1908	Chi-A	5	7	.417	23	13	8	1	2	136	127	2	18	21	9.7	2.71	85	.248	.276	10	.204	1	-5	-6	5	0.1
1909	Chi-A	0	1	.000	1	1	1	0	0	9	16	0	1	2	17.0	5.00	47	.485	.500	0	.000	-0	-3	-3	-0	-0.3
	Was-A	1	3	.250	9	5	2	0	0	38	55	0	5	9	14.4	5.45	45	.333	.357	1	.053	-1	-13	-13	0	-1.3
	Yr	1	4	.200	10	6	3	0	0	47	71	0	6	11	14.9	5.36	45	.359	.380	1	.045	-1	-15	-15	1	-1.6
1912	Was-A	0	1	.000	1	1	0	0	0	1	3	0	2	0	27.0	18.00	19	.429	.429	0	.000	-0	-2	-2	-0	-0.9
1913	Was-A	0	0	—	4	0	0	0	0	9	7	0	4	2	12.0	5.00	59	.184	.279	0	.000	-0	-2	-2	0	-0.4
1914	Was-A	0	0	—	1	0	0	0	0	1	3	0	1	0	27.0			.750	.750	0	—	-0	-0	-0	-0	0.0
1915	Was-A	0	0	—	1	0	0	0	0	3	7	0	1	2	24.0	9.00	33	.438	.471	0	.000	0	-2	-2	-0	-0.2
1918	Was-A	1	2	.333	5	4	1	0	0	24	24	1	6	5	11.6	3.00	91	.279	.333	1	.125	0	-1	-1	0	-0.2
1919	Was-A	0	0	—	1	0	0	0	0	4	0	0	0	0		∞	—	1.000	1.000	0	—	0	-4	-4	0	-0.3
1924	Was-A	0	0	—	1	0	0	0	0	2	4	0	0	0	18.0			.500	.500	1	1.000	0	1	1	0	0.1
Total	16	83	75	.525	218	161	128	16	7	1514	1455	16	272	425	10.4	2.67	95	.254	.291	97	.176	1	2	-21	34	1.8

● **TAVO ALVAREZ** Alvarez, Cesar Octavio b: 11/25/71, Ciudad Obregon, Mexico BR/TR, 6'3", 245 lbs. Deb: 8/21/95

YEAR	TM/L	W	L	PCT	G	GS	CG	SH	SV	IP	H	HR	BB	SO	RAT	ERA	ERA+	OAV	OOB	BH	AVG	PB	PR	/A	PD	TPI
1995	Mon-N	1	5	.167	8	8	0	0	0	37¹	46	2	14	17	15.2	6.75	64	.297	.366	0	.000	-1	-11	-10	-0	-1.5
1996	Mon-N	2	1	.667	11	5	0	0	0	21	19	0	12	9	13.7	3.00	144	.235	.340	2	.500	1	3	3	-0	0.5
Total	2	3	6	.333	19	13	0	0	0	58¹	65	2	26	26	14.7	5.40	80	.275	.357	2	.125	-1	-8	-7	-0	-1.0

● **JOSE ALVAREZ** Alvarez, Jose Lino b: 4/12/56, Tampa, Fla. BR/TR, 5'10", 170 lbs. Deb: 10/1/81

YEAR	TM/L	W	L	PCT	G	GS	CG	SH	SV	IP	H	HR	BB	SO	RAT	ERA	ERA+	OAV	OOB	BH	AVG	PB	PR	/A	PD	TPI
1981	Atl-N	0	0	—	1	0	0	0	0	2	0	0	0	2	0.0	0.00	—	.000	.000	0	—	0	1	1	-0	0.0
1982	Atl-N	0	0	—	7	0	0	0	0	7²	8	1	2	6	11.7	4.70	79	.308	.357	0	—	0	-1	-1	-0	0.0
1988	Atl-N	5	6	.455	60	0	0	0	3	102¹	88	7	53	81	12.9	2.99	123	.240	.346	3	.375	-1	5	8	1	1.1
1989	Atl-N	3	3	.500	30	0	0	0	2	50¹	44	4	24	45	12.3	2.86	128	.237	.327	0	.000	-0	4	4	1	0.6
Total	4	8	9	.471	98	0	0	0	5	162¹	140	12	79	134	12.5	2.99	123	.240	.337	3	.273	-1	9	12	2	1.7

● **WILSON ALVAREZ** Alvarez, Wilson Eduardo (Fuenmayor) b: 3/24/70, Maracaibo, Venez. BL/TL, 6'1", 175 lbs. Deb: 7/24/89

YEAR	TM/L	W	L	PCT	G	GS	CG	SH	SV	IP	H	HR	BB	SO	RAT	ERA	ERA+	OAV	OOB	BH	AVG	PB	PR	/A	PD	TPI
1989	Tex-A	0	1	.000	1	1	0	0	0	0	3	2	2	0	—	∞	—	1.000	1.000	0	—	0	-3	-3	0	-0.3
1991	Chi-A	3	2	.600	10	9	1	0	0	56¹	47	9	29	32	12.1	3.51	113	.230	.326	0	—	0	-3	-3	-0	-0.3
1992	Chi-A	5	3	.625	34	9	0	0	1	100¹	103	12	65	66	15.4	5.20	74	.272	.384	0	—	0	-14	-15	-0	-1.1
1993	*Chi-A	15	8	.652	31	31	1	0	0	207²	168	14	122	155	12.9	2.95	142	.230	.346	0	—	0	32	28	-0	2.9
1994	Chi-A★	12	8	.600	24	24	2	1	0	161²	147	16	62	108	11.6	3.45	135	.241	.311	0	—	0	24	22	-2	2.2
1995	Chi-A	8	11	.421	29	29	3	0	0	175	171	21	93	118	13.7	4.32	103	.258	.351	0	—	0	8	3	1	0.5
1996	Chi-A	15	10	.600	35	35	0	0	0	217¹	216	21	97	181	13.1	4.22	111	.258	.338	0	—	0	19	11	0	1.4
Total	7	58	43	.574	164	138	8	1	1	918¹	855	95	470	660	13.2	3.91	112	.249	.343	0	—	0	69	50	-1	5.9

● **RED AMES** Ames, Leon Kessling b: 8/2/1882, Warren, Ohio d: 10/8/36, Warren, Ohio BB/TR, 5'10.5", 185 lbs. Deb: 9/14/03

YEAR	TM/L	W	L	PCT	G	GS	CG	SH	SV	IP	H	HR	BB	SO	RAT	ERA	ERA+	OAV	OOB	BH	AVG	PB	PR	/A	PD	TPI
1903	NY-N	2	0	1.000	2	2	1	0	0	14	8	0	14	8.4		1.29	260	.114	.250	0	.000	-1	3	3	-1	0.3
1904	NY-N	4	6	.400	16	13	11	1	3	115	94	2	38	93	10.6	2.27	120	.222	.291	5	.125	-1	6	6	-0	0.3
1905	*NY-N	22	8	.733	34	31	21	2	0	262²	220	2	105	198	11.2	2.74	107	.230	.308	14	.144	-1	6	8	0	0.5
1906	NY-N	12	10	.545	31	25	15	1	0	203¹	166	7	93	156	11.6	2.66	98	.223	.312	4	.066	-3	-0	-1	3	-0.1
1907	NY-N	10	12	.455	39	26	17	1	0	233¹	184	6	93	156	10.9	2.16	115	.219	.315	12	.174	2	8	8	3	1.3
1908	NY-N	7	4	.636	18	15	5	0	1	114¹	96	0	27	81	9.8	1.81	133	.232	.281	7	.194	-0	7	7	3	0.9
1909	NY-N	15	10	.600	34	26	20	2	0	244	217	2	81	156	11.1	2.69	95	.241	.306	6	.074	-5	-3	-4	7	-0.2
1910	NY-N	12	11	.522	33	23	13	3	0	190¹	161	9	63	94	10.9	2.22	133	.237	.308	11	.177	-1	17	16	4	2.1
1911	*NY-N	11	10	.524	34	23	13	1	2	205	170	0	54	118	10.0	2.68	126	.223	.277	6	.094	-3	16	16	3	1.4

YEAR TM/L	W	L	PCT	G	GS	CG	SH	SV	IP	H	HR	BB	SO	RAT	ERA	ERA+	OAV	OOB	BH	AVG	PB	PR	/A	PD	TPI
1912 *NY-N	11	5	.688	33	22	9	2	2	179	194	3	35	83	11.7	2.46	137	.281	.320	13	.224	1	19	18	2	1.8
1913 NY-N	2	1	.667	8	5	2	0	1	41^2	35	0	8	30	9.5	2.16	144	.241	.286	2	.154	-1	5	4	2	0.5
Cin-N	11	13	.458	31	24	12	1	2	187^1	185	7	70	80	12.5	2.88	113	.265	.336	6	.102	-4	7	8	0	0.5
Yr	13	14	.481	39	29	14	1	3	229	220	7	78	110	11.9	2.75	117	.261	.327	8	.111	-5	12	12	2	1.0
1914 Cin-N	15	23	.395	47	36	18	3	**6**	297	274	8	94	128	11.3	2.64	111	.248	.311	12	.128	-4	5	10	4	1.3
1915 Cin-N	2	4	.333	17	7	4	1	0	68	82	2	24	26	14.0	4.50	64	.311	.368	1	.050	-1	-13	-12	1	-1.1
StL-N	9	3	.750	15	14	8	2	1	113^1	93	1	32	48	9.9	2.46	113	.286	.282	4	.114	-2	4	4	2	0.4
Yr	11	7	.611	32	21	12	3	2	181^1	175	3	56	74	11.5	3.23	87	.259	.316	5	.091	-3	-10	-8	2	-0.7
1916 StL-N	11	16	.407	45	25	10	2	**8**	228	225	3	57	98	11.3	2.64	100	.263	.313	12	.176	-0	-1	0	-2	-0.2
1917 StL-N	15	10	.600	43	19	10	2	3	209	189	2	57	62	10.7	2.71	99	.249	.304	12	.188	2	-0	-0	4	0.7
1918 StL-N	9	14	.391	27	25	17	0	1	206^2	192	1	52	68	10.8	2.31	117	.252	.304	10	.156	-1	10	9	-1	0.9
1919 StL-N	3	5	.375	23	6	1	0	1	70	88	1	25	19	14.7	4.89	57	.314	.373	4	.222	-0	-15	-16	-2	-2.0
Phi-N	0	2	.000	3	2	1	0	0	16	26	1	0	3	16.3	6.19	52	.400	.426	2	.400	1	-6	-5	0	-2.6
Yr	3	7	.300	26	8	2	0	2	86	114	2	25	23	14.9	5.13	56	.329	.380	6	.261	1	-21	-22	-2	-2.6
Total 17	183	167	.523	533	369	209	26	36	3198	2896	42	1034	1702	11.2	2.63	108	.245	.310	143	.141	-21	77	77	32	8.7

● DOC AMOLE
Amole, Morris George b: 7/5/1878, Coatesville, Pa. d: 3/7/12, Wilmington, Del. BR/TL, 5'9", 165 lbs. Deb: 8/19/1897

YEAR TM/L	W	L	PCT	G	GS	CG	SH	SV	IP	H	HR	BB	SO	RAT	ERA	ERA+	OAV	OOB	BH	AVG	PB	PR	/A	PD	TPI
1897 Bal-N	4	4	.500	11	7	6	0	0	70	67	0	17	19	11.6	2.57	162	.250	.309	3	.107	-3	14	12	0	0.9
1898 Was-N	0	6	.000	7	5	4	0	0	49^1	83	0	22	11	20.3	7.84	47	.369	.439	2	.100	-2	-23	-23	1	-2.1
Total 2	4	10	.286	18	12	10	0	0	119^1	150	0	39	30	15.2	4.75	84	.304	.369	5	.104	-4	-10	-10	1	-1.2

● VICENTE AMOR
Amor, Vicente (Alvarez) b: 8/8/32, Havana, Cuba BR/TR, 6'3", 182 lbs. Deb: 4/16/55

YEAR TM/L	W	L	PCT	G	GS	CG	SH	SV	IP	H	HR	BB	SO	RAT	ERA	ERA+	OAV	OOB	BH	AVG	PB	PR	/A	PD	TPI
1955 Chi-N	0	1	.000	4	0	0	0	0	6	11	0	3	3	21.0	4.50	91	.407	.467	0	—	0	-0	-0	1	0.0
1957 Cin-N	1	2	.333	9	4	1	0	0	27^1	39	2	10	9	16.8	5.93	69	.345	.408	1	.167	-0	-6	-6	-0	-0.6
Total 2	1	3	.250	13	4	1	0	0	33^1	50	2	13	12	17.6	5.67	72	.357	.419	1	.167	-0	-7	-6	1	-0.6

● WALTER ANCKER
Ancker, Walter b: 4/10/1894, New York, N.Y. d: 2/13/54, Englewood, N.J. BR/TR, 6'1", 190 lbs. Deb: 9/3/15

YEAR TM/L	W	L	PCT	G	GS	CG	SH	SV	IP	H	HR	BB	SO	RAT	ERA	ERA+	OAV	OOB	BH	AVG	PB	PR	/A	PD	TPI
1915 Phi-A	0	0	—	4	1	0	0	0	17^2	17	1	4	17	19.9	3.57		.279	.443	0	.000	-1	-1	-1	0	-0.1

● LARRY ANDERSEN
Andersen, Larry Eugene b: 5/6/53, Portland, Ore. BR/TR, 6'3", 205 lbs. Deb: 9/5/75

YEAR TM/L	W	L	PCT	G	GS	CG	SH	SV	IP	H	HR	BB	SO	RAT	ERA	ERA+	OAV	OOB	BH	AVG	PB	PR	/A	PD	TPI
1975 Cle-A	0	0	—	3	0	0	0	0	5^2	4	0	2	4	9.5	4.76	79	.200	.273	0	—	0	-1	-1	0	0.0
1977 Cle-A	0	1	.000	11	0	0	0	0	14^1	10	1	9	8	11.9	3.14	126	.200	.322	0	—	0	1	1	1	0.2
1979 Cle-A	0	0	—	8	0	0	0	0	16^2	25	3	4	7	15.7	7.56	56	.357	.392	0	—	0	-6	-6	0	0.0
1981 Sea-A	3	3	.500	41	0	0	0	5	67^2	57	4	18	40	10.2	2.66	145	.228	.285	0	—	0	7	9	-0	0.7
1982 Sea-A	0	0	—	40	1	0	0	1	79^2	100	16	23	32	14.3	5.99	71	.311	.364	0	—	0	-17	-15	1	-0.1
1983 *Phi-N	1	0	1.000	17	0	0	0	0	26^1	19	0	9	14	9.6	2.39	149	.200	.269	0	.000	0	4	3	0	0.1
1984 Phi-N	3	7	.300	64	0	0	0	4	90^2	85	5	25	54	10.9	2.38	152	.248	.299	0	.000	0	12	13	0	1.4
1985 Phi-N	3	3	.500	57	0	0	0	3	73	78	5	26	50	13.2	4.32	85	.274	.341	0	.000	0	-6	-5	2	-0.3
1986 Phi-N	0	0	—	10	0	0	0	0	12^2	19	0	3	9	15.6	4.26	90	.388	.423	0	—	0	-1	-1	0	0.0
*Hou-N	2	1	.667	38	0	0	0	1	64^2	64	2	23	33	12.2	2.78	129	.276	.344	0	.000	-1	7	6	0	0.2
Yr	2	1	.667	48	0	0	0	1	77^1	83	2	26	42	12.8	3.03	120	.294	.356	0	.000	-1	6	5	0	0.2
1987 Hou-N	9	5	.643	67	0	0	0	5	101^2	95	7	41	94	12.2	3.45	113	.246	.322	1	.167	0	7	5	0	0.7
1988 Hou-N	2	4	.333	53	0	0	0	5	82^2	82	3	20	66	11.2	2.94	113	.254	.299	2	.333	1	5	3	-0	0.3
1989 Hou-N	4	4	.500	60	0	0	0	3	87^2	63	3	24	85	8.9	1.54	220	.198	.254	1	.333	1	**19**	18	1	1.8
1990 Hou-N	5	2	.714	50	0	0	0	6	73^2	61	2	24	68	10.5	1.95	190	.229	.296	0	.000	0	15	14	1	1.6
*Bos-A	0	0	—	15	0	0	0	1	22	18	0	3	25	9.0	1.23	332	.220	.256	0	—	0	7	7	-1	-0.2
1991 SD-N	3	4	.429	38	0	0	0	13	47	39	1	13	40	10.0	2.30	165	.231	.286	0	.000	0	7	8	0	1.5
1992 SD-N	1	1	.500	34	0	0	0	2	35	24	2	8	35	9.4	3.34	107	.202	.254	0	.000	0	1	1	0	0.1
1993 *Phi-N	3	2	.600	64	0	0	0	0	61^2	54	4	21	67	11.1	2.92	136	.233	.299	1	1.000	0	8	7	-1	0.5
1994 Phi-N	1	2	.333	29	0	0	0	0	32^2	33	2	15	27	13.2	4.41	97	.256	.333	0	—	0	-1	-0	0	0.0
Total 17	40	39	.506	699	1	0	0	49	995^1	932	58	311	758	11.4	3.15	119	.249	.309	6	.132	0	68	68	5	8.5

● ALLAN ANDERSON
Anderson, Allan Lee b: 1/7/64, Lancaster, Ohio BL/TL, 6', 186 lbs. Deb: 6/11/86

YEAR TM/L	W	L	PCT	G	GS	CG	SH	SV	IP	H	HR	BB	SO	RAT	ERA	ERA+	OAV	OOB	BH	AVG	PB	PR	/A	PD	TPI
1986 Min-A	3	6	.333	21	10	1	0	0	84^1	106	11	30	51	14.6	5.55	78	.316	.374	0	—	0	-13	-12	0	-1.0
1987 Min-A	1	0	1.000	4	2	0	0	0	12^1	20	3	10	3	21.9	10.95	42	.392	.492	0	—	0	-9	-9	-0	-0.7
1988 Min-A	16	9	.640	30	30	3	1	0	202^1	199	14	37	83	10.8	**2.45**	**166**	.261	.301	0	—	0	34	36	1	4.5
1989 Min-A	17	10	.630	33	33	4	1	0	196^2	214	15	53	69	12.5	3.80	109	.275	.327	0	.000	0	2	7	-1	0.9
1990 Min-A	7	18	.280	31	31	5	1	0	188^2	214	20	39	82	12.3	4.53	92	.289	.329	0	—	0	-13	-8	2	-1.1
1991 Min-A	5	11	.313	29	22	2	0	0	134^1	148	24	34	51	13.1	4.96	86	.289	.340	0	—	0	-13	-10	0	-1.1
Total 6	49	54	.476	148	128	15	3	0	818^2	901	87	211	339	12.5	4.11	101	.282	.331	0	.000	0	-12	5	2	1.5

● RED ANDERSON
Anderson, Arnold Revola b: 6/19/12, Lawton, Iowa d: 8/7/72, Sioux City, Iowa BR/TR, 6'3", 210 lbs. Deb: 9/19/37

YEAR TM/L	W	L	PCT	G	GS	CG	SH	SV	IP	H	HR	BB	SO	RAT	ERA	ERA+	OAV	OOB	BH	AVG	PB	PR	/A	PD	TPI
1937 Was-A	0	1	.000	2	1	0	0	0	10^2	11	0	4	3	19.4	6.75	66	.282	.451	0	.000	-0	-3	-3	0	-0.2
1940 Was-A	1	1	.500	2	2	0	0	0	14	12	0	5	3	10.9	3.86	108	.245	.315	3	.600	1	1	0	0	0.2
1941 Was-A	4	6	.400	32	6	3	0	0	112	127	7	53	34	14.7	4.18	97	.296	.377	8	.258	2	-0	-1	-1	0.0
Total 3	5	8	.385	36	9	3	0	0	136^2	150	7	62	40	14.7	4.35	94	.290	.378	11	.282	3	-2	-4	-1	0.0

● BRIAN ANDERSON
Anderson, Brian James b: 4/26/72, Portsmouth, Va. BL/TL, 6'1", 190 lbs. Deb: 9/10/93

YEAR TM/L	W	L	PCT	G	GS	CG	SH	SV	IP	H	HR	BB	SO	RAT	ERA	ERA+	OAV	OOB	BH	AVG	PB	PR	/A	PD	TPI
1993 Cal-A	0	0	—	4	1	0	0	0	11^1	11	1	2	4	10.3	3.97	113	.256	.289	0	—	0	0	1	-0	-0.3
1994 Cal-A	7	5	.583	18	18	0	0	0	101^2	120	13	27	47	13.5	5.22	94	.300	.352	0	—	0	-5	-4	-1	-1.4
1995 Cal-A	6	8	.429	18	17	1	0	0	99^2	110	24	30	45	12.9	5.87	80	.282	.338	0	—	0	-13	-13	-0	-1.4
1996 Cle-A	3	1	.750	10	9	0	0	0	51^1	58	9	14	21	12.6	4.91	100	.296	.343	0	—	0	0	-0	1	0.1
Total 4	16	14	.533	50	45	1	0	0	264	299	47	73	117	13.0	5.35	90	.291	.342	0	—	0	-17	-16	0	-2.2

● DAVE ANDERSON
Anderson, David S. b: 10/10/1868, Chester, Pa. d: 3/22/1897, Chester, Pa. TL, Deb: 8/24/1889

YEAR TM/L	W	L	PCT	G	GS	CG	SH	SV	IP	H	HR	BB	SO	RAT	ERA	ERA+	OAV	OOB	BH	AVG	PB	PR	/A	PD	TPI
1889 Phi-N	0	1	.000	5	2	1	0	0	23	30	2	14	8	17.2	7.43	59	.306	.393	2	.182	-0	-9	-8	0	-0.3
1890 Phi-N	1	1	.500	3	2	1	0	0	19^1	31	0	11	7	20.0	7.45	49	.352	.430	1	.111	-1	-8	-8	0	-0.7
Pit-N	2	11	.154	13	13	13	0	0	108	116	2	49	41	14.3	4.67	71	.266	.350	3	.071	-3	-13	-16	4	-1.6
Yr	3	12	.200	16	15	14	0	0	127^1	147	2	60	48	15.1	5.09	66	.280	.361	4	.078	-6	-21	-25	4	-2.3
Total 2	3	13	.188	21	17	15	0	0	150^1	177	4	74	56	15.5	5.45	64	.285	.368	6	.097	-6	-30	-33	4	-2.6

● JOHN ANDERSON
Anderson, John Charles b: 11/23/32, St.Paul, Minn. BR/TR, 6'1", 190 lbs. Deb: 8/17/58

YEAR TM/L	W	L	PCT	G	GS	CG	SH	SV	IP	H	HR	BB	SO	RAT	ERA	ERA+	OAV	OOB	BH	AVG	PB	PR	/A	PD	TPI
1958 Phi-N	0	0	—	5	1	0	0	0	16	26	5	4	9	17.4	7.88	50	.361	.403	0	.000	-0	-7	-7	-0	0.0
1960 Bal-A	0	0	—	4	0	0	0	0	4^2	8	0	4	3	23.1	13.50	28	.444	.545	0	—	0	-5	-5	0	0.0
1962 StL-N	0	0	—	5	0	0	0	0	6^1	6	1	3	6	9.9	1.42	300	.182	.280	0	—	0	2	2	0	0.0
Hou-N	0	0	—	10	0	0	0	0	17^2	24	0	6	7	14.8	5.09	73	.338	.363	0	.000	-0	-2	-3	1	0.0
Yr	0	0	—	15	0	0	0	0	24	30	1	9	13	13.5	4.13	94	.300	.340	0	.000	-0	-4	-5	2	0.0
Total 3	0	0	—	24	1	0	0	1	44^2	64	6	14	19	15.9	6.45	60	.339	.387	0	.000	-0	-12	-13	2	0.0

● FRED ANDERSON
Anderson, John Frederick b: 12/11/1885, Calahaln, N.C. d: 11/8/57, Winston-Salem, N.C. BR/TR, 6'2", 180 lbs. Deb: 9/25/09

YEAR TM/L	W	L	PCT	G	GS	CG	SH	SV	IP	H	HR	BB	SO	RAT	ERA	ERA+	OAV	OOB	BH	AVG	PB	PR	/A	PD	TPI
1909 Bos-A	0	0	—	1	1	0	0	0	8	3	0	1	5	4.5	1.13	222	.115	.148	0	.000	0	1	1	0	0.0
1913 Bos-A	0	6	.000	10	8	4	0	0	57^1	84	0	21	32	16.6	5.97	49	.350	.405	1	.050	-2	-19	-19	0	-2.0
1914 Buf-F	13	15	.464	37	28	21	2	0	260^1	243	8	64	144	10.7	3.08	96	.249	.297	17	.189	-3	-6	-3	-1	-0.7
1915 Buf-F	19	13	.594	36	28	14	5	0	240	192	9	72	142	10.0	2.51	111	.222	.285	12	.150	-5	6	8	-1	0.4
1916 NY-N	9	13	.409	38	27	13	2	2	188	206	7	38	98	11.9	3.40	72	.277	.316	8	.138	0	-16	-20	-2	-2.7
1917 *NY-N	8	8	.500	38	16	9	1	0	162	122	1	34	66	**8.8**	1.44	**177**	.209	**.255**	3	.071	-3	23	20	-1	1.7
1918 NY-N	4	2	.667	18	4	2	1	**3**	70^2	62	1	17	24	10.3	2.67	163	.246	.299	0	.000	-3	1	-0	3	0.0
Total 7	53	57	.482	178	114	62	11	8	986^1	912	22	247	514	10.7	2.86	95	.248	.298	41	.131	-16	-11	-15	-2	-3.3

● BUD ANDERSON
Anderson, Karl Adam b: 5/27/56, Westbury, N.Y. BR/TR, 6'3", 210 lbs. Deb: 6/11/82

YEAR TM/L	W	L	PCT	G	GS	CG	SH	SV	IP	H	HR	BB	SO	RAT	ERA	ERA+	OAV	OOB	BH	AVG	PB	PR	/A	PD	TPI
1982 Cle-A	3	4	.429	25	5	1	0	0	80^2	84	4	30	44	12.8	3.35	122	.268	.334	0	—	0	7	7	-0	0.5

YEAR	TM/L	W	L	PCT	G	GS	CG	SH	SV	IP	H	HR	BB	SO	RAT	ERA	ERA+	OAV	OOB	BH	AVG	PB	PR	/A	PD	TPI
1983	Cle-A	1	6	.143	39	1	0	0	7	68¹	64	8	32	32	12.6	4.08	104	.255	.339	0	—	0	-0	1	-1	0.0
Total	2	4	10	.286	64	6	1	0	7	149	148	12	62	76	12.7	3.68	113	.262	.337	0	—	0	6	8	-1	0.5

● **LARRY ANDERSON** Anderson, Lawrence Dennis b: 12/3/52, Maywood, Cal. BR/TR, 6'3", 190 lbs. Deb: 9/25/74

YEAR	TM/L	W	L	PCT	G	GS	CG	SH	SV	IP	H	HR	BB	SO	RAT	ERA	ERA+	OAV	OOB	BH	AVG	PB	PR	/A	PD	TPI
1974	Mil-A	0	0	—	2	0	0	0	0	2¹	2	0	1	3	11.6	0.00	—	.250	.333	0	—	0	1	1	0	0.0
1975	Mil-A	1	0	1.000	8	1	1	1	0	30¹	36	3	6	13	12.5	5.04	76	.298	.331	0	—	0	-4	-4	-0	-0.1
1977	Chi-A	1	3	.250	6	0	0	0	0	8²	10	1	15	7	26.0	9.35	44	.286	.500	0	—	0	-5	-5	-0	-1.8
Total	3	2	3	.400	16	1	1	1	0	41¹	48	4	22	23	15.2	5.66	68	.293	.376	0	—	0	-8	-8	-0	-1.9

● **MIKE ANDERSON** Anderson, Michael Allen b: 6/22/51, Florence, S.C. BR/TR, 6'2", 200 lbs. Deb: 9/2/71 F♦

YEAR	TM/L	W	L	PCT	G	GS	CG	SH	SV	IP	H	HR	BB	SO	RAT	ERA	ERA+	OAV	OOB	BH	AVG	PB	PR	/A	PD	TPI
1979	Phi-N	0	0	—	1	0	0	0	0	1	2	0	2	0	18.0	0.00	—	.400	.400	18	.231	0	0	0	0	0.0

● **MIKE ANDERSON** Anderson, Michael James b: 7/30/66, Austin, Tex. BR/TR, 6'3", 200 lbs. Deb: 9/7/93

YEAR	TM/L	W	L	PCT	G	GS	CG	SH	SV	IP	H	HR	BB	SO	RAT	ERA	ERA+	OAV	OOB	BH	AVG	PB	PR	/A	PD	TPI
1993	Cin-N	0	0	—	3	0	0	0	0	5¹	12	3	3	4	25.3	18.56	22	.444	.500	0	.000	-0	-9	-9	0	0.0

● **CRAIG ANDERSON** Anderson, Norman Craig b: 7/1/38, Washington, D.C. BR/TR, 6'2", 205 lbs. Deb: 6/23/61

YEAR	TM/L	W	L	PCT	G	GS	CG	SH	SV	IP	H	HR	BB	SO	RAT	ERA	ERA+	OAV	OOB	BH	AVG	PB	PR	/A	PD	TPI
1961	StL-N	4	3	.571	25	0	0	0	1	38²	38	3	12	21	11.9	3.26	135	.255	.315	3	.333	1	3	5	0	0.9
1962	NY-N	3	17	.150	50	14	2	0	4	131¹	150	18	63	62	14.9	5.35	78	.278	.359	3	.094	-2	-20	-17	3	-2.3
1963	NY-N	0	2	.000	3	2	0	0	0	9¹	17	0	3	6	19.3	8.68	40	.362	.400	1	.333	0	-6	-5	0	-0.2
1964	NY-N	0	1	.000	4	1	0	0	0	13	21	0	3	5	16.6	5.54	65	.382	.414	0	.000	-0	-3	-3	0	-0.2
Total	4	7	23	.233	82	17	2	0	5	192¹	226	21	81	94	14.6	5.10	81	.286	.357	7	.149	-1	-26	-20	3	-2.5

● **RICK ANDERSON** Anderson, Richard Arlen b: 11/29/56, Everett, Wash. BR/TR, 6', 175 lbs. Deb: 6/9/86

YEAR	TM/L	W	L	PCT	G	GS	CG	SH	SV	IP	H	HR	BB	SO	RAT	ERA	ERA+	OAV	OOB	BH	AVG	PB	PR	/A	PD	TPI
1986	NY-N	2	1	.667	15	5	0	0	1	49²	45	3	11	21	10.1	2.72	130	.245	.287	1	.091	-1	6	5	-1	0.2
1987	KC-A	0	2	.000	6	2	0	0	0	13	26	3	9	12	25.6	13.85	33	.394	.481	0	—	0	-14	-13	0	-1.6
1988	KC-A	2	1	.667	7	3	0	0	0	34	41	3	9	9	13.5	4.24	94	.308	.357	0	—	0	-1	-1	-1	-0.2
Total	3	4	4	.500	28	10	0	0	1	96²	112	9	29	42	13.4	4.75	81	.292	.347	1	.091	-1	-9	-10	-1	-1.6

● **RICK ANDERSON** Anderson, Richard Lee b: 12/25/53, Inglewood, Cal. d: 6/23/89, Wilmington, Cal. BR/TR, 6'2", 210 lbs. Deb: 9/18/79

YEAR	TM/L	W	L	PCT	G	GS	CG	SH	SV	IP	H	HR	BB	SO	RAT	ERA	ERA+	OAV	OOB	BH	AVG	PB	PR	/A	PD	TPI
1979	NY-A	0	0	—	1	0	0	0	0	2¹	1	0	4	0	19.3	3.86	106	.167	.500	0	—	0	0	0	0	0.1
1980	Sea-A	0	0	—	5	2	0	0	0	9²	8	1	10	7	16.8	3.72	111	.229	.400	0	—	0	0	0	-0	-0.1
Total	2	0	0	—	6	2	0	0	0	12	9	1	14	7	17.3	3.75	110	.220	.418	0	—	0	0	0	0	0.0

● **BOB ANDERSON** Anderson, Robert Carl b: 9/29/35, E.Chicago, Ind. BR/TR, 6'4.5", 210 lbs. Deb: 7/31/57

YEAR	TM/L	W	L	PCT	G	GS	CG	SH	SV	IP	H	HR	BB	SO	RAT	ERA	ERA+	OAV	OOB	BH	AVG	PB	PR	/A	PD	TPI
1957	Chi-N	0	1	.000	8	0	0	0	0	16¹	20	2	8	7	16.0	7.71	50	.317	.403	0	.000	-1	-7	-7	0	-0.4
1958	Chi-N	3	3	.500	17	8	2	0	0	65²	61	3	29	51	12.5	3.97	99	.255	.338	2	.118	-1	-0	-0	0	-0.1
1959	Chi-N	12	13	.480	37	36	7	1	0	235¹	245	21	77	113	12.5	4.13	96	.272	.333	6	.075	-4	-5	-1	-1	-0.8
1960	Chi-N	9	11	.450	38	30	5	0	1	203²	201	26	68	115	12.2	4.11	92	.255	.320	12	.169	-0	-8	-8	1	-0.6
1961	Chi-N	7	10	.412	57	12	1	0	8	152	162	14	56	96	13.0	4.26	98	.275	.340	6	.143	-0	-4	-1	4	-0.9
1962	Chi-N	2	7	.222	57	4	0	0	4	107²	111	9	60	82	14.7	5.02	83	.266	.364	3	.130	-1	-13	-10	-0	-0.9
1963	Det-N	3	1	.750	32	3	0	0	0	60	58	5	21	38	12.0	3.30	113	.258	.337	4	.444	2	3	0	1	0.3
Total	7	36	46	.439	246	93	15	1	13	840²	858	80	319	502	12.9	4.26	93	.266	.337	33	.134	-4	-34	-29	5	-2.3

● **SCOTT ANDERSON** Anderson, Scott Richard b: 8/1/62, Corvallis, Ore. BR/TR, 6'6", 190 lbs. Deb: 4/8/87

YEAR	TM/L	W	L	PCT	G	GS	CG	SH	SV	IP	H	HR	BB	SO	RAT	ERA	ERA+	OAV	OOB	BH	AVG	PB	PR	/A	PD	TPI
1987	Tex-A	0	1	.000	8	0	0	0	0	11¹	17	0	8	6	20.6	9.53	47	.347	.448	0	—	0	-6	-6	1	-0.4
1990	Mon-N	4	3	0	0	0	18	12	1	5	16	8.5	3.00	122	.188	.246	0	.000	-0	2	1	-0	0.0
1995	KC-A	1	0	1.000	6	4	0	0	0	25¹	29	3	8	6	13.5	5.33	90	.290	.349	0	—	0	-2	-2	-0	-0.1
Total	3	1	2	.333	18	7	0	0	0	54²	58	4	21	28	13.3	5.43	80	.272	.343	0	.000	-0	-7	-7	0	-0.5

● **VARNEY ANDERSON** Anderson, Varney Samuel "Varn" b: 6/18/1866, Geneva, Ill. d: 11/5/41, Rockford, Ill. BR/TR, 5'10", 165 lbs. Deb: 8/1/1889

YEAR	TM/L	W	L	PCT	G	GS	CG	SH	SV	IP	H	HR	BB	SO	RAT	ERA	ERA+	OAV	OOB	BH	AVG	PB	PR	/A	PD	TPI
1889	Ind-N	0	1	.000	2	1	1	0	0	12	13	0	9	3	18.8	4.50	93	.265	.410	0	.000	-1	-1	-0	0	-0.1
1894	Was-N	0	2	.000	2	2	1	0	0	14	15	0	6	3	14.1	7.07	74	.273	.355	3	.429	0	-3	-3	-0	-0.2
1895	Was-N	9	16	.360	29	25	18	0	0	204²	288	13	97	35	17.4	5.89	81	.327	.400	28	.289	3	-25	-25	1	-1.8
1896	Was-N	0	1	.000	2	2	1	0	0	9	23	0	3	0	26.0	13.00	34	.469	.500	3	.600	1	-9	-9	-1	-0.6
Total	4	9	20	.310	35	30	22	0	0	239²	339	13	115	41	17.6	6.16	78	.328	.402	34	.298	4	-37	-37	0	-2.7

● **WALTER ANDERSON** Anderson, Walter Carl "Lefty" b: 9/25/1897, Grand Rapids, Mich. d: 1/6/90, Battle Creek, Mich. BL/TL, 6'2", 160 lbs. Deb: 5/14/17

YEAR	TM/L	W	L	PCT	G	GS	CG	SH	SV	IP	H	HR	BB	SO	RAT	ERA	ERA+	OAV	OOB	BH	AVG	PB	PR	/A	PD	TPI
1917	Phi-A	0	0	—	14	2	0	0	0	38²	32	0	21	10	12.6	3.03	91	.246	.355	3	.429	1	-2	-1	0	0.1
1919	Phi-A	1	0	1.000	3	0	0	0	0	14	13	0	8	10	14.1	3.86	89	.245	.355	0	.000	-1	-1	-1	0	-0.1
Total	2	1	0	1.000	17	2	0	0	0	52²	45	0	29	20	13.0	3.25	90	.246	.355	3	.273	0	-3	-2	0	0.1

● **BILL ANDERSON** Anderson, William Edward "Lefty" b: 11/28/1895, Boston, Mass. d: 3/13/83, Medford, Mass. BR/TL, 6'1", 165 lbs. Deb: 9/10/25

YEAR	TM/L	W	L	PCT	G	GS	CG	SH	SV	IP	H	HR	BB	SO	RAT	ERA	ERA+	OAV	OOB	BH	AVG	PB	PR	/A	PD	TPI
1925	Bos-N	0	0	—	2	0	0	0	0	2²	4	1	2	1	23.6	10.13	40	.500	.583							0.0

● **WINGO ANDERSON** Anderson, Wingo Charlie b: 8/13/1886, Alvarado, Tex. d: 12/19/50, Fort Worth, Tex. BL/TL, 5'10.5", 150 lbs. Deb: 4/16/10

YEAR	TM/L	W	L	PCT	G	GS	CG	SH	SV	IP	H	HR	BB	SO	RAT	ERA	ERA+	OAV	OOB	BH	AVG	PB	PR	/A	PD	TPI
1910	Cin-N	0	0	—	7	2	0	0	0	17¹	16	0	17	11	17.7	4.67	62	.258	.425	1	.200	-0	-3	-3	-1	-0.1

● **JOHN ANDRE** Andre, John Edward b: 1/3/23, Brockton, Mass. d: 11/25/76, Centerville, Mass. BL/TR, 6'4", 200 lbs. Deb: 4/16/55

YEAR	TM/L	W	L	PCT	G	GS	CG	SH	SV	IP	H	HR	BB	SO	RAT	ERA	ERA+	OAV	OOB	BH	AVG	PB	PR	/A	PD	TPI
1955	Chi-N	0	1	.000	22	3	0	0	0	45	45	7	28	19	14.8	5.80	70	.259	.365	1	.111	-1	-9	-9	-0	-0.3

● **ELBERT ANDREWS** Andrews, Elbert De Vore b: 12/11/01, Greenwood, S.C. d: 11/25/79, Greenwood, S.C. BL/TR, 6', 175 lbs. Deb: 5/1/25

YEAR	TM/L	W	L	PCT	G	GS	CG	SH	SV	IP	H	HR	BB	SO	RAT	ERA	ERA+	OAV	OOB	BH	AVG	PB	PR	/A	PD	TPI
1925	Phi-A	0	0	—	6	0	0	0	0	8	12	0	11	0	25.9	10.13	46	.375	.535	0	—	0	-5	-5	-0	0.0

● **HUB ANDREWS** Andrews, Herbert Carl b: 8/31/22, Burbank, Okla. BR/TR, 6', 170 lbs. Deb: 4/20/47

YEAR	TM/L	W	L	PCT	G	GS	CG	SH	SV	IP	H	HR	BB	SO	RAT	ERA	ERA+	OAV	OOB	BH	AVG	PB	PR	/A	PD	TPI
1947	NY-N	0	0	—	7	0	0	0	0	8²	14	1	4	2	18.7	6.23	65	.368	.429	0	—	0	-2	-2	0	0.0
1948	NY-N	0	0	—	1	0	0	0	0	3	3	0	0	0	.300	.300	0	—	0	1	1	0	0.0			
Total	2	0	0	—	8	0	0	0	0	11²	17	1	4	2	16.2	4.63	87	.354	.404	0	—	0	-1	-1	0	0.0

● **IVY ANDREWS** Andrews, Ivy Paul "Poison" b: 5/6/07, Dora, Ala. d: 11/24/70, Birmingham, Ala. BR/TR, 6'1", 200 lbs. Deb: 8/15/31

YEAR	TM/L	W	L	PCT	G	GS	CG	SH	SV	IP	H	HR	BB	SO	RAT	ERA	ERA+	OAV	OOB	BH	AVG	PB	PR	/A	PD	TPI
1931	NY-A	2	0	1.000	7	3	1	0	0	34¹	36	3	8	10	11.5	4.19	95	.273	.314	2	.182	0	1	-1	-0	0.0
1932	NY-A	2	1	.667	4	1	1	0	0	24²	20	0	9	7	10.6	1.82	223	.215	.284	2	.222	1	7	6	0	0.8
	Bos-A	8	6	.571	25	19	8	0	0	141²	144	4	53	30	12.6	3.81	118	.262	.329	7	.137	-3	11	11	-1	0.5
	Yr	10	7	.588	29	20	9	0	0	166¹	164	4	62	37	12.3	3.52	126	.255	.322	9	.150	-2	18	17	0	1.3
1933	Bos-A	7	13	.350	34	17	5	0	1	140	157	8	61	39	14.1	4.95	88	.279	.350	9	.214	-0	-10	-9	-1	-1.2
1934	StL-A	4	11	.267	43	13	2	0	3	139	166	7	65	51	15.0	4.66	107	.301	.375	14	.350	3	-3	-5	-2	0.6
1935	StL-A	13	7	.650	50	20	10	0	1	213¹	231	10	53	43	12.0	3.54	135	.273	.317	9	.132	-5	22	30	-2	1.7
1936	StL-A	7	12	.368	36	25	11	0	1	191¹	221	19	50	33	12.7	4.84	111	.286	.330	10	.169	-1	4	11	-2	0.1
1937	Cle-A	3	4	.429	20	4	1	1	0	59²	76	7	9	16	12.8	4.37	105	.311	.336	3	.250	-1	2	5	-0	0.0
	*NY-A	3	2	.600	11	5	3	1	0	49	49	2	17	17	12.1	3.12	142	.259	.320	1	.067	-1	8	7	0	0.6
	Yr	6	6	.500	31	9	4	2	1	108²	125	9	26	33	12.5	3.81	119	.289	.329	4	.148	-1	10	9	-0	0.6
1938	NY-A	1	3	.250	19	1	1	0	0	48	51	3	17	13	12.8	3.00	151	.268	.329	0	.167	-0	10	8	0	0.6
Total	8	50	59	.459	249	108	43	2	8	1041	1151	59	342	257	12.9	4.14	115	.279	.335	59	.185	-6	51	70	-9	4.4

● **JOHN ANDREWS** Andrews, John Richard b: 2/9/49, Monterey Park, Cal. BL/TL, 5'10", 175 lbs. Deb: 4/8/73

YEAR	TM/L	W	L	PCT	G	GS	CG	SH	SV	IP	H	HR	BB	SO	RAT	ERA	ERA+	OAV	OOB	BH	AVG	PB	PR	/A	PD	TPI
1973	StL-N	1	1	.500	16	0	0	0	0	18¹	16	3	11	5	13.3	4.42	82	.235	.342	1	.500	0	-2	-2	-0	-0.2

● **NATE ANDREWS** Andrews, Nathan Hardy b: 9/30/13, Pembroke, N.C. d: 4/26/91, Winston-Salem, N.C. BR/TR, 6', 195 lbs. Deb: 5/1/37

YEAR	TM/L	W	L	PCT	G	GS	CG	SH	SV	IP	H	HR	BB	SO	RAT	ERA	ERA+	OAV	OOB	BH	AVG	PB	PR	/A	PD	TPI
1937	StL-N	0	0	—	4	0	0	0	0	9	12	1	4	6	15.0	4.00	100	.324	.375	0	—	0	-0	-0	0	0.1
1939	StL-N	1	2	.333	11	1	0	0	0	16	24	0	3	6	20.3	6.75	61	.343	.439	0	.000	-0	-5	-5	0	-0.8
1940	Cle-A	0	1	.000	6	0	0	0	0	12	16	1	4	3	16.5	6.00	70	.327	.400	0	—	0	-2	-2	1	-0.1
1941	Cle-A	0	0	—	2	0	0	0	0	2¹	4	0	1	1	19.3	11.57	34	.300	.417	0	—	0	-2	-2	-0	-0.1
1943	Bos-N	14	20	.412	36	34	23	3	0	283²	253	11	75	80	10.6	2.57	133	.238	.291	14	.156	-0	26	27	2	3.4
1944	Bos-N☆	16	15	.516	37	34	16	2	2	257¹	263	14	74	76	11.9	3.22	119	.261	.312	10	.114	-4	11	17	2	1.8

YEAR	TM/L	W	L	PCT	G	GS	CG	SH	SV	IP	H	HR	BB	SO	RAT	ERA	ERA+	OAV	OOB	BH	AVG	PB	PR	/A	PD	TPI
1945	Bos-N	7	12	.368	21	19	8	0	0	137²	160	9	52	26	13.9	4.58	84	.295	.356	9	.209	0	-12	-11	-0	-1.4
1946	Cin-N	2	4	.333	7	7	3	0	0	43¹	50	2	8	13	12.3	3.95	85	.281	.316	1	.071	-1	-3	-3	-0	-0.5
	NY-N	1	0	1.000	3	2	0	0	0	12	17	2	4	5	15.8	6.00	57	.362	.412	1	.500	1	-3	-3	-0	-0.2
	Yr	3	4	.429	10	9	3	0	0	55¹	67	4	12	18	12.8	4.39	77	.296	.332	2	.125	-0	-6	-6	-0	-0.7
Total 8		41	54	.432	127	97	50	5	2	773¹	798	40	236	216	12.1	3.46	106	.265	.321	35	.146	-4	10	17	4	2.3

● FRED ANDRUS   Andrus, Frederick Hotham   b: 8/23/1850, Washington, Mich.   d: 11/10/37, Detroit, Mich.   BR/TR, 6'2", 185 lbs.   Deb: 7/25/1876 ♦

YEAR	TM/L	W	L	PCT	G	GS	CG	SH	SV	IP	H	HR	BB	SO	RAT	ERA	ERA+	OAV	OOB	BH	AVG	PB	PR	/A	PD	TPI
1884	Chi-N	1	0	1.000	1	1	1	0	0	9	8	0	4	3	13.0	2.00	157	.297	.333	1	.200	0	1	1	0	0.1

● JOAQUIN ANDUJAR   Andujar, Joaquin   b: 12/21/52, San Pedro De Macoris, D.R.   BB/TR, 6', 180 lbs.   Deb: 4/8/76

YEAR	TM/L	W	L	PCT	G	GS	CG	SH	SV	IP	H	HR	BB	SO	RAT	ERA	ERA+	OAV	OOB	BH	AVG	PB	PR	/A	PD	TPI
1976	Hou-N	9	10	.474	28	25	9	4	0	172¹	163	8	75	59	12.3	3.60	89	.255	.334	8	.140	-0	-2	-8	-1	-0.9
1977	Hou-N☆	11	8	.579	26	25	4	0	0	158²	149	11	64	69	12.3	3.69	97	.251	.328	10	.189	2	4	-2	2	0.2
1978	Hou-N	5	7	.417	35	13	2	0	1	110²	88	3	58	55	12.2	3.42	97	.224	.330	3	.130	-2	-1	-2	0	0.1
1979	Hou-N★	12	12	.500	46	23	8	0	4	194	168	7	88	77	12.0	3.43	102	.233	.319	5	.088	-0	6	2	4	0.6
1980	*Hou-N	3	8	.273	35	14	0	0	2	122	132	8	43	75	12.9	3.91	84	.277	.337	5	.172	2	-4	-8	1	-0.3
1981	Hou-N	2	3	.400	9	3	0	0	0	23²	29	2	12	18	15.6	4.94	67	.296	.373	0	.000	-0	-4	-4	-1	-0.9
	StL-N	6	1	.857	11	8	1	0	0	55¹	56	4	11	19	10.9	3.74	95	.265	.302			-2	-2	-1	-0	-0.3
	Yr	8	4	.667	20	11	1	0	0	79	85	6	23	37	12.3	4.10	85	.273	.323	0	.000	-2	-5	-5	-0	-1.2
1982	*StL-N	15	10	.600	38	37	9	5	0	265²	237	11	50	137	10.1	2.47	146	.240	.282	15	.158	-1	33	34	2	3.2
1983	StL-N	6	16	.273	39	34	5	2	1	225	215	23	75	125	11.7	4.16	87	.253	.316	6	.082	-3	-13	-14	5	-1.0
1984	StL-N†	20	14	.588	36	36	12	4	0	261¹	218	20	70	147	10.2	3.34	104	.229	.286	11	.131	1	7	4	3	1.0
1985	*StL-N†	21	12	.636	38	38	10	2	0	269²	265	15	82	112	11.9	3.40	104	.260	.322	10	.106	-2	6	4	-1	0.2
1986	Oak-A	12	7	.632	28	26	7	1	1	155¹	139	23	56	72	11.5	3.82	101	.239	.310	0	—	0	6	1	0	0.1
1987	Oak-A	3	5	.375	13	13	1	0	0	60²	63	11	26	32	13.6	6.08	68	.269	.350	0	—	0	-11	-13	0	-1.3
1988	Hou-N	2	5	.286	23	10	0	0	0	78²	94	9	21	35	13.7	4.00	83	.297	.350	4	.211	2	-5	-6	-0	-0.3
Total 13		127	118	.518	405	305	68	19	9	2153	2016	155	731	1032	11.7	3.58	98	.250	.316	77	.127	-1	24	-13	18	0.4

● LUIS ANDUJAR   Andujar, Luis (Sanchez)   b: 11/22/72, Bani, D.R.   BR/TR, 6'2", 175 lbs.   Deb: 9/8/95

YEAR	TM/L	W	L	PCT	G	GS	CG	SH	SV	IP	H	HR	BB	SO	RAT	ERA	ERA+	OAV	OOB	BH	AVG	PB	PR	/A	PD	TPI
1995	Chi-A	2	1	.667	5	5	0	0	0	30¹	26	4	14	9	12.2	3.26	136	.230	.320	0	—	0	5	4	-1	0.5
1996	Chi-A	0	2	.000	5	5	0	0	0	23	32	4	15	6	18.4	8.22	57	.337	.427	0	—	0	-8	-9	-0	-0.2
	Tor-A	1	1	.500	3	2	0	0	0	14¹	14	4	1	5	10.0	5.02	101	.264	.291	0	—	0	-0	-1	-1	-0.1
	Yr	1	3	.250	8	7	0	0	0	37¹	46	8	16	11	15.2	6.99	69	.307	.377	0	—	0	-8	-9	-1	-0.3
Total 2		3	4	.429	13	12	0	0	0	67²	72	12	30	20	13.8	5.32	88	.276	.355	0	—	0	-3	-5	-2	0.2

● NORM ANGELINI   Angelini, Norman Stanley   b: 9/24/47, San Francisco, Cal.   BL/TL, 5'11", 175 lbs.   Deb: 7/22/72

YEAR	TM/L	W	L	PCT	G	GS	CG	SH	SV	IP	H	HR	BB	SO	RAT	ERA	ERA+	OAV	OOB	BH	AVG	PB	PR	/A	PD	TPI
1972	KC-A	2	1	.667	21	0	0	0	2	16	13	1	12	16	14.6	2.25	135	.228	.371	0	.000	-0	1	1	-0	0.3
1973	KC-A	0	0	—	7	0	0	0	0	3²	2	0	7	3	22.1	4.91	84	.200	.529	0	—	0	-0	-0	-1	-0.1
Total 2		2	1	.667	28	0	0	0	3	19²	15	1	19	19	16.0	2.75	117	.224	.402	0	.000	0	1	1	-0	0.2

● CAP ANSON   Anson, Adrian Constantine   b: 4/11/1852, Marshalltown, Iowa   d: 4/14/22, Chicago, Ill.   BR/TR, 6', 227 lbs.   Deb: 5/6/1871   MH♦

YEAR	TM/L	W	L	PCT	G	GS	CG	SH	SV	IP	H	HR	BB	SO	RAT	ERA	ERA+	OAV	OOB	BH	AVG	PB	PR	/A	PD	TPI
1883	Chi-N	0	0	—	2	0	0	0	1	3	1	0	1	0	6.0	0.00	—	.091	.167	127	.308	1	1	1	0	0.1
1884	Chi-N	0	1	.000	1	0	0	0	0	1	3	2	1	1	36.0	18.00	17	.375	.444	159	.335	0	-2	-2	0	-0.9
Total 2		0	1	.000	3	0	0	0	1	4	4	2	2	1	13.5	4.50	71	.211	.286	2995	.329	1	-1	-1	0	-0.8

● JOHNNY ANTONELLI   Antonelli, John August   b: 4/12/30, Rochester, N.Y.   BL/TL, 6', 190 lbs.   Deb: 7/4/48

YEAR	TM/L	W	L	PCT	G	GS	CG	SH	SV	IP	H	HR	BB	SO	RAT	ERA	ERA+	OAV	OOB	BH	AVG	PB	PR	/A	PD	TPI
1948	Bos-N	0	0	—	4	0	0	0	0	4	2	0	3	0	11.3	2.25	170	.143	.294	0	—	0	1	1	0	0.1
1949	Bos-N	3	7	.300	22	10	3	1	0	96	99	6	42	48	13.4	3.56	106	.273	.351	3	.120	-1	5	2	-1	0.0
1950	Bos-N	2	3	.400	20	6	2	1	0	57²	81	2	22	33	16.7	5.93	65	.335	.399	2	.125	-1	-11	-13	-0	-1.0
1953	Mil-N	12	12	.500	31	26	11	2	1	175¹	167	15	71	131	12.3	3.18	123	.242	.314	11	.177	0	22	14	1	1.9
1954	*NY-N★	21	7	.750	39	37	18	6	2	258²	209	22	94	152	10.7	2.30	176	.219	.293	16	.163	0	51	50	2	5.5
1955	NY-N	14	16	.467	38	34	14	2	1	235¹	206	24	82	143	11.4	3.33	121	.234	.307	17	.207	3	19	18	1	2.4
1956	NY-N★	20	13	.606	41	36	15	5	1	258¹	225	20	75	145	10.6	2.86	132	.234	.292	14	.157	1	26	27	1	3.6
1957	NY-N☆	12	18	.400	40	30	8	3	0	212¹	216	19	67	114	12.6	3.77	104	.276	.333	11	.153	3	3	4	-2	0.6
1958	SF-N☆	16	13	.552	41	34	13	0	3	241²	216	31	87	143	11.4	3.28	116	.239	.308	19	.226	4	18	14	-3	1.7
1959	SF-N★	19	10	.655	40	38	17	4	1	282	247	29	76	165	10.4	3.10	123	.233	.286	16	.158	-1	27	22	-1	2.2
1960	SF-N	6	7	.462	41	10	1	1	11	112¹	106	7	47	57	12.4	3.77	92	.253	.331	8	.235	2	-0	-4	-1	-0.3
1961	Cle-A	0	4	.000	11	7	0	0	0	48	68	8	18	23	16.3	6.56	60	.338	.395	4	.267	-0	-14	-14	1	-0.8
	Mil-N	1	0	1.000	9	0	0	0	0	10²	16	2	3	8	16.0	7.59	49	.340	.380	0	.000	-0	-4	-5	-0	-0.4
Total 12		126	110	.534	377	268	102	25	21	1992¹	1870	185	687	1162	11.7	3.34	116	.247	.313	121	.178	15	141	118	-1	15.7

● BOB APODACA   Apodaca, Robert John   b: 1/31/50, Los Angeles, Cal.   BR/TR, 5'11", 170 lbs.   Deb: 9/18/73   C

YEAR	TM/L	W	L	PCT	G	GS	CG	SH	SV	IP	H	HR	BB	SO	RAT	ERA	ERA+	OAV	OOB	BH	AVG	PB	PR	/A	PD	TPI
1973	NY-N	0	0	—	1	0	0	0	0	0	0	0	2	0	—	∞	—	1.000	0	—	0	-1	-1	-0	-0.1
1974	NY-N	6	6	.500	35	8	1	0	3	103	92	7	42	54	11.9	3.50	102	.241	.319	3	.120	0	1	1	-1	0.1
1975	NY-N	3	4	.429	46	0	0	0	13	84²	66	4	28	45	10.0	1.49	232	.222	.289	4	.364	2	20	18	2	2.6
1976	NY-N	3	7	.300	43	3	0	0	5	89²	71	4	29	45	10.3	2.81	117	.223	.293	2	.125	-0	7	5	1	0.7
1977	NY-N	4	8	.333	59	0	0	0	5	84	83	7	30	53	12.2	3.43	109	.255	.319	1	.167	-0	4	3	1	0.5
Total 5		16	25	.390	184	11	1	0	26	361¹	312	22	131	197	11.2	2.86	123	.236	.307	10	.172	2	32	26	4	3.8

● LUIS APONTE   Aponte, Luis Eduardo (Yuripe)   b: 6/14/53, ElTigre, Venez.   BR/TR, 6', 185 lbs.   Deb: 9/4/80

YEAR	TM/L	W	L	PCT	G	GS	CG	SH	SV	IP	H	HR	BB	SO	RAT	ERA	ERA+	OAV	OOB	BH	AVG	PB	PR	/A	PD	TPI
1980	Bos-A	0	0	—	4	0	0	0	0	7	6	2	1	10	10.3	1.29	328	.250	.308	0	—	0	2	2	0	-0.2
1981	Bos-A	0	1	.000	1	0	0	0	0	15²	11	0	3	11	8.0	0.57	674	.208	.250	0	—	0	5	6	1	0.4
1982	Bos-A	2	2	.500	40	0	0	0	3	85	78	5	44	50	10.9	3.18	136	.246	.301	0	—	0	8	11	2	0.5
1983	Bos-A	5	4	.556	34	0	0	0	3	62	74	7	23	32	14.4	3.63	120	.301	.365	0	—	0	3	5	1	0.7
1984	Cle-A	1	0	1.000	25	0	0	0	0	50¹	53	5	15	25	12.3	4.11	99	.269	.324	0	—	0	-1	-0	-1	-0.1
Total 5		9	6	.600	110	0	0	0	7	220	222	17	68	113	12.0	3.27	129	.265	.323	0	—	0	18	23	3	1.3

● KEVIN APPIER   Appier, Robert Kevin   b: 12/6/67, Lancaster, Cal.   BR/TR, 6'2", 180 lbs.   Deb: 6/14/89

YEAR	TM/L	W	L	PCT	G	GS	CG	SH	SV	IP	H	HR	BB	SO	RAT	ERA	ERA+	OAV	OOB	BH	AVG	PB	PR	/A	PD	TPI
1989	KC-A	1	4	.200	6	5	0	0	0	21²	34	3	12	10	19.1	9.14	42	.374	.447	0	—	0	-13	-13	-1	-2.2
1990	KC-A	12	8	.600	32	24	3	3	0	185²	179	13	54	127	11.6	2.76	139	.252	.310	0	—	0	24	22	-0	2.3
1991	KC-A	13	10	.565	34	31	6	3	0	207²	205	13	61	158	11.6	3.42	120	.255	.309	0	—	0	15	16	0	1.7
1992	KC-A	15	8	.652	30	30	3	0	0	208¹	167	10	68	150	10.2	2.46	165	.217	.282	0	—	0	34	37	0	3.8
1993	KC-A	18	8	.692	34	34	5	1	0	238²	183	8	81	186	10.0	2.56	179	.212	.280	0	—	0	47	53	-2	4.8
1994	KC-A	7	6	.538	23	23	1	0	0	155	137	11	63	145	11.8	3.83	131	.240	.320	0	—	0	17	20	-1	1.2
1995	KC-A★	15	10	.600	31	31	4	1	0	201¹	163	14	80	185	11.0	3.89	123	.221	.304	0	—	0	18	20	-0	2.1
1996	KC-A	14	11	.560	32	32	5	1	0	211¹	192	17	75	207	11.2	3.62	135	.245	.315	0	—	0	32	30	-1	2.3
Total 8		95	65	.594	222	210	27	9	0	1429²	1260	89	494	1168	11.2	3.28	136	.236	.305	0	—	0	174	186	-4	16.9

● FRED APPLEGATE   Applegate, Frederick Romaine   b: 5/9/1879, Williamsport, Pa.   d: 4/21/68, Williamsport, Pa.   BR/TR, 6'2", 180 lbs.   Deb: 9/30/04

YEAR	TM/L	W	L	PCT	G	GS	CG	SH	SV	IP	H	HR	BB	SO	RAT	ERA	ERA+	OAV	OOB	BH	AVG	PB	PR	/A	PD	TPI
1904	Phi-A	1	2	.333	3	3	3	0	0	21	29	0	8	12	16.3	6.43	42	.330	.392	2	.286	-0	-9	-9	0	-1.0

● ED APPLETON   Appleton, Edward Samuel "Whitey"   b: 2/29/1892, Arlington, Tex.   d: 1/27/32, Arlington, Tex.   BR/TR, 6'0.5", 173 lbs.   Deb: 4/16/15

YEAR	TM/L	W	L	PCT	G	GS	CG	SH	SV	IP	H	HR	BB	SO	RAT	ERA	ERA+	OAV	OOB	BH	AVG	PB	PR	/A	PD	TPI
1915	Bro-N	4	10	.286	34	10	5	0	1	138¹	133	3	66	50	13.5	3.32	84	.263	.357	7	.159	-0	-9	-8	-1	-0.9
1916	Bro-N	1	2	.333	14	3	1	0	1	47	49	1	18	14	13.0	3.06	88	.278	.349	2	.167	-0	-2	-1	-0	-0.3
Total 2		5	12	.294	48	13	6	0	1	185¹	182	4	84	64	13.4	3.25	85	.267	.355	9	.161	-1	-11	-10	-2	-1.2

● PETE APPLETON   Appleton, Peter William "Jake" (a.k.a. Jablonowski In 1927-33)   b: 5/20/04, Terryville, Conn.   d: 1/18/74, Trenton, N.J.   BR/TR, 5'11", 180 lbs.   Deb: 9/14/27

YEAR	TM/L	W	L	PCT	G	GS	CG	SH	SV	IP	H	HR	BB	SO	RAT	ERA	ERA+	OAV	OOB	BH	AVG	PB	PR	/A	PD	TPI
1927	Cin-N	2	1	.667	6	2	2	1	0	29²	29	0	17	13	14.0	1.82	208	.261	.359	6	.545	2	7	6	1	0.9
1928	Cin-N	3	4	.429	31	1	0	0	0	82²	101	7	22	20	13.6	4.68	85	.311	.358	10	.323	3	-6	-7	2	0.0
1930	Cle-A	8	7	.533	39	4	3	0	0	118²	122	6	35	45	13.7	4.02	120	.274	.357	8	.200	-1	8	11	2	1.2
1931	Cle-A	4	4	.500	29	4	3	0	0	79²	100	7	29	25	14.7	4.63	100	.293	.350	5	.208	0	-2	-0	-0	0.0
1932	Cle-A	0	0	—	4	0	0	0	0	5	11	1	3	1	25.2	16.20	29	.407	.467	0	—	0	-7	-6	0	0.0

YEAR	TM/L	W	L	PCT	G	GS	CG	SH	SV	IP	H	HR	BB	SO	RAT	ERA	ERA+	OAV	OOB	BH	AVG	PB	PR	/A	PD	TPI
	Bos-A	0	3	.000	11	3	0	0	0	46	49	2	26	15	15.1	4.11	109	.265	.362	3	.176	-0	2	2	2	0.3
	Yr	0	3	.000	15	3	0	0	0	51	60	3	29	16	16.1	5.29	85	.283	.374	3	.176	-0	-5	-4	2	0.3
1933	NY-A	0	0	—	1	0	0	0	0	2	3	0	1	0	18.0	0.00	—	.375	.444	0	—	0	1	1	0	0.0
1936	Was-A	14	9	.609	38	20	12	1	3	201²	199	7	77	77	12.5	3.53	135	.254	.324	19	.250	2	34	28	1	3.0
1937	Was-A	8	15	.348	35	18	7	4	2	168	167	16	72	62	13.1	4.39	101	.260	.339	11	.186	-2	4	1	3	0.2
1938	Was-A	7	9	.438	43	10	5	0	5	164¹	175	12	61	62	13.0	4.60	98	.270	.333	15	.254	3	-3	-2	-0	0.1
1939	Was-A	5	10	.333	40	4	2	0	6	102²	104	11	47	50	13.7	4.56	95	.265	.351	4	.160	-1	1	-2	0	-0.4
1940	Chi-A	4	0	1.000	25	0	0	0	5	57²	54	8	28	21	13.0	5.62	79	.248	.336	3	.176	-0	-8	-8	-0	-0.7
1941	Chi-A	0	3	.000	13	0	0	0	1	27¹	27	4	17	12	15.1	5.27	78	.257	.371	1	.250	0	-3	-4	0	-0.3
1942	Chi-A	0	0	—	4	0	0	0	0	4²	2	0	3	2	9.6	3.86	93	.133	.278	0	—	0	-0	-0	0	
	StL-A	1	1	.500	14	0	0	0	2	27¹	25	1	11	12	11.9	2.96	125	.243	.316	1	.167	1	2	2	1	0.4
	Yr	1	1	.500	18	0	0	0	2	32	27	1	14	14	11.5	3.09	119	.229	.311	1	.167	1	2	1	1	0.4
1945	StL-A	0	0	—	2	0	0	0	0	2¹	3	0	7	1	38.6	15.43	23	.273	.556	0	—	0	-3	-3	0	-0.1
	Was-A	1	0	1.000	6	2	1	0	1	21¹	16	1	11	12	11.4	3.38	92	.211	.310	1	.200	-0	-0	-1	-0	-0.1
	Yr	1	0	1.000	8	2	1	0	1	23²	19	1	18	13	14.1	4.56	69	.218	.352	1	.200	-0	-4	-4	-0	-0.1
Total	14	57	66	.463	341	71	34	6	26	1141	1187	76	486	420	13.4	4.30	104	.268	.343	87	.233	7	33	19	12	4.6

● LUIS AQUINO
Aquino, Luis Antonio (Colon)   b: 5/19/64, Santurce, P.R.   BR/TR, 6', 195 lbs.   Deb: 8/8/86

YEAR	TM/L	W	L	PCT	G	GS	CG	SH	SV	IP	H	HR	BB	SO	RAT	ERA	ERA+	OAV	OOB	BH	AVG	PB	PR	/A	PD	TPI
1986	Tor-A	1	1	.500	7	0	0	0	0	11¹	14	2	3	5	13.5	6.35	66	.304	.347	0	—	0	-3	-3	-0	-0.4
1988	KC-A	1	0	1.000	7	5	1	1	0	29	33	1	17	11	15.8	2.79	143	.282	.378	0	—	0	4	4	-0	0.1
1989	KC-A	6	8	.429	34	16	2	1	0	141¹	148	6	35	68	11.9	3.50	110	.271	.320	0	—	0	6	5	1	0.6
1990	KC-A	4	1	.800	20	3	1	0	0	68¹	59	6	27	28	11.9	3.16	121	.237	.321	0	—	0	6	5	0	0.4
1991	KC-A	8	4	.667	38	18	1	1	3	157	152	10	47	80	11.6	3.44	120	.253	.311	0	—	0	11	12	0	0.9
1992	KC-A	3	6	.333	15	13	0	0	0	67²	81	5	20	11	13.6	4.52	90	.303	.354	0	—	0	-4	-4	-0	-0.5
1993	Fla-N	6	8	.429	38	13	0	0	0	110²	115	6	40	67	13.0	3.42	126	.276	.346	2	.080	-2	8	11	4	1.5
1994	Fla-N	2	1	.667	29	1	0	0	0	50²	39	3	22	22	11.4	3.73	117	.210	.303	1	.167	0	3	4	1	0.3
1995	Mon-N	0	2	.000	29	0	0	0	2	37¹	47	4	11	22	14.7	3.86	111	.301	.359	1	.333	1	1	2	-0	0.1
	SF-N	0	1	.000	5	0	0	0	0	5	10	2	2	4	21.6	14.40	28	.400	.444	0	—	-0	-6	-6	-0	-0.9
	Yr	0	3	.000	34	0	0	0	2	42¹	57	6	13	26	14.9	5.10	84	.308	.354	1	.250	0	-4	-4	-0	-0.8
Total	9	31	32	.492	222	69	5	3	5	678¹	698	45	224	318	12.6	3.68	111	.267	.331	4	.114	-1	26	31	6	2.1

● FRED ARCHER
Archer, Frederick Marvin "Lefty"   b: 3/7/10, Johnson City, Tenn.   d: 10/31/81, Charlotte, N.C.   BL/TL, 6', 193 lbs.   Deb: 9/5/36

YEAR	TM/L	W	L	PCT	G	GS	CG	SH	SV	IP	H	HR	BB	SO	RAT	ERA	ERA+	OAV	OOB	BH	AVG	PB	PR	/A	PD	TPI
1936	Phi-A	2	3	.400	6	5	2	0	0	36²	41	3	15	9	14.5	6.38	80	.289	.369	4	.267	0	-5	-5	-0	-0.5
1937	Phi-A	0	0	—	1	0	0	0	0	3	4	0	0	2	12.0	6.00	79	.333	.333	0	—	0	-0	-0	0	
Total	2	2	3	.400	7	5	2	0	0	39²	45	3	15	11	14.3	6.35	80	.292	.366	4	.267	1	-6	-6	0	-0.5

● JIM ARCHER
Archer, James William   b: 5/25/32, Max Meadows, Va.   BR/TL, 6', 190 lbs.   Deb: 4/30/61

YEAR	TM/L	W	L	PCT	G	GS	CG	SH	SV	IP	H	HR	BB	SO	RAT	ERA	ERA+	OAV	OOB	BH	AVG	PB	PR	/A	PD	TPI
1961	KC-A	9	15	.375	39	27	9	2	5	205¹	204	11	60	110	11.8	3.20	131	.257	.313	4	.063	-5	19	22	-0	2.0
1962	KC-A	0	1	.000	18	1	0	0	0	27²	40	8	10	12	16.3	9.43	45	.342	.394	1	1.000	0	-17	-16	-0	-0.5
Total	2	9	16	.360	57	28	9	2	5	233	244	19	70	122	12.3	3.94	106	.268	.323	5	.078	-4	2	6	-1	1.5

● RUGGER ARDIZOIA
Ardizoia, Rinaldo Joseph   b: 11/20/19, Oleggio, Italy   BR/TR, 5'11", 180 lbs.   Deb: 4/30/47

YEAR	TM/L	W	L	PCT	G	GS	CG	SH	SV	IP	H	HR	BB	SO	RAT	ERA	ERA+	OAV	OOB	BH	AVG	PB	PR	/A	PD	TPI
1947	NY-A	0	0	—	1	0	0	0	0	2	4	1	1	0	22.5	9.00	39	.500	.556	0	—	0	-1	-1	0	0.0

● FRANK ARELLANES
Arellanes, Frank Julian   b: 1/28/1882, Santa Cruz, Cal.   d: 12/13/18, San Jose, Cal.   BR/TR, 6', 180 lbs.   Deb: 7/28/08

YEAR	TM/L	W	L	PCT	G	GS	CG	SH	SV	IP	H	HR	BB	SO	RAT	ERA	ERA+	OAV	OOB	BH	AVG	PB	PR	/A	PD	TPI
1908	Bos-A	4	3	.571	11	8	6	1	0	79	60	1	18	33	9.2	1.82	135	.205	.259	5	.167	0	5	6	-1	0.4
1909	Bos-A	16	12	.571	45	28	17	1	**8**	230²	192	3	43	82	9.4	2.18	114	.229	.270	13	.167	-1	8	8	0	0.9
1910	Bos-A	4	7	.364	18	13	2	0	0	100	106	1	24	33	12.0	2.88	89	.283	.332	6	.176	0	-4	-4	-0	-0.4
Total	3	24	22	.522	74	49	25	2	8	409²	358	5	85	148	10.0	2.28	110	.238	.283	24	.169	-1	9	10	-1	0.9

● RUDY ARIAS
Arias, Rodolfo (Martinez)   b: 6/6/31, Las Villas, Cuba   BL/TL, 5'10", 165 lbs.   Deb: 4/10/59

YEAR	TM/L	W	L	PCT	G	GS	CG	SH	SV	IP	H	HR	BB	SO	RAT	ERA	ERA+	OAV	OOB	BH	AVG	PB	PR	/A	PD	TPI
1959	Chi-A	2	0	1.000	34	0	0	0	2	44	49	7	20	28	14.3	4.09	92	.277	.354	0	.000	-1	-1	-2	1	-0.1

● DON ARLICH
Arlich, Donald Louis   b: 2/15/43, Wayne, Mich.   BL/TL, 6'2", 185 lbs.   Deb: 10/2/65

YEAR	TM/L	W	L	PCT	G	GS	CG	SH	SV	IP	H	HR	BB	SO	RAT	ERA	ERA+	OAV	OOB	BH	AVG	PB	PR	/A	PD	TPI
1965	Hou-N	0	0	—	1	1	0	0	0	6	5	0	1	0	9.0	3.00	112	.227	.261	0	.000	-0	0	0	-0	0.0
1966	Hou-N	0	1	.000	7	0	0	0	0	4	11	0	4	1	36.0	15.75	22	.478	.571	0	.000	-0	-5	-5	-0	-1.2
Total	2	0	1	.000	8	1	0	0	0	10	16	0	5	1	19.8	8.10	42	.356	.431	0	.000	-0	-5	-5	-0	-1.2

● STEVE ARLIN
Arlin, Stephen Ralph   b: 9/25/45, Seattle, Wash.   BR/TR, 6'3.5", 195 lbs.   Deb: 6/17/69

YEAR	TM/L	W	L	PCT	G	GS	CG	SH	SV	IP	H	HR	BB	SO	RAT	ERA	ERA+	OAV	OOB	BH	AVG	PB	PR	/A	PD	TPI
1969	SD-N	0	1	.000	4	1	0	0	0	10²	13	2	9	9	18.6	9.28	38	.289	.407	0	.000	-0	-7	-7	-0	-0.6
1970	SD-N	1	0	1.000	2	2	1	1	0	12²	11	0	8	13	13.5	2.84	140	.244	.358	0	.000	-1	2	2	0	0.1
1971	SD-N	9	19	.321	36	34	10	4	0	227²	211	9	103	156	12.7	3.48	95	.244	.329	9	.123	-1	-0	-5	-1	-0.8
1972	SD-N	10	21	.323	38	37	12	3	0	250	217	19	122	159	12.5	3.60	91	.237	.332	11	.153	3	-4	-9	-3	-2.0
1973	SD-N	11	14	.440	34	27	7	3	0	180	196	26	72	98	13.4	5.10	68	.278	.346	10	.167	1	-29	-33	-1	-3.9
1974	SD-N	1	7	.125	16	12	1	0	1	64	85	9	37	18	17.4	5.91	60	.326	.413	2	.111	-1	-16	-17	-0	-2.0
	Cle-A	2	5	.286	11	10	1	0	0	43²	59	1	22	20	16.7	6.60	55	.333	.407	0	—	0	-14	-14	-1	-2.0
Total	6	34	67	.337	141	123	32	11	1	788²	792	61	373	463	13.6	4.33	78	.263	.348	32	.139	1	-69	-82	-3	-10.0

● ORVILLE ARMBRUST
Armbrust, Orville Martin   b: 3/2/10, Beirne, Ark.   d: 10/2/67, Mobile, Ala.   BR/TR, 5'10", 195 lbs.   Deb: 9/18/34

YEAR	TM/L	W	L	PCT	G	GS	CG	SH	SV	IP	H	HR	BB	SO	RAT	ERA	ERA+	OAV	OOB	BH	AVG	PB	PR	/A	PD	TPI
1934	Was-A	1	0	1.000	3	2	0	0	0	12²	10	1	3	2	9.2	2.13	203	.208	.255	0	.000	-1	3	3	1	0.2

● HOWARD ARMSTRONG
Armstrong, Howard Elmer   b: 12/2/1889, E.Claridon, Ohio   d: 3/8/26, Canisteo, N.Y.   BR/TR, 5'9", 165 lbs.   Deb: 9/30/11

YEAR	TM/L	W	L	PCT	G	GS	CG	SH	SV	IP	H	HR	BB	SO	RAT	ERA	ERA+	OAV	OOB	BH	AVG	PB	PR	/A	PD	TPI
1911	Phi-A	0	1	.000	1	0	0	0	0	3	3	0	1	0	12.0	0.00	—	.273	.333				1	1	0	0.4

● JACK ARMSTRONG
Armstrong, Jack William   b: 3/7/65, Englewood, N.J.   BR/TR, 6'5", 220 lbs.   Deb: 6/21/88

YEAR	TM/L	W	L	PCT	G	GS	CG	SH	SV	IP	H	HR	BB	SO	RAT	ERA	ERA+	OAV	OOB	BH	AVG	PB	PR	/A	PD	TPI
1988	Cin-N	4	7	.364	14	13	0	0	0	65¹	63	8	38	45	13.9	5.79	62	.256	.356	2	.095	-1	-17	-16	1	-2.4
1989	Cin-N	2	3	.400	9	8	0	0	0	42²	40	5	21	23	12.9	4.64	78	.245	.332	0	.000	-1	-5	-5	0	-0.6
1990	*Cin-N★	12	9	.571	29	27	2	1	0	166	151	9	59	110	11.7	3.42	115	.241	.313	5	.106	-2	7	10	0	1.0
1991	Cin-N	7	13	.350	27	24	1	0	0	139²	158	25	54	93	13.8	5.48	69	.293	.359	4	.093	-2	-28	-26	-1	-3.4
1992	Cle-A	6	15	.286	35	23	1	0	0	166²	176	23	67	114	13.3	4.64	84	.269	.340		—	0	-13	-14	1	-1.3
1993	Fla-N	9	17	.346	36	33	0	0	0	196¹	210	29	78	118	13.5	4.49	96	.271	.343	10	.152	-2	-10	-4	-0	-0.6
1994	Tex-A	0	1	.000	2	2	0	0	0	10	9	3	2	7	9.9	3.60	134	.231	.268	0	—	0	1	1	0	0.1
Total	7	40	65	.381	152	130	4	1	0	786²	807	102	319	510	13.1	4.58	87	.265	.338	21	.114	-6	-65	-53	2	-7.2

● MIKE ARMSTRONG
Armstrong, Michael Dennis   b: 3/7/54, Glen Cove, N.Y.   BR/TR, 6'3", 206 lbs.   Deb: 8/12/80

YEAR	TM/L	W	L	PCT	G	GS	CG	SH	SV	IP	H	HR	BB	SO	RAT	ERA	ERA+	OAV	OOB	BH	AVG	PB	PR	/A	PD	TPI
1980	SD-N	0	0	—	11	0	0	0	0	14¹	16	1	13	14	18.2	5.65	61	.296	.433	0	.000	-0	-3	-4	-0	-0.1
1981	SD-N	0	2	.000	10	0	0	0	0	12	14	1	11	9	18.8	6.00	54	.311	.446	0	.000	-0	-3	-4	-0	-0.6
1982	KC-A	5	5	.500	52	0	0	0	6	112²	88	9	43	75	10.7	3.20	128	.215	.295	0	—	0	11	11	-1	0.9
1983	KC-A	10	7	.588	58	0	0	0	3	102²	86	11	45	52	11.7	3.86	106	.228	.315	0	—	0	3	4	0	0.3
1984	NY-A	3	2	.600	36	0	0	0	1	54¹	47	6	26	43	12.1	3.48	109	.239	.327	0	—	0	4	4	0	0.3
1985	NY-A	0	0	—	9	0	0	0	0	14²	9	2	4	11	6.8	3.07	130	.173	.204	0	—	0	2	2	0	0.1
1986	NY-A	0	0	—	7	1	0	0	0	8²	13	4	5	8	18.7	9.35	44	.351	.429	0	—	0	-5	-5	-0	-0.5
1987	Cle-A	1	0	1.000	14	0	0	0	0	18²	27	4	10	17	17.8	8.68	52	.333	.407	0	—	0	-9	-9	-0	-0.5
Total	8	19	17	.528	197	1	0	0	11	338	300	42	155	221	12.3	4.10	97	.240	.326	0	.000	-0	-2	-4	-3	0.3

● SCOTT ARNOLD
Arnold, Scott Gentry   b: 8/18/62, Lexington, Ky.   BR/TR, 6'2", 210 lbs.   Deb: 4/7/88

YEAR	TM/L	W	L	PCT	G	GS	CG	SH	SV	IP	H	HR	BB	SO	RAT	ERA	ERA+	OAV	OOB	BH	AVG	PB	PR	/A	PD	TPI
1988	StL-N	0	0	—	6	0	0	0	0	6²	9	0	4	8	17.6	5.40	64	.321	.406		—	0	-1	-1	0	0.0

● TONY ARNOLD
Arnold, Tony Dale   b: 5/3/59, ElPaso, Tex.   BR/TR, 5'11", 170 lbs.   Deb: 8/9/86

YEAR	TM/L	W	L	PCT	G	GS	CG	SH	SV	IP	H	HR	BB	SO	RAT	ERA	ERA+	OAV	OOB	BH	AVG	PB	PR	/A	PD	TPI
1986	Bal-A	0	2	.000	11	0	0	0	0	25¹	25	0	11	7	12.8	3.55	116	.278	.356	0	—	0	2	1	1	0.3
1987	Bal-A	0	0	—	27	0	0	0	0	53	71	8	17	18	15.3	5.77	76	.330	.385	0	—	0	-8	-8	2	0.2
Total	2	0	2	.000	38	0	0	0	0	78¹	96	8	28	25	14.5	5.06	85	.315	.376	0	—	0	-6	-6	3	0.5

YEAR	TM/L	W	L	PCT	G	GS	CG	SH	SV	IP	H	HR	BB	SO	RAT	ERA	ERA+	OAV	OOB	BH	AVG	PB	PR	/A	PD	TPI

● **BRAD ARNSBERG**   Arnsberg, Bradley James   b: 8/20/63, Seattle, Wash.   BR/TR, 6'4", 205 lbs.   Deb: 9/6/86

1986	NY-A	0	0	—	2	1	0	0	0	8	13	1	1	3	15.8	3.38	121	.342	.359	0	—	0	1	1	-0	0.0
1987	NY-A	1	3	.250	6	2	0	0	0	19¹	22	5	13	14	16.3	5.59	78	.289	.393	0	—	0	-2	-3	1	-0.4
1989	Tex-A	2	1	.667	16	1	0	0	1	48	45	6	22	26	13.1	4.13	96	.247	.338	0	—	0	-1	-1	1	0.0
1990	Tex-A	6	1	.857	53	0	0	0	5	62²	56	4	33	44	13.1	2.15	182	.235	.333	0	—	0	12	12	1	1.5
1991	Tex-A	0	1	.000	9	0	0	0	0	9²	10	5	8	5	14.0	8.38	48	.256	.341	0	—	0	-5	-5	-0	-0.4
1992	Cle-A	0	0	—	8	0	0	0	0	10²	13	6	11	5	21.9	11.81	33	.317	.481	0	—	0	-9	-9	-0	0.1
Total	6	9	6	.600	94	6	0	0	6	158¹	159	27	85	100	14.3	4.26	94	.259	.356	0	—	0	-5	-5	2	0.8

● **ORIE ARNTZEN**   Arntzen, Orie Edgar "Old Folks"   b: 10/18/09, Beverly, Ill.   d: 1/28/70, Cedar Rapids, Iowa   BR/TR, 6'1", 200 lbs.   Deb: 4/20/43

1943	Phi-A	4	13	.235	32	20	9	0	0	164¹	172	5	69	66	13.5	4.22	81	.277	.354	8	.160	-1	-17	-15	-3	-1.9

● **RENE AROCHA**   Arocha, Rene (Magaly)   b: 2/24/66, Havana, Cuba   BR/TR, 6', 180 lbs.   Deb: 4/9/93

1993	StL-N	11	8	.579	32	29	1	0	0	188	197	20	31	96	11.1	3.78	105	.271	.304	6	.103	-2	5	4	-1	0.1
1994	StL-N	4	4	.500	45	7	1	1	11	83	94	9	21	62	12.9	4.01	104	.286	.336	1	.111	0	2	1	-0	0.1
1995	StL-N	3	5	.375	41	0	0	0	0	49²	55	6	18	25	13.8	3.99	105	.297	.369	0	.000	-0	1	1	0	0.2
Total	3	18	17	.514	118	36	2	1	11	320²	346	35	70	183	12.0	3.87	104	.279	.322	7	.103	-2	8	6	-1	0.4

● **GERRY ARRIGO**   Arrigo, Gerald William   b: 6/12/41, Chicago, Ill.   BL/TL, 6'1", 195 lbs.   Deb: 6/12/61

1961	Min-A	0	1	.000	7	2	0	0	0	9²	9	0	10	6	19.6	10.24	41	.265	.457	1	.500	0	-7	-6	0	-0.5
1962	Min-A	0	0	—	1	0	0	0	0	1	1	1	1	1	36.0	18.00	23	.600	.667	0	.000	0	-2	-2	0	0.0
1963	Min-A	1	2	.333	5	1	0	0	0	15²	12	2	4	13	9.2	2.87	127	.211	.262	0	.000	-0	1	1	0	0.0
1964	Min-A	7	4	.636	41	12	3	2	1	105¹	97	11	45	96	12.3	3.84	93	.244	.324	5	.172	1	-3	-3	0	-0.2
1965	Cin-N	2	4	.333	27	5	0	0	2	54	75	4	30	43	17.8	6.17	61	.342	.426	2	.167	1	-16	-15	-1	-1.7
1966	Cin-N	0	0	—	3	0	0	0	0	7¹	7	2	3	3	12.3	4.91	79	.250	.323	0	.000	-0	-1	-1	-0	0.0
	NY-N	3	3	.500	17	5	0	0	0	43¹	47	5	16	28	13.1	3.74	97	.276	.339	5	.500	3	-1	-0	1	0.3
	Yr	3	3	.500	20	5	0	0	0	50²	54	7	19	31	13.0	3.91	94	.273	.336	5	.455	3	-2	-1	0	0.3
1967	Cin-N	6	6	.500	32	5	1	1	1	74	61	6	35	56	12.2	3.16	119	.232	.331	4	.211	1	2	5	-2	0.7
1968	Cin-N	12	10	.545	36	31	5	1	0	205¹	181	13	77	140	11.5	3.33	95	.237	.310	5	.075	-2	-8	-4	1	-0.5
1969	Cin-N	4	7	.364	20	16	1	0	0	91	89	9	61	35	15.6	4.15	91	.256	.379	5	.161	-0	-6	-4	-2	-0.7
1970	Chi-A	0	3	.000	5	3	0	0	0	13¹	14	2	9	12	22.3	12.83	30	.393	.471	0	.000	-0	-13	-13	-0	-2.2
Total	10	35	40	.467	194	80	9	3	4	620	605	56	291	433	13.3	4.14	85	.258	.345	27	.151	2	-52	-42	-3	-4.6

● **FERNANDO ARROYO**   Arroyo, Fernando   b: 3/21/52, Sacramento, Cal.   BR/TR, 6'3", 195 lbs.   Deb: 6/28/75

1975	Det-A	2	1	.667	14	1	0	0	0	53¹	56	5	22	25	13.3	4.56	88	.272	.345	0	—	0	-5	-3	1	-0.1
1977	Det-A	8	18	.308	38	28	8	1	0	209¹	227	23	52	60	12.0	4.17	103	.278	.321	0	—	0	-3	3	6	0.6
1978	Det-A	0	0	—	2	0	0	0	0	4¹	11	1	0	1	18.7	8.31	47	.400	.429	0	—	0	-2	-2	0	-0.1
1979	Det-A	1	1	.500	6	0	0	0	0	12	17	3	4	7	15.8	8.25	52	.340	.389	0	—	0	-5	-5	-0	-0.8
1980	Min-A	6	6	.500	21	11	1	1	0	92¹	97	7	32	27	12.8	4.68	93	.273	.337	0	—	0	-7	-3	-1	-1.0
1981	Min-A	7	10	.412	23	19	2	0	0	128¹	144	11	34	39	12.8	3.93	100	.290	.342	0	—	0	-4	0	0	-0.3
1982	Min-A	0	1	.000	6	0	0	0	0	13²	17	2	6	4	15.1	5.27	81	.321	.390	0	—	0	-2	-1	1	-0.2
	Oak-A	0	0	—	10	0	0	0	0	22¹	23	4	7	9	12.5	5.24	75	.271	.333	0	—	0	-3	-3	0	0.3
	Yr	0	1	.000	16	0	0	0	0	36	40	6	13	13	13.5	5.25	77	.288	.353	0	—	0	-5	-5	1	0.1
1986	Oak-A	0	0	—	1	0	0	0	0	0	0	0	3	0	—	—	—	—	1.000	—	—	—	0	0	0	0.5
Total	8	24	37	.393	121	60	12	3	0	535²	589	56	160	172	12.8	4.44	94	.283	.337	0	—	0	-30	-16	7	-1.1

● **LUIS ARROYO**   Arroyo, Luis Enrique   b: 2/18/27, Penuelas, P.R.   BL/TL, 5'8", 190 lbs.   Deb: 4/20/55

1955	StL-N☆	11	8	.579	35	24	9	1	0	159	162	22	63	68	12.8	4.19	97	.261	.331	13	.232	1	-3	-2	-2	-0.4
1956	Pit-N	3	3	.500	18	2	1	0	0	28²	36	5	12	17	15.1	4.71	80	.298	.361	2	.500	1	-3	-3	0	-0.5
1957	Pit-N	3	11	.214	54	10	0	0	1	130²	151	19	31	101	13.0	4.68	81	.282	.329	5	.156	-1	-12	-13	-2	-1.5
1959	Cin-N	1	0	1.000	10	0	0	0	0	13²	17	0	11	8	18.4	3.95	103	.321	.438	0	.000	-0	5	3	0	0.5
1960	*NY-A	5	1	.833	29	0	0	0	7	40²	30	2	22	29	11.5	2.88	125	.207	.311	0	.000	-0	5	3	0	0.5
1961	*NY-A☆	15	5	.750	65	0	0	0	29	119	83	5	49	87	10.2	2.19	169	.199	.288	7	.280	2	24	20	-1	4.3
1962	NY-A	1	3	.250	27	0	0	0	7	33²	33	5	17	21	13.6	4.81	78	.262	.354	2	.500	1	-3	-4	-1	-0.6
1963	NY-A	1	1	.500	6	0	0	0	0	6	12	0	3	5	22.5	13.50	26	.444	.500	0	—	0	-7	-7	-0	-1.8
Total	8	40	32	.556	244	36	10	1	44	531¹	524	58	208	336	12.6	3.93	98	.256	.329	29	.227	3	2	-5	-5	0.0

● **RUDY ARROYO**   Arroyo, Rudolph   b: 6/19/50, New York, N.Y.   BL/TL, 6'2", 195 lbs.   Deb: 6/1/71

1971	StL-N	0	1	.000	9	0	0	0	0	11²	18	2	5	5	17.7	5.40	67	.375	.434	0	.000	-0	-3	-3	0	-0.2

● **HARRY ARUNDEL**   Arundel, Harry   b: 2/1855, Philadelphia, Pa.   d: 3/25/04, Cleveland, Ohio   TR, 5'6", 145 lbs.   Deb: 7/19/1875

1875	Atl-n	0	1	.000	1	1	0	0	0	2¹	6	0	0	0	23.1	7.71	27	.400	.400	0	.000	-1	-1	-1		-0.4
1882	Pit-a	4	10	.286	14	14	13	0	0	120	155	3	23	47	13.4	4.65	56	.294	.323	10	.189	0	-26	-27	5	-2.0
1884	Pro-N	1	0	1.000	1	1	1	0	0	9	8	0	4	4	12.0	1.00	282	.250	.333	1	.333	0	2	2	-0	0.2
Total	2	5	10	.333	15	15	14	0	0	129	163	3	27	51	13.3	4.40	60	.291	.324	11	.196	-1	-24	-25	5	-1.8

● **KEN ASH**   Ash, Kenneth Lowther   b: 9/16/01, Anmoore, W.Va.   d: 11/15/79, Clarksburg, W.Va.   BR/TR, 5'11", 165 lbs.   Deb: 4/17/25

1925	Chi-A	0	0	—	2	0	0	0	0	4	7	0	2	0	15.8	9.00	46	.389	.389	0	—	0	-2	-2	-0	0.0
1928	Cin-N	3	3	.500	8	5	2	0	0	36	43	1	13	6	14.3	6.50	61	.314	.377	1	.071	-1	-10	-10	0	-1.4
1929	Cin-N	1	5	.167	29	7	2	0	2	82	91	2	30	26	13.8	4.83	95	.292	.363	4	.143	-1	7	6	1	-0.3
1930	Cin-N	2	0	1.000	16	1	1	0	0	39¹	37	3	16	15	12.1	3.43	141	.268	.344	2	.182	-1	7	6	1	0.3
Total	4	6	8	.429	55	13	5	0	2	161¹	178	6	59	47	13.6	4.96	90	.294	.363	6	.130	-3	-6	-9	1	-1.4

● **ANDY ASHBY**   Ashby, Andrew Jason   b: 7/11/67, Kansas City, Mo.   BR/TR, 6'5", 180 lbs.   Deb: 6/10/91

1991	Phi-N	1	5	.167	8	8	0	0	0	42	41	5	19	26	13.5	6.00	61	.256	.346	1	.083	-1	-11	-11	0	-1.4
1992	Phi-N	1	3	.250	10	8	0	0	0	37	42	6	21	24	15.6	7.54	46	.290	.383	1	.091	-0	-17	-17	0	-1.6
1993	Col-N	0	4	.000	20	9	0	0	0	54	89	6	32	33	20.7	8.50	56	.377	.458	4	.267	0	-27	-22	1	-1.4
	SD-N	3	6	.333	12	12	0	0	0	69	79	14	24	44	13.6	5.48	75	.295	.355	1	.048	-1	-11	-10	0	-1.2
	Yr	3	10	.231	32	21	0	0	0	123	168	19	56	77	16.5	6.80	65	.329	.397	5	.139	-1	-38	-33	1	-2.6
1994	SD-N	6	11	.353	24	24	4	0	0	164¹	145	16	43	121	10.5	3.40	121	.233	.286	8	.163	-0	15	13	0	1.2
1995	SD-N	12	10	.545	31	31	2	2	0	192²	180	17	62	150	11.8	2.94	137	.252	.322	8	.163	-0	26	23	-2	2.3
1996	*SD-N	9	5	.643	24	24	1	0	0	150²	147	17	34	85	11.0	3.23	124	.259	.305	11	.244	3	17	13	1	1.5
Total	6	32	44	.421	129	116	7	2	1	709²	723	80	235	483	12.5	4.20	97	.267	.331	34	.168	1	-7	-11	-0	-0.6

● **PAUL ASSENMACHER**   Assenmacher, Paul Andre   b: 12/10/60, Detroit, Mich.   BL/TL, 6'3", 195 lbs.   Deb: 4/12/86

1986	Atl-N	7	3	.700	61	0	0	0	7	68¹	61	5	26	56	11.5	2.50	159	.241	.312	0	.000	-0	9	11	1	1.9
1987	Atl-N	1	1	.500	52	0	0	0	2	54²	58	8	24	39	13.7	5.10	85	.260	.335	0	.000	-0	-6	-5	-1	-0.3
1988	Atl-N	8	7	.533	64	0	0	0	5	79¹	72	4	32	71	11.9	3.06	120	.251	.328	1	.333	1	3	5	0	1.2
1989	Atl-N	1	3	.250	49	0	0	0	0	57²	55	2	16	64	11.2	3.59	102	.249	.303	0	.000	-0	-1	0	0	0.0
	*Chi-N	2	1	.667	14	0	0	0	0	19	19	1	12	15	14.7	5.21	72	.275	.325	0	.000	-0	-4	-3	0	-0.5
	Yr	3	4	.429	63	0	0	0	0	76²	74	3	28	79	12.0	3.99	92	.253	.318	0	.000	-1	-4	-3	1	-0.5
1990	Chi-N	7	2	.778	74	0	0	0	10	103	90	10	36	95	11.1	2.80	146	.239	.308	0	.000	-1	11	15	1	1.5
1991	Chi-N	7	8	.467	75	0	0	0	15	102²	85	10	31	117	10.4	3.24	120	.223	.287	1	.250	-0	5	7	-1	1.2
1992	Chi-N	4	4	.500	70	0	0	0	8	68	72	6	26	67	13.4	4.10	88	.271	.342	0	.000	-0	-5	-4	-1	-0.6
1993	Chi-N	2	1	.667	46	0	0	0	0	38²	44	3	13	34	13.3	3.49	114	.288	.343	1	.500	3	1	2	-0	0.1
	NY-A	2	2	.500	26	0	0	0	0	17¹	10	0	9	11	10.4	3.12	133	.175	.299	0	—	0	5	4	0	0.4
1994	Chi-A	1	2	.333	44	0	0	0	1	33	26	3	13	29	10.9	3.55	132	.224	.308	0	—	0	5	6	0	0.7
1995	*Cle-A	6	2	.750	47	0	0	0	0	38¹	32	3	12	40	11.0	2.82	167	.225	.299	0	—	0	10	9	0	1.0
1996	*Cle-A	4	2	.667	63	0	0	0	1	46²	46	1	14	44	12.3	3.09	159	.260	.328	0	—	0	9	8	0	1.0
Total	11	52	38	.578	685	0	0	0	49	726²	670	57	264	682	11.8	3.38	120	.246	.317	3	.083	-0	41	54	0	7.7

YEAR	TM/L	W	L	PCT	G	GS	CG	SH	SV	IP	H	HR	BB	SO	RAT	ERA	ERA+	OAV	OOB	BH	AVG	PB	PR	/A	PD	TPI

● **PEDRO ASTACIO** Astacio, Pedro Julio (Pura) b: 11/28/69, Hato Mayor, D.R. BR/TR, 6'2", 174 lbs. Deb: 7/3/92

1992	LA-N	5	5	.500	11	11	4	4	0	82	80	1	20	43	11.2	1.98	174	.255	.304	3	.125	-1	14	13	-0	1.6
1993	LA-N	14	9	.609	31	31	3	2	0	186¹	165	14	68	122	11.5	3.57	107	.239	.312	10	.161	-1	10	5	-1	0.3
1994	LA-N	6	8	.429	23	23	3	1	0	149	142	18	47	108	11.7	4.29	91	.252	.314	3	.064	-3	-1	-6	-1	-0.9
1995	*LA-N	7	8	.467	48	11	1	1	0	104	103	12	29	80	11.8	4.24	91	.261	.318	3	.125	-0	-1	-5	0	-0.7
1996	*LA-N	9	8	.529	35	32	0	0	0	211²	207	18	67	130	12.0	3.44	112	.261	.326	6	.088	-3	18	10	1	0.4
Total	5	41	38	.519	148	108	11	8	0	733	697	63	231	483	11.7	3.60	106	.253	.316	25	.111	-8	40	17	-1	0.7

● **KEITH ATHERTON** Atherton, Keith Rowe b: 2/19/59, Newport News, Va. BR/TR, 6'4", 200 lbs. Deb: 7/14/83

1983	Oak-A	2	5	.286	29	0	0	0	4	68¹	53	7	23	40	10.1	2.77	139	.215	.285	0	.000	0	10	8	-1	0.8
1984	Oak-A	7	6	.538	57	0	0	0	2	104	110	13	39	58	13.1	4.33	86	.274	.341	0	—	0	-4	-7	-2	-1.0
1985	Oak-A	4	7	.364	56	0	0	0	3	104²	89	17	42	77	11.3	4.30	90	.231	.306	0	—	0	-2	-5	-2	-0.3
1986	Oak-A	1	2	.333	13	0	0	0	0	15¹	18	2	11	8	17.0	5.87	66	.295	.403	0	—	0	-3	-3	-0	-0.2
	Min-A	5	8	.385	47	0	0	0	10	81²	82	9	35	59	13.0	3.75	115	.264	.340	0	—	0	4	5	-0	0.7
	Yr	6	10	.375	60	0	0	0	10	97	100	11	46	67	13.6	4.08	104	.267	.349	0	—	0	1	2	-0	0.5
1987	*Min-A	7	5	.583	59	0	0	0	2	79¹	81	10	30	51	13.0	4.54	102	.262	.335	0	—	0	-1	1	-0	0.1
1988	Min-A	7	5	.583	49	0	0	0	3	74	65	10	22	43	10.8	3.41	119	.235	.296	0	—	0	5	5	-0	0.7
1989	Cle-A	0	3	.000	32	0	0	0	2	39	48	7	13	13	14.1	4.15	95	.293	.345	0	—	0	-1	-1	-1	-0.2
Total	7	33	41	.446	342	0	0	0	26	566¹	546	75	215	349	12.3	3.99	101	.253	.324	0	.000	0	8	3	-6	0.6

● **TOMMY ATKINS** Atkins, Francis Montgomery b: 12/9/1887, Ponca, Neb. d: 5/7/56, Cleveland, Ohio BL/TL, 5'10.5", 165 lbs. Deb: 10/2/09

1909	Phi-A	0	0	—	1	1	0	0	0	6	6	0	5	4	16.5	4.50	53	.261	.393	0	.000	-0	-1	-1	0	0.0
1910	Phi-A	3	2	.600	15	3	2	0	2	57	53	0	23	29	12.2	2.68	88	.254	.330	2	.118	-1	-1	-2	0	-0.3
Total	2	3	2	.600	16	4	2	0	2	63	59	0	28	33	12.6	2.86	83	.254	.337	2	.105	-1	-2	-3	0	-0.3

● **JAMES ATKINS** Atkins, James Curtis b: 3/10/21, Birmingham, Ala. BL/TR, 6'3", 205 lbs. Deb: 9/29/50

1950	Bos-A	0	0	—	1	0	0	0	0	4²	4	1	4	0	17.4	3.86	127	.235	.409	0	.000	-0	0	1	-0	0.0
1952	Bos-A	0	1	.000	3	1	0	0	0	10¹	11	0	7	2	15.7	3.48	113	.275	.383	2	.667	1	0	1	0	0.1
Total	2	0	1	.000	4	1	0	0	0	15	15	1	11	2	16.2	3.60	118	.263	.391	2	.400	1	1	1	0	0.1

● **AL ATKINSON** Atkinson, Albert Wright b: 3/9/1861, Clinton, Ill. d: 6/17/52, Elkhorn Township, Mo. BR/TR, 5'11.5", 165 lbs. Deb: 5/1/1884

1884	Phi-a	11	11	.500	22	22	20	1	0	184	186	3	21	93	10.6	4.21	80	.244	.274	16	.193	-1	-20	-17	0	-1.7
	CP-U	6	10	.375	16	16	16	1	0	140	127	1	21	104	9.5	2.76	88	.226	.253	14	.206	-5	-5	-5	1	-0.9
	Bal-U	3	5	.375	8	8	8	0	0	69²	60	4	12	50	9.3	2.33	115	.217	.249	4	.138	-4	1	3	0	-0.1
	Yr	9	15	.375	24	24	24	1	0	209²	187	5	33	154	9.4	2.62	96	.223	.252	18	.186	-9	-4	-2	1	-1.0
1886	Phi-a	25	17	.595	45	45	44	1	0	396²	414	11	101	154	12.2	3.95	89	.256	.308	18	.122	-6	-22	-20	-2	-2.4
1887	Phi-a	6	8	.429	15	15	11	0	0	124²	156	2	54	34	15.6	5.92	72	.292	.364	12	.203	-1	-22	-23	1	-1.8
Total	3	51	51	.500	106	106	99	3	0	915	943	21	209	435	11.7	3.96	85	.251	.297	64	.165	-16	-68	-61	-1	-6.9

● **BILL ATKINSON** Atkinson, William Cecil Glenn b: 10/4/54, Chatham, Ont., Can. BL/TR, 5'7", 165 lbs. Deb: 9/18/76

1976	Mon-N	0	0	—	4	0	0	0	0	5	3	0	1	4	7.2	0.00	—	.176	.222	0	—	0	2	2	0	0.0
1977	Mon-N	7	2	.778	55	0	0	0	7	83¹	72	12	29	56	10.9	3.35	114	.234	.300	1	.200	-0	5	4	1	0.6
1978	Mon-N	2	2	.500	29	0	0	0	3	45¹	45	5	28	32	14.7	4.37	81	.268	.376	2	.500	1	-4	-4	0	-0.3
1979	Mon-N	2	0	1.000	10	0	0	0	1	13²	9	0	4	7	8.6	1.98	186	.170	.228	0	.000	-0	3	3	-0	0.3
Total	4	11	4	.733	98	0	0	0	11	147¹	129	17	62	99	11.7	3.42	108	.236	.315	3	.300	1	6	5	1	0.6

● **DEREK AUCOIN** Aucoin, Derek Alfred b: 3/27/70, Lachine, Que., Can. BR/TR, 6'7", 235 lbs. Deb: 5/21/96

| 1996 | Mon-N | 0 | 1 | .000 | 2 | 0 | 0 | 0 | 0 | 2² | 3 | 0 | 1 | 3 | 13.5 | 3.38 | 128 | .300 | .364 | 0 | — | 0 | 0 | 0 | 0 | 0.1 |

● **DON AUGUST** August, Donald Glenn b: 7/3/63, Inglewood, Cal. BR/TR, 6'3", 190 lbs. Deb: 6/2/88

1988	Mil-A	13	7	.650	24	22	6	1	0	148¹	137	12	48	66	11.2	3.09	129	.245	.305	0	—	0	14	15	2	2.1
1989	Mil-A	12	12	.500	31	25	2	1	0	142¹	175	17	58	51	14.9	5.31	72	.302	.368	0	—	0	-23	-23	1	-3.3
1990	Mil-A	0	3	.000	5	0	0	0	0	11	13	0	5	2	14.7	6.55	59	.295	.367	0	—	0	-3	-3	0	-0.7
1991	Mil-A	9	8	.529	28	23	1	1	0	138¹	166	18	47	62	14.1	5.47	73	.301	.359	0	—	0	-21	-23	1	-2.3
Total	4	34	30	.531	88	70	9	3	0	440	491	47	158	181	13.4	4.64	85	.283	.345	0	—	0	-33	-35	4	-4.2

● **JERRY AUGUSTINE** Augustine, Gerald Lee b: 7/24/52, Kewaunee, Wis. BL/TL, 6', 185 lbs. Deb: 9/9/75

1975	Mil-A	2	0	1.000	5	3	1	0	0	26²	26	2	12	8	13.2	3.04	126	.274	.361	0	—	0	2	2	-0	0.1
1976	Mil-A	9	12	.429	39	24	5	3	0	171²	167	9	56	59	11.9	3.30	106	.261	.324	0	—	0	4	4	-2	0.3
1977	Mil-A	12	18	.400	33	33	10	1	0	209	222	16	72	68	12.8	4.48	91	.277	.339	0	—	0	-10	-10	-1	-1.2
1978	Mil-A	13	12	.520	35	30	9	2	0	188¹	204	14	61	59	12.9	4.54	83	.280	.339	0	—	0	-16	-16	2	-1.7
1979	Mil-A	9	6	.600	43	2	0	0	5	85²	95	6	30	41	13.2	3.47	120	.284	.344	0	—	0	7	7	-2	1.0
1980	Mil-A	4	3	.571	39	1	0	0	2	69²	83	5	36	22	15.6	4.52	86	.301	.385	0	—	0	-4	-5	0	-0.4
1981	Mil-A	2	2	.500	27	2	0	0	2	61¹	75	4	18	26	13.8	4.26	80	.300	.349	0	—	0	-4	-6	0	-0.3
1982	Mil-A	1	3	.250	20	2	1	0	0	62	63	13	26	22	13.2	5.08	74	.267	.345	0	—	0	-7	-9	-1	-0.2
1983	Mil-A	3	3	.500	34	7	1	0	2	64¹	89	11	25	40	16.1	5.74	65	.328	.387	0	—	0	-12	-14	0	-1.3
1984	Mil-A	0	0	—	3	0	0	0	0	5¹	4	0	4	3	15.2	0.00	—	.211	.375	0	—	0	2	2	0	0.2
Total	10	55	59	.482	279	104	27	6	11	944	1028	87	340	348	13.2	4.23	90	.281	.346	0	—	0	-37	-45	-3	-3.7

● **ELDEN AUKER** Auker, Elden Le Roy "Submarine" b: 9/21/10, Norcatur, Kan. BR/TR, 6'2", 194 lbs. Deb: 8/10/33

1933	Det-A	3	3	.500	15	6	2	1	0	55	63	3	25	17	14.7	5.24	82	.285	.363	2	.118	-1	-6	-6	-1	-0.7
1934	*Det-A	15	7	.682	43	18	10	2	1	205	234	9	56	86	12.9	3.42	128	.288	.336	11	.149	-2	24	22	3	2.1
1935	*Det-A	18	7	.720	36	25	13	2	0	195	213	13	61	63	13.1	3.83	109	.279	.340	16	.216	1	14	7	1	1.0
1936	Det-A	13	16	.448	35	31	14	2	0	215¹	263	11	83	66	14.6	4.89	101	.302	.365	24	.308	7	4	1	5	1.2
1937	Det-A	17	9	.654	39	32	19	1	1	252²	250	11	97	72	12.6	3.88	120	.260	.331	18	.198	-4	21	22	5	2.9
1938	Det-A	11	10	.524	27	24	12	1	0	160²	184	14	56	46	13.7	5.27	95	.284	.351	5	.088	-4	-9	-5	3	-0.6
1939	Bos-A	9	10	.474	31	25	6	1	0	151	183	14	61	43	14.6	5.36	88	.294	.358	12	.226	-2	-12	-11	2	-0.8
1940	StL-A	16	11	.593	38	35	20	2	0	263²	299	17	96	75	13.6	3.96	116	.281	.342	19	.213	3	12	18	2	2.1
1941	StL-A	14	15	.483	34	31	13	0	0	216	268	20	85	60	14.8	5.50	78	.303	.365	10	.125	-3	-32	-29	1	-3.3
1942	StL-A	14	13	.519	35	34	17	2	0	249	273	16	86	62	13.1	4.08	91	.277	.337	14	.161	-1	-12	-11	1	-1.1
Total	10	130	101	.563	333	261	126	14	2	1963¹	2230	129	706	594	13.6	4.42	101	.285	.347	131	.187	6	3	11	21	2.8

● **JOE AUSANIO** Ausanio, Joseph John b: 12/9/65, Kingston, N.Y. BR/TR, 6'1", 205 lbs. Deb: 7/14/94

1994	NY-A	2	1	.667	13	0	0	0	0	15²	16	3	6	15	12.6	5.17	80	.254	.319	0	—	0	-1	-1	0	0.0
1995	NY-A	2	0	1.000	28	0	0	0	1	37²	42	9	23	36	15.5	5.73	80	.286	.382	0	—	0	-4	-5	-0	-0.2
Total	2	4	1	.800	41	0	0	0	1	53¹	58	12	29	51	14.7	5.57	83	.276	.364	0	—	0	-5	-6	-0	-0.2

● **DENNIS AUST** Aust, Dennis Kay b: 11/25/40, Tecumseh, Neb. BR/TR, 5'11", 180 lbs. Deb: 9/6/65

1965	StL-N	0	0	—	6	0	0	0	1	7¹	6	0	2	7	9.8	4.91	78	.214	.267	0	.000	-0	-1	-1	0	0.0
1966	StL-N	0	1	.000	9	0	0	0	1	9²	12	1	6	7	16.8	6.52	55	.308	.400	0	.000	-0	-3	-3	-0	-0.4
Total	2	0	1	.000	15	0	0	0	2	17	18	1	8	14	13.8	5.82	64	.269	.347	0	.000	-0	-4	-4	0	-0.4

● **JIM AUSTIN** Austin, James Parker b: 12/7/63, Farmville, Va. BR/TR, 6'2", 200 lbs. Deb: 7/4/91

1991	Mil-A	0	0	—	5	0	0	0	0	8²	8	1	11	3	22.8	8.31	48	.276	.512	0	—	0	-4	-4	0	0.1
1992	Mil-A	5	2	.714	47	0	0	0	0	58¹	38	2	32	30	11.1	1.85	207	.191	.309	0	—	0	14	13	-1	1.5
1993	Mil-A	1	2	.333	31	0	0	0	0	33	28	3	13	15	11.5	3.82	111	.230	.309	0	—	0	2	2	-0	0.1
Total	3	6	4	.600	83	0	0	0	0	100	74	6	56	48	12.2	3.06	130	.211	.330	0	—	0	11	10	-1	1.7

● **RICK AUSTIN** Austin, Rick Gerald b: 10/27/46, Seattle, Wash. BR/TL, 6'4", 190 lbs. Deb: 6/21/70

1970	Cle-A	2	5	.286	31	8	1	1	3	67²	74	10	26	53	13.7	4.79	83	.281	.353	2	.111	0	-8	-6	1	-0.5
1971	Cle-A	0	0	—	23	0	0	0	2	23	25	3	20	20	18.8	5.09	75	.291	.440	0	.000	-0	-4	-3	0	0.0
1975	Mil-A	2	3	.400	32	0	0	0	2	40	32	3	32	30	14.6	4.05	95	.222	.367	0	—	0	-1	-1	-1	-0.2

YEAR TM/L	W	L	PCT	G	GS	CG	SH	SV	IP	H	HR	BB	SO	RAT	ERA	ERA+	OAV	OOB	BH	AVG	PB	PR	/A	PD	TPI
1976 Mil-A	0	0	—	3	0	0	0	0	5¹	10	1	0	3	18.6	5.06	69	.435	.458	0	—	0	-1	-1	0	0.0
Total 4	4	8	.333	89	8	1	1	0	136	141	17	78	106	15.0	4.63	84	.273	.377	2	.105	0	-14	-11	1	-0.7

● **AL AUTRY**   Autry, Albert   b: 2/29/52, Modesto, Cal.   BR/TR, 6'5", 225 lbs.   Deb: 9/14/76

YEAR TM/L	W	L	PCT	G	GS	CG	SH	SV	IP	H	HR	BB	SO	RAT	ERA	ERA+	OAV	OOB	BH	AVG	PB	PR	/A	PD	TPI
1976 Atl-N	1	0	1.000	1	1	0	0	0	5	4	2	3	2	12.6	5.40	70	.222	.333	0	.000	-0	-1	-1	-0	-0.2

● **STEVE AVERY**   Avery, Steven Thomas   b: 4/14/70, Trenton, Mich.   BL/TL, 6'4", 180 lbs.   Deb: 6/13/90

YEAR TM/L	W	L	PCT	G	GS	CG	SH	SV	IP	H	HR	BB	SO	RAT	ERA	ERA+	OAV	OOB	BH	AVG	PB	PR	/A	PD	TPI
1990 Atl-N	3	11	.214	21	20	1	1	0	99	121	7	45	75	15.3	5.64	72	.302	.375	4	.133	-1	-20	-18	2	-2.1
1991 ★Atl-N	18	8	.692	35	35	3	1	0	210¹	189	21	65	137	11.0	3.38	115	.240	.300	17	.215	3	-7	12	-0	1.8
1992 ★Atl-N	11	11	.500	35	35	2	2	0	233²	216	14	71	129	11.1	3.20	114	.246	.302	13	.171	2	8	12	-0	1.2
1993 ★Atl-N★	18	6	.750	35	35	3	1	0	223¹	216	14	43	125	10.4	2.94	136	.261	.297	12	.160	1	27	27	2	2.9
1994 Atl-N	8	3	.727	24	24	1	0	0	151²	127	15	55	122	11.0	4.04	105	.227	.301	5	.102	-2	3	3	0	0.1
1995 ★Atl-N	7	13	.350	29	29	3	1	0	173¹	165	22	52	141	11.6	4.67	91	.252	.312	11	.208	3	-10	-8	2	-0.3
1996 ★Atl-N	7	10	.412	24	23	1	0	0	131	146	10	40	86	13.1	4.47	99	.285	.341	11	.239	5	-4	-1	1	0.5
Total 7	72	62	.537	203	201	14	6	0	1222¹	1180	103	371	815	11.6	3.83	105	.255	.313	73	.179	11	12	28	7	4.1

● **JAY AVREA**   Avrea, James Epherium   b: 7/6/20, Cleburne, Tex.   d: 6/26/87, Dallas, Tex.   BR/TR, 6'1.5", 175 lbs.   Deb: 4/22/50

YEAR TM/L	W	L	PCT	G	GS	CG	SH	SV	IP	H	HR	BB	SO	RAT	ERA	ERA+	OAV	OOB	BH	AVG	PB	PR	/A	PD	TPI
1950 Cin-N	0	0	—	2	0	0	0	0	5¹	6	0	3	2	15.2	3.38	125	.273	.360	0	.000	-0	1	1	-0	0.0

● **BOBBY AYALA**   Ayala, Robert Joseph   b: 7/8/69, Ventura, Cal.   BR/TR, 6'2", 190 lbs.   Deb: 9/5/92

YEAR TM/L	W	L	PCT	G	GS	CG	SH	SV	IP	H	HR	BB	SO	RAT	ERA	ERA+	OAV	OOB	BH	AVG	PB	PR	/A	PD	TPI
1992 Cin-N	2	1	.667	5	5	0	0	0	29	33	1	13	23	14.6	4.34	83	.297	.376	0	.000	-1	-3	-2	1	-0.2
1993 Cin-N	7	10	.412	43	9	0	0	3	98	106	16	45	65	14.5	5.60	72	.274	.360	2	.095	-1	-17	-17	-1	-2.9
1994 Sea-A	4	3	.571	46	0	0	0	18	56²	42	4	26	76	10.8	2.86	171	.203	.292	0	—	0	12	13	-0	2.0
1995 ★Sea-A	6	5	.545	63	0	0	0	19	71	73	9	30	77	13.8	4.44	107	.262	.346	0	—	0	2	2	-0	0.4
1996 Sea-A	6	3	.667	50	0	0	0	3	67¹	65	10	25	61	12.3	5.88	84	.256	.327	0	—	0	-7	-7	0	-0.8
Total 5	25	22	.532	207	14	0	0	43	322	319	38	139	302	13.2	4.81	93	.258	.340	2	.067	-2	-12	-12	0	-1.5

● **JAKE AYDELOTT**   Aydelott, Jacob Stuart   b: 7/6/1861, N.Manchester, Ind.   d: 10/22/26, Detroit, Mich.   6', 180 lbs.   Deb: 5/15/1884

YEAR TM/L	W	L	PCT	G	GS	CG	SH	SV	IP	H	HR	BB	SO	RAT	ERA	ERA+	OAV	OOB	BH	AVG	PB	PR	/A	PD	TPI
1884 Ind-a	5	7	.417	12	12	11	0	0	106	129	6	29	30	13.4	4.92	67	.282	.324	5	.114	-3	-20	-19	-2	-2.0
1886 Phi-a	0	2	.000	2	2	2	0	0	18	21	0	12	5	16.5	4.00	88	.304	.407	0	.000	-1	-1	-1	-0	-0.2
Total 2	5	9	.357	14	14	13	0	0	124	150	0	41	35	13.9	4.79	69	.285	.336	5	.100	-4	-21	-20	-2	-2.2

● **BILL AYERS**   Ayers, William Oscar   b: 9/27/19, Newnan, Ga.   d: 9/24/80, Newnan, Ga.   BR/TR, 6'3", 185 lbs.   Deb: 4/17/47

YEAR TM/L	W	L	PCT	G	GS	CG	SH	SV	IP	H	HR	BB	SO	RAT	ERA	ERA+	OAV	OOB	BH	AVG	PB	PR	/A	PD	TPI
1947 NY-N	0	3	.000	13	4	0	0	1	35¹	46	7	14	22	15.5	8.15	50	.322	.386	2	.250	-0	-16	-16	1	-1.2

● **DOC AYERS**   Ayers, Yancy Wyatt   b: 5/20/1890, Fancy Gap, Va.   d: 5/26/68, Pulaski, Va.   BR/TR, 6'1", 185 lbs.   Deb: 9/9/13

YEAR TM/L	W	L	PCT	G	GS	CG	SH	SV	IP	H	HR	BB	SO	RAT	ERA	ERA+	OAV	OOB	BH	AVG	PB	PR	/A	PD	TPI
1913 Was-A	1	1	.500	4	2	1	1	1	17²	9	0	4	17	8.7	1.53	193	.182	.239	0	.000	-1	3	3	1	0.3
1914 Was-A	12	15	.444	49	32	8	3	3	265¹	221	5	54	148	9.6	2.54	111	.238	.286	14	.169	-0	6	8	-2	0.6
1915 Was-A	14	9	.609	40	16	8	2	3	211¹	178	1	38	96	9.5	2.21	134	.234	.276	12	.190	-1	17	18	-4	1.2
1916 Was-A	5	9	.357	43	17	7	0	2	157	173	4	52	69	13.1	3.78	74	.285	.346	6	.140	-2	-17	-17	-4	-2.2
1917 Was-A	11	10	.524	40	15	12	3	1	207²	192	3	59	78	11.2	2.17	121	.256	.317	13	.206	-4	11	11	-1	1.0
1918 Was-A	10	12	.455	40	24	11	4	3	219²	215	2	63	67	11.7	2.83	96	.261	.319	10	.152	-2	-1	-2	-0	-0.5
1919 Was-A	0	6	.000	11	5	0	1	0	43²	52	0	17	16	15.0	2.89	111	.317	.395	5	.417	2	2	2	1	0.4
Det-A	5	3	.625	24	5	3	1	0	93²	88	2	31	32	11.7	2.69	119	.254	.320	3	.125	-1	6	5	-0	0.3
Yr	5	9	.357	35	10	3	1	1	137¹	140	2	48	44	12.5	2.75	116	.272	.337	8	.222	1	7	7	0	0.7
1920 Det-A	7	14	.333	46	23	8	3	1	208²	217	6	62	103	12.4	3.88	96	.280	.340	9	.153	-2	-4	-4	-0	-0.6
1921 Det-A	0	0	—	2	1	0	0	0	4	9	0	2	0	24.8	9.00	47	.450	.500	0	—	-0	-2	-2	-0	0.0
Total 9	65	79	.451	299	140	58	17	15	1428²	1357	23	382	622	11.3	2.84	105	.259	.315	72	.171	-8	22	21	-10	0.5

● **BOB AYRAULT**   Ayrault, Robert Cunningham   b: 4/27/66, South Lake Tahoe, Cal.   BR/TR, 6'4", 230 lbs.   Deb: 6/7/92

YEAR TM/L	W	L	PCT	G	GS	CG	SH	SV	IP	H	HR	BB	SO	RAT	ERA	ERA+	OAV	OOB	BH	AVG	PB	PR	/A	PD	TPI
1992 Phi-N	2	2	.500	30	0	0	0	0	43¹	32	0	17	27	10.4	3.12	112	.209	.292	0	—	0	2	2	0	0.2
1993 Phi-N	2	0	1.000	10	0	0	0	0	10¹	18	1	10	8	25.3	9.58	41	.375	.492	0	.000	-0	-6	-6	-0	-1.1
Sea-A	1	1	.500	14	0	0	0	0	19²	18	1	6	7	11.0	3.20	137	.254	.312	0	—	0	3	3	0	0.2
Total 2	5	3	.625	54	0	0	0	0	73¹	68	2	33	42	12.6	4.05	94	.250	.336	0	.000	-0	-2	-2	-0	-0.7

● **BOB BABCOCK**   Babcock, Robert Ernest   b: 8/25/49, New Castle, Pa.   BR/TR, 6'5", 210 lbs.   Deb: 7/22/79

YEAR TM/L	W	L	PCT	G	GS	CG	SH	SV	IP	H	HR	BB	SO	RAT	ERA	ERA+	OAV	OOB	BH	AVG	PB	PR	/A	PD	TPI
1979 Tex-A	0	0	—	4	0	0	0	0	5¹	7	1	7	6	23.6	10.13	41	.318	.483	0	—	0	-4	-4	0	-0.1
1980 Tex-A	1	2	.333	19	0	0	0	0	23¹	20	3	8	15	11.6	4.63	84	.238	.319	0	—	0	-2	-2	-0	-0.2
1981 Tex-A	1	1	.500	16	1	0	0	0	28²	21	2	16	18	11.9	2.20	158	.219	.336	0	—	0	5	4	0	0.3
Total 3	2	3	.400	39	1	0	0	0	57¹	48	6	31	39	12.9	3.92	94	.238	.347	0	—	-0	-1	-1	0	0.1

● **JOHNNY BABICH**   Babich, John Charles   b: 5/14/13, Albion, Cal.   BR/TR, 6'1.5", 185 lbs.   Deb: 6/19/34

YEAR TM/L	W	L	PCT	G	GS	CG	SH	SV	IP	H	HR	BB	SO	RAT	ERA	ERA+	OAV	OOB	BH	AVG	PB	PR	/A	PD	TPI
1934 Bro-N	7	11	.389	25	19	7	0	1	135	148	5	51	62	13.4	4.20	93	.281	.347	7	.140	-3	-2	-4	2	-0.6
1935 Bro-N	7	14	.333	37	24	7	2	0	143¹	191	7	52	55	15.4	6.66	60	.317	.373	9	.184	-0	-42	-43	0	-5.1
1936 Bos-N	0	0	—	3	0	0	0	0	6	11	1	6	1	27.0	10.50	37	.440	.563	0	—	-0	-4	-4	-0	0.0
1940 Phi-A	14	13	.519	31	30	16	1	0	229¹	222	16	80	94	11.9	3.73	119	.248	.310	10	.116	-6	17	18	0	1.4
1941 Phi-A	2	7	.222	16	14	4	0	0	78¹	85	9	31	19	13.7	6.09	69	.281	.353	10	.400	4	-17	-17	1	-1.1
Total 5	30	45	.400	112	87	34	3	1	592	657	38	220	231	13.5	4.93	85	.279	.343	36	.171	-5	-49	-50	3	-5.4

● **LES BACKMAN**   Backman, Lester John   b: 3/20/1888, Cleves, Ohio   d: 11/8/75, Cincinnati, Ohio   BR/TR, 6'0.5", 195 lbs.   Deb: 7/3/09

YEAR TM/L	W	L	PCT	G	GS	CG	SH	SV	IP	H	HR	BB	SO	RAT	ERA	ERA+	OAV	OOB	BH	AVG	PB	PR	/A	PD	TPI
1909 StL-N	3	11	.214	21	15	8	0	0	128¹	146	1	39	35	13.2	4.14	61	.302	.357	4	.103	-1	-22	-23	-0	-2.5
1910 StL-N	6	7	.462	26	11	4	0	2	116	117	4	53	41	13.3	3.03	98	.284	.346	4	.114	0	-1	-1	-0	-0.1
Total 2	9	18	.333	47	26	12	0	2	244¹	263	5	92	76	13.3	3.61	76	.284	.352	8	.108	-1	-22	-24	-1	-2.6

● **EDDIE BACON**   Bacon, Edgar Suter   b: 4/8/1895, Franklin Co., Ky.   d: 10/2/63, Louisville, Ky.   Deb: 8/13/17 ◆

YEAR TM/L	W	L	PCT	G	GS	CG	SH	SV	IP	H	HR	BB	SO	RAT	ERA	ERA+	OAV	OOB	BH	AVG	PB	PR	/A	PD	TPI
1917 Phi-A	0	0	—	1	0	0	0	0	6	5	0	7	0	18.0	6.00	46	.238	.429	3	.500	1	-2	-2	1	0.3

● **MIKE BACSIK**   Bacsik, Michael James   b: 4/1/52, Dallas, Tex.   BR/TR, 6'1", 185 lbs.   Deb: 6/15/75

YEAR TM/L	W	L	PCT	G	GS	CG	SH	SV	IP	H	HR	BB	SO	RAT	ERA	ERA+	OAV	OOB	BH	AVG	PB	PR	/A	PD	TPI
1975 Tex-A	1	2	.333	7	3	0	0	0	26²	28	1	9	13	12.8	3.71	101	.275	.339	0	—	0	0	0	-0	0.0
1976 Tex-A	3	2	.600	23	0	0	0	0	55	66	3	26	21	15.4	4.25	84	.308	.388	0	—	0	-4	-4	-1	-0.4
1977 Tex-A	0	0	—	2	0	0	0	0	2¹	9	1	0	1	34.7	19.29	21	.563	.563	0	—	0	-4	-4	0	0.0
1979 Min-A	4	2	.667	31	0	0	0	0	65²	61	6	29	33	12.3	4.39	100	.249	.328	0	—	0	-1	-0	-0	-0.1
1980 Min-A	0	0	—	10	0	0	0	0	23	26	1	11	9	14.5	4.30	101	.286	.363	0	—	0	-0	-0	-0	-0.1
Total 5	8	6	.571	73	3	0	0	0	172²	190	12	75	77	14.0	4.43	91	.284	.359	0	—	-0	-10	-8	-1	-0.6

● **FRED BACZEWSKI**   Baczewski, Frederic John "Lefty"   b: 5/15/26, St.Paul, Minn.   d: 11/14/76, Culver City, Cal.   BL/TL, 6'2.5", 185 lbs.   Deb: 4/26/53

YEAR TM/L	W	L	PCT	G	GS	CG	SH	SV	IP	H	HR	BB	SO	RAT	ERA	ERA+	OAV	OOB	BH	AVG	PB	PR	/A	PD	TPI
1953 Chi-N	0	0	—	3	0	0	0	0	10	20	1	6	3	24.3	6.30	71	.435	.509	1	.500	-0	-2	-2	-0	0.0
Cin-N	11	4	.733	24	18	10	1	1	138¹	125	13	52	58	11.6	3.45	126	.244	.315	8	.178	-0	13	14	-3	1.1
Yr	11	4	.733	33	18	10	1	1	148¹	145	14	58	61	12.4	3.64	120	.259	.330	9	.191	-0	11	12	-3	1.1
1954 Cin-N	6	6	.500	29	22	4	1	0	130	159	22	53	43	14.7	5.26	80	.305	.370	3	.071	-3	-17	-15	-1	-1.7
1955 Cin-N	0	0	—	1	0	0	0	0	1	2	2	0	0	18.0	18.00	24	.400	.400	-0	—	-0	-2	-2	-0	0.0
Total 3	17	10	.630	63	40	14	2	1	279¹	306	38	111	104	13.5	4.45	96	.282	.351	12	.135	-3	-8	-5	-4	-0.6

● **LORE BADER**   Bader, Lore Verne "King"   b: 4/27/1888, Bader, Ill.   d: 6/2/73, LeRoy, Kan.   BL/TL, 6', 175 lbs.   Deb: 9/30/12 C

YEAR TM/L	W	L	PCT	G	GS	CG	SH	SV	IP	H	HR	BB	SO	RAT	ERA	ERA+	OAV	OOB	BH	AVG	PB	PR	/A	PD	TPI
1912 NY-N	2	0	1.000	3	0	0	0	0	10	9	0	5	3	14.4	0.90	376	.250	.372	0	.000	-0	3	3	0	0.5
1917 Bos-A	2	0	1.000	15	1	0	0	1	38¹	48	1	18	14	15.7	2.35	110	.306	.381	3	.300	1	1	1	0	0.2
1918 Bos-A	1	3	.250	4	5	4	2	1	0	27	26	1	12	10	13.7	3.33	81	.271	.369	1	.111	-1	-2	-1	-0	-0.5
Total 3	5	3	.625	22	6	3	1	0	75¹	83	2	36	27	14.8	2.51	109	.287	.376	4	.182	-0	2	2	0	0.2

● **ED BAECHT**   Baecht, Edward Joseph   b: 5/15/07, Paden, Okla.   d: 8/15/57, Grafton, Ill.   BR/TR, 6'3", 195 lbs.   Deb: 4/24/26

YEAR TM/L	W	L	PCT	G	GS	CG	SH	SV	IP	H	HR	BB	SO	RAT	ERA	ERA+	OAV	OOB	BH	AVG	PB	PR	/A	PD	TPI
1926 Phi-N	2	0	1.000	28	5	1	0	0	56	73	4	28	14	16.4	6.11	68	.324	.402	2	.143	-1	-14	-12	2	-0.3
1927 Phi-N	0	1	.000	1	1	0	0	0	6	12	0	2	1	21.0	12.00	34	.429	.467	0	.000	-0	-5	-5	0	-0.6
1928 Phi-N	1	1	.500	9	1	0	0	0	24	37	1	9	10	17.3	6.00	71	.385	.438	1	.143	-0	-5	-5	-0	-0.3

YEAR	TM/L	W	L	PCT	G	GS	CG	SH	SV	IP	H	HR	BB	SO	RAT	ERA	ERA+	OAV	OOB	BH	AVG	PB	PR	/A	PD	TPI
1931	Chi-N	2	4	.333	22	6	2	0	0	67	64	1	32	34	14.0	3.76	103	.250	.351	5	.278	1	1	1	1	0.2
1932	Chi-N	0	0	—	1	0	0	0	0	1	1	0	1	0	18.0	0.00	—	.333	.500	0	—	0	0	0	0	0.0
1937	StL-A	0	0	—	3	0	0	0	0	6¹	13	3	6	3	29.8	12.79	38	.419	.538	0	.000	-0	-6	-6	0	-0.3
Total	6	5	6	.455	64	9	3	0	0	160¹	200	9	78	61	16.2	5.56	73	.313	.397	8	.190	-1	-29	-27	3	-1.0

● JIM BAGBY
Bagby, James Charles Jacob Jr. b: 9/8/16, Cleveland, Ohio d: 9/2/88, Marietta, Ga. BR/TR, 6'2", 170 lbs. Deb: 4/18/38 F

YEAR	TM/L	W	L	PCT	G	GS	CG	SH	SV	IP	H	HR	BB	SO	RAT	ERA	ERA+	OAV	OOB	BH	AVG	PB	PR	/A	PD	TPI
1938	Bos-A	15	11	.577	43	25	10	1	2	198²	218	9	90	73	14.1	4.21	117	.283	.360	13	.191	-1	13	16	2	1.9
1939	Bos-A	5	5	.500	21	11	3	0	0	80	119	7	36	35	17.7	7.09	67	.347	.412	10	.294	3	-22	-21	-0	-1.9
1940	Bos-A	10	16	.385	36	21	6	1	2	182²	217	15	83	57	14.8	4.73	95	.296	.368	15	.203	-0	-7	-5	0	-0.6
1941	Cle-A	9	15	.375	33	27	12	0	2	200²	214	10	76	53	13.3	4.04	98	.273	.341	18	.243	2	2	2	0	0.1
1942	Cle-A☆	17	9	.654	38	35	16	4	1	270²	267	19	64	54	11.0	2.96	117	.258	.302	18	.189	1	21	15	0	1.5
1943	Cle-A☆	17	14	.548	36	33	16	3	1	273	248	15	80	70	10.9	3.10	100	.240	.296	30	.268	4	6	0	2	0.9
1944	Cle-A	4	5	.444	13	10	2	0	0	79	101	2	34	12	15.8	4.33	76	.312	.384	7	.226	1	-8	-9	-0	-0.8
1945	Cle-A	8	11	.421	25	19	11	3	1	159¹	171	3	59	38	13.1	3.73	87	.279	.344	17	.293	3	-6	-8	3	-0.3
1946	*Bos-A	7	6	.538	21	11	6	1	0	106²	117	4	49	16	14.1	3.71	99	.279	.356	5	.119	-2	-2	-1	-0	-0.3
1947	Pit-N	5	4	.556	37	6	2	0	0	115²	143	14	37	23	14.4	4.67	90	.304	.361	7	.219	1	-8	-6	1	-0.2
Total	10	97	96	.503	303	198	84	13	9	1666¹	1815	98	608	431	13.2	3.96	97	.278	.342	140	.226	12	-11	-23	10	0.3

● JIM BAGBY
Bagby, James Charles Jacob Sr. "Sarge" b: 10/5/1889, Barnett, Ga. d: 7/28/54, Marietta, Ga. BB/TR, 6', 170 lbs. Deb: 4/22/12 F

YEAR	TM/L	W	L	PCT	G	GS	CG	SH	SV	IP	H	HR	BB	SO	RAT	ERA	ERA+	OAV	OOB	BH	AVG	PB	PR	/A	PD	TPI
1912	Cin-N	2	1	.667	5	1	0	0	0	17¹	17	2	9	10	13.5	3.12	108	.270	.361	0	.000	-1	1	0	0	0.0
1916	Cle-A	16	16	.500	48	27	14	3	5	272²	253	2	67	88	10.8	2.61	115	.251	.303	15	.167	-1	7	12	-3	1.1
1917	Cle-A	23	13	.639	49	37	26	8	7	320²	277	6	73	83	10.0	1.96	144	.235	.283	25	.231	2	25	31	-3	3.8
1918	Cle-A	17	16	.515	45	31	23	2	6	271¹	274	0	78	57	11.7	2.69	112	.276	.330	21	.212	-0	3	10	-2	1.0
1919	Cle-A	17	11	.607	35	32	21	0	3	241¹	258	3	44	61	11.4	2.80	120	.275	.310	23	.258	5	12	15	-0	2.1
1920	*Cle-A	31	12	.721	48	38	30	3	0	339²	338	9	79	73	11.2	2.89	132	.266	.311	33	.252	6	34	34	-7	3.8
1921	Cle-A	14	12	.538	40	26	13	0	3	191²	238	14	44	37	13.4	4.70	91	.308	.348	15	.197	-9	-9	-9	-2	-1.4
1922	Cle-A	4	5	.444	25	10	4	0	1	98¹	134	5	39	25	16.1	6.32	63	.340	.404	11	.262	6	-25	-25	1	-1.7
1923	Pit-N	3	2	.600	21	6	2	0	3	68²	95	6	25	16	15.9	5.24	76	.336	.392	1	.050	-2	-9	-9	-15	-0.9
Total	9	127	88	.591	316	208	133	16	29	1821²	1884	47	458	450	11.7	3.11	110	.273	.321	144	.218	11	38	62	-15	7.8

● STAN BAHNSEN
Bahnsen, Stanley Raymond b: 12/15/44, Council Bluffs, Ia. BR/TR, 6'2", 203 lbs. Deb: 9/9/66

YEAR	TM/L	W	L	PCT	G	GS	CG	SH	SV	IP	H	HR	BB	SO	RAT	ERA	ERA+	OAV	OOB	BH	AVG	PB	PR	/A	PD	TPI
1966	NY-A	1	1	.500	4	3	1	0	1	23	15	3	7	16	8.6	3.52	94	.181	.244	1	.143	-0	-0	-1	-0	-0.1
1968	NY-A	17	12	.586	37	34	10	1	0	267¹	216	14	68	162	9.6	2.05	141	.221	.273	4	.049	-4	27	25	-2	2.2
1969	NY-A	9	16	.360	40	33	5	2	1	220²	222	28	90	130	12.7	3.83	91	.260	.331	5	.083	-3	-5	-9	1	-1.2
1970	NY-A	14	11	.560	36	35	6	2	0	232²	227	23	75	116	11.8	3.33	106	.256	.316	11	.149	-1	10	5	1	0.5
1971	NY-A	14	12	.538	36	34	14	3	0	242	221	20	72	110	11.1	3.35	97	.248	.308	12	.152	0	3	-3	3	0.0
1972	Chi-A	21	16	.568	43	41	5	1	0	252¹	263	22	73	157	12.2	3.60	87	.268	.323	14	.152	-1	-15	-13	2	-1.8
1973	Chi-A	18	21	.462	42	42	14	4	0	282¹	290	20	117	120	13.1	3.57	111	.269	.343	0	—	0	8	12	3	1.8
1974	Chi-A	12	15	.444	38	35	10	1	0	216¹	230	17	110	102	14.3	4.70	79	.277	.364	0	—	0	-26	-23	1	-2.6
1975	Chi-A	4	6	.400	12	12	2	0	0	67¹	78	9	40	31	16.2	6.01	64	.291	.389	0	—	0	-17	-16	-0	-2.0
	Oak-A	6	7	.462	21	16	2	0	0	100	88	6	37	49	11.5	3.24	112	.238	.313	0	.000	0	6	4	0	0.5
	Yr	10	13	.435	33	28	4	0	0	167¹	166	11	77	80	13.2	4.36	85	.259	.342	0	—	0	-11	-12	0	-1.5
1976	Oak-A	8	7	.533	35	14	1	0	0	143	124	13	43	82	10.6	3.34	101	.232	.292	0	—	0	3	0	1	0.1
1977	Oak-A	1	2	.333	11	2	0	0	1	22	24	5	13	21	15.5	6.14	66	.286	.388	0	—	0	-5	-5	-1	-0.7
	Mon-N	8	9	.471	23	22	3	1	0	127¹	142	14	38	58	12.7	4.81	79	.283	.333	5	.119	-1	-13	-14	-0	-1.7
1978	Mon-N	1	5	.167	44	1	0	0	7	75	74	9	31	44	12.6	3.84	92	.261	.334	1	.091	-0	-2	-3	-0	-0.4
1979	Mon-N	3	1	.750	55	0	0	0	5	94¹	80	10	42	71	11.6	3.15	116	.236	.320	1	.071	-0	6	5	0	0.2
1980	Mon-N	7	6	.538	57	0	0	0	4	91¹	80	7	33	48	11.1	3.05	117	.235	.302	1	.111	1	6	5	0	0.8
1981	*Mon-N	2	1	.667	25	3	0	0	0	49	45	7	24	28	12.9	4.96	70	.247	.338	1	.111	-0	-8	-8	1	-0.7
1982	Cal-A	0	1	.000	7	0	0	0	0	9²	13	0	6	5	19.6	4.66	87	.310	.420	0	—	-1	-1	-1	-0	-0.1
	Phi-N	0	0	—	8	0	0	0	0	13¹	8	0	3	9	7.4	1.35	271	.182	.234	0	—	0	3	3	-0	0.3
Total	16	146	149	.495	574	327	73	16	20	2529	2440	223	924	1359	12.1	3.60	97	.255	.323	56	.117	-9	-20	-35	4	-5.2

● ED BAHR
Bahr, Edson Garfield b: 10/16/19, Rouleau, Sask., Canada BR/TR, 6'1.5", 172 lbs. Deb: 5/1/46

YEAR	TM/L	W	L	PCT	G	GS	CG	SH	SV	IP	H	HR	BB	SO	RAT	ERA	ERA+	OAV	OOB	BH	AVG	PB	PR	/A	PD	TPI
1946	Pit-N	8	6	.571	27	14	7	0	0	136²	128	8	52	44	12.2	2.63	134	.254	.330	8	.178	-1	12	14	-0	1.3
1947	Pit-N	3	5	.375	19	11	1	0	0	82¹	82	5	43	25	14.0	4.59	92	.263	.358	2	.087	-2	-5	-3	-1	-0.6
Total	2	11	11	.500	46	25	8	0	0	219	210	13	95	69	12.9	3.37	112	.257	.341	10	.147	-3	7	10	-1	0.7

● GROVER BAICHLEY
Baichley, Grover Cleveland b: 1/7/1890, Toledo, Ill. d: 6/30/56, San Jose, Cal. BR/TR, 5'9.5", 165 lbs. Deb: 8/24/14

YEAR	TM/L	W	L	PCT	G	GS	CG	SH	SV	IP	H	HR	BB	SO	RAT	ERA	ERA+	OAV	OOB	BH	AVG	PB	PR	/A	PD	TPI
1914	StL-A	0	0	—	4	0	0	0	0	7	9	0	3	3	15.4	5.14	53	.346	.414	-0	—	-0	-2	-2	0	0.0

● SCOTT BAILES
Bailes, Scott Alan b: 12/18/61, Chillicothe, Ohio BL/TL, 6'2", 175 lbs. Deb: 4/9/86

YEAR	TM/L	W	L	PCT	G	GS	CG	SH	SV	IP	H	HR	BB	SO	RAT	ERA	ERA+	OAV	OOB	BH	AVG	PB	PR	/A	PD	TPI
1986	Cle-A	10	10	.500	62	10	0	0	7	112²	123	12	43	60	13.3	4.95	84	.276	.342	0	—	0	-10	-10	-1	-1.7
1987	Cle-A	7	8	.467	39	17	0	0	6	120¹	145	21	47	65	14.7	4.64	98	.296	.362	0	—	0	-2	-2	0	-0.2
1988	Cle-A	9	14	.391	37	21	5	2	0	145	149	22	46	53	12.2	4.90	84	.266	.324	0	—	0	-15	-13	-0	-1.9
1989	Cle-A	5	9	.357	34	11	0	0	0	113²	116	7	29	47	11.7	4.28	93	.269	.320	0	—	0	-5	-4	0	-0.5
1990	Cal-A	2	0	1.000	27	0	0	0	0	35¹	46	8	20	16	17.1	6.37	60	.315	.401	0	—	0	-10	-10	1	-0.3
1991	Cal-A	1	2	.333	42	0	0	0	0	51²	41	5	22	41	11.7	4.18	98	.218	.313	0	—	0	-0	-0	0	0.0
1992	Cal-A	3	1	.750	32	0	0	0	0	38²	59	7	28	25	20.5	7.45	53	.351	.447	0	—	0	-15	-15	-0	-1.4
Total	7	37	44	.457	273	59	5	2	13	617¹	679	82	235	307	13.6	4.93	84	.280	.347	0	—	0	-57	-54	-0	-6.0

● SWEETBREADS BAILEY
Bailey, Abraham Lincoln b: 2/12/1895, Joliet, Ill. d: 9/27/39, Joliet, Ill. BR/TR, 6', 184 lbs. Deb: 5/23/19

YEAR	TM/L	W	L	PCT	G	GS	CG	SH	SV	IP	H	HR	BB	SO	RAT	ERA	ERA+	OAV	OOB	BH	AVG	PB	PR	/A	PD	TPI
1919	Chi-N	3	5	.375	21	5	0	0	0	71¹	75	2	29	12.4	3.15	91	.288	.346	7	.389	3	-2	-2	2	0.3
1920	Chi-N	1	2	.333	21	1	0	0	0	36²	55	1	11	8	16.7	7.12	45	.359	.410	2	.143	-0	-16	-16	1	-1.2
1921	Chi-N	0	0	—	3	0	0	0	0	5	6	0	2	4	16.2	3.60	106	.300	.391	0	—	0	0	0	0	0.0
	Bro-N	0	0	—	7	0	0	0	0	24¹	35	1	7	6	15.9	5.18	75	.368	.417	0	.000	-0	-4	-3	-0	-0.1
	Yr	0	0	—	10	0	0	0	0	29¹	41	1	9	8	15.6	4.91	79	.353	.405	0	.000	-0	-4	-3	-0	-0.1
Total	3	4	7	.364	52	6	0	0	0	137¹	171	4	40	35	14.3	4.59	69	.324	.379	8	.267	2	-22	-22	2	-1.0

● ROGER BAILEY
Bailey, Charles Roger b: 10/3/70, Chattachoochee, Fla. BR/TR, 6'1", 180 lbs. Deb: 4/27/95

YEAR	TM/L	W	L	PCT	G	GS	CG	SH	SV	IP	H	HR	BB	SO	RAT	ERA	ERA+	OAV	OOB	BH	AVG	PB	PR	/A	PD	TPI
1995	Col-N	7	6	.538	39	6	0	0	0	81¹	88	9	39	33	14.2	4.98	108	.283	.365	2	.125	-1	-7	4	-0	0.4
1996	Col-N	2	3	.400	24	11	0	0	0	83²	94	7	52	45	15.8	6.24	87	.288	.388	5	.263	2	-19	-7	3	0.1
Total	2	9	9	.500	63	17	0	0	1	165	182	16	91	78	15.0	5.62	96	.286	.377	7	.200	1	-26	-4	3	0.5

● HARVEY BAILEY
Bailey, Harvey Francis b: 11/24/1876, Adrian, Mich. d: 7/10/22, Toledo, Ohio TL, 6', 160 lbs. Deb: 6/30/1899

YEAR	TM/L	W	L	PCT	G	GS	CG	SH	SV	IP	H	HR	BB	SO	RAT	ERA	ERA+	OAV	OOB	BH	AVG	PB	PR	/A	PD	TPI
1899	Bos-N	6	4	.600	12	11	8	0	0	86²	83	7	35	26	12.9	3.95	105	.252	.334	8	.235	0	-1	2	-1	0.1
1900	Bos-N	0	0	—	4	1	0	0	0	20	24	0	11	9	16.6	4.95	83	.296	.394	2	.222	0	-3	-2	1	0.1
Total	2	6	4	.600	16	12	8	0	0	106²	107	7	46	35	13.6	4.13	100	.260	.346	10	.233	0	-4	-0	-0	0.1

● HOWARD BAILEY
Bailey, Howard L b: 7/31/57, Grand Haven, Mich. BR/TL, 6', 195 lbs. Deb: 4/12/81

YEAR	TM/L	W	L	PCT	G	GS	CG	SH	SV	IP	H	HR	BB	SO	RAT	ERA	ERA+	OAV	OOB	BH	AVG	PB	PR	/A	PD	TPI
1981	Det-A	1	4	.200	9	5	0	0	0	36²	45	4	13	17	15.0	7.36	51	.308	.377	0	—	0	-15	-15	-0	-1.7
1982	Det-A	0	0	—	8	0	0	0	0	10	6	0	2	3	7.2	0.00	—	.182	.229	0	—	0	5	5	0	0.1
1983	Det-A	5	5	.500	33	3	0	0	1	72	69	11	25	21	12.0	4.88	80	.255	.322	0	—	0	-7	-8	0	-0.9
Total	3	6	9	.400	50	8	0	0	1	118²	120	15	40	41	12.5	5.23	74	.267	.333	0	—	0	-17	-18	1	-2.5

● JIM BAILEY
Bailey, James Hopkins b: 12/16/34, Strawberry Plains, Tenn. BB/TL, 6'2.5", 210 lbs. Deb: 9/10/59 F

YEAR	TM/L	W	L	PCT	G	GS	CG	SH	SV	IP	H	HR	BB	SO	RAT	ERA	ERA+	OAV	OOB	BH	AVG	PB	PR	/A	PD	TPI
1959	Cin-N	0	1	.000	3	1	0	0	0	11²	17	1	6	7	18.5	6.17	66	.333	.414	0	.000	-0	-3	-3	-0	-0.3

● KING BAILEY
Bailey, Linwood C. b: 11/1870, Virginia d: 11/19/17, Macon, Ga. BL/TL, 6' ", 185 lbs. Deb: 9/21/1895

YEAR	TM/L	W	L	PCT	G	GS	CG	SH	SV	IP	H	HR	BB	SO	RAT	ERA	ERA+	OAV	OOB	BH	AVG	PB	PR	/A	PD	TPI
1895	Cin-N	1	0	1.000	1	1	1	0	0	8	13	0	0	0	15.8	5.63	88	.361	.378	2	.500	1	-1	-1	0	0.0

YEAR	TM/L	W	L	PCT	G	GS	CG	SH	SV	IP	H	HR	BB	SO	RAT	ERA	ERA+	OAV	OOB	BH	AVG	PB	PR	/A	PD	TPI

● CORY BAILEY
Bailey, Phillip Cory   b: 1/24/71, Marion, Ill.   BR/TR, 6'1", 210 lbs.   Deb: 9/1/93

YEAR	TM/L	W	L	PCT	G	GS	CG	SH	SV	IP	H	HR	BB	SO	RAT	ERA	ERA+	OAV	OOB	BH	AVG	PB	PR	/A	PD	TPI
1993	Bos-A	0	1	.000	11	0	0	0	0	15²	12	0	12	11	13.8	3.45	134	.231	.375	0	—	0	2	2	1	-0.3
1994	Bos-A	0	1	.000	5	0	0	0	0	4¹	10	2	4	4	27.0	12.46	40	.476	.542	0	—	0	-4	-4	-0	-0.9
1995	StL-N	0	0	—	3	0	0	0	0	3²	2	0	2	5	9.8	7.36	57	.154	.267	0	—	0	-1	-1	0	0.0
1996	StL-N	5	2	.714	51	0	0	0	0	57	57	1	30	58	13.9	3.00	141	.263	.355	0	.000	1	8	8	-0	0.9
Total 4		5	4	.556	70	0	0	0	0	80²	81	3	47	58	14.4	3.79	115	.267	.368	0	.000	1	4	5	0	-0.3

● STEVE BAILEY
Bailey, Steven John   b: 2/12/42, Bronx, N.Y.   BR/TR, 6'1", 194 lbs.   Deb: 4/14/67

YEAR	TM/L	W	L	PCT	G	GS	CG	SH	SV	IP	H	HR	BB	SO	RAT	ERA	ERA+	OAV	OOB	BH	AVG	PB	PR	/A	PD	TPI
1967	Cle-A	2	5	.286	32	1	0	0	0	64²	62	5	42	46	14.9	3.90	84	.259	.377	0	.000	-1	-5	-5	0	-0.6
1968	Cle-A	0	1	.000	2	1	0	0	0	5	4	1	2	1	10.8	3.60	82	.235	.316	0	—	0	-0	-0	-0	-0.1
Total 2		2	6	.250	34	2	0	0	0	69²	66	6	44	47	14.6	3.88	84	.258	.373	0	.000	-1	-5	-5	0	-0.7

● BILL BAILEY
Bailey, William F.   b: 4/12/1889, Ft.Smith, Ark.   d: 11/2/26, Houston, Tex.   BL/TL, 5'11", 165 lbs.   Deb: 9/17/07

YEAR	TM/L	W	L	PCT	G	GS	CG	SH	SV	IP	H	HR	BB	SO	RAT	ERA	ERA+	OAV	OOB	BH	AVG	PB	PR	/A	PD	TPI
1907	StL-A	4	1	.800	6	5	3	0	0	48¹	39	0	15	17	10.8	2.42	104	.223	.299	3	.150	-1	1	0	-1	-0.2
1908	StL-A	3	5	.375	22	12	7	0	0	106²	85	2	50	42	11.6	3.04	79	.220	.314	3	.088	-2	-8	-8	-2	-1.1
1909	StL-A	9	10	.474	32	20	17	1	0	199	174	2	75	111	11.5	2.44	99	.248	.325	22	.286	5	1	-1	-1	0.5
1910	StL-A	3	18	.143	34	20	13	0	0	192¹	186	2	97	90	13.7	3.32	74	.262	.359	13	.206	-8	-17	-18	-1	-2.0
1911	StL-A	0	3	.000	7	2	2	0	0	31²	42	1	16	8	17.1	4.55	74	.339	.423	0	.000	-2	-4	-4	0	-0.5
1912	StL-A	0	1	.000	3	2	0	0	0	10²	15	0	10	2	21.1	9.28	36	.341	.463	1	.500	1	-7	-7	-1	-0.5
1914	Bal-F	7	9	.438	19	18	10	1	0	128²	106	2	68	131	12.7	3.08	99	.230	.338	7	.163	-1	-3	-1	3	0.1
1915	Bal-F	6	19	.240	36	23	11	2	0	190¹	179	8	115	98	14.3	4.63	62	.255	.366	15	.231	-0	-40	-37	-1	-4.6
	Chi-F	3	1	.750	5	5	3	3	0	33¹	23	1	10	24	8.9	2.16	116	.202	.266	2	.222	0	2	1	1	0.2
	Yr	9	20	.310	41	28	14	5	0	223²	202	9	125	122	13.2	4.27	66	.245	.344	17	.230	-0	-38	-36	-1	-4.4
1918	Det-A	1	2	.333	8	4	1	0	0	37²	53	0	26	13	19.1	5.97	45	.368	.468	1	.077	-1	-13	-14	1	-1.1
1921	StL-N	2	5	.286	19	6	3	1	0	74	95	1	22	20	14.5	4.26	86	.330	.381	2	.091	-2	-4	-5	1	-0.5
1922	StL-N	0	2	.000	12	0	0	0	0	31²	38	1	23	11	17.3	5.40	72	.325	.436	2	.286	-0	-5	-5	1	-0.2
Total 11		38	76	.333	203	117	70	8	0	1084¹	1035	20	527	570	13.3	3.57	77	.261	.354	71	.194	-3	-97	-98	-1	-9.9

● BOB BAILOR
Bailor, Robert Michael   b: 7/10/51, Connellsville, Pa.   BR/TR, 5'11", 170 lbs.   Deb: 9/6/75   C♦

YEAR	TM/L	W	L	PCT	G	GS	CG	SH	SV	IP	H	HR	BB	SO	RAT	ERA	ERA+	OAV	OOB	BH	AVG	PB	PR	/A	PD	TPI
1980	Tor-A	0	0	—	3	0	0	0	0	2¹	4	0	1	0	19.3	7.71	56	.364	.417	82	.236	2	-1	-1	-0	0.0

● LOREN BAIN
Bain, Herbert Loren   b: 7/4/22, Staples, Minn.   BR/TR, 6', 190 lbs.   Deb: 6/23/45

YEAR	TM/L	W	L	PCT	G	GS	CG	SH	SV	IP	H	HR	BB	SO	RAT	ERA	ERA+	OAV	OOB	BH	AVG	PB	PR	/A	PD	TPI
1945	NY-N	0	0	—	3	0	0	0	0	8	10	1	4	1	16.9	7.88	50	.323	.417	1	.333	0	-4	-4	-0	0.0

● DOUG BAIR
Bair, Charles Douglas   b: 8/22/49, Defiance, Ohio   BR/TR, 6', 180 lbs.   Deb: 9/13/76

YEAR	TM/L	W	L	PCT	G	GS	CG	SH	SV	IP	H	HR	BB	SO	RAT	ERA	ERA+	OAV	OOB	BH	AVG	PB	PR	/A	PD	TPI
1976	Pit-N	0	0	—	4	0	0	0	0	6¹	4	0	5	4	12.8	5.68	61	.174	.321	0	—	0	-2	-2	-0	0.0
1977	Oak-A	4	6	.400	45	0	0	0	8	83¹	78	11	57	68	14.6	3.46	116	.253	.370	0	—	0	6	5	1	0.9
1978	Cin-N	7	6	.538	70	0	0	0	28	100¹	87	6	38	91	11.2	1.97	180	.236	.307	2	.143	-0	18	18	-1	3.2
1979	*Cin-N	11	7	.611	65	0	0	0	16	94¹	93	7	51	86	14.0	4.29	87	.256	.353	0	.000	-1	-6	-6	-1	-1.4
1980	Cin-N	3	6	.333	61	0	0	0	0	85	91	7	39	62	13.9	4.24	84	.277	.355	0	.000	-0	-6	-6	2	-0.6
1981	Cin-N	2	2	.500	24	0	0	0	0	39	42	5	17	16	13.6	5.77	62	.271	.343	1	.333	-1	-10	-10	-1	-0.9
	StL-N	2	0	1.000	11	0	0	0	1	15²	13	0	2	14	8.6	3.45	103	.224	.250	0	—	0	0	0	-0	-0.0
	Yr	4	2	.667	35	0	0	0	1	54²	55	5	19	30	12.2	5.10	70	.258	.319	1	.167	-1	-10	-9	-1	-0.9
1982	*StL-N	5	3	.625	63	0	0	0	8	91²	69	7	36	68	10.4	2.55	142	.211	.291	1	.077	-1	11	11	0	1.0
1983	StL-N	1	1	.500	26	0	0	0	1	29²	24	4	13	21	11.2	3.03	119	.224	.308	0	—	0	2	2	-0	0.1
	Det-A	7	3	.700	27	1	0	0	4	55²	51	8	19	39	11.5	3.88	101	.242	.307	0	—	0	1	0	-0	0.2
1984	*Det-A	5	3	.625	47	1	0	0	4	93²	82	10	36	57	11.3	3.75	105	.238	.310	0	—	0	3	2	1	0.3
1985	Det-A	2	0	1.000	21	3	0	0	0	49	54	3	25	30	14.7	6.24	65	.281	.367	0	—	0	-11	-12	1	-0.3
	StL-N	0	0	—	2	0	0	0	0	2	2	0	2	0	13.5	0.00	—	.167	.375	0	—	0	1	1	-0	0.0
1986	Oak-A	2	3	.400	31	0	0	0	4	45	37	5	18	40	11.0	3.00	129	.224	.301	0	—	0	6	4	1	1.1
1987	Phi-N	0	0	1.000	11	0	0	0	0	13²	14	5	5	10	14.5	5.93	72	.309	.367	0	.000	-0	-3	-3	0	-0.4
1988	Tor-A	0	0	—	10	0	0	0	0	13¹	14	2	4	8	11.5	4.05	97	.280	.321	0	—	0	-0	-0	0	0.0
1989	Pit-N	2	3	.400	44	0	0	0	0	67¹	52	4	28	56	10.7	2.27	148	.211	.292	1	.200	0	8	8	1	0.7
1990	Pit-N	0	0	—	22	0	0	0	0	24¹	30	3	11	19	15.2	4.81	75	.306	.376	0	.000	-0	-3	-3	-0	0.0
Total 15		55	43	.561	584	5	0	0	81	909¹	839	86	405	689	12.4	3.63	103	.246	.328	5	.096	-2	15	10	2	3.9

● BOB BAIRD
Baird, Robert Allen   b: 1/16/40, Knoxville, Tenn.   d: 4/11/74, Chattanooga, Tenn.   BL/TL, 6'4", 195 lbs.   Deb: 9/3/62

YEAR	TM/L	W	L	PCT	G	GS	CG	SH	SV	IP	H	HR	BB	SO	RAT	ERA	ERA+	OAV	OOB	BH	AVG	PB	PR	/A	PD	TPI
1962	Was-A	0	1	.000	3	0	0	0	0	10²	13	0	8	3	17.7	6.75	60	.310	.420	0	.000	-0	-3	-3	-0	-0.3
1963	Was-A	0	3	.000	5	3	0	0	0	11²	12	1	7	7	15.4	7.71	48	.261	.370	1	.333	0	-6	-5	-0	-1.1
Total 2		0	4	.000	8	6	0	0	0	22¹	25	1	15	10	16.5	7.25	53	.284	.394	1	.167	0	-9	-8	-1	-1.4

● JERSEY BAKELY
Bakely, Edward Enoch (b: Edward Enoch Bakley)   b: 4/17/1864, Blackwood, N.J.   d: 2/17/15, Philadelphia, Pa.   BR/TR,   Deb: 5/11/1883

YEAR	TM/L	W	L	PCT	G	GS	CG	SH	SV	IP	H	HR	BB	SO	RAT	ERA	ERA+	OAV	OOB	BH	AVG	PB	PR	/A	PD	TPI
1883	Phi-a	5	3	.625	8	8	7	0	0	61¹	65	0	12	14	11.3	3.23	108	.255	.288	5	.192	1	1	2	0	0.2
1884	Phi-U	14	25	.359	39	38	38	1	0	344²	390	0	76	204	12.2	4.47	52	.267	.303	22	.132	-16	-77	-82	-3	-8.2
	Wil-U	0	2	.000	2	2	2	0	0	17	24	0	1	9	13.2	4.24	63	.312	.321	0	—	-1	-3	-3	-0	-0.3
	KC-U	2	3	.400	5	5	3	0	0	33	29	0	4	13	9.0	2.45	91	.220	.243	3	.150	-2	-0	-1	-1	-0.3
	Yr	16	30	.348	46	45	43	1	0	394²	443	0	81	226	11.9	4.29	54	.265	.299	25	.130	-18	-81	-86	-4	-8.8
1888	Cle-a	25	33	.431	61	61	60	4	0	532²	518	14	128	212	11.2	2.97	104	.246	.294	26	.134	-6	5	7	-1	0.1
1889	Cle-N	12	22	.353	36	34	33	2	0	304¹	296	9	106	105	12.1	2.96	136	.247	.313	15	.135	-1	36	36	2	3.4
1890	Cle-P	12	25	.324	43	38	32	0	0	326¹	412	13	147	67	15.6	4.47	89	.295	.365	28	.203	-2	-9	-18	-3	-1.8
1891	Was-a	2	10	.167	13	12	11	0	0	104¹	127	6	60	32	16.6	5.35	70	.291	.384	10	.222	-0	-19	-19	-2	-1.7
	Bal-a	4	2	.667	8	6	5	0	0	59	48	1	30	13	12.1	2.29	163	.214	.310	2	.095	-0	9	10	-1	0.8
	Yr	6	12	.333	21	18	16	0	0	163¹	175	7	90	45	14.7	4.24	88	.262	.351	12	.182	-0	-9	-9	-3	-0.9
Total 6		76	125	.378	215	204	191	7	0	1782²	1909	43	564	669	12.7	3.66	91	.262	.318	111	.153	-26	-57	-68	-7	-7.8

● DAVE BAKENHASTER
Bakenhaster, David Lee   b: 3/5/45, Columbus, O.   BR/TR, 5'10", 168 lbs.   Deb: 6/20/64

YEAR	TM/L	W	L	PCT	G	GS	CG	SH	SV	IP	H	HR	BB	SO	RAT	ERA	ERA+	OAV	OOB	BH	AVG	PB	PR	/A	PD	TPI
1964	StL-N	0	0	—	2	0	0	0	0	3	9	1	1	0	30.0	6.00	63	.474	.500	0	—	0	-1	-1	0	0.0

● AL BAKER
Baker, Albert Jones   b: 2/28/06, Batesville, Miss.   d: 11/6/82, Kenedy, Tex.   BR/TR, 5'11", 170 lbs.   Deb: 8/20/38

YEAR	TM/L	W	L	PCT	G	GS	CG	SH	SV	IP	H	HR	BB	SO	RAT	ERA	ERA+	OAV	OOB	BH	AVG	PB	PR	/A	PD	TPI
1938	Bos-A	0	0	—	3	0	0	0	0	7²	13	2	2	2	18.8	9.39	53	.371	.421	0	.000	-1	-4	-4	-0	-0.1

● BOCK BAKER
Baker, Charles "Smiling Bock"   b: 7/17/1878, Troy, N.Y.   d: 8/17/40, New York, N.Y.   TL, 5'9", 181 lbs.   Deb: 4/28/01

YEAR	TM/L	W	L	PCT	G	GS	CG	SH	SV	IP	H	HR	BB	SO	RAT	ERA	ERA+	OAV	OOB	BH	AVG	PB	PR	/A	PD	TPI
1901	Cle-A	0	1	.000	1	1	1	0	0	8	23	0	6	0	33.8	5.63	63	.500	.566	0	.000	-1	-2	-2	0	-0.2
	Phi-A	0	1	.000	1	1	0	0	0	6	6	0	5	1	18.0	10.50	36	.261	.414	1	.333	0	-5	-4	-0	-0.5
	Yr	0	2	.000	2	2	1	0	0	14	29	0	11	1	26.4	7.71	47	.414	.500	1	.143	-1	-6	-6	0	-0.7

● ERNIE BAKER
Baker, Earnest Gould   b: 8/8/1875, Concord, Mich.   d: 10/25/45, Homer, Mich.   BR/TR, 5'10", 160 lbs.   Deb: 8/18/05

YEAR	TM/L	W	L	PCT	G	GS	CG	SH	SV	IP	H	HR	BB	SO	RAT	ERA	ERA+	OAV	OOB	BH	AVG	PB	PR	/A	PD	TPI
1905	Cin-N	0	0	—	1	0	0	0	0	4	7	1	0	1	18.0	4.50	73	.412	.444	0	.000	-0	-1	-1	-0	-0.1

● JESSE BAKER
Baker, Jesse Ormond   b: 6/3/1888, Anderson Island, Wash.   d: 9/26/72, Tacoma, Wash.   BL/TL, 5'11", 188 lbs.   Deb: 4/23/11

YEAR	TM/L	W	L	PCT	G	GS	CG	SH	SV	IP	H	HR	BB	SO	RAT	ERA	ERA+	OAV	OOB	BH	AVG	PB	PR	/A	PD	TPI
1911	Chi-A	2	7	.222	22	8	3	0	1	94	101	3	30	51	12.9	3.93	82	.288	.351	3	.103	-2	-6	-7	1	-0.7

● KIRTLEY BAKER
Baker, Kirtley "Whitey"   b: 6/24/1869, Aurora, Ind.   d: 4/15/27, Covington, Ky.   BR/TR, 5'9", 160 lbs.   Deb: 5/7/1890 ♦

YEAR	TM/L	W	L	PCT	G	GS	CG	SH	SV	IP	H	HR	BB	SO	RAT	ERA	ERA+	OAV	OOB	BH	AVG	PB	PR	/A	PD	TPI
1890	Pit-N	3	19	.136	25	21	19	2	0	178¹	209	11	86	76	15.9	5.60	59	.284	.374	10	.147	-1	-40	-46	0	-4.3
1893	Bal-N	3	8	.273	15	12	8	0	0	91²	138	5	58	26	19.7	8.44	56	.337	.426	17	.298	2	-38	-38	3	-2.7
1894	Bal-N	0	1	.000	1	0	0	0	0	1	0	1	0	2	0.0	∞	—	1.000	1.000	0	.000	-0	-5	-5	-0	-0.3
1898	Was-N	2	3	.400	6	5	1	0	0	47	56	1	18	7	14.2	3.06	120	.293	.354	5	.278	1	-3	-3	-1	0.4
1899	Was-N	1	7	.125	11	6	6	0	0	54	79	3	22	6	17.8	6.83	57	.339	.410	3	.158	-1	-18	-18	2	-1.9
Total 5		9	38	.191	58	44	34	2	0	371	483	20	186	115	17.0	6.28	60	.307	.391	35	.211	1	-99	-103	4	-8.8

● NEAL BAKER
Baker, Neal Vernon   b: 4/30/04, LaPorte, Tex.   d: 1/5/82, Houston, Tex.   BR/TR, 6'1", 175 lbs.   Deb: 6/26/27

YEAR	TM/L	W	L	PCT	G	GS	CG	SH	SV	IP	H	HR	BB	SO	RAT	ERA	ERA+	OAV	OOB	BH	AVG	PB	PR	/A	PD	TPI
1927	Phi-A	0	0	—	5	2	0	0	0	17¹	27	2	7	3	17.7	5.71	75	.365	.420	1	.167	-0	-3	-3	0	0.0

YEAR TM/L	W	L	PCT	G	GS	CG	SH	SV	IP	H	HR	BB	SO	RAT	ERA	ERA+	OAV	OOB	BH	AVG	PB	PR	/A	PD	TPI

● NORM BAKER
Baker, Norman Leslie b: 10/14/1863, Philadelphia, Pa. d: 2/20/49, Hurffville, N.J. Deb: 5/21/1883

YEAR TM/L	W	L	PCT	G	GS	CG	SH	SV	IP	H	HR	BB	SO	RAT	ERA	ERA+	OAV	OOB	BH	AVG	PB	PR	/A	PD	TPI
1883 Pit-a	0	2	.000	3	3	2	0	0	19	24	0	11	5	16.6	3.32	97	.289	.372	0	.000	-2	-0	-0	-1	-0.2
1885 Lou-a	13	12	.520	25	24	24	1	0	217	210	3	69	79	12.0	3.40	95	.241	.304	18	.207	-1	-4	-4	-2	-0.6
1890 Bal-a	1	1	.500	2	2	2	0	0	17	16	0	6	10	11.6	3.71	109	.242	.306	0	.000	-1	0	1	0	0.0
Total 3	14	15	.483	30	29	28	1	0	253	250	3	86	94	12.3	3.42	96	.245	.309	18	.170	-3	-3	-4	-2	-0.8

● SCOTT BAKER
Baker, Scott b: 5/18/70, San Jose, Cal. BL/TL, 6'2", 175 lbs. Deb: 7/17/95

YEAR TM/L	W	L	PCT	G	GS	CG	SH	SV	IP	H	HR	BB	SO	RAT	ERA	ERA+	OAV	OOB	BH	AVG	PB	PR	/A	PD	TPI
1995 Oak-A	0	0	—	1	0	0	0	0	3²	5	0	5	3	27.0	9.82	46	.333	.524	0	—	-2	-2	-0	0.4

● STEVE BAKER
Baker, Steven Byrne b: 8/30/56, Eugene, Ore. BR/TR, 6', 185 lbs. Deb: 5/25/78

YEAR TM/L	W	L	PCT	G	GS	CG	SH	SV	IP	H	HR	BB	SO	RAT	ERA	ERA+	OAV	OOB	BH	AVG	PB	PR	/A	PD	TPI
1978 Det-A	2	4	.333	15	10	0	0	0	63¹	66	6	42	39	15.3	4.55	85	.276	.384	0	—	0	-6	-5	-1	-0.7
1979 Det-A	1	7	.125	21	12	0	0	1	84	97	13	51	54	16.5	6.64	65	.296	.400	0	—	0	-23	-22	-1	-2.0
1982 Oak-A	1	1	.500	5	3	0	0	0	25²	30	3	4	14	11.9	4.56	86	.288	.315	0	—	0	-1	-2	-0	-0.2
1983 Oak-A	3	3	.500	35	1	0	0	5	54	59	4	26	23	14.5	4.33	89	.282	.367	0	—	0	-2	-3	-1	-0.2
StL-N	0	1	.000	8	0	0	0	0	10	10	0	4	1	13.5	1.80	201	.286	.375	0	—	0	2	2	0	0.2
Total 4	7	16	.304	84	26	0	0	6	237	262	26	127	131	15.1	5.13	78	.286	.379	0	—	0	-29	-29	-3	-2.7

● TOM BAKER
Baker, Thomas Calvin "Rattlesnake" b: 6/11/13, Nursery, Tex. d: 1/3/91, Fort Worth, Tex. BR/TR, 6'1.5", 180 lbs. Deb: 8/15/35

YEAR TM/L	W	L	PCT	G	GS	CG	SH	SV	IP	H	HR	BB	SO	RAT	ERA	ERA+	OAV	OOB	BH	AVG	PB	PR	/A	PD	TPI
1935 Bro-N	1	0	1.000	11	1	1	0	0	42	48	2	20	10	14.6	4.29	93	.277	.352	9	.474	4	-1	-1	-0	0.2
1936 Bro-N	1	8	.111	35	8	2	0	2	87²	98	3	48	35	15.2	4.72	88	.288	.379	7	.233	1	-7	-6	0	-0.4
1937 Bro-N	0	1	.000	7	0	0	0	0	8¹	14	1	5	2	21.6	8.64	47	.378	.465	0	—	-0	-4	-4	0	-0.3
NY-N	1	0	1.000	13	0	0	0	0	31	30	0	16	11	13.4	4.06	96	.268	.359	2	.222	1	-1	-1	-0	-0.1
Yr	1	1	.500	20	0	0	0	0	39¹	44	1	21	13	14.9	5.03	78	.293	.380	2	.222	-0	-5	-5	-0	-0.5
1938 NY-N	0	0	—	2	0	0	0	0	4	5	0	3	0	18.0	6.75	56	.313	.421	0	—	0	-1	-1	0	0.0
Total 4	3	9	.250	68	9	3	0	2	173	195	6	92	58	15.1	4.73	85	.288	.375	18	.310	5	-14	-13	-1	-0.7

● TOM BAKER
Baker, Thomas Henry b: 5/6/34, Port Townsend, Wash. d: 3/9/80, Port Townsend, Wash. BL/TL, 6', 195 lbs. Deb: 8/2/63

YEAR TM/L	W	L	PCT	G	GS	CG	SH	SV	IP	H	HR	BB	SO	RAT	ERA	ERA+	OAV	OOB	BH	AVG	PB	PR	/A	PD	TPI
1963 Chi-N	0	1	.000	10	1	0	0	0	18	20	2	7	14	14.0	3.00	117	.282	.354	0	—	-0	1	1	0	0.0

● MIKE BALAS
Balas, Mitchell Francis (b: Mitchell Francis Balaski) b: 5/17/10, Lowell, Mass. BR/TR, 6', 195 lbs. Deb: 4/27/38

YEAR TM/L	W	L	PCT	G	GS	CG	SH	SV	IP	H	HR	BB	SO	RAT	ERA	ERA+	OAV	OOB	BH	AVG	PB	PR	/A	PD	TPI
1938 Bos-N	0	0	—	1	0	0	0	0	1¹	3	0	0	0	20.3	6.75	51	.375	.375	0	—	0	-0	-0	-0	0.0

● JACK BALDSCHUN
Baldschun, Jack Edward b: 10/16/36, Greenville, O. BR/TR, 6', 190 lbs. Deb: 4/28/61

YEAR TM/L	W	L	PCT	G	GS	CG	SH	SV	IP	H	HR	BB	SO	RAT	ERA	ERA+	OAV	OOB	BH	AVG	PB	PR	/A	PD	TPI
1961 Phi-N	5	3	.625	65	0	0	0	3	99²	90	7	49	59	13.0	3.88	105	.243	.339	0	.000	-1	2	2	0	0.1
1962 Phi-N	12	7	.632	67	0	0	0	13	112²	95	6	58	95	12.4	2.96	131	.231	.328	1	.063	-1	12	11	1	2.1
1963 Phi-N	11	7	.611	65	0	0	0	16	113²	99	7	42	89	11.4	2.30	141	.232	.306	0	.000	-2	13	12	1	2.2
1964 Phi-N	6	9	.400	71	0	0	0	21	118¹	111	8	40	78	11.7	3.12	111	.246	.312	4	.250	1	6	5	1	1.1
1965 Phi-N	5	8	.385	65	0	0	0	6	99	102	4	42	81	13.5	3.82	91	.273	.352	0	.000	-1	-3	-4	1	-0.6
1966 Cin-N	1	5	.167	42	0	0	0	0	57¹	71	4	25	44	15.7	5.49	71	.318	.397	1	.333	0	-12	-10	0	-0.9
1967 Cin-N	0	0	—	9	0	0	0	0	13	15	0	9	12	16.6	4.15	90	.283	.387	0	.000	-0	-1	-1	-0	-0.2
1969 SD-N	7	2	.778	61	0	0	0	6	77	80	7	29	67	13.0	4.79	74	.264	.332	1	.250	0	-10	-11	-0	-1.2
1970 SD-N	1	0	1.000	12	0	0	0	5	13¹	24	2	4	12	18.9	10.13	39	.375	.412	0	—	0	-9	-9	-0	-0.6
Total 9	48	41	.539	457	0	0	0	60	704	687	45	298	555	12.9	3.69	98	.257	.336	7	.090	-3	-3	-5	4	2.2

● LADY BALDWIN
Baldwin, Charles Busted b: 4/8/1859, Oramel, N.Y. d: 3/7/37, Hastings, Mich. BL/TL, 5'11", 160 lbs. Deb: 9/30/1884 ♦

YEAR TM/L	W	L	PCT	G	GS	CG	SH	SV	IP	H	HR	BB	SO	RAT	ERA	ERA+	OAV	OOB	BH	AVG	PB	PR	/A	PD	TPI
1884 Mil-U	1	1	.500	2	2	2	0	0	17	7	0	1	2	4.2	2.65	50	.117	.131	6	.222	-0	-0	-2	-0	-0.2
1885 Det-N	11	9	.550	21	20	19	1	1	179¹	137	2	28	135	8.3	1.86	153	.197	.228	30	.242	3	19	20	2	2.4
1886 *Det-N	42	13	.764	56	56	55	7	0	487	371	11	100	323	8.7	2.24	148	.202	.243	41	.201	3	58	58	4	6.1
1887 *Det-N	13	10	.565	24	24	24	1	0	211	225	8	61	60	12.4	3.84	105	.269	.323	23	.271	3	6	5	1	0.6
1888 Det-N	3	3	.500	6	6	5	0	0	53	76	5	15	26	15.6	5.43	51	.322	.365	6	.261	2	-15	-16	-1	-1.3
1890 Bro-N	1	0	1.000	2	1	0	0	0	7²	15	0	4	4	22.3	7.04	49	.395	.452	0	.000	-0	-3	-3	-0	-0.3
Buf-P	2	5	.286	7	7	7	0	0	62	90	5	24	13	17.0	4.50	91	.325	.385	8	.286	1	-2	-3	-0	-0.1
Total 6	73	41	.640	118	116	112	9	1	1017	921	31	233	582	10.3	2.85	118	.232	.276	114	.231	12	63	58	5	7.2

● KID BALDWIN
Baldwin, Clarence Geoghan b: 11/1/1864, Newport, Ky. d: 7/10/1897, Cincinnati, Ohio BR/TR, 5'6", 147 lbs. Deb: 7/27/1884 ♦

YEAR TM/L	W	L	PCT	G	GS	CG	SH	SV	IP	H	HR	BB	SO	RAT	ERA	ERA+	OAV	OOB	BH	AVG	PB	PR	/A	PD	TPI
1885 Cin-a	0	0	—	2	1	0	0	0	4	5	0	6	1	24.8	9.00	36	.294	.478	17	.135	-0	-3	-3	0	0.0

● DAVE BALDWIN
Baldwin, David George b: 3/30/38, Tucson, Ariz. BR/TR, 6'2", 200 lbs. Deb: 9/6/66

YEAR TM/L	W	L	PCT	G	GS	CG	SH	SV	IP	H	HR	BB	SO	RAT	ERA	ERA+	OAV	OOB	BH	AVG	PB	PR	/A	PD	TPI
1966 Was-A	0	0	—	4	0	0	0	0	7	8	1	4	11	11.6	3.86	90	.267	.290	0	—	0	-0	-0	-0	0.0
1967 Was-A	2	4	.333	58	0	0	0	12	68²	53	2	20	52	10.1	1.70	186	.215	.285	0	.000	-0	12	11	1	1.5
1968 Was-A	0	2	.000	40	0	0	0	6	42	40	7	12	30	11.1	4.07	72	.260	.313	0	.000	-0	-5	-5	-1	-0.4
1969 Was-A	2	4	.333	43	0	0	0	4	66²	57	9	34	51	13.0	4.05	90	.236	.342	0	.000	-1	-3	-4	-0	-0.6
1970 Mil-A	2	1	.667	28	0	0	0	0	35¹	25	4	18	26	11.0	2.55	149	.205	.307	1	.500	1	5	5	0	0.7
1973 Chi-A	0	0	—	3	0	0	0	0	5	7	0	4	1	19.8	3.60	110	.368	.478	0	—	0	0	0	0	0.0
Total 6	6	11	.353	176	0	0	0	22	224²	190	17	89	164	11.5	3.08	108	.234	.316	1	.067	-1	8	6	4	1.2

● HARRY BALDWIN
Baldwin, Howard Edward b: 6/3/1900, Baltimore, Md. d: 1/23/58, Baltimore, Md. BR/TR, 5'11", 160 lbs. Deb: 5/4/24

YEAR TM/L	W	L	PCT	G	GS	CG	SH	SV	IP	H	HR	BB	SO	RAT	ERA	ERA+	OAV	OOB	BH	AVG	PB	PR	/A	PD	TPI
1924 *NY-N	3	1	.750	10	2	1	0	0	33²	42	5	11	5	14.2	4.28	86	.309	.361	4	.364	1	-2	-2	-0	-0.2
1925 NY-N	0	0	—	1	0	0	0	0	1	3	0	1	0	36.0	9.00	45	.500	.571	0	—	0	-1	-1	-0	0.0
Total 2	3	1	.750	11	2	1	0	0	34²	45	5	12	5	14.8	4.41	83	.317	.370	4	.364	1	-2	-2	-0	-0.2

● JAMES BALDWIN
Baldwin, James J. b: 7/15/71, Southern Pines, N.C. BR/TR, 6'3", 210 lbs. Deb: 4/30/95

YEAR TM/L	W	L	PCT	G	GS	CG	SH	SV	IP	H	HR	BB	SO	RAT	ERA	ERA+	OAV	OOB	BH	AVG	PB	PR	/A	PD	TPI
1995 Chi-A	0	1	.000	6	4	0	0	0	14²	32	5	9	10	25.2	12.89	35	.444	.506	0	—	0	-13	-14	0	-0.5
1996 Chi-A	11	6	.647	28	28	0	0	0	169	168	24	57	127	12.2	4.42	106	.257	.320	0	—	0	11	5	-1	0.7
Total 2	11	7	.611	34	32	0	0	0	183²	200	30	66	137	13.2	5.10	92	.275	.339	0	—	0	-2	-8	-1	0.2

● MARK BALDWIN
Baldwin, Marcus Elmore "Fido" b: 10/29/1863, Pittsburgh, Pa. d: 11/10/29, Pittsburgh, Pa. BR/TR, 6', 190 lbs. Deb: 5/2/1887

YEAR TM/L	W	L	PCT	G	GS	CG	SH	SV	IP	H	HR	BB	SO	RAT	ERA	ERA+	OAV	OOB	BH	AVG	PB	PR	/A	PD	TPI
1887 Chi-N	18	17	.514	40	39	35	1	**1**	334	329	23	122	164	12.6	3.40	132	.248	.319	26	.187	-4	25	41	-3	2.6
1888 Chi-N	13	15	.464	30	30	27	2	0	251	224	13	99	157	12.7	2.76	110	.249	.327	16	.151	-1	2	7	2	0.8
1889 Col-a	27	34	.443	**63**	59	54	6	1	513²	458	9	274	**368**	13.2	3.61	100	.231	.331	39	.188	1	14	11	1	0.2
1890 Chi-P	**33**	24	.579	**58**	56	53	1	0	492	494	10	249	**206**	13.9	3.35	130	.250	.339	45	.212	-1	48	54	3	4.8
1891 Pit-N	22	28	.440	53	51	48	2	0	437²	385	10	227	197	13.1	2.76	119	.227	.327	27	.153	-3	29	26	1	2.1
1892 Pit-N	26	27	.491	56	53	45	0	0	440¹	447	11	194	157	13.6	3.47	95	.253	.334	18	.101	-12	-9	-2	-2	-2.1
1893 Pit-N	0	0	—	1	1	0	0	0	2¹	6	0	1	0	27.0	11.57	39	.462	.500	0	.000	-2	-2	-2	0	0.0
NY-N	16	20	.444	45	39	33	2	2	331¹	335	6	141	100	13.3	4.10	114	.255	.332	17	.127	-11	21	20	-3	0.5
Yr	16	20	.444	46	40	33	2	**2**	333²	341	6	142	100	13.4	4.15	112	.257	.331	17	.126	-11	19	19	-3	0.5
Total 7	155	165	.484	346	328	295	14	4	2802¹	2695	82	1307	1349	13.2	3.37	113	.244	.331	188	.163	-31	128	139	-1	8.9

● O. F. BALDWIN
Baldwin, Orson F. b: 11/3/1881, Carson City, Mich. d: 2/16/42, Los Angeles, Cal. TR, 185 lbs. Deb: 9/6/08

YEAR TM/L	W	L	PCT	G	GS	CG	SH	SV	IP	H	HR	BB	SO	RAT	ERA	ERA+	OAV	OOB	BH	AVG	PB	PR	/A	PD	TPI
1908 StL-N	1	3	.250	4	4	0	0	0	14²	16	0	11	5	18.4	6.14	38	.302	.448	0	.000	-1	-6	-6	-0	-1.5

● RICK BALDWIN
Baldwin, Rickey Alan b: 6/1/53, Fresno, Cal. BL/TR, 6'3", 180 lbs. Deb: 4/10/75

YEAR TM/L	W	L	PCT	G	GS	CG	SH	SV	IP	H	HR	BB	SO	RAT	ERA	ERA+	OAV	OOB	BH	AVG	PB	PR	/A	PD	TPI
1975 NY-N	3	5	.375	54	0	0	0	6	97¹	97	4	34	54	12.5	3.33	104	.263	.332	3	.200	0	3	1	1	0.2
1976 NY-N	0	0	—	11	0	0	0	0	22²	14	0	10	9	10.3	2.38	138	.189	.302	1	.333	0	3	2	0	0.0
1977 NY-N	1	2	.333	40	0	0	0	1	62²	62	6	31	23	14.1	4.45	84	.265	.363	2	.500	-1	-4	-5	1	-0.1
Total 3	4	7	.364	105	0	0	0	7	182²	173	10	75	86	12.8	3.60	98	.256	.339	6	.273	-1	2	-1	1	0.1

● JEFF BALLARD
Ballard, Jeffrey Scott b: 8/13/63, Billings, Mont. BL/TL, 6'2", 198 lbs. Deb: 5/9/87

YEAR TM/L	W	L	PCT	G	GS	CG	SH	SV	IP	H	HR	BB	SO	RAT	ERA	ERA+	OAV	OOB	BH	AVG	PB	PR	/A	PD	TPI
1987 Bal-A	2	8	.200	14	14	0	0	0	69²	100	15	27	27	17.4	6.59	67	.344	.414		—	0	-17	-17	0	-1.8
1988 Bal-A	8	12	.400	25	25	6	1	0	153¹	167	15	42	41	12.6	4.40	89	.278	.332		—	0	-7	-9	-2	-1.0
1989 Bal-A	18	8	.692	35	35	4	0	0	215¹	240	16	57	62	12.6	3.43	111	.287	.336		—	0	11	9	4	1.6
1990 Bal-A	2	11	.154	44	17	0	0	0	133¹	152	22	42	50	13.3	4.93	77	.289	.345		—	0	-15	-17	0	-1.3

YEAR	TM/L	W	L	PCT	G	GS	CG	SH	SV	IP	H	HR	BB	SO	RAT	ERA	ERA+	OAV	OOB	BH	AVG	PB	PR	/A	PD	TPI
1991	Bal-A	6	12	.333	26	22	0	0	0	123²	153	16	28	37	13.3	5.60	71	.302	.341	0	—	0	-21	-23	-1	-2.7
1993	Pit-N	4	1	.800	25	5	0	0	0	53²	70	3	15	16	14.6	4.86	83	.332	.382	4	.364	-1	-5	-5	1	-0.2
1994	Pit-N	1	1	.500	28	0	0	0	2	24¹	32	5	10	11	15.9	6.66	65	.323	.391	1	.500	0	-7	-6	-0	-0.5
Total	7	41	53	.436	197	118	10	2	2	773¹	914	92	229	244	13.5	4.71	83	.298	.350	5	.385	2	-60	-67	2	-5.9

● JAY BALLER
Baller, Jay Scot   b: 10/6/60, Stayton, Ore.   BR/TR, 6'7", 225 lbs.   Deb: 9/19/82

YEAR	TM/L	W	L	PCT	G	GS	CG	SH	SV	IP	H	HR	BB	SO	RAT	ERA	ERA+	OAV	OOB	BH	AVG	PB	PR	/A	PD	TPI
1982	Phi-N	0	0	—	4	1	0	0	0	8	7	1	2	7	11.3	3.38	109	.226	.294	0	—	0	0	-0	0.0
1985	Chi-N	2	3	.400	20	4	0	0	1	52	52	8	17	31	12.1	3.46	115	.260	.321	0	.000	-1	1	3	-0	0.2
1986	Chi-N	2	4	.333	36	0	0	0	5	53²	58	7	28	42	14.8	5.37	75	.275	.365	0	.000	-1	-10	-8	-1	-1.1
1987	Chi-N	0	1	.000	23	0	0	0	0	29¹	38	4	20	27	17.8	6.75	63	.325	.423	1	1.000	0	-9	-8	-0	-0.2
1990	KC-A	0	1	.000	3	0	0	0	0	2¹	4	1	2	1	27.0	15.43	25	.364	.500	0	—	-0	-3	-3	-0	-0.9
1992	Phi-N	0	0	—	8	0	0	0	0	11	10	5	10	9	16.4	8.18	43	.250	.400	0	—	0	-6	-6	-0	0.0
Total	6	4	9	.308	94	5	0	0	6	156¹	169	26	79	117	14.6	5.24	77	.277	.365	1	.071	-1	-26	-21	-2	-2.0

● MARK BALLINGER
Ballinger, Mark Alan   b: 1/31/49, Glendale, Cal.   BR/TR, 6'6", 205 lbs.   Deb: 8/6/71

YEAR	TM/L	W	L	PCT	G	GS	CG	SH	SV	IP	H	HR	BB	SO	RAT	ERA	ERA+	OAV	OOB	BH	AVG	PB	PR	/A	PD	TPI
1971	Cle-A	1	2	.333	18	0	0	0	0	34²	39	2	13	25	11.4	4.67	82	.233	.308	1	.200	-0	-5	-3	-0	-0.3

● WIN BALLOU
Ballou, Noble Winfield   b: 11/30/1897, Mount Morgan, Ky.   d: 1/30/63, San Francisco, Cal   BR/TL, 5'10.5", 170 lbs.   Deb: 8/24/25

YEAR	TM/L	W	L	PCT	G	GS	CG	SH	SV	IP	H	HR	BB	SO	RAT	ERA	ERA+	OAV	OOB	BH	AVG	PB	PR	/A	PD	TPI
1925	*Was-A	1	1	.500	10	1	0	0	0	27²	38	1	13	13	16.6	4.55	93	.342	.411	1	.143	-0	-0	-1	0	-0.1
1926	StL-A	11	10	.524	43	14	5	0	2	154	186	12	71	59	15.3	4.79	90	.311	.387	2	.048	-3	-13	-9	3	-1.0
1927	StL-A	5	6	.455	21	11	4	0	0	90¹	105	4	46	17	15.1	4.78	91	.309	.393	1	.036	-4	-6	-4	-0	-0.8
1929	Bro-N	2	3	.400	25	1	1	0	0	57²	69	5	38	20	16.7	6.71	69	.304	.404	1	.063	-2	-13	-13	2	-0.9
Total	4	19	20	.487	99	27	10	0	2	329²	398	22	168	109	15.6	5.11	86	.312	.394	5	.054	-9	-33	-27	5	-2.8

● TONY BALSAMO
Balsamo, Anthony Fred   b: 11/21/37, Brooklyn, N.Y.   BR/TR, 6'2", 185 lbs.   Deb: 4/14/62

YEAR	TM/L	W	L	PCT	G	GS	CG	SH	SV	IP	H	HR	BB	SO	RAT	ERA	ERA+	OAV	OOB	BH	AVG	PB	PR	/A	PD	TPI
1962	Chi-N	0	1	.000	18	0	0	0	0	29¹	34	1	20	27	16.9	6.44	64	.293	.401	1	.200	-1	-8	-7	1	-0.1

● GEORGE BAMBERGER
Bamberger, George Irvin   b: 8/1/25, Staten Island, N.Y.   BR/TR, 6', 175 lbs.   Deb: 4/19/51   MC

YEAR	TM/L	W	L	PCT	G	GS	CG	SH	SV	IP	H	HR	BB	SO	RAT	ERA	ERA+	OAV	OOB	BH	AVG	PB	PR	/A	PD	TPI
1951	NY-N	0	0	—	2	0	0	0	0	2	4	2	2	1	27.0	18.00	22	.444	.545	0	—	-0	-3	-3	-0	0.0
1952	NY-N	0	0	—	5	0	0	0	0	4	6	1	6	0	27.0	9.00	41	.353	.522	0	—	-0	-2	-2	-0	0.0
1959	Bal-A	0	0	—	3	1	0	0	1	8¹	15	1	2	2	18.4	7.56	50	.405	.436	0	.000	-0	-3	-3	-0	-0.1
Total	3	0	0	—	10	1	0	0	1	14¹	25	4	10	3	22.0	9.42	40	.397	.479	0	.000	-0	-9	-9	-0	-0.1

● SAL BANDO
Bando, Salvatore Leonard   b: 2/13/44, Cleveland, O.   BR/TR, 6', 205 lbs.   Deb: 9/3/66   FC♦

YEAR	TM/L	W	L	PCT	G	GS	CG	SH	SV	IP	H	HR	BB	SO	RAT	ERA	ERA+	OAV	OOB	BH	AVG	PB	PR	/A	PD	TPI
1979	Mil-A	0	0	—	1	0	0	0	0	3	3	0	0	0	9.0	6.00	69	.231	.231	117	.246	1	-1	-1	-0	-0.1

● EDDIE BANE
Bane, Edward Norman   b: 3/22/52, Chicago, Ill.   BR/TL, 5'9", 160 lbs.   Deb: 7/4/73

YEAR	TM/L	W	L	PCT	G	GS	CG	SH	SV	IP	H	HR	BB	SO	RAT	ERA	ERA+	OAV	OOB	BH	AVG	PB	PR	/A	PD	TPI
1973	Min-A	0	5	.000	23	6	0	0	2	60¹	62	5	30	42	14.0	4.92	80	.270	.359	0	—	0	-7	-6	1	-0.7
1975	Min-A	3	1	.750	4	4	0	0	0	28¹	28	5	15	14	14.0	2.86	134	.262	.358	0	—	0	3	3	-1	0.2
1976	Min-A	4	7	.364	17	15	1	0	0	79¹	92	6	39	24	14.9	5.11	70	.290	.368	0	—	0	-14	-13	-2	-2.0
Total	3	7	13	.350	44	25	1	0	2	168	182	13	84	80	14.4	4.66	81	.278	.363	0	—	0	-19	-17	-1	-2.5

● DICK BANEY
Baney, Richard Lee   b: 11/1/46, Fullerton, Cal.   BR/TR, 6', 185 lbs.   Deb: 7/11/69

YEAR	TM/L	W	L	PCT	G	GS	CG	SH	SV	IP	H	HR	BB	SO	RAT	ERA	ERA+	OAV	OOB	BH	AVG	PB	PR	/A	PD	TPI
1969	Sea-A	1	0	1.000	9	1	0	0	0	18²	21	2	7	9	13.5	3.86	94	.292	.354	0	.000	-0	-0	-0	-0	-0.1
1973	Cin-N	2	1	.667	11	1	0	0	2	30²	26	1	6	17	10.6	2.93	116	.234	.298	2	.222	1	2	2	-1	0.1
1974	Cin-N	1	0	1.000	22	1	0	0	1	41	51	4	17	12	14.9	5.49	64	.305	.370	0	.000	-1	-9	-9	-1	-0.4
Total	3	4	1	.800	42	3	0	0	3	90¹	98	7	30	38	13.2	4.28	81	.280	.344	2	.125	-0	-7	-8	-3	-0.4

● DAN BANKHEAD
Bankhead, Daniel Robert   b: 5/3/20, Empire, Ala.   d: 5/2/76, Houston, Tex.   BR/TR, 6'1", 184 lbs.   Deb: 8/26/47

YEAR	TM/L	W	L	PCT	G	GS	CG	SH	SV	IP	H	HR	BB	SO	RAT	ERA	ERA+	OAV	OOB	BH	AVG	PB	PR	/A	PD	TPI
1947	*Bro-N	0	0	—	4	0	0	0	0	10	15	1	8	6	21.6	7.20	57	.341	.453	1	.250	1	-3	-3	-0	0.0
1950	Bro-N	9	4	.692	41	12	2	1	3	129¹	119	16	88	96	14.5	5.50	75	.252	.371	9	.231	1	-19	-20	-1	-1.8
1951	Bro-N	0	1	.000	7	1	0	0	1	14	27	5	14	9	26.4	15.43	25	.422	.526	0	.000	-0	-18	-18	-0	-1.1
Total	3	9	5	.643	52	13	2	1	4	153¹	161	22	110	111	16.1	6.52	63	.277	.395	10	.222	2	-41	-41	-1	-2.9

● SCOTT BANKHEAD
Bankhead, Michael Scott   b: 7/31/63, Raleigh, N.C.   BR/TR, 5'10", 175 lbs.   Deb: 5/25/86

YEAR	TM/L	W	L	PCT	G	GS	CG	SH	SV	IP	H	HR	BB	SO	RAT	ERA	ERA+	OAV	OOB	BH	AVG	PB	PR	/A	PD	TPI
1986	KC-A	8	9	.471	24	17	0	0	0	121	121	14	37	94	12.0	4.61	92	.259	.318	0	—	0	-6	-5	-0	-0.7
1987	Sea-A	9	8	.529	27	25	2	0	0	149¹	168	35	37	95	12.5	5.42	87	.283	.329	0	—	0	-16	-12	-2	-1.5
1988	Sea-A	7	9	.438	21	21	1	0	1	135	115	8	38	102	10.3	3.07	136	.224	.278	0	—	0	13	16	-1	1.7
1989	Sea-A	14	6	.700	33	33	3	2	0	210¹	187	19	63	140	10.8	3.34	121	.239	.298	0	—	0	13	16	-2	1.3
1990	Sea-A	0	2	.000	4	4	0	0	0	13	18	2	7	4	17.3	11.08	36	.333	.410	0	—	0	-10	-10	-1	-1.3
1991	Sea-A	3	6	.333	17	9	0	0	0	60²	73	8	21	28	14.2	4.90	84	.297	.357	0	—	0	-5	-5	-0	-0.7
1992	Cin-N	10	4	.714	54	0	0	0	1	70²	57	4	29	53	11.3	2.93	123	.218	.304	2	.222	5	5	5	-2	0.9
1993	Bos-A	2	1	.667	40	0	0	0	0	64¹	59	7	29	47	12.3	3.50	132	.250	.332	0	—	0	6	8	-0	0.2
1994	Bos-A	3	2	.600	27	0	0	0	0	37²	34	5	12	25	11.0	4.54	111	.239	.299	0	—	0	1	2	-1	-0.1
1995	NY-A	1	1	.500	20	1	0	0	0	39	44	9	16	20	13.8	6.00	77	.278	.345	0	—	0	-6	-6	-1	-0.3
Total	10	57	48	.543	267	110	7	3	1	901	876	111	289	614	11.3	4.18	102	.254	.314	2	.222	5	-6	-11	-11	-0.5

● BILL BANKS
Banks, William John (b: William John Yerrick)   b: 2/26/1874, Danville, Pa.   d: 9/8/36, Danville, Pa.   BR/TR, 5'11", 150 lbs.   Deb: 9/27/1895

YEAR	TM/L	W	L	PCT	G	GS	CG	SH	SV	IP	H	HR	BB	SO	RAT	ERA	ERA+	OAV	OOB	BH	AVG	PB	PR	/A	PD	TPI
1895	Bos-N	1	0	1.000	1	1	1	0	0	7	7	0	4	4	14.1	0.00	—	.259	.355	0	.000	-1	4	4	0	0.5
1896	Bos-N	0	3	.000	4	3	2	0	0	23	42	2	13	6	22.3	10.57	43	.389	.463	3	.273	0	-16	-15	-1	-1.4
Total	2	1	3	.250	5	4	3	0	0	30	49	2	17	10	20.4	8.10	58	.363	.442	3	.214	-1	-12	-11	-1	-0.9

● WILLIE BANKS
Banks, Willie Anthony   b: 2/27/69, Jersey City, N.J.   BR/TR, 6'1", 190 lbs.   Deb: 7/31/91

YEAR	TM/L	W	L	PCT	G	GS	CG	SH	SV	IP	H	HR	BB	SO	RAT	ERA	ERA+	OAV	OOB	BH	AVG	PB	PR	/A	PD	TPI
1991	Min-A	1	1	.500	5	3	0	0	0	17¹	21	1	12	16	17.1	5.71	75	.288	.388	0	—	0	-3	-3	-1	-0.6
1992	Min-A	4	4	.500	16	12	0	0	0	71	80	6	37	37	15.1	5.70	71	.288	.375	0	—	0	-14	-13	-0	-1.5
1993	Min-A	11	12	.478	31	30	0	0	0	171¹	186	17	78	138	14.0	4.04	108	.280	.358	0	—	0	5	6	-1	0.6
1994	Chi-N	8	12	.400	23	23	1	1	0	138¹	139	16	56	91	12.8	5.40	77	.261	.333	5	.122	-1	-18	-19	-2	-2.6
1995	Chi-N	0	1	.000	10	0	0	0	0	11²	27	5	12	9	30.1	15.43	27	.458	.549	0	.000	-0	-15	-15	0	-1.0
	LA-N	0	2	.000	6	6	0	0	0	29	36	2	16	23	16.4	4.03	94	.303	.390	1	.125	0	0	-0	0	0.0
	Fla-N	2	3	.400	9	9	0	0	0	50	43	7	30	30	13.3	4.32	98	.235	.346	6	.353	2	-1	-1	-0	0.1
	Yr	2	6	.250	25	15	0	0	0	90²	106	14	58	62	16.4	5.66	72	.291	.390	7	.269	2	-15	-16	-0	-0.9
Total	5	26	35	.426	100	83	1	1	0	488²	532	54	241	344	14.4	5.03	83	.279	.362	12	.179	1	-45	-45	-4	-5.0

● FLOYD BANNISTER
Bannister, Floyd Franklin   b: 6/10/55, Pierre, S.D.   BL/TL, 6'1", 195 lbs.   Deb: 4/19/77

YEAR	TM/L	W	L	PCT	G	GS	CG	SH	SV	IP	H	HR	BB	SO	RAT	ERA	ERA+	OAV	OOB	BH	AVG	PB	PR	/A	PD	TPI
1977	Hou-N	8	9	.471	24	23	4	1	0	142³	138	11	68	112	13.2	4.04	88	.254	.341	9	.188	0	-2	-7	-1	-0.9
1978	Hou-N	3	9	.250	28	16	2	2	0	110¹	120	13	63	94	15.0	4.81	69	.280	.374	5	.161	-2	-15	-18	-2	-2.0
1979	Sea-A	10	15	.400	30	30	6	2	0	182¹	185	25	68	115	12.7	4.05	108	.260	.328	0	—	0	3	6	-2	0.4
1980	Sea-A	9	13	.409	32	32	8	0	0	217²	200	24	66	155	11.1	3.47	119	.239	.296	0	—	0	14	16	-1	1.4
1981	Sea-A	9	9	.500	21	21	2	0	0	121¹	128	14	39	85	12.6	4.45	87	.268	.327	0	—	0	-11	-8	-1	-1.3
1982	Sea-A★	12	13	.480	35	35	5	3	0	247	225	32	77	**209**	11.1	3.43	124	.243	.303	0	—	0	18	22	-1	1.9
1983	*Chi-A	16	10	.615	34	34	5	2	0	217¹	191	19	71	193	10.9	3.35	125	.233	.295	0	—	0	17	20	-1	1.9
1984	Chi-A	14	11	.560	34	34	4	0	0	218	211	30	80	152	12.3	4.83	86	.252	.322	0	.000	0	-20	-16	-2	-1.8
1985	Chi-A	10	14	.417	34	34	4	1	0	210²	211	30	100	198	13.5	4.87	89	.261	.346	0	—	0	-17	-13	-1	-1.5
1986	Chi-A	10	14	.417	28	27	6	1	0	165¹	162	17	48	92	11.5	3.54	122	.259	.314	0	—	0	12	14	-1	1.7
1987	Chi-A	16	11	.593	34	34	11	2	0	228²	216	38	49	124	10.4	3.58	128	.246	.286	0	—	0	22	25	-3	2.3
1988	KC-A	12	13	.480	31	31	2	0	0	189¹	182	22	68	113	12.1	4.33	92	.248	.316	0	—	0	-8	-7	-0	-0.9
1989	KC-A	4	1	.800	14	14	0	0	0	75¹	87	8	18	35	12.7	4.66	83	.290	.332	0	—	0	-7	-7	-1	-0.3
1991	Cal-A	0	0	—	16	0	0	0	0	25	25	5	10	16	12.6	3.96	104	.266	.337	0	—	0	0	-0	-0	0.0
1992	Tex-A	1	1	.500	36	0	0	0	0	37	39	3	21	30	15.3	6.32	60	.281	.387	0	—	0	-10	-10	-0	-0.3
Total	15	134	143	.484	431	363	62	16	0	2388	2320	291	846	1723	12.1	4.06	101	.253	.319	14	.175	-3	0	6	-0	0.6

YEAR	TM/L	W	L	PCT	G	GS	CG	SH	SV	IP	H	HR	BB	SO	RAT	ERA	ERA+	OAV	OOB	BH	AVG	PB	PR	/A	PD	TPI

● **JIMMY BANNON** Bannon, James Henry "Foxy Grandpa" b: 5/5/1871, Amesbury, Mass. d: 3/24/48, Glen Rock, N.J. BR/TR, 5'5", 160 lbs. Deb: 6/15/1893 F♦

1893	StL-N	0	1	.000	1	1	0	0	0	4	10	1	5	1	38.3	22.50	21	.455	.586	36	.336	0	-8	-8	-0	-1.0
1894	Bos-N	0	0	—	1	0	0	0	0	2	4	1	1	0	22.5	0.00	—	.400	.455	166	.336	0	1	1	0	0.0
1895	Bos-N	0	0	—	1	0	0	0	0	3	4	0	2	1	18.0	6.00	85	.308	.400	171	.350	0	-0	0	0	0.0
Total	3	0	1	.000	3	1	0	0	0	9	18	2	8	2	28.0	12.00	42	.400	.509	459	.320	1	-7	-7	-0	-1.0

● **JACK BANTA** Banta, Jackie Kay b: 6/24/25, Hutchinson, Kan. BL/TR, 6'2.5", 175 lbs. Deb: 9/18/47

1947	Bro-N	0	1	.000	3	1	0	0	0	7²	7	1	4	3	14.1	7.04	59	.226	.333	0	.000	-0	-3	-2	1	-0.2
1948	Bro-N	0	1	.000	2	1	0	0	0	3¹	5	0	5	1	27.0	8.10	49	.385	.556	0	.000	-0	-2	-2	-0	-0.4
1949	*Bro-N	10	6	.625	48	12	2	1	3	152¹	125	12	68	97	11.8	3.37	122	.223	.314	5	.109	-2	11	12	1	1.1
1950	Bro-N	4	4	.500	16	5	1	0	2	41³	39	2	36	15	17.0	4.35	94	.252	.402	2	.167	-0	-1	-1	-1	-0.3
Total	4	14	12	.538	69	19	3	1	5	204²	176	15	113	116	13.1	3.78	108	.232	.339	7	.115	-2	6	7	0	0.2

● **BRIAN BARBER** Barber, Brian Scott b: 3/4/73, Hamilton, Ohio BR/TR, 6'1", 170 lbs. Deb: 8/12/95

1995	StL-N	2	1	.667	9	4	0	0	0	29¹	31	4	16	27	14.4	5.22	80	.279	.370	1	.125	-0	-3	-3	-1	-0.4
1996	StL-N	0	0	—	1	1	0	0	0	3	4	0	6	1	33.0	15.00	28	.364	.611	0	—	0	-4	-4	-0	0.0
Total	2	2	1	.667	10	5	0	0	0	32¹	35	4	22	28	16.1	6.12	68	.287	.400	1	.125	-0	-7	-7	-1	-0.4

● **STEVE BARBER** Barber, Stephen David b: 2/22/39, Takoma Park, Md. BL/TL, 6', 200 lbs. Deb: 4/21/60

1960	Bal-A	10	7	.588	36	27	6	1	2	181²	148	10	113	112	13.1	3.22	118	.226	.343	3	.056	-4	13	12	0	0.7
1961	Bal-A	18	12	.600	37	34	14	**8**	1	248¹	194	13	130	150	11.8	3.33	115	.218	.319	13	.162	2	19	14	4	2.2
1962	Bal-A	9	6	.600	28	19	5	2	0	140¹	145	9	61	89	13.3	3.46	107	.262	.337	3	.071	-2	8	4	1	0.3
1963	Bal-A†	20	13	.606	39	36	11	6	0	258²	253	12	92	180	12.1	2.75	126	.258	.324	12	.138	-0	25	21	2	2.8
1964	Bal-A	9	13	.409	36	26	4	0	1	157	144	15	81	118	13.3	3.84	93	.248	.347	7	.149	1	-4	-5	3	-0.3
1965	Bal-A	15	10	.600	37	32	7	2	0	220¹	177	16	81	130	10.6	2.69	129	.224	.297	5	.077	-2	19	19	1	2.1
1966	Bal-A☆	10	5	.667	25	22	5	3	0	133¹	104	6	49	91	10.5	2.30	145	.218	.294	3	.068	-3	17	15	1	1.5
1967	Bal-A	4	9	.308	15	15	1	1	0	74²	47	5	61	48	13.6	4.10	77	.185	.353	2	.091	-1	-7	-8	-1	-1.3
	NY-A	6	9	.400	17	17	3	1	0	97²	103	4	54	70	14.7	4.05	77	.278	.375	5	.172	1	-9	-10	-1	-1.4
	Yr	10	18	.357	32	32	4	2	0	172¹	150	9	115	118	14.0	4.07	77	.238	.358	7	.137	1	-16	-18	-1	-2.7
1968	NY-A	6	5	.545	20	19	3	1	0	128¹	127	7	64	87	13.6	3.23	90	.256	.345	2	.051	-1	-4	-5	-0	-0.5
1969	Sea-A	4	7	.364	25	16	0	0	0	86¹	99	9	48	69	15.4	4.80	76	.292	.381	5	.200	1	-11	-11	0	-1.2
1970	Chi-N	0	1	.000	5	2	0	0	0	5²	10	1	6	3	25.4	9.53	47	.417	.533	0	—	0	-3	-3	-0	-0.5
	Atl-N	0	1	.000	5	2	0	0	0	14²	17	3	5	11	14.1	4.91	87	.288	.354	1	.250	0	-1	-1	-0	-0.1
	Yr	0	2	.000	10	2	0	0	0	20¹	27	3	11	14	17.3	6.20	70	.325	.411	1	.250	0	-5	-4	-0	-0.6
1971	Atl-N	3	1	.750	39	3	0	0	2	75	92	6	25	40	14.3	4.80	77	.301	.357	2	.154	-0	-11	-9	-0	-0.5
1972	Atl-N	0	0	—	5	0	0	0	0	15²	18	1	6	8	14.4	5.74	66	.290	.362	1	.200	0	-4	-3	1	0.1
	Cal-A	4	4	.500	34	3	0	0	2	58	37	4	30	34	10.6	2.02	144	.188	.298	1	.143	1	7	6	-1	0.9
1973	Cal-A	3	2	.600	50	1	0	0	4	89¹	90	5	32	58	12.6	3.53	101	.265	.333	0	—	0	3	0	-1	0.5
1974	SF-N	0	1	.000	13	0	0	0	0	13²	13	0	12	13	16.5	5.27	72	.255	.397	0	—	0	-3	-2	-1	-0.2
Total	15	121	106	.533	466	272	59	21	13	1999	1818	125	950	1309	12.7	3.36	105	.245	.334	65	.115	-6	54	34	10	5.1

● **STEVE BARBER** Barber, Steven Lee b: 3/13/48, Grand Rapids, Mich. BR/TR, 6'1", 190 lbs. Deb: 4/9/70

1970	Min-A	0	0	—	18	0	0	0	2	27¹	26	1	18	14	15.1	4.61	81	.263	.387	0	.000	-0	-3	-3	-0	-0.1
1971	Min-A	1	0	1.000	4	2	0	0	0	11²	8	2	13	4	16.2	6.17	58	.190	.382	0	.000	-1	-4	-3	-0	-0.3
Total	2	1	0	1.000	22	2	0	0	2	39	34	3	31	18	15.5	5.08	72	.241	.385	0	.000	-1	-6	-6	-1	-0.4

● **FRANK BARBERICH** Barberich, Frank Frederick b: 2/3/1882, Newtown, N.Y. d: 5/1/65, Ocala, Fla. BB/TR, 5'10.5", 175 lbs. Deb: 9/17/07

1907	Bos-N	1	1	.500	2	2	1	0	0	12¹	19	0	5	1	17.5	5.84	44	.358	.414	0	.000	-0	-5	-5	0	-0.7
1910	Bos-N	0	0	—	2	0	0	0	0	5	7	0	2	0	16.2	7.20	35	.350	.409	0	.000	-0	-3	-3	0	0.0
Total	2	1	1	.500	4	2	1	0	0	17¹	26	0	7	1	17.1	6.23	41	.356	.412	0	.000	-1	-7	-7	0	-0.7

● **CURT BARCLAY** Barclay, Curtis Cordell b: 8/22/31, Chicago, Ill. d: 3/25/85, Missoula, Montana BR/TR, 6'3", 210 lbs. Deb: 4/21/57

1957	NY-N	9	9	.500	37	28	5	2	0	183	196	21	48	67	12.1	3.44	114	.274	.321	11	.190	0	9	10	3	1.2
1958	SF-N	1	0	1.000	6	1	0	0	0	16	16	3	5	6	13.5	2.81	136	.258	.343	4	.667	2	2	2	0	0.3
1959	SF-N	0	0	—	1	0	0	0	0	0¹	2	0	2	0	108.0	54.00	7	.500	.667	0	—	0	-2	-2	-0	0.0
Total	3	10	9	.526	44	29	5	2	0	199¹	214	24	55	73	12.4	3.48	113	.274	.325	15	.234	2	9	10	3	1.5

● **RAY BARE** Bare, Raymond Douglas b: 4/15/49, Miami, Fla. d: 3/29/94, Miami, Fla. BR/TR, 6'2", 195 lbs. Deb: 7/30/72

1972	StL-N	0	1	.000	14	0	0	0	1	16²	18	0	6	5	13.0	0.54	590	.281	.343	0	—	0	5	5	-0	0.4
1974	StL-N	1	2	.333	10	3	0	0	0	24¹	25	2	9	6	12.6	5.92	60	.281	.347	1	.200	-0	-6	-6	1	-0.6
1975	Det-A	8	13	.381	29	21	6	1	0	150²	174	16	47	71	13.3	4.48	90	.293	.346	0	—	0	-12	-8	2	-1.1
1976	Det-A	7	8	.467	30	21	3	2	0	134	157	13	51	59	14.0	4.63	80	.293	.354	0	—	0	-17	-14	1	-1.4
1977	Det-A	0	2	.000	5	4	0	0	0	14¹	24	3	7	4	19.5	12.56	34	.381	.443	0	—	0	-14	-13	0	-1.6
Total	5	16	26	.381	88	49	9	3	2	340	398	28	120	145	13.7	4.79	80	.296	.354	1	.200	-0	-43	-36	4	-4.3

● **JOHN BARFIELD** Barfield, John David b: 10/15/64, Pine Bluff, Ark. BL/TL, 6'1", 185 lbs. Deb: 9/7/89

1989	Tex-A	0	1	.000	4	2	0	0	0	11²	15	0	9	14	14.7	6.17	64	.319	.373	0	—	0	-3	-3	-0	-0.3
1990	Tex-A	4	3	.571	33	0	0	0	1	44¹	42	2	13	17	11.4	4.67	84	.268	.327	0	—	0	-4	-4	-0	-0.5
1991	Tex-A	4	4	.500	28	9	0	0	1	83¹	96	11	22	27	12.7	4.54	89	.289	.333	0	—	0	-4	-5	-0	-0.4
Total	3	8	8	.500	65	11	0	0	2	139¹	153	13	39	53	12.5	4.72	85	.285	.335	0	—	0	-11	-11	-0	-1.2

● **CLYDE BARFOOT** Barfoot, Clyde Raymond "Foots" b: 7/8/1891, Richmond, Va. d: 3/11/71, Highland Park, Cal BR/TR, 6', 170 lbs. Deb: 4/13/22

1922	StL-N	4	5	.444	42	2	1	0	2	117²	139	2	30	19	13.7	4.21	92	.307	.363	12	.353	5	-1	-4	1	0.2
1923	StL-N	3	3	.500	33	2	1	1	1	101¹	112	7	27	23	12.4	3.73	105	.289	.337	7	.189	-1	3	2	0	0.0
1926	Det-A	1	2	.333	11	1	0	0	2	31¹	42	4	12	7	14.6	4.88	83	.318	.362	1	.200	-0	-3	-3	1	-0.2
Total	3	8	10	.444	86	5	2	1	5	250¹	293	13	66	49	13.3	4.10	95	.301	.353	20	.263	4	-1	-5	1	0.0

● **GREG BARGAR** Bargar, Greg Robert b: 1/27/59, Inglewood, Cal. BR/TR, 6'2", 185 lbs. Deb: 7/17/83

1983	Mon-N	2	0	1.000	8	3	0	0	0	20	23	6	8	9	14.4	6.75	53	.271	.340	1	.167	-0	-7	-7	-1	-0.7
1984	Mon-N	0	1	.000	3	1	0	0	0	8	8	1	7	2	16.9	7.88	43	.286	.429	0	.000	-0	-4	-4	0	-0.4
1986	StL-N	0	2	.000	22	0	0	0	0	27¹	36	3	10	12	16.1	5.60	65	.330	.402	0	.000	-0	-6	-6	1	-0.4
Total	3	2	3	.400	33	4	0	0	0	55¹	67	10	25	23	15.6	6.34	57	.302	.382	1	.111	-0	-16	-17	0	-1.5

● **CY BARGER** Barger, Eros Bolivar b: 5/18/1885, Jamestown, Ky. d: 9/23/64, Columbia, Ky. BL/TR, 6', 160 lbs. Deb: 8/30/06

1906	NY-A	0	0	—	2	1	0	0	0	5¹	7	0	3	3	16.9	10.13	29	.318	.400	1	.333	0	-4	-4	-0	-0.2
1907	NY-A	0	0	—	1	0	0	0	0	6	10	0	1	0	18.0	3.00	93	.370	.414	0	.000	-0	-0	-0	-1	-0.1
1910	Bro-N	15	15	.500	35	30	25	2	1	271²	267	2	107	87	12.6	2.88	105	.275	.351	24	.231	3	5	5	2	0.2
1911	Bro-N	11	15	.423	30	30	21	1	0	217¹	224	9	71	60	12.5	3.52	95	.279	.342	33	.228	1	-3	-4	1	-0.2
1912	Bro-N	1	9	.100	16	11	6	0	0	94	120	4	42	30	15.9	5.46	61	.326	.401	7	.189	-0	-21	-22	1	-1.9
1914	Pit-F	10	16	.385	33	26	18	1	1	228¹	252	7	63	70	12.7	4.34	66	.290	.342	17	.205	-1	-37	-37	-2	-4.0
1915	Pit-F	9	8	.529	34	13	8	1	6	153	130	1	47	47	10.6	2.29	118	.238	.303	15	.278	2	7	7	-1	0.9
Total	7	46	63	.422	151	111	78	5	9	975²	1010	18	334	297	12.7	3.56	85	.280	.346	97	.227	5	-54	-56	-0	-4.5

● **BRIAN BARK** Bark, Brian Stuart b: 8/26/68, Baltimore, Md. BL/TL, 5'9", 170 lbs. Deb: 7/6/95

| 1995 | Bos-A | 0 | 0 | — | 3 | 0 | 0 | 0 | 0 | 2¹ | 2 | 0 | 1 | 0 | 11.6 | 0.00 | — | .286 | .375 | 0 | — | 0 | 1 | 1 | -0 | -0.1 |

● **LEN BARKER** Barker, Leonard Harold b: 7/7/55, Fort Knox, Ky. BR/TR, 6'5", 225 lbs. Deb: 9/14/76

1976	Tex-A	1	0	1.000	2	2	1	0	0	15	7	0	9	12	9.6	2.40	149	.149	.273	—	—	0	2	2	-0	0.1
1977	Tex-A	4	1	.800	15	3	0	0	1	47¹	36	1	24	51	11.6	2.66	153	.217	.319	—	—	0	7	7	1	0.8
1978	Tex-A	1	5	.167	29	0	0	0	4	52¹	63	6	29	33	16.2	4.82	78	.304	.395	—	—	0	-6	-6	-0	-0.7
1979	Cle-A	6	6	.500	29	19	2	0	0	137¹	146	6	70	93	14.3	4.92	87	.277	.364	—	—	0	-11	-10	-1	-0.9
1980	Cle-A	19	12	.613	36	36	8	1	0	246¹	237	17	92	**187**	12.1	4.17	98	.252	.320	—	—	0	-4	-3	-2	-0.5

YEAR TM/L	W	L	PCT	G	GS	CG	SH	SV	IP	H	HR	BB	SO	RAT	ERA	ERA+	OAV	OOB	BH	AVG	PB	PR	/A	PD	TPI
1981 Cle-A★	8	7	.533	22	22	9	3	0	154¹	150	7	46	**127**	11.5	3.91	93	.249	.303	0	—	0	-4	-5	-0	-0.4
1982 Cle-A	15	11	.577	33	33	10	1	0	244²	211	17	88	187	11.1	3.90	105	.232	.301	0	—	0	5	5	-0	0.5
1983 Cle-A	8	13	.381	24	24	4	1	0	149²	150	16	52	105	12.3	5.11	83	.266	.330	0	—	0	-17	-15	-1	-2.0
Atl-N	1	3	.250	6	6	0	0	0	33	31	0	14	21	12.3	3.82	102	.248	.324	1	.125	-0	-1	0	1	0.1
1984 Atl-N	7	8	.467	21	20	1	0	0	126¹	120	10	38	95	11.4	3.85	100	.254	.312	2	.053	-1	-4	-4	3	0.1
1985 Atl-N	2	9	.182	20	18	0	0	0	73²	84	10	37	47	14.9	6.35	61	.288	.370	0	.000	-2	-23	-21	-1	-3.0
1987 Mil-A	2	1	.667	11	11	0	0	0	43²	54	6	17	22	15.0	5.36	85	.303	.371	0	—	0	-4	-4	-0	-0.4
Total 11	74	76	.493	248	194	35	7	5	1323²	1289	96	513	975	12.4	4.34	95	.256	.327	3	.048	-3	-59	-48	-1	-6.2

● JEFF BARKLEY
Barkley, Jeffrey Carver   b: 11/21/59, Hickory, N.C.   BB/TR, 6'3", 185 lbs.   Deb: 9/16/84

YEAR TM/L	W	L	PCT	G	GS	CG	SH	SV	IP	H	HR	BB	SO	RAT	ERA	ERA+	OAV	OOB	BH	AVG	PB	PR	/A	PD	TPI
1984 Cle-A	0	0	—	3	0	0	0	0	4	6	1	4	4	15.8	6.75	61	.353	.389	0	—	0	-1	-1	0	-0.1
1985 Cle-A	0	3	.000	21	0	0	0	1	41	37	5	15	30	11.4	5.27	78	.243	.311	0	—	0	-5	-5	0	-0.3
Total 2	0	3	.000	24	0	0	0	1	45	43	6	16	34	11.8	5.40	76	.254	.319	0	—	0	-6	-6	0	-0.4

● MIKE BARLOW
Barlow, Michael Roswell   b: 4/30/48, Stamford, N.Y.   BL/TR, 6'6", 215 lbs.   Deb: 6/18/75

YEAR TM/L	W	L	PCT	G	GS	CG	SH	SV	IP	H	HR	BB	SO	RAT	ERA	ERA+	OAV	OOB	BH	AVG	PB	PR	/A	PD	TPI
1975 StL-N	0	0	—	9	0	0	0	0	7²	11	0	3	2	17.6	4.70	80	.355	.429	0	—	0	-1	-1	-0	0.0
1976 Hou-N	2	2	.500	16	0	0	0	0	22	27	0	17	11	18.0	4.50	71	.318	.431	0	.000	-0	-2	-3	1	-0.5
1977 Cal-A	4	2	.667	20	1	0	0	0	59	53	3	27	25	12.8	4.58	86	.249	.344	0	—	0	-3	-4	-0	-0.1
1978 Cal-A	0	0	—	1	0	0	0	0	2	3	0	0	1	13.5	4.50	80	.375	.375	0	—	0	-0	-0	-0	0.0
1979 *Cal-A	1	1	.500	35	0	0	0	0	86	106	8	30	33	14.7	5.13	79	.314	.376	0	—	0	-9	-10	-0	-0.1
1980 Tor-A	3	1	.750	40	1	0	0	5	55	57	4	21	19	13.1	4.09	105	.273	.345	0	—	0	-0	1	-0	-0.1
1981 Tor-A	0	0	—	12	0	0	0	0	15	22	1	6	5	19.2	4.20	94	.338	.427	0	—	0	-1	-0	0	0.0
Total 7	10	6	.625	133	2	0	0	6	246²	279	16	104	96	14.5	4.63	86	.294	.373	0	.000	-0	-17	-18	-0	-0.7

● CHARLIE BARNABE
Barnabe, Charles Edward   b: 6/12/1900, Russell Gulch, Colo.   d: 8/16/77, Waco, Tex.   BL/TL, 5'11.5", 164 lbs.   Deb: 4/14/27

YEAR TM/L	W	L	PCT	G	GS	CG	SH	SV	IP	H	HR	BB	SO	RAT	ERA	ERA+	OAV	OOB	BH	AVG	PB	PR	/A	PD	TPI
1927 Chi-A	0	5	.000	17	4	1	0	0	61	86	2	20	5	16.4	5.31	76	.351	.411	3	.158	1	-8	-9	1	-0.4
1928 Chi-A	0	2	.000	7	2	0	0	0	9²	17	0	3	3	16.8	6.52	62	.395	.409	4	.500	2	-3	-3	1	-0.2
Total 2	0	7	.000	24	6	1	0	0	70²	103	2	23	8	16.4	5.48	74	.358	.411	7	.259	3	-11	-11	1	-0.6

● BRIAN BARNES
Barnes, Brian Keith   b: 3/25/67, Roanoke Rapids, N.C.   BL/TL, 5'9", 170 lbs.   Deb: 9/14/90

YEAR TM/L	W	L	PCT	G	GS	CG	SH	SV	IP	H	HR	BB	SO	RAT	ERA	ERA+	OAV	OOB	BH	AVG	PB	PR	/A	PD	TPI
1990 Mon-N	1	1	.500	4	4	1	0	0	28	25	2	7	23	10.3	2.89	126	.236	.283	0	.000	-1	3	2	0	0.1
1991 Mon-N	5	8	.385	28	27	1	0	0	160	135	16	84	117	12.7	4.22	86	.233	.336	4	.082	-1	-10	-11	1	-0.7
1992 Mon-N	6	6	.500	21	17	0	0	0	100	77	9	46	65	11.3	2.97	117	.213	.307	8	.276	2	6	6	0	0.9
1993 Mon-N	2	6	.250	52	8	0	0	3	100	105	9	48	60	13.8	4.41	95	.274	.355	3	.150	-0	-4	-3	-0	-0.2
1994 Cle-A	0	1	.000	6	0	0	0	0	13¹	12	2	15	11	18.2	5.40	87	.235	.409	0	—	0	-1	-1	-0	-0.1
LA-N				5	0	0	0	0	5	10	1	4	5	25.2	7.20	54	.400	.483	0	—	0	-2	-2	0	-0.1
Total 5	14	22	.389	116	56	2	0	3	406¹	364	39	204	275	12.8	3.94	95	.242	.335	15	.140	1	-7	-8	1	0.0

● FRANK BARNES
Barnes, Frank   b: 8/26/26, Longwood, Miss.   BR/TR, 6', 170 lbs.   Deb: 9/22/57

YEAR TM/L	W	L	PCT	G	GS	CG	SH	SV	IP	H	HR	BB	SO	RAT	ERA	ERA+	OAV	OOB	BH	AVG	PB	PR	/A	PD	TPI
1957 StL-N	0	1	.000	3	1	0	0	0	10	13	0	9	5	19.8	4.50	88	.317	.440	0	.000	-0	-1	-1	-0	-0.1
1958 StL-N	1	1	.500	8	1	0	0	0	19	19	3	16	17	17.5	7.58	54	.260	.407	1	.167	-0	-8	-7	-0	-0.7
1960 StL-N	0	1	.000	4	1	0	0	1	7²	9	1	9	8	21.1	3.52	116	.267	.450	0	—	0	-0	-0	-0	-0.0
Total 3	1	3	.250	15	3	0	0	1	36²	40	4	34	30	18.9	5.89	69	.278	.425	1	.100	-1	-8	-7	-1	-0.8

● FRANK BARNES
Barnes, Frank Samuel "Lefty"   b: 1/9/1900, Dallas, Tex.   d: 9/27/67, Houston, Tex.   BL/TL, 6'2.5", 195 lbs.   Deb: 4/18/29

YEAR TM/L	W	L	PCT	G	GS	CG	SH	SV	IP	H	HR	BB	SO	RAT	ERA	ERA+	OAV	OOB	BH	AVG	PB	PR	/A	PD	TPI
1929 Det-A	0	1	.000	4	1	0	0	0	5	10	3	3	0	25.2	7.20	60	.400	.482	0	.000	-0	-2	-2	0	-0.3
1930 NY-A	0	1	.000	2	2	0	0	0	12¹	13	0	13	2	19.7	8.03	54	.283	.450	2	.333	1	-5	-5	1	-0.1
Total 2	0	2	.000	6	3	0	0	0	17¹	23	0	16	2	21.3	7.79	55	.324	.461	2	.286	1	-6	-7	2	-0.4

● JESSE BARNES
Barnes, Jesse Lawrence "Nubby"   b: 8/26/1892, Perkins, Okla.   d: 9/9/61, Santa Rosa, N.Mex.   BR/TR, 6', 170 lbs.   Deb: 7/30/15   F

YEAR TM/L	W	L	PCT	G	GS	CG	SH	SV	IP	H	HR	BB	SO	RAT	ERA	ERA+	OAV	OOB	BH	AVG	PB	PR	/A	PD	TPI
1915 Bos-N	3	0	1.000	9	3	2	0	0	45¹	41	1	10	16	10.9	1.39	186	.244	.302	3	.176	0	7	6	-1	0.3
1916 Bos-N	6	15	.286	33	18	9	3	1	163	154	3	37	55	10.8	2.37	105	.254	.302	9	.188	0	4	2	4	0.7
1917 Bos-N	13	21	.382	50	33	27	2	1	295	261	3	50	107	9.6	2.68	95	.241	.277	24	.238	4	1	-4	3	0.3
1918 NY-N	6	1	.857	9	9	4	2	0	54²	53	0	13	12	10.9	1.81	145	.255	.299	4	.222	0	6	5	2	0.9
1919 NY-N	**25**	9	.735	38	34	23	4	1	295²	263	8	35	92	9.1	2.40	117	.236	.260	32	.267	5	17	13	3	2.4
1920 NY-N	20	15	.571	43	34	23	2	0	292²	271	9	56	63	10.1	2.64	113	.250	.288	22	.204	-2	16	11	3	1.3
1921 *NY-N	15	9	.625	42	31	15	1	0	258²	298	13	44	56	12.0	3.10	118	.299	.331	19	.207	-1	20	16	1	1.4
1922 *NY-N	13	8	.619	37	29	14	2	0	212²	236	10	38	52	11.7	3.51	114	.299	.311	14	.182	-1	14	12	3	1.2
1923 NY-N	3	1	.750	12	4	1	0	1	36	48	1	13	12	15.3	6.25	61	.329	.384	3	.273	-0	-9	-10	1	-0.8
Bos-N	10	14	.417	31	23	12	5	2	195¹	204	8	43	41	11.4	2.76	144	.270	.310	10	.147	-4	27	27	3	2.9
Yr	13	15	.464	43	27	13	5	3	231¹	252	9	56	53	12.0	3.31	120	.280	.322	13	.165	-4	18	17	4	2.1
1924 Bos-N	15	20	.429	37	32	21	**4**	0	267²	292	7	53	49	11.6	3.23	118	.284	.319	20	.222	1	19	18	1	2.1
1925 Bos-N	11	16	.407	32	28	17	0	0	216¹	255	14	63	55	13.3	4.53	88	.297	.346	16	.198	-2	-6	-13	-2	-1.5
1926 Bro-N	10	11	.476	31	24	10	1	1	158	204	6	35	29	13.7	5.24	73	.321	.358	14	.237	-0	-25	-25	-1	-2.0
1927 Bro-N	2	10	.167	18	10	2	1	0	78²	106	5	25	14	15.0	5.72	69	.331	.380	5	.217	-0	-16	-15	-0	-0.9
Total 13	152	150	.503	422	312	180	26	13	2569²	2686	88	515	653	11.3	3.22	104	.273	.310	195	.214		74	41	20	6.3

● JUNIE BARNES
Barnes, Junie Shoaf "Lefty"   b: 12/1/11, Linwood, N.C.   d: 12/31/63, Jacksonville, N.C.   BL/TL, 5'11.5", 170 lbs.   Deb: 9/12/34

YEAR TM/L	W	L	PCT	G	GS	CG	SH	SV	IP	H	HR	BB	SO	RAT	ERA	ERA+	OAV	OOB	BH	AVG	PB	PR	/A	PD	TPI
1934 Cin-N	0	0	—	2	0	0	0	0	0¹	0	0	1	0	27.0	0.00	—	.000	.500	0	—	0	0	0	0	0.0

● RICH BARNES
Barnes, Richard Monroe   b: 7/21/59, Palm Beach, Fla.   BR/TL, 6'4", 186 lbs.   Deb: 7/18/82

YEAR TM/L	W	L	PCT	G	GS	CG	SH	SV	IP	H	HR	BB	SO	RAT	ERA	ERA+	OAV	OOB	BH	AVG	PB	PR	/A	PD	TPI
1982 Chi-A	0	2	.000	6	2	0	0	1	17	21	1	4	6	14.3	4.76	85	.292	.346	0	—	0	-1	-1	0	-0.1
1983 Cle-A	1	1	.500	4	2	0	0	0	11²	18	0	10	2	21.6	6.94	61	.375	.483	0	—	0	-4	-4	-0	-0.7
Total 2	1	3	.250	10	4	0	0	1	28²	39	1	14	8	17.3	5.65	73	.325	.404	0	—	0	-5	-5	0	-0.8

● BOB BARNES
Barnes, Robert Avery "Lefty"   b: 1/6/02, Washburn, Ill.   d: 12/8/93, Peoria, Ill.   BL/TL, 5'11.5", 150 lbs.   Deb: 7/8/24

YEAR TM/L	W	L	PCT	G	GS	CG	SH	SV	IP	H	HR	BB	SO	RAT	ERA	ERA+	OAV	OOB	BH	AVG	PB	PR	/A	PD	TPI
1924 Chi-A	0	0	—	2	0	0	0	0	4²	14	1	0	1	27.0	19.29	21	.519	.519	0	.000	-0	-8	-8	0	0.0

● ROSS BARNES
Barnes, Roscoe Charles   b: 5/8/1850, Mount Morris, N.Y.   d: 2/5/15, Chicago, Ill.   BR/TR, 5'8.5", 145 lbs.   Deb: 5/5/1871   U♦

YEAR TM/L	W	L	PCT	G	GS	CG	SH	SV	IP	H	HR	BB	SO	RAT	ERA	ERA+	OAV	OOB	BH	AVG	PB	PR	/A	PD	TPI
1876 Chi-N	0	0	—	1	0	0	0	0	1¹	7	0	0	0	47.3	20.25	12	.538	.538	138	.429	1	-3	-3	0	0.0

● VIRGIL BARNES
Barnes, Virgil Jennings "Zeke"   b: 3/5/1897, Ontario, Kan.   d: 7/24/58, Wichita, Kan.   BR/TR, 6', 165 lbs.   Deb: 9/25/19   F

YEAR TM/L	W	L	PCT	G	GS	CG	SH	SV	IP	H	HR	BB	SO	RAT	ERA	ERA+	OAV	OOB	BH	AVG	PB	PR	/A	PD	TPI
1919 NY-N	0	0	—	1	1	0	0	0	2	1	0	1	2	31.5	18.00	16	.545	.583	0	—	0	-3	-3	-0	0.0
1920 NY-N	0	1	.000	1	0	0	0	0	7	9	0	1	2	12.9	3.86	78	.310	.333	0	.000	-0	-1	-1	-0	-0.1
1922 NY-N	1	0	1.000	22	2	1	0	2	51²	46	1	11	16	9.9	3.48	115	.243	.285	2	.167	-1	4	3	0	0.1
1923 *NY-N	2	3	.400	23	5	2	0	0	53	59	2	19	16	13.2	3.91	98	.285	.345	0	.000	-2	-1	-0	-0	-0.2
1924 *NY-N	16	10	.615	35	29	15	1	3	229¹	239	10	57	59	11.6	3.06	120	.270	.314	14	.182	-2	21	15	2	1.6
1925 NY-N	15	11	.577	32	27	17	1	2	221²	242	13	53	53	12.0	3.53	114	.281	.323	9	.101	-9	18	12	0	0.4
1926 NY-N	8	13	.381	31	25	9	1	2	185	183	4	56	54	11.8	2.87	131	.261	.318	5	.054	-7	20	18	-1	1.1
1927 NY-N	14	11	.560	35	29	12	2	2	228²	251	14	51	66	12.0	3.98	97	.283	.325	9	.108	-7	-1	-3	-1	-1.1
1928 NY-N	3	3	.500	10	9	3	0	0	55¹	71	3	18	11	14.5	5.04	78	.330	.382	2	.091	-2	-6	-7	-1	-0.9
Bos-N	2	7	.222	16	10	1	0	0	60¹	86	3	26	7	16.7	5.82	67	.344	.406	1	.059	-2	-12	-13	-1	-1.8
Yr	5	10	.333	26	19	4	1	0	115²	157	6	44	18	15.6	5.45	72	.338	.395	3	.077	-3	-19	-20	-1	-2.7
Total 9	61	59	.508	205	134	58	7	11	1094	1192	46	293	275	12.3	3.66	105	.282	.329	40	.108	-31	38	22	1	-0.9

● REX BARNEY
Barney, Rex Edward   b: 12/19/24, Omaha, Neb.   BR/TR, 6'3", 185 lbs.   Deb: 8/18/43

YEAR TM/L	W	L	PCT	G	GS	CG	SH	SV	IP	H	HR	BB	SO	RAT	ERA	ERA+	OAV	OOB	BH	AVG	PB	PR	/A	PD	TPI
1943 Bro-N	2	2	.500	9	8	1	0	0	45¹	36	4	41	23	15.7	6.35	53	.217	.378	1	.056	-2	-15	-15	-0	-1.4
1946 Bro-N	2	5	.286	16	9	1	0	0	53²	46	7	51	36	16.3	5.87	58	.240	.399	4	.235	1	-15	-15	-1	-1.7
1947 *Bro-N	5	2	.714	28	9	0	0	0	77²	66	4	59	36	14.7	4.75	87	.240	.378	3	.111	-1	-6	-5	-0	-0.6
1948 Bro-N	15	13	.536	44	34	12	4	0	246²	193	17	122	138	11.7	3.10	129	.217	.315	14	.167	-2	23	25	-4	1.9
1949 *Bro-N	9	8	.529	38	20	6	2	0	140²	108	15	89	80	12.8	4.41	93	.216	.338	10	.213	0	-6	-5	-3	-0.8

YEAR	TM/L	W	L	PCT	G	GS	CG	SH	SV	IP	H	HR	BB	SO	RAT	ERA	ERA+	OAV	OOB	BH	AVG	PB	PR	/A	PD	TPI
1950	Bro-N	2	1	.667	20	1	0	0	0	33²	25	6	48	23	20.0	6.42	64	.214	.449	1	.125	0	-9	-9	-1	-0.7
Total	6	35	31	.530	155	81	20	6	1	597²	474	48	410	336	15.3	4.31	91	.221	.350	33	.164	-4	-26	-24	-9	-3.3

● EDGAR BARNHART
Barnhart, Edgar Vernon b: 9/16/04, Providence, Mo. d: 9/14/84, Columbia, Mo. BL/TR, 5'10", 160 lbs. Deb: 9/23/24

YEAR	TM/L	W	L	PCT	G	GS	CG	SH	SV	IP	H	HR	BB	SO	RAT	ERA	ERA+	OAV	OOB	BH	AVG	PB	PR	/A	PD	TPI
1924	StL-A	0	0	—	1	0	0	0	0	1	0	0	2	0	18.0			.000	.400	0	—	0	0	1	0	0.0

● LES BARNHART
Barnhart, Leslie Earl "Barney" b: 2/23/05, Hoxie, Kan. d: 10/7/71, Scottsdale, Ariz. BR/TR, 6', 180 lbs. Deb: 9/22/28

YEAR	TM/L	W	L	PCT	G	GS	CG	SH	SV	IP	H	HR	BB	SO	RAT	ERA	ERA+	OAV	OOB	BH	AVG	PB	PR	/A	PD	TPI
1928	Cle-A	0	1	.000	2	1	0	0	0	9	13	1	4	1	17.0	7.00	59	.325	.386	1	.500	1	-3	-3	1	-0.3
1930	Cle-A	1	0	1.000	1	1	0	0	0	8¹	12	0	4	1	17.3	6.48	74	.364	.432	0	.000	-1	-2	-2	0	-0.2
Total	2	1	1	.500	3	2	0	0	0	17¹	25	1	8	2	17.1	6.75	66	.342	.407	1	.200	-1	-5	-4	-0	-0.5

● GEORGE BARNICLE
Barnicle, George Bernard "Barney" b: 8/26/17, Fitchburg, Mass. d: 10/10/90, Largo, Fla. BR/TR, 6'2", 175 lbs. Deb: 9/6/39

YEAR	TM/L	W	L	PCT	G	GS	CG	SH	SV	IP	H	HR	BB	SO	RAT	ERA	ERA+	OAV	OOB	BH	AVG	PB	PR	/A	PD	TPI
1939	Bos-N	2	2	.500	6	1	0	0	0	18¹	16	1	8	15	11.8	4.91	75	.235	.316	0	.000	-1	-2	-2	0	-0.5
1940	Bos-N	1	0	1.000	13	2	1	0	0	32²	28	1	31	11	17.9	7.44	50	.233	.414	0	.000	-1	-13	-14	1	-0.5
1941	Bos-N	0	1	.000	1	1	0	0	0	6²	5	0	4	2	13.5	6.75	54	.238	.385	0	.000	-0	-2	-2	0	-0.3
Total	3	3	3	.500	20	4	1	0	0	57²	49	2	43	28	15.5	6.55	56	.234	.382	0	.000	-2	-17	-18	1	-1.3

● ED BARNOWSKI
Barnowski, Edward Anthony b: 8/23/43, Scranton, Pa. BR/TR, 6'2", 195 lbs. Deb: 9/8/65

YEAR	TM/L	W	L	PCT	G	GS	CG	SH	SV	IP	H	HR	BB	SO	RAT	ERA	ERA+	OAV	OOB	BH	AVG	PB	PR	/A	PD	TPI
1965	Bal-A	0	0	—	4	0	0	0	0	4¹	3	0	7	6	20.8	2.08	167	.200	.455	0	—	0	0	0	-0	0.0
1966	Bal-A	0	0	—	2	0	0	0	0	3	4	0	1	2	15.0	3.00	111	.364	.417	0	—	0	0	0	0	0.0
Total	2	0	0	—	6	0	0	0	0	7¹	7	0	8	8	18.4	2.45	139	.269	.441	0	—	0	0	1	0	0.0

● SALOME BAROJAS
Barojas, Salome (Romero) b: 6/16/57, Cordoba, Mex. BR/TR, 5'9", 188 lbs. Deb: 4/11/82

YEAR	TM/L	W	L	PCT	G	GS	CG	SH	SV	IP	H	HR	BB	SO	RAT	ERA	ERA+	OAV	OOB	BH	AVG	PB	PR	/A	PD	TPI
1982	Chi-A	6	6	.500	61	0	0	0	21	106²	96	9	46	56	12.1	3.54	114	.244	.324	0	—	0	6	6	3	1.2
1983	*Chi-A	3	3	.500	52	0	0	0	12	87¹	70	2	32	38	11.0	2.47	169	.224	.306	0	—	0	15	17	0	1.3
1984	Chi-A	2	3	.600	24	0	0	0	1	39¹	48	3	19	18	15.3	4.58	91	.310	.385	0	—	0	-3	-2	1	-0.3
	Sea-A	6	5	.545	19	14	0	0	1	95¹	88	12	41	37	12.5	3.97	101	.249	.332	0	—	0	0	1	1	0.1
	Yr	9	7	.563	43	14	0	0	2	134²	136	15	60	55	13.3	4.14	97	.268	.349	0	—	0	-2	-2	2	-0.2
1985	Sea-A	0	5	.000	17	4	0	0	0	52²	66	5	33	27	16.7	5.98	70	.305	.398	0	—	0	-11	-10	0	-0.9
1988	Phi-N	0	0	—	6	0	0	0	0	8²	7	1	8	1	15.6	8.31	43	.250	.417	0	—	0	-5	-5	-0	0.0
Total	5	18	21	.462	179	18	0	0	35	390	374	33	179	177	13.0	3.95	103	.257	.342	0	—	0	4	6	5	1.4

● JIM BARR
Barr, James Leland b: 2/10/48, Lynwood, Cal. BR/TR, 6'3", 205 lbs. Deb: 7/31/71

YEAR	TM/L	W	L	PCT	G	GS	CG	SH	SV	IP	H	HR	BB	SO	RAT	ERA	ERA+	OAV	OOB	BH	AVG	PB	PR	/A	PD	TPI
1971	*SF-N	1	1	.500	17	0	0	0	0	35¹	33	3	5	16	9.9	3.57	95	.254	.287	0	.000	-0	-0	-1	1	0.0
1972	SF-N	8	10	.444	44	18	8	2	2	179	166	16	41	86	10.6	2.87	122	.246	.292	9	.184	1	12	12	1	1.4
1973	SF-N	11	17	.393	41	33	8	3	2	231¹	240	24	49	88	11.4	3.81	100	.268	.310	10	.152	-1	-4	-0	-1	-0.1
1974	SF-N	13	9	.591	44	27	11	5	2	239²	223	17	47	84	10.2	2.74	139	.251	.290	18	.254	-4	23	28	1	3.1
1975	SF-N	13	14	.481	35	33	12	6	0	244	244	17	58	77	11.3	3.06	124	.265	.310	9	.118	-3	15	20	3	2.2
1976	SF-N	15	12	.556	37	37	8	3	0	252¹	260	18	60	75	11.5	2.89	126	.266	.310	12	.162	-2	17	21	3	2.8
1977	SF-N	12	16	.429	38	38	6	2	0	234¹	286	18	56	97	13.3	4.76	82	.306	.347	10	.132	-2	-22	-22	3	-2.3
1978	SF-N	8	11	.421	32	25	5	2	1	163	180	7	35	44	11.9	3.53	98	.281	.319	5	.100	-3	1	-2	1	-0.4
1979	Cal-A	10	12	.455	36	25	5	0	0	197	217	22	55	69	12.6	4.20	97	.287	.338	0	—	0	-0	-3	2	0.1
1980	Cal-A	1	4	.200	24	7	0	0	1	68	90	12	23	22	15.4	5.56	71	.323	.380	0	—	0	-12	-12	-1	-0.8
1982	SF-N	4	3	.571	53	9	1	1	2	128²	125	9	20	47	10.4	3.29	109	.262	.297	8	.250	1	4	4	0	0.4
1983	SF-N	5	3	.625	53	0	0	0	2	92²	106	7	20	47	12.3	3.98	89	.294	.332	2	.133	-0	-4	-5	2	-0.4
Total	12	101	112	.474	454	252	64	20	12	2065¹	2170	161	469	741	11.6	3.56	105	.273	.316	83	.162	-0	31	42	12	6.0

● BOB BARR
Barr, Robert Alexander b: 3/12/08, Newton, Mass. BR/TR, 6', 175 lbs. Deb: 9/11/35

YEAR	TM/L	W	L	PCT	G	GS	CG	SH	SV	IP	H	HR	BB	SO	RAT	ERA	ERA+	OAV	OOB	BH	AVG	PB	PR	/A	PD	TPI
1935	Bro-N	0	0	—	2	0	0	0	0	2¹	5	0	2	0	27.0	3.86	103	.385	.467	0	—	0	0	0	-0	0.0

● BOB BARR
Barr, Robert McClelland b: 12/1856, Washington, D.C. d: 3/11/30, Washington, D.C. BR/TR, 6'1", 192 lbs. Deb: 6/23/1883

YEAR	TM/L	W	L	PCT	G	GS	CG	SH	SV	IP	H	HR	BB	SO	RAT	ERA	ERA+	OAV	OOB	BH	AVG	PB	PR	/A	PD	TPI
1883	Pit-a	6	18	.250	26	23	19	0	1	203¹	263	5	28	81	12.9	4.38	73	.294	.294	3	.246	3	-24	-26	1	-2.1
1884	Was-a	9	23	.281	32	32	32	2	0	281	311	9	31	138	11.4	3.46	88	.258	.284	20	.148	-2	-7	-13	-1	-1.5
	Ind-a	3	11	.214	16	16	15	0	0	132	160	2	19	69	12.5	4.98	66	.275	.304	12	.185	0	-25	-25	-1	-2.1
	Yr	12	34	.261	48	48	47	2	0	413	471	11	50	207	11.5	3.94	79	.262	.284	32	.160	-2	-32	-38	-2	-3.6
1886	Was-N	3	18	.143	23	23	21	1	0	191²	221	7	54	80	12.9	4.41	74	.280	.326	13	.165	-2	-23	-24	-1	-2.4
1890	Roc-a	28	24	.538	57	54	52	3	0	493¹	458	7	219	209	12.6	3.25	110	.239	.321	36	.179	-1	34	17	3	1.6
1891	NY-N	0	4	.000	5	4	2	0	0	27	47	1	12	11	20.7	5.33	60	.367	.434	1	.091	-0	-6	-6	-0	-0.7
Total	5	49	98	.333	159	152	141	6	1	1328¹	1460	31	363	588	12.6	3.85	87	.265	.314	117	.185	-3	-52	-77	1	-7.2

● STEVE BARR
Barr, Steven Charles b: 9/8/51, St.Louis, Mo. BL/TL, 6'4", 200 lbs. Deb: 10/1/74

YEAR	TM/L	W	L	PCT	G	GS	CG	SH	SV	IP	H	HR	BB	SO	RAT	ERA	ERA+	OAV	OOB	BH	AVG	PB	PR	/A	PD	TPI
1974	Bos-A	1	0	1.000	1	1	1	0	0	9	7	0	6	3	13.0	4.00	96	.212	.333	0	—	0	-0	-0	0	-0.4
1975	Bos-A	0	1	.000	3	2	0	0	0	7	11	1	7	2	23.1	2.57	158	.367	.486	0	—	0	1	1	-0	-0.5
1976	Tex-A	2	6	.250	20	10	3	0	0	67²	70	10	44	27	15.2	5.59	64	.269	.375	0	—	0	-16	-15	0	-1.6
Total	3	3	7	.300	24	13	4	0	0	83²	88	11	57	32	15.6	5.16	71	.272	.382	0	—	0	-15	-14	0	-2.5

● RED BARRETT
Barrett, Charles Henry b: 2/14/15, Santa Barbara, Cal d: 7/28/90, Wilson, N.C. BR/TR, 5'11", 183 lbs. Deb: 9/15/37

YEAR	TM/L	W	L	PCT	G	GS	CG	SH	SV	IP	H	HR	BB	SO	RAT	ERA	ERA+	OAV	OOB	BH	AVG	PB	PR	/A	PD	TPI
1937	Cin-N	0	0	—	1	0	0	0	0	6¹	5	0	2	1	9.9	1.42	263	.227	.292	0	.000	-0	2	2	-0	-0.1
1938	Cin-N	2	0	1.000	6	2	0	0	0	28²	28	2	15	5	13.5	3.14	116	.257	.347	1	.143	-0	6	7	1	0.0
1939	Cin-N	0	0	—	2	0	0	0	0	5¹	5	0	1	5	10.1	1.69	227	.263	.300	0	.000	-0	1	1	0	0.0
1940	Cin-N	1	0	1.000	3	0	0	0	0	2²	5	0	1	2	20.3	6.75	56	.455	.500	0	—	0	-1	-1	0	-0.3
1943	Bos-N	12	18	.400	38	31	14	3	0	255	240	11	63	64	10.8	3.18	107	.250	.298	11	.136	-4	6	7	1	0.4
1944	Bos-N	9	16	.360	42	30	11	1	2	230¹	257	13	63	54	12.6	4.06	94	.279	.327	13	.173	-1	-12	-6	2	-0.4
1945	Bos-N	2	3	.400	9	5	2	0	2	38	43	6	13	16	14.2	4.74	81	.281	.353	2	.222	-0	-4	-4	1	-0.4
	StL-N†	21	9	.700	36	29	22	3	0	246²	244	12	38	60	10.3	2.74	137	.256	.285	10	.112	-5	29	28	-1	2.5
	Yr	23	12	.657	45	34	24	3	2	284²	287	18	54	76	10.8	3.00	125	.259	.294	12	.122	-5	25	24	0	2.1
1946	StL-N	3	2	.600	23	9	1	1	2	67	75	5	24	22	13.6	4.03	86	.282	.346	1	.059	-1	-5	-4	1	-0.4
1947	Bos-N	11	12	.478	36	30	12	3	1	210²	200	16	53	53	10.9	3.55	110	.244	.292	8	.111	-2	12	8	0	0.5
1948	*Bos-N	7	8	.467	34	13	0	0	0	128¹	132	9	26	40	11.1	3.65	105	.268	.305	7	.179	-1	4	3	0	0.1
1949	Bos-N	1	1	.500	23	0	0	0	0	44¹	44	7	10	17	14.2	5.68	66	.326	.368	1	.200	-0	-8	-9	1	-0.3
Total	11	69	69	.500	253	149	67	11	7	1263¹	1292	78	312	333	11.5	3.53	105	.264	.309	54	.136	-16	28	26	5	1.6

● FRANK BARRETT
Barrett, Francis Joseph "Red" b: 7/1/13, Ft.Lauderdale, Fla BR/TR, 6'2", 173 lbs. Deb: 10/1/39

YEAR	TM/L	W	L	PCT	G	GS	CG	SH	SV	IP	H	HR	BB	SO	RAT	ERA	ERA+	OAV	OOB	BH	AVG	PB	PR	/A	PD	TPI
1939	StL-N	0	1	.000	1	0	0	0	0	1²	1	0	1	3	10.8	5.40	76	.167	.286	0	—	0	-0	-0	-1	-0.1
1944	Bos-A	8	7	.533	38	2	0	0	8	90¹	93	5	42	40	13.5	3.69	92	.271	.352	4	.143	-1	-3	-3	-0	-0.6
1945	Bos-A	4	3	.571	37	0	0	0	3	86	77	0	29	35	11.1	2.62	130	.249	.314	5	.250	1	7	8	1	0.7
1946	Bos-N	2	4	.333	23	0	0	0	1	35¹	35	2	17	12	13.5	5.09	67	.252	.338	0	—	0	-7	-7	1	-1.0
1950	Pit-N	1	2	.333	5	0	0	0	0	4¹	5	1	1	0	12.5	4.15	106	.357	.400	0	—	0	-0	-0	0	0.1
Total	5	15	17	.469	104	2	0	0	12	217²	211	8	90	90	12.5	3.51	98	.260	.336	9	.167	-1	-2	-2	1	-0.9

● TIM BARRETT
Barrett, Timothy Wayne b: 1/24/61, Huntingburg, Ind. BL/TR, 6'1", 185 lbs. Deb: 7/18/88

YEAR	TM/L	W	L	PCT	G	GS	CG	SH	SV	IP	H	HR	BB	SO	RAT	ERA	ERA+	OAV	OOB	BH	AVG	PB	PR	/A	PD	TPI
1988	Mon-N	0	0	—	4	0	0	0	0	9¹	6	1	6	3	5.79	62	.270	.308	0	.000	-0	-2	-2	-0	-0.1		

● DICK BARRETT
Barrett, Tracy Souter "Kewpie Dick" (a.k.a. Richard Oliver 1933 And Richard Oliver Barrett 1934-43)
b: 9/28/06, Montoursville, Pa d: 10/30/66, Seattle, Wash. BR/TR, 5'9", 175 lbs. Deb: 6/27/33

YEAR	TM/L	W	L	PCT	G	GS	CG	SH	SV	IP	H	HR	BB	SO	RAT	ERA	ERA+	OAV	OOB	BH	AVG	PB	PR	/A	PD	TPI
1933	Phi-A	4	4	.500	15	7	3	0	0	70¹	74	2	49	26	15.9	5.76	74	.272	.385	6	.286	2	-12	-12	0	-0.9
1934	Bos-N	1	3	.250	15	4	1	0	0	32¹	50	2	12	6	17.3	6.68	57	.361	.416	1	.143	-0	-9	-10	-1	-1.0
1943	Chi-N	0	4	.000	15	4	0	0	0	45	52	2	28	20	16.2	4.80	70	.291	.389	1	.111	-1	-7	-7	-0	-0.7
	Phi-N	10	9	.526	23	20	10	2	1	169¹	137	5	51	65	10.1	2.39	141	.221	.282	7	.143	-0	19	18	0	2.2
	Yr	10	13	.435	38	24	10	2	1	214¹	189	7	79	85	11.3	2.90	116	.236	.306	8	.138	-1	12	11	0	1.5
1944	Phi-N	12	18	.400	37	27	11	1	0	221²	223	7	88	74	12.8	3.86	94	.262	.333	16	.216	2	-6	-6	2	-0.3

YEAR	TM/L	W	L	PCT	G	GS	CG	SH	SV	IP	H	HR	BB	SO	RAT	ERA	ERA+	OAV	OOB	BH	AVG	PB	PR	/A	PD	TPI
1945	Phi-N	8	20	.286	36	30	8	0	1	190²	217	11	92	72	14.9	5.38	71	.281	.363	9	.145	-1	-33	-33	1	-4.2
Total 5		35	58	.376	141	91	32	3	2	729	753	29	320	271	13.4	4.28	86	.266	.343	40	.180	1	-49	-50	4	-4.9

● **BILL BARRETT**　Barrett, William Joseph "Whispering Bill"　b: 5/28/1900, Cambridge, Mass.　d: 1/26/51, Cambridge, Mass.　BR/TR, 6′, 175 lbs.　Deb: 5/13/21　♦

YEAR	TM/L	W	L	PCT	G	GS	CG	SH	SV	IP	H	HR	BB	SO	RAT	ERA	ERA+	OAV	OOB	BH	AVG	PB	PR	/A	PD	TPI
1921	Phi-A	1	0	1.000	4	0	0	0	0	5	2	0	9	2	19.8	7.20	62	.133	.458	7	.233	0	-2	-2	-0	-0.2

● **FRANCISCO BARRIOS**　Barrios, Francisco Javier (Jimenez)　b: 6/10/53, Hermosillo, Mex.　d: 4/9/82, Hermosillo, Mexico　BR/TR, 6′3″, 195 lbs.　Deb: 8/18/74

YEAR	TM/L	W	L	PCT	G	GS	CG	SH	SV	IP	H	HR	BB	SO	RAT	ERA	ERA+	OAV	OOB	BH	AVG	PB	PR	/A	PD	TPI
1974	Chi-A	0	0	—	2	0	0	0	0	2	7	0	2	2	40.5	27.00	14	.538	.600	0	—	0	-5	-5	-0	-0.2
1976	Chi-A	5	9	.357	35	14	6	0	3	141²	136	13	46	81	11.8	4.32	83	.255	.318	0	—	0	-13	-12	-1	-1.3
1977	Chi-A	14	7	.667	33	31	9	0	0	231¹	241	22	58	119	11.8	4.12	99	.267	.315	0	—	0	-2	-1	-1	-0.1
1978	Chi-A	9	15	.375	33	32	9	2	0	195²	180	13	85	79	12.5	4.05	94	.246	.330	0	—	0	-6	-5	2	-0.4
1979	Chi-A	8	3	.727	15	15	2	0	0	94²	88	9	33	28	12.0	3.61	118	.242	.314	0	—	0	6	7	-1	0.6
1980	Chi-A	1	1	.500	3	3	0	0	0	16¹	21	4	8	2	16.5	4.96	81	.323	.405	0	—	0	-2	-2	-0	-0.2
1981	Chi-A	1	3	.250	8	7	1	0	0	36¹	45	3	14	12	14.9	3.96	95	.292	.355	0	—	0	-1	-2	-0	-0.2
Total 7		38	38	.500	129	102	27	2	3	718	718	64	246	323	12.4	4.15	94	.260	.326	0	—	0	-22	-20	-1	-1.8

● **FRANK BARRON**　Barron, Frank John　b: 8/6/1890, St.Marys, W.Va.　d: 9/18/64, St.Marys, W.Va.　BL/TL, 6′1″, 175 lbs.　Deb: 8/19/14

YEAR	TM/L	W	L	PCT	G	GS	CG	SH	SV	IP	H	HR	BB	SO	RAT	ERA	ERA+	OAV	OOB	BH	AVG	PB	PR	/A	PD	TPI
1914	Was-A	0	0	—	1	0	0	0	0	1	1	0	1	0	9.0			.333	.333	0	—	0				

● **ED BARRY**　Barry, Edward "Jumbo"　b: 10/2/1882, Madison, Wis.　d: 6/19/20, Montague, Mass.　TL, 6′3″, 185 lbs.　Deb: 8/21/05

YEAR	TM/L	W	L	PCT	G	GS	CG	SH	SV	IP	H	HR	BB	SO	RAT	ERA	ERA+	OAV	OOB	BH	AVG	PB	PR	/A	PD	TPI
1905	Bos-A	1	2	.333	7	5	2	0	0	40²	38	2	15	18	12.6	2.88	94	.248	.331	1	.091	-0	-1	-1	-2	-0.3
1906	Bos-A	0	3	.000	3	3	3	0	0	21	23	3	5	10	13.3	6.00	46	.280	.344	1	.111	-0	-8	-8	0	-0.9
1907	Bos-A	0	1	.000	2	2	1	0	0	17¹	13	1	5	6	9.9	2.08	124	.210	.279	0	.000	-0	1	1	-0	0.0
Total 3		1	6	.143	12	10	6	0	0	79	74	5	25	34	12.2	3.53	76	.249	.324	2	.087	-1	-8	-7	-2	-1.2

● **HARDIN BARRY**　Barry, Hardin "Finn"　b: 3/26/1891, Susanville, Cal.　d: 11/5/69, Carson City, Nev.　BR/TR, 6′, 185 lbs.　Deb: 6/21/12

YEAR	TM/L	W	L	PCT	G	GS	CG	SH	SV	IP	H	HR	BB	SO	RAT	ERA	ERA+	OAV	OOB	BH	AVG	PB	PR	/A	PD	TPI
1912	Phi-A	0	0	—	3	0	0	0	0	13	18	0	4	3	15.9	7.62	40	.360	.418	0	.000	-0	-6	-7	-0	-0.1

● **TOM BARRY**　Barry, Thomas Arthur　b: 4/10/1879, St.Louis, Mo.　d: 6/4/46, St.Louis, Mo.　TR, 5′9″, 155 lbs.　Deb: 4/15/04

YEAR	TM/L	W	L	PCT	G	GS	CG	SH	SV	IP	H	HR	BB	SO	RAT	ERA	ERA+	OAV	OOB	BH	AVG	PB	PR	/A	PD	TPI
1904	Phi-N	0	1	.000	1	1	0	0	0	0²	6	0	1	1	94.5	40.50	7	.667	.700	0	—	0	-3	-3	0	-1.7

● **BOB BARTHELSON**　Barthelson, Robert Edward　b: 7/15/24, New Haven, Conn.　BR/TR, 6′, 185 lbs.　Deb: 7/4/44

YEAR	TM/L	W	L	PCT	G	GS	CG	SH	SV	IP	H	HR	BB	SO	RAT	ERA	ERA+	OAV	OOB	BH	AVG	PB	PR	/A	PD	TPI
1944	NY-N	1	1	.500	7	1	0	0	0	9²	13	2	5	4	16.8	4.66	79	.310	.383	0	—	0	-1	-1	-0	-0.2

● **JOHN BARTHOLD**　Barthold, John Francis "Hans"　b: 4/14/1882, Philadelphia, Pa.　d: 11/4/46, Fairview Village, Pa.　BB/TR, 5′11″, 180 lbs.　Deb: 5/17/04

YEAR	TM/L	W	L	PCT	G	GS	CG	SH	SV	IP	H	HR	BB	SO	RAT	ERA	ERA+	OAV	OOB	BH	AVG	PB	PR	/A	PD	TPI
1904	Phi-A	0	0	—	4	0	0	0	0	10²	12	0	8	5	17.7	5.06	53	.286	.412	1	.333	1	-3	-3	-0	0.1

● **LES BARTHOLOMEW**　Bartholomew, Lester Justin　b: 4/4/03, Madison, Wis.　d: 9/19/72, Barrington, Ill.　BR/TL, 5′11.5″, 195 lbs.　Deb: 4/11/28

YEAR	TM/L	W	L	PCT	G	GS	CG	SH	SV	IP	H	HR	BB	SO	RAT	ERA	ERA+	OAV	OOB	BH	AVG	PB	PR	/A	PD	TPI
1928	Pit-N	0	0	—	6	0	0	0	0	22²	31	2	9	6	15.9	7.15	57	.356	.417	1	.143	-0	-8	-8	-0	0.0
1932	Chi-A	0	0	—	3	0	0	0	0	5¹	5	0	6	1	18.6	5.06	85	.250	.423	0	.000	-0	-0	-0	-0	0.0
Total 2		0	0	—	9	0	0	0	0	28	36	2	15	7	16.4	6.75	61	.336	.418	1	.125	-0	-8	-8	-0	0.0

● **BILL BARTLEY**　Bartley, William Jackson　b: 1/8/1885, Cincinnati, Ohio　d: 5/17/65, Cincinnati, Ohio　BR/TR, 5′11.5″, 190 lbs.　Deb: 9/15/03

YEAR	TM/L	W	L	PCT	G	GS	CG	SH	SV	IP	H	HR	BB	SO	RAT	ERA	ERA+	OAV	OOB	BH	AVG	PB	PR	/A	PD	TPI
1903	NY-N	0	0	—	1	0	0	0	0	3	3	0	4	2	21.0	0.00	—	.273	.467	0	.000	-0	1	1	0	0.0
1906	Phi-A	0	0	—	3	0	0	0	1	8²	10	0	6	6	16.6	9.35	29	.294	.400	1	.333	1	-6	-6	1	-0.1
1907	Phi-A	0	1	.000	15	3	2	0	0	56¹	44	0	19	16	10.1	2.24	116	.218	.285	2	.095	-2	2	2	-0	-0.1
Total 3		0	1	.000	19	3	2	0	1	68	57	0	29	24	11.4	3.04	87	.231	.312	3	.120	-1	-3	-3	0	-0.1

● **SHAWN BARTON**　Barton, Shawn Edward　b: 5/14/63, Los Angeles, Cal.　BR/TL, 6′3″, 195 lbs.　Deb: 8/6/92

YEAR	TM/L	W	L	PCT	G	GS	CG	SH	SV	IP	H	HR	BB	SO	RAT	ERA	ERA+	OAV	OOB	BH	AVG	PB	PR	/A	PD	TPI
1992	Sea-A	1	0	1.000	14	0	0	0	0	12¹	10	1	7	4	12.4	2.92	136	.238	.347	0	—	0	1	1	0	0.1
1995	SF-N	4	1	.800	52	0	0	0	1	44¹	37	3	19	22	11.8	4.26	96	.237	.328	0	—	0	-0	-1	1	0.0
1996	SF-N	0	0	—	7	0	0	0	0	8¹	19	2	1	3	21.6	9.72	42	.442	.455	0	—	0	-5	-5	0	0.0
Total 3		4	2	.667	73	0	0	0	1	65	66	6	27	29	13.2	4.71	86	.274	.352	0	—	0	-4	-5	1	0.1

● **CHARLIE BARTSON**　Bartson, Charles Franklin　b: 3/13/1865, Peoria, Ill.　d: 6/9/36, Peoria, Ill.　6′, 170 lbs.　Deb: 5/14/1890

YEAR	TM/L	W	L	PCT	G	GS	CG	SH	SV	IP	H	HR	BB	SO	RAT	ERA	ERA+	OAV	OOB	BH	AVG	PB	PR	/A	PD	TPI
1890	Chi-P	9	10	.474	26	20	17	0	1	197	226	8	66	52	13.9	4.11	106	.276	.339	13	.167	-3	3	5	5	0.6

● **JIM BASKETTE**　Baskette, James Blaine "Big Jim"　b: 12/10/1887, Athens, Tenn.　d: 7/30/42, Athens, Tenn.　BR/TR, 6′2″, 185 lbs.　Deb: 9/22/11

YEAR	TM/L	W	L	PCT	G	GS	CG	SH	SV	IP	H	HR	BB	SO	RAT	ERA	ERA+	OAV	OOB	BH	AVG	PB	PR	/A	PD	TPI
1911	Cle-A	1	2	.333	4	2	2	0	0	21¹	21	0	9	8	13.1	3.38	101	.273	.356	2	.333	1	-0	0	-0	0.0
1912	Cle-A	8	4	.667	29	11	7	1	1	116	109	4	46	51	12.6	3.18	107	.252	.334	5	.125	-1	2	3	-3	-0.1
1913	Cle-A	0	0	—	2	1	0	0	0	4²	8	1	2	0	19.3	5.79	52	.400	.455	1	1.000	-1	-1	-1	0	0.1
Total 3		9	6	.600	35	14	9	1	1	142	138	5	57	59	12.9	3.30	103	.261	.342	8	.170	1	0	2	-3	0.0

● **NORM BASS**　Bass, Norman Delaney　b: 1/21/39, Laurel, Miss.　BR/TR, 6′3″, 205 lbs.　Deb: 4/23/61

YEAR	TM/L	W	L	PCT	G	GS	CG	SH	SV	IP	H	HR	BB	SO	RAT	ERA	ERA+	OAV	OOB	BH	AVG	PB	PR	/A	PD	TPI
1961	KC-A	11	11	.500	40	23	6	2	0	170²	164	17	82	74	13.2	4.69	89	.255	.343	7	.119	-2	-13	-10	-3	-1.6
1962	KC-A	2	6	.250	22	10	0	0	0	75¹	96	7	46	33	17.0	6.09	69	.317	.407	1	.045	-2	-18	-16	1	-1.5
1963	KC-A	0	0	—	3	1	0	0	0	7²	11	2	9	4	23.5	11.74	33	.333	.476	0	.000	-0	-7	-7	-0	0.0
Total 3		13	17	.433	65	34	6	2	0	253²	271	26	137	111	14.6	5.32	79	.277	.368	8	.098	-4	-37	-32	-2	-3.1

● **DICK BASS**　Bass, Richard William　b: 7/7/06, Rogersville, Tenn.　d: 2/3/89, Graceville, Fla.　BR/TR, 6′2″, 175 lbs.　Deb: 9/21/39

YEAR	TM/L	W	L	PCT	G	GS	CG	SH	SV	IP	H	HR	BB	SO	RAT	ERA	ERA+	OAV	OOB	BH	AVG	PB	PR	/A	PD	TPI
1939	Was-A	0	1	.000	1	1	0	0	0	8	7	0	6	1	15.8	6.75	64	.241	.389	0	.000	0	-2	-2	-0	-0.2

● **CHARLIE BASTIAN**　Bastian, Charles J.　b: 7/4/1860, Philadelphia, Pa.　d: 1/18/32, Pennsauken, N.J.　BR/TR, 5′6.5″, 145 lbs.　Deb: 8/18/1884　♦

YEAR	TM/L	W	L	PCT	G	GS	CG	SH	SV	IP	H	HR	BB	SO	RAT	ERA	ERA+	OAV	OOB	BH	AVG	PB	PR	/A	PD	TPI
1884	Wil-U	0	0	—	1	0	0	0	0	6	6	0	0	4	9.0	3.00	89	.240	.240	12	.200	-0	-0	-0	-0	0.0

● **JOE BATCHELDER**　Batchelder, Joseph Edmund "Win"　b: 7/11/1898, Wenham, Mass.　d: 5/5/89, Beverly, Mass.　BR/TL, 5′7″, 165 lbs.　Deb: 9/29/23

YEAR	TM/L	W	L	PCT	G	GS	CG	SH	SV	IP	H	HR	BB	SO	RAT	ERA	ERA+	OAV	OOB	BH	AVG	PB	PR	/A	PD	TPI
1923	Bos-N	1	0	1.000	4	1	1	0	0	9	12	2	1	2	14.0	7.00	57	.353	.389	0	.000	-0	-3	-3	-0	-0.3
1924	Bos-N	0	0	—	3	0	0	0	0	4²	4	0	2	2	11.6	3.86	99	.235	.316	0	.000	-0	-0	-0	-0	0.0
1925	Bos-N	0	0	—	4	0	0	0	0	7	10	0	1	2	14.1	5.14	78	.357	.379	0	.000	-0	-1	-1	0	0.0
Total 3		1	0	1.000	11	1	1	0	0	20²	26	2	4	6	14.1	5.66	70	.329	.369	0	.000	-0	-4	-4	0	-0.3

● **RICH BATCHELOR**　Batchelor, Richard Anthony　b: 4/8/67, Florence, S.C.　BR/TR, 6′1″, 195 lbs.　Deb: 9/3/93

YEAR	TM/L	W	L	PCT	G	GS	CG	SH	SV	IP	H	HR	BB	SO	RAT	ERA	ERA+	OAV	OOB	BH	AVG	PB	PR	/A	PD	TPI
1993	StL-N	0	0	—	9	0	0	0	0	10	14	1	3	4	15.3	8.10	49	.359	.405	0	—	0	-5	-5	-0	-0.5
1996	StL-N	2	0	1.000	11	0	0	0	0	15	9	0	1	11	6.0	1.20	353	.173	.189	0	.000	-0	5	5	-0	0.6
Total 2		2	0	1.000	20	0	0	0	0	25	23	1	4	15	9.7	3.96	104	.253	.284	0	.000	-0	-0	-0	-0	0.6

● **DICK BATES**　Bates, Charles Richard　b: 10/7/45, McArthur, Ohio　BL/TR, 6′, 190 lbs.　Deb: 4/27/69

YEAR	TM/L	W	L	PCT	G	GS	CG	SH	SV	IP	H	HR	BB	SO	RAT	ERA	ERA+	OAV	OOB	BH	AVG	PB	PR	/A	PD	TPI
1969	Sea-A	0	0	—	1	0	0	0	0	1²	4	1	3	3	32.4	27.00	13	.375	.545			0	-4	-4	0	

● **FRANK BATES**　Bates, Creed Frank　b: Chattanooga, Tenn.　Deb: 10/7/1898

YEAR	TM/L	W	L	PCT	G	GS	CG	SH	SV	IP	H	HR	BB	SO	RAT	ERA	ERA+	OAV	OOB	BH	AVG	PB	PR	/A	PD	TPI
1898	Cle-N	2	1	.667	4	4	4	0	0	29	30	0	11	5	13.0	3.10	117	.265	.336	1	.111	0	2	2	-0	0.1
1899	StL-N	0	0	—	2	0	0	0	0	8²	7	0	5	0	12.5	1.04	383	.219	.324	1	.333	1	3	3	-0	0.0
	Cle-N	1	18	.053	20	19	17	0	0	153	239	6	105	13	21.6	7.24	51	.355	.458	14	.215	1	-57	-60	-0	-5.3
	Yr	1	18	.053	22	19	17	0	0	161²	246	6	110	13	21.1	6.90	54	.348	.452	15	.221	2	-55	-58	-0	-5.3
Total 2		3	19	.136	26	23	21	0	0	190²	276	6	121	18	19.9	6.33	58	.337	.437	16	.208	2	-53	-56	-0	-5.2

● **JOHN BATES**　Bates, John William　b: 5/28/1868, Ohio　d: 3/24/19, Oakland, Cal.　Deb: 8/25/1889

YEAR	TM/L	W	L	PCT	G	GS	CG	SH	SV	IP	H	HR	BB	SO	RAT	ERA	ERA+	OAV	OOB	BH	AVG	PB	PR	/A	PD	TPI
1889	KC-a	0	1	.000	1	1	1	0	0	8	15	0	5	3	22.5	13.50	31	.385	.455	0	.000	-1	-9	-8	-0	-0.7

● **MIGUEL BATISTA**　Batista, Miguel Jerez (Decartes)　b: 2/19/71, Santo Domingo, D.R.　BR/TR, 6′, 160 lbs.　Deb: 4/11/92

YEAR	TM/L	W	L	PCT	G	GS	CG	SH	SV	IP	H	HR	BB	SO	RAT	ERA	ERA+	OAV	OOB	BH	AVG	PB	PR	/A	PD	TPI
1992	Pit-N	0	0	—	1	0	0	0	0	2	4	1	3	1	31.5	9.00	38	.400	.538	0	—	0	-1	-1	-0	0.0
1996	Fla-N	0	0	—	9	0	0	0	0	11¹	9	0	7	6	12.7	5.56	73	.231	.348	0	—	0	-2	-2	-0	0.0
Total 2		0	0	—	10	0	0	0	0	13¹	13	1	10	7	15.5	6.08	65	.265	.390	0	—	0	-3	-3	-0	0.0

YEAR TM/L	W	L	PCT	G	GS	CG	SH	SV	IP	H	HR	BB	SO	RAT	ERA	ERA+	OAV	OOB	BH	AVG	PB	PR	/A	PD	TPI

● JOE BATTIN   Battin, Joseph V.   b: 11/11/1851, Philadelphia, Pa.   d: 12/10/37, Akron, Ohio   BR/TR,   Deb: 8/11/1871   MU ♦

1877 StL-N	0	0	—	1	0	0	0	0	3²	3	0	1	1	9.8	4.91	53	.200	.250	45	.199	0	-1	-1	-0	0.0
1883 Pit-a	0	0	—	2	0	0	0	0	4	9	0	1	0	22.5	2.25	143	.429	.455	83	.214	0	-0	-0	-0	0.0
Total 2	0	0	—	3	0	0	0	0	7²	12	0	2	1	16.4	3.52	83	.333	.368	313	.218	0	-0	-1	-0	0.0

● CHRIS BATTON   Batton, Christopher Sean   b: 8/24/54, Los Angeles, Cal.   BR/TR, 6'4", 195 lbs.   Deb: 9/19/76

| 1976 Oak-A | 0 | 0 | — | 2 | 1 | 0 | 0 | 0 | 4 | 5 | 1 | 3 | 4 | 18.0 | 9.00 | 37 | .313 | .421 | 0 | — | 0 | -2 | -3 | -0 | 0.1 |

● LOU BAUER   Bauer, Louis Walter   b: 11/30/1898, Egg Harbor City, N.J.   d: 2/4/79, Pomona, N.J.   BR/TR, 6', 175 lbs.   Deb: 8/13/18

| 1918 Phi-A | 0 | 0 | — | 1 | 0 | 0 | 0 | 0 | 0 | 0 | 0 | 2 | 0 | — | ∞ | — | — | 1.000 | 0 | — | 0 | -1 | -1 | 0 | -0.1 |

● AL BAUERS   Bauers, Albert J.   b: 1850, Columbus, Ohio   d: 9/6/13, Wilkes-Barre, Pa.   TL,   Deb: 9/22/1884   U

1884 Col-a	1	2	.333	3	3	3	0	0	25	22	1	14	13	13.0	4.68	65	.224	.321	3	.273	0	-4	-5	0	-0.4
1886 StL-N	0	4	.000	4	4	3	0	0	28²	31	1	27	13	18.2	5.97	54	.267	.406	2	.167	-1	-8	-9	-1	-1.0
Total 2	1	6	.143	7	7	6	0	0	53²	53	2	41	26	15.8	5.37	58	.248	.369	5	.217	-0	-12	-13	-1	-1.4

● RUSS BAUERS   Bauers, Russell Lee   b: 5/10/14, Townsend, Wis.   d: 1/1/95, Hines, Ill.   BL/TR, 6'3", 195 lbs.   Deb: 8/20/36

1936 Pit-N	0	0	—	1	0	0	0	0	1¹	2	0	4	0	47.3	33.75	12	.500	.778	0	—	0	-4	-4	-0	0.0
1937 Pit-N	13	6	.684	34	19	11	2	1	187²	174	2	80	118	12.4	2.88	134	.245	.325	15	.217	1	22	21	3	2.3
1938 Pit-N	13	14	.481	40	34	12	2	3	243	207	7	99	117	11.6	3.07	124	.233	.314	21	.239	4	19	20	-3	2.1
1939 Pit-N	2	4	.333	15	8	1	0	1	53²	46	4	25	12	12.1	3.35	114	.240	.330	4	.211	0	3	3	-1	0.2
1940 Pit-N	0	2	.000	15	2	0	0	0	30²	29	2	18	11	18.2	7.63	50	.323	.413	2	.286	0	-13	-13	0	-0.7
1941 Pit-N	1	3	.250	8	5	1	0	0	37¹	40	1	25	20	15.7	5.54	65	.267	.371	5	.357	1	-8	-8	-1	-0.8
1946 Chi-N	2	1	.667	15	3	2	0	1	43¹	45	1	19	22	13.5	3.53	94	.273	.351	3	.300	1	-1	-1	-0	0.1
1950 StL-A	0	0	—	1	0	0	0	0	2	6	0	1	0	31.5	4.50	110	.600	.636	0	—	0	0	0	0	0.0
Total 8	31	30	.508	129	71	27	4	6	599	562	17	271	300	12.7	3.53	107	.250	.334	50	.242	7	19	17	-2	3.2

● FRANK BAUMANN   Baumann, Frank Matt "The Beau"   b: 7/1/33, St.Louis, Mo.   BL/TL, 6'1", 210 lbs.   Deb: 7/31/55

1955 Bos-A	2	1	.667	7	5	0	0	0	34	38	2	17	27	14.8	5.82	74	.281	.366	3	.231	-0	-7	-6	0	-0.4
1956 Bos-A	2	1	.667	7	1	0	0	0	24²	22	3	14	18	13.1	3.28	141	.234	.333	3	.333	1	2	4	-1	0.4
1957 Bos-A	1	0	1.000	4	1	0	0	0	12	13	1	3	7	12.8	3.75	106	.277	.333	1	.500	0	0	0	0	0.0
1958 Bos-A	2	2	.500	10	7	2	0	0	52¹	56	4	27	31	15.0	4.47	90	.276	.372	3	.214	1	-4	-3	-1	-0.2
1959 Bos-A	6	4	.600	26	10	3	0	1	95²	96	11	55	48	14.3	4.05	100	.259	.357	6	.207	1	-2	0	1	0.1
1960 Chi-A	13	6	.684	47	20	7	2	3	185¹	169	11	53	71	10.8	**2.67**	142	.247	.302	8	.154	1	25	23	-2	2.1
1961 Chi-A	10	13	.435	53	23	5	1	3	187²	249	22	59	75	14.9	5.61	70	.318	.368	16	.262	-6	-33	-35	1	-3.1
1962 Chi-A	7	6	.538	40	10	3	1	0	119²	117	10	36	55	11.7	3.38	115	.258	.316	8	.267	8	7	0	1	1.2
1963 Chi-A	2	1	.667	24	1	0	0	0	50¹	52	2	17	31	12.3	3.04	115	.265	.324	1	.091	0	3	3	0	0.1
1964 Chi-A	0	3	.000	22	0	0	0	1	32	40	4	16	19	15.8	6.19	56	.320	.397	0	.000	0	-9	-10	-0	-1.0
1965 Chi-N	0	1	.000	4	0	0	0	0	3²	4	0	3	2	17.2	7.36	50	.286	.412	0	—	0	-2	-1	0	-0.4
Total 11	45	38	.542	244	78	19	4	13	797¹	856	70	300	384	13.2	4.11	95	.276	.342	49	.218	14	-19	-19	-2	-1.2

● GEORGE BAUMGARDNER   Baumgardner, George Washington   b: 7/22/1891, Barboursville, W.Va.   d: 12/13/70, Barboursville, W.Va.   BL/TR, 5'11", 178 lbs.   Deb: 4/14/12

1912 StL-A	11	13	.458	30	27	18	2	0	218¹	222	1	79	102	12.9	3.38	98	.274	.346	11	.145	0	-2	-2	-0	-0.1
1913 StL-A	10	19	.345	38	31	23	2	1	253¹	267	6	84	78	12.3	3.13	94	.283	.348	13	.167	2	-5	-5	-2	-0.5
1914 StL-A	14	13	.519	45	18	9	3	3	183²	152	3	84	93	12.0	2.79	97	.229	.323	7	.132	-1	-1	-2	-1	-0.5
1915 StL-A	0	2	.000	7	1	1	0	0	22¹	29	0	11	6	16.1	4.43	65	.358	.435	0	.000	-1	-4	-4	1	-0.4
1916 StL-A	1	0	1.000	4	2	0	0	0	8	12	0	5	4	19.1	7.88	35	.364	.447	0	.000	-0	-4	-5	-1	-0.6
Total 5	36	47	.434	124	79	51	7	4	685²	682	10	263	283	12.8	3.22	93	.269	.345	31	.144	-0	-16	-17	-2	-2.1

● ROSS BAUMGARTEN   Baumgarten, Ross   b: 5/27/55, Highland Park, Ill.   BL/TL, 6'1", 180 lbs.   Deb: 8/16/78

1978 Chi-A	2	2	.500	7	4	1	0	0	23	29	3	9	15	15.3	5.87	65	.315	.382	0	—	0	-5	-5	-0	-0.8
1979 Chi-A	13	8	.619	28	28	4	3	0	190²	175	18	83	72	12.2	3.54	120	.243	.322	0	—	0	14	15	-0	1.5
1980 Chi-A	2	12	.143	24	23	3	1	0	136	127	10	52	66	11.9	3.44	117	.256	.327	0	—	0	9	9	2	1.1
1981 Chi-A	5	9	.357	19	19	2	1	0	101²	101	9	40	52	12.6	4.07	88	.260	.331	0	—	0	-5	-6	-0	-0.7
1982 Pit-N	0	5	.000	12	10	0	0	0	44	60	3	27	17	17.8	6.55	57	.347	.435	1	.083	-1	-14	-14	0	-1.5
Total 5	22	36	.379	90	84	10	6	0	495¹	492	43	211	222	12.8	4.00	100	.263	.339	1	.083	-1	-1	-1	2	-0.4

● HARRY BAUMGARTNER   Baumgartner, Harry E.   b: 10/8/1892, S.Pittsburg, Tenn.   d: 12/3/30, Augusta, Ga.   BR/TR, 5'11", 175 lbs.   Deb: 9/6/20

| 1920 Det-A | 0 | 1 | .000 | 9 | 0 | 0 | 0 | 0 | 18 | 18 | 1 | 7 | 4 | 12.0 | 4.00 | 93 | .273 | .333 | 1 | .250 | -0 | -1 | 0 | 0.0 |

● STAN BAUMGARTNER   Baumgartner, Stanwood Fulton   b: 12/14/1894, Houston, Tex.   d: 10/4/55, Philadelphia, Pa.   BL/TL, 6', 175 lbs.   Deb: 6/26/14

1914 Phi-N	2	2	.500	15	3	2	1	0	60¹	60	0	16	24	11.6	3.28	90	.270	.325	1	.053	-1	-3	-2	-1	-0.4
1915 Phi-N	0	0	—	16	1	0	0	0	48¹	38	2	23	27	11.5	2.42	113	.226	.323	1	.083	-1	2	2	1	0.1
1916 Phi-N	0	0	—	1	0	0	0	0	4	5	0	1	0	13.5	2.25	118	.333	.375	0	.000	0	0	0	0	0.0
1921 Phi-N	3	6	.333	22	7	2	0	0	66²	103	8	22	13	17.1	7.02	60	.355	.404	6	.200	0	-24	-21	-1	-2.4
1922 Phi-N	1	1	.500	6	1	0	0	0	9²	18	1	5	2	21.4	6.52	72	.409	.469	1	.333	-0	-3	-2	0	-0.3
1924 Phi-A	13	6	.684	36	16	12	1	4	181	181	6	73	45	12.8	2.88	149	.271	.347	13	.217	-0	27	28	-2	2.5
1925 Phi-A	6	3	.667	37	12	2	1	3	113¹	120	2	35	18	12.9	3.57	130	.275	.338	7	.233	-0	10	14	-1	0.9
1926 Phi-A	1	1	.500	10	1	0	0	0	22¹	28	0	10	10	15.3	4.03	103	.326	.396	1	.333	0	0	0	0	0.1
Total 8	26	21	.553	143	41	18	3	7	505²	553	19	185	129	13.4	3.70	109	.287	.354	30	.190	-2	9	19	-3	0.5

● GEORGE BAUSEWINE   Bausewine, George W.   b: 3/22/1869, Philadelphia, Pa.   d: 7/29/47, Norristown, Pa.   6'2", 207 lbs.   Deb: 9/14/1889   U

| 1889 Phi-a | 1 | 4 | .200 | 7 | 6 | 6 | 0 | 0 | 55¹ | 64 | 1 | 33 | 18 | 17.2 | 3.90 | 97 | .281 | .393 | 1 | .048 | -2 | -0 | -1 | 0 | -0.2 |

● ED BAUTA   Bauta, Eduardo (Galvez)   b: 1/6/35, Florida, Cuba   BR/TR, 6'3", 200 lbs.   Deb: 7/6/60

1960 StL-N	0	0	—	9	0	0	0	1	15²	14	4	11	6	14.9	6.32	65	.237	.366	0	.000	-0	-4	-4	-0	-0.1
1961 StL-N	2	0	1.000	13	0	0	0	5	19¹	12	2	5	12	7.9	1.40	315	.171	.227	2	.500	1	6	6	-0	1.1
1962 StL-N	1	0	1.000	20	0	0	0	0	32¹	28	5	21	25	13.9	5.01	85	.239	.360	1	.250	0	-4	-3	-0	-0.1
1963 StL-N	3	4	.429	38	0	0	0	3	52²	55	2	21	30	13.3	3.93	90	.279	.355	0	.000	-1	-4	-2	-1	-0.5
NY-N	0	0	—	9	0	0	0	0	19	22	0	9	13	14.7	5.21	67	.289	.365	0	.000	-0	-4	-4	0	-0.4
Yr	3	4	.429	47	0	0	0	3	71²	77	2	30	43	13.4	4.27	83	.278	.349	0	.000	-1	-8	-6	-1	-0.5
1964 NY-N	0	2	.000	8	0	0	0	1	10	17	1	3	8	18.0	5.40	66	.395	.435	0	—	0	-2	-2	0	-0.4
Total 5	6	6	.500	97	0	0	0	11	149	148	14	70	89	13.4	4.35	89	.263	.349	3	.176	-0	-13	-8	-1	-0.2

● JOSE BAUTISTA   Bautista, Jose Joaquin (Arias)   b: 7/25/64, Bani, D.R.   BR/TR, 6'1", 205 lbs.   Deb: 4/9/88

1988 Bal-A	6	15	.286	33	25	3	0	0	171²	171	21	45	76	11.7	4.30	91	.258	.311	0	—	0	-6	-8	-1	-0.7
1989 Bal-A	3	4	.429	15	10	0	0	0	78	84	17	15	30	11.5	5.31	71	.274	.310	0	—	0	-12	-13	-1	-1.1
1990 Bal-A	1	0	1.000	22	0	0	0	0	26²	28	4	7	15	11.8	4.05	94	.272	.318	0	—	0	-0	0	-0	-0.1
1991 Bal-A	0	1	.000	5	0	0	0	0	5¹	13	1	3	3	32.1	16.88	23	.464	.559	0	—	0	-8	-8	-0	-1.1
1993 Chi-N	10	3	.769	58	7	1	0	2	111²	105	11	27	63	11.0	2.82	141	.250	.303	4	.190	0	15	14	1	1.7
1994 Chi-N	4	5	.444	58	0	0	0	1	69¹	75	10	17	45	12.3	3.89	107	.284	.335	0	.000	-0	2	2	-0	0.2
1995 SF-N	3	8	.273	52	6	0	0	0	100²	120	24	26	45	13.5	6.44	63	.295	.345	0	.000	-2	-25	-26	-1	-2.8
1996 SF-N	3	4	.429	37	0	0	0	0	69²	66	10	15	28	10.7	3.36	122	.249	.294	1	.111	-0	7	6	0	0.5
Total 8	30	40	.429	280	49	4	0	3	633	662	98	157	305	12.0	4.44	89	.269	.318	5	.100	-2	-27	-33	-2	-3.4

● BILL BAYNE   Bayne, William Lear "Beverly"   b: 4/18/1899, Pittsburgh, Pa.   d: 5/22/81, St.Louis, Mo.   BL/TL, 5'9", 160 lbs.   Deb: 9/20/19

1919 StL-A	1	1	.500	2	2	1	0	0	12	16	0	6	6	16.5	5.25	69	.320	.393	2	.400	0	-3	-3	-0	-0.3
1920 StL-A	5	6	.455	18	13	6	1	0	99²	102	8	41	38	13.5	3.70	106	.279	.363	6	.171	-2	1	2	-2	-0.2
1921 StL-A	11	5	.688	47	14	6	1	3	164	167	8	80	82	13.8	4.72	95	.270	.358	18	.300	5	-8	-4	-1	1.0
1922 StL-A	4	5	.444	26	8	2	0	0	92²	86	5	37	38	12.8	4.56	91	.249	.338	7	.233	-1	-2	0	-1	-0.6
1923 StL-A	2	2	.500	19	2	0	0	0	46	49	4	31	15	16.2	4.50	93	.287	.405	3	.231	-1	-3	-2	-1	-0.2

YEAR TM/L	W	L	PCT	G	GS	CG	SH	SV	IP	H	HR	BB	SO	RAT	ERA	ERA+	OAV	OOB	BH	AVG	PB	PR	/A	PD	TPI
1924 StL-A	1	3	.250	22	3	0	0	0	50²	47	4	29	20	14.9	4.44	102	.250	.373	6	.429	2	-1	0	-1	0.2
1928 Cle-A	2	5	.286	37	6	3	0	3	108²	128	3	43	39	15.0	5.13	81	.309	.388	11	.367	3	-13	-12	2	-0.4
1929 Bos-A	5	5	.500	27	6	2	0	0	84¹	111	9	29	26	15.8	6.72	64	.326	.392	8	.320	2	-23	-23	1	-1.9
1930 Bos-A	0	0	—	1	0	0	0	0	4	5	1	1	1	13.5	4.50	102	.294	.333	1	.500	0	0	0	0	0.0
Total 9	31	32	.492	199	55	21	2	8	662	711	37	297	259	14.4	4.84	87	.283	.370	62	.290	10	-55	-45	-3	-3.4

● **WALTER BEALL**   Beall, Walter Esau b: 7/29/1899, Washington, D.C. d: 1/28/59, Suitland, Md. BR/TR, 5'10", 178 lbs. Deb: 9/3/24

YEAR TM/L	W	L	PCT	G	GS	CG	SH	SV	IP	H	HR	BB	SO	RAT	ERA	ERA+	OAV	OOB	BH	AVG	PB	PR	/A	PD	TPI
1924 NY-A	2	0	1.000	4	2	1	0	0	23	19	2	17	18	14.1	3.52	118	.237	.371	1	.143	-1	2	2	-1	0.0
1925 NY-A	0	1	.000	8	1	0	0	0	11¹	11	0	19	6	26.2	12.71	34	.282	.541	0	.000	-1	-10	-11	0	-0.8
1926 NY-A	2	4	.333	20	9	1	0	1	81²	71	2	68	56	16.0	3.53	109	.240	.392	3	.136	0	4	3	1	0.3
1927 NY-A	0	0	—	1	0	0	0	0	1	1	0	0	0	9.0	9.00	43	.333	.333	0	—	-1	-1	-1	0	0.0
1929 Was-A	1	0	1.000	3	0	0	0	0	7¹	8	0	7	5	19.3	3.86	110	.348	.500	0	—	-1	0	0	0	0.0
Total 5	5	5	.500	36	12	1	0	1	124	110	4	111	85	16.7	4.43	90	.249	.410	4	.114	-1	-4	-6	0	-0.5

● **ALEX BEAM**   Beam, Alexander Rodger b: 11/21/1870, Johnstown, Pa. d: 4/17/38, Nogales, Ariz. Deb: 5/25/1889

YEAR TM/L	W	L	PCT	G	GS	CG	SH	SV	IP	H	HR	BB	SO	RAT	ERA	ERA+	OAV	OOB	BH	AVG	PB	PR	/A	PD	TPI
1889 Pit-N	1	1	.500	2	2	2	0	0	18	11	0	15	1	13.0	6.50	58	.172	.329	1	.167	0	-5	-6	-0	-0.4

● **ERNIE BEAM**   Beam, Ernest Joseph b: 3/17/1867, Mansfield, Ohio d: 9/12/18, Mansfield, Ohio TR, 6'0.5", 185 lbs. Deb: 5/2/1895

YEAR TM/L	W	L	PCT	G	GS	CG	SH	SV	IP	H	HR	BB	SO	RAT	ERA	ERA+	OAV	OOB	BH	AVG	PB	PR	/A	PD	TPI
1895 Phi-N	0	2	.000	9	1	1	0	**3**	24²	33	1	25	3	21.5	11.31	42	.314	.450	2	.182	-1	-18	-18	-0	-1.4

● **CHARLIE BEAMON**   Beamon, Charles Alfonzo Sr. b: 12/25/34, Oakland, Cal. BR/TR, 5'11", 195 lbs. Deb: 9/26/56 F

YEAR TM/L	W	L	PCT	G	GS	CG	SH	SV	IP	H	HR	BB	SO	RAT	ERA	ERA+	OAV	OOB	BH	AVG	PB	PR	/A	PD	TPI
1956 Bal-A	2	0	1.000	2	1	1	0	0	13	9	0	8	14	11.8	1.38	283	.191	.309	0	.000	-1	4	4	0	0.5
1957 Bal-A	0	0	—	4	1	0	0	0	8²	8	1	7	5	16.6	5.19	69	.229	.372	0	.000	-0	-1	-2	-0	0.0
1958 Bal-A	1	3	.250	21	3	0	1	0	49²	47	3	21	26	13.4	4.35	83	.266	.363	0	.000	-1	-3	-4	2	-0.2
Total 3	3	3	.500	27	5	1	1	0	71¹	64	4	36	45	13.5	3.91	93	.247	.354	0	.000	-2	-1	-2	2	0.3

● **BELVE BEAN**   Bean, Beveric Benton "Bill" b: 4/23/05, Mullin, Tex. d: 6/1/88, Comanche, Tex. BR/TR, 6'1.5", 197 lbs. Deb: 5/30/30

YEAR TM/L	W	L	PCT	G	GS	CG	SH	SV	IP	H	HR	BB	SO	RAT	ERA	ERA+	OAV	OOB	BH	AVG	PB	PR	/A	PD	TPI
1930 Cle-A	3	3	.500	23	3	1	0	2	74¹	99	7	32	19	15.9	5.45	89	.331	.396	9	.346	-0	-7	-5	0	-0.2
1931 Cle-A	0	1	.000	4	0	0	0	0	7	11	0	4	3	20.6	6.43	72	.379	.471	0	.000	-0	-2	-1	0	-0.2
1933 Cle-A	1	2	.333	27	2	0	0	0	70¹	80	6	20	41	12.9	5.25	85	.300	.351	4	.182	-1	-8	-6	1	-0.2
1934 Cle-A	5	1	.833	21	1	0	0	0	51¹	53	2	21	20	13.5	3.86	118	.265	.344	3	.200	-0	4	4	1	0.5
1935 Cle-A	0	0	—	1	0	0	0	0	1	2	1	0	1	18.0	9.00	50	.400	.400	0	—	0	-1	-0	-0	0.0
Was-A	2	0	1.000	10	2	0	0	0	31	43	5	19	6	18.0	7.26	60	.339	.425	3	.375	3	-10	-10	-1	-0.4
Yr	2	0	1.000	11	2	0	0	0	32	45	6	19	6	18.0	7.31	59	.341	.424	3	.375	3	-10	-11	-1	-0.4
Total 5	11	7	.611						235	288	21	96	89	14.9	5.32	86	.311	.378	19	.264	4	-22	-19	1	-0.5

● **DAVE BEARD**   Beard, Charles David b: 10/2/59, Atlanta, Ga. BL/TR, 6'5", 215 lbs. Deb: 7/16/80

YEAR TM/L	W	L	PCT	G	GS	CG	SH	SV	IP	H	HR	BB	SO	RAT	ERA	ERA+	OAV	OOB	BH	AVG	PB	PR	/A	PD	TPI
1980 Oak-A	0	1	.000	13	0	0	0	1	16	12	0	7	12	11.3	3.38	112	.218	.317	0	—	0	1	1	-0	0.4
1981 *Oak-A	1	1	.500	13	0	0	0	3	13	9	1	4	15	9.7	2.77	126	.191	.269	0	—	0	1	1	0	0.2
1982 Oak-A	10	9	.526	54	2	0	0	11	91²	85	9	35	73	11.9	3.44	114	.244	.315	0	—	0	6	5	-0	1.3
1983 Oak-A	5	5	.500	43	0	0	0	10	61	55	8	36	40	13.7	5.61	69	.246	.355	0	—	0	-10	-12	-1	-1.8
1984 Sea-A	3	2	.600	43	0	0	0	5	76	88	15	33	40	14.8	5.80	69	.291	.369	0	—	0	-15	-15	-0	-1.0
1985 Chi-N	0	0	—	9	0	0	0	0	12²	16	2	7	4	16.3	6.39	62	.314	.397	0	—	0	-4	-3	-0	-0.2
1989 Det-A	0	2	.000	2	1	0	0	0	5¹	9	2	2	1	20.3	5.06	75	.375	.444	0	—	0	-1	-1	0	-0.2
Total 7	19	20	.487	172	3	0	0	30	275²	274	37	124	185	13.3	4.70	83	.261	.344	0	—	0	-21	-25	-2	-1.1

● **MIKE BEARD**   Beard, Michael Richard b: 6/21/50, Little Rock, Ark. BL/TL, 6'1", 185 lbs. Deb: 9/7/74

YEAR TM/L	W	L	PCT	G	GS	CG	SH	SV	IP	H	HR	BB	SO	RAT	ERA	ERA+	OAV	OOB	BH	AVG	PB	PR	/A	PD	TPI
1974 Atl-N	0	0	—	6	0	0	0	0	9¹	5	1	1	7	6.8	2.89	131	.156	.206	0	—	0	1	1	0	0.2
1975 Atl-N	4	1	1.000	34	2	0	0	0	70¹	71	4	28	27	12.9	3.20	118	.265	.339	1	.111	-0	3	4	0	0.2
1976 Atl-N	0	2	.000	30	0	0	0	1	33²	38	1	14	8	13.9	4.28	89	.299	.369	0	.000	-0	-3	-2	1	0.0
1977 Atl-N	0	0	—	4	0	0	0	0	4²	14	3	2	1	30.9	9.64	46	.452	.485	0	—	0	-3	-3	0	0.0
Total 4	4	2	.667	74	2	0	0	1	118	128	9	45	43	13.4	3.74	102	.279	.348	1	.100	-1	-2	-0	1	0.2

● **RALPH BEARD**   Beard, Ralph William b: 2/11/29, Cincinnati, Ohio BR/TR, 6'5", 200 lbs. Deb: 6/29/54

YEAR TM/L	W	L	PCT	G	GS	CG	SH	SV	IP	H	HR	BB	SO	RAT	ERA	ERA+	OAV	OOB	BH	AVG	PB	PR	/A	PD	TPI
1954 StL-N	0	4	.000	13	10	0	0	0	58	62	2	28	17	14.3	3.72	110	.278	.364	1	.059	-1	2	2	-1	-0.1

● **GENE BEARDEN**   Bearden, Henry Eugene b: 9/5/20, Lexa, Ark. BL/TL, 6'3", 204 lbs. Deb: 5/10/47

YEAR TM/L	W	L	PCT	G	GS	CG	SH	SV	IP	H	HR	BB	SO	RAT	ERA	ERA+	OAV	OOB	BH	AVG	PB	PR	/A	PD	TPI
1947 Cle-A	0	0	—	1	0	0	0	0	0¹	2	0	1	0	81.0	81.00	4	.667	.750	0	—	0	-3	-3	0	0.0
1948 *Cle-A	20	7	.741	37	29	15	6	1	229²	187	9	106	80	11.6	**2.43**	**167**	.229	.320	23	.256	5	47	**42**	3	5.5
1949 Cle-A	8	8	.500	32	19	5	0	0	127	140	6	92	41	16.6	5.10	78	.286	.401	5	.111	-3	-13	-16	4	-1.6
1950 Cle-A	1	3	.250	13	3	0	0	0	45¹	57	5	32	10	17.7	6.15	70	.328	.432	2	.154	-1	-8	-9	-1	-0.7
Was-A	3	5	.375	12	9	4	0	0	68¹	81	1	33	20	15.3	4.21	107	.297	.377	5	.227	1	0	-0	0	0.3
Yr	4	8	.333	26	12	4	0	0	113²	138	6	65	30	16.2	4.99	89	.309	.399	7	.200	2	-5	-7	-0	-0.4
1951 Was-A	0	0	—	1	1	0	0	0	2²	6	0	2	1	27.0	16.88	24	.429	.500	0	—	-0	-4	-4	-0	0.0
Det-A	3	4	.429	37	4	2	1	0	106	112	6	58	38	14.5	4.33	96	.275	.366	6	.188	1	-2	-2	0	0.0
Yr	3	4	.429	38	5	2	1	0	108²	118	6	60	39	14.8	4.64	90	.280	.371	6	.188	1	-6	-6	-0	0.0
1952 StL-A	7	8	.467	34	16	3	0	0	150²	158	13	78	45	14.2	4.30	91	.270	.357	23	.354	6	-10	-6	1	0.1
1953 Chi-A	3	3	.500	25	3	0	0	0	58¹	48	8	33	24	12.5	2.93	137	.223	.327	4	.190	-1	7	7	0	0.6
Total 7	45	38	.542	193	84	29	7	1	788¹	791	48	435	259	14.1	3.96	103	.266	.361	68	.236	10	17	12	7	4.2

● **GARY BEARE**   Beare, Gary Ray b: 8/22/52, San Diego, Cal. BR/TR, 6'4", 205 lbs. Deb: 9/7/76

YEAR TM/L	W	L	PCT	G	GS	CG	SH	SV	IP	H	HR	BB	SO	RAT	ERA	ERA+	OAV	OOB	BH	AVG	PB	PR	/A	PD	TPI
1976 Mil-A	2	3	.400	6	5	2	0	0	41	43	4	15	32	12.7	3.29	106	.274	.337	0	—	0	1	1	-0	0.2
1977 Mil-A	3	3	.500	17	6	0	0	0	58²	63	6	38	32	15.6	6.44	63	.276	.382	0	—	0	-16	-15	2	-1.2
Total 2	5	6	.455	23	11	2	0	0	99²	106	10	53	64	14.4	5.15	74	.275	.364	0	—	0	-15	-15	1	-1.0

● **LARRY BEARNARTH**   Bearnarth, Lawrence Donald b: 9/11/41, New York, N.Y. BR/TR, 6'2", 203 lbs. Deb: 4/16/63 C

YEAR TM/L	W	L	PCT	G	GS	CG	SH	SV	IP	H	HR	BB	SO	RAT	ERA	ERA+	OAV	OOB	BH	AVG	PB	PR	/A	PD	TPI
1963 NY-N	3	8	.273	58	2	0	0	4	126¹	127	7	47	48	12.8	3.42	102	.268	.340	6	.200	1	-2	-1	2	0.5
1964 NY-N	5	5	.500	44	1	0	0	4	78	79	6	38	31	13.7	4.15	86	.271	.360	2	.143	-0	-5	-5	3	-0.4
1965 NY-N	3	5	.375	40	3	0	0	1	60²	75	6	28	16	15.9	4.60	77	.304	.384	1	.111	0	-7	-7	-0	-0.8
1966 NY-N	2	3	.400	29	1	0	0	0	54²	59	11	20	27	13.2	4.45	82	.281	.346	1	.111	-0	-5	-5	-1	-0.3
1971 Mil-A	0	0	—	2	0	0	0	0	3	10	1	2	2	36.0	18.00	19	.556	.600	0	—	0	-5	-5	0	0.0
Total 5	13	21	.382	173	7	0	0	8	322²	350	31	135	124	13.9	4.13	86	.282	.358	10	.161	1	-24	-21	7	-1.0

● **KEVIN BEARSE**   Bearse, Kevin Gerard b: 11/7/65, Jersey City, N.J. BL/TL, 6'2", 195 lbs. Deb: 4/15/90

YEAR TM/L	W	L	PCT	G	GS	CG	SH	SV	IP	H	HR	BB	SO	RAT	ERA	ERA+	OAV	OOB	BH	AVG	PB	PR	/A	PD	TPI
1990 Cle-A	0	2	.000	3	3	0	0	0	7²	16	2	5	2	27.0	12.91	30	.421	.511	0	—	0	-8	-8	-0	-1.4

● **CHRIS BEASLEY**   Beasley, Christopher Charles b: 6/23/62, Jackson, Tenn. BR/TR, 6'2", 190 lbs. Deb: 7/20/91

YEAR TM/L	W	L	PCT	G	GS	CG	SH	SV	IP	H	HR	BB	SO	RAT	ERA	ERA+	OAV	OOB	BH	AVG	PB	PR	/A	PD	TPI
1991 Cal-A	0	1	.000	22	0	0	0	0	26²	26	2	10	14	12.5	3.38	122	.257	.330	0	—	0	2	2	0	0.1

● **ED BEATIN**   Beatin, Ebenezer Ambrose b: 8/10/1866, Baltimore, Md. d: 5/9/25, Baltimore, Md. BR/TL, 5'9", 162 lbs. Deb: 8/2/1887

YEAR TM/L	W	L	PCT	G	GS	CG	SH	SV	IP	H	HR	BB	SO	RAT	ERA	ERA+	OAV	OOB	BH	AVG	PB	PR	/A	PD	TPI
1887 Det-N	1	1	.500	2	2	2	0	0	18	13	2	8	6	11.0	4.00	101	.203	.301	0	.000	-1	0	0	-0	-0.1
1888 Det-N	5	7	.417	12	12	12	1	0	107	111	6	16	44	10.9	2.86	97	.251	.280	14	.250	5	-0	-1	0	0.4
1889 Cle-N	20	15	.571	36	36	35	3	0	317²	316	12	141	155	13.1	3.57	113	.251	.339	14	.116	-6	16	16	-4	0.9
1890 Cle-N	22	30	.423	54	54	53	1	0	474¹	518	11	186	155	13.6	3.83	93	.269	.339	27	.141	-9	-14	-13	3	-1.7
1891 Cle-N	0	3	.000	5	4	2	1	0	29	39	1	21	4	20.5	5.28	66	.310	.431	1	.077	-1	-6	-6	0	-0.6
Total 5	48	56	.462	109	108	104	5	0	946	997	32	372	335	13.3	3.68	99	.261	.332	56	.144	-12	-4	-4	-1	-1.1

● **JIM BEATTIE**   Beattie, James Louis b: 7/4/54, Hampton, Va. BR/TR, 6'6", 220 lbs. Deb: 4/25/78

YEAR TM/L	W	L	PCT	G	GS	CG	SH	SV	IP	H	HR	BB	SO	RAT	ERA	ERA+	OAV	OOB	BH	AVG	PB	PR	/A	PD	TPI
1978 *NY-A	6	9	.400	25	22	0	0	0	128	118	8	51	65	12.8	3.73	97	.255	.336	0	—	0	-2	-1	0	-0.1
1979 NY-A	3	6	.333	15	13	1	1	0	76	85	9	41	32	14.9	5.21	78	.294	.382	0	—	0	-8	-10	-1	-0.8
1980 Sea-A	5	15	.250	33	29	3	0	0	187¹	205	19	98	67	14.7	4.85	85	.286	.375	0	—	0	-17	-15	0	-1.4
1981 Sea-A	3	2	.600	13	9	6	1	0	66²	59	2	18	36	10.7	2.97	130	.232	.288	0	—	0	7	7	0	0.5
1982 Sea-A	8	12	.400	28	26	6	1	0	172¹	149	13	65	140	11.2	3.34	127	.233	.305	0	—	0	14	17	1	1.7

YEAR	TM/L	W	L	PCT	G	GS	CG	SH	SV	IP	H	HR	BB	SO	RAT	ERA	ERA+	OAV	OOB	BH	AVG	PB	PR	/A	PD	TPI
1983	Sea-A	10	15	.400	30	29	8	2	0	196²	197	12	66	132	12.2	3.84	111	.259	.321	0	—	0	5	9	3	1.1
1984	Sea-A	12	16	.429	32	32	12	2	0	211	206	13	75	119	12.2	3.41	117	.260	.328	0	—	0	14	13	1	1.9
1985	Sea-A	5	6	.455	18	15	1	1	0	70¹	93	9	33	45	16.5	7.29	58	.316	.391	0	—	0	-25	-24	-1	-3.2
1986	Sea-A	0	6	.000	9	7	0	0	0	40¹	54	7	14	24	16.5	6.02	70	.341	.402	0	—	0	-8	-8	1	-1.0
Total	9	52	87	.374	203	182	31	7	1	1148²	1174	88	461	660	13.0	4.17	98	.267	.341	0	—	0	-20	-12	7	-1.3

● **BLAINE BEATTY** Beatty, Gordon Blaine b: 4/25/64, Victoria, Tex. BL/TL, 6'2", 185 lbs. Deb: 9/16/89

YEAR	TM/L	W	L	PCT	G	GS	CG	SH	SV	IP	H	HR	BB	SO	RAT	ERA	ERA+	OAV	OOB	BH	AVG	PB	PR	/A	PD	TPI
1989	NY-N	0	0	—	2	1	0	0	0	6	5	1	2	3	10.5	1.50	218	.217	.280	1	.500	0	1	1	0	0.0
1991	NY-N	0	0	—	5	0	0	0	0	9²	9	0	4	7	12.1	2.79	130	.250	.325	0	—	0	1	1	0	0.0
Total	2	0	0	—	7	1	0	0	0	15²	14	1	6	10	11.5	2.30	152	.237	.308	1	.500	0	2	2	0	0.0

● **JOHNNY BEAZLEY** Beazley, John Andrew "Nig" b: 5/25/18, Nashville, Tenn. d: 4/21/90, Nashville, Tenn. BR/TR, 6'1.5", 190 lbs. Deb: 9/28/41

YEAR	TM/L	W	L	PCT	G	GS	CG	SH	SV	IP	H	HR	BB	SO	RAT	ERA	ERA+	OAV	OOB	BH	AVG	PB	PR	/A	PD	TPI
1941	StL-N	1	0	1.000	1	1	0	0	0	9	10	0	3	4	13.0	1.00	376	.294	.351	0	.000	-0	3	3	-0	0.3
1942	*StL-N	21	6	.778	43	23	13	3	3	215¹	181	4	73	91	10.7	2.13	161	.226	.293	10	.137	-1	28	31	0	4.0
1946	*StL-N	7	5	.583	19	18	5	0	0	103	109	6	55	36	14.7	4.46	77	.275	.368	8	.242	1	-12	-11	-1	-1.2
1947	Bos-N	2	0	1.000	9	2	2	0	0	28²	30	1	19	12	15.4	4.40	89	.273	.380	0	.000	-1	-1	-2	-0	-0.2
1948	Bos-N	0	1	.000	3	2	0	0	0	16	19	2	7	4	14.6	4.50	85	.284	.351	0	.000	-1	-1	-1	-0	-0.1
1949	Bos-N	0	0	—	1	0	0	0	0	2	0	0	0	0	0.0	0.00	—	.000	.000	0	—	-0	1	1	0	0.0
Total	6	31	12	.721	76	46	21	3	3	374	349	13	157	147	12.3	3.01	116	.247	.325	18	.150	-2	18	20	-1	2.8

● **BUCK BECANNON** Becannon, James Melvin b: 8/22/1859, New York, N.Y. d: 11/5/23, New York, N.Y. 5'10", 165 lbs. Deb: 10/15/1884 ♦

YEAR	TM/L	W	L	PCT	G	GS	CG	SH	SV	IP	H	HR	BB	SO	RAT	ERA	ERA+	OAV	OOB	BH	AVG	PB	PR	/A	PD	TPI
1884	*NY-a	1	0	1.000	1	1	1	0	0	6	2	0	2	2	6.0	1.50	208	.091	.167	0	.000	-0	1	1	0	0.1
1885	NY-a	2	8	.200	10	10	10	0	0	85	108	5	24	13	14.5	6.25	47	.296	.348	10	.303	2	-28	-31	0	-2.4
Total	2	3	8	.273	11	11	11	0	0	91	110	5	26	15	13.9	5.93	50	.284	.337	10	.244	2	-27	-30	0	-2.3

● **GEORGE BECHTEL** Bechtel, George A. b: 1848, Philadelphia, Pa. 5'11", 165 lbs. Deb: 5/20/1871 ♦

YEAR	TM/L	W	L	PCT	G	GS	CG	SH	SV	IP	H	HR	BB	SO	RAT	ERA	ERA+	OAV	OOB	BH	AVG	PB	PR	/A	PD	TPI
1871	Ath-n	1	2	.333	3	3	3	2	0	26	43	0	11	1	18.7	7.96	51	.319	.370	33	.351	1	-11	-11		-0.6
1873	Phi-n	0	2	.000	3	3	1	0	0	16	27	0	4	0	16.3	4.50	73	.318	.333	63	.244	0	-2	-2		-0.2
1874	Phi-n	3	1	.250	6	4	4	0	0	39	57	0	1	0	13.4	1.62	137	.297	.301	42	.278	1	2	3		0.2
1875	Cen-n	2	12	.143	14	14	14	0	0	126	169	0	5	6	12.4	2.71	80	.274	.280	17	.279	3	-7	-8		-0.4
	Ath-n	3	1	.750	4	4	4	0	0	36	41	0	3	3	11.0	2.50	96	.279	.293	46	.280		-1	-0		-0.1
	Yr	5	13	.278	18	18	18	0	0	162	210	0	8	9	12.1	2.67	83	.275	.283	4	.280		-8	-8		-0.4
Total	4 n	7	20	.259	30	27	25	0	0	243	337	0	22	10	13.3	3.19	70	.287	.300	275	.282	6	-26	-26		-1.0

● **GEORGE BECK** Beck, Ernest George B. b: 2/21/1890, South Bend, Ind. d: 10/29/73, South Bend, Ind. BR/TR, 5'11", 165 lbs. Deb: 5/15/14

YEAR	TM/L	W	L	PCT	G	GS	CG	SH	SV	IP	H	HR	BB	SO	RAT	ERA	ERA+	OAV	OOB	BH	AVG	PB	PR	/A	PD	TPI
1914	Cle-A	0	0	—	1	0	0	0	0	1	1	0	0	0	18.0	0.00	—	.250	.400	0	—	0	0	0	-0	0.0

● **FRANK BECK** Beck, Frank J. (b: Frank J. Hengstebeck) b: 4/29/1860, Poughkeepsie, N.Y. d: 2/8/41, Detroit, Mich. TR, 5'9", 141 lbs. Deb: 5/2/1884 ♦

YEAR	TM/L	W	L	PCT	G	GS	CG	SH	SV	IP	H	HR	BB	SO	RAT	ERA	ERA+	OAV	OOB	BH	AVG	PB	PR	/A	PD	TPI
1884	Pit-a	0	3	.000	3	3	3	0	0	25	33	0	6	11	15.8	6.12	55	.306	.370	4	.333	-1	-8	-8	0	-0.6
	Bal-U	0	2	.000	2	2	1	0	0	9	17	0	4	7	21.0	8.00	34	.378	.429	2	.100	-1	-6	-5	0	-0.8
Total	1	0	5	.000	5	5	4	0	0	34	50	0	10	18	17.2	6.62	48	.327	.387	6	.188	-0	-14	-13	0	-1.4

● **RICH BECK** Beck, Richard Henry b: 1/21/41, Pasco, Wash. BB/TR, 6'3", 190 lbs. Deb: 9/14/65

YEAR	TM/L	W	L	PCT	G	GS	CG	SH	SV	IP	H	HR	BB	SO	RAT	ERA	ERA+	OAV	OOB	BH	AVG	PB	PR	/A	PD	TPI
1965	NY-A	2	1	.667	3	3	1	1	0	21	22	1	7	10	12.4	2.14	159	.275	.333	1	.000	-0	3	3	0	0.4

● **ROD BECK** Beck, Rodney Roy b: 8/3/68, Burbank, Cal. BR/TR, 6'1", 215 lbs. Deb: 5/6/91

YEAR	TM/L	W	L	PCT	G	GS	CG	SH	SV	IP	H	HR	BB	SO	RAT	ERA	ERA+	OAV	OOB	BH	AVG	PB	PR	/A	PD	TPI
1991	SF-N	1	1	.500	31	0	0	0	1	52¹	53	4	13	38	11.5	3.78	95	.273	.322	1	.500	0	-1	-1	0	0.0
1992	SF-N	3	3	.500	65	0	0	0	17	92	62	4	15	87	7.7	1.76	188	.190	.230	1	.500	0	18	16	-0	1.6
1993	SF-N★	3	1	.750	76	0	0	0	48	79¹	57	11	13	86	8.3	2.16	181	.201	.243	0	.000	-0	17	15	-1	2.2
1994	SF-N★	2	4	.333	48	0	0	0	28	48²	49	10	13	39	11.5	2.77	144	.261	.308	0	.000	0	8	7	0	1.3
1995	SF-N	5	6	.455	60	0	0	0	33	58²	60	6	21	42	12.7	4.45	92	.267	.335	1	.333	0	-2	-2	-0	-0.6
1996	SF-N	0	9	.000	63	0	0	0	35	62	56	9	10	48	9.7	3.34	122	.238	.272	1	.333	0	6	5	-1	1.1
Total	6	14	24	.368	343	0	0	0	162	393	337	45	85	340	9.9	2.89	131	.232	.279	4	.235	1	46	39	-2	5.6

● **BOOM-BOOM BECK** Beck, Walter William b: 10/16/04, Decatur, Ill. d: 5/7/87, Champaign, Ill. BR/TR, 6'2", 200 lbs. Deb: 9/22/24 C

YEAR	TM/L	W	L	PCT	G	GS	CG	SH	SV	IP	H	HR	BB	SO	RAT	ERA	ERA+	OAV	OOB	BH	AVG	PB	PR	/A	PD	TPI
1924	StL-A	0	0	—	1	0	0	0	0	2	2	1	0	0	27.0	0.00	—	.667	.750			0	0	1	0	0.0
1927	StL-A	1	0	1.000	3	1	1	0	0	11¹	15	0	5	6	16.7	5.56	78	.333	.412	1	.250	-2	-2	-2	-0	-0.1
1928	StL-A	2	3	.400	16	4	2	0	0	49	52	4	20	17	14.0	4.41	95	.289	.373	6	.429	1	-2	-1	-0	-0.1
1933	Bro-N	12	20	.375	43	35	15	3	1	257	270	9	69	89	12.3	3.54	91	.267	.321	18	.189	0	-6	-9	-0	-1.1
1934	Bro-N	2	6	.250	22	9	2	0	0	57	72	6	32	24	17.2	7.42	53	.301	.395	4	.235	1	-21	-22	1	-2.4
1939	Phi-N	7	14	.333	34	16	12	0	3	182²	203	11	64	77	13.3	4.73	85	.280	.345	9	.132	-3	-16	-15	0	-1.8
1940	Phi-N	4	9	.308	29	15	4	0	0	129¹	147	13	41	38	13.7	4.31	90	.286	.349	2	.056	-3	-7	-6	1	-0.7
1941	Phi-N	1	9	.100	34	7	2	0	0	95¹	104	8	35	34	13.3	4.63	80	.286	.341	4	.120	-2	-11	-10	-3	-1.4
1942	Phi-N	0	1	.000	26	1	0	0	1	53	69	4	17	10	14.8	4.75	70	.325	.378	4	.333	1	-8	-9	-1	-0.1
1943	Phi-N	0	0	—	4	0	0	0	0	13²	24	1	3	3	20.4	9.88	34	.393	.456	2	.500	1	-10	-10	-0	-0.5
1944	Det-A	1	2	.333	28	2	0	0	1	74	67	5	27	25	11.8	3.89	92	.243	.317	7	.318	2	-4	-3	-2	-0.1
1945	Cin-N	2	4	.333	11	5	2	0	1	47²	42	0	12	9	10.4	3.40	111	.236	.288	3	.214	-0	2	2	0	0.2
	Pit-N	6	1	.857	14	5	4	0	0	63	54	2	14	20	9.7	2.14	184	.234	.278	2	.125	-1	12	13	-1	1.2
	Yr	8	5	.615	25	10	6	0	1	110²	96	2	26	29	9.9	2.68	144	.234	.280	5	.167	-1	14	15	-0	1.4
Total	12	38	69	.355	265	100	44	3	6	1034	1121	63	342	352	13.1	4.30	86	.277	.340	61	.187	-2	-72	-71	-5	-6.3

● **CHARLIE BECKER** Becker, Charles S. "Buck" b: 10/14/1888, Washington, D.C. d: 7/30/28, Washington, D.C. BL/TL, 6'2", 180 lbs. Deb: 8/2/11

YEAR	TM/L	W	L	PCT	G	GS	CG	SH	SV	IP	H	HR	BB	SO	RAT	ERA	ERA+	OAV	OOB	BH	AVG	PB	PR	/A	PD	TPI
1911	Was-A	3	5	.375	11	5	5	1	0	71¹	80	2	23	31	13.9	4.04	81	.268	.335	5	.227		-5	-6	1	-0.6
1912	Was-A	0	0	—	4	0	0	0	0	9	8	0	6	5	14.0	3.00	111	.258	.378	1	.500	1	0	0	0	0.0
Total	2	3	5	.375	15	5	5	1	0	80¹	88	2	29	36	13.9	3.92	84	.267	.340	6	.250		-5	-6	1	-0.6

● **BOB BECKER** Becker, Robert Charles b: 8/15/1875, Syracuse, N.Y. d: 10/11/51, Syracuse, N.Y. TL Deb: 9/6/1897

YEAR	TM/L	W	L	PCT	G	GS	CG	SH	SV	IP	H	HR	BB	SO	RAT	ERA	ERA+	OAV	OOB	BH	AVG	PB	PR	/A	PD	TPI
1897	Phi-N	0	2	.000	5	2	2	0	0	24	32	1	9	10	15.0	5.63	75	.317	.367	1	.111	-0	-3	-4	-0	-0.3
1898	Phi-N	0	0	—	1	0	0	0	0	5	6	0	1	0	19.8	10.80	32	.300	.440	0	.000	-0	-4	-4	-0	0.0
Total	2	0	2	.000	6	2	2	0	0	29	38	1	10	10	15.8	6.52	62	.314	.381	1	.100	-0	-7	-8	-0	-0.3

● **ROBBIE BECKETT** Beckett, Robert Joseph b: 7/16/72, Austin, Tex. BR/TL, 6'5", 235 lbs. Deb: 9/12/96

YEAR	TM/L	W	L	PCT	G	GS	CG	SH	SV	IP	H	HR	BB	SO	RAT	ERA	ERA+	OAV	OOB	BH	AVG	PB	PR	/A	PD	TPI
1996	Col-N	0	0	—	5	0	0	0	0	5¹	6	3	6	2	25.3	13.50	40	.286	.500			0	-6	-5	0	0.0

● **JAKE BECKLEY** Beckley, Jacob Peter "Eagle Eye" b: 8/4/1867, Hannibal, Mo. d: 6/25/18, Kansas City, Mo. BL/TL, 5'10", 200 lbs. Deb: 6/20/1888 H♦

YEAR	TM/L	W	L	PCT	G	GS	CG	SH	SV	IP	H	HR	BB	SO	RAT	ERA	ERA+	OAV	OOB	BH	AVG	PB	PR	/A	PD	TPI
1902	Cin-N	0	1	.000	2	0	0	0	0	4	9	0	1	2	22.5	6.75	44	.450	.476	175	.330		-2	-2	1	-0.2

● **JIM BECKMAN** Beckman, James Joseph (b: Reinhardt Boeckman) b: 3/1/05, Cincinnati, Ohio d: 12/5/74, Montgomery, Ohio BR/TR, 5'10", 172 lbs. Deb: 7/27/27

YEAR	TM/L	W	L	PCT	G	GS	CG	SH	SV	IP	H	HR	BB	SO	RAT	ERA	ERA+	OAV	OOB	BH	AVG	PB	PR	/A	PD	TPI
1927	Cin-N	0	1	.000	4	1	0	0	0	12¹	18	2	9	6	18.2	5.84	65	.340	.417	0	.000	-0	-3	-3	-1	-0.3
1928	Cin-N	0	1	.000	6	0	0	0	0	15¹	19	1	9	6	16.4	5.87	68	.306	.394	0	.000	-0	-3	-3	-0	-0.3
Total	2	0	2	.000	10	1	0	0	0	27²	37	3	15	4	17.2	5.86	66	.321	.405	0	.000	-0	-6	-6	-1	-0.6

● **BILL BECKMANN** Beckmann, William Aloysius b: 12/8/07, Clayton, Mo. d: 1/2/90, Florissant, Mo. BR/TR, 6', 175 lbs. Deb: 5/2/39

YEAR	TM/L	W	L	PCT	G	GS	CG	SH	SV	IP	H	HR	BB	SO	RAT	ERA	ERA+	OAV	OOB	BH	AVG	PB	PR	/A	PD	TPI
1939	Phi-A	7	11	.389	27	19	7	2	0	155¹	198	15	41	20	13.9	5.39	87	.312	.355	13	.250	0	-13	-12	-2	-1.2
1940	Phi-A	8	4	.667	34	9	6	2	1	127¹	132	11	35	47	11.9	4.17	107	.265	.314	8	.205	-1	3	4	-2	0.1
1941	Phi-A	5	9	.357	22	15	4	0	0	130	141	11	33	28	12.2	4.57	92	.270	.315	9	.191	-0	-6	-6	-3	-0.8
1942	Phi-A	0	1	.000	5	1	0	0	0	20¹	24	1	9	3	14.6	7.08	53	.289	.359	2	.500	1	-3	-7	-1	-0.2
	StL-N	1	0	1.000	2	0	0	0	0	7	4	0	1	0	6.4	0.00	—	.200	.238	0	.000	-0	3	3	-0	0.4
Total	4	21	25	.457	90	44	17	4	1	440	499	38	119	108	12.7	4.79	92	.284	.330	32	.224	1	-22	-18	-7	-1.7

● **JOE BECKWITH** Beckwith, Thomas Joseph b: 1/28/55, Opelika, Ala. BL/TR, 6'3", 200 lbs. Deb: 7/21/79

YEAR	TM/L	W	L	PCT	G	GS	CG	SH	SV	IP	H	HR	BB	SO	RAT	ERA	ERA+	OAV	OOB	BH	AVG	PB	PR	/A	PD	TPI
1979	LA-N	1	2	.333	17	0	0	0	2	37¹	74	4	15	28	13.7	4.34	84	.284	.350	1	.000	-1	-3	-0	0	-0.3
1980	LA-N	3	3	.500	38	0	0	0	0	59²	60	7	23	40	12.7	1.96	178	.263	.333	0	.000	-0	11	10	-1	0.9

YEAR TM/L	W	L	PCT	G	GS	CG	SH	SV	IP	H	HR	BB	SO	RAT	ERA	ERA+	OAV	OOB	BH	AVG	PB	PR	/A	PD	TPI
1982 LA-N	2	1	.667	19	1	0	0	1	40	38	2	14	33	11.7	2.70	128	.252	.315	0	.000	-1	4	3	-1	0.1
1983 *LA-N	3	4	.429	42	3	0	0	1	71	73	5	35	50	13.8	3.55	101	.264	.348	1	.200	0	1	0	1	0.1
1984 KC-A	8	4	.667	49	1	0	0	2	100²	92	13	25	75	10.6	3.40	119	.247	.298	0	—	0	7	7	0	0.8
1985 *KC-A	1	5	.167	49	0	0	0	1	95	99	9	32	80	12.7	4.07	102	.269	.333	0	—	0	1	1	0	0.0
1986 LA-N	0	0	—	15	0	0	0	0	18¹	28	5	6	13	16.7	6.87	50	.350	.395	0	—	0	-6	-7	-1	-0.1
Total 7	18	19	.486	229	5	0	0	7	422	432	39	150	319	12.6	3.54	107	.266	.331	1	.053	-1	14	12	-0	1.5

● JULIO BECQUER
Becquer, Julio (Villegas) b: 12/20/31, Havana, Cuba BL/TL, 5'11.5", 178 lbs. Deb: 9/13/55 ♦

YEAR TM/L	W	L	PCT	G	GS	CG	SH	SV	IP	H	HR	BB	SO	RAT	ERA	ERA+	OAV	OOB	BH	AVG	PB	PR	/A	PD	TPI
1960 Was-A	0	0	—	1	0	0	0	0	1	1	1	0	0	9.0	9.00	43	.250	.250	75	.252	0	-1	-1	-0	0.0
1961 Min-A	0	0	—	1	0	0	0	0	1¹	4	0	1	0	33.8	20.25	21	.500	.556	20	.238	0	-2	-2	-0	0.0
Total 2	0	0	—	2	0	0	0	0	2¹	5	1	1	0	23.1	15.43	26	.417	.462	238	.244	0	-3	-3	-0	0.0

● PHIL BEDGOOD
Bedgood, Phillip Burlette b: 3/8/1898, Harrison, Ga. d: 11/8/27, Fort Pierce, Fla. BR/TR, 6'3", 218 lbs. Deb: 9/20/22

YEAR TM/L	W	L	PCT	G	GS	CG	SH	SV	IP	H	HR	BB	SO	RAT	ERA	ERA+	OAV	OOB	BH	AVG	PB	PR	/A	PD	TPI
1922 Cle-A	1	0	1.000	1	1	0	0	0	9	7	0	4	5	14.0	4.00	100	.233	.378	0	.000	-0	0	0	-0	0.0
1923 Cle-A	0	2	.000	9	2	0	0	0	18²	16	0	14	7	15.4	5.30	75	.246	.395	1	.250	0	-3	-3	-0	-0.2
Total 2	1	2	.333	10	3	1	0	0	27²	23	0	18	12	15.0	4.88	82	.242	.390	1	.167	0	-3	-3	-0	-0.2

● HUGH BEDIENT
Bedient, Hugh Carpenter b: 10/23/1889, Gerry, N.Y. d: 7/21/65, Jamestown, N.Y. BR/TR, 6', 185 lbs. Deb: 4/26/12

YEAR TM/L	W	L	PCT	G	GS	CG	SH	SV	IP	H	HR	BB	SO	RAT	ERA	ERA+	OAV	OOB	BH	AVG	PB	PR	/A	PD	TPI
1912 *Bos-A	20	9	.690	41	28	19	0	2	231	206	6	55	122	10.3	2.92	116	.240	.288	14	.192	1	10	12	1	1.6
1913 Bos-A	15	14	.517	43	28	15	1	5	259	255	0	67	122	11.4	2.78	106	.261	.312	10	.125	-3	4	5	-4	-0.3
1914 Bos-A	8	12	.400	42	16	7	1	2	177¹	187	4	45	70	12.0	3.60	75	.281	.331	5	.100	-2	-17	-18	-1	-2.3
1915 Buf-F	16	18	.471	53	30	16	2	**10**	269¹	284	5	69	106	11.9	3.17	88	.274	.321	9	.108	-5	-13	-11	-2	-2.2
Total 4	59	53	.527	179	102	57	4	19	936²	932	15	236	420	11.4	3.08	96	.263	.312	38	.133	-9	-16	-12	-7	-3.2

● ANDY BEDNAR
Bednar, Andrew Jackson b: 8/16/08, Streator, Ill. d: 11/26/37, Graham, Tex. BR/TR, 5'10.5", 180 lbs. Deb: 9/6/30

YEAR TM/L	W	L	PCT	G	GS	CG	SH	SV	IP	H	HR	BB	SO	RAT	ERA	ERA+	OAV	OOB	BH	AVG	PB	PR	/A	PD	TPI
1930 Pit-N	0	0	—	2	0	0	0	0	1¹	4	0	1	1	33.8	27.00	18	.500	.556	0	—	0	-3	-3	0	0.0
1931 Pit-N	0	0	—	3	0	0	0	0	4	10	1	0	2	22.5	11.25	34	.476	.476	0	—	0	-3	-3	0	0.0
Total 2	0	0	—	5	0	0	0	0	5¹	14	1	1	3	25.3	15.19	27	.483	.500	0	—	0	-7	-7	0	0.0

● STEVE BEDROSIAN
Bedrosian, Stephen Wayne b: 12/6/57, Methuen, Mass. BR/TR, 6'3", 200 lbs. Deb: 8/14/81

YEAR TM/L	W	L	PCT	G	GS	CG	SH	SV	IP	H	HR	BB	SO	RAT	ERA	ERA+	OAV	OOB	BH	AVG	PB	PR	/A	PD	TPI
1981 Atl-N	1	2	.333	15	1	0	0	0	24¹	15	2	15	9	11.5	4.44	81	.169	.295	0	.000	-0	-3	-2	-0	-0.3
1982 *Atl-N	8	6	.571	64	3	0	0	11	137²	102	7	57	123	10.7	2.42	154	.206	.293	1	.038	-2	18	20	-0	2.0
1983 Atl-N	9	10	.474	70	1	0	0	19	120	100	11	51	114	11.6	3.60	108	.229	.315	2	.105	-1	0	4	0	0.6
1984 Atl-N	9	6	.600	40	4	0	0	11	83²	65	5	33	81	10.6	2.37	163	.210	.289	2	.118	-1	11	14	-1	2.6
1985 Atl-N	7	15	.318	37	37	0	0	0	206²	198	17	111	134	13.7	3.83	100	.254	.351	5	.078	-4	-6	0	-2	-0.5
1986 Phi-N	8	6	.571	68	0	0	0	29	90¹	79	12	34	82	11.3	3.39	114	.232	.301	1	.200	-0	3	5	-1	0.9
1987 Phi-N★	5	3	.625	65	0	0	0	**40**	89	79	11	28	74	10.9	2.83	150	.237	.298	0	.000	-0	12	14	-1	2.1
1988 Phi-N	6	6	.500	57	0	0	0	28	74¹	75	6	27	61	12.3	3.75	95	.257	.320	0	.000	-0	-3	-2	-0	-0.4
1989 Phi-N	2	3	.400	28	0	0	0	6	33²	21	7	17	24	10.4	3.21	110	.183	.293	0	—	0	1	1	0	0.2
*SF-N	1	4	.200	40	0	0	0	17	51	35	5	22	34	10.1	2.65	127	.192	.279	1	.167	-0	5	4	-1	0.5
Yr	3	7	.300	68	0	0	0	23	84²	56	12	39	58	10.1	2.87	120	.187	.280	1	.167	-0	6	5	-2	0.7
1990 SF-N	9	9	.500	68	0	0	0	17	79¹	72	6	44	43	13.4	4.20	87	.241	.342	2	.500	1	-4	-5	-0	-1.1
1991 *Min-A	5	3	.625	56	0	0	0	6	77¹	70	11	35	44	12.6	4.42	96	.243	.331	0	—	0	-3	-1	-1	-0.3
1993 Atl-N	5	2	.714	49	0	0	0	0	49²	34	4	14	33	9.1	1.63	246	.194	.262	0	—	0	13	13	-0	1.6
1994 Atl-N	0	2	.000	46	0	0	0	0	46	41	4	18	43	11.9	3.33	128	.243	.323	1	.500	0	5	5	-0	0.2
1995 Atl-N	1	2	.333	29	0	0	0	0	28	40	6	12	22	17.0	6.11	70	.354	.421	0	—	0	-6	-6	-0	-0.6
Total 14	76	79	.490	732	46	0	0	184	1191	1026	114	518	921	11.9	3.38	114	.232	.317	15	.098	-7	46	64	-9	7.5

● FRED BEEBE
Beebe, Frederick Leonard b: 12/31/1880, Lincoln, Neb. d: 10/30/57, Elgin, Ill. BR/TR, 6'1", 190 lbs. Deb: 4/17/06

YEAR TM/L	W	L	PCT	G	GS	CG	SH	SV	IP	H	HR	BB	SO	RAT	ERA	ERA+	OAV	OOB	BH	AVG	PB	PR	/A	PD	TPI
1906 Chi-N	6	1	.857	14	6	4	0	1	70	56	1	32	55	12.0	2.70	98	.210	.306	3	.103	-1	-1	-0	-1	-0.3
StL-N	9	9	.500	20	19	16	1	0	160²	115	1	68	116	10.8	3.02	87	.208	.305	10	.172	0	-7	-7	-0	-0.8
Yr	15	10	.600	34	25	20	1	1	230²	171	2	100	**171**	10.9	2.93	90	.207	.300	13	.149	-1	-7	-8	-1	-1.1
1907 StL-N	7	19	.269	31	29	24	4	0	238¹	192	1	109	141	11.7	2.72	92	.230	.326	11	.128	-3	-7	-6	1	-0.8
1908 StL-N	5	13	.278	29	19	12	0	0	174¹	134	3	66	72	10.5	2.63	90	**.193**	.267	7	.125	-2	-5	-5	2	-0.6
1909 StL-N	15	21	.417	44	34	18	1	1	287²	256	5	104	105	11.5	2.82	90	.229	.299	18	.167	-2	-7	-9	1	-1.3
1910 Cin-N	12	14	.462	35	26	11	2	0	214¹	193	9	94	93	12.3	3.07	95	.246	.333	12	.164	-2	-1	-4	3	-0.3
1911 Phi-N	3	3	.500	9	8	3	0	0	48¹	52	2	24	20	14.7	4.47	77	.297	.391	5	.263	2	-6	-6	1	-0.3
1916 Cle-A	5	3	.625	20	12	5	1	0	100²	92	1	37	32	11.6	2.41	125	.251	.321	6	.214	1	5	7	-0	0.6
Total 7	62	83	.428	202	153	93	9	4	1294¹	1090	17	534	634	11.6	2.86	93	.227	.311	72	.158	-8	-28	-30	6	-3.8

● MATT BEECH
Beech, Lucas Matthew b: 1/20/72, Oakland, Cal. BL/TL, 6'2", 190 lbs. Deb: 8/8/96

YEAR TM/L	W	L	PCT	G	GS	CG	SH	SV	IP	H	HR	BB	SO	RAT	ERA	ERA+	OAV	OOB	BH	AVG	PB	PR	/A	PD	TPI
1996 Phi-N	1	4	.200	8	8	0	0	0	41¹	49	8	11	33	13.7	6.97	63	.306	.362	1	.071	-1	-13	-12	-0	-1.3

● ED BEECHER
Beecher, Edward Harry b: 7/2/1860, Guilford, Conn. d: 9/12/35, Hartford, Conn. BL/TL, 5'10", 185 lbs. Deb: 6/28/1887 ♦

YEAR TM/L	W	L	PCT	G	GS	CG	SH	SV	IP	H	HR	BB	SO	RAT	ERA	ERA+	OAV	OOB	BH	AVG	PB	PR	/A	PD	TPI
1890 Buf-P	0	0	—	1	0	0	0	0	6	10	0	3	0	19.5	12.00	34	.357	.419	159	.297	0	-5	-5	-0	0.0

● ROY BEECHER
Beecher, Leroy "Colonel" b: 5/10/1884, Swanton, Ohio d: 10/11/52, Toledo, Ohio BL/TR, 6'2", 180 lbs. Deb: 9/29/07

YEAR TM/L	W	L	PCT	G	GS	CG	SH	SV	IP	H	HR	BB	SO	RAT	ERA	ERA+	OAV	OOB	BH	AVG	PB	PR	/A	PD	TPI
1907 NY-N	0	2	.000	2	2	2	0	0	14	17	0	6	5	14.8	2.57	96	.293	.359	0	.000	-1	-0	-0	-0	-0.1
1908 NY-N	0	0	—	2	0	0	0	0	5²	11	0	3	0	22.2	7.94	30	.440	.500	1	.333	-1	-4	-3	0	-0.1
Total 2	0	2	.000	4	2	2	0	1	19²	28	0	9	5	16.9	4.12	60	.337	.402	1	.125	-0	-4	-4	0	-0.2

● FRED BEENE
Beene, Freddy Ray b: 11/24/42, Angleton, Tex. BB/TR, 5'9", 160 lbs. Deb: 9/18/68

YEAR TM/L	W	L	PCT	G	GS	CG	SH	SV	IP	H	HR	BB	SO	RAT	ERA	ERA+	OAV	OOB	BH	AVG	PB	PR	/A	PD	TPI
1968 Bal-A	0	0	—	1	0	0	0	0	1	2	0	1	1	27.0	9.00	33	.500	.600	0	—	0	-1	-1	-0	0.0
1969 Bal-A	0	0	—	2	0	0	0	0	2²	2	0	1	2	10.1	0.00	—	.200	.273	0	—	0	1	1	0	0.0
1970 Bal-A	0	0	—	4	0	0	0	0	6	8	1	5	4	19.5	6.00	61	.320	.433	0	—	0	-2	-2	-0	0.0
1972 NY-A	1	3	.250	29	1	0	0	3	57²	55	3	24	37	12.5	2.34	126	.256	.333	0	.000	-1	5	4	0	0.2
1973 NY-A	6	0	1.000	19	4	0	0	1	91	67	5	27	49	9.4	1.68	218	.209	.273	0	—	0	22	20	1	1.6
1974 NY-A	0	0	—	6	0	0	0	0	10	9	1	2	10	10.8	2.70	131	.231	.286	0	—	0	1	1	0	0.2
Cle-A	4	4	.500	32	0	0	0	2	73	68	7	26	35	11.7	4.93	73	.246	.314	0	—	0	-11	-11	1	-1.0
Yr	4	4	.500	38	0	0	0	3	83	77	8	28	45	11.5	4.66	77	.244	.307	0	—	0	-10	-10	1	-0.8
1975 Cle-A	1	0	1.000	19	1	0	0	0	46²	63	4	25	20	17.6	6.94	54	.323	.408	0	—	0	-16	-16	0	-0.4
Total 7	12	7	.632	112	6	0	0	8	288	274	21	111	156	12.3	3.63	97	.253	.326	0	.000	-1	-1	-3	2	0.6

● ANDY BEENE
Beene, Ramon Andrew b: 10/13/56, Freeport, Tex. BR/TR, 6'3", 205 lbs. Deb: 9/22/83

YEAR TM/L	W	L	PCT	G	GS	CG	SH	SV	IP	H	HR	BB	SO	RAT	ERA	ERA+	OAV	OOB	BH	AVG	PB	PR	/A	PD	TPI
1983 Mil-A	0	0	—	1	0	0	0	0	2	3	1	0	0	18.0	4.50	83	.333	.400	0	—	0	-0	-0	-0	0.8
1984 Mil-A	0	2	.000	5	3	0	0	0	18²	28	0	9	11	18.8	11.09	35	.350	.429	0	—	0	-15	-15	0	-1.0
Total 2	0	2	.000	6	3	0	0	0	20²	31	1	10	11	18.7	10.45	37	.348	.426	0	—	0	-15	-15	0	-0.2

● CLARENCE BEERS
Beers, Clarence Scott b: 12/9/18, ElDorado, Kan. BR/TR, 6', 175 lbs. Deb: 5/2/48

YEAR TM/L	W	L	PCT	G	GS	CG	SH	SV	IP	H	HR	BB	SO	RAT	ERA	ERA+	OAV	OOB	BH	AVG	PB	PR	/A	PD	TPI
1948 StL-N	0	0	—	1	0	0	0	0	0²	3	0	1	0	54.0	13.50	30	.500	.571	0	—	0	-1	-1	-0	0.0

● JOE BEGGS
Beggs, Joseph Stanley "Fireman" b: 11/4/10, Rankin, Pa. d: 7/19/83, Indianapolis, Ind BR/TR, 6'1", 182 lbs. Deb: 4/19/38

YEAR TM/L	W	L	PCT	G	GS	CG	SH	SV	IP	H	HR	BB	SO	RAT	ERA	ERA+	OAV	OOB	BH	AVG	PB	PR	/A	PD	TPI
1938 NY-A	3	2	.600	14	9	4	0	0	58¹	69	7	20	8	13.7	5.40	84	.299	.355	5	.250	1	-4	-6	2	-0.2
1940 *Cin-N	12	3	.800	37	1	0	0	**7**	76²	68	1	21	25	10.6	2.00	190	.243	.298	4	.190	-1	**16**	**15**	1	3.3
1941 Cin-N	4	3	.571	37	0	0	0	6	57	57	2	27	19	13.3	3.79	95	.313	.402	3	.300	-1	-1	-1	-0	-0.1
1942 Cin-N	6	5	.545	38	0	0	0	8	88²	65	4	33	24	10.0	2.13	154	.206	.283	0	.000	-3	12	11	3	1.6
1943 Cin-N	7	6	.538	39	4	2	0	6	115¹	121	0	25	28	11.4	2.34	142	.276	.315	5	.143	-1	**13**	**12**	1	1.5
1944 Cin-N	1	0	1.000	1	1	1	0	0	9	8	0	2	0	8.0	2.00	174	.222	.222	0	.000	-1	2	1	0	0.1
1946 Cin-N	12	10	.545	28	22	14	2	1	190	175	6	39	60	10.2	2.32	144	.247	.287	14	.222	2	23	22	1	2.9
1947 Cin-N	0	3	.000	11	4	0	0	0	32¹	42	4	6	11	13.4	5.29	78	.316	.345	1	.091	-1	-4	-4	-1	-0.4
NY-N	3	3	.500	32	0	0	0	2	66	81	6	18	23	13.6	4.23	96	.300	.346	1	.077	-1	-1	-1	-0	-0.2
Yr	3	6	.333	43	4	0	0	2	98¹	123	10	24	34	13.5	4.58	89	.305	.346	2	.083	-2	-6	-5	0	-0.6

YEAR	TM/L	W	L	PCT	G	GS	CG	SH	SV	IP	H	HR	BB	SO	RAT	ERA	ERA+	OAV	OOB	BH	AVG	PB	PR	/A	PD	TPI
1948	NY-N	0	0	—	1	0	0	0	0	0¹	2	0	0	0	54.0	0.00	—	.667	.667	0	—	0	0	0	0	0.0
Total	9	48	35	.578	238	41	23	4	29	693²	688	39	189	178	11.4	2.96	122	.265	.316	33	.167	-3	55	50	8	8.5

● **ED BEGLEY**   Begley, Edward N. (b: Edward N. Bagley)   b: 1863, New York, N.Y.   d: 7/24/19, Waterbury, Conn.   Deb: 5/3/1884

YEAR	TM/L	W	L	PCT	G	GS	CG	SH	SV	IP	H	HR	BB	SO	RAT	ERA	ERA+	OAV	OOB	BH	AVG	PB	PR	/A	PD	TPI
1884	NY-N	12	18	.400	31	30	30	0	0	266	296	9	99	104	13.4	4.16	72	.263	.323	22	.182	-3	-35	-35	-2	-3.4
1885	NY-a	4	9	.308	15	14	10	0	0	115	131	5	48	44	14.6	4.93	60	.278	.355	9	.173	-0	-21	-25	1	-2.1
Total	2	16	27	.372	46	44	40	0	0	381	427	14	147	148	13.7	4.39	68	.268	.333	31	.179	-3	-56	-60	-1	-5.5

● **PETIE BEHAN**   Behan, Charles Frederick   b: 12/11/1887, Dallas City, Pa.   d: 1/22/57, Bradford, Pa.   BR/TR, 5'10", 160 lbs.   Deb: 9/16/21

YEAR	TM/L	W	L	PCT	G	GS	CG	SH	SV	IP	H	HR	BB	SO	RAT	ERA	ERA+	OAV	OOB	BH	AVG	PB	PR	/A	PD	TPI
1921	Phi-N	0	1	.000	2	2	1	0	0	10²	17	0	1	3	15.2	5.91	72	.354	.367	0	—	-1	-3	-2	-0	-0.2
1922	Phi-N	4	2	.667	7	5	3	1	0	47¹	49	3	14	13	12.2	2.47	189	.259	.314	5	.250	-0	9	12	-1	1.3
1923	Phi-N	3	12	.200	31	17	5	0	2	131	182	11	57	27	16.5	5.50	84	.336	.401	8	.186	-2	-22	-13	-1	-1.5
Total	3	7	15	.318	40	24	9	1	2	189	248	14	72	43	15.3	4.76	97	.319	.378	13	.194	-3	-16	-3	-2	-0.4

● **RICK BEHENNA**   Behenna, Richard Kipp   b: 3/6/60, Miami, Fla.   BR/TR, 6'2", 170 lbs.   Deb: 4/12/83

YEAR	TM/L	W	L	PCT	G	GS	CG	SH	SV	IP	H	HR	BB	SO	RAT	ERA	ERA+	OAV	OOB	BH	AVG	PB	PR	/A	PD	TPI
1983	Atl-N	3	3	.500	14	6	0	0	0	37¹	37	7	12	17	12.1	4.58	85	.255	.316	4	.333	2	-4	-3	-0	-0.3
	Cle-A	0	2	.000	5	4	0	0	0	26	22	0	14	9	12.8	4.15	102	.232	.336	0	—	0	-0	0	0	-0.2
1984	Cle-A	0	3	.000	3	3	0	0	0	9²	17	5	8	6	24.2	13.97	29	.386	.491	0	—	0	-11	-11	0	-2.1
1985	Cle-A	0	2	.000	4	4	0	0	0	19²	29	3	8	4	16.9	7.78	53	.354	.411	0	—	0	-8	-8	-1	-0.7
Total	3	3	10	.231	26	17	0	0	0	92²	105	15	42	36	14.6	6.12	66	.287	.365	4	.333	2	-23	-21	-1	-3.3

● **MEL BEHNEY**   Behney, Melvin Brian   b: 9/2/47, Newark, N.J.   BL/TL, 6'2", 180 lbs.   Deb: 8/14/70

YEAR	TM/L	W	L	PCT	G	GS	CG	SH	SV	IP	H	HR	BB	SO	RAT	ERA	ERA+	OAV	OOB	BH	AVG	PB	PR	/A	PD	TPI
1970	Cin-N	0	2	.000	5	1	0	0	0	10	15	1	8	2	20.7	4.50	90	.341	.442	0	.000	-0	-1	-1	-0	-0.1

● **HANK BEHRMAN**   Behrman, Henry Bernard   b: 6/27/21, Brooklyn, N.Y.   d: 1/20/87, New York, N.Y.   BR/TR, 5'11", 174 lbs.   Deb: 4/17/46

YEAR	TM/L	W	L	PCT	G	GS	CG	SH	SV	IP	H	HR	BB	SO	RAT	ERA	ERA+	OAV	OOB	BH	AVG	PB	PR	/A	PD	TPI
1946	Bro-N	11	5	.688	47	11	2	0	4	150²	138	3	69	78	12.5	2.93	115	.241	.325	4	.095	-3	8	8	-2	0.3
1947	*Bro-N	0	0	—	2	0	0	0	0	3²	3	1	4	2	17.2	9.82	42	.231	.412	0	—	0	-2	-2	0	-0.0
	Pit-N	0	2	.000	10	2	0	0	0	24²	33	4	17	11	19.0	9.12	46	.347	.456	0	.000	-1	-14	-13	-1	-1.1
	*Bro-N	5	3	.625	38	6	0	0	8	88¹	94	9	44	31	14.1	5.30	78	.274	.357	6	.231	1	-12	-11	-1	-1.2
	Yr	5	5	.500	50	8	0	0	8	116²	130	16	65	44	15.0	6.25	66	.287	.376	6	.188	-0	-28	-27	-2	-2.3
1948	Bro-N	5	4	.556	34	4	2	1	7	91	95	7	42	42	13.8	4.05	99	.268	.350	3	.107	-2	-1	-1	-0	-0.3
1949	NY-N	3	3	.500	43	4	1	1	0	71¹	64	5	52	25	14.6	4.92	81	.239	.363	1	.077	-1	-7	-7	-0	-0.6
Total	4	24	17	.585	174	27	5	2	19	429²	427	31	228	189	13.9	4.40	87	.259	.352	14	.122	-5	-28	-28	-5	-2.9

● **TIM BELCHER**   Belcher, Timothy Wayne   b: 10/19/61, Mount Gilead, Ohio   BR/TR, 6'3", 210 lbs.   Deb: 9/6/87

YEAR	TM/L	W	L	PCT	G	GS	CG	SH	SV	IP	H	HR	BB	SO	RAT	ERA	ERA+	OAV	OOB	BH	AVG	PB	PR	/A	PD	TPI
1987	LA-N	4	2	.667	6	5	0	0	0	34	30	2	7	23	9.8	2.38	166	.240	.280	2	.200	0	6	6	-0	1.0
1988	*LA-N	12	6	.667	36	27	4	4	1	179²	143	8	51	152	9.8	2.91	115	.217	.275	4	.071	-2	11	8	-1	0.6
1989	LA-N	15	12	.556	39	30	**10**	**8**	1	230	182	20	80	200	10.5	2.82	121	.217	.291	7	.100	-2	17	15	-2	1.4
1990	LA-N	9	9	.500	24	24	5	2	0	153	136	17	48	102	10.9	4.00	91	.240	.302	7	.163	1	-4	-6	-2	-0.7
1991	LA-N	10	9	.526	33	33	2	1	0	209¹	189	10	75	156	11.4	2.62	137	.240	.307	8	.119	-2	25	23	-2	1.6
1992	Cin-N	15	14	.517	35	34	2	1	0	227²	201	17	80	149	11.2	3.91	92	.238	.307	8	.105	-2	-10	-8	-0	-1.2
1993	Cin-N	9	6	.600	22	22	4	2	0	137	134	11	47	101	12.4	4.47	90	.254	.324	10	.200	1	-6	-7	-1	-0.7
	*Chi-A	3	5	.375	12	11	1	1	0	71²	64	8	27	34	11.6	4.40	95	.242	.314	0	—	0	-1	-2	-1	-0.2
1994	Det-A	7	15	.318	25	25	3	0	0	162	192	21	78	76	15.2	5.89	82	.290	.368	0	—	0	-20	-19	1	-1.9
1995	*Sea-A	10	12	.455	28	28	1	0	0	179¹	188	19	88	96	14.1	4.52	105	.269	.354	0	—	0	4	4	-1	0.4
1996	KC-A	15	11	.577	35	35	4	1	0	238²	262	28	68	113	12.7	3.92	125	.281	.334	0	—	0	28	26	-0	2.6
Total	10	109	101	.519	295	274	36	17	5	1822¹	1721	161	649	1202	11.9	3.80	105	.249	.317	46	.124	-5	51	41	-8	2.9

● **STAN BELINDA**   Belinda, Stanley Peter   b: 8/6/66, Huntingdon, Pa.   BR/TR, 6'3", 185 lbs.   Deb: 9/8/89

YEAR	TM/L	W	L	PCT	G	GS	CG	SH	SV	IP	H	HR	BB	SO	RAT	ERA	ERA+	OAV	OOB	BH	AVG	PB	PR	/A	PD	TPI
1989	Pit-N	0	1	.000	8	0	0	0	0	10¹	13	0	2	10	13.1	6.10	55	.295	.326	0	—	0	-3	-3	-0	-0.3
1990	*Pit-N	3	4	.429	55	0	0	0	8	58¹	48	4	29	55	12.0	3.55	102	.227	.324	0	.000	-1	2	0	-1	-0.1
1991	*Pit-N	7	5	.583	60	0	0	0	16	78¹	50	10	35	71	10.2	3.45	104	.184	.286	0	.000	-0	2	1	-1	0.1
1992	*Pit-N	6	4	.600	59	0	0	0	18	71¹	58	8	29	57	11.0	3.15	109	.223	.301	2	.667	1	3	2	-1	0.3
1993	Pit-N	3	1	.750	40	0	0	0	19	42¹	35	4	11	30	10.0	3.61	112	.224	.280	0	.000	-0	2	2	-0	0.3
	KC-A	1	1	.500	23	0	0	0	0	27¹	30	2	6	25	12.2	4.28	107	.280	.325	0	—	0	1	1	-0	0.0
1994	KC-A	2	2	.500	37	0	0	0	1	49	47	6	24	37	14.0	5.14	97	.250	.350	0	—	0	-2	-1	-1	-0.2
1995	*Bos-A	8	1	.889	63	0	0	0	10	69²	51	5	28	57	10.7	3.10	157	.205	.295	0	—	0	12	14	-1	1.6
1996	Bos-A	2	1	.667	31	0	0	0	2	28²	33	3	20	18	17.3	6.59	78	.272	.399	0	—	0	-5	-5	-0	-0.7
Total	8	32	20	.615	376	0	0	0	74	435¹	363	42	184	360	11.7	3.89	106	.227	.314	2	.125	0	11	11	-5	1.1

● **BO BELINSKY**   Belinsky, Robert   b: 12/7/36, New York, N.Y.   BL/TL, 6'2", 191 lbs.   Deb: 4/18/62

YEAR	TM/L	W	L	PCT	G	GS	CG	SH	SV	IP	H	HR	BB	SO	RAT	ERA	ERA+	OAV	OOB	BH	AVG	PB	PR	/A	PD	TPI
1962	LA-A	10	11	.476	33	31	5	3	1	187¹	149	12	122	145	13.6	3.56	109	.216	.344	10	.167	1	9	6	-0	0.7
1963	LA-A	2	9	.182	13	13	2	0	0	76²	78	12	35	60	13.7	5.75	60	.262	.347	2	.074	-2	-18	-20	1	-2.5
1964	LA-A	9	8	.529	23	22	4	1	0	135¹	120	8	49	91	11.6	2.86	115	.240	.315	4	.095	-1	11	6	-1	0.5
1965	Phi-N	4	9	.308	30	14	3	0	1	109²	103	13	48	71	12.9	4.84	71	.248	.334	6	.188	1	-16	-17	-1	-2.0
1966	Phi-N	0	2	.000	9	1	0	0	0	15¹	14	3	5	8	12.9	2.93	123	.250	.344	1	.333	0	1	1	0	0.2
1967	Hou-N	3	9	.250	27	18	0	0	0	115¹	112	12	54	80	13.6	4.68	71	.255	.347	3	.077	-2	-17	-18	-2	-2.1
1969	Pit-N	0	3	.000	8	3	0	0	0	17²	17	1	14	15	16.8	4.58	76	.266	.412	0	.000	-0	-2	-2	-0	-0.4
1970	Cin-N	0	0	—	3	0	0	0	0	10	6	0	6	6	18.0	4.50	90	.294	.400	1	1.000	1	-0	-0	-0	0.1
Total	8	28	51	.354	146	102	14	4	2	665¹	603	61	333	476	13.2	4.10	86	.247	.340	27	.131	-2	-32	-43	-4	-5.5

● **CHARLIE BELL**   Bell, Charles C.   b: 8/12/1868, Cincinnati, Ohio   d: 2/7/37, Cincinnati, Ohio   TR ,   Deb: 10/13/1889   F♦

YEAR	TM/L	W	L	PCT	G	GS	CG	SH	SV	IP	H	HR	BB	SO	RAT	ERA	ERA+	OAV	OOB	BH	AVG	PB	PR	/A	PD	TPI
1889	KC-a	1	0	1.000	1	1	1	0	0	9	4	0	3	3	8.0	1.00	418	.129	.229	1	.167	0	3	3	1	0.4
1891	Lou-a	2	6	.250	10	9	8	0	0	77	93	4	20	16	14.1	4.68	78	.289	.346	1	.036	-2	-8	-9	-2	-1.0
	Cin-a	1	0	1.000	1	1	1	0	0	9	2	0	3	1	6.0	0.00	—	.069	.182	2	.500	4	4	0	0	0.5
	Yr	3	6	.333	11	10	9	0	0	86	95	4	23	17	12.5	4.19	88	.265	.311	3	.094	-2	-4	-5	-1	-0.5
Total	2	4	6	.400	12	11	10	0	0	95	99	4	26	20	12.8	3.88	97	.259	.323	4	.105	-2	-2	-1	-0	-0.1

● **ERIC BELL**   Bell, Eric Alvin   b: 10/27/63, Modesto, Cal.   BL/TL, 6'3", 195 lbs.   Deb: 9/24/85

YEAR	TM/L	W	L	PCT	G	GS	CG	SH	SV	IP	H	HR	BB	SO	RAT	ERA	ERA+	OAV	OOB	BH	AVG	PB	PR	/A	PD	TPI
1985	Bal-A	0	0	—	4	0	0	0	0	5²	4	1	4	4	12.7	4.76	85	.200	.333	0	—	0	-0	-0	0	0.1
1986	Bal-A	1	2	.333	4	4	0	0	0	23¹	23	4	14	18	14.3	5.01	82	.258	.359	0	—	0	-2	-2	-1	-0.3
1987	Bal-A	10	13	.435	33	29	2	0	0	165	174	32	78	111	13.9	5.45	81	.271	.351	0	—	0	-18	-19	-2	-2.3
1991	Cle-A	4	0	1.000	10	0	0	0	0	18	5	0	5	7	5.5	0.50	830	.091	.180	0	—	0	7	7	-0	1.6
1992	Cle-A	0	0	.000	7	1	0	0	0	15¹	12	1	9	10	18.8	7.63	51	.349	.438	0	—	0	-6	-6	1	-0.6
1993	Hou-N	0	1	.000	10	0	0	0	0	7¹	10	0	2	2	14.7	6.14	63	.313	.353	0	—	0	-2	-2	-0	-0.3
Total	6	15	18	.455	68	34	2	0	0	234²	238	38	112	152	13.6	5.18	83	.264	.348	0	—	0	-22	-23	-2	-1.8

● **GARY BELL**   Bell, Gary   b: 11/17/36, San Antonio, Tex.   BR/TR, 6'1", 198 lbs.   Deb: 6/1/58

YEAR	TM/L	W	L	PCT	G	GS	CG	SH	SV	IP	H	HR	BB	SO	RAT	ERA	ERA+	OAV	OOB	BH	AVG	PB	PR	/A	PD	TPI
1958	Cle-A	12	10	.545	33	23	10	0	1	182	141	14	73	110	10.8	3.31	110	.213	.296	11	.196	2	9	7	-2	0.7
1959	Cle-A	16	11	.593	44	28	12	1	5	234	208	28	105	136	12.2	4.04	91	.238	.323	18	.240	3	-5	-9	-2	-0.9
1960	Cle-A★	9	10	.474	28	23	6	2	1	154²	139	15	82	109	13.3	4.13	90	.242	.344	7	.149	-0	-4	-7	-1	-0.7
1961	Cle-A	12	16	.429	34	34	11	2	0	228¹	214	32	100	163	12.6	4.10	96	.245	.326	16	.198	1	-4	-6	-1	-0.4
1962	Cle-A	10	9	.526	57	6	1	0	12	107²	104	14	52	80	13.3	4.26	94	.264	.354	5	.208	1	-4	-5	-1	-0.8
1963	Cle-A	8	5	.615	58	7	0	0	8	119	91	14	52	98	11.1	2.95	123	.208	.298	3	.115	-1	9	9	1	1.0
1964	Cle-A	8	6	.571	56	2	0	0	6	106	106	15	53	89	13.8	4.33	83	.260	.351	6	.375	2	-9	-11	-0	-1.0
1965	Cle-A	6	5	.545	60	1	0	0	17	103²	86	7	50	86	12.0	3.04	115	.226	.319	1	.063	-0	5	5	-1	0.6
1966	Cle-A☆	14	15	.483	40	37	12	0	0	254¹	211	19	79	194	10.4	3.22	107	.228	.291	10	.132	-1	6	6	2	0.8
1967	Cle-A	1	5	.167	9	9	0	0	0	60²	50	7	24	39	11.1	3.71	88	.234	.314	0	.000	-1	3	1	-0	0.1
	*Bos-A	12	8	.600	29	24	8	0	3	165¹	143	14	47	115	10.6	3.16	110	.231	.290	12	.203	1	1	1	1	0.8
	Yr	13	13	.500	38	33	8	0	3	226	193	21	71	154	10.7	3.31	104	.231	.295	12	.162	-1	-2	3	0	0.4
1968	Bos-A☆	11	11	.500	35	27	5	3	1	191¹	177	7	68	103	11.3	3.12	101	.239	.308	13	.220	2	-3	-1	0	0.3
1969	Sea-A	2	6	.250	13	11	1	0	2	61¹	76	8	34	30	16.4	4.70	77	.305	.393	3	.214	1	-7	-7	0	-0.7

YEAR	TM/L	W	L	PCT	G	GS	CG	SH	SV	IP	H	HR	BB	SO	RAT	ERA	ERA+	OAV	OOB	BH	AVG	PB	PR	/A	PD	TPI
	Chi-A	0	0	—	23	2	0	0	0	38²	48	8	23	26	17.0	6.28	61	.308	.403	0	.000	-0	-11	-10	0	0.0
	Yr	2	6	.250	36	13	1	1	2	100	124	16	57	56	16.5	5.31	70	.302	.390	3	.158	1	-19	-18	0	-0.7
Total	12	121	117	.508	519	233	71	9	51	2015	1794	206	842	1378	12.0	3.68	98	.239	.320	105	.185	9	-17	-18	-3	-0.7

● GEORGE BELL
Bell, George Glenn "Farmer" b: 11/2/1874, Greenwood, N.Y. d: 12/25/41, New York, N.Y. BR/TR, 6', 195 lbs. Deb: 4/17/07

YEAR	TM/L	W	L	PCT	G	GS	CG	SH	SV	IP	H	HR	BB	SO	RAT	ERA	ERA+	OAV	OOB	BH	AVG	PB	PR	/A	PD	TPI
1907	Bro-N	8	16	.333	35	27	20	3	1	263²	222	1	77	88	10.4	2.25	104	.238	.300	8	.095	-2	6	3	2	0.3
1908	Bro-N	4	15	.211	29	19	12	2	1	155¹	162	3	45	63	12.1	3.59	65	.270	.324	8	.170	-1	-21	-22	1	-2.4
1909	Bro-N	16	15	.516	33	30	29	6	1	256	236	5	73	95	11.0	2.71	96	.251	.307	15	.167	-1	-3	-3	2	-0.1
1910	Bro-N	10	27	.270	44	36	25	4	1	310	267	4	82	102	10.2	2.64	115	.241	.296	13	.134	-4	13	13	-3	0.7
1911	Bro-N	5	6	.455	19	12	6	2	0	101	123	2	28	28	13.6	4.28	78	.315	.364	4	.121	-1	-10	-11	2	-1.0
Total	5	43	79	.352	160	124	92	17	4	1086	1010	15	305	376	11.0	2.85	94	.254	.310	48	.137	-6	-14	-20	4	-2.5

● HI BELL
Bell, Herman S b: 7/16/1897, Mt.Sherman, Ky. d: 6/7/49, Glendale, Cal. BR/TR, 6', 185 lbs. Deb: 4/16/24

YEAR	TM/L	W	L	PCT	G	GS	CG	SH	SV	IP	H	HR	BB	SO	RAT	ERA	ERA+	OAV	OOB	BH	AVG	PB	PR	/A	PD	TPI
1924	StL-N	3	8	.273	28	10	5	0	1	113¹	124	5	29	29	12.5	4.92	77	.292	.344	2	.065	-2	-13	-14	0	-1.5
1926	*StL-N	6	6	.500	27	7	3	0	2	85	82	1	17	27	10.7	3.18	123	.255	.296	3	.120	-1	6	7	-1	0.6
1927	StL-N	1	3	.250	25	1	0	0	0	57¹	71	5	22	31	14.8	3.92	101	.317	.381	1	.091	-1	-0	-0	-1	-0.1
1929	StL-N	0	2	.000	7	0	0	0	0	13	19	1	4	4	15.9	6.92	67	.339	.383	0	.000	-0	-3	-3	-0	-0.5
1930	*StL-N	4	3	.571	39	9	2	0	8	115¹	143	4	23	42	13.1	3.90	129	.299	.334	2	.077	-3	14	14	1	0.7
1932	NY-N	8	4	.667	35	10	3	0	2	120	132	12	16	25	11.3	3.68	101	.280	.307	4	.088	-2	3	4	-1	-0.3
1933	*NY-N	6	5	.545	38	7	1	1	5	105¹	100	4	20	24	10.4	2.05	157	.246	.285	4	.138	-1	15	14	-1	1.3
1934	NY-N	4	3	.571	22	2	0	0	0	54	72	2	12	9	14.2	3.67	105	.319	.358	2	.105	-1	2	1	0	0.0
Total	8	32	34	.485	221	46	14	1	24	663¹	743	34	143	191	12.2	3.69	107	.285	.326	17	.096	-12	23	19	-4	0.2

● JERRY BELL
Bell, Jerry Houston b: 10/6/47, Madison, Tenn. BB/TR, 6'4", 190 lbs. Deb: 9/6/71

YEAR	TM/L	W	L	PCT	G	GS	CG	SH	SV	IP	H	HR	BB	SO	RAT	ERA	ERA+	OAV	OOB	BH	AVG	PB	PR	/A	PD	TPI
1971	Mil-A	2	1	.667	8	0	0	0	0	14²	10	0	6	8	9.8	3.07	113	.200	.286	0	—	-1	1	1	1	0.1
1972	Mil-A	5	1	.833	25	3	0	0	0	70²	50	1	33	20	11.0	1.66	183	.209	.313	1	.071	-1	11	11	1	0.9
1973	Mil-A	9	9	.500	31	25	8	0	1	183²	185	14	70	57	12.7	3.97	95	.263	.334	0	—	-3	-4	-1	-1	-0.1
1974	Mil-A	1	0	1.000	5	0	0	0	0	14	17	2	5	4	14.1	2.57	141	.315	.373	0	—	-0	2	2	-0	0.1
Total	4	17	11	.607	69	28	8	0	1	283	262	17	114	89	12.2	3.28	109	.250	.329	1	.071	-1	10	9	1	1.0

● RALPH BELL
Bell, Ralph Albert "Lefty" b: 11/6/1890, Kahoka, Mo. d: 10/18/59, Burlington, Iowa BL/TL, 5'11.5", 170 lbs. Deb: 7/16/12

YEAR	TM/L	W	L	PCT	G	GS	CG	SH	SV	IP	H	HR	BB	SO	RAT	ERA	ERA+	OAV	OOB	BH	AVG	PB	PR	/A	PD	TPI
1912	Chi-A	0	0	—	3	0	0	0	0	6	8	1	8	5	24.0	9.00	36	.333	.500	0	.000	-0	-4	-4	0	0.0

● BILL BELL
Bell, William Samuel "Ding Dong" b: 10/24/33, Goldsboro, N.C. d: 10/11/62, Durham, N.C. BR/TR, 6'3", 200 lbs. Deb: 9/5/52

YEAR	TM/L	W	L	PCT	G	GS	CG	SH	SV	IP	H	HR	BB	SO	RAT	ERA	ERA+	OAV	OOB	BH	AVG	PB	PR	/A	PD	TPI
1952	Pit-N	0	1	.000	4	1	0	0	0	15²	16	3	13	4	16.7	4.60	87	.254	.382	0	.000	-0	-2	-1	0	-0.1
1955	Pit-N	0	0	—	1	0	0	0	0	1	0	0	1	0	9.0	0.00	—	.000	.250	0	—	-0	1	0	-0	0.0
Total	2	0	1	.000	5	1	0	0	0	16²	16	3	14	4	16.2	4.32	93	.242	.375	0	.000	-0	-1	-1	0	-0.1

● CHIEF BENDER
Bender, Charles Albert b: 5/5/1884, Crow Wing Co., Minn d: 5/22/54, Philadelphia, Pa. BR/TR, 6'2", 185 lbs. Deb: 4/20/03 CH

YEAR	TM/L	W	L	PCT	G	GS	CG	SH	SV	IP	H	HR	BB	SO	RAT	ERA	ERA+	OAV	OOB	BH	AVG	PB	PR	/A	PD	TPI
1903	Phi-A	17	14	.548	36	33	29	2	0	270	239	6	65	127	11.0	3.07	100	.237	.299	22	.183	-1	-3	-0	-1	-0.2
1904	Phi-A	10	11	.476	29	20	18	4	0	203²	167	1	59	149	10.2	2.87	93	.225	.285	18	.228	3	-6	-4	-2	-0.4
1905	*Phi-A	18	11	.621	35	23	18	4	0	229	193	6	90	142	11.6	2.83	94	.230	.313	20	.217	2	-4	-4	3	-0.1
1906	Phi-A	15	10	.600	36	27	24	0	3	238¹	208	5	48	159	10.0	2.53	108	.238	.284	23	.253	7	4	5	-1	1.3
1907	Phi-A	16	8	.667	33	24	20	4	3	219¹	185	1	34	112	9.1	2.05	127	.231	.265	23	.230	3	12	13	-2	1.7
1908	Phi-A	8	9	.471	18	17	14	1	0	138²	121	1	21	85	9.4	1.75	146	.236	.270	11	.220	2	10	12	-2	1.8
1909	Phi-A	18	8	.692	34	29	24	5	1	250	196	2	47	161	8.9	1.66	145	.214	.254	25	.215	4	23	21	2	2.9
1910	*Phi-A	23	5	.821	30	28	25	3	0	250	182	1	47	155	8.6	1.58	150	.207	.255	25	.269	8	26	22	2	3.8
1911	*Phi-A	17	5	.773	31	24	16	2	3	216¹	198	2	58	114	10.8	2.16	146	.252	.307	13	.165	-3	28	24	1	2.0
1912	Phi-A	13	8	.619	27	19	12	1	2	171	169	1	33	90	10.7	2.74	113	.277	.315	9	.150	-1	11	7	-2	0.4
1913	*Phi-A	21	10	.677	48	21	14	2	13	236²	208	2	59	135	10.2	2.21	125	.228	.277	12	.154	0	19	15	-2	1.9
1914	*Phi-A	17	3	.850	28	23	14	7	2	179	159	4	55	107	10.8	2.26	115	.240	.299	9	.145	-0	10	7	-0	0.8
1915	Bal-F	4	16	.200	26	23	15	0	1	178¹	198	5	37	89	12.2	3.99	72	.298	.342	16	.267	-1	-25	-22	-1	-2.1
1916	Phi-N	7	7	.500	27	13	4	0	3	122²	137	3	34	43	13.3	3.74	71	.287	.347	12	.279	4	-15	-15	2	-1.3
1917	Phi-N	8	2	.800	20	10	8	4	2	113	84	1	26	43	9.3	1.67	168	.215	.277	8	.205	1	13	14	-2	1.3
1925	Chi-A	0	0	—	1	0	0	0	0	1	3	0	1	0	18.0	18.00	20	.333	.500	0	—	-0	-2	-0	0	0.0
Total	16	212	127	.625	459	334	255	40	34	3017	2645	40	712	1711	10.3	2.46	111	.239	.291	243	.212	33	101	94	-5	13.8

● ALAN BENES
Benes, Alan Paul b: 1/21/72, Evansville, Ind. BR/TR, 6'5", 215 lbs. Deb: 9/19/95 F

YEAR	TM/L	W	L	PCT	G	GS	CG	SH	SV	IP	H	HR	BB	SO	RAT	ERA	ERA+	OAV	OOB	BH	AVG	PB	PR	/A	PD	TPI
1995	StL-N	1	2	.333	3	3	0	0	0	16	24	4	20	20	16.3	8.44	50	.343	.387	0	.000	-1	-8	-8	-0	-1.1
1996	*StL-N	13	10	.565	34	32	3	1	0	191	192	27	87	131	13.5	4.90	86	.266	.350	9	.148	-0	-15	-14	-2	-1.7
Total	2	14	12	.538	37	35	3	1	0	207	216	29	91	151	13.7	5.17	82	.273	.354	9	.134	-1	-22	-22	-2	-2.8

● ANDY BENES
Benes, Andrew Charles b: 8/20/67, Evansville, Ind. BR/TR, 6'6", 235 lbs. Deb: 8/11/89 F

YEAR	TM/L	W	L	PCT	G	GS	CG	SH	SV	IP	H	HR	BB	SO	RAT	ERA	ERA+	OAV	OOB	BH	AVG	PB	PR	/A	PD	TPI
1989	SD-N	6	3	.667	10	10	0	0	0	66²	51	7	31	66	11.2	3.51	100	.213	.305	6	.250	2	-0	-0	0	0.2
1990	SD-N	10	11	.476	32	31	2	0	0	192¹	177	18	69	140	11.6	3.60	106	.242	.309	6	.100	-2	4	5	-3	0.0
1991	SD-N	15	11	.577	33	33	4	1	0	223	194	23	59	167	10.4	3.03	125	.232	.286	2	.032	-2	16	19	-1	1.9
1992	SD-N	13	14	.481	34	34	2	2	0	231¹	230	14	61	169	11.5	3.35	107	.264	.316	10	.149	-2	4	6	-0	0.9
1993	SD-N★	15	15	.500	34	34	4	2	0	230²	200	23	86	179	11.3	3.78	109	.232	.305	9	.125	-0	7	9	-3	0.7
1994	SD-N	6	14	.300	25	25	2	2	0	172¹	155	20	51	189	10.8	3.86	106	.237	.294	8	.163	-0	7	5	1	0.6
1995	SD-N	4	7	.364	19	19	1	1	0	118²	121	10	45	126	12.9	4.17	97	.262	.333	6	.150	-0	0	-2	-1	-0.3
	*Sea-A	7	2	.778	12	12	0	0	0	63	72	8	33	45	15.3	5.86	81	.287	.374	0	—	0	-8	-8	-0	-1.0
1996	*StL-N	18	10	.643	36	34	3	1	0	230¹	215	28	77	160	11.6	3.83	111	.247	.312	11	.151	-0	10	10	-3	0.9
Total	8	94	87	.519	235	232	18	9	0	1528¹	1415	151	512	1241	11.5	3.70	107	.245	.310	58	.130	-1	39	44	-9	3.9

● RAY BENGE
Benge, Raymond Adelphia b: 4/22/02, Jacksonville, Tex. BR/TR, 5'9.5", 160 lbs. Deb: 9/26/25

YEAR	TM/L	W	L	PCT	G	GS	CG	SH	SV	IP	H	HR	BB	SO	RAT	ERA	ERA+	OAV	OOB	BH	AVG	PB	PR	/A	PD	TPI
1925	Cle-A	1	0	1.000	2	2	1	1	0	11²	9	0	3	3	9.3	1.54	286	.205	.255	2	.400	0	4	4	-1	0.3
1926	Cle-A	1	0	1.000	8	0	0	0	0	11²	15	0	4	3	14.7	3.86	105	.313	.365	1	.333	0	0	0	0	0.1
1928	Phi-N	8	18	.308	40	28	12	1	1	201²	219	15	88	68	13.9	4.55	94	.286	.363	12	.207	-0	-13	-6	-2	-0.9
1929	Phi-N	11	15	.423	38	27	9	2	4	199	255	24	77	78	15.2	6.29	83	.322	.385	15	.203	-3	-35	-24	-3	-3.0
1930	Phi-N	11	15	.423	38	29	14	0	1	225²	305	22	81	70	15.4	5.70	96	.328	.382	18	.205	-3	-18	-6	-1	-0.9
1931	Phi-N	14	18	.438	38	31	16	2	2	247	251	12	61	117	11.6	3.17	134	.262	.310	18	.205	-3	19	30	-2	3.3
1932	Phi-N	13	12	.520	41	28	13	2	6	222²	247	15	58	89	12.5	4.05	109	.281	.329	13	.173	-3	-4	9	-1	0.6
1933	Bro-N	10	17	.370	37	30	16	2	1	228²	238	11	55	74	11.8	3.42	94	.268	.315	14	.184	0	-2	-5	-3	-0.9
1934	Bro-N	14	12	.538	36	32	14	1	0	227	252	11	61	64	12.5	4.32	90	.272	.319	15	.169	-1	-7	-11	-1	-1.3
1935	Bro-N	9	9	.500	23	17	5	1	0	124²	142	12	47	39	13.7	4.48	89	.289	.353	9	.191	-1	-6	-7	-2	-1.1
1936	Bos-N	7	9	.438	21	19	2	0	0	115	161	6	38	32	15.7	5.79	66	.333	.382	6	.140	-3	-23	-25	-2	-3.2
	Phi-N	1	4	.200	15	6	0	0	0	45²	70	3	19	13	17.5	4.73	96	.350	.406	0	.000	-1	-4	-1	-2	-0.4
	Yr	8	13	.381	36	25	2	0	0	160²	231	9	57	45	16.1	5.49	73	.337	.388	6	.113	-4	-26	-26	-4	-3.6
1938	Cin-N	1	1	.500	9	0	0	0	0	15¹	13	1	6	5	11.2	4.11	89	.228	.302	1	.333	0	-1	-0	0	-0.1
Total	12	101	130	.437	346	249	102	12	19	1875¹	2177	142	598	655	13.5	4.52	95	.292	.347	124	.188	-17	-89	-46	-18	-7.5

● ARMANDO BENITEZ
Benitez, Armando German b: 11/3/72, Ramon Santana, D.R. BR/TR, 6'4", 180 lbs. Deb: 7/28/94

YEAR	TM/L	W	L	PCT	G	GS	CG	SH	SV	IP	H	HR	BB	SO	RAT	ERA	ERA+	OAV	OOB	BH	AVG	PB	PR	/A	PD	TPI
1994	Bal-A	0	0	—	3	0	0	0	0	10	8	0	4	14	11.7	0.90	556	.216	.310	0	—	0	4	5	0	-0.1
1995	Bal-A	1	5	.167	44	0	0	0	2	47²	37	8	37	56	14.9	5.66	84	.213	.366	0	—	0	-5	-5	-1	-0.7
1996	*Bal-A	1	0	1.000	18	0	0	0	4	14¹	7	2	6	20	8.2	3.77	130	.143	.236	0	—	0	2	2	0	0.2
Total	3	2	5	.286	65	0	0	0	6	72	52	10	47	90	13.1	4.63	104	.200	.335	0	—	0	2	1	-1	-0.6

● HENRY BENN
Benn, Henry Omer b: 1/25/1890, Viola, Wis. d: 6/4/67, Madison, Wis. BR/TR, 6', 190 lbs. Deb: 9/24/14

YEAR	TM/L	W	L	PCT	G	GS	CG	SH	SV	IP	H	HR	BB	SO	RAT	ERA	ERA+	OAV	OOB	BH	AVG	PB	PR	/A	PD	TPI
1914	Cle-A	0	0	—	1	0	0	0	0	1	0	0	0	1	0.0	0.00	—	.000	.000	0	—	0	0	0	-0	0.0

● DAVE BENNETT
Bennett, David Hans b: 11/7/45, Berkeley, Cal. BR/TR, 6'5", 195 lbs. Deb: 6/12/64 F

YEAR	TM/L	W	L	PCT	G	GS	CG	SH	SV	IP	H	HR	BB	SO	RAT	ERA	ERA+	OAV	OOB	BH	AVG	PB	PR	/A	PD	TPI
1964	Phi-N	0	0	—	1	0	0	0	0	1	2	0	1	0	18.0	9.00	39	.400	.400	0	—	0	-1	-1	0	0.0

YEAR	TM/L	W	L	PCT	G	GS	CG	SH	SV	IP	H	HR	BB	SO	RAT	ERA	ERA+	OAV	OOB	BH	AVG	PB	PR	/A	PD	TPI

● DENNIS BENNETT
Bennett, Dennis John b: 10/5/39, Oakland, Cal. BL/TL, 6'5", 205 lbs. Deb: 5/12/62 F

YEAR	TM/L	W	L	PCT	G	GS	CG	SH	SV	IP	H	HR	BB	SO	RAT	ERA	ERA+	OAV	OOB	BH	AVG	PB	PR	/A	PD	TPI
1962	Phi-N	9	9	.500	31	24	7	2	3	174²	144	17	68	149	11.2	3.81	102	.224	.304	8	.127	-1	3	1	-1	0.0
1963	Phi-N	9	5	.643	23	16	6	1	1	119¹	102	12	33	82	10.5	2.64	122	.231	.290	9	.225	3	9	8	0	1.3
1964	Phi-N	12	14	.462	41	32	7	2	1	208	222	23	58	125	12.3	3.68	94	.280	.333	13	.197	3	-3	-5	-1	-0.3
1965	Bos-A	5	7	.417	34	18	3	0	0	141²	152	15	53	85	13.4	4.38	85	.279	.350	7	.179	2	-15	-10	-1	-0.7
1966	Bos-A	3	3	.500	16	13	0	0	0	75	75	9	23	47	11.9	3.24	117	.261	.318	3	.130	1	2	5	-1	0.3
1967	Bos-A	4	3	.571	13	11	4	1	0	69²	72	12	22	34	12.4	3.88	90	.268	.328	3	.120	-0	-5	-3	-0	-0.4
	NY-N	1	1	.500	8	6	0	0	0	26¹	37	4	7	14	15.4	5.13	66	.336	.381	2	.250	-0	-5	-5	-0	-0.3
1968	Cal-A	0	5	.000	16	7	1	0	1	48¹	46	6	17	36	12.5	3.54	82	.250	.327	1	.077	-1	-3	-3	1	-0.4
Total	7	43	47	.478	182	127	28	6	6	863	850	98	281	572	12.1	3.69	96	.260	.324	46	.166	7	-18	-13	-2	-0.5

● ERIK BENNETT
Bennett, Erik Hans b: 9/13/68, Yreka, Cal. BR/TR, 6'2", 205 lbs. Deb: 5/15/95

YEAR	TM/L	W	L	PCT	G	GS	CG	SH	SV	IP	H	HR	BB	SO	RAT	ERA	ERA+	OAV	OOB	BH	AVG	PB	PR	/A	PD	TPI
1995	Cal-A	0	0	—	1	0	0	0	0	0¹	0	0	0	0	0.0		—	.000	.000	0	—	0	0	0	0	0.0
1996	Min-A	2	0	1.000	24	0	0	0	1	27¹	33	7	16	13	16.8	7.90	65	.306	.405	0	—	0	-9	-8	0	-0.5
Total	2	2	0	1.000	25	0	0	0	1	27²	33	7	16	13	16.6	7.81	66	.303	.402	0	—	0	-9	-8	0	-0.5

● FRANK BENNETT
Bennett, Francis Allen "Chip" b: 10/27/04, Mardela Springs, Md. d: 3/18/66, Wilmington, Del. BR/TR, 5'10.5", 163 lbs. Deb: 9/17/27

YEAR	TM/L	W	L	PCT	G	GS	CG	SH	SV	IP	H	HR	BB	SO	RAT	ERA	ERA+	OAV	OOB	BH	AVG	PB	PR	/A	PD	TPI
1927	Bos-A	0	1	.000	4	1	0	0	0	12¹	15	0	6	1	15.3	2.92	145	.333	.412	0	.000	-1	2	2	0	0.1
1928	Bos-A	0	0	—	1	0	0	0	0	1	1	0	0	0	9.0	0.00	—	.250	.250	0	—	0	0	0	0	0.0
Total	2	0	1	.000	5	1	0	0	0	13¹	16	0	6	1	14.9	2.70	156	.327	.400	0	.000	-1	2	2	0	0.1

● ALLEN BENSON
Benson, Allen Wilbert "Bullet Ben" b: 7/12/08, Hurley, S.Dak. BR/TR, 6'1", 185 lbs. Deb: 8/19/34

YEAR	TM/L	W	L	PCT	G	GS	CG	SH	SV	IP	H	HR	BB	SO	RAT	ERA	ERA+	OAV	OOB	BH	AVG	PB	PR	/A	PD	TPI
1934	Was-A	0	1	.000	2	2	0	0	0	9²	19	0	5	4	24.2	12.10	36	.413	.491	0	.000	-0	-8	-8	-0	-0.7

● CY BENTLEY
Bentley, Clytus G. b: 11/23/1850, East Haven, Conn. d: 2/26/1873, Middletown, Conn. Deb: 4/26/1872

YEAR	TM/L	W	L	PCT	G	GS	CG	SH	SV	IP	H	HR	BB	SO	RAT	ERA	ERA+	OAV	OOB	BH	AVG	PB	PR	/A	PD	TPI
1872	Man-n	2	15	.118	18	17	15	0	0	149	272	4	12	5	17.2	6.10	59	.338	.348	27	.235	-2	-41	-42		-2.8

● JACK BENTLEY
Bentley, John Needles b: 3/8/1895, Sandy Spring, Md. d: 10/24/69, Olney, Md. BL/TL, 5'11.5", 200 lbs. Deb: 9/6/13 ♦

YEAR	TM/L	W	L	PCT	G	GS	CG	SH	SV	IP	H	HR	BB	SO	RAT	ERA	ERA+	OAV	OOB	BH	AVG	PB	PR	/A	PD	TPI
1913	Was-A	1	0	1.000	3	1	0	0	1	11	5	0	2	5	5.7	0.00	—	.147	.194	0	.000	-0	4	4	0	0.4
1914	Was-A	5	7	.417	30	11	3	2	4	125¹	110	3	53	55	11.9	2.37	119	.249	.334	11	.275	-0	2	5	-1	0.8
1915	Was-A	0	2	.000	4	2	0	0	0	11¹	8	0	3	0	8.7	0.79	374	.200	.256	0	.000	-0	3	3	-0	0.4
1916	Was-A	0	0	—	2	0	0	0	0	1¹	1	0	1	1	6.8	0.00	—	.000	.250	0	—	0	0	0	0	0.0
1923	*NY-N	13	8	.619	31	26	12	1	3	183	198	10	67	80	13.3	4.48	85	.277	.343	38	.427	16	-10	-13	-1	0.0
1924	*NY-N	16	5	.762	28	24	13	1	1	188	196	11	56	60	12.3	3.78	97	.273	.329	26	.265	4	-2	-1	-1	0.0
1925	NY-N	11	9	.550	28	22	11	0	0	157	200	10	59	47	14.9	5.04	80	.323	.383	20	.303	6	-14	-13	-1	-0.9
1926	Phi-N	0	2	.000	7	3	0	0	0	25¹	37	2	10	7	16.7	8.17	51	.327	.382	62	.258	1	-12	-11	-0	-0.7
	NY-N	0	0	—	1	0	0	0	0	2	0	0	2	1	9.0	0.00	—	.000	.250	1	.250	-0	1	1	-0	0.0
	Yr	0	2	.000	8	3	0	0	0	27¹	37	2	12	8	16.1	7.57	54	.311	.374	63	.258	1	-11	-11	-0	-0.7
1927	NY-N	0	0	—	4	0	0	0	0	9²	7	1	10	3	16.8	2.79	138	.206	.400	2	.222	1	1	0	0	0.1
Total	9	46	33	.582	138	89	39	4	9	714	761	37	263	259	13.1	4.01	91	.280	.346	170	.291	28	-20	-28	-3	0.1

● AL BENTON
Benton, John Alton b: 3/18/11, Noble, Okla. d: 4/14/68, Lynwood, Cal. BR/TR, 6'4", 215 lbs. Deb: 4/18/34

YEAR	TM/L	W	L	PCT	G	GS	CG	SH	SV	IP	H	HR	BB	SO	RAT	ERA	ERA+	OAV	OOB	BH	AVG	PB	PR	/A	PD	TPI
1934	Phi-A	7	9	.438	32	21	7	0	1	155	145	7	88	58	13.6	4.88	90	.249	.349	6	.109	-4	-7	-9	0	-1.1
1935	Phi-A	3	4	.429	27	9	0	0	0	78¹	110	7	47	42	18.2	7.70	59	.328	.413	1	.040	-3	-28	-27	-1	-2.3
1938	Det-A	5	3	.625	19	10	6	0	0	95¹	93	10	39	33	12.6	3.30	151	.259	.333	4	.121	-3	16	18	1	1.1
1939	Det-A	6	8	.429	37	16	3	0	5	150	182	11	58	67	14.5	4.56	107	.294	.355	4	.091	-0	1	5	0	0.1
1940	Det-A	6	10	.375	42	0	0	0	17	79¹	93	5	36	50	14.6	4.42	107	.294	.366	0	.000	-3	-0	3	-0	-0.4
1941	Det-A☆	15	6	.714	38	14	7	1	7	157²	130	11	65	63	11.3	2.97	153	.221	.302	3	.060	-5	21	28	-0	3.1
1942	Det-A★	7	13	.350	35	30	9	1	2	226²	210	9	84	110	11.7	2.90	136	.246	.314	5	.075	-5	19	26	-1	1.6
1945	*Det-A	13	8	.619	31	27	12	5	3	191²	175	7	63	76	11.3	2.02	174	.241	.303	4	.063	-6	29	32	2	3.2
1946	Det-A	11	7	.611	28	15	6	1	1	140²	132	9	58	60	12.2	3.65	100	.245	.319	9	.184	-1	-2	0	1	0.0
1947	Det-A	6	7	.462	36	14	4	0	7	133	147	11	61	33	14.1	4.40	86	.288	.365	6	.154	-1	-10	-9	-0	-1.1
1948	Det-A	2	2	.500	30	0	0	0	3	44¹	45	4	36	18	16.6	5.68	77	.273	.406	2	.182	-0	-7	-6	-0	-0.6
1949	Cle-A	9	6	.600	40	11	4	2	10	135²	116	7	51	41	11.1	2.12	188	.238	.312	5	.132	-0	31	28	-2	2.9
1950	Cle-A	4	2	.667	36	0	0	0	4	63	57	7	30	26	12.6	3.57	121	.243	.331	1	.083	-1	7	5	-1	0.4
1952	Bos-A	4	3	.571	24	0	0	0	6	37²	37	1	17	20	12.9	2.39	165	.268	.348	0	.000	-1	5	6	-0	1.2
Total	14	98	88	.527	455	167	58	10	66	1688¹	1672	106	733	697	12.9	3.66	115	.259	.336	50	.098	-39	74	102	-1	8.9

● RUBE BENTON
Benton, John Clebon b: 6/27/1887, Clinton, N.C. d: 12/12/37, Dothan, Ala. BL/TL, 6'1", 190 lbs. Deb: 6/28/10

YEAR	TM/L	W	L	PCT	G	GS	CG	SH	SV	IP	H	HR	BB	SO	RAT	ERA	ERA+	OAV	OOB	BH	AVG	PB	PR	/A	PD	TPI
1910	Cin-N	0	1	.000	12	2	0	0	0	38	44	1	23	15	16.1	4.74	62	.282	.378	1	.091	-1	-7	-8	1	-0.2
1911	Cin-N	3	3	.500	6	6	5	0	0	44²	44	0	23	28	14.1	2.01	164	.270	.370	2	.143	-0	7	6	-1	0.7
1912	Cin-N	18	20	.474	50	39	22	2	2	302	316	2	118	162	13.5	3.10	108	.278	.356	14	.135	-6	10	9	2	0.5
1913	Cin-N	11	7	.611	23	22	9	1	0	144¹	140	4	60	68	13.0	3.49	93	.265	.350	10	.208	1	-5	-4	1	-0.4
1914	Cin-N	16	18	.471	41	31	16	5	2	271	223	3	95	121	10.9	2.96	99	.228	.303	13	.143	-3	-5	-0	4	-0.4
1915	Cin-N	6	13	.316	35	21	6	2	4	176¹	165	2	67	83	12.6	3.32	86	.257	.340	11	.208	-0	-11	-9	2	-0.8
	NY-N	3	5	.375	10	7	3	0	1	60²	57	0	9	26	10.5	2.82	91	.253	.297	5	.217	1	-0	-2	-0	-0.1
	Yr	9	18	.333	45	28	9	2	5	237	222	2	76	109	11.5	3.19	87	.257	.332	16	.211	1	-12	-11	2	-0.9
1916	NY-N	16	8	.667	38	29	15	3	2	238²	210	5	58	115	10.5	2.87	85	.241	.296	7	.090	-4	-7	-11	-1	-1.8
1917	*NY-N	15	9	.625	35	25	14	3	3	215	190	5	41	70	10.0	2.72	94	.238	.281	12	.167	-1	-0	-4	-2	-0.8
1918	NY-N	1	2	.333	3	3	2	0	0	24	17	0	3	9	7.5	1.88	140	.202	.230	1	.143	1	2	2	0	0.4
1919	NY-N	17	11	.607	35	28	11	1	2	209	181	5	52	53	10.2	2.63	107	.237	.289	13	.194	-1	7	4	-1	0.4
1920	NY-N	9	16	.360	33	25	12	4	2	193¹	222	8	31	52	11.9	3.03	128	.291	.321	6	.092	-7	7	4	1	-0.3
1921	NY-N	5	2	.714	18	9	3	1	0	72	72	2	17	11	11.1	2.88	128	.266	.309	3	.143	-2	7	6	-1	0.4
1923	Cin-N	14	10	.583	33	26	15	0	1	219	243	10	57	59	12.5	3.66	106	.284	.333	23	.287	4	13	11	2	2.0
1924	Cin-N	7	9	.438	32	19	6	1	1	162²	166	2	24	42	10.7	2.77	136	.266	.297	12	.261	6	20	18	1	2.0
1925	Cin-N	9	10	.474	33	16	6	1	1	146²	182	3	34	36	13.3	4.05	102	.307	.342	9	.200	1	4	1	-1	0.1
Total	15	150	144	.510	437	308	145	24	21	2517¹	2472	52	712	950	11.7	3.09	102	.261	.319	142	.172	-14	33	13	4	0.6

● LARRY BENTON
Benton, Lawrence James b: 11/20/1897, St.Louis, Mo. d: 4/3/53, Amberley, Ohio BR/TR, 5'11", 165 lbs. Deb: 4/25/23

YEAR	TM/L	W	L	PCT	G	GS	CG	SH	SV	IP	H	HR	BB	SO	RAT	ERA	ERA+	OAV	OOB	BH	AVG	PB	PR	/A	PD	TPI
1923	Bos-N	5	9	.357	35	9	1	0	0	128	141	4	57	42	14.2	4.99	80	.293	.373	5	.161	-1	-14	-14	1	-1.3
1924	Bos-N	5	7	.417	30	13	4	0	0	128	129	4	64	41	13.8	4.15	92	.274	.365	3	.091	-3	-4	-5	-0	-0.7
1925	Bos-N	14	7	.667	31	21	16	2	1	183¹	170	6	70	49	11.9	3.09	130	.249	.320	14	.241	2	24	19	-1	2.2
1926	Bos-N	14	14	.500	43	27	12	1	1	231²	244	10	81	103	12.9	3.85	92	.280	.346	12	.154	-4	-1	-8	-3	-1.4
1927	Bos-N	4	2	.667	11	10	3	0	0	60¹	72	3	27	25	15.1	4.48	83	.310	.387	4	.222	-1	-4	-5	-1	-0.4
	NY-N	13	5	.722	29	23	8	1	2	173	183	9	54	65	12.4	3.95	98	.275	.331	8	.160	-2	-1	-2	-0	-0.4
	Yr	17	7	.708	40	33	11	1	2	233¹	255	12	81	90	13.0	4.09	93	.284	.344	12	.176	-1	-4	-7	-1	-0.8
1928	NY-N	25	9	.735	42	35	28	2	4	310¹	299	14	71	90	10.7	2.73	144	.258	.300	16	.143	-3	44	41	-0	3.9
1929	NY-N	11	17	.393	39	30	14	3	0	237	276	16	61	63	12.8	4.14	111	.297	.340	9	.155	-6	15	12	1	0.9
1930	NY-N	1	3	.250	8	4	1	0	1	30	42	8	14	16	16.8	7.80	61	.323	.389	3	.300	-1	-9	-10	-1	-1.0
	Cin-N	7	12	.368	35	22	9	0	1	177²	246	7	45	47	14.7	5.12	94	.337	.375	11	.177	-2	-3	-6	-3	-0.9
	Yr	8	15	.348	43	26	10	0	2	207²	288	15	59	63	15.0	5.50	87	.334	.377	14	.194	-0	-12	-16	-3	-1.9
1931	Cin-N	10	15	.400	38	23	12	2	2	204¹	240	6	53	35	12.9	3.35	112	.299	.343	11	.167	-1	12	9	1	1.0
1932	Cin-N	6	13	.316	35	21	7	0	2	179²	201	10	29	35	11.4	4.31	90	.285	.311	11	.204	-0	-9	-9	-1	-0.9
1933	Cin-N	10	11	.476	34	19	7	2	2	152²	160	5	36	33	11.7	3.71	91	.271	.316	9	.170	-1	6	2	-1	0.6
1934	Cin-N	0	1	.000	16	1	0	0	0	29	53	4	7	5	18.6	6.52	63	.393	.423	2	.286	0	-8	-8	-0	-0.3
1935	Bos-N	2	3	.400	17	1	0	0	0	72	100	2	24	11	16.0	6.88	55	.338	.388	4	.200	1	-23	-25	-1	-1.5
Total	13	127	128	.498	455	258	122	13	22	2297	2559	109	691	670	12.8	4.03	98	.288	.341	122	.165	-17	14	-16	-8	-2.2

● SID BENTON
Benton, Sidney Wright b: 8/4/1895, Buckner, Ark. d: 3/8/77, Fayetteville, Ark. BR/TR, 6'1", 170 lbs. Deb: 4/18/22

YEAR	TM/L	W	L	PCT	G	GS	CG	SH	SV	IP	H	HR	BB	SO	RAT	ERA	ERA+	OAV	OOB	BH	AVG	PB	PR	/A	PD	TPI
1922	StL-N	0	0	—	1	0	0	0	0	0	0	0	2	0	—		—	—	1.000	0	—	0	0	0	0	0.0

YEAR TM/L	W	L	PCT	G	GS	CG	SH	SV	IP	H	HR	BB	SO	RAT	ERA	ERA+	OAV	OOB	BH	AVG	PB	PR	/A	PD	TPI

● JOE BENZ   Benz, Joseph Louis "Blitzen" or "Butcher Boy"   b: 1/21/1886, New Alsace, Ind.   d: 4/22/57, Chicago, Ill.   BR/TR, 6'1.5", 196 lbs.   Deb: 8/16/11

YEAR TM/L	W	L	PCT	G	GS	CG	SH	SV	IP	H	HR	BB	SO	RAT	ERA	ERA+	OAV	OOB	BH	AVG	PB	PR	/A	PD	TPI
1911 Chi-A	3	2	.600	12	6	1	0	0	55²	52	0	13	28	10.8	2.26	142	.251	.302	1	.059	-2	7	6	1	0.4
1912 Chi-A	13	17	.433	42	31	12	3	0	238²	231	5	90	97	11.7	2.90	110	.259	.319	10	.132	-5	11	8	1	0.5
1913 Chi-A	7	10	.412	33	17	6	1	1	151	146	1	59	79	12.3	2.74	107	.254	.325	9	.180	-1	3	4	0	0.7
1914 Chi-A	14	19	.424	48	35	16	4	2	283²	245	4	66	142	9.9	2.26	119	.236	.282	12	.130	-3	15	14	6	2.0
1915 Chi-A	15	11	.577	39	28	17	2	0	238²	209	4	43	81	9.6	2.11	141	.238	.276	10	.127	-5	22	23	3	2.2
1916 Chi-A	9	5	.643	28	16	6	4	0	142	108	1	32	57	9.1	2.03	136	.214	.265	3	.065	-4	13	12	1	0.8
1917 Chi-A	7	3	.700	19	13	7	2	0	94²	76	1	23	25	9.6	2.47	120	.220	.272	5	.167	-1	2	2	0	0.1
1918 Chi-A	8	8	.500	29	17	10	1	0	154	156	1	28	30	10.9	2.63	104	.269	.304	11	.216	-1	3	2	3	0.5
1919 Chi-A	0	0	—	1	0	0	0	0	2	2	0	0	0	9.0	0.00	—	.250	.250	0	—	0	1	1	0	0.2
Total 9	76	75	.503	251	163	75	17	3	1359²	1225	16	334	539	10.5	2.43	119	.243	.294	61	.138	-21	76	70	19	7.2

● JASON BERE   Bere, Jason Phillip   b: 5/26/71, Cambridge, Mass.   BR/TR, 6'3", 185 lbs.   Deb: 5/27/93

YEAR TM/L	W	L	PCT	G	GS	CG	SH	SV	IP	H	HR	BB	SO	RAT	ERA	ERA+	OAV	OOB	BH	AVG	PB	PR	/A	PD	TPI
1993 *Chi-A	12	5	.706	24	24	1	0	0	142²	109	12	81	129	12.3	3.47	120	.210	.323	0	—	0	13	11	-0	1.4
1994 Chi-A★	12	2	.857	24	24	1	0	0	141²	119	17	80	127	12.7	3.81	122	.229	.333	0	—	0	16	13	-1	1.1
1995 Chi-A	8	15	.348	27	27	1	0	0	137²	151	21	106	110	17.2	7.19	62	.277	.400	0	—	0	-38	-42	-1	-5.2
1996 Chi-A	0	1	.000	5	5	0	0	0	16²	26	3	18	19	23.8	10.26	46	.356	.484	0	—	0	-10	-10	-0	-0.4
Total 4	32	23	.582	80	80	2	0	0	438²	405	53	285	385	14.4	5.01	89	.245	.360	0	—	0	-19	-27	-1	-3.1

● JUAN BERENGUER   Berenguer, Juan Bautista   b: 11/30/54, Aguadulce, Pan.   BR/TR, 5'11", 215 lbs.   Deb: 8/17/78

YEAR TM/L	W	L	PCT	G	GS	CG	SH	SV	IP	H	HR	BB	SO	RAT	ERA	ERA+	OAV	OOB	BH	AVG	PB	PR	/A	PD	TPI
1978 NY-N	0	2	.000	5	3	0	0	0	13	17	1	11	8	20.1	8.31	42	.327	.453	0	.000	-0	-7	-7	-0	-1.0
1979 NY-N	1	1	.500	5	5	0	0	0	30²	28	2	12	25	12.0	2.93	124	.252	.331	1	.143	0	3	2	-1	0.1
1980 NY-N	0	1	.000	9	1	0	0	0	9¹	9	1	10	7	18.3	5.79	61	.250	.413	0	—	0	-2	-2	0	-0.2
1981 KC-A	0	4	.000	8	3	0	0	0	19²	22	4	16	20	18.3	8.69	41	.289	.426	0	—	0	-11	-11	-1	-1.9
Tor-A	2	9	.182	12	11	1	0	0	71	62	7	35	29	12.7	4.31	91	.235	.331	0	—	0	-5	-3	-1	-0.6
Yr	2	13	.133	20	14	1	0	0	90²	84	11	51	49	13.7	5.26	73	.243	.346	0	—	0	-2	-2	0	-2.5
1982 Det-A	0	0	—	2	1	0	0	0	6²	5	0	9	8	18.9	6.75	60	.200	.412	0	—	0	-2	-2	-0	0.0
1983 Det-A	9	5	.643	37	19	2	1	1	157²	110	19	71	129	10.7	3.14	124	.193	.289	0	—	0	16	13	-2	1.0
1984 Det-A	11	10	.524	31	27	2	1	0	168¹	146	14	79	118	12.3	3.48	113	.232	.323	0	—	0	10	8	-1	0.8
1985 Det-A	5	6	.455	31	13	0	0	0	95	96	12	48	82	13.7	5.59	73	.259	.346	0	—	0	-15	-16	-1	-1.6
1986 SF-N	2	3	.400	46	4	0	0	4	73¹	64	4	44	72	13.5	2.70	130	.242	.354	1	.143	-0	8	7	-1	0.4
1987 *Min-A	8	1	.889	47	6	0	0	4	112	100	10	47	110	11.8	3.94	117	.238	.315	0	—	0	6	8	-1	0.4
1988 Min-A	8	4	.667	57	0	0	0	2	100	74	7	61	99	12.2	3.96	103	.207	.325	0	—	0	1	0	0	0.0
1989 Min-A	9	3	.750	56	0	0	0	3	106	96	11	47	93	12.3	3.48	119	.246	.330	0	—	0	5	8	-1	0.6
1990 Min-A	8	5	.615	51	0	0	0	0	100¹	85	9	58	77	13.0	3.41	122	.232	.340	0	—	0	6	8	-2	0.8
1991 Atl-N	0	3	.000	49	0	0	0	17	64¹	43	5	20	53	9.2	2.24	174	.189	.263	0	.000	-1	10	12	-0	1.0
1992 Atl-N	3	1	.750	28	0	0	0	1	33¹	37	5	16	19	14.0	5.13	71	.290	.354	0	—	0	-6	-5	-0	-0.7
KC-A	1	4	.200	19	0	0	0	0	44²	42	3	20	26	12.7	5.64	72	.247	.330	0	—	0	-8	-8	-1	-0.8
Total 15	67	62	.519	490	95	5	2	32	1205¹	1034	116	604	975	12.5	3.90	103	.232	.328	2	.083	-1	7	14	-11	-1.7

● BRUCE BERENYI   Berenyi, Bruce Michael   b: 8/21/54, Bryan, Ohio   BR/TR, 6'3", 215 lbs.   Deb: 7/5/80

YEAR TM/L	W	L	PCT	G	GS	CG	SH	SV	IP	H	HR	BB	SO	RAT	ERA	ERA+	OAV	OOB	BH	AVG	PB	PR	/A	PD	TPI
1980 Cin-N	2	2	.500	6	6	0	0	0	27²	34	1	23	19	18.5	7.81	46	.318	.438	0	.000	-1	-13	-12	-1	-1.6
1981 Cin-N	9	6	.600	21	20	5	3	0	126	97	3	77	106	13.4	3.50	101	.211	.324	8	.190	1	-0	1	-1	0.1
1982 Cin-N	9	18	.333	34	34	4	1	0	222¹	208	8	96	157	12.4	3.36	110	.255	.335	15	.242	3	6	8	2	1.5
1983 Cin-N	9	14	.391	32	31	4	1	0	186¹	173	9	102	151	13.4	3.86	98	.247	.345	12	.218	-2	-5	-1	3	0.3
1984 Cin-N	3	7	.300	13	11	0	0	0	51	63	6	42	53	18.5	6.00	63	.306	.423	1	.063	-1	-14	-13	-0	-2.2
NY-N	9	6	.600	19	19	0	0	0	115	100	6	53	81	12.1	3.76	94	.238	.325	9	.243	2	-2	-3	-1	-0.3
Yr	12	13	.480	32	30	0	0	0	166	163	6	95	134	14.0	4.45	81	.260	.358	10	.189	0	-16	-15	-1	-2.5
1985 NY-N	1	0	1.000	3	3	0	0	0	13²	8	0	10	10	12.5	2.63	131	.170	.328	1	.250	0	1	1	0	0.2
1986 NY-N	2	2	.500	14	7	0	0	0	39²	47	5	24	30	15.9	6.35	56	.299	.389	0	.000	-1	-12	-12	-0	-1.2
Total 7	44	55	.444	142	131	13	5	0	781²	730	32	425	607	13.4	4.03	91	.251	.347	46	.197	4	-38	-32	3	-3.2

● HEINIE BERGER   Berger, Charles   b: 1/7/1882, LaSalle, Ill.   d: 2/10/54, Lakewood, Ohio   TR, 5'9",   Deb: 5/6/07

YEAR TM/L	W	L	PCT	G	GS	CG	SH	SV	IP	H	HR	BB	SO	RAT	ERA	ERA+	OAV	OOB	BH	AVG	PB	PR	/A	PD	TPI
1907 Cle-A	3	3	.500	14	7	5	1	0	87¹	74	0	20	50	9.8	2.99	84	.232	.279	5	.179	0	-4	-5	-1	-0.5
1908 Cle-A	13	8	.619	29	24	16	0	0	199¹	152	1	66	101	10.0	2.12	113	.219	.290	8	.108	-4	6	6	-0	0.1
1909 Cle-A	13	14	.481	34	29	19	4	1	247	221	2	58	162	10.6	2.73	94	.256	.312	11	.133	-1	-7	-5	-0	-0.7
1910 Cle-A	3	4	.429	13	8	2	0	0	65¹	57	0	32	24	12.7	3.03	85	.243	.341	3	.143	-1	-4	-3	-1	-0.5
Total 4	32	29	.525	90	68	42	5	1	599	504	3	176	337	10.5	2.60	96	.239	.303	27	.131	-6	-9	-7	-2	-1.6

● SEAN BERGMAN   Bergman, Sean Frederick   b: 4/11/70, Joliet, Ill.   BR/TR, 6'4", 205 lbs.   Deb: 7/7/93

YEAR TM/L	W	L	PCT	G	GS	CG	SH	SV	IP	H	HR	BB	SO	RAT	ERA	ERA+	OAV	OOB	BH	AVG	PB	PR	/A	PD	TPI
1993 Det-A	1	4	.200	9	6	1	0	0	39²	47	6	23	19	16.1	5.67	76	.294	.386	0	—	0	-6	-6	0	-0.6
1994 Det-A	2	1	.667	3	3	0	0	0	17²	22	2	7	12	15.3	5.60	86	.301	.370	0	—	0	-2	-1	-0	-0.2
1995 Det-A	7	10	.412	28	28	1	1	0	135¹	169	19	67	86	16.0	5.12	93	.307	.386	0	—	0	-6	-5	-1	-0.7
1996 SD-N	6	8	.429	41	14	0	0	0	113¹	119	14	33	85	12.2	4.37	91	.274	.328	3	.100	-1	-2	-5	-0	-0.5
Total 4	16	23	.410	81	51	2	1	0	306	357	41	130	202	14.6	4.94	89	.293	.365	3	.100	-1	-16	-18	-2	-2.0

● JACK BERLY   Berly, John Chambers   b: 5/24/03, Natchitoches, La.   d: 6/26/77, Houston, Tex.   BR/TR, 5'11.5", 190 lbs.   Deb: 4/22/24

YEAR TM/L	W	L	PCT	G	GS	CG	SH	SV	IP	H	HR	BB	SO	RAT	ERA	ERA+	OAV	OOB	BH	AVG	PB	PR	/A	PD	TPI
1924 StL-N	0	0	—	4	0	0	0	0	8	8	2	4	2	13.5	5.63	67	.267	.353	0	.000	-0	-2	-2	0	0.0
1931 NY-N	7	8	.467	27	11	4	1	0	111¹	114	6	51	45	13.7	3.88	95	.270	.354	6	.171	-1	-0	-2	1	-0.2
1932 Phi-N	1	2	.333	21	1	1	0	2	46	61	4	21	15	16.2	7.63	58	.333	.405	0	.000	-1	-19	-16	1	-1.1
1933 Phi-N	2	3	.400	13	6	1	1	0	50	62	5	22	4	15.5	5.04	76	.307	.381	4	.308	0	-9	-7	1	-0.5
Total 4	10	13	.435	65	18	6	2	2	215¹	245	17	98	66	14.6	5.02	78	.292	.371	10	.167	-2	-30	-27	3	-1.8

● VICTOR BERNAL   Bernal, Victor Hugo   b: 10/6/53, Los Angeles, Cal.   BR/TR, 6'1", 175 lbs.   Deb: 4/6/77

YEAR TM/L	W	L	PCT	G	GS	CG	SH	SV	IP	H	HR	BB	SO	RAT	ERA	ERA+	OAV	OOB	BH	AVG	PB	PR	/A	PD	TPI
1977 SD-N	1	1	.500	15	0	0	0	0	20¹	23	4	9	6	14.2	5.31	67	.287	.360	0	.000	-0	-3	-4	-0	-0.4

● DWIGHT BERNARD   Bernard, Dwight Vern   b: 5/31/52, Mt. Vernon, Ill.   BR/TR, 6'2", 170 lbs.   Deb: 6/29/78

YEAR TM/L	W	L	PCT	G	GS	CG	SH	SV	IP	H	HR	BB	SO	RAT	ERA	ERA+	OAV	OOB	BH	AVG	PB	PR	/A	PD	TPI
1978 NY-N	1	4	.200	30	1	0	0	3	48	54	4	27	26	15.2	4.31	81	.297	.388	1	.200	-1	-4	-4	0	-0.4
1979 NY-N	0	3	.000	32	1	0	0	0	44	59	2	26	20	17.4	4.70	77	.331	.417	0	—	0	-5	-4	-0	-0.3
1981 *Mil-A	0	0	—	6	0	0	0	0	5	5	0	6	1	19.8	3.60	95	.263	.440	0	—	0	-0	-0	-0	0.1
1982 *Mil-A	3	1	.750	47	0	0	0	6	79	78	4	27	45	12.1	3.76	101	.263	.326	1	—	0	3	0	-1	0.1
Total 4	4	8	.333	115	2	0	0	9	176	196	10	86	92	14.5	4.14	88	.290	.371	1	.200	-1	-6	-9	-0	-0.5

● JOE BERNARD   Bernard, Joseph Carl "J.C."   b: 3/24/1882, Brighton, Ill.   d: 9/22/60, Springfield, Ill.   BR/TR, 6'1", 175 lbs.   Deb: 9/23/09

YEAR TM/L	W	L	PCT	G	GS	CG	SH	SV	IP	H	HR	BB	SO	RAT	ERA	ERA+	OAV	OOB	BH	AVG	PB	PR	/A	PD	TPI
1909 StL-N	0	0	—	1	0	0	0	0	1	0	2	2	27.0	0.00	—	.250	.500	0	—	0	0	0	0	0.0

● BILL BERNHARD   Bernhard, William Henry "Strawberry Bill"   b: 3/16/1871, Clarence, N.Y.   d: 3/30/49, San Diego, Cal.   BB/TR, 6'1", 205 lbs.   Deb: 4/24/1899

YEAR TM/L	W	L	PCT	G	GS	CG	SH	SV	IP	H	HR	BB	SO	RAT	ERA	ERA+	OAV	OOB	BH	AVG	PB	PR	/A	PD	TPI
1899 Phi-N	6	6	.500	21	12	10	1	0	132¹	120	3	36	23	11.0	2.65	139	.242	.301	13	.241	0	18	15	-0	1.2
1900 Phi-N	15	10	.600	32	27	20	0	2	218²	284	4	74	49	14.9	4.77	76	.313	.368	14	.154	-5	-26	-28	1	-2.9
1901 Phi-A	17	10	.630	31	27	26	1	0	257	328	6	50	58	13.3	4.52	84	.307	.339	20	.187	-1	-24	-21	4	-1.6
1902 Phi-A	1	0	1.000	1	1	1	0	0	9	7	0	3	1	10.0	1.00	367	.212	.278	0	.000	-1	3	3	-1	0.1
Cle-A	17	5	.773	27	24	22	3	1	217	169	4	34	57	8.6	2.20	157	.216	.253	18	.200	-1	33	30	1	2.8
Yr	18	5	.783	28	25	23	3	1	226	176	4	37	58	8.7	2.15	161	.215	.254	18	.191	-2	36	33	1	2.9
1903 Cle-A	14	6	.700	20	19	18	3	0	165²	151	1	21	60	9.3	2.12	135	.242	.267	12	.185	-1	16	14	1	1.6
1904 Cle-A	23	13	.639	38	37	35	4	0	320²	323	2	55	130	10.7	2.13	119	.263	.296	22	.177	-1	17	14	-1	1.4
1905 Cle-A	7	13	.350	22	19	17	0	0	174¹	185	4	34	56	11.4	3.36	78	.274	.309	6	.087	-6	-14	-14	0	-2.1
1906 Cle-A	16	15	.516	31	30	23	2	0	255¹	235	4	45	88	10.5	2.54	103	.248	.287	21	.212	2	4	2	0	0.7
1907 Cle-A	0	4	.000	7	5	3	0	0	42	58	0	11	19	14.8	3.21	78	.330	.369	3	.200	-0	-3	-3	-0	-0.3
Total 9	116	82	.586	231	200	175	14	3	1792	1860	26	365	545	11.3	3.04	102	.268	.307	129	.180	-13	23	11	7	0.9

YEAR	TM/L	W	L	PCT	G	GS	CG	SH	SV	IP	H	HR	BB	SO	RAT	ERA	ERA+	OAV	OOB	BH	AVG	PB	PR	/A	PD	TPI

● WALTER BERNHARDT
Bernhardt, Walter Jacob b: 5/20/1893, Pleasant Village, Pa. d: 7/26/58, Watertown, N.Y. BR/TR, 6'2", 175 lbs. Deb: 7/16/18

| 1918 | NY-A | 0 | 0 | — | 1 | 0 | 0 | 0 | 0 | 0² | 0 | 0 | 0 | 1 | 0.0 | 0.00 | — | .000 | .000 | 0 | — | 0 | 0 | 0 | 0 | 0.0 |

● JOE BERRY
Berry, Jonas Arthur "Jittery Joe" b: 12/16/04, Huntsville, Ark. d: 9/27/58, Anaheim, Cal. BL/TR, 5'10.5", 145 lbs. Deb: 9/6/42

1942	Chi-N	0	0	—	2	0	0	0	0	2	7	0	2	1	40.5	18.00	18	.538	.600	0	—	0	-3	-3	0	0.0
1944	Phi-A	10	8	.556	53	0	0	0	**12**	111¹	78	4	23	44	8.3	1.94	179	.192	.238	3	.120	-1	18	**19**	2	3.6
1945	Phi-A	8	7	.533	**52**	0	0	0	5	130¹	114	5	38	51	10.5	2.35	146	.232	.287	5	.143	-1	15	16	1	2.0
1946	Phi-A	0	1	.000	5	0	0	0	0	13	15	1	3	5	13.2	2.77	128	.288	.339	1	.333	0	1	1	0	0.1
	Cle-A	3	6	.333	21	0	0	0	1	37¹	32	4	21	16	12.8	3.38	98	.235	.338	2	.286	0	1	-0	-1	0.1
	Yr	3	7	.300	26	0	0	0	1	50¹	47	5	24	21	12.7	3.22	105	.249	.333	3	.300	0	2	1	-0	0.0
Total	4	21	22	.488	133	0	0	0	18	294	246	14	87	117	10.3	2.45	140	.224	.282	11	.157	-2	31	32	3	5.6

● FRANK BERTAINA
Bertaina, Frank Louis b: 4/14/44, San Francisco, Cal. BL/TL, 5'11", 180 lbs. Deb: 8/1/64

1964	Bal-A	1	0	1.000	6	4	1	1	0	26	18	3	13	18	10.7	2.77	129	.198	.298	0	.000	-1	2	2	0	0.1
1965	Bal-A	0	0	—	2	1	0	0	0	6	9	0	4	5	19.5	6.00	58	.360	.448	0	.000	-0	-2	-2	0	0.0
1966	Bal-A	2	5	.286	16	9	0	0	0	63¹	52	3	36	46	13.1	3.13	107	.226	.341	2	.105	-1	2	1	-2	-0.1
1967	Bal-A	1	1	.500	5	2	0	0	0	21²	17	4	14	19	12.9	3.32	95	.224	.344	1	.111	-0	-0	-0	-0	-0.1
	Was-A	6	5	.545	18	17	4	4	0	95²	90	8	37	67	11.9	2.92	108	.251	.322	2	.057	-3	3	3	-1	0.0
	Yr	7	6	.538	23	19	4	4	0	117¹	107	12	51	86	12.1	2.99	106	.246	.328	3	.068	-3	3	2	-1	-0.1
1968	Was-A	7	13	.350	27	23	1	0	0	127¹	133	15	69	81	14.7	4.66	63	.273	.369	5	.132	-0	-24	-25	-0	-3.7
1969	Was-A	1	3	.250	14	5	0	0	0	35²	43	3	22	25	16.7	6.56	53	.291	.386	4	.364	2	-12	-12	-0	-1.0
	Bal-A	0	0	—	3	0	0	0	0	6	1	0	3	5	6.0	0.00	—	.053	.211	1	1.000	0	2	2	-0	0.1
	Yr	1	3	.250	17	5	0	0	0	41²	44	3	26	30	15.1	5.62	62	.267	.366	5	.417	3	-9	-10	-0	-0.9
1970	StL-N	1	2	.333	8	5	0	0	0	31¹	36	1	15	14	14.6	3.16	130	.293	.370	1	.143	-0	3	3	0	0.3
Total	7	19	29	.396	99	66	6	5	0	413	399	42	214	280	13.6	3.84	85	.257	.350	16	.127	-1	-24	-27	-2	-4.4

● MIKE BERTOTTI
Bertotti, Michael David b: 1/18/70, Jersey City, N.J. BL/TL, 6'1", 185 lbs. Deb: 7/29/95

1995	Chi-A	1	1	.500	4	4	0	0	0	14¹	23	6	11	15	23.2	12.56	35	.365	.481	0	—	0	-12	-13	-0	-1.1
1996	Chi-A	2	0	1.000	15	2	0	0	0	28	28	5	20	19	15.4	5.14	91	.257	.372	0	—	0	-0	-1	-0	0.4
Total	2	3	1	.750	19	6	0	0	0	42¹	51	11	31	34	18.1	7.65	60	.297	.413	0	—	0	-13	-14	-0	-0.7

● LEFTY BERTRAND
Bertrand, Roman Mathias b: 2/28/09, Cobden, Minn. BR/TL, 6', 180 lbs. Deb: 4/15/36

| 1936 | Phi-N | 0 | 0 | — | 1 | 0 | 0 | 0 | 0 | 2 | 3 | 1 | 2 | 1 | 22.5 | 9.00 | 50 | .333 | .455 | 0 | — | 0 | -1 | -1 | -0 | 0.0 |

● ANDRES BERUMEN
Berumen, Andres b: 4/5/71, Tijuana, Mexico BR/TR, 6'2", 210 lbs. Deb: 4/27/95

1995	SD-N	2	3	.400	37	0	0	0	1	44¹	37	3	36	42	15.4	5.68	71	.226	.374	0	.000	-0	-7	-8	-1	-0.9
1996	SD-N	0	0	—	3	0	0	0	0	3¹	3	1	2	4	16.2	5.40	74	.231	.375	0	—	0	-0	-1	-0	0.0
Total	2	2	3	.400	40	0	0	0	1	47²	40	4	38	46	15.5	5.66	71	.226	.374	0	.000	-0	-8	-9	-1	-0.9

● FRED BESANA
Besana, Frederick Cyril b: 4/5/31, Lincoln, Cal. BR/TL, 6'3.5", 200 lbs. Deb: 4/18/56

| 1956 | Bal-A | 1 | 0 | 1.000 | 7 | 2 | 0 | 0 | 0 | 17² | 22 | 1 | 14 | 7 | 19.4 | 5.60 | 70 | .310 | .437 | 0 | .000 | -0 | -3 | -3 | 1 | -0.1 |

● HERMAN BESSE
Besse, Herman A. b: 8/16/11, St.Louis, Mo. d: 8/13/72, Los Angeles, Cal. BL/TL, 6'2", 190 lbs. Deb: 4/19/40

1940	Phi-A	0	3	.000	17	5	0	0	0	53	70	10	34	19	18.2	8.83	50	.315	.413	5	.263	2	-26	-26	-1	-1.1
1941	Phi-A	2	0	1.000	6	2	1	0	0	19²	28	4	12	8	18.3	10.07	42	.329	.412	1	.200	-0	-13	-13	0	-1.0
1942	Phi-A	2	9	.182	30	14	4	0	1	133	163	7	69	78	16.0	6.16	61	.300	.383	12	.226	2	-37	-35	-2	-2.6
1943	Phi-A	1	1	.500	5	1	0	0	0	16¹	18	2	4	3	12.7	3.31	103	.295	.348	0	.000	-1	-0	0	-0	-0.1
1946	Phi-A	0	2	.000	7	3	0	0	1	20²	19	1	9	10	12.2	5.23	68	.247	.326	0	.000	-0	-4	-4	-0	-0.4
Total	5	5	15	.250	65	25	5	0	2	242²	298	24	128	118	16.1	6.79	58	.302	.386	18	.200	2	-80	-77	-3	-5.2

● DON BESSENT
Bessent, Fred Donald b: 3/13/31, Jacksonville, Fla. d: 7/7/90, Jacksonville, Fla. BR/TR, 6', 175 lbs. Deb: 7/17/55

1955	*Bro-N	8	1	.889	24	2	1	0	3	63¹	51	7	21	29	10.2	2.70	150	.220	.285	2	.100	-2	9	10	-0	1.2
1956	*Bro-N	4	3	.571	38	0	0	0	9	79¹	63	5	31	52	10.7	2.50	159	.221	.297	2	.111	-1	11	13	-1	1.2
1957	Bro-N	1	3	.250	27	0	0	0	0	44	58	5	19	24	15.8	5.73	73	.328	.393	1	.250	-0	-9	-8	-0	-0.7
1958	LA-N	1	0	1.000	19	0	0	0	0	24¹	24	3	17	13	15.5	3.33	123	.270	.393	0	.000	-0	2	2	1	0.1
Total	4	14	7	.667	108	2	1	0	12	211	196	20	88	118	12.2	3.33	122	.250	.327	5	.114	-3	13	17	-1	1.8

● KARL BEST
Best, Karl Jon b: 3/6/59, Aberdeen, Wash. BR/TR, 6'4", 210 lbs. Deb: 8/19/83

1983	Sea-A	0	1	.000	4	0	0	0	0	5¹	14	2	5	3	35.4	13.50	32	.483	.583	0	—	0	-6	-5	-0	-1.0
1984	Sea-A	1	1	.500	5	0	0	0	0	6	7	0	4	6	10.5	3.00	133	.292	.292	0	—	0	1	1	-0	0.3
1985	Sea-A	2	1	.667	15	0	0	0	4	32¹	25	1	6	32	8.9	1.95	216	.207	.250	0	—	0	8	8	-0	0.8
1986	Sea-A	2	3	.400	26	0	0	0	1	35²	35	3	21	23	14.4	4.04	105	.255	.358	0	—	0	1	1	-0	0.1
1988	Min-A	0	0	—	11	0	0	0	0	12	15	1	7	9	16.5	6.00	68	.306	.393	0	—	0	-3	-3	-0	-0.1
Total	5	5	6	.455	61	0	0	0	5	91¹	96	7	39	73	13.7	4.04	104	.267	.345	0	—	0	1	2	-2	0.0

● JIM BETHKE
Bethke, James Charles b: 11/5/46, Falls City, Neb. BR/TR, 6'3", 185 lbs. Deb: 4/12/65

| 1965 | NY-N | 2 | 0 | 1.000 | 25 | 0 | 0 | 0 | 1 | 40 | 41 | 3 | 22 | 19 | 15.5 | 4.27 | 83 | .266 | .379 | 0 | .000 | -0 | -3 | -3 | 1 | -0.1 |

● JEFF BETTENDORF
Bettendorf, Jeffrey Allen b: 12/10/60, Lompoc, Cal. BR/TR, 6'3", 180 lbs. Deb: 4/8/84

| 1984 | Oak-A | 0 | 0 | — | 3 | 0 | 0 | 0 | 1 | 9² | 9 | 3 | 5 | 5 | 13.0 | 4.66 | 80 | .243 | .333 | 0 | — | 0 | -1 | -1 | -0 | 0.4 |

● HARRY BETTS
Betts, Harold Matthew "Chubby" or "Ginger" b: 6/19/1881, Alliance, Ohio d: 5/22/46, San Antonio, Tex. BR/TR, 5'10", 200 lbs. Deb: 9/22/03

1903	StL-N	0	1	.000	1	1	1	0	0	9	11	0	5	2	18.0	10.00	33	.297	.409	0	.000	-0	-7	-7	-0	-0.5
1913	Cin-N	0	0	—	1	0	0	0	0	3¹	1	0	3	0	13.5	2.70	120	.143	.455	0	.000	-0	0	0	-0	0.0
Total	2	0	1	.000	2	1	1	0	0	12¹	12	0	8	2	16.8	8.03	41	.273	.418	0	.000	-0	-7	-7	-0	-0.5

● HUCK BETTS
Betts, Walter Martin b: 2/18/1897, Millsboro, Del. d: 6/13/87, Millsboro, Del. BR/TR, 5'11", 170 lbs. Deb: 4/26/20

1920	Phi-N	1	1	.500	27	4	1	0	0	88¹	86	9	33	18	12.3	3.57	96	.261	.332	2	.080	-2	-4	-1	-1	-0.3
1921	Phi-N	3	7	.300	32	7	1	0	4	100²	141	8	14	28	14.2	4.47	95	.337	.365	8	.267	0	-8	-3	0	-0.2
1922	Phi-N	1	0	1.000	7	0	0	0	0	15	23	3	8	4	18.6	9.60	48	.349	.419	0	.000	-0	-9	-8	-0	-0.5
1923	Phi-N	2	4	.333	19	4	3	0	1	84¹	100	7	14	18	12.6	3.09	149	.314	.351	3	.097	-3	9	14	0	0.6
1924	Phi-N	7	10	.412	37	9	2	0	2	144¹	160	8	42	46	12.9	4.30	104	.286	.341	7	.156	-2	-7	-3	-2	-0.1
1925	Phi-N	4	5	.444	35	7	1	0	1	97¹	146	10	38	28	17.3	5.55	86	.342	.400	10	.294	2	-14	-8	-1	-0.4
1932	Bos-N	13	11	.542	31	27	16	3	1	221²	229	8	35	32	10.7	2.80	134	.267	.295	19	.241	-2	27	24	-2	2.4
1933	Bos-N	11	11	.500	35	26	17	4	4	242	225	9	55	40	10.4	2.79	110	.248	.290	17	.224	4	15	7	4	1.4
1934	Bos-N	17	10	.630	40	27	10	2	3	213	258	10	47	42	12.8	4.06	94	.286	.330	13	.188	1	-0	-6	-2	-0.7
1935	Bos-N	2	9	.182	44	19	2	1	0	159²	213	9	40	40	14.4	5.47	69	.321	.362	7	.159	-0	-26	-30	1	-1.7
Total	10	61	68	.473	307	125	53	8	16	1366¹	1581	83	321	323	12.7	3.93	98	.292	.334	86	.197	-2	-18	-9	-0	0.5

● BILL BEVENS
Bevens, Floyd Clifford b: 10/21/16, Hubbard, Ore. d: 10/26/91, Salem, Ore. BR/TR, 6'3.5", 210 lbs. Deb: 5/12/44

1944	NY-A	4	1	.800	8	5	3	0	0	43²	44	4	13	16	12.0	2.68	130	.274	.331	1	.063	-2	4	4	-0	0.2
1945	NY-A	13	9	.591	29	25	14	2	0	184	174	12	68	76	11.9	3.67	94	.254	.322	7	.111	-4	-6	-4	1	-0.9
1946	NY-A	16	13	.552	31	31	18	3	0	249²	213	11	78	120	10.5	2.23	154	.232	.293	7	.083	-4	35	34	-4	3.0
1947	*NY-A	7	13	.350	28	23	11	1	0	165	167	13	77	77	13.4	3.82	93	.264	.345	7	.121	-3	-2	-5	-0	-0.9
Total	4	40	36	.526	96	84	46	6	0	642¹	598	40	236	289	11.7	3.08	113	.250	.318	22	.100	-13	31	29	-4	1.4

● BRIAN BEVIL
Bevil, Brian Scott b: 9/5/71, Houston, Tex. BR/TR, 6'3", 190 lbs. Deb: 6/17/96

| 1996 | KC-A | 1 | 0 | 1.000 | 3 | 1 | 0 | 0 | 0 | 11 | 9 | 2 | 5 | 7 | 11.5 | 5.73 | 85 | .237 | .326 | 0 | — | 0 | -1 | -0 | 0 | 0.1 |

● LOU BEVIL
Bevil, Louis Eugene (b: Louis Eugene Bevilacqua) b: 11/27/22, Nelson, Ill. d: 2/1/73, Dixon, Ill. BB/TR, 5'11.5", 190 lbs. Deb: 9/2/42

| 1942 | Was-A | 0 | 1 | .000 | 4 | 1 | 0 | 0 | 0 | 9² | 9 | 0 | 11 | 2 | 19.6 | 6.52 | 56 | .265 | .457 | 0 | .000 | -0 | -3 | -3 | -0 | -0.3 |

YEAR TM/L	W	L	PCT	G	GS	CG	SH	SV	IP	H	HR	BB	SO	RAT	ERA	ERA+	OAV	OOB	BH	AVG	PB	PR	/A	PD	TPI
● **BEN BEVILLE** Beville, Clarence Benjamin b: 8/28/1877, Colusa, Cal. d: 1/5/37, Yountville, Cal. BR/TR, 5'9", 190 lbs. Deb: 5/24/01																								
1901 Bos-A	0	2	.000	2	2	1	0	0	9	8	0	9	1	18.0	4.00	88	.235	.409	2	.286	0	-0	-0	-0	-0.1
● **JIM BIBBY** Bibby, James Blair b: 10/29/44, Franklinton, N.C. BR/TR, 6'5", 235 lbs. Deb: 9/4/72																								
1972 StL-N	1	3	.250	6	6	0	0	0	40¹	29	4	19	28	10.9	3.35	102	.206	.304	1	.125	0	0	0	0	0.1
1973 StL-N	0	2	.000	6	5	0	0	0	16	19	2	17	12	21.4	9.56	38	.306	.469	0	.000	0	-10	-11	0	-1.1
Tex-A	9	10	.474	26	23	11	2	1	180¹	121	14	106	155	11.6	3.24	115	**.192**	.314	0	—	0	11	10	-2	0.8
1974 Tex-A	19	19	.500	41	41	11	5	0	264	255	25	113	149	12.9	4.74	75	.255	.336	0	—	0	-33	-34	1	-4.3
1975 Tex-A	2	6	.250	12	12	4	1	0	68¹	73	2	28	31	13.6	5.00	75	.274	.348	0	—	0	-9	-9	-1	-1.0
Cle-A	5	9	.357	24	12	2	0	1	112²	99	7	50	62	11.9	3.20	118	.235	.316	0	—	0	7	7	1	0.9
Yr	7	15	.318	36	24	6	1	1	181	172	9	78	93	12.4	3.88	97	.248	.324	0	—	0	-2	-2	-0	-0.1
1976 Cle-A	13	7	.650	34	21	4	3	1	163¹	162	6	56	84	12.1	3.20	109	.266	.329	0	—	0	6	5	-1	0.5
1977 Cle-A	12	13	.480	37	30	9	2	2	206²	197	17	73	141	11.9	3.57	110	.250	.317	0	—	0	11	9	-2	0.8
1978 Pit-N	8	7	.533	34	14	3	2	1	107	100	10	39	72	11.9	3.53	105	.246	.315	4	.129	1	1	2	0	0.4
1979 *Pit-N	12	4	.750	34	17	4	1	0	137²	110	9	47	103	10.5	2.81	138	.218	.290	8	.178	2	14	16	-2	1.8
1980 Pit-N★	19	6	**.760**	35	34	6	1	0	238¹	210	20	88	144	11.5	3.32	110	.238	.312	12	.156	2	7	8	-2	0.8
1981 Pit-N	6	3	.667	14	14	2	2	0	93²	79	4	26	48	10.3	2.50	144	.225	.282	4	.143	1	10	11	-1	1.1
1983 Pit-N	5	12	.294	29	12	0	0	2	78	92	10	51	44	16.6	6.69	55	.297	.398	2	.111	-1	-27	-26	-0	-5.0
1984 Tex-A	0	0	—	8	0	0	0	0	16¹	11	1	10	6	16.0	4.41	94	.297	.392	0	—	-0	-1	-0	-0	-0.1
Total 12	111	101	.524	340	239	56	19	8	1722²	1565	131	723	1079	12.2	3.76	98	.243	.323	31	.148	5	-11	-11	-8	-4.3
● **VERN BICKFORD** Bickford, Vernon Edgell b: 8/17/20, Hellier, Ky. d: 5/6/60, Concord, Va. BR/TR, 6', 185 lbs. Deb: 4/24/48																								
1948 *Bos-N	11	5	.688	33	22	10	1	1	146	125	8	63	60	11.8	3.27	117	.226	.309	10	.204	1	11	9	-1	0.9
1949 Bos-N★	16	11	.593	37	36	15	2	0	230²	246	20	106	101	14.0	4.25	89	.273	.354	15	.185	-1	-5	-12	2	-1.1
1950 Bos-N	19	14	.576	40	39	**27**	2	0	311²	293	25	122	126	12.2	3.47	111	.248	.321	16	.138	-4	23	13	-1	0.7
1951 Bos-N	11	9	.550	25	20	12	3	0	164²	146	7	76	76	12.5	3.12	118	.240	.330	6	.115	-2	15	10	3	1.2
1952 Bos-N	7	12	.368	26	22	7	1	0	161¹	165	7	64	62	12.9	3.74	97	.269	.340	9	.176	-0	-0	-2	1	-0.2
1953 Mil-N	2	5	.286	20	9	2	0	1	58	60	8	35	25	15.1	5.28	74	.279	.385	1	.067	-1	-6	-9	1	-0.9
1954 Bal-A	0	1	.000	1	1	0	0	0	4	5	0	1	0	13.5	9.00	40	.333	.375	-0	.000	-0	-2	-2	0	-0.4
Total 7	66	57	.537	182	149	73	9	2	1076¹	1040	76	467	450	12.8	3.71	102	.254	.335	57	.156	-7	36	7	3	0.2
● **DAN BICKHAM** Bickham, Daniel Denison b: 10/31/1864, Dayton, Ohio d: 3/3/51, Dayton, Ohio BR/TR, 5'10", 160 lbs. Deb: 8/13/1886																								
1886 Cin-a	1	0	1.000	1	1	1	0	0	9	13	0	3	6	16.0	3.00	117	.351	.400	1	.333	0	0	1	0	0.1
● **CHARLIE BICKNELL** Bicknell, Charles Stephen "Bud" b: 7/27/28, Plainfield, N.J. BR/TR, 5'11", 170 lbs. Deb: 4/22/48																								
1948 Phi-N	0	1	.000	17	1	0	0	0	25²	29	5	17	5	16.1	5.96	66	.287	.390	0	.000	-1	-6	-6	-1	-0.3
1949 Phi-N	0	0	—	13	0	0	0	0	28¹	32	3	17	4	16.2	7.62	52	.291	.395	0	.000	1	-11	-12	-0	-0.1
Total 2	0	1	.000	30	1	0	0	0	54	61	8	34	9	16.2	6.83	58	.289	.393	0	.000	-0	-17	-17	-1	-0.3
● **MIKE BIELECKI** Bielecki, Michael Joseph b: 7/31/59, Baltimore, Md. BR/TR, 6'3", 200 lbs. Deb: 9/14/84																								
1984 Pit-N	0	0	—	4	4	0	0	0	4¹	4	0	1	0	8.3	0.00	—	.250	.250	0	—	0	2	2	0	0.0
1985 Pit-N	2	3	.400	12	7	0	0	0	45²	45	5	31	22	15.2	4.53	79	.257	.372	0	.000	-1	-5	-5	-1	-0.5
1986 Pit-N	6	11	.353	31	27	0	0	0	148²	149	10	83	83	15.2	4.66	82	.262	.358	3	.063	-3	-16	-14	-1	-1.8
1987 Pit-N	2	3	.400	8	8	2	0	0	45²	43	6	12	25	11.0	4.73	87	.250	.303	1	.063	-0	-3	-3	-0	-0.4
1988 Chi-N	2	2	.500	19	5	0	0	0	48¹	55	4	16	33	13.2	3.35	108	.284	.338	1	.100	-0	1	1	-0	0.0
1989 *Chi-N	18	7	**.720**	33	33	4	3	0	212¹	187	16	81	147	11.4	3.14	120	.237	.308	3	.043	-5	8	15	-1	1.0
1990 Chi-N	8	11	.421	36	29	0	0	1	168	188	13	70	103	14.1	4.93	83	.287	.361	7	.163	-0	-21	-16	3	-1.4
1991 Chi-N	13	11	.542	39	25	0	0	0	172	169	18	54	72	11.8	4.50	86	.262	.321	3	.065	-2	-16	-12	1	-1.7
Atl-N	0	0	—	2	0	0	0	0	1²	2	0	2	3	21.6	0.00	—	.286	.444	0	—	0	1	1	0	0.0
Yr	13	11	.542	41	25	0	0	0	173²	171	18	56	75	11.8	4.46	87	.259	.317	3	.065	-2	-15	-11	1	-1.7
1992 Atl-N	2	4	.333	19	14	1	1	0	80²	77	7	27	62	11.7	2.57	143	.254	.317	3	.125	-1	8	10	1	0.7
1993 Cle-A	4	5	.444	13	13	0	0	0	68²	90	8	23	38	15.1	5.90	73	.310	.365	0	—	0	-12	-12	-0	-1.2
1994 Atl-N	2	0	1.000	19	1	0	0	0	27	28	2	12	18	13.7	4.00	106	.277	.360	0	.000	-0	1	1	0	0.0
1995 Cal-A	4	6	.400	22	11	0	0	0	75¹	80	15	31	45	13.6	5.97	79	.273	.349	0	—	0	-11	-11	-1	-1.1
1996 *Atl-N	4	3	.571	40	5	0	0	2	75¹	63	8	33	71	11.5	2.63	167	.224	.306	1	.100	0	13	15	1	1.4
Total 13	67	66	.504	297	178	7	4	3	1173²	1180	107	475	723	12.8	4.19	95	.263	.336	22	.079	-14	-49	-27	3	-5.0
● **HARRY BIEMILLER** Biemiller, Harry Lee b: 10/9/1897, Baltimore, Md. d: 5/25/65, Orlando, Fla. BR/TR, 6'1", 171 lbs. Deb: 8/26/20																								
1920 Was-A	1	0	1.000	5	2	1	0	0	17	21	1	13	10	18.0	4.76	78	.318	.430	0	.000	-1	-2	-2	1	-0.1
1925 Cin-N	0	1	.000	23	1	0	0	2	47	45	2	21	9	14.0	4.02	102	.280	.386	0	.000	-0	1	0	2	0.1
Total 2	1	1	.500	28	3	1	0	2	64	66	3	34	19	15.0	4.22	95	.291	.399	0	.000	-1	-1	-1	2	0.0
● **LOU BIERBAUER** Bierbauer, Louis W. b: 9/28/1865, Erie, Pa. d: 1/31/26, Erie, Pa. BL/TR, 5'8", 140 lbs. Deb: 4/17/1886 ◆																								
1886 Phi-a	0	0	—	2	0	0	0	0	10²	8	0	5	1	11.0	4.22	83	.178	.260	118	.226	-0	-1	-1	-1	0.0
1887 Phi-a	0	0	—	1	0	0	0	0	1	0	0	0	0	0.00	—	.000	.000	144	.272	0	1	0	0	0.1
1888 Phi-a	0	0	—	1	0	0	0	0	3	5	0	0	3	15.0	0.00	—	.357	.357	143	.267	0	1	0	0	0.1
Total 3	0	0	—	4	0	0	0	0	14²	13	0	5	4	11.0	3.07	112	.210	.269	1521	.267	0	1	1	-1	0.1
● **LYLE BIGBEE** Bigbee, Lyle Randolph "Al" b: 8/22/1893, Sweet Home, Ore. d: 8/5/42, Portland, Ore. BL/TR, 6', 180 lbs. Deb: 4/15/20 F◆																								
1920 Phi-A	0	3	.000	12	2	0	0	0	45	66	5	25	12	18.2	8.00	50	.369	.446	14	.187	-0	-21	-20	-1	-1.1
1921 Pit-N	0	0	—	5	0	0	0	0	8	4	1	4	1	9.0	1.13	341	.154	.267	0	.000	-0	2	2	-0	0.1
Total 2	0	3	.000	17	2	0	0	0	53	70	5	29	13	16.8	6.96	57	.341	.423	14	.182	-0	-19	-17	0	-1.1
● **CHARLIE BIGGS** Biggs, Charles Orval b: 9/15/06, French Lick, Ind. d: 5/24/54, French Lick, Ind. BR/TR, 6'1", 185 lbs. Deb: 9/3/32																								
1932 Chi-A	1	1	.500	6	4	0	0	0	24²	32	2	12	11	17.1	6.93	62	.314	.402	1	.111	-0	-7	-7	-0	-0.5
● **LARRY BIITTNER** Biittner, Lawrence David b: 7/27/45, Pocahontas, Ia. BL/TL, 6'2", 205 lbs. Deb: 7/17/70 ◆																								
1977 Chi-N	0	0	—	1	0	0	0	0	1¹	5	3	1	3	40.5	40.50	11	.556	.600	147	.298	-0	-5	-5	0	-0.4
● **JIM BILBREY** Bilbrey, James Melvin b: 4/20/24, Rickman, Tenn. d: 12/26/85, Toledo, Ohio BR/TR, 6'2.5", 205 lbs. Deb: 5/17/49																								
1949 StL-A	0	0	—	1	0	0	0	0	1	0	3	0	0	36.0	18.00	25	.250	.571	2	—	0	-2	-1	0	0.0
● **EMIL BILDILLI** Bildilli, Emil "Hill Billy" b: 9/16/12, Diamond, Ind. d: 9/16/46, Hartford City, Ind. BR/TL, 5'10", 170 lbs. Deb: 8/24/37																								
1937 StL-A	0	1	.000	4	1	0	0	0	8	12	1	3	2	16.9	10.13	48	.353	.405	0	.000	-0	-5	-5	1	-0.4
1938 StL-A	1	2	.333	5	3	2	0	0	21²	33	3	11	11	18.3	7.06	70	.359	.427	2	.250	-0	-5	-5	-0	-0.5
1939 StL-A	1	1	.500	2	2	2	0	0	19	21	0	6	8	12.8	3.32	147	.266	.318	0	.000	-0	3	3	0	0.3
1940 StL-A	2	4	.333	28	11	3	0	1	97	113	12	52	32	15.5	5.57	82	.298	.386	6	.200	-1	-13	-11	3	-0.4
1941 StL-A	0	0	—	2	0	0	0	0	2¹	5	0	3	2	30.9	11.57	37	.417	.533	0	—	-0	-2	-2	0	0.0
Total 5	4	8	.333	41	17	7	0	1	148	184	16	75	55	15.9	5.84	80	.309	.388	8	.178	-2	-22	-19	4	-1.0
● **HARRY BILLIARD** Billiard, Harry Pree "Pree" b: 11/11/1883, Monroe, Ind. d: 6/3/23, Wooster, Ohio BR/TR, 6', 190 lbs. Deb: 7/31/08																								
1908 NY-A	0	0	—	3	1	0	0	0	17	15	1	14	10	18.0	2.65	94	.234	.410	1	.167	-0	-0	-1	0	-0.1
1914 Ind-F	8	7	.533	32	16	5	0	2	125²	117	4	63	45	13.4	3.72	84	.255	.356	7	.184	-1	-12	-8	-2	-1.3
1915 New-F	0	1	.000	14	2	0	0	0	28¹	32	0	28	7	20.0	5.72	66	.291	.447	2	.333	-0	-9	-10	1	-0.3
Total 3	8	8	.500	52	18	5	0	2	171	164	5	105	62	14.1	3.95	75	.260	.379	10	.200	-2	-22	-19	-2	-1.7
● **JACK BILLINGHAM** Billingham, John Eugene b: 2/21/43, Orlando, Fla. BR/TR, 6'4", 215 lbs. Deb: 4/11/68																								
1968 LA-N	3	0	1.000	50	1	0	0	8	70²	54	0	30	46	11.0	2.17	128	.215	.304	0	.000	0	6	5	1	0.4
1969 Hou-N	6	7	.462	52	4	1	0	2	82²	92	12	29	71	13.7	4.25	83	.290	.359	1	.071	-0	-6	-6	-0	-1.0
1970 Hou-N	13	9	.591	46	24	8	2	0	187²	190	10	63	134	12.6	3.98	99	.259	.326	6	.103	-2	1	-2	1	-0.3
1971 Hou-N	10	16	.385	33	33	8	5	0	228¹	205	9	68	139	11.4	3.39	99	.243	.311	9	.123	-3	2	-1	0	-0.4
1972 *Cin-N	12	12	.500	36	31	8	4	1	217²	197	18	64	137	11.1	3.18	101	.241	.301	5	.070	-4	7	1	-0	-0.4

YEAR	TM/L	W	L	PCT	G	GS	CG	SH	SV	IP	H	HR	BB	SO	RAT	ERA	ERA+	OAV	OOB	BH	AVG	PB	PR	/A	PD	TPI
1973	*Cin-N☆	19	10	.655	40	40	16	**7**	0	**293**¹	257	20	95	155	11.1	3.04	112	.236	.303	6	.065	-5	20	12	2	0.8
1974	Cin-N	19	11	.633	36	35	8	3	0	212¹	233	16	64	103	12.8	3.94	88	.288	.345	5	.075	-5	-8	-11	1	-1.9
1975	*Cin-N	15	10	.600	33	32	5	0	0	208	222	22	76	79	13.3	4.11	87	.279	.348	7	.108	-1	-11	-12	-2	-1.6
1976	*Cin-N	12	10	.545	34	29	5	2	1	177	190	17	62	76	13.0	4.32	81	.279	.343	14	.237	-1	-16	-16	-1	-1.6
1977	Cin-N	10	10	.500	36	23	3	2	0	161²	195	16	56	76	14.5	5.23	75	.306	.371	9	.161	-1	-24	-22	-2	-2.4
1978	Det-A	15	8	.652	30	30	10	4	0	201²	218	16	65	59	13.0	3.88	100	.284	.346	0	—	0	-3	-0	-1	-0.2
1979	Det-A	10	7	.588	35	19	2	0	3	158	163	13	60	59	13.1	3.30	131	.275	.348	0	—	0	16	18	-1	1.7
1980	Det-A	0	0	—	8	0	0	0	0	7¹	11	1	6	3	20.9	7.36	56	.355	.459	0	—	0	-3	-3	-0	-0.1
	Bos-A	1	3	.250	7	4	0	0	0	24¹	45	6	12	4	22.6	11.10	38	.413	.488	0	—	0	-19	-19	-0	-2.4
	Yr	1	3	.250	15	4	0	0	0	31²	56	7	18	7	22.2	10.23	41	.397	.479	0	—	0	-22	-21	-0	-2.5
Total	13	145	113	.562	476	305	74	27	15	2230²	2272	176	750	1141	12.6	3.83	94	.268	.335	62	.111	-17	-37	-59	-7	-9.4

● **JOSH BILLINGS**   Billings, Haskell Clark b: 9/27/07, New York, N.Y. d: 12/26/83, Greenbrae, Cal. BR/TR, 5'11", 180 lbs. Deb: 8/17/27

YEAR	TM/L	W	L	PCT	G	GS	CG	SH	SV	IP	H	HR	BB	SO	RAT	ERA	ERA+	OAV	OOB	BH	AVG	PB	PR	/A	PD	TPI
1927	Det-A	5	4	.556	10	9	5	0	0	67	64	3	39	18	14.6	4.84	87	.259	.373	7	.259	0	-5	-5	-1	-0.5
1928	Det-A	5	10	.333	21	16	3	1	0	110²	118	4	59	48	14.8	5.12	80	.276	.371	10	.286	3	-13	-12	-0	-1.2
1929	Det-A	0	1	.000	8	0	0	0	0	19¹	27	0	9	1	17.2	5.12	84	.365	.440	0	.000	-1	-2	-2	1	-0.1
Total	3	10	15	.400	39	25	8	1	0	197	209	7	107	67	15.0	5.03	83	.277	.378	17	.250	2	-20	-19	-0	-1.8

● **DOUG BIRD**   Bird, James Douglas b: 3/5/50, Corona, Cal. BR/TR, 6'4", 180 lbs. Deb: 4/29/73

YEAR	TM/L	W	L	PCT	G	GS	CG	SH	SV	IP	H	HR	BB	SO	RAT	ERA	ERA+	OAV	OOB	BH	AVG	PB	PR	/A	PD	TPI
1973	KC-A	4	4	.500	54	0	0	0	20	102¹	81	10	30	83	9.9	2.99	137	.217	.279	0	—	0	9	13	-2	1.0
1974	KC-A	7	6	.538	55	1	1	0	10	92¹	100	6	27	62	12.5	2.73	140	.286	.339	0	—	0	9	11	1	1.8
1975	KC-A	9	6	.600	51	4	0	0	11	105¹	100	7	40	81	12.1	3.25	119	.258	.331	0	—	0	6	7	-1	1.0
1976	*KC-A	12	10	.545	39	27	2	1	2	197²	191	17	31	107	10.2	3.37	104	.251	.283	0	—	0	3	3	-2	0.1
1977	*KC-A	11	4	.733	53	5	0	0	14	118¹	120	14	29	83	11.6	3.88	104	.270	.319	0	—	0	-2	-1	-2	0.2
1978	*KC-A	6	6	.500	40	6	0	0	8	98²	110	8	31	48	13.0	5.29	72	.284	.340	0	—	0	-17	-16	-0	-1.9
1979	Phi-N	2	0	1.000	32	1	0	0	0	61	73	7	16	33	13.4	5.16	74	.305	.354	1	.167	0	-10	-9	-1	-0.4
1980	NY-A	3	0	1.000	22	1	0	0	1	50²	47	3	14	17	11.0	2.66	147	.257	.313	0	—	0	8	7	1	0.5
1981	NY-A	5	1	.833	17	4	0	0	0	53¹	58	5	16	28	12.5	2.70	132	.280	.332	0	—	0	6	5	0	0.6
	Chi-N	4	5	.444	12	12	2	1	0	75¹	72	5	16	34	10.6	3.58	103	.254	.297	2	.100	-1	-1	1	-1	-0.1
1982	Chi-N	9	14	.391	35	33	2	1	0	191	230	26	30	71	12.4	5.14	73	.297	.325	8	.143	-2	-33	-30	-2	-3.5
1983	Bos-A	1	4	.200	22	6	0	0	1	67²	91	14	16	33	14.5	6.65	65	.324	.365	0	—	0	-19	-17	-0	-1.3
Total	11	73	60	.549	432	100	8	3	60	1213²	1273	122	296	680	11.8	3.99	96	.272	.319	11	.134	-2	-36	-23	-8	-2.0

● **RED BIRD**   Bird, James Edward b: 4/25/1890, Stephenville, Tex. d: 3/23/72, Murfreesboro, Ark. BL/TL, 5'11", 170 lbs. Deb: 9/17/21

YEAR	TM/L	W	L	PCT	G	GS	CG	SH	SV	IP	H	HR	BB	SO	RAT	ERA	ERA+	OAV	OOB	BH	AVG	PB	PR	/A	PD	TPI
1921	Was-A	0	0	—	1	0	0	0	0	5	5	0	1	2	12.6	5.40	76	.294	.368	0	.000	-0	-1	-1	0	0.0

● **MIKE BIRKBECK**   Birkbeck, Michael Lawrence b: 3/10/61, Orrville, Ohio BR/TR, 6'1", 190 lbs. Deb: 8/17/86

YEAR	TM/L	W	L	PCT	G	GS	CG	SH	SV	IP	H	HR	BB	SO	RAT	ERA	ERA+	OAV	OOB	BH	AVG	PB	PR	/A	PD	TPI
1986	Mil-A	1	1	.500	7	4	0	0	0	22	24	0	12	13	14.7	4.50	96	.282	.371	0	—	0	-1	-0	-0	-0.1
1987	Mil-A	1	4	.200	10	10	1	0	0	45	63	8	19	25	16.4	6.20	74	.335	.396	0	—	0	-9	-8	1	-0.7
1988	Mil-A	10	8	.556	23	23	0	0	0	124	141	10	37	64	13.0	4.72	84	.285	.336	0	—	0	-10	-10	2	-1.1
1989	Mil-A	0	4	.000	9	9	1	0	0	44²	57	4	22	31	16.5	5.44	71	.310	.392	0	—	0	-8	-8	-0	-0.7
1992	NY-N	0	1	.000	1	1	0	0	0	7	12	3	1	2	16.7	9.00	39	.387	.406	0	.000	-0	-4	-4	-0	-0.5
1995	NY-N	0	1	.000	4	4	0	0	0	27²	22	2	2	14	7.8	1.63	249	.220	.235	2	.333	1	8	7	-0	0.4
Total	6	12	19	.387	54	51	2	0	0	270¹	319	27	93	149	13.8	4.86	84	.295	.353	2	.250	1	-24	-24	2	-2.7

● **RALPH BIRKOFER**   Birkofer, Ralph Joseph "Lefty" b: 11/5/08, Cincinnati, Ohio d: 3/16/71, Cincinnati, Ohio BL/TL, 5'11", 213 lbs. Deb: 4/25/33

YEAR	TM/L	W	L	PCT	G	GS	CG	SH	SV	IP	H	HR	BB	SO	RAT	ERA	ERA+	OAV	OOB	BH	AVG	PB	PR	/A	PD	TPI
1933	Pit-N	4	2	.667	9	8	3	1	0	50²	43	1	17	20	10.8	2.31	144	.234	.296	7	.318	1	6	6	-0	0.8
1934	Pit-N	11	12	.478	41	24	11	0	1	204	227	11	66	71	13.1	4.10	100	.277	.335	17	.227	1	-1	0	-0	-0.1
1935	Pit-N	9	7	.563	37	18	8	1	1	150¹	173	5	42	80	13.2	4.07	101	.283	.335	14	.241	2	-1	1	-3	0.0
1936	Pit-N	7	5	.583	34	13	2	0	0	109¹	130	4	44	48	14.5	4.69	86	.295	.362	9	.220	-0	-8	-8	-3	-1.0
1937	Bro-N	0	2	.000	11	1	0	0	0	29²	45	3	6	5	16.4	6.67	60	.341	.383	1	.273	1	-9	-9	-1	-0.5
Total	5	31	28	.525	132	64	24	2	2	544	618	24	175	224	13.4	4.19	96	.282	.340	50	.242	5	-13	-10	-8	-0.8

● **BABE BIRRER**   Birrer, Werner Joseph b: 7/4/28, Buffalo, N.Y. BR/TR, 6', 195 lbs. Deb: 6/5/55

YEAR	TM/L	W	L	PCT	G	GS	CG	SH	SV	IP	H	HR	BB	SO	RAT	ERA	ERA+	OAV	OOB	BH	AVG	PB	PR	/A	PD	TPI
1955	Det-A	4	3	.571	36	3	1	0	3	80¹	77	9	29	28	11.9	4.15	93	.248	.313	3	.158	2	-2	-3	-1	-0.1
1956	Bal-A	0	0	—	4	0	0	0	0	5¹	9	0	1	1	16.9	6.75	58	.360	.385	0	.000	-0	-2	-2	-0	0.0
1958	LA-N	0	0	—	16	0	0	0	0	34	43	4	7	16	13.5	4.50	91	.309	.347	4	.571	2	-2	-1	-0	0.1
Total	3	4	3	.571	56	3	1	0	4	119²	129	13	37	45	12.6	4.36	90	.272	.326	7	.259	4	-5	-6	-1	0.0

● **TIM BIRTSAS**   Birtsas, Timothy Dean b: 9/5/60, Pontiac, Mich. BL/TL, 6'7", 240 lbs. Deb: 5/3/85

YEAR	TM/L	W	L	PCT	G	GS	CG	SH	SV	IP	H	HR	BB	SO	RAT	ERA	ERA+	OAV	OOB	BH	AVG	PB	PR	/A	PD	TPI
1985	Oak-A	10	6	.625	29	25	2	0	0	141¹	124	18	91	94	13.9	4.01	96	.238	.354	0	—	0	-2	-3	-3	-0.3
1986	Oak-A	0	0	—	2	0	0	0	0	2	4	1	4	1	27.0	22.50	17	.286	.545	0	—	0	-4	-4	-0	-0.5
1988	Cin-N	1	3	.250	36	4	0	0	0	64¹	61	6	24	38	12.3	4.20	85	.250	.325	0	.000	-1	-5	-4	-1	-0.5
1989	Cin-N	2	2	.500	42	1	0	0	1	69²	68	5	27	57	12.7	3.75	96	.261	.337	1	.250	1	-2	-1	-1	0.0
1990	Cin-N	1	3	.250	29	0	0	0	0	51¹	69	7	24	41	16.5	3.86	102	.325	.397	0	.000	-0	0	0	0	0.0
Total	5	14	14	.500	138	30	2	0	1	328²	324	37	170	231	13.8	4.08	93	.260	.354	1	.056	-0	-10	-11	-4	-0.6

● **FRANK BISCAN**   Biscan, Frank Stephen "Porky" b: 3/13/20, Mt.Olive, Ill. d: 5/22/59, St.Louis, Mo. BL/TL, 5'11", 190 lbs. Deb: 5/3/42

YEAR	TM/L	W	L	PCT	G	GS	CG	SH	SV	IP	H	HR	BB	SO	RAT	ERA	ERA+	OAV	OOB	BH	AVG	PB	PR	/A	PD	TPI
1942	StL-A	0	1	.000	11	0	0	0	1	27	13	1	11	10	8.0	2.33	159	.143	.235	0	.000	-0	4	4	0	0.1
1946	StL-A	1	1	.500	16	0	0	0	1	22²	28	3	22	9	19.9	5.16	72	.318	.455	0	.000	-0	-4	-4	-0	-0.4
1948	StL-A	6	7	.462	47	4	1	0	2	98²	129	3	71	45	19.1	6.11	75	.322	.435	5	.192	1	-20	-17	-2	-1.9
Total	3	7	9	.438	74	4	1	0	4	148¹	170	4	104	64	17.2	5.28	81	.294	.409	5	.143	-0	-20	-17	-0	-2.2

● **CHARLIE BISHOP**   Bishop, Charles Tuller b: 1/1/24, Atlanta, Ga. d: 7/5/93, Lawrenceville, Ga. BR/TR, 6'2", 195 lbs. Deb: 8/22/52

YEAR	TM/L	W	L	PCT	G	GS	CG	SH	SV	IP	H	HR	BB	SO	RAT	ERA	ERA+	OAV	OOB	BH	AVG	PB	PR	/A	PD	TPI
1952	Phi-A	2	2	.500	6	5	1	0	0	30²	29	2	24	11	15.6	6.46	61	.238	.363	1	.111	-0	-9	-9	-0	-0.9
1953	Phi-A	3	14	.176	39	20	1	1	2	160²	174	15	86	66	14.8	5.66	76	.282	.375	5	.089	-4	-30	-24	2	-2.5
1954	Phi-A	4	6	.400	20	12	4	0	1	96	98	10	50	34	14.3	4.41	89	.275	.372	4	.121	-2	-7	-5	-2	-0.8
1955	KC-A	1	0	1.000	4	0	0	0	0	6²	6	1	8	10	23.0	5.40	77	.261	.500	1	.500	-0	-1	-0	-0	-0.1
Total	4	10	22	.313	69	37	6	1	3	294	307	28	168	121	14.9	5.33	77	.275	.376	11	.110	-6	-47	-39	1	-4.3

● **JIM BISHOP**   Bishop, James Morton b: 1/28/1898, Montgomery City, Mo. d: 9/20/73, Montgomery City, Mo. BR/TR, 6', 195 lbs. Deb: 4/26/23

YEAR	TM/L	W	L	PCT	G	GS	CG	SH	SV	IP	H	HR	BB	SO	RAT	ERA	ERA+	OAV	OOB	BH	AVG	PB	PR	/A	PD	TPI
1923	Phi-N	0	3	.000	15	0	0	0	1	32²	48	3	11	5	17.1	6.34	73	.353	.413	0	.000	-2	-8	-6	1	-0.6
1924	Phi-N	0	1	.000	7	1	0	0	0	16²	24	3	7	3	16.7	6.48	69	.348	.408	1	.200	-0	-5	-4	0	-0.2
Total	2	0	4	.000	22	1	0	0	1	49¹	72	6	18	8	17.0	6.39	71	.351	.412	1	.067	-2	-13	-10	1	-0.8

● **LLOYD BISHOP**   Bishop, Lloyd Clifton b: 4/25/1890, Conway Springs, Kan. d: 6/18/68, Wichita, Kan. BR/TR, 6', 180 lbs. Deb: 9/5/14

YEAR	TM/L	W	L	PCT	G	GS	CG	SH	SV	IP	H	HR	BB	SO	RAT	ERA	ERA+	OAV	OOB	BH	AVG	PB	PR	/A	PD	TPI
1914	Cle-A	0	1	.000	3	1	0	0	0	8	14	0	3	1	19.1	5.63	51	.389	.436	0	.000	-0	-3	-2	-0	-0.3

● **BILL BISHOP**   Bishop, William Henry "Lefty" b: 10/22/1900, Houtzdale, Pa. d: 2/14/56, St.Joseph, Mo. BL/TL, 5'8", 170 lbs. Deb: 9/15/21

YEAR	TM/L	W	L	PCT	G	GS	CG	SH	SV	IP	H	HR	BB	SO	RAT	ERA	ERA+	OAV	OOB	BH	AVG	PB	PR	/A	PD	TPI
1921	Phi-A	0	0	—	2	0	0	0	0	7	8	0	4	0	23.1	9.00	50	.267	.450	0	.000	-1	-4	-4	0	0.0

● **BILL BISHOP**   Bishop, William Robinson b: 12/27/1869, Adamsburg, Pa. d: 12/15/32, Pittsburgh, Pa. Deb: 9/13/1886

YEAR	TM/L	W	L	PCT	G	GS	CG	SH	SV	IP	H	HR	BB	SO	RAT	ERA	ERA+	OAV	OOB	BH	AVG	PB	PR	/A	PD	TPI
1886	Pit-a	0	1	.000	2	2	2	0	0	17	17	0	11	4	15.4	3.18	107	.221	.326	1	.143	-1	1	0	-1	-0.1
1887	Pit-N	0	3	.000	3	3	3	0	0	27	45	2	22	4	22.0	13.33	29	.354	.457	0	.000	-0	-28	-28	-0	-1.9
1889	Chi-N	0	0	—	2	0	0	0	2	3	6	0	6	1	36.0	18.00	23	.400	.571	0	.000	-0	-5	-5	-0	-0.4
Total	3	0	4	.000	7	5	5	0	2	47	68	2	39	9	21.1	9.96	37	.311	.421	1	.059	-2	-32	-33	-1	-2.5

● **HI BITHORN**   Bithorn, Hiram Gabriel (Sosa) b: 3/18/16, Santurce, P.R. d: 1/1/52, ElMante, Mex. BR/TR, 6'1", 200 lbs. Deb: 4/15/42

YEAR	TM/L	W	L	PCT	G	GS	CG	SH	SV	IP	H	HR	BB	SO	RAT	ERA	ERA+	OAV	OOB	BH	AVG	PB	PR	/A	PD	TPI
1942	Chi-N	9	14	.391	38	16	9	0	2	171¹	191	8	81	65	14.3	3.68	87	.296	.374	7	.123	-0	-7	-9	-1	-1.4
1943	Chi-N	18	12	.600	39	30	19	**7**	2	249²	227	8	65	86	10.6	2.60	129	.244	.294	16	.174	-0	22	21	1	2.6
1946	Chi-N	6	5	.545	26	7	2	1	1	86²	97	5	25	34	12.7	3.84	86	.283	.332	5	.179	1	-1	-2	-0	-0.7

YEAR	TM/L	W	L	PCT	G	GS	CG	SH	SV	IP	H	HR	BB	SO	RAT	ERA	ERA+	OAV	OOB	BH	AVG	PB	PR	/A	PD	TPI
1947	Chi-A	1	0	1.000	2	0	0	0	0	2	2	0	1	2	9.0	0.00	—	.286	.286	0	—	0	1	1	-0	0.4
Total	4	34	31	.523	105	53	30	8	5	509²	517	21	171	185	12.0	3.16	104	.268	.328	28	.158	-2	12	7	-0	0.9

● **JOE BITKER**   Bitker, Joseph Anthony   b: 2/12/64, Glendale, Cal.   BR/TR, 6'1", 175 lbs.   Deb: 7/31/90

YEAR	TM/L	W	L	PCT	G	GS	CG	SH	SV	IP	H	HR	BB	SO	RAT	ERA	ERA+	OAV	OOB	BH	AVG	PB	PR	/A	PD	TPI
1990	Oak-A	0	0	—	1	0	0	0	0	3	1	0	2	6	6.0	0.00	—	.111	.200	0	—	0	1	1	0	0.2
	Tex-A	0	0	—	5	0	0	0	0	9	7	0	3	6	11.0	3.00	131	.212	.297	0	—	0	1	1	0	0.0
	Yr	0	0	—	6	0	0	0	0	12	8	0	4	8	9.8	2.25	172	.190	.277	0	—	0	2	2	0	0.2
1991	Tex-A	1	0	1.000	9	0	0	0	0	14²	17	4	8	16	15.3	6.75	60	.274	.357	0	—	0	-4	-4	-0	-0.2
Total	2	1	0	1.000	15	0	0	0	0	26²	25	4	12	24	12.8	4.73	84	.240	.325	0	—	0	-2	-2	0	0.0

● **JEFF BITTIGER**   Bittiger, Jeffrey Scott   b: 4/13/62, Jersey City, N.J.   BR/TR, 5'10", 175 lbs.   Deb: 9/2/86

YEAR	TM/L	W	L	PCT	G	GS	CG	SH	SV	IP	H	HR	BB	SO	RAT	ERA	ERA+	OAV	OOB	BH	AVG	PB	PR	/A	PD	TPI
1986	Phi-N	1	1	.500	3	3	0	0	0	14²	16	2	7	8	14.7	5.52	70	.271	.358	1	.333	1	-3	-3	0	-0.2
1987	Min-A	1	0	1.000	3	1	0	0	0	8¹	17	2	6	3	13.0	5.40	85	.314	.333	0	—	0	-1	-1	0	-0.1
1988	Chi-A	2	4	.333	25	7	0	0	0	61²	59	11	29	33	12.8	4.23	94	.255	.338	0	—	0	-2	-2	-1	-0.2
1989	Chi-A	0	1	.000	2	1	0	0	0	9²	3	2	6	9	14.0	6.52	58	.257	.366	0	—	0	-3	-3	-0	-0.3
Total	4	4	6	.400	33	12	0	0	0	94¹	95	17	42	53	13.3	4.77	84	.264	.344	1	.333	1	-8	-8	-1	-0.8

● **JIM BIVIN**   Bivin, James Nathaniel   b: 12/11/09, Jackson, Miss.   d: 11/7/82, Pueblo, Colo.   BR/TR, 6', 155 lbs.   Deb: 4/16/35

YEAR	TM/L	W	L	PCT	G	GS	CG	SH	SV	IP	H	HR	BB	SO	RAT	ERA	ERA+	OAV	OOB	BH	AVG	PB	PR	/A	PD	TPI
1935	Phi-N	2	9	.182	47	14	0	0	1	161²	220	20	65	54	16.0	5.79	78	.316	.377	7	.146	-1	-32	-23	-1	-1.5

● **DAVE BLACK**   Black, David   b: 4/19/1892, Chicago, Ill.   d: 10/27/36, Pittsburgh, Pa.   BL/TR, 6'2", 175 lbs.   Deb: 5/2/14

YEAR	TM/L	W	L	PCT	G	GS	CG	SH	SV	IP	H	HR	BB	SO	RAT	ERA	ERA+	OAV	OOB	BH	AVG	PB	PR	/A	PD	TPI
1914	Chi-F	1	0	1.000	8	1	0	0	0	25	28	1	4	19	11.5	6.12	43	.311	.340	2	.286	1	-9	-10	0	-0.3
1915	Chi-F	6	7	.462	25	10	2	0	0	121¹	104	3	33	43	10.6	2.45	103	.241	.304	4	.108	-3	4	1	2	-0.1
	Bal-F	1	3	.250	8	4	1	0	0	34	32	2	15	10	13.0	3.71	77	.260	.350	3	.250	0	-4	-3	1	-0.3
	Yr	7	10	.412	33	14	3	0	0	155¹	136	5	48	53	10.8	2.72	95	.243	.305	7	.143	-3	0	-2	2	-0.4
1923	Bos-A	0	0	—	2	0	0	0	0	1	2	0	0	0	18.0	0.00	—	.500	.500	0	—	0	0	0	0	0.0
Total	3	8	10	.444	43	15	4	0	0	181¹	166	6	52	72	11.2	3.18	82	.256	.319	9	.161	-2	-8	-11	2	-0.7

● **DON BLACK**   Black, Donald Paul   b: 7/20/16, Salix, Iowa   d: 4/21/59, Cuyahoga Falls, O.   BR/TR, 6', 185 lbs.   Deb: 4/24/43

YEAR	TM/L	W	L	PCT	G	GS	CG	SH	SV	IP	H	HR	BB	SO	RAT	ERA	ERA+	OAV	OOB	BH	AVG	PB	PR	/A	PD	TPI
1943	Phi-A	6	16	.273	33	26	12	1	1	208	193	8	110	65	13.4	4.20	81	.247	.344	13	.188	-1	-21	-19	0	-1.9
1944	Phi-A	10	12	.455	29	27	8	0	0	177¹	177	6	75	78	13.0	4.06	86	.259	.336	11	.186	-1	-12	-11	-0	-1.4
1945	Phi-A	5	11	.313	26	18	8	0	0	125¹	154	5	69	47	16.0	5.17	66	.307	.391	6	.162	-2	-25	-24	-1	-3.1
1946	Cle-A	1	2	.333	18	4	0	0	0	43²	45	5	21	15	13.8	4.53	73	.273	.358	2	.200	-0	-5	-6	1	-0.3
1947	Cle-A	10	12	.455	30	28	8	3	0	190²	177	17	85	72	12.4	3.92	89	.249	.330	12	.182	-1	-5	-9	1	-1.0
1948	Cle-A	2	2	.500	18	10	1	0	0	52	57	5	40	16	17.0	5.37	76	.282	.403	3	.200	-0	-6	-8	-0	-0.5
Total	6	34	55	.382	154	113	37	4	1	797	803	46	400	293	13.7	4.35	82	.264	.352	47	.184	-4	-74	-76	0	-8.2

● **BUD BLACK**   Black, Harry Ralston   b: 6/30/57, San Mateo, Cal.   BL/TL, 6'2", 180 lbs.   Deb: 9/5/81

YEAR	TM/L	W	L	PCT	G	GS	CG	SH	SV	IP	H	HR	BB	SO	RAT	ERA	ERA+	OAV	OOB	BH	AVG	PB	PR	/A	PD	TPI
1981	Sea-A	0	0	—	2	0	0	0	0	1	2	0	3	2	45.0	0.00	—	.500	.714	0	—	0	0	0	0	-0.2
1982	KC-A	4	6	.400	22	14	0	0	0	88¹	92	10	34	40	13.1	4.58	89	.269	.340	0	—	0	-5	-5	-0	-0.5
1983	KC-A	10	7	.588	24	24	3	0	0	161¹	159	19	43	58	11.4	3.79	107	.257	.308	0	—	0	5	5	2	0.7
1984	*KC-A	17	12	.586	35	35	8	1	0	257	226	22	64	140	**10.3**	3.12	129	.233	**.283**	0	—	0	25	26	3	3.1
1985	*KC-A	10	15	.400	33	33	5	2	0	205²	216	17	59	122	12.4	4.33	96	.268	.324	0	—	0	-4	-4	-1	-0.5
1986	KC-A	5	10	.333	56	4	0	0	9	121	100	14	43	68	11.2	3.20	133	.225	.303	0	—	0	13	14	1	1.8
1987	KC-A	8	6	.571	29	18	0	0	1	122¹	126	16	35	61	12.2	3.60	126	.265	.322	0	—	0	12	13	-0	1.3
1988	KC-A	2	1	.667	17	0	0	0	0	22	29	3	11	19	13.9	4.91	81	.267	.351	0	—	0	-2	-2	-0	-0.3
	Cle-A	2	3	.400	16	7	0	0	1	59	59	6	23	44	13.1	5.03	82	.262	.341	0	—	0	-7	-6	1	-0.4
	Yr	4	4	.500	33	7	0	0	1	81	82	8	34	63	13.3	5.00	82	.264	.344	0	—	0	-9	-8	0	-0.7
1989	Cle-A	12	11	.522	33	32	6	3	0	222¹	213	14	52	88	10.8	3.36	118	.252	.296	0	—	0	13	15	-1	1.4
1990	Cle-A	11	10	.524	29	29	5	2	0	191	171	16	58	103	11.0	3.53	111	.236	.296	0	—	0	8	8	0	0.8
	Tor-A	2	1	.667	3	2	0	0	0	15²	10	2	3	3	8.0	4.02	98	.189	.246	0	—	0	-0	0	0	0.0
	Yr	13	11	.542	32	31	5	2	0	206²	181	19	61	106	10.6	3.57	110	.230	.286	0	—	0	8	8	0	0.8
1991	SF-N	12	16	.429	34	34	3	3	0	214¹	201	25	71	104	11.6	3.99	90	.251	.315	13	.183	1	-7	-10	2	-0.9
1992	SF-N	10	12	.455	28	28	2	1	0	177	178	23	59	82	12.1	3.97	83	.263	.323	3	.056	-3	-9	-13	1	-1.6
1993	SF-N	8	2	.800	16	16	0	0	0	93²	89	13	33	45	11.9	3.56	110	.256	.325	9	.243	2	5	4	1	0.7
1994	SF-N	4	2	.667	10	10	0	0	0	54¹	50	7	16	28	11.4	4.47	90	.245	.309	1	.059	-1	-2	-3	-0	-0.4
1995	Cle-A	4	2	.667	11	10	0	0	0	47¹	63	8	16	34	15.0	6.85	69	.317	.367	0	—	0	-11	-11	0	-1.2
Total	15	121	116	.511	398	296	32	12	11	2053¹	1978	217	623	1039	11.6	3.84	103	.253	.312	26	.145	-1	33	30	9	3.8

● **JOE BLACK**   Black, Joseph   b: 2/8/24, Plainfield, N.J.   BR/TR, 6'2", 220 lbs.   Deb: 5/1/52

YEAR	TM/L	W	L	PCT	G	GS	CG	SH	SV	IP	H	HR	BB	SO	RAT	ERA	ERA+	OAV	OOB	BH	AVG	PB	PR	/A	PD	TPI
1952	*Bro-N	15	4	.789	56	2	1	0	15	142¹	102	9	41	85	9.1	2.15	169	.201	.262	5	.139	-1	**25**	**24**	-2	3.3
1953	*Bro-N	6	3	.667	34	3	0	0	5	72²	74	12	27	42	12.6	5.33	80	.259	.325	4	.235	0	-8	-9	-0	-1.1
1954	Bro-N	0	0	—	5	0	0	0	0	7	11	3	5	3	20.6	11.57	35	.355	.444	0	—	0	-6	-6	-0	0.0
1955	Bro-N	1	0	1.000	6	0	0	0	0	15¹	15	1	5	9	11.7	2.93	138	.273	.333	1	.333	0	2	2	-0	0.1
	Cin-N	5	2	.714	32	11	1	0	3	102¹	106	13	25	54	11.5	4.22	100	.263	.306	3	.100	-2	-2	0	-1	-0.3
	Yr	6	2	.750	38	11	1	0	3	117²	121	14	30	63	11.5	4.05	104	.264	.309	4	.121	-2	-0	2	-1	-0.2
1956	Cin-N	3	2	.600	32	0	0	0	2	61²	61	11	25	27	12.6	4.52	88	.256	.327	0	.000	-0	-5	-4	-1	-0.5
1957	Was-A	0	1	.000	7	0	0	0	0	12²	22	4	1	2	16.3	7.11	55	.393	.404	0	—	0	-5	-5	-0	-0.3
Total	6	30	12	.714	172	16	2	0	25	414	391	53	129	222	11.3	3.91	102	.248	.306	13	.135	-5	1	3	-3	1.2

● **BOB BLACK**   Black, Robert Benjamin   b: 12/10/1862, Cincinnati, Ohio   d: 3/21/33, Sioux City, Iowa   5'5.5", 155 lbs.   Deb: 8/19/1884   ♦

YEAR	TM/L	W	L	PCT	G	GS	CG	SH	SV	IP	H	HR	BB	SO	RAT	ERA	ERA+	OAV	OOB	BH	AVG	PB	PR	/A	PD	TPI
1884	KC-U	4	9	.308	16	15	13	0	0	123	127	1	17	93	10.5	3.22	69	.249	.273	36	.247	1	-11	-13	2	-0.8

● **BUD BLACK**   Black, William Carroll   b: 7/9/32, St.Louis, Mo.   BR/TR, 6'3", 197 lbs.   Deb: 9/13/52

YEAR	TM/L	W	L	PCT	G	GS	CG	SH	SV	IP	H	HR	BB	SO	RAT	ERA	ERA+	OAV	OOB	BH	AVG	PB	PR	/A	PD	TPI
1952	Det-A	0	1	.000	2	2	0	0	0	8	14	0	5	0	21.4	10.13	38	.389	.463	0	.000	-0	-6	-6	-0	-0.6
1955	Det-A	1	1	.500	3	2	1	1	0	14	12	0	1	8	14.1	1.29	299	.231	.355	1	.250	-0	4	4	0	0.6
1956	Det-A	1	1	.500	5	1	0	0	0	10	10	2	5	7	13.5	3.60	114	.256	.341	0	.000	-0	1	1	0	0.1
Total	3	2	3	.400	10	5	1	1	0	32	36	2	18	15	15.2	4.22	93	.283	.381	1	.111	-1	-1	-1	0	0.1

● **CHARLIE BLACKBURN**   Blackburn, Foster Edwin   b: 1/6/1895, Chicago, Ill.   d: 3/9/84, New Port Richey, Fla.   BR/TR, 6'1", 165 lbs.   Deb: 4/17/15

YEAR	TM/L	W	L	PCT	G	GS	CG	SH	SV	IP	H	HR	BB	SO	RAT	ERA	ERA+	OAV	OOB	BH	AVG	PB	PR	/A	PD	TPI
1915	KC-F	0	1	1.000	7	2	0	0	0	15²	19	2	13	7	18.4	8.62	31	.306	.427	0	.000	-0	-10	-10	0	-0.6
1921	Chi-A	0	0	—	1	0	0	0	0	1	0	0	1	0	9.0	0.00	—	.000	.333	0	—	0	-0	-0	-0	0.0
Total	2	0	1	1.000	8	2	0	0	0	16²	19	2	14	7	17.8	8.10	34	.297	.423	0	.000	-0	-10	-10	0	-0.6

● **GEORGE BLACKBURN**   Blackburn, George W. "Smiling George"   b: 9/21/1871, Ozark, Mo.   TR , 5'11", 184 lbs.   Deb: 7/6/1897

YEAR	TM/L	W	L	PCT	G	GS	CG	SH	SV	IP	H	HR	BB	SO	RAT	ERA	ERA+	OAV	OOB	BH	AVG	PB	PR	/A	PD	TPI
1897	Bal-N	2	2	.500	5	4	3	0	0	33	34	2	12	1	12.8	6.82	61	.264	.331	1	.077	-2	-9	-10	-0	-1.0

● **JIM BLACKBURN**   Blackburn, James Ray "Bones"   b: 6/19/24, Warsaw, Ky.   d: 10/26/69, Cincinnati, Ohio   BR/TR, 6'4", 175 lbs.   Deb: 7/24/48

YEAR	TM/L	W	L	PCT	G	GS	CG	SH	SV	IP	H	HR	BB	SO	RAT	ERA	ERA+	OAV	OOB	BH	AVG	PB	PR	/A	PD	TPI
1948	Cin-N	0	2	.000	16	0	0	0	0	32¹	38	1	14	10	14.5	4.18	94	.302	.371	0	.000	-0	-1	-1	-0	-0.1
1951	Cin-N	0	0	—	2	0	0	0	0	3²	8	0	1	1	29.5	17.18	24	.444	.545	0	—	0	-5	-5	0	0.0
Total	2	0	2	.000	18	0	0	0	0	36	46	1	15	11	16.0	5.50	71	.319	.395	0	.000	-0	-6	-6	-0	-0.1

● **RON BLACKBURN**   Blackburn, Ronald Hamilton   b: 4/23/35, Mt.Airy, N.C.   BR/TR, 6'0.5", 160 lbs.   Deb: 4/15/58

YEAR	TM/L	W	L	PCT	G	GS	CG	SH	SV	IP	H	HR	BB	SO	RAT	ERA	ERA+	OAV	OOB	BH	AVG	PB	PR	/A	PD	TPI
1958	Pit-N	2	1	.667	38	6	0	0	3	63²	61	7	27	31	12.9	3.39	114	.261	.345	2	.286	1	4	3	1	0.4
1959	Pit-N	1	1	.500	26	6	0	0	1	44¹	50	5	15	19	13.6	3.65	106	.286	.349	1	.200	1	1	1	-1	0.1
Total	2	3	2	.600	64	6	0	0	4	108	111	12	42	50	13.2	3.50	110	.271	.346	3	.250	2	5	4	0	0.5

● **LENA BLACKBURNE**   Blackburne, Russell Aubrey "Slats"   b: 10/23/1886, Clifton Heights, Pa.   d: 2/29/68, Riverside, N.J.   BR/TR, 5'11", 160 lbs.   Deb: 4/14/10   MC♦

YEAR	TM/L	W	L	PCT	G	GS	CG	SH	SV	IP	H	HR	BB	SO	RAT	ERA	ERA+	OAV	OOB	BH	AVG	PB	PR	/A	PD	TPI
1929	Chi-A	0	0	—	1	0	0	0	0	1	0	0	2	0	27.0	0.00	—	1.000	.000	0	—	0	0	0	0	0.0

● **EWELL BLACKWELL**   Blackwell, Ewell "The Whip"   b: 10/23/22, Fresno, Cal.   d: 10/29/96, Hendersonville, N.C.   BR/TR, 6'6", 195 lbs.   Deb: 4/21/42

YEAR	TM/L	W	L	PCT	G	GS	CG	SH	SV	IP	H	HR	BB	SO	RAT	ERA	ERA+	OAV	OOB	BH	AVG	PB	PR	/A	PD	TPI
1942	Cin-N	0	0	—	2	0	0	0	0	3	3	0	3	1	18.0	6.00	55	.231	.375	0	.000	-0	-1	-1	0	0.0

YEAR	TM/L	W	L	PCT	G	GS	CG	SH	SV	IP	H	HR	BB	SO	RAT	ERA	ERA+	OAV	OOB	BH	AVG	PB	PR	/A	PD	TPI
1946	Cin-N★	9	13	.409	33	25	10	**5**	0	194¹	160	1	79	100	11.3	2.45	136	.226	.307	6	.107	-3	21	19	4	2.3
1947	Cin-N★	**22**	8	.733	33	33	**23**	6	0	273	227	10	95	**193**	10.7	2.47	166	.234	.304	13	.123	-5	48	49	5	**5.2**
1948	Cin-N★	7	9	.438	22	20	4	1	1	138²	134	12	52	114	12.3	4.54	86	.251	.323	11	.229	1	-9	-10	4	-0.5
1949	Cin-N★	5	5	.500	30	4	0	0	1	76²	80	7	34	55	13.7	4.23	99	.271	.352	4	.211	-0	-2	-0	1	0.1
1950	Cin-N★	17	15	.531	40	32	18	1	4	261	203	12	112	188	11.3	2.97	143	**.210**	.301	13	.146	-2	34	**37**	2	4.3
1951	Cin-N★	16	15	.516	38	32	11	2	2	232²	204	16	97	120	12.0	3.44	118	.233	.315	24	.293	7	13	16	0	2.9
1952	Cin-N	3	12	.200	23	17	3	0	0	102	107	6	60	48	15.2	5.38	70	.275	.379	5	.156	-0	-19	-18	-0	-2.4
	*NY-A	1	0	1.000	5	2	0	0	1	16	12	0	12	7	13.5	0.56	591	.203	.338	1	.200	-0	6	5	-0	0.4
1953	NY-A	2	0	1.000	8	4	0	0	1	19²	17	2	13	11	14.2	3.66	101	.233	.356	0	.000	-1	1	0	-0	-0.1
1955	KC-A	0	1	.000	2	0	0	0	0	4	3	1	5	2	20.3	6.75	62	.200	.500	0	—	0	-1	-1	-0	-0.3
Total	10	82	78	.512	236	169	69	15	10	1321	1150	67	562	839	12.0	3.30	120	.235	.319	77	.174	-3	91	96	16	11.9

● **GEORGE BLAEHOLDER**   Blaeholder, George Franklin b: 1/26/04, Orange, Cal. d: 12/29/47, Garden Grove, Cal. BR/TR, 5'11", 175 lbs. Deb: 4/20/25

YEAR	TM/L	W	L	PCT	G	GS	CG	SH	SV	IP	H	HR	BB	SO	RAT	ERA	ERA+	OAV	OOB	BH	AVG	PB	PR	/A	PD	TPI
1925	StL-A	0	0	—	2	0	0	0	0	2	6	3	1	1	36.0	31.50	15	.600	.667	0	—	-0	-6	-6	-0	0.0
1927	StL-A	0	1	.000	1	1	1	0	0	9	8	1	4	2	13.0	5.00	87	.258	.361	1	.333	-1	-1	-0	0	0.0
1928	StL-A	10	15	.400	38	26	9	1	3	214¹	235	23	52	87	12.1	4.37	96	.280	.324	15	.211	2	-8	-4	5	0.2
1929	StL-A	14	15	.483	42	24	13	**4**	2	222	237	18	61	72	12.1	4.18	106	.275	.323	9	.122	-4	2	6	6	0.9
1930	StL-A	11	13	.458	37	23	10	1	4	191¹	235	20	46	70	13.3	4.61	106	.280	.343	12	.185	-1	1	6	-1	0.4
1931	StL-A	11	15	.423	35	32	13	1	0	226³	280	15	56	79	13.4	4.53	102	.295	.335	11	.143	-3	-4	3	3	0.3
1932	StL-A	14	14	.500	42	36	16	1	0	258¹	304	19	76	80	13.3	4.70	103	.290	.340	12	.136	-4	-6	4	0	0.1
1933	StL-A	15	19	.441	38	36	14	3	0	255²	283	24	69	63	12.4	4.72	99	.280	.326	14	.182	-1	-12	-2	3	0.0
1934	StL-A	14	18	.438	39	33	14	1	0	234³	276	16	68	66	13.2	4.22	118	.296	.343	7	.093	-5	7	20	0	1.9
1935	StL-A	1	1	.500	6	2	0	0	0	17²	25	3	6	2	15.8	7.13	67	.342	.392	0	.000	-1	-5	-5	1	-0.4
	Phi-N	6	10	.375	23	22	10	1	0	149	173	10	49	22	13.4	3.99	114	.289	.343	2	.043	-6	8	9	2	0.4
	Yr	7	11	.389	29	24	10	1	0	166²	198	13	55	22	13.7	4.32	106	.295	.348	2	.040	-7	3	5	2	0.0
1936	Cle-A	8	4	.667	35	16	6	1	0	134¹	158	21	47	30	13.9	5.09	99	.295	.356	6	.130	-3	-1	-1	2	-0.2
Total	11	104	125	.454	338	251	106	14	12	1914¹	2220	173	535	572	13.0	4.54	103	.290	.337	89	.142	-25	-26	30	20	3.6

● **DENNIS BLAIR**   Blair, Dennis Herman b: 6/5/54, Middletown, Ohio BR/TR, 6'5", 182 lbs. Deb: 5/26/74

YEAR	TM/L	W	L	PCT	G	GS	CG	SH	SV	IP	H	HR	BB	SO	RAT	ERA	ERA+	OAV	OOB	BH	AVG	PB	PR	/A	PD	TPI
1974	Mon-N	11	7	.611	22	22	4	1	0	146	113	7	76	76	11.7	3.27	117	.210	.308	6	.118	-2	6	9	3	1.2
1975	Mon-N	8	15	.348	30	27	4	1	0	163¹	150	14	106	82	14.3	3.80	101	.251	.366	7	.143	-1	-3	-0	-1	-0.2
1976	Mon-N	0	2	.000	5	4	0	0	0	15²	21	1	11	9	19.5	4.02	92	.300	.410	0	.000	-0	-1	-1	-0	-0.1
1980	SD-N	0	1	.000	5	1	0	0	0	14	18	3	3	11	13.5	6.43	53	.310	.344	1	.200	0	-4	-5	-1	-0.3
Total	4	19	25	.432	62	54	6	1	0	339	302	25	192	178	13.4	3.69	103	.239	.344	14	.128	-4	-3	4	1	0.6

● **WILLIE BLAIR**   Blair, William Allen b: 12/18/65, Paintsville, Ky. BR/TR, 6'1", 185 lbs. Deb: 4/11/90

YEAR	TM/L	W	L	PCT	G	GS	CG	SH	SV	IP	H	HR	BB	SO	RAT	ERA	ERA+	OAV	OOB	BH	AVG	PB	PR	/A	PD	TPI
1990	Tor-A	3	5	.375	27	6	0	0	0	68²	66	4	28	43	12.5	4.06	97	.250	.324	0	—	0	-1	-1	-1	-0.3
1991	Cle-A	2	3	.400	11	5	0	0	0	36	58	7	10	13	17.3	6.75	62	.377	.418	0	—	0	-11	-10	-0	-1.3
1992	Hou-N	5	7	.417	29	8	0	0	0	78²	74	5	25	48	11.6	4.00	84	.249	.312	1	.059	-1	-4	-6	-1	-1.0
1993	Col-N	6	10	.375	46	18	1	0	0	146	184	20	42	84	14.1	4.75	100	.306	.354	4	.111	-2	-11	0	-4	-0.2
1994	Col-N	0	5	.000	47	1	0	0	3	77²	98	9	39	68	16.3	5.79	86	.308	.391	0	.000	-1	-14	-7	-1	-0.6
1995	SD-N	7	5	.583	40	12	0	0	0	114	112	11	45	83	12.6	4.34	93	.262	.335	0	.000	-0	-2	-4	-1	-0.7
1996	*SD-N	2	6	.250	60	0	0	0	1	88	80	13	29	67	11.9	4.60	87	.240	.314	0	.000	-0	-4	-6	-2	-0.7
Total	7	25	41	.379	260	50	1	0	4	609	672	69	218	406	13.4	4.73	89	.280	.345	5	.058	-6	-47	-34	-6	-4.8

● **BILL BLAIR**   Blair, William Ellsworth b: 9/17/1863, Pittsburgh, Pa. d: 2/22/1890, Pittsburgh, Pa. BL/TL, 5'8.5", 172 lbs. Deb: 7/19/1888

YEAR	TM/L	W	L	PCT	G	GS	CG	SH	SV	IP	H	HR	BB	SO	RAT	ERA	ERA+	OAV	OOB	BH	AVG	PB	PR	/A	PD	TPI
1888	Phi-a	1	3	.250	4	4	3	0	0	31	29	0	8	16	11.0	2.61	114	.238	.290	4	.308	1	2	1	0	0.3

● **DICK BLAISDELL**   Blaisdell, Howard Carleton b: 6/18/1862, Bradford, Mass. d: 8/20/1886, Malden, Mass. Deb: 7/9/1884

YEAR	TM/L	W	L	PCT	G	GS	CG	SH	SV	IP	H	HR	BB	SO	RAT	ERA	ERA+	OAV	OOB	BH	AVG	PB	PR	/A	PD	TPI
1884	KC-U	0	3	.000	3	3	3	0	0	26	49	0	4	8	18.3	8.65	26	.377	.396	5	.313	0	-18	-19	-1	-1.4

● **ED BLAKE**   Blake, Edward James b: 12/23/25, E.St.Louis, Ill. BR/TR, 5'11", 175 lbs. Deb: 5/1/51

YEAR	TM/L	W	L	PCT	G	GS	CG	SH	SV	IP	H	HR	BB	SO	RAT	ERA	ERA+	OAV	OOB	BH	AVG	PB	PR	/A	PD	TPI
1951	Cin-N	0	0	—	3	0	0	0	0	4	10	3	1	1	24.8	11.25	36	.476	.500	0	—	0	-3	-3	0	0.0
1952	Cin-N	0	0	—	2	0	0	0	0	3	3	0	0	0	9.0	0.00	—	.250	.250	0	—	0	1	1	0	0.0
1953	Cin-N	0	0	—	1	0	0	0	0	0	1	0	1	0	—	∞	—	1.000	1.000	0	—	0	-2	-2	-0	-0.2
1957	KC-A	0	0	—	2	0	0	0	0	1²	1	1	2	0	16.2	5.40	73	.167	.375	0	—	0	-0	-0	-0	0.0
Total	4	0	0	—	8	0	0	0	0	8²	15	4	4	1	19.7	8.31	48	.375	.432	0	—	0	-4	-4	1	-0.2

● **SHERIFF BLAKE**   Blake, John Frederick b: 9/17/1899, Ansted, W.Va. d: 10/31/82, Beckley, W.Va. BB/TR, 6', 180 lbs. Deb: 6/29/20

YEAR	TM/L	W	L	PCT	G	GS	CG	SH	SV	IP	H	HR	BB	SO	RAT	ERA	ERA+	OAV	OOB	BH	AVG	PB	PR	/A	PD	TPI
1920	Pit-N	0	0	—	6	0	0	0	0	13¹	21	0	6	7	18.9	8.10	40	.368	.438	1	.250	-0	-7	-7	0	0.0
1924	Chi-N	6	6	.500	29	11	4	0	1	106¹	123	3	44	42	14.3	4.57	85	.299	.370	8	.290	1	-8	-8	1	-0.6
1925	Chi-N	10	18	.357	36	31	14	0	2	231¹	260	17	114	93	14.7	4.86	89	.287	.370	12	.152	-4	-15	-14	0	-1.8
1926	Chi-N	11	12	.478	39	27	11	4	1	197²	204	7	92	95	13.8	3.60	117	.272	.366	14	.215	-1	5	5	2	0.7
1927	Chi-N	13	14	.481	32	27	13	2	0	224³	238	5	82	64	13.0	3.29	117	.282	.348	16	.193	-2	16	14	3	1.6
1928	Chi-N	17	11	.607	34	29	16	**4**	1	240²	209	4	101	78	11.7	2.47	156	.240	.321	19	.216	0	41	37	-2	3.8
1929	*Chi-N	14	13	.519	35	30	13	1	1	218¹	244	8	103	70	14.4	4.29	108	.291	.370	14	.173	-2	10	8	-2	0.5
1930	Chi-N	10	14	.417	34	24	7	0	0	186²	213	14	99	80	15.2	4.82	101	.291	.378	15	.227	-1	3	1	3	0.0
1931	Chi-N	0	4	.000	16	5	0	0	0	50	64	4	26	29	16.4	5.22	74	.312	.392	8	.500	3	-8	-7	1	-0.2
	Phi-N	4	5	.444	14	9	1	0	0	71	90	2	35	31	16.2	5.58	76	.305	.384	6	.240	-1	-13	-11	2	-0.9
	Yr	4	9	.308	30	14	1	0	0	121	154	6	61	60	16.2	5.43	75	.307	.386	14	.341	3	-21	-18	3	-1.1
1937	StL-A	2	2	.500	15	1	0	0	1	36²	55	5	20	12	18.4	7.61	63	.350	.424	1	.100	-1	-12	-11	0	-1.1
	StL-A	0	3	.000	14	2	2	0	0	43²	71	4	18	20	13.0	3.71	107	.335	.342	3	.300	0	1	1	0	0.2
Total	10	87	102	.460	304	196	81	11	8	1620	1766	68	740	621	14.1	4.13	101	.284	.363	118	.211	-6	12	9	9	2.5

● **AL BLANCHE**   Blanche, Prosby Albert (b: Prosper Belangio) b: 9/21/09, Somerville, Mass. BR/TR, 6', 178 lbs. Deb: 8/23/35

YEAR	TM/L	W	L	PCT	G	GS	CG	SH	SV	IP	H	HR	BB	SO	RAT	ERA	ERA+	OAV	OOB	BH	AVG	PB	PR	/A	PD	TPI
1935	Bos-N	0	0	—	6	0	0	0	0	17¹	14	0	5	4	9.9	1.56	243	.230	.288	1	.167	-0	5	4	0	0.0
1936	Bos-N	0	1	.000	11	0	0	0	0	16	20	1	8	4	16.3	6.19	62	.303	.387	1	.250	-0	-4	-4	1	-0.2
Total	2	0	1	.000	17	0	0	0	0	33¹	34	1	13	8	13.0	3.78	101	.268	.340	2	.200	-0	1	0	1	-0.2

● **GIL BLANCO**   Blanco, Gilbert Henry b: 12/15/45, Phoenix, Ariz. BL/TL, 6'5", 205 lbs. Deb: 4/24/65

YEAR	TM/L	W	L	PCT	G	GS	CG	SH	SV	IP	H	HR	BB	SO	RAT	ERA	ERA+	OAV	OOB	BH	AVG	PB	PR	/A	PD	TPI
1965	NY-A	1	1	.500	17	1	0	0	0	20¹	16	1	12	14	12.8	3.98	85	.232	.354	0	—	0	-1	-1	-1	-0.2
1966	KC-A	2	4	.333	11	8	0	0	0	38¹	31	3	36	21	16.7	4.70	72	.237	.415	2	.167	-0	-5	-6	0	-0.8
Total	2	3	5	.375	28	9	0	0	0	58²	47	4	48	35	15.3	4.45	76	.235	.395	2	.167	-0	-7	-7	-0	-1.0

● **FRED BLANDING**   Blanding, Frederick James "Fritz" b: 2/8/1888, Redlands, Cal. d: 7/16/50, Salem, Va. BR/TR, 6', 185 lbs. Deb: 9/15/10

YEAR	TM/L	W	L	PCT	G	GS	CG	SH	SV	IP	H	HR	BB	SO	RAT	ERA	ERA+	OAV	OOB	BH	AVG	PB	PR	/A	PD	TPI
1910	Cle-A	2	2	.500	6	5	4	0	0	45¹	42	0	12	25	11.7	2.78	93	.254	.319	2	.111	-0	1	1	-1	-0.3
1911	Cle-A	7	11	.389	29	16	11	0	2	176	190	5	60	80	13.1	3.68	93	.283	.347	17	.262	2	-7	-5	0	-0.3
1912	Cle-A	18	14	.563	39	31	23	1	1	262	259	4	79	75	11.7	2.92	117	.267	.324	21	.226	1	12	14	0	1.8
1913	Cle-A	15	10	.600	41	22	14	3	0	215	234	6	73	63	12.9	2.55	119	.282	.341	21	.244	4	9	12	-2	1.5
1914	Cle-A	3	9	.250	29	12	5	0	1	116	133	0	54	35	14.6	3.96	91	.301	.378	4	.103	-2	-16	-14	1	-1.5
Total	5	45	46	.495	144	86	57	5	4	814¹	859	15	277	278	12.7	3.13	102	.279	.341	65	.216	4	-3	6	-2	1.2

● **FRED BLANK**   Blank, Frederick August b: 6/18/1874, DeSoto, Mo. d: 2/5/36, St.Louis, Mo. BL/TL, 6'0.5", 175 lbs. Deb: 6/20/1894

YEAR	TM/L	W	L	PCT	G	GS	CG	SH	SV	IP	H	HR	BB	SO	RAT	ERA	ERA+	OAV	OOB	BH	AVG	PB	PR	/A	PD	TPI
1894	Cin-N	0	1	.000	1	1	1	0	0	8	5	0	9	1	15.8	4.50	124	.179	.378	0	.000	-1	1	1	1	0.1

● **HOMER BLANKENSHIP**   Blankenship, Homer "Si" b: 8/4/02, Bonham, Tex. d: 6/22/74, Longview, Tex. BR/TR, 6', 185 lbs. Deb: 9/6/22 F

YEAR	TM/L	W	L	PCT	G	GS	CG	SH	SV	IP	H	HR	BB	SO	RAT	ERA	ERA+	OAV	OOB	BH	AVG	PB	PR	/A	PD	TPI
1922	Chi-A	0	0	—	4	0	0	0	0	13	21	1	5	3	18.0	4.85	84	.389	.441	0	.000	-0	-1	-1	0	-0.1
1923	Chi-A	1	1	.500	4	0	0	0	0	5	9	0	1	1	18.0	3.60	110	.429	.455	0	—	0	0	0	0	0.1
1928	Pit-N	0	2	.000	5	2	0	0	0	21²	27	1	9	6	15.0	5.82	70	.321	.387	3	.375	1	-4	-4	1	-0.2
Total	3	1	3	.250	13	2	0	0	0	39²	57	2	15	10	16.3	5.22	78	.358	.414	3	.250	-0	-5	-5	1	-0.2

YEAR TM/L	W	L	PCT	G	GS	CG	SH	SV	IP	H	HR	BB	SO	RAT	ERA	ERA+	OAV	OOB	BH	AVG	PB	PR	/A	PD	TPI
● **KEVIN BLANKENSHIP** Blankenship, Kevin De Wayne b: 1/26/63, Anaheim, Cal. BR/TR, 6′, 180 lbs. Deb: 9/20/88																									
1988 Atl-N	0	1	.000	2	2	0	0	0	10²	7	0	7	5	12.7	3.38	109	.194	.341	0	.000	-0	0	0	-0	0.0
Chi-N	1	0	1.000	1	1	0	0	0	5	7	2	1	4	14.4	7.20	50	.318	.348	0	.000	-0	-2	-2	-0	-0.4
Yr	1	1	.500	3	3	0	0	0	15²	14	2	8	9	12.6	4.60	79	.237	.328	0	.000	-1	-2	-2	-1	-0.4
1989 Chi-N	0	0	—	2	0	0	0	0	5¹	4	0	2	2	10.1	1.69	223	.200	.273	0	.000	-0	1	1	-0	0.0
1990 Chi-N	0	2	.000	3	2	0	0	0	12¹	13	1	6	5	13.9	5.84	70	.265	.345	0	.000	-0	-3	-2	-0	-0.4
Total 3	1	3	.250	8	5	0	0	0	33¹	31	3	16	16	13.0	4.59	83	.244	.333	0	.000	-1	-4	-3	-1	-0.8
● **TED BLANKENSHIP** Blankenship, Theodore b: 5/10/01, Bonham, Tex. d: 1/14/45, Atoka, Okla. BR/TR, 6′1″, 170 lbs. Deb: 7/2/22 F																									
1922 Chi-A	8	10	.444	24	15	7	0	1	127²	124	4	47	42	12.2	3.81	107	.266	.335	7	.171	-1	3	4	0	0.4
1923 Chi-A	9	14	.391	44	23	9	1	0	204²	219	8	100	57	14.2	4.35	91	.287	.372	16	.211	2	-8	-9	-1	-0.8
1924 Chi-A	7	6	.538	25	11	7	0	1	129¹	167	1	38	36	14.3	5.01	82	.317	.364	15	.326	6	-11	-13	-2	-0.8
1925 Chi-A	17	8	.680	40	23	16	3	1	232	218	11	69	81	11.1	3.03	137	.253	.308	18	.205	2	35	29	-4	2.5
1926 Chi-A	13	10	.565	29	26	15	1	1	209²	217	13	65	66	12.2	3.61	107	.273	.328	10	.132	-2	10	6	-2	0.1
1927 Chi-A	12	17	.414	37	34	11	3	0	236²	280	14	74	51	13.5	5.06	80	.299	.352	15	.188	3	-24	-27	-3	-2.6
1928 Chi-A	9	11	.450	27	22	8	0	0	158	186	9	80	36	15.3	4.61	88	.306	.388	-2	.169	-2	-10	-10	-2	-1.4
1929 Chi-A	0	2	.000	8	1	0	0	0	18¹	28	3	9	7	18.2	8.84	48	.359	.425	1	.250	-1	-9	-9	-1	-0.9
1930 Chi-A	2	1	.667	7	1	0	0	0	14²	23	0	7	2	19.0	9.20	50	.371	.443	1	.200	-0	-7	-7	-1	-1.2
Total 9	77	79	.494	241	156	73	8	4	1330²	1462	63	489	378	13.3	4.55	94	.287	.351	93	.196	7	-22	-36	-15	-4.7
● **CY BLANTON** Blanton, Darrell Elijah b: 7/6/08, Waurika, Okla. d: 9/13/45, Norman, Okla. BL/TR, 5′11.5″, 180 lbs. Deb: 9/23/34																									
1934 Pit-N	0	1	.000	1	1	0	0	0	8	5	1	4	5	11.3	3.38	122	.161	.278	0	.000	0	1	1	0	0.1
1935 Pit-N	18	13	.581	35	31	23	**4**	1	254¹	220	3	55	142	**9.8**	2.58	159	.229	.272	13	.134	-4	41	43	2	4.7
1936 Pit-N	13	15	.464	44	32	15	**4**	3	235²	235	9	55	127	11.2	3.51	115	.257	.301	13	.155	-3	13	14	1	1.3
1937 Pit-N★	14	12	.538	34	34	14	4	0	242²	250	13	76	143	12.3	3.30	117	.266	.324	14	.165	-0	17	15	-0	1.4
1938 Pit-N	11	7	.611	29	26	10	1	0	172²	190	13	46	80	12.4	3.70	103	.281	.329	13	.203	-1	2	2	2	0.3
1939 Pit-N	2	3	.400	10	6	1	0	0	42	45	4	10	11	11.8	4.29	90	.266	.307	4	.286	1	-2	-2	-0	-0.2
1940 Phi-N	4	3	.571	13	10	5	0	0	77	82	7	21	24	12.2	4.32	90	.272	.322	2	.083	-1	-4	-4	0	-0.4
1941 Phi-N☆	6	13	.316	28	25	7	1	0	163²	186	11	57	64	13.5	4.51	82	.284	.344	6	.118	-2	-16	-15	-3	-2.0
1942 Phi-N	0	4	.000	6	3	0	0	0	22¹	30	3	13	15	17.7	5.64	59	.345	.436	1	.125	-0	-6	-6	0	-1.0
Total 9	68	71	.489	202	168	75	14	4	1218¹	1243	64	337	611	11.8	3.55	110	.262	.314	66	.154	-11	45	49	2	4.2
● **WADE BLASINGAME** Blasingame, Wade Allen b: 11/22/43, Deming, N.Mex. BL/TL, 6′1″, 185 lbs. Deb: 9/17/63																									
1963 Mil-N	0	0	—	2	0	0	0	0	3	7	0	2	6	27.0	12.00	27	.467	.529	0	—	0	-3	-3	0	0.0
1964 Mil-N	9	5	.643	28	13	3	1	2	116²	113	15	54	70	12.7	4.24	83	.257	.334	7	.175	3	-9	-9	0	-0.7
1965 Mil-N	16	10	.615	38	36	10	1	1	224²	200	17	116	117	12.9	3.77	94	.244	.341	15	.185	3	-6	-6	1	-0.2
1966 Atl-N	3	7	.300	16	12	0	0	0	67²	71	5	25	34	13.0	5.32	68	.272	.340	5	.217	1	-13	-13	-0	-1.6
1967 Atl-N	1	0	1.000	10	4	0	0	0	25¹	27	1	21	20	17.4	4.62	72	.287	.422	1	.143	0	-4	-4	0	-2.7
Hou-N	4	7	.364	15	14	0	0	0	77	91	9	27	46	14.0	5.96	56	.298	.359	4	.182	2	-22	-23	-0	-2.7
Yr	5	7	.417	25	18	0	0	0	102²	118	10	48	66	14.8	5.63	59	.295	.373	5	.172	2	-26	-26	0	-2.7
1968 Hou-N	1	2	.333	22	2	0	0	1	36	45	3	10	22	13.8	4.75	62	.308	.353	0	.000	0	-7	-7	1	-0.5
1969 Hou-N	0	5	.000	26	5	0	0	1	52	66	4	33	33	17.5	5.37	66	.306	.402	0	.000	-0	-10	-10	0	-1.1
1970 Hou-N	3	3	.500	13	13	1	0	0	77²	76	4	23	55	11.7	3.48	112	.261	.320	2	.083	-0	5	3	0	0.3
1971 Hou-N	9	11	.450	30	28	3	0	0	158¹	177	11	45	93	13.4	4.60	73	.285	.346	10	.204	4	-20	-22	1	-2.0
1972 Hou-N	0	0	—	10	0	0	0	0	8¹	4	1	8	9	15.1	8.64	39	.148	.378	0	—	0	-5	-5	0	0.0
NY-A	0	1	.000	12	1	0	0	0	17	14	5	11	7	13.8	4.24	70	.250	.382	0	.000	0	-2	-2	1	0.0
Total 10	46	51	.474	222	128	16	2	5	863²	891	75	372	512	13.5	4.52	77	.271	.350	44	.166	14	-96	-101	4	-8.5
● **STEVE BLASS** Blass, Stephen Robert b: 4/18/42, Canaan, Conn. BR/TR, 6′, 165 lbs. Deb: 5/10/64																									
1964 Pit-N	5	8	.385	24	13	3	1	0	104²	107	9	45	67	13.2	4.04	87	.266	.341	2	.067	-1	-6	-6	0	-0.8
1966 Pit-N	11	7	.611	34	25	1	0	0	155²	173	12	46	76	12.8	3.87	92	.284	.336	12	.231	1	-5	-5	-3	-0.7
1967 Pit-N	6	8	.429	32	16	2	0	0	126²	126	12	47	72	12.4	3.55	95	.261	.329	5	.128	-1	-3	-3	0	-0.3
1968 Pit-N	18	6	**.750**	33	31	12	7	0	220¹	191	13	57	132	10.3	2.12	138	.234	.288	11	.138	-1	21	20	-1	2.1
1969 Pit-N	16	10	.615	38	32	9	0	2	210	207	21	86	147	12.8	4.46	78	.258	.335	21	.250	6	-20	-23	3	-1.8
1970 Pit-N	10	12	.455	31	31	6	1	0	196²	187	14	73	120	12.1	3.52	111	.254	.326	8	.114	-2	11	8	0	0.6
1971 *Pit-N	15	8	.652	33	33	12	**5**	0	240	226	16	68	136	11.1	2.85	119	.249	.303	10	.120	-3	16	14	1	1.1
1972 *Pit-N★	19	8	.704	32	32	11	2	0	249²	227	16	84	117	11.4	2.49	134	.246	.311	15	.183	1	27	23	2	2.9
1973 Pit-N	3	9	.250	23	18	1	0	0	88²	109	11	84	27	20.8	9.85	36	.313	.462	10	.417	4	-61	-62	1	-6.3
1974 Pit-N	0	0	—	1	1	0	0	0	5	7	2	7	2	21.6	9.00	38	.238	.429	0	.000	-0	-3	-3	0	0.0
Total 10	103	76	.575	282	231	57	16	2	1597¹	1558	128	597	896	12.4	3.63	94	.258	.328	94	.172	4	-21	-37	3	-3.2
● **STEVE BLATERIC** Blateric, Stephen Lawrence b: 3/20/44, Denver, Colo. BR/TR, 6′3″, 200 lbs. Deb: 9/17/71																									
1971 Cin-N	0	0	—	2	0	0	0	0	2²	5	2	0	4	20.3	13.50	25	.385	.429	0	—	0	-3	-3	0	0.0
1972 NY-A	0	0	—	1	0	0	0	0	4	2	0	0	4	4.5	0.00	—	.143	.143	0	.000	-0	1	1	0	0.0
1975 Cal-A	0	0	—	2	0	0	0	0	4¹	9	0	1	5	20.8	6.23	57	.429	.455	0	—	0	-1	-1	-0	0.4
Total 3	0	0	—	5	0	0	0	0	11	16	2	1	13	14.7	5.73	57	.333	.360	0	.000	-0	-3	-3	0	0.4
● **HENRY BLAUVELT** Blauvelt, Henry Russell b: 4/8/1873, Nyack, N.Y. d: 12/28/26, Portland, Ore. Deb: 6/22/1890																									
1890 Roc-a	0	0	—	2	0	0	0	0	12¹	19	0	8	5	19.7	10.22	35	.339	.422	3	.500	1	-9	-9	0	0.1
● **GARY BLAYLOCK** Blaylock, Gary Nelson b: 10/11/31, Clarkton, Mo. BR/TR, 6′, 196 lbs. Deb: 4/10/59 C																									
1959 StL-N	4	5	.444	26	12	3	0	0	100	117	14	43	61	14.6	5.13	83	.298	.371	4	.118	0	-13	-10	1	-0.7
NY-A	0	1	.000	15	1	0	0	0	25²	30	0	15	20	16.1	3.51	104	.306	.404	1	.500	1	1	0	-0	0.0
Total 1	4	6	.400	41	13	3	0	0	125²	147	14	58	81	14.9	4.80	86	.300	.377	5	.139	1	-12	-10	0	-0.7
● **BOB BLAYLOCK** Blaylock, Robert Edward b: 6/28/35, Chattanooga, Okla BR/TR, 6′1″, 185 lbs. Deb: 7/22/56																									
1956 StL-N	1	6	.143	14	6	0	0	0	41	45	7	24	39	15.1	6.37	59	.276	.369	1	.091	-1	-12	-12	0	-1.8
1959 StL-N	0	1	.000	3	1	0	0	0	9	8	1	3	3	11.0	4.00	106	.229	.289	0	.000	-0	-0	-0	0	0.0
Total 2	1	7	.125	17	7	0	0	0	50	53	8	27	42	14.4	5.94	65	.268	.356	1	.083	-1	-12	-12	0	-1.8
● **RON BLAZIER** Blazier, Ronald Patrick b: 7/30/71, Altoona, Pa. BR/TR, 6′6″, 215 lbs. Deb: 5/31/96																									
1996 Phi-N	3	1	.750	27	0	0	0	0	38¹	49	6	10	25	13.9	5.87	74	.310	.351	1	1.000	0	-7	-6	-1	-0.6
● **RAY BLEMKER** Blemker, Raymond b: 8/9/37, Huntingburg, Ind. d: 2/15/94, Evansville, Ind BR/TL, 5′11″, 190 lbs. Deb: 7/3/60																									
1960 KC-A	0	0	—	1	0	0	0	0	1²	3	1	2	0	32.4	27.00	15	.375	.545	0	—	0	-4	-4	-0	0.0
● **CLARENCE BLETHEN** Blethen, Clarence Waldo "Climax" b: 7/11/1893, Dover-Foxcroft, Maine d: 4/11/73, Frederick, Md. BL/TR, 5′11″, 165 lbs. Deb: 9/17/23																									
1923 Bos-A	0	0	—	5	0	0	0	0	17²	29	0	7	2	18.3	7.13	58	.382	.434	0	.000	-1	-6	-6	0	-0.2
1929 Bro-N	0	0	—	2	0	0	0	0	2	4	0	3	0	31.5	9.00	51	.444	.583	0	—	0	-1	-1	0	0.0
Total 2	0	0	—	7	0	0	0	0	19²	33	0	10	2	19.7	7.32	57	.388	.453	0	.000	-1	-7	-7	-1	-0.2
● **BOB BLEWETT** Blewett, Robert Lawrence b: 6/28/1877, Fond Du Lac, Wis. d: 3/17/58, Sedro Woolley, Wash. BL/TL, 5′11″, 170 lbs. Deb: 6/17/02																									
1902 NY-N	0	2	.000	5	3	2	0	0	28	39	0	7	8	15.1	4.82	58	.328	.370	0	.000	-1	-6	-6	-1	-0.6
● **ELMER BLISS** Bliss, Elmer Ward b: 3/9/1875, Penfield, Pa. d: 3/18/62, Bradford, Pa. BL/TR, 6′, 180 lbs. Deb: 9/28/03 ♦																									
1903 NY-A	1	0	1.000	1	1	1	0	0	7	4	0	3	2	5.1	0.00	—	.167	.167	0	.000	-0	2	2	-0	0.3
● **TERRY BLOCKER** Blocker, Terry Fennell b: 8/18/59, Columbia, S.C. BL/TL, 6′2″, 195 lbs. Deb: 4/11/85 ♦																									
1989 Atl-N			—	1	0	0	0	0	1	0	0	0	2	18.0	0.00	—	.000	.500	7	.226	0	0	0	0	0.0

YEAR	TM/L	W	L	PCT	G	GS	CG	SH	SV	IP	H	HR	BB	SO	RAT	ERA	ERA+	OAV	OOB	BH	AVG	PB	PR	/A	PD	TPI

● **BEN BLOMDAHL**   Blomdahl, Benjamin Earl b: 12/30/70, Long Beach, Cal. BR/TR, 6'2", 185 lbs. Deb: 4/28/95

| 1995 | Det-A | 0 | 0 | — | 14 | 0 | 0 | 0 | 1 | 24¹ | 36 | 5 | 13 | 15 | 18.1 | 7.77 | 61 | .356 | .430 | 0 | — | 0 | -8 | -8 | 1 | 0.0 |

● **JOE BLONG**   Blong, Joseph Myles b: 9/17/1853, St.Louis, Mo. d: 9/16/1892, St.Louis, Mo. BR/TR, Deb: 5/4/1875 ♦

1875	RS-n	3	12	.200	15	15	12	1	0	129	169	0	2	14	11.9	3.07	71	.284	.286	10	.147	-4	-12	-13	1	-1.1
1876	StL-N	0	0	—	1	0	0	0	0	4	2	0	1	0	6.8	0.00	—	.154	.214	62	.235	-0	1	1	0	0.0
1877	StL-N	10	9	.526	25	21	17	0	0	187¹	203	0	38	51	11.6	2.74	95	.262	.296	47	.216	0	1	-3	-2	-0.4
Total	2	10	9	.526	26	21	17	0	0	191¹	205	0	39	51	11.5	2.68	97	.260	.295	109	.226	0	2	-2	-1	-0.4

● **VIDA BLUE**   Blue, Vida Rochelle b: 7/28/49, Mansfield, La. BB/TL, 6', 189 lbs. Deb: 7/20/69

1969	Oak-A	1	1	.500	12	4	0	0	0	42	49	13	18	24	14.4	6.64	52	.290	.358	0	.000	-0	-14	-15	-1	-0.8
1970	Oak-A	2	0	1.000	6	6	2	2	0	38²	20	0	12	35	7.7	2.09	169	.152	.228	3	.200	2	7	6	0	0.9
1971	*Oak-A★	24	8	.750	39	39	24	**8**	0	312	209	19	88	301	8.7	**1.82**	183	**.189**	**.252**	12	.118	-2	57	53	-4	4.9
1972	*Oak-A	6	10	.375	25	23	5	4	0	151	117	11	48	111	9.9	2.80	101	.215	.280	2	.044	-2	4	1	-2	-0.4
1973	*Oak-A	20	9	.690	37	37	13	4	0	263²	214	26	105	158	11.0	3.28	108	.224	.303	0	.000	0	16	8	-2	0.5
1974	*Oak-A	17	15	.531	40	40	12	1	0	282¹	246	17	98	174	11.0	3.25	102	.236	.303	0	—	0	11	2	-5	-0.1
1975	*Oak-A★	22	11	.667	39	38	13	2	1	278	243	21	99	189	11.2	3.01	120	.236	.307	0	—	0	24	19	-2	2.0
1976	Oak-A	18	13	.581	37	37	20	6	0	298¹	268	9	63	166	10.0	2.35	143	.239	.280	0	—	0	**39**	33	-3	3.1
1977	Oak-A†	14	19	.424	38	38	16	1	0	279²	284	23	86	157	11.9	3.83	105	.264	.319	0	.000	-1	7	6	-1	0.5
1978	SF-N★	18	10	.643	35	35	9	4	0	258	233	12	70	171	10.6	2.79	124	.246	.298	6	.076	-2	23	19	-2	2.0
1979	SF-N	14	14	.500	34	34	10	0	0	237	246	23	111	138	13.6	5.01	77	.272	.352	10	.120	0	-34	-40	2	-3.9
1980	SF-N†	14	10	.583	31	31	8	1	0	224	202	14	61	129	10.6	2.97	119	.242	.294	5	.074	-4	16	14	2	1.3
1981	SF-N★	8	6	.571	18	18	1	0	0	124²	97	7	54	63	11.0	2.45	140	.217	.303	7	.200	2	14	14	2	2.0
1982	KC-A	13	12	.520	31	31	6	2	0	181	163	20	80	103	12.1	3.78	108	.238	.318	0	—	0	6	6	-0	-1.0
1983	KC-A	0	5	.000	19	14	1	0	0	85¹	96	12	35	53	14.0	6.01	68	.286	.357	0	—	0	-18	-18	-0	-1.0
1985	SF-N	8	8	.500	33	20	1	0	0	131	115	17	80	103	13.5	4.47	77	.240	.350	4	.133	1	-13	-15	0	-1.6
1986	SF-N	10	10	.500	28	28	0	0	0	156²	137	17	77	100	12.3	3.27	107	.239	.329	4	.093	1	8	4	-1	0.5
Total	17	209	161	.565	502	473	143	37	2	3343¹	2939	263	1185	2175	11.2	3.27	108	.237	.305	53	.104	-1	152	95	-17	10.2

● **JIM BLUEJACKET**   Bluejacket, James (b: James Smith) b: 7/8/1887, Adair, Okla. d: 3/26/47, Pekin, Ill. BR/TR, 6'2.5", 200 lbs. Deb: 8/6/14 F

1914	Bro-F	4	5	.444	17	7	3	1	0	67	77	2	19	29	12.9	3.76	76	.302	.350	3	.136	-1	-7	-7	1	-0.8
1915	Bro-F	10	11	.476	24	21	10	2	0	162²	155	2	75	48	12.7	3.15	86	.258	.340	8	.131	-5	-8	-8	-4	-1.8
1916	Cin-N	0	1	.000	3	2	0	0	1	7	12	0	3	1	19.3	7.71	34	.400	.455	0	.000	-0	-4	-4	-0	-0.6
Total	3	14	17	.452	44	30	13	3	1	236²	244	4	97	78	13.0	3.46	80	.275	.347	11	.129	-6	-18	-18	-3	-3.2

● **JAIME BLUMA**   Bluma, James Andrew b: 5/18/72, Beaufort, S.C. BR/TR, 5'11", 195 lbs. Deb: 8/9/96

| 1996 | KC-A | 0 | 0 | — | 17 | 0 | 0 | 0 | 5 | 20 | 18 | 2 | 4 | 14 | 10.8 | 3.60 | 136 | .247 | .304 | 0 | — | 0 | 3 | 3 | 1 | 0.4 |

● **CLINT BLUME**   Blume, Clinton Willis b: 10/17/1898, Brooklyn, N.Y. d: 6/12/73, Islip, N.Y. BR/TR, 5'11", 175 lbs. Deb: 9/30/22

1922	NY-N	1	0	1.000	1	1	0	0	0	9	7	0	1	2	8.0	1.00	400	.212	.235	1	1.000	1	3	3	-1	0.4
1923	NY-N	2	0	1.000	12	1	0	0	0	24	22	0	20	2	16.5	3.75	102	.265	.419	0	.000	-0	1	0	-1	-0.1
Total	2	3	0	1.000	13	2	1	0	0	33	29	0	21	4	14.2	3.00	129	.250	.374	1	.167	1	4	3	-1	0.3

● **BERT BLYLEVEN**   Blyleven, Rik Aalbert b: 4/6/51, Zeist, Holland BR/TR, 6'3", 207 lbs. Deb: 6/5/70

1970	*Min-A	10	9	.526	27	25	5	1	0	164	143	17	47	135	10.5	3.18	117	.232	.289	7	.140	-1	10	10	-2	0.8
1971	Min-A	16	15	.516	38	38	17	5	0	278¹	267	21	59	224	10.7	2.81	126	.255	.298	12	.132	-3	20	23	-0	2.2
1972	Min-A	17	17	.500	39	38	11	3	0	287¹	247	22	69	228	10.2	2.73	118	.233	.286	15	.160	-1	11	15	1	2.0
1973	Min-A★	20	17	.541	40	40	25	**9**	0	325	296	16	67	258	10.3	2.52	**157**	.242	.287	0	—	0	**47**	52	-2	5.7
1974	Min-A	17	17	.500	37	37	19	3	0	281	244	14	77	249	10.6	2.66	140	.233	.292	0	—	0	30	33	0	4.0
1975	Min-A	15	10	.600	35	35	20	3	0	275²	219	24	84	233	10.0	3.00	127	.219	.283	0	—	0	24	25	3	2.4
1976	Min-A	4	5	.444	12	12	4	0	0	95¹	101	3	35	75	13.2	3.12	115	.283	.354	0	—	0	4	5	0	0.5
	Tex-A	9	11	.450	24	24	14	6	0	202¹	182	11	46	144	10.5	2.76	130	.242	.293	0	—	0	17	19	2	2.0
	Yr	13	16	.448	36	36	18	6	0	297²	283	14	81	219	11.2	2.87	125	.254	.309	0	—	0	21	23	2	2.5
1977	Tex-A	14	12	.538	30	30	15	5	0	234²	181	20	69	182	**9.9**	2.72	150	.214	.279	0	—	0	35	35	0	3.8
1978	Pit-N	14	10	.583	34	34	11	4	0	243²	217	17	66	182	10.7	3.03	122	.235	.290	11	.129	-2	15	18	1	1.6
1979	*Pit-N	12	5	.706	37	37	4	0	0	237¹	238	21	92	172	12.7	3.60	108	.265	.338	9	.129	-3	3	7	-2	0.0
1980	Pit-N	8	13	.381	34	32	5	2	0	216²	219	20	59	168	11.5	3.82	95	.262	.311	5	.082	-4	-5	-4	-0	-0.8
1981	Cle-A	11	7	.611	20	20	9	1	0	159¹	145	9	40	107	10.7	2.88	126	.245	.298	0	—	0	14	13	-2	1.4
1982	Cle-A	2	2	.500	4	4	0	0	0	20¹	16	2	11	19	12.4	4.87	84	.211	.310	0	—	0	-2	-2	-0	-0.3
1983	Cle-A	7	10	.412	24	24	5	1	0	156¹	160	11	44	123	12.3	3.91	108	.267	.328	0	—	0	3	6	1	0.6
1984	Cle-A	19	7	.731	33	32	12	4	0	245	204	19	74	170	10.4	2.87	143	.224	.287	0	—	0	31	33	0	3.4
1985	Cle-A★	9	11	.450	23	23	15	4	0	179²	163	14	49	129	11.4	3.26	121	.240	.298	0	—	0	18	17	-1	1.7
	Min-A	8	5	.615	14	14	9	1	0	114	101	9	26	77	10.2	3.00	147	.237	.284	0	—	0	15	18	-0	1.8
	Yr	17	16	.515	37	37	**24**	**5**	0	293²	264	23	75	**206**	10.5	3.16	134	.239	.286	0	—	0	32	35	-1	3.5
1986	Min-A	17	14	.548	36	36	16	3	0	**271²**	262	50	58	215	10.9	4.01	107	.250	.295	0	—	0	5	9	-1	0.9
1987	*Min-A	15	12	.556	37	37	8	1	0	267	249	46	101	196	12.1	4.01	115	.249	.323	0	—	0	13	18	2	1.7
1988	Min-A	10	17	.370	33	33	7	0	0	207¹	240	21	51	145	13.3	5.43	75	.294	.348	0	—	0	-34	-31	-1	-3.6
1989	Cal-A	17	5	.773	33	33	8	**5**	0	241	225	14	44	131	10.3	2.73	140	.248	.289	0	—	0	31	29	1	2.7
1990	Cal-A	8	7	.533	23	23	2	0	0	134	163	23	25	69	13.1	5.24	73	.303	.342	0	—	0	-20	-21	2	-2.0
1992	Cal-A	8	12	.400	25	24	1	0	0	133	150	17	29	70	12.5	4.74	84	.285	.329	0	—	0	-12	-11	-1	-1.6
Total	22	287	250	.534	692	685	242	60	0	4970	4632	430	1322	3701	11.1	3.31	117	.247	.303	59	.131	-13	271	317	1	30.8

● **MIKE BLYZKA**   Blyzka, Michael John b: 12/25/28, Hamtramck, Mich. BR/TR, 5'11.5", 190 lbs. Deb: 4/21/53

1953	StL-A	2	6	.250	33	9	1	0	1	94¹	110	6	56	23	15.8	6.39	66	.292	.383	0	.000	-3	-25	-23	-1	-2.0
1954	Bal-A	1	5	.167	37	0	0	0	1	86¹	83	2	51	35	14.0	4.69	76	.254	.354	2	.133	-1	-9	-11	0	-0.8
Total	2	3	11	.214	70	9	2	0	1	180²	193	8	107	58	14.9	5.58	70	.274	.370	2	.053	-4	-34	-34	-0	-2.8

● **CHARLIE BOARDMAN**   Boardman, Charles Louis b: 4/27/1893, Seneca Falls, N.Y. d: 8/10/68, Sacramento, Cal. BL/TL, 6'2.5", 194 lbs. Deb: 9/26/13

1913	Phi-A	0	2	.000	2	1	0	0	0	9	10	0	6	4	16.0	2.00	138	.294	.400	0	.000	-0	1	1	-0	0.1
1914	Phi-A	0	0	—	2	0	0	0	0	7¹	10	0	4	2	17.2	4.91	53	.357	.438	0	.000	-0	-2	-2	0	0.0
1915	StL-N	1	0	1.000	3	1	1	0	0	19	12	0	15	7	12.8	2.84	98	.188	.342	2	.286	1	-0	-0	-0	0.0
Total	3	1	2	.333	7	2	1	0	0	35¹	32	0	25	13	14.5	3.06	90	.254	.377	2	.167	1	-1	-1	-1	0.1

● **DOUG BOCHTLER**   Bochtler, Douglas Eugene b: 7/5/70, W.Palm Beach, Fla. BR/TR, 6'3", 205 lbs. Deb: 5/5/95

1995	SD-N	4	4	.500	34	0	0	0	1	45¹	38	5	19	45	11.3	3.57	113	.239	.320	0	.000	-0	3	2	0	0.4
1996	*SD-N	2	4	.333	63	0	0	0	4	65²	45	6	39	68	11.6	3.02	132	.195	.314	0	—	0	9	7	-1	0.5
Total	2	6	8	.429	97	0	0	0	5	111	83	11	58	113	11.5	3.25	123	.213	.316	0	.000	-0	12	9	-1	0.9

● **RANDY BOCKUS**   Bockus, Randy Walter b: 10/5/60, Canton, Ohio BL/TR, 6'2", 190 lbs. Deb: 9/10/86

1986	SF-N	0	0	—	5	0	0	0	0	4	4	0	4	4	16.7	2.57	137	.241	.371	0	.000	-0	1	1	0	0.0
1987	SF-N	1	0	1.000	12	0	0	0	0	17¹	17	2	4	9	10.9	3.63	106	.266	.309	0	.000	-0	1	1	0	0.0
1988	SF-N	1	1	.500	20	0	0	0	0	32	35	2	13	18	13.8	4.78	68	.277	.371	1	.167	-0	-5	-5	-0	-0.3
1989	Det-A	0	0	—	2	0	0	0	0	5¹	7	0	2	2	15.2	5.06	75	.333	.391	0	—	0	-1	-1	-0	0.0
Total	4	2	1	.667	39	0	0	0	0	61²	75	5	25	33	13.4	4.23	83	.284	.357	1	.125	-0	-4	-5	1	-0.3

● **MIKE BODDICKER**   Boddicker, Michael James b: 8/23/57, Cedar Rapids, Iowa BR/TR, 5'11", 172 lbs. Deb: 10/4/80

1980	Bal-A	0	1	.000	1	1	0	0	0	7¹	8	1	5	4	13.5	6.14	64	.207	.324	0	—	0	-2	-2	-0	-0.2
1981	Bal-A	0	0	—	2	0	0	0	0	5²	6	1	2	12	12.7	4.76	76	.261	.320	0	—	0	0	-0	-0	0.0
1982	Bal-A	1	0	1.000	7	0	0	0	0	25²	21	2	12	20	13.0	3.51	115	.258	.339	0	—	0	2	2	0	0.1
1983	*Bal-A	16	8	.667	27	26	10	**5**	0	179	141	13	52	120	9.7	2.77	143	**.216**	.274	0	—	0	26	24	3	3.4
1984	Bal-A☆	**20**	11	.645	34	34	16	4	0	261¹	218	23	81	128	10.5	**2.79**	139	.228	.292	0	—	0	**35**	31	6	**4.2**

BODDICKER (continued)

YEAR	TM/L	W	L	PCT	G	GS	CG	SH	SV	IP	H	HR	BB	SO	RAT	ERA	ERA+	OAV	OOB	BH	AVG	PB	PR	/A	PD	TPI
1985	Bal-A	12	17	.414	32	32	9	2	0	203¹	227	13	89	135	14.2	4.07	99	.286	.361	0	—	0	2	-1	6	0.4
1986	Bal-A	14	12	.538	33	33	7	0	0	218¹	214	30	74	175	12.3	4.70	88	.255	.323	0	—	0	-13	-14	3	-1.0
1987	Bal-A	10	12	.455	33	33	7	2	0	226	212	29	78	152	11.8	4.18	105	.248	.316	0	—	0	7	5	4	0.8
1988	Bal-A	6	12	.333	21	21	4	0	0	147	149	14	51	100	12.9	3.86	101	.265	.338	0	—	0	2	1	-1	0.0
	*Bos-A	7	3	.700	15	14	1	0	0	89	85	3	26	56	11.5	2.63	156	.257	.317	0	—	0	13	15	2	1.8
	Yr	13	15	.464	36	35	5	1	0	236	234	17	77	156	12.0	3.39	117	.256	.316	0	—	0	15	15	1	1.8
1989	Bos-A	15	11	.577	34	34	3	2	0	211²	217	19	71	145	12.7	4.00	103	.267	.333	0	—	0	-3	2	1	0.4
1990	*Bos-A	17	8	.680	34	34	4	0	0	228	225	16	69	143	12.0	3.36	121	.258	.319	0	—	0	14	18	1	1.9
1991	KC-A	12	12	.500	30	29	1	0	0	180²	188	13	59	79	13.0	4.08	101	.272	.340	0	—	0	0	1	2	0.3
1992	KC-A	1	4	.200	29	8	0	0	3	86²	92	5	37	47	14.2	4.98	81	.269	.354	0	—	0	-10	-9	1	-0.4
1993	Mil-A	3	5	.375	10	10	1	0	0	54	77	6	15	24	16.0	5.67	75	.338	.389	0	—	0	-8	-9	0	-1.0
Total	14	134	116	.536	342	309	63	16	3	2123²	2082	188	721	1330	12.2	3.80	107	.257	.325	0	—	0	64	65	28	10.7

● **GEORGE BOEHLER**   Boehler, George Henry   b: 1/2/1892, Lawrenceburg, Ind.   d: 6/23/58, Lawrenceburg, Ind   BR/TR, 6'2", 180 lbs.   Deb: 9/13/12

YEAR	TM/L	W	L	PCT	G	GS	CG	SH	SV	IP	H	HR	BB	SO	RAT	ERA	ERA+	OAV	OOB	BH	AVG	PB	PR	/A	PD	TPI
1912	Det-A	0	2	.000	5	4	2	0	0	32	50	0	14	15	18.6	6.47	50	.365	.431	1	.100	-1	-11	-11	1	-0.6
1913	Det-A	0	1	.000	1	1	0	0	0	8	11	0	6	2	21.4	6.75	43	.355	.487	1	.333		-3	-3	1	-0.3
1914	Det-A	2	3	.400	18	6	2	0	0	63	54	1	48	37	15.7	3.57	79	.242	.394	3	.176	1	-6	-5	-0	-0.4
1915	Det-A	1	1	.500	8	0	0	0	0	15	19	0	4	7	14.4	1.80	168	.328	.381	3	.750	2	2	2	-0	0.4
1916	Det-A	1	1	.500	5	2	1	0	0	13¹	12	0	9	8	15.5	4.73	61	.261	.404	0	.000		-3	-3	1	-0.3
1920	StL-A	0	1	.000	3	1	0	0	0	7	10	1	4	2	18.0	7.71	51	.303	.378	0	.000		-3	-3	0	-0.3
1921	StL-A	0	0	—	1	0	0	0	0	1	1	0	0	1	9.0	0.00	—	.500	.500	0	—		0	0	0	0.0
1923	Pit-N	1	3	.250	10	3	1	0	0	28¹	33	1	26	12	19.1	6.04	66	.314	.455	3	.300	1	-6	-6	-0	-0.7
1926	Bro-N	1	0	1.000	10	1	0	0	0	34²	42	1	23	10	17.7	4.41	87	.302	.412	3	.250		-2	-2	-1	-0.1
Total	9	6	12	.333	61	18	7	0	0	202¹	232	4	134	93	17.1	4.71	70	.300	.415	14	.233	3	-33	-32	1	-2.3

● **JOE BOEHLING**   Boehling, John Joseph   b: 3/20/1891, Richmond, Va.   d: 9/8/41, Richmond, Va.   BL/TL, 5'11", 168 lbs.   Deb: 6/20/12

YEAR	TM/L	W	L	PCT	G	GS	CG	SH	SV	IP	H	HR	BB	SO	RAT	ERA	ERA+	OAV	OOB	BH	AVG	PB	PR	/A	PD	TPI
1912	Was-A	0	0	—	3	0	0	0	0	5	4	0	2	2	21.6	7.20	46	.235	.480	0	—	0	-2	-2	0	0.0
1913	Was-A	17	7	.708	38	25	18	3	4	235¹	197	3	82	110	11.0	2.14	138	.229	.303	19	.221	1	21	21	2	2.6
1914	Was-A	12	8	.600	27	24	14	2	1	196	180	3	76	91	12.2	3.03	93	.258	.339	17	.239	4	-6	-5	2	0.1
1915	Was-A	14	13	.519	40	32	14	2	0	229²	217	5	119	108	13.5	3.22	92	.255	.352	13	.173	0	-7	-6	2	-0.4
1916	Was-A	9	11	.450	27	19	7	2	0	139²	134	1	54	52	12.3	3.09	90	.260	.333	7	.171	1	-4	-5	4	-0.2
	Cle-A	2	4	.333	12	9	3	0	0	60²	63	0	23	18	13.1	2.67	113	.281	.353	5	.263	1	1	1	2	0.4
	Yr	11	15	.423	39	28	10	2	0	200¹	197	1	77	70	12.4	2.97	96	.265	.336	12	.200	1	-3	-2	4	0.2
1917	Cle-A	1	6	.143	12	7	1	0	0	46¹	50	1	16	11	13.4	4.66	61	.291	.361	3	.188	-0	-10	-9	-0	-1.4
1920	Cle-A	0	1	.000	3	2	0	0	0	13	16	0	4	4	18.0	4.85	78	.333	.448	2	.500	1	-2	-2	0	0.0
Total	7	55	50	.524	162	118	57	9	5	925¹	861	6	386	396	12.5	2.97	98	.254	.337	66	.212	7	-10	-5	11	1.1

● **BRIAN BOEHRINGER**   Boehringer, Brian Edward   b: 1/8/69, St.Louis, Mo.   BB/TR, 6'2", 180 lbs.   Deb: 4/30/95

YEAR	TM/L	W	L	PCT	G	GS	CG	SH	SV	IP	H	HR	BB	SO	RAT	ERA	ERA+	OAV	OOB	BH	AVG	PB	PR	/A	PD	TPI
1995	NY-A	0	3	.000	7	3	0	0	0	17²	24	5	22	10	23.9	13.75	34	.320	.480	0	—	0	-18	-18	-1	-2.2
1996	*NY-A	2	4	.333	15	3	0	0	0	46¹	46	6	21	37	13.2	5.44	93	.260	.342	0	—	0	-2	-2	-0	-0.3
Total	2	2	7	.222	22	6	0	0	0	64	70	11	43	47	16.2	7.73	64	.278	.387	0	—	0	-20	-20	-1	-2.5

● **LARRY BOERNER**   Boerner, Lawrence Hyer   b: 1/21/05, Staunton, Va.   d: 10/16/69, Staunton, Va.   BR/TR, 6'4.5", 175 lbs.   Deb: 6/30/32

YEAR	TM/L	W	L	PCT	G	GS	CG	SH	SV	IP	H	HR	BB	SO	RAT	ERA	ERA+	OAV	OOB	BH	AVG	PB	PR	/A	PD	TPI
1932	Bos-A	0	4	.000	21	5	0	0	0	61	71	2	37	19	16.4	5.02	90	.302	.404	0	.000	-3	-4	-4	0	-0.4

● **JOE BOEVER**   Boever, Joseph Martin   b: 10/4/60, Kirkwood, Mo.   BR/TR, 6'1", 200 lbs.   Deb: 7/19/85

YEAR	TM/L	W	L	PCT	G	GS	CG	SH	SV	IP	H	HR	BB	SO	RAT	ERA	ERA+	OAV	OOB	BH	AVG	PB	PR	/A	PD	TPI
1985	StL-N	0	0	—	13	0	0	0	0	16¹	17	3	4	20	11.6	4.41	80	.270	.313	0	—	0	-1	-2	-0	0.0
1986	StL-N	0	1	.000	11	0	0	0	0	21²	19	2	11	8	12.5	1.66	219	.232	.323	1	.500	0	5	5	-0	0.2
1987	Atl-N	1	0	1.000	14	0	0	0	0	18¹	29	4	12	18	20.1	7.36	59	.367	.451	0	—	0	-7	-6	-0	-0.3
1988	Atl-N	0	2	.000	16	0	0	0	1	20¹	12	1	7	6	6.2	1.77	208	.182	.206	0	—	0	4	4	0	0.5
1989	Atl-N	4	11	.267	66	0	0	0	21	82¹	78	6	34	68	12.4	3.94	93	.252	.328	0	.000	-0	-4	-3	1	-0.5
1990	Atl-N	1	3	.250	33	0	0	0	6	42¹	40	6	35	35	15.9	4.68	86	.252	.387	0	.000	-0	-4	-3	-1	-0.5
	Phi-N	2	3	.400	34	0	0	0	8	46	37	0	16	40	10.4	2.15	178	.215	.282	0	.000	0	8	9	-1	1.1
	Yr	3	6	.333	67	0	0	0	14	88¹	77	6	51	75	13.0	3.36	117	.231	.333	0	.000	-0	4	6	-1	0.6
1991	Phi-N	3	5	.375	68	0	0	0	0	98¹	90	10	54	89	13.2	3.84	95	.245	.341	1	.333		-2	-2	-1	-0.2
1992	Hou-N	3	6	.333	**81**	0	0	0	2	111¹	103	3	45	67	12.3	2.51	134	.248	.327	0	.000	-1	12	11	0	0.8
1993	Oak-A	4	2	.667	42	0	0	0	0	79¹	87	8	33	49	14.1	3.86	106	.280	.356	0	—	0	4	2	0	0.5
	Det-A	2	1	.667	19	0	0	0	3	23	14	1	14	9	9.8	2.74	156	.179	.281	0	—	-0	4	4	-0	0.6
	Yr	6	3	.667	61	0	0	0	3	102¹	101	9	44	63	12.8	3.61	114	.255	.330	0	—	0	8	6	-0	1.1
1994	Det-A	9	2	.818	46	0	0	0	3	81¹	80	7	35	37	13.2	3.98	122	.263	.347	0	—	0	7	8	1	1.0
1995	Det-A	5	7	.417	60	0	0	0	3	98²	128	17	44	71	16.0	6.39	74	.319	.391	0	—	-0	-18	-18	-1	-1.9
1996	Pit-N	0	2	.000	13	0	0	0	2	15	17	2	6	14	14.4	5.40	81	.288	.364	0	.000	-0	-2	-2	-0	-0.3
Total	12	34	45	.430	516	0	0	0	49	754¹	751	75	343	541	13.2	3.93	102	.262	.344	2	.118	-1	7	7	-2	1.0

● **JOHN BOGART**   Bogart, John Renzie "Big John"   b: 9/21/1900, Bloomsburg, Pa.   d: 12/7/86, Clarence, N.Y.   BR/TR, 6'2", 195 lbs.   Deb: 9/17/20

YEAR	TM/L	W	L	PCT	G	GS	CG	SH	SV	IP	H	HR	BB	SO	RAT	ERA	ERA+	OAV	OOB	BH	AVG	PB	PR	/A	PD	TPI
1920	Det-A	2	1	.667	4	2	0	0	0	23²	16	0	18	5	12.9	3.04	122	.195	.340	2	.250		2	2	-1	0.1

● **RAY BOGGS**   Boggs, Raymond Joseph "Lefty"   b: 12/12/04, Reamsville, Kan.   d: 11/27/89, Grand Junction, Colo.   BL/TL, 6'0.5", 170 lbs.   Deb: 9/1/28

YEAR	TM/L	W	L	PCT	G	GS	CG	SH	SV	IP	H	HR	BB	SO	RAT	ERA	ERA+	OAV	OOB	BH	AVG	PB	PR	/A	PD	TPI
1928	Bos-N	0	0	—	4	0	0	0	0	5	2	0	7	2	21.6	5.40	72	.167	.545	0	—	0	-1	-1	-0	0.0

● **TOMMY BOGGS**   Boggs, Thomas Winton   b: 10/25/55, Poughkeepsie, N.Y.   BR/TR, 6'2", 200 lbs.   Deb: 7/19/76

YEAR	TM/L	W	L	PCT	G	GS	CG	SH	SV	IP	H	HR	BB	SO	RAT	ERA	ERA+	OAV	OOB	BH	AVG	PB	PR	/A	PD	TPI
1976	Tex-A	1	7	.125	13	13	3	0	0	90¹	87	7	34	36	12.2	3.49	103	.257	.326	0	—	0	0	1	-1	-0.1
1977	Tex-A	0	3	.000	6	6	0	0	0	27¹	40	1	12	15	17.5	5.93	69	.351	.417	0	—	0	-6	-6	-0	-0.6
1978	Atl-N	2	8	.200	16	12	1	1	0	59	80	8	26	21	16.3	6.71	60	.323	.389	3	.167		-21	-17	-2	-2.7
1979	Atl-N	0	2	.000	3	3	0	0	0	12²	21	0	4	1	18.5	6.39	63	.362	.413	1	.250		-4	-3	-0	-0.4
1980	Atl-N	12	9	.571	32	26	4	3	0	192¹	180	14	46	84	10.8	3.42	109	.249	.298	10	.159	-2	4	7	-2	0.3
1981	Atl-N	3	13	.188	25	24	2	0	0	142²	140	11	54	81	12.4	4.10	87	.265	.336	7	.152	-1	-10	-8	-1	-1.0
1982	Atl-N	2	2	.500	10	10	0	0	0	46¹	43	2	22	29	13.0	3.30	113	.253	.345	4	.235	-1	2	2	-0	0.2
1983	Atl-N	0	0	—	5	0	0	0	0	6¹	8	1	1	6	12.8	5.68	68	.320	.346	0	—	0	-1	-1	-0	-0.1
1985	Tex-A	0	0	—	4	0	0	0	0	7	13	3	2	6	19.3	11.57	37	.382	.417	0	—	0	-6	-6	0	-0.4
Total	9	20	44	.313	114	94	10	4	0	584	612	47	201	278	12.7	4.22	89	.273	.337	25	.169	-2	-41	-31	-5	-4.3

● **WARREN BOGLE**   Bogle, Warren Frederick   b: 10/19/46, Passaic, N.J.   BL/TL, 6'4", 220 lbs.   Deb: 7/31/68

YEAR	TM/L	W	L	PCT	G	GS	CG	SH	SV	IP	H	HR	BB	SO	RAT	ERA	ERA+	OAV	OOB	BH	AVG	PB	PR	/A	PD	TPI
1968	Oak-A	0	0	—	16	1	0	0	0	23	26	3		26	13.3	4.30	65	.283	.340	0	.000	-1	-3	-4	1	0.0

● **BRIAN BOHANON**   Bohanon, Brian Edward   b: 8/1/68, Denton, Tex.   BL/TL, 6'2", 210 lbs.   Deb: 4/10/90

YEAR	TM/L	W	L	PCT	G	GS	CG	SH	SV	IP	H	HR	BB	SO	RAT	ERA	ERA+	OAV	OOB	BH	AVG	PB	PR	/A	PD	TPI
1990	Tex-A	0	3	.000	11	6	0	0	0	34	40	6	18	15	15.9	6.62	59	.296	.387	0	—	0	-10	-10	1	-0.7
1991	Tex-A	4	3	.571	11	11	1	0	0	61¹	66	4	23	34	13.4	4.84	83	.274	.342	0	—	0	-5	-6	-1	-0.5
1992	Tex-A	1	1	.500	18	7	0	0	0	45²	57	7	25	29	16.4	6.31	60	.297	.381	0	—	0	-12	-13	-0	-0.3
1993	Tex-A	4	4	.500	36	8	0	0	0	92²	107	8	46	45	15.2	4.76	87	.296	.382	0	—	0	-5	-6	1	-0.1
1994	Tex-A	2	2	.500	11	5	0	0	0	37¹	51	7	8	26	14.5	7.23	67	.321	.357	0	—	0	-10	-10	-0	-0.8
1995	Det-A	1	1	.500	52	10	0	0	0	105²	121	10	41	63	14.1	5.54	86	.285	.354	0	—	0	-10	-9	-0	-0.1
1996	Tor-A	0	1	.000	20	0	0	0	0	22	27	4	19	17	19.6	7.77	65	.303	.436	0	—	0	-7	-7	0	-0.3
Total	7	12	15	.444	159	47	1	0	0	398²	469	46	180	229	15.0	5.71	76	.293	.370	0	—	0	-58	-61	1	-2.8

● **PAT BOHEN**   Bohen, Leo Ignatius   b: 9/30/1891, Oakland, Iowa   d: 4/8/42, Napa, Cal.   BR/TR, 5'10.5", 155 lbs.   Deb: 10/1/13

YEAR	TM/L	W	L	PCT	G	GS	CG	SH	SV	IP	H	HR	BB	SO	RAT	ERA	ERA+	OAV	OOB	BH	AVG	PB	PR	/A	PD	TPI
1913	Phi-A	0	1	.000	1	1	1	0	0	8	3	0	2	5	5.6	1.13	246	.115	.179	0	.000	-0	2	1	-0	0.1
1914	Pit-N	0	0	—	1	0	0	0	0	1	2	0	0	2	45.0	18.00	15	.500	.714	0	.000	-0	-2	-2	-0	0.0
Total	2	0	1	.000	2	1	1	0	0	9	5	0	2	7	10.0	3.00	92	.167	.286	0	.000	-1	-0	-0	-0	0.1

● **CHARLIE BOHN**   Bohn, Charles   b: 1857, Cleveland, Ohio   d: 8/1/03, Cleveland, Ohio   BR/TR, 5'9", 165 lbs.   Deb: 6/20/1882 ◆

YEAR	TM/L	W	L	PCT	G	GS	CG	SH	SV	IP	H	HR	BB	SO	RAT	ERA	ERA+	OAV	OOB	BH	AVG	PB	PR	/A	PD	TPI
1882	Lou-a	1	1	.500	2	2	2	0	0	18	21	0	3	1	12.0	3.00	83	.273	.300	2	.154	-0	-1	-1	0	-0.1

YEAR TM/L	W	L	PCT	G	GS	CG	SH	SV	IP	H	HR	BB	SO	RAT	ERA	ERA+	OAV	OOB	BH	AVG	PB	PR	/A	PD	TPI

● **JOHN BOHNET**   Bohnet, John Kelly   b: 1/18/61, Pasadena, Cal.   BB/TL, 6', 175 lbs.   Deb: 5/10/82

YEAR TM/L	W	L	PCT	G	GS	CG	SH	SV	IP	H	HR	BB	SO	RAT	ERA	ERA+	OAV	OOB	BH	AVG	PB	PR	/A	PD	TPI
1982 Cle-A	0	0	—	3	0	0	0	0	11²	11	4	7	4	14.7	6.94	59	.250	.365	0	—	0	-4	-4	0	0.0

● **DAN BOITANO**   Boitano, Danny Jon   b: 3/22/53, Sacramento, Cal.   BR/TR 6', 185 lbs.   Deb: 10/1/78

YEAR TM/L	W	L	PCT	G	GS	CG	SH	SV	IP	H	HR	BB	SO	RAT	ERA	ERA+	OAV	OOB	BH	AVG	PB	PR	/A	PD	TPI
1978 Phi-N	0	0	—	1	0	0	0	0	1	0	0	1	0	9.0	0.00	—	.000	.250	0	—	0	0	0	0	0.0
1979 Mil-A	0	0	—	5	0	0	0	0	6	6	1	3	5	13.5	1.50	278	.273	.360	0	—	0	2	2	0	0.0
1980 Mil-A	0	1	.000	11	0	0	0	0	17²	26	7	6	11	16.8	8.15	47	.342	.398	0	—	0	-8	-8	0	-0.2
1981 NY-N	2	1	.667	15	0	0	0	0	16¹	21	2	5	8	15.4	5.51	63	.309	.373	0	—	0	-4	-4	0	-0.6
1982 Tex-A	0	0	—	19	0	0	0	0	30¹	33	5	13	28	14.2	5.34	72	.280	.361	0	—	0	-4	-5	-0	0.2
Total 5	2	2	.500	51	0	0	0	0	71¹	86	15	28	52	15.0	5.68	67	.300	.372	0	—	0	-14	-15	-0	-0.6

● **DICK BOKELMANN**   Bokelmann, Richard Werner   b: 10/26/26, Arlington Heights, Ill.   BR/TR, 6'0.5", 180 lbs.   Deb: 8/3/51

YEAR TM/L	W	L	PCT	G	GS	CG	SH	SV	IP	H	HR	BB	SO	RAT	ERA	ERA+	OAV	OOB	BH	AVG	PB	PR	/A	PD	TPI
1951 StL-N	3	3	.500	20	1	0	0	3	52¹	49	2	31	22	13.9	3.78	105	.245	.349	0	.000	-2	1	1	-1	-0.1
1952 StL-N	0	1	.000	11	0	0	0	0	12²	20	0	7	5	19.2	9.24	40	.357	.429	0	—	0	-8	-8	1	-0.5
1953 StL-N	0	0	—	3	0	0	0	0	3	4	0	0	0	12.0	6.00	71	.308	.308	0	—	0	-1	-1	0	0.0
Total 3	3	4	.429	34	1	0	0	3	68	73	2	38	27	14.8	4.90	80	.271	.364	0	.000	-2	-7	-7	0	-0.6

● **JOE BOKINA**   Bokina, Joseph   b: 4/4/10, Northampton, Mass.   d: 10/25/91, Chattanooga, Tenn.   BR/TR, 6', 184 lbs.   Deb: 4/16/36

YEAR TM/L	W	L	PCT	G	GS	CG	SH	SV	IP	H	HR	BB	SO	RAT	ERA	ERA+	OAV	OOB	BH	AVG	PB	PR	/A	PD	TPI
1936 Was-A	0	2	.000	5	1	0	0	0	8¹	15	0	6	2	22.7	8.64	55	.395	.477	0	.000	-0	-3	-4	-0	-0.7

● **BERNIE BOLAND**   Boland, Bernard Anthony   b: 1/21/1892, Rochester, N.Y.   d: 9/12/73, Detroit, Mich.   BR/TR, 5'8.5", 168 lbs.   Deb: 4/14/15

YEAR TM/L	W	L	PCT	G	GS	CG	SH	SV	IP	H	HR	BB	SO	RAT	ERA	ERA+	OAV	OOB	BH	AVG	PB	PR	/A	PD	TPI
1915 Det-A	13	7	.650	45	18	8	1	2	202²	167	2	75	72	11.0	3.11	98	.230	.307	11	.175	-1	-4	-2	0	-0.2
1916 Det-A	10	3	.769	46	9	5	1	3	130¹	111	1	73	59	13.0	3.94	73	.240	.349	8	.250	2	-16	-15	-3	-1.7
1917 Det-A	16	11	.593	43	28	13	3	6	238	192	0	95	89	11.1	2.68	99	.226	.308	4	.056	-5	-1	-1	0	-0.7
1918 Det-A	14	10	.583	29	25	14	4	0	204	176	1	67	63	11.0	2.65	101	.236	.304	12	.174	0	3	0	-1	-0.1
1919 Det-A	14	16	.467	35	30	18	1	1	242²	222	7	80	71	11.3	3.04	105	.253	.318	8	.108	-3	5	4	-2	0.0
1920 Det-A	0	2	.000	4	3	1	0	0	17¹	23	0	14	4	20.3	7.79	48	.348	.476	1	.143	-0	-8	-8	-0	-0.7
1921 StL-A	1	4	.200	7	6	0	0	0	27	34	2	28	6	21.0	9.33	48	.309	.453	1	.100	-1	-15	-15	-0	-2.0
Total 7	68	53	.562	209	119	59	10	12	1062	925	13	432	364	11.7	3.25	91	.241	.322	45	.138	-8	-35	-36	-5	-5.4

● **BILL BOLDEN**   Bolden, William Horace "Big Bill"   b: 5/9/1893, Dandridge, Tenn.   d: 12/8/66, Jefferson City, Tenn.   BR/TR, 6'4", 200 lbs.   Deb: 6/27/19

YEAR TM/L	W	L	PCT	G	GS	CG	SH	SV	IP	H	HR	BB	SO	RAT	ERA	ERA+	OAV	OOB	BH	AVG	PB	PR	/A	PD	TPI
1919 StL-N	0	1	.000	3	1	0	0	0	12	17	0	4	4	16.5	5.25	53	.340	.400	1	.333	0	-3	-3	0	-0.2

● **STEW BOLEN**   Bolen, Stewart O'Neal   b: 10/12/02, Jackson, Ala.   d: 8/30/69, Mobile, Ala.   BL/TL, 5'11", 180 lbs.   Deb: 4/15/26

YEAR TM/L	W	L	PCT	G	GS	CG	SH	SV	IP	H	HR	BB	SO	RAT	ERA	ERA+	OAV	OOB	BH	AVG	PB	PR	/A	PD	TPI
1926 StL-A	0	0	—	5	0	0	0	0	14²	21	2	6	7	16.6	6.14	70	.356	.415	2	.500	1	-3	-3	-0	-0.3
1927 StL-A	0	1	.000	3	1	0	0	0	9²	14	0	5	7	17.7	8.38	52	.368	.442	1	.333	1	-5	-4	0	-0.3
1931 Phi-N	3	12	.200	28	16	2	0	0	98¹	117	5	63	55	16.8	6.39	66	.297	.399	5	.156	-1	-28	-23	0	-3.1
1932 Phi-N	0	0	—	5	0	0	0	0	16	18	0	10	3	16.9	2.81	157	.281	.395	1	.143	-0	2	3	-0	-0.1
Total 4	3	13	.188	41	17	3	0	0	139	170	7	84	72	16.8	6.09	75	.306	.403	9	.196	-0	-34	-28	-0	-3.5

● **BOBBY BOLIN**   Bolin, Bobby Donald   b: 1/29/39, Hickory Grove, S.C.   BR/TR, 6'4", 200 lbs.   Deb: 4/18/61

YEAR TM/L	W	L	PCT	G	GS	CG	SH	SV	IP	H	HR	BB	SO	RAT	ERA	ERA+	OAV	OOB	BH	AVG	PB	PR	/A	PD	TPI
1961 SF-N	2	2	.500	37	1	0	0	5	48	37	6	37	48	14.4	3.19	120	.210	.356	2	.286	0	5	3	-1	0.3
1962 *SF-N	7	3	.700	41	5	2	0	5	92	84	10	35	74	12.1	3.62	105	.243	.321	6	.261	2	3	2	-1	0.3
1963 SF-N	10	6	.625	47	12	2	0	7	137¹	128	13	57	134	12.6	3.28	98	.242	.324	5	.143	2	0	-1	-2	-0.2
1964 SF-N	6	9	.400	38	23	5	3	1	174²	143	16	77	146	11.9	3.25	110	.220	.313	5	.100	0	6	6	0	0.5
1965 SF-N	14	6	.700	45	13	2	0	2	163	125	17	56	135	10.2	2.76	130	.214	.288	9	.167	1	14	15	-2	1.8
1966 SF-N	11	10	.524	36	34	10	4	1	224¹	174	25	70	143	10.2	2.89	127	.211	.281	13	.171	3	18	19	-2	1.9
1967 SF-N	6	8	.429	37	15	0	0	0	120	120	16	50	69	13.0	4.88	67	.258	.333	8	.242	2	-20	-21	-1	-2.2
1968 SF-N	10	5	.667	34	19	6	3	0	176²	128	9	46	126	9.1	1.99	148	.200	.258	5	.091	-1	20	19	-1	1.5
1969 SF-N	7	7	.500	30	22	2	0	0	146¹	149	17	49	102	12.6	4.43	79	.260	.326	6	.154	3	-14	-15	-1	-1.1
1970 Mil-A	5	11	.313	32	20	3	0	1	132	131	20	67	81	13.8	4.91	77	.256	.346	7	.194	2	-18	-16	-1	-1.7
Bos-A	2	0	1.000	6	0	0	0	2	8	2	0	5	8	9.0	0.00	—	.080	.258	0	.000	-0	3	4	0	1.1
Yr	7	11	.389	38	20	3	0	3	140	133	20	72	89	13.2	4.63	82	.243	.332	7	.189	2	-14	-13	-1	-0.6
1971 Bos-A	5	3	.625	52	0	0	0	6	69²	74	5	24	51	12.7	4.26	87	.273	.332	3	.250	0	-6	-4	-1	-0.6
1972 Bos-A	0	1	.000	21	0	0	0	5	30²	24	3	11	27	10.6	2.93	109	.209	.283	0	—	0	0	1	-0	0.0
1973 Bos-A	3	4	.429	39	0	0	0	15	53¹	45	5	13	31	10.0	2.70	149	.232	.284	0	—	0	7	8	1	1.6
Total 13	88	75	.540	495	164	32	10	50	1576	1364	164	597	1175	11.5	3.40	103	.231	.308	69	.163	15	18	19	-13	3.2

● **GREG BOLLO**   Bollo, Gregory Gene   b: 11/16/43, Detroit, Mich.   BR/TR, 6'4", 183 lbs.   Deb: 5/9/65

YEAR TM/L	W	L	PCT	G	GS	CG	SH	SV	IP	H	HR	BB	SO	RAT	ERA	ERA+	OAV	OOB	BH	AVG	PB	PR	/A	PD	TPI
1965 Chi-A	0	0	—	15	0	0	0	0	22²	12	5	9	16	9.1	3.57	89	.152	.256	0	—	0	-0	-1	0	0.0
1966 Chi-A	0	1	.000	3	1	0	0	0	7	7	0	3	4	14.1	2.57	123	.269	.367	0	.000	0	1	0	0	0.0
Total 2	0	1	.000	18	1	0	0	0	29²	19	5	12	20	10.3	3.34	96	.181	.283	0	.000	0	1	/0	0	0.0

● **RODNEY BOLTON**   Bolton, Rodney Earl   b: 9/23/68, Chattanooga, Tenn.   BR/TR, 6'2", 190 lbs.   Deb: 4/10/93

YEAR TM/L	W	L	PCT	G	GS	CG	SH	SV	IP	H	HR	BB	SO	RAT	ERA	ERA+	OAV	OOB	BH	AVG	PB	PR	/A	PD	TPI
1993 Chi-A	2	6	.250	9	8	0	0	0	42¹	55	4	16	17	15.3	7.44	56	.314	.375	0	—	0	-15	-15	1	-2.0
1995 Chi-A	0	2	.000	8	3	0	0	0	22	33	4	14	10	19.2	8.18	54	.351	.435	0	—	0	-8	-9	0	-0.4
Total 2	2	8	.200	17	11	0	0	0	64¹	88	8	30	27	16.6	7.69	56	.327	.397	0	—	0	-23	-24	1	-2.4

● **TOM BOLTON**   Bolton, Thomas Edward   b: 5/6/62, Nashville, Tenn.   BL/TL, 6'3", 175 lbs.   Deb: 5/17/87

YEAR TM/L	W	L	PCT	G	GS	CG	SH	SV	IP	H	HR	BB	SO	RAT	ERA	ERA+	OAV	OOB	BH	AVG	PB	PR	/A	PD	TPI
1987 Bos-A	1	0	1.000	29	0	0	0	0	61²	83	5	27	49	16.3	4.38	104	.329	.399	0	—	0	1	1	0	-0.2
1988 Bos-A	1	3	.250	30	0	0	0	1	30¹	35	1	14	21	14.5	4.75	87	.285	.358	0	—	0	-3	-2	1	-0.5
1989 Bos-A	0	4	.000	28	4	0	0	0	17¹	21	1	10	9	16.1	8.31	49	.292	.378	0	—	0	-9	-8	-0	-1.8
1990 *Bos-A	10	5	.667	21	16	3	0	0	119²	111	6	47	65	12.1	3.38	120	.251	.327	0	—	0	7	9	1	0.7
1991 Bos-A	8	9	.471	25	19	0	0	0	110	136	6	51	64	15.4	5.24	82	.308	.381	0	—	0	-14	-11	-1	-1.9
1992 Bos-A	1	2	.333	21	4	0	0	0	29	34	0	14	23	15.5	3.41	123	.286	.370	0	—	0	2	3	0	-0.2
Cin-N	3	3	.500	16	8	0	0	0	46¹	52	9	23	27	15.0	5.24	69	.284	.370	0	.000	-1	-9	-8	0	-1.1
1993 Det-A	6	6	.500	43	8	0	0	0	102²	113	5	45	66	14.5	4.47	96	.282	.364	0	—	0	-2	-2	0	-0.5
1994 Bal-A	1	2	.333	22	0	0	0	0	23¹	29	3	13	12	16.2	5.40	93	.309	.393	0	—	0	-2	-1	0	-0.4
Total 8	31	34	.477	209	56	3	0	1	540¹	614	46	244	336	14.6	4.56	93	.289	.366	0	.000	-1	-28	-20	2	-5.5

● **MARK BOMBACK**   Bomback, Mark Vincent   b: 4/14/53, Portsmouth, Va.   BR/TR, 5'11", 170 lbs.   Deb: 9/12/78

YEAR TM/L	W	L	PCT	G	GS	CG	SH	SV	IP	H	HR	BB	SO	RAT	ERA	ERA+	OAV	OOB	BH	AVG	PB	PR	/A	PD	TPI
1978 Mil-A	0	0	—	2	1	0	0	0	1²	5	1	1	1	32.4	16.20	23	.500	.545	0	—	0	-2	-2	-0	0.0
1980 NY-N	10	8	.556	36	25	2	1	0	162²	191	17	49	68	13.5	4.09	87	.297	.350	10	.233	3	-9	-10	2	-0.4
1981 Tor-A	5	5	.500	20	11	0	0	0	90¹	84	6	35	33	12.0	3.89	101	.251	.323	0	—	0	-2	-1	0	0.1
1982 Tor-A	1	5	.167	16	8	0	0	0	59²	87	10	25	22	17.3	6.03	74	.343	.408	0	—	0	-13	-10	1	-1.3
Total 4	16	18	.471	74	45	2	1	0	314¹	367	34	110	124	13.9	4.44	86	.295	.356	10	.233	3	-27	-22	3	-1.6

● **TOMMY BOND**   Bond, Thomas Henry   b: 4/2/1856, Granard, Ireland   d: 1/24/41, Boston, Mass.   BR/TR, 5'7.5", 160 lbs.   Deb: 5/5/1874   MU♦

YEAR TM/L	W	L	PCT	G	GS	CG	SH	SV	IP	H	HR	BB	SO	RAT	ERA	ERA+	OAV	OOB	BH	AVG	PB	PR	/A	PD	TPI
1874 Atl-n	22	32	.407	55	55	55	1	0	497	606	16	8	39	11.1	2.03	101	.266	.268	54	.220	-0	8	1		0.9
1875 Har-n	19	16	.543	40	39	37	6	0	352	302	3	7	70	7.9	1.41	167	.216	.219	77	.266	3	32	37		3.7
1876 Har-N	31	13	.705	45	45	45	6	0	408	355	2	18	88	8.1	1.68	141	.220	.227	50	.275	1	29	32	5	3.2
1877 Bos-N	40	17	.702	58	58	58	6	0	521	530	5	36	170	9.8	2.11	133	.249	.261	59	.228	-4	41	41	3	3.5
1878 Bos-N	40	19	.678	59	59	57	9	0	532²	571	5	33	182	10.2	2.06	115	.269	.280	50	.212	-4	15	18	2	1.3
1879 Bos-N	43	19	.694	64	64	59	11	0	555¹	543	8	24	155	9.2	1.96	126	.251	.259	62	.241	2	33	32	7	3.8
1880 Bos-N	26	29	.473	63	57	49	3	0	493	559	1	45	118	11.0	2.67	85	.274	.290	62	.220	-2	-16	-22	10	-1.4
1881 Bos-N	0	3	.000	3	3	2	0	0	25¹	40	3	2	2	14.9	4.26	62	.360	.372	2	.200	-2	-4	-5	1	-0.4
1882 Wor-N	0	1	.000	2	1	1	0	0	12¹	12	0	7	2	13.9	4.38	71	.218	.306	4	.133	-1	-2	-2	1	-0.1
1884 Bos-U	13	9	.591	23	21	19	0	0	189	185	3	14	128	9.5	3.00	78	.239	.253	48	.296	-0	-12	-13	3	-1.0
Ind-a	0	5	.000	5	5	5	0	0	43	62	0	4	15	14.2	5.65	58	.310	.320	3	.130	-1	-11	-11	-1	-1.1
Total 2 n	41	48	.461	95	94	92	7	0	849	908	18	15	109	9.8	1.77	123	.247	.250	131	.245	2	41	38		4.6
Total 8	193	115	.627	322	314	294	35	0	2779²	2857	32	178	860	9.8	2.25	123	.255	.267	340	.236	-9	71	70	30	7.7

YEAR	TM/L	W	L	PCT	G	GS	CG	SH	SV	IP	H	HR	BB	SO	RAT	ERA	ERA+	OAV	OOB	BH	AVG	PB	PR	/A	PD	TPI

● RICKY BONES   Bones, Ricardo Ricky b: 4/7/69, Salinas, P.R.   BR/TR, 5'10", 175 lbs.   Deb: 8/11/91

YEAR	TM/L	W	L	PCT	G	GS	CG	SH	SV	IP	H	HR	BB	SO	RAT	ERA	ERA+	OAV	OOB	BH	AVG	PB	PR	/A	PD	TPI
1991	SD-N	4	6	.400	11	11	0	0	0	54	57	3	18	31	12.5	4.83	79	.269	.326	1	.077	-0	-7	-6	-1	-1.2
1992	Mil-A	9	10	.474	31	28	0	0	0	163¹	169	27	48	65	12.5	4.57	84	.264	.324	0	—	0	-12	-13	-1	-1.4
1993	Mil-A	11	11	.500	32	31	3	0	0	203²	222	28	63	63	12.9	4.86	87	.278	.336	0	—	0	-12	-14	-1	-1.2
1994	Mil-A☆	10	9	.526	24	24	4	1	0	170²	166	17	45	57	11.3	3.43	147	.255	.306	0	—	0	26	30	-3	2.5
1995	Mil-A	10	12	.455	32	31	3	0	0	200¹	218	26	83	77	13.7	4.63	108	.281	.353	0	—	0	2	8	2	0.5
1996	Mil-A	7	14	.333	32	23	0	0	0	145	170	28	62	59	15.0	5.83	90	.294	.371	0	—	0	-14	-9	-2	-1.6
	NY-A	0	0	—	4	1	0	0	0	7	14	2	6	4	27.0	14.14	36	.438	.538	0	—	-0	-7	-7	-0	-0.1
	Yr	7	14	.333	36	24	0	0	0	152	184	30	68	63	15.0	6.22	84	.295	.365	0	—	0	-21	-16	-2	-1.7
Total	6	51	62	.451	166	149	10	1	0	944	1016	131	325	356	13.1	4.72	97	.275	.340	1	.077	-0	-23	-13	-6	-2.5

● JULIO BONETTI   Bonetti, Julio Giacomo b: 7/14/11, Genoa, Italy d: 6/17/52, Belmont, Cal.   BR/TR, 6', 180 lbs.   Deb: 4/22/37

YEAR	TM/L	W	L	PCT	G	GS	CG	SH	SV	IP	H	HR	BB	SO	RAT	ERA	ERA+	OAV	OOB	BH	AVG	PB	PR	/A	PD	TPI
1937	StL-A	4	11	.267	28	16	7	0	1	143¹	190	13	60	43	15.8	5.84	83	.321	.385	7	.149	-2	-19	-16	2	-1.3
1938	StL-A	2	3	.400	17	0	0	0	0	28¹	41	1	13	7	17.2	6.35	78	.350	.415	0	.000	-1	-5	-4	0	-0.7
1940	Chi-N	0	0	—	1	0	0	0	0	1¹	3	0	4	0	47.3	20.25	19	.429	.636	0	—	0	-2	-2	-0	0.0
Total	3	6	14	.300	46	16	7	0	1	173	234	14	77	50	16.3	6.03	80	.327	.394	7	.127	-3	-27	-23	2	-2.0

● HANK BONEY   Boney, Henry Tate "Haney" b: 10/28/03, Wallace, N.C.   BR/TR, 5'11", 176 lbs.   Deb: 6/28/27

YEAR	TM/L	W	L	PCT	G	GS	CG	SH	SV	IP	H	HR	BB	SO	RAT	ERA	ERA+	OAV	OOB	BH	AVG	PB	PR	/A	PD	TPI
1927	NY-N	0	0	—	3	0	0	0	0	4	4	0	2	0	13.5	2.25	171	.267	.353	0	—	0	1	1	-0	0.0

● TINY BONHAM   Bonham, Ernest Edward b: 8/16/13, Ione, Cal. d: 9/15/49, Pittsburgh, Pa.   BR/TR, 6'2", 215 lbs.   Deb: 8/5/40

YEAR	TM/L	W	L	PCT	G	GS	CG	SH	SV	IP	H	HR	BB	SO	RAT	ERA	ERA+	OAV	OOB	BH	AVG	PB	PR	/A	PD	TPI
1940	NY-A	9	3	.750	12	12	10	3	0	99¹	83	4	13	37	8.7	1.90	212	.224	.250	7	.189	0	27	24	-2	2.5
1941	*NY-A	9	6	.600	23	14	7	1	2	126²	118	12	31	43	10.7	2.98	132	.246	.294	8	.160	-1	16	13	-3	1.1
1942	*NY-A☆	21	5	**.808**	28	27	**22**	**6**	0	226	199	11	24	71	**8.9**	2.27	152	.237	**.259**	9	.122	-2	**35**	29	-4	2.6
1943	*NY-A☆	15	8	.652	28	26	17	4	1	225²	197	13	52	71	10.0	2.27	142	.236	.282	15	.197	0	26	24	-5	2.0
1944	NY-A	12	9	.571	26	25	17	1	0	213²	228	14	41	54	11.3	2.99	116	.273	.307	10	.133	-3	10	12	-3	0.5
1945	NY-A	8	11	.421	23	23	12	0	0	180²	186	11	22	42	10.5	3.29	105	.265	.288	15	.238	3	2	4	-3	0.3
1946	NY-A	5	8	.385	18	14	6	2	3	104²	97	6	23	30	10.3	3.70	93	.243	.284	4	.129	-0	-2	-3	-2	-0.6
1947	Pit-N	11	8	.579	33	18	7	3	3	149²	167	17	35	63	12.3	3.85	110	.277	.319	7	.156	-0	3	6	-3	0.4
1948	Pit-N	6	10	.375	22	20	7	0	0	135²	145	18	23	42	11.3	4.31	94	.276	.310	8	.163	-2	-5	-4	-4	-0.9
1949	Pit-N	7	4	.636	18	14	5	1	0	89	81	11	23	25	10.5	4.25	99	.246	.295	1	.045	-1	-0	-2	-2	-0.3
Total	10	103	72	.589	231	193	110	21	9	1551	1501	117	287	478	10.4	3.06	120	.254	.289	84	.161	-7	110	105	-29	7.6

● BILL BONHAM   Bonham, William Gordon b: 10/1/48, Glendale, Cal.   BR/TR, 6'3", 195 lbs.   Deb: 4/7/71

YEAR	TM/L	W	L	PCT	G	GS	CG	SH	SV	IP	H	HR	BB	SO	RAT	ERA	ERA+	OAV	OOB	BH	AVG	PB	PR	/A	PD	TPI
1971	Chi-N	2	1	.667	33	2	0	0	0	60	63	6	36	41	15.6	4.65	85	.281	.392	2	.167	-0	-8	-5	1	-0.1
1972	Chi-N	1	1	.500	19	4	0	0	0	57²	56	4	25	49	12.8	3.12	122	.260	.340	4	.286	1	2	4	0	0.4
1973	Chi-N	7	5	.583	44	15	3	0	6	152	126	10	64	121	11.5	3.02	131	.230	.315	4	.093	-3	11	16	4	1.4
1974	Chi-N	11	22	.333	44	36	10	2	1	242²	246	13	109	191	13.4	3.86	99	.263	.343	12	.143	-3	-6	-1	5	0.1
1975	Chi-N	13	15	.464	38	36	7	2	0	229¹	254	15	109	165	14.4	4.71	82	.281	.361	15	.183	-0	-28	-22	1	-2.3
1976	Chi-N	9	13	.409	32	31	3	0	0	196	215	11	96	110	14.4	4.27	90	.283	.365	13	.200	1	-17	-9	0	-0.8
1977	Chi-N	10	13	.435	34	34	1	0	0	214²	207	15	82	134	12.2	4.36	101	.254	.324	15	.231	1	-11	1	3	0.5
1978	Cin-N	11	5	.688	23	23	1	0	0	140¹	151	9	50	83	13.0	3.53	101	.276	.337	8	.186	1	5	3	0	0.6
1979	Cin-N	9	7	.563	29	29	2	0	0	175²	173	14	60	78	12.3	3.79	98	.261	.330	8	.140	-1	-1	-1	0	-0.2
1980	Cin-N	2	1	.667	4	4	0	0	0	19	21	1	5	13	12.4	4.74	75	.276	.321	0	.000	-0	-2	-2	-0	-0.4
Total	10	75	83	.475	300	214	27	4	11	1487¹	1512	98	636	985	13.2	4.01	97	.266	.343	81	.172	-2	-59	-20	18	-0.8

● JOE BONIKOWSKI   Bonikowski, Joseph Peter b: 1/16/41, Philadelphia, Pa.   BR/TR, 6', 175 lbs.   Deb: 4/12/62

YEAR	TM/L	W	L	PCT	G	GS	CG	SH	SV	IP	H	HR	BB	SO	RAT	ERA	ERA+	OAV	OOB	BH	AVG	PB	PR	/A	PD	TPI
1962	Min-A	5	7	.417	30	13	3	0	2	99²	95	6	38	45	12.1	3.88	105	.255	.325	4	.148	-1	1	2	1	0.3

● BILL BONNESS   Bonness, William John "Lefty" b: 12/15/23, Cleveland, Ohio d: 12/3/77, Detroit, Mich.   BR/TL, 6'4", 200 lbs.   Deb: 9/26/44

YEAR	TM/L	W	L	PCT	G	GS	CG	SH	SV	IP	H	HR	BB	SO	RAT	ERA	ERA+	OAV	OOB	BH	AVG	PB	PR	/A	PD	TPI
1944	Cle-A	0	1	.000	2	1	0	0	0	7	11	0	5	1	23.1	7.71	43	.367	.486	0	.000	-0	-3	-3	0	-0.4

● GUS BONO   Bono, Adlai Wendell b: 8/29/1894, Doe Run, Mo. d: 12/3/48, Dearborn, Mich.   BR/TR, 5'11", 175 lbs.   Deb: 9/13/20

YEAR	TM/L	W	L	PCT	G	GS	CG	SH	SV	IP	H	HR	BB	SO	RAT	ERA	ERA+	OAV	OOB	BH	AVG	PB	PR	/A	PD	TPI
1920	Was-A	0	2	.000	4	1	0	0	0	12¹	17	0	6	4	16.8	8.76	43	.315	.383	0	.000	-0	-7	-7	0	-0.9

● GREG BOOKER   Booker, Gregory Scott b: 6/22/60, Lynchburg, Va.   BR/TR, 6'6", 233 lbs.   Deb: 9/11/83

YEAR	TM/L	W	L	PCT	G	GS	CG	SH	SV	IP	H	HR	BB	SO	RAT	ERA	ERA+	OAV	OOB	BH	AVG	PB	PR	/A	PD	TPI
1983	SD-N	0	1	.000	6	1	0	0	0	11²	18	2	9	5	20.8	7.71	45	.375	.474	0	.000	-0	-5	-5	0	-0.4
1984	*SD-N	1	1	.500	32	1	0	0	0	57¹	67	4	27	28	14.8	3.30	108	.295	.370	2	.286	1	2	2	0	0.1
1985	SD-N	0	1	.000	17	0	0	0	0	22¹	20	3	17	7	15.3	6.85	52	.247	.384	0	.000	-0	-8	-8	-0	-0.4
1986	SD-N	1	0	1.000	9	0	0	0	0	11	10	2	4	5	11.5	1.64	233	.233	.298	0	—	0	3	2	-0	0.2
1987	SD-N	1	1	.500	44	0	0	0	1	68¹	62	5	30	17	12.5	3.16	125	.246	.333	0	.000	-1	7	6	-0	0.1
1988	SD-N	2	2	.500	34	2	0	0	0	63²	68	5	19	43	12.4	3.39	100	.278	.332	2	.250	1	0	1	1	0.1
1989	SD-N	0	1	.000	11	0	0	0	0	19	15	2	10	8	11.8	4.26	82	.224	.325	0	—	0	0	0	-0	-0.1
	Min-A	0	0	—	6	0	0	0	0	8²	11	1	2	6	13.5	4.15	100	.306	.342	0	—	-0	-0	-1	-0	-0.5
1990	SF-N	0	0	—	2	0	0	0	0	2	7	1	2	1	31.5	13.50	27	.538	.538	0	—	-0	-2	-2	-0	-0.2
Total	8	5	7	.417	161	4	0	0	2	264	278	24	118	119	13.7	3.89	94	.275	.353	4	.174	1	-6	-7	1	-0.9

● RED BOOLES   Booles, Seabron Jesse b: 7/14/1880, Bernice, La. d: 3/16/55, Monroe, La.   BL/TL, 5'10", 150 lbs.   Deb: 7/30/09

YEAR	TM/L	W	L	PCT	G	GS	CG	SH	SV	IP	H	HR	BB	SO	RAT	ERA	ERA+	OAV	OOB	BH	AVG	PB	PR	/A	PD	TPI
1909	Cle-A	0	1	.000	4	1	0	0	0	22²	20	0	8	6	11.5	1.99	129	.235	.309	1	.167	0	1	1	-0	0.1

● DANNY BOONE   Boone, Daniel Hugh b: 1/14/54, Long Beach, Cal.   BL/TL, 5'8", 150 lbs.   Deb: 4/11/81 F

YEAR	TM/L	W	L	PCT	G	GS	CG	SH	SV	IP	H	HR	BB	SO	RAT	ERA	ERA+	OAV	OOB	BH	AVG	PB	PR	/A	PD	TPI
1981	SD-N	1	0	1.000	37	0	0	0	2	63¹	63	2	21	43	12.1	2.84	113	.267	.329	2	.500	1	5	3	1	0.3
1982	SD-N	1	0	1.000	10	0	0	0	0	16	21	3	4	8	13.5	5.63	61	.323	.353	1	.200	0	-4	-4	0	-0.2
	Hou-N	0	1	.000	12	0	0	0	0	12²	7	1	4	4	7.8	3.55	93	.171	.244	0	.000	-0	0	-0	0	0.0
	Yr	1	1	.500	22	0	0	0	0	28²	28	4	8	12	11.0	4.71	72	.264	.310	1	.167	0	-4	-4	0	-0.2
1990	Bal-A	0	0	—	4	1	0	0	0	9²	12	1	3	2	14.9	2.79	136	.308	.372	0	—	0	1	1	0	0.3
Total	3	2	1	.667	61	1	0	0	4	101²	103	6	31	57	12.0	3.36	99	.270	.329	3	.300	1	2	0	1	0.4

● GEORGE BOONE   Boone, George Morris b: 3/1/1871, Louisville, Ky. d: 9/24/10, Louisville, Ky.   Deb: 4/23/1891

YEAR	TM/L	W	L	PCT	G	GS	CG	SH	SV	IP	H	HR	BB	SO	RAT	ERA	ERA+	OAV	OOB	BH	AVG	PB	PR	/A	PD	TPI
1891	Lou-a	0	0	—	4	1	0	0	1	15	15	0	9	4	14.4	7.80	47	.250	.348	2	.333	0	-7	-7	-0	-0.1

● DAN BOONE   Boone, James Albert b: 1/19/1895, Samantha, Ala. d: 5/11/68, Tuscaloosa, Ala.   BR/TR, 6'2", 190 lbs.   Deb: 9/10/19

YEAR	TM/L	W	L	PCT	G	GS	CG	SH	SV	IP	H	HR	BB	SO	RAT	ERA	ERA+	OAV	OOB	BH	AVG	PB	PR	/A	PD	TPI
1919	Phi-A	0	1	.000	3	2	0	0	0	14²	24	0	10	1	20.9	6.75	51	.375	.459	0	.000	-1	-6	-5	1	-0.3
1921	Det-A	0	0	—	1	0	0	0	0	2	3	0	0	1	13.5	0.00	—	.200	.429	0	.000	-0	1	1	0	0.1
1922	Cle-A	4	6	.400	11	10	4	2	0	75¹	87	3	19	9	12.8	4.06	99	.298	.343	5	.192	-1	-0	-0	-1	-0.1
1923	Cle-A	4	6	.400	27	4	2	0	0	70¹	93	3	31	15	16.3	6.01	66	.322	.393	4	.211	-0	-16	-16	3	-1.6
Total	4	8	13	.381	42	16	6	2	0	162¹	205	6	62	25	15.0	5.10	77	.315	.378	9	.180	-1	-21	-21	4	-2.0

● AMOS BOOTH   Booth, Amos Smith "Darling" b: 9/14/1853, Cincinnati, O. d: 7/1/21, Miamisburg, Ohio   BR/TR, 5'9", 159 lbs.   Deb: 4/25/1876 ♦

YEAR	TM/L	W	L	PCT	G	GS	CG	SH	SV	IP	H	HR	BB	SO	RAT	ERA	ERA+	OAV	OOB	BH	AVG	PB	PR	/A	PD	TPI
1876	Cin-N	0	1	.000	3	1	0	0	0	9²	22	0	1	0	20.5	9.31	24	.431	.431	71	.261	♦	-8	-8	-0	-0.6
1877	Cin-N	1	7	.125	12	8	6	0	0	86	114	1	13	18	13.3	3.56	74	.296	.319	27	.172	-1	-7	-9	-1	-0.8
Total	2	1	8	.111	15	9	6	0	0	95²	136	1	13	18	14.0	4.14	63	.312	.332	98	.224	-1	-15	-16	-1	-1.4

● EDDIE BOOTH   Booth, Edward H. b: Brooklyn, N.Y.   Deb: 4/26/1872 ♦

YEAR	TM/L	W	L	PCT	G	GS	CG	SH	SV	IP	H	HR	BB	SO	RAT	ERA	ERA+	OAV	OOB	BH	AVG	PB	PR	/A	PD	TPI
1876	NY-N	0	0	—	1	0	0	0	0	5	16	0	0	0	28.8	10.80	20	.471	.471	49	.215	-0	-5	-5	-0	0.0

● JOHN BOOZER   Boozer, John Morgan b: 7/6/38, Columbia, S.C. d: 1/24/86, Lexington, S.C.   BR/TR, 6'3", 205 lbs.   Deb: 7/22/62

YEAR	TM/L	W	L	PCT	G	GS	CG	SH	SV	IP	H	HR	BB	SO	RAT	ERA	ERA+	OAV	OOB	BH	AVG	PB	PR	/A	PD	TPI
1962	Phi-N	0	0	—	9	0	0	0	0	20¹	22	3	10	13	14.2	5.75	67	.282	.364	0	.000	-0	-4	-4	-0	0.0
1963	Phi-N	3	4	.429	21	11	1	0	0	83	67	11	33	69	11.0	2.93	110	.227	.307	3	.143	-0	3	3	-2	0.0
1964	Phi-N	3	4	.429	22	3	0	0	0	60¹	64	6	18	51	12.5	5.07	68	.271	.328	1	.077	-1	-10	-11	1	-1.2
1966	Phi-N	0	0	—	2	0	0	0	0	5¹	8	1	3	5	18.6	6.75	53	.348	.423	0	.000	-0	-2	-2	-0	-0.2
1967	Phi-N	5	4	.556	28	7	1	0	1	74²	86	6	24	48	13.4	4.10	83	.292	.347	4	.211	1	-6	-6	-0	-0.6

YEAR	TM/L	W	L	PCT	G	GS	CG	SH	SV	IP	H	HR	BB	SO	RAT	ERA	ERA+	OAV	OOB	BH	AVG	PB	PR	/A	PD	TPI
1968	Phi-N	2	2	.500	38	0	0	0	5	68²	76	3	15	49	12.2	3.67	82	.279	.322	1	.111	-0	-5	-5	-0	-0.4
1969	Phi-N	1	2	.333	46	2	0	0	6	82	91	12	36	47	13.9	4.28	83	.283	.356	3	.333	1	-6	-7	-1	-0.3
Total	7	14	16	.467	171	22	3	0	15	394¹	414	42	139	282	12.8	4.09	82	.272	.336	12	.162	-0	-30	-31	-2	-2.5

● PEDRO BORBON
Borbon, Pedro (Rodriguez)   b: 12/2/46, Valverde, Mao, D.R.   BR/TR, 6'2", 185 lbs.   Deb: 4/9/69   F

YEAR	TM/L	W	L	PCT	G	GS	CG	SH	SV	IP	H	HR	BB	SO	RAT	ERA	ERA+	OAV	OOB	BH	AVG	PB	PR	/A	PD	TPI
1969	Cal-A	2	3	.400	22	0	0	0	0	41	55	5	11	20	15.4	6.15	57	.324	.378	0	.000	-0	-12	-12	-0	-1.4
1970	Cin-N	0	2	.000	12	1	0	0	0	17¹	21	2	6	6	15.6	6.75	60	.309	.390	0	.000	-0	-5	-5	2	-0.4
1971	Cin-N	0	0	—	3	0	0	0	0	4¹	3	1	1	4	8.3	4.15	81	.200	.250	0	—	0	-0	-0	-0	-0.1
1972	*Cin-N	8	3	.727	62	2	0	0	11	122	115	5	32	48	11.1	3.17	101	.254	.307	1	.048	-1	4	1	-1	-0.1
1973	*Cin-N	11	4	.733	80	0	0	0	14	121	137	4	35	60	12.9	2.16	158	.298	.349	5	.333	1	**20**	17	-0	2.6
1974	Cin-N	10	7	.588	73	0	0	0	14	139	133	11	32	53	10.9	3.24	108	.255	.303	5	.192	-0	6	4	-1	0.4
1975	*Cin-N	9	5	.643	67	0	0	0	5	125	145	6	21	29	12.2	2.95	122	.301	.334	7	.292	-0	9	9	-1	1.1
1976	*Cin-N	4	3	.571	69	1	0	0	8	121	135	4	31	53	12.6	3.35	105	.292	.342	4	.222	0	2	2	-0	0.1
1977	Cin-N	10	5	.667	73	0	0	0	18	127	131	7	24	48	11.2	3.19	123	.268	.307	4	.182	-0	10	10	-2	1.3
1978	Cin-N	8	2	.800	62	0	0	0	4	99¹	102	6	27	35	12.0	4.98	71	.274	.328	2	.182	-0	-16	-16	-0	-1.7
1979	Cin-N	2	2	.500	30	0	0	0	2	44²	48	2	8	23	11.3	3.43	109	.277	.309	2	.333	0	2	2	-0	0.2
	SF-N	4	3	.571	30	0	0	0	3	46	56	7	13	26	13.5	4.89	71	.303	.348	1	.333	0	-6	-7	-1	-1.1
	Yr	6	5	.545	60	0	0	0	5	90²	104	9	21	49	12.4	4.17	87	.287	.326	3	.333	1	-4	-5	-1	-0.9
1980	StL-N	1	0	1.000	10	0	0	0	0	19	17	3	10	4	12.8	3.79	97	.250	.346	1	.250	0	-0	-0	-0	0.0
Total	12	69	39	.639	593	4	0	0	80	1026²	1098	63	251	409	12.1	3.52	101	.280	.328	32	.205	2	14	3	-4	1.0

● PEDRO BORBON
Borbon, Pedro Felix (Marte)   b: 11/15/67, Mao, D.R.   BR/TL, 6'1", 205 lbs.   Deb: 10/2/92   F

YEAR	TM/L	W	L	PCT	G	GS	CG	SH	SV	IP	H	HR	BB	SO	RAT	ERA	ERA+	OAV	OOB	BH	AVG	PB	PR	/A	PD	TPI
1992	Atl-N	0	1	.000	2	0	0	0	0	1¹	2	0	1	2	20.3	6.75	54	.333	.429	0	—	-0	-0	-0	0	-0.3
1993	Atl-N	0	0	—	3	0	0	0	0	1²	3	0	3	2	32.4	21.60	19	.429	.600	0	—	-0	-3	-3	-0	0.0
1995	*Atl-N	2	2	.500	41	0	0	0	2	32	29	6	17	33	13.2	3.09	138	.240	.338	0	.000	-0	4	4	0	0.5
1996	Atl-N	3	0	1.000	43	0	0	0	1	36	26	1	7	31	8.5	2.75	166	.200	.246	1	1.000	-0	6	7	0	0.6
Total	4	5	3	.625	89	0	0	0	3	71	60	7	28	67	11.4	3.42	126	.227	.306	1	.500	-0	7	8	1	0.8

● GEORGE BORCHERS
Borchers, George Benard "Chief"   b: 4/18/1869, Sacramento, Cal.   d: 10/24/38, Sacramento, Cal.   BB/TR, 5'10", 180 lbs.   Deb: 5/18/1888

YEAR	TM/L	W	L	PCT	G	GS	CG	SH	SV	IP	H	HR	BB	SO	RAT	ERA	ERA+	OAV	OOB	BH	AVG	PB	PR	/A	PD	TPI
1888	Chi-N	4	4	.500	10	10	7	1	0	67	67	2	29	26	13.7	3.49	87	.251	.338	2	.061	-2	-5	-3	-0	-0.5
1895	Lou-N	0	1	.000	1	1	0	0	0	0²	1	0	3	0	54.0	27.00	17	.333	.667	0	—	0	-2	-2	-0	-1.1
Total	2	4	5	.444	11	11	7	1	0	67²	68	2	32	26	14.1	3.72	82	.252	.344	2	.061	-2	-6	-5	-0	-1.6

● JOE BORDEN
Borden, Joseph Emley (a.k.a. Joseph Emley Josephs In 1875)   b: 5/9/1854, Jacobstown, N.J.   d: 10/14/29, Yeadon, Pa.   BR/TR, 5'9", 140 lbs.   Deb: 7/24/1875

YEAR	TM/L	W	L	PCT	G	GS	CG	SH	SV	IP	H	HR	BB	SO	RAT	ERA	ERA+	OAV	OOB	BH	AVG	PB	PR	/A	PD	TPI
1875	Phi-n	2	4	.333	7	7	7	2	0	66	47	0	7	9	**7.4**	1.50	152	**.181**	**.203**	3	.107	-3	5	6		0.1
1876	Bos-N	11	12	.478	29	24	16	2	1	218¹	257	4	51	34	12.7	2.89	78	.276	.313	25	.207	-3	-14	-15	-2	-1.7

● RICH BORDI
Bordi, Richard Albert   b: 4/18/59, San Francisco, Cal.   BR/TR, 6'7", 220 lbs.   Deb: 7/16/80

YEAR	TM/L	W	L	PCT	G	GS	CG	SH	SV	IP	H	HR	BB	SO	RAT	ERA	ERA+	OAV	OOB	BH	AVG	PB	PR	/A	PD	TPI
1980	Oak-A	0	0	—	1	0	0	0	0	2	4	0	0	0	18.0	4.50	84	.400	.400	0	—	0	-0	-0	-0	0.0
1981	Oak-A	0	0	—	2	0	0	0	0	2	1	0	1	0	9.0	0.00	—	.143	.250	0	—	0	1	1	-0	0.0
1982	Sea-A	0	2	.000	7	2	0	0	0	13	18	4	1	10	13.8	8.31	51	.310	.333	0	—	0	-6	-6	-0	-0.9
1983	Chi-N	0	2	.000	11	1	0	0	1	25¹	34	2	12	20	16.3	4.97	76	.321	.390	0	.000	-0	-4	-3	-0	-0.3
1984	Chi-N	5	2	.714	31	7	0	0	4	83¹	78	11	20	41	10.6	3.46	113	.242	.287	1	.053	-1	1	4	-1	0.1
1985	NY-A	6	8	.429	51	3	0	0	0	98	95	5	29	64	11.5	3.21	124	.253	.308	0	—	0	10	9	-1	1.2
1986	Bal-A	6	4	.600	52	1	0	0	3	107	105	13	41	83	12.6	4.46	93	.254	.327	0	—	0	-3	-4	1	-0.2
1987	NY-A	3	1	.750	16	1	0	0	0	33	42	7	12	23	14.7	7.64	57	.309	.365	0	—	0	-12	-12	-1	-1.2
1988	Oak-A	0	1	.000	2	0	0	0	0	7²	6	0	5	6	12.9	4.70	84	.214	.333	0	—	0	-1	-1	-0	-0.1
Total	9	20	20	.500	173	17	0	0	10	371¹	383	42	121	247	12.4	4.34	93	.263	.322	1	.043	-1	-13	-12	-2	-1.4

● BILL BORDLEY
Bordley, William Clarke   b: 1/9/58, Los Angeles, Cal.   BR/TL, 6'3", 185 lbs.   Deb: 6/30/80

YEAR	TM/L	W	L	PCT	G	GS	CG	SH	SV	IP	H	HR	BB	SO	RAT	ERA	ERA+	OAV	OOB	BH	AVG	PB	PR	/A	PD	TPI
1980	SF-N	2	3	.400	8	6	0	0	0	30²	34	3	11	16	16.1	4.70	75	.288	.396	1	.167	-0	-4	-4	-1	-0.5

● PAUL BORIS
Boris, Paul Stanley   b: 12/13/55, Irvington, N.J.   BR/TR, 6'2", 200 lbs.   Deb: 5/21/82

YEAR	TM/L	W	L	PCT	G	GS	CG	SH	SV	IP	H	HR	BB	SO	RAT	ERA	ERA+	OAV	OOB	BH	AVG	PB	PR	/A	PD	TPI
1982	Min-A	1	2	.333	23	0	0	0	0	49²	46	8	19	30	12.1	3.99	106	.246	.322	0	—	0	0	1	-1	-0.2

● FRANK BORK
Bork, Frank Bernard   b: 7/13/40, Buffalo, N.Y.   BR/TL, 6'2", 175 lbs.   Deb: 4/15/64

YEAR	TM/L	W	L	PCT	G	GS	CG	SH	SV	IP	H	HR	BB	SO	RAT	ERA	ERA+	OAV	OOB	BH	AVG	PB	PR	/A	PD	TPI
1964	Pit-N	2	2	.500	33	2	0	0	0	42	51	6	11	31	13.5	4.07	86	.295	.341	1	.200	0	-2	-3	0	-0.2

● TOM BORLAND
Borland, Thomas Bruce "Spike"   b: 2/14/33, ElDorado, Kan.   BL/TL, 6'3", 172 lbs.   Deb: 5/15/60

YEAR	TM/L	W	L	PCT	G	GS	CG	SH	SV	IP	H	HR	BB	SO	RAT	ERA	ERA+	OAV	OOB	BH	AVG	PB	PR	/A	PD	TPI
1960	Bos-A	0	4	.000	26	4	0	0	3	51	67	4	23	32	15.9	6.53	62	.322	.390	0	.000	-2	-15	-14	-0	-1.3
1961	Bos-A	0	0	—	1	0	0	0	0	1	3	0	0	0	27.0	18.00	23	.500	.500	0	—	0	-2	-2	-0	-0.1
Total	2	0	4	.000	27	4	0	0	3	52	70	4	23	32	16.1	6.75	60	.327	.392	0	.000	-2	-17	-16	-0	-1.3

● TOBY BORLAND
Borland, Toby Shawn   b: 5/29/69, Ruston, La.   BR/TR, 6'6", 186 lbs.   Deb: 5/27/94

YEAR	TM/L	W	L	PCT	G	GS	CG	SH	SV	IP	H	HR	BB	SO	RAT	ERA	ERA+	OAV	OOB	BH	AVG	PB	PR	/A	PD	TPI
1994	Phi-N	1	0	1.000	24	0	0	0	0	34¹	31	1	14	26	12.8	2.36	182	.248	.343	0	.000	-0	7	5	0	0.2
1995	Phi-N	1	3	.250	50	0	0	0	6	74	81	3	37	59	15.0	3.77	112	.277	.368	1	.200	-0	3	4	-1	0.2
1996	Phi-N	7	3	.700	69	0	0	0	1	90²	83	9	43	76	12.8	4.07	107	.239	.327	0	.000	-0	1	5	-1	0.1
Total	3	9	6	.600	143	0	0	0	7	199	195	13	94	161	13.6	3.66	117	.255	.346	1	.083	-1	12	14	-2	0.5

● JOE BOROWSKI
Borowski, Joseph Thomas   b: 5/4/71, Bayonne, N.J.   BR/TR, 6'2", 225 lbs.   Deb: 7/9/95

YEAR	TM/L	W	L	PCT	G	GS	CG	SH	SV	IP	H	HR	BB	SO	RAT	ERA	ERA+	OAV	OOB	BH	AVG	PB	PR	/A	PD	TPI
1995	Bal-A	0	0	—	6	0	0	0	0	7¹	5	0	4	3	11.0	1.23	387	.192	.300	0	—	0	3	3	0	-0.1
1996	Atl-N	2	4	.333	22	0	0	0	0	26	33	4	13	15	16.3	4.85	91	.330	.412	0	.000	-0	-2	-1	2	-0.1
Total	2	2	4	.333	28	0	0	0	0	33¹	38	4	17	18	15.1	4.05	111	.302	.389	0	.000	-0	1	2	2	-0.2

● HANK BOROWY
Borowy, Henry Ludwig   b: 5/12/16, Bloomfield, N.J.   BR/TR, 6', 175 lbs.   Deb: 4/18/42

YEAR	TM/L	W	L	PCT	G	GS	CG	SH	SV	IP	H	HR	BB	SO	RAT	ERA	ERA+	OAV	OOB	BH	AVG	PB	PR	/A	PD	TPI
1942	*NY-A	15	4	.789	25	21	13	4	1	178¹	157	6	66	85	11.3	2.52	136	.233	.301	11	.157	-1	22	18	1	1.9
1943	*NY-A	14	9	.609	29	27	14	3	0	217¹	195	11	72	113	11.1	2.82	114	.241	.305	15	.203	3	12	10	1	1.4
1944	NY-A★	17	12	.586	35	30	19	3	2	252²	224	15	88	107	11.1	2.64	132	.236	.301	12	.133	-3	22	24	1	2.5
1945	NY-A†	10	5	.667	18	18	7	1	0	132¹	107	6	58	35	11.3	3.13	111	.221	.305	11	.220	1	3	5	-1	0.8
	*Chi-N	11	2	.846	15	14	11	1	1	122¹	105	2	47	47	11.2	**2.13**	171	.231	.303	7	.171	-0	23	21	-1	2.1
1946	Chi-N	12	10	.545	32	28	8	1	0	201	220	9	61	95	12.6	3.76	88	.274	.326	13	.181	-1	-8	-10	-0	-0.9
1947	Chi-N	8	12	.400	40	25	9	0	2	183	190	19	63	75	12.5	4.38	90	.267	.328	7	.125	-1	-6	-9	-0	-0.9
1948	Chi-N	5	10	.333	39	17	2	1	1	127	156	9	40	54	14.5	4.89	80	.308	.369	8	.222	2	-13	-14	-1	-1.1
1949	Phi-N	12	12	.500	28	28	13	2	0	193¹	188	19	63	43	11.7	4.19	94	.259	.319	11	.213	-0	-3	-5	-2	-0.4
1950	Phi-N	0	0	—	3	0	0	0	0	6¹	5	0	4	3	12.8	5.68	71	.250	.375	0	—	-0	-1	-1	-0	-0.0
	Pit-N	1	3	.250	11	3	0	0	0	25¹	32	6	9	9	14.9	6.39	69	.311	.372	1	.167	-0	-6	-6	-0	-0.8
	Yr	1	3	.250	14	3	0	0	0	31²	37	6	13	12	14.5	6.25	69	.301	.372	1	.167	-0	-7	-7	-0	-0.8
	Det-A	1	1	.500	13	2	1	0	0	32²	23	3	16	12	10.7	3.31	142	.205	.305	1	.143	0	5	5	0	0.2
1951	Det-A	2	2	.500	14	2	1	0	0	45¹	58	3	21	16	17.1	6.95	60	.314	.404	0	.000	-0	-14	-14	-1	-1.1
Total	10	108	82	.568	314	214	94	16	7	1717	1660	108	623	690	12.0	3.50	104	.254	.320	99	.173	3	35	24	5	3.7

● CHRIS BOSIO
Bosio, Christopher Louis   b: 4/3/63, Carmichael, Cal.   BR/TR, 6'3", 235 lbs.   Deb: 8/3/86

YEAR	TM/L	W	L	PCT	G	GS	CG	SH	SV	IP	H	HR	BB	SO	RAT	ERA	ERA+	OAV	OOB	BH	AVG	PB	PR	/A	PD	TPI
1986	Mil-A	0	4	.000	10	4	0	0	0	34²	41	9	13	29	14.0	7.01	62	.293	.353		—	0	-11	-10	0	-1.1
1987	Mil-A	11	8	.579	46	19	2	1	2	170	187	18	50	150	12.6	5.24	87	.276	.327		—	0	-15	-13	1	-1.3
1988	Mil-A	7	15	.318	38	22	9	1	6	182	190	13	38	84	11.4	3.36	118	.268	.307		—	0	12	13	3	1.8
1989	Mil-A	15	10	.600	33	33	8	2	0	234²	225	16	48	173	10.7	2.95	130	.249	.291		—	0	24	23	1	2.5
1990	Mil-A	4	9	.308	20	20	4	1	0	132²	131	15	38	76	11.7	4.00	97	.258	.313		—	0	-1	-2	0	-0.0
1991	Mil-A	14	10	.583	32	32	5	0	0	204²	187	15	58	117	11.0	3.25	122	.244	.304		—	0	19	16	-1	1.8
1992	Mil-A	16	6	.727	33	33	4	2	0	231¹	223	21	44	120	10.5	3.62	106	.254	.293		—	0	8	6	0	0.7
1993	Sea-A	9	9	.500	29	24	3	1	1	164¹	138	14	59	119	11.1	3.45	128	.229	.304		—	0	16	15	0	1.7
1994	Sea-A	4	10	.286	19	19	4	0	0	125	137	15	40	67	12.9	4.32	113	.277	.333		—	0	7	8	2	0.8

YEAR TM/L	W	L	PCT	G	GS	CG	SH	SV	IP	H	HR	BB	SO	RAT	ERA	ERA+	OAV	OOB	BH	AVG	PB	PR	/A	PD	TPI
1995 *Sea-A	10	8	.556	31	31	0	0	0	170	211	18	69	85	15.1	4.92	96	.312	.380	0	—	0	-4	-4	0	-0.4
1996 Sea-A	4	4	.500	18	9	0	0	0	60^2	72	8	24	39	14.8	5.93	83	.299	.372	0	—	0	-6	-7	0	-0.7
Total 11	94	93	.503	309	246	39	9	9	1710	1742	162	481	1059	11.9	3.96	106	.264	.318	0	—	0	49	47	9	5.8

● SHAWN BOSKIE
Boskie, Shawn Kealoha   b: 3/28/67, Hawthorne, Nev.   BR/TR, 6'3", 205 lbs.   Deb: 5/20/90

YEAR TM/L	W	L	PCT	G	GS	CG	SH	SV	IP	H	HR	BB	SO	RAT	ERA	ERA+	OAV	OOB	BH	AVG	PB	PR	/A	PD	TPI
1990 Chi-N	5	6	.455	15	15	0	0	0	97^2	99	8	31	49	12.1	3.69	111	.265	.323	8	.222	1	1	4	0	0.6
1991 Chi-N	4	9	.308	28	20	0	0	0	129	150	14	52	62	14.4	5.23	74	.294	.364	7	.171	2	-22	-19	1	-1.5
1992 Chi-N	5	11	.313	23	18	0	0	0	91^2	96	14	36	39	13.4	5.01	72	.284	.360	5	.185	1	-15	-14	1	-2.1
1993 Chi-N	5	3	.625	39	2	0	0	0	65^2	63	7	21	39	12.5	3.43	116	.258	.335	3	.273	1	4	4	-1	0.4
1994 Chi-N	0	0	—	2	0	0	0	0	3^2	3	0	0	2	7.4	0.00	—	.214	.214	0	—	0	2	2	0	0.0
Phi-N	4	6	.400	18	14	1	0	0	84^1	85	14	29	59	12.5	5.23	82	.258	.323	3	.115	1	-10	-9	0	-0.8
Yr	4	6	.400	20	14	1	0	0	88	88	14	29	61	12.3	5.01	85	.256	.319	3	.115	1	-8	-7	1	-0.8
Sea-A	0	1	.000	2	1	0	0	0	2^2	4	1	1	0	16.9	6.75	72	.333	.385	0	—	0	-1	-1	0	-0.3
1995 Cal-A	7	7	.500	20	20	1	0	0	111^2	127	16	25	51	12.8	5.64	83	.281	.329	0	—	0	-12	-12	0	-1.1
1996 Cal-A	12	11	.522	37	28	1	0	0	189^1	226	40	67	133	14.5	5.32	92	.294	.360	0	—	0	-7	-9	0	-0.7
Total 7	42	54	.438	184	118	4	0	0	775^2	853	114	262	434	12.5	4.92	88	.280	.345	26	.184	5	-59	-53	2	-5.5

● DICK BOSMAN
Bosman, Richard Allen   b: 2/17/44, Kenosha, Wis.   BR/TR, 6'3", 208 lbs.   Deb: 6/1/66   C

YEAR TM/L	W	L	PCT	G	GS	CG	SH	SV	IP	H	HR	BB	SO	RAT	ERA	ERA+	OAV	OOB	BH	AVG	PB	PR	/A	PD	TPI
1966 Was-A	2	6	.250	13	7	0	0	0	39	60	4	12	20	16.6	7.62	45	.361	.404	3	.250	0	-18	-18	-1	-3.1
1967 Was-A	3	1	.750	7	7	2	1	0	51^1	38	3	10	25	8.4	1.75	180	.204	.245	3	.200	0	8	8	-1	0.7
1968 Was-A	2	9	.182	46	10	0	0	1	139	139	8	35	63	11.5	3.69	79	.262	.312	6	.200	1	-11	-12	-0	-0.9
1969 Was-A	14	5	.737	31	26	5	2	1	193	156	11	39	99	9.2	**2.19**	**158**	.220	.262	6	.094	-1	31	27	1	2.7
1970 Was-A	16	12	.571	36	34	7	3	0	230^2	212	16	71	134	11.1	3.00	118	.245	.304	11	.138	-2	18	14	0	1.4
1971 Was-A	12	16	.429	35	35	7	1	0	236^2	245	16	71	113	12.2	3.73	89	.272	.329	7	.093	-1	-7	-11	-2	-1.6
1972 Tex-A	8	10	.444	29	29	1	1	0	173^1	183	11	48	105	12.3	3.63	83	.273	.327	5	.094	-1	-11	-12	1	-1.3
1973 Tex-A	2	5	.286	7	7	1	1	0	40^1	42	6	17	14	13.4	4.24	88	.268	.343	0	—	0	-2	-2	-0	-0.4
Cle-A	1	8	.111	22	17	2	0	0	97	130	19	29	41	15.3	6.22	63	.320	.374	0	—	0	-26	-25	-1	-2.1
Yr	3	13	.188	29	24	3	1	0	137^1	172	25	46	55	14.7	5.64	69	.304	.363	0	—	0	-28	-27	-1	-2.5
1974 Cle-A	7	5	.583	25	18	2	1	0	127^1	126	13	29	56	11.0	4.10	88	.255	.298	0	—	0	-7	-7	-2	-0.8
1975 Cle-A	0	2	.000	6	3	0	0	0	28^2	33	3	8	11	13.8	4.08	93	.292	.351	0	—	0	-1	-1	-0	-0.1
*Oak-A	11	4	.733	22	21	2	0	0	122^2	112	12	24	42	10.2	3.52	103	.240	.281	0	—	0	3	1	-1	0.2
Yr	11	6	.647	28	24	2	0	0	151^1	145	15	32	53	10.7	3.63	101	.248	.290	0	—	0	3	0	-1	0.1
1976 Oak-A	4	2	.667	27	15	0	0	0	112	118	13	19	34	11.1	4.10	82	.274	.306	0	—	0	-7	-9	0	-0.4
Total 11	82	85	.491	306	229	29	10	2	1591	1594	149	412	757	11.5	3.67	93	.261	.312	41	.125	-5	-29	-46	-5	-5.7

● MEL BOSSER
Bosser, Melvin Edward   b: 2/8/20, Johnstown, Pa.   BR/TR, 6', 173 lbs.   Deb: 4/29/45

YEAR TM/L	W	L	PCT	G	GS	CG	SH	SV	IP	H	HR	BB	SO	RAT	ERA	ERA+	OAV	OOB	BH	AVG	PB	PR	/A	PD	TPI
1945 Cin-N	2	0	1.000	7	2	0	0	0	16	9	0	17	3	14.6	3.38	111	.158	.351	0	.000	-1	1	1	-0	0.0

● ANDY BOSWELL
Boswell, Andrew Cottrell   b: 9/5/1874, New Gretna, N.J.   d: 2/3/36, Ocean City, N.J.   TR, 6'1", 165 lbs.   Deb: 5/10/1895

YEAR TM/L	W	L	PCT	G	GS	CG	SH	SV	IP	H	HR	BB	SO	RAT	ERA	ERA+	OAV	OOB	BH	AVG	PB	PR	/A	PD	TPI
1895 NY-N	2	2	.500	5	4	3	0	0	34	41	1	22	18	17.5	5.82	80	.293	.400	3	.188	-1	-4	-4	-1	-0.5
Was-N	1	2	.333	6	3	3	0	0	30	44	1	19	12	19.5	6.00	80	.336	.428	4	.286	-1	-4	-4	-0	-0.3
Yr	3	4	.429	11	7	6	0	0	64	85	2	41	30	18.0	5.91	80	.310	.404	7	.233	-1	-8	-8	-1	-0.8

● DAVE BOSWELL
Boswell, David Wilson   b: 1/20/45, Baltimore, Md.   BR/TR, 6'3", 185 lbs.   Deb: 9/18/64

YEAR TM/L	W	L	PCT	G	GS	CG	SH	SV	IP	H	HR	BB	SO	RAT	ERA	ERA+	OAV	OOB	BH	AVG	PB	PR	/A	PD	TPI
1964 Min-A	2	0	1.000	4	4	0	0	0	23^1	21	4	12	25	12.7	4.24	84	.236	.327	2	.222	0	-2	-2	1	-0.1
1965 *Min-A	6	5	.545	27	12	1	0	0	106	77	20	46	85	10.9	3.40	105	.204	.298	12	.316	4	1	2	-1	0.5
1966 Min-A	12	5	.706	28	21	8	1	0	169^1	120	19	65	173	10.1	3.14	115	.197	.280	9	.143	-1	6	9	1	0.8
1967 Min-A	14	12	.538	37	32	11	3	0	222^2	162	14	107	204	11.2	3.27	106	.202	.302	16	.219	4	-1	5	-1	0.8
1968 Min-A	10	13	.435	34	28	7	2	0	190	148	19	87	143	11.5	3.32	93	.213	.307	16	.233	5	-7	-5	-2	-0.3
1969 *Min-A	20	12	.625	39	38	10	0	0	256^1	215	18	99	190	11.3	3.23	113	.226	.304	16	.170	3	11	12	-2	1.5
1970 Min-A	3	7	.300	18	15	0	0	0	68^2	80	12	44	45	16.5	6.42	58	.292	.394	4	.160	-0	-21	-21	-1	-2.7
1971 Det-A	0	0	—	3	0	0	0	0	4^1	3	0	4	3	18.7	6.23	58	.200	.429	0	—	-1	-1	-1	0	0.0
Bal-A	1	2	.333	15	1	0	0	0	24^2	32	4	15	14	17.1	4.38	77	.305	.392	1	.200	-1	-3	-3	0	-0.3
Yr	1	2	.333	18	1	0	0	0	29	35	4	21	17	17.4	4.66	73	.289	.394	1	.200	-1	-4	-4	0	-0.3
Total 8	68	56	.548	205	151	37	6	0	1065^1	858	110	481	882	11.6	3.52	99	.219	.310	74	.202	13	-17	-4	-4	0.2

● DEREK BOTELHO
Botelho, Derek Wayne   b: 8/2/56, Long Beach, Cal.   BR/TR, 6'2", 180 lbs.   Deb: 7/18/82

YEAR TM/L	W	L	PCT	G	GS	CG	SH	SV	IP	H	HR	BB	SO	RAT	ERA	ERA+	OAV	OOB	BH	AVG	PB	PR	/A	PD	TPI
1982 KC-A	2	1	.667	8	4	0	0	0	24	25	4	8	12	12.4	4.13	99	.275	.333	0	—	0	-1	-1	-0	-0.0
1985 Chi-N	1	3	.250	11	7	1	0	0	44	52	8	23	23	15.8	5.32	75	.299	.387	2	.143	-0	-8	-6	-0	-0.6
Total 2	3	4	.429	19	11	1	0	0	68	77	12	31	35	14.6	4.90	82	.291	.369	2	.143	-0	-9	-7	-1	-0.6

● RICKY BOTTALICO
Bottalico, Ricky Paul   b: 8/26/69, New Britain, Conn.   BL/TR, 6'1", 200 lbs.   Deb: 7/29/94

YEAR TM/L	W	L	PCT	G	GS	CG	SH	SV	IP	H	HR	BB	SO	RAT	ERA	ERA+	OAV	OOB	BH	AVG	PB	PR	/A	PD	TPI
1994 Phi-N	0	0	—	3	0	0	0	0	3	3	0	1	3	12.0	0.00	—	.250	.308	0	—	0	1	1	-0	0.1
1995 Phi-N	5	3	.625	62	0	0	0	1	87^2	50	7	42	87	9.9	2.46	171	.167	.277	0	.000	-1	17	17	-1	1.3
1996 Phi-N★	4	5	.444	61	0	0	0	34	67^2	47	6	23	74	9.6	3.19	137	.197	.274	1	.333	1	8	9	-1	1.8
Total 3	9	8	.529	126	0	0	0	35	158^1	100	13	66	164	9.8	2.73	157	.182	.277	1	.125	-0	26	27	-1	3.1

● KENT BOTTENFIELD
Bottenfield, Kent Dennis   b: 11/14/68, Portland, Ore.   BB/TR, 6'3", 225 lbs.   Deb: 7/6/92

YEAR TM/L	W	L	PCT	G	GS	CG	SH	SV	IP	H	HR	BB	SO	RAT	ERA	ERA+	OAV	OOB	BH	AVG	PB	PR	/A	PD	TPI
1992 Mon-N	1	2	.333	10	4	0	0	1	32^1	26	1	11	14	10.6	2.23	156	.217	.288	3	.375	1	5	4	-1	0.5
1993 Mon-N	2	5	.286	23	11	0	0	0	83	93	11	33	33	14.2	4.12	101	.288	.363	4	.167	-0	-1	0	-0	0.0
Col-N	3	5	.375	14	14	1	0	0	76^2	86	13	38	30	14.7	6.10	78	.302	.386	7	.269	1	-18	-11	2	-0.8
Yr	5	10	.333	37	25	1	0	0	159^2	179	24	71	63	14.1	5.07	88	.292	.386	11	.220	1	-18	-11	2	-0.8
1994 Col-N	3	1	.750	15	1	0	0	1	24^2	28	1	10	15	14.6	5.84	85	.283	.360	0	.000	-0	-4	-2	-1	-0.4
SF-N	0	0	—	1	0	0	0	0	1^2	5	1	0	2	27.0	10.80	37	.556	.556	0	—	0	-1	-1	-0	-0.1
Yr	3	1	.750	16	1	0	0	1	26^1	33	2	10	17	14.7	6.15	80	.300	.368	0	—	-0	-6	-4	-1	-0.4
1996 Chi-N	3	5	.375	48	0	0	0	0	61^2	59	7	19	33	11.8	2.63	162	.255	.320	1	.500	1	11	11	1	1.5
Total 4	12	18	.400	111	30	1	0	3	280	297	30	111	125	13.5	4.31	101	.278	.353	15	.246	2	-9	1	1	0.8

● RALPH BOTTING
Botting, Ralph Wayne   b: 5/12/55, Houlton, Maine   BL/TL, 6', 195 lbs.   Deb: 6/28/79

YEAR TM/L	W	L	PCT	G	GS	CG	SH	SV	IP	H	HR	BB	SO	RAT	ERA	ERA+	OAV	OOB	BH	AVG	PB	PR	/A	PD	TPI
1979 Cal-A	2	0	1.000	12	1	0	0	0	29^2	46	6	15	22	18.8	8.80	46	.362	.434	0	—	0	-15	-16	-0	-0.9
1980 Cal-A	0	3	.000	6	6	0	0	0	26^1	40	1	13	12	18.1	5.81	68	.348	.414	0	—	0	-5	-6	-0	-0.5
Total 2	2	3	.400	18	7	0	0	0	56	86	7	28	34	18.5	7.39	54	.355	.424	0	—	0	-20	-21	-0	-1.4

● BOB BOTZ
Botz, Robert Allen   b: 4/28/35, Milwaukee, Wis.   BR/TR, 5'11", 170 lbs.   Deb: 5/8/62

YEAR TM/L	W	L	PCT	G	GS	CG	SH	SV	IP	H	HR	BB	SO	RAT	ERA	ERA+	OAV	OOB	BH	AVG	PB	PR	/A	PD	TPI
1962 LA-A	2	1	.667	35	0	0	0	0	63	71	7	11	24	12.0	3.43	113	.285	.321	0	.000	-1	4	3	-1	-0.1

● DENIS BOUCHER
Boucher, Denis   b: 3/7/68, Montreal, Que., Can.   BR/TL, 6'1", 195 lbs.   Deb: 4/12/91

YEAR TM/L	W	L	PCT	G	GS	CG	SH	SV	IP	H	HR	BB	SO	RAT	ERA	ERA+	OAV	OOB	BH	AVG	PB	PR	/A	PD	TPI
1991 Tor-A	0	3	.000	7	7	0	0	0	35^1	39	6	16	16	14.5	4.58	92	.279	.361	0	—	0	-2	-1	1	-0.2
Cle-A	1	4	.200	5	5	0	0	0	22^2	35	6	8	13	17.1	8.34	50	.350	.398	0	—	0	-11	-11	0	-1.7
Yr	1	7	.125	12	12	0	0	0	58	74	12	24	29	15.2	6.05	69	.305	.367	0	—	0	-13	-12	1	-1.9
1992 Cle-A	2	2	.500	8	7	0	0	0	41	48	9	20	17	15.1	6.37	61	.302	.383	0	—	0	-11	-11	-0	-0.9
1993 Mon-N	3	1	.750	5	5	0	0	0	28^1	24	1	3	14	8.6	1.91	219	.229	.250	1	.167	0	7	7	-0	1.0
1994 Mon-N	0	1	.000	10	2	0	0	0	18^2	24	6	7	17	14.9	6.75	63	.324	.383	1	.333	1	-5	-5	0	-0.2
Total 4	6	11	.353	35	26	0	0	0	146	170	28	54	77	14.0	5.42	76	.294	.357	2	.222	1	-22	-21	0	-2.0

● CARL BOULDIN
Bouldin, Carl Edward   b: 9/17/39, Germantown, Ky.   BB/TR, 6'2", 180 lbs.   Deb: 9/2/61

YEAR TM/L	W	L	PCT	G	GS	CG	SH	SV	IP	H	HR	BB	SO	RAT	ERA	ERA+	OAV	OOB	BH	AVG	PB	PR	/A	PD	TPI
1961 Was-A	0	1	.000	2	1	0	0	0	3	5	2	9	5	29.7	16.20	25	.500	.550	0	.000	-0	-5	-5	-0	-0.9
1962 Was-A	1	2	.333	2	1	0	0	0	20	26	0	9	12	16.2	5.85	69	.321	.396	0	.000	-1	-4	-4	-0	-0.6
1963 Was-A	2	2	.500	10	3	0	0	0	23^1	31	3	8	15	15.0	5.79	64	.307	.358	0	.000	-1	-6	-5	-0	-0.9
1964 Was-A	0	3	.000	9	3	0	0	0	25	30	2	11	12	15.5	5.40	69	.294	.374	0	.000	-2	-5	-5	-0	-0.6
Total 4	3	8	.273	27	10	0	0	0	71^2	96	7	30	36	16.2	6.15	62	.318	.385	0	.000	-2	-19	-19	-0	-3.0

YEAR	TM/L	W	L	PCT	G	GS	CG	SH	SV	IP	H	HR	BB	SO	RAT	ERA	ERA+	OAV	OOB	BH	AVG	PB	PR	/A	PD	TPI

● JAKE BOULTES   Boultes, Jacob John b: 8/6/1884, St.Louis, Mo. d: 12/24/55, St.Louis, Mo. TR , 6'3", Deb: 4/18/07

1907	Bos-N	5	9	.357	24	12	11	0	0	139²	140	1	50	49	12.8	2.71	94	.266	.338	9	.132	-2	-4	-2	4	0.0
1908	Bos-N	3	5	.375	17	5	1	0	0	74²	80	7	8	28	10.7	3.01	80	.274	.296	3	.143	-0	-5	-5	-0	-0.7
1909	Bos-N	0	0	—	1	0	0	0	0	8	9	2	0	1	11.3	6.75	42	.290	.313	1	.333	0	-4	-3	-0	0.0
Total	3	8	14	.364	42	17	12	0	0	222¹	229	10	58	78	12.0	2.96	85	.269	.324	13	.141	-2	-13	-11	4	-0.7

● STEVE BOURGEOIS   Bourgeois, Steven James b: 8/4/72, Lutcher, La. BR/TR, 6'1", 220 lbs. Deb: 4/3/96

| 1996 | SF-N | 1 | 3 | .250 | 15 | 5 | 0 | 0 | 0 | 40 | 60 | 4 | 21 | 17 | 19.1 | 6.30 | 65 | .355 | .438 | 3 | .273 | 2 | -9 | -10 | 0 | -0.6 |

● JIM BOUTON   Bouton, James Alan b: 3/8/39, Newark, N.J. BR/TR, 6', 185 lbs. Deb: 4/22/62

1962	NY-A	7	7	.500	36	16	3	1	2	133	124	9	59	71	12.4	3.99	94	.254	.334	2	.063	-2	-0	-4	-0	-0.5
1963	*NY-A★	21	7	.750	40	30	12	6	1	249¹	191	18	87	148	10.1	2.53	139	.212	.284	6	.072	-6	31	27	-1	2.3
1964	*NY-A	18	13	.581	38	37	11	4	0	271¹	227	32	60	125	9.7	3.02	120	.225	.273	13	.130	-3	18	18	-3	1.3
1965	NY-A	4	15	.211	30	25	4	0	0	151¹	158	23	60	97	13.3	4.82	71	.269	.342	4	.093	-0	-23	-24	-0	-2.8
1966	NY-A	3	8	.273	24	19	3	0	1	120¹	117	13	38	65	11.7	2.69	123	.257	.315	4	.105	-2	10	8	1	0.7
1967	NY-A	1	0	1.000	17	1	0	0	0	44¹	47	5	18	31	13.4	4.67	67	.275	.347	0	.000	-0	-7	-8	-0	-0.2
1968	NY-A	1	1	.500	12	3	1	0	0	44	49	5	9	24	12.3	3.68	79	.287	.330	0	.000	-0	-3	-4	1	-0.1
1969	Sea-A	2	1	.667	57	1	0	0	1	92	77	12	38	68	11.4	3.91	93	.219	.299	0	.000	-1	-3	-3	1	-0.1
	Hou-N	0	2	.000	16	1	1	0	1	30²	32	1	12	32	13.5	4.11	86	.267	.343	0	.000	-0	-2	-2	-0	-0.2
1970	Hou-N	4	6	.400	29	6	1	0	0	73¹	84	5	33	49	14.5	5.40	72	.285	.359	6	.353	2	-11	-12	-1	-1.3
1978	Atl-N	1	3	.250	5	5	1	0	0	29	25	4	21	10	14.3	4.97	82	.234	.359	0	.000	-0	-4	-3	-0	-0.5
Total	10	62	63	.496	304	144	34	11	6	1238²	1131	127	435	720	11.5	3.57	90	.243	.311	35	.101	-13	5	-5	-1	-1.4

● RYAN BOWEN   Bowen, Ryan Eugene b: 2/10/68, Hanford, Cal. BR/TR, 6', 185 lbs. Deb: 7/22/91

1991	Hou-N	6	4	.600	14	13	0	0	0	71²	73	4	36	49	14.1	5.15	68	.268	.360	4	.182	1	-12	-13	-1	-1.6
1992	Hou-N	0	7	.000	11	9	0	0	0	33²	48	8	30	22	21.4	10.96	31	.333	.455	1	.111	-0	-28	-28	-1	-4.6
1993	Fla-N	8	12	.400	27	27	2	1	0	156²	156	11	87	98	14.1	4.42	98	.263	.360	6	.118	-1	-7	-2	-0	-0.3
1994	Fla-N	1	5	.167	8	8	1	0	0	47¹	50	9	19	32	13.5	4.94	88	.273	.348	5	.357	2	-4	-3	-1	-0.2
1995	Fla-N	2	0	1.000	4	3	0	0	0	16²	23	3	12	15	18.9	3.78	111	.329	.427	2	.333	0	1	1	-0	0.1
Total	5	17	28	.378	64	60	3	1	0	326	350	35	184	216	15.0	5.30	76	.277	.373	18	.176	2	-49	-46	-4	-6.6

● CY BOWEN   Bowen, Sutherland McCoy b: 2/17/1871, Kingston, Ind. d: 1/25/25, Greensburg, Ind. BR/TR, 6', 175 lbs. Deb: 4/28/1896

| 1896 | NY-N | 0 | 1 | .000 | 2 | 1 | 1 | 0 | 0 | 12 | 12 | 0 | 9 | 3 | 18.0 | 6.00 | 70 | .261 | .414 | 1 | .333 | 0 | -2 | -2 | 0 | -0.1 |

● FRANK BOWERMAN   Bowerman, Frank Eugene "Mike" b: 12/5/1868, Romeo, Mich. d: 11/30/48, Romeo, Mich. BR/TR, 6'2", 190 lbs. Deb: 8/24/1895 M♦

| 1904 | NY-N | 0 | 0 | — | 1 | 0 | 0 | 0 | 0 | 1 | 3 | 0 | 1 | 0 | 36.0 | 9.00 | 30 | .429 | .500 | 67 | .232 | M | -1 | -1 | -0 | 0.0 |

● STEW BOWERS   Bowers, Stewart Cole "Doc" b: 2/26/15, New Freedom, Pa. BB/TR, 6', 170 lbs. Deb: 8/5/35 ♦

1935	Bos-A	2	1	.667	10	2	1	0	0	23²	26	1	17	5	16.4	3.42	139	.283	.394	1	.200	-0	1	1	-0	0.4
1936	Bos-A	0	0	—	5	0	0	0	0	5²	10	1	2	0	19.1	9.53	56	.370	.414	0	—	-0	-3	-3	-0	0.0
Total	2	2	1	.667	15	2	1	0	0	29¹	36	2	19	5	16.9	4.60	106	.303	.399	1	.200	-0	1	1	-0	0.4

● GRANT BOWLER   Bowler, Grant Tierney "Moose" b: 10/24/07, Denver, Col. d: 6/25/68, Denver, Colo. BR/TR, 6', 190 lbs. Deb: 8/21/31

1931	Chi-A	0	1	.000	13	3	1	0	0	35¹	40	1	24	15	16.3	5.35	80	.288	.393	1	.100	-0	-4	-4	-1	-0.2
1932	Chi-A	0	0	—	4	0	0	0	0	6¹	15	1	3	2	25.6	15.63	28	.484	.529	0	.000	-0	-8	-8	-0	-0.2
Total	2	0	1	.000	17	3	1	0	0	41²	55	2	27	17	17.7	6.91	62	.324	.416	1	.083	-1	-12	-12	-1	-0.2

● CHARLIE BOWLES   Bowles, Charles James b: 3/15/17, Norwood, Mass. BR/TR, 6'3", 180 lbs. Deb: 9/25/43

1943	Phi-A	1	1	.500	2	2	2	0	0	18	17	0	4	6	10.5	3.00	113	.258	.300	1	.125	-1	1	1	0	0.0
1945	Phi-A	0	3	.000	8	4	1	0	0	33¹	35	3	23	11	15.7	5.13	67	.273	.384	5	.238	1	-7	-6	0	-0.5
Total	2	1	4	.200	10	6	3	0	0	51¹	52	3	27	17	13.9	4.38	78	.268	.357	6	.207	-0	-6	-5	0	-0.5

● EMMETT BOWLES   Bowles, Emmett Jerome "Chief" b: 8/2/1898, Wanette, Okla. d: 9/3/59, Flagstaff, Ariz. BR/TR, 6', 180 lbs. Deb: 9/12/22

| 1922 | Chi-A | 0 | 0 | — | 1 | 0 | 0 | 0 | 0 | 1 | 2 | 0 | 1 | 0 | 27.0 | 27.00 | 15 | .500 | .600 | 0 | — | 0 | -3 | -3 | -0 | 0.0 |

● ABE BOWMAN   Bowman, Alvah Edson b: 1/25/1893, Greenup, Ill. d: 10/11/79, Longview, Tex. BR/TR, 6'1", 190 lbs. Deb: 5/19/14

1914	Cle-A	2	7	.222	22	10	2	1	0	72²	74	0	45	27	15.2	4.46	65	.277	.389	1	.048	-2	-14	-13	-0	-1.7
1915	Cle-A	0	1	.000	2	1	0	0	0	1¹	1	0	3	0	27.0	20.25	15	.250	.571	0	—	-0	-3	-3	1	-1.2
Total	2	2	8	.200	24	11	2	1	0	74	75	0	48	27	15.4	4.74	61	.277	.393	1	.048	-2	-16	-15	-0	-2.9

● JOE BOWMAN   Bowman, Joseph Emil b: 6/17/10, Kansas City, Kan. d: 11/22/90, Kansas City, Mo. BL/TR, 6'2", 190 lbs. Deb: 4/18/32 ♦

1932	Phi-A	0	1	.000	7	0	0	0	0	11	14	2	6	4	18.8	8.18	55	.318	.434	1	1.000	0	-5	-4	1	-0.2
1934	NY-N	5	4	.556	30	10	3	0	3	107¹	119	2	36	36	13.2	3.61	107	.279	.338	5	.172	-0	5	3	-0	0.2
1935	Phi-N	7	10	.412	33	17	6	1	1	148¹	157	13	56	58	13.2	4.25	107	.269	.337	13	.194	-0	-4	-5	-0	-0.3
1936	Phi-N	9	20	.310	40	28	12	0	1	203²	243	14	53	80	13.4	5.04	90	.289	.337	15	.195	-1	-23	-11	-2	-1.7
1937	Pit-N	8	8	.500	30	19	7	0	1	128	161	11	35	38	13.9	4.57	85	.306	.351	7	.333	2	-6	-6	-1	-0.5
1938	Pit-N	3	4	.429	17	1	0	0	0	60	68	2	20	25	13.2	4.65	82	.285	.340	7	.333	2	-6	-6	-1	-0.5
1939	Pit-N	10	14	.417	37	27	10	1	1	184²	217	15	43	58	13.0	4.48	86	.292	.336	33	.344	12	-12	-13	-0	-0.3
1940	Pit-N	9	10	.474	32	24	10	0	2	187²	209	10	66	57	13.5	4.46	85	.274	.337	22	.244	9	-13	-14	-0	-0.3
1941	Pit-N	3	2	.600	18	7	1	1	1	69¹	77	3	28	22	13.8	2.99	121	.278	.346	8	.258	1	5	4	0	0.5
1944	Bos-A	12	8	.600	26	24	10	1	0	168¹	175	14	64	53	12.9	4.81	71	.269	.336	20	.244	3	-26	-26	-2	-2.7
1945	Bos-A	0	2	.000	3	3	0	0	0	11²	18	1	9	0	20.8	9.26	37	.360	.458	2	.222	0	-8	-8	-1	-1.0
	Cin-N	11	13	.458	25	24	15	1	0	185²	198	8	68	71	13.2	3.59	105	.270	.338	5	.070	-5	4	4	-2	-0.2
Total	11	77	96	.445	298	184	74	5	11	1465²	1656	102	484	502	13.4	4.40	89	.282	.341	141	.221	24	-89	-77	-7	-6.7

● BOB BOWMAN   Bowman, Robert James b: 10/3/10, Keystone, W.Va. d: 9/4/72, Bluefield, W.Va. BR/TR, 5'10.5", 160 lbs. Deb: 4/21/39

1939	StL-N	13	5	.722	51	15	4	2	**9**	169¹	141	8	60	78	10.7	2.60	158	.232	.302	4	.085	-3	25	28	-1	2.7
1940	StL-N	7	5	.583	28	17	7	0	0	114¹	118	9	43	43	13.0	4.33	92	.267	.337	2	.061	-2	-6	-4	-0	-0.7
1941	NY-N	6	7	.462	29	6	2	0	1	80¹	100	10	36	25	15.3	5.71	65	.302	.372	1	.048	-1	-19	-18	1	-2.6
1942	Chi-N	0	0	—	1	0	0	0	0	1	1	0	0	0	9.0	0.00	—	.250	.250	0	—	0	0	0	-0	0.0
Total	4	26	17	.605	109	38	13	2	10	365	360	27	139	146	12.5	3.82	104	.260	.330	7	.069	-5	0	6	-1	-0.6

● BOB BOWMAN   Bowman, Robert Leroy b: 5/10/31, Laytonville, Cal. BR/TR, 6'1", 195 lbs. Deb: 4/16/55 ♦

| 1959 | Phi-N | 0 | 1 | .000 | 5 | 0 | 0 | 0 | 0 | 6 | 5 | 1 | 6 | 0 | 15.0 | 6.00 | 68 | .227 | .370 | 10 | .127 | -0 | -1 | -1 | 0 | -0.2 |

● ROGER BOWMAN   Bowman, Roger Clinton b: 8/18/27, Amsterdam, N.Y. BR/TL, 6', 175 lbs. Deb: 9/22/49

1949	NY-N	0	0	—	2	2	0	0	0	6¹	6	1	7	4	18.5	4.26	93	.261	.433	0	.000	-0	-0	-0	1	0.0
1951	NY-N	2	4	.333	9	5	0	0	0	26¹	35	2	24	19	19.8	6.15	64	.297	.411	0	.000	-0	-6	-7	-1	-1.3
1952	NY-N	0	1	.000	3	0	0	0	0	3	6	0	3	4	30.0	12.00	31	.429	.556	0	.000	-0	-3	-3	-0	-0.5
1953	Pit-N	0	4	.000	30	2	0	0	0	65¹	65	9	26	39	13.1	4.82	93	.261	.341	2	.286	-0	-4	-3	-0	-0.1
1955	Pit-N	0	3	.000	7	0	0	0	0	16²	25	2	10	8	19.4	8.64	48	.347	.434	1	.500	0	-9	-8	-0	-1.2
Total	5	2	11	.154	50	9	0	0	0	117²	137	14	71	75	16.2	5.81	73	.288	.385	3	.167	-0	-22	-20	-1	-2.6

● SUMNER BOWMAN   Bowman, Sumner Sallade b: 2/9/1867, Millersburg, Pa. d: 1/11/54, Millersburg, Pa. BL/TL, 6', 160 lbs. Deb: 6/11/1890

1890	Phi-N	0	0	—	1	1	0	0	0	8	11	0	2	4	15.8	7.88	46	.314	.368	2	.500	1	-4	-4	0	0.0
	Pit-N	2	5	.286	9	7	6	0	0	70²	100	1	50	22	20.5	6.62	50	.324	.435	10	.278	-2	-24	-26	-0	-1.7
	Yr	2	5	.286	10	8	6	0	0	78²	111	1	52	24	19.9	6.75	49	.322	.426	12	.300	-2	-28	-30	-0	-1.7
1891	Phi-a	2	5	.286	8	8	8	0	0	68	73	0	37	22	15.2	3.44	111	.265	.363	13	.241	0	2	3	-1	0.2
Total	2	4	10	.286	18	16	14	0	0	146²	184	1	89	46	17.8	5.22	68	.297	.400	25	.266	-2	-26	-27	-1	-1.5

● TED BOWSFIELD   Bowsfield, Edward Oliver b: 1/10/35, Vernon, B.C., Canada BR/TL, 6'1", 190 lbs. Deb: 7/20/58

| 1958 | Bos-A | 4 | 2 | .667 | 16 | 10 | 2 | 0 | 0 | 65² | 58 | 3 | 36 | 38 | 13.0 | 3.84 | 104 | .233 | .332 | 4 | .154 | -1 | -1 | 1 | 1 | 0.1 |
| 1959 | Bos-A | 0 | 1 | .000 | 5 | 2 | 0 | 0 | 0 | 9 | 12 | 2 | 9 | 4 | 25.0 | 15.00 | 27 | .390 | .500 | 0 | .000 | -0 | -11 | -11 | -0 | -1.0 |

YEAR	TM/L	W	L	PCT	G	GS	CG	SH	SV	IP	H	HR	BB	SO	RAT	ERA	ERA+	OAV	OOB	BH	AVG	PB	PR	/A	PD	TPI
1960	Bos-A	1	2	.333	17	2	0	0	2	21	20	1	13	18	14.6	5.14	79	.260	.374	1	.250	-0	-3	-3	1	-0.3
	Cle-A	3	4	.429	11	6	1	1	0	40²	47	1	20	14	14.8	5.09	73	.296	.374	-0	.100	-0	-5	-6	1	-0.9
	Yr	4	6	.400	28	8	1	1	2	61²	67	2	33	32	14.6	5.11	75	.280	.368	2	.143	-0	-8	-9	1	-1.2
1961	LA-A	11	8	.579	41	21	4	1	0	157	154	18	63	88	12.5	3.73	121	.255	.327	7	.137	-1	5	14	-1	1.3
1962	LA-A	9	8	.529	34	25	1	0	1	139	154	12	40	52	12.7	4.40	88	.277	.328	6	.162	1	-7	-8	-3	-1.1
1963	KC-A	5	7	.417	41	11	2	1	3	111¹	115	14	47	67	13.3	4.45	88	.269	.345	1	.043	-1	-10	-7	-2	-0.6
1964	KC-A	4	7	.364	50	9	2	1	0	118²	135	12	31	45	12.9	4.10	93	.285	.334	2	.095	-1	-6	-4	0	-0.4
Total	7	37	39	.487	215	86	12	4	6	662¹	699	63	259	326	13.2	4.35	93	.270	.339	22	.127	-3	-38	-24	1	-2.9

● OIL CAN BOYD
Boyd, Dennis Ray b: 10/6/59, Meridian, Miss. BR/TR, 6'1", 155 lbs. Deb: 9/13/82

YEAR	TM/L	W	L	PCT	G	GS	CG	SH	SV	IP	H	HR	BB	SO	RAT	ERA	ERA+	OAV	OOB	BH	AVG	PB	PR	/A	PD	TPI
1982	Bos-A	0	1	.000	3	1	0	0	0	8¹	11	2	2	2	14.0	5.40	80	.314	.351	0	—	0	-1	-1	-0	-0.1
1983	Bos-A	4	8	.333	15	13	5	0	0	98²	103	9	23	43	11.6	3.28	132	.269	.312	0	—	0	9	12	-1	0.8
1984	Bos-A	12	12	.500	29	26	10	3	0	197²	207	18	53	134	11.9	4.37	95	.269	.317	0	—	0	-8	-5	-2	-0.3
1985	Bos-A	15	13	.536	35	35	13	3	0	272¹	273	26	67	154	11.4	3.70	116	.261	.308	0	—	0	13	18	3	1.9
1986	*Bos-A	16	10	.615	30	30	10	0	0	214¹	222	32	45	129	11.3	3.78	110	.265	.304	0	—	0	9	9	1	1.1
1987	Bos-A	1	3	.250	7	7	0	0	0	36²	47	6	9	12	14.2	5.89	77	.315	.363	0	—	0	-6	-6	1	-0.5
1988	Bos-A	9	7	.563	23	23	1	0	0	129²	147	25	41	71	13.2	5.34	77	.289	.344	0	—	0	-20	-18	-1	-2.1
1989	Bos-A	3	2	.600	10	10	0	0	0	59	57	8	19	26	11.6	4.42	93	.253	.311	0	—	0	-4	-2	-1	-0.3
1990	Mon-N	10	6	.625	31	31	3	3	0	190²	164	19	52	113	10.3	2.93	125	.233	.289	3	.051	-4	18	15	-1	0.6
1991	Mon-N	6	8	.429	19	19	1	1	0	120¹	115	9	40	82	11.6	3.52	103	.256	.316	3	.083	-1	2	1	-1	-0.1
	Tex-A	2	7	.222	12	12	0	0	0	62	81	12	17	33	14.2	6.68	60	.314	.356	0	—	0	-18	-18	-1	-2.2
Total	10	78	77	.503	214	207	43	10	0	1389²	1427	166	368	799	11.7	4.04	101	.266	.315	6	.063	-5	-5	5	3	-1.2

● GARY BOYD
Boyd, Gary Lee b: 8/22/46, Pasadena, Cal. BR/TR, 6'4", 200 lbs. Deb: 8/1/69

YEAR	TM/L	W	L	PCT	G	GS	CG	SH	SV	IP	H	HR	BB	SO	RAT	ERA	ERA+	OAV	OOB	BH	AVG	PB	PR	/A	PD	TPI
1969	Cle-A	0	2	.000	8	3	0	0	1	18	11	8	1	14	18.0	9.00	42	.205	.415	0	.000	0	-7	-6	-0	-1.0

● JAKE BOYD
Boyd, Jacob Henry b: 1/19/1874, Martinsburg, W.Va. d: 8/12/32, Gettysburg, Pa. TL, 160 lbs. Deb: 9/20/1894 ♦

YEAR	TM/L	W	L	PCT	G	GS	CG	SH	SV	IP	H	HR	BB	SO	RAT	ERA	ERA+	OAV	OOB	BH	AVG	PB	PR	/A	PD	TPI
1894	Was-N	0	3	.000	3	3	3	0	0	19	37	1	14	3	24.6	8.53	62	.402	.486	3	.143	-1	-7	-7	0	-0.7
1895	Was-N	2	11	.154	14	12	8	0	0	85¹	126	1	35	16	18.0	7.07	68	.338	.409	42	.268	2	-22	-21	1	-2.1
1896	Was-N	1	2	.333	4	2	2	0	0	32	45	0	15	6	18.0	6.75	65	.328	.418	1	.077	-1	-8	-8	0	-0.6
Total	3	3	16	.158	21	17	13	0	0	136²	208	2	64	25	19.1	7.20	66	.346	.423	46	.241	-1	-37	-37	2	-3.4

● RAY BOYD
Boyd, Raymond C. b: 2/11/1887, Hortonville, Ind. d: 2/11/20, Hortonville, Ind. BR/TR, 5'10", 160 lbs. Deb: 9/24/10

YEAR	TM/L	W	L	PCT	G	GS	CG	SH	SV	IP	H	HR	BB	SO	RAT	ERA	ERA+	OAV	OOB	BH	AVG	PB	PR	/A	PD	TPI
1910	StL-A	0	2	.000	3	2	1	0	0	14¹	16	0	6	6	13.8	4.40	56	.286	.355	1	.200	-0	-3	-3	-1	-0.5
1911	Cin-N	2	2	.500	7	4	3	0	1	44	34	0	18	20	11.3	2.66	124	.206	.296	1	.083	-0	4	3	-0	0.2
Total	2	2	4	.333	10	6	4	0	1	58¹	50	0	24	26	11.3	3.09	101	.226	.310	2	.118	-0	1	0	-1	-0.3

● BILL BOYD
Boyd, William J. b: 12/22/1852, New York, N.Y. d: 9/30/12, Jamaica, N.Y. Deb: 4/22/1872 MU♦

YEAR	TM/L	W	L	PCT	G	GS	CG	SH	SV	IP	H	HR	BB	SO	RAT	ERA	ERA+	OAV	OOB	BH	AVG	PB	PR	/A	PD	TPI
1875	Atl-n	0	0	—	1	0	0	0	0	1²	4	0	0	0	21.6	0.00		.444	.444	44	.291	0	0			0.0

● CLOYD BOYER
Boyer, Cloyd Victor "Junior" b: 9/1/27, Alba, Mo. BR/TR, 6'1", 188 lbs. Deb: 4/23/49 FC

YEAR	TM/L	W	L	PCT	G	GS	CG	SH	SV	IP	H	HR	BB	SO	RAT	ERA	ERA+	OAV	OOB	BH	AVG	PB	PR	/A	PD	TPI
1949	StL-N	0	0	—	4	1	0	0	0	3¹	5	0	7	0	32.4	10.80	39	.357	.571	0	—	0	-3	-2	0	0.0
1950	StL-N	7	7	.500	36	14	6	1	1	120¹	105	15	49	82	11.7	3.52	122	.233	.312	6	.182	0	8	10	-1	1.1
1951	StL-N	2	5	.286	19	8	1	0	1	63¹	68	9	46	40	16.6	5.26	75	.286	.408	4	.200	0	-9	-9	-2	-1.1
1952	StL-N	6	6	.500	23	14	4	2	0	110¹	108	11	47	44	13.0	4.24	88	.258	.338	8	.211	2	-6	-6	-2	-0.6
1955	KC-A	5	5	.500	30	11	2	0	0	98¹	107	21	69	32	16.7	6.22	67	.282	.402	2	.069	-2	-25	-22	-1	-2.2
Total	5	20	23	.465	112	48	13	3	2	395²	393	56	218	198	14.3	4.73	86	.262	.362	20	.167	1	-34	-30	-4	-2.8

● HENRY BOYLE
Boyle, Henry J. "Handsome Henry" b: 9/20/1860, Philadelphia, Pa. d: 5/25/32, Philadelphia, Pa. TR , Deb: 7/9/1884 ♦

YEAR	TM/L	W	L	PCT	G	GS	CG	SH	SV	IP	H	HR	BB	SO	RAT	ERA	ERA+	OAV	OOB	BH	AVG	PB	PR	/A	PD	TPI
1884	StL-U	15	3	.833	19	16	16	2	1	150	118	3	10	88	7.7	1.74	138	.202	.215	68	.260	-1	12	11	1	0.8
1885	StL-N	16	24	.400	42	39	39	1	0	366²	346	2	100	133	10.9	2.75	100	.239	.288	52	.202	1	3	-0	-1	0.0
1886	StL-N	9	15	.375	25	24	23	2	0	210	183	5	46	101	9.8	1.76	184	.220	.261	27	.250	4	36	34	1	3.9
1887	Ind-N	13	24	.351	38	38	37	0	0	328	356	11	69	85	12.0	3.65	110	.265	.307	27	.191	-1	15	18	-4	1.2
1888	Ind-N	15	22	.405	37	37	36	3	0	323	315	11	58	98	10.7	3.26	91	.245	.283	18	.144	-3	-15	-11	3	-1.1
1889	Ind-N	21	23	.477	46	45	38	2	0	378²	422	14	95	97	12.6	3.92	106	.273	.321	38	.245	5	4	11	-5	1.1
Total	6	89	111	.445	207	199	189	10	1	1756¹	1740	46	378	602	11.0	3.06	110	.247	.289	230	.219	5	56	61	-7	5.9

● HARRY BOYLES
Boyles, Harry "Stretch" b: 11/29/11, Granite City, Ill. BR/TR, 6'5", 185 lbs. Deb: 8/3/38

YEAR	TM/L	W	L	PCT	G	GS	CG	SH	SV	IP	H	HR	BB	SO	RAT	ERA	ERA+	OAV	OOB	BH	AVG	PB	PR	/A	PD	TPI
1938	Chi-A	0	4	.000	9	2	1	0	1	29¹	31	2	25	18	17.8	5.22	94	.263	.400	1	.125	-1	-1	-1	1	-0.1
1939	Chi-A	0	0	—	2	0	0	0	0	3¹	4	0	6	1	27.0	10.80	44	.308	.526	0	.000	-0	-2	-2	-0	0.0
Total	2	0	4	.000	11	2	1	0	1	32²	35	2	31	19	18.7	5.79	84	.267	.415	1	.111	-1	-4	-4	1	-0.1

● MARSHALL BOZE
Boze, Marshall Wayne b: 5/23/71, San Manuel, Ariz. BR/TR, 6'1", 214 lbs. Deb: 4/28/96

YEAR	TM/L	W	L	PCT	G	GS	CG	SH	SV	IP	H	HR	BB	SO	RAT	ERA	ERA+	OAV	OOB	BH	AVG	PB	PR	/A	PD	TPI
1996	Mil-A	0	2	.000	25	0	0	0	1	31¹	47	5	25	19	21.7	7.79	68	.362	.484	0	—	0	-10	-9	1	-0.5

● GENE BRABENDER
Brabender, Eugene Mathew b: 8/16/41, Madison, Wis. BR/TR, 6'5.5", 225 lbs. Deb: 5/11/66

YEAR	TM/L	W	L	PCT	G	GS	CG	SH	SV	IP	H	HR	BB	SO	RAT	ERA	ERA+	OAV	OOB	BH	AVG	PB	PR	/A	PD	TPI
1966	Bal-A	4	3	.571	31	1	0	0	2	71	57	4	29	62	11.0	3.55	94	.229	.312	1	.077	-1	-1	-2	0	-0.2
1967	Bal-A	6	4	.600	14	14	3	1	0	94	77	6	23	71	9.7	3.35	94	.220	.270	2	.071	-1	-1	-2	-0	-0.3
1968	Bal-A	6	7	.462	37	15	3	2	3	125	116	9	48	92	12.0	3.31	88	.248	.322	3	.086	-0	-5	-5	-1	-0.7
1969	Sea-A	13	14	.481	40	29	7	1	0	202¹	193	26	103	139	13.7	4.36	83	.254	.353	9	.129	-1	-17	-16	-3	-2.4
1970	Mil-A	6	15	.286	29	21	2	0	1	128¹	127	8	79	76	14.5	6.02	63	.255	.359	4	.098	-2	-33	-32	-0	-4.7
Total	5	35	43	.449	151	80	15	4	6	621	570	53	282	440	12.6	4.25	80	.245	.332	19	.102	-5	-56	-58	-3	-8.3

● JACK BRACKEN
Bracken, John James b: 4/14/1881, Cleveland, Ohio d: 7/16/54, Highland Park, Mich. BR/TR, 5'11", 175 lbs. Deb: 8/7/01

YEAR	TM/L	W	L	PCT	G	GS	CG	SH	SV	IP	H	HR	BB	SO	RAT	ERA	ERA+	OAV	OOB	BH	AVG	PB	PR	/A	PD	TPI
1901	Cle-A	4	8	.333	12	12	12	0	0	100	137	4	31	18	16.0	6.21	57	.322	.381	10	.227	-0	-28	-30	-1	-2.6

● JOHN BRACKENRIDGE
Brackenridge, John Givler b: 12/24/1880, Harrisburg, Pa. d: 3/20/53, Harrisburg, Pa. BR/TR, 6', Deb: 4/15/04

YEAR	TM/L	W	L	PCT	G	GS	CG	SH	SV	IP	H	HR	BB	SO	RAT	ERA	ERA+	OAV	OOB	BH	AVG	PB	PR	/A	PD	TPI
1904	Phi-N	0	1	.000	7	1	0	0	0	34	37	4	16	11	15.1	5.56	48	.298	.396	2	.154	-0	-11	-11	2	-0.1

● DON BRADEY
Bradey, Donald Eugene b: 10/4/34, Charlotte, N.C. BR/TR, 5'9", 180 lbs. Deb: 9/25/64

YEAR	TM/L	W	L	PCT	G	GS	CG	SH	SV	IP	H	HR	BB	SO	RAT	ERA	ERA+	OAV	OOB	BH	AVG	PB	PR	/A	PD	TPI
1964	Hou-N	0	2	.000	3	1	0	0	0	2¹	6	0	3	2	34.7	19.29	18	.429	.529	0	—	0	-4	-4	-0	-2.2

● LARRY BRADFORD
Bradford, Larry b: 12/21/49, Chicago, Ill. BR/TL, 6'1", 200 lbs. Deb: 9/24/77

YEAR	TM/L	W	L	PCT	G	GS	CG	SH	SV	IP	H	HR	BB	SO	RAT	ERA	ERA+	OAV	OOB	BH	AVG	PB	PR	/A	PD	TPI
1977	Atl-N	0	0	—	2	0	0	0	0	2²	3	1	4	3	10.1	3.38	132	.273	.273	0	.000	0	0	0	0	0.0
1979	Atl-N	1	0	1.000	21	0	0	0	0	19	11	0	10	11	10.4	0.95	427	.172	.293	0	.000	-0	6	7	0	0.5
1980	Atl-N	3	4	.429	56	0	0	0	4	55¹	49	5	22	32	11.7	2.44	153	.243	.320	0	.000	-0	7	8	-0	1.1
1981	Atl-N	2	0	1.000	25	0	0	0	3	26²	26	1	12	14	12.8	3.71	96	.268	.349	1	1.000	0	-1	-0	0	0.0
Total	4	6	4	.600	104	0	0	0	7	103²	89	7	48	58	11.7	2.52	150	.238	.321	1	.200	-0	13	14	1	1.6

● BILL BRADFORD
Bradford, William D b: 8/28/21, Choctaw, Ark. BR/TR, 6'2", 180 lbs. Deb: 4/24/56

YEAR	TM/L	W	L	PCT	G	GS	CG	SH	SV	IP	H	HR	BB	SO	RAT	ERA	ERA+	OAV	OOB	BH	AVG	PB	PR	/A	PD	TPI
1956	KC-A	0	0	—	2	0	0	0	0	2	2	0	1	2	13.5	9.00	48	.250	.333	0	—	0	-1	-1	0	0.0

● FRED BRADLEY
Bradley, Fred Langdon b: 7/31/20, Parsons, Kan. BR/TR, 6'1", 180 lbs. Deb: 5/1/48

YEAR	TM/L	W	L	PCT	G	GS	CG	SH	SV	IP	H	HR	BB	SO	RAT	ERA	ERA+	OAV	OOB	BH	AVG	PB	PR	/A	PD	TPI
1948	Chi-A	0	0	—	8	0	0	0	0	15²	11	2	4	9	9.2	4.60	93	.190	.254	0	.000	-0	-1	-1	0	0.0
1949	Chi-A	0	0	—	1	0	0	0	0	2	4	0	3	0	31.5	13.50	31	.444	.583	0	.000	-0	-2	-2	0	0.0
Total	2	0	0	—	9	0	0	0	0	17²	15	2	7	9	11.2	5.60	76	.224	.307	0	.000	-0	-3	-3	0	0.0

● FOGHORN BRADLEY
Bradley, George H. b: 7/1/1855, Milford, Mass. d: 4/3/1900, Philadelphia, Pa. BR/TR, Deb: 8/23/1876 U

YEAR	TM/L	W	L	PCT	G	GS	CG	SH	SV	IP	H	HR	BB	SO	RAT	ERA	ERA+	OAV	OOB	BH	AVG	PB	PR	/A	PD	TPI
1876	Bos-N	9	10	.474	22	17	17	3	0	173¹	201	1	16	31	11.3	2.49	91	.263	.279	19	.232	-1	-4	-5	-1	-0.5

● GEORGE BRADLEY
Bradley, George Washington "Grin" b: 7/13/1852, Reading, Pa. d: 10/2/31, Philadelphia, Pa. BR/TR, 5'10.5", 175 lbs. Deb: 5/4/1875 ♦

YEAR	TM/L	W	L	PCT	G	GS	CG	SH	SV	IP	H	HR	BB	SO	RAT	ERA	ERA+	OAV	OOB	BH	AVG	PB	PR	/A	PD	TPI
1875	StL-n	33	26	.559	60	60	57	5	0	535²	540	3	17	60	9.4	2.13	94	.241	.247	62	.244	7	5	-7		0.1
1876	StL-N	45	19	.703	64	64	63	**16**	0	573	470	3	38	103	**8.0**	**1.23**	**174**	**.211**	**.224**	66	.249	4	**69**	58	1	5.8

YEAR	TM/L	W	L	PCT	G	GS	CG	SH	SV	IP	H	HR	BB	SO	RAT	ERA	ERA+	OAV	OOB	BH	AVG	PB	PR	/A	PD	TPI
1877	Chi-N	18	23	.439	50	44	35	2	0	394	452	4	39	59	11.2	3.31	90	.269	.286	52	.243	0	-22	-15	1	-1.3
1879	Tro-N	13	40	.245	54	54	53	3	0	487	590	12	26	133	11.4	2.85	88	.275	.284	62	.247	4	-19	-19	4	-0.7
1880	Pro-N	13	8	.619	28	20	16	4	1	196	158	2	6	54	7.5	1.38	160	.210	.217	70	.227	1	22	18	1	1.9
1881	Cle-N	2	4	.333	6	6	5	0	0	51	70	2	3	6	12.9	3.88	67	.320	.329	60	.249	0	-6	-7	-1	-0.7
1882	Cle-N	6	9	.400	18	16	15	0	0	147	164	5	22	32	11.4	3.73	75	.264	.289	21	.183	-3	-14	-15	3	-1.2
1883	Phi-a	16	7	.696	26	23	22	0	0	214¹	215	7	22	56	10.0	3.15	110	.244	.263	73	.234	0	4	8	-1	0.5
1884	Cin-U	25	15	.625	41	38	36	3	0	342	350	7	23	168	9.8	2.71	95	.248	.260	43	.190	-12	-10	-6	2	-1.4
Total	8	138	125	.525	287	265	245	28	1	2404¹	2469	42	179	611	9.9	2.50	103	.248	.262	456	.228	-5	23	19	11	2.9

● **HERB BRADLEY**   Bradley, Herbert Theodore b: 1/3/03, Agenda, Kan. d: 10/16/59, Clay Center, Kan. BR/TR, 6', 170 lbs. Deb: 5/9/27

YEAR	TM/L	W	L	PCT	G	GS	CG	SH	SV	IP	H	HR	BB	SO	RAT	ERA	ERA+	OAV	OOB	BH	AVG	PB	PR	/A	PD	TPI
1927	Bos-A	1	1	.500	6	2	2	0	0	23	16	0	7	6	9.8	3.13	135	.198	.278	3	.429	1	3	3	-0	0.3
1928	Bos-A	0	3	.000	15	5	1	1	0	47¹	64	2	16	14	15.6	7.23	57	.339	.396	2	.154	-1	-17	-16	1	-0.8
1929	Bos-A	0	0	—	3	0	0	0	0	4	7	1	2	0	20.3	6.75	63	.438	.500	0	—	-0	-1	-1	0	-0.0
Total	3	1	4	.200	24	7	3	1	0	74¹	87	3	25	20	14.0	5.93	70	.304	.368	5	.238	-0	-15	-15	1	-0.5

● **BERT BRADLEY**   Bradley, Steven Bert b: 12/23/56, Athens, Ga. BB/TR, 6'1", 190 lbs. Deb: 9/3/83

YEAR	TM/L	W	L	PCT	G	GS	CG	SH	SV	IP	H	HR	BB	SO	RAT	ERA	ERA+	OAV	OOB	BH	AVG	PB	PR	/A	PD	TPI
1983	Oak-A	0	0	—	6	0	0	0	0	8¹	14	1	4	3	19.4	6.48	59	.400	.462	0	—	0	-2	-2	1	0.1

● **TOM BRADLEY**   Bradley, Thomas William b: 3/16/47, Asheville, N.C. BR/TR, 6'3", 185 lbs. Deb: 9/9/69

YEAR	TM/L	W	L	PCT	G	GS	CG	SH	SV	IP	H	HR	BB	SO	RAT	ERA	ERA+	OAV	OOB	BH	AVG	PB	PR	/A	PD	TPI
1969	Cal-A	0	1	.000	3	0	0	0	0	2	9	1	0	2	40.5	27.00	13	.600	.600	0	—	0	-5	-5	0	-1.8
1970	Cal-A	2	5	.286	17	11	1	1	0	69²	71	3	33	53	13.6	4.13	87	.270	.354	3	.167	0	-3	-4	-0	-0.3
1971	Chi-A	15	15	.500	45	39	7	6	2	285²	273	16	74	206	11.0	2.96	121	.248	.297	15	.156	-1	16	20	-2	1.8
1972	Chi-A	15	14	.517	40	40	11	2	0	260	225	19	65	209	10.1	2.98	105	.231	.280	12	.132	-2	2	4	-0	0.2
1973	SF-N	13	12	.520	35	34	6	1	0	224	212	26	69	136	11.4	3.90	98	.246	.304	15	.195	1	-6	-2	-2	-0.3
1974	SF-N	8	11	.421	30	21	2	0	0	134¹	152	15	52	72	13.7	5.16	74	.282	.346	3	.075	-2	-23	-20	-1	-2.9
1975	SF-N	2	3	.400	13	6	0	0	0	42	57	6	13	13	16.3	6.21	61	.326	.392	0	.000	-1	-12	-11	0	-1.2
Total	7	55	61	.474	183	151	27	10	2	1017²	999	86	311	691	11.7	3.72	96	.254	.311	48	.145	-5	-31	-19	-5	-4.5

● **BILL BRADLEY**   Bradley, William Joseph b: 2/13/1878, Cleveland, Ohio d: 3/11/54, Cleveland, Ohio BR/TR, 6', 185 lbs. Deb: 8/26/1899 M♦

YEAR	TM/L	W	L	PCT	G	GS	CG	SH	SV	IP	H	HR	BB	SO	RAT	ERA	ERA+	OAV	OOB	BH	AVG	PB	PR	/A	PD	TPI
1901	Cle-A	0	0	—	1	0	0	0	0	1	0	0	0	0	36.0	0.00	—	.571	.571	151	.293	0	0	0	-0	0.0

● **JOE BRADSHAW**   Bradshaw, Joe Siah b: 8/17/1897, RoEllen, Tenn. d: 1/30/85, Tavares, Fla. BR/TR, 6'2.5", 200 lbs. Deb: 5/9/29

YEAR	TM/L	W	L	PCT	G	GS	CG	SH	SV	IP	H	HR	BB	SO	RAT	ERA	ERA+	OAV	OOB	BH	AVG	PB	PR	/A	PD	TPI
1929	Bro-N	0	0	—	2	0	0	0	0	4	3	0	4	2	20.3	4.50	103	.231	.474	0	—	0	0	0	0	0.0

● **NEAL BRADY**   Brady, Cornelius Joseph b: 3/4/1897, Covington, Ky. d: 6/19/47, Fort Mitchell, Ky BR/TR, 6'0.5", 197 lbs. Deb: 9/25/15

YEAR	TM/L	W	L	PCT	G	GS	CG	SH	SV	IP	H	HR	BB	SO	RAT	ERA	ERA+	OAV	OOB	BH	AVG	PB	PR	/A	PD	TPI
1915	NY-A	0	0	—	2	1	0	0	0	8²	9	1	7	6	16.6	3.12	94	.281	.410	1	.000	-1	-0	-0	-0	-0.1
1917	NY-A	1	0	1.000	2	1	0	0	0	9	6	1	5	4	11.0	2.00	134	.188	.297	1	.500	0	1	1	0	0.2
1925	Cin-N	1	3	.250	20	3	2	0	1	63²	73	4	20	12	13.7	4.66	88	.289	.350	6	.240	1	-3	-4	0	-0.1
Total	3	2	3	.400	24	5	2	0	1	81¹	88	4	32	22	13.7	4.20	91	.278	.351	7	.226	1	-2	-3	1	0.0

● **JIM BRADY**   Brady, James Joseph "Diamond Jim" b: 3/2/36, Jersey City, N.J. BL/TL, 6'2", 185 lbs. Deb: 5/12/56

YEAR	TM/L	W	L	PCT	G	GS	CG	SH	SV	IP	H	HR	BB	SO	RAT	ERA	ERA+	OAV	OOB	BH	AVG	PB	PR	/A	PD	TPI
1956	Det-A	0	0	—	6	0	0	0	0	6¹	15	3	11	3	36.9	28.42	14	.484	.619	0	—	0	-17	-17	0	0.0

● **KING BRADY**   Brady, James Ward b: 5/28/1881, Elmer, N.J. d: 8/21/47, Albany, N.Y. BR/TR, 6', 190 lbs. Deb: 9/21/05

YEAR	TM/L	W	L	PCT	G	GS	CG	SH	SV	IP	H	HR	BB	SO	RAT	ERA	ERA+	OAV	OOB	BH	AVG	PB	PR	/A	PD	TPI
1905	Phi-N	1	1	.500	2	2	2	0	0	13	19	0	0	3	14.5	3.46	84	.333	.356	1	.200	-0	-1	-1	-0	-0.1
1906	Pit-N	1	1	.500	3	2	1	0	0	23	30	0	4	14	13.3	2.35	114	.313	.340	1	.100	1	1	1	-1	-0.1
1907	Pit-N	0	0	—	1	0	0	0	0	2	0	0	1	0	13.5	0.00	—	.286	.375	0	—	0	1	1	-0	0.0
1908	Bos-A	1	0	1.000	1	1	1	1	0	9	8	0	0	3	8.0	0.00	—	.242	.242	0	.000	0	2	2	0	0.2
1912	Bos-N	0	0	—	1	0	0	0	0	2²	5	0	3	0	27.0	20.25	18	.313	.421	0	—	-0	-5	-5	0	0.0
Total	5	3	2	.600	8	5	4	1	0	49²	64	0	10	20	13.4	3.08	89	.306	.338	2	.111	-1	-2	-2	-1	0.0

● **BILL BRADY**   Brady, William Aloysius "King" b: 8/18/1889, New York, N.Y. TR, 6'2", Deb: 7/9/12

YEAR	TM/L	W	L	PCT	G	GS	CG	SH	SV	IP	H	HR	BB	SO	RAT	ERA	ERA+	OAV	OOB	BH	AVG	PB	PR	/A	PD	TPI
1912	Bos-N	0	0	—	1	0	0	0	0	1	2	0	0	0	18.0	0.00	—	.500	.500	0	—	0	0	0	-0	0.0

● **DICK BRAGGINS**   Braggins, Richard Realf b: 12/25/1879, Mercer, Pa. d: 8/16/63, Lake Wales, Fla. BR/TR, 5'11", 170 lbs. Deb: 5/16/01

YEAR	TM/L	W	L	PCT	G	GS	CG	SH	SV	IP	H	HR	BB	SO	RAT	ERA	ERA+	OAV	OOB	BH	AVG	PB	PR	/A	PD	TPI
1901	Cle-A	1	2	.333	4	3	2	0	0	32	44	1	15	1	16.9	4.78	74	.324	.395	2	.154	-1	-4	-4	0	-0.4

● **ASA BRAINARD**   Brainard, Asa "Count" b: 1841, Albany, N.Y. d: 12/29/1888, Denver, Colo. TR, 5'8.5", 150 lbs. Deb: 5/5/1871 ♦

YEAR	TM/L	W	L	PCT	G	GS	CG	SH	SV	IP	H	HR	BB	SO	RAT	ERA	ERA+	OAV	OOB	BH	AVG	PB	PR	/A	PD	TPI
1871	Oly-n	12	15	.444	30	30	30	0	0	264	361	4	37	13	13.6	4.50	93	.308	.308	30	.224	-6	-8	-10	-1	-1.0
1872	Oly-n	2	7	.222	9	9	9	0	0	79	148	0	5	1	17.4	6.38	56	.333	.341	16	.372	4	-24	-24	-1	-1.3
	Man-n	0	2	.000	2	2	1	0	0	8	13	0	0	0	14.6	5.63	64	.260	.260	5	.200	-0	-2	-2	0	-0.5
	Yr	2	9	.182	11	11	10	0	0	87	161	0	5	1	17.2	6.31	57	.326	.333	21	.309	3	-26	-26	-1	-1.8
1873	Bal-n	5	7	.417	14	14	12	0	0	108²	182	0	9	3	15.8	4.14	79	.323	.334	18	.261	0	-11	-11	-1	-0.8
1874	Bal-n	5	22	.185	30	27	25	0	0	240	405	1	27	8	16.2	3.68	60	.326	.341	47	.240	-1	-40	-39	-1	-3.2
Total	4 n	24	53	.312	85	82	77	0	0	699²	1109	5	78	25	15.3	4.39	61	.312	.327	116	.248	-4	-171	-169	-4	-6.8

● **AL BRAITHWOOD**   Braithwood, Alfred b: 2/15/1892, Braceville, Ill. d: 11/24/60, Rowlesburg, W.Va. BR/TL, 6'1.5", 145 lbs. Deb: 9/1/15

YEAR	TM/L	W	L	PCT	G	GS	CG	SH	SV	IP	H	HR	BB	SO	RAT	ERA	ERA+	OAV	OOB	BH	AVG	PB	PR	/A	PD	TPI
1915	Pit-F	0	0	—	2	0	0	0	0	4	4	0	0	0	9.0	0.00	—	.000	.000	0	—	0	1	1	0	0.1

● **ERV BRAME**   Brame, Ervin Beckham b: 10/12/01, Big Rock, Tenn. d: 11/22/49, Hopkinsville, Ky. BL/TR, 6'2", 190 lbs. Deb: 4/14/28

YEAR	TM/L	W	L	PCT	G	GS	CG	SH	SV	IP	H	HR	BB	SO	RAT	ERA	ERA+	OAV	OOB	BH	AVG	PB	PR	/A	PD	TPI
1928	Pit-N	7	4	.636	24	11	6	0	0	95²	110	5	44	22	14.6	5.08	80	.291	.366	13	.265	4	-12	-11	-1	-0.8
1929	Pit-N	16	11	.593	37	28	19	1	0	229²	250	17	71	68	12.6	4.55	105	.278	.331	36	.310	12	4	6	-4	1.2
1930	Pit-N	17	8	.680	32	29	**22**	0	1	235²	291	21	56	55	13.4	4.70	106	.305	.346	41	.353	11	7	7	-3	1.3
1931	Pit-N	9	13	.409	26	21	15	2	0	179²	211	14	45	33	12.8	4.21	91	.295	.336	26	.274	6	-7	-7	-2	-0.4
1932	Pit-N	3	1	.750	23	3	0	0	0	51	84	6	16	10	17.6	7.41	51	.365	.407	5	.250	1	-20	-20	-1	-1.4
Total	5	52	37	.584	142	92	62	3	1	791²	946	63	232	188	13.5	4.76	94	.298	.347	121	.306	33	-27	-25	-11	-0.1

● **RALPH BRANCA**   Branca, Ralph Theodore Joseph "Hawk" b: 1/6/26, Mt.Vernon, N.Y. BR/TR, 6'3", 220 lbs. Deb: 6/12/44

YEAR	TM/L	W	L	PCT	G	GS	CG	SH	SV	IP	H	HR	BB	SO	RAT	ERA	ERA+	OAV	OOB	BH	AVG	PB	PR	/A	PD	TPI
1944	Bro-N	0	2	.000	21	1	0	0	1	44²	46	2	32	16	16.7	7.05	50	.274	.405	0	.000	—	-17	-17	-0	-0.9
1945	Bro-N	5	6	.455	16	15	7	0	1	109²	73	4	79	69	12.5	3.04	124	.189	.327	4	.100	-3	9	9	0	0.6
1946	Bro-N	3	1	.750	24	10	2	2	3	67¹	62	4	41	42	13.8	3.88	87	.246	.352	2	.111	0	-3	-4	-1	-0.3
1947	*Bro-N☆	21	12	.636	43	36	15	4	1	280	251	22	98	148	11.4	2.67	155	.240	.309	12	.133	-3	43	46	-4	4.4
1948	Bro-N★	14	9	.609	36	28	11	1	1	215²	189	24	80	122	11.4	3.51	114	.232	.304	15	.203	1	11	12	-4	0.8
1949	*Bro-N☆	13	5	.722	34	27	9	2	1	186²	181	21	91	109	13.2	4.39	93	.253	.339	5	.081	-2	-7	-6	-4	-1.1
1950	Bro-N	7	9	.438	43	15	5	0	7	142	152	24	55	100	13.1	4.69	82	.271	.336	4	.118	1	-9	-11	-1	-1.0
1951	Bro-N	13	12	.520	42	27	13	3	3	204	180	19	85	118	11.8	3.26	120	.237	.316	11	.175	-1	16	15	-3	1.4
1952	Bro-N	4	2	.667	16	7	2	0	0	61	52	8	21	26	11.4	3.84	95	.232	.309	3	.158	-0	-1	-1	-1	-0.2
1953	Bro-N	0	0	—	7	0	0	0	0	11	15	4	5	6	18.0	9.82	43	.341	.431	0	—	-0	-7	-7	0	0.0
	Det-A	4	7	.364	17	14	7	0	0	102	98	7	31	50	11.6	4.15	98	.253	.311	4	.118	-1	-2	-1	-0	-0.3
1954	Det-A	3	3	.500	17	5	0	0	0	45¹	63	10	30	15	18.9	5.76	64	.330	.426	4	.308	1	-10	-10	-1	-1.1
	NY-A	1	0	1.000	5	1	0	0	0	12²	9	0	12	7	16.3	2.84	121	.200	.404	2	.500	1	1	1	-0	-0.1
	Yr	4	3	.571	22	6	0	0	0	58	72	10	42	22	18.0	5.12	71	.304	.413	6	.353	2	-9	-10	-1	-1.2
1956	Bro-N	0	0	—	1	0	0	0	0	2	1	0	2	2	13.5	0.00	—	.143	.333	0	—	0	1	1	0	0.0
Total	12	88	68	.564	322	188	71	12	19	1484	1372	149	663	829	12.5	3.79	104	.245	.328	66	.142	-6	25	27	-18	2.4

● **HARVEY BRANCH**   Branch, Harvey Alfred b: 2/8/39, Memphis, Tenn. BR/TL, 6', 175 lbs. Deb: 9/18/62

YEAR	TM/L	W	L	PCT	G	GS	CG	SH	SV	IP	H	HR	BB	SO	RAT	ERA	ERA+	OAV	OOB	BH	AVG	PB	PR	/A	PD	TPI
1962	StL-N	0	1	.000	3	1	0	0	0	5	5	2	9	3	18.0	5.40	79	.263	.417	0	.000	-0	-1	-1	0	-0.1

● **NORM BRANCH**   Branch, Norman Downs "Red" b: 3/22/15, Spokane, Wash. d: 11/21/71, Navasota, Tex. BR/TR, 6'3", 200 lbs. Deb: 5/5/41

YEAR	TM/L	W	L	PCT	G	GS	CG	SH	SV	IP	H	HR	BB	SO	RAT	ERA	ERA+	OAV	OOB	BH	AVG	PB	PR	/A	PD	TPI
1941	NY-A	5	1	.833	27	0	0	0	2	47	37	2	26	28	12.1	2.87	137	.224	.330	0	.000	-1	7	6	1	0.6
1942	NY-A	0	1	.000	10	0	0	0	2	15²	18	3	16	13	19.5	6.32	54	.290	.436	1	.333	0	-5	-5	0	-0.4
Total	2	5	2	.714	37	0	0	0	4	62²	55	5	42	41	13.9	3.73	102	.242	.361	1	.077	-1	2	1	0	0.2

YEAR	TM/L	W	L	PCT	G	GS	CG	SH	SV	IP	H	HR	BB	SO	RAT	ERA	ERA+	OAV	OOB	BH	AVG	PB	PR	/A	PD	TPI
● ROY BRANCH										Branch, Roy b: 7/12/53, St.Louis, Mo. BR/TR, 6′, 175 lbs. Deb: 9/11/79																
1979	Sea-A	0	1	.000	2	2	0	0	0	11¹	12	2	7	6	15.1	7.94	55	.273	.373	0	—	0	-5	-5	-0	-0.4
● MARK BRANDENBURG										Brandenburg, Mark Clay b: 7/14/70, Houston, Tex. BR/TR, 6′, 180 lbs. Deb: 7/20/95																
1995	Tex-A	0	1	.000	11	0	0	0	0	27¹	36	5	7	21	14.5	5.93	81	.316	.361	0	—	0	-4	-3	-0	-0.2
1996	Tex-A	1	3	.250	26	0	0	0	0	47²	48	3	25	37	14.2	3.21	165	.262	.357	0	—	0	9	11	-1	0.5
	Bos-A	4	2	.667	29	0	0	0	0	28¹	28	5	8	29	11.8	3.81	135	.250	.306	0	—	0	4	4	0	0.7
	Yr	5	5	.500	55	0	0	0	0	76	76	8	33	66	13.6	3.43	153	.254	.330	0	—	0	13	15	-1	1.2
Total	2	5	6	.455	66	0	0	0	0	103¹	112	13	40	87	13.6	4.09	125	.274	.344	0	—	0	9	12	-1	1.0
● CHICK BRANDOM										Brandom, Chester Milton b: 3/31/1887, Coldwater, Kan. d: 10/7/58, Santa Ana, Cal. BR/TR, 5′8″, 161 lbs. Deb: 9/3/08																
1908	Pit-N	1	0	1.000	3	1	1	0	1	17	13	0	4	8	9.5	0.53	435	.228	.290	1	.143	-0	3	3	0	0.3
1909	Pit-N	1	0	1.000	13	2	0	0	2	40²	33	0	10	21	9.7	1.11	246	.239	.295	1	.100	-1	7	7	1	0.3
1915	New-F	1	1	.500	16	1	1	0	0	50¹	55	0	15	15	12.7	3.40	75	.293	.348	2	.200	-1	-4	-5	1	-0.1
Total	3	3	1	.750	32	4	2	0	3	108	101	0	29	44	11.1	2.08	124	.264	.320	4	.148	-0	6	6	2	0.5
● BUCKY BRANDON										Brandon, Darrell G b: 7/8/40, Nacogdoches, Tex. BR/TR, 6′2″, 200 lbs. Deb: 4/19/66																
1966	Bos-A	8	8	.500	40	17	5	2	2	157²	129	13	70	101	11.6	3.31	115	.222	.310	8	.182	1	2	9	0	1.1
1967	Bos-A	5	11	.313	39	19	2	0	3	157²	147	21	59	96	12.2	4.17	84	.245	.320	8	.186	1	-16	-12	0	-1.2
1968	Bos-A	0	0	—	8	0	0	0	0	12²	19	1	9	10	20.6	6.39	49	.333	.433	0	.000	-0	-5	-5	0	-0.5
1969	Sea-A	0	1	.000	15	1	0	0	0	15	15	4	16	9	19.8	8.40	43	.250	.423	0	—	0	-8	-8	-0	-0.5
	Min-A	0	0	—	3	0	0	0	0	3¹	5	1	3	2	21.6	2.70	135	.357	.471	0	.000	-0	0	-0	-0	0.0
	Yr	0	1	.000	11	1	0	0	0	18¹	20	5	19	11	19.1	7.36	49	.263	.411	0	.000	-0	-8	-8	-0	-0.5
1971	Phi-N	6	6	.500	52	0	0	0	4	83	81	5	47	44	13.9	3.90	90	.264	.362	2	.154	-0	-4	-4	-1	-0.6
1972	Phi-N	7	7	.500	42	6	0	0	2	104¹	106	9	46	67	13.6	3.45	104	.268	.353	1	.067	-1	0	2	-2	-0.1
1973	Phi-N	2	4	.333	36	0	0	0	2	56¹	54	5	25	25	13.1	5.43	70	.261	.349	1	.200	0	-11	-10	0	-1.1
Total	7	28	37	.431	228	43	7	2	13	590	556	59	275	354	13.0	4.04	90	.250	.339	20	.164	1	-42	-27	-2	-2.4
● ED BRANDT										Brandt, Edward Arthur "Big Ed" b: 2/17/05, Spokane, Wash. d: 11/1/44, Spokane, Wash. BL/TL, 6′1″, 190 lbs. Deb: 4/26/28																
1928	Bos-N	9	21	.300	38	31	12	1	0	225¹	234	22	109	84	14.0	5.07	77	.273	.359	17	.243	5	-27	-29	2	-2.6
1929	Bos-N	8	13	.381	26	21	13	0	0	167²	196	12	83	50	15.2	5.53	85	.302	.385	15	.234	2	-15	-16	2	-1.2
1930	Bos-N	4	11	.267	41	13	4	1	1	147¹	168	15	59	65	13.9	5.01	99	.291	.356	12	.240	1	-1	-1	2	0.1
1931	Bos-N	18	11	.621	33	29	23	3	2	250	228	11	77	112	11.1	2.92	130	.244	.324	21	.256	5	26	24	3	3.6
1932	Bos-N	16	16	.500	35	31	19	2	1	254	271	11	57	79	11.8	3.97	95	.275	.318	19	.207	-0	-3	-6	1	-0.5
1933	Bos-N	18	14	.563	41	32	23	4	4	287²	256	10	77	104	10.5	2.60	118	.245	.298	30	.309	9	24	15	-0	2.7
1934	Bos-N	16	14	.533	40	28	20	3	5	255	249	13	81	66	11.9	3.53	108	.240	.310	23	.240	4	15	8	-3	1.1
1935	Bos-N	5	19	.208	29	25	12	0	0	174²	224	12	66	61	13.0	5.00	76	.319	.378	13	.210	-0	-19	-24	1	-2.6
1936	Bro-N	11	13	.458	38	29	12	1	2	234	246	14	65	104	12.1	3.50	118	.268	.319	16	.190	0	14	16	-2	1.3
1937	Pit-N	11	10	.524	33	25	7	2	2	176¹	177	11	67	74	12.6	3.11	124	.263	.332	10	.169	1	16	15	1	1.8
1938	Pit-N	5	4	.556	24	13	5	1	0	96¹	93	3	35	38	12.0	3.46	110	.250	.314	11	.297	2	4	4	-1	0.5
Total	11	121	146	.453	378	277	150	18	17	2268¹	2342	134	778	877	12.5	3.86	101	.269	.332	187	.236	30	34	5	6	4.2
● BILL BRANDT										Brandt, William George b: 3/21/15, Aurora, Ind. d: 5/16/68, Fort Wayne, Ind. BR/TR, 5′8.5″, 170 lbs. Deb: 9/20/41																
1941	Pit-N	0	1	.000	2	1	0	0	0	7	5	1	3	4	10.3	3.86	94	.200	.286	0	.000	-0	-0	-0	-0	-0.1
1942	Pit-N	1	1	.500	3	1	1	0	0	16¹	23	1	5	4	15.4	4.96	68	.343	.389	1	.143	-0	-3	-3	-0	-0.4
1943	Pit-N	4	1	.800	29	3	0	0	0	57¹	57	3	19	17	12.1	3.14	111	.248	.308	1	.143	-0	2	2	-0	0.1
Total	3	5	3	.625	34	7	1	0	0	80²	85	4	27	21	12.6	3.57	97	.264	.323	2	.133	-1	-2	-1	-1	-0.4
● CLIFF BRANTLEY										Brantley, Clifford b: 4/12/68, Staten Island, N.Y. BR/TR, 6′1″, 190 lbs. Deb: 9/3/91																
1991	Phi-N	2	2	.500	6	5	0	0	0	31²	26	0	19	25	13.4	3.41	107	.228	.348	0	.000	-1	1	1	0	0.0
1992	Phi-N	2	6	.250	28	9	0	0	0	76¹	71	6	58	32	15.7	4.60	76	.251	.386	3	.214	1	-9	-9	0	-0.8
Total	2	4	8	.333	34	14	0	0	0	108	97	6	77	57	15.0	4.25	83	.244	.375	3	.136	0	-8	-9	0	-0.8
● JEFF BRANTLEY										Brantley, Jeffrey Hoke b: 9/5/63, Florence, Ala. BR/TR, 5′11″, 180 lbs. Deb: 8/5/88																
1988	SF-N	0	1	.000	9	1	0	0	1	20²	22	2	6	11	12.6	5.66	58	.275	.333	1	.500	0	-5	-6	1	-0.2
1989	*SF-N	7	1	.875	59	1	0	0	0	97¹	101	10	37	69	12.9	4.07	83	.271	.340	1	.083	-1	-6	-8	0	-0.6
1990	SF-N★	5	3	.625	55	0	0	0	19	86²	77	3	33	61	11.7	1.56	234	.240	.317	2	.286	1	22	20	0	2.7
1991	SF-N	5	2	.714	67	0	0	0	15	95¹	78	8	52	81	12.7	2.45	146	.225	.335	0	.000	0	13	12	-1	1.1
1992	SF-N	7	7	.500	56	4	0	0	7	91²	67	8	45	86	11.3	2.95	112	.207	.310	1	.111	0	6	4	-0	0.5
1993	SF-N	5	6	.455	53	12	0	0	0	113²	112	16	46	76	13.1	4.28	91	.259	.340	3	.107	-1	-3	-5	-2	-0.7
1994	Cin-N	6	6	.500	50	0	0	0	15	65¹	46	6	28	63	10.2	2.48	167	.202	.289	0	.000	0	13	12	0	2.5
1995	*Cin-N	3	2	.600	56	0	0	0	28	70¹	53	11	20	62	9.5	2.82	146	.206	.266	0	.000	0	11	10	-1	1.9
1996	Cin-N	1	2	.333	66	0	0	0	44	71	54	7	28	76	10.4	2.41	172	.215	.294	0	.000	0	14	14	-1	1.9
Total	9	39	30	.565	471	18	0	0	129	712	610	74	295	585	11.7	3.05	122	.234	.316	8	.118	-2	63	54	-3	8.5
● KITTY BRASHEAR										Brashear, Norman C. b: 8/27/1877, Mansfield, Ohio d: 12/22/34, Los Angeles, Cal. BR/TR, Deb: 6/25/1899 F																
1899	Lou-N	1	0	1.000	3	0	0	0	0	8	8	2	5	2	12.4	4.50	86	.258	.324	1	.500	0	-1	-1	0	0.0
● JOHN BRAUN										Braun, John Paul b: 12/26/39, Madison, Wis. BR/TR, 6′5″, 218 lbs. Deb: 10/2/64																
1964	Mil-N	0	0	—	1	0	0	0	0	2	1	0	1	3	13.5	0.00	—	.286	.375	0	—	0	1	1	0	0.2
● GARLAND BRAXTON										Braxton, Edgar Garland b: 6/10/1900, Snow Camp, N.C. d: 2/25/66, Norfolk, Va. BB/TL, 5′11″, 152 lbs. Deb: 5/27/21																
1921	Bos-N	1	3	.250	17	2	0	0	0	37¹	44	0	17	16	15.2	4.82	76	.310	.391	0	.000	-1	-4	-5	1	-0.5
1922	Bos-N	1	2	.333	25	5	2	0	0	66²	75	3	24	15	13.9	3.38	118	.286	.355	1	.063	-2	5	5	-1	0.0
1925	NY-A	1	1	.500	3	2	0	0	0	19¹	26	1	5	11	14.9	6.52	65	.338	.386	2	.333	0	-5	-5	-0	-0.4
1926	NY-A	5	1	.833	37	1	0	0	0	67¹	71	7	19	30	12.0	2.67	144	.275	.325	6	.300	1	10	9	0	0.9
1927	Was-A	10	9	.526	58	2	0	0	13	155¹	144	5	33	96	10.4	2.95	138	.246	.289	9	.231	0	20	19	-2	2.2
1928	Was-A	13	11	.542	38	24	15	2	6	218¹	177	7	44	94	9.3	2.51	160	.222	.267	9	.125	-4	37	36	-0	3.5
1929	Was-A	12	10	.545	37	20	9	0	4	182	219	6	51	59	13.5	4.85	88	.299	.346	8	.148	-1	-12	-12	-1	-1.5
1930	Was-A	3	2	.600	15	0	0	0	5	27¹	22	3	9	10	10.2	3.29	140	.222	.287	0	.000	-1	4	4	0	0.6
	Chi-A	4	10	.286	19	10	2	0	1	90²	127	9	33	44	16.0	6.45	72	.333	.388	2	.087	-2	-18	-18	-1	-2.5
	Yr	7	12	.368	34	10	2	0	6	118	149	12	42	51	14.6	5.72	81	.310	.367	2	.071	-2	-14	-14	-2	-1.9
1931	Chi-A	0	3	.000	17	3	0	0	0	47¹	71	4	29	28	18.3	6.85	62	.338	.409	1	.091	-1	-13	-14	1	-0.8
	StL-A	0	0	—	11	1	0	0	1	18	27	1	7	19	19.0	10.50	44	.370	.452	2	.667	1	-12	-12	0	0.1
	Yr	0	3	.000	28	4	0	0	1	65¹	98	5	36	47	18.2	7.85	56	.344	.414	3	.214	-0	-25	-25	0	-0.7
1933	StL-A	0	1	.000	5	0	0	0	0	8¹	11	0	5	5	21.6	9.72	48	.289	.426	0	.000	-0	-5	-5	-0	-0.5
Total	10	50	53	.485	282	71	28	2	32	938	1014	38	276	412	12.6	4.13	101	.291	.332	40	.156	-8	8	8	-5	1.1
● AL BRAZLE										Brazle, Alpha Eugene "Cotton" b: 10/19/13, Loyal, Okla. d: 10/24/73, Grand Junction, Colo. BL/TL, 6′2″, 185 lbs. Deb: 7/25/43																
1943	*StL-N	8	2	.800	13	9	8	1	0	88	74	0	29	26	10.5	1.53	219	.231	.295	9	.281	2	18	18	0	2.4
1946	*StL-N	11	10	.524	37	15	6	2	0	153¹	152	11	55	58	12.3	3.29	105	.261	.327	11	.212	-0	2	3	0	0.3
1947	StL-N	14	8	.636	44	19	7	0	4	168	186	7	48	85	12.6	2.84	146	.284	.335	14	.219	1	23	24	3	3.4
1948	StL-N	10	6	.625	42	23	6	2	1	156¹	171	8	50	55	12.7	3.80	108	.281	.335	8	.145	-2	3	5	0	0.6
1949	StL-N	14	8	.636	39	25	9	1	0	206¹	208	18	61	75	12.0	3.18	131	.263	.321	11	.134	-4	20	22	-0	1.7
1950	StL-N	11	9	.550	46	12	3	0	6	164²	188	12	80	47	14.9	4.10	105	.296	.378	13	.213	-1	4	3	0	0.3
1951	StL-N	6	5	.545	56	8	5	0	7	154¹	139	13	60	66	11.9	3.09	128	.245	.322	5	.109	-3	15	15	-2	0.6
1952	StL-N	12	5	.706	46	6	3	1	16	109¹	75	7	42	55	9.7	2.72	137	.198	.280	4	.125	-1	12	12	-2	1.9
1953	StL-N	6	7	.462	60	0	0	0	18	92	101	8	43	55	14.3	4.21	101	.280	.360	5	.333	1	1	1	0	0.3
1954	StL-N	4	4	.556	58	0	0	0	0	84¹	93	10	24	32	12.8	4.16	99	.288	.343	0	.000	-2	-1	-0	-1	-0.3
Total	10	97	64	.602	441	117	47	7	60	1376²	1387	84	492	554	12.4	3.31	120	.266	.332	80	.177	-9	93	103	3	11.3

YEAR	TM/L	W	L	PCT	G	GS	CG	SH	SV	IP	H	HR	BB	SO	RAT	ERA	ERA+	OAV	OOB	BH	AVG	PB	PR	/A	PD	TPI

● HARRY BRECHEEN   Brecheen, Harry David "Harry The Cat"   b: 10/14/14, Broken Bow, Okla.   BL/TL, 5'10", 160 lbs.   Deb: 4/22/40   C

YEAR	TM/L	W	L	PCT	G	GS	CG	SH	SV	IP	H	HR	BB	SO	RAT	ERA	ERA+	OAV	OOB	BH	AVG	PB	PR	/A	PD	TPI
1940	StL-N	0	0	—	3	0	0	0	0	3¹	2	0	2	4	10.8	0.00	—	.167	.286	0	—	0	1	1	0	0.0
1943	*StL-N	9	6	.600	29	13	8	1	4	135¹	98	4	39	68	9.3	2.26	149	.206	.270	8	.190	1	17	17	-1	2.1
1944	*StL-N	16	5	.762	30	22	13	3	0	189¹	174	8	46	88	10.6	2.85	124	.242	.290	11	.162	1	16	14	-0	1.5
1945	StL-N	15	4	**.789**	24	18	13	3	2	157¹	136	5	44	63	10.6	2.52	149	.238	.298	7	.123	-1	22	21	-1	2.3
1946	StL-N	15	15	.500	36	30	14	**5**	3	231¹	212	8	67	117	11.0	2.49	139	.244	.301	11	.133	-3	24	25	2	3.1
1947	StL-N★	16	11	.593	29	28	18	1	1	223¹	220	20	66	89	11.6	3.30	125	.260	.316	20	.241	5	19	21	1	2.9
1948	StL-N☆	20	7	.741	33	30	21	**7**	1	233¹	193	6	49	**149**	9.4	**2.24**	**183**	.222	**.265**	12	.146	-1	45	**48**	1	**5.5**
1949	StL-N	14	11	.560	32	31	14	2	1	214²	207	18	65	88	11.7	3.35	124	.252	.312	21	.273	5	16	19	-1	2.5
1950	StL-N	8	11	.421	27	23	12	2	1	163¹	151	18	45	80	11.0	3.80	113	.244	.298	14	.241	8	3	6	-0	1.2
1951	StL-N	8	4	.667	24	16	5	0	2	138²	134	11	54	57	12.3	3.25	122	.256	.327	12	.218	-2	11	11	-0	1.1
1952	StL-N	7	5	.583	25	13	4	1	2	100¹	82	12	28	54	10.1	3.32	112	.223	.283	6	.207	1	5	4	2	0.9
1953	StL-A	5	13	.278	26	16	3	0	1	117¹	122	7	31	44	12.0	3.07	137	.269	.320	7	.179	-1	12	15	2	2.3
Total	12	133	92	.591	318	240	125	25	18	1907²	1731	117	536	901	10.9	2.92	133	.242	.298	129	.192	11	194	205	6	25.4

● BILL BRECKINRIDGE   Breckinridge, William Robertson   b: 10/16/07, Tulsa, Okla.   d: 8/23/58, Tulsa, Okla.   BR/TR, 5'11", 175 lbs.   Deb: 6/30/29

| 1929 | Phi-A | 0 | 0 | — | 3 | 1 | 0 | 0 | 0 | 10 | 10 | 0 | 16 | 2 | 23.4 | 8.10 | 52 | .270 | .491 | 0 | .000 | -1 | -4 | -4 | -1 | -0.1 |

● FRED BREINING   Breining, Fred Lawrence   b: 11/15/55, San Francisco, Cal.   BR/TR, 6'4", 185 lbs.   Deb: 9/4/80

1980	SF-N	0	0	—	5	0	0	0	0	6²	8	0	4	3	17.6	5.40	65	.333	.448	0	—	0	-1	-1	-0	0.0
1981	SF-N	5	2	.714	45	1	0	0	1	77²	66	4	38	37	12.3	2.55	135	.243	.340	0	.000	-1	8	8	0	0.5
1982	SF-N	11	6	.647	54	9	2	0	0	143¹	146	6	52	98	12.5	3.08	117	.269	.334	6	.207	1	8	8	1	1.2
1983	SF-N	11	12	.478	32	32	6	0	0	202²	202	15	60	117	11.9	3.82	93	.259	.316	10	.149	1	-4	-6	-1	-0.6
1984	Mon-N	0	0	—	4	0	0	0	0	6²	4	0	5	5	12.2	1.35	254	.190	.346	0	.000	-0	2	2	-0	0.0
Total	5	27	20	.574	140	42	8	0	1	437	426	25	159	260	12.2	3.34	106	.260	.329	16	.148	1	12	10	-0	1.1

● ALONZO BREITENSTEIN   Breitenstein, Alonzo   b: 11/9/1857, Utica, N.Y.   d: 6/19/32, Utica, N.Y.   Deb: 7/7/1883

| 1883 | Phi-N | 0 | 1 | .000 | 1 | 1 | 0 | 0 | 0 | 5 | 8 | 0 | 2 | 0 | 18.0 | 9.00 | 34 | .320 | .370 | 0 | .000 | — | -3 | -3 | -0 | -0.5 |

● TED BREITENSTEIN   Breitenstein, Theodore P. "Theo"   b: 6/1/1869, St.Louis, Mo.   d: 5/3/35, St.Louis, Mo.   BL/TL, 5'9", 167 lbs.   Deb: 4/28/1891

1891	StL-a	2	0	1.000	6	1	1	1	1	28²	15	2	14	13	9.1	2.20	191	.150	.254	1	.000	-2	5	6	-1	0.2
1892	StL-N	9	19	.321	39	32	28	1	1	282²	280	8	148	126	13.6	4.69	68	.248	.339	16	.122	-3	-44	-47	3	-3.7
1893	StL-N	19	24	.442	48	42	38	1	1	382²	359	8	156	102	12.3	**3.18**	**149**	.241	.316	29	.181	-5	63	66	2	5.5
1894	StL-N	27	23	.540	**56**	50	**46**	1	0	**447**¹	497	21	191	140	14.1	4.79	113	.278	.352	40	.220	-1	27	31	3	2.6
1895	StL-N	19	30	.388	54	50	**46**	1	0	429²	458	16	178	127	13.6	4.44	109	.269	.343	42	.193	7	16	19	3	1.3
1896	StL-N	18	26	.409	44	43	37	1	0	339²	376	12	138	102	13.8	4.48	97	.278	.347	42	.259	3	-4	-5	4	0.1
1897	Cin-N	23	12	.657	40	39	32	2	0	320¹	345	3	91	98	12.5	3.62	126	.273	.326	33	.266	1	25	33	-0	3.1
1898	Cin-N	20	14	.588	39	37	32	3	0	315²	313	1	123	68	12.7	3.42	112	.257	.330	26	.215	1	7	15	3	1.7
1899	Cin-N	13	9	.591	26	24	21	0	0	210²	219	2	71	59	12.8	3.59	109	.268	.333	37	.352	9	6	8	-0	1.5
1900	Cin-N	10	10	.500	24	20	18	1	0	192¹	205	4	79	39	13.9	3.65	101	.272	.352	24	.190	-0	1	2	2	0.2
1901	StL-N	0	3	.000	3	3	1	0	0	15	24	1	14	3	22.8	6.60	48	.358	.469	2	.333	-1	-5	-6	1	-0.8
Total	11	160	170	.485	379	341	300	12	3	2964¹	3091	79	1203	889	13.3	4.04	109	.265	.338	291	.216	-3	96	121	20	11.7

● AD BRENNAN   Brennan, Addison Foster   b: 7/18/1881, LaHarpe, Kan.   d: 1/7/62, Kansas City, Mo.   BL/TL, 5'11", 170 lbs.   Deb: 5/19/10

1910	Phi-N	2	0	1.000	19	5	2	0	0	73¹	72	2	28	28	12.6	2.33	134	.264	.339	7	.280	1	6	6	-2	0.1
1911	Phi-N	2	1	.667	5	3	1	0	0	22²	22	0	12	12	13.9	3.57	96	.259	.357	2	.222	-0	-0	-0	-0	0.0
1912	Phi-N	11	9	.550	27	19	13	1	2	174	185	4	49	78	12.3	3.57	102	.274	.326	15	.254	4	-3	1	2	0.7
1913	Phi-N	14	12	.538	40	25	12	1	1	207	204	5	46	94	11.1	2.39	139	.268	.314	11	.164	-2	19	22	0	2.5
1914	Chi-F	5	5	.500	16	11	5	1	0	85²	84	6	21	31	11.2	3.57	74	.256	.305	8	.250	1	-7	-9	-1	-0.9
1915	Chi-F	3	9	.250	19	13	7	2	0	106	117	4	30	40	13.1	3.74	67	.287	.346	5	.185	-2	-12	-14	-2	-1.7
1918	Was-A	0	0	—	2	1	0	0	0	5¹	7	0	5	2	21.9	5.06	54	.241	.371	0	.000	-1	-1	-1	0	0.0
	Cle-A	0	0	—	1	0	0	0	0	3	3	0	3	0	18.0	3.00	100	.333	.500	0	—	-0	-0	-0	-0	0.0
	Yr	0	0	—	3	1	0	0	0	8¹	10	0	8	2	19.4	4.32	65	.256	.383	0	.000	-0	-1	-0	0	0.0
Total	7	37	36	.507	129	77	40	5	3	677	694	21	194	283	12.1	3.11	102	.270	.327	48	.218	4	1	5	-1	0.7

● DON BRENNAN   Brennan, James Donald   b: 12/2/03, Augusta, Maine   d: 4/26/53, Boston, Mass.   BR/TR, 6', 210 lbs.   Deb: 4/16/33

1933	NY-A	5	1	.833	18	10	3	0	3	85	92	4	47	46	14.7	4.98	78	.275	.365	7	.259	2	-7	-10	1	-0.4
1934	Cin-N	4	3	.571	28	7	2	0	2	78	89	3	35	31	14.4	3.81	107	.290	.364	5	.227	0	2	2	-1	0.2
1935	Cin-N	5	5	.500	38	5	2	1	5	114¹	101	4	44	48	11.7	3.15	126	.242	.320	3	.100	-1	11	11	-2	0.6
1936	Cin-N	6	2	.714	41	4	0	0	9	94¹	117	2	35	40	14.6	4.39	87	.305	.364	2	.080	-3	-4	-6	-0	-0.8
1937	Cin-N	1	1	.500	10	0	0	0	0	16	25	1	10	9	19.7	6.75	55	.347	.427	1	—	-5	-5	-5	0	-0.6
	*NY-N	1	0	1.000	6	0	0	0	0	9¹	12	0	9	7	21.2	6.75	58	.316	.458	0	.000	-3	-3	-3	-0	-0.3
	Yr	2	1	.667	16	0	0	0	0	25¹	37	1	19	7	20.3	6.75	56	.336	.438	1	.000	-8	-8	-8	-0	-0.9
Total	5	21	12	.636	141	26	7	1	19	397	436	14	180	172	14.1	4.19	94	.281	.358	17	.155	-2	-5	-12	-2	-1.3

● TOM BRENNAN   Brennan, Thomas Martin   b: 10/30/52, Chicago, Ill.   BR/TR, 6'1", 180 lbs.   Deb: 9/5/81

1981	Cle-A	2	2	.500	7	6	1	0	0	48¹	49	5	14	15	11.7	3.17	114	.259	.310	0	—	0	3	2	1	0.3
1982	Cle-A	4	2	.667	30	4	0	0	2	92²	112	9	10	46	12.0	4.27	95	.300	.322	0	-2	-2	-0	-0.1
1983	Cle-A	2	2	.500	11	5	1	1	0	39²	45	3	8	21	12.3	3.86	110	.288	.327	0	—	-0	1	1	0	0.1
1984	Chi-A	0	1	.000	4	1	0	0	0	6²	8	1	3	3	14.9	4.05	103	.308	.379	0	—	-0	-0	-0	-0	0.0
1985	LA-N	1	3	.250	12	4	0	0	0	31²	41	2	11	17	14.8	7.39	47	.333	.388	1	.125	-0	-13	-14	1	-1.4
Total	5	9	10	.474	64	20	2	1	2	219	255	20	46	102	12.5	4.40	89	.294	.332	1	.125	-0	-12	-12	3	-1.1

● WILLIAM BRENNAN   Brennan, William Raymond   b: 1/15/63, Tampa, Fla.   BR/TR, 6'3", 200 lbs.   Deb: 7/19/88

1988	LA-N	0	1	.000	4	2	0	0	0	9¹	13	0	6	7	18.3	6.75	49	.342	.432	0	.000	-0	-3	-4	-0	-0.3
1993	Chi-N	2	1	.667	8	1	0	0	0	15	16	2	8	11	15.0	4.20	95	.291	.391	0	.000	-0	-0	-0	0	0.0
Total	2	2	2	.500	12	3	0	0	0	24¹	29	2	14	18	16.3	5.18	72	.312	.407	0	.000	-0	-4	-4	-0	-0.3

● JIM BRENNEMAN   Brenneman, James Leroy   b: 2/13/41, San Diego, Cal.   BR/TR, 6'2", 180 lbs.   Deb: 7/9/65

| 1965 | NY-A | 0 | 0 | — | 3 | 0 | 0 | 0 | 0 | 2 | 5 | 1 | 3 | 2 | 36.0 | 18.00 | 19 | .455 | .571 | 0 | — | 0 | -3 | -3 | -0 | 0.0 |

● BERT BRENNER   Brenner, Delbert Henry "Dutch"   b: 7/18/1887, Minneapolis, Minn   d: 4/11/71, St.Louis Park, Minn.   BR/TR, 6', 175 lbs.   Deb: 9/21/12

| 1912 | Cle-A | 1 | 0 | 1.000 | 2 | 1 | 0 | 0 | 0 | 13 | 14 | 0 | 4 | 3 | 12.5 | 2.77 | 123 | .286 | .340 | 0 | .000 | -1 | 1 | 1 | 0 | 0.0 |

● LYNN BRENTON   Brenton, Lynn Davis "Buck" or "Herb"   b: 10/7/1890, Peoria, Ill.   d: 10/14/68, Los Angeles, Cal.   BR/TR, 5'10", 165 lbs.   Deb: 8/10/13

1913	Cle-A	0	0	—	1	0	0	0	0	2	4	0	2	0	18.0	9.00	34	.400	.400	0	—	-1	-1	-1	-0	0.0
1915	Cle-A	2	3	.400	11	5	1	1	0	51	60	1	20	18	14.5	3.35	91	.308	.378	2	.118	-1	-2	-2	-1	-0.4
1920	Cin-N	2	1	.667	5	1	1	0	1	18¹	17	0	4	13	10.3	4.91	62	.236	.276	2	.250	-0	-4	-4	2	-0.5
1921	Cin-N	1	8	.111	17	9	2	0	1	60	80	3	17	19	14.7	4.05	88	.342	.389	2	.133	-0	-2	-3	2	-0.2
Total	4	5	12	.294	34	15	4	1	2	131¹	161	4	41	52	14.0	3.97	83	.315	.369	6	.150	-0	-9	-10	3	-1.1

● ROGER BRESNAHAN   Bresnahan, Roger Philip "The Duke Of Tralee"   b: 6/11/1879, Toledo, Ohio   d: 12/4/44, Toledo, Ohio   BR/TR, 5'9", 200 lbs.   Deb: 8/27/1897   MCH♦

1897	Was-N	4	0	1.000	6	5	3	1	0	41	52	1	10	12	14.3	3.95	110	.306	.355	6	.375	1	2	2	-0	0.2
1901	Bal-A	0	1	.000	2	1	0	0	0	6	10	0	4	3	21.0	6.00	64	.370	.452	79	.266	-2	-1	-0	2	0.1
1910	StL-N	0	0	—	1	0	0	0	0	3¹	6	0	1	0	18.9	0.00	—	.400	.438	65	.278	0	1	1	-0	0.0
Total	3	4	1	.800	9	6	3	1	0	50¹	68	1	15	15	15.4	3.93	107	.321	.374	1252	.279	-1	1	1	0	0.1

● RUBE BRESSLER   Bressler, Raymond Bloom   b: 10/23/1894, Coder, Pa.   d: 11/7/66, Cincinnati, Ohio   BR/TL, 6', 187 lbs.   Deb: 4/24/14   ♦

1914	Phi-A	10	4	.714	29	10	8	1	2	147²	112	1	56	96	10.5	1.77	148	.220	.302	11	.216	4	16	14	-2	1.5
1915	Phi-A	4	17	.190	32	20	7	1	0	178¹	183	3	118	69	15.5	5.20	56	.283	.399	8	.145	1	-45	-45	0	-4.5
1916	Phi-A	2	0	.000	15	5	0	0	0	45	16	0	14	18	19.2	6.60	43	.296	.457	1	.200	1	-6	-6	-0	-0.7

YEAR TM/L	W	L	PCT	G	GS	CG	SH	SV	IP	H	HR	BB	SO	RAT	ERA	ERA+	OAV	OOB	BH	AVG	PB	PR	/A	PD	TPI
1917 Cin-N	0	0	—	2	1	0	0	0	9	15	0	5	2	20.0	6.00	44	.429	.500	1	.200	-0	-3	-3	-0	0.0
1918 Cin-N	8	5	.615	17	13	10	0	0	128	124	3	39	37	11.5	2.46	108	.261	.318	17	.274	4	4	3	3	1.1
1919 Cin-N	2	4	.333	13	4	1	0	0	41²	37	1	8	13	9.7	3.46	80	.248	.287	34	.206	2	-3	-3	1	-0.3
1920 Cin-N	2	0	1.000	10	2	1	0	0	20¹	24	0	2	4	11.5	1.77	172	.300	.317	8	.267	0	3	3	0	0.3
Total 7	26	32	.448	107	52	27	3	2	540	511	8	242	229	12.8	3.40	81	.262	.348	1170	.301	12	-34	-38	1	-2.6

● HERB BRETT
Brett, Herbert James "Duke" b: 5/23/1900, Lawrenceville, Va. d: 11/25/74, St.Petersburg, Fla BR/TR, 6', 175 lbs. Deb: 8/8/24

YEAR TM/L	W	L	PCT	G	GS	CG	SH	SV	IP	H	HR	BB	SO	RAT	ERA	ERA+	OAV	OOB	BH	AVG	PB	PR	/A	PD	TPI
1924 Chi-N	0	0	—	1	1	0	0	0	5¹	6	0	7	1	21.9	5.06	77	.300	.481	0	.000	-0	-1	-0	0	-0.1
1925 Chi-N	1	1	.500	10	1	0	0	0	17¹	12	0	3	6	8.3	3.63	119	.194	.242	0	.000	-0	1	1	1	0.2
Total 2	1	1	.500	11	2	0	0	0	22²	18	0	10	7	11.5	3.97	106	.220	.312	0	.000	-0	1	1	0	0.1

● KEN BRETT
Brett, Kenneth Alven b: 9/18/48, Brooklyn, N.Y. BL/TL, 5'11", 195 lbs. Deb: 9/27/67 F

YEAR TM/L	W	L	PCT	G	GS	CG	SH	SV	IP	H	HR	BB	SO	RAT	ERA	ERA+	OAV	OOB	BH	AVG	PB	PR	/A	PD	TPI
1967 *Bos-A	0	0	—	1	0	0	0	0	2	3	0	0	2	13.5	4.50	77	.375	.375	0	—	0	-0	-0	-0	0.0
1969 Bos-A	2	3	.400	8	8	0	0	0	39¹	41	6	22	23	15.1	5.26	72	.275	.379	3	.300	2	-7	-6	0	-0.5
1970 Bos-A	8	9	.471	41	14	1	0	2	139¹	118	17	79	155	12.9	4.07	97	.223	.327	13	.317	6	-6	-2	1	0.5
1971 Bos-A	0	3	.000	29	2	0	0	1	59	57	7	35	57	14.2	5.34	69	.253	.356	2	.200	-0	-12	-11	-0	-0.6
1972 Mil-A	7	12	.368	26	22	2	1	0	133	121	13	49	74	11.6	4.53	67	.242	.311	10	.227	2	-22	-22	-2	-3.0
1973 Phi-N	13	9	.591	31	25	10	1	0	211²	206	19	74	111	11.9	3.44	110	.259	.322	20	.250	8	5	8	2	1.9
1974 *Pit-N★	13	9	.591	27	27	10	3	0	191	192	9	52	96	11.6	3.30	104	.257	.308	27	.310	11	7	3	0	1.5
1975 *Pit-N	9	5	.643	23	16	4	1	0	118	110	10	43	47	11.8	3.36	106	.250	.320	12	.231	4	3	2	0	0.7
1976 NY-A	0	0	—	2	0	0	0	1	2¹	2	0	0	1	7.7	0.00	—	.222	.222	0	—	0	1	1	-0	0.1
Chi-A	10	12	.455	27	26	16	1	1	200²	171	5	76	91	11.2	3.32	107	.234	.308	1	.083	2	4	5	1	0.6
Yr	10	12	.455	29	26	16	1	2	203	173	5	76	92	11.2	3.28	109	.233	.307	1	.083	2	5	6	0	0.7
1977 Chi-A	6	4	.600	13	13	2	0	0	82²	101	10	15	39	12.7	5.01	82	.305	.337	0	—	0	-9	-8	-0	-0.9
Cal-A	7	10	.412	21	21	5	0	0	142	157	15	38	41	12.5	4.25	92	.287	.337	0	—	0	-3	-5	2	0.0
Yr	13	14	.481	34	34	7	0	0	224²	258	25	53	80	12.6	4.53	89	.293	.335	0	—	0	-12	-14	2	-0.9
1978 Cal-A	3	5	.375	31	10	1	1	1	100	100	12	42	43	12.9	4.95	73	.262	.336	0	—	0	-13	-15	2	-0.7
1979 Min-A	0	0	—	9	0	0	0	0	12²	16	1	6	3	15.6	4.97	88	.320	.393	0	—	0	-1	-0	-0	-0.3
LA-N	4	3	.571	30	0	0	0	2	47	52	1	12	13	12.4	3.45	105	.277	.323	3	.273	1	1	1	2	0.4
1980 KC-A	0	0	—	8	0	0	0	1	13¹	8	0	5	4	9.5	0.00	—	.174	.269	0	—	0	6	6	0	0.1
1981 KC-A	1	1	.500	22	0	0	0	2	32¹	35	2	14	7	13.9	4.18	86	.282	.360	0	—	0	-2	-2	-0	-0.1
Total 14	83	85	.494	349	184	51	8	11	1526¹	1490	127	562	807	12.2	3.93	93	.257	.325	91	.262	35	-47	-46	8	-0.3

● MARV BREUER
Breuer, Marvin Howard "Baby Face" b: 4/29/14, Rolla, Mo. d: 1/17/91, Rolla, Mo. BR/TR, 6'2", 185 lbs. Deb: 5/4/39

YEAR TM/L	W	L	PCT	G	GS	CG	SH	SV	IP	H	HR	BB	SO	RAT	ERA	ERA+	OAV	OOB	BH	AVG	PB	PR	/A	PD	TPI
1939 NY-A	0	0	—	1	0	0	0	0	1	2	0	1	0	27.0	9.00	48	.667	.750	0	—	0	-0	-1	0	0.0
1940 NY-A	8	9	.471	27	22	10	0	0	164	175	8	61	71	13.0	4.55	89	.267	.329	2	.037	-5	-3	-10	-1	-1.3
1941 *NY-A	9	7	.563	26	18	7	1	2	141	131	10	49	77	11.6	4.09	96	.243	.308	4	.087	-3	1	-2	-1	-0.6
1942 *NY-A	8	9	.471	27	19	6	0	1	164¹	157	11	37	72	10.7	3.07	112	.252	.295	3	.056	-3	11	7	-2	0.1
1943 NY-A	0	1	.000	5	1	0	0	0	14	22	0	6	6	18.0	8.36	39	.349	.406	1	.333	0	-8	-8	0	-0.5
Total 5	25	26	.490	86	60	23	1	3	484¹	487	41	154	226	12.0	4.03	94	.258	.315	10	.064	-11	0	-13	-3	-2.3

● JIM BREWER
Brewer, James Thomas b: 11/17/37, Merced, Cal. d: 11/16/87, Tyler, Tex. BL/TL, 6'2", 195 lbs. Deb: 7/17/60 C

YEAR TM/L	W	L	PCT	G	GS	CG	SH	SV	IP	H	HR	BB	SO	RAT	ERA	ERA+	OAV	OOB	BH	AVG	PB	PR	/A	PD	TPI
1960 Chi-N	0	3	.000	5	4	0	0	0	21²	25	2	6	7	13.3	5.82	65	.272	.323	1	.167	0	-5	-5	0	-0.6
1961 Chi-N	1	7	.125	36	11	0	0	0	86²	116	17	21	57	14.3	5.82	72	.321	.360	4	.182	0	-17	-16	-2	-1.4
1962 Chi-N	0	1	.000	6	1	0	0	0	5²	10	2	3	1	20.6	9.53	44	.435	.500	0	—	0	-4	-3	-0	-0.5
1963 Chi-N	3	2	.600	29	1	0	0	0	49²	59	10	15	35	13.4	4.89	72	.294	.343	0	.000	0	-9	-8	-1	-0.8
1964 LA-N	4	3	.571	34	5	1	1	1	93	79	5	25	63	10.1	3.00	108	.232	.284	6	.273	2	6	2	-1	0.2
1965 *LA-N	3	2	.600	19	2	0	0	2	49¹	33	1	28	31	11.1	1.82	179	.196	.311	0	.000	-1	9	8	0	0.3
1966 *LA-N	2	2	.000	13	0	0	0	2	22	17	0	11	8	11.5	3.68	90	.221	.318	0	—	0	-0	-1	0	-0.1
1967 LA-N	5	4	.556	30	11	0	0	1	100²	78	8	31	74	9.8	2.68	116	.218	.283	1	.045	-1	8	5	-1	0.2
1968 LA-N	8	3	.727	54	0	0	0	14	76¹	59	5	33	75	10.8	2.48	112	.219	.304	2	.222	0	4	2	0	0.5
1969 LA-N	7	6	.538	59	0	0	0	20	88¹	71	5	41	92	11.8	2.55	131	.221	.317	1	.091	0	10	8	0	1.5
1970 LA-N	7	6	.538	58	0	0	0	24	89	66	10	33	91	10.0	3.13	122	.207	.281	1	.083	-0	9	7	0	1.3
1971 LA-N	6	5	.545	51	0	0	0	22	81¹	55	4	24	66	8.7	1.88	172	.194	.257	3	.333	1	14	12	1	2.6
1972 LA-N	8	7	.533	51	0	0	0	17	78¹	41	6	25	69	7.8	1.26	264	.157	.236	0	.000	0	19	18	-0	4.5
1973 LA-N★	6	8	.429	56	0	0	0	20	71²	58	8	25	56	10.4	3.01	114	.229	.299	2	.400	1	5	3	0	0.9
1974 *LA-N	4	4	.500	39	0	0	0	18	39¹	29	5	10	26	8.9	2.52	135	.207	.260	0	.000	-0	5	4	-1	0.7
1975 LA-N	3	1	.750	21	0	0	0	2	33	44	2	12	21	15.5	5.18	66	.333	.393	0	.000	0	-6	-7	0	-0.8
Cal-A	1	0	1.000	21	0	0	0	5	34²	38	2	11	22	12.7	1.82	195	.279	.333	0	—	0	8	7	1	0.9
1976 Cal-A	3	1	.750	21	0	0	0	3	20	16	0	6	16	11.7	2.70	123	.256	.310	0	—	0	2	1	0	0.3
Total 17	69	65	.515	584	35	1	1	132	1040²	898	92	360	810	11.0	3.07	111	.236	.303	21	.150	1	59	38	-4	10.2

● JACK BREWER
Brewer, John Herndon "Buddy" b: 7/21/19, Los Angeles, Cal. BR/TR, 6'2", 170 lbs. Deb: 7/15/44

YEAR TM/L	W	L	PCT	G	GS	CG	SH	SV	IP	H	HR	BB	SO	RAT	ERA	ERA+	OAV	OOB	BH	AVG	PB	PR	/A	PD	TPI
1944 NY-N	1	4	.200	14	7	2	0	0	55	66	8	16	21	13.9	5.56	66	.288	.343	4	.211	0	-12	-12	-1	-1.0
1945 NY-N	8	6	.571	28	21	8	0	0	159²	162	14	58	49	12.6	3.83	102	.260	.326	10	.179	-1	-1	1	-3	-0.3
1946 NY-N	0	0	—	1	0	0	0	0	2	3	0	2	3	22.5	13.50	50	.333	.455	0	—	0	-2	-2	0	-0.0
Total 3	9	10	.474	43	28	10	0	0	216²	231	22	76	73	13.0	4.36	88	.268	.332	14	.187	-1	-15	-12	-3	-1.3

● ROD BREWER
Brewer, Rodney Lee b: 2/24/66, Eustis, Fla. BL/TL, 6'3", 210 lbs. Deb: 9/5/90 ♦

YEAR TM/L	W	L	PCT	G	GS	CG	SH	SV	IP	H	HR	BB	SO	RAT	ERA	ERA+	OAV	OOB	BH	AVG	PB	PR	/A	PD	TPI
1993 StL-N	0	0	—	1	0	0	0	0	1	3	1	2	1	45.0	45.00	9	.500	.625	42	.286	0	-5	-5	0	0.0

● TOM BREWER
Brewer, Thomas Austin b: 9/3/31, Wadesboro, N.C. BR/TR, 6'1", 175 lbs. Deb: 4/18/54

YEAR TM/L	W	L	PCT	G	GS	CG	SH	SV	IP	H	HR	BB	SO	RAT	ERA	ERA+	OAV	OOB	BH	AVG	PB	PR	/A	PD	TPI
1954 Bos-A	10	9	.526	33	23	7	0	0	162²	152	15	95	69	14.1	4.65	88	.249	.356	16	.267	3	-17	-10	-2	-1.0
1955 Bos-A	11	10	.524	31	28	9	2	0	192²	198	21	87	91	13.7	4.20	102	.263	.346	11	.151	-2	-5	2	3	0.3
1956 Bos-A★	19	9	.679	32	32	15	4	0	244¹	200	14	112	127	11.7	3.50	132	.220	.309	28	.298	4	18	30	4	4.1
1957 Bos-A	16	13	.552	32	32	15	2	0	238¹	225	24	93	128	12.3	3.85	103	.250	.325	19	.202	-1	-2	4	6	0.9
1958 Bos-A	12	12	.500	33	32	10	1	0	227¹	227	21	93	124	13.0	3.72	108	.259	.335	16	.195	-0	1	7	4	1.1
1959 Bos-A	10	12	.455	36	32	11	3	2	215¹	219	14	88	121	12.9	3.76	108	.265	.338	8	.111	-4	2	7	4	0.7
1960 Bos-A	10	15	.400	34	29	8	1	1	186²	220	13	72	60	14.4	4.82	84	.301	.368	12	.194	0	-20	-16	3	-1.7
1961 Bos-A	3	2	.600	10	9	0	0	0	42	37	4	29	13	14.1	3.43	122	.242	.363	4	.286	1	3	3	1	0.2
Total 8	91	82	.526	241	217	75	13	3	1509¹	1478	126	669	733	13.1	4.00	104	.257	.338	114	.207	1	-19	27	22	5.0

● BILLY BREWER
Brewer, William Robert b: 4/15/68, Fort Worth, Tex. BL/TL, 6'1", 175 lbs. Deb: 4/8/93

YEAR TM/L	W	L	PCT	G	GS	CG	SH	SV	IP	H	HR	BB	SO	RAT	ERA	ERA+	OAV	OOB	BH	AVG	PB	PR	/A	PD	TPI
1993 KC-A	2	2	.500	46	0	0	0	0	39	31	6	20	28	11.8	3.46	132	.230	.329	0	—	0	4	5	-1	0.0
1994 KC-A	4	1	.800	50	0	0	0	0	38²	28	4	16	25	10.7	2.56	159	.207	.301	0	—	0	10	10	0	1.3
1995 KC-A	2	3	.333	48	0	0	0	0	45¹	54	9	20	31	15.1	5.56	86	.290	.365	0	—	0	-4	-4	-0	-0.5
1996 NY-A	1	0	1.000	4	0	0	0	0	5²	7	0	8	8	23.8	9.53	53	.292	.469	0	—	0	-3	-3	0	-0.4
Total 4	9	7	.563	148	0	0	0	0	128²	120	19	64	92	13.2	4.20	114	.250	.343	0	—	0	6	9	-0	0.4

● JAMIE BREWINGTON
Brewington, Jamie Chancellor b: 9/28/71, Greenville, N.C. BR/TR, 6'4", 180 lbs. Deb: 7/24/95

YEAR TM/L	W	L	PCT	G	GS	CG	SH	SV	IP	H	HR	BB	SO	RAT	ERA	ERA+	OAV	OOB	BH	AVG	PB	PR	/A	PD	TPI
1995 SF-N	6	4	.600	13	13	0	0	0	48	45	8	45	45	14.0	4.54	90	.245	.359	5	.217	0	-3	-4	-0	-0.4

● ALAN BRICE
Brice, Alan Healey b: 10/1/37, New York, N.Y. BR/TR, 6'5", 215 lbs. Deb: 9/22/61

YEAR TM/L	W	L	PCT	G	GS	CG	SH	SV	IP	H	HR	BB	SO	RAT	ERA	ERA+	OAV	OOB	BH	AVG	PB	PR	/A	PD	TPI
1961 Chi-A	0	1	.000	3	0	0	0	0	3¹	4	0	3	2	18.9	0.00	—	.308	.438	0	—	0	1	1	-0	0.4

● RALPH BRICKNER
Brickner, Ralph Harold "Brick" b: 5/2/25, Cincinnati, Ohio d: 5/9/94, Port Jefferson, N.Y. BR/TR, 6'3.5", 215 lbs. Deb: 5/4/52

YEAR TM/L	W	L	PCT	G	GS	CG	SH	SV	IP	H	HR	BB	SO	RAT	ERA	ERA+	OAV	OOB	BH	AVG	PB	PR	/A	PD	TPI
1952 Bos-A	3	1	.750	14	1	0	0	1	33	32	1	11	9	11.7	2.18	181	.264	.326	2	.250	0	5	6	-1	0.8

● MARSHALL BRIDGES
Bridges, Marshall "Sheriff" b: 6/2/31, Jackson, Miss. d: 9/3/90, Jackson, Miss. BB/TL, 6'1", 180 lbs. Deb: 6/17/59

YEAR TM/L	W	L	PCT	G	GS	CG	SH	SV	IP	H	HR	BB	SO	RAT	ERA	ERA+	OAV	OOB	BH	AVG	PB	PR	/A	PD	TPI
1959 StL-N	6	3	.667	27	4	1	0	1	76	67	10	37	76	12.3	4.26	99	.240	.329	5	.217	2	-3	-0	-2	0.0
1960 StL-N	2	2	.500	20	1	0	0	1	31¹	33	2	16	27	14.4	3.45	119	.266	.355	0	.000	-0	1	2	-0	0.2
Cin-N	4	0	1.000	14	0	0	0	2	25¹	14	1	7	26	7.5	1.07	359	.161	.223	1	.250	0	8	8	-0	1.4

YEAR	TM/L	W	L	PCT	G	GS	CG	SH	SV	IP	H	HR	BB	SO	RAT	ERA	ERA+	OAV	OOB	BH	AVG	PB	PR	/A	PD	TPI
	Yr	6	2	.750	34	1	0	0	3	56²	47	3	23	53	11.1	2.38	167	.220	.295	1	.100	-0	9	10	-1	1.6
1961	Cin-N	0	1	.000	13	0	0	0	0	20²	26	4	11	17	16.5	7.84	52	.317	.404	0	.000	-0	-9	-9	-0	-0.4
1962	*NY-A	8	4	.667	52	0	0	0	18	71²	49	4	48	66	12.2	3.14	119	.194	.323	0	.000	-2	7	5	2	1.0
1963	NY-A	2	0	1.000	23	0	0	0	1	33	27	2	30	35	15.8	3.82	92	.237	.400	0	—	-0	-1	-1	2	0.1
1964	Was-A	0	3	.000	17	0	0	0	2	30	37	3	17	16	16.2	5.70	65	.303	.388	0	.000	-0	-7	-7	-0	-0.7
1965	Was-A	1	2	.333	40	0	0	0	0	57¹	62	5	25	39	13.7	2.67	130	.268	.340	1	.143	0	5	5	-0	0.3
Total	7	23	15	.605	206	5	1	0	25	345¹	315	29	191	302	13.3	3.75	102	.244	.343	7	.119	-0	1	3	1	1.9

● TOMMY BRIDGES
Bridges, Thomas Jefferson Davis   b: 12/28/06, Gordonsville, Tenn   d: 4/19/68, Nashville, Tenn.   BR/TR, 5'10.5", 155 lbs.   Deb: 8/13/30   C

YEAR	TM/L	W	L	PCT	G	GS	CG	SH	SV	IP	H	HR	BB	SO	RAT	ERA	ERA+	OAV	OOB	BH	AVG	PB	PR	/A	PD	TPI
1930	Det-A	3	2	.600	8	5	2	0	0	37²	28	4	23	17	12.2	4.06	118	.215	.333	1	.300	1	2	3	-0	0.4
1931	Det-A	8	16	.333	35	23	8	2	0	173	182	13	108	105	15.1	4.99	92	.263	.363	8	.148	-2	-12	-8	-1	-1.2
1932	Det-A	14	12	.538	34	26	10	**4**	1	201	174	14	119	108	13.2	3.36	140	.233	.339	11	.164	-1	25	30	-1	3.2
1933	Det-A	14	12	.538	33	28	17	2	2	233	192	8	110	120	11.9	3.09	140	**.226**	.319	16	.205	2	31	32	1	3.5
1934	*Det-A☆	22	11	.667	36	35	23	3	1	275	249	16	104	151	11.7	3.67	120	.241	.312	12	.122	-4	25	22	-2	1.7
1935	*Det-A☆	21	10	.677	36	34	23	4	1	274¹	277	22	113	**163**	12.9	3.51	119	.259	.332	26	.239	3	29	20	-1	2.1
1936	Det-A†	**23**	11	.676	39	38	26	5	0	294²	289	21	115	**175**	12.3	3.60	137	.255	.326	25	.212	-0	47	44	2	4.4
1937	Det-A★	15	12	.556	34	31	18	3	0	245¹	267	16	91	138	13.2	4.07	115	.274	.338	23	.240	2	15	16	1	1.8
1938	Det-A	13	9	.591	25	20	13	0	1	151	171	14	58	101	13.8	4.59	109	.287	.353	7	.130	-1	3	7	-1	0.6
1939	Det-A★	17	7	.708	29	26	16	2	2	198	186	11	61	129	11.5	3.50	140	.243	.304	10	.197	0	25	31	-0	3.3
1940	*Det-A☆	12	9	.571	29	28	12	2	0	197²	171	11	88	133	11.8	3.37	141	.229	.311	12	.176	-2	22	30	-1	2.6
1941	Det-A	9	12	.429	25	22	10	1	0	147²	169	8	75	97	13.3	3.41	133	.233	.320	4	.085	-3	12	19	2	2.3
1942	Det-A	9	7	.563	23	22	11	2	1	174	164	6	61	97	11.8	2.74	144	.246	.313	6	.095	-2	18	23	1	1.9
1943	Det-A	12	7	.632	25	22	11	3	0	191²	159	9	61	124	10.3	2.39	147	.226	.287	14	.219	2	19	24	-1	2.6
1945	*Det-A	1	0	1.000	4	1	0	0	0	11	14	2	4	6	13.1	3.27	107	.311	.340	0	.000	0	0	0	1	0.0
1946	Det-A	1	1	.500	9	1	0	0	1	21¹	24	5	8	17	13.9	5.91	62	.279	.347	0	.000	0	-6	-5	-0	-0.5
Total	16	194	138	.584	424	362	200	33	10	2826¹	2675	181	1192	1674	12.4	3.57	126	.248	.325	181	.180	-5	256	291	-3	28.7

● BUTTONS BRIGGS
Briggs, Herbert Theodore   b: 7/8/1875, Poughkeepsie, N.Y.   d: 2/18/11, Cleveland, Ohio   BR/TR, 6'1", 180 lbs.   Deb: 4/23/1896

YEAR	TM/L	W	L	PCT	G	GS	CG	SH	SV	IP	H	HR	BB	SO	RAT	ERA	ERA+	OAV	OOB	BH	AVG	PB	PR	/A	PD	TPI
1896	Chi-N	12	8	.600	26	21	19	0	1	194	202	6	108	84	15.1	4.31	105	.266	.368	10	.128	-6	1	5	-3	-0.4
1897	Chi-N	4	17	.190	22	22	21	0	0	186²	246	6	85	60	16.4	5.26	85	.315	.388	13	.160	-6	-20	-16	-1	-2.0
1898	Chi-N	1	3	.250	4	4	3	0	0	30	38	0	10	14	14.7	5.70	63	.306	.363	6	.429	1	-7	-7	-0	-0.6
1904	Chi-N	19	11	.633	34	30	28	3	3	277	252	3	77	112	10.9	2.05	130	.246	.304	16	.170	-0	21	19	-4	1.6
1905	Chi-N	8	8	.500	20	20	13	5	0	168	141	1	52	68	10.7	2.14	139	.237	.304	3	.053	-4	16	16	-2	0.7
Total	5	44	47	.484	106	97	84	8	4	855²	879	16	332	338	13.1	3.41	104	.268	.342	48	.148	-15	12	14	-10	-0.7

● JOHN BRIGGS
Briggs, Jonathan Tift   b: 1/24/34, Natoma, Cal.   BR/TR, 5'10", 175 lbs.   Deb: 4/17/56

YEAR	TM/L	W	L	PCT	G	GS	CG	SH	SV	IP	H	HR	BB	SO	RAT	ERA	ERA+	OAV	OOB	BH	AVG	PB	PR	/A	PD	TPI
1956	Chi-N	0	0	—	3	0	0	0	0	5¹	5	1	4	1	20.3	1.69	223	.238	.429	0		0	1	1	0	0.0
1957	Chi-N	0	1	.000	3	0	0	0	0	4¹	7	2	3	1	20.8	12.46	31	.368	.455	0	—	-0	-4	-4	-0	-0.8
1958	Chi-N	5	5	.500	20	17	3	1	0	95²	99	12	45	46	13.6	4.52	87	.270	.352	9	.257	2	-6	-6	-1	-0.5
1959	Cle-A	0	1	.000	4	1	0	0	0	12²	12	1	3	5	10.7	2.13	173	.245	.288	0	.000	-0	2	2	-0	0.1
1960	Cle-A	4	2	.667	21	2	0	0	1	36¹	32	4	15	19	11.9	4.46	84	.250	.333	1	.125	-0	-2	-3	-0	-0.6
	KC-A	0	2	.000	8	1	0	0	0	11¹	19	3	12	8	24.6	12.71	31	.380	.500	0	.000	-0	-11	-11	-0	-1.6
	Yr	4	4	.500	29	3	0	0	1	47²	51	7	27	27	14.7	6.42	59	.282	.375	1	.091	-1	-13	-14	-1	-2.2
Total	5	9	11	.450	59	21	3	1	1	165²	174	23	82	80	14.2	5.00	77	.275	.363	10	.208	1	-20	-21	-2	-3.4

● NELSON BRILES
Briles, Nelson Kelley   b: 8/5/43, Dorris, Cal.   BR/TR, 5'11", 200 lbs.   Deb: 4/19/65

YEAR	TM/L	W	L	PCT	G	GS	CG	SH	SV	IP	H	HR	BB	SO	RAT	ERA	ERA+	OAV	OOB	BH	AVG	PB	PR	/A	PD	TPI
1965	StL-N	3	3	.500	37	2	0	0	4	82¹	79	4	26	52	12.1	3.50	110	.258	.328	2	.133	-0	0	3	-1	0.1
1966	StL-N	4	15	.211	49	17	0	0	6	154	162	14	54	100	13.0	3.21	112	.279	.348	3	.079	-2	7	6	-1	0.7
1967	*StL-N	14	5	.737	49	14	4	2	6	155¹	139	8	40	94	10.7	2.43	135	.236	.290	6	.150	0	16	15	-2	1.8
1968	*StL-N	19	11	.633	33	33	13	4	0	243²	251	18	55	141	11.6	2.81	103	.266	.311	11	.138	1	5	2	-2	0.1
1969	StL-N	15	13	.536	36	33	10	3	0	227²	218	17	63	126	11.2	3.52	102	.251	.303	8	.105	-1	2	1	-1	-0.1
1970	StL-N	6	7	.462	30	19	1	1	0	106²	129	14	36	59	14.1	6.24	66	.297	.353	7	.179	1	-26	-25	-2	-2.7
1971	*Pit-N	8	4	.667	37	14	4	2	1	136	132	12	35	76	11.2	3.04	111	.250	.301	10	.256	4	6	5	-1	0.7
1972	*Pit-N	14	11	.560	28	27	9	2	0	195²	185	14	43	120	10.5	3.08	108	.249	.291	11	.157	-0	8	5	-1	0.6
1973	Pit-N	14	13	.519	33	33	7	1	0	218²	201	19	51	94	10.4	2.84	124	.244	.288	14	.194	3	20	16	0	2.3
1974	KC-A	5	7	.417	18	17	3	0	0	103	118	9	21	41	12.3	4.02	95	.293	.331	0	—	-0	-5	-2	-1	-0.7
1975	KC-A	6	6	.500	24	16	3	0	0	112	127	9	25	73	12.6	4.26	90	.285	.330	0	—	-0	-6	-5	-0	-0.6
1976	Tex-A	11	9	.550	32	31	7	1	1	210	224	15	47	99	11.7	3.26	110	.273	.314	6	8	-3	0.3
1977	Tex-A	6	4	.600	28	15	2	1	1	108¹	114	13	30	57	12.5	4.24	94	.275	.333	0	—	-0	-2	-2	-1	-0.3
	Bal-A	0	0	—	2	0	0	0	1	4	5	2	0	2	11.3	6.75	56	.294	.294	0	—	-0	-1	-1	-0	0.0
	Yr	6	4	.600	30	15	2	1	2	112¹	119	15	30	59	11.9	4.33	94	.271	.318	0	—	-0	-3	-3	-1	-0.3
1978	Bal-A	4	4	.500	16	8	1	0	0	54¹	58	6	21	30	13.4	4.64	75	.276	.351	0	—	-0	-5	-7	-1	-1.0
Total	14	129	112	.535	452	279	64	17	22	2111²	2141	186	547	1163	11.7	3.44	102	.264	.314	72	.154	5	25	19	-14	1.2

● FRANK BRILL
Brill, Francis Hasbrouck (b: Francis Hasbrouck Briell)   b: 3/30/1864, Astoria, N.Y.   d: 11/19/44, Flushing, N.Y.   BR/TR, 5'8", 155 lbs.   Deb: 6/23/1884

YEAR	TM/L	W	L	PCT	G	GS	CG	SH	SV	IP	H	HR	BB	SO	RAT	ERA	ERA+	OAV	OOB	BH	AVG	PB	PR	/A	PD	TPI
1884	Det-N	2	10	.167	12	12	12	1	0	103	148	7	26	18	15.2	5.50	53	.312	.348	6	.136	-3	-29	-30	-2	-2.9

● JIM BRILLHEART
Brillheart, James Benson   b: 9/28/03, Dublin, Va.   d: 9/2/72, Radford, Va.   BR/TL, 5'11", 170 lbs.   Deb: 4/17/22

YEAR	TM/L	W	L	PCT	G	GS	CG	SH	SV	IP	H	HR	BB	SO	RAT	ERA	ERA+	OAV	OOB	BH	AVG	PB	PR	/A	PD	TPI
1922	Was-A	4	6	.400	31	10	3	0	1	119²	120	3	72	47	15.0	3.61	107	.275	.388	3	.083	-4	6	3	-2	-0.3
1923	Was-A	0	1	.000	12	0	0	0	0	18	27	1	12	8	20.0	7.00	54	.360	.455	0	.000	-0	-6	-6	0	-0.3
1927	Chi-N	4	2	.667	32	12	4	0	0	128²	140	4	38	36	12.7	4.13	94	.286	.343	1	.023	-5	-3	-4	-1	-0.8
1931	Bos-A	0	0	—	11	1	0	0	0	19²	27	2	15	7	19.2	5.49	78	.325	.429	2	.500	2	-3	-3	1	0.2
Total	4	8	9	.471	86	23	7	0	1	286	314	10	137	98	14.6	4.19	93	.290	.376	6	.070	-8	-6	-9	-2	-1.2

● BRAD BRINK
Brink, Bradford Albert   b: 1/20/65, Roseville, Cal.   BR/TR, 6'2", 195 lbs.   Deb: 5/17/92

YEAR	TM/L	W	L	PCT	G	GS	CG	SH	SV	IP	H	HR	BB	SO	RAT	ERA	ERA+	OAV	OOB	BH	AVG	PB	PR	/A	PD	TPI
1992	Phi-N	0	4	.000	8	7	0	0	0	41¹	53	2	13	16	14.6	4.14	84	.308	.360	1	.083	-0	-3	-3	-0	-0.3
1993	Phi-N	0	0	—	2	0	0	0	0	6	3	1	3	8	9.0	3.00	132	.143	.250	0	—	-0	1	1	-0	0.0
1994	SF-N	0	0	—	4	0	0	0	0	8¹	4	1	4	3	8.6	1.08	371	.143	.250	0	.000	-0	3	3	0	0.0
Total	3	0	4	.000	14	7	0	0	0	55²	60	4	20	27	13.1	3.56	102	.271	.335	1	.071	-1	1	0	-0	-0.3

● JOHN BRISCOE
Briscoe, John Eric   b: 9/22/67, LaGrange, Ill.   BR/TR, 6'3", 185 lbs.   Deb: 4/18/91

YEAR	TM/L	W	L	PCT	G	GS	CG	SH	SV	IP	H	HR	BB	SO	RAT	ERA	ERA+	OAV	OOB	BH	AVG	PB	PR	/A	PD	TPI
1991	Oak-A	0	0	—	11	0	0	0	0	14	12	3	10	14	14.1	7.07	54	.235	.361	0	—	-0	-5	-5	-0	0.3
1992	Oak-A	0	0	—	2	0	0	0	0	7	12	0	9	4	27.0	6.43	58	.400	.538	0	—	-0	-2	-2	-0	-0.2
1993	Oak-A	1	0	1.000	17	0	0	0	0	24²	26	3	26	24	19.0	8.03	51	.277	.433	0	—	-0	-10	-11	-0	0.1
1994	Oak-A	4	2	.667	37	0	0	0	1	49¹	31	9	39	45	13.0	4.01	110	.185	.341	0	—	-0	4	2	-1	0.2
1995	Oak-A	0	1	.000	16	0	0	0	0	18¹	25	4	21	19	23.6	8.35	54	.347	.505	0	—	-0	-7	-8	-0	-0.2
1996	Oak-A	0	1	.000	17	0	0	0	0	26¹	18	2	24	14	14.4	3.76	128	.205	.375	0	—	-0	4	3	-0	0.1
Total	6	5	5	.500	100	2	0	0	2	139²	124	21	129	115	16.5	5.67	77	.247	.403	0	—	-0	-16	-21	-1	0.3

● LOU BRISSIE
Brissie, Leland Victor   b: 6/5/24, Anderson, S.C.   BL/TL, 6'4", 215 lbs.   Deb: 9/28/47

YEAR	TM/L	W	L	PCT	G	GS	CG	SH	SV	IP	H	HR	BB	SO	RAT	ERA	ERA+	OAV	OOB	BH	AVG	PB	PR	/A	PD	TPI
1947	Phi-A	0	1	.000	1	1	0	0	0	7	9	1	5	4	18.0	6.43	59	.310	.412	0	.000	-0	-2	-2	-0	-0.3
1948	Phi-A	14	10	.583	39	25	11	0	5	194	202	6	95	127	13.9	4.13	104	.269	.352	18	.237	-0	3	3	-2	0.2
1949	Phi-A★	16	11	.593	34	29	18	0	3	229¹	220	20	118	118	13.5	4.28	96	.251	.344	24	.267	3	-4	-4	-4	-0.5
1950	Phi-A	7	19	.269	46	31	15	2	8	246	237	22	117	101	13.1	4.02	113	.253	.338	15	.172	-3	15	14	-0	1.1
1951	Phi-A	0	2	.000	2	2	0	0	0	13¹	20	0	8	3	18.9	6.75	63	.357	.438	1	.200	-0	-4	-4	-0	-0.5
	Cle-A	4	3	.571	54	4	1	0	9	112¹	90	5	61	50	12.3	3.20	118	.223	.329	6	.261	0	11	7	-2	0.4
	Yr	4	5	.444	56	6	1	0	9	125²	110	5	69	53	13.0	3.58	107	.239	.342	7	.250	-0	7	3	-2	-0.1
1952	Cle-A	3	2	.600	42	1	0	0	5	82²	68	5	34	28	11.1	3.48	96	.221	.299	2	.250	-1	2	-1	1	0.1
1953	Cle-A	0	0	—	16	0	0	0	2	13	21	3	13	5	23.5	7.62	49	.389	.507	0	—	-0	-5	-6	-0	-0.2
Total	7	44	48	.478	234	93	45	2	29	897²	867	61	451	436	13.4	4.07	102	.254	.343	67	.227	1	19	8	-7	0.3

YEAR	TM/L	W	L	PCT	G	GS	CG	SH	SV	IP	H	HR	BB	SO	RAT	ERA	ERA+	OAV	OOB	BH	AVG	PB	PR	/A	PD	TPI

● JIM BRITT Britt, James Edward b: 2/25/1856, Brooklyn, N.Y. d: 2/28/23, San Francisco, Cal Deb: 5/2/1872

1872	Atl-n	9	28	.243	37	37	37	0	0	336	570	6	19	13	15.8	4.34	104	.328	.335	40	.256	-8	-26	6		-1.6
1873	Atl-n	17	36	.321	54	54	51	1	0	480²	696	6	40	15	13.8	3.89	78	.300	.312	47	.196	-3	-34	-46		-3.5
Total	2 n	26	64	.289	91	91	88	1	0	816²	1266	12	59	28	14.6	4.08	74	.312	.322	87	.220	-11	-75	-95		-5.1

● JACK BRITTIN Brittin, John Albert b: 3/4/24, Athens, Ill. d: 1/5/94, Springfield, Ill. BR/TR, 5'11", 175 lbs. Deb: 9/15/50

1950	Phi-N	0	0	—	3	0	0	0	0	4	2	0	3	3	11.3	4.50	90	.143	.294	0	—	0	-0	-0	0	0.0
1951	Phi-N	0	0	—	3	0	0	0	0	4	5	0	6	3	24.8	9.00	43	.294	.478	0	—	0	-2	-2	0	0.0
Total	2	0	0	—	6	0	0	0	0	8	7	0	9	6	18.0	6.75	58	.226	.400	0	—	0	-2	-2	0	0.0

● JIM BRITTON Britton, James Allan b: 3/25/44, N.Tonawanda, N.Y. BR/TR, 6'5", 225 lbs. Deb: 9/20/67

1967	Atl-N	0	2	.000	2	2	0	0	0	13¹	15	2	4	4	11.5	6.08	55	.278	.304	0	.000	-0	-4	-4	-0	-0.6
1968	Atl-N	4	6	.400	34	9	2	2	3	90	81	1	34	61	11.7	3.10	97	.245	.320	3	.143	-0	-1	-1	-0	-0.2
1969	*Atl-N	7	5	.583	24	13	2	1	1	88	69	10	49	60	12.1	3.78	95	.218	.323	4	.190	-0	-2	-2	-1	-0.3
1971	Mon-N	2	3	.400	16	6	0	0	0	45²	49	10	27	23	15.4	5.72	62	.274	.375	0	.000	-1	-11	-11	-1	-1.3
Total	4	13	16	.448	76	30	4	3	4	237	214	23	112	148	12.5	4.03	83	.243	.332	7	.127	-2	-18	-18	-2	-2.4

● TONY BRIZZOLARA Brizzolara, Anthony John b: 1/14/57, Santa Monica, Cal. BR/TR, 6'5", 215 lbs. Deb: 5/19/79

1979	Atl-N	6	9	.400	20	19	2	0	0	107¹	133	6	33	64	14.2	5.28	77	.303	.356	1	.029	-3	-18	-15	-0	-2.1
1983	Atl-N	1	0	1.000	14	0	0	0	1	20¹	22	2	6	17	12.4	3.54	109	.278	.329	0		-0	0	1	-0	0.0
1984	Atl-N	1	2	.333	10	4	0	0	0	29	33	4	11	14	14.3	5.28	73	.284	.357	0	.000	-1	-5	-5	-0	-0.5
Total	3	8	11	.421	44	23	2	0	1	156²	188	12	50	95	14.0	5.06	79	.297	.353	1	.024	-4	-24	-19	-0	-2.6

● JOHNNY BROACA Broaca, John Joseph b: 10/3/09, Lawrence, Mass. d: 5/16/85, Lawrence, Mass. BR/TR, 5'11", 190 lbs. Deb: 6/2/34

1934	NY-A	12	9	.571	26	24	13	1	0	177¹	203	9	65	74	13.7	4.16	98	.284	.344	2	.030	-7	7	-2	-2	-1.0
1935	NY-A	15	7	.682	29	27	14	2	0	201	199	16	79	78	12.4	3.58	113	.254	.323	12	.150	-4	19	10	-3	0.3
1936	NY-A	12	7	.632	37	27	12	1	3	206	235	16	66	84	13.2	4.24	110	.284	.337	9	.110	-6	18	10	-2	-0.1
1937	NY-A	1	4	.200	7	6	3	0	0	44	58	5	17	9	15.3	4.70	94	.324	.383	0	.000	-2	-0	-1	-1	-0.4
1939	Cle-A	4	2	.667	22	2	0	0	0	46	53	5	28	13	15.8	4.70	94	.288	.382	0	.000	-2	-0	-1	-0	-0.3
Total	5	44	29	.603	121	86	42	4	3	674¹	748	51	255	258	13.4	4.08	105	.278	.341	23	.091	-21	44	15	-8	-1.5

● PETE BROBERG Broberg, Peter Sven b: 3/2/50, W.Palm Beach, Fla. BR/TR, 6'3", 205 lbs. Deb: 6/20/71

1971	Was-A	5	9	.357	18	18	7	1	0	124²	104	10	53	89	12.1	3.47	95	.228	.322	5	.114	0	-0	-2	-1	-0.3
1972	Tex-A	5	12	.294	39	25	3	2	1	176¹	153	14	85	133	12.8	4.29	70	.237	.338	4	.078	-2	-24	-25	1	-2.5
1973	Tex-A	5	9	.357	22	20	6	1	0	118²	130	8	66	57	15.2	5.61	66	.283	.379	0	—	0	-24	-25	-0	-2.6
1974	Tex-A	0	4	.000	12	2	0	0	0	29	29	7	13	15	13.3	8.07	44	.264	.347	0	—	0	-14	-15	-0	-1.6
1975	Mil-A	14	16	.467	38	32	7	2	0	220¹	219	17	106	100	13.9	4.13	93	.263	.357	0	—	0	-9	-7	-0	-0.9
1976	Mil-A	1	7	.125	20	11	6	0	0	92¹	99	6	72	28	17.1	4.97	70	.281	.409	0	—	0	-15	-15	-1	-1.3
1977	Chi-N	1	2	.333	22	0	0	0	0	36	34	8	18	20	13.0	4.75	92	.250	.344	0	.000	-1	-3	-1	-0	-0.2
1978	Oak-A	10	12	.455	35	26	2	0	0	165²	174	16	65	94	13.1	4.62	79	.269	.338	0	—	0	-16	-18	-1	-2.0
Total	8	41	71	.366	206	134	26	6	1	963	942	85	478	536	13.8	4.56	78	.259	.353	9	.089	-3	-105	-109	-1	-11.4

● DOUG BROCAIL Brocail, Douglas Keith b: 5/16/67, Clearfield, Pa. BL/TR, 6'5", 220 lbs. Deb: 9/8/92

1992	SD-N	0	0	—	3	3	0	0	0	14	17	2	5	15	14.1	6.43	56	.298	.355	1	.200	-0	-5	-4	-0	-0.5
1993	SD-N	4	13	.235	24	24	0	0	0	128¹	143	16	42	70	13.3	4.56	91	.282	.342	6	.182	-0	-7	-6	-0	-0.7
1994	SD-N	0	0	—	12	0	0	0	0	17	21	1	5	11	14.8	5.82	71	.304	.368	0	.000	-0	-3	-3	-0	0.0
1995	Hou-N	6	4	.600	36	7	0	0	1	77¹	87	10	22	39	13.2	4.19	92	.280	.335	4	.250	1	-0	-3	-0	-0.2
1996	Hou-N	1	5	.167	23	4	0	0	0	53	58	7	23	34	14.1	4.58	86	.289	.367	0	.000	-1	-2	-4	-0	-0.6
Total	5	11	22	.333	98	38	0	0	1	289²	326	36	97	169	13.5	4.63	86	.285	.347	11	.164	-0	-17	-21	-1	-1.5

● LEW BROCKETT Brockett, Lewis Albert "King" b: 7/23/1880, Brownsville, Ill. d: 9/19/60, Norris City, Ill. BR/TR, 5'10.5", 168 lbs. Deb: 4/25/07

1907	NY-A	1	2	.333	8	4	1	0	0	46¹	58	1	26	13	16.7	6.22	45	.309	.398	4	.182	-0	-19	-18	-1	-1.2
1909	NY-A	10	8	.556	26	18	10	3	1	170	148	3	59	70	11.3	2.12	119	.245	.318	17	.283	3	7	8	4	1.7
1911	NY-A	2	4	.333	16	8	2	0	0	75¹	73	3	39	25	14.0	4.66	77	.256	.356	12	.308	2	-11	-9	1	-0.4
Total	3	13	14	.481	50	30	13	3	1	291²	279	7	124	108	12.8	3.43	83	.259	.343	33	.273	5	-23	-19	3	0.1

● DICK BRODOWSKI Brodowski, Richard Stanley b: 7/26/32, Bayonne, N.J. BR/TR, 6'2", 190 lbs. Deb: 6/15/52

1952	Bos-A	5	5	.500	20	12	4	0	0	114²	111	12	50	42	12.9	4.40	90	.252	.333	8	.205	1	-9	-6	-0	-0.4
1955	Bos-A	1	0	1.000	16	0	0	0	0	32	36	5	25	10	17.4	5.63	76	.295	.419	5	.500	3	-6	-5	1	-0.2
1956	Was-A	0	3	.000	7	3	1	0	0	17²	31	5	12	8	21.9	9.17	47	.397	.478	0	.000	-1	-10	-10	-0	-1.3
1957	Was-A	0	1	.000	8	0	0	0	0	11¹	12	2	10	4	18.3	11.12	35	.261	.404	0	.000	-0	-9	-9	-0	-0.7
1958	Cle-A	1	0	1.000	5	0	0	0	0	10	3	0	6	12	8.1	0.00	—	.100	.250	0	.000	-0	4	4	-0	0.4
1959	Cle-A	2	2	.500	18	0	0	0	5	30	19	3	21	9	12.9	1.80	205	.181	.333	2	.333	0	7	6	-1	1.0
Total	6	9	11	.450	72	15	5	0	5	215²	212	27	124	85	14.4	4.76	84	.258	.361	15	.242	1	-23	-19	-0	-0.8

● ERNIE BROGLIO Broglio, Ernest Gilbert b: 8/27/35, Berkeley, Cal. BR/TR, 6'2", 200 lbs. Deb: 4/11/59

1959	StL-N	7	12	.368	35	25	6	3	0	181¹	174	20	89	133	13.1	4.72	90	.250	.335	6	.098	-3	-15	-10	-1	-1.1
1960	StL-N	21	9	.700	52	24	9	3	0	226¹	172	18	100	188	10.9	2.74	149	.213	.301	14	.206	2	26	34	1	4.8
1961	StL-N	9	12	.429	29	26	7	2	0	174²	166	19	75	113	12.5	4.12	107	.248	.325	9	.145	-2	-2	5	-1	0.3
1962	StL-N	12	9	.571	34	30	11	4	0	222¹	193	22	93	132	11.7	3.00	143	.237	.316	10	.139	-2	23	31	1	2.6
1963	StL-N	18	8	.692	39	35	11	5	0	250	202	24	90	145	10.7	2.99	119	.216	.287	10	.112	-3	8	16	0	1.3
1964	StL-N	3	5	.375	11	11	3	1	0	69¹	65	7	26	36	11.9	3.50	109	.247	.317	2	.095	-0	0	2	-0	0.2
	Chi-N	4	7	.364	18	16	3	0	1	100¹	111	12	30	46	12.6	4.04	92	.281	.332	10	.286	3	-6	-4	-1	-0.2
	Yr	7	12	.368	29	27	6	1	1	169²	176	19	56	82	12.3	3.82	98	.267	.324	12	.214	2	-5	-1	-2	0.0
1965	Chi-N	1	6	.143	26	6	0	0	0	50²	63	7	46	22	19.4	6.93	53	.313	.441	-0		-1	-19	-18	-1	-2.4
1966	Chi-N	2	6	.250	15	11	2	0	0	62¹	70	14	38	34	15.6	6.35	58	.290	.387	7	.368	3	-19	-19	2	-1.7
Total	8	77	74	.510	259	184	52	18	2	1337¹	1216	143	587	849	12.2	3.74	107	.242	.322	68	.158	-2	-3	39	1	3.8

● KEN BRONDELL Brondell, Kenneth Leroy b: 10/17/21, Bradshaw, Neb. BR/TR, 6'1", 195 lbs. Deb: 5/3/44

| 1944 | NY-N | 0 | 1 | .000 | 7 | 2 | 1 | 0 | 0 | 19¹ | 27 | 3 | 8 | 1 | 16.3 | 8.38 | 44 | .329 | .389 | 0 | .000 | -1 | -10 | -10 | -1 | -0.6 |

● JEFF BRONKEY Bronkey, Jacob Jeffrey b: 9/18/65, Kabul, Afghanistan BR/TR, 6'3", 215 lbs. Deb: 5/2/93

1993	Tex-A	1	1	.500	21	0	0	0	0	36	39	4	11	18	12.8	4.00	104	.285	.342	0	.000	0	1	1	1	0.1
1994	Mil-A	1	1	.500	16	0	0	0	0	20²	20	3	12	13	13.9	4.35	116	.247	.344	0	—	0	1	2	0	0.1
1995	Mil-A	0	0	—	8	0	0	0	0	12¹	15	0	6	5	15.3	3.65	137	.313	.389	0	.000	0	1	2	0	0.0
Total	3	2	2	.500	45	0	0	0	0	69	74	7	29	36	13.6	4.04	113	.278	.351	0	.000	0	4	4	1	0.2

● JIM BRONSTAD Bronstad, James Warren b: 6/22/36, Ft.Worth, Tex. BR/TR, 6'3", 196 lbs. Deb: 6/7/59

1959	NY-A	0	3	.000	16	3	0	0	2	29¹	34	2	13	14	14.7	5.22	70	.288	.364	0	—	-0	-4	-5	-0	-0.6
1963	Was-A	1	3	.250	25	0	0	0	0	57¹	66	9	22	22	14.0	5.65	66	.297	.363	0	.000	-1	-13	-12	1	-0.9
1964	Was-A	0	1	.000	4	0	0	0	0	7	10	0	2	9	15.4	5.14	72	.345	.387	0	—	-0	-1	-1	-0	-0.2
Total	3	1	7	.125	45	3	0	0	2	93²	110	11	37	45	14.3	5.48	67	.298	.365	0	.000	-2	-18	-19	1	-1.7

● IKE BROOKENS Brookens, Edward Dwain b: 1/3/49, Chambersburg, Pa. BR/TR, 6'5", 170 lbs. Deb: 6/17/75

| 1975 | Det-A | 0 | 0 | — | 3 | 0 | 0 | 0 | 0 | 10¹ | 14 | 2 | 8 | 1 | 18.3 | 5.23 | 77 | .282 | .378 | 0 | — | -0 | -2 | -1 | -0 | -0.1 |

● HARRY BROOKS Brooks, Harry Frank b: 11/30/1865, Philadelphia, Pa. d: 12/5/45, Philadelphia, Pa. Deb: 7/24/1886 ♦

| 1886 | NY-a | 0 | 1 | .000 | 1 | 1 | 0 | 0 | 0 | 2 | 9 | 0 | 2 | 0 | 49.5 | 36.00 | 9 | .429 | .478 | 0 | .000 | -0 | -7 | -7 | -0 | -1.5 |

● JIM BROSNAN Brosnan, James Patrick b: 10/24/29, Cincinnati, O. BR/TR, 6'4", 210 lbs. Deb: 4/15/54

| 1954 | Chi-N | 1 | 0 | 1.000 | 18 | 0 | 0 | 0 | 0 | 33¹ | 44 | 9 | 18 | 17 | 17.0 | 9.45 | 44 | .331 | .414 | 1 | .125 | -0 | -20 | -19 | 1 | -0.4 |
| 1956 | Chi-N | 5 | 9 | .357 | 30 | 10 | 1 | 1 | 1 | 95 | 95 | 9 | 45 | 51 | 13.3 | 3.79 | 100 | .270 | .353 | 4 | .182 | -0 | -0 | -0 | -1 | -0.1 |

YEAR	TM/L	W	L	PCT	G	GS	CG	SH	SV	IP	H	HR	BB	SO	RAT	ERA	ERA+	OAV	OOB	BH	AVG	PB	PR	/A	PD	TPI
1957	Chi-N	5	5	.500	41	5	1	0	0	98^2	79	11	46	73	11.5	3.38	115	.219	.310	5	.250	2	6	5	1	0.8
1958	Chi-N	3	4	.429	8	8	2	0	0	51^2	41	3	29	24	12.2	3.14	125	.225	.332	2	.105	-1	5	4	1	0.6
	StL-N	8	4	.667	33	12	2	0	7	115	107	10	50	65	12.4	3.44	120	.250	.330	3	.097	-1	6	9	0	0.9
	Yr	11	8	.579	41	20	4	0	7	166^2	148	13	79	89	12.3	3.35	121	.241	.329	5	.100	-2	11	13	1	1.5
1959	StL-N	1	3	.250	20	1	0	0	2	33	34	5	15	18	13.6	4.91	86	.276	.360	2	.286	1	-4	-2	1	-0.1
	Cin-N	8	3	.727	26	9	1	1	2	83^1	79	7	26	56	11.9	3.35	121	.248	.314	1	.043	-2	6	7	1	0.7
	Yr	9	6	.600	46	10	1	1	4	116^1	113	12	41	74	12.3	3.79	108	.255	.324	3	.100	-1	2	4	1	0.6
1960	Cin-N	7	2	.778	57	2	0	0	12	99	79	4	22	62	9.2	2.36	162	.225	.271	3	.200	-2	15	16	0	2.0
1961	*Cin-N	10	4	.714	53	0	0	0	16	80	77	7	18	40	10.7	3.04	134	.249	.291	2	.154	-0	9	9	1	1.9
1962	Cin-N	4	4	.500	48	0	0	0	13	64^2	76	6	18	51	13.1	3.34	120	.258	.338	0	.000	-1	4	5	-1	0.7
1963	Cin-N	0	1	.000	6	0	0	0	0	4^2	8	2	3	4	21.2	7.71	43	.421	.500	0	—	0	-2	-2	-0	-0.4
	Chi-A	3	8	.273	45	0	0	0	14	73	71	7	22	46	11.5	2.84	124	.263	.318	4	.308	1	6	5	-0	1.1
Total	9	55	47	.539	385	47	7	2	67	831^1	790	80	312	507	12.0	3.54	111	.254	.324	27	.153	1	31	36	3	7.7

● **TERRY BROSS** Bross, Terrence Paul b: 3/30/66, ElPaso, Tex. BR/TR, 6'9", 234 lbs. Deb: 9/4/91

YEAR	TM/L	W	L	PCT	G	GS	CG	SH	SV	IP	H	HR	BB	SO	RAT	ERA	ERA+	OAV	OOB	BH	AVG	PB	PR	/A	PD	TPI
1991	NY-N	0	0	—	8	0	0	0	0	10	7	1	3	5	9.0	1.80	202	.200	.263	0	—	0	2	2	-0	0.0
1993	SF-N	0	0	—	2	0	0	0	0	2	3	1	1	1	10.0	9.00	43	.333	.400	0	—	0	-1	-1	-0	0.0
Total	2	0	0	—	10	0	0	0	0	12	10	2	4	6	10.5	3.00	123	.227	.292	0	—	0	1	1	-1	0.0

● **FRANK BROSSEAU** Brosseau, Franklin Lee b: 7/31/44, Drayton, N.D. BR/TR, 6'1", 180 lbs. Deb: 9/10/69

YEAR	TM/L	W	L	PCT	G	GS	CG	SH	SV	IP	H	HR	BB	SO	RAT	ERA	ERA+	OAV	OOB	BH	AVG	PB	PR	/A	PD	TPI
1969	Pit-N	0	0	—	2	0	0	0	0	1^2	1	0	2	2	21.6	10.80	32	.286	.444	0	—	0	-1	-1	-0	0.0
1971	Pit-N	0	0	—	1	0	0	0	0	2	2	0	0	0	4.5	0.00	—	.200	.200	0	—	0	1	1	0	0.0
Total	2	0	0	—	3	0	0	0	0	3^2	3	0	2	2	12.3	4.91	70	.250	.357	0	—	0	-1	-1	-0	0.0

● **DAN BROUTHERS** Brouthers, Dennis Joseph "Big Dan" b: 5/8/1858, Sylvan Lake, N.Y. d: 8/2/32, E.Orange, N.J. BL/TL, 6'2", 207 lbs. Deb: 6/23/1879 H♦

YEAR	TM/L	W	L	PCT	G	GS	CG	SH	SV	IP	H	HR	BB	SO	RAT	ERA	ERA+	OAV	OOB	BH	AVG	PB	PR	/A	PD	TPI
1879	Tro-N	0	2	.000	3	2	2	0	0	21	35	0	8	6	18.4	5.57	45	.343	.391	46	.274	1	-7	-7	-1	-0.5
1883	Buf-N	0	0	—	1	0	0	0	0	2	9	0	3	2	54.0	31.50	10	.643	.706	159	.374	1	-6	-6	-0	-0.0
Total	2	0	2	.000	4	2	2	0	0	23	44	0	11	8	21.5	7.83	33	.379	.433	2296	.342	1	-13	-13	-1	-0.5

● **SCOTT BROW** Brow, Scott John b: 3/17/69, Butte, Mont. BR/TR, 6'3", 200 lbs. Deb: 4/28/93

YEAR	TM/L	W	L	PCT	G	GS	CG	SH	SV	IP	H	HR	BB	SO	RAT	ERA	ERA+	OAV	OOB	BH	AVG	PB	PR	/A	PD	TPI
1993	Tor-A	1	1	.500	6	3	0	0	0	18	19	2	10	7	15.0	6.00	72	.275	.375	0	—	0	-3	-3	1	-0.2
1994	Tor-A	0	3	.000	18	0	0	0	2	29	34	4	19	15	16.8	5.90	82	.288	.391	0	—	0	-4	-3	0	-0.4
1996	Tor-A	1	0	1.000	18	1	0	0	0	38^2	45	5	25	23	16.3	5.59	90	.294	.393	0	—	0	-3	-2	-0	-0.1
Total	3	2	4	.333	42	4	0	0	2	85^2	98	11	54	45	16.2	5.78	83	.288	.389	0	—	0	-9	-9	1	-0.7

● **FRANK BROWER** Brower, Frank Willard "Turkeyfoot" b: 3/26/1893, Gainesville, Va. d: 11/20/60, Baltimore, Md. BL/TR, 6'2", 180 lbs. Deb: 8/14/20 ♦

YEAR	TM/L	W	L	PCT	G	GS	CG	SH	SV	IP	H	HR	BB	SO	RAT	ERA	ERA+	OAV	OOB	BH	AVG	PB	PR	/A	PD	TPI
1924	Cle-A	0	0	—	4	0	0	0	0	9^2	7	0	4	6	11.2	0.93	459	.212	.316	30	.280	-0	4	4	-0	0.0

● **ALTON BROWN** Brown, Alton Leo "Deacon" b: 4/16/25, Norfolk, Va. BR/TR, 6'2", 195 lbs. Deb: 4/21/51

YEAR	TM/L	W	L	PCT	G	GS	CG	SH	SV	IP	H	HR	BB	SO	RAT	ERA	ERA+	OAV	OOB	BH	AVG	PB	PR	/A	PD	TPI
1951	Was-A	0	0	—	7	0	0	0	0	11^2	14	1	12	7	20.8	9.26	44	.298	.450	0	.000	-0	-7	-7	-0	0.0

● **BOARDWALK BROWN** Brown, Carroll William b: 2/20/1887, Woodbury, N.J. d: 2/8/77, Burlington, N.J. BR/TR, 6'1.5", 178 lbs. Deb: 9/27/11

YEAR	TM/L	W	L	PCT	G	GS	CG	SH	SV	IP	H	HR	BB	SO	RAT	ERA	ERA+	OAV	OOB	BH	AVG	PB	PR	/A	PD	TPI
1911	Phi-A	0	1	.000	2	1	1	0	0	12	12	0	2	6	10.5	4.50	70	.267	.298	0	.000	-1	-2	-2	-0	-0.2
1912	Phi-A	13	11	.542	34	24	15	3	0	199	204	2	87	64	13.6	3.66	84	.283	.367	11	.145	-3	-8	-13	3	-1.4
1913	Phi-A	17	11	.607	43	35	11	3	1	235^1	200	6	87	70	11.4	2.94	94	.219	.294	13	.159	-1	-0	-5	-2	-0.9
1914	Phi-A	1	6	.143	15	8	2	0	0	66	64	1	26	20	12.3	4.09	64	.268	.340	0	.000	-2	-10	-11	0	-1.3
	NY-A	5	5	.500	20	14	8	0	0	122^1	123	2	42	57	12.2	3.24	85	.271	.334	8	.182	1	-7	-6	3	-0.1
	Yr	6	11	.353	35	22	10	0	1	188^1	187	3	68	77	12.2	3.54	77	.270	.336	8	.125	-0	-17	-17	3	-1.4
1915	NY-A	2	6	.250	19	11	5	0	1	96^2	95	4	47	34	13.7	4.10	72	.275	.370	6	.188	-1	-12	-12	-0	-1.1
Total	5	38	40	.487	133	93	42	6	3	731^1	698	15	291	251	12.5	3.47	83	.257	.334	38	.147	-6	-39	-49	4	-5.0

● **CHARLIE BROWN** Brown, Charles E. b: 1878, Baltimore, Md. TL, 6', 180 lbs. Deb: 8/4/1897

YEAR	TM/L	W	L	PCT	G	GS	CG	SH	SV	IP	H	HR	BB	SO	RAT	ERA	ERA+	OAV	OOB	BH	AVG	PB	PR	/A	PD	TPI
1897	Cle-N	1	2	.333	4	4	2	0	0	24^1	30	2	17	8	19.2	7.77	58	.300	.426	3	.273	0	-9	-9	-0	-0.8

● **BUSTER BROWN** Brown, Charles Edward "Yank" b: 8/31/1881, Boone, Iowa d: 2/9/14, Sioux City, Iowa BR/TR, 6', 180 lbs. Deb: 6/22/05

YEAR	TM/L	W	L	PCT	G	GS	CG	SH	SV	IP	H	HR	BB	SO	RAT	ERA	ERA+	OAV	OOB	BH	AVG	PB	PR	/A	PD	TPI
1905	StL-N	8	11	.421	23	21	17	3	0	178^2	172	5	62	57	12.3	2.97	100	.260	.332	6	.092	-3	1	0	3	0.0
1906	StL-N	8	16	.333	32	27	21	0	0	238^1	208	2	112	109	12.5	2.64	99	.234	.327	14	.165	-0	-0	-2	2	0.2
1907	StL-N	1	6	.143	9	8	6	0	0	63^2	57	2	45	17	15.1	3.39	74	.263	.401	7	.269	-2	-7	-6	1	-0.3
	Phi-N	9	6	.600	21	16	13	4	0	130	118	3	56	38	12.5	2.42	100	.246	.333	10	.189	2	1	-0	-1	0.1
	Yr	10	12	.455	30	24	19	4	0	193^2	175	5	101	55	13.1	2.74	89	.250	.349	17	.215	-0	-6	-6	1	-0.2
1908	Phi-N	0	0	—	3	0	0	0	0	7	9	0	5	4	19.3	2.57	94	.346	.469	1	.200	-0	-0	-1	1	0.1
1909	Phi-N	0	0	—	7	1	0	0	0	25	22	1	16	10	14.0	3.24	80	.259	.382	0	.000	-1	-2	-2	-0	-0.1
	Bos-N	4	8	.333	18	17	8	2	0	123^1	108	1	56	32	12.5	3.14	90	.244	.339	7	.146	-2	-7	-4	1	-0.5
	Yr	4	8	.333	25	18	8	2	0	148^1	130	2	72	42	12.7	3.16	88	.246	.344	7	.123	-2	-9	-6	1	-0.6
1910	Bos-N	9	23	.281	46	29	16	1	2	263	251	6	94	88	11.9	2.67	125	.268	.337	16	.198	0	11	19	1	2.5
1911	Bos-N	8	18	.308	42	25	13	0	2	241	258	11	116	76	14.3	4.29	89	.284	.371	21	.250	3	-24	-13	0	-0.9
1912	Bos-N	4	15	.211	31	21	9	0	0	168^1	146	7	66	68	11.4	4.01	89	.239	.315	13	.213	1	-11	-8	0	-0.7
1913	Bos-N	0	0	—	4	0	0	0	0	13^1	9	0	3	3	16.2	4.73	70	.396	.453	0	.000	-0	-2	-2	0	0.0
Total	9	51	103	.331	234	165	106	10	4	1451^2	1368	36	631	501	12.8	3.21	96	.258	.343	95	.182	-6	-42	-18	8	0.4

● **CURLY BROWN** Brown, Charles Roy "Lefty" b: 12/9/1888, Spring Hill, Kan. d: 6/10/68, Spring Hill, Kan. BL/TL, 5'10.5", 165 lbs. Deb: 9/8/11

YEAR	TM/L	W	L	PCT	G	GS	CG	SH	SV	IP	H	HR	BB	SO	RAT	ERA	ERA+	OAV	OOB	BH	AVG	PB	PR	/A	PD	TPI
1911	StL-A	1	2	.333	3	2	2	0	0	23	22	0	8	11	11.0	2.74	123	.247	.295	0	.000	-0	1	1	-0	0.1
1912	StL-A	1	3	.250	16	4	2	1	0	64^2	69	0	35	28	14.9	4.87	68	.277	.373	5	.208	-0	-11	-11	-3	-0.9
1913	StL-A	1	1	.500	2	2	0	0	0	14	12	0	4	3	10.3	2.57	114	.245	.302	2	.400	1	1	1	-0	0.1
1915	Cin-N	0	2	.000	7	3	0	0	0	27	26	2	6	13	11.3	4.67	61	.245	.298	4	.364	1	-6	-5	-1	-0.4
Total	4	3	8	.273	28	11	6	1	0	128^2	129	2	50	52	12.9	4.20	76	.262	.337	11	.224	-0	-15	-14	-4	-1.2

● **CLINT BROWN** Brown, Clinton Harold b: 7/8/03, Blackash, Pa. d: 12/31/55, Rocky River, Ohio BL/TR, 6'1", 190 lbs. Deb: 9/27/28

YEAR	TM/L	W	L	PCT	G	GS	CG	SH	SV	IP	H	HR	BB	SO	RAT	ERA	ERA+	OAV	OOB	BH	AVG	PB	PR	/A	PD	TPI
1928	Cle-A	0	2	.000	2	1	1	0	0	11	14	0	2	2	13.1	4.91	84	.304	.333	1	.200	-0	-1	-1	0	-0.1
1929	Cle-A	0	2	.000	3	1	0	0	0	16^1	18	0	6	1	13.2	3.31	134	.286	.348	0	.000	-1	2	2	1	0.2
1930	Cle-A	11	13	.458	35	31	16	3	1	213^2	271	14	51	54	13.7	4.97	97	.314	.356	18	.247	-2	-8	-3	2	0.0
1931	Cle-A	11	15	.423	39	33	12	2	0	233^1	284	10	55	50	13.1	4.71	98	.295	.333	15	.172	-2	-8	-2	4	0.0
1932	Cle-A	15	12	.556	37	32	21	1	1	262^2	298	14	50	59	12.1	4.08	116	.279	.314	25	.250	6	12	19	2	2.4
1933	Cle-A	11	12	.478	33	23	10	2	1	185	202	10	34	47	11.6	3.41	130	.276	.310	13	.145	3	18	21	3	2.4
1934	Cle-A	4	3	.571	17	2	0	0	0	50^1	83	3	14	15	17.3	5.90	77	.359	.396	5	.294	-0	-8	-8	-0	-0.8
1935	Cle-A	4	3	.571	23	5	1	0	2	49	61	3	14	20	14.0	5.14	88	.300	.349	2	.200	-0	-4	-4	1	-0.4
1936	Chi-A	6	2	.750	38	2	0	0	0	83	106	5	24	19	14.4	4.99	104	.315	.366	4	.160	-0	2	0	0	0.2
1937	Chi-A	7	7	.500	**53**	0	0	0	18	100	92	7	36	51	11.6	3.42	135	.242	.309	4	.222	1	**13**	**13**	0	2.3
1938	Chi-A	1	3	.250	29	0	0	0	3	13^2	16	0	6	6	16.5	4.61	106	.333	.439	1	.500	1	0	0	0	0.3
1939	Chi-A	11	10	.524	**61**	0	0	0	18	118^1	127	8	27	41	11.7	3.88	122	.281	.322	4	.211	0	10	11	2	2.3
1940	Chi-A	4	6	.400	37	0	0	0	10	66	75	5	16	23	12.7	3.68	120	.284	.330	1	.071	-0	5	5	0	0.8
1941	Chi-A	3	3	.500	41	0	0	0	5	74^1	71	3	28	22	12.8	3.27	120	.279	.348	2	.118	0	7	6	3	0.8
1942	Cle-A	1	1	.500	7	0	0	0	0	9	16	2	2	4	19.0	6.00	57	.356	.396	0	.000	-0	-2	-3	0	-0.6
Total	15	89	93	.489	434	130	62	8	64	1485^2	1740	84	368	410	12.9	4.26	109	.291	.335	91	.199	5	37	60	19	9.8

● **CURT BROWN** Brown, Curtis Steven b: 1/15/60, Ft.Lauderdale, Fla. BR/TR, 6'5", 200 lbs. Deb: 6/10/83

YEAR	TM/L	W	L	PCT	G	GS	CG	SH	SV	IP	H	HR	BB	SO	RAT	ERA	ERA+	OAV	OOB	BH	AVG	PB	PR	/A	PD	TPI
1983	Cal-A	1	1	.500	10	0	0	0	0	16	25	1	4	7	16.3	7.31	55	.368	.403	0	—	0	-6	-6	-0	-0.6
1984	NY-A	1	1	.500	13	0	0	0	0	16^2	14	1	4	10	11.9	2.70	140	.281	.324	0	—	0	2	2	-0	0.2
1986	Mon-N	0	1	.000	6	0	0	0	0	12	15	0	4	2	12.8	3.00	123	.319	.347	0	—	0	1	1	0	0.1
1987	Mon-N	0	1	.000	5	0	0	0	0	7	10	2	4	6	18.0	7.71	54	.333	.412	0	—	0	-3	-3	-0	-0.3
Total	4	2	4	.333	34	0	0	0	0	51^2	68	4	14	27	14.3	4.88	80	.325	.368	0	—	-0	-5	-6	-0	-0.5

YEAR	TM/L	W	L	PCT	G	GS	CG	SH	SV	IP	H	HR	BB	SO	RAT	ERA	ERA+	OAV	OOB	BH	AVG	PB	PR	/A	PD	TPI

● ED BROWN Brown, Edward P. b: Chicago, Ill. TR, 178 lbs. Deb: 8/19/1882 ♦

1882	StL-a	0	0	—	1	0	0	0	0	2	2	0	0	1	9.0	0.00	—	.250	.250	11	.183	-0	1	1	-0	0.0
1884	Tol-a	0	1	.000	1	1	1	0	0	9	19	0	4	1	24.0	9.00	38	.396	.453	27	.176	-0	-6	-6	-0	-0.4
Total	2	0	1	.000	2	1	1	0	0	11	21	0	4	2	21.3	7.36	45	.375	.426	38	.178	-0	-5	-5	-0	-0.4

● ELMER BROWN Brown, Elmer Young "Shook" b: 3/25/1883, Southport, Ind. d: 1/23/55, Indianapolis, Ind. BL/TR, 5'11.5", 172 lbs. Deb: 9/16/11

1911	StL-A	1	1	.500	5	3	1	1	0	16²	16	0	14	5	16.2	6.48	52	.242	.375	1	.125	-1	-6	-6	1	-0.6
1912	StL-A	5	8	.385	23	13	2	1	0	120¹	122	2	42	45	13.2	2.99	111	.280	.359	6	.167	-1	4	4	-1	0.3
1913	Bro-N	0	0	—	3	1	0	0	0	13	6	0	10	6	11.8	2.08	159	.158	.347	0	.000	-1	2	2	-0	-0.1
1914	Bro-N	1	2	.333	11	4	1	0	0	36²	33	2	23	22	15.5	3.93	73	.402	.563	1	.083	-1	-5	-4	1	-0.4
1915	Bro-N	0	0	—	1	0	0	0	0	2	4	0	3	1	31.5	9.00	31	.500	.636	0	—	0	-1	-1	0	-0.0
Total	5	7	11	.389	43	21	4	2	0	188²	181	4	92	79	14.0	3.48	93	.287	.395	8	.133	-3	-6	-5	-0	-0.8

● HAL BROWN Brown, Hector Harold "Skinny" b: 12/11/24, Greensboro, N.C. BR/TR, 6'2", 182 lbs. Deb: 4/19/51 C

1951	Chi-A	0	0	—	3	0	0	0	0	8²	15	3	4	4	19.7	9.35	40	.385	.442	2	1.000	1	-5	-5	0	0.0
1952	Chi-A	2	3	.400	24	8	1	0	0	72¹	82	8	21	31	12.8	4.23	86	.284	.332	3	.158	1	-4	-5	-0	-0.2
1953	Bos-A	11	6	.647	30	25	6	1	0	166¹	177	16	57	62	12.7	4.65	90	.269	.327	17	.293	5	-12	-8	-0	-0.4
1954	Bos-A	1	8	.111	40	5	1	0	0	118	126	6	41	66	13.0	4.12	100	.269	.331	3	.125	-0	-5	-0	1	0.0
1955	Bos-A	1	0	1.000	2	0	0	0	0	4	2	0	2	2	9.0	2.25	191	.143	.250	1	1.000	1	1	0	0	0.2
	Bal-A	0	4	.000	15	5	1	0	0	57	51	5	26	26	12.2	4.11	93	.241	.324	0	—	-1	-2	-1	-0	-0.3
	Yr	1	4	.200	17	5	1	0	0	61	53	5	28	28	12.0	3.98	97	.235	.319	1	.059	-1	-0	-1	-1	-0.1
1956	Bal-A	9	7	.563	35	14	4	1	2	151²	142	18	37	57	10.7	4.04	97	.247	.294	8	.190	1	2	-0	0	0.0
1957	Bal-A	7	8	.467	25	20	7	2	1	150	132	17	37	62	10.3	3.90	92	.236	.285	10	.208	2	-2	-5	-1	-0.4
1958	Bal-A	7	5	.583	19	17	4	2	1	96²	96	9	20	44	10.8	3.07	117	.259	.297	4	.148	-0	7	6	-0	0.4
1959	Bal-A	11	9	.550	31	21	2	0	3	164	158	16	32	81	10.5	3.79	100	.252	.290	2	.048	-3	-0	-3	-1	-0.3
1960	Bal-A	12	5	.706	30	20	6	1	0	159	155	14	22	66	**10.1**	3.06	125	.258	**.286**	8	.182	3	14	13	-1	1.5
1961	Bal-A	10	6	.625	27	23	6	3	1	166²	153	14	33	61	10.1	3.19	121	.247	.286	7	.140	-0	16	12	-0	1.0
1962	Bal-A	6	4	.600	22	11	0	0	1	85²	88	12	21	25	11.8	4.10	90	.268	.318	8	.286	2	-1	-4	-1	-0.4
	NY-A	0	1	.000	2	1	0	0	0	6²	9	3	2	2	14.9	6.75	56	.333	.379	0	.000	-0	-2	-2	-0	-0.3
	Yr	6	5	.545	24	12	0	0	1	92¹	97	15	23	27	11.7	4.29	86	.270	.314	8	.276	1	-3	-6	-1	-0.7
1963	Hou-N	5	11	.313	26	20	6	3	0	141¹	137	14	8	68	9.2	3.31	95	.255	.266	4	.093	-2	-0	-3	-0	-0.7
1964	Hou-N	3	15	.167	27	21	3	0	1	132	154	18	26	53	12.4	3.95	86	.292	.327	5	.128	-1	-6	-8	-2	-1.2
Total	14	85	92	.480	358	211	47	13	11	1680	1677	173	389	710	11.1	3.81	98	.260	.303	82	.169	8	2	-11	-10	-0.9

● JACKIE BROWN Brown, Jackie Gene b: 5/31/43, Holdenville, Okla. BR/TR, 6'1", 195 lbs. Deb: 7/2/70 FC

1970	Was-A	2	2	.500	24	5	1	0	0	57	49	8	37	47	13.6	3.95	90	.231	.345	2	.154	-0	-1	-2	-1	-0.3
1971	Was-A	3	4	.429	14	9	0	0	0	47	60	9	27	21	16.9	5.94	56	.316	.404	2	.133	-0	-13	-14	1	-1.8
1973	Tex-A	5	5	.500	25	3	2	1	2	66²	82	7	25	45	14.7	3.92	95	.309	.373	0	—	-1	-1	-1	-0	-0.3
1974	Tex-A	13	12	.520	35	26	9	2	0	216²	219	13	74	134	12.3	3.57	100	.265	.329	0	—	0	1	0	-1	-0.1
1975	Tex-A	5	5	.500	17	7	2	1	0	70¹	70	7	35	35	13.7	4.22	89	.266	.357	0	—	-3	-4	-2	-0	-0.6
	Cle-A	1	2	.333	25	3	1	0	1	69¹	72	9	29	41	13.1	4.28	88	.276	.348	0	—	-4	-4	-0	-0	-0.3
	Yr	6	7	.462	42	10	3	1	1	139²	142	16	64	76	13.3	4.25	89	.269	.349	0	—	-7	-8	-2	-0	-0.8
1976	Cle-A	9	11	.450	32	27	5	2	0	180	193	14	55	104	12.8	4.25	82	.276	.335	0	—	-5	-15	-1	-1	-1.6
1977	Mon-N	9	12	.429	42	25	6	2	0	185²	189	15	71	89	12.8	4.51	84	.264	.334	7	.125	-2	-12	-14	-2	-1.9
Total	7	47	53	.470	214	105	26	8	3	892²	934	82	353	516	13.2	4.18	87	.272	.343	11	.131	-3	-48	-55	-7	-6.8

● KEVIN BROWN Brown, James Kevin b: 3/14/65, Milledgeville, Ga. BR/TR, 6'4", 195 lbs. Deb: 9/30/86

1986	Tex-A	1	0	1.000	1	1	0	0	0	5	6	0	0	4	10.8	3.60	119	.316	.316	0	—	0	0	0	0	0.1
1988	Tex-A	1	1	.500	4	4	1	0	0	23¹	33	2	8	12	16.2	4.24	96	.330	.385	0	—	0	-1	-0	-0	-0.1
1989	Tex-A	12	9	.571	28	28	7	0	0	191	167	10	70	104	11.4	3.35	118	.234	.305	0	—	0	11	13	3	1.7
1990	Tex-A	12	10	.545	26	26	6	2	0	180	175	13	60	88	11.9	3.60	109	.255	.318	0	.000	0	6	6	-0	0.7
1991	Tex-A	9	12	.429	33	33	0	0	0	210²	233	17	90	96	14.4	4.40	92	.284	.364	0	—	0	-7	-9	1	-0.7
1992	Tex-A★	**21**	11	.656	35	35	11	1	0	**265²**	262	11	76	173	11.8	3.32	114	.260	.318	0	—	0	18	14	2	1.9
1993	Tex-A	15	12	.556	34	34	12	3	0	233	228	14	74	142	12.2	3.59	115	.252	.319	0	—	0	19	14	4	2.0
1994	Tex-A	7	9	.438	26	25	3	0	0	170	218	18	50	123	14.5	4.82	100	.314	.365	0	—	0	-9	-11	0	0.3
1995	Bal-A	10	9	.526	26	26	3	1	0	172¹	155	10	48	117	11.1	3.60	132	.241	.303	0	—	0	21	22	7	2.7
1996	Fla-N★	17	11	.607	32	32	5	**3**	0	233	187	8	33	159	9.1	**1.89**	**214**	.220	.263	9	.120	-1	**60**	**56**	6	**7.2**
Total	10	105	84	.556	245	244	48	10	0	1684	1664	103	509	1018	12.1	3.52	118	.259	.320	9	.118	-1	128	117	25	15.8

● JIM BROWN Brown, James W. H. b: 12/12/1860, Clinton Co., Pa. d: 4/6/08, Williamsport, Pa. Deb: 4/17/1884 ♦

1884	Alt-U	1	9	.100	11	11	7	0	0	74	99	4	36	39	16.4	5.35	50	.301	.370	22	.250	-2	-24	-22	0	-2.2
	NY-N	0	1	.000	1	1	1	0	0	9	10	0	8	2	18.0	5.00	60	.263	.391	0	.000	-1	-2	-2	-0	-0.2
	StP-U	1	4	.200	6	6	4	1	0	36	43	1	14	20	14.3	3.75	35	.277	.337	5	.313	-4	-5	-10	-0	-0.8
1886	Phi-a	0	1	.000	1	1	1	0	0	8¹	9	0	3	4	13.0	3.24	108	.265	.324	0	.000	-0	-0	-0	-0	-0.0
Total	2	2	15	.118	19	19	13	1	0	127¹	161	5	61	65	15.7	4.74	50	.290	.360	27	.245	-1	-31	-34	0	-3.2

● JOHN BROWN Brown, John J. "Ad" b: Trenton, N.J. Deb: 8/11/1897

| 1897 | Bro-N | 0 | 1 | .000 | 1 | 1 | 0 | 0 | 0 | 5 | 7 | 0 | 4 | 0 | 25.2 | 7.20 | 57 | .333 | .500 | 1 | .500 | 0 | -2 | -2 | 0 | -0.2 |

● JOPHERY BROWN Brown, Jophery Clifford b: 1/22/45, Grambling, La. BL/TR, 6'2", 190 lbs. Deb: 9/21/68

| 1968 | Chi-N | 0 | 0 | — | 1 | 0 | 0 | 0 | 0 | 2 | 2 | 0 | 1 | 0 | 13.5 | 4.50 | 70 | .286 | .375 | 0 | — | -0 | -0 | -0 | 0 | 0.0 |

● JOE BROWN Brown, Joseph E. b: 4/4/1859, Warren, Pa. d: 6/28/1888, Warren, Pa. 5'10", 162 lbs. Deb: 8/16/1884 ♦

1884	Chi-N	4	2	.667	7	6	5	0	0	50	56	4	7	27	11.3	4.68	67	.258	.281	13	.213	-1	-9	-9	-0	-0.9
1885	Bal-a	0	4	.000	4	4	4	0	0	38	52	0	4	9	13.3	5.68	57	.306	.322	3	.158	-1	-10	-10	-0	-0.9
Total	2	4	6	.400	11	10	9	0	0	88	108	4	11	36	12.2	5.11	62	.279	.299	16	.200	-2	-20	-19	-1	-1.8

● JOE BROWN Brown, Joseph Henry b: 7/3/1900, Little Rock, Ark. d: 3/7/50, Los Angeles, Cal. BR/TR, 6', 176 lbs. Deb: 5/17/27

| 1927 | Chi-a | 0 | 0 | — | 1 | 1 | 0 | 0 | 0 | 2 | 0 | 1 | 0 | — | ∞ | — | 1.000 | 1.000 | 0 | — | 0 | -3 | -3 | 0 | -0.2 |

● KEITH BROWN Brown, Keith Edward b: 2/14/64, Flagstaff, Ariz. BB/TR, 6'4", 215 lbs. Deb: 8/25/88

1988	Cin-N	2	1	.667	4	3	0	0	0	16¹	14	1	4	6	9.9	2.76	130	.237	.286	0	.000	-0	1	1	0	0.2
1990	Cin-N	0	0	—	11	1	0	0	0	11¹	12	2	3	8	11.9	4.76	83	.286	.333	0	—	0	-1	-1	0	-0.1
1991	Cin-N	0	0	—	11	0	0	0	0	12	15	0	6	4	15.8	2.25	169	.306	.382	0	—	0	2	0	0	0.1
1992	Cin-N	0	1	.000	2	2	0	0	0	8	10	2	5	5	16.9	4.50	80	.313	.405	0	—	0	-1	-1	-0	-0.1
Total	4	2	2	.500	25	6	0	0	0	47²	51	5	18	23	13.0	3.40	110	.280	.345	0	.000	-0	1	0	0	0.1

● KEVIN BROWN Brown, Kevin Dewayne b: 3/5/66, Oroville, Cal. BL/TL, 6'1", 185 lbs. Deb: 7/27/90

1990	NY-N	0	0	—	2	0	0	0	0	2	1	0	1	0	13.5	0.00	—	.250	.333	0	—	0	1	1	0	0.0
	Mil-A	1	1	.500	5	3	0	0	0	21	14	1	7	12	9.4	2.57	151	.182	.259	0	—	0	3	3	1	0.3
1991	Mil-A	2	4	.333	15	10	0	0	0	63²	66	6	34	30	14.3	5.51	72	.270	.362	0	—	0	-10	-11	0	-0.8
1992	Sea-A	0	0	—	2	0	0	0	0	3	4	1	3	2	21.0	9.00	44	.333	.467	0	—	0	-2	-2	0	0.0
Total	3	3	5	.375	24	13	0	0	0	89²	86	8	45	44	13.3	4.82	82	.252	.343	0	—	0	-8	-9	1	-0.5

● LEW BROWN Brown, Lewis J. "Blower" b: 2/1/1858, Leominster, Mass. d: 1/16/1889, Boston, Mass. BR/TR, 5'10.5", 185 lbs. Deb: 6/17/1876 ♦

1878	Pro-N	0	0	—	1	0	0	0	0	1	4	0	1	0	36.0	18.00	12	.500	.500	74	.305	-2	-2	-0	0	-0.0
1884	Bos-U	0	0	—	1	0	0	0	0	1	6	0	4	0	63.0	36.00	6	.667	.700	75	.231	-0	-4	-4	-0	-0.6
Total	2	0	0	—	2	0	0	0	0	2	10	0	5	0	49.5	27.00	8	.462	.611	379	.248	-0	-5	-5	-0	-0.6

● LLOYD BROWN Brown, Lloyd Andrew "Gimpy" b: 12/25/04, Beeville, Tex. d: 1/14/74, Opa-Locka, Fla. BL/TL, 5'9", 170 lbs. Deb: 7/17/25

| 1925 | Bro-N | 0 | 3 | .000 | 17 | 5 | 1 | 0 | 0 | 63¹ | 79 | 1 | 25 | 23 | 15.1 | 4.12 | 101 | .319 | .385 | 2 | .087 | -2 | 1 | 0 | 0 | -0.2 |
| 1928 | Was-A | 4 | 4 | .500 | 27 | 10 | 2 | 0 | 1 | 107 | 112 | 7 | 40 | 38 | 13.0 | 4.04 | 99 | .273 | .341 | 5 | .161 | 0 | -0 | -3 | 3 | 0.3 |

YEAR	TM/L	W	L	PCT	G	GS	CG	SH	SV	IP	H	HR	BB	SO	RAT	ERA	ERA+	OAV	OOB	BH	AVG	PB	PR	/A	PD	TPI
1929	Was-A	8	7	.533	40	15	7	1	0	168	186	7	69	48	13.7	4.18	101	.297	.368	11	.220	3	1	1	2	0.5
1930	Was-A	16	12	.571	38	22	10	1	0	197	220	6	59	59	13.2	4.25	108	.293	.354	14	.215	2	9	8	3	1.4
1931	Was-A	15	14	.517	42	32	15	1	0	258²	256	13	79	79	11.7	3.20	134	.257	.311	22	.229	4	34	31	1	3.4
1932	Was-A	15	12	.556	46	24	10	2	5	202²	239	11	55	53	13.1	4.44	97	.296	.342	7	.100	-5	1	-3	1	-0.7
1933	StL-A	1	6	.143	8	6	0	0	0	39	57	1	17	7	17.1	7.15	65	.350	.411	3	.273	1	-12	-11	1	-1.4
	Bos-A	8	11	.421	33	21	9	2	1	163¹	180	4	64	37	13.4	4.02	109	.281	.347	16	.281	6	5	6	4	1.7
	Yr	9	17	.346	41	27	9	2	1	202¹	237	5	81	44	14.1	4.63	96	.295	.360	19	.279	7	-8	-4	5	0.3
1934	Cle-A	5	10	.333	38	15	5	0	6	117	116	7	51	39	13.0	3.85	118	.263	.342	7	.233	1	8	9	0	1.2
1935	Cle-A	8	7	.533	42	8	4	2	4	122	123	6	37	45	12.0	3.61	125	.265	.323	4	.108	-2	11	12	1	1.2
1936	Cle-A	8	10	.444	24	16	12	1	1	140¹	166	13	45	34	13.7	4.17	121	.294	.349	10	.222	2	14	14	1	1.7
1937	Cle-A	2	6	.250	31	5	2	0	0	77	107	4	27	32	16.0	6.55	70	.329	.386	4	.167	-1	-16	-17	1	-1.4
1940	Phi-N	1	3	.250	18	2	0	0	3	37²	58	3	16	16	17.7	6.21	63	.354	.411	1	.077	-1	-10	-10	0	-1.2
Total	12	91	105	.464	404	181	77	10	21	1693	1899	83	590	510	13.3	4.20	105	.288	.348	106	.192	6	45	42	19	6.5

● MACE BROWN
Brown, Mace Stanley b: 5/21/09, North English, Ia. BR/TR, 6'1", 190 lbs. Deb: 5/21/35 C

YEAR	TM/L	W	L	PCT	G	GS	CG	SH	SV	IP	H	HR	BB	SO	RAT	ERA	ERA+	OAV	OOB	BH	AVG	PB	PR	/A	PD	TPI
1935	Pit-N	4	1	.800	18	5	2	0	0	72²	84	5	22	28	13.1	3.59	114	.287	.337	4	.167	-0	3	4	2	0.3
1936	Pit-N	10	11	.476	47	10	3	0	3	165	178	8	55	56	12.8	3.87	105	.275	.332	10	.167	-2	3	3	1	0.3
1937	Pit-N	7	2	.778	50	2	0	0	7	107²	109	2	45	60	13.0	4.18	92	.261	.334	9	.300	2	-3	-4	-1	-0.2
1938	Pit-N★	15	9	.625	**51**	2	0	0	5	132²	155	5	44	55	13.5	3.80	100	.294	.349	5	.132	-2	-0	-0	-0	-0.2
1939	Pit-N	9	13	.409	47	19	8	1	7	200¹	232	8	52	71	12.8	3.37	114	.293	.338	7	.109	-4	12	10	1	0.8
1940	Pit-N	10	9	.526	48	17	5	1	**7**	173	181	5	49	73	12.1	3.49	109	.267	.318	6	.115	-1	7	6	1	0.7
1941	Pit-N	0	0	—	1	0	0	0	0	1¹	1	0	0	0	13.5	0.00	—	.333	.333	0	—	0	1	1	0	0.1
	Bro-N	3	2	.600	24	0	0	0	3	42²	31	3	26	22	12.2	3.16	116	.208	.330	0	.000	-1	2	2	1	0.3
	Yr	3	2	.600	25	0	0	0	3	44	33	3	26	22	12.3	3.07	119	.213	.330	0	.000	-1	3	3	1	0.3
1942	Bos-A	9	3	.750	34	0	0	0	6	60¹	56	4	28	20	12.5	3.43	109	.255	.339	1	.067	-1	4	5	0	0.4
1943	Bos-A	6	6	.500	**49**	0	0	0	9	93¹	71	2	51	40	11.8	2.12	156	.222	.329	1	.059	-1	**12**	**12**	0	1.7
1946	*Bos-A	3	1	.750	18	0	0	0	1	26¹	26	2	16	10	14.4	2.05	179	.268	.372	0	.000	-1	4	5	1	0.7
Total	10	76	57	.571	387	55	18	2	48	1075¹	1125	44	388	435	12.7	3.46	110	.271	.335	43	.137	-11	43	43	6	4.9

● MARK BROWN
Brown, Mark Anthony b: 7/13/59, Bellows Falls, Vt. BB/TR, 6'2", 190 lbs. Deb: 8/9/84

YEAR	TM/L	W	L	PCT	G	GS	CG	SH	SV	IP	H	HR	BB	SO	RAT	ERA	ERA+	OAV	OOB	BH	AVG	PB	PR	/A	PD	TPI
1984	Bal-A	1	2	.333	9	0	0	0	0	23	22	7	7	10	11.7	3.91	99	.256	.319	0	—	0	0	-0	-0	0.0
1985	Min-A	0	0	—	6	0	0	0	0	15²	21	1	7	5	16.1	6.89	64	.333	.400	0	—	0	-5	-4	0	-0.1
Total	2	1	2	.333	15	0	0	0	0	38²	43	8	14	15	13.5	5.12	80	.289	.354	0	—	0	-5	-4	-1	-0.1

● MIKE BROWN
Brown, Michael Gary b: 3/4/59, Camden County, N.J. BR/TR, 6'2", 195 lbs. Deb: 9/16/82

YEAR	TM/L	W	L	PCT	G	GS	CG	SH	SV	IP	H	HR	BB	SO	RAT	ERA	ERA+	OAV	OOB	BH	AVG	PB	PR	/A	PD	TPI
1982	Bos-A	1	0	1.000	3	0	0	0	0	6	7	0	1	4	12.0	0.00	—	.304	.333	0	—	0	3	3	-0	0.4
1983	Bos-A	6	6	.500	19	18	0	0	0	104	110	12	43	35	13.4	4.67	93	.276	.350	0	—	0	-7	-4	-1	-0.5
1984	Bos-A	1	8	.111	15	11	0	0	0	67	104	9	19	32	16.9	6.85	61	.347	.391	0	—	0	-21	-20	1	-2.3
1985	Bos-A	0	0	—	2	1	0	0	0	3¹	9	0	3	3	32.4	21.60	20	.500	.571	0	—	0	-6	-6	-0	-0.1
1986	Bos-A	4	4	.500	15	10	0	0	0	57¹	72	10	25	32	15.4	5.34	78	.316	.386	0	—	0	-7	-7	0	-0.9
	Sea-A	0	2	.000	6	2	0	0	0	15²	19	4	11	9	17.2	7.47	57	.302	.405	0	—	0	-6	-6	-0	-0.6
	Yr	4	6	.400	21	12	0	0	0	73	91	14	36	41	15.7	5.79	72	.308	.384	0	—	0	-13	-13	1	-1.5
1987	Sea-A	0	0	—	1	0	0	0	0	0¹	3	0	0	0	81.0	54.00	9	.750	.750	0	—	0	-2	-2	-0	-0.2
Total	6	12	20	.375	61	42	3	1	0	253²	324	35	102	115	15.3	5.75	74	.313	.378	0	—	0	-47	-42	0	-4.2

● MORDECAI BROWN
Brown, Mordecai Peter Centennial "Three Finger" or "Miner"
b: 10/19/1876, Nyesville, Ind. d: 2/14/48, Terre Haute, Ind. BR/TR, 5'10", 175 lbs. Deb: 4/19/03 MH

YEAR	TM/L	W	L	PCT	G	GS	CG	SH	SV	IP	H	HR	BB	SO	RAT	ERA	ERA+	OAV	OOB	BH	AVG	PB	PR	/A	PD	TPI
1903	StL-N	9	13	.409	26	24	19	1	0	201	231	7	59	83	13.3	2.60	126	.293	.347	15	.195	-0	15	15	2	1.6
1904	Chi-N	15	10	.600	26	23	21	4	1	212¹	155	1	50	81	**8.9**	1.86	143	**.199**	**.253**	19	.213	1	21	19	-1	2.3
1905	Chi-N	18	12	.600	30	24	24	4	0	249	219	3	44	89	9.5	2.17	138	.235	.271	13	.140	-1	23	23	-0	2.4
1906	*Chi-N	26	6	.813	36	32	27	**9**	3	277¹	198	1	61	144	**8.5**	**1.04**	254	.202	**.252**	20	.204	-1	**49**	49	-2	**6.8**
1907	*Chi-N	20	6	.769	34	27	20	6	3	233	180	2	40	107	8.7	1.39	179	.221	.262	13	.153	-0	28	29	4	**4.0**
1908	*Chi-N	29	9	.763	44	31	27	9	**5**	312¹	214	1	49	123	7.7	1.47	160	.195	.232	25	.207	1	31	31	-1	4.1
1909	Chi-N	**27**	9	.750	**50**	34	**32**	8	7	342²	246	1	53	172	8.0	1.31	193	.202	.239	22	.176	1	**49**	47	-1	5.4
1910	*Chi-N	25	14	.641	46	31	**27**	6	7	295¹	256	3	64	143	**9.9**	1.86	155	.232	**.277**	18	.175	-0	39	34	3	4.9
1911	Chi-N	21	11	.656	**53**	27	21	0	**13**	270	267	5	55	129	10.9	2.80	118	.262	.303	23	.253	5	18	15	-4	1.9
1912	Chi-N	5	6	.455	15	8	5	2	0	88²	92	2	20	34	11.5	2.64	126	.274	.317	9	.290	2	8	7	-2	0.8
1913	Cin-N	11	12	.478	39	16	11	1	6	173¹	174	7	44	41	11.4	2.91	112	.277	.325	11	.204	-0	6	7	-1	0.7
1914	StL-F	12	6	.667	26	18	13	2	0	175	172	7	43	81	11.2	3.20	92	.254	.302	15	.254	1	-8	-5	-2	-0.6
	Bro-F	2	5	.286	9	8	5	0	0	57²	63	1	18	32	12.6	4.21	68	.276	.329	4	.211	-1	-9	-9	-1	-1.0
	Yr	14	11	.560	35	26	18	2	0	232²	235	8	61	113	11.4	3.52	85	.259	.306	19	.244	-0	-16	-13	-3	-1.6
1915	Chi-F	17	8	.680	35	25	17	3	4	236¹	189	2	64	95	9.9	2.09	120	.220	.279	24	.293	5	17	11	3	2.0
1916	Chi-N	2	3	.400	12	4	2	0	0	48¹	52	0	9	21	12.1	3.91	74	.289	.337	6	.250	1	-7	-5	-0	-0.5
Total	14	239	130	.648	481	332	271	55	49	3172¹	2708	43	673	1375	9.8	2.06	137	.233	.278	235	.206	15	279	267	1	34.8

● MYRL BROWN
Brown, Myrl Lincoln b: 10/10/1894, Waynesboro, Pa. d: 2/23/81, Harrisburg, Pa. BR/TR, 5'11", 172 lbs. Deb: 8/19/22

YEAR	TM/L	W	L	PCT	G	GS	CG	SH	SV	IP	H	HR	BB	SO	RAT	ERA	ERA+	OAV	OOB	BH	AVG	PB	PR	/A	PD	TPI
1922	Pit-N	3	1	.750	7	5	2	0	0	34²	42	2	13	9	14.3	5.97	68	.296	.355	3	.273	1	-7	-7	0	-0.6

● NORM BROWN
Brown, Norman Ladelle b: 2/1/19, Evergreen, N.C. d: 5/31/95, Bennettsville, S.C. BB/TR, 6'3", 180 lbs. Deb: 10/3/43

YEAR	TM/L	W	L	PCT	G	GS	CG	SH	SV	IP	H	HR	BB	SO	RAT	ERA	ERA+	OAV	OOB	BH	AVG	PB	PR	/A	PD	TPI
1943	Phi-A	0	0	—	1	1	0	0	0	7	5	0	1	6	6.4	0.00	—	.185	.185	0	.000	-0	3	3	0	0.0
1946	Phi-A	0	1	.000	4	0	0	0	0	7¹	8	2	6	3	17.2	6.14	58	.267	.389	0	.000	-0	-2	-2	-0	-0.3
Total	2	0	1	.000	5	1	0	0	0	14¹	13	2	6	4	11.9	3.14	111	.228	.302	0	.000	-0	1	1	0	-0.3

● PAUL BROWN
Brown, Paul Dwayne b: 6/18/41, Ft.Smith, Ark. BR/TR, 6'1", 190 lbs. Deb: 7/23/61 F

YEAR	TM/L	W	L	PCT	G	GS	CG	SH	SV	IP	H	HR	BB	SO	RAT	ERA	ERA+	OAV	OOB	BH	AVG	PB	PR	/A	PD	TPI
1961	Phi-N	0	1	.000	5	1	0	0	0	10	13	3	4	7	19.8	8.10	50	.325	.449	1	.500	0	-5	-4	-0	-0.4
1962	Phi-N	0	6	.000	23	9	0	0	0	63²	74	9	35	29	15.5	5.94	65	.298	.387	2	.154	-2	-14	-15	-1	-1.3
1963	Phi-N	0	1	.000	6	2	0	0	0	15¹	15	2	5	11	12.9	4.11	79	.238	.314	1	.500	0	-1	-1	0	-0.1
1968	Phi-N	0	0	—	2	0	0	0	0	4	6	0	1	4	15.8	9.00	30	.353	.389	0	—	0	-3	-3	-0	-0.1
Total	4	0	8	.000	36	12	0	0	1	93	108	14	47	45	15.6	6.00	63	.293	.382	4	.235	1	-23	-23	-0	-1.7

● RAY BROWN
Brown, Paul Percival b: 1/31/1889, Chicago, Ill. d: 5/29/55, Los Angeles, Cal. BR/TR, 6'1", 172 lbs. Deb: 9/29/09

YEAR	TM/L	W	L	PCT	G	GS	CG	SH	SV	IP	H	HR	BB	SO	RAT	ERA	ERA+	OAV	OOB	BH	AVG	PB	PR	/A	PD	TPI
1909	Chi-N	1	0	1.000	1	1	1	0	0	9	5	0	4	2	9.0	2.00	127	.172	.273	0	.000	-0	1	1	0	0.0

● STUB BROWN
Brown, Richard P. b: 8/3/1870, Baltimore, Md. d: 3/11/48, Baltimore, Md. TL, 6'2", 220 lbs. Deb: 8/15/1893

YEAR	TM/L	W	L	PCT	G	GS	CG	SH	SV	IP	H	HR	BB	SO	RAT	ERA	ERA+	OAV	OOB	BH	AVG	PB	PR	/A	PD	TPI
1893	Bal-N	0	0	—	2	0	0	0	0	9	13	0	16	4	19.0	6.00	79	.325	.413	1	.200	-0	-1	-1	-0	-0.1
1894	Bal-N	4	0	1.000	9	6	3	0	0	49²	59	3	24	8	15.2	4.89	112	.292	.370	2	.087	-4	3	3	-1	-0.2
1897	Cin-N	0	1	.000	2	1	1	0	0	13	17	1	8	2	17.3	4.15	110	.315	.403	0	.000	-1	0	1	0	-0.1
Total	3	4	1	.800	13	7	4	0	0	71²	89	4	37	10	16.1	4.90	106	.301	.382	3	.091	-5	1	2	-1	-0.4

● BOB BROWN
Brown, Robert Murray b: 4/1/11, Dorchester, Mass. d: 8/3/90, Pembroke, Mass. BR/TR, 6'0.5", 190 lbs. Deb: 4/21/30

YEAR	TM/L	W	L	PCT	G	GS	CG	SH	SV	IP	H	HR	BB	SO	RAT	ERA	ERA+	OAV	OOB	BH	AVG	PB	PR	/A	PD	TPI
1930	Bos-N	0	0	—	3	0	0	0	0	6	10	0	8	1	27.0	10.50	47	.417	.563	0	.000	-0	-4	-4	0	0.0
1931	Bos-N	0	1	.000	3	1	0	0	0	6¹	9	0	3	2	17.1	8.53	44	.375	.444	1	.500	0	-3	-3	-0	-0.4
1932	Bos-N	14	7	.667	35	28	9	0	1	213	187	6	104	110	12.4	3.30	114	.238	.329	13	.194	-0	14	11	-1	0.9
1933	Bos-N	0	0	—	3	0	0	0	0	6²	6	0	3	1	12.2	2.70	114	.250	.333	0	.000	-0	1	1	0	0.1
1934	Bos-N	1	3	.250	16	8	2	1	0	58¹	59	2	36	21	15.1	5.71	67	.262	.371	5	.238	0	-11	-12	-1	-0.8
1935	Bos-N	1	8	.111	15	10	2	0	0	65	79	2	36	17	15.9	6.37	59	.302	.386	2	.105	-1	-17	-19	-1	-2.3
1936	Bos-N	0	2	.000	4	2	0	0	0	8¹	10	1	3	1	14.0	5.40	71	.278	.333	0	.000	-0	-1	-1	0	-0.3
Total	7	16	21	.432	79	49	13	2	1	363²	360	11	193	159	13.8	4.84	84	.261	.354	21	.183	-2	-22	-28	-3	-2.9

● SCOTT BROWN
Brown, Scott Edward b: 8/30/56, DeQuincy, La. BR/TR, 6'2", 220 lbs. Deb: 8/11/81

YEAR	TM/L	W	L	PCT	G	GS	CG	SH	SV	IP	H	HR	BB	SO	RAT	ERA	ERA+	OAV	OOB	BH	AVG	PB	PR	/A	PD	TPI
1981	Cin-N	1	0	1.000	10	0	0	0	0	13	16	0	7	1	11.8	2.77	128	.314	.327	0	.000	-0	1	1	-0	0.1

YEAR	TM/L	W	L	PCT	G	GS	CG	SH	SV	IP	H	HR	BB	SO	RAT	ERA	ERA+	OAV	OOB	BH	AVG	PB	PR	/A	PD	TPI

● **STEVE BROWN**   Brown, Steven Elbert   b: 2/12/57, San Francisco, Cal.   BR/TR, 6'5", 200 lbs.   Deb: 8/1/83

1983	Cal-A	2	3	.400	12	4	2	1	0	46	45	4	16	23	11.9	3.52	114	.256	.318	0	—	0	3	3	-0	0.2
1984	Cal-A	0	1	.000	3	3	0	0	0	11	16	0	9	5	20.5	9.00	44	.340	.446	0	—	0	-6	-6	-0	-0.5
Total	2	2	4	.333	15	7	2	1	0	57	61	4	25	28	13.6	4.58	87	.274	.347	0		0	-3	-4	-0	-0.3

● **TOM BROWN**   Brown, Thomas Dale   b: 8/10/49, Lafayette, La.   BR/TR, 6'1", 170 lbs.   Deb: 9/14/78

| 1978 | Sea-A | 0 | 0 | — | 6 | 0 | 0 | 0 | 0 | 13 | 14 | 2 | 4 | 8 | 12.5 | 4.15 | 92 | .286 | .340 | | | | -1 | -1 | 0 | 0.0 |

● **TOM BROWN**   Brown, Thomas Tarlton   b: 9/21/1860, Liverpool, England   d: 10/25/27, Washington, D.C.   BL/TR, 5'10", 168 lbs.   Deb: 7/6/1882   MU♦

1882	Bal-a	0	0	—	2	0	0	0	0	8¹	13	0	6	2	20.5	1.08	255	.333	.422	55	.304	1	1	2	-1	0.0
1883	Col-a	0	1	.000	3	1	1	0	0	14	14	0	10	6	15.4	5.79	53	.246	.358	115	.274	1	-4	-4	-1	-0.2
1884	Col-a	2	1	.667	4	0	0	0	0	19	27	0	7	16	16.1	7.11	43	.281	.330	123	.273	1	-8	-9	-1	-1.0
1885	Pit-a	0	0	—	2	0	0	0	0	6	0	0	3	2	9.0	3.00	107	.000	.207	134	.307	1	0	0	-0	0.0
1886	Pit-a	0	0	—	1	0	0	0	0	2	2	0	5	1	31.5	9.00	38	.125	.333	131	.285	0	-1	-1	0	0.0
Total	5	2	2	.500	12	1	1	0	0	49¹	56	0	31	16	16.4	5.29	57	.242	.340	1951	.265	4	-12	-12	-2	-1.2

● **JUMBO BROWN**   Brown, Walter George   b: 4/30/07, Greene, R.I.   d: 10/2/66, Freeport, N.Y.   BR/TR, 6'4", 295 lbs.   Deb: 8/26/25

1925	Chi-N	0	0	—	2	0	0	0	0	6	5	0	4	0	13.5	3.00	144	.217	.333	0	.000	-0	1	1	0	0.0
1927	Cle-A	0	2	.000	8	0	0	0	0	18²	19	3	26	8	22.2	6.27	67	.284	.489	2	.667	1	-4	-4	-0	-0.2
1928	Cle-A	0	1	.000	5	0	0	0	0	14²	19	0	15	12	20.9	6.75	61	.365	.507	2	.667	1	-4	-4	-0	-0.1
1932	NY-A	5	2	.714	19	3	3	1	1	55²	58	1	30	31	14.6	4.53	90	.270	.364	4	.174	-1	-0	-3	1	-0.2
1933	NY-A	7	5	.583	21	8	1	0	0	74	78	3	52	55	15.8	5.23	74	.269	.380	5	.179	-1	-8	-11	-0	-1.5
1935	NY-A	6	5	.545	20	8	3	1	0	87¹	94	2	37	41	13.5	3.61	112	.279	.350	10	.313	3	8	4	0	0.8
1936	NY-A	1	4	.200	20	3	0	0	1	64	93	0	29	19	17.2	5.91	79	.352	.416	0	.000	-3	-6	-9	1	-0.8
1937	Cin-N	1	0	1.000	4	1	0	0	0	9²	16	0	3	4	17.7	8.38	45	.390	.432	0	.000	0	-5	-5	-0	-0.5
	NY-N	1	0	1.000	4	0	0	0	0	8²	5	0	5	4	10.4	1.04	374	.172	.294	0	—	0	3	3	1	0.4
	Yr	2	0	1.000	8	1	0	0	0	18¹	21	0	8	8	14.2	4.91	78	.300	.372	0	.000	-0	-2	-2	0	-0.1
1938	NY-N	5	3	.625	43	0	0	0	5	90	65	5	28	42	9.4	1.80	209	.204	.271	3	.188	1	**20**	**20**	-1	1.8
1939	NY-N	4	0	1.000	31	0	0	0	7	56¹	69	1	25	24	15.2	4.15	95	.304	.375	4	.364	-1	-1	-1	-0	0.0
1940	NY-N	2	4	.333	41	0	0	0	**7**	55¹	49	5	25	31	12.0	3.42	114	.232	.314	1	.100	-1	3	3	-1	0.2
1941	NY-N	1	5	.167	31	0	0	0	**8**	57	49	2	21	30	11.1	3.32	111	.238	.308	1	.111	-1	2	1	0	0.2
Total	12	33	31	.516	249	23	7	2	29	597¹	619	26	300	301	13.9	4.07	99	.271	.357	32	.204	2	7	-4	-0	0.1

● **WALTER BROWN**   Brown, Walter Irving   b: 4/23/15, Jamestown, N.Y.   d: 2/3/91, Westfield, N.Y.   BR/TR, 5'11", 175 lbs.   Deb: 5/16/47

| 1947 | StL-A | 1 | 0 | 1.000 | 19 | 0 | 0 | 0 | 0 | 46 | 50 | 3 | 28 | 10 | 15.3 | 4.89 | 79 | .294 | .394 | 0 | .000 | -1 | -6 | -5 | 0 | -0.2 |

● **CAL BROWNING**   Browning, Calvin Duane   b: 3/16/38, Burns Flat, Okla.   BL/TL, 5'11", 190 lbs.   Deb: 6/12/60

| 1960 | StL-N | 0 | 0 | — | 1 | 0 | 0 | 0 | 0 | 0² | 5 | 1 | 0 | 0 | 81.0 | 40.50 | 10 | .714 | .750 | | | 0 | -3 | -3 | -0 | 0.0 |

● **FRANK BROWNING**   Browning, Frank "Dutch"   b: 10/29/1882, Falmouth, Ky.   d: 5/19/48, San Antonio, Tex.   BR/TR, 5'5", 145 lbs.   Deb: 4/16/10

| 1910 | Det-A | 2 | 2 | .500 | 11 | 6 | 2 | 0 | 3 | 49 | 51 | 0 | 10 | 16 | 11.2 | 2.57 | 102 | .262 | .298 | 0 | .000 | -2 | -0 | 0 | 1 | 0.0 |

● **PETE BROWNING**   Browning, Louis Rogers "The Gladiator"   b: 6/17/1861, Louisville, Ky.   d: 9/10/05, Louisville, Ky.   BR/TR, 6', 180 lbs.   Deb: 5/2/1882 ♦

| 1884 | Lou-a | 0 | 1 | .000 | 2 | 0 | 0 | 0 | 0 | 2 | 2 | 0 | 2 | 0 | 135.0 | 54.00 | 6 | 1.000 | 1.000 | 150 | .336 | 1 | -2 | -2 | 0 | -1.9 |

● **TOM BROWNING**   Browning, Thomas Leo   b: 4/28/60, Casper, Wyoming   BL/TL, 6'1", 190 lbs.   Deb: 9/9/84

1984	Cin-N	1	0	1.000	3	3	0	0	0	23¹	27	0	5	14	12.3	1.54	245	.303	.340	1	.143	-0	5	6	-0	0.2
1985	Cin-N	20	9	.690	38	38	6	4	0	261¹	242	29	73	155	11.0	3.55	107	.245	.299	17	.193	2	1	7	-2	0.8
1986	Cin-N	14	13	.519	39	39	4	2	0	243¹	225	26	70	147	10.9	3.81	102	.245	.299	14	.163	-1	-3	-2	-3	-0.2
1987	Cin-N	10	13	.435	32	31	2	0	0	183	201	27	61	117	13.1	5.02	85	.284	.345	8	.154	0	-19	-16	-2	-1.8
1988	Cin-N	18	5	.783	36	36	5	2	0	250²	205	36	64	124	9.9	3.41	105	.224	.280	12	.145	0	1	5	-3	0.2
1989	Cin-N	15	12	.556	37	37	9	2	0	249²	241	31	64	118	11.1	3.39	106	.255	.304	7	.090	-3	3	6	-1	0.1
1990	*Cin-N	15	9	.625	35	35	2	1	0	227²	235	24	52	99	11.5	3.80	104	.266	.311	7	.093	-3	-0	4	-2	-0.2
1991	Cin-N☆	14	14	.500	36	36	1	0	0	230¹	241	32	56	115	11.8	4.18	91	.266	.312	12	.171	2	-13	-10	-3	-1.3
1992	Cin-N	6	5	.545	16	16	0	0	0	87	108	6	28	33	14.3	5.07	71	.311	.366	7	.226	1	-15	-14	0	-1.5
1993	Cin-N	7	7	.500	21	20	0	0	0	114	159	16	20	53	14.2	4.74	85	.333	.361	8	.216	-3	-9	-9	1	-0.6
1994	Cin-N	3	1	.750	7	7	2	1	0	40²	34	8	13	22	10.6	4.20	98	.222	.287	2	.143	-0	-0	-0	-0	-0.1
1995	KC-A	0	2	.000	2	2	0	0	0	10	13	2	5	3	16.2	8.10	59	.302	.375	0	—	0	-4	-4	-0	-0.5
Total	12	123	90	.577	302	300	31	12	0	1921	1931	236	511	1000	11.6	3.94	97	.262	.312	95	.153	2	-51	-24	-15	-4.9

● **BRUCE BRUBAKER**   Brubaker, Bruce Ellsworth   b: 12/29/41, Harrisburg, Pa.   BR/TR, 6'1", 198 lbs.   Deb: 4/15/67

1967	LA-N	0	0	—	1	0	0	0	0	1¹	3	1	0	2	20.3	20.25	15	.429	.429	0		0	-3	-3	0	0.0
1970	Mil-A	0	0	—	1	0	0	0	0	2	2	1	1	0	13.5	9.00	42	.250	.333	0		0	-1	-1	-0	0.0
Total	2	0	0	—	2	0	0	0	0	3¹	5	2	1	2	16.2	13.50	26	.333	.375	0		0	-4	-4	0	0.0

● **LOU BRUCE**   Bruce, Louis R.   b: 1/16/1877, St.Regis, N.Y.   d: 2/9/68, Ilion, N.Y.   BL/TR, 5'5", 145 lbs.   Deb: 6/22/04 ♦

| 1904 | Phi-A | 0 | 0 | — | 2 | 0 | 0 | 0 | 0 | 11 | 11 | 1 | 2 | 2 | 10.6 | 4.91 | 55 | .262 | .295 | 27 | .267 | 0 | -3 | -3 | 0 | 0.1 |

● **BOB BRUCE**   Bruce, Robert James   b: 5/16/33, Detroit, Mich.   BR/TR, 6'3", 210 lbs.   Deb: 9/14/59

1959	Det-A	0	1	.000	2	1	0	0	0	2	2	1	3	1	22.5	9.00	45	.250	.455	0	—	0	-1	-1	-0	-0.4
1960	Det-A	4	7	.364	34	15	1	0	0	130	127	16	56	76	13.0	3.74	106	.250	.331	7	.179	2	3	3	1	0.3
1961	Det-A	1	2	.333	14	6	0	0	0	44²	57	6	24	25	16.7	4.43	92	.320	.407	1	.111	0	-2	-2	-1	-0.2
1962	Hou-N	10	9	.526	32	27	6	0	0	175	164	16	82	135	13.3	4.06	92	.248	.342	11	.200	5	-2	-6	-0	-0.1
1963	Hou-N	5	9	.357	30	25	1	1	0	170¹	162	7	60	123	12.2	3.59	88	.250	.321	7	.127	2	-6	-8	-1	-0.6
1964	Hou-N	15	9	.625	35	29	9	4	0	202¹	191	8	33	135	10.1	2.76	124	.246	.279	12	.190	-2	18	15	-0	2.0
1965	Hou-N	9	18	.333	35	34	7	1	0	229²	241	25	38	145	11.3	3.72	90	.270	.307	9	.122	-1	-5	-9	0	-1.1
1966	Hou-N	3	13	.188	25	23	1	0	0	129²	160	16	29	71	13.7	5.34	64	.301	.346	3	.077	-2	-25	-28	-3	-3.2
1967	Atl-N	2	3	.400	12	7	1	0	1	38²	42	3	15	22	13.5	4.89	68	.269	.337	2	.167	0	-7	-7	-1	-0.9
Total	9	49	71	.408	219	167	26	6	1	1122¹	1146	95	340	733	12.3	3.85	91	.263	.323	52	.150	6	-28	-43	-2	-4.2

● **FRED BRUCKBAUER**   Bruckbauer, Frederick John   b: 5/27/38, New Ulm, Minn.   BR/TR, 6'1", 185 lbs.   Deb: 4/25/61

| 1961 | Min-A | 0 | 0 | — | 1 | 0 | 0 | 0 | 0 | 0 | 3 | 0 | 1 | 0 | — | ∞ | — | 1.000 | 1.000 | 0 | | 0 | -3 | -3 | 0 | -0.3 |

● **ANDY BRUCKMILLER**   Bruckmiller, Andrew   b: 1/1/1882, McKeesport, Pa.   d: 1/12/70, McKeesport, Pa.   BR/TR, 5'11", 175 lbs.   Deb: 6/26/05

| 1905 | Det-A | 0 | 0 | — | 1 | 0 | 0 | 0 | 0 | 1 | 4 | 0 | 1 | 1 | 45.0 | 27.00 | 10 | .571 | .625 | 0 | .000 | -0 | -3 | -3 | -0 | 0.0 |

● **MIKE BRUHERT**   Bruhert, Michael Edwin   b: 6/24/51, Jamaica, N.Y.   BR/TR, 6'6", 220 lbs.   Deb: 4/9/78

| 1978 | NY-N | 4 | 11 | .267 | 27 | 22 | 1 | 1 | 0 | 133² | 171 | 6 | 34 | 56 | 13.9 | 4.78 | 73 | .317 | .359 | 3 | .075 | -3 | -18 | -19 | -0 | -2.2 |

● **DUFF BRUMLEY**   Brumley, Duff Lechaun   b: 8/25/70, Cleveland, Tenn.   BR/TR, 6'4", 195 lbs.   Deb: 6/1/94

| 1994 | Tex-A | 0 | 0 | — | 2 | 0 | 0 | 0 | 0 | 3¹ | 5 | 1 | 4 | 3 | 29.7 | 16.20 | 30 | .400 | .550 | 0 | | 0 | -4 | -4 | -0 | -0.4 |

● **GREG BRUMMETT**   Brummett, Gregory Scott   b: 4/20/67, Wichita, Kan.   BR/TR, 6', 180 lbs.   Deb: 5/29/93

1993	SF-N	2	3	.400	8	8	0	0	0	46	53	9	13	20	12.9	4.70	83	.294	.342	0	.000	-1	-3	-4	0	-0.5
	Min-A	2	1	.667	5	5	0	0	0	26²	29	3	15	10	14.9	5.74	76	.299	.393	0	—	0	-4	-4	-1	-0.4
Total	1	4	4	.500	13	13	0	0	0	72²	82	12	28	30	13.6	5.08	80	.296	.361	0	.000	-1	-8	-8	-1	-0.9

● **JACK BRUNER**   Bruner, Jack Raymond   b: 7/1/24, Waterloo, Iowa   BL/TL, 6'1", 185 lbs.   Deb: 9/16/49

1949	Chi-A	1	2	.333	4	2	0	0	0	7²	7	0	8	4	21.1	8.22	51	.357	.500	0	—	-0	-3	-3	-0	-1.1
1950	Chi-A	0	0	—	9	0	0	0	0	12¹	7	0	14	8	16.1	3.65	123	.184	.415	0		0	1	1	0	0.0
	StL-A	1	2	.333	13	1	0	0	1	35	36	4	23	16	15.7	4.63	107	.267	.381	0		-1	-1	-1	0	-0.1
	Yr	1	2	.333	22	1	0	0	1	47¹	43	4	37	24	15.6	4.37	110	.247	.385	0	.000	-1	1	2	-1	-0.1
Total	2	2	4	.333	26	3	0	0	1	55	53	4	45	28	16.5	4.91	96	.264	.406	0	.000	-1	-2	-1	-1	-1.2

YEAR	TM/L	W	L	PCT	G	GS	CG	SH	SV	IP	H	HR	BB	SO	RAT	ERA	ERA+	OAV	OOB	BH	AVG	PB	PR	/A	PD	TPI

● ROY BRUNER   Bruner, Walter Roy   b: 2/10/17, Cecilia, Ky.   d: 11/30/86, St.Matthews, Ky.   BR/TR, 6′, 165 lbs.   Deb: 9/14/39

1939	Phi-N	0	4	.000	4	4	2	0	0	27	38	3	13	11	17.0	6.67	60	.339	.408	1	.111	-1	-8	-8	-1	-1.0
1940	Phi-N	0	0	—	2	0	0	0	0	6¹	5	2	6	4	15.6	5.68	69	.227	.393	1	.500	-1	-1	-1	0	-0.1
1941	Phi-N	0	3	.000	13	1	0	0	0	29¹	37	1	25	13	19.0	4.91	75	.336	.459	0	.000	-0	-4	-4	0	-0.5
Total	3	0	7	.000	19	5	2	0	0	62²	80	6	44	28	17.8	5.74	67	.328	.431	2	.118	-1	-14	-13	-1	-1.4

● GEORGE BRUNET   Brunet, George Stuart "Lefty"   b: 6/8/35, Houghton, Mich.   d: 10/25/91, Poza Rica, Mex.   BR/TL, 6′1″, 210 lbs.   Deb: 9/14/56

1956	KC-A	0	0	—	6	1	0	0	0	9	10	1	11	5	21.0	7.00	62	.286	.457	0	.000	-0	-3	-3	0	0.0
1957	KC-A	0	1	.000	4	2	0	0	0	11¹	13	2	4	3	13.5	5.56	71	.277	.333	0	.000	-0	-2	-2	-0	-0.2
1959	KC-A	0	0	—	2	0	0	0	0	4²	10	2	7	7	34.7	11.57	35	.435	.581	0	—	-0	-4	-4	1	0.1
1960	KC-A	0	2	.000	3	2	0	0	0	10¹	12	0	10	4	20.0	4.35	91	.308	.460	0	.000	-0	-1	-0	1	0.0
	Mil-N	2	0	1.000	17	6	0	0	0	49²	53	6	22	39	13.8	5.07	68	.275	.352	1	.091	-1	-7	-9	0	-0.4
1961	Mil-N	0	0	—	5	0	0	0	0	5	7	1	2	0	16.2	5.40	69	.412	.474	0	—	-0	-1	-0	0	0.0
1962	Hou-N	2	4	.333	17	11	2	0	0	54	62	2	21	36	13.8	4.50	83	.291	.355	1	.059	-1	-3	-5	1	-0.5
1963	Hou-N	0	3	.000	5	2	0	0	0	12²	24	2	6	11	21.3	7.11	44	.393	.448	0	.000	-0	-5	-6	0	-1.1
	Bal-A	0	1	.000	16	0	0	0	1	20	25	3	9	13	15.7	5.40	64	.301	.376	0	.000	-0	-4	-4	0	-1.2
1964	LA-A	2	2	.500	10	7	0	0	0	42¹	38	2	25	36	13.4	3.61	91	.237	.341	2	.182	-0	0	-2	-0	-0.1
1965	Cal-A	9	11	.450	41	26	8	3	2	197	149	9	69	141	10.1	2.56	133	.209	.282	3	.054	-2	20	18	-1	1.4
1966	Cal-A	13	13	.500	41	32	8	2	0	212	183	21	106	148	12.5	3.31	101	.234	.329	7	.103	-2	3	1	-0	0.0
1967	Cal-A	11	19	.367	40	37	7	2	1	250	203	19	90	165	10.7	3.31	95	.223	.295	6	.077	-4	-2	-5	-2	-1.2
1968	Cal-A	13	17	.433	39	36	8	5	0	245¹	191	19	68	132	9.6	2.86	102	.215	.273	6	.081	-3	3	1	-2	-0.5
1969	Cal-A	6	7	.462	23	19	2	2	0	100²	98	15	39	56	12.3	3.84	91	.255	.325	1	.037	-1	-2	-4	1	-0.7
	Sea-A	2	5	.286	12	11	2	0	0	63²	70	11	28	37	13.9	5.37	68	.280	.353	3	.150	1	-12	-12	1	-1.1
	Yr		8	12	.400	35	30	4	2	0	164¹	168	26	67	93	12.9	4.44	80	.264	.334	4	.085	-0	-15	-16	-0	-1.8
1970	Was-A	8	6	.571	24	20	2	1	0	118	124	10	48	67	13.2	4.42	80	.275	.346	6	.158	1	-9	-11	-1	-1.2
	Pit-N	1	1	.500	12	1	0	0	0	16²	19	1	9	17	15.7	2.70	144	.311	.408	0	.000	-0	2	2	0	0.2
1971	StL-N	0	1	.000	7	0	0	0	0	9¹	12	3	7	4	18.3	5.79	62	.316	.422	1	.333	-1	-2	-2	0	-0.2
Total	15	69	93	.426	324	213	39	15	4	1431²	1303	133	581	921	12.0	3.62	92	.244	.320	37	.089	-14	-31	-46	-4	-5.7

● TOM BRUNO   Bruno, Thomas Michael   b: 1/26/53, Chicago, Ill.   BR/TR, 6′5″, 210 lbs.   Deb: 8/1/76

1976	KC-A	1	0	1.000	12	0	0	0	0	17¹	20	3	9	11	15.1	6.75	52	.290	.372	0	—	-0	-6	-6	-0	-0.4
1977	Tor-A	0	1	.000	12	0	0	0	0	18¹	30	4	13	9	21.6	7.85	53	.366	.458	0	—	0	-8	-7	0	-0.4
1978	StL-N	4	3	.571	18	3	0	0	1	49²	38	3	17	33	10.0	1.99	176	.209	.276	1	.083	-1	9	8	-1	1.1
1979	StL-N	2	3	.400	27	1	0	0	0	38¹	37	1	22	27	14.3	4.23	89	.253	.359	1	.200	-1	-2	-2	-0	-0.2
Total	4	7	7	.500	69	4	0	0	1	123²	125	11	61	80	13.8	4.22	87	.261	.348	2	.118	-1	-7	-7	-1	0.1

● JIM BRUSKE   Bruske, James Scott   b: 10/7/64, E.St.Louis, Ill.   BR/TR, 6′1″, 185 lbs.   Deb: 8/25/95

1995	LA-N	0	0	—	9	0	0	0	1	10	12	0	4	5	15.3	4.50	84	.300	.378		—	0	-0	-1	0	0.0
1996	LA-N	0	0	—	11	0	0	0	0	12²	17	2	3	12	14.9	5.68	68	.315	.362		—	0	-2	-3	0	0.0
Total	2	0	0	—	20	0	0	0	1	22²	29	2	7	17	15.1	5.16	74	.309	.369		—	0	-2	-3	-0	0.0

● WARREN BRUSSTAR   Brusstar, Warren Scott   b: 2/2/52, Oakland, Cal.   BR/TR, 6′3″, 200 lbs.   Deb: 5/6/77

1977	*Phi-N	7	2	.778	46	0	0	0	3	71¹	64	7	24	46	11.2	2.65	151	.250	.317	0	.000	-1	10	11	1	1.4
1978	*Phi-N	6	3	.667	58	0	0	0	0	88²	74	0	30	60	10.9	2.33	153	.239	.312	1	.143	-1	12	12	2	1.4
1979	Phi-N	1	0	1.000	13	0	0	0	0	14¹	23	1	4	9	16.3	6.91	55	.383	.422	0	—	-0	-5	-5	0	-0.4
1980	Phi-N	2	2	.500	26	0	0	0	0	38²	42	3	13	21	12.8	3.72	102	.286	.344	0	.000	-0	-1	-0	0	-0.1
1981	*Phi-N	0	1	.000	14	0	0	0	0	12¹	12	0	10	8	16.8	4.38	83	.250	.390	0	—	-0	-1	-1	0	-0.1
1982	Phi-N	2	3	.400	22	0	0	0	2	22²	31	2	5	11	14.7	4.76	77	.348	.389	0	.000	-0	-3	-3	-0	-0.6
	Chi-A	2	0	1.000	10	0	0	0	0	18¹	19	2	3	8	11.3	3.44	117	.257	.295	0	—	0	1	1	1	0.2
1983	Chi-N	3	1	.750	59	0	0	0	1	80¹	67	1	37	46	11.9	2.35	161	.234	.326	0	.000	-0	11	13	0	0.6
1984	*Chi-N	1	1	.500	41	0	0	0	3	63²	57	4	21	36	11.2	3.11	126	.247	.312	1	.200	-1	3	6	-0	0.3
1985	Chi-N	4	3	.571	51	0	0	0	4	74¹	87	8	36	34	15.3	6.05	66	.292	.374	1	.143	-1	-20	-17	-2	-1.9
Total	9	28	16	.636	340	0	0	0	14	484²	476	28	183	273	12.5	3.51	109	.265	.337	3	.094	-1	8	17	2	0.9

● CLAY BRYANT   Bryant, Claiborne Henry   b: 11/16/11, Madison Heights, Va.   BR/TR, 6′2.5″, 195 lbs.   Deb: 4/19/35   C

1935	Chi-N	1	2	.333	9	1	0	0	2	22²	34	1	7	13	16.3	5.16	76	.358	.402	2	.333	2	-3	-3	-0	-0.2
1936	Chi-N	2	1	.667	26	0	0	0	2	57¹	57	0	24	35	13.0	3.30	121	.259	.337	5	.417	1	**5**	**4**	1	0.4
1937	Chi-N	9	3	.750	38	9	4	1	3	135¹	117	1	78	75	13.0	4.26	94	.232	.336	14	.311	5	-5	-4	-3	-0.2
1938	*Chi-N	19	11	.633	44	30	17	3	2	270¹	235	6	125	**135**	12.0	3.10	124	.235	.321	24	.226	4	21	22	-3	2.4
1939	Chi-N	2	1	.667	4	4	2	0	0	31¹	42	3	14	9	16.4	5.74	69	.307	.375	3	.214	-0	-6	-6	-1	-0.5
1940	Chi-N	0	1	.000	8	0	0	0	0	26¹	26	2	14	5	13.7	4.78	78	.265	.357	3	.333	1	-3	-3	0	0.0
Total	6	32	20	.615	129	44	23	4	7	543¹	511	13	262	272	12.9	3.73	104	.249	.335	51	.266	13	8	10	-6	1.9

● RON BRYANT   Bryant, Ronald Raymond   b: 11/12/47, Redlands, Cal.   BB/TL, 6′, 190 lbs.   Deb: 9/29/67

1967	SF-N	0	0	—	1	0	0	0	0	4	3	0	0	2	9.0	4.50	73	.200	.250	0	.000	-0	-1	-1	0	0.0
1969	SF-N	4	3	.571	16	8	0	0	1	57²	60	8	25	30	13.6	4.37	80	.271	.351	3	.188	1	-5	-6	0	-0.6
1970	SF-N	5	8	.385	34	11	1	0	0	96	103	7	38	66	13.4	4.78	83	.274	.344	3	.111	-1	-8	-9	1	-1.0
1971	*SF-N	7	10	.412	27	22	3	2	0	140	146	6	49	79	12.7	3.79	90	.272	.336	10	.200	-1	-5	-6	0	-0.6
1972	SF-N	14	7	.667	35	28	11	4	0	214	176	20	77	107	10.7	2.90	120	.224	.295	12	.171	1	13	14	-4	1.2
1973	SF-N	**24**	12	.667	41	39	8	0	0	270	240	23	115	143	12.1	3.53	108	.234	.316	16	.168	1	4	9	0	1.2
1974	SF-N	3	15	.167	41	23	0	0	0	126²	142	11	68	75	15.2	5.61	68	.286	.376	4	.129	-1	-28	-26	-0	-3.4
1975	StL-N	0	1	.000	10	1	0	0	0	8²	20	2	7	7	28.0	16.62	23	.444	.519	0	.000	-1	-13	-12	0	-1.2
Total	8	57	56	.504	205	132	23	6	1	917	890	80	379	509	12.7	4.02	91	.254	.331	48	.165	-0	-42	-36	-4	-4.7

● T.R. BRYDEN   Bryden, Thomas Ray   b: 1/17/59, Moses Lake, Wash.   BR/TR, 6′4″, 190 lbs.   Deb: 4/10/86

| 1986 | Cal-A | 2 | 1 | .667 | 16 | 0 | 0 | 0 | 0 | 34¹ | 38 | 4 | 21 | 25 | 16.0 | 6.55 | 63 | .290 | .396 | 1 | — | 0 | -9 | -9 | 0 | -0.6 |

● TOD BRYNAN   Brynan, Charles Ruley   b: 7/1863, Philadelphia, Pa.   d: 5/10/25, Philadelphia, Pa.   BR/TR,   Deb: 6/22/1888

1888	Chi-N	2	1	.667	3	3	2	0	0	25	29	2	7	11	13.7	6.48	47	.271	.328	2	.182	0	-10	-10	-1	-0.9
1891	Bos-N	0	1	.000	1	1	0	0	0	1	4	0	3	0	63.0	54.00	7	.571	.700	0	—	-0	-6	-6	-0	-1.9
Total	2	2	2	.500	4	4	2	0	0	26	33	2	10	11	15.6	8.31	37	.289	.357	2	.182	-0	-16	-15	-1	-2.8

● JIM BUCHANAN   Buchanan, James Forrest   b: 7/1/1876, Chatham Hill, Va.   d: 6/15/49, Norfolk, Neb.   BL/TR, 5′10″, 165 lbs.   Deb: 4/16/05

| 1905 | StL-A | 5 | 9 | .357 | 22 | 15 | 12 | 1 | **2** | 141¹ | 140 | 3 | 72 | 54 | 11.3 | 3.70 | 73 | .272 | .309 | 7 | .152 | -0 | -13 | -15 | 0 | -1.5 |

● BOB BUCHANAN   Buchanan, Robert Gordon   b: 5/3/61, Ridley Park, Pa.   BL/TL, 6′1″, 185 lbs.   Deb: 7/13/85

1985	Cin-N	1	0	1.000	14	0	0	0	0	16	25	4	9	3	19.1	8.44	45	.368	.442	0	.000	-0	-9	-9	-0	-0.5
1989	KC-A	0	0	—	2	0	0	0	0	3¹	5	1	3	3	21.6	16.20	24	.333	.444	0	—	-0	-5	-5	0	-0.1
Total	2	1	0	1.000	16	0	0	0	0	19¹	30	5	12	6	19.6	9.78	39	.361	.442	0	.000	-0	-13	-13	-0	-0.5

● GARY BUCKELS   Buckels, Gary Scott   b: 7/22/65, LaMirada, Cal.   BR/TR, 6′, 185 lbs.   Deb: 7/23/94

| 1994 | StL-N | 0 | 0 | — | 16 | 0 | 0 | 0 | 0 | 23² | 25 | 2 | 13 | 9 | 14.1 | 4.56 | 81 | .275 | .367 | 0 | .000 | -3 | 3 | 0 | 0 | 0.2 |

● GARLAND BUCKEYE   Buckeye, Garland Maiers "Gob"   b: 10/16/1897, Heron Lake, Minn.   d: 11/14/75, Stone Lake, Wis.   BB/TL, 6′, 260 lbs.   Deb: 6/19/18

1918	Was-A	0	0	—	1	0	0	0	0	2	3	0	2	0	22.5	18.00	15	.333	.600	0	—	0	-3	-3	0	-0.2
1925	Cle-A	13	8	.619	30	18	11	1	0	153	161	3	58	49	13.2	3.65	121	.267	.338	14	.226	7	13	13	-1	1.7
1926	Cle-A	6	9	.400	32	18	5	1	0	165²	160	3	69	36	12.8	3.10	131	.264	.345	12	.200	8	17	18	-2	1.4
1927	Cle-A	10	17	.370	35	25	13	2	1	204²	231	6	74	38	13.6	3.96	106	.296	.362	12	.171	16	6	7	-1	1.0
1928	Cle-A	1	5	.167	9	6	0	0	0	35	58	3	11	8	16.7	6.69	62	.389	.417	1	.111	-1	-10	-10	-0	-1.4
	NY-N	0	0	—	1	0	0	0	0	3²	9	1	0	2	27.0	14.73	27	.409	.458	1	.500	1	-4	-4	0	0.1
Total	5	30	39	.435	108	67	29	4	1	564	622	15	214	134	13.6	3.91	108	.287	.356	47	.230	7	16	19	-3	2.6

YEAR TM/L	W	L	PCT	G	GS	CG	SH	SV	IP	H	HR	BB	SO	RAT	ERA	ERA+	OAV	OOB	BH	AVG	PB	PR	/A	PD	TPI
● **ED BUCKINGHAM** Buckingham, Edward Taylor b: 5/12/1874, Metuchen, N.J. d: 7/30/42, Bridgeport, Conn. Deb: 8/30/1895																									
1895 Was-N	0	0	—	1	1	0	0	0	3	6	0	2	1	24.0	6.00	80	.400	.471	0	.000	-0	-0	-0	0	0.0
● **JESS BUCKLES** Buckles, Jesse Robert "Jim" b: 5/20/1890, LaVerne, Cal. d: 8/2/75, Westminster, Cal. BL/TL, 6'2.5", 205 lbs. Deb: 9/17/16																									
1916 NY-A	0	0	—	2	0	0	0	0	4	3	0	1	2	9.0	2.25	128	.188	.235	-0	—	-0	0	0	-0	0.0
● **JOHN BUCKLEY** Buckley, John Edward b: 3/20/1869, Marlborough, Mass. d: 5/3/42, Westborough, Mass. BL/TR, 6'1", 200 lbs. Deb: 7/15/1890																									
1890 Buf-P	1	3	.250	4	4	4	0	0	34	49	5	16	4	17.2	7.68	53	.325	.389	0	.000	-2	-13	-14	0	-1.1
● **MIKE BUDNICK** Budnick, Michael Joe b: 9/15/19, Astoria, Ore. BR/TR, 6'1", 200 lbs. Deb: 4/18/46																									
1946 NY-N	2	3	.400	35	7	1	1	3	88¹	75	13	48	36	12.5	3.16	109	.231	.330	6	.300	3	2	3	1	0.5
1947 NY-N	0	0	—	7	1	0	0	0	12	16	0	9	6	19.5	10.50	39	.314	.426	1	.250	-0	-9	-9	0	0.0
Total 2	2	3	.400	42	8	1	1	3	100¹	91	13	58	42	13.4	4.04	87	.242	.343	7	.292	3	-6	-6	1	0.5
● **CHARLIE BUFFINTON** Buffinton, Charles G. b: 6/14/1861, Fall River, Mass. d: 9/23/07, Fall River, Mass. BR/TR, 6'1", 180 lbs. Deb: 5/17/1882 M♦																									
1882 Bos-N	2	3	.400	5	5	4	1	0	42	53	2	14	11	14.4	4.07	70	.296	.347	13	.260	-8	-5	-6	1	-0.5
1883 Bos-N	25	14	.641	43	41	34	4	1	333	346	4	51	188	10.7	3.03	102	.254	.281	81	.238	0	4	3	-1	0.1
1884 Bos-N	48	16	.750	67	67	63	8	0	587	506	15	76	417	8.9	2.15	135	.219	.244	94	.267	12	54	48	3	5.7
1885 Bos-N	22	27	.449	51	50	49	6	0	434¹	425	10	112	242	11.1	2.88	93	.246	.292	81	.240	5	-3	-9	6	0.0
1886 Bos-N	7	10	.412	18	17	16	0	0	151	203	4	39	47	14.4	4.59	70	.308	.346	51	.290	4	-21	-23	-1	-1.8
1887 Phi-N	21	17	.553	40	38	35	1	0	332¹	352	16	92	160	12.1	3.66	116	.264	.313	72	.268	2	15	21	7	2.6
1888 Phi-N	28	17	.622	46	46	43	6	0	400¹	324	6	59	199	8.7	1.91	155	.213	.244	29	.181	-1	42	47	10	**5.8**
1889 Phi-N	28	16	.636	47	43	37	2	0	380	390	10	121	153	12.2	3.24	134	.257	.315	32	.208	-3	33	47	2	4.3
1890 Phi-P	19	15	.559	36	33	28	0	1	283¹	312	8	126	89	14.1	3.81	112	.268	.343	41	.273	4	13	15	1	1.6
1891 Bos-a	29	9	**.763**	48	43	33	2	1	363²	303	8	120	158	**10.6**	2.55	137	.219	**.284**	34	.188	-0	47	38	6	3.6
1892 Bal-N	4	8	.333	13	13	9	0	0	97	130	4	30	16.6	4.92	70	.309	.381	15	.349	4	-18	-16	2	-1.1	
Total 11	233	152	.605	414	396	351	30	3	3404	3344	87	856	1700	11.2	2.96	114	.246	.292	543	.245	27	162	161	35	20.3
● **BOB BUHL** Buhl, Robert Ray b: 8/12/28, Saginaw, Mich. BR/TR, 6'2", 190 lbs. Deb: 4/17/53																									
1953 Mil-N	13	8	.619	30	18	8	3	0	154¹	133	9	73	83	12.2	2.97	132	.235	.326	6	.113	-3	23	16	1	1.8
1954 Mil-N	2	7	.222	31	14	2	1	3	110¹	117	6	65	57	15.0	4.00	93	.277	.376	1	.032	-3	1	-3	-0	-0.6
1955 Mil-N	13	11	.542	38	27	11	1	1	201²	168	13	109	117	12.4	3.21	117	.227	.327	6	.105	-4	18	12	-1	0.9
1956 Mil-N	18	8	.692	38	33	13	2	0	216²	190	19	105	86	12.3	3.32	104	.236	.326	7	.096	-4	11	3	0	0.0
1957 *Mil-N	18	7	**.720**	34	31	14	2	0	216²	191	15	121	117	13.0	2.74	128	.241	.341	6	.082	-3	27	18	-2	1.4
1958 Mil-N	5	2	.714	11	10	3	0	1	73	74	5	30	27	12.9	3.45	102	.260	.332	5	.200	-2	4	1	1	0.2
1959 Mil-N	15	9	.625	31	25	12	**4**	0	198	181	9	74	105	11.7	2.86	124	.243	.313	4	.057	-5	24	15	3	1.5
1960 Mil-N★	16	9	.640	36	33	11	2	0	238²	202	23	103	121	11.6	3.09	111	.229	.312	14	.157	-2	18	9	3	1.0
1961 Mil-N	9	10	.474	32	29	9	1	0	188¹	180	23	98	77	13.5	4.11	91	.256	.351	4	.067	-4	-2	-8	-1	-1.0
1962 Mil-N	0	1	.000	1	1	0	0	0	2	6	0	4	1	45.0	22.50	17	.545	.667	0	—	-0	-4	-4	-0	-1.1
Chi-N	12	13	.480	34	30	8	1	0	212	204	23	94	109	12.9	3.69	104	.255	.338	8	.000	-6	6	11	-2	0.4
Yr	12	14	.462	35	31	8	1	0	214	210	23	98	110	13.2	3.87	107	.259	.343	8	.000	-6	2	7	-2	-0.7
1963 Chi-N	11	14	.440	37	34	6	0	0	226	219	24	62	108	11.3	3.38	104	.259	.312	8	.108	-3	2	3	1	0.1
1964 Chi-N	15	14	.517	36	35	11	3	0	227²	208	22	68	107	11.1	3.83	97	.244	.303	7	.096	-2	-8	-3	2	-0.3
1965 Chi-N	13	11	.542	32	31	2	0	0	184¹	207	26	57	92	12.9	4.39	84	.284	.335	4	.060	-4	-17	-15	0	-2.2
1966 Chi-N	0	0	—	1	1	0	0	0	2¹	4	1	1	1	19.3	15.43	24	.400	.455	0	—	-3	-3	-3	0	0.0
Phi-N	6	8	.429	32	18	1	0	1	132	156	6	39	59	13.6	4.77	75	.298	.351	4	.098	-2	-17	-17	1	-1.8
Yr	6	8	.429	33	19	1	0	1	134¹	160	11	40	60	13.7	4.96	73	.299	.352	4	.095	-2	-20	-20	1	-1.8
1967 Phi-N	0	0	—	3	0	0	0	0	3	6	2	2	1	24.0	12.00	28	.462	.533	0	—	0	-3	-3	0	0.0
Total 15	166	132	.557	457	369	111	20	6	2587	2446	238	1105	1268	12.5	3.55	103	.251	.330	76	.089	-43	75	36	8	0.3
● **DE WAYNE BUICE** Buice, De Wayne Allison b: 8/20/57, Lynwood, Cal. BR/TR, 6', 170 lbs. Deb: 4/25/87																									
1987 Cal-A	6	7	.462	57	0	0	0	17	114	87	12	40	109	10.2	3.39	127	.213	.287	0	—	0	13	11	0	1.5
1988 Cal-A	2	4	.333	32	0	0	0	3	41¹	45	5	19	38	13.9	5.88	66	.287	.364	0	—	-9	-9	-9	0	-1.2
1989 Tor-A	1	0	1.000	7	0	0	0	0	17	13	2	13	10	13.8	5.82	65	.220	.361	0	—	-4	-4	-4	0	-0.2
Total 3	9	11	.450	96	0	0	0	20	172¹	145	19	72	157	11.4	4.23	98	.232	.314	0	—	0	1	-2	0	0.1
● **CY BUKER** Buker, Cyril Owen b: 2/5/19, Greenwood, Wis. BL/TR, 5'11", 190 lbs. Deb: 5/17/45																									
1945 Bro-N	7	2	.778	42	4	0	0	5	87¹	90	2	45	48	14.0	3.30	114	.268	.356	3	.188	-0	5	4	-1	0.4
● **JIM BULLINGER** Bullinger, James Eric b: 8/21/65, New Orleans, La. BR/TR, 6'2", 185 lbs. Deb: 5/27/92																									
1992 Chi-N	2	8	.200	39	9	1	0	7	85	72	9	54	36	13.8	4.66	77	.233	.354	5	.250	2	-11	-10	2	-0.8
1993 Chi-N	1	0	1.000	15	0	0	0	0	16²	18	1	9	10	14.6	4.32	92	.277	.365	0	.000	-0	-1	-1	-0	-0.1
1994 Chi-N	6	2	.750	33	10	1	0	2	100	87	6	34	72	11.0	3.60	115	.235	.300	3	.136	1	7	6	-1	0.4
1995 Chi-N	12	8	.600	24	24	1	1	0	150	152	14	65	93	13.6	4.14	99	.265	.349	6	.128	1	-1	-1	0	0.1
1996 Chi-N	6	10	.375	37	20	1	0	1	129¹	144	15	68	90	15.3	6.54	65	.283	.376	8	.250	6	-33	-33	1	-2.8
Total 5	27	28	.491	148	63	4	2	11	481	473	45	230	301	13.6	4.77	85	.259	.349	22	.180	9	-37	-38	3	-3.2
● **RED BULLOCK** Bullock, Malton Joseph b: 10/12/11, Biloxi, Miss. d: 6/27/88, Pascagoula, Miss. BL/TL, 6'1", 192 lbs. Deb: 5/19/36																									
1936 Phi-A	0	2	.000	12	2	0	0	0	16²	19	0	37	7	30.2	14.04	36	.271	.523	0	.000	-1	-17	-17	1	-1.5
● **MELVIN BUNCH** Bunch, Melvin Lynn b: 11/4/71, Texarkana, Tex. BR/TR, 6'1", 165 lbs. Deb: 5/6/95																									
1995 KC-A	1	3	.250	13	5	0	0	0	40	42	11	14	19	12.6	5.62	85	.261	.320	—	0	-4	-4	-1	-0.5	
● **WALLY BUNKER** Bunker, Wallace Edward b: 1/25/45, Seattle, Wash. BR/TR, 6'2", 197 lbs. Deb: 9/29/63																									
1963 Bal-A	0	1	.000	1	1	0	0	0	4	10	1	3	4	29.3	13.50	26	.476	.542	1	.500	0	-4	-4	-0	-0.7
1964 Bal-A	19	5	**.792**	29	29	12	6	1	214	161	17	62	96	9.5	2.69	133	.207	.269	5	.069	-2	22	21	1	2.2
1965 Bal-A	10	8	.556	34	27	4	1	2	189	170	16	58	84	11.0	3.38	103	.242	.303	4	.073	-1	2	2	-1	-0.1
1966 *Bal-A	10	6	.625	29	24	3	0	0	142²	151	14	48	84	12.7	4.29	78	.269	.329	5	.104	-1	-14	-15	-1	-1.7
1967 Bal-A	3	7	.300	29	9	1	0	1	88	83	7	31	51	11.9	4.09	77	.254	.322	2	.077	-2	-8	-9	1	-1.1
1968 Bal-A	2	0	1.000	18	10	2	1	0	71	54	4	14	44	9.4	2.41	121	.225	.267	2	.111	-0	5	4	-0	0.1
1969 KC-A	12	11	.522	35	31	10	1	2	222²	198	29	62	130	10.7	3.23	114	.238	.294	10	.143	0	10	11	3	1.5
1970 KC-A	2	11	.154	24	15	2	0	0	121²	109	16	50	59	11.8	4.22	89	.238	.313	2	.065	-0	-7	-6	-1	-0.8
1971 KC-A	2	3	.400	7	6	0	0	0	32¹	35	7	6	15	11.4	5.01	68	.271	.304	0	.000	-1	-6	-6	-0	-0.9
Total 9	60	52	.536	206	152	34	5	5	1085¹	976	113	334	569	11.0	3.51	99	.240	.300	31	.094	-5	-1	-1	3	-1.5
● **JIM BUNNING** Bunning, James Paul David b: 10/23/31, Southgate, Ky. BR/TR, 6'3", 195 lbs. Deb: 7/20/55 H																									
1955 Det-A	3	5	.375	15	6	3	0	1	51	59	6	32	37	16.6	6.35	60	.291	.395	3	.200	-0	-14	-14	0	-1.9
1956 Det-A	5	1	.833	15	3	0	0	1	53¹	55	6	28	34	14.0	3.71	111	.257	.343	6	.333	3	3	2	-1	0.4
1957 Det-A★	**20**	8	.714	45	30	14	1	1	267¹	214	33	72	182	10.0	2.69	143	.218	.279	20	.213	3	**33**	**35**	-5	3.3
1958 Det-A	14	12	.538	35	34	10	3	0	219²	188	29	79	177	11.3	3.52	115	.228	.304	14	.187	-1	6	12	-3	1.0
1959 Det-A★	17	13	.567	40	35	14	1	1	249²	220	37	75	**201**	11.0	3.89	104	.234	.298	17	.191	-1	-1	-5	-0	0.1
1960 Det-A★	11	14	.440	36	34	10	3	0	252	217	20	64	**201**	10.4	2.79	**142**	.236	.293	13	.160	-2	**30**	33	-1	2.6
1961 Det-A★	17	11	.607	38	37	12	4	1	268	232	25	71	194	10.5	3.19	128	.229	.285	13	.130	-4	25	27	-2	2.0
1962 Det-A★	19	10	.655	41	35	12	2	6	258	262	28	74	184	12.1	3.59	113	.261	.320	23	.242	4	11	14	-5	1.4
1963 Det-A	12	13	.480	39	35	6	2	1	248¹	245	38	69	196	11.6	3.88	97	.254	.307	13	.155	-9	-7	-4	-2	-0.6
1964 Phi-N★	19	8	.704	41	39	13	5	2	284¹	248	23	46	219	9.7	2.63	132	.233	.274	12	.121	-2	29	27	-4	1.8
1965 Phi-N	19	9	.679	39	39	15	7	0	291	253	23	62	268	10.1	2.60	133	.232	.281	22	.214	4	30	28	0	3.1
1966 Phi-N★	19	14	.576	43	41	16	**5**	1	314	260	26	55	252	9.2	2.41	149	.223	.270	19	.179	1	42	41	3	4.1
1967 Phi-N	17	15	.531	40	40	16	**6**	0	302¹	241	36	73	**253**	9.7	2.29	149	.217	.273	17	.163	2	**36**	**38**	-3	4.1
1968 Pit-N	4	14	.222	27	24	3	1	0	160	168	14	48	95	12.6	3.88	75	.272	.333	5	.098	-2	-16	-19	-2	-2.3
1969 Pit-N	10	9	.526	25	25	4	1	0	156	147	10	49	124	11.7	3.81	99	.249	.313	2	.043	-3	-4	-6	-1	-1.3
LA-N	3	1	.750	9	9	1	0	0	56¹	65	5	10	33	12.1	3.36	99	.288	.321	2	.111	-1	0	-1	0	-0.2

YEAR	TM/L	W	L	PCT	G	GS	CG	SH	SV	IP	H	HR	BB	SO	RAT	ERA	ERA+	OAV	OOB	BH	AVG	PB	PR	/A	PD	TPI
	Yr	13	10	.565	34	34	5	0	0	212¹	212	15	59	157	11.5	3.69	93	.257	.307	4	.062	-4	-2	-6	-4	-1.5
1970	Phi-N	10	15	.400	34	33	4	0	0	219	233	19	56	147	12.2	4.11	97	.274	.325	9	.127	-2	-2	-3	-1	-0.6
1971	Phi-N	5	12	.294	29	16	1	0	1	110	126	11	37	58	13.8	5.48	64	.297	.362	3	.120	-0	-25	-24	-0	-3.4
Total	17	224	184	.549	591	519	151	40	16	3760¹	3433	372	1000	2855	11.0	3.27	114	.242	.299	213	.167	-1	179	192	-41	13.6

● DAVE BURBA
Burba, David Allen b: 7/7/66, Dayton, Ohio BR/TR, 6'4", 220 lbs. Deb: 9/8/90

YEAR	TM/L	W	L	PCT	G	GS	CG	SH	SV	IP	H	HR	BB	SO	RAT	ERA	ERA+	OAV	OOB	BH	AVG	PB	PR	/A	PD	TPI
1990	Sea-A	0	0	—	6	0	0	0	0	8	8	0	2	4	12.4	4.50	88	.267	.333		0	-1	-0	0	0.0	
1991	Sea-A	2	2	.500	22	2	0	0	1	36²	34	6	14	16	11.8	3.68	112	.245	.314	0	—	0	2	2	-0	0.1
1992	SF-N	2	7	.222	23	11	0	0	0	70²	80	4	31	47	14.4	4.97	67	.287	.362	1	.067	-1	-11	-13	-1	-1.7
1993	SF-N	10	3	.769	54	5	0	0	0	95¹	95	14	37	88	12.7	4.25	92	.265	.338	5	.294	2	-2	-4	-0	-0.3
1994	SF-N	3	6	.333	57	0	0	0	0	74	59	5	45	84	13.4	4.38	91	.221	.346	0	.000	-0	-1	-3	-1	-0.4
1995	SF-N	4	2	.667	37	0	0	0	0	43¹	38	5	25	46	13.1	4.98	82	.235	.337	0	—	0	-4	-4	-0	-0.6
	*Cin-N	6	2	.750	15	9	1	1	0	63¹	52	4	26	50	11.1	3.27	126	.223	.301	1	.067	-0	6	6	-1	0.6
	Yr	10	4	.714	52	9	1	1	0	106²	90	9	51	96	11.9	3.97	103	.227	.315	1	.067	-0	3	2	-1	0.0
1996	Cin-N	11	13	.458	34	33	0	0	0	195	179	18	97	148	12.8	3.83	108	.244	.334	7	.104	-1	8	7	-2	0.5
Total	7	38	35	.521	248	60	1	1	1	586¹	545	56	277	483	12.8	4.13	96	.248	.335	14	.120		-3	-10	-5	-1.8

● BILL BURBACH
Burbach, William David b: 8/22/47, Dickeyville, Wis. BR/TR, 6'4", 215 lbs. Deb: 4/11/69

YEAR	TM/L	W	L	PCT	G	GS	CG	SH	SV	IP	H	HR	BB	SO	RAT	ERA	ERA+	OAV	OOB	BH	AVG	PB	PR	/A	PD	TPI
1969	NY-A	6	8	.429	31	24	2	1	0	140²	112	15	102	82	13.8	3.65	95	.219	.351	4	.100	-1	-0	-3	-1	-0.4
1970	NY-A	0	2	.000	4	4	0	0	0	16²	23	2	9	10	17.8	10.26	34	.324	.407	0	.000	-1	-12	-12	-0	-1.2
1971	NY-A	0	1	.000	2	0	0	0	0	3¹	6	0	5	3	29.7	10.80	30	.400	.550	0	.000	-0	-3	-3	-0	-0.7
Total	3	6	11	.353	37	28	2	1	0	160²	141	17	116	95	14.6	4.48	78	.236	.363	4	.085	-2	-15	-18	-1	-2.3

● LARRY BURCHART
Burchart, Larry Wayne b: 2/8/46, Tulsa, Okla. BR/TR, 6'3", 205 lbs. Deb: 4/10/69

YEAR	TM/L	W	L	PCT	G	GS	CG	SH	SV	IP	H	HR	BB	SO	RAT	ERA	ERA+	OAV	OOB	BH	AVG	PB	PR	/A	PD	TPI
1969	Cle-A	0	2	.000	29	0	0	0	0	42¹	42	7	24	26	14.2	4.25	89	.266	.366	0	—	0	-3	-2	-1	-0.2

● FRED BURCHELL
Burchell, Frederick Duff b: 7/14/1879, Perth Amboy, N.J. d: 11/20/51, Jordan, N.Y. BR/TL, 5'11", 190 lbs. Deb: 4/17/03

YEAR	TM/L	W	L	PCT	G	GS	CG	SH	SV	IP	H	HR	BB	SO	RAT	ERA	ERA+	OAV	OOB	BH	AVG	PB	PR	/A	PD	TPI
1903	Phi-N	0	3	.000	6	3	2	0	0	44	48	0	14	12	13.1	2.86	114	.293	.356	3	.188	-1	2	2	-0	0.0
1907	Bos-A	0	1	.000	2	1	0	0	0	10	8	0	2	6	9.9	2.70	95	.222	.282	1	.200	-0	-0	-0	-0	0.0
1908	Bos-A	10	8	.556	31	19	9	0	0	179²	161	2	65	94	11.9	2.96	83	.247	.326	17	.246	1	-11	-10	-2	-1.1
1909	Bos-A	3	3	.500	10	5	1	0	0	52	51	1	11	12	11.1	2.94	85	.271	.318	3	.158	-0	-3	-3	1	-0.3
Total	4	13	15	.464	49	28	12	0	0	285²	268	3	92	124	11.8	2.93	89	.258	.328	24	.220	-0	-12	-10	-2	-1.4

● FREDDIE BURDETTE
Burdette, Freddie Thomason b: 9/15/36, Moultrie, Ga. BR/TR, 6'1", 170 lbs. Deb: 9/5/62

YEAR	TM/L	W	L	PCT	G	GS	CG	SH	SV	IP	H	HR	BB	SO	RAT	ERA	ERA+	OAV	OOB	BH	AVG	PB	PR	/A	PD	TPI
1962	Chi-N	0	0	—	8	0	0	0	1	9²	5	2	8	5	12.1	3.72	111	.161	.333	0	—	0	0	-0	0	0.0
1963	Chi-N	0	0	—	4	0	0	0	0	4²	5	1	2	1	13.5	3.86	91	.313	.389	0	—	0	-0	-0	0	0.0
1964	Chi-N	1	0	1.000	18	0	0	0	0	20	17	2	10	4	12.6	3.15	118	.243	.346	1	1.000	-0	1	-1	-0	0.1
Total	3	1	0	1.000	30	0	0	0	1	34¹	27	5	20	10	12.6	3.41	112	.231	.348	1	.500	-0	1	-0	0	0.1

● LEW BURDETTE
Burdette, Selva Lewis b: 11/22/26, Nitro, W.Va. BR/TR, 6'2", 190 lbs. Deb: 9/26/50 C

YEAR	TM/L	W	L	PCT	G	GS	CG	SH	SV	IP	H	HR	BB	SO	RAT	ERA	ERA+	OAV	OOB	BH	AVG	PB	PR	/A	PD	TPI
1950	NY-A	0	0	—	2	0	0	0	0	1¹	3	0	0	0	20.3	6.75	64	.500	.500		0	-0	-0	0	0.0	
1951	Bos-N	0	0	—	3	0	0	0	0	4¹	6	0	5	1	24.9	6.23	59	.375	.545	0	.000	-0	-1	-1	0	0.0
1952	Bos-N	6	11	.353	45	9	5	0	7	137	138	8	47	47	12.3	3.61	100	.265	.328	4	.114	-0	2	-0	1	0.0
1953	Mil-N	15	5	.750	46	13	6	1	8	175	177	7	56	58	12.2	3.24	121	.264	.326	9	.170	-1	20	13	2	1.5
1954	Mil-N	15	14	.517	38	32	13	4	0	238	224	17	62	79	11.0	2.76	135	.251	.302	7	.089	-5	35	26	1	2.5
1955	Mil-N	13	8	.619	42	33	11	2	0	230	253	19	73	70	13.0	4.03	93	.280	.337	20	.233	1	0	-7	2	-0.1
1956	Mil-N	19	10	.655	39	35	16	**6**	1	256¹	234	22	52	110	10.1	**2.70**	128	.241	.282	16	.186	1	30	22	1	2.6
1957	*Mil-N★	17	9	.654	37	33	14	1	0	256²	260	25	59	78	11.3	3.72	94	.264	.307	13	.148	1	5	-6	2	-0.3
1958	*Mil-N★	20	10	**.667**	40	36	19	3	0	275¹	279	18	50	113	10.9	2.91	121	.264	.301	24	.242	9	**32**	19	3	3.1
1959	Mil-N★	**21**	9	.583	41	39	20	**4**	1	289²	312	38	38	105	10.9	4.07	87	.273	.297	21	.202	6	-4	-17	0	-1.3
1960	Mil-N	19	13	.594	45	32	**18**	4	4	275²	277	19	35	83	10.3	3.36	102	.260	.287	16	.176	5	12	2	5	1.2
1961	Mil-N	18	11	.621	40	36	14	3	0	**272**	295	31	33	92	10.9	4.00	94	.273	.296	21	.204	5	1	-8	2	0.0
1962	Mil-N	10	9	.526	37	19	6	1	2	143²	172	26	23	59	12.3	4.89	78	.298	.327	9	.176	-0	-15	-17	1	-1.9
1963	Mil-N	6	5	.545	15	13	4	1	0	84	71	15	24	28	10.3	3.64	88	.228	.285	1	.038	-0	-3	-4	-0	-0.6
	StL-N	3	8	.273	21	14	3	0	2	98	106	6	16	45	11.8	3.77	94	.278	.319	3	.097	-1	-5	-2	-2	-0.5
	Yr	9	13	.409	36	27	7	1	2	182	177	21	40	73	11.1	3.71	92	.255	.302	4	.070	-2	-9	-6	-2	-1.1
1964	StL-N	1	0	1.000	8	0	0	0	0	10	10	1	3	3	11.7	1.80	211	.256	.310	0	.000	-0	2	0	-0	0.2
	Chi-N	9	9	.500	28	17	8	2	0	131	152	15	19	40	11.4	4.88	76	.292	.319	12	.279	6	-20	-17	-2	-1.4
	Yr	10	9	.526	36	17	8	2	0	141	162	16	22	43	11.8	4.66	80	.289	.317	12	.273	6	-18	-15	-2	-1.1
1965	Chi-N	0	2	.000	7	3	0	0	0	20¹	26	3	4	5	13.7	5.31	69	.299	.337	2	.333	1	-4	-4	-0	-0.2
	Phi-N	3	3	.500	19	9	1	1	0	70²	95	5	17	23	14.9	5.48	63	.329	.376	6	.300	1	-15	-16	-1	-1.1
	Yr	3	5	.375	26	12	1	1	0	91	121	8	21	28	14.5	5.44	65	.321	.365	8	.308	2	-19	-20	-1	-1.3
1966	Cal-A	7	2	.778	54	0	0	0	5	79²	80	4	12	27	10.5	3.39	99	.268	.298	1	.125	0	-0	-1	-0	-0.1
1967	Cal-A	1	0	1.000	19	0	0	0	1	18¹	16	4	0	8	8.3	4.91	64	.232	.243	0	—	0	-3	-4	-0	-0.2
Total	18	203	144	.585	626	373	158	33	31	3067¹	3186	289	628	1074	11.4	3.66	99	.268	.308	185	.183	30	68	-8	19	3.4

● BILL BURDICK
Burdick, William Byron b: 10/11/1859, Austin, Minn. d: 10/23/49, Spokane, Wash. BR/TR, Deb: 7/23/1888

YEAR	TM/L	W	L	PCT	G	GS	CG	SH	SV	IP	H	HR	BB	SO	RAT	ERA	ERA+	OAV	OOB	BH	AVG	PB	PR	/A	PD	TPI
1888	Ind-N	10	10	.500	20	20	20	0	0	176	168	12	43	55	11.1	2.81	105	.242	.292	10	.147	-2	1	3	-0	0.0
1889	Ind-N	2	4	.333	10	4	2	0	1	45²	58	7	13	16	14.0	4.53	92	.301	.345	2	.118	-0	-3	-2	-0	-0.2
Total	2	12	14	.462	30	24	22	0	1	221²	226	19	56	71	11.7	3.17	101	.255	.304	12	.141	-3	-2	1	-0	-0.2

● TOM BURGMEIER
Burgmeier, Thomas Henry b: 8/2/43, St.Paul, Minn. BL/TL, 5'11", 185 lbs. Deb: 4/10/68 C

YEAR	TM/L	W	L	PCT	G	GS	CG	SH	SV	IP	H	HR	BB	SO	RAT	ERA	ERA+	OAV	OOB	BH	AVG	PB	PR	/A	PD	TPI
1968	Cal-A	1	4	.200	56	2	0	0	5	72²	66	5	24	33	11.0	4.33	67	.250	.313	0	.000	0	-11	-12	4	-0.6
1969	KC-A	3	1	.750	31	0	0	0	1	54	67	5	21	23	14.8	4.17	88	.316	.380	3	.167	-0	-3	-3	2	-0.3
1970	KC-A	6	6	.500	41	0	0	0	1	68¹	59	3	43	43	10.8	3.16	118	.236	.300	2	.143	-0	4	4	2	0.9
1971	KC-A	9	7	.563	67	0	0	0	17	88¹	71	3	30	44	11.0	1.73	198	.223	.303	5	.250	2	17	17	3	4.4
1972	KC-A	6	2	.750	51	0	0	0	9	55¹	67	0	33	18	16.4	4.23	72	.313	.407	4	.333	1	-7	-7	1	-1.2
1973	KC-A	0	0	—	6	0	0	0	0	10	13	2	4	4	16.2	5.40	76	.310	.383	0	—	0	-2	-1	-0	-0.4
1974	Min-A	5	3	.625	50	0	0	0	4	91²	92	7	26	34	11.8	4.52	83	.270	.325	0	—	0	-9	-8	3	-0.6
1975	Min-A	5	8	.385	46	0	0	0	11	75²	76	7	23	41	11.9	3.09	124	.264	.321	0	—	0	6	6	0	1.2
1976	Min-A	8	1	.889	57	0	0	0	1	115¹	95	11	29	45	9.8	2.50	143	.226	.279	0	—	0	13	14	2	1.2
1977	Min-A	6	4	.600	61	0	0	0	0	97¹	113	15	33	35	13.7	5.09	78	.299	.358	0	—	0	-11	-12	1	-1.1
1978	Bos-A	2	1	.667	35	1	0	0	0	61¹	74	7	23	24	14.7	4.40	93	.302	.369	0	—	0	-4	-2	1	-0.2
1979	Bos-A	3	2	.600	44	0	0	0	2	88²	91	6	16	60	11.1	2.74	161	.263	.304	0	—	0	15	16	1	0.6
1980	Bos-A☆	5	4	.556	62	0	0	0	24	99	87	3	20	54	9.9	2.00	211	.241	.285	0	—	0	22	24	3	3.7
1981	Bos-A	4	5	.444	32	0	0	0	6	59²	61	5	17	14	12.4	2.87	135	.268	.329	0	—	0	5	7	1	1.0
1982	Bos-A	7	0	1.000	40	0	0	0	2	102¹	98	6	22	44	10.7	2.29	188	.259	.303	0	—	0	20	23	2	1.4
1983	Oak-A	6	7	.462	49	0	0	0	0	96	89	2	32	39	11.3	2.81	137	.244	.305	0	—	0	13	11	2	1.7
1984	Oak-A	3	0	1.000	17	0	0	0	2	23	15	2	8	8	9.0	2.35	159	.190	.264	0	—	0	4	4	0	0.8
Total	17	79	55	.590	745	3	0	0	102	1258²	1231	94	384	584	11.8	3.23	118	.261	.321	14	.212	2	72	81	27	12.8

● ENRIQUE BURGOS
Burgos, Enrique (Calles) b: 10/7/65, Chorrera, Panama BL/TL, 6'4", 195 lbs. Deb: 7/15/93

YEAR	TM/L	W	L	PCT	G	GS	CG	SH	SV	IP	H	HR	BB	SO	RAT	ERA	ERA+	OAV	OOB	BH	AVG	PB	PR	/A	PD	TPI
1993	KC-A	0	1	.000	5	0	0	0	0	5	5	0	6	12	21.6	9.00	51	.238	.429	0	—	0	-3	-2	-0	-0.8
1995	SF-N	0	0	—	5	0	0	0	0	8¹	14	1	6	6	22.7	8.64	47	.378	.477	0	—	0	-4	-4	-0	-0.1
Total	2	0	1	.000	10	0	0	0	0	13¹	19	1	12	18	22.3	8.78	49	.328	.458	0	—	0	-7	-7	-0	-0.8

● SANDY BURK
Burk, Charles Sanford b: 4/22/1887, Columbus, Ohio d: 10/11/34, Brooklyn, N.Y. BR/TR, 5'8", 155 lbs. Deb: 9/12/10

YEAR	TM/L	W	L	PCT	G	GS	CG	SH	SV	IP	H	HR	BB	SO	RAT	ERA	ERA+	OAV	OOB	BH	AVG	PB	PR	/A	PD	TPI
1910	Bro-N	0	3	.000	4	3	1	0	0	19¹	17	0	27	14	21.4	6.05	50	.258	.484		-6	-6	-0	-0.9	
1911	Bro-N	1	3	.250	13	7	1	0	0	58	54	1	47	15	16.1	5.12	65	.261	.405	2	.105	-1	-11	-12	-0	-1.6
1912	Bro-N	0	0	—	2	0	0	0	0	8¹	9	0	3	2	13.0	3.24	103	.273	.333	1	.250	0	1	0	0	0.0
	StL-N	1	3	.250	12	4	2	0	1	44²	37	0	12	17	10.1	2.42	142	.236	.294	0	.000	-2	5	5	-1	0.2
	Yr	1	3	.250	14	4	2	0	1	53	46	0	15	19	10.5	2.55	134	.242	.301	1	.067	-1	5	5	-1	0.2

YEAR	TM/L	W	L	PCT	G	GS	CG	SH	SV	IP	H	HR	BB	SO	RAT	ERA	ERA⁺	OAV	OOB	BH	AVG	PB	PR	/A	PD	TPI
1913	StL-N	0	2	.000	19	5	0	0	1	70	81	1	33	29	15.4	5.14	63	.290	.377	2	.091	-2	-15	-15	-0	-0.6
1915	Pit-F	2	0	1.000	2	2	1	0	0	18	8	0	11	9	9.5	1.00	271	.140	.279	1	.167	-0	3	3	-1	0.3
Total	5	4	11	.267	52	21	5	0	2	218¹	206	2	133	86	14.5	4.25	76	.258	.372	6	.090	-6	-24	-24	-2	-1.8

● **ELMER BURKART**   Burkart, Elmer Robert "Swede"   b: 2/1/17, Torresdale, Pa.   d: 2/6/95, Baltimore, Md.   BR/TR, 6'2", 190 lbs.   Deb: 9/14/36

YEAR	TM/L	W	L	PCT	G	GS	CG	SH	SV	IP	H	HR	BB	SO	RAT	ERA	ERA⁺	OAV	OOB	BH	AVG	PB	PR	/A	PD	TPI
1936	Phi-N	0	0	—	2	2	0	0	0	7²	4	0	12	2	18.8	3.52	129	.160	.432	0	.000	-0	0	1	0	0.0
1937	Phi-N	0	0	—	7	0	0	0	0	16	20	0	9	4	16.3	6.19	70	.323	.408	0	.000	-1	-4	-3	0	-0.1
1938	Phi-N	0	1	.000	2	1	1	0	0	10	12	0	3	1	14.4	4.50	86	.286	.348	0	.000	-0	-1	-1	-0	-0.1
1939	Phi-N	1	0	1.000	5	0	0	0	0	8¹	11	0	2	2	14.0	4.32	93	.344	.382	1	1.000	1	-0	-0	0	0.0
Total	4	1	1	.500	16	3	1	0	0	42	47	0	26	9	15.9	4.93	85	.292	.394	1	.083	-1	-5	-3	-0	-0.2

● **JAMES BURKE**   Burke, James   b: Attleboro, Mass.   Deb: 6/10/1882

YEAR	TM/L	W	L	PCT	G	GS	CG	SH	SV	IP	H	HR	BB	SO	RAT	ERA	ERA⁺	OAV	OOB	BH	AVG	PB	PR	/A	PD	TPI
1882	Buf-N	0	1	.000	1	1	0	0	0	4	10	0	0	0	22.5	11.25	26	.435	.435	0	.000	-1	-4	-4	1	-0.6
1883	Buf-N	0	0	—	1	1	0	0	0	8	9	0	3	1	13.5	5.63	56	.243	.300	1	.200	-0	-2	-2	0	-0.0
1884	Bos-U	19	15	.559	38	36	34	0	0	322	326	10	31	255	10.0	2.85	84	.245	.263	41	.223	-7	-15	-17	-4	-2.3
Total	3	19	16	.543	40	38	34	0	0	334	345	10	34	256	10.2	3.02	80	.249	.267	42	.218	-8	-21	-23	-4	-2.9

● **JOHN BURKE**   Burke, John C.   b: 2/9/70, Durango, Colo.   BB/TR, 6'4", 220 lbs.   Deb: 8/13/96

YEAR	TM/L	W	L	PCT	G	GS	CG	SH	SV	IP	H	HR	BB	SO	RAT	ERA	ERA⁺	OAV	OOB	BH	AVG	PB	PR	/A	PD	TPI
1996	Col-N	2	1	.667	11	0	0	0	0	15²	21	3	7	19	16.7	7.47	73	.318	.392	1	.500	0	-6	-4	0	-0.6

● **JOHN BURKE**   Burke, John Patrick   b: 1/27/1877, Hazleton, Pa.   d: 8/4/50, Jersey City, N.J.   BR/TR,   Deb: 6/27/02 ♦

YEAR	TM/L	W	L	PCT	G	GS	CG	SH	SV	IP	H	HR	BB	SO	RAT	ERA	ERA⁺	OAV	OOB	BH	AVG	PB	PR	/A	PD	TPI
1902	NY-N	0	1	.000	2	1	0	0	0	14	21	0	3	5	15.4	5.79	48	.344	.375	2	.154	-0	-5	-5	0	-0.3

● **BOBBY BURKE**   Burke, Robert James "Lefty"   b: 1/23/07, Joliet, Ill.   d: 2/8/71, Joliet, Ill.   BL/TL, 6'0.5", 150 lbs.   Deb: 4/16/27

YEAR	TM/L	W	L	PCT	G	GS	CG	SH	SV	IP	H	HR	BB	SO	RAT	ERA	ERA⁺	OAV	OOB	BH	AVG	PB	PR	/A	PD	TPI
1927	Was-A	3	2	.600	36	6	1	0	1	100	91	6	32	20	11.7	3.96	103	.245	.316	3	.125	-2	2	1	0	-0.2
1928	Was-A	2	4	.333	26	7	2	1	0	85¹	87	1	18	27	11.3	3.90	103	.277	.320	5	.250	1	1	1	0	0.2
1929	Was-A	6	8	.429	37	17	4	0	0	141	154	6	55	51	13.6	4.79	89	.279	.349	6	.140	-3	-8	-9	-2	-1.2
1930	Was-A	3	4	.429	24	4	2	0	3	74¹	62	2	29	35	11.4	3.63	127	.229	.310	4	.174	-1	8	8	-1	0.5
1931	Was-A	8	3	.727	30	13	3	1	2	128²	124	6	50	38	12.3	4.27	101	.255	.327	10	.213	-0	2	0	0	0.0
1932	Was-A	3	6	.333	22	10	2	0	0	91	94	4	44	32	14.1	5.14	84	.272	.353	5	.200	0	-7	-8	-1	-0.8
1933	Was-A	4	3	.571	25	6	4	1	0	64	64	4	31	28	13.6	3.23	129	.256	.343	4	.235	0	7	7	0	0.7
1934	Was-A	8	8	.500	37	15	7	1	0	168	155	2	72	52	12.2	3.21	134	.245	.323	13	.228	1	24	21	0	1.9
1935	Was-A	1	8	.111	15	10	2	0	0	66¹	90	7	27	16	16.1	7.46	58	.327	.391	4	.182	-0	-22	-23	1	-2.4
1937	Phi-N	0	0	—	2	0	0	0	0	0	1	0	2	0	—	∞	—	.500	.750	0	—	-0	-1	-1	0	-0.1
Total	10	38	46	.452	254	88	27	4	5	918²	926	35	360	299	12.8	4.29	99	.263	.336	54	.194	-3	6	-3	-3	-1.4

● **STEVE BURKE**   Burke, Steven Michael   b: 3/5/55, Stockton, Cal.   BB/TR, 6'2", 200 lbs.   Deb: 9/10/77

YEAR	TM/L	W	L	PCT	G	GS	CG	SH	SV	IP	H	HR	BB	SO	RAT	ERA	ERA⁺	OAV	OOB	BH	AVG	PB	PR	/A	PD	TPI
1977	Sea-A	0	1	.000	6	0	0	0	0	15²	12	0	7	6	10.9	2.87	143	.226	.317	0	—	0	2	2	0	0.2
1978	Sea-A	0	1	.000	18	0	0	0	0	49	46	2	24	16	13.0	3.49	109	.258	.350	0	—	0	1	2	0	0.1
Total	2	0	2	.000	24	0	0	0	0	64²	58	2	31	22	12.5	3.34	116	.251	.342	0	—	0	4	4	0	0.3

● **TIM BURKE**   Burke, Timothy Philip   b: 2/19/59, Omaha, Neb.   BR/TR, 6'3", 205 lbs.   Deb: 4/8/85

YEAR	TM/L	W	L	PCT	G	GS	CG	SH	SV	IP	H	HR	BB	SO	RAT	ERA	ERA⁺	OAV	OOB	BH	AVG	PB	PR	/A	PD	TPI
1985	Mon-N	9	4	.692	**78**	0	0	0	8	120¹	86	9	44	87	10.2	2.39	142	.204	.290	1	.100	-0	**16**	13	1	1.6
1986	Mon-N	9	7	.563	68	2	0	0	4	101¹	103	7	46	82	13.6	2.93	126	.262	.345	0	.000	-0	9	9	1	1.4
1987	Mon-N	7	0	1.000	55	0	0	0	18	91	64	3	17	58	8.0	1.19	354	.196	.235	0	.000	-1	29	**30**	1	3.2
1988	Mon-N	3	5	.375	61	0	0	0	18	82	84	7	25	42	12.3	3.40	106	.272	.332	0	.000	-0	2	2	0	0.3
1989	Mon-N★	9	3	.750	68	0	0	0	28	84²	68	6	22	54	9.6	2.55	138	.225	.278	0	.000	-0	9	9	1	1.9
1990	Mon-N	3	3	.500	58	0	0	0	20	75	71	6	21	47	11.3	2.52	145	.247	.303	1	.167	-0	11	9	2	1.4
1991	Mon-N	3	4	.429	37	0	0	0	5	46	41	3	14	25	11.5	4.11	88	.243	.316	0	.000	-0	-2	-3	0	-0.4
	NY-N	3	3	.500	35	0	0	0	1	55²	55	5	12	34	10.8	2.75	132	.255	.294	0	.000	-0	6	6	1	0.6
	Yr	6	7	.462	72	0	0	0	6	101²	96	8	26	59	10.8	3.36	108	.246	.293	0	.000	-1	4	3	1	0.2
1992	NY-N	1	2	.333	15	0	0	0	0	15²	26	1	3	7	16.7	5.74	60	.366	.392	0	—	0	-4	-4	0	-0.7
	NY-A	2	2	.500	23	0	0	0	0	27²	26	2	15	8	13.3	3.25	120	.250	.350	0	—	0	2	2	1	0.4
Total	8	49	33	.598	498	2	0	0	102	699¹	624	49	219	444	11.1	2.72	135	.240	.304	2	.045	-2	76	74	7	9.7

● **BILLY BURKE**   Burke, William Ignatius   b: 7/11/1889, Clinton, Mass.   d: 2/9/67, Worcester, Mass.   BL/TL, 5'10", 165 lbs.   Deb: 4/30/10

YEAR	TM/L	W	L	PCT	G	GS	CG	SH	SV	IP	H	HR	BB	SO	RAT	ERA	ERA⁺	OAV	OOB	BH	AVG	PB	PR	/A	PD	TPI
1910	Bos-N	1	0	1.000	19	1	1	0	0	64	68	1	29	22	13.9	4.08	82	.302	.387	4	.190	-1	-7	-5	-1	-0.2
1911	Bos-N	0	1	.000	2	1	0	0	0	3¹	6	0	5	1	29.7	18.90	20	.429	.579	1	1.000	0	-6	-6	-0	-1.1
Total	2	1	1	.500	21	2	1	0	0	67¹	74	1	34	23	14.7	4.81	78	.310	.400	5	.227	-1	-13	-11	-2	-1.3

● **BILL BURKE**   Burke, William R.   b: 11/1865, Cincinnati, Ohio   d: 3/17/39, Atchison, Kan.   6', 200 lbs.   Deb: 7/20/1887

YEAR	TM/L	W	L	PCT	G	GS	CG	SH	SV	IP	H	HR	BB	SO	RAT	ERA	ERA⁺	OAV	OOB	BH	AVG	PB	PR	/A	PD	TPI
1887	Det-N	0	1	.000	2	2	1	0	0	15	21	0	5	3	16.8	6.00	67	.318	.384	2	.250	-0	-3	-3	-0	-0.2

● **JESSE BURKETT**   Burkett, Jesse Cail "Crab"   b: 12/4/1868, Wheeling, W.Va.   d: 5/27/53, Worcester, Mass.   BL/TL, 5'8", 155 lbs.   Deb: 4/22/1890   CH♦

YEAR	TM/L	W	L	PCT	G	GS	CG	SH	SV	IP	H	HR	BB	SO	RAT	ERA	ERA⁺	OAV	OOB	BH	AVG	PB	PR	/A	PD	TPI
1890	NY-N	3	10	.231	21	14	6	0	0	118	134	3	92	82	18.3	5.57	63	.277	.407	124	.309	8	-26	-27	2	-1.7
1894	Cle-N	0	0	—	1	0	0	0	0	4	6	0	1	0	15.8	4.50	121	.333	.368	187	.358	0	0	0	0	0.0
1902	StL-A	0	1	.000	1	0	0	0	0	1	4	0	1	2	45.0	9.00	39	.571	.625	169	.306	1	-1	-1	0	-0.4
Total	3	3	11	.214	23	14	6	0	0	123	144	3	94	84	18.4	5.56	64	.283	.408	2850	.338	9	-26	-27	2	-2.1

● **JOHN BURKETT**   Burkett, John David   b: 11/28/64, New Brighton, Pa.   BR/TR, 6'2", 205 lbs.   Deb: 9/15/87

YEAR	TM/L	W	L	PCT	G	GS	CG	SH	SV	IP	H	HR	BB	SO	RAT	ERA	ERA⁺	OAV	OOB	BH	AVG	PB	PR	/A	PD	TPI
1987	SF-N	0	0	—	3	0	0	0	0	6	7	2	3	5	16.5	4.50	85	.304	.407	0	.000	-0	-0	-0	0	0.0
1990	SF-N	14	7	.667	33	32	2	0	1	204	201	18	61	118	11.7	3.79	96	.257	.314	3	.048	-3	-0	-3	-1	-0.7
1991	SF-N	12	11	.522	36	34	3	1	0	206²	223	19	60	131	12.8	4.18	86	.277	.335	5	.091	-1	-11	-14	-1	-1.6
1992	SF-N	13	9	.591	32	32	3	1	0	189²	194	13	45	107	11.5	3.84	86	.264	.310	1	.018	-3	-7	-11	-3	-1.8
1993	SF-N★	**22**	7	.759	34	34	2	1	0	231²	224	18	40	145	10.7	3.65	107	.255	.296	9	.118	-1	10	7	1	0.8
1994	SF-N	6	8	.429	25	25	0	0	0	159¹	176	14	36	85	12.4	3.62	111	.286	.332	3	.059	-4	11	7	0	0.2
1995	Fla-N	14	14	.500	30	30	4	1	0	188¹	208	22	57	126	13.0	4.30	98	.282	.339	7	.106	-2	-3	-2	0	-0.4
1996	Fla-N	6	10	.375	24	24	1	0	0	154	154	15	42	108	11.6	4.32	94	.263	.316	9	.173	-2	-5	-0	-0	-0.4
	*Tex-A	5	2	.714	10	10	1	1	0	68²	75	4	16	47	12.2	4.06	131	.280	.325	0	—	0	7	10	-1	0.2
Total	8	92	68	.575	227	221	16	4	1	1408¹	1462	125	360	872	12.0	3.96	98	.269	.320	37	.088	-15	4	-14	-3	-3.7

● **KEN BURKHART**   Burkhart, Kenneth William (b: Kenneth William Burkhardt)   b: 11/18/16, Knoxville, Tenn.   BR/TR, 6'1", 190 lbs.   Deb: 4/21/45   U

YEAR	TM/L	W	L	PCT	G	GS	CG	SH	SV	IP	H	HR	BB	SO	RAT	ERA	ERA⁺	OAV	OOB	BH	AVG	PB	PR	/A	PD	TPI
1945	StL-N	18	8	.692	42	22	12	4	2	217¹	206	9	66	67	11.4	2.90	129	.251	.309	13	.181	1	22	20	-1	2.2
1946	StL-N	6	3	.667	25	13	5	2	2	100	111	4	36	32	13.4	2.88	120	.282	.346	5	.147	-0	6	6	-2	0.4
1947	StL-N	3	6	.333	34	6	1	0	1	95	108	7	23	44	12.8	5.21	79	.292	.340	3	.125	-1	-12	-11	1	-1.0
1948	StL-N	0	0	—	20	0	0	0	0	37¹	50	4	14	16	15.9	5.54	74	.331	.395	1	.250	-0	-7	-6	1	-0.0
	Cin-N	0	3	.000	16	0	0	0	1	41²	42	3	16	14	12.7	6.91	57	.255	.324	3	.333	-2	-14	-14	-0	-0.7
	Yr	0	3	.000	36	0	0	0	1	79	92	7	30	30	14.0	6.27	64	.289	.352	4	.308	-2	-20	-20	0	-0.7
1949	Cin-N	0	0	—	11	0	0	0	0	28¹	29	2	10	8	13.2	3.18	132	.282	.345	2	.286	0	3	3	0	0.1
Total	5	27	20	.574	148	41	18	6	7	519²	546	35	165	181	12.5	3.84	99	.273	.332	27	.180	-2	-1	-2	1	1.0

● **WALLY BURNETTE**   Burnette, Wallace Harper   b: 6/20/29, Blairs, Va.   BR/TR, 6'0.5", 178 lbs.   Deb: 7/15/56

YEAR	TM/L	W	L	PCT	G	GS	CG	SH	SV	IP	H	HR	BB	SO	RAT	ERA	ERA⁺	OAV	OOB	BH	AVG	PB	PR	/A	PD	TPI
1956	KC-A	6	8	.429	18	14	4	1	0	121¹	115	13	39	54	11.6	2.89	150	.252	.314	2	.051	-4	17	19	-1	1.5
1957	KC-A	7	12	.368	38	9	1	0	1	113	115	4	44	57	12.7	4.30	92	.268	.338	8	.250	1	-6	-4	2	-0.4
1958	KC-A	1	1	.500	12	4	0	0	0	28¹	29	2	14	11	13.7	3.49	112	.264	.347	1	.167	0	1	1	-0	0.0
Total	3	14	21	.400	68	27	5	1	1	262²	259	23	97	122	12.3	3.56	116	.260	.328	11	.143	-4	11	16	1	1.1

● **DENNIS BURNS**   Burns, Dennis   b: 5/24/1898, Tiff City, Mo.   d: 5/21/69, Tulsa, Okla.   BR/TR, 5'10", 180 lbs.   Deb: 9/22/23

YEAR	TM/L	W	L	PCT	G	GS	CG	SH	SV	IP	H	HR	BB	SO	RAT	ERA	ERA⁺	OAV	OOB	BH	AVG	PB	PR	/A	PD	TPI
1923	Phi-A	2	1	.667	4	3	2	0	0	27	21	1	7	8	9.3	2.00	205	.210	.262	1	.111	-1	6	6	-0	0.6
1924	Phi-A	6	8	.429	37	17	4	0	1	154	191	3	68	26	15.2	5.08	84	.314	.384	6	.143	-2	-15	-14	-0	-1.3
Total	2	8	9	.471	41	20	6	0	1	181	212	4	75	34	14.3	4.62	92	.299	.367	7	.136	-3	-7	-7	-0	-0.7

YEAR	TM/L	W	L	PCT	G	GS	CG	SH	SV	IP	H	HR	BB	SO	RAT	ERA	ERA+	OAV	OOB	BH	AVG	PB	PR	/A	PD	TPI

● **FARMER BURNS**   Burns, James "Slab" b: Ashtabula, Ohio   TR , 5'7", 168 lbs.   Deb: 7/6/01

YEAR	TM/L	W	L	PCT	G	GS	CG	SH	SV	IP	H	HR	BB	SO	RAT	ERA	ERA+	OAV	OOB	BH	AVG	PB	PR	/A	PD	TPI
1901	StL-N	0	0	—	1	0	0	0	0	1	2	0	1	0	36.0	9.00	35	.400	.571	0	—	0	-1	-1	-0	0.0

● **DICK BURNS**   Burns, Richard Simon b: 12/26/1863, Holyoke, Mass. d: 11/16/37, Holyoke, Mass.   BL/TL, 5'7", 140 lbs.   Deb: 5/3/1883 ♦

YEAR	TM/L	W	L	PCT	G	GS	CG	SH	SV	IP	H	HR	BB	SO	RAT	ERA	ERA+	OAV	OOB	BH	AVG	PB	PR	/A	PD	TPI
1883	Det-N	2	12	.143	17	13	13	0	0	127²	172	8	33	30	14.5	4.51	69	.301	.339	26	.186	-2	-19	-20	-0	-1.8
1884	Cin-U	23	15	.605	40	40	34	1	0	329²	298	7	47	167	9.4	2.46	104	.225	.252	107	.306	3	-1	4	-0	0.6
1885	StL-N	0	0	—	1	0	0	0	0	3	3	0	0	2	9.0	9.00	31	.250	.250	12	.222	1	-2	-2	1	0.1
Total	3	25	27	.481	58	53	47	1	0	460¹	473	15	80	199	11.8	3.07	89	.248	.278	145	.267	2	-22	-18	1	-1.1

● **BRITT BURNS**   Burns, Robert Britt b: 6/8/59, Houston, Tex.   BL/TL, 6'5", 218 lbs.   Deb: 8/5/78

YEAR	TM/L	W	L	PCT	G	GS	CG	SH	SV	IP	H	HR	BB	SO	RAT	ERA	ERA+	OAV	OOB	BH	AVG	PB	PR	/A	PD	TPI
1978	Chi-A	0	2	.000	2	2	0	0	0	7²	14	2	3	3	20.0	12.91	29	.378	.425	0	—	0	-8	-8	0	-1.3
1979	Chi-A	0	0	—	6	0	0	0	0	5	10	1	1	2	19.8	5.40	79	.435	.458	0	—	0	-1	-1	-0	0.0
1980	Chi-A	15	13	.536	34	32	11	1	0	238	213	19	63	133	10.6	2.84	142	.241	.295	0	—	0	32	31	-1	3.5
1981	Chi-A☆	10	6	.625	24	23	5	1	0	156²	139	14	49	108	11.1	2.64	135	.238	.303	0	—	0	18	16	-4	1.3
1982	Chi-A	13	5	.722	28	28	5	1	0	169¹	168	12	67	116	12.6	4.04	100	.257	.329	0	—	0	1	-0	-3	-0.3
1983	*Chi-A	10	11	.476	29	26	8	4	0	173²	165	14	55	115	11.7	3.58	117	.249	.311	0	—	0	9	12	-2	1.0
1984	Chi-A	4	12	.250	34	16	2	0	3	117	130	7	45	85	13.8	5.00	83	.280	.349	0	—	0	-13	-11	-0	-1.4
1985	Chi-A	18	11	.621	36	34	8	4	0	227	206	26	79	172	11.4	3.96	109	.242	.308	0	—	0	5	9	-1	0.8
Total	8	70	60	.538	193	161	39	11	3	1094¹	1045	93	362	734	11.8	3.66	111	.251	.315	0	—	0	42	49	-11	3.6

● **TOM BURNS**   Burns, Thomas Everett b: 3/30/1857, Honesdale, Pa. d: 3/19/02, Jersey City, N.J.   BR/TR, 5'7", 152 lbs.   Deb: 5/1/1880   MU♦

YEAR	TM/L	W	L	PCT	G	GS	CG	SH	SV	IP	H	HR	BB	SO	RAT	ERA	ERA+	OAV	OOB	BH	AVG	PB	PR	/A	PD	TPI
1880	Chi-N	0	0	—	1	0	0	0	0	1¹	2	0	1	0	27.0	0.00	—	.250	.400	103	.309		0	0		0.0

● **OYSTER BURNS**   Burns, Thomas P. b: 9/6/1864, Philadelphia, Pa. d: 11/11/28, Brooklyn, N.Y.   BR/TR, 5'8", 183 lbs.   Deb: 8/18/1884 ♦

YEAR	TM/L	W	L	PCT	G	GS	CG	SH	SV	IP	H	HR	BB	SO	RAT	ERA	ERA+	OAV	OOB	BH	AVG	PB	PR	/A	PD	TPI
1884	Bal-a	0	0	—	2	0	0	0	0	9	12	0	2	6	14.0	3.00	116	.343	.378	39	.298	1	0	-0		0.0
1885	Bal-a	7	4	.636	15	11	10	1	**3**	105²	112	2	21	30	12.4	3.58	91	.266	.321	74	.231	3	-4	-4	-1	-0.2
1887	Bal-a	1	0	1.000	3	0	0	0	0	11¹	16	0	4	2	18.3	9.53	43	.371	.441	188	.341	2	-7	-7	-1	-0.4
1888	Bal-a	0	1	.000	5	0	0	0	0	12²	12	0	3	2	10.7	4.26	70	.240	.283	97	.298	2	-2	-0	-1	-0.1
Total	4	8	5	.615	25	11	10	1	4	138²	152	2	30	40	12.9	4.09	81	.271	.326	1389	.300	7	-12	-12	-2	-0.7

● **TODD BURNS**   Burns, Todd Edward b: 7/6/63, Maywood, Cal.   BR/TR, 6'2", 186 lbs.   Deb: 5/31/88

YEAR	TM/L	W	L	PCT	G	GS	CG	SH	SV	IP	H	HR	BB	SO	RAT	ERA	ERA+	OAV	OOB	BH	AVG	PB	PR	/A	PD	TPI
1988	*Oak-A	8	2	.800	17	14	2	0	1	102²	93	8	34	57	11.2	3.16	120	.241	.304	0	—	0	9	7	-1	0.8
1989	*Oak-A	6	5	.545	50	2	0	0	8	96¹	66	3	28	49	8.9	2.24	164	.196	.260	0	—	0	18	15	-1	2.0
1990	*Oak-A	3	3	.500	43	2	0	0	3	78²	78	8	32	43	12.6	2.97	125	.263	.334	0	—	0	8	6	-1	0.7
1991	Oak-A	1	0	1.000	9	0	0	0	0	13¹	10	2	4	3	12.2	3.38	114	.217	.333	0	—	0	1	1	0	0.4
1992	Tex-A	3	5	.375	35	10	0	0	1	103	97	8	32	55	11.6	3.84	99	.248	.311	0	—	0	-1	-1	-1	-0.1
1993	Tex-A	0	4	.000	25	5	0	0	0	65	63	6	32	35	13.4	4.57	91	.253	.343	0	—	0	-2	-3	-1	-0.5
	StL-N	0	4	.000	24	0	0	0	0	30²	38	8	9	10	12.0	6.16	64	.274	.325	0	.000	-0	-7	-7	-1	-1.0
Total	6	21	23	.477	203	33	2	0	13	489²	439	43	175	252	11.4	3.47	110	.241	.310	0	.000	-0	28	19	-6	2.8

● **BILL BURNS**   Burns, William Thomas "Sleepy Bill" b: 1/29/1880, San Saba, Tex. d: 6/6/53, Ramona, Cal.   BB/TL, 6'2", 195 lbs.   Deb: 4/18/08

YEAR	TM/L	W	L	PCT	G	GS	CG	SH	SV	IP	H	HR	BB	SO	RAT	ERA	ERA+	OAV	OOB	BH	AVG	PB	PR	/A	PD	TPI
1908	Was-A	6	11	.353	23	19	11	2	0	164	135	3	18	55	8.6	1.70	134	.229	.257	8	.148	-1	13	11	3	1.4
1909	Was-A	1	1	.500	6	4	1	0	0	29¹	25	0	7	13	10.7	1.23	198	.229	.294	3	.273	0	4	4	0	0.4
	Chi-A	7	13	.350	23	19	10	3	0	168	161	2	34	50	10.9	2.04	115	.264	.312	9	.153	1	8	6	1	0.9
	Yr	8	14	.364	29	23	11	3	0	197¹	186	2	41	63	10.7	1.92	123	.258	.305	12	.171	1	12	10	1	1.3
1910	Chi-A	0	0	—	1	0	0	0	0	0¹	0	0	1	0	27.0	0.00	—	.000	.500	0	—	0	0	0	0	0.0
	Cin-N	8	13	.381	31	21	13	2	0	178²	183	3	49	57	12.3	3.48	84	.262	.333	16	.262	2	-9	-11	1	-0.9
1911	Cin-N	1	0	1.000	6	3	0	0	1	17²	17	1	3	6	11.7	3.06	108	.254	.315	3	.429	2	1	0	1	0.3
	Phi-N	6	10	.375	21	14	8	3	1	121	132	5	26	47	12.2	3.42	101	.287	.333	6	.150	-1	-0	-2	1	0.3
	Yr	7	10	.412	27	17	8	3	2	138²	149	6	29	52	11.9	3.38	102	.281	.326	9	.191	0	0	1	3	0.3
1912	Det-A	1	4	.200	6	5	2	0	0	38²	52	0	14	9	14.7	5.35	61	.338	.382	3	.231	-1	-9	-9	-0	-0.6
Total	5	30	52	.366	117	85	45	10	2	717²	705	14	147	233	11.2	2.72	100	.265	.313	48	.196	4	8	0	7	1.3

● **PETE BURNSIDE**   Burnside, Peter Willits b: 7/2/30, Evanston, Ill.   BR/TR, 6'2", 190 lbs.   Deb: 9/20/55

YEAR	TM/L	W	L	PCT	G	GS	CG	SH	SV	IP	H	HR	BB	SO	RAT	ERA	ERA+	OAV	OOB	BH	AVG	PB	PR	/A	PD	TPI
1955	NY-N	1	0	1.000	2	2	1	0	0	12²	10	1	9	2	13.5	2.84	142	.204	.328	1	.200	0	2	2	-0	0.1
1957	NY-N	1	4	.200	10	9	1	1	0	30²	47	5	13	18	17.9	8.80	45	.356	.418	0	.000	-1	-17	-17	-0	-2.3
1958	SF-N	0	0	—	6	1	0	0	0	10²	20	3	5	4	21.1	6.75	56	.400	.455	0	—	0	-3	-3	-0	-0.4
1959	Det-A	1	3	.250	30	0	0	0	1	62	55	7	25	49	11.9	3.77	108	.237	.317	0	.000	-1	1	2	0	0.1
1960	Det-A	7	7	.500	31	15	2	0	2	113²	122	14	50	71	13.9	4.28	93	.277	.356	4	.148	-1	-5	-4	-1	-0.6
1961	Was-A	4	9	.308	33	16	4	2	2	113¹	106	11	51	56	12.7	4.53	89	.251	.335	2	.059	-1	-6	-6	-1	-1.0
1962	Was-A	5	11	.313	40	20	6	2	0	149²	152	20	51	74	12.3	4.45	91	.263	.325	2	.057	-1	-8	-7	-2	-1.1
1963	Bal-A	0	1	.000	6	0	0	0	0	7¹	11	0	2	6	17.2	4.91	74	.344	.400	0	.000	-0	-1	-1	-0	-0.2
	Was-A	1	0	1.000	38	1	0	0	5	67¹	84	12	24	23	14.4	6.15	60	.308	.364	1	.091	-1	-19	-18	-1	-0.4
	Yr	1	1	.500	44	1	0	0	5	74²	95	12	26	29	14.6	6.03	61	.310	.364	1	.083	-1	-20	-19	-2	-0.6
Total	8	19	36	.345	196	64	14	3	7	567¹	607	73	230	303	13.5	4.91	82	.275	.347	10	.076	-8	-57	-53	-6	-5.4

● **SHELDON BURNSIDE**   Burnside, Sheldon John b: 12/22/54, South Bend, Ind.   BR/TL, 6'5", 200 lbs.   Deb: 9/4/78

YEAR	TM/L	W	L	PCT	G	GS	CG	SH	SV	IP	H	HR	BB	SO	RAT	ERA	ERA+	OAV	OOB	BH	AVG	PB	PR	/A	PD	TPI
1978	Det-A	0	0	—	2	0	0	0	0	4	4	2	3	3	13.5	9.00	43	.250	.333	0	—	0	-2	-2	-0	-0.2
1979	Det-A	1	1	.500	10	0	0	0	0	21¹	28	2	8	13	15.6	6.33	68	.333	.398	0	—	0	-5	-5	-0	-0.6
1980	Cin-N	1	0	1.000	7	0	0	0	0	4²	6	1	2	2	13.5	1.93	185	.333	.368	0	.000	-0	1	1	0	0.2
Total	3	2	1	.667	19	0	0	0	0	30	38	5	11	18	15.0	6.00	69	.322	.385	0	.000	-0	-6	-6	-1	-0.6

● **GEORGE BURPO**   Burpo, George Harvie b: 6/19/22, Jenkins, Ky.   BR/TL, 6', 195 lbs.   Deb: 6/9/46

YEAR	TM/L	W	L	PCT	G	GS	CG	SH	SV	IP	H	HR	BB	SO	RAT	ERA	ERA+	OAV	OOB	BH	AVG	PB	PR	/A	PD	TPI
1946	Cin-N	0	0	—	2	0	0	0	0	2¹	4	0	5	1	34.7	15.43	22	.400	.600	0	—	0	-3	-3	-0	0.0

● **HARRY BURRELL**   Burrell, Harry J. b: 5/26/1869, Bethel, Vt. d: 12/11/14, Omaha, Neb.   BR/TL,   Deb: 9/13/1891

YEAR	TM/L	W	L	PCT	G	GS	CG	SH	SV	IP	H	HR	BB	SO	RAT	ERA	ERA+	OAV	OOB	BH	AVG	PB	PR	/A	PD	TPI
1891	StL-a	4	2	.667	7	4	3	0	0	43	51	4	21	19	15.5	4.81	87	.285	.366	5	.227	-0	-5	-3	-0	-0.4

● **AL BURRIS**   Burris, Alva Burton b: 1/28/1874, Warwick, Md. d: 3/24/38, Salisbury, Md.   BR/TR,   Deb: 6/22/1894

YEAR	TM/L	W	L	PCT	G	GS	CG	SH	SV	IP	H	HR	BB	SO	RAT	ERA	ERA+	OAV	OOB	BH	AVG	PB	PR	/A	PD	TPI
1894	Phi-N	0	0	—	1	0	0	0	0	5	14	0	2	0	28.8	18.00	28	.500	.533	2	.500	1	-7	-7	0	0.0

● **RAY BURRIS**   Burris, Bertram Ray b: 8/22/50, Idabel, Okla.   BR/TR, 6'5", 200 lbs.   Deb: 4/8/73   C

YEAR	TM/L	W	L	PCT	G	GS	CG	SH	SV	IP	H	HR	BB	SO	RAT	ERA	ERA+	OAV	OOB	BH	AVG	PB	PR	/A	PD	TPI
1973	Chi-N	1	1	.500	31	1	0	0	1	64²	65	2	27	57	12.8	2.92	135	.261	.333	1	.143	0	5	7	1	0.3
1974	Chi-N	3	5	.375	40	5	0	0	0	75	91	8	26	40	14.5	6.60	58	.300	.363	1	.077	-1	-25	-23	-1	-2.5
1975	Chi-N	15	10	.600	36	35	8	2	0	238¹	259	25	73	108	12.7	4.12	93	.281	.337	15	.183	1	-13	-14	-4	-1.0
1976	Chi-N	15	13	.536	37	36	10	4	0	249	251	20	70	112	11.8	3.11	124	.263	.317	9	.111	-4	11	21	0	1.9
1977	Chi-N	14	16	.467	39	39	5	1	0	221	270	22	67	105	13.8	4.72	93	.305	.356	12	.174	1	-20	-8	3	-0.7
1978	Chi-N	7	13	.350	40	32	4	1	1	198²	210	15	79	94	13.5	4.76	85	.274	.349	7	.115	1	-26	-16	2	-1.5
1979	Chi-N	0	0	—	14	0	0	0	0	21²	23	0	16	10	16.2	6.23	66	.284	.402	0	.000	0	-6	-5	0	0.1
	NY-A	1	3	.250	15	0	0	0	0	27²	40	5	10	19	16.3	6.18	63	.342	.394	0	—	0	-6	-5	-0	-0.6
	NY-N	0	2	.000	4	0	0	0	0	21²	21	2	6	10	11.6	3.32	109	.247	.304	0	.167	0	1	1	0	0.1
1980	NY-N	7	13	.350	29	29	1	0	0	170¹	181	20	54	83	12.6	4.02	88	.277	.336	5	.098	-2	-8	-9	-1	-1.3
1981	*Mon-N	9	7	.563	22	21	4	0	0	135²	117	9	41	52	10.7	3.05	114	.235	.297	7	.189	1	7	7	0	0.8
1982	Mon-N	4	14	.222	37	15	2	0	0	123²	143	14	53	55	14.4	4.73	77	.297	.369	5	.179	-1	-16	-15	-1	-2.0
1983	Mon-N	4	7	.364	40	17	2	1	0	154	139	13	56	100	11.5	3.68	97	.244	.314	9	.231	3	-1	-2	0	0.2
1984	Oak-A	13	10	.565	34	28	5	1	0	211²	193	15	90	93	12.4	3.15	119	.244	.327	0	—	0	20	14	-3	1.9
1985	Mil-A	9	13	.409	29	28	8	0	0	170¹	182	25	53	81	12.6	4.81	87	.272	.328	0	—	0	-13	-12	-1	-1.4
1986	StL-N	4	5	.444	23	10	0	0	0	82	92	13	32	36	13.6	5.60	65	.287	.359	4	.148	0	-17	-18	-1	-1.8
1987	Mil-A	2	2	.500	10	2	0	0	0	23	33	4	12	8	17.6	5.87	78	.351	.425	0	—	0	-4	-3	-0	-0.6
Total	15	108	134	.446	480	302	47	10	4	2188¹	2310	221	764	1065	12.9	4.17	93	.274	.338	76	.151	-1	-110	-75	-6	-9.0

YEAR	TM/L	W	L	PCT	G	GS	CG	SH	SV	IP	H	HR	BB	SO	RAT	ERA	ERA+	OAV	OOB	BH	AVG	PB	PR	/A	PD	TPI
● **JOHN BURROWS**				Burrows, John b: 10/30/13, Winnfield, La. d: 4/27/87, Coal Run, Ohio BR/TL, 5'10", 200 lbs. Deb: 4/25/43																						
1943	Phi-A	0	1	.000	4	1	0	0	0	7²	8	0	9	3	21.1	8.22	41	.276	.462	0	.000	-0	-4	-4	-0	-0.5
	Chi-N	0	2	.000	23	1	0	0	2	32²	25	0	16	18	11.8	3.86	87	.205	.307	2	.667	1	-2	-2	0	0.0
1944	Chi-N	0	0	—	3	0	0	0	0	3	7	0	3	1	30.0	18.00	20	.467	.556	0	—	-0	-5	-5	0	0.0
Total	2	0	3	.000	30	2	0	0	2	43¹	40	0	28	22	14.7	5.61	60	.241	.360	2	.500	1	-11	-11	0	-0.5
● **TERRY BURROWS**				Burrows, Terry Dale b: 11/28/68, Lake Charles, La. BL/TL, 6'1", 185 lbs. Deb: 6/12/94																						
1994	Tex-A	0	0	—	1	0	0	0	0	1	1	1	1	1	18.0	9.00	54	.250	.400	0	—	0	-0	-0	-0	0.0
1995	Tex-A	2	2	.500	28	3	0	0	1	44²	60	11	19	22	16.3	6.45	75	.323	.391	0	—	0	-9	-8	-1	-0.7
1996	Mil-A	2	0	1.000	8	0	0	0	0	12²	12	2	10	5	16.3	2.84	185	.261	.404	0	—	0	3	3	-0	0.4
Total	3	4	2	.667	37	3	0	0	1	58¹	73	14	30	27	16.4	5.71	86	.309	.394	0	—	0	-6	-5	-1	-0.3
● **JIM BURTON**				Burton, Jim Scott b: 10/27/49, Royal Oak, Mich. BR/TL, 6'3", 195 lbs. Deb: 6/10/75																						
1975	*Bos-A	1	2	.333	29	4	0	0	1	53	58	6	19	39	13.1	2.89	141	.276	.336	0	—	0	5	7	0	-0.3
1977	Bos-A	0	0	—	1	0	0	0	0	2²	2	0	1	3	10.1	0.00	—	.200	.273	0	—	0	1	1	-0	-0.7
Total	2	1	2	.333	30	4	0	0	1	55²	60	6	20	42	12.9	2.75	149	.273	.333	0	—	0	6	8	-0	-1.0
● **MOE BURTSCHY**				Burtschy, Edward Frank b: 4/18/22, Cincinnati, Ohio BR/TR, 6'3", 208 lbs. Deb: 6/17/50																						
1950	Phi-A	0	1	.000	9	1	0	0	0	19	22	2	21	12	20.8	7.11	64	.289	.449	0	.000	-0	-5	-5	0	-0.2
1951	Phi-A	0	0	—	7	0	0	0	0	17	18	0	12	4	16.4	5.29	81	.277	.397	1	.333	0	-2	-2	-0	0.0
1954	Phi-A	5	4	.556	46	0	0	0	4	94²	80	7	53	54	13.4	3.80	103	.234	.350	2	.118	-1	-1	-1	0	0.0
1955	KC-A	2	0	1.000	7	0	0	0	0	11¹	17	0	10	9	22.2	10.32	40	.354	.475	1	.333	0	-8	-8	-0	-1.1
1956	KC-A	3	1	.750	21	0	0	0	0	43¹	41	6	30	18	15.4	3.95	110	.263	.392	1	.125	-1	1	2	2	0.3
Total	5	10	6	.625	90	1	0	0	4	185¹	178	15	126	97	15.4	4.71	88	.259	.385	5	.139	-1	-15	-12	1	-1.0
● **DENNIS BURTT**				Burtt, Dennis Allen b: 11/29/57, San Diego, Cal. BB/TR, 6', 180 lbs. Deb: 9/4/85																						
1985	Min-A	2	2	.500	5	2	0	0	0	28¹	20	2	7	9	8.6	3.81	116	.200	.252	0	—	0	1	2	0	0.1
1986	Min-A	0	0	—	3	0	0	0	0	2	7	1	3	1	45.0	31.50	14	.538	.625	0	—	0	-6	-6	-0	-0.1
Total	2	2	2	.500	8	2	0	0	0	30¹	27	3	10	10	11.0	5.64	78	.239	.301	0	—	0	-5	-4	0	0.0
● **DICK BURWELL**				Burwell, Richard Matthew b: 1/23/40, Alton, Ill. BR/TR, 6'1", 190 lbs. Deb: 9/13/60																						
1960	Chi-N	0	0	—	3	1	0	0	0	9²	11	2	7	1	17.7	5.59	68	.306	.432	1	.333	0	-2	-2	0	0.0
1961	Chi-N	0	0	—	2	0	0	0	0	4	6	0	4	0	22.5	9.00	46	.375	.500	0	.000	-0	-2	-2	0	0.0
Total	2	0	0	—	5	1	0	0	0	13²	17	2	11	1	19.1	6.59	59	.327	.453	1	.250	0	-4	-4	0	0.0
● **BILL BURWELL**				Burwell, William Edwin b: 3/27/1895, Jarbalo, Kan. d: 6/11/73, Ormond Beach, Fla BL/TR, 5'11", 175 lbs. Deb: 5/1/20 MC																						
1920	StL-A	6	4	.600	33	2	0	0	2	113¹	133	6	42	30	14.2	3.65	107	.303	.369	7	.167	-2	2	3	-0	0.1
1921	StL-A	2	4	.333	33	3	1	0	2	84¹	102	2	29	17	14.2	5.12	87	.309	.368	6	.240	-0	-8	-6	-1	-0.5
1928	Pit-N	1	0	1.000	4	1	0	0	0	20²	18	2	8	2	11.3	5.23	78	.234	.306	2	.222	-0	-3	-3	1	-0.1
Total	3	9	8	.529	70	6	1	0	6	218¹	253	9	79	49	13.9	4.37	95	.299	.363	15	.197	-2	-9	-5	-1	-0.5
● **MIKE BUSBY**				Busby, Michael James b: 12/27/72, Lomita, Cal. BR/TR, 6'4", 210 lbs. Deb: 4/7/96																						
1996	StL-N	0	1	.000	1	1	0	0	0	4	9	4	4	4	31.5	18.00	24	.409	.519	1	.500	0	-6	-6	0	-0.8
● **STEVE BUSBY**				Busby, Steven Lee b: 9/29/49, Burbank, Cal. BR/TR, 6'2", 205 lbs. Deb: 9/8/72																						
1972	KC-A	3	1	.750	5	5	3	0	0	40	28	1	8	31	8.1	1.57	192	.200	.243	3	.200	0	7	6	-1	0.7
1973	KC-A	16	15	.516	37	37	7	1	0	238¹	246	18	105	174	13.5	4.23	97	.271	.350	0	—	0	-11	-3	2	-0.7
1974	KC-A☆	22	14	.611	38	38	20	3	0	292¹	284	14	92	198	11.9	3.39	113	.258	.320	0	—	0	8	14	3	1.5
1975	KC-A★	18	12	.600	34	34	18	3	0	260¹	233	18	81	160	11.0	3.08	125	.242	.303	0	—	0	20	22	4	2.6
1976	KC-A	3	3	.500	13	13	1	0	0	71²	58	7	49	29	13.8	4.40	80	.218	.346	0	—	0	-7	-7	-0	-0.6
1978	KC-A	1	0	1.000	7	5	0	0	0	21¹	24	2	15	10	17.3	7.59	50	.282	.402	0	—	0	-9	-9	-0	-0.6
1979	KC-A	6	6	.500	22	12	4	0	0	94¹	71	10	64	49	12.9	3.63	118	.220	.349	0	—	0	6	7	2	0.8
1980	KC-A	1	3	.250	11	6	0	0	0	42¹	59	3	19	6	16.6	6.17	66	.335	.406	0	—	0	-10	-10	-0	-0.9
Total	8	70	54	.565	167	150	53	7	0	1060²	1003	73	433	659	12.4	3.72	105	.253	.330	3	.200	0	4	20	10	2.8
● **DON BUSCHHORN**				Buschhorn, Donald Lee b: 4/29/46, Independence, Mo. BR/TR, 6', 170 lbs. Deb: 5/15/65																						
1965	KC-A	0	1	.000	12	3	0	0	0	31	36	7	8	9	13.1	4.35	80	.295	.344	2	.500	1	-3	-3	-0	0.0
● **GUY BUSH**				Bush, Guy Terrell "The Mississippi Mudcat" b: 8/23/01, Aberdeen, Miss. d: 7/2/85, Shannon, Miss. BR/TR, 6', 175 lbs. Deb: 9/17/23																						
1923	Chi-N	0	0	—	1	0	0	0	0	2	2	0	0	0	9.0	0.00	—	.250	.250	0	—	0	0	0	0	0.0
1924	Chi-N	2	5	.286	16	8	4	0	0	80²	91	7	24	36	13.1	4.02	97	.285	.339	4	.154	-1	-1	-1	-2	-0.4
1925	Chi-N	6	13	.316	42	15	5	0	4	182	213	15	52	76	13.3	4.30	101	.300	.350	11	.193	-2	-1	0	4	0.2
1926	Chi-N	13	9	.591	35	16	7	2	2	157¹	149	3	42	32	11.1	2.86	134	.258	.311	8	.167	-2	17	17	1	1.9
1927	Chi-N	10	10	.500	36	22	9	1	2	193¹	177	3	79	62	12.2	3.03	128	.250	.330	8	.123	-4	19	18	0	1.3
1928	Chi-N	15	6	.714	42	24	9	2	2	204¹	229	10	86	61	14.1	3.83	100	.293	.367	6	.082	-6	4	0	-1	-0.6
1929	*Chi-N	18	7	.720	**50**	29	18	0	**8**	270²	277	16	107	82	12.9	3.66	126	.265	.335	15	.165	-4	32	29	2	2.0
1930	Chi-N	15	10	.600	46	25	11	0	3	225	291	22	86	75	15.2	6.20	79	.316	.376	22	.282	3	-31	-33	1	-2.5
1931	Chi-N	16	8	.667	39	24	14	1	2	180¹	190	9	66	54	12.9	4.49	86	.268	.332	7	.123	-1	-13	-13	-0	-1.3
1932	*Chi-N	19	11	.633	40	30	15	1	0	238²	262	13	70	73	12.8	3.21	118	.278	.332	15	.179	-1	18	15	1	1.8
1933	Chi-N	20	12	.625	41	32	20	4	2	259	261	9	68	84	11.5	2.75	119	.257	.304	11	.125	-1	17	15	4	2.1
1934	Chi-N	18	10	.643	40	27	15	1	0	209¹	213	15	54	75	11.5	3.83	101	.262	.309	16	.229	1	5	1	1	0.3
1935	Pit-N	11	11	.500	41	25	8	1	2	204¹	237	16	40	42	12.4	4.32	95	.285	.321	8	.127	-1	-7	-5	-1	-0.6
1936	Pit-N	1	3	.250	16	0	0	0	2	34²	49	3	11	10	15.6	5.97	68	.336	.382	3	.333	‘0	-8	-7	1	-0.7
	Bos-N	4	5	.444	15	11	3	0	0	90¹	98	2	20	28	11.8	3.39	113	.281	.320	3	.120	-1	6	4	1	0.4
	Yr	5	8	.385	31	11	3	0	2	125	147	5	31	38	12.8	4.10	95	.297	.338	6	.176	-0	-1	-3	1	-0.3
1937	Bos-N	8	15	.348	32	20	11	1	1	180²	201	8	48	56	12.4	3.54	101	.282	.328	6	.111	-2	1	1	0	0.0
1938	StL-N	0	1	.000	6	0	0	0	0	6	6	1	3	1	13.5	4.50	88	.286	.375	0	—	0	-0	-0	-0	-0.1
1945	Cin-N	0	0	—	4	0	0	0	0	4¹	7	0	3	1	16.6	8.31	45	.350	.407	0	—	0	-2	-2	-0	-0.1
Total	17	176	136	.564	542	308	151	16	34	2722	2950	152	859	850	12.9	3.86	103	.277	.334	143	.161	-22	64	41	12	3.7
● **JOE BUSH**				Bush, Leslie Ambrose "Bullet Joe" b: 11/27/1892, Brainerd, Minn. d: 11/1/74, Ft.Lauderdale, Fla. BR/TR, 5'9", 173 lbs. Deb: 9/30/12																						
1912	Phi-A	0	0	—	1	1	0	0	0	8	14	0	4	3	20.3	7.88	39	.368	.429	1	.500	1	-4	-4	-0	0.1
1913	*Phi-A	15	6	.714	39	16	6	1	3	200¹	199	3	66	81	12.1	3.82	79	.248	.310	11	.157	-0	-20	-23	4	-2.0
1914	*Phi-A	16	12	.571	38	22	14	2	3	206	184	2	81	109	11.9	3.06	85	.242	.322	14	.189	2	-7	-10	-1	-1.2
1915	Phi-A	5	15	.250	25	18	8	0	0	145²	137	3	89	89	14.2	4.14	71	.263	.375	7	.143	-3	-19	-20	0	-2.7
1916	Phi-A	15	24	.385	40	33	25	8	0	286²	222	4	130	157	11.1	2.57	111	.219	.310	14	.140	-4	8	9	5	1.4
1917	Phi-A	11	17	.393	37	31	17	4	2	233¹	203	3	111	121	12.3	2.47	111	.241	.328	16	.200	1	5	7	0	1.1
1918	*Bos-A	15	15	.500	36	31	26	7	2	272²	241	3	91	125	11.1	2.11	127	.242	.307	27	.276	6	20	17	3	3.1
1919	Bos-A	0	0	—	3	3	0	0	0	9	11	0	4	3	15.0	5.00	60	.324	.395	2	.400	1	-2	-2	0	0.1
1920	Bos-A	15	15	.500	35	32	18	0	1	243²	287	3	94	88	14.4	4.25	86	.300	.369	25	.245	-2	-12	-16	3	-1.4
1921	Bos-A	16	9	.640	37	32	21	3	1	254¹	244	6	93	96	12.1	3.50	121	.260	.330	39	.325	6	22	20	1	2.7
1922	*NY-A	26	7	**.788**	39	30	20	0	1	255¹	240	16	85	92	11.5	3.31	121	.252	.314	31	.326	8	21	20	1	3.1
1923	*NY-A	19	15	.559	37	30	22	3	0	275²	263	7	117	125	12.6	3.43	115	.260	.340	31	.277	7	17	16	1	2.6
1924	NY-A	17	16	.515	39	31	19	3	1	252	262	9	109	80	13.5	3.57	116	.273	.352	42	.339	14	18	16	2	3.4
1925	StL-A	14	14	.500	33	30	15	2	0	208²	230	18	91	63	13.9	5.09	92	.284	.357	26	.255	3	-16	-10	-2	-0.4
1926	Was-A	1	8	.111	19	9	3	0	0	71¹	83	5	35	27	15.5	6.69	58	.292	.380	7	.233	-1	-21	-22	0	-2.2
	Pit-N	6	6	.500	19	11	9	2	1	110²	97	7	35	38	10.9	3.01	131	.236	.299	13	.265	2	10	11	-1	1.3
1927	Pit-N	1	2	.333	5	3	0	0	0	6²	14	1	5	1	25.7	13.50	30	.412	.487	3	.600	-1	-7	-7	0	-2.1
	NY-N	1	1	.500	5	2	0	0	0	12	18	1	5	6	17.3	7.50	51	.340	.397	2	.500	1	-5	-5	-0	-0.6
	Yr	2	3	.400	10	5	0	0	0	18²	32	2	10	7	20.3	9.64	39	.368	.433	5	.556	1	-12	-12	-0	-2.7

YEAR TM/L	W	L	PCT	G	GS	CG	SH	SV	IP	H	HR	BB	SO	RAT	ERA	ERA+	OAV	OOB	BH	AVG	PB	PR	/A	PD	TPI
1928 Phi-A	2	1	.667	11	2	1	0	1	35¹	39	1	18	15	14.8	5.09	79	.300	.389	1	.067	-1	-4	-4	1	-0.4
Total 17	195	183	.516	489	368	225	35	20	3087¹	2992	96	1263	1319	12.6	3.51	99	.259	.335	313	.253	49	4	-8	21	5.9

● **JACK BUSHELMAN**   Bushelman, John Francis   b: 8/29/1885, Cincinnati, Ohio   d: 10/26/55, Roanoke, Va.   BR/TR, 6'2", 175 lbs.   Deb: 10/5/09

YEAR TM/L	W	L	PCT	G	GS	CG	SH	SV	IP	H	HR	BB	SO	RAT	ERA	ERA+	OAV	OOB	BH	AVG	PB	PR	/A	PD	TPI
1909 Cin-N	0	1	.000	1	1	1	0	0	7	7	1	4	3	14.1	2.57	101	.241	.333	0	.000	-0	0	0	-0	-0.1
1911 Bos-A	0	1	.000	3	1	1	0	0	12	8	0	10	5	14.3	3.00	109	.186	.352	0	.000	-0	0	0	-0	0.0
1912 Bos-A	1	0	1.000	3	0	0	0	0	7²	9	0	5	5	16.4	4.70	72	.310	.412	0	.000	-0	-1	-1	-0	-0.1
Total 3	1	2	.333	7	2	2	0	0	26²	24	1	19	13	14.9	3.38	93	.238	.364	0	.000	-1	-1	-1	-0	-0.2

● **FRANK BUSHEY**   Bushey, Francis Clyde   b: 8/1/06, Wheaton, Kan.   d: 3/18/72, Topeka, Kan.   BR/TR, 6', 180 lbs.   Deb: 9/17/27

YEAR TM/L	W	L	PCT	G	GS	CG	SH	SV	IP	H	HR	BB	SO	RAT	ERA	ERA+	OAV	OOB	BH	AVG	PB	PR	/A	PD	TPI
1927 Bos-A	0	0	—	1	0	0	0	0	1¹	2	0	2	0	27.0	6.75	63	.500	.667	0	—	0	-0	-0	-0	0.0
1930 Bos-A	0	1	.000	11	0	0	0	0	30	34	1	13	6	15.3	6.30	73	.306	.398	1	.111	-0	-6	-6	-0	-0.2
Total 2	0	1	.000	12	0	0	0	0	31¹	36	1	15	6	15.8	6.32	73	.320	.410	1	.111	-0	-6	-6	-0	-0.2

● **CHRIS BUSHING**   Bushing, Christopher Shaun   b: 11/4/67, Rockville Centre, N.Y.   BR/TR, 6', 190 lbs.   Deb: 9/3/93

YEAR TM/L	W	L	PCT	G	GS	CG	SH	SV	IP	H	HR	BB	SO	RAT	ERA	ERA+	OAV	OOB	BH	AVG	PB	PR	/A	PD	TPI
1993 Cin-N	0	0	—	6	0	0	0	0	4¹	9	1	4	3	27.0	12.46	32	.450	.542	0	—	0	-4	-4	-0	0.0

● **TOM BUSKEY**   Buskey, Thomas William   b: 2/20/47, Harrisburg, Pa.   BR/TR, 6'3", 220 lbs.   Deb: 8/5/73

YEAR TM/L	W	L	PCT	G	GS	CG	SH	SV	IP	H	HR	BB	SO	RAT	ERA	ERA+	OAV	OOB	BH	AVG	PB	PR	/A	PD	TPI
1973 NY-A	0	1	.000	8	0	0	0	1	16²	18	2	4	8	12.4	5.40	68	.286	.338	0	—	0	-3	-3	-0	0.0
1974 NY-A	0	1	.000	4	0	0	0	1	5²	10	1	3	3	22.2	6.35	55	.400	.483	0	—	0	-2	-2	-0	-0.3
Cle-A	2	6	.250	51	0	0	0	17	93	93	10	33	40	12.3	3.19	113	.263	.327	0	—	0	4	4	1	0.7
Yr	2	7	.222	55	0	0	0	18	98²	103	11	36	43	12.8	3.38	107	.271	.336	0	—	0	3	3	1	0.4
1975 Cle-A	5	3	.625	50	0	0	0	7	77	69	7	29	29	11.6	2.57	147	.252	.326	0	—	0	10	10	2	1.4
1976 Cle-A	5	4	.556	39	0	0	0	6	94¹	88	9	34	32	11.9	3.63	96	.256	.328	0	—	0	-1	-1	1	0.0
1977 Cle-A	0	0	—	21	0	0	0	0	34	45	6	8	15	14.3	5.29	74	.313	.353	0	—	0	-5	-5	-0	0.2
1978 Tor-A	0	1	.000	8	0	0	0	0	13¹	14	1	5	7	12.8	3.38	116	.275	.339	0	—	0	1	1	1	0.0
1979 Tor-A	6	10	.375	44	0	0	0	7	78²	74	10	25	44	11.4	3.43	126	.249	.310	0	—	0	7	8	2	1.7
1980 Tor-A	3	1	.750	33	0	0	0	0	66²	68	11	26	34	12.7	4.45	97	.278	.347	0	—	0	-3	-1	-0	-0.4
Total 8	21	27	.438	258	0	0	0	34	479¹	479	57	167	212	12.3	3.66	105	.267	.332	0	—	0	9	11	5	3.3

● **MAX BUTCHER**   Butcher, Albert Maxwell   b: 9/21/10, Holden, W.Va.   d: 9/15/57, Man, W.Va.   BR/TR, 6'2", 220 lbs.   Deb: 4/20/36

YEAR TM/L	W	L	PCT	G	GS	CG	SH	SV	IP	H	HR	BB	SO	RAT	ERA	ERA+	OAV	OOB	BH	AVG	PB	PR	/A	PD	TPI
1936 Bro-N	6	6	.500	38	15	5	0	2	147²	154	11	59	55	13.0	3.96	104	.268	.337	6	.125	-3	1	3	-2	-0.2
1937 Bro-N	11	15	.423	39	24	8	1	0	191²	203	12	75	57	13.4	4.27	94	.280	.354	10	.161	-1	-8	-5	3	-0.4
1938 Bro-N	5	4	.556	24	8	3	0	2	72²	104	9	39	21	17.8	6.56	59	.334	.410	4	.160	0	-22	-21	1	-2.3
Phi-N	4	8	.333	12	12	11	0	0	98¹	94	6	31	29	11.6	2.93	133	.253	.314	9	.257	1	9	10	0	1.3
Yr	9	12	.429	36	20	14	0	2	171	198	15	70	50	14.2	4.47	87	.290	.358	13	.217	1	-13	-11	2	-1.0
1939 Phi-N	2	13	.133	19	16	3	0	0	104¹	131	6	10	51	27	15.8	5.61	71	.308	.383	7	.184	-1	-20	-19	-2	-2.5
Pit-N	4	4	.500	14	12	5	2	0	86²	104	2	23	21	13.2	3.43	112	.290	.340	3	.097	-2	5	4	2	0.3
Yr	6	17	.261	33	28	8	2	0	191	235	12	74	48	14.6	4.62	85	.302	.363	10	.145	-3	-15	-15	-0	-2.2
1940 Pit-N	8	9	.471	35	24	6	2	2	136¹	161	14	46	40	13.7	6.01	63	.290	.346	15	.300	4	-33	-33	1	-3.2
1941 Pit-N	17	12	.586	33	32	19	0	0	236	249	11	66	61	12.1	3.05	118	.265	.314	15	.183	-1	15	15	0	1.7
1942 Pit-N	5	8	.385	24	18	9	0	1	150²	144	7	44	49	11.3	2.93	116	.247	.303	7	.143	-2	6	8	0	0.5
1943 Pit-N	10	8	.556	33	21	10	2	1	193²	191	4	57	45	11.6	2.60	134	.262	.317	10	.164	-1	17	19	0	1.6
1944 Pit-N	13	11	.542	35	27	13	5	1	199	216	8	46	43	11.9	3.12	119	.273	.314	12	.190	-0	11	13	3	1.7
1945 Pit-N	10	8	.556	28	20	12	0	0	169¹	184	7	46	37	12.4	3.03	130	.277	.328	12	.222	0	15	17	1	1.8
Total 10	95	106	.473	334	229	104	14	9	1786¹	1935	100	583	485	12.8	3.73	101	.276	.333	110	.184	-6	-3	11	8	0.3

● **JOHN BUTCHER**   Butcher, John Daniel   b: 3/8/57, Glendale, Cal.   BR/TR, 6'4", 190 lbs.   Deb: 9/8/80

YEAR TM/L	W	L	PCT	G	GS	CG	SH	SV	IP	H	HR	BB	SO	RAT	ERA	ERA+	OAV	OOB	BH	AVG	PB	PR	/A	PD	TPI
1980 Tex-A	3	3	.500	6	6	1	0	0	35¹	34	2	13	27	12.0	4.08	96	.248	.313	0	—	0	-0	-1	0	0.2
1981 Tex-A	1	2	.333	6	6	1	1	0	27²	18	0	8	19	8.5	1.63	213	.186	.248	0	—	0	6	6	0	0.9
1982 Tex-A	1	5	.167	18	13	2	0	1	94¹	102	10	34	39	13.2	4.87	80	.280	.345	0	—	0	-8	-10	2	-0.4
1983 Tex-A	6	6	.500	38	6	1	1	5	123	128	8	41	58	12.4	3.51	114	.270	.329	0	—	0	8	7	0	0.8
1984 Min-A	13	11	.542	34	34	8	1	0	225	242	18	53	83	12.0	3.44	122	.276	.320	0	—	0	14	19	-1	1.6
1985 Min-A	11	14	.440	34	33	4	1	0	207²	239	24	43	92	12.5	4.98	88	.289	.328	0	—	0	-19	-13	0	-1.5
1986 Min-A	0	3	.000	16	10	1	0	0	70	82	11	24	29	13.8	6.30	68	.294	.352	0	—	0	-17	-16	0	-0.7
Cle-A	1	5	.167	13	8	1	1	0	50²	86	6	13	16	18.1	6.93	60	.381	.421	0	—	0	-15	-16	-1	-1.5
Yr	1	8	.111	29	18	2	1	0	120²	168	17	37	45	15.5	6.56	65	.330	.379	0	—	0	-32	-31	-1	-2.2
Total 7	36	49	.424	164	113	22	6	6	833²	931	79	229	363	12.7	4.42	94	.284	.334	0	—	0	-32	-24	1	-0.6

● **MIKE BUTCHER**   Butcher, Michael Dana   b: 5/10/65, Davenport, Iowa   BR/TR, 6'1", 200 lbs.   Deb: 7/6/92

YEAR TM/L	W	L	PCT	G	GS	CG	SH	SV	IP	H	HR	BB	SO	RAT	ERA	ERA+	OAV	OOB	BH	AVG	PB	PR	/A	PD	TPI
1992 Cal-A	2	2	.500	19	0	0	0	0	27²	29	3	13	24	14.3	3.25	122	.264	.352	0	—	0	2	2	-0	0.3
1993 Cal-A	1	0	1.000	23	0	0	0	8	28¹	21	2	15	24	12.1	2.86	158	.204	.317	0	—	0	5	5	-1	0.3
1994 Cal-A	2	1	.667	33	0	0	0	1	29²	31	2	23	19	17.0	6.67	73	.274	.406	0	—	0	-6	-6	1	-0.5
1995 Cal-A	6	1	.857	40	0	0	0	0	51¹	49	7	31	29	14.2	4.73	99	.257	.363	0	—	0	-0	-1	-1	-0.1
Total 4	11	4	.733	115	0	0	0	9	137	130	14	82	96	14.4	4.47	102	.251	.361	0	—	0	1	1	-0	0.0

● **SAL BUTERA**   Butera, Salvatore Philip   b: 9/25/52, Richmond Hill, N.Y   BR/TR, 6', 190 lbs.   Deb: 4/10/80   ♦

YEAR TM/L	W	L	PCT	G	GS	CG	SH	SV	IP	H	HR	BB	SO	RAT	ERA	ERA+	OAV	OOB	BH	AVG	PB	PR	/A	PD	TPI
1985 Mon-N	0	0	—	1	0	0	0	0	1	0	0	0	0	0.00	—	.000	.000	24	.200	0	0	0	-0	0.0
1986 Cin-N	0	0	—	1	0	0	0	0	1	0	0	1	1	9.0	0.00	—	.000	.250	27	.239	0	0	0	-0	0.0
Total 2	0	0	—	2	0	0	0	0	2	0	0	1	1	4.5	0.00	—	.000	.143	182	.227	0	1	1	-0	0.0

● **BILL BUTLAND**   Butland, Wilburn Rue   b: 3/22/18, Terre Haute, Ind.   BR/TL, 6'5", 185 lbs.   Deb: 5/29/40

YEAR TM/L	W	L	PCT	G	GS	CG	SH	SV	IP	H	HR	BB	SO	RAT	ERA	ERA+	OAV	OOB	BH	AVG	PB	PR	/A	PD	TPI
1940 Bos-A	1	2	.333	3	3	1	0	0	21	27	4	10	5	15.9	5.57	81	.307	.378	0	.000	-1	-3	-3	1	-0.3
1942 Bos-A	7	1	.875	23	10	6	2	1	111¹	85	8	33	46	9.8	2.51	149	.206	.270	1	.036	-1	14	15	0	1.0
1946 Bos-A	1	0	1.000	5	2	0	0	0	16¹	23	3	13	10	19.8	11.02	33	.343	.450	1	.250	-0	-14	-13	0	-0.7
1947 Bos-A	0	0	—	1	0	0	0	0	2	3	0	0	1	13.5	4.50	86	.333	.333	0	—	0	-0	-0	-0	0.0
Total 4	9	3	.750	32	15	7	2	1	150²	138	11	56	62	11.8	3.88	99	.240	.310	2	.051	-2	-2	-1	1	0.0

● **CECIL BUTLER**   Butler, Cecil Dean "Slewfoot"   b: 10/23/37, Dallas, Ga.   BR/TR, 6'4", 195 lbs.   Deb: 4/23/62

YEAR TM/L	W	L	PCT	G	GS	CG	SH	SV	IP	H	HR	BB	SO	RAT	ERA	ERA+	OAV	OOB	BH	AVG	PB	PR	/A	PD	TPI
1962 Mil-N	2	0	1.000	9	2	1	0	0	31	26	4	9	22	10.2	2.61	145	.217	.271	0	.000	-1	5	4	0	0.2
1964 Mil-N	0	0	—	2	0	0	0	0	4¹	7	2	0	2	14.5	8.31	42	.368	.368	0	—	0	-2	-2	0	0.0
Total 2	2	0	1.000	11	2	1	0	0	35¹	33	6	9	24	10.7	3.31	114	.237	.284	0	.000	-1	2	2	0	0.2

● **CHARLIE BUTLER**   Butler, Charles Thomas   b: 5/12/06, Green Cove Springs, Fla.   d: 5/10/64, Brunswick, Ga.   BR/TL, 6'1.5", 210 lbs.   Deb: 5/1/33

YEAR TM/L	W	L	PCT	G	GS	CG	SH	SV	IP	H	HR	BB	SO	RAT	ERA	ERA+	OAV	OOB	BH	AVG	PB	PR	/A	PD	TPI
1933 Phi-N	0	0	—	1	0	0	0	0	1	1	0	2	0	27.0	9.00	42	.250	.500	0	—	0	-1	-1	-0	0.0

● **IKE BUTLER**   Butler, Isaac Burr   b: 8/22/1873, Langston, Mich.   d: 3/17/48, Oakland, Cal.   TR, 6', 175 lbs.   Deb: 8/5/02

YEAR TM/L	W	L	PCT	G	GS	CG	SH	SV	IP	H	HR	BB	SO	RAT	ERA	ERA+	OAV	OOB	BH	AVG	PB	PR	/A	PD	TPI
1902 Bal-A	1	10	.091	16	14	12	0	0	116¹	168	1	45	13	16.6	5.34	71	.337	.394	6	.113	-3	-23	-20	-1	-1.9

● **BILL BUTLER**   Butler, William Franklin   b: 3/12/47, Hyattsville, Md.   BL/TL, 6'2", 210 lbs.   Deb: 4/9/69

YEAR TM/L	W	L	PCT	G	GS	CG	SH	SV	IP	H	HR	BB	SO	RAT	ERA	ERA+	OAV	OOB	BH	AVG	PB	PR	/A	PD	TPI
1969 KC-A	9	10	.474	34	29	5	4	0	193²	174	19	91	156	12.5	3.90	94	.240	.328	3	.050	-4	-5	-5	-3	-1.1
1970 KC-A	4	12	.250	25	25	2	1	0	140²	117	17	87	75	13.1	3.77	99	.229	.342	2	.045	-3	-1	-1	-2	-0.6
1971 KC-A	1	2	.333	14	6	0	0	0	44¹	45	6	18	32	12.8	3.45	99	.268	.339	1	.083	-1	0	-0	-0	-0.1
1972 Cle-A	0	0	—	6	2	0	0	0	11²	9	1	10	6	14.7	1.54	208	.220	.373	0	.000	-0	2	1	0	0.2
1974 Min-A	4	6	.400	26	12	2	0	0	98²	91	9	56	79	13.5	4.10	91	.251	.353	0	—	0	-5	-4	-2	-0.8
1975 Min-A	5	4	.556	23	8	1	0	0	81²	100	12	35	55	14.9	5.95	64	.301	.368	0	—	0	-20	-19	-0	-2.0
1977 Min-A	0	1	.000	6	4	0	0	1	21	19	1	15	5	14.6	6.86	58	.244	.372	0	—	0	-7	-7	-1	-0.4
Total 7	23	35	.397	134	86	10	5	1	591²	555	65	312	408	13.3	4.21	88	.250	.345	6	.051	-7	-37	-33	-9	-4.8

● **TOM BUTTERS**   Butters, Thomas Arden   b: 4/8/38, Delaware, O.   BR/TR, 6'2", 195 lbs.   Deb: 9/8/62

YEAR TM/L	W	L	PCT	G	GS	CG	SH	SV	IP	H	HR	BB	SO	RAT	ERA	ERA+	OAV	OOB	BH	AVG	PB	PR	/A	PD	TPI
1962 Pit-N	0	0	—	4	0	0	0	0	6	5	0	6	10	18.0	1.50	262	.238	.429	0	—	0	2	2	0	0.0
1963 Pit-N	0	0	—	6	1	0	0	0	16¹	15	1	8	11	13.8	4.41	75	.259	.368	1	.333	0	-2	-2	-0	0.0

YEAR	TM/L	W	L	PCT	G	GS	CG	SH	SV	IP	H	HR	BB	SO	RAT	ERA	ERA+	OAV	OOB	BH	AVG	PB	PR	/A	PD	TPI
1964	Pit-N	2	2	.500	28	4	0	0	0	64¹	52	3	37	58	12.5	2.38	148	.221	.327	2	.182	0	8	8	-1	0.4
1965	Pit-N	0	1	.000	5	0	0	0	0	9	9	2	5	6	14.0	7.00	50	.250	.341	0	.000	-0	-3	-3	0	-0.4
Total	4	2	3	.400	43	5	0	0	0	95²	81	6	56	85	13.2	3.10	113	.231	.342	3	.200	0	4	4	-1	0.0

● **FRANK BUTTERY**   Buttery, Frank   b: 5/13/1851, Silvermine, Conn.   d: 12/16/02, Silvermine, Conn.   Deb: 4/26/1872 ♦

1872	Man-n	3	2	.600	7	5	5	0	0	54	88	1	2	0	15.0	4.50	80	.326	.331	24	.258	-1	-5	-5		-0.5

● **RALPH BUXTON**   Buxton, Ralph Stanley "Buck"   b: 6/7/11, Weyburn, Sask., Canada   d: 1/6/88, San Leandro, Cal.   BR/TR, 5'11.5", 163 lbs.   Deb: 9/11/38

1938	Phi-A	0	1	.000	5	0	0	0	0	9¹	12	1	5	9	16.4	4.82	100	.324	.405	0	.000	-0	-0	0	-0	0.0
1949	NY-A	0	1	.000	14	0	0	0	2	26²	22	3	16	14	12.8	4.05	100	.229	.339	0	.000	-0	-0	-0	-0	-0.1
Total	2	0	2	.000	19	0	0	0	2	36	34	4	21	23	13.8	4.25	100	.256	.357	0	.000	-1	0	-0	-0	-0.1

● **JOHN BUZHARDT**   Buzhardt, John William   b: 8/17/36, Prosperity, S.C.   BR/TR, 6'2", 198 lbs.   Deb: 9/10/58

1958	Chi-N	3	0	1.000	6	2	1	0	0	24¹	16	2	7	9	8.5	1.85	212	.184	.245	1	.125	-0	6	6	1	0.7
1959	Chi-N	4	5	.444	31	10	1	1	0	101¹	107	12	29	33	12.2	4.97	79	.271	.322	2	.069	-1	-12	-12	1	-1.0
1960	Phi-N	5	16	.238	30	29	5	0	0	200¹	198	14	68	73	12.0	3.86	100	.259	.321	10	.161	-1	-2	0	-1	-0.1
1961	Phi-N	6	18	.250	41	27	6	1	0	202¹	200	28	65	92	12.1	4.49	91	.263	.326	6	.105	-2	-10	-9	0	-1.2
1962	Chi-A	8	12	.400	28	25	8	2	0	152¹	156	16	59	64	12.9	4.19	93	.264	.335	6	.118	-2	-4	-5	2	-0.6
1963	Chi-A	9	4	.692	19	18	6	3	0	126¹	100	8	31	59	9.7	2.42	145	.216	.273	4	.083	-3	17	15	1	1.4
1964	Chi-A	10	8	.556	31	25	8	3	0	160	150	13	35	97	10.6	2.98	116	.250	.295	11	.204	2	11	8	0	1.2
1965	Chi-A	13	8	.619	32	30	4	1	1	188¹	167	12	56	108	11.0	3.01	106	.242	.305	7	.125	0	10	4	-1	0.3
1966	Chi-A	6	11	.353	33	22	5	4	1	150¹	144	15	30	66	10.7	3.83	83	.248	.289	5	.116	-1	-7	-11	3	-1.0
1967	Chi-A	3	9	.250	28	7	0	0	0	88²	100	11	37	33	14.5	3.96	78	.294	.373	4	.200	0	-7	-8	0	-1.1
	Bal-A	0	1	.000	7	1	0	0	0	11²	14	1	5	7	14.7	4.63	68	.298	.365	0	.000	-0	-2	-2	0	0.0
	Yr	3	10	.231	35	8	0	0	0	100¹	114	12	42	40	14.0	4.04	77	.288	.356	4	.190	0	-9	-10	1	-1.2
1968	Hou-N	0	0	—	1	0	0	0	0	0²	0	0	0	0	0.0	0.00	—	.000	.000	0	—	0	0	0	0	0.0
	Hou-N	4	4	.500	39	4	0	0	5	88²	73	8	15	37	12.0	3.12	95	.239	.325	4	.250	1	-1	-2	1	0.0
Total	11	71	96	.425	326	200	44	15	7	1490²	1425	130	457	678	11.6	3.66	97	.253	.314	60	.135	-7	-1	-16	7	-1.5

● **BUD BYERLY**   Byerly, Eldred William   b: 10/26/20, Webster Groves, Mo   BR/TR, 6'2.5", 185 lbs.   Deb: 9/26/43

1943	StL-N	1	0	1.000	2	2	0	0	0	13	14	0	5	6	13.2	3.46	97	.280	.345	0	.000	-0	-0	-0	-0	-0.1
1944	*StL-N	2	2	.500	9	4	2	0	0	42¹	37	2	20	13	12.1	3.40	104	.228	.313	2	.167	-0	1	1	1	0.1
1945	StL-N	4	5	.444	33	8	2	0	0	95	111	3	41	39	14.5	4.74	79	.288	.358	5	.217	1	-10	-10	2	-0.6
1950	Cin-N	0	1	.000	4	1	0	0	0	14²	12	1	4	5	9.8	2.45	173	.218	.271	0	.000	-0	3	3	0	0.1
1951	Cin-N	2	1	.667	40	1	0	0	0	66	69	6	25	28	13.1	3.27	125	.267	.337	0	.000	-0	5	6	1	0.3
1952	Cin-N	0	1	.000	12	2	0	0	1	24²	29	0	7	14	13.1	5.11	74	.309	.356	1	.200	-0	-4	-4	-0	-0.2
1956	Was-A	2	4	.333	25	0	0	0	4	51²	45	6	14	24	10.6	2.96	146	.243	.303	1	.091	-1	7	8	0	0.9
1957	Was-A	6	6	.500	47	1	0	0	1	95	94	6	22	39	11.1	3.13	125	.264	.309	1	.067	-1	7	8	1	1.1
1958	Was-A	2	0	1.000	17	0	0	1	0	24	34	4	11	13	17.3	6.75	56	.347	.418	0	.000	-1	-8	-8	-0	-0.7
	Bos-A	1	2	.333	18	0	0	0	0	30¹	31	1	7	16	11.6	1.78	225	.272	.320	0	.000	-1	7	7	-0	0.6
	Yr	3	2	.600	35	0	0	0	1	54¹	65	5	18	29	13.9	3.98	99	.302	.359	0	.000	-1	-0	-0	-0	-0.1
1959	SF-N	1	0	1.000	11	0	0	0	0	13	11	2	5	4	11.1	1.38	275	.234	.308	0	—	-0	4	4	1	0.3
1960	SF-N	1	0	1.000	19	0	0	0	2	22	32	3	6	13	16.0	5.32	65	.340	.386	0	.000	-0	-4	-4	0	-0.3
Total	11	22	22	.500	237	17	4	0	14	491²	519	34	167	209	12.7	3.70	105	.273	.335	10	.118	-4	8	10	4	1.5

● **HARRY BYRD**   Byrd, Harry Gladwin   b: 2/3/25, Darlington, S.C.   d: 5/14/85, Darlington, S.C.   BR/TR, 6'1", 188 lbs.   Deb: 4/21/50

1950	Phi-A	0	0	—	6	0	0	0	0	10²	25	3	9	2	30.4	16.88	27	.481	.571	0	.000	-0	-15	-15	-0	-1.8
1952	Phi-A	15	15	.500	37	28	15	3	2	228¹	244	12	98	116	13.8	3.31	120	.274	.351	10	.133	-3	9	16	0	1.8
1953	Phi-A	11	20	.355	40	37	11	2	0	236²	279	23	115	122	15.5	5.51	78	.294	.379	18	.222	-1	-40	-32	-1	-3.8
1954	NY-A	9	7	.563	25	21	5	1	0	132¹	131	10	43	52	12.3	2.99	115	.258	.324	9	.196	1	11	7	-1	0.7
1955	Bal-A	3	2	.600	14	8	1	1	0	65¹	64	7	28	25	13.6	4.55	84	.261	.354	3	.158	-0	-4	-5	-1	-0.4
	Chi-A	4	6	.400	25	12	1	1	1	91	85	10	30	44	11.6	4.65	85	.251	.315	2	.067	-3	-7	-7	0	-1.0
	Yr	7	8	.467	39	20	2	2	2	156¹	149	17	58	69	12.0	4.61	85	.251	.320	5	.102	-3	-11	-12	-1	-1.4
1956	Chi-A	0	1	.000	3	1	0	0	0	4¹	9	0	4	0	27.0	10.38	39	.474	.565	0	.000	-0	-3	-3	-0	-0.6
1957	Det-A	4	3	.571	37	1	0	0	5	59	53	6	28	20	12.7	3.36	115	.249	.342	0	.000	-1	3	3	-1	0.3
Total	7	46	54	.460	187	108	33	8	9	827²	890	71	355	381	14.0	4.35	91	.277	.356	42	.160	-8	-46	-36	-3	-3.0

● **JEFF BYRD**   Byrd, Jeffrey Alan   b: 11/11/56, LaMesa, Cal.   BR/TR, 6'3", 195 lbs.   Deb: 6/20/77

1977	Tor-A	2	13	.133	17	17	1	0	0	87¹	79	11	68	41	17.1	6.18	68	.286	.404	0	—	0	-21	-19	1	-2.8

● **PAUL BYRD**   Byrd, Paul Gregory   b: 12/3/70, Louisville, Ky.   BR/TR, 6'1", 185 lbs.   Deb: 7/28/95

1995	NY-N	2	0	1.000	17	0	0	0	0	22	18	1	7	26	10.6	2.05	198	.222	.292	1	1.000	0	5	5	0	0.4
1996	NY-N	1	2	.333	38	0	0	0	0	46²	48	7	21	31	13.3	4.24	92	.265	.342	0	.000	-0	-0	-2	0	-0.1
Total	2	3	2	.600	55	0	0	0	0	68²	66	8	28	57	12.5	3.54	112	.252	.326	1	.333	0	5	3	-0	0.3

● **JERRY BYRNE**   Byrne, Gerald Wilford   b: 2/2/07, Parnell, Mich.   d: 8/11/55, Lansing, Mich.   BR/TR, 6', 170 lbs.   Deb: 8/31/29

1929	Chi-A	1	0	1.000	3	1	0	0	0	7¹	14	1	6	1	20.9	7.36	58	.379	.486	0	.000	-0	-3	-3	-0	-0.3

● **TOMMY BYRNE**   Byrne, Thomas Joseph   b: 12/31/19, Baltimore, Md.   BL/TL, 6'1", 182 lbs.   Deb: 4/27/43

1943	NY-A	2	1	.667	11	2	0	0	0	31²	28	1	35	22	18.8	6.54	49	.248	.437	1	.091	-0	-11	-12	0	-1.0
1946	NY-A	0	1	.000	4	1	0	0	0	9¹	7	1	8	5	15.4	5.79	60	.194	.356	2	.222	0	-2	-2	0	-0.2
1947	NY-A	0	0	—	4	1	0	0	0	4¹	5	0	6	2	22.8	4.15	85	.294	.478	0	—	0	-0	-0	0	-0.0
1948	NY-A	8	5	.615	31	11	5	1	2	133²	79	8	101	93	12.7	3.30	124	.172	.332	15	.326	6	15	12	-1	1.5
1949	*NY-A	15	7	.682	32	30	12	3	0	196	125	11	179	129	14.6	3.72	109	**.183**	.362	16	.193	1	10	7	-3	0.5
1950	NY-A☆	15	9	.625	31	31	10	2	0	203¹	188	23	160	118	16.2	4.74	91	.245	.387	22	.272	7	-4	-10	-2	-0.5
1951	NY-A	2	1	.667	9	3	0	0	0	21	16	0	36	14	23.6	6.86	56	.213	.482	2	.222	1	-6	-7	-0	-0.8
	StL-A	4	10	.286	19	17	7	2	0	122²	104	5	114	57	16.9	3.82	115	.235	.404	16	.281	4	4	8	-1	1.1
	Yr	6	11	.353	28	20	7	2	0	143²	120	5	150	71	17.7	4.26	101	.230	.413	18	.273	5	-2	1	-1	0.3
1952	StL-A	7	14	.333	29	24	14	0	0	196	182	16	112	91	14.0	4.68	84	.247	.354	21	.250	5	-22	-17	-4	-1.5
1953	Chi-A	2	0	1.000	6	6	0	0	0	16	18	0	26	4	24.8	10.13	40	.295	.506	3	.167	1	-11	-11	0	-1.0
	Was-A	0	5	.000	6	5	2	0	0	33²	35	3	22	22	15.5	4.28	91	.276	.387	1	.059	-1	-1	-1	0	-0.2
	Yr	2	5	.286	12	11	2	0	0	49²	53	3	48	26	18.5	6.16	64	.282	.430	4	.114	-1	-12	-12	1	-1.2
1954	NY-A	3	2	.600	5	5	4	0	0	40	36	1	19	24	12.4	2.70	127	.240	.325	7	.368	4	5	3	0	0.9
1955	*NY-A	16	5	**.762**	27	22	9	3	2	160	137	17	87	76	13.0	3.15	119	.237	.344	16	.205	4	14	11	-1	1.6
1956	*NY-A	7	3	.700	37	8	1	0	6	109²	99	9	72	52	14.9	3.36	115	.262	.374	14	.269	6	10	6	1	1.2
1957	*NY-A	4	6	.400	30	9	1	0	0	84²	70	7	60	57	14.6	4.36	82	.227	.364	7	.189	4	-5	-7	-1	-0.5
Total	13	85	69	.552	281	170	65	12	12	1362	1138	98	1037	766	14.9	4.11	97	.229	.371	143	.238	41	-5	-20	-11	1.1

● **MARTY BYSTROM**   Bystrom, Martin Eugene   b: 7/26/58, Coral Gables, Fla.   BR/TR, 6'5", 200 lbs.   Deb: 9/7/80

1980	*Phi-N	5	0	1.000	6	5	1	1	0	36	26	1	9	21	8.8	1.50	252	.195	.246	1	.071	-1	8	9	1	1.4
1981	Phi-N	4	3	.571	9	9	1	0	0	53²	55	3	16	24	12.1	3.35	108	.264	.320	2	.118	-1	1	2	1	0.1
1982	Phi-N	5	6	.455	19	16	1	0	0	89	93	2	35	50	13.4	4.85	76	.277	.354	3	.125	-0	-12	-12	-1	-1.5
1983	*Phi-N	6	9	.400	24	23	1	1	0	119¹	136	6	44	87	14.1	4.60	77	.285	.353	9	.237	2	-13	-14	-1	-1.5
1984	Phi-N	4	4	.500	11	11	0	0	0	56²	66	5	22	36	14.0	5.08	71	.283	.345	2	.158	-0	-9	-9	-0	-1.2
	NY-A	2	2	.500	7	7	0	0	0	39¹	34	3	13	24	11.0	2.97	127	.230	.296	0	—	0	4	4	1	0.6
1985	NY-A	3	2	.600	8	8	0	0	0	41	44	8	19	16	14.0	5.71	70	.280	.362	0	—	0	-7	-8	0	-0.6
Total	6	29	26	.527	84	79	4	2	0	435	454	28	158	258	13.0	4.26	86	.268	.336	18	.161	0	-28	-28	1	-2.7

● **GREG CADARET**   Cadaret, Gregory James   b: 2/27/62, Detroit, Mich.   BL/TL, 6'3", 205 lbs.   Deb: 7/5/87

1987	Oak-A	6	2	.750	29	0	0	0	0	39²	37	6	24	30	14.1	4.54	91	.252	.360	0	—	0	-0	-2	1	0.3
1988	*Oak-A	5	2	.714	58	0	0	0	3	71²	60	2	36	64	12.2	2.89	131	.226	.320	0	—	0	9	7	0	0.7
1989	Oak-A	0	0	—	26	0	0	0	0	27²	21	0	19	14	13.0	2.28	162	.214	.342	0	—	0	5	4	1	0.1

YEAR	TM/L	W	L	PCT	G	GS	CG	SH	SV	IP	H	HR	BB	SO	RAT	ERA	ERA+	OAV	OOB	BH	AVG	PB	PR	/A	PD	TPI
	NY-A	5	5	.500	20	13	3	1	0	92¹	109	7	38	66	14.5	4.58	84	.298	.367	0	—	0	-7	-7	0	-0.7
	Yr	5	5	.500	46	13	3	1	0	120	130	7	57	80	14.2	4.05	94	.279	.360	0	—	0	-2	-3	1	-0.6
1990	NY-A	5	4	.556	54	6	0	0	3	121¹	120	8	64	80	13.7	4.15	96	.268	.361	0	—	0	-3	-2	2	0.0
1991	NY-A	8	6	.571	68	5	0	0	3	121²	110	8	59	105	12.6	3.62	114	.246	.337	0	—	0	6	7	1	0.8
1992	NY-A	4	8	.333	46	11	1	1	0	103²	104	12	74	73	15.6	4.25	92	.267	.387	0	—	0	-4	-4	1	-0.3
1993	Cin-N	2	1	.667	34	0	0	0	1	32²	40	3	23	23	17.6	4.96	81	.305	.413	0	.000	-0	-3	-3	-0	0.3
	KC-A	1	1	.500	13	0	0	0	0	15¹	14	0	7	12	12.9	2.93	156	.264	.361	0		0	2	3	0	0.3
1994	Tor-A	0	1	.000	21	0	0	0	0	20	24	4	17	15	18.4	5.85	82	.289	.410	0	—	0	-2	-2	-0	-0.1
	Det-A	1	0	1.000	17	0	0	0	2	20	17	0	16	14	14.8	3.60	135	.227	.363	0	—	0	3	3	1	0.2
	Yr	1	1	.500	38	0	0	0	2	40	41	4	33	29	16.6	4.72	102	.259	.387	0	—	0	0	0	1	0.1
Total	8	37	30	.552	386	35	4	2	13	666	656	50	377	486	14.1	3.99	101	.262	.361	0	.000	-0	5	3	6	1.0

● LEON CADORE   Cadore, Leon Joseph "Caddy" b: 11/20/1890, Chicago, Ill. d: 3/16/58, Spokane, Wash. BR/TR, 6'1", 190 lbs. Deb: 4/28/15

YEAR	TM/L	W	L	PCT	G	GS	CG	SH	SV	IP	H	HR	BB	SO	RAT	ERA	ERA+	OAV	OOB	BH	AVG	PB	PR	/A	PD	TPI
1915	Bro-N	0	2	.000	7	2	1	0	0	21	28	0	8	12	16.3	5.57	50	.337	.409	0	.000	-1	-7	-7	0	-0.7
1916	Bro-N	0	0	—	1	0	0	0	0	6	10	0	0	2	15.0	4.50	60	.370	.370	0	.000	-0	-1	-1	0	-0.1
1917	Bro-N	13	13	.500	37	30	21	1	3	264	231	3	63	115	10.3	2.45	114	.241	.292	24	.261	5	8	10	-2	1.4
1918	Bro-N	1	0	1.000	2	1	1	1	0	17	6	0	2	5	4.8	0.53	526	.115	.164	0	.000	-0	4	4	0	0.2
1919	Bro-N	14	12	.538	35	27	16	3	0	250²	228	5	39	94	9.8	2.37	125	.245	.280	14	.161	-3	15	17	-3	1.0
1920	*Bro-N	15	14	.517	35	30	16	4	0	254¹	256	4	56	79	11.1	2.62	122	.270	.313	20	.220	2	15	17	1	2.3
1921	Bro-N	13	14	.481	35	30	12	1	0	211²	243	17	46	79	12.5	4.17	93	.292	.334	14	.187	-1	-9	-7	-1	-1.0
1922	Bro-N	8	15	.348	29	21	13	0	0	190¹	224	11	57	49	13.3	4.35	94	.299	.349	19	.268	4	-5	-6	-3	-0.5
1923	Bro-N	4	1	.800	8	4	3	0	0	36	39	2	13	5	13.0	4.25	96	.289	.354	1	.077	-1	3	3	-1	0.1
	Chi-A	0	1	.000	1	1	0	0	0	2¹	6	0	2	3	30.9	23.14	17	.500	.571	0	—	0	-5	-5	-0	-1.1
1924	NY-N	0	0	—	2	0	0	0	0	4	2	0	3	2	11.3	0.00	—	.154	.313	0	—	0	2	2	0	0.0
Total	10	68	72	.486	192	147	83	10	3	1257¹	1273	44	289	445	11.4	3.14	106	.269	.314	92	.208	5	19	27	-8	1.7

● CHARLIE CADY   Cady, Charles B. b: 12/1865, Chicago, Ill. d: 6/7/09, Kankakee, Ill. 5'11", 180 lbs. Deb: 9/5/1883 ♦

YEAR	TM/L	W	L	PCT	G	GS	CG	SH	SV	IP	H	HR	BB	SO	RAT	ERA	ERA+	OAV	OOB	BH	AVG	PB	PR	/A	PD	TPI
1883	Cle-N	0	1	.000	1	1	1	0	0	8	13	0	4	5	19.1	7.88	40	.361	.425	0	.000	-1	-4	-4	-0	-0.4
1884	CP-U	3	1	.750	4	4	4	0	0	35	37	0	13	15	12.9	2.83	86	.253	.314	2	.100	-1	-2	-2	-0	-0.3
Total	2	3	2	.600	5	5	5	0	0	43	50	0	17	20	14.0	3.77	68	.275	.337	2	.059	-2	-6	-6	-0	-0.7

● JOHN CAHILL   Cahill, John Patrick Parnell "Patsy" b: 4/30/1865, San Francisco, Cal d: 10/31/01, Pleasanton, Cal. BR/TR, 5'7.5", 168 lbs. Deb: 5/31/1884 ♦

YEAR	TM/L	W	L	PCT	G	GS	CG	SH	SV	IP	H	HR	BB	SO	RAT	ERA	ERA+	OAV	OOB	BH	AVG	PB	PR	/A	PD	TPI
1884	Col-a	1	0	1.000	2	1	1	0	0	16	15	0	4	1	12.4	5.06	60	.211	.282	46	.219	0	-3	-4	-0	-0.2
1886	StL-N	1	0	1.000	2	0	0	0	0	12	11	0	7	3	10.5	3.00	108	.268	.318	92	.199	-0	0	0	0	0.0
1887	Ind-N	0	2	.000	6	1	1	0	0	22	40	2	15	4	14.32	14.32	29	.430	.535	54	.205	-1	-25	-25	-1	-1.6
Total	3	2	2	.500	10	2	2	0	0	50	66	2	26	8	17.5	8.64	41	.322	.411	192	.205	-1	-28	-28	-1	-1.8

● LES CAIN   Cain, Leslie b: 1/13/48, San Luis Obispo, Cal. BL/TL, 6'1", 200 lbs. Deb: 4/28/68

YEAR	TM/L	W	L	PCT	G	GS	CG	SH	SV	IP	H	HR	BB	SO	RAT	ERA	ERA+	OAV	OOB	BH	AVG	PB	PR	/A	PD	TPI
1968	Det-A	1	0	1.000	8	4	0	0	0	24	25	1	20	13	16.9	3.00	100	.269	.398	1	.143	0	-0	0	0	0.1
1970	Det-A	12	7	.632	29	29	5	0	0	180²	167	19	98	156	13.5	3.84	97	.247	.349	11	.162	0	-2	-2	-0	-0.4
1971	Det-A	10	9	.526	26	26	3	1	0	144²	121	14	91	118	13.6	4.35	82	.228	.348	8	.145	-0	-14	-12	-0	-1.6
1972	Det-A	0	3	.000	5	5	0	0	0	23²	18	2	16	16	12.9	3.80	83	.209	.333	1	.143	-0	-2	-2	-0	-0.3
Total	4	23	19	.548	68	64	8	1	0	373	331	32	225	303	13.7	3.98	90	.239	.351	21	.153	-0	-19	-16	-1	-2.0

● SUGAR CAIN   Cain, Merritt Patrick b: 4/5/07, Macon, Ga. d: 4/3/75, Atlanta, Ga. BL/TR, 5'11", 190 lbs. Deb: 4/15/32

YEAR	TM/L	W	L	PCT	G	GS	CG	SH	SV	IP	H	HR	BB	SO	RAT	ERA	ERA+	OAV	OOB	BH	AVG	PB	PR	/A	PD	TPI
1932	Phi-A	3	4	.429	10	6	3	0	0	45	42	1	28	24	14.0	5.00	90	.256	.365	1	.250	1	-3	-2	-0	-0.3
1933	Phi-A	13	12	.520	38	32	16	1	1	218	244	18	137	43	15.9	4.25	101	.280	.379	16	.200	-1	1	1	-1	-0.1
1934	Phi-A	9	17	.346	36	32	15	0	0	230²	235	15	128	66	14.3	4.41	99	.266	.360	13	.159	-3	2	-1	-1	-0.4
1935	Phi-A	0	5	.000	6	5	0	0	0	26	39	1	19	5	20.1	6.58	69	.382	.479	0	.000	-1	-6	-6	-0	-1.0
	StL-A	9	8	.529	31	24	8	1	0	167²	197	7	104	68	16.4	5.26	91	.290	.388	11	.193	-1	-15	-9	-3	-1.2
	Yr	9	13	.409	37	29	8	1	0	193²	236	8	123	73	16.9	5.44	88	.302	.400	11	.169	-4	-21	-15	-3	-2.2
1936	StL-A	1	1	.500	4	3	1	0	0	16¹	20	0	9	8	16.0	6.61	81	.286	.367	2	.286	0	-3	-2	-0	-0.2
	Chi-A	14	10	.583	30	26	14	1	0	195¹	228	18	75	42	14.2	4.75	110	.293	.359	7	.103	-4	6	10	-3	0.4
	Yr	15	11	.577	34	29	15	1	0	211²	248	18	84	50	14.3	4.89	107	.292	.360	9	.120	-4	3	8	-3	0.2
1937	Chi-A	4	2	.667	18	6	1	0	0	68²	88	7	51	17	18.2	6.16	75	.325	.432	4	.182	-1	-12	-12	-0	-0.9
1938	Chi-A	0	1	.000	5	3	0	0	0	19²	26	0	18	6	20.1	4.58	107	.321	.444	0	.000	-0	0	1	-1	-0.2
Total	7	53	60	.469	178	137	58	2	1	987¹	1119	67	569	279	15.5	4.83	96	.287	.380	56	.163	-13	-29	-21	-9	-3.9

● BOB CAIN   Cain, Robert Max "Sugar" b: 10/16/24, Longford, Kan. BL/TL, 6', 165 lbs. Deb: 9/18/49 ♦

YEAR	TM/L	W	L	PCT	G	GS	CG	SH	SV	IP	H	HR	BB	SO	RAT	ERA	ERA+	OAV	OOB	BH	AVG	PB	PR	/A	PD	TPI
1949	Chi-A	0	0	—	6	0	0	0	0	11	7	0	5	5	9.8	2.45	170	.179	.273	0	.000	-0	2	2	-0	0.0
1950	Chi-A	9	12	.429	34	23	11	1	2	171²	153	12	109	77	14.0	3.93	114	.244	.361	12	.197	-0	12	11	-0	1.1
1951	Chi-A	1	2	.333	4	4	1	0	0	26¹	25	3	13	3	14.0	3.76	107	.248	.350	3	.333	1	1	1	-0	0.1
	Det-A	11	10	.524	35	22	6	1	2	149¹	135	12	82	58	13.7	4.70	89	.239	.347	13	.245	2	-10	-9	-0	-0.9
	Yr	12	12	.500	39	26	7	1	2	175²	160	15	95	61	13.6	4.56	91	.240	.344	16	.258	3	-9	-8	-0	-0.8
1952	StL-A	12	10	.545	29	27	8	1	2	170	169	15	62	70	12.3	4.13	95	.264	.331	8	.138	-1	-9	-4	-2	-0.8
1953	StL-A	4	10	.286	32	13	1	0	1	99²	129	8	45	36	15.8	6.23	67	.310	.379	6	.200	-0	-25	-22	-2	-2.9
Total	5	37	44	.457	140	89	27	3	8	628	618	50	316	249	13.7	4.50	93	.259	.351	42	.196	1	-27	-21	-4	-3.4

● CHARLIE CALDWELL   Caldwell, Charles William "Chuck" b: 8/2/01, Bristol, Va. d: 11/1/57, Princeton, N.J. BR/TR, 5'10", 180 lbs. Deb: 7/7/25

YEAR	TM/L	W	L	PCT	G	GS	CG	SH	SV	IP	H	HR	BB	SO	RAT	ERA	ERA+	OAV	OOB	BH	AVG	PB	PR	/A	PD	TPI
1925	NY-A	0	0	—	3	0	0	0	0	2²	7	0	3	1	33.8	16.88	25	.467	.556	0	—	0	-4	-4	0	0.0

● EARL CALDWELL   Caldwell, Earl Welton "Teach" b: 4/9/05, Sparks, Tex. d: 9/15/81, Mission, Tex. BR/TR, 6'1", 178 lbs. Deb: 9/8/28

YEAR	TM/L	W	L	PCT	G	GS	CG	SH	SV	IP	H	HR	BB	SO	RAT	ERA	ERA+	OAV	OOB	BH	AVG	PB	PR	/A	PD	TPI
1928	Phi-N	1	4	.200	5	5	1	1	0	34²	46	5	17	6	16.4	5.71	75	.348	.423	1	.111	-0	-7	-6	0	-0.7
1935	StL-A	3	2	.600	5	2	1	0	0	36²	34	2	17	5	12.5	3.68	130	.245	.327	2	.182	-0	3	5	1	0.6
1936	StL-A	7	16	.304	41	25	10	2	2	189	252	26	83	59	16.7	6.00	99	.319	.394	11	.190	-0	-20	-13	-1	-1.4
1937	StL-A	0	0	—	9	2	0	0	0	29	39	3	13	8	16.8	6.83	71	.317	.391	2	.222	0	-7	-6	-0	-0.7
1945	Chi-A	6	7	.462	27	11	5	1	4	105¹	108	8	37	45	12.6	3.59	92	.265	.331	8	.216	-0	-3	-3	-3	-0.1
1946	Chi-A	13	4	.765	39	0	0	0	8	90²	60	2	29	42	8.9	2.08	164	.186	.255	3	.167	1	**14**	**13**	1	3.0
1947	Chi-A	1	4	.200	40	0	0	0	8	54¹	53	4	30	22	13.9	3.64	100	.261	.359	0	.000	-1	0	0	-1	-0.2
1948	Chi-A	1	5	.167	25	1	0	0	3	39	53	3	22	10	17.8	5.31	80	.335	.423	0	.000	-0	-4	-5	-0	-0.7
	Bos-A	1	1	.500	8	0	0	0	0	9	11	2	11	5	23.0	13.00	34	.333	.511	1	.333	-0	-9	-9	-0	-1.5
	Yr	2	6	.250	33	1	0	0	3	48	64	5	33	15	18.4	6.75	63	.332	.432	1	.125	-0	-13	-13	-0	-2.2
Total	8	*33	43	.434	200	49	18	5	25	587²	656	44	259	202	14.4	4.69	92	.284	.358	28	.178	-2	-32	-25	3	-1.0

● RALPH CALDWELL   Caldwell, Ralph Grant "Lefty" b: 1/18/1884, Philadelphia, Pa. d: 8/5/69, W.Trenton, N.J. BL/TL, 5'9", 155 lbs. Deb: 9/10/04

YEAR	TM/L	W	L	PCT	G	GS	CG	SH	SV	IP	H	HR	BB	SO	RAT	ERA	ERA+	OAV	OOB	BH	AVG	PB	PR	/A	PD	TPI
1904	Phi-N	2	2	.500	6	5	5	0	0	41	40	1	15	30	12.5	4.17	64	.242	.313	8	.444	3	-7	-7	-0	-0.3
1905	Phi-N	1	3	.250	7	2	1	0	0	34	44	1	7	29	14.3	4.24	69	.321	.367	0	.000	-2	-5	-5	-1	-0.8
Total	2	3	5	.375	13	7	6	0	0	75	84	2	22	59	13.3	4.20	66	.278	.337	8	.242	1	-11	-12	-1	-1.1

● MIKE CALDWELL   Caldwell, Ralph Michael b: 1/22/49, Tarboro, N.C. BR/TL, 6', 185 lbs. Deb: 9/4/71

YEAR	TM/L	W	L	PCT	G	GS	CG	SH	SV	IP	H	HR	BB	SO	RAT	ERA	ERA+	OAV	OOB	BH	AVG	PB	PR	/A	PD	TPI
1971	SD-N	1	0	1.000	6	0	0	0	0	6²	4	0	3	5	9.5	0.00	—	.174	.269	1	1.000	1	3	2	0	0.5
1972	SD-N	7	11	.389	42	20	4	2	2	163²	183	10	49	102	13.0	4.01	82	.282	.337	7	.140	-1	-10	-13	2	-1.1
1973	SD-N	5	14	.263	55	13	3	1	10	149	146	8	53	86	12.1	3.74	93	.260	.326	5	.143	-1	-1	-5	2	-0.5
1974	SF-N	14	5	.737	31	27	6	2	0	189¹	176	17	63	83	11.6	2.95	139	.249	.314	9	.143	-2	14	18	4	2.0
1975	SF-N	7	13	.350	38	21	4	0	1	163¹	194	16	48	57	13.6	4.79	79	.296	.348	7	.159	-0	-21	-18	2	-1.9
1976	SF-N	1	7	.125	50	9	0	0	2	107¹	145	5	20	55	14.0	4.86	75	.324	.356	3	.158	-0	-16	-15	1	-1.0
1977	Cin-N	0	0	—	13	0	0	0	0	24²	25	1	8	11	12.0	4.01	98	.260	.317	2	.500	1	-0	-0	0	0.1
	Mil-A	5	8	.385	21	12	2	0	0	94¹	101	6	36	38	13.3	4.58	89	.271	.338	0	—	0	-5	-5	3	-0.4
1978	Mil-A	22	9	.710	37	34	**23**	6	1	293¹	258	14	54	131	9.8	2.36	159	.234	.274	0	—	0	46	45	1	5.0
1979	Mil-A	16	6	**.727**	30	30	16	4	0	235	252	18	39	89	11.3	3.29	126	.278	.311	0	—	0	24	23	5	2.4
1980	Mil-A	13	11	.542	34	33	11	2	1	225¹	248	29	56	74	12.2	4.03	96	.285	.330	0	—	0	-4	0	0	-0.4

YEAR TM/L	W	L	PCT	G	GS	CG	SH	SV	IP	H	HR	BB	SO	RAT	ERA	ERA+	OAV	OOB	BH	AVG	PB	PR	/A	PD	TPI
1981 *Mil-A	11	9	.550	24	23	3	0	0	144^1	151	18	38	41	11.8	3.93	87	.272	.319	0	—	0	-4	-8	-0	-1.0
1982 *Mil-A	17	13	.567	35	34	12	3	0	258	269	30	58	75	11.4	3.91	97	.271	.311	0	—	0	5	-4	2	0.1
1983 Mil-A	12	11	.522	32	32	10	2	0	228^1	269	35	51	58	12.7	4.53	82	.296	.334	0	—	0	-12	-20	-0	-1.5
1984 Mil-A	6	13	.316	26	19	4	1	0	126	160	11	21	34	13.0	4.64	83	.314	.343	0	—	0	-9	-11	1	-1.4
Total 14	137	130	.513	475	307	98	23	18	2408^2	2581	218	597	939	12.0	3.81	99	.276	.322	34	.157	-2	11	-14	24	0.9

● **RAY CALDWELL** Caldwell, Raymond Benjamin "Rube" or "Sum" b: 4/26/1888, Corydon, Pa. d: 8/17/67, Salamanca, N.Y. BL/TR, 6'2", 190 lbs. Deb: 9/9/10 ◆

YEAR TM/L	W	L	PCT	G	GS	CG	SH	SV	IP	H	HR	BB	SO	RAT	ERA	ERA+	OAV	OOB	BH	AVG	PB	PR	/A	PD	TPI
1910 NY-A	1	0	1.000	6	2	1	0	1	19^1	19	1	9	17	13.0	3.72	71	.260	.341	0	.000	—	-3	-2	-0	-0.3
1911 NY-A	14	14	.500	41	26	19	1	1	255	240	7	79	145	11.7	3.35	107	.260	.327	40	.272	3	-0	7	-3	0.8
1912 NY-A	8	16	.333	30	26	13	3	0	183^1	196	1	67	95	13.2	4.47	80	.277	.344	18	.237	1	-23	-18	-1	-1.7
1913 NY-A	9	8	.529	27	16	15	2	1	164^1	131	5	60	87	11.0	2.41	124	.219	.299	28	.289	3	10	11	-1	1.7
1914 NY-A	17	9	.654	31	23	22	5	1	213	153	5	51	92	8.8	1.94	142	.205	.260	22	.195	1	19	19	-2	2.5
1915 NY-A	19	16	.543	36	35	31	3	0	305	266	6	107	130	11.2	2.89	101	.244	.315	35	.243	8	2	1	-3	0.6
1916 NY-A	5	12	.294	21	18	14	1	0	165^2	142	6	65	76	11.7	2.99	97	.243	.327	19	.204	-0	-3	-2	-1	-0.3
1917 NY-A	13	16	.448	32	29	21	1	0	236	199	8	76	102	10.7	2.86	94	.234	.302	32	.258	6	-5	-5	-1	0.3
1918 NY-A	9	8	.529	24	21	14	1	1	176^2	173	2	62	59	12.0	3.06	93	.261	.325	44	.291	4	-5	-4	-3	-0.1
1919 Bos-A	7	4	.636	18	12	6	1	0	86^1	92	1	31	23	13.1	3.96	76	.279	.346	13	.271	1	-7	-9	-2	-1.0
Cle-A	5	1	.833	6	6	4	1	0	52^2	33	1	19	24	9.2	1.71	196	.181	.266	8	.348	2	9	10	-1	1.3
Yr	12	5	.706	24	18	10	2	0	139	125	2	50	47	11.5	3.11	101	.243	.312	21	.296	4	2	1	-3	0.3
1920 *Cle-A	20	10	.667	34	33	20	1	0	237^2	286	9	63	80	13.4	3.86	98	.303	.350	19	.213	1	-2	-3	-3	-0.5
1921 Cle-A	6	6	.500	37	12	4	1	4	147	159	4	49	76	12.9	4.90	87	.275	.333	11	.208	0	-10	-10	-0	-0.8
Total 12	133	120	.526	343	259	184	21	5	2242	2089	59	738	1006	11.6	3.22	99	.253	.319	289	.248	31	-20	-4	-19	2.5

● **JEFF CALHOUN** Calhoun, Jeffrey Wilton b: 4/11/58, LaGrange, Ga. BL/TL, 6'2", 190 lbs. Deb: 9/2/84

YEAR TM/L	W	L	PCT	G	GS	CG	SH	SV	IP	H	HR	BB	SO	RAT	ERA	ERA+	OAV	OOB	BH	AVG	PB	PR	/A	PD	TPI
1984 Hou-N	0	1	.000	9	0	0	0	0	15^1	5	0	2	11	4.1	1.17	283	.100	.135	0	—	0	4	4	0	0.2
1985 Hou-N	2	5	.286	44	0	0	0	0	63^2	56	2	24	47	11.3	2.54	136	.243	.315	0	.000	-0	7	6	0	0.8
1986 *Hou-N	1	0	1.000	20	0	0	0	0	26^2	28	3	12	14	13.5	3.71	97	.264	.339	0	—	0	-0	-1	-1	-0.1
1987 Phi-N	3	1	.750	42	0	0	0	1	42^2	25	1	26	31	11.0	1.48	287	.168	.295	0	.000	0	12	13	1	1.2
1988 Phi-N	0	0	—	3	0	0	0	0	2^1	6	2	1	1	27.0	15.43	23	.462	.500	0	—	0	-3	-3	-0	0.0
Total 5	6	7	.462	118	0	0	0	5	150^2	120	8	65	104	11.1	2.51	147	.219	.303	0	.000	-0	21	20	-0	2.1

● **FRED CALIGIURI** Caligiuri, Frederick John b: 10/22/18, W.Hickory, Pa. BR/TR, 6', 190 lbs. Deb: 9/3/41

YEAR TM/L	W	L	PCT	G	GS	CG	SH	SV	IP	H	HR	BB	SO	RAT	ERA	ERA+	OAV	OOB	BH	AVG	PB	PR	/A	PD	TPI
1941 Phi-A	2	2	.500	5	5	4	0	0	43	45	2	14	7	12.3	2.93	143	.257	.312	4	.200	1	6	6	-1	0.5
1942 Phi-A	0	3	.000	13	2	0	0	0	36^2	45	2	18	20	16.0	6.38	59	.300	.382	1	.083	-0	-11	-11	-0	-0.9
Total 2	2	5	.286	18	7	4	0	1	79^2	90	4	32	27	14.0	4.52	89	.277	.345	5	.156	1	-5	-5	-1	-0.4

● **WILL CALIHAN** Calihan, William T. (b: William T. Callahan) b: 1869, Oswego, N.Y. d: 12/20/17, Rochester, N.Y. 5'8", 150 lbs. Deb: 4/17/1890

YEAR TM/L	W	L	PCT	G	GS	CG	SH	SV	IP	H	HR	BB	SO	RAT	ERA	ERA+	OAV	OOB	BH	AVG	PB	PR	/A	PD	TPI
1890 Roc-a	18	15	.545	37	36	31	0	0	296^1	276	4	125	127	12.7	3.28	109	.239	.322	23	.145	-3	19	9	3	0.8
1891 Phi-a	6	6	.500	13	11	11	0	0	112	151	7	47	28	16.9	6.43	59	.312	.387	11	.196	-1	-34	-32	2	-2.4
Total 2	24	21	.533	50	47	42	0	0	408^1	427	11	172	155	13.8	4.14	88	.261	.341	34	.158	-5	-14	-23	4	-1.6

● **BEN CALLAHAN** Callahan, Benjamin Franklin b: 5/19/57, Mt.Airy, N.C. BR/TR, 6'7", 230 lbs. Deb: 6/22/83

YEAR TM/L	W	L	PCT	G	GS	CG	SH	SV	IP	H	HR	BB	SO	RAT	ERA	ERA+	OAV	OOB	BH	AVG	PB	PR	/A	PD	TPI
1983 Oak-A	1	2	.333	4	2	0	0	0	9^1	18	0	5	2	22.2	12.54	31	.400	.460	0	—	0	-9	-9	0	-1.8

● **NIXEY CALLAHAN** Callahan, James Joseph b: 3/18/1874, Fitchburg, Mass. d: 10/4/34, Boston, Mass. BR/TR, 5'10.5", 180 lbs. Deb: 5/12/1894 M◆

YEAR TM/L	W	L	PCT	G	GS	CG	SH	SV	IP	H	HR	BB	SO	RAT	ERA	ERA+	OAV	OOB	BH	AVG	PB	PR	/A	PD	TPI
1894 Phi-N	1	2	.333	9	2	1	0	2	33^2	64	3	17	9	23.0	9.89	52	.398	.470	5	.238	-1	-17	-18	1	-1.3
1897 Chi-N	12	9	.571	23	22	21	1	0	189^2	221	6	55	52	13.5	4.03	111	.289	.343	105	.292	3	6	9	1	1.2
1898 Chi-N	20	10	.667	31	31	30	2	0	274^1	267	2	71	73	11.4	2.46	146	.253	.307	43	.262	4	35	34	3	3.9
1899 Chi-N	21	12	.636	35	34	33	3	0	294^1	327	5	76	77	13.1	3.06	123	.281	.338	39	.260	4	26	23	5	3.0
1900 Chi-N	13	16	.448	32	32	32	2	0	285^1	347	5	74	77	14.0	3.82	94	.299	.353	27	.235	2	-4	-7	6	0.2
1901 Chi-A	15	8	.652	27	22	20	1	0	215^1	195	4	50	70	10.6	2.42	144	.239	.290	39	.331	8	30	25	6	3.9
1902 Chi-A	16	14	.533	35	31	29	2	0	282^1	287	8	89	75	12.3	3.60	94	.264	.326	51	.234	3	-1	-7	6	0.2
1903 Chi-A	1	2	.333	3	3	3	0	0	28	40	0	5	12	14.8	4.50	82	.333	.365	128	.292	1	-5	-5	1	-0.3
Total 8	99	73	.576	195	177	169	11	2	1603	1748	33	437	445	12.8	3.39	109	.276	.332	901	.273	25	70	54	26	10.8

● **JIM CALLAHAN** Callahan, James W. b: Moberly, Mo. Deb: 9/3/1898

YEAR TM/L	W	L	PCT	G	GS	CG	SH	SV	IP	H	HR	BB	SO	RAT	ERA	ERA+	OAV	OOB	BH	AVG	PB	PR	/A	PD	TPI
1898 StL-N	0	2	.000	2	2	1	0	0	8^1	18	2	7	2	29.2	16.20	23	.429	.529	0	.000	-1	-12	-11	0	-1.6

● **JOE CALLAHAN** Callahan, Joseph Thomas b: 10/8/16, E.Boston, Mass. d: 5/24/49, S.Boston, Mass. BR/TR, 6'2", 170 lbs. Deb: 9/13/39

YEAR TM/L	W	L	PCT	G	GS	CG	SH	SV	IP	H	HR	BB	SO	RAT	ERA	ERA+	OAV	OOB	BH	AVG	PB	PR	/A	PD	TPI
1939 Bos-N	1	0	1.000	4	1	0	0	0	17^1	17	0	3	8	10.9	3.12	119	.250	.292	0	.000	0	2	1	0	0.1
1940 Bos-N	0	2	.000	6	2	0	0	0	15	20	1	13	3	9.8	10.20	36	.351	.471	0	.000	-1	-11	-11	1	-1.2
Total 2	1	2	.333	10	3	1	0	0	32^1	37	1	16	11	15.0	6.40	58	.296	.380	0	.000	-1	-9	-10	1	-1.1

● **RAY CALLAHAN** Callahan, Raymond James "Pat" b: 8/29/1891, Ashland, Wis. d: 1/23/73, Olympia, Wash. BL/TL, 5'10.5", 170 lbs. Deb: 9/12/15

YEAR TM/L	W	L	PCT	G	GS	CG	SH	SV	IP	H	HR	BB	SO	RAT	ERA	ERA+	OAV	OOB	BH	AVG	PB	PR	/A	PD	TPI
1915 Cin-N	0	0	—	3	0	0	0	0	6^1	12	1	4	1	18.5	8.53	34	.364	.382	1	.333	-0	-4	-4	-0	0.0

● **DICK CALMUS** Calmus, Richard Lee b: 1/7/44, Los Angeles, Cal. BR/TR, 6'4", 187 lbs. Deb: 4/22/63

YEAR TM/L	W	L	PCT	G	GS	CG	SH	SV	IP	H	HR	BB	SO	RAT	ERA	ERA+	OAV	OOB	BH	AVG	PB	PR	/A	PD	TPI
1963 LA-N	3	1	.750	21	1	0	0	0	44	32	3	16	25	9.8	2.66	114	.204	.277	0	.000	-1	3	2	-1	0.0
1967 Chi-N	0	0	—	1	1	0	0	0	4^1	5	2	0	1	10.4	8.31	43	.278	.278	1	.500	-0	-2	-2	0	0.0
Total 2	3	1	.750	22	2	0	0	0	48^1	37	5	16	26	9.9	3.17	97	.211	.277	1	.125	-0	1	-1	-1	0.0

● **MARK CALVERT** Calvert, Mark b: 9/29/56, Tulsa, Okla. BR/TR, 6'1", 195 lbs. Deb: 4/17/83

YEAR TM/L	W	L	PCT	G	GS	CG	SH	SV	IP	H	HR	BB	SO	RAT	ERA	ERA+	OAV	OOB	BH	AVG	PB	PR	/A	PD	TPI
1983 SF-N	1	4	.200	18	4	0	0	0	37^1	46	2	34	14	20.0	6.27	56	.307	.444	0	.000	-1	-11	-11	1	-1.4
1984 SF-N	2	4	.333	10	5	1	0	0	32	40	4	9	5	14.1	5.06	69	.303	.352	0	.000	-0	-5	-6	0	-1.0
Total 2	3	8	.273	28	9	1	0	0	69^1	86	6	43	19	17.3	5.71	62	.305	.404	0	.000	-1	-16	-17	1	-2.4

● **PAUL CALVERT** Calvert, Paul Leo Emile b: 10/6/17, Montreal, Que., Can. BR/TR, 6', 185 lbs. Deb: 9/24/42

YEAR TM/L	W	L	PCT	G	GS	CG	SH	SV	IP	H	HR	BB	SO	RAT	ERA	ERA+	OAV	OOB	BH	AVG	PB	PR	/A	PD	TPI
1942 Cle-A	0	0	—	1	0	0	0	0	1	0	0	0	0	9.0	0.00	—	.000	.286	0	—	0	1	1	-0	0.0
1943 Cle-A	0	0	—	5	0	0	0	0	8^1	6	0	6	2	14.0	4.32	72	.200	.351	0	.000	-0	-1	-1	0	0.0
1944 Cle-A	1	3	.250	35	4	0	0	0	77	89	4	38	31	14.8	4.56	72	.289	.367	4	.267	1	-10	-11	2	-0.2
1945 Cle-A	0	0	—	1	0	0	0	0	1^1	3	0	1	1	27.0	13.50	24	.429	.500	0	—	0	-2	-2	0	0.0
1949 Was-A	6	17	.261	34	23	5	0	1	160^2	175	11	86	52	14.7	5.43	78	.279	.368	7	.137	-2	-22	-21	3	-2.5
1950 Det-A	2	2	.500	32	0	0	0	4	51^1	71	7	25	14	17.2	6.31	74	.324	.398	0	.000	-0	-10	-9	1	-0.7
1951 Det-A	0	0	—	1	0	0	0	0	1	1	0	0	0	9.0	0.00	—	.250	.250	0	—	0	0	0	0	0.0
Total 7	9	22	.290	109	27	5	0	5	301^2	345	22	158	102	15.2	5.31	76	.287	.373	11	.149	-2	-43	-43	5	-3.4

● **ERNIE CAMACHO** Camacho, Ernest Carlos b: 2/1/55, Salinas, Cal. BR/TR, 6'1", 180 lbs. Deb: 5/22/80

YEAR TM/L	W	L	PCT	G	GS	CG	SH	SV	IP	H	HR	BB	SO	RAT	ERA	ERA+	OAV	OOB	BH	AVG	PB	PR	/A	PD	TPI
1980 Oak-A	0	0	—	5	0	0	0	0	11^2	20	2	5	9	20.1	6.94	54	.364	.426	0	—	0	-4	-4	-0	0.0
1981 Pit-N	0	1	.000	9	0	0	0	0	21^2	23	0	15	11	15.8	4.98	72	.295	.409	0	.000	-0	-4	-3	-0	-0.2
1983 Cle-A	0	1	.000	4	0	0	0	0	5^1	5	1	2	3	13.5	5.06	84	.250	.348	0	—	0	-1	-0	0	-0.3
1984 Cle-A	5	9	.357	69	0	0	0	23	100	83	6	37	48	10.9	2.43	168	.229	.303	0	—	0	17	18	0	3.2
1985 Cle-A	0	0	—	1	0	0	0	0	3^1	4	0	1	2	18.8	8.10	51	.333	.385	0	—	0	-1	-1	0	0.0
1986 Cle-A	2	4	.333	51	0	0	0	20	57^1	60	1	31	36	14.6	4.08	101	.269	.363	0	—	0	1	1	0	0.1
1987 Cle-A	0	0	—	15	0	0	0	1	13^2	21	1	5	9	19.2	9.22	49	.350	.426	0	—	0	-7	-7	1	-0.5
1988 Hou-N	0	3	.000	13	0	0	0	0	17^2	25	1	12	13	18.8	7.64	43	.352	.446	0	.000	-0	-8	-8	-1	-1.4
1989 SF-N	3	0	1.000	13	0	0	0	0	16^1	10	1	11	14	11.6	2.76	122	.175	.309	0	.000	-0	1	1	3	0.3
1990 SF-N	0	0	—	10	0	0	0	0	10	9	1	3	8	11.7	3.60	101	.256	.310	0	—	0	-0	-0	0	0.0
StL-N	0	0	—	6	0	0	0	0	5^2	7	2	6	7	20.6	7.94	48	.318	.464	0	—	0	-3	-3	0	0.0
Yr	0	0	—	14	0	0	0	0	15^2	17	3	9	15	14.9	5.17	72	.279	.371	0	—	0	-2	-3	0	0.0
Total 10	10	10	.333	193	0	0	0	45	262^2	268	16	128	155	13.8	4.21	94	.268	.356	0	.000	-0	-8	-8	1	0.9

YEAR	TM/L	W	L	PCT	G	GS	CG	SH	SV	IP	H	HR	BB	SO	RAT	ERA	ERA+	OAV	OOB	BH	AVG	PB	PR	/A	PD	TPI

● **FRED CAMBRIA**   Cambria, Frederick Dennis   b: 1/22/48, Cambria Heights, N.Y.   BR/TR, 6'2", 195 lbs.   Deb: 8/26/70

| 1970 | Pit-N | 1 | 2 | .333 | 6 | 5 | 0 | 0 | 0 | 33¹ | 37 | 2 | 12 | 14 | 13.5 | 3.51 | 111 | .272 | .336 | 2 | .200 | 1 | 2 | 1 | 0 | 0.2 |

● **JACK CAMERON**   Cameron, John William "Happy Jack"   b: 9/1884, Nova Scotia, Can.   d: 8/17/51, Boston, Mass.   Deb: 9/13/06 ♦

| 1906 | Bos-N | 0 | 0 | — | 2 | 1 | 0 | 0 | 0 | 6 | 4 | 0 | 6 | 2 | 15.0 | 3.00 | — | .211 | .400 | 11 | .180 | -0 | 2 | 2 | 0 | 0.0 |

● **HARRY CAMNITZ**   Camnitz, Henry Richardson   b: 10/26/1884, McKinney, Ky.   d: 1/6/51, Louisville, Ky.   BR/TR, 6'1", 168 lbs.   Deb: 4/14/09   F

1909	Pit-N	0	0	—	1	0	0	0	0	4	6	0	1	1	15.8	4.50	60	.353	.389	0	.000	-0	-1	-1	0	0.0
1911	StL-N	1	0	1.000	2	0	0	0	0	2	0	0	1	2	4.5	0.00	—	.000	.143	0	—	-0	1	1	-0	0.4
Total	2	1	0	1.000	3	0	0	0	0	6	6	0	2	3	12.0	3.00	98	.261	.320	0	.000	-0	-0	-0	0	0.4

● **HOWIE CAMNITZ**   Camnitz, Samuel Howard "Red"   b: 8/22/1881, Covington, Ky.   d: 3/2/60, Louisville, Ky.   BR/TR, 5'9", 169 lbs.   Deb: 4/22/04   F

1904	Pit-N	1	4	.200	10	2	2	0	0	49	48	0	20	21	13.0	4.22	65	.259	.341	1	.063	-1	-3	-8	-1	-1.0
1906	Pit-N	1	0	1.000	2	1	1	1	0	9	6	0	5	5	13.0	2.00	134	.188	.297	0	.000	-0	1	1	-0	0.0
1907	Pit-N	13	8	.619	31	19	15	4	1	180	135	0	59	85	9.9	2.15	113	.211	.281	3	.050	-5	6	6	-0	0.0
1908	Pit-N	16	9	.640	38	26	17	3	2	236²	182	6	69	118	9.7	1.56	148	.210	.272	6	.083	-3	21	20	-1	1.7
1909	*Pit-N	25	6	**.806**	41	30	20	6	3	283	207	1	68	133	9.0	1.62	168	.211	.267	12	.138	-0	31	35	-3	3.7
1910	Pit-N	12	13	.480	38	31	16	1	2	260	246	1	61	120	11.0	3.22	96	.256	.308	11	.125	-3	-5	-3	-2	-0.9
1911	Pit-N	20	15	.571	40	33	18	1	1	267²	245	8	84	139	11.2	3.13	110	.248	.309	12	.143	-3	8	9	-3	0.4
1912	Pit-N	22	12	.647	41	32	22	2	2	276²	256	8	82	121	11.4	2.83	115	.251	.315	23	.235	1	18	13	-3	1.2
1913	Pit-N	6	17	.261	36	21	5	1	2	192¹	203	7	84	64	13.8	3.74	81	.282	.363	9	.153	-1	-12	-16	1	-1.8
	Phi-N	3	3	.500	9	5	1	0	1	49	49	1	23	21	13.0	3.67	91	.268	.356	1	.063	-1	-3	-2	-1	-0.5
	Yr	9	20	.310	45	26	6	1	3	241¹	252	8	107	85	13.5	3.73	83	.277	.354	10	.133	-3	-14	-17	-0	-2.3
1914	Pit-F	14	19	.424	36	34	20	1	1	262	256	8	90	82	12.2	3.23	89	.258	.324	14	.161	-5	-10	-11	-5	-2.1
1915	Pit-F	0	0	—	4	2	0	0	0	20	19	1	11	6	13.5	4.50	60	.257	.353	0	.000	-1	-4	-4	-1	-0.2
Total	11	133	106	.556	326	236	137	20	15	2085¹	1852	41	656	915	11.1	2.75	106	.242	.307	92	.136	-24	43	40	-18	0.5

● **RICK CAMP**   Camp, Rick Lamar   b: 6/10/53, Trion, Ga.   BR/TR, 6', 198 lbs.   Deb: 9/15/76

1976	Atl-N	0	1	.000	5	1	0	0	0	11¹	13	0	2	6	11.9	6.35	60	.302	.333	0	.000	-0	-4	-3	1	-0.2
1977	Atl-N	6	3	.667	54	0	0	0	10	78²	89	6	47	51	15.7	4.00	111	.283	.377	0	.000	-1	4	4	-0	0.4
1978	Atl-N	2	4	.333	42	4	0	0	6	74¹	99	5	32	23	16.2	3.75	108	.329	.399	0	.000	-1	-1	2	-0	0.1
1980	Atl-N	6	4	.600	77	0	0	0	22	108¹	92	3	29	33	10.4	1.91	196	.235	.294	1	.111	-0	20	22	4	3.3
1981	Atl-N	9	3	.750	48	0	0	0	17	76	68	5	12	47	9.6	1.78	202	.239	.272	0	.000	-1	14	**15**	0	3.0
1982	*Atl-N	11	13	.458	51	21	3	0	5	177¹	199	18	52	68	12.8	3.65	102	.291	.342	1	.024	-3	-1	1	-5	-0.1
1983	Atl-N	10	9	.526	40	16	1	0	0	140	146	16	38	61	12.1	3.79	102	.270	.323	3	.077	-2	-3	1	0	-0.1
1984	Atl-N	8	6	.571	31	21	1	0	0	148²	134	11	63	69	12.0	3.27	118	.245	.325	5	.111	-2	5	10	0	0.7
1985	Atl-N	4	6	.400	66	2	0	0	3	127²	130	8	61	49	13.8	3.95	97	.263	.349	3	.231	1	-5	-1	-2	-0.2
Total	9	56	49	.533	414	65	5	0	57	942¹	970	72	336	407	12.7	3.37	114	.269	.335	13	.074	-8	25	51	3	7.0

● **KID CAMP**   Camp, Winfield Scott   b: 1870, Columbus, Ohio   d: 3/2/1895, Omaha, Neb.   TR, 6', 160 lbs.   Deb: 5/3/1892   F

1892	Pit-N	0	1	.000	4	1	1	0	0	23	31	4	9	6	16.0	6.26	53	.310	.373	1	.091	-1	-8	-8	-1	-0.5
1894	Chi-N	0	1	.000	3	2	2	0	0	22	34	0	12	6	19.2	6.55	86	.351	.427	0	.000	-3	-3	-2	-0	-0.2
Total	2	0	2	.000	7	3	3	0	0	45	65	4	21	12	17.6	6.40	69	.330	.400	1	.045	-4	-11	-10	-1	-0.7

● **BERT CAMPANERIS**   Campaneris, Dagoberto (Blanco) "Campy" (b: Dagoberto Campaneria (Blanco))   b: 3/9/42, Pueblo Nuevo, Cuba   BR/TR, 5'10", 160 lbs.   Deb: 7/23/64 ♦

| 1965 | KC-A | 0 | 0 | — | 1 | 0 | 0 | 0 | 0 | 1 | 2 | 1 | 2 | 1 | 27.0 | 9.00 | 39 | .333 | .600 | 156 | .270 | 0 | -1 | -1 | 0 | 0.0 |

● **ARCHIE CAMPBELL**   Campbell, Archibald Stewart "Iron Man"   b: 10/20/03, Maplewood, N.J.   d: 12/22/89, Sparks, Nevada   BR/TR, 6', 180 lbs.   Deb: 4/21/28

1928	NY-A	0	1	.000	13	1	0	0	2	24	30	0	11	9	15.4	5.25	72	.288	.357	1	.250	-4	-3	-4	-1	-0.3
1929	Was-A	0	1	.000	4	0	0	0	2	4	10	1	5	1	33.8	15.75	27	.500	.600	0	—	-0	-5	-5	0	-0.9
1930	Cin-N	2	4	.333	23	3	1	0	2	58	71	2	31	19	16.0	5.43	89	.311	.396	4	.267	-0	-3	-4	2	-0.2
Total	3	2	6	.250	40	4	1	0	6	86	111	3	47	29	16.6	5.86	77	.315	.398	5	.263	-4	-11	-13	2	-1.4

● **DAVE CAMPBELL**   Campbell, David Alan   b: 9/3/51, Princeton, Ind.   BR/TR, 6'3", 210 lbs.   Deb: 5/6/77

1977	Atl-N	0	6	.000	65	0	0	0	13	88²	78	7	33	42	11.6	3.05	146	.239	.315	1	.083	-1	9	14	-2	1.0
1978	Atl-N	4	4	.500	53	0	0	0	1	69¹	67	10	49	45	15.7	4.80	84	.258	.385	0	—	0	-9	-6	-0	-0.7
Total	2	4	10	.286	118	0	0	0	14	158	145	17	82	87	13.4	3.82	112	.247	.348	1	.083	-1	-1	8	-2	0.3

● **HUGH CAMPBELL**   Campbell, Hugh F.   b: 1846, Ireland   d: 3/1/1881, Elizabeth, N.J.   Deb: 4/28/1873   F

| 1873 | Res-n | 2 | 16 | .111 | 19 | 18 | 18 | 0 | 0 | 165 | 250 | 6 | 7 | 5 | 14.0 | 2.84 | 118 | .296 | .302 | 13 | .149 | -5 | 8 | 9 | | 0.5 |

● **JIM CAMPBELL**   Campbell, James Marcus   b: 5/19/66, Santa Maria, Cal.   BL/TL, 5'11", 175 lbs.   Deb: 8/21/90

| 1990 | KC-A | 1 | 0 | 1.000 | 2 | 2 | 0 | 0 | 0 | 9² | 15 | 1 | 1 | 2 | 14.9 | 8.38 | 46 | .349 | .364 | 0 | — | | -5 | -5 | -0 | -0.3 |

● **JOHN CAMPBELL**   Campbell, John Millard   b: 9/13/07, Washington, D.C.   d: 4/24/95, Daytona Beach, Fla.   BR/TR, 6'1.5", 184 lbs.   Deb: 7/23/33

| 1933 | Was-A | 0 | 0 | — | 1 | 0 | 0 | 0 | 0 | 1 | 1 | 0 | 1 | 0 | 18.0 | 0.00 | — | .200 | .333 | 0 | | 0 | 0 | 0 | -0 | 0.0 |

● **KEVIN CAMPBELL**   Campbell, Kevin Wade   b: 12/6/64, Marianna, Ark.   BR/TR, 6'2", 255 lbs.   Deb: 7/19/91

1991	Oak-A	1	0	1.000	14	0	0	0	0	23	13	1	14	16	11.0	2.74	140	.167	.301	0	—	0	3	3	0	0.2
1992	Oak-A	2	3	.400	32	5	0	0	1	65	66	4	45	38	15.4	5.12	73	.267	.380	0	—	0	-9	-10	-1	-0.7
1993	Oak-A	0	0	—	11	0	0	0	0	16	20	1	11	9	18.0	7.31	56	.313	.421	0	—	0	-5	-6	-0	-0.3
1994	Min-A	1	0	1.000	14	0	0	0	0	24²	20	2	15	9	9.5	2.92	167	.233	.283	0	—	0	5	5	1	0.2
1995	Min-A	0	0	—	6	0	0	0	0	9²	8	0	5	12	12.1	4.66	102	.235	.333	0	—	0	-0	-0	-0	-0.0
Total	5	4	3	.571	77	5	0	0	1	138¹	127	8	91	80	13.7	4.55	89	.250	.355	0	—	0	-5	-6	-1	-0.3

● **MIKE CAMPBELL**   Campbell, Michael Thomas   b: 2/17/64, Seattle, Wash.   BR/TR, 6'3", 210 lbs.   Deb: 7/4/87

1987	Sea-A	1	4	.200	9	9	1	0	0	49¹	41	9	25	35	12.4	4.74	99	.224	.324	0	—	0	-2	-0	0	-0.4
1988	Sea-A	6	10	.375	20	20	2	0	0	114²	128	18	43	63	13.4	5.89	71	.280	.342	0	—	0	-24	-22	-1	-2.8
1989	Sea-A	1	2	.333	5	5	0	0	0	21	28	4	10	6	16.3	7.29	58	.301	.369	0	—	0	-8	-8	-0	-1.1
1992	Tex-A	0	1	.000	1	0	0	0	0	3²	3	1	2	2	12.3	9.82	39	.231	.333	0	—	0	-2	-0	-0	-0.4
1994	SD-N	1	1	.500	22	0	0	0	0	8²	13	5	10	10	19.4	12.96	32	.351	.429	1	.333	0	-8	-8	-0	-1.4
1996	Chi-N	3	1	.750	13	6	0	0	0	36¹	29	7	10	19	9.7	4.46	73	.216	.271	4	.364	2	-1	-1	-0	0.0
Total	6	12	19	.387	51	41	3	0	0	233¹	242	44	95	135	13.1	5.86	73	.264	.334	5	.357	2	-45	-41	-2	-6.1

● **BILLY CAMPBELL**   Campbell, William James   b: 11/5/1873, Pittsburgh, Pa.   d: 10/6/57, Cincinnati, Ohio   BL/TL, 5'10", 165 lbs.   Deb: 4/17/05

1905	StL-N	1	1	.500	2	2	2	0	0	17	27	0	7	3	18.0	7.41	40	.365	.420	1	.143	-0	-8	-8	1	-0.7
1907	Cin-N	3	0	1.000	3	3	2	0	0	21	19	0	3	4	9.4	2.14	121	.244	.272	2	.250	0	1	1	1	0.2
1908	Cin-N	12	13	.480	35	24	19	2	2	221¹	203	3	44	73	10.5	2.60	89	.252	.299	6	.083	-3	-6	-7	4	-0.8
1909	Cin-N	7	11	.389	30	15	7	0	2	148¹	162	0	39	37	12.7	2.67	97	.288	.344	6	.140	-1	-1	-1	2	0.0
Total	4	23	25	.479	70	44	31	2	4	407²	411	3	93	116	11.2	2.80	88	.270	.324	15	.115	-4	-15	-16	8	-1.3

● **BILL CAMPBELL**   Campbell, William Richard   b: 8/9/48, Highland Park, Mich.   BR/TR, 6'3", 190 lbs.   Deb: 7/14/73

1973	Min-A	3	3	.500	28	2	0	0	7	51²	44	5	20	42	11.3	3.14	126	.226	.301		—	0	4	5	0	0.4
1974	Min-A	8	7	.533	63	0	0	0	19	120¹	109	4	55	89	12.4	2.62	142	.242	.327		—	0	13	15	1	2.2
1975	Min-A	4	6	.400	47	7	2	1	5	121	119	13	46	76	12.4	3.79	101	.262	.333	0	.000	0	1	1	0	0.1
1976	Min-A	17	5	**.773**	**78**	0	0	0	20	167²	145	9	62	115	11.4	3.01	119	.234	.309	0	—	0	10	11	-0	1.5
1977	Bos-A★	13	9	.591	69	0	0	0	**31**	140	112	13	60	114	11.4	2.96	152	.224	.313		—	0	17	24	2	3.9
1978	Bos-A	7	5	.583	29	0	0	0	4	50²	62	3	17	38	14.0	3.91	105	.308	.362		—	0	1	1	-0	-0.1
1979	Bos-A	3	4	.429	41	0	0	0	9	54²	55	7	23	43	13.0	4.28	103	.262	.338		—	0	-2	-2	1	-0.4
1980	Bos-A	4	0	1.000	23	0	0	0	0	41¹	44	4	22	17	14.4	4.79	88	.284	.373		—	0	-3	-3	-0	-0.4
1981	Bos-A	1	1	.500	30	0	0	0	7	48¹	45	5	20	37	12.1	3.17	122	.245	.319		—	0	3	4	0	0.2

YEAR	TM/L	W	L	PCT	G	GS	CG	SH	SV	IP	H	HR	BB	SO	RAT	ERA	ERA+	OAV	OOB	BH	AVG	PB	PR	/A	PD	TPI
1982	Chi-N	3	6	.333	62	0	0	0	8	100	89	6	40	71	11.6	3.69	101	.245	.319	1	.143	-0	-1	0	2	0.3
1983	Chi-N	6	8	.429	**82**	0	0	0	8	122¹	128	4	49	97	13.1	4.49	84	.275	.346	1	.100	-1	-12	-9	2	-1.0
1984	Phi-N	6	5	.545	57	0	0	0	0	81¹	68	2	35	52	11.4	3.43	106	.222	.302	0	.000	-0	1	2	-1	0.1
1985	*StL-N	5	3	.625	50	0	0	0	4	64¹	51	5	21	41	10.9	3.50	101	.230	.298	2	.333	1	1	0	-1	0.0
1986	Det-A	3	6	.333	34	0	0	0	3	55²	46	5	21	37	11.0	3.88	106	.230	.306	0	—	0	2	1	-1	0.2
1987	Mon-N	0	0	—	7	0	0	0	0	10	18	2	4	4	19.8	8.10	52	.360	.407	0	.000	-0	-4	-4	0	0.0
Total 15		83	68	.550	700	9	2	1	126	1229¹	1139	82	495	864	12.1	3.54	110	.248	.324	4	.154	-8	28	47	5	7.5

● **CARDELL CAMPER**   Camper, Cardell   b: 7/6/52, Boley, Okla.   BR/TR, 6'3", 208 lbs.   Deb: 9/11/77

YEAR	TM/L	W	L	PCT	G	GS	CG	SH	SV	IP	H	HR	BB	SO	RAT	ERA	ERA+	OAV	OOB	BH	AVG	PB	PR	/A	PD	TPI
1977	Cle-A	1	0	1.000	3	1	0	0	0	9¹	7	0	4	9	10.6	3.86	102	.200	.282	0	—	0	0	0	-0	0.2

● **SAL CAMPFIELD**   Campfield, William Holton   b: 2/19/1868, Meadville, Pa.   d: 5/16/52, Meadville, Pa.   BR/TR, 6'0.5",   Deb: 5/15/1896

YEAR	TM/L	W	L	PCT	G	GS	CG	SH	SV	IP	H	HR	BB	SO	RAT	ERA	ERA+	OAV	OOB	BH	AVG	PB	PR	/A	PD	TPI
1896	NY-N	1	1	.500	6	2	2	0	0	27	31	1	6	6	13.0	4.00	105	.284	.333	2	.167	-0	-1	-1	0	0.0

● **SAL CAMPISI**   Campisi, Salvatore John   b: 8/11/42, Brooklyn, N.Y.   BR/TR, 6'2", 210 lbs.   Deb: 8/15/69

YEAR	TM/L	W	L	PCT	G	GS	CG	SH	SV	IP	H	HR	BB	SO	RAT	ERA	ERA+	OAV	OOB	BH	AVG	PB	PR	/A	PD	TPI
1969	StL-N	1	0	1.000	7	0	0	0	0	9²	4	0	6	7	9.3	0.93	384	.121	.256	0	—	0	3	3	0	0.3
1970	StL-N	2	2	.500	37	0	0	0	4	49¹	53	2	37	26	17.0	2.92	141	.282	.408	0	.000	-0	6	7	-0	0.6
1971	Min-A	0	0	—	6	0	0	0	0	4¹	5	1	4	2	18.7	4.15	86	.294	.429	0	—	0	-0	-0	0	0.0
Total 3		3	2	.600	50	0	0	0	4	63¹	62	3	47	35	15.9	2.70	148	.261	.389	0	.000	-0	9	9	0	0.9

● **HUGH CANAVAN**   Canavan, Hugh Edward "Hugo"   b: 5/13/1897, Worcester, Mass.   d: 9/4/67, Boston, Mass.   BL/TL, 5'8", 160 lbs.   Deb: 4/23/18

YEAR	TM/L	W	L	PCT	G	GS	CG	SH	SV	IP	H	HR	BB	SO	RAT	ERA	ERA+	OAV	OOB	BH	AVG	PB	PR	/A	PD	TPI
1918	Bos-N	0	4	.000	11	3	3	0	0	46²	70	0	15	18	17.4	6.36	42	.366	.427	2	.095	-0	-19	-19	1	-1.4

● **JOHN CANDELARIA**   Candelaria, John Robert "Candy Man"   b: 11/6/53, New York, N.Y.   BL/TL, 6'7", 232 lbs.   Deb: 6/8/75

YEAR	TM/L	W	L	PCT	G	GS	CG	SH	SV	IP	H	HR	BB	SO	RAT	ERA	ERA+	OAV	OOB	BH	AVG	PB	PR	/A	PD	TPI
1975	*Pit-N	8	6	.571	18	18	4	1	0	120²	95	8	36	95	9.9	2.76	128	.212	.273	6	.140	-0	12	10	-1	1.0
1976	Pit-N	16	7	.696	32	31	11	4	1	220	173	12	60	138	9.6	3.15	111	.216	.273	14	.184	3	9	8	-1	1.1
1977	Pit-N☆	20	5	**.800**	33	33	6	1	0	230²	197	29	50	133	9.7	**2.34**	**170**	.232	.276	18	.225	4	**40**	42	-2	4.7
1978	Pit-N	12	11	.522	30	29	3	1	1	189	191	15	49	94	11.7	3.24	114	.261	.312	9	.173	3	7	10	-2	1.3
1979	*Pit-N	14	9	.609	33	30	8	0	0	207	201	25	41	101	10.7	3.22	121	.253	.292	9	.132	-1	12	15	0	1.5
1980	Pit-N	11	14	.440	35	34	7	0	1	233¹	246	14	50	97	11.5	4.01	91	.276	.317	15	.195	2	-11	-10	-1	-0.8
1981	Pit-N	2	2	.500	6	6	0	0	0	40²	42	3	11	14	11.7	3.54	101	.271	.319	3	.231	0	-0	-0	0	0.0
1982	Pit-N	12	7	.632	31	30	1	1	1	174²	166	13	37	133	10.7	2.94	126	.255	.299	12	.222	3	13	15	-1	1.8
1983	Pit-N	15	8	.652	33	32	2	0	0	197²	191	15	45	157	10.8	3.23	115	.257	.302	9	.138	-0	9	10	-2	0.9
1984	Pit-N	12	11	.522	33	28	3	1	2	185¹	179	19	34	133	10.4	2.72	132	.256	.291	8	.129	1	18	18	-2	2.1
1985	Pit-N	2	4	.333	37	0	0	0	9	54¹	57	7	14	47	11.9	3.64	98	.275	.324	0	.000	-0	-0	-0	-1	-0.1
	Cal-A	7	3	.700	13	13	1	1	0	71	70	7	24	53	12.3	3.80	108	.262	.330	0	—	0	3	2	-1	0.3
1986	*Cal-A	10	2	.833	16	16	1	1	0	91²	68	4	26	81	9.5	2.55	161	.206	.270	0	—	0	17	16	-1	1.9
1987	Cal-A	8	6	.571	20	20	0	0	0	116²	127	17	20	74	11.4	4.71	91	.279	.311	0	—	0	-3	-5	1	-0.2
	NY-N	2	0	1.000	3	3	0	0	0	12¹	17	1	3	14	14.6	5.84	65	.333	.370	1	.200	0	-2	-3	0	-0.4
1988	NY-A	13	7	.650	25	24	6	2	1	157	150	18	23	121	10.0	3.38	116	.248	.278	0	—	0	10	10	-0	1.2
1989	NY-A	3	3	.500	10	6	1	0	0	49	49	8	12	37	11.2	5.14	75	.258	.302	0	—	0	-7	-7	-0	-0.8
	Mon-N	0	2	.000	12	0	0	0	0	16¹	17	3	4	14	11.6	3.31	107	.283	.328	0	—	0	0	0	0	0.0
1990	Min-A	7	3	.700	34	1	0	0	4	58¹	55	9	9	44	9.9	3.39	122	.244	.274	0	—	0	3	5	-1	0.7
	Tor-A	0	3	.000	13	2	0	0	1	21¹	32	2	11	19	19.0	5.48	72	.356	.437	0	—	0	-4	-4	1	-0.4
	Yr	7	6	.538	47	3	0	0	5	79²	87	11	20	63	12.3	3.95	104	.274	.321	0	—	0	-0	1	-0	0.3
1991	LA-N	1	1	.500	59	0	0	0	2	33²	31	3	11	38	11.2	3.74	96	.252	.313	0	—	0	2	0	-1	-0.1
1992	LA-N	2	5	.286	50	0	0	0	5	25¹	20	1	13	23	11.7	2.84	121	.220	.317	0	—	0	2	2	0	0.6
1993	Pit-N	0	3	.000	24	0	0	0	1	19²	25	3	9	17	16.0	8.24	49	.313	.389	0	—	0	-9	-9	-1	-1.4
Total 19		177	122	.592	600	356	54	13	29	2525²	2399	245	592	1673	10.8	3.33	114	.251	.298	104	.174	15	117	126	-13	14.9

● **MILO CANDINI**   Candini, Mario Cain   b: 8/3/17, Manteca, Cal.   BR/TR, 6', 187 lbs.   Deb: 5/1/43

YEAR	TM/L	W	L	PCT	G	GS	CG	SH	SV	IP	H	HR	BB	SO	RAT	ERA	ERA+	OAV	OOB	BH	AVG	PB	PR	/A	PD	TPI
1943	Was-A	11	7	.611	28	21	8	3	1	166	144	3	65	67	11.4	2.49	128	.238	.313	9	.161	-1	15	13	1	1.4
1944	Was-A	6	7	.462	28	10	4	2	1	103	110	3	49	31	14.0	4.11	79	.276	.357	10	.313	3	-8	-10	-0	-0.9
1946	Was-A	2	0	1.000	9	0	0	0	1	21²	15	1	4	6	7.9	2.08	161	.192	.232	2	.333	1	3	3	-0	0.4
1947	Was-A	3	4	.429	38	2	0	0	1	87	96	5	35	31	13.6	5.17	72	.273	.339	3	.167	-0	-14	-14	0	-1.0
1948	Was-A	2	3	.400	35	4	1	0	3	94¹	96	4	63	23	15.3	5.15	84	.267	.378	8	.364	-0	-9	-8	-0	-0.2
1949	Was-A	0	0	—	3	0	0	0	0	5²	4	0	1	1	7.9	4.76	89	.200	.238	1	1.000	0	-0	-0	-0	0.0
1950	Phi-N	1	0	1.000	18	0	0	0	1	30	32	2	15	10	14.1	2.70	150	.281	.364	1	.167	-0	5	4	1	0.4
1951	Phi-N	1	0	1.000	15	0	0	0	0	30	33	3	18	14	15.3	6.00	64	.275	.370	1	.333	1	-7	-7	0	-0.1
Total 8		26	21	.553	174	37	13	5	8	537²	530	18	250	183	13.1	3.92	92	.259	.341	35	.243	7	-15	-19	1	-0.2

● **TOM CANDIOTTI**   Candiotti, Thomas Caesar   b: 8/31/57, Walnut Creek, Cal.   BR/TR, 6'3", 205 lbs.   Deb: 8/8/83

YEAR	TM/L	W	L	PCT	G	GS	CG	SH	SV	IP	H	HR	BB	SO	RAT	ERA	ERA+	OAV	OOB	BH	AVG	PB	PR	/A	PD	TPI
1983	Mil-A	4	4	.500	10	8	2	1	0	55²	62	4	16	21	12.9	3.23	116	.291	.346	0	—	0	5	3	-1	0.5
1984	Mil-A	2	2	.500	8	6	0	0	0	32¹	38	5	10	23	13.4	5.29	73	.277	.327	0	—	0	-5	-5	-1	-0.6
1986	Cle-A	16	12	.571	36	34	**17**	3	0	252¹	234	18	106	167	12.4	3.57	116	.246	.326	0	—	0	17	16	3	1.9
1987	Cle-A	7	18	.280	32	32	7	2	0	201²	193	28	93	111	12.9	4.78	95	.250	.333	0	—	0	-6	-0	-0	-0.6
1988	Cle-A	14	8	.636	31	31	11	1	0	216²	225	15	53	137	11.8	3.28	125	.272	.321	0	—	0	16	20	2	2.1
1989	Cle-A	13	10	.565	31	31	4	0	0	206	188	10	55	124	10.8	3.10	128	.242	.295	0	—	0	18	20	4	2.5
1990	Cle-A	15	11	.577	31	29	3	1	0	202	207	23	55	128	11.9	3.65	107	.263	.316	0	—	0	6	3	1	1.0
1991	Cle-A	7	6	.538	15	15	3	0	0	108¹	88	6	28	86	9.8	2.24	185	.218	.272	0	—	0	22	23	-0	2.7
	*Tor-A	6	7	.462	19	19	3	0	0	129²	114	6	45	81	11.3	2.98	141	.236	.306	0	—	0	16	18	-0	1.7
	Yr	13	13	.500	34	34	6	0	0	238	202	12	73	167	10.6	2.65	158	.225	.287	0	—	0	38	41	-0	4.4
1992	LA-N	11	15	.423	32	30	6	2	0	203²	177	19	63	152	10.7	3.00	115	.237	.299	6	.107	-1	11	10	1	1.2
1993	LA-N	8	10	.444	33	32	2	0	0	213²	192	12	71	155	11.3	3.12	122	.241	.308	8	.133	-1	22	17	-0	1.7
1994	LA-N	7	7	.500	23	22	5	0	0	153	149	9	54	102	12.2	4.12	95	.259	.328	7	.140	-1	2	-3	1	-0.3
1995	LA-N	7	14	.333	30	30	1	1	0	190¹	187	18	58	141	12.0	3.50	108	.255	.318	6	.109	-1	14	6	-0	0.4
1996	*LA-N	9	11	.450	28	27	1	0	0	152¹	172	18	43	79	12.9	4.49	86	.288	.339	4	.089	-2	-5	-11	3	-1.1
Total 13		126	135	.483	359	346	65	11	0	2317²	2226	185	750	1507	11.8	3.53	112	.253	.316	31	.117	-6	133	114	16	12.6

● **JOHN CANEIRA**   Caneira, John Cascaes   b: 10/7/52, Waterbury, Conn.   BR/TR, 6'3", 180 lbs.   Deb: 9/10/77

YEAR	TM/L	W	L	PCT	G	GS	CG	SH	SV	IP	H	HR	BB	SO	RAT	ERA	ERA+	OAV	OOB	BH	AVG	PB	PR	/A	PD	TPI
1977	Cal-A	2	2	.500	6	4	0	0	0	28²	27	5	16	17	13.5	4.08	96	.252	.350	0	—	0	-0	-1	-1	0.2
1978	Cal-A	0	0	—	2	2	0	0	0	7²	8	2	3	0	12.9	7.04	51	.286	.355	0	—	0	-3	-3	-0	0.1
Total 2		2	2	.500	8	6	0	0	0	36¹	35	7	19	17	13.4	4.71	82	.259	.351	0	—	0	-3	-3	-1	0.3

● **JOHN CANGELOSI**   Cangelosi, John Anthony   b: 3/10/63, Brooklyn, N.Y.   BB/TL, 5'8", 150 lbs.   Deb: 6/3/85 ♦

YEAR	TM/L	W	L	PCT	G	GS	CG	SH	SV	IP	H	HR	BB	SO	RAT	ERA	ERA+	OAV	OOB	BH	AVG	PB	PR	/A	PD	TPI
1988	Pit-N	0	0	—	1	0	0	0	0	2	1	0	0	0	4.5	0.00	—	.143	.143	30	.254	0	1	1	-0	0.0
1995	Hou-N	0	0	—	1	0	0	0	0	1	0	0	1	0	9.0	0.00	—	.000	.250	64	.318	0	0	0	0	0.0
Total 2		0	0	—	2	0	0	0	0	3	1	0	1	0	6.0	0.00	—	.100	.182	410	.251	1	1	1	0	0.0

● **JOSE CANO**   Cano, Joselito (Soriano)   b: 3/7/62, Boca De Soco, D.R.   BR/TR, 6'3", 175 lbs.   Deb: 8/28/89

YEAR	TM/L	W	L	PCT	G	GS	CG	SH	SV	IP	H	HR	BB	SO	RAT	ERA	ERA+	OAV	OOB	BH	AVG	PB	PR	/A	PD	TPI
1989	Hou-N	1	1	.500	6	3	1	0	0	23	24	2	7	8	12.1	5.09	67	.267	.320	0	.000	-1	-4	-4	-0	-0.4

● **JOSE CANSECO**   Canseco, Jose (Capas)   b: 7/2/64, Havana, Cuba   BR/TR, 6'3", 240 lbs.   Deb: 9/2/85   F♦

YEAR	TM/L	W	L	PCT	G	GS	CG	SH	SV	IP	H	HR	BB	SO	RAT	ERA	ERA+	OAV	OOB	BH	AVG	PB	PR	/A	PD	TPI
1993	Tex-A	0	0	—	1	0	0	0	0	1	2	0	3	0	45.0	27.00	15	.500	.714	39	.255	1	-3	-3	0	-0.4

● **GUY CANTRELL**   Cantrell, Guy Dewey "Gunner"   b: 4/9/04, Clarita, Okla.   d: 1/31/61, McAlester, Okla.   BR/TR, 6', 190 lbs.   Deb: 8/18/25

YEAR	TM/L	W	L	PCT	G	GS	CG	SH	SV	IP	H	HR	BB	SO	RAT	ERA	ERA+	OAV	OOB	BH	AVG	PB	PR	/A	PD	TPI
1925	Bro-N	1	0	1.000	14	3	1	0	0	36	42	0	14	13	14.3	3.00	139	.294	.361	4	.294	-1	5	5	1	0.1
1927	Bro-N	0	0	—	7	1	0	0	0	10	10	0	6	5	14.4	2.70	147	.250	.348	1	.333	0	1	1	0	0.0
	Phi-A	0	2	.000	1	1	1	0	0	18	25	0	7	7	16.0	5.00	85	.338	.395	1	.167	0	-2	-1	0	-0.2
1930	Det-A	1	5	.167	16	2	1	0	0	35	38	5	20	20	15.2	5.66	85	.271	.366	0	.000	-2	-4	-3	1	-0.5
Total 3		2	7	.222	38	7	4	0	0	99	115	5	47	45	14.9	4.27	103	.290	.368	6	.074	-3	-0	-0	2	-0.6

YEAR	TM/L	W	L	PCT	G	GS	CG	SH	SV	IP	H	HR	BB	SO	RAT	ERA	ERA+	OAV	OOB	BH	AVG	PB	PR	/A	PD	TPI

● **BEN CANTWELL**   Cantwell, Benjamin Caldwell   b: 4/13/02, Milan, Tenn.   d: 12/4/62, Salem, Mo.   BR/TR, 6'1", 168 lbs.   Deb: 8/19/27

1927	NY-N	1	1	.500	5	2	1	0	0	19²	26	1	2	6	13.3	4.12	94	.313	.337	2	.250	-0	-0	-1	-0	-0.1
1928	NY-N	1	0	1.000	7	1	0	0	1	18¹	20	1	4	0	12.3	4.42	89	.282	.329	1	.500	-1	-1	-1	1	0.1
	Bos-N	3	3	.500	22	9	3	0	0	90	112	7	36	18	15.0	5.10	77	.304	.369	5	.172	-1	-11	-12	1	-0.7
	Yr	4	3	.571	29	10	3	0	1	108¹	132	8	40	18	14.5	4.98	79	.300	.361	7	.212	-0	-12	-13	2	-0.6
1929	Bos-N	4	13	.235	27	20	8	0	2	157	171	11	52	25	12.9	4.47	105	.280	.338	9	.180	-0	4	4	4	0.7
1930	Bos-N	9	15	.375	31	21	10	0	2	173¹	213	16	45	43	13.4	4.88	101	.312	.355	19	.302	2	2	1	4	0.7
1931	Bos-N	7	9	.438	33	16	9	2	2	156¹	160	4	34	32	11.2	3.63	104	.262	.301	13	.228	0	4	3	3	0.6
1932	Bos-N	13	11	.542	37	9	3	1	5	146	133	6	33	33	10.5	2.96	127	.247	.296	14	.280	2	15	13	3	2.6
1933	Bos-N	20	10	.667	40	29	18	2	2	254²	242	12	54	57	10.6	2.62	117	.249	.291	12	.141	-1	20	13	4	1.8
1934	Bos-N	5	11	.313	27	19	6	1	5	143¹	163	8	34	45	12.5	4.33	88	.285	.327	12	.279	1	-4	-8	2	-0.5
1935	Bos-N	4	25	.138	39	24	13	0	0	210²	235	15	44	34	12.0	4.61	82	.282	.320	19	.284	-1	-14	-19	2	-1.7
1936	Bos-N	9	9	.500	34	12	4	0	0	133¹	127	8	35	42	11.2	3.04	126	.252	.306	8	.195	-1	15	12	3	1.7
1937	NY-N	0	1	.000	1	1	0	0	0	4	6	1	1	1	15.8	9.00	43	.375	.412	0	—	0	-2	-2	0	-0.4
	Bro-N	0	0	—	13	0	0	0	0	27¹	32	1	8	12	13.2	4.61	88	.288	.336	1	.167	-0	-2	-2	2	0.2
	Yr	0	1	.000	14	1	0	0	0	31¹	38	2	9	13	13.5	5.17	78	.299	.346	1	.167	-0	-4	-4	2	-0.2
Total	11	76	108	.413	316	163	75	6	21	1534	1640	90	382	348	12.1	3.91	100	.275	.321	116	.231	8	25	-2	28	5.0

● **MIKE CANTWELL**   Cantwell, Michael Joseph   b: 1/15/1896, Washington, D.C.   d: 1/5/53, Oteen, N.C.   BL/TL, 5'10", 155 lbs.   Deb: 8/17/16   F

1916	NY-A	0	0	—	1	0	0	0	0	2	0	0	2	0	9.00	0.00	—	.000	.333	0	—	1	1	-0	0.0
1919	Phi-N	1	3	.250	5	3	2	0	0	27¹	36	1	9	6	15.5	5.60	58	.343	.405	2	.222	-0	-8	-7	-1	-1.0
1920	Phi-N	0	3	.000	5	1	0	0	0	23¹	25	1	15	8	16.6	3.86	89	.284	.406	1	.143	-1	-2	-1	0	-0.2
Total	3	1	6	.143	11	4	2	0	0	52²	61	2	26	14	15.7	4.61	71	.310	.404	3	.188	-1	-9	-8	-1	-1.2

● **TOM CANTWELL**   Cantwell, Thomas Aloysius   b: 12/23/1888, Washington, D.C.   d: 4/1/68, Washington, D.C.   BL/TR, 6', 170 lbs.   Deb: 5/19/09   F

1909	Cin-N	1	0	1.000	6	1	1	0	0	21²	16	0	7	10	10.0	1.66	156	.205	.279	3	.600	1	2	2	-0	0.3
1910	Cin-N	0	0	—	2	0	0	0	0	1¹	2	0	3	0	33.8	13.50	22	.400	.625	0	—	0	-2	-2	-0	0.0
Total	2	1	0	1.000	8	1	1	0	0	23	18	0	10	10	12.5	2.35	111	.217	.309	3	.600	1	1	1	-0	0.3

● **MIKE CAPEL**   Capel, Michael Lee   b: 10/13/61, Marshall, Tex.   BR/TR, 6'1", 175 lbs.   Deb: 5/7/88

1988	Chi-N	2	1	.667	22	0	0	0	0	29¹	34	5	13	19	15.3	4.91	73	.293	.379	0	.000	-0	-5	-4	-0	-0.5
1990	Mil-A	0	0	—	2	0	0	0	0	0¹	6	0	1	1	216.0	135.00	3	.857	.889	0	—	-0	-5	-5	-0	-0.5
1991	Hou-N	1	3	.250	25	0	0	0	0	32²	33	3	15	23	13.2	3.03	116	.266	.345	0	—	0	2	2	0	0.2
Total	3	3	4	.429	49	0	0	0	0	62¹	73	8	29	43	15.3	4.62	77	.296	.379	0	.000	-0	-7	-7	-0	-0.7

● **DOUG CAPILLA**   Capilla, Douglas Edmund   b: 1/7/52, Honolulu, Hawaii   BL/TL, 5'8", 175 lbs.   Deb: 9/12/76

1976	StL-N	1	0	1.000	7	0	0	0	0	8¹	9	1	4	5	13.0	5.40	65	.242	.324	0	—	-2	-2	-0	-0.2
1977	StL-N	0	0	—	2	0	0	0	0	2¹	2	0	2	1	15.4	15.43	25	.222	.364	0	—	-3	-3	-0	-0.3
	Cin-N	7	8	.467	22	16	1	0	0	106¹	94	10	59	74	13.1	4.23	93	.237	.338	2	.059	-3	-4	-4	-1	-0.8
	Yr	7	8	.467	24	16	1	0	0	108²	96	10	61	75	13.2	4.47	88	.236	.339	2	.059	-3	-7	-7	-1	-0.8
1978	Cin-N	0	1	.000	6	3	0	0	0	11	14	1	11	9	20.5	9.82	36	.318	.455	0	.000	-0	-8	-8	-0	-0.7
1979	Cin-N	1	0	1.000	5	0	0	0	0	6¹	7	1	5	6	18.5	8.53	44	.269	.406	1	1.000	0	-3	-3	-0	-0.4
	Chi-N	1	0	.000	13	1	0	0	0	17¹	14	1	7	10	10.9	2.60	159	.206	.280	0	—	0	2	3	0	0.2
	Yr	1	1	.500	18	1	0	0	0	23²	21	2	12	10	12.5	4.18	96	.221	.308	1	1.000	0	-1	-0	1	-0.2
1980	Chi-N	2	8	.200	39	11	0	0	0	89²	82	7	51	51	13.7	4.12	95	.253	.360	4	.190	0	-5	-2	1	-0.1
1981	Chi-N	1	0	1.000	42	0	0	0	0	51	52	1	34	28	15.5	3.18	116	.284	.402	0	.000	-0	2	3	0	0.0
Total	6	12	18	.400	136	31	1	0	0	292¹	273	21	173	178	14.0	4.34	89	.252	.359	7	.115	-3	-21	-15	0	-2.0

● **GEORGE CAPPUZZELLO**   Cappuzzello, George Angelo   b: 1/15/54, Youngstown, Ohio   BR/TL, 6', 175 lbs.   Deb: 5/31/81

1981	Det-A	1	1	.500	18	3	0	0	1	33²	28	2	18	19	12.8	3.48	108	.222	.329	0	—	0	1	1	-0	0.0
1982	Hou-N	0	1	.000	17	0	0	0	0	19¹	16	2	7	13	12.1	2.79	119	.232	.329	0	.000	-0	2	1	0	0.1
Total	2	1	2	.333	35	3	0	0	1	53	44	4	25	32	12.6	3.23	112	.226	.329	0	.000	-0	2	2	0	0.1

● **BUZZ CAPRA**   Capra, Lee William   b: 10/1/47, Chicago, Ill.   BR/TR, 5'10", 168 lbs.   Deb: 9/15/71

1971	NY-N	0	1	.000	3	0	0	0	0	5¹	3	0	5	6	13.5	8.44	40	.167	.348	0	.000	-0	-3	-3	0	-0.5
1972	NY-N	3	2	.600	14	6	0	0	0	53	50	7	27	45	13.1	4.58	73	.253	.342	3	.250	1	-7	-7	1	-0.4
1973	NY-N	2	7	.222	24	0	0	0	4	42	35	4	28	35	13.9	3.86	94	.233	.361	0	.000	-0	-1	-1	0	-0.2
1974	Atl-N☆	16	8	.667	39	27	11	5	1	217	163	13	84	137	10.4	2.28	166	.208	.287	11	.164	0	32	36	-3	3.7
1975	Atl-N	4	7	.364	12	12	5	0	0	78¹	77	8	28	69	12.2	4.25	89	.257	.322	1	.043	-2	-5	-4	1	-0.7
1976	Atl-N	0	1	.000	5	0	0	0	0	9¹	14	1	7	6	14.5	8.68	44	.265	.375	0	—	-0	-5	-5	-0	-0.5
1977	Atl-N	6	11	.353	45	16	0	0	0	139¹	142	8	80	100	14.6	5.36	83	.263	.362	4	.111	-2	-22	-14	-1	-1.7
Total	7	31	37	.456	142	61	16	5	5	544¹	479	50	258	362	12.4	3.87	100	.237	.326	19	.135	-2	-12	-1	0	-0.3

● **PAT CARAWAY**   Caraway, Cecil Bradford Patrick   b: 9/26/05, Erath Co., Tex.   d: 6/9/74, El Paso, Tex.   BL/TL, 6'4", 175 lbs.   Deb: 4/19/30

1930	Chi-A	10	10	.500	38	21	9	1	1	193¹	194	11	57	83	11.8	3.86	120	.267	.323	11	.172	-1	17	16	3	1.6
1931	Chi-A	10	24	.294	51	32	11	1	2	220	268	17	101	55	15.4	6.22	68	.295	.370	14	.194	-1	-45	-48	-1	-6.1
1932	Chi-A	2	6	.250	19	9	1	0	0	64²	80	6	37	13	16.7	6.82	63	.304	.396	3	.143	-1	-17	-18	0	-1.8
Total	3	22	40	.355	108	62	21	2	3	478	542	34	195	151	14.1	5.35	83	.286	.356	28	.178	-3	-45	-50	2	-6.3

● **JOHN CARDEN**   Carden, John Bruton   b: 5/19/21, Killeen, Tex.   d: 2/8/49, Mexia, Tex.   BR/TR, 6'5", 210 lbs.   Deb: 5/18/46

| 1946 | NY-N | 0 | 0 | — | 1 | 0 | 0 | 0 | 0 | 2 | 4 | 0 | 4 | 1 | 40.5 | 22.50 | 15 | .400 | .600 | 0 | — | 0 | -4 | -4 | 0 | 0.0 |

● **CONRAD CARDINAL**   Cardinal, Conrad Seth   b: 3/30/42, Brooklyn, N.Y.   BR/TR, 6'1", 190 lbs.   Deb: 4/11/63

| 1963 | Hou-N | 0 | 1 | .000 | 6 | 1 | 0 | 0 | 0 | 13¹ | 15 | 0 | 7 | 7 | 14.9 | 6.08 | 52 | .283 | .367 | 0 | .000 | -0 | -4 | -4 | 0 | -0.3 |

● **BEN CARDONI**   Cardoni, Armand Joseph "Big Ben"   b: 8/21/20, Jessup, Pa.   d: 4/2/69, Jessup, Pa.   BR/TR, 6'3", 195 lbs.   Deb: 8/22/43

1943	Bos-N	0	0	—	11	0	0	0	1	28	38	1	14	9	17.0	6.43	53	.336	.414	0	.000	-1	-9	-9	-0	-0.2
1944	Bos-N	0	6	.000	22	5	1	0	0	75²	83	5	37	24	14.4	3.93	97	.284	.367	4	.235	-0	-3	-1	-1	-0.1
1945	Bos-N	0	0	—	3	0	0	0	0	4	6	0	3	5	22.5	9.00	43	.300	.417	0	—	-0	-2	-2	-0	0.0
Total	3	0	6	.000	36	5	1	0	1	107²	127	6	54	34	15.4	4.76	78	.299	.382	4	.167	-1	-14	-13	-1	-0.3

● **DON CARDWELL**   Cardwell, Donald Eugene   b: 12/7/35, Winston-Salem, N.C.   BR/TR, 6'4", 210 lbs.   Deb: 4/21/57

1957	Phi-N	4	8	.333	30	19	5	1	1	128¹	122	17	42	92	11.8	4.91	78	.251	.316	7	.200	1	-15	-16	-0	-1.2
1958	Phi-N	4	8	.333	16	14	3	0	0	107²	99	16	37	77	11.5	4.51	88	.241	.307	8	.211	1	-7	-7	-0	-0.4
1959	Phi-N	9	10	.474	25	22	5	0	0	153	135	22	65	106	12.0	4.06	101	.238	.320	2	.055	-3	-1	1	-3	-0.5
1960	Phi-N	1	2	.333	5	4	0	0	0	28¹	28	4	11	21	12.7	4.45	87	.262	.336	2	.250	-2	-2	-0	-0	-0.1
	Chi-N	8	14	.364	31	26	6	1	0	177	166	19	68	129	12.2	4.37	86	.249	.323	14	.203	3	-12	-12	-2	-1.1
	Yr	9	16	.360	36	30	6	1	0	205¹	194	23	79	150	12.2	4.38	87	.250	.324	16	.208	5	-14	-13	-2	-1.1
1961	Chi-N	15	14	.517	39	38	13	3	0	259¹	243	26	88	156	11.8	3.82	110	.246	.314	10	.105	-1	6	10	2	1.2
1962	Chi-N	7	16	.304	41	29	6	1	4	195²	205	27	60	104	12.6	4.92	84	.267	.327	9	.148	-0	-21	-17	1	-1.7
1963	Pit-N	13	15	.464	33	32	7	2	0	213²	195	21	52	112	11.1	3.07	107	.245	.305	6	.085	-2	5	5	-1	0.4
1964	Pit-N	1	2	.333	4	4	1	0	0	19¹	15	1	7	10	11.6	2.79	126	.217	.316	1	.143	-0	2	2	0	0.3
1965	Pit-N	13	10	.565	37	34	13	2	1	240¹	214	21	59	107	10.7	3.18	110	.239	.295	12	.162	3	10	9	2	1.3
1966	Pit-N	6	6	.500	32	14	1	0	0	101²	112	15	27	60	12.8	4.60	78	.282	.337	3	.103	-1	-11	-12	-1	-1.1
1967	NY-N	5	9	.357	26	16	3	0	0	118¹	112	8	39	71	12.0	3.57	95	.249	.319	6	.158	-0	-3	-2	0	-0.2
1968	NY-N	7	13	.350	29	25	5	1	0	179²	156	19	50	82	10.8	2.96	102	.233	.296	5	.049	-3	1	1	-3	0.1
1969	*NY-N	8	10	.444	30	21	4	0	0	152¹	145	15	47	60	11.6	3.01	121	.252	.314	8	.170	-1	10	11	2	1.6
1970	NY-N	0	2	.000	16	1	0	0	0	25	31	6	11	8	14.4	6.48	62	.306	.374	0	.000	-0	-7	-7	0	-0.5
	Atl-N	2	1	.667	16	2	1	0	0	23	31	5	13	16	17.6	9.00	48	.326	.413	2	.400	-1	-12	-12	1	-1.2
	Yr	2	3	.400	32	3	1	0	0	48	62	11	24	24	15.4	7.69	54	.312	.374	2	.200	-0	-19	-19	1	-1.7
Total	14	102	138	.425	410	301	72	17	7	2122²	2009	225	671	1211	11.8	3.92	95	.250	.315	94	.135	2	-59	-47	10	-2.7

YEAR	TM/L	W	L	PCT	G	GS	CG	SH	SV	IP	H	HR	BB	SO	RAT	ERA	ERA+	OAV	OOB	BH	AVG	PB	PR	/A	PD	TPI

● **TEX CARLETON**   Carleton, James Otto b: 8/19/06, Comanche, Tex. d: 1/11/77, Fort Worth, Tex.   BB/TR, 6'1.5", 180 lbs. Deb: 4/17/32

1932	StL-N	10	13	.435	44	22	9	3	0	196¹	198	12	70	113	12.4	4.08	96	.261	.326	9	.150	-2	-4	-3	2	-0.3
1933	StL-N	17	11	.607	44	33	15	4	3	277	263	15	97	147	11.8	3.38	103	.249	.315	17	.187	1	-1	3	-1	0.3
1934	*StL-N	16	11	.593	40	31	16	0	2	240²	260	14	52	103	11.9	4.26	99	.271	.314	11	.193	1	-5	-1	-0	-0.1
1935	*Chi-N	11	8	.579	31	22	8	0	1	171	169	17	60	84	12.2	3.89	101	.257	.322	8	.129	-3	2	1	2	0.0
1936	Chi-N	14	10	.583	35	26	12	4	1	197¹	204	14	67	88	12.6	3.65	109	.268	.332	14	.233	6	8	7	2	1.6
1937	Chi-N	16	8	.667	32	27	18	4	0	208¹	183	10	94	105	12.1	3.15	126	.236	.321	12	.169	1	18	19	1	2.2
1938	Chi-N	10	9	.526	33	24	9	0	0	167²	213	11	74	80	15.8	5.42	71	.307	.381	15	.231	3	-30	-30	-0	-2.7
1940	Bro-N	6	6	.500	34	17	4	1	2	149	140	12	47	88	11.5	3.81	105	.245	.305	8	.186	-0	1	3	-1	0.1
Total	8	100	76	.568	293	202	91	16	9	1607¹	1630	105	561	808	12.5	3.91	100	.261	.326	100	.185	6	-13	-0	6	1.1

● **CISCO CARLOS**   Carlos, Francisco Manuel b: 9/17/40, Monrovia, Cal.   BR/TR, 6'3", 205 lbs. Deb: 8/25/67

1967	Chi-A	2	0	1.000	8	7	1	1	0	41²	23	0	9	27	7.1	0.86	359	.161	.216	1	.063	-1	11	10	0	0.4
1968	Chi-A	4	14	.222	29	21	0	0	0	122¹	121	13	37	57	12.4	3.90	78	.258	.326	2	.065	-1	-13	-12	2	-1.7
1969	Chi-A	4	3	.571	25	4	0	0	0	49¹	52	4	23	28	14.6	5.66	68	.274	.367	0	.000	-1	-11	-10	1	-1.3
	Was-A	1	1	.500	6	4	0	0	0	17²	23	2	6	5	14.8	4.58	76	.348	.403	1	.200	-1	-2	-2	-0	-0.1
	Yr	5	4	.556	31	8	0	0	0	67	75	6	29	33	14.0	5.37	70	.287	.359	1	.067	-0	-13	-12	1	-1.4
1970	Was-A	0	0	—	5	0	0	0	0	6	3	0	4	2	10.5	1.50	237	.150	.292	0	—	0	1	1	0	0.0
Total	4	11	18	.379	73	36	1	1	0	237	222	19	79	119	12.0	3.72	88	.250	.322	4	.065	-3	-13	-12	3	-2.7

● **DON CARLSEN**   Carlsen, Donald Herbert b: 10/15/26, Chicago, Ill.   BR/TR, 6'1", 175 lbs. Deb: 4/28/48

1948	Chi-N	0	0	—	1	0	0	0	0	1	5	0	2	1	63.0	36.00	11	.625	.700	0	—	0	-4	-4	0	0.0
1951	Pit-N	2	3	.400	7	6	0	0	0	43	50	4	14	20	13.6	4.19	101	.292	.349	4	.250	-1	-1	0	-1	0.0
1952	Pit-N	0	1	.000	5	1	0	0	0	10	20	1	5	2	22.5	10.80	37	.417	.472	1	.333	0	-8	-8	1	-0.6
Total	3	2	4	.333	13	7	0	0	0	54	75	5	21	23	16.2	6.00	70	.330	.390	5	.263	-1	-12	-11	0	-0.6

● **DAN CARLSON**   Carlson, Daniel Steven b: 1/26/70, Portland, Ore.   BR/TR, 6'1", 185 lbs. Deb: 9/15/96

| 1996 | SF-N | 1 | 0 | 1.000 | 5 | 0 | 0 | 0 | 0 | 10 | 13 | 2 | 4 | 13 | 13.5 | 2.70 | 151 | .310 | .341 | 0 | .000 | -0 | 2 | 2 | -0 | 0.1 |

● **HAL CARLSON**   Carlson, Harold Gust b: 5/17/1892, Rockford, Ill. d: 5/28/30, Chicago, Ill.   BR/TR, 6', 180 lbs. Deb: 4/13/17

1917	Pit-N	7	11	.389	34	17	9	1	1	161¹	140	0	49	68	10.8	2.90	98	.241	.304	6	.122	-2	-3	-1	2	-0.2
1918	Pit-N	0	1	.000	3	2	0	0	0	12	12	1	5	5	12.8	3.75	77	.286	.362	1	.200	-1	-1	-1	0	-0.1
1919	Pit-N	8	10	.444	22	14	7	1	0	141	114	0	39	49	9.9	2.23	135	.243	.303	7	.163	-1	11	12	1	1.7
1920	Pit-N	14	13	.519	39	31	16	3	3	246²	262	4	63	62	12.1	3.36	96	.281	.331	23	.271	3	-6	-4	-5	-0.6
1921	Pit-N	4	8	.333	31	10	3	0	4	109²	121	6	23	37	12.0	4.27	90	.290	.330	15	.294	1	-6	-5	1	-0.4
1922	Pit-N	9	12	.429	39	18	6	0	2	145¹	193	10	58	64	15.8	5.70	75	.323	.386	15	.268	3	-26	-26	2	-2.7
1923	Pit-N	0	0	—	4	0	0	0	0	13¹	19	1	4	14	14.9	4.73	85	.358	.393	0	.000	-0	-1	-1	0	-0.1
1924	Phi-N	8	17	.320	38	23	12	1	2	203²	267	9	55	66	14.4	4.86	92	.329	.374	21	.276	2	-22	-9	-1	-0.8
1925	Phi-N	13	14	.481	35	32	18	4	0	234	281	19	52	80	13.0	4.23	113	.298	.338	17	.183	-2	1	14	-1	1.1
1926	Phi-N	17	12	.586	35	34	20	3	0	267¹	293	9	47	55	11.5	3.23	128	.281	.313	23	.240	2	18	27	-4	2.6
1927	Phi-N	4	5	.444	11	9	4	0	1	63²	80	7	18	13	13.9	5.23	79	.316	.362	4	.240	-0	-9	-8	-1	-1.0
	Chi-N	12	8	.600	27	22	15	2	0	184¹	201	9	27	27	11.2	3.17	122	.280	.307	11	.164	-3	15	14	-0	1.0
	Yr	16	13	.552	38	31	19	2	1	248	281	16	45	40	11.9	3.70	106	.289	.322	17	.185	-3	6	6	-1	0.0
1928	Chi-N	3	2	.600	20	5	2	0	0	56¹	74	4	15	11	14.2	5.91	65	.329	.371	5	.263	-0	-12	-13	0	-1.1
1929	*Chi-N	11	5	.688	31	14	6	2	0	111²	131	11	31	35	13.1	5.16	90	.292	.340	9	.231	0	-5	-7	2	-0.6
1930	Chi-N	4	2	.667	8	6	3	0	0	51²	68	5	14	14	14.5	5.05	97	.313	.358	5	.250	-0	-0	-1	1	0.0
Total	14	114	120	.487	377	237	121	17	19	2002	2256	93	498	590	12.5	3.97	99	.291	.337	159	.223	4	-49	-0	-0	-1.1

● **LEON CARLSON**   Carlson, Leon Alton "Swede" b: 2/17/1895, Jamestown, N.Y. d: 9/15/61, Jamestown, N.Y.   BR/TR, 6'3", 195 lbs. Deb: 5/31/20

| 1920 | Was-A | 0 | 0 | — | 3 | 0 | 0 | 0 | 0 | 12¹ | 14 | 1 | 2 | 3 | 11.7 | 3.65 | 102 | .292 | .320 | 1 | .167 | -0 | 0 | 0 | -0 | -0.1 |

● **STEVE CARLTON**   Carlton, Steven Norman "Lefty" b: 12/22/44, Miami, Fla.   BL/TL, 6'4", 210 lbs. Deb: 4/12/65   H

1965	StL-N	0	0	—	15	2	0	0	0	25	27	3	8	21	13.0	2.52	153	.287	.350	0	.000	-0	3	4	1	0.0
1966	StL-N	3	3	.500	9	9	2	1	0	52	56	2	18	25	12.8	3.12	115	.280	.339	4	.267	1	3	3	0	0.4
1967	*StL-N	14	9	.609	30	28	11	2	1	193	173	10	62	168	11.1	2.98	110	.238	.300	11	.153	1	8	6	0	0.8
1968	*StL-N	13	11	.542	34	33	10	5	0	231²	214	11	61	162	10.8	2.99	97	.246	.298	12	.164	2	-0	-2	-1	-0.1
1969	StL-N★	17	11	.607	31	31	12	2	0	236¹	185	15	93	210	10.7	2.17	165	.216	.295	17	.213	5	37	37	-1	4.9
1970	StL-N	10	19	.345	34	33	13	2	0	253²	239	25	109	193	12.4	3.73	110	.251	.329	16	.200	2	9	11	-1	1.2
1971	StL-N☆	20	9	.690	37	36	18	4	0	273¹	275	23	98	172	12.4	3.56	101	.262	.328	17	.177	1	-3	1	-0	0.2
1972	Phi-N★	27	10	.730	41	41	30	8	0	346¹	257	17	87	310	9.0	1.97	182	.206	.259	23	.197	4	57	62	-2	7.4
1973	Phi-N	13	20	.394	40	40	18	3	0	293¹	293	29	113	223	12.5	3.90	97	.260	.329	25	.245	2	-8	-3	-1	-0.4
1974	Phi-N☆	16	13	.552	39	39	17	1	0	291	249	21	136	240	12.1	3.22	117	.234	.323	25	.245	2	13	18	-1	1.9
1975	Phi-N	15	14	.517	37	37	14	3	0	255²	217	24	104	192	11.4	3.56	105	.233	.312	14	.156	-0	2	5	-1	0.4
1976	*Phi-N☆	20	7	.741	35	35	13	2	0	252²	224	19	72	195	10.6	3.13	113	.237	.291	20	.217	2	10	12	-1	1.0
1977	*Phi-N☆	23	10	.697	36	36	17	2	0	283	229	25	89	198	10.2	2.64	151	.223	.287	26	.268	8	40	43	1	6.0
1978	Phi-N	16	13	.552	34	34	12	3	0	247¹	228	30	63	161	10.7	2.84	126	.246	.297	25	.291	7	20	20	1	3.3
1979	Phi-N★	18	11	.621	35	35	13	4	0	251	202	25	89	213	10.6	3.62	106	.219	.292	21	.223	3	6	-1	0	0.9
1980	*Phi-N☆	24	9	.727	38	38	13	3	0	304	243	15	90	286	9.9	2.34	162	.218	.278	19	.188	-1	43	49	-1	5.3
1981	*Phi-N☆	13	4	.765	24	24	10	1	0	190	152	9	62	179	10.2	2.42	150	.222	.288	9	.134	-0	23	26	-1	2.2
1982	Phi-N★	23	11	.676	38	38	19	6	0	295²	253	17	86	286	10.3	3.10	118	.232	.289	22	.218	4	16	18	-1	2.4
1983	*Phi-N	15	16	.484	37	37	8	3	0	283²	277	20	84	275	11.5	3.11	115	.258	.314	19	.196	3	16	14	-1	1.7
1984	Phi-N	13	7	.650	33	33	1	0	0	229	214	14	79	163	11.5	3.58	102	.246	.309	16	.190	2	0	-1	-3	0.0
1985	Phi-N	1	8	.111	16	16	0	0	0	92	84	6	53	48	13.4	3.33	111	.249	.350	5	.179	0	3	4	1	0.4
1986	Phi-N	4	8	.333	16	16	0	0	0	83	102	15	45	62	15.9	6.18	62	.297	.379	7	.206	1	-23	-21	-1	-2.7
	SF-N	1	3	.250	6	6	0	0	0	30	36	4	16	18	15.9	5.10	69	.303	.390	2	.182	1	-5	-5	1	-0.5
	Yr	5	11	.313	22	22	0	0	0	113	138	19	61	80	15.9	5.89	64	.297	.380	9	.200	2	-27	-27	-1	-3.2
	Chi-A	4	3	.571	10	10	0	0	0	63¹	58	6	25	40	11.8	3.69	117	.252	.325	0	—	0	3	4	-1	0.1
1987	Cle-A	5	9	.357	23	14	3	0	0	109	111	17	63	71	14.5	5.37	84	.266	.364	0	—	0	-11	-10	-0	-1.2
	Min-A	1	5	.167	9	7	0	0	0	43	54	7	23	20	16.5	6.70	69	.310	.397	0	—	0	-11	-10	-0	-1.3
	Yr	6	14	.300	32	21	3	0	0	152	165	24	86	91	15.0	5.74	79	.276	.369	0	—	0	-22	-20	-0	-2.5
1988	Min-A	0	1	.000	4	1	0	0	0	9²	20	5	5	5	23.3	16.76	24	.408	.463	0	—	0	-14	-14	-0	-1.1
Total	24	329	244	.574	741	709	254	55	2	5217¹	4672	414	1833	4136	11.3	3.22	115	.240	.308	346	.201	49	236	277	-18	33.2

● **DON CARMAN**   Carman, Donald Wayne b: 8/14/59, Oklahoma City, Okla   BL/TL, 6'3", 195 lbs. Deb: 10/1/83

1983	Phi-N	0	0	—	1	0	0	0	1	1	0	0	0	0	0.00	—	.000	.000	0	—	0	0	0	0	0.1
1984	Phi-N	0	1	.000	11	0	0	0	0	13¹	14	2	6	16	13.5	5.40	67	.255	.328	0	.000	-0	-3	-3	-0	-0.2
1985	Phi-N	9	4	.692	71	0	0	0	7	86¹	52	6	38	87	9.6	2.08	177	.178	.277	0	.000	-0	14	15	0	2.5
1986	Phi-N	10	5	.667	50	14	2	1	1	134¹	113	11	52	98	11.3	3.22	120	.234	.313	0	.000	-3	7	9	2	0.9
1987	Phi-N	13	11	.542	35	35	3	2	0	211	194	34	69	125	11.4	4.22	100	.244	.308	5	.082	-3	0	-3	-0	-0.6
1988	Phi-N	10	14	.417	36	32	2	0	0	201¹	211	20	70	116	12.7	4.29	83	.270	.333	3	.048	-5	-19	-16	-3	-2.6
1989	Phi-N	5	15	.250	49	20	0	0	0	149¹	152	21	86	81	14.5	5.24	68	.260	.358	1	.029	-3	-29	-28	-1	-3.9
1990	Phi-N	6	2	.750	59	1	0	0	1	86²	69	13	38	58	11.5	4.15	92	.218	.310	3	.273	1	-3	-3	-0	-0.2
1991	Cin-N	0	2	.000	28	0	0	0	0	36	40	3	19	15	15.0	5.25	72	.286	.375	0	.000	-0	-6	-6	0	-0.3
1992	Tex-A	0	0	—	2	0	0	0	0	2¹	4	0	0	2	15.4	7.71	49	.364	.364	0	—	0	-1	-1	-0	-0.1
Total	10	53	54	.495	342	102	7	3	11	921²	849	115	378	598	12.2	4.11	92	.245	.323	12	.057	-14	-42	-32	-5	-4.3

● **CHET CARMICHAEL**   Carmichael, Chester Keller b: 1/9/1888, Muncie, Ind. d: 8/22/60, Rochester, N.Y.   BR/TR, 5'11.5", 200 lbs. Deb: 9/5/09

| 1909 | Cin-N | 0 | 0 | — | 2 | 0 | 0 | 0 | 0 | 7 | 9 | 0 | 3 | 2 | 18.0 | 0.00 | — | .321 | .424 | 0 | .000 | -0 | 2 | 2 | -0 | -0.1 |

● **RAFAEL CARMONA**   Carmona, Rafael b: 10/2/72, Rio Piedras, P.R.   BL/TR, 6'2", 185 lbs. Deb: 5/18/95

| 1995 | Sea-A | 2 | 4 | .333 | 15 | 3 | 0 | 0 | 1 | 47² | 55 | 9 | 34 | 28 | 17.2 | 5.66 | 84 | .293 | .406 | 0 | — | 0 | -5 | -5 | 0 | -0.6 |

YEAR	TM/L	W	L	PCT	G	GS	CG	SH	SV	IP	H	HR	BB	SO	RAT	ERA	ERA+	OAV	OOB	BH	AVG	PB	PR	/A	PD	TPI
1996	Sea-A	8	3	.727	53	1	0	0	1	90¹	95	11	55	62	15.2	4.28	115	.273	.377	0	—	0	7	6	-0	0.7
Total	2	10	7	.588	138					150	150	20	89	90	15.9	4.76	102	.280	.387	0	—	0	2	2	0	0.1

● EDDIE CARNETT
Carnett, Edwin Elliott "Lefty" b: 10/21/16, Springfield, Mo.   BL/TL, 6', 185 lbs.   Deb: 4/19/41 ◆

YEAR	TM/L	W	L	PCT	G	GS	CG	SH	SV	IP	H	HR	BB	SO	RAT	ERA	ERA+	OAV	OOB	BH	AVG	PB	PR	/A	PD	TPI
1941	Bos-N	0	0	—	2	0	0	0	0	1¹	4	0	3	2	47.3	20.25	18	.500	.636	0	—	0	-2	-2	-0	0.0
1944	Chi-A	0	0	—	2	0	0	0	0	2	3	1	0	2	13.5	9.00	38	.333	.333	126	.276	1	-1	-1	0	0.0
1945	Cle-A	0	0	—	2	0	0	0	0	2	0	0	0	1	0.00	0.00	—	.000	.000	16	.219	0	1	1	0	0.0
Total	3	0	0	—	6	0	0	0	0	5¹	7	1	3	4	16.9	8.44	40	.304	.385	142	.268	1	-3	-3	0	0.0

● PAT CARNEY
Carney, Patrick Joseph "Doc" b: 8/7/1876, Holyoke, Mass.   d: 1/9/53, Worcester, Mass.   BL/TL, 6', 200 lbs.   Deb: 9/20/01 ◆

YEAR	TM/L	W	L	PCT	G	GS	CG	SH	SV	IP	H	HR	BB	SO	RAT	ERA	ERA+	OAV	OOB	BH	AVG	PB	PR	/A	PD	TPI
1902	Bos-N	0	1	.000	2	1	0	0	0	5	6	1	3	3	18.0	9.00	31	.300	.417	141	.270	0	-3	-3	-0	-0.6
1903	Bos-N	4	5	.444	10	9	9	0	0	78	93	2	31	29	14.5	4.04	79	.284	.349	94	.240	1	-7	-7	-0	-0.6
1904	Bos-N	0	4	.000	4	3	1	0	0	26¹	40	1	12	5	18.1	5.81	47	.364	.431	57	.204	0	-9	-9	-0	-1.1
Total	3	4	10	.286	16	13	10	0	0	109¹	139	4	46	37	15.6	4.69	66	.303	.372	308	.247	2	-19	-20	-1	-2.3

● CRIS CARPENTER
Carpenter, Cris Howell b: 4/5/65, St.Augustine, Fla.   BR/TR, 6'1", 195 lbs.   Deb: 5/14/88

YEAR	TM/L	W	L	PCT	G	GS	CG	SH	SV	IP	H	HR	BB	SO	RAT	ERA	ERA+	OAV	OOB	BH	AVG	PB	PR	/A	PD	TPI
1988	StL-N	2	3	.400	8	8	1	0	0	47²	56	3	9	24	12.5	4.72	74	.298	.333	2	.143	-0	-7	-7	-0	-0.7
1989	StL-N	4	4	.500	36	5	0	0	0	68	70	4	26	35	13.0	3.18	114	.262	.332	4	.444	1	2	3	0	0.5
1990	StL-N	0	0	—	4	0	0	0	0	8	5	2	2	6	7.9	4.50	85	.167	.219	0	.000	-0	-1	-1	-0	0.0
1991	StL-N	10	4	.714	59	0	0	0	0	66	53	6	20	47	10.0	4.23	88	.220	.280	1	.333	1	-4	-4	-0	-0.7
1992	StL-N	5	4	.556	73	0	0	0	1	88	69	10	27	46	10.2	2.97	114	.220	.291	1	.333	0	5	4	-1	0.4
1993	Fla-N	0	1	.000	29	0	0	0	0	37¹	29	1	13	26	10.6	2.89	149	.212	.289	0	—	0	5	6	1	0.2
	Tex-A	4	1	.800	27	0	0	0	1	32	35	4	12	27	13.8	4.22	98	.289	.363	0	—	0	0	0	0	0.2
1994	Tex-A	2	5	.286	47	0	0	0	5	59	69	7	20	39	13.6	5.03	96	.291	.346	0	—	0	-2	-1	-0	-0.2
1996	Mil-A	0	0	—	8	0	0	0	0	8¹	12	1	2	2	15.1	7.56	70	.333	.368	0	—	0	-2	-2	-0	-0.3
Total	8	27	22	.551	291	13	1	0	7	414¹	398	38	131	252	11.7	3.91	99	.254	.315	8	.267	1	-2	-1	-1	-0.8

● LEW CARPENTER
Carpenter, Lewis Emmett b: 8/16/13, Woodstock, Ga.   d: 4/25/79, Marietta, Ga.   BR/TR, 6'2", 195 lbs.   Deb: 5/1/43

YEAR	TM/L	W	L	PCT	G	GS	CG	SH	SV	IP	H	HR	BB	SO	RAT	ERA	ERA+	OAV	OOB	BH	AVG	PB	PR	/A	PD	TPI
1943	Was-A	0	0	—	4	0	0	0	0	3¹	1	0	4	1	16.2	0.00	—	.125	.462	0	—	0	1	1	-0	0.0

● PAUL CARPENTER
Carpenter, Paul Calvin b: 8/12/1894, Granville, Ohio   d: 3/14/68, Newark, Ohio   BR/TR, 5'11", 165 lbs.   Deb: 7/26/16

YEAR	TM/L	W	L	PCT	G	GS	CG	SH	SV	IP	H	HR	BB	SO	RAT	ERA	ERA+	OAV	OOB	BH	AVG	PB	PR	/A	PD	TPI
1916	Pit-N	0	0	—	5	0	0	0	0	7²	8	0	4	5	14.1	1.17	229	.258	.343	0	.000	-0	1	1	0	0.0

● BOB CARPENTER
Carpenter, Robert Louis b: 12/12/17, Chicago, Ill.   BR/TR, 6'3", 195 lbs.   Deb: 9/12/40

YEAR	TM/L	W	L	PCT	G	GS	CG	SH	SV	IP	H	HR	BB	SO	RAT	ERA	ERA+	OAV	OOB	BH	AVG	PB	PR	/A	PD	TPI
1940	NY-N	2	0	1.000	5	3	2	0	0	33	29	2	14	25	11.7	2.73	142	.238	.316	1	.100	-0	4	4	-0	0.2
1941	NY-N	11	6	.647	29	19	8	1	2	131²	138	15	42	42	12.4	3.83	97	.265	.323	7	.156	-0	-3	-2	-3	-0.5
1942	NY-N	11	10	.524	28	25	12	2	0	185²	192	13	51	62	11.8	3.15	107	.263	.312	12	.185	-1	3	4	-3	0.1
1946	NY-N	1	3	.250	12	6	1	1	0	39	37	7	18	13	12.7	4.85	71	.245	.325	1	.100	0	-6	-6	-1	-0.7
1947	NY-N	0	0	—	2	0	0	0	0	3	5	0	3	0	24.0	12.00	34	.385	.500	0	—	0	-3	-3	-0	0.0
	Chi-N	0	1	.000	4	1	0	0	0	7¹	10	1	4	1	17.2	4.91	80	.323	.400	1	1.000	0	-1	-1	0	0.0
	Yr	0	1	.000	6	1	0	0	0	10¹	15	1	7	1	19.2	6.97	57	.341	.431	1	1.000	0	-3	-3	0	0.0
Total	5	25	20	.556	80	54	23	4	2	399²	411	38	132	134	12.3	3.60	98	.262	.321	22	.168	-1	-5	-3	-6	-0.9

● FRANK CARPIN
Carpin, Frank Dominic b: 9/14/38, Brooklyn, N.Y.   BL/TL, 5'10", 172 lbs.   Deb: 5/25/65

YEAR	TM/L	W	L	PCT	G	GS	CG	SH	SV	IP	H	HR	BB	SO	RAT	ERA	ERA+	OAV	OOB	BH	AVG	PB	PR	/A	PD	TPI
1965	Pit-N	3	1	.750	39	0	0	0	4	39²	35	0	24	27	14.1	3.18	111	.243	.363	0	.000	-0	2	1	1	0.3
1966	Hou-N	1	0	1.000	10	0	0	0	0	6	9	0	6	2	22.5	7.50	46	.346	.469	0	—	0	-3	-3	-0	-0.5
Total	2	4	1	.800	49	0	0	0	4	45²	44	0	30	29	15.2	3.74	93	.259	.379	0	.000	-0	-1	-1	1	-0.2

● GIOVANNI CARRARA
Carrara, Giovanni (Jimenez) b: 3/4/68, Edo Anzoategui, Venez.   BR/TR, 6'2", 210 lbs.   Deb: 7/29/95

YEAR	TM/L	W	L	PCT	G	GS	CG	SH	SV	IP	H	HR	BB	SO	RAT	ERA	ERA+	OAV	OOB	BH	AVG	PB	PR	/A	PD	TPI
1995	Tor-A	2	4	.333	12	7	1	0	0	48²	64	10	25	27	16.6	7.21	65	.320	.398	0	—	0	-14	-14	-1	-1.4
1996	Tor-A	0	1	.000	11	0	0	0	0	15	23	5	12	10	21.0	11.40	44	.359	.461	0	—	0	-11	-11	-0	-0.6
	Cin-N	1	0	1.000	8	5	0	0	0	23	31	6	13	13	18.0	5.87	71	.323	.414	0	.000	-1	-4	-4	-0	-0.2
Total	2	3	5	.375	31	12	1	0	0	86²	118	21	50	50	17.8	7.58	61	.328	.414	0	.000	-1	-28	-29	-1	-2.2

● HECTOR CARRASCO
Carrasco, Hector (Pacheco) b: 10/22/69, San Pedro De Macoris, D.R.   BR/TR, 6'2", 175 lbs.   Deb: 4/4/94

YEAR	TM/L	W	L	PCT	G	GS	CG	SH	SV	IP	H	HR	BB	SO	RAT	ERA	ERA+	OAV	OOB	BH	AVG	PB	PR	/A	PD	TPI
1994	Cin-N	5	6	.455	45	0	0	0	6	56¹	42	3	30	41	11.8	2.24	185	.210	.319	0	.000	-1	12	12	-0	2.2
1995	*Cin-N	2	7	.222	64	0	0	0	5	87¹	86	1	46	64	13.8	4.12	100	.257	.350	0	.000	-1	1	-0	-1	-0.2
1996	Cin-N	4	3	.571	56	0	0	0	0	74¹	58	6	45	59	12.6	3.75	111	.214	.328	1	.200	0	4	3	0	0.3
Total	3	11	16	.407	165	0	0	0	11	218	186	10	121	164	12.9	3.51	118	.231	.335	1	.056	-1	17	15	-1	2.3

● ALEX CARRASQUEL
Carrasquel, Alejandro Eloy (Aparicio) b: 7/24/12, Caracas, Venez.   d: 8/19/69, Caracas, Venez.   BR/TR, 6'1", 182 lbs.   Deb: 4/23/39

YEAR	TM/L	W	L	PCT	G	GS	CG	SH	SV	IP	H	HR	BB	SO	RAT	ERA	ERA+	OAV	OOB	BH	AVG	PB	PR	/A	PD	TPI
1939	Was-A	5	9	.357	40	17	7	0	2	159¹	165	7	68	41	13.2	4.69	93	.266	.340	7	.167	1	-1	-6	0	-0.3
1940	Was-A	6	2	.750	28	0	0	0	0	48	42	4	29	19	13.3	4.88	86	.240	.348	0	.000	-1	-3	-4	0	-0.6
1941	Was-A	6	2	.750	35	5	4	0	0	96²	103	7	49	30	14.2	3.44	117	.278	.364	2	.095	1	8	6	4	0.9
1942	Was-A	7	7	.500	35	15	7	1	4	152¹	161	7	53	40	12.7	3.43	107	.267	.327	6	.136	-0	4	4	1	0.5
1943	Was-A	11	7	.611	39	13	4	1	5	144¹	160	3	54	48	13.4	3.68	87	.279	.342	8	.186	1	-6	-8	1	-0.8
1944	Was-A	8	7	.533	43	7	3	0	2	134	143	8	50	35	13.1	3.43	95	.273	.339	7	.194	0	-3	-1	0	0.0
1945	Was-A	7	5	.583	35	7	5	2	1	122²	105	5	40	38	10.6	2.71	114	.228	.289	3	.083	-2	9	5	0	0.3
1949	Chi-A	0	0	—	3	0	0	0	0	3²	8	1	4	1	29.5	14.73	28	.421	.522	0	—	0	-4	-4	-0	-0.4
Total	8	50	39	.562	258	64	30	4	16	861	887	42	347	252	13.0	3.73	98	.265	.335	33	.144	0	6	-9	8	-0.0

● AMALIO CARRENO
Carreno, Amalio Rafael (Adrian) b: 4/11/64, Chacachacare, Ven.   BR/TR, 6', 170 lbs.   Deb: 7/7/91

YEAR	TM/L	W	L	PCT	G	GS	CG	SH	SV	IP	H	HR	BB	SO	RAT	ERA	ERA+	OAV	OOB	BH	AVG	PB	PR	/A	PD	TPI
1991	Phi-N	0	0	—	3	0	0	0	0	3¹	5	1	3	2	27.0	16.20	23	.333	.500	0	.000	-0	-5	-5	-0	-0.4

● BILL CARRICK
Carrick, William Martin "Doughnut Bill" b: 9/5/1873, Erie, Pa.   d: 3/7/32, Philadelphia, Pa.   TR ,   Deb: 7/30/1898

YEAR	TM/L	W	L	PCT	G	GS	CG	SH	SV	IP	H	HR	BB	SO	RAT	ERA	ERA+	OAV	OOB	BH	AVG	PB	PR	/A	PD	TPI
1898	NY-N	3	1	.750	5	4	4	0	0	39²	39	0	21	10	14.7	3.40	102	.255	.363	3	.167	-1	1	0	1	0.0
1899	NY-N	16	27	.372	44	43	**40**	3	0	361²	485	4	122	60	15.6	4.65	81	.320	.378	18	.138	-6	-32	-36	-2	-3.7
1900	NY-N	19	22	.463	**45**	41	32	1	0	341²	415	7	92	63	13.7	3.53	102	.299	.348	20	.174	-3	6	-3	-0	0.0
1901	Was-A	14	22	.389	42	37	34	0	0	324	367	12	93	70	13.3	3.75	98	.282	.339	20	.159	-5	-3	-3	-0	-0.7
1902	Was-A	11	17	.393	31	30	28	0	0	257²	344	10	72	36	14.8	4.86	76	.320	.368	20	.185	-2	-37	-33	-3	-3.3
Total	5	63	89	.414	167	155	138	4	0	1324²	1650	33	400	239	14.4	4.14	89	.304	.359	81	.163	-16	-64	-68	-0	-7.7

● DON CARRITHERS
Carrithers, Donald George b: 9/15/49, Lynwood, Cal.   BR/TR, 6'2", 180 lbs.   Deb: 8/1/70

YEAR	TM/L	W	L	PCT	G	GS	CG	SH	SV	IP	H	HR	BB	SO	RAT	ERA	ERA+	OAV	OOB	BH	AVG	PB	PR	/A	PD	TPI
1970	SF-N	2	1	.667	11	2	0	0	0	22	31	5	14	14	18.4	7.36	54	.333	.421	0	.000	-0	-8	-8	-0	-1.0
1971	*SF-N	5	3	.625	22	12	2	1	1	80¹	77	6	37	41	13.0	4.03	84	.254	.339	3	.176	-0	-5	-6	-1	-0.5
1972	SF-N	4	8	.333	25	14	2	1	0	90	108	10	42	42	15.5	5.80	60	.296	.376	6	.207	1	-23	-23	0	-2.8
1973	SF-N	1	2	.333	25	3	0	0	0	58	64	2	35	36	16.0	4.81	79	.278	.383	4	.250	0	-7	-6	-1	-0.1
1974	Mon-N	5	2	.714	22	3	0	0	0	60	56	6	17	31	11.4	3.00	128	.249	.310	4	.286	0	4	6	1	0.8
1975	Mon-N	5	3	.625	19	14	5	2	0	101	90	7	38	47	11.8	3.30	116	.240	.317	6	.176	0	4	6	2	0.7
1976	Mon-N	6	12	.333	34	19	2	0	0	140¹	153	9	78	71	15.3	4.43	84	.286	.384	1	.108	-1	-14	-11	-2	-1.3
1977	Min-A	0	1	.000	7	0	0	0	0	14¹	16	2	6	4	14.4	6.91	58	.271	.348	0	—	0	-5	-5	-0	-0.2
Total	8	28	32	.467	165	67	11	3	3	566	595	47	267	275	14.1	4.45	83	.272	.358	27	.176	0	-55	-48	5	-4.4

● CLAY CARROLL
Carroll, Clay Palmer "Hawk" b: 5/2/41, Clanton, Ala.   BR/TR, 6'1", 200 lbs.   Deb: 9/2/64

YEAR	TM/L	W	L	PCT	G	GS	CG	SH	SV	IP	H	HR	BB	SO	RAT	ERA	ERA+	OAV	OOB	BH	AVG	PB	PR	/A	PD	TPI
1964	Mil-N	2	0	1.000	11	0	0	0	0	20¹	15	1	3	17	8.0	1.77	199	.200	.231	0	.000	-0	4	4	1	0.5
1965	Mil-N	0	1	.000	19	1	0	0	1	34²	35	3	13	16	12.7	4.41	80	.269	.340	0	.000	-1	-3	-3	-0	-0.2
1966	Atl-N	8	7	.533	**73**	1	0	0	11	144¹	127	8	29	67	10.0	2.37	154	.236	.280	3	.100	-2	20	20	1	2.3
1967	Atl-N	6	12	.333	42	7	1	0	0	93	111	8	29	35	13.8	5.52	66	.304	.360	1	.063	1	-22	-23	1	-4.0
1968	Atl-N	0	1	.000	10	0	0	0	0	22¹	26	1	4	12	12.9	4.84	62	.310	.356	0	.000	-0	-5	-5	-0	-0.2
	Cin-N	7	7	.500	58	1	0	0	17	122	102	3	32	59	10.2	2.29	128	.230	.290	6	.250	0	7	7	3	1.2
	Yr	7	8	.467	68	1	0	0	17	144	128	4	38	71	10.8	2.69	117	.242	.300	6	.207	0	1	5	7	2.0
1969	Cin-N	12	6	.667	71	4	0	0	7	150²	149	9	78	90	14.0	3.52	107	.262	.358	6	.207	2	1	4	3	1.0

YEAR	TM/L	W	L	PCT	G	GS	CG	SH	SV	IP	H	HR	BB	SO	RAT	ERA	ERA+	OAV	OOB	BH	AVG	PB	PR	/A	PD	TPI
1970	*Cin-N	9	4	.692	65	0	0	0	16	104^1	104	4	27	63	11.5	2.59	156	.259	.309	1	.071	-1	17	17	1	2.5
1971	Cin-N☆	10	4	.714	61	0	0	0	15	93^2	78	5	42	64	11.7	2.50	134	.234	.324	1	.100	-1	10	9	4	2.0
1972	*Cin-N☆	6	4	.600	**65**	0	0	0	**37**	96	89	5	32	51	11.4	2.25	143	.256	.321	2	.182	0	13	10	1	2.2
1973	*Cin-N	8	8	.500	53	5	0	0	14	92^2	111	5	34	41	14.6	3.69	92	.307	.374	3	.214	0	-0	-3	1	-0.5
1974	Cin-N	12	5	.706	57	3	0	0	6	100^2	96	3	30	46	11.3	2.15	163	.256	.311	3	.167	-0	16	15	2	2.8
1975	*Cin-N	7	5	.583	56	2	0	0	7	96^1	93	2	32	44	12.0	2.62	137	.255	.320	0	—	-2	11	10	-1	1.1
1976	Chi-A	4	4	.500	29	0	0	0	0	77^1	67	1	24	38	10.8	2.56	139	.242	.307	0	—	0	8	9	0	1.0
1977	StL-N	4	2	.667	51	1	0	0	1	90	77	8	24	34	10.2	2.50	154	.238	.293	1	.091	-1	14	13	1	1.0
	Chi-A	1	3	.250	8	0	0	0	1	11^1	14	3	4	4	14.3	4.76	86	.311	.367	0	—	0	-1	-1	0	-0.3
1978	Pit-N	0	0	—	2	0	0	0	0	4	2	0	3	0	11.3	2.25	164	.143	.294	0	—	0	1	1	0	0.0
Total 15		96	73	.568	731	28	1	0	143	1353^1	1296	67	442	681	11.5	2.94	120	.257	.321	27	.130	-5	93	90	17	13.4

● ED CARROLL
Carroll, Edgar Fleischer b: 7/27/07, Baltimore, Md. d: 10/13/84, Rossville, Md. BR/TR, 6'3", 185 lbs. Deb: 5/1/29

YEAR	TM/L	W	L	PCT	G	GS	CG	SH	SV	IP	H	HR	BB	SO	RAT	ERA	ERA+	OAV	OOB	BH	AVG	PB	PR	/A	PD	TPI
1929	Bos-A	1	0	1.000	24	0	0	0	0	67^1	77	6	20	13	13.5	5.61	76	.291	.349	1	.063	-2	-10	-10	0	-0.3

● OWNIE CARROLL
Carroll, Owen Thomas b: 11/11/02, Kearny, N.J. d: 6/8/75, Orange, N.J. BR/TR, 5'10.5", 165 lbs. Deb: 6/20/25

YEAR	TM/L	W	L	PCT	G	GS	CG	SH	SV	IP	H	HR	BB	SO	RAT	ERA	ERA+	OAV	OOB	BH	AVG	PB	PR	/A	PD	TPI
1925	Det-A	2	2	.500	10	4	1	0	0	40^2	46	1	28	12	16.8	3.76	114	.293	.406	6	.375	1	3	2	-2	0.2
1927	Det-A	10	6	.625	31	15	8	0	0	172	186	5	73	41	13.9	3.98	106	.281	.358	12	.174	-2	3	4	2	0.3
1928	Det-A	16	12	.571	34	28	19	2	2	231	219	6	87	51	12.2	3.27	126	.262	.337	19	.194	-0	20	21	1	2.4
1929	Det-A	9	17	.346	34	26	12	0	1	202	249	10	86	54	15.3	4.63	93	.310	.383	17	.230	2	-9	-8	2	-0.5
1930	Det-A	0	5	.000	9	9	0	0	0	20^1	30	3	14	9	17.3	10.62	45	.333	.394	1	.143	-1	-13	-13	0	-2.2
	NY-A	0	1	1.000	10	1	0	0	0	32^2	49	2	18	8	19.6	6.61	65	.374	.464	2	.200	-0	-7	-8	1	-0.1
	Yr	0	6	.000	16	4	0	0	0	53	79	5	27	12	18.7	8.15	55	.357	.437	3	.176	-0	-21	-22	1	-2.3
	Cin-N	0	1	.000	3	2	1	0	0	14	17	3	3	0	12.9	4.50	107	.309	.345	1	.200	-0	1	1	0	0.0
1931	Cin-N	3	9	.250	29	12	4	0	0	107^1	135	6	51	24	15.9	5.53	67	.314	.392	7	.206	0	-20	-21	1	-1.9
1932	Cin-N	10	19	.345	32	26	15	0	1	210	245	7	44	55	12.8	4.50	86	.286	.328	16	.208	2	-14	-15	-1	-1.7
1933	Bro-N	13	15	.464	33	31	11	0	0	226^1	248	6	54	45	12.3	3.78	85	.281	.327	11	.149	-1	-11	-14	3	-1.4
1934	Bro-N	1	3	.250	26	5	0	0	1	74^1	108	9	33	17	17.2	6.42	61	.342	.406	6	.240	1	-19	-21	3	-0.6
Total 9		64	90	.416	248	153	71	2	5	1330^2	1532	61	486	311	14.0	4.43	89	.294	.359	98	.200	2	-68	-72	11	-5.5

● DICK CARROLL
Carroll, Richard Thomas "Shadow" b: 7/21/1884, Cleveland, Ohio d: 11/22/45, Cleveland, Ohio BR/TR, 6'2", Deb: 9/25/09

YEAR	TM/L	W	L	PCT	G	GS	CG	SH	SV	IP	H	HR	BB	SO	RAT	ERA	ERA+	OAV	OOB	BH	AVG	PB	PR	/A	PD	TPI
1909	NY-A	0	0	—	2	1	0	0	0	5	7	1	1	1	14.4	3.60	70	.292	.320	1	.500	0	-1	-1	-0	0.0

● TOM CARROLL
Carroll, Thomas Michael b: 11/5/52, Utica, N.Y. BL/TR, 6'3", 190 lbs. Deb: 7/7/74

YEAR	TM/L	W	L	PCT	G	GS	CG	SH	SV	IP	H	HR	BB	SO	RAT	ERA	ERA+	OAV	OOB	BH	AVG	PB	PR	/A	PD	TPI
1974	Cin-N	4	3	.571	16	13	0	0	0	78^1	68	11	44	37	12.9	3.68	95	.231	.331	4	.154	-1	-1	-2	-1	-0.3
1975	Cin-N	4	1	.800	12	7	0	0	0	47	52	1	26	14	15.3	4.98	72	.284	.379	0	.000	-2	-7	-7	-1	-0.9
Total 2		8	4	.667	28	20	0	0	0	125^1	120	12	70	51	13.8	4.16	85	.252	.350	4	.100	-2	-8	-9	-2	-1.2

● KID CARSEY
Carsey, Wilfred b: 10/22/1870, New York, N.Y. d: 3/29/60, Miami, Fla. BL/TR, 5'7", 168 lbs. Deb: 4/8/1891 ♦

YEAR	TM/L	W	L	PCT	G	GS	CG	SH	SV	IP	H	HR	BB	SO	RAT	ERA	ERA+	OAV	OOB	BH	AVG	PB	PR	/A	PD	TPI
1891	Was-a	14	37	.275	54	53	46	1	0	415	513	17	161	174	15.2	4.99	75	.293	.362	28	.150	-5	-58	-57	6	-5.1
1892	Phi-N	19	16	.543	43	36	30	1	1	317^2	320	6	104	76	12.4	3.12	104	.251	.314	20	.153	-3	6	5	2	0.3
1893	Phi-N	20	15	.571	39	35	30	1	1	318^1	375	7	124	50	14.6	4.81	95	.285	.355	27	.186	-7	-5	-8	2	-1.2
1894	Phi-N	18	12	.600	35	31	26	0	0	277	349	22	102	41	15.2	5.56	92	.304	.370	34	.272	3	-7	-14	2	-0.7
1895	Phi-N	24	16	.600	44	40	35	0	1	342^1	460	14	118	64	15.7	4.92	97	.317	.376	41	.291	3	-5	-5	-1	-0.3
1896	Phi-N	11	11	.500	27	21	18	1	1	187^1	273	4	72	36	17.0	5.62	77	.337	.397	18	.222	1	-26	-27	1	-2.2
1897	Phi-N	2	1	.667	4	4	2	0	0	28	35	0	16	1	16.7	5.14	82	.304	.394	3	.231	-1	-3	-3	-0	-0.3
	StL-N	3	8	.273	12	11	11	0	0	99	133	5	31	14	15.3	6.00	73	.319	.372	13	.302	2	-19	-18	1	-1.2
	Yr	5	9	.357	16	15	13	0	0	127	168	5	47	15	15.5	5.81	75	.315	.375	16	.286	2	-21	-20	1	-1.5
1898	StL-N	2	12	.143	20	13	10	0	0	123^2	177	2	37	10	16.3	6.33	60	.333	.387	21	.200	-0	-37	-35	2	-3.0
1899	Cle-N	1	8	.111	10	9	8	0	0	77^2	109	2	24	11	15.6	5.68	65	.330	.379	10	.278	1	-16	-17	1	-1.3
	Was-N	1	2	.333	4	3	2	0	0	29	27	0	4	3	9.9	3.72	105	.248	.281	0	.000	-2	0	1	1	-0.1
	Yr	2	10	.167	14	12	10	0	0	106^2	136	2	28	14	13.9	5.15	73	.308	.351	10	.213	-1	-15	-17	1	-1.4
1901	Bro-N	1	0	1.000	2	0	0	0	0	7	9	1	3	4	16.7	10.29	33	.310	.394	0	.000	-0	-2	-5	-0	-0.6
Total 10		116	138	.457	294	256	218	4	3	2222	2780	80	796	484	15.0	4.95	85	.300	.363	221	.213	-8	-175	-183	14	-15.7

● AL CARSON
Carson, Albert James "Soldier" b: 8/22/1882, Chicago, Ill. d: 11/26/62, San Diego, Cal. TR , Deb: 5/6/10

YEAR	TM/L	W	L	PCT	G	GS	CG	SH	SV	IP	H	HR	BB	SO	RAT	ERA	ERA+	OAV	OOB	BH	AVG	PB	PR	/A	PD	TPI
1910	Chi-N	0	0	—	2	0	0	0	0	6^2	6	0	1	2	9.5	4.05	71	.240	.269	0	.000	0	-1	-1	0	0.0

● ANDY CARTER
Carter, Andrew Godfrey b: 11/9/68, Philadelphia, Pa. BL/TL, 6'5", 200 lbs. Deb: 5/3/94

YEAR	TM/L	W	L	PCT	G	GS	CG	SH	SV	IP	H	HR	BB	SO	RAT	ERA	ERA+	OAV	OOB	BH	AVG	PB	PR	/A	PD	TPI
1994	Phi-N	0	2	.000	20	0	0	0	0	34^1	34	5	12	18	13.6	4.46	96	.268	.359	0	.000	-1	-1	-1	-1	-0.2
1995	Phi-N	0	0	—	4	0	0	0	0	7^1	4	3	2	6	8.6	6.14	69	.167	.259	1	1.000	0	-2	-2	-0	-0.0
Total 2		0	2	.000	24	0	0	0	0	41^2	38	8	14	24	12.7	4.75	90	.252	.343	1	.143	-0	-3	-2	-1	-0.2

● ARNOLD CARTER
Carter, Arnold Lee "Hook" or "Lefty" b: 3/14/18, Rainelle, W.Va. d: 4/12/89, Louisville, Ky. BL/TL, 5'10", 170 lbs. Deb: 4/29/44

YEAR	TM/L	W	L	PCT	G	GS	CG	SH	SV	IP	H	HR	BB	SO	RAT	ERA	ERA+	OAV	OOB	BH	AVG	PB	PR	/A	PD	TPI
1944	Cin-N	11	7	.611	33	18	9	3	3	148^2	143	1	40	33	11.3	2.60	134	.256	.309	12	.250	-1	17	15	1	2.4
1945	Cin-N	2	4	.333	13	6	2	1	0	46^2	54	2	13	4	13.3	3.09	122	.286	.338	3	.176	0	4	3	0	0.5
Total 2		13	11	.542	46	24	11	4	3	195^1	197	3	53	37	11.7	2.72	131	.264	.317	15	.231	-1	20	18	1	2.9

● NICK CARTER
Carter, Conrad Powell b: 5/19/1879, Oatlands, Va. d: 11/23/61, Grasonville, Md. BL/TR, 5'8", 140 lbs. Deb: 4/14/08

YEAR	TM/L	W	L	PCT	G	GS	CG	SH	SV	IP	H	HR	BB	SO	RAT	ERA	ERA+	OAV	OOB	BH	AVG	PB	PR	/A	PD	TPI
1908	Phi-A	2	5	.286	14	4	2	0	0	60^2	58	1	17	11	11.4	2.97	86	.270	.329	2	.100	-2	-4	-3	1	-0.4

● JEFF CARTER
Carter, Jeffrey Allen b: 12/3/64, Tampa, Fla. BR/TR, 6'3", 195 lbs. Deb: 7/31/91

YEAR	TM/L	W	L	PCT	G	GS	CG	SH	SV	IP	H	HR	BB	SO	RAT	ERA	ERA+	OAV	OOB	BH	AVG	PB	PR	/A	PD	TPI
1991	Chi-A	0	1	.000	5	0	0	0	0	12	8	1	5	2	9.8	5.25	76	.182	.265	0	—	0	-2	-2	-0	-0.2

● LARRY CARTER
Carter, Larry Gene b: 5/22/65, Charleston, W.Va. BR/TR, 6'5", 195 lbs. Deb: 9/6/92

YEAR	TM/L	W	L	PCT	G	GS	CG	SH	SV	IP	H	HR	BB	SO	RAT	ERA	ERA+	OAV	OOB	BH	AVG	PB	PR	/A	PD	TPI
1992	SF-N	1	5	.167	6	6	0	0	0	33	34	6	18	21	14.2	4.64	71	.270	.361	2	.200	1	-4	-5	-1	-0.8

● PAUL CARTER
Carter, Paul Warren "Nick" b: 5/1/1894, Lake Park, Ga. d: 9/11/84, Lake Park, Ga. BL/TR, 6'3", 175 lbs. Deb: 9/15/14

YEAR	TM/L	W	L	PCT	G	GS	CG	SH	SV	IP	H	HR	BB	SO	RAT	ERA	ERA+	OAV	OOB	BH	AVG	PB	PR	/A	PD	TPI
1914	Cle-A	1	3	.250	5	4	1	0	0	24^2	35	0	5	9	14.6	2.92	99	.340	.370	0	.000	-1	-0	-1	-0	-0.1
1915	Cle-A	1	1	.500	11	2	2	0	0	42	44	1	18	14	13.3	3.21	95	.272	.344	3	.214	-1	-1	-1	1	0.1
1916	Chi-N	2	2	.500	8	5	2	0	0	36	26	1	17	16	10.8	2.75	106	.203	.297	2	.167	-0	-1	1	1	0.2
1917	Chi-N	5	8	.385	23	13	6	2	0	113^1	115	2	19	34	10.9	3.26	89	.276	.313	6	.171	-0	-7	-5	-1	-0.7
1918	Chi-N	3	2	.600	21	4	1	0	2	73	78	2	19	13	12.0	2.71	103	.290	.339	6	.240	0	0	1	2	0.2
1919	Chi-N	4	4	.556	28	7	2	0	1	85	81	1	28	17	11.8	2.65	109	.252	.316	7	.269	1	3	2	-0	0.3
1920	Chi-N	3	6	.333	31	8	2	0	0	106	131	3	36	14	14.6	4.67	69	.324	.387	6	.171	-1	-18	-17	-2	-1.7
Total 7		20	26	.435	127	43	16	2	3	480	510	10	142	115	12.4	3.32	89	.283	.339	30	.195	-1	-24	-19	1	-1.7

● SOL CARTER
Carter, Solomon Mobley "Buck" b: 12/23/08, Picayune, Miss. BR/TR, 6', 178 lbs. Deb: 4/15/31

YEAR	TM/L	W	L	PCT	G	GS	CG	SH	SV	IP	H	HR	BB	SO	RAT	ERA	ERA+	OAV	OOB	BH	AVG	PB	PR	/A	PD	TPI
1931	Phi-A	0	0	—	2	0	0	0	0	2^1	1	0	4	1	19.3	19.29	23	.143	.455	0	—	0	-4	-4	1	0.0

● BOB CARUTHERS
Caruthers, Robert Lee "Parisian Bob" b: 1/5/1864, Memphis, Tenn. d: 8/5/11, Peoria, Ill. BL/TR, 5'7", 138 lbs. Deb: 9/7/1884 MU♦

YEAR	TM/L	W	L	PCT	G	GS	CG	SH	SV	IP	H	HR	BB	SO	RAT	ERA	ERA+	OAV	OOB	BH	AVG	PB	PR	/A	PD	TPI
1884	StL-a	7	2	.778	13	7	7	0	0	82^2	61	1	15	58	8.6	2.61	125	.189	.232	22	.268	2	6	6	-1	0.6
1885	*StL-a	**40**	13	.755	53	53	53	6	0	482^1	430	3	57	190	9.4	**2.07**	158	.230	.260	50	.225	6	**63**	64	0	6.6
1886	*StL-a	30	14	.682	44	43	42	2	0	387^1	323	3	86	166	9.7	2.32	148	.217	.263	106	.334	26	48	48	-2	6.8
1887	*StL-a	29	9	.763	39	39	39	2	0	341	337	6	61	74	10.9	3.30	138	.247	.287	130	.357	20	38	47	7	6.2
1888	Bro-a	29	15	.659	44	43	42	4	0	391^2	337	4	53	140	9.2	2.39	125	.224	.255	77	.230	10	29	26	1	3.5
1889	*Bro-a	**40**	11	.784	56	50	46	7	1	445	444	16	104	118	11.3	3.13	119	.252	.298	43	.250	17	35	29	2	4.2
1890	*Bro-N	23	11	.676	37	33	30	1	0	300	292	9	87	64	11.7	3.09	111	.247	.305	63	.265	11	16	12	3	2.2
1891	Bro-N	18	14	.563	38	32	29	2	1	297	323	7	107	69	13.4	3.12	106	.267	.333	48	.281	11	7	6	1	1.7
1892	StL-N	2	10	.167	18	10	10	0	0	101^2	108	7	29	21	14.5	5.84	55	.277	.350	142	.277	6	-29	-30	0	-2.4
Total 9		218	99	.688	340	310	298	24	3	2828^2	2678	59	597	900	10.7	2.83	128	.240	.285	695	.282	111	214	206	11	29.4

YEAR	TM/L	W	L	PCT	G	GS	CG	SH	SV	IP	H	HR	BB	SO	RAT	ERA	ERA+	OAV	OOB	BH	AVG	PB	PR	/A	PD	TPI

● CHUCK CARY   Cary, Charles Douglas b: 3/3/60, Whittier, Cal.   BL/TL, 6'4", 210 lbs.   Deb: 8/22/85

1985	Det-A	0	1	.000	16	0	0	0	2	23²	16	2	8	22	9.9	3.42	119	.190	.277	0	—	0	2	2	-0	0.1
1986	Det-A	1	2	.333	22	0	0	0	0	31²	33	3	15	21	13.6	3.41	121	.273	.353	0	—	0	3	3	-0	0.2
1987	Atl-N	1	1	.500	13	0	0	0	0	16²	17	3	4	15	11.9	3.78	115	.266	.319	0	.000	-0	1	1	-0	0.1
1988	Atl-N	0	0	—	7	0	0	0	0	8¹	8	1	4	7	14.0	6.48	57	.250	.351	0	—	0	-3	-3	-0	0.0
1989	NY-A	4	4	.500	22	11	2	0	0	99¹	78	13	29	79	9.7	3.26	119	.209	.266	0	—	0	7	7	-2	0.4
1990	NY-A	6	12	.333	28	27	2	0	0	156²	155	21	55	134	12.1	4.19	95	.260	.323	0	—	0	-5	-4	-1	-0.5
1991	NY-A	1	6	.143	10	9	0	0	0	53¹	61	6	32	34	15.7	5.91	70	.285	.378	0	—	0	-11	-10	-0	-1.2
1993	Chi-A	1	0	1.000	16	0	0	0	0	20²	22	1	11	10	15.7	5.23	80	.286	.396	0	—	0	-2	-2	-0	0.1
Total	8	14	26	.350	134	47	4	0	3	410¹	390	50	158	322	12.2	4.17	96	.250	.322	0	.000	-0	-9	-7	-4	-0.8

● SCOTT CARY   Cary, Scott Russell "Red" b: 4/11/23, Kendallville, Ind.   BL/TL, 5'11.5", 168 lbs.   Deb: 5/1/47

| 1947 | Was-A | 3 | 1 | .750 | 23 | 3 | 1 | 0 | 0 | 54² | 73 | 5 | 20 | 25 | 15.5 | 5.93 | 63 | .312 | .369 | 1 | .077 | -1 | -13 | -13 | -1 | -1.0 |

● JERRY CASALE   Casale, Jerry Joseph b: 9/27/33, Brooklyn, N.Y.   BR/TR, 6'2", 200 lbs.   Deb: 9/14/58

1958	Bos-A	0	0	—	2	0	0	0	0	3	1	0	2	3	9.0	0.00	—	.111	.273	0	—	0	1	1	0	0.0
1959	Bos-A	13	8	.619	31	26	9	3	0	179²	162	20	89	93	12.8	4.31	94	.238	.331	10	.169	3	-9	-5	-4	-0.7
1960	Bos-A	2	9	.182	29	14	1	0	0	96¹	113	14	67	54	16.9	6.17	66	.294	.400	9	.273	4	-25	-23	-0	-2.0
1961	LA-A	1	5	.167	13	7	0	0	1	42²	52	9	25	35	16.5	6.54	69	.297	.388	6	.462	3	-12	-10	-0	-0.9
	Det-A	0	0	—	3	1	0	0	0	12	15	3	3	6	13.5	5.25	78	.313	.353	0	.000	-0	-2	-2	0	0.0
	Yr	1	5	.167	16	8	0	0	1	54²	67	12	28	41	15.6	6.26	71	.298	.375	6	.375	3	-14	-11	-0	-0.9
1962	Det-A	1	2	.333	18	1	0	0	0	36²	33	5	18	16	12.5	4.66	87	.236	.323	0	.000	-1	-3	-2	-0	-0.2
Total	5	17	24	.415	96	49	10	3	1	370¹	376	51	204	207	14.3	5.08	81	.262	.356	25	.216	7	-49	-40	-5	-3.8

● JOE CASCARELLA   Cascarella, Joseph Thomas "Crooning Joe" b: 6/28/07, Philadelphia, Pa.   BR/TR, 5'10.5", 175 lbs.   Deb: 4/17/34

1934	Phi-A	12	15	.444	42	22	9	2	1	194¹	214	8	104	71	14.9	4.68	94	.288	.377	6	.094	-4	-4	-6	2	-0.9
1935	Phi-A	1	6	.143	9	3	1	0	0	32¹	29	1	22	15	14.2	5.29	86	.252	.372	1	.125	-1	-3	-3	2	-0.4
	Bos-A	0	3	.000	6	4	0	0	0	17	25	3	11	9	19.1	6.88	69	.329	.414	0	.000	-0	-5	-4	0	-0.6
	Yr	1	9	.100	15	7	1	0	0	49¹	54	4	33	24	15.9	5.84	79	.283	.388	1	.100	-1	-8	-7	2	-1.0
1936	Bos-A	0	2	.000	10	1	0	0	0	20²	27	0	9	7	15.7	6.97	76	.329	.396	0	.000	-1	-4	-4	0	-0.3
	Was-A	9	8	.529	22	16	7	1	1	139¹	147	7	54	34	13.4	4.07	117	.276	.349	7	.143	-2	15	11	-2	0.7
	Yr	9	10	.474	32	17	7	1	1	160	174	7	63	41	13.7	4.44	109	.283	.355	7	.132	-3	11	7	-2	0.4
1937	Was-A	0	5	.000	10	4	1	0	1	32¹	50	3	23	10	20.6	8.07	55	.347	.440	2	.222	-0	-12	-13	-1	-1.6
	Cin-N	1	2	.333	11	3	2	0	1	43²	44	1	22	16	13.6	3.92	95	.263	.349	1	.091	-1	-0	-1	-1	-0.1
1938	Cin-N	4	7	.364	33	1	0	0	0	61	66	2	22	30	13.0	4.57	80	.275	.336	3	.167	-1	-5	-6	-0	-1.2
Total	5	27	48	.360	143	54	20	3	8	540²	602	25	267	192	14.6	4.84	91	.287	.370	20	.121	-9	-19	-26	1	-4.4

● CHARLIE CASE   Case, Charles Emmett b: 9/7/1879, Smith Landing, O.   d: 4/16/64, Clermont Co., Ohio   BR/TR, 6', 170 lbs.   Deb: 7/5/01

1901	Cin-N	1	2	.333	3	3	3	0	0	27	34	0	6	5	13.3	4.67	69	.306	.342	1	.100	-1	-4	-4	-0	-0.5
1904	Pit-N	10	5	.667	18	17	14	3	0	141	129	0	31	49	10.5	2.94	93	.243	.290	9	.170	-1	-3	-3	1	-0.2
1905	Pit-N	11	11	.500	31	24	18	3	1	217	202	6	66	57	11.7	2.57	117	.251	.319	1	.103	-2	10	10	-3	0.5
1906	Pit-N	1	1	.500	2	2	1	0	0	11	8	0	5	3	11.5	5.73	47	.190	.292	1	.500	-1	-4	-4	0	-0.5
Total	4	23	19	.548	54	46	36	6	1	396	373	6	108	114	11.4	2.93	99	.251	.311	12	.185	-1	-0	-1	-3	-0.7

● DAN CASEY   Casey, Daniel Maurice b: 11/20/1862, Binghamton, N.Y.   d: 2/8/43, Washington, D.C.   BR/TL, 6', 180 lbs.   Deb: 8/18/1884   F

1884	Wil-U	1	1	.500	2	2	2	0	0	18	23	0	4	10	13.5	1.00	266	.291	.325	1	.167	-1	3	3	-0	0.2
1885	Det-N	4	8	.333	12	12	12	1	0	104	105	1	35	79	12.1	3.29	86	.256	.315	5	.116	-3	-5	-5	1	-0.7
1886	Phi-N	24	18	.571	44	44	39	4	0	369	326	8	104	193	10.5	2.41	137	.223	.275	23	.152	-5	37	36	-1	2.9
1887	Phi-N	28	13	.683	45	45	43	4	0	390¹	377	15	115	119	11.7	**2.86**	**148**	.246	.305	27	.165	-11	53	60	-2	3.7
1888	Phi-N	14	18	.438	33	33	31	2	0	285²	298	6	48	108	11.1	3.15	94	.259	.291	18	.153	-4	-10	-6	1	-0.9
1889	Phi-N	6	10	.375	20	20	15	1	0	152¹	170	4	72	65	14.7	3.77	115	.273	.356	15	.221	-2	4	10	0	0.7
1890	Syr-a	19	22	.463	45	42	40	2	0	360²	365	8	165	169	13.6	4.14	85	.255	.337	26	.162	-6	-11	-24	-2	-2.3
Total	7	96	90	.516	201	198	182	14	0	1680¹	1664	42	543	743	12.0	3.18	113	.249	.309	115	.162	-27	71	75	1	3.6

● HUGH CASEY   Casey, Hugh Thomas b: 10/14/13, Atlanta, Ga.   d: 7/3/51, Atlanta, Ga.   BR/TR, 6'1", 207 lbs.   Deb: 4/29/35

1935	Chi-N	0	0	—	13	0	0	0	0	25²	29	1	14	10	15.1	3.86	102	.279	.364	1	.167	-0	0	0	0	0.0
1939	Bro-N	15	10	.600	40	25	15	0	1	227¹	228	13	54	79	11.6	2.93	137	.260	.311	15	.203	-0	25	28	2	3.1
1940	Bro-N	11	8	.579	44	10	5	2	2	154	136	13	51	53	11.3	3.62	110	.237	.306	9	.250	2	4	6	1	1.0
1941	*Bro-N	14	11	.560	45	18	4	1	7	162	155	8	57	61	11.8	3.89	94	.251	.316	6	.120	-1	-5	-4	2	-0.6
1942	Bro-N	6	3	.667	50	2	0	0	13	112	91	3	44	54	11.0	2.25	145	.221	.300	4	.148	-0	13	13	-1	1.2
1946	Bro-N	11	5	.688	46	1	0	0	5	99²	101	6	33	31	12.3	1.99	170	.267	.329	3	.136	-1	**16**	**15**	3	2.9
1947	*Bro-N	10	4	.714	46	0	0	0	18	76²	75	7	29	40	12.4	3.99	104	.260	.331	1	.056	-1	1	1	0	0.6
1948	Bro-N	3	0	1.000	22	0	0	0	4	36	59	6	17	9	19.5	8.00	50	.391	.459	0	.000	-1	-16	-16	-0	-1.6
1949	Pit-N	4	1	.800	33	0	0	0	5	38²	50	4	14	9	15.1	4.66	90	.314	.374	1	.333	1	-3	-2	-0	-0.4
	NY-A	1	0	1.000	4	0	0	0	0	7²	11	0	8	5	22.3	8.22	49	.324	.452	0	.000	-0	-3	-4	-0	-0.4
Total	9	75	42	.641	343	56	24	3	55	939²	935	58	321	349	12.3	3.45	110	.260	.325	40	.164	-2	32	38	6	5.3

● BILL CASEY   Casey, William B. b: St.Louis, Mo.   Deb: 8/17/1887

| 1887 | Phi-a | 0 | 0 | — | 1 | 0 | 0 | 0 | 0 | 1 | 4 | 0 | 1 | 0 | 45.0 | 18.00 | 24 | .667 | .714 | 0 | — | 0 | -2 | -2 | -0 | 0.0 |

● CARL CASHION   Cashion, Jay Carl b: 6/6/1891, Mecklenburg Co., N.C.   d: 11/17/35, Lake Millicent, Wis.   BL/TR, 6'2", 200 lbs.   Deb: 8/4/11

1911	Was-A	1	5	.167	11	9	5	0	0	71¹	67	4	47	26	15.3	4.16	79	.220	.338	12	.324	2	-6	-7	1	-0.2
1912	Was-A	10	6	.625	26	17	13	1	1	170¹	150	4	103	84	13.6	3.17	105	.250	.365	22	.214	2	3	3	-1	0.5
1913	Was-A	1	1	.500	4	3	0	0	0	9	7	0	14	3	24.0	6.00	49	.269	.558	3	.250	0	-3	-4	0	-0.5
1914	Was-A	0	1	.000	2	1	0	0	0	5	4	0	6	1	19.8	10.80	26	.250	.478	0	.000	-0	-4	-4	0	-0.7
Total	4	12	13	.480	43	30	18	1	1	255²	228	8	170	114	14.6	3.70	89	.241	.366	37	.242	5	-11	-11	1	-0.9

● LARRY CASIAN   Casian, Lawrence Paul b: 10/28/65, Lynwood, Cal.   BR/TL, 6', 170 lbs.   Deb: 9/9/90

1990	Min-A	2	1	.667	5	3	0	0	0	22¹	26	2	4	11	12.1	3.22	129	.306	.337	0	—	0	2	2	-0	0.3
1991	Min-A	0	0	—	15	0	0	0	0	18¹	28	4	7	6	17.7	7.36	58	.354	.414	0	—	0	-7	-6	-0	-0.3
1992	Min-A	1	0	1.000	6	0	0	0	0	6²	7	0	1	2	10.8	2.70	150	.259	.286	0	—	0	1	1	0	-0.1
1993	Min-A	5	3	.625	54	0	0	0	1	56²	59	1	14	31	11.8	3.02	144	.268	.315	0	—	0	8	8	-1	1.0
1994	Min-A	1	3	.250	33	0	0	0	0	40²	57	11	12	18	15.7	7.08	69	.343	.394	0	—	0	-10	-10	-1	-0.8
	Cle-A	0	2	.000	7	0	0	0	0	8¹	16	1	4	2	21.6	8.64	55	.421	.476	0	—	0	-4	-4	-0	-0.7
	Yr	1	5	.167	40	0	0	0	0	49	73	12	16	20	16.3	7.35	66	.351	.397	0	—	0	-14	-14	-1	-1.5
1995	Chi-N	1	0	1.000	42	0	0	0	1	23¹	22	1	15	11	14.7	1.93	213	.258	.365	0	.000	0	6	6	0	0.5
1996	Chi-N	1	1	.500	35	0	0	0	0	24	14	2	11	12	9.8	1.88	227	.187	.299	0	—	0	6	6	0	0.5
Total	7	11	10	.524	197	3	0	0	3	200¹	230	22	68	96	13.6	4.22	104	.295	.356	0	—	0	2	4	1	0.1

● CRAIG CASKEY   Caskey, Craig Douglas b: 12/11/49, Visalia, Cal.   BB/TL, 5'11", 185 lbs.   Deb: 7/19/73

| 1973 | Mon-N | 0 | 0 | — | 9 | 0 | 0 | 0 | 0 | 14 | 15 | 3 | 4 | 8 | 12.6 | 5.65 | 67 | .278 | .339 | 0 | — | 0 | -3 | -3 | -0 | 0.1 |

● ED CASSIAN   Cassian, Edwin b: Connecticut   TR, 5'8", 160 lbs.   Deb: 6/26/1891

1891	Phi-N	1	3	.250	6	4	3	0	0	38	40	1	16	10	14.0	2.84	120	.260	.341	2	.118	-1	2	2	1	0.1
	Was-a	2	4	.333	7	5	5	0	0	53	73	3	35	14	19.2	5.60	67	.316	.417	9	.346	2	-11	-11	0	-0.7
Total	1	3	7	.300	13	9	8	0	0	91	113	4	51	24	17.0	4.45	81	.294	.387	11	.256	1	-9	-9	1	-0.6

● JOHN CASSIDY   Cassidy, John P. b: 1857, Brooklyn, N.Y.   d: 7/2/1891, Brooklyn, N.Y.   BR/TL, 5'8", 168 lbs.   Deb: 4/24/1875   ◆

| 1875 | Atl-n | 1 | 21 | .045 | 30 | 22 | 18 | 0 | 0 | 213² | 284 | 3 | 11 | 9 | 12.4 | 3.03 | 69 | .277 | .285 | 29 | .175 | -3 | -19 | -23 | | -1.9 |
| 1877 | Har-n | 1 | 1 | .500 | 2 | 2 | 2 | 0 | 0 | 18 | 24 | 0 | 1 | 2 | 12.5 | 5.00 | 49 | .320 | .329 | 95 | .378 | 1 | -4 | -5 | -0 | -0.4 |

YEAR TM/L	W	L	PCT	G	GS	CG	SH	SV	IP	H	HR	BB	SO	RAT	ERA	ERA+	OAV	OOB	BH	AVG	PB	PR	/A	PD	TPI

● GEORGE CASTER Caster, George Jasper "Ug" b: 8/4/07, Colton, Cal. d: 12/18/55, Lakewood, Cal. BR/TR, 6'1.5", 180 lbs. Deb: 9/10/34

1934 Phi-A	3	2	.600	5	3	2	0	0	37	32	3	14	15	11.9	3.41	129	.235	.320	4	.267	0	4	4	1	0.6
1935 Phi-A	1	4	.200	25	1	0	0	1	63¹	86	8	37	24	17.8	6.25	73	.322	.408	5	.227	0	-13	-12	2	-0.7
1937 Phi-A	12	19	.387	34	33	19	3	0	231²	227	23	107	100	13.1	4.43	106	.258	.339	19	.211	-1	5	7	0	0.8
1938 Phi-A	16	20	.444	42	40	20	2	1	281¹	310	25	117	112	13.8	4.35	111	.277	.347	20	.198	1	14	15	-2	1.6
1939 Phi-A	9	9	.500	28	17	7	1	0	136	144	16	45	59	12.7	4.90	96	.276	.337	9	.209	-1	-4	-3	0	-0.4
1940 Phi-A	4	19	.174	36	24	11	0	2	178¹	234	18	69	75	15.4	6.56	68	.312	.372	8	.129	-3	-43	-42	-1	-4.7
1941 StL-A	3	7	.300	32	9	3	0	3	104¹	105	12	37	36	12.4	5.00	86	.259	.324	3	.103	-2	-10	-8	1	-0.8
1942 StL-A	8	2	.800	39	0	0	0	5	80	62	3	39	34	11.7	2.81	132	.217	.317	1	.067	-1	8	8	1	1.0
1943 StL-A	6	8	.429	35	0	0	0	6	76¹	69	4	41	43	13.1	2.12	157	.246	.345	3	.136	-1	10	10	0	2.1
1944 StL-A	6	6	.500	42	0	0	0	**12**	81	91	5	33	46	13.8	2.44	147	.284	.351	5	.250	0	9	10	-0	1.9
1945 StL-A	1	2	.333	10	0	0	0	1	15²	20	0	7	9	15.5	6.89	51	.308	.375	1	.333	0	-6	-6	-0	-1.1
*Det-A	5	1	.833	22	0	0	0	2	51¹	47	3	27	23	13.3	3.86	91	.250	.350	2	.182	-0	-3	-2	-0	-0.2
Yr	6	3	.667	32	0	0	0	3	67	67	3	34	32	13.8	4.57	77	.265	.356	3	.214	-0	-9	-8	-0	-1.3
1946 Det-A	2	1	.667	26	0	0	0	4	41¹	42	1	24	16	14.6	5.66	65	.264	.364	1	.143	-0	-10	-9	1	-0.8
Total 12	76	100	.432	376	127	62	6	39	1377²	1469	121	597	595	13.7	4.54	96	.273	.349	81	.184	-7	-39	-27	2	-0.7

● TONY CASTILLO Castillo, Antonio Jose (Jimenez) b: 3/1/63, Quibor, Venez. BL/TL, 5'10", 177 lbs. Deb: 8/14/88

1988 Tor-A	1	0	1.000	14	0	0	0	1	15	10	2	2	14	7.2	3.00	131	.200	.231	0	—	0	2	2	0	0.1
1989 Tor-A	1	1	.500	17	0	0	0	0	17²	23	0	10	10	17.3	6.11	62	.333	.425	0	—	0	-4	-5	-0	-0.4
Atl-N	0	1	.000	12	0	0	0	0	9¹	8	0	4	5	11.6	4.82	76	.222	.300	0	.000	-0	-1	-1	0	-0.1
1990 Atl-N	5	1	.833	52	3	0	0	0	76²	93	5	20	64	13.4	4.23	95	.302	.347	1	.143	-0	-4	-2	1	0.0
1991 Atl-N	1	1	.500	10	3	0	0	0	8²	13	3	5	8	18.7	7.27	53	.342	.419	0	—	-0	-3	-3	-0	-0.7
NY-N	1	0	1.000	10	3	0	0	0	23²	27	1	6	10	12.5	1.90	191	.281	.324	0	.000	-0	5	5	0	0.2
Yr	2	1	.667	17	3	0	0	0	32¹	40	4	11	18	14.2	3.34	111	.299	.352	0	.000	-0	2	2	-0	-0.5
1993 *Tor-A	3	2	.600	51	0	0	0	0	50²	44	4	22	28	11.7	3.38	128	.242	.324	0	—	0	5	5	0	0.5
1994 Tor-A	5	2	.714	41	0	0	0	1	68	66	7	28	43	12.8	2.51	192	.260	.340	0	—	0	17	17	1	1.7
1995 Tor-A	1	5	.167	55	0	0	0	13	72²	64	7	24	38	11.3	3.22	146	.243	.314	0	—	0	12	12	-0	1.2
1996 Tor-A	2	3	.400	40	0	0	0	1	72¹	72	9	20	48	11.7	4.23	119	.260	.314	0	—	-0	6	7	1	0.5
Chi-A	3	1	.750	15	0	0	0	1	22²	23	1	4	9	11.1	1.59	296	.267	.308	0	—	0	9	8	-0	1.3
Yr	5	4	.556	55	0	0	0	2	95	95	10	24	57	11.4	3.60	138	.259	.306	0	—	0	15	14	1	1.8
Total 8	23	17	.575	314	6	0	0	18	437¹	443	39	145	277	12.3	3.54	126	.267	.330	1	.083	-0	43	45	3	4.3

● MANNY CASTILLO Castillo, Esteban Manuel Antonio (Cabrera) b: 4/1/57, Santo Domingo, D.R. BB/TR, 5'9", 160 lbs. Deb: 9/1/80 ♦

| 1983 Sea-A | 0 | 0 | — | 1 | 0 | 0 | 0 | 0 | 2² | 8 | 3 | 3 | 2 | 40.5 | 23.63 | 18 | .533 | .632 | 42 | .207 | 1 | -6 | -6 | -0 | 0.0 |

● FRANK CASTILLO Castillo, Frank Anthony b: 4/1/69, ElPaso, Tex. BR/TR, 6'1", 180 lbs. Deb: 6/27/91

1991 Chi-N	6	7	.462	18	18	4	0	0	111²	107	5	33	73	11.3	4.35	89	.252	.306	5	.143	-0	-8	-6	-0	-0.7
1992 Chi-N	10	11	.476	33	33	0	0	0	205	179	19	63	135	10.9	3.46	104	.232	.295	6	.092	-2	1	3	-1	0.0
1993 Chi-N	5	8	.385	29	25	2	0	0	141¹	162	20	39	84	13.4	4.84	82	.293	.349	7	.163	-0	-13	-13	3	-0.9
1994 Chi-N	2	1	.667	4	4	1	0	0	23	25	3	5	19	11.7	4.30	96	.278	.316	0	.000	-1	-0	-0	-0	-0.1
1995 Chi-N	11	10	.524	29	29	2	2	0	188	179	22	52	135	11.3	3.21	128	.248	.303	6	.102	-2	20	19	-1	1.6
1996 Chi-N	7	16	.304	33	33	1	1	0	182¹	209	46	46	139	11.3	5.28	81	.288	.337	5	.088	-3	-22	-21	0	-2.5
Total 6	41	53	.436	146	142	10	3	0	851²	861	97	238	585	11.9	4.16	95	.262	.317	29	.108	-9	-21	-18	-0	-2.6

● JUAN CASTILLO Castillo, Juan Francisco (Azdura) b: 6/23/70, Caracas, Venez. BR/TR, 6'5", 205 lbs. Deb: 7/26/94

| 1994 NY-N | 0 | 0 | — | 2 | 2 | 0 | 0 | 0 | 11² | 17 | 2 | 5 | 1 | 17.0 | 6.94 | 60 | .362 | .423 | 1 | .200 | 0 | -4 | -4 | 1 | 0.1 |

● BOBBY CASTILLO Castillo, Robert Ernie b: 4/18/55, Los Angeles, Cal. BR/TR, 5'10", 170 lbs. Deb: 9/10/77

1977 LA-N	1	0	1.000	6	0	0	0	0	11¹	12	2	2	7	11.1	3.97	96	.279	.311	0	.000	-0	-0	-0	0	0.0
1978 LA-N	0	4	.000	18	0	0	0	1	34	28	2	33	30	16.1	3.97	88	.239	.407	0	.000	-1	-1	-2	0	-0.3
1979 LA-N	2	0	1.000	19	0	0	0	7	24¹	26	0	13	25	14.8	1.11	328	.277	.370	0	.000	-0	7	7	0	0.9
1980 LA-N	8	6	.571	61	0	0	0	5	98¹	70	4	45	60	10.6	2.75	127	.206	.301	1	.111	-0	9	8	1	1.2
1981 *LA-N	2	4	.333	34	1	0	0	5	50²	50	5	24	35	13.1	5.33	62	.262	.344	4	.444	2	-10	-11	-1	-1.3
1982 Min-A	13	11	.542	40	25	6	1	0	218²	194	26	85	123	11.5	3.66	116	.241	.313	0	—	0	10	14	-2	1.2
1983 Min-A	8	12	.400	27	25	3	0	0	158¹	170	17	65	90	13.4	4.77	89	.278	.348	0	—	0	-13	-9	1	-1.0
1984 Min-A	2	1	.667	10	0	0	0	0	25¹	14	2	19	7	11.7	1.78	237	.177	.337	0	—	0	6	7	-0	0.6
1985 *LA-N	2	2	.500	35	5	0	0	0	68	59	9	41	57	13.4	5.43	64	.230	.339	1	.100	-0	-14	-15	0	-0.8
Total 9	38	40	.487	250	59	9	1	18	689	623	67	327	434	12.5	3.94	99	.246	.333	6	.154	0	-6	-2	-1	0.5

● SLICK CASTLEMAN Castleman, Clydell b: 9/8/13, Donelson, Tenn. BR/TR, 6', 185 lbs. Deb: 5/9/34

1934 NY-N	1	0	1.000	7	1	0	0	0	16²	18	1	10	5	15.1	5.40	72	.277	.373	1	.250	1	-2	-3	1	0.0
1935 NY-N	15	6	.714	29	25	9	1	0	173²	186	14	64	64	13.0	4.09	94	.268	.330	12	.179	-0	-1	-5	1	-0.4
1936 *NY-N	4	7	.364	29	12	2	1	1	111²	148	6	56	54	16.8	5.64	69	.323	.403	5	.128	-1	-20	-22	1	-1.9
1937 NY-N	11	6	.647	23	23	10	2	0	160¹	148	19	33	78	10.2	3.31	117	.247	.287	4	.070	-5	11	10	-3	0.3
1938 NY-N	4	5	.444	21	14	4	0	0	90²	108	4	37	18	14.7	4.17	90	.296	.365	3	.097	-2	-4	-4	-1	-0.6
1939 NY-N	1	2	.333	12	4	0	0	0	33²	36	1	23	6	15.8	4.54	86	.286	.396	3	.333	1	-2	-2	-1	-0.2
Total 6	36	26	.581	121	79	25	4	1	586²	644	45	223	225	13.4	4.25	91	.279	.345	28	.135	-6	-19	-25	-2	-2.8

● ROY CASTLETON Castleton, Royal Eugene b: 7/26/1885, Salt Lake City, Utah d: 6/24/67, Los Angeles, Cal. BR/TL, 5'11", 167 lbs. Deb: 4/16/07

1907 NY-A	1	1	.500	3	2	1	0	0	16	11	1	3	3	7.9	2.81	99	.196	.237	0	.000	-1	-0	-0	-0	-0.1
1909 Cin-N	1	1	.500	4	1	1	0	0	14	14	0	6	5	14.1	1.93	135	.275	.373	2	.667	1	1	1	0	0.3
1910 Cin-N	1	2	.333	4	2	1	0	0	13²	15	0	6	5	14.5	3.29	89	.288	.373	0	.000	-1	-0	-1	0	-0.2
Total 3	3	4	.429	11	5	3	0	0	43²	40	1	15	13	12.0	2.68	104	.252	.328	2	.154	-0	0	0	0	0.0

● PAUL CASTNER Castner, Paul Henry "Lefty" b: 2/16/1897, St.Paul, Minn. d: 3/3/86, St.Paul, Minn. BL/TL, 5'11", 187 lbs. Deb: 8/6/23

| 1923 Chi-A | 0 | 0 | — | 6 | 0 | 0 | 0 | 0 | 10 | 14 | 0 | 5 | 0 | 17.1 | 6.30 | 63 | .326 | .396 | 0 | .000 | -0 | -3 | -3 | 0 | 0.0 |

● BILL CASTRO Castro, William Radhames (Checo) b: 12/13/53, Santiago, D.R. BR/TR, 5'11", 170 lbs. Deb: 8/20/74 C

1974 Mil-A	0	0	—	8	0	0	0	0	18	19	2	5	10	12.0	4.00	80	.264	.312	0	—	0	-2	-2	0	0.0
1975 Mil-A	3	2	.600	18	5	0	0	0	75	78	3	17	25	11.6	2.52	152	.271	.316	0	—	0	10	11	0	0.7
1976 Mil-A	4	6	.400	39	0	0	0	8	70¹	70	4	19	23	11.8	3.45	101	.265	.322	0	—	0	1	0	-0	0.2
1977 Mil-A	8	6	.571	51	0	0	0	13	69¹	76	7	23	28	13.1	4.15	98	.293	.356	0	—	0	-1	-1	1	0.0
1978 Mil-A	5	4	.556	42	0	0	0	1	49²	43	2	14	17	11.4	1.81	207	.234	.309	0	—	0	11	11	0	2.3
1979 Mil-A	3	1	.750	39	0	0	0	2	44¹	40	7	13	10	10.8	2.03	205	.244	.299	0	—	0	11	11	-1	1.1
1980 Mil-A	2	4	.333	56	0	0	0	9	84¹	89	2	17	32	11.5	2.77	139	.274	.314	0	—	0	12	10	1	1.2
1981 NY-A	1	1	.500	11	0	0	0	0	19	26	2	5	4	14.7	3.79	94	.329	.369	0	—	-0	-0	-0	0	0.0
1982 KC-A	3	2	.600	21	4	0	0	1	75²	72	8	20	37	11.2	3.45	118	.243	.296	0	—	0	5	5	-1	0.2
1983 KC-A	2	0	1.000	18	0	0	0	1	40¹	51	4	12	17	15.6	6.64	61	.300	.364	0	—	0	-12	-12	0	-0.5
Total 10	31	26	.544	303	9	0	0	45	546¹	564	36	145	203	12.0	3.33	117	.268	.322	0	—	0	35	34	0	5.2

● ELI CATES Cates, Eli Eldo b: 1/26/1877, Greens Fork, Ind. d: 5/29/64, Anderson, Ind. BR/TR, 5'9.5", 175 lbs. Deb: 4/20/08 ♦

| 1908 Was-A | 4 | 8 | .333 | 19 | 11 | 8 | 0 | 0 | 113² | 112 | 1 | 32 | 33 | 11.5 | 2.53 | 90 | .261 | .314 | 11 | .186 | 1 | -2 | -3 | 1 | 0.0 |

● TED CATHER Cather, Theodore Physick b: 5/20/1889, Chester, Pa. d: 4/9/45, Elkton, Md. BR/TR, 5'10.5", 178 lbs. Deb: 9/23/12 ♦

| 1913 StL-N | 0 | 0 | — | 1 | 0 | 0 | 0 | 0 | 0¹ | 1 | 0 | 2 | 0 | 108.0 | 54.00 | 6 | .500 | .800 | 39 | .213 | 0 | -2 | -2 | 0 | 0.0 |

● HARDIN CATHEY Cathey, Hardin "Lil Abner" b: 7/6/19, Burns, Tenn. BR/TR, 6'4", 190 lbs. Deb: 4/16/42

| 1942 Was-A | 1 | 1 | .500 | 12 | 2 | 0 | 0 | 0 | 30¹ | 44 | 1 | 16 | 8 | 17.8 | 7.42 | 49 | .341 | .414 | 3 | .375 | 1 | -13 | -13 | -0 | -0.7 |

● KEEFE CATO Cato, John Keefe b: 5/6/58, Yonkers, N.Y. BR/TR, 6'1", 185 lbs. Deb: 6/13/83

| 1983 Cin-N | 1 | 0 | 1.000 | 4 | 0 | 0 | 0 | 0 | 3² | 2 | 0 | 1 | 3 | 7.4 | 2.45 | 155 | .154 | .214 | 0 | — | 0 | 1 | -0 | 0.1 |

YEAR	TM/L	W	L	PCT	G	GS	CG	SH	SV	IP	H	HR	BB	SO	RAT	ERA	ERA+	OAV	OOB	BH	AVG	PB	PR	/A	PD	TPI
1984	Cin-N	0	1	.000	8	0	0	0	1	15²	22	5	4	12	14.9	8.04	47	.344	.382	2	.500	1	-8	-7	0	-0.4
Total	2	1	1	.500	12	0	0	0	1	19¹	24	5	5	15	13.5	6.98	54	.312	.354	2	.500	1	-7	-7	0	-0.3

● JOHN CATTANACH
Cattanach, John Leckie b: 5/10/1863, Providence, R.I. d: 11/10/26, Providence, R.I. 5'10", 190 lbs. Deb: 6/5/1884

YEAR	TM/L	W	L	PCT	G	GS	CG	SH	SV	IP	H	HR	BB	SO	RAT	ERA	ERA+	OAV	OOB	BH	AVG	PB	PR	/A	PD	TPI
1884	Pro-N	0	0	—	1	1	0	0	0	5	2	0	4	2	10.8	9.00	31	.100	.250	0	.000	-1	-3	-3	-0	-0.1
	StL-U	1	1	.500	2	2	2	0	0	17	12	0	4	13	8.5	2.12	113	.185	.232	0	.000	-2	1	1	0	-0.1
Total	1	1	1	.500	3	3	2	0	0	22	14	0	8	15	9.0	3.68	68	.165	.237	0	.000	-2	-3	-3	-0	-0.2

● BILL CAUDILL
Caudill, William Holland b: 7/13/56, Santa Monica, Cal. BR/TR, 6'1", 210 lbs. Deb: 5/12/79

YEAR	TM/L	W	L	PCT	G	GS	CG	SH	SV	IP	H	HR	BB	SO	RAT	ERA	ERA+	OAV	OOB	BH	AVG	PB	PR	/A	PD	TPI
1979	Chi-N	1	7	.125	29	12	0	0	0	90	89	16	41	104	13.4	4.80	86	.255	.340	1	.059	-1	-11	-7	1	-0.7
1980	Chi-N	4	6	.400	72	2	0	0	1	127²	100	10	59	112	11.3	2.19	179	.223	.314	2	.222	0	20	**25**	-1	1.8
1981	Chi-N	1	5	.167	30	10	0	0	0	71	87	9	45	45	15.2	5.83	63	.301	.373	2	.143	0	-18	-17	-1	-1.4
1982	Sea-A	12	9	.571	70	0	0	0	26	95²	65	9	35	111	9.5	2.35	180	.192	.270	0	—	0	18	20	-1	5.1
1983	Sea-A	2	8	.200	63	0	0	0	26	72²	70	10	38	73	13.6	4.71	90	.257	.353	0	—	0	-5	-4	-1	-1.1
1984	Oak-A★	9	7	.563	68	0	0	0	36	96¹	77	9	31	89	10.1	2.71	138	.218	.281	0	.000	0	14	11	-2	2.4
1985	Tor-A	4	6	.400	67	0	0	0	14	69¹	53	9	35	46	11.7	2.99	141	.209	.310	0	—	0	9	9	-1	1.4
1986	Tor-A	2	4	.333	40	0	0	0	2	36¹	36	6	17	32	13.6	6.19	68	.254	.342	0	—	0	-8	-8	-1	-1.3
1987	Oak-A	0	0	—	6	0	0	0	1	8	10	3	1	8	12.4	9.00	46	.294	.314	0	—	0	-4	-4	-0	0.1
Total	9	35	52	.402	445	24	0	0	106	667	587	81	288	620	12.0	3.68	110	.237	—	5	.122	-1	14	26	-7	6.3

● RED CAUSEY
Causey, Cecil Algernon b: 8/11/1893, Georgetown, Fla. d: 11/11/60, Avon Park, Fla. BR/TR, 6'1", 160 lbs. Deb: 4/26/18

YEAR	TM/L	W	L	PCT	G	GS	CG	SH	SV	IP	H	HR	BB	SO	RAT	ERA	ERA+	OAV	OOB	BH	AVG	PB	PR	/A	PD	TPI
1918	NY-N	11	6	.647	29	18	10	2	2	158¹	143	1	42	48	10.9	2.79	94	.245	.304	6	.125	-3	-0	-3	-1	-0.7
1919	NY-N	9	3	.750	19	16	6	0	0	105	99	5	38	25	11.9	3.69	76	.251	.320	5	.132	-1	-9	-10	-1	-1.3
	Bos-N	4	5	.444	10	10	3	0	0	69	81	1	20	14	13.3	4.57	63	.308	.359	2	.095	-2	-13	-13	-0	-1.7
	Yr	13	8	.619	29	26	9	0	0	174	180	6	58	39	12.4	4.03	70	.273	.333	7	.119	-3	-22	-23	-1	-3.0
1920	Phi-N	7	14	.333	35	26	11	1	3	181¹	203	4	79	30	14.2	4.32	79	.299	.376	11	.186	-2	-24	-18	-2	-2.4
1921	Phi-N	3	3	.500	7	7	4	0	0	50²	58	4	11	9	12.4	2.84	149	.294	.335	3	.150	-1	5	8	-0	0.8
	NY-N	1	1	.500	7	1	0	0	0	14²	13	0	6	1	11.7	2.45	149	.228	.302	1	.333	-1	2	2	-0	0.2
	Yr	4	4	.500	14	8	4	0	0	65¹	71	4	17	10	12.1	2.76	149	.278	.324	4	.174	-1	7	10	-0	1.0
1922	NY-N	4	3	.571	24	2	1	0	1	70²	69	2	34	13	13.1	3.18	126	.267	.347	5	.238	-0	7	6	1	0.6
Total	5	39	35	.527	131	80	35	3	6	649²	666	18	230	139	12.6	3.59	89	.273	.340	33	.157	-9	-31	-29	-3	-4.5

● PUG CAVET
Cavet, Tiller H. b: 12/26/1889, McGregor, Tex. d: 8/4/66, San Luis Obispo, Cal. BL/TL, 6'3", 176 lbs. Deb: 4/25/11

YEAR	TM/L	W	L	PCT	G	GS	CG	SH	SV	IP	H	HR	BB	SO	RAT	ERA	ERA+	OAV	OOB	BH	AVG	PB	PR	/A	PD	TPI
1911	Det-A	0	0	—	1	1	0	0	0	4	6	1	3	1	15.8	4.50	77	.316	.350	0	.000	-0	-2	-2	-0	-0.0
1914	Det-A	7	7	.500	31	14	6	1	2	151¹	129	2	44	51	10.8	2.44	115	.238	.306	5	.106	-2	5	6	1	0.5
1915	Det-A	4	2	.667	17	7	2	0	1	71	83	1	22	26	13.6	4.06	75	.300	.355	6	.231	-0	-8	-6	-0	-0.5
Total	3	11	9	.550	49	22	8	1	3	226¹	218	3	67	78	11.8	2.98	97	.260	.323	11	.153	-0	-4	-2	1	0.0

● ART CECCARELLI
Ceccarelli, Arthur Edward "Chic" b: 4/2/30, New Haven, Conn. BR/TL, 6', 190 lbs. Deb: 5/3/55

YEAR	TM/L	W	L	PCT	G	GS	CG	SH	SV	IP	H	HR	BB	SO	RAT	ERA	ERA+	OAV	OOB	BH	AVG	PB	PR	/A	PD	TPI
1955	KC-A	4	7	.364	31	16	3	1	0	123²	123	20	71	68	14.1	5.31	79	.258	.354	3	.079	-3	-19	-16	-2	-1.7
1956	KC-A	0	1	.000	3	2	0	0	0	10	13	3	4	2	16.2	7.20	60	.317	.391	0	.000	-0	-3	-3	-1	-0.2
1957	Bal-A	0	5	.000	20	8	1	0	0	58	62	3	31	30	14.7	4.50	80	.278	.371	0	.000	-2	-5	-6	-1	-0.7
1959	Chi-N	5	5	.500	18	15	4	2	0	102	95	19	37	56	11.7	4.76	83	.245	.312	3	.091	-1	-9	-9	-1	-1.0
1960	Chi-N	0	0	—	7	1	0	0	0	13	16	1	4	10	13.8	5.54	68	.296	.345	0	—	0	-3	-3	-0	0.0
Total	5	9	18	.333	79	42	8	3	0	306²	309	46	147	166	13.5	5.05	79	.261	.345	6	.068	-6	-38	-37	-3	-3.6

● JOSE CECENA
Cecena, Jose Isabel (Lugo) b: 8/20/63, Ciudad Obregon, Mexico BR/TR, 5'11", 180 lbs. Deb: 4/6/88

YEAR	TM/L	W	L	PCT	G	GS	CG	SH	SV	IP	H	HR	BB	SO	RAT	ERA	ERA+	OAV	OOB	BH	AVG	PB	PR	/A	PD	TPI
1988	Tex-A	0	0	—	22	0	0	0	1	26¹	20	2	23	27	15.4	4.78	85	.213	.378	0	—	0	-2	-2	-0	-0.1

● REX CECIL
Cecil, Rex Rolston b: 10/8/16, Lindsay, Okla. d: 10/30/66, Long Beach, Cal. BL/TR, 6'3", 195 lbs. Deb: 8/13/44

YEAR	TM/L	W	L	PCT	G	GS	CG	SH	SV	IP	H	HR	BB	SO	RAT	ERA	ERA+	OAV	OOB	BH	AVG	PB	PR	/A	PD	TPI
1944	Bos-A	4	5	.444	11	9	4	0	0	61	72	5	33	33	15.6	5.16	66	.286	.371	5	.278	2	-12	-12	-0	-1.4
1945	Bos-A	2	5	.286	7	7	1	0	0	45	46	4	27	30	14.6	5.20	66	.261	.360	6	.300	1	-9	-9	1	-1.1
Total	2	6	10	.375	18	16	5	0	0	106	118	9	60	63	15.2	5.18	66	.276	.366	11	.289	2	-21	-21	1	-2.5

● PETE CENTER
Center, Marvin Earl b: 4/22/12, Hazel Green, Ky. BR/TR, 6'4", 190 lbs. Deb: 9/11/42

YEAR	TM/L	W	L	PCT	G	GS	CG	SH	SV	IP	H	HR	BB	SO	RAT	ERA	ERA+	OAV	OOB	BH	AVG	PB	PR	/A	PD	TPI
1942	Cle-A	0	0	—	1	0	0	0	0	3¹	7	0	4	0	32.4	16.20	21	.438	.571	0	.000	-0	-5	-5	-0	0.0
1943	Cle-A	1	2	.333	24	1	0	0	1	42¹	29	3	18	10	10.0	2.76	112	.201	.290	0	.000	-1	3	2	-1	0.0
1945	Cle-A	6	3	.667	31	8	2	0	1	85²	89	2	28	34	12.4	3.99	81	.270	.329	2	.091	-2	-6	-7	-2	-1.1
1946	Cle-A	0	2	.000	21	0	0	0	1	29	29	2	20	6	15.5	4.97	67	.269	.388	0	—	-0	-5	-5	-0	-0.4
Total	4	7	7	.500	77	9	2	0	3	160¹	154	7	70	50	12.7	4.10	79	.258	.338	2	.065	-3	-13	-16	-3	-1.5

● RICK CERONE
Cerone, Richard Aldo b: 5/19/54, Newark, N.J. BR/TR, 5'11", 192 lbs. Deb: 8/17/75 ♦

YEAR	TM/L	W	L	PCT	G	GS	CG	SH	SV	IP	H	HR	BB	SO	RAT	ERA	ERA+	OAV	OOB	BH	AVG	PB	PR	/A	PD	TPI
1987	NY-A	0	0	—	2	0	0	0	0	2	0	0	1	1	4.5	0.00	—	.000	.143	69	.243	2	1	1	-0	0.0

● JOHN CERUTTI
Cerutti, John Joseph b: 4/28/60, Albany, N.Y. BL/TL, 6'2", 200 lbs. Deb: 9/1/85

YEAR	TM/L	W	L	PCT	G	GS	CG	SH	SV	IP	H	HR	BB	SO	RAT	ERA	ERA+	OAV	OOB	BH	AVG	PB	PR	/A	PD	TPI
1985	Tor-A	0	2	.000	4	1	0	0	0	6²	10	1	4	5	20.3	5.40	78	.323	.417		0	—	-1	-1	0	-0.3
1986	Tor-A	9	4	.692	34	20	2	1	1	145¹	150	25	47	89	12.3	4.15	102	.268	.326		0	—	0	1	0	-0.1
1987	Tor-A	11	4	.733	44	21	2	0	0	151¹	144	30	59	92	12.1	4.40	102	.251	.322		0	—	1	2	-2	-0.1
1988	Tor-A	6	7	.462	46	12	0	0	1	123²	120	12	42	65	12.0	3.13	126	.256	.322		0	—	11	13	1	1.4
1989	*Tor-A	11	11	.500	33	31	3	1	0	205¹	214	19	53	69	12.0	3.07	123	.273	.323		0	—	19	16	3	2.0
1990	Tor-A	9	9	.500	30	23	0	0	0	140	162	23	49	49	13.8	4.76	83	.297	.359		0	—	-13	-13	-0	-1.5
1991	Det-A	3	6	.333	38	8	1	0	2	88²	94	9	37	29	13.5	4.57	91	.276	.351		0	—	-5	-4	1	-0.2
Total	7	49	43	.533	229	116	8	2	4	861	894	119	291	398	12.6	3.94	103	.271	.333		0	—	13	12	4	1.2

● RAY CHADWICK
Chadwick, Ray Charles b: 11/17/62, Durham, N.C. BB/TR, 6'2", 180 lbs. Deb: 7/29/86

YEAR	TM/L	W	L	PCT	G	GS	CG	SH	SV	IP	H	HR	BB	SO	RAT	ERA	ERA+	OAV	OOB	BH	AVG	PB	PR	/A	PD	TPI
1986	Cal-A	0	5	.000	7	7	0	0	0	27¹	39	5	15	9	18.1	7.24	57	.336	.417		0	—	-9	-10	0	-1.3

● LEON CHAGNON
Chagnon, Leon Wilbur "Shag" b: 9/28/02, Pittsfield, N.H. d: 7/30/53, Amesbury, Mass. BR/TR, 6', 182 lbs. Deb: 10/5/29

YEAR	TM/L	W	L	PCT	G	GS	CG	SH	SV	IP	H	HR	BB	SO	RAT	ERA	ERA+	OAV	OOB	BH	AVG	PB	PR	/A	PD	TPI
1929	Pit-N	0	0	—	1	1	0	0	0	7	11	1	4	4	15.4	9.00	53	.333	.353	0	.000	-0	-3	-3	0	0.0
1930	Pit-N	0	3	.000	18	4	1	0	0	62	92	9	23	27	17.4	6.82	73	.355	.418	4	.200	-1	-13	-13	0	-0.5
1932	Pit-N	9	6	.600	30	10	4	1	0	128	140	10	34	52	12.4	3.94	97	.276	.324	9	.225	0	-1	-2	-2	-0.2
1933	Pit-N	6	4	.600	39	5	1	0	1	100	100	2	17	35	10.8	3.69	90	.259	.296	1	.048	-2	-4	-4	-1	-0.7
1934	Pit-N	4	1	.800	33	1	0	0	1	58	68	5	24	19	14.4	4.81	88	.288	.356	3	.231	0	-5	-4	1	-0.2
1935	NY-N	0	2	.000	14	1	0	0	1	38¹	32	7	16	16	8.7	3.52	109	.232	.259	0	.000	-1	2	1	0	0.0
Total	6	19	16	.543	135	22	8	1	3	393¹	443	34	104	153	12.8	4.51	87	.284	.333	17	.162	-2	-24	-25	-1	-1.6

● BOB CHAKALES
Chakales, Robert Edward "Chick" b: 8/10/27, Asheville, N.C. BR/TR, 6'1", 185 lbs. Deb: 4/21/51

YEAR	TM/L	W	L	PCT	G	GS	CG	SH	SV	IP	H	HR	BB	SO	RAT	ERA	ERA+	OAV	OOB	BH	AVG	PB	PR	/A	PD	TPI
1951	Cle-A	3	4	.429	17	10	2	1	0	68¹	80	3	43	32	16.2	4.74	80	.292	.388	7	.350	2	-5	-7	-0	-0.5
1952	Cle-A	1	2	.333	5	1	0	0	0	12	19	2	8	7	20.3	9.75	34	.388	.474	2	.500	1	-8	-9	-1	-1.6
1953	Cle-A	0	2	.000	7	3	1	0	0	27	28	2	10	6	13.0	2.67	141	.283	.355	2	.286	0	4	3	0	0.3
1954	Cle-A	2	0	1.000	10¹	4	0	2	3	13.9	0.87	422	.114	.340				1	.333	1	3	3	-0	0.7
	Bal-A	3	7	.300	38	6	0	0	3	89¹	81	8	43	44	12.6	3.73	96	.245	.333	8	.364	2	-0	-1	0	0.1
	Yr	5	7	.417	41	6	0	0	3	99²	85	9	55	47	12.7	3.43	105	.232	.334	9	.360	3	3	2	0	0.8
1955	Chi-A	0	0	—	7	0	0	0	0	12¹	11	2	6	6	12.4	1.46	276	.231	.256	0	.000	-0	3	3	-0	0.3
	Was-A	2	3	.400	29	6	1	0	1	54²	55	4	25	28	13.3	5.27	73	.263	.345	0	.000	-1	-8	-9	1	-0.8
	Yr	2	3	.400	36	6	1	0	1	67	66	6	31	34	13.2	4.57	84	.262	.345	0	.000	-1	-5	-5	1	-0.8
1956	Was-A	4	4	.500	43	1	0	0	1	96	94	3	57	33	14.4	4.03	107	.268	.375	3	.150	-1	3	1	-0	0.3
1957	Was-A	0	1	.000	4	2	0	0	0	18¹	20	2	10	12	14.7	5.40	72	.274	.361	1	.143	-0	-3	-3	0	-0.1
	Bos-A	0	2	.000	18	0	0	0	3	32	53	5	11	16	18.3	8.16	49	.379	.428	2	.667	-1	-16	-15	-1	-1.1
	Yr	0	3	.000	22	2	0	0	3	50¹	73	7	21	28	17.0	7.15	55	.341	.403	3	.300	-1	-19	-18	-0	-1.2
Total	7	15	25	.375	171	23	3	1	10	420¹	445	31	225	187	14.5	4.54	87	.277	.369	26	.271	5	-28	-31	-2	-2.7

YEAR	TM/L	W	L	PCT	G	GS	CG	SH	SV	IP	H	HR	BB	SO	RAT	ERA	ERA+	OAV	OOB	BH	AVG	PB	PR	/A	PD	TPI

● GEORGE CHALMERS　　Chalmers, George W. "Dut"　b: 6/7/1888, Edinburgh, Scot.　d: 8/5/60, Bronx, N.Y.　BR/TR, 6'1", 189 lbs.　Deb: 9/21/10

1910	Phi-N	1	1	.500	4	3	2	0	0	22	21	0	11	12	13.5	5.32	59	.280	.379	1	.143	-0	-6	-5	1	-0.3
1911	Phi-N	13	10	.565	38	22	11	3	4	208²	196	5	101	101	13.0	3.11	111	.256	.346	13	.178	-1	7	8	-1	0.6
1912	Phi-N	3	4	.429	12	8	3	0	0	57²	64	4	37	22	16.1	3.28	111	.296	.404	3	.188	-0	1	2	-2	0.0
1913	Phi-N	3	10	.231	26	14	4	0	1	116	133	4	51	46	14.7	4.81	69	.296	.374	7	.212	-1	-21	-19	1	-1.9
1914	Phi-N	0	3	.000	3	2	1	0	0	18	23	0	15	6	19.5	5.50	53	.324	.448	0	.000	-1	-5	-5	0	-0.8
1915	*Phi-N	8	9	.471	26	20	13	1	1	170¹	159	3	45	82	10.8	2.48	110	.255	.305	10	.169	-0	5	5	1	0.4
1916	Phi-N	1	4	.200	12	8	2	0	0	53²	49	2	19	21	11.7	3.19	83	.244	.315	0	.000	-2	-3	-3	0	-0.5
Total	7	29	41	.414	121	77	36	4	6	646¹	645	17	279	290	13.1	3.41	93	.269	.348	34	.163	-5	-22	-18	1	-2.5

● CRAIG CHAMBERLAIN　　Chamberlain, Craig Philip　b: 2/2/57, Hollywood, Cal.　BR/TR, 6'1", 190 lbs.　Deb: 8/12/79

1979	KC-A	4	4	.500	10	10	4	0	0	69²	68	7	18	30	11.2	3.75	114	.261	.311	0	—	0	4	4	-2	0.2
1980	KC-A	0	1	.000	5	0	0	0	0	9¹	10	3	5	3	14.5	6.75	60	.270	.357	0	—	0	-3	-3	0	-0.3
Total	2	4	5	.444	15	10	4	0	0	79	78	10	23	33	11.6	4.10	103	.262	.317	0	—	0	1	1	-2	-0.1

● ELTON CHAMBERLAIN　　Chamberlain, Elton P. "Icebox"　b: 11/5/1867, Buffalo, N.Y.　d: 9/22/29, Baltimore, Md.　BR/TR, 5'9", 168 lbs.　Deb: 9/13/1886

1886	Lou-a	0	3	.000	4	4	4	0	0	31¹	39	0	17	18	16.1	6.61	55	.287	.366	3	.158	-0	-11	-10	-0	-0.7
1887	Lou-a	18	16	.529	36	36	35	1	0	309	340	8	117	118	13.7	3.79	116	.274	.343	26	.198	-3	17	21	1	1.5
1888	Lou-a	14	9	.609	24	24	21	1	0	196	177	2	59	119	11.3	2.53	122	.232	.297	18	.191	0	12	12	1	1.4
	*StL-a	11	2	.846	14	14	13	1	0	112	61	1	27	57	7.6	1.61	203	.154	.220	5	.100	-3	18	21	-1	1.7
	Yr	25	11	.694	38	38	34	2	0	308	238	3	86	176	9.6	2.19	143	.204	.262	23	.160	-3	30	33	0	3.1
1889	StL-a	32	15	.681	53	51	44	3	1	421²	376	18	165	202	11.9	2.97	142	.231	.309	34	.199	-2	41	59	-3	4.7
1890	StL-a	3	1	.750	5	5	3	0	0	35	47	1	26	14	18.8	5.91	73	.311	.412	2	.133	-1	-8	-6	0	-0.6
	Col-a	12	6	.667	25	21	19	6	0	175	128	2	70	114	10.6	2.21	162	.198	.285	15	.231	3	32	27	-2	2.4
	Yr	15	7	.682	30	26	22	**6**	0	210	175	3	96	128	12.0	2.83	131	.220	.310	17	.213	1	24	21	-2	1.8
1891	Phi-a	22	23	.489	49	46	44	0	0	405²	397	3	206	204	13.6	4.22	91	.248	.338	33	.188	2	-22	-18	0	-1.4
1892	Cin-N	19	23	.452	52	49	43	2	0	406¹	391	4	170	169	12.8	3.39	96	.243	.322	36	.225	3	-5	-5	-4	-0.6
1893	Cin-N	16	12	.571	34	27	19	1	0	241	248	3	112	59	14.0	3.73	128	.258	.345	19	.196	-3	25	28	-2	2.0
1894	Cin-N	10	9	.526	23	22	18	1	0	177²	220	10	91	57	16.4	5.77	96	.301	.387	22	.314	4	-9	-4	-1	-0.1
1896	Cle-N	0	1	.000	2	2	1	0	0	11	21	1	5	2	22.1	7.36	62	.396	.458	0	.000	-0	-4	-3	-0	-0.3
Total	10	157	120	.567	321	301	264	16	1	2521²	2445	63	1065	1133	12.9	3.57	112	.246	.326	213	.203	-2	88	119	-11	10.0

● BILL CHAMBERLAIN　　Chamberlain, William Vincent　b: 4/21/09, Stoughton, Mass.　d: 2/6/94, Brockton, Mass.　BR/TL, 5'10.5", 173 lbs.　Deb: 8/2/32

| 1932 | Chi-A | 0 | 5 | .000 | 12 | 5 | 0 | 0 | 0 | 41¹ | 39 | 3 | 25 | 11 | 13.9 | 4.57 | 95 | .250 | .354 | 1 | .100 | -1 | -0 | -1 | -1 | -0.2 |

● CLIFF CHAMBERS　　Chambers, Clifford Day "Lefty"　b: 1/10/22, Portland, Ore.　BL/TL, 6'3", 208 lbs.　Deb: 4/24/48

1948	Chi-N	2	9	.182	29	12	3	1	0	103²	100	4	48	51	13.1	4.43	88	.254	.339	4	.133	-1	-5	-6	0	-0.6
1949	Pit-N	13	7	.650	34	21	10	1	0	177¹	186	15	58	93	12.6	3.96	106	.268	.329	13	.236	3	2	5	1	0.9
1950	Pit-N	12	15	.444	37	33	11	2	0	249¹	262	18	92	93	13.0	4.30	102	.265	.332	26	.289	7	-4	2	-2	0.7
1951	Pit-N	3	6	.333	10	10	2	1	0	59²	64	5	31	19	14.9	5.58	76	.276	.371	7	.333	2	-11	-9	-2	-1.1
	StL-N	11	6	.647	21	16	9	1	0	129¹	120	13	56	45	12.2	3.83	104	.251	.329	8	.163	0	2	2	-2	0.1
	Yr	14	12	.538	31	26	11	2	0	189	184	18	87	64	12.9	4.38	92	.257	.338	15	.214	2	-9	-7	-3	-1.0
1952	StL-N	4	4	.500	26	13	2	1	1	98¹	110	8	33	47	13.3	4.12	90	.285	.344	9	.281	3	-4	-4	0	0.0
1953	StL-N	3	6	.333	32	8	0	0	0	79²	82	7	43	26	14.2	4.86	88	.266	.358	2	.118	-1	-5	-5	0	-0.6
Total	6	48	53	.475	189	113	37	7	1	897¹	924	70	361	374	13.1	4.29	96	.266	.338	69	.235	13	-26	-16	-4	-0.6

● JOHNNIE CHAMBERS　　Chambers, Johnnie Monroe　b: 9/10/11, Copperhill, Tenn　d: 5/11/77, Palatka, Fla.　BL/TL, 6', 185 lbs.　Deb: 5/4/37

| 1937 | StL-N | 0 | 0 | — | 2 | 0 | 0 | 0 | 0 | 2 | 5 | 0 | 2 | 1 | 31.5 | 18.00 | 22 | .455 | .538 | 0 | — | 0 | -3 | -3 | -0 | 0.0 |

● ROME CHAMBERS　　Chambers, Richard Jerome　b: 8/31/1875, Weaverville, N.C.　d: 8/30/02, Weaverville, N.C.　BL/TL, 6'2", 173 lbs.　Deb: 5/7/00

| 1900 | Bos-N | 0 | 0 | — | 1 | 0 | 0 | 0 | 0 | 4 | 5 | 0 | 2 | 2 | 22.5 | 11.25 | 37 | .313 | .476 | 0 | .000 | -0 | -3 | -3 | -0 | -0.2 |

● BILL CHAMBERS　　Chambers, William Christopher　b: 9/13/1889, Cameron, W.Va.　d: 3/27/62, Fort Wayne, Ind.　BR/TR, 5'9", 185 lbs.　Deb: 7/11/10

| 1910 | StL-N | 0 | 0 | — | 1 | 0 | 0 | 0 | 0 | 1 | 1 | 0 | 1 | 0 | 9.0 | 0.00 | — | .250 | .250 | 0 | — | 0 | 0 | 0 | -0 | 0.0 |

● BILL CHAMPION　　Champion, Buford Billy　b: 9/18/47, Shelby, N.C.　BR/TR, 6'4", 188 lbs.　Deb: 6/4/69

1969	Phi-N	5	10	.333	23	20	4	2	1	116²	130	7	63	70	15.1	5.01	71	.286	.376	6	.171	0	-18	-19	1	-2.1
1970	Phi-N	0	2	.000	7	1	0	0	0	14	21	3	10	12	20.6	9.00	44	.375	.478	0	.000	-0	-8	-8	0	-0.9
1971	Phi-N	3	5	.375	37	9	0	0	0	108²	100	10	48	49	12.5	4.39	80	.249	.334	3	.111	-1	-11	-10	1	-0.8
1972	Phi-N	4	14	.222	30	22	3	0	0	132²	155	11	54	54	14.2	5.09	71	.301	.368	5	.147	0	-24	-22	1	-2.7
1973	Mil-A	5	8	.385	37	11	2	0	1	136¹	139	10	62	53	13.7	3.70	102	.267	.350	0	—	0	2	1	2	0.5
1974	Mil-A	11	4	.733	31	23	2	0	0	161²	168	12	49	60	12.1	3.62	100	.270	.323	0	—	0	-0	-1	1	-0.1
1975	Mil-A	6	6	.500	27	13	1	0	0	110	125	11	55	40	14.7	5.89	65	.290	.370	0	—	0	-26	-25	1	-2.4
1976	Mil-A	0	1	.000	10	3	0	0	0	24¹	35	0	13	18	18.1	7.03	50	.361	.441	0	—	0	-9	-10	1	-0.2
Total	8	34	50	.405	202	102	13	3	2	804³	873	64	354	360	13.9	4.69	78	.282	.358	14	.141	-1	-95	-93	4	-8.7

● DEAN CHANCE　　Chance, Wilmer Dean　b: 6/1/41, Wooster, Ohio　BR/TR, 6'3", 200 lbs.　Deb: 9/11/61

1961	LA-A	0	2	.000	5	4	0	0	0	18¹	33	5	11	19.1		6.87	66	.412	.453	0	.000	-1	-6	-5	1	-0.4
1962	LA-A	14	10	.583	50	24	6	2	8	206²	195	14	66	127	11.6	2.96	130	.250	.313	4	.062	-5	23	21	1	2.0
1963	LA-A	13	18	.419	45	35	6	2	3	248	229	10	90	168	11.9	3.19	107	.243	.316	12	.150	-1	12	6	1	0.8
1964	LA-A★	**20**	9	.690	46	35	**15**	**11**	4	278¹	194	7	86	207	9.1	**1.65**	**199**	.195	.261	7	.079	-5	**61**	**51**	-2	4.7
1965	Cal-A	15	10	.600	36	33	10	4	0	225²	197	12	101	164	12.2	3.15	108	.238	.328	7	.093	-2	8	6	3	0.8
1966	Cal-A	12	17	.414	41	37	11	2	1	259²	206	18	114	180	11.3	3.08	109	.222	.312	2	.026	-6	10	8	2	0.4
1967	Min-A★	20	14	.588	41	39	**18**	5	1	283²	244	17	68	220	10.1	2.73	127	.229	.279	3	.033	-6	16	23	2	2.4
1968	Min-A	16	16	.500	43	39	15	6	1	292	224	15	63	234	9.2	2.53	122	.211	.261	5	.054	-6	15	18	3	1.8
1969	*Min-A	5	4	.556	20	15	1	0	0	88¹	76	6	35	50	11.7	2.95	124	.233	.315	1	.042	-1	7	7	-1	0.4
1970	Cle-A	9	8	.529	45	19	1	1	4	155	172	18	59	109	13.8	4.24	93	.287	.357	3	.071	-3	-9	-5	-1	-0.9
	NY-N	0	1	.000	3	0	0	0	0	2	3	0	2	0	22.5	13.50	30	.500	.625	0	—	0	-2	-2	0	-1.0
1971	Det-A	4	6	.400	31	14	0	0	0	89²	91	5	50	64	14.6	3.51	102	.265	.364	0	.000	-2	-1	-1	-0	-0.2
Total	11	128	115	.527	406	294	83	33	23	2147¹	1864	122	739	1534	11.2	2.92	119	.234	.305	44	.066	-37	134	131	8	10.8

● ED CHANDLER　　Chandler, Edward Oliver　b: 2/17/22, Pinson, Ala.　BR/TR, 6'2", 190 lbs.　Deb: 4/18/47

| 1947 | Bro-N | 0 | 1 | .000 | 15 | 1 | 0 | 0 | 1 | 29² | 31 | 7 | 12 | 8 | 13.0 | 6.37 | 65 | .263 | .331 | 0 | .000 | 0 | -8 | -7 | 0 | -0.3 |

● SPUD CHANDLER　　Chandler, Spurgeon Ferdinand　b: 9/12/07, Commerce, Ga.　d: 1/9/90, S.Pasadena, Fla.　BR/TR, 6', 181 lbs.　Deb: 5/6/37　C

1937	NY-A	7	4	.636	12	10	6	2	0	82¹	79	8	20	31	10.9	2.84	156	.253	.300	4	.133	-2	16	15	2	1.7
1938	NY-A	14	5	.737	23	23	14	2	0	172	183	7	47	36	12.1	4.03	113	.271	.320	14	.203	2	15	10	4	1.5
1939	NY-A	3	0	1.000	11	0	0	0	0	19	26	0	9	14	16.6	2.84	153	.329	.398	2	.400	1	4	3	1	0.6
1940	NY-A	8	7	.533	27	24	9	1	0	172	184	4	60	56	13.1	4.60	88	.275	.341	9	.150	1	-4	-11	3	-0.4
1941	*NY-A	10	4	.714	28	20	11	4	4	163²	146	5	60	50	11.3	3.19	123	.239	.307	11	.183	-1	17	13	3	1.3
1942	*NY-A★	16	5	.762	24	24	17	3	0	200²	176	4	74	74	11.4	2.38	145	.237	.309	15	.211	4	29	24	3	3.2
1943	*NY-A☆	**20**	4	**.833**	30	30	**20**	5	0	253	197	5	54	134	**9.1**	**1.64**	**197**	.215	**.261**	25	.258	7	**47**	**44**	3	**5.7**
1944	NY-A	0	0	—	1	1	0	0	0	4	6	0	2	1	12.0	4.50	77	.300	.364	0	.000	-0	-1	-1	0	0.0
1945	NY-A	2	1	.667	4	4	1	0	0	31	30	2	7	14	10.7	4.65	75	.250	.291	4	.333	1	-4	-4	0	-0.3
1946	NY-A☆	20	8	.714	34	32	20	6	2	257¹	200	7	90	138	10.2	2.10	164	.218	.288	14	.149	4	40	39	4	4.8
1947	NY-A☆	9	5	.643	17	16	9	1	0	128	100	4	41	48	11.8	2.46	144	.214	.277	12	.245	4	18	15	3	2.3
Total	11	109	43	.717	211	184	109	26	6	1485	1327	64	463	614	11.0	2.84	132	.240	.301	110	.201	17	176	149	27	20.6

● ESTY CHANEY　　Chaney, Esty Clyon　b: 1/29/1891, Hadley, Pa.　d: 2/5/52, Cleveland, Ohio　BR/TR, 5'11", 170 lbs.　Deb: 8/2/13

1913	Bos-A	0	0	—	1	0	0	0	0	4	4	0	4	2	27.0	9.00	33	.200	.429	0	—	0	-1	-1	-0	0.0
1914	Bro-F	0	0	—	1	0	0	0	0	4	7	0	2	1	20.3	6.75	43	.389	.450	0	.000	-0	-2	-2	-0	0.0
Total	2	0	0	—	2	0	0	0	0	8	5	0	4	1	21.6	7.88	40	.348	.444	0	.000	-0	-2	-2	-0	0.0

YEAR TM/L	W	L	PCT	G	GS	CG	SH	SV	IP	H	HR	BB	SO	RAT	ERA	ERA+	OAV	OOB	BH	AVG	PB	PR	/A	PD	TPI

● DARRIN CHAPIN   Chapin, Darrin John   b: 2/1/66, Warren, Ohio   BR/TR, 6', 170 lbs.   Deb: 9/21/91

1991 NY-A	0	1	.000	3	0	0	0	0	5¹	3	0	6	5	15.2	5.06	82	.158	.360	0	—	0	-1	-1	0	-0.1
1992 Phi-N	0	0	—	1	0	0	0	0	2	2	1	0	1	9.0	9.00	39	.250	.250	0	—	0	-1	-1	-0	-0.1
Total 2	0	1	.000	4	0	0	0	0	7¹	5	1	6	6	13.5	6.14	65	.185	.333	0	—	0	-2	-2	0	-0.1

● TINY CHAPLIN   Chaplin, James Bailey   b: 7/13/05, Los Angeles, Cal.   d: 3/25/39, National City, Cal   BR/TR, 6'1", 195 lbs.   Deb: 4/13/28

1928 NY-N	0	2	.000	12	1	0	0	0	24	27	0	8	5	13.1	4.50	87	.284	.340	0	.000	-1	-1	-2	-1	-0.2
1930 NY-N	2	6	.250	19	8	3	0	1	73	89	8	16	20	13.4	5.18	91	.305	.349	2	.105	-2	-4	-0	-3	-0.3
1931 NY-N	3	0	1.000	16	3	1	0	1	42¹	39	2	16	7	12.1	3.19	116	.242	.318	2	.182	0	3	2	-1	0.1
1936 Bos-N	10	15	.400	40	31	14	0	2	231²	273	21	62	86	13.1	4.12	93	.294	.340	17	.202	-0	-3	-7	2	-0.6
Total 4	15	23	.395	87	43	18	0	4	371	428	31	102	118	13.1	4.25	94	.290	.340	21	.176	-1	-2	-10	1	-1.0

● ED CHAPMAN   Chapman, Edwin Volney   b: 11/28/05, Courtland, Miss.   BB/TR, 6'1", 185 lbs.   Deb: 8/6/33

1933 Was-A	0	0	—	6	1	0	0	0	9	10	2	12	4	18.0	8.00	52	.270	.308	0	.000	-0	-4	-4	-0	-0.1

● FRED CHAPMAN   Chapman, Frederick Joseph   b: 11/24/1872, Little Cooley, Pa.   d: 12/14/57, Union City, Pa.   BR/TR, 5'8", 165 lbs.   Deb: 7/22/1887

1887 Phi-a	0	0	—	1	1	1	0	0	5	8	0	2	4	18.0	7.20	60	.364	.417	0	.000	0	-2	-2	0	0.0

● BEN CHAPMAN   Chapman, William Benjamin   b: 12/25/08, Nashville, Tenn.   d: 7/7/93, Hoover, Ala.   BR/TR, 6', 190 lbs.   Deb: 4/15/30   MC♦

1944 Bro-N	5	3	.625	11	9	6	0	0	79¹	75	4	33	37	12.6	3.40	104	.242	.321	14	.368	6	2	1	-2	0.6
1945 Bro-N	3	3	.500	10	7	2	0	0	53²	64	3	32	23	16.6	5.53	68	.296	.394	3	.136	-1	-10	-11	1	-1.0
Phi-N	0	0	—	3	0	0	0	0	7	7	0	6	4	16.7	7.71	50	.259	.394	16	.314	0	-3	-3	-0	0.0
Yr	3	3	.500	13	7	2	0	0	60²	71	3	38	27	16.2	5.79	65	.289	.384	19	.260	-0	-13	-14	0	-1.0
1946 Phi-N	0	0	—	1	0	0	0	0	1	1	0	1	0	9.0	0.00	—	.200	.200	-0	—	0	0	0	0	0.0
Total 3	8	6	.571	25	16	8	0	0	141	147	7	71	65	14.3	4.40	83	.263	.353	1958	.302	6	-11	-12	-1	-0.4

● BILL CHAPPELLE   Chappelle, William Hogan "Big Bill"   b: 3/22/1884, Waterloo, N.Y.   d: 12/31/44, Mineola, N.Y.   BR/TR, 6'2", 206 lbs.   Deb: 8/20/08

1908 Bos-N	2	4	.333	13	6	3	1	0	70¹	60	0	17	23	10.4	1.79	135	.233	.290	1	.048	0	4	5	1	0.4
1909 Bos-N	1	1	.500	5	3	2	0	0	29	31	0	11	8	13.3	1.86	151	.279	.350	4	.364	2	2	3	1	0.6
Cin-N	0	0	—	1	0	0	0	0	4	5	0	2	0	18.0	2.25	115	.278	.381	0	.000	-0	0	0	-0	0.0
Yr	1	1	.500	6	3	2	0	0	33	36	0	13	8	13.6	1.91	146	.277	.347	4	.333	2	3	3	1	0.6
1914 Bro-F	4	4	.667	16	6	4	0	0	74¹	71	1	29	31	12.5	3.15	91	.255	.332	0	.000	-4	-2	-2	-1	-0.7
Total 3	7	7	.500	35	15	9	1	0	177²	167	1	59	62	11.9	2.38	113	.251	.321	5	.089	-3	5	6	1	0.3

● NORM CHARLTON   Charlton, Norman Wood   b: 1/6/63, Fort Polk, La.   BB/TL, 6'3", 195 lbs.   Deb: 8/19/88

1988 Cin-N	4	5	.444	10	10	0	0	0	61¹	60	6	20	39	12.0	3.96	90	.256	.320	0	.000	-1	-4	-3	-0	-0.5
1989 Cin-N	8	3	.727	69	0	0	0	0	95¹	67	5	40	98	10.3	2.93	123	.197	.285	0	.000	-1	6	7	0	0.7
1990 *Cin-N	12	9	.571	56	16	1	1	2	154¹	131	10	70	117	12.0	2.74	144	.231	.320	5	.135	0	18	21	1	2.8
1991 Cin-N	3	5	.375	39	11	0	0	1	108¹	92	6	34	77	11.0	2.91	131	.236	.307	1	.043	-2	9	11	1	0.7
1992 Cin-N★	4	2	.667	64	0	0	0	26	81¹	79	7	26	90	12.0	2.99	120	.262	.326	1	.200	0	5	6	-1	0.7
1993 Sea-A	1	3	.250	34	0	0	0	18	34²	22	4	17	48	10.1	2.34	188	.179	.279	0	—	0	8	8	-0	1.5
1995 Phi-N	2	5	.286	25	0	0	0	0	22	23	2	15	12	16.8	7.36	57	.280	.410	1	1.000	1	-8	-8	-1	-2.1
*Sea-A	2	1	.667	30	0	0	0	14	47²	23	2	16	58	7.6	1.51	314	.143	.225	0	—	0	17	17	0	1.8
1996 Sea-A	4	7	.364	70	0	0	0	20	75²	66	7	38	73	12.7	4.04	122	.244	.336	0	—	0	8	7	0	1.2
Total 8	40	40	.500	397	37	1	1	81	680²	565	49	276	612	11.4	3.12	128	.228	.311	8	.093	-2	59	67	-1	6.8

● PETE CHARTON   Charton, Frank Lane   b: 12/21/42, Jackson, Tenn.   BL/TR, 6'2", 190 lbs.   Deb: 4/19/64

1964 Bos-A	0	2	.000	25	5	0	0	0	65	67	12	24	37	12.7	5.26	73	.275	.342	1	.100	-0	-12	-10	2	-0.2

● HAL CHASE   Chase, Harold Homer "Prince Hal"   b: 2/13/1883, Los Gatos, Cal.   d: 5/18/47, Colusa, Cal.   BR/TL, 6', 175 lbs.   Deb: 4/14/05   M♦

1908 NY-A	0	0	—	1	0	0	0	0	0¹	0	0	0	0	0.0	0.00	—	.000	.000	104	.257	0	0	0	0	0.0

● KEN CHASE   Chase, Kendall Fay "Lefty"   b: 10/6/13, Oneonta, N.Y.   d: 1/16/85, Oneonta, N.Y.   BL/TL, 6'2", 210 lbs.   Deb: 4/23/36

1936 Was-A	0	0	—	1	0	0	0	0	2¹	2	0	4	1	23.1	11.57	41	.250	.500	1	1.000	1	-2	-2	-0	0.0
1937 Was-A	14	9	4	—	.571	9	0	43		76¹	74	4	60	15.8	4.13	107	.257	.385	1	.034	-4	-4	3	-0	-0.2
1938 Was-A	9	10	.474	32	21	7	0	1	150	151	4	113	64	16.1	5.58	81	.268	.394	10	.208	-1	-13	-18	1	-1.7
1939 Was-A	10	19	.345	32	31	15	1	0	232	215	10	114	118	12.8	3.80	114	.243	.330	15	.169	-3	21	14	0	1.3
1940 Was-A	15	17	.469	35	34	20	1	0	261²	260	14	143	129	14.0	3.23	129	.261	.357	15	.163	-1	33	27	-1	2.8
1941 Was-A	6	18	.250	33	30	8	1	0	205²	228	11	115	98	15.1	5.08	80	.280	.371	11	.149	-1	-21	-24	1	-2.4
1942 Bos-A	5	1	.833	13	10	4	0	0	80¹	82	5	41	34	13.8	3.81	98	.263	.348	6	.182	1	-1	-1	-1	-0.1
1943 Bos-A	0	4	.000	7	5	0	0	0	27¹	36	0	30	7	21.7	6.91	46	.316	.458	1	.091	-1	-11	-11	0	-1.4
NY-N	4	12	.250	21	20	4	1	0	129¹	140	7	74	86	15.0	4.11	84	.275	.369	4	.214	-0	-10	-9	-1	-1.2
Total 8	53	84	.387	188	160	62	4	1	1165	1188	55	694	582	14.7	4.27	97	.265	.365	69	.165	-8	-19	-19	-0	-2.9

● JIM CHATTERTON   Chatterton, James M.   b: 10/14/1864, Brooklyn, N.Y.   d: 12/15/44, Tewksbury, Mass.   Deb: 6/7/1884   ♦

1884 KC-U	0	1	.000	1	1	0	0	0	5	11	0	2	1	23.4	3.60	62	.407	.448	2	.133	-0	-1	-1	0	-0.1

● NESTOR CHAVEZ   Chavez, Nestor Isais (Silva)   b: 7/6/47, Chacao, Venez.   d: 3/16/69, Maracaibo, Venez.   BR/TR, 6', 170 lbs.   Deb: 9/9/67

1967 SF-N	1	0	1.000	2	0	0	0	0	5	4	0	3	3	12.6	0.00	—	.211	.318	0	.000	-0	2	2	0	0.4

● DAVE CHEADLE   Cheadle, David Baird   b: 2/19/52, Greensboro, N.C.   BL/TL, 6'2", 203 lbs.   Deb: 9/16/73

1973 Atl-N	0	1	.000	2	0	0	0	0	2	1	3	2	2	22.5	18.00	22	.250	.455	0	—	0	-3	-3	-0	-1.1

● CHARLIE CHECH   Chech, Charles William   b: 4/27/1878, Madison, Wis.   d: 1/31/38, Los Angeles, Cal.   BR/TR, 5'11.5", 190 lbs.   Deb: 4/14/05

1905 Cin-N	14	14	.500	39	25	20	1	0	267²	300	4	77	79	13.0	2.89	114	.288	.344	17	.191	1	3	12	-0	1.2
1906 Cin-N	1	4	.200	11	5	5	0	3	66	59	1	24	21	12.1	2.32	119	.243	.326	5	.200	1	2	3	0	0.4
1908 Cle-A	11	7	.611	27	20	14	4	0	165²	136	2	34	51	9.6	1.74	137	.229	.279	5	.104	-1	12	12	1	1.4
1909 Bos-A	7	5	.583	17	13	6	1	0	106²	107	3	27	40	11.7	2.95	85	.260	.314	3	.083	-0	-6	-5	-0	-0.9
Total 4	33	30	.524	94	63	45	6	3	606	602	10	162	187	11.8	2.52	113	.263	.320	30	.152	-1	12	21	1	2.1

● VIRGIL CHEEVES   Cheeves, Virgil Earl "Chief"   b: 2/12/01, Oklahoma City, Okla.   d: 5/5/79, Dallas, Tex.   BR/TR, 6', 195 lbs.   Deb: 9/7/20

1920 Chi-N	0	0	—	5	2	0	0	0	18	16	0	7	3	11.5	3.50	92	.250	.324	0	.000	-0	-1	-1	-1	-0.1
1921 Chi-N	11	12	.478	37	22	9	1	0	163	192	8	47	39	13.7	4.64	82	.309	.366	8	.167	-2	-15	-15	-3	-2.2
1922 Chi-N	12	11	.522	39	22	9	1	2	182²	195	8	76	40	13.8	4.09	103	.281	.360	13	.210	1	-4	-4	2	0.2
1923 Chi-N	3	4	.429	19	8	0	0	0	71¹	89	8	37	16	16.3	6.18	65	.314	.399	4	.174	-1	-17	-17	-1	-1.6
1924 Cle-A	0	0	—	8	0	0	0	0	17¹	26	2	7	2	22.8	7.79	55	.388	.518	1	.250	0	-7	-7	0	0.0
1927 NY-N	0	0	—	3	0	0	0	0	6¹	9	2	1	2	17.1	4.26	90	.333	.429	0	—	-0	-0	-0	0	0.0
Total 6	26	27	.491	111	55	18	2	2	458²	526	28	188	98	14.5	4.73	84	.300	.375	26	.184	-1	-40	-38	-5	-3.7

● ITALO CHELINI   Chelini, Italo Vincent "Chilly" or "Lefty"   b: 10/10/14, San Francisco, Cal   d: 8/25/72, San Francisco, Cal   BL/TL, 5'10.5", 175 lbs.   Deb: 9/12/35

1935 Chi-A	0	0	—	2	0	0	0	0	5	7	1	4	1	21.6	12.60	37	.350	.480	1	.500	0	-5	-4	0	0.0
1936 Chi-A	4	3	.571	18	6	5	0	0	83²	100	8	30	16	14.0	4.95	105	.291	.348	5	.156	-1	1	2	-1	-0.1
1937 Chi-A	0	1	.000	4	0	0	0	0	8²	15	2	0	3	16.6	10.38	44	.405	.421	0	—	0	-6	-6	-0	-0.5
Total 3	4	4	.500	24	6	5	0	0	97¹	122	11	34	20	14.6	5.83	88	.304	.362	6	.171	-1	-9	-8	-1	-0.6

● LARRY CHENEY   Cheney, Laurance Russell   b: 5/2/1886, Belleville, Kan.   d: 1/6/69, Daytona Beach, Fla.   BR/TR, 6'1.5", 185 lbs.   Deb: 9/9/11

1911 Chi-N	1	0	1.000	3	1	0	0	0	10	8	0	9	11	9.9	0.00	—	.229	.289	1	.250	0	4	4	1	0.5
1912 Chi-N	26	10	.722	42	38	28	4	0	303¹	262	5	111	140	11.3	2.85	117	.234	.307	24	.226	5	19	16	-2	2.0
1913 Chi-N	21	14	.600	54	36	25	2	11	305	271	7	98	136	11.1	2.57	124	.241	.306	20	.192	2	22	21	-0	2.6
1914 Chi-N	20	18	.526	50	40	21	6	5	311¹	239	4	140	157	11.2	2.54	109	.215	.308	18	.180	3	9	8	-1	1.4
1915 Chi-N	8	9	.471	25	18	6	1	0	131¹	120	1	55	68	12.3	3.56	78	.246	.327	6	.150	-1	-12	-11	2	-1.4
Bro-N	2	2	.000	5	4	1	0	0	27	16	0	17	11	11.7	1.67	167	.174	.315	1	.143	0	3	3	0	0.3

YEAR	TM/L	W	L	PCT	G	GS	CG	SH	SV	IP	H	HR	BB	SO	RAT	ERA	ERA+	OAV	OOB	BH	AVG	PB	PR	/A	PD	TPI
	Yr	8	11	.421	30	22	7	2	0	158¹	136	1	72	79	11.9	3.24	86	.233	.319	7	.149	-1	-9	-8	2	-1.1
1916	*Bro-N	18	12	.600	41	32	15	5	0	253	178	5	105	166	10.4	1.92	140	**.198**	.289	9	.114	-3	20	21	-1	2.3
1917	Bro-N	8	12	.400	35	24	14	1	2	210¹	185	4	73	102	11.3	2.35	119	.239	.309	14	.206	-2	8	10	-1	1.2
1918	Bro-N	11	13	.458	32	21	15	0	1	200²	177	2	74	83	11.7	3.00	93	.241	.319	16	.242	2	-5	-5	1	-0.2
1919	Bro-N	1	3	.250	9	4	2	0	0	39	45	1	14	14	14.1	4.15	72	.300	.367	2	.182	-0	-5	-5	-0	-0.6
	Bos-N	0	2	.000	8	2	0	0	0	33	35	0	15	14	13.6	3.55	81	.294	.373	2	.182	-0	-2	-3	0	-0.1
	Phi-N	2	5	.286	9	6	5	0	0	57¹	69	2	28	25	15.4	4.55	71	.315	.395	2	.095	-2	-10	-8	-1	-1.2
	Yr	3	10	.231	26	12	7	0	0	129¹	149	3	57	52	14.4	4.18	73	.304	.378	6	.140	-2	-18	-16	-1	-1.9
Total 9		116	100	.537	313	225	132	20	19	1881¹	1605	36	733	926	11.5	2.70	109	.234	.313	115	.186	9	49	52	0	6.8

● **TOM CHENEY** Cheney, Thomas Edgar b: 10/14/34, Morgan, Ga. BR/TR, 6', 180 lbs. Deb: 4/21/57

YEAR	TM/L	W	L	PCT	G	GS	CG	SH	SV	IP	H	HR	BB	SO	RAT	ERA	ERA+	OAV	OOB	BH	AVG	PB	PR	/A	PD	TPI
1957	StL-N	0	1	.000	4	3	0	0	0	9	6	0	15	10	21.0	5.00	79	.207	.477	0	.000	-0	-1	-1	0	-0.1
1959	StL-N	0	1	.000	11	2	0	0	0	11²	17	2	11	8	23.1	6.94	61	.354	.492	0	—	0	-4	-4	0	-0.3
1960	*Pit-N	2	2	.500	11	8	1	1	0	52	44	5	33	35	13.3	3.98	94	.238	.353	3	.176	-0	-1	-1	-2	-0.2
1961	Pit-N	0	0	—	1	0	0	0	0	0	1	1	4	0	—	∞	—	.500	.833	0	—	0	-4	-4	0	-0.3
	Was-A	1	3	.250	10	7	0	0	0	29²	32	8	26	20	17.6	8.80	46	.283	.417	4	.500	-2	-16	-16	-1	-1.6
1962	Was-A	7	9	.438	37	23	8	3	1	173¹	134	12	97	147	12.1	3.17	127	.213	.320	1	.063	-3	15	17	0	1.1
1963	Was-A	8	9	.471	23	21	7	4	0	136¹	99	14	40	97	9.2	2.71	137	.202	.264	5	.109	-3	14	15	-2	1.3
1964	Was-A	1	3	.250	15	6	1	0	1	48²	45	10	13	25	10.7	3.70	100	.245	.294	3	.250	0	-0	-0	-0	0.0
1966	Was-A	0	1	.000	3	1	0	0	0	5¹	4	1	6	3	18.6	5.06	68	.222	.440	0	—	0	-1	-1	0	-0.1
Total 8		19	29	.396	115	71	13	8	2	466	382	53	245	345	12.2	3.77	103	.225	.325	18	.135	-3	2	5	-4	-0.2

● **JACK CHESBRO** Chesbro, John Dwight "Happy Jack" b: 6/5/1874, N.Adams, Mass. d: 11/6/31, Conway, Mass. BR/TR, 5'9", 180 lbs. Deb: 7/12/1899 CH

YEAR	TM/L	W	L	PCT	G	GS	CG	SH	SV	IP	H	HR	BB	SO	RAT	ERA	ERA+	OAV	OOB	BH	AVG	PB	PR	/A	PD	TPI
1899	Pit-N	6	9	.400	19	17	15	0	0	149	165	3	59	28	14.2	4.11	93	.280	.357	9	.155	-3	-4	-5	-3	-0.9
1900	Pit-N	15	13	.536	32	26	20	3	1	215²	220	4	79	56	13.0	3.67	99	.264	.336	15	.176	-1	1	-1	-2	-0.4
1901	Pit-N	21	10	**.677**	36	28	26	**6**	1	287²	261	4	52	129	11.2	2.38	137	.240	.284	25	.216	3	30	28	-3	2.7
1902	Pit-N	**28**	6	**.824**	35	33	31	**8**	5	286¹	242	6	62	136	10.2	2.17	126	.229	.285	20	.179	-2	19	18	-2	1.6
1903	NY-A	21	15	.583	40	36	33	1	0	324²	300	7	74	147	10.6	2.77	113	.245	.293	23	.185	-1	7	13	2	1.4
1904	NY-A	**41**	12	.774	55	51	48	6	0	454²	338	4	88	239	8.6	1.82	149	**.208**	.252	41	.236	6	39	**45**	5	**6.9**
1905	NY-A	19	15	.559	41	38	24	5	0	303¹	262	5	71	156	10.1	2.20	134	.235	.284	21	.188	0	15	25	1	3.0
1906	NY-A	23	17	.575	**49**	42	24	4	1	325	314	2	75	152	11.0	2.96	100	.257	.305	26	.208	-1	-10	0	-0	-0.1
1907	NY-A	10	10	.500	30	25	17	1	0	206	192	0	46	78	10.7	2.53	110	.249	.297	15	.197	-1	0	6	1	0.6
1908	NY-A	14	20	.412	45	31	20	3	1	288²	276	6	67	124	11.1	2.93	85	.256	.307	18	.176	-2	-17	-15	1	-1.8
1909	NY-A	0	4	.000	9	4	2	0	0	49²	70	2	13	17	15.6	6.34	40	.347	.394	1	.176	-0	-21	-21	1	-1.5
	Bos-A	0	1	.000	1	1	0	0	0	6	7	1	4	3	16.5	4.50	56	.318	.423	1	.500	-0	-1	-1	-0	-0.2
	Yr	0	5	.000	10	5	2	0	0	55²	77	3	17	20	15.2	6.14	41	.339	.385	2	.211	-0	-23	-22	1	-1.7
Total 11		198	132	.600	392	332	260	35	5	2896²	2647	39	690	1265	10.7	2.68	111	.244	.297	217	.197	-2	58	96	-1	11.3

● **BOB CHESNES** Chesnes, Robert Vincent b: 5/6/21, Oakland, Cal. d: 5/23/79, Everett, Wash. BB/TR, 6', 180 lbs. Deb: 5/6/48

YEAR	TM/L	W	L	PCT	G	GS	CG	SH	SV	IP	H	HR	BB	SO	RAT	ERA	ERA+	OAV	OOB	BH	AVG	PB	PR	/A	PD	TPI
1948	Pit-N	14	6	.700	25	23	11	4	0	194¹	180	13	90	69	12.7	3.57	114	.247	.333	25	.275	7	8	11	3	2.1
1949	Pit-N	7	13	.350	27	25	8	1	1	145¹	153	15	82	49	14.9	5.88	71	.276	.374	17	.250	6	-30	-27	3	-2.4
1950	Pit-N	3	3	.500	9	7	2	0	0	39	44	7	17	12	14.8	5.54	79	.293	.376	2	.154	-0	-6	-5	2	-0.5
Total 3		24	22	.522	61	55	21	1	1	378²	377	35	189	130	13.7	4.66	89	.263	.354	44	.256	12	-27	-21	8	-0.8

● **MITCH CHETKOVICH** Chetkovich, Mitchell b: 7/21/17, Fairpoint, Ohio d: 8/24/71, Grass Valley, Cal. BR/TR, 6'3.5", 208 lbs. Deb: 4/19/45

YEAR	TM/L	W	L	PCT	G	GS	CG	SH	SV	IP	H	HR	BB	SO	RAT	ERA	ERA+	OAV	OOB	BH	AVG	PB	PR	/A	PD	TPI
1945	Phi-N	0	0	—	4	0	0	0	0	3	2	0	3	0	15.0	0.00	—	.182	.357	0	—	0	1	1	-0	0.0

● **TONY CHEVEZ** Chevez, Silvio Antonio (b: Silvio Antonio Aguilera (Chevez)) b: 6/20/54, Telica, Nicaragua BR/TR, 5'11", 177 lbs. Deb: 5/31/77

YEAR	TM/L	W	L	PCT	G	GS	CG	SH	SV	IP	H	HR	BB	SO	RAT	ERA	ERA+	OAV	OOB	BH	AVG	PB	PR	/A	PD	TPI
1977	Bal-A	0	0	—	4	0	0	0	0	8	10	3	8	7	22.5	12.38	31	.294	.455	0	—	0	-7	-8	-0	0.5

● **SCOTT CHIAMPARINO** Chiamparino, Scott Michael b: 8/22/66, San Mateo, Cal. BR/TR, 6'2", 190 lbs. Deb: 9/5/90

YEAR	TM/L	W	L	PCT	G	GS	CG	SH	SV	IP	H	HR	BB	SO	RAT	ERA	ERA+	OAV	OOB	BH	AVG	PB	PR	/A	PD	TPI
1990	Tex-A	1	2	.333	6	6	0	0	0	37²	36	1	12	19	11.9	2.63	149	.250	.316	0	—	0	5	5	-1	0.3
1991	Tex-A	1	0	1.000	5	5	0	0	0	22¹	26	1	12	8	15.3	4.03	100	.295	.380	0	—	0	0	-0	-1	-0.1
1992	Tex-A	0	4	.000	4	4	0	0	0	25¹	25	2	5	13	10.7	3.55	107	.260	.297	0	—	0	1	1	-0	0.3
Total 3		2	6	.250	15	15	0	0	0	85¹	87	4	29	40	12.4	3.27	120	.265	.329	0	—	0	7	6	-2	0.5

● **FLOYD CHIFFER** Chiffer, Floyd John b: 4/20/56, Glen Cove, N.Y. BR/TR, 6'2", 185 lbs. Deb: 4/7/82

YEAR	TM/L	W	L	PCT	G	GS	CG	SH	SV	IP	H	HR	BB	SO	RAT	ERA	ERA+	OAV	OOB	BH	AVG	PB	PR	/A	PD	TPI
1982	SD-N	4	3	.571	51	0	0	0	4	79¹	73	9	34	48	12.6	2.95	116	.247	.333	0	.000	-1	6	4	-0	0.3
1983	SD-N	0	2	.000	15	0	0	0	1	22²	17	0	10	15	10.7	3.18	110	.210	.297	0	.000	-0	1	1	0	0.1
1984	SD-N	1	0	1.000	15	0	0	0	0	28	42	1	16	20	18.6	7.71	46	.347	.423	0	—	-0	-13	-13	-1	-0.5
Total 3		5	5	.500	81	0	0	0	5	130	132	10	60	83	13.6	4.02	86	.266	.349	0	.000	-1	-6	-8	-1	-0.1

● **HARRY CHILD** Child, Harry Stephen Patrick (b: Harry Stephen Patrick Chesley) b: 5/23/05, Baltimore, Md. d: 11/8/72, Alexandria, Va. BB/TR, 5'11", 187 lbs. Deb: 7/16/30

YEAR	TM/L	W	L	PCT	G	GS	CG	SH	SV	IP	H	HR	BB	SO	RAT	ERA	ERA+	OAV	OOB	BH	AVG	PB	PR	/A	PD	TPI
1930	Was-A	0	0	—	5	0	0	0	0	10	11	5	4	5	13.5	6.30	73	.263	.349	1	.250	-0	-2	-2	0	0.0

● **BILL CHILDERS** Childers, William b: St.Louis, Mo. Deb: 7/27/1895

YEAR	TM/L	W	L	PCT	G	GS	CG	SH	SV	IP	H	HR	BB	SO	RAT	ERA	ERA+	OAV	OOB	BH	AVG	PB	PR	/A	PD	TPI
1895	Lou-N	0	0	—	1	1	0	0	0	0	2	0	6	0	—	∞	—	1.000	1.000	0	—	0	-6	-6	0	-0.4

● **ROCKY CHILDRESS** Childress, Rodney Osborne b: 2/18/62, Santa Rosa, Cal. BR/TR, 6'2", 195 lbs. Deb: 5/17/85

YEAR	TM/L	W	L	PCT	G	GS	CG	SH	SV	IP	H	HR	BB	SO	RAT	ERA	ERA+	OAV	OOB	BH	AVG	PB	PR	/A	PD	TPI
1985	Phi-N	0	1	.000	16	1	0	0	0	33¹	45	3	9	14	14.6	6.21	59	.326	.367	1	.167	-0	-10	-9	-0	-0.3
1986	Phi-N	0	0	—	2	0	0	0	0	2²	4	0	1	1	16.9	6.75	57	.364	.417	0	—	-0	-1	-1	-0	-0.0
1987	Hou-N	1	2	.333	32	0	0	0	0	48¹	46	4	18	26	11.9	2.98	131	.260	.328	0	.000	-0	6	5	-0	0.2
1988	Hou-N	1	0	1.000	11	0	0	0	0	23¹	26	3	9	24	13.9	6.17	54	.280	.350	1	.250	-0	-7	-7	-1	-0.3
Total 4		2	3	.400	61	1	0	0	0	107²	121	10	37	65	13.1	4.76	78	.289	.348	2	.167	-0	-12	-13	-1	-0.4

● **BOB CHIPMAN** Chipman, Robert Howard "Mr. Chips" b: 10/11/18, Brooklyn, N.Y. d: 11/8/73, Huntington, N.Y. BL/TL, 6'2", 190 lbs. Deb: 9/28/41

YEAR	TM/L	W	L	PCT	G	GS	CG	SH	SV	IP	H	HR	BB	SO	RAT	ERA	ERA+	OAV	OOB	BH	AVG	PB	PR	/A	PD	TPI
1941	Bro-N	1	0	1.000	3	0	0	0	0	5	3	0	1	3	7.2	0.00	—	.150	.190	0	.000	-0	2	2	-0	0.4
1942	Bro-N	0	0	—	2	0	0	0	0	1¹	1	0	2	1	20.3	0.00	—	.250	.500	0	—	0	0	0	0	0.0
1943	Bro-N	0	0	—	1	0	0	0	0	1²	2	0	2	2	21.6	0.00	—	.400	.571	0	—	0	1	1	0	0.0
1944	Bro-N	3	1	.750	11	3	1	0	0	36¹	38	1	24	20	15.4	4.21	84	.270	.376	2	.182	-0	-2	-3	0	-0.3
	Chi-N	9	9	.500	26	21	8	1	2	129	147	9	40	41	13.0	3.49	101	.288	.340	5	.104	-3	2	1	-0	-0.2
	Yr	12	10	.545	37	24	9	1	2	165¹	185	10	64	61	13.6	3.65	97	.284	.348	7	.119	-3	-1	-2	-0	-0.5
1945	*Chi-N	4	5	.444	25	10	3	0	0	72	63	4	34	29	12.3	3.50	104	.230	.317	3	.176	-1	2	1	-0	-0.2
1946	Chi-N	6	5	.545	34	10	3	3	2	109¹	103	8	54	44	13.0	3.13	106	.255	.344	2	.061	-3	3	3	-1	-0.2
1947	Chi-N	7	6	.538	32	17	5	1	0	134²	135	6	66	51	13.4	3.68	107	.264	.348	4	.091	-3	6	4	1	0.2
1948	Chi-N	2	1	.667	34	3	0	0	0	60¹	73	5	24	16	14.5	3.58	109	.293	.355	4	.250	-0	3	2	1	0.4
1949	Chi-N	7	8	.467	38	11	0	1	1	113¹	110	7	63	46	13.9	3.97	102	.248	.344	3	.125	-0	1	1	-1	-0.1
1950	Bos-N	7	7	.500	27	12	4	1	0	124	122	9	46	35	12.6	4.43	87	.262	.319	6	.154	-1	-4	-3	-3	-1.1
1951	Bos-N	4	3	.571	33	6	1	0	0	52	59	5	19	17	13.8	4.85	76	.284	.349	1	.100	-1	-5	-7	-0	-1.0
1952	Bos-N	1	1	.500	29	0	0	0	0	41²	28	2	20	14	10.4	2.81	129	.188	.284	2	.400	-1	4	4	0	0.3
Total 12		51	46	.526	293	87	29	7	14	880²	889	60	386	322	13.1	3.72	100	.261	.338	32	.128	-8	13	13	-2	-1.4

● **STEVE CHITREN** Chitren, Stephen Vincent b: 6/8/67, Tokyo, Japan BR/TR, 6', 180 lbs. Deb: 9/15/90

YEAR	TM/L	W	L	PCT	G	GS	CG	SH	SV	IP	H	HR	BB	SO	RAT	ERA	ERA+	OAV	OOB	BH	AVG	PB	PR	/A	PD	TPI
1990	Oak-A	1	0	1.000	8	0	0	0	0	17²	7	0	4	19	5.6	1.02	365	.117	.172	0	—	0	6	5	0	0.4
1991	Oak-A	1	4	.200	56	0	0	0	4	60¹	59	8	32	47	14.2	4.33	89	.258	.358	0	—	0	-2	-3	-0	-0.3
Total 2		2	4	.333	64	0	0	0	4	78	66	8	36	66	12.2	3.58	106	.228	.322	0	—	0	4	2	-0	0.1

● **NELSON CHITTUM** Chittum, Nelson Boyd b: 3/25/33, Harrisonburg, Va. BR/TR, 6'1", 180 lbs. Deb: 8/17/58

YEAR	TM/L	W	L	PCT	G	GS	CG	SH	SV	IP	H	HR	BB	SO	RAT	ERA	ERA+	OAV	OOB	BH	AVG	PB	PR	/A	PD	TPI
1958	StL-N	0	1	.000	13	2	0	0	0	29¹	31	5	7	13	12.0	6.44	64	.265	.312	1	.250	-0	-8	-8	0	-0.2
1959	Bos-A	3	0	1.000	21	0	0	0	0	30¹	29	0	11	12	11.9	1.19	342	.200	.333	1	.200	0	9	10	1	1.0

YEAR	TM/L	W	L	PCT	G	GS	CG	SH	SV	IP	H	HR	BB	SO	RAT	ERA	ERA+	OAV	OOB	BH	AVG	PB	PR	/A	PD	TPI
1960	Bos-A	0	0	—	6	0	0	0	0	8¹	8	0	6	5	15.1	4.32	94	.242	.359	0	.000	-0	-0	-0	0	0.0
Total	3	3	1	.750	40	2	0	0	0	68	68	5	24	30	12.3	3.84	106	.263	.327	2	.200	0	0	2	1	0.8

● **BOB CHLUPSA**   Chlupsa, Robert Joseph b: 9/16/45, New York, N.Y. BR/TR, 6'7", 215 lbs. Deb: 7/16/70

YEAR	TM/L	W	L	PCT	G	GS	CG	SH	SV	IP	H	HR	BB	SO	RAT	ERA	ERA+	OAV	OOB	BH	AVG	PB	PR	/A	PD	TPI
1970	StL-N	0	2	.000	14	0	0	0	0	16¹	26	2	9	10	19.3	8.82	47	.366	.438	0	—	0	-9	-9	1	-0.8
1971	StL-N	0	0	—	1	0	0	0	0	2	3	0	1	1	13.5	9.00	40	.333	.333	0	—	0	-1	-1	0	-0.1
Total	2	0	2	.000	15	0	0	0	0	18¹	29	2	9	11	18.7	8.84	46	.363	.427	0	—	0	-10	-10	1	-0.8

● **DON CHOATE**   Choate, Donald Leon b: 7/2/38, Potosi, Mo. BR/TR, 6', 185 lbs. Deb: 9/12/60

YEAR	TM/L	W	L	PCT	G	GS	CG	SH	SV	IP	H	HR	BB	SO	RAT	ERA	ERA+	OAV	OOB	BH	AVG	PB	PR	/A	PD	TPI
1960	SF-N	0	0	—	4	0	0	0	0	8	7	0	4	7	12.4	2.25	155	.233	.324	0	—	0	1	1	0	0.0

● **BOBBY CHOUINARD**   Chouinard, Robert William b: 5/1/72, Manila, Philippines BR/TR, 6'1", 188 lbs. Deb: 5/26/96

YEAR	TM/L	W	L	PCT	G	GS	CG	SH	SV	IP	H	HR	BB	SO	RAT	ERA	ERA+	OAV	OOB	BH	AVG	PB	PR	/A	PD	TPI
1996	Oak-A	4	2	.667	13	11	0	0	0	59	75	10	32	32	16.8	6.10	79	.316	.404	0	—	0	-7	-8	1	-0.6

● **CHIEF CHOUNEAU**   Chouneau, William (b: William Cadreau) b: 9/2/1889, Cloquet, Minn. d: 9/17/48, Cloquet, Minn. BR/TR, 5'9", 150 lbs. Deb: 10/9/10

YEAR	TM/L	W	L	PCT	G	GS	CG	SH	SV	IP	H	HR	BB	SO	RAT	ERA	ERA+	OAV	OOB	BH	AVG	PB	PR	/A	PD	TPI
1910	Chi-A	0	1	.000	1	1	0	0	0	5¹	7	0	1	0	11.8	3.38	71	.292	.292	0	.000	1	-1	-1	-0	-0.1

● **MIKE CHRIS**   Chris, Michael b: 10/8/57, Santa Monica, Cal. BL/TL, 6'3", 180 lbs. Deb: 7/31/79

YEAR	TM/L	W	L	PCT	G	GS	CG	SH	SV	IP	H	HR	BB	SO	RAT	ERA	ERA+	OAV	OOB	BH	AVG	PB	PR	/A	PD	TPI
1979	Det-A	3	3	.500	13	8	0	0	0	39	46	3	21	31	15.5	6.92	62	.297	.381	0	—	0	-12	-11	1	-1.4
1982	SF-N	0	2	.000	9	6	0	0	0	26	23	2	26	10	17.3	4.85	74	.245	.413	1	.143	-0	-4	-4	1	-0.2
1983	SF-N	0	0	—	7	0	0	0	0	13¹	16	1	16	5	23.0	8.10	44	.308	.486	0	.000	-0	-7	-7	-0	-0.1
Total	3	3	5	.375	29	14	0	0	0	78¹	85	6	63	46	17.3	6.43	61	.282	.411	1	.111	-0	-22	-22	1	-1.7

● **GARY CHRISTENSON**   Christenson, Gary Richard b: 5/5/53, Mineola, N.Y. BL/TL, 6'5", 200 lbs. Deb: 9/1/79

YEAR	TM/L	W	L	PCT	G	GS	CG	SH	SV	IP	H	HR	BB	SO	RAT	ERA	ERA+	OAV	OOB	BH	AVG	PB	PR	/A	PD	TPI
1979	KC-A	0	0	—	6	0	0	0	0	10²	10	1	2	4	10.1	3.38	126	.250	.286	0	—	0	1	1	0	0.0
1980	KC-A	3	0	1.000	24	0	0	0	1	31¹	35	4	18	16	15.8	5.17	78	.278	.377	0	—	0	-4	-4	1	-0.4
Total	2	3	0	1.000	30	0	0	0	1	42	45	5	20	20	14.4	4.71	87	.271	.356	0	—	0	-3	-3	1	-0.4

● **LARRY CHRISTENSON**   Christenson, Larry Richard b: 11/10/53, Everett, Wash. BR/TR, 6'4", 215 lbs. Deb: 4/13/73

YEAR	TM/L	W	L	PCT	G	GS	CG	SH	SV	IP	H	HR	BB	SO	RAT	ERA	ERA+	OAV	OOB	BH	AVG	PB	PR	/A	PD	TPI
1973	Phi-N	1	4	.200	10	9	1	0	0	34¹	53	3	20	11	19.4	6.55	58	.366	.446	0	.000	-1	-11	-11	-0	-1.4
1974	Phi-N	1	1	.500	10	1	0	0	2	23	20	2	15	18	13.7	4.30	88	.241	.357	0	.000	-1	-2	-1	-0	-0.2
1975	Phi-N	11	6	.647	29	26	5	2	1	171²	149	12	45	88	10.2	3.67	102	.236	.288	14	.246	5	1	1	-3	0.2
1976	Phi-N	13	8	.619	32	29	2	0	0	168²	199	8	42	54	12.9	3.68	96	.297	.339	10	.196	4	-3	-3	-3	-0.2
1977	*Phi-N	19	6	.760	34	34	5	1	0	219¹	229	21	69	118	12.5	4.06	98	.268	.327	10	.135	1	-4	-2	-2	-0.3
1978	*Phi-N	13	14	.481	33	33	9	3	0	228	209	16	47	131	10.1	3.24	110	.244	.284	5	.075	-2	9	8	-0	0.7
1979	Phi-N	5	10	.333	19	17	2	0	0	106	118	9	30	53	12.7	4.50	85	.291	.342	9	.290	5	-9	-8	-0	-0.6
1980	*Phi-N	5	1	.833	14	14	0	0	0	73²	62	4	27	44	11.2	4.03	94	.227	.304	7	.368	3	-4	-2	1	0.3
1981	*Phi-N	4	7	.364	20	15	0	0	0	106²	108	8	30	70	11.7	3.54	102	.267	.319	3	.100	-1	-1	-1	-1	-0.1
1982	Phi-N	9	10	.474	33	33	3	0	0	223	212	15	53	145	10.8	3.47	106	.253	.300	5	.075	-3	3	5	-1	0.2
1983	Phi-N	2	4	.333	9	9	0	0	0	48¹	42	2	17	44	11.2	3.91	91	.233	.303	1	.059	-1	-2	-2	1	-0.2
Total	11	83	71	.539	243	220	27	6	4	1402²	1401	100	395	781	11.7	3.79	98	.262	.315	64	.150	10	-24	-12	-8	-1.6

● **CLAY CHRISTIANSEN**   Christiansen, Clay C. b: 6/28/58, Wichita, Kan. BR/TR, 6'5", 205 lbs. Deb: 5/10/84

YEAR	TM/L	W	L	PCT	G	GS	CG	SH	SV	IP	H	HR	BB	SO	RAT	ERA	ERA+	OAV	OOB	BH	AVG	PB	PR	/A	PD	TPI
1984	NY-A	2	4	.333	24	6	0	0	0	38²	50	4	12	27	14.7	6.05	63	.309	.360	0	—	0	-9	-10	-0	-1.4

● **JASON CHRISTIANSEN**   Christiansen, Jason Samuel b: 9/21/69, Omaha, Neb. BR/TL, 6'5", 230 lbs. Deb: 4/26/95

YEAR	TM/L	W	L	PCT	G	GS	CG	SH	SV	IP	H	HR	BB	SO	RAT	ERA	ERA+	OAV	OOB	BH	AVG	PB	PR	/A	PD	TPI
1995	Pit-N	1	3	.250	63	0	0	0	0	56¹	49	5	34	53	13.7	4.15	104	.234	.350	0	.000	-0	0	1	-0	0.0
1996	Pit-N	3	3	.500	33	0	0	0	0	44¹	56	7	19	38	15.4	6.70	65	.311	.380	0	.000	-0	-12	-11	0	-1.4
Total	2	4	6	.400	96	0	0	0	0	100²	105	12	53	91	14.5	5.27	82	.270	.363	0	.000	-1	-12	-11	-0	-1.4

● **MIKE CHRISTOPHER**   Christopher, Michael Wayne b: 11/3/63, Petersburg, Va. BR/TR, 6'5", 205 lbs. Deb: 9/10/91

YEAR	TM/L	W	L	PCT	G	GS	CG	SH	SV	IP	H	HR	BB	SO	RAT	ERA	ERA+	OAV	OOB	BH	AVG	PB	PR	/A	PD	TPI
1991	LA-N	0	0	—	3	0	0	0	0	4	2	0	3	2	11.3	0.00	—	.167	.333	0	—	0	2	2	0	0.1
1992	Cle-A	0	0	—	10	0	0	0	0	18	17	2	10	13	13.5	3.00	130	.254	.351	0	—	0	2	2	0	0.1
1993	Cle-A	0	0	—	9	0	0	0	0	11²	14	3	2	8	12.3	3.86	112	.286	.314	0	—	0	1	1	0	0.0
1995	Det-A	4	0	1.000	36	0	0	0	1	61¹	71	6	14	34	12.8	3.82	125	.292	.336	0	—	0	6	6	0	0.4
1996	Det-A	1	1	.500	13	0	0	0	0	30	47	12	11	19	17.4	9.30	54	.351	.400	0	—	0	-14	-14	-0	-0.8
Total	5	5	1	.833	71	0	0	0	1	125	151	25	40	76	13.9	4.90	94	.299	.353	0	—	0	-4	-4	-1	-0.3

● **RUSS CHRISTOPHER**   Christopher, Russell Ormand b: 9/12/17, Richmond, Cal. d: 12/5/54, Richmond, Cal. BR/TR, 6'3", 180 lbs. Deb: 4/14/42 F

YEAR	TM/L	W	L	PCT	G	GS	CG	SH	SV	IP	H	HR	BB	SO	RAT	ERA	ERA+	OAV	OOB	BH	AVG	PB	PR	/A	PD	TPI
1942	Phi-A	4	13	.235	30	18	10	0	1	165	154	8	99	58	14.0	3.82	99	.254	.362	5	.089	-3	-3	-1	6	0.2
1943	Phi-A	5	8	.385	24	15	5	0	2	133	120	3	58	56	12.2	3.45	109	.242	.325	7	.156	-1	-2	-1	-5	0.6
1944	Phi-A	14	14	.500	35	24	13	1	1	215¹	200	6	63	84	11.4	2.97	117	.245	.306	18	.222	1	11	12	5	2.6
1945	Phi-A†	13	13	.500	33	27	17	2	2	227¹	213	9	75	100	11.8	3.17	108	.251	.319	13	.171	-1	5	7	7	1.5
1946	Phi-A	5	7	.417	30	13	1	0	0	119¹	119	5	44	79	12.5	4.30	82	.254	.322	5	.139	-0	-11	-14	4	-0.5
1947	Phi-A	10	7	.588	44	0	0	0	12	80²	70	4	33	33	11.5	2.90	131	.236	.313	2	.125	-0	7	8	1	2.0
1948	*Cle-A	3	2	.600	45	0	0	0	17	59	55	3	27	14	12.5	2.90	140	.247	.328	0	.000	-0	9	8	0	1.0
Total	7	54	64	.458	241	97	46	3	35	999²	931	38	399	424	12.2	3.37	106	.248	.325	50	.158	-3	17	24	31	7.4

● **BUBBA CHURCH**   Church, Emory Nicholas b: 9/12/24, Birmingham, Ala. BR/TR, 6', 180 lbs. Deb: 4/30/50

YEAR	TM/L	W	L	PCT	G	GS	CG	SH	SV	IP	H	HR	BB	SO	RAT	ERA	ERA+	OAV	OOB	BH	AVG	PB	PR	/A	PD	TPI
1950	Phi-N	8	6	.571	31	18	8	2	1	142	113	12	56	50	10.7	2.73	149	.225	.303	8	.182	0	22	21	-0	1.9
1951	Phi-N	15	11	.577	38	33	15	4	1	247	246	17	90	104	12.3	3.53	109	.261	.326	22	.256	5	12	9	-2	1.1
1952	Phi-N	0	0	—	2	1	0	0	0	5	11	0	1	3	23.4	10.80	34	.440	.481	0	.000	-0	-4	-4	0	0.0
	Cin-N	5	9	.357	29	22	5	1	0	153¹	173	21	48	47	13.1	4.34	87	.301	.358	12	.240	3	-10	-10	-1	-0.6
	Yr	5	9	.357	31	23	5	1	0	158¹	184	21	49	50	13.4	4.55	83	.306	.361	12	.235	3	-14	-14	-1	-0.6
1953	Cin-N	3	3	.500	11	7	2	0	0	43²	55	9	19	12	15.7	5.98	73	.318	.392	4	.267	1	-8	-8	-0	-0.8
	Chi-N	4	5	.444	27	11	1	0	1	104¹	115	16	49	47	14.3	5.00	89	.276	.355	7	.212	1	-8	-6	-1	-0.5
	Yr	7	8	.467	38	18	3	0	1	148	170	25	68	59	14.6	5.29	84	.288	.363	11	.229	2	-17	-14	-1	-1.3
1954	Chi-N	1	3	.250	7	3	1	0	0	14²	21	8	13	8	20.9	9.82	43	.350	.466	0	.000	-1	-9	-9	-0	-2.0
1955	Chi-N	0	0	—	2	0	0	0	1	3¹	4	1	1	3	13.5	5.40	76	.286	.333	0	.000	-0	-1	-0	-0	-0.1
Total	6	36	37	.493	147	95	32	7	4	713¹	738	84	277	274	12.9	4.10	97	.272	.342	53	.226	9	-7	-8	-4	-1.0

● **LEN CHURCH**   Church, Leonard b: 3/21/42, Chicago, Ill. d: 4/22/88, Richardson, Tex. BB/TR, 6', 190 lbs. Deb: 8/27/66

YEAR	TM/L	W	L	PCT	G	GS	CG	SH	SV	IP	H	HR	BB	SO	RAT	ERA	ERA+	OAV	OOB	BH	AVG	PB	PR	/A	PD	TPI
1966	Chi-N	0	1	.000	4	0	0	0	0	6	10	1	7	3	25.5	7.50	49	.400	.531	0	—	0	-3	-3	0	-0.4

● **CHUCK CHURN**   Churn, Clarence Nottingham b: 2/1/30, Bridgetown, Va. BR/TR, 6'3", 205 lbs. Deb: 4/18/57

YEAR	TM/L	W	L	PCT	G	GS	CG	SH	SV	IP	H	HR	BB	SO	RAT	ERA	ERA+	OAV	OOB	BH	AVG	PB	PR	/A	PD	TPI
1957	Pit-N	0	0	—	5	0	0	0	0	8¹	9	1	4	4	14.0	4.32	88	.333	.419	0	.000	-0	-0	-0	1	0.1
1958	Cle-A	0	0	—	6	0	0	0	0	8²	12	1	5	4	17.7	6.23	59	.343	.425	0	—	0	-2	-2	-0	-0.1
1959	*LA-N	3	2	.600	14	0	0	0	1	30²	28	2	10	24	11.4	4.99	85	.255	.322	1	.167	-0	-4	-3	0	-0.3
Total	3	3	2	.600	25	0	0	0	1	47²	49	4	19	32	13.0	5.10	79	.285	.359	1	.143	-0	-6	-6	1	-0.2

● **MARK CIARDI**   Ciardi, Mark Thomas b: 8/19/61, New Brunswick, N.J. BR/TR, 6' ", 180 lbs. Deb: 4/9/87

YEAR	TM/L	W	L	PCT	G	GS	CG	SH	SV	IP	H	HR	BB	SO	RAT	ERA	ERA+	OAV	OOB	BH	AVG	PB	PR	/A	PD	TPI
1987	Mil-A	1	1	.500	4	3	0	0	0	16¹	26	5	9	8	19.3	9.37	49	.361	.432	0	—	0	-9	-9	-0	-0.9

● **AL CICOTTE**   Cicotte, Alva Warren "Bozo" b: 12/23/29, Melvindale, Mich. d: 11/29/82, Westland, Mich. BR/TR, 6'3", 185 lbs. Deb: 4/22/57

YEAR	TM/L	W	L	PCT	G	GS	CG	SH	SV	IP	H	HR	BB	SO	RAT	ERA	ERA+	OAV	OOB	BH	AVG	PB	PR	/A	PD	TPI
1957	NY-A	2	2	.500	20	2	0	0	2	65¹	57	5	30	36	12.1	3.03	118	.237	.325	3	.150	-0	6	4	0	0.4
1958	Was-A	0	3	.000	8	4	0	0	0	28	36	3	14	14	16.1	4.82	79	.316	.391	2	.200	-0	-3	-3	-1	-0.4
	Det-A	3	1	.750	14	2	0	0	0	43	50	1	15	21	13.6	3.56	113	.307	.365	3	.176	-1	2	1	1	0.3
	Yr	3	4	.429	22	6	0	0	0	71	86	4	29	35	14.6	4.06	97	.309	.375	5	.185	-1	-2	-1	-1	-0.1
1959	Cle-A	3	1	.750	26	1	0	0	0	44	46	4	25	23	14.9	5.32	69	.299	.403	1	.333	-0	-7	-8	0	-0.6
1961	StL-N	2	6	.250	29	7	0	0	0	75	83	16	34	51	14.3	5.28	83	.283	.362	6	.286	1	-10	-7	0	-0.6
1962	Hou-N	0	0	—	5	0	0	0	0	4²	8	1	2	4	17.4	3.86	97	.381	.409	0	—	0	-0	-0	-0	0.0
Total	5	10	13	.435	102	16	0	0	4	260	280	30	119	149	14.0	4.36	90	.284	.364	15	.211	0	-14	-12	-0	-1.1

YEAR	TM/L	W	L	PCT	G	GS	CG	SH	SV	IP	H	HR	BB	SO	RAT	ERA	ERA+	OAV	OOB	BH	AVG	PB	PR	/A	PD	TPI

● EDDIE CICOTTE Cicotte, Edward Victor "Knuckles" b: 6/19/1884, Springwells, Mich. d: 5/5/69, Detroit, Mich. BB/TR, 5'9", 175 lbs. Deb: 9/3/05

1905	Det-A	1	1	.500	3	1	1	0	0	18	25	5	6	6	15.0	3.50	78	.329	.370	3	.429	1	-2	-2	-1	-0.2
1908	Bos-A	11	12	.478	39	24	17	2	2	207¹	198	0	59	95	11.6	2.43	101	.256	.318	17	.236	2	-1	1	0	0.4
1909	Bos-A	13	5	.722	27	17	10	1	2	159¹	117	3	56	82	9.8	1.98	126	.210	.283	12	.235	3	9	9	-0	1.4
1910	Bos-A	15	11	.577	36	30	20	3	0	250	213	4	86	104	11.2	2.74	93	.233	.308	12	.141	-1	-6	-5	3	-0.4
1911	Bos-A	11	15	.423	35	25	16	1	0	220	236	2	73	106	12.8	2.82	116	.282	.342	10	.141	-2	13	11	1	1.0
1912	Bos-A	1	3	.250	9	6	2	0	0	46	58	0	15	20	14.5	5.67	60	.319	.374	2	.154	0	-12	-12	1	-0.8
	Chi-A	9	7	.563	20	18	13	1	0	152	159	3	37	70	11.6	2.84	113	.277	.320	13	.245	1	8	6	2	1.0
	Yr	10	10	.500	29	24	15	1	0	198	217	3	52	90	12.2	3.50	93	.286	.332	15	.227	1	-6	-3	3	0.2
1913	Chi-A	18	12	.600	41	30	18	3	1	268	224	2	73	121	10.1	1.58	185	.226	.281	13	.143	-3	40	40	7	5.2
1914	Chi-A	11	16	.407	45	30	15	4	3	269¹	220	0	72	102	9.9	2.04	132	.232	.288	14	.163	-1	21	19	7	2.7
1915	Chi-A	13	12	.520	39	26	15	1	3	223¹	216	2	48	106	10.9	3.02	99	.261	.306	14	.209	1	-2	-1	-0	0.0
1916	Chi-A	15	7	**.682**	44	19	11	2	5	187	138	1	70	91	10.1	1.78	155	.218	.296	12	.211	2	22	20	1	2.9
1917	*Chi-A	**28**	12	.700	49	35	29	7	4	**346²**	246	2	70	150	**8.3**	**1.53**	**174**	**.203**	**.248**	20	.179	1	**44**	**43**	-1	**5.4**
1918	Chi-A	12	19	.387	38	30	24	1	2	266	275	2	40	104	10.7	2.77	99	.271	.300	14	.163	2	-0	-1	-0	0.0
1919	*Chi-A	**29**	7	**.806**	40	35	**30**	5	1	**306²**	256	5	49	110	**9.0**	1.82	175	.228	.261	20	.202	1	48	46	-4	5.2
1920	Chi-A	21	10	.677	37	35	28	4	2	303¹	316	6	74	87	11.6	3.26	115	.275	.320	22	.196	-3	18	17	0	1.4
Total	14	208	149	.583	502	361	249	36	25	3223	2897	32	827	1374	10.5	2.38	123	.245	.297	198	.186	4	200	194	15	25.2

● PETE CIMINO Cimino, Peter William b: 10/17/42, Philadelphia, Pa. BR/TR, 6'2", 195 lbs. Deb: 9/22/65

1965	Min-A	0	0	—	1	0	0	0	0	1	1	0	0	0	0.0	0.00	—	.000	.000	0	—	-0	0	0	-0	0.0
1966	Min-A	2	5	.286	35	0	0	0	4	64²	53	4	30	57	11.7	2.92	123	.222	.311	0	.000	-0	4	5	-1	0.5
1967	Cal-A	3	3	.500	46	1	0	0	1	88¹	73	12	31	80	10.8	3.26	96	.229	.301	5	.417	2	-0	-1	-1	-0.1
1968	Cal-A	0	0	—	4	0	0	0	0	7	7	0	4	2	14.1	2.57	113	.259	.355	0	—	-0	0	0	-0	0.0
Total	4	5	8	.385	86	1	0	0	5	161	133	16	65	139	11.2	3.07	108	.226	.306	5	.278	1	4	4	-2	0.4

● FRANK CIMORELLI Cimorelli, Frank Thomas b: 8/2/68, Poughkeepsie, N.Y. BR/TR, 6', 175 lbs. Deb: 4/30/94

| 1994 | StL-N | 0 | 0 | — | 11 | 0 | 0 | 0 | 1 | 13¹ | 20 | 0 | 10 | 1 | 21.6 | 8.78 | 47 | .345 | .457 | 0 | .000 | -0 | -7 | -7 | -1 | -0.2 |

● LOU CIOLA Ciola, Louis Alexander b: 9/6/22, Norfolk, Va. d: 10/18/81, Austin, Minn. BR/TR, 5'9", 165 lbs. Deb: 7/25/43

| 1943 | Phi-A | 1 | 3 | .250 | 12 | 3 | 2 | 0 | 0 | 43² | 48 | 2 | 22 | 7 | 14.6 | 5.56 | 61 | .273 | .357 | 3 | .167 | -1 | -11 | -11 | -0 | -1.0 |

● GALEN CISCO Cisco, Galen Bernard b: 3/7/36, St.Marys, Ohio BR/TR, 5'11", 215 lbs. Deb: 6/11/61 C

1961	Bos-A	2	4	.333	17	8	0	0	0	52¹	67	5	28	26	16.3	6.71	62	.325	.406	1	.100	-0	-16	-15	0	-1.5
1962	Bos-A	4	7	.364	23	9	1	0	0	83	95	11	50	43	16.0	6.72	61	.292	.392	2	.080	-1	-25	-24	1	-2.6
	NY-N	1	1	.500	4	2	1	0	0	19¹	15	0	13	13	13.5	3.26	128	.208	.337	0	.000	-1	2	2	-0	0.1
1963	NY-N	7	15	.318	51	17	1	0	0	155²	165	15	64	81	13.6	4.34	80	.273	.349	5	.132	-0	-18	-15	-0	-2.0
1964	NY-N	6	19	.240	36	25	5	2	0	191²	182	17	54	78	11.4	3.62	99	.256	.313	6	.111	-0	-2	-1	2	-0.1
1965	NY-N	4	8	.333	35	17	1	1	0	112¹	119	12	51	58	13.7	4.49	79	.272	.349	7	.259	2	-12	-12	-2	-1.1
1967	Bos-A	1	1	.500	11	0	0	0	1	22¹	21	4	8	8	11.7	3.63	96	.266	.333	0	.000	-1	-0	-0	-0	-0.1
1969	KC-A	1	1	.500	15	0	0	0	1	22¹	17	4	15	18	12.9	3.63	102	.215	.340	0	—	-0	-0	0	-0	-0.1
Total	7	25	56	.309	192	78	9	3	2	659	681	68	281	325	13.4	4.56	81	.271	.349	21	.128	0	-72	-64	1	-7.0

● RALPH CITARELLA Citarella, Ralph Alexander b: 2/7/58, East Orange, N.J. BR/TR, 6', 180 lbs. Deb: 9/13/83

1983	StL-N	0	0	—	6	0	0	0	0	11	5	1	6	5	9.0	1.64	221	.205	.262	0	.000	-0	2	2	-0	0.0
1984	StL-N	0	1	.000	10	0	0	0	0	22¹	20	0	7	15	12.1	3.63	96	.238	.319	1	.250	-0	-0	-0	-0	-0.0
1987	Chi-A	0	0	—	5	0	0	0	0	11	13	4	4	9	15.5	7.36	62	.302	.388	0	—	-0	-4	-3	-0	-0.1
Total	3	0	1	.000	21	0	0	0	0	44¹	41	4	14	28	12.2	4.06	93	.247	.324	1	.200	-0	-1	-1	-0	-0.1

● BOBBY CLACK Clack, Robert S. "Gentlemanly Bob" (b: Robert S. Clark) b: 6/1850, England d: 10/22/33, Danvers, Mass. BR/TR, 5'9", 153 lbs. Deb: 5/13/1874 ♦

| 1876 | Cin-N | 0 | 0 | — | 1 | 0 | 0 | 0 | 0 | 2 | 2 | 0 | 0 | 0 | 9.0 | 4.50 | 49 | .250 | .250 | 19 | .161 | -0 | -0 | -1 | 0 | 0.0 |

● JIM CLANCY Clancy, James b: 12/18/55, Chicago, Ill. BR/TR, 6'4", 220 lbs. Deb: 7/26/77

1977	Tor-A	4	9	.308	13	13	4	1	0	76²	80	7	47	44	14.9	5.05	83	.280	.381	0	—	0	-8	-7	1	-1.0
1978	Tor-A	10	12	.455	31	30	7	0	0	193²	199	10	91	106	13.5	4.09	96	.270	.351	0	—	0	-7	-4	1	-0.4
1979	Tor-A	2	7	.222	12	11	2	0	0	63²	65	8	31	33	13.6	5.51	79	.272	.356	0	—	0	-9	-8	0	-1.0
1980	Tor-A	13	16	.448	34	34	15	2	0	250²	217	19	128	152	12.5	3.30	130	.233	.327	0	—	0	20	28	-0	2.7
1981	Tor-A	6	12	.333	22	22	2	0	0	125	126	12	64	56	14.0	4.90	80	.262	.355	0	—	0	-17	-13	-2	-2.1
1982	Tor-A★	16	14	.533	40	40	11	3	0	266²	251	26	77	139	11.1	3.71	121	.248	.302	0	—	0	11	23	-2	2.1
1983	Tor-A	15	11	.577	34	34	11	1	0	223	238	23	61	99	12.1	3.91	110	.271	.319	0	—	0	4	10	-2	0.8
1984	Tor-A	13	15	.464	36	36	5	0	0	219²	249	25	88	118	13.9	5.12	80	.287	.355	0	—	0	-28	-25	0	-2.7
1985	*Tor-A	9	6	.600	23	23	1	0	0	128²	117	15	37	66	10.8	3.78	111	.241	.295	0	—	0	5	6	-1	0.6
1986	Tor-A	14	14	.500	34	34	6	0	0	219¹	202	24	63	126	11.0	3.94	107	.243	.299	0	—	0	6	7	1	0.8
1987	Tor-A	15	11	.577	37	37	5	1	0	241¹	234	24	80	180	11.7	3.54	127	.255	.315	0	—	0	24	25	2	2.6
1988	Tor-A	11	13	.458	36	31	4	0	1	196¹	207	16	47	118	12.1	4.49	87	.272	.322	0	—	0	-11	-12	-1	-1.4
1989	Hou-N	7	14	.333	33	26	1	0	0	147	155	13	66	91	13.5	5.08	66	.269	.344	6	.146	-0	-26	-24	-3	-3.8
1990	Hou-N	2	8	.200	33	10	0	0	0	76	100	4	33	44	16.1	6.51	57	.322	.392	3	.214	0	-23	-24	1	-2.7
1991	Hou-N	0	3	.000	30	0	0	0	5	55	37	5	20	33	9.3	2.78	126	.193	.269	0	.000	-0	6	4	-1	0.1
	*Atl-N	3	2	.600	24	0	0	0	3	34²	36	3	14	17	13.2	5.71	68	.267	.340	0	.000	-0	-8	-7	-0	-1.1
	Yr	3	5	.375	54	0	0	0	8	89²	73	8	34	50	10.8	3.91	93	.222	.297	0	.000	-1	-2	-3	-1	-1.0
Total	15	140	167	.456	472	381	74	11	10	2517¹	2513	244	947	1422	12.5	4.23	98	.261	.329	9	.148	-0	-62	-26	-8	-6.5

● BRYAN CLARK Clark, Bryan Donald b: 7/12/56, Madera, Cal. BL/TL, 6'2", 185 lbs. Deb: 4/11/81

1981	Sea-A	2	5	.286	29	9	1	0	2	93¹	92	3	55	52	14.3	4.34	89	.261	.363	0	—	0	-7	-5	1	-0.3
1982	Sea-A	5	2	.714	37	5	1	1	0	114²	104	6	58	70	12.7	2.75	154	.241	.331	0	—	0	17	19	1	1.2
1983	Sea-A	7	10	.412	41	17	2	0	0	162¹	160	14	72	76	13.0	3.94	108	.261	.342	0	—	0	6	3	6	0.8
1984	Tor-A	1	2	.333	20	3	0	0	0	45²	66	6	22	21	17.5	5.91	69	.342	.412	0	—	0	-10	-9	1	-0.4
1985	Cle-A	3	4	.429	31	3	0	0	2	62²	78	8	34	24	16.1	6.32	65	.311	.393	0	—	0	-15	-15	1	-1.5
1986	Chi-A	0	0	—	5	0	0	0	0	8	8	0	2	6	11.3	4.50	96	.276	.323	0	—	0	-0	-0	-0	-0.1
1987	Chi-A	0	0	—	11	0	0	0	0	18²	19	1	8	8	13.0	2.41	190	.297	.375	0	—	0	4	4	-1	0.1
1990	Sea-A	2	0	1.000	12	0	0	0	0	11	9	0	10	3	15.5	3.27	121	.237	.396	0	—	0	1	1	0	0.2
Total	8	20	23	.465	186	37	4	1	4	516¹	536	38	261	259	14.0	4.15	100	.272	.359	0	—	0	-8	-1	7	-0.2

● ED CLARK Clark, Edward C. b: Cincinnati, Ohio Deb: 7/4/1886

1886	Phi-a	0	1	.000	1	1	1	0	0	8	10	2	2	2	15.8	6.75	52	.294	.368	0	.000	-0	-3	-3	-0	-0.3
1891	Col-a	0	0	—	1	0	0	0	0	2	2	0	0	1	9.0	0.00	—	.250	.250	1	1.000	0	1	1	0	0.0
Total	2	0	1	.000	2	1	1	0	0	10	12	2	2	3	14.4	5.40	65	.286	.348	0	.000	-0	-2	-2	-0	-0.3

● GEORGE CLARK Clark, George Myron b: 5/19/1891, Smithland, Iowa d: 11/14/40, Sioux City, Iowa BR/TL, 6', 190 lbs. Deb: 5/16/13

| 1913 | NY-A | 0 | 1 | .000 | 11 | 0 | 0 | 0 | 0 | 19 | 22 | 1 | 19 | 5 | 20.8 | 9.00 | 33 | .272 | .427 | 1 | .500 | 1 | -13 | -13 | -0 | -0.5 |

● GINGER CLARK Clark, Harvey Daniel b: 3/7/1879, Wooster, Ohio d: 5/10/43, Lake Charles, La. BR/TR, 5'11", 165 lbs. Deb: 8/11/02

| 1902 | Cle-A | 1 | 0 | 1.000 | 1 | 1 | 1 | 0 | 0 | 6 | 10 | 0 | 3 | 1 | 21.0 | 6.00 | 57 | .370 | .452 | 2 | .500 | 1 | -2 | -2 | 0 | -0.1 |

● MARK CLARK Clark, Mark Willard b: 5/12/68, Bath, Ill. BR/TR, 6'5", 225 lbs. Deb: 9/6/91

1991	StL-N	1	1	.500	7	2	0	0	0	22¹	17	3	11	13	11.3	4.03	92	.215	.311	0	.000	-1	-1	-1	-0	-0.2
1992	StL-N	3	10	.231	20	20	1	0	0	113¹	117	4	36	44	12.2	4.45	76	.265	.321	5	.139	-2	-12	-13	-2	-1.7
1993	Cle-A	7	5	.583	26	15	1	0	0	109¹	119	8	25	57	11.9	4.28	101	.279	.321	0	—	0	-1	-2	-0	-0.1
1994	Cle-A	11	3	.786	20	20	4	1	0	127¹	133	14	40	60	12.5	3.82	124	.273	.333	0	—	0	14	13	1	1.3
1995	Cle-A	9	7	.563	22	21	2	0	0	124²	143	13	42	68	13.6	5.27	89	.288	.348	0	—	0	-8	-8	-0	-0.9

YEAR	TM/L	W	L	PCT	G	GS	CG	SH	SV	IP	H	HR	BB	SO	RAT	ERA	ERA+	OAV	OOB	BH	AVG	PB	PR	/A	PD	TPI
1996	NY-N	14	11	.560	32	32	0	2	0	212¹	217	20	48	142	11.4	3.43	114	.265	.308	3	.043	-5	18	12	-2	0.6
Total	6	45	37	.549	127	110	10	2	0	709¹	746	80	202	384	12.2	4.14	101	.271	.324	8	.071	-7	12	2	-5	-1.0

● **MIKE CLARK**   Clark, Michael John   b: 2/12/22, Camden, N.J.   BR/TR, 6'4", 190 lbs.   Deb: 7/27/52

1952	StL-N	2	0	1.000	12	4	0	0	1	25¹	32	2	14	10	16.3	6.04	61	.311	.393	0	.000	-1	-6	-7	0	-0.5
1953	StL-N	1	0	1.000	23	2	0	0	1	35²	46	2	21	17	17.4	4.79	89	.315	.408	0	.000	-1	-2	-1	1	-0.1
Total	2	3	0	1.000	35	6	0	0	1	61	78	4	35	27	17.0	5.31	76	.313	.402	0	.000	-1	-9	-9	1	-0.6

● **SPIDER CLARK**   Clark, Owen F.   b: 9/16/1867, Brooklyn, N.Y.   d: 2/8/1892, Brooklyn, N.Y.   TR, 5'10", 150 lbs.   Deb: 5/2/1889 ◆

| 1890 | Buf-P | 0 | 0 | — | 1 | 0 | 0 | 0 | 0 | 4 | 8 | 0 | 2 | 2 | 22.5 | 6.75 | 61 | .400 | .455 | 69 | .265 | 0 | -1 | -1 | -0 | |

● **PHIL CLARK**   Clark, Philip James   b: 10/3/32, Albany, Ga.   BR/TR, 6'3", 210 lbs.   Deb: 4/15/58

1958	StL-N	0	1	.000	7	0	0	0	1	7²	11	2	3	1	16.4	3.52	117	.355	.412	0	.000	-0	-1	-0	0	
1959	StL-N	0	1	.000	7	0	0	0	0	7	8	0	8	5	20.6	12.86	33	.286	.444	0	—	0	-7	-7	0	-0.8
Total	2	0	2	.000	14	0	0	0	1	14²	19	2	11	6	18.4	7.98	52	.322	.429	0	.000	-0	-7	-6	0	-0.8

● **RICKEY CLARK**   Clark, Rickey Charles   b: 3/21/46, Mt.Clemens, Mich.   BR/TR, 6'2", 170 lbs.   Deb: 4/22/67

1967	Cal-A	12	11	.522	32	30	1	1	0	174	144	15	69	81	11.3	2.59	121	.224	.305	2	.040	-4	12	11	1	1.1
1968	Cal-A	1	11	.083	21	17	0	0	0	94¹	74	4	54	60	12.3	3.53	82	.217	.326	3	.107	-1	-6	-6	1	-0.9
1969	Cal-A	0	0	—	6	1	0	0	0	9²	12	2	7	6	17.7	5.59	62	.300	.404	1	.500	0	-2	-2	-1	0.0
1971	Cal-A	2	1	.667	11	7	1	1	1	44	36	6	28	28	13.5	2.86	113	.220	.340	4	.267	1	3	2	-1	0.2
1972	Cal-A	4	9	.308	26	15	2	0	1	109²	105	10	55	61	13.3	4.51	64	.261	.352	3	.097	-1	-18	-20	1	-2.3
Total	5	19	32	.373	96	70	4	2	2	431²	371	37	213	236	12.4	3.38	90	.233	.328	13	.103	-5	-10	-16	1	-1.9

● **BOB CLARK**   Clark, Robert William   b: 8/22/1897, Newport, Pa.   d: 5/18/44, Carlsbad, N.Mex.   BR/TR, 6'3", 188 lbs.   Deb: 5/26/20

1920	Cle-A	1	2	.333	11	2	2	1	0	42	59	0	8	5	15.6	3.43	111	.383	.435	2	.200	-0	0	-0	0	0.0
1921	Cle-A	0	0	—	5	0	0	0	0	9¹	23	2	6	2	28.9	14.46	29	.511	.577	0	.000	-1	-11	-11	-0	-0.1
Total	2	1	2	.333	16	2	2	1	0	51¹	82	2	9	10	18.1	5.44	71	.412	.468	2	.154	-1	-9	-9	-1	-0.1

● **TERRY CLARK**   Clark, Terry Lee   b: 10/18/60, Los Angeles, Cal.   BR/TR, 6'2", 190 lbs.   Deb: 7/7/88

1988	Cal-A	6	6	.500	15	15	2	1	0	94	120	8	31	39	14.5	5.07	76	.323	.375	0	—	0	-12	-13	0	-1.2
1989	Cal-A	0	2	.000	4	2	0	0	0	11	13	0	3	7	13.1	4.91	78	.310	.356	0	—	0	-1	-0	-0	-0.2
1990	Hou-N	0	0	—	1	1	0	0	0	4	9	0	3	2	27.0	13.50	27	.429	.500	1	.500	0	-4	-4	-0	0.0
1995	Atl-N	0	0	—	3	0	0	0	0	3²	3	0	5	2	19.6	4.91	87	.231	.444	0	—	-0	-0	-0	0	0.0
	Bal-A	2	5	.286	38	0	0	0	1	39	40	3	15	18	12.9	3.46	137	.276	.348	0	—	0	5	6	-1	0.8
1996	KC-A	1	1	.500	12	0	0	0	0	17¹	28	3	7	12	18.2	7.79	63	.350	.402	0	—	0	-5	-6	-0	-0.5
	Hou-N	0	2	.000	5	0	0	0	0	6¹	16	1	2	5	27.0	11.37	34	.471	.514	0	—	-0	-5	-5	1	-1.2
Total	5	9	16	.360	78	18	2	1	1	175¹	229	15	66	85	15.2	5.39	77	.324	.383	1	.500	0	-22	-24	-0	-2.3

● **OTIE CLARK**   Clark, William Otis   b: 5/22/18, Boscobel, Wis.   BR/TR, 6'1.5", 190 lbs.   Deb: 4/17/45

| 1945 | Bos-A | 4 | 4 | .500 | 12 | 9 | 4 | 1 | 0 | 82 | 86 | 6 | 19 | 20 | 11.6 | 3.07 | 111 | .268 | .311 | 5 | .208 | 0 | 3 | 3 | -2 | 0.1 |

● **WATTY CLARK**   Clark, William Watson "Lefty"   b: 5/16/02, St.Joseph, La.   d: 3/4/72, Clearwater, Fla.   BL/TL, 6'0.5", 175 lbs.   Deb: 5/28/24

1924	Cle-A	1	3	.250	12	1	0	0	0	25²	38	0	14	6	18.9	7.01	61	.345	.429	2	.222	-1	-8	-8	-0	-1.0
1927	Bro-N	7	2	.778	27	3	1	0	2	73²	74	2	19	32	11.4	2.32	171	.265	.312	3	.143	-1	13	13	0	1.5
1928	Bro-N	12	9	.571	40	19	10	2	3	194²	193	4	50	85	11.3	2.68	148	.259	.306	10	.152	-2	28	28	1	2.7
1929	Bro-N	16	19	.457	41	36	19	3	1	**279**	295	14	71	140	11.9	3.74	123	.270	.316	16	.165	-3	30	27	2	2.5
1930	Bro-N	13	13	.500	44	29	9	1	6	200	209	20	38	81	11.1	4.18	117	.271	.306	14	.206	0	17	16	0	1.9
1931	Bro-N	14	10	.583	34	28	16	3	1	233¹	243	4	52	96	11.4	3.20	119	.267	.308	21	.250	4	17	16	-3	1.6
1932	Bro-N	20	12	.625	40	36	19	2	0	273	282	10	49	99	11.4	3.49	109	.264	.299	21	.216	1	12	10	1	1.3
1933	Bro-N	2	4	.333	11	8	4	1	1	50²	61	2	6	14	12.4	4.80	67	.303	.333	2	.154	-0	-8	-9	-0	-1.0
	NY-N	3	4	.429	16	5	0	0	0	44	58	3	11	11	14.3	4.70	68	.317	.359	3	.273	1	-7	-7	1	-0.9
	Yr	5	8	.385	27	13	4	1	1	94²	119	5	17	25	13.0	4.75	68	.307	.338	5	.208	1	-15	-16	1	-1.9
1934	NY-N	1	2	.333	5	4	1	0	0	18²	23	5	6	6	13.5	6.75	57	.295	.337	1	.167	-0	-6	-6	0	-0.7
	Bro-N	2	0	1.000	17	1	0	0	0	25¹	40	0	9	10	17.8	5.33	73	.345	.397	1	.125	-1	-4	-4	0	-0.4
	Yr	3	2	.600	22	5	1	0	0	44	63	5	14	16	16.0	5.93	66	.325	.373	2	.143	-0	-9	-10	-1	-1.1
1935	Bro-N	13	8	.619	33	25	11	1	0	207	215	11	28	35	10.6	3.30	120	.264	.289	14	.177	0	16	15	2	1.6
1936	Bro-N	7	11	.389	33	16	1	1	2	120	162	11	28	28	14.3	4.43	93	.316	.351	9	.231	0	-5	-4	-0	-0.5
1937	Bro-N	0	0	—	2	0	0	0	0	2¹	4	0	3	0	27.0	7.71	52	.308	.438	0	—	-0	-1	-1	0	-0.1
Total	12	111	97	.534	355	206	91	14	16	1747¹	1897	86	383	643	11.8	3.66	112	.275	.315	117	.196	0	96	87	1	8.6

● **LEFTY CLARKE**   Clarke, Alan Thomas   b: 3/8/1896, Clarksville, Md.   d: 3/11/75, Cheverly, Md.   BB/TL, 5'11", 180 lbs.   Deb: 10/2/21

| 1921 | Cin-N | 0 | 1 | .000 | 1 | 1 | 1 | 0 | 0 | 5 | 7 | 2 | 1 | 6 | 16.2 | 5.40 | 66 | .304 | .360 | 0 | .000 | -0 | -1 | -1 | -0 | -0.2 |

● **HENRY CLARKE**   Clarke, Henry Tefft   b: 8/28/1875, Bellevue, Neb.   d: 3/28/50, Colorado Springs, Colo.   BR/TR,   Deb: 6/26/1897 ◆

1897	Cle-N	0	4	.000	5	4	3	0	0	30²	32	4	12	3	13.8	6.16	73	.267	.348	7	.280	-0	-6	-6	-1	-0.6
1898	Chi-N	1	0	1.000	1	1	1	0	0	9	8	0	5	1	14.0	2.00	179	.235	.350	1	.250	0	2	2	-0	0.2
Total	2	1	4	.200	6	5	4	0	0	39²	40	4	17	4	13.8	5.22	82	.260	.349	8	.276	0	-5	-4	-1	-0.4

● **RUFE CLARKE**   Clarke, Rufus Rivers   b: 4/13/1900, Estill, S.C.   d: 2/8/83, Columbia, S.C.   BR/TR, 6'1", 203 lbs.   Deb: 9/3/23 F

1923	Det-A	1	1	.500	5	0	0	0	0	6	6	0	6	2	19.5	4.50	86	.300	.481	0	.000	-0	-0	-0	-1	-0.1
1924	Det-A	0	0	—	2	0	0	0	0	5¹	3	0	5	1	15.2	3.38	122	.158	.360	0	.000	0	1	0	-0	0.0
Total	2	1	1	.500	7	0	0	0	0	11¹	9	0	11	3	17.5	3.97	100	.231	.423	0	.000	-0	0	-0	-1	-0.1

● **STAN CLARKE**   Clarke, Stanley Martin   b: 8/9/60, Toledo, Ohio   BL/TL, 6'1", 180 lbs.   Deb: 6/7/83

1983	Tor-A	1	1	.500	10	0	0	0	0	11	10	2	5	7	12.3	3.27	131	.256	.341	0	—	0	1	1	0	0.0
1985	Tor-A	0	0	—	4	0	0	0	0	4	3	1	2	2	11.3	4.50	94	.214	.313	0	—	-0	-0	-0	0	0.0
1986	Tor-A	0	1	.000	10	0	0	0	0	12²	18	4	10	9	19.9	9.24	46	.375	.483	0	—	-0	-7	-7	0	-0.5
1987	Sea-A	2	2	.500	22	0	0	0	0	23	31	7	10	13	16.0	5.48	86	.333	.398	0	—	0	-3	-2	-0	-0.4
1989	KC-A	0	2	.000	2	0	0	0	0	7	14	2	4	5	23.1	15.43	25	.438	.500	0	—	0	-9	-9	-1	-1.5
1990	StL-N	0	0	—	2	0	0	0	0	3¹	2	0	0	3	5.4	2.70	141	.167	.167	0	—	0	0	0	-0	0.0
Total	6	3	6	.333	50	0	0	0	0	61	78	16	31	36	16.1	6.79	64	.328	.405	0	—	-0	-18	-17	-0	-2.4

● **WEBBO CLARKE**   Clarke, Vibert Ernesto   b: 6/8/28, Colon, Panama   d: 6/14/70, Cristobal, C.Z.   BL/TL, 6', 165 lbs.   Deb: 9/4/55

| 1955 | Was-A | 0 | 0 | — | 7 | 2 | 0 | 0 | 0 | 21¹ | 17 | 2 | 14 | 9 | 13.1 | 4.64 | 83 | .221 | .341 | 1 | .167 | -0 | -2 | -2 | -0 | 0.0 |

● **DAD CLARKE**   Clarke, William H.   b: 1/7/1865, Oswego, N.Y.   d: 6/3/11, Lorain, Ohio   BB/TR,   Deb: 4/23/1888

1888	Chi-N	1	0	1.000	2	2	1	0	0	16	23	2	6	6	17.4	5.06	60	.315	.383	2	.286	2	-4	-4	0	0.0
1891	Col-a	1	2	.333	4	3	2	0	0	21	30	1	16	2	20.1	6.86	50	.326	.431	1	.111	0	-7	-8	0	-0.8
1894	NY-N	3	4	.429	15	6	5	0	1	84	114	3	26	15	15.3	4.93	106	.320	.371	8	.216	-0	4	3	0	0.1
1895	NY-N	18	15	.545	37	30	27	1	1	281²	336	5	60	67	13.0	3.39	137	.304	.333	29	.240	-2	44	39	-3	3.1
1896	NY-N	17	24	.415	48	40	33	1	1	351	431	9	60	66	12.9	4.26	99	.300	.332	30	.204	-4	4	3	-3	0.5
1897	NY-N	2	1	.667	6	4	2	0	0	31	43	1	11	10	16.3	6.10	68	.326	.386	1	.167	-1	-6	-7	-0	-0.6
	Lou-N	2	4	.333	7	6	2	0	0	54²	74	3	10	7	14.2	3.95	108	.320	.354	5	.227	-1	2	2	-0	0.1
	Yr	4	5	.444	13	10	4	0	0	85²	117	4	21	17	14.7	4.73	89	.321	.361	6	.200	-2	-4	-5	-0	-0.5
1898	Lou-N	0	1	.000	1	1	1	0	0	9	10	0	2	1	14.0	5.00	72	.278	.350	0	.000	-1	-1	-1	-0	-0.2
Total	7	44	51	.463	120	92	77	2	3	848¹	1061	24	191	174	13.6	4.33	106	.302	.344	78	.214	-6	35	23	-6	0.9

● **DAD CLARKSON**   Clarkson, Arthur Hamilton   b: 8/31/1866, Cambridge, Mass.   d: 2/5/11, Somerville, Mass.   BR/TR, 5'10", 165 lbs.   Deb: 8/20/1891 F

1891	NY-N	1	2	.333	5	2	1	0	0	28	24	0	18	11	14.5	2.89	111	.222	.349	4	.444	2	1	1	0	0.3
1892	Bos-N	1	0	1.000	7	0	0	0	0	7	5	0	3	2	10.3	1.29	273	.192	.276	0	.000	-0	2	2	0	0.2
1893	StL-N	12	9	.571	24	21	17	1	0	186¹	194	4	79	37	13.9	3.48	136	.260	.342	10	.133	-5	25	26	1	1.8
1894	StL-N	8	17	.320	32	32	24	1	0	233¹	318	9	117	46	17.2	6.36	85	.321	.399	16	.182	-4	-27	-25	1	-2.0

YEAR	TM/L	W	L	PCT	G	GS	CG	SH	SV	IP	H	HR	BB	SO	RAT	ERA	ERA+	OAV	OOB	BH	AVG	PB	PR	/A	PD	TPI
1895	StL-N	1	6	.143	7	7	7	0	0	61	91	7	26	9	17.6	7.38	66	.340	.402	1	.043	-3	-18	-17	-1	-1.6
	Bal-N	12	3	.800	20	14	10	0	0	142	169	5	64	23	15.0	3.87	123	.291	.365	8	.140	-4	14	14	2	0.9
	Yr	13	9	.591	27	21	17	0	0	203	260	12	90	32	15.7	4.92	97	.306	.375	9	.112	-7	-3	-3	1	-0.7
1896	Bal-N	4	2	.667	7	4	3	0	0	47	72	1	18	7	17.6	4.98	86	.348	.405	5	.278	0	-3	-4	-0	-0.4
Total	6	39	39	.500	96	81	63	2	0	704²	873	26	325	133	15.8	4.90	99	.298	.376	44	.161	-14	-6	-3	2	-0.8

● **JOHN CLARKSON**   Clarkson, John Gibson b: 7/1/1861, Cambridge, Mass. d: 2/4/09, Belmont, Mass.   BR/TR, 5'10", 155 lbs.   Deb: 5/2/1882 FH

YEAR	TM/L	W	L	PCT	G	GS	CG	SH	SV	IP	H	HR	BB	SO	RAT	ERA	ERA+	OAV	OOB	BH	AVG	PB	PR	/A	PD	TPI
1882	Wor-N	1	2	.333	3	3	2	0	0	24	49	0	2	3	19.1	4.50	69	.392	.402	4	.364	1	-4	-4	0	-0.3
1884	Chi-N	10	3	.769	14	13	12	0	0	118	94	10	25	102	9.1	2.14	147	.208	.249	22	.262	4	11	13	3	1.8
1885	*Chi-N	**53**	16	.768	**70**	70	**68**	**10**	0	**623**	497	21	97	**308**	8.6	1.85	164	.208	.239	61	.216	2	**67**	**82**	8	**8.9**
1886	*Chi-N	36	17	.679	55	55	50	3	0	466²	419	20	86	313	9.7	2.41	151	.229	.264	49	.233	1	47	**64**	4	6.5
1887	Chi-N	**38**	21	.644	60	59	56	2	0	523	513	20	92	237	10.5	3.08	146	.246	.281	52	.242	2	58	82	9	8.3
1888	Bos-N	33	20	.623	54	54	53	3	0	483¹	448	17	119	223	10.7	2.76	103	.236	.284	40	.195	3	5	5	3	0.9
1889	Bos-N	49	19	**.721**	**73**	72	**68**	8	1	620	589	16	203	284	**11.7**	**2.73**	153	.243	**.306**	54	.206	5	**89**	**99**	11	**10.1**
1890	Bos-N	26	18	.591	44	44	43	2	0	383	370	14	140	138	12.4	3.27	115	.246	.317	43	.249	3	13	21	-1	2.0
1891	Bos-N	33	19	.635	55	51	47	3	**3**	460²	435	18	154	141	11.8	2.79	131	.240	.305	42	.225	3	28	44	4	4.8
1892	Bos-N	8	6	.571	16	16	15	4	0	145²	115	4	60	48	11.1	2.35	150	.208	.292	13	.228	1	15	19	0	1.7
	*Cle-N	17	10	.630	29	28	27	1	1	243¹	235	4	72	91	11.5	2.55	133	.244	.299	14	.139	-5	20	23	-1	1.5
	Yr	25	16	.610	45	44	42	5	1	389	350	8	132	139	11.2	2.48	139	.230	.293	27	.171	-4	35	41	-1	3.2
1893	Cle-N	16	17	.485	36	35	31	0	0	295	358	11	95	62	14.0	4.45	110	.291	.344	27	.206	-4	7	14	3	1.1
1894	Cle-N	8	10	.444	22	18	13	1	0	150²	173	6	46	28	13.1	4.42	124	.285	.335	11	.200	-2	15	17	2	1.4
Total	12	328	178	.648	531	518	485	37	5	4536¹	4295	161	1191	1978	11.0	2.81	134	.240	.291	432	.219	9	371	480	46	48.7

● **WALTER CLARKSON**   Clarkson, Walter Hamilton b: 11/3/1878, Cambridge, Mass. d: 10/10/46, Cambridge, Mass.   BR/TR, 5'10", 150 lbs.   Deb: 7/2/04 F

YEAR	TM/L	W	L	PCT	G	GS	CG	SH	SV	IP	H	HR	BB	SO	RAT	ERA	ERA+	OAV	OOB	BH	AVG	PB	PR	/A	PD	TPI
1904	NY-A	1	2	.333	13	4	2	0	1	66¹	63	3	25	43	13.3	5.02	54	.251	.343	7	.269	2	-18	-17	-1	-0.8
1905	NY-A	3	3	.500	9	4	3	0	0	46	40	1	13	35	10.8	3.91	75	.235	.297	1	.053	-2	-6	-5	-1	-0.9
1906	NY-A	9	4	.692	32	16	9	3	0	151	135	6	55	64	11.6	2.32	128	.242	.316	8	.157	-1	6	11	-1	0.7
1907	NY-A	1	1	.500	5	2	0	0	0	17¹	19	1	8	3	15.1	6.23	45	.279	.372	2	.286	0	-7	-7	-0	-0.7
	Cle-A	4	6	.400	17	10	9	1	0	90²	77	1	29	32	10.8	1.99	126	.232	.299	1	.036	-3	6	5	-0	0.1
	Yr	5	7	.417	22	12	9	1	0	108	96	2	37	35	11.3	2.67	96	.239	.308	3	.086	-3	-1	-1	-0	-0.6
1908	Cle-A	0	0	—	2	1	0	0	0	3¹	6	0	2	1	27.0	10.80	22	.400	.526	1	1.000	-0	-3	-3	-0	0.0
Total	5	18	16	.529	78	37	23	4	1	374²	340	12	132	178	11.9	3.17	88	.244	.320	20	.152	-4	-23	-16	-4	-1.6

● **BILL CLARKSON**   Clarkson, William Henry "Blackie" b: 9/27/1898, Portsmouth, Va. d: 8/27/71, Raleigh, N.C.   BR/TR, 5'11", 160 lbs.   Deb: 5/2/27

YEAR	TM/L	W	L	PCT	G	GS	CG	SH	SV	IP	H	HR	BB	SO	RAT	ERA	ERA+	OAV	OOB	BH	AVG	PB	PR	/A	PD	TPI
1927	NY-N	3	9	.250	26	7	2	0	2	86²	92	3	52	28	15.1	4.36	88	.280	.380	1	.050	-1	-4	-5	0	-0.7
1928	NY-N	0	0	—	4	0	0	0	0	5²	10	1	3	1	17.5	7.94	49	.455	.478	0	—	0	-2	-3	-0	0.0
	Bos-N	0	2	.000	19	1	0	0	0	34²	53	2	20	10	19.7	6.75	58	.349	.434	0	.000	-0	-11	-11	1	-0.5
	Yr	0	2	.000	23	1	0	0	0	40¹	63	3	23	11	19.4	6.92	57	.362	.439	0	.000	-0	-13	-13	1	-0.5
1929	Bos-N	0	1	.000	2	1	0	0	0	7	16	0	4	0	25.7	10.29	45	.485	.541	1	.500	-0	-4	-4	0	-0.4
Total	3	3	12	.200	51	9	2	0	2	134	171	5	79	39	16.9	5.44	72	.319	.408	2	.080	-1	-22	-22	1	-1.6

● **MARTY CLARY**   Clary, Martin Keith b: 4/3/62, Detroit, Mich.   BR/TR, 6'4", 190 lbs.   Deb: 9/5/87

YEAR	TM/L	W	L	PCT	G	GS	CG	SH	SV	IP	H	HR	BB	SO	RAT	ERA	ERA+	OAV	OOB	BH	AVG	PB	PR	/A	PD	TPI
1987	Atl-N	0	1	.000	7	1	0	0	0	14²	20	2	4	7	15.3	6.14	71	.328	.379	0	.000	-0	-3	-3	-0	-0.2
1989	Atl-N	4	3	.571	18	17	2	1	0	108²	103	6	31	30	11.2	3.15	116	.249	.303	5	.161	-3	4	6	0	0.5
1990	Atl-N	1	10	.091	33	14	0	0	0	101²	128	9	39	44	14.9	5.67	71	.308	.368	0	.000	-3	-21	-18	1	-2.0
Total	3	5	14	.263	58	32	2	1	0	225	251	17	74	81	13.1	4.48	86	.282	.339	5	.083	-2	-20	-15	1	-1.7

● **GOWELL CLASET**   Claset, Gowell Sylvester "Lefty" b: 11/26/07, Battle Creek, Mich d: 3/8/81, St.Petersburg, Fla.   BB/TL, 6'3.5", 210 lbs.   Deb: 4/12/33

YEAR	TM/L	W	L	PCT	G	GS	CG	SH	SV	IP	H	HR	BB	SO	RAT	ERA	ERA+	OAV	OOB	BH	AVG	PB	PR	/A	PD	TPI
1933	Phi-A	2	0	1.000	8	1	0	0	0	11¹	23	1	11	1	27.0	9.53	45	.426	.523	1	.500	1	-7	-7	0	-0.8

● **FRITZ CLAUSEN**   Clausen, Frederick William b: 4/26/1869, New York, N.Y. d: 2/11/60, Memphis, Tenn.   BR/TL, 5'11", 190 lbs.   Deb: 7/23/1892

YEAR	TM/L	W	L	PCT	G	GS	CG	SH	SV	IP	H	HR	BB	SO	RAT	ERA	ERA+	OAV	OOB	BH	AVG	PB	PR	/A	PD	TPI
1892	Lou-N	9	13	.409	24	24	24	2	0	200	181	3	87	94	12.2	3.06	100	.232	.311	13	.155	-3	5	0	-1	-0.3
1893	Lou-N	1	4	.200	5	5	3	0	0	33	41	2	22	4	17.5	6.00	73	.295	.395	3	.214	-1	-5	-6	-0	-0.7
	Chi-N	6	2	.750	10	9	8	0	1	76	71	1	39	31	13.6	3.08	150	.240	.338	4	.121	-3	13	13	0	0.8
	Yr	7	6	.538	15	14	11	0	1	109	112	3	61	35	14.7	3.96	115	.257	.355	7	.149	-4	8	7	0	0.1
1894	Chi-N	0	1	.000	1	1	0	0	0	4¹	5	0	3	1	16.6	10.38	54	.294	.400	0	.000	-0	-2	-2	-0	-0.3
1896	Lou-N	0	2	.000	2	2	1	0	0	11	17	1	6	4	21.3	6.55	66	.347	.448	0	.000	-1	-3	-3	-0	-0.4
Total	4	16	22	.421	42	41	36	2	1	324¹	315	7	157	134	13.4	3.58	101	.246	.334	20	.147	-8	8	2	-0	-0.9

● **AL CLAUSS**   Clauss, Albert Stanley "Lefty" b: 6/24/1891, New Haven, Conn. d: 9/13/52, New Haven, Conn.   BR/TL, 5'10.5", 178 lbs.   Deb: 4/22/13

YEAR	TM/L	W	L	PCT	G	GS	CG	SH	SV	IP	H	HR	BB	SO	RAT	ERA	ERA+	OAV	OOB	BH	AVG	PB	PR	/A	PD	TPI
1913	Det-A	0	1	.000	5	1	0	0	0	13¹	11	0	12	1	16.9	4.73	62	.220	.391	0	.000	-1	-3	-3	-0	-0.3

● **DANNY CLAY**   Clay, Danny Bruce b: 10/24/61, Sun Valley, Cal.   BR/TR, 6'1", 190 lbs.   Deb: 5/1/88

YEAR	TM/L	W	L	PCT	G	GS	CG	SH	SV	IP	H	HR	BB	SO	RAT	ERA	ERA+	OAV	OOB	BH	AVG	PB	PR	/A	PD	TPI
1988	Phi-N	0	1	.000	17	0	0	0	0	24	27	5	21	12	18.0	6.00	59	.303	.436	0	.000	-0	-7	-7	-1	-0.3

● **KEN CLAY**   Clay, Kenneth Earl b: 4/6/54, Lynchburg, Va.   BR/TR, 6'3", 195 lbs.   Deb: 6/7/77

YEAR	TM/L	W	L	PCT	G	GS	CG	SH	SV	IP	H	HR	BB	SO	RAT	ERA	ERA+	OAV	OOB	BH	AVG	PB	PR	/A	PD	TPI
1977	*NY-A	2	3	.400	21	3	0	0	1	55²	53	6	24	20	12.6	4.37	90	.251	.331	0	—	0	-2	-3	0	-0.2
1978	*NY-A	3	4	.429	28	6	0	0	0	75²	89	5	21	32	13.3	4.28	85	.291	.340	0	—	0	-4	-6	-1	-0.5
1979	NY-A	1	7	.125	32	5	0	0	2	78¹	88	12	25	28	13.2	5.40	75	.291	.350	0	—	0	-10	-12	0	-1.1
1980	Tex-A	2	3	.400	8	8	0	0	0	43	43	4	29	17	15.7	4.60	85	.256	.375	0	—	0	-3	-3	-1	-0.3
1981	Sea-A	2	7	.222	22	14	0	0	0	101	116	10	42	32	14.3	4.63	83	.294	.366	0	—	0	-11	-9	-2	-0.9
Total	5	10	24	.294	111	36	0	0	3	353²	389	35	141	129	13.8	4.68	83	.281	.353	0	—	0	-30	-32	-3	-3.0

● **MARK CLEAR**   Clear, Mark Alan b: 5/27/56, Los Angeles, Cal.   BR/TR, 6'4", 215 lbs.   Deb: 4/4/79

YEAR	TM/L	W	L	PCT	G	GS	CG	SH	SV	IP	H	HR	BB	SO	RAT	ERA	ERA+	OAV	OOB	BH	AVG	PB	PR	/A	PD	TPI
1979	*Cal-A★	11	5	.688	52	0	0	0	14	109	87	6	68	98	13.0	3.63	112	.219	.337	0	—	0	7	5	-1	0.8
1980	Cal-A	11	11	.500	55	0	0	0	9	106¹	82	6	65	105	12.9	3.30	119	.216	.338	0	—	0	9	7	-1	1.6
1981	Bos-A	8	3	.727	34	0	0	0	9	76²	69	11	51	82	14.3	4.11	94	.239	.357	0	—	0	-4	-2	-1	-0.5
1982	Bos-A☆	14	9	.609	55	0	0	0	14	105	92	11	61	109	13.7	3.00	144	.238	.352	0	—	0	13	15	-0	3.5
1983	Bos-A	4	5	.444	48	0	0	0	4	96	101	10	68	81	16.1	6.28	69	.273	.390	0	—	0	-24	-21	-1	-2.2
1984	Bos-A	8	3	.727	47	0	0	0	8	67	47	2	70	76	16.0	4.03	103	.198	.385	0	—	0	-0	1	0	0.1
1985	Bos-A	1	3	.250	41	0	0	0	1	55²	45	1	50	55	16.2	3.72	115	.225	.392	0	—	0	3	3	1	0.3
1986	Mil-A	5	5	.500	59	0	0	0	16	73²	53	4	36	85	11.0	2.20	197	.201	.299	0	—	0	16	17	-0	2.8
1987	Mil-A	8	5	.615	58	0	0	0	6	78¹	70	9	55	81	14.9	4.48	102	.239	.368	0	—	0	-0	1	1	0.2
1988	Mil-A	0	1	.000	25	0	0	0	0	29	23	4	21	26	13.7	2.79	142	.215	.344	0	—	0	4	4	-0	0.0
1990	Cal-A	0	0	—	4	0	0	0	0	7²	5	0	9	6	18.8	5.87	65	.200	.444	0	—	0	-2	-2	-0	0.0
Total	11	71	49	.592	481	0	0	0	83	804¹	674	60	554	804	14.1	3.85	109	.228	.357	0	—	0	21	30	-3	6.6

● **JOE CLEARY**   Cleary, Joseph Christopher "Fire" b: 12/3/18, Cork, Ireland   BR/TR, 5'9", 150 lbs.   Deb: 8/4/45

YEAR	TM/L	W	L	PCT	G	GS	CG	SH	SV	IP	H	HR	BB	SO	RAT	ERA	ERA+	OAV	OOB	BH	AVG	PB	PR	/A	PD	TPI
1945	Was-A	0	0	—	1	0	0	0	0	0¹	5	0	3	1	216.0	189.00	2	.833	.889	0	—	0	-7	-7	0	0.0

● **ROGER CLEMENS**   Clemens, William Roger b: 8/4/62, Dayton, Ohio   BR/TR, 6'4", 215 lbs.   Deb: 5/15/84

YEAR	TM/L	W	L	PCT	G	GS	CG	SH	SV	IP	H	HR	BB	SO	RAT	ERA	ERA+	OAV	OOB	BH	AVG	PB	PR	/A	PD	TPI
1984	Bos-A	9	4	.692	21	20	5	1	0	133¹	146	13	29	126	11.9	4.32	94	.271	.311	0	—	0	-5	-2	0	-0.3
1985	Bos-A	7	5	.583	15	15	3	1	0	98¹	83	5	37	74	11.3	3.29	130	.228	.304	0	—	0	9	11	0	1.2
1986	*Bos-A★	24	4	**.857**	33	33	10	1	0	254	179	21	67	238	**8.9**	**2.48**	168	**.195**	**.253**	0	—	0	48	48	-1	4.9
1987	Bos-A	20	9	**.690**	36	36	**18**	**7**	0	281²	248	19	83	256	10.9	2.97	153	.235	.296	0	—	0	46	49	-2	4.4
1988	*Bos-A★	18	12	.600	35	35	**14**	8	0	264	217	17	62	291	9.7	2.93	140	.220	.270	0	—	0	30	35	-2	3.3
1989	Bos-A	17	11	.607	35	35	8	3	0	253¹	215	20	93	230	11.2	3.13	131	.231	.307	0	—	0	21	27	-1	2.6
1990	*Bos-A☆	21	6	.778	31	31	7	4	0	228¹	193	7	54	209	**1.93**	**211**	.202	.280	0	—	0	**50**	**54**	1	**6.7**
1991	Bos-A	18	10	.643	35	35	13	**4**	0	**271**	219	15	65	241	9.6	2.62	164	.221	.272	0	—	0	44	51	1	4.8
1992	Bos-A★	18	11	.621	32	32	11	**5**	0	246²	203	11	62	208	10.0	**2.41**	175	.224	.280	0	—	0	42	49	-0	5.8
1993	Bos-A	11	14	.440	29	29	2	1	0	191²	175	17	67	160	11.9	4.46	103	.244	.318	0	—	0	-3	4	-1	0.3
1994	Bos-A	9	7	.563	24	24	3	1	0	170²	124	15	71	168	10.5	2.85	**177**	**.203**	.291	0	—	0	37	41	-0	3.1

YEAR	TM/L	W	L	PCT	G	GS	CG	SH	SV	IP	H	HR	BB	SO	RAT	ERA	ERA+	OAV	OOB	BH	AVG	PB	PR	/A	PD	TPI
1995	*Bos-A	10	5	.667	23	23	0	0	0	140	141	15	60	132	13.8	4.18	117	.259	.348	0	—	0	8	11	1	0.9
1996	Bos-A	10	13	.435	34	34	6	2	0	242²	216	19	106	**257**	12.1	3.63	141	.237	.319	1	1.000	0	37	41	-1	3.2
Total	13	192	111	.634	383	382	100	38	0	2776	2359	194	856	2590	10.7	3.06	144	.229	.293	1	1.000	0	366	418	-4	40.9

● BILL CLEMENSEN
Clemensen, William Melville b: 6/20/19, New Brunswick, N.J. d: 2/18/94, Alta, Cal. BR/TR, 6'1", 193 lbs. Deb: 5/22/39

YEAR	TM/L	W	L	PCT	G	GS	CG	SH	SV	IP	H	HR	BB	SO	RAT	ERA	ERA+	OAV	OOB	BH	AVG	PB	PR	/A	PD	TPI
1939	Pit-N	0	1	.000	12	1	0	0	0	27	32	0	20	13	18.3	7.33	52	.311	.437	2	.333	1	-10	-10	1	-0.1
1941	Pit-N	1	0	1.000	2	1	1	0	0	13	7	0	7	4	9.7	2.77	130	.159	.275	0	.000	-1	1	1	-0	0.0
1946	Pit-N	0	0	—	1	0	0	0	0	2	0	0	0	2	0.0	0.00	—	.000	.000	0	—	0	1	1	-0	0.0
Total	3	1	1	.500	15	2	1	0	0	42	39	0	27	19	14.8	5.57	67	.255	.377	2	.200	0	-8	-8	1	-0.1

● PAT CLEMENTS
Clements, Patrick Brian b: 2/2/62, McCloud, Cal. BR/TL, 6', 180 lbs. Deb: 4/9/85

YEAR	TM/L	W	L	PCT	G	GS	CG	SH	SV	IP	H	HR	BB	SO	RAT	ERA	ERA+	OAV	OOB	BH	AVG	PB	PR	/A	PD	TPI
1985	Cal-A	5	0	1.000	41	0	0	0	0	62	47	4	25	19	10.7	3.34	123	.218	.305	0	—	0	6	5	1	0.5
	Pit-N	0	2	.000	27	0	0	0	2	34¹	39	2	15	17	14.2	3.67	97	.289	.360	1	.333	0	-0	-1	-0	-0.1
1986	Pit-N	0	4	.000	65	0	0	0	2	61	53	1	32	31	12.8	2.80	137	.251	.355	0	.000	-1	6	7	1	0.6
1987	NY-A	3	3	.500	55	0	0	0	7	80	91	4	30	36	13.9	4.95	89	.299	.368	0	—	0	-4	-5	1	-0.3
1988	NY-A	0	0	—	6	1	0	0	0	8¹	12	1	4	3	17.3	6.48	61	.343	.410	0	—	0	-2	-2	0	0.1
1989	SD-N	4	1	.800	23	1	0	0	0	39	39	4	15	18	12.5	3.92	89	.267	.335	0	.000	-1	-2	-2	0	-0.3
1990	SD-N	0	0	—	9	0	0	0	0	13	20	1	7	6	18.7	4.15	92	.357	.429	0	—	0	-1	-0	0	0.0
1991	SD-N	1	0	1.000	12	0	0	0	0	14¹	13	0	9	8	13.8	3.77	101	.255	.367	0	.000	-0	0	0	0	0.0
1992	SD-N	2	1	.667	27	0	0	0	0	23²	25	0	12	11	14.8	2.66	134	.281	.379	0	.000	-0	2	2	1	0.3
	Bal-A	2	0	1.000	23	0	0	0	0	24²	23	0	11	9	13.1	3.28	122	.258	.353	0	—	0	2	2	1	0.2
Total	8	17	11	.607	288	2	0	0	12	360¹	362	17	160	158	13.7	3.77	105	.272	.355	1	.059	-1	6	7	4	0.9

● LANCE CLEMONS
Clemons, Lance Levis b: 7/6/47, Philadelphia, Pa. BL/TL, 6'2", 205 lbs. Deb: 8/12/71

YEAR	TM/L	W	L	PCT	G	GS	CG	SH	SV	IP	H	HR	BB	SO	RAT	ERA	ERA+	OAV	OOB	BH	AVG	PB	PR	/A	PD	TPI
1971	KC-A	1	0	1.000	10	3	0	0	0	24	26	2	12	20	14.6	4.13	83	.263	.348	2	.286	2	-2	-2	0	0.2
1972	StL-N	0	1	.000	3	1	0	0	0	5¹	8	1	5	2	23.6	10.13	34	.364	.500	0	.000	-0	-4	-4	0	-0.6
1974	Bos-A	1	0	1.000	6	0	0	0	0	6¹	8	1	4	1	18.5	9.95	39	.296	.406	0	—	0	-4	-4	0	-0.6
Total	3	2	1	.667	19	4	0	0	0	35²	42	4	21	23	16.7	6.06	58	.284	.384	2	.250	2	-10	-10	0	-1.0

● REGGIE CLEVELAND
Cleveland, Reginald Leslie b: 5/23/48, Swift Current, Sask., Canada BR/TR, 6'1", 195 lbs. Deb: 10/1/69

YEAR	TM/L	W	L	PCT	G	GS	CG	SH	SV	IP	H	HR	BB	SO	RAT	ERA	ERA+	OAV	OOB	BH	AVG	PB	PR	/A	PD	TPI
1969	StL-N	0	0	—	1	1	0	0	0	4	7	0	1	3	18.0	9.00	40	.368	.400	0	.000	-0	-2	-2	-0	-0.2
1970	StL-N	0	4	.000	16	1	0	0	0	26	31	3	18	22	17.0	7.62	54	.298	.402	1	.250	0	-10	-10	-1	-1.4
1971	StL-N	12	12	.500	34	34	10	0	0	222	238	20	53	148	12.0	4.01	90	.271	.317	14	.171	-1	-14	-10	-0	-1.1
1972	StL-N	14	15	.483	33	33	11	3	0	230²	229	21	60	153	11.5	3.94	86	.258	.308	17	.239	1	-13	-14	-1	-1.5
1973	StL-N	14	10	.583	32	32	6	3	0	224	211	16	61	122	11.1	3.01	121	.246	.300	17	.230	4	16	16	-2	1.8
1974	Bos-A	12	14	.462	41	27	10	0	0	221¹	234	25	69	103	12.7	4.31	89	.271	.332	0	—	0	-17	-12	1	-1.2
1975	*Bos-A	13	9	.591	31	20	3	1	0	170²	173	19	52	78	12.0	4.43	92	.263	.320	0	—	0	-12	-7	-0	-0.8
1976	Bos-A	10	9	.526	41	14	3	0	2	170	159	8	61	76	11.9	3.07	127	.246	.315	0	—	0	8	16	-0	0.8
1977	Bos-A	11	8	.579	36	27	9	1	2	190¹	211	20	43	85	12.2	4.26	105	.281	.323	0	—	0	-4	5	-1	-0.1
1978	Bos-A	0	1	.000	1	0	0	0	0	0¹	1	0	0	0	27.0	0.00	—	.333	.333	0	—	0	0	0	0	0.2
	Tex-A	5	7	.417	53	0	0	0	12	75²	65	5	23	46	10.8	3.09	121	.236	.301	0	—	0	6	5	0	1.0
	Yr	5	8	.385	54	0	0	0	12	76	66	5	23	46	10.9	3.08	122	.237	.302	0	—	0	6	6	1	1.2
1979	Mil-A	1	5	.167	29	1	0	0	4	55	77	9	23	22	16.4	6.71	62	.344	.405	0	—	0	-15	-16	-1	-1.8
1980	Mil-A	11	9	.550	45	13	5	2	4	154¹	150	9	49	54	11.9	3.73	104	.254	.317	0	—	0	5	2	-1	0.3
1981	Mil-A	2	3	.400	35	0	0	0	1	62¹	57	5	30	18	12.2	5.15	66	.239	.327	0	—	0	-11	-12	-1	-1.0
Total	13	105	106	.498	428	203	57	12	25	1809	1843	152	543	930	12.1	4.01	95	.264	.321	49	.211	6	-63	-38	-9	-4.8

● TEX CLEVENGER
Clevenger, Truman Eugene b: 7/9/32, Visalia, Cal. BR/TR, 6'1", 180 lbs. Deb: 4/18/54

YEAR	TM/L	W	L	PCT	G	GS	CG	SH	SV	IP	H	HR	BB	SO	RAT	ERA	ERA+	OAV	OOB	BH	AVG	PB	PR	/A	PD	TPI
1954	Bos-A	2	4	.333	23	8	1	0	0	67²	67	9	29	43	13.0	4.79	86	.262	.341	3	.214	0	-8	-5	0	-0.4
1956	Was-A	0	0	—	20	1	0	0	0	31²	34	4	21	17	15.3	5.40	80	.264	.370	0	.000	-0	-4	-4	-0	-0.4
1957	Was-A	7	6	.538	52	9	2	0	8	139²	139	11	47	75	12.2	4.19	93	.261	.326	7	.212	1	-6	-5	1	-0.2
1958	Was-A	9	9	.500	**55**	4	0	0	6	124	119	12	50	70	12.3	4.35	88	.251	.324	3	.136	0	-8	-7	3	-0.8
1959	Was-A	8	5	.615	50	7	2	2	8	117¹	114	9	51	71	12.8	3.91	100	.256	.335	4	.174	1	-1	0	4	0.5
1960	Was-A	5	11	.313	53	11	0	0	7	128²	150	10	49	49	14.1	4.20	93	.298	.363	2	.091	-1	-5	-4	-1	-0.7
1961	LA-A	2	1	.667	12	0	0	0	1	16	13	1	13	11	14.6	1.69	267	.220	.361	0	.000	-0	4	5	1	1.0
	NY-A	1	1	.500	21	0	0	0	0	31²	35	3	21	14	16.2	4.83	77	.287	.396	1	.250	0	-3	-4	1	-0.1
	Yr	3	2	.600	33	0	0	0	1	47²	48	4	34	25	15.7	3.78	105	.265	.384	1	.143	0	1	1	1	0.9
1962	NY-A	2	0	1.000	21	0	0	0	0	38	36	3	17	11	12.8	2.84	132	.248	.331	0	.000	-0	5	4	0	0.1
Total	8	36	37	.493	307	40	6	2	30	694²	706	62	298	361	13.2	4.18	94	.265	.342	20	.157	1	-26	-20	8	-0.6

● STEW CLIBURN
Cliburn, Stewart Walker b: 12/19/56, Jackson, Miss. BR/TR, 6', 195 lbs. Deb: 9/17/84 F

YEAR	TM/L	W	L	PCT	G	GS	CG	SH	SV	IP	H	HR	BB	SO	RAT	ERA	ERA+	OAV	OOB	BH	AVG	PB	PR	/A	PD	TPI
1984	Cal-A	0	0	—	1	0	0	0	0	2	3	0	1	1	18.0	13.50	29	.333	.400	0	—	0	-2	-2	0	0.0
1985	Cal-A	9	3	.750	44	0	0	0	6	99	87	5	26	48	10.4	2.09	197	.241	.294	0	—	0	23	22	1	2.9
1988	Cal-A	4	2	.667	40	1	0	0	0	84	83	11	32	42	13.0	4.07	95	.266	.346	0	—	0	-1	-2	0	0.1
Total	3	13	5	.722	85	1	0	0	6	185	173	16	59	91	11.6	3.31	128	.254	.320	0	—	0	20	18	2	3.0

● JIM CLINTON
Clinton, James Lawrence "Big Jim" b: 8/10/1850, New York, N.Y. d: 9/3/21, Brooklyn, N.Y. BR/TR, 5'8.5", 174 lbs. Deb: 5/18/1872 MU◆

YEAR	TM/L	W	L	PCT	G	GS	CG	SH	SV	IP	H	HR	BB	SO	RAT	ERA	ERA+	OAV	OOB	BH	AVG	PB	PR	/A	PD	TPI
1875	Atl-n	1	13	.071	17	14	9	0	0	123	141	0	5	7	10.7	2.41	86	.262	.268	10	.123	-5	-3	-5	—	-0.7
1876	Lou-N	0	1	.000	1	1	1	0	0	9	12	0	0	1	12.0	6.00	45	.279	.279	22	.338	0	-4	-3	0	-0.2

● TONY CLONINGER
Cloninger, Tony Lee b: 8/13/40, Lincoln Co., N.C. BR/TR, 6', 210 lbs. Deb: 6/15/61 C

YEAR	TM/L	W	L	PCT	G	GS	CG	SH	SV	IP	H	HR	BB	SO	RAT	ERA	ERA+	OAV	OOB	BH	AVG	PB	PR	/A	PD	TPI
1961	Mil-N	7	2	.778	19	10	3	0	0	84	84	16	33	51	12.6	5.25	71	.258	.328	5	.167	-0	-11	-14	1	-1.3
1962	Mil-N	8	3	.727	24	15	4	1	0	111	113	16	46	69	13.0	4.30	88	.264	.337	4	.103	-2	-4	-6	0	-0.7
1963	Mil-N	9	11	.450	41	18	4	2	1	145¹	131	17	63	100	12.1	3.78	85	.239	.320	5	.135	-2	-8	-9	-2	-1.4
1964	Mil-N	19	14	.576	38	34	15	3	2	242²	206	29	82	163	10.8	3.56	99	.231	.298	21	.241	-1	-1	-1	-0	0.2
1965	Mil-N	24	11	.686	40	38	16	1	1	279	247	20	119	211	11.9	3.29	107	.236	.316	17	.162	2	8	7	-1	0.9
1966	Atl-N	14	11	.560	39	38	11	1	1	257²	253	29	116	178	13.1	4.12	88	.258	.340	26	.234	10	-15	-14	-0	-0.3
1967	Atl-N	4	7	.364	16	16	1	0	0	76²	85	13	31	55	13.6	5.17	64	.285	.353	5	.200	1	-15	-16	-0	-2.0
1968	Atl-N	1	3	.250	8	1	0	0	0	19	15	0	11	7	12.3	4.26	70	.227	.338	0	.000	-0	-3	-3	-0	-0.6
	Cin-N	4	3	.571	17	17	2	2	0	91¹	81	7	48	65	13.0	4.04	78	.233	.331	7	.206	3	-11	-9	-0	-0.4
	Yr	5	6	.455	25	18	2	2	0	110¹	96	7	59	72	12.9	4.08	77	.231	.331	7	.184	2	-13	-12	-1	-1.0
1969	Cin-N	11	17	.393	35	34	6	2	0	189²	184	24	103	103	13.9	5.03	75	.250	.346	12	.167	1	-30	-27	-2	-3.6
1970	*Cin-N	9	7	.563	30	18	0	0	0	148	136	10	78	56	13.3	3.83	105	.249	.347	10	.213	3	4	3	2	0.8
1971	Cin-N	3	6	.333	28	9	1	0	0	97¹	79	12	49	51	12.2	3.88	86	.230	.332	7	.259	1	-5	-6	0	-0.3
1972	StL-N	0	0	—	17	0	0	0	0	26	29	2	19	11	17.0	5.19	66	.293	.412	0	.000	-0	-5	-5	1	-0.3
Total	12	113	97	.538	352	247	63	13	6	1767²	1643	180	798	1120	12.6	4.07	88	.247	.330	119	.192	21	-96	-98	-2	-9.0

● BRAD CLONTZ
Clontz, John Bradley b: 4/25/71, Stuart, Va. BR/TR, 6'1", 180 lbs. Deb: 4/26/95

YEAR	TM/L	W	L	PCT	G	GS	CG	SH	SV	IP	H	HR	BB	SO	RAT	ERA	ERA+	OAV	OOB	BH	AVG	PB	PR	/A	PD	TPI
1995	*Atl-N	8	1	.889	59	0	0	0	4	69	71	5	22	55	12.6	3.65	117	.269	.334	0	.000	-0	4	5	0	0.6
1996	*Atl-N	6	3	.667	**81**	0	0	0	1	80²	78	11	33	49	12.6	5.69	77	.255	.331	0	.000	-0	-13	-12	1	-1.1
Total	2	14	4	.778	140	0	0	0	5	149²	149	16	55	104	12.6	4.75	91	.261	.333	0	.000	-0	-9	-7	1	-0.5

● AL CLOSTER
Closter, Alan Edward b: 6/15/43, Creighton, Neb. BL/TL, 6'2", 190 lbs. Deb: 4/19/66

YEAR	TM/L	W	L	PCT	G	GS	CG	SH	SV	IP	H	HR	BB	SO	RAT	ERA	ERA+	OAV	OOB	BH	AVG	PB	PR	/A	PD	TPI
1966	Was-A	0	0	—	1	0	0	0	0	0¹	1	0	0	0	81.0	0.00	—	.500	.750	0	—	0	0	0	0	0.0
1971	NY-A	2	2	.500	14	1	0	0	0	28¹	33	4	13	22	15.2	5.08	64	.289	.372	0	.000	-1	-5	-6	1	-0.8
1972	NY-A	0	0	—	2	0	0	0	0	2¹	2	1	4	2	23.1	11.57	25	.250	.500	0	—	0	-2	-2	0	-0.3
1973	Atl-N	0	0	—	4	0	0	0	0	4¹	7	1	4	2	22.8	14.54	27	.389	.500	0	—	0	-5	-5	0	-0.7
Total	4	2	2	.500	21	1	0	0	0	35¹	43	6	23	26	17.3	6.62	50	.303	.407	0	.000	-1	-12	-13	1	-0.8

● ED CLOUGH
Clough, Edgar George "Big Ed" or "Spec" b: 10/28/06, Wiconisco, Pa. d: 1/30/44, Harrisburg, Pa. BL/TL, 6', 188 lbs. Deb: 8/28/24 ◆

YEAR	TM/L	W	L	PCT	G	GS	CG	SH	SV	IP	H	HR	BB	SO	RAT	ERA	ERA+	OAV	OOB	BH	AVG	PB	PR	/A	PD	TPI
1925	StL-N	0	1	.000	3	1	0	0	0	10	11	1	5	3	15.3	8.10	53	.289	.386	1	.250	-0	-4	-4	-0	-0.4

YEAR TM/L	W	L	PCT	G	GS	CG	SH	SV	IP	H	HR	BB	SO	RAT	ERA	ERA+	OAV	OOB	BH	AVG	PB	PR	/A	PD	TPI
1926 StL-N	0	0	—	1	0	0	0	0	2	5	1	3	0	40.5	22.50	17	.556	.692	0	.000	-0	-4	-4	-0	0.0
Total 2	0	1	.000	4	1	0	0	0	12	16	1	8	3	19.5	10.50	40	.340	.456	2	.105	-0	-8	-8	-0	-0.4

● **BILL CLOWERS**   Clowers, William Perry   b: 8/14/1898, San Marcos, Tex.   d: 1/13/78, Sweeny, Tex.   BL/TL, 5'11", 175 lbs.   Deb: 7/20/26

YEAR TM/L	W	L	PCT	G	GS	CG	SH	SV	IP	H	HR	BB	SO	RAT	ERA	ERA+	OAV	OOB	BH	AVG	PB	PR	/A	PD	TPI
1926 Bos-A	0	0	—	2	0	0	0	0	1²	2	0	0	0	10.8	0.00	—	.333	.333	0	—	0	1	1	0	0.0

● **BRYAN CLUTTERBUCK**   Clutterbuck, Bryan Richard   b: 12/17/59, Detroit, Mich.   BR/TR, 6'4", 223 lbs.   Deb: 7/18/86

YEAR TM/L	W	L	PCT	G	GS	CG	SH	SV	IP	H	HR	BB	SO	RAT	ERA	ERA+	OAV	OOB	BH	AVG	PB	PR	/A	PD	TPI
1986 Mil-A	0	1	.000	20	0	0	0	0	56²	68	8	16	38	13.7	4.29	101	.296	.347	0	—	0	-1	0	-0	0.0
1989 Mil-A	2	5	.286	14	11	1	0	0	67¹	73	11	16	29	11.9	4.14	93	.269	.310	0	—	0	-2	-2	-2	-0.4
Total 2	2	6	.250	34	11	1	0	0	124	141	19	32	67	12.7	4.21	96	.281	.327	0	—	0	-3	-2	-2	-0.4

● **DAVID CLYDE**   Clyde, David Eugene   b: 4/22/55, Kansas City, Kan.   BL/TL, 6'1", 185 lbs.   Deb: 6/27/73

YEAR TM/L	W	L	PCT	G	GS	CG	SH	SV	IP	H	HR	BB	SO	RAT	ERA	ERA+	OAV	OOB	BH	AVG	PB	PR	/A	PD	TPI
1973 Tex-A	4	8	.333	18	18	0	0	0	93¹	106	8	54	74	15.8	5.01	74	.293	.390	0	—	0	-12	-13	-0	-1.3
1974 Tex-A	3	9	.250	28	21	4	0	0	117	129	14	47	52	13.8	4.38	81	.286	.359	0	—	0	-10	-11	-2	-1.2
1975 Tex-A	0	1	.000	1	1	0	0	0	7	6	0	6	2	15.4	2.57	146	.273	.429	0	—	0	1	1	-0	0.1
1978 Cle-A	8	11	.421	28	25	5	0	0	153¹	166	4	60	83	13.4	4.28	87	.280	.350	0	—	0	-9	-9	-1	-1.1
1979 Cle-A	3	4	.429	9	8	1	0	0	45²	50	7	13	17	12.6	5.91	72	.279	.332	0	—	0	-9	-8	-0	-1.1
Total 5	18	33	.353	84	73	10	0	0	416¹	457	33	180	228	14.0	4.63	81	.285	.361	0	—	0	-39	-41	-4	-4.6

● **TOM CLYDE**   Clyde, Thomas Knox   b: 8/17/23, Wachapreague, Va.   BR/TR, 6'3", 195 lbs.   Deb: 5/31/43

YEAR TM/L	W	L	PCT	G	GS	CG	SH	SV	IP	H	HR	BB	SO	RAT	ERA	ERA+	OAV	OOB	BH	AVG	PB	PR	/A	PD	TPI
1943 Phi-A	0	0	—	4	0	0	0	0	6	7	1	4	0	18.0	9.00	38	.304	.429	0	.000	-0	-4	-4	-0	-0.1

● **ANDY COAKLEY**   Coakley, Andrew James (a.k.a. Jack McAllister in 1902)   b: 11/20/1882, Providence, R.I.   d: 9/27/63, New York, N.Y.   BL/TR, 6', 165 lbs.   Deb: 9/17/02

YEAR TM/L	W	L	PCT	G	GS	CG	SH	SV	IP	H	HR	BB	SO	RAT	ERA	ERA+	OAV	OOB	BH	AVG	PB	PR	/A	PD	TPI
1902 Phi-A	2	1	.667	3	3	3	0	0	27	25	0	9	9	12.0	2.67	138	.245	.319	3	.375	1	3	3	0	0.5
1903 Phi-A	0	3	.000	6	3	2	0	0	37²	48	2	11	20	14.6	5.50	56	.310	.363	3	.200	-0	-11	-10	-0	-0.8
1904 Phi-A	4	3	.571	8	8	7	2	0	62	48	1	23	33	10.6	1.89	142	.215	.294	2	.087	-2	5	5	-0	0.3
1905 *Phi-A	18	8	.692	35	31	21	3	0	255	227	6	73	145	10.8	1.84	145	.240	.299	13	.138	-3	23	23	-1	1.9
1906 Phi-A	7	8	.467	22	16	10	0	0	149	144	6	44	59	11.5	3.14	87	.257	.314	7	.143	-2	-7	-7	-3	-1.1
1907 Cin-N	17	16	.515	37	30	21	1	1	265¹	269	1	79	89	12.0	2.34	111	.274	.332	6	.071	-6	4	8	-3	0.0
1908 Cin-N	8	18	.308	32	28	20	4	0	242¹	219	3	64	61	10.7	1.86	124	.249	.303	7	.092	-4	14	12	-4	0.4
Chi-N	2	0	1.000	4	3	2	1	0	20¹	14	0	6	7	8.9	0.89	266	.192	.253	0	.000	-1	3	3	-0	0.2
Yr	10	18	.357	36	31	22	5	2	262²	233	3	70	68	10.4	1.78	130	.244	.295	7	.085	-5	17	15	-5	0.6
1909 Chi-N	0	1	.000	1	1	0	0	0	2	7	0	3	1	45.0	18.00	14	.583	.667	0	—	0	-3	-3	-0	-1.0
1911 NY-A	0	1	.000	2	1	1	0	0	11²	20	1	4	4	17.0	5.40	67	.377	.400	1	.250	-0	-3	-2	0	-0.2
Total 9	58	59	.496	150	124	87	11	3	1072¹	1021	9	314	428	11.4	2.35	111	.256	.315	42	.117	-16	28	32	-12	0.2

● **JIM COATES**   Coates, James Alton   b: 8/4/32, Farnham, Va.   BR/TR, 6'4", 192 lbs.   Deb: 9/21/56

YEAR TM/L	W	L	PCT	G	GS	CG	SH	SV	IP	H	HR	BB	SO	RAT	ERA	ERA+	OAV	OOB	BH	AVG	PB	PR	/A	PD	TPI
1956 NY-A	0	0	—	2	0	0	0	0	2	1	0	4	0	27.0	13.50	29	.167	.545	0	—	0	-2	-2	0	0.0
1959 NY-A	6	1	.857	37	4	2	0	0	100¹	89	10	36	64	11.5	2.87	127	.234	.305	2	.095	-1	11	9	0	0.4
1960 *NY-A★	13	3	.813	35	18	6	2	1	149	139	16	66	73	12.5	4.28	84	.248	.330	12	.250	-4	-7	-12	-2	-1.0
1961 *NY-A	11	5	.688	43	11	4	1	5	141¹	128	15	53	80	12.0	3.44	108	.243	.321	1	.029	-3	9	4	0	0.1
1962 *NY-A	7	6	.538	50	6	0	0	6	117²	119	9	50	67	13.3	4.44	84	.263	.343	4	.125	-1	-6	-9	-2	-1.3
1963 Was-A	2	4	.333	20	2	0	0	0	44¹	51	4	21	31	15.2	5.28	70	.297	.383	0	.000	-0	-8	-8	0	-1.0
Cin-N	0	0	—	9	0	0	0	0	16¹	21	2	7	11	15.4	5.51	61	.313	.378	0	—	-0	-4	-4	0	-0.1
1965 Cal-A	2	0	1.000	17	0	0	0	0	28	23	1	16	15	12.5	3.54	96	.228	.333	0	.000	-0	-0	-0	-0	-0.1
1966 Cal-A	1	1	.500	9	4	1	0	0	31²	32	3	10	16	11.9	3.98	84	.258	.313	1	.091	-0	-2	-2	-0	-0.2
1967 Cal-A	1	2	.333	25	1	0	0	0	52¹	47	5	23	39	12.7	4.30	73	.244	.336	1	.333	1	-6	-7	0	-0.3
Total 9	43	22	.662	247	46	13	4	15	683¹	650	65	286	396	12.7	4.00	90	.252	.332	21	.131	-3	-15	-30	-4	-3.4

● **GEORGE COBB**   Cobb, George Woodworth   b: 9/25/1865, Independence, Ia.   d: 8/19/26, Pomona, Cal.   6', 168 lbs.   Deb: 4/15/1892

YEAR TM/L	W	L	PCT	G	GS	CG	SH	SV	IP	H	HR	BB	SO	RAT	ERA	ERA+	OAV	OOB	BH	AVG	PB	PR	/A	PD	TPI
1892 Bal-N	10	37	.213	53	47	42	0	0	394¹	495	21	140	159	14.9	4.86	71	.295	.356	36	.209	5	-69	-63	2	-5.3

● **HERB COBB**   Cobb, Herbert Edward   b: 8/6/04, Pinetops, N.C.   d: 1/8/80, Tarboro, N.C.   BR/TR, 5'11", 150 lbs.   Deb: 4/21/29

YEAR TM/L	W	L	PCT	G	GS	CG	SH	SV	IP	H	HR	BB	SO	RAT	ERA	ERA+	OAV	OOB	BH	AVG	PB	PR	/A	PD	TPI
1929 StL-A	0	0	—	1	0	0	0	0	1	3	1	0	0	36.0	36.00	12	.600	.667	0	—	0	-4	-4	-0	0.0

● **TY COBB**   Cobb, Tyrus Raymond "The Georgia Peach"   b: 12/18/1886, Narrows, Ga.   d: 7/17/61, Atlanta, Ga.   BL/TR, 6'1", 175 lbs.   Deb: 8/30/05   MH♦

YEAR TM/L	W	L	PCT	G	GS	CG	SH	SV	IP	H	HR	BB	SO	RAT	ERA	ERA+	OAV	OOB	BH	AVG	PB	PR	/A	PD	TPI
1918 Det-A	0	0	—	2	0	0	0	1	4	6	0	2	0	18.0	4.50	59	.400	.471	161	.382	1	-1	-1	-0	0.0
1925 Det-A	0	0	—	1	0	0	0	0	1	0	0	0	0	0.0	0.00	—	.000	.000	157	.378	1	0	0	-0	0.1
Total 2	0	0	—	3	0	0	0	1	5	6	0	2	0	14.4	3.60	83	.333	.400	4189	.366	2	-0	-0	-0	0.1

● **JAIME COCANOWER**   Cocanower, James Stanley   b: 2/14/57, San Juan, P.R.   BR/TR, 6'4", 200 lbs.   Deb: 9/7/83

YEAR TM/L	W	L	PCT	G	GS	CG	SH	SV	IP	H	HR	BB	SO	RAT	ERA	ERA+	OAV	OOB	BH	AVG	PB	PR	/A	PD	TPI
1983 Mil-A	2	0	1.000	5	3	1	0	0	30	21	1	12	8	10.2	1.80	208	.200	.288	0	—	0	8	6	0	0.7
1984 Mil-A	8	16	.333	33	27	1	0	0	174²	188	13	78	65	14.2	4.02	96	.279	.362	0	—	0	-1	-3	1	-0.2
1985 Mil-A	6	8	.429	24	15	3	1	0	116¹	122	6	73	44	15.7	4.33	96	.274	.386	0	—	0	-2	-2	0	-0.2
1986 Mil-A	0	1	.000	17	2	0	0	0	44²	40	1	38	22	16.1	4.43	98	.248	.398	0	—	0	-1	-1	1	0.1
Total 4	16	25	.390	79	47	5	1	0	365²	371	21	201	139	14.6	3.99	100	.268	.369	0	—	0	3	0	3	0.4

● **GOAT COCHRAN**   Cochran, Alvah Jackson "Al" or "Goat"   b: 1/31/1891, Concord, Ga.   d: 5/23/47, Atlanta, Ga.   BR/TR, 5'10", 175 lbs.   Deb: 8/25/15

YEAR TM/L	W	L	PCT	G	GS	CG	SH	SV	IP	H	HR	BB	SO	RAT	ERA	ERA+	OAV	OOB	BH	AVG	PB	PR	/A	PD	TPI
1915 Cin-N	0	0	—	1	0	0	0	0	2	5	0	1	0	22.5	9.00	32	.455	.455	0	—	0	-1	-1	-0	0.0

● **GENE COCREHAM**   Cocreham, Eugene   b: 11/14/1884, Luling, Tex.   d: 12/27/45, Luling, Tex.   BR/TR, 6'3.5", 192 lbs.   Deb: 9/25/13

YEAR TM/L	W	L	PCT	G	GS	CG	SH	SV	IP	H	HR	BB	SO	RAT	ERA	ERA+	OAV	OOB	BH	AVG	PB	PR	/A	PD	TPI
1913 Bos-N	0	1	.000	1	1	0	0	0	8¹	13	0	4	3	19.4	7.56	43	.371	.450	0	.000	-1	-4	-4	0	-0.4
1914 Bos-N	3	4	.429	15	3	1	0	0	44²	48	2	27	15	15.1	4.84	57	.296	.397	1	.100	-0	-10	-10	-1	-1.7
1915 Bos-N	0	0	—	1	0	0	0	0	1²	3	0	0	0	16.2	5.40	48	.429	.429	0	—	-0	-1	-0	0	0.0
Total 3	3	5	.375	17	4	1	0	0	54²	64	2	31	18	15.8	5.27	54	.314	.407	1	.071	-1	-15	-15	-2	-2.1

● **CHRIS CODIROLI**   Codiroli, Christopher Allen   b: 3/26/58, Oxnard, Cal.   BR/TR, 6'1", 160 lbs.   Deb: 9/11/82

YEAR TM/L	W	L	PCT	G	GS	CG	SH	SV	IP	H	HR	BB	SO	RAT	ERA	ERA+	OAV	OOB	BH	AVG	PB	PR	/A	PD	TPI
1982 Oak-A	1	2	.333	3	3	0	0	0	16²	16	1	4	5	10.8	4.32	90	.246	.290	0	—	0	-0	-1	0	0.0
1983 Oak-A	12	12	.500	37	31	7	2	1	205²	208	17	72	85	12.6	4.46	86	.264	.331	0	—	0	-9	-14	-2	-1.5
1984 Oak-A	6	6	.600	28	14	1	0	0	89¹	111	16	34	44	14.9	5.84	64	.304	.368	0	—	0	-18	-21	-0	-2.0
1985 Oak-A	14	14	.500	37	37	4	0	0	226	228	23	78	111	12.3	4.46	86	.259	.321	0	—	0	-8	-15	-1	-1.7
1986 Oak-A	5	8	.385	16	16	1	0	0	91²	91	15	38	46	12.9	4.03	96	.250	.324	0	—	0	2	-2	-1	-0.1
1987 Oak-A	2	0	—	3	3	0	0	0	11¹	12	1	4	10	16.7	8.74	47	.273	.396	0	—	0	-5	-6	-0	-0.7
1988 Cle-A	0	0	—	14	2	0	0	0	19¹	32	2	10	12	20.9	9.31	44	.372	.455	0	—	0	-11	-11	-0	-2.2
1990 KC-A	0	0	—	10	1	0	0	0	13¹	13	1	16	9	29.6	9.58	40	.325	.557	0	—	0	-7	-7	-0	-0.6
Total 8	38	47	.447	144	108	13	2	3	670¹	711	76	261	312	13.4	4.87	79	.270	.341	0	—	0	-58	-76	-2	-8.8

● **SLICK COFFMAN**   Coffman, George David   b: 12/11/10, Veto, Ala.   BR/TR, 6', 155 lbs.   Deb: 5/21/37   F

YEAR TM/L	W	L	PCT	G	GS	CG	SH	SV	IP	H	HR	BB	SO	RAT	ERA	ERA+	OAV	OOB	BH	AVG	PB	PR	/A	PD	TPI
1937 Det-A	7	5	.583	28	5	1	0	0	101	121	8	39	22	14.5	4.37	107	.295	.361	5	.172	3	3	3	-1	0.3
1938 Det-A	4	4	.500	39	6	1	0	0	95²	120	6	48	31	15.8	6.02	88	.310	.386	4	.167	-0	-13	-11	-0	-0.9
1939 Det-A	2	1	.667	23	1	0	0	0	42¹	51	4	22	10	15.7	6.38	77	.295	.378	0	.000	-0	-8	-7	0	-0.5
1940 StL-A	2	2	.500	31	4	1	0	0	74²	108	5	23	26	15.8	6.27	73	.334	.379	3	.200	-0	-16	-14	1	-0.6
Total 4	15	12	.556	121	16	3	0	3	313²	400	23	132	89	15.4	5.60	85	.309	.375	12	.164	-0	-34	-28	-1	-1.7

● **KEVIN COFFMAN**   Coffman, Kevin Reese   b: 1/19/65, Austin, Tex.   BR/TR, 6'2", 175 lbs.   Deb: 9/5/87

YEAR TM/L	W	L	PCT	G	GS	CG	SH	SV	IP	H	HR	BB	SO	RAT	ERA	ERA+	OAV	OOB	BH	AVG	PB	PR	/A	PD	TPI
1987 Atl-N	2	3	.400	5	5	0	0	0	25¹	31	2	22	14	19.9	4.62	94	.313	.452	1	.100	-0	-2	-1	1	-0.1
1988 Atl-N	2	6	.250	18	11	0	0	0	67	62	3	54	24	16.1	5.78	64	.251	.393	5	.227	2	-17	-16	1	-1.5
1990 Chi-N	0	2	.000	8	2	0	0	0	18¹	26	0	19	9	22.1	11.29	36	.333	.464	1	.200	-0	-15	-15	0	-1.3
Total 3	4	11	.267	31	18	0	0	0	110²	119	5	95	47	18.0	6.42	61	.281	.420	7	.189	1	-34	-31	2	-2.9

● **DICK COFFMAN**   Coffman, Samuel Richard   b: 12/18/06, Veto, Ala.   d: 3/24/72, Athens, Ala.   BR/TR, 6'2", 195 lbs.   Deb: 4/28/27   F

YEAR TM/L	W	L	PCT	G	GS	CG	SH	SV	IP	H	HR	BB	SO	RAT	ERA	ERA+	OAV	OOB	BH	AVG	PB	PR	/A	PD	TPI
1927 Was-A	0	1	.000	5	2	0	0	0	16	20	0	2	5	13.5	3.38	120	.313	.353	1	.333	0	1	1	0	0.1

YEAR	TM/L	W	L	PCT	G	GS	CG	SH	SV	IP	H	HR	BB	SO	RAT	ERA	ERA+	OAV	OOB	BH	AVG	PB	PR	/A	PD	TPI
1928	StL-A	4	5	.444	29	7	3	0	1	85²	122	7	37	25	16.8	6.09	69	.359	.423	1	.043	-3	-20	-18	0	-1.9
1929	StL-A	1	1	.500	27	3	1	1	1	52²	61	3	14	11	13.3	5.98	74	.295	.348	0	—	-10	-9	0	-0.4
1930	StL-A	8	18	.308	38	30	12	1	1	196	250	14	69	54	14.9	5.14	95	.311	.369	9	.136	-5	-11	-6	-1	-1.1
1931	StL-A	9	13	.409	32	17	11	2	1	169¹	159	10	51	39	11.3	3.88	119	.241	.298	4	.078	-5	9	14	-2	1.0
1932	StL-A	5	3	.625	9	6	3	0	0	61	66	3	21	14	13.1	3.10	157	.277	.341	2	.045	-2	9	12	-1	1.1
	Was-A	1	6	.143	22	9	2	1	0	76¹	92	2	31	17	14.6	4.83	89	.307	.373	2	.091	-1	-3	-4	-1	-0.5
	Yr	6	9	.400	31	15	5	1	0	137¹	158	5	52	31	13.8	4.06	112	.293	.356	3	.068	-3	6	7	-2	0.6
1933	StL-A	3	7	.300	21	13	3	1	1	81	114	9	39	19	17.2	5.89	79	.329	.399	1	.037	-3	-14	-11	0	-1.4
1934	StL-A	9	10	.474	40	21	6	1	3	173	212	11	59	55	14.2	4.53	110	.303	.358	11	.216	-1	-1	9	0	0.8
1935	StL-A	5	11	.313	41	18	5	0	2	143²	206	14	46	34	15.9	6.14	78	.335	.383	6	.146	-1	-27	-21	-1	-2.2
1936	*NY-N	7	5	.583	42	2	0	0	7	101²	119	7	23	26	12.7	3.90	100	.296	.354	4	.200	-0	1	0	1	0.1
1937	*NY-N	8	3	.727	42	1	0	0	3	80	93	4	31	30	14.4	3.04	128	.289	.359	7	.368	2	**8**	8	0	1.3
1938	NY-N	8	4	.667	**51**	3	1	1	**12**	111¹	116	3	21	21	11.3	3.48	108	.268	.306	2	.071	-3	4	4	-2	0.0
1939	NY-N	1	2	.333	28	0	0	0	3	38	50	1	6	9	14.0	3.08	128	.316	.353	0	.000	-1	4	4	0	0.2
1940	Bos-N	1	5	.167	31	0	0	0	3	48¹	63	4	6	11	14.2	5.40	69	.323	.365	1	.083	-1	-8	-9	-1	-1.2
1945	Phi-N	2	1	.667	14	0	0	0	0	26¹	39	0	2	4	14.0	5.13	75	.351	.363	1	.250	-1	-4	-4	1	-0.2
Total	15	72	95	.431	472	132	47	8	38	1460¹	1782	92	463	372	14.1	4.65	96	.302	.357	51	.127	-22	-61	-33	-2	-4.3

● **DICK COGAN** Cogan, Richard Henry b: 12/5/1871, Paterson, N.J. d: 5/2/48, Paterson, N.J. BR/TR, 5'7", 150 lbs. Deb: 5/10/1897

YEAR	TM/L	W	L	PCT	G	GS	CG	SH	SV	IP	H	HR	BB	SO	RAT	ERA	ERA+	OAV	OOB	BH	AVG	PB	PR	/A	PD	TPI
1897	Bal-N	0	0	—	1	0	0	0	0	2	4	0	2	0	31.5	13.50	31	.400	.538	0	.000	-0	-2	-2	-0	-0.2
1899	Chi-N	2	3	.400	5	5	5	0	0	44	54	1	24	9	16.8	4.30	87	.302	.396	5	.200	1	-2	-3	-1	-0.2
1900	NY-N	0	0	—	2	0	0	0	0	8	10	0	6	1	18.0	6.75	54	.303	.410	1	.125	-0	-3	-3	-0	0.0
Total	3	2	3	.400	8	5	5	0	0	54	68	1	32	10	17.5	5.00	75	.306	.405	6	.176	0	-7	-8	-1	0.0

● **HY COHEN** Cohen, Hyman b: 1/29/31, Brooklyn, N.Y. BR/TR, 6'5", 220 lbs. Deb: 4/17/55

YEAR	TM/L	W	L	PCT	G	GS	CG	SH	SV	IP	H	HR	BB	SO	RAT	ERA	ERA+	OAV	OOB	BH	AVG	PB	PR	/A	PD	TPI
1955	Chi-N	0	0	—	7	1	0	0	0	17	28	2	10	4	20.6	7.94	51	.378	.459	0	.000	-0	-7	-7	-0	-0.1

● **SYD COHEN** Cohen, Sydney Harry b: 5/7/06, Baltimore, Md. d: 4/9/88, ElPaso, Tex. BB/TL, 5'11", 180 lbs. Deb: 9/18/34 F

YEAR	TM/L	W	L	PCT	G	GS	CG	SH	SV	IP	H	HR	BB	SO	RAT	ERA	ERA+	OAV	OOB	BH	AVG	PB	PR	/A	PD	TPI
1934	Was-A	1	1	.500	3	2	1	0	0	18	25	2	6	6	15.5	7.50	58	.333	.383	3	.273	0	-6	-6	1	-0.4
1936	Was-A	0	2	.000	19	1	0	0	1	36	44	4	14	21	15.3	5.25	91	.303	.377	0	.000	-1	-1	-2	2	0.0
1937	Was-A	2	4	.333	33	0	1	0	4	55	64	1	17	22	13.3	3.11	142	.299	.351	2	.143	-1	9	8	2	0.9
Total	3	3	7	.300	55	3	2	0	5	109	133	7	37	49	14.3	4.54	100	.306	.365	5	.152	-2	2	-0	5	0.5

● **ROCKY COLAVITO** Colavito, Rocco Domenico b: 8/10/33, New York, N.Y. BR/TR, 6'3", 190 lbs. Deb: 9/10/55 C♦

YEAR	TM/L	W	L	PCT	G	GS	CG	SH	SV	IP	H	HR	BB	SO	RAT	ERA	ERA+	OAV	OOB	BH	AVG	PB	PR	/A	PD	TPI
1958	Cle-A	0	0	—	1	0	0	0	0	3	0	0	3	1	9.0	0.00	—	.000	.273	148	.303	1	1	1	0	0.0
1968	NY-A	1	0	1.000	1	0	0	0	0	2²	1	0	2	1	10.1	0.00	—	.111	.273	20	.220	0	1	1	-0	0.4
Total	2	1	0	1.000	2	0	0	0	0	5²	1	0	5	2	9.5	0.00	—	.059	.273	1730	.266	1	2	2	0	0.4

● **VINCE COLBERT** Colbert, Vincent Norman b: 12/20/45, Washington, D.C. BR/TR, 6'4", 200 lbs. Deb: 5/19/70

YEAR	TM/L	W	L	PCT	G	GS	CG	SH	SV	IP	H	HR	BB	SO	RAT	ERA	ERA+	OAV	OOB	BH	AVG	PB	PR	/A	PD	TPI
1970	Cle-A	1	1	.500	23	0	0	0	2	31	37	4	16	17	15.7	7.26	55	.298	.383	0	.000	-0	-12	-11	0	-0.8
1971	Cle-A	7	6	.538	50	10	2	0	2	142²	140	11	71	74	13.7	3.97	96	.265	.358	4	.138	-1	-8	-2	0	-0.2
1972	Cle-A	1	7	.125	22	11	1	1	0	74²	74	8	38	36	14.3	4.58	70	.267	.370	4	.200	1	-13	-11	0	-1.1
Total	3	9	14	.391	95	21	3	1	4	248¹	251	23	125	127	14.1	4.57	80	.270	.365	8	.157	0	-33	-25	1	-2.1

● **JIM COLBORN** Colborn, James William b: 5/22/46, Santa Paula, Cal. BR/TR, 6', 191 lbs. Deb: 7/13/69

YEAR	TM/L	W	L	PCT	G	GS	CG	SH	SV	IP	H	HR	BB	SO	RAT	ERA	ERA+	OAV	OOB	BH	AVG	PB	PR	/A	PD	TPI
1969	Chi-N	1	0	1.000	6	2	0	0	0	14²	15	2	9	4	15.3	3.07	131	.283	.397	0	.000	-0	1	2	0	0.1
1970	Chi-N	3	1	.750	34	5	0	0	4	72²	88	3	23	50	13.9	3.59	125	.298	.351	1	.067	-1	4	7	1	0.4
1971	Chi-N	0	1	.000	14	0	0	0	0	10¹	18	1	3	2	18.3	6.97	56	.383	.420	0	—	-0	-4	-3	0	-0.3
1972	Mil-A	7	7	.500	39	12	4	1	0	147²	135	14	43	97	11.0	3.11	97	.245	.302	3	.081	-1	-1	-1	-1	-0.4
1973	Mil-A☆	20	12	.625	43	36	22	4	1	314¹	297	21	87	135	11.1	3.18	118	.251	.304	0	—	0	22	20	2	2.2
1974	Mil-A	10	13	.435	33	31	10	1	0	224	230	27	60	83	11.9	4.06	89	.268	.320	0	—	0	-11	-11	0	-1.0
1975	Mil-A	11	13	.458	36	29	8	1	0	206¹	215	18	65	79	12.4	4.27	90	.270	.329	0	—	0	-11	-10	1	-1.0
1976	Mil-A	9	15	.375	32	32	7	0	0	225²	232	20	54	101	11.5	3.71	94	.268	.312	0	—	0	-5	-5	0	-0.6
1977	KC-A	18	14	.563	36	35	6	1	0	239	233	22	81	103	12.3	3.62	112	.255	.324	0	—	0	12	11	1	1.4
1978	KC-A	1	2	.333	8	3	0	0	0	28¹	31	4	12	8	14.3	4.76	80	.282	.363	0	—	-0	-3	-3	1	-0.3
	Sea-A	3	10	.231	20	19	3	0	0	114¹	125	21	38	26	13.3	5.35	71	.279	.343	0	—	0	-20	-20	3	-1.7
	Yr	4	12	.250	28	22	3	0	0	142²	156	25	50	34	13.4	5.24	73	.279	.344	0	—	0	-23	-23	3	-2.0
Total	10	83	88	.485	301	204	60	8	7	1597¹	1619	153	475	688	12.0	3.80	98	.265	.322	4	.073	-3	-17	-14	7	-1.2

● **TOM COLCOLOUGH** Colcolough, Thomas Bernard b: 10/8/1870, Charleston, S.C. d: 12/10/19, Charleston, S.C. BR/TR, 5'10.5", 180 lbs. Deb: 8/1/1893

YEAR	TM/L	W	L	PCT	G	GS	CG	SH	SV	IP	H	HR	BB	SO	RAT	ERA	ERA+	OAV	OOB	BH	AVG	PB	PR	/A	PD	TPI
1893	Pit-N	1	0	1.000	8	3	1	0	**2**	43²	45	1	32	7	15.9	4.12	110	.259	.374	2	.143	-1	3	2	-1	0.0
1894	Pit-N	8	5	.615	22	14	11	0	0	148²	207	5	70	29	17.1	7.08	74	.326	.397	14	.200	-3	-29	-30	0	-1.9
1895	Pit-N	1	1	.500	6	5	2	0	0	35¹	38	1	21	15	16.3	5.60	81	.271	.386	5	.333	3	-3	-4	-1	0.0
1899	NY-N	4	5	.444	11	8	7	0	0	81²	85	1	41	14	14.2	3.97	95	.268	.357	10	.270	1	-1	-2	1	0.0
Total	4	14	11	.560	47	30	21	0	2	309¹	375	8	164	65	16.1	5.67	82	.296	.383	31	.228	1	-31	-35	0	-1.9

● **BERT COLE** Cole, Albert George b: 7/1/1896, San Francisco, Cal. d: 5/30/75, San Mateo, Cal. BL/TL, 6'1", 180 lbs. Deb: 4/19/21

YEAR	TM/L	W	L	PCT	G	GS	CG	SH	SV	IP	H	HR	BB	SO	RAT	ERA	ERA+	OAV	OOB	BH	AVG	PB	PR	/A	PD	TPI
1921	Det-A	7	4	.636	20	11	7	1	1	109²	134	3	36	22	14.3	4.27	100	.305	.363	13	.283	3	0	0	-1	0.2
1922	Det-A	1	6	.143	23	5	2	1	0	79¹	105	4	39	21	16.4	4.88	80	.313	.387	4	.160	-1	-7	-9	0	-0.7
1923	Det-A	13	5	.722	52	13	6	1	5	163	183	9	61	32	13.7	4.14	93	.284	.351	14	.255	2	-3	-5	-1	-0.4
1924	Det-A	3	9	.250	28	12	2	1	0	109¹	135	4	35	16	14.4	4.69	88	.314	.371	10	.270	1	-6	-7	1	-0.5
1925	Det-A	2	3	.400	14	2	1	0	0	33²	44	2	15	7	16.0	5.88	73	.336	.408	3	.273	1	-6	-6	1	-0.7
	Cle-A	1	1	.500	13	2	0	0	2	44	55	1	25	9	16.6	6.14	72	.322	.411	2	.154	-0	-8	-8	-0	-0.4
	Yr	3	4	.429	27	4	1	0	2	77²	99	3	40	16	16.2	6.03	73	.327	.407	5	.208	1	-14	-14	1	-1.1
1927	Chi-A	1	4	.200	27	2	0	0	0	66²	79	3	19	12	13.6	4.72	86	.309	.363	3	.167	-1	-4	-5	2	-0.3
Total	6	28	32	.467	177	47	18	4	10	605²	735	26	230	119	14.6	4.67	89	.305	.370	49	.239	4	-34	-40	2	-2.8

● **DAVE COLE** Cole, David Bruce b: 8/29/30, Williamsport, Md. BR/TR, 6'2", 175 lbs. Deb: 9/9/50

YEAR	TM/L	W	L	PCT	G	GS	CG	SH	SV	IP	H	HR	BB	SO	RAT	ERA	ERA+	OAV	OOB	BH	AVG	PB	PR	/A	PD	TPI
1950	Bos-N	0	1	.000	4	0	0	0	0	8	7	0	3	8	12.4	1.13	342	.259	.355	0	.000	-0	3	2	0	0.2
1951	Bos-N	2	4	.333	23	7	1	0	0	67²	64	3	64	33	17.3	4.26	86	.254	.409	6	.353	4	-2	-4	0	0.0
1952	Bos-N	1	1	.500	22	3	0	0	0	44²	38	2	42	22	16.7	4.03	90	.241	.409	0	—	-1	-2	-2	-0	-0.2
1953	Mil-N	0	1	.000	10	0	0	0	0	14²	17	1	14	13	19.0	8.59	46	.279	.413	1	.500	-0	-7	-8	0	-0.2
1954	Chi-N	3	8	.273	18	14	2	1	0	84	74	7	62	37	14.7	5.36	78	.241	.370	6	.214	-1	-12	-11	0	-1.1
1955	Phi-N	0	3	.000	7	3	0	0	0	18¹	21	3	14	6	17.2	6.38	62	.304	.422	1	.200	-1	-5	-5	0	-0.7
Total	6	6	18	.250	84	27	3	1	0	237¹	221	16	199	119	16.2	4.93	79	.253	.395	14	.230	1	-25	-27	1	-2.1

● **ED COLE** Cole, Edward William (b: Edward William Kisleauskas) b: 3/22/09, Wilkes-Barre, Pa. BR/TR, 5'11", 170 lbs. Deb: 4/22/38

YEAR	TM/L	W	L	PCT	G	GS	CG	SH	SV	IP	H	HR	BB	SO	RAT	ERA	ERA+	OAV	OOB	BH	AVG	PB	PR	/A	PD	TPI
1938	StL-A	1	5	.167	36	1	0	0	3	88²	116	8	48	26	17.2	5.18	96	.313	.399	3	.143	-1	-4	-2	-1	-0.3
1939	StL-A	0	2	.000	6	0	0	0	0	6¹	8	1	6	5	19.9	7.11	68	.308	.438	0	.000	-0	-2	-2	0	-0.4
Total	2	1	7	.125	42	1	0	0	3	95	124	9	54	31	17.3	5.31	94	.313	.401	3	.136	-1	-6	-4	-1	-0.7

● **KING COLE** Cole, Leonard Leslie b: 4/15/1886, Toledo, Iowa d: 1/6/16, Bay City, Mich. BR/TR, 6'1", 170 lbs. Deb: 10/6/09

YEAR	TM/L	W	L	PCT	G	GS	CG	SH	SV	IP	H	HR	BB	SO	RAT	ERA	ERA+	OAV	OOB	BH	AVG	PB	PR	/A	PD	TPI
1909	Chi-N	1	0	1.000	1	1	1	1	0	9	6	0	3	1	9.0	0.00	—	.194	.265	3	.750	0	1	2	0	0.7
1910	*Chi-N	20	4	**.833**	33	29	21	4	1	239²	174	4	130	114	11.8	1.80	**160**	**.211**	.325	21	.231	2	33	29	-1	3.0
1911	Chi-N	18	7	.720	32	27	13	2	0	221¹	188	3	99	101	12.0	3.13	106	.236	.328	12	.152	-2	7	4	-2	0.0
1912	Chi-N	2	2	.333	12	3	0	0	0	19	36	2	8	10	21.8	10.89	31	.409	.469	2	.400	1	-16	-16	0	-1.7
	Pit-N	2	2	.500	12	5	2	0	0	49	61	5	18	11	14.9	6.43	51	.330	.395	4	.133	-1	-16	-17	-1	-1.3
	Yr	3	4	.429	24	8	2	0	0	68	97	7	26	21	16.5	7.68	43	.353	.413	6	.194	0	-32	-33	-1	-3.2
1914	NY-A	11	9	.550	33	15	8	2	0	141²	151	3	51	43	12.9	3.30	84	.288	.352	2	.048	-3	-9	-9	-0	-0.3
1915	NY-A	3	3	.500	10	6	2	0	0	51	41	3	22	19	11.6	3.18	92	.224	.317	1	.077	-0	-1	-1	-0	-0.3
Total	6	56	27	.675	129	86	47	9	2	730²	657	13	331	298	12.5	3.12	97	.250	.340	43	.173	-2	-0	-7	-6	-1.7

YEAR TM/L	W	L	PCT	G	GS	CG	SH	SV	IP	H	HR	BB	SO	RAT	ERA	ERA+	OAV	OOB	BH	AVG	PB	PR	/A	PD	TPI

● **VICTOR COLE**   Cole, Victor Alexander   b: 1/23/68, Leningrad, Russia   BB/TR, 5'10", 160 lbs.   Deb: 6/6/92

YEAR TM/L	W	L	PCT	G	GS	CG	SH	SV	IP	H	HR	BB	SO	RAT	ERA	ERA+	OAV	OOB	BH	AVG	PB	PR	/A	PD	TPI
1992 Pit-N	0	2	.000	8	4	0	0	0	23	23	1	14	12	14.5	5.48	63	.261	.363	0	.000	-0	-5	-5	0	-0.5

● **JOHN COLEMAN**   Coleman, John   b: Bristol, Pa.   TR ,   Deb: 6/23/1890

YEAR TM/L	W	L	PCT	G	GS	CG	SH	SV	IP	H	HR	BB	SO	RAT	ERA	ERA+	OAV	OOB	BH	AVG	PB	PR	/A	PD	TPI
1890 Phi-N	0	1	.000	1	1	0	0	0	1²	4	0	3	2	37.8	21.60	17	.444	.583	0	—	0	-3	-3	-0	-1.0

● **JOHN COLEMAN**   Coleman, John   b: 1874, Lees Summit, Mo.   TL , 5'10", 174 lbs.   Deb: 9/25/1895

YEAR TM/L	W	L	PCT	G	GS	CG	SH	SV	IP	H	HR	BB	SO	RAT	ERA	ERA+	OAV	OOB	BH	AVG	PB	PR	/A	PD	TPI
1895 StL-N	0	1	.000	1	1	1	0	0	8	12	1	8	5	23.6	13.50	36	.343	.477	1	.200	-0	-8	-8	0	-0.6

● **JOHN COLEMAN**   Coleman, John Francis   b: 3/6/1863, Saratoga Springs, N.Y.   d: 5/31/22, Detroit, Mich.   BL/TR, 5'9.5", 170 lbs.   Deb: 5/1/1883 ◆

YEAR TM/L	W	L	PCT	G	GS	CG	SH	SV	IP	H	HR	BB	SO	RAT	ERA	ERA+	OAV	OOB	BH	AVG	PB	PR	/A	PD	TPI
1883 Phi-N	12	48	.200	65	61	59	3	0	538¹	772	17	48	159	13.7	4.87	63	.309	.322	83	.234	4	-103	-106	1	-8.1
1884 Phi-N	5	15	.250	21	19	14	1	0	154¹	216	9	22	37	13.9	4.90	61	.308	.329	42	.246	2	-33	-33	1	-2.9
Phi-a	0	2	.000	3	2	2	0	0	21	28	0	2	5	14.6	3.43	99	.304	.347	22	.206	0	-0	-0	0	0.0
1885 Phi-a	2	2	.500	8	3	3	0	0	60¹	82	0	5	12	13.0	3.43	100	.366	.380	119	.299	2	-1	0	-0	0.2
1886 Phi-a	1	1	.500	3	1	1	0	0	20²	18	1	5	2	10.5	2.61	134	.225	.279	121	.246	0	2	2	-0	0.2
1889 Phi-a	3	2	.600	5	5	4	0	0	34	38	2	14	6	14.0	2.91	130	.273	.344	1	.053	-2	4	3	1	0.2
1890 Pit-N	0	2	.000	2	2	1	0	0	14	28	1	6	3	21.9	9.64	34	.406	.453	2	.182	0	-9	-10	-0	-0.9
Total 6	23	72	.242	107	93	84	4	0	842²	1182	30	102	224	13.8	4.68	67	.311	.330	645	.257	7	-142	-144	3	-11.3

● **JOE COLEMAN**   Coleman, Joseph Howard   b: 2/3/47, Boston, Mass.   BR/TR, 6'3", 195 lbs.   Deb: 9/28/65   FC

YEAR TM/L	W	L	PCT	G	GS	CG	SH	SV	IP	H	HR	BB	SO	RAT	ERA	ERA+	OAV	OOB	BH	AVG	PB	PR	/A	PD	TPI
1965 Was-A	2	0	1.000	2	2	2	0	0	18	9	0	8	7	8.5	1.50	232	.153	.254	0	.000	-1	4	4	1	0.5
1966 Was-A	1	0	1.000	1	1	1	0	0	9	6	0	2	4	8.0	2.00	173	.188	.235	0	.000	-0	1	1	0	0.2
1967 Was-A	8	9	.471	28	22	3	0	0	134	154	6	47	77	14.1	4.63	68	.291	.359	2	.056	-1	-21	-22	-2	-2.9
1968 Was-A	12	16	.429	33	33	12	2	0	223	212	19	51	139	11.1	3.27	89	.250	.302	9	.129	-1	-7	-9	-1	-1.3
1969 Was-A	12	13	.480	40	36	12	4	1	247²	222	26	100	182	11.9	3.27	106	.243	.322	9	.107	-2	10	5	1	0.3
1970 Was-A	8	12	.400	39	29	6	1	0	218²	190	25	89	152	11.6	3.58	99	.233	.311	8	.119	-2	3	-1	0	0.2
1971 Det-A	20	9	.690	39	38	16	3	0	286	241	17	96	236	10.8	3.15	114	.229	.298	9	.094	-3	10	14	-2	0.8
1972 *Det-A†	19	14	.576	40	39	9	3	0	280	216	23	110	222	10.8	2.80	112	.214	.297	9	.110	-0	8	11	-1	0.9
1973 Det-A	23	15	.605	40	40	13	2	0	288¹	283	32	93	202	12.0	3.53	116	.258	.322	0	—	0	9	18	-0	1.9
1974 Det-A	14	12	.538	41	41	11	2	0	285²	272	30	158	177	13.9	4.32	88	.254	.356	0	—	0	-22	-16	2	-1.3
1975 Det-A	10	18	.357	31	31	6	1	0	201	234	27	85	125	14.7	5.55	72	.291	.366	0	—	0	-40	-34	0	-4.1
1976 Det-A	2	5	.286	12	12	1	0	0	66²	80	1	34	38	16.1	4.86	76	.308	.398	0	—	0	-10	-9	2	-0.7
Chi-N	2	8	.200	39	4	0	0	4	79	72	9	35	66	12.4	4.10	94	.246	.330	2	.154	-0	-5	-2	-1	-0.3
1977 Oak-A	4	4	.500	43	12	2	0	2	127²	114	11	49	55	11.6	2.96	136	.241	.314	0	—	0	16	15	-0	0.9
1978 Oak-A	3	0	1.000	10	0	0	0	0	19²	12	1	5	4	7.8	1.37	265	.185	.243	0	—	0	5	5	0	0.8
Tor-A	2	0	1.000	31	0	0	0	0	60²	67	6	30	28	14.5	4.60	85	.286	.370	0	—	0	-6	-5	-1	-0.3
Yr	5	0	1.000	41	0	0	0	0	80¹	79	7	35	32	12.9	3.81	101	.263	.342	0	—	0	-0	-0	-1	0.5
1979 SF-N	0	0	—	5	0	0	0	0	3²	3	0	2	0	14.7	0.00	—	.231	.375	0	—	0	2	1	-0	0.2
Pit-N	0	0	—	10	0	0	0	0	20²	29	1	6	14	17.0	6.10	64	.326	.394	1	.200	0	-5	-5	-1	-0.3
Yr	0	0	—	15	0	0	0	0	24¹	32	1	8	14	16.3	5.18	74	.308	.379	1	.200	0	-4	-4	-1	-0.2
Total 15	142	135	.513	484	340	94	18	7	2569¹	2416	234	1003	1728	12.3	3.70	97	.250	.327	49	.106	-10	-48	-28	-2	-4.4

● **JOE COLEMAN**   Coleman, Joseph Patrick   b: 7/30/22, Medford, Mass.   BR/TR, 6'2.5", 200 lbs.   Deb: 9/19/42   F

YEAR TM/L	W	L	PCT	G	GS	CG	SH	SV	IP	H	HR	BB	SO	RAT	ERA	ERA+	OAV	OOB	BH	AVG	PB	PR	/A	PD	TPI
1942 Phi-A	0	1	.000	1	0	0	0	0	6	8	0	1	4	13.5	3.00	126	.308	.333	0	.000	-1	0	1	-0	0.0
1946 Phi-A	0	2	.000	4	2	0	0	0	13	19	1	8	8	18.7	5.54	64	.345	.429	2	.400	1	-3	-3	-0	-0.4
1947 Phi-A	6	12	.333	32	21	9	2	1	160¹	171	17	62	65	13.1	4.32	88	.275	.341	7	.146	-1	-11	-9	-2	-1.3
1948 Phi-A★	14	13	.519	33	29	13	3	0	215²	224	11	90	86	13.1	4.09	105	.269	.341	9	.122	-4	5	5	-1	0.4
1949 Phi-A	13	14	.481	33	30	18	1	1	240¹	249	12	127	109	14.2	3.86	107	.271	.361	14	.177	0	9	7	-5	0.3
1950 Phi-A	0	5	.000	15	6	2	0	0	54	74	9	50	12	20.7	8.50	54	.332	.454	1	.059	-1	-24	-24	-2	-1.9
1951 Phi-A	1	6	.143	28	9	1	0	0	96¹	117	12	59	34	16.7	5.98	72	.305	.402	7	.259	1	-20	-18	-1	-1.2
1953 Phi-A	3	4	.429	21	9	2	1	0	90	85	8	49	18	13.5	4.00	107	.254	.352	8	.286	1	-0	-3	-2	0.2
1954 Bal-A	13	17	.433	33	32	15	4	0	221¹	184	16	96	103	11.5	3.50	102	.232	.317	13	.176	2	6	2	1	0.7
1955 Bal-A	0	1	.000	6	2	0	0	0	11²	19	5	10	4	23.1	10.80	35	.373	.484	2	.667	1	-9	-9	-0	-0.6
Det-A	2	1	.667	17	0	0	0	3	25¹	22	1	14	5	13.1	3.20	120	.239	.346	3	.750	1	2	2	0	0.4
Yr	2	2	.500	23	2	0	0	3	37	41	6	24	9	16.1	5.59	69	.281	.386	5	.714	3	-7	-7	0	-0.2
Total 10	52	76	.406	223	140	60	11	6	1134	1172	92	566	444	13.9	4.38	92	.271	.357	66	.182	2	-44	-44	-12	-3.8

● **PERCY COLEMAN**   Coleman, Pierce D.   b: 10/15/1876, Mason, Ohio   d: 2/16/48, Van Nuys, Cal.   TR ,   Deb: 7/2/1897

YEAR TM/L	W	L	PCT	G	GS	CG	SH	SV	IP	H	HR	BB	SO	RAT	ERA	ERA+	OAV	OOB	BH	AVG	PB	PR	/A	PD	TPI
1897 StL-N	1	2	.333	12	4	2	0	0	57¹	99	0	32	10	21.7	8.16	54	.375	.455	6	.214	-1	-25	-24	1	-0.9
1898 Cin-N	0	1	.000	1	1	1	0	0	9	13	0	3	2	17.0	3.00	128	.333	.395	0	.000	-1	1	1	-0	0.0
Total 2	1	3	.250	13	5	3	0	0	66¹	112	0	35	12	21.0	7.46	58	.370	.448	6	.194	-1	-24	-23	1	-0.9

● **RIP COLEMAN**   Coleman, Walter Gary   b: 7/31/31, Troy, N.Y.   BL/TL, 6'2", 185 lbs.   Deb: 8/15/55

YEAR TM/L	W	L	PCT	G	GS	CG	SH	SV	IP	H	HR	BB	SO	RAT	ERA	ERA+	OAV	OOB	BH	AVG	PB	PR	/A	PD	TPI
1955 *NY-A	2	1	.667	10	6	0	0	1	29	40	2	16	15	17.7	5.28	71	.331	.413	2	.200	1	-4	-5	0	-0.4
1956 NY-A	3	5	.375	29	9	0	0	2	88¹	97	6	42	42	14.3	3.67	105	.285	.366	1	.042	-5	5	2	0	-0.1
1957 KC-A	0	7	.000	19	6	1	1	0	41	53	5	25	15	17.1	5.93	67	.325	.415	0	.000	-1	-10	-9	0	-1.4
1959 KC-A	2	10	.167	29	11	2	0	2	81	85	8	34	54	13.3	4.56	88	.273	.347	2	.080	-2	-6	-5	0	-0.9
Bal-A	0	0	—	3	0	0	0	0	4	4	0	2	4	13.5	0.00	—	.267	.353	0	—	0	2	2	1	0.1
Yr	2	10	.167	32	11	2	0	2	85	89	8	36	58	13.2	4.34	92	.271	.342	2	.080	-2	-5	-3	1	-0.8
1960 Bal-A	0	2	.000	5	1	0	0	0	4	8	0	5	0	31.5	11.25	34	.444	.583	0	.000	-0	-3	-3	0	-1.3
Total 5	7	25	.219	95	33	3	1	5	247¹	287	21	124	130	15.1	4.58	85	.296	.379	5	.072	-5	-17	-18	2	-4.0

● **ALLAN COLLAMORE**   Collamore, Allan Edward   b: 6/5/1887, Worcester, Mass.   d: 8/8/80, Battle Creek, Mich.   BR/TR, 6', 170 lbs.   Deb: 4/15/11

YEAR TM/L	W	L	PCT	G	GS	CG	SH	SV	IP	H	HR	BB	SO	RAT	ERA	ERA+	OAV	OOB	BH	AVG	PB	PR	/A	PD	TPI
1911 Phi-A	0	1	.000	2	0	0	0	0	2	6	0	3	1	49.5	36.00	9	.600	.733	0	—	0	-7	-7	-0	-1.9
1914 Cle-A	3	7	.300	27	8	3	0	0	105¹	100	3	49	32	13.2	3.25	89	.264	.357	3	.094	-2	-6	-4	-1	-0.7
1915 Cle-A	2	5	.286	11	6	5	2	0	64¹	52	0	22	15	10.4	2.38	128	.235	.305	4	.174	0	4	5	1	0.6
Total 3	5	13	.278	40	14	8	2	0	171²	158	3	74	48	12.6	3.30	89	.259	.347	7	.127	-1	-9	-7	-0	-2.0

● **HAP COLLARD**   Collard, Earl Clinton   b: 8/29/1898, Williams, Ariz.   d: 7/9/68, Jamestown, Cal.   BR/TR, 6', 170 lbs.   Deb: 4/23/27

YEAR TM/L	W	L	PCT	G	GS	CG	SH	SV	IP	H	HR	BB	SO	RAT	ERA	ERA+	OAV	OOB	BH	AVG	PB	PR	/A	PD	TPI
1927 Cle-A	0	0	—	4	0	0	0	0	5¹	8	0	3	2	18.6	5.06	83	.333	.422	0	—	0	-1	-1	-0	0.0
1928 Cle-A	0	0	—	1	0	0	0	0	4	4	0	4	1	18.0	2.25	184	.250	.400	1	1.000	0	1	1	-0	0.0
1930 Phi-N	6	12	.333	30	15	4	0	0	127	188	15	39	25	16.3	6.80	80	.350	.397	9	.205	-2	-26	-19	1	-2.1
Total 3	6	12	.333	35	15	4	0	0	136¹	200	15	46	28	16.4	6.60	81	.347	.398	10	.222	-1	-26	-19	1	-2.1

● **ORLIN COLLIER**   Collier, Orlin Edward   b: 2/17/07, E.Prairie, Mo.   d: 9/9/44, Memphis, Tenn.   BR/TR, 5'11.5", 180 lbs.   Deb: 9/11/31

YEAR TM/L	W	L	PCT	G	GS	CG	SH	SV	IP	H	HR	BB	SO	RAT	ERA	ERA+	OAV	OOB	BH	AVG	PB	PR	/A	PD	TPI
1931 Det-A	0	1	.000	2	2	0	0	0	10¹	17	0	7	3	20.9	7.84	59	.362	.444	0	.000	0	-4	-4	-0	-0.3

● **HARRY COLLIFLOWER**   Colliflower, James Harry "Collie"   b: 3/11/1869, Petersville, Md.   d: 8/12/61, Washington, D.C.   BL/TL, 5'11.5", 175 lbs.   Deb: 7/21/1899   U

YEAR TM/L	W	L	PCT	G	GS	CG	SH	SV	IP	H	HR	BB	SO	RAT	ERA	ERA+	OAV	OOB	BH	AVG	PB	PR	/A	PD	TPI
1899 Cle-N	1	11	.083	14	12	11	0	0	98	152	6	41	8	18.7	8.17	45	.353	.422	23	.303	2	-47	-49	0	-4.0

● **DAN COLLINS**   Collins, Daniel Thomas   b: 7/12/1854, St.Louis, Mo.   d: 9/21/1883, New Orleans, La.   Deb: 6/8/1874 ◆

YEAR TM/L	W	L	PCT	G	GS	CG	SH	SV	IP	H	HR	BB	SO	RAT	ERA	ERA+	OAV	OOB	BH	AVG	PB	PR	/A	PD	TPI
1874 Chi-n	1	1	.500	2	2	1	0	0	11	22	0	2	0	19.6	4.91	45	.386	.407	1	.083	-1	-3	-3	-0	-0.4

● **DON COLLINS**   Collins, Donald Edward   b: 9/15/52, Lyons, Ga.   BR/TL, 6'2", 195 lbs.   Deb: 5/4/77

YEAR TM/L	W	L	PCT	G	GS	CG	SH	SV	IP	H	HR	BB	SO	RAT	ERA	ERA+	OAV	OOB	BH	AVG	PB	PR	/A	PD	TPI
1977 Atl-N	3	9	.250	40	6	0	0	2	70²	82	9	41	27	15.8	5.09	87	.299	.392	0	.000	-1	-9	-5	-1	-1.1
1980 Cle-A	0	0	—	4	0	0	0	0	6	9	0	7	0	24.0	7.50	54	.346	.485	0	—	0	-2	-2	-0	0.0
Total 2	3	9	.250	44	6	0	0	2	76²	91	9	48	27	16.4	5.28	84	.303	.401	0	.000	-1	-12	-7	-1	-1.1

● **RIP COLLINS**   Collins, Harry Warren   b: 2/26/1896, Weatherford, Tex.   d: 5/27/68, Bryan, Tex.   BR/TR, 6'1", 205 lbs.   Deb: 4/19/20

YEAR TM/L	W	L	PCT	G	GS	CG	SH	SV	IP	H	HR	BB	SO	RAT	ERA	ERA+	OAV	OOB	BH	AVG	PB	PR	/A	PD	TPI
1920 NY-A	14	8	.636	36	18	10	2	1	187¹	171	6	79	66	12.7	3.22	119	.247	.337	8	.129	-4	12	13	1	0.8
1921 *NY-A	11	5	.688	28	16	7	2	0	137¹	158	6	78	64	16.1	5.44	78	.293	.392	11	.196	-1	-18	-18	-1	-2.0

YEAR	TM/L	W	L	PCT	G	GS	CG	SH	SV	IP	H	HR	BB	SO	RAT	ERA	ERA+	OAV	OOB	BH	AVG	PB	PR	/A	PD	TPI
1922	Bos-A	14	11	.560	32	29	15	3	0	210²	219	4	103	69	14.2	3.76	109	.274	.364	12	.158	-3	7	8	-1	0.5
1923	Det-A	3	7	.300	17	14	3	1	0	92¹	104	3	22	25	13.3	4.87	79	.284	.342	3	.111	-2	-9	-10	0	-1.1
1924	Det-A	14	7	.667	34	30	11	1	0	216	199	6	63	75	11.1	3.21	128	.249	.307	11	.145	-5	25	22	0	1.4
1925	Det-A	6	11	.353	26	20	5	0	0	140	149	7	52	33	13.3	4.56	94	.281	.352	5	.119	-4	-3	-4	4	-0.4
1926	Det-A	8	8	.500	30	13	5	3	1	122	128	4	44	44	13.2	2.73	149	.278	.350	6	.154	-1	17	18	1	2.2
1927	Det-A	13	7	.650	30	25	10	1	0	172²	207	5	59	37	14.3	4.69	90	.312	.375	11	.204	-0	-11	-9	5	-0.5
1929	StL-A	11	6	.647	26	20	10	1	1	155¹	162	16	73	47	14.0	4.00	111	.270	.355	17	.274	4	7	0	1	1.1
1930	StL-A	9	7	.563	35	20	6	1	2	171²	168	11	63	75	12.4	4.35	112	.259	.330	7	.130	-2	6	10	-0	0.6
1931	StL-A	5	5	.500	17	14	2	0	0	107	130	5	38	34	14.2	3.79	122	.307	.366	5	.147	-1	7	10	1	0.9
Total	11	108	82	.568	311	219	84	15	5	1712¹	1795	73	674	569	13.4	3.99	106	.275	.351	96	.165	-18	38	45	9	3.5

● ORTH COLLINS
Collins, Orth Stein "Buck" b: 4/27/1880, Lafayette, Ind. d: 12/13/49, Ft.Lauderdale, Fla BL/TR, 6′, 150 lbs. Deb: 6/1/04 ♦

1909	Was-A	0	0	—	1	0	0	0	0	1	0	0	1	0	0.00	—	.000	.000	0	.000	-0	0	-0	-0	0.0

● PHIL COLLINS
Collins, Philip Eugene "Fidgety Phil" b: 8/27/01, Chicago, Ill. d: 8/14/48, Chicago, Ill. BR/TR, 5′11″, 175 lbs. Deb: 10/7/23

1923	Chi-N	1	0	1.000	1	1	0	0	0	5	8	0	1	2	16.2	3.60	111	.400	.429	-0	—	0	0	0	1	0.1
1929	Phi-N	9	7	.563	43	11	3	0	5	153¹	172	18	83	61	15.2	5.75	90	.284	.374	11	.190	-0	-18	-10	-1	-1.0
1930	Phi-N	16	11	.593	47	25	17	1	3	239	287	22	86	87	14.4	4.78	114	.299	.363	22	.253	3	5	18	-2	1.8
1931	Phi-N	12	16	.429	42	27	16	2	4	240¹	268	14	83	73	13.3	3.86	110	.283	.344	16	.168	-4	0	10	1	0.8
1932	Phi-N	14	12	.538	43	21	6	0	3	184¹	231	21	65	66	14.7	5.27	84	.314	.375	18	.265	2	-29	-18	-0	-2.0
1933	Phi-N	8	13	.381	42	13	5	1	6	151	178	9	50	44	14.4	4.11	93	.293	.360	7	.132	-0	-13	-5	-1	-1.1
1934	Phi-N	13	18	.419	45	32	15	0	1	254	277	30	87	72	13.0	4.18	93	.273	.333	15	.170	-5	-3	15	-3	0.9
1935	Phi-N	0	2	.000	3	3	0	0	0	14²	24	5	9	4	20.3	11.66	39	.348	.423	0	.000	-1	-12	-12	0	-1.2
	StL-N	7	6	.538	26	8	2	0	2	82²	96	6	26	18	13.6	4.57	90	.290	.347	4	.160	-1	-5	-4	-1	-0.8
	Yr	7	8	.467	29	11	2	0	2	97¹	120	11	35	22	14.6	5.64	74	.300	.361	4	.129	-2	-18	-16	-1	-2.0
Total	8	80	85	.485	292	141	64	4	24	1324¹	1541	125	497	423	14.1	4.66	100	.291	.356	93	.193	-8	-75	-3	-7	-2.5

● RAY COLLINS
Collins, Raymond Williston b: 2/11/1887, Colchester, Vt. d: 1/9/70, Burlington, Vt. BL/TL, 6′1″, 185 lbs. Deb: 7/19/09

1909	Bos-A	4	3	.571	12	8	4	2	0	73²	70	2	18	31	10.8	2.81	89	.269	.317	3	.130	-0	-3	-3	1	-0.2
1910	Bos-A	13	11	.542	35	26	18	4	1	244²	205	1	41	109	9.1	1.62	158	.229	.264	15	.179	-1	25	25	-4	2.1
1911	Bos-A	11	12	.478	31	24	14	0	1	194²	184	1	44	86	10.7	2.40	136	.256	.302	9	.150	0	20	19	-3	1.7
1912	*Bos-A	13	8	.619	27	24	17	4	0	199¹	192	4	42	82	10.7	2.53	135	.256	.297	11	.169	0	17	19	-3	1.6
1913	Bos-A	19	8	.704	30	30	19	3	0	246²	242	3	37	88	10.3	2.63	112	.263	.293	12	.150	2	8	9	-4	0.7
1914	Bos-A	20	13	.606	39	30	16	6	0	272¹	252	3	56	72	10.2	2.51	107	.258	.298	11	.139	-0	7	5	-6	0.0
1915	Bos-A	4	7	.364	25	9	2	0	0	104²	101	1	31	43	11.4	4.30	65	.261	.317	8	.286	5	-16	-18	-3	-1.7
Total	7	84	62	.575	199	151	90	19	4	1336	1246	15	269	511	10.3	2.51	115	.254	.294	69	.165	6	59	58	-22	4.2

● JACKIE COLLUM
Collum, Jack Dean b: 6/21/27, Victor, Ia. BL/TL, 5′7″, 163 lbs. Deb: 9/21/51

1951	StL-N	2	1	.667	3	2	1	1	0	17	11	0	10	5	11.1	1.59	250	.204	.328	3	.429	1	4	4	0	1.0
1952	StL-N	0	0	—	2	0	0	0	0	3	2	0	1	0	9.0	0.00	—	.200	.273	0	—	0	1	1	0	0.0
1953	StL-N	0	0	—	7	0	0	0	0	11¹	15	1	4	5	15.1	6.35	67	.326	.380	-0	—	-0	-3	-3	1	0.1
	Cin-N	7	11	.389	30	12	4	1	3	124²	123	8	39	51	12.1	3.75	116	.263	.328	10	.278	3	7	8	1	1.4
	Yr	7	11	.389	37	12	4	1	3	136	138	9	43	56	12.4	3.97	109	.269	.333	10	.256	2	5	6	2	1.5
1954	Cin-N	7	3	.700	36	2	1	0	0	79	86	8	32	28	14.0	3.76	112	.283	.361	3	.231	2	3	4	3	0.9
1955	Cin-N	9	8	.529	32	17	5	0	1	134	128	17	49	49	11.2	3.63	117	.254	.308	2	.250	0	6	9	-0	1.3
1956	StL-N	6	2	.750	38	1	0	0	7	60	63	6	27	17	13.8	4.20	90	.281	.364	3	.214	1	-3	-3	1	-0.3
1957	Chi-N	1	1	.500	9	0	0	0	1	10²	9	1	9	7	15.2	6.75	57	.211	.375	0	—	0	-3	-3	0	-0.6
	Bro-N	0	0	—	3	0	0	0	0	4¹	7	1	1	3	16.6	8.31	50	.368	.400	0	—	0	-2	-2	-0	-0.0
	Yr	1	1	.500	12	0	0	0	1	15	15	1	10	10	15.0	7.20	55	.254	.362	0	—	0	-6	-5	-0	-0.6
1958	LA-N	0	0	—	2	0	0	0	0	3¹	4	2	2	0	16.2	8.10	51	.308	.400	0	.000	-0	-2	-1	0	0.0
1962	Min-A	0	2	.000	8	3	0	0	0	15¹	29	1	11	5	23.5	11.15	37	.414	.494	0	.000	0	-12	-12	-0	-1.3
	Cle-A	0	0	—	1	0	0	0	0	1¹	4	0	1	0	27.0	13.50	29	.571	.571	0	—	0	-1	-1	0	0.0
	Yr	0	2	.000	9	3	0	0	0	16²	33	1	11	6	23.8	11.34	36	.418	.489	0	.000	-0	-14	-13	-0	-1.3
Total	9	32	28	.533	171	37	11	2	12	464	480	44	173	171	13.0	4.15	101	.273	.344	29	.246	8	-4	1	6	2.5

● DICK COLPAERT
Colpaert, Richard Charles b: 1/3/44, Fraser, Mich. BR/TR, 5′10″, 182 lbs. Deb: 7/21/70

1970	Pit-N	1	0	1.000	8	0	0	0	0	10²	9	3	8	6	14.3	5.91	66	.237	.370	0	—	0	-2	-2	-0	-0.2

● LOYD COLSON
Colson, Loyd Albert b: 11/4/47, Wellington, Tex. BR/TR, 6′1″, 190 lbs. Deb: 9/25/70

1970	NY-A	0	0	—	1	0	0	0	0	2	3	0	3	3	13.5	4.50	78	.333	.333	0	—	0	-0	-0	-0	0.0

● LARRY COLTON
Colton, Lawrence Robert b: 6/8/42, Los Angeles, Cal. BL/TR, 6′3″, 200 lbs. Deb: 5/6/68

1968	Phi-N	0	0	—	1	0	0	0	0	2	3	0	0	2	13.5	4.50	67	.333	.333	0	—	0	-0	-0	-0	0.0

● GEOFF COMBE
Combe, Geoffrey Wade b: 2/1/56, Melrose, Mass. BR/TR, 6′2″, 185 lbs. Deb: 9/2/80

1980	Cin-N	0	0	—	4	0	0	0	0	6²	9	0	4	10	17.6	10.80	33	.346	.433	0	—	0	-5	-5	-0	-0.5
1981	Cin-N	1	0	1.000	14	0	0	0	0	17²	27	3	10	9	18.3	7.64	46	.370	.446	0	—	0	-8	-8	-0	-0.5
Total	2	1	0	1.000	18	0	0	0	0	24¹	36	3	14	19	18.5	8.51	42	.364	.442	0	—	0	-13	-13	-0	-0.5

● PAT COMBS
Combs, Patrick Dennis b: 10/29/66, Newport, R.I. BL/TL, 6′3″, 200 lbs. Deb: 9/5/89

1989	Phi-N	4	0	1.000	6	6	1	1	0	38²	36	2	6	30	9.8	2.09	169	.248	.278	2	.167	0	6	6	-1	0.7
1990	Phi-N	10	10	.500	32	31	3	2	0	183¹	179	12	86	108	13.2	4.07	94	.257	.342	9	.150	0	-6	-5	-0	-0.5
1991	Phi-N	2	6	.250	14	13	1	0	0	64¹	64	7	43	41	15.2	4.90	75	.254	.367	2	.133	1	-9	-9	-1	-1.0
1992	Phi-N	1	1	.500	4	4	0	0	0	18²	20	0	12	11	15.4	7.71	45	.278	.381	1	.125	0	-9	-9	1	-0.7
Total	4	17	17	.500	56	54	5	3	0	305	299	21	147	190	13.3	4.22	88	.257	.343	14	.147	2	-17	-16	-1	-1.5

● JORGE COMELLAS
Comellas, Jorge (Pous) "Pancho" b: 12/7/16, Havana, Cuba BR/TR, 6′, 190 lbs. Deb: 4/19/45

1945	Chi-N	0	2	.000	7	1	0	0	0	12	11	1	6	6	12.8	4.50	81	.244	.333	0	.000	0	-1	-1	1	-0.1

● STEVE COMER
Comer, Steven Michael b: 1/13/54, Minneapolis, Minn. BB/TR, 6′3″, 205 lbs. Deb: 4/15/78 C

1978	Tex-A	11	5	.688	30	11	3	2	1	117¹	107	5	37	65	11.1	2.30	163	.249	.310	0	—	0	19	19	1	2.6
1979	Tex-A	17	12	.586	36	36	6	1	0	242¹	230	24	84	86	12.0	3.68	113	.252	.320	0	—	0	14	13	-0	1.4
1980	Tex-A	2	4	.333	12	11	0	0	0	41²	65	5	22	9	17.9	7.99	49	.367	.443	0	—	0	-18	-19	-0	-2.2
1981	Tex-A	8	2	.800	36	1	0	0	6	77¹	70	1	31	22	11.9	2.56	135	.241	.317	0	—	0	9	8	1	1.3
1982	Tex-A	1	6	.143	37	3	0	0	6	97	133	11	36	22	15.9	5.10	76	.342	.400	0	—	0	-11	-13	-0	-0.8
1983	Phi-N	1	0	1.000	3	1	0	0	0	8²	11	0	3	1	14.5	5.19	69	.314	.368	0	.000	0	-2	-2	-0	-0.2
1984	Cle-A	4	8	.333	22	20	2	0	0	117¹	146	11	39	39	14.5	5.68	72	.309	.366	0	—	0	-22	-21	-1	-1.9
Total	7	44	37	.543	176	83	11	3	13	701²	762	57	252	245	13.2	4.13	95	.281	.347	0	.000	-0	-10	-15	1	0.2

● CHARLIE COMISKEY
Comiskey, Charles Albert "Commy" or "The Old Roman"
b: 8/15/1859, Chicago, Ill. d: 10/26/31, Eagle River, Wis. BR/TR, 6′, 180 lbs. Deb: 5/2/1882 MH♦

1882	StL-a	0	1	.000	2	1	1	0	0	8	12	0	3	2	16.9	0.00	—	.324	.375	80	.243	0	2	2	0	0.3
1884	StL-a	0	0	—	1	0	0	0	0	4	1	0	0	4	2.3	2.25	145	.059	.059	109	.237	0	0	0	-0	0.0
1889	StL-a	0	0	—	1	0	0	0	0	0¹	0	0	0	0	0.0	0.00	—	.000	.000	168	.286	0	0	0	-0	0.0
Total	3	0	1	.000	4	1	1	0	0	12¹	13	0	3	6	11.7	0.73	410	.236	.276	1530	.264	0	3	3	0	0.3

● JACK COMPTON
Compton, Harry Leroy b: 3/9/1882, Lancaster, Ohio d: 7/4/74, Lancaster, Ohio BR/TR, 5′9″, 157 lbs. Deb: 9/7/11

1911	Cin-N	0	1	.000	8	3	0	0	1	25¹	19	0	15	6	12.4	3.91	85	.204	.321	2	.333	0	-1	-2	-0	-0.1

● CLINT COMPTON
Compton, Robert Clinton b: 11/1/50, Montgomery, Ala. BL/TL, 5′11″, 185 lbs. Deb: 10/3/72

1972	Chi-N	0	0	—	1	0	0	0	0	2	2	0	2	0	18.0	9.00	42	.286	.444	0	—	0	-1	-1	-0	0.0

YEAR	TM/L	W	L	PCT	G	GS	CG	SH	SV	IP	H	HR	BB	SO	RAT	ERA	ERA+	OAV	OOB	BH	AVG	PB	PR	/A	PD	TPI

● **KEITH COMSTOCK** Comstock, Keith Martin b: 12/23/55, San Francisco, Cal. BL/TL, 6', 175 lbs. Deb: 4/3/84

1984	Min-A	0	0	—	4	0	0	0	0	6¹	6	2	4	2	14.2	8.53	49	.261	.370	0	—	0	-3	-3	0	-0.2
1987	SF-N	2	0	1.000	15	0	0	0	1	20²	19	1	10	21	12.6	3.05	126	.253	.341	0	.000	-0	2	2	0	0.2
	SD-N	0	1	.000	26	0	0	0	0	36	33	4	21	38	13.5	5.50	72	.252	.355	0	.000	-0	-6	-6	-1	-0.2
	Yr	2	1	.667	41	0	0	0	1	56²	52	5	31	59	13.2	4.61	85	.251	.349	0	.000	-0	-3	-4	-1	0.0
1988	SD-N	0	0	—	7	0	0	0	0	8	8	1	3	9	12.4	6.75	50	.250	.314	0	—	0	-3	-3	0	0.2
1989	Sea-A	1	2	.333	31	0	0	0	0	25²	26	1	10	22	12.6	2.81	144	.268	.336	0	—	0	3	3	-0	0.2
1990	Sea-A	7	4	.636	60	0	0	0	2	56	40	4	26	50	10.6	2.89	137	.206	.300	0	—	0	6	7	1	1.3
1991	Sea-A	0	0	—	1	0	0	0	0	0¹	2	0	1	0	81.0	54.00	8	.667	.750	0	—	0	-2	-2	0	0.0
Total	6	10	7	.588	144	0	0	0	3	153	134	14	75	142	12.3	4.06	97	.241	.332	0	.000	-0	-2	-2	0	1.3

● **RALPH COMSTOCK** Comstock, Ralph Remick "Commy" b: 11/24/1890, Sylvania, Ohio d: 9/13/66, Toledo, Ohio BR/TR, 5'10", 168 lbs. Deb: 8/26/13

1913	Det-A	2	5	.286	10	7	1	0	1	60¹	90	0	16	37	16.0	5.37	54	.344	.384	5	.227	1	-16	-16	-0	-1.6
1915	Bos-A	1	0	1.000	3	0	0	0	0	9	10	2	2	1	12.0	2.00	139	.294	.333	0	.000	0	1	1	0	0.1
	Pit-F	3	3	.500	12	7	3	0	2	52²	44	3	7	18	8.9	3.25	83	.237	.268	0	.000	-2	-3	-3	-0	-0.6
1918	Pit-N	5	6	.455	15	8	6	0	1	81	78	0	14	44	10.4	3.00	96	.259	.297	5	.192	-0	-2	-1	-0	-0.2
Total	3	11	14	.440	40	22	10	0	4	203	222	5	39	100	11.7	3.72	76	.284	.321	10	.152	-2	-21	-20	-0	-2.3

● **DAVE CONCEPCION** Concepcion, David Ismael (Benitez) b: 6/17/48, Aragua, Venez. BR/TR, 6'1", 180 lbs. Deb: 4/6/70 ♦

| 1988 | Cin-N | 0 | 0 | — | 1 | 0 | 0 | 0 | 0 | 1¹ | 2 | 0 | 1 | 0 | 13.5 | — | | .333 | .333 | 39 | .198 | | 1 | 1 | 0 | 0.0 |

● **DAVID CONE** Cone, David Brian b: 1/2/63, Kansas City, Mo. BL/TR, 6'1", 185 lbs. Deb: 6/8/86

1986	KC-A	0	0	—	11	0	0	0	0	22²	29	2	13	21	17.1	5.56	76	.309	.398	0	—	0	-3	-3	-0	-0.1
1987	NY-N	5	6	.455	21	13	1	0	1	99¹	87	11	44	68	12.3	3.71	102	.239	.329	2	.065	-1	4	1	-0	-0.1
1988	*NY-N★	20	3	.870	35	28	8	4	0	231¹	178	10	80	213	10.2	2.22	145	.213	.285	12	.150	-1	32	26	-1	2.5
1989	NY-N	14	8	.636	34	33	7	2	0	219²	183	20	74	190	10.7	3.52	93	.223	.290	18	.234	4	-1	-6	-2	-0.4
1990	NY-N	14	10	.583	31	30	6	2	0	211²	177	21	65	233	10.3	3.23	116	.226	.286	14	.200	3	13	12	-0	1.6
1991	NY-N	14	14	.500	34	34	5	2	0	232²	204	13	73	241	10.9	3.29	111	.235	.298	9	.125	-1	10	9	0	1.0
1992	NY-N★	13	7	.650	27	27	7	5	0	196²	162	12	82	214	11.6	2.88	120	.223	.309	6	.092	-2	14	13	-0	1.1
	*Tor-A	4	3	.571	8	7	0	0	0	53	39	3	29	47	12.1	2.55	160	.206	.321	0	—	0	8	9	-1	1.1
1993	KC-A	11	14	.440	34	34	6	1	0	254	205	20	114	191	11.7	3.33	137	.223	.315	0	—	0	28	35	-1	3.0
1994	KC-A★	16	5	.762	23	23	4	3	0	171²	130	15	54	132	10.0	2.94	170	.209	.279	0	—	0	36	39	0	**4.4**
1995	Tor-A	9	6	.600	17	17	5	2	0	130¹	113	12	41	102	11.0	3.38	139	.232	.298	0	—	0	19	19	0	2.0
	*NY-A	9	2	.818	13	13	1	0	0	99	82	12	47	89	11.8	3.82	121	.223	.313	0	—	0	10	9	-1	0.8
	Yr	18	8	.692	30	30	6	2	0	229¹	195	24	88	191	11.1	3.57	131	.226	.299	0	—	0	29	28	-1	2.8
1996	*NY-A	7	2	.778	11	11	1	0	0	72	50	3	34	71	10.8	2.88	198	.198	.298	0	—	0	17	17	-1	1.9
Total	11	136	80	.630	299	270	51	21	1	1994	1639	161	750	1812	11.0	3.16	125	.223	.300	61	.154	5	186	177	-7	18.8

● **BOB CONE** Cone, Robert Earl b: 2/27/1894, Galveston, Tex. d: 5/24/55, Galveston, Tex. BR/TR, 6'2", 172 lbs. Deb: 7/25/15

| 1915 | Phi-A | 0 | 0 | — | 1 | 1 | 0 | 0 | 0 | 0² | 5 | 0 | 0 | 0 | 67.5 | 40.50 | 7 | .714 | .714 | 0 | — | 0 | -3 | -3 | -0 | 0.0 |

● **DICK CONGER** Conger, Richard b: 4/3/21, Los Angeles, Cal. d: 2/16/70, Los Angeles, Cal. BR/TR, 6', 185 lbs. Deb: 4/22/40

1940	Det-A	1	0	1.000	2	0	0	0	0	3	2	0	3	1	15.0	3.00	159	.200	.385	0	—	0	0	1	-0	0.2
1941	Pit-N	0	0	—	2	1	0	0	0	4	3	0	3	2	13.5	0.00	—	.214	.353	0	—	0	2	2	-0	0.2
1942	Pit-N	0	0	—	2	1	0	0	0	8¹	9	0	5	3	15.1	2.16	157	.290	.389	0	.000	-0	1	1	1	0.0
1943	Phi-N	2	7	.222	13	10	2	0	0	54²	72	3	24	18	16.6	6.09	55	.327	.406	1	.063	-1	-16	-17	-0	-2.4
Total	4	3	7	.300	19	12	2	0	0	70	86	3	35	24	16.2	5.14	67	.313	.400	1	.053	-1	-13	-13	0	-2.2

● **ALLEN CONKWRIGHT** Conkwright, Allen Howard "Red" b: 12/4/1896, Sedalia, Mo. d: 7/30/91, LaMesa, Cal. BR/TR, 5'10", 170 lbs. Deb: 9/16/20

| 1920 | Det-A | 2 | 1 | .667 | 5 | 3 | 0 | 0 | 1 | 19¹ | 29 | 0 | 16 | 4 | 20.9 | 6.98 | 53 | .397 | .506 | 1 | .200 | 1 | -7 | -7 | 0 | -0.9 |

● **GENE CONLEY** Conley, Donald Eugene b: 11/10/30, Muskogee, Okla. BR/TR, 6'8", 225 lbs. Deb: 4/17/52

1952	Bos-N	0	3	.000	4	3	0	0	0	12²	23	4	9	6	24.2	7.82	46	.397	.493	2	.400	1	-6	-6	-0	-1.1
1954	Mil-N★	14	9	.609	28	27	12	6	0	194¹	171	17	79	113	11.9	2.96	126	.240	.322	12	.156	-2	24	16	-1	1.5
1955	Mil-N★	11	7	.611	22	21	10	0	0	158	152	23	52	107	11.7	4.16	90	.254	.315	11	.204	-1	-2	-7	-0	-0.8
1956	Mil-N	8	9	.471	31	19	5	1	3	158¹	169	13	52	68	12.7	3.13	111	.276	.335	7	.156	-1	11	6	-1	0.5
1957	*Mil-N	9	9	.500	35	18	6	1	1	148	133	9	64	61	12.1	3.16	111	.244	.325	9	.196	1	12	6	-0	0.7
1958	Mil-N	0	6	.000	26	7	0	0	2	72	89	8	17	53	13.8	4.88	72	.309	.356	3	.188	1	-7	-11	-0	-0.8
1959	Phi-N★	12	7	.632	25	22	12	3	1	180	159	13	42	100	10.1	3.00	**137**	.235	.281	16	.239	2	19	22	-0	2.5
1960	Phi-N	8	14	.364	29	25	9	2	0	183¹	192	10	42	117	11.6	3.68	105	.272	.314	8	.127	-1	2	4	-2	0.2
1961	Bos-A	11	14	.440	33	30	6	2	1	199²	229	33	65	113	13.4	4.91	85	.287	.343	16	.219	4	-20	-17	-1	-1.5
1962	Bos-A	15	14	.517	34	33	9	2	1	241²	238	28	68	134	11.6	3.95	105	.256	.310	18	.207	3	1	5	-1	0.8
1963	Bos-A	3	4	.429	9	9	0	0	0	40²	51	4	21	14	16.2	6.64	57	.305	.386	3	.200	-1	-14	-13	-1	-1.9
Total	11	91	96	.487	276	214	69	13	9	1588²	1606	162	511	888	12.2	3.82	101	.264	.324	105	.192	8	20	6	-6	0.1

● **ED CONLEY** Conley, Edward J. b: 7/10/1864, Sandwich, Mass. d: 10/16/1894, Cumberland, R.I. 5'8", 142 lbs. Deb: 7/20/1884

| 1884 | Pro-N | 4 | 4 | .500 | 8 | 8 | 8 | 1 | 0 | 71 | 63 | 4 | 22 | 33 | 10.8 | 2.15 | 131 | .223 | .280 | 4 | .143 | -2 | 7 | 5 | -1 | 0.2 |

● **SNIPE CONLEY** Conley, James Patrick b: 4/25/1894, Cressona, Pa. d: 1/7/78, DeSoto, Tex. BR/TR, 5'11.5", 179 lbs. Deb: 5/20/14

1914	Bal-F	4	6	.400	35	11	4	2	1	125	112	2	47	86	11.9	2.52	120	.259	.340	4	.114	-3	5	7	-1	0.1
1915	Bal-F	1	4	.200	25	6	4	0	0	86	97	5	32	40	13.9	4.29	67	.314	.386	6	.250	1	-15	-14	-1	-0.7
1918	Cin-N	2	0	1.000	5	0	0	0	1	13²	17	2	5	2	14.5	5.27	51	.321	.379	1	.250	0	-4	-4	0	-0.6
Total	3	7	10	.412	65	17	8	2	2	224²	226	9	84	128	12.8	3.36	88	.284	.360	11	.175	-1	-14	-10	-1	-1.2

● **BOB CONLEY** Conley, Robert Burns b: 2/1/34, Mousie, Ky. BR/TR, 6'1", 188 lbs. Deb: 9/11/58

| 1958 | Phi-N | 0 | 0 | — | 2 | 2 | 0 | 0 | 0 | 8¹ | 9 | 0 | 1 | 0 | 7.56 | 52 | | .273 | .294 | 0 | — | 0 | -3 | -3 | -0 | 0.0 |

● **BERT CONN** Conn, Albert Thomas b: 9/22/1879, Philadelphia, Pa. d: 11/2/44, Philadelphia, Pa. TR, Deb: 9/16/1898 ♦

1898	Phi-N	0	1	.000	1	1	0	0	0	7	13	1	2	3	19.3	6.43	53	.394	.429	1	.333	1	-2	-2	-0	-0.2
1900	Phi-N	0	2	.000	4	1	1	0	0	17¹	29	0	16	2	26.5	8.31	44	.372	.510	3	.333	1	-9	-9	-1	-0.8
Total	2	0	3	.000	5	2	1	0	0	24¹	42	1	18	5	24.4	7.77	46	.378	.489	8	.267	2	-11	-11	-1	-1.0

● **SARGE CONNALLY** Connally, George Walter b: 8/31/1898, McGregor, Tex. d: 1/27/78, Temple, Tex. BR/TR, 5'11", 170 lbs. Deb: 9/10/21

1921	Chi-A	0	1	.000	5	2	0	0	0	22¹	29	0	10	6	16.1	6.45	66	.330	.404	4	.500	2	-5	-5	0	0.0
1923	Chi-A	0	0	—	8²	7	0	0	0	8²	7	0	12	3	20.8	6.23	64	.241	.476	1	.333	0	-2	-2	-0	0.0
1924	Chi-A	7	13	.350	44	13	6	0	6	160	177	4	68	55	14.3	4.05	102	.290	.369	11	.220	-1	3	1	3	0.3
1925	Chi-A	6	7	.462	40	2	0	0	8	104²	122	2	58	46	15.6	4.64	89	.310	.402	7	.250	-1	-3	-6	3	-0.3
1926	Chi-A	6	5	.545	31	8	5	0	0	108¹	128	5	35	47	13.7	3.16	122	.300	.356	5	.156	-1	10	9	2	0.9
1927	Chi-A	10	15	.400	43	18	11	1	5	198¹	217	8	83	58	14.0	4.08	99	.292	.370	22	.328	4	1	-1	1	0.4
1928	Chi-A	5	5	.286	28	5	1	0	0	74¹	89	1	29	28	14.8	4.84	84	.313	.385	2	.105	-1	-7	-7	-0	-0.7
1929	Chi-A	0	0	—	11	0	0	0	0	11¹	13	0	8	3	16.7	4.76	90	.317	.429	0	—	0	-1	-1	-0	0.0
1931	Cle-A	5	5	.500	17	9	5	0	1	85²	87	7	50	37	15.0	4.20	110	.256	.361	5	.185	-0	2	5	0	0.6
1932	Cle-A	8	6	.571	35	7	4	1	0	112¹	119	6	42	32	13.1	4.33	110	.266	.333	7	.175	-0	2	5	0	0.5
1933	Cle-A	5	3	.625	41	3	1	0	0	103	112	4	49	30	14.3	4.89	91	.271	.353	6	.231	1	-7	-5	-2	-0.5
1934	Cle-A	0	0	—	1	0	0	0	0	1²	4	0	0	0	15.2	5.06	90	.222	.391	0	.000	-0	-0	-0	0	0.0
Total	12	49	60	.450	303	67	33	2	31	994¹	1104	32	449	345	14.4	4.30	98	.288	.368	70	.233	5	-7	-8	5	1.1

● **BILL CONNELLY** Connelly, William Wirt "Wild Bill" b: 6/29/25, Alberta, Va. d: 11/27/80, Richmond, Va. BL/TR, 6', 175 lbs. Deb: 8/22/45

1945	Phi-A	1	1	.500	2	1	0	0	0	8	7	0	8	0	16.9	4.50	76	.259	.429	0	.000	0	-1	-1	-0	-0.2
1950	Chi-A	0	0	—	2	0	0	0	0	2¹	5	1	1	0	23.1	11.57	39	.455	.500	0	—	0	-2	-2	-0	0.0
	Det-A	0	0	—	2	0	0	0	0	4	4	1	2	1	13.5	6.75	69	.250	.333	0	.000	-0	-1	-1	0	0.0
	Yr	0	0	—	4	0	0	0	0	6¹	9	2	3	1	17.1	8.53	54	.333	.400	0	.000	-0	-3	-3	-0	0.0

YEAR	TM/L	W	L	PCT	G	GS	CG	SH	SV	IP	H	HR	BB	SO	RAT	ERA	ERA+	OAV	OOB	BH	AVG	PB	PR	/A	PD	TPI
1952	NY-N	5	0	1.000	11	4	0	0	0	31²	22	4	25	22	13.4	4.55	81	.208	.359	4	.364	3	-3	-3	1	-0.1
1953	NY-N	0	1	.000	8	3	0	0	0	20¹	33	4	17	11	22.1	11.07	39	.371	.472	0	.000	-1	-15	-15	-0	-0.7
Total	4	6	2	.750	25	7	0	0	0	66¹	71	10	53	34	16.8	6.92	57	.285	.411	4	.211	3	-22	-22	-0	-1.0

● **ED CONNOLLY**   Connolly, Edward Joseph Jr. b: 12/3/39, Brooklyn, N.Y.   BL/TL, 6'1", 190 lbs.   Deb: 4/19/64 F

YEAR	TM/L	W	L	PCT	G	GS	CG	SH	SV	IP	H	HR	BB	SO	RAT	ERA	ERA+	OAV	OOB	BH	AVG	PB	PR	/A	PD	TPI
1964	Bos-A	4	11	.267	27	15	1	1	0	80²	80	3	64	73	16.7	4.91	79	.261	.398	3	.167	0	-12	-9	-1	-1.7
1967	Cle-A	2	1	.667	15	4	0	0	0	49¹	63	6	34	45	17.9	7.48	46	.315	.417	2	.182	-0	-23	-23	-0	-1.3
Total	2	6	12	.333	42	19	1	1	0	130	143	9	98	118	17.2	5.88	62	.282	.405	5	.172	-0	-35	-33	-2	-3.0

● **JOHN CONNOR**   Connor, John b: 8/1854, Scotland   d: 10/13/32, Boston, Mass.   Deb: 7/26/1884

YEAR	TM/L	W	L	PCT	G	GS	CG	SH	SV	IP	H	HR	BB	SO	RAT	ERA	ERA+	OAV	OOB	BH	AVG	PB	PR	/A	PD	TPI
1884	Bos-N	1	4	.200	7	7	7	0	0	60	70	1	18	29	13.2	3.15	92	.275	.322	2	.080	-3	-1	-2	-0	-0.3
1885	Buf-N	0	1	.000	1	1	1	0	0	9	14	0	2	0	16.0	4.00	75	.378	.410	0	.000	-0	-1	-1	-1	-0.2
	Lou-a	1	3	.250	4	4	4	0	0	35	43	0	12	19	14.7	4.89	66	.295	.356	1	.143	-1	-6	-6	-1	-0.7
Total	2	2	8	.200	12	12	12	0	0	104	127	1	32	48	13.9	3.81	79	.290	.341	4	.095	-4	-9	-9	-1	-1.2

● **JOE CONNORS**   Connors, Joseph P.   b: Paterson, N.J.   Deb: 5/3/1884 ♦

YEAR	TM/L	W	L	PCT	G	GS	CG	SH	SV	IP	H	HR	BB	SO	RAT	ERA	ERA+	OAV	OOB	BH	AVG	PB	PR	/A	PD	TPI
1884	Alt-U	0	1	.000	1	1	1	0	0	9	18	0	5	0	23.0	7.00	38	.391	.451	1	.091	-1	-5	-4	0	-0.4
	KC-U	0	1	.000	2	1	1	0	0	12	24	1	0	1	18.0	4.50	50	.393	.393	1	.091	-1	-3	-3	-1	-0.3
	Yr	0	2	.000	3	2	2	0	0	21	42	1	5	1	20.1	5.57	43	.393	.420	2	.091	-2	-7	-7	-0	-0.7

● **BILL CONNORS**   Connors, William Joseph b: 11/2/41, Schenectady, N.Y.   BR/TR, 6'1", 180 lbs.   Deb: 5/3/66 C

YEAR	TM/L	W	L	PCT	G	GS	CG	SH	SV	IP	H	HR	BB	SO	RAT	ERA	ERA+	OAV	OOB	BH	AVG	PB	PR	/A	PD	TPI
1966	Chi-N	0	1	.000	11	0	0	0	0	16	20	4	7	3	15.2	7.31	50	.308	.375	0	—	0	-7	-6	-0	-0.4
1967	NY-N	0	0	—	6	1	0	0	0	13	8	3	5	13	9.7	6.23	54	.170	.264	0	.000	-0	-4	-4	-0	-0.1
1968	NY-N	0	1	.000	9	0	0	0	0	14	21	0	7	8	18.6	9.00	34	.339	.414	1	1.000	1	-9	-9	-0	-0.6
Total	3	0	2	.000	26	1	0	0	0	43	49	7	19	24	14.7	7.53	45	.282	.359	1	.500	1	-20	-20	-1	-1.1

● **TED CONOVAR**   Conovar, Theodore "Huck" b: 3/10/1868, Lexington, Ky.   d: 7/27/10, Paris, Ky.   BR/TR, 5'10.5", 165 lbs.   Deb: 5/26/1889

YEAR	TM/L	W	L	PCT	G	GS	CG	SH	SV	IP	H	HR	BB	SO	RAT	ERA	ERA+	OAV	OOB	BH	AVG	PB	PR	/A	PD	TPI
1889	Cin-a	0	0	—	1	0	0	0	1	2	4	0	2	1	27.0	13.50	29	.400	.500			0	-2	-2	-0	-0.2

● **TIM CONROY**   Conroy, Timothy James b: 4/3/60, McKeesport, Pa.   BL/TL, 5'11", 185 lbs.   Deb: 6/23/78

YEAR	TM/L	W	L	PCT	G	GS	CG	SH	SV	IP	H	HR	BB	SO	RAT	ERA	ERA+	OAV	OOB	BH	AVG	PB	PR	/A	PD	TPI
1978	Oak-A	0	0	—	2	2	0	0	0	4²	3	0	9	0	25.1	7.71	47	.188	.500	0	—	0	-2	-2	-0	0.1
1982	Oak-A	2	2	.500	5	5	1	0	0	25¹	20	1	18	17	13.5	3.55	110	.222	.352	0	—	1	1	-0	-0	0.2
1983	Oak-A	7	10	.412	39	18	3	1	0	162¹	141	17	98	112	13.4	3.94	98	.232	.340	0	—	2	-1	-2	-2	-0.2
1984	Oak-A	1	6	.143	38	14	0	0	0	93	82	11	63	69	14.2	5.23	72	.236	.356	0	—	-0	-13	-15	-1	-0.9
1985	Oak-A	0	1	.000	16	2	0	0	0	25¹	22	3	15	8	13.5	4.26	90	.237	.349	0	—	-0	-0	-1	-0	0.0
1986	StL-N	5	11	.313	25	21	1	0	0	115¹	122	15	56	79	14.1	5.23	70	.275	.360	4	.138	1	-19	-20	-1	-2.5
1987	StL-N	3	2	.600	10	9	0	0	0	40²	48	0	22	22	16.4	5.53	75	.306	.404	0	.000	-0	-7	-6	-1	-0.8
Total	7	18	32	.360	135	71	5	1	0	466²	438	47	284	307	14.1	4.80	85	.249	.357	4	.091	-1	-37	-46	-6	-4.1

● **JIM CONSTABLE**   Constable, Jimmy Lee "Sheriff" b: 6/14/33, Jonesborough, Tenn.   BB/TL, 6'1", 185 lbs.   Deb: 6/24/56

YEAR	TM/L	W	L	PCT	G	GS	CG	SH	SV	IP	H	HR	BB	SO	RAT	ERA	ERA+	OAV	OOB	BH	AVG	PB	PR	/A	PD	TPI
1956	NY-N	0	0	—	3	0	0	0	0	4¹	9	0	7	1	35.3	14.54	26	.429	.586	0	—	0	-5	-5	-0	0.1
1957	NY-N	1	1	.500	16	0	0	0	0	28¹	27	2	7	13	12.1	2.86	138	.262	.333	0	.000	-0	3	3	-0	0.1
1958	SF-N	1	0	1.000	9	0	0	0	1	8	10	1	3	4	14.6	5.63	68	.323	.382	1	1.000	1	-1	-1	-0	-0.1
	Cle-A	0	1	.000	6	2	0	0	0	9¹	17	1	4	3	21.2	11.57	32	.415	.478	2	1.000	4	-8	-8	-1	-0.7
	Was-A	0	1	.000	15	2	0	0	0	27²	29	3	15	25	14.6	4.88	78	.271	.366	1	.250	1	-3	-3	-0	-0.1
	Yr	1	2	.000	21	4	0	0	0	37	46	4	19	28	16.1	6.57	57	.309	.391	3	.500	1	-12	-11	-1	-0.8
1962	Mil-N	1	1	.500	3	2	1	1	0	18	14	1	4	12	9.0	2.00	190	.222	.269	0	.000	-0	4	4	-1	0.4
1963	SF-N	0	0	—	4	0	0	0	0	2¹	3	0	1	1	15.4	3.86	83	.333	.400	0	—	0	-0	-0	-0	0.0
Total	5	3	4	.429	56	6	1	1	1	98	109	8	41	59	14.4	4.87	78	.291	.371	4	.235	2	-11	-11	-1	-0.4

● **SANDY CONSUEGRA**   Consuegra, Sandalio Simeon (Castello) b: 9/3/20, Potrerillos, Cuba   BR/TR, 5'10", 165 lbs.   Deb: 6/10/50

YEAR	TM/L	W	L	PCT	G	GS	CG	SH	SV	IP	H	HR	BB	SO	RAT	ERA	ERA+	OAV	OOB	BH	AVG	PB	PR	/A	PD	TPI
1950	Was-A	7	8	.467	21	18	8	2	2	124²	132	6	57	38	13.7	4.40	102	.270	.347	7	.175	-1	2	1	0	0.1
1951	Was-A	7	8	.467	40	12	5	0	3	146	140	10	63	31	12.5	4.01	102	.251	.327	10	.233	-0	2	1	1	0.2
1952	Was-A	6	0	1.000	30	2	0	0	5	73²	80	2	27	19	13.1	3.05	116	.276	.338	3	.176	-0	5	4	-1	0.3
1953	Was-A	0	0	—	4	0	0	0	0	5	9	0	5	0	23.4	10.80	36	.391	.481	0	—	-0	-4	-4	-0	0.0
	Chi-A	7	5	.583	29	13	5	1	3	124	122	9	28	30	11.0	2.54	158	.258	.302	2	.057	-4	20	20	3	1.9
	Yr	7	5	.583	33	13	5	1	3	129	131	9	32	30	11.5	2.86	141	.264	.311	2	.057	-4	16	17	3	1.9
1954	Chi-A★	16	3	**.842**	39	17	3	2	3	154	142	9	35	31	10.3	2.69	139	.248	.292	11	.229	1	18	18	1	2.4
1955	Chi-A	6	5	.545	44	7	3	0	7	126¹	120	4	18	35	10.0	2.64	150	.256	.286	3	.103	-2	**19**	18	-0	1.5
1956	Chi-A	1	2	.333	28	1	0	0	3	38¹	45	0	11	6	13.4	5.17	79	.296	.348	0	.000	-1	-4	-5	-0	-0.5
	Bal-A	1	1	.500	4	1	0	0	0	8²	10	2	2	2	12.5	4.15	94	.294	.333	1	.500	1	-0	-0	-0	0.0
	Yr	2	3	.400	32	2	0	0	3	47	55	2	13	8	13.2	4.98	82	.293	.338	1	.167	-0	-4	-5	-0	-0.5
1957	Bal-A	0	0	—	5	0	0	0	0	5	4	0	1	1	9.0	1.80	200	.211	.211	0	—	0	1	1	0	0.0
	NY-N	0	0	—	4	0	0	0	0	3²	7	1	1	0	19.6	2.45	160	.438	.421	0	—	0	1	0	0	0.0
Total	8	51	32	.614	248	71	24	5	26	809¹	811	43	246	193	11.8	3.37	119	.262	.318	37	.170	-5	59	57	4	5.9

● **NARDI CONTRERAS**   Contreras, Arnaldo Juan b: 9/19/51, Tampa, Fla.   BB/TR, 6'2", 193 lbs.   Deb: 5/23/80 C

YEAR	TM/L	W	L	PCT	G	GS	CG	SH	SV	IP	H	HR	BB	SO	RAT	ERA	ERA+	OAV	OOB	BH	AVG	PB	PR	/A	PD	TPI
1980	Chi-A	0	0	—	8	0	0	0	0	13²	18	1	7	8	17.8	5.93	68	.333	.429	0	—	0	-3	-3	0	0.0

● **JIM CONVERSE**   Converse, James Daniel b: 8/17/71, San Francisco, Cal.   BL/TR, 5'9", 180 lbs.   Deb: 5/22/93

YEAR	TM/L	W	L	PCT	G	GS	CG	SH	SV	IP	H	HR	BB	SO	RAT	ERA	ERA+	OAV	OOB	BH	AVG	PB	PR	/A	PD	TPI
1993	Sea-A	1	3	.250	4	4	0	0	0	20¹	23	3	14	10	16.4	5.31	83	.295	.402	0	—	0	-2	-2	1	-0.3
1994	Sea-A	0	5	.000	13	8	0	0	0	48²	73	5	40	39	21.1	8.69	56	.353	.460	0	—	0	-21	-21	-0	-1.7
1995	Sea-A	0	3	.000	6	1	0	0	0	11	16	2	9	8	19.6	7.36	64	.348	.444	0	—	0	-3	-3	-0	-0.9
	KC-A	1	0	1.000	9	0	0	0	1	12¹	12	0	5	6	14.6	5.84	82	.267	.377	0	—	0	-2	-1	-0	-0.1
	Yr	1	3	.250	15	1	0	0	1	23¹	28	2	14	14	17.0	6.56	73	.304	.419	0	—	0	-5	-5	-0	-0.9
Total	3	2	11	.154	32	13	0	0	1	92¹	124	10	68	63	17.6	7.41	64	.330	.436	0	—	0	-28	-27	1	-2.9

● **JIM CONWAY**   Conway, James P. b: 10/8/1858, Clifton Heights, Pa.   TR,   Deb: 5/5/1884 F

YEAR	TM/L	W	L	PCT	G	GS	CG	SH	SV	IP	H	HR	BB	SO	RAT	ERA	ERA+	OAV	OOB	BH	AVG	PB	PR	/A	PD	TPI
1884	Bro-a	3	9	.250	13	13	10	0	0	105¹	132	4	15	25	12.8	4.44	75	.289	.316	6	.128	-4	-14	-13	-2	-1.6
1885	Phi-a	0	1	.000	2	2	1	0	0	12¹	19	0	2	0	15.3	7.30	47	.358	.382	0	.000	-0	-6	-5	-0	-0.4
1889	KC-a	19	19	.500	41	37	33	0	0	335	334	12	90	115	11.8	3.25	129	.252	.306	31	.208	-6	22	35	1	2.7
Total	3	22	29	.431	56	52	44	0	0	452²	485	16	107	140	12.1	3.64	109	.264	.311	37	.183	-10	3	16	-1	0.7

● **JERRY CONWAY**   Conway, Jerome Patrick b: 6/7/01, Holyoke, Mass.   d: 4/16/80, Holyoke, Mass.   BL/TL, 6'2", 190 lbs.   Deb: 8/31/20

YEAR	TM/L	W	L	PCT	G	GS	CG	SH	SV	IP	H	HR	BB	SO	RAT	ERA	ERA+	OAV	OOB	BH	AVG	PB	PR	/A	PD	TPI
1920	Was-A	0	0	—	1	0	0	0	0	2	1	0	1	0	9.0	0.00	—	.167	.286	0	—	0	1	1	-0	0.0

● **PETE CONWAY**   Conway, Peter J. b: 10/30/1866, Burmont, Pa.   d: 1/13/03, Clifton Heights, Pa.   BR/TR, 5'10.5", 162 lbs.   Deb: 8/10/1885 F♦

YEAR	TM/L	W	L	PCT	G	GS	CG	SH	SV	IP	H	HR	BB	SO	RAT	ERA	ERA+	OAV	OOB	BH	AVG	PB	PR	/A	PD	TPI
1885	Buf-N	10	17	.370	27	27	26	1	0	210	256	10	44	94	12.9	4.67	64	.287	.320	10	.111	-4	-43	-39	1	-4.2
1886	KC-N	5	15	.250	23	20	19	0	0	180	236	6	61	81	14.9	5.75	66	.294	.343	47	.242	0	-49	-39	-2	-3.4
	Det-N	6	5	.545	11	11	11	0	0	91	93	1	25	35	11.7	3.36	99	.255	.303	8	.186	1	-1	-0	-0	-0.1
	Yr	11	20	.355	34	31	30	0	0	271	329	7	86	116	13.8	4.95	73	.282	.331	55	.232	1	-49	-40	-2	-3.5
1887	*Det-N	8	9	.471	17	17	16	0	0	146	132	3	47	40	11.3	2.90	140	.235	.300	22	.232	0	19	19	3	1.9
1888	Det-N	30	14	.682	45	45	43	4	0	391	315	11	57	176	8.9	2.26	123	.208	**.243**	46	.275	15	26	22	3	3.9
1889	Pit-N	2	1	.667	3	3	2	0	0	22	26	1	16	2	17.2	4.91	76	.286	.393	1	.100	-0	-2	-3	-0	-0.2
Total	5	61	61	.500	126	123	117	5	0	1040	1058	32	250	428	11.5	3.59	90	.255	.295	134	.263	12	-50	-42	4	-2.1

● **DICK CONWAY**   Conway, Richard Butler b: 4/25/1865, Lowell, Mass.   d: 9/9/26, Lowell, Mass.   BL/TR, 5'7.5", 140 lbs.   Deb: 7/22/1886 F

YEAR	TM/L	W	L	PCT	G	GS	CG	SH	SV	IP	H	HR	BB	SO	RAT	ERA	ERA+	OAV	OOB	BH	AVG	PB	PR	/A	PD	TPI
1886	Bal-a	2	7	.222	9	9	8	0	0	76²	106	6	43	64	17.8	6.81	50	.312	.394	7	.206	1	-29	-29	2	-2.2
1887	Bos-N	9	15	.375	26	26	25	0	0	222¹	249	10	86	45	13.8	4.66	87	.276	.343	36	.248	2	-14	-15	-1	-1.0
1888	Bos-N	4	2	.667	6	6	6	0	0	53	49	2	8	12	10.4	2.38	120	.240	.282	4	.160	-1	3	3	-0	0.2
Total	3	15	24	.385	41	41	39	0	0	352	404	18	137	121	14.2	4.78	78	.279	.347	47	.230	2	-40	-41	2	-3.0

YEAR TM/L	W	L	PCT	G	GS	CG	SH	SV	IP	H	HR	BB	SO	RAT	ERA	ERA+	OAV	OOB	BH	AVG	PB	PR	/A	PD	TPI
● **JOE CONZELMAN** Conzelman, Joseph Harrison b: 7/14/1885, Bristol, Conn. d: 4/17/79, Mountain Brook, Ala. BR/TR, 6′, 170 lbs. Deb: 5/1/13																									
1913 Pit-N	0	1	.000	3	2	1	0	0	15	13	0	5	9	11.4	1.20	251	.245	.322	0	.000	-1	3	3	0	0.1
1914 Pit-N	5	6	.455	33	9	4	1	2	101	88	2	40	39	11.7	2.94	90	.254	.337	3	.111	-2	-2	-3	2	-0.4
1915 Pit-N	1	1	.500	18	1	0	0	0	47¹	41	0	20	22	12.2	3.42	80	.248	.340	1	.091	-1	-4	-4	1	-0.2
Total 3	6	8	.429	54	12	5	1	2	163¹	142	2	65	70	11.8	2.92	93	.252	.336	4	.095	-3	-2	-4	2	-0.5
● **ANDY COOK** Cook, Andrew Bernard b: 8/30/67, Memphis, Tenn. BR/TR, 6′5″, 215 lbs. Deb: 5/9/93																									
1993 NY-A	0	1	.000	4	0	0	0	0	5¹	4	1	7	4	18.6	5.06	82	.200	.407	0	—	0	-0	-1	0	0.0
● **DENNIS COOK** Cook, Dennis Bryan b: 10/4/62, LaMarque, Tex. BL/TL, 6′3″, 185 lbs. Deb: 9/12/88																									
1988 SF-N	2	1	.667	4	4	1	1	0	22	9	1	11	13	8.2	2.86	114	.125	.241	0	.000	1	1	1	-0	0.1
1989 SF-N	1	0	1.000	2	2	1	0	0	15	13	1	5	9	10.8	1.80	187	.245	.310	1	.167	1	3	3	0	0.3
Phi-N	6	8	.429	21	16	1	1	0	106	97	17	33	58	11.2	3.99	89	.243	.304	8	.222	1	-6	-5	-1	-0.7
Yr	7	8	.467	23	18	2	1	0	121	110	18	38	67	11.2	3.72	95	.243	.305	9	.214	2	-3	-3	-1	-0.4
1990 Phi-N	8	3	.727	42	13	2	1	0	141²	132	13	54	58	11.9	3.56	107	.250	.322	13	.310	4	4	4	-0	0.7
LA-N	1	1	.500	5	3	0	0	0	14¹	23	7	2	6	15.7	7.53	49	.365	.385	2	.286	1	-6	-6	-0	-0.6
Yr	9	4	.692	47	16	2	1	0	156	155	20	56	64	12.2	3.92	97	.259	.323	15	.306	5	-2	-2	-0	0.1
1991 LA-N	1	0	1.000	20	1	0	0	0	17²	12	0	7	8	9.7	0.51	705	.203	.288	0	.000	-0	6	6	0	0.3
1992 Cle-A	5	7	.417	32	25	1	0	0	158	156	29	50	96	11.8	3.82	102	.255	.314	0	—	0	2	2	-2	-0.1
1993 Cle-A	5	5	.500	25	6	0	0	0	54	62	9	16	34	13.3	5.67	76	.295	.351	0	—	0	-8	-8	-1	-1.3
1994 Chi-A	3	1	.750	38	0	0	0	0	33	29	4	14	26	11.7	3.55	132	.230	.307	0	—	0	5	4	-0	0.4
1995 Cle-A	0	0	—	11	0	0	0	0	12²	16	3	10	13	19.2	6.39	73	.320	.443	0	—	0	-2	-2	0	0.0
Tex-A	0	0	—	35	1	0	0	2	45	47	6	16	40	12.8	4.00	121	.280	.346	0	—	0	4	4	-1	0.1
Yr	0	2	.000	46	1	0	0	2	57²	63	9	26	53	14.0	4.53	106	.288	.366	0	—	0	1	2	-1	0.1
1996 *Tex-A	5	2	.714	60	0	0	0	0	70¹	53	2	35	64	12.2	4.09	130	.214	.328	0	—	0	7	10	-1	0.6
Total 9	37	30	.552	295	71	6	3	3	689²	649	92	253	425	12.0	3.93	104	.251	.322	24	.250	7	9	11	-6	-0.2
● **EARL COOK** Cook, Earl Davis b: 12/10/08, Stouffville, Ont., Canada BR/TR, 6′, 195 lbs. Deb: 9/12/41																									
1941 Det-A	0	0	—	1	0	0	0	0	2	4	0	1	0	18.0	4.50	101	.400	.400	0	—	0	-0	0	-0	0.0
● **GLEN COOK** Cook, Glen Patrick b: 9/8/59, Buffalo, N.Y. BR/TR, 5′11″, 180 lbs. Deb: 6/23/85																									
1985 Tex-A	2	3	.400	9	7	0	0	0	40	53	12	18	19	16.6	9.45	45	.327	.404	0	—	0	-24	-23	-1	-2.3
● **MIKE COOK** Cook, Michael Horace b: 8/14/63, Charleston, S.C. BR/TR, 6′3″, 200 lbs. Deb: 7/1/86																									
1986 Cal-A	0	2	.000	5	1	0	0	0	9	13	3	7	6	20.0	9.00	46	.333	.435	0	—	0	-5	-5	0	-0.8
1987 Cal-A	1	2	.333	16	1	0	0	0	34¹	34	7	18	27	13.6	5.50	78	.264	.354	0	—	0	-4	-5	1	-0.2
1988 Cal-A	0	1	.000	3	0	0	0	0	3²	4	0	1	2	14.7	4.91	79	.308	.400	0	—	0	-0	-0	-1	-0.1
1989 Min-A	0	1	.000	15	0	0	0	0	21³	22	1	17	15	16.9	5.06	82	.268	.400	0	—	0	-3	-2	-1	-0.6
1993 Bal-A	0	0	—	2	0	0	0	0	3	1	0	2	3	9.0	0.00	—	.091	.231	0	—	0	1	1	-0	-0.1
Total 5	1	6	.143	41	2	0	0	0	71¹	74	11	45	53	15.3	5.55	76	.270	.377	0	—	0	-11	-11	0	-1.8
● **ROLLIN COOK** Cook, Rollin Edward b: 10/5/1890, Toledo, Ohio d: 8/11/75, Toledo, Ohio BR/TR, 5′9″, 152 lbs. Deb: 7/6/15																									
1915 StL-A	0	0	—	5	0	0	0	0	13²	16	0	9	7	17.1	7.24	40	.276	.382	1	.250	0	-7	-7	0	0.0
● **RON COOK** Cook, Ronald Wayne b: 7/11/47, Jefferson, Tex. BL/TL, 6′1″, 175 lbs. Deb: 4/10/70																									
1970 Hou-N	4	4	.500	41	7	0	0	0	82¹	80	4	42	50	13.7	3.72	104	.274	.371	4	.235	2	3	1	-0	0.3
1971 Hou-N	0	4	.000	5	4	0	0	0	25²	23	2	8	10	11.2	4.91	69	.237	.302	2	.250	0	-4	-4	0	-0.6
Total 2	4	8	.333	46	11	0	0	0	108	103	6	50	60	13.1	4.00	94	.265	.354	6	.240	2	-1	-3	-0	-0.3
● **STEVE COOKE** Cooke, Steven Montague b: 1/14/70, Lihue, Hawaii BR/TL, 6′6″, 220 lbs. Deb: 7/28/92																									
1992 Pit-N	2	0	1.000	11	0	0	0	0	23	22	2	4	10	10.2	3.52	98	.253	.286	1	.333	0	-0	-0	-0	0.0
1993 Pit-N	10	10	.500	32	32	3	1	0	210²	207	22	59	132	11.5	3.89	104	.258	.312	11	.155	-1	4	4	-2	0.0
1994 Pit-N	4	11	.267	25	23	2	0	0	134¹	157	21	46	74	13.9	5.02	86	.298	.360	8	.190	-0	-12	-11	-1	-1.1
1996 Pit-N	0	0	—	3	0	0	0	0	8¹	11	1	5	7	17.3	7.56	58	.314	.400	-0	.000	-0	-3	-3	-0	0.0
Total 4	16	21	.432	71	55	5	1	1	376¹	397	46	114	223	12.4	4.35	94	.274	.330	20	.171	-0	-12	-10	-4	-1.1
● **DANNY COOMBS** Coombs, Daniel Bernard b: 3/23/42, Lincoln, Me. BR/TL, 6′5″, 210 lbs. Deb: 9/27/63																									
1963 Hou-N	0	0	—	1	0	0	0	0	0¹	3	0	0	0	81.0	27.00	12	.750	.750	0	—	0	-1	-1	-0	0.0
1964 Hou-N	1	1	.500	7	1	0	0	0	18	21	1	10	14	16.0	5.00	68	.300	.395	0	.000	-0	-3	-3	-0	-0.4
1965 Hou-N	0	2	.000	26	3	0	0	0	47	54	3	23	35	15.3	4.79	70	.292	.379	1	.111	-0	-7	-7	1	-0.2
1966 Hou-N	0	0	—	2	0	0	0	0	2²	4	1	1	1	13.5	3.38	101	.333	.333	0	.000	-0	-0	-0	-0	0.0
1967 Hou-N	3	0	1.000	6	2	0	0	0	24¹	21	0	9	23	11.1	3.33	99	.233	.303	1	.125	-0	-0	-0	-0	0.0
1968 Hou-N	4	3	.571	40	2	0	0	0	46²	52	4	17	29	13.5	3.28	90	.286	.350	4	.400	-1	-2	-2	-0	-0.1
1969 Hou-N	1	1	.500	8	0	0	0	0	8	12	0	2	3	16.9	6.75	52	.364	.417	0	.000	-0	-3	-3	-0	-0.4
1970 SD-N	10	14	.417	35	27	5	1	0	188¹	185	12	76	105	12.6	3.30	121	.256	.329	5	.096	-2	16	14	-2	1.3
1971 SD-N	1	6	.143	19	7	0	0	0	57²	81	10	25	37	16.5	6.24	53	.327	.388	3	.214	-1	-18	-19	-1	-1.9
Total 9	19	27	.413	144	42	5	1	2	393	433	26	162	249	13.8	4.08	88	.290	.350	14	.140	-0	-17	-21	-0	-1.7
● **JACK COOMBS** Coombs, John Wesley "Colby Jack" b: 11/18/1882, LeGrand, Iowa d: 4/15/57, Palestine, Tex. BB/TR, 6′, 185 lbs. Deb: 7/5/06 MC♦																									
1906 Phi-A	10	10	.500	23	18	13	1	0	173	144	0	68	90	11.4	2.50	109	.229	.312	16	.239	1	4	4	-0	0.6
1907 Phi-A	6	9	.400	23	17	10	2	2	132²	109	2	64	73	12.3	3.12	83	.227	.329	8	.167	-1	-8	-8	0	-1.0
1908 Phi-A	7	5	.583	26	18	10	4	0	153	130	1	64	80	11.6	2.00	128	.233	.316	56	.255	4	7	10	0	1.1
1909 Phi-A	12	11	.522	30	24	18	6	1	205²	156	1	73	97	10.3	2.32	104	.213	.289	14	.169	1	4	2	-0	0.3
1910 *Phi-A	**31**	9	.775	**45**	38	35	**13**	1	353	248	0	115	224	9.4	1.30	183	.201	.273	29	.220	4	48	42	-5	4.8
1911 *Phi-A	**28**	12	.700	47	40	26	1	2	336²	360	8	119	185	13.2	3.53	89	.280	.348	45	.319	14	-7	-14	-3	-0.5
1912 Phi-A	21	10	.677	40	32	23	1	2	262²	227	5	94	120	11.4	3.29	93	.241	.316	28	.255	6	-1	-6	-1	-0.1
1913 Phi-A	0	0	—	2	2	0	0	0	5¹	5	0	6	0	20.3	10.13	27	.250	.444	1	.333	1	-4	-4	-0	0.0
1914 Phi-A	0	1	.000	2	2	0	0	0	8	8	0	3	1	13.5	4.50	58	.267	.353	2	.273	1	-2	-2	-0	-0.2
1915 Bro-N	15	10	.600	29	24	17	2	0	195²	166	1	91	56	12.6	2.58	108	.236	.337	21	.280	4	4	4	-4	0.5
1916 *Bro-N	13	8	.619	27	20	10	3	0	159	136	3	44	47	10.3	2.66	101	.239	.296	11	.180	-0	-1	0	-6	-0.6
1917 Bro-N	7	11	.389	31	14	9	0	0	141	147	7	49	34	13.0	3.96	71	.284	.355	10	.227	2	-20	-18	-3	-2.4
1918 Bro-N	8	14	.364	27	20	16	2	0	189	191	10	49	44	11.5	3.81	73	.266	.315	19	.168	-0	-22	-22	-3	-2.7
1920 Det-A	0	0	—	2	0	0	0	0	5²	7	0	2	1	14.3	3.18	117	.318	.375	0	.000	-0	0	0	-0	0.0
Total 14	158	110	.590	354	269	187	35	8	2320	2034	38	841	1052	11.5	2.78	99	.241	.316	261	.235	36	3	-8	-25	-0.2
● **BOBBY COOMBS** Coombs, Raymond Franklin b: 2/2/08, Goodwins Mills, Me. d: 10/21/91, Ogunquit, Me. BR/TR, 5′9.5″, 160 lbs. Deb: 6/8/33																									
1933 Phi-A	0	1	.000	21	0	0	0	2	31¹	47	4	20	8	19.2	7.47	57	.348	.432	2	.400	1	-11	-11	-0	-0.4
1943 NY-N	0	1	.000	9	0	0	0	0	16	33	4	8	5	23.1	12.94	27	.423	.477	0	.000	0	-17	-17	-0	-0.9
Total 2	0	2	.000	30	0	0	0	2	47¹	80	8	28	13	20.5	9.32	43	.376	.448	2	.286	1	-28	-28	-0	-1.3
● **WILLIAM COON** Coon, William K. b: 3/21/1855, Pennsylvania d: 8/30/15, Burlington, N.J. Deb: 9/4/1875 ♦																									
1876 Phi-N	0	0	—	2	0	0	0	0	7	9	0	0	0	11.6	5.14	47	.257	.257	50	.227	-0	-2	-2	-0	0.0
● **JOHNNY COONEY** Cooney, John Walter b: 3/18/01, Cranston, R.I. d: 7/8/86, Sarasota, Fla. BR/TL, 5′10″, 165 lbs. Deb: 4/19/21 FMC♦																									
1921 Bos-N	0	1	.000	8	1	0	0	0	20²	19	3	10	9	12.6	3.92	93	.241	.326	1	.200	0	-0	-1	0	0.0
1922 Bos-N	1	2	.333	4	3	1	0	0	25	19	0	9	4	9.4	2.16	185	.224	.283	0	.000	-1	5	5	0	0.4
1923 Bos-N	3	5	.375	23	8	5	2	0	98	92	3	22	23	10.7	3.31	121	.246	.293	25	.379	4	8	7	-2	0.7
1924 Bos-N	8	9	.471	34	19	12	2	0	181	176	4	50	70	11.4	3.18	120	.260	.314	33	.254	2	14	13	-1	1.1
1925 Bos-N	14	14	.500	31	29	20	2	0	245²	267	15	50	65	11.7	3.48	115	.274	.312	33	.320	5	22	14	1	2.4
1926 Bos-N	3	3	.500	19	8	3	0	0	83¹	106	6	29	23	15.3	4.00	89	.320	.387	38	.302	3	-2	-4	0	0.1
1928 Bos-N	3	7	.300	24	6	2	0	0	89²	106	7	31	18	13.8	4.32	91	.303	.360	7	.171	-0	-3	-4	3	-0.1
1929 Bos-N	2	3	.400	14	2	1	0	0	45	57	4	21	10	15.0	5.00	94	.315	.389	23	.319	1	-1	-2	1	0.1

YEAR	TM/L	W	L	PCT	G	GS	CG	SH	SV	IP	H	HR	BB	SO	RAT	ERA	ERA+	OAV	OOB	BH	AVG	PB	PR	/A	PD	TPI
1930	Bos-N	0	0	—	2	0	0	0	0	7	16	2	3	1	25.7	18.00	27	.471	.526	0	.000	-1	-10	-10	1	0.0
Total	9	34	44	.436	159	76	44	7	6	795¹	858	41	223	224	12.4	3.72	106	.278	.331	965	.286	15	32	19	4	4.7

● BOB COONEY
Cooney, Robert Daniel b: 7/12/07, Glens Falls, N.Y. d: 5/4/76, Glens Falls, N.Y. BR/TR, 5'11", 160 lbs. Deb: 9/6/31

YEAR	TM/L	W	L	PCT	G	GS	CG	SH	SV	IP	H	HR	BB	SO	RAT	ERA	ERA+	OAV	OOB	BH	AVG	PB	PR	/A	PD	TPI
1931	StL-A	0	3	.000	5	4	1	0	0	39¹	46	1	29	12	15.3	4.12	113	.291	.374	5	.385	1	2	0	-0	0.2
1932	StL-A	1	2	.333	23	3	1	0	1	71	94	8	30	23	16.7	6.97	70	.324	.402	0	.000	-3	-20	-17	-2	-1.0
Total	2	1	5	.167	28	7	2	0	1	110¹	140	9	56	36	16.2	5.95	80	.313	.393	5	.143	-2	-19	-14	-2	-0.8

● BILL COONEY
Cooney, William A. "Cush" b: 4/7/1883, Boston, Mass. d: 11/6/28, Roxbury, Mass. TR, Deb: 9/22/09 ♦

YEAR	TM/L	W	L	PCT	G	GS	CG	SH	SV	IP	H	HR	BB	SO	RAT	ERA	ERA+	OAV	OOB	BH	AVG	PB	PR	/A	PD	TPI
1909	Bos-N	0	0	—	3	0	0	0	0	6¹	4	0	2	3	8.5	1.42	198	.182	.250	3	.300	0	1	1	-0	0.0

● WILBUR COOPER
Cooper, Arley Wilbur b: 2/24/1892, Bearsville, W.Va. d: 8/7/73, Encino, Cal. BR/TL, 5'11", 175 lbs. Deb: 8/29/12

YEAR	TM/L	W	L	PCT	G	GS	CG	SH	SV	IP	H	HR	BB	SO	RAT	ERA	ERA+	OAV	OOB	BH	AVG	PB	PR	/A	PD	TPI
1912	Pit-N	3	0	1.000	6	4	3	2	0	38	32	1	15	30	11.1	1.66	197	.227	.301	2	.154	-0	7	7	-0	0.4
1913	Pit-N	5	3	.625	30	9	3	1	0	93	98	0	45	39	14.0	3.29	92	.276	.361	3	.077	-1	-1	-3	-2	-0.5
1914	Pit-N	16	15	.516	40	34	19	0	0	266²	246	4	79	102	11.1	2.13	125	.254	.313	19	.207	1	20	16	0	2.0
1915	Pit-N	5	16	.238	38	21	11	1	4	185²	180	4	52	71	11.7	3.30	83	.262	.323	7	.117	-3	-11	-12	1	-1.5
1916	Pit-N	12	11	.522	42	23	16	2	2	246	189	4	74	111	9.8	1.87	144	.215	.279	17	.215	0	21	22	3	2.2
1917	Pit-N	17	11	.607	40	34	23	7	1	297²	276	4	54	99	10.1	2.36	120	.258	.297	21	.204	2	12	16	-3	1.5
1918	Pit-N	19	14	.576	38	29	26	2	3	273¹	219	2	65	117	9.7	2.11	136	.242	.279	23	.242	3	20	23	-2	1.3
1919	Pit-N	19	13	.594	35	32	27	4	1	286²	229	10	74	106	10.0	2.67	113	.225	.287	29	.287	6	8	11	-5	1.4
1920	Pit-N	24	15	.615	44	37	28	3	2	327	307	5	52	114	10.2	2.39	134	.253	.290	25	.221	1	27	30	3	3.2
1921	Pit-N	**22**	14	.611	38	38	29	2	0	**327**	341	9	80	134	11.9	3.25	118	.272	.320	31	.254	4	19	21	-3	2.2
1922	Pit-N	23	14	.622	41	36	**27**	4	0	294²	330	13	61	129	12.2	3.18	128	.286	.326	29	.269	9	**30**	**29**	-2	**4.0**
1923	Pit-N	17	19	.472	39	38	26	1	0	294²	331	11	71	77	12.6	3.57	112	.288	.335	28	.262	4	14	14	-1	1.7
1924	Pit-N	20	14	.588	38	35	25	**4**	1	268²	296	13	40	62	11.4	3.28	117	.283	.330	36	.346	10	17	17	-4	2.5
1925	Chi-N	12	14	.462	32	26	13	0	0	212¹	249	18	61	41	13.3	4.28	101	.291	.341	17	.207	1	-0	1	-2	-0.1
1926	Chi-N	2	1	.667	8	8	3	2	0	55	65	6	21	18	14.1	4.42	87	.311	.374	7	.389	3	-4	-4	-1	0.0
	Det-A	0	4	.000	8	3	0	0	0	13²	27	0	9	2	25.7	11.20	36	.443	.534	0	.000	-1	-11	-11	0	-2.4
Total	15	216	178	.548	517	407	279	35	14	3480	3415	103	853	1252	11.3	2.89	116	.262	.312	293	.239	39	168	180	-27	19.7

● CAL COOPER
Cooper, Calvin Asa b: 8/11/22, Great Falls, S.C. d: 7/4/94, Clinton, S.C. BR/TR, 6'2.5", 180 lbs. Deb: 9/14/48

YEAR	TM/L	W	L	PCT	G	GS	CG	SH	SV	IP	H	HR	BB	SO	RAT	ERA	ERA+	OAV	OOB	BH	AVG	PB	PR	/A	PD	TPI
1948	Was-A	0	0	—	1	0	0	0	0	1	5	1	5	1	54.0	45.00	10	.625	.667	0	—	0	-5	-5	-0	0.0

● DON COOPER
Cooper, Donald James b: 1/15/57, New York, N.Y. BR/TR, 6'1", 185 lbs. Deb: 4/9/81

YEAR	TM/L	W	L	PCT	G	GS	CG	SH	SV	IP	H	HR	BB	SO	RAT	ERA	ERA+	OAV	OOB	BH	AVG	PB	PR	/A	PD	TPI
1981	Min-A	1	5	.167	27	2	0	0	0	58²	61	9	32	33	14.4	4.30	92	.274	.367	0	—	-4	-4	-2	-1	-0.6
1982	Min-A	0	1	.000	6	1	0	0	0	11¹	14	2	10	5	19.9	9.53	45	.311	.446	0	—	-2	-7	-7	-0	-0.7
1983	Tor-A	0	0	—	4	0	0	0	0	5¹	8	3	0	5	13.5	6.75	64	.348	.348	0	—	-2	-2	-1	-0	-0.5
1985	NY-A	0	0	—	7	0	0	0	0	10	12	2	3	4	13.5	5.40	74	.300	.349	0	—	-1	-1	-2	-0	0.2
Total	4	1	6	.143	44	3	0	0	0	85¹	95	14	46	47	15.0	5.27	76	.287	.376	0	—	-9	-14	-12	-2	-1.6

● GUY COOPER
Cooper, Guy Evans "Rebel" b: 1/28/1893, Rome, Ga. d: 8/2/51, Santa Monica, Cal. BB/TR, 6'1", 185 lbs. Deb: 5/2/14

YEAR	TM/L	W	L	PCT	G	GS	CG	SH	SV	IP	H	HR	BB	SO	RAT	ERA	ERA+	OAV	OOB	BH	AVG	PB	PR	/A	PD	TPI
1914	NY-A	0	0	—	3	0	0	0	0	3	3	0	2	3	15.0	9.00	31	.273	.385	0	.000	-0	-2	-2	-0	0.0
	Bos-A	1	0	1.000	9	1	0	0	0	22	23	1	9	5	14.3	5.32	51	.299	.393	0	.000	-1	-6	-6	-1	-0.5
	Yr	1	0	1.000	10	1	0	0	0	25	26	1	11	8	14.4	5.76	47	.295	.392	0	.000	-1	-8	-8	-1	-0.5
1915	Bos-A	0	0	—	1	0	0	0	0	2	0	0	2	0	9.0	0.00	—	.000	.286	0	—	0	1	1	-0	0.0
Total	2	1	0	1.000	11	1	0	0	0	27	26	1	13	8	14.0	5.33	51	.280	.385	0	.000	-1	-8	-8	-1	-0.5

● MORT COOPER
Cooper, Morton Cecil b: 3/2/13, Atherton, Mo. d: 11/17/58, Little Rock, Ark. BR/TR, 6'2", 210 lbs. Deb: 9/14/38 F

YEAR	TM/L	W	L	PCT	G	GS	CG	SH	SV	IP	H	HR	BB	SO	RAT	ERA	ERA+	OAV	OOB	BH	AVG	PB	PR	/A	PD	TPI
1938	StL-N	2	1	.667	4	3	1	0	1	23²	17	1	12	11	11.4	3.04	130	.195	.300	2	.222	0	2	2	1	0.4
1939	StL-N	12	6	.667	45	26	7	2	4	210²	208	6	97	130	13.1	3.25	127	.232	.342	16	.232	3	16	20	-3	1.6
1940	StL-N	11	12	.478	38	29	16	3	3	230²	225	12	86	95	12.3	3.63	110	.253	.321	13	.157	-2	-6	-3	-2	0.4
1941	StL-N	13	9	.591	29	25	12	0	0	186²	175	15	69	118	11.9	3.91	96	.244	.313	13	.186	-0	-6	-3	-1	-0.5
1942	*StL-N★	**22**	7	.759	37	35	22	**10**	0	278²	207	9	68	152	**9.0**	**1.78**	**193**	.204	**.258**	19	.184	-4	**48**	**51**	-3	**5.0**
1943	*StL-N★	**21**	8	**.724**	37	32	24	6	1	274	228	5	79	141	10.2	2.30	146	.226	.286	17	.170	-1	33	32	-2	3.2
1944	*StL-N	22	7	.759	34	33	22	**7**	1	252¹	227	6	60	97	10.4	2.46	143	.239	.288	19	.202	2	32	30	-5	3.0
1945	StL-N	2	0	1.000	4	3	1	0	0	23²	20	1	7	14	10.6	1.52	246	.247	.292	2	.333	1	6	6	-1	0.5
	Bos-N†	7	4	.636	20	11	4	1	1	78	77	4	27	45	12.1	3.35	115	.257	.320	6	.231	1	4	4	0	0.7
	Yr	9	4	.692	24	14	5	1	1	101²	97	5	34	59	11.7	2.92	130	.249	.311	8	.250	2	10	10	-0	1.2
1946	Bos-N☆	13	11	.542	28	27	15	4	1	199	181	16	39	83	**9.9**	3.12	110	.209	**.276**	14	.209	1	6	7	-3	0.6
1947	Bos-N	2	5	.286	10	7	2	0	0	46²	48	7	13	15	12.4	4.05	96	.271	.328	0	.000	-1	0	-1	-3	-0.3
	NY-N	1	5	.167	8	8	2	0	0	36²	51	7	13	12	15.7	7.12	57	.323	.374	6	.429	-1	-12	-12	-1	-1.4
	Yr	3	10	.231	18	15	4	0	0	83¹	99	9	26	27	13.5	5.40	74	.300	.344	6	.222	2	-12	-13	-2	-1.7
1949	Chi-N	0	0	—	1	0	0	0	0	0²	2	1	1	0	—	∞	—	1.000	1.000	0	—	0	-3	-3	-0	-0.3
Total	11	128	75	.631	295	239	128	33	14	1840²	1666	85	571	913	11.1	2.97	123	.240	.300	127	.194	6	132	143	-20	12.9

● PAT COOPER
Cooper, Orge Patterson b: 11/26/17, Albemarle, N.C. d: 3/15/93, Charlotte, N.C. BR/TR, 6'3", 180 lbs. Deb: 5/11/46 ♦

YEAR	TM/L	W	L	PCT	G	GS	CG	SH	SV	IP	H	HR	BB	SO	RAT	ERA	ERA+	OAV	OOB	BH	AVG	PB	PR	/A	PD	TPI
1946	Phi-A	0	0	—	1	0	0	0	0	1	1	0	1	0	18.0	0.00	—	.250	.400		—	0	0	0	-0	0.0

● MAYS COPELAND
Copeland, Mays b: 8/31/13, Mountain View, Ark d: 11/29/82, Indio, Cal. BR/TR, 6', 180 lbs. Deb: 4/27/35

YEAR	TM/L	W	L	PCT	G	GS	CG	SH	SV	IP	H	HR	BB	SO	RAT	ERA	ERA+	OAV	OOB	BH	AVG	PB	PR	/A	PD	TPI
1935	StL-N	0	0	—	1	0	0	0	0	0²	2	0	2	0	27.0	13.50	30	.667	.667		—	-1	-1	-1	0	0.0

● ROCKY COPPINGER
Coppinger, John Thomas b: 3/19/74, ElPaso, Tex. BR/TR, 6'5", 245 lbs. Deb: 6/11/96

YEAR	TM/L	W	L	PCT	G	GS	CG	SH	SV	IP	H	HR	BB	SO	RAT	ERA	ERA+	OAV	OOB	BH	AVG	PB	PR	/A	PD	TPI
1996	Bal-A†	10	6	.625	23	22	0	0	0	125	126	25	60	104	13.5	5.18	94	.263	.348	0	—	-3	-3	-4	-2	-0.5

● HENRY COPPOLA
Coppola, Henry Peter b: 8/6/12, E.Douglas, Mass. d: 7/10/90, Norfolk, Mass. BR/TR, 5'11", 175 lbs. Deb: 4/19/35

YEAR	TM/L	W	L	PCT	G	GS	CG	SH	SV	IP	H	HR	BB	SO	RAT	ERA	ERA+	OAV	OOB	BH	AVG	PB	PR	/A	PD	TPI
1935	Was-A	3	4	.429	19	5	2	1	0	59¹	72	6	29	19	15.5	5.92	73	.300	.378	1	.071	-0	-10	-11	-0	-1.1
1936	Was-A	0	0	—	6	0	0	1	0	14	17	1	12	2	18.6	4.50	106	.315	.439	1	.333	1	1	0	0	0.1
Total	2	3	4	.429	25	5	2	1	0	73¹	89	7	41	21	16.1	5.65	78	.303	.390	2	.118	1	-9	-11	-0	-1.0

● DOUG CORBETT
Corbett, Douglas Mitchell b: 11/4/52, Sarasota, Fla. BR/TR, 6'1", 185 lbs. Deb: 4/10/80

YEAR	TM/L	W	L	PCT	G	GS	CG	SH	SV	IP	H	HR	BB	SO	RAT	ERA	ERA+	OAV	OOB	BH	AVG	PB	PR	/A	PD	TPI
1980	Min-A	8	6	.571	73	0	0	0	23	136¹	102	7	42	89	9.6	1.98	220	.213	.278	0	—	0	**31**	**36**	3	4.5
1981	Min-A☆	2	6	.250	**54**	0	0	0	17	87²	80	5	34	60	11.7	2.57	154	.239	.309	0	—	0	11	13	2	1.6
1982	Min-A	0	2	.000	10	0	0	0	3	22	27	3	10	15	15.1	5.32	80	.300	.370	0	—	0	-3	-3	1	-0.4
	Cal-A	1	7	.125	33	0	0	0	8	57	46	8	25	37	11.2	5.05	80	.223	.307	0	—	0	-6	-6	-0	-0.9
	Yr	1	9	.100	43	0	0	0	11	79	73	11	35	52	12.3	5.13	80	.247	.326	0	—	0	-9	-9	-1	-1.3
1983	Cal-A	1	1	.500	8	0	0	0	1	17¹	26	1	4	18	16.1	3.63	110	.351	.392	0	—	0	1	1	-0	0.1
1984	Cal-A	5	1	.833	45	0	0	0	4	85	76	2	30	48	11.4	2.12	174	.244	.314	0	—	0	18	17	0	1.9
1985	Cal-A	3	3	.500	30	0	0	0	0	46	49	7	20	24	13.7	4.89	84	.274	.350	0	—	0	-4	-4	0	-0.4
1986	*Cal-A	4	2	.667	46	0	0	0	10	78²	66	11	22	36	10.2	3.66	112	.231	.288	0	—	0	5	4	1	0.6
1987	Bal-A	0	2	.000	11	0	0	0	1	23	25	5	13	16	14.9	7.83	56	.281	.373	0	—	0	-9	-9	1	-0.6
Total	8	24	30	.444	313	1	0	0	66	553	497	49	200	343	11.4	3.32	125	.242	.312	0	—	0	43	50	8	5.9

● JOE CORBETT
Corbett, Joseph A. b: 12/4/1875, San Francisco, Cal. d: 5/2/45, San Francisco, Cal. BR/TR, 5'10", Deb: 8/23/1895

YEAR	TM/L	W	L	PCT	G	GS	CG	SH	SV	IP	H	HR	BB	SO	RAT	ERA	ERA+	OAV	OOB	BH	AVG	PB	PR	/A	PD	TPI
1895	Was-N	0	2	.000	3	3	3	0	0	19	26	3	9	3	17.5	5.68	84	.321	.402	2	.133	-1	-2	-2	-0	-0.2
1896	*Bal-N	3	0	1.000	8	3	3	0	1	41	31	0	17	28	11.6	2.20	195	.208	.310	6	.273	1	10	9	-1	0.6
1897	*Bal-N	24	8	.750	37	37	34	1	0	313	330	2	115	149	13.4	3.11	134	.269	.341	37	.247	1	42	37	2	3.1
1904	StL-N	5	8	.385	14	14	12	0	0	108²	110	2	51	68	14.0	4.39	61	.240	.327	9	.209	1	-20	-20	0	-2.0
Total	4	32	18	.640	62	57	52	1	1	481²	497	7	192	248	13.5	3.42	113	.260	.338	54	.235	2	30	24	2	1.5

● SHERMAN CORBETT
Corbett, Sherman Stanley b: 11/3/62, New Braunfels, Tex. BL/TL, 6'4", 205 lbs. Deb: 5/29/88

YEAR	TM/L	W	L	PCT	G	GS	CG	SH	SV	IP	H	HR	BB	SO	RAT	ERA	ERA+	OAV	OOB	BH	AVG	PB	PR	/A	PD	TPI
1988	Cal-A	2	1	.667	34	0	0	0	1	45²	47	2	23	28	13.8	4.14	93	.273	.359	0	—	-1	-1	-1	-0	0.0
1989	Cal-A	0	0	—	4	0	0	0	0	5¹	3	1	1	3	6.8	3.38	113	.158	.200	0	—	0	0	0	-0	0.0

YEAR TM/L	W	L	PCT	G	GS	CG	SH	SV	IP	H	HR	BB	SO	RAT	ERA	ERA+	OAV	OOB	BH	AVG	PB	PR	/A	PD	TPI
1990 Cal-A	0	0	—	4	0	0	0	0	5	8	0	3	2	19.8	9.00	42	.364	.440	0	—	0	-3	-3	-0	0.0
Total 3	2	1	.667	42	0	0	0	0	56	58	3	27	33	13.7	4.50	86	.272	.354	0	—	0	-3	-4	-1	0.0

● RAY CORBIN
Corbin, Alton Ray b: 2/12/49, Live Oak, Fla. BR/TR, 6'2", 200 lbs. Deb: 4/6/71

YEAR TM/L	W	L	PCT	G	GS	CG	SH	SV	IP	H	HR	BB	SO	RAT	ERA	ERA+	OAV	OOB	BH	AVG	PB	PR	/A	PD	TPI
1971 Min-A	8	11	.421	52	11	2	0	3	140¹	141	19	70	83	13.7	4.10	87	.265	.353	7	.206	1	-10	-9	1	-1.0
1972 Min-A	8	9	.471	31	19	5	3	0	161²	135	12	53	83	10.8	2.62	123	.230	.300	4	.082	-2	8	11	-2	0.7
1973 Min-A	8	5	.615	51	7	1	0	14	148¹	124	7	60	83	11.5	3.03	130	.229	.311	0	—	0	13	15	-1	1.4
1974 Min-A	7	6	.538	29	15	1	0	0	112¹	133	8	40	50	14.1	5.29	70	.294	.356	0	—	0	-21	-19	1	-2.1
1975 Min-A	5	7	.417	18	11	3	0	0	89²	105	13	38	49	14.6	5.12	75	.295	.366	0	—	0	-13	-13	1	-1.5
Total 5	36	38	.486	181	63	12	3	17	652¹	638	59	261	348	12.7	3.84	95	.258	.334	11	.133	-2	-23	-15	-0	-2.5

● ARCHIE CORBIN
Corbin, Archie Ray b: 12/30/67, Beaumont, Tex. BR/TR, 6'4", 190 lbs. Deb: 9/10/91

YEAR TM/L	W	L	PCT	G	GS	CG	SH	SV	IP	H	HR	BB	SO	RAT	ERA	ERA+	OAV	OOB	BH	AVG	PB	PR	/A	PD	TPI
1991 KC-A	0	0	—	2	0	0	0	0	2¹	3	0	2	1	19.3	3.86	107	.300	.417	0	—	0	0	0	-0	0.0
1996 Bal-A	2	0	1.000	18	0	0	0	0	27¹	22	2	22	20	14.8	2.30	212	.222	.369	0	—	0	8	8	-1	0.5
Total 2	2	0	1.000	20	0	0	0	0	29²	25	2	24	21	15.2	2.43	199	.229	.373	0	—	0	8	8	-1	0.5

● JACK CORCORAN
Corcoran, John H. b: 1860, Lowell, Mass. Deb: 5/1/1884 ♦

YEAR TM/L	W	L	PCT	G	GS	CG	SH	SV	IP	H	HR	BB	SO	RAT	ERA	ERA+	OAV	OOB	BH	AVG	PB	PR	/A	PD	TPI
1884 Bro-a	0	0	—	1	0	0	0	0	1	0	0	1	0	9.0	0.00	—	.000	.091	39	.211	0	0	0	-0	0.0

● LARRY CORCORAN
Corcoran, Lawrence J. b: 8/10/1859, Brooklyn, N.Y. d: 10/14/1891, Newark, N.J. BL/TR, 120 lbs. Deb: 5/1/1880 F ♦

YEAR TM/L	W	L	PCT	G	GS	CG	SH	SV	IP	H	HR	BB	SO	RAT	ERA	ERA+	OAV	OOB	BH	AVG	PB	PR	/A	PD	TPI
1880 Chi-N	43	14	.754	63	60	57	4	2	536¹	404	6	99	268	8.4	1.95	124	.199	.236	66	.231	-0	25	28	6	3.1
1881 Chi-N	31	14	.689	45	44	43	4	0	396²	380	10	78	150	10.4	2.31	118	.242	.278	42	.222	-1	20	19	-2	1.4
1882 Chi-N	27	12	**.692**	39	39	38	3	0	355²	281	5	63	170	**8.7**	**1.95**	**147**	**.200**	**.234**	35	.207	-2	38	36	1	3.1
1883 Chi-N	34	20	.630	56	53	51	3	0	473²	483	7	82	216	10.7	2.49	128	.247	.277	55	.209	-1	34	37	1	3.3
1884 Chi-N	35	23	.603	60	59	57	7	0	516²	473	35	116	272	10.3	2.40	130	.229	.270	61	.243	7	33	42	7	4.6
1885 Chi-N	5	2	.714	7	7	6	1	0	59¹	63	2	24	10	13.2	3.64	83	.259	.326	6	.273	2	-5	-4	0	-0.3
NY-N	2	1	.667	3	3	2	0	0	25	24	1	11	10	12.6	2.88	93	.241	.321	5	.357	1	-1	-1	0	0.1
Yr	7	3	.700	10	10	8	1	0	84¹	87	3	35	20	13.0	3.42	86	.255	.324	11	.306	3	-6	-5	1	-0.2
1886 Was-N	0	1	.000	2	1	1	0	0	14	16	0	4	3	12.9	5.79	57	.271	.317	15	.185	0	-4	-4	1	-0.2
1887 Ind-N	0	2	.000	2	2	1	0	0	15	23	3	19	4	26.4	12.60	33	.338	.494	2	.200	-0	-14	-14	0	-1.1
Total 8	177	89	.665	277	268	256	22	2	2392¹	2147	69	496	1103	10.0	2.36	122	.226	.264	287	.223	1	127	139	14	14.0

● MIKE CORCORAN
Corcoran, Michael b: Brooklyn, N.Y. Deb: 7/15/1884 F

YEAR TM/L	W	L	PCT	G	GS	CG	SH	SV	IP	H	HR	BB	SO	RAT	ERA	ERA+	OAV	OOB	BH	AVG	PB	PR	/A	PD	TPI
1884 Chi-N	0	1	.000	1	1	1	0	0	9	16	1	7	2	23.0	4.00	78	.372	.460	0	.000	-0	-1	-1	-0	-0.1

● FRANCISCO CORDOVA
Cordova, Francisco b: 4/26/72, Veracruz, Mex. BR/TR, 5'11", 165 lbs. Deb: 4/2/96

YEAR TM/L	W	L	PCT	G	GS	CG	SH	SV	IP	H	HR	BB	SO	RAT	ERA	ERA+	OAV	OOB	BH	AVG	PB	PR	/A	PD	TPI
1996 Pit-N	4	7	.364	59	6	0	0	12	99	103	11	20	95	11.4	4.09	107	.263	.303	2	.125	-1	1	3	1	0.4

● ED COREY
Corey, Edward Norman "Ike" (b: Abraham Simon Cohen) b: 7/13/1899, Chicago, Ill. d: 9/17/70, Kenosha, Wis. BR/TR, 6', 170 lbs. Deb: 7/2/18

YEAR TM/L	W	L	PCT	G	GS	CG	SH	SV	IP	H	HR	BB	SO	RAT	ERA	ERA+	OAV	OOB	BH	AVG	PB	PR	/A	PD	TPI
1918 Chi-A	0	0	—	1	0	0	0	0	2	2	0	1	0	13.5	4.50	61	.333	.429	0	.000	-0	-0	-0	0	0.0

● FRED COREY
Corey, Frederick Harrison b: 1857, S.Kingston, R.I. d: 11/27/12, Providence, R.I. BR/TR, Deb: 5/1/1878 ♦

YEAR TM/L	W	L	PCT	G	GS	CG	SH	SV	IP	H	HR	BB	SO	RAT	ERA	ERA+	OAV	OOB	BH	AVG	PB	PR	/A	PD	TPI
1878 Pro-N	1	2	.333	5	5	2	0	0	23	22	0	7	7	11.3	2.35	94	.250	.305	3	.143	-1	-0	-0	-1	-0.1
1880 Wor-N	8	9	.471	25	17	9	2	2	148¹	131	6	16	47	8.9	2.43	107	.219	.239	24	.174	-3	-1	3	-3	-0.2
1881 Wor-N	6	15	.286	23	21	20	1	0	188²	231	3	31	33	12.5	3.72	81	.299	.326	45	.222	-1	-20	-15	-1	-1.5
1882 Wor-N	1	13	.071	21	14	12	0	0	139	180	5	19	36	12.9	3.56	87	.286	.307	63	.247	0	-10	-7	1	-0.4
1883 Phi-a	10	7	.588	18	16	15	0	0	148¹	182	3	24	42	12.5	3.40	102	.283	.309	77	.258	2	-2	1	1	0.3
1885 Phi-a	1	0	1.000	1	1	1	0	0	9	18	2	1	3	19.0	7.00	49	.419	.432	94	.245	-0	-4	-4	0	-0.3
Total 6	27	46	.370	93	74	59	3	2	656¹	764	19	98	168	11.8	3.32	91	.276	.300	427	.246	-3	-36	-21	-2	-2.2

● POP CORKHILL
Corkhill, John Stewart b: 4/11/1858, Parkesburg, Pa. d: 4/4/21, Pennsauken, N.J. BL/TR, 5'10", 180 lbs. Deb: 5/1/1883 ♦

YEAR TM/L	W	L	PCT	G	GS	CG	SH	SV	IP	H	HR	BB	SO	RAT	ERA	ERA+	OAV	OOB	BH	AVG	PB	PR	/A	PD	TPI
1884 Cin-a	1	0	1.000	1	0	0	0	0	5	1	0	2	4	5.4	1.80	185	.063	.167	124	.274	0	1	1	-0	0.1
1885 Cin-a	1	4	.200	8	1	0	0	1	37	36	2	10	12	11.4	3.65	89	.243	.296	111	.252	1	-2	-2	0	-0.1
1886 Cin-a	0	0	—	1	0	0	0	0	0²	1	0	0	1	13.5	13.50	26	.125	.125	143	.265	0	-1	-1	0	0.0
1887 Cin-a	1	0	1.000	5	0	0	0	0	14²	22	1	3	1	16.6	5.52	79	.324	.370	168	.311	1	-2	-2	-0	-0.1
1888 Cin-a	0	0	—	2	0	0	0	1	5	8	0	2	3	14.4	10.80	29	.348	.348	133	.271	1	-4	-4	-0	-0.2
Total 5	3	4	.429	17	1	0	0	2	62¹	68	3	17	21	12.4	4.62	76	.259	.306	1120	.254	3	-8	-8	-0	-0.3

● MIKE CORKINS
Corkins, Michael Patrick b: 5/25/46, Riverside, Cal. BR/TR, 6'1", 200 lbs. Deb: 9/8/69

YEAR TM/L	W	L	PCT	G	GS	CG	SH	SV	IP	H	HR	BB	SO	RAT	ERA	ERA+	OAV	OOB	BH	AVG	PB	PR	/A	PD	TPI
1969 SD-N	1	3	.250	6	4	0	0	0	17	27	3	8	13	18.5	8.47	42	.370	.432	0	.000	-0	-9	-9	-0	-1.7
1970 SD-N	5	6	.455	24	18	1	0	0	111	109	11	79	75	15.6	4.62	86	.258	.379	8	.216	2	-7	-8	-1	-0.6
1971 SD-N	0	0	—	8	0	0	0	0	13	14	1	6	16	13.8	3.46	95	.280	.357	0	—	0	0	0	0	0.0
1972 SD-N	6	9	.400	47	9	2	1	6	140	125	14	62	108	12.3	3.54	93	.240	.325	9	.237	3	-1	-4	-0	-0.1
1973 SD-N	5	8	.385	47	11	2	0	0	122	130	12	61	82	14.9	4.50	77	.274	.370	7	.212	4	-11	-14	-2	-1.2
1974 SD-N	2	2	.500	25	2	0	0	0	56¹	53	5	32	41	13.7	4.79	74	.255	.357	0	.000	-0	-7	-8	-1	-0.6
Total 6	19	28	.404	157	44	5	1	9	459¹	458	46	248	335	14.2	4.39	81	.262	.360	24	.202	10	-36	-42	-4	-4.2

● RHEAL CORMIER
Cormier, Rheal Paul b: 4/23/67, Moncton, N.B., Can. BL/TL, 5'10", 185 lbs. Deb: 8/15/91

YEAR TM/L	W	L	PCT	G	GS	CG	SH	SV	IP	H	HR	BB	SO	RAT	ERA	ERA+	OAV	OOB	BH	AVG	PB	PR	/A	PD	TPI
1991 StL-N	4	5	.444	11	10	2	0	0	67²	74	5	8	38	11.2	4.12	90	.277	.303	5	.238	1	-3	-3	-1	-0.4
1992 StL-N	10	10	.500	31	30	3	0	0	186	194	15	33	117	11.2	3.68	92	.269	.306	6	.102	-2	-4	-6	1	-0.7
1993 StL-N	7	6	.538	38	21	1	0	0	145¹	163	18	27	75	12.0	4.33	91	.284	.321	11	.234	2	-5	-6	1	-0.2
1994 StL-N	3	2	.600	7	7	0	0	0	39²	40	6	7	26	11.3	5.45	76	.256	.301	4	.286	1	-5	-6	-1	-0.5
1995 *Bos-A	7	5	.583	48	12	0	0	0	115	131	12	31	69	12.9	4.07	120	.294	.344	0	—	0	8	10	1	0.8
1996 Mon-N	7	10	.412	33	27	1	1	0	159²	165	16	41	100	12.1	4.17	103	.270	.325	8	.186	1	1	2	3	0.6
Total 6	38	38	.500	168	107	7	1	0	713	767	72	147	425	11.9	4.13	97	.276	.319	34	.185	3	-8	-9	4	-0.4

● MARDIE CORNEJO
Cornejo, Nieves Mardie b: 8/5/51, Wellington, Kan. BR/TR, 6'3", 200 lbs. Deb: 4/8/78

YEAR TM/L	W	L	PCT	G	GS	CG	SH	SV	IP	H	HR	BB	SO	RAT	ERA	ERA+	OAV	OOB	BH	AVG	PB	PR	/A	PD	TPI
1978 NY-N	4	2	.667	25	0	0	0	3	36²	37	1	14	17	13.3	2.45	142	.285	.367	0	—	0	5	4	-0	0.7

● REID CORNELIUS
Cornelius, Jonathan Reid b: 6/2/70, Thomasville, Ala. BR/TR, 6', 200 lbs. Deb: 4/29/95

YEAR TM/L	W	L	PCT	G	GS	CG	SH	SV	IP	H	HR	BB	SO	RAT	ERA	ERA+	OAV	OOB	BH	AVG	PB	PR	/A	PD	TPI
1995 Mon-N	0	0	—	8	0	0	0	0	9	11	3	5	4	18.0	8.00	54	.306	.419	0	—	0	-4	-4	0	0.0
NY-N	3	7	.300	10	10	0	0	0	57²	64	8	25	35	14.0	5.15	79	.284	.359	2	.100	-1	-6	-7	1	-1.1
Yr	3	7	.300	18	10	0	0	0	66²	75	11	30	39	14.3	5.54	74	.285	.361	2	.100	-1	-10	-11	1	-1.1

● JEFF CORNELL
Cornell, Jeffery Ray b: 2/10/57, Kansas City, Mo. BB/TR, 5'11", 170 lbs. Deb: 6/2/84

YEAR TM/L	W	L	PCT	G	GS	CG	SH	SV	IP	H	HR	BB	SO	RAT	ERA	ERA+	OAV	OOB	BH	AVG	PB	PR	/A	PD	TPI
1984 SF-N	1	3	.250	23	0	0	0	0	38¹	51	4	22	19	17.4	6.10	57	.340	.428	0	.000	-0	-11	-11	-1	-1.2

● BRAD CORNETT
Cornett, Brad Byron b: 2/4/69, Lamesa, Tex. BR/TR, 6'3", 190 lbs. Deb: 6/8/94

YEAR TM/L	W	L	PCT	G	GS	CG	SH	SV	IP	H	HR	BB	SO	RAT	ERA	ERA+	OAV	OOB	BH	AVG	PB	PR	/A	PD	TPI
1994 Tor-A	1	3	.250	9	4	0	0	0	31	40	1	11	22	15.7	6.68	72	.331	.400	0	—	0	-6	-6	0	-0.7
1995 Tor-A	0	0	—	5	0	0	0	0	5	9	1	3	4	23.4	9.00	52	.429	.520	0	—	0	-2	-2	0	0.1
Total 2	1	3	.250	14	4	0	0	0	36	49	2	14	26	16.8	7.00	69	.345	.419	0	—	0	-9	-9	0	-0.6

● TERRY CORNUTT
Cornutt, Terry Stanton b: 10/2/52, Roseburg, Ore. BR/TR, 6'2", 195 lbs. Deb: 4/9/77

YEAR TM/L	W	L	PCT	G	GS	CG	SH	SV	IP	H	HR	BB	SO	RAT	ERA	ERA+	OAV	OOB	BH	AVG	PB	PR	/A	PD	TPI
1977 SF-N	1	2	.333	28	1	0	0	0	44¹	38	4	22	23	12.2	3.86	101	.229	.319	0	.000	-0	1	1	-1	-0.1
1978 SF-N	0	0	—	1	0	0	0	0	3	1	0	0	0	3.0	3.00	—	.100	.100	0	—	0	1	1	0	0.0
Total 2	1	2	.333	29	1	0	0	0	47¹	39	4	22	23	11.6	3.61	107	.222	.308	0	.000	-0	1	1	-1	-0.1

● ED CORREA
Correa, Edwin Josue (Andino) b: 4/29/66, Hato Rey, P.R. BR/TR, 6'2", 192 lbs. Deb: 9/18/85

YEAR TM/L	W	L	PCT	G	GS	CG	SH	SV	IP	H	HR	BB	SO	RAT	ERA	ERA+	OAV	OOB	BH	AVG	PB	PR	/A	PD	TPI
1985 Chi-A	1	0	1.000	5	1	0	0	0	10¹	7	2	11	10	19.2	6.97	62	.275	.431	0	—	0	-3	-3	-0	-0.6
1986 Tex-A	12	14	.462	32	32	4	2	0	202¹	167	15	126	189	13.2	4.23	102	.223	.337	0	—	0	-1	2	3	0.3
1987 Tex-A	3	5	.375	15	15	0	0	0	70	83	17	52	61	17.9	7.59	59	.296	.414	0	—	0	-24	-24	-0	-2.2
Total 3	16	19	.457	52	48	4	2	0	282²	261	34	189	260	14.6	5.16	80	.244	.361	0	—	0	-29	-26	2	-2.5

YEAR TM/L	W	L	PCT	G	GS	CG	SH	SV	IP	H	HR	BB	SO	RAT	ERA	ERA+	OAV	OOB	BH	AVG	PB	PR	/A	PD	TPI

● **FRANK CORRIDON** Corridon, Frank J. "Fiddler" b: 11/25/1880, Newport, R.I. d: 2/21/41, Syracuse, N.Y. BR/TR, 6', 170 lbs. Deb: 4/15/04

1904	Chi-N	5	5	.500	12	10	9	0	0	100¹	88	2	37	34	11.8	3.05	87	.240	.321	13	.224	0	-3	-4	3	-0.1
	Phi-N	6	5	.545	12	11	11	1	0	94¹	88	2	28	44	11.8	2.19	122	.250	.320	6	.171	-0	6	5	3	0.8
	Yr	11	10	.524	24	21	20	1	0	194²	176	4	65	78	11.5	2.64	101	.242	.312	19	.204	0	2	1	6	0.7
1905	Phi-N	10	12	.455	35	26	18	1	1	212	203	2	57	79	11.7	3.48	84	.257	.319	15	.208	4	-11	-13	2	-0.6
1907	Phi-N	18	14	.563	37	32	23	3	2	274	228	0	89	131	10.7	2.46	98	.230	.299	16	.165	0	-1	-5	4	0.4
1908	Phi-N	14	10	.583	27	24	18	2	1	208¹	178	0	48	50	10.0	2.51	97	.239	.290	9	.123	-2	-3	-3	0	-0.1
1909	Phi-N	11	7	.611	27	19	11	3	0	171	147	0	61	69	11.3	2.11	123	.242	.313	11	.186	0	9	9	5	1.6
1910	StL-N	6	14	.300	30	18	9	0	3	156	168	1	55	51	13.4	3.81	78	.283	.353	10	.196	-0	-13	-14	3	-1.5
Total	6	70	67	.511	180	140	99	10	7	1216	1100	7	375	458	11.4	2.80	95	.247	.315	80	.180	3	-16	-20	24	0.5

● **JIM CORSI** Corsi, James Bernard b: 9/9/61, Newton, Mass. BR/TR, 6'1", 210 lbs. Deb: 6/28/88

1988	Oak-A	0	1	.000	11	1	0	0	0	21¹	20	1	6	10	11.0	3.80	100	.260	.313	0	—	0	0	-0	-0	0.1
1989	Oak-A	1	2	.333	22	0	0	0	0	38¹	26	2	10	21	8.7	1.88	196	.194	.255	0	—	0	9	8	-0	0.6
1991	Hou-N	0	5	.000	47	0	0	0	0	77²	76	6	23	53	11.5	3.71	95	.259	.312	0	.000	-0	-0	-2	1	0.0
1992	*Oak-A	4	2	.667	32	0	0	0	0	44	44	2	18	19	12.7	1.43	261	.273	.346	0	—	0	12	11	1	1.7
1993	Fla-N	0	2	.000	15	0	0	0	0	20¹	28	1	10	7	16.8	6.64	65	.337	.409	0	—	-0	-6	-5	-0	-0.4
1995	Oak-A	2	4	.333	38	0	0	0	2	45	31	2	26	26	11.8	2.20	203	.203	.326	0	—	0	13	11	1	1.5
1996	Oak-A	6	0	1.000	56	0	0	0	3	73²	71	6	34	43	13.2	4.03	119	.269	.359	0	.000	-0	8	6	2	0.9
Total	7	13	16	.448	221	1	0	0	5	320¹	296	20	127	179	12.0	3.23	126	.254	.330	0	.000	-0	36	30	5	4.4

● **BARRY CORT** Cort, Barry Lee b: 4/15/56, Toronto, Ont., Can. BR/TR, 6'5", 210 lbs. Deb: 4/22/77

| 1977 | Mil-A | 1 | 1 | .500 | 7 | 3 | 1 | 0 | 0 | 24¹ | 25 | 1 | 9 | 17 | 12.9 | 3.33 | 122 | .281 | .354 | 0 | — | 0 | 2 | 2 | 0 | 0.2 |

● **AL CORWIN** Corwin, Elmer Nathan b: 12/3/26, Newburgh, N.Y. BR/TR, 6'1", 170 lbs. Deb: 7/25/51

1951	*NY-N	5	1	.833	15	8	3	1	1	59	49	7	21	30	10.7	3.66	107	.222	.289	1	.050	-2	2	2	-2	-0.2
1952	NY-N	6	1	.857	21	7	1	0	2	67²	58	5	36	36	12.5	2.66	139	.237	.335	2	.095	-1	8	8	-1	0.6
1953	NY-N	6	4	.600	48	7	2	1	2	106²	122	17	68	49	16.3	4.98	86	.290	.393	9	.281	4	-8	-8	-1	-0.4
1954	NY-N	1	3	.250	20	0	0	0	0	31¹	35	4	14	14	14.1	4.02	100	.297	.371	0	.000	-0	0	0	-1	-0.1
1955	NY-N	0	1	.000	13	0	0	0	0	24²	25	3	17	13	15.3	4.01	100	.263	.375	0	.000	0	0	0	-0	-0.1
Total	5	18	10	.643	117	22	6	2	5	289	36	156	142	13.9	3.98	101	.263	.356	12	.152	0	2	1	-6	-0.2

● **MIKE COSGROVE** Cosgrove, Michael John b: 2/17/51, Phoenix, Ariz. BL/TL, 6'1", 180 lbs. Deb: 9/10/72

1972	Hou-N	0	1	.000	7	0	0	0	1	13²	16	2	3	7	12.5	4.61	73	.286	.322	0	.000	-0	-2	-2	-1	-0.2
1973	Hou-N	1	1	.500	13	1	0	0	1	10	11	1	8	9	17.1	1.80	202	.282	.404	0	—	0	2	2	-0	0.3
1974	Hou-N	7	3	.700	45	0	0	0	2	90	76	2	39	47	11.6	3.50	99	.232	.316	1	.056	-1	1	-0	-1	-0.2
1975	Hou-N	1	2	.333	32	3	1	0	5	71¹	62	7	37	32	12.5	3.03	111	.245	.341	2	.154	0	5	3	-0	0.2
1976	Hou-N	3	4	.429	22	16	1	1	0	89²	106	6	58	34	16.7	5.52	58	.303	.405	2	.087	-1	-20	-23	-0	-1.7
Total	5	12	11	.522	119	20	2	1	8	274²	271	13	145	122	13.7	4.03	83	.264	.357	5	.089	-2	-14	-21	-2	-1.6

● **JIM COSMAN** Cosman, James Henry b: 2/19/43, Brockport, N.Y. BR/TR, 6'4.5", 211 lbs. Deb: 10/2/66

1966	StL-N	1	0	1.000	1	1	1	1	0	9	2	0	2	5	5.0	0.00	—	.074	.167	0	.000	-0	4	4	-0	0.4
1967	StL-N	1	0	1.000	10	5	0	0	0	31¹	21	3	24	11	14.4	3.16	104	.198	.370	1	.125	-0	1	0	-1	-0.1
1970	Chi-N	0	0	—	1	0	0	0	0	1	3	1	1	0	36.0	27.00	17	.600	.667	0	—	-0	-3	-2	0	0.0
Total	3	2	0	1.000	12	6	1	1	0	41¹	26	4	27	16	12.8	3.05	111	.188	.345	1	.091	-0	1	-1	-1	0.3

● **JOHN COSTELLO** Costello, John Reilly b: 12/24/60, Bronx, N.Y. BR/TR, 6'1", 190 lbs. Deb: 6/2/88

1988	StL-N	5	2	.714	36	0	0	0	1	49²	44	3	25	38	12.5	1.81	192	.235	.325	0	.000	-0	9	9	-1	1.2
1989	StL-N	5	4	.556	48	0	0	0	3	62¹	48	5	20	40	10.1	3.32	109	.213	.283	0	.000	-1	1	2	-1	0.1
1990	StL-N	0	0	—	4	0	0	0	0	4¹	7	1	4	2	18.7	6.23	61	.368	.429	0	—	-0	-1	-0	-0	0.00
	Mon-N	0	0	—	4	0	0	0	0	6¹	5	2	1	4	8.5	5.68	64	.208	.240	0	—	-0	-1	-1	-0	0.0
	Yr	0	0	—	8	0	0	0	0	10²	12	3	2	2	11.8	5.91	63	.273	.304	0	—	-0	-3	-3	-0	0.0
1991	SD-N	1	0	1.000	27	0	0	0	0	35	37	2	17	24	13.9	3.09	123	.276	.358	0	.000	-0	2	3	-0	0.0
Total	4	11	6	.647	119	0	0	0	4	157²	141	13	64	104	11.9	2.97	122	.239	.317	0	.000	-1	11	11	-3	1.3

● **DAN COTTER** Cotter, Daniel Joseph b: 4/14/1867, Boston, Mass. d: 9/4/35, Boston, Mass. BR/TR, Deb: 7/16/1890

| 1890 | Buf-P | 0 | 1 | .000 | 1 | 1 | 1 | 0 | 0 | 9 | 18 | 1 | 7 | 0 | 25.0 | 14.00 | 29 | .400 | .481 | 0 | .000 | -1 | -10 | -10 | -0 | -0.7 |

● **ENSIGN COTTRELL** Cottrell, Ensign Stover b: 8/29/1888, Hoosick Falls, N.Y. d: 2/27/47, Syracuse, N.Y. BL/TL, 5'9.5", 173 lbs. Deb: 6/21/11

1911	Pit-N	0	0	—	1	0	0	0	0	1	4	0	1	0	45.0	9.00	38	.667	.714	0	—	0	-1	-1	-0	0.0
1912	Chi-N	0	0	—	1	0	0	0	0	4	8	0	1	1	20.3	9.00	37	.444	.474	0	—	-0	-2	-3	-0	0.0
1913	Phi-A	1	0	1.000	3	1	0	0	0	10	15	0	2	3	15.3	5.40	51	.326	.354	1	.250	1	-3	-3	-0	-0.2
1914	Bos-N	0	1	.000	1	1	0	0	0	1	2	0	3	1	45.0	9.00	31	.333	.556	0	—	-0	-1	-1	-0	-0.5
1915	NY-A	0	1	.000	7	0	0	0	0	21¹	29	2	7	7	15.6	3.38	87	.330	.385	0	.000	-0	-1	-1	-0	-0.1
Total	5	1	2	.333	12	2	1	0	0	37¹	58	2	14	12	17.6	4.82	61	.354	.408	1	.083	-0	-8	-8	-0	-0.8

● **JOHNNY COUCH** Couch, John Daniel b: 3/31/1891, Vaughn, Mont. d: 12/8/75, San Mateo, Cal. BL/TR, 6', 180 lbs. Deb: 4/11/17

1917	Det-A	0	0	—	3	0	0	0	0	13¹	13	0	1	9	9.5	2.70	98	.255	.269	0	.000	-0	-0	-0	-1	0.0
1922	Cin-N	16	9	.640	43	33	18	2	1	264	301	13	56	45	12.3	3.89	103	.289	.328	12	.132	-3	6	3	1	0.0
1923	Cin-N	2	7	.222	19	8	1	0	0	69¹	98	2	15	14	14.7	5.97	65	.334	.377	4	.174	-1	-15	-16	-1	-1.9
	Phi-N	2	4	.333	11	7	2	0	0	65	91	4	21	18	15.9	5.26	87	.335	.389	6	.250	-0	-9	-5	-0	-0.5
	Yr	4	11	.267	30	15	3	0	0	134¹	189	6	36	32	15.3	5.63	75	.339	.383	10	.213	-1	-24	-21	-1	-2.4
1924	Phi-N	4	8	.333	37	7	3	0	3	137	170	13	39	23	13.8	4.73	94	.306	.352	10	.204	-1	-13	-4	-1	-0.3
1925	Phi-N	5	6	.455	34	6	1	2	2	94¹	112	9	39	11	14.5	5.44	88	.298	.365	5	.161	-2	-12	-7	-1	-0.7
Total	5	29	34	.460	147	62	26	3	6	643	785	41	171	112	13.5	4.63	91	.304	.350	37	.167	-6	-43	-29	2	-3.4

● **MIKE COUCHEE** Couchee, Michael Eugene b: 12/4/57, San Jose, Cal. BR/TR, 6', 190 lbs. Deb: 4/5/83 C

| 1983 | SD-N | 0 | 1 | .000 | 8 | 0 | 0 | 0 | 0 | 14 | 12 | 1 | 6 | 5 | 11.6 | 5.14 | 68 | .214 | .290 | 1 | .500 | 0 | -2 | -3 | -0 | -0.2 |

● **ED COUGHLIN** Coughlin, Edward E. b: 8/5/1861, Hartford, Conn. d: 12/25/52, Hartford, Conn. Deb: 5/15/1884 ◆

| 1884 | Buf-N | 0 | 1 | .000 | 1 | 0 | 0 | 0 | 0 | — | 6 | 1 | 9 | 0 | ∞ | — | .600 | 1 | .250 | -0 | -3 | -3 | 0 | -0.2 |

● **ROSCOE COUGHLIN** Coughlin, William Edward b: 3/15/1868, Walpole, Mass. d: 3/20/51, Chelsea, Mass. TR, 5'10", 160 lbs. Deb: 4/22/1890

1890	Chi-N	4	6	.400	11	10	10	0	0	95	102	3	40	29	13.8	4.26	86	.286	.342	10	.256	1	-7	-6	1	-0.4
1891	NY-N	3	4	.429	8	7	6	0	0	61	74	5	23	22	14.8	3.84	83	.289	.355	3	.130	1	-3	-4	1	-0.2
Total	2	7	10	.412	19	17	16	0	0	156	176	8	63	51	14.2	4.10	85	.275	.347	13	.210	2	-11	-11	2	-0.6

● **FRITZ COUMBE** Coumbe, Frederick Nicholas b: 12/13/1889, Antrim, Pa. d: 3/21/78, Paradise, Cal. BL/TL, 6', 152 lbs. Deb: 4/22/14

1914	Bos-A	1	2	.333	17	5	1	0	1	62¹	49	0	16	21	9.4	1.44	186	.224	.274	2	.111	-1	9	9	0	0.4
	Cle-A	1	5	.167	14	5	2	0	0	55¹	59	0	16	22	12.8	3.25	89	.288	.351	6	.261	-1	-3	-2	1	0.0
	Yr	2	7	.222	31	10	3	0	1	117²	108	0	32	39	11.0	2.29	121	.254	.312	8	.195	0	6	6	1	0.3
1915	Cle-A	4	7	.364	30	12	4	1	2	114	123	1	37	37	12.9	3.47	88	.279	.355	10	.270	1	-7	-5	3	-0.2
1916	Cle-A	7	5	.583	29	13	7	2	0	120¹	121	1	27	39	11.1	2.02	149	.279	.323	1	.057	-3	11	13	5	1.5
1917	Cle-A	8	6	.571	34	10	4	1	5	134¹	119	0	35	30	10.5	2.14	132	.251	.307	6	.154	-1	8	10	3	1.3
1918	Cle-A	13	7	.650	30	17	9	0	3	150	164	4	52	41	13.0	3.06	98	.286	.347	12	.214	-1	-5	-5	3	-0.3
1919	Cle-A	1	1	.500	23	2	0	0	0	23²	32	2	9	7	15.6	5.32	63	.348	.406	3	.500	-1	-6	-5	0	-0.3
1920	Cin-N	0	1	.000	3	0	0	0	0	14²	17	0	4	7	12.9	4.91	62	.304	.350	3	.231	-1	-3	-3	0	-0.1
1921	Cin-N	3	4	.429	13	6	3	0	2	86²	89	2	21	12	11.1	3.22	111	.280	.332	7	.226	1	0	1	1	0.1
Total	8	38	38	.500	193	70	30	4	13	761¹	773	10	217	212	11.9	2.80	108	.277	.332	52	.206	-5	10	20	20	3.5

● **HARRY COURTNEY** Courtney, Henry Seymour b: 11/19/1898, Asheville, N.C. d: 12/11/54, Lyme, Conn. BL/TL, 6'4", 185 lbs. Deb: 9/13/19

| 1919 | Was-A | 3 | 0 | 1.000 | 4 | 3 | 2 | 1 | 0 | 26¹ | 25 | 0 | 19 | 6 | 15.0 | 2.73 | 117 | .269 | .393 | 2 | .200 | -0 | 1 | 1 | -1 | 0.0 |

YEAR TM/L	W	L	PCT	G	GS	CG	SH	SV	IP	H	HR	BB	SO	RAT	ERA	ERA+	OAV	OOB	BH	AVG	PB	PR	/A	PD	TPI
1920 Was-A	8	11	.421	37	24	10	1	0	188	223	6	77	48	14.8	4.74	79	.298	.371	16	.232	4	-20	-21	-3	-1.8
1921 Was-A	6	9	.400	30	15	3	0	1	132²	159	7	71	26	16.1	5.63	73	.305	.397	14	.298	2	-20	-22	-1	-1.9
1922 Was-A	0	1	.000	5	0	0	0	0	10	11	0	9	4	18.0	3.60	107	.306	.444	1	.000	-1	0	0	-0	0.0
Chi-A	5	6	.455	18	11	5	0	0	86²	100	5	37	28	14.3	4.98	82	.299	.371	9	.273	3	-9	-9	-1	-0.7
Yr	5	7	.417	23	11	5	0	0	96²	111	5	46	32	14.7	4.84	84	.300	.379	9	.243	2	-9	-8	-1	-0.7
Total 4	22	27	.449	94	53	20	2	1	443²	518	18	213	112	15.2	4.91	79	.299	.382	41	.252	7	-47	-50	-5	-4.4

● **JOHN COURTRIGHT**   Courtright, John Charles   b: 5/30/70, Marion, Ohio   BL/TL, 6'2", 185 lbs.   Deb: 5/6/95

YEAR TM/L	W	L	PCT	G	GS	CG	SH	SV	IP	H	HR	BB	SO	RAT	ERA	ERA+	OAV	OOB	BH	AVG	PB	PR	/A	PD	TPI
1995 Cin-N	0	0	—	1	0	0	0	0	1	2	0	0		18.0	9.00	46	.500	.500	0	—	0	-1	-1	-0	0.0

● **HARRY COVELESKI**   Coveleski, Harry Frank "The Giant Killer" (b: Harry Frank Kowalewski)
b: 4/23/1886, Shamokin, Pa.   d: 8/4/50, Shamokin, Pa.   BB/TL, 6', 180 lbs.   Deb: 9/10/07   F

YEAR TM/L	W	L	PCT	G	GS	CG	SH	SV	IP	H	HR	BB	SO	RAT	ERA	ERA+	OAV	OOB	BH	AVG	PB	PR	/A	PD	TPI
1907 Phi-N	1	0	1.000	4	0	0	0	0	20	10	0	3	6	6.3	0.00	—	.147	.194	0	.000	-0	5	5	-0	0.2
1908 Phi-N	4	1	.800	6	5	5	2	0	43²	29	0	12	22	8.9	1.24	196	.196	.265	2	.133	-0	5	6	1	0.8
1909 Phi-N	6	10	.375	24	17	8	2	1	121²	109	0	49	56	12.1	2.74	95	.247	.329	4	.108	-2	-2	-2	1	-0.4
1910 Cin-N	1	1	.500	7	4	2	0	0	39¹	35	1	42	27	18.5	5.26	55	.246	.431	1	.063	1	-10	-10	1	-0.5
1914 Det-A	22	12	.647	44	36	23	5	2	303¹	251	4	100	124	10.8	2.49	113	.227	.298	23	.242	5	8	11	7	2.3
1915 Det-A	22	13	.629	50	38	20	1	4	312²	271	2	87	150	10.9	2.45	124	.233	.298	18	.175	-2	17	20	4	2.4
1916 Det-A	21	11	.656	44	39	22	3	2	324¹	278	6	63	108	9.8	1.97	145	.232	.282	25	.212	1	31	32	4	3.9
1917 Det-A	4	6	.400	16	11	2	0	0	69	70	0	14	15	11.2	2.61	101	.265	.307	5	.227	-0	0	0	2	-0.1
1918 Det-A	0	1	.000	3	1	1	0	0	14	17	0	6	3	14.8	3.86	69	.315	.383	1	.250	-0	-2	-2	1	-0.1
Total 9	81	55	.596	198	151	83	13	9	1248	1070	13	376	511	10.8	2.39	118	.235	.301	79	.189	-0	54	61	20	8.8

● **STAN COVELESKI**   Coveleski, Stanley Anthony (b: Stanislaus Kowalewski)
b: 7/13/1889, Shamokin, Pa.   d: 3/20/84, South Bend, Ind.   BR/TR, 5'11", 166 lbs.   Deb: 9/10/12   FH

YEAR TM/L	W	L	PCT	G	GS	CG	SH	SV	IP	H	HR	BB	SO	RAT	ERA	ERA+	OAV	OOB	BH	AVG	PB	PR	/A	PD	TPI
1912 Phi-A	2	1	.667	5	2	2	1	0	21	18	0	4	9	9.9	3.43	90	.231	.277	1	.143	-0	-0	-1	-1	-0.2
1916 Cle-A	15	13	.536	45	27	11	1	3	232	247	6	58	76	11.9	3.41	88	.278	.323	13	.173	-0	-15	-10	2	-1.1
1917 Cle-A	19	14	.576	45	36	24	**9**	4	298¹	202	3	94	133	9.0	1.81	157	**.194**	.261	13	.134	-4	28	34	4	3.1
1918 Cle-A	22	13	.629	38	33	25	2	1	311	261	2	76	87	9.9	1.82	165	.229	.279	21	.191	-3	33	41	-0	4.6
1919 Cle-A	24	12	.667	43	34	24	4	4	286	286	2	60	118	11.0	2.61	128	.267	.308	20	.213	4	20	23	3	3.6
1920 *Cle-A	24	14	.632	41	38	26	3	2	315	284	6	65	**133**	10.1	2.49	153	**.243**	**.285**	25	.225	3	**46**	46	3	**5.9**
1921 Cle-A	23	13	.639	43	40	28	2	2	315	341	6	84	99	12.3	3.37	126	.280	.329	18	.155	-6	32	31	7	3.2
1922 Cle-A	17	14	.548	35	33	21	3	2	276²	292	14	64	98	11.6	3.32	121	.274	.316	10	.101	-7	22	21	1	1.5
1923 Cle-A	13	14	.481	33	31	17	**5**	2	228	251	8	42	54	11.6	**2.76**	**143**	.282	.316	7	.089	-8	**31**	30	3	2.9
1924 Cle-A	15	16	.484	37	33	18	2	0	240¹	286	6	73	58	13.6	4.04	106	.294	.346	11	.134	-5	5	6	-0	0.2
1925 *Was-A	20	5	**.800**	32	32	15	3	0	241	230	7	73	58	11.4	**2.84**	**149**	.255	.312	9	.111	-8	42	37	0	2.6
1926 Was-A	14	11	.560	36	34	11	3	1	245¹	272	1	81	50	12.9	3.12	124	.286	.342	17	.207	1	25	20	1	2.1
1927 Was-A	2	1	.667	5	4	0	0	0	14¹	13	0	8	3	13.2	3.14	129	.250	.350	2	.333	1	0	2	1	0.3
1928 NY-A	2	1	.833	12	8	2	0	0	58	72	5	20	5	14.3	5.74	66	.323	.379	1	.053	-2	-11	-13	1	-1.2
Total 14	215	142	.602	450	385	224	38	21	3082	3055	66	802	981	11.4	2.89	128	.262	.311	168	.159	-34	259	276	16	27.5

● **CHET COVINGTON**   Covington, Chester Rogers "Chesty"   b: 11/6/10, Cairo, Ill.   d: 6/11/76, Pembroke Park, Fla.   BB/TL, 6'2", 195 lbs.   Deb: 4/23/44

YEAR TM/L	W	L	PCT	G	GS	CG	SH	SV	IP	H	HR	BB	SO	RAT	ERA	ERA+	OAV	OOB	BH	AVG	PB	PR	/A	PD	TPI
1944 Phi-N	1	1	.500	19	0	0	0	0	38²	46	2	8	13	12.6	4.66	78	.297	.331	0	.000	-1	-4	-4	-0	-0.3

● **TEX COVINGTON**   Covington, William Wilkes   b: 3/19/1887, Henryville, Tenn.   d: 12/10/31, Denison, Tex.   BL/TR, 6'1", 175 lbs.   Deb: 4/25/11   F

YEAR TM/L	W	L	PCT	G	GS	CG	SH	SV	IP	H	HR	BB	SO	RAT	ERA	ERA+	OAV	OOB	BH	AVG	PB	PR	/A	PD	TPI
1911 Det-A	7	1	.875	17	6	5	0	0	83²	94	2	33	29	14.7	4.09	85	.297	.381	6	.188	-1	-7	-6	-1	-0.7
1912 Det-A	3	4	.429	14	9	2	1	0	63¹	58	0	30	19	12.9	4.12	79	.253	.347	2	.133	0	-6	-6	-1	-0.6
Total 2	10	5	.667	31	15	7	1	0	147	152	2	63	48	14.0	4.10	82	.278	.367	8	.170	-1	-13	-12	-2	-1.3

● **JOE COWLEY**   Cowley, Joseph Alan   b: 8/15/58, Lexington, Ky.   BR/TR, 6'5", 210 lbs.   Deb: 4/13/82

YEAR TM/L	W	L	PCT	G	GS	CG	SH	SV	IP	H	HR	BB	SO	RAT	ERA	ERA+	OAV	OOB	BH	AVG	PB	PR	/A	PD	TPI
1982 Atl-N	1	2	.333	17	8	0	0	0	52¹	53	6	16	27	12.0	4.47	83	.265	.323	3	.200	-0	-5	-4	-0	-0.2
1984 NY-A	9	2	.818	16	11	3	1	0	83¹	75	12	31	71	11.7	3.56	106	.234	.305	0	—	0	4	2	0	0.6
1985 NY-A	12	6	.667	30	26	1	0	0	159²	132	29	85	97	12.6	3.95	101	.224	.328	0	—	0	1	1	-0	0.2
1986 Chi-A	11	11	.500	27	27	4	0	0	162¹	133	20	83	132	12.1	3.88	111	.223	.321	0	—	0	5	8	-1	0.9
1987 Phi-N	0	4	.000	5	4	0	0	0	11²	21	2	17	5	30.9	15.43	27	.389	.548	1	.333	1	-15	-15	-1	-3.2
Total 5	33	25	.569	95	76	8	1	0	469¹	414	69	232	332	12.7	4.20	96	.235	.329	4	.222	-1	-7	-8	-1	-1.7

● **DANNY COX**   Cox, Danny Bradford   b: 9/21/59, Northampton, England   BR/TR, 6'4", 235 lbs.   Deb: 8/6/83

YEAR TM/L	W	L	PCT	G	GS	CG	SH	SV	IP	H	HR	BB	SO	RAT	ERA	ERA+	OAV	OOB	BH	AVG	PB	PR	/A	PD	TPI
1983 StL-N	3	6	.333	12	12	0	0	0	83	92	6	23	36	12.5	3.25	111	.286	.333	2	.074	-2	3	3	1	0.2
1984 StL-N	9	11	.450	29	27	1	1	0	156¹	171	9	54	70	13.4	4.03	86	.289	.355	7	.132	0	-8	-10	1	-1.1
1985 *StL-N	18	9	.667	35	35	10	4	0	241	226	19	64	131	10.9	2.88	123	.251	.303	12	.152	1	19	18	-1	1.9
1986 StL-N	12	13	.480	32	32	8	0	0	220	189	14	60	108	10.3	2.90	125	.234	.289	5	.077	-3	20	18	-5	1.1
1987 *StL-N	11	9	.550	31	31	2	0	0	199¹	224	17	71	101	13.5	3.88	107	.290	.352	8	.116	-2	4	4	-1	0.3
1988 StL-N	3	8	.273	13	13	0	0	0	86	89	6	25	47	12.0	3.98	87	.272	.326	1	.043	-2	-5	-5	0	-0.7
1991 Phi-N	4	6	.400	23	17	0	0	0	102¹	98	14	39	46	12.1	4.57	80	.258	.329	3	.103	-1	-10	-10	-1	-1.0
1992 Phi-N	2	2	.500	9	7	0	0	0	38¹	46	3	19	30	15.3	5.40	65	.299	.376	1	.091	-1	-8	-7	-1	-0.8
*Pit-N	3	1	.750	16	0	0	0	3	24¹	20	2	8	18	10.4	3.33	103	.225	.289	0	.000	-0	0	0	-0	-0.0
Yr	5	3	.625	25	7	0	0	3	62²	66	5	27	48	13.4	4.60	76	.269	.342	1	.071	-1	-8	-8	-1	-0.8
1993 *Tor-A	7	6	.538	44	0	0	0	2	83²	73	6	29	84	11.0	3.12	138	.230	.294	0	—	0	11	11	-1	1.5
1994 Tor-A	1	1	.500	10	0	0	0	0	18²	7	0	7	14	7.2	1.45	333	.113	.214	0	—	0	7	7	-0	0.8
1995 Tor-A	1	3	.250	24	0	0	0	0	45	57	4	33	38	18.2	7.40	64	.317	.425	0	—	0	-13	-13	-0	-1.0
Total 11	74	75	.497	278	174	21	5	8	1298	1292	102	432	723	12.1	3.64	103	.263	.325	39	.109	-9	21	17	-6	1.2

● **ERNIE COX**   Cox, Ernest Thompson   b: 2/19/1894, Birmingham, Ala.   d: 4/29/74, Birmingham, Ala.   BL/TR, 6'1", 180 lbs.   Deb: 5/5/22

YEAR TM/L	W	L	PCT	G	GS	CG	SH	SV	IP	H	HR	BB	SO	RAT	ERA	ERA+	OAV	OOB	BH	AVG	PB	PR	/A	PD	TPI
1922 Chi-A	0	0	—	1	0	0	0	0	1	1	0	2	0	27.0	18.00	23	.250	.500	0	—	0	-2	-2	-0	0.0

● **GEORGE COX**   Cox, George Melvin   b: 11/15/04, Sherman, Tex.   BR/TR, 6'1", 170 lbs.   Deb: 4/12/28

YEAR TM/L	W	L	PCT	G	GS	CG	SH	SV	IP	H	HR	BB	SO	RAT	ERA	ERA+	OAV	OOB	BH	AVG	PB	PR	/A	PD	TPI
1928 Chi-A	1	2	.333	26	2	0	0	0	89	110	6	39	22	15.3	5.26	77	.313	.385	2	.077	-2	-12	-12	2	-0.4

● **GLENN COX**   Cox, Glenn Melvin   b: 2/3/31, Montebello, Cal.   BR/TR, 6'2", 210 lbs.   Deb: 9/20/55

YEAR TM/L	W	L	PCT	G	GS	CG	SH	SV	IP	H	HR	BB	SO	RAT	ERA	ERA+	OAV	OOB	BH	AVG	PB	PR	/A	PD	TPI
1955 KC-A	0	2	.000	2	2	0	0	0	2¹	11	0	1	2	46.3	30.86	14	.611	.632	0	.000	-0	-7	-7	0	-2.7
1956 KC-A	0	2	.000	3	3	1	0	0	23¹	15	2	22	14	14.3	4.24	102	.203	.385	0	.000	-1	-0	0	-1	-0.2
1957 KC-A	1	0	1.000	10	0	0	0	0	14¹	18	1	9	8	17.0	5.02	79	.321	.415	0	.000	-0	-2	-2	0	-0.1
1958 KC-A	0	0	—	2	0	0	0	0	3²	6	1	3	1	22.1	9.82	40	.400	.500	0	.000	-0	-2	-2	-0	-0.2
Total 4	1	4	.200	17	5	1	0	0	43²	50	4	35	25	17.5	6.39	65	.307	.429	0	.000	-1	-12	-11	-1	-3.0

● **CASEY COX**   Cox, Joseph Casey   b: 7/3/41, Long Beach, Cal.   BR/TR, 6'5", 200 lbs.   Deb: 4/15/66

YEAR TM/L	W	L	PCT	G	GS	CG	SH	SV	IP	H	HR	BB	SO	RAT	ERA	ERA+	OAV	OOB	BH	AVG	PB	PR	/A	PD	TPI
1966 Was-A	4	5	.444	66	0	0	0	7	113	104	6	35	46	11.4	3.50	99	.250	.314	0	.000	-1	-1	-1	0	-0.1
1967 Was-A	7	4	.636	54	0	0	0	1	73	54	2	21	32	11.3	2.96	107	.250	.314	0	.000	-0	2	2	0	0.2
1968 Was-A	0	1	.000	4	0	0	0	0	7²	7	0	4	4	8.2	2.35	124	.250	.250	0	—	0	1	1	-0	0.0
1969 Was-A	12	7	.632	52	13	4	0	0	171²	161	15	64	73	11.8	2.78	125	.251	.320	5	.106	-2	16	13	-1	1.1
1970 Was-A	8	12	.400	37	30	1	0	1	192¹	211	27	44	68	12.1	4.45	80	.329	.329	7	.121	-2	-16	-19	-2	-2.2
1971 Was-A	5	7	.417	54	11	0	0	0	124¹	131	9	40	43	12.9	3.98	83	.273	.338	2	.077	-1	-7	-9	-1	-1.2
1972 Tex-A	3	5	.375	35	4	0	0	4	65¹	73	6	27	27	13.8	4.41	68	.277	.344	1	.111	1	-10	-12	-1	-1.3
NY-A	0	1	.000	5	1	0	0	0	11²	13	0	2	4	13.9	4.63	64	.271	.333	0	—	0	-2	-0	-0	-0.2
Yr	3	6	.333	40	5	0	0	4	77	86	6	29	31	13.7	4.44	68	.276	.341	1	.111	1	-12	-12	-1	-1.5
1973 NY-A	0	0	—	1	0	0	0	0	3	5	0	1	0	24.0	6.00	61	.357	.471	0	—	0	-1	-1	0	0.1
Total 8	39	42	.481	308	59	5	0	20	762	772	66	234	297	12.2	3.70	91	.266	.327	15	.099	-6	-17	-27	-3	-3.6

● **LES COX**   Cox, Leslie Warren   b: 8/14/05, Junction, Tex.   d: 10/14/34, San Angelo, Tex.   BR/TR, 6', 164 lbs.   Deb: 9/11/26

YEAR TM/L	W	L	PCT	G	GS	CG	SH	SV	IP	H	HR	BB	SO	RAT	ERA	ERA+	OAV	OOB	BH	AVG	PB	PR	/A	PD	TPI
1926 Chi-A	0	1	.000	2	0	0	0	0	5	6	2	5	3	19.8	5.40	72	.261	.393	1	.500	0	-1	-1	0	-0.2

YEAR TM/L	W	L	PCT	G	GS	CG	SH	SV	IP	H	HR	BB	SO	RAT	ERA	ERA+	OAV	OOB	BH	AVG	PB	PR	/A	PD	TPI

● **RED COX** Cox, Plateau Rex b: 2/16/1895, Laurel Springs, N.C. d: 10/15/84, Roanoke, Va. BL/TR, 6'2", 190 lbs. Deb: 4/17/20

| 1920 Det-A | 0 | 0 | — | 3 | 0 | 0 | 0 | 0 | 5 | 9 | 0 | 3 | 1 | 21.6 | 5.40 | 69 | .375 | .444 | 0 | .000 | -0 | -1 | -1 | -0 | 0.0 |

● **TERRY COX** Cox, Terry Lee b: 3/30/49, Odessa, Tex. BR/TR, 6'5", 215 lbs. Deb: 9/7/70

| 1970 Cal-A | 0 | 0 | — | 3 | 0 | 0 | 0 | 0 | 2¹ | 4 | 0 | 0 | 3 | 15.4 | 3.86 | 94 | .400 | .400 | 0 | — | 0 | -0 | -0 | 0 | 0.0 |

● **BILL COX** Cox, William Donald b: 6/23/13, Ashmore, Ill. d: 2/16/88, Charleston, Ill. BR/TR, 6'1", 185 lbs. Deb: 6/6/36

1936 StL-N	0	0	—	2	0	0	0	0	2²	4	0	1	1	16.9	6.75	58	.333	.385	0	—	-1	-1	-0	0.0
1937 Chi-A	1	0	1.000	3	2	1	1	0	12²	9	0	5	8	9.9	0.71	648	.200	.280	1	.250	0	6	5	-0	0.4
1938 Chi-A	0	2	.000	7	1	0	0	0	11²	11	0	13	5	18.5	6.94	70	.244	.414	0	.000	-0	-3	-3	-0	-0.4
StL-A	1	4	.200	22	7	1	0	0	63	81	8	35	16	16.6	7.00	71	.315	.397	1	.059	-1	-15	-14	-0	-1.0
Yr	1	6	.143	29	8	1	0	0	74²	92	8	48	21	16.9	6.99	71	.305	.400	1	.053	-2	-18	-17	-0	-1.4
1939 StL-A	0	2	.000	4	2	1	0	0	9¹	10	0	4	8	17.4	9.64	50	.256	.383	0	.000	-0	-5	-5	1	-0.8
1940 StL-A	0	1	.000	12	0	0	0	0	17¹	23	3	12	7	18.2	7.27	63	.333	.432	0	.000	-0	-6	-5	-0	-0.2
Total 5	2	9	.182	50	12	3	1	0	116²	138	11	74	45	16.4	6.56	74	.296	.392	2	.080	-2	-24	-22	1	-2.0

● **BILL COYLE** Coyle, William Claude b: Pittsburgh, Pa. TR, Deb: 7/7/1893

| 1893 Bos-N | 0 | 1 | .000 | 2 | 1 | 0 | 0 | 0 | 8 | 14 | 1 | 3 | 2 | 19.1 | 9.00 | 55 | .368 | .415 | 0 | .000 | -1 | -4 | -4 | 0 | -0.4 |

● **CHARLIE COZART** Cozart, Charles Rhubin b: 10/17/19, Lenoir, N.C. BR/TL, 6', 190 lbs. Deb: 4/17/45

| 1945 Bos-N | 1 | 0 | 1.000 | 5 | 0 | 0 | 0 | 0 | 8 | 10 | 2 | 15 | 4 | 28.1 | 10.13 | 38 | .303 | .521 | 0 | .000 | -0 | -6 | -6 | 1 | -0.5 |

● **ROY CRABB** Crabb, James Roy b: 8/23/1890, Monticello, Iowa d: 3/30/40, Lewistown, Mont. BR/TR, 5'11", 160 lbs. Deb: 8/10/12

1912 Chi-A	0	1	.000	2	1	0	0	0	8²	6	0	4	3	10.4	1.04	308	.214	.313	0	.000	-0	2	2	0	0.2
Phi-A	2	4	.333	7	7	3	0	0	43¹	48	0	17	12	14.3	3.74	82	.287	.367	0	.000	-3	-2	-3	-0	-0.6
Yr	2	5	.286	9	8	3	0	0	52	54	0	21	15	13.7	3.29	94	.277	.359	0	.000	-3	0	-1	-0	-0.4

● **GEORGE CRABLE** Crable, George E. b: 12/1885, Nebraska BL/TL, 6'1", 190 lbs. Deb: 8/3/10

| 1910 Bro-N | 0 | 0 | — | 2 | 1 | 0 | 0 | 0 | 7¹ | 5 | 0 | 5 | 3 | 14.7 | 4.91 | 62 | .217 | .400 | 0 | .000 | 0 | -2 | -2 | 0 | 0.0 |

● **TIM CRABTREE** Crabtree, Timothy Lyle b: 10/13/69, Jackson, Mich. BR/TR, 6'4", 205 lbs. Deb: 6/23/95

1995 Tor-A	0	2	.000	31	0	0	0	0	32	30	1	13	21	12.7	3.09	152	.240	.321	0	—	0	6	6	1	0.4
1996 Tor-A	5	3	.625	53	0	0	0	1	67¹	59	4	22	57	11.2	2.54	199	.231	.300	0	—	0	18	19	0	1.9
Total 2	5	5	.500	84	0	0	0	1	99¹	89	5	35	78	11.7	2.72	182	.234	.307	0	—	0	24	25	1	2.3

● **WALT CRADDOCK** Craddock, Walter Anderson b: 3/25/32, Pax, W.Va. d: 7/6/80, Parma Heights, O. BR/TL, 5'11.5", 176 lbs. Deb: 9/3/55

1955 KC-A	0	2	.000	4	2	0	0	0	15	18	3	10	9	16.8	7.80	54	.300	.400	0	.000	-1	-6	-6	-0	-0.7
1956 KC-A	0	2	.000	2	2	0	0	0	9¹	9	1	10	8	18.3	6.75	64	.265	.432	0	.000	-0	-3	-3	-0	-0.5
1958 KC-A	0	3	.000	23	1	0	0	0	36²	41	4	20	22	15.2	5.89	66	.289	.380	0	.000	-0	-9	-8	0	-0.6
Total 3	0	7	.000	29	5	0	0	0	61	68	8	40	39	16.1	6.49	62	.288	.394	0	.000	-1	-18	-17	0	-1.8

● **MOLLY CRAFT** Craft, Maurice Montague b: 11/28/1895, Portsmouth, Va. d: 10/25/78, Los Angeles, Cal. BR/TR, 6'2", 165 lbs. Deb: 8/8/16

1916 Was-A	0	1	.000	2	1	0	0	0	11	12	0	6	9	14.7	3.27	85	.316	.409	0	.000	-0	-1	-1	0	0.0
1917 Was-A	0	0	—	8	0	0	0	1	14	17	0	8	2	16.1	3.86	68	.315	.403	1	.500	0	-2	-2	0	0.0
1918 Was-A	0	0	—	3	0	0	0	0	7	5	0	1	5	7.7	1.29	212	.208	.240	0	.000	-0	1	1	0	0.0
1919 Was-A	0	3	.000	16	2	0	0	1	48²	59	2	18	17	14.6	3.88	83	.309	.374	2	.111	-2	-4	-4	-0	-0.4
Total 4	0	4	.000	29	3	1	0	2	80²	93	2	33	33	14.3	3.57	83	.309	.374	3	.115	-2	-5	-5	1	-0.4

● **HOWARD CRAGHEAD** Craghead, Howard Oliver "Judge" b: 5/25/08, Selma, Cal. d: 7/15/62, San Diego, Cal. BR/TR, 6'2", 200 lbs. Deb: 4/30/31

1931 Cle-A	0	0	—	4	0	0	0	0	5²	8	0	2	0	15.9	6.35	73	.320	.370	0	—	-1	-1	-1	0	0.0
1933 Cle-A	0	0	—	11	0	0	0	0	17¹	19	1	10	2	15.6	6.23	71	.292	.395	0	.000	-0	-4	-3	0	0.0
Total 2	0	0	—	15	0	0	0	0	23	27	1	12	2	15.7	6.26	72	.300	.388	0	.000	-1	-5	-5	0	0.0

● **GEORGE CRAIG** Craig, George McCarthy "Lefty" b: 11/15/1887, Philadelphia, Pa. d: 4/23/11, Indianapolis, Ind. TL, Deb: 7/19/07

| 1907 Phi-A | 0 | 0 | — | 2 | 0 | 0 | 0 | 0 | 5 | 9 | 0 | 6 | 0 | 37.8 | 10.80 | 24 | .286 | .583 | 0 | — | -2 | -2 | -2 | -0 | 0.0 |

● **PETE CRAIG** Craig, Peter Joel b: 7/10/40, LaSalle, Ontario, Canada BL/TR, 6'5", 220 lbs. Deb: 9/6/64

1964 Was-A	0	0	—	2	1	0	0	0	1²	8	1	4	0	64.8	48.60	8	.667	.750	0	—	-8	-8	-0	0.0
1965 Was-A	0	3	.000	3	3	0	0	0	14¹	18	1	8	6	16.3	8.16	43	.321	.406	2	.667	1	-7	-7	1	-1.1
1966 Was-A	0	0	—	1	0	0	0	0	2	2	0	1	1	13.5	4.50	77	.250	.333	0	—	-0	-0	-0	0	0.0
Total 3	0	3	.000	6	4	0	0	0	18	28	2	13	7	20.5	11.50	30	.368	.461	2	.667	1	-16	-16	0	-1.1

● **ROGER CRAIG** Craig, Roger Lee b: 2/17/30, Durham, N.C. BR/TR, 6'4", 191 lbs. Deb: 7/17/55 MC

1955 *Bro-N	5	3	.625	21	10	3	0	2	90²	81	8	43	48	12.4	2.78	146	.238	.325	2	.077	-2	13	13	-1	0.8
1956 *Bro-N	12	11	.522	35	32	8	2	1	199	169	25	87	109	11.8	3.71	107	.231	.316	1	.016	-5	1	6	-2	-0.2
1957 Bro-N	6	9	.400	32	13	1	0	0	111¹	102	18	47	69	12.2	4.61	90	.249	.329	4	.138	-1	-9	-5	-1	-0.7
1958 LA-N	2	1	.667	9	2	1	0	0	32	30	3	12	16	11.8	4.50	91	.242	.309	0	—	-2	-1	-1	-1	-0.3
1959 *LA-N	11	5	.688	29	17	4	**4**	0	152²	122	13	45	76	9.9	2.06	205	.217	.276	3	.058	-4	32	**37**	-1	3.2
1960 LA-N	8	3	.727	21	15	6	1	0	115²	99	8	43	69	11.3	3.27	121	.230	.305	2	.056	-2	6	9	-0	0.5
1961 LA-N	5	6	.455	40	14	2	0	2	112³	130	22	52	63	14.9	6.15	71	.288	.367	4	.148	-0	-27	-23	-1	-2.2
1962 NY-N	10	24	.294	42	33	13	0	3	233¹	261	35	70	118	13.0	4.51	93	.288	.343	4	.053	-5	-15	-9	4	-1.3
1963 NY-N	5	22	.185	46	31	14	0	2	236	249	28	58	108	11.9	3.78	92	.267	.314	6	.087	-2	-13	-8	-3	-0.8
1964 *StL-N	7	9	.438	39	19	3	0	5	166	180	16	35	84	11.9	3.25	117	.276	.317	10	.208	4	5	10	2	1.4
1965 Cin-N	1	4	.200	40	1	0	0	3	64¹	74	6	25	30	14.3	3.64	103	.289	.359	2	.182	-0	-1	1	0	0.1
1966 Phi-N	2	1	.667	14	0	0	0	1	22¹	31	4	5	13	14.3	5.56	65	.330	.360	0	—	-0	-5	-5	1	-0.6
Total 12	74	98	.430	368	186	58	7	19	1536¹	1528	186	522	803	12.2	3.83	104	.259	.323	38	.085	-22	-13	25	4	-0.1

● **JERRY CRAM** Cram, Gerald Allen b: 12/9/47, Los Angeles, Cal. BR/TR, 6', 180 lbs. Deb: 9/3/69

1969 KC-A	0	1	.000	5	2	0	0	0	16²	15	0	6	10	11.3	3.24	114	.231	.296	0	.000	-0	1	1	-0	0.2
1974 NY-N	0	1	.000	10	0	0	0	0	22¹	22	1	4	8	10.5	1.61	221	.275	.310	1	.333	0	5	5	0	0.2
1975 NY-N	0	1	.000	4	0	0	0	0	5	7	2	2	2	16.2	5.40	64	.333	.391	0	—	-0	-1	-1	0	-0.2
1976 KC-A	0	0	—	4	0	0	0	0	4¹	8	0	1	2	18.7	6.23	56	.421	.450	0	—	-0	-1	-1	-0	0.0
Total 4	0	3	.000	23	2	0	0	0	48¹	52	3	13	22	12.1	2.98	120	.281	.328	1	.167	-0	3	3	0	0.2

● **DOC CRAMER** Cramer, Roger Maxwell "Flit" b: 7/22/05, Beach Haven, N.J. d: 9/9/90, Manahawkin, N.J. BL/TR, 6'2", 185 lbs. Deb: 9/18/29 C◆

| 1938 Bos-A★ | 0 | 0 | — | 1 | 0 | 0 | 0 | 0 | 4 | 3 | 0 | 1 | 1 | 13.5 | 4.50 | 110 | .214 | .353 | 198 | .301 | 0 | 0 | 0 | 0 | 0.0 |

● **BILL CRAMER** Cramer, William Wendell b: 5/21/1891, Bedford, Ind. d: 9/11/66, Fort Wayne, Ind. BR/TR, 6', 175 lbs. Deb: 6/25/12

| 1912 Cin-N | 0 | 0 | — | 1 | 0 | 0 | 0 | 0 | 2¹ | 6 | 0 | 2 | 2 | 23.1 | 0.00 | — | .500 | .500 | 0 | .000 | -0 | 1 | 1 | -0 | 0.0 |

● **DOC CRANDALL** Crandall, James Otis b: 10/8/1887, Wadena, Ind. d: 8/17/51, Bell, Cal. BR/TR, 5'10.5", 180 lbs. Deb: 4/24/08 ◆

1908 NY-N	12	12	.500	32	24	13	0	0	214²	198	3	59	77	11.2	2.93	82	.248	.307	16	.222	5	-14	-12	-1	-1.1
1909 NY-N	6	4	.600	30	8	4	0	6	122	117	5	33	55	11.3	2.88	89	.252	.305	10	.244	3	-4	-4	2	0.1
1910 NY-N	17	4	.810	42	18	13	2	5	207²	194	10	43	73	10.4	2.56	116	.246	.289	25	.342	10	11	9	-1	1.9
1911 *NY-N	15	5	.750	41	15	9	2	5	198²	199	10	51	94	11.6	2.63	128	.256	.307	27	.239	4	17	16	2	2.3
1912 *NY-N	13	7	.650	37	10	7	0	5	162	181	3	35	60	12.1	3.61	94	.286	.326	25	.313	6	-4	-4	0	0.2
1913 NY-N	2	4	.333	24	2	1	0	3	55¹	61	2	13	28	12.2	3.09	101	.293	.338	7	.280	2	1	1	0	0.3
*NY-N	2	0	1.000	11	1	1	0	3	42¹	41	1	11	14	11.1	2.55	122	.248	.295	8	.364	3	3	3	1	0.5
Yr	4	4	.500	35	3	2	0	6	97²	102	3	24	42	11.6	2.86	109	.273	.317	15	.319	5	4	3	1	0.8
1914 StL-F	13	9	.591	27	21	18	1	0	196	194	8	52	84	11.4	3.54	86	.256	.305	86	.309	7	-5	-1	0	-0.4
1915 StL-F	21	15	.583	51	33	22	4	1	312²	307	5	77	117	11.3	2.59	111	.263	.314	40	.284	12	5	10	1	2.6
1916 StL-A	0	0	—	2	0	0	0	0	1¹	7	0	1	0	60.8	27.00	10	.636	.692	BH	.083	-0	-4	-4	0	-0.1

YEAR	TM/L	W	L	PCT	G	GS	CG	SH	SV	IP	H	HR	BB	SO	RAT	ERA	ERA+	OAV	OOB	BH	AVG	PB	PR	/A	PD	TPI
1918	Bos-N	1	2	.333	5	3	3	0	0	34	39	1	4	4	11.6	2.38	113	.307	.333	8	.286	1	1	1	0	0.3
Total	10	102	62	.622	302	135	91	9	25	1546²	1538	52	379	606	11.4	2.92	101	.261	.310	253	.285	54	-1	5	1	6.6

● **ED CRANE** Crane, Edward Nicholas "Cannon-Ball" b: 5/27/1862, Boston, Mass. d: 9/19/1896, Rochester, N.Y. BR/TR, 5'10.5", 204 lbs. Deb: 4/17/1884 ♦

YEAR	TM/L	W	L	PCT	G	GS	CG	SH	SV	IP	H	HR	BB	SO	RAT	ERA	ERA+	OAV	OOB	BH	AVG	PB	PR	/A	PD	TPI
1884	Bos-U	0	2	.000	4	2	1	0	0	18	17	1	6	13	11.5	4.00	60	.233	.291	122	.285	0	-3	-3	1	-0.2
1886	Was-N	1	7	.125	10	8	7	1	0	70	91	5	53	39	18.5	7.20	46	.313	.419	50	.171	-1	-30	-30	-0	-2.5
1888	*NY-N	5	6	.455	12	11	11	2	1	92²	70	3	40	58	10.9	2.43	113	.193	.277	6	.162	1	4	3	1	0.5
1889	*NY-N	14	10	.583	29	25	23	0	0	230	221	10	136	130	14.4	3.68	107	.245	.350	21	.204	3	9	7	-4	0.4
1890	NY-P	16	19	.457	43	35	28	0	0	330¹	323	12	208	116	14.7	4.63	98	.245	.352	46	.315	8	-15	-3	-3	0.0
1891	Cin-a	14	14	.500	32	31	25	1	0	250	216	3	139	122	13.3	**2.45**	**168**	.225	.332	17	.155	-6	35	46	-2	3.5
	Cin-N	4	8	.333	14	11	11	0	0	116²	134	3	64	51	15.5	4.09	83	.277	.365	5	.109	-3	-10	-9	-0	-1.0
1892	NY-N	16	24	.400	47	42	35	2	1	364¹	350	10	189	174	13.6	3.80	85	.243	.335	40	.245	4	-21	-24	-0	-1.8
1893	NY-N	2	4	.333	10	7	4	0	0	68¹	84	2	41	11	17.3	5.93	79	.294	.393	12	.462	4	-10	-10	-1	-0.3
	Bro-N	0	2	.000	2	2	1	0	0	10	19	2	9	5	26.1	13.50	33	.388	.492	2	.400	1	-10	-10	-0	-1.1
	Yr	2	6	.250	12	9	5	0	0	78¹	103	4	50	16	17.7	6.89	67	.302	.393	14	.452	5	-19	-20	-1	-1.4
Total	8	72	96	.429	204	176	146	7	2	1550¹	1525	51	885	719	14.3	3.99	95	.247	.347	335	.238	11	-49	-35	-9	-2.5

● **CARLOS CRAWFORD** Crawford, Carlos Lamonte b: 10/4/71, Charlotte, N.C. BR/TR, 6'1", 185 lbs. Deb: 6/7/96

YEAR	TM/L	W	L	PCT	G	GS	CG	SH	SV	IP	H	HR	BB	SO	RAT	ERA	ERA+	OAV	OOB	BH	AVG	PB	PR	/A	PD	TPI
1996	Phi-N	0	1	.000	1	1	0	0	0	3²	7	1	2	4	24.5	4.91	89	.389	.476	0	.000	-0	-0	-0	-1	-0.1

● **LARRY CRAWFORD** Crawford, Charles Lowrie b: 4/27/14, Swissvale, Pa. d: 12/20/94, Hanover, Pa. BL/TL, 6'1", 165 lbs. Deb: 7/21/37

YEAR	TM/L	W	L	PCT	G	GS	CG	SH	SV	IP	H	HR	BB	SO	RAT	ERA	ERA+	OAV	OOB	BH	AVG	PB	PR	/A	PD	TPI
1937	Phi-N	0	0		6	0	0	0	0	6	12	2	1	2	19.5	15.00	29	.387	.406	0		0	-7	-7	-0	-0.1

● **JIM CRAWFORD** Crawford, James Frederick "Catfish" b: 9/29/50, Chicago, Ill. BL/TL, 6'3", 200 lbs. Deb: 4/6/73

YEAR	TM/L	W	L	PCT	G	GS	CG	SH	SV	IP	H	HR	BB	SO	RAT	ERA	ERA+	OAV	OOB	BH	AVG	PB	PR	/A	PD	TPI
1973	Hou-N	2	4	.333	48	0	0	0	6	70	69	7	33	56	13.4	4.50	81	.256	.341	3	.231	1	-7	-7	1	-0.5
1975	Hou-N	3	5	.375	44	2	0	0	4	86²	92	6	37	37	13.6	3.63	93	.280	.356	5	.294	2	-0	-3	0	0.0
1976	Det-A	1	8	.111	32	5	1	0	2	109¹	115	4	43	68	13.0	4.53	82	.275	.343	0	—	0	-12	-10	5	-0.6
1977	Det-A	7	8	.467	37	7	0	0	1	126	156	13	50	91	14.8	4.79	90	.310	.373	0	—	0	-10	-7	1	-0.7
1978	Det-A	2	3	.400	20	0	0	0	0	39¹	45	3	19	24	15.1	4.35	89	.292	.377	0	—	0	-3	-2	-0	-0.4
Total	5	15	28	.349	181	14	1	0	13	431¹	477	27	182	276	13.9	4.40	86	.285	.357	8	.267	3	-32	-29	6	-2.2

● **STEVE CRAWFORD** Crawford, Steven Ray b: 4/29/58, Pryor, Okla. BR/TR, 6'5", 225 lbs. Deb: 9/2/80

YEAR	TM/L	W	L	PCT	G	GS	CG	SH	SV	IP	H	HR	BB	SO	RAT	ERA	ERA+	OAV	OOB	BH	AVG	PB	PR	/A	PD	TPI
1980	Bos-A	2	0	1.000	6	4	2	0	0	32¹	41	3	8	10	13.6	3.62	117	.306	.345	0	—	0	1	2	0	-0.1
1981	Bos-A	0	5	.000	14	11	0	0	0	57²	69	10	16	29	14.0	4.99	77	.301	.360	0	—	0	-9	-7	0	-0.6
1982	Bos-A	1	0	1.000	5	0	0	0	0	9	14	0	0	2	14.0	2.00	215	.341	.341	0	—	0	2	2	0	0.2
1984	Bos-A	5	0	1.000	35	0	0	0	1	62	69	6	21	21	13.2	3.34	125	.286	.346	0	—	0	4	6	-0	0.1
1985	Bos-A	6	5	.545	44	1	0	0	12	91	103	8	28	58	13.0	3.76	114	.289	.340	0	—	0	4	5	1	0.3
1986	*Bos-A	0	2	.000	40	0	0	0	4	57¹	69	5	19	32	13.8	3.92	106	.308	.362	0	—	0	2	2	0	0.1
1987	Bos-A	5	4	.556	29	0	0	0	0	72²	91	13	32	43	15.5	5.33	85	.314	.386	0	—	0	-7	-6	1	-0.7
1989	KC-A	3	1	.750	25	0	0	0	0	54	48	2	19	33	11.7	2.83	136	.242	.318	0	—	0	6	6	2	0.6
1990	KC-A	5	4	.556	46	0	0	0	1	80	79	7	23	54	11.8	4.16	92	.254	.312	0	—	0	-2	-3	-1	-0.1
1991	KC-A	3	2	.600	33	0	0	0	1	46²	92	6	18	38	15.2	5.98	69	.311	.373	0	—	0	-10	-10	-0	-1.0
Total	10	30	23	.566	277	16	2	0	19	562²	643	54	186	320	13.5	4.17	99	.290	.348	0	—	0	-8	-3	3	-1.0

● **DOUG CREEK** Creek, Paul Douglas b: 3/1/69, Winchester, Va. BL/TL, 5'10", 205 lbs. Deb: 9/17/95

YEAR	TM/L	W	L	PCT	G	GS	CG	SH	SV	IP	H	HR	BB	SO	RAT	ERA	ERA+	OAV	OOB	BH	AVG	PB	PR	/A	PD	TPI
1995	StL-N	0	0	—	6	0	0	0	0	6²	2	0	3	10	6.8	0.00	—	.095	.208	0		0	3	3	-0	0.0
1996	SF-N	0	2	.000	63	0	0	0	0	48¹	45	11	32	38	14.7	6.52	63	.243	.361	0	.000	-0	-12	-13	-1	-0.6
Total	2	0	2	.000	69	0	0	0	0	55	47	11	35	48	13.7	5.73	72	.228	.346	0	.000	-0	-9	-9	-1	-0.6

● **JACK CREEL** Creel, Jack Dalton "Tex" b: 4/23/16, Kyle, Tex. BR/TR, 6', 165 lbs. Deb: 4/22/45

YEAR	TM/L	W	L	PCT	G	GS	CG	SH	SV	IP	H	HR	BB	SO	RAT	ERA	ERA+	OAV	OOB	BH	AVG	PB	PR	/A	PD	TPI
1945	StL-N	5	4	.556	26	8	2	0	2	87	78	5	45	34	13.3	4.14	90	.245	.349	2	.077	-2	-3	-4	0	-0.5

● **KEITH CREEL** Creel, Steven Keith b: 2/4/59, Dallas, Tex. BR/TR, 6'2", 180 lbs. Deb: 5/25/82

YEAR	TM/L	W	L	PCT	G	GS	CG	SH	SV	IP	H	HR	BB	SO	RAT	ERA	ERA+	OAV	OOB	BH	AVG	PB	PR	/A	PD	TPI
1982	KC-A	1	4	.200	9	6	0	0	0	41²	43	8	25	13	14.7	5.40	76	.267	.366	0	—	0	-6	-6	0	-0.6
1983	KC-A	2	5	.286	25	10	1	0	0	89¹	116	17	35	31	15.4	6.35	64	.320	.382	0	—	0	-23	-23	-1	-1.6
1985	Cle-A	2	5	.286	15	8	0	0	0	62	73	7	23	31	14.2	4.79	86	.296	.360	0	—	0	-4	-5	-1	-0.5
1987	Tex-A	0	0	—	6	0	0	0	0	9²	12	2	5	5	15.8	4.66	96	.293	.370	0	—	0	-0	-0	0	0.0
Total	4	5	14	.263	55	24	1	0	0	202²	244	34	88	80	14.9	5.60	74	.300	.372	0	—	0	-33	-33	-2	-2.7

● **BOB CREMINS** Cremins, Robert Anthony "Lefty" or "Crooked Arm" b: 2/15/06, Pelham Manor, N.Y. BL/TL, 5'11", 178 lbs. Deb: 8/17/27

YEAR	TM/L	W	L	PCT	G	GS	CG	SH	SV	IP	H	HR	BB	SO	RAT	ERA	ERA+	OAV	OOB	BH	AVG	PB	PR	/A	PD	TPI
1927	Bos-A	0	0	—	4	0	0	0	0	5¹	5	0	3	0	13.5	5.06	83	.250	.348	0	—	0	-1	-0	0	0.0

● **WALKER CRESS** Cress, Walker James "Foots" b: 3/6/17, Ben Hur, Va. d: 4/21/96, Baton Rouge, La. BR/TR, 6'5", 205 lbs. Deb: 4/27/48

YEAR	TM/L	W	L	PCT	G	GS	CG	SH	SV	IP	H	HR	BB	SO	RAT	ERA	ERA+	OAV	OOB	BH	AVG	PB	PR	/A	PD	TPI
1948	Cin-N	0	1	.000	30	2	1	0	0	60	60	2	42	33	15.5	4.50	87	.271	.390	4	.500	2	-4	-4	-1	0.0
1949	Cin-N	0	0	—	3	0	0	0	0	2	2	0	3	0	22.5	0.00	—	.286	.500	0		0	1	1	-0	0.0
Total	2	0	1	.000	33	2	1	0	0	62	62	2	45	33	15.7	4.35	90	.272	.394	4	.500	2	-3	-3	-1	0.0

● **TIM CREWS** Crews, Stanley Timothy b: 4/3/61, Tampa, Fla. d: 3/23/93, Orlando, Fla. BR/TR, 6', 190 lbs. Deb: 7/27/87

YEAR	TM/L	W	L	PCT	G	GS	CG	SH	SV	IP	H	HR	BB	SO	RAT	ERA	ERA+	OAV	OOB	BH	AVG	PB	PR	/A	PD	TPI
1987	LA-N	1	1	.500	20	0	0	0	3	29	30	2	8	20	12.4	2.48	160	.268	.328	0	.000	-0	5	5	0	0.4
1988	LA-N	4	0	1.000	42	0	0	0	0	71²	77	3	16	45	11.7	3.14	106	.278	.317	1	.200	0	2	2	-1	0.2
1989	LA-N	0	1	.000	44	0	0	0	1	61²	69	7	23	56	13.7	3.21	106	.284	.351	0	—	0	2	1	-0	0.0
1990	LA-N	4	5	.444	66	2	0	0	5	107¹	98	9	24	76	10.3	2.77	132	.238	.282	0	.000	-1	12	11	-1	0.7
1991	LA-N	2	3	.400	60	0	0	0	6	76	75	7	19	53	11.1	3.43	105	.256	.301	0	.000	0	2	1	0	0.1
1992	LA-N	0	3	.000	49	2	0	0	0	78	95	6	20	43	13.5	5.19	66	.310	.357	2	.286	0	-15	-15	-1	-0.6
Total	6	11	13	.458	281	4	0	0	15	423²	444	34	110	293	11.9	3.44	103	.270	.319	3	.136	-0	9	5	-3	0.6

● **JERRY CRIDER** Crider, Jerry Stephen b: 9/2/41, Sioux Falls, S.D. BR/TR, 6'2", 200 lbs. Deb: 5/21/69

YEAR	TM/L	W	L	PCT	G	GS	CG	SH	SV	IP	H	HR	BB	SO	RAT	ERA	ERA+	OAV	OOB	BH	AVG	PB	PR	/A	PD	TPI
1969	Min-A	1	0	1.000	21	1	0	0	1	28²	32	3	15	16	15.1	4.71	78	.284	.381	4	.444	2	-3	-3	0	0.1
1970	Chi-A	4	7	.364	32	8	0	0	4	91	101	13	34	40	13.5	4.45	88	.288	.354	2	.083	-1	-7	-6	-2	-1.0
Total	2	5	7	.417	53	9	0	0	5	119²	132	16	49	56	13.9	4.51	85	.287	.361	6	.182	-0	-11	-9	-2	-0.9

● **CHUCK CRIM** Crim, Charles Robert b: 7/23/61, Van Nuys, Cal. BR/TR, 6', 190 lbs. Deb: 4/8/87

YEAR	TM/L	W	L	PCT	G	GS	CG	SH	SV	IP	H	HR	BB	SO	RAT	ERA	ERA+	OAV	OOB	BH	AVG	PB	PR	/A	PD	TPI
1987	Mil-A	6	8	.429	53	5	0	0	12	130	133	15	39	56	12.1	3.67	125	.266	.323	0	—	0	11	13	-0	1.4
1988	Mil-A	7	6	.538	70	0	0	0	9	105	95	11	28	58	10.7	2.91	136	.247	.302	0	—	0	12	12	0	1.6
1989	Mil-A	9	7	.563	76	0	0	0	7	117²	114	7	36	59	11.6	2.83	136	.259	.318	0	—	0	14	13	-1	1.7
1990	Mil-A	3	5	.375	67	0	0	0	11	85²	88	7	23	39	11.9	3.47	112	.261	.312	0	—	0	4	4	0	0.5
1991	Mil-A	8	5	.615	66	0	0	0	3	91¹	115	9	25	39	14.0	4.63	86	.305	.351	0	—	0	-5	-7	0	-0.8
1992	Cal-A	7	6	.538	57	0	0	0	1	87	100	11	29	30	14.0	5.17	77	.293	.359	0	—	0	-12	-12	0	-1.6
1993	Cal-A	2	2	.500	11	0	0	0	0	15¹	17	2	5	10	14.1	5.87	77	.298	.375	0	—	0	-3	-2	1	-0.5
1994	Chi-N	5	4	.556	49	1	0	0	2	64¹	69	9	24	43	13.2	4.48	93	.271	.336	0	.000	-0	-2	-2	0	-0.3
Total	8	47	43	.522	449	6	0	0	45	696¹	731	71	209	334	12.4	3.83	107	.272	.329	0	.000	0	20	19	-0	2.0

● **JACK CRIMIAN** Crimian, John Melvin b: 2/17/26, Philadelphia, Pa. BR/TR, 5'10", 180 lbs. Deb: 7/3/51

YEAR	TM/L	W	L	PCT	G	GS	CG	SH	SV	IP	H	HR	BB	SO	RAT	ERA	ERA+	OAV	OOB	BH	AVG	PB	PR	/A	PD	TPI
1951	StL-N	1	0	1.000	11	0	0	0	1	17	24	3	8	5	16.9	9.00	44	.338	.405	1	.333	0	-10	-10	-0	-0.6
1952	StL-N	0	0	—	5	0	0	0	0	8¹	15	4	4	4	20.5	9.72	38	.417	.475	0	.000	0	-6	-6	-0	-0.4
1956	KC-A	4	8	.333	54	7	0	0	1	129	129	19	49	59	12.8	5.51	79	.265	.339	5	.227	1	-19	-17	-1	-1.4
1957	Det-A	0	1	.000	4	0	0	0	0	5²	9	1	4	1	20.6	12.71	30	.375	.464	0		0	-6	-6	-0	-0.4
Total	4	5	9	.357	74	7	0	0	2	160	177	27	65	69	13.9	6.36	67	.287	.360	6	.231	1	-40	-38	-1	-2.8

● **DODE CRISS** Criss, Dode b: 3/12/1885, Sherman, Miss. d: 9/8/55, Sherman, Miss. BL/TL, 6'2", 200 lbs. Deb: 4/20/08 ♦

YEAR	TM/L	W	L	PCT	G	GS	CG	SH	SV	IP	H	HR	BB	SO	RAT	ERA	ERA+	OAV	OOB	BH	AVG	PB	PR	/A	PD	TPI
1908	StL-A	0	1	.000	9	1	0	0	0	18	15	1	13	9	15.5	6.50	37	.250	.408	28	.341	1	-8	-8	-1	-0.4
1909	StL-A	1	5	.167	11	6	3	0	0	55¹	53	0	32	43	14.2	3.42	71	.262	.369	14	.292	5	-6	-6	-1	-0.1
1910	StL-A	2	1	.667	6	0	0	0	0	19¹	12	0	9	9	11.6	1.40	177	.176	.309	21	.231	1	2	2	-0	0.5

YEAR TM/L	W	L	PCT	G	GS	CG	SH	SV	IP	H	HR	BB	SO	RAT	ERA	ERA+	OAV	OOB	BH	AVG	PB	PR	/A	PD	TPI
1911 StL-A	0	2	.000	4	2	0	0	0	18¹	24	0	10	9	17.7	8.35	40	.333	.429	21	.253	0	-10	-10	0	-0.8
Total	4	3	9	.250	30	9	3	0	0	111	104	1	64	70	14.5	4.38	59	.259	.375	84	.276	8	-22	-22	-2	-0.8

● BILL CRISTALL
Cristall, William Arthur "Lefty" b: 9/12/1878, Odessa, Russia d: 1/28/39, Buffalo, N.Y. BL/TL, 5'7", 145 lbs. Deb: 9/3/01

YEAR TM/L	W	L	PCT	G	GS	CG	SH	SV	IP	H	HR	BB	SO	RAT	ERA	ERA+	OAV	OOB	BH	AVG	PB	PR	/A	PD	TPI
1901 Cle-A	1	5	.167	6	6	5	1	0	47	54	1	30	12	16.4	4.84	73	.280	.388	7	.350	2	-6	-7	2	-0.3

● LEO CRISTANTE
Cristante, Dante Leo b: 12/10/26, Detroit, Mich. d: 8/24/77, Dearborn, Mich. BR/TR, 6'1", 195 lbs. Deb: 4/21/51

YEAR TM/L	W	L	PCT	G	GS	CG	SH	SV	IP	H	HR	BB	SO	RAT	ERA	ERA+	OAV	OOB	BH	AVG	PB	PR	/A	PD	TPI
1951 Phi-N	1	1	.500	10	1	0	0	0	22	28	3	9	6	15.5	4.91	78	.318	.388	1	.167	-0	-2	-3	0	-0.2
1955 Det-A	0	1	.000	20	1	0	0	0	36²	37	1	14	9	12.5	3.19	120	.261	.327	0	.000	-1	3	3	-1	-0.2
Total 2	1	2	.333	30	2	0	0	0	58²	65	4	23	15	13.7	3.84	100	.283	.350	1	.077	-1	1	0	-1	-0.4

● MORRIE CRITCHLEY
Critchley, Morris Arthur b: 3/26/1850, New London, Conn. d: 3/6/10, Pittsburgh, Pa. 6'1", 190 lbs. Deb: 5/8/1882

YEAR TM/L	W	L	PCT	G	GS	CG	SH	SV	IP	H	HR	BB	SO	RAT	ERA	ERA+	OAV	OOB	BH	AVG	PB	PR	/A	PD	TPI
1882 Pit-a	1	0	1.000	1	1	1	1	0	9	7	0	1	3	8.0	0.00	—	.200	.222	0	.000	-1	3	3	0	0.2
StL-a	0	4	.000	4	4	4	0	0	34	43	3	7	2	13.2	4.24	66	.289	.321	3	.214	-0	-6	-5	-1	-0.6
Yr	1	4	.200	5	5	5	1	0	43	50	3	8	5	12.1	3.35	83	.272	.302	3	.158	-1	-3	-3	-1	-0.4

● CLAUDE CROCKER
Crocker, Claude Arthur b: 7/20/24, Caroleen, N.C. BR/TR, 6'2", 185 lbs. Deb: 8/1/44

YEAR TM/L	W	L	PCT	G	GS	CG	SH	SV	IP	H	HR	BB	SO	RAT	ERA	ERA+	OAV	OOB	BH	AVG	PB	PR	/A	PD	TPI
1944 Bro-N	0	0	—	2	0	0	0	0	3¹	6	0	5	1	29.7	10.80	33	.400	.550	1	1.000	0	-3	-3	-0	0.1
1945 Bro-N	0	0	—	1	0	0	0	1	2	2	0	1	1	13.5	0.00	—	.286	.375	0	—	0	1	1	-0	0.1
Total 2	0	0	—	3	0	0	0	1	5¹	8	0	6	2	23.6	6.75	54	.364	.500	1	1.000	0	-2	-2	0	0.2

● RAY CRONE
Crone, Raymond Hayes b: 8/7/31, Memphis, Tenn. BR/TR, 6'2", 185 lbs. Deb: 4/13/54

YEAR TM/L	W	L	PCT	G	GS	CG	SH	SV	IP	H	HR	BB	SO	RAT	ERA	ERA+	OAV	OOB	BH	AVG	PB	PR	/A	PD	TPI
1954 Mil-N	1	0	1.000	19	2	1	0	1	49	44	6	24	33	11.8	2.02	184	.247	.323	2	.200	-0	11	9	-0	0.2
1955 Mil-N	10	9	.526	33	15	6	1	0	140¹	117	11	42	76	10.2	3.46	108	.227	.285	7	.159	-1	9	5	0	0.4
1956 Mil-N	11	10	.524	35	21	6	0	2	169²	173	19	44	73	11.6	3.87	89	.263	.311	6	.122	1	-2	-8	-1	-0.9
1957 Mil-N	3	1	.750	11	5	2	0	0	42¹	54	8	15	15	14.7	4.46	78	.312	.367	2	.182	1	-3	-5	1	-0.2
NY-N	4	8	.333	25	17	2	0	1	120²	131	11	40	56	13.0	4.33	91	.272	.331	1	.025	-4	-6	-5	2	-0.6
Yr	7	9	.438	36	22	4	0	1	163	185	19	55	71	13.4	4.36	88	.282	.340	-3	.059	-3	-9	-10	3	-0.8
1958 SF-N	1	2	.333	14	1	0	0	0	24	35	5	13	7	18.0	6.75	56	.354	.429	0	.000	-0	-7	-8	0	-0.9
Total 5	30	30	.500	137	61	17	1	4	546	554	60	173	260	12.1	3.87	95	.263	.325	18	.115	-3	2	-12	2	-2.0

● JACK CRONIN
Cronin, John J. b: 5/26/1874, Staten Island, N.Y d: 7/12/29, Middletown, N.Y. BR/TR, 6' ", 200 lbs. Deb: 8/24/1895

YEAR TM/L	W	L	PCT	G	GS	CG	SH	SV	IP	H	HR	BB	SO	RAT	ERA	ERA+	OAV	OOB	BH	AVG	PB	PR	/A	PD	TPI
1895 Bro-N	0	0	—	2	0	0	0	2	5	10	0	3	1	23.4	10.80	41	.417	.481	1	.500	1	-3	-4	0	-0.2
1898 Pit-N	2	2	.500	4	4	2	1	0	28	35	0	8	9	13.8	3.54	101	.304	.350	1	.100	-0	0	0	-0	0.0
1899 Cin-N	2	2	.500	5	5	5	0	0	41	56	2	16	9	16.9	5.49	71	.324	.397	2	.118	-1	-7	-7	-1	-0.7
1901 Det-A	13	15	.464	30	28	21	0	0	219²	261	6	42	62	12.9	3.89	99	.292	.331	21	.247	2	-6	-1	-3	-0.2
1902 Det-A	0	0	—	4	0	0	0	0	17¹	26	1	8	5	19.2	9.35	39	.347	.430	0	.000	-1	-11	-11	0	-0.1
Bal-A	3	5	.375	10	8	8	0	0	75²	86	1	24	20	10.7	2.62	144	.236	.296	4	.148	-1	8	10	2	1.1
Yr	3	5	.375	14	8	8	0	0	93	92	2	32	25	12.0	3.87	97	.257	.318	4	.118	-2	-3	-1	3	1.0
NY-N	5	6	.455	13	12	11	0	0	114	105	3	18	52	9.7	2.45	115	.245	.275	11	.169	-1	4	5	0	0.3
1903 NY-N	6	4	.600	20	11	8	0	1	115²	130	5	37	50	13.5	3.81	88	.284	.345	9	.196	0	-7	-6	0	-0.5
1904 Bro-N	12	23	.343	40	34	33	4	0	307	284	10	79	110	11.0	2.70	102	.245	.300	17	.157	-3	1	2	0	-0.1
Total 7	43	57	.430	128	102	88	6	3	923¹	973	28	235	318	12.1	3.40	96	.270	.321	66	.180	-5	-20	-13	-1	-0.4

● GEORGE CROSBY
Crosby, George Washington b: 1860, Iowa d: 1/9/13, San Francisco, Cal. Deb: 5/22/1884

YEAR TM/L	W	L	PCT	G	GS	CG	SH	SV	IP	H	HR	BB	SO	RAT	ERA	ERA+	OAV	OOB	BH	AVG	PB	PR	/A	PD	TPI
1884 Chi-N	1	2	.333	3	3	3	0	0	28	27	3	12	11	12.5	3.54	89	.227	.298	4	.308	1	-2	-1	1	0.0

● KEN CROSBY
Crosby, Kenneth Stewart b: 12/15/47, New Denver, B.C., Canada BR/TR, 6'2", 179 lbs. Deb: 8/5/75

YEAR TM/L	W	L	PCT	G	GS	CG	SH	SV	IP	H	HR	BB	SO	RAT	ERA	ERA+	OAV	OOB	BH	AVG	PB	PR	/A	PD	TPI
1975 Chi-N	1	0	1.000	9	0	0	0	0	8¹	10	0	7	6	18.4	3.24	119	.294	.415	0	—	0	0	1	0	0.1
1976 Chi-N	0	0	—	7	1	0	0	0	12	20	3	8	5	21.0	12.00	32	.377	.459	1	.500	1	-11	-11	0	0.0
Total 2	1	0	1.000	16	1	0	0	0	20¹	30	3	15	11	19.9	8.41	46	.345	.441	1	.500	1	-11	-10	0	0.1

● LEM CROSS
Cross, George Lewis b: 1/9/1872, Sanbornton, N.H. d: 10/9/30, Manchester, N.H. TR, 5'9", 155 lbs. Deb: 8/6/1893

YEAR TM/L	W	L	PCT	G	GS	CG	SH	SV	IP	H	HR	BB	SO	RAT	ERA	ERA+	OAV	OOB	BH	AVG	PB	PR	/A	PD	TPI
1893 Cin-N	0	2	.000	3	3	2	0	0	21	24	3	9	7	14.1	5.57	86	.279	.347	2	.333	1	-2	-2	0	0.0
1894 Cin-N	3	4	.429	8	7	3	0	0	53	94	8	21	11	20.4	8.49	65	.381	.440	6	.231	-1	-19	-17	-1	-1.5
Total 2	3	6	.333	11	10	5	0	0	74	118	11	30	18	18.6	7.66	70	.354	.416	8	.250	-0	-21	-19	-0	-1.5

● DOUG CROTHERS
Crothers, Douglas b: 11/16/1859, Natchez, Miss. d: 3/29/07, St.Louis, Mo. BR/TR, Deb: 8/3/1884

YEAR TM/L	W	L	PCT	G	GS	CG	SH	SV	IP	H	HR	BB	SO	RAT	ERA	ERA+	OAV	OOB	BH	AVG	PB	PR	/A	PD	TPI
1884 KC-U	1	2	.333	3	3	3	0	0	25	26	0	6	11	11.5	1.80	124	.250	.291	2	.133	-2	2	1	-1	-0.1
1885 NY-a	7	11	.389	18	18	18	1	0	154	192	4	49	40	14.2	5.08	58	.293	.344	8	.157	0	-31	-36	0	-3.1
Total 2	8	13	.381	21	21	21	1	0	179	218	4	55	51	13.8	4.63	62	.287	.337	10	.152	-1	-30	-35	-0	-3.2

● BILL CROUCH
Crouch, William Henry "Skip" b: 12/3/1886, Marshallton, Del. d: 12/22/45, Highland Park, Mich. BL/TL, 6'1", 210 lbs. Deb: 7/12/10 F

YEAR TM/L	W	L	PCT	G	GS	CG	SH	SV	IP	H	HR	BB	SO	RAT	ERA	ERA+	OAV	OOB	BH	AVG	PB	PR	/A	PD	TPI
1910 StL-A	0	0	—	1	1	1	0	0	8	6	0	7	2	14.6	3.38	73	.231	.394	0	.000	-1	-1	-1	-0	-0.1

● BILL CROUCH
Crouch, Wilmer Elmer b: 8/20/10, Wilmington, Del. d: 12/26/80, Howell, Mich. BB/TR, 6'1", 180 lbs. Deb: 5/9/39 F

YEAR TM/L	W	L	PCT	G	GS	CG	SH	SV	IP	H	HR	BB	SO	RAT	ERA	ERA+	OAV	OOB	BH	AVG	PB	PR	/A	PD	TPI
1939 Bro-N	4	0	1.000	6	3	3	0	0	38¹	37	3	14	10	12.0	2.58	156	.255	.321	1	.133	-1	6	6	-1	0.5
1941 Phi-N	2	3	.400	20	5	1	0	1	59	65	4	17	26	12.5	4.42	84	.286	.336	1	.091	-0	-5	-5	2	-0.3
StL-N	1	2	.333	18	4	0	0	6	45	45	2	14	15	11.8	3.00	125	.271	.328	0	.000	-1	3	4	-1	0.1
Yr	3	5	.375	38	9	1	0	7	104	110	6	31	41	12.2	3.81	98	.280	.333	1	.042	-2	-2	-1	1	-0.2
1945 StL-N	1	0	1.000	6	0	0	0	0	13¹	12	1	7	4	13.5	3.38	111	.255	.364	0	.000	0	1	1	0	0.0
Total 3	8	5	.615	50	12	4	0	7	155²	159	10	52	55	12.3	3.47	110	.272	.332	3	.073	-3	4	6	0	0.3

● ZACH CROUCH
Crouch, Zachary Quinn b: 10/26/65, Folsom, Cal. BL/TL, 6'3", 180 lbs. Deb: 6/4/88

YEAR TM/L	W	L	PCT	G	GS	CG	SH	SV	IP	H	HR	BB	SO	RAT	ERA	ERA+	OAV	OOB	BH	AVG	PB	PR	/A	PD	TPI
1988 Bos-A	0	0	—	3	0	0	0	0	1¹	4	0	2	0	40.5	6.75	61	.571	.667	0	—	0	-0	-0	0	-0.2

● ALVIN CROWDER
Crowder, Alvin Floyd "General" b: 1/11/1899, Winston-Salem, N.C d: 4/3/72, Winston-Salem, N.C. BL/TR, 5'10", 170 lbs. Deb: 7/24/26

YEAR TM/L	W	L	PCT	G	GS	CG	SH	SV	IP	H	HR	BB	SO	RAT	ERA	ERA+	OAV	OOB	BH	AVG	PB	PR	/A	PD	TPI
1926 Was-A	7	4	.636	19	12	6	0	1	100	97	3	60	26	14.3	3.96	98	.261	.367	9	.237	1	-1	-1	1	0.1
1927 Was-A	4	7	.364	15	11	4	2	0	67¹	58	3	42	22	13.6	4.54	89	.232	.347	3	.136	-1	-3	-4	-1	-0.7
StL-A	3	5	.375	21	8	2	1	3	73²	71	3	42	30	13.9	5.01	87	.260	.361	6	.261	0	-7	-5	-1	-0.6
Yr	7	12	.368	36	19	6	3	3	141	129	6	84	52	13.7	4.79	88	.246	.351	9	.200	-1	-10	-9	-2	-1.3
1928 StL-A	21	5	.808	41	31	19	1	4	244	228	11	91	99	12.2	3.69	114	.258	.325	15	.188	-2	10	14	-5	0.7
1929 StL-A	17	15	.531	40	34	19	4	4	266²	272	22	93	79	12.3	3.92	113	.271	.332	18	.188	-3	10	15	-2	1.1
1930 StL-A	3	7	.300	13	10	5	1	0	77¹	85	11	27	42	13.2	4.66	105	.283	.345	4	.160	-2	-0	2	1	0.0
Was-A	15	9	.625	27	25	20	0	1	202¹	191	6	69	65	11.6	3.60	128	.249	.312	13	.171	-2	24	22	-4	1.7
Yr	18	16	.529	40	35	25	1	1	279²	276	17	96	107	12.0	3.89	120	.259	.325	17	.168	-4	23	24	-3	1.8
1931 Was-A	18	11	.621	44	26	13	1	6	234¹	255	13	72	85	12.6	3.88	111	.275	.328	19	.216	-1	13	11	-3	0.7
1932 Was-A	26	13	.667	50	39	21	3	1	327	319	11	77	100	10.9	3.33	130	.252	.295	21	.221	2	42	36	-2	3.5
1933 *Was-A★	24	15	.615	52	35	17	0	4	299¹	311	14	81	110	11.9	3.97	105	.267	.316	19	.186	1	10	7	-3	0.5
1934 Was-A	4	10	.286	29	13	4	0	3	100²	142	9	38	39	16.1	6.79	64	.326	.380	7	.219	-2	-26	-28	-1	-3.2
*Det-A	5	1	.833	9	9	3	1	0	66²	81	3	20	30	13.6	4.18	105	.295	.342	4	.133	-2	2	2	-1	-0.2
Yr	9	11	.450	38	22	7	1	3	167¹	223	12	58	69	15.1	5.75	76	.314	.365	11	.177	-4	-23	-26	-2	-3.4
1935 *Det-A	16	10	.615	33	32	16	2	0	241	269	16	67	59	12.7	4.26	98	.285	.335	17	.183	-2	5	-3	-3	-0.7
1936 Det-A	3	4	.571	9	7	1	0	0	44	54	5	21	10	17.4	8.39	59	.342	.409	3	.150	-1	-16	-17	-0	-2.0
Total 11	167	115	.592	402	292	150	16	22	2344¹	2453	136	800	799	12.5	4.12	105	.270	.330	164	.194	-12	64	52	-24	1.0

● CAP CROWELL
Crowell, Minot Joy b: 9/5/1892, Roxbury, Mass. d: 9/30/62, Central Falls, R.I. BR/TR, 6'1", 178 lbs. Deb: 6/23/15

YEAR TM/L	W	L	PCT	G	GS	CG	SH	SV	IP	H	HR	BB	SO	RAT	ERA	ERA+	OAV	OOB	BH	AVG	PB	PR	/A	PD	TPI
1915 Phi-A	2	6	.250	10	8	4	0	0	54¹	56	1	47	15	17.9	5.47	54	.292	.443	5	.227	-0	-15	-15	-0	-2.0
1916 Phi-A	0	5	.000	9	6	1	0	0	39²	43	0	34	15	17.9	4.99	57	.289	.427	0	.000	-1	-10	-9	-1	-1.3
Total 2	2	11	.154	19	14	5	0	0	94	99	1	81	30	17.9	5.27	55	.290	.436	5	.147	-1	-25	-24	-1	-3.3

● BILLY CROWELL
Crowell, William Theodore b: 11/6/1865, Cincinnati, Ohio d: 7/24/35, Ft.Worth, Tex. BR/TR, 5'8.5", 160 lbs. Deb: 4/20/1887

YEAR TM/L	W	L	PCT	G	GS	CG	SH	SV	IP	H	HR	BB	SO	RAT	ERA	ERA+	OAV	OOB	BH	AVG	PB	PR	/A	PD	TPI
1887 Cle-a	14	31	.311	45	45	45	1	0	389¹	541	9	138	72	16.2	4.88	89	.327	.386	22	.141	-13	-25	-23	-3	-3.1

YEAR	TM/L	W	L	PCT	G	GS	CG	SH	SV	IP	H	HR	BB	SO	RAT	ERA	ERA+	OAV	OOB	BH	AVG	PB	PR	/A	PD	TPI
1888	Cle-a	5	13	.278	18	18	16	0	0	150²	212	8	61	61	16.8	5.79	53	.320	.385	5	.086	-5	-46	-45	-1	-4.4
	Lou-a	0	1	.000	1	1	1	0	0	9	12	1	6	5	19.0	6.00	51	.308	.413	0	.000	-0	-3	-3	0	-0.2
	Yr	5	14	.263	19	19	17	0	0	159²	224	9	67	66	16.5	5.81	53	.315	.375	5	.082	-5	-49	-48	-1	-4.6
Total	2	19	45	.297	64	64	62	1	0	549	765	18	205	138	16.4	5.15	77	.325	.386	27	.124	-18	-74	-71	-4	-7.7

● WOODY CROWSON　　Crowson, Thomas Woodrow　b: 9/9/18, Fuquay Sprgs., N.C　d: 8/14/47, Mayodan, N.C.　BR/TR, 6'2", 185 lbs.　Deb: 4/17/45

YEAR	TM/L	W	L	PCT	G	GS	CG	SH	SV	IP	H	HR	BB	SO	RAT	ERA	ERA+	OAV	OOB	BH	AVG	PB	PR	/A	PD	TPI
1945	Phi-A	0	0	—	1	0	0	0	0	3	2	0	3	2	15.0	6.00	57	.200	.385	0	.000	-0	-1	-1	0	0.0

● CAL CRUM　　Crum, Calvin N.　b: 7/27/1890, Cooks Mills, Ill.　d: 12/7/45, Tulsa, Okla.　BR/TR, 6'1", 175 lbs.　Deb: 4/17/17

1917	Bos-N	0	0	—	1	0	0	0	0	1	1	0	1	0	18.0	—		.250	.400	0	—	0	0	0	0	0.0
1918	Bos-N	0	1	.000	1	1	0	0	0	2¹	6	0	3	0	38.6	15.43	17	.600	.714	0	.000	-0	-3	-3	0	-0.9
Total	2	0	1	.000	2	1	0	0	0	3¹	7	0	4	0	32.4	10.80	24	.500	.632	0	.000	-0	-3	-3	1	-0.9

● ROY CRUMPLER　　Crumpler, Roy Maxton　b: 7/8/1896, Clinton, N.C.　d: 10/6/69, Fayetteville, N.C.　BL/TL, 6'1", 195 lbs.　Deb: 9/16/20

1920	Det-A	1	0	1.000	2	2	1	0	0	13	17	2	11	2	20.1	5.54	67	.315	.439	3	.333	1	-3	-3	-0	-0.1
1925	Phi-N	0	0	—	3	1	0	0	0	4²	8	0	2	1	19.3	7.71	62	.381	.435	0	.000	-0	-2	-2	0	-0.0
Total	2	1	0	1.000	5	3	1	0	0	17²	25	2	13	3	19.9	6.11	65	.333	.438	3	.273	1	-4	-4	-0	-0.1

● DICK CRUTCHER　　Crutcher, Richard Louis　b: 11/25/1889, Frankfort, Ky.　d: 6/19/52, Frankfort, Ky.　BR/TR, 5'9", 148 lbs.　Deb: 4/14/14

1914	Bos-N	5	7	.417	33	15	5	1	0	158²	169	4	66	48	13.7	3.46	80	.293	.371	8	.148	-1	-12	-12	1	-0.9
1915	Bos-N	2	2	.500	14	4	1	0	2	43²	50	1	16	17	14.0	4.33	60	.309	.378	3	.231	1	-8	-8	0	-0.7
Total	2	7	9	.438	47	19	6	1	2	202¹	219	5	82	65	13.7	3.65	75	.296	.373	11	.164	-0	-19	-21	1	-1.6

● TODD CRUZ　　Cruz, Todd Ruben　b: 11/23/55, Highland Park, Mich　BR/TR, 6', 175 lbs.　Deb: 9/4/78　◆

| 1984 | Bal-A | 0 | 0 | — | 1 | 0 | 0 | 0 | 0 | 1 | 0 | 0 | 0 | 0 | 0.0 | 0.00 | | .000 | .000 | 31 | .218 | 0 | 0 | 0 | 0 | 0.0 |

● VICTOR CRUZ　　Cruz, Victor Manuel (b: Victor Manuel De La Cruz (Gil))　b: 12/24/57, Rancho Viejo La Vega, D.R.　BR/TR, 5'9", 200 lbs.　Deb: 6/24/78

1978	Tor-A	7	3	.700	32	0	0	0	9	47¹	28	0	35	51	12.2	1.71	229	.179	.333	0	—	-0	11	12	-0	2.8
1979	Cle-A	3	9	.250	61	0	0	0	10	78²	70	10	44	63	13.2	4.23	100	.244	.346	0	—	-0	-0	6	-2	-0.2
1980	Cle-A	6	7	.462	55	0	0	0	12	86	71	10	27	88	10.6	3.45	118	.229	.297	0	—	-0	6	6	-1	0.8
1981	Pit-N	1	1	.500	22	0	0	0	1	34	33	6	15	28	13.0	2.65	136	.264	.348	0	.000	-0	3	4	0	0.2
1983	Tex-A	1	3	.250	17	0	0	0	5	25	16	2	10	18	9.7	1.44	278	.184	.276	0	—	-0	7	7	-0	1.4
Total	5	18	23	.439	187	0	0	0	37	271	218	28	131	248	11.8	3.09	131	.226	.323	0	.000	-0	27	28	-4	5.0

● COOKIE CUCCURULLO　　Cuccurullo, Arthur Joseph　b: 2/8/18, Asbury Park, N.J.　d: 1/23/83, W.Orange, N.J.　BL/TL, 5'10", 168 lbs.　Deb: 10/3/43

1943	Pit-N	1	1	.000	1	1	0	0	0	7	10	3	3	3	16.7	6.43	54	.357	.419	0	—	1	-2	-2	0	-0.2
1944	Pit-N	2	1	.667	32	4	0	0	4	106¹	110	5	44	31	13.3	4.06	91	.270	.346	14	.368	5	-5	-4	1	0.4
1945	Pit-N	1	3	.250	29	4	0	0	5	56²	68	2	34	17	16.6	5.24	75	.305	.399	3	.214	-0	-9	-8	0	-0.6
Total	3	3	5	.375	62	9	0	0	5	170	188	7	81	51	14.5	4.55	83	.286	.367	17	.327	5	-17	-15	1	-0.3

● JIM CUDWORTH　　Cudworth, James Alaric "Cuddy"　b: 8/22/1858, Fairhaven, Mass.　d: 12/21/43, Middleboro, Mass.　BR/TR, 6', 165 lbs.　Deb: 7/27/1884　◆

| 1884 | KC-U | 0 | 0 | — | 2 | 1 | 1 | 0 | 0 | 17 | 19 | 1 | 3 | 6 | 11.6 | 4.24 | 53 | .264 | .293 | 17 | .147 | -0 | -3 | -4 | -1 | -0.1 |

● CHARLIE CUELLAR　　Cuellar, Jesus Patracis　b: 9/24/17, Ybor City, Fla.　d: 10/11/94, Tampa, Fla.　BR/TR, 5'11", 183 lbs.　Deb: 7/2/50

| 1950 | Chi-A | 0 | 0 | — | 2 | 0 | 0 | 0 | 0 | 1¹ | 6 | 0 | 3 | 1 | 60.8 | 33.75 | 13 | .600 | .692 | 0 | — | 0 | -4 | -4 | 0 | 0.0 |

● MIKE CUELLAR　　Cuellar, Miguel Angel (Santana)　b: 5/8/37, Las Villas, Cuba　BL/TL, 5'11", 175 lbs.　Deb: 4/18/59

1959	Cin-N	0	0		2	0	0	0	0	4	7	1	4	5	24.8	15.75	26	.368	.478	0	.000	-0	-5	-5	-0	-0.9
1964	StL-N	5	5	.500	32	7	1	0	4	72	80	8	33	56	14.3	4.50	85	.288	.365	0	.000	-2	-8	-6	1	-0.9
1965	Hou-N	1	4	.200	25	4	0	0	2	56	55	3	21	46	12.4	3.54	95	.262	.332	0	.000	-1	0	-1	-0	-0.2
1966	Hou-N	12	10	.545	38	28	11	1	2	227¹	193	10	52	175	9.7	2.22	154	.229	.274	8	.113	-0	35	30	0	2.9
1967	Hou-N★	16	11	.593	36	32	16	3	1	246¹	233	16	63	203	10.9	3.03	109	.248	.296	13	.140	1	9	8	-0	0.9
1968	Hou-N	8	11	.421	28	24	11	2	1	170²	152	8	45	133	10.4	2.74	108	.237	.289	11	.193	2	5	4	-0	0.7
1969	*Bal-A	23	11	.676	39	39	18	5	0	290²	213	19	79	182	9.1	2.38	149	.204	**.261**	12	.117	-3	**40**	**38**	-0	4.1
1970	*Bal-A☆	**24**	**8**	**.750**	40	40	**21**	4	0	297²	273	34	69	190	10.4	3.48	105	.242	.286	10	.089	-8	8	6	-3	-0.2
1971	*Bal-A★	20	9	.690	38	38	21	4	0	292¹	250	30	78	124	10.1	3.08	109	.234	.287	11	.103	-4	12	9	1	0.5
1972	Bal-A	18	12	.600	35	35	17	4	0	248¹	197	21	71	132	9.7	2.57	119	.220	.277	11	.126	-1	13	14	0	1.6
1973	Bal-A	18	13	.581	38	38	17	2	0	267	265	29	84	140	11.8	3.27	114	.258	.314	0	—	-0	16	14	0	1.6
1974	*Bal-A☆	22	10	**.688**	38	38	20	5	0	269¹	253	17	86	106	11.4	3.11	111	.252	.312	0	—	-0	15	10	-3	0.9
1975	Bal-A	14	12	.538	36	36	17	5	0	256	229	17	84	105	11.0	3.66	96	.244	.313	0	—	-0	3	-4	-2	-2.7
1976	Bal-A	4	13	.235	26	19	2	1	1	107	129	8	50	32	15.2	4.96	74	.307	.383	0	—	-0	-17	-20	-0	-2.7
1977	Cal-A	0	1	.000	2	1	0	0	0	3¹	7	2	3	2	32.4	18.90	21	.500	.571	0	—	-0	-5	-6	-0	-1.0
Total	15	185	130	.587	453	379	172	36	11	2808	2538	222	822	1632	10.8	3.14	109	.243	.299	76	.115	-13	122	92	-2	8.1

● BOBBY CUELLAR　　Cuellar, Robert　b: 8/20/52, Alice, Tex.　BR/TR, 5'11", 188 lbs.　Deb: 9/9/77

| 1977 | Tex-A | 0 | 0 | — | 4 | 0 | 0 | 0 | 0 | 6² | 4 | 1 | 2 | 3 | 8.1 | 1.35 | 302 | .182 | .250 | 0 | — | -0 | 2 | 2 | -0 | -0.1 |

● BERT CUETO　　Cueto, Dagoberto (Concepcion)　b: 8/14/37, San Luis, Cuba　BR/TR, 6'4", 170 lbs.　Deb: 6/18/61

| 1961 | Min-A | 1 | 3 | .250 | 7 | 5 | 0 | 0 | 0 | 21¹ | 27 | 1 | 10 | 5 | 16.0 | 7.17 | 59 | .300 | .376 | 0 | .000 | -0 | -7 | -7 | 0 | -1.1 |

● JACK CULLEN　　Cullen, John Patrick　b: 10/6/39, Newark, N.J.　BR/TR, 5'11", 170 lbs.　Deb: 9/9/62

1962	NY-A	0	0	—	2	0	0	0	1	3	2	0	2	2	12.0	0.00	—	.182	.308	0	—	0	1	1	-0	0.1
1965	NY-A	3	4	.429	12	9	2	1	0	59	59	2	21	25	12.2	3.05	112	.262	.325	3	.150	-0	3	2	1	0.3
1966	NY-A	1	0	1.000	5	0	0	0	0	11¹	11	0	5	7	12.7	3.97	84	.256	.333	0	.000	-0	-1	-1	-0	-0.1
Total	3	4	4	.500	19	9	2	1	1	73¹	72	2	28	34	12.3	3.07	111	.258	.326	3	.130	-1	3	3	0	0.3

● NICK CULLOP　　Cullop, Henry Nicholas "Tomato Face" (b: Heinrich Nicholas Kolop)　b: 10/16/1900, St.Louis, Mo.　d: 12/8/78, Westerville, Ohio　BR/TR, 6', 200 lbs.　Deb: 4/14/26　◆

| 1927 | Cle-A | 0 | 0 | — | 1 | 0 | 0 | 0 | 0 | 1 | 3 | 0 | 0 | 0 | 27.0 | 9.00 | 47 | .600 | .600 | 16 | .235 | 0 | -1 | -1 | 0 | 0.0 |

● NICK CULLOP　　Cullop, Norman Andrew　b: 9/17/1887, Chilhowie, Va.　d: 4/15/61, Tazewell, Va.　BL/TL, 5'11.5", 172 lbs.　Deb: 5/20/13

1913	Cle-A	3	7	.300	23	8	4	0	0	97¹	105	3	35	30	13.2	4.42	69	.291	.358	4	.129	-1	-16	-15	1	-1.5
1914	Cle-A	0	1	.000	1	0	0	0	0	3¹	4	0	1	2	13.5	2.70	107	.364	.417	0	.000	-0	0	0	0	0.0
	KC-F	14	19	.424	44	36	22	4	1	295²	256	6	87	149	10.8	2.34	119	.235	.299	14	.141	-5	18	14	1	1.1
1915	KC-F	22	11	.667	44	36	22	3	2	302¹	278	6	77	111	10.5	2.44	108	.249	.297	18	.188	-1	10	6	6	1.2
1916	NY-A	13	6	.684	28	22	9	1	0	167	151	4	32	77	10.0	2.05	141	.243	.284	6	.109	-3	14	16	-5	1.0
1917	NY-A	5	9	.357	30	18	5	2	1	146¹	161	2	31	27	11.9	3.32	81	.307	.348	7	.159	-1	-11	-10	-1	-1.1
1921	StL-A	0	2	.000	4	1	0	0	1	11²	18	1	6	3	18.5	8.49	53	.340	.407	0	.000	-0	-5	-5	0	-0.7
Total	6	57	55	.509	174	121	62	9	5	1024	973	24	259	400	11.1	2.73	102	.258	.310	49	.149	-12	10	6	3	0.0

● BUD CULLOTON　　Culloton, Bernard Aloysius　b: 5/19/1897, Kingston, N.Y.　d: 11/9/76, Kingston, N.Y.　BR/TR, 5'11", 180 lbs.　Deb: 4/16/25

1925	Pit-N	0	1	.000	9	0	0	0	1	21	19	1	3	8	8.6	2.57	173	.241	.250	0	.000	-0	4	4	0	0.1
1926	Pit-N	0	0	—	4	0	0	0	0	3²	3	0	6	1	22.1	7.36	53	.214	.450	0	—	-0	-1	-1	0	0.0
Total	2	0	1	.000	13	0	0	0	1	24²	22	1	7	4	10.6	3.28	133	.237	.290	0	.000	-0	3	3	0	0.1

● RAY CULP　　Culp, Raymond Leonard　b: 8/6/41, Elgin, Tex.　BR/TR, 6', 200 lbs.　Deb: 4/10/63

1963	Phi-N★	14	11	.560	34	30	10	6	1	203¹	148	15	102	176	11.3	2.97	109	.206	.309	9	.136	-0	7	6	-0	0.7
1964	Phi-N	8	7	.533	30	19	3	1	0	135	139	15	56	96	13.3	4.13	84	.263	.340	5	.114	-1	-9	-10	-1	-1.2
1965	Phi-N	14	10	.583	33	30	11	2	0	204¹	188	19	78	134	12.2	3.22	108	.243	.322	6	.088	-2	7	6	-1	0.3
1966	Phi-N	7	4	.636	34	12	1	0	1	110²	106	19	53	100	13.5	5.04	71	.246	.338	2	.077	-2	-18	-18	-1	-1.9
1967	Chi-N	8	11	.421	30	22	4	0	0	152²	128	22	59	111	11.7	3.89	91	.239	.311	5	.098	-1	-9	-6	-1	-0.9
1968	Bos-A	16	6	.727	35	30	11	6	0	216¹	166	18	82	190	10.7	2.91	108	.210	.292	8	.114	-1	2	6	-0	0.4
1969	Bos-A★	17	8	.680	32	32	9	2	0	227	195	25	79	172	11.1	3.81	100	.231	.302	12	.152	-5	-1	0	0	0.0

YEAR	TM/L	W	L	PCT	G	GS	CG	SH	SV	IP	H	HR	BB	SO	RAT	ERA	ERA+	OAV	OOB	BH	AVG	PB	PR	/A	PD	TPI
1970	Bos-A	17	14	.548	33	33	15	1	0	251¹	211	22	91	197	11.2	3.04	130	.224	.300	12	.124	-3	19	26	-1	2.6
1971	Bos-A	14	16	.467	35	35	12	3	0	242²	236	21	67	151	11.4	3.60	103	.253	.307	8	.118	-2	-4	2	-2	-0.1
1972	Bos-A	5	8	.385	16	16	4	1	0	105	104	8	53	52	13.7	4.46	72	.260	.351	7	.212	1	-16	-15	0	-1.7
1973	Bos-A	2	6	.250	10	9	0	0	0	50¹	46	9	32	32	14.7	4.47	90	.247	.369	0	—	0	-4	-3	-0	-0.4
Total 11		122	101	.547	322	268	80	22	1	1898¹	1677	188	752	1411	11.8	3.58	99	.235	.314	74	.123	-11	-29	-5	-8	-2.2

● **BILL CULP** Culp, William Edward b: 6/11/1887, Bellaire, Ohio d: 9/3/69, Arnold, Pa. BB/TR, 6'1.5", 165 lbs. Deb: 9/8/10

YEAR	TM/L	W	L	PCT	G	GS	CG	SH	SV	IP	H	HR	BB	SO	RAT	ERA	ERA+	OAV	OOB	BH	AVG	PB	PR	/A	PD	TPI
1910	Phi-N	0	0	—	4	0	0	0	1	6²	8	0	4	4	16.2	8.10	39	.333	.429	0	.000	-0	-4	-4	1	-0.1

● **GEORGE CULVER** Culver, George Raymond b: 7/8/43, Salinas, Cal. BR/TR, 6'2", 185 lbs. Deb: 9/7/66

YEAR	TM/L	W	L	PCT	G	GS	CG	SH	SV	IP	H	HR	BB	SO	RAT	ERA	ERA+	OAV	OOB	BH	AVG	PB	PR	/A	PD	TPI
1966	Cle-A	0	2	.000	5	1	0	0	0	9²	15	1	7	6	21.4	8.38	41	.357	.460	0	.000	-0	-5	-5	0	-0.9
1967	Cle-A	7	3	.700	53	1	0	0	3	75	71	2	31	41	13.0	3.96	82	.258	.346	1	.250	-0	-6	-6	1	-0.7
1968	Cin-N	11	16	.407	42	35	5	2	2	226²	229	8	84	114	13.0	3.22	98	.264	.339	8	.121	-1	-6	-2	2	-0.1
1969	Cin-N	5	7	.417	32	13	0	0	4	101¹	117	8	52	58	15.8	4.26	88	.291	.384	3	.097	-2	-8	-6	2	-0.7
1970	StL-N	3	3	.500	11	7	2	0	0	56²	64	6	24	23	14.1	4.61	89	.284	.356	3	.176	-0	-4	-3	2	-0.1
	Hou-N	3	3	.500	32	0	0	0	3	45	44	1	21	31	13.6	3.20	121	.254	.345	1	.250	-0	4	3	-1	0.4
	Yr	6	6	.500	43	7	2	0	3	101²	108	7	45	54	13.8	3.98	101	.270	.348	4	.190	0	1	0	1	0.3
1971	Hou-N	5	8	.385	59	0	0	0	7	95¹	89	4	38	57	12.2	2.64	127	.257	.334	1	.091	-1	9	8	1	1.2
1972	Hou-N	6	2	.750	45	0	0	0	0	97¹	73	7	43	82	11.2	3.05	110	.212	.309	3	.158	-0	4	3	-0	0.3
1973	LA-N	4	4	.500	28	0	0	0	2	42	45	4	21	23	14.4	3.00	115	.292	.381	0	.000	-0	3	2	1	0.5
	Phi-N	3	1	.750	14	0	0	0	0	18²	26	0	15	7	19.8	4.82	79	.342	.451	0	—	-0	-2	-2	0	-0.4
	Yr	7	5	.583	42	0	0	0	2	60²	71	4	36	30	15.9	3.56	100	.305	.398	0	—	0	1	-0	2	0.1
1974	Phi-N	1	0	1.000	14	0	0	0	0	21²	20	1	16	9	15.4	6.65	57	.267	.402	0	.000	-0	-7	-7	-0	-0.4
Total 9		48	49	.495	335	57	7	2	23	789	793	42	352	451	13.6	3.62	96	.266	.352	20	.124	-4	-18	-13	8	-0.9

● **JOHN CUMBERLAND** Cumberland, John Sheldon b: 5/10/47, Westbrook, Me. BR/TL, 6', 190 lbs. Deb: 9/27/68 C

YEAR	TM/L	W	L	PCT	G	GS	CG	SH	SV	IP	H	HR	BB	SO	RAT	ERA	ERA+	OAV	OOB	BH	AVG	PB	PR	/A	PD	TPI
1968	NY-A	0	0	—	1	0	0	0	0	2	3	1	1	1	18.0	9.00	32	.333	.400	0	—	0	-1	-1	0	0.0
1969	NY-A	0	0	—	2	0	0	0	0	4	3	0	4	0	15.8	4.50	77	.231	.412	0	—	0	-0	-0	0	0.0
1970	NY-A	3	4	.429	15	8	1	0	0	64	62	9	15	38	10.8	3.94	89	.252	.295	1	.059	-1	-2	-3	-1	-0.5
	SF-N	2	0	1.000	7	0	0	0	0	11	6	0	4	6	8.2	0.82	486	.158	.238	0	—	0	4	4	0	0.6
1971	*SF-N	9	6	.600	45	21	5	2	2	185	153	22	55	65	10.1	2.92	116	.223	.281	7	.119	-2	11	10	-3	0.7
1972	SF-N	0	4	.000	9	6	0	0	0	25	38	6	7	8	16.2	8.64	40	.336	.375	1	.111	-0	-14	-14	-1	-2.1
	StL-N	1	1	.500	14	1	0	0	0	21²	23	6	7	7	12.5	6.65	51	.291	.349	0	.000	-1	-8	-8	-1	-0.8
	Yr	1	5	.167	23	7	0	0	0	46²	61	12	14	15	14.5	7.71	45	.316	.362	1	.071	-1	-22	-22	-2	-2.9
1974	Cal-A	0	1	.000	17	0	0	0	0	21²	24	2	10	12	14.1	3.74	92	.289	.366	0	—	0	-0	-1	-0	-0.1
Total 6		15	16	.484	110	36	6	2	2	334¹	312	46	103	127	11.8	3.82	90	.246	.303	9	.099	-5	-11	-14	-6	-2.7

● **JOHN CUMMINGS** Cummings, John Russell b: 5/10/69, Torrance, Cal. BL/TL, 6'3", 200 lbs. Deb: 4/10/93

YEAR	TM/L	W	L	PCT	G	GS	CG	SH	SV	IP	H	HR	BB	SO	RAT	ERA	ERA+	OAV	OOB	BH	AVG	PB	PR	/A	PD	TPI
1993	Sea-A	0	6	.000	10	8	1	0	0	46¹	59	6	16	19	15.0	6.02	73	.316	.376	0	—	0	-9	-8	0	-0.9
1994	Sea-A	2	4	.333	17	8	0	0	0	64	66	7	37	33	14.5	5.63	87	.270	.367	0	—	0	-6	-5	-1	-0.5
1995	Sea-A	0	0	—	4	0	0	0	0	5¹	7	4	7	4	25.3	11.81	40	.400	.556	0	—	0	-4	-4	0	0.0
	*LA-N	3	1	.750	35	0	0	0	0	39	38	3	10	21	11.1	3.00	126	.250	.296	0	.000	-0	5	3	0	0.2
1996	LA-N	0	1	.000	4	0	0	0	0	5¹	12	1	2	5	23.6	6.75	57	.462	.500	0	—	0	-2	-2	0	-0.3
	Det-A	3	3	.500	21	0	0	0	0	31²	36	3	20	24	16.5	5.12	99	.283	.389	0	—	0	-0	-0	-0	0.0
Total 4		8	15	.348	91	16	1	0	0	191²	219	20	92	106	14.8	5.31	85	.290	.370	0	.000	-0	-16	-16	-1	-1.5

● **STEVE CUMMINGS** Cummings, Steven Brent b: 7/15/64, Houston, Tex. BB/TR, 6'2", 200 lbs. Deb: 6/24/89

YEAR	TM/L	W	L	PCT	G	GS	CG	SH	SV	IP	H	HR	BB	SO	RAT	ERA	ERA+	OAV	OOB	BH	AVG	PB	PR	/A	PD	TPI
1989	Tor-A	2	0	1.000	5	2	0	0	0	21	18	1	11	8	12.9	3.00	126	.231	.333	0	—	0	2	2	-0	0.1
1990	Tor-A	0	0	—	6	2	0	0	0	12¹	22	4	5	4	20.4	5.11	77	.431	.491	0	—	0	-2	-2	-0	-0.1
Total 2		2	0	1.000	11	4	0	0	0	33¹	40	5	16	12	15.7	3.78	101	.310	.395	0	—	0	-0	-0	-0	0.0

● **CANDY CUMMINGS** Cummings, William Arthur b: 10/18/1848, Ware, Mass. d: 5/16/24, Toledo, Ohio BR/TR, 5'9", 120 lbs. Deb: 4/22/1872 H

YEAR	TM/L	W	L	PCT	G	GS	CG	SH	SV	IP	H	HR	BB	SO	RAT	ERA	ERA+	OAV	OOB	BH	AVG	PB	PR	/A	PD	TPI
1872	Mut-n	33	20	.623	55	55	53	3	0	497	605	2	30	43	11.5	2.97	113	.273	.283	52	.208	-4	37	22		3.1
1873	Bal-n	28	14	.667	42	42	42	1	0	382	475	4	33	34	12.0	2.66	122	.274	.287	48	.250	2	25	25		1.7
1874	Phi-n	28	26	.519	54	54	52	3	0	483	616	4	18	61	11.8	1.96	113	.276	.282	52	.225	-4	12	14		0.4
1875	Har-n	35	12	.745	48	47	46	7	0	416	397	0	4	82	8.7	1.60	146	.235	.236	44	.199	-5	29	34		2.8
1876	Har-N	16	8	.667	24	24	24	5	0	216	215	0	14	26	9.5	1.67	142	.239	.251	17	.162	-8	15	17	-2	0.6
1877	Cin-N	5	14	.263	19	19	16	0	0	155²	219	2	13	11	13.4	4.34	61	.315	.327	14	.200	-0	-26	-29	0	-2.6
Total 4 n		124	72	.633	199	198	193	14	0	1778	2093	10	85	220	11.0	2.31	126	.266	.274	196	.219	-10	103	100		8.0
Total 2		21	22	.488	43	43	40	5	0	371²	434	2	27	37	11.2	2.78	90	.272	.284	31	.177	-7	-11	-12	-2	-2.0

● **BRUCE CUNNINGHAM** Cunningham, Bruce Lee b: 9/29/05, San Francisco, Cal. d: 3/8/84, Hayward, Cal. BR/TR, 5'10.5", 165 lbs. Deb: 5/7/29

YEAR	TM/L	W	L	PCT	G	GS	CG	SH	SV	IP	H	HR	BB	SO	RAT	ERA	ERA+	OAV	OOB	BH	AVG	PB	PR	/A	PD	TPI
1929	Bos-N	4	6	.400	17	8	4	0	1	91²	100	7	32	22	13.2	4.52	104	.282	.344	4	.148	-0	2	2	1	0.2
1930	Bos-N	5	6	.455	36	6	2	0	0	106²	121	7	41	28	13.7	5.48	90	.289	.352	6	.194	-0	-6	-6	3	-0.2
1931	Bos-N	3	12	.200	33	16	6	1	1	136²	157	7	54	32	14.0	4.48	85	.296	.363	3	.071	-4	-9	-10	4	-1.0
1932	Bos-N	1	0	1.000	18	3	0	0	0	47	50	1	19	21	14.0	3.45	109	.281	.363	2	.222	4	2	2	1	0.3
Total 4		13	24	.351	104	33	12	1	2	382	428	22	146	103	13.7	4.64	93	.289	.356	15	.138	-2	-11	-14	9	-0.7

● **BERT CUNNINGHAM** Cunningham, Ellsworth Elmer b: 11/25/1865, Wilmington, Del. d: 5/14/52, Cragmere, Del. BR/TR, 187 lbs. Deb: 9/15/1887 U

YEAR	TM/L	W	L	PCT	G	GS	CG	SH	SV	IP	H	HR	BB	SO	RAT	ERA	ERA+	OAV	OOB	BH	AVG	PB	PR	/A	PD	TPI
1887	Bro-a	0	2	.000	3	3	3	0	0	23	26	0	13	8	16.8	5.09	85	.263	.371	0	—	0	-2	-2	-0	-0.2
1888	Bal-a	22	29	.431	51	51	50	0	0	453¹	412	8	157	186	11.9	3.39	88	.233	.307	33	.186	-2	-17	-21	0	-2.1
1889	Bal-a	16	19	.457	39	33	29	0	1	279¹	306	11	141	140	14.9	4.87	81	.270	.358	27	.206	-3	-32	-29	-0	-2.9
1890	Phi-P	3	9	.250	14	11	11	0	0	108²	133	0	67	33	17.1	5.22	82	.289	.387	6	.115	-4	-12	-11	-1	-1.1
	Buf-P	9	15	.375	25	25	24	2	0	211	251	8	134	78	16.7	5.84	70	.283	.381	23	.228	1	-38	-41	-1	-3.1
	Yr	12	24	.333	39	36	35	2	0	319²	384	8	201	111	16.6	5.63	74	.285	.383	29	.190	-4	-50	-52	0	-4.2
1891	Bal-a	11	14	.440	30	25	21	0	0	237²	241	18	118	59	14.8	4.01	93	.254	.356	15	.150	-2	-8	-7	2	-0.6
1895	Lou-N	11	16	.407	31	28	24	1	0	231	299	6	104	49	15.9	4.75	97	.309	.378	30	.300	6	1	-3	2	0.4
1896	Lou-N	7	14	.333	27	20	17	0	1	189¹	242	6	74	37	15.8	5.09	85	.300	.380	22	.250	3	-16	-16	2	-0.9
1897	Lou-N	14	13	.519	29	27	25	0	0	234²	286	2	72	49	14.2	4.14	103	.298	.355	22	.237	-0	-1	-5	-1	-0.2
1898	Lou-N	28	15	.651	44	42	41	0	0	362	387	8	65	34	11.7	3.16	113	.272	.313	32	.229	2	18	17	-1	1.8
1899	Lou-N	17	17	.500	39	37	33	1	0	323²	385	4	75	36	13.2	3.84	101	.295	.360	40	.266	3	1	1	6	0.8
1900	Chi-N	4	3	.571	8	7	7	0	0	64	84	0	21	19	15.3	4.36	83	.316	.375	4	.148	-1	-5	-5	-0	-0.6
1901	Chi-N	0	1	.000	1	1	1	0	0	9	11	0	3	2	14.0	5.00	85	.297	.350	0	.000	-0	-2	-2	1	-0.1
Total 12		142	167	.460	341	310	286	4	2	2726²	3063	61	1064	718	14.1	4.22	91	.277	.349	254	.217	-1	-105	-117	12	-8.1

● **GEORGE CUNNINGHAM** Cunningham, George Harold b: 7/13/1894, Sturgeon Lake, Minn. d: 3/10/72, Chattanooga, Tenn. BR/TR, 5'11", 185 lbs. Deb: 4/14/16 ♦

YEAR	TM/L	W	L	PCT	G	GS	CG	SH	SV	IP	H	HR	BB	SO	RAT	ERA	ERA+	OAV	OOB	BH	AVG	PB	PR	/A	PD	TPI
1916	Det-A	7	10	.412	35	14	5	0	2	150¹	146	0	74	68	13.4	2.75	104	.269	.360	11	.268	5	1	2	1	0.9
1917	Det-A	2	7	.222	44	8	4	0	4	139	113	2	51	49	10.9	2.91	91	.227	.304	6	.176	1	-4	-0	0	-0.2
1918	Det-A	6	7	.462	27	14	10	0	1	140	131	0	38	39	11.2	3.15	84	.255	.312	25	.223	8	-6	-8	0	-0.3
1919	Det-A	1	1	.500	17	0	0	0	0	47²	54	0	15	11	14.0	4.91	65	.292	.361	5	.217	2	-9	-9	0	-0.1
Total 4		16	25	.390	123	36	19	0	8	477	444	2	178	167	12.1	3.13	89	.255	.330	47	.224	11	-17	-19	2	0.3

● **MIKE CUNNINGHAM** Cunningham, Mody b: 6/14/1882, Lancaster, S.C. d: 12/10/69, Lancaster, S.C. BR/TR, 5'10.5", 175 lbs. Deb: 8/31/06

YEAR	TM/L	W	L	PCT	G	GS	CG	SH	SV	IP	H	HR	BB	SO	RAT	ERA	ERA+	OAV	OOB	BH	AVG	PB	PR	/A	PD	TPI
1906	Phi-N	1	0	1.000	5	1	1	0	0	28	29	0	9	15	12.5	3.21	85	.271	.333	4	.333	1	-2	-2	-0	0.0

● **NIG CUPPY** Cuppy, George Joseph (b: George Koppe) b: 7/3/1869, Logansport, Ind. d: 7/27/22, Elkhart, Ind. BR/TR, 5'7", 160 lbs. Deb: 4/16/1892

YEAR	TM/L	W	L	PCT	G	GS	CG	SH	SV	IP	H	HR	BB	SO	RAT	ERA	ERA+	OAV	OOB	BH	AVG	PB	PR	/A	PD	TPI
1892	*Cle-N	28	13	.683	47	42	38	1	0	376	333	9	121	103	11.1	2.51	135	.228	.291	36	.214	0	32	37	3	3.8
1893	Cle-N	17	10	.630	31	30	24	0	0	243²	316	9	75	39	14.8	4.47	109	.305	.357	22	.248	1	5	11	-1	0.8
1894	Cle-N	24	15	.615	43	43	39	3	0	316	381	11	128	61	14.8	4.56	120	.295	.363	35	.259	1	27	32	1	2.9
1895	*Cle-N	26	14	.650	47	40	36	1	1	353	384	9	95	91	12.4	3.54	141	.273	.323	40	.286	7	49	57	4	5.8
1896	*Cle-N	25	14	.641	46	40	35	1	1	358	388	8	75	86	11.8	3.12	146	.274	.314	38	.270	6	50	56	4	5.8

YEAR	TM/L	W	L	PCT	G	GS	CG	SH	SV	IP	H	HR	BB	SO	RAT	ERA	ERA+	OAV	OOB	BH	AVG	PB	PR	/A	PD	TPI
1897	Cle-N	10	6	.625	19	17	13	1	0	138	150	3	26	23	11.8	3.20	141	.275	.314	8	.145	-4	17	20	-1	1.5
1898	Cle-N	9	8	.529	18	15	13	1	0	128	147	4	25	27	12.5	3.30	110	.286	.327	5	.104	-4	4	4	-2	0.0
1899	StL-N	11	8	.579	21	21	18	1	0	171²	203	3	26	23	12.3	3.15	127	.294	.324	13	.186	-3	14	16	0	1.3
1900	Bos-N	8	4	.667	17	13	9	0	1	105¹	107	8	24	23	11.7	3.08	134	.263	.314	11	.262	1	7	12	-1	1.2
1901	Bos-A	4	6	.400	9	9	7	0	0	93¹	111	1	19	22	12.2	4.15	85	.292	.321	10	.204	0	-5	-6	-2	-0.7
Total	10	162	98	.623	302	262	224	9	5	2283	2520	62	609	504	12.6	3.48	127	.275	.325	223	.233	6	200	239	6	22.4

● SAMMY CURRAN
Curran, Simon Francis   b: 10/30/1874, Dorchester, Mass.   d: 5/19/36, Dorchester, Mass.   TL ,   Deb: 8/1/02

YEAR	TM/L	W	L	PCT	G	GS	CG	SH	SV	IP	H	HR	BB	SO	RAT	ERA	ERA+	OAV	OOB	BH	AVG	PB	PR	/A	PD	TPI
1902	Bos-N	0	0	—	1	0	0	0	0	6²	6	0	3		8.1	1.35	209	.240	.240	0	.000	-0	1	1	-0	-0.1

● LAFAYETTE CURRENCE
Currence, Delancy Lafayette   b: 12/3/51, Rock Hill, S.C.   BB/TL, 5'11", 175 lbs.   Deb: 7/24/75

| 1975 | Mil-A | 0 | 2 | .000 | 8 | 1 | 0 | 0 | 0 | 18² | 25 | 5 | 14 | 7 | 18.8 | 7.71 | 50 | .316 | .419 | 0 | — | 0 | -8 | -8 | -1 | -0.8 |

● MURPHY CURRIE
Currie, Archibald Murphy   b: 8/31/1893, Fayetteville, N.C.   d: 6/22/39, Asheboro, N.C.   BR/TR, 5'11.5", 185 lbs.   Deb: 8/31/16

| 1916 | StL-N | 0 | 0 | — | 6 | 0 | 0 | 0 | 0 | 14¹ | 7 | 1 | 9 | 8 | 10.0 | 1.88 | 140 | .149 | .286 | 0 | .000 | -0 | 1 | 1 | -1 | -0.1 |

● CLARENCE CURRIE
Currie, Clarence Franklin   b: 12/30/1878, Glencoe, Ont., Can.   d: 7/15/41, Little Chute, Wis   BR/TR,   Deb: 4/25/02

YEAR	TM/L	W	L	PCT	G	GS	CG	SH	SV	IP	H	HR	BB	SO	RAT	ERA	ERA+	OAV	OOB	BH	AVG	PB	PR	/A	PD	TPI
1902	Cin-N	3	4	.429	10	7	6	1	0	65¹	70	1	17	20	12.3	3.72	81	.273	.324	2	.083	-2	-7	-5	1	-0.7
	StL-N	7	5	.583	15	12	10	2	0	124²	125	0	35	30	12.0	2.60	105	.261	.319	9	.196	-0	3	2	2	0.4
	Yr	10	9	.526	25	19	16	3	0	190	195	1	52	50	12.0	2.98	95	.265	.318	11	.157	-2	-4	-3	3	-0.3
1903	StL-N	4	12	.250	22	16	13	1	1	148	155	7	60	52	13.7	4.01	81	.281	.342	4	.085	-3	-12	-12	4	-1.1
	Chi-N	1	2	.333	6	3	2	0	1	33¹	35	1	9	9	12.7	2.97	106	.254	.313	5	.417	1	1	1	0	0.3
	Yr	5	14	.263	28	19	15	1	2	181¹	190	8	69	61	13.0	3.82	85	.271	.339	9	.153	-1	-11	-12	5	-0.8
Total	2	15	23	.395	53	38	31	4	2	371¹	385	9	121	111	12.8	3.39	89	.270	.336	20	.155	-4	-15	-15	8	-1.1

● BILL CURRIE
Currie, William Cleveland   b: 11/29/28, Leary, Ga.   BR/TR, 6', 175 lbs.   Deb: 4/13/55

| 1955 | Was-A | 0 | 0 | — | 3 | 0 | 0 | 0 | 0 | 4¹ | 7 | 3 | 2 | 2 | 20.8 | 12.46 | 31 | .350 | .435 | 0 | — | -0 | -4 | -4 | 0 | -0.3 |

● GEORGE CURRY
Curry, George James "Soldier Boy"   b: 12/21/1888, Bridgeport, Conn.   d: 10/5/63, West Haven, Conn.   BR/TR, 6', 185 lbs.   Deb: 7/16/11

| 1911 | StL-A | 0 | 3 | .000 | 9 | 4 | 1 | 0 | 0 | 15² | 19 | 0 | 24 | 2 | 24.7 | 7.47 | 45 | .339 | .538 | 0 | .000 | -1 | -7 | -7 | -0 | -1.1 |

● STEVE CURRY
Curry, Stephen Thomas   b: 9/13/65, Winter Park, Fla.   BR/TR, 6'6", 217 lbs.   Deb: 7/10/88

| 1988 | Bos-A | 0 | 1 | .000 | 3 | 3 | 0 | 0 | 0 | 11 | 15 | 0 | 14 | 4 | 23.7 | 8.18 | 50 | .357 | .518 | 0 | — | 0 | -5 | -5 | 0 | -0.4 |

● WES CURRY
Curry, Wesley   b: 4/1/1860, Wilmington, Del.   d: 5/19/33, Philadelphia, Pa.   Deb: 8/6/1884   U

| 1884 | Ric-a | 0 | 2 | .000 | 2 | 2 | 2 | 0 | 0 | 16 | 15 | 2 | 3 | 1 | 10.7 | 5.06 | 66 | .221 | .264 | 2 | .250 | -0 | -3 | -3 | -0 | -0.3 |

● CLIFF CURTIS
Curtis, Clifton Garfield   b: 7/3/1883, Delaware, Ohio   d: 4/23/43, Utica, Ohio   BR/TR, 6'2", 180 lbs.   Deb: 8/23/09

YEAR	TM/L	W	L	PCT	G	GS	CG	SH	SV	IP	H	HR	BB	SO	RAT	ERA	ERA+	OAV	OOB	BH	AVG	PB	PR	/A	PD	TPI
1909	Bos-N	4	5	.444	10	9	8	2	0	83	53	1	30	22	9.2	1.41	200	.191	.275	1	.034	-3	11	13	1	1.3
1910	Bos-N	6	24	.200	43	37	12	2	2	251	251	9	124	75	13.9	3.55	94	.277	.371	12	.146	-4	-14	-6	6	-0.6
1911	Bos-N	1	8	.111	12	9	5	0	0	77	79	4	34	23	13.4	4.44	86	.265	.344	7	.250	-0	-9	-5	1	-0.5
	Chi-N	1	2	.333	4	1	0	0	0	7	7	0	5	4	19.3	3.86	86	.241	.405	1	.500	-0	-0	0	0	-0.1
	Phi-N	2	1	.667	8	5	3	1	0	45	45	0	15	13	12.2	2.60	132	.260	.323	4	.267	0	4	4	-0	0.2
	Yr	4	11	.267	24	15	8	1	0	129	131	4	54	40	13.0	3.77	97	.259	.332	12	.267	0	-5	-1	0	-0.4
1912	Phi-N	2	5	.286	10	8	2	0	0	50	55	3	17	20	13.7	3.24	112	.286	.357	0	.000	-1	1	2	1	0.2
	Bro-N	4	7	.364	19	9	3	0	1	80	72	4	37	22	12.9	3.94	85	.250	.347	8	.308	1	-5	-5	-0	-0.5
	Yr	6	12	.333	29	17	5	0	1	130	127	7	54	42	12.9	3.67	94	.262	.344	8	.195	-1	-4	-3	1	-0.3
1913	Bro-N	8	9	.471	30	16	6	0	2	151²	145	1	55	57	12.3	3.26	101	.255	.328	6	.122	-3	-1	3	-1	-0.1
Total	5	28	61	.315	136	94	39	5	5	744²	707	22	317	236	12.8	3.31	101	.259	.344	39	.159	-10	-13	3	9	-0.1

● JACK CURTIS
Curtis, Jack Patrick   b: 1/11/37, Rhodhiss, N.C.   BL/TL, 5'10", 175 lbs.   Deb: 4/22/61

YEAR	TM/L	W	L	PCT	G	GS	CG	SH	SV	IP	H	HR	BB	SO	RAT	ERA	ERA+	OAV	OOB	BH	AVG	PB	PR	/A	PD	TPI
1961	Chi-N	10	13	.435	31	27	6	0	0	180¹	220	23	51	57	13.6	4.89	85	.303	.350	10	.167	3	-17	-14	0	-1.2
1962	Chi-N	0	2	.000	4	3	0	0	0	18	18	2	6	8	12.0	3.50	118	.277	.338	1	.250	0	1	1	-0	0.1
	Mil-N	4	4	.500	30	5	0	0	1	75²	82	8	27	40	13.2	4.16	91	.282	.347	4	.222	2	-2	-3	-1	-0.2
	Yr	4	6	.400	34	8	0	0	1	93²	100	10	33	48	13.0	4.04	96	.280	.344	5	.227	2	-1	-2	-1	-0.1
1963	Cle-A	0	0	—	4	0	0	0	0	5	8	0	5	3	25.2	18.00	20	.348	.483	0	—	0	-8	-8	0	0.0
Total	3	14	19	.424	69	35	6	0	1	279	328	33	89	108	13.6	4.84	84	.297	.352	15	.183	5	-26	-24	-1	-1.3

● JACK CURTIS
Curtis, John Duffield   b: 3/9/48, Newton, Mass.   BL/TL, 6'2", 185 lbs.   Deb: 8/13/70

YEAR	TM/L	W	L	PCT	G	GS	CG	SH	SV	IP	H	HR	BB	SO	RAT	ERA	ERA+	OAV	OOB	BH	AVG	PB	PR	/A	PD	TPI
1970	Bos-A	0	0	—	1	0	0	0	0	2¹	4	1	1	1	19.3	11.57	34	.333	.385	0	—	-0	-2	-2	0	0.0
1971	Bos-A	2	2	.500	5	3	1	0	0	26	30	3	6	19	12.5	3.12	119	.291	.330	1	.111	-0	1	2	-1	0.1
1972	Bos-A	11	8	.579	26	21	8	3	0	154¹	161	8	50	106	12.3	3.73	86	.271	.328	5	.094	-2	-12	-9	-0	-1.4
1973	Bos-A	13	13	.500	35	30	10	4	0	221³	225	24	83	101	12.6	3.58	112	.264	.331	0	—	0	6	11	-1	1.0
1974	StL-N	10	14	.417	33	29	5	2	1	195	199	15	83	89	13.1	3.78	94	.267	.342	10	.159	-0	-4	-5	-0	-0.6
1975	StL-N	8	9	.471	39	18	4	0	1	146²	151	13	65	67	13.4	3.44	109	.268	.346	8	.211	2	3	5	2	0.9
1976	StL-N	6	11	.353	37	15	3	1	1	134	139	11	65	50	13.7	4.50	79	.276	.359	7	.200	2	-15	-14	-0	-1.5
1977	SF-N	3	3	.500	43	9	1	1	1	77	95	5	48	47	16.8	5.49	71	.314	.409	3	.231	1	-14	-14	1	-0.7
1978	SF-N	4	3	.571	46	0	0	0	0	63	60	1	29	38	12.7	3.71	93	.262	.345	0	.000	-0	-1	-2	0	-0.2
1979	SF-N	10	9	.526	27	18	3	2	0	120²	121	15	46	85	12.2	4.18	84	.257	.318	5	.147	1	-6	-9	-1	-1.3
1980	SD-N	10	8	.556	30	27	6	0	0	187	184	9	67	71	12.2	3.51	98	.262	.329	12	.194	1	2	-1	1	0.0
1981	SD-N	2	6	.250	28	8	0	0	0	66²	70	11	30	31	13.6	5.13	63	.275	.353	1	.077	-1	-12	-14	-1	-1.7
1982	SD-N	8	6	.571	26	18	1	1	0	116¹	121	15	46	54	13.0	4.10	83	.262	.341	11	.297	3	-6	-9	-1	-0.8
	Cal-A	0	1	.000	8	0	0	0	0	12	16	0	3	10	14.3	6.00	68	.320	.358	0	—	0	-3	-3	-0	-0.3
1983	Cal-A	1	2	.333	37	3	0	0	5	90	89	5	40	36	13.1	3.80	106	.258	.339	0	—	0	3	2	-1	0.0
1984	Cal-A	1	2	.333	17	0	0	0	0	28²	30	4	11	18	12.9	4.40	90	.263	.328	0	—	-0	-1	-1	0	0.0
Total	15	89	97	.478	438	199	42	14	11	1641	1695	140	669	825	13.0	3.96	91	.270	.341	63	.175	5	-61	-63	-1	-6.6

● VERN CURTIS
Curtis, Vernon Eugene "Turk"   b: 5/24/20, Cairo, Ill.   d: 6/24/92, Cairo, Ill.   BR/TR, 6', 170 lbs.   Deb: 9/6/43

YEAR	TM/L	W	L	PCT	G	GS	CG	SH	SV	IP	H	HR	BB	SO	RAT	ERA	ERA+	OAV	OOB	BH	AVG	PB	PR	/A	PD	TPI
1943	Was-A	0	0	—	4	1	0	0	0	4	3	0	6	1	20.3	6.75	47	.200	.429	0	—	0	-2	-2	-0	0.0
1944	Was-A	0	1	.000	3	1	0	0	0	9²	8	0	3	2	10.2	2.79	117	.235	.297	0	.000	-0	1	0	-0	0.0
1946	Was-A	0	0	—	11	0	0	0	0	16¹	19	1	10	7	16.0	7.16	47	.297	.392	0	.000	-0	-7	-7	0	0.0
Total	3	0	1	.000	16	1	0	0	0	30	30	1	19	10	14.7	5.70	58	.265	.371	0	.000	-1	-7	-8	0	0.0

● ED CUSHMAN
Cushman, Edgar Leander   b: 3/27/1852, Eagleville, Ohio   d: 9/26/15, Erie, Pa.   BR/TL, 6', 177 lbs.   Deb: 7/6/1883

YEAR	TM/L	W	L	PCT	G	GS	CG	SH	SV	IP	H	HR	BB	SO	RAT	ERA	ERA+	OAV	OOB	BH	AVG	PB	PR	/A	PD	TPI
1883	Buf-N	3	3	.500	7	7	5	0	0	50¹	61	4	17	34	13.9	3.93	81	.285	.338	5	.217	-0	-4	-4	-0	-0.4
1884	Mil-U	4	0	1.000	4	4	4	2	0	36	10	0	3	47	3.3	1.00	132	.082	.104	1	.091	-2	6	1	-1	-0.1
1885	Phi-a	3	7	.300	10	10	10	0	0	87	101	1	17	37	12.5	3.52	98	.269	.306	7	.189	-1	-3	-1	-1	-0.3
	NY-a	8	14	.364	22	22	22	0	0	191	158	2	33	133	9.1	2.78	106	.210	.246	10	.145	-1	10	4	-2	0.1
	Yr	11	21	.344	32	32	32	0	0	278	259	3	50	170	10.1	3.01	103	.221	.263	17	.160	-2	7	3	-3	-0.2
1886	NY-a	17	21	.447	38	38	37	2	0	325²	278	6	99	167	10.4	3.12	109	.220	.277	19	.151	-7	12	10	0	0.4
1887	NY-a	10	15	.400	26	26	25	0	0	220	310	3	83	64	16.4	5.97	71	.325	.384	23	.247	-1	-41	-42	-1	-3.1
1890	Tol-a	17	21	.447	40	38	34	0	1	315²	346	5	107	125	13.2	4.19	94	.277	.331	13	.100	-9	-11	-8	-5	-2.0
Total	6	62	81	.434	147	145	137	4	1	1225²	1264	23	359	607	12.1	3.86	92	.254	.308	78	.160	-17	-32	-43	-10	-5.4

● HARVEY CUSHMAN
Cushman, Harvey Barnes   b: 7/10/1877, Rockland, Me.   d: 12/27/20, Emsworth, Pa.   Deb: 8/24/02

| 1902 | Pit-N | 0 | 4 | .000 | 4 | 4 | 3 | 0 | 0 | 25² | 30 | 1 | 31 | 12 | 22.1 | 7.36 | 37 | .291 | .463 | 2 | .200 | -1 | -13 | -13 | -1 | -1.6 |

● MIKE CVENGROS
Cvengros, Michael John   b: 12/1/01, Pana, Ill.   d: 8/2/70, Hot Springs, Ark.   BL/TL, 5'8", 159 lbs.   Deb: 9/30/22

YEAR	TM/L	W	L	PCT	G	GS	CG	SH	SV	IP	H	HR	BB	SO	RAT	ERA	ERA+	OAV	OOB	BH	AVG	PB	PR	/A	PD	TPI
1922	NY-N	0	1	.000	1	1	0	0	0	9	6	1	3	3	10.0	4.00	100	.194	.286	0	.000	-0	0	0	0	0.0
1923	Chi-A	12	13	.480	40	26	14	0	3	214¹	216	6	107	86	14.1	4.41	90	.265	.203	-1		.203	-1	-10	-11	0	-1.2
1924	Chi-A	3	12	.200	26	15	2	0	0	105²	119	5	67	36	16.1	5.88	70	.300	.405	6	.200	-2	-19	-21	0	-2.2
1925	Chi-A	3	9	.250	22	11	4	0	0	104²	109	4	55	32	14.4	4.30	97	.278	.371	5	.152	-0	-2	-2	-0	-0.3
1927	*Pit-N	2	1	.667	23	4	0	0	1	53²	55	3	24	21	13.4	3.35	123	.271	.351	3	.158	-0	3	5	1	0.3

YEAR	TM/L	W	L	PCT	G	GS	CG	SH	SV	IP	H	HR	BB	SO	RAT	ERA	ERA+	OAV	OOB	BH	AVG	PB	PR	/A	PD	TPI
1929	Chi-N	5	4	.556	32	2	0	0	2	64	82	2	29	23	15.8	4.64	99	.319	.390	6	.400	2	1	-0	0	0.2
Total	6	25	40	.385	144	59	21	0	6	551¹	587	24	285	201	14.6	4.59	90	.282	.374	35	.201	1	-24	-28	1	-3.2

● JIM CZAJKOWSKI
Czajkowski, James Mark   b: 12/18/63, Parma, Ohio   BB/TR, 6'4", 215 lbs.   Deb: 7/29/94

YEAR	TM/L	W	L	PCT	G	GS	CG	SH	SV	IP	H	HR	BB	SO	RAT	ERA	ERA+	OAV	OOB	BH	AVG	PB	PR	/A	PD	TPI
1994	Col-N	0	0	—	5	0	0	0	0	8²	9	2	6	2	18.7	4.15	120	.281	.439	0	—	0	0	1	0	0.0

● OMAR DAAL
Daal, Omar Jesus (Cordero)   b: 3/1/72, Maracaibo, Venez.   BL/TL, 6'3", 160 lbs.   Deb: 4/24/93

YEAR	TM/L	W	L	PCT	G	GS	CG	SH	SV	IP	H	HR	BB	SO	RAT	ERA	ERA+	OAV	OOB	BH	AVG	PB	PR	/A	PD	TPI
1993	LA-N	2	3	.400	47	0	0	0	0	35¹	36	5	21	19	14.5	5.09	75	.277	.377	0	—	0	-4	-5	0	-0.6
1994	LA-N	0	0	—	24	0	0	0	0	13²	12	1	5	9	11.2	3.29	119	.245	.315	0	—	0	1	1	-0	0.0
1995	LA-N	4	0	1.000	28	0	0	0	0	20	9	1	15	11	20.2	7.20	53	.354	.459	0	—	0	-7	-8	-0	-1.3
1996	Mon-N	4	5	.444	64	6	0	0	0	87¹	74	10	37	82	11.5	4.02	107	.228	.309	0	.000	-1	2	3	1	0.2
Total	4	10	8	.556	163	6	0	0	0	156¹	151	17	78	121	13.3	4.61	89	.258	.347	0	.000	-1	-8	-9	1	-1.7

● JOHN D'ACQUISTO
D'Acquisto, John Francis   b: 12/24/51, San Diego, Cal.   BR/TR, 6'2", 205 lbs.   Deb: 9/2/73

YEAR	TM/L	W	L	PCT	G	GS	CG	SH	SV	IP	H	HR	BB	SO	RAT	ERA	ERA+	OAV	OOB	BH	AVG	PB	PR	/A	PD	TPI
1973	SF-N	1	1	.500	7	3	1	0	0	27²	24	4	19	29	13.7	3.58	107	.219	.339	0	.000	-1	0	1	-0	-0.1
1974	SF-N	12	14	.462	38	36	5	1	0	215	182	13	124	167	13.1	3.77	101	.227	.334	8	.113	-1	-4	1	-4	-0.4
1975	SF-N	2	4	.333	10	6	0	0	0	28	29	5	34	22	20.9	10.29	37	.264	.445	0	.000	-0	-21	-20	-1	-3.4
1976	SF-N	3	8	.273	28	19	0	0	0	106	93	5	102	53	16.8	5.35	68	.243	.406	7	.269	2	-22	-20	-0	-1.8
1977	StL-N	0	0	—	3	2	0	0	0	8¹	5	0	10	9	17.3	4.32	89	.185	.421	0	.000	-0	-0	-0	-1	-0.0
	SD-N	1	2	.333	17	12	0	0	0	44	49	3	47	45	19.8	6.95	51	.297	.455	0	.000	-1	-15	-17	0	-1.0
	Yr	1	2	.333	20	14	0	0	0	52¹	54	3	57	54	19.3	6.54	55	.278	.444	0	.000	-1	-15	-17	0	-1.0
1978	SD-N	4	3	.571	45	3	0	0	10	93	60	2	56	104	11.3	2.13	156	.185	.307	4	.190	1	15	12	-1	1.2
1979	SD-N	9	13	.409	51	11	1	1	2	133²	140	15	86	97	15.4	4.92	72	.275	.383	4	.129	1	-18	-21	-2	-3.2
1980	SD-N	2	3	.400	39	0	0	0	1	67	67	2	36	44	14.0	3.76	91	.270	.365	0	.000	-0	-1	-2	-0	-0.3
	Mon-N	0	2	.000	11	0	0	0	2	20²	14	0	9	15	10.0	2.18	164	.206	.299	0	—	0	3	3	0	0.4
	Yr	2	5	.286	50	0	0	0	3	87²	81	2	45	59	12.9	3.39	102	.252	.343	0	.000	-1	2	1	-0	0.1
1981	Cal-A	0	0	—	6	0	0	0	0	19¹	26	2	12	8	18.2	10.71	34	.338	.433	0	—	0	-15	-15	-0	0.0
1982	Oak-A	0	1	.000	11	0	0	0	0	17	20	1	9	7	15.4	5.29	74	.290	.372	0	—	0	-2	-3	-0	0.1
Total	10	34	51	.400	266	92	7	2	15	779²	708	52	544	600	14.7	4.56	79	.245	.368	23	.127	0	-79	-81	-9	-8.5

● JOHN DAGENHARD
Dagenhard, John Douglas   b: 4/25/17, Magnolia, Ohio   BR/TR, 6'2", 195 lbs.   Deb: 9/28/43

YEAR	TM/L	W	L	PCT	G	GS	CG	SH	SV	IP	H	HR	BB	SO	RAT	ERA	ERA+	OAV	OOB	BH	AVG	PB	PR	/A	PD	TPI
1943	Bos-N	1	0	1.000	2	1	1	0	0	11	9	0	4	2	12.3	0.00	—	.225	.326	0	.000	-0	4	4	1	0.5

● PETE DAGLIA
Daglia, Peter George   b: 2/28/06, Napa, Cal.   d: 3/11/52, Willits, Cal.   BR/TR, 6'1", 200 lbs.   Deb: 6/8/32

YEAR	TM/L	W	L	PCT	G	GS	CG	SH	SV	IP	H	HR	BB	SO	RAT	ERA	ERA+	OAV	OOB	BH	AVG	PB	PR	/A	PD	TPI
1932	Chi-A	2	4	.333	12	5	2	0	0	50	67	4	20	16	16.4	5.76	75	.324	.394	1	.077	-1	-7	-8	-1	-0.9

● JAY DAHL
Dahl, Jay Steven   b: 12/6/45, San Bernardino, Cal.   d: 6/20/65, Salisbury, N.C.   BB/TL, 5'10", 183 lbs.   Deb: 9/27/63

YEAR	TM/L	W	L	PCT	G	GS	CG	SH	SV	IP	H	HR	BB	SO	RAT	ERA	ERA+	OAV	OOB	BH	AVG	PB	PR	/A	PD	TPI
1963	Hou-N	0	1	.000	1	1	0	0	0	2²	7	0	3	1	23.6	16.88	19	.438	.438	0	—	0	-4	-4	-0	-0.9

● JERRY DAHLKE
Dahlke, Jerome Alexander "Joe"   b: 6/8/30, Marathon, Wis.   BR/TR, 6', 180 lbs.   Deb: 5/6/56

YEAR	TM/L	W	L	PCT	G	GS	CG	SH	SV	IP	H	HR	BB	SO	RAT	ERA	ERA+	OAV	OOB	BH	AVG	PB	PR	/A	PD	TPI
1956	Chi-A	0	0	—	5	0	0	0	0	2¹	5	0	6	1	42.4	19.29	21	.455	.647	0	—	0	-4	-4	-0	0.0

● SAM DAILEY
Dailey, Samuel Laurence   b: 3/31/04, Oakford, Ill.   d: 12/2/79, Columbia, Mo.   BL/TR, 5'11", 168 lbs.   Deb: 7/4/29

YEAR	TM/L	W	L	PCT	G	GS	CG	SH	SV	IP	H	HR	BB	SO	RAT	ERA	ERA+	OAV	OOB	BH	AVG	PB	PR	/A	PD	TPI
1929	Phi-N	2	2	.500	20	5	0	0	0	51¹	74	5	23	18	17.2	7.54	69	.349	.415	1	.059	-2	-16	-13	-1	-1.1

● VINCE DAILEY
Dailey, Vincent Perry   b: 12/25/1864, Osceola, Pa.   d: 11/14/19, Hornell, N.Y.   6', 200 lbs.   Deb: 4/21/1890 ♦

YEAR	TM/L	W	L	PCT	G	GS	CG	SH	SV	IP	H	HR	BB	SO	RAT	ERA	ERA+	OAV	OOB	BH	AVG	PB	PR	/A	PD	TPI
1890	Cle-N	0	1	.000	2	1	0	0	0	7	12	0	7	0	24.4	7.71	46	.364	.475	71	.289	1	-3	-3	0	-0.3

● BILL DAILEY
Dailey, William Garland   b: 5/13/35, Arlington, Va.   BR/TR, 6'3", 185 lbs.   Deb: 8/17/61

YEAR	TM/L	W	L	PCT	G	GS	CG	SH	SV	IP	H	HR	BB	SO	RAT	ERA	ERA+	OAV	OOB	BH	AVG	PB	PR	/A	PD	TPI
1961	Cle-A	1	0	1.000	12	0	0	0	0	19	16	0	6	7	10.4	0.95	415	.232	.293	0	.000	-0	6	6	0	0.3
1962	Cle-A	2	2	.500	27	0	0	0	1	42²	44	3	11	24	13.1	3.59	108	.270	.348	0	.000	-0	2	1	-0	0.1
1963	Min-A	6	3	.667	66	0	0	0	21	108²	80	9	19	72	8.2	1.99	183	.208	.246	5	.238	2	20	20	2	3.0
1964	Min-A	1	2	.333	14	0	0	0	0	15¹	23	3	17	6	25.8	8.22	44	.377	.537	0	—	0	-8	-8	0	-1.4
Total	4	10	7	.588	119	0	0	0	22	185²	163	15	53	109	11.0	2.76	135	.241	.308	5	.192	1	20	20	3	2.0

● ED DAILY
Daily, Edward M.   b: 9/7/1862, Providence, R.I.   d: 10/21/1891, Washington, D.C.   BR/TR, 5'10.5", 174 lbs.   Deb: 5/4/1885   F♦

YEAR	TM/L	W	L	PCT	G	GS	CG	SH	SV	IP	H	HR	BB	SO	RAT	ERA	ERA+	OAV	OOB	BH	AVG	PB	PR	/A	PD	TPI
1885	Phi-N	26	23	.531	50	50	49	6	0	440	370	12	90	140	9.4	2.21	126	.217	.256	38	.207	-0	30	28	-4	2.4
1886	Phi-N	16	9	.640	27	23	22	1	0	218	211	7	59	95	11.1	3.06	108	.242	.290	70	.227	3	6	6	2	0.8
1887	Phi-N	0	4	.000	6	5	4	0	0	41¹	52	2	25	7	16.8	7.19	59	.289	.367	30	.283	1	-14	-14	1	-0.8
	Was-N	0	1	.000	1	1	1	0	0	7	5	0	6	3	14.1	7.71	53	.208	.367	78	.251	0	-3	-3	0	-0.3
	Yr	0	5	.000	7	6	5	0	0	48¹	57	2	31	10	16.4	7.26	58	.279	.374	108	.259	1	-17	-16	1	-1.1
1888	Was-N	2	7	.222	9	8	8	0	0	73²	84	7	19	20	13.4	4.89	57	.278	.325	102	.225	1	-17	-17	0	-1.5
1889	Col-a	0	0	—	2	0	0	0	0	1²	1	0	4	2	27.0	21.60	17	.167	.500	148	.256	0	-3	-3	-0	-0.4
1890	Bro-a	10	15	.400	27	27	27	0	0	235²	252	3	93	82	13.9	4.05	96	.265	.342	94	.239	3	-5	-4	2	0.1
	NY-N	2	0	1.000	2	1	1	0	0	16	6	0	6	9	9.0	2.25	156	.113	.254	2	.133	-1	2	2	1	0.2
	*Lou-a	6	3	.667	12	10	9	1	0	93	83	2	30	31	11.3	1.94	199	.232	.298	20	.250	2	20	20	2	2.1
1891	Lou-a	4	8	.333	15	14	11	0	0	111¹	149	6	45	27	16.6	5.74	64	.310	.382	16	.250	2	-25	-26	1	-1.9
Total	7	66	70	.485	151	139	132	6	1	1237²	1217	39	380	407	11.9	3.39	98	.246	.305	616	.239	12	-8	-11	5	0.7

● HUGH DAILY
Daily, Hugh Ignatius "One Arm" (b: Harry Criss)   b: 1857, Baltimore, Md.   BR/TR, 6'2", 180 lbs.   Deb: 5/1/1882

YEAR	TM/L	W	L	PCT	G	GS	CG	SH	SV	IP	H	HR	BB	SO	RAT	ERA	ERA+	OAV	OOB	BH	AVG	PB	PR	/A	PD	TPI
1882	Buf-N	15	14	.517	29	29	29	0	0	255²	246	6	70	116	11.1	2.99	98	.234	.282	18	.164	-6	-3	-2	-5	-1.1
1883	Cle-N	23	19	.548	45	43	40	4	0	378²	360	6	99	171	10.9	2.42	130	.243	.291	18	.127	-10	30	31	-1	1.8
1884	CP-U	27	27	.500	56	56	54	5	0	484²	430	11	71	469	9.3	2.43	100	.222	.249	43	.219	-11	1	1	1	-0.8
	Was-U	1	1	.500	2	2	2	0	0	16	16	0	1	14	9.6	2.25	107	.242	.254	-0	—	-1	0	0	0	-0.1
	Yr	28	28	.500	58	58	56	5	0	500²	446	11	72	483	9.3	2.43	101	.223	.250	43	.214	-12	1	1	1	-0.9
1885	StL-N	3	8	.273	11	11	10	1	0	91¹	92	5	31	44	13.4	3.94	70	.252	.333	3	.086	-3	-11	-12	-0	-1.4
1886	Was-N	0	6	.000	6	6	6	0	0	49	69	2	40	15	20.0	7.35	45	.332	.440	2	.125	-1	-22	-22	-0	-1.9
1887	Cle-a	4	12	.250	16	16	16	0	0	139²	181	1	44	30	14.7	3.67	118	.311	.362	4	.069	-8	10	10	-1	0.0
Total	6	73	87	.456	165	163	157	10	0	1415	1394	30	369	846	11.2	2.92	101	.245	.291	88	.157	-39	5	6	-6	-3.4

● BRUCE DalCANTON
DalCanton, John Bruce   b: 6/15/42, California, Pa.   BR/TR, 6'2", 205 lbs.   Deb: 9/3/67   C

YEAR	TM/L	W	L	PCT	G	GS	CG	SH	SV	IP	H	HR	BB	SO	RAT	ERA	ERA+	OAV	OOB	BH	AVG	PB	PR	/A	PD	TPI
1967	Pit-N	2	1	.667	8	2	1	0	0	24	19	1	10	13	11.3	1.88	179	.211	.297	2	.333	1	4	4	-1	0.5
1968	Pit-N	1	1	.500	7	0	0	0	2	17	7	0	6	8	7.9	2.12	138	.127	.238	0	.000	-0	2	2	-1	0.1
1969	Pit-N	8	2	.800	57	0	0	0	5	86¹	79	3	49	56	13.3	3.34	105	.252	.353	3	.300	2	2	1	-0	0.4
1970	Pit-N	9	4	.692	41	6	1	0	1	84²	94	7	39	53	14.2	4.57	85	.282	.359	0	.000	-2	-5	-6	-1	-1.0
1971	KC-A	8	6	.571	25	22	2	0	0	141¹	144	8	44	58	12.0	3.44	100	.262	.317	4	.087	-3	-0	-2	-4	-0.4
1972	KC-A	6	6	.500	35	16	1	0	0	132¹	135	7	29	75	11.2	3.40	89	.265	.306	4	.098	-2	-5	-5	-0	-0.4
1973	KC-A	4	3	.571	32	3	1	0	3	97¹	108	4	46	38	14.6	4.81	85	.284	.351	0	—	0	-11	-8	-0	-0.7
1974	KC-A	8	10	.444	31	22	9	2	0	175¹	135	5	82	96	11.4	3.13	122	.211	.306	0	—	0	9	13	0	1.4
1975	KC-A	0	2	.000	4	2	0	0	0	8²	23	0	6	5	32.2	15.58	25	.479	.554	0	—	0	-11	-11	-0	-1.8
	Atl-N	2	7	.222	26	9	0	0	0	67	63	2	35	40	13.6	3.36	112	.248	.327	2	.105	-1	3	3	0	0.4
1976	Atl-N	3	5	.375	42	1	0	0	2	73¹	67	6	42	36	13.6	3.56	106	.244	.348	2	.222	0	1	1	0	0.3
1977	Chi-A	0	2	.000	8	0	0	0	2	24	20	1	13	9	12.4	3.75	109	.230	.330	0	—	0	1	1	-0	0.1
Total	11	51	49	.510	316	83	15	2	19	931¹	894	48	391	485	12.6	3.67	99	.253	.331	17	.113	-3	-12	-5	-3	-1.7

● GENE DALE
Dale, Emmett Eugene   b: 6/16/1889, St.Louis, Mo.   d: 3/20/58, St.Louis, Mo.   BR/TR, 6'3", 179 lbs.   Deb: 9/19/11

YEAR	TM/L	W	L	PCT	G	GS	CG	SH	SV	IP	H	HR	BB	SO	RAT	ERA	ERA+	OAV	OOB	BH	AVG	PB	PR	/A	PD	TPI
1911	StL-N	0	2	.000	5	2	0	0	0	14²	13	0	16	13	19.0	6.75	50	.250	.443	2	.400	0	-5	-5	0	-0.6
1912	StL-N	0	5	.000	19	3	1	0	0	61²	76	4	51	37	19.0	6.57	52	.311	.436	6	.273	1	-22	-22	1	-1.5
1915	Cin-N	18	17	.514	49	35	20	4	3	296²	256	6	107	104	11.2	2.46	116	.243	.316	20	.220	2	10	13	1	1.7
1916	Cin-N	3	4	.429	17	5	2	0	0	69²	80	3	33	23	14.9	5.17	50	.304	.386	3	.143	-0	-20	-20	1	-1.8
Total	4	21	28	.429	90	45	23	4	3	442²	425	13	207	177	13.1	3.60	81	.263	.352	31	.223	3	-37	-34	2	-2.2

YEAR	TM/L	W	L	PCT	G	GS	CG	SH	SV	IP	H	HR	BB	SO	RAT	ERA	ERA+	OAV	OOB	BH	AVG	PB	PR	/A	PD	TPI

● BUD DALEY   Daley, Leavitt Leo   b: 10/7/32, Orange, Cal.   BL/TL, 6'1", 185 lbs.   Deb: 9/10/55

1955	Cle-A	0	1	.000	2	1	0	0	0	7	10	1	1	2	14.1	6.43	62	.333	.355	0	.000	-0	-2	-2	0	-0.2
1956	Cle-A	1	0	1.000	14	0	0	0	0	20¹	21	2	14	13	17.7	6.20	68	.273	.417	0	.000	-0	-5	-5	1	-0.1
1957	Cle-A	2	8	.200	34	10	1	0	2	87¹	99	7	40	54	15.4	4.43	84	.279	.368	4	.200	0	-6	-7	1	-0.6
1958	KC-A	3	2	.600	26	5	1	0	0	70²	67	5	19	39	11.7	3.31	118	.249	.313	2	.125	-1	4	5	1	0.3
1959	KC-A★	16	13	.552	39	29	12	2	1	216¹	212	24	62	125	11.9	3.16	127	.257	.317	23	.295	4	17	20	-0	3.1
1960	KC-A★	16	16	.500	37	35	13	1	0	231	234	27	96	126	13.2	4.56	87	.263	.341	12	.160	1	-18	-15	1	-1.6
1961	KC-A	4	8	.333	16	10	2	0	1	63²	84	6	22	36	15.7	4.95	84	.319	.383	2	.111	-1	-7	-5	1	-0.9
	*NY-A	8	9	.471	23	17	7	0	0	129²	127	17	51	83	12.6	3.96	94	.257	.331	6	.133	-1	1	-3	-1	-0.6
	Yr	12	17	.414	39	27	9	0	1	193¹	211	23	73	119	13.4	4.28	90	.275	.341	8	.127	-2	-6	-9	-0	-1.5
1962	*NY-A	7	5	.583	43	6	0	0	4	105¹	105	8	21	55	11.2	3.59	104	.258	.303	5	.185	-0	4	2	-0	0.2
1963	NY-A	0	0	—	1	0	0	0	1	1	2	0	0	0	9.0	0.00	—	.667	.667	0	—	0	-0	-0	0	0.1
1964	NY-A	3	2	.600	13	3	0	0	1	35	37	3	25	16	17.0	4.63	78	.274	.402	2	.250	1	-4	-5	1	-0.4
Total	10	60	64	.484	248	116	36	3	10	967¹	998	100	351	549	13.1	4.03	97	.266	.339	56	.192	3	-15	-14	4	-0.7

● BILL DALEY   Daley, William   b: 6/27/1868, Poughkeepsie, N.Y.   d: 5/4/22, Poughkeepsie, N.Y.   TL,   Deb: 7/17/1889

1889	Bos-N	3	3	.500	9	7	4	0	0	48	34	1	43	40	14.8	4.31	97	.193	.357	3	.150	-1	-2	-1	3	0.1
1890	Bos-P	18	7	**.720**	34	25	19	2	2	235	246	7	167	110	14.8	3.60	123	.258	.373	17	.155	-5	17	21	-1	1.1
1891	Bos-a	8	6	.571	19	11	10	0	**2**	126²	119	6	81	68	14.7	2.98	117	.240	.354	10	.169	-3	10	7	1	0.4
Total	3	29	16	.644	62	43	33	2	4	409²	399	14	291	218	15.6	3.49	117	.245	.366	30	.159	-8	25	27	3	1.6

● MIKE DALTON   Dalton, Michael Edward   b: 3/27/63, Palo Alto, Cal.   BR/TL, 6', 215 lbs.   Deb: 5/31/91

| 1991 | Det-A | 0 | 0 | — | 4 | 0 | 0 | 0 | 0 | 8 | 8 | 0 | 5 | 5 | 16.9 | 3.38 | 123 | .333 | .368 | 0 | — | 0 | 1 | 1 | 0 | -0.1 |

● GEORGE DALY   Daly, George Josephs "Pecks"   b: 7/28/1887, Buffalo, N.Y.   d: 12/12/57, Buffalo, N.Y.   BR/TR, 5'10.5", 175 lbs.   Deb: 9/26/09

| 1909 | NY-N | 0 | 3 | .000 | 3 | 3 | 3 | 0 | 0 | 21 | 31 | 0 | 8 | 8 | 17.1 | 6.00 | 43 | .341 | .400 | 1 | .111 | -1 | -8 | -8 | -1 | -1.1 |

● JEFF D'AMICO   D'Amico, Jeffrey Charles   b: 12/27/75, St.Petersburg, Fla.   BR/TR, 6'7", 250 lbs.   Deb: 6/28/96

| 1996 | Mil-A | 6 | 6 | .500 | 17 | 17 | 0 | 0 | 0 | 86 | 88 | 21 | 31 | 53 | 12.5 | 5.44 | 97 | .267 | .330 | 0 | — | 0 | -4 | -2 | -1 | -0.4 |

● BILL DAMMANN   Dammann, William Henry "Wee Willie"   b: 8/9/1872, Chicago, Ill.   d: 12/6/48, Lynnhaven, Va.   BL/TL, 5'7", 155 lbs.   Deb: 4/24/1897

1897	Cin-N	6	4	.600	16	11	7	0	0	95	122	3	37	21	15.5	4.74	96	.309	.375	5	.161	-1	-4	-2	1	-0.1
1898	Cin-N	16	10	.615	35	22	16	2	2	224²	277	3	67	51	14.1	3.61	106	.301	.353	16	.195	1	0	6	-3	0.4
1899	Cin-N	2	1	.667	9	5	3	1	1	48	74	0	11	2	16.1	4.88	80	.351	.386	1	.056	-2	-5	-5	0	-0.4
Total	3	24	15	.615	60	38	26	4	3	367²	473	5	115	74	14.7	4.06	99	.310	.363	22	.168	-1	-10	-1	-2	-0.1

● ART DANEY   Daney, Arthur Lee   b: 7/9/04, Talihina, Okla.   d: 3/11/88, Phoenix, Ariz.   BR/TR, 5'11", 165 lbs.   Deb: 5/25/28

| 1928 | Phi-A | 0 | 0 | — | 1 | 0 | 0 | 0 | 0 | 1 | 1 | 0 | 0 | 0 | 9.0 | 0.00 | — | .250 | .250 | 0 | — | 0 | 0 | 0 | 0 | 0.0 |

● DAVE DANFORTH   Danforth, David Charles "Dauntless Dave"   b: 3/7/1890, Granger, Tex.   d: 9/19/70, Baltimore, Md.   BL/TL, 6', 167 lbs.   Deb: 8/1/11

1911	Phi-A	4	1	.800	14	2	1	0	1	33²	29	1	17	21	13.1	3.74	84	.240	.348	1	.167	0	-1	-2	-0	-0.3
1912	Phi-A	0	0	—	3	0	0	0	0	20¹	26	0	12	8	16.8	3.98	77	.338	.427	1	.250	-2	-2	-0	0	-0.3
1916	Chi-A	6	5	.545	28	8	1	0	2	93²	87	1	37	49	12.2	3.27	85	.259	.338	2	.087	-1	-5	-5	1	-0.6
1917	*Chi-A	11	6	.647	**50**	9	1	1	**9**	173	155	1	74	79	12.1	2.65	100	.244	.325	6	.130	0	0	-0	-3	-0.3
1918	Chi-A	6	15	.286	39	11	5	0	2	139	148	1	40	48	12.5	3.43	80	.288	.345	6	.143	-2	-10	-11	0	-1.8
1919	Chi-A	1	2	.333	15	1	0	0	0	41²	58	1	20	17	17.1	7.78	41	.333	.405	1	.111	0	-21	-21	-0	-1.5
1922	StL-A	5	2	.714	20	10	3	0	1	79²	93	1	38	48	14.9	3.28	127	.304	.383	2	.087	-2	7	8	-1	0.3
1923	StL-A	16	14	.533	38	29	16	0	1	226¹	221	4	87	96	12.7	3.94	106	.262	.340	15	.211	2	1	6	-0	0.9
1924	StL-A	15	12	.556	41	27	11	1	4	219²	246	16	69	65	13.0	4.51	100	.292	.348	13	.171	4	-7	0	-3	-0.4
1925	StL-A	7	9	.438	38	15	5	0	2	159	172	19	61	53	13.4	4.36	107	.284	.353	8	.174	-2	1	6	-4	-0.1
Total	10	71	66	.518	286	112	43	2	23	1186	1235	45	455	484	13.1	3.89	95	.277	.349	56	.160	-6	-37	-25	-10	-3.8

● CHUCK DANIEL   Daniel, Charles Edward   b: 9/17/33, Bluffton, Ark.   BR/TR, 6'2", 195 lbs.   Deb: 9/21/57

| 1957 | Det-A | 0 | 0 | — | 1 | 0 | 0 | 0 | 0 | 2¹ | 3 | 1 | 0 | 2 | 11.6 | 7.71 | 50 | .333 | .333 | 0 | — | 0 | -1 | -1 | -0 | 0.0 |

● BENNIE DANIELS   Daniels, Bennie   b: 6/17/32, Tuscaloosa, Ala.   BL/TR, 6'1.5", 193 lbs.   Deb: 9/24/57

1957	Pit-N	0	1	.000	1	1	0	0	0	7	5	0	3	2	10.3	1.29	295	.208	.296	0	.000	-0	2	2	1	0.3
1958	Pit-N	0	3	.000	8	5	1	0	0	27²	32	3	15	15	15.3	5.53	70	.290	.382	1	.125	-0	-5	-5	1	-0.4
1959	Pit-N	7	9	.438	34	12	5	0	1	100²	115	9	39	67	13.9	5.45	71	.287	.353	9	.310	6	-17	-18	-1	-2.0
1960	Pit-N	1	3	.250	10	6	0	0	1	40¹	52	4	16	16	15.4	7.81	48	.311	.375	3	.188	-0	-18	-18	1	-1.5
1961	Was-A	12	11	.522	32	28	12	1	0	212	184	14	80	110	11.3	3.44	117	.237	.331	15	.197	3	14	14	1	1.8
1962	Was-A	7	16	.304	44	21	3	1	2	161¹	172	14	68	66	13.5	4.85	83	.280	.354	6	.130	-1	-16	-15	5	-1.5
1963	Was-A	5	10	.333	35	24	6	1	0	168²	163	19	58	88	11.8	4.38	85	.250	.312	7	.152	1	-14	-12	3	-0.6
1964	Was-A	8	10	.444	33	24	3	0	0	163	147	20	64	73	11.7	3.70	100	.245	.317	6	.128	0	-1	0	3	0.3
1965	Was-A	5	13	.278	33	18	1	1	1	116¹	135	16	39	42	13.5	4.72	74	.290	.345	4	.133	0	-16	-16	-0	-2.3
Total	9	45	76	.372	230	139	26	5	5	997	1004	99	383	471	12.6	4.44	86	.264	.332	51	.170	9	-72	-69	12	-5.9

● CHARLIE DANIELS   Daniels, Charles L.   b: 7/1/1861, Roxbury, Mass.   d: 2/9/38, Boston, Mass.   Deb: 4/18/1884

| 1884 | Bos-U | 0 | 2 | .000 | 2 | 2 | 2 | 0 | 0 | 16² | 20 | 0 | 2 | 12 | 11.9 | 4.32 | 55 | .278 | .297 | 3 | .273 | 0 | -3 | -4 | -0 | -0.3 |

● PETE DANIELS   Daniels, Peter J. "Smiling Pete"   b: 4/8/1864, County Cavan, Ireland   d: 2/13/28, Indianapolis, Ind.   BL/TL,   Deb: 4/19/1890

1890	Pit-N	1	2	.333	4	4	3	0	0	28	40	1	12	8	17.7	7.07	47	.325	.399	4	.333	1	-11	-12	-0	-0.8
1898	StL-N	1	6	.143	10	6	3	0	0	54²	62	0	14	13	13.0	3.62	105	.283	.335	3	.176	-0	-0	1	-0	0.1
Total	2	2	8	.200	14	10	6	0	0	82²	102	1	26	21	14.6	4.79	76	.298	.358	7	.241	1	-11	-11	-0	-0.7

● GEORGE DARBY   Darby, George William "Deacon"   b: 2/6/1869, Kansas City, Mo.   d: 2/25/37, Sacramento, Cal.   BR/TR, 5'10.5", 160 lbs.   Deb: 4/28/1893

| 1893 | Cin-N | 1 | 1 | .500 | 4 | 3 | 2 | 0 | 0 | 29 | 41 | 2 | 18 | 6 | 19.2 | 7.76 | 62 | .323 | .419 | 3 | .300 | 0 | -10 | -10 | 1 | -0.4 |

● PAT DARCY   Darcy, Patrick Leonard   b: 5/12/50, Troy, Ohio   BL/TR, 6'3", 175 lbs.   Deb: 9/12/74

1974	Cin-N	1	0	1.000	6	2	0	0	0	17	17	2	8	14	13.2	3.71	94	.262	.342	1	.333	0	-0	-0	-0	0.0
1975	*Cin-N	11	5	.688	27	22	1	0	1	130²	134	4	59	46	13.3	3.58	100	.269	.346	4	.085	-3	1	0	-0	-0.3
1976	Cin-N	2	3	.400	11	4	0	0	1	39	41	2	22	15	14.5	6.23	56	.279	.373	2	.182	1	-12	-12	-1	-1.5
Total	3	14	8	.636	44	28	1	0	3	186²	192	8	89	75	13.5	4.15	86	.270	.352	7	.115	-2	-11	-12	-1	-1.8

● ALVIN DARK   Dark, Alvin Ralph "Blackie"   b: 1/7/22, Comanche, Okla.   BR/TR, 5'11", 185 lbs.   Deb: 7/14/46   MC♦

| 1953 | NY-N | 0 | 0 | — | 1 | 1 | 0 | 0 | 1 | 4 | 4 | 1 | 0 | 0 | 18.0 | 18.00 | 24 | .250 | .400 | 194 | .300 | - | -2 | -2 | -0 | 0.0 |

● RON DARLING   Darling, Ronald Maurice   b: 8/19/60, Honolulu, Hawaii   BR/TR, 6'3", 195 lbs.   Deb: 9/6/83

1983	NY-N	1	3	.250	5	5	1	0	0	35¹	31	0	17	23	13.0	2.80	129	.248	.352	1	.100	-1	3	3	0	0.3
1984	NY-N	12	9	.571	33	33	2	2	0	205²	179	17	104	136	12.6	3.81	93	.235	.331	10	.149	-1	-5	-6	2	-0.5
1985	NY-N☆	16	6	.727	36	35	4	2	0	248	214	21	114	167	12.0	2.90	119	.235	.323	13	.171	2	19	15	3	1.9
1986	*NY-N	15	6	.714	34	34	4	2	0	237	203	21	81	184	10.9	2.81	126	.234	.302	8	.099	-2	24	19	3	1.8
1987	NY-N	12	8	.600	32	32	2	0	0	207²	183	24	96	167	12.2	4.29	88	.233	.319	1	.123	1	-5	-12	4	-0.6
1988	*NY-N	17	9	.654	34	34	7	4	0	240²	218	24	60	161	10.6	3.25	99	.245	.297	18	.220	6	5	-1	0	0.5
1989	NY-N	14	14	.500	33	33	4	1	0	217¹	214	19	70	153	11.9	3.52	93	.258	.318	9	.123	1	-1	-6	2	-0.5
1990	NY-N	7	9	.438	33	18	1	0	0	126	135	20	44	99	13.1	4.50	83	.273	.338	4	.129	1	-10	-11	1	-1.1
1991	NY-N	5	6	.455	17	16	0	0	0	102¹	96	9	28	58	11.4	3.87	94	.251	.313	4	.118	-0	-2	-5	-0	-0.3
	Mon-N	0	2	.000	3	3	0	0	0	17	25	6	5	11	16.4	7.41	49	.333	.383	1	.167	0	-7	-7	-0	-0.7
	Yr	5	8	.385	20	20	0	0	0	119¹	121	15	33	69	11.7	4.37	83	.259	.309	5	.125	-0	-9	-10	-1	-1.0
	Oak-A	3	7	.300	12	12	0	0	0	75	64	7	38	60	12.5	4.08	94	.237	.335	0	—	0	-1	-3	0	0.2
1992	*Oak-A	15	10	.600	33	33	4	3	0	206¹	198	15	72	99	12.0	3.66	102	.253	.319	0	—	0	6	2	-1	0.3
1993	Oak-A	5	9	.357	31	29	3	0	0	178	198	22	72	95	13.9	5.16	79	.281	.352	0	—	0	-17	-21	-2	-1.4

YEAR	TM/L	W	L	PCT	G	GS	CG	SH	SV	IP	H	HR	BB	SO	RAT	ERA	ERA+	OAV	OOB	BH	AVG	PB	PR	/A	PD	TPI
1994	Oak-A	10	11	.476	25	25	4	0	0	160	162	18	59	108	12.8	4.50	98	.267	.339	0	.000	0	5	-1	0	-0.1
1995	Oak-A	4	7	.364	21	21	1	0	0	104	124	16	46	69	15.1	6.23	72	.296	.371	0	—	0	-18	-20	2	-1.6
Total	13	136	116	.540	382	364	37	13	0	2360¹	2244	239	906	1590	12.2	3.87	95	.252	.325	76	.144	6	-1	-51	15	-1.8

● BOB DARNELL
Darnell, Robert Jack b: 11/6/30, Wewoka, Okla. BR/TR, 5'10", 175 lbs. Deb: 8/10/54

YEAR	TM/L	W	L	PCT	G	GS	CG	SH	SV	IP	H	HR	BB	SO	RAT	ERA	ERA+	OAV	OOB	BH	AVG	PB	PR	/A	PD	TPI
1954	Bro-N	0	0	—	6	1	0	0	0	14¹	15	2	7	5	13.8	3.14	130	.278	.361	0	.000	-0	1	2	0	0.0
1956	Bro-N	0	0	—	1	0	0	0	0	1¹	1	0	0	6	6.8	0.00	—	.200	.200	0	—	-0	1	1	-0	0.0
Total	2	0	0	—	7	1	0	0	0	15²	16	2	7	5	13.2	2.87	142	.271	.348	0	.000	-0	2	2	0	0.0

● MIKE DARR
Darr, Michael Edward b: 3/23/56, Pomona, Cal. BR/TR, 6'4", 190 lbs. Deb: 9/6/77

YEAR	TM/L	W	L	PCT	G	GS	CG	SH	SV	IP	H	HR	BB	SO	RAT	ERA	ERA+	OAV	OOB	BH	AVG	PB	PR	/A	PD	TPI
1977	Tor-A	0	1	.000	1	1	0	0	0	1¹	3	1	4	1	54.0	33.75	12	.429	.667	0	—	0	-4	-4	0	-1.5

● GEORGE DARROW
Darrow, George Oliver b: 7/12/03, Beloit, Kan. d: 3/24/83, Sun City, Ariz. BL/TL, 6', 180 lbs. Deb: 4/22/34

YEAR	TM/L	W	L	PCT	G	GS	CG	SH	SV	IP	H	HR	BB	SO	RAT	ERA	ERA+	OAV	OOB	BH	AVG	PB	PR	/A	PD	TPI
1934	Phi-N	2	6	.250	17	8	2	0	1	49	57	4	28	14	16.3	5.51	86	.302	.403	2	.133	0	-8	-4	0	-0.6

● BOBBY DARWIN
Darwin, Arthur Bobby Lee b: 2/16/43, Los Angeles, Cal. BR/TR, 6'2", 200 lbs. Deb: 9/30/62 ♦

YEAR	TM/L	W	L	PCT	G	GS	CG	SH	SV	IP	H	HR	BB	SO	RAT	ERA	ERA+	OAV	OOB	BH	AVG	PB	PR	/A	PD	TPI
1962	LA-A	0	1	.000	1	1	0	0	0	3¹	8	0	4	6	32.4	10.80	36	.421	.522	0	.000	-0	-3	-3	-0	-0.5
1969	LA-N	0	0	—	3	0	0	0	0	3²	4	0	5	0	27.0	9.82	34	.333	.579	0	—	-0	-3	-3	0	0.0
Total	2	0	1	.000	4	1	0	0	0	7	12	0	9	6	29.6	10.29	35	.387	.548	559	.251	-0	-5	-5	-0	-0.5

● DANNY DARWIN
Darwin, Daniel Wayne b: 10/25/55, Bonham, Tex. BR/TR, 6'3", 190 lbs. Deb: 9/8/78 F

YEAR	TM/L	W	L	PCT	G	GS	CG	SH	SV	IP	H	HR	BB	SO	RAT	ERA	ERA+	OAV	OOB	BH	AVG	PB	PR	/A	PD	TPI
1978	Tex-A	1	0	1.000	3	1	0	0	0	8²	11	0	1	8	12.5	4.15	90	.324	.343	0	—	-0	-0	-0	-0	-0.1
1979	Tex-A	4	4	.500	20	6	1	0	0	78	50	5	30	58	9.8	4.04	103	.186	.280	0	—	0	2	1	-1	0.0
1980	Tex-A	13	4	.765	53	2	0	0	8	109²	98	4	50	104	12.3	2.63	148	.243	.329	0	—	0	17	15	-0	2.6
1981	Tex-A	9	9	.500	22	22	6	2	0	146	115	12	57	98	11.0	3.64	95	.218	.302	0	—	0	-0	-3	-1	-0.2
1982	Tex-A	10	8	.556	56	1	0	0	7	89	95	6	37	61	13.6	3.44	113	.279	.354	0	—	0	3	5	1	1.3
1983	Tex-A	8	13	.381	28	26	9	2	0	183	175	9	62	92	11.8	3.49	115	.250	.313	0	—	0	12	10	-1	1.0
1984	Tex-A	8	12	.400	35	32	5	1	0	223²	249	19	54	123	12.4	3.94	105	.279	.323	0	—	0	1	5	-2	0.1
1985	Mil-A	8	18	.308	39	29	11	1	2	217²	212	34	65	125	11.6	3.80	109	.254	.311	0	—	0	8	9	-3	0.7
1986	Mil-A	6	8	.429	27	14	5	1	0	130¹	120	13	35	80	10.9	3.52	123	.246	.300	0	—	0	9	12	1	1.1
	Hou-N	5	2	.714	12	8	1	0	0	54¹	50	7	9	40	9.8	2.32	155	.239	.271	1	.063	-1	8	8	-1	0.8
1987	Hou-N	9	10	.474	33	30	3	1	0	195²	184	17	69	134	11.9	3.59	109	.246	.314	12	.182	1	11	7	-2	0.7
1988	Hou-N	8	13	.381	44	20	3	0	3	192	189	20	48	129	11.4	3.84	86	.259	.311	4	.071	-1	-8	-11	2	-1.1
1989	Hou-N	11	4	.733	68	0	0	0	7	122	92	9	33	104	9.4	2.36	143	.212	.271	2	.118	-1	15	14	-1	1.6
1990	Hou-N	11	4	.733	48	17	3	0	2	162²	136	11	31	109	9.5	2.21	168	.225	.267	5	.132	1	29	27	-1	2.4
1991	Bos-A	3	6	.333	12	12	0	0	0	68	71	15	15	42	11.9	5.16	83	.263	.311	0	—	0	-8	-7	-0	-1.0
1992	Bos-A	9	9	.500	51	15	2	0	3	161¹	159	11	53	124	12.1	3.96	106	.257	.321	0	—	0	-0	4	-1	0.1
1993	Bos-A	15	11	.577	34	34	2	1	0	229¹	196	31	49	130	9.7	3.26	142	.230	.274	0	—	0	27	35	-0	3.4
1994	Bos-A	7	5	.583	13	13	0	0	0	75²	101	13	24	54	15.0	6.30	80	.317	.366	0	—	0	-13	-11	-2	-1.4
1995	Tor-A	1	8	.111	13	11	0	0	0	65	91	13	24	36	16.3	7.62	62	.340	.400	0	—	0	-21	-21	-1	-2.4
	Tex-A	2	2	.500	7	4	0	0	0	34	40	12	7	22	12.7	7.15	68	.292	.331	0	—	0	-9	-9	-0	-0.9
	Yr	3	10	.231	20	15	0	0	0	99	131	25	31	58	14.8	7.45	64	.317	.366	0	—	0	-30	-30	-2	-3.3
1996	Pit-N	7	9	.438	19	19	0	0	0	122¹	117	9	16	69	10.2	3.02	145	.253	.287	8	.205	2	16	19	1	2.6
	Hou-N	3	2	.600	15	6	0	0	0	42¹	43	7	11	27	12.8	5.95	64	.267	.337	1	.100	-0	-8	-10	-1	-1.1
	Yr	10	11	.476	34	25	0	0	0	164²	160	16	27	96	10.5	3.77	112	.253	.290	9	.184	2	8	9	0	1.5
Total	19	158	161	.495	652	322	52	9	32	2710²	2594	272	780	1769	11.5	3.72	109	.252	.309	33	.136	2	94	97	-12	10.2

● JEFF DARWIN
Darwin, Jeffrey Scott b: 7/6/69, Sherman, Tex. BR/TR, 6'3", 180 lbs. Deb: 6/13/94 F

YEAR	TM/L	W	L	PCT	G	GS	CG	SH	SV	IP	H	HR	BB	SO	RAT	ERA	ERA+	OAV	OOB	BH	AVG	PB	PR	/A	PD	TPI
1994	Sea-A	0	0	—	2	0	0	0	0	4	7	1	3	1	24.8	13.50	36	.389	.500	0	—	0	-4	-4	-0	0.0
1996	Chi-A	0	1	.000	22	0	0	0	0	30²	26	5	9	15	10.9	2.93	160	.232	.301	0	—	0	7	6	-0	0.5
Total	2	0	1	.000	24	0	0	0	0	34²	33	6	12	16	12.5	4.15	114	.254	.331	0	—	0	3	2	-1	0.5

● DOUG DASCENZO
Dascenzo, Douglas Craig b: 6/30/64, Cleveland, Ohio BB/TL, 5'7", 150 lbs. Deb: 9/2/88 ♦

YEAR	TM/L	W	L	PCT	G	GS	CG	SH	SV	IP	H	HR	BB	SO	RAT	ERA	ERA+	OAV	OOB	BH	AVG	PB	PR	/A	PD	TPI
1990	Chi-N	0	0	—	1	0	0	0	0	1	1	0	0	1	9.0	0.00	—	.333	.333	61	.253	0	0	0	0	0.0
1991	Chi-N	0	0	—	3	0	0	0	0	4	2	0	2	2	9.0	0.00	—	.154	.267	61	.255	1	2	2	-0	0.0
Total	2	0	0	—	4	0	0	0	0	5	3	0	2	3	9.0	0.00	—	.188	.278	287	.234	1	2	2	-0	0.0

● LEE DASHNER
Dashner, Lee Claire "Lefty" b: 4/25/1887, Renault, Ill. d: 12/16/59, ElDorado, Kan. BB/TL, 5'11.5", 192 lbs. Deb: 8/4/13

YEAR	TM/L	W	L	PCT	G	GS	CG	SH	SV	IP	H	HR	BB	SO	RAT	ERA	ERA+	OAV	OOB	BH	AVG	PB	PR	/A	PD	TPI
1913	Cle-A	0	0	—	1	0	0	0	0	1²	1	0	0	0	5.40	56		.000	.000	0		0	-0	-0	-0	-0.0

● FRANK DASSO
Dasso, Francis Joseph Nicholas b: 8/31/17, Chicago, Ill. BR/TR, 5'11.5", 185 lbs. Deb: 4/22/45

YEAR	TM/L	W	L	PCT	G	GS	CG	SH	SV	IP	H	HR	BB	SO	RAT	ERA	ERA+	OAV	OOB	BH	AVG	PB	PR	/A	PD	TPI
1945	Cin-N	4	5	.444	16	12	6	0	0	95²	89	9	53	39	13.4	3.67	102	.253	.351	5	.161	-1	1	1	0	0.1
1946	Cin-N	0	0	—	2	0	0	0	0	1	2	0	2	1	36.0	27.00	12	.400	.571	0	—	-0	-3	-3	0	0.0
Total	2	4	5	.444	18	12	6	0	0	96²	91	9	55	40	13.6	3.91	96	.255	.354	5	.161	-1	1	1	0	0.1

● DAN DAUB
Daub, Daniel William "Mickey" b: 1/12/1868, Middletown, Ohio d: 3/25/51, Bradenton, Fla. BR/TR, 5'10", 160 lbs. Deb: 8/31/1892

YEAR	TM/L	W	L	PCT	G	GS	CG	SH	SV	IP	H	HR	BB	SO	RAT	ERA	ERA+	OAV	OOB	BH	AVG	PB	PR	/A	PD	TPI
1892	Cin-N	1	2	.333	4	3	2	0	0	25	23	0	13	7	13.7	2.88	113	.235	.336	0	.000	-1	1	1	0	0.0
1893	Bro-N	6	6	.500	12	12	12	0	0	103	104	3	61	25	14.9	3.84	115	.254	.358	8	.190	-2	9	7	3	0.7
1894	Bro-N	10	12	.455	34	27	15	0	0	224	291	6	91	45	16.1	6.11	81	.311	.383	18	.189	-6	-19	-29	-1	-2.4
1895	Bro-N	10	10	.500	25	21	16	0	0	184²	212	4	51	36	13.4	4.29	102	.284	.339	14	.197	-2	10	2	2	0.2
1896	Bro-N	12	11	.522	32	24	18	0	0	225	255	6	63	53	13.0	3.60	115	.283	.335	19	.226	2	19	13	4	1.5
1897	Bro-N	6	11	.353	19	16	11	0	0	137²	180	8	48	19	15.6	6.08	67	.313	.376	11	.224	-2	-27	-30	-2	-2.5
Total	6	45	52	.464	126	103	74	0	0	899¹	1065	26	327	185	14.5	4.75	93	.291	.357	70	.201	-6	-7	-36	8	-2.5

● HOOKS DAUSS
Dauss, George August (b: George August Daus)
b: 9/22/1889, Indianapolis, Ind d: 7/27/63, St.Louis, Mo. BR/TR, 5'10.5", 168 lbs. Deb: 9/28/12

YEAR	TM/L	W	L	PCT	G	GS	CG	SH	SV	IP	H	HR	BB	SO	RAT	ERA	ERA+	OAV	OOB	BH	AVG	PB	PR	/A	PD	TPI
1912	Det-A	1	1	.500	2	2	2	0	0	17	11	0	9	7	12.2	3.18	103	.186	.324	1	.250	1	0	1	0	0.2
1913	Det-A	13	12	.520	33	29	22	2	1	225	188	3	82	107	11.3	2.48	118	.228	.308	14	.177	3	11	11	-1	1.5
1914	Det-A	18	15	.545	45	35	22	3	4	302	286	3	87	150	11.7	2.86	98	.257	.321	21	.216	6	-4	-2	1	0.4
1915	Det-A	24	13	.649	46	35	27	1	2	309²	261	11	115	132	11.2	2.50	121	.235	.313	15	.146	0	15	18	9	3.2
1916	Det-A	19	12	.613	39	29	18	4	1	238²	220	9	90	95	12.3	3.21	89	.257	.339	16	.222	8	-10	-9	-2	-0.1
1917	Det-A	17	14	.548	37	31	22	6	2	270²	243	3	87	102	11.2	2.43	109	.245	.311	11	.126	-1	7	7	4	1.1
1918	Det-A	12	16	.429	33	24	21	1	3	249²	243	3	58	73	11.4	2.99	89	.263	.313	14	.182	3	-6	-9	2	-0.5
1919	Det-A	21	9	.700	34	32	22	2	0	256¹	262	6	63	73	11.6	3.55	90	.267	.315	14	.144	-3	-9	-10	6	-0.8
1920	Det-A	13	21	.382	38	32	18	0	0	270¹	308	11	84	83	13.3	3.56	105	.289	.345	14	.169	1	7	5	8	1.5
1921	Det-A	10	15	.400	32	28	16	1	0	233	275	11	81	68	14.3	4.33	99	.297	.362	23	.261	2	-1	-1	5	0.6
1922	Det-A	13	13	.500	39	25	12	1	4	218²	251	7	59	78	13.0	4.20	92	.289	.339	15	.208	3	-4	-8	1	0.1
1923	Det-A	21	13	.618	50	39	22	4	3	316	331	10	78	105	11.8	3.62	107	.272	.319	24	.231	5	13	9	2	1.4
1924	Det-A	12	11	.522	40	10	5	0	6	131¹	155	6	40	44	13.4	4.50	90	.302	.354	12	.132	-2	-5	-7	-0	-1.2
1925	Det-A	16	11	.593	35	30	16	1	1	228	238	7	85	58	12.9	3.16	136	.272	.339	15	.185	2	31	29	-1	3.8
1926	Det-A	12	6	.667	35	5	0	0	9	124¹	135	6	49	27	13.3	4.20	97	.287	.354	10	.238	4	-2	-2	-0	0.1
Total	15	222	182	.550	538	388	245	22	40	3390²	3407	87	1067	1201	12.2	3.30	103	.266	.329	212	.189	32	44	33	38	9.9

● VIC DAVALILLO
Davalillo, Victor Jose (Romero) b: 7/31/36, Cabimas, Venez. BL/TL, 5'7", 155 lbs. Deb: 4/9/63 F♦

YEAR	TM/L	W	L	PCT	G	GS	CG	SH	SV	IP	H	HR	BB	SO	RAT	ERA	ERA+	OAV	OOB	BH	AVG	PB	PR	/A	PD	TPI
1969	StL-N	0	0	—	2	0	0	0	0	2	2	0	2	0	—	∞		1.000	1.000	26	.265	-0	-1	-1	0	-0.1

● CLAUDE DAVENPORT
Davenport, Claude Edwin "Big Dave"
b: 5/28/1898, Runge, Tex. d: 6/13/76, Corpus Christi, Tex. BR/TR, 6'6", 193 lbs. Deb: 10/2/20 F

YEAR	TM/L	W	L	PCT	G	GS	CG	SH	SV	IP	H	HR	BB	SO	RAT	ERA	ERA+	OAV	OOB	BH	AVG	PB	PR	/A	PD	TPI
1920	NY-N	0	0	—	1	0	0	0	0	2	2	1	1	0	13.5	4.50	67	.250	.333	0	.000	-0	-0	-0	-0	-0.1

● DAVE DAVENPORT
Davenport, David W. b: 2/20/1890, DeRidder, La. d: 10/16/54, ElDorado, Ark. BR/TR, 6'6", 220 lbs. Deb: 4/17/14 F

YEAR	TM/L	W	L	PCT	G	GS	CG	SH	SV	IP	H	HR	BB	SO	RAT	ERA	ERA+	OAV	OOB	BH	AVG	PB	PR	/A	PD	TPI
1914	Cin-N	2	2	.500	10	6	3	1	2	54	38	1	30	22	11.8	2.50	117	.202	.321	2	.111	-1	2	3	-0	0.1
	StL-F	8	13	.381	33	26	13	2	4	215²	204	3	80	142	12.1	3.46	98	.251	.324	6	.088	-6	-14	-10	1	-1.4

YEAR	TM/L	W	L	PCT	G	GS	CG	SH	SV	IP	H	HR	BB	SO	RAT	ERA	ERA+	OAV	OOB	BH	AVG	PB	PR	/A	PD	TPI
1915	StL-F	22	18	.550	**55**	46	**30**	**10**	1	392²	300	5	96	**229**	9.2	2.20	131	**.215**	.268	12	.092	-11	23	**30**	-8	0.9
1916	StL-A	12	11	.522	**59**	31	13	1	2	290²	267	4	100	129	11.6	2.85	96	.256	.326	10	.137	3	-1	-3	-3	-0.3
1917	StL-A	17	17	.500	47	39	20	2	2	280²	273	5	105	100	12.4	3.08	84	.260	.331	9	.098	-6	-13	-15	-1	-2.5
1918	StL-A	10	11	.476	31	22	12	2	1	180	182	0	69	60	12.9	3.25	84	.273	.347	7	.135	1	-9	-10	2	-0.9
1919	StL-A	2	11	.154	24	16	5	0	0	123¹	135	4	41	37	13.0	3.94	84	.280	.339	3	.077	-4	-10	-9	1	-1.1
Total	6	73	83	.468	259	186	96	18	12	1537	1399	22	521	719	11.5	2.93	97	.248	.316	49	.104	-24	-22	-15	-9	-5.2

● LUM DAVENPORT   Davenport, Joubert Lum   b: 6/27/1900, Tucson, Ariz.   d: 4/21/61, Dallas, Tex.   BL/TL, 6'1", 165 lbs.   Deb: 5/2/21

YEAR	TM/L	W	L	PCT	G	GS	CG	SH	SV	IP	H	HR	BB	SO	RAT	ERA	ERA+	OAV	OOB	BH	AVG	PB	PR	/A	PD	TPI
1921	Chi-A	0	3	.000	13	2	0	0	0	35¹	41	1	32	9	18.8	6.88	62	.318	.457	7	.412	2	-10	-10	-0	-0.6
1922	Chi-A	1	1	.500	9	1	0	0	0	16²	14	2	13	9	14.6	10.80	38	.233	.370	0	.000	-0	-13	-12	0	-1.2
1923	Chi-A	0	0	—	2	0	0	0	0	4¹	7	0	4	1	22.8	6.23	64	.438	.550	1	1.000	0	-1	-1	0	0.0
1924	Chi-A	0	0	—	1	0	0	0	0	2	1	0	2	1	13.5	0.00	—	.125	.300	0	—	0	1	1	0	0.0
Total	4	1	4	.200	25	3	0	0	0	58¹	63	3	51	20	17.7	7.71	54	.296	.434	8	.381	2	-23	-23	-0	-1.8

● MIKE DAVEY   Davey, Michael Gerard   b: 6/2/52, Spokane, Wash.   BR/TL, 6'2", 190 lbs.   Deb: 8/13/77

YEAR	TM/L	W	L	PCT	G	GS	CG	SH	SV	IP	H	HR	BB	SO	RAT	ERA	ERA+	OAV	OOB	BH	AVG	PB	PR	/A	PD	TPI
1977	Atl-N	0	0	—	16	0	0	0	2	16	19	1	9	7	15.8	5.06	88	.302	.389	0	.000	-0	-2	-1	-0	-0.1
1978	Atl-N	0	0	—	3	0	0	0	0	2²	1	0	1	0	6.8	0.00	—	.125	.222	0	—	0	1	1	0	0.0
Total	2	0	0	—	19	0	0	0	2	18²	20	1	10	7	14.5	4.34	101	.282	.370	0	.000	-0	-1	0	-0	-0.1

● RAY DAVIAULT   Daviault, Raymond Joseph Robert   b: 5/27/34, Montreal, Que., Can   BR/TR, 6'1", 170 lbs.   Deb: 4/13/62

YEAR	TM/L	W	L	PCT	G	GS	CG	SH	SV	IP	H	HR	BB	SO	RAT	ERA	ERA+	OAV	OOB	BH	AVG	PB	PR	/A	PD	TPI
1962	NY-N	1	5	.167	36	3	0	0	0	81	92	14	48	51	16.0	6.22	67	.288	.388	1	.067	-1	-21	-18	-1	-1.4

● BOB DAVIDSON   Davidson, Robert Banks   b: 1/6/63, Bad Kurznach, W.Ger.   BR/TR, 6', 185 lbs.   Deb: 7/15/89

YEAR	TM/L	W	L	PCT	G	GS	CG	SH	SV	IP	H	HR	BB	SO	RAT	ERA	ERA+	OAV	OOB	BH	AVG	PB	PR	/A	PD	TPI
1989	NY-A	0	0	—	1	0	0	0	0	1	1	1	1	0	18.00	18.00	21	.250	.400	0	—	0	-2	-2	0	0.0

● TED DAVIDSON   Davidson, Thomas Eugene   b: 10/4/39, Las Vegas, Nev.   BR/TL, 6', 192 lbs.   Deb: 7/24/65

YEAR	TM/L	W	L	PCT	G	GS	CG	SH	SV	IP	H	HR	BB	SO	RAT	ERA	ERA+	OAV	OOB	BH	AVG	PB	PR	/A	PD	TPI
1965	Cin-N	4	3	.571	24	1	0	0	1	68²	57	5	17	54	10.0	2.23	168	.233	.288	0	.000	-2	10	12	1	1.0
1966	Cin-N	5	4	.556	54	0	0	0	4	85¹	82	11	23	54	11.2	3.90	100	.253	.305	0	.000	-1	-3	-0	-0	-0.2
1967	Cin-N	1	0	1.000	9	0	0	0	0	13	13	0	3	6	11.1	4.15	90	.250	.291	0	—	0	-1	-1	0	0.0
1968	Cin-N	1	0	1.000	23	0	0	0	0	21²	27	3	7	7	14.1	6.23	51	.307	.358	0	.000	-0	-8	-7	0	-0.4
	Atl-N	0	0	—	4	0	0	0	0	6²	10	2	4	3	18.9	6.75	44	.345	.424	0	—	0	-3	-3	0	0.0
	Yr	1	0	1.000	27	0	0	0	0	28	37	5	11	10	15.2	6.35	49	.316	.375	0	.000	0	-11	-10	0	-0.4
Total	4	11	7	.611	114	1	0	0	5	195¹	189	21	54	124	11.3	3.69	101	.256	.309	0	.000	-3	-5	1	1	0.4

● JERRY DAVIE   Davie, Gerald Lee   b: 2/10/33, Detroit, Mich.   BR/TR, 6', 180 lbs.   Deb: 4/14/59

YEAR	TM/L	W	L	PCT	G	GS	CG	SH	SV	IP	H	HR	BB	SO	RAT	ERA	ERA+	OAV	OOB	BH	AVG	PB	PR	/A	PD	TPI
1959	Det-A	2	2	.500	11	5	1	0	0	36²	40	8	17	20	15.0	4.17	97	.265	.355	4	.400	2	-1	-0	1	0.2

● GEORGE DAVIES   Davies, George Washington   b: 2/22/1868, Portage, Wis.   d: 9/22/06, Waterloo, Wis.   180 lbs.   Deb: 8/18/1891

YEAR	TM/L	W	L	PCT	G	GS	CG	SH	SV	IP	H	HR	BB	SO	RAT	ERA	ERA+	OAV	OOB	BH	AVG	PB	PR	/A	PD	TPI
1891	Mil-a	7	5	.583	12	12	12	1	0	102	94	2	35	61	11.6	2.65	166	.237	.303	9	.243	1	12	20	-1	1.9
1892	Cle-N	10	16	.385	26	26	23	0	0	215²	201	4	69	95	11.5	2.59	131	.237	.299	12	.138	-5	17	19	3	1.7
1893	Cle-N	0	2	.000	3	3	1	0	0	15	28	1	0	3	22.8	11.40	36	.389	.463	2	.333	-0	-11	-11	0	-0.9
	NY-N	1	1	.500	5	1	0	0	0	36¹	41	1	13	7	13.4	6.19	75	.275	.333	4	.333	2	-6	-6	0	-0.1
	Yr	1	3	.250	8	4	2	0	0	51¹	69	2	23	10	16.1	7.71	61	.312	.377	6	.333	2	-17	-17	-1	-0.9
Total	3	18	24	.429	46	42	37	1	0	369	364	8	127	166	12.2	3.32	116	.248	.312	27	.190	-3	12	22	2	2.7

● CHICK DAVIES   Davies, Lloyd Garrison   b: 3/6/1892, Peabody, Mass.   d: 9/5/73, Middletown, Conn.   BL/TL, 5'8", 145 lbs.   Deb: 7/11/14 ◆

YEAR	TM/L	W	L	PCT	G	GS	CG	SH	SV	IP	H	HR	BB	SO	RAT	ERA	ERA+	OAV	OOB	BH	AVG	PB	PR	/A	PD	TPI
1914	Phi-A	1	0	1.000	9	1	0	0	0	9	8	0	3	4	11.0	1.00	261	.258	.324	11	.239	0	2	2	0	0.3
1915	Phi-A	1	2	.333	4	1	0	0	0	15¹	20	1	0	12	19.4	8.80	33	.339	.458	24	.182	0	-10	-10	1	-1.5
1925	NY-N	0	0	—	2	1	0	0	0	7¹	13	0	4	5	20.9	6.14	66	.361	.425	0	.000	-0	-2	-2	0	0.0
1926	NY-N	2	4	.333	38	1	0	0	**6**	89	96	3	35	27	13.2	3.94	95	.277	.344	4	.222	1	-1	-2	1	0.0
Total	4	4	6	.400	45	5	1	0	6	120²	137	3	54	38	14.3	4.48	80	.290	.364	39	.193	-3	-11	-12	2	-1.2

● CHILI DAVIS   Davis, Charles Theodore   b: 1/17/60, Kingston, Jamaica   BB/TR, 6'3", 195 lbs.   Deb: 4/10/81 ◆

YEAR	TM/L	W	L	PCT	G	GS	CG	SH	SV	IP	H	HR	BB	SO	RAT	ERA	ERA+	OAV	OOB	BH	AVG	PB	PR	/A	PD	TPI
1993	Cal-A	0	0	—	1	0	0	0	0	2	0	0	0	0	4.5	0.00	—	.000	.143	139	.243	1	1	1	-0	0.0

● CURT DAVIS   Davis, Curtis Benton "Coonskin"   b: 9/7/03, Greenfield, Mo.   d: 10/13/65, Covina, Cal.   BR/TR, 6'2", 185 lbs.   Deb: 4/21/34

YEAR	TM/L	W	L	PCT	G	GS	CG	SH	SV	IP	H	HR	BB	SO	RAT	ERA	ERA+	OAV	OOB	BH	AVG	PB	PR	/A	PD	TPI
1934	Phi-N	19	17	.528	**51**	31	18	3	5	274¹	283	14	60	99	11.5	2.95	160	.269	.313	20	.211	-2	34	54	9	**7.8**
1935	Phi-N	16	14	.533	44	27	19	3	2	231	264	14	47	74	12.4	3.66	124	.285	.324	13	.173	-1	9	22	7	2.8
1936	Phi-N	2	4	.333	10	8	3	0	0	60¹	71	6	19	18	13.6	4.62	98	.291	.345	4	.154	-1	-4	-1	0	-0.2
	Chi-N★	11	9	.550	24	20	10	0	1	153	146	11	31	52	10.5	3.00	133	.251	.290	8	.151	-2	17	17	3	2.1
	Yr	13	13	.500	34	28	13	0	1	213¹	217	17	50	70	11.3	3.46	120	.263	.306	12	.152	-3	13	16	3	1.9
1937	Chi-N	10	5	.667	28	14	8	0	0	123²	138	7	30	32	12.6	4.08	98	.286	.334	10	.300	4	-2	-1	2	0.4
1938	StL-N	12	8	.600	40	21	8	2	2	173¹	187	9	27	36	11.2	3.63	109	.272	.301	13	.228	2	1	8	4	1.1
1939	StL-N☆	22	16	.579	49	31	13	3	7	248	279	18	48	70	12.0	3.63	113	.280	.315	40	.381	12	8	13	1	3.3
1940	StL-N	0	4	.000	14	7	0	0	1	54	73	4	19	12	15.5	5.17	77	.327	.383	0	.000	-2	-8	-7	1	-0.6
	Bro-N	8	7	.533	22	18	9	0	2	137	135	13	19	46	10.2	3.81	105	.256	.283	6	.128	-1	3	3	1	0.3
	Yr	8	11	.421	36	25	9	0	3	191	208	17	38	58	11.6	4.19	95	.277	.312	6	.091	-3	-7	-4	2	-0.3
1941	*Bro-N	13	7	.650	28	16	10	5	2	154¹	141	6	27	50	9.9	2.97	123	.244	.280	11	.186	2	11	12	4	2.1
1942	Bro-N	15	6	.714	32	26	13	5	2	206	179	10	51	60	10.4	2.36	138	.233	.287	12	.176	-0	22	21	3	2.5
1943	Bro-N	10	13	.435	31	21	8	2	3	164¹	182	8	39	47	12.2	3.78	89	.281	.324	9	.164	-1	-7	-8	2	-0.9
1944	Bro-N	10	11	.476	31	23	14	1	4	194	207	12	39	49	11.6	3.34	106	.270	.310	10	.159	-1	6	5	2	0.5
1945	Bro-N	10	10	.500	24	18	10	0	0	149²	171	9	21	39	11.7	3.25	116	.280	.308	7	.137	-1	6	8	0	1.0
1946	Bro-N	0	0	—	1	0	0	0	0	2	3	1	2	0	27.0	13.50	25	.375	.545	0	—	0	-2	-2	0	0.0
Total	13	158	131	.547	429	281	141	24	33	2325	2459	142	479	684	11.6	3.42	116	.270	.310	165	.203	7	96	139	31	22.1

● DIXIE DAVIS   Davis, Frank Talmadge   b: 10/12/1890, Wilsons Mills, N.C.   d: 2/4/44, Raleigh, N.C.   BR/TR, 5'11", 155 lbs.   Deb: 7/12/12

YEAR	TM/L	W	L	PCT	G	GS	CG	SH	SV	IP	H	HR	BB	SO	RAT	ERA	ERA+	OAV	OOB	BH	AVG	PB	PR	/A	PD	TPI
1912	Cin-N	0	1	.000	7	0	0	0	0	26²	25	0	16	12	14.2	2.70	124	.258	.368	2	.200	-0	2	2	-1	0.0
1915	Chi-A	0	0	—	2	0	0	0	0	3	2	0	2	2	15.0	0.00	—	.250	.455	0	—	0	1	1	0	0.0
1918	Phi-N	0	2	.000	17	2	1	0	0	47	43	1	30	18	14.0	3.06	98	.247	.358	0	.000	-0	-2	-0	-1	-0.2
1920	StL-A	18	12	.600	38	31	22	0	0	269¹	250	10	149	85	13.6	3.17	123	.256	.359	25	.266	3	19	22	-4	0.3
1921	StL-A	16	16	.500	40	36	20	2	0	265¹	279	12	123	100	14.1	4.44	101	.281	.366	20	.211	-3	-5	1	-1	-0.3
1922	StL-A	11	6	.647	25	25	7	2	0	174¹	162	10	87	65	13.3	4.08	102	**.250**	.345	8	.136	-3	-1	-1	-0	-0.3
1923	StL-A	4	6	.400	19	17	5	1	0	109¹	106	4	63	36	14.3	3.62	115	.259	.365	10	.250	0	4	7	-2	0.3
1924	StL-A	11	13	.458	29	24	11	5	0	160¹	159	9	72	45	13.3	4.10	110	.263	.347	7	.152	-2	7	7	-1	0.7
1925	StL-A	12	7	.632	35	22	9	0	0	180¹	192	10	106	58	15.2	4.59	102	.279	.380	11	.172	-4	-4	-1	-0	-0.1
1926	StL-A	3	8	.273	27	7	2	0	2	83	93	7	40	39	14.5	4.66	92	.282	.372	4	.167	-0	-3	-0	-0	-0.5
Total	10	75	71	.514	239	164	77	10	2	1318²	1311	63	688	460	14.0	3.97	107	.267	.362	87	.197	-10	12	39	-10	1.6

● GEORGE DAVIS   Davis, George Allen "Iron"   b: 3/9/1890, Lancaster, N.Y.   d: 6/4/61, Buffalo, N.Y.   BB/TR, 5'10.5", 175 lbs.   Deb: 7/16/12

YEAR	TM/L	W	L	PCT	G	GS	CG	SH	SV	IP	H	HR	BB	SO	RAT	ERA	ERA+	OAV	OOB	BH	AVG	PB	PR	/A	PD	TPI
1912	NY-A	1	4	.200	10	7	3	0	0	54	61	5	28	22	15.3	6.50	55	.293	.385	2	.111	-1	-19	-17	-2	-1.6
1913	Bos-N	0	0	—	2	0	0	0	0	8	7	1	5	3	13.5	4.50	73	.241	.353	0	.000	-0	-1	-0	-1	-0.1
1914	Bos-N	3	3	.500	9	4	1	0	0	55²	42	1	26	26	11.5	3.40	81	.215	.317	3	.167	-0	-4	-4	-2	-0.6
1915	Bos-N	3	3	.500	15	9	4	1	0	73¹	85	2	19	26	13.3	3.80	68	.304	.356	6	.261	1	-9	-10	-3	-0.6
Total	4	7	10	.412	36	20	8	1	0	191	195	9	78	77	13.3	4.48	66	.274	.354	11	.180	-0	-33	-33	-3	-2.9

● STORM DAVIS   Davis, George Earl   b: 12/26/61, Dallas, Tex.   BR/TR, 6'4", 207 lbs.   Deb: 4/29/82

YEAR	TM/L	W	L	PCT	G	GS	CG	SH	SV	IP	H	HR	BB	SO	RAT	ERA	ERA+	OAV	OOB	BH	AVG	PB	PR	/A	PD	TPI
1982	Bal-A	8	4	.667	29	8	1	0	0	100²	96	8	28	67	11.1	3.49	116	.257	.308	0	—	0	7	6	-0	0.7
1983	*Bal-A	13	7	.650	34	29	6	1	0	200¹	180	14	64	125	11.1	3.59	110	.238	.299	0	—	0	10	8	-2	0.7
1984	Bal-A	14	9	.609	35	31	10	2	0	225	205	7	71	105	11.2	3.12	124	.247	.310	0	—	0	22	19	-3	1.7
1985	Bal-A	10	8	.556	31	28	6	1	0	175	172	11	70	93	12.5	4.53	89	.256	.327	0	—	0	-7	-10	-1	-0.7
1986	Bal-A	9	12	.429	25	25	2	0	0	154	166	16	49	96	12.6	3.62	114	.275	.330	0	—	0	9	9	2	1.3
1987	SD-N	2	7	.222	21	10	0	0	0	62²	70	5	36	37	15.5	6.18	64	.280	.375	1	.063	-1	-15	-15	0	-2.0

YEAR	TM/L	W	L	PCT	G	GS	CG	SH	SV	IP	H	HR	BB	SO	RAT	ERA	ERA+	OAV	OOB	BH	AVG	PB	PR	/A	PD	TPI
	Oak-A	1	1	.500	5	5	0	0	0	30¹	28	3	11	28	11.6	3.26	126	.241	.307	0	—	0	4	3	-1	0.7
1988	*Oak-A	16	7	.696	33	33	1	0	0	201²	211	16	91	127	13.5	3.70	102	.274	.352	0	—	0	6	2	-2	0.4
1989	*Oak-A	19	7	.731	31	31	1	0	0	169¹	187	19	68	91	13.7	4.36	84	.288	.358	0	—	0	-9	-13	-2	-1.7
1990	KC-A	7	10	.412	21	20	0	0	0	112	129	9	35	62	13.2	4.74	81	.281	.332	0	—	0	-10	-11	-1	-1.5
1991	KC-A	3	9	.250	51	9	1	1	2	114¹	140	11	46	53	14.7	4.96	83	.306	.370	0	—	0	-11	-11	-1	-1.2
1992	Bal-A	7	3	.700	48	2	0	0	4	89¹	79	5	36	53	11.8	3.43	117	.244	.323	0	—	0	5	6	1	0.7
1993	Oak-A	2	6	.250	19	8	0	0	0	62²	68	5	33	37	14.8	6.18	66	.276	.367	0	—	0	-13	-16	-0	-1.5
	Det-A	0	2	.000	24	0	0	0	4	35¹	25	4	15	36	10.4	3.06	140	.198	.289	0	—	0	5	5	-0	0.3
	Yr	2	8	.200	43	8	0	0	4	98	93	9	48	73	13.0	5.05	82	.247	.334	0	—	0	-8	-10	0	-1.2
1994	Det-A	2	4	.333	35	0	0	0	0	48	36	3	34	38	13.1	3.56	136	.207	.337	0	—	0	7	7	1	0.8
Total	13	113	96	.541	442	239	30	5	11	1780²	1792	136	687	1048	12.6	4.02	99	.263	.332	1	.063	-1	10	-11	-8	-1.7

● **GEORGE DAVIS**   Davis, George Stacey   b: 8/23/1870, Cohoes, N.Y.   d: 10/17/40, Philadelphia, Pa.   BB/TR, 5'9", 180 lbs.   Deb: 4/19/1890   M♦

YEAR	TM/L	W	L	PCT	G	GS	CG	SH	SV	IP	H	HR	BB	SO	RAT	ERA	ERA+	OAV	OOB	BH	AVG	PB	PR	/A	PD	TPI
1891	Cle-N	0	1	.000	3	0	0	0	1	4	8	0	3	4	24.8	15.75	22	.400	.478	165	.289	1	-6	-5	-0	-1.1

● **JIM DAVIS**   Davis, James Bennett   b: 9/15/24, Red Bluff, Cal.   d: 12/6/95, San Mateo, Cal.   BB/TL, 6', 180 lbs.   Deb: 4/18/54

YEAR	TM/L	W	L	PCT	G	GS	CG	SH	SV	IP	H	HR	BB	SO	RAT	ERA	ERA+	OAV	OOB	BH	AVG	PB	PR	/A	PD	TPI
1954	Chi-N	11	7	.611	46	12	2	0	4	127²	114	12	51	58	11.8	3.52	119	.247	.326	2	.063	-1	8	10	1	1.3
1955	Chi-N	7	11	.389	42	16	0	0	3	133²	122	16	58	62	12.3	4.44	92	.246	.327	1	.027	-4	-6	-5	-1	-1.1
1956	Chi-N	5	7	.417	46	11	2	1	2	120¹	116	11	59	66	13.5	3.66	103	.256	.349	5	.179	-0	1	1	1	0.2
1957	StL-N	0	1	.000	10	0	0	0	0	13²	18	1	6	11	15.8	5.27	75	.340	.407	0	.000	-0	-2	-2	0	-0.2
	NY-N	1	0	1.000	10	0	0	0	0	11	13	2	5	6	14.7	6.55	60	.283	.353	1	1.000	0	-3	-3	0	-0.2
	Yr	1	1	.500	20	0	0	0	1	24²	31	3	11	11	15.3	5.84	68	.310	.378	1	.500	-0	-5	-5	0	-0.4
Total	4	24	26	.480	154	39	4	1	10	406¹	383	42	179	197	12.7	4.01	100	.253	.337	9	.091	-5	-2	-0	1	-0.0

● **JOEL DAVIS**   Davis, Joel Clark   b: 1/30/65, Jacksonville, Fla.   BL/TR, 6'5", 205 lbs.   Deb: 8/11/85

YEAR	TM/L	W	L	PCT	G	GS	CG	SH	SV	IP	H	HR	BB	SO	RAT	ERA	ERA+	OAV	OOB	BH	AVG	PB	PR	/A	PD	TPI
1985	Chi-A	3	3	.500	12	11	1	0	0	71¹	71	6	26	37	12.4	4.16	104	.256	.322	0	—	0	-0	1	-2	-0.4
1986	Chi-A	4	5	.444	19	19	1	0	0	105¹	115	9	51	54	14.3	4.70	92	.280	.361	0	—	0	-6	-5	-1	-0.5
1987	Chi-A	1	5	.167	13	9	1	0	0	55	56	7	29	25	13.9	5.73	80	.264	.353	0	—	0	-8	-7	-1	-0.9
1988	Chi-A	0	1	.000	5	2	0	0	0	16	21	4	5	10	14.6	6.75	59	.328	.377	0	—	0	-5	-5	-0	-0.3
Total	4	8	14	.364	49	41	3	0	0	247²	263	26	111	126	13.7	4.91	89	.273	.349	0	—	0	-19	-15	-3	-2.1

● **DAISY DAVIS**   Davis, John Henry Albert   b: 11/28/1858, Boston, Mass.   d: 11/5/02, Lynn, Mass.   TR,   Deb: 5/6/1884

YEAR	TM/L	W	L	PCT	G	GS	CG	SH	SV	IP	H	HR	BB	SO	RAT	ERA	ERA+	OAV	OOB	BH	AVG	PB	PR	/A	PD	TPI
1884	StL-a	10	12	.455	25	24	20	1	0	198¹	196	1	35	143	11.1	2.90	112	.249	.293	15	.172	-2	8	8	-1	0.4
	Bos-N	1	3	.250	4	4	3	0	0	31	50	0	8	13	16.8	7.84	37	.355	.389	1	.000	-3	-17	-17	0	-1.6
1885	Bos-N	5	6	.455	11	11	10	1	0	94¹	110	2	28	30	13.2	4.29	63	.280	.328	7	.189	-1	-15	-17	-1	-1.7
Total	2	16	21	.432	40	39	33	2	0	323²	356	3	71	186	12.3	3.78	81	.269	.313	22	.157	-5	-24	-26	-2	-2.9

● **JOHN DAVIS**   Davis, John Kirk   b: 1/5/63, Chicago, Ill.   BR/TR, 6'7", 215 lbs.   Deb: 7/24/87

YEAR	TM/L	W	L	PCT	G	GS	CG	SH	SV	IP	H	HR	BB	SO	RAT	ERA	ERA+	OAV	OOB	BH	AVG	PB	PR	/A	PD	TPI
1987	KC-A	5	2	.714	27	0	0	0	2	43²	29	0	26	24	11.7	2.27	201	.195	.322	0	—	0	11	11	0	1.5
1988	Chi-A	2	5	.286	34	1	0	0	1	63²	77	5	50	37	18.5	6.64	60	.297	.419	0	—	0	-19	-19	-0	-1.9
1989	Chi-A	0	1	.000	4	0	0	0	1	6	5	2	2	5	10.5	4.50	85	.217	.280	0	—	0	-0	-0	0	0.1
1990	SD-N	0	1	.000	6	0	0	0	0	9¹	9	1	4	7	12.5	5.79	66	.257	.333	0	.000	-0	-2	-2	-0	-0.2
Total	4	7	9	.438	71	1	0	0	4	122²	120	8	82	73	15.3	4.92	85	.258	.375	0	.000	-0	-11	-10	-0	-0.5

● **BUD DAVIS**   Davis, John Wilbur "Country"   b: 12/7/1896, Merry Point, Va.   d: 5/26/67, Williamsburg, Va.   BL/TR, 6', 207 lbs.   Deb: 4/19/15

YEAR	TM/L	W	L	PCT	G	GS	CG	SH	SV	IP	H	HR	BB	SO	RAT	ERA	ERA+	OAV	OOB	BH	AVG	PB	PR	/A	PD	TPI
1915	Phi-A	0	2	.000	18	2	2	0	0	66²	65	1	59	18	17.6	4.05	72	.273	.429	8	.308	2	-8	-8	-1	0.0

● **MARK DAVIS**   Davis, Mark William   b: 10/19/60, Livermore, Cal.   BL/TL, 6'4", 205 lbs.   Deb: 9/12/80

YEAR	TM/L	W	L	PCT	G	GS	CG	SH	SV	IP	H	HR	BB	SO	RAT	ERA	ERA+	OAV	OOB	BH	AVG	PB	PR	/A	PD	TPI
1980	Phi-N	0	0	—	2	1	0	0	0	7	4	0	5	5	11.6	2.57	147	.160	.300	1	.500	0	1	1	-0	0.1
1981	Phi-N	1	4	.200	9	9	0	0	0	43	49	7	24	29	15.3	7.74	47	.299	.388	1	.091	-0	-20	-20	-0	-2.0
1983	SF-N	6	4	.600	20	20	2	2	0	111	93	14	50	83	11.8	3.49	101	.227	.315	4	.133	-1	2	1	-1	0.4
1984	SF-N	5	17	.227	46	27	1	0	0	174²	201	25	54	124	13.4	5.36	65	.293	.349	6	.130	-0	-34	-36	-2	-4.2
1985	SF-N	5	12	.294	77	1	0	0	7	114¹	89	13	41	131	10.5	3.54	97	.219	.295	3	.250	1	-1	-1	-1	-0.2
1986	SF-N	5	7	.417	67	2	0	0	4	84¹	63	6	34	90	10.5	2.99	118	.212	.295	1	.125	0	7	5	-0	0.7
1987	SF-N	4	5	.444	20	11	1	0	0	70²	72	9	28	51	13.2	4.71	82	.273	.351	5	.217	-1	-5	-7	-1	-0.7
	SD-N	5	3	.625	43	0	0	0	2	62¹	51	5	31	47	12.1	3.18	124	.224	.322	2	.286	0	6	5	0	0.7
	Yr	9	8	.529	63	11	1	0	2	133	123	14	59	98	12.5	3.99	98	.247	.329	7	.233	2	1	-1	-0	0.0
1988	SD-N★	5	10	.333	62	0	0	0	28	98¹	70	2	42	102	10.3	2.01	169	.199	.284	2	.200	1	16	15	2	3.6
1989	SD-N★	4	3	.571	70	0	0	0	**44**	92²	66	6	31	92	9.6	1.85	189	.200	.273	0	.000	-1	17	17	-1	2.6
1990	KC-A	2	7	.222	53	3	0	0	6	68²	71	7	52	73	16.6	5.11	75	.259	.385	0	—	0	-9	-10	-1	-1.3
1991	KC-A	6	3	.667	29	5	0	0	1	62²	55	6	39	47	13.6	4.45	93	.240	.353	0	—	0	-2	-2	-0	-0.3
1992	KC-A	1	3	.250	13	6	0	0	0	36¹	42	6	28	19	17.3	7.18	56	.294	.409	0	—	0	-13	-13	-0	-1.4
	Atl-N	1	0	1.000	14	0	0	0	0	16²	22	3	13	15	19.4	7.02	52	.314	.429	0	.000	-0	-7	-6	-0	-0.4
1993	Phi-N	1	2	.333	25	0	0	0	0	31¹	35	4	24	28	17.2	5.17	77	.273	.392	1	.333	-0	-4	-4	-0	-0.4
	SD-N	0	3	.000	35	0	0	0	4	38¹	44	6	20	42	15.0	3.52	117	.295	.379	0	.000	-0	2	3	0	0.2
	Yr	1	5	.167	60	0	0	0	4	69²	79	10	44	70	15.9	4.26	95	.284	.382	1	.250	-0	-2	-2	-0	-0.2
1994	SD-N	0	1	.000	20	0	0	0	0	18	20	4	13	15	18.2	8.82	47	.299	.412	0	—	0	-9	-9	-0	-0.4
Total	14	51	84	.378	605	85	4	2	96	1128²	1047	125	529	993	12.8	4.15	88	.248	.335	26	.156	5	-52	-61	-4	-3.4

● **BOB DAVIS**   Davis, Robert Edward   b: 9/11/33, New York, N.Y.   BR/TR, 6', 170 lbs.   Deb: 7/26/58

YEAR	TM/L	W	L	PCT	G	GS	CG	SH	SV	IP	H	HR	BB	SO	RAT	ERA	ERA+	OAV	OOB	BH	AVG	PB	PR	/A	PD	TPI
1958	KC-A	0	4	.000	8	4	0	0	0	31	45	5	12	22	17.1	7.84	50	.346	.410	1	.167	-0	-14	-14	0	-1.5
1960	KC-A	0	0	—	21	0	0	0	1	32	31	1	22	28	15.2	3.66	109	.263	.383	1	.250	-1	1	1	1	0.1
Total	2	0	4	.000	29	4	0	0	1	63	76	6	34	50	16.1	5.71	69	.306	.396	2	.200	-1	-13	-12	2	-1.4

● **RON DAVIS**   Davis, Ronald Gene   b: 8/6/55, Houston, Tex.   BR/TR, 6'4", 207 lbs.   Deb: 7/29/78

YEAR	TM/L	W	L	PCT	G	GS	CG	SH	SV	IP	H	HR	BB	SO	RAT	ERA	ERA+	OAV	OOB	BH	AVG	PB	PR	/A	PD	TPI
1978	NY-A	0	0	—	5	0	0	0	0	2¹	3	0	3	0	23.1	11.57	31	.333	.500	0	—	0	-2	-2	-0	0.1
1979	NY-A	14	2	.875	44	0	0	0	9	85¹	84	5	28	43	11.9	2.85	143	.262	.323	0	.000	0	13	12	1	2.3
1980	*NY-A	9	3	.750	53	0	0	0	7	131	121	9	32	65	10.9	2.95	133	.246	.299	0	.000	0	16	14	0	1.4
1981	*NY-A★	4	5	.444	43	0	0	0	6	73	47	9	25	83	8.9	2.71	132	.186	.259	0	—	0	8	7	-1	0.9
1982	Min-A	3	9	.250	63	0	0	0	22	106	106	16	44	89	13.1	4.42	96	.261	.339	0	—	0	-4	-2	-0	-0.3
1983	Min-A	5	8	.385	66	0	0	0	30	89	89	6	33	84	12.6	3.34	127	.266	.338	0	—	0	7	9	-2	1.4
1984	Min-A	7	11	.389	64	0	0	0	29	83	79	11	41	74	13.2	4.55	92	.253	.344	0	—	0	-5	-3	-0	-1.1
1985	Min-A	2	6	.250	57	0	0	0	25	64²	55	7	35	72	13.1	3.48	127	.230	.338	0	—	0	5	7	0	0.8
1986	Min-A	4	6	.250	36	0	0	0	2	38²	54	7	29	30	20.5	9.08	46	.340	.451	0	—	0	-21	-21	-0	-3.8
	Chi-N	0	2	.000	17	0	0	0	0	20	31	3	10	16	15.3	7.65	53	.356	.378	0	.000	-0	-9	-8	-1	-0.8
1987	Chi-N	0	0	—	21	0	0	0	0	32¹	43	8	12	31	15.3	5.85	71	.328	.385	0	—	0	-6	-6	-1	-0.1
	LA-N	0	0	—	4	0	0	0	0	4	7	1	6	1	31.5	6.75	59	.412	.583	0	—	0	-2	-2	0	-0.1
	Yr	0	0	—	25	0	0	0	0	36¹	50	9	18	32	17.1	5.94	71	.336	.411	0	—	0	-8	-7	-0	-0.1
1988	SF-N	1	1	.500	25	0	0	0	0	17¹	15	4	9	15	11.4	4.67	70	.234	.310	0	.000	0	-1	-3	-0	-0.3
Total	11	47	53	.470	481	0	0	0	130	746²	735	82	300	597	12.7	4.05	101	.260	.336	0	.000	0	-3	-3	-0	0.5

● **PEACHES DAVIS**   Davis, Roy Thomas   b: 5/31/05, Glen Rose, Tex.   d: 4/28/95, Duncan, Okla.   BL/TR, 6'3.5", 190 lbs.   Deb: 7/11/36

YEAR	TM/L	W	L	PCT	G	GS	CG	SH	SV	IP	H	HR	BB	SO	RAT	ERA	ERA+	OAV	OOB	BH	AVG	PB	PR	/A	PD	TPI
1936	Cin-N	8	8	.500	26	15	5	0	5	125²	139	7	36	32	12.7	3.58	107	.280	.331	7	.163	-1	6	3	0	0.3
1937	Cin-N	11	13	.458	42	24	11	1	3	218	252	5	51	59	12.6	3.59	104	.295	.337	10	.128	-4	8	3	-3	0.3
1938	Cin-N	7	12	.368	29	19	11	1	1	167²	193	9	40	28	12.6	3.97	92	.290	.331	15	.246	1	-3	-6	-3	-0.8
1939	Cin-N	1	0	1.000	20	0	0	0	2	30²	43	5	11	4	16.1	6.46	59	.341	.399	1	.333	-0	-9	-9	-0	-0.2
Total	4	27	33	.450	117	58	27	2	11	542	627	26	138	123	12.8	3.87	96	.293	.337	33	.178	-4	2	-8	-6	-1.1

● **STEVE DAVIS**   Davis, Steven Kennon   b: 8/4/60, San Antonio, Tex.   BL/TL, 6'1", 195 lbs.   Deb: 8/25/85

YEAR	TM/L	W	L	PCT	G	GS	CG	SH	SV	IP	H	HR	BB	SO	RAT	ERA	ERA+	OAV	OOB	BH	AVG	PB	PR	/A	PD	TPI
1985	Tor-A	2	1	.667	10	5	0	0	0	28	23	5	13	22	11.6	3.54	119	.223	.310	0	—	0	2	2	-0	0.0
1986	Tor-A	0	0	—	3	0	0	0	0	3²	8	2	5	5	31.9	17.18	25	.471	.591	0	—	0	-5	-5	-0	-0.2

YEAR TM/L	W	L	PCT	G	GS	CG	SH	SV	IP	H	HR	BB	SO	RAT	ERA	ERA+	OAV	OOB	BH	AVG	PB	PR	/A	PD	TPI
1989 Cle-A	1	1	.500	12	0	0	0	0	25²	34	4	14	12	16.8	8.06	49	.318	.397	0	—	0	-12	-12	-0	-0.9
Total 3	3	2	.600	25	7	0	0	0	57¹	65	9	32	39	15.2	6.44	64	.286	.375	0	—	0	-15	-15	-1	-1.1

● **TIM DAVIS**   Davis, Timothy Howard b: 7/14/70, Marianna, Fla.   BL/TL, 5'11", 165 lbs.   Deb: 4/4/94

1994 Sea-A	2	2	.500	42	1	0	0	0	49¹	57	4	25	28	15.1	4.01	122	.295	.379	0	—	0	4	5	0	0.4
1995 Sea-A	2	1	.667	5	5	0	0	0	24	30	2	18	19	18.0	6.38	74	.306	.414	0	—	0	-4	-4	1	-0.4
1996 Sea-A	2	2	.500	40	0	0	0	2	42²	43	4	17	34	13.1	4.01	123	.259	.335	0	—	0	5	4	0	0.3
Total 3	6	5	.545	87	6	0	0	2	116	130	10	60	81	15.0	4.50	108	.284	.371	0	—	0	5	5	1	0.3

● **WILEY DAVIS**   Davis, Wiley Anderson b: 8/1/1875, Seymour, Tenn. d: 9/22/42, Detroit, Mich.   BR/TR, 5'10", 165 lbs.   Deb: 4/18/1896

1896 Cin-N	1	1	.500	2	0	0	0	0	4¹	8	0	2	1	20.8	8.31	55	.400	.455	0	.000	0	-2	-2	1	-0.5

● **WOODY DAVIS**   Davis, Woodrow Wilson "Babe" b: 4/25/13, Nicholls, Ga.   BL/TR, 6'1", 200 lbs.   Deb: 5/2/38

1938 Det-A	0	0	—	2	0	0	0	0	6	3	0	4	1	10.5	1.50	333	.158	.304	0	.000	-0	2	2	-0	0.0

● **MIKE DAVISON**   Davison, Michael Lynn b: 8/4/45, Galesburg, Ill.   BL/TL, 6'1", 170 lbs.   Deb: 10/1/69

1969 SF-N	0	0	—	1	0	0	0	0	2	2	0	0	2	9.0	4.50	78	.250	.250		—	0	-0	-0	-0	0.0
1970 SF-N	3	5	.375	31	0	0	0	1	36	46	4	22	21	17.0	6.50	61	.324	.415	0	.000	0	-10	-10	1	-1.9
Total 2	3	5	.375	32	0	0	0	1	38	48	4	22	23	16.6	6.39	62	.320	.407	0	.000	0	-10	-10	1	-1.9

● **SCOTT DAVISON**   Davison, Scotty Ray b: 10/16/70, Inglewood, Cal.   BR/TR, 6', 190 lbs.   Deb: 9/4/95

1995 Sea-A	0	0	—	3	0	0	0	0	4¹	7	1	1	3	16.6	6.23	76	.350	.381	0	—	0	-1	-1	0	0.0
1996 Sea-A	0	0	—	5	0	0	0	0	9	11	6	3	9	14.0	9.00	55	.297	.350	0	—	0	-4	-4	0	0.0
Total 2	0	0	—	8	0	0	0	0	13¹	18	7	4	12	14.9	8.10	60	.316	.361	0	—	0	-5	-5	0	0.0

● **BILL DAWLEY**   Dawley, William Chester b: 2/6/58, Norwich, Conn.   BR/TR, 6'4", 240 lbs.   Deb: 4/15/83

1983 Hou-N★	6	6	.500	48	0	0	0	14	79²	51	9	22	60	8.4	2.82	120	.185	.247	2	.222	0	7	5	-1	0.8
1984 Hou-N	11	4	.733	60	0	0	0	5	98	82	5	35	47	10.7	1.93	172	.234	.303	3	.333	2	18	15	-1	2.5
1985 Hou-N	5	3	.625	49	0	0	0	2	81	76	7	37	48	12.6	3.56	97	.259	.341	2	.200	0	-1	0	0	0.6
1986 Chi-A	0	7	.000	46	0	0	0	2	97²	91	10	28	66	11.1	3.32	130	.247	.302	0	.000	0	9	11	-1	0.6
1987 StL-N	5	8	.385	60	0	0	0	2	96²	93	15	38	65	12.3	4.47	93	.259	.332	2	.167	0	-4	-3	1	-0.3
1988 Phi-N	0	2	.000	8	0	0	0	0	8²	16	3	4	2	20.8	13.50	26	.381	.435	0	—	0	-10	-10	-0	-1.9
1989 Oak-A	0	0	—	4	0	0	0	0	9	11	0	2	3	14.0	4.00	92	.297	.350	0	—	0	-0	-0	-1	0.0
Total 7	27	30	.474	275	0	0	0	25	470²	420	49	166	292	11.3	3.42	109	.243	.311	9	.214	3	21	16	-2	1.7

● **JOE DAWSON**   Dawson, Ralph Fenton b: 3/9/1897, Bow, Wash. d: 1/4/78, Longview, Tex.   BR/TR, 5'11", 182 lbs.   Deb: 7/4/24

1924 Cle-A	1	2	.333	4	4	0	0	0	20¹	24	0	21	7	20.4	6.64	64	.300	.451	2	.286		-5	-5	1	-0.6
1927 *Pit-N	3	7	.300	20	7	4	0	0	80²	80	2	32	17	12.5	4.46	92	.268	.338	5	.200	-1	-5	-3	-1	-0.5
1928 Pit-N	7	7	.500	31	7	1	0	3	128²	116	6	56	36	12.1	3.29	124	.242	.322	12	.279	3	10	11	-3	1.2
1929 Pit-N	0	1	.000	4	0	0	0	0	8²	13	2	3	2	16.6	8.31	57	.342	.390	1	.500	1	-3	-3	-0	-0.3
Total 4	11	17	.393	59	18	5	0	3	238¹	233	10	112	62	13.1	4.15	99	.260	.343	20	.260	3	-4	-1	-3	-0.2

● **REX DAWSON**   Dawson, Rexford Paul b: 2/10/1889, Skagit Co., Wash. d: 10/20/58, Indianapolis, Ind.   BL/TL, 6', 185 lbs.   Deb: 10/3/13

1913 Was-A	0	0	—	1	0	0	0	0	1	1	0	1	0	9.0	0.00	—	.250	.250		—	0	0	0	-0	0.0

● **PEA RIDGE DAY**   Day, Clyde Henry b: 8/26/1899, Pea Ridge, Ark. d: 3/21/34, Kansas City, Mo.   BR/TR, 6', 190 lbs.   Deb: 9/19/24

1924 StL-N	1	1	.500	3	3	0	0	0	17²	22	0	6	3	14.3	4.58	82	.306	.359	1	.125	-1	-1	-2	-0	-0.3
1925 StL-N	2	4	.333	17	4	1	0	1	40	53	5	7	13	14.2	6.30	69	.325	.364	2	.154	-1	-9	-9	-1	-1.3
1926 Cin-N	0	0	—	4	0	0	0	0	7¹	13	1	2	2	18.4	7.36	50	.406	.441	0	.000	-0	-3	-3	-0	-0.1
1931 Bro-N	2	2	.500	22	2	1	0	1	57¹	75	5	13	30	13.8	4.55	84	.315	.351	4	.222	0	-4	-5	-1	-0.4
Total 4	5	7	.417	46	9	3	0	2	122¹	163	11	28	48	14.3	5.30	75	.323	.362	7	.171	-2	-18	-18	-2	-2.1

● **BILL DAY**   Day, William M. b: 7/28/1867, Wilmington, Del. d: 8/16/23, Wilmington, Del.   TR , 5'8", 150 lbs.   Deb: 8/20/1889

1889 Phi-N	0	3	.000	4	3	2	0	0	19	16	0	23	20	18.5	5.21	83	.222	.411	0	.000		-3	-2	-0	-0.4
1890 Phi-N	1	1	.500	4	2	2	0	0	23²	26	0	12	9	14.5	3.04	120	.271	.352	1	.100	-1	1	2	-1	-0.1
Pit-N	0	6	.000	6	6	6	0	0	50	66	1	24	10	16.4	5.22	63	.308	.381	1	.043	-4	-9	-11	1	-1.1
Yr	1	7	.125	10	8	8	0	0	73²	92	1	36	19	15.8	4.52	75	.297	.372	2	.061	-5	-8	-9	1	-1.2
Total 2	1	10	.091	14	11	10	0	0	92²	108	1	59	39	16.3	4.66	77	.283	.380	2	.047	-6	-10	-11	1	-1.6

● **KEN DAYLEY**   Dayley, Kenneth Grant b: 2/25/59, Jerome, Idaho   BL/TL, 6', 175 lbs.   Deb: 5/13/82

1982 Atl-N	5	6	.455	20	11	0	0	0	71¹	79	9	25	34	13.1	4.54	82	.286	.346	5	.250	1	-7	-6	-2	-1.0
1983 Atl-N	5	8	.385	24	16	0	0	0	104²	100	12	39	70	12.1	4.30	90	.257	.328	7	.219	1	-5	-2	-0	-0.7
1984 Atl-N	0	3	.000	4	4	0	0	0	18²	28	5	6	10	16.9	5.30	73	.341	.393	2	.500	1	-4	-A	-0	-0.4
StL-N	0	2	.000	3	2	0	0	0	5	16	1	5	0	37.8	18.00	19	.615	.677	0	—	0	-8	-8	-0	-2.1
Yr	0	5	.000	7	6	0	0	0	23²	44	6	11	10	20.9	7.99	47	.404	.458	2	.500	1	-12	-11	0	-2.5
1985 *StL-N	4	4	.500	57	0	0	0	11	65¹	65	2	18	62	11.4	2.76	128	.263	.313	2	.400	1	6	6	1	1.1
1986 StL-N	0	3	.000	31	0	0	0	5	38²	42	1	11	33	12.6	3.26	112	.275	.327	1	.200	0	2	2	0	0.2
1987 *StL-N	9	5	.643	53	0	0	0	4	61	52	2	33	63	12.8	2.66	156	.234	.339	0	—	0	10	10	-1	2.2
1988 *StL-N	2	7	.222	54	0	0	0	5	55¹	48	2	19	38	11.1	2.77	126	.239	.308	0	.000	0	4	4	-0	0.7
1989 StL-N	4	3	.571	71	0	0	0	12	75¹	63	3	30	40	11.1	2.87	127	.228	.304	0	.000	-1	5	6	-2	0.5
1990 StL-N	4	4	.500	58	0	0	0	2	73¹	63	5	30	51	11.4	3.56	107	.233	.310	0	.000	-1	2	2	-0	0.1
1991 Tor-A	0	0	—	8	0	0	0	0	4¹	7	0	5	3	27.0	6.23	67	.368	.520	0	—	0	-1	-1	0	0.0
1993 Tor-A	0	0	—	8	0	0	0	0	0²	1	0	4	2	67.5	0.00	—	.333	.714	0	—	0	0	0	0	0.0
Total 11	33	45	.423	385	33	0	0	39	573²	564	42	225	406	12.5	3.66	101	.261	.332	17	.210	3	17	19	-5	0.6

● **REN DEAGLE**   Deagle, Lorenzo Burroughs b: 6/26/1858, New York, N.Y. d: 12/24/36, Kansas City, Mo.   BR/TR, 5'9", 190 lbs.   Deb: 5/17/1883

1883 Cin-a	10	8	.556	18	18	17	1	0	148	136	0	34	48	10.3	2.31	141	.229	.270	-5	16	15	-1	0.9		
1884 Cin-a	3	1	.750	4	4	4	1	0	34	39	0	9	12	13.2	5.03	66	.322	.374	0	.000	-2	-7	-6	-0	-0.7
Lou-a	4	6	.400	12	12	8	0	0	87¹	80	0	13	23	10.3	2.58	120	.238	.281	6	.133	-3	7	5	1	0.3
Yr	7	7	.500	16	16	12	1	0	121¹	119	0	22	35	11.0	3.26	97	.260	.304	6	.103	-5	-0	-1	1	-0.4
Total 2	17	15	.531	34	34	29	2	0	269¹	255	0	56	83	10.7	2.74	117	.242	.286	15	.117	-9	16	14	-1	0.4

● **COT DEAL**   Deal, Ellis Fergason b: 1/23/23, Arapaho, Okla.   BB/TR, 5'10.5", 185 lbs.   Deb: 9/11/47   C

1947 Bos-A	0	1	.000	5	2	0	0	0	12²	20	0	7	6	19.2	9.24	42	.364	.435	2	.500	1	-8	-8	0	-0.5
1948 Bos-A	1	0	1.000	4	0	0	0	0	4	3	0	3	2	13.5	0.00	—	.200	.333	0	—	0	2	2	0	0.5
1950 StL-N	0	0	—	1	0	0	0	0	1	3	0	2	1	45.0	18.00	24	.500	.625	0	—	0	-2	-2	-0	-0.0
1954 StL-N	2	3	.400	33	0	0	0	1	71²	85	14	36	25	15.7	6.28	65	.297	.383	2	.100	0	-18	-17	0	-1.1
Total 4	3	4	.429	45	2	0	0	1	89¹	111	14	48	34	16.4	6.55	63	.307	.394	4	.167	1	-25	-24	-0	-1.1

● **CHUBBY DEAN**   Dean, Alfred Lovill b: 8/24/16, Mt.Airy, N.C. d: 12/21/70, Riverside, Cal.   BL/TL, 5'11", 181 lbs.   Deb: 4/14/36 ◆

1937 Phi-A	1	0	1.000	2	1	0	0	0	9	7	0	6	4	13.0	4.00	118	.219	.342	81	.262	0	1	0	0	0.1
1938 Phi-A	2	1	.667	6	1	0	0	0	23	22	3	15	3	14.5	3.52	117	.250	.359	6	.300	2	3	3	1	0.6
1939 Phi-A	5	8	.385	54	11	0	0	0	116²	132	8	80	39	16.4	5.25	90	.289	.395	27	.351	8	-8	-7	1	0.2
1940 Phi-A	6	13	.316	30	19	8	1	1	159¹	220	21	63	38	16.6	6.61	67	.324	.381	26	.289	4	-39	-38	-1	-2.9
1941 Phi-A	2	4	.333	18	7	2	0	0	75²	90	9	24	21	14.9	6.19	68	.294	.367	9	.243	2	-17	-17	0	-0.9
Cle-A	1	4	.200	8	8	4	0	0	53¹	57	3	24	14	13.7	4.39	90	.282	.358	4	.160	0	-3	-3	-1	-0.1
Yr	3	8	.273	26	15	6	0	0	129	147	12	59	36	14.4	5.44	75	.289	.363	13	.210	2	-19	-19	1	-1.0
1942 Cle-A	8	11	.421	27	22	8	0	0	172²	170	7	66	46	12.3	3.81	91	.261	.329	27	.267	8	-3	-7	-3	-0.2
1943 Cle-A	5	5	.500	17	0	0	0	0	76	83	1	29	21	13.3	4.50	69	.281	.358	99	.196	1	-10	-12	-1	-1.4
Total 7	30	46	.395	162	68	23	1	9	685²	781	51	323	195	14.5	5.08	79	.288	.364	287	.274	25	-75	-80	-4	-4.6

● **DORY DEAN**   Dean, Charles Wilson b: 11/6/1852, Cincinnati, Ohio d: 5/4/35, Nashville, Tenn.   BR/TR, Deb: 6/22/1876

1876 Cin-N	4	26	.133	30	30	26	0	0	262²	397	1	24	22	14.4	3.73	59	.322	.335	36	.261	1	-42	-45	-1	-3.7

YEAR TM/L	W	L	PCT	G	GS	CG	SH	SV	IP	H	HR	BB	SO	RAT	ERA	ERA+	OAV	OOB	BH	AVG	PB	PR	/A	PD	TPI
● **HARRY DEAN** Dean, James Harry b: 5/12/15, Rockmart, Ga. d: 6/1/60, Rockmart, Ga. BR/TR, 6'4", 185 lbs. Deb: 4/16/41																									
1941 Was-A	0	0	—	2	0	0	0	0	2	2	0	3	0	27.0	4.50	90	.250	.500	0	—	0	-0	-0	-0	0.0
● **DIZZY DEAN** Dean, Jay Hanna b: 1/16/10, Lucas, Ark. d: 7/17/74, Reno, Nevada BR/TR, 6'2", 182 lbs. Deb: 9/28/30 FCH																									
1930 StL-N	1	0	1.000	1	1	1	0	0	9	3	0	3	5	6.0	1.00	502	.103	.188	1	.333	0	4	4	1	0.5
1932 StL-N	18	15	.545	46	33	16	**4**	2	**286**	280	14	102	**191**	12.2	3.30	119	.260	.327	25	.258	5	18	20	-1	2.5
1933 StL-N	20	18	.526	**48**	34	**26**	3	4	293	279	11	64	**199**	10.7	3.04	114	.250	.293	19	.181	1	10	14	-5	1.4
1934 *StL-N★	30	7	.811	50	33	24	**7**	7	311²	288	14	75	**195**	10.7	2.66	159	.241	.289	24	.246	4	49	54	-2	6.4
1935 StL-N★	28	12	.700	50	36	**29**	3	5	**325¹**	324	16	77	**190**	11.2	3.04	135	.256	.300	30	.234	4	35	38	-5	4.3
1936 StL-N★	24	13	.649	**51**	34	**28**	2	11	315	310	21	53	195	10.5	3.17	124	.253	.285	27	.223	1	30	27	-4	2.8
1937 StL-N★	13	10	.565	27	25	17	4	1	197¹	200	9	33	120	10.7	2.69	148	.259	.291	15	.227	2	27	28	-3	3.0
1938 *Chi-N	7	1	.875	13	10	3	1	0	74²	63	2	8	22	8.7	1.81	212	.226	.250	5	.192	-0	16	17	-1	1.6
1939 Chi-N	6	4	.600	19	13	7	2	0	96¹	98	4	17	27	10.8	3.36	117	.261	.294	5	.147	-1	6	6	-1	0.4
1940 Chi-N	3	3	.500	10	9	3	0	0	54	68	4	20	18	14.7	5.17	73	.306	.364	4	.222	0	-8	-9	1	-0.7
1941 Chi-N	0	0	—	1	1	0	0	0	1	3	0	1	0	27.0	18.00	19	.429	.429	0	—	0	-2	-2	0	0.0
1947 StL-A	0	0	—	1	1	0	0	0	4	3	0	1	0	9.0	0.00	—	.231	.286	1	1.000	0	2	2	-0	0.0
Total 12	150	83	.644	317	230	154	26	30	1967¹	1919	95	453	1163	11.0	3.02	130	.253	.298	161	.225	15	187	201	-20	22.2
● **PAUL DEAN** Dean, Paul Dee "Daffy" b: 8/14/13, Lucas, Ark. d: 3/17/81, Springdale, Ark. BR/TR, 6', 175 lbs. Deb: 4/18/34 F																									
1934 *StL-N	19	11	.633	39	26	16	5	2	233¹	225	19	52	150	10.9	3.43	123	.248	.292	20	.241	1	16	21	-6	1.9
1935 StL-N	19	12	.613	46	33	19	2	5	269²	261	16	55	143	10.8	3.37	122	.249	.292	12	.133	-5	19	22	-6	1.2
1936 StL-N	5	5	.500	17	14	5	0	1	92	113	3	20	28	13.1	4.60	86	.300	.337	2	.059	-4	-6	-7	-3	-1.3
1937 StL-N	0	0	—	1	0	0	0	0	0	1	0	2	0	—	∞	—	1.000	1.000	0	—	0	-3	-3	0	-0.3
1938 StL-N	3	1	.750	5	4	2	1	0	31	37	3	5	14	12.2	2.61	151	.298	.326	2	.182	-0	4	5	-1	0.5
1939 StL-N	1	0	1.000	16	2	0	0	0	43	54	4	10	16	13.6	6.07	68	.310	.351	1	.111	-1	-10	-9	-0	-0.3
1940 NY-N	4	4	.500	27	7	2	0	0	99¹	110	8	29	32	12.6	3.90	100	.281	.330	3	.115	-2	-1	-0	-1	-0.3
1941 NY-N	0	0	—	5	0	0	0	0	5²	8	0	3	3	17.5	3.18	116	.320	.393	0	—	0	0	0	0	0.0
1943 StL-A	0	0	—	3	1	0	0	0	13¹	16	0	5	1	13.5	3.38	99	.296	.345	0	.000	-0	-0	-0	-0	-0.1
Total 9	50	34	.595	159	87	44	8	8	787¹	825	53	179	387	11.7	3.75	109	.266	.309	40	.156	-10	20	28	-18	1.3
● **WAYLAND DEAN** Dean, Wayland Ogden b: 6/20/02, Richwood, W.Va. d: 4/10/30, Huntington, W.Va. BB/TR, 6'1", 178 lbs. Deb: 4/17/24																									
1924 *NY-N	6	12	.333	26	20	6	0	0	125²	139	9	45	39	13.5	5.01	73	.280	.346	8	.200	1	-16	-19	3	-2.0
1925 NY-N	10	7	.588	33	14	6	1	1	151¹	169	13	50	53	13.3	4.64	87	.282	.342	12	.235	3	-6	-10	0	-0.7
1926 Phi-N	8	16	.333	33	26	15	1	0	203²	245	9	89	52	14.9	4.91	84	.307	.379	27	.265	5	-24	-17	-1	-1.4
1927 Phi-N	0	1	.000	2	0	0	0	0	3	6	0	2	1	24.0	12.00	34	.500	.571	2	.667	1	-3	-3	0	-0.5
Chi-N	0	0	—	2	0	0	0	0	2	0	0	2	2	13.5	0.00	—	.000	.429	0	—	0	1	1	0	0.0
Yr	0	1	.000	4	0	0	0	0	5	6	0	4	3	19.8	7.20	56	.375	.524	2	.667	1	-2	-2	0	-0.5
Total 4	24	36	.400	96	60	27	2	1	485²	559	31	188	147	14.1	4.87	82	.293	.360	49	.250	10	-48	-47	2	-4.6
● **DENNIS DeBARR** DeBarr, Dennis Lee b: 1/16/53, Cheyenne, Wyo. BL/TL, 6'2", 190 lbs. Deb: 5/14/77																									
1977 Tor-A	0	1	.000	14	0	0	0	0	21¹	29	1	8	10	15.6	5.91	71	.337	.394	0	—	0	-4	-4	-0	-0.2
● **JOE DeBERRY** DeBerry, Joseph Gaddy b: 11/29/1896, Mt.Gilead, N.C. d: 10/9/44, Southern Pines, N.C BL/TR, 6'1", 175 lbs. Deb: 8/24/20																									
1920 StL-A	2	4	.333	10	3	1	0	0	54²	65	2	20	12	14.3	4.94	79	.307	.372	3	.167	-1	-7	-6	0	-0.6
1921 StL-A	0	1	.000	10	0	0	0	0	12¹	15	0	10	1	18.2	6.57	68	.300	.417	0	.000	-0	-3	-3	0	-0.2
Total 2	2	5	.286	20	3	1	0	0	67	80	2	30	13	15.0	5.24	77	.305	.381	3	.150	-1	-10	-9	0	-0.8
● **DAVE DeBUSSCHERE** DeBusschere, David Albert b: 10/16/40, Detroit, Mich. BR/TR, 6'6", 225 lbs. Deb: 4/22/62																									
1962 Chi-A	0	0	—	12	0	0	0	0	18	5	1	23	8	14.5	2.00	195	.089	.363	0	—	0	4	4	0	0.0
1963 Chi-A	3	4	.429	24	10	1	1	0	84¹	80	9	34	53	12.6	3.09	113	.249	.329	1	.045	-2	5	4	0	0.2
Total 2	3	4	.429	36	10	1	1	0	102¹	85	10	57	61	12.9	2.90	123	.225	.335	1	.045	-2	9	8	0	0.2
● **ART DECATUR** Decatur, Arthur Rue b: 1/14/1894, Cleveland, Ohio d: 4/25/66, Talladega, Ala. BR/TR, 6'1", 190 lbs. Deb: 4/15/22																									
1922 Bro-N	3	4	.429	29	3	2	0	1	87²	87	3	29	31	12.0	2.77	147	.265	.327	2	.080	-2	13	13	-2	0.6
1923 Bro-N	3	3	.500	36	5	2	0	3	97²	101	3	32	25	12.4	2.58	150	.264	.325	0	.000	-3	**15**	**14**	-2	0.4
1924 Bro-N	10	9	.526	31	10	3	0	1	126¹	156	12	27	38	13.3	4.13	91	.308	.348	5	.114	-4	-4	-5	-2	-1.3
1925 Bro-N	0	0	—	1	0	0	0	0	1	3	0	0	0	27.0	18.00	23	.600	.600	0	—	-0	-2	-2	-0	0.0
Phi-N	4	13	.235	25	15	4	0	2	128	170	13	35	31	14.6	5.27	91	.316	.360	2	.049	-5	-14	-7	-2	-1.4
Yr	4	13	.235	26	15	4	0	2	129	173	13	35	31	14.7	5.37	89	.319	.362	2	.049	-6	-16	-9	-2	-1.4
1926 Phi-N	0	0	—	2	1	0	0	0	3	6	0	2	0	24.0	6.00	69	.375	.444	0	—	-1	-1	-0	0	0.0
1927 Phi-N	3	5	.375	29	3	0	0	0	94²	130	11	20	27	14.6	7.42	56	.334	.373	6	.222	-6	-37	-35	-2	-2.7
Total 6	23	34	.404	153	37	10	0	7	538¹	653	42	145	152	13.6	4.51	92	.302	.349	15	.094	-14	-29	-23	-10	-4.4
● **MARTY DECKER** Decker, Dee Martin b: 6/7/57, Upland, Cal. BR/TR, 5'10", 168 lbs. Deb: 9/20/83																									
1983 SD-N	0	0	—	4	0	0	0	0	8²	8	2	3	9	9.3	2.08	168	.167	.265	0	—	0	1	1	0	0.0
● **JOE DECKER** Decker, George Henry b: 6/16/47, Storm Lake, Ia. BR/TR, 6', 180 lbs. Deb: 9/18/69																									
1969 Chi-N	1	0	1.000	4	1	0	0	0	12¹	10	0	6	13	11.7	2.92	138	.222	.314	0	.000	-0	1	2	-0	0.1
1970 Chi-N	2	7	.222	24	17	1	0	0	108²	108	12	56	79	13.9	4.64	97	.263	.357	6	.176	1	-7	-2	-1	-0.1
1971 Chi-N	3	2	.600	21	4	0	0	0	45²	62	2	25	37	17.1	4.73	83	.343	.422	2	.250	1	-6	-4	1	-0.3
1972 Chi-N	1	0	1.000	5	1	0	0	0	12²	9	1	4	7	9.2	2.13	179	.188	.250	0	.000	-0	2	2	-0	0.1
1973 Min-A	10	10	.500	29	24	6	3	0	170¹	167	12	88	109	13.7	4.17	95	.260	.352	0	—	0	-7	-4	0	-0.4
1974 Min-A	16	14	.533	37	34	11	1	0	248²	234	24	97	158	12.1	3.29	113	.252	.324	0	—	0	9	12	-2	1.1
1975 Min-A	1	3	.250	10	7	1	0	0	26¹	25	2	36	8	20.8	8.54	45	.260	.462	0	—	0	-14	-14	-0	-1.8
1976 Min-A	2	7	.222	13	12	0	0	0	58	60	3	51	35	17.4	5.28	68	.273	.412	0	—	0	-11	-11	1	-1.5
1979 Sea-A	0	1	.000	9	2	0	0	0	27¹	27	2	14	12	13.5	4.28	102	.255	.342	0	—	0	-0	1	1	0.0
Total 9	36	44	.450	152	105	19	4	0	710	702	58	377	458	13.8	4.17	94	.262	.355	8	.174	1	-34	-19	-1	-2.8
● **JEFF DEDMON** Dedmon, Jeffrey Linden b: 3/4/60, Torrance, Cal. BL/TR, 6'2", 200 lbs. Deb: 9/2/83																									
1983 Atl-N	0	0	—	5	0	0	0	0	4	10	1	0	3	22.5	13.50	29	.455	.455	0	—	0	-4	-4	0	0.0
1984 Atl-N	4	3	.571	54	0	0	0	0	81	86	5	35	51	13.7	3.78	102	.277	.354	0	.000	-1	-2	1	2	0.2
1985 Atl-N	6	3	.667	60	0	0	0	0	86	84	5	49	41	14.0	4.08	94	.264	.364	1	.111	-0	-5	-2	3	0.1
1986 Atl-N	6	6	.500	57	0	0	0	3	99²	90	8	39	58	12.0	2.98	133	.242	.320	2	.125	-1	8	11	2	1.4
1987 Atl-N	3	4	.429	53	0	0	0	4	89²	82	7	42	40	12.5	3.91	111	.246	.332	4	.250	1	-1	1	1	0.5
1988 Cle-A	1	0	1.000	21	0	0	0	2	33²	35	3	21	17	15.8	4.54	90	.276	.391	0	—	0	-2	-2	1	0.1
Total 6	20	16	.556	250	0	0	0	12	394	387	30	186	210	13.3	3.84	105	.261	.348	7	.149	-0	-3	8	9	2.3
● **JIM DEDRICK** Dedrick, James Michael b: 4/4/68, Los Angeles, Cal. BB/TR, 6', 185 lbs. Deb: 8/12/95																									
1995 Bal-A	0	0	—	6	0	0	0	0	7²	8	1	6	3	17.6	2.35	202	.308	.455	0	—	0	2	2	0	0.0
● **DUMMY DEEGAN** Deegan, William John b: 11/16/1874, Bronx, N.Y. d: 5/17/57, Bronx, N.Y. Deb: 8/3/01																									
1901 NY-N	0	1	.000	2	1	1	0	0	17	27	0	6	8	17.5	6.35	52	.355	.402	0	.000	-1	-6	-6	0	-0.3
● **JOHN DEERING** Deering, John Thomas b: 6/25/1879, Lynn, Mass. d: 2/15/43, Beverly, Mass. BR/TR, 6', 180 lbs. Deb: 5/12/03																									
1903 Det-A	3	4	.429	10	8	5	0	0	60²	73	3	24	14	15.1	3.86	75	.308	.371	8	.333	2	-6	-6	-1	-0.5
NY-A	4	3	.571	9	7	6	1	0	60	59	0	18	14	11.7	3.75	83	.257	.313	1	.043	-3	-5	-4	-1	-0.8
Yr	7	7	.500	19	15	11	1	0	120²	136	3	42	28	13.4	3.80	79	.283	.342	9	.191	-0	-11	-11	-2	-1.3
● **MIKE DEGERICK** Degerick, Michael Arthur b: 4/1/43, New York, N.Y. BR/TR, 6'2", 178 lbs. Deb: 9/4/61																									
1961 Chi-A	0	0	—	1	0	0	0	0	1²	2	0	4	0	16.2	5.40	72	.400	.500	0	—	0	-0	-0	0	0.0
1962 Chi-A	0	0	—	1	0	0	0	0	1	1	0	0	2	18.0	0.00	—	.250	.400	0	—	0	0	0	0	0.0
Total 2	0	0	—	2	0	0	0	0	2²	3	0	2	2	16.9	3.38	116	.333	.455	0	—	0	0	0	0	0.0

YEAR	TM/L	W	L	PCT	G	GS	CG	SH	SV	IP	H	HR	BB	SO	RAT	ERA	ERA+	OAV	OOB	BH	AVG	PB	PR	/A	PD	TPI

● PEP DEININGER Deininger, Otto Charles b: 10/10/1877, Wasseralfingen, Germany d: 9/25/50, Boston, Mass. BL/TL, 5'8.5", 180 lbs. Deb: 4/26/02 ♦

1902	Bos-A	0	0	—	2	1	0	0	0	12	19	3	9	2	22.5	9.75	37	.358	.469	2	.333	1	-8	-8	-1	0.1

● JOSE DeJESUS DeJesus, Jose Luis b: 1/6/65, Brooklyn, N.Y. BR/TR, 6'5", 175 lbs. Deb: 9/9/88

1988	KC-A	0	1	.000	2	1	0	0	0	2²	6	0	5	2	37.1	27.00	15	.429	.579	0	—	0	-7	-7	-0	-1.5
1989	KC-A	0	0	—	8	1	0	0	0	8	7	1	6	2	16.9	4.50	85	.241	.405	0	—	0	-1	-1	-0	0.0
1990	Phi-N	7	8	.467	22	22	3	1	0	130	97	10	73	87	11.9	3.74	102	.210	.321	3	.079	-1	1	1	-1	0.0
1991	Phi-N	10	9	.526	31	29	3	0	1	181²	147	7	128	118	13.8	3.42	107	.224	.355	8	.129	-1	5	5	-3	0.1
1994	KC-A	3	1	.750	5	4	0	0	0	26²	27	2	13	12	13.5	4.73	106	.276	.360	0	—	0	1	1	-0	-0.1
Total 5		20	19	.513	63	57	6	1	1	349	284	20	227	221	13.3	3.84	100	.226	.347	11	.110	-2	-1	-1	-4	-1.5

● TOMMY de la CRUZ de la Cruz, Tomas (Rivero) b: 9/18/11, Marianao, Cuba d: 9/6/58, Havana, Cuba BR/TR, 6'2", 168 lbs. Deb: 4/20/44

| 1944 | Cin-N | 9 | 9 | .500 | 34 | 20 | 9 | 0 | 1 | 191¹ | 170 | 9 | 45 | 65 | 10.2 | 3.25 | 108 | .238 | .284 | 9 | .155 | -0 | 8 | 5 | -0 | 0.4 |

● JIM DELAHANTY Delahanty, James Christopher b: 6/20/1879, Cleveland, Ohio d: 10/17/53, Cleveland, Ohio BR/TR, 5'10.5", 170 lbs. Deb: 4/19/01 F♦

1904	Bos-N	0	0	—	1	0	0	0	0	3¹	5	0	1	0	16.2	0.00	—	.357	.400	142	.285	0	1	1	0	0.0
1905	Bos-N	0	0	—	1	1	0	0	0	2	5	1	0	0	22.5	4.50	69	.500	.500	119	.258	0	-1	-0	0	0.0
Total 2		0	0	—	2	1	0	0	0	5¹	10	1	1	0	18.6	1.69	171	.417	.440	1159	.283	1	1	1	0	0.0

● ART DELANEY Delaney, Arthur Dewey "Swede" (b: Arthur Dewey Helenius) b: 1/5/1895, Chicago, Ill. d: 5/2/70, Hayward, Cal. BR/TR, 5'10.5", 178 lbs. Deb: 4/16/24

1924	StL-N	1	0	1.000	8	1	1	0	0	20	19	0	6	2	11.2	1.80	210	.250	.305	2	.286	0	5	4	0	0.3
1928	Bos-N	9	17	.346	39	22	8	0	2	192¹	197	11	56	45	11.9	3.79	103	.267	.319	9	.143	-3	4	3	1	0.1
1929	Bos-N	3	5	.375	20	8	3	1	0	75	103	6	35	17	16.7	6.12	76	.336	.405	3	.143	0	-12	-12	-1	-1.0
Total 3		13	22	.371	67	31	12	1	2	287¹	319	17	97	64	13.1	4.26	96	.285	.343	14	.154	-2	-3	-5	0	-0.6

● FRANCISCO de la ROSA de la Rosa, Francisco (Jimenez) b: 3/3/66, LaRomana, D.R. BB/TR, 5'11", 185 lbs. Deb: 9/7/91

| 1991 | Bal-A | 0 | 0 | — | 2 | 0 | 0 | 0 | 0 | 4 | 6 | 0 | 2 | 1 | 18.0 | 4.50 | 88 | .353 | .421 | 0 | — | 0 | -0 | -0 | -0 | 0.3 |

● JOSE DeLEON DeLeon, Jose (Chestaro) b: 12/20/60, Rancho Viejo, D.R. BR/TR, 6'3", 215 lbs. Deb: 7/23/83

1983	Pit-N	7	3	.700	15	15	3	2	0	108	75	5	47	118	10.3	2.83	131	.196	.285	2	.059	-1	10	10	-1	0.8
1984	Pit-N	7	13	.350	30	28	5	1	0	192¹	147	10	92	153	11.3	3.74	96	.214	.310	5	.085	-4	-3	-3	-3	-0.9
1985	Pit-N	2	19	.095	31	25	1	0	3	162²	138	15	89	149	12.7	4.70	76	.231	.334	2	.056	-2	-20	-20	-1	-2.7
1986	Pit-N	1	3	.250	9	1	0	0	1	16¹	17	2	17	11	19.3	8.27	46	.266	.427	0	.000	0	-8	-8	0	-1.7
	Chi-A	4	5	.444	13	13	1	0	0	79	49	7	42	68	10.8	2.96	145	.179	.297	0	—	0	11	12	0	1.3
1987	Chi-A	11	12	.478	33	31	3	0	0	206	177	24	97	153	12.4	4.02	114	.230	.324	0	—	0	10	13	-3	0.8
1988	StL-N	13	10	.565	34	34	3	1	0	225¹	198	13	86	208	11.4	3.67	95	.237	.310	10	.139	-0	-6	-5	-2	-0.8
1989	StL-N	16	12	.571	36	36	5	3	0	244²	173	16	80	**201**	9.5	3.05	119	**.197**	.269	8	.096	-4	12	16	-4	0.9
1990	StL-N	7	19	.269	32	32	0	0	0	182²	168	16	86	164	12.8	4.43	86	.246	.335	6	.107	-1	-13	-13	-2	-1.9
1991	StL-N	5	9	.357	28	28	1	0	0	162²	144	15	61	118	11.7	2.71	137	.239	.315	2	.043	-4	18	18	-2	0.9
1992	StL-N	2	7	.222	29	15	0	0	0	102¹	95	7	43	72	12.3	4.57	74	.245	.324	1	.048	-1	-12	-13	-1	-1.3
	Phi-N	0	1	.000	3	3	0	0	0	15	16	0	5	7	12.6	3.00	116	.281	.339	2	.400	1	1	1	-0	0.1
	Yr	2	8	.200	32	18	0	0	0	117¹	111	7	48	79	12.2	4.37	78	.246	.318	3	.115	-0	-11	-13	-2	-1.2
1993	Phi-N	3	0	1.000	24	3	0	0	0	47	39	5	27	34	13.6	3.26	122	.229	.351	0	.000	-0	4	4	-1	0.1
	*Chi-A	0	0	—	11	0	0	0	0	10¹	5	2	3	6	7.8	1.74	240	.152	.243	0	—	0	3	3	0	0.3
1994	Chi-A	3	2	.600	42	0	0	0	2	67	48	5	31	67	11.4	3.36	139	.200	.307	0	—	0	11	10	-1	0.7
1995	Chi-A	5	3	.625	38	0	0	0	0	67²	60	10	28	53	12.5	5.19	86	.238	.329	0	—	0	-4	-6	-1	-0.6
	Mon-N	0	1	.000	7	0	0	0	0	8¹	7	2	7	12	16.2	7.56	57	.233	.395	0	—	0	-3	-3	-0	-0.3
Total 13		86	119	.420	415	264	21	7	6	1897¹	1556	153	841	1594	11.7	3.76	102	.224	.313	38	.091	-16	9	15	-22	-4.6

● LUIS DeLEON DeLeon, Luis Antonio (Tricoche) b: 8/19/58, Ponce, P.R. BR/TR, 6'1", 153 lbs. Deb: 9/6/81

1981	StL-N	0	1	.000	10	0	0	0	0	15¹	11	1	3	8	8.2	2.35	151	.200	.241	0	.000	-0	2	2	-0	0.1
1982	SD-N	9	5	.643	61	0	0	0	15	102	77	10	16	60	8.3	2.03	169	.212	.247	1	.091	-4	18	16	1	2.7
1983	SD-N	6	6	.500	63	0	0	0	13	111	89	6	27	90	9.5	2.68	130	.224	.275	2	.143	-0	12	10	-2	1.1
1984	SD-N	2	2	.500	32	0	0	0	0	42²	44	12	12	44	12.7	5.48	65	.256	.319	0	.000	-0	-9	-9	-0	-0.8
1985	SD-N	0	3	.000	29	0	0	0	3	38²	39	6	10	31	12.1	4.19	84	.267	.327	1	.200	1	-3	-3	-0	-0.3
1987	Bal-A	0	2	.000	11	0	0	0	1	20²	19	1	8	13	12.6	4.79	92	.253	.341	0	—	0	-1	-1	-1	0.1
1989	Sea-A	0	0	—	1	0	0	0	0	4	5	1	1	2	15.8	2.25	179	.313	.389	0	—	0	1	1	-0	-0.2
Total 7		17	19	.472	207	1	0	0	32	334¹	284	39	77	248	10.3	3.12	114	.232	.284	4	.114	-2	20	16	-2	2.7

● FLAME DELHI Delhi, Lee William b: 11/5/1892, Harqua Hala, Ariz. d: 5/9/66, San Rafael, Cal. BR/TR, 6'2.5", 198 lbs. Deb: 4/16/12

| 1912 | Chi-A | 0 | 0 | — | 1 | 0 | 0 | 0 | 0 | 2 | 3 | 0 | 3 | 0 | 30.0 | 9.00 | 36 | .412 | .500 | 0 | — | 0 | -2 | -2 | 0 | 0.0 |

● WHEEZER DELL Dell, William George b: 6/11/1887, Tuscarora, Nev. d: 8/24/66, Independence, Cal. BR/TR, 6'4", 210 lbs. Deb: 4/22/12

1912	StL-N	0	0	—	3	0	0	0	0	2¹	3	0	6	2	23.1	11.57	30	.188	.316	0	—	0	-3	-3	0	0.0
1915	Bro-N	11	10	.524	40	24	12	4	1	215	166	5	100	94	11.5	2.34	119	.218	.315	10	.152	-1	10	10	0	1.0
1916	*Bro-N	8	9	.471	32	16	9	2	1	155	143	2	43	76	11.0	2.26	118	.256	.314	4	.091	-2	6	7	-1	0.4
1917	Bro-N	0	4	.000	17	4	0	0	1	58	55	3	25	28	12.7	3.72	75	.263	.347	1	.063	-2	-7	-6	-1	-0.7
Total 4		19	23	.452	92	44	21	6	3	430¹	367	10	171	198	11.5	2.55	108	.237	.319	15	.119	-5	7	9	-2	0.7

● IKE DELOCK Delock, Ivan Martin b: 11/11/29, Highland Park, Mich. BR/TR, 5'11", 175 lbs. Deb: 4/17/52

1952	Bos-A	4	9	.308	39	7	1	1	5	95	88	9	50	46	13.3	4.26	92	.245	.341	1	.045	-1	-6	-3	-0	-0.6
1953	Bos-A	3	1	.750	23	1	0	0	1	48²	60	2	20	22	15.2	4.44	95	.308	.378	1	.100	-1	-2	-1	-0	-0.2
1955	Bos-A	9	7	.563	29	18	6	0	3	143²	136	16	61	88	12.6	3.76	114	.247	.326	7	.143	-1	3	8	-1	0.7
1956	Bos-A	13	7	.650	38	8	1	0	9	128¹	122	12	80	105	14.5	4.21	110	.252	.326	3	.103	-2	-1	6	-0	0.7
1957	Bos-A	9	8	.529	49	2	0	0	11	94	80	11	45	62	12.3	3.83	104	.230	.323	1	.048	-1	-0	2	-1	0.4
1958	Bos-A	14	8	.636	31	19	9	1	2	160	155	13	56	82	11.9	3.37	119	.252	.315	3	.063	-4	7	11	-1	1.0
1959	Bos-A	11	6	.647	28	17	4	0	0	134¹	129	12	62	55	12.3	2.95	138	.236	.322	3	.064	-3	14	17	-2	1.5
1960	Bos-A	9	10	.474	24	23	3	1	0	129¹	145	21	52	49	14.0	4.73	85	.283	.354	5	.116	-3	-12	-10	-2	-1.6
1961	Bos-A	6	9	.400	28	23	3	1	0	156	185	24	52	80	13.8	4.90	85	.293	.349	5	.104	-2	-15	-13	-2	-1.4
1962	Bos-A	5	4	.556	17	13	4	2	0	86¹	89	10	24	49	11.8	3.75	110	.268	.317	2	.087	-1	2	4	-0	0.1
1963	Bos-A	1	2	.333	10	6	0	0	0	32	31	4	12	23	12.1	4.50	84	.246	.312	0	.000	-0	-3	-3	-0	-0.4
	Bal-A	1	3	.250	7	5	0	0	0	30¹	25	7	16	11	12.2	5.04	69	.236	.336	0	.000	-0	-5	-5	-0	-0.7
	Yr	2	5	.286	13	11	1	0	0	62¹	56	11	28	34	12.1	4.76	76	.240	.322	0	.000	-3	-8	-8	-0	-1.1
Total 11		84	75	.528	329	147	32	6	31	1238	1236	141	530	672	13.0	4.03	102	.259	.336	31	.086	-20	-19	-13	-9	-0.8

● RAMON de los SANTOS de los Santos, Ramon (Genero) b: 1/19/49, Santo Domingo, D.R. BL/TL, 6'1", 175 lbs. Deb: 8/21/74

| 1974 | Hou-N | 1 | 1 | .500 | 12 | 0 | 0 | 0 | 0 | 12¹ | 11 | 0 | 9 | 7 | 14.6 | 2.19 | 158 | .234 | .357 | 0 | — | 0 | 2 | 2 | 0 | 0.3 |

● RICH DeLUCIA DeLucia, Richard Anthony b: 10/7/64, Reading, Pa. BR/TR, 6', 180 lbs. Deb: 9/8/90

1990	Sea-A	1	2	.333	5	5	1	0	0	36	30	2	9	20	9.8	2.00	198	.226	.275	0	—	0	8	8	-1	0.5
1991	Sea-A	12	13	.480	32	31	0	0	0	182	176	31	78	98	12.8	5.09	81	.260	.339	0	—	0	-20	-20	-2	-2.5
1992	Sea-A	3	6	.333	30	11	0	0	1	83²	100	13	35	66	14.7	5.49	72	.293	.362	0	—	0	-14	-14	-1	-1.5
1993	Sea-A	3	6	.333	30	1	0	0	0	42²	46	5	23	48	14.8	4.64	95	.272	.363	0	—	0	-2	-1	-1	-0.2
1994	Cin-N	0	0	—	10	0	0	0	0	10²	9	1	6	15	11.8	4.22	98	.214	.298	0	—	0	-0	-0	-0	-0.0
1995	StL-N	8	7	.533	56	1	0	0	0	82¹	63	9	36	76	11.1	3.39	124	.213	.304	2	.200	0	7	7	-0	1.3
1996	SF-N	3	6	.333	56	0	0	0	0	61²	62	8	31	55	14.0	5.84	70	.259	.352	1	.250	0	-11	-12	-1	-1.4
Total 7		30	40	.429	217	49	1	0	1	499	486	72	217	378	12.9	4.69	88	.256	.336	3	.214	1	-32	-32	-1	-3.8

● FRED DEMARAIS Demarais, Frederick b: 11/1/1866, Canada d: 3/6/19, Stamford, Conn. TR, 5'9", 168 lbs. Deb: 7/26/1890

| 1890 | Chi-N | 0 | 0 | — | 1 | 0 | 0 | 0 | 0 | 2 | 1 | 0 | 1 | 1 | 9.0 | 0.00 | — | .143 | .250 | 0 | — | -0 | 1 | 1 | 0 | 0.0 |

YEAR TM/L	W	L	PCT	G	GS	CG	SH	SV	IP	H	HR	BB	SO	RAT	ERA	ERA+	OAV	OOB	BH	AVG	PB	PR	/A	PD	TPI

● AL DEMAREE Demaree, Albert Wentworth b: 9/8/1884, Quincy, Ill. d: 4/30/62, Los Angeles, Cal. BL/TR, 6', 170 lbs. Deb: 9/26/12

1912 NY-N	1	0	1.000	2	2	1	1	0	16	17	0	2	11	10.7	1.69	200	.288	.311	0	.000	-1	3	3	0	0.1
1913 *NY-N	13	4	.765	31	24	11	2	2	199²	176	4	38	76	9.9	2.21	141	.243	.286	7	.106	-3	22	20	-3	0.9
1914 NY-N	10	17	.370	38	30	13	2	0	224	219	3	77	89	12.2	3.09	86	.263	.331	9	.132	-2	-8	-11	-1	-1.6
1915 Phi-N	14	11	.560	32	26	13	3	1	209²	201	4	58	69	11.2	3.05	90	.260	.314	12	.176	-0	-7	-7	-5	-1.3
1916 Phi-N	19	14	.576	39	35	25	4	1	285	252	4	48	130	9.7	2.62	101	.242	.281	11	.109	-4	0	1	-6	-1.1
1917 Chi-N	5	9	.357	24	18	6	1	1	141¹	125	5	37	43	10.4	2.55	114	.244	.297	5	.122	-1	3	5	1	0.4
NY-N	4	5	.444	15	11	1	0	0	78¹	70	1	17	23	10.1	2.64	97	.239	.283	2	.111	-1	1	-1	0	-0.2
Yr	9	14	.391	39	29	7	1	1	219²	195	6	54	66	10.2	2.58	107	.241	.290	7	.119	-2	3	5	1	0.2
1918 NY-N	8	6	.571	26	14	8	2	1	142	143	5	25	39	10.8	2.47	106	.262	.297	6	.128	-3	5	2	-0	-0.1
1919 Bos-N	6	6	.500	25	13	6	0	3	128	147	8	31	34	12.9	3.80	75	.300	.348	1	.048	-5	-13	-13	-2	-2.0
Total 8	80	72	.526	232	173	84	15	9	1424	1350	34	337	514	10.9	2.77	100	.256	.304	54	.118	-20	6	0	-16	-4.9

● LARRY DEMERY Demery, Lawrence Calvin b: 6/4/53, Bakersfield, Cal. BR/TR, 6', 170 lbs. Deb: 6/2/74

1974 *Pit-N	6	6	.500	19	15	2	0	0	95¹	95	12	51	51	13.8	4.25	81	.262	.354	5	.152	1	-7	-9	-1	-1.0
1975 *Pit-N	7	5	.583	45	8	1	0	4	114²	95	7	43	59	11.1	2.90	122	.230	.307	3	.125	1	9	8	-1	0.9
1976 Pit-N	10	7	.588	36	15	4	1	2	145	123	8	58	72	11.4	3.17	110	.234	.313	5	.125	-1	5	5	-0	0.5
1977 Pit-N	6	5	.545	39	8	0	0	1	90¹	100	13	47	35	14.6	5.08	78	.279	.363	3	.150	-0	-12	-11	-0	-1.3
Total 4	29	23	.558	139	46	7	1	7	445¹	413	40	199	217	12.5	3.72	97	.249	.331	16	.137	0	-4	-6	-2	-0.9

● HARRY DeMILLER DeMiller, Harry b: 11/12/1867, Wooster, Ohio d: 10/19/28, Santa Ana, Cal. BR/TL, Deb: 8/20/1892

| 1892 Chi-N | 1 | 1 | .500 | 4 | 2 | 2 | 0 | 0 | 24 | 29 | 1 | 16 | 15 | 17.3 | 6.38 | 52 | .287 | .390 | 3 | .300 | 1 | -8 | -8 | 0 | -0.4 |

● DON DeMOLA DeMola, Donald John b: 7/5/52, Glen Cove, N.Y. BR/TR, 6'2", 185 lbs. Deb: 4/13/74

1974 Mon-N	1	0	1.000	25	1	0	0	0	57²	46	7	21	47	10.5	3.12	123	.223	.295	0	.000	-1	3	5	-1	0.0
1975 Mon-N	4	7	.364	60	0	0	0	1	97²	92	8	42	63	12.7	4.15	92	.251	.335	0	.000	-1	-6	-4	-3	-0.8
Total 2	5	7	.417	85	1	0	0	1	155¹	138	15	63	110	11.9	3.77	102	.241	.321	0	.000	-3	-3	1	-3	-0.8

● BEN DeMOTT DeMott, Benyew Harrison b: 4/2/1889, Green Village, N.J. d: 7/5/63, Somerville, N.J. BR/TR, 6', 192 lbs. Deb: 8/12/10

1910 Cle-A	0	3	.000	6	4	1	0	0	28¹	45	4	8	13	17.2	5.40	48	.388	.432	3	.167	-0	-9	-9	-0	-0.9
1911 Cle-A	0	1	.000	1	1	0	0	0	3²	10	0	2	2	29.5	12.27	28	.588	.632	0	.000	-0	-4	-3	1	-0.6
Total 2	0	4	.000	7	5	1	0	0	32	55	4	10	15	18.6	6.19	43	.414	.458	3	.136	-0	-13	-12	1	-1.5

● CON DEMPSEY Dempsey, Cornelius Francis b: 9/16/23, San Francisco, Cal. BR/TR, 6'4", 190 lbs. Deb: 4/28/51

| 1951 Pit-N | 0 | 2 | .000 | 3 | 2 | 0 | 0 | 0 | 7 | 11 | 2 | 4 | 3 | 19.3 | 9.00 | 47 | .393 | .469 | 0 | .000 | -0 | -4 | -4 | 0 | -0.8 |

● RICK DEMPSEY Dempsey, John Rikard b: 9/13/49, Fayetteville, Tenn. BR/TR, 6', 190 lbs. Deb: 9/23/69 ♦

| 1991 Mil-A | 0 | 0 | — | 2 | 0 | 0 | 0 | 0 | 2 | 3 | 0 | 1 | 0 | 18.0 | 4.50 | 88 | .333 | .400 | 34 | .231 | 2 | -0 | -0 | -0 | 0.0 |

● MARK DEMPSEY Dempsey, Mark Steven b: 12/17/57, Dayton, Ohio BR/TR, 6'6", 220 lbs. Deb: 9/4/82

| 1982 SF-N | 0 | 0 | — | 3 | 1 | 0 | 0 | 0 | 5² | 11 | 1 | 2 | 4 | 20.6 | 7.94 | 45 | .440 | .481 | 0 | .000 | -0 | -3 | -3 | 0 | 0.0 |

● BILL DENEHY Denehy, William Francis b: 3/31/46, Middletown, Conn. BB/TR, 6'3", 200 lbs. Deb: 4/16/67

1967 NY-N	1	7	.125	15	8	0	0	0	53²	51	8	29	35	13.4	4.70	72	.248	.340	0	.000	-1	-8	-8	-1	-1.2
1968 Was-A	0	0	—	3	0	0	0	0	2	4	0	4	1	36.0	9.00	32	.444	.615	0	—	0	-1	-1	0	-0.1
1971 Det-A	0	3	.000	31	1	0	0	1	49	47	4	28	27	14.5	4.22	85	.250	.359	0	.000	-1	-4	-3	-0	-0.2
Total 3	1	10	.091	49	9	0	0	1	104²	102	12	61	63	14.4	4.56	76	.253	.357	0	.000	-2	-13	-13	-1	-1.4

● BRIAN DENMAN Denman, Brian John b: 2/12/56, Minneapolis, Minn. BR/TR, 6'4", 205 lbs. Deb: 8/22/82

| 1982 Bos-A | 3 | 4 | .429 | 9 | 9 | 2 | 1 | 0 | 49 | 55 | 6 | 9 | 11 | 11.8 | 4.78 | 90 | .282 | .314 | 0 | — | 0 | -4 | -3 | -0 | -0.6 |

● DON DENNIS Dennis, Donald Ray b: 3/3/42, Uniontown, Kan. BR/TR, 6'2", 190 lbs. Deb: 6/18/65

1965 StL-N	2	3	.400	41	0	0	0	0	55	47	3	16	29	10.5	2.29	168	.236	.296	2	.400	1	8	9	2	1.3
1966 StL-N	4	2	.667	38	1	0	0	2	59²	73	8	17	25	13.7	4.98	72	.302	.350	1	.083	-1	-9	-9	3	-0.7
Total 2	6	5	.545	79	1	0	0	2	114²	120	11	33	54	12.2	3.69	101	.272	.326	3	.176	-0	-1	0	4	0.6

● JERRY DENNY Denny, Jeremiah Dennis (b: Jeremiah Dennis Eldridge)
b: 3/16/1859, New York, N.Y. d: 8/16/27, Houston, Tex. BR/TR, 5'11.5", 180 lbs. Deb: 5/2/1881 ♦

| 1888 Ind-N | 0 | 0 | — | 1 | 0 | 0 | 0 | 0 | 4 | 5 | 1 | 4 | 2 | 20.3 | 9.00 | 33 | .278 | .409 | 137 | .261 | 0 | -3 | -3 | 0 | 0.0 |

● JOHN DENNY Denny, John Allen b: 11/8/52, Prescott, Ariz. BR/TR, 6'3", 190 lbs. Deb: 9/12/74

1974 StL-N	0	0	—	2	0	0	0	0	2	3	0	1	0	13.5	0.00	—	.273	.273	0	—	-1	1	-1	-0	0.0
1975 StL-N	10	7	.588	25	24	3	2	0	136	149	5	51	72	13.4	3.97	95	.280	.346	10	.227	1	-5	-3	2	-0.1
1976 StL-N	11	9	.550	30	30	8	3	0	207	189	11	74	74	11.8	**2.52**	**140**	.246	.318	15	.224	2	23	**23**	1	2.7
1977 StL-N	8	8	.500	26	26	3	1	0	149²	165	9	62	60	14.0	4.51	85	.281	.355	5	.098	-3	-10	-11	3	-1.0
1978 StL-N	14	11	.560	33	33	11	2	0	234	200	13	74	103	10.8	2.96	119	.234	.304	13	.178	2	16	14	8	2.7
1979 StL-N	8	11	.421	31	31	6	2	0	206	206	24	100	99	13.5	4.85	78	.264	.350	9	.129	-1	-26	-25	2	-2.1
1980 Cle-A	8	6	.571	16	16	4	1	0	108²	116	4	47	59	13.9	4.39	93	.284	.365	0	—	0	-4	-4	1	-0.4
1981 Cle-A	10	6	.625	19	19	6	3	0	145²	139	9	66	94	12.9	3.15	115	.254	.338	0	—	0	8	5	1	1.4
1982 Cle-A	6	11	.353	21	21	5	0	0	138¹	126	11	73	94	13.3	5.01	81	.240	.340	0	—	0	-14	-14	-1	-1.4
Phi-N	0	2	.000	4	4	0	0	0	22¹	18	1	9	19	11.3	4.03	91	.217	.301	1	.100	-1	-1	-1	0	0.1
1983 *Phi-N	19	6	**.760**	36	36	7	1	0	242²	229	9	53	139	10.6	2.37	150	.250	.294	13	.169	2	**34**	32	1	3.5
1984 Phi-N	7	7	.500	22	22	2	0	0	154¹	122	11	29	94	9.0	2.45	148	.214	.257	9	.191	2	20	20	4	2.3
1985 Phi-N	11	14	.440	33	33	6	2	0	230²	252	15	83	123	13.2	3.82	96	.282	.345	10	.123	-2	-6	-4	1	-0.4
1986 Cin-N	11	10	.524	37	27	2	1	0	171¹	179	15	56	115	12.6	4.20	92	.272	.333	12	.222	2	-9	-6	3	-0.3
Total 13	123	108	.532	325	322	62	18	0	2148²	2093	137	778	1146	12.3	3.59	104	.258	.327	97	.170	2	25	30	31	7.0

● EDDIE DENT Dent, Elliott Estill b: 12/8/1887, Baltimore, Md. d: 11/25/74, Birmingham, Ala. BR/TR, 6'1", 190 lbs. Deb: 8/31/09

1909 Bro-N	2	4	.333	6	5	4	0	0	42	47	5	17	13	13.3	4.29	60	.307	.369	1	.067	-1	-8	-8	-1	-1.2
1911 Bro-N	2	1	.667	5	3	1	0	0	31²	30	0	10	7	11.9	3.69	90	.256	.326	1	.100	-0	-1	-1	0	-0.1
1912 Bro-N	0	0	—	1	0	0	0	0	1	4	0	1	1	45.0	36.00	9	.571	.625	0	.000	-0	-4	-4	0	-0.0
Total 3	4	5	.444	12	8	5	0	0	74²	81	5	28	21	13.1	4.46	65	.292	.357	2	.077	-2	-13	-13	-0	-1.3

● ROGER DENZER Denzer, Roger "Peaceful Valley" b: 10/5/1871, LeSeur, Minn. d: 9/18/49, LeSeur, Minn. BL/TR, 6', 180 lbs. Deb: 4/24/1897

1897 Chi-N	2	8	.200	12	10	8	0	0	94²	125	4	34	17	15.3	5.13	87	.315	.372	6	.154	-3	-9	-7	-1	-0.9
1901 NY-N	2	6	.250	11	9	3	1	0	61²	69	2	5	22	11.1	3.36	99	.280	.300	2	.091	-1	-0	-1	-1	-0.3
Total 2	4	14	.222	23	19	11	1	0	156¹	194	6	39	39	13.6	4.43	90	.302	.345	8	.131	-4	-9	-8	-2	-1.2

● GEORGE DERBY Derby, George H. "Jonah" b: 7/6/1857, Webster, Mass. d: 7/4/25, Philadelphia, Pa. BL/TR, 6', 175 lbs. Deb: 5/2/1881

1881 Det-N	29	26	.527	56	55	55	**9**	0	494²	505	3	86	212	10.8	2.20	132	.251	.281	44	.186	-10	**32**	39	2	**3.0**
1882 Det-N	17	20	.459	40	39	38	3	0	362	386	8	81	182	11.6	3.26	90	.256	.294	29	.195	-6	-14	-13	1	-1.5
1883 Buf-N	2	10	.167	14	13	12	0	0	107²	173	3	15	34	15.7	5.85	54	.334	.353	14	.237	-1	-32	-32	1	-2.6
Total 3	48	56	.462	110	107	105	12	0	964¹	1064	14	182	428	11.6	3.01	98	.263	.295	87	.196	-17	-15	-5	4	-1.1

● PAUL DERRINGER Derringer, Samuel Paul "Duke" b: 10/17/06, Springfield, Ky. d: 11/17/87, Sarasota, Fla. BR/TR, 6'3.5", 205 lbs. Deb: 4/16/31

1931 *StL-N	18	8	**.692**	35	23	15	4	2	211²	225	9	65	134	12.5	3.36	117	.274	.330	7	.097	-6	12	14	-0	0.9
1932 StL-N	11	14	.440	39	30	14	1	0	233¹	296	6	67	78	14.1	4.05	97	.310	.356	13	.178	-0	-4	-3	-2	-0.5
1933 StL-N	0	2	.000	3	1	1	0	0	17	24	0	9	9	15.9	4.24	82	.353	.436	0	.000	-1	-2	-1	-0	-0.2
Cin-N	7	25	.219	33	31	16	2	1	231	240	4	51	86	11.5	3.23	105	.275	.315	14	.184	-1	2	1	0	0.5
Yr	7	27	.206	36	32	17	2	1	248	264	4	60	89	11.9	3.30	103	.281	.323	14	.173	-2	1	1	0	0.4
1934 Cin-N	15	21	.417	47	31	18	4	4	261	297	13	50	122	12.4	3.59	114	.283	.323	18	.196	1	14	14	-2	1.7
1935 Cin-N★	22	13	.629	45	33	20	3	0	276²	295	13	49	120	11.3	3.51	113	.271	.305	13	.140	-5	16	14	3	1.4
1936 Cin-N	19	19	.500	**51**	37	13	2	5	282¹	331	11	42	121	12.0	4.02	95	.289	.316	10	.200	-1	0	-6	-0	-0.8

YEAR	TM/L	W	L	PCT	G	GS	CG	SH	SV	IP	H	HR	BB	SO	RAT	ERA	ERA+	OAV	OOB	BH	AVG	PB	PR	/A	PD	TPI
1937	Cin-N	10	14	.417	43	26	12	1	1	222²	240	7	55	94	11.9	4.04	92	.271	.313	16	.200	1	-3	-8	1	-0.6
1938	Cin-N☆	21	14	.600	41	37	26	4	3	307	315	20	49	132	10.7	2.93	124	.262	.291	21	.176	-0	29	24	-2	2.4
1939	*Cin-N★	25	7	.781	38	35	28	5	0	301	321	15	35	128	10.7	2.93	131	.272	.295	23	.209	0	33	30	-3	2.7
1940	*Cin-N★	20	12	.625	37	37	26	3	0	296²	280	17	48	115	10.0	3.06	124	.246	.276	18	.167	-2	26	24	-4	1.8
1941	Cin-N★	12	14	.462	29	28	17	2	1	228¹	233	16	54	76	11.3	3.31	109	.266	.309	13	.155	-3	8	7	-1	0.4
1942	Cin-N†	10	11	.476	29	27	13	1	0	208²	203	4	49	68	11.0	3.06	107	.250	.296	9	.132	-2	6	5	-4	-0.1
1943	Chi-N	10	14	.417	32	25	10	2	3	174	184	7	39	75	11.5	3.57	93	.264	.303	13	.224	1	-4	-4	-4	-0.9
1944	Chi-N	7	13	.350	42	16	7	0	3	180	205	13	39	69	12.2	4.15	85	.284	.321	9	.158	-2	-11	-12	-1	-1.5
1945	*Chi-N	16	11	.593	35	30	15	1	4	213²	223	8	51	86	11.6	3.45	106	.265	.308	15	.200	0	8	5	-2	0.4
Total	15	223	212	.513	579	445	251	32	29	3645	3912	158	761	1507	11.6	3.46	108	.272	.310	220	.175	-20	131	108	-17	7.6

● **JIM DERRINGTON** Derrington, Charles James "Blackie" b: 11/29/39, Compton, Cal. BL/TL, 6'3", 190 lbs. Deb: 9/30/56

YEAR	TM/L	W	L	PCT	G	GS	CG	SH	SV	IP	H	HR	BB	SO	RAT	ERA	ERA+	OAV	OOB	BH	AVG	PB	PR	/A	PD	TPI
1956	Chi-A	0	1	.000	1	1	0	0	0	6	9	2	6	3	22.5	7.50	55	.375	.500	1	.500	0	-2	-2	-0	-0.3
1957	Chi-A	0	1	.000	20	5	0	0	0	37	29	4	29	14	14.4	4.86	77	.216	.360	0	.000	-0	-4	-5	-1	-0.3
Total	2	0	2	.000	21	6	0	0	0	43	38	6	35	17	15.5	5.23	72	.241	.381	1	.167	0	-7	-7	-1	-0.6

● **JIM DESHAIES** Deshaies, James Joseph b: 6/23/60, Massena, N.Y. BL/TL, 6'4", 225 lbs. Deb: 8/7/84

YEAR	TM/L	W	L	PCT	G	GS	CG	SH	SV	IP	H	HR	BB	SO	RAT	ERA	ERA+	OAV	OOB	BH	AVG	PB	PR	/A	PD	TPI
1984	NY-A	0	1	.000	2	2	0	0	0	7	14	1	7	5	27.0	11.57	33	.438	.538	0	—	0	-6	-6	0	-0.7
1985	Hou-N	0	0	—	2	0	0	0	0	3	1	0	2	3	3.0	0.00	—	.100	.100	0	—	0	1	1	-0	0.0
1986	Hou-N	12	5	.706	26	26	1	1	0	144	124	16	59	128	11.6	3.25	111	.234	.313	2	.047	-1	7	6	-2	0.3
1987	Hou-N	11	6	.647	26	25	1	0	0	152	149	22	57	104	12.2	4.62	85	.257	.324	5	.094	-0	-9	-12	-1	-1.2
1988	Hou-N	11	14	.440	31	31	3	2	0	207	164	20	72	127	10.3	3.00	111	.218	.288	3	.048	-4	10	7	-2	0.2
1989	Hou-N	15	10	.600	34	34	6	3	0	225²	180	15	79	153	10.5	2.91	116	.217	.288	9	.120	-2	15	12	-1	0.9
1990	Hou-N	7	12	.368	34	34	2	0	0	209¹	186	21	84	119	12.0	3.78	98	.245	.326	4	.063	-3	0	-2	-1	-0.6
1991	Hou-N	5	12	.294	28	28	1	0	0	161	156	19	72	98	12.8	4.98	70	.259	.339	4	.098	-1	-23	-26	-2	-2.7
1992	SD-N	4	7	.364	15	15	0	0	0	96	92	6	33	46	11.8	3.28	109	.258	.323	6	.207	1	2	3	1	0.5
1993	Min-A	11	13	.458	27	27	1	0	0	167¹	159	24	51	80	11.6	4.41	99	.254	.317	0	—	0	-2	-1	-1	-0.2
	SF-N	2	2	.500	5	4	0	0	0	17	24	2	6	5	16.4	4.24	92	.348	.408	0	.000	-1	-0	-1	-0	-0.2
1994	Min-A	6	12	.333	25	25	0	0	0	130¹	170	30	54	78	15.6	7.39	66	.321	.386	0	.000	-0	-37	-37	-1	-3.9
1995	Phi-N	0	1	.000	2	2	0	0	0	5¹	15	3	1	6	27.0	20.25	21	.484	.500	0	.000	-0	-10	-9	-0	-1.2
Total	12	84	95	.469	257	253	15	6	0	1525	1434	179	575	951	12.0	4.14	91	.251	.323	33	.088	-12	-51	-65	-9	-8.8

● **JIMMIE DeSHONG** DeShong, James Brooklyn b: 11/30/09, Harrisburg, Pa. d: 10/16/93, Lower Paxton Township, Pa. BR/TR, 5'11", 165 lbs. Deb: 4/12/32

YEAR	TM/L	W	L	PCT	G	GS	CG	SH	SV	IP	H	HR	BB	SO	RAT	ERA	ERA+	OAV	OOB	BH	AVG	PB	PR	/A	PD	TPI
1932	Phi-A	0	0	—	6	0	0	0	0	10	17	3	9	5	24.3	11.70	39	.378	.491	0	—	-0	-8	-8	0	-0.7
1934	NY-A	6	7	.462	31	12	6	0	3	133²	126	6	56	40	12.4	4.11	99	.243	.319	8	.190	2	6	-1	-0	0.1
1935	NY-A	4	1	.800	29	3	0	0	1	69	64	6	33	30	12.9	3.26	124	.242	.331	1	.071	-1	9	6	2	0.5
1936	Was-A	18	10	.643	34	31	16	2	2	223²	255	11	96	59	14.2	4.63	103	.285	.356	15	.190	2	10	4	-2	0.4
1937	Was-A	14	15	.483	37	34	20	0	1	264¹	290	15	124	86	14.2	4.90	90	.280	.359	19	.202	2	-8	-14	1	-1.0
1938	Was-A	5	8	.385	31	14	1	0	0	131¹	160	11	83	41	16.7	6.58	69	.310	.407	12	.261	3	-26	-30	0	-2.1
1939	Was-A	0	3	.000	7	6	1	0	0	40²	56	7	31	12	19.3	8.63	50	.337	.442	3	.200	0	-18	-19	1	-1.0
Total	7	47	44	.516	175	100	44	2	9	872²	968	59	432	273	14.6	5.08	87	.281	.363	58	.198	7	-35	-63	3	-3.1

● **JOHN DeSILVA** DeSilva, John Reed b: 9/30/67, Fort Bragg, Cal. BR/TR, 6', 193 lbs. Deb: 8/15/93

YEAR	TM/L	W	L	PCT	G	GS	CG	SH	SV	IP	H	HR	BB	SO	RAT	ERA	ERA+	OAV	OOB	BH	AVG	PB	PR	/A	PD	TPI
1993	Det-A	0	0	—	1	0	0	0	0	1	2	0	0	0	18.0	9.00	48	.667	.667	0	—	0	-1	-1	0	0.0
	LA-N	0	0	—	3	0	0	0	0	5¹	6	1	1	6	11.8	6.75	57	.273	.304	0	—	0	-2	-2	-0	-0.2
1995	Bal-A	1	0	1.000	2	2	0	0	0	8²	8	3	7	1	16.6	7.27	65	.258	.410	0	—	0	-2	-2	-0	-0.2
Total	2	1	0	1.000	6	2	0	0	0	15	16	3	8	7	15.0	7.20	61	.286	.385	0	—	0	-5	-5	0	-0.2

● **SHORTY DesJARDIEN** DesJardien, Paul Raymond b: 8/24/1893, Coffeyville, Kan. d: 3/7/56, Monrovia, Cal. BR/TR, 6'4.5", 205 lbs. Deb: 5/20/16

YEAR	TM/L	W	L	PCT	G	GS	CG	SH	SV	IP	H	HR	BB	SO	RAT	ERA	ERA+	OAV	OOB	BH	AVG	PB	PR	/A	PD	TPI
1916	Cle-A	0	0	—	1	0	0	0	0	1	1	0	1	0	18.0	18.00	17	.200	.333	0	—	0	-2	-2	-0	0.0

● **RUBE DESSAU** Dessau, Frank Rolland b: 3/29/1883, New Galilee, Pa. d: 5/6/52, York, Pa. BB/TR, 5'11", 175 lbs. Deb: 9/22/07

YEAR	TM/L	W	L	PCT	G	GS	CG	SH	SV	IP	H	HR	BB	SO	RAT	ERA	ERA+	OAV	OOB	BH	AVG	PB	PR	/A	PD	TPI
1907	Bos-N	0	1	.000	2	2	1	0	0	9¹	13	0	10	1	23.1	10.61	24	.394	.545	0	.000	-0	-8	-8	-0	-0.8
1910	Bro-N	2	3	.400	19	0	0	0	1	51¹	67	0	29	24	17.7	5.79	52	.328	.424	1	.067	-1	-16	-16	-1	-1.7
Total	2	2	4	.333	21	2	1	0	1	60²	80	0	39	25	18.5	6.53	45	.338	.443	1	.053	-1	-24	-24	-2	-2.5

● **ELMER DESSENS** Dessens, Elmer b: 1/13/72, Hermosillo, Mex. BR/TR, 6', 190 lbs. Deb: 6/24/96

YEAR	TM/L	W	L	PCT	G	GS	CG	SH	SV	IP	H	HR	BB	SO	RAT	ERA	ERA+	OAV	OOB	BH	AVG	PB	PR	/A	PD	TPI
1996	Pit-N	0	2	.000	15	3	0	0	0	25	40	2	4	13	15.8	8.28	53	.385	.407	2	.400	1	-11	-11	-0	-0.7

● **JOHN DETTMER** Dettmer, John Franklin b: 3/4/70, Centerville, Ill. BR/TR, 6', 185 lbs. Deb: 6/16/94

YEAR	TM/L	W	L	PCT	G	GS	CG	SH	SV	IP	H	HR	BB	SO	RAT	ERA	ERA+	OAV	OOB	BH	AVG	PB	PR	/A	PD	TPI
1994	Tex-A	0	6	.000	11	9	0	0	0	54	63	10	20	27	14.3	4.33	111	.286	.354	0	—	0	3	3	-0	0.3
1995	Tex-A	0	0	—	1	0	0	0	0	0¹	2	0	0	0	54.0	27.00	18	.667	.667	0	—	0	-1	-1	0	0.0
Total	2	0	6	.000	12	9	0	0	0	54¹	65	10	20	27	14.6	4.47	108	.291	.358	0	—	0	2	2	-0	0.3

● **TOM DETTORE** Dettore, Thomas Anthony b: 11/17/47, Canonsburg, Pa. BL/TR, 6'4", 200 lbs. Deb: 6/11/73

YEAR	TM/L	W	L	PCT	G	GS	CG	SH	SV	IP	H	HR	BB	SO	RAT	ERA	ERA+	OAV	OOB	BH	AVG	PB	PR	/A	PD	TPI
1973	Pit-N	0	1	.000	12	1	0	0	0	22²	33	1	14	13	19.9	5.96	59	.340	.439	0	.000	-0	-6	-6	-0	-0.3
1974	Chi-N	3	5	.375	16	9	0	0	0	64²	64	4	31	43	14.1	4.18	91	.255	.351	5	.250	1	-4	-3	-0	-0.1
1975	Chi-N	5	4	.556	36	5	0	0	0	85¹	88	8	31	46	13.5	5.38	71	.270	.350	6	.250	1	-17	-15	-1	-1.3
1976	Chi-N	0	1	.000	4	0	0	0	0	7	11	3	6	4	16.7	10.29	38	.355	.394	0	—	0	-5	-5	-0	-0.6
Total	4	8	11	.421	68	15	0	0	0	179²	196	16	78	106	14.6	5.21	73	.278	.365	11	.229	2	-32	-28	-2	-2.3

● **MEL DEUTSCH** Deutsch, Melvin Elliott b: 7/26/15, Caldwell, Tex. BR/TR, 6'4", 215 lbs. Deb: 4/21/46

YEAR	TM/L	W	L	PCT	G	GS	CG	SH	SV	IP	H	HR	BB	SO	RAT	ERA	ERA+	OAV	OOB	BH	AVG	PB	PR	/A	PD	TPI
1946	Bos-A	0	0	—	3	0	0	0	0	6¹	7	1	3	2	14.2	5.68	64	.280	.357	0	.000	-0	-1	-1	-0	0.0

● **CHARLIE DEVENS** Devens, Charles b: 1/1/10, Milton, Mass. BR/TR, 6'1", 180 lbs. Deb: 9/24/32

YEAR	TM/L	W	L	PCT	G	GS	CG	SH	SV	IP	H	HR	BB	SO	RAT	ERA	ERA+	OAV	OOB	BH	AVG	PB	PR	/A	PD	TPI
1932	NY-A	1	0	1.000	1	1	1	0	0	9	6	0	7	4	13.0	2.00	204	.200	.351	0	.000	0	2	2	0	0.2
1933	NY-A	3	3	.500	14	8	2	0	0	62	59	1	50	23	15.8	4.35	89	.250	.381	2	.095	-1	-1	-3	-1	-0.4
1934	NY-A	1	0	1.000	1	1	1	0	0	11	9	0	5	4	11.5	1.64	248	.225	.311	1	.500	1	3	3	0	0.5
Total	3	5	3	.625	16	10	4	0	0	82	74	1	62	31	14.9	3.73	105	.242	.370	3	.120	0	5	2	-1	0.4

● **ADRIAN DEVINE** Devine, Paul Adrian b: 12/2/51, Galveston, Tex. BR/TR, 6'4", 205 lbs. Deb: 6/27/73

YEAR	TM/L	W	L	PCT	G	GS	CG	SH	SV	IP	H	HR	BB	SO	RAT	ERA	ERA+	OAV	OOB	BH	AVG	PB	PR	/A	PD	TPI
1973	Atl-N	2	3	.400	24	1	0	0	4	32¹	45	6	12	15	16.4	6.40	61	.338	.401	1	.250	0	-10	-9	-1	-1.5
1975	Atl-N	1	0	1.000	5	2	0	0	0	16¹	19	2	7	8	14.9	4.41	86	.284	.360	0	.000	-1	-1	-0	-0	-0.2
1976	Atl-N	5	6	.455	48	1	0	0	9	73	72	3	26	48	12.2	3.21	118	.255	.320	0	.000	-2	2	5	-1	0.6
1977	Tex-A	11	6	.647	56	0	0	0	15	105²	102	8	31	67	11.7	3.58	114	.259	.319	0	—	0	6	6	2	1.2
1978	Atl-N	5	4	.556	64	0	0	0	3	65¹	84	3	25	26	15.0	5.92	68	.323	.382	1	.091	-1	-17	-14	-0	-1.9
1979	Atl-N	1	2	.333	40	0	0	0	0	66²	84	4	25	22	15.0	3.24	125	.311	.374	0	.000	-1	6	6	-1	0.1
1980	Tex-A	1	1	.500	13	0	0	0	0	28	49	4	9	8	19.0	4.82	81	.377	.421	0	—	0	-2	-3	-0	-0.4
Total	7	26	22	.542	217	12	0	0	31	387¹	455	34	135	194	14.0	4.21	95	.296	.357	2	.049	-3	-19	-9	0	-1.9

● **JIM DEVINE** Devine, Walter James b: 10/5/1858, Brooklyn, N.Y. d: 1/11/05, Syracuse, N.Y. TL. Deb: 5/9/1883 ♦

YEAR	TM/L	W	L	PCT	G	GS	CG	SH	SV	IP	H	HR	BB	SO	RAT	ERA	ERA+	OAV	OOB	BH	AVG	PB	PR	/A	PD	TPI
1883	Bal-a	1	1	.500	2	2	1	0	0	11	15	0	1	3	13.1	7.36	47	.306	.320	2	.222	-0	-5	-5	-1	-0.6

● **HAL DEVINEY** Deviney, Harold John b: 4/11/1893, Newton, Mass. d: 1/4/33, Westwood, Mass. TR. Deb: 7/30/20

YEAR	TM/L	W	L	PCT	G	GS	CG	SH	SV	IP	H	HR	BB	SO	RAT	ERA	ERA+	OAV	OOB	BH	AVG	PB	PR	/A	PD	TPI
1920	Bos-A	0	0	—	1	0	0	0	0	3	7	0	2	0	27.0	15.00	24	.500	.563	2	1.000	2	-4	-4	-0	0.2

● **JIM DEVLIN** Devlin, James Alexander b: 1849, Philadelphia, Pa. d: 10/10/1883, Philadelphia, Pa. BR/TR, 5'11", 175 lbs. Deb: 4/21/1873 ♦

YEAR	TM/L	W	L	PCT	G	GS	CG	SH	SV	IP	H	HR	BB	SO	RAT	ERA	ERA+	OAV	OOB	BH	AVG	PB	PR	/A	PD	TPI
1875	Chi-n	7	16	.304	28	24	24	0	0	224	254	0	12	23	10.7	1.93	118	.256	.265	92	.289	7	7	8	1	1.3
1876	Lou-N	30	35	.462	68	68	66	5	0	622	566	3	37	122	8.7	1.56	174	.224	.235	94	.315	2	51	80	1	7.3
1877	Lou-N	35	25	.583	61	61	61	4	0	559	617	4	41	141	10.6	2.25	147	.270	.283	72	.269	-2	34	65	2	5.9
Total	2	65	60	.520	129	129	127	9	0	1181	1183	7	78	263	9.6	1.89	159	.246	.258	166	.293	1	86	145	3	13.2

YEAR	TM/L	W	L	PCT	G	GS	CG	SH	SV	IP	H	HR	BB	SO	RAT	ERA	ERA+	OAV	OOB	BH	AVG	PB	PR	/A	PD	TPI
● JIM DEVLIN	Devlin, James H. b: 4/16/1866, Troy, N.Y. d: 12/14/1900, Troy, N.Y. TL , 5'7", 135 lbs. Deb: 6/28/1886																										
1886	NY-N	0	0	—	1	0	0	0	1	2	3	0	4	2	31.5	18.00	18	.250	.438	0	.000	-0	-3	-3	0	-0.3
1887	Phi-N	0	2	.000	2	2	2	0	0	18	20	0	10	6	16.5	6.00	71	.267	.375	2	.333	1	-4	-4	0	-0.2
1888	*StL-a	6	5	.545	11	11	10	0	0	90¹	82	3	20	45	11.0	3.19	102	.233	.289	11	.297	2	-1	1	0	0.2
1889	StL-a	5	3	.625	9	8	5	0	0	60	56	0	24	37	13.1	2.40	176	.239	.328	5	.192	-2	10	12	1	1.3
Total 4		11	10	.524	23	21	17	0	1	170¹	161	3	58	90	12.5	3.38	109	.239	.316	18	.257	1	1	6	2	1.0
● CHARLIE DEWALD	Dewald, Charles H. b: 9/1867, Newark, N.J. d: 8/22/04, Cleveland, Ohio TL , Deb: 9/2/1890																										
1890	Cle-P	2	0	1.000	2	2	2	0	0	14	13	0	5	6	11.6	0.64	618	.236	.300	3	.375	1	6	5	-0	0.6
● MARK DEWEY	Dewey, Mark Alan b: 1/3/65, Grand Rapids, Mich. BR/TR, 6', 185 lbs. Deb: 8/24/90																										
1990	SF-N	1	1	.500	14	0	0	0	0	22²	22	1	6	11	10.7	2.78	131	.259	.300	0	.000	-0	3	2	-0	0.2
1992	NY-N	1	0	1.000	20	0	0	0	0	33¹	37	2	10	24	12.7	4.32	80	.283	.331	0	.000	-0	-3	-3	0	-0.1
1993	Pit-N	1	2	.333	21	0	0	0	7	26²	14	0	14	14	9.1	2.36	171	.157	.265	0	—	0	5	5	0	0.8
1994	Pit-N	2	1	.667	45	0	0	0	1	51¹	61	4	19	30	14.6	3.68	117	.303	.372	1	1.000	-0	3	4	-1	0.2
1995	SF-N	1	0	1.000	27	0	0	0	0	31²	30	2	17	32	13.4	3.13	131	.254	.348	0	.000	-0	4	3	-0	0.1
1996	SF-N	6	3	.667	78	0	0	0	0	83¹	79	9	41	57	13.5	4.21	97	.257	.354	0	.000	-0	0	-1	2	0.0
Total 6		12	7	.632	205	0	0	0	8	249	243	18	102	168	12.9	3.65	110	.261	.341	1	.091	0	11	10	1	1.2
● CARLOS DIAZ	Diaz, Carlos Antonio b: 1/7/58, Kaneohe, Hawaii BR/TL, 6', 170 lbs. Deb: 6/30/82																										
1982	Atl-N	3	2	.600	19	0	0	0	1	25¹	31	3	9	16	14.2	4.62	81	.307	.364	0	.000	-0	-3	-3	-0	-0.5
	NY-N	0	0	—	4	0	0	0	0	3²	6	0	4	0	24.5	0.00	—	.353	.476	0	—	0	1	1	0	0.0
	Yr	3	2	.600	23	0	0	0	1	29	37	3	13	16	15.5	4.03	92	.311	.379	0	.000	-0	-1	-1	-0	-0.5
1983	NY-N	3	1	.750	54	0	0	0	1	83¹	62	1	35	64	10.6	2.05	177	.211	.297	0	.000	-0	15	15	1	0.8
1984	LA-N	1	0	1.000	37	0	0	0	1	41	47	4	24	36	15.6	5.49	64	.285	.376	0	.000	-0	-9	-9	-1	-1.0
1985	*LA-N	6	3	.667	46	0	0	0	0	79¹	70	7	18	73	10.0	2.61	133	.230	.273	0	.000	-0	9	8	-1	0.7
1986	LA-N	0	0	—	19	0	0	0	0	25¹	33	2	7	18	14.2	4.26	81	.317	.360	0	.000	-0	-2	-2	-0	-0.2
Total 5		13	6	.684	179	0	0	0	4	258	249	17	97	207	12.1	3.21	111	.253	.320	0	.000	-1	12	10	-0	0.7
● ROB DIBBLE	Dibble, Robert Keith b: 1/24/64, Bridgeport, Conn. BL/TR, 6'4", 230 lbs. Deb: 6/29/88																										
1988	Cin-N	1	1	.500	37	0	0	0	0	59¹	43	2	21	59	9.9	1.82	197	.207	.283	0	.000	-0	11	12	-1	0.2
1989	Cin-N	10	5	.667	74	0	0	0	2	99	62	4	39	141	9.5	2.09	172	.176	.264	0	.000	-1	15	17	-1	2.3
1990	*Cin-N★	8	3	.727	68	0	0	0	11	98	62	3	34	136	8.9	1.74	226	.183	.259	0	.000	-1	**22**	**24**	-0	3.0
1991	Cin-N★	3	5	.375	67	0	0	0	31	82¹	67	5	25	124	10.1	3.17	120	.223	.282	0	.000	0	3	4	-1	0.7
1992	Cin-N	3	5	.375	63	0	0	0	25	70¹	48	3	31	110	10.4	3.07	117	.193	.287	2	.400	1	3	4	-1	0.7
1993	Cin-N	1	4	.200	45	0	0	0	19	41²	34	8	42	49	16.8	6.48	62	.225	.400	1	1.000	0	-11	-11	-0	-2.0
1995	Chi-A	0	1	.000	16	0	0	0	1	14¹	7	1	17	26	23.2	6.28	71	.156	.493	0	—	-0	-2	-3	-0	-0.8
	Mil-A	1	1	.500	15	0	0	0	0	12	9	1	19	11	21.0	8.25	60	.225	.475	0	—	0	-5	-5	-0	-0.8
	Yr	1	2	.333	31	0	0	0	1	26¹	16	2	46	26	21.2	7.18	65	.178	.456	0	—	-0	-7	-7	-0	-0.8
Total 7		27	25	.519	385	0	0	0	89	477	332	27	238	645	11.0	2.98	128	.197	.301	3	.120	-1	38	44	-3	4.3
● PEDRO DIBUT	Dibut, Pedro (Villafana) b: 11/18/1892, Cienfuegos, Cuba d: 12/4/79, Hialeah, Fla. BR/TR, 5'8", 190 lbs. Deb: 5/1/24																										
1924	Cin-N	3	0	1.000	7	2	2	0	0	36²	24	1	12	15	8.8	2.21	170	.188	.257	3	.273	1	7	6	1	0.7
1925	Cin-N	0	0	—	1	0	0	0	0	0	3	0	0	0	—	∞	—	1.000	1.000	0	—	0	-2	-2	-0	-0.2
Total 2		3	0	1.000	8	2	2	0	0	36²	27	1	12	15	9.6	2.70	139	.206	.273	3	.273	1	5	4	1	0.5
● LEO DICKERMAN	Dickerman, Leo Louis b: 10/31/1896, DeSoto, Mo. d: 4/30/82, Atkins, Ark. BR/TR, 6'4", 192 lbs. Deb: 4/21/23																										
1923	Bro-N	8	12	.400	35	20	7	1	0	159²	180	4	72	58	14.3	3.72	104	.283	.357	13	.250	3	5	3	2	0.8
1924	Bro-N	0	0	—	7	2	0	0	0	19²	20	0	16	9	17.4	5.49	68	.263	.404	1	.167	-0	-4	-4	0	0.0
	StL-N	7	4	.636	18	13	8	1	0	119¹	108	6	51	28	12.0	2.41	157	.249	.328	9	.231	1	19	18	0	1.7
	Yr	7	4	.636	25	15	8	1	0	139¹	128	6	67	37	12.6	2.84	133	.250	.337	10	.222	1	16	14	1	1.7
1925	StL-N	4	11	.267	29	18	7	2	1	130²	135	10	79	40	14.9	5.58	77	.273	.376	5	.114	-3	-19	-18	4	-1.7
Total 3		19	27	.413	89	53	22	4	1	429²	443	20	218	135	14.0	4.00	99	.270	.358	28	.199	1	2	-1	6	0.8
● GEORGE DICKERSON	Dickerson, George Clark b: 12/1/1892, Renner, Tex. d: 7/9/38, Los Angeles, Cal. BR/TR, 6'1", 170 lbs. Deb: 8/2/17																										
1917	Cle-A	0	0	—	1	0	0	0	0	1	0	0	0	0	0.0	0.00	—	.000	.000	0	—	0	0	0	-0	0.0
● EMERSON DICKMAN	Dickman, George Emerson b: 11/12/14, Buffalo, N.Y. d: 4/27/81, New York, N.Y. BR/TR, 6'2", 175 lbs. Deb: 6/27/36																										
1936	Bos-A	0	0	—	1	0	0	0	0	2	4	0	4	1	27.0	9.00	59	.400	.500	0	—	0	-0	-0	0	0.0
1938	Bos-A	5	5	.500	32	11	3	1	0	104	117	9	54	22	15.1	5.28	93	.288	.377	10	.286	4	-6	-4	0	0.0
1939	Bos-A	8	3	.727	48	1	0	0	5	113²	126	10	43	46	13.6	4.43	107	.288	.349	2	.056	-4	2	4	3	0.2
1940	Bos-A	8	6	.571	35	9	2	0	3	100	121	15	38	40	14.7	6.03	75	.291	.356	3	.107	-2	-18	-17	2	-2.1
1941	Bos-A	1	1	.500	9	3	1	0	0	31	37	4	17	16	15.7	6.39	65	.301	.386	1	.091	-1	-8	-8	-1	-0.6
Total 5		22	15	.595	125	24	6	1	8	349²	403	38	153	126	14.6	5.33	88	.288	.363	16	.145	-2	-30	-25	4	-2.5
● JIM DICKSON	Dickson, James Edward b: 4/20/38, Portland, Ore. BL/TR, 6'1", 185 lbs. Deb: 7/2/63																										
1963	Hou-N	0	1	.000	13	0	0	0	2	14²	22	0	2	6	14.7	6.14	51	.344	.364	0	.000	-0	-5	-5	-0	-0.5
1964	Cin-N	1	0	1.000	4	0	0	0	0	5	8	0	2	6	23.4	7.20	50	.444	.565	0	—	0	-2	-2	-0	-0.4
1965	KC-A	3	2	.600	68	0	0	0	1	85²	68	6	47	54	12.3	3.47	101	.220	.327	0	.000	-0	-1	-1	-0	-0.1
1966	KC-A	1	0	1.000	24	1	0	0	0	37	37	4	26	20	14.6	5.35	63	.264	.368	1	.250	-0	-8	-8	-0	-0.3
Total 4		5	3	.625	109	1	0	0	3	142¹	135	10	77	86	13.5	4.36	79	.254	.351	1	.143	0	-15	-15	-1	-1.3
● JASON DICKSON	Dickson, Jason Royce b: 3/30/73, London, Ont., Can. BL/TR, 6', 190 lbs. Deb: 8/21/96																										
1996	Cal-A	1	4	.200	7	7	0	0	0	43¹	52	6	18	20	14.7	4.57	107	.306	.376	0	—	0	2	2	-0	0.1
● LANCE DICKSON	Dickson, Lance Michael b: 10/19/69, Fullerton, Cal. BR/TL, 6', 185 lbs. Deb: 8/9/90																										
1990	Chi-N	0	3	.000	3	3	0	0	0	13²	20	2	4	4	15.8	7.24	56	.370	.414	0	.000	-0	-5	-5	1	-0.8
● MURRY DICKSON	Dickson, Murry Monroe b: 8/21/16, Tracy, Mo. d: 9/21/89, Kansas City, Kan. BR/TR, 5'10.5", 157 lbs. Deb: 9/30/39																										
1939	StL-N	0	0	—	1	0	0	0	0	3²	1	0	1	2	4.9	0.00	—	.091	.167	0	.000	-0	2	2	-0	0.0
1940	StL-N	0	0	—	1	1	0	0	0	1²	5	0	1	0	32.4	16.20	25	.500	.545	0	—	0	-2	-2	-0	-0.2
1942	StL-N	6	3	.667	36	7	2	0	2	120²	91	1	61	66	11.4	2.91	118	.216	.316	8	.190	-0	5	7	1	0.6
1943	*StL-N	8	2	.800	31	7	2	0	0	115²	119	4	49	44	13.1	3.58	94	.269	.343	9	.265	1	-3	-0	-0	-0.2
1946	*StL-N	15	6	.714	47	19	12	2	1	184¹	160	8	56	82	10.7	2.88	120	.234	.295	18	.277	4	11	12	4	2.2
1947	StL-N	13	16	.448	47	25	11	4	3	231²	211	16	88	111	11.7	3.07	135	.243	.315	17	.213	1	25	27	1	3.4
1948	StL-N	12	16	.429	42	29	11	1	1	252¹	257	36	85	113	12.2	4.14	99	.265	.325	27	.281	4	-5	-1	1	0.3
1949	Pit-N	12	14	.462	44	20	11	2	0	224¹	216	17	80	89	12.1	3.29	128	.255	.324	17	.202	0	19	23	5	3.0
1950	Pit-N	10	15	.400	51	22	8	0	3	225	227	20	83	76	12.5	3.80	115	.260	.326	21	.256	3	9	15	2	2.0
1951	Pit-N	20	16	.556	45	35	19	3	2	288²	294	32	101	112	12.5	4.02	105	.262	.327	30	.273	5	-2	7	4	1.7
1952	Pit-N	14	21	.400	43	34	21	2	2	277²	278	26	76	112	11.5	3.57	112	.261	.311	24	.224	2	5	13	4	2.3
1953	Pit-N★	10	19	.345	45	26	10	1	4	200²	240	27	58	88	13.5	4.53	99	.298	.348	7	.115	-4	-5	-1	-0	-0.5
1954	Phi-N	10	20	.333	40	31	12	4	3	226¹	256	31	73	64	13.2	3.78	107	.286	.342	15	.190	-0	7	11	1	1.3
1955	Phi-N	12	11	.522	36	28	12	4	0	216	190	27	82	92	11.5	3.50	113	.238	.312	18	.220	1	13	11	1	1.3
1956	Phi-N	0	3	.000	3	3	0	0	0	23	20	1	2	1	12.5	5.09	73	.241	.337	3	.333	1	-3	-3	-0	-0.3
	StL-N	13	8	.619	28	27	12	3	0	196¹	175	20	57	109	10.7	3.07	123	.240	.296	19	.247	4	15	16	4	2.5
	Yr	13	11	.542	31	30	12	3	0	219¹	195	21	59	110	10.9	3.28	115	.240	.301	22	.256	4	12	14	4	2.2
1957	StL-N	5	3	.625	14	13	3	1	0	74	87	8	25	29	13.7	4.14	96	.296	.353	6	.222	1	-2	-1	2	0.1
1958	KC-A	9	5	.643	27	19	8	1	0	99	99	12	46	47	13.3	3.27	119	.258	.330	7	.179	0	6	7	2	0.8
	*NY-A	1	2	.333	6	2	0	0	1	20¹	18	1	12	8	13.7	5.75	61	.237	.348	4	.286	-0	-4	-5	-0	-0.7
	Yr	10	7	.588	33	11	8	1	1	119¹	117	13	58	55	12.1	3.70	104	.253	.318	11	.262	-0	1	2	2	0.7
1959	KC-A	2	1	.667	38	0	0	0	0	71	85	19	36	27	14.2	4.94	81	.290	.350	3	.176	-1	-9	-7	-0	-0.4
Total 18		172	181	.487	625	338	149	27	23	3052¹	3029	302	1058	1281	12.2	3.66	110	.260	.323	253	.231	25	81	120	32	19.7

YEAR TM/L	W	L	PCT	G	GS	CG	SH	SV	IP	H	HR	BB	SO	RAT	ERA	ERA+	OAV	OOB	BH	AVG	PB	PR	/A	PD	TPI
● **WALT DICKSON**				Dickson, Walter R. "Hickory" b: 12/3/1878, New Summerfield, Tex. d: 12/9/18, Ardmore, Okla. BR/TR, 5'11.5", 175 lbs. Deb: 4/26/10																				
1910 NY-N	1	0	1.000	12	1	0	0	0	29²	31	1	9	9	12.1	5.46	54	.272	.325	1	.250	0	-8	-8	-1	-0.3
1912 Bos-N	3	19	.136	36	20	9	1	1	189	233	2	61	47	14.1	3.86	93	.320	.375	10	.167	-1	-9	-6	-2	-0.6
1913 Bos-N	6	7	.462	19	15	8	0	0	128	118	4	45	47	11.5	3.23	102	.249	.316	8	.178	-1	-0	1	-1	-0.2
1914 Pit-F	9	19	.321	40	32	19	3	1	256²	262	5	74	63	11.9	3.16	91	.273	.327	7	.084	-9	-8	-8	-0	-1.8
1915 Pit-F	7	5	.583	27	11	4	0	0	96²	115	5	33	36	14.0	4.19	65	.316	.376	4	.129	-1	-16	-16	0	-1.9
Total 5	26	50	.342	134	79	40	4	2	700	759	17	222	202	12.7	3.60	86	.288	.345	30	.135	-12	-41	-38	0	-4.8
● **GEORGE DIEHL**				Diehl, George Krause b: 2/25/18, Emmaus, Pa. d: 8/24/86, Kingsport, Tenn. BR/TR, 6'2", 196 lbs. Deb: 4/19/42																				
1942 Bos-N	0	0	—	1	0	0	0	0	3²	2	0	2	0	12.3	2.45	136	.167	.333	0	.000	-0	0	0	0	0.0
1943 Bos-N	0	0	—	1	0	0	0	0	4	4	0	3	1	15.8	4.50	76	.267	.389	0	.000	-0	-0	-0	1	0.1
Total 2	0	0	—	2	0	0	0	0	7²	6	0	5	1	14.1	3.52	96	.222	.364	0	.000	-0	-0	-0	1	0.1
● **LARRY DIERKER**				Dierker, Lawrence Edward b: 9/22/46, Hollywood, Cal BR/TR, 6'4", 215 lbs. Deb: 9/22/64																				
1964 Hou-N	0	1	.000	3	1	0	0	0	9	7	1	3	5	10.0	2.00	171	.219	.286	0	.000	-0	2	1	-1	0.1
1965 Hou-N	7	8	.467	26	19	1	0	0	146²	135	16	37	109	10.7	3.50	96	.240	.290	5	.100	-1	1	-2	-2	-0.5
1966 Hou-N	10	8	.556	29	28	8	2	0	187	173	17	45	108	10.5	3.18	108	.240	.285	10	.149	1	9	5	-1	0.5
1967 Hou-N	6	5	.545	15	15	4	0	0	99	95	4	25	68	11.0	3.36	98	.252	.300	7	.226	2	0	-1	-1	0.0
1968 Hou-N	12	15	.444	32	32	10	1	0	233²	206	14	89	161	11.7	3.31	89	.240	.317	5	.068	-3	-9	-9	-2	-1.7
1969 Hou-N★	20	13	.606	39	37	20	4	0	305¹	240	18	72	232	9.2	2.33	152	.214	**.262**	17	.144	-1	43	41	-1	4.3
1970 Hou-N	16	12	.571	37	36	17	2	1	269²	263	31	82	191	11.7	3.87	100	.254	.313	16	.174	-0	-1	-1	-1	-0.1
1971 Hou-N†	12	6	.667	24	23	6	2	0	159	150	8	33	91	10.5	2.72	124	.248	.289	4	.074	-3	13	11	0	1.0
1972 Hou-N	15	8	.652	31	31	12	5	0	214²	209	14	51	115	11.1	3.40	99	.256	.304	13	.167	-0	1	-2	-0	-0.3
1973 Hou-N	1	1	.500	14	3	0	0	0	27	27	3	13	18	14.0	4.33	84	.265	.359	0	.000	-0	-2	-2	-0	-0.2
1974 Hou-N	11	10	.524	33	33	7	3	0	223²	189	18	82	150	11.1	2.90	120	.232	.307	14	.197	1	18	14	0	1.4
1975 Hou-N	14	16	.467	34	34	14	2	0	232	225	24	91	127	12.5	4.00	84	.260	.335	7	.092	-4	-10	-16	-1	-2.4
1976 Hou-N	13	14	.481	28	28	7	4	0	187²	171	9	72	112	11.9	3.69	86	.243	.319	9	.141	-1	-4	-10	-1	-1.6
1977 StL-N	2	6	.250	11	9	0	0	0	39¹	47	2	23	16	16.3	4.58	84	.267	.345	0	.000	-0	-3	-3	-0	-0.7
Total 14	139	123	.531	356	329	106	25	1	2333²	2130	184	711	1493	11.1	3.31	103	.243	.303	107	.136	-12	65	29	-12	-0.2
● **BILL DIETRICH**				Dietrich, William John "Bullfrog" b: 3/29/10, Philadelphia, Pa. d: 6/20/78, Philadelphia, Pa. BR/TR, 6', 185 lbs. Deb: 4/13/33																				
1933 Phi-A	0	1	.000	8	1	0	0	0	17	13	1	19	4	16.9	5.82	74	.236	.432	1	.333	1	-3	-3	0	0.0
1934 Phi-A	11	12	.478	39	23	14	4	3	207²	201	12	114	88	13.8	4.68	94	.255	.351	15	.208	3	-4	-7	-2	-0.5
1935 Phi-A	7	13	.350	43	15	8	1	3	185¹	203	7	101	59	14.8	5.39	84	.276	.364	5	.083	-6	-19	-17	-1	-2.2
1936 Phi-A	4	6	.400	21	4	0	0	3	71²	91	4	40	34	16.5	6.53	78	.305	.388	3	.111	-2	-12	-11	1	-1.3
Was-A	0	1	.000	5	0	0	0	0	8¹	13	0	6	4	20.5	9.72	49	.351	.442	0	—	0	-4	-5	0	-0.4
Chi-A	4	4	.500	14	11	6	1	0	82²	93	8	36	39	14.2	4.68	111	.284	.356	8	.267	1	3	5	-0	0.4
Yr	8	11	.421	40	15	6	1	3	162²	197	12	82	77	15.5	5.75	89	.297	.375	11	.193	-1	-13	-11	1	-1.3
1937 Chi-A	8	10	.444	29	20	7	1	1	143¹	162	15	72	62	14.7	4.90	94	.285	.366	8	.182	1	-4	-5	1	-0.3
1938 Chi-A	2	4	.333	8	7	1	0	0	48	47	9	31	11	15.0	5.44	90	.259	.364	1	.063	-1	-3	-3	-0	-0.4
1939 Chi-A	7	8	.467	25	19	2	0	0	127²	134	14	56	43	13.5	5.22	91	.272	.349	8	.216	2	-8	-7	-1	-0.5
1940 Chi-A	10	6	.625	23	17	6	1	0	149²	154	10	65	43	13.2	4.03	110	.266	.340	12	.240	3	6	7	-2	0.8
1941 Chi-A	5	8	.385	19	15	4	1	0	109¹	114	7	50	26	13.8	5.35	77	.263	.345	3	.088	0	-15	-12	-1	-1.6
1942 Chi-A	6	11	.353	26	23	6	0	0	160	173	16	70	39	13.9	4.89	74	.277	.355	5	.104	-1	-22	-23	-0	-2.3
1943 Chi-A	12	10	.545	26	26	12	2	0	186²	180	4	53	52	11.3	2.80	119	.253	.307	8	.143	0	10	11	1	1.5
1944 Chi-A	16	17	.485	36	36	15	2	0	246	269	15	68	70	12.4	3.62	95	.279	.328	9	.117	-3	-5	-5	-1	-1.0
1945 Chi-A	7	10	.412	18	16	6	3	0	122¹	136	4	36	43	12.7	4.19	79	.279	.329	6	.167	0	-11	-12	0	-1.4
1946 Chi-A	3	3	.500	11	9	3	0	1	62	63	4	24	20	12.6	2.61	131	.267	.335	1	.053	-2	6	6	1	0.5
1947 Phi-A	5	2	.714	11	9	2	1	0	60²	48	1	18	13	13.4	3.12	122	.223	.350	1	.063	-2	4	5	-1	0.3
1948 Phi-A	1	2	.333	4	2	0	0	0	15¹	21	0	4	5	17.6	5.87	73	.356	.441	0	.000	-0	-3	-3	0	-0.4
Total 16	108	128	.458	366	253	92	17	11	2003²	2117	128	890	660	13.6	4.48	92	.271	.348	94	.150	-5	-85	-84	-3	-8.8
● **DUTCH DIETZ**				Dietz, Lloyd Arthur b: 2/9/12, Cincinnati, Ohio d: 10/29/72, Beaumont, Tex. BR/TR, 5'11.5", 180 lbs. Deb: 4/26/40																				
1940 Pit-N	0	1	.000	4	2	0	0	0	15¹	22	2	4	8	15.3	5.87	65	.355	.394	1	.143	-0	-3	-4	-0	-0.3
1941 Pit-N	7	2	.778	33	6	4	1	1	100¹	88	6	33	22	11.0	2.33	155	.233	.298	4	.160	-1	15	14	0	1.2
1942 Pit-N	6	9	.400	40	13	3	0	3	134¹	139	8	57	35	13.2	3.95	86	.268	.342	7	.200	1	-10	-8	-2	-1.1
1943 Pit-N	0	3	.000	8	0	0	0	0	9	12	0	4	0	17.0	6.00	58	.324	.405	0	—	-0	-3	-3	1	-0.7
Phi-N	1	1	.500	21	0	0	0	2	36	42	2	15	10	14.3	6.50	52	.292	.358	1	.167	0	-12	-11	0	-0.8
Yr	1	4	.200	29	0	0	0	2	45	54	2	19	14	14.6	6.40	53	.297	.363	1	.167	0	-15	-15	0	-1.5
Total 4	14	16	.467	106	21	7	1	6	295	303	18	113	79	12.8	3.87	90	.266	.334	13	.178	-0	-14	-13	-1	-1.7
● **REESE DIGGS**				Diggs, Reese Wilson "Diggsy" b: 9/22/15, Mathews, Va. d: 10/30/78, Baltimore, Md. BB/TR, 6'2", 180 lbs. Deb: 9/15/34																				
1934 Was-A	1	2	.333	4	1	1	0	0	21	26	3	15	2	17.3	6.75	64	.313	.418	2	.250	-1	-5	-6	-0	-0.6
● **JACK DiLAURO**				DiLauro, Jack Edward b: 5/3/43, Akron, Ohio BB/TL, 6'2", 185 lbs. Deb: 5/15/69																				
1969 NY-N	1	4	.200	23	4	0	0	1	63²	54	4	18	27	10.6	2.40	152	.216	.272	0	.000	-1	9	8	-0	0.5
1970 Hou-N	1	3	.250	42	0	0	0	3	33²	34	4	17	23	13.6	4.28	91	.262	.347	0	.000	-0	-1	-1	-0	-0.2
Total 2	2	7	.222	65	4	0	0	4	97¹	84	8	35	50	11.0	3.05	122	.232	.300	0	.000	-2	8	7	-1	0.3
● **GORDON DILLARD**				Dillard, Gordon Lee b: 5/20/64, Salinas, Cal. BL/TL, 6'1", 190 lbs. Deb: 8/12/88																				
1988 Bal-A	0	0	—	2	1	0	0	0	3	3	1	4	2	21.0	6.00	65	.273	.467	0	—	-0	-1	-1	0	0.1
1989 Phi-N	0	0	—	5	0	0	0	0	4	7	0	0	2	15.8	6.75	53	.368	.368	0	—	-0	-1	-1	0	0.0
Total 2	0	0	—	7	1	0	0	0	7	10	1	4	4	18.0	6.43	58	.333	.412	0	—	-0	-2	-2	0	0.1
● **HARLEY DILLINGER**				Dillinger, Harley Hugh "Hoke" or "Lefty" b: 10/30/1894, Pomeroy, Ohio d: 1/8/59, Cleveland, Ohio BR/TL, 5'11", 175 lbs. Deb: 8/16/14																				
1914 Cle-A	0	1	.000	11	2	1	0	0	33²	41	0	25	11	17.9	4.54	64	.325	.441	0	.000	-1	-7	-6	-1	-0.4
● **BILL DILLMAN**				Dillman, William Howard b: 5/25/45, Trenton, N.J. BR/TR, 6'2", 180 lbs. Deb: 4/14/67																				
1967 Bal-A	5	9	.357	32	15	2	1	3	124	115	13	33	69	11.0	4.35	72	.249	.303	5	.161	-0	-15	-17	-1	-2.0
1970 Mon-N	2	3	.400	18	0	0	0	0	30²	28	4	18	17	13.8	5.28	78	.255	.364	0	.000	-0	-4	-4	0	-0.6
Total 2	7	12	.368	50	15	2	1	3	154²	143	17	51	86	11.6	4.54	74	.250	.316	5	.152	-1	-20	-21	-1	-2.6
● **STEVE DILLON**				Dillon, Stephen Edward b: 3/20/43, Yonkers, N.Y. BL/TL, 5'10", 160 lbs. Deb: 9/5/63																				
1963 NY-N	0	0	—	1	0	0	0	0	1²	1	0	1	0	16.2	10.80	32	.429	.429	0	—	0	-1	-1	0	0.0
1964 NY-N	0	0	—	2	0	0	0	0	3	4	1	2	3	18.0	9.00	40	.333	.429	0	—	-0	-2	-2	-0	0.0
Total 2	0	0	—	3	0	0	0	0	4²	7	1	2	3	17.4	9.64	37	.368	.429	0	—	-0	-3	-3	-0	0.0
● **FRANK DiMICHELE**				Dimichele, Frank Lawrence b: 2/16/65, Philadelphia, Pa. BR/TL, 6'3", 205 lbs. Deb: 4/8/88																				
1988 Cal-A	0	0	—	4	0	0	0	0	6²	8	2	2	3	13.5	9.64	40	.263	.333	0	—	-0	-3	-3	0	0.0
● **BILL DINNEEN**				Dinneen, William Henry "Big Bill" b: 4/5/1876, Syracuse, N.Y. d: 1/13/55, Syracuse, N.Y. BR/TR, 6'1", 190 lbs. Deb: 4/22/1898 U																				
1898 Was-N	9	16	.360	29	27	22	0	0	218¹	238	6	88	83	14.1	4.00	92	.275	.353	8	.100	-4	-9	-8	0	-1.2
1899 Was-N	14	20	.412	37	35	30	0	1	291	350	6	106	91	14.4	3.93	100	.297	.361	36	.303	5	-2	-0	4	0.8
1900 Bos-N	20	14	.588	40	37	33	1	0	320²	304	11	105	107	11.7	3.12	133	.250	.314	35	.280	2	21	**36**	2	**3.6**
1901 Bos-N	15	18	.455	37	34	31	0	0	309¹	295	8	77	141	11.4	2.94	122	.248	.299	31	.211	0	23	-1	2	2.1
1902 Bos-A	21	21	.500	42	42	39	2	0	371¹	348	9	99	136	11.0	2.93	122	.248	.302	18	.128	-6	27	-7	-6	1.3
1903 *Bos-A	21	13	.618	37	34	32	6	**2**	299	255	6	96	148	9.7	2.26	134	.230	.276	17	.160	-1	23	26	-1	2.6
1904 Bos-A	23	14	.622	37	37	37	5	0	335²	283	8	63	153	9.3	2.20	124	.230	.268	25	.208	-1	15	18	-2	1.7
1905 Bos-A	12	14	.462	31	29	23	2	1	243²	235	7	50	97	10.8	3.73	72	.255	.299	13	.148	-3	-29	-28	0	-3.2
1906 Bos-A	8	19	.296	28	27	22	1	0	218²	209	4	52	60	10.8	2.92	94	.255	.300	7	.111	-1	-6	-4	-3	-0.9
1907 Bos-A	0	4	.000	5	5	3	0	0	42²	41	0	16	8	14.3	5.23	49	.313	.361	0	.000	-0	-10	-10	-1	-1.2

YEAR TM/L	W	L	PCT	G	GS	CG	SH	SV	IP	H	HR	BB	SO	RAT	ERA	ERA+	OAV	OOB	BH	AVG	PB	PR	/A	PD	TPI
StL-A	7	10	.412	24	16	15	2	4	155.1	153	3	33	38	11.1	2.43	103	.260	.305	10	.204	2	2	1	-3	0.0
Yr	7	14	.333	29	21	18	2	4	188	195	8	41	46	11.5	2.92	86	.269	.313	10	.169	1	-8	-4	-4	-1.2
1908 StL-A	14	7	.667	27	16	11	2	0	167	133	2	53	39	10.2	2.10	114	.231	.300	12	.203	0	5	5	-3	0.4
1909 StL-A	6	7	.462	17	13	8	3	0	112	112	3	29	26	11.4	3.46	70	.267	.316	7	.194	2	-12	-13	-0	-1.3
Total 12	170	177	.490	391	352	306	24	7	3074.2	2957	78	829	1127	11.3	3.01	107	.254	.308	219	.192	-6	38	70	-15	4.7

● **RON DIORIO**   Diorio, Ronald Michael   b: 7/15/46, Waterbury, Conn.   BR/TR, 6'6", 212 lbs.   Deb: 8/9/73

YEAR TM/L	W	L	PCT	G	GS	CG	SH	SV	IP	H	HR	BB	SO	RAT	ERA	ERA+	OAV	OOB	BH	AVG	PB	PR	/A	PD	TPI
1973 Phi-N	0	0	—	23	0	0	0	1	19.1	18	1	6	11	11.2	2.33	163	.257	.316	0	—	0	3	3	-0	0.0
1974 Phi-N	0	0	—	2	0	0	0	0	1	2	1	1	0	27.0	18.00	21	.400	.500	0	—	0	-2	-2	0	0.0
Total 2	0	0	—	25	0	0	0	1	20.1	20	2	7	11	12.0	3.10	122	.267	.329	0	—	0	1	2	0	0.0

● **FRANK DiPINO**   DiPino, Frank Michael   b: 10/22/56, Syracuse, N.Y.   BL/TL, 6', 180 lbs.   Deb: 9/14/81

YEAR TM/L	W	L	PCT	G	GS	CG	SH	SV	IP	H	HR	BB	SO	RAT	ERA	ERA+	OAV	OOB	BH	AVG	PB	PR	/A	PD	TPI
1981 Mil-A	0	0	—	2	0	0	0	0	2.1	0	0	3	3	11.6	—	—	.000	.300	0	—	0	1	1	-0	0.2
1982 Hou-N	2	2	.500	6	6	0	0	0	28.1	32	1	11	25	13.7	6.04	55	.302	.368	0	.000	-1	-8	-9	-1	-1.2
1983 Hou-N	3	4	.429	53	0	0	0	20	71.1	52	2	20	67	9.2	2.65	128	.260	.265	1	.167	1	8	6	1	1.0
1984 Hou-N	4	9	.308	57	0	0	0	14	75.1	74	3	36	65	13.3	3.35	99	.260	.345	0	.000	-1	2	-0	0	-0.1
1985 Hou-N	3	7	.300	54	0	0	0	6	76	69	7	43	49	13.5	4.03	86	.248	.353	2	.167	-0	-4	-5	-2	-0.8
1986 Hou-N	1	3	.250	31	0	0	0	3	40.1	27	5	16	27	10.0	3.57	101	.189	.280	1	.200	1	1	0	0	-0.1
Chi-N	2	4	.333	30	0	0	0	0	40	47	6	14	43	13.7	5.17	78	.297	.355	0	.000	0	-6	-5	1	-0.6
Yr	3	7	.300	61	0	0	0	3	80.1	74	11	30	70	11.7	4.37	87	.243	.311	1	.167	-0	-6	-5	2	-0.5
1987 Chi-N	3	3	.500	69	0	0	0	3	80	75	7	34	61	12.4	3.15	136	.252	.330	1	.500	1	8	10	1	0.9
1988 Chi-N	2	3	.400	63	0	0	0	6	90.1	102	6	32	69	13.4	4.98	72	.285	.344	1	.100	-0	-15	-14	-0	-1.0
1989 StL-N	9	0	1.000	67	0	0	0	6	88.1	69	6	20	44	9.5	2.45	148	.227	.273	1	.077	-1	10	12	0	1.1
1990 StL-N	5	2	.714	62	0	0	0	3	81	92	8	31	49	13.8	4.56	84	.294	.359	1	.250	0	-7	-7	-1	-0.5
1992 StL-N	0	0	—	9	0	0	0	0	11	9	0	2	8	9.8	1.64	207	.220	.273	1	1.000	0	2	2	0	0.1
1993 KC-A	1	1	.500	11	0	0	0	0	15.2	21	2	6	5	16.7	6.89	66	.328	.403	0	—	0	-4	-4	0	-0.6
Total 12	35	38	.479	514	6	0	0	56	700	673	53	269	515	12.2	3.83	96	.256	.328	9	.125	-1	-12	-13	2	-1.4

● **JERRY DiPOTO**   DiPoto, Gerard Peter   b: 5/24/68, Jersey City, N.J.   BR/TR, 6'2", 200 lbs.   Deb: 5/11/93

YEAR TM/L	W	L	PCT	G	GS	CG	SH	SV	IP	H	HR	BB	SO	RAT	ERA	ERA+	OAV	OOB	BH	AVG	PB	PR	/A	PD	TPI
1993 Cle-A	4	4	.500	46	0	0	0	11	56.1	57	0	30	41	14.1	2.40	180	.270	.364	0	—	0	12	12	1	2.0
1994 Cle-A	0	0	—	7	0	0	0	0	15.2	26	1	10	9	21.3	8.04	59	.406	.493	0	—	0	-6	-6	-0	-0.6
1995 NY-N	4	6	.400	58	0	0	0	2	78.2	77	2	29	49	12.6	3.78	107	.267	.343	0	.000	-1	4	2	1	0.3
1996 NY-N	7	2	.778	57	0	0	0	0	77.1	91	5	45	52	16.2	4.19	94	.298	.394	0	.000	-0	0	-2	0	-0.2
Total 4	15	12	.556	168	0	0	0	13	228	251	8	114	151	14.8	3.87	106	.289	.377	0	.000	-1	10	6	1	2.1

● **GEORGE DISCH**   Disch, George Charles   b: 3/15/1879, Lincoln, Mo.   d: 8/25/50, Rapid City, S.D.   5'11",   Deb: 8/8/05

YEAR TM/L	W	L	PCT	G	GS	CG	SH	SV	IP	H	HR	BB	SO	RAT	ERA	ERA+	OAV	OOB	BH	AVG	PB	PR	/A	PD	TPI
1905 Det-A	0	2	.000	8	3	1	0	0	47.2	43	1	8	14	10.0	2.64	103	.243	.283	2	.105	-1	0	0	0	-0.1

● **GLENN DISHMAN**   Dishman, Glenelg Edward   b: 11/5/70, Baltimore, Md.   BR/TL, 6'1", 195 lbs.   Deb: 6/22/95

YEAR TM/L	W	L	PCT	G	GS	CG	SH	SV	IP	H	HR	BB	SO	RAT	ERA	ERA+	OAV	OOB	BH	AVG	PB	PR	/A	PD	TPI
1995 SD-N	4	8	.333	19	16	0	0	0	97	104	11	34	43	13.2	5.01	80	.278	.345	6	.200	1	-9	-11	-1	-1.1
1996 SD-N	0	0	—	3	0	0	0	0	2.1	3	0	1	0	15.4	7.71	52	.300	.364	0	—	0	-1	-1	-0	0.0
Phi-N	0	0	—	4	1	0	0	0	7	9	2	2	3	14.1	7.71	57	.321	.367	0	—	0	-3	-3	-0	0.0
Yr	0	0	—	7	1	0	0	0	9.1	12	2	3	3	14.5	7.71	55	.316	.366	0	—	0	-4	-4	-0	0.0
Total 2	4	8	.333	26	17	0	0	0	106.1	116	13	37	46	13.3	5.25	77	.282	.347	6	.200	1	-13	-14	-1	-1.1

● **ALEC DISTASO**   Distaso, Alec John   b: 12/23/48, Los Angeles, Cal.   BR/TR, 6'2", 200 lbs.   Deb: 4/20/69

YEAR TM/L	W	L	PCT	G	GS	CG	SH	SV	IP	H	HR	BB	SO	RAT	ERA	ERA+	OAV	OOB	BH	AVG	PB	PR	/A	PD	TPI
1969 Chi-N	0	0	—	2	0	0	0	0	4	6	0	1	4	13.5	3.86	104	.316	.350	0	—	0	-0	-0	0	0.0

● **ART DITMAR**   Ditmar, Arthur John   b: 4/3/29, Winthrop, Mass.   BR/TR, 6'2", 196 lbs.   Deb: 4/19/54

YEAR TM/L	W	L	PCT	G	GS	CG	SH	SV	IP	H	HR	BB	SO	RAT	ERA	ERA+	OAV	OOB	BH	AVG	PB	PR	/A	PD	TPI
1954 Phi-A	1	4	.200	14	5	0	0	0	39.1	50	4	36	14	19.9	6.41	61	.314	.444	1	.125	0	-12	-11	-0	-1.2
1955 KC-A	12	12	.500	35	22	7	1	1	175.1	180	23	86	79	14.0	5.03	83	.270	.360	13	.210	-0	-21	-17	1	-2.0
1956 KC-A	12	22	.353	44	34	14	2	1	254.1	254	30	108	126	13.1	4.42	98	.262	.340	13	.143	-4	-7	-3	-1	-0.8
1957 *NY-A	8	3	.727	46	11	0	0	6	127.1	128	9	35	64	11.7	3.25	110	.261	.313	7	.200	0	8	5	-1	0.3
1958 *NY-A	9	8	.529	38	13	4	0	4	139.2	124	14	38	52	10.8	3.42	103	.237	.295	11	.250	2	5	2	-2	0.2
1959 NY-A	13	9	.591	38	25	7	1	1	202	156	17	52	96	**9.6**	2.90	126	.211	**.270**	15	.197	-2	22	17	-1	1.8
1960 *NY-A	15	9	.625	34	28	8	1	0	200	195	25	56	65	11.3	3.06	117	.256	.308	11	.159	-2	18	12	-2	1.1
1961 NY-A	2	3	.400	12	8	1	0	0	54.1	59	9	14	24	12.4	4.64	80	.285	.336	1	.053	-2	-4	-6	1	-0.6
KC-A	0	5	.000	20	5	0	1	0	54	60	6	23	19	14.2	5.67	74	.286	.362	2	.167	-0	-10	-9	-0	-0.8
Yr	2	8	.200	32	13	1	1	0	108.1	119	15	37	43	13.1	5.15	77	.281	.341	3	.097	-2	-14	-14	1	-1.4
1962 KC-A	0	2	.000	6	5	0	0	0	21.2	31	1	13	19	19.1	6.65	64	.323	.414	1	.167	-0	-6	-6	-0	-0.5
Total 9	72	77	.483	287	156	41	5	14	1268	1237	138	461	552	12.3	3.98	97	.256	.326	75	.178	-3	-7	-16	-2	-2.5

● **SONNY DIXON**   Dixon, John Craig   b: 11/5/24, Charlotte, N.C.   BB/TR, 6'2.5", 205 lbs.   Deb: 4/20/53

YEAR TM/L	W	L	PCT	G	GS	CG	SH	SV	IP	H	HR	BB	SO	RAT	ERA	ERA+	OAV	OOB	BH	AVG	PB	PR	/A	PD	TPI
1953 Was-A	5	8	.385	43	6	3	0	3	120	123	13	31	40	11.7	3.75	104	.267	.316	4	.154	2	3	2	1	0.4
1954 Was-A	1	2	.333	16	0	0	0	1	29.2	26	3	12	7	11.5	3.03	117	.236	.311	0	.000	-1	2	2	1	0.2
Phi-A	5	7	.417	38	6	1	0	4	107.1	136	8	27	42	13.9	4.86	80	.308	.352	7	.250	2	-14	-11	3	-0.6
Yr	6	9	.400	**54**	6	1	0	5	137	162	11	39	49	13.4	4.47	86	.293	.343	7	.206	1	-11	-10	3	-0.6
1955 KC-A	0	0	—	1	0	0	0	0	1.2	6	1	0	0	32.4	16.20	26	.545	.545	0	—	0	-2	-2	0	0.0
1956 NY-A	0	1	.000	4	0	0	0	1	4.1	5	0	5	1	20.8	2.08	186	.294	.455	0	—	-1	1	1	0	0.2
Total 4	11	18	.379	102	12	4	0	9	263	296	25	75	90	12.9	4.17	93	.284	.335	11	.180	1	-9	-9	6	0.0

● **KEN DIXON**   Dixon, Kenneth John   b: 10/17/60, Monroe, Va.   BB/TR, 5'11", 166 lbs.   Deb: 9/22/84

YEAR TM/L	W	L	PCT	G	GS	CG	SH	SV	IP	H	HR	BB	SO	RAT	ERA	ERA+	OAV	OOB	BH	AVG	PB	PR	/A	PD	TPI
1984 Bal-A	0	1	.000	2	2	0	0	0	13	14	1	4	8	12.5	4.15	93	.269	.321	0	—	0	-0	-0	0	0.0
1985 Bal-A	8	4	.667	34	18	3	1	1	162	144	20	64	108	11.7	3.67	110	.237	.312	0	—	0	9	7	-1	0.3
1986 Bal-A	11	13	.458	35	33	2	0	0	202.1	194	33	83	170	12.4	4.58	90	.249	.322	0	—	0	-9	-10	-1	-1.1
1987 Bal-A	7	10	.412	34	15	0	0	5	105	128	31	27	91	13.4	6.43	68	.292	.334	0	—	0	-23	-24	-0	-3.3
Total 4	26	28	.481	105	68	5	1	6	482.1	480	85	178	377	12.4	4.66	89	.256	.322	0	—	0	-24	-28	-2	-4.1

● **STEVE DIXON**   Dixon, Steven Ross   b: 8/3/69, Cincinnati, Ohio   BL/TL, 6', 190 lbs.   Deb: 9/7/93

YEAR TM/L	W	L	PCT	G	GS	CG	SH	SV	IP	H	HR	BB	SO	RAT	ERA	ERA+	OAV	OOB	BH	AVG	PB	PR	/A	PD	TPI
1993 StL-N	0	0	—	4	0	0	0	0	2.2	7	1	5	2	40.5	33.75	12	.538	.667	0	—	0	-9	-9	0	0.0
1994 StL-N	0	0	—	2	0	0	0	0	2.1	3	0	8	1	43.4	23.14	18	.333	.647	0	—	0	-5	-5	0	0.0
Total 2	0	0	—	6	0	0	0	0	5	10	1	13	3	41.4	28.80	14	.455	.657	0	—	0	-14	-14	0	0.0

● **TOM DIXON**   Dixon, Thomas Earl   b: 4/23/55, Orlando, Fla.   BR/TR, 5'11", 175 lbs.   Deb: 7/30/77

YEAR TM/L	W	L	PCT	G	GS	CG	SH	SV	IP	H	HR	BB	SO	RAT	ERA	ERA+	OAV	OOB	BH	AVG	PB	PR	/A	PD	TPI
1977 Hou-N	1	0	1.000	9	4	0	0	0	30.1	40	0	7	15	14.2	3.26	109	.320	.361	0	.000	-1	2	1	0	0.0
1978 Hou-N	7	11	.389	30	19	3	2	1	140	140	8	40	66	11.6	3.99	83	.260	.318	4	.100	-2	-6	-11	-1	-1.5
1979 Hou-N	1	2	.333	19	1	0	0	0	25.2	39	2	6	9	18.9	6.66	53	.348	.425	1	1.000	1	-8	-9	-1	-0.8
1983 Mon-N	0	1	.000	4	0	0	0	0	3.2	6	1	1	4	19.6	9.82	37	.375	.444	0	—	0	-3	-3	-0	-0.6
Total 4	9	14	.391	62	24	4	2	1	199.2	225	11	63	94	13.1	4.33	78	.288	.343	5	.104	-2	-15	-21	-2	-2.9

● **BILL DOAK**   Doak, William Leopold "Spittin' Bill"   b: 1/28/1891, Pittsburgh, Pa.   d: 11/26/54, Bradenton, Fla.   BR/TR, 6'0.5", 165 lbs.   Deb: 9/1/12

YEAR TM/L	W	L	PCT	G	GS	CG	SH	SV	IP	H	HR	BB	SO	RAT	ERA	ERA+	OAV	OOB	BH	AVG	PB	PR	/A	PD	TPI
1912 Cin-N	0	0	—	1	1	0	0	0	2	4	0	1	2	22.5	4.50	75	.444	.500	0	—	0	-0	-0	0	0.0
1913 StL-N	2	8	.200	15	12	5	1	1	93	79	4	39	51	11.9	3.10	104	.236	.325	1	.032	-3	1	1	1	-0.1
1914 StL-N	19	6	.760	36	33	16	7	1	256	193	2	87	118	10.1	**1.72**	**162**	.216	.290	10	.118	-3	30	31	5	3.2
1915 StL-N	16	18	.471	38	36	19	3	1	276	263	4	85	124	11.6	2.64	106	.261	.323	15	.174	1	5	9	3	1.5
1916 StL-N	12	8	.600	29	26	11	2	0	192	177	6	55	82	11.0	2.63	101	.251	.308	8	.129	-2	-0	5	3	0.1
1917 StL-N	16	20	.444	44	37	16	3	2	281.2	257	6	85	111	11.2	3.10	87	.252	.312	12	.126	-4	-12	-13	-5	-1.6
1918 StL-N	9	15	.375	31	24	13	1	0	211	191	3	60	74	10.9	2.43	111	.249	.306	12	.182	1	8	7	1	1.5
1919 StL-N	13	14	.481	31	29	13	3	0	202.2	179	5	55	69	10.6	3.11	90	.246	.299	7	.109	-4	-4	-1	-0	-0.9
1920 StL-N	20	12	.625	39	37	20	5	1	270	256	7	80	90	11.4	2.53	129	.253	.312	11	.143	-6	18	14	0	0.9
1921 StL-N	15	6	**.714**	32	29	13	1	1	208.2	224	9	37	83	11.4	**2.59**	**142**	.278	.313	10	.143	-3	28	25	2	2.2
1922 StL-N	11	13	.458	37	29	8	2	2	180.1	222	12	69	73	14.7	5.54	70	.311	.374	7	.130	-3	-29	-34	-0	-3.9

YEAR	TM/L	W	L	PCT	G	GS	CG	SH	SV	IP	H	HR	BB	SO	RAT	ERA	ERA+	OAV	OOB	BH	AVG	PB	PR	/A	PD	TPI
1923	StL-N	8	13	.381	30	26	7	2	0	185	199	4	69	53	13.2	3.26	120	.279	.346	3	.045	-9	15	13	3	0.8
1924	StL-N	2	1	.667	11	1	0	0	3	22	25	0	14	7	16.0	3.27	116	.313	.415	1	.200	-0	1	1	1	0.2
	Bro-N	11	5	.688	21	16	8	2	0	149¹	130	8	35	32	10.1	3.07	122	.239	.289	10	.179	-1	13	11	3	1.3
	Yr	13	6	.684	32	17	8	2	3	171¹	155	8	49	39	10.9	3.10	121	.249	.307	11	.180	-1	15	12	3	1.5
1927	Bro-N	11	8	.579	27	20	6	1	0	145	153	6	40	37	12.2	3.48	114	.271	.322	6	.128	-3	7	8	1	0.8
1928	Bro-N	3	8	.273	28	12	4	1	3	99¹	104	1	35	12	13.0	3.26	122	.271	.340	3	.111	-2	8	8	3	0.9
1929	StL-N	1	2	.333	3	2	0	0	0	9	17	1	5	3	22.0	12.00	39	.415	.478	0	.000	0	-7	-7	-0	-1.6
Total	16	169	157	.518	453	369	162	34	16	2782²	2676	71	851	1014	11.6	2.98	107	.249	.319	115	.127	-42	80	64	43	5.3

● WALT DOANE   Doane, Walter Rudolph b: 3/12/1887, Bellevue, Idaho d: 10/19/35, W.Brandywine, Pa. BL/TR, 6', 165 lbs. Deb: 9/20/09 ◆

YEAR	TM/L	W	L	PCT	G	GS	CG	SH	SV	IP	H	HR	BB	SO	RAT	ERA	ERA+	OAV	OOB	BH	AVG	PB	PR	/A	PD	TPI
1909	Cle-A	0	1	.000	1	1	0	0	0	5	10	0	1	2	19.8	5.40	47	.400	.423	1	.111	-0	-2	-2	-0	-0.3
1910	Cle-A	0	0	—	6	0	0	0	0	17²	31	1	8	7	20.4	5.60	46	.413	.476	2	.286	1	-6	-6	-1	-0.0
Total	2	0	1	.000	7	1	0	0	0	22²	41	1	9	9	20.3	5.56	46	.410	.464	3	.188	1	-8	-8	-1	-0.3

● JOHN DOBB   Dobb, John Kenneth "Lefty" b: 11/15/01, Muskegon, Mich. d: 7/31/91, Muskegon, Mich. BR/TL, 6'2", 180 lbs. Deb: 8/13/24

YEAR	TM/L	W	L	PCT	G	GS	CG	SH	SV	IP	H	HR	BB	SO	RAT	ERA	ERA+	OAV	OOB	BH	AVG	PB	PR	/A	PD	TPI
1924	Chi-A	0	0	—	2	0	0	0	0	4	4	0	1	2	22.5	9.00	46	.400	.455	0	—	0	-1	-1	-0	0.0

● RAY DOBENS   Dobens, Raymond Joseph "Lefty" b: 7/28/06, Nashua, N.H. d: 4/21/80, Stuart, Fla. BL/TL, 5'8", 175 lbs. Deb: 7/7/29

YEAR	TM/L	W	L	PCT	G	GS	CG	SH	SV	IP	H	HR	BB	SO	RAT	ERA	ERA+	OAV	OOB	BH	AVG	PB	PR	/A	PD	TPI
1929	Bos-A	0	0	—	11	2	1	0	0	28¹	32	4	9	4	13.3	3.81	112	.302	.362	3	.375	1	1	1	-1	0.0

● JESS DOBERNIC   Dobernic, Andrew Joseph b: 11/20/17, Mt.Olive, Ill. BR/TR, 5'10", 170 lbs. Deb: 7/2/39

YEAR	TM/L	W	L	PCT	G	GS	CG	SH	SV	IP	H	HR	BB	SO	RAT	ERA	ERA+	OAV	OOB	BH	AVG	PB	PR	/A	PD	TPI
1939	Chi-A	0	1	.000	4	0	0	0	0	3¹	3	0	6	1	27.0	13.50	35	.231	.500	0	.000	-0	-3	-3	0	-0.7
1948	Chi-N	7	2	.778	54	0	0	0	1	85²	67	8	40	48	11.3	3.15	124	.213	.303	2	.200	-0	8	7	-2	0.5
1949	Chi-N	0	0	—	4	0	0	0	0	4	9	2	4	0	29.3	20.25	20	.450	.542	0	—	0	-7	-7	-0	0.0
	Cin-N	0	0	—	14	0	0	0	0	19¹	28	7	16	6	20.5	9.78	43	.329	.436	0	.000	-0	-12	-12	-0	0.0
	Yr	0	0	—	18	0	0	0	0	23¹	37	9	20	6	22.0	11.57	36	.352	.456	0	.000	-0	-20	-19	-0	0.0
Total	3	7	3	.700	76	0	0	0	1	112¹	107	17	66	55	14.0	5.21	76	.247	.349	2	.154	-0	-15	-15	-2	-0.2

● CHUCK DOBSON   Dobson, Charles Thomas b: 1/10/44, Kansas City, Mo. BR/TR, 6'4", 200 lbs. Deb: 4/19/66

YEAR	TM/L	W	L	PCT	G	GS	CG	SH	SV	IP	H	HR	BB	SO	RAT	ERA	ERA+	OAV	OOB	BH	AVG	PB	PR	/A	PD	TPI
1966	KC-A	4	6	.400	14	14	1	0	0	83²	71	7	50	61	13.2	4.09	83	.234	.346	3	.115	-1	-6	-6	1	-0.7
1967	KC-A	10	10	.500	32	29	4	1	0	197²	172	11	75	110	11.4	3.69	86	.233	.306	13	.181	-0	-10	-11	-0	-1.1
1968	Oak-A	12	14	.462	35	34	11	3	0	225¹	197	20	80	168	11.2	3.00	94	.234	.303	15	.200	2	-0	-4	2	-0.2
1969	Oak-A	15	13	.536	35	35	11	1	0	235¹	244	16	80	137	12.4	3.86	89	.270	.330	8	.101	-3	-6	-11	-2	-1.7
1970	Oak-A	16	15	.516	41	40	13	**5**	0	267	230	32	92	149	11.0	3.74	95	.229	.297	11	.118	-3	-1	-6	-2	-1.2
1971	Oak-A	15	5	.750	30	30	7	1	0	189	185	24	71	100	12.2	3.81	88	.259	.327	13	.197	3	-7	-10	0	-0.7
1973	Oak-A	1	0	1.000	1	1	0	0	0	2¹	6	1	3	2	30.9	7.71	46	.429	.500	0	—	0	-1	-1	-0	-0.3
1974	Cal-A	2	3	.400	5	5	2	0	0	30	39	3	13	16	15.6	5.70	60	.315	.380	0	—	0	-7	-8	-0	-1.0
1975	Cal-A	0	2	.000	9	2	0	0	0	28	30	5	14	14	14.5	6.75	58	.275	.363	0	—	0	-9	-10	-1	-0.7
Total	9	74	69	.517	202	190	49	11	0	1258¹	1174	125	476	758	11.9	3.78	87	.247	.318	63	.153	-2	-48	-68	-1	-7.6

● JOE DOBSON   Dobson, Joseph Gordon "Burrhead" b: 1/20/17, Durant, Okla. d: 6/23/94, Jacksonville, Fla. BR/TR, 6'2", 197 lbs. Deb: 4/26/39

YEAR	TM/L	W	L	PCT	G	GS	CG	SH	SV	IP	H	HR	BB	SO	RAT	ERA	ERA+	OAV	OOB	BH	AVG	PB	PR	/A	PD	TPI
1939	Cle-A	2	3	.400	35	3	0	0	1	78	87	3	51	27	16.0	5.88	75	.290	.395	1	.056	-0	-11	-13	1	-0.8
1940	Cle-A	3	7	.300	40	7	2	1	3	100	101	8	48	57	13.4	4.95	85	.268	.351	3	.125	-1	-6	-8	-0	-0.8
1941	Bos-A	12	5	.706	27	18	7	1	0	134¹	136	8	67	69	13.7	4.49	93	.262	.349	7	.149	-0	-5	-5	-2	-0.7
1942	Bos-A	11	9	.550	30	23	10	3	0	182²	155	9	68	72	11.1	3.30	113	.231	.303	10	.145	-1	7	9	2	0.9
1943	Bos-A	7	11	.389	25	20	9	3	0	164¹	144	4	57	63	11.0	3.12	106	.239	.305	5	.096	-3	3	4	-2	-0.2
1946	*Bos-A	13	7	.650	32	24	9	1	0	166²	148	11	68	91	11.7	3.24	113	.234	.309	5	.100	-2	5	8	2	0.9
1947	Bos-A	18	8	.692	33	31	15	1	1	228²	203	15	73	110	10.9	2.95	132	.238	**.299**	16	.208	1	19	24	-2	2.5
1948	Bos-A☆	16	10	.615	38	32	16	5	2	245	237	14	92	116	12.1	3.56	123	.253	.320	17	.202	1	20	23	-1	2.2
1949	Bos-A	14	12	.538	33	27	12	2	2	212²	219	12	97	87	13.5	3.85	113	.269	.348	10	.147	-1	8	12	-1	1.1
1950	Bos-A	15	10	.600	39	27	12	1	4	206²	217	15	81	81	13.0	4.18	117	.275	.343	15	.214	1	9	16	1	2.0
1951	Chi-A	7	6	.538	28	21	6	0	3	146²	136	17	51	67	11.5	3.62	111	.248	.312	3	.065	-6	8	7	0	0.0
1952	Chi-A	14	10	.583	29	25	11	3	1	200²	164	11	60	101	10.0	2.51	145	.222	.280	12	.190	0	26	25	-2	2.8
1953	Chi-A	5	5	.500	23	15	3	1	1	100²	96	10	37	50	11.9	3.67	110	.249	.314	2	.069	-2	4	4	-1	0.1
1954	Bos-A	0	0	—	2	0	0	0	0	2²	5	0	1	1	20.3	6.75	61	.385	.429	0	—	0	-1	-1	-0	0.0
Total	14	137	103	.571	414	273	112	22	18	2170	2048	137	851	992	12.1	3.62	112	.250	.322	106	.152	-15	86	105	-5	10.0

● PAT DOBSON   Dobson, Patrick Edward b: 2/12/42, Depew, N.Y. BR/TR, 6'3", 190 lbs. Deb: 5/31/67 C

YEAR	TM/L	W	L	PCT	G	GS	CG	SH	SV	IP	H	HR	BB	SO	RAT	ERA	ERA+	OAV	OOB	BH	AVG	PB	PR	/A	PD	TPI
1967	Det-A	1	2	.333	28	1	0	0	0	49¹	38	6	27	34	12.2	2.92	112	.216	.327	0	.000	-1	2	2	-1	0.0
1968	*Det-A	5	8	.385	47	10	1	0	7	125	89	13	48	93	10.0	2.66	113	.200	.281	4	.143	0	4	5	1	0.7
1969	Det-A	5	10	.333	49	9	1	0	9	105	100	10	39	64	12.0	3.60	104	.253	.322	2	.091	-1	0	2	0	0.1
1970	SD-N	14	15	.483	40	34	8	1	0	251	257	28	78	185	12.2	3.76	106	.265	.322	10	.141	-0	8	6	-0	0.5
1971	*Bal-A	20	8	.714	38	37	18	4	1	282¹	248	24	63	187	10.0	2.90	116	.235	.279	10	.110	-3	18	14	-1	0.9
1972	Bal-A☆	16	18	.471	38	36	13	3	0	268²	220	18	69	161	9.8	2.65	116	.224	.278	12	.141	-2	12	13	-2	1.3
1973	Atl-N	3	7	.300	12	10	1	1	0	57²	73	1	19	23	14.5	4.99	79	.315	.369	1	.067	-1	-9	-7	0	-1.2
	NY-A	9	8	.529	22	21	6	1	0	142²	150	22	34	70	11.8	4.17	88	.266	.311	0	—	0	-6	-8	0	-0.8
1974	NY-A	19	15	.559	39	39	12	2	0	281	282	23	75	157	11.6	3.07	115	.262	.312	0	—	0	17	14	-1	1.5
1975	NY-A	11	14	.440	33	30	7	1	0	207²	205	21	83	129	12.5	4.07	90	.261	.333	0	—	0	-7	-9	-0	-1.0
1976	Cle-A	16	12	.571	35	35	6	0	0	217¹	226	13	65	117	12.1	3.48	100	.272	.327	0	—	0	1	0	-1	0.0
1977	Cle-A	3	12	.200	35	17	1	0	0	133¹	155	23	48	81	14.9	6.14	64	.299	.378	0	—	0	-31	-33	0	-3.1
Total	11	122	129	.486	414	279	74	14	19	2120¹	2043	197	665	1301	11.6	3.54	100	.255	.314	39	.123	-8	10	-1	-3	-1.1

● GEORGE DOCKINS   Dockins, George Woodrow "Lefty" b: 5/5/17, Clyde, Kan. BL/TL, 6', 175 lbs. Deb: 5/5/45

YEAR	TM/L	W	L	PCT	G	GS	CG	SH	SV	IP	H	HR	BB	SO	RAT	ERA	ERA+	OAV	OOB	BH	AVG	PB	PR	/A	PD	TPI
1945	StL-N	8	6	.571	31	12	5	2	0	126¹	132	4	38	33	12.1	3.21	117	.269	.321	6	.176	1	8	8	-1	0.8
1947	Bro-N	0	0	—	4	0	0	0	0	5¹	10	2	2	1	20.3	11.81	35	.400	.444	0	.000	-0	-5	-5	0	0.0
Total	2	8	6	.571	35	12	5	2	0	131²	142	6	40	34	12.4	3.55	106	.275	.327	6	.171	1	4	3	-1	0.8

● SAM DODGE   Dodge, Samuel Edward b: 12/9/1889, Neath, Pa. d: 4/5/66, Utica, N.Y. BR/TR, 6'1", 170 lbs. Deb: 9/24/21

YEAR	TM/L	W	L	PCT	G	GS	CG	SH	SV	IP	H	HR	BB	SO	RAT	ERA	ERA+	OAV	OOB	BH	AVG	PB	PR	/A	PD	TPI
1921	Bos-A	0	0	—	1	0	0	0	0	1	1	0	1	0	18.0	9.00	47	.500	.667	0	—	-0	-1	-1	-0	0.0
1922	Bos-A	0	0	—	3	0	0	0	0	6	11	0	3	3	21.0	4.50	91	.379	.438	0	.000	-0	-0	-0	-0	0.0
Total	2	0	0	—	4	0	0	0	0	7	12	0	4	3	20.6	5.14	80	.387	.457	0	.000	-0	-1	-1	-0	0.0

● FRED DOE   Doe, Alfred George "Count" b: 4/18/1864, Rockport, Mass. d: 10/4/38, Quincy, Mass. BR/TR, 5'10", 165 lbs. Deb: 8/23/1890

YEAR	TM/L	W	L	PCT	G	GS	CG	SH	SV	IP	H	HR	BB	SO	RAT	ERA	ERA+	OAV	OOB	BH	AVG	PB	PR	/A	PD	TPI
1890	Buf-P	0	1	.000	1	1	1	0	0	6	10	0	7	2	25.5	12.00	34	.357	.486	1	.500	-0	-5	-5	-0	-0.5
	Pit-P	0	0	—	1	0	0	0	0	4	4	0	2	2	13.5	4.50	87	.250	.333	1	.500	-0	-0	-0	-0	0.0
	Yr	0	1	.000	2	1	1	0	0	10	14	0	9	4	20.7	9.00	45	.318	.434	1	.250	-0	-5	-6	-0	-0.5

● ED DOHENY   Doheny, Edwin Richard b: 11/24/1873, Northfield, Vt. d: 12/29/16, Medfield, Mass. BL/TL, 5'10.5", 165 lbs. Deb: 9/16/1895

YEAR	TM/L	W	L	PCT	G	GS	CG	SH	SV	IP	H	HR	BB	SO	RAT	ERA	ERA+	OAV	OOB	BH	AVG	PB	PR	/A	PD	TPI
1895	NY-N	0	3	.000	3	3	3	0	0	25²	37	2	19	9	20.7	6.66	70	.333	.444	1	.100	-1	-5	-6	-0	-0.5
1896	NY-N	6	7	.462	17	15	9	0	0	108¹	112	3	59	39	14.7	4.49	94	.265	.363	6	.150	-2	-1	-3	-0	-0.5
1897	NY-N	4	4	.500	10	10	10	0	0	85	69	0	45	37	12.9	2.12	196	.220	.333	7	.200	-1	21	19	3	1.6
1898	NY-N	7	19	.269	28	27	23	0	0	213	238	1	101	96	15.2	3.68	95	.280	.370	14	.163	-1	-2	-5	-3	-0.3
1899	NY-N	14	17	.452	35	33	30	1	0	265¹	282	2	156	115	16.1	4.51	83	.272	.386	27	.241	-0	-19	-22	5	-1.6
1900	NY-N	4	14	.222	20	18	12	0	0	133²	148	2	96	44	17.9	5.45	66	.280	.411	12	.222	-0	-26	-27	2	-2.7
1901	NY-N	2	5	.286	10	6	6	0	0	74	88	1	17	36	13.5	4.50	73	.293	.344	10	.345	3	-10	-10	-0	-0.5
	Pit-N	6	2	.750	11	10	6	1	0	76²	68	1	22	28	11.2	2.00	164	.236	.302	3	.115	0	11	11	-2	0.9
	Yr	8	7	.533	21	16	12	1	0	150²	156	2	39	64	11.9	3.23	102	.263	.313	13	.236	4	2	1	-1	0.4
1902	Pit-N	16	4	.800	22	21	19	2	0	188¹	161	0	61	57	11.3	2.53	108	.231	.307	12	.156	-2	5	4	-1	0.1
1903	Pit-N	16	8	.667	27	25	22	2	0	222²	209	1	89	75	12.8	3.19	101	.252	.338	19	.209	-1	5	3	-1	0.1
Total	9	75	83	.475	183	168	140	6	2	1392²	1412	13	665	567	14.3	3.75	94	.263	.359	111	.198	-3	-24	-37	15	-3.0

YEAR	TM/L	W	L	PCT	G	GS	CG	SH	SV	IP	H	HR	BB	SO	RAT	ERA	ERA+	OAV	OOB	BH	AVG	PB	PR	/A	PD	TPI
● JOHN DOHERTY				Doherty, John Harold b: 6/11/67, New York, N.Y. BR/TR, 6'4", 200 lbs. Deb: 4/8/92																					
1992	Det-A	7	4	.636	47	11	0	0	3	116	131	4	25	37	12.4	3.88	102	.287	.329	0	—	0	1	1	1	0.2
1993	Det-A	14	11	.560	32	31	3	2	0	184²	205	19	48	63	12.6	4.44	97	.286	.335	0	—	0	-2	-3	-2	-0.5
1994	Det-A	6	7	.462	18	17	2	0	0	101¹	139	13	26	28	14.9	6.48	75	.337	.380	0	—	0	-19	-18	2	-1.7
1995	Det-A	5	9	.357	48	2	0	0	6	113	130	10	37	46	13.8	5.10	93	.288	.350	0	—	0	-5	-4	1	-0.4
1996	Bos-A	0	0	—	3	0	0	0	0	6¹	8	1	4	3	18.5	5.68	90	.276	.382	0	—	0	-0	-0	1	-0.2
Total	5	32	31	.508	148	61	5	2	9	521¹	613	47	140	177	13.3	4.87	91	.296	.347	0	—	0	-26	-25	3	-2.6
● JOHN DOLAN				Dolan, John b: 9/12/1867, Newport, Ky. d: 5/8/48, Springfield, Ohio TR, 5'10", 170 lbs. Deb: 9/5/1890																					
1890	Cin-N	1	1	.500	2	2	2	0	0	18	17	3	10	9	14.0	4.50	79	.243	.346	1	.125	-1	-2	-2	-0	-0.2
1891	Col-a	12	11	.522	27	24	19	0	0	203¹	216	8	84	68	13.3	4.16	83	.263	.331	7	.090	-4	-10	-16	-2	-1.9
1892	Was-N	2	2	.500	5	4	3	0	0	37	39	0	15	4	13.4	4.38	74	.260	.331	3	.231	-1	-4	-5	-1	-0.4
1893	StL-N	0	1	.000	3	1	1	0	0	17¹	26	1	7	1	17.7	4.15	114	.338	.400	1	.143	0	1	1	-0	0.0
1895	Chi-N	0	1	.000	2	2	1	0	0	11	16	0	6	1	18.8	6.55	78	.333	.418	0	.000	-0	-2	-2	-0	-0.1
Total	5	15	16	.484	39	33	26	0	1	286²	314	12	122	87	13.8	4.30	83	.269	.341	12	.110	-5	-17	-23	-3	-2.6
● COZY DOLAN				Dolan, Patrick Henry b: 12/3/1872, Cambridge, Mass. d: 3/29/07, Louisville, Ky. BL/TL, 5'10", 160 lbs. Deb: 4/26/1895 ◆																					
1895	Bos-N	11	7	.611	25	21	18	3	1	198¹	215	11	67	47	13.4	4.27	120	.272	.340	20	.241	-1	11	18	4	1.5
1896	Bos-N	1	4	.200	6	5	3	0	0	41	55	1	27	14	18.7	4.83	94	.318	.419	2	.143	-1	-2	-1	-0	-0.3
1905	Bos-N	0	1	.000	2	0	0	0	0	4	7	2	1	1	18.0	9.00	34	.368	.400	119	.275	1	-3	-3	-0	-0.5
1906	Bos-N	0	1	.000	2	2	0	0	0	12	12	1	6	7	13.5	4.50	60	.300	.391	136	.248	0	-2	-2	-0	-0.2
Total	4	12	13	.480	35	26	21	3	1	255¹	289	15	101	69	14.3	4.44	109	.283	.357	855	.269	-2	4	12	3	0.5
● TOM DOLAN				Dolan, Thomas J. b: 1/10/1859, New York, N.Y. d: 1/16/13, St.Louis, Mo. BR/TR, Deb: 9/30/1879 ◆																					
1883	StL-a	0	0	—	1	0	0	0	0	4	4	0	1	0	9.0	4.50	97	.250	.250	63	.214	-0	-1	-0	0	0.0
● ART DOLL				Doll, Arthur James "Moose" b: 5/7/13, Chicago, Ill. d: 4/28/78, Calumet City, Ill. BR/TR, 6'1", 190 lbs. Deb: 9/21/35 ◆																					
1936	Bos-N	0	1	.000	1	1	0	0	0	8	11	1	2	4	15.8	3.38	114	.355	.412	0	.000	-0	1	1	0	0.0
1938	Bos-N	0	0	—	3	0	0	0	0	4	4	0	3	1	15.8	2.25	153	.286	.412	1	1.000	1	1	1	-0	0.1
Total	2	0	1	.000	4	1	0	0	0	12	15	1	5	5	15.8	3.00	123	.333	.412	2	.154	0	1	1	0	0.1
● RED DONAHUE				Donahue, Francis Rostell b: 1/23/1873, Waterbury, Conn. d: 8/25/13, Philadelphia, Pa. BR/TR, 6', 187 lbs. Deb: 5/6/1893																					
1893	NY-N	0	0	—	2	0	0	0	1	5	8	1	3	1	23.4	9.00	52	.348	.464	0	.000	-0	-2	-2	0	-0.1
1895	StL-N	0	1	.000	1	1	1	0	0	8	9	2	3	2	14.6	6.75	72	.281	.361	0	.000	-1	-2	-2	-0	-0.2
1896	StL-N	7	24	.226	32	32	28	0	0	267	376	6	98	70	16.4	5.80	75	.329	.389	17	.159	-8	-43	-43	-1	-4.3
1897	StL-N	10	35	.222	46	42	38	1	1	348	484	16	106	64	15.8	6.13	72	.326	.380	33	.213	-3	-70	-67	5	-6.1
1898	Phi-N	16	17	.485	35	35	31	1	0	284¹	327	7	80	37	13.3	3.55	97	.286	.340	16	.143	-7	-2	-3	-4	-0.7
1899	Phi-N	21	8	.724	35	31	27	4	0	279	292	6	63	51	11.8	3.39	109	.269	.316	20	.180	-5	15	9	3	0.6
1900	Phi-N	15	10	.600	32	24	21	2	0	240	299	6	50	41	13.4	3.60	100	.304	.344	20	.222	-1	3	0	-1	-0.2
1901	Phi-N	20	13	.606	34	33	33	1	0	295¹	299	2	59	88	11.2	2.59	131	.261	.302	11	.097	-9	24	27	-2	1.6
1902	StL-A	22	11	.667	35	34	33	3	0	316¹	322	7	65	63	11.2	2.76	128	.264	.306	11	.093	-9	29	27	7	2.2
1903	StL-A	8	7	.533	16	15	14	0	0	131	145	0	22	51	11.5	2.75	106	.279	.309	8	.157	-2	3	0	0	0.1
	Cle-A	7	9	.438	16	15	14	4	0	136²	142	3	12	45	10.5	2.44	117	.267	.291	8	.151	-1	8	6	1	0.7
	Yr	15	16	.484	32	30	28	4	0	267²	287	3	34	96	11.0	2.59	111	.273	.300	16	.154	-3	11	9	2	0.8
1904	Cle-A	19	14	.576	35	32	30	6	0	277	261	2	49	127	10.9	2.40	105	.264	.299	17	.168	-1	6	4	2	0.5
1905	Cle-A	6	12	.333	20	18	14	1	0	137²	132	2	25	45	10.6	3.40	77	.254	.295	4	.075	-5	-11	-12	1	-1.8
1906	Det-A	13	14	.481	28	28	26	3	0	241	276	6	54	82	12.0	2.73	101	.278	.323	10	.123	-4	-1	-1	-0	-0.3
Total	13	164	175	.484	367	340	312	25	3	2966¹	3376	61	689	787	12.7	3.61	96	.285	.331	175	.152	-56	-40	-52	18	-8.0
● DEACON DONAHUE				Donahue, John Stephen Michael b: 6/23/20, Chicago, Ill. BR/TR, 6', 180 lbs. Deb: 9/16/43																					
1943	Phi-N	0	0	—	2	0	0	0	0	4	4	0	1	1	13.5	4.50	75	.235	.316	0	—	-0	-1	0	0	0.0
1944	Phi-N	0	2	.000	6	0	0	0	0	9¹	18	0	2	2	19.3	7.71	47	.429	.455	0	.000	-0	-4	-4	0	-0.8
Total	2	0	2	.000	8	0	0	0	0	13¹	22	0	3	3	17.6	6.75	52	.373	.413	0	.000	-0	-5	-5	0	-0.8
● ATLEY DONALD				Donald, Richard Atley "Swampy" b: 8/19/10, Morton, Miss. d: 10/19/92, West Monroe, La. BL/TR, 6'1", 186 lbs. Deb: 4/21/38																					
1938	NY-A	0	1	.000	2	2	0	0	0	12	7	0	14	6	16.5	5.25	86	.175	.340	1	.167	-0	-1	-0	0	-0.1
1939	NY-A	13	3	.813	24	20	11	2	1	153	144	12	60	55	12.0	3.71	118	.247	.317	15	.250	3	16	11	-1	1.1
1940	NY-A	8	3	.727	24	11	6	1	0	118²	113	11	59	60	13.2	3.03	133	.249	.339	6	.146	-2	18	13	-3	0.6
1941	*NY-A	9	5	.643	22	20	10	0	0	159	141	11	69	71	12.1	3.57	110	.237	.320	4	.081	-4	10	6	-0	0.3
1942	*NY-A	11	3	.786	20	19	10	1	0	147²	133	6	45	53	10.8	3.11	111	.239	.296	9	.148	-1	9	5	-2	0.3
1943	NY-A	6	4	.600	22	15	2	0	0	119¹	134	10	38	57	13.0	4.60	70	.276	.329	8	.128	-1	-17	-18	-2	-1.9
1944	NY-A	13	10	.565	30	19	9	0	0	159	173	13	59	48	13.2	3.34	104	.280	.345	10	.182	-0	2	3	-1	0.2
1945	NY-A	5	4	.556	9	9	6	2	0	63²	62	3	25	19	12.3	2.97	117	.248	.316	5	.208	0	3	5	-1	0.3
Total	8	65	33	.663	153	115	54	6	1	932¹	907	66	369	369	12.4	3.52	107	.253	.325	57	.160	-7	39	24	-11	0.4
● ED DONALDS				Donalds, Edward Alexander "Erston" b: 6/22/1885, Bidwell, Ohio d: 7/3/50, Columbus, Ohio BR/TR, 5'11", 180 lbs. Deb: 9/1/12																					
1912	Cin-N	1	0	1.000	1	0	0	0	0	4	7	0	1	1	15.8	4.50	74	.438	.438	0	—	-0	-1	0	0	-0.1
● MIKE DONLIN				Donlin, Michael Joseph "Turkey Mike" b: 5/30/1878, Peoria, Ill. d: 9/24/33, Hollywood, Cal. BL/TL, 5'9", 170 lbs. Deb: 7/19/1899 ◆																					
1899	StL-N	0	1	.000	3	1	0	0	0	15¹	15	1	14	6	17.6	7.63	52	.254	.405	86	.323	1	-6	-6	1	-0.2
1902	Cin-N	0	0	—	1	0	0	0	0	1	1	0	0	0	9.00	0.00	—	.250	.250	41	.287	0	0	-0	-0	-0
Total	2	0	1	.000	4	1	0	0	0	16¹	16	1	14	6	17.1	7.16	55	.254	.397	1282	.333	1	-6	-6	1	-0.2
● ED DONNELLY				Donnelly, Edward "Big Ed" or "Ned" (b: Edward O'Donnell) b: 7/29/1880, Hampton, N.Y. d: 11/28/57, Rutland, Vt. BR/TR, 6'1", 205 lbs. Deb: 9/19/11																					
1911	Bos-N	3	2	.600	5	4	4	1	0	36²	33	0	9	16	10.8	2.45	156	.236	.291	1	.071	-1	4	6	-0	0.6
1912	Bos-N	5	10	.333	37	18	10	0	0	184¹	225	10	72	67	14.7	4.35	82	.304	.370	19	.275	3	-19	-16	1	-0.8
Total	2	8	12	.400	42	22	14	1	0	221	258	10	81	83	14.1	4.03	90	.293	.357	20	.241	2	-15	-10	1	-0.2
● ED DONNELLY				Donnelly, Edward Vincent b: 12/10/34, Allen, Mich. BR/TR, 6', 175 lbs. Deb: 8/1/59																					
1959	Chi-N	1	1	.500	9	0	0	0	0	14¹	18	1	9	4	17.0	3.14	126	.305	.397	0	—	0	1	1	0	0.2
● FRANK DONNELLY				Donnelly, Franklin Marion b: 10/7/1869, Tamaroa, Ill. d: 2/3/53, Canton, Ill. 5'6", 180 lbs. Deb: 8/15/1893																					
1893	Chi-N	3	1	.750	7	5	3	0	2	42	51	1	17	6	15.4	5.36	86	.291	.367	8	.444	4	-3	-3	-0	0.1
● BLIX DONNELLY				Donnelly, Sylvester Urban b: 1/21/14, Olivia, Minn. d: 6/20/76, Olivia, Minn. BR/TR, 5'10", 178 lbs. Deb: 5/6/44																					
1944	*StL-N	2	1	.667	27	4	2	1	2	76¹	61	2	34	45	11.4	2.12	166	.218	.307	1	.063	-1	13	12	1	0.5
1945	StL-N	8	10	.444	31	23	9	4	2	166¹	157	10	87	76	13.5	3.52	106	.250	.346	7	.130	-2	5	4	-4	-0.2
1946	StL-N	1	2	.333	13	0	0	0	0	13²	17	1	10	11	18.4	3.95	87	.347	.467	0	—	0	-0	-0	1	0.0
	Phi-N	3	4	.429	12	8	2	0	1	76¹	64	7	24	38	10.6	2.95	116	.220	.284	7	.280	2	4	4	-1	0.5
	Yr	4	6	.400	25	8	2	0	1	90	81	8	34	49	11.7	3.10	111	.238	.310	7	.280	2	3	3	-1	0.3
1947	Phi-N	4	6	.400	38	10	5	1	5	120²	113	6	46	30	12.1	2.98	134	.265	.340	2	.063	-2	14	14	-0	0.9
1948	Phi-N	5	7	.417	26	19	8	1	0	131²	125	13	49	46	11.9	3.69	107	.261	.330	10	.222	2	4	4	-3	0.3
1949	Phi-N	2	1	.667	23	1	0	0	0	78¹	84	7	40	36	14.4	5.06	78	.294	.382	4	.174	-1	-9	-10	-2	-0.6
1950	Phi-N	4	3	.333	14	1	0	0	0	21	30	5	10	10	17.1	4.29	94	.330	.396	1	.200	-0	-1	-1	0	-0.1
1951	Bos-N	0	1	.000	6	0	0	0	0	7¹	8	1	6	3	18.4	7.36	50	.286	.429	0	.000	-0	-3	-3	0	-0.4
Total	8	27	36	.429	190	75	27	7	12	691²	659	52	306	296	12.8	3.49	109	.257	.340	32	.159	-1	27	24	-8	0.7
● JIM DONOHUE				Donohue, James Thomas b: 10/31/38, St.Louis, Mo. BR/TR, 6'4", 190 lbs. Deb: 4/11/61																					
1961	Det-A	1	1	.500	14	0	0	0	0	20¹	23	2	15	20	16.8	3.54	116	.287	.400	0	.000	-0	1	1	-0	0.1
	LA-A	4	6	.400	38	7	0	0	5	100¹	93	16	50	79	12.8	4.31	105	.246	.334	4	.148	-1	-3	2	-0	0.1
	Yr	5	7	.417	52	7	0	0	6	120²	116	18	65	99	13.5	4.18	106	.253	.346	4	.143	-1	-2	4	-1	0.2

YEAR	TM/L	W	L	PCT	G	GS	CG	SH	SV	IP	H	HR	BB	SO	RAT	ERA	ERA+	OAV	OOB	BH	AVG	PB	PR	/A	PD	TPI
1962	LA-A	1	0	1.000	12	1	0	0	0	24¹	24	4	11	14	13.7	3.70	104	.258	.349	1	.250	0	1	0	-1	0.0
	Min-A	0	1	.000	6	1	0	0	1	10¹	12	2	6	3	15.7	6.97	59	.324	.419	0	.000	-0	-3	-3	1	-0.3
	Yr	1	1	.500	18	2	0	0	1	34²	36	6	17	17	13.8	4.67	84	.273	.356	1	.167	-0	-3	-3	-0	-0.3
Total	2	6	8	.429	70	9	0	0	7	155¹	152	24	82	116	13.7	4.29	101	.259	.351	5	.147	-1	-5	1	-1	-0.1

● PETE DONOHUE
Donohue, Peter Joseph   b: 11/5/1900, Athens, Tex.   d: 2/23/88, Ft.Worth, Tex.   BR/TR, 6'2", 185 lbs.   Deb: 7/1/21

YEAR	TM/L	W	L	PCT	G	GS	CG	SH	SV	IP	H	HR	BB	SO	RAT	ERA	ERA+	OAV	OOB	BH	AVG	PB	PR	/A	PD	TPI
1921	Cin-N	7	6	.538	21	11	7	0	1	118¹	117	5	26	44	10.9	3.35	107	.263	.304	8	.211	1	6	3	2	0.6
1922	Cin-N	18	9	.667	33	30	18	2	1	242	257	7	43	66	11.3	3.12	128	.276	.312	16	.182	-3	26	23	1	2.1
1923	Cin-N	21	15	.583	42	36	19	2	3	274¹	304	3	68	84	12.5	3.38	114	.278	.326	24	.250	3	19	15	1	2.0
1924	Cin-N	16	9	.640	35	31	16	3	0	221²	248	9	36	72	11.9	3.60	105	.285	.321	14	.192	-0	7	4	-1	0.2
1925	Cin-N	21	14	.600	42	38	**27**	3	2	**301**	310	3	49	78	10.9	3.08	133	.268	.299	32	.294	7	40	34	-3	4.0
1926	Cin-N	**20**	14	.588	47	38	17	**5**	2	**285²**	298	6	49	73	10.9	3.37	109	.268	.298	33	.311	9	14	10	-3	1.7
1927	Cin-N	6	16	.273	33	24	12	1	1	190²	253	3	32	48	13.5	4.11	92	.328	.366	16	.250	1	-4	-7	0	-0.6
1928	Cin-N	7	11	.389	23	18	8	0	0	150	180	10	32	37	12.9	4.74	83	.309	.348	7	.146	-0	-12	-13	1	-1.3
1929	Cin-N	10	13	.435	32	24	7	0	0	177²	243	12	51	30	15.1	5.42	84	.331	.377	20	.333	4	-14	-17	0	-1.3
1930	Cin-N	1	3	.250	8	5	2	0	1	34¹	53	0	13	4	17.6	6.29	77	.363	.419	1	.100	-1	-5	-6	1	-0.5
	NY-N	7	6	.538	18	11	4	0	1	86²	135	6	18	26	16.1	6.13	77	.360	.392	9	.273	1	-11	-13	-2	-1.6
	Yr	8	9	.471	26	16	6	0	2	121	188	6	31	30	16.4	6.17	77	.360	.398	10	.233	0	-16	-19	-0	-2.1
1931	NY-N	0	1	.000	4	1	0	0	0	11¹	14	2	4	4	14.3	5.56	66	.311	.367	0	.000	-0	-2	-2	-0	-0.2
	Cle-A	0	0	—	2	0	0	0	0	5¹	9	1	5	4	23.6	8.44	55	.429	.538	0	.000	-0	-2	-2	0	-0.0
1932	Bos-A	0	1	.000	4	0	0	0	0	12²	18	2	6	1	17.1	7.82	57	.340	.407	0	.000	-1	-5	-5	1	-0.3
Total	12	134	118	.532	344	269	137	16	12	2112¹	2439	68	422	571	12.4	3.87	103	.293	.330	180	.246	21	56	25	-1	4.8

● LINO DONOSO
Donoso, Lino (Galeta)   b: 9/23/22, Havana, Cuba   d: 10/13/90, Veracruz, Mexico   BL/TL, 5'11", 160 lbs.   Deb: 6/18/55

YEAR	TM/L	W	L	PCT	G	GS	CG	SH	SV	IP	H	HR	BB	SO	RAT	ERA	ERA+	OAV	OOB	BH	AVG	PB	PR	/A	PD	TPI
1955	Pit-N	4	6	.400	25	9	3	0	1	95	106	16	35	38	13.5	5.31	78	.287	.351	5	.185	-1	-13	-13	0	-1.2
1956	Pit-N	0	0	—	3	0	0	0	0	1²	2	0	1	1	16.2	0.00	—	.250	.333	0	—	-0	1	1	0	0.0
Total	2	4	6	.400	28	9	3	0	1	96²	108	16	36	39	13.5	5.21	79	.286	.350	5	.185	-1	-13	-12	0	-1.2

● DICK DONOVAN
Donovan, Richard Edward   b: 12/7/27, Boston, Mass.   BL/TR, 6'3", 205 lbs.   Deb: 4/24/50

YEAR	TM/L	W	L	PCT	G	GS	CG	SH	SV	IP	H	HR	BB	SO	RAT	ERA	ERA+	OAV	OOB	BH	AVG	PB	PR	/A	PD	TPI
1950	Bos-N	0	2	.000	10	3	0	0	0	29²	24	4	34	9	19.4	8.19	47	.255	.438	1	.167	-1	-13	-14	-0	-0.7
1951	Bos-N	0	0	—	8	2	0	0	1	13²	17	0	11	4	18.4	5.27	70	.298	.412	1	.333	1	-2	-2	0	-0.2
1952	Bos-N	0	2	.000	7	2	0	0	1	13	18	1	12	6	22.2	5.54	65	.346	.485	0	.000	-0	-3	-3	1	-0.4
1954	Det-A	0	0	—	2	0	0	0	0	6	9	1	5	2	21.0	10.50	35	.360	.467	0	.000	-0	-5	-5	-0	0.0
1955	Chi-A☆	15	9	.625	29	24	11	5	0	187	186	17	48	88	11.4	3.32	119	.261	.311	17	.224	5	13	13	1	2.1
1956	Chi-A	12	10	.545	34	31	14	3	0	234²	212	22	59	120	10.6	3.64	113	.240	.292	20	.222	8	13	12	2	1.9
1957	Chi-A	16	6	**.727**	28	28	**16**	2	0	220²	203	17	45	88	10.8	2.77	135	.247	.293	12	.145	2	25	24	0	2.5
1958	Chi-A	15	14	.517	34	34	16	4	0	248	240	23	53	127	10.9	3.01	121	.251	.295	9	.112	-1	21	17	-1	1.6
1959	*Chi-A	9	10	.474	31	29	5	1	0	179²	171	15	58	71	11.7	3.66	103	.247	.310	8	.131	1	4	2	-2	0.1
1960	Chi-A	6	1	.857	33	8	0	0	3	78²	87	13	25	30	12.8	5.38	70	.283	.337	3	.130	-0	-13	-14	1	-1.1
1961	Was-A★	10	10	.500	23	22	11	2	0	168²	138	10	35	62	9.4	**2.40**	**167**	.224	**.269**	10	.179	2	30	30	-1	3.7
1962	Cle-A★	20	10	.667	34	34	16	**5**	0	250²	255	23	47	94	10.9	3.59	108	.263	.299	16	.180	6	11	8	-1	1.4
1963	Cle-A	11	13	.458	30	30	7	3	0	206	211	27	28	84	10.7	4.24	85	.265	.295	9	.130	-1	-14	-14	-1	-1.7
1964	Cle-A	7	9	.438	30	23	5	0	1	158¹	181	19	29	83	12.1	4.55	79	.290	.324	7	.146	3	-16	-17	1	-1.2
1965	Cle-A	1	3	.250	12	3	0	0	0	22²	32	6	6	12	15.1	5.96	58	.333	.373	0	.000	-1	-6	-6	-0	-1.1
Total	15	122	99	.552	345	273	101	25	5	2017¹	1988	198	495	880	11.3	3.67	104	.258	.306	113	.163	24	45	31	-0	7.3

● TOM DONOVAN
Donovan, Thomas Joseph   b: 1/1/1873, West Troy, N.Y.   d: 3/25/33, Watervliet, N.Y.   BR/TR, 6'2", 168 lbs.   Deb: 9/10/01   F♦

YEAR	TM/L	W	L	PCT	G	GS	CG	SH	SV	IP	H	HR	BB	SO	RAT	ERA	ERA+	OAV	OOB	BH	AVG	PB	PR	/A	PD	TPI
1901	Cle-A	0	0	—	7	0	0	0	0	7	16	0	3	0	27.0	5.14	69	.444	.512	18	.254		-1	-1	-0	0.0

● BILL DONOVAN
Donovan, Willard Earl   b: 7/6/16, Maywood, Ill.   BB/TL, 6'2", 198 lbs.   Deb: 4/19/42

YEAR	TM/L	W	L	PCT	G	GS	CG	SH	SV	IP	H	HR	BB	SO	RAT	ERA	ERA+	OAV	OOB	BH	AVG	PB	PR	/A	PD	TPI
1942	Bos-N	3	6	.333	31	10	2	0	0	89¹	97	2	32	23	13.0	3.43	97	.283	.344	6	.240	-1	-1	-1	2	0.3
1943	Bos-N	1	0	1.000	7	0	0	0	0	14²	17	0	9	1	16.0	1.84	185	.304	.400	1	.333	0	3	3	1	0.3
Total	2	4	6	.400	38	10	2	0	0	104	114	2	41	24	13.4	3.20	105	.286	.352	7	.250	1	1	2	3	0.6

● BILL DONOVAN
Donovan, William Edward "Wild Bill"   b: 10/13/1876, Lawrence, Mass.   d: 12/9/23, Forsyth, N.Y.   BR/TR, 5'11", 190 lbs.   Deb: 4/22/1898   MC♦

YEAR	TM/L	W	L	PCT	G	GS	CG	SH	SV	IP	H	HR	BB	SO	RAT	ERA	ERA+	OAV	OOB	BH	AVG	PB	PR	/A	PD	TPI
1898	Was-N	1	6	.143	17	7	6	0	0	88	88	0	69	36	16.8	4.30	85	.259	.394	17	.165	-1	-7	-6	-0	-0.5
1899	Bro-N	1	2	.333	5	2	2	0	0	25	35	0	13	11	17.3	4.32	91	.330	.403	3	.231	-1	-1	-1	-0	-0.1
1900	Bro-N	1	2	.333	5	4	3	0	0	31	36	0	18	13	16.5	6.68	58	.290	.393	0	.000	-2	-10	-10	1	-0.8
1901	Bro-N	**25**	15	.625	**45**	38	36	2	**3**	351	324	1	152	226	12.4	2.77	121	.244	.325	23	.170	-1	22	23	-1	2.1
1902	Bro-N	17	15	.531	35	33	30	4	1	297²	250	1	111	170	11.1	2.78	99	.228	.303	28	.174	-0	-1	-1	0	0.0
1903	Det-A	17	16	.515	35	34	**34**	4	0	307	247	3	95	187	10.2	2.29	127	.220	.284	30	.242	4	23	21	-3	2.4
1904	Det-A	17	16	.515	34	34	30	3	0	293	251	5	94	137	10.9	2.46	104	.232	.300	38	.271	5	5	3	0	1.0
1905	Det-A	18	15	.545	34	32	27	5	0	280²	236	2	101	135	11.1	2.60	105	.230	.305	25	.192	1	2	4	-3	0.3
1906	Det-A	9	15	.375	25	25	22	0	0	211²	221	4	72	85	12.8	3.15	88	.272	.337	11	.121	-5	-11	-9	-0	-1.5
1907	*Det-A	25	4	**.862**	32	28	27	3	1	271	222	3	82	123	10.4	2.19	119	.226	.291	29	.266	7	11	12	-6	1.5
1908	*Det-A	18	7	.720	29	28	25	6	0	242²	210	7	53	141	10.0	2.08	116	.231	.278	13	.159	0	9	6	-6	0.2
1909	*Det-A	8	7	.533	21	17	13	4	2	140¹	121	0	60	76	12.0	2.31	109	.235	.322	9	.200	1	3	3	-2	0.1
1910	Det-A	17	7	.708	26	23	20	3	0	206²	184	4	61	107	11.0	2.44	108	.243	.305	15	.145	-2	2	4	-6	-0.4
1911	Det-A	10	9	.526	20	19	15	1	0	168¹	160	4	64	81	12.1	3.31	104	.250	.321	12	.200	3	1	3	-5	0.1
1912	Det-A	1	0	1.000	3	1	0	0	0	10	5	0	2	6	7.2	0.90	362	.147	.216	1	.077	-1	3	3	0	0.1
1915	NY-A	0	3	.000	9	1	0	0	0	33²	35	1	10	17	12.3	4.81	61	.278	.336	1	.083	-1	-7	-7	-1	-0.7
1916	NY-A	0	0	—	1	0	0	0	0	1	1	0	1	0	18.0	0.00	—	.250	.400	0	—	-0	0	0	0	0.0
1918	Det-A	1	0	1.000	2	1	0	0	0	6	5	0	1	1	9.0	1.50	177	.227	.261	1	.500	0	1	1	0	0.2
Total	18	186	139	.572	378	327	289	35	8	2964²	2631	30	1059	1552	11.5	2.69	106	.239	.310	251	.193	-2	43	54	-31	4.1

● JOHN DOPSON
Dopson, John Robert   b: 7/14/63, Baltimore, Md.   BL/TR, 6'4", 205 lbs.   Deb: 9/4/85

YEAR	TM/L	W	L	PCT	G	GS	CG	SH	SV	IP	H	HR	BB	SO	RAT	ERA	ERA+	OAV	OOB	BH	AVG	PB	PR	/A	PD	TPI
1985	Mon-N	0	2	.000	4	3	0	0	0	13	25	4	4	4	20.1	11.08	31	.379	.414	0	.000	0	-11	-11	-0	-1.3
1988	Mon-N	3	11	.214	26	26	1	0	0	168²	150	15	58	101	11.2	3.04	118	.235	.300	3	.059	-3	8	10	-3	0.3
1989	Bos-A	12	8	.600	29	28	2	0	0	169¹	166	14	69	95	12.6	3.99	103	.257	.330	0	—	0	-2	-2	3	0.5
1990	Bos-A	0	0	—	4	4	0	0	0	17²	13	2	9	9	11.2	2.04	200	.200	.297	0	—	0	4	4	1	0.0
1991	Bos-A	0	0	—	1	0	0	0	0	1	2	0	1	0	27.0	18.00	24	.500	.600	0	—	0	-2	-2	0	0.0
1992	Bos-A	7	11	.389	25	25	0	0	0	141¹	159	17	38	55	12.7	4.08	103	.287	.335	0	—	0	-2	-1	-1	-0.1
1993	Bos-A	7	11	.389	34	28	1	1	0	155¹	170	16	59	89	13.4	4.97	93	.281	.347	0	—	0	-11	-6	1	-0.9
1994	Cal-A	1	4	.200	21	5	0	0	1	58²	67	6	26	33	14.7	6.14	80	.288	.366	0	—	0	-9	-8	0	-0.6
Total	8	30	47	.390	144	119	4	1	1	725¹	752	74	264	386	12.7	4.27	98	.268	.333	3	.055	-3	-25	-8	3	-2.1

● JOHN DORAN
Doran, John F.   b: 1867, Chicago, Ill.   TL, 5'4", 160 lbs.   Deb: 4/11/1891

YEAR	TM/L	W	L	PCT	G	GS	CG	SH	SV	IP	H	HR	BB	SO	RAT	ERA	ERA+	OAV	OOB	BH	AVG	PB	PR	/A	PD	TPI
1891	Lou-a	5	10	.333	15	14	12	0	0	126	160	3	75	55	17.7	5.43	67	.299	.398	10	.189	-2	-24	-25	-0	-2.3

● MIKE DORGAN
Dorgan, Michael Cornelius   b: 10/2/1853, Middletown, Conn.   d: 4/26/09, Hartford, Conn.   BR/TR, 5'9", 180 lbs.   Deb: 5/8/1877   FM♦

YEAR	TM/L	W	L	PCT	G	GS	CG	SH	SV	IP	H	HR	BB	SO	RAT	ERA	ERA+	OAV	OOB	BH	AVG	PB	PR	/A	PD	TPI
1879	Syr-N	0	0	—	2	0	0	0	0	12	13	0	2	8	11.3	2.25	105	.260	.288	72	.267		0	0	0	0.0
1880	Pro-N	0	0	—	1	0	0	0	0	8	4	0	0	2	4.5	1.13	196	.138	.138	79	.246		1	1	0	0.0
1883	NY-N	0	1	.000	1	1	0	0	0	7	9	0	1	1	18.0	3.86	80	.286	.412	61	.234		-1	-1	-0	-0.1
1884	NY-N	8	6	.571	14	14	12	0	0	113	98	5	51	90	11.9	3.50	85	.215	.294	94	.276	2	-7	-7	1	-0.5
Total	4	8	7	.533	18	15	13	0	0	140	123	4	59	103	11.7	3.28	88	.218	.293	802	.274	3	-6	-6	1	-0.6

● HARRY DORISH
Dorish, Harry "Fritz"   b: 7/13/21, Swoyersville, Pa.   BR/TR, 5'11", 206 lbs.   Deb: 4/15/47   C

YEAR	TM/L	W	L	PCT	G	GS	CG	SH	SV	IP	H	HR	BB	SO	RAT	ERA	ERA+	OAV	OOB	BH	AVG	PB	PR	/A	PD	TPI
1947	Bos-A	7	8	.467	41	9	2	0	2	136	149	6	54	50	13.5	4.70	83	.283	.351	5	.143	-1	-15	-12	1	-1.3
1948	Bos-A	0	1	.000	9	0	0	0	0	14¹	18	1	6	5	15.1	5.65	78	.281	.343	-0	.250	-0	-2	-2	0	-0.1
1949	Bos-A	0	0	—	5	0	0	0	0	7²	7	1	1	6	9.4	2.35	186	.241	.267	0	—	0	2	2	0	0.0
1950	StL-A	4	9	.308	29	13	4	0	0	109	162	13	36	36	17.1	6.44	77	.337	.394	5	.161	-0	-23	-18	-1	-1.8
1951	Chi-A	5	6	.455	32	4	2	1	0	96²	101	6	31	29	12.3	3.54	114	.272	.328	8	.258	0	6	5	0	0.6

YEAR	TM/L	W	L	PCT	G	GS	CG	SH	SV	IP	H	HR	BB	SO	RAT	ERA	ERA+	OAV	OOB	BH	AVG	PB	PR	/A	PD	TPI
1952	Chi-A	8	4	.667	39	1	1	0	11	91	66	4	42	47	10.8	2.47	148	.208	.303	2	.091	-1	12	12	2	1.9
1953	Chi-A	10	6	.625	55	6	2	0	18	145²	140	4	52	69	12.2	3.40	118	.254	.325	7	.171	-2	10	10	2	1.3
1954	Chi-A	6	4	.600	37	6	2	1	6	109	88	9	29	48	9.7	2.72	137	.228	.284	3	.111	-2	12	12	-1	0.9
1955	Chi-A	2	0	1.000	13	0	0	0	1	17	16	0	9	6	13.2	1.59	249	.258	.352	1	.333	0	4	4	1	0.6
	Bal-A	3	3	.500	35	1	0	0	6	65²	58	4	28	22	11.9	3.15	121	.238	.319	0	.000	-1	6	5	1	0.4
	Yr	5	3	.625	48	1	0	0	7	82²	74	4	37	28	12.2	2.83	136	.242	.326	1	.077	-1	10	9	1	1.0
1956	Bal-A	0	0	—	13	0	0	0	0	19²	22	3	3	4	11.4	4.12	95	.297	.325	0	—	0	0	-0	1	0.1
	Bos-A	0	2	.000	15	0	0	0	0	22²	23	1	10	11	13.1	3.57	129	.277	.355	0	—	0	1	3	1	0.3
	Yr	0	2	.000	28	0	0	0	0	42¹	45	4	13	15	12.3	3.83	112	.283	.337	0	—	0	2	2	2	0.4
Total	10	45	43	.511	323	40	13	2	44	834¹	850	57	301	332	12.6	3.83	106	.267	.333	32	.157	-6	14	20	6	2.9

● GUS DORNER   Dorner, Augustus   b: 8/18/1876, Chambersburg, Pa.   d: 5/4/56, Chambersburg, Pa.   BR/TR, 5'10", 176 lbs.   Deb: 9/17/02

YEAR	TM/L	W	L	PCT	G	GS	CG	SH	SV	IP	H	HR	BB	SO	RAT	ERA	ERA+	OAV	OOB	BH	AVG	PB	PR	/A	PD	TPI
1902	Cle-A	3	1	.750	4	4	4	1	0	36	33	1	13	5	11.8	1.25	275	.244	.315	5	.385	2	9	9	-0	1.2
1903	Cle-A	4	5	.444	12	8	4	2	0	73²	83	4	24	28	13.2	4.52	63	.283	.340	2	.080	-2	-13	-14	0	-1.6
1906	Cin-N	0	1	.000	2	1	1	0	0	15	16	0	4	5	12.6	1.20	230	.276	.333	0	—	-1	3	0	0	0.1
	Bos-N	8	25	.242	34	32	29	0	0	273¹	264	5	103	104	12.6	3.65	74	.260	.338	14	.140	-4	-31	-29	3	-3.5
	Yr	8	26	.235	36	33	30	0	0	288¹	280	5	107	109	12.6	3.53	76	.261	.337	14	.133	-5	-29	-27	2	-3.4
1907	Bos-N	12	16	.429	36	31	24	2	0	271¹	253	4	92	85	11.9	3.12	82	.255	.327	12	.130	-3	-19	-17	-3	-2.4
1908	Bos-N	8	19	.296	38	28	14	3	0	216¹	176	3	77	41	11.1	3.54	68	.224	.305	12	.179	-2	-28	-27	2	-3.3
1909	Bos-N	1	2	.333	5	2	0	0	1	24²	17	1	17	7	13.1	2.55	110	.198	.343	1	.167	-0	0	1	-0	0.1
Total	6	36	69	.343	131	106	76	8	1	910¹	842	18	330	275	12.1	3.37	78	.250	.326	46	.149	-9	-80	-74	1	-9.5

● BERT DORR   Dorr, Charles Albert   b: 2/2/1862, New York   d: 6/16/14, Dickinson, N.Y.   Deb: 8/24/1882

YEAR	TM/L	W	L	PCT	G	GS	CG	SH	SV	IP	H	HR	BB	SO	RAT	ERA	ERA+	OAV	OOB	BH	AVG	PB	PR	/A	PD	TPI
1882	StL-a	2	6	.250	8	8	8	0	0	66	53	0	1	34	7.4	2.59	108	.205	.208	4	.154	-2	1	2	1	0.1

● CAL DORSETT   Dorsett, Calvin Leavelle "Preacher"   b: 6/10/13, Lone Oak, Tex.   d: 10/22/70, Elk City, Okla.   BR/TR, 6', 180 lbs.   Deb: 8/19/40

YEAR	TM/L	W	L	PCT	G	GS	CG	SH	SV	IP	H	HR	BB	SO	RAT	ERA	ERA+	OAV	OOB	BH	AVG	PB	PR	/A	PD	TPI
1940	Cle-A	0	0	—	1	0	0	0	0	1	1	1	0	0	9.0	9.00	47	.250	.250	0	—	-0	-1	-1	-0	0.0
1941	Cle-A	0	1	.000	5	2	0	0	0	11¹	21	0	10	5	24.6	10.32	38	.382	.477	0	.000	-0	-8	-8	-0	-0.6
1947	Cle-A	0	0	—	2	0	0	0	0	1¹	3	1	3	1	40.5	27.00	13	.500	.667	0	—	-0	-3	-3	-0	0.0
Total	3	0	1	.000	8	2	0	0	0	13²	25	2	13	6	25.0	11.85	33	.385	.487	0	—	-0	-12	-12	-0	-0.6

● JIM DORSEY   Dorsey, James Edward   b: 8/2/55, Oak Park, Ill.   BR/TR, 6'7", 190 lbs.   Deb: 9/2/80

YEAR	TM/L	W	L	PCT	G	GS	CG	SH	SV	IP	H	HR	BB	SO	RAT	ERA	ERA+	OAV	OOB	BH	AVG	PB	PR	/A	PD	TPI
1980	Cal-A	1	2	.333	4	4	0	0	0	15²	25	2	8	8	19.5	9.19	43	.368	.442	0	—	-0	-9	-9	-0	-1.3
1984	Bos-A	0	0	—	2	0	0	0	0	2²	6	0	2	4	10.13	41	.462	.533	0	—	-0	-2	-2	-0	0.0
1985	Bos-A	0	1	.000	2	1	0	0	0	5¹	12	1	8	2	37.1	20.25	21	.444	.595	0	—	-0	-10	-9	-0	-1.2
Total	3	1	3	.250	8	5	0	0	0	23²	43	4	20	14	24.3	11.79	34	.398	.496	0	—	-0	-20	-20	-0	-2.5

● JERRY DORSEY   Dorsey, Michael Jeremiah   b: 1854, Canada   d: 11/3/38, Auburn, N.Y.   Deb: 7/9/1884 ♦

YEAR	TM/L	W	L	PCT	G	GS	CG	SH	SV	IP	H	HR	BB	SO	RAT	ERA	ERA+	OAV	OOB	BH	AVG	PB	PR	/A	PD	TPI
1884	Bal-U	0	1	.000	1	1	1	0	0	4	7	1	0	3	15.8	9.00	30	.368	.368	0	.000	-1	-3	-3	0	-0.5

● JACK DOSCHER   Doscher, John Henry Jr.   b: 7/27/1880, Troy, N.Y.   d: 5/27/71, Park Ridge, N.J.   BL/TL, 6'1", 205 lbs.   Deb: 7/2/03   F

YEAR	TM/L	W	L	PCT	G	GS	CG	SH	SV	IP	H	HR	BB	SO	RAT	ERA	ERA+	OAV	OOB	BH	AVG	PB	PR	/A	PD	TPI
1903	Chi-N	0	1	.000	1	1	1	0	0	3	6	0	2	5	27.0	12.00	26	.429	.529	0	.000	-0	-3	-3	-0	-0.6
	Bro-N	0	0	—	3	0	0	0	0	8	8	1	9	4	23.1	7.71	41	.296	.486	0	.000	-0	-4	-4	-0	-0.1
	Yr	0	1	.000	4	1	1	0	0	10	14	1	11	9	23.4	9.00	35	.333	.481	0	.000	-1	-6	-6	-0	-0.7
1904	Bro-N	0	0	—	2	0	0	0	0	6¹	1	0	1	2	2.8	0.00	—	.053	.100	1	.500	0	2	2	0	0.2
1905	Bro-N	1	5	.167	12	7	6	0	0	71	60	1	30	33	11.8	3.17	91	.232	.318	2	.083	-2	-1	-2	-2	-0.5
1906	Bro-N	0	1	.000	2	1	1	0	0	14	12	0	4	10	10.3	1.29	196	.250	.308	0	.000	-1	2	2	-0	0.2
1908	Cin-N	1	3	.250	7	4	3	0	0	44¹	31	1	22	7	11.4	1.83	126	.196	.306	2	.133	0	3	3	0	0.2
Total	5	2	10	.167	27	13	10	0	0	145²	118	3	68	61	12.0	2.84	95	.225	.323	5	.100	-3	-1	-2	-3	-1.0

● RICHARD DOTSON   Dotson, Richard Elliott   b: 1/10/59, Cincinnati, Ohio   BR/TR, 6', 204 lbs.   Deb: 9/4/79

YEAR	TM/L	W	L	PCT	G	GS	CG	SH	SV	IP	H	HR	BB	SO	RAT	ERA	ERA+	OAV	OOB	BH	AVG	PB	PR	/A	PD	TPI
1979	Chi-A	2	0	1.000	5	5	1	1	0	24¹	28	0	6	13	12.6	3.70	115	.286	.327	0	—	0	1	0	-0	0.1
1980	Chi-A	12	10	.545	33	32	8	0	0	198	185	20	87	109	12.6	4.27	94	.247	.331	0	—	0	-5	-5	1	-0.4
1981	Chi-A	9	8	.529	24	24	5	4	0	141	145	13	49	73	12.6	3.77	95	.270	.336	0	—	0	-2	-3	-0	-0.4
1982	Chi-A	11	15	.423	34	31	3	1	0	196²	219	19	73	109	13.6	3.84	105	.282	.348	0	—	0	5	4	-1	0.4
1983	*Chi-A	22	7	**.759**	35	35	8	1	0	240	209	19	106	137	12.1	3.23	130	.240	.328	0	—	0	22	26	4	3.4
1984	Chi-A★	14	15	.483	32	32	14	1	0	245²	216	24	103	120	11.9	3.59	116	.238	.321	0	—	0	11	15	-0	1.7
1985	Chi-A	3	4	.429	9	9	0	0	0	52¹	53	5	17	33	12.6	4.47	97	.261	.327	0	—	0	-1	-0	-0	-0.1
1986	Chi-A	10	17	.370	34	34	3	1	0	197	226	24	69	110	13.6	5.48	79	.289	.348	0	—	0	-29	-26	-1	-3.1
1987	Chi-A	11	12	.478	31	31	7	2	0	211¹	201	26	86	114	12.2	4.17	110	.249	.321	0	—	0	7	10	2	1.1
1988	NY-A	12	9	.571	32	29	4	0	0	171	178	27	72	77	13.4	5.00	79	.266	.348	0	—	0	-20	-20	-1	-2.3
1989	NY-A	2	5	.286	11	9	1	0	0	51²	69	8	17	14	15.2	5.57	69	.317	.369	0	—	0	-10	-10	-1	-1.2
	Chi-A	3	7	.300	17	17	1	0	0	99²	112	8	41	55	13.8	3.88	98	.282	.349	0	—	0	0	0	-0	-0.1
	Yr	5	12	.294	28	26	2	0	0	151¹	181	16	58	69	14.2	4.46	86	.293	.354	0	—	0	-10	-10	-1	-1.3
1990	KC-A	0	4	.000	8	7	0	0	0	28²	43	3	14	9	17.9	8.48	45	.355	.422	0	—	0	-15	-15	-0	-1.7
Total	12	111	113	.496	305	295	55	11	0	1857¹	1884	194	740	973	12.9	4.23	97	.264	.337	0	—	0	-35	-25	2	-2.6

● GARY DOTTER   Dotter, Gary Richard   b: 8/7/42, St.Louis, Mo.   BL/TL, 6'1", 180 lbs.   Deb: 9/10/61

YEAR	TM/L	W	L	PCT	G	GS	CG	SH	SV	IP	H	HR	BB	SO	RAT	ERA	ERA+	OAV	OOB	BH	AVG	PB	PR	/A	PD	TPI
1961	Min-A	0	0	—	2	0	0	0	0	6	6	0	4	2	15.0	9.00	47	.273	.385	0	.000	-0	-3	-3	0	0.0
1963	Min-A	0	0	—	2	0	0	0	0	2	0	0	0	1	0.00	—	.000	.000	0	.000	-0	1	1	0	0.0
1964	Min-A	0	0	—	3	0	0	0	0	4¹	3	1	3	6	12.5	2.08	172	.188	.316	0	.000	-0	1	0	0	0.0
Total	3	0	0	—	7	0	0	0	0	12¹	9	1	7	10	11.7	5.11	76	.205	.314	0	.000	-0	-2	-2	0	0.0

● BABE DOTY   Doty, Elmer L.   b: 12/17/1867, Genoa, Ohio   d: 11/20/29, Toledo, Ohio   BL/TR, 6', 160 lbs.   Deb: 8/18/1890

YEAR	TM/L	W	L	PCT	G	GS	CG	SH	SV	IP	H	HR	BB	SO	RAT	ERA	ERA+	OAV	OOB	BH	AVG	PB	PR	/A	PD	TPI
1890	Tol-a	1	0	1.000	1	1	1	0	0	9	9	1	4	4	10.0	1.00	395	.250	.270	0	.000	-0	3	3	-0	0.2

● JIM DOUGHERTY   Dougherty, James E.   b: 3/8/68, Brentwood, N.Y.   BR/TR, 6', 210 lbs.   Deb: 4/27/95

YEAR	TM/L	W	L	PCT	G	GS	CG	SH	SV	IP	H	HR	BB	SO	RAT	ERA	ERA+	OAV	OOB	BH	AVG	PB	PR	/A	PD	TPI
1995	Hou-N	8	4	.667	56	0	0	0	0	67²	76	7	25	49	13.8	4.92	79	.292	.361	1	.125	-0	-6	-8	1	-1.1
1996	Hou-N	0	2	.000	12	0	0	0	0	13	14	2	11	6	18.0	9.00	42	.280	.419	0	—	-0	-7	-7	0	-1.0
Total	2	8	6	.571	68	0	0	0	0	80²	90	9	36	55	14.5	5.58	69	.290	.371	1	.125	-0	-12	-15	1	-2.1

● TOM DOUGHERTY   Dougherty, Thomas James "Sugar Boy"   b: 5/30/1881, Chicago, Ill.   d: 11/6/53, Milwaukee, Wis.   BL/TR, 195 lbs.   Deb: 4/24/04

YEAR	TM/L	W	L	PCT	G	GS	CG	SH	SV	IP	H	HR	BB	SO	RAT	ERA	ERA+	OAV	OOB	BH	AVG	PB	PR	/A	PD	TPI
1904	Chi-A	1	0	1.000	1	0	0	0	0	2	0	0	0	0	0.0	0.00	—	.000	.000	0	.000	-0	1	1	0	0.3

● WHAMMY DOUGLAS   Douglas, Charles William   b: 2/17/35, Carrboro, N.C.   BR/TR, 6'2", 185 lbs.   Deb: 7/29/57

YEAR	TM/L	W	L	PCT	G	GS	CG	SH	SV	IP	H	HR	BB	SO	RAT	ERA	ERA+	OAV	OOB	BH	AVG	PB	PR	/A	PD	TPI
1957	Pit-N	3	3	.500	11	8	0	0	0	47	48	5	30	28	15.5	3.26	114	.270	.384	1	.063	-1	3	3	-0	0.2

● LARRY DOUGLAS   Douglas, Lawrence Howard   b: 6/5/1890, Jellico, Tenn.   d: 11/4/49, Jellico, Tenn.   6'3", 175 lbs.   Deb: 6/17/15

YEAR	TM/L	W	L	PCT	G	GS	CG	SH	SV	IP	H	HR	BB	SO	RAT	ERA	ERA+	OAV	OOB	BH	AVG	PB	PR	/A	PD	TPI
1915	Bal-F	1	0	1.000	2	0	0	0	0	3	3	0	2	1	15.0	3.00	96	.273	.385	0	—	0	-0	-0	0	0.0

● PHIL DOUGLAS   Douglas, Phillip Brooks "Shufflin' Phil"   b: 6/17/1890, Cedartown, Ga.   d: 8/1/52, Sequatchie, Tenn.   BR/TR, 6'3", 190 lbs.   Deb: 8/30/12

YEAR	TM/L	W	L	PCT	G	GS	CG	SH	SV	IP	H	HR	BB	SO	RAT	ERA	ERA+	OAV	OOB	BH	AVG	PB	PR	/A	PD	TPI
1912	Chi-A	0	1	.000	3	1	0	0	0	12¹	21	0	6	7	19.7	7.30	44	.382	.443	0	.000	-1	-5	-6	0	-0.4
1914	Cin-N	11	18	.379	45	25	13	0	1	239¹	186	7	92	121	10.9	2.56	115	.223	.308	10	.183	-1	6	10	-2	0.7
1915	Cin-N	1	5	.167	8	7	0	0	0	46²	53	0	23	29	14.7	5.40	53	.299	.380	2	.118	-1	-14	-13	-1	-1.6
	Bro-N	5	5	.500	20	13	5	1	0	116²	104	1	17	63	9.7	2.62	106	.241	.278	6	.154	-1	3	2	0	0.1
	Chi-N	1	1	.500	4	4	2	1	0	25	17	0	7	18	9.0	2.16	129	.187	.253	0	.000	-0	3	2	0	0.1
	Yr	7	11	.389	32	24	7	2	0	188¹	174	1	47	110	10.6	3.25	86	.247	.295	8	.125	-3	-10	-9	-1	-1.4
1917	Chi-N	14	20	.412	**51**	37	20	5	1	293¹	269	13	50	151	10.0	2.55	114	.250	.287	11	.126	-4	5	11	4	1.4
1918	*Chi-N	10	9	.526	25	19	11	2	2	156²	145	3	34	68	10.3	2.13	131	.246	.285	14	.255	-1	15	15	5	2.0
1919	Chi-N	10	6	.625	25	19	8	0	0	161²	153	0	34	69	9.4	2.00	144	.250	.275	8	.157	-2	16	15	5	2.0
	NY-N	2	4	.333	8	6	4	0	0	51¹	53	0	6	21	10.5	2.10	133	.264	.288	0	.000	-2	5	5	0	0.2
	Yr	12	10	.545	33	25	12	4	0	213	186	0	40	84	9.6	2.03	141	.238	.276	8	.121	-4	21	20	5	2.2

YEAR TM/L	W	L	PCT	G	GS	CG	SH	SV	IP	H	HR	BB	SO	RAT	ERA	ERA+	OAV	OOB	BH	AVG	PB	PR	/A	PD	TPI
1920 NY-N	14	10	.583	46	21	10	3	2	226	225	6	55	71	11.2	2.71	111	.263	.309	11	.151	-4	11	7	1	0.4
1921 *NY-N	15	10	.600	40	27	13	3	2	221²	266	17	55	55	13.1	4.22	87	.308	.351	16	.198	0	-11	-14	1	-1.3
1922 NY-N	11	4	.733	24	21	9	1	0	157²	154	6	35	33	11.0	2.63	152	.257	.302	12	.207	1	26	24	0	2.1
Total 9	94	93	.503	299	200	95	20	8	1708¹	1626	52	411	683	10.9	2.80	111	.256	.305	90	.161	-16	53	58	13	5.6

● KIP DOWD   Dowd, James Joseph b: 2/16/1889, Holyoke, Mass. d: 12/20/60, Holyoke, Mass. BR/TR, 5'10.5", 160 lbs. Deb: 7/5/10

YEAR TM/L	W	L	PCT	G	GS	CG	SH	SV	IP	H	HR	BB	SO	RAT	ERA	ERA+	OAV	OOB	BH	AVG	PB	PR	/A	PD	TPI
1910 Pit-N	0	0	—	1	0	0	0	0	2	4	0	2	1	31.5	0.00	—	.400	.538	0	—	0	1	1	-0	0.0

● DAVE DOWLING   Dowling, David Barclay b: 8/23/42, Baton Rouge, La. BR/TL, 6'2", 181 lbs. Deb: 10/3/64

YEAR TM/L	W	L	PCT	G	GS	CG	SH	SV	IP	H	HR	BB	SO	RAT	ERA	ERA+	OAV	OOB	BH	AVG	PB	PR	/A	PD	TPI
1964 StL-N	0	0	—	1	0	0	0	0	1	2	0	0	0	18.0	0.00	—	.400	.400	0	—	-0	0	0	-0	0.0
1966 Chi-N	1	0	1.000	1	1	1	0	0	9	10	0	0	3	10.0	2.00	184	.270	.270	0	.000	-0	2	2	-0	0.1
Total 2	1	0	1.000	2	1	1	0	0	10	12	0	0	3	10.8	1.80	205	.286	.286	0	.000	-0	2	2	-0	0.1

● PETE DOWLING   Dowling, Henry Peter b: St.Louis, Mo. d: 6/30/05, Hot Lake, Ore. TL, 5'11". Deb: 7/17/1897

YEAR TM/L	W	L	PCT	G	GS	CG	SH	SV	IP	H	HR	BB	SO	RAT	ERA	ERA+	OAV	OOB	BH	AVG	PB	PR	/A	PD	TPI
1897 Lou-N	1	2	.333	4	4	2	0	0	26	39	0	8	3	18.3	5.88	72	.342	.414	2	.200	-0	-5	-5	-0	-0.4
1898 Lou-N	13	20	.394	36	32	30	0	0	285²	284	7	120	84	13.4	4.16	86	.257	.342	21	.196	1	-17	-18	-1	-1.7
1899 Lou-N	13	17	.433	34	32	29	0	0	289²	321	4	93	88	13.4	3.11	124	.280	.343	27	.233	-1	24	24	-0	2.0
1901 Mil-A	1	4	.200	10	4	3	0	0	49²	71	1	14	25	16.1	5.62	64	.332	.384	4	.211	1	-11	-11	-0	-0.8
Cle-A	11	22	.333	33	30	28	2	0	256¹	269	1	104	99	13.6	3.86	92	.267	.344	16	.162	-4	-6	-9	-0	-1.2
Yr	12	26	.316	43	34	31	2	1	306	340	2	118	124	13.9	4.15	86	.277	.348	20	.169	-3	-16	-20	1	-2.0
Total 4	39	65	.375	117	102	92	2	1	907¹	984	13	339	299	13.8	3.87	95	.274	.348	70	.199	-3	-14	-19	-1	-2.1

● AL DOWNING   Downing, Alphonso Erwin b: 6/28/41, Trenton, N.J. BR/TL, 5'11", 177 lbs. Deb: 7/19/61

YEAR TM/L	W	L	PCT	G	GS	CG	SH	SV	IP	H	HR	BB	SO	RAT	ERA	ERA+	OAV	OOB	BH	AVG	PB	PR	/A	PD	TPI
1961 NY-A	0	1	.000	5	1	0	0	0	9	7	0	12	12	20.0	8.00	46	.212	.435	0	.000	-0	-4	-4	0	-0.4
1962 NY-A	0	0	—	1	0	0	0	0	1	0	0	0	1	0.0	0.00	—	.000	.000	0	—	0	0	0	0	0.0
1963 *NY-A	13	5	.722	24	22	10	4	0	175²	114	7	80	171	9.9	2.56	137	.184	.277	6	.103	-2	21	19	-1	1.5
1964 *NY-A	13	8	.619	37	35	11	1	2	244	201	18	120	217	11.8	3.47	100	.223	.314	15	.176	1	4	4	0	0.4
1965 NY-A	12	14	.462	35	32	8	2	0	212	185	16	105	179	12.4	3.40	100	.237	.329	8	.108	-1	0	1	0	-1.1
1966 NY-A	10	11	.476	30	30	1	0	0	200	178	23	79	152	11.6	3.56	94	.235	.309	7	.100	-2	-3	-5	-4	-1.1
1967 NY-A★	14	10	.583	31	28	10	4	0	201²	158	13	61	171	10.0	2.63	119	.217	.283	8	.121	1	13	11	-1	1.3
1968 NY-A	3	3	.500	15	12	1	0	0	61¹	54	7	20	40	11.0	3.52	82	.237	.301	3	.176	0	-4	-4	-0	-0.4
1969 NY-A	7	5	.583	30	15	5	1	0	130²	117	12	49	85	11.4	3.38	103	.240	.309	6	.136	0	4	1	-2	-0.1
1970 Oak-A	3	3	.500	10	6	1	0	0	41	39	5	22	26	13.6	3.95	90	.252	.348	2	.182	-0	-1	-2	2	-0.1
Mil-A	2	10	.167	17	16	1	0	0	94¹	79	8	59	53	13.5	3.34	113	.232	.350	2	.083	-2	4	5	0	0.4
Yr	5	13	.278	27	22	2	0	0	135¹	118	13	81	79	13.4	3.52	105	.237	.347	4	.114	-2	3	3	2	0.3
1971 LA-N	20	9	.690	37	36	12	5	0	262¹	245	16	84	136	11.4	2.68	121	.247	.308	16	.174	2	23	16	-1	1.9
1972 LA-N	9	9	.500	31	30	7	4	0	202²	196	13	67	117	12.0	2.98	112	.254	.319	8	.121	-1	11	8	5	1.1
1973 LA-N	9	9	.500	30	28	5	2	0	193	155	19	68	124	10.4	3.31	104	.219	.289	5	.088	-1	7	3	1	0.2
1974 *LA-N	5	6	.455	21	16	1	1	0	98¹	94	7	45	63	13.0	3.66	93	.251	.341	5	.172	-0	-0	-3	1	-0.2
1975 LA-N	2	1	.667	22	6	0	0	1	74²	59	6	28	39	10.7	2.89	118	.215	.293	0	.000	-1	6	4	1	0.2
1976 LA-N	1	2	.333	17	3	0	0	0	46²	43	3	18	30	11.8	3.86	88	.250	.321	0	.000	-1	-2	-2	0	-0.2
1977 LA-N	0	1	.000	12	1	0	0	0	20	22	4	16	23	17.1	6.75	57	.278	.400	0	—	0	-6	-7	-0	-0.3
Total 17	123	107	.535	405	317	73	24	3	2268¹	1946	177	933	1639	11.5	3.22	105	.232	.311	91	.127	-7	75	44	2	4.2

● DAVE DOWNS   Downs, David Ralph b: 6/21/52, Logan, Utah BR/TR, 6'5", 220 lbs. Deb: 9/2/72 F

YEAR TM/L	W	L	PCT	G	GS	CG	SH	SV	IP	H	HR	BB	SO	RAT	ERA	ERA+	OAV	OOB	BH	AVG	PB	PR	/A	PD	TPI
1972 Phi-N	1	1	.500	4	4	1	0	0	23	25	1	3	5	11.3	2.74	131	.294	.326	2	.250	0	2	2	0	0.2

● KELLY DOWNS   Downs, Kelly Robert b: 10/25/60, Ogden, Utah BR/TR, 6'4", 200 lbs. Deb: 7/29/86 F

YEAR TM/L	W	L	PCT	G	GS	CG	SH	SV	IP	H	HR	BB	SO	RAT	ERA	ERA+	OAV	OOB	BH	AVG	PB	PR	/A	PD	TPI
1986 SF-N	4	4	.500	14	14	1	0	0	88¹	78	5	30	64	11.3	2.75	128	.236	.305	5	.172	0	9	8	0	0.6
1987 *SF-N	12	9	.571	41	28	4	3	1	186	185	14	67	137	12.4	3.63	106	.258	.324	8	.143	-0	9	4	-4	0.0
1988 SF-N	13	9	.591	27	26	6	3	0	168	140	11	47	118	10.2	3.32	98	.225	.283	9	.167	-2	-1	-0	-0	0.1
1989 *SF-N	4	8	.333	18	15	0	0	0	82²	82	7	26	49	11.9	4.79	70	.261	.320	2	.091	-1	-12	-13	-1	-1.9
1990 SF-N	3	2	.600	13	8	0	0	0	63	56	2	20	31	11.1	3.43	106	.233	.298	0	.000	-1	3	2	1	0.1
1991 SF-N	10	4	.714	45	11	0	0	0	111²	99	12	53	62	12.5	4.19	85	.239	.329	2	.087	-1	-6	-8	1	-0.9
1992 SF-N	1	2	.333	19	7	0	0	0	62¹	65	4	24	33	13.3	3.47	95	.275	.350	0	.000	-1	0	-1	1	-0.3
*Oak-A	5	5	.500	18	13	0	0	0	82	72	4	46	38	13.4	3.29	114	.237	.345	0	—	0	6	4	-1	0.6
1993 Oak-A	5	10	.333	42	12	0	0	0	119²	135	14	60	66	14.8	5.64	72	.287	.370	0	—	0	-18	-21	-2	-2.3
Total 8	57	53	.518	237	135	11	6	1	963²	912	73	373	598	12.2	3.86	94	.250	.324	26	.123	-2	-6	-26	-7	-4.0

● TOM DOWSE   Dowse, Thomas Joseph b: 8/12/1866, Ireland d: 12/14/46, Riverside, Cal. BR/TR, 5'11", 175 lbs. Deb: 4/21/1890 ♦

YEAR TM/L	W	L	PCT	G	GS	CG	SH	SV	IP	H	HR	BB	SO	RAT	ERA	ERA+	OAV	OOB	BH	AVG	PB	PR	/A	PD	TPI
1890 Cle-N	0	0	—	1	0	0	0	0	5	6	0	1	0	12.6	5.40	66	.286	.318	33	.208	-0	-1	-1	0	0.0

● JESS DOYLE   Doyle, Jesse Herbert b: 4/14/1898, Knoxville, Tenn. d: 4/15/61, Belleville, Ill. BR/TR, 5'11", 175 lbs. Deb: 4/14/25

YEAR TM/L	W	L	PCT	G	GS	CG	SH	SV	IP	H	HR	BB	SO	RAT	ERA	ERA+	OAV	OOB	BH	AVG	PB	PR	/A	PD	TPI
1925 Det-A	4	7	.364	45	3	0	0	8	118¹	158	6	50	31	16.2	5.93	73	.340	.410	8	.242	3	-20	-21	-1	-1.7
1926 Det-A	0	0	—	2	0	0	0	1	4¹	7	0	1	2	14.5	4.15	98	.316	.350	1	1.000	0	-0	-0	-0	0.0
1927 Det-A	0	0	—	7	0	0	0	0	12¹	16	0	5	0	15.3	8.03	52	.314	.375	1	.333	1	-5	-5	0	0.0
1931 StL-A	0	0	—	1	0	0	0	0	1	3	0	1	0	36.0	27.00	17	.500	.571	0	—	-0	-3	-2	-0	0.0
Total 4	4	7	.364	55	3	0	0	9	136	183	6	57	38	16.2	6.22	69	.338	.406	10	.270	4	-28	-29	-1	-1.7

● JOHN DOYLE   Doyle, John Aloysius b: 1858, Nova Scotia, Canada d: 12/24/15, Providence, R.I. Deb: 7/26/1882

YEAR TM/L	W	L	PCT	G	GS	CG	SH	SV	IP	H	HR	BB	SO	RAT	ERA	ERA+	OAV	OOB	BH	AVG	PB	PR	/A	PD	TPI
1882 StL-a	0	3	.000	3	3	3	0	0	24	41	0	3	5	16.5	2.63	107	.353	.370	2	.182	-0	0	0	-1	0.0

● SLOW JOE DOYLE   Doyle, Judd Bruce b: 9/15/1881, Clay Center, Kan. d: 11/21/47, Tannersville, N.Y. BR/TR, 5'8", 150 lbs. Deb: 8/25/06

YEAR TM/L	W	L	PCT	G	GS	CG	SH	SV	IP	H	HR	BB	SO	RAT	ERA	ERA+	OAV	OOB	BH	AVG	PB	PR	/A	PD	TPI
1906 NY-A	2	1	.667	9	6	3	2	0	45¹	34	1	13	28	9.5	2.38	124	.211	.274	3	.214	-0	2	3	0	0.2
1907 NY-A	11	11	.500	29	23	15	1	1	193²	169	2	67	94	11.2	2.65	105	.237	.308	8	.138	-1	-2	-3	-3	-0.1
1908 NY-A	1	1	.500	12	4	1	1	0	48	42	1	14	20	10.9	2.63	94	.235	.297	3	.214	-0	-1	-1	-2	-0.1
1909 NY-A	8	6	.571	17	15	8	3	0	125²	103	0	37	57	10.2	2.58	98	.232	.294	7	.167	-1	-1	-1	-4	-0.4
1910 NY-A	0	2	.000	3	2	1	0	0	12¹	19	0	5	6	18.3	8.03	33	.365	.431	1	.250	-0	-8	-7	1	-0.9
Cin-N	0	0	—	5	0	0	0	0	11¹	16	0	11	4	21.4	6.35	46	.327	.450	0	.000	0	-4	-4	1	-0.1
Total 5	22	21	.512	75	50	29	7	1	436¹	383	7	147	209	11.2	2.85	95	.240	.308	22	.163	-1	-15	-7	-7	-1.4

● PAUL DOYLE   Doyle, Paul Sinnott b: 10/2/39, Philadelphia, Pa. BL/TL, 5'11", 172 lbs. Deb: 5/28/69

YEAR TM/L	W	L	PCT	G	GS	CG	SH	SV	IP	H	HR	BB	SO	RAT	ERA	ERA+	OAV	OOB	BH	AVG	PB	PR	/A	PD	TPI
1969 *Atl-N	2	0	1.000	36	0	0	0	4	39	31	4	16	25	10.8	2.08	174	.231	.313	0	.000	-0	7	7	1	0.5
1970 Cal-A	3	1	.750	40	0	0	0	4	42	43	7	21	34	13.9	5.14	70	.267	.355	0	.000	-0	-7	-7	1	-0.7
SD-N	0	2	.000	9	0	0	0	2	7	7	0	6	2	19.3	6.43	62	.360	.484	0	—	0	-2	-2	1	-0.2
1972 Cal-A	0	0	—	2	0	0	0	1	2¹	4	0	3	4	19.3	0.00	—	.250	.455	0	—	-0	1	1	0	0.2
Total 3	5	3	.625	87	0	0	0	11	90¹	85	11	46	65	13.2	3.79	96	.259	.352	0	.000	-1	-1	-1	3	-0.2

● CARL DOYLE   Doyle, William Carl b: 7/30/12, Knoxville, Tenn. d: 9/4/51, Knoxville, Tenn. BR/TR, 6'1", 185 lbs. Deb: 8/5/35

YEAR TM/L	W	L	PCT	G	GS	CG	SH	SV	IP	H	HR	BB	SO	RAT	ERA	ERA+	OAV	OOB	BH	AVG	PB	PR	/A	PD	TPI
1935 Phi-A	2	7	.222	14	9	3	0	0	79²	86	4	72	34	18.1	5.99	76	.282	.422	4	.133	-2	-14	-13	1	-1.3
1936 Phi-A	0	3	.000	8	6	1	0	0	38²	66	4	29	12	23.3	10.94	47	.369	.469	4	.267	1	-25	-25	-1	-1.4
1939 Bro-N	1	2	.333	5	1	1	1	1	17²	18	1	7	7	16.3	7.65	395	.136	.227	1	.167	0	6	6	0	1.1
1940 Bro-N	0	0	—	3	0	0	0	0	5²	18	3	6	4	44.5	27.00	15	.545	.651	1	1.000	1	-15	-14	-0	-0.5
StL-N	3	3	.500	21	5	1	0	0	81	99	7	41	44	16.2	5.89	68	.294	.380	6	.200	2	-18	-17	-0	-1.0
Yr	3	3	.500	24	5	1	0	0	86²	117	10	47	48	17.7	7.27	55	.313	.398	7	.226	2	-33	-32	-0	-1.5
Total 4	6	15	.286	51	21	6	1	2	222²	277	18	155	101	18.1	6.95	63	.303	.414	16	.195	1	-66	-63	-0	-3.1

● TOM DOZIER   Dozier, Thomas Dean b: 9/5/61, San Pablo, Cal. BR/TR, 6'2", 190 lbs. Deb: 5/17/86

YEAR TM/L	W	L	PCT	G	GS	CG	SH	SV	IP	H	HR	BB	SO	RAT	ERA	ERA+	OAV	OOB	BH	AVG	PB	PR	/A	PD	TPI
1986 Oak-A	0	0	—	4	0	0	0	0	6¹	6	1	5	4	15.6	5.68	68	.261	.393	0	—	0	-1	-1	-0	0.6

● BUZZ DOZIER   Dozier, William Joseph b: 8/31/27, Waco, Tex. BR/TR, 6'3", 185 lbs. Deb: 9/12/47

YEAR TM/L	W	L	PCT	G	GS	CG	SH	SV	IP	H	HR	BB	SO	RAT	ERA	ERA+	OAV	OOB	BH	AVG	PB	PR	/A	PD	TPI
1947 Was-A	0	0	—	2	0	0	0	0	4²	2	0	1	2	5.8	0.00	—	.133	.188	0	.000	-0	2	2	0	0.0

YEAR	TM/L	W	L	PCT	G	GS	CG	SH	SV	IP	H	HR	BB	SO	RAT	ERA	ERA+	OAV	OOB	BH	AVG	PB	PR	/A	PD	TPI
1949	Was-A	0	0	—	2	0	0	0	0	6¹	12	0	6	1	25.6	11.37	37	.429	.529	0	.000	-0	-5	-5	-0	-0.1
Total	2	0	0	—	4	0	0	0	0	11	14	0	7	3	17.2	6.55	62	.326	.420	0	.000	-0	-3	-3	-0	-0.1

● **DOUG DRABEK**   Drabek, Douglas Dean   b: 7/25/62, Victoria, Tex.   BR/TR, 6'1", 185 lbs.   Deb: 5/30/86

YEAR	TM/L	W	L	PCT	G	GS	CG	SH	SV	IP	H	HR	BB	SO	RAT	ERA	ERA+	OAV	OOB	BH	AVG	PB	PR	/A	PD	TPI
1986	NY-A	7	8	.467	27	21	0	1	0	131²	126	13	50	76	12.2	4.10	100	.251	.323	0	—	0	1	-0	-1	-0.1
1987	Pit-N	11	12	.478	29	28	1	1	0	176¹	165	23	46	120	10.8	3.88	106	.247	.296	7	.119	-1	4	4	1	0.5
1988	Pit-N	15	7	.682	33	32	3	1	0	219¹	194	21	50	127	10.3	3.08	111	.239	.288	13	.171	3	9	8	-1	1.0
1989	Pit-N	14	12	.538	35	34	8	5	0	244¹	215	21	69	123	10.6	2.80	120	.238	.295	8	.104	-2	19	15	-0	1.3
1990	*Pit-N	**22**	6	**.786**	33	33	9	3	0	231¹	190	15	56	131	9.7	2.76	131	.225	.275	18	.214	5	26	22	2	3.4
1991	*Pit-N	15	14	.517	35	35	5	2	0	234²	245	16	62	142	11.9	3.07	116	.274	.323	15	.179	1	16	13	2	1.9
1992	*Pit-N	15	11	.577	34	34	10	4	0	256²	218	17	54	177	9.7	2.77	124	.231	.277	14	.157	1	21	19	1	2.1
1993	Hou-N	9	18	.333	34	34	7	1	0	237²	242	18	60	157	11.5	3.79	102	.267	.315	6	.085	-2	7	2	-0	0.1
1994	Hou-N★	12	6	.667	23	23	6	2	0	164²	132	14	45	121	9.8	2.84	139	.220	.277	14	.241	3	25	20	2	2.7
1995	Hou-N	10	9	.526	31	31	2	1	0	185	205	18	54	143	13.0	4.77	81	.282	.338	14	.233	4	-12	-19	0	-1.3
1996	Hou-N	7	9	.438	30	30	1	0	0	175¹	208	21	60	137	14.1	4.57	84	.298	.359	10	.179	0	-7	-15	0	-1.1
Total	11	137	112	.550	344	335	52	21	0	2257	2140	196	606	1454	11.1	3.41	108	.252	.305	119	.167	13	109	72	5	10.5

● **MOE DRABOWSKY**   Drabowsky, Myron Walter   b: 7/21/35, Ozanna, Poland   BR/TR, 6'2", 200 lbs.   Deb: 8/7/56   C

YEAR	TM/L	W	L	PCT	G	GS	CG	SH	SV	IP	H	HR	BB	SO	RAT	ERA	ERA+	OAV	OOB	BH	AVG	PB	PR	/A	PD	TPI
1956	Chi-N	2	4	.333	9	7	3	0	0	51	37	1	39	36	13.8	2.47	153	.207	.355	4	.250	0	7	7	-0	0.9
1957	Chi-N	13	15	.464	36	33	12	2	0	239²	214	22	94	170	11.9	3.53	110	.242	.321	15	.183	2	9	9	0	1.2
1958	Chi-N	9	11	.450	22	20	4	1	0	125²	118	19	73	77	14.0	4.51	87	.245	.350	7	.156	-1	-8	-8	-0	-1.3
1959	Chi-N	5	10	.333	31	23	3	1	0	141²	138	21	75	70	13.7	4.13	96	.251	.344	5	.111	-1	-3	-3	-0	-0.4
1960	Chi-N	3	1	.750	32	7	0	0	1	50¹	71	3	23	26	17.0	6.44	59	.338	.406	0	.000	-1	-15	-15	-1	-1.3
1961	Mil-N	0	2	.000	16	0	0	0	2	25¹	26	4	18	5	16.0	4.62	81	.277	.398	1	.250	0	-2	-2	-0	-0.2
1962	Cin-N	2	6	.250	23	10	1	0	1	83	84	13	31	61	13.1	4.99	81	.267	.344	0	.000	-2	-10	-9	-1	-1.0
	KC-A	1	1	.500	10	3	0	0	0	28	29	8	10	19	12.9	5.14	82	.266	.333	1	.167	0	-4	-3	-0	-0.2
1963	KC-A	7	13	.350	26	22	9	2	0	174¹	135	16	64	109	10.7	3.05	128	.214	.295	10	.161	1	11	17	-2	1.8
1964	KC-A	5	13	.278	53	21	1	0	1	168¹	176	24	72	119	13.7	5.29	72	.273	.353	1	.023	-4	-31	-28	1	-3.1
1965	KC-A	1	5	.167	14	5	0	0	0	38²	44	5	18	25	15.1	4.42	79	.291	.378	1	.091	-1	-4	-4	-0	-0.7
1966	*Bal-A	6	0	1.000	44	3	0	0	7	96	62	10	29	98	8.6	2.81	118	.181	.247	8	.364	4	7	6	-1	0.7
1967	Bal-A	7	5	.583	43	0	0	0	12	95¹	64	7	25	96	8.8	1.60	196	.194	.253	7	.350	2	17	16	0	2.9
1968	Bal-A	4	4	.500	45	0	0	0	7	61¹	35	3	25	46	9.4	1.91	153	.166	.267	2	.286	0	7	7	-0	1.2
1969	KC-A	11	9	.550	52	0	0	0	11	98	68	10	30	76	9.2	2.94	125	.190	.256	4	.235	1	7	8	1	2.0
1970	KC-A	1	2	.333	24	0	0	0	2	35²	36	3	12	38	10.6	3.28	114	.217	.294	1	.250	0	2	2	0	0.2
	*Bal-A	4	2	.667	21	0	0	0	1	33¹	30	7	15	21	12.4	3.78	96	.233	.317	0	.000	-1	-0	-0	-0	-0.2
	Yr	5	4	.556	45	0	0	0	3	69	58	10	27	59	11.2	3.52	105	.221	.296	1	.111	-1	1	1	0	0.1
1971	StL-N	6	1	.857	51	0	0	0	8	60¹	49	7	33	49	11.9	3.43	105	.207	.317	1	.167	0	3	-1	-1	0.1
1972	StL-N	1	1	.500	30	0	0	0	2	27²	29	4	14	22	14.3	2.60	131	.259	.346	0	.000	-0	3	2	1	0.0
	Chi-A	0	0	—	7	0	0	0	0	7¹	6	0	2	4	9.8	2.45	127	.240	.296	0	.000	-0	0	1	0	0.0
Total	17	88	105	.456	589	154	33	6	55	1641	1441	182	702	1162	12.1	3.71	101	.236	.321	68	.162	-0	-5	4	-5	2.7

● **DICK DRAGO**   Drago, Richard Anthony   b: 6/25/45, Toledo, Ohio   BR/TR, 6'1", 190 lbs.   Deb: 4/11/69

YEAR	TM/L	W	L	PCT	G	GS	CG	SH	SV	IP	H	HR	BB	SO	RAT	ERA	ERA+	OAV	OOB	BH	AVG	PB	PR	/A	PD	TPI
1969	KC-A	11	13	.458	41	26	10	2	1	200²	190	19	65	108	11.5	3.77	98	.248	.308	3	.058	-3	-3	-2	2	-0.3
1970	KC-A	9	15	.375	35	34	7	1	0	240	239	20	72	127	11.9	3.75	100	.266	.325	4	.053	-6	-1	-0	-1	-0.7
1971	KC-A	17	11	.607	35	34	15	4	0	241¹	251	14	46	109	11.4	2.98	115	.276	.318	10	.130	1	13	12	0	1.5
1972	KC-A	12	17	.414	34	33	11	2	0	239¹	230	22	51	135	10.8	3.01	101	.254	.298	4	.059	-2	1	1	-3	-0.5
1973	KC-A	12	14	.462	37	33	10	1	0	212²	252	16	76	98	14.2	4.23	97	.300	.363	0	—	0	-10	-3	1	-0.2
1974	Bos-A	7	10	.412	33	18	8	0	3	175²	165	17	56	90	11.6	3.48	110	.251	.315	0	—	0	3	7	-2	0.1
1975	*Bos-A	2	2	.500	40	2	0	0	15	72²	69	5	31	42	12.4	3.84	106	.247	.323	0	—	0	1	2	-0	-0.1
1976	Cal-A	7	8	.467	43	0	0	0	6	79¹	80	7	31	43	13.2	4.42	75	.264	.342	0	—	0	-8	-10	-2	-1.8
1977	Cal-A	0	1	.000	13	0	0	0	2	21	22	3	3	15	10.7	3.00	130	.272	.298	0	—	0	1	2	0	0.3
	Bal-A	6	3	.667	36	0	0	0	3	39²	49	2	15	20	14.7	3.63	104	.308	.371	0	—	0	3	-1	-1	0.5
	Yr	6	4	.600	49	0	0	0	5	60²	71	5	18	35	13.4	3.41	112	.293	.345	0	—	0	4	-3	-1	0.8
1978	Bos-A	4	4	.500	37	1	0	0	7	77¹	71	5	32	42	12.5	3.03	136	.246	.329	0	—	0	6	9	-1	1.0
1979	Bos-A	10	6	.625	53	1	0	0	13	89	85	6	21	67	11.0	3.03	145	.254	.304	0	—	0	12	14	-0	2.6
1980	Bos-A	7	7	.500	43	0	0	0	3	132²	127	17	44	63	11.9	4.14	102	.251	.317	0	.000	-1	-2	-1	-0	0.0
1981	Sea-A	4	6	.400	39	0	0	0	5	53²	71	4	15	27	14.4	5.53	70	.324	.368	0	—	0	-11	-10	-0	-1.9
Total	13	108	117	.480	519	189	62	10	58	1875	1901	157	558	987	12.1	3.62	103	.266	.324	21	.077	-10	4	23	-5	0.5

● **BRIAN DRAHMAN**   Drahman, Brian Stacy   b: 11/7/66, Kenton, Ky.   BR/TR, 6'3", 205 lbs.   Deb: 4/16/91

YEAR	TM/L	W	L	PCT	G	GS	CG	SH	SV	IP	H	HR	BB	SO	RAT	ERA	ERA+	OAV	OOB	BH	AVG	PB	PR	/A	PD	TPI
1991	Chi-A	3	2	.600	28	0	0	0	0	30²	21	4	13	18	10.0	3.23	123	.193	.279	0	—	0	3	3	-0	0.5
1992	Chi-A	0	0	—	5	0	0	0	0	7	6	0	2	1	10.3	2.57	150	.222	.276	0	—	0	1	1	0	0.0
1993	Chi-A	0	0	—	5	0	0	0	1	5¹	7	0	6	3	15.2	0.00	—	.333	.391	0	—	0	1	1	0	0.1
1994	Fla-N	0	0	—	9	0	0	0	0	13	15	2	6	7	14.5	6.23	70	.300	.375	0	—	0	-3	-3	0	-0.1
Total	4	3	2	.600	47	0	0	0	1	56	49	6	23	29	11.6	3.54	115	.237	.313	0	—	0	4	3	0	0.6

● **LOGAN DRAKE**   Drake, Logan Gaffney "L.G."   b: 12/26/1900, Spartanburg, S.C.   d: 6/1/40, Columbia, S.C.   BR/TR, 5'10.5", 165 lbs.   Deb: 9/21/22

YEAR	TM/L	W	L	PCT	G	GS	CG	SH	SV	IP	H	HR	BB	SO	RAT	ERA	ERA+	OAV	OOB	BH	AVG	PB	PR	/A	PD	TPI
1922	Cle-A	0	0	—	1	0	0	0	0	3	4	0	2	1	18.0	3.00	134	.364	.462	0	.000	0	0	0	0	0.0
1923	Cle-A	0	0	—	4	0	0	0	0	4¹	4	0	2	4	14.5	4.15	95	.133	.350	0	.000	0	0	0	0	0.0
1924	Cle-A	0	1	.000	5	1	0	0	0	11¹	18	0	10	8	23.0	10.32	41	.400	.518	0	.000	-0	-8	-8	-0	-0.6
Total	3	0	1	.000	10	1	0	0	0	18²	24	0	16	11	20.3	7.71	54	.338	.472	0	.000	-0	-7	-7	-0	-0.6

● **TOM DRAKE**   Drake, Thomas Kendall   b: 8/7/12, Birmingham, Ala.   d: 7/2/88, Birmingham, Ala.   BR/TR, 6'1", 185 lbs.   Deb: 4/24/39

YEAR	TM/L	W	L	PCT	G	GS	CG	SH	SV	IP	H	HR	BB	SO	RAT	ERA	ERA+	OAV	OOB	BH	AVG	PB	PR	/A	PD	TPI
1939	Cle-A	0	1	.000	8	1	0	0	0	15	23	2	19	1	26.4	9.00	49	.377	.537	0	.000	-0	-7	-8	0	-0.4
1941	Bro-N	1	1	.500	10	2	0	0	0	24²	26	2	9	12	12.8	4.38	84	.280	.343	2	.400	-0	-2	-2	-0	-0.1
Total	2	1	2	.333	18	3	0	0	0	39²	49	4	28	13	17.9	6.13	65	.318	.429	2	.286	-0	-9	-10	0	-0.5

● **MIKE DRAPER**   Draper, Michael Anthony   b: 9/14/66, Hagerstown, Md.   BR/TR, 6'2", 180 lbs.   Deb: 4/10/93

YEAR	TM/L	W	L	PCT	G	GS	CG	SH	SV	IP	H	HR	BB	SO	RAT	ERA	ERA+	OAV	OOB	BH	AVG	PB	PR	/A	PD	TPI
1993	NY-N	1	1	.500	29	1	0	0	0	42¹	53	2	14	16	14.2	4.25	94	.327	.381	2	.667	1	-1	-1	0	0.1

● **DAVE DRAVECKY**   Dravecky, David Francis   b: 2/14/56, Youngstown, Ohio   BR/TL, 6'1", 195 lbs.   Deb: 6/15/82

YEAR	TM/L	W	L	PCT	G	GS	CG	SH	SV	IP	H	HR	BB	SO	RAT	ERA	ERA+	OAV	OOB	BH	AVG	PB	PR	/A	PD	TPI
1982	SD-N	5	3	.625	31	10	0	0	2	105	86	3	33	59	10.3	2.57	133	.225	.288	3	.130	-0	12	10	2	0.9
1983	SD-N★	14	10	.583	28	28	5	3	0	183²	181	18	44	74	11.2	3.58	97	.262	.309	6	.098	-1	1	-2	1	-0.3
1984	*SD-N	9	8	.529	50	14	3	2	8	156²	125	12	51	71	10.3	2.93	122	.222	.291	4	.098	-1	11	11	-2	1.0
1985	SD-N	13	11	.542	34	31	7	2	0	214²	200	18	57	105	10.8	2.93	120	.249	.300	8	.116	-0	16	14	-1	1.4
1986	SD-N	9	11	.450	26	26	3	1	0	161²	149	17	54	87	11.4	3.07	119	.246	.318	7	.140	0	12	10	0	1.3
1987	SD-N	3	7	.300	30	10	1	0	0	79	71	10	31	60	12.0	3.76	105	.240	.318	3	.167	0	3	2	0	0.2
	*SF-N	7	5	.583	18	18	4	3	0	112¹	115	8	33	78	12.0	3.20	120	.272	.328	5	.132	0	11	8	1	0.9
	Yr	10	12	.455	48	28	5	3	0	191¹	186	18	64	138	11.9	3.43	113	.257	.319	8	.143	0	14	10	1	1.1
1988	SF-N	2	2	.500	7	7	1	0	0	37	33	4	8	19	10.0	3.16	103	.243	.285	1	.100	-0	1	0	-0	0.1
1989	SF-N	2	0	1.000	4	4	1	0	0	27²	21	3	8	19	9.5	3.46	97	.182	.265	1	.333	0	-1	-0	-0	0.1
Total	8	64	57	.529	226	146	28	9	10	1062²	968	97	315	558	11.0	3.13	115	.245	.304	38	.121	-2	67	54	1	5.5

● **TOM DREES**   Drees, Thomas Kent   b: 6/17/63, Des Moines, Iowa   BB/TL, 6'6", 210 lbs.   Deb: 9/3/91

YEAR	TM/L	W	L	PCT	G	GS	CG	SH	SV	IP	H	HR	BB	SO	RAT	ERA	ERA+	OAV	OOB	BH	AVG	PB	PR	/A	PD	TPI
1991	Chi-A	0	0	—	4	0	0	0	0	7¹	10	4	6	2	19.6	12.27	32	.345	.457	0	—	0	-7	-7	-0	0.1

● **DARREN DREIFORT**   Dreifort, Darren James   b: 5/18/72, Wichita, Kan.   BR/TR, 6'2", 205 lbs.   Deb: 4/7/94

YEAR	TM/L	W	L	PCT	G	GS	CG	SH	SV	IP	H	HR	BB	SO	RAT	ERA	ERA+	OAV	OOB	BH	AVG	PB	PR	/A	PD	TPI
1994	LA-N	0	5	.000	27	0	0	0	6	29	45	0	15	22	19.9	6.21	63	.357	.441	1	1.000	1	-6	-7	1	-1.2
1996	*LA-N	1	4	.200	19	0	0	0	0	23²	23	2	12	24	13.3	4.94	78	.256	.343	0	.000	-0	-2	-3	1	-0.5
Total	2	1	9	.100	46	0	0	0	6	52²	68	2	27	46	16.9	5.64	69	.315	.401	1	.250	0	-8	-10	1	-1.7

YEAR TM/L	W	L	PCT	G	GS	CG	SH	SV	IP	H	HR	BB	SO	RAT	ERA	ERA+	OAV	OOB	BH	AVG	PB	PR	/A	PD	TPI
● CLEM DREISEWERD								Dreisewerd, Clemens Johann "Steamboat" b: 1/24/16, Old Monroe, Mo. BL/TL, 6'1.5", 195 lbs. Deb: 8/29/44																
1944 Bos-A	2	4	.333	7	7	3	0	0	48²	52	2	9	9	11.3	4.07	84	.268	.300	3	.188	0	-3	-4	-1	-0.5
1945 Bos-A	0	1	.000	2	2	0	0	0	9²	13	0	2	3	14.9	4.66	73	.325	.372	0	.000	-0	-1	-1	-0	-0.2
1946 *Bos-A	4	1	.800	20	1	0	0	0	47¹	50	6	15	19	12.4	4.18	88	.276	.332	0	.000	-1	-4	-3	1	-0.3
1948 StL-A	0	2	.000	13	0	0	0	1	22¹	28	6	8	6	14.5	5.64	81	.318	.375	0	.000	-1	-3	-3	-0	-0.3
NY-N	0	0	—	4	0	0	0	1	12²	17	3	5	2	15.6	5.68	69	.321	.379	1	.250	-1	-2	-2	-0	0.0
Total 4	6	8	.429	46	10	3	0	2	140²	160	14	39	39	12.8	4.54	82	.288	.336	4	.105	-1	-14	-13	-1	-1.3
● KIRK DRESSENDORFER								Dressendorfer, Kirk Richard b: 4/8/69, Houston, Tex. BR/TR, 5'11", 190 lbs. Deb: 4/13/91																
1991 Oak-A	3	3	.500	7	7	0	0	0	34²	33	5	21	17	14.0	5.45	70	.244	.346	0	—	0	-5	-6	-0	-0.7
● BOB DRESSER								Dresser, Robert Nicholson b: 10/4/1878, Newton, Mass. d: 7/27/24, Duxbury, Mass. BL/TL, Deb: 8/13/02																
1902 Bos-N	0	1	.000	1	1	1	0	0	9	12	0	0	8	12.0	3.00	94	.316	.316	1	.250	0	-0	-0	-0	0.0
● ROB DRESSLER								Dressler, Robert Anthony b: 2/2/54, Portland, Ore. BR/TR, 6'3", 180 lbs. Deb: 9/7/75																
1975 SF-N	1	0	1.000	3	2	1	0	0	16¹	17	0	4	6	11.6	1.10	345	.274	.318	0	.000	-0	5	5	0	0.3
1976 SF-N	3	10	.231	25	19	0	0	0	107²	125	8	35	33	13.5	4.43	82	.291	.347	4	.129	-1	-11	-10	1	-1.1
1978 StL-N	0	1	.000	3	2	0	0	0	13	12	0	4	4	11.1	2.08	169	.267	.327	0	.000	-0	2	2	-0	0.1
1979 Sea-A	3	2	.600	21	11	2	0	0	104	134	11	22	36	13.5	4.93	88	.312	.345	0	—	-0	-8	-7	-0	-0.3
1980 Sea-A	4	10	.286	30	14	3	0	0	149¹	161	14	33	50	11.9	3.98	104	.280	.322	0	—	-0	1	3	1	0.3
Total 5	11	23	.324	82	48	6	0	0	390¹	449	33	98	129	12.7	4.17	96	.291	.335	4	.105	-1	-12	-7	2	-0.7
● DAVE DREW								Drew, David Deb: 5/14/1884 ◆																
1884 Phi-U	0	1	.000	1	0	0	0	0	7	7	0	0	2	9.0	3.86	60	.241	.241	4	.444	0	-1	-1	-0	-0.1
● KARL DREWS								Drews, Karl August b: 2/22/20, Staten Island, N.Y. d: 8/15/63, Dania, Fla. BR/TR, 6'4", 198 lbs. Deb: 9/8/46																
1946 NY-A	0	1	.000	3	1	0	0	0	6¹	6	0	6	4	18.5	8.53	40	.250	.419	0	.000	-0	-4	-4	-0	-0.5
1947 *NY-A	6	6	.500	30	10	0	0	1	91²	92	6	55	45	14.9	4.91	72	.264	.373	1	.037	-2	-12	-14	1	-1.9
1948 NY-A	2	3	.400	19	2	0	0	1	38	35	3	31	11	15.6	3.79	108	.248	.384	0	.000	-1	2	1	1	0.2
StL-A	3	2	.600	20	2	0	0	2	38	43	3	38	11	19.2	8.05	57	.289	.433	0	.000	-0	-16	-15	-0	-1.8
Yr	5	5	.500	39	4	0	0	3	76	78	6	69	22	17.4	5.92	73	.269	.409	0	.000	-1	-14	-14	1	-1.6
1949 StL-A	4	12	.250	31	23	3	1	0	139²	180	11	66	35	16.4	6.64	68	.317	.397	0	.000	-5	-38	-33	-1	-3.6
1951 Phi-N	1	0	1.000	5	3	1	0	0	23	29	2	7	13	15.7	6.26	61	.296	.367	2	.250	-1	-6	-6	-0	-0.2
1952 Phi-N	14	15	.483	33	30	15	5	0	228²	213	13	52	96	10.6	2.72	135	.252	.298	9	.110	-2	26	24	0	2.8
1953 Phi-N	9	10	.474	47	27	6	0	3	185¹	218	26	50	72	13.5	4.52	93	.293	.346	7	.119	-2	-5	-6	2	-0.7
1954 Phi-N	1	0	1.000	8	0	0	0	0	16	18	2	8	6	13.5	5.63	72	.300	.382	0	.000	-1	-3	-3	-0	-0.2
Cin-N	4	4	.500	22	9	1	1	0	60	79	6	19	29	15.0	6.00	70	.326	.380	2	.167	-1	-13	-12	-0	-1.3
Yr	5	4	.556	30	9	1	1	0	76	97	8	27	35	14.9	5.92	70	.320	.380	2	.125	1	-16	-15	-0	-1.5
Total 8	44	53	.454	218	107	26	7	7	826²	913	72	332	322	13.9	4.76	84	.284	.357	21	.083	-12	-68	-68	3	-7.2
● STEVE DREYER								Dreyer, Steven William b: 11/19/69, Ames, Iowa BR/TR, 6'3", 180 lbs. Deb: 8/8/93																
1993 Tex-A	3	3	.500	10	6	0	0	0	41	44	7	20	23	15.1	5.71	73	.291	.371	0	—	0	-6	-7	-0	-0.9
1994 Tex-A	1	1	.500	5	3	0	0	0	17¹	19	1	8	11	14.5	5.71	84	.271	.354	0	—	0	-2	-2	-0	-0.2
Total 2	4	4	.500	15	9	0	0	0	58¹	67	8	34	15.0	5.71	76	.285	.366	0	—	0	-8	-9	-1	-1.1
● DENNY DRISCOLL								Driscoll, John F. b: 11/19/1855, Lowell, Mass. d: 7/11/1886, Lowell, Mass. BL/TL, 5'10.5", 160 lbs. Deb: 7/1/1880 ◆																
1880 Buf-N	1	3	.250	6	4	4	0	0	41²	48	1	9	17	12.3	3.89	63	.270	.305	10	.154	-1	-7	-7	0	-0.6
1882 Pit-a	13	9	.591	23	23	23	0	0	201	162	0	12	59	7.8	1.21	216	.206	.218	11	.138	-2	33	31	-4	2.4
1883 Pit-a	18	21	.462	41	40	35	1	0	336¹	427	3	39	79	12.5	3.99	81	.290	.309	27	.182	-5	-26	-29	6	-2.5
1884 Lou-a	6	6	.500	13	13	10	0	0	102	110	3	7	16	10.5	3.44	90	.252	.267	12	.188	-2	-4	-2	4	-0.3
Total 4	38	39	.494	83	80	72	1	0	681	747	7	67	171	10.8	3.08	97	.260	.277	60	.167	-9	-2	-8	4	-1.0
● MICHAEL DRISCOLL								Driscoll, Michael Columbus b: 10/19/1892, Rockland, Mass. d: 3/22/53, Foxboro, Mass. BR/TR, 6'1", 160 lbs. Deb: 7/6/16																
1916 Phi-A	0	1	.000	1	0	0	0	0	5	6	0	2	0	14.4	5.40	53	.273	.333	0	—	-0	-1	-1	1	-0.2
● TOM DROHAN								Drohan, Thomas F b: 8/26/1887, Fall River, Mass. d: 9/17/26, Kewanee, Ill. BR/TR, 5'10", 175 lbs. Deb: 5/1/13																
1913 Was-A	0	0	—	2	0	0	0	0	2	5	1	0	2	22.5	9.00	33	.500	.500	0	—	0	-1	-1	0	0.0
● DICK DROTT								Drott, Richard Fred "Hummer" b: 7/1/36, Cincinnati, Ohio d: 8/16/85, Glendale Heights, Ill. BR/TR, 6', 185 lbs. Deb: 4/16/57																
1957 Chi-N	15	11	.577	38	32	7	3	0	229	200	22	129	170	13.2	3.58	108	.234	.340	8	.100	-5	8	8	-1	0.2
1958 Chi-N	7	11	.389	39	31	4	0	0	167¹	156	23	99	127	14.0	5.43	72	.245	.352	15	.273	3	-28	-28	1	-2.3
1959 Chi-N	1	2	.333	8	6	1	1	0	27¹	25	5	26	15	16.8	5.93	67	.245	.398	1	.125	-0	-6	-6	-0	-0.6
1960 Chi-N	0	6	.000	23	9	0	0	0	55¹	63	7	42	32	17.6	7.16	53	.296	.419	1	.100	-1	-21	-21	-0	-2.1
1961 Chi-N	1	4	.200	35	8	0	0	0	98	75	13	51	48	11.7	4.22	99	.215	.317	6	.273	1	-2	-0	-2	-0.1
1962 Hou-N	1	0	1.000	13	0	0	0	0	13	12	1	9	10	14.5	7.62	49	.240	.356	0	.000	-0	-5	-6	-0	-0.4
1963 Hou-N	2	12	.143	27	14	2	1	0	97²	95	13	49	58	13.8	4.98	63	.257	.353	3	.130	-1	-18	-20	-1	-2.8
Total 7	27	46	.370	176	101	14	5	0	687²	626	84	405	460	13.8	4.78	80	.243	.351	34	.168	-2	-72	-74	-5	-8.1
● LOUIS DRUCKE								Drucke, Louis Frank b: 12/3/1888, Waco, Tex. d: 9/22/55, Waco, Tex. BR/TR, 6'1", 188 lbs. Deb: 9/25/09																
1909 NY-N	2	1	.667	3	3	2	0	0	24	20	0	13	8	12.4	2.25	114	.227	.327	1	.125	-0	1	1	-0	0.0
1910 NY-N	12	10	.545	34	27	15	0	0	215¹	174	3	82	151	11.2	2.47	120	.228	.312	15	.214	4	14	12	2	1.7
1911 NY-N	4	4	.500	15	10	4	0	0	75²	83	1	41	42	15.7	4.04	83	.281	.384	2	.087	-1	-5	-6	1	-0.6
1912 NY-N	0	0	—	1	0	0	0	0	2	5	0	1	0	27.0	13.50	25	.417	.462	0	—	-0	-2	-2	0	-0.2
Total 4	18	15	.545	53	40	21	0	0	317	282	4	137	201	12.4	2.90	105	.243	.333	18	.178	2	7	5	2	0.9
● CARL DRUHOT								Druhot, Carl A. "Collie" b: 9/1/1882, Ohio d: 2/11/18, Portland, Ore. BL/TL, 5'7", 150 lbs. Deb: 4/18/06																
1906 Cin-N	2	2	.500	4	3	1	0	0	25	27	0	7	14	13.0	4.32	64	.270	.330	2	.222	0	-5	-4	-1	-0.7
StL-N	6	7	.462	15	13	12	1	0	130¹	117	1	46	45	11.6	2.62	100	.238	.310	13	.232	1	0	0	1	0.2
Yr	8	9	.471	19	16	13	1	0	155¹	144	1	53	59	11.7	2.90	91	.243	.310	15	.231	1	-5	-4	-0	-0.5
1907 StL-N	0	1	.000	1	0	0	0	0	2¹	3	0	4	1	30.9	15.43	16	.600	.800	0	—	0	-3	-3	0	-0.9
Total 2	8	10	.444	20	17	13	1	0	157²	147	1	57	60	12.1	3.08	86	.247	.321	15	.231	-0	-8	-7	-0	-1.4
● TIM DRUMMOND								Drummond, Timothy Darnell b: 12/24/64, LaPlata, Md. BR/TR, 6'3", 170 lbs. Deb: 9/12/87																
1987 Pit-N	0	0	—	6	0	0	0	0	6	5	0	3	5	12.0	4.50	91	.227	.320	0	—	-0	-0	-0	-0	0.0
1989 Min-A	0	0	—	8	0	0	0	1	16¹	16	0	8	9	14.3	3.86	107	.246	.347	0	.000	-0	0	1	0	-0.5
1990 Min-A	3	5	.375	35	4	0	0	0	91	104	8	36	49	13.9	4.35	95	.295	.362	0	—	-0	-5	-2	-0	-0.6
Total 3	3	5	.375	49	4	0	0	1	113¹	125	8	47	63	13.9	4.29	97	.284	.357	0	.000	-0	-5	-2	-1	-1.1
● DON DRYSDALE								Drysdale, Donald Scott b: 7/23/36, Van Nuys, Cal. d: 7/3/93, Montreal, Que., Canada BR/TR, 6'6", 216 lbs. Deb: 4/17/56 H																
1956 *Bro-N	5	5	.500	25	12	2	0	0	99	95	9	31	55	11.7	2.64	150	.255	.317	5	.192	-1	12	15	1	1.6
1957 Bro-N	17	9	.654	34	29	9	4	0	221	197	17	61	148	10.8	2.69	155	.236	.294	9	.123	-0	29	36	5	4.7
1958 LA-N	12	13	.480	44	29	6	1	0	211²	214	23	72	131	12.8	4.17	98	.263	.333	15	.227	8	-5	-2	3	1.0
1959 *LA-N★	17	13	.567	44	36	15	4	2	270²	237	26	93	242	11.6	3.46	122	.233	.308	15	.165	3	15	23	2	3.0
1960 LA-N	15	14	.517	41	36	15	5	2	269	214	27	72	246	9.9	2.84	140	.215	.275	13	.157	2	27	34	4	4.3
1961 LA-N☆	13	10	.565	40	37	10	3	0	244	236	29	83	182	12.5	3.69	118	.254	.329	16	.193	4	9	18	-1	1.8
1962 LA-N★	25	9	.735	43	41	19	2	1	314¹	272	21	78	232	10.3	2.83	128	.230	.283	22	.198	5	39	28	1	3.4
1963 *LA-N★	19	17	.528	42	42	17	3	0	315¹	287	25	57	251	10.1	2.63	115	.242	.283	16	.167	3	23	14	3	2.4
1964 *LA-N★	18	16	.529	40	40	21	5	0	321¹	242	16	68	237	8.8	2.18	148	.207	.262	19	.173	4	48	38	2	4.7
1965 *LA-N★	23	12	.657	44	42	20	7	1	308²	270	30	66	210	10.2	2.77	118	.232	.280	39	.300	22	26	17	4	4.4
1966 *LA-N	13	16	.448	40	40	11	3	0	273²	279	35	45	177	11.2	3.42	96	.265	.306	20	.189	4	6	-4	-1	-0.1
1967 LA-N	13	16	.448	38	38	9	3	0	282	269	19	60	196	10.8	2.74	113	.251	.296	12	.129	-0	20	11	3	1.4
1968 LA-N★	14	12	.538	31	31	12	8	0	239	201	11	56	155	10.1	2.15	129	.231	.286	14	.177	4	22	16	2	2.4

YEAR	TM/L	W	L	PCT	G	GS	CG	SH	SV	IP	H	HR	BB	SO	RAT	ERA	ERA+	OAV	OOB	BH	AVG	PB	PR	/A	PD	TPI
1969	LA-N	5	4	.556	12	12	1	1	0	62²	71	9	13	24	12.4	4.45	75	.291	.332	3	.136	0	-6	-8	0	-1.0
Total	14	209	166	.557	518	465	167	49	6	3432	3084	280	855	2486	10.7	2.95	121	.239	.294	218	.186	60	266	230	25	34.0

● MONK DUBIEL
Dubiel, Walter John b: 2/12/18, Hartford, Conn. d: 10/23/69, Hartford, Conn. BR/TR, 6′, 190 lbs. Deb: 4/19/44

YEAR	TM/L	W	L	PCT	G	GS	CG	SH	SV	IP	H	HR	BB	SO	RAT	ERA	ERA+	OAV	OOB	BH	AVG	PB	PR	/A	PD	TPI
1944	NY-A	13	13	.500	30	28	19	3	0	232	217	12	86	79	11.8	3.38	103	.248	.316	15	.181	-2	1	3	0	0.1
1945	NY-A	10	9	.526	26	20	9	1	0	151¹	157	9	62	45	13.0	4.64	75	.266	.335	16	.276	4	-21	-20	-2	-2.1
1948	Phi-N	8	10	.444	37	17	6	2	4	147	139	13	58	42	11.9	3.89	101	.248	.320	7	.167	0	1	1	-2	0.3
1949	Chi-N	6	9	.400	32	20	3	1	4	147²	142	16	54	52	12.0	4.14	97	.250	.317	10	.286	3	-2	-1	1	0.3
1950	Chi-N	6	10	.375	39	12	4	2	2	142²	152	12	67	51	13.9	4.16	101	.270	.348	9	.200	1	-0	1	2	0.3
1951	Chi-N	2	2	.500	22	0	0	0	1	54²	46	3	22	19	11.2	2.30	178	.232	.309	0	.000	-1	10	11	0	0.7
1952	Chi-N	0	0	—	1	0	0	0	0	0²	1	0	1	1	13.5	0.00	—	.333	.333	0	—	0	0	0	0	0.0
Total	7	45	53	.459	187	97	41	9	11	879¹	854	65	349	289	12.4	3.87	98	.254	.325	57	.207	5	-11	-6	-0	-0.7

● BRIAN DuBOIS
DuBois, Brian Andrew b: 4/18/67, Joliet, Ill. BL/TL, 5′10″, 195 lbs. Deb: 8/17/89

YEAR	TM/L	W	L	PCT	G	GS	CG	SH	SV	IP	H	HR	BB	SO	RAT	ERA	ERA+	OAV	OOB	BH	AVG	PB	PR	/A	PD	TPI
1989	Det-A	0	4	.000	6	5	0	0	1	36	29	2	17	13	12.0	1.75	218	.218	.316	0	—	0	9	8	-0	1.1
1990	Det-A	3	5	.375	12	11	0	0	0	58¹	70	9	22	34	14.3	5.09	78	.310	.373	0	—	0	-8	-7	-1	-1.0
Total	2	3	9	.250	18	16	0	0	1	94¹	99	11	39	47	13.5	3.82	102	.276	.352	0	—	0	1	1	-1	0.1

● JEAN DUBUC
Dubuc, Jean Joseph Octave Arthur "Chauncey" b: 9/15/1888, St.Johnsbury, Vt. d: 8/28/58, Fort Myers, Fla. BR/TR, 5′10.5″, 185 lbs. Deb: 6/25/08 C♦

YEAR	TM/L	W	L	PCT	G	GS	CG	SH	SV	IP	H	HR	BB	SO	RAT	ERA	ERA+	OAV	OOB	BH	AVG	PB	PR	/A	PD	TPI
1908	Cin-N	5	6	.455	15	9	7	1	0	85¹	62	2	41	32	11.4	2.74	84	.205	.309	4	.138	-1	-4	-4	1	-0.6
1909	Cin-N	2	5	.286	19	5	2	1	0	71¹	72	0	46	19	15.4	3.66	71	.269	.384	3	.167	0	-8	-8	0	-0.8
1912	Det-A	17	10	.630	37	26	23	2	3	250	217	2	109	97	12.0	2.77	118	.235	.321	29	.269	6	15	14	4	2.5
1913	Det-A	15	14	.517	36	28	22	1	2	242²	228	1	91	73	12.1	2.89	101	.252	.325	36	.267	5	1	1	8	1.9
1914	Det-A	13	14	.481	36	27	15	2	1	224	216	4	76	70	12.0	3.46	81	.257	.324	28	.226	7	-18	-16	3	-0.8
1915	Det-A	17	12	.586	39	33	19	5	2	258	231	6	88	74	11.5	3.21	94	.245	.316	23	.205	0	-8	-5	1	-0.4
1916	Det-A	10	10	.500	36	16	8	1	0	170¹	134	1	84	40	11.8	2.96	97	.233	.336	20	.256	5	-2	-2	4	0.8
1918	*Bos-A	0	1	.000	2	1	1	0	0	10²	11	1	5	1	13.5	4.22	64	.268	.348	1	.167	0	-2	-2	-0	-0.2
1919	NY-N	6	4	.600	36	5	1	0	3	132	119	4	37	32	10.8	2.66	105	.246	.303	6	.143	-1	4	2	2	0.2
Total	9	85	76	.528	256	150	101	12	13	1444¹	1290	20	577	438	11.9	3.04	96	.244	.324	150	.230	21	-22	-21	23	2.6

● JIM DUCKWORTH
Duckworth, James Raymond b: 5/24/39, National City, Cal. BR/TR, 6′4″, 194 lbs. Deb: 4/13/63

YEAR	TM/L	W	L	PCT	G	GS	CG	SH	SV	IP	H	HR	BB	SO	RAT	ERA	ERA+	OAV	OOB	BH	AVG	PB	PR	/A	PD	TPI
1963	Was-A	4	12	.250	37	15	2	0	0	120²	131	13	67	66	15.5	6.04	61	.278	.379	0	.000	-3	-32	-31	-1	-4.1
1964	Was-A	1	6	.143	30	2	0	0	3	56	52	9	25	56	12.9	4.34	85	.244	.332	2	.222	0	-4	-4	0	-0.4
1965	Was-A	2	2	.500	17	8	0	0	0	64	45	11	36	74	11.7	3.94	88	.202	.318	0	.000	-3	-3	-1	-5	-0.5
1966	Was-A	0	3	.000	5	4	0	0	0	14¹	14	2	10	14	15.7	5.02	69	.259	.385	0	.000	-0	-3	-2	0	-0.6
	KC-A	0	2	.000	8	0	0	0	1	12	14	2	14	10	18.8	9.00	38	.292	.424	0	—	0	-7	-7	-0	-1.3
	Yr	0	5	.000	13	4	0	0	1	26¹	28	4	20	24	16.7	6.84	50	.269	.392	0	.000	-1	-10	-10	-1	-1.9
Total	4	7	25	.219	97	29	2	0	4	267	256	37	148	220	14.2	5.26	69	.253	.358	2	.034	-5	-50	-49	-2	-6.9

● CLISE DUDLEY
Dudley, Elzie Clise b: 8/8/03, Graham, N.C. d: 1/12/89, Moncks Corner, S.C BL/TL, 6′1″, 195 lbs. Deb: 4/18/29

YEAR	TM/L	W	L	PCT	G	GS	CG	SH	SV	IP	H	HR	BB	SO	RAT	ERA	ERA+	OAV	OOB	BH	AVG	PB	PR	/A	PD	TPI
1929	Bro-N	6	14	.300	35	21	8	0	1	156²	202	9	64	33	15.9	5.69	81	.315	.385	5	.098	-1	-17	-19	2	-1.8
1930	Bro-N	2	4	.333	21	7	2	0	1	66²	103	3	27	18	17.8	6.35	77	.371	.458	5	.208	-0	-10	-11	1	-0.7
1931	Phi-N	8	14	.364	30	24	8	0	0	179	206	10	56	50	13.5	3.52	121	.287	.343	18	.214	0	7	14	1	1.8
1932	Phi-N	1	1	.500	13	0	0	0	1	17²	23	3	8	5	15.8	7.13	62	.329	.397	4	.286	3	-6	-5	0	-0.3
1933	Pit-N	0	0	—	1	0	0	0	0	0¹	6	0	1	0	189.0	135.00	2	.857	.875	0	—	0	-5	-5	0	0.0
Total	5	17	33	.340	100	52	18	1	2	420¹	540	25	156	106	15.3	5.03	90	.315	.378	32	.185	1	-31	-24	4	-1.0

● HAL DUES
Dues, Hal Joseph b: 9/22/54, LaMarque, Tex. BR/TR, 6′3″, 180 lbs. Deb: 9/9/77

YEAR	TM/L	W	L	PCT	G	GS	CG	SH	SV	IP	H	HR	BB	SO	RAT	ERA	ERA+	OAV	OOB	BH	AVG	PB	PR	/A	PD	TPI
1977	Mon-N	1	1	.500	6	4	0	0	0	23	26	2	9	9	13.7	4.30	88	.265	.327	0	.000	-1	-1	-1	0	-0.1
1978	Mon-N	5	6	.455	25	12	4	0	1	99	85	5	42	36	11.9	2.36	149	.240	.327	6	.194	0	13	13	-0	1.4
1980	Mon-N	0	1	.000	6	1	0	0	0	12¹	17	1	4	2	15.3	6.57	54	.333	.382	0	—	-0	-4	-4	0	-0.3
Total	3	6	8	.429	37	17	4	0	1	134¹	128	8	55	47	12.5	3.08	116	.254	.333	6	.154	-1	8	7	0	1.0

● LARRY DUFF
Duff, Cecil Elba b: 11/30/1897, Radersburg, Mont. d: 11/10/69, Bend, Ore. BL/TL, 6′1″, 175 lbs. Deb: 9/5/22

YEAR	TM/L	W	L	PCT	G	GS	CG	SH	SV	IP	H	HR	BB	SO	RAT	ERA	ERA+	OAV	OOB	BH	AVG	PB	PR	/A	PD	TPI
1922	Chi-A	1	1	.500	3	1	0	0	0	12²	16	1	3	7	13.5	4.97	82	.340	.380	2	.400	0	-1	-1	-0	-0.2

● JIM DUFFALO
Duffalo, James Francis b: 11/25/35, Helvetia, Pa. BR/TR, 6′1″, 175 lbs. Deb: 4/12/61

YEAR	TM/L	W	L	PCT	G	GS	CG	SH	SV	IP	H	HR	BB	SO	RAT	ERA	ERA+	OAV	OOB	BH	AVG	PB	PR	/A	PD	TPI
1961	SF-N	5	1	.833	24	4	1	0	1	61²	59	9	32	37	13.6	4.23	90	.257	.352	5	.294	3	-1	-3	-1	0.0
1962	SF-N	1	2	.333	24	2	0	0	0	42	42	3	23	29	13.9	3.64	104	.264	.348	0	.000	-0	-1	1	-1	0.0
1963	SF-N	4	2	.667	34	5	0	0	2	75¹	56	7	34	55	11.3	2.87	112	.209	.309	2	.111	-1	4	3	1	0.2
1964	SF-N	5	1	.833	35	3	1	0	3	74	57	9	31	55	10.9	2.92	122	.209	.294	1	.071	-1	5	5	-1	0.3
1965	SF-N	0	1	.000	2	0	0	0	0	0¹	1	0	2	0	81.0	27.00	13	.500	.750	0	—	0	-1	-1	0	-1.6
	Cin-N	0	1	.000	22	0	0	0	0	44¹	33	3	30	34	13.8	3.45	109	.212	.356	0	.000	-1	-0	1	1	-1.6
	Yr	0	2	.000	24	0	0	0	0	44²	34	3	32	34	14.3	3.63	103	.215	.364	0	.000	-1	-1	1	1	-1.6
Total	5	15	8	.652	141	14	2	0	6	297²	248	27	155	210	12.5	3.39	106	.227	.329	8	.127	-1	8	7	-1	-1.1

● JOHN DUFFIE
Duffie, John Brown b: 10/4/45, Greenwood, S.C. BR/TR, 6′7″, 210 lbs. Deb: 9/18/67

YEAR	TM/L	W	L	PCT	G	GS	CG	SH	SV	IP	H	HR	BB	SO	RAT	ERA	ERA+	OAV	OOB	BH	AVG	PB	PR	/A	PD	TPI
1967	LA-N	0	2	.000	1	1	0	0	0	4	6	1	3	2	20.2	6.75	49	.353	.450	0	.000	0	-2	-2	0	-0.2

● BERNIE DUFFY
Duffy, Bernard Allen b: 8/18/1893, Vinson, Okla. d: 2/9/62, Abilene, Tex. BR/TR, 5′11″, 180 lbs. Deb: 9/20/13

YEAR	TM/L	W	L	PCT	G	GS	CG	SH	SV	IP	H	HR	BB	SO	RAT	ERA	ERA+	OAV	OOB	BH	AVG	PB	PR	/A	PD	TPI
1913	Pit-N	0	0	—	3	2	0	0	0	11¹	18	0	3	8	16.7	5.56	54	.360	.396	1	.250	0	-3	-3	0	0.0

● DAN DUGAN
Dugan, Daniel Phillip b: 2/22/07, Plainfield, N.J. d: 6/25/68, Green Brook, N.J. BL/TL, 6′1.5″, 187 lbs. Deb: 9/5/28

YEAR	TM/L	W	L	PCT	G	GS	CG	SH	SV	IP	H	HR	BB	SO	RAT	ERA	ERA+	OAV	OOB	BH	AVG	PB	PR	/A	PD	TPI
1928	Chi-A	0	0	—	1	0	0	0	0	0¹	1	0	0	0	27.0	.000	—	.000	.000	0	—	0	0	0	0	0.0
1929	Chi-A	1	4	.200	19	2	0	0	0	65	77	9	19	15	13.6	6.65	64	.300	.353	5	.150	-1	-17	-17	-2	-1.4
Total	2	1	4	.200	20	2	0	0	0	65¹	77	9	19	15	13.5	6.61	65	.298	.351	5	.150	-1	-17	-17	-2	-1.4

● ED DUGAN
Dugan, Edward John b: 1864, Brooklyn, N.Y. Deb: 8/5/1884 F

YEAR	TM/L	W	L	PCT	G	GS	CG	SH	SV	IP	H	HR	BB	SO	RAT	ERA	ERA+	OAV	OOB	BH	AVG	PB	PR	/A	PD	TPI
1884	Ric-a	5	14	.263	20	20	20	0	0	166¹	196	5	15	60	11.5	4.49	74	.267	.284	8	.114	-4	-23	-22	-2	-2.4

● BILL DUGGLEBY
Duggleby, William James "Frosty Bill" b: 3/16/1874, Utica, N.Y. d: 8/30/44, Redfield, N.Y. TR, Deb: 4/21/1898

YEAR	TM/L	W	L	PCT	G	GS	CG	SH	SV	IP	H	HR	BB	SO	RAT	ERA	ERA+	OAV	OOB	BH	AVG	PB	PR	/A	PD	TPI
1898	Phi-N	3	3	.500	9	5	4	0	0	54	70	4	18	12	15.7	5.50	62	.311	.378	5	.238	2	-11	-12	1	-0.8
1901	Phi-N	20	12	.625	35	29	26	5	0	284²	302	9	41	95	11.2	2.88	118	.270	.302	19	.165	-3	14	17	5	1.9
1902	Phi-N	1	1	.500	2	2	2	0	0	17	19	0	4	4	12.2	3.18	116	.284	.324	0	.000	-1	1	1	1	0.1
	Phi-N	11	17	.393	33	27	25	0	1	258²	282	2	51	60	12.2	3.38	83	.277	.323	17	.173	-1	-17	-16	2	-1.5
1903	Phi-N	13	16	.448	36	30	28	3	2	264¹	318	4	79	57	13.9	3.75	87	.303	.358	24	.231	2	-14	-14	1	-1.0
1904	Phi-N	12	13	.480	32	27	22	2	1	223²	265	3	53	55	13.2	3.78	71	.292	.338	14	.171	0	-26	-27	-0	-2.7
1905	Phi-N	18	17	.514	38	36	27	1	0	289²	270	10	83	75	11.4	2.46	119	.253	.315	11	.109	-2	18	15	-2	1.3
1906	Phi-N	13	19	.406	42	30	22	5	0	280¹	241	6	66	83	10.2	2.25	116	.227	.287	14	.141	-2	12	11	1	1.2
1907	Phi-N	0	2	.000	5	2	0	0	0	29	43	2	11	8	18.3	7.45	33	.371	.447	1	.111	0	-16	-16	1	-0.9
	Pit-N	2	2	.500	9	3	1	0	0	40¹	34	0	12	4	10.7	2.68	91	.239	.308	2	.154	-0	-1	-1	-1	-0.1
	Yr	2	4	.333	14	5	1	0	0	69¹	77	2	23	12	13.2	4.67	52	.293	.354	3	.136	0	-17	-17	-2	-0.9
Total	8	93	102	.477	241	191	159	17	6	1741¹	1844	39	424	453	12.2	3.18	93	.272	.323	107	.165	-4	-41	-43	11	-2.4

● MARTIN DUKE
Duke, Martin F. "Duck" (b: Martin F. Duck) b: 1867, Zanesville, Ohio d: 12/31/1898, Minneapolis, Minn. TL, Deb: 8/24/1891

YEAR	TM/L	W	L	PCT	G	GS	CG	SH	SV	IP	H	HR	BB	SO	RAT	ERA	ERA+	OAV	OOB	BH	AVG	PB	PR	/A	PD	TPI
1891	Was-a	1	2	.333	4	4	2	0	0	23	36	0	19	21	21.5	7.43	50	.346	.447	1	.111	-1	-9	-9	-0	-0.9

● JAN DUKES
Dukes, Noble Jan b: 8/16/45, Cheyenne, Wyo. BL/TL, 5′11″, 175 lbs. Deb: 9/6/69

YEAR	TM/L	W	L	PCT	G	GS	CG	SH	SV	IP	H	HR	BB	SO	RAT	ERA	ERA+	OAV	OOB	BH	AVG	PB	PR	/A	PD	TPI
1969	Was-A	0	2	.000	8	0	0	0	0	11	8	0	4	3	9.8	2.45	141	.216	.293	0	.000	0	1	1	-0	0.2
1970	Was-A	0	0	—	5	0	0	0	0	6²	6	0	1	4	10.8	2.70	132	.240	.296	0	.000	0	1	1	0	0.0
1972	Tex-A	0	0	—	3	0	0	0	0	2¹	1	0	5	0	23.1	3.86	78	.167	.545	0	.000	-0	-2	-0	0	0.0
Total	3	0	2	.000	16	0	0	0	0	20	15	0	10	7	11.7	2.70	118	.221	.329	0	.000	0	1	1	-0	0.2

YEAR	TM/L	W	L	PCT	G	GS	CG	SH	SV	IP	H	HR	BB	SO	RAT	ERA	ERA+	OAV	OOB	BH	AVG	PB	PR	/A	PD	TPI

● **TOM DUKES**　Dukes, Thomas Earl　b: 8/31/42, Knoxville, Tenn.　BR/TR, 6'2", 185 lbs.　Deb: 8/15/67

YEAR	TM/L	W	L	PCT	G	GS	CG	SH	SV	IP	H	HR	BB	SO	RAT	ERA	ERA+	OAV	OOB	BH	AVG	PB	PR	/A	PD	TPI
1967	Hou-N	0	2	.000	17	0	0	0	1	23²	25	2	11	23	14.5	5.32	62	.275	.365	1	.500	0	-5	-5	-0	-0.5
1968	Hou-N	2	2	.500	43	0	0	0	4	52²	62	3	28	37	15.7	4.27	69	.291	.379	0	.000	-0	-8	-8	0	-0.7
1969	SD-N	1	0	1.000	13	0	0	0	1	22¹	26	2	10	15	14.5	7.25	49	.295	.367	0	.000	-0	-9	-9	-0	-0.5
1970	SD-N	1	6	.143	53	0	0	0	10	69	62	7	25	56	11.6	4.04	98	.246	.319	0	.000	-1	0	-1	-0	-0.2
1971	*Bal-A	1	5	.167	28	0	0	0	4	38¹	40	4	8	30	11.5	3.52	95	.263	.304	1	.143	-0	-1	-1	-1	-0.2
1972	Cal-A	0	1	.000	7	0	0	0	1	11	11	1	0	8	9.8	1.64	178	.262	.279	0	—	0	2	2	-1	0.1
Total	6	5	16	.238	161	0	0	0	21	217	226	19	82	169	13.1	4.35	79	.270	.341	2	.095	-1	-20	-22	-2	-2.0

● **BOB DULIBA**　Duliba, Robert John　b: 1/9/35, Glen Lyon, Pa.　BR/TR, 5'10", 185 lbs.　Deb: 8/11/59

YEAR	TM/L	W	L	PCT	G	GS	CG	SH	SV	IP	H	HR	BB	SO	RAT	ERA	ERA+	OAV	OOB	BH	AVG	PB	PR	/A	PD	TPI
1959	StL-N	0	1	.000	11	0	0	0	1	22³	19	2	12	14	12.3	2.78	153	.237	.337	0	.000	-0	3	4	1	0.2
1960	StL-N	4	4	.500	27	0	0	0	1	40²	49	6	16	23	14.4	4.20	97	.310	.374	1	.200	-0	-2	-0	-0	-0.1
1962	StL-N	2	0	1.000	28	0	0	0	2	39¹	33	3	17	22	11.4	2.06	207	.239	.323	0	.000	-0	8	10	0	0.5
1963	LA-A	1	1	.500	6	0	0	0	1	7²	3	0	6	4	10.6	1.17	292	.125	.300	0	.000	-0	2	2	-0	0.5
1964	LA-A	6	4	.600	58	0	0	0	9	72²	80	5	22	33	12.8	3.59	91	.287	.341	0	.000	-1	-0	-2	1	-0.4
1965	Bos-A	4	2	.667	39	0	0	0	1	64²	60	6	22	27	11.5	3.78	99	.248	.311	0	.000	-0	-2	-0	-0	-0.1
1967	KC-A	0	0	—	7	0	0	0	0	9²	13	3	1	6	13.0	6.52	49	.342	.359	0	—	0	-4	-4	-0	0.0
Total	7	17	12	.586	176	0	0	0	14	257	257	25	96	129	12.4	3.47	108	.268	.335	1	.038	-2	6	8	1	0.6

● **GEORGE DUMONT**　Dumont, George Henry "Pea Soup"　b: 11/13/1895, Minneapolis, Minn.　d: 10/13/56, Minneapolis, Minn.　BR/TR, 5'11", 163 lbs.　Deb: 9/14/15

YEAR	TM/L	W	L	PCT	G	GS	CG	SH	SV	IP	H	HR	BB	SO	RAT	ERA	ERA+	OAV	OOB	BH	AVG	PB	PR	/A	PD	TPI
1915	Was-A	2	1	.667	6	4	3	2	0	40	23	0	12	18	8.3	2.02	147	.169	.247	2	.167	-0	4	4	-1	0.2
1916	Was-A	2	3	.400	17	5	2	0	1	53	37	0	17	21	9.3	3.06	91	.194	.263	1	.071	-0	-1	-2	-1	-0.3
1917	Was-A	5	14	.263	37	23	8	2	2	204²	171	3	76	65	11.1	2.55	103	.227	.303	6	.203	-5	3	2	-3	-0.7
1918	Was-A	1	1	.500	4	1	1	0	0	14	18	0	6	12	15.4	5.14	53	.295	.358	1	.333	1	-4	-4	-0	-0.4
1919	Bos-A	0	4	.000	13	2	0	0	0	35¹	45	1	19	12	16.6	4.33	70	.326	.411	0	.000	-0	-4	-5	-0	-0.5
Total	5	10	23	.303	77	35	14	4	3	347	294	4	130	128	11.3	2.85	96	.230	.306	6	.064	-5	-3	-4	-5	-1.7

● **DAN DUMOULIN**　Dumoulin, Daniel Lynn　b: 8/20/53, Kokomo, Ind.　BR/TR, 6', 175 lbs.　Deb: 9/5/77

YEAR	TM/L	W	L	PCT	G	GS	CG	SH	SV	IP	H	HR	BB	SO	RAT	ERA	ERA+	OAV	OOB	BH	AVG	PB	PR	/A	PD	TPI
1977	Cin-N	0	0	—	5	0	0	0	0	5¹	12	3	3	5	25.3	13.50	29	.462	.517	0	—	0	-6	-6	0	0.0
1978	Cin-N	1	0	1.000	3	0	0	0	0	5	7	0	3	2	19.8	1.80	197	.368	.478	0	—	0	1	1	0	0.2
Total	2	1	0	1.000	8	0	0	0	0	10¹	19	0	6	7	22.6	7.84	48	.422	.500	0	—	0	-5	-5	0	0.2

● **NICK DUMOVICH**　Dumovich, Nicholas　b: 1/2/02, Sacramento, Cal.　d: 12/12/78, Laguna Hills, Cal.　BL/TL, 6', 170 lbs.　Deb: 4/20/23

YEAR	TM/L	W	L	PCT	G	GS	CG	SH	SV	IP	H	HR	BB	SO	RAT	ERA	ERA+	OAV	OOB	BH	AVG	PB	PR	/A	PD	TPI
1923	Chi-N	3	5	.375	28	8	1	0	1	94	118	4	45	23	15.0	4.60	87	.319	.397	7	.241	1	-6	-6	1	-0.2

● **MATT DUNBAR**　Dunbar, Matthew Marshall　b: 10/15/68, Tallahassee, Fla.　BL/TL, 6', 170 lbs.　Deb: 4/25/95

YEAR	TM/L	W	L	PCT	G	GS	CG	SH	SV	IP	H	HR	BB	SO	RAT	ERA	ERA+	OAV	OOB	BH	AVG	PB	PR	/A	PD	TPI
1995	Fla-N	0	1	.000	8	0	0	0	0	7	12	0	11	5	30.9	11.57	36	.387	.558	0	—	0	-6	-6	1	-0.6

● **ED DUNDON**　Dundon, Edward Joseph "Dummy"　b: 7/10/1859, Columbus, Ohio　d: 8/18/1893, Columbus, Ohio　TR,　Deb: 6/2/1883　♦

YEAR	TM/L	W	L	PCT	G	GS	CG	SH	SV	IP	H	HR	BB	SO	RAT	ERA	ERA+	OAV	OOB	BH	AVG	PB	PR	/A	PD	TPI
1883	Col-a	3	16	.158	20	19	16	0	0	166²	213	7	38	31	13.6	4.48	69	.292	.327	15	.161	-3	-22	-26	0	-2.5
1884	Col-a	6	4	.600	11	9	7	0	0	81	85	9	15	37	11.1	3.78	80	.249	.281	12	.140	-1	-5	-7	1	-0.6
Total	2	9	20	.310	31	28	23	0	0	247²	298	16	53	68	13.0	4.25	72	.278	.312	27	.151	-4	-27	-33	1	-3.1

● **JIM DUNEGAN**　Dunegan, James William　b: 8/6/47, Burlington, Iowa　BR/TR, 6'1", 205 lbs.　Deb: 5/28/70

YEAR	TM/L	W	L	PCT	G	GS	CG	SH	SV	IP	H	HR	BB	SO	RAT	ERA	ERA+	OAV	OOB	BH	AVG	PB	PR	/A	PD	TPI
1970	Chi-N	0	2	.000	7	0	0	0	0	13¹	13	2	12	3	16.9	4.73	95	.277	.424	1	.250	0	-1	-0	0	0.0

● **WILEY DUNHAM**　Dunham, Henry Huston　b: 1/30/1877, Piketon, Ohio　d: 1/16/34, Cleveland, Ohio　6'1", 180 lbs.　Deb: 5/24/02

YEAR	TM/L	W	L	PCT	G	GS	CG	SH	SV	IP	H	HR	BB	SO	RAT	ERA	ERA+	OAV	OOB	BH	AVG	PB	PR	/A	PD	TPI
1902	StL-N	2	3	.400	7	5	3	0	1	38	47	1	13	15	14.9	5.68	48	.303	.368	1	.083	-1	-12	-12	-0	-1.6

● **DAVEY DUNKLE**　Dunkle, Edward Perks　b: 8/30/1872, Philipsburg, Pa.　d: 11/19/41, Lock Haven, Pa.　BB/TR, 6'2", 220 lbs.　Deb: 8/28/1897

YEAR	TM/L	W	L	PCT	G	GS	CG	SH	SV	IP	H	HR	BB	SO	RAT	ERA	ERA+	OAV	OOB	BH	AVG	PB	PR	/A	PD	TPI
1897	Phi-N	5	2	.714	7	7	7	0	0	62	72	0	23	9	13.9	3.48	121	.288	.350	4	.174	-1	6	5	-1	0.3
1898	Phi-N	1	4	.200	12	7	4	0	0	68¹	83	1	38	21	17.1	6.98	49	.297	.399	6	.214	-0	-26	-27	-1	-1.7
1899	Was-N	0	2	.000	4	2	2	0	0	26	46	3	14	9	21.1	10.04	39	.383	.452	3	.273	-0	-18	-18	-0	-1.1
1903	Chi-A	4	4	.500	12	7	6	0	1	82	96	1	31	26	14.3	4.06	69	.291	.357	10	.303	2	-10	-11	-2	-1.0
	Was-A	5	9	.357	14	13	10	0	0	108¹	111	4	33	51	12.3	4.24	74	.264	.324	4	.098	-4	-15	-13	-2	-2.0
	Yr	9	13	.409	26	20	16	0	1	190¹	207	5	64	77	13.0	4.16	72	.275	.335	14	.189	-4	-25	-25	-4	-3.0
1904	Was-A	2	9	.182	12	11	7	0	0	74¹	95	1	23	23	14.7	4.96	54	.311	.366	4	.143	-2	-20	-19	-0	-2.7
Total	5	17	30	.362	61	47	36	0	1	421	503	10	162	139	14.7	5.02	65	.295	.364	31	.189	-4	-83	-83	-7	-8.1

● **FRED DUNLAP**　Dunlap, Frederick C. "Sure Shot"　b: 5/21/1859, Philadelphia, Pa.　d: 12/1/02, Philadelphia, Pa.　BR/TR, 5'8", 165 lbs.　Deb: 5/1/1880　M♦

YEAR	TM/L	W	L	PCT	G	GS	CG	SH	SV	IP	H	HR	BB	SO	RAT	ERA	ERA+	OAV	OOB	BH	AVG	PB	PR	/A	PD	TPI
1884	StL-U	0	0	—	1	0	0	0	1	0²	2	0	0	1	27.0	13.50	18	.500	.500	185	.412	1	-1	-1	0	-0.2
1887	*Det-N	0	0	—	1	0	0	0	1	2	4	0	0	1	18.0	4.50	90	.500	.500	72	.265	-0	-0	-0	-0	-0.0
Total	2	0	0	—	2	0	0	0	2	2²	6	0	0	2	20.3	6.75	54	.500	.500	1159	.292	1	-1	-1	0	-0.2

● **JACK DUNLEAVY**　Dunleavy, John Francis　b: 9/14/1879, Harrison, N.J.　d: 4/11/44, S.Norwalk, Conn.　TL, 5'6", 167 lbs.　Deb: 5/30/03　♦

YEAR	TM/L	W	L	PCT	G	GS	CG	SH	SV	IP	H	HR	BB	SO	RAT	ERA	ERA+	OAV	OOB	BH	AVG	PB	PR	/A	PD	TPI
1903	StL-N	6	8	.429	14	13	9	0	0	102	101	2	57	51	14.6	4.06	80	.264	.351	48	.249	2	-9	-9	1	-0.8
1904	StL-N	1	4	.200	7	5	5	0	0	55	63	4	23	28	14.2	4.42	61	.275	.344	40	.233	2	-10	-11	1	-0.7
Total	2	7	12	.368	21	18	14	0	0	157	164	6	80	79	14.5	4.18	73	.268	.361	193	.241	4	-19	-20	1	-1.5

● **JIM DUNN**　Dunn, James William "Bill"　b: 2/25/31, Valdosta, Ga.　BR/TR, 6'0.5", 185 lbs.　Deb: 8/26/52

YEAR	TM/L	W	L	PCT	G	GS	CG	SH	SV	IP	H	HR	BB	SO	RAT	ERA	ERA+	OAV	OOB	BH	AVG	PB	PR	/A	PD	TPI
1952	Pit-N	0	0	—	3	0	0	0	0	5¹	4	0	3	2	11.8	3.38	118	.190	.292	0	.000	-0	0	0	0	0.0

● **JACK DUNN**　Dunn, John Joseph　b: 10/6/1872, Meadville, Pa.　d: 10/22/28, Towson, Md.　BR/TR, 5'9", Deb: 5/6/1897　♦

YEAR	TM/L	W	L	PCT	G	GS	CG	SH	SV	IP	H	HR	BB	SO	RAT	ERA	ERA+	OAV	OOB	BH	AVG	PB	PR	/A	PD	TPI
1897	Bro-N	14	9	.609	35	21	21	0	0	216²	251	6	66	26	13.5	4.57	90	.288	.344	29	.221	-2	-6	-11	1	-1.0
1898	Bro-N	16	21	.432	41	37	31	0	0	322²	352	10	82	66	13.0	3.60	100	.275	.327	41	.246	0	1	0	1	-0.1
1899	Bro-N	23	13	.639	41	34	29	2	2	299¹	323	8	86	48	12.8	3.70	106	.275	.334	30	.246	0	5	7	3	1.0
1900	Bro-N	3	4	.429	10	7	5	0	0	63	88	1	28	6	17.1	5.57	69	.330	.401	6	.231	-0	-13	-12	1	-1.0
	Phi-N	5	5	.500	10	9	9	1	0	80	87	2	29	12	13.6	4.84	75	.276	.347	10	.303	-1	-10	-11	-1	-1.0
	Yr	8	9	.471	20	16	14	1	0	143	175	3	57	18	14.9	5.16	72	.299	.366	16	.271	1	-23	-23	1	-2.0
1901	Phi-N	0	1	.000	2	2	0	0	0	4²	11	0	7	1	38.6	21.21	16	.458	.606	1	.000	-9	-9	-0	1	-1.2
	Bal-A	3	3	.500	9	6	6	0	0	59²	74	2	21	5	14.5	3.62	107	.301	.358	90	.249	0	0	2	1	0.2
1902	NY-N	0	3	.000	3	2	2	0	0	26²	28	0	12	6	13.5	3.71	76	.269	.345	72	.211	3	-3	-3	1	-0.2
1904	NY-N	0	0	—	1	0	0	0	0	2	3	1	0	1	13.5	4.50	61	.167	.286	56	.309	1	-1	-0	0	-0.0
Total	7	64	59	.520	142	118	103	3	3	1076²	1217	30	334	171	13.4	4.11	92	.283	.342	397	.245	1	-36	-38	5	-3.3

● **MIKE DUNNE**　Dunne, Michael Dennis　b: 10/27/62, South Bend, Ind.　BR/TR, 6'4", 190 lbs.　Deb: 6/5/87

YEAR	TM/L	W	L	PCT	G	GS	CG	SH	SV	IP	H	HR	BB	SO	RAT	ERA	ERA+	OAV	OOB	BH	AVG	PB	PR	/A	PD	TPI
1987	Pit-N	13	6	.684	23	23	5	1	0	163¹	143	10	68	72	11.7	3.03	136	.240	.319	5	.094	-1	19	20	2	2.3
1988	Pit-N	7	11	.389	30	28	1	0	0	170	163	15	88	70	13.6	3.92	87	.255	.349	5	.109	-1	-9	-10	0	-1.0
1989	Pit-N	1	1	.500	3	3	0	0	0	14¹	21	1	9	4	19.5	7.53	45	.328	.419	1	.250	0	-6	-7	0	-0.7
	Sea-A	2	9	.182	15	15	1	0	0	85¹	104	7	37	38	15.1	5.27	76	.307	.378	0	—	0	-13	-12	0	-1.3
1990	SD-N	3	3	.500	10	6	0	0	0	28²	28	4	17	15	14.1	5.65	68	.241	.338	0	.000	-1	-6	-6	1	-0.6
1992	Chi-A	2	0	1.000	4	1	0	0	0	12²	12	0	6	6	13.5	4.26	91	.255	.352	0	—	0	-1	-1	0	-0.1
Total	5	25	30	.455	85	76	7	1	0	474¹	471	37	225	205	13.4	4.08	93	.261	.347	11	.101	-1	-16	-15	3	-1.4

● **ANDY DUNNING**　Dunning, Andrew Jackson　b: 8/12/1871, New York, N.Y.　d: 6/21/52, New York, N.Y.　BR/TR, 6', 175 lbs.　Deb: 5/23/1889

YEAR	TM/L	W	L	PCT	G	GS	CG	SH	SV	IP	H	HR	BB	SO	RAT	ERA	ERA+	OAV	OOB	BH	AVG	PB	PR	/A	PD	TPI
1889	Pit-N	0	2	.000	2	2	2	0	0	18	20	1	16	4	18.0	7.00	54	.274	.404	0	.000	-1	-6	-7	0	-0.6
1891	NY-N	0	1	.000	1	1	0	0	0	2	3	1	3	1	27.0	4.50	71	.333	.500	0	.000	-0	-0	-0	-0	-0.1
Total	2	0	3	.000	3	3	2	0	0	20	23	2	19	5	18.9	6.75	55	.287	.416	0	.000	-1	-6	-7	0	-0.7

● **STEVE DUNNING**　Dunning, Steven John　b: 5/15/49, Denver, Colo.　BR/TR, 6'2", 205 lbs.　Deb: 6/14/70

YEAR	TM/L	W	L	PCT	G	GS	CG	SH	SV	IP	H	HR	BB	SO	RAT	ERA	ERA+	OAV	OOB	BH	AVG	PB	PR	/A	PD	TPI
1970	Cle-A	4	9	.308	19	17	0	0	0	94¹	93	16	54	77	14.4	4.96	80	.261	.364	5	.161	-1	-13	-11	1	-1.2
1971	Cle-A	8	14	.364	31	29	3	1	1	184	173	25	109	132	14.0	4.50	85	.254	.361	10	.182	1	-21	-14	2	-1.2
1972	Cle-A	6	4	.600	16	16	1	0	0	105	98	16	43	52	12.1	3.26	99	.248	.322	9	.273	5	-2	-0	-1	0.5

YEAR	TM/L	W	L	PCT	G	GS	CG	SH	SV	IP	H	HR	BB	SO	RAT	ERA	ERA+	OAV	OOB	BH	AVG	PB	PR	/A	PD	TPI
1973	Cle-A	0	2	.000	4	3	0	0	0	18	17	2	13	10	15.0	6.50	60	.250	.370	0	—	0	-5	-5	-0	-0.5
	Tex-A	2	6	.250	23	12	2	0	0	94¹	101	11	52	38	14.7	5.34	70	.275	.367	0	—	0	-16	-17	-0	-1.3
	Yr	2	8	.200	27	15	2	0	0	112¹	118	13	65	48	14.7	5.53	68	.271	.367	0	—	0	-21	-22	-0	-1.8
1974	Tex-A	0	0	—	1	0	0	0	0	2¹	3	2	3	1	23.1	19.29	18	.333	.500	0	—	0	-4	-4	0	0.1
1976	Cal-A	0	0	—	4	0	0	0	0	6	9	2	6	4	22.5	7.50	44	.310	.429	0	—	0	-3	-3	0	0.2
	Mon-N	2	6	.250	32	7	1	0	0	91¹	93	6	33	72	12.6	4.14	90	.274	.342	2	.133	-0	-6	-4	-0	-0.3
1977	Oak-A	1	0	1.000	6	0	0	0	0	18¹	17	2	10	4	13.3	3.93	102	.254	.351	0	—	0	0	0	0	0.1
Total	7	23	41	.359	136	84	7	1	1	613²	604	82	323	390	13.8	4.56	82	.261	.355	26	.194	6	-71	-58	3	-3.6

● **FRANK DUPEE**   Dupee, Frank Oliver b: 4/29/1877, Monkton, Vt. d: 8/14/56, Portland, Me. TL , 6'1", 200 lbs. Deb: 8/24/01

| 1901 | Chi-A | 0 | 1 | .000 | 1 | 1 | 0 | 0 | 0 | 3 | 3 | 0 | 3 | 0 | — | ∞ | — | — | 1.000 | 0 | — | 0 | -3 | -3 | 0 | -0.2 |

● **MIKE DUPREE**   Dupree, Michael Dennis b: 5/29/53, Kansas City, Kan. BR/TR, 6'1", 185 lbs. Deb: 4/13/76

| 1976 | SD-N | 0 | 0 | — | 12 | 0 | 0 | 0 | 0 | 15² | 18 | 4 | 7 | 14 | 14.4 | 9.19 | 36 | .286 | .357 | 1 | 1.000 | 1 | -10 | -10 | 0 | 0.1 |

● **KID DURBIN**   Durbin, Blaine Alphonsus b: 9/10/1886, Lamar, Mo. d: 9/11/43, Kirkwood, Mo. BL/TL, 5'8", 155 lbs. Deb: 4/24/07 ♦

| 1907 | Chi-N | 0 | 1 | .000 | 5 | 1 | 1 | 0 | 1 | 16² | 14 | 0 | 10 | 5 | 13.5 | 5.40 | 46 | .233 | .352 | 6 | .333 | 1 | -5 | -5 | 0 | -0.3 |

● **RYNE DUREN**   Duren, Rinold George b: 2/22/29, Cazenovia, Wis. BR/TR, 6'1", 195 lbs. Deb: 9/25/54

1954	Bal-A	0	0	—	1	0	0	0	0	2	3	0	1	2	18.0	9.00	40	.333	.400	0	—	0	-1	-1	0	0.0
1957	KC-A	0	3	.000	14	6	0	0	1	42²	37	4	30	37	14.6	5.27	75	.236	.365	1	.071	0	-7	-6	0	-0.5
1958	*NY-A☆	6	4	.600	44	1	0	0	**20**	75²	40	4	43	87	10.7	2.02	175	.157	.296	1	.077	0	15	13	0	2.5
1959	NY-A★	3	6	.333	41	0	0	0	14	76²	49	6	43	96	11.2	1.88	194	.181	.301	0	.000	-1	17	15	-0	2.2
1960	*NY-A	3	4	.429	42	1	0	0	9	49	27	3	49	67	15.2	4.96	72	.160	.369	0	.000	0	-6	-7	-1	-1.3
1961	NY-A	0	1	.000	4	0	0	0	0	5	2	2	4	7	10.8	5.40	69	.125	.300	0	—	0	-1	-1	-0	-0.2
	LA-A☆	6	12	.333	40	14	1	1	2	99	87	13	75	108	15.0	5.18	87	.233	.366	1	.040	-2	-13	-7	-1	-1.5
	Yr	6	13	.316	44	14	1	1	2	104	89	15	79	115	14.8	5.19	86	.229	.363	1	.040	-2	-14	-8	-2	-1.7
1962	LA-A	2	9	.182	42	3	0	0	8	71¹	53	1	57	74	14.6	4.42	87	.206	.363	1	.067	-1	-4	-4	-0	-0.9
1963	Phi-N	6	2	.750	33	7	1	0	2	87¹	65	6	52	84	12.6	3.30	98	.210	.332	3	.143	-1	-0	-1	-1	-0.1
1964	Phi-N	0	0	—	2	0	0	0	0	3	5	0	1	5	21.0	6.00	58	.357	.438	0	—	0	-1	-1	-0	0.1
	Cin-N	0	2	.000	26	0	0	0	1	43²	41	6	15	39	12.2	2.89	125	.248	.322	0	.000	-0	3	4	-1	0.1
	Yr	0	2	.000	28	0	0	0	1	46²	46	6	16	44	12.5	3.09	117	.256	.327	0	.000	-0	2	3	-1	0.0
1965	Phi-N	0	0	—	6	0	0	0	0	11	10	0	4	6	12.3	3.27	106	.270	.357	0	.000	0	0	0	0	0.0
	Was-A	1	1	.500	16	0	0	0	1	23	24	0	18	18	17.6	6.65	52	.286	.429	0	—	0	-8	-8	-0	-0.7
Total	10	27	44	.380	311	32	2	1	57	589¹	443	60	392	630	13.4	3.83	98	.209	.344	5	.061	-5	-6	-4	-0.4

● **DON DURHAM**   Durham, Donald Gary b: 3/21/49, Yosemite, Ky. BR/TR, 6', 170 lbs. Deb: 7/16/72

1972	StL-N	2	7	.222	10	8	1	0	0	47²	42	1	22	35	12.1	4.34	78	.240	.325	7	.500	0	-5	-5	-1	-0.5
1973	Tex-A	0	4	.000	15	4	0	0	1	40¹	49	7	23	23	16.3	7.59	49	.304	.395	0	—	0	-17	-17	-0	-1.6
Total	2	2	11	.154	25	12	1	0	1	88	91	8	45	58	14.0	5.83	61	.271	.359	7	.500	4	-22	-22	-1	-2.1

● **ED DURHAM**   Durham, Edward Fant "Bull" b: 8/17/08, Chester, S.C. d: 4/27/76, Chester, S.C. BL/TR, 5'11", 170 lbs. Deb: 4/19/29

1929	Bos-A	1	0	1.000	14	1	0	0	0	22¹	34	2	14	6	19.3	9.27	46	.374	.457	0	.000	-0	-12	-12	-0	-0.5
1930	Bos-A	4	15	.211	33	12	6	1	1	140	144	9	43	28	12.2	4.69	98	.270	.326	4	.098	-4	-1	-1	-0	-0.6
1931	Bos-A	8	10	.444	38	15	7	2	0	165¹	175	9	50	53	12.5	4.25	101	.266	.322	3	.056	-6	2	1	-2	-0.6
1932	Bos-A	6	13	.316	34	22	4	0	0	175¹	187	13	49	62	12.3	3.80	118	.274	.327	7	.123	-3	13	14	1	1.0
1933	Chi-A	10	6	.625	24	21	6	0	0	138²	137	12	46	65	12.2	4.48	95	.256	.320	10	.217	0	-3	-4	-1	-0.5
Total	5	29	44	.397	143	71	23	3	1	641²	677	45	202	204	12.5	4.45	99	.271	.329	24	.119	-14	-0	-3	-3	-1.2

● **JOHN DURHAM**   Durham, John Garfield b: 10/7/1881, Douglass, Kan. d: 5/7/49, Coffeyville, Kan. BR/TR, 6', 175 lbs. Deb: 9/15/02

| 1902 | Chi-A | 1 | 1 | .500 | 3 | 3 | 3 | 0 | 0 | 20 | 21 | 0 | 16 | 3 | 16.6 | 5.85 | 58 | .269 | .394 | 1 | .067 | -1 | -5 | -5 | 0 | -0.5 |

● **BULL DURHAM**   Durham, Louis Raphael (b: Louis Raphael Staub) b: 6/27/1877, New Oxford, Pa. d: 6/28/60, Bentley, Kan. BR/TR, 5'10", Deb: 9/15/04

1904	Bro-N	2	0	1.000	2	2	1	0	0	11	10	0	5	1	12.3	3.27	84	.250	.333	1	.250	0	-1	-1	-0	-0.1
1907	Was-A	0	0	—	2	0	0	0	0	5	10	0	4	2	27.0	12.60	19	.417	.517	0	—	0	-6	-6	-0	-0.2
1908	NY-N	0	0	—	1	0	0	0	0	2	2	0	1	2	13.5	9.00	27	.250	.333	0	—	0	-1	-1	-0	-0.1
1909	NY-N	0	0	—	4	0	0	0	1	11	15	0	2	2	13.9	3.27	78	.326	.354	0	.000	0	-1	-1	-0	-0.1
Total	4	2	0	1.000	9	2	1	0	1	29	37	0	12	6	15.5	5.28	49	.314	.382	1	.143	0	-9	-9	-1	-0.4

● **RICH DURNING**   Durning, Richard Knott b: 10/10/1892, Louisville, Ky. d: 9/23/48, Castle Point, N.Y BL/TL, 6'2", 178 lbs. Deb: 4/16/17

1917	Bro-N	0	0	—	1	0	0	0	0	1	0	0	0	0	—	.000	—	.000	.000	0	—	0	0	0	-0	0.0
1918	Bro-N	0	0	—	1	0	0	0	0	2	4	0	4	0	31.5	13.50	21	.375	.583	0	—	0	-2	-2	-0	0.0
Total	2		0	0	—	2	0	0	0	0	3	4	0	4	0	21.0	9.00	31	.273	.467	0	—	0	-2	-2	-0	0.0

● **JESSE DURYEA**   Duryea, James Newton "Cyclone Jim" b: 9/7/1859, Osage, Iowa d: 8/19/42, Algona, Iowa BR/TR, 5'10", 175 lbs. Deb: 4/20/1889

1889	Cin-a	32	19	.627	53	48	38	2	1	401	372	9	127	183	11.6	2.56	153	.238	.302	44	.272	6	57	60	0	6.7
1890	Cin-N	16	12	.571	33	32	29	2	1	274	270	11	60	108	11.1	2.92	122	.250	.294	15	.152	1	20	19	0	1.7
1891	Cin-N	1	9	.100	10	10	8	0	0	77	101	4	25	13	15.5	5.38	63	.305	.366	1	.031	-5	-17	-17	-0	-2.0
	StL-a	1	1	.500	3	3	2	0	0	24	19	0	10	13	10.9	3.38	125	.211	.290	4	.364	1	2	2	-0	0.2
1892	Cin-N	2	5	.286	9	7	4	0	0	68	55	3	26	21	11.1	3.57	91	.212	.292	3	.111	-1	-2	-2	1	-0.2
	Was-N	3	11	.214	18	15	13	1	2	127	102	6	45	48	11.1	2.41	135	.211	.291	6	.120	-2	12	12	4	1.3
	Yr	5	16	.238	27	22	18	1	2	195	157	9	71	69	10.9	2.82	116	.211	.287	9	.117	-3	10	10	4	1.1
1893	Was-N	4	10	.286	17	15	9	0	0	117	182	8	56	20	19.3	7.54	61	.345	.420	13	.277	2	-37	-38	-0	-2.9
Total	5	59	67	.468	143	130	104	5	3	1088	1101	41	349	416	12.5	3.45	109	.254	.318	86	.201	1	34	36	5	4.8

● **ERV DUSAK**   Dusak, Ervin Frank "Four Sack" b: 7/29/20, Chicago, Ill. d: 11/6/94, Glendale Heights, Ill. BR/TR, 6'2", 185 lbs. Deb: 9/18/41 ♦

1948	StL-N	0	0	—	1	0	0	0	0	1	0	0	0	0	0.00	—	.000	.250	65	.244	-0	0	0	0	0.0
1950	StL-N	0	2	.000	14	2	0	0	1	36¹	27	2	27	16	13.6	3.72	116	.211	.353	1	.083	-0	2	2	0	0.1
1951	StL-N	0	0	—	5	0	0	0	0	10	14	0	7	4	18.9	7.20	55	.333	.429	1	.500	1	-4	-4	0	0.2
	Pit-N	0	1	.000	3	1	0	0	0	6²	9	2	9	2	27.0	12.15	35	.357	.526	12	.308	1	-6	-5	-0	-0.7
	Yr	0	1	.000	8	1	0	0	0	16²	24	2	16	10	22.1	9.18	44	.343	.471	13	.317	2	-10	-9	-0	-0.4
Total	3	0	3	.000	23	2	0	0	1	54	51	4	44	26	16.2	5.33	79	.254	.393	251	.243	2	-8	-7	0	-0.4

● **CARL DUSER**   Duser, Carl Robert b: 7/22/32, Hazleton, Pa. BL/TL, 6'1", 175 lbs. Deb: 9/15/56

1956	KC-A	1	1	.500	2	2	0	0	0	6	14	0	5	2	24.0	9.00	48	.452	.485	0	.000	—	-3	-3	0	-0.8
1958	KC-A	0	0	—	1	0	0	0	0	2	5	0	0	3	27.0	4.50	87	.500	.545	0	—	0	-0	-0	-0	0.0
Total	2	1	1	.500	3	2	0	0	0	8	19	0	5	5	24.8	7.88	54	.463	.500	0	.000	—	-3	-3	-0	-0.8

● **BOB DUSTAL**   Dustal, Robert Andrew b: 9/28/35, Sayreville, N.J. BR/TR, 6', 172 lbs. Deb: 4/9/63

| 1963 | Det-A | 0 | 1 | .000 | 7 | 0 | 0 | 0 | 0 | 6 | 10 | 1 | 6 | 4 | 22.5 | 9.00 | 42 | .357 | .455 | 0 | — | 0 | -4 | -4 | 1 | -0.5 |

● **BILL DUZEN**   Duzen, William George b: 2/21/1870, Buffalo, N.Y. d: 3/11/44, Buffalo, N.Y. BR/TR, 5'11", 165 lbs. Deb: 9/21/1890

| 1890 | Buf-P | 0 | 2 | .000 | 2 | 2 | 2 | 0 | 0 | 13 | 20 | 2 | 14 | 5 | 23.5 | 13.85 | 30 | .339 | .466 | 1 | .250 | — | -14 | -14 | -0 | -1.1 |

● **FRANK DWYER**   Dwyer, John Francis b: 3/25/1868, Lee, Mass. d: 2/4/43, Pittsfield, Mass. BR/TR, 5'8", 145 lbs. Deb: 9/20/1888 MC

1888	Chi-N	4	1	.800	5	5	5	1	0	42	32	1	9	17	8.8	1.07	283	.198	.240	4	.190	-0	8	9	0	1.0
1889	Chi-N	16	13	.552	32	30	27	0	0	276	307	14	72	63	12.6	3.59	116	.273	.321	27	.200	-2	13	17	-2	1.1
1890	Chi-P	3	6	.333	12	6	6	0	0	69¹	98	4	25	17	16.0	6.23	70	.319	.370	14	.264	-0	-15	-15	-1	-1.3
1891	Cin-a	13	19	.406	35	31	29	1	0	289	322	11	124	101	14.5	4.52	91	.279	.351	40	.307	-3	-13	-13	-1	-0.8
	Mil-a	6	4	.600	10	10	10	0	0	86	92	1	21	27	12.2	2.20	200	.264	.314	9	.225	4	15	21	0	1.9
	Yr	19	23	.452	45	41	39	1	0	375	424	12	145	128	13.8	3.98	105	.274	.337	49	.271	1	-11	8	1	1.1
1892	StL-N	2	8	.200	10	10	8	0	0	64	90	1	24	16	16.3	5.63	57	.319	.377	2	.080	-1	-17	-17	-1	-2.1
	Cin-N	20	10	.667	34	28	25	3	0	268¹	262	6	49	47	10.6	2.31	141	.246	.282	21	.159	-4	29	28	-1	2.2

YEAR	TM/L	W	L	PCT	G	GS	CG	SH	SV	IP	H	HR	BB	SO	RAT	ERA	ERA+	OAV	OOB	BH	AVG	PB	PR	/A	PD	TPI
	Yr	22	18	.550	44	38	31	3	1	332¹	352	7	73	63	11.6	2.95	110	.261	.301	23	.146	-6	12	11	-1	0.1
1893	Cin-N	18	15	.545	37	30	28	1	**2**	287¹	332	17	93	53	13.5	4.13	116	.281	.336	24	.200	-3	17	21	3	1.8
1894	Cin-N	19	21	.475	45	39	34	1	1	348	471	27	106	49	15.3	5.07	110	.320	.371	46	.267	1	10	19	1	1.7
1895	Cin-N	18	15	.545	37	31	23	2	0	280¹	355	10	74	46	14.2	4.24	117	.304	.353	30	.265	2	17	23	-0	2.1
1896	Cin-N	24	11	.686	36	34	30	3	1	288²	321	8	60	57	12.2	3.15	146	.279	.321	29	.264	4	39	47	-2	4.7
1897	Cin-N	18	13	.581	37	31	22	0	0	247¹	315	5	56	41	13.9	3.78	120	.307	.350	25	.266	0	15	21	-3	1.8
1898	Cin-N	16	10	.615	31	28	24	0	0	240	257	3	42	29	11.8	3.04	126	.272	.314	12	.141	-4	15	21	-2	1.4
1899	Cin-N	0	5	.000	5	5	2	0	0	32²	48	1	9	2	16.0	5.51	71	.340	.384	4	.364	1	-6	-6	0	-0.6
Total	12	177	151	.540	366	318	271	12	6	2819	3312	109	764	565	13.3	3.84	115	.286	.336	287	.229	-7	114	178	-4	14.9

● **BEN DYER**   Dyer, Benjamin Franklin   b: 2/13/1893, Chicago, Ill.   d: 8/7/59, Kenosha, Wis.   BR/TR, 5'10", 170 lbs.   Deb: 5/28/14 ♦

YEAR	TM/L	W	L	PCT	G	GS	CG	SH	SV	IP	H	HR	BB	SO	RAT	ERA	ERA+	OAV	OOB	BH	AVG	PB	PR	/A	PD	TPI
1918	Det-A	0	0	—	2	0	0	0	0	1²	0	0	0	0	0.0	0.00	—	.000	.000	5	.278	0	1	0	0	0.0

● **EDDIE DYER**   Dyer, Edwin Hawley   b: 10/11/1900, Morgan City, La.   d: 4/20/64, Houston, Tex.   BL/TL, 5'11.5", 168 lbs.   Deb: 7/8/22 M♦

YEAR	TM/L	W	L	PCT	G	GS	CG	SH	SV	IP	H	HR	BB	SO	RAT	ERA	ERA+	OAV	OOB	BH	AVG	PB	PR	/A	PD	TPI
1922	StL-N	0	0	—	2	0	0	0	0	3²	7	0	0	3	17.2	2.45	157	.412	.412	1	.333	1	1	1	0	0.1
1923	StL-N	2	1	.667	4	3	2	1	0	22	30	0	5	7	14.7	4.09	95	.333	.375	12	.267	-0	-0	-0	-0	0.0
1924	StL-N	8	11	.421	29	15	7	1	0	136²	174	6	51	23	15.1	4.61	82	.331	.395	18	.237	1	-11	-13	1	-1.2
1925	StL-N	4	3	.571	27	5	1	0	3	82¹	93	4	24	25	13.6	4.15	104	.278	.340	3	.097	-2	1	2	0	-0.1
1926	StL-N	1	0	1.000	6	0	0	0	0	9¹	7	0	14	4	21.2	11.57	34	.219	.468	1	.500	0	-8	-8	0	-0.7
1927	StL-N	0	0	—	1	0	0	0	0	2	5	1	2	1	31.5	18.00	22	.500	.583	0	—	-0	-3	-3	-0	0.0
Total	6	15	15	.500	69	23	10	2	3	256	316	11	96	63	14.9	4.75	84	.313	.380	35	.223	1	-21	-22	1	-1.9

● **MIKE DYER**   Dyer, Michael Lawrence   b: 9/8/66, Upland, Cal.   BR/TR, 6'3", 195 lbs.   Deb: 6/29/89

YEAR	TM/L	W	L	PCT	G	GS	CG	SH	SV	IP	H	HR	BB	SO	RAT	ERA	ERA+	OAV	OOB	BH	AVG	PB	PR	/A	PD	TPI
1989	Min-A	4	7	.364	16	12	1	0	0	71	74	2	37	37	14.3	4.82	86	.273	.365	0	—	-0	-7	-5	-1	-1.0
1994	Pit-N	1	1	.500	14	0	0	0	4	15¹	15	1	12	13	17.6	5.87	74	.268	.423	0	.000	-0	-3	-3	-0	-0.5
1995	Pit-N	4	5	.444	55	0	0	0	0	74²	81	9	30	53	14.0	4.34	99	.281	.359	4	.571	1	-1	-0	1	0.2
1996	Mon-N	5	5	.500	70	1	0	0	2	75²	79	7	34	51	14.0	4.40	98	.277	.364	0	.000	-1	-2	-1	1	-0.1
Total	4	14	18	.438	155	13	1	0	6	236²	249	19	113	154	14.3	4.60	93	.277	.367	4	.267	-0	-13	-9	-0	-1.4

● **JIMMY DYGERT**   Dygert, James Henry "Sunny Jim"   b: 7/5/1884, Utica, N.Y.   d: 2/8/36, New Orleans, La.   BR/TR, 5'10", 185 lbs.   Deb: 9/8/05

YEAR	TM/L	W	L	PCT	G	GS	CG	SH	SV	IP	H	HR	BB	SO	RAT	ERA	ERA+	OAV	OOB	BH	AVG	PB	PR	/A	PD	TPI
1905	Phi-A	1	4	.200	6	3	2	1	0	35¹	41	2	11	24	13.8	4.33	61	.291	.351	4	.267	0	-7	-7	2	-0.7
1906	Phi-A	11	13	.458	35	25	15	4	0	213²	175	1	91	106	11.6	2.70	101	.226	.316	13	.176	3	-0	1	1	0.1
1907	Phi-A	21	8	.724	42	28	18	5	0	261²	200	2	85	151	10.4	2.34	111	**.214**	.292	12	.128	-4	6	8	-1	0.3
1908	Phi-A	11	15	.423	41	28	15	5	1	238²	184	2	97	164	11.0	2.87	99	.220	.309	6	.080	-6	-13	-8	3	-1.3
1909	Phi-A	9	5	.643	32	13	6	1	0	137¹	117	1	70	117	11.7	2.42	99	.242	.327	9	.205	0	1	-0	-1	-0.1
1910	Phi-A	4	4	.500	19	8	6	1	0	99¹	81	0	49	59	12.1	2.54	94	.231	.331	3	.083	-2	-2	-2	-0	-0.6
Total	6	57	49	.538	175	105	62	16	2	986	798	9	383	583	11.3	2.65	97	.227	.312	47	.139	-11	-13	-8	1	-2.3

● **JIMMY DYKES**   Dykes, James Joseph   b: 11/10/1896, Philadelphia, Pa.   d: 6/15/76, Philadelphia, Pa.   BR/TR, 5'9", 185 lbs.   Deb: 5/6/18   MC♦

YEAR	TM/L	W	L	PCT	G	GS	CG	SH	SV	IP	H	HR	BB	SO	RAT	ERA	ERA+	OAV	OOB	BH	AVG	PB	PR	/A	PD	TPI
1927	Phi-A	0	0	—	2	0	0	0	1	2	2	0	1	0	13.5	4.50	95	.333	.429	135	.324	1	-0	-0	-0	0.0

● **ARNOLD EARLEY**   Earley, Arnold Carl   b: 6/4/33, Lincoln Park, Mich.   BL/TL, 6'1", 200 lbs.   Deb: 9/27/60

YEAR	TM/L	W	L	PCT	G	GS	CG	SH	SV	IP	H	HR	BB	SO	RAT	ERA	ERA+	OAV	OOB	BH	AVG	PB	PR	/A	PD	TPI
1960	Bos-A	0	1	.000	2	0	0	0	0	4	5	1	4	5	29.3	15.75	26	.429	.520	0	.000	0	-5	-5	-0	-0.9
1961	Bos-A	2	4	.333	33	1	0	0	7	49²	42	3	34	44	13.8	3.99	105	.226	.345	0	.000	-1	0	1	0	0.1
1962	Bos-A	4	5	.444	38	3	0	0	5	68¹	76	4	46	59	16.2	5.80	71	.281	.388	2	.200	0	-14	-13	1	-1.6
1963	Bos-A	3	7	.300	53	4	0	0	1	115²	124	13	43	97	13.6	4.75	80	.270	.343	5	.278	1	-14	-12	0	-0.9
1964	Bos-A	1	1	.500	25	3	1	0	1	50¹	51	3	18	45	12.5	2.68	144	.266	.332	1	.111	-0	5	7	1	0.4
1965	Bos-A	0	1	.000	57	0	0	0	0	74¹	79	5	29	47	13.4	3.63	103	.271	.344	0	.000	-0	-1	-1	0	-0.1
1966	Chi-N	2	1	.667	13	0	0	0	0	17²	14	1	9	12	11.7	3.57	103	.226	.324	0	.000	0	0	-0	-1	-0.1
1967	Hou-N	0	0	—	2	0	0	0	0	1¹	9	1	1	1	40.5	27.00	12	.625	.667	0	—	-0	-4	-4	-0	0.0
Total	8	12	20	.375	223	10	1	0	14	381¹	400	35	184	310	14.1	4.48	87	.269	.354	8	.157	0	-33	-25	1	-3.0

● **TOM EARLEY**   Earley, Thomas Francis Aloysius   b: 2/19/17, Roxbury, Mass.   d: 4/5/88, Nantucket, Mass.   BR/TR, 6', 180 lbs.   Deb: 9/27/38

YEAR	TM/L	W	L	PCT	G	GS	CG	SH	SV	IP	H	HR	BB	SO	RAT	ERA	ERA+	OAV	OOB	BH	AVG	PB	PR	/A	PD	TPI
1938	Bos-N	1	0	1.000	2	1	1	0	0	11	8	2	1	4	8.2	3.27	105	.186	.222	0	.000	-1	1	0	-0	-0.1
1939	Bos-N	1	4	.200	14	2	0	0	1	40	49	1	19	9	15.7	4.72	78	.304	.385	3	.300	1	-4	-5	1	-0.4
1940	Bos-N	2	0	1.000	4	1	1	1	0	16¹	16	1	3	5	11.6	3.86	96	.267	.323	2	.400	1	-0	-0	0	0.1
1941	Bos-N	6	8	.429	33	13	6	1	3	138²	120	9	46	54	11.0	2.53	141	.233	.300	11	.234	1	17	16	-1	1.7
1942	Bos-N	6	11	.353	27	18	6	0	1	112²	120	10	55	28	14.1	4.71	71	.276	.359	4	.118	-1	-18	-17	0	-2.4
1945	Bos-N	2	1	.667	11	2	1	0	0	41	36	4	19	4	12.1	4.61	83	.235	.320	3	.214	1	-4	-4	-0	-0.2
Total	6	18	24	.429	91	37	15	2	5	359²	349	27	143	104	12.5	3.78	94	.256	.330	23	.202	2	-7	-9	-0	-1.3

● **BILL EARLEY**   Earley, William Albert   b: 1/30/56, Cincinnati, Ohio   BR/TL, 6'4", 200 lbs.   Deb: 9/22/86

YEAR	TM/L	W	L	PCT	G	GS	CG	SH	SV	IP	H	HR	BB	SO	RAT	ERA	ERA+	OAV	OOB	BH	AVG	PB	PR	/A	PD	TPI
1986	StL-N	0	0	—	3	0	0	0	0	3	0	0	2	2	6.0	0.00	—	.000	.182	0	—	0	1	1	-0	0.0

● **GEORGE EARNSHAW**   Earnshaw, George Livingston "Moose"   b: 2/15/1900, New York, N.Y.   d: 12/1/76, Little Rock, Ark.   BR/TR, 6'4", 210 lbs.   Deb: 6/3/28   C

YEAR	TM/L	W	L	PCT	G	GS	CG	SH	SV	IP	H	HR	BB	SO	RAT	ERA	ERA+	OAV	OOB	BH	AVG	PB	PR	/A	PD	TPI
1928	Phi-A	7	7	.500	26	22	7	3	1	158¹	143	7	100	111	13.9	3.81	105	.240	.351	14	.246	1	4	4	-1	0.2
1929	*Phi-A	24	8	.750	44	33	13	3	1	254²	233	8	125	149	12.8	3.29	129	**.241**	.331	15	.172	-2	27	27	-3	2.4
1930	*Phi-A	22	13	.629	49	39	20	**3**	2	296	299	20	139	193	13.3	4.44	105	.266	.347	26	.228	1	7	8	-1	0.7
1931	*Phi-A	21	7	.750	43	30	23	3	6	281²	255	16	75	152	10.6	3.67	122	.236	.288	30	.263	6	22	26	0	2.9
1932	Phi-A	19	13	.594	36	33	21	0	0	245¹	262	28	94	109	13.2	4.77	95	.266	.336	26	.286	8	-8	-7	1	-0.3
1933	Phi-A	5	10	.333	21	18	4	0	0	117²	153	8	58	37	16.2	5.97	72	.311	.385	8	.182	-0	-22	-22	1	-2.2
1934	Chi-A	14	11	.560	33	30	16	2	0	227	242	28	104	97	13.9	4.52	105	.270	.349	16	.203	-0	-1	-5	-1	-0.9
1935	Chi-A	1	2	.333	3	3	0	0	0	18	26	2	11	8	18.5	9.00	51	.342	.425	2	.286	0	-9	-9	-0	-1.0
	Bro-N	8	12	.400	25	22	6	2	0	166	175	14	53	72	12.4	4.12	96	.270	.325	13	.217	1	-2	-3	0	-0.2
1936	Bro-N	4	9	.308	19	13	4	1	1	93	113	7	30	40	14.1	5.32	78	.297	.384	8	.242	-0	-13	-12	0	-1.5
	StL-N	2	1	.667	20	6	1	0	1	57²	80	4	20	28	16.1	6.40	62	.333	.392	4	.222	0	-15	-16	1	-0.7
	Yr	6	10	.375	39	19	5	1	2	150²	193	11	50	68	14.7	5.73	71	.310	.364	12	.235	0	-29	-28	1	-2.2
Total	9	127	93	.577	319	249	115	18	12	1915¹	1881	142	809	1002	13.2	4.38	100	.265	.339	162	.230	9	-10	-2	-2	0.8

● **LOGAN EASLEY**   Easley, Kenneth Logan   b: 11/4/61, Salt Lake City, Utah   BR/TR, 6'1", 185 lbs.   Deb: 4/9/87

YEAR	TM/L	W	L	PCT	G	GS	CG	SH	SV	IP	H	HR	BB	SO	RAT	ERA	ERA+	OAV	OOB	BH	AVG	PB	PR	/A	PD	TPI
1987	Pit-N	1	1	.500	17	0	0	0	0	26¹	23	5	17	21	14.0	5.47	75	.242	.363	0	.000	-0	-4	-4	1	-0.2
1989	Pit-N	1	0	1.000	10	0	0	0	1	12¹	8	1	7	6	11.7	4.38	77	.190	.320	0	.000	-0	-1	-1	-0	-0.2
Total	2	2	1	.667	27	0	0	0	1	38²	31	6	24	27	13.3	5.12	75	.226	.350	0	.000	-0	-5	-5	1	-0.4

● **MAL EASON**   Eason, Malcolm Wayne "Kid"   b: 3/13/1879, Brookville, Pa.   d: 4/16/70, Douglas, Ariz.   BR/TR, 6', 175 lbs.   Deb: 10/1/00   U

YEAR	TM/L	W	L	PCT	G	GS	CG	SH	SV	IP	H	HR	BB	SO	RAT	ERA	ERA+	OAV	OOB	BH	AVG	PB	PR	/A	PD	TPI
1900	Chi-N	1	0	1.000	1	1	1	0	0	9	7	0	3	2	12.0	1.00	361	.257	.316	0	.000	-1	3	3	-0	0.2
1901	Chi-N	8	17	.320	27	25	23	1	0	220²	246	9	60	68	13.0	3.59	90	.280	.335	12	.138	-5	-7	-9	-2	-1.5
1902	Chi-N	1	1	.500	2	2	2	0	0	18	21	0	4	2	11.5	1.00	270	.292	.311	1	.200	0	4	4	0	0.5
	Bos-N	9	12	.429	27	27	20	2	0	213¹	249	4	61	53	13.6	2.91	97	.291	.347	6	.083	-6	-3	-2	-1	-0.9
	Yr	10	13	.435	29	29	22	2	0	231¹	270	4	65	55	13.4	2.76	102	.291	.341	7	.091	-6	0	1	-1	-0.4
1903	Det-A	2	5	.286	7	6	6	1	0	56¹	60	1	19	21	13.1	3.36	87	.271	.337	2	.100	-2	-2	-3	-1	-0.3
1905	Bro-N	5	21	.192	34	26	18	3	0	207	230	5	72	64	13.3	4.30	67	.294	.354	14	.173	-1	-30	-32	1	-3.5
1906	Bro-N	10	17	.370	34	26	18	3	1	227	212	1	74	64	11.7	3.25	78	.256	.323	8	.091	-4	-16	-18	1	-2.5
Total	6	36	73	.330	125	114	90	10	1	951¹	1027	20	291	274	12.9	3.42	84	.279	.339	43	.121	-19	-51	-58	2	-8.0

● **CARL EAST**   East, Carlton William   b: 8/27/1894, Marietta, Ga.   d: 1/15/53, Whitesburg, Ga.   BL/TL, 6'2", 178 lbs.   Deb: 8/24/15 ♦

YEAR	TM/L	W	L	PCT	G	GS	CG	SH	SV	IP	H	HR	BB	SO	RAT	ERA	ERA+	OAV	OOB	BH	AVG	PB	PR	/A	PD	TPI
1915	StL-A	0	0	—	1	1	0	0	0	3¹	6	0	2	1	21.6	16.20	18	.400	.471	0	.000	-0	-5	-5	-0	0.0

● **HUGH EAST**   East, Gordon Hugh   b: 7/7/19, Birmingham, Ala.   d: 11/2/81, Charleston, S.C.   BR/TR, 6'2", 185 lbs.   Deb: 9/13/41

YEAR	TM/L	W	L	PCT	G	GS	CG	SH	SV	IP	H	HR	BB	SO	RAT	ERA	ERA+	OAV	OOB	BH	AVG	PB	PR	/A	PD	TPI
1941	NY-N	1	1	.500	2	2	0	0	0	15²	19	0	9	4	16.1	3.45	107	.297	.384	2	.222	0	0	-0	-0	0.1
1942	NY-N	0	2	.000	4	1	0	0	0	7¹	15	1	7	2	27.0	9.82	34	.429	.524	1	.500	0	-5	-5	-0	-1.0

YEAR	TM/L	W	L	PCT	G	GS	CG	SH	SV	IP	H	HR	BB	SO	RAT	ERA	ERA+	OAV	OOB	BH	AVG	PB	PR	/A	PD	TPI
1943	NY-N	1	3	.250	13	5	1	0	0	40¹	51	4	25	21	17.0	5.36	64	.298	.388	1	.077	-1	-9	-9	-1	-0.9
Total	3	2	6	.250	19	8	1	0	0	63¹	85	5	41	27	17.9	5.40	65	.315	.405	4	.167	1	-14	-13	-1	-1.8

● **JAMIE EASTERLY**   Easterly, James Morris b: 2/17/53, Houston, Tex.   BL/TL, 5'9", 180 lbs.   Deb: 4/6/74

YEAR	TM/L	W	L	PCT	G	GS	CG	SH	SV	IP	H	HR	BB	SO	RAT	ERA	ERA+	OAV	OOB	BH	AVG	PB	PR	/A	PD	TPI
1974	Atl-N	0	0	—	3	0	0	0	0	2²	6	0	4	0	33.8	16.88	22	.400	.526	0	—	0	-4	-4	0	0.0
1975	Atl-N	2	9	.182	21	13	0	0	0	68²	73	5	42	34	15.3	4.98	76	.275	.379	1	.056	-2	-10	-9	-1	-1.5
1976	Atl-N	1	1	.500	4	4	0	0	0	22	23	0	13	11	14.7	4.91	77	.280	.379	1	.111	0	-3	-3	0	-0.3
1977	Atl-N	2	4	.333	22	5	0	0	1	58²	72	5	30	37	16.1	6.14	72	.303	.387	4	.267	1	-15	-11	-1	-1.1
1978	Atl-N	3	6	.333	37	6	0	0	1	78	91	9	45	42	15.9	5.65	72	.299	.393	4	.211	0	-18	-14	0	-1.5
1979	Atl-N	0	0	—	4	0	0	0	0	2²	7	0	3	3	33.8	13.50	30	.467	.556	0	—	0	-3	-3	0	0.0
1981	*Mil-A	3	3	.500	44	0	0	0	4	62	46	0	34	31	11.6	3.19	107	.219	.328	0	—	0	3	2	0	0.2
1982	Mil-A	0	2	.000	28	0	0	0	2	30²	39	6	15	16	15.8	4.70	81	.312	.386	0	—	0	-2	-3	1	0.0
1983	Mil-A	0	1	.000	12	0	0	0	1	11²	14	0	10	6	20.1	3.86	97	.350	.500	0	.000	0	0	-0	-0	0.0
	Cle-A	4	2	.667	41	0	0	0	3	57	69	4	22	39	14.7	3.63	117	.309	.377	0	—	0	3	4	0	0.4
	Yr	4	3	.571	53	0	0	0	4	68²	83	4	32	45	15.3	3.67	113	.312	.390	0	.000	0	3	4	0	0.2
1984	Cle-A	3	1	.750	26	1	0	0	2	69¹	74	3	23	42	12.7	3.38	121	.273	.332	0	—	0	5	5	0	0.2
1985	Cle-A	4	1	.800	50	7	0	0	0	98²	96	9	53	58	14.0	3.92	105	.264	.363	0	—	0	2	2	0	0.2
1986	Cle-A	0	2	.000	13	0	0	0	0	17²	27	3	12	9	19.9	7.64	54	.365	.453	0	—	0	-7	-7	-0	-0.6
1987	Cle-A	1	1	.500	16	0	0	0	0	31²	26	4	13	22	11.4	4.55	99	.218	.301	0	—	0	-0	-0	-0	-0.0
Total	13	23	33	.411	321	36	0	0	14	611¹	663	48	319	350	14.7	4.62	87	.283	.373	10	.161	-1	-49	-40	-0	-4.0

● **JACK EASTON**   Easton, John S. b: 2/28/1867, Bridgeport, Ohio   d: 11/28/03, Steubenville, Ohio   Deb: 9/23/1889

YEAR	TM/L	W	L	PCT	G	GS	CG	SH	SV	IP	H	HR	BB	SO	RAT	ERA	ERA+	OAV	OOB	BH	AVG	PB	PR	/A	PD	TPI
1889	Col-a	1	0	1.000	4	1	1	0	0	18	13	0	21	7	18.5	3.50	104	.197	.411	0	—	-1	1	0	-0	-0.1
1890	Col-a	15	14	.517	37	29	23	0	1	255²	213	4	125	147	12.6	3.52	102	.220	.321	19	.178	0	10	2	1	0.3
1891	Col-a	5	10	.333	18	16	13	0	0	135¹	145	4	59	52	14.6	4.52	77	.265	.352	15	.238	2	-12	-16	1	-1.1
	StL-a	3	2	.600	7	6	4	0	0	47²	48	3	23	22	14.2	5.10	83	.253	.346	5	.179	1	-7	-5	-2	-0.6
	Col-a	0	2	.000	2	2	2	0	0	15	15	2	4	13	12.6	3.60	96	.250	.318	0	.000	-1	-0	-0	-1	-0.1
	Yr	8	14	.364	27	24	19	0	0	198	208	8	86	87	13.5	4.59	79	.255	.327	20	.196	-0	-19	-21	-1	-1.8
1892	StL-N	2	0	1.000	5	2	2	0	0	31	38	2	26	4	19.5	6.39	50	.290	.419	3	.176	-0	-11	-11	-0	-0.6
1894	Pit-N	0	1	.000	2	3	1	0	0	19²	26	0	4	1	15.1	4.12	127	.313	.367	0	.000	-1	3	2	-1	-0.1
Total	5	26	29	.473	76	57	46	0	2	522¹	498	14	262	246	14.0	4.12	89	.243	.343	42	.176	-2	-16	-27	-0	-2.3

● **RAWLY EASTWICK**   Eastwick, Rawlins Jackson b: 10/24/50, Camden, N.J.   BR/TR, 6'3", 180 lbs.   Deb: 9/12/74

YEAR	TM/L	W	L	PCT	G	GS	CG	SH	SV	IP	H	HR	BB	SO	RAT	ERA	ERA+	OAV	OOB	BH	AVG	PB	PR	/A	PD	TPI
1974	Cin-N	0	0	—	8	0	0	0	2	17²	12	1	5	14	8.7	2.04	171	.188	.246	0	.000	-0	3	3	-0	0.0
1975	*Cin-N	5	3	.625	58	0	0	0	**22**	90	77	6	25	61	10.4	2.60	138	.229	.287	0	.000	-0	10	10	-1	1.1
1976	*Cin-N	11	5	.688	71	0	0	0	**26**	107²	93	3	27	70	10.2	2.09	168	.232	.284	0	.000	-2	17	17	-2	3.1
1977	Cin-N	2	2	.500	23	0	0	0	4	43¹	40	7	8	17	10.0	2.91	135	.244	.279	1	.167	-0	5	5	-1	0.5
	StL-N	3	7	.300	41	1	0	0	4	53²	74	6	21	30	15.9	4.70	82	.332	.389	2	.400	1	-5	-5	-1	-0.9
	Yr	5	9	.357	64	1	0	0	11	97	114	9	29	47	13.3	3.90	100	.295	.344	3	.273	1	-0	-0	-2	-0.4
1978	NY-A	2	1	.667	8	0	0	0	2	24²	22	2	4	13	9.9	3.28	110	.232	.270	0	—	0	1	1	-0	0.2
	*Phi-N	2	1	.667	22	0	0	0	1	40¹	31	5	18	14	10.9	4.02	89	.209	.295	0	.000	-0	0	0	-2	-0.1
1979	Phi-N	3	6	.333	51	0	0	0	6	82²	90	8	45	47	12.6	4.90	78	.284	.338	0	.000	-1	-11	-10	-2	-1.4
1980	KC-A	0	1	.000	14	0	0	0	0	22	37	2	8	5	19.2	5.32	76	.363	.420	0	—	0	-3	-3	1	-0.1
1981	Chi-N	0	1	.000	30	0	0	0	6	43¹	43	2	15	24	12.0	2.28	162	.264	.326	0	.000	-0	6	7	0	0.5
Total	8	28	27	.509	326	1	0	0	68	525¹	519	38	156	295	11.7	3.31	112	.258	.314	4	.071	-3	22	22	-7	2.5

● **CRAIG EATON**   Eaton, Craig b: 9/7/54, Glendale, Ohio   BR/TR, 5'11", 175 lbs.   Deb: 9/5/79

YEAR	TM/L	W	L	PCT	G	GS	CG	SH	SV	IP	H	HR	BB	SO	RAT	ERA	ERA+	OAV	OOB	BH	AVG	PB	PR	/A	PD	TPI
1979	KC-A	0	0	—	5	0	0	0	0	10	8	0	3	4	9.9	2.70	158	.222	.282	0	—	0	2	2	0	0.0

● **ZEB EATON**   Eaton, Zebulon Vance "Red" b: 2/2/20, Cooleemee, N.C.   d: 12/17/89, W.Palm Beach, Fla.   BR/TR, 5'10", 185 lbs.   Deb: 4/18/44

YEAR	TM/L	W	L	PCT	G	GS	CG	SH	SV	IP	H	HR	BB	SO	RAT	ERA	ERA+	OAV	OOB	BH	AVG	PB	PR	/A	PD	TPI
1944	Det-A	0	0	—	6	0	0	0	0	15²	19	2	8	4	15.5	5.74	62	.322	.403	1	.100	-1	-4	-4	-0	-0.1
1945	*Det-A	4	2	.667	17	3	0	0	0	53¹	48	0	40	15	15.4	4.05	87	.247	.384	8	.250	2	-4	-3	0	-0.1
Total	2	4	2	.667	23	3	0	0	0	69	67	2	48	19	15.4	4.43	80	.265	.388	9	.214	0	-8	-7	-0	-0.1

● **GARY EAVE**   Eave, Gary Louis b: 7/22/63, Monroe, La.   BR/TR, 6'4", 200 lbs.   Deb: 4/12/88

YEAR	TM/L	W	L	PCT	G	GS	CG	SH	SV	IP	H	HR	BB	SO	RAT	ERA	ERA+	OAV	OOB	BH	AVG	PB	PR	/A	PD	TPI
1988	Atl-N	0	0	—	5	0	0	0	0	5	7	0	3	0	18.0	9.00	41	.333	.417	0	—	0	-3	-3	-0	0.0
1989	Atl-N	2	0	1.000	3	3	0	0	0	20²	15	0	12	9	12.2	1.31	279	.200	.318	0	.000	-1	5	5	-0	0.4
1990	Sea-A	0	3	.000	8	5	0	0	0	30	27	5	20	16	14.7	4.20	94	.241	.366	0	—	-1	-1	-0	-0	-0.1
Total	3	2	3	.400	16	8	0	0	0	55²	49	5	35	25	14.1	3.56	107	.236	.354	0	.000	-1	1	2	-1	0.3

● **VALLIE EAVES**   Eaves, Vallie Ennis "Chief" b: 9/6/11, Allen, Okla.   d: 4/19/60, Norman, Okla.   BR/TR, 6'2.5", 180 lbs.   Deb: 9/12/35

YEAR	TM/L	W	L	PCT	G	GS	CG	SH	SV	IP	H	HR	BB	SO	RAT	ERA	ERA+	OAV	OOB	BH	AVG	PB	PR	/A	PD	TPI
1935	Phi-A	1	2	.333	3	3	1	0	0	14	12	1	6	6	17.4	5.14	88	.240	.415	0	.000	-1	-1	-1	-0	-0.2
1939	Chi-A	0	1	.000	2	1	1	0	0	11²	11	1	8	5	15.4	4.63	102	.250	.377	2	.333	0	-0	-0	-0	0.0
1940	Chi-A	0	2	.000	5	3	0	0	0	18²	22	2	24	11	22.7	6.75	66	.301	.480	0	.000	-1	-5	-5	-1	-0.3
1941	Chi-N	3	3	.500	12	7	4	0	0	58²	56	4	21	24	12.3	3.53	99	.253	.327	2	.100	-1	1	-0	-1	-0.3
1942	Chi-N	0	0	—	2	0	0	0	0	3	4	0	2	0	21.0	9.00	36	.308	.438	0	—	-0	-2	-2	-0	0.0
Total	5	4	8	.333	24	14	6	0	0	106	105	7	70	46	15.4	4.58	86	.262	.379	4	.114	-3	-7	-8	-3	-1.0

● **EDDIE EAYRS**   Eayrs, Edwin b: 11/10/1890, Blackstone, Mass.   d: 11/30/69, Warwick, R.I.   BL/TL, 5'7", 160 lbs.   Deb: 6/30/13 ◆

YEAR	TM/L	W	L	PCT	G	GS	CG	SH	SV	IP	H	HR	BB	SO	RAT	ERA	ERA+	OAV	OOB	BH	AVG	PB	PR	/A	PD	TPI
1913	Pit-N	0	0	—	2	0	0	0	0	8	6	0	5	5	15.8	2.25	134	.267	.389	1	.167	-0	1	1	-0	0.0
1920	Bos-N	1	2	.333	7	3	0	0	0	26¹	36	1	12	7	17.1	5.47	56	.346	.424	80	.328	2	-7	-7	1	-0.5
1921	Bos-N	0	0	—	2	0	0	0	0	4²	11	0	9	1	34.7	17.36	51	.391	.563	1	.067	-2	-7	-7	-0	-0.2
Total	3	1	2	.333	11	3	0	0	0	39	53	1	27	13	18.9	6.23	50	.338	.441	83	.306	0	-13	-14	-0	-0.7

● **HARRY ECCLES**   Eccles, Harry Josiah "Bugs" b: 7/9/1893, Kennedy, N.Y.   d: 6/2/55, Jamestown, N.Y.   BL/TL, 6'2", 170 lbs.   Deb: 9/13/15

YEAR	TM/L	W	L	PCT	G	GS	CG	SH	SV	IP	H	HR	BB	SO	RAT	ERA	ERA+	OAV	OOB	BH	AVG	PB	PR	/A	PD	TPI
1915	Phi-A	0	1	.000	5	1	0	0	1	21	18	2	6	13	10.3	4.71	62	.240	.296	1	.167	-0	-4	-4	-1	-0.3

● **DENNIS ECKERSLEY**   Eckersley, Dennis Lee b: 10/3/54, Oakland, Cal.   BR/TR, 6'2", 190 lbs.   Deb: 4/12/75

YEAR	TM/L	W	L	PCT	G	GS	CG	SH	SV	IP	H	HR	BB	SO	RAT	ERA	ERA+	OAV	OOB	BH	AVG	PB	PR	/A	PD	TPI
1975	Cle-A	13	7	.650	34	24	6	2	2	186²	147	16	90	152	11.8	2.60	145	.215	.312	0	—	0	24	24	-3	2.3
1976	Cle-A	13	12	.520	36	30	9	3	1	199¹	155	13	78	200	10.7	3.43	102	.214	.295	0	—	0	2	1	-1	0.1
1977	Cle-A★	14	13	.519	33	33	12	3	0	247¹	214	31	54	191	10.0	3.53	112	.231	**.278**	0	—	0	15	11	-3	0.9
1978	Bos-A	20	8	.714	35	35	16	3	0	268¹	258	30	71	162	11.3	2.99	138	.251	.304	0	—	0	23	34	-2	2.8
1979	Bos-A	17	10	.630	33	33	17	2	0	246²	234	29	59	150	10.9	2.99	**148**	.251	.298	0	—	0	34	**39**	1	4.0
1980	Bos-A	12	14	.462	30	30	8	0	0	197²	188	25	44	121	10.7	4.28	99	.248	.291	0	—	0	-5	-1	-1	-0.1
1981	Bos-A	9	8	.529	23	23	8	2	0	154	160	9	35	79	11.6	4.27	91	.267	.310	0	—	0	-10	-7	-1	-0.8
1982	Bos-A★	13	13	.500	33	33	11	3	0	224¹	228	31	43	127	11.0	3.73	115	.261	.297	0	—	0	9	14	-1	1.1
1983	Bos-A	9	13	.409	28	28	2	0	0	176¹	223	27	39	77	13.7	5.61	77	.303	.343	0	—	0	-30	-25	-2	-2.7
1984	Bos-A	4	4	.500	9	9	2	0	0	64²	71	10	13	33	11.8	5.01	83	.284	.322	0	—	0	-7	-6	1	-0.9
	*Chi-N	10	8	.556	24	24	2	0	0	160¹	152	11	36	81	10.8	3.03	129	.250	.296	6	.109	-3	10	16	1	1.5
1985	Chi-N	11	7	.611	25	25	6	2	0	169¹	145	15	19	117	8.9	3.08	129	.229	.255	7	.125	-0	10	17	0	1.8
1986	Chi-N	6	11	.353	33	32	1	0	0	201	226	21	43	137	12.2	4.57	88	.285	.324	11	.159	-0	-19	-12	-0	-0.8
1987	Oak-A	6	8	.429	54	2	0	0	16	115²	99	11	17	113	9.3	3.03	136	.232	.262	0	—	0	18	14	-1	2.0
1988	*Oak-A★	4	2	.667	60	0	0	0	**45**	72²	52	5	11	70	7.9	2.35	161	.198	.233	0	—	0	13	12	-1	2.1
1989	Oak-A	4	0	1.000	51	0	0	0	33	57²	32	5	3	55	5.6	1.56	236	.162	.178	0	—	0	15	14	-0	2.4
1990	Oak-A	4	2	.667	63	0	0	0	48	73¹	41	2	4	73	5.5	0.61	605	.160	.172	0	—	0	27	25	-2	4.7
1991	Oak-A★	5	4	.556	67	0	0	0	43	76	60	11	9	87	8.3	2.96	129	.208	.235	0	—	0	10	7	0	1.6
1992	Oak-A★	7	1	.875	69	0	0	0	**51**	80	62	5	11	93	8.3	1.91	196	.211	.242	0	—	0	18	16	1	3.5
1993	Oak-A	2	4	.333	64	0	0	0	36	67	67	7	13	80	11.4	4.16	98	.261	.301	0	—	0	1	1	-0	0.1
1994	Oak-A	5	4	.556	45	0	0	0	19	44¹	49	5	13	47	12.8	4.26	104	.275	.328	0	—	0	-0	-0	-0	0.0
1995	Oak-A	4	6	.400	52	0	0	0	29	50¹	53	5	11	40	11.6	4.83	93	.269	.311	0	—	0	-2	-2	-1	-0.3
1996	*StL-N	0	6	.000	63	0	0	0	30	60	65	8	6	49	11.3	3.30	128	.274	.304	0	.000	-0	6	6	-1	1.0
Total	22	192	165	.538	964	361	100	20	353	3193	2981	332	722	2334	10.6	3.48	116	.245	.291	24	.133	-1	163	201	-15	26.5

YEAR TM/L	W	L	PCT	G	GS	CG	SH	SV	IP	H	HR	BB	SO	RAT	ERA	ERA+	OAV	OOB	BH	AVG	PB	PR	/A	PD	TPI
● **AL ECKERT**				Eckert, Albert George "Obbie" b: 5/17/06, Milwaukee, Wis. d: 4/20/74, Milwaukee, Wis. BL/TL, 5'10", 174 lbs. Deb: 4/21/30																				
1930 Cin-N	0	1	.000	2	1	0	0	0	5	7	0	4	1	19.8	7.20	67	.304	.407	0	.000	-0	-1	-1	0	-0.2
1931 Cin-N	0	1	.000	14	1	0	0	0	18²	26	3	9	5	16.9	9.16	41	.325	.393	1	.333	0	-11	-11	-0	-0.5
1935 StL-N	0	0	—	2	0	0	0	0	3	7	0	1	1	24.0	12.00	34	.467	.500	0	—	-0	-3	-3	-0	-0.0
Total 3	0	2	.000	18	2	0	0	0	26²	40	3	14	7	18.2	9.11	44	.339	.409	1	.250	0	-15	-15	0	-0.7
● **CHARLIE ECKERT**				Eckert, Charles William "Buzz" b: 8/8/1897, Philadelphia, Pa. d: 8/22/86, Trevose, Pa. BR/TR, 5'10.5", 165 lbs. Deb: 9/18/19																				
1919 Phi-A	0	1	.000	2	1	1	0	0	16	17	1	3	6	11.3	3.94	87	.270	.303	1	.167	-0	-1	-0	-0	-0.1
1920 Phi-A	0	0	—	2	0	0	0	0	5²	8	0	1	1	15.9	4.76	84	.421	.476	0	.000	-0	-1	-0	-0	-0.1
1922 Phi-A	0	2	.000	21	0	0	0	0	50	61	7	23	15	15.3	4.68	91	.319	.395	1	.091	-1	-4	-2	2	-0.1
Total 3	0	3	.000	25	1	1	0	0	71²	86	8	27	22	14.4	4.52	90	.315	.381	2	.111	-2	-5	-4	1	-0.3
● **CHRIS EDDY**				Eddy, Christopher Mark b: 11/27/69, Dallas, Tex. BL/TL, 6'3", 200 lbs. Deb: 4/26/95																				
1995 Oak-A	0	0	—	6	0	0	0	0	3²	7	0	2	2	27.0	7.36	61	.438	.550	0	—	-0	-1	-1	0	0.3
● **DON EDDY**				Eddy, Donald Eugene b: 10/25/46, Mason City, Iowa BR/TL, 5'11", 170 lbs. Deb: 9/7/70																				
1970 Chi-A	0	0	—	7	0	0	0	0	11²	10	0	6	9	12.3	2.31	168	.244	.340	0	—	0	2	2	0	0.0
1971 Chi-A	0	2	.000	22	0	0	0	0	22²	19	3	19	14	15.1	2.38	151	.232	.376	1	1.000	1	3	3	-1	0.3
Total 2	0	2	.000	29	0	0	0	0	34¹	29	3	25	23	14.2	2.36	157	.236	.365	1	1.000	1	5	5	-1	0.3
● **STEVE EDDY**				Eddy, Steven Allen b: 8/21/57, Sterling, Ill. BR/TR, 6'2", 185 lbs. Deb: 6/13/79																				
1979 Cal-A	1	1	.500	7	4	0	0	0	32¹	36	1	20	7	16.1	4.73	86	.290	.397	0	—	0	-2	-2	0	0.0
● **JOE EDELEN**				Edelen, Benny Joe b: 9/16/55, Durant, Okla. BR/TR, 6', 165 lbs. Deb: 4/18/81																				
1981 StL-N	1	0	1.000	13	0	0	0	0	17¹	29	2	3	10	17.1	9.35	38	.367	.398	1	.333	0	-11	-11	-0	-0.6
Cin-N	1	0	1.000	5	0	0	0	0	12²	5	1	0	5	3.6	0.71	500	.128	.128	0	.000	-0	4	4	-1	0.2
Yr	2	0	1.000	18	0	0	0	0	30	34	3	3	15	11.1	5.70	62	.283	.301	1	.200	0	-7	-7	-1	-0.4
1982 Cin-N	0	0	—	9	0	0	0	0	15¹	22	2	8	11	17.6	8.80	42	.344	.417	1	.500	0	-9	-9	-0	-0.1
Total 2	2	0	1.000	27	0	0	0	0	45¹	56	5	11	26	13.5	6.75	53	.308	.351	2	.286	0	-16	-16	-1	-0.4
● **ED EDELEN**				Edelen, Edward Joseph "Doc" b: 3/16/12, Bryantown, Md. d: 2/1/82, LaPlata, Md. BR/TR, 6', 191 lbs. Deb: 8/20/32																				
1932 Was-A	0	0	—	2	0	0	0	0	1	1	0	6	0	54.0	27.00	16	.000	.600	0	—	0	-3	-3	-0	0.0
● **JOHN EDELMAN**				Edelman, John Rogers b: 7/27/35, Philadelphia, Pa. BR/TR, 6'3", 185 lbs. Deb: 6/2/55																				
1955 Mil-N	0	0	—	5	0	0	0	0	5²	7	0	8	3	23.8	11.12	34	.304	.484	0	—	0	-4	-5	0	0.0
● **CHARLIE EDEN**				Eden, Charles M. b: 1/18/1855, Lexington, Ky. d: 9/17/20, Cincinnati, Ohio BL/TL, 168 lbs. Deb: 8/17/1877 ◆																				
1884 Pit-a	0	1	.000	2	1	1	0	0	12	12	1	3	3	12.0	6.00	56	.255	.314	33	.270	1	-4	-4	-1	-0.2
1885 Pit-a	1	2	.333	4	1	0	0	0	15²	22	0	3	5	14.4	5.17	62	.314	.342	103	.254	1	-3	-3	-1	-0.5
Total 2	1	3	.250	6	2	1	0	0	27²	34	1	6	8	13.3	5.53	59	.291	.331	244	.261	1	-7	-7	-1	-0.7
● **KEN EDENFIELD**				Edenfield, Kenneth Edward b: 3/18/67, Jesup, Ga. BR/TR, 6'1", 165 lbs. Deb: 5/11/95																				
1995 Cal-A	0	0	—	7	0	0	0	0	12²	15	1	5	6	14.2	4.26	110	.300	.364	0	—	1	1	1	-0	0.0
1996 Cal-A	0	0	—	2	0	0	0	0	4¹	10	2	2	4	27.0	10.38	47	.435	.500	0	—	0	-3	-3	-0	0.0
Total 2	0	0	—	9	0	0	0	0	17	25	3	7	10	17.5	5.82	81	.342	.407	0	—	0	-2	-2	-0	0.0
● **TOM EDENS**				Edens, Thomas Patrick b: 6/9/61, Ontario, Ore. BR/TR, 6'3", 185 lbs. Deb: 6/2/87																				
1987 NY-N	0	0	—	2	2	0	0	0	8	15	2	4	4	21.4	6.75	56	.417	.475	0	.000	-0	-2	-3	0	0.0
1990 Mil-A	4	5	.444	35	6	0	0	2	89	89	8	33	40	12.7	4.45	87	.262	.334	0	—	0	-5	-6	-1	-0.6
1991 Min-A	2	2	.500	8	6	0	0	0	33	34	2	10	19	12.0	4.09	104	.256	.308	0	—	0	1	0	0	0.1
1992 Min-A	6	3	.667	52	0	0	0	3	76¹	65	1	36	57	12.1	2.83	143	.236	.329	0	—	0	9	10	-1	1.1
1993 Hou-N	1	1	.500	38	0	0	0	0	49	47	4	19	21	12.1	3.12	124	.263	.333	0	.000	-0	5	4	0	0.2
1994 Hou-N	4	1	.800	39	0	0	0	1	50	55	3	17	38	13.3	4.50	88	.289	.354	0	.000	-0	-2	-3	1	-0.2
Phi-N	1	0	1.000	3	0	0	0	0	4	4	0	1	1	11.3	2.25	191	.267	.313	0	—	0	1	1	0	0.2
Yr	5	1	.833	42	0	0	0	1	54	59	3	18	39	12.8	4.33	92	.281	.338	0	.000	-0	-1	-2	1	-0.2
1995 Chi-N	1	0	1.000	5	0	0	0	0	3	6	0	3	2	27.0	6.00	68	.400	.500	0	—	0	-1	-1	0	-0.2
Total 7	19	12	.613	182	14	0	0	6	312¹	315	20	123	182	12.9	3.86	103	.266	.339	0	.000	-1	5	4	1	0.6
● **BUTCH EDGE**				Edge, Claude Lee b: 7/18/56, Houston, Tex. BR/TR, 6'3", 203 lbs. Deb: 8/13/79																				
1979 Tor-A	3	4	.429	9	9	1	0	0	51²	60	6	24	19	14.8	5.23	83	.283	.359	0	—	0	-6	-5	-0	-0.6
● **BILL EDGERTON**				Edgerton, William Albert b: 8/16/41, South Bend, Ind. BL/TL, 6'2", 185 lbs. Deb: 9/3/66																				
1966 KC-A	0	1	.000	6	1	0	0	0	8¹	7	0	7	3	18.4	3.24	105	.303	.425	0	—	0	0	0	0	0.0
1967 KC-A	1	0	1.000	7	0	0	0	0	8¹	11	1	3	6	16.2	2.16	147	.324	.395	0	—	0	1	1	0	0.1
1969 Sea-A	0	1	.000	4	0	0	0	0	4	10	1	0	2	24.8	13.50	27	.455	.478	0	—	0	-4	-4	0	-0.9
Total 3	1	2	.333	17	1	0	0	0	20²	31	2	10	11	18.2	4.79	70	.348	.426	0	—	0	-3	-3	1	-0.8
● **GEORGE EDMONDSON**				Edmondson, George Henderson "Big Ed" b: 5/18/1896, Waxahachie, Tex. d: 7/11/73, Waco, Tex. BR/TR, 6'1", 179 lbs. Deb: 8/15/22																				
1922 Cle-A	0	0	—	2	0	0	0	0	2	4	0	0	0	18.0	9.00	45	.444	.444	0	—	0	-1	-1	-0	0.0
1923 Cle-A	0	0	—	1	0	0	0	0	4	8	0	0	0	27.0	11.25	35	.444	.545	0	.000	-0	-3	-3	-0	0.0
1924 Cle-A	0	0	—	5	1	0	0	0	8	10	1	5	0	16.9	9.00	47	.294	.385	1	.333	-0	-4	-4	-0	0.0
Total 3	0	0	—	8	1	0	0	0	14	22	1	8	3	19.9	9.64	43	.361	.443	1	.250	-0	-9	-9	-0	0.0
● **PAUL EDMONDSON**				Edmondson, Paul Michael b: 2/12/43, Kansas City, Kan. d: 2/13/70, Santa Barbara, Cal. BR/TR, 6'5", 195 lbs. Deb: 6/20/69																				
1969 Chi-A	1	6	.143	14	13	1	0	0	87²	72	5	39	46	11.8	3.70	104	.227	.319	5	.172	-1	2	2	3	0.4
● **BOB EDMONDSON**				Edmondson, Robert E. b: 4/30/1879, Paris, Ky. d: 8/14/31, Lawrence, Kan. BR/TR, 5'11", 185 lbs. Deb: 9/15/06 ◆																				
1906 Was-A	0	1	.000	2	1	0	0	0	10	10	0	2	0	10.8	4.50	59	.263	.300	1	.333	0	-2	-2	0	-0.1
● **SAM EDMONSTON**				Edmonston, Samuel Sherwood "Big Sam" b: 8/30/1883, Washington, D.C. d: 4/12/79, Corpus Christi, Tex. BL/TL, 5'11.5", 185 lbs. Deb: 6/24/07																				
1907 Was-A	0	0	—	1	0	0	0	0	3	8	0	1	0	27.0	9.00	27	.500	.529	0	.000	0	-2	-2	0	0.0
● **EDWARDS**				Edwards Deb: 9/11/1875																				
1875 Atl-n	0	1	.000	1	1	0	0	0	2	4	0	0	0	18.0	4.50	46	.308	.308	1	.200		-1	-1		-0.2
● **FOSTER EDWARDS**				Edwards, Foster Hamilton "Eddie" b: 9/1/03, Holstein, Iowa d: 1/4/80, Orleans, Mass. BR/TR, 6'3", 175 lbs. Deb: 7/2/25																				
1925 Bos-N	0	0	—	1	0	0	0	0	2	5	0	0	1	31.5	9.00	45	.545	.583	0	—	0	-1	-1	-0	0.0
1926 Bos-N	2	0	1.000	3	3	1	0	0	25	20	0	13	4	11.9	0.72	492	.230	.330	0	.000	-2	9	8	-0	0.4
1927 Bos-N	2	8	.200	29	11	3	0	0	92	95	2	45	37	14.0	4.99	74	.274	.362	1	.045	-2	-11	-13	-1	-1.5
1928 Bos-N	2	1	.667	21	3	2	0	0	49¹	67	2	23	17	16.8	5.66	69	.327	.400	1	.091	-1	-9	-10	0	-0.6
1930 NY-A	0	0	—	2	0	0	0	0	1²	5	0	2	1	37.8	21.60	20	.500	.583	0	—	0	-3	-3	-0	0.0
Total 5	6	9	.400	56	17	6	0	0	170	193	4	84	60	14.9	4.76	79	.292	.377	2	.048	-5	-14	-19	-1	-1.7
● **JIM JOE EDWARDS**				Edwards, James Corbette "Little Joe" b: 12/14/1894, Banner, Miss. d: 1/19/65, Sarepta, Miss. BR/TL, 6'2", 185 lbs. Deb: 5/14/22																				
1922 Cle-A	3	8	.273	25	7	0	0	0	92²	113	1	40	44	15.3	4.47	90	.313	.389	2	.087	-2	-4	-5	-1	-0.8
1923 Cle-A	10	10	.500	38	21	8	1	1	179¹	200	5	75	68	14.1	3.71	107	.286	.359	7	.119	-5	5	5	-1	-0.1
1924 Cle-A	4	3	.571	10	7	5	0	0	57	64	3	34	15	15.5	2.84	150	.305	.402	3	.150	-1	9	9	0	0.9
1925 Cle-A	0	3	.000	13	3	1	0	0	36	60	0	23	12	21.0	8.25	54	.382	.464	1	.111	-1	-15	-15	-1	-1.0
Chi-A	1	2	.333	9	4	1	0	0	45¹	46	1	23	20	13.9	3.97	105	.263	.352	3	.176	-1	2	1	0	0.0
Yr	1	5	.167	22	7	2	0	0	81¹	106	1	46	32	16.9	5.86	73	.318	.403	4	.154	-2	-13	-14	2	-1.0
1926 Chi-A	6	9	.400	32	16	8	3	1	142	140	6	63	41	12.9	4.18	104	.264	.343	5	.109	-5	1	1		-0.9

YEAR	TM/L	W	L	PCT	G	GS	CG	SH	SV	IP	H	HR	BB	SO	RAT	ERA	ERA+	OAV	OOB	BH	AVG	PB	PR	/A	PD	TPI
1928	Cin-N	2	2	.500	18	1	0	0	2	32	43	1	20	11	17.7	7.59	52	.347	.438	3	.300	0	-13	-13	-1	-1.6
Total 6		26	37	.413	145	59	23	6	4	584¹	666	18	278	211	14.7	4.37	92	.295	.376	24	.130	-13	-19	-23	-1	-3.5

● **SHERMAN EDWARDS**   Edwards, Sherman Stanley b: 7/25/09, Mt.Ida, Ark. d: 3/8/92, ElDorado, Ark. BR/TR, 6', 165 lbs. Deb: 9/21/34

YEAR	TM/L	W	L	PCT	G	GS	CG	SH	SV	IP	H	HR	BB	SO	RAT	ERA	ERA+	OAV	OOB	BH	AVG	PB	PR	/A	PD	TPI
1934	Cin-N	0	0	—	1	0	0	0	0	3	4	0	1	1	15.0	3.00	136	.333	.385	0	.000	-0	0	0	0	0.0

● **WAYNE EDWARDS**   Edwards, Wayne Maurice b: 3/7/64, Burbank, Cal. BL/TL, 6'5", 185 lbs. Deb: 9/11/89

YEAR	TM/L	W	L	PCT	G	GS	CG	SH	SV	IP	H	HR	BB	SO	RAT	ERA	ERA+	OAV	OOB	BH	AVG	PB	PR	/A	PD	TPI
1989	Chi-A	0	0	—	7	0	0	0	0	7¹	7	1	3	9	12.3	3.68	103	.269	.345	0	—	0	0	0	0	0.1
1990	Chi-A	5	3	.625	42	5	0	0	2	95	81	6	41	63	11.8	3.22	119	.234	.321	0	—	0	7	6	0	0.6
1991	Chi-A	0	2	.000	13	0	0	0	0	23¹	22	2	17	12	15.0	3.86	103	.259	.382	0	—	0	1	0	-0	0.0
Total 3		5	5	.500	62	5	0	0	2	125²	110	9	61	84	12.5	3.37	114	.241	.334	0	—	0	8	7	0	0.7

● **HARRY EELLS**   Eells, Harry Archibald "Slippery" b: 2/14/1881, Ida Grove, Iowa d: 10/15/40, Los Angeles, Cal. BR/TR, 6'1", 195 lbs. Deb: 4/22/06

YEAR	TM/L	W	L	PCT	G	GS	CG	SH	SV	IP	H	HR	BB	SO	RAT	ERA	ERA+	OAV	OOB	BH	AVG	PB	PR	/A	PD	TPI
1906	Cle-A	4	5	.444	14	8	6	1	0	86¹	77	1	48	35	13.3	2.61	100	.242	.347	6	.188	1	1	0	1	0.1

● **WISH EGAN**   Egan, Aloysius Jerome b: 6/16/1881, Evart, Mich. d: 4/13/51, Detroit, Mich. BR/TR, 6'3", 185 lbs. Deb: 9/3/02

YEAR	TM/L	W	L	PCT	G	GS	CG	SH	SV	IP	H	HR	BB	SO	RAT	ERA	ERA+	OAV	OOB	BH	AVG	PB	PR	/A	PD	TPI
1902	Det-A	0	2	.000	3	3	2	0	0	22	23	0	6	11	11.9	2.86	127	.271	.319	2	.250	-0	2	2	1	0.2
1905	StL-N	6	15	.286	23	19	18	0	0	171¹	189	2	39	29	12.4	3.57	83	.285	.333	6	.102	-3	-11	-11	5	-1.1
1906	StL-N	2	9	.182	16	12	7	0	0	86¹	97	3	27	23	13.1	4.59	57	.278	.333	2	.069	-2	-19	-19	1	-2.3
Total 3		8	26	.235	42	34	27	0	0	279²	309	5	72	52	12.6	3.83	76	.282	.332	10	.104	-5	-28	-28	6	-3.2

● **JIM EGAN**   Egan, James K. "Troy Terrier" b: 1858, Derby, Conn. d: 9/26/1884, New Haven, Conn. TL, Deb: 5/15/1882 ◆

YEAR	TM/L	W	L	PCT	G	GS	CG	SH	SV	IP	H	HR	BB	SO	RAT	ERA	ERA+	OAV	OOB	BH	AVG	PB	PR	/A	PD	TPI
1882	Tro-N	4	6	.400	12	10	10	0	0	100	133	2	24	20	14.1	4.14	68	.315	.352	23	.200	-2	-14	-15	-2	-1.4

● **RIP EGAN**   Egan, John Joseph b: 7/9/1871, Philadelphia, Pa. d: 12/22/50, Cranston, R.I. TR, 5'11", 168 lbs. Deb: 4/30/1894 U

YEAR	TM/L	W	L	PCT	G	GS	CG	SH	SV	IP	H	HR	BB	SO	RAT	ERA	ERA+	OAV	OOB	BH	AVG	PB	PR	/A	PD	TPI
1894	Was-N	0	0	—	1	0	0	0	0	5	8	1	2	0	18.0	10.80	49	.364	.417	0	.000	-0	-3	-3	0	0.0

● **DICK EGAN**   Egan, Richard Wallis b: 3/24/37, Berkeley, Cal. BL/TL, 6'4", 193 lbs. Deb: 4/9/63 C

YEAR	TM/L	W	L	PCT	G	GS	CG	SH	SV	IP	H	HR	BB	SO	RAT	ERA	ERA+	OAV	OOB	BH	AVG	PB	PR	/A	PD	TPI
1963	Det-A	0	1	.000	20	0	0	0	0	21	25	4	3	16	12.0	5.14	73	.287	.311	0	—	0	-4	-3	-1	-0.1
1964	Det-A	0	0	—	23	0	0	0	2	34¹	33	4	17	21	13.4	4.46	82	.246	.336	0	.000	-0	-3	-3	1	0.0
1966	Cal-A	0	0	—	11	0	0	0	0	14¹	17	2	6	11	14.4	4.40	76	.309	.377	0	.000	-0	-2	-2	-0	0.0
1967	LA-N	1	1	.500	20	0	0	0	0	31²	34	3	15	20	15.1	6.25	50	.272	.368	0	.000	-0	-10	-11	-1	-0.7
Total 4		1	2	.333	74	0	0	0	2	101¹	109	13	41	68	13.8	5.15	67	.272	.347	0	.000	-1	-18	-19	0	-0.8

● **BRUCE EGLOFF**   Egloff, Bruce Edward b: 4/10/65, Denver, Colo. BR/TR, 6'2", 215 lbs. Deb: 4/13/91

YEAR	TM/L	W	L	PCT	G	GS	CG	SH	SV	IP	H	HR	BB	SO	RAT	ERA	ERA+	OAV	OOB	BH	AVG	PB	PR	/A	PD	TPI
1991	Cle-A	0	0	—	6	0	0	0	0	5²	8	0	4	8	19.1	4.76	87	.333	.429	0	—	0	-0	-0	-0	0.0

● **HOWARD EHMKE**   Ehmke, Howard Jonathan "Bob" b: 4/24/1894, Silver Creek, N.Y. d: 3/17/59, Philadelphia, Pa. BR/TR, 6'3", 190 lbs. Deb: 4/12/15

YEAR	TM/L	W	L	PCT	G	GS	CG	SH	SV	IP	H	HR	BB	SO	RAT	ERA	ERA+	OAV	OOB	BH	AVG	PB	PR	/A	PD	TPI
1915	Buf-F	0	2	.000	18	2	0	0	0	53²	69	2	25	18	16.6	5.53	51	.325	.409	0	.000	-2	-17	-16	2	-0.6
1916	Det-A	3	1	.750	5	4	4	0	0	37¹	34	0	15	15	11.8	3.13	91	.252	.327	1	.143	-1	-1	-1	1	-0.1
1917	Det-A	10	15	.400	35	25	13	4	2	206	174	3	88	90	11.7	2.97	89	.243	.330	17	.246	2	-7	-7	2	-0.4
1919	Det-A	17	10	.630	33	31	20	2	0	248²	255	5	107	79	13.3	3.18	100	.274	.353	23	.253	3	1	0	4	0.7
1920	Det-A	15	18	.455	38	33	23	2	3	268¹	250	8	124	98	13.0	3.25	115	.253	.344	25	.238	-2	16	14	6	2.4
1921	Det-A	13	14	.481	30	22	13	1	0	196¹	220	15	81	68	14.4	4.54	94	.286	.364	21	.284	-2	-6	-6	1	-0.4
1922	Det-A	17	17	.500	45	29	16	1	1	279²	299	12	101	108	13.6	4.22	92	.281	.356	16	.157	-4	-5	-10	2	-1.3
1923	Bos-A	20	17	.541	43	39	28	3	1	316²	318	12	119	121	13.0	3.78	109	.272	.349	25	.223	-2	17	12	5	1.6
1924	Bos-A	19	17	.528	45	36	26	4	4	**315**	324	14	119	119	11.9	3.46	126	.265	.316	28	.222	-4	27	32	2	3.3
1925	Bos-A	9	20	.310	34	31	22	0	1	260²	285	8	85	95	13.2	3.73	122	.285	.348	13	.148	-5	19	24	5	2.2
1926	Bos-A	3	10	.231	14	14	7	1	0	97¹	115	9	45	38	15.2	5.46	75	.303	.382	5	.147	-1	-16	-15	1	-1.6
	Phi-A	12	4	.750	20	18	10	1	0	147¹	125	1	50	55	10.9	2.81	148	.232	.302	7	.152	-2	20	22	0	2.1
	Yr	15	14	.517	34	32	17	2	0	244²	240	4	95	93	13.1	3.86	107	.261	.339	12	.150	-3	4	7	1	0.5
1927	Phi-A	12	10	.545	30	27	10	1	0	189²	200	13	60	68	13.0	4.22	101	.281	.349	14	.206	-1	-2	1	3	0.2
1928	Phi-A	9	8	.529	23	18	5	1	0	139¹	135	6	44	34	11.8	3.62	111	.254	.316	11	.239	1	7	6	0	0.8
1929	*Phi-A	7	2	.778	11	8	2	0	0	54²	44	5	15	20	10.5	3.29	129	.233	.288	2	.105	-2	6	6	0	0.7
1930	Phi-A	0	1	.000	3	1	0	0	0	10	22	4	2	4	24.3	11.70	40	.458	.509	1	.333	0	-8	-8	0	-0.5
Total 15		166	166	.500	427	338	199	20	14	2820²	2873	103	1042	1030	12.9	3.75	104	.271	.343	210	.208	-11	42	52	32	9.1

● **RED EHRET**   Ehret, Philip Sydney b: 8/31/1868, Louisville, Ky. d: 7/28/40, Cincinnati, Ohio BR/TR, 6', 175 lbs. Deb: 7/7/1888 ◆

YEAR	TM/L	W	L	PCT	G	GS	CG	SH	SV	IP	H	HR	BB	SO	RAT	ERA	ERA+	OAV	OOB	BH	AVG	PB	PR	/A	PD	TPI
1888	KC-a	3	2	.600	7	6	5	0	0	52	58	1	22	12	14.4	3.98	86	.272	.349	12	.190	-1	-5	-3	1	-0.2
1889	Lou-a	10	29	.256	45	38	35	1	0	364	441	11	115	135	14.2	4.80	80	.290	.347	65	.252	2	-38	-38	3	-2.7
1890	*Lou-a	25	14	.641	43	38	35	4	2	359	351	5	79	174	11.2	2.53	152	.248	.296	31	.212	-3	53	53	3	4.3
1891	Lou-a	13	13	.500	26	24	23	2	0	220²	225	2	70	76	12.5	3.47	105	.255	.318	22	.242	1	5	0	0	0.5
1892	Pit-N	16	20	.444	39	36	32	0	0	316	290	7	83	101	11.3	2.65	124	.234	.294	34	.258	3	22	23	-4	3.0
1893	Pit-N	18	18	.500	39	35	32	4	0	314¹	322	3	115	70	13.2	3.44	133	.257	.331	24	.176	-6	43	39	1	3.0
1894	Pit-N	19	21	.475	46	38	31	0	1	346²	441	12	128	102	15.0	5.14	102	.306	.367	23	.170	-11	7	4	-1	-0.6
1895	StL-N	6	19	.240	37	32	18	0	0	231²	360	11	88	55	17.8	6.02	80	.349	.405	21	.219	-3	-32	-30	1	-2.5
1896	Cin-N	18	14	.563	34	33	29	2	0	276²	298	5	74	60	12.4	3.42	135	.273	.324	20	.196	-3	29	37	1	3.1
1897	Cin-N	8	10	.444	34	19	11	0	2	184¹	256	7	47	43	15.4	4.78	95	.326	.374	13	.197	-3	-10	-5	-1	-0.7
1898	Lou-N	3	7	.300	12	10	9	0	0	89	130	3	20	20	15.5	5.76	62	.348	.375	9	.225	1	-21	-22	-1	-1.9
Total 11		139	167	.454	362	309	260	14	4	2754¹	3172	63	841	848	13.6	4.02	105	.282	.339	274	.217	-22	55	62	-4	4.4

● **RUBE EHRHARDT**   Ehrhardt, Welton Claude b: 11/20/1894, Beecher, Ill. d: 4/27/80, Chicago Heights, Ill. BR/TR, 6'2", 190 lbs. Deb: 7/18/24

YEAR	TM/L	W	L	PCT	G	GS	CG	SH	SV	IP	H	HR	BB	SO	RAT	ERA	ERA+	OAV	OOB	BH	AVG	PB	PR	/A	PD	TPI
1924	Bro-N	5	3	.625	15	9	6	2	0	83²	71	5	17	13	9.6	2.26	166	.232	.275	4	.138	-2	15	14	-2	0.8
1925	Bro-N	10	14	.417	36	25	12	0	1	207²	239	10	62	47	13.2	5.03	83	.293	.345	15	.211	2	-17	-20	4	-1.4
1926	Bro-N	2	5	.286	44	1	0	0	4	97	101	5	35	25	12.6	3.90	98	.275	.338	6	.250	-0	-1	-1	-2	-0.2
1927	Bro-N	3	7	.300	46	5	4	0	5	95²	90	7	27	12	12.2	3.57	111	.264	.341	6	.250	1	4	3	0	0.7
1928	Bro-N	1	3	.250	28	2	1	1	0	54	74	1	27	12	17.0	4.67	85	.352	.429	4	.286	0	-4	-4	1	-0.2
1929	Cin-N	1	2	.333	24	1	1	0	0	49¹	58	2	22	19	14.8	4.74	96	.305	.380	2	.182	-0	-0	-1	0	0.0
Total 6		22	34	.393	193	41	22	3	10	587¹	633	26	200	128	12.9	4.15	97	.284	.345	37	.214	0	-4	-7	5	-0.3

● **HACK EIBEL**   Eibel, Henry Hack b: 12/6/1893, Brooklyn, N.Y. d: 10/16/45, Macon, Ga. BL/TL, 5'11", 220 lbs. Deb: 6/13/12 ◆

YEAR	TM/L	W	L	PCT	G	GS	CG	SH	SV	IP	H	HR	BB	SO	RAT	ERA	ERA+	OAV	OOB	BH	AVG	PB	PR	/A	PD	TPI
1920	Bos-A	0	0	—	3	0	0	0	0	10¹	10	0	3	5	11.3	3.48	105	.270	.325	8	.186	-0	0	0	-0	0.0

● **JUAN EICHELBERGER**   Eichelberger, Juan Tyrone b: 10/21/53, St.Louis, Mo. BR/TR, 6'3", 205 lbs. Deb: 9/7/78

YEAR	TM/L	W	L	PCT	G	GS	CG	SH	SV	IP	H	HR	BB	SO	RAT	ERA	ERA+	OAV	OOB	BH	AVG	PB	PR	/A	PD	TPI
1978	SD-N	0	0	—	3	0	0	0	0	3¹	4	0	2	2	16.2	10.80	31	.267	.353	0	—	0	-3	-3	0	0.0
1979	SD-N	1	1	.500	3	3	1	0	0	21	15	1	11	12	11.1	3.43	103	.211	.317	2	.400	1	1	-0	0	0.1
1980	SD-N	4	2	.667	15	13	0	0	0	88²	73	8	55	43	13.1	3.65	94	.233	.350	3	.111	-1	-1	-2	-1	-0.3
1981	SD-N	8	8	.500	25	24	3	1	0	141¹	136	5	74	81	13.6	3.50	93	.259	.353	4	.087	-3	-0	-4	-1	-0.6
1982	SD-N	7	14	.333	31	24	8	0	0	177²	171	23	72	74	12.4	4.20	81	.251	.325	5	.091	-2	-12	-15	-1	-1.9
1983	Cle-A	4	11	.267	28	15	2	0	0	134	132	16	59	56	13.0	4.90	86	.259	.338	0	—	0	-13	-10	-1	-1.1
1988	Atl-N	2	0	1.000	20	0	0	0	0	37¹	44	3	10	13	13.0	3.86	95	.297	.342	0	.000	0	-0	-1	-0	0.0
Total 7		26	36	.419	125	79	14	1	0	603¹	575	50	283	281	12.9	4.10	87	.254	.339	14	.103	-4	-29	-35	-2	-3.8

● **MARK EICHHORN**   Eichhorn, Mark Anthony b: 11/21/60, San Jose, Cal. BR/TR, 6'4", 200 lbs. Deb: 8/30/82

YEAR	TM/L	W	L	PCT	G	GS	CG	SH	SV	IP	H	HR	BB	SO	RAT	ERA	ERA+	OAV	OOB	BH	AVG	PB	PR	/A	PD	TPI
1982	Tor-A	0	3	.000	7	7	0	0	0	38	40	4	14	16	12.8	5.45	82	.260	.321	0	—	0	-6	-4	-1	-0.5
1986	Tor-A	14	6	.700	69	0	0	0	10	157	105	8	45	166	9.0	1.72	245	.191	.261	0	—	0	43	44	2	**5.7**
1987	Tor-A	10	6	.625	**89**	0	0	0	4	127²	110	14	52	96	11.8	3.17	142	.234	.318	0	—	0	18	19	2	2.2
1988	Tor-A	0	3	.000	37	0	0	0	1	66²	79	7	27	28	15.1	4.18	94	.304	.382	0	—	0	-2	-0	0	0.0
1989	Atl-N	5	5	.500	45	0	0	0	0	68¹	70	6	22	49	11.9	4.35	84	.271	.332	0	—	0	-4	-5	-1	-0.5
1990	Cal-A	2	5	.286	60	0	0	0	13	84²	98	7	23	69	13.5	3.08	124	.289	.345	0	—	0	8	11	0	0.9
1991	Cal-A	3	3	.500	70	0	0	0	1	81²	63	8	13	49	8.6	1.98	207	.219	.257	0	—	0	19	19	2	1.5
1992	Cal-A	2	4	.333	42	0	0	0	1	56²	51	2	18	42	11.0	2.38	167	.238	.297	0	—	0	10	10	1	1.1

YEAR TM/L	W	L	PCT	G	GS	CG	SH	SV	IP	H	HR	BB	SO	RAT	ERA	ERA+	OAV	OOB	BH	AVG	PB	PR	/A	PD	TPI
*Tor-A	2	0	1.000	23	0	0	0	0	31	35	1	7	19	12.8	4.35	94	.285	.333	0	—	0	-1	-1	1	-0.1
Yr	4	4	.500	65	0	0	0	2	87²	86	3	25	61	11.6	3.08	130	.253	.308	0	—	0	8	9	2	1.0
1993 *Tor-A	3	1	.750	54	0	0	0	0	72²	76	3	22	47	12.5	2.72	158	.272	.332	0	—	0	13	13	2	0.8
1994 Bal-A	6	5	.545	43	0	0	0	1	71	62	1	19	35	10.9	2.15	232	.240	.305	0	—	0	**21**	**22**	2	3.2
1996 Cal-A	1	2	.333	24	0	0	0	0	30¹	36	3	11	24	14.5	5.04	97	.308	.377	0	—	0	-0	-1	1	0.0
Total 11	48	43	.527	563	7	0	0	32	885²	825	49	270	640	11.5	3.00	141	.249	.314	0	.000	-0	116	121	15	14.4

● **DAVE EILAND** Eiland, David William b: 7/5/66, Dade City, Fla. BR/TR, 6'3", 210 lbs. Deb: 8/3/88

YEAR TM/L	W	L	PCT	G	GS	CG	SH	SV	IP	H	HR	BB	SO	RAT	ERA	ERA+	OAV	OOB	BH	AVG	PB	PR	/A	PD	TPI
1988 NY-A	0	0	—	3	3	0	0	0	12²	15	6	4	7	14.9	6.39	62	.294	.368	0	—	0	-3	-3	0	0.0
1989 NY-A	1	3	.250	6	6	0	0	0	34¹	44	5	13	11	15.5	5.77	67	.328	.396	0	—	0	-7	-7	-1	-0.8
1990 NY-A	2	1	.667	5	5	0	0	0	30¹	31	2	5	16	10.7	3.56	111	.254	.283	0	—	0	1	1	-0	0.1
1991 NY-A	2	5	.286	18	13	0	0	0	72²	87	10	23	18	14.0	5.33	78	.302	.360	0	—	0	-10	-10	-2	-1.0
1992 SD-N	0	2	.000	7	7	0	0	0	27	33	1	5	10	12.7	5.67	63	.287	.317	1	.111	-1	-6	-6	0	-0.4
1993 SD-N	0	3	.000	10	9	0	0	0	48¹	58	5	17	14	14.2	5.21	79	.297	.357	1	.083	-1	-6	-6	0	-0.4
1995 NY-A	1	1	.500	4	1	0	0	0	10	16	1	3	6	18.0	6.30	73	.348	.400	0	—	0	-2	-2	0	-0.3
Total 7	6	15	.286	53	44	0	0	0	235¹	284	30	70	82	13.9	5.28	76	.299	.352	2	.095	-0	-34	-33	-2	-2.8

● **DAVE EILERS** Eilers, David Louis b: 12/3/36, Oldenburg, Tex. BR/TR, 5'11", 188 lbs. Deb: 7/27/64

YEAR TM/L	W	L	PCT	G	GS	CG	SH	SV	IP	H	HR	BB	SO	RAT	ERA	ERA+	OAV	OOB	BH	AVG	PB	PR	/A	PD	TPI
1964 Mil-N	0	0	—	6	0	0	0	0	7²	11	1	1	1	15.3	4.70	75	.333	.371	0	—	0	-1	-1	-0	0.0
1965 Mil-N	0	0	—	6	0	0	0	0	3²	8	1	1	2	19.6	12.27	29	.421	.421	0	—	0	-4	-4	-0	-0.1
NY-N	1	1	.500	11	0	0	0	2	18	20	2	4	9	13.0	4.00	88	.274	.329	1	1.000	-0	-1	-1	-0	-0.1
Yr	1	1	.500	17	0	0	0	2	21²	28	3	4	10	14.1	5.40	65	.304	.347	1	1.000	-0	-4	-5	-0	-0.1
1966 NY-N	1	1	.500	23	0	0	0	0	34²	39	7	7	14	12.2	4.67	78	.287	.326	0	.000	-0	-4	-4	1	-0.2
1967 Hou-N	6	4	.600	35	0	0	0	1	59¹	68	3	17	27	13.3	3.94	84	.296	.352	0	.000	-1	-4	-4	-0	-0.8
Total 4	8	6	.571	81	0	0	0	3	123¹	146	14	29	52	13.3	4.45	78	.297	.345	1	.111	-0	-13	-14	-0	-1.1

● **JOEY EISCHEN** Eischen, Joseph Raymond b: 5/25/70, West Covina, Cal. BL/TL, 6'1", 190 lbs. Deb: 6/19/94

YEAR TM/L	W	L	PCT	G	GS	CG	SH	SV	IP	H	HR	BB	SO	RAT	ERA	ERA+	OAV	OOB	BH	AVG	PB	PR	/A	PD	TPI
1994 Mon-N	0	0	—	1	0	0	0	0	0²	4	0	1	0	67.5	54.00	8	.667	.714	0	—	0	-4	-4	-0	-0.2
1995 LA-N	0	0	—	17	0	0	0	0	20¹	19	1	11	15	14.2	3.10	122	.232	.337	0	.000	-0	2	2	-0	0.2
1996 LA-N	0	1	.000	28	0	0	0	0	43¹	48	4	20	36	15.0	4.78	81	.282	.371	0	.000	-1	-3	-4	-1	-0.2
Det-A	1	1	.500	24	0	0	0	0	25	27	3	14	16	14.8	3.24	156	.284	.376	0	—	0	5	5	1	0.4
Total 3	1	2	.333	70	0	0	0	0	89¹	98	8	45	67	15.1	4.33	96	.278	.370	0	.000	-1	1	-2	-0	0.2

● **JAKE EISENHART** Eisenhart, Jacob Henry b: 10/3/22, Perkasie, Pa. d: 12/20/87, Huntingdon, Pa. BL/TL, 6'3.5", 195 lbs. Deb: 6/10/44

YEAR TM/L	W	L	PCT	G	GS	CG	SH	SV	IP	H	HR	BB	SO	RAT	ERA	ERA+	OAV	OOB	BH	AVG	PB	PR	/A	PD	TPI
1944 Cin-N	0	0	—	1	0	0	0	0	0¹	0	0	1	0	27.0	0.00	—	.000	.500	0	—	0	0	0	0	0.0

● **HARRY EISENSTAT** Eisenstat, Harry b: 10/10/15, Brooklyn, N.Y. BL/TL, 5'11", 185 lbs. Deb: 5/19/35

YEAR TM/L	W	L	PCT	G	GS	CG	SH	SV	IP	H	HR	BB	SO	RAT	ERA	ERA+	OAV	OOB	BH	AVG	PB	PR	/A	PD	TPI
1935 Bro-N	0	1	.000	2	0	0	0	0	4²	9	0	2	2	21.2	13.50	29	.429	.478	1	.000	-0	-5	-5	1	-0.7
1936 Bro-N	1	2	.333	5	2	1	0	0	14¹	22	1	6	11	17.6	5.65	73	.344	.400	1	.333	-0	-3	-3	-0	-0.4
1937 Bro-N	3	3	.500	13	5	0	0	0	47²	61	2	11	12	13.8	3.97	102	.308	.348	0	.000	-1	-0	-1	0	-0.1
1938 Det-A	9	6	.600	32	9	5	0	4	125¹	131	7	29	37	11.6	3.73	134	.266	.308	5	.139	-1	15	18	1	1.8
1939 Det-A	2	2	.500	10	2	1	0	0	29²	39	3	9	6	14.6	6.98	70	.315	.361	3	.375	1	-8	-7	1	-0.6
Cle-A	6	7	.462	26	11	4	1	2	103²	109	8	23	38	11.5	3.30	133	.265	.304	8	.250	1	15	13	-1	1.4
Yr	8	9	.471	36	13	5	1	2	133¹	148	11	32	44	12.2	4.12	110	.277	.317	11	.275	1	7	6	-0	0.8
1940 Cle-A	1	4	.200	27	3	0	0	4	71²	78	6	12	27	11.3	3.14	134	.282	.311	3	.273	-0	**10**	9	-0	0.7
1941 Cle-A	1	1	.500	21	0	0	0	0	34	43	2	16	11	16.1	4.24	93	.312	.391	2	.333	1	-0	-1	-1	-0.1
1942 Cle-A	2	1	.667	29	1	0	0	2	47²	58	1	6	19	12.1	2.45	140	.304	.325	1	.250	1	6	5	-0	0.3
Total 8	25	27	.481	165	33	11	1	14	478²	550	30	114	157	12.6	3.84	114	.287	.328	26	.211	1	30	29	0	2.4

● **ED EITELJORGE** Eiteljorge, Edward Henry b: 10/14/1871, Berlin, Germany d: 12/5/42, Greencastle, Ind. BR/TR, 6'2", 190 lbs. Deb: 5/2/1890

YEAR TM/L	W	L	PCT	G	GS	CG	SH	SV	IP	H	HR	BB	SO	RAT	ERA	ERA+	OAV	OOB	BH	AVG	PB	PR	/A	PD	TPI
1890 Chi-N	0	1	.000	2	1	0	0	0	2	5	0	1	0	27.0	22.50	16	.455	.500	0	.000	-0	-4	-4	-0	-1.0
1891 Was-a	1	5	.167	8	7	6	0	0	61¹	79	3	41	23	18.9	6.16	61	.303	.415	5	.192	-1	-17	-17	2	-1.1
Total 2	1	6	.143	9	8	6	0	0	63¹	84	3	42	24	19.2	6.68	56	.309	.424	5	.185	-1	-21	-21	1	-2.1

● **HEINIE ELDER** Elder, Henry Knox b: 8/23/1890, Seattle, Wash. d: 11/13/58, Long Beach, Cal. BL/TL, 6'2", 200 lbs. Deb: 7/7/13

YEAR TM/L	W	L	PCT	G	GS	CG	SH	SV	IP	H	HR	BB	SO	RAT	ERA	ERA+	OAV	OOB	BH	AVG	PB	PR	/A	PD	TPI
1913 Det-A	0	0	—	1	0	0	0	0	3¹	4	0	5	2	24.3	8.10	36	.286	.474	0	—	0	-2	-2	-0	0.0

● **CAL ELDRED** Eldred, Calvin John b: 11/24/67, Cedar Rapids, Iowa BR/TR, 6'4", 215 lbs. Deb: 9/24/91

YEAR TM/L	W	L	PCT	G	GS	CG	SH	SV	IP	H	HR	BB	SO	RAT	ERA	ERA+	OAV	OOB	BH	AVG	PB	PR	/A	PD	TPI
1991 Mil-A	2	0	1.000	3	3	0	0	0	16	20	1	6	10	14.6	4.50	88	.299	.356	0	—	0	-1	-1	-0	0.0
1992 Mil-A	11	2	.846	14	14	2	1	0	100¹	76	4	23	62	9.1	1.79	214	.207	.257	0	—	0	24	23	-0	3.1
1993 Mil-A	16	16	.500	36	36	8	1	0	**258**	232	32	91	180	11.6	4.01	106	.239	.311	0	—	0	9	7	-0	0.7
1994 Mil-A	11	11	.500	25	25	6	0	0	179	158	23	84	98	12.4	4.68	108	.236	.325	0	—	0	2	7	1	0.8
1995 Mil-A	1	1	.500	4	4	0	0	0	23²	24	4	10	18	13.3	3.42	146	.261	.340	0	—	0	3	4	0	0.3
1996 Mil-A	4	4	.500	15	15	0	0	0	84²	82	8	38	50	13.2	4.46	118	.259	.345	0	—	0	5	7	-1	0.5
Total 6	45	34	.570	97	97	16	2	0	661²	592	73	252	418	11.8	3.90	116	.239	.314	0	—	0	43	46	-1	5.4

● **HOD ELLER** Eller, Horace Owen b: 7/5/1894, Muncie, Ind. d: 7/18/61, Indianapolis, Ind BR/TR, 5'11.5", 185 lbs. Deb: 4/16/17

YEAR TM/L	W	L	PCT	G	GS	CG	SH	SV	IP	H	HR	BB	SO	RAT	ERA	ERA+	OAV	OOB	BH	AVG	PB	PR	/A	PD	TPI
1917 Cin-N	10	5	.667	37	11	7	1	1	152¹	131	2	37	77	10.1	2.36	111	.239	.290	6	.133	-2	6	4	-2	0.0
1918 Cin-N	16	12	.571	37	22	14	0	1	217²	205	1	59	84	11.2	2.36	113	.253	.309	11	.157	-2	10	8	-4	0.3
1919 *Cin-N	19	9	.679	38	30	16	7	2	248¹	216	7	50	137	9.8	2.39	116	.238	.281	26	.280	7	14	11	-3	1.6
1920 Cin-N	13	12	.520	35	23	15	1	0	210¹	208	6	52	76	11.3	2.95	103	.266	.315	22	.253	1	4	2	-1	0.2
1921 Cin-N	2	2	.500	13	3	0	0	1	34¹	46	3	15	7	16.0	4.98	72	.322	.386	3	.231	0	-5	-5	-1	-0.7
Total 5	60	40	.600	160	89	52	9	5	863	806	19	213	381	10.8	2.62	108	.253	.303	68	.221	5	30	19	-11	1.4

● **JOE ELLICK** Ellick, Joseph J. b: 4/3/1854, Cincinnati, Ohio d: 4/21/23, Kansas City, Kan. 5'10", 162 lbs. Deb: 5/13/1875 MU♦

YEAR TM/L	W	L	PCT	G	GS	CG	SH	SV	IP	H	HR	BB	SO	RAT	ERA	ERA+	OAV	OOB	BH	AVG	PB	PR	/A	PD	TPI
1878 Mil-N	0	1	.000	1	0	0	0	0	3	1	0	1	0	6.0	3.00	88	.100	.182	2	.154	-0	-0	-0	-0	-0.1

● **BRUCE ELLINGSEN** Ellingsen, Harold Bruce b: 4/26/49, Pocatello, Idaho BL/TL, 6', 180 lbs. Deb: 7/4/74

YEAR TM/L	W	L	PCT	G	GS	CG	SH	SV	IP	H	HR	BB	SO	RAT	ERA	ERA+	OAV	OOB	BH	AVG	PB	PR	/A	PD	TPI
1974 Cle-A	1	1	.500	16	1	0	0	0	42	45	5	17	16	13.3	3.21	102	.278	.346	0	—	0	2	2	-0	0.1

● **CLAUDE ELLIOTT** Elliott, Claude Judson "Chaucer" or "Old Pardee" b: 11/17/1879, Pardeeville, Wis. d: 6/21/23, Pardeeville, Wis. BR/TR, 6', 190 lbs. Deb: 4/16/04

YEAR TM/L	W	L	PCT	G	GS	CG	SH	SV	IP	H	HR	BB	SO	RAT	ERA	ERA+	OAV	OOB	BH	AVG	PB	PR	/A	PD	TPI
1904 Cin-N	3	1	.750	9	6	4	1	0	57²	53	1	23	19	12.5	2.97	99	.247	.331	5	.208	-1	-1	-0	0	0.1
NY-N	0	1	.000	3	1	1	0	0	15	21	1	3	8	14.4	3.00	91	.328	.358	1	.200	1	-0	-0	-1	-0.1
Yr	3	2	.600	12	7	5	1	0	72²	74	3	26	27	12.4	2.97	97	.261	.324	6	.207	1	-2	-1	-1	0.0
1905 NY-N	0	1	.000	10	2	2	0	**6**	38	41	3	12	20	12.8	4.03	73	.270	.327	3	.188	0	-4	-5	1	-0.3
Total 2	3	3	.500	22	9	7	1	6	110²	115	6	38	47	12.8	3.33	87	.267	.333	9	.200	1	-6	-5	-0	-0.3

● **DONNIE ELLIOTT** Elliott, Donald Glenn b: 9/20/68, Pasadena, Tex. BR/TR, 6'4", 190 lbs. Deb: 4/23/94

YEAR TM/L	W	L	PCT	G	GS	CG	SH	SV	IP	H	HR	BB	SO	RAT	ERA	ERA+	OAV	OOB	BH	AVG	PB	PR	/A	PD	TPI
1994 SD-N	0	1	.000	30	0	0	0	0	33	31	3	21	24	14.5	3.27	125	.250	.363	0	.000	-0	3	3	-0	0.1
1995 SD-N	0	0	—	1	0	0	0	0	2	2	0	1	3	13.5	0.00	—	.250	.333	0	—	0	1	1	-0	0.0
Total 2	0	1	.000	31	0	0	0	0	35	33	3	22	27	14.4	3.09	133	.250	.361	0	.000	-0	4	4	-0	0.1

● **HAL ELLIOTT** Elliott, Harold William b: 5/29/1899, Mt.Clemens, Mich. d: 4/25/63, Honolulu, Hawaii BR/TR, 6'1.5", 170 lbs. Deb: 4/19/29

YEAR TM/L	W	L	PCT	G	GS	CG	SH	SV	IP	H	HR	BB	SO	RAT	ERA	ERA+	OAV	OOB	BH	AVG	PB	PR	/A	PD	TPI
1929 Phi-N	3	7	.300	40	8	2	0	0	114¹	146	5	59	32	16.1	6.06	86	.313	.390	5	.167	-1	-17	-11	-2	-0.8
1930 Phi-N	6	11	.353	**48**	11	2	0	0	117¹	191	7	58	37	19.2	7.67	71	.382	.447	3	.094	-3	-35	-29	2	-3.3
1931 Phi-N	0	2	.000	16	4	0	0	0	33	46	5	19	16	18.0	9.55	44	.338	.423	1	.111	-0	-21	-19	-0	-1.3
1932 Phi-N	2	4	.333	16	7	0	0	0	57²	70	5	38	13	16.9	5.77	76	.297	.394	3	.167	-0	-12	-9	-1	-0.9
Total 4	11	24	.314	120	30	4	0	0	322¹	453	22	174	90	17.6	6.95	73	.338	.415	12	.135	-5	-85	-68	2	-6.3

● **GLENN ELLIOTT** Elliott, Herbert Glenn "Lefty" b: 11/11/19, Sapulpa, Okla d: 7/27/69, Portland, Ore. BB/TL, 5'10", 170 lbs. Deb: 4/17/47

YEAR TM/L	W	L	PCT	G	GS	CG	SH	SV	IP	H	HR	BB	SO	RAT	ERA	ERA+	OAV	OOB	BH	AVG	PB	PR	/A	PD	TPI
1947 Bos-N	0	1	.000	11	0	0	0	1	19	18	4	11	8	13.7	4.74	82	.269	.372	1	.500	0	-1	-2	0	0.0
1948 Bos-N	1	0	1.000	1	1	0	0	0	3	5	0	1	2	18.0	3.00	128	.357	.400	0	.000	0	-0	-0	-0	0.0

YEAR	TM/L	W	L	PCT	G	GS	CG	SH	SV	IP	H	HR	BB	SO	RAT	ERA	ERA+	OAV	OOB	BH	AVG	PB	PR	/A	PD	TPI
1949	Bos-N	3	4	.429	22	6	1	0	0	68¹	70	7	27	15	12.8	3.95	96	.269	.338	1	.059	-1	1	-1	1	-0.2
Total	3	4	5	.444	34	7	1	0	1	90¹	93	11	39	25	13.2	4.08	93	.273	.347	2	.095	-1	-0	-3	1	-0.2

● JUMBO ELLIOTT
Elliott, James Thomas b: 10/22/1900, St.Louis, Mo. d: 1/7/70, Terre Haute, Ind. BR/TL, 6'3", 235 lbs. Deb: 4/21/23

YEAR	TM/L	W	L	PCT	G	GS	CG	SH	SV	IP	H	HR	BB	SO	RAT	ERA	ERA+	OAV	OOB	BH	AVG	PB	PR	/A	PD	TPI
1923	StL-A	0	0	—	1	0	0	0	0	1	1	0	3	0	36.0	27.00	15	.333	.667	0	—	0	-3	-3	-0	0.0
1925	Bro-N	0	2	.000	3	1	0	0	0	10²	17	0	9	3	22.8	8.44	50	.362	.474	1	.000	-1	-5	-5	-0	-0.8
1927	Bro-N	6	13	.316	30	21	12	2	3	188¹	188	5	60	99	11.9	3.30	120	.269	.327	9	.141	-1	13	14	-4	0.8
1928	Bro-N	9	14	.391	41	21	7	2	1	192	194	8	64	74	12.4	3.89	102	.268	.332	12	.176	2	2	-2	-3	0.1
1929	Bro-N	1	2	.333	6	3	0	0	0	19	21	2	16	7	18.0	6.63	70	.280	.413	1	.250	0	-4	-4	-0	-0.5
1930	Bro-N	10	7	.588	35	21	6	2	1	198¹	204	16	70	59	12.7	3.95	124	.271	.337	10	.147	-2	23	21	-3	1.1
1931	Phi-N	**19**	14	.576	**52**	30	12	2	5	249	288	15	83	99	13.6	4.27	100	.287	.344	11	.122	-6	-11	-1	-5	-1.2
1932	Phi-N	11	10	.524	39	22	8	0	0	166	210	14	67	62	14.0	5.42	81	.300	.346	12	.197	-2	-28	-19	-2	-2.3
1933	Phi-N	6	10	.375	35	21	6	0	2	161²	188	8	49	43	13.4	3.84	99	.295	.348	12	.231	-0	-9	-0	-4	-0.4
1934	Phi-N	0	1	.000	3	1	0	0	0	5¹	8	0	4	1	21.9	10.13	47	.333	.448	0	.000	-0	-3	-3	-0	-0.5
	Bos-N	1	1	.500	7	3	0	0	0	15¹	19	2	9	6	17.0	5.87	65	.284	.377	1	.250	-1	-3	-3	-0	-0.4
	Yr	1	2	.333	10	4	0	0	0	20²	27	2	13	7	17.9	6.97	58	.293	.387	1	.200	-1	-7	-7	-0	-0.9
Total	10	63	74	.460	252	144	51	8	12	1206²	1338	70	414	453	13.3	4.24	100	.283	.344	68	.163	-8	-29	2	-21	-4.1

● DOCK ELLIS
Ellis, Dock Phillip b: 3/11/45, Los Angeles, Cal. BB/TR, 6'3", 210 lbs. Deb: 6/18/68

YEAR	TM/L	W	L	PCT	G	GS	CG	SH	SV	IP	H	HR	BB	SO	RAT	ERA	ERA+	OAV	OOB	BH	AVG	PB	PR	/A	PD	TPI
1968	Pit-N	6	5	.545	26	10	2	0	0	104	82	4	38	52	10.5	2.51	117	.213	.285	2	.069	-1	5	5	0	0.4
1969	Pit-N	11	17	.393	35	33	8	2	0	218²	206	14	76	173	11.8	3.58	97	.250	.316	6	.088	-3	0	-2	1	-0.5
1970	*Pit-N	13	10	.565	30	30	9	4	0	201²	194	9	87	128	13.0	3.21	121	.257	.342	7	.100	-3	19	15	2	1.5
1971	*Pit-N★	19	9	.679	31	31	11	2	0	226²	207	15	63	137	10.8	3.06	111	.239	.292	16	.203	2	10	8	2	1.3
1972	*Pit-N	15	7	.682	25	25	4	1	0	163¹	156	6	33	96	10.6	2.70	123	.253	.294	9	.153	-1	14	11	-1	1.3
1973	Pit-N	12	14	.462	28	28	3	1	0	192	176	7	55	122	11.1	3.05	115	.240	.299	7	.108	-3	13	10	1	1.2
1974	Pit-N	12	9	.571	26	26	9	0	0	176²	163	13	41	91	10.7	3.16	109	.242	.292	12	.214	3	9	6	-1	0.9
1975	*Pit-N	8	9	.471	27	24	5	2	0	140	163	9	46	65	13.4	3.79	93	.292	.345	4	.111	-0	-3	-4	-1	-0.5
1976	*NY-A	17	8	.680	32	32	8	1	0	211²	195	14	76	65	11.7	3.19	107	.247	.316	0	—	0	5	5	-3	0.3
1977	NY-A	1	1	.500	3	3	1	0	0	19²	18	1	8	5	11.9	1.83	215	.237	.310	0	—	0	5	5	-0	0.5
	Oak-A	1	5	.167	7	7	0	0	0	26	35	1	14	11	17.3	9.69	42	.315	.397	0	—	0	-16	-16	-0	-2.7
	Tex-A	10	6	.625	23	22	7	1	1	167¹	158	13	42	90	10.8	2.90	140	.254	.301	0	—	0	21	22	-2	1.8
	Yr	12	12	.500	33	32	8	1	1	213	211	19	64	106	11.6	3.63	112	.260	.314	0	—	0	10	10	-2	-0.4
1978	Tex-A	9	7	.563	22	22	3	0	0	141¹	131	15	46	45	11.4	4.20	89	.245	.307	0	—	0	-7	-7	-0	-0.7
1979	Tex-A	1	5	.167	10	9	0	0	0	46²	64	16	5	16	15.4	5.98	69	.323	.374	0	—	0	-9	-9	-0	-1.0
	NY-N	3	7	.300	17	14	1	0	0	85	110	9	34	41	15.4	6.04	60	.320	.383	2	.077	-1	-22	-23	-1	-2.4
	Pit-N	0	0	—	3	1	0	0	0	7	9	1	2	1	14.1	2.57	151	.346	.393	0	—	0	1	1	0	0.0
	Yr	3	7	.300	20	15	1	0	0	92	119	10	36	42	15.2	5.77	63	.316	.375	2	.074	-2	-21	-22	-1	-2.4
Total	12	138	119	.537	345	317	71	14	1	2127²	2067	140	674	1136	11.8	3.46	103	.255	.315	65	.133	-7	49	26	-3	1.4

● JIM ELLIS
Ellis, James Russell b: 3/25/45, Tulare, Cal. BR/TL, 6'2", 185 lbs. Deb: 8/11/67

YEAR	TM/L	W	L	PCT	G	GS	CG	SH	SV	IP	H	HR	BB	SO	RAT	ERA	ERA+	OAV	OOB	BH	AVG	PB	PR	/A	PD	TPI
1967	Chi-N	1	1	.500	8	1	0	0	0	16²	20	1	9	8	15.7	3.24	109	.313	.397	1	.200	0	0	1	-0	0.1
1969	StL-N	0	0	—	2	1	0	0	0	5¹	7	0	3	0	16.9	1.69	212	.318	.400	0	—	0	1	1	-0	0.0
Total	2	1	1	.500	10	2	0	0	0	22	27	1	12	8	16.0	2.86	124	.314	.398	1	.200	0	1	2	-1	0.1

● ROBERT ELLIS
Ellis, Robert Randolph b: 12/15/70, Baton Rouge, La. BR/TR, 6'5", 220 lbs. Deb: 9/12/96

YEAR	TM/L	W	L	PCT	G	GS	CG	SH	SV	IP	H	HR	BB	SO	RAT	ERA	ERA+	OAV	OOB	BH	AVG	PB	PR	/A	PD	TPI
1996	Cal-A	0	0	—	3	0	0	0	0	5	0	0	4	5	7.2	0.00	—	.000	.211	0	—	0	3	3	-0	0.0

● SAMMY ELLIS
Ellis, Samuel Joseph b: 2/11/41, Youngstown, Ohio BL/TR, 6'1", 180 lbs. Deb: 4/14/62 C

YEAR	TM/L	W	L	PCT	G	GS	CG	SH	SV	IP	H	HR	BB	SO	RAT	ERA	ERA+	OAV	OOB	BH	AVG	PB	PR	/A	PD	TPI
1962	Cin-N	2	2	.500	8	4	0	0	0	28	29	6	29	27	19.0	6.75	60	.269	.428	2	.200	-0	-9	-8	-0	-1.0
1964	Cin-N	10	3	.769	52	5	2	0	14	122¹	101	9	28	125	9.6	2.57	140	.223	.270	2	.083	-0	13	14	0	1.9
1965	Cin-N☆	22	10	.688	44	39	15	2	2	263²	222	22	104	183	11.3	3.79	99	.226	.304	12	.125	-1	-7	-1	-3	-0.6
1966	Cin-N	12	19	.387	41	36	7	0	0	221	226	35	64	154	12.5	5.29	74	.264	.328	8	.114	-2	-41	-34	-3	-4.7
1967	Cin-N	8	11	.421	32	27	8	1	0	175²	197	18	67	80	13.7	3.84	98	.286	.353	4	.082	-2	-9	-4	-0	-0.5
1968	Cal-A	9	10	.474	42	24	3	0	2	164	150	22	56	93	11.6	3.95	74	.244	.313	2	.045	-3	-18	-19	-2	-2.8
1969	Chi-A	0	3	.000	10	5	0	0	0	29¹	42	6	15	16	18.1	5.83	66	.336	.415	1	.167	-0	-7	-6	-0	-0.5
Total	7	63	58	.521	229	140	35	3	18	1004	967	118	378	677	12.3	4.15	88	.253	.323	31	.104	-8	-78	-58	-9	-8.2

● GEORGE ELLISON
Ellison, George Russell b: 1/24/1895, California d: 1/20/78, San Francisco, Cal. BR/TR, 6'3", 185 lbs. Deb: 8/21/20

YEAR	TM/L	W	L	PCT	G	GS	CG	SH	SV	IP	H	HR	BB	SO	RAT	ERA	ERA+	OAV	OOB	BH	AVG	PB	PR	/A	PD	TPI
1920	Cle-A	0	0	—	1	0	0	0	0	1	0	0	2	1	18.0	0.00	—	.000	.400	0	—	0	0	0	0	0.0

● DICK ELLSWORTH
Ellsworth, Richard Clark b: 3/22/40, Lusk, Wyo. BL/TL, 6'4", 195 lbs. Deb: 6/22/58 F

YEAR	TM/L	W	L	PCT	G	GS	CG	SH	SV	IP	H	HR	BB	SO	RAT	ERA	ERA+	OAV	OOB	BH	AVG	PB	PR	/A	PD	TPI
1958	Chi-N	0	1	.000	1	1	0	0	0	2¹	4	0	3	1	30.9	15.43	25	.364	.533	0	.000	-0	-3	-3	-0	-0.8
1960	Chi-N	7	13	.350	31	27	6	0	0	176²	170	12	72	94	12.4	3.72	102	.257	.332	2	.042	-3	1	1	-0	-0.2
1961	Chi-N	10	11	.476	37	31	7	1	0	186²	213	23	48	91	12.7	3.86	108	.292	.338	2	.036	-5	4	7	3	0.5
1962	Chi-N	9	20	.310	37	33	6	0	1	208²	241	23	77	113	13.9	5.09	81	.291	.355	7	.113	1	-27	-22	0	-2.5
1963	Chi-N	22	10	.688	37	37	19	4	0	290²	223	14	75	185	9.3	2.11	**167**	.210	.263	9	.096	-2	38	45	2	5.2
1964	Chi-N☆	14	18	.438	37	36	16	1	0	256²	267	34	71	148	12.0	3.75	99	.266	.317	4	.046	-5	-6	-1	2	-0.5
1965	Chi-N	14	15	.483	36	34	8	1	0	222¹	227	26	57	130	11.7	3.81	97	.265	.313	7	.096	-2	-11	-9	2	-0.4
1966	Chi-N	8	22	.267	38	37	9	0	1	269¹	321	28	51	144	12.6	3.98	92	.294	.328	14	.156	-1	-11	-9	2	-0.8
1967	Phi-N	6	7	.462	32	21	3	1	0	125¹	152	16	36	45	13.9	4.38	78	.306	.359	4	.108	-1	-14	-14	2	-1.3
1968	Bos-A	16	7	.696	31	28	10	1	0	196	196	16	37	106	11.0	3.03	104	.260	.301	4	.056	-5	-1	3	-0	0.0
1969	Bos-A	0	0	—	2	0	0	0	0	12	16	1	4	4	15.0	3.75	101	.320	.370	0	.000	-0	-0	-0	-0	0.0
	Cle-A	6	9	.400	34	22	3	1	0	135	162	10	40	48	13.8	4.13	91	.301	.354	6	.133	-1	-8	-6	-0	-0.7
	Yr	6	9	.400	36	24	3	1	0	147	178	11	44	52	13.9	4.10	92	.302	.356	6	.125	-2	-8	-5	-0	-0.7
1970	Cle-A	3	3	.500	29	1	0	0	0	43²	49	4	14	13	13.2	4.53	87	.299	.358	0	.000	-0	-3	-4	1	-0.3
	Mil-A	0	0	—	14	0	0	0	0	15²	11	0	3	9	8.6	1.72	220	.196	.250	-0	—	-0	3	4	0	0.5
	Yr	3	3	.500	43	1	0	0	0	59¹	60	4	17	22	11.8	3.79	103	.269	.324	0	.000	-0	-1	1	-1	-0.3
1971	Mil-A	0	1	.000	11	0	0	0	0	14²	22	1	7	10	18.4	4.91	71	.361	.435	0	.000	-0	-2	-2	-0	-0.2
Total	13	115	137	.456	407	310	87	9	5	2155²	2274	194	595	1140	12.2	3.72	100	.272	.324	59	.088	-25	-37	-2	12	-2.2

● STEVE ELLSWORTH
Ellsworth, Steven Clark b: 7/30/60, Chicago, Ill. BR/TR, 6'8", 220 lbs. Deb: 4/7/88 F

YEAR	TM/L	W	L	PCT	G	GS	CG	SH	SV	IP	H	HR	BB	SO	RAT	ERA	ERA+	OAV	OOB	BH	AVG	PB	PR	/A	PD	TPI
1988	Bos-A	1	6	.143	8	7	0	0	0	36	47	7	16	16	16.0	6.75	61	.315	.386			0	-11	-11	-0	-1.8

● DON ELSTON
Elston, Donald Ray b: 4/6/29, Campbellstown, Ohio d: 1/2/95, Evanston, Ill. BR/TR, 6', 170 lbs. Deb: 9/17/53

YEAR	TM/L	W	L	PCT	G	GS	CG	SH	SV	IP	H	HR	BB	SO	RAT	ERA	ERA+	OAV	OOB	BH	AVG	PB	PR	/A	PD	TPI
1953	Chi-N	0	1	.000	2	1	0	0	0	5	11	1	2	2	19.8	14.40	31	.458	.458	0	.000	-0	-6	-6	-0	-0.8
1957	Bro-N	0	0	—	1	0	0	0	0	1	1	0	1	0	9.0	0.00	—	.250	.250	0	—	0	0	0	0	0.0
	Chi-N	6	7	.462	39	14	2	0	8	144	139	16	55	102	12.4	3.56	109	.259	.334	4	.108	-2	5	5	0	0.3
	Yr	6	7	.462	40	14	2	0	8	145	140	16	55	103	12.4	3.54	109	.259	.333	4	.108	-2	5	5	0	0.3
1958	Chi-N	9	8	.529	**69**	0	0	0	10	97	75	9	39	84	10.7	2.88	136	.214	.294	5	.357	1	**12**	**11**	1	2.4
1959	Chi-N★	10	8	.556	**65**	0	0	0	13	97²	77	11	46	82	11.6	3.32	119	.218	.313	4	.211	0	7	5	2	1.3
1960	Chi-N	8	9	.471	60	0	0	0	11	127	109	17	55	85	11.9	3.40	111	.231	.316	3	.125	-0	5	5	-2	0.5
1961	Chi-N	6	7	.462	58	0	0	0	6	93¹	108	11	45	59	15.3	5.59	75	.297	.383	2	.182	-0	-16	-15	-0	-2.1
1962	Chi-N	4	8	.333	57	0	0	0	9	66¹	57	6	32	37	12.2	2.44	170	.247	.341	0	.000	-1	11	13	1	2.5
1963	Chi-N	4	1	.800	51	0	0	0	6	70	57	6	21	41	10.3	2.83	124	.226	.291	0	.000	-0	5	5	-1	0.3
1964	Chi-N	2	5	.286	48	0	0	0	6	54¹	68	4	34	26	17.4	5.30	70	.330	.432	1	.167	-0	-11	-10	1	-1.1
Total	9	49	54	.476	755²	702	80	72	90	755²	702	80	327	519	12.6	3.69	106	.251	.335	19	.153	-3	11	17	1	3.3

● NARCISO ELVIRA
Elvira, Narciso Chicho (Delgado) b: 10/29/67, Veracruz, Mex. BL/TL, 5'10", 160 lbs. Deb: 9/9/90

YEAR	TM/L	W	L	PCT	G	GS	CG	SH	SV	IP	H	HR	BB	SO	RAT	ERA	ERA+	OAV	OOB	BH	AVG	PB	PR	/A	PD	TPI
1990	Mil-A	0	0	—	4	0	0	0	0	5	6	0	5	4	19.8	5.40	72	.300	.440	0	—	0	-1	-1	0	0.1

● HARRY ELY
Ely, Harry Deb: 9/24/1892

YEAR	TM/L	W	L	PCT	G	GS	CG	SH	SV	IP	H	HR	BB	SO	RAT	ERA	ERA+	OAV	OOB	BH	AVG	PB	PR	/A	PD	TPI
1892	Bal-N	0	1	.000	1	1	1	0	0	7	14	0	7	0	29.6	7.71	44	.400	.523	0	.000	-0	-3	-3	-0	-0.4

YEAR	TM/L	W	L	PCT	G	GS	CG	SH	SV	IP	H	HR	BB	SO	RAT	ERA	ERA+	OAV	OOB	BH	AVG	PB	PR	/A	PD	TPI

● **BONES ELY**   Ely, William Frederick   b: 6/7/1863, N.Girard, Pa.   d: 1/10/52, Berkeley, Cal.   BR/TR, 6'1", 155 lbs.   Deb: 6/19/1884 ◆

1884	Buf-N	0	1	.000	1	1	0	0	0	5	17	1	5	4	39.6	14.40	22	.500	.564	0	.000	-1	-6	-6	-0	-0.7
1886	Lou-a	0	4	.000	6	4	4	0	1	44	53	0	26	28	16.2	5.32	68	.280	.367	-1	.156	-1	-9	-8	-0	-0.7
1890	Syr-a	0	0	—	1	0	0	0	0	2	7	0	0	0	31.5	22.50	16	.538	.538	130	.262	0	-4	-4	0	0.0
1894	StL-N	0	0	—	1	0	0	0	0	1	0	3	0	0	27.0	0.00	—	.000	.500	156	.306	0	1	1	0	0.0
Total	4	0	5	.000	9	5	4	0	1	52	77	1	34	32	19.2	6.75	54	.322	.407	1331	.258	-1	-19	-18	0	-1.4

● **ALAN EMBREE**   Embree, Alan Duane   b: 1/23/70, Vancouver, Wash.   BL/TL, 6'2", 185 lbs.   Deb: 9/15/92

1992	Cle-A	0	2	.000	4	4	0	0	0	18	19	3	8	12	14.0	7.00	56	.271	.354	0	—	0	-6	-6	-1	-0.6
1995	*Cle-A	3	2	.600	23	0	0	0	1	24²	23	2	16	23	14.2	5.11	92	.253	.364	0	—	0	-1	-1	-0	-0.2
1996	*Cle-A	1	1	.500	24	0	0	0	0	31	30	10	21	33	14.8	6.39	77	.259	.372	0	—	0	-5	-5	-0	-0.3
Total	3	4	5	.444	51	4	0	0	1	73²	72	15	45	68	14.4	6.11	75	.260	.365	0	—	0	-12	-12	-1	-1.1

● **RED EMBREE**   Embree, Charles Willard   b: 8/30/17, ElMonte, Cal.   d: 9/24/96, Eugene, Ore.   BR/TR, 6', 165 lbs.   Deb: 9/10/41

1941	Cle-A	0	1	.000	1	1	0	0	0	4	7	0	3	4	24.8	6.75	58	.438	.550	0	.000	-0	-1	-1	-0	-0.3
1942	Cle-A	3	4	.429	19	6	2	0	0	63	58	0	31	44	13.0	3.86	89	.242	.333	2	.133	-0	-1	-3	-0	-0.3
1944	Cle-A	0	1	.000	3	1	0	0	0	3¹	2	0	5	4	18.9	13.50	24	.167	.412	0	—	-0	-4	-4	-0	-0.9
1945	Cle-A	4	4	.500	8	8	5	1	0	70	56	3	26	42	10.5	1.93	168	.215	.287	3	.143	-1	11	10	1	1.2
1946	Cle-A	8	12	.400	28	26	8	0	0	200	170	15	79	87	11.3	3.47	95	.227	.302	13	.186	1	1	-3	-1	-0.3
1947	Cle-A	8	10	.444	27	21	6	0	0	162²	137	13	67	56	11.3	3.15	110	.233	.313	9	.173	-1	10	6	1	0.5
1948	NY-A	5	3	.625	20	8	4	0	0	76²	77	6	30	25	12.7	3.76	109	.261	.331	4	.148	-1	5	3	-1	0.0
1949	StL-N	3	13	.188	35	19	4	0	1	127¹	146	13	89	24	16.8	5.37	84	.294	.405	6	.162	-1	-17	-12	-0	-1.4
Total	8	31	48	.392	141	90	29	1	1	707	653	50	330	286	12.6	3.72	98	.246	.331	37	.166	-4	4	-5	-2	-1.5

● **SLIM EMBREY**   Embrey, Charles Akin   b: 8/17/01, Columbia, Tenn.   d: 10/10/47, Nashville, Tenn.   BR/TR, 6'2", 184 lbs.   Deb: 10/1/23

| 1923 | Chi-A | 0 | 0 | — | 1 | 0 | 0 | 0 | 0 | 2² | 7 | 0 | 2 | 1 | 30.4 | 10.13 | 39 | .500 | .563 | | | 0 | -2 | -2 | 0 | 0.0 |

● **CHARLIE EMIG**   Emig, Charles Henry   b: 4/5/1875, Cincinnati, Ohio   d: 10/2/75, Oklahoma City, Okla.   TL ,   Deb: 9/4/1896

| 1896 | Lou-N | 0 | 1 | .000 | 1 | 1 | 1 | 0 | 0 | 8 | 12 | 1 | 7 | 1 | 24.8 | 7.88 | 55 | .343 | .489 | 0 | .000 | -1 | -3 | -3 | 1 | -0.3 |

● **SLIM EMMERICH**   Emmerich, William Peter   b: 9/29/19, Allentown, Pa.   BR/TR, 6'1", 170 lbs.   Deb: 5/14/45

1945	NY-N	4	4	.500	31	7	1	0	0	100	111	8	33	27	13.1	4.86	80	.278	.334	3	.120	-2	-12	-11	-0	-0.9
1946	NY-N	0	0	—	2	0	0	0	0	4	6	1	0	1	13.5	4.50	76	.400	.400	0	-0	-0	-0	0	0.0
Total	2	4	4	.500	33	7	1	0	0	104	117	9	33	28	13.1	4.85	80	.282	.336	3	.120	-2	-12	-11	-0	-0.9

● **BOB EMSLIE**   Emslie, Robert Daniel   b: 1/27/1859, Guelph, Ont., Can.   d: 4/26/43, St.Thomas, Ont., Canada   BR/TR, 5'11",   Deb: 7/25/1883   U

1883	Bal-a	9	13	.409	24	23	21	1	0	201¹	188	3	41	62	10.2	3.17	110	.231	.268	16	.165	-3	3	7	2	0.5
1884	Bal-a	32	17	.653	50	50	50	4	0	455¹	419	5	88	264	10.3	2.75	126	.224	.264	37	.190	-5	25	36	-1	2.8
1885	Bal-a	3	10	.231	13	13	11	0	0	107	131	0	30	27	14.0	4.29	76	.298	.350	12	.235	0	-12	-12	-1	-1.2
	Phi-a	0	4	.000	4	4	3	0	0	28²	37	1	6	9	13.5	6.28	55	.291	.323	1	.083	-1	-10	-9	1	-1.0
	Yr	3	14	.176	17	17	14	0	0	135²	168	1	36	36	13.5	4.71	70	.294	.336	13	.206	-1	-22	-21	-1	-2.2
Total	3	44	44	.500	91	90	85	5	0	792¹	775	9	165	362	11.1	3.19	108	.239	.279	66	.186	-9	6	22	0	1.1

● **LUIS ENCARNACION**   Encarnacion, Luis Martin Lora (b: Luis Martin Lora (Encarcnacion))
b: 10/20/63, Santo Domingo, D.R.   BR/TR, 5'10", 178 lbs.   Deb: 7/27/90

| 1990 | KC-A | 0 | 0 | — | 4 | 0 | 0 | 0 | 0 | 10¹ | 14 | 1 | 4 | 8 | 15.7 | 7.84 | 49 | .311 | .367 | 0 | — | 0 | -5 | -5 | -0 | 0.1 |

● **JOE ENGEL**   Engel, Joseph William   b: 3/12/1893, Washington, D.C.   d: 6/12/69, Chattanooga, Tenn   BR/TL, 6'1.5", 183 lbs.   Deb: 5/30/12

1912	Was-A	2	5	.286	17	10	2	0	1	75	70	2	50	29	14.9	3.96	84	.253	.375	1	.059	-1	-5	-5	1	-0.5
1913	Was-A	8	9	.471	36	24	6	2	0	164²	124	2	85	70	12.0	3.06	97	.207	.317	3	.061	-5	-2	-2	-1	-0.8
1914	Was-A	7	5	.583	35	15	1	0	3	124¹	108	2	75	41	13.6	2.97	95	.254	.372	3	.107	-1	-3	-2	-1	-0.2
1915	Was-A	0	3	.000	11	3	0	0	0	33²	30	0	19	9	13.9	3.21	93	.261	.380	0	.000	-1	-0	-1	0	-0.1
1917	Cin-N	0	1	.000	1	1	1	0	0	8	12	0	4	2	20.3	5.63	47	.353	.450	0	.000	-0	-3	-3	-0	-0.3
1919	Cle-A	0	0	—	1	0	0	0	0	0	0	0	3	0	—	∞	—	—	1.000	0	.000	-0	-2	-2	-0	-0.2
1920	Was-A	0	0	—	1	0	0	0	0	1²	0	0	4	0	27.0	21.60	17	.000	.556	0	.000	-0	-3	-3	-0	0.0
Total	7	17	23	.425	102	53	10	2	4	407¹	344	6	242	151	13.5	3.38	88	.237	.355	7	.067	-6	-20	-18	-0	-2.1

● **STEVE ENGEL**   Engel, Steven Michael   b: 12/31/61, Cincinnati, Ohio   BR/TL, 6'3", 216 lbs.   Deb: 7/30/85

| 1985 | Chi-N | 1 | 5 | .167 | 11 | 8 | 1 | 0 | 1 | 51² | 61 | 10 | 26 | 29 | 15.2 | 5.57 | 72 | .298 | .377 | 3 | .188 | -1 | -11 | -9 | -0 | -0.9 |

● **RICK ENGLE**   Engle, Richard Douglas   b: 4/7/57, Corbin, Ky.   BR/TL, 5'11.5", 181 lbs.   Deb: 9/2/81

| 1981 | Mon-N | 0 | 0 | — | 1 | 0 | 0 | 0 | 0 | 2 | 6 | 0 | 1 | 2 | 31.5 | 18.00 | 19 | .500 | .538 | 0 | — | -0 | -2 | -2 | 1 | -0.2 |

● **JACK ENRIGHT**   Enright, Jackson Percy   b: 11/29/1895, Fort Worth, Tex.   d: 8/18/75, Pompano Beach, Fla   BR/TR, 5'11", 177 lbs.   Deb: 9/26/17

| 1917 | NY-A | 0 | 1 | .000 | 1 | 1 | 0 | 0 | 0 | 5 | 5 | 0 | 3 | 1 | 14.4 | 5.40 | 50 | .294 | .400 | 0 | .000 | -0 | -2 | -1 | 1 | -0.2 |

● **TERRY ENYART**   Enyart, Terry Gene   b: 10/10/50, Ironton, Ohio   BR/TL, 6'2", 190 lbs.   Deb: 6/17/74

| 1974 | Mon-N | 0 | 0 | — | 2 | 0 | 0 | 0 | 0 | 1² | 4 | 0 | 4 | 2 | 43.2 | 16.20 | 24 | .444 | .615 | 0 | — | 0 | -2 | -2 | -0 | 0.0 |

● **JOHNNY ENZMANN**   Enzmann, John "Gentleman John"   b: 3/4/1890, Brooklyn, N.Y.   d: 3/14/84, Riverhead, N.Y.   BR/TR, 5'10", 165 lbs.   Deb: 7/10/14

1914	Bro-N	1	0	1.000	7	1	0	0	0	19	21	1	8	5	15.2	4.74	60	.300	.395	0	—	-1	-4	-4	1	-0.2
1918	Cle-A	5	7	.417	30	14	8	0	2	136²	130	1	29	38	10.8	2.37	127	.263	.310	7	.149	-2	6	10	-0	0.6
1919	Cle-A	3	2	.600	14	4	2	0	0	55¹	67	0	6	13	12.5	2.28	147	.312	.342	2	.133	-0	6	7	-1	0.4
1920	Phi-N	2	3	.400	16	2	1	0	0	58²	79	1	16	35	15.3	3.84	89	.320	.373	4	.167	-1	-5	-3	-0	-0.2
Total	4	11	12	.478	67	21	11	0	2	269²	297	4	61	91	12.4	2.84	111	.289	.338	13	.141	-3	3	10	-0	0.6

● **AL EPPERLY**   Epperly, Albert Paul "Tub" or "Pard"   b: 5/7/18, Glidden, Iowa   BL/TR, 6'2", 194 lbs.   Deb: 4/25/38

1938	Chi-N	2	0	1.000	9	4	1	0	0	27	28	1	15	10	14.3	3.67	104	.264	.355	2	.250	1	0	-0	-0	0.1
1950	Bro-N	0	0	—	5	0	0	0	0	9	14	1	5	3	19.0	5.00	82	.378	.452	0	—	-1	-1	-0	-0	0.0
Total	2	2	0	1.000	14	4	1	0	0	36	42	2	20	13	15.5	4.00	97	.294	.380	2	.250	-0	-0	-0	-0	0.1

● **GREG ERARDI**   Erardi, Joseph Gregory   b: 5/31/54, Syracuse, N.Y.   BR/TR, 6'1", 190 lbs.   Deb: 9/6/77

| 1977 | Sea-A | 0 | 1 | .000 | 5 | 0 | 0 | 0 | 0 | 9 | 12 | 3 | 6 | 5 | 18.0 | 4.00 | 69 | .300 | .391 | 0 | — | -0 | -2 | -2 | -0 | -0.2 |

● **EDDIE ERAUTT**   Erautt, Edward Lorenz Sebastian   b: 9/26/24, Portland, Ore.   BR/TR, 6', 186 lbs.   Deb: 4/16/47   F

1947	Cin-N	4	9	.308	36	10	2	0	0	119	146	5	53	43	15.2	5.07	81	.307	.379	2	.069	-1	-13	-13	-1	-1.3
1948	Cin-N	0	0	—	2	0	0	0	0	3	3	0	1	0	12.0	6.00	65	.250	.308	0	—	-1	-1	-0	-0	0.0
1949	Cin-N	4	11	.267	39	9	1	0	0	112²	99	9	61	43	13.0	3.36	125	.241	.351	4	.174	-0	**9**	**10**	-1	1.2
1950	Cin-N	4	2	.667	33	2	1	0	1	65¹	82	9	22	35	15.2	5.65	75	.307	.373	2	.154	-0	-11	-10	-0	-0.9
1951	Cin-N	0	0	—	30	0	0	0	0	39¹	51	2	23	20	17.4	5.72	71	.314	.411	0	.000	-1	-8	-7	1	0.0
1953	Cin-N	0	0	—	4	0	0	0	0	4²	11	1	3	2	27.0	5.79	75	.500	.560	0	.000	-1	-1	-0	0	0.0
	StL-N	3	1	.750	20	1	0	0	0	35²	43	6	16	15	15.4	6.31	67	.299	.377	1	.167	-1	-8	-8	-0	-0.8
	Yr	3	1	.750	24	1	0	0	0	40¹	54	7	19	16	16.7	6.25	68	.325	.401	1	.143	-1	-9	-9	-0	-0.8
Total	6	15	23	.395	164	22	4	0	2	379²	434	34	179	157	14.9	4.86	86	.293	.376	9	.120	-4	-33	-29	-0	-1.8

● **JOHN ERICKS**   Ericks, John Edward   b: 6/16/67, Tinley Park, Ill.   BR/TR, 6'7", 220 lbs.   Deb: 6/24/95

1995	Pit-N	3	9	.250	19	18	1	0	0	106	108	7	50	80	13.6	4.58	94	.263	.346	2	.097	-2	-5	-3	-1	-0.6
1996	Pit-N	4	5	.444	28	4	0	0	8	46²	56	11	19	46	14.5	5.79	76	.292	.355	1	.000	-1	-8	-7	-1	-1.6
Total	2	7	14	.333	47	22	1	0	8	152²	164	18	69	126	13.9	4.95	87	.272	.349	3	.083	-2	-13	-11	-2	-2.2

● **DON ERICKSON**   Erickson, Don Lee   b: 12/13/31, Springfield, Ill.   BR/TR, 6', 175 lbs.   Deb: 9/1/58

| 1958 | Phi-N | 0 | 1 | .000 | 9 | 0 | 0 | 0 | 1 | 11² | 11 | 3 | 9 | 9 | 15.4 | 4.63 | 86 | .244 | .370 | 0 | .000 | -0 | -1 | /A | -0 | -0.1 |

YEAR TM/L	W	L	PCT	G	GS	CG	SH	SV	IP	H	HR	BB	SO	RAT	ERA	ERA+	OAV	OOB	BH	AVG	PB	PR	/A	PD	TPI
● ERIC ERICKSON Erickson, Eric George Adolph b: 3/13/1895, Goteborg, Sweden d: 5/19/65, Jamestown, N.Y. BR/TR, 6'2", 190 lbs. Deb: 10/6/14																									
1914 NY-N	0	1	.000	1	1	0	0	0	5	8	0	3	3	19.8	0.00	—	.364	.440	0	.000	-0	2	1	-0	0.3
1916 Det-A	0	0	—	8	0	0	0	0	16	13	0	8	7	12.4	2.81	102	.220	.324	-0	.000	-1	0	0	-1	-0.1
1918 Det-A	4	5	.444	12	9	8	0	1	94¹	81	2	29	48	10.8	2.48	107	.240	.306	4	.121	-3	3	2	-3	-0.4
1919 Det-A	0	2	.000	3	2	0	0	0	14²	17	0	10	4	17.2	6.75	47	.293	.406	1	.200	-0	-6	-6	0	-0.7
Was-A	6	11	.353	20	15	7	1	0	132	130	7	63	86	13.6	3.95	81	.254	.344	7	.146	-1	-11	-11	-3	-1.7
Yr	6	13	.316	23	17	7	1	0	146²	147	7	73	90	13.9	4.23	76	.258	.349	8	.151	-2	-16	-17	-3	-2.4
1920 Was-A	12	16	.429	39	27	12	0	1	239¹	231	13	128	87	13.9	3.84	97	.264	.365	23	.277	4	-1	-3	-4	-0.3
1921 Was-A	8	10	.444	32	22	9	3	0	179	181	7	65	71	12.8	3.62	114	.269	.341	9	.150	-3	13	10	-3	0.2
1922 Was-A	4	12	.250	30	17	6	2	2	141²	144	8	73	61	14.0	4.96	78	.279	.372	6	.133	-2	-14	-17	-2	-2.1
Total 7	34	57	.374	145	93	42	6	4	822	805	37	379	367	13.3	3.85	93	.264	.352	50	.179	-6	-14	-23	-15	-4.8
● HAL ERICKSON Erickson, Harold James b: 7/17/19, Portland, Ore. BR/TR, 6'5", 230 lbs. Deb: 4/14/53																									
1953 Det-A	0	1	.000	18	0	0	0	1	32¹	43	4	10	19	15.3	4.73	86	.323	.379	0	.000	-1	-3	-2	-0	-0.2
● PAUL ERICKSON Erickson, Paul Walford "Li'L Abner" b: 12/14/15, Zion, Ill. BR/TR, 6'2", 200 lbs. Deb: 6/29/41																									
1941 Chi-N	5	7	.417	32	15	7	1	1	141	126	2	64	85	12.3	3.70	95	.234	.318	7	.152	0	-1	-3	-1	-0.3
1942 Chi-N	1	6	.143	18	7	1	0	0	63	70	4	41	26	15.9	5.43	59	.288	.391	3	.143	-1	-15	-16	0	-1.7
1943 Chi-N	1	3	.250	15	4	0	0	0	42²	47	4	22	24	15.0	6.12	55	.280	.370	3	.200	-0	-13	-13	-1	-1.2
1944 Chi-N	5	9	.357	33	15	5	3	1	124¹	113	5	67	82	13.0	3.55	100	.243	.338	2	.056	-1	1	-0	2	0.0
1945 *Chi-N	7	4	.636	28	9	3	0	3	108¹	94	5	48	53	12.4	3.32	110	.233	.325	5	.156	-0	6	4	-0	0.4
1946 Chi-N	9	7	.563	32	14	5	1	0	137	119	6	70	69	12.3	2.43	137	.232	.321	2	.050	-4	15	14	-1	1.0
1947 Chi-N	7	12	.368	40	20	6	0	1	174	179	17	93	82	14.3	4.34	91	.268	.362	15	.250	3	-8	-7	-1	-0.4
1948 Chi-N	0	0	—	3	0	0	0	0	5²	7	0	6	4	20.6	6.35	61	.292	.433	0	.000	-0	-2	-2	-0	-0.2
Phi-N	2	0	1.000	4	2	0	0	0	17¹	19	2	17	5	18.7	5.19	76	.292	.439	1	.143	-0	-2	-2	-0	-0.2
NY-N	0	0	—	2	0	0	0	0	1	0	0	2	1	18.0	0.00	—	.000	.400	0	—	-0	1	1	0	0.0
Yr	2	0	1.000	9	2	0	0	0	24	26	2	25	10	19.1	5.25	75	.283	.436	1	.125	-0	-3	-4	-0	-0.2
Total 8	37	48	.435	207	86	27	5	6	814¹	774	41	425	432	13.5	3.86	93	.250	.345	38	.147	-2	-16	-26	-0	-2.4
● RALPH ERICKSON Erickson, Ralph Lief b: 6/25/02, Dubois, Idaho BL/TL, 6'1", 175 lbs. Deb: 9/11/29																									
1929 Pit-N	0	0	—	1	0	0	0	0	1	2	0	2	0	36.0	27.00	18	.500	.667	0	—	-0	-2	-2	-0	0.0
1930 Pit-N	1	0	1.000	7	0	0	0	0	14	21	1	10	2	19.9	7.07	70	.375	.470	1	.250	-0	-3	-3	-0	-0.2
Total 2	1	0	1.000	8	0	0	0	0	15	23	1	12	2	21.0	8.40	59	.383	.486	1	.250	-0	-6	-6	-0	-0.2
● ROGER ERICKSON Erickson, Roger Farrell b: 8/30/56, Springfield, Ill. BR/TR, 6'3", 190 lbs. Deb: 4/6/78																									
1978 Min-A	14	13	.519	37	37	14	0	0	265²	268	19	79	121	12.0	3.96	96	.263	.321	0	—	0	-6	-4	-0	-0.4
1979 Min-A	3	10	.231	24	21	0	0	0	123	154	17	48	47	14.9	5.63	78	.310	.372	0	—	0	-19	-17	-0	-1.7
1980 Min-A	7	13	.350	32	27	7	0	0	191¹	198	13	56	97	12.1	3.25	134	.268	.322	0	—	0	17	24	-0	2.3
1981 Min-A	3	8	.273	14	14	1	0	0	91¹	93	7	31	44	12.2	3.84	103	.262	.321	0	—	0	-2	1	-0	-0.1
1982 Min-A	4	3	.571	7	7	2	0	0	40²	56	6	12	12	15.3	4.87	87	.326	.373	0	—	0	-4	-3	-1	-0.4
NY-A	4	5	.444	16	11	0	0	1	70²	86	5	17	37	13.1	4.46	89	.301	.340	0	—	0	-3	-4	-1	-0.5
Yr	8	8	.500	23	18	2	0	1	111¹	142	11	29	49	13.8	4.61	89	.308	.349	0	—	0	-7	-7	-1	-0.9
1983 NY-A	0	1	.000	5	0	0	0	0	16²	13	1	8	7	11.3	4.32	90	.213	.304	0	—	0	-1	0	0	0.2
Total 6	35	53	.398	135	117	24	0	1	799¹	868	68	251	365	12.8	4.13	99	.277	.334	0	—	0	-18	-4	-1	-0.6
● SCOTT ERICKSON Erickson, Scott Gavin b: 2/2/68, Long Beach, Cal. BR/TR, 6'4", 220 lbs. Deb: 6/25/90																									
1990 Min-A	8	4	.667	19	17	1	0	0	113	108	9	51	53	13.1	2.87	145	.256	.343	0	—	0	13	16	-0	1.6
1991 *Min-A	**20**	8	**.714**	32	32	5	3	0	204	189	13	71	108	11.7	3.18	134	.248	.317	0	—	0	21	25	1	3.1
1992 Min-A	13	12	.520	32	32	5	3	0	212	197	18	83	101	12.2	3.40	119	.252	.330	0	—	0	13	15	2	1.8
1993 Min-A	8	19	.296	34	34	1	0	0	218²	266	17	71	116	14.3	5.19	84	.305	.364	0	—	0	-21	-20	1	-2.0
1994 Min-A	8	11	.421	23	23	2	1	0	144	173	15	59	104	15.1	5.44	90	.299	.372	0	—	0	-10	-9	1	-0.9
1995 Min-A	4	6	.400	15	15	0	0	0	87²	102	11	32	45	14.2	5.95	80	.291	.357	0	—	0	-12	-12	2	-0.9
Bal-A	9	4	.692	17	16	7	2	0	108²	111	7	35	61	12.2	3.89	122	.273	.332	0	—	0	10	10	3	1.3
Yr	13	10	.565	32	31	7	2	0	196¹	213	18	67	106	12.9	4.81	99	.279	.338	0	—	0	-2	-1	4	0.4
1996 *Bal-A	13	12	.520	34	34	6	0	0	222¹	262	21	66	100	13.7	5.02	98	.297	.354	0	—	0	-1	-3	4	0.2
Total 7	83	76	.522	206	203	27	9	0	1310¹	1408	111	468	688	13.3	4.33	104	.279	.346	0	—	0	13	24	13	4.2
● DICK ERRICKSON Errickson, Richard Merriwell "Lief" b: 3/5/14, Vineland, N.J. BL/TR, 6'1", 175 lbs. Deb: 4/27/38																									
1938 Bos-N	9	7	.563	34	10	6	1	6	122²	113	1	56	40	12.5	3.15	109	.246	.330	4	.114	-1	9	4	2	0.5
1939 Bos-N	6	9	.400	28	11	3	0	1	128¹	143	6	54	33	13.9	4.00	92	.293	.365	10	.227	1	-1	-4	2	-0.2
1940 Bos-N	12	13	.480	34	29	17	3	4	236¹	241	8	90	34	12.6	3.16	118	.270	.338	13	.157	-2	18	15	1	1.4
1941 Bos-N	6	12	.333	38	23	5	2	2	165²	192	12	62	45	14.0	4.78	75	.287	.351	8	.178	-0	-21	-22	1	-2.2
1942 Bos-N	2	5	.286	21	4	0	0	1	59¹	76	8	20	15	14.6	5.01	67	.309	.361	2	.125	-1	-11	-11	-1	-1.4
Chi-N	1	1	.500	13	0	0	0	0	24	39	1	8	9	18.0	4.13	78	.411	.462	0	.000	-1	-2	-1	1	-0.2
Yr	3	6	.333	34	4	0	0	1	83¹	115	9	28	24	15.6	4.75	69	.337	.389	2	.095	-1	-13	-13	-0	-1.6
Total 5	36	47	.434	168	77	31	6	13	736¹	804	36	290	176	13.5	3.85	94	.282	.350	37	.162	-5	-9	-21	5	-2.1
● CARL ERSKINE Erskine, Carl Daniel "Oisk" b: 12/13/26, Anderson, Ind. BR/TR, 5'10", 165 lbs. Deb: 7/25/48																									
1948 Bro-N	6	3	.667	17	9	3	0	0	64	51	5	35	29	12.2	3.23	124	.231	.339	2	.095	-2	5	5	-1	0.4
1949 *Bro-N	8	1	.889	22	3	2	0	0	79²	68	6	51	49	13.7	4.63	89	.235	.354	3	.115	-2	-5	-5	0	-0.6
1950 Bro-N	7	6	.538	22	13	3	0	1	103	109	15	35	50	12.7	4.72	87	.273	.333	9	.243	-2	-7	-7	-1	-0.7
1951 Bro-N	16	12	.571	46	19	7	0	4	189²	206	23	78	95	13.6	4.46	88	.283	.351	8	.131	-2	-11	-11	-0	-1.8
1952 *Bro-N	14	6	.700	33	26	10	4	2	206²	167	17	71	131	10.5	2.70	135	.220	.289	10	.152	-0	24	22	2	2.3
1953 *Bro-N	20	6	**.769**	39	33	16	4	3	246²	213	21	95	187	11.3	3.54	120	.230	.304	20	.215	-0	20	20	2	1.7
1954 Bro-N★	18	15	.545	38	37	12	2	1	260¹	239	21	92	166	11.6	4.15	98	.243	.311	14	.159	-1	-2	-2	-0	-0.4
1955 *Bro-N	11	8	.579	31	29	7	2	1	194²	185	29	64	84	11.5	3.79	107	.253	.313	15	.203	-0	5	6	-2	0.3
1956 *Bro-N	13	11	.542	31	28	6	1	0	186¹	189	25	57	95	11.9	4.25	93	.264	.320	8	.121	-3	-10	-6	-1	-1.0
1957 Bro-N	5	3	.625	15	7	1	0	0	66	62	8	20	26	11.2	3.55	118	.248	.304	2	.091	-2	5	5	-1	0.2
1958 LA-N	4	4	.500	31	9	2	1	0	98¹	115	14	35	54	13.7	5.13	80	.297	.355	1	.037	-3	-13	-11	-1	-1.0
1959 LA-N	0	3	.000	10	3	0	0	0	23¹	33	5	13	15	17.7	7.71	55	.320	.397	0	.000	-1	-10	-9	-0	-1.2
Total 12	122	78	.610	335	216	71	14	13	1718²	1637	199	646	981	12.0	4.00	101	.252	.321	92	.156	-13	0	6	-4	-1.8
● CHICO ESCARREGA Escarrega, Ernesto (Acosta) b: 12/27/49, Los Mochis, Mex. BR/TR, 5'11", 185 lbs. Deb: 4/26/82																									
1982 Chi-A	1	3	.250	38	2	0	0	1	73²	73	3	16	33	10.9	3.67	110	.263	.303	0	—	0	3	3	-1	0.1
● VAUGHN ESHELMAN Eshelman, Vaughn Michael b: 5/22/69, Philadelphia, Pa. BL/TL, 6'3", 205 lbs. Deb: 5/2/95																									
1995 Bos-A	6	3	.667	23	14	0	0	0	81²	86	3	36	41	13.6	4.85	100	.272	.348	0	—	0	-1	0	-1	-0.1
1996 Bos-A	6	3	.667	39	10	0	0	0	87²	112	13	58	59	17.7	7.08	73	.311	.410	0	—	0	-20	-19	-0	-1.6
Total 2	12	6	.667	62	24	0	0	0	169¹	198	16	94	100	15.7	6.01	83	.293	.382	0	—	0	-21	-19	-0	-1.7
● DUKE ESPER Esper, Charles H. b: 7/28/1868, Salem, N.J. d: 8/31/10, Philadelphia, Pa. TL, 5'11.5", 185 lbs. Deb: 4/18/1890																									
1890 Phi-a	8	9	.471	18	16	14	1	0	143²	176	1	67	61	15.5	4.89	78	.292	.368	18	.295	4	-16	-17	1	-1.1
Pit-N	0	2	.000	2	2	1	0	0	17	18	0	10	9	15.4	5.29	62	.265	.367	1	.143	-1	-3	-4	0	-0.3
Phi-N	5	0	1.000	5	5	4	0	0	41	40	1	16	18	12.3	3.07	119	.248	.316	3	.158	-1	2	2	0	0.1
Yr	5	2	.714	7	7	6	0	0	58	58	1	26	27	13.0	3.72	95	.252	.328	4	.154	-2	-1	-1	1	-0.1
1891 Phi-N	20	15	.571	39	36	25	1	1	296	302	8	121	108	13.1	3.56	96	.254	.327	27	.220	1	-5	-1	-5	-0.4
1892 Phi-N	11	6	.647	21	18	14	1	0	160¹	171	2	58	45	12.9	3.42	95	.262	.323	17	.243	2	-7	-2	-2	-0.2
Pit-N	2	0	1.000	3	3	1	0	0	18¹	18	0	12	5	14.7	5.40	61	.247	.353	0	.000	-1	-4	-4	-0	-0.5
Yr	13	6	.684	24	21	15	0	1	178²	189	2	70	50	13.0	3.63	90	.260	.325	17	.215	0	-7	-1	-1	-0.7
1893 Was-N	12	28	.300	42	36	34	0	0	334¹	442	14	156	78	16.4	4.71	98	.309	.395	14	.287	2	1	5	0	0.4
1894 Was-N	5	10	.333	18	14	7	0	0	116	177	8	39	24	16.9	7.45	71	.346	.395	14	.259	1	-27	-28	0	-2.3

YEAR	TM/L	W	L	PCT	G	GS	CG	SH	SV	IP	H	HR	BB	SO	RAT	ERA	ERA+	OAV	OOB	BH	AVG	PB	PR	/A	PD	TPI
	*Bal-N	10	2	.833	16	9	8	0	2	101	107	1	36	25	12.8	3.92	139	.269	.331	10	.222	-1	16	17	1	1.5
	Yr	15	12	.556	34	23	15	0	2	217	284	9	75	49	14.9	5.81	92	.312	.365	24	.242	0	-12	-11	1	-0.8
1895	*Bal-N	10	12	.455	34	25	16	1	1	218¹	248	2	79	39	13.5	3.92	122	.281	.341	16	.178	-6	21	20	-2	0.8
1896	Bal-N	14	5	.737	20	18	14	1	0	155²	168	3	39	19	12.1	3.58	119	.273	.319	13	.197	-2	13	12	-2	0.7
1897	StL-N	1	6	.143	8	8	7	0	0	61¹	95	5	12	8	15.8	5.28	83	.351	.380	8	.320	1	-7	-6	1	-0.3
1898	StL-N	3	5	.375	10	8	6	0	0	64²	86	1	22	14	15.0	5.98	63	.316	.367	10	.370	2	-17	-16	0	-1.4
Total	9	101	100	.502	236	198	152	4	5	1727²	2048	46	667	453	14.3	4.39	96	.288	.351	178	.241	5	-33	-33	1	-2.9

● **NINO ESPINOSA** Espinosa, Arnulfo Acevedo (b: Arnulfo Acevedo (Espinosa))
b: 8/15/53, Villa Altagracia, D.R. d: 12/24/87, Villa Altagracia, D.R. BR/TR, 6'1", 192 lbs. Deb: 9/13/74

YEAR	TM/L	W	L	PCT	G	GS	CG	SH	SV	IP	H	HR	BB	SO	RAT	ERA	ERA+	OAV	OOB	BH	AVG	PB	PR	/A	PD	TPI
1974	NY-N	0	0	—	2	1	0	0	0	9	12	1	0	2	12.0	5.00	71	.324	.324	1	.500	0	-1	-1	0	0.0
1975	NY-N	0	1	.000	2	0	0	0	0	3	8	0	1	2	27.0	18.00	19	.471	.500	0	—	0	-5	-5	-0	-1.1
1976	NY-N	4	4	.500	12	5	0	0	0	41²	41	3	13	30	11.7	3.67	90	.265	.321	0	.000	-1	-1	-2	-1	-0.5
1977	NY-N	10	13	.435	32	29	7	1	0	200	188	17	55	105	11.2	3.42	109	.249	.304	8	.129	-1	11	7	-0	0.6
1978	NY-N	11	15	.423	32	32	6	1	0	203²	230	24	75	76	13.6	4.73	74	.292	.355	14	.209	2	-26	-28	2	-2.8
1979	Phi-N	14	12	.538	33	33	8	3	0	212	211	20	65	88	11.8	3.65	105	.262	.319	14	.194	2	2	4	0	0.6
1980	Phi-N	3	5	.375	12	12	1	0	0	76¹	73	9	19	13	11.1	3.77	100	.250	.300	3	.115	-1	-1	-0	-1	-0.2
1981	Phi-N	2	5	.286	14	14	2	0	0	73²	98	11	24	22	15.0	6.11	59	.333	.386	4	.200	-1	-21	-20	-1	-1.8
	Tor-A	0	0	—	1	0	0	0	0	1	4	0	0	0	36.0	9.00	44	.667	.667	0	—	0	-1	-1	-0	-0.2
Total	8	44	55	.444	140	126	24	5	0	820¹	865	85	252	338	12.4	4.17	88	.275	.331	44	.171	1	-44	-46	0	-5.4

● **ALVARO ESPINOZA** Espinoza, Alvaro Alberto b: 2/19/62, Valencia, Venez. BR/TR, 6', 170 lbs. Deb: 9/14/84 ♦

YEAR	TM/L	W	L	PCT	G	GS	CG	SH	SV	IP	H	HR	BB	SO	RAT	ERA	ERA+	OAV	OOB	BH	AVG	PB	PR	/A	PD	TPI
1991	NY-A	0	0	—	1	0	0	0	0	0²	0	0	0	0	0.0	0.00	—	.000	.000	123	.256	1	0	0	0	0.0

● **MARK ESSER** Esser, Mark Gerald b: 4/1/56, Erie, Pa. BR/TL, 6'1", 190 lbs. Deb: 4/22/79

YEAR	TM/L	W	L	PCT	G	GS	CG	SH	SV	IP	H	HR	BB	SO	RAT	ERA	ERA+	OAV	OOB	BH	AVG	PB	PR	/A	PD	TPI
1979	Chi-A	0	0	—	2	0	0	0	0	1²	2	0	4	1	32.4	16.20	26	.286	.545	0	—	0	-2	-2	-0	0.0

● **BILL ESSICK** Essick, William Earl "Vinegar Bill" b: 12/18/1881, Grand Ridge, Ill. d: 10/12/51, Los Angeles, Cal. TR, 5'10", 175 lbs. Deb: 9/12/06

YEAR	TM/L	W	L	PCT	G	GS	CG	SH	SV	IP	H	HR	BB	SO	RAT	ERA	ERA+	OAV	OOB	BH	AVG	PB	PR	/A	PD	TPI
1906	Cin-N	2	2	.500	6	4	3	0	0	39¹	39	1	16	16	13.0	2.97	93	.273	.354	1	.077	-1	-1	-1	-1	-0.3
1907	Cin-N	0	2	.000	3	2	2	0	0	21²	23	0	8	7	13.3	2.91	89	.274	.344	0	.000	-1	-1	-1	1	-0.1
Total	2	2	4	.333	9	6	5	0	0	61	62	1	24	23	13.1	2.95	91	.273	.350	1	.048	-2	-3	-2	0	-0.4

● **DICK ESTELLE** Estelle, Richard Henry b: 1/18/42, Lakewood, N.J. BB/TL, 6'2", 170 lbs. Deb: 9/4/64

YEAR	TM/L	W	L	PCT	G	GS	CG	SH	SV	IP	H	HR	BB	SO	RAT	ERA	ERA+	OAV	OOB	BH	AVG	PB	PR	/A	PD	TPI
1964	SF-N	1	2	.333	6	6	0	0	0	41²	39	3	23	23	13.4	3.02	118	.247	.343	1	.067	-1	2	3	-1	0.0
1965	SF-N	0	0	—	6	1	0	0	0	11¹	12	0	8	6	16.7	3.97	91	.261	.382	0	.000	-0	-1	-0	0	0.0
Total	2	1	2	.333	12	7	0	0	0	53	51	3	31	29	14.1	3.23	111	.250	.352	1	.063	-1	1	2	-1	0.0

● **SHAWN ESTES** Estes, Aaron Shawn b: 2/18/73, San Bernardino, Cal. BB/TL, 6'2", 185 lbs. Deb: 9/16/95

YEAR	TM/L	W	L	PCT	G	GS	CG	SH	SV	IP	H	HR	BB	SO	RAT	ERA	ERA+	OAV	OOB	BH	AVG	PB	PR	/A	PD	TPI
1995	SF-N	0	3	.000	3	3	0	0	0	17¹	16	2	5	14	11.4	6.75	60	.229	.289	0	.000	-1	-5	-5	-0	-0.8
1996	SF-N	3	5	.375	11	11	0	0	0	70	63	3	39	60	13.4	3.60	114	.243	.347	3	.158	-0	5	4	0	0.4
Total	2	3	8	.273	14	14	0	0	0	87¹	79	5	44	74	13.0	4.23	97	.240	.335	3	.125	-1	-0	-1	-0	-0.4

● **GEORGE ESTOCK** Estock, George John b: 11/2/24, Stirling, N.J. BR/TR, 6', 185 lbs. Deb: 4/21/51

YEAR	TM/L	W	L	PCT	G	GS	CG	SH	SV	IP	H	HR	BB	SO	RAT	ERA	ERA+	OAV	OOB	BH	AVG	PB	PR	/A	PD	TPI
1951	Bos-N	0	1	.000	36	0	0	0	3	60	56	7	27	18	12.8	4.33	85	.258	.366	2	.286	1	-4	-4	0	-0.1

● **CHUCK ESTRADA** Estrada, Charles Leonard b: 2/15/38, San Luis Obispo, Cal. BR/TR, 6'1", 185 lbs. Deb: 4/21/60 C

YEAR	TM/L	W	L	PCT	G	GS	CG	SH	SV	IP	H	HR	BB	SO	RAT	ERA	ERA+	OAV	OOB	BH	AVG	PB	PR	/A	PD	TPI
1960	Bal-A★	**18**	11	.621	36	25	12	1	2	208²	162	18	101	144	12.0	3.58	106	**.218**	.323	9	.141	-0	7	5	-0	0.6
1961	Bal-A	15	9	.625	33	31	6	1	0	212	159	19	132	160	12.8	3.69	104	**.207**	.331	8	.114	-3	8	4	-2	-0.2
1962	Bal-A	9	17	.346	34	33	6	0	0	223¹	199	24	121	165	13.3	3.83	97	.240	.343	10	.152	-0	3	-3	-3	-0.6
1963	Bal-A	3	2	.600	8	7	0	0	0	31¹	26	2	19	16	13.2	4.60	76	.226	.341	1	.100	-1	-3	-4	-1	-0.7
1964	Bal-A	3	2	.600	17	6	0	0	0	54²	62	8	21	32	14.0	5.27	68	.282	.350	2	.143	-0	-10	-10	-1	-1.0
1966	Chi-N	1	1	.500	9	1	0	0	0	12¹	16	2	5	3	16.1	7.30	50	.314	.386	0	.000	-0	-5	-5	-0	-0.8
1967	NY-N	1	2	.333	9	2	0	0	0	22	28	5	17	15	18.8	9.41	36	.326	.442	0	—	-1	-15	-15	-0	-1.8
Total	7	50	44	.532	146	105	24	2	2	764¹	652	78	416	535	13.0	4.07	92	.232	.339	30	.129	-5	-15	-28	-8	-4.5

● **OSCAR ESTRADA** Estrada, Oscar b: 2/15/04, Havana, Cuba d: 1/2/78, Havana, Cuba BL/TL, 5'8", 160 lbs. Deb: 4/21/29

YEAR	TM/L	W	L	PCT	G	GS	CG	SH	SV	IP	H	HR	BB	SO	RAT	ERA	ERA+	OAV	OOB	BH	AVG	PB	PR	/A	PD	TPI
1929	StL-A	0	0	—	1	0	0	0	0	1	1	0	1	0	18.0	0.00	—	.250	.400	0	—	0	0	0	0	0.0

● **MARK ETTLES** Ettles, Mark Edward b: 10/30/66, Perth, Australia BR/TR, 6', 178 lbs. Deb: 6/5/93

YEAR	TM/L	W	L	PCT	G	GS	CG	SH	SV	IP	H	HR	BB	SO	RAT	ERA	ERA+	OAV	OOB	BH	AVG	PB	PR	/A	PD	TPI
1993	SD-N	1	0	1.000	14	0	0	0	0	18	23	4	4	9	13.5	6.50	64	.307	.342	0	—	-0	-5	-5	0	-0.2

● **JOHN EUBANK** Eubank, John Franklin "Honest John" b: 9/9/1872, Servia, Ind. d: 11/3/58, Bellevue, Mich. BR/TR, 6'2", 215 lbs. Deb: 9/19/05

YEAR	TM/L	W	L	PCT	G	GS	CG	SH	SV	IP	H	HR	BB	SO	RAT	ERA	ERA+	OAV	OOB	BH	AVG	PB	PR	/A	PD	TPI
1905	Det-A	1	0	1.000	3	2	0	0	0	17¹	13	0	3	1	8.8	2.08	132	.210	.258	5	.357	1	1	1	-1	0.2
1906	Det-A	4	10	.286	24	12	7	1	2	135	147	4	35	38	12.7	3.53	78	.280	.335	13	.206	0	-13	-12	1	-1.1
1907	Det-A	3	3	.500	15	8	4	1	0	81	88	0	20	17	12.0	2.67	98	.279	.322	4	.129	-1	-1	-1	1	-0.1
Total	3	8	13	.381	42	22	11	2	2	233¹	248	0	58	56	12.1	3.12	87	.275	.325	22	.204	0	-13	-11	1	-1.0

● **UEL EUBANKS** Eubanks, Uel Melvin "Poss" b: 2/14/03, Quinlan, Tex. d: 11/21/54, Dallas, Tex. BR/TR, 6'3", 175 lbs. Deb: 7/20/22

YEAR	TM/L	W	L	PCT	G	GS	CG	SH	SV	IP	H	HR	BB	SO	RAT	ERA	ERA+	OAV	OOB	BH	AVG	PB	PR	/A	PD	TPI
1922	Chi-N	0	0	—	2	0	0	0	0	1²	5	0	4	1	48.6	27.00	16	.556	.692	1	1.000	1	-4	-4	0	0.1

● **FRANK EUFEMIA** Eufemia, Frank Anthony b: 12/23/59, Bronx, N.Y. BR/TR, 5'11", 185 lbs. Deb: 5/21/85

YEAR	TM/L	W	L	PCT	G	GS	CG	SH	SV	IP	H	HR	BB	SO	RAT	ERA	ERA+	OAV	OOB	BH	AVG	PB	PR	/A	PD	TPI
1985	Min-A	4	2	.667	39	0	0	0	2	61²	56	7	21	30	11.2	3.79	116	.250	.314	0	—	0	2	4	1	0.4

● **CHICK EVANS** Evans, Charles Franklin b: 10/15/1889, Arlington, Vt. d: 9/2/16, Schenectady, N.Y. BR/TR, Deb: 9/19/09

YEAR	TM/L	W	L	PCT	G	GS	CG	SH	SV	IP	H	HR	BB	SO	RAT	ERA	ERA+	OAV	OOB	BH	AVG	PB	PR	/A	PD	TPI
1909	Bos-N	0	3	.000	4	3	1	0	0	21²	25	0	14	11	16.2	4.57	62	.305	.406	0	.000	-1	-5	-4	-0	-0.7
1910	Bos-N	1	1	.500	13	1	0	0	2	31	33	1	27	12	16.8	5.23	64	.275	.439	1	.100	-1	-8	-7	0	-0.5
Total	2	1	4	.200	17	4	1	0	2	52²	58	1	41	23	16.6	4.96	63	.288	.425	1	.053	-2	-12	-11	-0	-1.2

● **ROY EVANS** Evans, Roy b: 3/19/1874, Knoxville, Tenn. d: 8/15/15, Galveston, Tex. BR/TR, 6', 180 lbs. Deb: 5/15/1897

YEAR	TM/L	W	L	PCT	G	GS	CG	SH	SV	IP	H	HR	BB	SO	RAT	ERA	ERA+	OAV	OOB	BH	AVG	PB	PR	/A	PD	TPI
1897	StL-N	0	0	—	3	0	0	0	0	13	33	1	13	4	31.8	9.69	45	.471	.554	0	.000	—	-8	-8	-0	0.0
	Lou-N	5	4	.556	9	8	6	0	0	59¹	66	4	24	20	14.9	4.10	104	.280	.366	3	.130	-2	1	1	-1	-0.1
	Yr	5	4	.556	12	8	6	0	0	72¹	99	5	37	24	17.9	5.10	84	.324	.410	3	.115	-2	-6	-7	-1	-0.1
1898	Was-N	3	3	.500	7	6	4	0	0	50²	50	0	25	11	14.6	3.38	109	.256	.361	1	.053	-2	1	2	-1	0.0
1899	Was-N	3	4	.429	7	7	6	0	0	54	60	1	25	27	14.2	5.67	69	.280	.356	4	.200	-1	-11	-11	0	-1.1
1902	NY-N	8	13	.381	23	17	17	0	0	176	186	2	58	48	12.9	3.17	89	.271	.336	8	.148	-1	-8	-7	-2	-0.7
	Bro-N	5	6	.455	13	11	11	2	0	97¹	91	0	33	35	11.7	2.68	103	.247	.313	9	.265	2	1	1	-3	0.0
	Yr	13	19	.406	36	28	28	2	0	273²	277	2	91	83	12.2	3.00	93	.261	.320	17	.193	1	-7	-6	-2	-0.7
1903	Bro-N	9	9	.357	15	12	9	0	0	110	121	1	41	42	13.8	3.27	98	.297	.371	5	.172	-0	-1	-1	-1	-0.2
	StL-A	0	4	.000	7	7	4	0	0	54	66	0	14	24	13.8	4.17	70	.300	.350	2	.105	-1	-7	-8	0	-0.6
Total	5	29	43	.403	84	68	57	2	0	614¹	673	10	233	211	13.8	3.66	88	.281	.353	32	.159	-4	-30	-30	-5	-2.8

● **RED EVANS** Evans, Russell Edison b: 11/12/06, Chicago, Ill. d: 6/14/82, Lakeview, Ark. BR/TR, 5'11", 168 lbs. Deb: 4/24/36

YEAR	TM/L	W	L	PCT	G	GS	CG	SH	SV	IP	H	HR	BB	SO	RAT	ERA	ERA+	OAV	OOB	BH	AVG	PB	PR	/A	PD	TPI
1936	Chi-A	0	3	.000	17	0	0	0	1	47¹	70	4	22	19	17.5	7.61	68	.338	.402	2	.133	-1	-14	-13	1	-0.7
1939	Bro-N	1	8	.111	24	6	0	0	1	64¹	74	4	26	28	14.0	5.18	78	.284	.359	4	.308	1	-9	-8	1	-0.8
Total	2	1	11	.083	41	6	0	0	2	111²	144	8	48	47	15.5	6.21	73	.308	.372	6	.214	-0	-23	-21	3	-1.5

● **JAKE EVANS** Evans, Uriah L. P. "Bloody Jake" b: 9/1856, Baltimore, Md. d: 1/16/07, Baltimore, Md. TR, 5'8", 154 lbs. Deb: 5/1/1879 ♦

YEAR	TM/L	W	L	PCT	G	GS	CG	SH	SV	IP	H	HR	BB	SO	RAT	ERA	ERA+	OAV	OOB	BH	AVG	PB	PR	/A	PD	TPI
1880	Tro-N	0	0	—	1	0	0	0	0	4	11	0	0	0	24.8	13.50	19	.524	.524	46	.256	0	-5	-5	0	0.0
1882	Wor-N	0	1	.000	1	1	1	0	0	8	13	1	0	2	14.6	5.63	55	.317	.317	71	.213	-0	-2	-2	-0	-0.2
1883	Cle-N	0	0	—	1	0	0	0	0	3	0	0	0	1	3.0	0.00	—	.000	.000	79	.238	0	1	1	0	0.1
Total	3	0	1	.000	3	1	1	0	0	15	24	1	0	3	14.4	6.60	45	.338	.338	435	.238	-0	-6	-6	1	-0.1

YEAR TM/L	W	L	PCT	G	GS	CG	SH	SV	IP	H	HR	BB	SO	RAT	ERA	ERA+	OAV	OOB	BH	AVG	PB	PR	/A	PD	TPI
● **ART EVANS** Evans, William Arthur b: 8/3/11, Elvins, Mo. d: 1/8/52, Wichita, Kan. BB/TL, 6'1.5", 181 lbs. Deb: 6/20/32																								
1932 Chi-A	0	0	—	7	0	0	0	0	18	19	1	10	6	14.5	3.00	144	.257	.345	0	.000	-0	3	3	1	0.0
● **BILL EVANS** Evans, William James b: 2/10/1894, Reidsville, N.C. d: 12/21/46, Burlington, N.C. BR/TR, 6', 175 lbs. Deb: 8/13/16																								
1916 Pit-N	2	5	.286	13	7	3	0	0	63	57	2	16	21	10.9	3.00	89	.249	.306	3	.150	-1	-3	-2	2	-0.1
1917 Pit-N	0	4	.000	8	2	1	0	0	26²	24	0	14	5	13.2	3.38	84	.231	.328	1	.111	-0	-2	-2	-1	-0.3
1919 Pit-N	0	4	.000	7	3	2	0	0	36²	41	1	18	15	14.5	5.65	54	.297	.378	0	.000	-1	-11	-11	-1	-1.1
Total 3	2	13	.133	28	12	6	0	0	126¹	122	3	48	41	12.4	3.85	73	.259	.333	4	.100	-2	-16	-14	2	-1.5
● **BILL EVANS** Evans, William Lawrence b: 3/25/19, Quanah, Texas d: 11/30/83, Grand Junction, Colo. BR/TR, 6'2", 180 lbs. Deb: 4/21/49																								
1949 Chi-A	0	1	.000	4	0	0	0	0	6¹	6	0	8	1	19.9	7.11	59	.261	.452	0	.000	-0	-2	-2	-0	-0.3
1951 Bos-A	0	0	—	9	0	0	0	0	15¹	15	0	8	3	13.5	4.11	109	.268	.359	0	.000	-1	0	1	-0	-0.1
Total 2	0	1	.000	13	0	0	0	0	21²	21	0	16	4	15.4	4.98	88	.266	.389	0	.000	-1	-2	-1	-1	-0.4
● **LEON EVERITT** Everitt, Edward Leon b: 1/12/47, Marshall, Tex. BL/TR, 6'1.5", 195 lbs. Deb: 4/21/69																								
1969 SD-N	0	1	.000	5	0	0	0	0	15²	18	2	12	11	17.8	8.04	44	.300	.425	0	.000	-0	-8	-8	0	-0.4
● **BRYAN EVERSGERD** Eversgerd, Bryan David b: 2/11/69, Centralia, Ill. BR/TL, 6'1", 190 lbs. Deb: 4/30/94																								
1994 StL-N	2	3	.400	40	1	0	0	0	67²	75	8	20	47	12.9	4.52	92	.295	.351	0	.000	-1	-2	-3	1	-0.2
1995 Mon-N	0	0	—	25	0	0	0	0	21	22	2	9	8	13.7	5.14	83	.268	.348	0	.000	-0	-2	-2	-0	0.0
Total 2	2	3	.400	65	1	0	0	0	88²	97	10	29	55	13.1	4.67	90	.289	.351	0	.000	-1	-5	-5	0	-0.2
● **BOB EWING** Ewing, George Lemuel "Long Bob" b: 4/24/1873, New Hampshire, O. d: 6/20/47, Wapakoneta, Ohio BR/TR, 6'1.5", 170 lbs. Deb: 4/19/02																								
1902 Cin-N	5	6	.455	15	12	10	0	0	117²	126	1	47	44	13.5	2.98	100	.273	.344	12	.169	-1	-3	0	-1	-0.2
1903 Cin-N	14	13	.519	29	28	27	1	1	246²	254	3	64	104	12.0	2.77	128	.265	.317	24	.253	4	14	22	4	2.9
1904 Cin-N	11	13	.458	26	24	22	0	0	212	198	3	58	99	11.0	2.46	119	.253	.308	25	.258	5	7	11	-1	1.6
1905 Cin-N	20	11	.645	40	34	30	4	0	311²	284	5	79	164	10.8	2.51	132	.246	.301	14	.139	-3	8	12	1	0.8
1906 Cin-N	13	14	.481	33	32	26	2	0	287²	248	4	60	145	9.7	2.38	116	.238	.281	14	.149	-3	8	12	1	0.8
1907 Cin-N	17	19	.472	41	37	32	2	0	332²	279	2	85	147	10.0	1.73	150	.231	.286	19	.154	-1	27	32	-6	2.9
1908 Cin-N	17	15	.531	37	32	23	4	3	293²	247	5	57	95	9.5	2.21	105	.241	.284	14	.149	0	5	3	-3	-0.1
1909 Cin-N	11	12	.478	31	29	14	2	0	218¹	195	1	63	86	10.9	2.43	107	.238	.298	8	.110	-4	4	4	-4	-0.5
1910 Phi-N	16	14	.533	34	32	19	0	0	255¹	235	5	86	102	11.6	3.00	104	.251	.318	20	.222	2	1	-4	-2	-0.4
1911 Phi-N	0	1	.000	8	3	1	0	0	24	29	2	14	12	16.1	7.88	44	.309	.398	2	.333	0	-12	-12	0	-0.4
1912 StL-N	0	0	—	1	1	0	0	0	1¹	2	0	1	0	20.3	0.00	—	.333	.429	0	.000	0	1	1	0	0.0
Total 11	124	118	.512	291	264	205	19	4	2301	2097	31	614	998	10.8	2.49	116	.247	.302	170	.195	7	69	102	-16	10.1
● **JOHN EWING** Ewing, John "Long Jong" b: 6/1/1863, Cincinnati, Ohio d: 4/23/1895, Denver, Colo. TR , Deb: 6/18/1883 F♦																								
1888 Lou-a	8	13	.381	21	21	21	2	0	191	175	3	34	87	10.2	2.83	109	.235	.276	16	.203	-2	5	5	0	0.4
1889 Lou-a	6	30	.167	40	39	37	1	0	331	407	6	147	155	15.4	4.87	79	.293	.367	23	.172	-6	-37	-37	2	-3.3
1890 NY-P	18	12	.600	35	31	27	1	2	267¹	294	6	104	145	13.9	4.24	107	.267	.339	24	.211	-3	-0	9	0	0.5
1891 NY-N	21	8	**.724**	33	30	28	5	0	269¹	237	2	105	138	11.8	2.27	141	.227	.305	23	.204	-2	32	28	0	2.3
Total 4	53	63	.457	129	121	113	9	2	1058²	1113	17	390	525	13.2	3.68	101	.260	.329	87	.192	-12	1	3	3	-0.1
● **BUCK EWING** Ewing, William b: 10/17/1859, Hoagland, Ohio d: 10/20/06, Cincinnati, Ohio BR/TR, 5'10", 188 lbs. Deb: 9/9/1880 FMH♦																								
1882 Tro-N	0	0	—	1	0	0	0	0	1	2	0	1	0	27.0	9.00	31	.400	.500	89	.271	0	-1	-1	0	0.0
1884 NY-N	0	1	.000	1	1	1	0	0	8	7	0	4	3	12.4	1.13	265	.241	.333	106	.277	0	2	2	-0	0.2
1885 NY-N	0	1	.000	1	0	0	0	0	2	4	0	3	0	31.5	4.50	59	.444	.583	104	.304	0	-0	-0	-1	-0.2
1888 *NY-N	0	0	—	2	0	0	0	0	7	8	1	4	6	16.7	2.57	107	.174	.255	127	.306	1	0	0	0	0.0
1889 *NY-N	2	0	1.000	3	2	0	0	0	20	23	0	8	12	13.9	4.05	97	.280	.344	133	.327	2	0	1	0	0.1
1890 NY-P	0	1	.000	1	1	1	0	0	9	11	1	3	2	14.0	4.00	114	.289	.341	119	.338	0	-0	-0	0	0.1
Total 6	2	3	.400	9	4	4	0	0	47	55	2	23	23	15.1	3.45	105	.263	.339	1625	.303	4	1	1	-1	0.1
● **GEORGE EYRICH** Eyrich, George Lincoln b: 3/3/25, Reading, Pa. BR/TR, 5'11", 175 lbs. Deb: 6/13/43																								
1943 Phi-N	0	0	—	9	0	0	0	0	18²	27	1	9	5	17.4	3.38	100	.342	.409	0	.000	-0	0	-0	-0	0.0
● **RED FABER** Faber, Urban Charles b: 9/6/1888, Cascade, Iowa d: 9/25/76, Chicago, Ill. BB/TR, 6'2", 180 lbs. Deb: 4/17/14 CH																								
1914 Chi-A	10	9	.526	40	19	11	2	**4**	181¹	154	3	64	88	11.4	2.68	100	.239	.319	8	.145	2	1	0	2	0.3
1915 Chi-A	24	14	.632	**50**	32	21	2	2	299²	264	3	99	182	11.2	2.55	117	.240	.309	11	.131	2	13	14	-0	2.1
1916 Chi-A	17	9	.654	35	25	15	3	1	205¹	167	1	61	87	10.2	2.02	137	.228	.292	6	.095	-3	19	17	2	2.0
1917 *Chi-A	16	13	.552	41	29	16	3	3	248	224	1	85	84	11.6	1.92	138	.245	.319	4	.058	-4	20	20	2	1.2
1918 Chi-A	4	1	.800	11	9	5	1	1	80²	70	3	23	26	10.4	1.23	223	.245	.301	1	.042	-0	14	14	1	0.8
1919 Chi-A	11	9	.550	25	20	9	0	0	162¹	185	7	45	45	13.2	3.83	83	.287	.341	10	.185	-0	-11	-12	0	-1.3
1920 Chi-A	23	13	.639	40	39	28	2	1	319	332	8	88	108	12.2	2.99	126	.277	.328	11	.106	-4	29	28	-1	1.9
1921 Chi-A	25	15	.625	43	39	**32**	4	1	330²	293	10	87	124	**10.5**	2.48	**171**	.242	.297	16	.148	-0	**66**	65	1	**7.0**
1922 Chi-A	21	17	.553	43	38	**31**	4	2	**352**	334	10	83	148	**10.8**	2.81	145	.252	**.299**	25	.200	-2	48	49	-1	4.9
1923 Chi-A	14	11	.560	32	31	15	2	0	232¹	233	6	62	91	11.7	3.41	116	.259	.311	15	.217	3	15	14	2	1.9
1924 Chi-A	9	11	.450	21	20	9	0	0	161¹	173	5	58	47	13.0	3.85	107	.282	.346	8	.148	-2	7	5	-2	0.6
1925 Chi-A	12	11	.522	34	32	16	1	0	238	266	8	59	71	12.4	3.78	110	.289	.333	4	.104	-4	16	10	1	0.6
1926 Chi-A	15	9	.625	27	25	13	1	0	184²	203	3	57	65	12.8	3.56	109	.281	.335	9	.150	-0	9	6	-3	-0.2
1927 Chi-A	4	7	.364	18	17	6	0	0	110²	131	2	41	39	14.4	4.55	89	.312	.380	10	.270	-2	-5	-6	2	-0.2
1928 Chi-A	13	9	.591	27	27	16	2	0	201¹	223	11	68	43	13.2	3.75	108	.286	.347	8	.114	-3	6	7	1	0.4
1929 Chi-A	13	13	.500	31	31	15	1	0	234	241	10	61	68	12.0	3.88	110	.271	.327	10	.123	-3	9	10	2	0.6
1930 Chi-A	8	13	.381	29	26	10	0	1	169	188	7	49	62	12.9	4.21	110	.283	.337	2	.041	-5	8	8	2	0.6
1931 Chi-A	10	14	.417	44	19	5	1	1	184	210	11	57	49	13.2	3.82	112	.285	.339	4	.075	-3	12	9	1	0.6
1932 Chi-A	2	11	.154	42	5	0	0	1	106	123	0	38	26	13.8	3.74	116	.290	.350	4	.222	1	**9**	7	-0	0.3
1933 Chi-A	3	4	.429	36	2	0	0	5	86¹	78	2	28	18	12.6	3.44	123	.275	.332	0	.000	-1	7	6	-1	0.3
Total 20	254	213	.544	669	483	273	29	28	4086²	4106	111	1213	1471	11.9	3.15	119	.266	.323	170	.134	-31	294	274	11	27.0
● **ROY FACE** Face, Elroy Leon b: 2/20/28, Stephentown, N.Y. BR/TR, 5'8", 155 lbs. Deb: 4/16/53																								
1953 Pit-N	6	8	.429	41	13	2	0	0	119	145	19	30	56	13.4	6.58	68	.297	.340	4	.133	-1	-30	-28	-1	-3.0
1955 Pit-N	5	7	.417	42	10	4	0	5	125²	128	10	40	84	12.0	3.58	115	.268	.325	3	.115	-1	6	7	1	0.5
1956 Pit-N	12	13	.480	**68**	3	0	0	6	135¹	131	16	42	96	11.6	3.52	107	.256	.314	5	.192	-0	4	4	1	0.6
1957 Pit-N	4	6	.400	59	1	0	0	10	93²	97	9	24	53	11.7	3.07	123	.270	.318	2	.125	-1	8	7	-2	0.7
1958 Pit-N	5	2	.714	57	0	0	0	**20**	84	77	6	22	47	10.6	2.89	134	.244	.293	0	.000	-1	10	9	1	1.2
1959 Pit-N★	18	1	**.947**	57	0	0	0	10	93¹	91	5	25	69	11.3	2.70	143	.266	.318	3	.231	0	13	12	0	2.6
1960 *Pit-N★	10	8	.556	**68**	0	0	0	24	114²	93	11	29	72	9.6	2.90	129	.226	.277	7	.412	2	11	11	1	2.5
1961 Pit-N★	6	12	.333	62	0	0	0	**17**	92	94	12	10	55	10.3	3.82	105	.267	.289	3	.273	0	2	2	0	0.1
1962 Pit-N	8	7	.533	63	0	0	0	**28**	91	74	7	18	45	9.2	1.88	209	.231	.274	1	.083	-1	**21**	21	-1	4.5
1963 Pit-N	3	9	.250	56	0	0	0	16	69²	75	6	19	41	12.5	3.23	102	.285	.340	2	.250	-0	0	1	0	0.2
1964 Pit-N	3	3	.500	55	0	0	0	4	79²	82	11	27	63	12.4	5.20	68	.269	.325	0	.000	-0	-15	-15	0	-1.2
1965 Pit-N	5	2	.714	16	0	0	0	0	20¹	20	1	7	19	12.0	2.66	132	.263	.325	0	.000	-0	2	1	-0	0.1
1966 Pit-N	6	6	.500	54	0	0	0	18	70	68	9	24	67	12.0	2.70	132	.262	.326	1	.143	-1	7	6	1	0.5
1967 Pit-N	5	5	.583	61	0	0	0	17	74¹	62	5	22	41	10.2	2.42	139	.230	.288	0	.000	-1	7	8	-1	0.5
1968 Pit-N	2	4	.333	43	0	0	0	13	52	46	3	7	34	9.5	2.60	113	.238	.272	0	.000	-1	2	1	0	0.3
Det-A	0	0	—	2	0	0	0	0	2	2	0	0	0	9.0	0.00	—	.250	.600	1	.500	0	-2	-2	-1	-0.2
1969 Mon-N	1	2	.667	44	0	0	0	5	59¹	62	11	15	34	11.7	3.94	93	.263	.307	1	.500	0	-2	-2	-1	-0.2
Total 16	104	95	.523	848	27	6	0	193	1375	1347	141	362	877	11.3	3.48	109	.260	.310	31	.160	-4	48	48	0	13.2
● **TONY FAETH** Faeth, Anthony Joseph b: 7/9/1893, Aberdeen, S.D. d: 12/22/82, St.Paul, Minn. BR/TR, 6', 180 lbs. Deb: 8/10/19																								
1919 Cle-A	0	0	—	6	0	0	0	1	18¹	13	0	10	7	11.3	0.49	682	.224	.338	0	.000	-1	6	6	-0	-0.1

YEAR	TM/L	W	L	PCT	G	GS	CG	SH	SV	IP	H	HR	BB	SO	RAT	ERA	ERA+	OAV	OOB	BH	AVG	PB	PR	/A	PD	TPI
1920	Cle-A	0	0	—	13	0	0	0	0	25	31	0	20	14	18.7	4.32	88	.333	.456	0	.000	-1	-1	-1	-0	-0.1
Total	2	0	0	—	19	0	0	0	0	43¹	44	0	30	21	15.6	2.70	134	.291	.412	0	.000	-1	4	4	-0	-0.2

● EVERETT FAGAN
Fagan, Everett Joseph b: 1/13/18, Pottersville, N.J. d: 2/16/83, Morristown, N.J. BR/TR, 6′, 195 lbs. Deb: 4/24/43

YEAR	TM/L	W	L	PCT	G	GS	CG	SH	SV	IP	H	HR	BB	SO	RAT	ERA	ERA+	OAV	OOB	BH	AVG	PB	PR	/A	PD	TPI
1943	Phi-A	2	6	.250	18	2	0	0	3	37¹	41	4	14	9	13.7	6.27	54	.283	.354	0	.000	-0	-12	-12	-0	-2.5
1946	Phi-A	0	1	.000	20	0	0	0	0	45	47	2	24	12	14.8	4.80	74	.264	.361	4	.286	1	-6	-6	-0	-0.1
Total	2	2	7	.222	38	2	0	0	3	82¹	88	6	38	21	14.3	5.47	64	.272	.358	4	.190	1	-19	-18	-0	-2.6

● BILL FAGAN
Fagan, William A. "Clinkers" b: 2/15/1869, Troy, N.Y. d: 3/21/30, Troy, N.Y. TL, 5′11″, 165 lbs. Deb: 9/15/1887

YEAR	TM/L	W	L	PCT	G	GS	CG	SH	SV	IP	H	HR	BB	SO	RAT	ERA	ERA+	OAV	OOB	BH	AVG	PB	PR	/A	PD	TPI
1887	NY-a	1	4	.200	6	6	6	0	0	45	55	1	24	12	16.2	4.00	106	.306	.393	3	.143	-2	1	1	0	-0.1
1888	KC-a	5	11	.313	17	17	15	0	0	142¹	179	4	75	49	16.1	5.69	60	.296	.375	14	.215	-1	-42	-36	1	-3.0
Total	2	6	15	.286	23	23	21	0	0	187¹	234	5	99	61	16.1	5.28	69	.298	.379	17	.198	-3	-40	-34	1	-3.1

● FRANK FAHEY
Fahey, Francis Raymond b: 1/22/1896, Milford, Mass. d: 3/19/54, Boston, Mass. BB/TR, 6′1″, 190 lbs. Deb: 4/25/18 ◆

YEAR	TM/L	W	L	PCT	G	GS	CG	SH	SV	IP	H	HR	BB	SO	RAT	ERA	ERA+	OAV	OOB	BH	AVG	PB	PR	/A	PD	TPI
1918	Phi-A	0	0	—	3	0	0	0	0	9	5	0	14	1	20.0	6.00	49	.200	.500	3	.176	-0	-3	-3	-1	-0.1

● JERRY FAHR
Fahr, Gerald Warren b: 12/9/24, Marmaduke, Ark. BR/TR, 6′5″, 185 lbs. Deb: 4/29/51

YEAR	TM/L	W	L	PCT	G	GS	CG	SH	SV	IP	H	HR	BB	SO	RAT	ERA	ERA+	OAV	OOB	BH	AVG	PB	PR	/A	PD	TPI
1951	Cle-A	0	0	—	5	0	0	0	0	5²	11	0	2	0	20.6	4.76	80	.500	.542	0	—	-0	-0	-1	-0	0.0

● PETE FAHRER
Fahrer, Clarence Willie b: 3/10/1890, Holgate, Ohio d: 6/10/67, Fremont, Mich. BL/TR, 6′, 190 lbs. Deb: 8/17/14

YEAR	TM/L	W	L	PCT	G	GS	CG	SH	SV	IP	H	HR	BB	SO	RAT	ERA	ERA+	OAV	OOB	BH	AVG	PB	PR	/A	PD	TPI
1914	Cin-N	0	0	—	5	0	0	0	0	8	4	0	2	2	13.5	1.13	260	.308	.400	0	.000	-0	1	2	0	0.0

● JIM FAIRBANK
Fairbank, James Lee "Lee" or "Smoky" b: 3/17/1881, Deansboro, N.Y. d: 12/27/55, Utica, N.Y. BR/TR, 5′10″, 185 lbs. Deb: 9/18/03

YEAR	TM/L	W	L	PCT	G	GS	CG	SH	SV	IP	H	HR	BB	SO	RAT	ERA	ERA+	OAV	OOB	BH	AVG	PB	PR	/A	PD	TPI
1903	Phi-A	1	1	.500	4	1	1	0	0	24	33	1	12	10	16.9	4.88	63	.327	.398	1	.100	-1	-5	-5	1	-0.3
1904	Phi-A	0	1	.000	3	1	1	0	0	17	19	0	13	6	18.0	6.35	42	.284	.415	0	.000	-1	-7	-7	1	-0.4
Total	2	1	2	.333	7	2	2	0	0	41	52	1	25	16	17.3	5.49	53	.310	.405	1	.063	-1	-12	-12	2	-0.7

● RAGS FAIRCLOTH
Faircloth, James Lamar b: 8/19/1892, Kenton, Tenn. d: 10/5/53, Tucson, Ariz. BR/TR, 5′11″, 160 lbs. Deb: 5/6/19

YEAR	TM/L	W	L	PCT	G	GS	CG	SH	SV	IP	H	HR	BB	SO	RAT	ERA	ERA+	OAV	OOB	BH	AVG	PB	PR	/A	PD	TPI
1919	Phi-N	0	0	—	2	0	0	0	0	2	5	0	2	0	22.5	9.00	36	.625	.625	0	—	-0	-1	-1	0	0.0

● HECTOR FAJARDO
Fajardo, Hector (Nabaratte) b: 11/16/70, Sahuayo, Mexico BR/TR, 6′4″, 185 lbs. Deb: 8/10/91

YEAR	TM/L	W	L	PCT	G	GS	CG	SH	SV	IP	H	HR	BB	SO	RAT	ERA	ERA+	OAV	OOB	BH	AVG	PB	PR	/A	PD	TPI
1991	Pit-N	0	0	—	2	0	0	0	0	6¹	10	0	7	8	24.2	9.95	36	.357	.486	0	.000	-0	-4	-4	-0	0.0
	Tex-A	0	2	.000	4	3	0	0	0	19	25	2	4	15	14.2	5.68	71	.329	.370	0	—	0	-3	-3	-0	-0.3
1993	Tex-A	0	0	—	1	0	0	0	0	0²	0	0	0	1	0.0	0.00	—	.000	.000	0	—	0	0	0	0	0.1
1994	Tex-A	5	7	.417	18	12	0	0	0	83¹	95	15	26	45	13.3	6.91	70	.284	.340	0	—	0	-20	-19	-0	-2.2
1995	Tex-A	0	0	—	5	2	0	0	0	15	19	2	5	9	15.0	7.80	62	.311	.373	0	—	0	-5	-5	-0	-0.1
Total	4	5	9	.357	30	17	0	0	0	124¹	149	19	42	78	14.1	6.95	67	.297	.356	0	.000	-0	-32	-32	-0	-2.5

● PETE FALCONE
Falcone, Peter Frank b: 10/1/53, Brooklyn, N.Y. BL/TL, 6′2″, 185 lbs. Deb: 4/13/75

YEAR	TM/L	W	L	PCT	G	GS	CG	SH	SV	IP	H	HR	BB	SO	RAT	ERA	ERA+	OAV	OOB	BH	AVG	PB	PR	/A	PD	TPI
1975	SF-N	12	11	.522	34	32	3	1	0	190	171	16	111	131	13.5	4.17	91	.244	.350	4	.062	-5	-12	-8	-1	-1.4
1976	StL-N	12	16	.429	32	32	9	2	0	212	173	12	93	138	11.4	3.23	110	.222	.306	8	.129	-1	6	7	-4	0.3
1977	StL-N	4	8	.333	27	22	1	1	1	124	130	19	61	75	14.1	5.44	71	.273	.359	10	.244	2	-21	-22	-1	-1.8
1978	StL-N	2	7	.222	19	14	0	0	0	75	94	9	48	28	17.3	5.76	61	.319	.417	5	.238	1	-18	-19	-2	-2.1
1979	NY-N	6	14	.300	33	31	1	1	0	184	194	24	76	113	13.3	4.16	88	.276	.347	9	.173	-0	-9	-11	-3	-1.3
1980	NY-N	7	10	.412	37	23	1	0	1	157¹	163	16	58	109	12.8	4.52	79	.269	.335	6	.146	-1	-16	-17	-3	-2.1
1981	NY-N	5	3	.625	35	9	3	1	1	95¹	84	3	36	56	11.3	2.55	137	.241	.312	4	.182	1	10	10	-2	0.8
1982	NY-N	8	10	.444	40	23	2	0	2	171	159	24	71	101	12.2	3.84	94	.252	.329	6	.113	-2	-5	-4	-3	-0.9
1983	Atl-N	9	4	.692	33	15	2	0	0	106²	102	14	60	59	13.8	3.63	107	.256	.355	3	.115	-1	0	3	-2	0.0
1984	Atl-N	5	7	.417	35	16	2	1	2	120	115	15	57	55	12.9	4.13	93	.252	.335	7	.212	1	-7	-4	-1	-0.4
Total	10	70	90	.438	325	217	25	7	7	1435¹	1385	152	671	865	13.0	4.07	90	.257	.341	62	.149	-6	-71	-63	-20	-8.9

● CHET FALK
Falk, Chester Emanuel "Spot" b: 5/15/05, Austin, Tex. d: 1/7/82, Austin, Tex. BL/TL, 6′2″, 170 lbs. Deb: 4/20/25 F

YEAR	TM/L	W	L	PCT	G	GS	CG	SH	SV	IP	H	HR	BB	SO	RAT	ERA	ERA+	OAV	OOB	BH	AVG	PB	PR	/A	PD	TPI
1925	StL-A	0	0	—	13	6	0	0	0	25	38	2	17	7	19.8	8.28	56	.362	.451	5	.625	2	-11	-10	0	0.3
1926	StL-A	4	4	.500	18	8	3	0	0	74	95	1	27	5	15.6	5.35	80	.338	.408	6	.194	-1	-11	-9	-1	-0.9
1927	StL-A	1	0	1.000	9	0	0	0	0	15²	25	1	10	2	20.1	5.74	76	.352	.432	1	.200	-0	-3	-2	0	-0.1
Total	3	5	4	.556	40	14	3	0	0	114²	158	4	54	16	17.1	6.04	73	.346	.422	12	.273	1	-25	-21	0	-0.7

● CY FALKENBERG
Falkenberg, Frederick Peter b: 12/17/1880, Chicago, Ill. d: 4/14/61, San Francisco, Cal BR/TR, 6′5″, 180 lbs. Deb: 4/21/03

YEAR	TM/L	W	L	PCT	G	GS	CG	SH	SV	IP	H	HR	BB	SO	RAT	ERA	ERA+	OAV	OOB	BH	AVG	PB	PR	/A	PD	TPI
1903	Pit-N	1	5	.167	10	6	3	0	0	56	65	0	32	24	15.9	3.86	84	.295	.390	4	.190	-0	-4	-4	2	-0.2
1905	Was-A	7	2	.778	12	10	6	2	0	75¹	71	1	31	35	12.4	3.82	69	.251	.335	4	.125	-2	-10	-10	-1	-1.4
1906	Was-A	14	20	.412	40	36	30	2	1	298²	277	1	108	178	12.0	2.86	92	.249	.323	18	.170	1	-6	-8	2	-0.5
1907	Was-A	6	17	.261	32	24	17	1	1	233²	195	0	77	100	10.8	2.35	103	.229	.299	12	.140	-3	5	2	2	0.1
1908	Was-A	6	2	.750	17	8	5	1	0	82²	70	0	21	34	10.1	1.96	117	.236	.291	6	.222	0	4	3	1	0.4
	Cle-A	2	4	.333	8	7	3	0	0	46¹	52	1	10	17	12.4	3.88	62	.284	.328	2	.118	-1	-8	-8	-1	-1.1
	Yr	8	6	.571	25	15	7	1	0	129	122	3	31	51	10.8	2.65	88	.253	.301	8	.182	-1	-4	-5	0	-0.7
1909	Cle-A	10	9	.526	24	18	13	2	0	165	135	0	50	82	10.4	2.40	107	.231	.297	9	.173	-1	1	3	3	0.5
1910	Cle-A	14	13	.519	37	29	18	3	1	256²	246	3	75	107	11.5	2.95	88	.261	.320	15	.183	-0	-12	-10	3	-0.8
1911	Cle-A	8	5	.615	15	13	7	0	0	106²	117	0	24	46	12.2	3.29	104	.282	.326	7	.175	-1	1	1	0	0.1
1913	Cle-A	23	10	.697	39	36	23	6	0	276	238	2	88	166	10.8	2.22	137	.235	.299	10	.119	-2	22	25	-2	2.5
1914	Ind-F	25	16	.610	49	43	33	9	3	377¹	332	5	89	236	10.2	2.22	141	.236	.284	21	.168	-4	28	38	3	3.8
1915	New-F	9	11	.450	25	21	14	0	1	172	175	6	47	76	12.1	3.24	79	.268	.326	3	.053	-7	-10	-13	1	-2.1
	Bro-F	3	3	.500	7	7	5	1	0	48	31	1	12	20	8.3	1.50	181	.189	.249	1	.067	-2	7	7	0	0.6
	Yr	12	14	.462	32	28	19	1	1	220	206	7	59	96	10.9	2.86	91	.250	.301	4	.056	-9	-3	-7	1	-1.5
1917	Phi-A	0	2	.250	11	5	3	0	0	80²	86	1	25	12	12.5	3.35	82	.293	.350	5	.185	-0	-6	-5	1	-0.3
Total	12	130	123	.514	330	266	180	27	8	2275	2090	23	690	1164	11.3	2.68	103	.248	.310	117	.152	-23	13	20	13	1.6

● ED FALLENSTEIN
Fallenstein, Edward Joseph "Jack" (b: Edward Joseph Valestin)
b: 12/22/08, Newark, N.J. d: 11/24/71, Orange, N.J. BR/TR, 6′3″, 180 lbs. Deb: 4/16/31

YEAR	TM/L	W	L	PCT	G	GS	CG	SH	SV	IP	H	HR	BB	SO	RAT	ERA	ERA+	OAV	OOB	BH	AVG	PB	PR	/A	PD	TPI
1931	Phi-N	0	0	—	24	0	0	0	0	41²	56	2	26	15	17.7	7.13	60	.333	.423	1	.200	0	-15	-13	0	0.0
1933	Bos-N	2	1	.667	9	4	1	1	0	35	43	1	13	5	14.7	3.60	85	.305	.368	3	.375	1	-1	-2	-0	-0.1
Total	2	2	1	.667	33	4	1	1	0	76²	99	3	39	20	16.3	5.52	67	.320	.398	4	.308	1	-16	-16	0	-0.1

● BOB FALLON
Fallon, Robert Joseph b: 2/18/60, Bronx, N.Y. BL/TL, 6′3″, 200 lbs. Deb: 4/26/84

YEAR	TM/L	W	L	PCT	G	GS	CG	SH	SV	IP	H	HR	BB	SO	RAT	ERA	ERA+	OAV	OOB	BH	AVG	PB	PR	/A	PD	TPI
1984	Chi-A	0	0	—	3	3	0	0	0	14²	12	0	11	10	14.1	3.68	113	.235	.371	0	—	0	1	1	0	0.0
1985	Chi-A	0	0	—	10	0	0	0	0	16	25	5	16	17	19.1	6.19	70	.342	.436	0	—	0	-4	-3	-1	-0.3
Total	2	0	0	—	13	3	0	0	0	30²	37	5	27	27	16.7	4.99	85	.308	.407	0	—	0	-3	-1	-1	-0.3

● CLIFF FANNIN
Fannin, Clifford Bryson "Mule" b: 5/13/24, Louisa, Ky. d: 12/11/66, Sandusky, Ohio BL/TR, 6′, 170 lbs. Deb: 9/2/45

YEAR	TM/L	W	L	PCT	G	GS	CG	SH	SV	IP	H	HR	BB	SO	RAT	ERA	ERA+	OAV	OOB	BH	AVG	PB	PR	/A	PD	TPI
1945	StL-A	0	0	—	7	0	0	0	0	10¹	8	0	5	5	11.3	2.61	135	.222	.317	0	.000	-0	1	1	0	0.0
1946	StL-A	5	2	.714	27	7	4	1	2	86²	76	4	32	52	12.4	3.01	124	.236	.326	5	.161	-1	5	7	0	0.5
1947	StL-A	6	8	.429	26	18	6	2	1	145²	134	10	77	77	13.1	3.58	108	.245	.340	9	.196	-2	3	5	0	0.5
1948	StL-A	10	14	.417	34	29	10	3	1	213²	198	14	104	102	12.8	4.17	109	.245	.332	11	.169	-4	3	9	-2	0.4
1949	StL-A	8	14	.364	30	25	5	0	1	143	177	15	93	57	17.0	6.17	73	.308	.404	9	.164	-2	-31	-26	-3	-3.7
1950	StL-A	5	9	.357	25	16	3	0	1	102	116	18	57	42	15.4	6.53	76	.280	.369	6	.176	-2	-22	-18	-0	-2.2
1951	StL-A	0	2	.000	7	1	0	0	0	15¹	20	6	5	11	14.7	6.46	68	.317	.368	1	.250	-1	-4	-4	0	-0.4
1952	StL-A	0	2	.000	8	2	0	0	0	16¹	34	5	20	6	23.7	12.67	31	.453	.512	0	.000	-0	-16	-16	-1	-1.7
Total	8	34	51	.400	164	98	28	6	6	733	763	72	393	352	14.2	4.85	89	.269	.358	41	.173	-5	-63	-42	-6	-6.3

● JACK FANNING
Fanning, John Jacob b: 1863, S.Orange, N.J. d: 6/10/17, Aberdeen, Wash. TR, 5′9″, 163 lbs. Deb: 9/20/1889

YEAR	TM/L	W	L	PCT	G	GS	CG	SH	SV	IP	H	HR	BB	SO	RAT	ERA	ERA+	OAV	OOB	BH	AVG	PB	PR	/A	PD	TPI
1889	Ind-N	0	1	.000	1	1	0	0	0	1	3	0	9	0	45.0	18.00	23	.500	.625	0	.000	-0	-2	-2	0	-0.8
1894	Phi-N	1	3	.250	5	4	2	0	0	32¹	45	4	20	7	18.6	8.07	63	.326	.419	2	.154	-1	-10	-11	0	-0.9
Total	2	1	4	.200	6	5	2	0	0	33¹	48	4	22	7	19.4	8.37	61	.333	.429	2	.143	-1	-11	-12	0	-1.7

YEAR	TM/L	W	L	PCT	G	GS	CG	SH	SV	IP	H	HR	BB	SO	RAT	ERA	ERA+	OAV	OOB	BH	AVG	PB	PR	/A	PD	TPI

● HARRY FANOK   Fanok, Harry Michael "The Flame Thrower"   b: 5/11/40, Whippany, N.J.   BB/TR, 6', 180 lbs.   Deb: 4/16/63

1963	StL-N	2	1	.667	12	0	0	0	1	25²	24	3	21	25	16.1	5.26	67	.255	.397	2	.400	1	-6	-5	-0	-0.5
1964	StL-N	0	0	—	4	0	0	0	0	7²	5	0	3	10	9.4	5.87	65	.179	.258	0	.000	-0	-2	-2	-0	0.0
Total	2	2	1	.667	16	0	0	0	1	33¹	29	3	24	35	14.6	5.40	67	.238	.367	2	.333	1	-8	-7	-0	-0.5

● FRANK FANOVICH   Fanovich, Frank Joseph "Lefty"   b: 1/11/22, New York, N.Y.   BL/TL, 5'11", 180 lbs.   Deb: 4/25/49

1949	Cin-N	0	2	.000	29	1	0	0	0	43¹	44	2	28	27	15.4	5.40	77	.257	.368	0	.000	-0	-7	-6	-0	-0.2
1953	Phi-A	0	3	.000	26	3	0	0	0	61²	62	5	37	37	15.3	5.55	77	.273	.389	2	.182	-0	-11	-9	-1	-0.5
Total	2	0	5	.000	55	4	0	0	0	105	106	7	65	64	15.3	5.49	77	.266	.380	2	.133	-1	-17	-14	-0	-0.7

● STAN FANSLER   Fansler, Stanley Robert   b: 2/12/65, Elkins, W.Va.   BR/TR, 5'11", 180 lbs.   Deb: 9/6/86

| 1986 | Pit-N | 0 | 3 | .000 | 5 | 5 | 0 | 0 | 0 | 24 | 20 | 1 | 15 | 13 | 13.1 | 3.75 | 102 | .247 | .365 | 1 | .167 | -0 | -0 | -0 | -0 | 0.0 |

● HARRY FANWELL   Fanwell, Harry Clayton   b: 10/16/1886, Patapsco, Md.   d: 7/15/65, Baltimore, Md.   BB/TR, 6', 175 lbs.   Deb: 7/23/10

| 1910 | Cle-A | 2 | 9 | .182 | 17 | 11 | 5 | 1 | 0 | 92 | 87 | 0 | 38 | 30 | 12.8 | 3.62 | 71 | .260 | .347 | 1 | .033 | -3 | -11 | -11 | 1 | -1.4 |

● ED FARMER   Farmer, Edward Joseph   b: 10/18/49, Evergreen Park, Ill   BR/TR, 6'5", 210 lbs.   Deb: 6/9/71

1971	Cle-A	5	4	.556	43	4	0	0	4	78²	77	9	41	48	13.8	4.35	88	.263	.359	1	.071	-1	-8	-5	-0	-0.7
1972	Cle-A	2	5	.286	46	1	0	0	7	61¹	51	10	27	33	11.6	4.40	73	.231	.317	1	.143	-0	-9	-8	0	-1.1
1973	Cle-A	0	2	.000	16	0	0	0	1	17¹	25	4	5	10	15.6	4.67	84	.325	.366	0	—	0	-2	-1	-0	-0.2
	Det-A	3	0	1.000	24	0	0	0	2	45	52	3	27	28	16.2	5.00	82	.292	.391	0	—	0	-6	-5	-1	-0.4
	Yr	3	2	.600	40	0	0	0	3	62¹	77	7	32	38	16.0	4.91	82	.301	.383	0	—	0	-8	-6	-1	-0.6
1974	Phi-N	2	1	.667	14	3	0	0	0	31	41	5	27	20	19.7	8.42	45	.323	.442	1	.111	-1	-17	-16	-0	-1.5
1977	Bal-A	0	0	—	1	0	0	0	0	1	1	0	1	0	18.0	∞		1.000	1.000	0	—	0	-1	-1	0	0.3
1978	Mil-A	1	0	1.000	3	0	0	0	1	11	7	1	4	6	9.0	0.82	459	.175	.250	0	—	0	4	4	-0	0.4
1979	Tex-A	2	0	1.000	11	2	0	0	0	33	30	2	19	25	13.9	4.36	95	.252	.364	0	—	0	-1	-1	-0	0.0
	Chi-A	3	7	.300	42	3	0	0	14	81¹	66	2	34	48	11.2	2.43	175	.219	.301	0	—	0	16	16	0	2.5
	Yr	5	7	.417	53	5	0	0	14	114¹	96	4	53	73	11.8	2.99	141	.226	.314	0	—	0	16	16	0	2.5
1980	Chi-A★	7	9	.438	64	0	0	0	30	99²	92	6	56	54	13.5	3.34	127	.244	.343	0	—	0	8	8	1	1.7
1981	Chi-A	3	3	.500	42	0	0	0	10	52²	53	5	34	42	15.0	4.61	78	.262	.371	0	—	0	-6	-6	-1	-0.8
1982	Phi-N	2	6	.250	47	4	0	0	6	76	66	4	50	58	13.7	4.86	75	.234	.349	1	.000	-1	-11	-10	0	-1.3
1983	Phi-N	0	6	.000	12	3	0	0	0	26²	35	2	20	16	18.9	6.08	59	.307	.415	1	.167	-0	-7	-7	-0	-1.5
	Oak-A	0	0	—	5	1	0	0	0	10¹	15	1	0	7	13.1	3.48	111	.366	.366	0	—	0	1	0	-0	0.0
Total	11	30	43	.411	370	21	0	0	75	624	611	52	345	395	14.0	4.30	89	.257	.355	4	.085	-3	-38	-31	-0	-2.6

● HOWARD FARMER   Farmer, Howard Earl   b: 11/18/66, Gary, Ind.   BR/TR, 6'3", 185 lbs.   Deb: 7/2/90   F

| 1990 | Mon-N | 0 | 3 | .000 | 6 | 4 | 0 | 0 | 0 | 23 | 26 | 9 | 10 | 14 | 14.1 | 7.04 | 52 | .302 | .375 | 2 | .400 | 1 | -8 | -9 | 1 | -0.8 |

● MIKE FARMER   Farmer, Michael Anthony   b: 7/3/68, Gary, Ind.   BB/TL, 6'1", 193 lbs.   Deb: 5/4/96   F

| 1996 | Col-N | 0 | 1 | .000 | 7 | 4 | 0 | 0 | 0 | 28 | 32 | 8 | 13 | 16 | 14.5 | 7.71 | 70 | .286 | .360 | 4 | .400 | 1 | -11 | -7 | -0 | -0.2 |

● JIM FARR   Farr, James Alfred   b: 5/18/56, Waverly, N.Y.   BR/TR, 6'1", 195 lbs.   Deb: 9/7/82

| 1982 | Tex-A | 0 | 0 | — | 5 | 0 | 0 | 0 | 0 | 18 | 20 | 0 | 7 | 6 | 13.5 | 2.50 | 155 | .278 | .342 | 0 | — | 0 | 3 | 3 | -0 | 0.0 |

● STEVE FARR   Farr, Steven Michael   b: 12/12/56, LaPlata, Md.   BR/TR, 5'11", 198 lbs.   Deb: 5/16/84

1984	Cle-A	3	11	.214	31	16	0	0	1	116	106	14	46	83	12.2	4.58	89	.245	.325	0	—	0	-8	-6	1	-0.6
1985	*KC-A	2	1	.667	16	3	0	0	1	37²	34	2	20	36	13.4	3.11	134	.245	.348	0	—	0	4	4	0	0.4
1986	KC-A	8	4	.667	56	0	0	0	8	109¹	90	10	39	83	10.9	3.13	136	.228	.304	0	—	0	13	14	1	1.5
1987	KC-A	4	3	.571	47	0	0	0	1	91	97	9	44	88	14.1	4.15	110	.270	.353	0	—	0	3	4	-1	0.0
1988	KC-A	5	4	.556	62	1	0	0	20	82²	74	5	30	72	11.5	2.50	159	.240	.312	0	—	0	13	14	-1	1.8
1989	KC-A	2	5	.286	51	2	0	0	18	63¹	75	5	22	56	13.9	4.12	93	.300	.355	0	—	0	-2	-2	-0	-0.3
1990	KC-A	13	7	.650	57	6	1	1	1	127	99	6	48	94	10.8	1.98	193	.220	.302	0	—	0	**27**	**26**	0	4.1
1991	NY-A	5	5	.500	60	0	0	0	23	70	57	4	20	60	10.5	2.19	189	.219	.288	0	—	0	15	15	1	3.0
1992	NY-A	2	2	.500	50	0	0	0	30	52	34	2	19	37	9.5	1.56	251	.186	.270	0	—	0	14	14	-1	2.3
1993	NY-A	2	2	.500	49	0	0	0	25	47	44	8	28	39	14.2	4.21	99	.253	.363	0	—	0	1	-0	1	-0.2
1994	Cle-A	1	1	.500	19	0	0	0	4	15¹	17	3	15	12	20.0	5.28	89	.279	.436	0	—	0	-1	-1	-0	-0.2
	Bos-A	1	0	1.000	11	0	0	0	0	13	24	2	3	8	18.7	6.23	81	.407	.435	0	—	0	-2	-2	-0	-0.2
	Yr	2	1	.667	30	0	0	0	4	28¹	41	5	18	20	18.7	5.72	85	.333	.418	0	—	0	-3	-3	-0	-0.4
Total	11	48	45	.516	509	28	1	1	132	824¹	751	70	334	668	12.2	3.25	127	.244	.325	0	—	0	78	79	1	12.0

● JOHN FARRELL   Farrell, John Edward   b: 8/4/62, Monmouth Beach, N.J.   BR/TR, 6'4", 210 lbs.   Deb: 8/18/87

1987	Cle-A	5	1	.833	10	9	1	0	0	69	68	7	22	28	12.4	3.39	133	.256	.324	0	—	0	8	9	-0	0.6
1988	Cle-A	14	10	.583	31	30	4	0	0	210¹	216	15	67	92	12.5	4.24	97	.269	.332	0	—	0	-6	-3	-0	-0.5
1989	Cle-A	9	14	.391	31	31	7	2	0	208	196	14	71	132	11.9	3.63	109	.244	.311	0	—	0	6	8	-2	0.3
1990	Cle-A	4	5	.444	17	17	1	0	0	96²	108	10	33	44	13.2	4.28	91	.286	.345	0	—	0	-4	-4	-0	-0.5
1993	Cal-A	3	12	.200	21	17	0	0	0	90²	110	22	44	45	16.0	7.35	61	.301	.387	0	—	0	-30	-29	-0	-3.9
1994	Cal-A	1	2	.333	3	3	0	0	0	13	16	2	8	10	17.3	9.00	54	.308	.410	0	—	0	-6	-6	1	-0.8
1995	Cle-A	0	0	—	1	0	0	0	0	4²	7	0	4	3	13.5	3.86	122	.368	.368	0	—	0	0	0	-0	0.0
1996	Det-A	0	2	.000	2	2	0	0	0	7²	11	2	5	0	24.2	14.21	36	.367	.515	0	—	0	-6	-6	-0	-1.2
Total	8	36	46	.439	116	109	13	2	0	698²	732	72	250	355	13.0	4.56	91	.270	.338	0	—	0	-39	-31	-2	-5.7

● KERBY FARRELL   Farrell, Major Kerby   b: 9/3/13, Leapwood, Tenn.   d: 12/17/75, Nashville, Tenn.   BL/TL, 5'11", 172 lbs.   Deb: 4/24/43   MC◆

| 1943 | Bos-N | 0 | 1 | .000 | 5 | 0 | 0 | 0 | 0 | 23 | 24 | 1 | 9 | 4 | 12.9 | 4.30 | 79 | .276 | .344 | 75 | .268 | 1 | -2 | -2 | -0 | 0.0 |

● TURK FARRELL   Farrell, Richard Joseph   b: 4/8/34, Boston, Mass.   d: 6/10/77, Great Yarmouth, England   BR/TR, 6'4", 220 lbs.   Deb: 9/21/56

1956	Phi-N	0	1	.000	1	1	0	0	0	4¹	6	0	3	0	20.8	12.46	30	.353	.476	0	.000	-0	-4	-4	0	-0.6
1957	Phi-N	10	2	.833	52	0	0	0	10	83¹	74	2	36	54	12.1	2.38	160	.242	.326	1	.111	0	**14**	13	0	2.2
1958	Phi-N★	8	9	.471	54	0	0	0	11	94	84	7	40	73	11.9	3.35	118	.244	.323	5	.208	-0	6	6	-2	1.1
1959	Phi-N	1	6	.143	38	0	0	0	6	57	61	9	25	31	13.6	4.74	87	.288	.363	1	.167	-0	-5	-4	-0	-0.6
1960	Phi-N	10	6	.625	59	0	0	0	11	103¹	88	9	29	70	10.5	2.70	144	.239	.302	3	.200	1	12	14	-1	2.2
1961	Phi-N	2	1	.667	12	0	0	0	0	9²	10	3	6	10	15.8	6.52	63	.270	.386	1	.500	-1	-3	-3	-0	-0.7
	LA-N	6	6	.500	50	0	0	0	10	89	107	12	43	80	15.3	5.06	86	.296	.373	0	.000	-2	-10	-7	-2	-1.4
	Yr	8	7	.533	62	0	0	0	10	98²	117	15	49	90	15.2	5.20	83	.294	.372	1	.050	-2	-13	-10	-2	-2.1
1962	Hou-N★	10	20	.333	43	29	11	2	4	241²	210	21	55	203	10.1	3.02	124	.233	.280	14	.179	2	25	19	2	2.3
1963	Hou-N	14	13	.519	34	26	12	0	1	202¹	161	12	35	141	8.8	3.02	104	.219	.256	9	.143	1	6	3	-2	-0.1
1964	Hou-N★	11	10	.524	32	27	7	0	0	198¹	196	21	52	117	11.4	3.27	105	.261	.311	5	.072	-3	6	3	-1	-0.5
1965	Hou-N★	11	11	.500	33	29	8	3	1	208¹	202	18	35	122	10.4	3.50	96	.252	.286	10	.135	-1	1	-3	-1	-0.6
1966	Hou-N	6	10	.375	32	21	3	0	2	152²	167	23	28	101	11.5	4.60	74	.278	.310	7	.146	-0	-2	-20	-2	-2.2
1967	Hou-N	1	0	1.000	11	2	0	0	0	11²	11	0	7	4	14.7	4.63	72	.244	.358	0	.000	-0	-2	-2	-0	-0.6
	Phi-N	9	6	.600	50	0	0	0	12	92	76	6	15	68	9.0	2.05	166	.228	.263	2	.105	-1	14	14	2	2.6
	Yr	10	6	.625	57	2	0	0	12	103²	87	6	22	78	9.5	2.34	145	.229	.273	2	.100	-0	12	12	-1	2.4
1968	Phi-N	4	6	.400	54	0	0	0	12	83	83	7	32	57	12.7	3.47	87	.271	.344	1	.167	-0	-4	-4	-0	-0.6
1969	Phi-N	3	4	.429	46	0	0	0	3	74¹	92	8	27	40	14.5	4.00	89	.307	.366	0	.000	-0	-3	-4	-2	-0.6
Total	14	106	111	.488	590	134	41	5	83	1705	1628	152	468	1177	11.2	3.45	103	.254	.307	59	.135	-9	35	21	-17	3.2

● JEFF FASSERO   Fassero, Jeffrey Joseph   b: 1/5/63, Springfield, Ill.   BL/TL, 6'1", 180 lbs.   Deb: 5/4/91

1991	Mon-N	2	5	.286	51	0	0	0	8	55¹	39	1	17	42	9.3	2.44	148	.196	.263	0	.000	-0	8	7	1	1.1
1992	Mon-N	8	7	.533	70	0	0	0	1	85²	81	1	34	63	12.3	2.84	122	.249	.324	1	.143	-0	6	6	0	1.1
1993	Mon-N	12	5	.706	56	15	0	0	1	149²	119	7	54	140	10.4	2.29	183	.216	.286	2	.063	0	**29**	**31**	0	3.1
1994	Mon-N	8	6	.571	21	21	1	0	0	138²	119	13	40	119	10.4	2.99	141	.229	.286	3	.068	0	19	19	3	1.9
1995	Mon-N	13	14	.481	30	30	1	0	0	189	207	15	74	164	13.5	4.33	99	.283	.351	4	.070	-3	-3	-1	1	-0.3

YEAR TM/L	W	L	PCT	G	GS	CG	SH	SV	IP	H	HR	BB	SO	RAT	ERA	ERA+	OAV	OOB	BH	AVG	PB	PR	/A	PD	TPI
1996 Mon-N	15	11	.577	34	34	5	1	0	231²	217	20	55	222	10.7	3.30	131	.244	.291	6	.094	-1	23	26	3	2.9
Total 6	58	48	.547	262	100	8	6	1	850	782	57	274	750	11.3	3.20	129	.243	.305	16	.077	-8	82	88	8	9.8

● **FAST**   Fast   b: Milwaukee, Wis.

YEAR TM/L	W	L	PCT	G	GS	CG	SH	SV	IP	H	HR	BB	SO	RAT	ERA	ERA+	OAV	OOB	BH	AVG	PB	PR	/A	PD	TPI
1887 Ind-N	0	1	.000	4	2	1	0	1	15²	25	1	8	0	20.1	10.34	40	.347	.427	2	.182	-1	-11	-11	0	-0.6

● **DARCY FAST**   Fast, Darcy Rae   b: 3/10/47, Dallas, Ore.   BL/TL, 6'3", 195 lbs.   Deb: 6/15/68

YEAR TM/L	W	L	PCT	G	GS	CG	SH	SV	IP	H	HR	BB	SO	RAT	ERA	ERA+	OAV	OOB	BH	AVG	PB	PR	/A	PD	TPI
1968 Chi-N	0	1	.000	8	0	0	0	0	10	8	1	8	10	14.4	5.40	59	.216	.356	0	.000	-0	-3	-2	0	-0.3

● **JACK FASZHOLZ**   Faszholz, John Edward "Preacher"   b: 4/11/27, St.Louis, Mo.   BR/TR, 6'3", 205 lbs.   Deb: 4/25/53

YEAR TM/L	W	L	PCT	G	GS	CG	SH	SV	IP	H	HR	BB	SO	RAT	ERA	ERA+	OAV	OOB	BH	AVG	PB	PR	/A	PD	TPI
1953 StL-N	0	0	—	4	1	0	0	0	11²	16	3	1	7	13.9	6.94	61	.327	.353	0	.000	-0	-3	-3	-1	-0.1

● **BILL FAUL**   Faul, William Alvan   b: 4/21/40, Cincinnati, Ohio   BR/TR, 5'10", 190 lbs.   Deb: 9/19/62

YEAR TM/L	W	L	PCT	G	GS	CG	SH	SV	IP	H	HR	BB	SO	RAT	ERA	ERA+	OAV	OOB	BH	AVG	PB	PR	/A	PD	TPI
1962 Det-A	0	0	—	1	0	0	0	0	1²	4	1	3	2	43.2	32.40	13	.444	.615	0	—	0	-5	-5	-0	0.0
1963 Det-A	5	6	.455	28	10	2	0	1	97	93	14	48	64	13.5	4.64	81	.251	.343	4	.148	-0	-11	-10	-2	-1.2
1964 Det-A	0	0	—	1	1	0	0	0	5	5	2	2	1	12.6	10.80	34	.250	.318	0	.000	-0	-4	-4	-0	0.0
1965 Chi-N	6	6	.500	17	15	5	3	0	96²	83	12	18	59	9.7	3.54	104	.232	.275	3	.100	-1	0	2	-2	-0.1
1966 Chi-N	1	4	.200	17	6	1	0	0	51¹	47	12	18	32	12.1	5.08	72	.242	.319	0	.000	-2	-8	-8	-1	-0.9
1970 SF-N	0	0	—	7	0	0	0	1	9²	15	1	6	6	19.6	7.45	53	.357	.438	0	—	-0	-4	-4	-0	-0.1
Total 6	12	16	.429	71	33	8	3	2	261¹	247	42	95	164	12.2	4.72	79	.249	.322	7	.097	-2	-32	-29	-5	-2.3

● **JIM FAULKNER**   Faulkner, James Leroy "Lefty"   b: 7/27/1899, Beatrice, Neb.   d: 6/1/62, W.Palm Beach, Fla.   BB/TL, 6'3", 190 lbs.   Deb: 9/15/27

YEAR TM/L	W	L	PCT	G	GS	CG	SH	SV	IP	H	HR	BB	SO	RAT	ERA	ERA+	OAV	OOB	BH	AVG	PB	PR	/A	PD	TPI
1927 NY-N	1	0	1.000	3	1	0	0	0	9²	13	0	5	2	17.7	3.72	104	.317	.404	1	.500	1	0	0	-0	0.1
1928 NY-N	9	8	.529	38	8	3	0	2	117¹	131	5	41	32	13.4	3.53	111	.289	.351	9	.231	1	6	5	1	0.8
1930 Bro-N	0	0	—	2	1	0	0	1	0¹	2	1	1	0	81.0	81.00	6	.667	.750	0	—	0	-3	-3	-0	-1.2
Total 3	10	8	.556	43	10	3	0	2	127¹	146	6	47	34	13.9	3.75	104	.293	.359	10	.244	2	2	2	1	-0.3

● **BUCK FAUSETT**   Fausett, Robert Shaw "Leaky"   b: 4/8/08, Sheridan, Ark.   d: 5/2/94, College Station, Tex.   BL/TR, 5'10", 170 lbs.   Deb: 4/18/44   ◆

YEAR TM/L	W	L	PCT	G	GS	CG	SH	SV	IP	H	HR	BB	SO	RAT	ERA	ERA+	OAV	OOB	BH	AVG	PB	PR	/A	PD	TPI
1944 Cin-N	0	0	—	2	0	0	0	0	10²	13	0	7	3	18.6	5.91	59	.295	.415	3	.097	-0	-3	-3	0	0.0

● **CHARLIE FAUST**   Faust, Charles Victor "Victory"   b: 10/9/1880, Marion, Kan.   d: 6/18/15, Fort Steilacoom, Wash.   BR/TR, 6'2",   Deb: 10/7/11

YEAR TM/L	W	L	PCT	G	GS	CG	SH	SV	IP	H	HR	BB	SO	RAT	ERA	ERA+	OAV	OOB	BH	AVG	PB	PR	/A	PD	TPI
1911 NY-N	0	0	—	2	0	0	0	0	2	1	0	1	0	9.0	4.50	75	.250	.250	0	—	-0	-0	-0	-0	0.1

● **CLAY FAUVER**   Fauver, Clayton King "Cayt"   b: 8/1/1872, N.Eaton, Ohio   d: 3/3/42, Chatsworth, Ga.   BB/TR, 5'10",   Deb: 9/7/1899

YEAR TM/L	W	L	PCT	G	GS	CG	SH	SV	IP	H	HR	BB	SO	RAT	ERA	ERA+	OAV	OOB	BH	AVG	PB	PR	/A	PD	TPI
1899 Lou-N	1	0	1.000	1	1	0	0	0	9	11	0	2	1	13.0	1.00	—	.297	.333	0	.000	-1	4	4	-0	0.3

● **VERN FEAR**   Fear, Luvern Carl   b: 8/21/24, Everly, Iowa   d: 9/6/76, Spencer, Iowa   BB/TR, 6', 170 lbs.   Deb: 8/3/52

YEAR TM/L	W	L	PCT	G	GS	CG	SH	SV	IP	H	HR	BB	SO	RAT	ERA	ERA+	OAV	OOB	BH	AVG	PB	PR	/A	PD	TPI
1952 Chi-N	0	0	—	4	0	0	0	0	8	9	1	3	4	14.6	7.88	49	.290	.371	0	.000	-0	-4	-4	-0	-0.4

● **JACK FEE**   Fee, John   b: 12/23/1867, Carbondale, Pa.   d: 3/3/13, Carbondale, Pa.   Deb: 9/14/1889

YEAR TM/L	W	L	PCT	G	GS	CG	SH	SV	IP	H	HR	BB	SO	RAT	ERA	ERA+	OAV	OOB	BH	AVG	PB	PR	/A	PD	TPI
1889 Ind-N	2	2	.500	7	3	2	0	0	40	39	2	31	10	17.1	4.27	98	.248	.392	3	.143	-2	-1	-0	1	-0.1

● **HARRY FELDMAN**   Feldman, Harry   b: 11/10/19, New York, N.Y.   d: 3/16/62, Fort Smith, Ark.   BR/TR, 6', 175 lbs.   Deb: 9/10/41

YEAR TM/L	W	L	PCT	G	GS	CG	SH	SV	IP	H	HR	BB	SO	RAT	ERA	ERA+	OAV	OOB	BH	AVG	PB	PR	/A	PD	TPI
1941 NY-N	1	1	.500	3	3	1	1	0	20¹	21	0	6	9	12.0	3.98	93	.280	.333	1	.167	0	-1	-1	-0	-0.1
1942 NY-N	7	1	.875	31	6	2	1	0	114	100	5	73	49	13.7	3.16	106	.236	.350	2	.282	3	2	3	-0	0.5
1943 NY-N	4	5	.444	31	10	1	0	0	104²	114	7	58	49	15.1	4.30	80	.279	.374	4	.133	-1	-11	-10	0	-0.9
1944 NY-N	11	13	.458	40	27	8	1	2	205¹	214	18	91	70	13.5	4.16	88	.266	.342	15	.205	-0	-13	-11	-2	-1.4
1945 NY-N	12	13	.480	35	30	10	3	1	217²	213	14	69	74	11.7	3.27	120	.251	.308	7	.097	-3	13	16	-2	1.1
1946 NY-N	0	2	.000	3	2	0	0	0	4	9	1	3	3	27.0	18.00	19	.474	.545	0	.000	-0	-6	-6	-0	-2.1
Total 6	35	35	.500	143	78	22	6	3	666	671	45	300	254	13.2	3.80	96	.260	.339	38	.172	-1	-16	-10	-5	-2.9

● **HARRY FELIX**   Felix, Harry   b: 1870, Brooklyn, N.Y.   d: 10/17/61, Miami, Fla.   BR/TR, 5'7.5", 160 lbs.   Deb: 10/5/01

YEAR TM/L	W	L	PCT	G	GS	CG	SH	SV	IP	H	HR	BB	SO	RAT	ERA	ERA+	OAV	OOB	BH	AVG	PB	PR	/A	PD	TPI
1901 NY-N	0	0	—	1	0	0	0	0	2	3	0	0	0	13.5	0.00	—	.333	.333	0	.000	-0	1	1	-0	0.0
1902 Phi-N	1	3	.250	9	5	3	0	0	45	61	1	11	10	14.4	5.60	50	.323	.360	5	.135	-1	-14	-14	-1	-1.2
Total 2	1	3	.250	10	5	3	0	0	47	64	1	11	10	14.4	5.36	53	.323	.359	5	.132	-1	-13	-13	-1	-1.2

● **BOB FELLER**   Feller, Robert William Andrew "Rapid Robert" (b: Robert William Feller)   b: 11/3/18, Van Meter, Iowa   BR/TR, 6', 185 lbs.   Deb: 7/19/36   H

YEAR TM/L	W	L	PCT	G	GS	CG	SH	SV	IP	H	HR	BB	SO	RAT	ERA	ERA+	OAV	OOB	BH	AVG	PB	PR	/A	PD	TPI
1936 Cle-A	5	3	.625	14	8	5	0	1	62	52	1	47	76	15.0	3.34	151	.229	.371	3	.136	-2	12	12	-1	1.1
1937 Cle-A	9	7	.563	26	19	9	0	1	148²	116	4	106	150	13.6	3.39	136	.218	.351	9	.170	-1	20	20	1	1.9
1938 Cle-A☆	17	11	.607	39	36	20	2	1	277²	225	13	208	**240**	14.3	4.08	114	**.220**	.356	17	.181	-2	22	17	-2	1.4
1939 Cle-A★	**24**	9	.727	39	35	**24**	4	1	**296²**	227	13	142	**246**	11.3	2.85	154	**.210**	.303	21	.212	**5**	**58**	51	0	**5.6**
1940 Cle-A★	**27**	11	.711	**43**	37	**31**	**4**	4	**320¹**	245	13	118	**261**	10.3	**2.61**	161	**.210**	**.285**	18	.157	-4	**63**	57	-4	**6.1**
1941 Cle-A★	**25**	13	.658	**44**	40	28	**6**	2	**343**	284	15	194	**260**	12.7	3.15	125	.226	.332	18	.150	-3	38	30	-1	3.2
1945 Cle-A	5	3	.625	9	9	7	1	0	72	50	1	35	59	10.9	2.50	130	.192	.293	4	.160	-0	7	6	-1	0.5
1946 Cle-A★	**26**	15	.634	**48**	42	**36**	**10**	4	**371¹**	277	11	153	**348**	10.5	2.18	152	.208	.291	16	.129	-2	**55**	46	-1	4.9
1947 Cle-A†	**20**	11	.645	42	37	20	**5**	3	**299**	230	17	127	**196**	10.9	2.68	130	.215	.300	18	.184	-3	**34**	27	2	3.1
1948 *Cle-A†	19	15	.559	44	38	18	2	3	280¹	255	20	116	**164**	12.0	3.56	114	.241	.317	9	.095	-8	23	15	-1	0.7
1949 Cle-A	15	14	.517	36	28	15	0	0	211	198	18	84	108	12.1	3.75	106	.248	.320	17	.236	-4	10	6	-4	0.7
1950 Cle-A★	16	11	.593	35	34	16	3	0	247	230	20	103	119	12.3	3.43	126	.247	.325	10	.120	-2	32	25	-4	1.7
1951 Cle-A	**22**	8	**.733**	33	32	16	4	0	249²	239	22	95	111	12.3	3.50	108	.253	.325	4	.123	-4	17	8	-3	0.1
1952 Cle-A	9	13	.409	30	30	11	0	0	191²	219	18	83	81	14.3	4.74	71	.288	.360	7	.117	1	-23	-30	-4	-3.0
1953 Cle-A	10	7	.588	25	25	10	1	0	175²	163	16	60	60	11.6	3.59	105	.251	.317	6	.107	3	8	3	1	0.1
1954 Cle-A	13	3	.813	19	19	9	1	0	140	127	13	39	59	10.9	3.09	119	.239	.294	9	.188	-2	10	9	-2	0.9
1955 Cle-A	4	4	.500	25	11	2	1	0	83	71	7	31	25	11.2	3.47	115	.235	.308	1	.048	-2	5	5	-1	0.1
1956 Cle-A	0	4	.000	19	4	2	0	0	58	63	7	23	18	13.3	4.97	85	.280	.347	0	.000	-2	-5	-5	-1	-0.6
Total 18	266	162	.621	570	484	279	44	21	3827	3271	224	1764	2581	12.0	3.25	122	.231	.319	193	.151	-7	385	301	-22	28.5

● **TERRY FELTON**   Felton, Terry Lane   b: 10/29/57, Texarkana, Ark.   BR/TR, 6'1", 180 lbs.   Deb: 9/28/79

YEAR TM/L	W	L	PCT	G	GS	CG	SH	SV	IP	H	HR	BB	SO	RAT	ERA	ERA+	OAV	OOB	BH	AVG	PB	PR	/A	PD	TPI
1979 Min-A	0	0	—	1	0	0	0	0	2	1	0	1	1	9.00	0.00	—	.000	.000	0	—	0	1	1	-0	-0.2
1980 Min-A	0	3	.000	5	4	0	0	0	17²	20	2	9	14	15.3	7.13	61	.286	.375	0	—	0	-6	-5	-0	-0.8
1981 Min-A	0	0	—	1	1	0	0	0	1¹	2	1	2	1	40.5	40.50	10	.500	.600	0	—	0	-5	-5	-0	-0.1
1982 Min-A	0	13	.000	48	6	0	0	3	117¹	99	18	76	92	13.7	4.99	85	.230	.351	0	—	0	-12	-10	-2	-1.2
Total 4	0	16	.000	55	10	0	0	3	138¹	123	21	87	108	14.0	5.53	77	.240	.355	0	—	0	-22	-20	-2	-2.3

● **HOD FENNER**   Fenner, Horace Alfred   b: 7/12/1897, Martin, Mich.   d: 11/20/54, Detroit, Mich.   BR/TR, 5'10.5", 165 lbs.   Deb: 9/9/21

YEAR TM/L	W	L	PCT	G	GS	CG	SH	SV	IP	H	HR	BB	SO	RAT	ERA	ERA+	OAV	OOB	BH	AVG	PB	PR	/A	PD	TPI
1921 Chi-A	0	0	—	2	1	0	0	0	7	14	0	3	1	21.9	7.71	55	.452	.500	0	.000	-0	-3	-3	-0	-0.1

● **STAN FERENS**   Ferens, Stanley "Lefty"   b: 3/5/15, Wendel, Pa.   d: 10/7/94, Hempfield Township, Pa.   BB/TL, 5'11", 170 lbs.   Deb: 6/10/42

YEAR TM/L	W	L	PCT	G	GS	CG	SH	SV	IP	H	HR	BB	SO	RAT	ERA	ERA+	OAV	OOB	BH	AVG	PB	PR	/A	PD	TPI
1942 StL-A	3	4	.429	19	3	1	0	0	69	76	2	21	23	12.7	3.78	98	.279	.331	3	.143	-1	-1	-1	-0	-0.1
1946 StL-A	2	9	.182	34	6	1	0	0	88	100	3	38	28	14.4	4.50	83	.293	.369	4	.167	-1	-10	-8	-1	-1.0
Total 2	5	13	.278	53	9	2	0	0	157	176	5	59	51	13.6	4.18	89	.287	.353	7	.156	-1	-11	-8	-1	-1.1

● **CHARLIE FERGUSON**   Ferguson, Charles Augustus   b: 5/10/1875, Okemos, Mich.   d: 5/17/31, Sault Ste.Marie, Mich.   TR, 5'11",   Deb: 9/20/01

YEAR TM/L	W	L	PCT	G	GS	CG	SH	SV	IP	H	HR	BB	SO	RAT	ERA	ERA+	OAV	OOB	BH	AVG	PB	PR	/A	PD	TPI
1901 Chi-N	0	0	—	1	0	0	0	0	2	1	0	2	0	13.5	0.00	—	.143	.333	0	.000	-0	1	1	-0	0.0

● **CHARLIE FERGUSON**   Ferguson, Charles J.   b: 4/17/1863, Charlottesville, Va.   d: 4/29/1888, Philadelphia, Pa.   BB/TR, 6', 165 lbs.   Deb: 5/1/1884

YEAR TM/L	W	L	PCT	G	GS	CG	SH	SV	IP	H	HR	BB	SO	RAT	ERA	ERA+	OAV	OOB	BH	AVG	PB	PR	/A	PD	TPI
1884 Phi-N	21	25	.457	50	47	46	2	1	416²	443	13	93	194	11.6	3.54	84	.253	.291	50	.246	7	-26	-26	-2	-1.7
1885 Phi-N	26	20	.565	48	45	45	5	0	405	345	5	81	197	9.5	2.22	126	.219	.257	72	.306	17	27	26	1	4.3
1886 Phi-N	30	9	.769	48	45	43	4	**2**	395²	317	11	69	212	8.8	1.98	167	.210	.244	66	.253	12	**59**	58	5	**6.5**
1887 Phi-N	22	10	.688	37	33	31	2	**1**	297¹	297	13	47	125	10.7	3.00	141	.254	.289	89	.337	14	36	41	3	4.7
Total 4	99	64	.607	183	170	165	13	4	1514²	1402	42	290	728	10.1	2.67	122	.233	.270	277	.288	49	95	97	6	13.8

YEAR TM/L	W	L	PCT	G	GS	CG	SH	SV	IP	H	HR	BB	SO	RAT	ERA	ERA+	OAV	OOB	BH	AVG	PB	PR	/A	PD	TPI
● **JOCKO FIELDS** Fields, John Joseph b: 10/20/1864, Cork, Ireland d: 10/14/50, Jersey City, N.J. BR/TR, 5'10", 160 lbs. Deb: 5/31/1887 ◆																								
1887 Pit-N	0	0	—	1	0	0	0	0	1	0	0	2	0	18.0	0.00	—	.000	.286	44	.268	0	0	0	-0	0.0
● **LOU FIENE** Fiene, Louis Henry "Big Finn" b: 12/29/1884, Ft.Dodge, Iowa d: 12/22/64, Chicago, Ill. BR/TR, 6', 175 lbs. Deb: 5/7/06																								
1906 Chi-A	1	1	.500	6	2	1	0	0	31	35	0	9	12	13.9	2.90	87	.287	.356	2	.200	0	-1	-1	0	-0.1
1907 Chi-A	0	1	.000	6	1	1	0	0	26	30	0	7	15	13.5	4.15	58	.291	.348	2	.182	0	-5	-5	0	-0.3
1908 Chi-A	0	1	.000	1	1	1	0	0	9	9	0	1	3	10.0	4.00	58	.257	.278	0	—	-0	-2	-2	-0	-0.2
1909 Chi-A	2	5	.286	13	6	4	0	0	72	75	1	18	24	12.3	4.13	57	.284	.341	2	.069	-2	-13	-14	1	-1.4
Total 4	3	8	.273	26	10	7	0	1	138	149	1	35	54	12.7	3.85	62	.284	.342	6	.113	-2	-20	-22	2	-2.0
● **DANNY FIFE** Fife, Danny Wayne b: 10/5/49, Harrisburg, Ill. BR/TR, 6'3", 175 lbs. Deb: 8/18/73																								
1973 Min-A	3	2	.600	10	7	1	0	0	51²	54	4	29	18	15.0	4.35	91	.270	.371	0	—	-0	-3	-2	-0	-0.2
1974 Min-A	0	0	—	4	0	0	0	0	4²	10	4	3	28.9	17.36	21	.417	.517	0	—	-0	-7	-7	-0	-0.1
Total 2	3	2	.600	14	7	1	0	0	56¹	64	2	33	21	16.1	5.43	72	.286	.387	0	—	-0	-10	-9	-0	-0.2
● **JACK FIFIELD** Fifield, John Proctor b: 10/5/1871, Enfield, N.H. d: 11/27/39, Syracuse, N.Y. BR/TR, 5'11", 160 lbs. Deb: 4/28/1897																								
1897 Phi-N	5	18	.217	27	26	21	0	0	210²	263	8	80	38	15.0	5.51	76	.303	.368	18	.234	3	-28	-31	1	-2.2
1898 Phi-N	11	9	.550	21	21	18	2	0	171¹	170	2	60	31	13.0	3.31	104	.257	.336	7	.109	-6	2	-3	-3	-0.4
1899 Phi-N	3	8	.273	14	11	9	1	1	92²	110	0	36	14	14.6	4.08	90	.294	.362	9	.257	-1	-2	-4	-1	-0.3
Was-N	2	4	.333	6	6	6	0	0	47	73	1	17	12	17.6	6.13	64	.353	.407	4	.200	-0	-12	-12	-1	-1.2
Yr	5	12	.294	20	17	15	1	1	139²	183	1	53	26	15.3	4.77	79	.313	.382	13	.236	1	-14	-16	-0	-1.5
Total 3	21	39	.350	68	64	54	3	1	521²	616	11	193	89	14.5	4.59	83	.292	.360	38	.194	-2	-36	-44	-2	-4.1
● **FRANK FIGGEMEIER** Figgemeier, Frank Y. b: 4/22/1874, St.Louis, Mo. d: 4/15/15, St.Louis, Mo. Deb: 9/25/1894																								
1894 Phi-N	0	1	.000	1	1	1	0	0	8	12	1	4	2	21.4	11.25	45	.343	.452	1	.333	0	-5	-5	0	-0.4
● **ED FIGUEROA** Figueroa, Eduardo (Padilla) b: 10/14/48, Ciales, P.R. BR/TR, 6'1", 190 lbs. Deb: 4/9/74																								
1974 Cal-A	2	8	.200	25	12	5	1	0	105¹	119	3	36	49	13.6	3.67	94	.294	.357	0	—	0	-1	-3	0	-0.2
1975 Cal-A	16	13	.552	33	32	16	2	0	244²	213	14	84	139	11.1	2.91	122	.233	.301	0	—	0	24	17	1	2.1
1976 *NY-A	19	10	.655	34	34	14	4	0	256²	237	13	94	119	11.7	3.02	113	.246	.315	0	—	0	14	11	-3	0.9
1977 *NY-A	16	11	.593	32	32	12	2	0	239¹	228	19	75	104	11.5	3.57	110	.252	.312	0	—	0	13	10	-2	0.9
1978 *NY-A	20	9	.690	35	35	12	1	0	253	233	22	77	92	11.1	2.99	121	.248	.307	0	—	0	22	18	-0	2.0
1979 NY-A	4	6	.400	16	16	4	1	0	104²	109	6	35	42	12.4	4.13	99	.275	.333	0	—	0	1	-1	0	0.1
1980 NY-A	3	3	.500	15	9	0	0	1	58	90	3	24	16	17.8	6.98	56	.363	.421	0	—	0	-19	-20	0	-1.7
Tex-A	0	7	.000	8	8	0	0	0	39²	62	9	12	9	16.8	5.90	66	.367	.407	0	—	0	-8	-9	-1	-1.2
Yr	3	10	.231	23	17	0	0	1	97²	152	12	36	25	17.3	6.54	60	.360	.410	0	—	0	-27	-29	-1	-2.9
1981 Oak-A	0	0	—	2	1	0	0	0	8¹	8	1	6	1	15.1	5.40	64	.258	.378	0	—	0	-2	-2	0	0.0
Total 8	80	67	.544	200	179	63	12	1	1309²	1299	90	443	571	12.1	3.51	104	.261	.324	0	—	0	44	23	-4	2.9
● **TOM FILER** Filer, Thomas Carson b: 12/1/56, Philadelphia, Pa. BR/TR, 6'1", 198 lbs. Deb: 6/8/82																								
1982 Chi-N	1	2	.333	8	8	0	0	0	40²	50	5	18	15	15.0	5.53	67	.301	.370	1	.083	-0	-9	-8	2	-0.4
1985 Tor-A	7	0	1.000	11	9	0	0	0	48²	38	6	18	24	10.4	3.88	108	.222	.296	0	—	0	1	2	-1	0.1
1988 Mil-A	5	8	.385	19	16	2	1	0	101²	108	8	33	39	12.6	4.43	90	.281	.339	0	—	0	-5	-5	3	-0.3
1989 Mil-A	7	3	.700	13	13	0	0	0	72¹	74	6	23	20	12.6	3.61	106	.271	.337	0	—	0	2	1	-0	0.1
1990 Mil-A	2	3	.400	7	4	0	0	0	22	26	2	9	14	14.3	6.14	63	.289	.354	0	—	0	-5	-6	-1	-1.0
1992 NY-N	0	1	.000	9	1	0	0	0	22	18	2	6	9	9.8	2.05	170	.222	.276	0	.000	-0	4	3	0	0.1
Total 6	22	17	.564	67	51	2	1	0	307¹	314	29	107	115	12.5	4.25	92	.269	.333	1	.067	-1	-12	-12	5	-1.2
● **EDDIE FILES** Files, Charles Edward b: 5/19/1883, Portland, Me. d: 5/10/54, Cornish, Maine BR/TR, Deb: 10/3/08																								
1908 Phi-A	0	0	—	2	0	0	0	0	9	8	0	4	3	13.0	6.00	40	.286	.394	0	.000	-0	-4	-3	-0	-0.1
● **MARC FILLEY** Filley, Marcus Lucius b: 2/28/12, Lansingburgh, N.Y. d: 1/20/95, Yarmouth, Maine BR/TR, 5'11", 172 lbs. Deb: 4/19/34																								
1934 Was-A	0	0	—	1	0	0	0	0	0¹	2	0	0	0	54.0	27.00	16	.667	.667	—		0	-1	-1	0	0.0
● **DANA FILLINGIM** Fillingim, Dana b: 11/6/1893, Columbus, Ga. d: 2/3/61, Tuskegee, Ala. BL/TR, 5'10", 175 lbs. Deb: 8/2/15																								
1915 Phi-A	0	5	.000	8	4	3	0	0	39¹	42	3	32	17	17.2	3.43	85	.313	.449	2	.167	-0	-2	-2	-0	-0.3
1918 Bos-N	7	6	.538	14	13	10	4	0	113	99	0	28	29	10.5	2.23	120	.243	.300	9	.214	0	7	6	-0	0.7
1919 Bos-N	6	13	.316	32	18	9	0	2	186¹	185	2	39	50	10.9	3.38	85	.270	.312	16	.246	1	-10	-11	2	-0.7
1920 Bos-N	12	21	.364	37	31	22	2	0	272	292	8	79	66	12.4	3.11	98	.287	.340	16	.174	-2	1	-2	5	0.2
1921 Bos-N	15	10	.600	44	23	11	3	1	239²	249	10	56	54	11.5	3.45	106	.272	.326	21	.247	5	9	5	-1	0.8
1922 Bos-N	5	9	.357	25	12	5	1	2	117	143	6	37	25	13.9	4.54	86	.311	.363	6	.158	-2	-6	-7	-1	-1.0
1923 Bos-N	1	9	.100	35	12	4	0	0	100¹	141	4	36	27	16.0	5.20	77	.345	.399	7	.226	1	-13	-14	2	-1.1
1925 Phi-N	1	0	1.000	5	1	0	0	0	9	19	1	6	2	26.0	10.38	46	.432	.500	0	.000	-0	-6	-5	-0	-0.5
Total 8	47	73	.392	200	114	59	10	5	1076¹	1170	32	313	270	12.5	3.56	98	.287	.340	77	.209	4	-21	-30	5	-1.8
● **PETE FILSON** Filson, William Peter b: 9/28/58, Darby, Pa. BB/TL, 6'2", 195 lbs. Deb: 5/15/82																								
1982 Min-A	0	2	.000	5	3	0	0	0	12¹	17	2	8	10	18.2	8.76	48	.321	.410	0	—	0	-6	-6	-0	-0.9
1983 Min-A	4	1	.800	26	8	0	0	1	90	87	9	29	49	11.7	3.40	125	.252	.312	0	—	0	7	8	-2	0.3
1984 Min-A	6	5	.545	55	7	0	0	1	118²	106	14	54	59	12.4	4.10	103	.238	.325	0	—	0	0	3	-1	-0.1
1985 Min-A	4	5	.444	40	6	1	0	2	95²	93	13	30	42	11.6	3.67	120	.251	.307	0	—	0	5	8	-1	0.6
1986 Min-A	0	0	—	4	0	0	0	0	6¹	13	1	2	4	22.7	5.68	76	.406	.457	0	—	0	-1	-1	0	0.0
Chi-A	0	1	.000	3	1	0	0	0	11²	14	4	5	4	14.7	6.17	70	.286	.352	0	—	0	-2	-2	-0	-0.2
Yr	0	1	.000	7	1	0	0	0	18	27	5	7	8	17.0	6.00	72	.329	.382	0	—	0	-4	-3	-1	-0.2
1987 NY-A	1	0	1.000	7	2	0	0	0	22	26	2	9	10	14.7	3.27	134	.299	.371	0	—	0	3	4	0	0.2
1990 KC-A	0	4	.000	8	7	0	0	0	35	42	6	13	9	14.7	5.91	65	.282	.348	0	—	0	-5	-6	-0	-0.7
Total 7	15	18	.455	148	34	1	0	4	391²	398	51	150	187	12.8	4.18	102	.260	.329	0	—	0	-5	3	-4	-0.8
● **JOEL FINCH** Finch, Joel D b: 8/20/56, South Bend, Ind. BR/TR, 6'2", 175 lbs. Deb: 6/12/79																								
1979 Bos-A	0	3	.000	15	7	0	0	0	57¹	65	5	25	25	14.3	4.87	91	.289	.363	0	.000	0	-4	-3	1	-0.1
● **BILL FINCHER** Fincher, William Allen b: 5/26/1894, Atlanta, Ga. d: 5/7/46, Shreveport, La. BR/TR, 6'1", 180 lbs. Deb: 4/23/16																								
1916 StL-A	0	1	.000	12	1	0	0	0	21	22	0	7	5	12.4	2.14	128	.282	.341	1	.250	0	2	1	1	0.2
● **TOMMY FINE** Fine, Thomas Morgan b: 10/10/14, Cleburne, Tex. BB/TR, 6', 180 lbs. Deb: 4/26/47																								
1947 Bos-A	1	2	.333	9	7	1	0	0	36	41	1	19	10	15.3	5.50	71	.285	.372	3	.333	1	-7	-6	2	-0.2
1950 StL-A	0	1	.000	14	0	0	0	0	36²	53	6	25	6	19.1	8.10	61	.342	.433	4	.333	1	-14	-13	-0	-0.2
Total 2	1	3	.250	23	7	1	0	0	72²	94	6	44	16	17.2	6.81	65	.314	.404	7	.333	2	-22	-19	1	-0.4
● **ROLLIE FINGERS** Fingers, Roland Glen b: 8/25/46, Steubenville, Ohio BR/TR, 6'4", 195 lbs. Deb: 9/15/68 H																								
1968 Oak-A	0	0	—	1	0	0	0	0	1¹	4	1	1	0	40.5	27.00	10	.571	.667	0	—	0	-4	-4	-0	0.0
1969 Oak-A	6	7	.462	60	8	1	1	12	119	116	13	41	61	12.2	3.71	93	.257	.325	5	.200	-1	-4	-2	-0	-0.2
1970 Oak-A	7	9	.438	45	19	1	0	2	148	137	13	48	79	11.4	3.65	97	.250	.312	4	.103	-0	-1	-2	1	-0.2
1971 *Oak-A	4	6	.400	48	8	2	1	17	129¹	94	14	30	98	9.2	2.99	111	.207	.268	7	.212	1	7	5	2	0.8
1972 *Oak-A	11	9	.550	65	2	0	0	21	111¹	85	8	32	113	9.5	2.51	113	.212	.272	6	.316	3	7	7	-1	1.0
1973 *Oak-A★	7	8	.467	62	2	0	0	22	126²	107	5	39	110	10.7	1.92	185	.226	.290	0	—	0	27	23	-1	3.4
1974 *Oak-A★	9	5	.643	76	0	0	0	18	119	104	5	29	95	10.1	2.65	125	.240	.289	0	—	0	13	9	2	1.6
1975 Oak-A☆	10	6	.625	75	0	0	0	24	126²	95	13	33	115	9.5	2.98	122	.213	.276	0	.000	0	9	6	0	1.4
1976 Oak-A☆	13	11	.542	70	0	0	0	20	134²	118	6	40	113	11.0	2.47	136	.243	.310	0	—	0	16	13	2	3.0
1977 SD-N	8	9	.471	78	0	0	0	35	132¹	123	6	36	113	10.9	2.99	118	.248	.300	1	.050	-0	13	8	0	2.2
1978 SD-N★	6	13	.316	67	0	0	0	37	107¹	84	4	29	72	9.6	2.52	132	.212	.267	3	.167	-0	13	10	-0	2.2
1979 SD-N	9	9	.500	54	0	0	0	13	83²	91	7	37	65	13.9	4.52	78	.281	.356	1	.083	-1	-7	-9	-1	-2.2
1980 SD-N	11	9	.550	66	0	0	0	23	103	101	3	32	69	11.6	2.80	123	.263	.320	5	.278	2	9	7	-1	1.9

YEAR TM/L	W	L	PCT	G	GS	CG	SH	SV	IP	H	HR	BB	SO	RAT	ERA	ERA+	OAV	OOB	BH	AVG	PB	PR	/A	PD	TPI
1981 *Mil-A★	6	3	.667	47	0	0	0	28	78	55	3	13	61	8.0	1.04	330	.198	.236	0	—	0	**23**	**21**	0	**4.2**
1982 Mil-A★	5	6	.455	50	0	0	0	29	79²	63	5	20	71	9.5	2.60	146	.220	.273	0	—	0	13	11	0	2.3
1984 Mil-A	1	2	.333	33	0	0	0	23	46	38	5	13	40	10.0	1.96	197	.213	.267	0	—	0	10	10	-0	1.7
1985 Mil-A	1	6	.143	47	0	0	0	17	55¹	59	9	19	24	12.7	5.04	83	.272	.331	0	—	0	-6	-5	1	-0.8
Total 17	114	118	.491	944	37	4	2	341	1701¹	1474	123	492	1299	10.6	2.90	119	.235	.295	31	.172	3	145	105	6	21.7

● HERMAN FINK
Fink, Herman Adam   b: 8/22/11, Concord, N.C.   d: 8/24/80, Salisbury, N.C.   BR/TR, 6'2", 198 lbs.   Deb: 9/16/35

YEAR TM/L	W	L	PCT	G	GS	CG	SH	SV	IP	H	HR	BB	SO	RAT	ERA	ERA+	OAV	OOB	BH	AVG	PB	PR	/A	PD	TPI
1935 Phi-A	0	3	.000	5	3	0	0	0	15²	18	0	10	2	16.7	9.19	49	.290	.397	1	.200	-0	-8	-8	-0	-1.2
1936 Phi-A	8	16	.333	34	24	9	0	3	188²	222	18	78	53	14.3	5.39	95	.294	.360	8	.125	-4	-7	-6	-2	-1.1
1937 Phi-A	2	1	.667	28	3	1	0	1	80	82	6	35	18	13.3	4.05	116	.263	.339	5	.208	-1	5	6	-0	0.1
Total 3	10	20	.333	67	30	10	0	4	284¹	322	24	123	73	14.1	5.22	95	.285	.356	14	.151	-5	-11	-8	-2	-2.2

● PEMBROKE FINLAYSON
Finlayson, Pembroke   b: 7/31/1888, Cheraw, S.C.   d: 3/6/12, Brooklyn, N.Y.   BR/TR,   Deb: 6/6/08

YEAR TM/L	W	L	PCT	G	GS	CG	SH	SV	IP	H	HR	BB	SO	RAT	ERA	ERA+	OAV	OOB	BH	AVG	PB	PR	/A	PD	TPI
1908 Bro-N	0	0	—	1	0	0	0	0	0¹	0	0	4	0	108.0	135.00	2	.000	.800	0	—	0	-5	-5	-0	0.0
1909 Bro-N	0	0	—	1	0	0	0	0	7	7	0	4	2	14.1	5.14	50	.212	.297	0	.000	-0	-2	-2	-0	-0.1
Total 2	0	0	—	2	0	0	0	0	7¹	7	0	8	2	14.3	11.05	23	.206	.357	0	.000	-0	-7	-7	-0	-0.1

● CHUCK FINLEY
Finley, Charles Edward   b: 11/26/62, Monroe, La.   BL/TL, 6'6", 220 lbs.   Deb: 5/29/86

YEAR TM/L	W	L	PCT	G	GS	CG	SH	SV	IP	H	HR	BB	SO	RAT	ERA	ERA+	OAV	OOB	BH	AVG	PB	PR	/A	PD	TPI
1986 *Cal-A	3	1	.750	25	0	0	0	0	46¹	40	4	23	37	12.4	3.30	124	.235	.330	0	—	0	4	4	1	0.4
1987 Cal-A	2	7	.222	35	3	0	0	0	90²	102	7	43	63	14.7	4.67	92	.287	.369	0	—	0	-2	-4	-0	-0.3
1988 Cal-A	9	15	.375	31	31	2	0	0	194¹	191	15	82	111	12.9	4.17	93	.263	.343	0	—	0	-4	-7	-1	-0.8
1989 Cal-A☆	16	9	.640	29	29	9	1	0	199²	171	13	82	156	11.5	2.57	148	.233	.312	0	—	0	29	28	-3	3.0
1990 Cal-A★	18	9	.667	32	32	7	2	0	236	210	17	81	177	11.2	2.40	159	.243	.309	0	—	0	39	37	-2	4.1
1991 Cal-A	18	9	.667	34	34	4	2	0	227¹	205	23	101	171	12.4	3.80	108	.244	.331	0	—	0	7	8	-3	0.6
1992 Cal-A	7	12	.368	31	31	4	1	0	204¹	212	24	98	124	13.8	3.96	100	.277	.362	0	—	0	-1	0	-3	-0.3
1993 Cal-A	16	14	.533	35	35	**13**	0	0	251¹	243	22	82	187	11.9	3.15	143	.253	.316	0	—	0	33	38	-2	3.7
1994 Cal-A	10	10	.500	25	25	7	2	0	**183**¹	178	21	71	148	12.4	4.32	113	.260	.332	0	—	0	10	12	-2	0.8
1995 Cal-A☆	15	12	.556	32	32	2	1	0	203	192	20	93	195	12.9	4.21	111	.249	.335	0	—	0	11	11	-2	1.1
1996 *Cal-A★	15	16	.484	35	35	4	1	0	238	241	27	94	215	13.1	4.16	118	.263	.339	0	—	0	22	19	-1	2.1
Total 11	129	114	.531	344	287	52	12	0	2074¹	1985	191	850	1584	12.5	3.65	117	.255	.332	0	—	0	149	146	-17	14.4

● HAPPY FINNERAN
Finneran, Joseph Ignatius "Smokey Joe"   b: 10/29/1891, E.Orange, N.J.   d: 2/3/42, Orange, N.J.   BR/TR, 5'10.5", 169 lbs.   Deb: 8/20/12

YEAR TM/L	W	L	PCT	G	GS	CG	SH	SV	IP	H	HR	BB	SO	RAT	ERA	ERA+	OAV	OOB	BH	AVG	PB	PR	/A	PD	TPI
1912 Phi-N	0	2	.000	14	4	0	0	1	46¹	50	2	10	10	11.8	2.53	144	.282	.324	2	.200	0	5	6	-0	0.3
1913 Phi-N	0	0	—	3	0	0	0	0	5	12	0	2	0	25.2	7.20	46	.462	.500	1	.667	1	-6	-5	-0	-0.1
1914 Bro-F	12	11	.522	27	23	13	2	1	175¹	153	6	60	54	11.2	3.18	90	.237	.308	7	.127	-5	-6	-6	-1	-1.3
1915 Bro-F	10	12	.455	37	24	12	1	2	215¹	197	2	87	68	12.2	2.80	97	.249	.331	11	.149	-5	-2	-2	-1	-0.7
1918 Det-A	0	2	.000	5	2	0	0	1	13²	22	0	8	2	19.8	9.88	27	.393	.469	0	.000	-0	-11	-11	1	-1.5
NY-A	3	6	.333	23	13	4	0	0	114¹	134	7	35	34	13.5	3.78	75	.305	.359	9	.231	1	-13	-12	-1	-0.9
Yr	3	8	.273	28	15	4	0	1	128	156	7	43	36	14.1	4.43	63	.315	.372	9	.214	0	-23	-23	-0	-2.4
Total 5	25	33	.431	109	66	29	3	5	570	568	17	202	168	12.4	3.30	87	.266	.335	31	.168	-7	-29	-28	-2	-4.0

● GAR FINNVOLD
Finnvold, Anders Gar   b: 3/11/68, Boynton Beach, Fla.   BR/TR, 6'5", 195 lbs.   Deb: 5/10/94

YEAR TM/L	W	L	PCT	G	GS	CG	SH	SV	IP	H	HR	BB	SO	RAT	ERA	ERA+	OAV	OOB	BH	AVG	PB	PR	/A	PD	TPI
1994 Bos-A	0	4	.000	8	8	0	0	0	36¹	45	4	15	17	15.6	5.94	85	.304	.380	0	—	0	-5	-4	-1	-0.7

● STEVE FIREOVID
Fireovid, Stephen John   b: 6/6/57, Bryan, Ohio   BB/TR, 6'2", 195 lbs.   Deb: 9/6/81

YEAR TM/L	W	L	PCT	G	GS	CG	SH	SV	IP	H	HR	BB	SO	RAT	ERA	ERA+	OAV	OOB	BH	AVG	PB	PR	/A	PD	TPI
1981 SD-N	0	1	.000	5	4	0	0	0	26¹	30	2	7	11	12.6	2.73	119	.294	.339	1	.143	-0	2	2	0	0.0
1983 SD-N	0	0	—	3	0	0	0	0	5	4	0	2	1	10.8	1.80	194	.235	.316	0	—	0	1	1	0	0.0
1984 Phi-N	0	0	—	6	0	0	0	0	5²	4	0	2	3	6.4	1.59	229	.200	.200	0	—	0	1	1	0	0.0
1985 Chi-A	0	0	—	4	0	0	0	0	7	17	0	2	2	24.4	5.14	84	.472	.500	0	—	0	-1	-1	-0	-0.1
1986 Sea-A	2	0	1.000	10	1	0	0	0	21	28	1	4	10	14.1	4.29	99	.333	.371	0	—	0	-0	-0	-0	0.0
1992 Tex-A	1	0	1.000	3	0	0	0	0	6²	10	0	4	0	18.9	4.05	94	.370	.452	0	—	0	-0	-0	-0	0.3
Total 6	3	1	.750	31	5	0	0	0	71²	93	3	19	27	14.2	3.39	110	.325	.369	1	.143	0	3	3	0	0.2

● TED FIRTH
Firth, John E.   b: 1856, Massachusetts   d: 6/23/02, Tewksbury, Mass.   Deb: 8/15/1884

YEAR TM/L	W	L	PCT	G	GS	CG	SH	SV	IP	H	HR	BB	SO	RAT	ERA	ERA+	OAV	OOB	BH	AVG	PB	PR	/A	PD	TPI
1884 Ric-a	0	1	.000	1	1	1	0	0	9	14	0	5	0	19.0	8.00	41	.326	.396	1	.333	0	-5	-5	-0	-0.4

● CARL FISCHER
Fischer, Charles William   b: 11/5/05, Medina, N.Y.   d: 12/10/63, Medina, N.Y.   BR/TL, 6', 180 lbs.   Deb: 7/19/30

YEAR TM/L	W	L	PCT	G	GS	CG	SH	SV	IP	H	HR	BB	SO	RAT	ERA	ERA+	OAV	OOB	BH	AVG	PB	PR	/A	PD	TPI
1930 Was-A	1	1	.500	8	4	1	0	1	33¹	37	0	18	21	15.4	4.86	95	.285	.380	0	.000	-1	-1	-1	-1	-0.1
1931 Was-A	13	9	.591	46	23	7	0	3	191	207	12	80	96	13.6	4.38	98	.273	.344	8	.121	-5	-0	-2	-4	-1.0
1932 Was-A	3	2	.600	12	7	1	1	1	50²	54	4	31	23	15.6	4.97	87	.282	.378	3	.200	1	-3	-4	-2	-0.4
StL-A	3	7	.300	24	11	4	0	0	97	122	12	45	35	15.5	5.57	87	.310	.380	9	.265	0	-12	-8	-1	-0.7
Yr	6	9	.400	36	18	5	1	1	147²	179	16	76	58	15.5	5.36	87	.300	.379	12	.245	1	-15	-11	-3	-1.1
1933 Det-A	11	15	.423	35	22	9	0	3	182²	176	5	84	93	13.0	3.55	122	.251	.334	3	.145	-3	15	15	-2	1.5
1934 Det-A	6	4	.600	20	15	4	1	1	95	107	5	38	39	13.8	4.36	101	.288	.360	2	.065	-3	1	0	-2	-0.4
1935 Det-A	0	1	.000	3	1	0	0	0	12	16	2	5	7	16.5	6.00	69	.320	.393	0	.000	-0	-2	-2	-0	-0.2
Chi-A	5	5	.500	24	11	3	1	0	88²	102	7	39	31	14.5	6.19	75	.283	.356	4	.190	-0	-17	-15	-1	-1.6
Yr	5	6	.455	27	12	3	1	0	100²	118	9	44	38	14.7	6.17	74	.286	.358	4	.174	-1	-19	-18	-1	-1.8
1937 Cle-A	0	1	.000	2	0	0	0	0	0²	2	0	1	1	40.5	27.00	17	.667	.750	0	.000	-0	-2	-2	-0	-1.4
Was-A	4	5	.444	17	11	2	0	2	72	74	6	31	30	13.1	4.38	101	.270	.344	3	.136	-1	2	0	-0	-0.2
Yr	4	6	.400	19	11	2	0	2	72²	76	6	32	31	13.4	4.58	97	.274	.350	3	.136	-1	-0	-2	-1	-1.6
Total 7	46	50	.479	191	105	31	3	11	823	900	53	372	376	14.0	4.63	96	.277	.354	38	.145	-12	-18	-18	-14	-4.5

● HANK FISCHER
Fischer, Henry William "Bulldog"   b: 1/11/40, Yonkers, N.Y.   BR/TR, 6', 190 lbs.   Deb: 4/16/62

YEAR TM/L	W	L	PCT	G	GS	CG	SH	SV	IP	H	HR	BB	SO	RAT	ERA	ERA+	OAV	OOB	BH	AVG	PB	PR	/A	PD	TPI
1962 Mil-N	2	3	.400	29	0	0	0	4	37¹	43	4	20	29	15.2	5.30	72	.291	.375	0	.000	-0	-6	-6	-0	-0.9
1963 Mil-N	4	3	.571	31	6	1	0	0	74¹	74	8	28	49	12.5	4.96	65	.262	.340	2	.105	-0	-14	-14	-1	-1.4
1964 Mil-N	11	10	.524	37	28	9	5	2	168¹	177	17	39	99	11.7	4.01	88	.265	.309	8	.154	1	-9	-9	-1	-1.1
1965 Mil-N	8	9	.471	31	19	2	0	0	122¹	126	18	30	79	12.3	3.89	91	.270	.331	4	.108	-1	-5	-5	-2	-1.0
1966 Atl-N	3	4	.400	14	8	0	0	0	48¹	55	3	14	22	13.0	3.91	93	.296	.348	0	.000	-2	-2	-1	-1	-0.4
Cin-N	0	6	.000	11	9	0	0	0	38	53	3	15	24	16.8	6.63	59	.331	.399	1	.091	-1	-13	-12	-0	-1.7
Yr	2	9	.182	25	17	0	0	0	86¹	108	6	29	46	14.6	5.11	73	.309	.366	1	.042	-2	-14	-13	-2	-2.1
Bos-A	2	3	.400	6	5	1	0	0	31	35	4	11	26	13.6	2.90	131	.287	.351	2	.222	0	2	3	0	0.6
1967 Bos-A	1	2	.333	9	2	1	0	0	26²	24	3	8	18	11.1	2.36	148	.229	.289	1	.143	-0	3	3	0	0.4
Total 6	30	39	.435	168	77	14	5	7	546²	587	60	174	369	12.8	4.23	84	.275	.334	18	.118	-3	-43	-41	-5	-5.5

● JEFF FISCHER
Fischer, Jeffrey Thomas   b: 8/17/63, W.Palm Beach, Fla.   BR/TR, 6'3", 185 lbs.   Deb: 6/19/87

YEAR TM/L	W	L	PCT	G	GS	CG	SH	SV	IP	H	HR	BB	SO	RAT	ERA	ERA+	OAV	OOB	BH	AVG	PB	PR	/A	PD	TPI
1987 Mon-N	0	1	.000	4	2	0	0	0	13²	21	3	5	9	17.1	8.56	49	.362	.413	1	.200	0	-7	-7	-0	-0.4
1989 LA-N	0	0	—	2	0	0	0	0	3¹	7	1	0	2	18.9	13.50	25	.438	.438	0	—	0	-4	-4	-0	0.0
Total 2	0	1	.000	6	2	0	0	0	17	28	4	5	11	17.5	9.53	42	.378	.418	1	.200	0	-11	-10	-0	-0.4

● RUBE FISCHER
Fischer, Reuben Walter   b: 9/19/16, Carlock, S.D.   BR/TR, 6'4", 190 lbs.   Deb: 9/12/41

YEAR TM/L	W	L	PCT	G	GS	CG	SH	SV	IP	H	HR	BB	SO	RAT	ERA	ERA+	OAV	OOB	BH	AVG	PB	PR	/A	PD	TPI
1941 NY-N	1	0	1.000	2	1	1	0	0	11	10	0	6	9	13.1	2.45	151	.238	.333	1	.333	0	1	2	-0	0.1
1943 NY-N	5	10	.333	22	17	4	0	1	130²	140	4	59	47	13.8	4.61	75	.281	.360	11	.256	3	-18	-17	-2	-1.7
1944 NY-N	6	14	.300	38	18	2	1	2	128²	128	7	87	39	15.5	5.18	71	.266	.384	5	.125	-2	-22	-22	-2	-3.4
1945 NY-N	3	8	.273	31	4	0	0	1	76²	90	6	49	27	16.4	5.63	69	.288	.387	4	.211	2	-16	-15	-1	-1.8
1946 NY-N	1	2	.333	15	1	0	0	0	35²	48	3	21	14	17.4	6.31	55	.316	.399	1	.111	-1	-11	-11	-0	-0.9
Total 5	16	34	.320	108	41	7	1	4	382²	416	20	222	136	15.2	5.10	71	.280	.377	22	.193	-2	-66	-63	-5	-7.7

● TODD FISCHER
Fischer, Todd Richard   b: 9/15/60, Columbus, Ohio   BR/TR, 5'10", 170 lbs.   Deb: 5/29/86

YEAR TM/L	W	L	PCT	G	GS	CG	SH	SV	IP	H	HR	BB	SO	RAT	ERA	ERA+	OAV	OOB	BH	AVG	PB	PR	/A	PD	TPI
1986 Cal-A	0	0	—	9	0	0	0	0	17	18	4	8	7	13.8	4.24	97	.286	.366	0	—	0	-0	-0	-0	0.0

● BILL FISCHER
Fischer, William Charles   b: 10/11/30, Wausau, Wis.   BR/TR, 6', 190 lbs.   Deb: 4/21/56   C

YEAR TM/L	W	L	PCT	G	GS	CG	SH	SV	IP	H	HR	BB	SO	RAT	ERA	ERA+	OAV	OOB	BH	AVG	PB	PR	/A	PD	TPI
1956 Chi-A	0	0	—	3	0	0	0	0	1²	6	0	1	2	37.8	21.60	19	.545	.583	0	—	0	-3	-3	0	0.0

YEAR	TM/L	W	L	PCT	G	GS	CG	SH	SV	IP	H	HR	BB	SO	RAT	ERA	ERA+	OAV	OOB	BH	AVG	PB	PR	/A	PD	TPI
1957	Chi-A	7	8	.467	33	11	3	1	1	124	139	1	35	48	12.8	3.48	107	.291	.344	6	.150	-2	4	3	-1	0.1
1958	Chi-A	2	3	.400	17	3	0	0	0	36¹	43	6	13	16	13.9	6.69	54	.301	.359	1	.143	-0	-12	-12	1	-1.4
	Det-A	2	4	.333	22	0	0	0	2	30²	46	6	13	16	17.3	7.63	53	.362	.421	1	.000	-0	-13	-12	0	-2.2
	Was-A	0	3	.000	3	3	0	0	0	21	24	1	5	10	12.9	3.86	99	.320	.370	1	.200	-0	-0	-0	0	0.1
	Yr	4	10	.286	42	6	0	0	2	88	113	13	31	42	14.8	6.34	60	.325	.382	2	.154	-0	-25	-25	2	-3.5
1959	Was-A	9	11	.450	34	29	6	1	0	187¹	211	16	43	62	12.4	4.28	92	.281	.324	7	.130	-2	-9	-8	4	-0.5
1960	Was-A	3	5	.375	20	7	1	0	0	77	85	7	17	31	11.9	4.91	79	.281	.320	3	.158	1	-9	-9	1	-0.6
	Det-A	5	3	.625	20	6	1	0	0	55	50	6	18	24	11.1	3.44	115	.244	.305	4	.364	2	3	3	0	0.7
	Yr	8	8	.500	40	13	2	0	0	132	135	13	35	55	11.6	4.30	91	.265	.313	7	.233	3	-6	-6	2	0.1
1961	Det-A	3	2	.600	26	1	0	0	3	46²	54	10	17	18	13.7	5.01	82	.292	.351	0	.000	-1	-5	-5	-0	-0.6
	KC-A	1	0	1.000	15	0	0	0	2	21	26	2	6	12	13.7	3.86	108	.321	.368	0	.000	-0	1	0	0	-0.0
	Yr	4	2	.667	41	1	0	0	5	67²	80	12	23	30	13.7	4.66	89	.301	.356	0	.000	-1	-5	-4	0	-0.6
1962	KC-A	4	12	.250	34	16	5	0	2	127²	150	16	8	38	11.2	3.95	107	.293	.305	4	.105	-2	0	-1	0	0.2
1963	KC-A	9	6	.600	45	2	0	0	3	95²	86	13	29	34	11.1	3.57	109	.242	.305	1	.067	-0	1	3	-1	0.3
1964	Min-A	0	1	.000	9	0	0	0	0	7¹	16	2	5	2	25.8	7.36	49	.471	.538	0	—	0	-3	-3	0	-0.4
Total	9	45	58	.437	281	78	16	2	13	831¹	936	86	210	313	12.5	4.34	91	.287	.333	27	.136	-4	-46	-37	5	-4.2

● **LEO FISHEL** Fishel, Leo b: 12/13/1877, Babylon, N.Y. d: 5/19/60, Hempstead, N.Y. BR/TR, 6', 175 lbs. Deb: 5/3/1899

YEAR	TM/L	W	L	PCT	G	GS	CG	SH	SV	IP	H	HR	BB	SO	RAT	ERA	ERA+	OAV	OOB	BH	AVG	PB	PR	/A	PD	TPI
1899	NY-N	0	1	.000	1	1	1	0	0	9	9	0	6	4	17.0	6.00	63	.257	.395	1	.250	-0	-2	-2	0	-0.2

● **FISHER** Fisher b: Johnstown, Pa. Deb: 7/17/1884

1884	Phi-U	1	7	.125	8	8	8	0	0	70²	76	0	13	42	11.3	3.57	65	.257	.288	8	.222	-1	-9	-10	-1	-1.0

● **FISHER** Fisher b: Philadelphia, Pa. Deb: 8/6/1885

1885	Buf-N	0	1	.000	1	1	1	0	0	9	10	0	2	4	12.0	5.00	60	.256	.293	0	.000	-1	-2	-2	0	-0.2

● **BRIAN FISHER** Fisher, Brian Kevin b: 3/18/62, Honolulu, Hawaii BR/TR, 6'4", 210 lbs. Deb: 5/7/85

YEAR	TM/L	W	L	PCT	G	GS	CG	SH	SV	IP	H	HR	BB	SO	RAT	ERA	ERA+	OAV	OOB	BH	AVG	PB	PR	/A	PD	TPI
1985	NY-A	4	4	.500	55	0	0	0	14	98¹	77	4	29	85	9.7	2.38	168	.216	.275	0	—	0	19	18	0	1.8
1986	NY-A	9	5	.643	62	0	0	0	6	96²	105	14	37	67	13.3	4.93	83	.277	.343	0	—	0	-8	-9	-1	-1.4
1987	Pit-N	11	9	.550	37	26	6	3	0	185¹	185	27	72	117	12.7	4.52	91	.262	.334	11	.190	5	-8	-8	-1	-0.6
1988	Pit-N	8	10	.444	33	22	1	1	1	146¹	157	13	57	66	13.5	4.61	74	.277	.348	2	.048	-2	-19	-20	-2	-2.7
1989	Pit-N	0	3	.000	9	3	0	0	1	17	25	2	10	8	18.5	7.94	42	.329	.407	0	.000	-1	-8	-9	-0	-1.5
1990	Hou-N	0	0	—	4	0	0	0	0	5	9	1	0	1	16.2	7.20	52	.409	.409	0	—	0	-2	-2	-0	-0.5
1992	Sea-A	4	3	.571	22	14	0	0	1	91¹	80	9	47	26	12.6	4.53	88	.234	.328	0	—	0	-6	-6	-0	-0.5
Total	7	36	34	.514	222	65	7	4	23	640	638	70	252	370	12.7	4.39	89	.261	.332	13	.124	2	-33	-36	-5	-4.9

● **CHAUNCEY FISHER** Fisher, Chauncey Burr "Peach" or "Whoa Bill" b: 1/8/1872, Anderson, Ind. d: 4/27/39, Los Angeles, Cal. BR/TR, 5'11", 175 lbs. Deb: 9/20/1893 F

YEAR	TM/L	W	L	PCT	G	GS	CG	SH	SV	IP	H	HR	BB	SO	RAT	ERA	ERA+	OAV	OOB	BH	AVG	PB	PR	/A	PD	TPI
1893	Cle-N	0	2	.000	2	2	0	0	0	18	26	0	9	9	17.5	5.50	89	.329	.398	2	.250	-0	-2	-1	0	-0.1
1894	Cle-N	0	2	.000	3	2	0	0	0	11	22	0	5	0	22.9	11.45	48	.407	.467	0	.000	-1	-7	-7	1	-0.8
	Cin-N	2	8	.200	11	11	10	0	0	91	134	4	44	14	17.6	7.32	76	.338	.405	10	.233	-1	-20	-18	-1	-1.5
	Yr	2	10	.167	14	13	10	0	0	102	156	4	49	14	18.1	7.76	71	.346	.410	10	.213	-2	-28	-25	-1	-2.3
1896	Cin-N	10	7	.588	27	15	13	2	2	159²	199	9	36	25	13.5	4.45	104	.303	.344	14	.246	0	-2	3	-0	0.2
1897	Bro-N	9	7	.563	20	13	11	1	1	149	184	5	43	31	13.8	4.23	97	.301	.349	12	.203	-1	-2	-2	-0	-0.4
1901	NY-N	0	0	—	1	1	0	0	0	4	11	0	2	1	29.3	15.75	21	.500	.542	0	—	-0	-6	-6	-0	-0.1
	StL-N	0	0	—	1	0	0	0	0	3	7	0	1	0	24.0	15.00	21	.438	.471	0	—	-0	-4	-4	0	0.0
	Yr	0	0	—	2	1	0	0	0	7	18	0	3	1	27.0	15.43	21	.474	.512	0	.000	-0	-9	-9	-0	-0.1
Total	5	21	26	.447	65	44	36	3	3	435²	583	18	140	80	15.1	5.37	86	.318	.368	38	.218	-3	-39	-35	-2	-2.7

● **CLARENCE FISHER** Fisher, Clarence Henry b: 8/27/1898, Letart, W.Va. d: 11/2/65, Point Pleasant, W.Va. BR/TR, 6', 174 lbs. Deb: 9/14/19

YEAR	TM/L	W	L	PCT	G	GS	CG	SH	SV	IP	H	HR	BB	SO	RAT	ERA	ERA+	OAV	OOB	BH	AVG	PB	PR	/A	PD	TPI
1919	Was-A	0	0	—	2	0	0	0	0	4	8	0	1	2	24.8	13.50	24	.421	.500	0	—	-0	-5	-5	0	0.0
1920	Was-A	0	1	.000	2	0	0	0	0	3²	5	0	5	0	24.5	9.82	38	.714	.833	0	.000	-0	-2	-1	1	-0.5
Total	2	0	1	.000	4	0	0	0	0	7²	13	0	8	1	24.7	11.74	29	.500	.618	0	.000	-0	-7	-7	1	-0.5

● **DON FISHER** Fisher, Donald Raymond b: 2/6/16, Cleveland, Ohio d: 7/29/73, Mayfield Heights, Ohio BR/TR, 6', 210 lbs. Deb: 8/25/45

1945	NY-N	1	0	1.000	2	1	1	0	0	18	12	0	4	10	10.5	2.00	196	.190	.292	1	.143	-0	4	4	0	0.2

● **EDDIE FISHER** Fisher, Eddie Gene b: 7/16/36, Shreveport, La. BR/TR, 6'2.5", 200 lbs. Deb: 6/22/59

YEAR	TM/L	W	L	PCT	G	GS	CG	SH	SV	IP	H	HR	BB	SO	RAT	ERA	ERA+	OAV	OOB	BH	AVG	PB	PR	/A	PD	TPI
1959	SF-N	2	6	.250	17	5	0	0	1	40	57	8	9	15	14.8	7.87	48	.339	.373	0	.000	-1	-17	-18	-1	-3.1
1960	SF-N	1	0	1.000	3	1	0	0	0	12²	11	2	7	9	9.2	3.55	98	.224	.277	3	.600	1	-0	-0	0	0.1
1961	SF-N	0	2	.000	15	1	0	0	0	33²	36	7	9	16	12.0	5.35	71	.267	.313	1	.143	-0	-5	-6	0	-0.3
1962	Chi-A	9	5	.643	57	12	2	1	5	182²	169	17	45	88	10.6	3.10	126	.245	.293	6	.130	-0	18	16	0	1.2
1963	Chi-A	9	8	.529	33	15	2	1	0	120²	114	14	28	67	10.7	3.95	89	.244	.290	5	.139	-1	-4	-6	1	-0.8
1964	Chi-A	6	3	.667	59	2	0	0	9	125	86	13	32	74	8.7	3.02	114	.192	.250	2	.167	-0	8	6	0	0.5
1965	Chi-A★	15	7	.682	**82**	0	0	0	24	165¹	118	13	43	90	**8.9**	2.40	133	.205	.262	4	.138	0	20	15	1	2.5
1966	Chi-A	1	3	.250	23	0	0	0	6	35¹	27	1	17	18	11.5	2.29	138	.214	.313	0	.000	-0	4	3	0	0.5
	Bal-A	5	3	.625	44	0	0	0	13	71²	60	4	19	39	10.2	2.64	126	.226	.282	2	.154	0	6	6	0	0.8
	Yr	6	6	.500	**67**	0	0	0	19	107	87	5	36	57	10.5	2.52	130	.221	.289	2	.133	-0	11	9	-0	1.3
1967	Bal-A	4	3	.571	46	0	0	0	1	89²	87	7	26	53	11.2	3.61	87	.245	.307	1	.200	-1	-4	-5	-1	-0.4
1968	Cle-A	4	2	.667	54	0	0	0	4	94²	87	8	17	42	10.1	2.85	104	.248	.286	0	.000	-0	1	1	1	0.2
1969	Cal-A	3	2	.600	52	0	0	0	2	96²	100	9	34	47	12.0	3.63	96	.272	.326	1	.091	-1	-0	-2	0	-0.2
1970	Cal-A	4	4	.500	67	0	0	0	8	130¹	117	15	35	74	10.6	3.04	119	.239	.292	1	.091	-1	10	8	1	0.7
1971	Cal-A	10	8	.556	57	3	0	0	3	119	92	11	50	82	10.9	2.72	119	.211	.295	1	.063	-1	10	7	0	0.9
1972	Cal-A	4	5	.444	43	1	0	0	4	81¹	73	6	31	32	11.5	3.76	77	.247	.319	2	.118	-1	-6	-8	-1	-1.1
	Chi-A	0	1	.000	6	0	0	0	0	22¹	31	1	9	10	16.1	4.43	70	.348	.408	0	—	0	-3	-3	-0	-0.2
	Yr	4	6	.400	49	1	0	0	4	103²	104	7	40	42	12.5	3.91	76	.267	.336	2	.083	-1	-10	-11	-1	-1.3
1973	Chi-A	6	7	.462	26	16	2	0	0	110²	135	12	38	57	14.3	4.88	81	.301	.360	0	—	0	-13	-13	-1	-1.2
	StL-N	2	1	.667	6	0	0	0	0	14	7	0	6	8	6.4	1.29	283	.192	.192	1	1.000	0	2	2	0	0.8
Total	15	85	70	.548	690	63	7	2	81	1538²	1398	149	438	812	10.9	3.41	101	.243	.299	30	.122	-5	26	5	3	0.8

● **ED FISHER** Fisher, Edward Fredrick b: 10/31/1876, Wayne, Mich. d: 7/24/51, Spokane, Wash. BR/TR, 6'2", 200 lbs. Deb: 9/5/02

1902	Det-A	0	0	—	1	0	0	0	0	4	4	0	1	0	11.3	—	.267	.313	0	.000	-0	2	2	-0	-0.1

● **FRITZ FISHER** Fisher, Frederick Brown b: 11/28/41, Adrian, Mich. BL/TL, 6'1", 180 lbs. Deb: 4/19/64

1964	Det-A	0	0	—	1	0	0	0	0	0¹	2	0	2	1	108.0	108.00	3	.667	.800	0	—	0	-4	-4	0	0.0

● **HARRY FISHER** Fisher, Harry Devereux b: 1/3/26, Newbury, Ont., Can. d: 9/20/81, Waterloo, Ont., Canada BL/TR, 6', 180 lbs. Deb: 9/16/51 ♦

1952	Pit-N	1	2	.333	8	3	0	0	0	18¹	17	4	13	5	15.7	6.87	58	.266	.405	5	.333	1	-6	-6	-1	-0.8

● **JACK FISHER** Fisher, John Howard "Fat Jack" b: 3/4/39, Frostburg, Md. BR/TR, 6'2", 215 lbs. Deb: 4/14/59

YEAR	TM/L	W	L	PCT	G	GS	CG	SH	SV	IP	H	HR	BB	SO	RAT	ERA	ERA+	OAV	OOB	BH	AVG	PB	PR	/A	PD	TPI
1959	Bal-A	1	6	.143	27	7	1	1	2	88²	76	7	38	52	11.7	3.05	124	.230	.311	3	.130	-1	8	7	-1	0.4
1960	Bal-A	12	11	.522	40	20	8	3	2	197²	174	13	78	99	11.6	3.41	111	.241	.317	11	.183	2	10	9	0	1.2
1961	Bal-A	10	13	.435	36	25	10	1	1	196	205	17	75	118	13.0	3.90	111	.270	.339	5	.089	-2	3	-1	-3	-0.6
1962	Bal-A	7	9	.438	32	25	4	0	1	152	173	23	56	81	13.7	5.09	73	.284	.346	5	.102	-1	-19	-24	-1	-2.3
1963	SF-N	6	10	.375	36	12	0	0	1	116	132	12	38	57	13.6	4.58	70	.284	.344	3	.103	-1	-17	-18	-2	-2.3
1964	NY-N	10	17	.370	40	34	8	1	0	227²	256	23	56	115	12.7	4.23	85	.283	.331	12	.158	1	-18	-16	-1	-1.8
1965	NY-N	8	24	.250	43	36	10	0	0	253²	252	22	68	116	11.5	3.94	90	.259	.310	12	.154	0	-1	-2	0	-0.3
1966	NY-N	11	14	.440	38	33	10	2	0	230	229	26	54	127	11.4	3.68	99	.260	.309	6	.090	-2	-2	-1	3	0.0
1967	NY-N	9	18	.333	39	30	7	1	0	220¹	251	21	64	117	13.0	4.70	72	.287	.339	7	.100	-1	-32	-32	1	-3.7
1968	Chi-A	8	13	.381	35	28	2	0	0	180²	176	14	48	80	11.5	2.99	101	.257	.307	2	.091	-1	4	4	1	0.4
1969	Cin-N	4	4	.500	34	15	0	0	0	113	137	15	30	55	13.7	5.50	68	.295	.345	4	.121	-1	-24	-22	-2	-1.8
Total	11	86	139	.382	400	265	62	9	9	1975²	2061	193	605	1017	12.4	4.06	88	.269	.326	74	.125	-6	-102	-108	-1	-12.2

YEAR TM/L	W	L	PCT	G	GS	CG	SH	SV	IP	H	HR	BB	SO	RAT	ERA	ERA+	OAV	OOB	BH	AVG	PB	PR	/A	PD	TPI
● **MAURICE FISHER** Fisher, Maurice Wayne b: 2/16/31, Uniondale, Ind. BR/TR, 6'5", 210 lbs. Deb: 4/16/55																									
1955 Cin-N	0	0	—	1	0	0	0	0	2²	5	1	2	1	23.6	6.75	63	.385	.467	0	.000	-0	-1	-1	-0	0.0
● **RAY FISHER** Fisher, Ray Lyle "Pick" b: 10/4/1887, Middlebury, Vt. d: 11/3/82, Ann Arbor, Mich. BR/TR, 5'11.5", 180 lbs. Deb: 7/2/10																									
1910 NY-A	5	3	.625	17	7	3	0	1	92¹	95	0	18	42	11.3	2.92	91	.274	.315	3	.103	-2	-4	-3	1	-0.3
1911 NY-A	10	11	.476	29	22	8	2	0	171²	178	3	55	99	12.5	3.25	111	.269	.330	7	.119	-3	2	7	4	0.8
1912 NY-A	2	8	.200	17	13	5	0	0	90¹	107	2	32	47	14.0	5.88	61	.312	.374	2	.065	-4	-26	-23	3	-2.2
1913 NY-A	12	16	.429	43	31	14	1	1	246¹	244	6	71	92	11.8	3.18	94	.261	.319	22	.278	3	-7	-5	2	0.0
1914 NY-A	10	12	.455	29	26	17	2	1	209	177	2	61	86	10.4	2.28	121	.241	.303	9	.138	-2	11	11	4	1.3
1915 NY-A	18	11	.621	30	28	20	4	0	247²	219	7	62	97	10.4	2.11	139	.243	.295	9	.108	-5	23	23	-0	2.1
1916 NY-A	11	8	.579	31	21	9	1	2	179	191	4	51	56	12.4	3.17	91	.285	.339	11	.177	1	-7	-5	-1	-0.6
1917 NY-A	8	9	.471	23	18	12	3	0	144	126	3	43	64	10.7	2.19	123	.243	.304	9	.180	-0	8	8	1	1.1
1919 *Cin-N	14	5	.737	26	20	12	5	1	174¹	141	5	38	41	9.3	2.17	128	.226	.271	16	.271	3	14	12	3	2.1
1920 Cin-N	10	11	.476	33	21	10	1	1	201	189	5	50	56	11.1	2.73	111	.249	.302	17	.243	1	9	7	2	1.1
Total 10	100	94	.515	278	207	110	19	7	1755²	1667	34	481	680	11.2	2.82	106	.257	.312	105	.179	-8	23	30	19	5.4
● **TOM FISHER** Fisher, Thomas Chalmers "Red" b: 11/1/1880, Anderson, Ind. d: 9/3/72, Anderson, Ind. BR/TR, 5'10.5", 185 lbs. Deb: 4/17/04 F																									
1904 Bos-N	6	16	.273	31	21	19	2	0	214	257	5	82	84	14.7	4.25	65	.302	.370	21	.212	3	-36	-35	-5	-3.4
● **TOM FISHER** Fisher, Thomas Gene b: 4/4/42, Cleveland, Ohio BR/TR, 6', 180 lbs. Deb: 9/20/67																									
1967 Bal-A	0	0	—	2	0	0	0	0	3¹	2	0	2	1	10.8	0.00		.182	.308	0	—	0	1	1	-0	0.0
● **CHEROKEE FISHER** Fisher, William Charles b: 12/1845, Philadelphia, Pa. d: 9/26/12, New York, N.Y. BR/TR, 5'9", 164 lbs. Deb: 5/6/1871 ♦																									
1871 Rok-n	4	16	.200	24	24	22	1	0	213	295	3	31	15	13.8	4.35	94	.281	.302	28	.228	-3	-3	-6		-0.3
1872 Bal-n	10	1	.909	19	11	9	1	1	110	93	0	11	20	**8.5**	1.80	204	**.197**	**.216**	52	.231	-1	22	23		0.9
1873 Ath-n	3	4	.429	13	5	5	0	2	84¹	90	1	10	14	**10.7**	1.81	188	**.227**	**.246**	66	.261	1	13	15		0.8
1874 Har-n	13	23	.361	39	35	31	0	0	322¹	417	1	13	20	12.0	2.26	102	.278	.284	54	.224	-1	-3	-1		-0.4
1875 Phi-n	22	19	.537	41	41	36	2	0	358	345	6	9	18	8.9	1.99	115	.229	.233	41	.232	-1	10	11		0.5
1876 Cin-N	4	20	.167	28	24	22	0	0	229¹	294	6	6	29	11.8	3.02	73	.285	.289	32	.248	-1	-18	-21	-2	-1.9
1878 Pro-N	0	1	.000	1	1	1	0	0	7	14	0	0	2	14.0	4.00	55	.304	.304	0	.000	-0	-2	-2	-0	-0.2
Total 5 n	52	63	.452	136	116	103	4	3	1087²	1240	11	74	87	10.9	2.50	115	.252	.263	241	.237	-8	40	47		1.5
Total 2	4	21	.160	29	25	23	0	0	238¹	308	6	6	31	11.9	3.06	72	.285	.289	32	.235	-2	-20	-23	-2	-2.1
● **MAX FISKE** Fiske, Maximilian Patrick "Ski" b: 10/12/1888, Chicago, Ill. d: 5/15/28, Chicago, Ill. BR/TR, 5'11", 185 lbs. Deb: 4/19/14																									
1914 Chi-F	12	12	.500	38	22	7	0	0	198	161	7	59	87	10.3	3.14	85	.231	.298	16	.235	0	-6	-11	-0	-1.2
● **PAUL FITTERY** Fittery, Paul Clarence b: 10/10/1887, Lebanon, Pa. d: 1/28/74, Cartersville, Ga. BR/TL, 5'8.5", 156 lbs. Deb: 9/5/14																									
1914 Cin-N	0	2	.000	8	4	2	0	0	43²	41	0	12	21	11.1	3.09	95	.246	.300	1	.059	-1	-1	-0	0	-0.2
1917 Phi-N	1	1	.500	17	2	1	0	0	55²	69	1	27	13	16.3	4.53	62	.317	.404	2	.091	-1	-11	-11	1	-0.3
Total 2	1	3	.250	25	6	3	0	0	99¹	110	1	39	34	14.0	3.90	73	.286	.360	3	.077	-2	-13	-11	2	-0.5
● **JOHN FITZGERALD** Fitzgerald, John Francis b: 9/15/33, Brooklyn, N.Y. BL/TL, 6'3", 190 lbs. Deb: 9/28/58																									
1958 SF-N	0	0	—	1	1	0	0	0	3	1	1	1	3	6.0	3.00	127	.111	.200	0	.000	-0	0	0	0	0.0
● **JOHN FITZGERALD** Fitzgerald, John H. b: 5/30/1870, Natick, Mass. d: 3/31/21, Boston, Mass. Deb: 7/18/1891																									
1891 Bos-a	1	1	.500	6	3	2	0	1	32	49	2	11	16	17.4	5.63	62	.340	.395	1	.071	-2	-7	-8	0	-0.5
● **JOHN FITZGERALD** Fitzgerald, John J. Deb: 4/18/1890																									
1890 Roc-a	3	8	.273	11	11	8	1	0	78	77	0	45	35	14.8	4.04	88	.250	.357	6	.194	-0	-1	-4	1	-0.4
● **JOHN FITZGERALD** Fitzgerald, John T. b: Leadville, Col. Deb: 6/4/1891																									
1891 Lou-a	14	18	.438	33	32	29	3	0	276	280	6	95	111	12.7	3.59	102	.254	.321	19	.170	-1	4	2	-4	-0.1
1892 Lou-N	1	3	.250	4	4	4	0	0	34	45	2	11	3	15.1	4.24	72	.306	.358	2	.133	-0	-4	-4	-1	-0.5
Total 2	15	21	.417	37	36	33	3	0	310	325	8	106	114	12.9	3.66	98	.260	.325	21	.165	-0	1	-2	-4	-0.6
● **PAUL FITZKE** Fitzke, Paul Frederick Herman "Bob" b: 7/30/1900, LaCrosse, Wis. d: 6/30/50, Sacramento, Cal. BR/TR, 5'11.5", 185 lbs. Deb: 9/1/24																									
1924 Cle-A	1	0	1.000	1	0	0	0	0	4	3	0	1	3	18.0	4.50	95	.313	.421	0	.000	0	1	1	-0	0.0
● **AL FITZMORRIS** Fitzmorris, Alan James b: 3/21/46, Buffalo, N.Y. BB/TR, 6'2", 190 lbs. Deb: 9/8/69																									
1969 KC-A	1	1	.500	7	0	0	0	2	10²	9	1	4	3	11.0	4.22	87	.237	.310	0	.000	-	-1	-0	-0	-0.2
1970 KC-A	8	5	.615	43	11	2	0	1	117²	112	14	52	47	12.5	4.44	84	.254	.333	9	.290	4	-9	-9	1	-0.5
1971 KC-A	7	5	.583	36	15	2	1	0	127¹	112	6	55	53	11.9	4.17	82	.245	.327	11	.250	2	-10	-10	2	-0.6
1972 KC-A	2	5	.286	38	2	0	0	0	101	99	10	28	51	11.4	3.74	81	.252	.303	4	.174	1	-8	-8	2	-0.3
1973 KC-A	8	3	.727	15	13	3	1	0	89	88	5	25	26	11.4	2.83	145	.259	.310	0	—	0	10	13	1	1.1
1974 KC-A	13	6	.684	34	27	9	4	1	190	189	8	63	53	11.9	2.79	137	.260	.319	0	—	0	17	23	3	2.3
1975 KC-A	16	12	.571	35	35	11	3	0	242	239	16	76	78	11.9	3.57	108	.262	.322	0	—	0	6	7	1	0.8
1976 KC-A	15	11	.577	35	33	8	2	0	220¹	227	6	56	80	11.6	3.06	114	.273	.320	0	—	0	11	11	3	1.6
1977 Cle-A	6	10	.375	29	21	1	0	0	133	164	12	53	54	14.8	5.41	73	.306	.369	0	—	0	-20	-22	-0	-2.0
1978 Cle-A	0	1	.000	7	0	0	0	0	14¹	19	3	7	5	17.0	6.28	59	.333	.415	0	—	0	-4	-4	-0	-0.2
Cal-A	1	0	1.000	9	0	0	0	0	31²	26	2	14	8	11.4	1.71	212	.236	.323	0	—	0	7	7	-0	0.5
Yr	1	1	.500	16	0	0	0	0	46	45	5	21	13	12.9	3.13	117	.268	.349	0	—	0	3	3	-0	0.3
Total 10	77	59	.566	288	159	36	11	7	1277	1284	83	433	458	12.2	3.65	101	.265	.327	24	.242	7	-1	5	12	2.5
● **FREDDIE FITZSIMMONS** Fitzsimmons, Frederick Landis "Fat Freddie" b: 7/28/01, Mishawaka, Ind. d: 11/18/79, Yucca Valley, Cal. BR/TR, 5'11", 185 lbs. Deb: 8/12/25 MC																									
1925 NY-N	6	3	.667	10	8	6	1	0	74²	70	4	18	17	10.6	2.65	152	.248	.293	9	.310	2	13	12	2	1.6
1926 NY-N	14	10	.583	37	26	12	0	0	219	224	7	58	48	11.8	2.88	130	.272	.322	11	.128	-6	23	21	3	1.8
1927 NY-N	17	10	.630	42	31	14	1	3	244²	260	15	67	78	12.2	3.72	104	.275	.325	18	.207	-0	6	4	2	0.6
1928 NY-N	20	9	.690	40	32	16	1	1	261¹	264	13	65	67	11.5	3.68	106	.268	.322	18	.191	1	9	7	2	0.9
1929 NY-N	15	11	.577	37	31	19	4	1	221²	242	14	66	55	12.6	4.10	112	.285	.338	15	.183	-2	15	12	4	1.4
1930 NY-N	19	7	**.731**	41	29	17	1	1	224¹	230	26	59	76	11.6	4.25	111	.266	.314	22	.265	5	18	12	7	2.2
1931 NY-N	18	11	.621	35	33	19	4	0	253²	246	16	62	78	10.8	3.05	121	.251	.296	21	.228	9	23	18	8	**3.7**
1932 NY-N	11	11	.500	35	31	11	0	0	237²	287	18	83	65	14.1	4.43	84	.299	.356	19	.221	4	-15	-19	7	-0.6
1933 *NY-N	16	11	.593	36	35	13	1	0	251²	243	14	72	65	11.3	2.90	111	.251	.305	19	.200	3	12	9	6	1.8
1934 NY-N	18	14	.563	38	37	14	3	0	263¹	266	12	51	73	10.9	3.04	127	.261	.297	22	.232	5	30	24	5	3.7
1935 NY-N	4	8	.333	18	15	6	**4**	0	94	104	7	22	23	12.2	4.02	96	.281	.323	8	.258	1	-0	-2	1	0.0
1936 *NY-N	10	7	.588	28	17	7	0	2	141	147	6	39	35	11.9	3.32	117	.274	.323	7	.149	-2	11	9	1	0.0
1937 NY-N	2	2	.500	6	4	1	1	0	27¹	28	3	8	13	11.9	4.61	84	.272	.324	3	.300	-2	-2	-0	-1	-0.1
Bro-N	4	8	.333	13	14	7	0	0	90²	91	2	32	29	12.3	4.27	95	.263	.327	5	.167	-1	-4	-5	-0	-0.3
Yr	6	10	.375	19	18	8	1	0	118	119	5	40	42	12.2	4.35	92	.265	.327	8	.200	-1	-6	-5	-1	-0.4
1938 Bro-N	11	8	.579	27	26	13	6	0	202²	205	8	43	38	11.1	3.02	129	.264	.306	12	.171	-1	17	20	6	2.3
1939 Bro-N	7	9	.438	27	20	5	0	3	151¹	178	8	28	44	12.4	3.87	104	.293	.327	11	.234	3	1	3	6	1.3
1940 Bro-N	16	2	**.889**	20	18	11	4	0	134¹	120	7	25	35	9.8	2.81	142	.233	.269	5	.106	-2	15	18	1	2.2
1941 *Bro-N	6	1	.857	13	12	3	1	0	82²	78	3	26	19	11.5	2.07	177	.245	.305	4	.143	-0	14	15	2	1.5
1942 Bro-N	0	0	—	3	0	0	0	0	3	6	1	2	1	21.0	15.00	22	.400	.438	1	.500	-0	-4	-0	0	0.0
1943 Bro-N	3	4	.429	11	7	1	0	0	44²	50	6	12	14	14.5	5.44	62	.281	.360	1	.071	-1	-10	-10	-1	-1.5
Total 19	217	146	.598	513	426	186	29	13	3223²	3335	186	846	870	11.8	3.51	111	.268	.316	231	.200	21	174	144	60	23.1
● **PATSY FLAHERTY** Flaherty, Patrick Joseph b: 6/29/1876, Mansfield, Pa. d: 1/23/68, Alexandria, La. BL/TL, 5'8", 165 lbs. Deb: 9/8/1899 ♦																									
1899 Lou-N	2	3	.400	5	4	4	0	0	39	41	0	5	5	10.8	2.31	167	.270	.297	5	.208	1	7	7	-1	0.7
1900 Pit-N	0	0	—	4	1	0	0	0	22	30	0	4	5	14.0	6.14	59	.323	.411	1	.111	-1	-6	-6	1	-0.4
1903 Chi-A	11	25	.306	40	34	29	2	1	293²	338	9	50	65	12.3	3.74	75	.288	.324	14	.137	-3	-25	-30	3	-3.4

YEAR	TM/L	W	L	PCT	G	GS	CG	SH	SV	IP	H	HR	BB	SO	RAT	ERA	ERA+	OAV	OOB	BH	AVG	PB	PR	/A	PD	TPI
1904	Chi-A	1	2	.333	5	5	4	0	0	43	36	1	10	14	9.8	2.09	117	.228	.278	4	.333	2	2	2	1	0.5
	Pit-N	19	9	.679	29	28	28	5	0	242	210	3	59	54	10.4	2.05	134	.232	.287	22	.212	5	19	19	5	3.4
1905	Pit-N	10	10	.500	27	20	15	0	1	187²	197	2	49	44	12.1	3.50	86	.272	.324	15	.197	2	-10	-10	2	-0.6
1907	Bos-N	12	15	.444	27	25	23	0	0	217	197	4	59	34	10.9	2.70	95	.248	.306	22	.191	2	-5	-3	2	0.1
1908	Bos-N	12	18	.400	31	31	21	0	0	244	221	6	81	50	11.4	3.25	74	.236	.303	12	.140	-0	-24	-23	2	-2.6
1910	Phi-N	0	0	—	1	0	0	0	0	0¹	1	0	1	0	54.0	0.00	—	.333	.500	1	.500	-0	-0	-0	-0	0.0
1911	Bos-N	0	2	.000	4	2	1	0	0	14	21	1	8	0	20.6	7.07	54	.350	.451	27	.287	1	-6	-5	-0	-0.6
Total	9	67	84	.444	173	150	125	7	2	1302²	1292	25	331	271	11.6	3.10	89	.259	.312	123	.197	10	-49	-50	14	-2.5

● **MIKE FLANAGAN**   Flanagan, Michael Kendall b: 12/16/51, Manchester, N.H. BL/TL, 6', 195 lbs. Deb: 9/5/75

YEAR	TM/L	W	L	PCT	G	GS	CG	SH	SV	IP	H	HR	BB	SO	RAT	ERA	ERA+	OAV	OOB	BH	AVG	PB	PR	/A	PD	TPI
1975	Bal-A	0	1	.000	2	1	0	0	0	9²	9	0	6	7	14.0	2.79	126	.250	.357	0	—	0	1	1	0	0.0
1976	Bal-A	3	5	.375	20	10	4	0	0	85	83	7	33	56	12.3	4.13	79	.260	.330	0	—	0	-6	-8	0	-0.3
1977	Bal-A	15	10	.600	36	33	15	2	1	235	235	17	70	149	11.8	3.64	104	.256	.321	0	—	0	11	4	-0	0.8
1978	Bal-A☆	19	15	.559	40	40	17	2	0	281¹	271	22	87	167	11.5	4.03	87	.257	.315	0	—	0	-8	-17	-2	-1.5
1979	*Bal-A	**23**	9	.719	39	38	16	**5**	0	265²	245	23	70	190	10.8	3.08	130	.245	.297	0	—	0	33	27	-0	3.2
1980	Bal-A	16	13	.552	37	37	12	2	0	251¹	278	27	71	128	12.6	4.12	96	.287	.337	0	—	0	-2	-5	0	-0.5
1981	Bal-A	9	6	.600	20	20	3	2	0	116	108	11	37	72	11.4	4.19	87	.244	.305	0	—	0	-7	-7	1	-0.5
1982	Bal-A	15	11	.577	36	35	11	1	0	236	233	24	76	103	11.9	3.97	102	.259	.319	0	—	0	3	2	0	0.2
1983	*Bal-A	12	4	.750	20	20	3	1	0	125¹	135	10	31	50	12.1	3.30	120	.278	.324	0	—	0	11	9	-1	1.1
1984	Bal-A	13	13	.500	34	34	10	2	0	226²	213	24	81	115	11.7	3.53	110	.250	.316	0	—	0	11	8	-1	0.9
1985	Bal-A	4	5	.444	15	15	1	0	0	86	101	14	28	42	13.7	5.13	79	.297	.354	0	—	0	-9	-10	-0	-0.8
1986	Bal-A	7	11	.389	29	28	2	0	0	172	179	15	66	96	12.9	4.24	98	.270	.337	0	—	0	-1	-2	-2	-0.3
1987	Bal-A	3	6	.333	16	16	4	0	0	94²	102	9	36	50	13.1	4.94	89	.278	.342	0	—	0	-5	-6	-0	-0.3
	Tor-A	3	2	.600	7	7	0	0	0	49¹	46	3	15	43	11.1	2.37	189	.237	.292	0	—	0	11	12	-0	0.9
	Yr	6	8	.429	23	23	4	0	0	144	148	12	51	93	12.4	4.06	109	.263	.325	0	—	0	6	6	-1	0.6
1988	Tor-A	13	13	.500	34	34	2	1	0	211	220	23	80	99	13.1	4.18	94	.271	.341	0	—	0	-5	-6	1	-0.6
1989	*Tor-A	8	10	.444	30	30	1	1	0	171²	186	10	47	47	12.5	3.93	96	.283	.335	0	—	0	-1	-3	1	-0.1
1990	Tor-A	2	2	.500	5	5	0	0	0	20¹	28	5	8	9	15.9	5.31	74	.329	.387	0	—	0	-3	-3	-0	-0.6
1991	Bal-A	2	7	.222	64	1	0	0	3	98¹	84	6	25	55	10.3	2.38	166	.236	.292	0	—	0	19	17	2	2.0
1992	Bal-A	0	0	—	42	0	0	0	0	34²	50	3	23	17	20.3	8.05	50	.338	.443	0	—	0	-16	-16	1	0.1
Total	18	167	143	.539	526	404	101	19	4	2770	2806	251	890	1491	12.1	3.90	100	.266	.325	0	—	0	36	-3	-1	3.7

● **RAY FLANIGAN**   Flanigan, Raymond Arthur b: 1/8/23, Morgantown, W.Va. d: 3/28/93, Baltimore, Md. BR/TR, 6', 190 lbs. Deb: 9/20/46

YEAR	TM/L	W	L	PCT	G	GS	CG	SH	SV	IP	H	HR	BB	SO	RAT	ERA	ERA+	OAV	OOB	BH	AVG	PB	PR	/A	PD	TPI
1946	Cle-A	0	1	.000	3	1	0	0	0	9	11	1	8	2	19.0	11.00	30	.289	.413	1	.500	1	-7	-8	0	-0.6

● **TOM FLANIGAN**   Flanigan, Thomas Anthony b: 9/6/34, Cincinnati, Ohio BR/TL, 6'3", 175 lbs. Deb: 4/14/54

YEAR	TM/L	W	L	PCT	G	GS	CG	SH	SV	IP	H	HR	BB	SO	RAT	ERA	ERA+	OAV	OOB	BH	AVG	PB	PR	/A	PD	TPI
1954	Chi-A	0	0	—	2	0	0	0	0	1²	1	0	1	0	10.8	0.00	—	.200	.333	0	—	0	0	0	0	0.0
1958	StL-N	0	0	—	1	0	0	0	0	1	2	1	1	0	27.0	9.00	46	.500	.600	0	—	0	-1	-1	-0	0.0
Total	2	0	0	—	3	0	0	0	0	2²	3	1	2	0	16.9	3.38	115	.333	.455	0	—	0	0	0	0	0.0

● **JACK FLATER**   Flater, John William b: 9/22/1880, Sandymount, Md. d: 3/20/70, Westminster, Md. BR/TR, 5'10", 175 lbs. Deb: 9/18/08

YEAR	TM/L	W	L	PCT	G	GS	CG	SH	SV	IP	H	HR	BB	SO	RAT	ERA	ERA+	OAV	OOB	BH	AVG	PB	PR	/A	PD	TPI
1908	Phi-A	1	3	.250	5	3	3	0	0	39¹	35	0	12	8	11.2	2.06	124	.252	.320	2	.133	-0	1	2	2	0.4

● **JOHN FLAVIN**   Flavin, John Thomas b: 5/7/42, Albany, Cal. BL/TL, 6'2", 208 lbs. Deb: 8/25/64

YEAR	TM/L	W	L	PCT	G	GS	CG	SH	SV	IP	H	HR	BB	SO	RAT	ERA	ERA+	OAV	OOB	BH	AVG	PB	PR	/A	PD	TPI
1964	Chi-N	0	1	.000	5	1	0	0	0	4²	5	0	4	7	27.0	13.50	28	.500	.560	0	.000	-0	-5	-5	0	-1.0

● **FRANK FLEET**   Fleet, Frank H. b: 1848, New York, N.Y. d: 6/13/1900, New York, N.Y. Deb: 10/18/1871 ♦

YEAR	TM/L	W	L	PCT	G	GS	CG	SH	SV	IP	H	HR	BB	SO	RAT	ERA	ERA+	OAV	OOB	BH	AVG	PB	PR	/A	PD	TPI
1871	Mut-n	0	1	.000	1	1	1	0	0	9	20	0	1	1	23.0	10.00	38	.370	.404	2	.333	0	-6	-6		-0.3
1873	Res-n	0	3	.000	3	3	3	0	0	24	57	0	0	1	21.4	5.63	60	.399	.399	23	.256	0	-6	-6		-0.4
1875	StL-n	2	1	.667	3	3	3	0	0	27	33	0	3	2	12.0	3.33	60	.277	.295	1	.063	-1	-3	-4		-0.4
	Atl-n	0	1	.000	2	1	1	0	0	15¹	26	0	0	1	15.3	4.70	44	.333	.333	25	.225	-0	-4	-4		-0.2
	Yr	2	2	.500	5	4	4	0	0	42¹	59	0	3	3	13.2	3.83	53	.299	.310	26	.205	-1	-8	-8		-0.6
Total	3 n	2	6	.250	9	8	7	0	0	75¹	136	0	4	4	17.0	5.14	40	.345	.355	86	.231	-1	-24	-26		-1.3

● **DAVE FLEMING**   Fleming, David Anthony b: 11/7/69, Jackson Heights, N.Y. BL/TL, 6'3", 200 lbs. Deb: 8/6/91

YEAR	TM/L	W	L	PCT	G	GS	CG	SH	SV	IP	H	HR	BB	SO	RAT	ERA	ERA+	OAV	OOB	BH	AVG	PB	PR	/A	PD	TPI
1991	Sea-A	1	0	1.000	9	3	0	0	0	17²	19	3	11	11	12.7	6.62	62	.284	.342	0	—	0	-5	-5	1	-0.1
1992	Sea-A	17	10	.630	33	33	7	4	0	228¹	225	13	60	112	11.4	3.39	117	.257	.307	0	—	0	14	15	-0	1.6
1993	Sea-A	12	5	.706	26	26	1	1	0	167¹	189	15	67	75	14.1	4.36	101	.290	.361	0	—	0	-1	1	1	0.0
1994	Sea-A	7	11	.389	23	23	0	0	0	117	152	17	65	65	16.8	6.46	76	.311	.394	0	—	0	-22	-20	0	-2.5
1995	Sea-A	1	5	.167	16	7	0	0	0	48	57	15	34	26	17.1	7.50	63	.294	.399	0	—	0	-15	-15	0	-1.5
	KC-A	0	1	.000	9	5	0	0	0	32	27	4	19	14	13.5	3.66	131	.230	.345	0	—	0	4	4	0	0.1
	Yr	1	6	.143	25	12	1	0	0	80	84	19	53	40	15.6	5.96	80	.267	.376	0	—	0	-11	-11	0	-1.4
Total	5	38	32	.543	116	97	9	5	0	610¹	669	67	248	303	13.8	4.67	93	.279	.351	0	—	0	-24	-21	2	-2.3

● **BILL FLEMING**   Fleming, Leslie Fletchard b: 7/31/13, Rowland, Cal. BR/TR, 6', 190 lbs. Deb: 8/21/40

YEAR	TM/L	W	L	PCT	G	GS	CG	SH	SV	IP	H	HR	BB	SO	RAT	ERA	ERA+	OAV	OOB	BH	AVG	PB	PR	/A	PD	TPI
1940	Bos-A	1	2	.333	10	4	1	0	0	46¹	53	4	20	24	14.6	4.86	·93	.290	.366	0	.000	-2	-2	-2	-1	-0.3
1941	Bos-A	1	1	.500	8	1	0	0	1	41¹	32	4	24	20	12.2	3.92	106	.212	.320	2	.222	1	1	1	-1	0.2
1942	Chi-N	5	6	.455	33	14	4	2	2	134¹	117	9	63	59	12.3	3.01	106	.230	.318	-4	.051	-4	3	3	-1	-0.1
1943	Chi-N	0	1	.000	11	0	0	0	0	32¹	41	2	12	12	15.6	6.40	52	.311	.381	0	.000	-1	-11	-11	0	-0.3
1944	Chi-N	9	10	.474	39	18	9	1	0	158¹	163	6	62	42	12.8	3.13	113	.270	.339	9	.170	-1	9	7	1	0.8
1946	Chi-N	0	1	.000	14	1	0	0	0	29¹	37	2	12	10	15.3	6.14	54	.301	.368	-0	.000	-0	-9	-9	0	-0.3
Total	6	16	21	.432	123	40	14	3	3	442	443	27	193	167	13.2	3.79	94	.260	.339	13	.104	-7	-8	-11	1	-0.2

● **HUCK FLENER**   Flener, Gregory Alan b: 2/25/69, Austin, Tex. BB/TL, 5'11", 185 lbs. Deb: 9/14/93

YEAR	TM/L	W	L	PCT	G	GS	CG	SH	SV	IP	H	HR	BB	SO	RAT	ERA	ERA+	OAV	OOB	BH	AVG	PB	PR	/A	PD	TPI
1993	Tor-A	0	0	—	6	0	0	0	0	6²	7	0	4	2	14.9	4.05	107	.269	.367	0	—	0	0	0	0	0.0
1996	Tor-A	3	2	.600	15	11	0	0	0	70²	68	9	33	44	13.0	4.58	110	.251	.334	0	—	0	3	4	1	0.3
Total	2	3	2	.600	21	11	0	0	0	77¹	75	9	37	46	13.2	4.54	110	.253	.337	0	—	0	3	4	1	0.3

● **VAN FLETCHER**   Fletcher, Alfred Vanoide b: 8/6/24, East Bend, N.C. BR/TR, 6'2", 185 lbs. Deb: 4/12/55

YEAR	TM/L	W	L	PCT	G	GS	CG	SH	SV	IP	H	HR	BB	SO	RAT	ERA	ERA+	OAV	OOB	BH	AVG	PB	PR	/A	PD	TPI
1955	Det-A	0	0	—	9	0	0	0	0	12	13	1	2	4	11.3	3.00	128	.260	.288	0	—	0	1	1	-0	0.0

● **PAUL FLETCHER**   Fletcher, Edward Paul b: 1/14/67, Gallipolis, Ohio BR/TR, 6'1", 185 lbs. Deb: 7/11/93

YEAR	TM/L	W	L	PCT	G	GS	CG	SH	SV	IP	H	HR	BB	SO	RAT	ERA	ERA+	OAV	OOB	BH	AVG	PB	PR	/A	PD	TPI
1993	Phi-N	0	0	—	1	0	0	0	0	0¹	0	0	0	0	0.00	0.00	—	.000	.000	0	—	0	0	0	0	0.0
1995	Phi-N	1	0	1.000	10	0	0	0	0	13¹	15	2	9	10	16.9	5.40	78	.288	.403	0	—	0	-2	-2	-0	-0.1
1996	Oak-A	0	0	—	1	0	0	0	0	1¹	6	0	1	0	47.3	20.25	24	.667	.700	0	—	0	-2	-2	-0	0.1
Total	3	1	0	1.000	12	0	0	0	0	15	21	2	10	10	19.2	6.60	65	.339	.438	0	—	0	-4	-4	0	0.0

● **SAM FLETCHER**   Fletcher, Samuel S. b: Altoona, Pa. TR, 6'2", 210 lbs. Deb: 10/6/09

YEAR	TM/L	W	L	PCT	G	GS	CG	SH	SV	IP	H	HR	BB	SO	RAT	ERA	ERA+	OAV	OOB	BH	AVG	PB	PR	/A	PD	TPI
1909	Bro-N	0	1	.000	1	1	1	0	0	9	13	0	2	3	15.0	8.00	32	.351	.385	0	.000	-0	-5	-5	-0	-0.5
1912	Cin-N	0	0	—	2	0	0	0	0	9²	15	1	11	3	24.2	12.10	28	.366	.500	2	.500	1	-9	-9	0	-0.4
Total	2	0	1	.000	3	1	1	0	0	18²	28	1	13	6	19.8	10.13	30	.359	.451	2	.286	1	-15	-15	0	-0.4

● **TOM FLETCHER**   Fletcher, Thomas Wayne b: 6/28/42, Elmira, N.Y. BB/TL, 6', 170 lbs. Deb: 9/12/62 F

YEAR	TM/L	W	L	PCT	G	GS	CG	SH	SV	IP	H	HR	BB	SO	RAT	ERA	ERA+	OAV	OOB	BH	AVG	PB	PR	/A	PD	TPI
1962	Det-A	0	0	—	1	0	0	0	0	2	2	0	2	1	18.0	0.00	—	.250	.400	0	—	0	1	1	-0	0.0

● **JOHN FLINN**   Flinn, John Richard b: 9/2/54, Merced, Cal. BR/TR, 6', 175 lbs. Deb: 5/6/78

YEAR	TM/L	W	L	PCT	G	GS	CG	SH	SV	IP	H	HR	BB	SO	RAT	ERA	ERA+	OAV	OOB	BH	AVG	PB	PR	/A	PD	TPI
1978	Bal-A	1	1	.500	13	1	0	0	0	15²	24	3	13	8	21.3	8.04	43	.348	.451	0	—	0	-7	-8	1	-0.5
1979	Bal-A	0	0	—	4	0	0	0	0	2²	2	1	0	2	10.1	0.00	—	.222	.300	0	—	0	1	1	0	0.1
1980	Mil-A	2	0	.667	20	1	0	0	2	37	31	3	20	15	12.4	3.89	99	.220	.317	0	—	0	-0	-0	-0	0.0
1982	Bal-A	2	0	1.000	5	0	0	0	0	13²	13	1	3	13	10.5	1.32	306	.260	.302	0	—	0	4	4	-0	0.6
Total	4	5	2	.714	42	2	0	0	2	69	70	7	36	14.0	14.0	4.17	92	.260	.350	0	—	0	-3	-3	-0	0.0

YEAR	TM/L	W	L	PCT	G	GS	CG	SH	SV	IP	H	HR	BB	SO	RAT	ERA	ERA+	OAV	OOB	BH	AVG	PB	PR	/A	PD	TPI

● HILLY FLITCRAFT   Flitcraft, Hildreth Milton   b: 8/21/23, Woodstown, N.J.   BL/TL, 6'2", 180 lbs.   Deb: 8/31/42

| 1942 | Phi-N | 0 | 0 | — | 3 | 0 | 0 | 0 | 0 | 3¹ | 6 | 0 | 2 | 1 | 21.6 | 8.10 | 41 | .429 | .500 | 0 | — | 0 | -2 | -2 | 0 | 0.0 |

● MORT FLOHR   Flohr, Moritz Herman "Dutch"   b: 8/15/11, Canisteo, N.Y.   d: 6/2/94, Hornell, N.Y.   BL/TL, 6', 173 lbs.   Deb: 6/8/34

| 1934 | Phi-A | 0 | 2 | .000 | 14 | 3 | 0 | 0 | 0 | 30² | 34 | 3 | 33 | 6 | 20.0 | 5.87 | 75 | .296 | .456 | 4 | .333 | 1 | -5 | -5 | 1 | -0.1 |

● DON FLORENCE   Florence, Donald Emery   b: 3/16/67, Manchester, N.H.   BR/TL, 6', 195 lbs.   Deb: 8/8/95

| 1995 | NY-N | 3 | 0 | 1.000 | 14 | 0 | 0 | 0 | 0 | 12 | 17 | 0 | 6 | 5 | 17.3 | 1.50 | 270 | .340 | .411 | 0 | .000 | -0 | 4 | 3 | 0 | 0.8 |

● JESSE FLORES   Flores, Jesse (Sandoval)   b: 11/2/14, Guadalajara, Mexico   d: 12/17/91, Orange, Cal.   BR/TR, 5'10", 175 lbs.   Deb: 4/16/42

1942	Chi-N	0	1	.000	4	0	0	0	0	5¹	5	1	2	6	11.8	3.38	95	.227	.292	0	—	-0	-0	-0	0	0.0
1943	Phi-A	12	14	.462	31	27	13	0	0	231¹	208	13	70	113	11.0	3.11	109	.240	.301	14	.175	-0	5	7	1	0.9
1944	Phi-A	9	11	.450	27	25	11	2	0	185²	172	8	49	65	10.9	3.39	103	.245	.298	11	.172	-0	1	2	-1	0.1
1945	Phi-A	7	10	.412	29	24	9	4	1	191¹	180	6	63	52	11.6	3.43	100	.250	.314	9	.148	-2	-1	-0	-3	-0.5
1946	Phi-A	9	7	.563	29	15	8	4	1	155	147	8	38	48	10.8	2.32	153	.249	.295	11	.250	3	20	21	-2	2.3
1947	Phi-A	4	13	.235	28	20	4	0	0	151¹	139	10	59	41	11.8	3.39	112	.244	.315	10	.227	1	5	7	-1	0.8
1950	Cle-A	3	3	.500	28	2	1	1	4	53	53	3	25	27	13.4	3.74	116	.261	.345	-2	.000	-2	5	4	-2	0.1
Total	7	44	59	.427	176	113	46	11	6	973	904	49	306	352	11.3	3.18	112	.246	.307	55	.181	-0	35	41	-7	3.7

● BRYCE FLORIE   Florie, Bryce Bettencourt   b: 5/21/70, Charleston, S.C.   BR/TR, 6', 185 lbs.   Deb: 7/17/94

1994	SD-N	0	0	—	9	0	0	0	0	9¹	8	1	8	10	10.6	0.96	426	.242	.306	0	—	0	3	3	1	0.1
1995	SD-N	2	2	.500	47	0	0	0	1	68²	49	8	38	68	11.9	3.01	134	.202	.320	0	.000	-0	9	8	0	0.4
1996	SD-N	2	2	.500	39	0	0	0	0	49¹	45	1	27	51	14.2	4.01	99	.239	.353	0	.000	-0	1	-0	0	0.0
	Mil-A	1	1	.000	15	0	0	0	0	19	20	3	13	12	15.6	6.63	79	.270	.379	0	.000	0	-3	-3	-0	-0.3
Total	3	4	5	.444	110	0	0	0	1	146¹	122	12	81	139	13.5	3.69	113	.227	.339	0	.000	-1	10	8	1	0.2

● BEN FLOWERS   Flowers, Bennett   b: 6/15/27, Wilson, N.C.   BR/TR, 6'4", 195 lbs.   Deb: 9/29/51

1951	Bos-A	0	0	—	1	0	0	0	0	3	2	0	1	2	9.0	0.00	—	.200	.273	0	.000	-0	1	1	-0	0.1
1953	Bos-A	1	4	.200	32	6	1	1	3	79¹	87	6	24	36	12.7	3.86	109	.280	.333	3	.158	-0	1	3	1	0.2
1955	Det-A	0	0	—	4	0	0	0	0	6	5	1	2	2	10.5	6.00	64	.238	.304	0	.000	-0	-1	-1	0	-0.1
	StL-N	1	0	1.000	4	4	0	0	0	27¹	27	1	12	19	12.8	3.62	112	.255	.331	1	.100	-1	1	1	-0	-0.1
1956	StL-N	1	1	.500	3	3	0	0	0	11²	15	1	5	5	15.4	6.94	54	.341	.408	0	.000	-0	-4	-4	0	-0.6
	Phi-N	0	2	.000	32	0	0	0	0	41	54	9	10	22	14.3	5.71	65	.331	.374	0	.000	-0	-9	-9	1	-0.3
	Yr	1	3	.250	35	3	0	0	0	52²	69	10	15	27	14.5	5.98	62	.330	.378	0	.000	-0	-13	-13	1	-0.9
Total	4	3	7	.300	76	13	1	1	3	168¹	190	18	54	86	13.2	4.49	90	.290	.346	4	.111	-2	-10	-9	1	-0.8

● DICKIE FLOWERS   Flowers, Charles Richard   b: 1850, Philadelphia, Pa.   d: 10/5/1892, Philadelphia, Pa.   Deb: 6/3/1871 ◆

| 1871 | Tro-n | 0 | 0 | — | 1 | 0 | 0 | 0 | 0 | 1 | 1 | 0 | 0 | 0 | 9.0 | 0.00 | — | .333 | .333 | 33 | .314 | 0 | 0 | 0 | | 0.0 |

● WES FLOWERS   Flowers, Charles Wesley   b: 8/13/13, Vanndale, Ark.   d: 12/31/88, Wynne, Ark.   BL/TL, 6'1.5", 190 lbs.   Deb: 8/8/40

1940	Bro-N	1	1	.500	5	2	0	0	0	21	23	2	10	8	15.4	3.43	117	.299	.400	1	.200	-0	1	1	0	0.1
1944	Bro-N	1	1	.500	9	1	0	0	0	17¹	26	3	13	3	20.8	7.79	46	.333	.435	3	.600	1	-8	-8	-0	-0.7
Total	2	2	2	.500	14	3	0	0	0	38¹	49	5	23	11	17.8	5.40	70	.316	.418	4	.400	1	-7	-7	-0	-0.6

● CARNEY FLYNN   Flynn, Cornelius Francis Xavier   b: 1/23/1875, Cincinnati, Ohio   d: 2/10/47, Cincinnati, Ohio   BL/TL, 5'11", 165 lbs.   Deb: 7/17/1894

1894	Cin-N	0	2	.000	2	1	0	0	0	7²	16	4	10	4	31.7	17.61	32	.421	.551	0	.000	-1	-10	-10	-0	-1.4
1896	NY-N	0	2	.000	3	2	1	0	0	10²	18	0	8	4	26.2	11.81	36	.367	.500	2	.500	2	-9	-9	-0	-1.0
	Was-N	0	1	.000	4	1	1	0	0	20	43	0	10	3	24.7	8.55	52	.430	.491	2	.250	-0	-9	-9	-1	-0.4
	Yr	0	3	.000	7	3	2	0	0	30²	61	0	18	7	23.8	9.68	45	.396	.466	4	.333	1	-18	-18	-1	-1.4
Total	2	0	5	.000	9	4	2	0	0	38¹	77	4	28	11	26.5	11.27	41	.412	.507	4	.267	1	-29	-29	-1	-2.8

● JOCKO FLYNN   Flynn, John A.   b: 6/30/1864, Lawrence, Mass.   d: 12/30/07, Lawrence, Mass.   TR , 5'6.5", 143 lbs.   Deb: 5/1/1886

| 1886 | Chi-N | 23 | 6 | **.793** | 32 | 29 | 28 | 2 | 1 | 257 | 207 | 9 | 63 | 146 | 9.5 | 2.24 | 163 | .210 | .257 | 41 | .200 | 1 | 31 | 40 | 2 | 4.1 |

● STU FLYTHE   Flythe, Stuart McGuire   b: 12/5/11, Conway, N.C.   d: 10/18/63, Durham, N.C.   BR/TR, 6'2", 175 lbs.   Deb: 5/31/36

| 1936 | Phi-A | 0 | 0 | — | 17 | 3 | 0 | 0 | 0 | 39¹ | 49 | 4 | 61 | 14 | 25.9 | 13.04 | 39 | .302 | .500 | 4 | .267 | -0 | -35 | -35 | 0 | 0.0 |

● GENE FODGE   Fodge, Gene Arlan "Suds"   b: 7/9/31, South Bend, Ind.   BR/TR, 6', 175 lbs.   Deb: 4/20/58

| 1958 | Chi-N | 1 | 1 | .500 | 16 | 4 | 1 | 0 | 0 | 39² | 47 | 5 | 11 | 15 | 13.2 | 4.76 | 82 | .296 | .341 | 0 | .000 | -1 | -4 | -4 | 0 | -0.2 |

● JIM FOGARTY   Fogarty, James G.   b: 2/12/1864, San Francisco, Cal   d: 5/20/1891, Philadelphia, Pa.   BR/TR, 5'10.5", 180 lbs.   Deb: 5/1/1884   FM◆

1884	Phi-N	0	0	—	1	0	0	0	0	1	2	0	0	1	18.0	0.00	—	.333	.333	80	.212	0	0	0		0.0
1886	Phi-N	0	1	.000	1	0	0	0	0	6	7	1	0	4	10.5	0.00	—	.250	.250	82	.293	0	2	2	0	0.4
1887	Phi-N	0	0	—	1	0	0	0	0	3	3	0	1	0	12.0	9.00	47	.200	.250	129	.261	0	-2	-2	-0	0.0
1889	Phi-N	0	0	—	4	0	0	0	0	4	4	2	2	0	13.5	9.00	48	.250	.333	129	.259	1	-2	-2	-0	0.0
Total	4	0	1	.000	7	0	0	0	0	14	16	1	3	5	12.2	4.50	48	.246	.279	709	.246	2	-1	-1	0	0.4

● CURRY FOLEY   Foley, Charles Joseph   b: 1/14/1856, Milltown, Ireland   d: 10/20/1898, Boston, Mass.   TL , 5'10", 160 lbs.   Deb: 5/13/1879 ◆

1879	Bos-N	9	9	.500	21	16	16	1	0	161²	175	1	15	57	10.6	2.51	99	.252	.268	46	.315	5	-0	-0	-2	0.2
1880	Bos-N	14	14	.500	36	28	21	1	0	238	264	1	40	68	11.5	3.89	58	.274	.303	97	.292	8	-40	-43	1	-3.6
1881	Buf-N	3	4	.429	10	6	2	0	0	41	70	1	5	12	16.5	5.27	53	.337	.352	96	.256	1	-11	-11	-0	-1.5
1882	Buf-N	0	0	—	1	0	0	0	0	1	2	0	0	0	18.0	18.00	16	.333	.333	104	.305	0	-2	-2	-0	0.0
1883	Buf-N	1	0	1.000	1	0	0	0	0	1	0	0	4	0	36.0	0.00	—	.000	.667	30	.270	0	0	0	0	0.3
Total	5	27	27	.500	69	50	39	2	0	442²	511	3	64	127	11.7	3.54	68	.273	.297	373	.286	14	-53	-56	-2	-4.6

● JOHN FOLEY   Foley, John J   b: Hannibal, Mo.   TL ,   Deb: 9/18/1885

| 1885 | Pro-N | 0 | 0 | — | 1 | 0 | 0 | 0 | 0 | 8 | 6 | 0 | 5 | 2 | 12.4 | 4.50 | 59 | .188 | .297 | 0 | .000 | -0 | -1 | -2 | 0 | -0.2 |

● TOM FOLEY   Foley, Thomas Michael   b: 9/9/59, Columbus, Ga.   BL/TR, 6'1", 175 lbs.   Deb: 4/9/83 ◆

| 1989 | Mon-N | 0 | 0 | — | 1 | 0 | 0 | 0 | 0 | 0¹ | 1 | 1 | 0 | 0 | 27.0 | 27.00 | 13 | .500 | .500 | 86 | .229 | 0 | -1 | -1 | 0 | 0.0 |

● RICH FOLKERS   Folkers, Richard Nevin   b: 10/17/46, Waterloo, Iowa   BL/TL, 6'2", 180 lbs.   Deb: 6/10/70

1970	NY-N	0	2	.000	16	0	0	0	0	29¹	36	6	25	15	18.7	6.44	62	.313	.436	2	.333	0	-8	-8	1	-0.4
1972	StL-N	1	0	1.000	9	0	0	0	0	13¹	12	0	5	7	11.5	3.38	101	.240	.309	0	.000	-0	0	-0	0	0.0
1973	StL-N	4	4	.500	34	9	1	0	3	82¹	74	10	34	44	12.1	3.61	101	.239	.321	2	.100	-1	0	0	-0	-0.1
1974	StL-N	6	2	.750	55	0	0	0	6	90	65	4	38	57	10.5	3.00	119	.207	.297	6	.100	1	6	6	-1	0.3
1975	SD-N	6	11	.353	45	15	4	0	0	142	155	8	39	87	12.4	4.18	83	.278	.327	6	.167	1	-9	-11	-0	-1.1
1976	SD-N	2	3	.400	33	3	0	0	0	59²	67	10	25	26	14.2	5.28	62	.279	.352	0	.000	-0	-12	-13	-0	-1.1
1977	Mil-A	0	1	.000	3	0	0	0	0	6¹	7	2	4	6	15.6	4.26	95	.269	.367	0	—	-0	-0	-0	-0	0.0
Total	7	19	23	.452	195	28	5	0	7	423	416	40	170	242	12.6	4.11	86	.258	.332	11	.143	-1	-22	-27	-1	-2.4

● LEW FONSECA   Fonseca, Lewis Albert   b: 1/21/1899, Oakland, Cal.   d: 11/26/89, Ely, Iowa   BR/TR, 5'10.5", 180 lbs.   Deb: 4/13/21   M◆

| 1932 | Chi-A | 0 | 0 | — | 1 | 0 | 0 | 0 | 0 | 1 | 0 | 0 | 0 | 0 | 0.0 | 0.00 | — | .000 | .000 | 5 | .135 | -0 | 0 | 0 | 0 | 0.0 |

● RAY FONTENOT   Fontenot, Silton Ray   b: 8/8/57, Lake Charles, La.   BL/TL, 6', 175 lbs.   Deb: 6/30/83

1983	NY-A	8	2	.800	15	15	3	1	0	97¹	101	3	25	27	11.7	3.33	117	.266	.314	0	—	0	8	6	1	0.8
1984	NY-A	8	9	.471	35	24	0	0	0	169¹	189	8	58	85	13.3	3.61	105	.290	.351	0	—	-0	7	3	0	0.4
1985	Chi-N	6	10	.375	38	23	0	0	0	154²	177	23	45	70	12.9	4.36	91	.294	.343	2	.049	-3	-13	-6	2	-0.8
1986	Chi-N	3	5	.375	42	0	0	0	2	56	57	5	21	24	12.6	3.86	105	.266	.332	1	.167	-0	1	-1	-1	0.1
	Min-A	0	0	—	15	0	0	0	0	16¹	27	3	4	10	18.2	9.92	43	.360	.407	0	—	-0	-10	-10	0	-0.2
Total	4	25	26	.490	145	62	3	1	2	493²	551	42	153	216	12.9	4.03	98	.287	.341	3	.063	-3	-10	-5	2	0.5

YEAR	TM/L	W	L	PCT	G	GS	CG	SH	SV	IP	H	HR	BB	SO	RAT	ERA	ERA+	OAV	OOB	BH	AVG	PB	PR	/A	PD	TPI

● **JIM FOOR** Foor, James Emerson b: 1/13/49, St.Louis, Mo. BL/TL, 6'2", 170 lbs. Deb: 4/9/71

1971	Det-A	0	0	—	3	0	0	0	0	1	2	0	4	2	54.0	18.00	20	.400	.667	0	—	0	-2	-2	0	0.0
1972	Det-A	1	0	1.000	7	0	0	0	0	3²	6	1	6	2	29.5	14.73	21	.353	.522	0	—	0	-5	-5	0	-1.2
1973	Pit-N	0	0	—	3	0	0	0	0	1¹	2	0	1	1	20.3	0.00	—	.286	.375	0	—	0	1	1	0	0.0
Total	3	1	0	1.000	13	0	0	0	0	6	10	1	11	5	31.5	12.00	28	.345	.525	0	—	0	-6	-6	0	-1.2

● **DAVY FORCE** Force, David W. "Wee Davy" or "Tom Thumb" b: 7/27/1849, New York, N.Y. d: 6/21/18, Englewood, N.J. BR/TR, 5'4", 130 lbs. Deb: 5/5/1871 ◆

1873	Bal-n	1	1	.500	3	1	1	0	0	18	23	0	0	0	11.5	3.50	93	.264	.264	86	.368	1	-0	-0		0.0
1874	Chi-n	0	0	—	1	0	0	0	0	7	22	4	0	0	28.3	15.43	14	.431	.431	92	.313	1	-10	-10		0.0
Total	2 n	1	1	.500	4	1	1	0	0	25	45	4	0	0	16.2	6.84	32	.326	.326	437	.336	2	-13	-13		0.0

● **DAVE FORD** Ford, David Alan b: 12/29/56, Cleveland, Ohio BR/TR, 6'4", 190 lbs. Deb: 9/2/78

1978	Bal-A	1	0	1.000	2	1	0	0	0	15	10	0	2	5	7.2	0.00	—	.196	.226	0	—	0	6	6	-0	1.1
1979	Bal-A	2	1	.667	9	2	0	0	2	30	23	2	7	7	9.0	2.10	191	.219	.268	0	—	0	7	6	0	1.0
1980	Bal-A	1	3	.250	25	3	0	0	0	69²	66	11	13	22	10.5	4.26	93	.251	.291	0	—	0	-2	-2	-1	-0.2
1981	Bal-A	1	2	.333	15	2	0	0	0	40	61	2	10	12	16.0	6.52	56	.359	.394	0	—	0	-13	-13	-0	-0.9
Total	4	5	6	.455	51	8	0	0	2	154²	160	15	32	46	11.3	4.02	96	.272	.311	0	—	0	-1	-3	-1	1.0

● **WHITEY FORD** Ford, Edward Charles "Chairman Of The Board" b: 10/21/28, New York, N.Y. BL/TL, 5'10", 181 lbs. Deb: 7/1/50 CH

1950	*NY-A	9	1	.900	20	12	7	2	1	112	87	7	52	59	11.3	2.81	153	.216	.309	7	.194	0	22	18	-0	1.5
1953	*NY-A	18	6	.750	32	30	11	3	0	207	187	13	110	110	13.1	3.00	123	.245	.344	20	.267	6	23	16	0	2.3
1954	NY-A★	16	8	.667	34	28	11	3	1	210²	170	10	101	125	11.6	2.82	122	.227	.319	10	.161	2	21	14	1	1.8
1955	NY-A★	**18**	7	.720	39	33	**18**	5	2	253²	188	20	113	137	10.7	2.63	143	.208	.297	14	.163	2	38	31	0	3.1
1956	*NY-A★	19	6	**.760**	31	30	18	2	1	225²	187	13	84	141	11.0	**2.47**	156	.228	.303	17	.218	3	42	35	5	4.5
1957	*NY-A	11	5	.688	24	17	5	0	0	129¹	114	10	53	84	11.7	2.57	139	.237	.313	6	.143	-1	17	15	2	1.8
1958	*NY-A☆	14	7	.667	30	29	15	**7**	1	219¹	174	14	62	145	**9.8**	**2.01**	176	.217	**.276**	15	.205	4	**43**	37	1	**3.9**
1959	NY-A★	16	10	.615	35	29	9	2	1	204	194	13	89	114	12.5	3.04	120	.250	.328	15	.231	7	19	14	4	2.8
1960	NY-A★	12	9	.571	33	29	8	**4**	0	192²	168	15	65	85	10.9	3.08	116	.235	.299	8	.151	2	17	11	1	1.4
1961	*NY-A★	**25**	4	**.862**	39	39	11	3	0	**283**	242	23	92	209	11.0	3.21	116	.229	.292	17	.177	3	26	16	0	1.8
1962	*NY-A	17	8	.680	38	37	7	0	0	257²	243	22	69	160	11.0	2.90	129	.246	.298	10	.118	-1	31	24	4	2.6
1963	*NY-A	**24**	7	**.774**	38	37	13	3	1	**269¹**	240	26	56	189	10.0	2.74	128	.241	.283	13	.141	0	27	23	-0	2.5
1964	*NY-A☆	17	6	.739	39	36	12	8	1	244²	212	10	57	172	10.0	2.13	170	.230	.276	8	.119	1	41	40	2	4.2
1965	NY-A	16	13	.552	37	36	9	2	1	244¹	241	22	50	162	10.8	3.24	105	.258	.297	15	.183	2	6	4	2	0.9
1966	NY-A	2	5	.286	22	9	0	0	0	73	79	8	24	43	12.7	2.47	135	.277	.333	0	.000	-0	8	7	3	0.8
1967	NY-A	2	4	.333	7	7	1	0	0	44	40	2	9	21	10.0	1.64	191	.247	.287	2	.154	-0	8	7	1	1.3
Total	16	236	106	.690	498	438	156	45	10	3170¹	2766	228	1086	1956	11.0	2.75	133	.235	.301	177	.173	27	386	315	26	37.2

● **GENE FORD** Ford, Eugene Matthew b: 6/23/12, Ft.Dodge, Iowa d: 9/7/70, Emmetsburg, Iowa BR/TR, 6'2", 195 lbs. Deb: 6/17/36

1936	Bos-N	0	0	—	2	1	0	0	0	2	2	0	3	0	22.5	13.50	28	.250	.455	0	—	0	-2	-2	0	0.0
1938	Chi-A	0	0	—	4	0	0	0	0	14	21	1	12	2	21.2	10.29	44	.350	.458	1	.167	-0	-9	-8	0	0.0
Total	2	0	0	—	6	1	0	0	0	16	23	1	15	2	21.4	10.69	44	.338	.458	1	.167	-0	-11	-11	0	0.0

● **GENE FORD** Ford, Eugene Wyman b: 4/16/1881, Milton, N.S., Can. d: 8/23/73, Dunedin, Fla. BR/TR, 6', 170 lbs. Deb: 5/5/05 F

| 1905 | Det-A | 0 | 1 | .000 | 7 | 1 | 0 | 0 | 0 | 35 | 51 | 0 | 14 | 20 | 17.2 | 5.66 | 48 | .340 | .404 | 0 | .000 | -1 | -12 | -11 | 0 | -0.4 |

● **WENTY FORD** Ford, Percival Edmund Wentworth b: 11/25/46, Nassau, Bahamas d: 7/8/80, Nassau, Bahamas BR/TR, 5'11", 165 lbs. Deb: 9/10/73

| 1973 | Atl-N | 1 | 2 | .333 | 4 | 2 | 1 | 0 | 0 | 16¹ | 17 | 3 | 8 | 4 | 14.3 | 5.51 | 71 | .279 | .371 | 2 | .400 | 1 | -3 | -3 | 0 | -0.4 |

● **RUSS FORD** Ford, Russell William b: 4/25/1883, Brandon, Man., Can. d: 1/24/60, Rockingham, N.C. BR/TR, 5'11", 175 lbs. Deb: 4/28/09 F

1909	NY-A	0	0	—	1	0	0	0	0	3	4	0	4	2	33.0	9.00	28	.333	.579	0	.000	—	-2	-2	0	0.0
1910	NY-A	26	6	.813	36	33	29	8	1	299²	194	4	70	209	8.6	1.65	161	.188	.245	20	.208	4	29	34	-3	4.0
1911	NY-A	22	11	.667	37	33	26	1	0	281¹	251	3	76	158	10.6	2.27	158	.237	.291	20	.196	-2	34	41	-1	4.3
1912	NY-A	13	21	.382	36	35	30	0	0	291²	317	10	79	112	12.4	3.55	101	.280	.329	32	.286	5	-7	1	0.9
1913	NY-A	12	18	.400	33	28	15	1	2	237	244	9	58	72	11.6	2.66	113	.275	.322	12	.162	0	7	9	-4	0.8
1914	Buf-F	21	6	**.778**	35	26	19	5	**6**	247¹	190	11	41	123	8.7	1.82	**163**	.214	.254	10	.128	-4	29	31	0	3.1
1915	Buf-F	5	9	.357	21	15	7	0	0	127¹	140	7	48	34	13.5	4.52	62	.285	.352	12	.279	3	-25	-24	-2	-2.2
Total	7	99	71	.582	199	170	126	15	9	1487¹	1340	44	376	710	10.6	2.59	121	.243	.296	106	.209	5	64	89	-5	10.9

● **TOM FORD** Ford, Thomas Walter b: 1866, Chattanooga, Tenn. d: 5/27/17, Chattanooga, Tenn. 5'10.5", 155 lbs. Deb: 5/6/1890

1890	Col-a	0	0	—	1	0	0	0	0	2	0	0	3	0	13.5	0.00	—	.000	.333	0	—	-0	1	1	0	0.0
	Bro-a	0	6	.000	7	6	6	0	0	49	70	2	32	12	18.7	5.14	76	.326	.413	1	.033	-3	-7	-7	-0	-0.8
	Yr	0	6	.000	8	6	6	0	0	51	70	2	35	12	18.5	4.94	79	.317	.410	1	.032	-3	-6	-6	-1	-0.8

● **HAPPY FOREMAN** Foreman, August b: 7/20/1897, Memphis, Tenn. d: 2/13/53, New York, N.Y. BL/TL, 5'7", 160 lbs. Deb: 9/3/24

1924	Chi-A	0	0	—	3	0	0	0	0	4	7	0	4	0	24.8	2.25	183	.467	.579	0	.000	-0	1	1	-0	-0.1
1926	Bos-A	0	0	—	3	0	0	0	0	7¹	3	0	5	3	9.8	3.68	111	.130	.286	0	.000	-0	0	1	0	0.0
Total	2	0	0	—	6	0	0	0	0	11¹	10	0	9	3	15.1	3.18	129	.263	.404	0	.000	-0	1	1	-0	-0.1

● **FRANK FOREMAN** Foreman, Francis Isaiah "Monkey" b: 5/1/1863, Baltimore, Md. d: 11/19/57, Baltimore, Md. BL/TL, 6', 160 lbs. Deb: 5/15/1884 F ◆

1884	CP-U	1	2	.333	3	1	1	0	0	18	12	0	2	10	12.5	4.00	61	.291	.309	1	.091	-2	-3	-3	0	-0.5
	KC-U	0	1	.000	1	1	1	0	0	8	17	0	2	5	21.4	5.63	40	.405	.432	0	.000	-1	-3	-3	1	-0.3
	Yr	1	3	.250	4	4	2	0	0	26	40	0	4	15	15.2	4.50	53	.331	.352	1	.071	-3	-6	-6	1	-0.8
1885	Bal-a	2	1	.667	3	3	2	0	0	27	33	0	9	11	14.3	6.00	54	.284	.341	4	.286	1	-8	-8	-0	-0.6
1889	Bal-a	23	21	.523	51	48	43	5	0	414	364	8	137	180	11.8	3.52	112	.229	.306	26	.144	-10	15	19	-2	0.5
1890	Cin-N	13	10	.565	25	24	20	0	0	198¹	201	6	89	57	14.1	3.95	90	.255	.345	10	.133	-0	-8	-9	-3	-1.1
1891	Was-a	18	20	.474	43	41	39	1	1	345¹	381	9	142	170	14.8	3.73	104	.271	.355	34	.222	9	-0	-0	0.9
1892	Was-N	2	4	.333	11	7	4	0	0	60	53	3	37	16	14.3	3.30	99	.227	.345	13	.464	8	-0	-1	0.6
	Bal-N	0	3	.000	4	3	2	0	0	25	40	4	11	5	18.7	6.84	50	.348	.409	4	.174	0	-10	-9	-0	-0.8
	Yr	2	7	.222	15	10	6	0	0	85	93	7	48	21	15.6	4.34	76	.263	.353	17	.333	8	-10	-10	-1	-0.2
1893	NY-N	0	1	.000	2	1	0	0	0	5²	19	1	10	0	47.6	27.00	17	.528	.638	0	.000	-1	-14	-14	-0	-1.4
1895	Cin-N	11	14	.440	32	27	19	0	1	219	253	11	92	55	14.8	4.11	121	.285	.362	29	.309	4	16	21	3	1.9
1896	Cin-N	14	7	.667	27	22	17	1	0	185²	212	2	62	33	13.7	3.97	116	.285	.346	18	.243	-1	8	13	-1	1.0
1901	Bos-A	0	1	.000	1	1	0	0	0	2	2	0	3	1	13.5	9.00	39	.258	.343	1	.000	-1	-5	-5	0	-0.5
	Bal-A	12	6	.667	24	22	18	1	0	191¹	225	2	58	41	13.6	3.67	105	.290	.344	26	.325	5	-4	-3	0	-0.0
	Yr	12	7	.632	25	23	19	1	1	199¹	228	2	60	42	13.6	3.88	99	.288	.341	26	.310	4	-5	-1	-0	-0.3
1902	Bal-A	0	2	.000	2	2	1	0	0	16¹	28	0	9	9	18.7	6.06	62	.378	.425	3	.429	1	-4	-4	0	-0.3
Total	11	96	93	.508	229	205	169	7	4	1721²	1857	47	659	586	13.9	3.97	100	.268	.344	169	.224	12	-17	1	-14	-0.1

● **BROWNIE FOREMAN** Foreman, John Davis b: 8/6/1875, Baltimore, Md. d: 10/10/26, Baltimore, Md. BL/TL, 5'8", 150 lbs. Deb: 7/18/1895 F

1895	Pit-N	8	6	.571	19	16	12	0	2	139²	131	0	64	54	13.8	3.22	140	**.244**	.346	3	.065	-6	24	20	2	1.3
1896	Pit-N	3	3	.500	9	9	5	0	0	61²	73	4	35	16	16.9	6.57	64	.292	.396	2	.150	0	-15	-16	1	-1.1
	Cin-N	1	3	.250	4	4	3	0	0	23	41	2	16	9	23.1	11.35	41	.383	.472	2	.200	-0	-18	-17	-0	-1.9
	Yr	4	6	.400	13	13	8	0	0	84²	114	6	51	27	17.8	7.87	55	.312	.400	5	.167	-0	-33	-33	1	-3.0
Total	2	12	12	.500	32	29	20	1	2	224¹	245	6	115	81	15.6	4.97	89	.274	.375	8	.105	-6	-9	-13	3	-1.7

● **BILL FORMAN** Forman, William Orange b: 10/10/1886, Venango, Pa. d: 10/3/58, Uniontown, Pa. BB/TR, 5'11", 180 lbs. Deb: 9/20/09

1909	Was-A	0	2	.000	2	2	0	0	0	11	6	0	3	3	13.9	4.91	50	.211	.362	1	.333	0	-3	-3	1	-0.4
1910	Was-A	0	0	—	1	0	0	0	0	2	5	0	1	0	13.50	13.50	18	.333	.333	1	.333	-0	-4	-4	-1	-0.0
Total	2	0	2	.000	3	2	1	0	0	11²	11	0	4	3	13.9	5.40	45	.220	.360	1	.333	-0	-4	-4	1	-0.4

● **MIKE FORNIELES** Fornieles, Jose Miguel (Torres) b: 1/18/32, Havana, Cuba BR/TR, 5'11", 172 lbs. Deb: 9/2/52

| 1952 | Was-A | 2 | 2 | .500 | 4 | 2 | 1 | 1 | 0 | 26¹ | 13 | 1 | 11 | 15 | 8.2 | 1.37 | 260 | .143 | .235 | 0 | .000 | -1 | 7 | 6 | -0 | 0.8 |

YEAR	TM/L	W	L	PCT	G	GS	CG	SH	SV	IP	H	HR	BB	SO	RAT	ERA	ERA+	OAV	OOB	BH	AVG	PB	PR	/A	PD	TPI
1953	Chi-A	8	7	.533	39	16	5	0	3	153	160	8	61	72	13.1	3.59	112	.270	.340	4	.098	-3	7	7	2	0.6
1954	Chi-A	1	2	.333	15	6	0	0	1	42	41	4	14	18	11.8	4.29	87	.252	.311	3	.273	0	-3	-3	1	-0.1
1955	Chi-A	6	3	.667	26	9	2	0	2	86¹	84	12	29	23	12.0	3.86	102	.255	.319	3	.103	-2	1	1	0	-0.1
1956	Chi-A	0	1	.000	6	0	0	0	0	15²	22	1	6	6	16.1	4.60	89	.306	.359	1	.200	0	-1	-1	-0	0.0
	Bal-A	4	7	.364	30	11	1	1	1	111	109	7	25	53	10.9	3.97	99	.266	.308	5	.167	-1	2	-1	2	0.1
	Yr	4	8	.333	36	11	1	1	1	126²	131	8	31	59	11.5	4.05	97	.271	.315	6	.171	-1	2	-2	2	0.1
1957	Bal-A	2	6	.250	15	4	1	1	0	57	57	4	17	43	11.7	4.26	84	.257	.310	5	.278	1	-3	-4	-1	-0.4
	Bos-A	8	7	.533	25	18	7	1	2	125¹	136	7	38	64	12.7	3.52	113	.271	.327	6	.136	-2	4	7	-1	0.4
	Yr	10	13	.435	40	22	8	2	2	182¹	193	11	55	107	12.4	3.75	103	.267	.321	11	.177	-1	1	2	-1	0.0
1958	Bos-A	4	6	.400	37	7	1	0	1	110²	123	10	33	49	13.2	4.96	81	.284	.343	6	.207	-0	-15	-12	-0	-1.1
1959	Bos-A	5	3	.625	46	0	0	0	11	82	77	6	29	54	11.7	3.07	132	.254	.321	3	.158	-1	7	9	-0	0.7
1960	Bos-A	10	5	.667	**70**	0	0	0	**14**	109	86	6	49	64	11.6	2.64	153	.219	.315	6	.400	2	15	17	1	2.9
1961	Bos-A★	9	8	.529	57	2	1	0	15	119¹	121	18	54	70	13.3	4.68	89	.265	.345	6	.156	0	-9	-7	2	-0.9
1962	Bos-A	3	6	.333	42	1	0	0	5	82¹	96	14	37	36	15.4	5.36	77	.303	.390	3	.188	-0	-13	-11	-0	-1.3
1963	Bos-A	0	0	—	9	0	0	0	0	14	16	0	5	5	13.5	6.43	59	.286	.344	1	.333	1	-4	-4	-0	-0.3
	Min-A	1	1	.500	11	0	0	0	0	22²	24	0	13	7	15.5	4.76	76	.273	.379	1	.167	0	-3	-3	-1	-0.3
	Yr	1	1	.500	20	0	0	0	0	36²	40	0	18	12	14.7	5.40	68	.276	.364	2	.222	1	-7	-7	-1	-0.3
Total	12	63	64	.496	432	76	20	4	55	1156²	1165	98	421	576	12.6	3.96	100	.263	.332	52	.169	-6	-7	2	4	1.6

● KEN FORSCH
Forsch, Kenneth Roth b: 9/8/46, Sacramento, Cal. BR/TR, 6'4", 210 lbs. Deb: 9/7/70 F

YEAR	TM/L	W	L	PCT	G	GS	CG	SH	SV	IP	H	HR	BB	SO	RAT	ERA	ERA+	OAV	OOB	BH	AVG	PB	PR	/A	PD	TPI
1970	Hou-N	1	2	.333	4	4	1	0	0	24	28	1	5	13	12.4	5.63	69	.298	.333	0	.000	-1	-4	-5	-1	-0.6
1971	Hou-N	8	8	.500	33	23	7	2	0	188¹	162	8	53	131	10.5	2.53	133	.230	.288	8	.136	-1	20	17	-2	1.1
1972	Hou-N	6	8	.429	30	24	1	0	0	156¹	163	19	62	113	13.0	3.91	86	.273	.341	6	.146	-1	-8	-10	-3	-1.1
1973	Hou-N	9	12	.429	46	26	5	0	4	201¹	197	18	74	149	12.3	4.20	86	.257	.325	4	.065	-4	-12	-13	-2	-1.9
1974	Hou-N	8	7	.533	70	0	0	0	10	103¹	98	3	37	48	12.1	2.79	124	.255	.326	0	.000	-1	10	8	-0	1.2
1975	Hou-N	4	8	.333	34	9	2	0	2	109	114	9	30	54	12.1	3.22	105	.277	.330	1	.045	-1	5	2	-0	0.1
1976	Hou-N★	4	3	.571	52	0	0	0	19	92	76	5	26	49	10.2	2.15	148	.226	.286	1	.091	-0	14	11	1	1.3
1977	Hou-N	5	8	.385	42	5	0	0	8	86	80	2	28	45	11.5	2.72	131	.246	.310	1	.077	-1	11	8	1	1.3
1978	Hou-N	10	6	.625	52	6	4	2	7	133¹	136	2	37	71	11.7	2.70	123	.268	.319	5	.185	-0	13	9	1	1.2
1979	Hou-N	11	6	.647	26	24	10	2	0	177²	155	14	35	58	**9.6**	3.04	116	.236	**.275**	8	.138	-0	14	9	2	1.1
1980	*Hou-N	12	13	.480	32	32	6	3	0	222¹	230	15	41	84	11.3	3.20	103	.266	.304	18	.234	4	10	2	1	0.8
1981	Cal-A★	11	7	.611	20	20	10	**4**	0	153	143	7	27	55	10.2	2.88	126	.250	.289	0	—	0	13	13	1	1.6
1982	Cal-A	13	11	.542	37	35	12	4	0	228	225	25	57	73	11.6	3.87	105	.258	.311	0	—	0	5	5	-2	0.3
1983	Cal-A	11	12	.478	31	31	11	1	0	219¹	226	21	61	81	11.9	4.06	99	.266	.318	0	—	0	-0	-1	-1	-0.2
1984	Cal-A	1	1	.500	2	2	1	0	0	16¹	14	2	3	10	9.4	2.20	180	.237	.274	0	—	0	3	3	1	0.5
1986	Cal-A	0	1	.000	10	0	0	0	1	17	24	4	10	13	19.1	9.53	43	.343	.439	0	—	0	-10	-10	-0	-0.6
Total	16	114	113	.502	521	241	70	18	51	2127¹	2071	155	586	1047	11.4	3.37	106	.257	.311	52	.136	-5	83	48	-3	6.1

● BOB FORSCH
Forsch, Robert Herbert b: 1/13/50, Sacramento, Cal. BR/TR, 6'4", 200 lbs. Deb: 7/7/74 F

YEAR	TM/L	W	L	PCT	G	GS	CG	SH	SV	IP	H	HR	BB	SO	RAT	ERA	ERA+	OAV	OOB	BH	AVG	PB	PR	/A	PD	TPI
1974	StL-N	7	4	.636	19	14	5	2	0	100	84	5	34	39	10.7	2.97	120	.230	.298	7	.241	1	7	7	-0	0.9
1975	StL-N	15	10	.600	34	34	7	4	0	230	213	14	70	108	11.2	2.86	131	.244	.303	24	.308	9	20	23	2	3.7
1976	StL-N	8	10	.444	33	32	2	0	0	194	209	17	71	76	13.1	3.94	90	.277	.341	11	.177	1	-10	-9	1	-0.6
1977	StL-N	20	7	.741	35	35	8	2	0	217¹	210	20	69	95	11.7	3.48	111	.251	.311	12	.167	0	10	9	-1	0.9
1978	StL-N	11	17	.393	34	34	7	3	0	233²	205	14	97	114	11.8	3.70	95	.238	.318	15	.181	3	-3	-5	1	-0.1
1979	StL-N	11	11	.500	33	32	7	1	0	218²	215	16	52	92	11.1	3.83	98	.262	.309	8	.110	-0	-2	-2	1	-0.1
1980	StL-N	11	10	.524	31	31	8	0	0	214²	225	12	43	87	11.0	3.77	98	.273	.304	23	.295	9	-4	-2	2	1.0
1981	StL-N	10	5	.667	20	20	7	0	0	124¹	106	7	29	41	10.1	3.18	112	.232	.284	5	.122	-1	4	5	0	0.5
1982	*StL-N	15	9	.625	36	34	6	2	1	233	238	16	54	69	11.4	3.48	104	.268	.313	15	.205	3	3	4	-2	0.5
1983	StL-N	10	12	.455	34	30	6	2	0	187	190	23	54	56	11.9	4.28	85	.266	.320	13	.241	4	-14	-14	-0	-1.1
1984	StL-N	2	5	.286	16	11	7	0	0	52¹	64	6	19	21	14.3	6.02	58	.303	.361	4	.250	1	-14	-15	-0	-1.6
1985	*StL-N	9	6	.600	34	19	3	1	2	136	132	11	47	48	12.0	3.90	91	.258	.323	11	.244	4	-5	-6	-0	-0.2
1986	StL-N	14	10	.583	33	33	3	0	0	230	211	19	68	104	11.0	3.25	112	.247	.304	13	.171	3	12	10	-1	1.3
1987	*StL-N	11	7	.611	33	30	2	1	0	179	189	15	45	89	12.0	4.32	96	.273	.321	17	.298	8	-5	-3	1	0.4
1988	StL-N	9	4	.692	30	12	1	0	0	108²	111	8	38	40	12.4	3.73	93	.270	.333	7	.280	2	-3	-3	-2	-0.3
	Hou-N	1	4	.200	6	6	0	0	0	27²	42	2	6	14	16.3	6.51	51	.359	.400	1	.143	0	-9	-10	-0	-1.5
	Yr	10	8	.556	36	18	1	0	0	136¹	153	10	44	54	13.1	4.29	80	.287	.344	8	.250	2	-13	-13	-2	-1.8
1989	Hou-N	4	5	.444	37	15	0	0	0	108¹	133	10	46	40	15.0	5.32	64	.303	.370	4	.167	-0	-22	-23	-1	-1.9
Total	16	168	136	.553	498	422	67	19	3	2794²	2777	216	832	1133	11.8	3.76	97	.261	.318	190	.213	48	-35	-33	-3	1.8

● TERRY FORSTER
Forster, Terry Jay b: 1/14/52, Sioux Falls, S.D. BL/TL, 6'3", 210 lbs. Deb: 4/11/71

YEAR	TM/L	W	L	PCT	G	GS	CG	SH	SV	IP	H	HR	BB	SO	RAT	ERA	ERA+	OAV	OOB	BH	AVG	PB	PR	/A	PD	TPI
1971	Chi-A	2	3	.400	45	3	0	0	1	49²	46	5	23	48	12.7	3.99	90	.241	.326	2	.400	1	-3	-2	0	-0.1
1972	Chi-A	6	5	.545	62	6	0	0	29	100	75	0	44	104	11.0	2.25	139	.208	.300	10	.526	4	9	10	1	2.5
1973	Chi-A	6	11	.353	51	12	4	0	16	172²	174	7	78	120	13.1	3.23	122	.266	.344	0	.000	0	11	14	5	2.1
1974	Chi-A	7	8	.467	59	1	0	0	**24**	134¹	120	6	48	105	11.8	3.62	103	.245	.322	0	—	0	2	3	6	0.6
1975	Chi-A	3	3	.500	17	1	0	0	4	37	30	0	24	32	13.1	2.19	177	.236	.358	0	—	0	7	7	2	1.4
1976	Chi-A	2	12	.143	29	16	1	0	0	111¹	126	7	41	70	13.6	4.37	82	.288	.351	0	—	0	-10	-10	2	-1.0
1977	Pit-N	6	4	.600	33	6	0	0	1	87¹	90	7	32	58	12.8	4.43	90	.269	.337	9	.346	5	-5	-4	-0	-0.2
1978	*LA-N	5	4	.556	47	0	0	0	22	65¹	56	7	23	46	10.9	1.93	182	.233	.300	4	.500	1	12	11	-0	2.6
1979	LA-N	1	2	.333	17	0	0	0	2	16¹	18	0	11	8	16.0	5.51	66	.295	.403	0	—	0	-3	-3	1	-0.6
1980	LA-N	0	0	—	9	0	0	0	0	11²	10	0	4	2	10.9	3.09	113	.222	.286	0	—	0	1	1	0	0.0
1981	*LA-N	0	1	.000	21	0	0	0	0	30²	37	1	15	17	15.3	4.11	81	.308	.385	0	.000	-0	-2	-3	1	0.0
1982	LA-N	5	6	.455	56	0	0	0	3	83	66	3	31	52	11.0	3.04	114	.221	.302	0	.000	-0	5	4	1	0.5
1983	Atl-N	3	2	.600	56	0	0	0	13	79¹	60	3	31	54	10.6	2.16	180	.217	.301	4	.500	2	13	15	1	1.6
1984	Atl-N	2	0	1.000	25	0	0	0	5	26²	30	1	7	10	12.5	2.70	143	.297	.343	2	.667	1	3	3	0	0.5
1985	Atl-N	2	3	.400	46	0	0	0	1	59¹	49	7	28	37	11.7	2.28	169	.222	.309	0	.000	-0	8	8	0	0.8
1986	Cal-A	4	1	.800	41	0	0	0	5	41	47	2	17	28	14.7	3.51	117	.297	.376	0	—	0	3	3	1	0.5
Total	16	54	65	.454	614	39	5	0	127	1105²	1034	51	457	791	12.3	3.23	114	.251	.330	31	.397	11	48	57	16	11.3

● TIM FORTUGNO
Fortugno, Timothy Shawn b: 4/11/62, Clinton, Mass. BL/TL, 6'1", 195 lbs. Deb: 7/20/92

YEAR	TM/L	W	L	PCT	G	GS	CG	SH	SV	IP	H	HR	BB	SO	RAT	ERA	ERA+	OAV	OOB	BH	AVG	PB	PR	/A	PD	TPI
1992	Cal-A	1	1	.500	14	5	1	1	1	41²	37	5	19	31	12.1	5.18	77	.236	.318	0	—	0	-6	-6	-0	-0.3
1994	Cin-N	1	0	1.000	25	0	0	0	0	30	32	2	14	29	14.7	4.20	98	.288	.383	1	.333	0	0	-1	1	0.1
1995	Chi-A	1	3	.250	37	0	0	0	0	38²	30	7	19	24	11.4	5.59	80	.213	.306	0	—	0	-4	-5	-0	-0.4
Total	3	3	4	.429	76	5	1	1	1	110¹	99	14	52	84	12.6	5.06	83	.242	.332	1	.333	-0	-9	-11	0	-0.6

● GARY FORTUNE
Fortune, Garrett Reese b: 10/11/1894, High Point, N.C. d: 9/23/55, Washington, D.C. BB/TR, 5'11.5", 176 lbs. Deb: 10/5/16

YEAR	TM/L	W	L	PCT	G	GS	CG	SH	SV	IP	H	HR	BB	SO	RAT	ERA	ERA+	OAV	OOB	BH	AVG	PB	PR	/A	PD	TPI
1916	Phi-N	0	1	.000	1	1	0	0	0	5	2	0	4	3	10.8	3.60	74	.118	.286	0	.000	-0	-1	-1	-0	-0.2
1918	Phi-N	0	2	.000	5	2	1	0	0	31	41	2	19	10	17.7	8.13	37	.333	.427	1	.200	-0	-18	-18	-0	-1.0
1920	Bos-A	0	2	.000	14	3	1	0	0	41²	46	0	23	10	14.9	5.83	63	.282	.371	2	.167	-0	-9	-10	-1	-0.5
Total	3	0	5	.000	20	6	2	0	0	77²	89	2	46	23	15.8	6.61	51	.294	.389	4	.167	-0	-28	-28	-1	-1.7

● JERRY FOSNOW
Fosnow, Gerald Eugene b: 9/21/40, Deshler, Ohio BR/TL, 6'4", 195 lbs. Deb: 6/29/64

YEAR	TM/L	W	L	PCT	G	GS	CG	SH	SV	IP	H	HR	BB	SO	RAT	ERA	ERA+	OAV	OOB	BH	AVG	PB	PR	/A	PD	TPI
1964	Min-A	0	1	.000	7	0	0	0	0	10²	13	3	8	9	17.7	10.97	38	.302	.412	0	—	0	-9	-9	-0	-0.8
1965	Min-A	3	3	.500	29	0	0	0	2	46²	33	7	25	35	11.4	4.44	80	.193	.299	0	.000	-1	-5	-5	0	-0.6
Total	2	3	4	.429	36	0	0	0	2	57¹	46	10	33	44	12.6	5.65	63	.215	.323	0	.000	-1	-14	-13	0	-1.4

● LARRY FOSS
Foss, Larry Curtis b: 4/18/36, Castleton, Kan. BR/TR, 6'2", 187 lbs. Deb: 9/18/61

YEAR	TM/L	W	L	PCT	G	GS	CG	SH	SV	IP	H	HR	BB	SO	RAT	ERA	ERA+	OAV	OOB	BH	AVG	PB	PR	/A	PD	TPI
1961	Pit-N	1	1	.500	3	3	0	0	0	15¹	15	3	11	9	16.4	5.87	68	.273	.412	1	.167	-0	-3	-3	-0	-0.4
1962	NY-N	0	1	.000	5	1	0	0	0	11²	17	2	7	3	19.3	4.63	90	.362	.455	0	.000	-0	-1	-1	-0	-0.1
Total	2	1	2	.333	8	4	0	0	0	27	32	5	18	12	17.7	5.33	76	.314	.431	1	.143	-0	-4	-4	-0	-0.5

YEAR TM/L	W	L	PCT	G	GS	CG	SH	SV	IP	H	HR	BB	SO	RAT	ERA	ERA+	OAV	OOB	BH	AVG	PB	PR	/A	PD	TPI
● TONY FOSSAS			Fossas, Emilio Antonio (Morejon) b: 9/23/57, Havana, Cuba BL/TL, 6′, 195 lbs. Deb: 5/15/88																					
1988 Tex-A	0	0	—	5	0	0	0	0	5²	11	0	2	0	20.6	4.76	86	.423	.464	0	—	0	-1	-0	0	-0.2
1989 Mil-A	2	2	.500	51	0	0	0	1	61	57	3	22	42	11.8	3.54	108	.256	.325	0	—	0	2	2	0	0.2
1990 Mil-A	2	3	.400	32	0	0	0	0	29¹	44	5	10	24	16.6	6.44	60	.331	.378	0	—	0	-8	-8	-0	-1.3
1991 Bos-A	3	2	.600	64	0	0	0	1	57	49	3	28	29	12.6	3.47	124	.236	.335	0	—	0	4	5	1	0.5
1992 Bos-A	1	2	.333	60	0	0	0	2	29²	31	1	14	19	14.0	2.43	174	.279	.365	0	—	0	5	6	1	0.3
1993 Bos-A	1	1	.500	71	0	0	0	0	40	38	4	15	39	12.4	5.17	89	.242	.316	0	—	0	-4	-2	0	-0.5
1994 Bos-A	2	0	1.000	44	0	0	0	1	34	35	6	15	31	13.5	4.76	106	.263	.342	0	—	0	0	1	-0	-0.1
1995 StL-N	3	0	1.000	58	0	0	0	0	36²	28	1	10	40	9.6	1.47	284	.214	.275	0	—	0	11	11	0	0.8
1996 *StL-N	0	4	.000	65	0	0	0	2	47	43	7	21	36	12.3	2.68	158	.231	.309	0	.000	-0	8	8	0	0.7
Total 9	14	14	.500	450	0	0	0	7	340¹	336	30	137	260	12.7	3.68	116	.257	.331	0	.000	-0	18	22	1	0.4
● ALAN FOSTER			Foster, Alan Benton b: 12/8/46, Pasadena, Cal. BR/TR, 6′, 180 lbs. Deb: 4/25/67																					
1967 LA-N	0	1	.000	4	2	0	0	0	16²	10	0	3	15	7.0	2.16	143	.169	.210	0	.000	-0	2	2	0	0.1
1968 LA-N	1	1	.500	3	3	0	0	0	15²	11	1	2	10	7.5	1.72	160	.200	.228	1	.250	0	2	2	-0	0.3
1969 LA-N	3	9	.250	24	15	2	2	0	102²	119	11	29	59	13.3	4.38	76	.290	.342	2	.074	-1	-9	-12	-0	-1.4
1970 LA-N	10	13	.435	33	33	7	1	0	198²	200	22	81	83	12.8	4.26	90	.264	.337	7	.109	-2	-5	-9	-1	-1.2
1971 Cle-A	8	12	.400	36	26	3	0	0	181²	158	19	82	97	12.1	4.16	92	.232	.318	2	.039	-4	-14	-7	-4	-1.6
1972 Cal-A	0	1	.000	8	0	0	0	0	12²	12	3	6	11	14.2	4.97	59	.245	.351	0	—	0	-3	-3	0	-0.2
1973 StL-N	13	9	.591	35	29	6	2	0	203²	195	17	63	106	11.6	3.14	116	.254	.315	13	.191	-1	12	11	-2	1.1
1974 StL-N	7	10	.412	31	25	5	1	0	162¹	167	16	61	78	12.8	3.88	92	.268	.336	8	.167	-1	-5	-6	-1	-0.7
1975 SD-N	3	1	.750	17	4	1	0	0	44²	41	7	21	20	12.5	2.42	144	.244	.328	1	.091	-1	6	5	0	0.4
1976 SD-N	3	6	.333	26	11	2	0	0	86²	75	9	35	22	11.5	3.22	102	.235	.313	1	.056	-0	3	0	-1	-0.1
Total 10	48	63	.432	217	148	26	6	0	1025¹	988	99	383	501	12.2	3.74	96	.254	.324	35	.119	-8	-10	-15	-9	-3.3
● ED FOSTER			Foster, Eddy Lee "Slim" b: Georgia d: 3/1/29, Montgomery, Ala. BR/TR, 6′1″, Deb: 7/31/08																					
1908 Cle-A	1	0	1.000	6	1	1	0	2	21	16	1	12	11	12.9	2.14	111	.229	.357	0	.000	-0	1	1	-1	-0.1
● RUBE FOSTER			Foster, George b: 1/5/1888, Lehigh, Okla d: 3/1/76, Bokoshe, Okla. BR/TR, 5′7.5″, 170 lbs. Deb: 4/10/13																					
1913 Bos-A	3	4	.429	19	8	4	1	0	68¹	64	1	28	36	12.6	3.16	93	.249	.332	2	.095	-1	-2	-2	-0	-0.4
1914 Bos-A	14	8	.636	32	27	17	5	0	211²	164	2	52	89	9.5	1.70	158	.218	.274	11	.175	0	24	23	-0	2.6
1915 *Bos-A	19	8	.704	37	33	21	5	1	255¹	217	3	86	82	11.0	2.11	131	.237	.310	23	.277	7	23	19	1	2.8
1916 *Bos-A	14	7	.667	33	19	9	3	2	182¹	173	0	86	53	13.0	3.06	90	.263	.352	11	.177	0	-5	-6	2	-0.5
1917 Bos-A	8	7	.533	17	16	9	1	0	124²	108	0	53	34	11.5	2.53	102	.243	.329	11	.268	2	2	1	1	0.4
Total 5	58	34	.630	138	103	60	15	3	842¹	726	6	305	294	11.3	2.36	116	.240	.315	58	.215	9	43	35	2	4.9
● KEVIN FOSTER			Foster, Kevin Christopher b: 1/13/69, Evanston, Ill. BR/TR, 6′1″, 160 lbs. Deb: 9/12/93																					
1993 Phi-N	0	1	.000	2	1	0	0	0	6²	13	3	7	6	27.0	14.85	27	.394	.500	0	.000	-0	-8	-8	-0	-0.9
1994 Chi-N	3	4	.429	13	13	0	0	0	81	70	7	35	75	11.8	2.89	144	.234	.316	2	.074	-2	12	11	-1	0.6
1995 Chi-N	12	11	.522	30	28	0	0	0	167²	149	32	65	146	11.8	4.51	91	.240	.317	15	.250	5	-6	-8	0	-0.6
1996 Chi-N	7	6	.538	17	16	1	0	0	87	98	16	35	53	14.0	6.21	69	.288	.358	8	.296	5	-19	-19	1	-1.8
Total 4	22	22	.500	62	58	1	0	0	342¹	330	58	142	280	12.6	4.76	87	.255	.333	25	.216	8	-22	-23	-3	-2.7
● LARRY FOSTER			Foster, Larry Lynn b: 12/24/37, Lansing, Mich. BL/TR, 6′, 185 lbs. Deb: 9/18/63																					
1963 Det-A	0	0	—	1	0	0	0	0	2	4	0	1	2	22.5	13.50	28	.364	.417	0	—	0	-2	-2	0	0.0
● STEVE FOSTER			Foster, Stephen Eugene b: 8/16/66, Dallas, Tex. BR/TR, 6′, 180 lbs. Deb: 8/22/91																					
1991 Cin-N	0	0	—	11	0	0	0	0	14	7	1	4	11	7.1	1.93	197	.143	.208	0	—	0	3	3	-0	0.0
1992 Cin-N	1	1	.500	31	1	0	0	2	50	52	4	13	34	11.7	2.88	125	.275	.322	1	.200	0	3	4	1	0.3
1993 Cin-N	2	2	.500	17	0	0	0	2	25²	23	1	5	16	10.2	1.75	230	.235	.279	0	—	0	7	6	-1	0.9
Total 3	3	3	.500	59	1	0	0	2	89²	82	6	22	61	10.5	2.41	156	.244	.292	1	.200	0	13	13	0	1.2
● STEVE FOUCAULT			Foucault, Steven Raymond b: 10/3/49, Duluth, Minn. BL/TR, 6′, 205 lbs. Deb: 4/7/73																					
1973 Tex-A	2	4	.333	32	0	0	0	8	55²	54	6	31	28	14.2	3.88	96	.262	.367	0	—	0	-0	-1	1	0.2
1974 Tex-A	8	9	.471	69	0	0	0	12	144¹	123	8	40	106	10.5	2.24	159	.234	.295	0	—	0	22	21	1	2.9
1975 Tex-A	8	4	.667	59	0	0	0	10	107	96	10	55	56	13.0	4.12	91	.249	.349	0	—	0	-4	-4	-1	-0.6
1976 Tex-A	8	8	.500	46	0	0	0	5	75²	68	9	25	41	11.5	3.33	108	.249	.321	0	—	0	2	2	0	0.6
1977 Det-A	7	7	.500	44	0	0	0	13	74¹	64	7	17	58	9.8	3.15	136	.226	.270	0	—	0	8	9	-1	1.9
1978 Det-A	2	4	.333	24	0	0	0	4	37¹	48	1	21	16	16.9	3.13	123	.324	.412	0	—	0	3	3	-1	0.3
KC-A	0	0	—	3	0	0	0	0	2¹	5	0	1	0	23.1	3.86	99	.417	.462	0	—	0	-0	-0	0	-0.2
Yr	2	4	.333	27	0	0	0	4	39²	53	1	22	16	17.0	3.18	122	.323	.403	0	—	0	3	3	-0	0.1
Total 6	35	36	.493	277	0	0	0	52	496²	458	41	190	307	12.1	3.21	117	.244	.318	0	—	0	29	30	1	5.1
● JACK FOURNIER			Fournier, John Frank b: 9/28/1889, AuSable, Mich. d: 9/5/73, Tacoma, Wash. BL/TR, 6′, 195 lbs. Deb: 4/13/12 ♦																					
1922 StL-N	0	0	—	1	0	0	0	0	1	0	0	0	0	0.0	—	—	.000	.000	119	.295	0	0	0	0	0.2
● HENRY FOURNIER			Fournier, Julius Henry "Frenchy" b: 8/8/1865, Syracuse, N.Y. d: 12/8/45, Detroit, Mich. TL , Deb: 8/22/1894																					
1894 Cin-N	1	3	.250	6	4	4	0	0	45	71	4	20	5	18.6	5.40	103	.353	.417	2	.105	-3	-0	1	0	-0.1
● DAVE FOUTZ			Foutz, David Luther "Scissors" b: 9/7/1856, Carroll Co., Md. d: 3/5/1897, Waverly, Ind. BR/TR, 6′2″, 161 lbs. Deb: 7/29/1884 FM ♦																					
1884 StL-a	15	6	.714	25	25	19	2	0	206²	167	7	36	95	9.2	2.18	150	.212	.255	27	.227	1	25	25	3	2.5
1885 *StL-a	33	14	.702	47	46	46	2	0	407²	351	8	92	147	10.2	2.63	125	.227	.278	59	.248	5	28	29	7	3.8
1886 *StL-a	41	16	.719	59	57	55	11	1	504	418	5	144	283	10.2	2.11	163	.216	.274	116	.280	11	75	75	2	8.1
1887 *StL-a	25	12	.676	40	38	36	1	0	339¹	369	7	90	106	12.4	3.87	117	.258	.306	151	.357	15	16	25	3	3.1
1888 Bro-a	12	7	.632	23	19	19	0	0	176	146	3	35	73	9.5	2.51	119	.218	.262	156	.277	6	11	9	3	1.5
1889 *Bro-a	0	1	.000	12	4	3	0	0	59²	70	2	19	21	13.4	4.37	85	.283	.335	152	.275	3	-3	-4	1	0.1
1890 *Bro-N	2	1	.667	5	2	2	0	2	29	29	0	6	4	11.2	1.86	185	.252	.295	154	.303	2	6	5	-1	0.6
1891 Bro-N	3	2	.600	6	5	3	0	0	52	51	1	16	14	11.8	3.29	100	.246	.304	134	.257	1	-0	0	0	0.1
1892 Bro-N	13	8	.619	27	20	17	0	1	203	210	3	63	56	12.3	3.41	93	.256	.313	41	.186	-5	-3	-6	3	-0.3
1893 Bro-N	0	0	—	6	0	0	0	0	18	28	2	8	3	18.0	7.50	59	.346	.404	137	.246	1	-6	-6	1	0.1
1894 Bro-N	0	0	—	2	0	0	0	0	2	4	0	1	0	22.5	13.50	37	.400	.455	90	.307	0	-2	-0	0	0.0
Total 11	147	66	.690	251	216	202	16	4	1997¹	1843	38	510	790	10.9	2.84	124	.235	.286	1253	.276	45	147	148	18	19.6
● JESSE FOWLER			Fowler, Jesse Peter "Pete" b: 10/30/1898, Spartanburg, S.C. d: 9/23/73, Columbia, S.C. BR/TL, 5′10.5″, 158 lbs. Deb: 7/29/24 F																					
1924 StL-N	1	1	.500	13	3	0	0	0	32²	28	0	18	13	13.2	4.41	86	.226	.333	2	.222	-1	-2	-2	-1	-0.2
● ART FOWLER			Fowler, John Arthur b: 7/3/22, Converse, S.C. BR/TR, 5′11″, 180 lbs. Deb: 4/17/54 FC																					
1954 Cin-N	12	10	.545	40	29	8	5	0	227²	256	20	85	93	13.6	3.83	109	.286	.351	6	.100	-1	6	9	-1	0.5
1955 Cin-N	11	10	.524	46	28	8	3	2	207²	198	20	63	94	11.4	3.90	109	.250	.306	12	.205	0	3	8	-1	0.6
1956 Cin-N	11	11	.500	45	23	8	1	0	177²	191	15	35	86	11.4	4.05	98	.278	.313	7	.146	0	-6	-1	-1	-0.1
1957 Cin-N	3	0	1.000	33	7	1	0	0	87²	111	11	24	45	14.1	6.47	64	.310	.357	3	.176	0	-25	-23	0	-0.7
1959 LA-N	4	4	.429	36	0	0	0	2	61	70	8	23	47	13.7	5.31	80	.294	.356	1	.083	-1	-9	-7	0	-0.9
1961 LA-A	5	8	.385	53	3	0	0	11	89	68	12	29	61	9.8	3.64	124	.209	.274	1	.077	-1	4	9	1	1.1
1962 LA-A	4	3	.571	48	0	0	0	5	77	67	6	25	58	10.9	2.81	138	.234	.298	3	.273	1	10	9	0	0.9
1963 LA-A	5	3	.625	57	0	0	0	10	89¹	70	5	19	53	9.0	2.42	142	.219	.263	2	.222	0	12	10	-1	1.0
1964 LA-A	0	2	.000	4	0	0	0	0	7	8	2	5	6	18.0	10.29	32	.296	.424	0	.000	-0	-5	-5	0	-1.3
Total 9	54	51	.514	362	90	25	4	32	1024	1039	99	308	539	11.9	4.03	102	.265	.320	35	.152	-2	-10	7	-3	1.1
● DICK FOWLER			Fowler, Richard John b: 3/30/21, Toronto, Ont., Can. d: 5/22/72, Oneonta, N.Y. BR/TR, 6′4.5″, 215 lbs. Deb: 9/13/41																					
1941 Phi-A	1	2	.333	4	3	1	0	0	24	26	4	8	8	12.8	3.38	124	.289	.347	0	.000	-0	2	2	-0	0.1
1942 Phi-A	6	11	.353	31	17	4	1	1	140	159	13	45	38	13.1	4.95	76	.287	.341	8	.160	-1	-20	-18	-2	-2.3
1945 Phi-A	1	2	.333	7	3	2	1	0	37¹	41	1	18	21	14.2	4.82	71	.283	.362	8	.444	3	-6	-6	-1	-0.1

YEAR	TM/L	W	L	PCT	G	GS	CG	SH	SV	IP	H	HR	BB	SO	RAT	ERA	ERA+	OAV	OOB	BH	AVG	PB	PR	/A	PD	TPI
1946	Phi-A	9	16	.360	32	28	14	1	0	205²	213	16	75	89	12.7	3.28	108	.263	.327	13	.183	-1	5	6	-1	0.5
1947	Phi-A	12	11	.522	36	31	16	3	0	227¹	210	12	85	75	11.8	2.81	136	.249	.319	14	.171	-3	23	25	-2	2.0
1948	Phi-A	15	8	.652	29	26	16	2	0	204²	221	15	76	50	13.2	3.78	113	.281	.348	12	.171	-2	12	12	-1	0.8
1949	Phi-A	15	11	.577	31	28	15	4	1	213²	210	13	115	43	13.8	3.75	110	.262	.357	18	.234	3	11	9	1	1.3
1950	Phi-A	1	5	.167	11	9	2	0	0	66²	75	7	56	15	18.1	6.48	70	.300	.434	5	.192	-1	-14	-14	-0	-1.1
1951	Phi-A	5	11	.313	22	22	4	0	0	125	141	11	72	29	15.4	5.62	76	.291	.384	8	.190	-0	-21	-19	-1	-2.1
1952	Phi-A	1	2	.333	18	3	1	0	0	58²	71	4	28	14	15.8	6.44	61	.302	.386	0	.000	-2	-18	-16	-1	-0.9
Total	10	66	79	.455	221	170	75	11	4	1303	1367	96	578	382	13.6	4.11	97	.273	.351	88	.186	-6	-27	-19	-6	-1.8

● ALAN FOWLKES   Fowlkes, Alan Kim b: 8/8/58, Brawley, Cal. BR/TR, 6'2", 190 lbs. Deb: 4/7/82

YEAR	TM/L	W	L	PCT	G	GS	CG	SH	SV	IP	H	HR	BB	SO	RAT	ERA	ERA+	OAV	OOB	BH	AVG	PB	PR	/A	PD	TPI
1982	SF-N	4	2	.667	21	15	1	0	0	85	111	12	24	50	14.8	5.19	69	.321	.373	3	.115	-1	-15	-15	-0	-1.1
1985	Cal-A	0	0	—	2	0	0	0	0	7	8	4	4	5	15.4	9.00	46	.276	.364	0	—	0	-4	-4	0	0.0
Total	2	4	2	.667	23	15	1	0	0	92	119	16	28	55	14.9	5.48	66	.317	.373	3	.115	-1	-19	-19	-0	-1.1

● HENRY FOX   Fox, Henry (b: Henry Fuchs) b: 11/18/1874, Scranton, Pa. d: 6/6/27, Scranton, Pa. Deb: 9/4/02

YEAR	TM/L	W	L	PCT	G	GS	CG	SH	SV	IP	H	HR	BB	SO	RAT	ERA	ERA+	OAV	OOB	BH	AVG	PB	PR	/A	PD	TPI
1902	Phi-N	0	0	—	1	0	0	0	1	2	4	0	1	1	27.0	18.00	16	.400	.500	0	—	0	-2	-2	0	-0.3

● HOWIE FOX   Fox, Howard Francis b: 3/1/21, Coburg, Ore. d: 10/9/55, San Antonio, Tex. BR/TR, 6'3", 210 lbs. Deb: 9/28/44

YEAR	TM/L	W	L	PCT	G	GS	CG	SH	SV	IP	H	HR	BB	SO	RAT	ERA	ERA+	OAV	OOB	BH	AVG	PB	PR	/A	PD	TPI
1944	Cin-N	0	0	—	2	0	0	0	0	2¹	2	0	0	0	7.7	0.00	—	.222	.222	0	.000	-0	1	1	-0	0.0
1945	Cin-N	8	13	.381	45	15	7	0	0	164¹	169	6	77	54	13.8	4.93	76	.268	.353	13	.283	3	-21	-21	4	-1.7
1946	Cin-N	0	0	—	4	0	0	0	0	5	12	2	5	1	30.6	18.00	19	.462	.548	0	—	-0	-8	-8	0	0.0
1948	Cin-N	6	9	.400	34	24	9	0	1	171	185	14	62	63	13.1	4.53	86	.280	.343	12	.200	1	-11	-12	1	-0.7
1949	Cin-N	6	19	.240	38	30	9	0	0	215	221	13	77	60	12.6	3.98	105	.265	.330	17	.236	1	2	5	6	1.3
1950	Cin-N	11	8	.579	34	22	10	1	1	187	196	14	85	64	13.6	4.33	98	.269	.347	11	.175	-0	-4	-2	3	0.1
1951	Cin-N	9	14	.391	40	30	9	4	2	228	239	15	69	57	12.2	3.83	107	.272	.326	8	.114	1	3	6	1	0.4
1952	Phi-N	2	7	.222	13	11	2	0	0	62	70	8	26	16	13.9	5.08	72	.287	.356	1	.048	-2	-9	-10	1	-1.3
1954	Bal-A	1	2	.333	38	0	0	0	2	73²	80	2	34	27	14.2	3.67	98	.289	.371	4	.250	1	0	1	1	0.2
Total	9	43	72	.374	248	132	42	5	6	1108¹	1174	71	435	342	13.2	4.33	92	.274	.343	66	.189	1	-46	-42	17	-1.7

● JOHN FOX   Fox, John Joseph b: 2/7/1859, Roxbury, Mass. d: 4/18/1893, Boston, Mass. Deb: 6/2/1881

YEAR	TM/L	W	L	PCT	G	GS	CG	SH	SV	IP	H	HR	BB	SO	RAT	ERA	ERA+	OAV	OOB	BH	AVG	PB	PR	/A	PD	TPI
1881	Bos-N	6	8	.429	17	16	12	0	0	124¹	144	0	39	30	13.2	3.33	80	.279	.329	21	.178	-4	-8	-9	1	-1.1
1883	Bal-a	6	13	.316	20	19	18	0	0	165¹	209	3	32	49	13.1	4.03	86	.289	.320	14	.152	-4	-13	-10	-1	-1.3
1884	Pit-a	1	6	.143	7	7	7	0	0	59	76	2	16	22	14.5	5.64	60	.291	.339	6	.240	0	-16	-15	1	-1.2
1886	Was-N	0	1	.000	1	1	1	0	0	8	11	0	11	3	24.8	9.00	37	.314	.478	1	.333	1	-5	-5	0	-0.4
Total	4	13	28	.317	45	43	38	0	0	356²	440	4	98	104	13.7	4.16	76	.287	.331	42	.176	-8	-42	-40	0	-4.0

● TERRY FOX   Fox, Terrence Edward b: 7/31/35, Chicago, Ill. BR/TR, 6', 175 lbs. Deb: 9/4/60

YEAR	TM/L	W	L	PCT	G	GS	CG	SH	SV	IP	H	HR	BB	SO	RAT	ERA	ERA+	OAV	OOB	BH	AVG	PB	PR	/A	PD	TPI
1960	Mil-N	0	0	—	5	0	0	0	0	8¹	6	0	6	5	13.0	4.32	79	.200	.333	0	.000	-0	-1	-1	-0	0.0
1961	Det-A	5	2	.714	39	0	0	0	12	57¹	42	6	16	32	9.6	1.41	290	.200	.266	2	.167	-1	17	17	1	2.8
1962	Det-A	3	1	.750	44	0	0	0	16	58	48	2	16	23	10.1	1.71	238	.227	.285	2	.250	2	15	15	0	2.1
1963	Det-A	8	6	.571	46	0	0	0	11	80¹	81	9	20	35	11.5	3.59	104	.263	.312	1	.091	-0	0	1	0	0.3
1964	Det-A	4	3	.571	32	0	0	0	5	61	77	4	16	28	13.9	3.39	108	.316	.360	3	.250	1	2	2	1	0.4
1965	Det-A	6	4	.600	42	0	0	0	10	77²	59	7	31	34	10.8	2.78	125	.214	.300	0	.000	-1	6	6	2	1.0
1966	Det-A	0	1	.000	4	0	0	0	1	10	9	3	2	4	9.9	6.30	55	.243	.282	0	.000	-0	-3	-3	-0	-0.3
	Phi-N	3	2	.600	36	0	0	0	4	44¹	57	3	17	22	15.4	4.47	80	.322	.388	0	.000	-1	-4	-4	0	-0.6
Total	7	29	19	.604	248	0	0	0	59	397	379	34	124	185	11.7	2.99	125	.254	.316	8	.123	1	31	33	4	5.7

● BILL FOXEN   Foxen, William Aloysius b: 5/31/1884, Tenafly, N.J. d: 4/17/37, Brooklyn, N.Y. BL/TL, 5'11.5", 165 lbs. Deb: 5/5/08

YEAR	TM/L	W	L	PCT	G	GS	CG	SH	SV	IP	H	HR	BB	SO	RAT	ERA	ERA+	OAV	OOB	BH	AVG	PB	PR	/A	PD	TPI
1908	Phi-N	7	7	.500	22	16	10	2	0	147¹	126	2	53	52	11.4	1.95	124	.240	.319	5	.094	-3	7	8	2	0.6
1909	Phi-N	3	7	.300	18	7	5	1	0	83¹	65	0	32	37	10.9	3.35	78	.219	.303	5	.208	3	-7	-7	4	0.0
1910	Phi-N	5	5	.500	16	9	5	0	0	77²	73	2	40	33	13.4	2.55	123	.268	.368	4	.174	-1	4	5	2	0.7
	Chi-N	0	0	—	2	0	0	0	0	5	7	0	3	2	18.0	9.00	32	.350	.435	0	.000	-0	-3	-3	-0	0.0
	Yr	5	5	.500	18	9	5	0	0	82²	80	2	43	35	13.4	2.94	106	.271	.364	4	.160	-1	1	2	1	0.7
1911	Chi-N	1	1	.500	3	1	0	0	0	13	12	0	12	6	16.6	2.08	160	.255	.407	1	.250	1	3	4	1	0.4
Total	4	16	20	.444	61	33	20	3	0	326¹	283	4	140	130	12.1	2.56	104	.244	.333	15	.142	-1	3	4	8	1.7

● JIMMIE FOXX   Foxx, James Emory "Beast" or "Double X" b: 10/22/07, Sudlersville, Md. d: 7/21/67, Miami, Fla. BR/TR, 6', 195 lbs. Deb: 5/1/25 CH◆

YEAR	TM/L	W	L	PCT	G	GS	CG	SH	SV	IP	H	HR	BB	SO	RAT	ERA	ERA+	OAV	OOB	BH	AVG	PB	PR	/A	PD	TPI
1939	Bos-A☆	0	0	—	1	0	0	0	0	1	0	0	1	0	0.0	0.00	—	.000	.000	168	.360	1	1	1	0	0.0
1945	Phi-N	1	0	1.000	9	2	0	0	0	22²	13	0	14	10	11.1	1.59	241	.171	.308	60	.268	2	6	6	-1	0.3
Total	2	1	0	1.000	10	2	0	0	0	23²	13	0	14	10	10.6	1.52	254	.165	.298	2646	.325	3	6	6	-1	0.3

● PAUL FOYTACK   Foytack, Paul Eugene b: 11/16/30, Scranton, Pa. BR/TR, 5'11", 180 lbs. Deb: 4/21/53

YEAR	TM/L	W	L	PCT	G	GS	CG	SH	SV	IP	H	HR	BB	SO	RAT	ERA	ERA+	OAV	OOB	BH	AVG	PB	PR	/A	PD	TPI
1953	Det-A	0	0	—	6	0	0	0	0	9²	15	1	9	7	23.3	11.17	36	.375	.500	0	.000	-0	-8	-8	-0	0.0
1955	Det-A	0	1	.000	22	1	0	0	0	49²	48	4	36	38	15.2	5.26	73	.259	.380	1	.091	-1	-7	-8	-0	-0.2
1956	Det-A	15	13	.536	43	33	16	1	1	256	211	24	142	184	12.5	3.59	115	.226	.330	11	.122	-6	16	15	-1	0.8
1957	Det-A	14	11	.560	38	27	8	1	1	212	175	19	104	118	12.0	3.14	123	.226	.321	14	.222	1	15	17	-2	1.7
1958	Det-A	15	13	.536	39	33	16	2	1	230	198	23	77	135	10.9	3.44	117	.233	.299	18	.240	2	8	15	-2	1.8
1959	Det-A	14	14	.500	39	37	11	2	1	240¹	239	34	64	110	11.4	4.64	87	.259	.308	9	.111	-4	-21	-16	-2	-2.1
1960	Det-A	2	11	.154	28	13	1	0	2	96²	108	11	49	38	14.6	6.14	64	.286	.369	7	.280	2	-24	-23	-2	-2.8
1961	Det-A	11	10	.524	32	20	6	0	0	169²	152	27	56	89	11.1	3.93	104	.238	.301	12	.222	2	3	3	-2	-0.2
1962	Det-A	10	7	.588	29	21	5	1	0	143²	145	18	86	63	14.5	4.39	93	.259	.359	6	.143	-1	-7	-5	0	-0.6
1963	Det-A	0	1	.000	9	0	0	0	0	17²	18	4	9	7	13.2	8.53	43	.265	.342	0	.000	-0	-10	-10	-0	-0.7
	LA-A	5	5	.500	25	8	0	0	0	70¹	68	9	29	37	12.4	3.71	92	.255	.328	4	.267	1	-1	-2	-1	-0.2
	Yr	5	6	.455	34	8	0	0	0	88	86	13	37	44	12.6	4.70	74	.256	.330	4	.211	1	-11	-12	-1	-0.9
1964	LA-A	0	1	.000	2	0	0	0	0	2¹	3	0	2	2	23.1	15.43	21	.364	.462	0	—	-0	-3	-3	-0	-1.0
Total	11	86	87	.497	312	193	63	7	7	1498	1381	174	662	827	12.4	4.14	90	.247	.327	82	.178	-3	-39	-24	-13	-3.1

● KEN FRAILING   Frailing, Kenneth Douglas b: 1/19/48, Marion, Wis. BL/TL, 6', 190 lbs. Deb: 9/1/72

YEAR	TM/L	W	L	PCT	G	GS	CG	SH	SV	IP	H	HR	BB	SO	RAT	ERA	ERA+	OAV	OOB	BH	AVG	PB	PR	/A	PD	TPI
1972	Chi-A	1	0	1.000	4	0	0	0	0	3	3	1	1	1	12.0	3.00	104	.250	.308	0	—	0	0	0	0	0.0
1973	Chi-A	0	0	—	10	0	0	0	0	18¹	18	1	7	15	12.8	1.96	202	.254	.329	0	—	0	4	4	-0	-0.2
1974	Chi-N	6	9	.400	55	16	1	0	1	125¹	150	11	43	71	13.9	3.88	98	.296	.353	8	.258	1	-4	-1	0	-0.2
1975	Chi-N	2	5	.286	41	0	0	0	0	53	61	6	26	39	15.1	5.43	71	.293	.377	1	.143	1	-11	-9	2	-1.0
1976	Chi-N	1	2	.333	6	3	0	0	0	18²	20	0	5	10	12.1	2.41	160	.274	.321	1	.000	0	2	3	0	0.4
Total	5	10	16	.385	116	19	1	0	2	218¹	252	19	82	136	13.9	3.96	97	.290	.354	9	.220	1	-8	-3	2	-0.8

● OSSIE FRANCE   France, Osman Beverly "O. B." b: 10/4/1858, Greensburg, Ohio d: 5/2/47, Akron, Ohio BL/TL, 5'8", 155 lbs. Deb: 7/14/1890

YEAR	TM/L	W	L	PCT	G	GS	CG	SH	SV	IP	H	HR	BB	SO	RAT	ERA	ERA+	OAV	OOB	BH	AVG	PB	PR	/A	PD	TPI
1890	Chi-N	0	0	—	2	0	0	0	0	9	10	0	3	2	22.5	13.50	27	.333	.455	0	.000	-0	-2	-2	-0	0.0

● EARL FRANCIS   Francis, Earl Coleman b: 7/14/35, Slab Fork, W.Va. BR/TR, 6'2", 215 lbs. Deb: 6/30/60

YEAR	TM/L	W	L	PCT	G	GS	CG	SH	SV	IP	H	HR	BB	SO	RAT	ERA	ERA+	OAV	OOB	BH	AVG	PB	PR	/A	PD	TPI
1960	Pit-N	1	0	1.000	18	14	0	0	0	18	14	0	9	8	9.5	2.20	188	.222	.279	0	.000	-1	4	4	-0	0.1
1961	Pit-N	2	8	.200	23	15	0	0	0	102²	110	6	47	53	13.9	4.21	95	.274	.351	3	.107	-1	-2	-3	0	-0.2
1962	Pit-N	9	8	.529	36	23	5	1	0	176	153	8	83	121	12.2	3.07	128	.235	.323	10	.164	1	17	17	1	1.7
1963	Pit-N	4	6	.400	33	13	0	0	0	97¹	107	6	43	72	14.2	4.53	73	.284	.363	8	.308	3	-13	-13	1	-1.0
1964	Pit-N	0	1	.000	2	2	0	0	0	6¹	7	2	1	6	12.8	8.53	41	.269	.321	0	.000	-0	-4	-4	-0	-0.5
1965	StL-N	0	0	—	2	0	0	0	0	5	7	3	3	3	19.8	5.06	76	.318	.400	0	—	-1	-1	-0	0	0.1
Total	6	16	23	.410	103	52	5	1	0	405²	398	21	181	263	13.0	3.77	100	.258	.340	21	.172	2	1	1	1	0.1

● RAY FRANCIS   Francis, Ray James b: 3/8/1893, Sherman, Tex. d: 7/6/34, Atlanta, Ga. BL/TL, 6'1.5", 182 lbs. Deb: 4/18/22

YEAR	TM/L	W	L	PCT	G	GS	CG	SH	SV	IP	H	HR	BB	SO	RAT	ERA	ERA+	OAV	OOB	BH	AVG	PB	PR	/A	PD	TPI
1922	Was-A	7	18	.280	39	26	15	2	2	225	265	7	66	64	13.5	4.28	90	.303	.356	13	.167	-2	-6	-10	-1	-1.3
1923	Det-A	5	8	.385	33	6	0	0	1	79¹	95	2	28	27	14.4	4.42	87	.308	.374	3	.143	-2	-4	-5	-0	-0.9
1925	NY-A	0	0	—	2	0	0	0	0	4²	5	0	3	1	17.4	7.71	55	.278	.409	0	—	-2	-2	-2	-0	-0.6
	Bos-A	0	2	.000	6	4	0	0	0	28	44	3	13	4	18.6	7.71	59	.373	.439	1	.125	-0	-10	-10	0	-0.6

YEAR	TM/L	W	L	PCT	G	GS	CG	SH	SV	IP	H	HR	BB	SO	RAT	ERA	ERA+	OAV	OOB	BH	AVG	PB	PR	/A	PD	TPI
	Yr	0	2	.000	10	4	0	0	0	32²	49	3	16	5	18.2	7.71	58	.358	.429	1	.125	-0	-12	-12	-0	-0.6
Total	3	12	28	.300	82	36	15	2	3	337	409	12	110	96	14.2	4.65	84	.310	.368	17	.159	-4	-22	-27	-1	-2.8

● JOHN FRANCO
Franco, John Anthony   b: 9/17/60, Brooklyn, N.Y.   BL/TL, 5'10", 180 lbs.   Deb: 4/24/84

YEAR	TM/L	W	L	PCT	G	GS	CG	SH	SV	IP	H	HR	BB	SO	RAT	ERA	ERA+	OAV	OOB	BH	AVG	PB	PR	/A	PD	TPI
1984	Cin-N	6	2	.750	54	0	0	0	4	79¹	74	3	36	55	12.7	2.61	145	.256	.343	0	.000	-0	9	10	1	1.1
1985	Cin-N	12	3	.800	67	0	0	0	12	99	83	5	40	61	11.3	2.18	173	.234	.314	2	.333	0	16	**18**	2	3.3
1986	Cin-N☆	6	6	.500	74	0	0	0	29	101	90	7	44	84	12.1	2.94	132	.242	.325	0	.000	-0	9	10	1	1.8
1987	Cin-N★	8	5	.615	68	0	0	0	32	82	76	6	27	61	11.3	2.52	168	.245	.306	0	.000	-0	14	16	1	3.3
1988	Cin-N	6	6	.500	70	0	0	0	**39**	86	60	3	27	46	9.1	1.57	228	.198	.264	0	.000	-0	**18**	**19**	1	**4.5**
1989	Cin-N☆	4	8	.333	60	0	0	0	32	80²	77	3	36	60	12.6	3.12	115	.258	.337	1	.333	0	3	4	1	1.1
1990	NY-N★	5	3	.625	55	0	0	0	33	67²	66	4	21	56	11.6	2.53	148	.252	.307	0	—	-1	10	9	1	1.9
1991	NY-N	5	9	.357	52	0	0	0	30	55¹	61	2	18	45	13.0	2.93	124	.271	.328	0	.000	-0	5	4	1	1.5
1992	NY-N	6	2	.750	31	0	0	0	15	33	24	1	11	20	9.5	1.64	212	.209	.278	0	.000	-0	7	7	2	2.4
1993	NY-N	4	3	.571	35	0	0	0	10	36¹	46	6	19	29	16.3	5.20	77	.313	.395	0	.000	-0	-5	-5	1	-1.0
1994	NY-N	1	4	.200	47	0	0	0	**30**	50	47	2	19	42	12.1	2.70	155	.244	.315	0	.000	-0	8	8	0	1.6
1995	NY-N	5	3	.625	48	0	0	0	29	51²	48	4	17	41	11.3	2.44	166	.251	.313	0	—	0	10	9	0	2.3
1996	NY-N	4	3	.571	51	0	0	0	28	54	54	4	21	48	12.5	1.83	214	.260	.328	0	—	0	14	13	0	2.6
Total	13	72	57	.558	712	0	0	0	323	876	806	48	336	648	11.8	2.57	149	.247	.318	3	.097	-2	117	123	9	26.4

● TERRY FRANCONA
Francona, Terry Jon   b: 4/22/59, Aberdeen, S.D.   BL/TL, 6'1", 190 lbs.   Deb: 8/19/81   FC♦

YEAR	TM/L	W	L	PCT	G	GS	CG	SH	SV	IP	H	HR	BB	SO	RAT	ERA	ERA+	OAV	OOB	BH	AVG	PB	PR	/A	PD	TPI
1989	Mil-A	0	0	—	1	0	0	0	0	1	0	0	1	0	9.0	0.00	—	.000	.000	54	.232	1	0	0	0	0.0

● CHARLIE FRANK
Frank, Charles   b: 5/30/1870, Mobile, Ala.   d: 5/24/22, Memphis, Tenn.   5'10", 170 lbs.   Deb: 8/18/1893   ♦

YEAR	TM/L	W	L	PCT	G	GS	CG	SH	SV	IP	H	HR	BB	SO	RAT	ERA	ERA+	OAV	OOB	BH	AVG	PB	PR	/A	PD	TPI
1894	StL-N	0	0	—	2	0	0	0	0	3	6	1	7	1	39.0	15.00	36	.400	.591	89	.279	-0	-3	-3	-0	0.0

● FRED FRANKHOUSE
Frankhouse, Frederick Meloy   b: 4/9/04, Port Royal, Pa.   d: 8/17/04, Port Royal, Pa.   BR/TR, 5'11", 175 lbs.   Deb: 9/11/27

YEAR	TM/L	W	L	PCT	G	GS	CG	SH	SV	IP	H	HR	BB	SO	RAT	ERA	ERA+	OAV	OOB	BH	AVG	PB	PR	/A	PD	TPI
1927	StL-N	5	1	.833	6	6	5	1	0	50	41	2	16	20	10.4	2.70	146	.218	.283	5	.250	0	7	7	-1	0.7
1928	StL-N	3	2	.600	21	10	3	0	1	84	91	6	36	29	14.1	3.96	101	.277	.358	5	.185	1	0	0	1	0.2
1929	StL-N	7	2	.778	30	12	6	0	1	133¹	149	9	43	37	13.2	4.12	113	.289	.349	15	.288	4	9	8	3	1.0
1930	StL-N	3	2	.400	8	1	0	0	0	19²	31	1	4	9	7.32	7.32	69	.373	.447	0	.000	-0	-5	-5	-0	-1.0
	Bos-N	7	6	.538	27	11	3	1	0	110²	138	13	43	30	14.9	5.61	88	.313	.377	14	.359	-4	-8	-8	-0	-0.4
	Yr	9	9	.500	35	12	3	1	0	130¹	169	14	54	34	15.5	5.87	84	.323	.388	14	.318	3	-13	-13	0	-1.4
1931	Bos-N	8	8	.500	26	15	6	0	1	127¹	125	4	43	50	12.1	4.03	94	.252	.315	6	.150	-2	-2	-3	1	-0.3
1932	Bos-N	4	6	.400	37	6	3	0	0	108²	113	7	45	35	13.3	3.56	106	.278	.355	3	.100	-1	4	2	3	0.4
1933	Bos-N	16	15	.516	43	30	14	2	2	244²	249	12	77	83	12.1	3.16	97	.267	.324	19	.237	4	5	-3	4	0.5
1934	Bos-N★	17	9	.654	37	31	13	2	1	233²	239	10	77	78	12.3	3.20	120	.262	.322	17	.200	2	22	16	-0	1.8
1935	Bos-N	11	15	.423	40	29	10	1	0	230²	278	12	81	64	14.2	4.76	80	.293	.352	20	.263	4	-19	-25	3	-1.4
1936	Bro-N	13	10	.565	41	31	9	1	2	234¹	236	18	89	62	12.6	3.65	113	.257	.325	13	.143	-4	10	13	1	0.8
1937	Bro-N	10	13	.435	33	25	9	1	0	179¹	214	8	78	64	14.9	4.27	95	.297	.369	11	.190	-0	-7	-5	3	-0.3
1938	Bro-N	3	5	.375	30	8	2	1	0	93²	92	6	44	32	13.5	4.04	97	.256	.344	4	.154	-1	-3	-1	-0	-0.1
1939	Bos-N	0	2	.000	23	0	0	0	0	38	37	3	18	12	13.3	2.61	142	.253	.339	0	.000	-1	6	5	-1	0.2
Total	13	106	97	.522	402	215	81	10	12	1888	2033	111	701	622	13.2	3.92	100	.275	.341	132	.208	12	18	-0	18	2.1

● JACK FRANKLIN
Franklin, Jack Wilford   b: 10/20/19, Paris, Ill.   d: 11/15/91, Panama City, Fla.   BR/TR, 5'11.5", 170 lbs.   Deb: 6/12/44

YEAR	TM/L	W	L	PCT	G	GS	CG	SH	SV	IP	H	HR	BB	SO	RAT	ERA	ERA+	OAV	OOB	BH	AVG	PB	PR	/A	PD	TPI
1944	Bro-N	0	0	—	1	0	0	0	0	2	2	1	4	0	36.0	13.50	26	.250	.571	0	—	0	-2	-2	-0	0.0

● JAY FRANKLIN
Franklin, John William   b: 3/16/53, Arlington, Va.   BR/TR, 6'2", 180 lbs.   Deb: 9/4/71

YEAR	TM/L	W	L	PCT	G	GS	CG	SH	SV	IP	H	HR	BB	SO	RAT	ERA	ERA+	OAV	OOB	BH	AVG	PB	PR	/A	PD	TPI
1971	SD-N	0	1	.000	3	1	0	0	0	5²	5	3	4	4	14.3	6.35	52	.250	.375	0	.000	-0	-2	-2	0	-0.3

● JOHN FRASCATORE
Frascatore, John Vincent   b: 2/4/70, Ozone Park, N.Y.   BR/TR, 6'1", 200 lbs.   Deb: 7/21/94

YEAR	TM/L	W	L	PCT	G	GS	CG	SH	SV	IP	H	HR	BB	SO	RAT	ERA	ERA+	OAV	OOB	BH	AVG	PB	PR	/A	PD	TPI
1994	StL-N	0	1	.000	1	1	0	0	0	3¹	7	2	4	4	24.3	16.20	26	.438	.500	0	.000	-0	-4	-4	0	-0.8
1995	StL-N	1	1	.500	14	4	0	0	0	32²	39	3	16	21	15.7	4.41	95	.298	.383	0	.000	-0	-1	-1	-1	-0.1
Total	2	1	2	.333	15	5	0	0	0	36	46	5	18	23	16.5	5.50	76	.313	.395	0	.000	-0	-5	-5	-0	-0.9

● CHICK FRASER
Fraser, Charles Carrolton   b: 3/17/1871, Chicago, Ill.   d: 5/8/40, Wendell, Idaho   BR/TR, 5'10.5", 188 lbs.   Deb: 4/19/1896   C

YEAR	TM/L	W	L	PCT	G	GS	CG	SH	SV	IP	H	HR	BB	SO	RAT	ERA	ERA+	OAV	OOB	BH	AVG	PB	PR	/A	PD	TPI
1896	Lou-N	12	27	.308	43	38	36	0	1	349¹	396	9	166	91	15.2	4.87	89	.283	.371	22	.151	-9	-20	-21	3	-2.2
1897	Lou-N	15	19	.441	35	34	32	0	0	286¹	332	11	133	70	15.3	4.09	104	.288	.372	18	.161	-4	7	6	6	0.7
1898	Lou-N	7	17	.292	26	26	20	1	0	203	230	4	100	58	15.7	5.32	67	.283	.378	13	.167	-2	-39	-39	4	-3.5
	Cle-N	2	3	.400	6	6	6	0	0	42	49	2	12	19	14.4	5.57	65	.290	.358	4	.250	-0	-9	-9	-0	-0.8
	Yr	9	20	.310	32	32	26	1	0	245	279	6	112	77	14.6	5.36	67	.278	.354	17	.181	-2	-48	-48	4	-4.3
1899	Phi-N	21	12	.636	35	33	29	4	0	270²	278	1	85	68	12.8	3.36	110	.265	.333	21	.179	-2	15	10	2	1.0
1900	Phi-N	15	9	.625	29	26	22	1	0	223¹	250	7	93	58	14.3	3.14	115	.282	.358	22	.259	4	14	12	3	1.7
1901	Phi-A	22	16	.579	40	37	35	4	0	331	344	6	132	110	13.8	3.81	99	.265	.347	26	.187	-3	-5	-1	2	-0.3
1902	Phi-N	12	13	.480	27	26	24	3	0	224	238	2	74	97	13.1	3.42	82	.272	.339	15	.174	-0	-16	-15	-0	-1.5
1903	Phi-N	12	17	.414	31	29	26	1	0	250	260	6	97	104	13.4	4.50	73	.267	.344	19	.204	4	-34	-34	2	-2.7
1904	Phi-N	14	24	.368	42	36	32	2	1	302	287	5	100	127	11.9	3.25	82	.246	.311	17	.155	-1	-17	-19	2	-2.1
1905	Bos-N	14	21	.400	39	37	35	2	0	334¹	320	8	149	130	13.0	3.28	94	.254	.340	35	.224	3	-10	-7	-1	-0.3
1906	Cin-N	10	20	.333	31	28	25	2	0	236	221	1	80	58	11.8	2.67	103	.259	.329	14	.171	-1	-1	2	1	0.2
1907	Chi-N	8	5	.615	22	15	9	2	1	138¹	112	1	46	41	10.5	2.28	110	.229	.299	3	.067	-3	3	3	0	0.3
1908	Chi-N	11	9	.550	26	17	11	2	2	162²	141	4	61	66	11.5	2.27	104	.244	.323	6	.120	-2	2	2	4	0.4
1909	Chi-N	0	0	—	1	0	0	0	0	3	2	0	4	1	18.0	0.00	—	.222	.462	0	.000	-0	1	1	0	0.0
Total	14	175	212	.452	433	388	342	22	6	3356	3460	69	1332	1098	13.4	3.68	92	.267	.345	235	.179	-15	-109	-108	29	-9.4

● WILLIE FRASER
Fraser, William Patrick   b: 5/26/64, New York, N.Y.   BR/TR, 6'1", 208 lbs.   Deb: 9/10/86

YEAR	TM/L	W	L	PCT	G	GS	CG	SH	SV	IP	H	HR	BB	SO	RAT	ERA	ERA+	OAV	OOB	BH	AVG	PB	PR	/A	PD	TPI
1986	Cal-A	0	0	—	1	1	0	0	0	4¹	6	1	2	1	14.5	8.31	49	.353	.389	0	—	0	-2	-2	-0	0.1
1987	Cal-A	10	10	.500	36	23	5	1	1	176²	160	26	63	106	11.7	3.92	110	.240	.312	0	—	0	10	7	-3	0.7
1988	Cal-A	12	13	.480	34	32	2	0	1	194²	203	33	80	86	13.5	5.41	71	.267	.344	0	—	0	-31	-34	-1	-3.7
1989	Cal-A	4	7	.364	44	0	0	0	0	91²	80	6	23	46	10.6	3.24	118	.235	.293	0	—	0	7	6	-0	0.7
1990	Cal-A	5	4	.556	45	0	0	0	0	76	69	4	24	32	11.0	3.08	124	.241	.300	0	—	0	6	6	-0	0.6
1991	Tor-A	0	2	.000	13	1	0	0	0	26¹	33	4	11	12	16.1	6.15	68	.303	.382	0	—	0	-6	-6	-0	-0.7
	StL-N	3	3	.500	35	0	0	0	0	49¹	44	9	21	25	12.4	4.93	75	.242	.330	0	.000	-0	-7	-7	-1	-0.9
1994	Fla-N	0	1	0.000	12	1	0	0	0	12¹	20	1	6	7	19.0	5.84	75	.370	.433	0	—	0	-2	-2	-0	-0.3
1995	Mon-N	2	1	.667	22	0	0	0	0	25²	25	6	9	12	13.0	5.61	76	.248	.327	0	—	0	-4	-4	-0	-0.5
Total	8	38	40	.487	239	57	7	1	7	657	640	89	238	328	12.4	4.47	90	.254	.326	0	.000	-0	-28	-34	-6	-4.0

● VIC FRASIER
Frasier, Victor Patrick   b: 8/5/04, Ruston, La.   d: 1/10/77, Jacksonville, Tex.   BR/TR, 6', 182 lbs.   Deb: 4/18/31

YEAR	TM/L	W	L	PCT	G	GS	CG	SH	SV	IP	H	HR	BB	SO	RAT	ERA	ERA+	OAV	OOB	BH	AVG	PB	PR	/A	PD	TPI
1931	Chi-A	13	15	.464	46	29	13	2	4	254	258	11	127	87	13.8	4.46	95	.259	.345	18	.209	1	-2	-6	-1	-0.6
1932	Chi-A	3	13	.188	29	21	4	0	0	146	180	14	70	33	15.7	6.23	69	.297	.374	4	.091	-3	-28	-31	2	-2.8
1933	Chi-A	1	1	.500	10	1	0	0	0	20¹	32	2	11	4	19.0	8.85	48	.368	.439	0	.000	-1	-10	-10	1	-0.8
	Det-A	5	5	.500	20	14	4	0	0	104¹	129	9	56	26	16.3	6.64	65	.312	.399	7	.189	-0	-27	-27	2	-2.1
	Yr	6	6	.500	30	15	4	0	0	124²	161	11	70	30	16.7	7.00	61	.321	.406	7	.171	-1	-38	-37	2	-2.9
1934	Det-A	1	3	.250	8	2	0	0	0	22²	30	1	6	12	17.1	5.96	74	.313	.394	2	.286	-0	-4	-4	-0	-0.4
1937	Bos-N	0	0	—	3	0	0	0	0	8	12	1	9	2	14.6	5.63	64	.364	.382	0	.000	-0	-2	-2	-0	-0.2
1939	Chi-A	0	1	.000	10	1	0	0	0	23²	45	10	9	7	21.3	10.27	46	.405	.459	2	.286	-0	-15	-15	-0	-0.5
Total	6	23	38	.377	126	68	21	2	4	579	686	37	291	170	15.4	5.77	75	.293	.373	33	.177	-3	-88	-94	4	-7.2

● GEORGE FRAZIER
Frazier, George Allen   b: 10/13/54, Oklahoma City, Okla.   BR/TR, 6'5", 205 lbs.   Deb: 5/25/78

YEAR	TM/L	W	L	PCT	G	GS	CG	SH	SV	IP	H	HR	BB	SO	RAT	ERA	ERA+	OAV	OOB	BH	AVG	PB	PR	/A	PD	TPI
1978	StL-N	0	3	.000	14	0	0	0	0	22	22	2	6	8	11.5	4.09	86	.260	.298	1	.333	-0	-1	0	-0	-0.2
1979	StL-N	2	4	.333	25	0	0	0	0	30¹	33	2	16	12	13.4	4.45	84	.278	.345	0	—	0	-3	-2	-0	-0.4
1980	StL-N	1	4	.200	22	0	0	0	3	23	24	3	7	11	12.1	2.74	135	.273	.326	0	—	0	2	2	0	0.6
1981	*NY-A	0	1	.000	16	0	0	0	3	27²	26	1	11	17	12.0	1.63	220	.245	.316	0	—	0	6	6	-0	0.4
1982	NY-A	4	4	.500	63	0	0	0	1	111²	103	7	39	69	11.8	3.47	115	.252	.325	0	—	0	8	6	-0	0.5

YEAR	TM/L	W	L	PCT	G	GS	CG	SH	SV	IP	H	HR	BB	SO	RAT	ERA	ERA+	OAV	OOB	BH	AVG	PB	PR	/A	PD	TPI
1983	NY-A	4	4	.500	61	0	0	0	8	115¹	94	5	45	78	11.1	3.43	113	.227	.307	0	—	0	8	6	0	0.7
1984	Cle-A	3	2	.600	22	0	0	0	1	44¹	45	3	14	24	12.0	3.65	112	.259	.314	0	—	0	2	2	-1	0.0
	*Chi-N	6	3	.667	37	0	0	0	3	63²	53	4	26	58	11.3	4.10	95	.221	.300	2	.286	—	-4	-1	-1	-0.3
1985	Chi-N	7	8	.467	51	0	0	0	2	76	88	11	52	46	16.9	6.39	62	.299	.410	0	.000	-1	-24	-20	-0	-3.8
1986	Chi-N	2	4	.333	35	0	0	0	0	51²	63	5	34	41	17.1	5.40	75	.310	.412	0	.000	-0	-10	-8	-1	-1.0
	Min-A	1	1	.500	15	0	0	0	6	26²	23	2	16	25	13.2	4.39	98	.232	.339	0	—	-0	-1	-0	-0	-0.2
1987	*Min-A	5	5	.500	54	0	0	0	2	81¹	77	9	51	58	14.4	4.98	93	.258	.369	0	—	0	-5	-3	-1	-0.7
Total	10	35	43	.449	415	0	0	0	29	675²	653	54	313	449	13.1	4.20	96	.257	.342	3	.143	-1	-20	-14	-4	-4.4

● **SCOTT FREDRICKSON**   Fredrickson, Scott Eric   b: 8/19/67, Manchester, N.H.   BR/TR, 6'3", 215 lbs.   Deb: 4/30/93

| 1993 | Col-N | 0 | 1 | .000 | 25 | 0 | 0 | 0 | 3 | 29 | 33 | 3 | 17 | 20 | 15.8 | 6.21 | 77 | .287 | .383 | 0 | .000 | -0 | -7 | -5 | -0 | -0.2 |

● **BUCK FREEMAN**   Freeman, Alexander Vernon   b: 7/5/1893, Mart, Tex.   d: 2/21/53, Fort Sam Houston, Tex.   BB/TR, 5'10", 167 lbs.   Deb: 4/13/21

1921	Chi-N	9	10	.474	38	20	6	0	3	177¹	189	12	70	42	13.6	4.11	93	.281	.356	11	.208	-0	-6	-6	-1	-0.7
1922	Chi-N	0	1	.000	11	1	0	0	1	25²	47	0	10	10	20.7	8.77	48	.412	.468	1	.125	-0	-13	-13	1	-0.5
Total	2	9	11	.450	49	21	6	0	4	203	236	12	80	52	14.5	4.70	82	.300	.372	12	.197	-0	-20	-19	-0	-1.2

● **HARVEY FREEMAN**   Freeman, Harvey Bayard "Buck"   b: 12/22/1897, Mottville, Mich.   d: 1/10/70, Kalamazoo, Mich.   BR/TR, 5'10", 160 lbs.   Deb: 7/10/21

| 1921 | Phi-A | 1 | 4 | .200 | 18 | 4 | 2 | 0 | 0 | 48 | 65 | 2 | 35 | 5 | 19.7 | 7.69 | 58 | .346 | .461 | 1 | .083 | -2 | -18 | -17 | 1 | -1.5 |

● **HERSH FREEMAN**   Freeman, Hershell Baskin "Buster"   b: 7/1/28, Gadsden, Ala.   BR/TR, 6'3", 220 lbs.   Deb: 9/10/52

1952	Bos-A	1	0	1.000	4	1	1	0	0	13²	13	1	5	5	12.5	3.29	120	.260	.339	2	.500	1	1	1	0	0.2
1953	Bos-A	1	4	.200	18	2	0	0	0	39	50	2	17	11	15.5	5.54	76	.316	.383	1	.091	-1	-7	-6	-0	-0.8
1955	Bos-A	0	0	—	2	0	0	0	0	1²	1	1	0	1	10.8	0.00	—	.200	.333	0	—	0	1	1	-0	0.0
	Cin-N	7	4	.636	52	0	0	0	11	91²	94	3	30	37	12.4	2.16	196	.276	.338	3	.167	1	**19**	**21**	1	3.1
1956	Cin-N	14	5	.737	64	0	0	0	18	108²	112	2	34	50	12.2	3.40	117	.274	.331	1	.056	-1	5	7	-0	1.3
1957	Cin-N	7	2	.778	52	0	0	0	8	83²	90	14	14	36	11.5	4.52	91	.277	.313	2	.200	-0	-6	-4	-1	-0.5
1958	Cin-N	0	0	—	3	0	0	0	0	7²	4	0	5	7	10.6	3.52	118	.154	.290	0	.000	-0	0	1	0	0.0
	Chi-N	0	1	.000	9	0	0	0	0	13	23	3	3	7	18.0	8.31	47	.354	.382	0	.000	0	-6	-6	0	-0.4
	Yr	0	1	.000	12	0	0	0	0	20²	27	3	8	14	15.7	6.53	61	.293	.350	0	.000	-0	-6	-6	0	-0.4
Total	6	30	16	.652	204	3	1	0	37	359	387	25	109	158	12.6	3.74	110	.281	.336	9	.143	-0	6	15	1	2.9

● **JIMMY FREEMAN**   Freeman, Jimmy Lee   b: 6/29/51, Carlsbad, N.Mex.   BL/TL, 6'4", 180 lbs.   Deb: 9/1/72

1972	Atl-N	2	2	.500	6	6	1	0	0	36	40	5	22	18	15.5	6.00	63	.278	.373	1	.077	-0	-10	-9	-1	-1.0
1973	Atl-N	0	2	.000	13	5	0	1	1	37¹	50	7	25	20	18.1	7.71	51	.327	.421	2	.154	-0	-17	-16	-1	-0.9
Total	2	2	4	.333	19	11	1	0	1	73¹	90	12	47	38	16.8	6.87	56	.303	.398	3	.115	-0	-27	-25	-2	-1.9

● **BUCK FREEMAN**   Freeman, John Frank   b: 10/30/1871, Catasauqua, Pa.   d: 6/25/49, Wilkes-Barre, Pa.   BL/TL, 5'9", 169 lbs.   Deb: 6/27/1891 ♦

1891	Was-a	3	2	.600	5	4	4	0	0	44	35	0	33	28	14.7	3.89	96	.211	.355	4	.222	-1	-1	-1	-0	0.0
1899	Was-N	0	0	—	2	0	0	0	0	7	15	3	3	0	27.0	7.71	51	.429	.512	187	.318	1	-3	-3	0	0.0
Total	2	3	2	.600	7	4	4	0	0	51	50	3	36	28	16.4	4.41	85	.249	.381	1235	.293	1	-4	-4	-0	0.0

● **JULIE FREEMAN**   Freeman, Julius Benjamin   b: 11/7/1868, Missouri   d: 6/10/21, St.Louis, Mo.   BR, ,   Deb: 10/10/1888

| 1888 | StL-a | 0 | 1 | .000 | 1 | 1 | 0 | 0 | 0 | 6¹ | 7 | 0 | 4 | 1 | 17.1 | 4.26 | 77 | .269 | .387 | 1 | .333 | 0 | -1 | -1 | -0 | -0.1 |

● **MARK FREEMAN**   Freeman, Mark Price   b: 12/7/30, Memphis, Tenn.   BR/TR, 6'4", 220 lbs.   Deb: 4/18/59

1959	KC-A	0	0	—	3	0	0	0	0	3²	6	0	3	1	22.1	9.82	41	.375	.474	0	—	0	-2	-2	-0	0.0
	NY-A	0	0	—	1	1	0	0	0	7	6	0	2	4	11.6	2.57	142	.240	.321	0	.000	-0	1	1	-0	0.0
	Yr	0	0	—	4	1	0	0	0	10²	12	0	5	5	15.2	5.06	74	.286	.375	0	.000	-0	-1	-2	-0	0.0
1960	Chi-N	3	3	.500	30	8	1	0	1	76²	70	10	33	50	12.7	5.63	67	.240	.327	3	.150	-0	-16	-16	-2	-1.4
Total	2	3	3	.500	34	9	1	0	1	87¹	82	10	38	55	13.0	5.56	68	.246	.334	3	.136	-1	-17	-17	-2	-1.4

● **MARVIN FREEMAN**   Freeman, Marvin   b: 4/10/63, Chicago, Ill.   BR/TR, 6'7", 200 lbs.   Deb: 9/16/86

1986	Phi-N	2	0	1.000	3	3	0	0	0	16	6	0	8	9	9.0	2.25	171	.120	.267	0	.000	-1	3	3	-0	0.2
1988	Phi-N	2	3	.400	11	11	0	0	0	51²	55	2	43	37	17.2	6.10	58	.276	.407	3	.214	-0	-15	-15	-0	-1.2
1989	Phi-N	0	0	—	1	1	0	0	0	3	2	0	5	0	21.0	6.00	59	.182	.438	0	.000	-0	-1	-1	0	-0.5
1990	Phi-N	0	2	.000	16	3	0	0	1	32¹	34	5	14	26	14.2	5.57	69	.264	.349	0	.000	-1	-6	-6	-0	-0.5
	Atl-N	1	0	1.000	9	0	0	0	0	15²	7	0	3	12	6.9	1.72	234	.130	.203	0	—	0	4	4	-0	0.2
	Yr	1	2	.333	25	3	0	0	1	48	41	5	17	38	11.3	4.31	90	.220	.293	0	.000	-1	-3	-2	-0	-0.3
1991	Atl-N	1	0	1.000	34	0	0	0	1	48	37	2	13	34	9.8	3.00	130	.214	.277	0	.000	-0	4	5	-1	0.0
1992	*Atl-N	7	5	.583	58	0	0	0	3	64¹	61	7	29	41	12.7	3.22	114	.251	.333	2	.500	1	2	3	-1	0.5
1993	Atl-N	2	0	1.000	21	0	0	0	0	23²	24	1	10	25	13.3	6.08	66	.261	.340	0	—	0	-5	-5	-0	-0.5
1994	Col-N	10	2	.833	19	18	0	0	0	112²	113	10	23	67	11.3	2.80	178	.266	.307	4	.111	-0	18	27	1	2.8
1995	Col-N	3	7	.300	22	18	0	0	0	94²	122	15	41	61	15.7	5.89	91	.318	.386	2	.087	-1	-18	-5	-1	-0.7
1996	Col-N	7	9	.438	26	23	0	0	0	129²	151	21	57	71	14.9	6.04	90	.294	.372	5	.122	-2	-26	-9	1	-1.1
	Chi-A	0	0	—	1	1	0	0	0	2	4	0	1	2	22.5	13.50	35	.364	.417	0	—	0	-2	-2	-0	0.0
Total	10	35	28	.556	221	78	0	0	5	593²	616	63	249	383	13.5	4.64	99	.269	.346	16	.114	-5	-44	-3	-2	-0.3

● **JAKE FREEZE**   Freeze, Carl Alexander   b: 4/25/1900, Huntington, Ark.   d: 4/9/83, San Angelo, Tex.   BR/TR, 5'8", 150 lbs.   Deb: 7/1/25

| 1925 | Chi-A | 0 | 0 | — | 2 | 0 | 0 | 0 | 0 | 3² | 5 | 1 | 3 | 1 | 19.6 | 2.45 | 169 | .333 | .444 | 0 | .000 | -0 | 1 | 1 | -0 | 0.0 |

● **DAVE FREISLEBEN**   Freisleben, David James   b: 10/31/51, Coraopolis, Pa.   BR/TR, 5'11", 200 lbs.   Deb: 4/26/74

1974	SD-N	9	14	.391	33	31	6	2	0	211²	194	13	112	130	13.3	3.66	97	.241	.339	11	.172	2	-1	-2	-0	0.0
1975	SD-N	5	14	.263	36	27	4	1	0	181	206	11	82	77	14.7	4.28	81	.289	.368	4	.083	-1	-13	-16	0	-1.7
1976	SD-N	10	13	.435	34	24	6	3	1	172	163	10	66	81	13.8	3.51	93	.248	.321	7	.189	1	-0	-5	2	-0.2
1977	SD-N	7	9	.438	33	23	1	0	0	138²	140	21	71	72	13.8	4.61	77	.266	.356	5	.135	0	-11	-16	-2	-1.9
1978	SD-N	0	3	.000	12	6	0	0	0	26²	41	3	16	18	19.6	6.08	55	.363	.438	0	.000	-0	-16	-17	-0	-0.9
	Cle-A	1	4	.200	12	10	0	0	0	44¹	52	4	31	19	17.3	7.11	53	.299	.411	0	—	0	-16	-17	-1	-1.6
1979	Tor-A	2	3	.400	42	2	0	0	3	91	101	6	53	35	15.4	4.95	88	.294	.391	0	—	0	-7	-6	-1	-0.4
Total	6	34	60	.362	202	121	17	6	4	865¹	897	67	430	430	14.1	4.30	83	.269	.357	27	.141	2	-56	-71	-2	-6.7

● **TONY FREITAS**   Freitas, Antonio   b: 5/5/08, Mill Valley, Cal.   d: 3/13/94, Orangevale, Cal.   BR/TL, 5'8", 161 lbs.   Deb: 5/31/32

1932	Phi-A	12	5	.706	23	18	10	1	0	150¹	150	11	48	31	12.1	3.83	118	.263	.325	8	.148	-1	11	12	1	1.1
1933	Phi-A	2	4	.333	19	9	2	0	1	64¹	90	8	24	15	16.2	7.27	59	.337	.396	1	.063	-1	-21	-21	0	-1.8
1934	Cin-N	6	12	.333	30	18	5	0	1	152²	194	6	25	37	13.1	4.01	102	.311	.341	9	.191	0	1	1	2	0.4
1935	Cin-N	5	10	.333	31	18	5	1	0	143²	174	6	38	51	13.4	4.57	87	.295	.340	6	.130	-0	-9	-9	1	-0.8
1936	Cin-N	0	2	.000	4	0	0	0	0	7²	6	0	2	1	10.3	1.29	297	.240	.296	0	.000	-0	2	2	0	0.5
Total	5	25	33	.431	107	63	22	1	4	518	614	31	137	135	13.2	4.48	94	.296	.343	24	.145	-2	-16	-16	4	-0.6

● **LARRY FRENCH**   French, Lawrence Herbert   b: 11/1/07, Visalia, Cal.   d: 2/9/87, San Diego, Cal.   BR/TL, 6'1", 195 lbs.   Deb: 4/18/29

1929	Pit-N	7	5	.583	30	13	6	0	1	123	130	10	62	49	14.3	4.90	97	.276	.364	8	.190	-1	-3	-2	1	-0.1
1930	Pit-N	17	18	.486	42	35	21	3	1	274²	325	20	89	90	13.8	4.36	114	.295	.351	22	.242	-1	19	19	-1	1.9
1931	Pit-N	15	13	.536	39	33	20	1	1	275²	301	9	70	73	12.1	3.26	118	.278	.322	17	.179	-1	18	18	-1	1.5
1932	Pit-N	18	16	.529	47	33	19	3	4	274¹	301	12	67	72	11.9	3.02	126	.276	.316	19	.207	-1	26	24	-4	2.5
1933	Pit-N	18	13	.581	47	35	21	5	1	291¹	290	9	55	88	10.8	2.72	122	.257	.294	15	.149	-2	20	19	-4	1.3
1934	Pit-N	12	18	.400	49	35	16	3	1	263²	299	16	59	103	12.3	3.58	115	.281	.321	16	.190	-0	14	16	-3	1.3
1935	*Chi-N	17	10	.630	42	30	16	**4**	2	246¹	279	10	44	90	11.9	2.96	133	.286	.318	12	.141	-4	29	27	1	2.4
1936	Chi-N	18	9	.667	43	28	16	**4**	3	252¹	262	16	54	104	11.5	3.39	118	.266	.308	18	.212	-0	18	17	-3	1.3
1937	Chi-N	16	10	.615	42	28	11	6	2	208	229	17	65	100	12.8	3.98	100	.274	.327	9	.127	-4	-2	0	2	-0.2
1938	*Chi-N	10	19	.345	43	27	10	3	1	201¹	210	12	67	84	12.3	3.80	101	.273	.326	11	.146	-4	-1	1	0	0.4
1939	Chi-N	15	8	.652	36	21	10	2	1	194	205	7	50	98	11.9	3.29	120	.269	.314	14	.192	-1	13	14	2	1.8
1940	Chi-N★	14	14	.500	40	33	18	3	2	246	240	12	64	107	11.3	3.29	114	.256	.306	14	.165	1	15	12	2	1.7

YEAR	TM/L	W	L	PCT	G	GS	CG	SH	SV	IP	H	HR	BB	SO	RAT	ERA	ERA+	OAV	OOB	BH	AVG	PB	PR	/A	PD	TPI
1941	Chi-N	5	14	.263	26	18	6	1	0	138	161	10	43	60	13.4	4.63	76	.285	.338	9	.191	1	-15	-17	-1	-2.1
	*Bro-N	0	0	—	6	1	0	0	0	15²	16	1	4	8	12.1	3.45	106	.267	.323	1	.250	0	0	0	-0	0.0
	Yr	5	14	.263	32	19	6	1	0	153²	177	11	47	68	13.2	4.51	78	.282	.333	10	.196	1	-15	-17	-1	-2.1
1942	Bro-N	15	4	**.789**	38	14	8	4	0	147²	127	1	36	62	10.2	1.83	178	.233	.287	12	.300	4	24	24	-1	3.4
Total	14	197	171	.535	570	384	198	40	17	3152	3375	164	819	1187	12.1	3.44	114	.272	.320	199	.188	0	178	171	-7	17.2

● BILL FRENCH
French, William b: Baltimore, Md. Deb: 4/14/1873 ♦

YEAR	TM/L	W	L	PCT	G	GS	CG	SH	SV	IP	H	HR	BB	SO	RAT	ERA	ERA+	OAV	OOB	BH	AVG	PB	PR	/A	PD	TPI
1873	Mar-n	0	1	.000	1	1	1	0	0	9	30	0	0	0	30.0	12.00	27	.462	.462	4	.222	-0	-9	-9		-0.5

● BENNY FREY
Frey, Benjamin Rudolph b: 4/6/06, Dexter, Mich. d: 11/1/37, Spring Arbor Township, Mich. BR/TR, 5'10", 165 lbs. Deb: 9/18/29

YEAR	TM/L	W	L	PCT	G	GS	CG	SH	SV	IP	H	HR	BB	SO	RAT	ERA	ERA+	OAV	OOB	BH	AVG	PB	PR	/A	PD	TPI
1929	Cin-N	1	2	.333	3	3	2	0	0	24	29	2	8	1	13.9	4.13	111	.302	.356	3	.375		2	1	1	0.3
1930	Cin-N	11	18	.379	44	28	14	2	1	245	295	6	62	43	13.2	4.70	103	.305	.349	25	.284	4	7	3	6	1.3
1931	Cin-N	8	12	.400	34	17	7	1	2	133²	166	2	36	19	13.7	4.92	76	.319	.365	14	.318	4	-16	-18	-4	-1.6
1932	StL-N	0	2	.000	2	0	0	0	0	3	6	0	2	0	24.0	12.00	33	.600	.667	1	.000	-0	-3	-3	-0	-1.2
	Cin-N	4	10	.286	28	15	5	0	0	131¹	159	10	30	27	13.0	4.32	89	.299	.338	9	.205	-0	-6	-7	3	-0.4
	Yr	4	12	.250	30	15	5	0	0	134¹	165	10	32	27	13.3	4.49	86	.305	.345	9	.200	-0	-9	-9	2	-1.6
1933	Cin-N	6	4	.600	37	9	1	1	0	132	144	4	21	12	11.3	3.82	89	.281	.309	11	.262	3	-7	-6	2	0.1
1934	Cin-N	11	16	.407	39	30	12	2	2	245¹	288	10	42	33	12.2	3.52	116	.289	.319	14	.171	-0	15	15	4	1.9
1935	Cin-N	6	10	.375	38	13	3	1	3	114¹	164	6	32	24	15.7	6.85	58	.335	.381	11	.344	4	-36	-36	2	-3.9
1936	Cin-N	10	8	.556	31	12	5	0	0	131¹	164	4	30	20	13.3	4.25	90	.296	.332	11	.250	7	-3	-6	-0	-0.5
Total	8	57	82	.410	256	127	49	7	8	1160	1415	54	263	179	13.1	4.50	90	.303	.341	98	.255	17	-47	-55	21	-4.0

● STEVE FREY
Frey, Steven Francis b: 7/29/63, Meadowbrook, Pa. BR/TL, 5'9", 170 lbs. Deb: 5/10/89

YEAR	TM/L	W	L	PCT	G	GS	CG	SH	SV	IP	H	HR	BB	SO	RAT	ERA	ERA+	OAV	OOB	BH	AVG	PB	PR	/A	PD	TPI
1989	Mon-N	3	2	.600	20	0	0	0	0	21¹	29	4	11	15	17.3	5.48	64	.326	.406	0	—	-0	-5	-5	-0	-1.0
1990	Mon-N	8	2	.800	51	0	0	0	9	55²	44	4	29	29	12.0	2.10	174	.219	.320	0	.000	-0	10	10	-0	1.9
1991	Mon-N	0	1	.000	31	0	0	0	1	39²	43	3	23	21	15.2	4.99	72	.281	.379	0	.000	-0	-6	-6	-1	-0.2
1992	Cal-A	4	2	.667	51	0	0	0	4	45¹	39	6	22	24	12.5	3.57	111	.238	.335	0	—	0	2	2	0	0.3
1993	Cal-A	2	3	.400	55	0	0	0	13	48¹	41	1	26	22	13.0	2.98	151	.230	.338	0	—	0	7	8	0	0.9
1994	SF-N	1	0	1.000	44	0	0	0	0	31	37	6	15	20	15.7	4.94	81	.322	.409	0	—	-0	-2	-3	-0	-0.1
1995	SF-N	0	1	.000	9	0	0	0	0	6¹	7	1	2	5	12.8	4.26	96	.280	.333	0	—	-0	-0	-0	-0	-0.0
	Sea-A	0	3	.000	13	0	0	0	0	11¹	16	0	6	7	18.3	4.76	99	.356	.442	0	—	-0	-0	-0	1	-0.1
	Phi-N	0	0	—	9	0	0	0	0	10²	3	1	2	2	4.2	0.84	501	.091	.143	0	.000	-0	4	4	0	0.4
1996	Phi-N	0	1	.000	31	0	0	0	1	34¹	38	4	18	12	14.7	4.72	92	.295	.381	0	—	-0	-2	-1	1	0.0
Total	8	18	15	.545	314	0	0	0	28	304	297	30	154	157	13.7	3.76	107	.262	.356	0	.000	-0	8	8	-1	1.8

● BERNIE FRIBERG
Friberg, Bernard Albert (b: Gustaf Bernhard Friberg)
b: 8/18/1899, Manchester, N.H. d: 12/8/58, Lynn, Mass. BR/TR, 5'11", 178 lbs. Deb: 8/20/19 ♦

YEAR	TM/L	W	L	PCT	G	GS	CG	SH	SV	IP	H	HR	BB	SO	RAT	ERA	ERA+	OAV	OOB	BH	AVG	PB	PR	/A	PD	TPI
1925	Phi-N	0	0	—	1	0	0	0	0	4	4	0	3	1	15.8	4.50	106	.286	.412	82	.270	0	-0	/0	-0	0.0

● MARION FRICANO
Fricano, Marion John b: 7/15/23, Brant, N.Y. d: 5/18/76, Tijuana, Mex. BR/TR, 6', 170 lbs. Deb: 9/6/52

YEAR	TM/L	W	L	PCT	G	GS	CG	SH	SV	IP	H	HR	BB	SO	RAT	ERA	ERA+	OAV	OOB	BH	AVG	PB	PR	/A	PD	TPI
1952	Phi-A	1	0	1.000	2	0	0	0	0	5	5	0	1	0	10.8	1.80	224	.238	.273	0	—		1	1	0	0.2
1953	Phi-A	9	12	.429	39	23	10	0	0	211	206	21	90	67	12.9	3.88	110	.257	.337	10	.145	-3	3	10	-2	0.4
1954	Phi-A	5	11	.313	37	20	4	0	0	151²	163	17	64	43	13.7	5.16	76	.275	.349	4	.098	-3	-24	-21	-2	-2.5
1955	KC-A	0	0	—	10	0	0	0	0	20	19	2	9	5	13.5	3.15	133	.253	.333	2	.667	1	2	2	0	0.1
Total	4	15	23	.395	88	43	14	0	0	387²	393	40	164	115	13.2	4.32	96	.264	.341	16	.142	-5	-19	-8	-3	-1.8

● SKIPPER FRIDAY
Friday, Grier William b: 10/26/1897, Gastonia, N.C. d: 8/25/62, Gastonia, N.C. BR/TR, 5'11", 170 lbs. Deb: 6/17/23

YEAR	TM/L	W	L	PCT	G	GS	CG	SH	SV	IP	H	HR	BB	SO	RAT	ERA	ERA+	OAV	OOB	BH	AVG	PB	PR	/A	PD	TPI
1923	Was-A	0	1	.000	7	2	1	0	0	30	35	2	22	9	17.7	6.90	55	.313	.434	2	.222	0	-10	-10	1	-0.2

● CY FRIED
Fried, Arthur Edwin b: 7/23/1897, San Antonio, Tex. d: 10/10/70, San Antonio, Tex. BL/TL, 5'11.5", 150 lbs. Deb: 9/17/20

YEAR	TM/L	W	L	PCT	G	GS	CG	SH	SV	IP	H	HR	BB	SO	RAT	ERA	ERA+	OAV	OOB	BH	AVG	PB	PR	/A	PD	TPI
1920	Det-A	0	0	—	2	0	0	0	0	1²	3	0	4	0	37.8	16.20	23	.500	.700	0	—	0	-2	-2	0	0.0

● BOB FRIEDRICHS
Friedrichs, Robert George b: 8/30/06, Cincinnati, Ohio BR/TR, 5'11.5", 165 lbs. Deb: 5/17/32

YEAR	TM/L	W	L	PCT	G	GS	CG	SH	SV	IP	H	HR	BB	SO	RAT	ERA	ERA+	OAV	OOB	BH	AVG	PB	PR	/A	PD	TPI
1932	Was-A	0	0	—	2	0	0	0	0	4	4	0	7	2	27.0	11.25	38	.250	.500	0	.000	-0	-3	-3	-0	0.0

● BILL FRIEL
Friel, William Edward b: 4/1/1876, Renovo, Pa. d: 12/24/59, St.Louis, Mo. BL/TR, 5'10", 165 lbs. Deb: 5/3/01 FUC♦

YEAR	TM/L	W	L	PCT	G	GS	CG	SH	SV	IP	H	HR	BB	SO	RAT	ERA	ERA+	OAV	OOB	BH	AVG	PB	PR	/A	PD	TPI
1902	StL-A	0	0	—	1	0	0	0	0	4	4	0	0	0	9.0	4.50	78	.267	.267	64	.240		-0	-0	-0	0.0

● DANNY FRIEND
Friend, Daniel Sebastian b: 4/18/1873, Cincinnati, Ohio d: 6/1/42, Chillicothe, Ohio TL, 5'9", 175 lbs. Deb: 9/10/1895

YEAR	TM/L	W	L	PCT	G	GS	CG	SH	SV	IP	H	HR	BB	SO	RAT	ERA	ERA+	OAV	OOB	BH	AVG	PB	PR	/A	PD	TPI
1895	Chi-N	2	2	.500	5	5	5	0	0	41	50	5	14	10	14.7	5.27	97	.296	.360	4	.235	-1	-2	-1	0	-0.1
1896	Chi-N	18	14	.563	36	33	28	1	0	290²	298	11	139	86	14.7	4.74	96	.263	.363	30	.238	-1	-12	-6	-2	-0.8
1897	Chi-N	12	11	.522	24	24	23	0	0	203	244	5	86	58	15.4	4.52	99	.295	.373	25	.284	-1	-5	-1	-2	-0.1
1898	Chi-N	0	2	.000	2	2	2	0	0	17	20	1	10	4	16.4	5.29	68	.290	.387	2	.286	-0	-3	-3	2	-0.1
Total	4	32	29	.525	67	64	58	1	0	551²	612	22	249	158	15.0	4.71	96	.279	.368	61	.256	-2	-22	-12	-2	-1.1

● BOB FRIEND
Friend, Robert Bartmess "Warrior" b: 11/24/30, Lafayette, Ind. BR/TR, 6', 190 lbs. Deb: 4/28/51

YEAR	TM/L	W	L	PCT	G	GS	CG	SH	SV	IP	H	HR	BB	SO	RAT	ERA	ERA+	OAV	OOB	BH	AVG	PB	PR	/A	PD	TPI
1951	Pit-N	6	10	.375	34	22	3	1	0	149²	173	12	68	41	14.5	4.27	99	.293	.366	4	.091	-2	-5	-1	0	-0.3
1952	Pit-N	7	17	.292	35	23	6	1	0	185	186	15	84	75	13.3	4.18	95	.258	.338	3	.058	-4	-9	-4	-1	-0.8
1953	Pit-N	8	11	.421	32	24	8	0	0	170²	193	18	57	66	13.3	4.90	91	.286	.344	7	.135	-2	-12	-8	-1	-0.9
1954	Pit-N	7	12	.368	35	20	4	2	2	170¹	204	16	58	73	13.9	5.07	83	.302	.358	14	.275	5	-19	-17	-1	-1.2
1955	Pit-N	14	9	.609	44	20	9	2	2	200¹	178	18	52	98	10.4	**2.83**	**145**	.242	.294	10	.164	-2	**27**	**29**	3	3.3
1956	Pit-N★	17	17	.500	49	42	19	4	3	314¹	310	25	85	166	11.4	3.46	109	.258	.308	16	.165	-1	11	11	-1	0.9
1957	Pit-N	14	18	.438	40	38	17	3	0	277	273	28	68	143	11.1	3.38	112	.257	.303	16	.184	1	15	13	-1	1.4
1958	Pit-N★	**22**	14	.611	38	38	16	1	0	274	299	25	61	135	12.0	3.68	105	.281	.322	10	.106	-4	8	6	-0	0.3
1959	Pit-N	8	19	.296	35	35	7	2	0	234²	267	19	52	104	12.5	4.03	96	.283	.325	12	.164	-0	-2	-4	-0	-0.4
1960	*Pit-N★	18	12	.600	38	37	16	4	1	275²	266	16	45	183	10.2	3.00	125	.251	.281	6	.068	-5	23	23	0	1.9
1961	Pit-N	14	19	.424	41	35	10	1	0	236	271	16	45	108	12.2	3.85	104	.289	.324	11	.139	-3	5	4	-1	0.1
1962	Pit-N	18	14	.563	39	36	13	**5**	1	261²	280	23	53	144	11.5	3.06	129	.273	.310	11	.121	-3	26	25	0	2.5
1963	Pit-N	17	16	.515	39	38	12	4	0	268²	236	13	44	144	9.5	2.34	141	.233	.269	9	.105	-3	28	28	-1	3.1
1964	Pit-N	13	18	.419	35	35	13	3	0	240¹	253	10	50	128	11.5	3.33	105	.271	.310	5	.070	-3	5	6	0	0.4
1965	Pit-N	8	12	.400	34	34	6	2	0	222	221	17	47	74	11.2	3.24	108	.260	.305	3	.042	-5	7	7	0	0.0
1966	NY-A	1	4	.200	12	8	0	0	0	44²	61	9	2	24	14.1	4.84	69	.330	.361	0	.000	-1	-7	-7	1	-0.8
	NY-N	5	8	.385	22	12	2	1	1	86	101	11	16	50	12.5	4.40	83	.289	.322	1	.034	-3	-8	-7	-2	-1.5
Total	16	197	230	.461	602	497	163	36	11	3611	3772	286	894	1734	11.7	3.58	107	.269	.315	138	.121	-36	94	100	2	8.0

● PETE FRIES
Fries, Peter Martin b: 10/30/1857, Scranton, Pa. d: 7/30/37, Chicago, Ill. BL/TL, 5'8", 160 lbs. Deb: 8/10/1883 ♦

YEAR	TM/L	W	L	PCT	G	GS	CG	SH	SV	IP	H	HR	BB	SO	RAT	ERA	ERA+	OAV	OOB	BH	AVG	PB	PR	/A	PD	TPI
1883	Col-a	0	3	.000	3	3	3	0	0	25	34	1	14	7	17.3	6.48	48	.304	.381	3	.300	1	-9	-9	0	-0.7

● JOHN FRILL
Frill, John Edmond b: 4/3/1879, Reading, Pa. d: 9/28/18, Westerly, R.I. BR/TL, 5'10.5", 170 lbs. Deb: 4/16/10

YEAR	TM/L	W	L	PCT	G	GS	CG	SH	SV	IP	H	HR	BB	SO	RAT	ERA	ERA+	OAV	OOB	BH	AVG	PB	PR	/A	PD	TPI
1910	NY-A	2	2	.500	10	5	3	1	1	48¹	55	1	5	27	11.4	4.47	59	.289	.311	2	.111	-1	-10	-10	0	-0.9
1912	StL-A	0	1	.000	3	3	0	0	0	4¹	16	1	2	4	37.4	20.77	16	.571	.600	1	.500	-0	-8	-8	0	-1.3
	Cin-N	1	0	1.000	3	2	0	0	0	15	19	0	1	2	13.2	6.00	56	.345	.379	1	.250	-0	-4	-4	0	-0.2
Total	2	3	3	.500	16	10	3	1	1	67²	90	2	7	33	13.4	5.85	49	.330	.356	4	.167	-1	-23	-22	0	-2.4

● DANNY FRISELLA
Frisella, Daniel Vincent "Bear" b: 3/4/46, San Francisco, Cal. d: 1/1/77, Phoenix, Ariz. BL/TR, 6', 195 lbs. Deb: 7/27/67

YEAR	TM/L	W	L	PCT	G	GS	CG	SH	SV	IP	H	HR	BB	SO	RAT	ERA	ERA+	OAV	OOB	BH	AVG	PB	PR	/A	PD	TPI
1967	NY-N	1	6	.143	14	11	0	0	0	74	68	6	33	51	12.3	3.41	100	.249	.330	2	.087	-1	-0	-0	-0	-0.1
1968	NY-N	2	4	.333	19	4	0	0	0	50²	53	5	17	47	12.4	3.91	77	.275	.329	1	.083	-1	-5	-5	0	-0.7
1969	NY-N	0	0	—	3	0	0	0	0	4²	8	1	3	5	21.2	7.71	47	.381	.458	0	.000	-0	-2	-2	-0	-0.3
1970	NY-N	8	3	.727	30	1	0	0	0	65²	49	4	34	54	11.4	3.02	130	.204	.303	4	.308	-1	5	5	1	1.3
1971	NY-N	8	5	.615	53	0	0	0	12	90²	74	4	40	93	10.8	1.99	172	.227	.296	3	.231	-1	15	14	1	2.6
1972	NY-N	5	8	.385	39	0	0	0	9	67¹	63	8	20	46	11.1	3.34	101	.243	.297	2	.286	1	1	1	1	0.1
1973	Atl-N	1	2	.333	42	0	0	0	8	45	40	6	23	27	12.8	4.20	94	.241	.337	1	.500	0	-3	-1	-0	-0.1
1974	Atl-N	3	4	.429	36	1	0	0	6	41²	37	4	28	34	14.0	5.18	73	.240	.357	0	.000	-0	-7	-7	-0	-1.2

YEAR	TM/L	W	L	PCT	G	GS	CG	SH	SV	IP	H	HR	BB	SO	RAT	ERA	ERA+	OAV	OOB	BH	AVG	PB	PR	/A	PD	TPI
1975	SD-N	1	6	.143	65	0	0	0	9	97²	86	7	51	67	12.8	3.13	111	.242	.340	1	.200	0	5	4	-0	0.3
1976	StL-N	0	0	—	18	0	0	0	1	22²	19	3	13	11	12.7	3.97	89	.232	.337	0	.000	-0	-1	-1	0	0.0
	Mil-A	5	2	.714	32	0	0	0	0	49¹	30	4	34	43	11.9	2.74	128	.175	.316	0	—	0	4	4	0	0.8
Total	10	34	40	.459	351	17	0	0	57	609¹	529	53	286	471	12.1	3.32	106	.235	.323	14	.179	1	14	13	0	3.1

● **EMIL FRISK**   Frisk, John Emil   b: 10/15/1874, Kalkaska, Mich.   d: 1/27/22, Seattle, Wash.   BL/TR, 6'1", 190 lbs.   Deb: 9/2/1899 ◆

YEAR	TM/L	W	L	PCT	G	GS	CG	SH	SV	IP	H	HR	BB	SO	RAT	ERA	ERA+	OAV	OOB	BH	AVG	PB	PR	/A	PD	TPI
1899	Cin-N	3	6	.333	9	9	9	0	0	68¹	81	1	17	17	13.7	3.95	99	.295	.349	7	.280	1	-1	-0	0	0.1
1901	Det-A	5	4	.556	11	7	6	0	0	74²	94	1	26	22	14.7	4.34	89	.304	.362	15	.313	2	-6	-4	3	0.1
Total	2	8	10	.444	20	16	15	0	0	143	175	2	43	39	14.2	4.15	94	.300	.356	135	.267	3	-6	-4	2	0.2

● **CHARLIE FRITZ**   Fritz, Charles Cornelius   b: 6/18/1882, Mobile, Ala.   d: 7/30/43, Mobile, Ala.   TL,   Deb: 10/5/07

YEAR	TM/L	W	L	PCT	G	GS	CG	SH	SV	IP	H	HR	BB	SO	RAT	ERA	ERA+	OAV	OOB	BH	AVG	PB	PR	/A	PD	TPI
1907	Phi-A	0	0	—	1	1	0	0	0	3	0	0	3	1	12.0	3.00	87	.000	.333	0	.000	-0	-0	-0	-0	0.0

● **BILL FROATS**   Froats, William John   b: 10/20/30, New York, N.Y.   BL/TL, 6', 180 lbs.   Deb: 4/22/55

YEAR	TM/L	W	L	PCT	G	GS	CG	SH	SV	IP	H	HR	BB	SO	RAT	ERA	ERA+	OAV	OOB	BH	AVG	PB	PR	/A	PD	TPI
1955	Det-A	0	0	—	1	0	0	0	0	2	0	0	2	0	9.0	0.00	—	.000	.333	0	—	0	1	1	0	0.0

● **SAM FROCK**   Frock, Samuel William   b: 12/23/1882, Baltimore, Md.   d: 11/3/25, Baltimore, Md.   BR/TR, 6', 168 lbs.   Deb: 9/21/07

YEAR	TM/L	W	L	PCT	G	GS	CG	SH	SV	IP	H	HR	BB	SO	RAT	ERA	ERA+	OAV	OOB	BH	AVG	PB	PR	/A	PD	TPI
1907	Bos-N	1	2	.333	5	3	3	1	0	33¹	28	1	11	12	11.1	2.97	86	.243	.320	1	.071	-1	-2	-2	-2	-0.4
1909	Pit-N	2	1	.667	8	4	3	0	1	36¹	44	0	4	11	12.6	2.48	110	.299	.331	2	.143	-1	0	1	0	0.0
1910	Pit-N	0	0	—	1	0	0	0	0	2	2	0	2	1	22.5	4.50	69	.400	.625	—	—	0	-0	-0	0	0.0
	Bos-N	12	19	.387	45	29	13	2	0	255¹	245	8	91	170	12.0	3.21	104	.262	.330	16	.190	-3	-5	3	1	0.2
	Yr	12	19	.387	46	29	13	2	0	257¹	247	8	93	171	12.0	3.22	103	.263	.332	16	.190	-3	-5	3	2	0.2
1911	Bos-N	0	1	.000	4	1	1	0	0	16	29	1	0	5	19.7	5.63	68	.426	.473	1	.200	-0	-4	-3	0	-0.2
Total	4	15	23	.395	63	37	20	3	3	343	348	9	113	202	12.4	3.23	99	.274	.339	20	.171	-5	-11	-1	-0	-0.4

● **TODD FROHWIRTH**   Frohwirth, Todd Gerard   b: 9/28/62, Milwaukee, Wis.   BR/TR, 6'4", 190 lbs.   Deb: 8/10/87

YEAR	TM/L	W	L	PCT	G	GS	CG	SH	SV	IP	H	HR	BB	SO	RAT	ERA	ERA+	OAV	OOB	BH	AVG	PB	PR	/A	PD	TPI
1987	Phi-N	1	0	1.000	10	0	0	0	0	11	12	0	2	9	11.5	0.00	—	.293	.326	0	.000	-0	5	5	0	0.4
1988	Phi-N	1	2	.333	12	0	0	0	0	12	16	2	11	9	20.3	8.25	43	.327	.450	0	—	0	-6	-6	1	-1.4
1989	Phi-N	1	0	1.000	45	0	0	0	0	62²	56	4	18	39	11.1	3.59	99	.240	.303	0	.000	-0	-1	-0	0	0.0
1990	Phi-N	0	1	.000	5	0	0	0	0	1	3	0	6	1	81.0	18.00	21	.500	.750	0	—	0	-2	-2	0	-1.3
1991	Bal-A	7	3	.700	51	0	0	0	3	96¹	64	2	29	77	8.8	1.87	211	.190	.256	0	—	0	**24**	**22**	3	2.9
1992	Bal-A	4	3	.571	65	0	0	0	4	106	97	4	41	58	12.0	2.46	163	.247	.323	0	—	0	17	18	3	1.5
1993	Bal-A	6	7	.462	70	0	0	0	3	96¹	91	7	44	50	12.9	3.83	117	.256	.343	0	—	0	5	7	2	0.7
1994	Bos-A	0	3	.000	22	0	0	0	1	26²	40	3	17	13	19.9	10.80	47	.339	.431	0	—	0	-18	-17	1	-1.9
1996	Cal-A	0	0	—	4	0	0	0	0	5²	10	1	4	3	23.8	11.12	44	.370	.469	0	—	0	-4	-4	0	0.0
Total	9	20	19	.513	284	0	0	0	11	417²	389	23	172	259	12.4	3.60	114	.250	.329	0	.000	-0	21	23	9	0.9

● **ART FROMME**   Fromme, Arthur Henry   b: 9/3/1883, Quincy, Ill.   d: 8/24/56, Los Angeles, Cal.   BR/TR, 6', 178 lbs.   Deb: 9/14/06

YEAR	TM/L	W	L	PCT	G	GS	CG	SH	SV	IP	H	HR	BB	SO	RAT	ERA	ERA+	OAV	OOB	BH	AVG	PB	PR	/A	PD	TPI
1906	StL-N	1	2	.333	3	3	3	1	0	25	19	0	10	11	10.8	1.44	183	.221	.309	2	.222	0	3	3	1	0.5
1907	StL-N	5	13	.278	23	16	13	2	0	145²	138	3	67	67	12.9	2.90	86	.256	.343	10	.182	1	-7	-6	0	-0.7
1908	StL-N	5	13	.278	20	14	9	2	0	116	102	1	50	62	11.9	2.72	87	.218	.296	5	.139	-1	-5	-5	-0	-0.9
1909	Cin-N	19	13	.594	37	34	22	4	2	279¹	195	3	101	126	9.6	1.90	137	.201	.278	18	.191	2	22	22	2	3.1
1910	Cin-N	3	4	.429	11	5	1	0	0	49¹	44	2	39	10	15.3	2.92	100	.260	.402	2	.133	-1	1	-0	0	-0.1
1911	Cin-N	10	11	.476	38	26	11	1	0	208	190	8	79	107	12.3	3.46	96	.248	.331	14	.189	-1	-1	-3	1	-0.4
1912	Cin-N	16	18	.471	43	37	23	3	0	296	285	7	88	120	11.7	2.74	123	.260	.321	9	.087	-9	22	21	1	1.2
1913	Cin-N	1	4	.200	9	7	2	0	0	56	55	1	21	24	12.7	4.18	78	.274	.351	3	.143	-0	-6	-6	-1	-0.6
	NY-N	11	6	.647	26	12	3	0	0	112¹	112	5	29	50	11.5	4.01	78	.260	.310	6	.171	-0	-10	-11	1	-1.4
	Yr	12	10	.545	35	19	5	0	0	168¹	167	6	50	74	11.7	4.06	78	.263	.319	9	.161	-1	-16	-17	1	-2.0
1914	NY-N	9	5	.643	38	12	3	1	2	138	142	7	44	57	12.6	3.20	83	.283	.349	7	.226	1	-6	-8	3	-0.4
1915	NY-N	0	1	.000	4	1	0	0	0	12¹	15	1	2	4	12.4	5.84	44	.306	.333	1	.333	1	-4	-4	-0	-0.3
Total	10	80	90	.471	252	167	90	14	4	1438	1297	37	530	638	11.7	2.90	100	.246	.320	77	.162	-8	8	2	8	-0.0

● **DAVE FROST**   Frost, Carl David   b: 11/17/52, Long Beach, Cal.   BR/TR, 6'6", 235 lbs.   Deb: 9/11/77

YEAR	TM/L	W	L	PCT	G	GS	CG	SH	SV	IP	H	HR	BB	SO	RAT	ERA	ERA+	OAV	OOB	BH	AVG	PB	PR	/A	PD	TPI
1977	Chi-A	1	1	.500	4	3	0	0	0	23²	30	4	3	15	12.9	3.04	134	.323	.351	0	—	0	3	3	-0	0.2
1978	Cal-A	5	4	.556	11	10	2	1	0	80¹	71	6	24	30	10.9	2.58	140	.240	.301	0	—	0	11	9	1	1.5
1979	*Cal-A	16	10	.615	36	33	12	2	1	239¹	226	16	77	107	11.6	3.57	114	.251	.314	0	—	0	17	13	-1	1.2
1980	Cal-A	4	8	.333	15	15	2	0	0	78¹	97	8	21	28	13.8	5.29	74	.308	.355	0	—	0	-11	-12	-1	-1.6
1981	Cal-A	1	8	.111	12	9	0	0	0	47¹	44	3	19	16	12.2	5.51	66	.250	.327	0	—	0	-10	-10	0	-1.6
1982	KC-A	6	6	.500	21	14	0	0	0	81²	103	4	30	26	15.0	5.51	74	.313	.376	0	—	0	-13	-13	-1	-1.8
Total	6	33	37	.471	99	84	16	3	1	550²	571	41	174	222	12.4	4.10	96	.271	.330	0	—	0	-3	-9	-3	-2.1

● **JOHNSON FRY**   Fry, Johnson "Jay"   b: 11/21/01, Huntington, W.Va.   d: 4/7/59, Carmi, Ill.   BR/TR, 6'1", 150 lbs.   Deb: 8/24/23

YEAR	TM/L	W	L	PCT	G	GS	CG	SH	SV	IP	H	HR	BB	SO	RAT	ERA	ERA+	OAV	OOB	BH	AVG	PB	PR	/A	PD	TPI
1923	Cle-A	0	0	—	1	0	0	0	0	3²	6	0	4	0	24.5	12.27	32	.353	.476	1	1.000	1	-3	-3	-0	0.1

● **CHARLIE FRYE**   Frye, Charles Andrew   b: 7/17/14, Hickory, N.C.   d: 5/25/45, Hickory, N.C.   BR/TR, 6'1", 175 lbs.   Deb: 7/28/40

YEAR	TM/L	W	L	PCT	G	GS	CG	SH	SV	IP	H	HR	BB	SO	RAT	ERA	ERA+	OAV	OOB	BH	AVG	PB	PR	/A	PD	TPI
1940	Phi-N	0	6	.000	15	5	1	0	0	50¹	58	3	26	18	15.0	4.65	84	.291	.373	5	.263	1	-4	-4	-1	-0.4

● **WOODIE FRYMAN**   Fryman, Woodrow Thompson   b: 4/15/40, Ewing, Ky.   BR/TL, 6'2", 205 lbs.   Deb: 4/15/66

YEAR	TM/L	W	L	PCT	G	GS	CG	SH	SV	IP	H	HR	BB	SO	RAT	ERA	ERA+	OAV	OOB	BH	AVG	PB	PR	/A	PD	TPI
1966	Pit-N	12	9	.571	36	28	9	3	1	181²	182	13	47	105	11.4	3.81	94	.261	.309	10	.159	-1	-4	-5	2	-0.8
1967	Pit-N	3	8	.273	28	18	3	1	1	113¹	121	12	44	74	13.4	4.05	83	.276	.348	4	.118	-1	-9	-9	2	-0.7
1968	Phi-N☆	12	14	.462	34	32	10	5	0	213²	198	12	64	151	11.3	2.78	108	.246	.306	6	.085	-2	5	5	-1	0.2
1969	Phi-N	12	15	.444	36	35	10	1	0	228¹	243	15	89	150	13.5	4.41	80	.270	.343	9	.118	-2	-21	-22	-1	-2.6
1970	Phi-N	8	6	.571	27	20	4	3	0	127²	122	11	43	97	11.7	4.09	98	.253	.315	5	.128	-2	-1	-1	-0	-0.3
1971	Phi-N	10	7	.588	37	17	3	2	2	149¹	133	7	46	104	11.0	3.38	104	.242	.304	7	.189	0	1	2	2	0.6
1972	Phi-N	4	10	.286	23	17	3	2	1	119²	131	9	39	69	12.9	4.36	82	.279	.337	5	.152	1	-12	-10	1	-1.0
	*Det-A	10	3	.769	16	14	6	1	0	113²	93	6	31	72	10.4	2.06	153	.220	.285	-2	.125	-2	13	14	1	1.4
1973	Det-A	6	13	.316	34	29	1	0	0	169²	200	23	64	119	14.2	5.36	76	.294	.357	0	—	0	-29	-24	2	-2.4
1974	Det-A	6	9	.400	27	22	4	1	0	141²	120	16	67	92	12.1	4.32	88	.233	.326	0	—	0	-11	-8	-1	-1.0
1975	Mon-N	9	12	.429	38	20	7	3	3	157	141	9	68	118	12.3	3.32	115	.239	.323	10	.204	1	5	9	1	1.4
1976	Mon-N☆	13	13	.500	34	32	4	2	0	216¹	218	14	76	123	12.6	3.37	110	.263	.332	7	.109	-3	3	8	-0	0.6
1977	Cin-N	5	5	.500	17	12	0	0	1	75¹	83	13	45	57	15.3	5.38	73	.292	.393	7	.318	2	-12	-12	1	-1.2
1978	Chi-N	2	4	.333	13	9	0	0	0	55²	64	6	37	28	16.3	5.17	78	.309	.414	1	.063	-1	-10	-7	1	-0.7
	Mon-N	5	7	.417	19	17	4	3	1	94²	93	4	37	53	12.6	3.61	98	.260	.334	2	.059	-2	-0	-1	-0	-0.4
	Yr	7	11	.389	32	26	4	3	1	150¹	157	10	74	81	14.0	4.19	89	.276	.362	3	.060	-3	-10	-8	1	-1.1
1979	Mon-N	3	6	.333	44	0	0	0	10	58	52	4	22	44	11.9	2.79	131	.248	.328	0	.000	-1	0	1	1	0.4
1980	Mon-N	7	4	.636	61	0	0	0	17	80	61	1	30	59	10.5	2.25	158	.209	.287	2	.167	-0	12	12	1	2.0
1981	*Mon-N	5	3	.625	35	0	0	0	7	43	38	1	14	25	11.1	1.88	185	.247	.314	2	.667	1	8	8	0	1.8
1982	Mon-N	9	4	.692	60	0	0	0	12	69²	66	3	26	46	12.0	3.75	97	.259	.330	2	.222	-0	-1	-1	1	0.0
1983	Mon-N	0	3	.000	6	0	0	0	0	6	11	1	1	1	27.0	21.00	17	.571	.600	0	—	0	-6	-6	0	-3.8
Total	18	141	155	.476	625	322	68	27	58	2411¹	2367	187	890	1587	12.4	3.77	96	.259	.329	84	.138	-12	-63	-43	4	-5.9

● **CHARLIE FUCHS**   Fuchs, Charles Thomas   b: 11/18/13, Union City, N.J.   d: 6/10/69, Weehawken, N.J.   BB/TR, 5'8", 168 lbs.   Deb: 4/17/42

YEAR	TM/L	W	L	PCT	G	GS	CG	SH	SV	IP	H	HR	BB	SO	RAT	ERA	ERA+	OAV	OOB	BH	AVG	PB	PR	/A	PD	TPI
1942	Det-A	3	3	.500	9	4	1	1	0	36²	43	5	19	15	15.5	6.63	60	.285	.368	1	.077	-1	-12	-11	1	-1.5
1943	Phi-N	2	7	.222	17	9	4	1	0	77²	76	4	34	12	13.1	4.29	79	.266	.350	2	.091	-2	-8	-8	-1	-1.1
	StL-A	0	0	—	13	0	0	0	0	35²	42	4	11	9	13.6	4.04	82	.294	.348	0	.000	-1	-3	-3	0	-0.1
1944	Bro-N	1	0	1.000	8	0	0	0	1	15²	25	2	9	5	20.1	5.74	62	.347	.427	0	.000	-0	-4	-4	1	-0.2
Total	3	6	10	.375	47	13	5	2	1	165²	186	15	73	41	14.4	4.89	72	.285	.363	3	.070	-4	-27	-25	0	-2.9

● **MIGUEL FUENTES**   Fuentes, Miguel (Pinet)   b: 5/10/46, Loiza Aldea, P.R.   d: 1/29/70, Loiza Aldea, P.R.   BR/TR, 6', 160 lbs.   Deb: 9/1/69

YEAR	TM/L	W	L	PCT	G	GS	CG	SH	SV	IP	H	HR	BB	SO	RAT	ERA	ERA+	OAV	OOB	BH	AVG	PB	PR	/A	PD	TPI
1969	Sea-A	1	3	.250	8	4	1	0	0	26	29	1	16	14	15.6	5.19	70	.284	.381	2	.333	0	-5	-5	-1	-0.6

YEAR	TM/L	W	L	PCT	G	GS	CG	SH	SV	IP	H	HR	BB	SO	RAT	ERA	ERA+	OAV	OOB	BH	AVG	PB	PR	/A	PD	TPI

● OSCAR FUHR Fuhr, Oscar Lawrence b: 8/22/1893, Defiance, Mo. d: 3/27/75, Dallas, Tex. BL/TL, 6'0.5", 176 lbs. Deb: 4/19/21

YEAR	TM/L	W	L	PCT	G	GS	CG	SH	SV	IP	H	HR	BB	SO	RAT	ERA	ERA+	OAV	OOB	BH	AVG	PB	PR	/A	PD	TPI
1921	Chi-N	0	0	—	1	0	0	0	0	4	11	1	0	2	24.8	9.00	42	.500	.500	0	.000	-0	-2	-2	0	0.0
1924	Bos-A	3	6	.333	23	10	4	1	0	80¹	100	1	39	30	16.1	5.94	74	.310	.392	4	.182	-1	-15	-14	1	-1.3
1925	Bos-A	0	6	.000	39	5	0	0	0	91¹	138	7	30	27	16.9	6.60	69	.364	.415	5	.250	0	-22	-21	1	-1.0
Total	3	3	12	.200	63	15	4	1	0	175²	249	9	69	59	16.7	6.35	70	.344	.407	9	.209	-1	-40	-37	2	-2.3

● JOHN FULGHAM Fulgham, John Thomas b: 6/9/56, St.Louis, Mo. BR/TR, 6'2", 205 lbs. Deb: 6/19/79

YEAR	TM/L	W	L	PCT	G	GS	CG	SH	SV	IP	H	HR	BB	SO	RAT	ERA	ERA+	OAV	OOB	BH	AVG	PB	PR	/A	PD	TPI
1979	StL-N	10	6	.625	20	19	10	2	0	146	123	10	26	75	9.4	2.53	149	.227	.267	6	.143	1	20	20	-2	2.0
1980	StL-N	4	6	.400	15	14	4	1	0	85¹	66	7	32	48	10.4	3.38	109	.219	.296	0	.000	-3	2	3	-0	0.0
Total	2	14	12	.538	35	33	14	3	0	231¹	189	17	58	123	9.8	2.84	132	.224	.277	6	.087	-2	22	23	-2	2.0

● ED FULLER Fuller, Edward Ashton b: 3/22/1868, Washington, D.C. d: 3/16/35, Hyattsville, Md. BR/TR, 6', 158 lbs. Deb: 7/17/1886

YEAR	TM/L	W	L	PCT	G	GS	CG	SH	SV	IP	H	HR	BB	SO	RAT	ERA	ERA+	OAV	OOB	BH	AVG	PB	PR	/A	PD	TPI
1886	Was-N	0	1	.000	2	1	1	0	0	13	15	0	5	3	13.8	6.92	47	.375	.444	1	.143	-0	-5	-5	-0	-0.3

● CURT FULLERTON Fullerton, Curtis Hooper b: 9/13/1898, Ellsworth, Me. d: 1/2/75, Winthrop, Mass. BL/TR, 6', 162 lbs. Deb: 4/14/21

YEAR	TM/L	W	L	PCT	G	GS	CG	SH	SV	IP	H	HR	BB	SO	RAT	ERA	ERA+	OAV	OOB	BH	AVG	PB	PR	/A	PD	TPI
1921	Bos-A	0	1	.000	4	1	1	0	0	15¹	22	3	10	4	19.4	8.80	48	.355	.452	0	.000	-0	-8	-8	-1	-0.5
1922	Bos-A	1	4	.200	31	3	0	0	0	64¹	70	4	35	17	15.4	5.46	75	.290	.391	4	.250	1	-10	-10	1	-0.4
1923	Bos-A	2	15	.118	37	15	6	0	1	143¹	167	9	71	37	15.3	5.09	81	.300	.385	11	.297	2	-18	-16	-2	-1.6
1924	Bos-A	7	12	.368	33	20	9	0	2	152	166	1	73	33	14.5	4.32	101	.283	.368	3	.071	-3	-2	-1	-0	-0.3
1925	Bos-A	0	3	.000	4	2	0	0	0	22²	22	1	9	3	13.1	3.18	143	.259	.344	2	.200	-0	3	3	1	0.4
1933	Bos-A	0	2	.000	6	2	0	0	0	25¹	36	1	13	10	17.8	8.53	51	.364	.442	1	.222	-0	-12	-12	-1	-0.7
Total	6	10	37	.213	115	43	18	0	3	423	483	15	211	104	15.2	5.11	83	.296	.384	20	.182	-1	-46	-40	-1	-3.1

● CHICK FULMER Fulmer, Charles John b: 2/12/1851, Philadelphia, Pa. d: 2/15/40, Philadelphia, Pa. BR/TR, 6', 158 lbs. Deb: 8/23/1871 FU♦

YEAR	TM/L	W	L	PCT	G	GS	CG	SH	SV	IP	H	HR	BB	SO	RAT	ERA	ERA+	OAV	OOB	BH	AVG	PB	PR	/A	PD	TPI
1873	Phi-n	0	0	—	2	0	0	0	0	5	7	0	1	0	14.4	3.60	92	.304	.333	66	.280	0	-0	-0		0.0

● CHRIS FULMER Fulmer, Christopher b: 7/4/1858, Tamaqua, Pa. d: 11/9/31, Tamaqua, Pa. BR/TR, 5'8", 165 lbs. Deb: 8/4/1884 ♦

YEAR	TM/L	W	L	PCT	G	GS	CG	SH	SV	IP	H	HR	BB	SO	RAT	ERA	ERA+	OAV	OOB	BH	AVG	PB	PR	/A	PD	TPI
1886	Bal-a	0	0	—	1	0	0	0	0	2	2	0	1	0	13.5	4.50	76	.250	.333	66	.244	-0	-0	-0	-0	0.0

● BILL FULTON Fulton, William David b: 10/22/63, Pittsburgh, Pa. BR/TR, 6'3", 195 lbs. Deb: 9/12/87

YEAR	TM/L	W	L	PCT	G	GS	CG	SH	SV	IP	H	HR	BB	SO	RAT	ERA	ERA+	OAV	OOB	BH	AVG	PB	PR	/A	PD	TPI
1987	NY-A	1	0	1.000	3	0	0	0	0	4²	9	4	1	2	21.2	11.57	38	.409	.458	0	—	0	-4	-4	0	-0.6

● FRANK FUNK Funk, Franklin Ray b: 8/30/35, Washington, D.C. BR/TR, 6', 175 lbs. Deb: 9/3/60 C

YEAR	TM/L	W	L	PCT	G	GS	CG	SH	SV	IP	H	HR	BB	SO	RAT	ERA	ERA+	OAV	OOB	BH	AVG	PB	PR	/A	PD	TPI
1960	Cle-A	4	2	.667	9	0	0	0	1	31²	27	3	9	18	10.2	1.99	188	.248	.305	1	.111	-0	7	6	0	1.2
1961	Cle-A	11	11	.500	56	0	0	0	11	92¹	79	9	31	62	11.9	3.31	119	.234	.306	1	.059	-1	7	6	0	1.4
1962	Cle-A	2	1	.667	47	0	0	0	9	80²	62	11	32	49	10.9	3.24	120	.212	.298	1	.067	-0	7	6	0	0.1
1963	Mil-N	3	3	.500	25	0	0	0	1	43²	42	3	13	19	11.5	2.68	120	.258	.316	0	.000	-0	3	3	-1	0.2
Total	4	20	17	.541	137	0	0	0	18	248¹	210	26	85	150	11.0	3.01	135	.233	.305	3	.067	-2	23	21	-1	2.9

● TOM FUNK Funk, Thomas James b: 3/13/62, Kansas City, Mo. BL/TL, 6'2", 210 lbs. Deb: 7/24/86

YEAR	TM/L	W	L	PCT	G	GS	CG	SH	SV	IP	H	HR	BB	SO	RAT	ERA	ERA+	OAV	OOB	BH	AVG	PB	PR	/A	PD	TPI
1986	Hou-N	0	0	—	8	0	0	0	0	8¹	10	1	6	2	17.3	6.48	56	.286	.390	0	.000	-0	-3	-3	0	0.0

● EDDIE FUSSELBACK Fusselback, Edward L. b: 7/17/1856, Philadelphia, Pa. d: 4/14/26, Philadelphia, Pa. 5'6", 156 lbs. Deb: 5/3/1882 ♦

YEAR	TM/L	W	L	PCT	G	GS	CG	SH	SV	IP	H	HR	BB	SO	RAT	ERA	ERA+	OAV	OOB	BH	AVG	PB	PR	/A	PD	TPI
1882	StL-a	1	2	.333	4	2	2	0	**1**	23	34	0	2	3	14.1	4.70	60	.321	.333	31	.228		-5	-5	-1	-0.6

● FRED FUSSELL Fussell, Frederick Morris "Moonlight Ace" b: 10/7/1895, Sheridan, Mo. d: 10/23/66, Syracuse, N.Y. BL/TL, 5'10", 155 lbs. Deb: 9/23/22

YEAR	TM/L	W	L	PCT	G	GS	CG	SH	SV	IP	H	HR	BB	SO	RAT	ERA	ERA+	OAV	OOB	BH	AVG	PB	PR	/A	PD	TPI
1922	Chi-N	1	1	.500	3	2	1	0	0	19	24	3	6	8	15.2	4.74	89	.333	.400	0	.000	-0	-1	-1	0	-0.1
1923	Chi-N	3	5	.375	28	2	1	0	3	76¹	90	2	31	38	14.6	5.54	72	.298	.369	4	.200	-0	-13	-13	0	-1.2
1928	Pit-N	8	9	.471	28	20	9	2	1	159²	183	6	41	43	12.7	3.61	113	.295	.340	7	.121	3	7	8	-3	0.2
1929	Pit-N	2	2	.500	21	3	0	0	1	39²	68	8	8	18	17.5	8.62	55	.389	.418	4	.250	2	-17	-17	-0	-1.3
Total	4	14	17	.452	80	27	11	2	5	294²	365	16	88	103	14.0	4.86	85	.312	.363	15	.150	-2	-25	-23	-2	-2.4

● MIKE FYHRIE Fyhrie, Michael Edwin b: 12/9/69, Long Beach, Cal. BR/TR, 6'2", 190 lbs. Deb: 9/14/96

YEAR	TM/L	W	L	PCT	G	GS	CG	SH	SV	IP	H	HR	BB	SO	RAT	ERA	ERA+	OAV	OOB	BH	AVG	PB	PR	/A	PD	TPI
1996	NY-N	0	1	.000	4	0	0	0	0	3	4	0	3	0	27.0	15.43	25	.364	.500	0	—	-0	-3	-3	0	-0.9

● FRANK GABLER Gabler, Frank Harold "The Great Gabbo" b: 11/6/11, E.Highlands, Cal. d: 11/1/67, Long Beach, Cal. BR/TR, 6'1", 175 lbs. Deb: 4/19/35

YEAR	TM/L	W	L	PCT	G	GS	CG	SH	SV	IP	H	HR	BB	SO	RAT	ERA	ERA+	OAV	OOB	BH	AVG	PB	PR	/A	PD	TPI
1935	NY-N	2	1	.667	26	1	0	0	0	60	79	6	20	24	14.9	5.70	68	.315	.365	2	.125	-1	-11	-12	0	-0.6
1936	*NY-N	9	8	.529	43	14	5	0	6	161²	170	11	34	46	11.5	3.12	125	.274	.315	10	.208	2	16	14	-1	1.5
1937	NY-N	0	0	—	6	0	0	0	0	9	20	1	2	3	22.0	10.00	39	.455	.478	0	—	0	-6	-6	-0	0.0
	Bos-N	4	7	.364	19	9	2	1	2	76	84	7	16	19	11.8	5.09	70	.283	.319	4	.182	-0	-10	-13	-1	-1.6
	Yr	4	7	.364	25	9	2	1	2	85	104	8	18	22	12.9	5.61	64	.305	.340	4	.182	-0	-16	-19	-1	-1.6
1938	Bos-N	0	0	—	1	0	0	0	0	4	3	0	1	0	9	81.00	♦	1.000	1.000	0	—	-0	-3	-3	0	0.0
	Chi-A	1	7	.125	18	7	3	0	0	69¹	101	12	34	17	17.7	9.09	54	.348	.418	5	.238	-0	-33	-32	-1	-2.9
Total	4	16	23	.410	113	31	10	1	8	376¹	457	37	107	109	13.6	5.26	76	.303	.351	21	.196	1	-47	-53	-2	-3.6

● GABE GABLER Gabler, John Richard b: 10/2/30, Kansas City, Mo. BB/TR, 6'2", 165 lbs. Deb: 9/18/59

YEAR	TM/L	W	L	PCT	G	GS	CG	SH	SV	IP	H	HR	BB	SO	RAT	ERA	ERA+	OAV	OOB	BH	AVG	PB	PR	/A	PD	TPI
1959	NY-A	1	1	.500	3	1	0	0	0	19¹	21	1	10	11	14.9	2.79	130	.284	.376	0	.000	-1	2	2	0	0.1
1960	NY-A	3	3	.500	21	4	0	0	1	52	46	2	32	19	13.5	4.15	86	.242	.351	1	.091	-0	-2	-3	-0	-0.4
1961	Was-A	3	8	.273	29	9	0	0	4	92²	104	5	37	33	13.8	4.86	83	.283	.351	5	.200	1	-9	-9	1	-0.8
Total	3	7	12	.368	53	14	0	0	5	164	171	8	79	63	13.8	4.39	87	.271	.354	6	.143	-0	-8	-10	1	-1.1

● KEN GABLES Gables, Kenneth Harlin "Coral" b: 1/31/19, Walnut Grove, Mo. d: 1/2/60, Walnut Grove, Mo. BR/TR, 5'11", 210 lbs. Deb: 4/18/45

YEAR	TM/L	W	L	PCT	G	GS	CG	SH	SV	IP	H	HR	BB	SO	RAT	ERA	ERA+	OAV	OOB	BH	AVG	PB	PR	/A	PD	TPI
1945	Pit-N	11	7	.611	29	16	6	0	1	138²	139	5	46	49	12.3	4.15	95	.256	.319	4	.103	-3	-5	-3	-2	-0.9
1946	Pit-N	2	4	.333	32	7	0	0	1	100²	113	3	52	39	14.8	5.27	67	.281	.365	6	.250	1	-21	-20	-2	-1.2
1947	Pit-N	0	0	—	1	0	0	0	0	0¹	3	1	0	0	81.0	54.00	8	.750	.750	0	—	-0	-2	-2	0	0.0
Total	3	13	11	.542	62	23	6	0	2	239²	255	9	98	88	13.4	4.69	80	.269	.340	10	.159	-1	-28	-25	-4	-2.1

● JOHN GADDY Gaddy, John Wilson "Sheriff" b: 2/5/14, Wadesboro, N.C. d: 5/3/66, Albemarle, N.C. BR/TR, 6'0.5", 182 lbs. Deb: 9/27/38

YEAR	TM/L	W	L	PCT	G	GS	CG	SH	SV	IP	H	HR	BB	SO	RAT	ERA	ERA+	OAV	OOB	BH	AVG	PB	PR	/A	PD	TPI
1938	Bro-N	2	0	1.000	2	1	0	0	0	13	4	0	3	2	12.5	0.69	564	.255	.321	0	.000	-1	4	5	-0	0.7

● BRENT GAFF Gaff, Brent Allen b: 10/5/58, Fort Wayne, Ind. BR/TR, 6'2", 200 lbs. Deb: 7/7/82

YEAR	TM/L	W	L	PCT	G	GS	CG	SH	SV	IP	H	HR	BB	SO	RAT	ERA	ERA+	OAV	OOB	BH	AVG	PB	PR	/A	PD	TPI
1982	NY-N	0	3	.000	7	5	0	0	0	31²	41	3	10	14	14.8	4.55	80	.323	.377	0	.000	-0	-3	-3	-0	-0.3
1983	NY-N	1	0	1.000	4	0	0	0	0	10¹	18	0	1	4	16.5	6.10	59	.360	.373	0	.000	-0	-3	-3	-0	-0.3
1984	NY-N	3	2	.600	47	0	0	0	1	84¹	77	3	36	42	12.2	3.63	97	.247	.327	0	.000	-1	-0	-1	-0	-0.1
Total	3	4	5	.444	58	5	0	0	1	126¹	136	7	47	60	13.2	4.06	88	.278	.344	0	.000	-1	-7	-7	-0	-0.7

● CHARLIE GAGUS Gagus, Charles Frederick (b: Charles Frederick Geggus) b: 3/25/1862, San Francisco, Cal d: 1/16/17, San Francisco, Cal Deb: 8/7/1884

YEAR	TM/L	W	L	PCT	G	GS	CG	SH	SV	IP	H	HR	BB	SO	RAT	ERA	ERA+	OAV	OOB	BH	AVG	PB	PR	/A	PD	TPI
1884	Was-U	10	9	.526	23	21	19	0	0	177¹	143	2	38	156	9.2	2.54	95	.206	.247	38	.247	-3	-2	-3	1	-0.4

● NEMO GAINES Gaines, Willard Roland b: 12/23/1897, Alexandria, Va. d: 1/26/79, Warrenton, Va. BL/TL, 6', 180 lbs. Deb: 6/26/21

YEAR	TM/L	W	L	PCT	G	GS	CG	SH	SV	IP	H	HR	BB	SO	RAT	ERA	ERA+	OAV	OOB	BH	AVG	PB	PR	/A	PD	TPI
1921	Was-A	0	0	—	4	0	0	0	0	4²	5	0	4	1	13.5	0.00	—	.294	.368	0	.000	-0	1	1	0	0.0

● FRED GAISER Gaiser, Frederick Jacob b: 8/31/1885, Stuttgart, Germany d: 10/9/18, Trenton, N.J. Deb: 9/3/08

YEAR	TM/L	W	L	PCT	G	GS	CG	SH	SV	IP	H	HR	BB	SO	RAT	ERA	ERA+	OAV	OOB	BH	AVG	PB	PR	/A	PD	TPI
1908	StL-N	0	0	—	1	0	0	0	0	2¹	4	0	3	2	27.0	7.71	31	.444	.583	0	.000	-0	-1	-1	0	0.0

● DAN GAKELER Gakeler, Daniel Michael b: 5/1/64, Mt.Holly, N.J. BR/TR, 6'6", 215 lbs. Deb: 6/9/91

YEAR	TM/L	W	L	PCT	G	GS	CG	SH	SV	IP	H	HR	BB	SO	RAT	ERA	ERA+	OAV	OOB	BH	AVG	PB	PR	/A	PD	TPI
1991	Det-A	1	4	.200	31	7	0	0	2	73²	73	5	39	43	13.8	5.74	72	.256	.348	0		0	-13	-13	-0	-0.9

● BOB GALASSO Galasso, Robert Joseph b: 1/13/52, Connellsville, Pa. BL/TR, 6'1", 205 lbs. Deb: 7/24/77

YEAR	TM/L	W	L	PCT	G	GS	CG	SH	SV	IP	H	HR	BB	SO	RAT	ERA	ERA+	OAV	OOB	BH	AVG	PB	PR	/A	PD	TPI
1977	Sea-A	0	6	.000	11	7	0	0	0	35	57	8	19	21	19.0	9.00	46	.365	.407		0	-19	-19	-0	-2.5
1979	Mil-A	3	1	.750	31	0	0	0	4	51¹	64	5	26	28	15.8	4.38	95	.299	.375		0	-1	-1	-0	-0.1
1981	Sea-A	1	1	.500	13	1	0	0	0	31²	32	2	13	14	12.8	4.83	80	.264	.336		0	-4	-3	-0	-0.3
Total	3	4	8	.333	55	8	0	0	4	118	153	15	47	63	15.5	5.87	69	.312	.375		0	-24	-24	-1	-2.9

YEAR TM/L	W	L	PCT	G	GS	CG	SH	SV	IP	H	HR	BB	SO	RAT	ERA	ERA+	OAV	OOB	BH	AVG	PB	PR	/A	PD	TPI
● **MILT GALATZER** Galatzer, Milton b: 5/4/07, Chicago, Ill. d: 1/29/76, San Francisco, Cal BL/TL, 5'10", 168 lbs. Deb: 6/25/33 ♦																									
1936 Cle-A	0	0	—	1	0	0	0	0	6	7	0	5	3	18.0	4.50	112	.292	.414	23	.237	0	0	0	0	0.0
● **RICH GALE** Gale, Richard Blackwell b: 1/19/54, Littleton, N.H. BR/TR, 6'7", 225 lbs. Deb: 4/30/78 C																									
1978 KC-A	14	8	.636	31	30	9	3	0	192¹	171	10	100	88	12.8	3.09	124	.244	.340	0	—	0	14	16	-2	1.5
1979 KC-A	9	10	.474	34	31	2	1	0	181²	197	19	99	103	14.9	5.65	75	.278	.369	0	—	0	-29	-28	-1	-2.5
1980 *KC-A	13	9	.591	32	28	6	1	1	190²	169	16	78	97	11.8	3.92	103	.239	.316	0	—	0	2	3	-1	0.2
1981 KC-A	6	6	.500	19	15	2	0	0	101²	107	14	38	47	13.0	5.40	67	.270	.336	0	—	0	-20	-20	-2	-2.3
1982 SF-N	7	14	.333	33	29	2	0	0	170¹	193	9	81	102	14.7	4.23	85	.294	.376	6	.125	1	-12	-12	-1	-1.2
1983 Cin-N	4	6	.400	33	7	0	0	1	89²	103	8	43	53	14.8	5.82	65	.286	.364	3	.150	1	-22	-20	-1	-2.1
1984 Bos-A	2	3	.400	13	4	0	0	0	43²	57	6	18	28	15.7	5.56	75	.315	.380	0	—	0	-8	-7	-0	-0.7
Total 7	55	56	.495	195	144	21	5	2	970	997	82	457	518	13.7	4.54	86	.269	.351	9	.132	2	-73	-69	-5	-7.1
● **DENNY GALEHOUSE** Galehouse, Dennis Ward b: 12/7/11, Marshallville, Ohio BR/TR, 6'1", 195 lbs. Deb: 4/30/34																									
1934 Cle-A	0	0	—	1	0	0	0	0	1	2	0	1	0	27.0	18.00	25	.500	.600	0	—	0	-2	-1	-0	0.0
1935 Cle-A	1	0	1.000	5	1	1	0	0	13	16	1	9	8	18.0	9.00	50	.314	.426	1	.250	-0	-7	-6	-0	-0.4
1936 Cle-A	8	7	.533	36	15	5	0	1	148¹	161	5	68	71	14.0	4.85	104	.280	.358	8	.170	-1	3	3	-2	0.0
1937 Cle-A	9	14	.391	36	29	7	0	3	200²	238	11	83	78	14.4	4.57	101	.302	.369	15	.208	-1	1	1	1	0.0
1938 Cle-A	7	8	.467	36	12	5	1	3	114	119	12	65	66	14.6	4.34	107	.275	.371	6	.154	-1	6	4	0	0.3
1939 Bos-A	9	10	.474	30	18	6	1	0	146²	160	6	52	68	13.1	4.54	104	.276	.337	3	.064	-3	1	3	0	0.1
1940 Bos-A	6	6	.500	25	20	5	0	0	120	155	10	41	44	14.7	5.18	87	.313	.366	3	.077	-4	-11	-9	1	-1.0
1941 StL-A	9	10	.474	30	24	11	2	0	190¹	183	10	68	61	12.1	3.64	118	.253	.320	13	.193	-0	11	14	1	1.3
1942 StL-A	12	12	.500	32	28	12	3	1	192¹	193	5	79	75	12.9	3.60	103	.262	.337	14	.194	1	1	1	2	0.4
1943 StL-A	11	11	.500	31	28	14	2	1	224	217	8	74	114	11.7	2.77	120	.255	.315	9	.125	-3	13	14	-3	0.7
1944 *StL-A	9	10	.474	24	19	6	2	0	153	162	6	44	80	12.2	3.12	115	.266	.316	3	.063	-4	5	8	-2	0.3
1946 StL-A	8	12	.400	30	24	11	2	0	180	194	9	52	90	12.3	3.65	102	.273	.322	5	.091	-3	-3	-2	-2	-0.4
1947 StL-A	1	3	.250	9	4	0	1	0	32¹	42	3	16	11	16.1	6.12	63	.311	.384	0	.000	-1	-9	-8	0	-1.0
Bos-A	11	7	.611	21	21	11	3	0	149	150	7	34	38	11.1	3.32	117	.260	.301	5	.096	-4	6	9	-1	0.6
Yr	12	10	.545	30	25	11	3	1	181¹	192	10	50	49	12.0	3.82	102	.269	.317	5	.083	-5	-2	-1	-1	-0.4
1948 Bos-A	8	8	.500	27	15	6	1	3	137¹	152	10	46	38	13.1	4.00	110	.282	.341	7	.167	-0	4	6	-2	0.5
1949 Bos-A	0	0	—	2	0	0	0	0	2	4	1	3	0	31.5	13.50	32	.400	.538	0	—	0	-2	-2	-0	0.0
Total 15	109	118	.480	375	258	100	17	13	2004	2148	104	735	851	13.0	3.97	105	.275	.338	92	.138	-25	20	40	-8	1.4
● **DOUG GALLAGHER** Gallagher, Douglas Eugene b: 2/21/40, Fremont, Ohio BR/TL, 6'3.5", 195 lbs. Deb: 4/9/62																									
1962 Det-A	0	4	.000	9	2	0	0	0	25	31	2	15	14	16.6	4.68	87	.290	.377	2	.333	1	-2	-2	0	-0.1
● **ED GALLAGHER** Gallagher, Edward Michael "Lefty" b: 11/28/10, Dorchester, Mass. d: 12/22/81, Hyannis, Mass. BB/TL, 6'2", 197 lbs. Deb: 7/8/32																									
1932 Bos-A	0	3	.000	9	3	0	0	0	23²	30	3	28	6	22.1	12.55	36	.323	.479	0	.000	-1	-21	-21	0	-2.1
● **BILL GALLAGHER** Gallagher, William John b: Philadelphia, Pa. TL, Deb: 5/2/1883 ♦																									
1883 Bal-a	0	5	.000	7	5	4	0	0	51²	79	0	6	19	14.8	5.40	64	.331	.347	10	.164	-1	-12	-11	-1	-0.9
1884 Phi-U	1	2	.333	3	3	3	0	0	25	32	3	4	12	13.0	3.24	72	.291	.316	1	.091	-2	-2	-3	-0	-0.4
Total 2	1	7	.125	10	8	7	0	0	76²	111	3	10	31	14.2	4.70	66	.318	.337	11	.138	-3	-14	-14	-1	-1.3
● **BERT GALLIA** Gallia, Melvin Allys b: 10/14/1891, Beeville, Tex. d: 3/19/76, Devine, Tex. BR/TR, 6', 165 lbs. Deb: 9/4/12																									
1912 Was-A	0	0	—	2	0	0	0	0	2	0	0	3	0	13.5	0.00	—	.000	.333	0	—	0	1	1	-0	0.0
1913 Was-A	1	5	.167	31	4	0	0	3	96	85	2	46	46	12.9	4.13	72	.222	.317	2	.087	-2	-13	-12	2	-0.8
1914 Was-A	0	0	—	2	0	0	0	0	6	3	0	4	4	10.5	4.50	63	.120	.241	0	.000	-0	-1	-1	-0	-0.1
1915 Was-A	17	11	.607	43	29	14	3	1	259²	220	2	64	130	10.0	2.29	130	.234	.286	14	.165	-2	19	20	-2	1.7
1916 Was-A	17	12	.586	49	31	13	1	2	283²	278	3	99	120	12.2	2.76	101	.266	.334	18	.194	1	2	1	-3	-0.2
1917 Was-A	9	13	.409	42	23	9	1	1	207²	191	1	93	84	12.5	2.99	88	.258	.344	14	.209	-1	-8	-8	-1	-0.8
1918 StL-A	8	6	.571	19	17	10	1	0	124	126	1	61	48	14.0	3.48	79	.268	.359	6	.130	-3	-10	-10	0	-1.4
1919 StL-A	12	14	.462	34	25	14	1	1	221¹	220	10	92	83	13.0	3.60	92	.264	.343	11	.153	-2	-9	-7	2	-0.8
1920 StL-A	0	1	.000	2	1	0	0	0	3²	8	0	3	0	27.0	7.36	53	.400	.478	0	.000	-0	-1	-1	-0	-0.3
Phi-N	2	6	.250	18	5	1	0	2	72	79	2	29	35	13.9	4.50	76	.287	.362	4	.174	-1	-11	-9	-1	-1.1
Total 9	66	68	.493	242	135	61	7	10	1277	1210	21	494	550	12.3	3.14	94	.256	.331	69	.167	-7	-31	-28	-3	-3.8
● **PHIL GALLIVAN** Gallivan, Philip Joseph b: 5/29/07, Seattle, Wash. d: 11/24/69, St.Paul, Minn. BR/TR, 6', 170 lbs. Deb: 4/21/31																									
1931 Bro-N	0	1	.000	6	1	0	0	0	15¹	23	2	7	1	17.6	5.28	72	.354	.417	0	.000	-0	-2	-3	1	-0.1
1932 Chi-A	1	3	.250	13	1	0	0	0	33¹	49	3	24	12	20.0	7.56	57	.338	.435	3	.375	1	-11	-12	-0	-1.1
1934 Chi-A	4	7	.364	35	7	3	0	1	126²	155	14	64	55	15.6	5.61	84	.295	.373	9	.225	1	-16	-12	-1	-0.9
Total 3	5	11	.313	54	9	3	0	1	175¹	227	19	95	68	16.6	5.95	77	.309	.389	12	.235	1	-30	-27	-1	-2.1
● **BALVINO GALVEZ** Galvez, Balvino (Jerez) b: 3/31/64, San Pedro De Macoris, D.R. BR/TR, 6', 170 lbs. Deb: 5/7/86																									
1986 LA-N	0	1	.000	10	0	0	0	0	20²	19	3	12	11	13.5	3.92	88	.241	.341	0	.000	-0	-0	-1	-0	-0.1
● **PUD GALVIN** Galvin, James Francis "Jim", "Gentle Jeems" or "The Little Steam Engine" b: 12/25/1856, St.Louis, Mo. d: 3/7/02, Pittsburgh, Pa. BR/TR, 5'8", 190 lbs. Deb: 5/22/1875 MUH																									
1875 StL-n	4	2	.667	8	7	7	0	1	62	53	0	1	8	7.8	**1.16**	**173**	.209	.212	6	.130	-1	7	6	0.5
1879 Buf-N	37	27	.578	66	66	65	6	0	593	585	3	31	136	9.3	2.28	115	.243	.253	66	.249	5	14	22	3	2.8
1880 Buf-N	20	35	.364	58	54	46	5	0	458²	528	5	32	128	11.0	2.71	91	.273	.284	51	.212	-4	-17	-13	1	-1.5
1881 Buf-N	28	24	.538	56	53	48	5	0	474	546	4	46	136	11.2	2.37	117	.274	.291	50	.212	-1	21	21	7	2.6
1882 Buf-N	28	23	.549	52	51	48	3	0	445¹	476	8	40	162	10.4	3.17	93	.256	.272	44	.214	-5	-13	-12	1	-1.6
1883 Buf-N	46	29	.613	76	75	72	5	0	656¹	676	9	50	279	10.0	2.72	117	.251	.265	71	.220	-8	31	34	-0	2.6
1884 Buf-N	46	22	.676	72	72	71	12	0	636¹	566	23	63	369	8.9	1.99	158	.227	.246	49	.179	-14	70	82	7	6.8
1885 Buf-N	13	19	.406	33	32	31	3	1	284	356	8	37	93	12.5	4.09	73	.292	.313	23	.189	-2	-40	-35	4	-3.0
Pit-a	3	7	.300	11	11	9	0	0	88¹	97	2	7	27	10.6	3.67	88	.266	.280	4	.105	-4	-4	-4	-1	-0.7
1886 Pit-a	29	21	.580	50	50	49	2	0	434²	457	3	71	72	10.7	2.67	127	.263	.296	49	.253	3	38	33	3	3.6
1887 Pit-N	28	21	.571	49	48	47	3	0	440²	490	12	67	76	11.6	3.29	118	.269	.299	41	.212	-2	38	29	8	3.0
1888 Pit-N	23	25	.479	50	50	49	6	0	437¹	446	9	53	107	10.4	2.63	101	.255	.280	25	.143	-6	10	2	4	-0.1
1889 Pit-N	23	16	.590	41	40	38	4	0	341	392	19	78	77	12.7	4.17	90	.296	.322	28	.187	-1	-6	-16	1	-1.3
1890 Pit-P	12	13	.480	26	25	23	1	0	217	275	3	49	35	13.8	4.35	90	.296	.337	20	.206	-0	-3	-11	4	-0.7
1891 Pit-N	14	14	.500	33	30	23	2	0	246²	256	10	62	46	12.1	2.88	114	.258	.310	18	.165	-4	13	11	0	0.6
1892 Pit-N	5	6	.455	12	12	10	0	0	96	104	3	28	29	12.4	2.63	126	.265	.314	5	.122	-3	7	7	-0	0.4
StL-N	5	6	.455	12	12	10	0	0	92	102	4	26	27	12.8	3.23	99	.270	.322	2	.051	-5	1	-0	-2	-0.6
Yr	10	12	.455	24	24	20	0	0	188	206	4	54	56	12.6	2.92	111	.268	.318	7	.087	-7	8	7	-2	-0.2
Total 14	360	308	.539	697	681	639	57	3	5941¹	6352	122	744	1799	10.8	2.87	109	.261	.284	546	.202	-48	160	162	39	12.9
● **LOU GALVIN** Galvin, Louis J. b: 4/1862, St.Paul, Minn. d: 6/17/1895, Deb: 10/1/1884																									
1884 StP-U	0	2	.000	3	3	3	0	0	25	21	0	10	17	11.2	2.88	46	.212	.284	2	.222	-1	-1	-4	-1	-0.4
● **BOB GAMBLE** Gamble, Robert J. b: 2/1867, Hazleton, Pa. TR, 5'10", 155 lbs. Deb: 5/2/1888																									
1888 Phi-a	0	1	.000	1	1	1	0	0	9	6	1	3	0	10.0	8.00	37	.270	.325	1	.333	0	-5	-5	0	-0.4
● **GUSSIE GANNON** Gannon, James Edward b: 11/26/1873, Erie, Pa. d: 4/12/66, Erie, Pa. BL/TL, 5'11", 154 lbs. Deb: 6/15/1895																									
1895 Pit-N	0	0	—	1	0	0	0	0	5	7	0	2	0	16.2	1.80	251	.333	.391	0	.000	-0	2	2	0	-0.1
● **JOE GANNON** Gannon, Joseph b: St.Louis, Mo. Deb: 8/28/1898																									
1898 StL-N	0	1	.000	1	1	1	0	0	9	13	0	5	2	19.0	11.00	34	.333	.422	0	.000	-1	-7	-7	-0	-0.5
● **JIM GANTNER** Gantner, James Elmer b: 1/5/53, Fond Du Lac, Wis. BL/TR, 6', 180 lbs. Deb: 9/3/76 C♦																									
1979 Mil-A	0	0	—	1	0	0	0	0	1	2	0	0	0	18.0	—		.400	.400	59	.284	1	0	0	0	0.0

YEAR	TM/L	W	L	PCT	G	GS	CG	SH	SV	IP	H	HR	BB	SO	RAT	ERA	ERA+	OAV	OOB	BH	AVG	PB	PR	/A	PD	TPI
● KEITH GARAGOZZO	Garagozzo, Keith John b: 10/25/69, Camden, N.J. BL/TL, 6′, 170 lbs. Deb: 4/5/94																								
1994	Min-A	0	0	—	7	0	0	0	0	9¹	9	3	13	3	21.2	9.64	50	.273	.478	0	—	0	-5	-5	0	0.0
● GENE GARBER	Garber, Henry Eugene b: 11/13/47, Lancaster, Pa. BR/TR, 5′10″, 175 lbs. Deb: 6/17/69																								
1969	Pit-N	0	0	—	2	1	0	0	0	5	6	3	1	3	12.6	5.40	65	.333	.368	0	.000	-0	-1	-1	-0	0.0
1970	Pit-N	0	3	.000	14	0	0	0	0	22¹	22	4	10	7	13.7	5.24	74	.275	.370	2	.667	1	-3	-3	1	-0.2
1972	Pit-N	0	0	—	4	0	0	0	0	6¹	7	3	3	3	14.2	7.11	47	.269	.345	0	.000	-0	-3	-3	0	0.0
1973	KC-A	9	9	.500	48	8	4	0	11	152²	164	14	49	60	12.7	4.24	97	.283	.341	0	—	0	-7	-2	1	-0.2
1974	KC-A	1	2	.333	17	0	0	0	1	28	35	3	13	14	15.8	4.82	79	.313	.389	0	—	0	-4	-3	-0	-0.7
	Phi-N	4	0	1.000	34	0	0	0	4	48	39	1	31	27	13.3	2.06	183	.236	.360	0	.000	-0	8	9	0	0.9
1975	Phi-N	10	12	.455	**71**	0	0	0	14	110	104	13	27	69	10.9	3.60	104	.254	.304	2	.167	-0	0	2	-0	0.3
1976	*Phi-N	9	3	.750	59	0	0	0	11	92²	78	4	30	92	9.2	2.82	126	.228	.298	2	.286	1	7	8	1	1.4
1977	*Phi-N	8	6	.571	64	0	0	0	19	103¹	82	6	23	78	9.3	2.35	170	.220	.270	0	.000	-1	18	19	2	3.2
1978	Phi-N	2	1	.667	22	0	0	0	3	38²	26	1	11	24	9.3	1.40	256	.191	.267	0	—	-0	9	9	-0	0.8
	Atl-N	4	4	.500	43	0	0	0	22	78¹	58	11	13	61	8.4	2.53	160	.204	.244	1	.091	-0	9	13	1	2.2
	Yr	6	5	.545	65	0	0	0	25	117	84	12	24	85	8.5	2.15	181	.199	.245	1	.071	-1	18	**23**	1	3.0
1979	Atl-N	6	16	.273	68	0	0	0	25	106	121	10	24	56	12.7	4.33	94	.283	.328	3	.300	1	-7	-3	1	-0.6
1980	Atl-N	5	5	.500	68	0	0	0	7	82¹	95	6	24	51	13.0	3.83	98	.288	.336	1	.500	-0	-2	-1	2	0.1
1981	Atl-N	4	6	.400	35	0	0	0	2	58²	49	2	20	34	10.6	2.61	137	.214	.277	0	.000	-1	6	6	2	1.3
1982	*Atl-N	8	10	.444	69	0	0	0	30	119¹	100	4	32	68	10.1	2.34	160	.231	.288	2	.133	0	17	18	2	3.9
1983	Atl-N	4	5	.444	43	0	0	0	9	60²	72	8	23	45	14.4	4.60	84	.300	.366	0	.000	-0	-7	-5	2	-0.6
1984	Atl-N	3	6	.333	62	0	0	0	11	106	103	7	24	55	11.0	3.06	126	.254	.299	2	.143	-0	6	9	1	1.0
1985	Atl-N	6	6	.500	59	0	0	0	6	97¹	98	8	25	66	11.6	3.61	107	.263	.313	1	.200	0	4	7	0	0.4
1986	Atl-N	5	5	.500	61	0	0	0	24	78	76	3	20	56	11.2	2.54	157	.260	.310	1	.167	1	10	12	1	2.4
1987	Atl-N	8	10	.444	49	0	0	0	10	69¹	87	7	28	48	15.1	4.41	88	.311	.375	0	.000	-0	-3	-1	2	0.0
	KC-A	0	0	—	13	0	0	0	6	14¹	13	1	1	3	9.4	2.51	181	.245	.273	0	—	0	3	3	0	0.3
1988	KC-A	0	4	.000	26	0	0	0	6	32²	29	4	13	20	12.1	3.58	111	.238	.321	0	—	0	1	1	0	0.2
Total	19	96	113	.459	931	9	4	0	218	1510	1464	123	445	940	11.6	3.34	116	.257	.314	17	.148	-0	59	92	20	16.1
● BOB GARBER	Garber, Robert Mitchell b: 9/10/28, Hunker, Pa. BR/TR, 6′1″, 190 lbs. Deb: 5/13/56																								
1956	Pit-N	0	0	—	2	0	0	0	0	4	3	1	3	3	13.5	2.25	168	.200	.333	0	—	0	1	1	-0	0.0
● RICH GARCES	Garces, Richard Aron (Mendoza) b: 5/18/71, Maracay, Venez. BR/TR, 6′, 187 lbs. Deb: 9/18/90																								
1990	Min-A	0	0	—	5	0	0	0	2	5²	4	0	4	1	12.7	1.59	261	.200	.333	0	—	0	1	2	0	-0.2
1993	Min-A	0	0	—	3	0	0	0	0	4	4	0	2	3	13.5	0.00	—	.250	.333	0	—	0	2	2	0	-0.0
1995	Chi-N	0	0	—	7	0	0	0	0	11	11	0	3	6	11.5	3.27	125	.256	.304	0	—	0	1	1	0	0.0
	Fla-N	0	2	.000	11	0	0	0	0	13¹	14	1	8	16	14.9	5.40	78	.264	.361	0	—	0	-2	-2	-0	-0.3
	Yr	0	2	.000	18	0	0	0	0	24¹	25	1	11	22	13.3	4.44	94	.260	.336	0	.000	0	-1	-1	-0	-0.3
1996	Bos-A	3	2	.600	37	0	0	0	2	44	42	5	33	55	15.3	4.91	105	.251	.375	0	—	0	1	1	0	-0.1
Total	4	3	4	.429	63	0	0	0	2	78	75	6	50	81	14.4	4.27	111	.251	.358	0	.000	-0	3	4	0	-0.6
● MIKE GARCIA	Garcia, Edward Miguel "The Big Bear" b: 11/17/23, San Gabriel, Cal. d: 1/13/86, Fairview Park, O. BR/TR, 6′1″, 200 lbs. Deb: 10/3/48																								
1948	Cle-A	0	0	—	1	0	0	0	0	2	3	0	1	1	13.5	0.00	—	.333	.333	0	—	0	1	1	0	0.0
1949	Cle-A	14	5	.737	41	20	8	5	2	175²	154	6	60	94	11.1	**2.36**	**169**	.241	.308	12	.235	3	36	32	1	3.6
1950	Cle-A	11	11	.500	33	29	11	0	0	184	191	15	74	76	13.0	3.86	112	.266	.334	13	.200	-1	15	10	2	1.1
1951	Cle-A	20	13	.606	47	30	15	1	6	254	239	10	82	118	11.5	3.15	120	.246	.307	18	.212	1	27	18	1	2.4
1952	Cle-A☆	22	11	.667	46	36	19	**6**	4	292¹	284	9	87	143	11.6	2.37	141	.253	.310	13	.137	-2	42	32	2	3.6
1953	Cle-A★	18	9	.667	38	35	21	3	0	271²	260	18	81	134	11.4	3.25	116	.250	.307	24	.250	4	23	15	-0	1.7
1954	*Cle-A†	19	8	.704	45	34	13	**5**	5	258²	220	6	71	129	**10.2**	**2.64**	**139**	.229	**.284**	11	.136	-2	31	**30**	1	2.9
1955	Cle-A	11	13	.458	38	31	6	2	3	210²	230	17	56	120	12.3	4.02	99	.278	.327	15	.217	2	-1	-1	-1	0.0
1956	Cle-A	11	12	.478	35	30	8	4	0	197²	213	18	74	119	13.3	3.78	111	.272	.339	7	.115	-3	8	9	-0	0.6
1957	Cle-A	12	8	.600	38	27	9	1	0	211¹	221	14	73	110	12.8	3.75	99	.269	.333	12	.160	-1	-1	-2	0	-0.4
1958	Cle-A	1	0	1.000	6	1	0	0	0	8	15	2	7	2	25.9	9.00	41	.395	.500	0	.000	-0	-5	-5	0	-0.5
1959	Cle-A	3	6	.333	29	8	1	0	1	72	72	4	31	49	12.9	4.00	92	.265	.340	1	.071	-1	-1	-3	-0	-0.4
1960	Chi-A	0	0	—	15	0	0	0	0	17²	23	2	10	8	16.8	4.58	82	.338	.423	1	.333	0	-1	-1	0	-0.1
1961	Was-A	0	1	.000	16	0	0	0	0	19	23	1	13	14	17.5	4.74	85	.287	.394	0	—	0	-2	-2	-1	-0.1
Total	14	142	97	.594	428	281	111	27	23	2174²	2148	122	719	1117	12.0	3.27	117	.257	.319	127	.182	1	174	134	2	14.5
● MIGUEL GARCIA	Garcia, Miguel Angel (Silfontes) b: 4/3/67, Caracas, Venez. BL/TL, 5′11″, 173 lbs. Deb: 4/30/87																								
1987	Cal-A	0	0	—	1	0	0	0	0	1²	3	0	3	0	32.4	16.20	27	.375	.545	0	—	0	-2	-2	0	0.1
	Pit-N	0	0	—	1	0	0	0	0	0²	0	0	0	0	0.0	.000	—	.000	.000	0	—	-0	0	0	-0	0.0
1988	Pit-N	0	0	—	1	0	0	0	0	2	3	1	2	0	27.0	4.50	76	.375	.545	0	—	0	0	0	-0	0.0
1989	Pit-N	0	2	.000	11	0	0	0	0	16	25	2	7	9	18.0	8.44	40	.357	.416	1	1.000	0	-9	-9	-0	-1.0
Total	3	0	2	.000	14	0	0	0	0	20¹	31	3	12	11	19.5	8.41	41	.352	.436	1	1.000	0	-11	-11	-0	-0.9
● RALPH GARCIA	Garcia, Ralph b: 12/14/48, Los Angeles, Cal. BR/TR, 6′, 195 lbs. Deb: 9/26/72																								
1972	SD-N	0	0	—	3	0	0	0	0	5	4	0	3	3	12.6	1.80	183	.211	.318	0	—	0	1	1	0	0.0
1974	SD-N	0	0	—	8	0	0	0	0	10¹	15	1	7	9	19.2	6.10	58	.357	.449	0	—	0	-3	-3	0	-0.3
Total	2	0	0	—	11	0	0	0	0	15¹	19	1	10	12	17.0	4.70	74	.311	.408	0	—	0	-2	-2	0	-0.2
● RAMON GARCIA	Garcia, Ramon (Garcia) b: 3/5/24, LaEsperanza, Cuba BR/TR, 5′10″, 170 lbs. Deb: 4/19/48																								
1948	Was-A	0	0	—	4	0	0	0	0	3²	11	0	4	2	39.3	17.18	25	.524	.615	1	1.000	0	-5	-5	0	0.1
● RAMON GARCIA	Garcia, Ramon Antonio (Fortunato) b: 12/9/69, Guanare, Venez. BR/TR, 6′2″, 200 lbs. Deb: 5/31/91																								
1991	Chi-A	4	4	.500	16	15	0	0	0	78¹	79	13	31	40	12.9	5.40	74	.269	.343	0	—	0	-11	-12	1	-0.9
1996	Mil-A	4	4	.500	37	2	0	0	4	75²	84	17	21	40	13.2	6.66	79	.287	.347	0	—	0	-14	-12	-0	-1.5
Total	2	8	8	.500	53	17	0	0	4	154	163	30	52	80	13.0	6.02	76	.278	.345	0	—	0	-25	-25	1	-2.4
● ART GARDINER	Gardiner, Arthur Cecil b: 12/26/1899, Brooklyn, N.Y. d: 10/21/54, Copiague, N.Y. BR/TR, Deb: 9/25/23																								
1923	Phi-N	0	0	—	1	0	0	0	0	1	0	1	0	1	0.0	—	—	1.000	1.000	0	—	0	0	0	0	0.0
● MIKE GARDINER	Gardiner, Michael James b: 10/19/65, Sarnia, Ont., Can. BB/TR, 6′, 185 lbs. Deb: 9/8/90																								
1990	Sea-A	0	2	.000	5	3	0	0	0	12²	22	1	5	6	20.6	10.66	37	.379	.446	0	—	0	-10	-9	0	-1.2
1991	Bos-A	9	10	.474	22	22	0	0	0	130	140	18	47	91	12.9	4.85	89	.274	.335	0	—	0	-11	-8	-0	-1.3
1992	Bos-A	4	10	.286	28	18	0	0	0	130²	126	21	58	79	12.8	4.75	89	.253	.333	0	—	0	-12	-8	-0	-0.9
1993	Mon-N	2	3	.400	24	2	0	0	0	38	40	3	19	21	14.2	5.21	80	.268	.355	0	.000	0	-5	-4	0	-0.6
	Det-A	0	0	—	10	0	0	0	0	11¹	12	0	7	4	15.1	3.97	108	.279	.380	0	—	0	0	0	0	0.0
1994	Det-A	2	2	.500	38	1	0	0	0	58²	53	10	23	31	11.7	4.14	117	.233	.304	0	—	0	4	5	0	0.2
1995	Det-A	0	0	—	9	0	0	0	0	12¹	27	5	2	7	21.2	14.59	33	.458	.475	0	—	0	-14	-13	0	-1.0
Total	6	17	27	.386	136	46	0	0	0	393²	420	49	161	239	13.4	5.21	83	.272	.342	0	.000	0	-46	-38	-1	-3.8
● CHRIS GARDNER	Gardner, Christopher John b: 3/30/69, Long Beach, Cal. BR/TR, 6′, 175 lbs. Deb: 9/10/91																								
1991	Hou-N	1	2	.333	5	4	0	0	0	25	5	14	12	12.2	4.01	97	.218	.327	0	—	-0	1	1	1	-0.1
● GID GARDNER	Gardner, Frank Washington b: 6/9/1859, Attleboro, Mass. d: 8/1/14, Cambridge, Mass. 165 lbs. Deb: 8/23/1879 ♦																								
1879	Tro-N	0	2	.000	2	2	2	0	0	14	27	0	3	3	17.4	5.79	43	.365	.365	1	.167	-0	-5	-5	-1	-0.6
1880	Cle-N	1	8	.111	9	9	9	0	0	77	80	2	20	21	11.7	2.57	91	.254	.299	6	.188	-0	-2	-2	-0	-0.2
1883	Bal-a	1	0	1.000	2	0	0	0	0	7	5	1	2	1	12.9	5.14	68	.290	.333	44	.273	1	-2	-2	-0	-0.1
1884	CP-U	0	1	.000	1	1	0	0	0	6	10	0	1	4	16.5	6.00	41	.345	.367	38	.255	-0	-2	-2	-0	-0.2
1885	Bal-a	0	1	.000	1	1	1	0	0	9	16	2	2	6	23.0	10.00	33	.372	.460	37	.218	-0	-7	-7	-0	-0.5
Total	5	2	12	.143	15	13	12	0	0	113	142	4	28	33	13.6	3.90	64	.289	.328	178	.233	-1	-17	-17	-1	-1.6

YEAR	TM/L	W	L	PCT	G	GS	CG	SH	SV	IP	H	HR	BB	SO	RAT	ERA	ERA+	OAV	OOB	BH	AVG	PB	PR	/A	PD	TPI

● **HARRY GARDNER** — Gardner, Harry Ray b: 6/1/1887, Quincy, Mich. d: 8/2/61, Canby, Ore. BR/TR, 6'2", 180 lbs. Deb: 4/17/11

YEAR	TM/L	W	L	PCT	G	GS	CG	SH	SV	IP	H	HR	BB	SO	RAT	ERA	ERA+	OAV	OOB	BH	AVG	PB	PR	/A	PD	TPI
1911	Pit-N	1	1	.500	13	3	2	0	2	42	39	2	20	24	13.1	4.50	76	.244	.335	3	.214	0	-5	-5	-1	-0.3
1912	Pit-N	0	0	—	1	0	0	0	0	0¹	3	0	1	0	108.0	0.00	—	.500	.571	0	—	0	0	0	0	0.0
Total 2		1	1	.500	14	3	2	0	2	42¹	42	2	21	24	13.8	4.46	77	.253	.344	3	.214	0	-5	-5	-1	-0.3

● **JIM GARDNER** — Gardner, James Anderson b: 10/4/1874, Pittsburgh, Pa. d: 4/24/05, Pittsburgh, Pa. TR, Deb: 6/20/1895

YEAR	TM/L	W	L	PCT	G	GS	CG	SH	SV	IP	H	HR	BB	SO	RAT	ERA	ERA+	OAV	OOB	BH	AVG	PB	PR	/A	PD	TPI
1895	Pit-N	8	2	.800	11	10	8	0	0	85¹	99	1	27	31	13.9	2.64	171	.286	.348	9	.265	1	20	18	-1	1.6
1897	Pit-N	5	5	.500	14	11	8	0	0	95¹	115	4	32	35	14.7	5.19	80	.296	.363	12	.158	-1	-9	-11	-0	-0.9
1898	Pit-N	10	13	.435	25	22	19	1	0	185¹	179	3	48	41	11.4	3.21	111	.252	.306	14	.154	-2	8	7	-2	0.4
1899	Pit-N	1	0	1.000	6	3	0	0	0	32¹	52	1	13	2	18.1	7.52	51	.361	.414	3	.231	1	-13	-13	-2	-0.4
1902	Chi-N	1	2	.333	3	3	2	0	0	25	23	0	10	6	11.9	2.88	94	.245	.317	2	.200	-0	-0	-0	0	0.0
Total 5		25	22	.532	59	49	37	1	0	423¹	468	9	130	115	13.2	3.85	100	.278	.338	40	.179	-1	6	1	-4	0.7

● **MARK GARDNER** — Gardner, Mark Allan b: 3/1/62, Los Angeles, Cal. BR/TR, 6'1", 190 lbs. Deb: 5/16/89

YEAR	TM/L	W	L	PCT	G	GS	CG	SH	SV	IP	H	HR	BB	SO	RAT	ERA	ERA+	OAV	OOB	BH	AVG	PB	PR	/A	PD	TPI
1989	Mon-N	0	3	.000	7	4	0	0	0	26¹	26	2	11	21	13.3	5.13	69	.250	.333	1	.167	-0	-5	-5	-0	-0.5
1990	Mon-N	7	9	.438	27	26	3	3	0	152²	129	13	61	135	11.7	3.42	107	.230	.315	5	.114	-1	6	4	2	0.5
1991	Mon-N	9	11	.450	27	27	0	0	0	168¹	139	17	75	107	11.7	3.85	94	.230	.319	5	.091	-2	-3	-4	-2	-0.9
1992	Mon-N	12	10	.545	33	30	0	0	0	179²	179	15	60	132	12.4	4.36	80	.259	.327	7	.140	1	-17	-18	-1	-2.1
1993	KC-A	4	6	.400	17	16	0	0	0	91²	92	17	36	54	13.0	6.19	74	.271	.348	0	—	-0	-19	-16	-2	-1.9
1994	Fla-N	4	4	.500	20	14	0	0	0	92¹	97	14	30	57	12.5	4.87	90	.276	.335	1	.040	-2	-7	-5	-1	-0.7
1995	Fla-N	5	5	.500	39	11	1	1	1	102¹	109	14	43	87	13.8	4.49	94	.272	.350	4	.190	-0	-3	-3	-1	-0.4
1996	SF-N	12	7	.632	30	28	4	1	0	179¹	200	28	57	145	13.3	4.42	93	.283	.344	11	.162	-0	-4	-7	-2	-0.8
Total 8		53	55	.491	200	156	8	5	1	992²	971	120	373	738	12.6	4.39	89	.259	.332	34	.126	-4	-52	-55	-7	-6.8

● **GLENN GARDNER** — Gardner, Miles Glenn b: 1/25/16, Burnsville, N.C. d: 7/7/64, Rochester, N.Y. BR/TR, 5'11", 180 lbs. Deb: 7/21/45

YEAR	TM/L	W	L	PCT	G	GS	CG	SH	SV	IP	H	HR	BB	SO	RAT	ERA	ERA+	OAV	OOB	BH	AVG	PB	PR	/A	PD	TPI
1945	StL-N	3	1	.750	17	4	2	1	1	54²	50	2	27	20	12.7	3.29	114	.242	.329	7	.333	2	3	3	-1	0.3

● **ROB GARDNER** — Gardner, Richard Frank b: 12/19/44, Binghamton, N.Y. BR/TL, 6'1", 176 lbs. Deb: 9/1/65

YEAR	TM/L	W	L	PCT	G	GS	CG	SH	SV	IP	H	HR	BB	SO	RAT	ERA	ERA+	OAV	OOB	BH	AVG	PB	PR	/A	PD	TPI
1965	NY-N	0	2	.000	5	4	0	0	0	28	23	4	7	19	9.6	3.21	110	.217	.265	0	.000	-1	1	1	0	0.0
1966	NY-N	4	8	.333	41	17	3	0	1	133²	147	15	64	74	14.4	5.12	71	.285	.367	7	.171	-0	-22	-22	0	-1.9
1967	Chi-N	0	2	.000	18	5	0	0	0	31²	33	2	6	16	11.1	3.98	89	.260	.293	0	.000	-0	-2	-2	-0	-0.1
1968	Cle-A	0	0	—	5	0	0	0	0	2²	5	0	2	6	23.6	6.75	44	.417	.500	0	—	-0	-1	-1	-0	0.0
1970	NY-A	1	0	1.000	1	1	0	0	0	7¹	8	2	4	6	14.7	4.91	72	.276	.364	1	.333	1	-1	-1	-0	-0.1
1971	Oak-A	0	0	—	4	1	0	0	0	7²	8	1	3	5	12.9	2.35	142	.267	.333	1	.500	1	1	1	0	0.1
	NY-A	0	0	—	2	0	0	0	0	3	3	0	2	2	15.0	3.00	108	.273	.385	0	—	0	0	0	0	0.0
	Yr	0	0	—	6	1	0	0	0	10²	11	1	5	7	13.5	2.53	131	.268	.348	1	.500	1	1	1	0	0.1
1972	NY-A	8	5	.615	20	14	1	0	0	97	91	9	28	58	11.0	3.06	96	.243	.296	3	.107	-1	-0	-1	-0	-0.4
1973	Oak-A	0	0	—	3	0	0	0	0	7¹	10	2	4	2	17.2	4.91	72	.370	.452	0	—	0	-1	-1	-0	0.4
	Mil-A	1	1	.500	10	0	0	0	0	12²	17	0	13	5	22.0	9.95	38	.327	.470	0	—	0	-9	-9	-0	-1.2
	Yr	1	1	.500	13	0	0	0	0	20	27	2	17	7	20.2	8.10	45	.342	.464	0	—	0	-10	-10	-0	-0.8
Total 8		14	18	.438	109	42	4	0	2	331	345	35	133	193	13.1	4.35	78	.269	.339	12	.138	-2	-34	-35	-0	-3.2

● **WES GARDNER** — Gardner, Wesley Brian b: 4/29/61, Benton, Ark. BR/TR, 6'4", 197 lbs. Deb: 7/29/84

YEAR	TM/L	W	L	PCT	G	GS	CG	SH	SV	IP	H	HR	BB	SO	RAT	ERA	ERA+	OAV	OOB	BH	AVG	PB	PR	/A	PD	TPI
1984	NY-N	1	1	.500	21	0	0	0	0	25¹	34	3	8	19	14.9	6.39	55	.321	.368	0	.000	-0	-8	-8	-0	-0.7
1985	NY-N	0	2	.000	9	0	0	0	0	12	18	1	8	11	19.5	5.25	66	.375	.464	0	—	-0	-2	-2	-0	-0.3
1986	Bos-A	0	0	—	1	0	0	0	0	1	1	0	0	1	9.0	9.00	46	.333	.333	0	—	-0	-1	-1	-0	0.0
1987	Bos-A	3	6	.333	49	1	0	0	10	89²	98	17	42	70	14.3	5.42	84	.279	.359	0	—	0	-10	-9	-1	-1.2
1988	*Bos-A	8	6	.571	36	18	1	0	0	149	119	17	64	106	11.2	3.50	117	.220	.305	0	—	0	8	10	-0	0.8
1989	Bos-A	3	7	.300	22	16	0	0	0	86	97	10	47	81	15.2	5.97	69	.287	.376	0	—	0	-20	-18	-2	-2.2
1990	Bos-A	3	3	.300	34	9	0	0	0	77¹	77	6	35	58	13.3	4.89	83	.259	.341	0	—	0	-8	-7	-1	-1.0
1991	SD-N	0	1	.000	14	0	0	0	0	20¹	27	1	12	9	17.3	7.08	54	.310	.394	0	.000	-0	-8	-7	-0	-0.4
	KC-A	0	0	—	3	0	0	0	0	5²	5	0	2	3	11.1	1.59	259	.208	.269	0	—	0	2	2	0	0.0
Total 8		18	30	.375	189	44	1	0	14	466¹	476	52	218	358	13.5	4.90	84	.265	.347	0	.000	-0	-47	-40	-2	-5.0

● **BILL GARDNER** — Gardner, William A. b: 9/1868, Baltimore, Md. Deb: 8/9/1887

YEAR	TM/L	W	L	PCT	G	GS	CG	SH	SV	IP	H	HR	BB	SO	RAT	ERA	ERA+	OAV	OOB	BH	AVG	PB	PR	/A	PD	TPI
1887	Bal-a	0	1	.000	3	2	1	0	0	13	23	1	0	3	23.5	11.08	37	.426	.523	3	.273	0	-10	-10	-0	-0.5

● **BILL GARFIELD** — Garfield, William Milton b: 10/26/1867, Sheffield, Ohio d: 12/16/41, Danville, Ill. BR/TR, 5'11.5", 160 lbs. Deb: 7/10/1889

YEAR	TM/L	W	L	PCT	G	GS	CG	SH	SV	IP	H	HR	BB	SO	RAT	ERA	ERA+	OAV	OOB	BH	AVG	PB	PR	/A	PD	TPI
1889	Pit-N	0	2	.000	4	2	2	0	0	29	45	2	17	4	19.6	7.76	48	.344	.423	0	.000	-2	-12	-13	-0	-0.8
1890	Cle-N	1	7	.125	9	8	2	0	0	70	91	3	35	16	17.9	4.89	73	.305	.393	4	.154	-1	-10	-10	-0	-1.0
Total 2		1	9	.100	13	10	9	0	0	99	136	5	52	20	17.9	5.73	63	.317	.402	4	.103	-3	-22	-23	-0	-1.8

● **BOB GARIBALDI** — Garibaldi, Robert Roy b: 3/3/42, Stockton, Cal. BL/TR, 6'4", 210 lbs. Deb: 7/15/62

YEAR	TM/L	W	L	PCT	G	GS	CG	SH	SV	IP	H	HR	BB	SO	RAT	ERA	ERA+	OAV	OOB	BH	AVG	PB	PR	/A	PD	TPI
1962	SF-N	0	0	—	9	0	0	0	1	12¹	13	1	5	9	13.1	5.11	74	.265	.333	0	.000	-0	-2	-2	0	0.0
1963	SF-N	0	1	.000	4	0	0	0	0	8	8	0	4	4	14.6	1.13	284	.276	.382	0	.000	0	2	2	0	0.3
1966	SF-N	0	0	—	1	0	0	0	0	1	1	0	2	0	9.0	0.00	—	.250	.250	0	—	0	0	0	0	0.0
1969	SF-N	0	1	.000	1	1	0	0	1	5	6	0	2	1	14.4	1.80	194	.316	.381	0	.000	-0	1	1	0	0.2
Total 4		0	2	.000	15	1	0	0	2	26¹	28	1	11	14	13.7	3.08	116	.277	.354	0	.000	-0	2	1	0	0.5

● **LOU GARLAND** — Garland, Louis Lyman b: 7/16/05, Archie, Mo. d: 8/30/90, Idaho Falls, Idaho BR/TR, 6'2.5", 200 lbs. Deb: 8/31/31

YEAR	TM/L	W	L	PCT	G	GS	CG	SH	SV	IP	H	HR	BB	SO	RAT	ERA	ERA+	OAV	OOB	BH	AVG	PB	PR	/A	PD	TPI
1931	Chi-A	0	2	.000	7	2	0	0	0	16²	30	2	14	4	24.3	10.26	41	.400	.500	0	.000	-0	-11	-11	1	-1.0

● **WAYNE GARLAND** — Garland, Marcus Wayne b: 10/26/50, Nashville, Tenn. BR/TR, 6', 195 lbs. Deb: 9/13/73

YEAR	TM/L	W	L	PCT	G	GS	CG	SH	SV	IP	H	HR	BB	SO	RAT	ERA	ERA+	OAV	OOB	BH	AVG	PB	PR	/A	PD	TPI
1973	Bal-A	0	1	.000	4	1	0	0	0	16	14	1	7	10	11.8	3.94	95	.233	.313	0	—	0	-0	-0	-0	0.0
1974	*Bal-A	5	5	.500	20	6	0	0	1	91	68	5	26	40	9.6	2.97	116	.211	.276	0	—	0	7	5	-1	0.6
1975	Bal-A	2	5	.286	29	1	0	0	0	87¹	80	7	31	46	11.5	3.71	95	.252	.321	0	—	0	1	-0	-0	0.0
1976	Bal-A	20	7	.741	38	25	14	4	1	232¹	224	10	64	113	11.4	2.67	122	.255	.309	0	—	0	22	15	2	2.1
1977	Cle-A	13	19	.406	38	38	21	1	0	282²	281	23	88	118	11.8	3.60	110	.261	.318	0	—	0	14	11	-0	1.1
1978	Cle-A	2	3	.400	6	6	0	0	0	29²	43	6	16	13	18.2	7.89	47	.347	.426	0	—	0	-14	-14	-1	-1.8
1979	Cle-A	4	10	.286	18	14	2	0	0	94²	120	11	34	40	14.9	5.23	81	.318	.379	0	—	0	-11	-10	-1	-1.4
1980	Cle-A	6	9	.400	25	20	4	1	0	150¹	163	18	48	55	13.0	4.61	88	.276	.337	0	—	0	-10	-9	-1	-0.9
1981	Cle-A	3	7	.300	12	10	2	1	0	56	69	8	14	15	16.6	5.79	63	.374	.409	0	—	0	-13	-13	-0	-2.0
Total 9		55	66	.455	190	121	43	7	6	1040	1082	89	328	450	12.4	3.89	96	.272	.330	0	—	0	-4	-18	-2	-2.3

● **MIKE GARMAN** — Garman, Michael Douglas b: 9/16/49, Caldwell, Idaho BR/TR, 6'3", 215 lbs. Deb: 9/22/69

YEAR	TM/L	W	L	PCT	G	GS	CG	SH	SV	IP	H	HR	BB	SO	RAT	ERA	ERA+	OAV	OOB	BH	AVG	PB	PR	/A	PD	TPI
1969	Bos-A	1	0	1.000	2	2	0	0	0	12¹	13	0	10	10	16.8	4.38	87	.277	.404	2	.400	1	-1	-1	0	0.0
1971	Bos-A	1	1	.500	3	3	0	0	0	18²	15	3	9	6	12.1	3.86	96	.217	.316	2	.333	0	-1	-0	-1	-0.1
1972	Bos-A	0	1	.000	3	1	0	0	0	3¹	4	1	2	1	16.2	10.80	30	.286	.375	0	—	0	-3	-3	-0	-0.7
1973	Bos-A	0	0	—	12	0	0	0	0	22	32	1	15	19	19.2	5.32	76	.352	.443	0	—	0	-4	-3	-0	-0.4
1974	StL-N	7	2	.778	64	0	0	0	6	81²	66	4	27	45	10.5	2.64	135	.227	.297	1	.100	-1	9	8	0	1.0
1975	StL-N	3	8	.273	66	0	0	0	10	79	73	4	48	48	13.9	2.39	157	.245	.352	0	.000	-0	11	12	-1	1.8
1976	Chi-N	2	4	.333	47	2	0	0	0	76¹	79	7	35	37	13.8	4.95	78	.273	.358	0	—	-1	-12	-9	-0	-0.8
1977	*LA-N	4	4	.500	49	0	0	0	12	62²	60	7	22	29	12.1	2.73	140	.254	.323	0	—	-1	8	8	-1	1.1
1978	LA-N	0	1	.000	10	0	0	0	0	16¹	15	3	3	9	9.9	4.41	80	.259	.295	0	—	-0	-2	-2	-0	-0.1
	Mon-N	4	6	.400	47	0	0	0	13	61¹	54	5	31	23	12.5	4.40	80	.238	.329	0	.000	-1	-6	-6	-0	-1.3
	Yr	4	7	.364	57	0	0	0	13	77²	69	8	34	32	11.8	4.40	80	.242	.323	0	—	-1	-7	-8	-1	-1.4
Total 9		22	27	.449	303	8	0	0	42	433²	411	34	202	213	12.9	3.63	102	.254	.340	5	.119	-2	-0	4	-3	0.5

● **WILLIE GARONI** — Garoni, William b: 7/28/1877, Ft.Lee, N.J. d: 9/9/14, Ft.Lee, N.J. BR/TR, 6'1", 165 lbs. Deb: 9/7/1899

YEAR	TM/L	W	L	PCT	G	GS	CG	SH	SV	IP	H	HR	BB	SO	RAT	ERA	ERA+	OAV	OOB	BH	AVG	PB	PR	/A	PD	TPI
1899	NY-N	0	1	.000	3	1	0	0	0	10	12	0	2	2	12.6	4.50	83	.300	.333	0	.000	-1	-1	-1	0	-0.1

YEAR TM/L	W	L	PCT	G	GS	CG	SH	SV	IP	H	HR	BB	SO	RAT	ERA	ERA+	OAV	OOB	BH	AVG	PB	PR	/A	PD	TPI

● **SCOTT GARRELTS** Garrelts, Scott William b: 10/30/61, Urbana, Ill. BR/TR, 6'4", 195 lbs. Deb: 10/2/82

YEAR TM/L	W	L	PCT	G	GS	CG	SH	SV	IP	H	HR	BB	SO	RAT	ERA	ERA+	OAV	OOB	BH	AVG	PB	PR	/A	PD	TPI
1982 SF-N	0	0	—	1	0	0	0	0	2	3	0	2	4	22.5	13.50	27	.333	.455	0	—	0	-2	-2	0	0.0
1983 SF-N	2	2	.500	5	5	1	1	0	35²	33	4	19	16	13.6	2.52	140	.254	.358	2	.222	0	4	4	0	0.5
1984 SF-N	2	3	.400	21	3	0	0	0	43	45	6	34	32	16.7	5.65	62	.274	.402	1	.100	-0	-10	-10	-1	-1.2
1985 SF-N☆	9	6	.600	74	0	0	0	13	105²	76	2	58	106	11.7	2.30	149	.198	.308	2	.222	1	15	13	2	2.4
1986 SF-N	13	9	.591	53	18	2	0	10	173²	144	17	74	125	11.4	3.11	113	.231	.314	8	.178	2	12	8	2	1.5
1987 *SF-N	11	7	.611	64	0	0	0	12	106¹	70	10	55	127	10.6	3.22	119	.192	.298	2	.200	1	10	7	-1	1.3
1988 SF-N	5	9	.357	65	0	0	0	13	98	80	3	46	86	11.8	3.58	91	.226	.318	1	.077	-1	-1	-3	-1	-0.7
1989 *SF-N	14	5	.737	30	29	2	1	0	193¹	149	11	46	119	**9.1**	2.28	148	.212	**.260**	9	.136	1	26	23	-0	2.3
1990 SF-N	12	11	.522	31	31	4	2	0	182	190	16	70	80	13.0	4.15	88	.272	.341	4	.061	-3	-7	-10	-1	-1.6
1991 SF-N	1	1	.500	8	3	0	0	0	19²	25	5	9	8	15.6	6.41	56	.313	.391	0	.000	-0	-6	-6	-0	-0.6
Total 10	69	53	.566	352	89	9	4	48	959¹	815	74	413	703	11.6	3.29	107	.232	.315	29	.125	-1	41	24	1	3.9

● **CLARENCE GARRETT** Garrett, Clarence Raymond "Laz" b: 3/6/1891, Reader, W.Va. d: 2/11/77, Moundsville, W.Va. BR/TR, 6'5.5", 185 lbs. Deb: 9/13/15

YEAR TM/L	W	L	PCT	G	GS	CG	SH	SV	IP	H	HR	BB	SO	RAT	ERA	ERA+	OAV	OOB	BH	AVG	PB	PR	/A	PD	TPI
1915 Cle-A	2	2	.500	4	4	2	0	0	23¹	19	1	6	5	10.0	2.31	132	.224	.283	0	.000	-0	2	2	1	0.4

● **GREG GARRETT** Garrett, Gregory b: 3/12/48, Atascadero, Cal. BB/TL, 6', 200 lbs. Deb: 4/24/70

YEAR TM/L	W	L	PCT	G	GS	CG	SH	SV	IP	H	HR	BB	SO	RAT	ERA	ERA+	OAV	OOB	BH	AVG	PB	PR	/A	PD	TPI
1970 Cal-A	5	6	.455	32	7	0	0	0	74²	48	6	44	53	11.2	2.65	136	.190	.312	1	.067	-1	9	8	-0	1.0
1971 Cin-N	0	1	.000	2	1	0	0	0	8²	7	0	10	2	17.7	1.04	323	.250	.447	1	.333	0	2	2	-0	0.3
Total 2	5	7	.417	34	8	0	0	0	83¹	55	6	54	55	11.9	2.48	144	.196	.320	2	.111	-1	11	10	-0	1.3

● **CLIFF GARRISON** Garrison, Clifford William b: 8/13/06, Belmont, Okla. d: 8/25/94, Woodland, Cal. BR/TR, 6', 180 lbs. Deb: 4/16/28

YEAR TM/L	W	L	PCT	G	GS	CG	SH	SV	IP	H	HR	BB	SO	RAT	ERA	ERA+	OAV	OOB	BH	AVG	PB	PR	/A	PD	TPI
1928 Bos-A	0	0	—	6	0	0	0	0	16	22	2	6	0	15.8	7.88	52	.361	.418	0	.000	-0	-7	-7	1	0.0

● **JIM GARRY** Garry, James Thomas b: 9/21/1869, Great Barrington, Mass. d: 1/15/17, Pittsfield, Mass. TL, Deb: 5/2/1893

YEAR TM/L	W	L	PCT	G	GS	CG	SH	SV	IP	H	HR	BB	SO	RAT	ERA	ERA+	OAV	OOB	BH	AVG	PB	PR	/A	PD	TPI
1893 Bos-N	0	1	.000	1	1	0	0	0	5	4	2	4	2	81.0	63.00	8	.625	.750	0	.000	-0	-6	-6	0	-2.1

● **NED GARVER** Garver, Ned Franklin b: 12/25/25, Ney, Ohio BR/TR, 5'10.5", 180 lbs. Deb: 4/28/48

YEAR TM/L	W	L	PCT	G	GS	CG	SH	SV	IP	H	HR	BB	SO	RAT	ERA	ERA+	OAV	OOB	BH	AVG	PB	PR	/A	PD	TPI
1948 StL-A	7	11	.389	38	24	7	0	5	198	200	14	95	75	13.5	3.41	134	.268	.352	19	.288	4	19	25	1	2.7
1949 StL-A	12	17	.414	41	32	16	1	3	223²	245	14	102	70	14.1	3.98	114	.277	.354	14	.187	1	5	14	0	1.8
1950 StL-A	13	18	.419	37	31	**22**	2	0	260	264	18	108	85	13.0	3.39	**146**	.264	.338	26	.286	4	**34**	**45**	2	**5.7**
1951 StL-A★	20	12	.625	33	30	**24**	1	0	246	237	17	96	84	12.4	3.73	118	.255	.328	29	.305	7	11	18	1	3.1
1952 StL-A	7	10	.412	21	21	7	2	0	148²	130	14	55	60	11.4	3.69	106	.235	.309	9	.184	-0	-4	-4	-0	0.4
Det-A	1	0	1.000	1	1	1	0	0	9	9	1	3	3	12.0	2.00	190	.265	.324	0	.000	0	2	2	0	0.3
Yr	8	10	.444	22	22	8	2	0	157²	139	15	58	63	11.2	3.60	109	.235	.304	9	.176	0	1	5	0	0.7
1953 Det-A	11	11	.500	30	26	13	0	1	198¹	228	16	66	69	13.4	4.45	91	.290	.347	11	.153	-1	-10	-8	-1	-0.8
1954 Det-A	14	11	.560	35	32	16	3	1	246¹	216	20	62	93	10.3	2.81	131	.236	.287	13	.165	-0	25	24	2	2.5
1955 Det-A	12	16	.429	33	32	16	1	0	230²	251	21	67	77	12.6	3.98	97	.279	.333	17	.224	5	-4	-4	-0	0.1
1956 Det-A	0	2	.000	6	3	1	0	0	17²	15	2	13	6	14.8	4.08	101	.234	.372	0	.000	-0	0	0	1	0.0
1957 KC-A	6	13	.316	24	23	6	1	0	145¹	120	13	55	61	11.1	3.84	103	.223	.301	8	.182	0	-1	2	-0	0.2
1958 KC-A	12	11	.522	31	28	10	3	1	201	192	24	66	72	11.6	4.03	97	.244	.304	12	.174	1	-6	-3	5	0.3
1959 KC-A	10	13	.435	32	30	9	2	1	201¹	214	22	42	61	11.6	3.71	108	.270	.309	20	.282	6	3	7	-0	1.3
1960 KC-A	4	9	.308	28	15	5	2	0	122¹	110	15	35	50	10.8	3.83	104	.240	.296	2	.074	-1	1	2	-0	0.1
1961 LA-A	0	3	.000	12	2	0	0	0	29	40	4	16	9	17.4	5.59	81	.348	.427	0	.000	-1	-5	-3	1	-0.3
Total 14	129	157	.451	402	330	153	18	12	2477¹	2471	213	881	881	12.3	3.73	112	.260	.325	180	.218	24	78	122	14	17.4

● **JERRY GARVIN** Garvin, Theodore Jared b: 10/21/55, Oakland, Cal. BL/TL, 6'3", 195 lbs. Deb: 4/10/77

YEAR TM/L	W	L	PCT	G	GS	CG	SH	SV	IP	H	HR	BB	SO	RAT	ERA	ERA+	OAV	OOB	BH	AVG	PB	PR	/A	PD	TPI
1977 Tor-A	10	18	.357	34	34	12	1	0	244²	247	33	85	127	12.4	4.19	100	.264	.328	0	—	0	-4	0	5	0.4
1978 Tor-A	4	12	.250	26	22	3	0	0	144²	189	20	48	67	15.0	5.54	71	.319	.374	0	—	0	-29	-26	1	-2.5
1979 Tor-A	0	1	.000	8	1	0	0	0	22²	15	2	10	14	10.7	2.78	156	.197	.307	0	—	0	4	4	-0	0.1
1980 Tor-A	4	7	.364	61	0	0	0	8	82²	70	6	27	52	10.6	2.29	188	.233	.296	0	—	0	16	19	1	2.7
1981 Tor-A	1	2	.333	35	4	0	0	0	53	46	3	23	25	11.7	3.40	116	.240	.321	0	—	0	2	3	0	0.2
1982 Tor-A	1	1	.500	32	4	0	0	0	58¹	81	10	26	35	16.7	7.25	62	.335	.401	0	—	0	-21	-18	2	-1.0
Total 6	20	41	.328	196	65	15	1	8	606	648	74	219	320	13.0	4.43	94	.277	.342	0	—	0	-32	-18	9	-0.1

● **NED GARVIN** Garvin, Virgil Lee b: 1/1/1874, Navasota, Tex. d: 6/16/08, Fresno, Cal. TR, 6'3.5", 160 lbs. Deb: 7/13/1896

YEAR TM/L	W	L	PCT	G	GS	CG	SH	SV	IP	H	HR	BB	SO	RAT	ERA	ERA+	OAV	OOB	BH	AVG	PB	PR	/A	PD	TPI
1896 Phi-N	0	1	.000	2	1	1	0	0	13	19	0	7	4	18.0	7.62	57	.339	.413	0	.000	-1	-5	-5	-0	-0.4
1899 Chi-N	9	13	.409	24	23	22	4	0	199	202	1	42	69	11.6	2.85	132	.263	.311	11	.155	-5	22	20	1	1.5
1900 Chi-N	10	18	.357	30	28	25	1	0	246¹	225	4	63	107	11.2	2.41	150	.243	.304	14	.154	-5	**35**	33	4	3.1
1901 Mil-A	7	20	.259	37	27	22	1	2	257¹	258	6	90	122	12.7	3.46	104	.258	.328	10	.108	-9	6	4	-0	-0.2
1902 Chi-A	10	10	.500	23	19	16	2	0	175¹	169	3	43	55	11.3	2.21	153	.254	.307	9	.153	-2	27	23	3	2.4
Bro-N	1	1	.500	2	2	1	0	0	18	15	0	4	7	9.5	1.00	276	.227	.271	1	.143	-0	4	4	0	0.2
1903 Bro-N	15	18	.455	38	34	30	2	2	298	277	2	84	154	11.3	3.08	104	.248	.308	8	.075	-8	6	4	0	0.2
1904 Bro-N	5	15	.250	23	22	16	2	0	181²	141	6	78	86	11.1	1.68	163	.218	.308	8	.127	-4	21	21	4	2.4
NY-A	1	0	1.000	2	1	1	0	0	12	14	0	2	8	12.0	2.25	121	.292	.320	0	.000	-1	0	1	1	0.1
Total 7	57	97	.370	181	158	134	13	4	1400²	1320	20	413	612	11.6	2.72	125	.249	.312	61	.122	-35	117	104	24	9.5

● **HARRY GASPAR** Gaspar, Harry Lambert b: 4/28/1883, Kingsley, Iowa d: 5/14/40, Orange, Cal. BR/TR, 6', 180 lbs. Deb: 4/21/09

YEAR TM/L	W	L	PCT	G	GS	CG	SH	SV	IP	H	HR	BB	SO	RAT	ERA	ERA+	OAV	OOB	BH	AVG	PB	PR	/A	PD	TPI
1909 Cin-N	19	11	.633	44	29	19	4	2	260	228	0	57	65	10.2	2.01	129	.242	.291	10	.122	-3	17	17	-5	1.1
1910 Cin-N	15	17	.469	48	31	16	4	**7**	275	257	6	75	74	11.4	2.59	113	.255	.317	10	.115	-3	14	10	-2	0.6
1911 Cin-N	11	17	.393	44	32	11	2	4	253²	272	9	69	76	12.6	3.30	100	.283	.340	13	.153	-2	3	-0	-1	-0.4
1912 Cin-N	1	3	.250	7	6	2	1	0	36²	38	0	16	13	13.5	4.17	81	.277	.357	3	.250	-1	-3	-3	-0	-0.3
Total 4	46	48	.489	143	98	48	11	13	825¹	795	15	217	228	11.5	2.69	110	.261	.318	36	.135	-9	31	24	-8	1.0

● **CHARLIE GASSAWAY** Gassaway, Charles Cason "Sheriff" b: 8/12/18, Gassaway, Ga. d: 1/15/92, Miami, Fla. BL/TL, 6'2.5", 210 lbs. Deb: 9/25/44

YEAR TM/L	W	L	PCT	G	GS	CG	SH	SV	IP	H	HR	BB	SO	RAT	ERA	ERA+	OAV	OOB	BH	AVG	PB	PR	/A	PD	TPI
1944 Chi-N	0	1	.000	2	2	0	0	0	11²	20	3	10	7	23.1	7.71	46	.385	.484	1	.250	-0	-5	-5	-0	-0.4
1945 Phi-A	4	7	.364	24	11	4	0	0	118	114	4	55	50	13.0	3.74	92	.252	.336	6	.154	-2	-5	-4	-1	-0.7
1946 Cle-A	1	1	.500	13	6	0	0	0	50²	54	2	26	23	14.9	3.91	85	.273	.368	1	.067	-1	-2	-3	0	-0.2
Total 3	5	9	.357	39	19	4	0	0	180¹	188	9	91	80	14.2	4.04	84	.268	.357	8	.138	-3	-12	-13	-2	-1.3

● **MILT GASTON** Gaston, Nathaniel Milton b: 1/27/1896, Ridgefield Park, N.J. d: 4/26/96, Hyannis, Mass. BR/TR, 6'1", 185 lbs. Deb: 4/20/24 F

YEAR TM/L	W	L	PCT	G	GS	CG	SH	SV	IP	H	HR	BB	SO	RAT	ERA	ERA+	OAV	OOB	BH	AVG	PB	PR	/A	PD	TPI
1924 NY-A	5	3	.625	29	2	0	0	1	86	92	3	44	24	14.9	4.50	92	.286	.382	1	.222	-1	-3	-3	-1	-0.5
1925 StL-A	15	14	.517	42	29	16	0	1	238²	284	8	101	84	14.7	4.41	106	.305	.376	21	.262	2	-0	7	-2	0.8
1926 StL-A	10	18	.357	32	28	14	1	0	214¹	227	13	101	39	13.9	4.33	99	.283	.366	13	.167	-2	-7	-1	-1	-0.3
1927 StL-A	13	17	.433	37	30	21	0	1	254	257	18	100	77	13.4	5.00	87	.281	.350	25	.260	5	-24	-18	1	-1.2
1928 Was-A	6	12	.333	28	22	8	3	0	148²	179	4	53	45	14.0	5.51	73	.302	.360	7	.143	-3	-24	-25	1	-2.7
1929 Bos-A	12	19	.387	39	29	20	1	0	243²	265	15	81	83	12.9	3.73	115	.289	.348	15	.192	0	14	15	-1	1.6
1930 Bos-A	13	20	.394	38	34	20	2	2	273	272	16	98	99	12.2	3.92	117	.259	.323	20	.204	-4	22	21	1	1.9
1931 Bos-A	2	13	.133	23	18	4	0	0	119	137	4	41	33	13.5	4.46	96	.291	.348	6	.158	-2	-1	-2	-0	-0.4
1932 Chi-A	7	17	.292	28	25	7	1	1	166²	183	10	73	44	13.9	4.00	108	.279	.332	14	.233	2	9	6	2	1.1
1933 Chi-A	12	8	.400	30	25	7	1	0	167	170	6	60	39	12.8	4.85	87	.272	.334	8	.154	-0	-11	-11	-1	-1.2
1934 Chi-A	6	19	.240	29	28	10	1	0	194	247	16	84	48	15.4	5.85	81	.313	.379	10	.147	-3	-29	-24	0	-2.5
Total 11	97	164	.372	355	270	127	10	8	2105	2338	114	836	615	13.7	4.55	97	.287	.355	145	.200	-5	-54	-35	0	-3.4

● **WELCOME GASTON** Gaston, Welcome Thornburg b: 12/19/1872, Guernsey Co., Ohio d: 12/13/44, Columbus, Ohio TL, Deb: 10/6/1898

YEAR TM/L	W	L	PCT	G	GS	CG	SH	SV	IP	H	HR	BB	SO	RAT	ERA	ERA+	OAV	OOB	BH	AVG	PB	PR	/A	PD	TPI
1898 Bro-N	1	1	.500	2	2	2	0	0	16	17	0	9	0	14.6	2.81	128	.270	.361	1	.125	-0	1	1	-0	0.1
1899 Bro-N	0	0	—	1	0	0	0	0	3	3	0	4	0	24.0	3.00	130	.250	.471	1	1.000	-0	1	0	0	0.1
Total 2	1	1	.500	3	2	2	0	0	19	20	0	13	0	16.1	2.84	128	.267	.382	2	.222	1	2	1	-0	0.2

● **HANK GASTRIGHT** Gastright, Henry Carl (b: Henry Carl Gastreich) b: 3/29/1865, Covington, Ky. d: 10/9/37, Cold Spring, Ky. BR/TR, 6'2", 190 lbs. Deb: 4/19/1889

YEAR TM/L	W	L	PCT	G	GS	CG	SH	SV	IP	H	HR	BB	SO	RAT	ERA	ERA+	OAV	OOB	BH	AVG	PB	PR	/A	PD	TPI
1889 Col-a	10	16	.385	32	26	21	0	1	222²	255	8	104	115	14.7	4.57	79	.279	.355	17	.181	-4	-18	-23	-0	-2.4

YEAR	TM/L	W	L	PCT	G	GS	CG	SH	SV	IP	H	HR	BB	SO	RAT	ERA	ERA+	OAV	OOB	BH	AVG	PB	PR	/A	PD	TPI
1890	Col-a	30	14	.682	48	45	41	4	0	401^1	312	8	135	199	10.4	2.94	122	.208	.281	36	.213	3	42	29	-4	2.4
1891	Col-a	12	19	.387	35	33	28	1	0	283^2	280	7	136	109	13.5	3.78	92	.249	.336	23	.197	2	-2	-10	1	-0.6
1892	Was-N	3	3	.500	11	8	6	0	0	79^2	94	3	38	32	15.3	5.08	64	.282	.361	4	.138	-4	-16	-16	-1	-1.1
1893	Pit-N	3	1	.750	9	5	3	0	0	59	74	3	39	12	17.7	6.25	73	.297	.399	1	.042	-4	-10	-11	1	-0.8
	Bos-N	12	4	.750	19	18	16	0	0	156	179	9	76	27	15.2	5.13	96	.279	.364	13	.191	-3	-8	-3	-2	-0.6
	Yr	15	5	**.750**	28	23	19	0	0	215	253	12	115	39	15.8	5.44	89	.283	.371	14	.152	-6	-19	-15	-1	-1.4
1894	Bro-N	2	6	.250	16	8	6	1	2	93	135	1	55	20	19.0	6.39	77	.335	.422	7	.171	-3	-11	-15	-1	-1.2
1896	Cin-N	0	0	—	1	0	0	0	0	6	8	0	1	3	13.5	4.50	102	.320	.346	0	.000	-0	-0	-0	-0	0.0
Total 7		72	63	.533	171	143	121	6	2	1301^1	1337	39	584	514	13.7	4.20	92	.258	.339	101	.186	-8	-23	-51	-7	-4.3

● **AUBREY GATEWOOD**   Gatewood, Aubrey Lee   b: 11/17/38, Little Rock, Ark.   BR/TR, 6'1", 170 lbs.   Deb: 9/11/63

YEAR	TM/L	W	L	PCT	G	GS	CG	SH	SV	IP	H	HR	BB	SO	RAT	ERA	ERA+	OAV	OOB	BH	AVG	PB	PR	/A	PD	TPI
1963	LA-A	1	1	.500	4	3	1	0	0	24	12	0	16	13	10.5	1.50	228	.148	.289	0	.000	-1	6	5	-0	0.3
1964	LA-A	3	3	.500	15	7	0	0	0	60^1	59	4	12	25	10.7	2.24	147	.258	.298	2	.100	-1	9	7	-0	0.5
1965	Cal-A	4	5	.444	46	3	0	0	0	92	91	5	37	37	12.6	3.42	90	.266	.339	3	.214	1	-0	-0	-1	0.0
1970	Atl-N	0	0	—	3	0	0	0	0	2	4	0	2	0	31.5	4.50	95	.364	.500	0	—	-0	-0	-0	-0	0.0
Total 4		8	9	.471	68	13	1	0	0	178^1	166	9	67	75	11.9	2.78	122	.250	.322	5	.119	-1	15	12	-1	0.8

● **CHIPPY GAW**   Gaw, George Joseph   b: 3/13/1892, W.Newton, Mass.   d: 5/26/68, Boston, Mass.   BR/TR, 5'11", 180 lbs.   Deb: 4/20/20

YEAR	TM/L	W	L	PCT	G	GS	CG	SH	SV	IP	H	HR	BB	SO	RAT	ERA	ERA+	OAV	OOB	BH	AVG	PB	PR	/A	PD	TPI
1920	Chi-N	1	1	.500	6	1	0	0	0	13	16	1	3	4	13.8	4.85	66	.320	.370	1	.250	-0	-2	-2	-0	-0.4

● **DALE GEAR**   Gear, Dale Dudley   b: 2/2/1872, Lone Elm, Kan.   d: 9/23/51, Topeka, Kan.   BR/TR, 5'11", 165 lbs.   Deb: 8/15/1896 ♦

YEAR	TM/L	W	L	PCT	G	GS	CG	SH	SV	IP	H	HR	BB	SO	RAT	ERA	ERA+	OAV	OOB	BH	AVG	PB	PR	/A	PD	TPI
1896	Cle-N	0	2	.000	3	2	2	0	0	23	35	1	6	6	16.8	5.48	83	.347	.394	6	.400		-3	-2		-0.1
1901	Was-A	4	11	.267	24	16	14	1	1	163	199	9	22	35	12.4	4.03	91	.297	.324	47	.236	0	-4	-7	2	-0.3
Total 2		4	13	.235	27	18	16	1	1	186	234	10	28	41	13.0	4.21	90	.304	.333	57	.239	2	-9	-9	2	-0.4

● **DINTY GEARIN**   Gearin, Dennis John   b: 10/15/1897, Providence, R.I.   d: 3/11/59, Providence, R.I.   BL/TL, 5'4", 148 lbs.   Deb: 8/6/23

YEAR	TM/L	W	L	PCT	G	GS	CG	SH	SV	IP	H	HR	BB	SO	RAT	ERA	ERA+	OAV	OOB	BH	AVG	PB	PR	/A	PD	TPI
1923	*NY-N	1	1	.500	6	2	1	0	0	24	23	1	10	9	12.4	3.38	113	.264	.340	2	.286	0	-2	-1	-0	0.1
1924	NY-N	1	2	.333	6	3	2	0	0	29	30	3	16	4	14.3	2.48	148	.275	.368	3	.333	0	4	4	-0	0.4
	Bos-N	0	1	.000	1	1	0	0	0	0	3	0	2	0	—	∞	—	1.000	1.000	0	—	0	-5	-5	0	-0.4
	Yr	1	3	.250	7	4	2	0	0	29	33	3	18	4	15.8	4.03	91	.295	.392	3	.333	0	-1	-1	-0	0.0
Total 2		2	4	.333	13	6	3	0	0	53	56	4	28	13	14.3	3.74	100	.281	.370	5	.313	1	0	-1	-0	0.1

● **BOB GEARY**   Geary, Robert Norton "Speed"   b: 5/10/1891, Cincinnati, Ohio   d: 1/3/80, Cincinnati, Ohio   BR/TR, 5'11", 168 lbs.   Deb: 4/25/18

YEAR	TM/L	W	L	PCT	G	GS	CG	SH	SV	IP	H	HR	BB	SO	RAT	ERA	ERA+	OAV	OOB	BH	AVG	PB	PR	/A	PD	TPI
1918	Phi-A	2	5	.286	16	7	6	2	4	87	94	0	31	24	13.2	2.69	109	.289	.357	4	.148	-1	1	2	-1	0.1
1919	Phi-A	0	3	.000	9	2	1	0	0	32^1	32	1	18	9	13.9	4.73	72	.264	.360	5	.500	2	-5	-5	-0	-0.2
1921	Cin-N	1	1	.500	10	1	0	0	0	29	38	1	2	10	12.4	4.34	82	.333	.345	2	.250	-0	-2	-0		-0.2
Total 3		3	9	.250	35	10	7	2	4	148^1	164	2	51	41	13.2	3.46	92	.293	.355	11	.244	1	-6	-5	-1	-0.3

● **BOB GEBHARD**   Gebhard, Robert Henry   b: 1/3/43, Lamberton, Minn.   BR/TR, 6'2", 210 lbs.   Deb: 8/2/71   C

YEAR	TM/L	W	L	PCT	G	GS	CG	SH	SV	IP	H	HR	BB	SO	RAT	ERA	ERA+	OAV	OOB	BH	AVG	PB	PR	/A	PD	TPI
1971	Min-A	1	2	.333	17	0	0	0	0	18	17	0	11	14	14.5	3.00	118	.243	.354	0	—	0	1	1	1	0.3
1972	Min-A	0	1	.000	13	0	0	0	0	21	36	3	13	13	21.9	8.57	57	.371	.455	0	—	0	-13	-13	1	-0.6
1974	Mon-N	0	0	—	1	0	0	0	0	2	5	1	0	2	22.5	4.50	85	.500	.500	0	—	-0	-0	-0	-0	0.0
Total 3		1	3	.250	31	0	0	0	1	41	58	4	24	26	18.7	5.93	57	.328	.417	0	—	0	-12	-12	1	-0.3

● **PETE GEBRIAN**   Gebrian, Peter "Gabe"   b: 8/10/23, Bayonne, N.J.   BR/TR, 6', 170 lbs.   Deb: 5/6/47

YEAR	TM/L	W	L	PCT	G	GS	CG	SH	SV	IP	H	HR	BB	SO	RAT	ERA	ERA+	OAV	OOB	BH	AVG	PB	PR	/A	PD	TPI
1947	Chi-A	2	3	.400	27	4	0	0	5	66^1	61	7	33	17	13.0	4.48	82	.247	.340	0	.000	-2	-6	-6	-1	-0.8

● **JIM GEDDES**   Geddes, James Lee   b: 3/23/49, Columbus, Ohio   BR/TR, 6'2", 200 lbs.   Deb: 4/28/72

YEAR	TM/L	W	L	PCT	G	GS	CG	SH	SV	IP	H	HR	BB	SO	RAT	ERA	ERA+	OAV	OOB	BH	AVG	PB	PR	/A	PD	TPI
1972	Chi-A	0	0	—	5	1	0	0	0	10^1	12	1	10	3	20.0	6.97	45	.293	.442	0	.000	-0	-4	-4	-0	0.0
1973	Chi-A	0	0	—	6	1	0	0	0	15^2	14	0	14	7	17.8	2.87	138	.255	.431	0	—	0	2	2	0	0.0
Total 2		0	0	—	11	2	0	0	0	26	26	1	24	10	18.7	4.50	81	.271	.435	0	.000	-0	-3	-3	0	0.0

● **JOE GEDEON**   Gedeon, Elmer Joseph   b: 12/5/1893, Sacramento, Cal.   d: 5/19/41, San Francisco, Cal   BR/TR, 6', 167 lbs.   Deb: 5/13/13 ♦

YEAR	TM/L	W	L	PCT	G	GS	CG	SH	SV	IP	H	HR	BB	SO	RAT	ERA	ERA+	OAV	OOB	BH	AVG	PB	PR	/A	PD	TPI
1913	Was-A	0	0	—	1	0	0	0	1	0^1	0	0	0	0	0.0	0.00	—	.000	.000	13	.183	0	0	0	0	0.1

● **COUNT GEDNEY**   Gedney, Alfred W.   b: 5/10/1849, Brooklyn, N.Y.   d: 3/26/22, Hackensack, N.J.   5'9", 140 lbs.   Deb: 4/27/1872 ♦

YEAR	TM/L	W	L	PCT	G	GS	CG	SH	SV	IP	H	HR	BB	SO	RAT	ERA	ERA+	OAV	OOB	BH	AVG	PB	PR	/A	PD	TPI
1875	Mut-n	1	0	1.000	2	1	1	0	0	11	7	0	1	2	6.5	0.82	285	.167	.186	55	.206	-0	2	2		0.2

● **JOHNNY GEE**   Gee, John Alexander "Whiz"   b: 12/7/15, Syracuse, N.Y.   d: 1/23/88, Cortland, N.Y.   BL/TL, 6'9", 225 lbs.   Deb: 9/17/39

YEAR	TM/L	W	L	PCT	G	GS	CG	SH	SV	IP	H	HR	BB	SO	RAT	ERA	ERA+	OAV	OOB	BH	AVG	PB	PR	/A	PD	TPI
1939	Pit-N	1	2	.333	3	3	1	0	0	19^2	20	0	10	16	13.7	4.12	93	.253	.337	0	.000	-1	-0	1	1	-0.1
1941	Pit-N	0	2	.000	4	4	0	0	0	7^1	10	0	10	8	18.4	6.14	59	.294	.385	1	.333	0	-2	-1	0	-0.5
1943	Pit-N	4	4	.500	15	10	4	1	0	82	89	6	27	18	12.7	4.28	81	.280	.336	3	.115	-1	-8	-7	-3	-1.0
1944	Pit-N	0	0	—	4	0	0	0	0	11^1	20	0	5	3	19.9	7.15	52	.377	.431	1	.500	0	-4	-4	-0	0.0
	NY-N	0	0	—	4	0	0	0	0	4^2	5	0	0	3	9.6	0.00	—	.263	.263	0	—	0	2	2	0	0.0
	Yr	0	0	—	8	0	0	0	0	16	25	0	5	6	16.9	5.06	73	.347	.390	1	.500	0	-3	-2	0	0.0
1945	NY-N	0	0	—	2	0	0	0	0	3	5	0	2	1	21.0	9.00	43	.385	.467	0	.000	-0	-2	-2	-0	-0.1
1946	NY-N	2	4	.333	13	6	0	0	0	47^1	60	3	15	22	14.6	3.99	86	.308	.363	3	.231	0	-3	-3	-1	-0.4
Total 6		7	12	.368	44	21	4	0	1	175^1	209	8	64	65	14.1	4.41	80	.294	.354	8	.157	-1	-18	-17	-3	-2.1

● **BILLY GEER**   Geer, William Henry Harrison (b: George Harrison Geer)   b: 8/13/1849, Syracuse, N.Y.   TR, 5'8", 160 lbs.   Deb: 10/15/1874 ♦

YEAR	TM/L	W	L	PCT	G	GS	CG	SH	SV	IP	H	HR	BB	SO	RAT	ERA	ERA+	OAV	OOB	BH	AVG	PB	PR	/A	PD	TPI
1884	Bro-a	0	0	—	2	0	0	0	0	5	14	0	3	1	30.6	12.60	26	.609	.654	82	.210	0	-5	-5	-0	0.0

● **HENRY GEHRING**   Gehring, Henry   b: 1/24/1881, St.Paul, Minn.   d: 4/18/12, Kansas City, Mo.   BR/TR,   Deb: 7/16/07

YEAR	TM/L	W	L	PCT	G	GS	CG	SH	SV	IP	H	HR	BB	SO	RAT	ERA	ERA+	OAV	OOB	BH	AVG	PB	PR	/A	PD	TPI
1907	Was-A	3	7	.300	15	9	8	2	0	87	92	1	14	31	11.1	3.31	73	.274	.305	9	.205		-7	-9	-2	-0.8
1908	Was-A	0	1	.000	3	1	0	0	0	5	9	0	2		23.4	14.40	16	.450	.542	3	.600	2	-7	-7	0	-0.9
Total 2		3	8	.273	18	10	8	2	0	92	101	1	16		11.7	3.91	62	.284	.320	12	.245	5	-14	-15	-2	-1.7

● **PAUL GEHRMAN**   Gehrman, Paul Arthur "Dutch"   b: 5/3/12, Marquam, Ore.   d: 10/23/86, Bend, Ore.   BR/TR, 6', 195 lbs.   Deb: 9/15/37

YEAR	TM/L	W	L	PCT	G	GS	CG	SH	SV	IP	H	HR	BB	SO	RAT	ERA	ERA+	OAV	OOB	BH	AVG	PB	PR	/A	PD	TPI
1937	Cin-N	0	1	.000	2	1	0	0	0	9^1	11	0	5	1	15.4	2.89	129	.282	.364	0	.000	-0	1	1	0	0.1

● **GARY GEIGER**   Geiger, Gary Merle   b: 4/4/37, Sand Ridge, Ill.   d: 4/24/96, Murphysboro, Ill.   BL/TR, 6', 168 lbs.   Deb: 4/15/58 ♦

YEAR	TM/L	W	L	PCT	G	GS	CG	SH	SV	IP	H	HR	BB	SO	RAT	ERA	ERA+	OAV	OOB	BH	AVG	PB	PR	/A	PD	TPI
1958	Cle-A	0	0	—	1	0	0	0	0	2	2	0	1	2	13.5	9.00	41	.286	.375	45	.231	0	-1	-1	0	0.0

● **EMIL GEIS**   Geis, Emil Michael   b: 3/1861, Villmar, Germany   BR/TR, 5'11", 170 lbs.   Deb: 7/19/1882

YEAR	TM/L	W	L	PCT	G	GS	CG	SH	SV	IP	H	HR	BB	SO	RAT	ERA	ERA+	OAV	OOB	BH	AVG	PB	PR	/A	PD	TPI
1882	Bal-a	4	9	.308	13	13	10	1	0	95^2	110	4	22	10	10.0	4.80	57	.220	.263	6	.146	-2	-22	-22	-3	-2.5

● **BILL GEIS**   Geis, William J. (b: William J. Geiss)   b: 7/15/1858, Chicago, Ill.   d: 9/18/24, Chicago, Ill.   5'10", 164 lbs.   Deb: 5/1/1884 F♦

YEAR	TM/L	W	L	PCT	G	GS	CG	SH	SV	IP	H	HR	BB	SO	RAT	ERA	ERA+	OAV	OOB	BH	AVG	PB	PR	/A	PD	TPI
1884	Det-N	0	0	—	1	0	0	0	0	5	14	0	1		28.8	14.40	20	.424	.457	50	.177	-0	-6	-6	-0	0.0

● **DAVE GEISEL**   Geisel, John David   b: 1/18/55, Windber, Pa.   BL/TL, 6'3", 210 lbs.   Deb: 6/13/78

YEAR	TM/L	W	L	PCT	G	GS	CG	SH	SV	IP	H	HR	BB	SO	RAT	ERA	ERA+	OAV	OOB	BH	AVG	PB	PR	/A	PD	TPI
1978	Chi-N	1	0	1.000	18	0	0	0	0	23^1	27	0	11	15	14.7	4.24	95	.278	.352	0	.000	-0	-2	-1	-0	-0.1
1979	Chi-N	0	0	—	7	0	0	0	0	15	10	0	4	5	9.0	0.60	686	.189	.259	0	.000	0	5	6	0	0.4
1981	Tor-A	2	0	1.000	16	0	0	0	0	16	11	0	10	7	11.8	0.56	657	.204	.328	0	.000	0	6	6	0	0.7
1982	Tor-A	1	1	.500	16	2	0	0	0	31^2	32	6	17	22	14.5	3.98	113	.260	.359	0	—	0	2	2	-0	-0.3
1983	Tor-A	0	3	.000	47	0	0	0	5	52^1	47	4	31	50	13.8	4.64	93	.240	.349	0	—	0	-3	-2	-1	-0.4
1984	Sea-A	1	1	.500	20	3	0	0	0	43^1	44	9	28	12	16.1	4.15	96	.273	.317	0	—	0	-2	-1	-0	-0.1
1985	Sea-A	0	0	—	12	0	0	0	0	27	35	3	15	17	16.7	6.33	67	.310	.391	0	—	-1	-6	-6	-0	-0.1
Total 7		5	5	.500	131	8	0	0	8	208^2	209	15	97	144	13.5	4.01	104	.259	.343	0	.000	-1	-2	4	-3	-0.2

● **VERN GEISHERT**   Geishert, Vernon William   b: 1/10/46, Madison, Wis.   BR/TR, 6'1", 215 lbs.   Deb: 8/26/69

YEAR	TM/L	W	L	PCT	G	GS	CG	SH	SV	IP	H	HR	BB	SO	RAT	ERA	ERA+	OAV	OOB	BH	AVG	PB	PR	/A	PD	TPI
1969	Cal-A	1	1	.500	11	3	0	0	0	31	32	4	7	18	11.6	4.65	75	.267	.313	0	.000	-1	-4	-4	0	-0.3

● **EMIL GEISS**   Geiss, Emil August   b: 3/20/1867, Chicago, Ill.   d: 10/4/11, Chicago, Ill.   BR/TR, 5'11", 170 lbs.   Deb: 5/18/1887 F♦

YEAR	TM/L	W	L	PCT	G	GS	CG	SH	SV	IP	H	HR	BB	SO	RAT	ERA	ERA+	OAV	OOB	BH	AVG	PB	PR	/A	PD	TPI
1887	Chi-N	0	1	.000	1	1	1	0	0	9	10	0	3	4	20.0	8.00	56	.395	.435	1	.083	-1	-4	-4	0	-0.3

YEAR TM/L	W	L	PCT	G	GS	CG	SH	SV	IP	H	HR	BB	SO	RAT	ERA	ERA+	OAV	OOB	BH	AVG	PB	PR	/A	PD	TPI
● **CHARLIE GELBERT** Gelbert, Charles Magnus b: 1/26/06, Scranton, Pa. d: 1/13/67, Easton, Pa. BR/TR, 5'11", 170 lbs. Deb: 4/16/29 ♦																									
1940 Was-A	0	0	—	2	0	0	0	0	4	5	2	3	1	18.0	9.00	46	.278	.381	20	.370	1	-2	-2	0	0.0
● **JOHN GELNAR** Gelnar, John Richard b: 6/25/43, Granite, Okla BR/TR, 6'1.5", 190 lbs. Deb: 8/4/64																									
1964 Pit-N	0	0	—	7	0	0	0	0	9	11	2	1	4	12.0	5.00	70	.314	.333	0	—	0	-1	-1	-0	0.0
1967 Pit-N	0	1	.000	10	1	0	0	0	19	30	4	11	5	20.4	8.05	42	.375	.462	1	.167	0	-10	-10	-0	-0.5
1969 Sea-A	3	10	.231	39	10	0	0	3	108²	103	7	26	69	11.1	3.31	110	.250	.302	1	.053	-2	4	4	-0	0.3
1970 Mil-A	4	3	.571	53	0	0	0	4	92¹	98	7	23	48	12.3	4.19	90	.277	.330	1	.083	-1	-5	-4	1	-0.2
1971 Mil-A	0	0	—	2	0	0	0	0	1¹	3	0	1	0	27.0	13.50	26	.429	.500	0	—	0	-1	-1	0	0.0
Total 5	7	14	.333	111	11	0	0	7	230¹	245	20	62	126	12.5	4.18	88	.276	.332	3	.081	-2	-14	-13	1	-0.4
● **JOE GENEWICH** Genewich, Joseph Edward b: 1/15/1897, Elmira, N.Y. d: 12/21/85, Lockport, N.Y. BR/TR, 6', 174 lbs. Deb: 9/13/22																									
1922 Bos-N	0	2	.000	6	2	1	0	0	23	29	2	11	4	15.7	7.04	57	.319	.392	1	.167	-0	-8	-8	-0	-0.6
1923 Bos-N	13	14	.481	43	24	12	1	1	227¹	272	15	46	54	12.9	3.72	107	.303	.341	19	.247	2	7	7	2	1.1
1924 Bos-N	10	19	.345	34	27	11	2	1	200¹	258	4	65	43	14.9	5.21	73	.329	.386	10	.167	-2	-30	-31	-0	-4.0
1925 Bos-N	12	10	.545	34	21	10	0	0	169	185	4	41	34	12.4	3.99	100	.279	.327	15	.273	1	5	0	-1	0.1
1926 Bos-N	8	16	.333	37	26	12	2	1	216	239	6	63	59	12.8	3.88	92	.288	.342	11	.164	-1	-1	-8	-1	-0.8
1927 Bos-N	11	8	.579	40	19	7	0	1	181	199	7	54	38	12.7	3.83	97	.279	.332	11	.193	-1	2	-2	0	-0.3
1928 Bos-N	3	7	.300	13	11	4	0	0	80²	88	14	18	15	12.2	4.13	95	.280	.325	1	.038	-1	-1	-2	-1	-0.4
NY-N	11	4	.733	26	18	10	2	3	158¹	136	10	54	37	10.9	3.18	123	.232	.298	13	.203	-1	14	13	1	1.1
Yr	14	11	.560	39	29	14	2	3	239	224	24	72	52	11.2	3.50	112	.248	.304	14	.156	-4	13	11	2	0.7
1929 NY-N	3	7	.300	21	9	1	0	1	85	133	9	30	19	17.4	6.78	68	.359	.409	12	.375	3	-19	-21	-0	-1.7
1930 NY-N	2	5	.286	18	9	3	0	1	61	71	6	20	13	13.6	5.61	84	.297	.354	3	.150	-1	-4	-6	-2	-0.5
Total 9	73	92	.442	272	166	71	7	12	1401²	1610	77	402	316	13.1	4.29	91	.293	.345	96	.207	-4	-35	-58	5	-6.0
● **GARY GENTRY** Gentry, Gary Edward b: 10/6/46, Phoenix, Ariz. BR/TR, 6', 183 lbs. Deb: 4/10/69																									
1969 *NY-N	13	12	.520	35	35	6	3	0	233²	192	24	81	154	10.7	3.43	107	.222	.293	6	.081	-4	4	6	1	0.3
1970 NY-N	9	9	.500	32	29	5	2	1	188¹	155	19	86	134	11.9	3.68	109	.224	.318	4	.068	-2	8	7	-2	0.2
1971 NY-N	12	11	.522	32	31	8	3	0	203¹	167	16	82	155	11.3	3.23	105	.224	.305	5	.074	-5	5	4	-1	-0.2
1972 NY-N	7	10	.412	32	26	3	0	0	164	153	20	75	120	12.8	4.01	84	.250	.338	5	.104	-1	-10	-12	2	-1.1
1973 Atl-N	4	6	.400	16	14	3	0	1	86²	74	7	35	42	11.4	3.43	115	.231	.308	7	.233	-1	2	5	-1	0.5
1974 Atl-N	0	0	—	3	1	0	0	0	6²	11	2	1	0	9.5	1.35	280	.167	.259	0	.000	-0	2	2	-0	0.3
1975 Atl-N	1	1	.500	7	2	0	0	0	20	25	3	8	10	14.8	4.95	76	.313	.375	0	.000	-1	-3	-3	-0	-0.3
Total 7	46	49	.484	157	138	25	8	2	902²	770	90	369	615	11.6	3.56	103	.231	.312	27	.095	-12	8	9	-1	-0.6
● **RUFE GENTRY** Gentry, James Ruffus b: 5/18/18, Daisy Station, N.C. BR/TR, 6'1", 180 lbs. Deb: 9/10/43 F																									
1943 Det-A	1	3	.250	4	4	2	0	0	29¹	30	2	12	8	13.5	3.68	96	.268	.349	0	.000	-1	-1	-1	-0	-0.2
1944 Det-A	12	14	.462	37	30	10	3	0	203²	211	9	108	68	14.3	4.24	84	.273	.365	15	.197	-1	-18	-15	1	-1.8
1946 Det-A	0	0	—	2	0	0	0	0	3	3	0	7	1	33.0	15.00	24	.333	.579	0	—	0	-4	-4	-0	0.0
1947 Det-A	0	0	—	1	0	0	0	0	0¹	1	0	2	0	81.0	81.00	5	.500	.750	0	—	0	-3	-3	-0	0.0
1948 Det-A	0	0	—	4	0	0	0	0	6²	5	0	5	1	14.9	2.70	162	.208	.367	1	1.000	0	1	1	-0	0.0
Total 5	13	17	.433	48	34	12	3	0	243	251	11	134	78	14.5	4.37	82	.272	.368	16	.184	-1	-25	-21	0	-2.0
● **CHRIS GEORGE** George, Christopher Sean b: 9/24/66, Pittsburgh, Pa. BR/TR, 6'2", 200 lbs. Deb: 10/1/91																									
1991 Mil-A	0	0	—	2	0	0	0	0	6	8	0	2	2	12.0	3.00	132	.333	.333	0	—	0	1	1	-0	0.1
● **LEFTY GEORGE** George, Thomas Edward b: 8/13/1886, Pittsburgh, Pa. d: 5/13/55, York, Pa. BL/TL, 6', 155 lbs. Deb: 4/14/11																									
1911 StL-A	4	9	.308	27	13	6	1	0	116¹	136	3	51	23	15.2	4.18	81	.256	.332	5	.114	-3	-11	-10	-1	-1.4
1912 Cle-A	0	5	.000	11	5	2	0	0	44¹	69	1	18	18	18.1	4.87	70	.373	.434	3	.214	1	-8	-7	0	-0.6
1915 Cin-N	2	2	.500	5	3	1	1	0	28	24	1	8	11	11.9	3.86	74	.242	.330	4	.333	2	-3	-3	1	-0.2
1918 Bos-N	1	5	.167	9	5	4	0	0	54¹	56	0	21	22	13.3	2.32	116	.281	.359	2	.091	-2	3	2	1	0.3
Total 4	7	21	.250	52	26	14	2	0	243	285	5	98	74	14.9	3.85	82	.281	.355	14	.152	-2	-19	-19	1	-1.9
● **BILL GEORGE** George, William M. b: 1/27/1865, Bellaire, Ohio d: 8/23/16, Wheeling, W.Va. BR/TR, 5'8", 165 lbs. Deb: 5/11/1887 ♦																									
1887 NY-N	3	9	.250	13	13	11	0	0	108	126	1	89	49	19.1	5.25	72	.292	.428	9	.170	-4	-14	-18	2	-1.6
1888 *NY-N	2	1	.667	4	3	3	1	0	33²	18	0	11	26	8.0	1.34	205	.149	.226	9	.231	1	6	5	-0	0.5
1889 Col-a	0	0	—	2	0	0	0	0	8	11	1	3	3	15.8	7.88	46	.314	.368	4	.235	-0	-4	-4	0	-0.0
Total 3	5	10	.333	19	16	14	1	0	149²	155	2	103	78	16.4	4.51	78	.264	.387	26	.210	-3	-12	-16	2	-1.1
● **OSCAR GEORGY** Georgy, Oscar John b: 11/25/16, New Orleans, La. BR/TR, 6'3.5", 180 lbs. Deb: 6/4/38																									
1938 NY-N	0	0	—	1	0	0	0	0	1	2	0	1	0	27.0	18.00	21	.400	.500	0	—	0	-2	-2	-0	0.0
● **DAVE GERARD** Gerard, David Frederick b: 8/6/36, New York, N.Y. BR/TR, 6'2", 205 lbs. Deb: 4/10/62																									
1962 Chi-N	2	3	.400	39	0	0	0	3	58²	67	10	28	30	14.7	4.91	84	.289	.368	1	.375	1	-6	-5	-0	-0.4
● **GEORGE GERBERMAN** Gerberman, George Alois b: 3/8/42, ElCampo, Tex. BR/TR, 6', 180 lbs. Deb: 9/23/62																									
1962 Chi-N	0	0	—	1	1	0	0	0	5¹	1	1	5	1	13.5	1.69	246	.158	.333	0	.000	0	1	1	-0	0.1
● **RUSTY GERHARDT** Gerhardt, Allen Russell b: 8/13/50, Baltimore, Md. BB/TL, 5'9", 175 lbs. Deb: 7/27/74																									
1974 SD-N	2	1	.667	23	1	0	0	1	35²	44	1	17	22	15.9	7.07	50	.308	.389	1	.167	-0	-14	-14	-0	-1.2
● **AL GERHEAUSER** Gerheauser, Albert "Lefty" b: 6/24/17, St.Louis, Mo. d: 5/28/72, Springfield, Mo. BL/TL, 6'3", 190 lbs. Deb: 4/24/43																									
1943 Phi-N	10	19	.345	38	31	11	2	0	215	222	10	70	92	12.3	3.60	94	.263	.321	8	.113	-3	-5	-5	-1	-1.1
1944 Phi-N	8	16	.333	30	29	10	2	0	182²	210	8	65	66	13.6	4.58	79	.285	.344	15	.231	3	-20	-20	-2	-2.1
1945 Pit-N	5	10	.333	32	14	5	1	0	140¹	170	5	54	55	14.4	3.91	101	.304	.366	12	.250	3	-2	-1	2	0.5
1946 Pit-N	2	2	.500	35	3	1	0	0	81²	92	7	25	32	13.0	3.97	89	.286	.339	4	.333	2	-5	-4	1	0.1
1948 StL-A	0	3	.000	14	2	0	0	0	23¹	32	0	10	10	16.6	7.33	62	.317	.384	2	.333	0	-8	-7	-0	-0.8
Total 5	25	50	.333	149	79	27	4	1	643	726	25	224	255	13.4	4.13	88	.283	.342	44	.209	5	-40	-36	-0	-3.4
● **STEVE GERKIN** Gerkin, Stephen Paul "Splinter" b: 11/19/12, Grafton, W.Va. d: 11/9/78, Bay Pines, Fla. BR/TR, 6'1", 162 lbs. Deb: 5/13/45																									
1945 Phi-A	0	12	.000	21	12	3	0	0	102	112	4	27	25	12.5	3.62	95	.285	.336	2	.059	-4	-3	-2	-0	-0.6
● **LES GERMAN** German, Lester Stanley b: 6/1/1869, Baltimore, Md. d: 6/10/34, Germantown, Md. BR/TR, 5'8", 165 lbs. Deb: 8/27/1890																									
1890 Bal-a	5	11	.313	17	16	15	0	0	132¹	147	3	54	37	14.6	4.83	84	.273	.353	6	.118	-2	-14	-11	-2	-1.4
1893 NY-N	8	8	.500	20	18	14	0	0	152	162	6	70	35	14.3	4.14	112	.265	.349	23	.311	2	9	9	-1	0.8
1894 NY-N	9	8	.529	23	15	10	0	1	134	178	7	66	17	17.1	5.78	91	.316	.397	17	.298	-0	-7	-8	2	-0.5
1895 NY-N	7	11	.389	25	18	16	0	0	178¹	243	7	78	36	16.7	5.96	78	.320	.390	29	.261	3	-23	-26	-1	-1.7
1896 NY-N	0	0	—	1	0	0	0	0	2²	6	0	0	0	33.8	13.50	31	.529	.556	0	.000	-0	-3	-3	-0	0.0
Was-N	2	20	.091	28	20	14	0	1	166²	240	6	74	20	17.2	6.32	70	.334	.400	16	.229	-0	-36	-35	1	-3.3
Yr	2	20	.091	29	20	14	0	1	169¹	249	6	75	20	17.5	6.43	68	.339	.404	16	.225	-0	-39	-38	1	-3.3
1897 Was-N	3	5	.375	15	5	4	0	0	83²	117	2	33	12	16.9	5.59	78	.328	.395	15	.341	2	-12	-12	-1	-0.7
Total 6	34	63	.351	129	92	73	0	2	849²	1096	30	376	147	16.2	5.49	83	.307	.382	106	.260	5	-86	-86	-0	-6.8
● **ED GERNER** Gerner, Edwin Frederick "Lefty" b: 7/22/1897, Philadelphia, Pa. d: 5/15/70, Philadelphia, Pa. BL/TL, 5'8.5", 175 lbs. Deb: 5/14/19																									
1919 Cin-N	1	0	1.000	5	1	0	0	0	17	22	0	3	2	14.3	3.18	87	.333	.380	1	.167	0	-0	-1	-0	0.0
● **LEFTY GERVAIS** Gervais, Lucien Edward b: 7/6/1890, Grover, Wis. d: 10/19/50, Los Angeles, Cal. BL/TL, 5'10", 165 lbs. Deb: 4/17/13																									
1913 Bos-N	0	1	.000	5	2	1	0	0	15²	18	0	4	1	12.6	5.74	57	.383	.431	0	.000	-0	-4	-4	-0	-0.3
● **CHARLIE GESSNER** Gessner, Charles J. b: Philadelphia, Pa. Deb: 7/19/1886																									
1886 Phi-a	0	1	.000	1	1	1	0	0	8	13	0	5	0	22.5	9.00	39	.351	.455	1	.250	-0	-5	-5	-0	-0.4

YEAR	TM/L	W	L	PCT	G	GS	CG	SH	SV	IP	H	HR	BB	SO	RAT	ERA	ERA+	OAV	OOB	BH	AVG	PB	PR	/A	PD	TPI

● AL GETTEL
Gettel, Allen Jones b: 9/17/17, Norfolk, Va.   BR/TR, 6'3.5", 200 lbs.   Deb: 4/20/45

YEAR	TM/L	W	L	PCT	G	GS	CG	SH	SV	IP	H	HR	BB	SO	RAT	ERA	ERA+	OAV	OOB	BH	AVG	PB	PR	/A	PD	TPI
1945	NY-A	9	8	.529	27	17	9	0	3	154²	141	11	53	67	11.7	3.90	89	.243	.314	16	.281	2	-9	-7	-1	-0.8
1946	NY-A	6	7	.462	26	11	6	5	2	103	89	6	40	54	11.4	2.97	116	.229	.305	4	.125	-2	6	5	0	0.5
1947	Cle-A	11	10	.524	31	21	9	2	0	149	122	12	62	64	11.3	3.20	109	.229	.313	15	.294	4	8	5	1	1.1
1948	Cle-A	0	1	.000	5	2	0	0	0	7²	15	2	10	4	30.5	17.61	23	.385	.520	-0	.000	-0	-11	-12	-0	-1.2
	Chi-A	8	10	.444	22	19	7	0	1	148	154	7	60	49	13.3	4.01	106	.268	.342	13	.241	-0	5	4	-1	0.4
	Yr	8	11	.421	27	21	7	0	1	155²	169	9	70	53	14.0	4.68	91	.275	.353	13	.228	-0	-7	-7	-1	-0.8
1949	Chi-A	2	5	.286	19	7	1	1	1	63	69	12	26	22	13.9	6.43	65	.283	.357	3	.167	-0	-16	-16	-1	-1.6
	Was-A	0	2	.000	16	1	0	0	1	34²	43	4	24	7	17.4	5.45	78	.314	.416	0	.000	-1	-5	-5	-1	-0.3
	Yr	2	7	.222	35	8	1	1	2	97²	112	16	50	29	14.9	6.08	69	.292	.374	3	.115	-1	-20	-20	-0	-1.9
1951	NY-N	1	2	.333	30	1	0	0	0	57¹	52	12	25	36	12.1	4.87	80	.240	.318	1	.083	-1	-6	-6	1	-0.3
1955	StL-N	1	0	1.000	8	0	0	0	0	17	26	6	10	7	19.1	9.00	45	.361	.439	3	.500	-1	-9	-9	-0	-0.4
Total	7	38	45	.458	184	79	31	5	6	734¹	711	72	310	310	12.7	4.28	88	.255	.334	55	.228	3	-37	-40	-1	-2.6

● CHARLIE GETTIG
Gettig, Charles Henry b: 12/1870, Baltimore, Md.   d: 4/11/35, Baltimore, Md.   BR, 5'10", 172 lbs.   Deb: 8/5/1896 ♦

YEAR	TM/L	W	L	PCT	G	GS	CG	SH	SV	IP	H	HR	BB	SO	RAT	ERA	ERA+	OAV	OOB	BH	AVG	PB	PR	/A	PD	TPI
1896	NY-N	1	0	1.000	4	1	1	0	1	14	20	0	8	5	19.3	9.64	44	.333	.429	3	.333	1	-8	-8	0	-0.5
1897	NY-N	1	1	.500	3	2	2	0	0	19	23	0	9	7	16.1	5.21	80	.295	.382	15	.200	-0	-2	-2	0	-0.2
1898	NY-N	6	3	.667	17	8	7	0	0	115	141	4	39	14	14.7	3.83	91	.299	.363	49	.250	2	-3	-5	1	0.0
1899	NY-N	7	8	.467	18	15	12	0	0	128	161	3	54	25	15.4	4.43	85	.307	.376	24	.247	1	-8	-10	-1	-0.8
Total	4	15	12	.556	42	26	22	0	1	276	345	4	110	51	15.4	4.50	82	.304	.374	91	.241	4	-21	-25	1	-1.5

● TOM GETTINGER
Gettinger, Lewis Thomas Leyton (b: Lewis Thomas Leyton Gittinger)   b: 12/11/1868, Frederick, Md.   d: 7/26/43, Pensacola, Fla.   BL/TL, 5'10", 180 lbs.   Deb: 9/21/1889 ♦

YEAR	TM/L	W	L	PCT	G	GS	CG	SH	SV	IP	H	HR	BB	SO	RAT	ERA	ERA+	OAV	OOB	BH	AVG	PB	PR	/A	PD	TPI
1895	Lou-N	0	0	—	2	0	0	0	0	6¹	13	1	1	0	19.9	7.11	65	.419	.438	70	.269	0	-2	-2	0	0.0

● CHARLIE GETZIEN
Getzien, Charles H. "Pretzels" b: 2/14/1864, Germany   d: 6/19/32, Chicago, Ill.   BR/TR, 5'10", 172 lbs.   Deb: 8/13/1884

YEAR	TM/L	W	L	PCT	G	GS	CG	SH	SV	IP	H	HR	BB	SO	RAT	ERA	ERA+	OAV	OOB	BH	AVG	PB	PR	/A	PD	TPI
1884	Det-N	5	12	.294	17	17	17	1	0	147¹	118	2	25	107	8.7	1.95	184	.204	.237	6	.109	-4	17	15	-2	1.0
1885	Det-N	12	25	.324	37	37	37	1	0	330	360	8	92	110	12.3	3.03	94	.264	.311	29	.212	-1	-8	-7	-2	-0.9
1886	Det-N	30	11	.732	43	43	42	1	0	386²	388	6	85	172	11.0	3.03	110	.250	.288	29	.176	-3	12	12	-2	0.8
1887	*Det-N	29	13	.690	43	42	41	2	0	366²	373	24	106	135	11.8	3.73	109	.254	.305	29	.186	-2	14	13	0	0.8
1888	Det-N	19	25	.432	46	46	45	2	0	404	411	13	54	202	10.5	3.05	91	.251	.279	41	.246	10	-9	-13	-2	-0.6
1889	Ind-N	18	22	.450	45	44	36	0	1	349	395	27	100	139	13.0	4.54	92	.277	.328	25	.180	-2	-20	-14	-3	-1.3
1890	Bos-N	23	17	.575	40	40	39	4	0	350	342	5	82	140	11.0	3.19	118	.248	.292	34	.231	5	15	22	-2	2.2
1891	Bos-N	4	5	.444	11	9	7	0	0	89	112	4	23	29	13.7	3.84	95	.296	.337	7	.171	1	-5	-2	1	0.0
	Cle-N	0	1	.000	1	1	1	0	0	9	12	1	4	4	16.0	8.00	43	.308	.372	0	.000	-1	-5	-5	-1	-0.4
	Yr	4	6	.400	12	10	8	0	0	98	124	5	27	33	13.9	4.22	86	.297	.340	7	.156	0	-10	-6	0	-0.4
1892	StL-N	5	8	.385	13	13	12	0	0	108	159	5	31	32	16.3	5.67	56	.329	.377	18	.200	-0	-29	-30	-1	-2.7
Total	9	145	139	.511	296	292	277	11	1	2539²	2670	95	602	1070	11.7	3.46	99	.259	.302	209	.198	8	-17	-9	-13	-1.5

● RUBE GEYER
Geyer, Jacob Bowman b: 3/26/1884, Allegheny, Pa.   d: 10/12/62, Ford Township, Minn.   BR/TR, 5'10", 170 lbs.   Deb: 4/24/10

YEAR	TM/L	W	L	PCT	G	GS	CG	SH	SV	IP	H	HR	BB	SO	RAT	ERA	ERA+	OAV	OOB	BH	AVG	PB	PR	/A	PD	TPI
1910	StL-N	0	1	.000	4	0	0	0	0	4	5	0	3	5	18.0	4.50	66	.294	.400	0	.000	-0	-1	-1	-0	-0.2
1911	StL-N	9	6	.600	29	11	7	1	0	148²	141	7	56	46	12.3	3.27	103	.259	.335	13	.228	1	2	2	-1	0.1
1912	StL-N	7	14	.333	41	18	5	0	0	181	191	4	84	61	13.9	3.28	104	.288	.371	11	.208	-0	3	3	0	0.3
1913	StL-N	1	5	.167	30	4	2	0	1	78²	83	7	38	21	14.1	5.26	61	.282	.368	2	.091	-2	-18	-18	-1	-1.5
Total	4	17	26	.395	104	33	14	1	1	412¹	420	17	181	133	13.4	3.67	92	.276	.358	26	.195	-1	-14	-14	-2	-1.3

● TONY GHELFI
Ghelfi, Anthony Paul b: 8/23/61, LaCrosse, Wis.   BR/TR, 6'3", 185 lbs.   Deb: 9/1/83

YEAR	TM/L	W	L	PCT	G	GS	CG	SH	SV	IP	H	HR	BB	SO	RAT	ERA	ERA+	OAV	OOB	BH	AVG	PB	PR	/A	PD	TPI
1983	Phi-N	1	1	.500	3	3	0	0	0	14¹	12	3	6	6	12.6	3.14	114	.268	.339	1	.250	—	1	1	1	0.2

● BOB GIALLOMBARDO
Giallombardo, Robert Paul b: 5/20/37, Brooklyn, N.Y.   BL/TL, 6', 175 lbs.   Deb: 6/21/58

YEAR	TM/L	W	L	PCT	G	GS	CG	SH	SV	IP	H	HR	BB	SO	RAT	ERA	ERA+	OAV	OOB	BH	AVG	PB	PR	/A	PD	TPI
1958	LA-N	1	1	.500	6	5	0	0	0	26¹	29	3	15	14	15.0	3.76	109	.284	.376	1	.167	-0	1	1	0	0.1

● JOE GIARD
Giard, Joseph Oscar "Peco" b: 10/7/1898, Ware, Mass.   d: 7/10/56, Worcester, Mass.   BL/TL, 5'10.5", 170 lbs.   Deb: 4/18/25

YEAR	TM/L	W	L	PCT	G	GS	CG	SH	SV	IP	H	HR	BB	SO	RAT	ERA	ERA+	OAV	OOB	BH	AVG	PB	PR	/A	PD	TPI
1925	StL-A	10	5	.667	30	21	9	4	0	160²	179	13	87	43	15.2	5.04	93	.295	.388	3	.057	-6	-12	-7	2	-0.9
1926	StL-A	3	10	.231	22	15	2	0	0	90	113	7	67	18	18.1	7.00	61	.318	.428	8	.276	0	-30	-27	-1	-3.2
1927	NY-A	0	0	—	16	0	0	0	0	27	38	1	19	10	19.0	8.00	48	.352	.449	2	.286	-0	-12	-12	-0	-0.0
Total	3	13	15	.464	68	36	11	4	0	277²	330	21	173	71	16.5	5.96	75	.309	.408	13	.146	-6	-53	-46	0	-4.1

● JOE GIBBON
Gibbon, Joseph Charles b: 4/10/35, Hickory, Miss.   BR/TL, 6'4", 210 lbs.   Deb: 4/17/60

YEAR	TM/L	W	L	PCT	G	GS	CG	SH	SV	IP	H	HR	BB	SO	RAT	ERA	ERA+	OAV	OOB	BH	AVG	PB	PR	/A	PD	TPI
1960	*Pit-N	4	2	.667	27	9	0	0	0	80¹	87	5	31	60	13.2	4.03	93	.277	.342	4	.211	1	-2	-3	0	-0.1
1961	Pit-N	13	10	.565	30	29	7	3	0	195¹	185	16	57	145	11.3	3.32	120	.251	.309	8	.136	-2	16	15	-0	1.4
1962	Pit-N	3	4	.429	19	8	0	0	0	57	53	4	24	26	12.2	3.63	108	.250	.326	3	.176	-0	2	1	0	0.3
1963	Pit-N	5	12	.294	37	22	5	0	1	147¹	147	7	54	110	12.6	3.30	100	.258	.328	4	.093	-2	-0	-1	-1	-0.1
1964	Pit-N	10	7	.588	28	24	3	0	0	146²	145	10	54	97	12.6	3.68	95	.262	.334	12	.255	3	-2	-3	1	0.1
1965	Pit-N	4	9	.308	31	15	1	0	0	105²	85	7	34	63	10.5	4.51	78	.221	.291	3	.115	-0	-11	-12	1	-1.4
1966	SF-N	4	6	.400	37	10	1	0	1	81	86	4	16	48	11.6	3.67	100	.275	.314	3	.200	-1	-0	1	0	0.2
1967	SF-N	6	2	.750	28	10	3	1	1	82	65	4	33	63	11.1	3.07	107	.220	.305	1	.042	-1	3	2	0	0.3
1968	SF-N	1	2	.333	29	0	1	0	1	40	33	3	19	22	12.1	1.57	187	.234	.333	0	.000	-0	6	6	0	0.5
1969	SF-N	1	3	.250	16	0	1	0	0	20	15	1	13	9	13.0	3.60	97	.211	.341	0	.000	-0	-0	-1	0	0.0
	Pit-N	5	1	.833	35	0	0	0	11	51¹	38	5	17	35	10.0	1.93	181	.208	.282	0	.000	-1	9	9	1	1.4
	Yr	6	4	.600	51	0	1	0	11	71¹	53	6	30	44	10.7	2.40	146	.208	.296	0	.000	-1	9	8	1	1.4
1970	*Pit-N	0	1	.000	41	0	0	0	5	41	44	2	24	26	15.4	4.83	81	.280	.383	0	.000	-4	-4	-4	0	-0.2
1971	Cin-N	5	6	.455	50	0	0	0	11	64¹	54	3	32	34	12.2	2.94	114	.239	.336	0	.000	-0	4	3	1	0.7
1972	Cin-N	0	0	—	2	0	0	0	0	0¹	3	1	1	1	108.0	54.00	6	.750	.800	0	—	-0	-2	-2	0	-0.0
	Hou-N	0	0	—	9	0	0	0	0	7¹	13	2	5	4	23.3	9.82	34	.394	.487	0	—	-0	-5	-5	1	0.1
	Yr	0	0	—	11	0	0	0	0	7²	16	3	6	5	26.3	11.74	29	.432	.523	0	—	-0	-7	-7	1	0.1
Total	13	61	65	.484	419	127	20	4	32	1119²	1053	74	414	743	12.1	3.52	102	.251	.323	38	.144	-3	12	8	11	3.2

● NORWOOD GIBSON
Gibson, Norwood Ringold "Gibby" b: 3/11/1877, Peoria, Ill.   d: 7/7/59, Peoria, Ill.   BR/TR, 5'10", 165 lbs.   Deb: 4/29/03

YEAR	TM/L	W	L	PCT	G	GS	CG	SH	SV	IP	H	HR	BB	SO	RAT	ERA	ERA+	OAV	OOB	BH	AVG	PB	PR	/A	PD	TPI
1903	Bos-A	13	9	.591	24	21	17	2	0	183¹	166	2	65	76	11.7	3.19	95	.241	.313	17	.266	5	-5	-3	0	0.1
1904	Bos-A	17	14	.548	33	32	29	1	0	273	216	8	81	112	9.9	2.21	121	.219	.281	6	.065	-6	12	14	-3	0.6
1905	Bos-A	4	7	.364	23	17	9	0	0	134	118	9	55	67	12.0	3.69	73	.238	.321	4	.095	-2	-15	-15	-2	-1.6
1906	Bos-A	0	2	.000	5	2	1	0	0	18²	25	2	7	3	15.4	5.30	52	.325	.381	1	.200	-0	-5	-5	0	-0.5
Total	4	34	32	.515	85	72	56	3	0	609	525	21	208	258	11.1	2.93	95	.233	.303	28	.138	-4	-14	-9	-5	-1.4

● PAUL GIBSON
Gibson, Paul Marshall b: 1/4/60, Southampton, N.Y.   BR/TL, 6', 165 lbs.   Deb: 4/8/88

YEAR	TM/L	W	L	PCT	G	GS	CG	SH	SV	IP	H	HR	BB	SO	RAT	ERA	ERA+	OAV	OOB	BH	AVG	PB	PR	/A	PD	TPI
1988	Det-A	4	2	.667	40	1	0	0	0	92	83	6	34	50	11.6	2.93	130	.240	.312	0	—	0	11	9	0	0.7
1989	Det-A	4	8	.333	45	13	0	0	0	132	129	11	57	77	13.1	4.64	82	.259	.342	0	—	0	-11	-12	-0	-1.0
1990	Det-A	5	4	.556	61	0	0	0	0	97¹	99	10	44	56	13.3	3.05	130	.269	.349	0	—	0	9	10	0	0.9
1991	Det-A	5	7	.417	68	0	0	0	8	96	112	10	48	52	15.3	4.59	90	.297	.381	0	—	0	-5	-5	-0	-0.7
1992	NY-N	0	1	.000	43	1	0	0	0	62	70	7	25	49	13.8	5.23	66	.287	.353	0	.000	0	-12	-12	-1	-0.3
1993	NY-N	1	1	.500	8	0	0	0	0	8²	14	1	2	12	16.6	5.19	77	.350	.381	0	—	0	-1	-1	0	-0.2
	NY-N	2	0	1.000	20	0	0	0	0	35¹	31	4	9	25	10.2	3.06	136	.238	.288	0	—	0	4	5	0	0.4
1994	NY-A	1	1	.500	30	0	0	0	0	29	26	5	17	21	13.7	4.97	92	.236	.344	0	—	0	-1	-1	0	0.1
1996	NY-A	0	0	—	4	0	0	0	0	4¹	6	1	0	3	12.5	6.23	81	.316	.316	0	—	0	-1	-1	0	-0.1
Total	8	22	24	.478	319	15	0	0	8	556²	570	51	236	345	13.2	4.07	97	.267	.344	0	.000	0	-6	-9	-1	-0.2

● BOB GIBSON
Gibson, Robert (b: Pack Robert Gibson) b: 11/9/35, Omaha, Neb.   BR/TR, 6'1.5", 195 lbs.   Deb: 4/15/59   CH

YEAR	TM/L	W	L	PCT	G	GS	CG	SH	SV	IP	H	HR	BB	SO	RAT	ERA	ERA+	OAV	OOB	BH	AVG	PB	PR	/A	PD	TPI
1959	StL-N	3	5	.375	13	9	2	1	0	75²	77	4	39	48	13.9	3.33	127	.274	.363	3	.115	-1	5	8	-0	0.7
1960	StL-N	3	6	.333	27	12	2	0	0	86²	97	7	48	69	15.2	5.61	73	.284	.374	5	.179	-0	-18	-15	1	-1.3
1961	StL-N	13	12	.520	35	27	10	2	1	211¹	186	13	119	166	13.2	3.24	136	.239	.344	13	.197	2	19	27	1	3.3
1962	StL-N★	15	13	.536	32	30	15	5	1	233²	174	15	95	208	10.7	2.85	150	.204	.291	20	.263	6	28	37	1	5.0

YEAR TM/L	W	L	PCT	G	GS	CG	SH	SV	IP	H	HR	BB	SO	RAT	ERA	ERA+	OAV	OOB	BH	AVG	PB	PR	/A	PD	TPI
1963 StL-N	18	9	.667	36	33	14	2	0	254^2	224	19	96	204	11.8	3.39	105	.233	.311	18	.207	7	-3	4	-2	1.0
1964 *StL-N	19	12	.613	40	36	17	2	1	287^1	250	25	86	245	10.8	3.01	121	.232	.294	15	.156	1	17	26	-1	2.7
1965 StL-N★	20	12	.625	38	36	20	6	1	299	243	34	103	270	10.7	3.07	125	.222	.295	25	.240	8	16	26	-2	3.6
1966 StL-N†	21	12	.636	35	35	20	**5**	0	280^1	210	20	78	225	9.4	2.44	147	.207	.267	20	.200	3	36	36	-1	4.4
1967 *StL-N★	13	7	.650	24	24	10	2	0	175^1	151	10	40	147	10.0	2.98	110	.231	.278	8	.133	1	8	6	0	0.8
1968 *StL-N☆	22	9	.710	34	34	28	**13**	0	304^2	198	11	62	**268**	**7.9**	**1.12**	**258**	**.184**	**.233**	16	.170	4	**63**	**60**	-3	**7.3**
1969 StL-N★	20	13	.606	35	35	**28**	4	0	314	251	12	95	269	10.2	2.18	164	.219	.285	29	.246	8	49	49	-2	**6.0**
1970 StL-N★	**23**	7	**.767**	34	34	23	3	0	294	262	13	88	274	10.8	3.12	132	.237	.296	33	.303	12	30	32	-1	4.2
1971 StL-N	16	13	.552	31	31	20	**5**	0	245^2	215	14	76	185	10.5	3.04	118	.232	.296	15	.172	2	12	15	0	2.1
1972 StL-N★	19	11	.633	34	34	23	4	0	278	226	14	88	208	10.3	2.46	138	.224	.288	20	.194	7	31	29	2	4.2
1973 StL-N	12	10	.545	25	25	13	1	0	195	159	12	57	142	10.1	2.77	132	.224	.284	12	.185	2	19	19	-1	2.3
1974 StL-N	11	13	.458	33	33	9	1	0	240	236	24	104	129	12.9	3.83	93	.259	.338	17	.210	3	-6	-7	-1	-0.6
1975 StL-N	3	10	.231	22	14	1	0	2	109	120	10	62	60	15.4	5.04	75	.287	.384	5	.179	0	-17	-16	-0	-1.7
Total 17	251	174	.591	528	482	255	56	6	3884^1	3279	257	1336	3117	10.9	2.91	127	.228	.299	274	.206	65	290	335	-10	44.0

● **BOB GIBSON**   Gibson, Robert Louis b: 6/19/57, Philadelphia, Pa. BR/TR, 6', 195 lbs. Deb: 4/13/83

YEAR TM/L	W	L	PCT	G	GS	CG	SH	SV	IP	H	HR	BB	SO	RAT	ERA	ERA+	OAV	OOB	BH	AVG	PB	PR	/A	PD	TPI
1983 Mil-A	3	4	.429	27	7	0	0	2	80^2	71	6	46	46	13.2	3.90	96	.237	.340	0	—	0	1	-2	-0	0.2
1984 Mil-A	2	5	.286	18	9	1	0	0	69	71	6	47	54	14.1	4.96	78	.236	.354	0	—	0	-7	-9	-0	-0.4
1985 Mil-A	6	7	.462	41	1	0	0	11	92^1	86	10	49	53	13.3	3.90	107	.260	.357	0	—	0	3	3	-0	0.4
1986 Mil-A	1	2	.333	11	1	0	0	0	26^2	23	7	23	11	15.5	4.73	92	.232	.377	0	—	0	-2	-1	-0	-0.3
1987 NY-N	0	0	—	1	0	0	0	0	1	0	0	1	2	9.0	0.00	—	.000	.250	0	—	0	0	0	0	0.0
Total 5	12	18	.400	98	18	1	1	13	269^2	241	29	166	166	13.7	4.24	94	.243	.353	0	—	0	-5	-8	-1	-0.1

● **ROBERT GIBSON**   Gibson, Robert Murray b: 8/20/1869, Duncansville, Pa. d: 12/19/49, Pittsburgh, Pa. BR/TR, 6'3", 185 lbs. Deb: 6/4/1890

YEAR TM/L	W	L	PCT	G	GS	CG	SH	SV	IP	H	HR	BB	SO	RAT	ERA	ERA+	OAV	OOB	BH	AVG	PB	PR	/A	PD	TPI
1890 Chi-N	1	0	1.000	1	1	1	0	0	9	6	0	2	1	8.0	0.00	—	.182	.229	0	.000	-0	4	4	0	0.4
Pit-N	0	3	.000	3	3	2	0	0	12	24	1	23	0	37.5	17.25	19	.400	.581	3	.231	-0	-18	-19	-1	-2.5
Yr	1	3	.250	4	4	3	0	0	21	30	1	25	1	24.9	9.86	35	.323	.479	3	.176	-1	-15	-15	-0	-2.1

● **SAM GIBSON**   Gibson, Samuel Braxton b: 8/5/1899, King, N.C. d: 1/31/83, High Point, N.C. BL/TR, 6'2", 198 lbs. Deb: 4/19/26

YEAR TM/L	W	L	PCT	G	GS	CG	SH	SV	IP	H	HR	BB	SO	RAT	ERA	ERA+	OAV	OOB	BH	AVG	PB	PR	/A	PD	TPI
1926 Det-A	12	9	.571	35	24	16	2	2	196^1	199	6	75	61	12.8	3.48	117	.269	.341	18	.250	2	12	13	0	1.4
1927 Det-A	11	12	.478	33	26	11	0	0	184^2	201	9	86	76	14.4	3.80	111	.285	.369	14	.212	-1	7	8	-1	0.6
1928 Det-A	5	8	.385	20	18	5	1	0	119^2	155	4	53	29	16.2	5.42	76	.322	.397	12	.286	-2	-18	-17	-1	-1.5
1930 NY-A	0	1	.000	2	2	0	0	0	6	14	1	6	3	30.0	15.00	29	.424	.513	1	.333	0	-7	-7	-0	-0.8
1932 NY-N	4	8	.333	41	5	1	1	3	81^2	107	7	30	39	15.3	4.85	77	.322	.382	5	.263	-0	-9	-10	-1	-1.4
Total 5	32	38	.457	131	75	33	4	5	588^1	676	27	250	208	14.5	4.28	95	.295	.370	50	.248	3	-15	-14	-3	-1.7

● **GEORGE GICK**   Gick, George Edward b: 10/18/15, Dunnington, Ind. BB/TR, 6', 190 lbs. Deb: 10/3/37

YEAR TM/L	W	L	PCT	G	GS	CG	SH	SV	IP	H	HR	BB	SO	RAT	ERA	ERA+	OAV	OOB	BH	AVG	PB	PR	/A	PD	TPI
1937 Chi-A	0	0	—	1	0	0	0	1	2	0	0	0	1	0.0	0.00	—	.000	.000	0	—	0	1	1	-0	0.1
1938 Chi-A	0	0	—	1	0	0	0	0	1	3	0	0	2	9.0	0.00	—	.000	.250	0	—	0	1	1	0	0.0
Total 2	0	0	—	2	0	0	0	1	3	3	0	0	2	3.0	0.00	—	.000	.100	0	—	0	2	2	-0	0.1

● **BRETT GIDEON**   Gideon, Byron Brett b: 8/8/63, Ozona, Tex. BR/TR, 6'2", 200 lbs. Deb: 7/5/87

YEAR TM/L	W	L	PCT	G	GS	CG	SH	SV	IP	H	HR	BB	SO	RAT	ERA	ERA+	OAV	OOB	BH	AVG	PB	PR	/A	PD	TPI
1987 Pit-N	1	5	.167	29	0	0	0	3	36^2	34	6	10	31	11.0	4.66	88	.243	.298	1	1.000	1	-2	-2	-0	-0.3
1989 Mon-N	0	0	—	4	0	0	0	0	4^2	5	1	2	2	19.3	1.93	183	.294	.455	0	—	0	1	1	0	0.0
1990 Mon-N	0	0	—	1	0	0	0	0	1	2	0	4	0	54.0	9.00	41	.500	.750	0	—	0	-1	-1	-0	0.0
Total 3	1	5	.167	34	0	0	0	3	42^1	41	7	19	33	13.0	4.46	90	.255	.337	1	1.000	1	-2	-2	-0	-0.3

● **JIM GIDEON**   Gideon, James Leslie b: 9/26/53, Taylor, Tex. BR/TR, 6'3", 190 lbs. Deb: 9/14/75

YEAR TM/L	W	L	PCT	G	GS	CG	SH	SV	IP	H	HR	BB	SO	RAT	ERA	ERA+	OAV	OOB	BH	AVG	PB	PR	/A	PD	TPI
1975 Tex-A	0	0	—	1	1	0	0	0	5^2	7	1	5	2	19.1	7.94	47	.292	.414	0	—	0	-3	-3	-0	0.0

● **FLOYD GIEBELL**   Giebell, Floyd George b: 12/10/09, Pennsboro, W.Va. BL/TR, 6'2.5", 172 lbs. Deb: 4/21/39

YEAR TM/L	W	L	PCT	G	GS	CG	SH	SV	IP	H	HR	BB	SO	RAT	ERA	ERA+	OAV	OOB	BH	AVG	PB	PR	/A	PD	TPI
1939 Det-A	1	1	.500	9	0	0	0	0	15^1	19	1	12	9	18.2	2.93	167	.317	.431	0	.000	-0	3	3	-0	0.3
1940 Det-A	2	0	1.000	2	2	2	1	0	18	14	2	4	11	9.0	1.00	476	.206	.250	0	—	-1	7	8	-0	0.7
1941 Det-A	0	0	—	17	2	0	0	0	34^1	45	3	26	10	18.6	6.03	75	.313	.418	2	.333	-0	-7	-6	-0	-0.0
Total 3	3	1	.750	28	4	2	1	0	67^2	78	6	42	30	16.0	3.99	117	.287	.382	2	.143	-1	2	5	-1	1.0

● **PAUL GIEL**   Giel, Paul Robert b: 2/29/32, Winona, Minn. BR/TR, 5'11", 185 lbs. Deb: 7/10/54

YEAR TM/L	W	L	PCT	G	GS	CG	SH	SV	IP	H	HR	BB	SO	RAT	ERA	ERA+	OAV	OOB	BH	AVG	PB	PR	/A	PD	TPI
1954 NY-N	0	0	—	6	0	0	0	0	4^1	8	0	2	4	20.8	8.31	49	.421	.476	0	—	0	-2	-2	-0	0.0
1955 NY-N	4	4	.500	34	2	0	0	0	82^1	70	8	50	47	13.3	3.39	119	.233	.346	1	.053	-2	6	6	-1	0.3
1958 SF-N	4	5	.444	29	9	0	0	0	92	89	12	55	55	14.3	4.70	81	.259	.365	2	.074	-2	-8	-9	1	-0.8
1959 Pit-N	0	0	—	4	0	0	0	0	7^2	17	0	6	3	27.0	14.09	27	.472	.548	0	—	0	-9	-9	-0	0.0
1960 Pit-N	2	0	1.000	16	0	0	0	0	33	35	3	15	21	13.6	5.73	65	.276	.352	0	—	-1	-7	-7	-1	-0.5
1961 Min-A	1	0	1.000	12	0	0	0	0	19^1	24	6	17	14	19.1	9.78	43	.289	.410	1	.500	-0	-12	-12	-0	-0.5
KC-A	0	0	—	1	0	0	0	0	1^2	6	1	3	1	48.6	37.80	11	.600	.692	0	—	-0	-6	-6	-0	-0.0
Yr	1	0	1.000	13	0	0	0	0	21	30	7	20	15	21.4	12.00	35	.319	.439	1	.500	-0	-19	-18	-0	-0.5
Total 6	11	9	.550	102	11	0	0	0	240^1	249	30	148	145	15.0	5.39	73	.271	.374	4	.073	-4	-38	-39	-0	-1.5

● **BOB GIGGIE**   Giggie, Robert Thomas b: 8/13/33, Dorchester, Mass. BR/TR, 6'1", 200 lbs. Deb: 4/18/59

YEAR TM/L	W	L	PCT	G	GS	CG	SH	SV	IP	H	HR	BB	SO	RAT	ERA	ERA+	OAV	OOB	BH	AVG	PB	PR	/A	PD	TPI
1959 Mil-N	1	0	1.000	13	0	0	0	1	20	24	3	10	15	15.3	4.05	87	.316	.395	0	.000	-0	-0	-1	1	0.0
1960 Mil-N	0	0	—	3	0	0	0	0	4^1	5	0	4	5	18.7	4.15	83	.278	.409	0	—	-0	-0	-0	-0	-0.0
KC-A	1	0	1.000	10	0	0	0	0	18^2	24	1	15	8	18.8	5.79	69	.333	.448	0	.000	-0	-4	-4	0	-0.2
1962 KC-A	1	1	.500	4	2	0	0	0	14^1	17	5	3	4	13.2	6.28	67	.293	.339	0	.000	-0	-4	-3	-1	-0.5
Total 3	3	1	.750	30	2	0	0	1	57	70	9	32	32	16.2	5.18	74	.313	.401	0	.000	-1	-8	-8	-0	-0.7

● **BILL GILBERT**   Gilbert, Alfred Gideon b: 3/13/1868, Havre De Grace, Md 6', 180 lbs. Deb: 9/15/1892

YEAR TM/L	W	L	PCT	G	GS	CG	SH	SV	IP	H	HR	BB	SO	RAT	ERA	ERA+	OAV	OOB	BH	AVG	PB	PR	/A	PD	TPI
1892 Bal-N	0	1	.000	2	1	1	0	0	14	14	1	17	5	19.9	5.79	59	.250	.425	2	.333	1	-4	-4	-1	-0.2

● **JOE GILBERT**   Gilbert, Joe Dennis b: 4/20/52, Jasper, Tex. BR/TL, 6'1", 167 lbs. Deb: 4/30/72

YEAR TM/L	W	L	PCT	G	GS	CG	SH	SV	IP	H	HR	BB	SO	RAT	ERA	ERA+	OAV	OOB	BH	AVG	PB	PR	/A	PD	TPI
1972 Mon-N	0	1	.000	22	0	0	0	1	33	41	3	18	25	16.1	8.45	42	.306	.388	0	.000	-0	-18	-18	-1	-0.6
1973 Mon-N	1	2	.333	21	0	0	0	1	29	30	1	19	17	15.2	4.97	77	.270	.377	0	.000	-0	-4	-4	0	-0.4
Total 2	1	3	.250	43	0	0	0	2	62	71	4	37	42	15.7	6.82	54	.290	.383	0	.000	-0	-23	-22	-0	-1.0

● **BILL GILBRETH**   Gilbreth, William Freeman b: 9/3/47, Abilene, Tex. BL/TL, 6', 180 lbs. Deb: 6/25/71

YEAR TM/L	W	L	PCT	G	GS	CG	SH	SV	IP	H	HR	BB	SO	RAT	ERA	ERA+	OAV	OOB	BH	AVG	PB	PR	/A	PD	TPI
1971 Det-A	2	1	.667	9	5	2	0	0	30	28	4	21	14	15.3	4.80	75	.264	.395	2	.182	-0	-4	-4	-0	-0.4
1972 Det-A	0	0	—	2	0	0	0	0	5	10	1	4	2	25.2	16.20	19	.476	.560	0	.000	-0	-7	-7	-0	0.0
1974 Cal-A	0	0	—	3	0	0	0	0	1^1	2	0	1	0	20.3	13.50	25	.400	.500	0	—	0	-1	-1	-0	0.0
Total 3	2	1	.667	14	5	2	0	0	36^1	40	5	26	16	16.8	6.69	53	.303	.425	2	.167	-0	-13	-13	-0	-0.4

● **BOB GILKS**   Gilks, Robert James b: 7/2/1864, Cincinnati, Ohio d: 8/21/44, Brunswick, Ga. BR/TR, 5'8", 178 lbs. Deb: 8/25/1887 ♦

YEAR TM/L	W	L	PCT	G	GS	CG	SH	SV	IP	H	HR	BB	SO	RAT	ERA	ERA+	OAV	OOB	BH	AVG	PB	PR	/A	PD	TPI
1887 Cle-a	7	5	.583	13	13	12	1	0	108	104	1	42	28	12.9	3.08	141	.245	.326	26	.313	2	15	15	2	1.6
1888 Cle-a	0	2	.000	4	2	2	0	**1**	21	26	1	8	7	15.0	8.14	38	.292	.357	111	.229	0	-12	-12	-0	-0.9
1890 Cle-N	2	2	.500	4	3	3	0	0	31^2	34	0	9	5	13.4	4.26	84	.266	.333	116	.213	-0	-2	-1	-1	-0.3
Total 3	9	9	.500	21	18	17	1	1	160^2	164	2	59	36	13.3	3.98	101	.256	.332	320	.231	2	0	2	0	0.4

● **ED GILL**   Gill, Edward James b: 8/7/1895, Somerville, Mass. d: 10/10/95, Brockton, Mass. BL/TR, 5'10", 165 lbs. Deb: 7/5/19

YEAR TM/L	W	L	PCT	G	GS	CG	SH	SV	IP	H	HR	BB	SO	RAT	ERA	ERA+	OAV	OOB	BH	AVG	PB	PR	/A	PD	TPI
1919 Was-A	1	1	.500	16	2	0	0	0	37^1	38	0	21	7	14.7	4.82	67	.260	.361	0	.000	-1	-7	-7	-1	-0.5

● **GEORGE GILL**   Gill, George Lloyd b: 2/13/09, Catchings, Miss. BR/TR, 6'1", 185 lbs. Deb: 5/4/37

YEAR TM/L	W	L	PCT	G	GS	CG	SH	SV	IP	H	HR	BB	SO	RAT	ERA	ERA+	OAV	OOB	BH	AVG	PB	PR	/A	PD	TPI
1937 Det-A	11	4	.733	31	10	4	1	1	127^2	146	11	42	40	13.3	4.51	104	.285	.340	7	.140	-3	2	2	1	0.1
1938 Det-A	9	7	.571	24	23	13	1	0	164	195	15	50	30	13.6	4.12	121	.286	.348	6	.105	-4	12	16	-1	1.3
1939 Det-A	0	1	.000	3	1	0	0	0	8^2	14	1	3	1	17.7	8.31	59	.368	.415	0	.000	-0	-4	-3	-0	-0.3
StL-A	1	12	.077	27	11	5	0	0	95	139	10	34	24	16.7	7.11	68	.343	.398	4	.154	-2	-26	-24	1	-2.6

YEAR	TM/L	W	L	PCT	G	GS	CG	SH	SV	IP	H	HR	BB	SO	RAT	ERA	ERA+	OAV	OOB	BH	AVG	PB	PR	/A	PD	TPI
	Yr	1	13	.071	30	12	5	0	0	103²	153	11	37	25	16.8	7.21	68	.345	.400	4	.143	-2	-30	-27	1	-2.9
Total	3	24	26	.480	85	45	22	2	1	395¹	494	37	129	95	14.3	5.05	96	.306	.360	17	.126	-9	-16	-9	2	-1.5

● **HADDIE GILL**   Gill, Harold Edward b: 1/23/1899, Brockton, Mass. d: 8/1/32, Brockton, Mass. BL/TL, 5'11", 165 lbs. Deb: 8/16/23

YEAR	TM/L	W	L	PCT	G	GS	CG	SH	SV	IP	H	HR	BB	SO	RAT	ERA	ERA+	OAV	OOB	BH	AVG	PB	PR	/A	PD	TPI
1923	Cin-N	0	0	—	1	0	0	0	0	1	1	0	1	1	18.0	—	—	.333	.500	0	—	0	0	0	0	0.0

● **CLARAL GILLENWATER**   Gillenwater, Claral Lewis b: 5/20/1900, Sims, Ind. d: 2/26/78, Bradenton, Fla. BR/TR, 6', 187 lbs. Deb: 8/20/23

YEAR	TM/L	W	L	PCT	G	GS	CG	SH	SV	IP	H	HR	BB	SO	RAT	ERA	ERA+	OAV	OOB	BH	AVG	PB	PR	/A	PD	TPI
1923	Chi-A	1	3	.250	5	3	1	1	0	21¹	28	2	6	2	14.8	5.48	72	.337	.389	0	.000	-1	-4	-4	0	-0.6

● **TOM GILLES**   Gilles, Thomas Bradford b: 7/2/62, Peoria, Ill. BR/TR, 6'1", 185 lbs. Deb: 6/7/90

YEAR	TM/L	W	L	PCT	G	GS	CG	SH	SV	IP	H	HR	BB	SO	RAT	ERA	ERA+	OAV	OOB	BH	AVG	PB	PR	/A	PD	TPI
1990	Tor-A	1	0	1.000	2	0	0	0	0	1¹	2	0	0	1	13.5	6.75	58	.333	.333	0	—	0	-0	-0	0	-0.3

● **JOHN GILLESPIE**   Gillespie, John Patrick "Silent John" b: 2/25/1900, Oakland, Cal. d: 2/15/54, Vallejo, Cal. BR/TR, 5'11.5", 172 lbs. Deb: 4/12/22

YEAR	TM/L	W	L	PCT	G	GS	CG	SH	SV	IP	H	HR	BB	SO	RAT	ERA	ERA+	OAV	OOB	BH	AVG	PB	PR	/A	PD	TPI
1922	Cin-N	3	3	.500	31	4	1	0	0	77²	84	2	29	21	13.6	4.52	88	.294	.367	2	.133	-1	-4	-5	1	-0.3

● **BOB GILLESPIE**   Gillespie, Robert William "Bunch" b: 10/8/18, Columbus, Ohio BR/TR, 6'4", 187 lbs. Deb: 5/11/44

YEAR	TM/L	W	L	PCT	G	GS	CG	SH	SV	IP	H	HR	BB	SO	RAT	ERA	ERA+	OAV	OOB	BH	AVG	PB	PR	/A	PD	TPI
1944	Det-A	0	1	.000	7	0	0	0	0	11	7	0	12	4	15.5	6.55	54	.194	.396	0	.000	-0	-4	-4	0	-0.3
1947	Chi-A	5	8	.385	25	17	1	0	0	118	133	4	53	36	14.3	4.73	77	.291	.366	2	.061	+3	-13	-14	3	-1.4
1948	Chi-A	0	4	.000	25	6	1	0	0	72	81	3	33	19	14.4	5.13	83	.287	.364	0	.000	-2	-7	-7	0	-0.6
1950	Bos-A	0	0	—	1	0	0	0	0	1¹	2	1	4	0	40.5	20.25	24	.333	.600	0	—	0	-2	-2	-0	0.0
Total	4	5	13	.278	58	23	2	0	0	202¹	223	8	102	59	14.5	5.07	76	.286	.369	2	.039	-5	-26	-27	3	-2.3

● **PAUL GILLIFORD**   Gilliford, Paul Gant "Gorilla" b: 1/12/45, Bryn Mawr, Pa. BR/TL, 5'11", 210 lbs. Deb: 9/20/67

YEAR	TM/L	W	L	PCT	G	GS	CG	SH	SV	IP	H	HR	BB	SO	RAT	ERA	ERA+	OAV	OOB	BH	AVG	PB	PR	/A	PD	TPI
1967	Bal-A	0	0	—	2	0	0	0	0	3	6	1	1	2	21.0	12.00	26	.429	.467	0	—	0	-3	-3	0	0.0

● **JACK GILLIGAN**   Gilligan, John Patrick b: 10/18/1884, Chicago, Ill. d: 11/19/80, Modesto, Cal. BB/TR, 6', 190 lbs. Deb: 9/16/09

YEAR	TM/L	W	L	PCT	G	GS	CG	SH	SV	IP	H	HR	BB	SO	RAT	ERA	ERA+	OAV	OOB	BH	AVG	PB	PR	/A	PD	TPI
1909	StL-A	1	2	.333	3	3	3	0	0	23	28	1	9	4	15.3	5.48	44	.315	.390	1	.111	-1	-8	-8	-1	-1.0
1910	StL-A	0	3	.000	9	5	2	0	0	39¹	67	0	28	10	15.1	3.66	68	.253	.377	3	.200	-0	-5	-5	0	-0.4
Total	2	1	5	.167	12	8	5	0	0	62¹	65	1	37	14	15.2	4.33	57	.277	.382	4	.167	-1	-13	-13	-0	-1.4

● **GEORGE GILLPATRICK**   Gillpatrick, George F. b: 2/28/1875, Holden, Mo. d: 12/15/41, Kansas City, Mo. Deb: 5/22/1898

YEAR	TM/L	W	L	PCT	G	GS	CG	SH	SV	IP	H	HR	BB	SO	RAT	ERA	ERA+	OAV	OOB	BH	AVG	PB	PR	/A	PD	TPI
1898	StL-N	0	2	.000	7	3	1	0	0	35	42	0	19	12	16.2	6.94	55	.296	.387	2	.125	-2	-13	-12	-1	-0.8

● **FRANK GILMORE**   Gilmore, Frank T. "Shadow" b: 4/27/1864, Webster, Mass. d: 7/21/29, Hartford, Conn. BR Deb: 9/11/1886

YEAR	TM/L	W	L	PCT	G	GS	CG	SH	SV	IP	H	HR	BB	SO	RAT	ERA	ERA+	OAV	OOB	BH	AVG	PB	PR	/A	PD	TPI
1886	Was-N	4	4	.500	9	9	9	1	0	75	57	3	22	75	9.5	2.52	130	.200	.257	0	.000	-4	7	6	-1	0.1
1887	Was-N	7	20	.259	28	27	27	1	0	234²	247	3	92	114	13.5	3.87	105	.262	.336	6	.065	-11	5	5	-3	-0.8
1888	Was-N	1	9	.100	12	11	10	0	0	95²	131	4	29	23	15.7	6.59	43	.323	.378	1	.024	-5	-40	-40	-2	-3.7
Total	3	12	33	.267	49	47	46	2	0	405¹	435	14	143	212	13.3	4.26	85	.266	.333	7	.043	-20	-28	-29	-6	-4.4

● **LEN GILMORE**   Gilmore, Leonard Preston "Meow" b: 11/3/17, Fairview Park, Ind. BR/TR, 6'3", 175 lbs. Deb: 10/1/44

YEAR	TM/L	W	L	PCT	G	GS	CG	SH	SV	IP	H	HR	BB	SO	RAT	ERA	ERA+	OAV	OOB	BH	AVG	PB	PR	/A	PD	TPI
1944	Pit-N	0	1	.000	1	1	1	0	0	8	13	2	0	0	14.6	7.88	47	.361	.361	0	.000	-0	-4	-4	1	-0.3

● **JOHN GILROY**   Gilroy, John M. b: 10/26/1869, Washington, D.C. d: 8/4/1897, Norfolk, Va. Deb: 8/30/1895

YEAR	TM/L	W	L	PCT	G	GS	CG	SH	SV	IP	H	HR	BB	SO	RAT	ERA	ERA+	OAV	OOB	BH	AVG	PB	PR	/A	PD	TPI
1895	Was-N	1	4	.200	8	4	2	0	0	41¹	63	3	24	2	19.8	6.53	73	.344	.431	7	.241	-1	-8	-8	1	-0.7
1896	Was-N	0	0	—	1	0	0	0	0	2	0	0	1	0	4.5	0.00	—	.000	.143	0	.000	-0	1	1	0	0.0
Total	2	1	4	.200	9	4	2	0	0	43¹	63	3	25	2	19.1	6.23	77	.333	.422	7	.233	-1	-7	-7	1	-0.7

● **HAL GILSON**   Gilson, Harold "Lefty" b: 2/9/42, Los Angeles, Cal. BR/TL, 6'5", 195 lbs. Deb: 4/14/68

YEAR	TM/L	W	L	PCT	G	GS	CG	SH	SV	IP	H	HR	BB	SO	RAT	ERA	ERA+	OAV	OOB	BH	AVG	PB	PR	/A	PD	TPI
1968	StL-N	0	2	.000	13	0	0	0	2	21²	27	1	11	19	15.8	4.57	63	.310	.388	0	.000	-0	-4	-4	-1	-0.6
	Hou-N	0	0	—	2	0	0	0	0	3²	7	0	1	1	22.1	7.36	40	.412	.474	0	—	0	-2	-2	0	0.0
	Yr	0	2	.000	15	0	0	0	2	25¹	34	1	12	20	16.7	4.97	58	.327	.402	0	—	-0	-6	-6	-1	-0.6

● **BILLY GING**   Ging, William Joseph b: 11/7/1872, Elmira, N.Y. d: 9/14/50, Elmira, N.Y. BR/TR, 5'10", 170 lbs. Deb: 9/25/1899

YEAR	TM/L	W	L	PCT	G	GS	CG	SH	SV	IP	H	HR	BB	SO	RAT	ERA	ERA+	OAV	OOB	BH	AVG	PB	PR	/A	PD	TPI
1899	Bos-N	1	0	1.000	1	1	1	0	0	8	5	0	5	2	11.3	1.13	370	.179	.303	0	.000	-1	2	3	-0	0.2

● **JOE GINGRAS**   Gingras, Joseph Elzead John b: 1/10/1894, New York, N.Y. d: 9/6/47, Jersey City, N.J. BR/TR, 6'2", 188 lbs. Deb: 6/18/15

YEAR	TM/L	W	L	PCT	G	GS	CG	SH	SV	IP	H	HR	BB	SO	RAT	ERA	ERA+	OAV	OOB	BH	AVG	PB	PR	/A	PD	TPI
1915	KC-F	0	0	—	2	0	0	0	0	4	6	0	1	2	15.8	6.75	39	.353	.389	0	.000	-0	-2	-2	-0	0.0

● **CHARLIE GIRARD**   Girard, Charles August b: 12/16/1884, Brooklyn, N.Y. d: 8/6/36, Brooklyn, N.Y. BR/TR, 5'10", 175 lbs. Deb: 9/14/10

YEAR	TM/L	W	L	PCT	G	GS	CG	SH	SV	IP	H	HR	BB	SO	RAT	ERA	ERA+	OAV	OOB	BH	AVG	PB	PR	/A	PD	TPI
1910	Phi-N	1	2	.333	7	1	0	0	1	26²	33	2	12	11	15.9	6.41	49	.308	.388	1	.125	-0	-10	-10	-1	-1.2

● **DAVE GIUSTI**   Giusti, David John b: 11/27/39, Seneca Falls, N.Y. BR/TR, 5'11", 195 lbs. Deb: 4/13/62

YEAR	TM/L	W	L	PCT	G	GS	CG	SH	SV	IP	H	HR	BB	SO	RAT	ERA	ERA+	OAV	OOB	BH	AVG	PB	PR	/A	PD	TPI
1962	Hou-N	2	3	.400	22	5	0	0	0	73²	82	7	30	43	13.7	5.62	66	.280	.347	7	.292	3	-14	-15	1	-0.6
1964	Hou-N	0	0	—	8	0	0	0	0	25²	24	1	8	16	11.2	3.16	108	.253	.311	2	.286	1	1	1	1	0.2
1965	Hou-N	8	7	.533	38	13	4	1	3	131¹	132	13	46	92	12.3	4.32	78	.259	.321	6	.171	2	-11	-14	1	-1.2
1966	Hou-N	15	14	.517	34	33	9	4	0	210	215	23	54	131	11.2	4.20	81	.260	.310	17	.230	5	-14	-18	-1	-1.9
1967	Hou-N	11	15	.423	37	33	8	1	1	221²	231	20	58	157	11.9	4.18	79	.265	.313	13	.155	3	-20	-21	-2	-2.2
1968	Hou-N	11	14	.440	37	34	12	2	1	251	226	15	67	186	10.6	3.19	93	.239	.293	15	.183	2	-6	-7	3	-0.1
1969	StL-N	3	7	.300	22	12	2	1	0	99²	96	7	37	62	12.1	3.61	99	.255	.323	5	.200	1	-0	-1	1	0.2
1970	*Pit-N	9	3	.750	66	1	0	0	26	103	98	7	39	85	12.0	3.06	128	.259	.328	3	.188	2	11	10	0	1.7
1971	*Pit-N	5	6	.455	58	0	0	0	**30**	86	79	5	31	55	11.6	2.93	115	.241	.308	1	.059	-1	5	4	-1	0.7
1972	*Pit-N	7	4	.636	54	0	0	0	22	74²	59	3	20	54	9.5	1.93	172	.219	.273	0	.000	-1	13	12	1	2.5
1973	Pit-N★	9	2	.818	67	0	0	0	20	98²	89	9	37	64	11.5	2.37	148	.241	.310	4	.308	1	14	13	-2	1.8
1974	*Pit-N	7	5	.583	64	2	0	0	12	105²	101	2	40	53	12.0	3.32	104	.258	.327	1	.111	-0	3	1	1	0.3
1975	*Pit-N	5	4	.556	61	0	0	0	17	91²	79	3	42	38	11.9	2.95	120	.237	.322	3	.300	1	7	6	0	0.9
1976	Pit-N	5	4	.556	40	0	0	0	6	58¹	59	7	24	28	13.3	4.32	81	.267	.347	0	—	-0	-5	-5	-0	-0.9
1977	Oak-A	3	3	.500	40	0	0	0	6	60¹	54	4	20	28	11.0	2.98	135	.245	.308	0	—	-0	7	7	0	0.9
	Chi-N	0	2	.000	22	0	0	0	0	27	36	3	15	13	16.6	6.04	73	.297	.383	0	—	-0	-6	-5	-0	-0.4
Total	15	100	93	.518	668	133	35	9	145	1716²	1654	126	570	1103	11.7	3.60	95	.253	.315	77	.187	18	-14	-33	2	1.9

● **BRIAN GIVENS**   Givens, Brian Allen b: 11/6/65, Lompoc, Cal. BR/TL, 6'6", 220 lbs. Deb: 6/24/95

YEAR	TM/L	W	L	PCT	G	GS	CG	SH	SV	IP	H	HR	BB	SO	RAT	ERA	ERA+	OAV	OOB	BH	AVG	PB	PR	/A	PD	TPI
1995	Mil-A	5	7	.417	19	19	1	0	0	107¹	116	11	54	73	14.5	4.95	101	.275	.361	0		0	-3	0	-1	-0.1
1996	Mil-A	1	3	.250	4	4	0	0	0	14	32	3	7	10	25.1	12.86	41	.438	.488	0		0	-12	-12	-1	-2.3
Total	2	6	10	.375	23	23	1	0	0	121¹	148	14	61	83	15.7	5.86	86	.299	.379	0		0	-15	-11	-2	-2.4

● **DAN GLADDEN**   Gladden, Clinton Daniel b: 7/7/57, San Jose, Cal. BR/TR, 5'11", 180 lbs. Deb: 9/5/83 ◆

YEAR	TM/L	W	L	PCT	G	GS	CG	SH	SV	IP	H	HR	BB	SO	RAT	ERA	ERA+	OAV	OOB	BH	AVG	PB	PR	/A	PD	TPI
1988	Min-A	0	0	—	1	0	0	0	0	1	1	0	0	0	9.0	—	—	.000	.000	155	.269	1	0	0	0	0.0
1989	Min-A	0	0	—	1	0	0	0	0	1	2	0	1	0	27.0	9.00	46	.400	.500	136	.295	1	-1	-1	0	0.0
Total	2	0	0	—	2	0	0	0	0	2	2	0	1	0	13.5	4.50	91	.250	.333	1215	.270	2	-0	-0	0	0.0

● **FRED GLADDING**   Gladding, Fred Earl b: 6/28/36, Flat Rock, Mich. BL/TR, 6', 225 lbs. Deb: 7/1/61 C

YEAR	TM/L	W	L	PCT	G	GS	CG	SH	SV	IP	H	HR	BB	SO	RAT	ERA	ERA+	OAV	OOB	BH	AVG	PB	PR	/A	PD	TPI
1961	Det-A	1	0	1.000	8	0	0	0	0	16¹	18	1	11	11	17.1	3.31	124	.286	.408	0	.000	-0	1	1	-0	0.0
1962	Det-A	0	0	—	6	0	0	0	0	5	3	1	4	2	9.0	—	.176	.263	0	.000	-0	2	2	0	0.0
1963	Det-A	1	1	.500	22	0	0	0	5	27¹	19	1	14	24	10.9	1.98	189	.198	.300	0	.000	-0	5	5	0	0.7
1964	Det-A	7	4	.636	42	0	0	0	7	67¹	57	7	27	59	11.5	3.07	119	.233	.314	0	.000	-0	4	4	1	0.7
1965	Det-A	6	2	.750	46	0	0	0	6	70	63	6	29	43	12.3	2.83	123	.239	.323	0	.000	-1	5	5	-1	0.5
1966	Det-A	5	0	1.000	51	0	0	0	5	74	62	6	29	57	11.2	3.28	106	.230	.307	0	.000	-0	1	1	-1	0.0
1967	Det-A	6	4	.600	42	1	0	0	12	77	64	4	19	64	9.9	1.99	164	.227	.287	0	.000	-0	11	11	-0	1.6
1968	Hou-N	0	0	—	7	0	0	0	0	4¹	8	0	3	2	24.9	14.54	20	.421	.522	0	—	-0	-6	-6	-0	-0.6
1969	Hou-N	4	8	.333	57	0	0	0	**29**	72²	83	2	27	46	13.7	4.21	84	.289	.352	1	.100	-1	-5	-5	-0	-1.4
1970	Hou-N	4	6	.636	63	0	0	0	18	71	69	4	26	35	12.4	4.06	96	.293	.354	0	.000	-1	-1	-1	-1	-0.2
1971	Hou-N	4	5	.444	48	0	0	0	12	51¹	51	0	22	17	14.0	2.10	160	.268	.365	0	.000	-0	8	7	-1	1.5
1972	Hou-N	5	6	.455	42	0	0	0	14	48²	38	1	12	18	9.6	2.77	121	.222	.281	0	.000	-1	4	3	-1	0.8

YEAR	TM/L	W	L	PCT	G	GS	CG	SH	SV	IP	H	HR	BB	SO	RAT	ERA	ERA+	OAV	OOB	BH	AVG	PB	PR	/A	PD	TPI
1973	Hou-N	2	0	1.000	16	0	0	0	1	16	18	4	4	9	12.4	4.50	81	.290	.333	0	—	0	-1	-2	0	-0.2
Total	13	48	34	.585	450	1	0	0	109	601	566	38	223	394	12.2	3.13	113	.252	.327	1	.016	-6	29	28	-2	3.4

● FRED GLADE
Glade, Frederick Monroe "Lucky"   b: 1/25/1876, Dubuque, Iowa   d: 11/21/34, Grand Island, Neb.   BR/TR, 5'10", 175 lbs.   Deb: 5/27/02

YEAR	TM/L	W	L	PCT	G	GS	CG	SH	SV	IP	H	HR	BB	SO	RAT	ERA	ERA+	OAV	OOB	BH	AVG	PB	PR	/A	PD	TPI
1902	Chi-N	0	1	.000	1	1	1	0	0	8	13	0	3	3	19.1	9.00	30	.361	.425	1	.333	1	-6	-6	0	-0.4
1904	StL-A	18	15	.545	35	34	30	6	1	289	248	2	58	156	9.9	2.27	109	.233	.281	19	.186	1	10	7	1	1.1
1905	StL-A	6	25	.194	32	32	28	2	0	275	257	3	58	127	10.7	2.81	90	.249	.296	9	.092	-6	-5	-8	4	-1.2
1906	StL-A	15	14	.517	35	32	28	4	1	266²	215	4	59	96	9.6	2.36	109	.224	.276	13	.137	-4	10	7	-3	0.0
1907	StL-A	13	9	.591	24	22	18	2	0	202	187	2	45	71	10.7	2.67	94	.248	.298	4	.205	-2	-3	-4	-4	-0.6
1908	NY-A	0	4	.000	5	5	2	0	0	32	30	0	14	11	13.5	4.22	59	.275	.378	0	.000	-1	-6	-6	-1	-0.9
Total	6	52	68	.433	132	126	107	14	2	1072²	950	11	237	464	10.4	2.62	97	.240	.291	57	.150	-7	0	-10	-3	-2.0

● JOHN GLAISER
Glaiser, John Burke "Bert"   b: 7/28/1894, Yoakum, Tex.   d: 3/7/59, Houston, Tex.   BL/TR, 5'8", 165 lbs.   Deb: 4/20/20

YEAR	TM/L	W	L	PCT	G	GS	CG	SH	SV	IP	H	HR	BB	SO	RAT	ERA	ERA+	OAV	OOB	BH	AVG	PB	PR	/A	PD	TPI
1920	Det-A	0	0	—	9	1	0	0	1	17	23	1	8	3	16.9	6.35	59	.354	.432	0	.000	-0	-5	-5	1	0.0

● TOM GLASS
Glass, Thomas Joseph   b: 4/29/1898, Greensboro, N.C.   d: 12/15/81, Greensboro, N.C.   BR/TR, 6'3", 170 lbs.   Deb: 6/12/25

YEAR	TM/L	W	L	PCT	G	GS	CG	SH	SV	IP	H	HR	BB	SO	RAT	ERA	ERA+	OAV	OOB	BH	AVG	PB	PR	/A	PD	TPI
1925	Phi-A	1	0	1.000	2	0	0	0	0	5	9	0	2	0	16.2	5.40	86	.409	.409	0	.000	-0	-1	-0	-0	-0.1

● JACK GLASSCOCK
Glasscock, John Wesley "Pebbly Jack"   b: 7/22/1859, Wheeling, W.Va.   d: 2/24/47, Wheeling, W.Va.   BR/TR, 5'8", 160 lbs.   Deb: 5/1/1879   M♦

YEAR	TM/L	W	L	PCT	G	GS	CG	SH	SV	IP	H	HR	BB	SO	RAT	ERA	ERA+	OAV	OOB	BH	AVG	PB	PR	/A	PD	TPI
1884	Cle-N	0	0	—	2	0	0	0	0	5	8	0	2	1	18.0	5.40	58	.333	.385	70	.249	0	-1	-1	0	0.1
1887	Ind-N	0	0	—	1	0	0	0	0	1	0	0	1	0	0.00	—	.000	.000	142	.294	0	0	0	0	0.0
1888	Ind-N	0	0	—	1	0	0	0	0	0¹	1	0	2	1	108.0	54.00	5	1.000	1.000	119	.269	0	-2	-2	0	0.0
1889	Ind-N	0	0	—	1	0	0	0	0	0²	3	0	3	0	81.0	0.00	—	.600	.750	205	.352	0	0	0	0	0.0
Total	4	0	0	—	5	0	0	0	0	7	12	0	7	3	25.7	6.43	53	.364	.488	2040	.290	1	-2	-2	1	0.1

● LUKE GLAVENICH
Glavenich, Luke Frank   b: 1/17/1893, Jackson, Cal.   d: 5/22/35, Stockton, Cal.   BR/TR, 5'9.5", 189 lbs.   Deb: 4/12/13

YEAR	TM/L	W	L	PCT	G	GS	CG	SH	SV	IP	H	HR	BB	SO	RAT	ERA	ERA+	OAV	OOB	BH	AVG	PB	PR	/A	PD	TPI
1913	Cle-A	0	0	—	1	0	0	0	0	3	4	1	3	1	54.0	9.00	34	.500	.667	1	—					

● TOM GLAVINE
Glavine, Thomas Michael   b: 3/25/66, Concord, Mass.   BL/TL, 6'1", 190 lbs.   Deb: 8/17/87

YEAR	TM/L	W	L	PCT	G	GS	CG	SH	SV	IP	H	HR	BB	SO	RAT	ERA	ERA+	OAV	OOB	BH	AVG	PB	PR	/A	PD	TPI
1987	Atl-N	2	4	.333	9	9	0	0	0	50¹	55	5	33	20	16.3	5.54	78	.279	.391	2	.125	-0	-8	-7	1	-0.7
1988	Atl-N	7	17	.292	34	34	1	0	0	195¹	201	12	63	84	12.5	4.56	81	.270	.333	11	.183	1	-24	-19	2	-1.9
1989	Atl-N	14	8	.636	29	29	6	4	0	186	172	20	40	90	10.4	3.68	99	.243	.285	10	.149	0	-4	-1	1	0.1
1990	Atl-N	10	12	.455	33	33	1	0	0	214²	232	18	78	129	13.1	4.28	94	.281	.343	7	.113	0	-12	-6	1	-0.4
1991	*Atl-N★	**20**	11	.645	34	34	**9**	1	0	246²	201	17	69	192	9.9	2.55	**152**	.222	.279	17	.230	4	31	**37**	3	**5.5**
1992	*Atl-N★	**20**	8	.714	33	33	7	**5**	0	225	197	6	70	129	10.8	2.76	133	.235	.295	19	.247	4	19	22	-0	3.3
1993	*Atl-N☆	**22**	6	.786	36	36	4	2	0	239¹	236	16	90	120	12.3	3.20	126	.259	.327	14	.173	1	22	22	0	2.5
1994	Atl-N	13	9	.591	25	25	2	0	0	165¹	173	10	70	140	13.3	3.97	107	.268	.341	10	.179	1	4	5	2	0.9
1995	*Atl-N★	16	7	.696	29	29	3	1	0	198²	182	9	66	127	11.5	3.08	138	.246	.312	14	.222	3	24	26	3	3.5
1996	*Atl-N★	15	10	.600	36	36	1	0	0	235³	222	14	85	181	11.7	2.98	148	.249	.314	22	.289	6	32	37	4	4.8
Total	10	139	92	.602	298	298	34	13	0	1956¹	1871	127	664	1212	11.8	3.45	116	.253	.316	126	.199	21	85	117	17	17.6

● RALPH GLAZE
Glaze, Daniel Ralph   b: 3/13/1882, Denver, Col.   d: 10/31/68, Atascadero, Cal.   BR/TR, 5'9", 165 lbs.   Deb: 6/1/06

YEAR	TM/L	W	L	PCT	G	GS	CG	SH	SV	IP	H	HR	BB	SO	RAT	ERA	ERA+	OAV	OOB	BH	AVG	PB	PR	/A	PD	TPI
1906	Bos-A	4	6	.400	19	10	7	0	0	123	110	4	32	56	10.8	3.59	77	.242	.299	10	.182	0	-12	-11	0	-0.8
1907	Bos-A	9	13	.409	32	21	11	1	0	182¹	150	4	48	68	10.0	2.32	111	.227	.283	11	.180	0	5	5	-4	0.2
1908	Bos-A	2	2	.500	10	3	2	0	0	34²	43	1	5	13	12.5	3.38	73	.253	.274	1	.077	-1	-4	-4	-1	-0.6
Total	3	15	21	.417	61	34	20	1	0	340	303	9	85	137	10.5	2.89	91	.236	.288	22	.171	-1	-11	-10	-4	-1.2

● WHITEY GLAZNER
Glazner, Charles Franklin   b: 9/17/1893, Sycamore, Ala.   d: 6/6/89, Orlando, Fla.   BR/TR, 5'9", 165 lbs.   Deb: 9/26/20

YEAR	TM/L	W	L	PCT	G	GS	CG	SH	SV	IP	H	HR	BB	SO	RAT	ERA	ERA+	OAV	OOB	BH	AVG	PB	PR	/A	PD	TPI
1920	Pit-N	0	0	—	2	0	0	0	0	8²	9	0	2	1	11.4	3.12	103	.300	.344	0	.000	-0	-0	-0	-0	-0.1
1921	Pit-N	14	5	.737	36	25	15	0	1	234	214	9	58	88	10.9	2.77	139	**.250**	.306	10	.132	-3	26	28	-4	1.4
1922	Pit-N	11	12	.478	34	26	10	1	1	193	238	9	52	77	13.6	4.38	93	.309	.354	16	.246	3	-6	-7	0	-0.4
1923	Pit-N	2	1	.667	7	4	1	1	0	30	29	5	11	8	12.0	3.30	122	.250	.315	4	.333	2	2	2	0	0.4
	Phi-N	7	14	.333	28	23	12	2	1	161¹	195	11	63	51	14.7	4.69	98	.304	.371	9	.170	-1	-12	-11	0	-0.3
	Yr	9	15	.375	35	27	13	3	2	191¹	224	16	74	59	14.3	4.47	101	.296	.363	13	.200	1	-10	1	0	0.1
1924	Phi-N	7	16	.304	35	24	8	2	0	156²	210	14	63	41	15.9	5.92	75	.339	.403	8	.157	-4	-36	-25	1	-3.4
Total	5	41	48	.461	142	102	46	6	4	783²	895	44	249	266	13.4	4.21	99	.295	.353	47	.181	-3	-25	-3	-3	-2.4

● JOE GLEASON
Gleason, Joseph Paul   b: 7/9/1895, Phelps, N.Y.   d: 9/8/90, Phelps, N.Y.   BR/TR, 5'10.5", 175 lbs.   Deb: 9/11/20

YEAR	TM/L	W	L	PCT	G	GS	CG	SH	SV	IP	H	HR	BB	SO	RAT	ERA	ERA+	OAV	OOB	BH	AVG	PB	PR	/A	PD	TPI
1920	Was-A	0	0	—	3	0	0	0	0	8	14	2	6	2	23.6	13.50	28	.326	.420	0	.000	1	-9	-9	0	0.1
1922	Was-A	2	2	.500	8	5	3	0	0	40²	53	3	18	12	15.9	4.65	83	.319	.389	2	.143	-0	-3	-4	-0	-0.3
Total	2	2	2	.500	11	5	3	0	0	48²	67	5	24	14	17.2	6.10	63	.321	.396	2	.125	1	-11	-12	0	-0.3

● BILL GLEASON
Gleason, William   b: 1868, Cleveland, Ohio   d: 12/2/1893, Cleveland, Ohio   Deb: 4/24/1890

YEAR	TM/L	W	L	PCT	G	GS	CG	SH	SV	IP	H	HR	BB	SO	RAT	ERA	ERA+	OAV	OOB	BH	AVG	PB	PR	/A	PD	TPI
1890	Cle-P	0	1	.000	1	1	0	0	0	4	14	1	4	0	45.0	27.00	15	.538	.625	0	.000	-0	-10	-10	-0	-1.2

● KID GLEASON
Gleason, William J.   b: 10/26/1866, Camden, N.J.   d: 1/2/33, Philadelphia, Pa.   BB/TR, 5'7", 158 lbs.   Deb: 4/20/1888   FMC♦

YEAR	TM/L	W	L	PCT	G	GS	CG	SH	SV	IP	H	HR	BB	SO	RAT	ERA	ERA+	OAV	OOB	BH	AVG	PB	PR	/A	PD	TPI
1888	Phi-N	7	16	.304	24	23	23	0	0	199²	199	11	53	89	11.9	2.84	105	.252	.309	17	.205	4	0	3	-3	0.0
1889	Phi-N	9	15	.375	29	21	15	0	1	205	242	8	97	64	15.3	5.58	78	.285	.364	25	.253	2	-36	-28	1	-2.3
1890	Phi-N	38	17	.691	60	55	54	6	**2**	506	479	8	167	222	11.8	2.63	139	.242	.306	47	.210	-6	53	58	-0	4.6
1891	Phi-N	24	22	.522	53	44	40	1	1	418	431	10	165	100	13.1	3.51	97	.256	.328	53	.248	6	-8	-5	-3	-0.2
1892	StL-N	20	24	.455	47	45	43	2	0	400	389	11	151	133	12.4	3.33	96	.245	.314	50	.215	8	-2	-6	5	0.7
1893	StL-N	21	22	.488	48	45	37	1	1	380¹	436	18	187	86	15.0	4.61	103	.279	.360	51	.256	4	2	5	1	0.8
1894	StL-N	2	6	.250	8	8	6	0	0	58	75	2	21	9	15.4	6.05	89	.310	.372	7	.250	-0	-5	-4	1	-0.3
	*Bal-N	15	5	.750	21	20	19	0	1	172	224	3	44	35	14.2	4.45	123	.312	.354	30	.349	4	17	19	-2	1.8
	Yr	17	11	.607	29	28	25	0	1	230	299	5	65	44	14.4	4.85	112	.310	.356	37	.313	4	12	15	-0	1.5
1895	*Bal-N	2	4	.333	9	5	3	0	0	50¹	77	4	21	6	18.1	6.97	68	.345	.409	130	.309	-2	-12	-12	-0	-1.0
Total	8	138	131	.513	299	266	240	10	6	2389¹	2552	75	906	744	13.3	3.79	103	.265	.333	1944	.261	20	10	29	-2	4.1

● JERRY DON GLEATON
Gleaton, Jerry Don   b: 9/14/57, Brownwood, Tex.   BL/TL, 6'3", 210 lbs.   Deb: 7/11/79

YEAR	TM/L	W	L	PCT	G	GS	CG	SH	SV	IP	H	HR	BB	SO	RAT	ERA	ERA+	OAV	OOB	BH	AVG	PB	PR	/A	PD	TPI
1979	Tex-A	0	1	.000	5	2	0	0	0	9²	15	0	2	2	16.8	6.52	64	.375	.419	0	—	0	-2	-3	0	-0.2
1980	Tex-A	0	0	—	5	0	0	0	0	7	5	0	4	2	11.6	2.57	151	.208	.321	0	—	0	1	0	0	0.1
1981	Sea-A	4	7	.364	20	13	1	0	0	85¹	88	10	38	31	13.5	4.75	81	.273	.354	0	—	0	-10	-11	-1	-1.2
1982	Sea-A	0	0	—	3	0	0	0	0	4²	7	3	2	1	19.3	13.50	31	.333	.417	0	—	0	-5	-5	-0	-0.1
1984	Chi-A	1	2	.333	11	1	0	0	2	18¹	20	2	6	4	13.3	3.44	121	.286	.351	0	—	0	2	1	-0	0.1
1985	Chi-A	1	0	1.000	31	0	0	0	1	29²	39	3	13	22	15.2	5.76	75	.316	.385	0	—	0	-5	-5	-0	-0.2
1987	KC-A	4	4	.500	48	0	0	0	5	50²	38	4	28	44	11.7	4.26	107	.216	.324	0	—	0	1	2	1	0.2
1988	KC-A	0	4	.000	42	0	0	0	3	38	33	2	17	29	12.6	3.55	112	.232	.327	0	—	0	2	2	0	0.1
1989	KC-A	0	0	—	15	0	0	0	0	14¹	20	1	6	9	16.3	5.65	68	.345	.406	0	—	0	-3	-3	-0	-0.2
1990	Det-A	1	3	.250	57	0	0	0	13	82²	62	5	25	56	9.8	2.94	135	.213	.282	0	—	0	9	9	0	0.6
1991	Det-A	3	2	.600	47	0	0	0	2	75¹	74	7	39	47	13.5	4.06	102	.269	.360	0	—	0	0	0	0	-0.0
1992	Pit-N	1	0	1.000	23	0	0	0	0	31²	34	4	19	18	15.1	4.26	81	.283	.381	0	.000	0	-3	-3	0	-0.1
Total	12	15	23	.395	307	16	1	0	26	447¹	433	40	199	265	12.9	4.25	95	.261	.345	0	—	0	-14	-10	-0	-0.9

● MARTIN GLENDON
Glendon, Martin J.   b: 2/8/1877, Milwaukee, Wis.   d: 11/6/50, Norwood Park, Ill.   5'8", 165 lbs.   Deb: 4/18/02

YEAR	TM/L	W	L	PCT	G	GS	CG	SH	SV	IP	H	HR	BB	SO	RAT	ERA	ERA+	OAV	OOB	BH	AVG	PB	PR	/A	PD	TPI
1902	Cin-N	0	1	.000	1	1	0	0	0	4	9	0	4	0	27.0	12.00	36	.357	.500	0	.000	-0	-3	-3	0	-0.7
1903	Cle-A	1	2	.333	3	3	3	0	0	27²	20	0	7	9	8.8	0.98	292	.202	.255	0	.000	-1	6	6	1	0.6
Total	2	1	3	.250	4	4	3	0	0	30²	25	0	11	9	10.6	2.05	140	.221	.290	0	.000	-1	3	3	1	-0.1

● BOB GLENN
Glenn, Burdette   b: 6/16/1894, W.Sunbury, Pa.   d: 6/3/77, Richmond, Cal.   Deb: 7/27/20

YEAR	TM/L	W	L	PCT	G	GS	CG	SH	SV	IP	H	HR	BB	SO	RAT	ERA	ERA+	OAV	OOB	BH	AVG	PB	PR	/A	PD	TPI
1920	StL-N	0	0	—	2	0	0	0	0	4	4	1	2	0	9.0	0.00	—	.222	.222	0	—	0	1	1	0	0.0

● SAL GLIATTO
Gliatto, Salvador Michael   b: 5/7/02, Chicago, Ill.   d: 11/2/95, Tyler, Tex.   BB/TR, 5'8.5", 150 lbs.   Deb: 4/19/30

YEAR	TM/L	W	L	PCT	G	GS	CG	SH	SV	IP	H	HR	BB	SO	RAT	ERA	ERA+	OAV	OOB	BH	AVG	PB	PR	/A	PD	TPI
1930	Cle-A	0	0	—	8	0	0	0	2	15	21	1	9	7	19.2	6.60	73	.328	.427	0	.000	-0	-3	-3	-0	-0.2

YEAR TM/L	W	L	PCT	G	GS	CG	SH	SV	IP	H	HR	BB	SO	RAT	ERA	ERA+	OAV	OOB	BH	AVG	PB	PR	/A	PD	TPI

● GEORGE GLINATSIS
Glinatsis, George b: 6/29/69, Youngstown, Ohio BR/TR, 6'4", 195 lbs. Deb: 7/18/94

YEAR TM/L	W	L	PCT	G	GS	CG	SH	SV	IP	H	HR	BB	SO	RAT	ERA	ERA+	OAV	OOB	BH	AVG	PB	PR	/A	PD	TPI
1994 Sea-A	0	1	.000	2	2	0	0	0	5¹	9	2	6	1	25.3	13.50	36	.429	.556	0	—	0	-5	-5	-0	-0.7

● ED GLYNN
Glynn, Edward Paul b: 6/3/53, Flushing, N.Y. BR/TL, 6'2", 180 lbs. Deb: 9/19/75

YEAR TM/L	W	L	PCT	G	GS	CG	SH	SV	IP	H	HR	BB	SO	RAT	ERA	ERA+	OAV	OOB	BH	AVG	PB	PR	/A	PD	TPI
1975 Det-A	0	2	.000	3	1	0	0	0	14²	11	1	8	8	11.7	4.30	93	.220	.328	0	—	0	-1	-0	-0	-0.1
1976 Det-A	1	3	.250	5	4	1	0	0	23²	22	3	20	17	16.0	6.08	61	.265	.408	0	—	0	-7	-6	-1	-1.0
1977 Det-A	2	1	.667	8	3	0	0	0	27¹	36	3	12	13	15.8	5.27	81	.316	.381	0	—	0	-4	-3	-0	-0.7
1978 Det-A	0	0	—	14	0	0	0	0	14²	11	3	4	9	9.2	3.07	126	.208	.263	0	—	0	1	1	1	0.1
1979 NY-N	1	4	.200	46	0	0	0	7	60	57	3	40	32	14.9	3.00	121	.259	.378	0	.000	-0	5	4	-1	0.3
1980 NY-N	3	3	.500	38	0	0	0	1	52¹	49	5	23	32	12.4	4.13	86	.246	.324	0	.000	-1	-3	-3	1	-0.4
1981 Cle-A	0	0	—	7	0	0	0	0	7²	5	0	4	4	10.6	1.17	309	.192	.300	0	—	0	2	2	-0	0.0
1982 Cle-A	5	2	.714	47	0	0	0	4	49²	43	6	30	54	13.2	4.17	98	.232	.340	0	—	0	-1	-0	-0	-0.1
1983 Cle-A	0	2	.000	11	0	0	0	0	12¹	22	2	6	13	20.4	5.84	73	.373	.431	0	—	0	-2	-2	-0	-0.5
1985 Mon-N	0	0	—	3	0	0	0	0	2¹	5	0	4	2	34.7	19.29	18	.455	.600	0	—	0	-4	-4	-0	0.0
Total 10	12	17	.414	175	8	1	0	12	264²	261	26	151	184	14.1	4.25	90	.261	.359	0	.000	-1	-13	-12	-2	-2.4

● JOT GOAR
Goar, Joshua Mercer b: 1/31/1870, New Lisbon, Ind. d: 4/4/47, New Castle, Ind. BR/TR, 5'9", 160 lbs. Deb: 4/18/1896

YEAR TM/L	W	L	PCT	G	GS	CG	SH	SV	IP	H	HR	BB	SO	RAT	ERA	ERA+	OAV	OOB	BH	AVG	PB	PR	/A	PD	TPI
1896 Pit-N	0	1	.000	3	0	0	0	0	13¹	36	1	8	3	30.4	16.88	25	.486	.542	1	.167	-1	-19	-19	-1	-1.0
1898 Cin-N	0	0	—	1	0	0	0	0	2	4	0	1	0	22.5	9.00	43	.400	.455	0	—	0	-1	-1	0	0.0
Total 2	0	1	.000	4	0	0	0	0	15¹	40	1	9	3	29.3	15.85	26	.476	.532	1	.167	-1	-20	-20	-1	-1.0

● GEORGE GOETZ
Goetz, George Burt b: Greencastle, Pa. 6'2", 180 lbs. Deb: 6/17/1889

YEAR TM/L	W	L	PCT	G	GS	CG	SH	SV	IP	H	HR	BB	SO	RAT	ERA	ERA+	OAV	OOB	BH	AVG	PB	PR	/A	PD	TPI
1889 Bal-a	1	0	1.000	1	1	1	0	0	9	12	0	2	2	12.0	4.00	99	.308	.308	0	.000	-1	-0	-1	0	-0.1

● JOHN GOETZ
Goetz, John Hardy b: 10/24/37, Goetzville, Mich. BR/TR, 6', 185 lbs. Deb: 4/16/60

YEAR TM/L	W	L	PCT	G	GS	CG	SH	SV	IP	H	HR	BB	SO	RAT	ERA	ERA+	OAV	OOB	BH	AVG	PB	PR	/A	PD	TPI
1960 Chi-N	0	0	—	4	0	0	0	0	6¹	10	2	4	6	19.9	12.79	30	.370	.452	0	.000	-0	-6	-6	0	0.0

● BILL GOGOLEWSKI
Gogolewski, William Joseph b: 10/26/47, Oshkosh, Wis. BL/TR, 6'4", 190 lbs. Deb: 9/3/70

YEAR TM/L	W	L	PCT	G	GS	CG	SH	SV	IP	H	HR	BB	SO	RAT	ERA	ERA+	OAV	OOB	BH	AVG	PB	PR	/A	PD	TPI
1970 Was-A	2	2	.500	8	6	0	0	0	33²	33	2	25	19	15.8	4.81	74	.260	.386	0	.000	-0	-4	-5	1	-0.5
1971 Was-A	6	5	.545	27	17	4	1	0	124¹	112	5	39	70	11.1	2.75	120	.241	.302	5	.156	1	10	8	-0	0.7
1972 Tex-A	4	11	.267	36	21	3	1	2	150²	136	9	58	95	11.9	4.24	71	.239	.316	5	.125	-1	-20	-21	2	-2.2
1973 Tex-A	3	6	.333	49	1	0	0	6	123²	139	10	48	77	13.7	4.22	88	.286	.351	0	—	0	-6	-7	2	-0.3
1974 Cle-A	0	0	—	5	0	0	0	0	13²	15	1	2	3	11.9	4.61	78	.283	.321	0	—	0	-2	-2	1	0.1
1975 Chi-A	0	0	—	19	0	0	0	2	55	61	5	28	37	14.7	5.24	74	.292	.378	0	—	0	-9	-8	1	0.0
Total 6	15	24	.385	144	44	6	2	10	501	496	32	200	301	12.7	4.02	85	.260	.334	10	.127	-1	-30	-34	5	-2.2

● GREG GOHR
Gohr, Gregory James b: 10/29/67, Santa Clara, Cal. BR/TR, 6'3", 205 lbs. Deb: 4/7/93

YEAR TM/L	W	L	PCT	G	GS	CG	SH	SV	IP	H	HR	BB	SO	RAT	ERA	ERA+	OAV	OOB	BH	AVG	PB	PR	/A	PD	TPI
1993 Det-A	0	0	—	16	0	0	0	0	22²	26	1	14	23	16.7	5.96	72	.289	.396	0	—	0	-4	-4	-0	0.0
1994 Det-A	2	2	.500	8	6	0	0	0	34	36	3	21	21	15.1	4.50	108	.263	.361	0	—	0	1	1	-1	0.0
1995 Det-A	1	0	1.000	10	0	0	0	0	10¹	9	0	3	12	10.5	0.87	546	.243	.300	0	—	0	4	4	-0	0.4
1996 Det-A	4	8	.333	17	16	0	0	0	91²	129	24	34	60	16.3	7.17	71	.328	.386	0	—	0	-22	-21	-1	-2.2
Cal-A	1	1	.500	15	0	0	0	0	24	34	7	10	16	16.5	7.50	65	.337	.396	0	—	0	-7	-7	-0	-0.4
Yr	5	9	.357	32	16	0	0	0	115²	163	31	44	75	16.1	7.24	69	.326	.381	0	—	0	-29	-28	-1	-2.6
Total 4	8	11	.421	66	22	0	0	1	182²	234	35	82	131	15.8	6.21	79	.309	.380	0	—	0	-27	-27	-2	-2.2

● JIM GOLDEN
Golden, James Edward b: 3/20/36, Eldon, Mo. BL/TR, 6', 175 lbs. Deb: 9/30/60

YEAR TM/L	W	L	PCT	G	GS	CG	SH	SV	IP	H	HR	BB	SO	RAT	ERA	ERA+	OAV	OOB	BH	AVG	PB	PR	/A	PD	TPI
1960 LA-N	1	0	1.000	1	1	0	0	0	7	6	1	4	4	12.9	6.43	62	.240	.345	1	.333	-0	-2	-2	-0	-0.2
1961 LA-N	1	1	.500	28	0	0	0	0	42	52	7	20	18	15.4	5.79	75	.306	.379	0	.000	-0	-8	-7	-0	-0.3
1962 Hou-N	7	11	.389	37	18	5	2	1	152²	163	13	50	88	12.6	4.07	92	.270	.326	12	.222	4	-2	-6	1	-0.2
1963 Hou-N	0	1	.000	3	1	0	0	0	6¹	12	0	2	5	19.9	5.68	55	.429	.467	0	—	0	-2	-2	-0	-0.3
Total 4	9	13	.409	69	20	5	2	1	208	233	21	76	115	13.4	4.54	85	.282	.343	13	.217	4	-14	-16	0	-1.0

● MIKE GOLDEN
Golden, Michael Henry b: 9/11/1851, Shirley, Mass. d: 1/11/29, Rockford, Ill. BR/TR, 5'8", 168 lbs. Deb: 5/5/1875 ♦

YEAR TM/L	W	L	PCT	G	GS	CG	SH	SV	IP	H	HR	BB	SO	RAT	ERA	ERA+	OAV	OOB	BH	AVG	PB	PR	/A	PD	TPI
1875 Wes-n	1	12	.077	13	13	13	0	0	113	111	0	12	20	9.8	1.83	133	.225	.243	6	.130	-4	5	8		0.3
Chi-n	6	7	.462	14	14	12	1	0	119	129	0	8	14	10.4	1.89	120	.247	.258	40	.258	1	4	5		0.4
Yr	7	19	.269	27	27	25	1	0	232	240	0	20	34	10.1	1.86	126	.236	.251	46	.229	-3	9	13		0.7
1878 Mil-N	3	13	.188	22	18	15	0	0	161	217	1	33	52	14.0	4.14	63	.295	.325	44	.206	-2	-33	-27	0	-2.2

● ROY GOLDEN
Golden, Roy Kramer b: 7/12/1888, Madisonville, O. d: 10/4/61, Norwood, Ohio BR/TR, 6'1", 195 lbs. Deb: 9/7/10

YEAR TM/L	W	L	PCT	G	GS	CG	SH	SV	IP	H	HR	BB	SO	RAT	ERA	ERA+	OAV	OOB	BH	AVG	PB	PR	/A	PD	TPI
1910 StL-N	2	3	.400	7	6	3	0	0	42²	44	3	33	31	16.7	4.43	67	.286	.418	4	.267	1	-7	-7	1	-0.6
1911 StL-N	4	9	.308	30	25	6	0	0	148²	127	6	129	81	15.8	5.02	67	.240	.394	5	.114	-1	-27	-27	-0	-2.2
Total 2	6	12	.333	37	31	9	0	0	191¹	171	9	162	112	16.0	4.89	67	.250	.399	9	.153	-1	-33	-34	1	-2.8

● FRED GOLDSMITH
Goldsmith, Fred Ernest b: 5/15/1856, New Haven, Conn. d: 3/28/39, Berkley, Mich. BR/TR, 6'1", 195 lbs. Deb: 10/23/1875 U♦

YEAR TM/L	W	L	PCT	G	GS	CG	SH	SV	IP	H	HR	BB	SO	RAT	ERA	ERA+	OAV	OOB	BH	AVG	PB	PR	/A	PD	TPI
1879 Tro-N	2	4	.333	8	7	7	0	0	63	61	0	1	31	8.9	1.57	159	.237	.240	9	.237	0	6	6	-0	0.6
1880 Chi-N	21	3	**.875**	26	24	22	4	1	210¹	189	2	18	90	8.9	1.75	138	.231	.247	37	.261	2	14	16	2	1.9
1881 Chi-N	24	13	.649	39	39	37	5	0	330	328	4	44	76	10.1	2.59	106	.247	.271	38	.241	3	7	5	1	1.1
1882 Chi-N	28	17	.622	45	45	45	4	0	405	377	7	38	109	9.2	2.42	119	.236	.254	42	.230	-1	22	20	-2	1.4
1883 Chi-N	25	19	.568	46	45	40	2	0	383¹	456	14	39	82	11.6	3.15	101	.277	.294	52	.221	-0	-2	-1	3	0.2
1884 Chi-N	9	11	.450	21	21	20	1	0	188	245	11	29	34	13.1	4.26	74	.298	.322	11	.136	-2	-27	-24	-3	-2.4
Bal-a	3	1	.750	4	4	3	0	0	30	29	0	2	11	9.6	2.70	128	.238	.256	2	.143	-0	2	3	0	0.3
Total 6	112	68	.622	189	185	174	16	1	1609²	1685	38	171	433	10.4	2.73	106	.256	.275	191	.224	-1	24	28	4	3.1

● HAL GOLDSMITH
Goldsmith, Harold Eugene b: 8/18/1898, Peconic, N.Y. d: 10/20/85, Riverhead, N.Y. BR/TR, 6', 174 lbs. Deb: 6/23/26

YEAR TM/L	W	L	PCT	G	GS	CG	SH	SV	IP	H	HR	BB	SO	RAT	ERA	ERA+	OAV	OOB	BH	AVG	PB	PR	/A	PD	TPI
1926 Bos-N	5	7	.417	19	15	5	0	0	101	135	2	28	16	14.6	4.37	81	.333	.377	8	.211	0	-6	-9	1	-0.8
1927 Bos-N	1	3	.250	22	5	1	0	1	71²	83	4	26	13	13.7	3.52	106	.289	.348	5	.238	0	3	2	0	0.1
1928 Bos-N	0	0	—	4	0	0	0	0	8¹	14	1	1	1	16.2	3.24	121	.359	.375	0	.000	-0	1	1	0	0.0
1929 StL-N	0	0	—	2	0	0	0	0	4	3	1	1	0	9.0	6.75	69	.214	.267	0	.000	-0	-1	-1	-0	0.0
Total 4	6	10	.375	47	20	6	0	1	185	235	8	56	30	14.2	4.04	90	.315	.364	13	.210	-0	-3	-8	1	-0.7

● IZZY GOLDSTEIN
Goldstein, Isidore b: 6/6/08, Odessa, Russia d: 9/24/93, Delray Beach, Fla. BB/TR, 6', 160 lbs. Deb: 4/24/32

YEAR TM/L	W	L	PCT	G	GS	CG	SH	SV	IP	H	HR	BB	SO	RAT	ERA	ERA+	OAV	OOB	BH	AVG	PB	PR	/A	PD	TPI
1932 Det-A	3	2	.600	16	6	0	0	0	56¹	63	2	41	14	17.1	4.47	105	.276	.393	5	.294	1	0	1	0	0.2

● DAVE GOLTZ
Goltz, David Allan b: 6/23/49, Pelican Rapids, Minn. BR/TR, 6'4", 215 lbs. Deb: 7/18/72

YEAR TM/L	W	L	PCT	G	GS	CG	SH	SV	IP	H	HR	BB	SO	RAT	ERA	ERA+	OAV	OOB	BH	AVG	PB	PR	/A	PD	TPI
1972 Min-A	3	3	.500	15	11	1	0	0	91	75	5	26	38	10.0	2.67	120	.224	.280	3	.103	-1	4	5	-0	0.3
1973 Min-A	6	4	.600	32	10	1	0	1	106¹	138	11	32	66	14.6	5.25	75	.318	.368	0	—	0	-17	-15	1	-1.3
1974 Min-A	10	10	.500	28	24	5	1	0	174¹	192	14	45	89	12.6	3.25	115	.282	.333	0	—	0	7	9	1	1.1
1975 Min-A	14	14	.500	32	32	15	1	0	243	235	18	72	128	11.6	3.67	104	.255	.313	0	—	0	3	4	1	0.5
1976 Min-A	14	14	.500	36	35	13	4	0	249¹	239	14	91	133	12.1	3.36	107	.254	.323	0	—	0	4	6	0	0.6
1977 Min-A	**20**	11	.645	39	39	19	2	0	303	284	26	91	186	11.2	3.36	119	.247	.304	0	—	0	24	21	-1	2.0
1978 Min-A	15	10	.600	29	29	13	2	0	220¹	209	12	67	116	11.3	2.49	153	.253	.309	0	—	0	31	32	0	3.7
1979 Min-A	14	13	.519	36	35	12	1	0	250²	282	22	69	132	12.6	4.16	105	.288	.336	0	—	0	1	4	1	0.5
1980 LA-N	7	11	.389	35	27	2	2	1	171¹	198	12	59	91	13.5	4.31	81	.299	.356	6	.128	-0	-13	-15	-0	-1.5
1981 *LA-N	2	7	.222	26	8	0	0	1	77	83	4	25	48	12.6	4.09	81	.288	.345	1	.059	-1	-5	-7	1	-0.8
1982 LA-N	0	1	.000	2	1	0	0	0	3²	4	1	2	3	14.7	4.91	71	.353	.353	0	.000	-0	-1	-0	-2	-0.1
*Cal-A	8	5	.615	28	7	1	0	3	86	82	4	32	49	12.0	4.08	99	.252	.320	0	—	0	-1	-0	-2	-0.2
1983 Cal-A	0	6	.000	15	6	0	0	0	63²	81	10	37	27	16.8	6.22	65	.315	.403	0	—	0	-15	-16	0	-1.2
Total 12	113	109	.509	353	264	83	13	8	2039²	2104	149	646	1105	12.2	3.69	104	.269	.327	10	.106	-1	23	31	0	3.6

● LUIS GOMEZ
Gomez, Luis (Sanchez) b: 8/19/51, Guadalajara, Mex. BR/TR, 5'9", 150 lbs. Deb: 4/28/74 ♦

YEAR TM/L	W	L	PCT	G	GS	CG	SH	SV	IP	H	HR	BB	SO	RAT	ERA	ERA+	OAV	OOB	BH	AVG	PB	PR	/A	PD	TPI
1981 Atl-N	0	0	—	1	0	0	0	0	1	3	0	2	0	45.0	27.00	13	.500	.625	7	.200	0	-3	-3	-0	0.0

YEAR	TM/L	W	L	PCT	G	GS	CG	SH	SV	IP	H	HR	BB	SO	RAT	ERA	ERA+	OAV	OOB	BH	AVG	PB	PR	/A	PD	TPI
● **PAT GOMEZ**					Gomez, Patrick Alexander b: 3/17/68, Roseville, Cal. BL/TL, 5'11", 185 lbs. Deb: 4/6/93																					
1993	SD-N	1	2	.333	27	1	0	0	0	31²	35	2	19	26	15.3	5.12	81	.292	.388	0	.000	-1	-4	-3	-1	-0.4
1994	SF-N	0	1	.000	26	0	0	0	0	33¹	23	2	20	14	11.6	3.78	106	.211	.333	0	.000	-0	2	1	-1	-0.1
1995	SF-N	0	0	—	18	0	0	0	0	14	16	2	12	15	18.0	5.14	79	.276	.400	0	.000	-0	-1	-2	-0	-0.1
Total	3	1	3	.250	71	1	0	0	0	79	74	6	51	55	14.2	4.56	89	.258	.370	0	.000	-1	-4	-4	-1	-0.5
● **RUBEN GOMEZ**					Gomez, Ruben (Colon) b: 7/13/27, Arroyo, P.R. BR/TR, 6', 175 lbs. Deb: 4/17/53																					
1953	NY-N	13	11	.542	29	26	13	3	0	204	166	17	101	113	12.0	3.40	126	.218	.313	15	.208	-0	20	20	2	2.3
1954	*NY-N	17	9	.654	37	32	10	4	0	221²	202	20	109	106	12.9	2.88	140	.244	.337	14	.173	0	29	28	2	3.2
1955	NY-N	9	10	.474	33	31	9	3	1	185¹	207	20	63	79	13.5	4.56	88	.285	.348	18	.300	4	-11	-11	3	-0.4
1956	NY-N	7	17	.292	40	31	4	2	0	196¹	191	19	77	76	12.7	4.58	83	.259	.337	11	.183	-0	-18	-17	2	-1.7
1957	NY-N	15	13	.536	38	36	16	1	0	238¹	233	28	71	92	11.7	3.78	104	.254	.311	16	.184	1	3	4	2	0.8
1958	SF-N	10	12	.455	42	30	8	1	1	207²	204	21	77	112	12.5	4.38	87	.261	.334	14	.200	1	-10	-13	2	-0.9
1959	Phi-L	3	8	.273	20	12	2	1	1	72¹	90	12	24	37	14.2	6.10	67	.300	.352	3	.176	0	-17	-16	2	-2.0
1960	Phi-N	0	3	.000	22	1	0	0	1	52¹	68	7	9	24	13.4	5.33	73	.321	.351	1	.083	0	-9	-8	-1	-0.6
1962	Cle-A	1	2	.333	15	4	0	0	1	45¹	50	5	25	21	15.3	4.37	89	.292	.389	3	.231	0	-2	-2	1	-0.1
	Min-A	1	1	.500	6	2	1	0	0	19¹	17	3	11	8	13.0	4.66	88	.254	.359	0	.000	-0	-1	-1	0	-0.1
	Yr	2	3	.400	21	6	1	0	1	64²	67	8	36	29	14.3	4.45	88	.276	.369	3	.167	-0	-3	-4	1	-0.2
1967	Phi-N	0	0	—	7	0	0	0	0	11¹	8	2	7	9	11.9	3.97	86	.211	.333	0	—	0	-1	-1	1	0.1
Total	10	76	86	.469	289	205	63	15	5	1454	1436	154	574	677	12.7	4.09	97	.259	.334	95	.199	6	-17	-18	14	0.6
● **LEFTY GOMEZ**					Gomez, Vernon Louis "Goofy" b: 11/26/08, Rodeo, Cal. d: 2/17/89, Greenbrae, Cal. BL/TL, 6'2", 173 lbs. Deb: 4/29/30 H																					
1930	NY-A	2	5	.286	15	6	2	0	1	60	66	12	28	22	14.3	5.55	78	.280	.358	3	.150	-2	-6	-8	1	-0.8
1931	NY-A	21	9	.700	40	26	17	1	3	243	206	7	85	150	10.9	2.67	149	.226	.295	11	.133	-3	46	35	1	3.5
1932	*NY-A	24	7	.774	37	31	21	1	1	265¹	266	23	105	176	12.7	4.21	97	.259	.329	18	.173	-1	8	-4	-3	-0.8
1933	NY-A★	16	10	.615	35	30	14	4	2	234²	218	16	106	**163**	12.4	3.18	122	.240	.319	9	.112	-3	29	18	-4	1.1
1934	NY-A★	**26**	5	**.839**	38	33	**25**	**6**	1	**281²**	223	12	96	158	**10.2**	**2.33**	174	**.215**	**.282**	13	.131	-3	**68**	54	-2	4.8
1935	NY-A	12	15	.444	34	30	15	2	1	246	223	18	86	138	11.4	3.18	127	.242	.309	10	.120	-6	35	24	1	1.6
1936	*NY-A☆	13	7	.650	31	30	10	0	0	188²	184	6	122	105	14.6	4.39	106	.254	.362	10	.145	3	14	6	-1	0.1
1937	*NY-A★	**21**	11	.656	34	34	25	**6**	0	278¹	233	10	93	**194**	10.6	**2.33**	191	**.223**	.287	21	.200	-1	**71**	65	-3	**6.5**
1938	*NY-A☆	18	12	.600	32	32	20	**4**	0	239	239	7	99	129	12.8	3.35	135	.260	.332	13	.151	-2	38	31	2	3.3
1939	*NY-A☆	12	8	.600	26	26	14	2	0	198	173	11	84	102	11.8	3.41	128	.235	.316	11	.151	-2	27	21	-1	1.5
1940	NY-A	3	3	.500	9	5	0	0	0	27¹	37	2	18	14	18.4	6.59	61	.325	.421	0	.000	-1	-7	-8	-1	-1.5
1941	NY-A	15	5	**.750**	23	23	8	1	0	156¹	151	10	103	76	14.7	3.74	105	.250	.360	9	.153	-1	7	3	-4	-0.1
1942	NY-A	6	4	.600	13	13	2	0	0	80	67	4	65	41	15.1	4.27	80	.237	.383	5	.152	-1	-5	-7	2	-1.1
1943	Was-A	0	1	.000	1	1	0	0	0	4²	4	0	5	0	17.4	5.79	55	.250	.429	0	.000	-0	-1	-1	1	-0.2
Total	14	189	102	.649	368	320	173	28	9	2503	2290	138	1095	1468	12.2	3.34	125	.242	.321	133	.147	-30	322	229	-15	17.9
● **JOE GONZALES**					Gonzales, Joe Madrid "Smokey" b: 3/19/15, San Francisco, Cal BR/TR, 5'9", 175 lbs. Deb: 8/28/37																					
1937	Bos-A	1	2	.333	8	2	2	0	0	31	37	1	11	13	13.9	4.35	109	.291	.348	0	.000	-2	1	1	0	0.0
● **RENE GONZALES**					Gonzales, Rene Adrian b: 9/3/60, Austin, Tex. BR/TR, 6'3", 191 lbs. Deb: 7/27/84 ◆																					
1993	Cal-A	0	0	—	1	0	0	0	0	1	0	0	0	0	0.0	0.00	—	.000	.000	84	.251	1	0	1	0	0.0
● **VINCE GONZALES**					Gonzales, Wenceslao (O'Reilly) b: 9/28/25, Quivican, Cuba d: 3/11/81, Ciudad Del Carmen, Campeche, Mexico BL/TL, 6'1", 165 lbs. Deb: 4/13/55																					
1955	Was-A	0	0	—	1	0	0	0	0	2	6	0	3	1	40.5	27.00	14	.500	.600	0	—	0	-5	-5	-0	0.0
● **GERMAN GONZALEZ**					Gonzalez, German Jose (Caraballo) b: 3/7/62, Rio Caribe, Venez. BR/TR, 6', 170 lbs. Deb: 8/5/88																					
1988	Min-A	0	0	—	16	0	0	0	1	21¹	20	4	8	19	12.2	3.38	121	.244	.319	0	—	0	1	2	0	-0.1
1989	Min-A	3	2	.600	22	0	0	0	0	29	32	2	11	25	14.6	4.66	89	.274	.356	0	—	0	-2	-0	-0	-0.3
Total	2	3	2	.600	38	0	0	0	1	50¹	52	6	19	44	13.6	4.11	100	.261	.341	0	—	0	-1	-0	0	-0.4
● **JULIO GONZALEZ**					Gonzalez, Julio Enrique (Herrera) b: 12/20/20, Banes, Cuba d: 2/15/91, Banes, Cuba BR/TR, 5'11", 150 lbs. Deb: 8/9/49																					
1949	Was-A	0	0	—	13	0	0	0	0	34¹	33	4	27	5	16.0	4.72	90	.256	.389	1	.200	0	-2	-2	-0	0.0
● **RALPH GOOD**					Good, Ralph Nelson "Holy" b: 4/25/1886, Monticello, Me. d: 11/24/65, Waterville, Maine BR/TR, 6', 165 lbs. Deb: 7/1/10																					
1910	Bos-N	0	0	—	2	0	0	0	0	9	6	0	2	4	10.0	2.00	166	.188	.278	0	.000	-0	1	1	0	0.0
● **WILBUR GOOD**					Good, Wilbur David "Lefty" b: 9/28/1885, Punxsutawney, Pa. d: 12/30/63, Brooksville, Fla. BL/TL, 5'6", 165 lbs. Deb: 8/18/05 ◆																					
1905	NY-A	0	2	.000	5	2	0	0	0	19	18	1	14	13	15.2	4.74	62	.250	.372	1	.375	1	-4	-4	0	-0.3
● **HERB GOODALL**					Goodall, Herbert Frank b: 3/10/1870, Mansfield, Pa. d: 1/20/38, Mansfield, Pa. BR/TR, 5'9", 180 lbs. Deb: 4/29/1890																					
1890	Lou-a	8	5	.615	18	13	8	1	4	109	94	2	51	46	12.8	3.39	114	.225	.324	19	.422	6	6	1	1	1.2
● **JOHN GOODELL**					Goodell, John Henry William "Lefty" b: 4/5/07, Muskogee, Okla. d: 9/21/93, Mesquite, Tex. BR/TL, 5'10", 165 lbs. Deb: 4/19/28																					
1928	Chi-A	0	0	—	2	0	0	0	0	3	6	0	2	0	18.00	23	.500	.600	0	—	0	-5	-5	0	0.0
● **DWIGHT GOODEN**					Gooden, Dwight Eugene "Doc" b: 11/16/64, Tampa, Fla. BR/TR, 6'3", 198 lbs. Deb: 4/7/84																					
1984	NY-N★	17	9	.654	31	31	7	3	0	218	161	7	73	**276**	**9.7**	2.60	136	**.202**	**.270**	14	.200	1	24	23	1	2.9
1985	NY-N☆	**24**	4	.857	35	35	**16**	8	0	276²	198	13	69	**268**	8.8	**1.53**	226	.201	.254	21	.226	6	**63**	59	2	**7.3**
1986	*NY-N★	17	6	.739	33	33	12	2	0	250	197	17	80	200	10.1	2.84	124	.215	.280	7	.086	-3	24	19	2	1.7
1987	NY-N	15	7	**.682**	25	25	7	3	0	179²	162	11	53	148	11.0	3.21	118	.244	.301	14	.219	2	17	11	-0	1.5
1988	*NY-N★	18	9	.667	34	34	10	3	0	248¹	242	8	57	175	11.1	3.19	101	.256	.303	16	.178	3	7	1	5	0.9
1989	NY-N	9	4	.692	19	17	0	0	0	118¹	93	9	47	101	10.8	2.89	113	.211	.290	8	.200	2	8	7	0	0.7
1990	NY-N	19	7	.731	34	34	2	1	0	232²	229	10	70	223	11.8	3.83	98	.258	.317	14	.187	-1	-2	-2	0	0.6
1991	NY-N	13	7	.650	27	27	3	1	0	190	185	12	56	150	11.6	3.60	101	.257	.313	15	.238	4	7	4	0	1.0
1992	NY-N	10	13	.435	31	31	3	0	0	206	197	11	70	145	11.8	3.67	95	.255	.319	19	.264	7	-4	-5	1	0.8
1993	NY-N	12	15	.444	29	29	7	2	0	208²	188	16	61	149	11.1	3.45	116	.242	.304	14	.200	4	14	13	0	2.0
1994	NY-N	3	4	.429	7	7	0	0	0	41¹	46	9	15	40	13.5	6.31	66	.282	.346	2	.167	-0	-10	-10	1	-1.3
1996	NY-A	11	7	.611	29	29	1	1	0	170²	169	19	88	126	14.0	5.01	101	.259	.355	0	—	0	-0	1	0	-0.0
Total	12	168	92	.646	334	332	68	24	1	2340¹	2067	142	739	2001	11.0	3.24	114	.237	.300	144	.197	29	145	115	15	16.9
● **ART GOODWIN**					Goodwin, Arthur Ingram b: 2/27/1877, Whiteley Twnshp., Pa. d: 6/19/43, Franklin Township, Pa. TR, 5'8", 195 lbs. Deb: 10/7/05																					
1905	NY-A	0	0	—	1	0	0	0	0	0¹	2	0	2	0	108.0	81.00	4	.667	.800	0	—	0	-3	-3	0	0.0
● **CLYDE GOODWIN**					Goodwin, Clyde Samuel b: 11/12/1886, Shade, Ohio d: 10/12/63, Dayton, Ohio BR/TR, 5'11", 145 lbs. Deb: 9/18/06																					
1906	Was-A	0	2	.000	4	3	1	0	0	22¹	20	0	13	9	13.7	4.43	59	.244	.354	1	.200	-0	-4	-4	-1	-0.4
● **JIM GOODWIN**					Goodwin, James Patrick b: 8/15/26, St.Louis, Mo. BL/TL, 6'1", 170 lbs. Deb: 4/24/48																					
1948	Chi-A	0	0	—	8	1	0	0	1	10¹	9	0	12	3	19.2	8.71	49	.237	.431	1	.500	0	-5	-5	0	-0.1
● **MARV GOODWIN**					Goodwin, Marvin Mardo b: 1/16/1891, Gordonsville, Va. d: 10/21/25, Houston, Tex. BR/TR, 5'11", 168 lbs. Deb: 9/7/16																					
1916	Was-A	0	0	—	3	0	0	0	0	5²	5	0	3	1	12.7	3.18	88	.231	.308	0	.000	-0	-0	-0	0	0.0
1917	StL-N	6	4	.600	14	12	6	3	0	85¹	70	1	19	38	9.4	2.21	122	.222	.266	4	.174	-0	5	5	2	0.7
1919	StL-N	11	9	.550	33	17	7	3	0	179	163	6	33	48	10.3	2.51	111	.245	.289	12	.200	1	8	6	-1	0.7
1920	StL-N	3	8	.273	32	4	2	0	1	116¹	153	1	28	23	14.4	4.95	60	.314	.357	7	.200	-0	-23	-25	-3	-2.5
1921	StL-N	1	2	.333	14	4	1	0	0	36¹	47	1	9	7	14.1	3.72	99	.315	.358	-0	.000	-1	-1	-1	-0	-0.1
1922	StL-N	0	0	—	2	0	0	0	0	4	3	0	6	0	13.5	2.25	172	.250	.400	0	—	0	1	0	0	0.1
1925	Cin-N	0	2	.000	4	2	0	0	0	20	26	0	2	4	13.1	4.79	86	.317	.364	1	.250	0	-1	-2	0	-0.1
Total	7	21	25	.457	102	48	19	3	2	447¹	467	8	100	121	11.7	3.30	90	.269	.315	24	.186	0	-11	-17	0	-1.1

YEAR	TM/L	W	L	PCT	G	GS	CG	SH	SV	IP	H	HR	BB	SO	RAT	ERA	ERA+	OAV	OOB	BH	AVG	PB	PR	/A	PD	TPI

● RAY GORDINIER
Gordinier, Raymond Cornelius "Gordy" b: 4/11/1892, Rochester, N.Y. d: 11/15/60, Rochester, N.Y. BB/TR, 5'8.5", 170 lbs. Deb: 9/17/21

YEAR	TM/L	W	L	PCT	G	GS	CG	SH	SV	IP	H	HR	BB	SO	RAT	ERA	ERA+	OAV	OOB	BH	AVG	PB	PR	/A	PD	TPI
1921	Bro-N	1	0	1.000	3	3	0	0	0	12	10	0	8	4	13.5	5.25	74	.227	.346	1	.250	0	-2	-2	0	-0.1
1922	Bro-N	0	0	—	5	0	0	0	0	11¹	13	3	8	5	16.7	8.74	47	.289	.396	0	.000	-0	-6	-6	-0	0.0
Total	2	1	0	1.000	8	3	0	0	0	23¹	23	3	16	9	15.0	6.94	57	.258	.371	1	.167	-0	-8	-8	0	-0.1

● DON GORDON
Gordon, Donald Thomas b: 10/10/59, New York, N.Y. BR/TR, 6'1", 175 lbs. Deb: 4/10/86

YEAR	TM/L	W	L	PCT	G	GS	CG	SH	SV	IP	H	HR	BB	SO	RAT	ERA	ERA+	OAV	OOB	BH	AVG	PB	PR	/A	PD	TPI
1986	Tor-A	0	1	.000	14	0	0	0	1	21²	28	1	8	13	15.4	7.06	60	.311	.374	0	—	0	-7	-7	-1	-0.4
1987	Tor-A	0	0	—	5	0	0	0	0	11	8	2	3	3	9.0	4.09	110	.200	.256	0	—	-0	0	0	-0	0.0
	Cle-A	0	3	.000	21	0	0	0	0	39²	49	3	12	20	14.7	4.08	111	.295	.357	0	—	0	2	2	1	0.2
	Yr	0	3	.000	26	0	0	0	0	50²	57	5	15	23	13.5	4.09	111	.277	.338	0	—	0	2	2	1	0.2
1988	Cle-A	3	4	.429	38	0	0	0	1	59¹	65	5	19	20	13.2	4.40	93	.284	.347	0	—	0	-3	-2	1	-0.2
Total	3	3	8	.273	78	0	0	0	2	131²	150	11	42	56	13.7	4.72	91	.286	.348	0	—	0	-8	-6	1	-0.4

● TOM GORDON
Gordon, Thomas b: 11/18/67, Sebring, Fla. BR/TR, 5'9", 160 lbs. Deb: 9/8/88

YEAR	TM/L	W	L	PCT	G	GS	CG	SH	SV	IP	H	HR	BB	SO	RAT	ERA	ERA+	OAV	OOB	BH	AVG	PB	PR	/A	PD	TPI
1988	KC-A	0	2	.000	5	2	0	0	0	15²	16	1	7	18	13.2	5.17	77	.267	.343	0	—	0	-2	-2	0	-0.2
1989	KC-A	17	9	.654	49	16	1	1	1	163	122	10	86	153	11.5	3.64	106	.210	.312	0	—	0	4	4	3	0.8
1990	KC-A	12	11	.522	32	32	6	1	0	195¹	192	17	99	175	13.5	3.73	103	.257	.347	0	—	0	4	2	1	0.3
1991	KC-A	9	14	.391	45	14	1	1	0	158	129	16	87	167	12.5	3.87	106	.221	.325	0	—	0	4	4	0	0.6
1992	KC-A	6	10	.375	40	11	0	0	0	117²	116	9	55	98	13.4	4.59	88	.258	.344	0	—	0	-9	-7	1	-1.0
1993	KC-A	12	6	.667	48	14	2	0	1	155²	125	11	77	143	11.7	3.58	128	.223	.318	0	—	0	13	17	1	1.5
1994	KC-A	11	7	.611	24	24	0	0	0	155¹	136	6	87	126	13.1	4.35	115	.237	.340	0	—	0	8	11	2	1.3
1995	KC-A	12	12	.500	31	31	2	0	0	189	204	12	89	119	14.1	4.43	108	.279	.360	0	—	0	6	7	1	0.9
1996	Bos-A	12	9	.571	34	34	4	1	0	215²	249	28	105	171	14.9	5.59	92	.284	.363	0	—	0	-14	-11	1	-1.0
Total	9	91	80	.532	308	178	16	3	3	1365¹	1289	119	692	1170	13.2	4.27	104	.250	.341	0	—	0	14	25	9	3.2

● CHARLIE GORIN
Gorin, Charles Perry b: 2/6/28, Waco, Tex. BL/TL, 5'10", 165 lbs. Deb: 5/29/54

YEAR	TM/L	W	L	PCT	G	GS	CG	SH	SV	IP	H	HR	BB	SO	RAT	ERA	ERA+	OAV	OOB	BH	AVG	PB	PR	/A	PD	TPI
1954	Mil-N	0	1	.000	5	0	0	0	0	9²	5	0	6	12	10.2	1.86	200	.152	.282	0	.000	-0	2	2	-0	0.1
1955	Mil-N	0	0	—	2	0	0	0	0	0¹	1	0	3	0	108.0	54.00	7	.500	.800	0	—	-0	-2	-2	-0	0.0
Total	2	0	1	.000	7	0	0	0	0	10	6	0	9	12	13.5	3.60	103	.171	.341	0	.000	-0	1	0	-0	0.1

● JACK GORMAN
Gorman, John F. "Stooping Jack" b: 1859, St.Louis, Mo. d: 9/9/1889, St.Louis, Mo. Deb: 7/1/1883 ◆

YEAR	TM/L	W	L	PCT	G	GS	CG	SH	SV	IP	H	HR	BB	SO	RAT	ERA	ERA+	OAV	OOB	BH	AVG	PB	PR	/A	PD	TPI
1884	Pit-a	1	2	.333	3	3	3	0	0	25	22	0	5	10	10.1	4.68	72	.212	.255	4	.148	-0	-4	-4	0	-0.4

● TOM GORMAN
Gorman, Thomas Aloysius b: 1/4/25, New York, N.Y. d: 12/26/92, Valley Stream, N.Y. BR/TR, 6'1", 190 lbs. Deb: 7/16/52

YEAR	TM/L	W	L	PCT	G	GS	CG	SH	SV	IP	H	HR	BB	SO	RAT	ERA	ERA+	OAV	OOB	BH	AVG	PB	PR	/A	PD	TPI
1952	*NY-A	6	2	.750	12	6	1	1	1	60²	63	8	22	31	12.9	4.60	72	.272	.340	2	.087	-1	-6	-9	-0	-1.2
1953	*NY-A	4	5	.444	40	1	0	0	6	77	65	5	32	38	12.0	3.39	109	.226	.317	2	.133	-1	5	3	-0	0.2
1954	NY-A	0	0	—	23	0	0	0	0	36²	30	1	14	31	11.0	2.21	156	.222	.300	0	.000	-1	6	5	-0	0.6
1955	KC-A	7	6	.538	57	0	0	0	18	109	98	11	36	46	11.4	3.55	118	.246	.314	2	.083	-1	5	8	-1	0.9
1956	KC-A	9	10	.474	52	13	1	0	3	171¹	176	23	68	56	12.5	3.83	113	.258	.330	2	.051	-4	6	9	-0	0.6
1957	KC-A	5	9	.357	38	12	3	1	3	124²	125	18	33	66	11.5	3.83	103	.261	.310	4	.121	-2	1	3	-0	0.2
1958	KC-A	4	4	.500	50	1	0	0	8	89²	86	8	20	44	10.9	3.51	111	.258	.306	2	.118	-1	3	4	-1	0.2
1959	KC-A	1	0	1.000	17	0	0	0	1	20	15	2	14	9	13.1	7.08	57	.293	.402	0	—	-0	-7	-7	-1	-0.5
Total	8	36	36	.500	289	33	5	2	42	689¹	659	77	239	321	12.0	3.77	105	.254	.321	14	.090	-10	11	14	-4	0.2

● TOM GORMAN
Gorman, Thomas David "Big Tom" b: 3/16/16, New York, N.Y. d: 8/11/86, Closter, N.J. BR/TL, 6'2", 200 lbs. Deb: 9/14/39 U

YEAR	TM/L	W	L	PCT	G	GS	CG	SH	SV	IP	H	HR	BB	SO	RAT	ERA	ERA+	OAV	OOB	BH	AVG	PB	PR	/A	PD	TPI
1939	NY-N	0	0	—	4	0	0	0	0	5	7	0	1	2	14.4	7.20	55	.350	.381	0	.000	-0	-2	-2	-0	0.0

● TOM GORMAN
Gorman, Thomas Patrick b: 12/16/57, Portland, Ore. BL/TL, 6'4", 200 lbs. Deb: 9/2/81

YEAR	TM/L	W	L	PCT	G	GS	CG	SH	SV	IP	H	HR	BB	SO	RAT	ERA	ERA+	OAV	OOB	BH	AVG	PB	PR	/A	PD	TPI
1981	Mon-N	0	0	—	9	0	0	0	0	15	12	0	6	13	11.4	4.20	83	.222	.311	0	—	0	-1	-1	1	0.1
1982	Mon-N	1	0	1.000	5	0	0	0	0	7	8	0	4	6	15.4	5.14	71	.286	.375	0	—	0	-1	-1	-0	-0.1
	NY-N	0	1	.000	3	1	0	0	0	9¹	8	0	1	5	7.7	0.96	376	.235	.235	0	.000	-0	3	3	0	0.3
	Yr	1	1	.500	8	1	0	0	0	16¹	16	0	4	13	11.0	2.76	132	.254	.299	0	.000	-0	2	2	0	0.2
1983	NY-N	1	4	.200	25	4	0	0	0	49¹	45	3	15	30	10.9	4.93	74	.245	.302	1	.250	-0	-7	-7	-0	-0.7
1984	NY-N	6	0	1.000	36	0	0	0	0	57²	51	6	13	40	10.1	2.97	119	.238	.285	0	—	-0	4	4	0	0.3
1985	NY-N	4	4	.500	34	2	0	0	0	52²	56	8	18	32	12.6	5.13	67	.277	.336	0	.000	-1	-9	-10	1	-1.3
1986	Phi-N	0	1	.000	8	0	0	0	0	11²	21	0	5	8	20.1	7.71	50	.382	.433	0	.000	-0	-5	-5	-0	-0.4
1987	SD-N	0	0	—	6	0	0	0	0	11	11	1	5	8	13.1	4.09	97	.262	.340	0	—	0	-0	-0	-0	-0.0
Total	7	12	10	.545	126	7	0	0	0	213²	212	18	66	144	11.8	4.34	83	.261	.318	1	.071	-1	-17	-18	2	-1.8

● JOE GORMLEY
Gormley, Joseph b: 12/20/1866, Summit Hill, Pa. d: 7/2/50, Summit Hill, Pa. BL/TL, Deb: 6/16/1891

YEAR	TM/L	W	L	PCT	G	GS	CG	SH	SV	IP	H	HR	BB	SO	RAT	ERA	ERA+	OAV	OOB	BH	AVG	PB	PR	/A	PD	TPI
1891	Phi-N	0	1	.000	1	1	1	0	0	8	10	0	5	2	16.9	5.63	61	.294	.385	0	.000	-1	-2	-2	0	-0.2

● HANK GORNICKI
Gornicki, Henry Frank b: 1/14/11, Niagara Falls, N.Y d: 2/16/96, Riviera Beach, Fla BR/TR, 6'1", 145 lbs. Deb: 4/17/41

YEAR	TM/L	W	L	PCT	G	GS	CG	SH	SV	IP	H	HR	BB	SO	RAT	ERA	ERA+	OAV	OOB	BH	AVG	PB	PR	/A	PD	TPI
1941	StL-N	1	0	1.000	4	1	1	1	0	11¹	6	0	9	6	12.7	3.18	118	.158	.333	1	.250	0	1	1	-0	0.0
	Chi-N	0	0	—	1	0	0	0	0	2	3	0	2	2	13.5	4.50	78	.375	.375	0	—	-0	-0	-0	-0	0.0
	Yr	1	0	1.000	5	1	1	1	0	13¹	9	0	11	8	12.2	3.38	110	.191	.321	1	.250	0	0	1	-0	0.0
1942	Pit-N	5	6	.455	25	14	7	2	2	112	89	2	40	48	10.4	2.57	132	.215	.286	4	.114	-1	9	10	-1	0.8
1943	Pit-N	9	13	.409	42	18	4	1	4	147	165	10	47	63	13.1	3.98	87	.286	.342	7	.175	-1	-10	-8	-1	-1.4
1946	Pit-N	0	0	—	7	0	0	0	0	12²	12	0	11	4	16.3	3.55	99	.255	.397	0	.000	-0	-0	-0	-1	-0.1
Total	4	15	19	.441	79	33	12	4	6	285	275	12	107	123	12.2	3.38	102	.254	.323	12	.146	-2	-0	2	-2	-0.7

● JOHNNY GORSICA
Gorsica, John Joseph Perry (b: John Joseph Perry Gorczyca) b: 3/29/15, Bayonne, N.J. BR/TR, 6'2", 180 lbs. Deb: 4/22/40

YEAR	TM/L	W	L	PCT	G	GS	CG	SH	SV	IP	H	HR	BB	SO	RAT	ERA	ERA+	OAV	OOB	BH	AVG	PB	PR	/A	PD	TPI
1940	*Det-A	7	7	.500	29	20	5	2	0	160	170	10	57	68	13.0	4.33	110	.272	.337	12	.194	-0	1	8	5	1.1
1941	Det-A	9	11	.450	33	21	8	1	2	171	193	14	55	59	13.2	4.47	102	.281	.336	17	.298	4	-6	1	4	0.9
1942	Det-A	3	2	.600	28	0	0	0	4	53	63	2	26	19	15.6	4.75	83	.310	.397	1	.100	-0	-6	-5	4	-0.1
1943	Det-A	4	5	.444	35	4	1	0	5	96¹	88	3	40	45	12.1	3.36	105	.247	.327	4	.174	0	-1	2	3	0.5
1944	Det-A	6	14	.300	34	19	8	1	4	162	192	4	55	32	12.7	4.11	87	.296	.333	7	.135	-1	-12	-10	3	-1.0
1946	Det-A	0	0	—	14	0	0	0	0	23²	28	5	11	14	14.8	4.56	80	.301	.375	2	.667	1	-3	-2	-0	0.2
1947	Det-A	2	0	1.000	31	0	0	0	2	57²	64	5	26	20	11.2	3.75	101	.208	.300	2	.200	0	1	1	-0	0.2
Total	7	31	39	.443	204	64	22	4	17	723²	778	44	247	272	13.0	4.18	98	.276	.338	45	.207	4	-28	-7	20	1.6

● RICH GOSSAGE
Gossage, Richard Michael "Goose" b: 7/5/51, Colorado Springs, Colo. BR/TR, 6'3", 217 lbs. Deb: 4/16/72

YEAR	TM/L	W	L	PCT	G	GS	CG	SH	SV	IP	H	HR	BB	SO	RAT	ERA	ERA+	OAV	OOB	BH	AVG	PB	PR	/A	PD	TPI
1972	Chi-A	7	1	.875	36	1	0	0	2	80	72	6	44	57	13.5	4.27	73	.247	.353	0	.000	-2	-11	-10	-1	-1.3
1973	Chi-A	0	4	.000	20	4	1	0	0	49²	57	9	37	33	17.6	7.43	53	.311	.435	0	—	0	-20	-19	-0	-1.4
1974	Chi-A	4	6	.400	39	3	0	0	1	89¹	92	4	47	64	14.2	4.13	90	.272	.364	0	—	0	-5	-4	-0	-0.5
1975	Chi-A★	9	8	.529	62	0	0	0	**26**	141²	99	3	70	130	11.1	1.84	210	.201	.306	0	.000	-0	**30**	**32**	1	5.2
1976	Chi-A☆	9	17	.346	31	29	15	0	1	224	214	16	90	135	12.6	3.94	91	.254	.333	0	—	0	-10	-9	-1	-1.1
1977	Pit-N★	11	9	.550	72	0	0	0	26	133	78	4	49	151	8.7	1.62	245	.170	.253	5	.217	1	**34**	35	-1	**6.4**
1978	*NY-A★	10	11	.476	63	0	0	0	**27**	134¹	87	6	59	122	9.9	2.01	180	.187	.281	0	—	0	**26**	24	-1	4.7
1979	NY-A	5	3	.625	36	0	0	0	18	58	48	5	19	41	10.3	2.62	155	.227	.291	0	—	0	10	9	-1	1.8
1980	*NY-A★	6	2	.750	64	0	0	0	**33**	99	74	6	37	103	10.2	2.27	173	.211	.288	0	—	0	19	18	-1	2.7
1981	*NY-A†	3	2	.600	32	0	0	0	20	46²	22	2	14	48	7.1	0.77	463	.141	.216	0	—	0	15	15	0	3.1
1982	NY-A☆	4	5	.444	56	0	0	0	30	93	63	8	28	102	8.8	2.23	179	.196	.261	0	—	0	19	18	-1	2.9
1983	NY-A	13	5	.722	57	0	0	0	22	87¹	82	5	25	90	11.1	2.27	172	.248	.303	0	—	0	17	16	-2	3.7
1984	*SD-N★	10	6	.625	62	0	0	0	25	102¹	75	4	36	84	9.9	2.90	123	.204	.277	4	.182	-0	8	8	-1	1.4
1985	SD-N★	5	3	.625	50	0	0	0	26	79	64	1	17	52	9.3	1.82	194	.226	.272	0	.000	-0	16	15	-1	2.3
1986	SD-N	5	7	.417	45	0	0	0	21	64²	69	8	20	63	12.7	4.45	82	.273	.331	0	.000	-1	-5	-6	-1	-1.5
1987	SD-N	5	5	.556	40	0	0	0	11	52	47	5	19	44	11.4	3.12	127	.244	.311	0	.000	-0	6	5	-1	0.8
1988	Chi-N	4	4	.500	46	0	0	0	13	43²	50	8	19	30	13.7	4.33	83	.291	.358	0	.000	-0	-4	-4	-0	-0.8
1989	SF-N	2	1	.667	31	0	0	0	4	43²	32	2	27	24	12.2	2.68	126	.212	.331	0	—	-0	4	3	-1	0.2
	NY-A	1	0	1.000	11	0	0	0	1	14¹	14	0	3	6	11.3	3.77	103	.275	.327	0	—	0	0	0	0	0.0

YEAR	TM/L	W	L	PCT	G	GS	CG	SH	SV	IP	H	HR	BB	SO	RAT	ERA	ERA+	OAV	OOB	BH	AVG	PB	PR	/A	PD	TPI
1991	Tex-A	4	2	.667	44	0	0	0	1	40¹	33	4	16	28	11.6	3.57	113	.228	.317	0	—	0	2	2	-1	0.2
1992	Oak-A	0	2	.000	30	0	0	0	0	38	32	5	19	26	12.6	2.84	132	.230	.331	0	—	0	5	4	-0	0.6
1993	Oak-A	4	5	.444	39	0	0	0	1	47²	49	6	26	40	14.3	4.53	90	.266	.360	0	—	0	-1	-2	-1	0.0
1994	Sea-A	3	0	1.000	36	0	0	0	1	47¹	44	6	15	29	11.8	4.18	117	.251	.321	0	—	0	3	4	-1	0.1
Total	22	124	107	.537	1002	37	16	0	310	1809¹	1497	119	732	1502	11.3	3.01	125	.228	.310	9	.106	-3	158	154	-14	29.5

● JIM GOTT
Gott, James William b: 8/3/59, Hollywood, Cal. BR/TR, 6'4", 220 lbs. Deb: 4/9/82

YEAR	TM/L	W	L	PCT	G	GS	CG	SH	SV	IP	H	HR	BB	SO	RAT	ERA	ERA+	OAV	OOB	BH	AVG	PB	PR	/A	PD	TPI
1982	Tor-A	5	10	.333	30	23	1	1	0	136	134	15	66	82	13.4	4.43	101	.255	.341	0	—	-0	-5	-1	-0	0.0
1983	Tor-A	9	14	.391	34	30	6	1	0	176²	195	15	68	121	13.7	4.74	91	.280	.349	0	—	0	-13	-9	-1	-1.1
1984	Tor-A	7	6	.538	35	12	1	1	2	109²	93	7	49	73	11.9	4.02	102	.233	.322	0	—	-0	-0	1	-1	-0.3
1985	SF-N	7	10	.412	26	26	2	0	0	148¹	144	10	51	78	11.9	3.88	89	.254	.317	10	.196	4	-5	-7	1	-0.3
1986	SF-N	0	0	—	9	2	0	0	1	13	16	0	4	9	20.1	7.62	46	.314	.453	0	.000	-0	-6	-6	-0	-0.1
1987	SF-N	1	0	1.000	30	3	0	0	0	56	53	4	32	63	14.0	4.50	85	.244	.347	1	.100	1	-3	-4	0	0.0
	Pit-N	0	2	.000	25	0	0	0	13	31	28	0	8	27	10.5	1.45	283	.233	.281	0	—	-0	9	9	-0	1.2
	Yr	1	2	.333	55	3	0	0	13	87	81	4	40	90	12.5	3.41	115	.238	.318	1	.091	0	6	5	-0	1.2
1988	Pit-N	6	6	.500	67	0	0	0	34	77¹	68	9	22	76	10.7	3.49	97	.243	.303	0	.000	-0	-0	-1	-0	-0.2
1989	Pit-N	0	0	—	1	0	0	0	0	0²	1	0	1	1	27.0	0.00	—	.333	.500	0	—	-0	0	0	-0	0.0
1990	LA-N	3	5	.375	50	0	0	0	3	62	59	5	34	44	13.5	2.90	126	.257	.352	0	.000	-0	6	5	-0	0.6
1991	LA-N	4	3	.571	55	0	0	0	2	76	63	5	32	73	11.4	2.96	121	.223	.305	1	.500	0	6	5	1	0.6
1992	LA-N	3	3	.500	68	0	0	0	6	88	72	4	41	75	11.7	2.45	140	.225	.315	1	.500	0	10	10	1	0.9
1993	LA-N	4	8	.333	62	0	0	0	25	77²	71	6	17	67	10.3	2.32	165	.248	.293	0	.000	-0	15	13	0	2.5
1994	LA-N	5	3	.625	37	0	0	0	2	36¹	46	3	20	29	17.1	5.94	66	.322	.416	0	—	-0	-7	-8	-0	-1.6
1995	Pit-N	2	4	.333	25	0	0	0	3	31¹	38	2	14	19	14.6	6.03	71	.288	.352	0	.000	-0	-6	-6	-0	-1.1
Total	14	56	74	.431	554	96	10	3	91	1120	1081	85	466	837	12.6	3.87	101	.254	.331	13	.178	5	1	2	0	1.1

● TED GOULAIT
Goulait, Theodore Lee b: 8/12/1889, St.Clair, Mich. d: 7/15/36, St.Clair, Mich. BR/TR, 5'9.5", 172 lbs. Deb: 9/28/12

YEAR	TM/L	W	L	PCT	G	GS	CG	SH	SV	IP	H	HR	BB	SO	RAT	ERA	ERA+	OAV	OOB	BH	AVG	PB	PR	/A	PD	TPI
1912	NY-N	0	0	—	1	1	1	0	0	7	11	0	4	4	19.3	6.43	53	.367	.441	1	.500	0	-2	-2	0	0.0

● AL GOULD
Gould, Albert Frank "Pudgy" b: 1/20/1893, Muscatine, Iowa d: 8/8/82, San Jose, Cal. BR/TR, 5'6.5", 160 lbs. Deb: 7/11/16

YEAR	TM/L	W	L	PCT	G	GS	CG	SH	SV	IP	H	HR	BB	SO	RAT	ERA	ERA+	OAV	OOB	BH	AVG	PB	PR	/A	PD	TPI
1916	Cle-A	5	7	.417	30	9	6	1	1	106²	101	0	40	41	12.2	2.53	119	.256	.329	3	.103	-2	4	6	-1	0.4
1917	Cle-A	4	4	.500	27	7	1	0	0	94	95	1	52	24	14.4	3.64	78	.281	.382	5	.208	1	-10	-8	2	-0.5
Total	2	9	11	.450	57	16	7	1	1	200²	196	1	92	65	13.2	3.05	96	.267	.354	8	.151	-1	-7	-3	1	-0.1

● CHARLIE GOULD
Gould, Charles Harvey b: 8/21/1847, Cincinnati, Ohio d: 4/10/17, Flushing, N.Y. BR/TR, 6', 172 lbs. Deb: 5/5/1871 M♦

YEAR	TM/L	W	L	PCT	G	GS	CG	SH	SV	IP	H	HR	BB	SO	RAT	ERA	ERA+	OAV	OOB	BH	AVG	PB	PR	/A	PD	TPI
1876	Cin-N	0	0	—	2	0	0	0	0	4¹	10	0	4	0	20.8	0.00	—	.400	.400	65	.252	0	1	1	-0	0.0

● LARRY GOWELL
Gowell, Lawrence Clyde b: 5/2/48, Lewiston, Me. BR/TR, 6'2", 182 lbs. Deb: 9/21/72

YEAR	TM/L	W	L	PCT	G	GS	CG	SH	SV	IP	H	HR	BB	SO	RAT	ERA	ERA+	OAV	OOB	BH	AVG	PB	PR	/A	PD	TPI
1972	NY-A	0	1	.000	2	1	0	0	0	7	3	0	2	7	6.4	1.29	229	.143	.217	1	1.000	1	1	1	0	0.3

● MAURO GOZZO
Gozzo, Mauro Paul b: 3/7/66, New Britain, Conn. BR/TR, 6'2", 210 lbs. Deb: 8/8/89

YEAR	TM/L	W	L	PCT	G	GS	CG	SH	SV	IP	H	HR	BB	SO	RAT	ERA	ERA+	OAV	OOB	BH	AVG	PB	PR	/A	PD	TPI
1989	Tor-A	4	1	.800	9	3	0	0	0	31²	35	1	9	10	12.8	4.83	78	.289	.344	0	—	-0	-3	-4	-0	-0.5
1990	Cle-A	0	0	—	2	0	0	0	0	2	0	0	2	2	12.0	0.00	—	.182	.308	0	—	0	1	1	-0	0.0
1991	Cle-A	0	0	—	2	2	0	0	0	4²	9	2	0	7	30.9	19.29	22	.450	.593	0	—	-0	-8	-8	-0	0.0
1992	Min-A	0	0	—	2	0	0	0	0	1²	7	2	0	1	37.8	27.00	15	.583	.583	0	—	-0	-4	-4	-0	-0.2
1993	NY-N	0	1	.000	10	0	0	0	1	14	11	1	5	6	10.3	2.57	156	.212	.281	0	—	0	2	2	-1	0.1
1994	NY-N	3	5	.375	23	8	0	0	0	69	86	3	28	33	15.0	4.83	86	.304	.369	4	.250	1	-5	-5	-0	-0.4
Total	6	7	7	.500	48	13	0	0	1	124	150	9	51	55	14.7	5.30	76	.301	.368	4	.250	1	-17	-17	-2	-1.0

● AL GRABOWSKI
Grabowski, Alfons Francis b: 9/6/01, Syracuse, N.Y. d: 10/29/66, Memphis, N.Y. BL/TL, 5'11.5", 175 lbs. Deb: 9/11/29 F

YEAR	TM/L	W	L	PCT	G	GS	CG	SH	SV	IP	H	HR	BB	SO	RAT	ERA	ERA+	OAV	OOB	BH	AVG	PB	PR	/A	PD	TPI
1929	StL-N	3	2	.600	6	6	4	2	0	50	44	0	8	22	9.4	2.52	185	.227	.257	4	.250	2	12	12	-0	1.2
1930	StL-N	6	4	.600	33	8	1	0	1	107	122	7	49	43	14.6	4.79	105	.295	.373	12	.364	3	2	3	-0	0.4
Total	2	9	6	.600	39	14	5	2	1	157	166	7	57	65	13.0	4.07	120	.273	.338	16	.327	4	14	15	-0	1.6

● REGGIE GRABOWSKI
Grabowski, Reginald John b: 7/16/07, Syracuse, N.Y. d: 4/2/55, Syracuse, N.Y. BR/TR, 6'0.5", 185 lbs. Deb: 4/15/32 F

YEAR	TM/L	W	L	PCT	G	GS	CG	SH	SV	IP	H	HR	BB	SO	RAT	ERA	ERA+	OAV	OOB	BH	AVG	PB	PR	/A	PD	TPI
1932	Phi-N	2	2	.500	14	2	0	0	0	34¹	38	2	22	15	16.3	3.67	120	.278	.380	0	.000	-1	3	3	-1	0.2
1933	Phi-N	1	3	.250	10	5	4	1	0	48	38	4	10	9	9.2	2.44	157	.220	.266	2	.125	-1	5	7	-1	0.4
1934	Phi-N	1	3	.250	27	5	0	0	0	65¹	114	13	23	13	19.3	9.23	51	.384	.433	1	.056	-2	-38	-33	-1	-2.0
Total	3	4	8	.333	51	12	4	1	0	147²	190	19	55	37	15.3	5.73	76	.312	.375	3	.075	-3	-32	-23	-3	-1.4

● MIKE GRACE
Grace, Michael James b: 6/20/70, Joliet, Ill. BR/TR, 6'4", 210 lbs. Deb: 9/1/95

YEAR	TM/L	W	L	PCT	G	GS	CG	SH	SV	IP	H	HR	BB	SO	RAT	ERA	ERA+	OAV	OOB	BH	AVG	PB	PR	/A	PD	TPI
1995	Phi-N	1	1	.500	2	2	0	0	0	11¹	10	0	4	7	11.1	3.18	133	.238	.304	0	.000	-0	1	1	-0	0.2
1996	Phi-N	7	2	.778	12	12	1	1	0	80	72	9	16	49	10.0	3.49	125	.238	.279	4	.138	-0	6	8	1	0.9
Total	2	8	3	.727	14	14	1	1	0	91¹	82	9	20	56	10.1	3.45	126	.238	.282	4	.129	-0	8	9	1	1.1

● JOHN GRAFF
Graff, John F. b: Philadelphia, Pa. Deb: 7/19/1893

YEAR	TM/L	W	L	PCT	G	GS	CG	SH	SV	IP	H	HR	BB	SO	RAT	ERA	ERA+	OAV	OOB	BH	AVG	PB	PR	/A	PD	TPI
1893	Was-N	0	1	.000	2	1	1	0	0	12	21	2	13	4	26.3	11.25	41	.368	.493	1	.200	-0	-9	-9	-0	-0.5

● PEACHES GRAHAM
Graham, George Frederick b: 3/23/1877, Aledo, Ill. d: 7/25/39, Long Beach, Cal. BR/TR, 5'9", 180 lbs. Deb: 9/14/02 F♦

YEAR	TM/L	W	L	PCT	G	GS	CG	SH	SV	IP	H	HR	BB	SO	RAT	ERA	ERA+	OAV	OOB	BH	AVG	PB	PR	/A	PD	TPI
1903	Chi-N	0	1	.000	1	1	0	0	0	9	9	0	3	4	23.4	5.40	58	.429	.520	0	.000	—	-1	-1	0	-0.2

● SKINNY GRAHAM
Graham, Kyle b: 8/14/1899, Oak Grove, Ala. d: 12/1/73, Oak Grove, Ala. BR/TR, 6'2", 172 lbs. Deb: 9/3/24

YEAR	TM/L	W	L	PCT	G	GS	CG	SH	SV	IP	H	HR	BB	SO	RAT	ERA	ERA+	OAV	OOB	BH	AVG	PB	PR	/A	PD	TPI
1924	Bos-N	0	4	.000	5	4	1	0	0	33	33	0	11	15	12.0	3.82	100	.287	.349	0	.000	-1	0	0	-0	-0.1
1925	Bos-N	7	12	.368	34	23	5	0	1	157	177	6	62	32	13.9	4.41	91	.296	.365	6	.136	-2	-3	-7	-2	-1.1
1926	Bos-N	3	3	.500	15	4	1	0	0	36¹	54	3	19	7	18.6	7.93	45	.370	.449	2	.167	-1	-17	-18	-0	-2.4
1929	Det-A	1	3	.250	13	6	2	0	1	51²	70	2	33	7	18.5	5.57	77	.340	.438	2	.105	-1	-8	-7	-1	-0.7
Total	4	11	22	.333	67	37	9	0	2	278	334	11	125	61	15.1	5.02	79	.314	.390	10	.122	-5	-27	-32	-3	-4.3

● OSCAR GRAHAM
Graham, Oscar M. b: 7/20/1878, Plattsmouth, Neb. d: 10/15/31, Moline, Ill. BL/TL, 6'0.5", Deb: 4/16/07

YEAR	TM/L	W	L	PCT	G	GS	CG	SH	SV	IP	H	HR	BB	SO	RAT	ERA	ERA+	OAV	OOB	BH	AVG	PB	PR	/A	PD	TPI
1907	Was-A	4	9	.308	20	14	6	0	0	104	116	3	29	44	13.4	3.98	61	.284	.347	11	.229	3	-17	-18	0	-1.7

● BILL GRAHAM
Graham, William Albert b: 1/21/37, Flemingsburg, Ky. BR/TR, 6'3", 217 lbs. Deb: 10/2/66

YEAR	TM/L	W	L	PCT	G	GS	CG	SH	SV	IP	H	HR	BB	SO	RAT	ERA	ERA+	OAV	OOB	BH	AVG	PB	PR	/A	PD	TPI
1966	Det-A	0	0	—	1	0	0	0	0	2	2	0	0	0	9.0	0.00	—	.250	.250	0	—	0	1	1	-0	0.0
1967	NY-N	1	2	.333	5	3	1	0	0	27¹	20	3	11	14	10.2	2.63	129	.200	.279	1	.125	-0	2	2	-1	0.1
Total	2	1	2	.333	6	3	1	0	0	29¹	22	3	11	16	10.1	2.45	138	.204	.277	1	.125	-0	3	3	-1	0.1

● BILL GRAHAME
Grahame, William James b: 7/22/1884, Owosso, Mich. d: 2/15/36, Holt, Mich. TL, 6', Deb: 4/18/08

YEAR	TM/L	W	L	PCT	G	GS	CG	SH	SV	IP	H	HR	BB	SO	RAT	ERA	ERA+	OAV	OOB	BH	AVG	PB	PR	/A	PD	TPI
1908	StL-A	6	7	.462	21	13	7	0	0	117¹	104	0	32	47	11.4	2.30	104	.240	.310	5	.119	-3	1	1	-0	-0.2
1909	StL-A	8	14	.364	34	21	13	3	1	187¹	171	3	60	82	11.3	3.12	77	.256	.322	10	.159	-0	-13	-15	1	-1.7
1910	StL-A	0	8	.000	9	6	1	0	0	43	46	2	13	12	13.2	3.56	70	.297	.366	2	.154	-5	-5	-5	-2	-1.1
Total	3	14	29	.326	64	40	21	3	1	347²	321	5	105	141	11.6	2.90	83	.256	.323	17	.144	-8	-17	-19	-1	-3.0

● JOE GRAHE
Grahe, Joseph Milton b: 8/14/67, W.Palm Beach, Fla. BR/TR, 6'1", 196 lbs. Deb: 8/4/90

YEAR	TM/L	W	L	PCT	G	GS	CG	SH	SV	IP	H	HR	BB	SO	RAT	ERA	ERA+	OAV	OOB	BH	AVG	PB	PR	/A	PD	TPI
1990	Cal-A	3	4	.429	8	8	0	0	0	43¹	51	3	23	25	16.0	4.98	77	.293	.385	0	—	0	-5	-6	1	-0.7
1991	Cal-A	3	7	.300	18	10	1	0	0	73	84	2	33	40	14.5	4.81	85	.288	.366	0	—	0	-6	-6	0	-0.7
1992	Cal-A	5	6	.455	46	7	0	0	21	94²	85	5	39	39	12.4	3.52	113	.246	.332	0	—	0	4	5	0	0.5
1993	Cal-A	4	1	.800	45	0	0	0	11	56²	54	5	25	31	12.9	2.86	158	.251	.335	0	—	0	9	10	1	1.0
1994	Cal-A	2	5	.286	40	0	0	0	13	43¹	68	5	18	26	19.1	6.65	74	.362	.434	0	—	0	-9	-9	-1	-1.5
1995	Col-N	4	3	.571	17	9	0	0	0	56²	69	6	27	27	15.7	5.08	106	.301	.382	5	.417	1	-6	2	1	0.4
Total	6	21	26	.447	174	34	1	0	45	367²	411	26	165	188	14.7	4.46	98	.285	.367	5	.417	1	-12	-3	4	-0.8

● TOMMY GRAMLY
Gramly, Bert Thomas b: 4/19/45, Dallas, Tex. BR/TR, 6'3", 175 lbs. Deb: 4/18/68

YEAR	TM/L	W	L	PCT	G	GS	CG	SH	SV	IP	H	HR	BB	SO	RAT	ERA	ERA+	OAV	OOB	BH	AVG	PB	PR	/A	PD	TPI
1968	Cle-A	0	1	.000	3	0	0	0	0	3¹	3	0	2	1	13.5	2.70	110	.250	.357	0	—	0	0	0	0	0.0

YEAR	TM/L	W	L	PCT	G	GS	CG	SH	SV	IP	H	HR	BB	SO	RAT	ERA	ERA+	OAV	OOB	BH	AVG	PB	PR	/A	PD	TPI

● HANK GRAMPP   Grampp, Henry Erchardt   b: 9/28/03, New York, N.Y.   d: 3/24/86, New York, N.Y.   BR/TR, 6'1", 185 lbs.   Deb: 6/2/27

	1927	Chi-N	0	0	—	2	0	0	0	0	3	4	0	1	3	15.0	9.00	43	.333	.385	0	—	0	-2	-2	0	0.0
	1929	Chi-N	0	1	.000	1	1	0	0	0	2	4	0	3	0	36.0	27.00	17	.500	.667	0	—	0	-5	-5	-0	-1.2
	Total	2	0	1	.000	3	1	0	0	0	5	8	0	4	3	23.4	16.20	26	.400	.520	0	—	0	-7	-7	0	-1.2

● JACK GRANEY   Graney, John Gladstone   b: 6/10/1886, St.Thomas, Ont., Can.   d: 4/20/78, Louisiana, Mo.   BL/TL, 5'9", 180 lbs.   Deb: 4/30/08 ◆

| 1908 | Cle-A | 0 | 0 | — | 2 | 0 | 0 | 0 | 0 | 3¹ | 6 | 0 | 1 | 0 | 18.9 | 5.40 | 44 | .400 | .438 | 0 | — | 0 | -1 | -1 | -0 | 0.0 |

● JEFF GRANGER   Granger, Jeffrey Adam   b: 12/16/71, San Pedro, Cal.   BR/TL, 6'4", 200 lbs.   Deb: 9/16/93

1993	KC-A	0	0	—	1	0	0	0	0	1	3	0	2	1	45.0	27.00	17	.500	.625	0	—	0	-3	-2	0	-0.3
1994	KC-A	0	1	.000	2	2	0	0	0	9¹	14	2	6	3	18.3	6.75	74	.325	.413	0	—	0	-2	-2	0	-0.2
1996	KC-A	0	0	—	15	0	0	0	0	16¹	21	3	10	11	18.2	6.61	74	.313	.418	0	—	0	-3	-3	0	0.2
Total	3	0	1	.000	18	2	0	0	0	26²	37	5	18	15	19.2	7.43	66	.327	.429	0	—	0	-7	-7	0	-0.3

● WAYNE GRANGER   Granger, Wayne Allan   b: 3/15/44, Springfield, Mass.   BR/TR, 6'2", 165 lbs.   Deb: 6/5/68

1968	*StL-N	4	2	.667	34	0	0	0	4	44	40	2	12	27	11.0	2.25	129	.238	.297	1	.200	0	4	3	2	0.7
1969	Cin-N	9	6	.600	**90**	0	0	0	27	144²	143	16	40	68	11.8	2.80	134	.262	.320	2	.095	-0	13	15	1	2.3
1970	*Cin-N	6	5	.545	67	0	0	0	**35**	84²	79	5	27	38	11.4	2.66	152	.252	.313	1	.100	-1	13	13	2	2.8
1971	Cin-N	7	6	.538	**70**	0	0	0	11	100	94	8	28	51	11.1	3.33	101	.251	.304	1	.143	1	2	0	3	0.5
1972	Min-A	4	6	.400	63	0	0	0	19	89²	83	7	28	49	11.3	3.01	107	.243	.304	2	.200	0	0	2	-0	0.3
1973	StL-N	2	4	.333	33	0	0	0	5	46²	50	3	21	14	14.1	4.24	86	.284	.367	0	.000	-0	-3	-3	-0	-0.5
	NY-A	0	1	.000	7	0	0	0	0	15¹	19	1	3	10	13.5	1.76	208	.279	.319	0	—	0	4	3	-1	0.2
1974	Chi-A	0	0	—	5	0	0	0	0	7²	16	1	3	4	22.3	8.22	45	.432	.475	0	—	0	-4	-4	0	-0.2
1975	Hou-N	2	5	.286	55	0	0	0	5	74	76	7	23	30	12.5	3.65	92	.264	.327	0	.000	-1	-0	-2	1	-0.2
1976	Mon-N	1	0	1.000	27	0	0	0	2	32	32	3	16	14	14.1	3.66	92	.264	.360	0	—	0	-1	-0	-0	0.0
Total	9	35	35	.500	451	0	0	0	108	638²	632	47	201	303	12.0	3.14	113	.260	.322	7	.103	-1	27	28	8	6.1

● GEORGE GRANT   Grant, George Addison   b: 1/6/03, E.Tallassee, Ala.   d: 3/25/86, Montgomery, Ala.   BR/TR, 5'11.5", 175 lbs.   Deb: 9/17/23

1923	StL-A	0	0	—	4	0	0	0	0	8²	15	0	3	2	18.7	5.19	80	.395	.439	0	.000	-0	-1	-1	0	0.0
1924	StL-A	1	2	.333	22	2	0	0	0	51¹	69	4	25	11	16.7	6.31	72	.325	.399	0	.000	-2	-12	-10	-1	-0.8
1925	StL-A	0	2	.000	12	0	0	0	0	16¹	26	2	8	7	18.7	6.06	77	.400	.466	1	.250	-0	-3	-3	0	-0.2
1927	Cle-A	4	6	.400	25	3	2	0	1	74²	85	1	40	19	15.1	4.46	94	.300	.387	2	.095	-2	-3	-2	0	-0.4
1928	Cle-A	10	8	.556	28	18	6	1	0	155¹	196	7	76	39	15.9	5.04	82	.319	.395	11	.183	-2	-17	-15	2	-1.5
1929	Cle-A	0	2	.000	12	0	0	0	0	24	41	2	23	5	24.0	10.50	42	.414	.525	0	.000	-0	-17	-16	0	-1.1
1931	Pit-N	0	0	—	11	0	0	0	0	17	28	0	7	6	19.1	7.41	52	.364	.424	0	—	0	-7	-7	0	0.0
Total	7	15	20	.429	114	23	8	1	1	347¹	460	16	182	89	16.7	5.65	75	.331	.410	14	.135	-8	-59	-54	3	-4.0

● JIM GRANT   Grant, James Ronald   b: 8/4/1894, Coalville, Iowa   d: 11/30/85, Des Moines, Iowa   BR/TL, 5'11", 180 lbs.   Deb: 4/21/23

| 1923 | Phi-N | 0 | 0 | — | 2 | 0 | 0 | 0 | 0 | 4 | 10 | 1 | 4 | 0 | 33.8 | 13.50 | 34 | .588 | .682 | 0 | .000 | -0 | -4 | -4 | 0 | 0.0 |

● MUDCAT GRANT   Grant, James Timothy "Jim"   b: 8/13/35, Lacoochee, Fla.   BR/TR, 6'1", 186 lbs.   Deb: 4/17/58

1958	Cle-A	10	11	.476	44	28	11	1	4	204	173	20	104	111	12.3	3.84	95	.228	.321	5	.076	-4	-2	-4	-2	-1.0
1959	Cle-A	10	7	.588	38	19	6	1	1	165¹	140	23	81	85	12.1	4.14	89	.232	.325	11	.200	1	-5	-8	-0	-0.7
1960	Cle-A	9	8	.529	33	19	5	0	0	159²	147	26	78	75	12.8	4.40	85	.243	.332	16	.281	4	-9	-12	-1	-0.9
1961	Cle-A	15	9	.625	35	35	11	3	0	244³	207	32	109	146	11.7	3.86	102	.227	.312	15	.170	1	4	2	1	0.3
1962	Cle-A	7	10	.412	26	23	6	1	0	149²	128	24	81	90	12.6	4.27	91	.233	.331	8	.151	-0	-5	-7	-0	-0.7
1963	Cle-A☆	13	14	.481	38	32	10	2	1	229¹	213	30	87	157	11.9	3.69	98	.243	.314	13	.188	3	-2	-3	-3	-0.2
1964	Cle-A	3	4	.429	13	9	1	0	0	62	82	11	25	43	15.7	5.95	60	.324	.387	6	.273	4	-16	-16	0	-1.2
	Min-A	11	9	.550	26	23	10	1	1	166	162	21	36	75	10.7	2.82	127	.248	.288	10	.167	0	15	14	0	1.7
	Yr	14	13	.519	39	32	11	1	1	228	244	32	61	118	12.0	3.67	98	.269	.315	16	.195	4	-1	-2	1	0.5
1965	*Min-A★	21	7	**.750**	41	39	14	**6**	0	270¹	252	34	61	142	10.4	3.30	108	.247	.289	15	.155	2	5	8	1	1.1
1966	Min-A	13	13	.500	35	35	10	3	0	249	248	23	49	110	11.0	3.25	111	.260	.300	15	.192	2	5	10	2	1.4
1967	Min-A	5	6	.455	27	14	2	0	0	95¹	121	10	17	50	13.1	4.72	73	.315	.346	5	.179	0	-16	-13	-2	-1.7
1968	LA-N	6	4	.600	37	4	1	0	3	94²	77	1	19	35	9.7	2.09	132	.226	.279	4	.129	0	9	7	1	0.9
1969	Mon-N	1	6	.143	11	10	1	0	0	50²	64	7	14	20	14.0	4.80	77	.299	.345	2	.125	-1	-7	-6	-0	-0.8
	StL-N	7	5	.583	30	3	1	0	7	63¹	62	9	22	35	12.2	4.12	87	.252	.319	5	.294	2	-4	-4	-1	-0.7
	Yr	8	11	.421	41	13	2	0	7	114	126	16	36	55	12.9	4.42	82	.273	.328	7	.212	1	-10	-10	-1	-1.5
1970	Oak-A	6	2	.750	72	0	0	0	24	123¹	104	8	30	54	10.0	1.82	194	.235	.288	2	.222	2	**26**	**24**	1	2.6
	Pit-N	2	1	.667	8	0	0	0	0	12	8	2	4	7	7.5	2.25	173	.190	.227	0	.000	-0	2	2	0	0.5
1971	Pit-N	5	3	.625	42	0	0	0	7	75	79	8	28	22	13.0	3.60	94	.274	.341	2	.250	-1	-1	-2	-1	-0.1
	*Oak-A	1	0	1.000	15	0	0	0	3	27¹	25	3	6	13	10.2	1.98	169	.243	.284	1	.333	0	5	4	-0	0.3
Total	14	145	119	.549	571	293	89	18	53	2441²	2292	292	849	1267	11.7	3.63	100	.248	.313	135	.178	16	5	-/A	-3	0.8

● MARK GRANT   Grant, Mark Andrew   b: 10/24/63, Aurora, Ill.   BR/TR, 6'2", 205 lbs.   Deb: 4/27/84

1984	SF-N	1	4	.200	11	10	0	0	1	53²	56	6	19	32	12.7	6.37	59	.272	.336	0	.000	-2	-17	-17	-0	-1.6
1986	SF-N	1	0	1.000	4	1	0	0	0	10	6	1	5	9	9.9	3.60	98	.176	.282	0	.000	-0	0	0	0	0.0
1987	SF-N	1	2	.333	16	8	0	0	1	61	66	6	21	32	13.0	3.54	109	.282	.344	1	.083	-0	4	2	-1	0.0
	SD-N	6	7	.462	17	17	2	1	0	102¹	104	16	52	58	13.7	4.66	85	.263	.348	3	.094	-1	-7	-8	-1	-1.0
	Yr	7	9	.438	33	25	2	1	1	163¹	170	22	73	90	13.4	4.24	92	.269	.345	4	.091	-1	-3	-6	-1	-1.0
1988	SD-N	2	8	.200	33	11	0	0	0	97²	97	14	36	61	12.4	3.69	92	.268	.338	0	—	-1	-3	-3	0	-0.4
1989	SD-N	8	2	.800	50	0	0	0	2	116¹	105	11	32	69	10.8	3.33	105	.248	.305	1	.050	-0	2	2	-0	0.1
1990	SD-N	1	1	.500	26	0	0	0	0	39	47	5	19	29	15.2	4.85	79	.305	.382	1	.500	0	-5	-4	1	-0.1
	Atl-N	1	2	.333	33	1	0	0	3	52¹	61	4	18	40	13.8	4.64	87	.293	.352	1	.250	1	-5	-4	-0	-0.2
	Yr	2	3	.400	59	1	0	0	3	91¹	108	9	37	69	14.4	4.73	83	.296	.362	2	.333	1	-10	-8	0	-0.3
1992	Sea-A	4	3	.333	23	10	0	0	0	81	100	6	22	42	13.8	3.89	102	.311	.358	0	—	-1	0	1	-1	-0.1
1993	Hou-N	0	0	—	6	0	0	0	0	11	11	0	5	6	13.1	0.82	473	.275	.356	0	—	0	4	4	-0	0.1
	Col-N	0	1	.000	14	0	0	0	1	14¹	23	4	6	8	18.2	12.56	38	.377	.433	0	—	0	-14	-12	-0	-0.9
	Yr	0	1	.000	20	0	0	0	1	25¹	34	4	11	14	16.0	7.46	59	.333	.398	0	—	0	-10	-9	-0	-0.8
Total	8	22	32	.407	233	58	2	1	8	638²	676	72	235	382	13.0	4.31	87	.277	.343	7	.067	-3	-39	-40	-2	-4.1

● RICK GRAPENTHIN   Grapenthin, Richard Ray   b: 4/16/58, Linn Grove, Iowa   BR/TR, 6'2", 205 lbs.   Deb: 5/3/83

1983	Mon-N	0	1	.000	1	0	0	0	0	4	4	2	1	3	11.3	9.00	40	.267	.313	0	.000	-0	-2	-2	0	-0.4
1984	Mon-N	1	2	.333	13	1	0	0	2	23	19	7	9	10.2	3.52	97	.235	.295	1	.200	0	0	-0	0	0.0
1985	Mon-N	0	0	—	5	0	0	0	0	7	13	0	8	4	28.3	14.14	24	.394	.524	1	1.000	1	-8	-8	-0	-0.4
Total	3	1	3	.250	19	1	0	0	2	34	36	5	16	16	14.0	6.35	54	.279	.363	2	.286	1	-10	-11	0	-0.4

● LOU GRASMICK   Grasmick, Louis Junior   b: 9/11/24, Baltimore, Md.   BR/TR, 6', 195 lbs.   Deb: 4/22/48

| 1948 | Phi-N | 0 | 0 | — | 2 | 0 | 0 | 0 | 0 | 5 | 3 | 1 | 8 | 2 | 19.8 | 7.20 | 55 | .176 | .440 | 1 | 1.000 | 0 | -2 | -2 | 0 | 0.1 |

● DON GRATE   Grate, Donald "Buckeye"   b: 8/27/23, Greenfield, Ohio   BR/TR, 6'2.5", 180 lbs.   Deb: 7/6/45

1945	Phi-N	0	1	.000	4	2	0	0	0	8¹	18	0	12	6	32.4	17.28	22	.439	.566	0	.000	-0	-12	-12	-0	-1.2
1946	Phi-N	1	0	1.000	3	0	0	0	0	8	4	0	2	6	6.8	1.13	305	.160	.222	0	.000	-0	2	2	0	0.2
Total	2	1	1	.500	7	2	0	0	0	16¹	22	0	14	12	19.8	9.37	39	.333	.450	0	.000	-0	-10	-10	-1	-1.0

● MARK GRATER   Grater, Mark Anthony   b: 1/19/64, Rochester, Pa.   BR/TR, 5'10", 205 lbs.   Deb: 6/12/91

1991	StL-N	0	0	—	3	0	0	0	0	3	5	0	2	1	21.0	0.00	—	.385	.467	0	—	0	1	1	-0	0.1
1993	Det-A	0	0	—	6	0	0	0	0	5	6	0	4	4	18.0	5.40	79	.286	.400	0	—	-0	-1	-1	-0	-0.1
Total	2	0	0	—	9	0	0	0	0	8	11	0	6	4	19.1	3.38	121	.324	.425	0	—	0	1	1	0	0.0

● DANNY GRAVES   Graves, Daniel Peter   b: 8/7/73, Saigon, Vietnam   BR/TR, 5'11", 200 lbs.   Deb: 7/13/96

| 1996 | Cle-A | 2 | 0 | 1.000 | 15 | 0 | 0 | 0 | 0 | 29² | 29 | 2 | 10 | 22 | 11.8 | 4.55 | 108 | .246 | .305 | 0 | — | 0 | 1 | 1 | -0 | 0.0 |

YEAR	TM/L	W	L	PCT	G	GS	CG	SH	SV	IP	H	HR	BB	SO	RAT	ERA	ERA+	OAV	OOB	BH	AVG	PB	PR	/A	PD	TPI
● FRANK GRAVES	Graves, Frank M. b: 11/2/1860, Cincinnati, Ohio 6', 163 lbs. Deb: 5/10/1886 ♦																									
1886	StL-N	0	0	—	1	0	0	0	0	7	10	0	1	2	14.1	9.00	36	.323	.344	21	.152	-0	-4	-4	-0	0.0
● CHARLIE GRAY	Gray, Charles b: 1867, Indianapolis, Ind. Deb: 4/23/1890																									
1890	Pit-N	1	4	.200	5	4	3	0	0	31	48	1	0	24	10	21.2	7.55	44	.343	.442	3	.200	-0	-14	-15	-1	-1.7
● DAVE GRAY	Gray, David Alexander b: 1/7/43, Ogden, Utah BR/TR, 6'1", 190 lbs. Deb: 6/14/64																									
1964	Bos-A	0	0	—	9	1	0	0	0	17	26.3					9.00	43	.321	.500	1	1.000	0	-8	-7	0	0.1
● CHUMMY GRAY	Gray, George Edward b: 7/17/1873, Rockland, Me. d: 8/14/13, Rockland, Maine TR, 5'11.5", 163 lbs. Deb: 9/14/1899																									
1899	Pit-N	3	3	.500	9	7	6	0	0	70²	85	1	24	9	14.4	3.44	111	.297	.360	-3	.038	-3	3	3	2	0.1
● JEFF GRAY	Gray, Jeffrey Edward b: 4/10/63, Richmond, Va. BR/TR, 6'1", 175 lbs. Deb: 6/21/88																									
1988	Cin-N	0	0	—	5	0	0	0	0	9¹	12	0	4	5	15.4	3.86	93	.333	.400	0	.000	-0	-0	-0	-0	0.0
1990	*Bos-A	2	4	.333	41	0	0	0	9	50²	53	3	15	50	12.3	4.44	92	.268	.322	0	—	-0	-3	-2	-0	-0.3
1991	Bos-A	2	3	.400	50	0	0	0	1	61²	39	7	10	41	7.3	2.34	184	.181	.220	0	—	-0	12	13	1	1.1
Total	3	4	7	.364	96	0	0	0	10	121²	104	10	29	96	10.0	3.33	125	.231	.281	0	.000	-0	9	11	1	0.8
● JOHNNY GRAY	Gray, John Leonard b: 12/11/27, W.Palm Beach, Fla. BR/TR, 6'4", 226 lbs. Deb: 7/18/54																									
1954	Phi-A	3	12	.200	18	16	5	0	0	105	111	10	91	51	17.3	6.51	60	.273	.406	1	.029	-4	-33	-30	0	-3.9
1955	KC-A	0	3	.000	8	5	0	0	0	26²	28	2	24	11	17.9	6.41	65	.277	.421	1	.125	-0	-7	-7	-1	-0.7
1957	Cle-A	1	3	.250	7	3	1	1	0	20	21	1	13	3	15.3	5.85	64	.288	.395	0	.000	-1	-5	-5	-0	-0.9
1958	Phi-N	0	0	—	15	0	0	0	0	17¹	12	3	14	10	13.5	4.15	95	.222	.382	0	.000	-0	-0	-0	-0	-0.0
Total	4	4	18	.182	48	24	6	1	0	169	172	16	142	75	16.8	6.18	64	.271	.405	2	.043	-5	-45	-42	-1	-5.5
● SAM GRAY	Gray, Samuel David "Sad Sam" b: 10/15/1897, Van Alstyne, Tex. d: 4/16/53, McKinney, Tex. BR/TR, 5'10", 175 lbs. Deb: 4/19/24																									
1924	Phi-A	8	7	.533	34	19	8	2	2	151²	169	5	89	54	15.7	3.98	108	.284	.383	10	.175	-2	4	5	-1	0.2
1925	Phi-A	16	8	.667	32	28	14	4	3	203²	199	11	63	80	11.7	3.27	142	.260	.319	12	.179	-2	25	31	-3	2.8
1926	Phi-A	11	12	.478	38	18	5	0	0	150²	164	5	50	82	13.0	3.64	114	.279	.340	11	.216	1	6	9	-2	1.1
1927	Phi-A	9	6	.600	37	13	3	1	3	133¹	153	4	51	49	14.0	4.59	93	.295	.362	8	.190	-1	-7	-5	-0	-0.6
1928	StL-A	20	12	.625	35	31	21	2	3	262²	256	11	86	102	11.8	3.19	132	.260	.320	19	.188	-2	25	30	-1	3.5
1929	StL-A	18	15	.545	43	37	23	**4**	1	305	336	16	96	109	12.8	3.72	119	.285	.340	19	.184	-2	18	24	-1	2.0
1930	StL-A	4	15	.211	27	24	7	0	0	167²	215	17	52	51	14.6	6.28	78	.316	.368	11	.204	-2	-30	-26	-1	-2.5
1931	StL-A	11	24	.314	43	37	13	0	2	258	323	20	54	88	13.3	5.09	91	.297	.332	14	.177	-1	-20	-13	-1	-1.7
1932	StL-A	7	12	.368	52	18	7	3	4	206²	250	9	53	79	13.2	4.53	107	.294	.336	13	.210	-0	-1	7	-1	0.5
1933	StL-A	7	4	.636	38	6	0	0	4	112	131	7	45	36	14.2	4.10	114	.301	.368	7	.219	-1	2	7	-1	0.7
Total	10	111	115	.491	379	231	101	16	22	1951¹	2196	111	639	730	13.2	4.18	108	.286	.343	124	.191	-10	23	68	-8	6.0
● TED GRAY	Gray, Ted Glenn b: 12/31/24, Detroit, Mich. BB/TL, 5'11", 175 lbs. Deb: 5/15/46																									
1946	Det-A	0	2	.000	3	2	0	0	0	11²	17	4	5	5	17.0	8.49	43	.340	.400	0	.000	-0	-6	-6	-0	-1.0
1948	Det-A	6	2	.750	26	11	3	1	0	85¹	73	2	72	60	15.6	4.22	104	.236	.385	7	.241	1	1	1	-0	0.1
1949	Det-A	10	10	.500	34	27	8	3	1	195	163	14	103	96	13.0	3.51	119	.227	.328	8	.127	-3	15	14	1	1.1
1950	Det-A★	10	7	.588	27	21	7	0	1	149¹	139	22	72	102	12.8	4.40	107	.248	.335	7	.140	-3	3	5	-2	0.1
1951	Det-A	7	14	.333	34	28	9	1	1	197¹	194	17	95	131	13.5	4.06	103	.256	.343	9	.143	-3	1	3	-1	-0.2
1952	Det-A	12	17	.414	35	32	13	2	0	224	212	21	101	138	12.7	4.14	92	.249	.331	13	.171	-2	-12	-9	1	-1.1
1953	Det-A	10	15	.400	30	28	8	0	0	176	166	25	76	115	12.7	4.60	88	.252	.336	14	.230	2	-12	-10	-1	-1.2
1954	Det-A	3	5	.375	19	10	2	0	0	72	70	8	56	29	16.0	5.38	69	.268	.401	1	.045	2	-13	-13	-1	-1.7
1955	Chi-A	0	0	—	2	1	0	0	0	3	9	0	2	1	33.0	18.00	22	.500	.550	0	—	-0	-5	-5	0	0.0
	Cle-A	0	0	—	2	0	0	0	0	2	5	1	2	1	31.5	18.00	22	.455	.538	0	—	-0	-3	-3	0	0.0
	NY-A	0	0	—	1	0	0	0	0	3	3	0	1	0	9.0	3.00	125	.300	.300	0	.000	-0	0	0	-0	0.0
	Bal-A	1	2	.333	9	1	0	0	0	15¹	21	3	11	8	18.8	8.22	46	.344	.444	0	.000	-0	-7	-8	1	-1.2
	Yr	1	2	.333	14	3	0	0	0	23¹	38	4	15	11	20.4	9.64	40	.376	.457	0	.000	-0	-15	-15	1	-1.2
Total	9	59	74	.444	222	162	50	7	4	1134	1072	114	595	687	13.5	4.37	94	.251	.346	59	.159	-10	-38	-30	-4	-5.1
● DOLLY GRAY	Gray, William Denton b: 12/3/1878, Houghton, Mich. d: 4/4/56, Yuba City, Cal. BL/TL, 6'2", 160 lbs. Deb: 4/13/09																									
1909	Was-A	5	19	.208	36	26	19	0	0	218	210	1	77	87	12.2	3.59	68	.258	.329	13	.146	-1	-27	-28	-1	-3.2
1910	Was-A	8	19	.296	34	29	21	3	0	229	216	3	65	84	11.4	2.63	95	.249	.309	21	.247	4	-3	-4	2	0.2
1911	Was-A	2	13	.133	28	15	6	0	0	121	160	4	40	42	15.1	5.06	65	.331	.385	10	.227	1	-23	-24	1	-2.3
Total	3	15	51	.227	98	70	46	3	0	568	586	8	182	213	12.5	3.52	75	.271	.333	44	.202	3	-53	-56	2	-5.3
● ELI GRBA	Grba, Eli b: 8/9/34, Chicago, Ill. BR/TR, 6'2", 207 lbs. Deb: 7/10/59																									
1959	NY-A	2	5	.286	19	6	0	0	0	50¹	52	6	39	23	16.3	6.44	57	.269	.392	3	.214	1	-14	-16	-0	-1.8
1960	*NY-A	6	4	.600	24	9	1	0	1	80²	65	9	46	32	12.6	3.68	97	.226	.337	5	.238	2	2	-1	-1	0.1
1961	LA-A	11	13	.458	40	30	8	0	2	211²	197	26	114	105	13.5	4.25	106	.242	.340	15	.234	4	-5	6	-1	0.9
1962	LA-A	8	9	.471	40	29	1	0	0	176¹	185	19	75	90	13.4	4.54	85	.267	.340	12	.207	4	-11	-13	-1	-0.8
1963	LA-A	1	2	.333	12	1	0	0	0	17¹	14	2	10	5	13.0	4.67	73	.222	.338	0	.000	-0	-2	-2	-0	-0.4
Total	5	28	33	.459	135	75	10	0	4	536¹	513	62	284	255	13.6	4.48	90	.250	.345	35	.219	10	-31	-27	-1	-2.0
● BILL GREASON	Greason, William Henry "Booster" b: 9/3/24, Atlanta, Ga. BR/TR, 5'10", 170 lbs. Deb: 5/31/54																									
1954	StL-N	0	1	.000	3	2	0	0	0	4	6	3	4	3	27.0	13.50	30	.421	.522	0	.000	-0	-4	-4	0	-0.8
● CHRIS GREEN	Green, Christopher De Wayne b: 9/5/60, Los Angeles, Cal. BL/TL, 6'2", 214 lbs. Deb: 4/17/84																									
1984	Pit-N	0	0	—	4	0	0	0	0	3	5	0	1	3	18.0	6.00	60	.417	.462	0	—	0	-1	-1	0	0.0
● ED GREEN	Green, Edward M. b: 1850, Philadelphia, Pa. Deb: 4/22/1890																									
1890	Phi-a	7	15	.318	25	22	20	1	1	191	267	4	94	56	17.3	5.80	66	.321	.393	15	.119	-4	-41	-42	3	-3.6
● FRED GREEN	Green, Fred Allen b: 9/14/33, Titusville, N.J. BR/TL, 6'4", 190 lbs. Deb: 4/15/59 F																									
1959	Pit-N	1	2	.333	17	1	0	0	0	37¹	37	2	15	20	13.0	3.13	123	.259	.329	0	.000	-1	3	3	0	0.2
1960	*Pit-N	8	4	.667	45	0	0	0	3	70	61	9	33	49	12.2	3.21	117	.243	.333	3	.375	3	4	4	-1	1.0
1961	Pit-N	0	0	—	13	0	0	0	0	20²	27	2	9	4	15.7	4.79	83	.321	.387	0	—	-2	-2	-1	0	-0.2
1962	Was-A	0	1	.000	5	0	0	0	0	7	7	3	6	2	16.7	6.43	63	.250	.382	0	—	-2	-2	-2	0	-0.2
1964	Pit-N	0	0	—	8	0	0	0	0	7¹	10	1	0	2	12.3	1.23	286	.323	.323	0	—	2	2	1	0	0.2
Total	5	9	7	.563	88	1	0	0	3	142¹	142	12	63	77	13.0	3.48	110	.264	.343	3	.176	-2	5	5	0	1.0
● DALLAS GREEN	Green, George Dallas b: 8/4/34, Newport, Del. BL/TR, 6'5", 210 lbs. Deb: 6/18/60 M																									
1960	Phi-N	3	6	.333	23	10	2	0	0	108²	100	10	44	51	12.1	4.06	96	.248	.325	7	.206	-0	-4	-2	-0	-0.1
1961	Phi-N	2	4	.333	42	10	1	1	1	128	160	8	47	45	14.7	4.85	84	.315	.375	5	.152	0	-12	-11	0	-0.4
1962	Phi-N	6	6	.500	37	10	2	1	0	129¹	145	10	43	58	13.4	3.83	101	.289	.352	2	.063	-1	2	2	0	0.2
1963	Phi-N	7	5	.583	40	14	0	0	0	120	134	8	30	68	13.1	3.23	100	.286	.342	3	.086	1	1	0	-0	0.0
1964	Phi-N	2	1	.667	25	0	0	0	0	42	63	4	14	21	16.9	5.79	60	.362	.416	0	—	0	-10	-11	-0	-0.8
1965	Was-A	0	0	—	14¹	14	0	3	2	6	14.4	3.14	114	.241	.279	0	—	0	1	0	0	0.0				
1966	NY-N	0	0	—	4	0	0	0	0	10	1	1	1	14.4	5.40	67	.333	.400	0	—	-0	-1	-1	0	-0.0
1967	Phi-N	0	0	—	15	0	0	0	0	15	25	3	6	12	19.2	9.00	38	.362	.421	0	—	-0	-9	-9	-0	-0.7
Total	8	20	22	.476	185	46	12	2	4	562¹	647	46	197	268	13.7	4.26	88	.294	.356	17	.120	-3	-33	-33	3	-1.1
● HARVEY GREEN	Green, Harvey George "Buck" b: 2/9/15, Kenosha, Wis. d: 7/24/70, Franklin, La. BB/TR, 6'2.5", 185 lbs. Deb: 9/12/35																									
1935	Bro-N	0	0	—	2	0	0	0	0	4	4	1	3	0	54.0	9.00	44	.400	.667	0	—	-0	-1	-1	-0	-0.1
● TYLER GREEN	Green, Tyler Scott b: 2/18/70, Springfield, Ohio BR/TR, 6'5", 185 lbs. Deb: 4/9/93																									
1993	Phi-N	0	0	—	3	2	0	0	0	7¹	16	1	5	7	25.8	7.36	54	.444	.512	0	.000	-0	-3	-3	-0	-0.1
1995	Phi-N★	8	9	.471	26	25	4	2	0	140²	157	15	66	85	14.5	5.31	80	.290	.371	8	.182	2	-18	-17	-1	-1.7
Total	2	8	9	.471	29	27	4	2	0	148	173	16	71	92	15.1	5.41	78	.299	.380	8	.174	2	-20	-20	-1	-1.8

YEAR	TM/L	W	L	PCT	G	GS	CG	SH	SV	IP	H	HR	BB	SO	RAT	ERA	ERA+	OAV	OOB	BH	AVG	PB	PR	/A	PD	TPI
● **TOMMY GREENE**				Greene, Ira Thomas				b: 4/6/67, Lumberton, N.C.			BR/TR, 6'5", 225 lbs.			Deb: 9/10/89											
1989	Atl-N	1	2	.333	4	4	1	1	0	26¹	22	5	6	17	9.6	4.10	89	.234	.280	1	.100	-1	-2	-1	-0	-0.2
1990	Atl-N	1	0	1.000	5	2	0	0	0	12¹	14	3	9	4	17.5	8.03	50	.286	.407	0	.000	-0	-6	-5	-0	-0.4
	Phi-N	2	3	.400	10	7	0	0	0	39	36	5	17	17	12.2	4.15	92	.247	.325	2	.182	-0	-2	-1	-0	-0.2
	Yr	3	3	.500	15	9	0	0	0	51¹	50	8	26	21	13.3	5.08	76	.255	.342	2	.167	0	-7	-7	-1	-0.6
1991	Phi-N	13	7	.650	36	27	3	2	0	207²	177	19	66	154	10.7	3.38	108	.230	.294	3	.268	1	7	7	-3	1.1
1992	Phi-N	3	3	.500	13	12	0	0	0	64¹	75	5	34	39	15.2	5.32	66	.291	.373	1	.125	-1	-13	-13	-1	-1.3
1993	*Phi-N	16	4	.800	31	30	7	2	0	200	175	12	62	167	10.8	3.42	116	.233	.294	16	.222	6	14	12	-1	1.6
1994	Phi-N	2	0	1.000	7	7	0	0	0	35²	37	5	22	28	14.9	4.54	94	.272	.373	5	.385	2	-1	-1	-0	0.1
1995	Phi-N	0	5	.000	11	6	0	0	0	33²	45	6	20	24	18.2	8.29	51	.319	.415	0	.000	-0	-15	-15	-0	-1.9
Total	7	38	24	.613	117	95	11	5	0	619	581	60	236	450	12.0	4.10	93	.248	.319	46	.219	14	-18	-19	-6	-1.2
● **JUNE GREENE**				Greene, Julius Foust			b: 6/25/1899, Ramseur, N.C.			d: 3/19/74, Glendora, Cal.		BL/TR, 6'2.5", 185 lbs.			Deb: 4/20/28	♦									
1928	Phi-N	0	0	—	1	0	0	0	0	2	5	0	0	2	22.5	9.00	47	.556	.556	3	.500	2	-1	-1	0	0.2
1929	Phi-N	0	0	—	5	0	0	0	0	13²	33	2	9	4	29.6	19.76	22	.465	.542	4	.211	0	-23	-22	0	0.0
Total	2	0	0	—	6	0	0	0	0	15²	38	2	9	4	28.7	18.38	28	.475	.543	7	.280	2	-24	-23	1	0.2
● **NELSON GREENE**				Greene, Nelson George "Lefty"			b: 9/20/1900, Philadelphia, Pa.		d: 4/6/83, Lebanon, Pa.		BL/TL, 6', 185 lbs.			Deb: 4/28/24										
1924	Bro-N	0	1	.000	4	1	0	0	0	9	14	1	2	3	16.0	4.00	94	.350	.381	0	.000	-0	-0	-0	0	0.0
1925	Bro-N	2	0	1.000	11	0	0	0	1	22	45	4	7	4	21.3	10.64	39	.417	.452	2	.286	-0	-16	-16	1	-1.3
Total	2	2	1	.667	15	1	0	0	1	31	59	5	9	7	19.7	8.71	47	.399	.433	2	.250	-0	-16	-16	1	-1.3
● **KENT GREENFIELD**				Greenfield, Kent			b: 7/1/02, Guthrie, Ky.		d: 3/14/78, Guthrie, Ky.		BR/TR, 6'1", 180 lbs.			Deb: 9/28/24										
1924	NY-N	0	1	.000	1	1	0	0	0	3	9	1	1	1	30.0	15.00	24	.500	.526	0	—	0	-4	-4	-0	-0.8
1925	NY-N	12	8	.600	29	20	12	0	0	171²	195	4	64	66	13.7	3.88	104	.288	.352	5	.081	-6	7	3	1	-0.2
1926	NY-N	13	12	.520	39	28	8	1	1	222²	206	17	82	74	11.8	3.96	95	.251	.322	6	.092	-5	-3	-5	-2	-1.2
1927	NY-N	2	2	.500	12	1	0	0	0	20	39	3	13	4	24.3	9.45	41	.411	.491	0	.000	-0	-12	-12	0	-2.0
	Bos-N	11	14	.440	27	26	11	1	0	190	203	3	59	59	12.6	3.84	97	.282	.341	11	.172	-2	2	-3	-0	-0.5
	Yr	13	16	.448	39	27	11	1	0	210	242	6	72	63	13.7	4.37	85	.297	.357	11	.167	-2	-11	-15	-0	-2.5
1928	Bos-N	3	11	.214	32	23	5	0	0	143²	173	6	60	30	14.9	5.32	73	.307	.378	2	.053	-4	-21	-23	1	-2.2
1929	Bos-N	0	0	—	6	2	0	0	0	15²	33	1	15	7	28.7	10.91	43	.465	.568	0	.000	-1	-11	-11	1	0.0
	Bro-N	0	0	—	6	0	0	0	0	8²	13	1	3	1	16.6	8.31	56	.382	.432	0	.000	-0	-3	-4	0	0.0
	Yr	0	0	—	12	2	0	0	0	24¹	46	2	18	8	23.7	9.99	47	.430	.512	0	.000	-1	-14	-14	1	0.0
Total	6	41	48	.461	152	101	36	2	1	775¹	871	36	297	242	13.8	4.54	85	.290	.358	24	.101	-18	-46	-58	-0	-6.9
● **JOHN GREENING**				Greening, John A. (b: John A. Greenig)			b: Philadelphia, Pa.			Deb: 5/9/1888														
1888	Was-N	0	1	.000	1	1	1	0	0	9	17	2	4	2	21.0	11.00	25	.405	.457	0	—	-0	-8	-8	-0	-0.6
● **BOB GREENWOOD**				Greenwood, Robert Chandler "Greenie"			b: 3/13/28, Cananea, Mexico			BR/TR, 6'5", 200 lbs.			Deb: 4/21/54										
1954	Phi-N	1	2	.333	11	4	0	0	0	36²	28	2	18	9	11.3	3.19	127	.209	.303	0	.000	-1	4	3	0	0.2
1955	Phi-N	0	0	—	1	0	0	0	0	2¹	7	1	0	0	27.0	15.43	26	.500	.500	0	.000	-0	-3	-3	-0	0.0
Total	2	1	2	.333	12	4	0	0	0	39	35	3	18	9	12.2	3.92	103	.236	.319	0	.000	-1	0	0	0	0.2
● **KENNY GREER**				Greer, Kenneth William			b: 5/12/67, Boston, Mass.			BR/TR, 6'2", 210 lbs.			Deb: 9/29/93										
1993	NY-N	1	0	1.000	1	0	0	0	0	1	0	0	0	2	0.0	0.00	—	.000	.000	0	—	-0	0	0	0	0.5
1995	SF-N	0	2	.000	8	0	0	0	0	12	15	3	5	7	15.8	5.25	78	.288	.362	0	.000	-0	-1	-2	0	-0.2
Total	2	1	2	.333	9	0	0	0	0	13	15	3	5	9	14.5	4.85	84	.273	.344	0	.000	-0	-1	-1	0	0.3
● **DAVE GREGG**				Gregg, David Charles "Highpockets"			b: 3/14/1891, Chehalis, Wash.			d: 11/12/65, Clarkston, Wash.		BR/TR, 6'1", 185 lbs.			Deb: 6/15/13	F								
1913	Cle-A	0	0	—	1	0	0	0	0	1	2	0	0	0	27.0	18.00	17	.400	.500	0	—	0	-2	-2	0	0.0
● **HAL GREGG**				Gregg, Harold Dana "Skeets"			b: 7/11/21, Anaheim, Cal.			d: 5/13/91, Bishop, Cal.		BR/TR, 6'3.5", 195 lbs.			Deb: 8/18/43									
1943	Bro-N	0	3	.000	5	4	0	0	0	18²	21	2	21	7	20.3	9.64	35	.304	.467	0	.000	-0	-13	-13	-0	-1.6
1944	Bro-N	9	16	.360	39	31	6	0	2	197²	201	12	137	92	15.8	5.46	65	.258	.376	14	.206	-0	-41	-42	-0	-4.7
1945	Bro-N†	18	13	.581	42	34	13	2	2	254¹	221	5	120	139	12.3	3.47	108	.232	.323	20	.220	3	9	8	-0	1.2
1946	Bro-N	6	4	.600	26	16	4	1	2	117¹	103	3	44	54	11.4	2.99	113	.236	.308	4	.125	-1	5	5	-2	0.1
1947	*Bro-N	4	5	.444	37	16	2	1	1	104¹	115	6	55	59	15.0	5.87	70	.272	.361	9	.265	2	-21	-20	1	-1.4
1948	Pit-N	2	4	.333	22	8	1	0	1	74¹	72	3	34	25	13.2	4.60	88	.255	.342	6	.273	2	-5	-4	-0	-0.2
1949	Pit-N	1	1	.500	8	1	0	0	0	18²	24	1	9	14	16.4	3.38	125	.303	.387	0	.000	-0	1	2	-0	0.1
1950	Pit-N	0	1	.000	5	1	0	0	0	5¹	10	2	7	3	30.4	13.50	32	.400	.545	0	.000	-0	-6	-5	0	-0.8
1952	NY-N	0	1	.000	16	4	1	0	1	36¹	42	7	17	13	15.1	4.71	79	.286	.367	1	.125	-0	-4	-4	-1	-0.2
Total	9	40	48	.455	200	115	27	4	9	827	805	41	443	401	13.9	4.54	84	.253	.350	54	.205	4	-73	-74	-3	-7.5
● **VEAN GREGG**				Gregg, Sylveanus Augustus			b: 4/13/1885, Chehalis, Wash.			d: 7/29/64, Aberdeen, Wash.		BR/TL, 6'1", 185 lbs.			Deb: 4/12/11	F								
1911	Cle-A	23	7	.767	34	26	22	5	0	244²	172	2	86	125	9.9	1.80	189	.205	.286	14	.165	-4	42	44	0	4.7
1912	Cle-A	20	13	.606	37	34	26	1	2	271¹	242	4	90	184	11.5	2.59	132	.246	.316	17	.175	-3	22	25	-2	2.4
1913	Cle-A	20	13	.606	44	34	23	3	3	285²	258	2	124	166	12.4	2.24	136	.246	.334	13	.131	-4	22	25	-3	2.1
1914	Cle-A	9	3	.750	17	12	6	1	0	96²	88	0	48	56	12.9	3.07	94	.251	.347	6	.176	1	-4	-2	-0	-0.3
	Bos-A	3	4	.429	12	9	4	0	0	68¹	71	0	37	24	14.2	3.95	68	.283	.375	4	.211	-0	-9	-10	-1	-1.0
	Yr	12	7	.632	29	21	10	1	0	165	159	0	85	80	13.3	3.44	82	.263	.354	10	.189	1	-13	-12	-2	-1.3
1915	Bos-A	4	2	.667	18	9	3	1	0	75	71	2	32	43	13.0	3.36	83	.260	.348	7	.350	2	-4	-5	0	-0.2
1916	Bos-A	2	5	.286	21	7	3	0	0	77²	71	0	30	41	12.1	3.01	92	.259	.339	2	.111	-1	-2	-4	-1	-0.3
1918	Phi-A	9	14	.391	30	25	17	3	2	199¹	180	4	67	63	11.4	3.12	94	.251	.320	12	.169	-3	-7	-4	-1	-0.9
1925	Was-A	2	2	.500	26	5	1	0	0	74¹	87	3	38	18	15.4	4.12	103	.318	.404	3	.214	0	2	1	-1	0.0
Total	8	92	63	.594	239	161	105	14	12	1393	1240	17	552	720	11.9	2.70	117	.248	.328	78	.171	-12	63	73	-8	6.5
● **FRANK GREGORY**				Gregory, Frank Ernst			b: 7/25/1888, Spring Valley Township, Wis.			d: 11/5/55, Beloit, Wis.		BR/TR, 5'11", 185 lbs.			Deb: 9/5/12								
1912	Cin-N	2	0	1.000	4	2	1	0	0	15²	19	0	7	4	15.5	4.60	73	.297	.375	1	.200	0	-2	-2	-1	-0.3
● **LEE GREGORY**				Gregory, Grover Leroy			b: 6/2/38, Bakersfield, Cal.			BL/TL, 6'1", 180 lbs.			Deb: 4/17/64										
1964	Chi-N	0	0	—	11	0	0	0	0	18	23	3	5	8	14.0	3.50	106	.333	.378	1	.077	0	0	0	0	0.0
● **HOWIE GREGORY**				Gregory, Howard Watterson			b: 11/18/1886, Hannibal, Mo.			d: 5/30/70, Tulsa, Okla.		BL/TR, 6', 175 lbs.			Deb: 4/16/11									
1911	StL-A	0	1	.000	3	1	0	0	0	7	11	0	4	1	19.3	5.14	66	.393	.469	0	.000	-0	-1	-1	-0	-0.2
● **PAUL GREGORY**				Gregory, Paul Edwin "Pop"			b: 6/9/08, Tomnolen, Miss.			BR/TR, 6'2", 180 lbs.			Deb: 4/20/32										
1932	Chi-A	5	3	.625	33	9	3	0	0	117²	125	8	51	39	13.6	4.51	96	.273	.348	3	.079	-3	-0	-0	3	-0.1
1933	Chi-A	4	11	.267	23	17	5	0	0	103²	124	10	47	18	14.9	4.95	86	.296	.368	5	.143	-1	-8	-8	1	-1.0
Total	2	9	14	.391	56	26	8	0	0	221¹	249	18	98	57	14.2	4.72	91	.284	.358	8	.110	-4	-8	-11	4	-1.1
● **BILL GREIF**				Greif, William Briley			b: 4/25/50, Ft.Stockton, Tex.			BR/TR, 6'5", 205 lbs.			Deb: 7/19/71										
1971	Hou-N	1	1	.500	7	3	0	0	0	16	18	1	8	14	15.8	5.06	66	.290	.389	1	.333	-2	-3	-3	-0	-0.3
1972	SD-N	5	16	.238	34	22	2	1	2	125¹	143	18	47	91	14.2	5.60	59	.287	.357	1	.030	-3	-30	-32	-2	-5.3
1973	SD-N	10	17	.370	36	31	9	3	1	199²	181	20	62	120	11.2	3.21	108	.246	.309	6	.098	-2	10	6	-1	0.5
1974	SD-N	9	19	.321	43	35	7	1	1	226	244	16	95	137	14.1	4.66	76	.279	.359	4	.071	-0	-26	-28	-0	-3.2
1975	SD-N	4	6	.400	59	5	0	0	9	72	74	7	38	43	14.6	3.88	90	.269	.368	0	.000	-2	-2	-3	-2	-0.7
1976	SD-N	1	3	.250	5	5	0	0	0	22¹	27	4	11	6	15.3	8.06	41	.297	.373	0	.000	-1	-11	-12	0	-1.7
	StL-N	1	5	.167	47	0	0	0	6	54²	60	5	26	31	14.5	4.12	86	.290	.374	0	.000	-0	-4	-4	-1	-0.5
	Yr	2	8	.200	52	5	0	0	6	77	87	9	37	37	14.7	5.26	66	.291	.373	0	.000	-1	-15	-15	-0	-2.2
Total	6	31	67	.316	231	97	18	5	19	715²	747	70	287	442	13.5	4.41	78	.272	.349	12	.072	-7	-66	-76	-5	-11.2

YEAR TM/L	W	L	PCT	G	GS	CG	SH	SV	IP	H	HR	BB	SO	RAT	ERA	ERA+	OAV	OOB	BH	AVG	PB	PR	/A	PD	TPI
● **BILL GREVELL**			Grevell, William J.		b: 3/5/1898, Williamstown, N.J.				d: 6/21/23, Philadelphia, Pa.			BR/TR, 5'11", 170 lbs.			Deb: 5/14/19										
1919 Phi-A	0	0	—	5	2	0	0	0	12	15	0	18	3	25.5	14.25	24	.306	.500	0	.000	-1	-15	-14	1	0.0
● **GREYSON**			Greyson TL ,			Deb: 8/27/1873																				
1873 Was-n	1	6	.143	7	7	7	0	0	63	112	3	7	3	17.0	5.43	62	.357	.371	4	.143	-2	-15	-15		-1.1
● **LEE GRIFFETH**			Griffeth, Leon Clifford		b: 5/20/25, Carmel, N.Y.			BB/TL, 5'11.5", 180 lbs.		Deb: 6/25/46																
1946 Phi-n	0	0	—	10	0	0	0	0	15¹	13	1	6	4	12.3	2.93	121	.232	.328	0	.000	0	1	1	-0	0.0
● **HANK GRIFFIN**			Griffin, James Linton "Pepper"		b: 7/11/1886, Whitehouse, Tex.			d: 2/11/50, Terrell, Tex.		BR/TR, 6', 165 lbs.		Deb: 5/5/11													
1911 Chi-N	0	0	—	1	1	0	0	0	1	1	1	3	1	36.0	18.00	18	.250	.571		0	-2	-2	0	0.0
Bos-N	0	6	.000	15	6	1	0	0	82²	96	3	34	30	14.8	5.23	73	.305	.383	7	.233	-0	-17	-13	-0	-0.8
Yr	0	6	.000	16	7	1	0	0	83²	97	4	37	31	15.1	5.38	71	.304	.387	7	.233	-0	-18	-14	-0	-0.8
1912 Bos-N	0	0	—	3	0	0	0	0	1²	3	0	3	0	37.8	27.00	13	.750	.875	0	—	-0	-4	-4	-0	0.0
Total 2	0	6	.000	19	7	1	0	0	85¹	100	4	40	31	15.5	5.80	66	.310	.397	7	.233	-0	-23	-19	0	-0.8
● **MARTY GRIFFIN**			Griffin, Martin John		b: 9/2/01, San Francisco, Cal.			d: 11/19/51, Los Angeles, Cal.		BR/TR, 6'2", 200 lbs.		Deb: 7/25/28													
1928 Bos-A	0	3	.000	11	3	0	0	0	37²	42	0	17	9	14.1	5.02	82	.300	.376	4	.308	1	-4	-4	-0	-0.2
● **MIKE GRIFFIN**			Griffin, Michael Leroy		b: 6/26/57, Colusa, Cal.			BR/TR, 6'5", 197 lbs.		Deb: 9/17/79															
1979 NY-A	0	0	—	3	0	0	0	1	4¹	5	0	2	5	14.5	4.15	98	.313	.389	0	—	-0	-0	-0	0	0.2
1980 NY-A	2	4	.333	13	9	0	0	0	54	64	6	23	25	14.7	4.83	81	.287	.356	0	—	-0	-5	-5	-0	-0.4
1981 NY-A	0	0	—	2	0	0	0	0	4¹	5	0	0	4	10.4	2.08	172	.278	.278	0	—	0	1	1	0	0.1
Chi-N	2	5	.286	16	9	0	0	1	52	64	4	9	20	12.6	4.50	82	.300	.330	2	.154	-0	-6	-5	0	-0.6
1982 SD-N	0	1	.000	7	0	0	0	0	10¹	9	0	3	4	10.5	3.48	98	.237	.293	0	.000	-0	0	-0	-0	0.0
1987 Bal-A	3	5	.375	23	6	1	0	1	74¹	78	9	33	42	13.8	4.36	101	.269	.350	0	—	0	1	0	-1	0.2
1989 Cin-N	0	0	—	3	0	0	0	0	4¹	10	0	3	1	27.0	12.46	29	.500	.565	1	1.000	-0	-4	-4	0	0.1
Total 6	7	15	.318	67	24	1	0	3	203²	235	19	73	101	13.8	4.60	87	.288	.349	3	.200	-0	-13	-13	-0	-0.4
● **PAT GRIFFIN**			Griffin, Patrick Richard		b: 5/6/1893, Niles, Ohio			d: 6/7/27, Youngstown, Ohio		BR/TR, 6'2", 180 lbs.		Deb: 7/23/14													
1914 Cin-N	0	0	—	1	0	0	0	0	1	3	0	2	0	45.0	9.00	33	.750	.833	0	—	-0	-1	-1	0	0.0
● **TOM GRIFFIN**			Griffin, Thomas James		b: 2/22/48, Los Angeles, Cal.			BR/TR, 6'3", 210 lbs.		Deb: 4/10/69															
1969 Hou-N	11	10	.524	31	31	6	3	0	188¹	156	19	93	200	12.2	3.54	100	.220	.317	9	.145	2	1	0	-2	0.1
1970 Hou-N	3	13	.188	23	20	2	1	0	111¹	118	9	72	72	15.6	5.74	68	.275	.383	2	.061	-2	-21	-23	-1	-3.1
1971 Hou-N	0	6	.000	10	6	0	0	0	37²	44	4	20	29	15.8	4.78	70	.288	.377	1	.111	-0	-5	-6	1	-0.8
1972 Hou-N	5	4	.556	39	5	1	1	3	94¹	92	7	38	83	12.7	3.24	104	.258	.334	7	.280	3	2	1	-1	0.4
1973 Hou-N	2	3	.400	25	12	4	0	0	99²	83	10	46	69	11.8	4.15	87	.229	.320	3	.107	-0	-5	-6	-0	-0.5
1974 Hou-N	14	10	.583	34	34	8	3	0	211	202	14	89	110	12.6	3.54	98	.250	.328	20	.294	8	2	-2	1	0.7
1975 Hou-N	3	8	.273	17	13	3	0	0	79¹	89	11	46	56	15.5	5.33	63	.288	.384	3	.136	-0	-15	-17	1	-2.1
1976 Hou-N	5	3	.625	20	2	0	0	0	41²	44	4	37	33	17.7	6.05	53	.278	.418	0	.000	-0	-12	-13	-0	-2.3
SD-N	4	3	.571	11	11	2	0	0	70¹	56	0	42	36	12.7	2.94	111	.222	.336	2	.077	-2	4	3	-0	0.0
Yr	9	6	.600	31	13	2	0	0	112	100	4	79	69	14.5	4.10	79	.242	.364	2	.065	-2	-7	-11	-0	-2.3
1977 SD-N	6	9	.400	38	20	0	0	0	151¹	144	17	88	79	14.1	4.46	79	.254	.359	6	.133	1	-9	-16	-2	-1.4
1978 Cal-A	3	4	.429	24	4	0	0	0	56	63	8	31	35	15.3	4.02	90	.279	.368	0	—	-0	-2	-3	-1	-0.2
1979 SF-N	5	6	.455	59	3	0	0	2	94¹	83	9	46	82	12.7	3.91	89	.237	.333	1	.071	-1	-2	-4	-2	-0.4
1980 SF-N	5	1	.833	42	4	0	0	0	107²	80	8	49	79	11.5	2.76	128	.212	.315	2	.111	0	10	9	0	0.5
1981 SF-N	8	8	.500	22	22	3	1	0	129¹	121	8	57	83	12.9	3.76	91	.249	.336	8	.195	2	-4	-5	2	-0.2
1982 Pit-N	1	3	.250	6	4	0	0	0	22¹	32	5	15	8	19.3	8.87	42	.330	.425	2	.222	0	-13	-13	0	-1.8
Total 14	77	94	.450	401	191	29	10	5	1494²	1407	133	769	1054	13.4	4.07	86	.249	.345	66	.163	12	-69	-94	1	-11.1
● **CLARK GRIFFITH**			Griffith, Clark Calvin "The Old Fox"																							
			b: 11/20/1869, Clear Creek, Mo.		d: 10/27/55, Washington, D.C.			BR/TR, 5'6.5", 156 lbs.		Deb: 4/11/1891 MH♦															
1891 StL-a	11	8	.579	27	17	12	0	0	186¹	195	8	58	68	12.9	3.33	126	.260	.326	12	.156	-3	8	18	0	1.2
Bos-a	3	1	.750	7	4	3	0	0	40	47	3	15	20	15.1	5.62	62	.283	.360	4	.174	2	-8	-9	-1	-0.6
Yr	14	9	.609	34	21	15	0	0	226¹	242	11	73	88	12.7	3.74	109	.260	.317	16	.160	-1	-0	9	-1	0.6
1893 Chi-N	1	2	.333	4	2	2	0	0	19²	24	1	5	9	13.7	5.03	92	.293	.341	2	.182	-1	-1	-1	1	-0.1
1894 Chi-N	21	14	.600	36	30	28	0	0	261¹	328	12	85	71	14.7	4.92	114	.303	.362	33	.232	-0	12	20	1	1.9
1895 Chi-N	26	14	.650	42	41	39	0	0	353	434	11	91	79	13.9	3.93	130	.298	.348	46	.319	5	34	46	1	4.5
1896 Chi-N	23	11	.676	36	35	35	0	0	317²	370	3	70	81	12.8	3.54	128	.289	.331	36	.267	3	29	35	1	3.3
1897 Chi-N	21	18	.538	41	38	**38**	7	0	343²	410	3	86	102	13.4	3.72	120	.293	.342	38	.235	3	23	28	3	3.0
1898 Chi-N	24	10	.706	38	38	36	4	0	325²	305	1	64	97	10.8	**1.88**	**191**	.246	.294	20	.164	-2	63	62	1	5.8
1899 Chi-N	22	14	.611	38	38	35	0	0	319²	329	5	65	73	11.5	2.79	134	.266	.310	31	.258	6	38	34	6	4.5
1900 Chi-N	14	13	.519	30	30	27	**4**	0	248	245	6	51	61	11.3	3.05	118	.258	.306	24	.253	5	18	15	-1	1.8
1901 Chi-A	24	7	**.774**	35	30	26	**5**	1	266²	275	4	50	67	11.1	2.67	131	.263	.299	27	.303	14	30	24	0	3.7
1902 Chi-A	15	9	.625	28	24	20	3	0	213	247	11	47	51	13.1	4.18	81	.290	.339	20	.217	-1	-14	-19	-1	-1.7
1903 NY-A	14	11	.560	25	24	22	2	0	213	201	3	33	69	10.1	2.70	116	.249	.283	11	.159	2	6	10	-3	1.0
1904 NY-A	7	5	.583	16	11	8	1	0	100¹	91	3	16	36	10.0	2.87	94	.243	.281	6	.143	-1	-3	-2	-1	-0.4
1905 NY-A	9	6	.600	25	7	4	2	1	101²	82	1	15	46	8.7	1.68	174	.223	.255	7	.219	-1	11	14	-2	2.1
1906 NY-A	2	2	.500	17	2	1	0	2	59²	58	0	15	16	11.6	3.02	98	.258	.316	2	.111	-1	-0	1	0	0.0
1907 NY-A	0	0	—	4	0	0	0	0	8¹	15	0	6	2	22.7	8.64	32	.395	.477	0	.000	-0	-6	-5	0	-0.3
1909 Cin-N	0	1	.000	1	1	0	0	0	6	11	0	2	3	19.5	6.00	43	.379	.419	0	.000	-0	-2	-1	0	-0.3
1912 Was-A	0	0	—	1	0	0	0	0	0	1	1	0	0	—	∞	—	1.000	1.000	0	—	-0	-1	-1	0	-0.1
1913 Was-A	0	0	—	1	0	0	0	0	1	1	0	0	0	9.0	0.00	—	.250	.250	1	1.000	1	0	0	0	0.1
1914 Was-A	0	0	—	1	0	0	0	0	1	1	0	0	0	9.0	0.00	—	.250	.250	1	1.000	1	0	0	0	0.1
Total 20	237	146	.619	453	372	337	22	6	3385²	3670	76	774	955	12.3	3.31	121	.274	.322	321	.233	35	233	266	7	29.7
● **FRANK GRIFFITH**			Griffith, Frank Wesley		b: 11/18/1872, Gilman, Ill.			d: 12/13/08, BL/TL,		Deb: 8/13/1892															
1892 Chi-N	0	1	.000	1	1	0	0	0	4	3	1	6	3	20.3	11.25	30	.200	.429	0	.000	-0	-4	-4	-0	-0.6
1894 Cle-N	1	2	.333	7	6	3	0	0	42¹	64	5	37	15	23.4	9.99	55	.344	.474	8	.333	2	-22	-21	-0	-0.9
Total 2	1	3	.250	8	7	3	0	0	46¹	67	6	43	18	23.1	10.10	52	.333	.470	8	.320	2	-25	-25	-0	-1.5
● **HAL GRIGGS**			Griggs, Harold Lloyd		b: 8/24/28, Shannon, Ga.			BR/TR, 6', 170 lbs.		Deb: 4/18/56															
1956 Was-A	1	6	.143	34	12	1	0	1	98²	120	14	76	48	18.0	6.02	72	.307	.421	0	.000	-1	-20	-19	1	-1.2
1957 Was-A	0	1	.000	2	0	0	0	0	13²	11	1	7	12	11.9	3.29	118	.229	.327	1	.250	0	1	1	0	0.1
1958 Was-A	3	11	.214	32	21	3	0	0	137	138	20	74	69	14.1	5.52	69	.262	.355	5	.122	-2	-27	-26	-0	-2.6
1959 Was-A	2	8	.200	37	10	2	1	2	97²	103	8	52	43	14.4	5.25	75	.270	.359	1	.056	-2	-15	-15	-0	-1.6
Total 4	6	26	.188	105	45	6	1	3	347	372	43	209	172	15.2	5.50	73	.276	.375	7	.089	-5	-61	-58	1	-5.3
● **GUIDO GRILLI**			Grilli, Guido John		b: 1/9/39, Memphis, Tenn.			BL/TL, 6', 188 lbs.		Deb: 4/12/66															
1966 Bos-A	0	1	.000	6	0	0	0	0	4²	5	1	9	4	27.0	7.71	49	.278	.519	1	.500	0	-2	-2	-0	-0.4
KC-A	0	1	.000	16	0	0	0	0	15²	19	0	11	8	19.0	6.89	49	.302	.429	0	—	0	-6	-6	-1	-0.5
Yr	0	2	.000	22	0	0	0	0	20¹	24	1	20	12	20.8	7.08	49	.296	.452	1	.500	0	-8	-8	-1	-0.9
● **STEVE GRILLI**			Grilli, Stephen Joseph		b: 5/2/49, Brooklyn, N.Y.			BR/TR, 6'2", 170 lbs.		Deb: 9/19/75															
1975 Det-A	0	0	—	3	0	0	0	0	6²	5	1	5	5	12.2	1.35	297	.136	.321	0	—	0	2	2	0	-0.2
1976 Det-A	3	1	.750	36	0	0	0	3	66	63	5	41	36	14.9	4.64	80	.258	.376	0	—	0	-8	-7	2	-0.3
1977 Det-A	1	2	.333	30	2	0	0	0	72²	71	8	49	49	15.2	4.83	89	.265	.384	0	—	-0	-6	-4	-1	-0.3
1979 Tor-A	0	0	—	1	0	0	0	0	2	1	0	1	1	9.0	4.50	—	.143	.143	0	—	-0	-0	-0	0	-0.1
Total 4	4	3	.571	70	2	0	0	3	147²	138	13	96	91	14.7	4.51	89	.255	.375	0	—	-0	-12	-8	1	-0.9

YEAR TM/L	W	L	PCT	G	GS	CG	SH	SV	IP	H	HR	BB	SO	RAT	ERA	ERA+	OAV	OOB	BH	AVG	PB	PR	/A	PD	TPI

● JOHN GRIM   Grim, John Helm b: 8/9/1867, Lebanon, Ky.   d: 7/28/61, Indianapolis, Ind   BR/TR, 6'2", 175 lbs.   Deb: 9/29/1888 ♦

| 1890 Roc-a | 0 | 0 | — | 1 | 0 | 0 | 0 | 0 | 3¹ | 3 | 0 | 4 | 3 | 18.9 | 0.00 | — | .231 | .412 | 51 | .266 | 0 | 1 | 1 | -0 | 0.0 |

● BOB GRIM   Grim, Robert Anton b: 3/8/30, New York, N.Y.   d: 10/23/96, Shawnee, Kan.   BR/TR, 6'1", 185 lbs.   Deb: 4/18/54

1954 NY-A	20	6	.769	37	20	8	1	0	199	175	9	85	108	11.9	3.26	106	.244	.327	10	.143	-1	10	4	-1	0.2
1955 *NY-A	7	5	.583	26	11	1	1	4	92¹	81	9	42	63	12.3	4.19	89	.238	.326	3	.120	-1	-2	-5	0	-0.7
1956 NY-A	6	1	.857	26	6	1	0	5	74²	64	5	31	48	11.7	2.77	139	.235	.318	1	.063	-0	11	9	-1	0.8
1957 *NY-A★	12	8	.600	46	0	0	0	19	72	60	5	36	52	12.0	2.63	137	.239	.334	1	.111	1	9	8	0	2.6
1958 NY-A	0	1	.000	11	0	0	0	0	16¹	12	3	10	11	12.7	5.51	64	.211	.338	0	.000	-0	-3	-4	-0	-0.2
KC-A	7	6	.538	26	14	5	1	0	113²	118	7	41	54	12.8	3.56	110	.269	.336	6	.188	-0	3	4	-1	0.3
Yr	7	7	.500	37	14	5	1	0	130	130	10	51	65	12.7	3.81	101	.262	.335	6	.182	-1	-1	1	-1	0.1
1959 KC-A	6	10	.375	40	9	3	1	4	125¹	124	10	57	65	13.2	4.09	98	.260	.343	3	.094	-1	-3	-1	-2	-0.4
1960 Cle-A	0	1	.000	3	0	0	0	0	2¹	6	0	1	2	27.0	11.57	32	.500	.538	0	—	0	-2	-2	0	-0.7
Cin-N	2	2	.500	26	0	0	0	2	30¹	32	3	10	22	12.5	4.45	86	.274	.331	0	.000	-0	-2	-2	-0	-0.3
StL-N	1	0	1.000	15	0	0	0	0	20²	22	1	9	15	13.5	3.05	134	.272	.344	0	.000	-0	2	2	0	0.1
Yr	3	2	.600	41	0	0	0	2	51	54	4	19	37	12.9	3.88	101	.267	.330	0	.000	-0	-1	-0	-0	-0.2
1962 KC-A	0	1	.000	12	0	0	0	3	13	14	0	9	3	15.2	6.23	68	.292	.393	0	.000	-0	-3	-3	1	-0.3
Total 8	61	41	.598	268	60	18	4	37	759²	708	50	330	443	12.5	3.61	104	.252	.334	24	.127	-4	19	11	-4	1.4

● BURLEIGH GRIMES   Grimes, Burleigh Arland "Ol' Stubblebeard"   b: 8/18/1893, Emerald, Wis.   d: 12/6/85, Clear Lake, Wis.   BR/TR, 5'10", 175 lbs.   Deb: 9/10/16   MCH

1916 Pit-N	2	3	.400	6	5	4	0	0	45²	40	1	10	20	9.9	2.36	114	.241	.284	3	.176	-0	1	2	1	0.2
1917 Pit-N	3	16	.158	37	17	8	1	0	194	186	5	70	72	12.2	3.53	81	.260	.331	16	.232	1	-18	-15	1	-1.1
1918 Bro-N	19	9	.679	40	30	19	7	1	269²	210	3	76	113	9.7	2.14	130	.216	.276	18	.200	0	19	19	4	2.6
1919 Bro-N	10	11	.476	25	21	13	1	0	181¹	179	2	60	82	12.2	3.47	86	.256	.321	17	.246	1	-11	-10	1	-0.9
1920 *Bro-N	23	11	**.676**	40	33	25	5	2	303²	271	5	67	131	10.1	2.22	144	.238	.282	34	.306	10	31	33	3	5.4
1921 Bro-N	**22**	13	.629	37	35	**30**	2	0	302¹	313	6	76	**136**	11.7	2.83	138	.274	.322	27	.237	2	32	**36**	4	**4.5**
1922 Bro-N	17	14	.548	36	34	18	1	1	259	324	17	84	99	14.4	4.76	85	.308	.363	22	.237	4	-19	-20	4	-1.2
1923 Bro-N	21	18	.538	39	38	**33**	2	0	**327**	356	16	100	119	12.9	3.58	108	.280	.338	30	.238	3	15	11	5	2.0
1924 Bro-N	22	13	.629	38	34	**30**	1	1	**310²**	351	15	91	135	13.0	3.82	98	.287	.339	37	.298	6	1	-3	5	0.9
1925 Bro-N	12	19	.387	33	31	19	0	0	246²	305	15	102	73	15.1	5.04	83	.309	.377	24	.250	5	-21	-23	8	-1.2
1926 Bro-N	12	13	.480	30	29	18	1	0	225¹	238	4	88	64	13.2	3.71	103	.276	.346	18	.222	1	3	3	3	0.6
1927 NY-N	19	8	.704	39	34	15	2	2	259²	274	12	87	102	12.7	3.54	109	.276	.337	18	.188	-0	11	9	5	1.3
1928 Pit-N	**25**	14	.641	48	37	**28**	**4**	3	**330²**	311	11	77	97	10.8	2.99	136	.248	.297	42	.321	11	37	39	6	6.1
1929 Pit-N	17	7	.708	33	29	18	2	2	232²	245	11	70	62	12.3	3.13	**152**	.269	.324	26	.286	6	**41**	**42**	3	**4.7**
1930 Bos-N	3	5	.375	11	9	1	0	0	49	72	4	22	15	17.8	7.35	67	.353	.424	3	.188	-0	-13	-13	0	-1.6
*StL-N	13	6	.684	22	19	10	1	0	152¹	174	5	43	58	13.1	3.01	166	.293	.345	15	.263	2	33	34	1	4.0
Yr	16	11	.593	33	28	11	1	0	201¹	246	9	65	73	14.1	4.07	123	.307	.362	18	.247	2	20	21	2	2.4
1931 *StL-N	17	9	.654	29	28	17	3	0	212¹	240	11	59	67	13.1	3.65	108	.286	.340	14	.184	-2	5	7	3	0.8
1932 *Chi-N	6	11	.353	30	18	5	1	1	141¹	174	8	50	36	14.3	4.78	79	.297	.354	11	.250	1	-14	-16	1	-1.5
1933 Chi-N	3	6	.333	17	7	3	1	3	69²	71	2	29	12	13.0	3.49	94	.277	.353	3	.150	-1	-1	-2	1	-0.2
StL-N	0	1	.000	4	3	0	0	1	13²	15	1	8	4	15.8	5.27	66	.263	.364	1	.200	0	-3	-3	-1	-0.3
Yr	3	7	.300	21	10	3	1	4	83¹	86	3	37	16	13.4	3.78	87	.274	.352	4	.160	-0	-4	-4	-0	-0.5
1934 StL-N	2	1	.667	4	0	0	0	0	7²	5	1	2	1	8.2	3.52	120	.179	.233	0	—	0	1	1	0	0.2
Pit-N	1	2	.333	8	4	0	0	0	27¹	36	4	10	9	15.5	7.24	57	.310	.370	1	.143	-0	-10	-10	1	-0.9
Yr	3	3	.500	12	4	0	0	0	35	41	1	12	10	13.9	6.43	64	.285	.344	1	.143	-0	-9	-9	1	-0.7
NY-A	1	2	.333	10	0	0	0	1	18	22	0	14	5	18.5	5.50	74	.319	.440	0	.000	-0	-2	-3	1	-0.4
Total 19	270	212	.560	616	497	314	35	18	4179²	4412	148	1295	1512	12.5	3.53	107	.273	.331	380	.248	52	118	122	58	24.0

● JOHN GRIMES   Grimes, John Thomas b: 4/17/1869, Woodstock, Md.   d: 1/17/64, San Francisco, Cal   BR/TR, 5'11", 160 lbs.   Deb: 7/28/1897

| 1897 StL-N | 0 | 2 | .000 | 3 | 1 | 1 | 0 | 0 | 19² | 24 | 0 | 8 | 4 | 17.4 | 5.95 | 74 | .300 | .404 | 2 | .286 | 1 | -4 | -3 | 1 | -0.1 |

● JASON GRIMSLEY   Grimsley, Jason Alan b: 8/7/67, Cleveland, Tex.   BR/TR, 6'3", 180 lbs.   Deb: 9/8/89

1989 Phi-N	1	3	.250	4	4	0	0	0	18¹	19	2	19	7	18.7	5.89	60	.268	.422	0	.000	-1	-5	-5	0	-0.9
1990 Phi-N	3	2	.600	11	11	0	0	0	57¹	47	1	43	41	14.4	3.30	116	.227	.365	3	.188	0	3	3	1	0.4
1991 Phi-N	1	7	.125	12	12	0	0	0	61	54	4	41	42	14.5	4.87	75	.242	.367	1	.059	-1	-8	-8	1	-0.9
1993 Cle-A	3	4	.429	10	6	0	0	0	42¹	52	3	20	27	15.5	5.31	81	.302	.378	0	—	0	-5	-5	-0	-0.7
1994 Cle-A	5	2	.714	14	13	1	0	0	82²	91	7	34	59	14.3	4.57	103	.283	.362	0	—	0	2	1	-0	0.1
1995 Cle-A	0	0	—	15	2	0	0	0	34	37	4	32	25	18.8	6.09	77	.289	.438	0	—	0	-5	-5	1	0.0
1996 Cal-A	5	7	.417	35	20	2	1	0	130¹	150	14	74	82	16.4	6.84	72	.286	.388	0	—	0	-27	-28	2	-1.8
Total 7	18	25	.419	101	68	3	1	1	426	450	35	263	283	15.6	5.39	82	.273	.382	4	.105	-1	-44	-46	4	-3.8

● ROSS GRIMSLEY   Grimsley, Ross Albert I b: 6/4/22, Americus, Kan.   d: 2/6/94, Memphis, Tenn.   BL/TL, 6', 175 lbs.   Deb: 9/3/51   F

| 1951 Chi-A | 0 | 0 | — | 7 | 0 | 0 | 0 | 0 | 14 | 12 | 1 | 10 | 8 | 14.1 | 3.86 | 105 | .235 | .361 | 0 | .000 | -0 | 0 | 0 | -1 | -0.1 |

● ROSS GRIMSLEY   Grimsley, Ross Albert II b: 1/7/50, Topeka, Kan.   BL/TL, 6'3", 200 lbs.   Deb: 5/16/71   F

1971 Cin-N	10	7	.588	26	26	6	3	0	161¹	151	15	43	67	10.9	3.57	94	.250	.302	6	.118	-1	-2	-4	-1	-0.6
1972 *Cin-N	14	8	.636	30	28	4	1	1	197²	194	18	50	79	11.1	3.05	105	.260	.307	8	.121	-2	9	4	-0	0.1
1973 *Cin-N	13	10	.565	38	36	8	1	1	242¹	245	24	68	90	11.6	3.23	105	.266	.317	5	.061	-6	12	5	-2	-0.4
1974 *Bal-A	18	13	.581	40	39	17	4	1	295²	267	26	76	158	10.5	3.07	112	.244	.295	0	—	0	18	12	0	1.4
1975 Bal-A	10	13	.435	35	32	8	1	0	197	210	29	47	89	11.8	4.07	86	.276	.319	0	—	0	-6	-12	0	-1.1
1976 Bal-A	8	7	.533	28	19	2	0	0	136²	143	8	35	41	11.8	3.95	83	.270	.317	0	—	0	-7	-10	-1	-1.1
1977 Bal-A	14	10	.583	34	34	11	2	0	218¹	230	24	74	53	12.6	3.96	96	.277	.337	0	—	0	2	-4	0	-0.2
1978 Mon-N☆	20	11	.645	36	36	19	3	0	263	237	17	67	84	10.5	3.05	116	.243	.293	13	.144	-1	15	14	1	1.6
1979 Mon-N	10	9	.526	32	27	2	0	0	151¹	199	16	41	42	14.5	5.35	68	.322	.367	11	.200	1	-27	-28	-1	-3.1
1980 Mon-N	2	4	.333	11	7	0	0	0	41¹	61	5	12	11	16.1	6.31	56	.351	.396	2	.222	0	-12	-13	0	-1.6
Cle-A	4	5	.444	14	11	2	0	0	74²	103	11	24	18	15.4	6.75	60	.331	.381	0	—	0	-23	-22	-1	-2.3
1982 Bal-A	2	4	.333	21	0	0	0	0	60	65	7	22	18	13.1	5.25	77	.283	.345	0	—	0	-8	-8	0	-0.3
Total 11	124	99	.556	345	295	79	15	3	2039¹	2105	202	559	750	11.8	3.81	92	.270	.320	45	.127	-10	-29	-67	-1	-7.6

● DAN GRINER   Griner, Donald Dexter "Rusty" b: 3/7/1888, Centerville, Tenn.   d: 6/3/50, Bishopville, S.C.   BL/TR, 6'1.5", 200 lbs.   Deb: 8/17/12

1912 StL-N	3	4	.429	12	7	2	0	0	54	54	3	15	20	12.8	3.17	108	.278	.335	1	.077	-1	1	2	-1	0.0
1913 StL-N	10	22	.313	34	34	18	1	0	225	279	3	66	79	14.2	5.08	64	.312	.366	21	.259	5	-47	-46	2	-5.0
1914 StL-N	9	13	.409	37	16	11	2	2	179	163	3	57	74	11.2	2.51	111	.254	.318	14	.255	4	5	6	-1	1.0
1915 StL-N	5	11	.313	37	18	9	3	3	150¹	137	4	46	46	11.4	2.81	99	.259	.328	14	.269	4	-1	-0	-2	0.0
1916 StL-N	0	0	—	4	0	0	0	0	11	15	0	3	3	15.5	4.09	65	.341	.396	1	.250	0	-2	-1	0	0.0
1918 Bro-N	1	5	.167	11	6	3	1	0	54¹	47	5	15	22	11.4	2.15	129	.267	.348	1	.071	-1	4	4	0	0.4
Total 6	28	55	.337	135	81	43	7	6	673²	700	22	202	244	12.5	3.49	86	.280	.342	52	.237	12	-39	-37	-2	-3.4

● LEE GRISSOM   Grissom, Lee Theo b: 10/23/07, Sherman, Tex.   BB/TL, 6'3", 200 lbs.   Deb: 9/2/34   F

1934 Cin-N	0	1	.000	4	1	0	0	0	7	13	0	7	4	25.7	15.43	26	.382	.488	0	.000	-0	-9	-9	-0	-1.0
1935 Cin-N	1	1	.500	3	3	1	0	0	21	31	0	4	13	15.0	3.86	103	.333	.361	0	.000	-1	0	0	-0	0.0
1936 Cin-N	1	1	.500	6	4	0	0	0	24¹	33	1	9	13	15.5	6.29	61	.320	.375	0	.000	-1	-6	-7	0	-0.6
1937 Cin-N★	12	17	.414	50	30	14	**5**	6	223²	193	7	93	149	11.7	3.26	114	.232	.313	7	.109	-3	16	12	-2	0.9
1938 Cin-N	3	4	.400	14	7	0	0	0	51	60	4	22	16	14.8	5.29	69	.300	.375	3	.188	-0	-9	-9	-0	-0.9
1939 *Cin-N	9	7	.563	33	21	3	0	0	153²	145	14	56	53	11.8	4.10	93	.249	.316	4	.085	-2	-3	-5	-2	-0.8
1940 NY-A	0	0	—	5	0	0	0	0	4²	4	2	0	1	11.6	0.00	—	.250	.333	0	—	0	1	1	-0	0.2
Bro-N	2	5	.286	14	10	0	0	0	73²	59	3	34	56	11.4	2.81	142	.215	.302	5	.217	0	9	10	-1	0.8
1941 Bro-N	0	0	—	4	1	0	0	0	11¹	10	2	4	5	14.3	2.38	154	.238	.360	1	.500	-0	2	2	-0	0.1
Phi-N	2	13	.133	29	15	4	0	0	131¹	120	4	70	74	13.2	3.97	93	.242	.338	-1	.167	-1	-5	-4	-1	-0.5

YEAR	TM/L	W	L	PCT	G	GS	CG	SH	SV	IP	H	HR	BB	SO	RAT	ERA	ERA+	OAV	OOB	BH	AVG	PB	PR	/A	PD	TPI
	Yr	2	13	.133	33	19	2	0	1	142²	130	6	78	79	13.2	3.85	96	.242	.340	7	.184	-0	-3	-2	-1	-0.4
Total	8	29	48	.377	162	95	23	6	7	701²	668	35	305	384	12.6	3.89	97	.250	.329	26	.127	-8	-3	-8	-6	-2.0

● **MARV GRISSOM**   Grissom, Marvin Edward b: 3/31/18, Los Molinos, Cal.   BR/TR, 6'3", 195 lbs.   Deb: 9/10/46 FC

YEAR	TM/L	W	L	PCT	G	GS	CG	SH	SV	IP	H	HR	BB	SO	RAT	ERA	ERA+	OAV	OOB	BH	AVG	PB	PR	/A	PD	TPI
1946	NY-N	0	2	.000	4	3	0	0	0	18²	17	1	13	9	14.9	4.34	79	.254	.383	1	.200	-0	-2	-2	1	-0.1
1949	Det-A	2	4	.333	27	3	0	0	0	39¹	56	6	34	17	20.8	6.41	65	.335	.450	2	.222	1	-10	-10	0	-1.2
1952	Chi-A	12	10	.545	28	24	7	1	0	166	156	6	79	97	12.9	3.74	98	.250	.337	8	.151	-1	-1	-2	-2	-0.5
1953	Bos-A	2	6	.250	13	11	1	1	0	59¹	61	5	30	31	14.0	4.70	89	.266	.354	0	.000	-3	-5	-3	-1	-0.7
	NY-N	4	2	.667	21	7	3	0	0	84¹	83	6	31	46	12.3	3.95	109	.255	.321	2	.074	-2	3	3	-1	0.1
1954	*NY-N★	10	7	.588	56	3	1	1	19	122¹	100	13	50	64	11.6	2.35	171	.226	.314	5	.156	-1	23	23	-0	3.6
1955	NY-N	5	4	.556	55	0	0	0	8	89¹	76	6	41	49	12.4	2.92	138	.237	.334	2	.154	-1	11	11	0	1.2
1956	NY-N	1	1	.500	43	0	0	0	7	80²	71	3	16	49	9.8	1.56	242	.241	.282	1	.091	-0	20	20	-1	0.8
1957	NY-N	4	4	.500	55	0	0	0	14	82²	74	6	23	51	10.8	2.61	151	.243	.301	2	.167	-1	12	12	1	1.7
1958	SF-N	7	5	.583	51	0	0	0	10	65¹	71	11	26	46	14.1	3.99	95	.287	.367	0	.000	-1	-0	-1	0	-0.3
1959	StL-N	0	0	—	3	0	0	0	0	2	6	2	0	0	27.0	22.50	19	.500	.500	0	—	0	-4	-4	0	-0.1
Total	10	47	45	.511	356	52	12	3	58	810	771	65	343	459	12.7	3.41	115	.254	.335	23	.122	-7	47	47	-0	4.6

● **CONNIE GROB**   Grob, Conrad George b: 11/9/32, Cross Plains, Wis.   BL/TR, 6'0.5", 180 lbs.   Deb: 4/22/56

YEAR	TM/L	W	L	PCT	G	GS	CG	SH	SV	IP	H	HR	BB	SO	RAT	ERA	ERA+	OAV	OOB	BH	AVG	PB	PR	/A	PD	TPI
1956	Was-A	4	5	.444	37	1	0	0	1	79¹	121	14	26	27	16.8	7.83	55	.353	.400	6	.333	1	-32	-31	1	-2.8

● **JOHNNY GRODZICKI**   Grodzicki, John "Grod" b: 2/26/17, Nanticoke, Pa.   BR/TR, 6'1.5", 200 lbs.   Deb: 4/18/41 C

YEAR	TM/L	W	L	PCT	G	GS	CG	SH	SV	IP	H	HR	BB	SO	RAT	ERA	ERA+	OAV	OOB	BH	AVG	PB	PR	/A	PD	TPI
1941	StL-N	2	1	.667	5	1	0	0	0	13¹	6	0	11	10	11.5	1.35	279	.130	.298	0	.000	0	3	4	-0	0.8
1946	StL-N	0	0	—	3	0	0	0	0	4	4	1	4	2	18.0	9.00	38	.250	.400	0	—	0	-2	-2	0	-0.1
1947	StL-N	0	1	.000	16	0	0	0	0	23¹	21	5	19	8	15.4	5.40	77	.253	.392	0	.000	-0	-3	-3	0	-0.1
Total	3	2	2	.500	24	1	0	0	0	40²	31	6	34	20	14.4	4.43	89	.214	.363	0	.000	-0	-3	-2	0	0.7

● **STEVE GROMEK**   Gromek, Stephen Joseph b: 1/15/20, Hamtramck, Mich.   BB/TR, 6'2", 180 lbs.   Deb: 8/18/41

YEAR	TM/L	W	L	PCT	G	GS	CG	SH	SV	IP	H	HR	BB	SO	RAT	ERA	ERA+	OAV	OOB	BH	AVG	PB	PR	/A	PD	TPI
1941	Cle-A	1	1	.500	9	2	1	0	2	23¹	25	0	11	19	13.9	4.24	93	.266	.343	1	.167	-0	-0	-1	-1	-0.2
1942	Cle-A	2	0	1.000	14	0	0	0	2	44¹	46	2	23	14	14.0	3.65	94	.267	.354	5	.333	3	0	-1	-1	0.2
1943	Cle-A	0	0	—	3	0	0	0	0	4	6	0	4	4	13.5	9.00	35	.353	.353	2	1.000	1	-3	-3	-0	0.1
1944	Cle-A	10	9	.526	35	21	12	2	1	203²	160	5	70	115	10.3	2.56	129	**.219**	.290	19	.260	5	20	17	-3	1.8
1945	Cle-A†	19	9	.679	33	30	21	3	1	251	229	6	66	101	10.7	2.55	128	.243	.295	21	.231	3	23	20	-3	2.2
1946	Cle-A	5	15	.250	29	21	5	2	4	153²	159	20	47	75	12.2	4.33	76	.264	.321	11	.196	-0	-14	-18	-1	-2.2
1947	Cle-A	3	5	.375	29	7	0	0	4	84¹	77	8	36	39	12.2	3.74	93	.240	.318	7	.318	-0	-2	-0	0	-0.1
1948	*Cle-A	9	3	.750	38	9	4	1	2	130	109	10	51	50	11.5	2.84	143	.226	.307	6	.146	-1	21	18	-1	1.3
1949	Cle-A	4	0	1.000	27	12	3	0	0	92	86	8	40	22	12.5	3.33	120	.250	.332	4	.167	-0	9	7	0	0.7
1950	Cle-A	10	7	.588	31	13	4	0	0	113¹	94	10	36	43	10.6	3.65	119	.226	.292	6	.158	-2	12	9	-0	1.5
1951	Cle-A	7	4	.636	27	8	4	0	1	107¹	98	6	29	40	11.0	2.77	137	.238	.295	8	.296	3	16	12	1	1.5
1952	Cle-A	7	7	.500	29	13	3	1	1	122²	109	14	28	65	10.2	3.67	91	.232	.278	3	.100	-0	0	-4	-3	-0.8
1953	Cle-A	1	1	.500	5	1	0	0	0	11	11	0	3	8	12.3	3.27	115	.268	.333	0	.000	-0	1	1	0	0.0
	Det-A	6	8	.429	19	17	6	1	1	125²	138	17	36	59	13.0	4.51	90	.276	.335	3	.073	-4	-7	-6	-1	-1.1
	Yr	7	9	.438	24	18	6	1	1	136²	149	17	39	67	12.9	4.41	92	.275	.333	3	.070	-4	-6	-6	-1	-1.1
1954	Det-A	18	16	.529	36	32	17	4	1	252²	236	26	57	102	10.9	2.74	135	.246	.297	15	.190	2	28	27	-3	3.4
1955	Det-A	13	10	.565	28	25	8	0	1	181	183	24	37	73	11.4	3.98	97	.261	.307	9	.167	4	-0	-3	-2	-0.1
1956	Det-A	8	6	.571	43	13	4	0	4	141	142	25	47	64	12.6	4.28	96	.263	.332	4	.148	-2	-2	-3	-2	-0.4
1957	Det-A	0	1	.000	15	1	0	0	1	23²	32	3	13	11	17.5	6.08	63	.333	.418	0	.000	-0	-6	-6	-1	-0.4
Total	17	123	108	.532	447	225	92	17	23	2064²	1940	186	630	904	11.5	3.41	108	.247	.309	124	.197	15	96	63	-21	6.9

● **BOB GROOM**   Groom, Robert b: 9/12/1884, Belleville, Ill. d: 2/19/48, Belleville, Ill.   BR/TR, 6'2", 175 lbs.   Deb: 4/13/09

YEAR	TM/L	W	L	PCT	G	GS	CG	SH	SV	IP	H	HR	BB	SO	RAT	ERA	ERA+	OAV	OOB	BH	AVG	PB	PR	/A	PD	TPI
1909	Was-A	7	26	.212	44	31	17	1	0	260²	218	2	105	131	11.6	2.87	85	.229	.314	8	.091	-6	-11	-13	4	-1.8
1910	Was-A	12	17	.414	34	30	22	3	0	257²	244	8	77	98	11.5	2.76	90	.260	.322	11	.120	-6	-7	-8	-2	-1.6
1911	Was-A	13	17	.433	37	32	20	2	0	254²	280	3	67	135	12.5	3.82	86	.282	.332	11	.134	-4	-13	-15	1	-1.9
1912	Was-A	24	13	.649	43	40	28	2	1	316	287	3	94	179	11.0	2.62	127	.246	.305	12	.117	-7	24	25	-2	1.9
1913	Was-A	16	16	.500	37	36	17	4	0	264¹	258	8	81	156	11.7	3.23	91	.254	.312	15	.163	1	-9	-8	2	-0.7
1914	StL-F	13	20	.394	42	34	23	1	1	280²	281	9	75	167	11.5	3.24	94	.262	.312	16	.160	-4	-11	-6	-1	-1.1
1915	StL-F	11	11	.500	37	26	11	4	2	209	200	6	73	111	11.8	3.27	88	.261	.327	10	.153	-3	-13	-9	0	-1.2
1916	StL-A	13	9	.591	41	26	8	1	4	217¹	174	1	98	92	11.4	2.57	107	.226	.315	7	.111	-2	6	4	2	0.4
1917	StL-A	8	19	.296	38	28	11	4	3	232²	193	3	95	82	11.3	2.94	88	.233	.315	8	.111	-4	-7	-9	-1	-1.6
1918	Cle-A	2	2	.500	14	5	0	0	0	43¹	70	0	18	8	18.5	7.06	43	.380	.438	1	.083	-1	-21	-20	1	-1.8
Total	10	119	150	.442	367	288	157	22	13	2336¹	2205	49	783	1159	11.7	3.10	93	.254	.319	98	.128	-35	-61	-58	2	-9.4

● **BUDDY GROOM**   Groom, Wedsel Gary b: 7/10/65, Dallas, Tex.   BL/TL, 6'2", 200 lbs.   Deb: 6/20/92

YEAR	TM/L	W	L	PCT	G	GS	CG	SH	SV	IP	H	HR	BB	SO	RAT	ERA	ERA+	OAV	OOB	BH	AVG	PB	PR	/A	PD	TPI
1992	Det-A	0	5	.000	12	7	0	0	1	38²	48	4	22	15	16.3	5.82	68	.320	.407	0	—	0	-8	-9	-1	-1.0
1993	Det-A	0	2	.000	19	3	0	0	0	36²	48	4	13	15	15.5	6.14	70	.322	.384	0	—	0	-7	-8	0	-0.3
1994	Det-A	0	1	.000	40	0	0	0	1	32	31	4	13	27	12.9	3.94	123	.256	.338	0	—	0	3	3	-1	0.0
1995	Det-A	1	3	.250	23	4	0	0	1	40²	55	6	26	23	18.4	7.52	63	.322	.417	0	—	0	-13	-13	-1	-1.1
	Fla-N	1	2	.333	14	0	0	0	0	15	26	2	6	12	19.2	7.20	59	.400	.451	0	—	0	-5	-5	0	-0.8
1996	Oak-A	5	0	1.000	72	1	0	0	2	77¹	85	8	34	57	14.2	3.84	125	.281	.360	0	—	0	10	8	-1	0.7
Total	5	7	13	.350	180	15	0	0	5	240¹	293	28	114	149	15.6	5.36	85	.306	.385	0	—	0	-20	-21	-3	-2.5

● **DON GROSS**   Gross, Donald John b: 6/30/31, Weidman, Mich.   BL/TL, 5'11", 186 lbs.   Deb: 7/21/55

YEAR	TM/L	W	L	PCT	G	GS	CG	SH	SV	IP	H	HR	BB	SO	RAT	ERA	ERA+	OAV	OOB	BH	AVG	PB	PR	/A	PD	TPI
1955	Cin-N	4	5	.444	17	11	2	1	0	67¹	79	11	16	33	12.8	4.14	102	.298	.340	3	.158	-1	-1	1	0	0.0
1956	Cin-N	3	0	1.000	19	7	2	0	0	69¹	69	4	20	47	11.7	1.95	204	.257	.310	2	.105	-1	14	16	1	0.7
1957	Cin-N	7	9	.438	43	16	5	0	1	148¹	152	21	33	73	11.4	4.31	95	.264	.307	5	.109	-2	-7	-3	-0	-0.6
1958	Pit-N	5	7	.417	40	2	0	0	7	74²	75	5	38	59	12.8	3.98	97	.241	.334	1	.056	-1	-0	-1	1	0.2
1959	Pit-N	1	1	.500	21	0	0	0	2	33	28	3	10	15	10.6	3.55	109	.238	.291	0	.000	0	1	1	0	0.2
1960	Pit-N	0	0	—	5	0	0	0	0	5¹	5	1	0	3	8.4	3.38	111	.238	.238	0	—	0	1	0	0	0.0
Total	6	20	22	.476	145	37	9	1	10	398	400	45	117	230	11.8	3.73	108	.261	.316	11	.106	-5	8	14	2	0.1

● **GREG GROSS**   Gross, Gregory Eugene b: 8/1/52, York, Pa.   BL/TL, 5'11", 175 lbs.   Deb: 9/5/73 ◆

YEAR	TM/L	W	L	PCT	G	GS	CG	SH	SV	IP	H	HR	BB	SO	RAT	ERA	ERA+	OAV	OOB	BH	AVG	PB	PR	/A	PD	TPI
1986	Phi-N	0	0	—	1	0	0	0	0	0²	1	0	1	2	27.0	0.00	—	.333	.500	25	.248	0	0	0	0	0.0
1989	Hou-N	0	0	—	1	0	0	0	0	1	3	0	1	1	36.0	18.00	19	.500	.571	15	.200	0	-2	-2	0	0.0
Total	2	0	0	—	2	0	0	0	0	1²	4	0	2	3	32.4	10.80	33	.444	.545	1073	.287	0	-1	-1	0	0.0

● **KEVIN GROSS**   Gross, Kevin Frank b: 6/8/61, Downey, Cal.   BR/TR, 6'5", 215 lbs.   Deb: 6/25/83

YEAR	TM/L	W	L	PCT	G	GS	CG	SH	SV	IP	H	HR	BB	SO	RAT	ERA	ERA+	OAV	OOB	BH	AVG	PB	PR	/A	PD	TPI
1983	Phi-N	4	6	.400	17	17	1	0	0	96	100	13	35	66	12.9	3.56	100	.265	.333	3	.091	-1	1	0	0	-0.1
1984	Phi-N	8	5	.615	44	14	1	0	1	129	140	8	44	84	13.2	4.12	88	.277	.341	2	.067	-2	-8	-7	1	-0.7
1985	Phi-N	15	13	.536	38	31	6	2	0	205²	194	11	81	151	12.3	3.41	108	.251	.328	9	.138	0	4	6	1	0.2
1986	Phi-N	12	12	.500	37	36	7	2	0	241²	240	28	94	154	12.7	4.02	96	.259	.333	18	.188	3	-8	-5	1	-0.2
1987	Phi-N	9	16	.360	34	33	3	1	0	200²	205	26	87	110	13.5	4.35	97	.267	.350	12	.190	-2	-6	-2	-2	-0.3
1988	Phi-N★	12	14	.462	33	33	5	1	0	231²	209	18	89	162	12.0	3.69	96	.239	.317	13	.173	1	-6	-0	-0	-0.5
1989	Mon-N	11	12	.478	31	31	4	0	0	201¹	188	20	88	158	12.6	4.38	81	.247	.330	9	.141	1	-20	-19	-0	-2.0
1990	Mon-N	9	12	.429	31	26	2	1	0	163¹	171	9	65	111	13.2	4.57	80	.272	.344	10	.200	4	-14	-17	-2	-1.8
1991	LA-N	10	11	.476	46	10	0	0	3	115²	123	10	50	95	13.6	3.58	100	.275	.351	7	.280	2	1	0	0	0.3
1992	LA-N	8	13	.381	34	30	4	1	0	204²	182	11	77	158	11.5	3.17	109	.241	.313	6	.095	-1	8	6	-1	0.4
1993	LA-N	13	13	.500	33	32	3	0	0	202¹	224	15	74	150	13.5	4.14	92	.281	.346	13	.203	5	-7	-9	-1	-0.1
1994	LA-N	9	7	.563	25	23	2	1	0	157¹	162	11	43	124	11.8	3.60	109	.263	.314	7	.149	1	11	6	2	0.9
1995	Tex-A	9	15	.375	31	30	4	0	0	183²	200	27	89	106	14.6	5.54	87	.279	.365	0	—	0	-17	-15	-1	-1.7
1996	Tex-A	11	8	.579	28	19	0	0	0	129¹	151	19	50	78	14.3	5.22	102	.293	.360	0	—	0	-3	1	0	-0.3
Total	14	140	157	.471	462	365	42	14	5	2462¹	2489	226	966	1707	12.9	4.09	95	.263	.336	106	.161	14	-60	-56	0	-5.0

YEAR TM/L	W	L	PCT	G	GS	CG	SH	SV	IP	H	HR	BB	SO	RAT	ERA	ERA+	OAV	OOB	BH	AVG	PB	PR	/A	PD	TPI

● **KIP GROSS** Gross, Kip Lee b: 8/24/64, Scottsbluff, Neb. BR/TR, 6'2", 195 lbs. Deb: 4/21/90

1990 Cin-N	0	0	—	5	0	0	0	0	6¹	6	0	2	3	11.4	4.26	93	.273	.333	0	—	0	-0	-0	-0	0.0
1991 Cin-N	6	4	.600	29	9	0	0	0	85²	93	8	40	40	14.0	3.47	110	.279	.357	2	.091	-1	2	3	0	0.2
1992 LA-N	1	1	.500	16	1	0	0	0	23²	32	1	10	14	16.0	4.18	82	.323	.385	2	1.000	1	-2	-2	1	0.0
1993 LA-N	0	0	—	10	0	0	0	0	15	13	0	4	12	10.2	0.60	636	.236	.288	0	—	0	6	5	-0	0.0
Total 4	7	5	.583	60	10	0	0	0	130²	144	9	56	69	13.8	3.31	113	.283	.354	4	.167	-0	6	6	0	0.2

● **WAYNE GROSS** Gross, Wayne Dale b: 1/14/52, Riverside, Cal. BL/TR, 6'2", 210 lbs. Deb: 8/21/76 ◆

| 1983 Oak-A | 0 | 0 | — | 1 | 0 | 0 | 0 | 0 | 2¹ | 2 | 0 | 1 | 0 | 15.4 | 0.00 | — | .222 | .364 | 79 | .233 | 1 | 1 | 1 | -0 | 0.0 |

● **HARLEY GROSSMAN** Grossman, Harley Joseph b: 5/5/30, Evansville, Ind. BR/TR, 6', 170 lbs. Deb: 4/22/52

| 1952 Was-A | 0 | 0 | — | 1 | 0 | 0 | 0 | 0 | 2 | 1 | 0 | 1 | 0 | 54.0 | 54.00 | 7 | .667 | .667 | 0 | — | 0 | -2 | -2 | 0 | 0.0 |

● **ERNIE GROTH** Groth, Ernest John "Dango" b: 12/24/1884, Cedarburg, Wis. d: 5/23/50, Milwaukee, Wis. BR/TR, 5'11", 175 lbs. Deb: 9/6/04

| 1904 Chi-N | 0 | 2 | .000 | 3 | 2 | 2 | 0 | 1 | 16 | 22 | 1 | 6 | 9 | 16.3 | 5.63 | 47 | .310 | .372 | 0 | .000 | -1 | -5 | -5 | -0 | -0.7 |

● **ERNEST GROTH** Groth, Ernest William b: 5/3/22, Beaver Falls, Pa. BR/TR, 5'9", 185 lbs. Deb: 9/11/47

1947 Cle-A	0	0	—	2	0	0	0	0	1¹	0	0	1	1	6.8	0.00	—	.000	.250	0	—	0	1	1	-0	0.0
1948 Cle-A	0	0	—	1	0	0	0	0	1	1	0	2	0	27.0	9.00	45	.250	.500	0	—	0	-1	-1	-0	0.0
1949 Chi-A	0	1	.000	3	0	0	0	0	5	2	2	3	1	10.8	5.40	77	.125	.300	0	—	0	-1	-1	-0	-0.1
Total 3	0	1	.000	6	0	0	0	0	7¹	3	2	6	2	12.3	4.91	82	.130	.333	0	—	0	-1	-1	-0	-0.1

● **MATT GROTT** Grott, Matthew Allen b: 12/5/67, LaPorte, Ind. BL/TL, 6'1", 210 lbs. Deb: 5/4/95

| 1995 Cin-N | 0 | 0 | — | 2 | 0 | 0 | 0 | 0 | 1² | 6 | 1 | 0 | 2 | 32.4 | 21.60 | 19 | .545 | .545 | 0 | — | 0 | -3 | -3 | 0 | 0.0 |

● **ORVAL GROVE** Grove, Orval Leroy b: 8/29/19, Mineral, Kan. d: 4/20/92, Carmichael, Cal. BR/TR, 6'3", 196 lbs. Deb: 5/28/40

1940 Chi-A	0	0	—	3	0	0	0	0	6	4	0	4	1	12.0	3.00	147	.182	.308	0	.000	-0	1	1	-0	0.0
1941 Chi-A	0	0	—	2	0	0	0	0	7	9	2	5	5	18.0	10.29	40	.321	.424	0	.000	-0	-5	-5	-0	0.0
1942 Chi-A	4	6	.400	12	8	4	0	0	66¹	77	1	33	21	15.1	5.16	70	.283	.363	5	.227	1	-11	-11	1	-1.3
1943 Chi-A	15	9	.625	32	25	18	3	2	216¹	192	9	72	76	11.1	2.75	122	.239	.304	12	.182	2	13	14	1	1.9
1944 Chi-A☆	14	15	.483	34	33	11	2	0	234²	237	11	71	105	12.1	3.72	92	.263	.322	8	.104	-3	-8	-8	4	-0.8
1945 Chi-A	14	12	.538	33	30	16	4	1	217	233	12	68	54	12.7	3.44	96	.273	.330	7	.099	-4	-2	-3	2	-0.6
1946 Chi-A	8	13	.381	33	26	10	1	0	205	213	10	78	60	12.9	3.02	113	.272	.340	7	.108	-2	11	9	2	0.8
1947 Chi-A	6	8	.429	25	19	6	1	0	135²	158	10	70	33	15.4	4.44	82	.296	.382	7	.146	-1	-11	-12	-1	-1.2
1948 Chi-A	2	10	.167	32	11	1	0	1	87²	110	6	42	18	15.9	6.16	69	.315	.393	2	.095	-2	-18	-19	2	-2.2
1949 Chi-A	0	0	—	1	0	0	0	0	0²	4	1	1	1	81.0	54.00	14	.667	.750	0	—	-0	-4	-4	0	0.0
Total 10	63	73	.463	207	152	66	11	4	1176²	1237	62	444	374	13.1	3.78	93	.272	.340	48	.129	-9	-33	-37	10	-3.4

● **LEFTY GROVE** Grove, Robert Moses b: 3/6/1900, Lonaconing, Md. d: 5/22/75, Norwalk, Ohio BL/TL, 6'3", 190 lbs. Deb: 4/14/25 H

1925 Phi-A	10	12	.455	45	18	5	0	1	197	207	11	131	**116**	15.7	4.75	98	.278	.390	8	.123	-6	-8	-2	2	-0.6
1926 Phi-A	13	13	.500	45	33	20	1	6	258	227	6	101	**194**	11.7	2.51	166	.244	.322	8	.099	-5	**43**	**48**	-1	4.0
1927 Phi-A	20	13	.606	51	28	14	1	9	262¹	251	6	79	**174**	11.4	3.19	134	.252	.309	10	.125	-3	28	31	-1	3.3
1928 Phi-A	**24**	8	.750	39	31	24	4	4	261²	228	10	64	**183**	10.1	2.58	156	.229	.277	15	.170	1	**43**	**42**	-3	**4.6**
1929 *Phi-A	20	6	**.769**	42	37	19	2	4	275¹	278	8	81	**170**	11.8	2.81	151	.262	.316	22	.216	1	**44**	**43**	-3	3.5
1930 *Phi-A	**28**	5	**.848**	50	32	22	2	**9**	291	273	8	60	**209**	10.5	2.54	184	.247	.288	22	.200	0	**68**	**69**	0	**7.3**
1931 *Phi-A	**31**	4	**.886**	41	30	**27**	**4**	5	288²	249	10	62	**175**	**9.7**	2.06	218	.229	**.271**	23	.200	-2	**74**	**78**	-2	**8.7**
1932 Phi-A	25	10	.714	44	30	**27**	**4**	7	291²	269	13	79	188	10.8	2.84	159	.241	**.292**	18	.168	0	**53**	**55**	-2	**5.9**
1933 Phi-A★	**24**	8	**.750**	45	28	**21**	2	6	275¹	280	12	83	114	12.0	3.20	134	.261	.316	9	.086	-7	33	33	0	2.9
1934 Bos-A	8	8	.500	22	12	5	0	0	109¹	149	5	32	43	15.0	6.50	74	.320	.365	6	.162	-0	-24	-21	-1	-2.5
1935 Bos-A☆	20	12	.625	35	30	23	2	1	273	269	6	65	121	**11.1**	2.70	176	.257	.302	7	.079	-5	**53**	**62**	2	6.4
1936 Bos-A★	17	12	.586	35	30	22	**6**	2	253¹	237	14	65	130	**10.9**	2.81	189	.246	**.297**	11	.138	-3	**63**	**71**	0	**7.0**
1937 Bos-A☆	17	9	.654	32	32	21	3	0	262	269	9	83	153	12.1	3.02	157	.261	.317	13	.143	-3	46	50	-1	4.0
1938 Bos-A★	14	4	.778	24	21	12	1	1	163²	169	8	52	99	12.2	**3.08**	160	.263	.319	8	.148	-1	31	34	-0	3.1
1939 Bos-A☆	15	4	**.789**	23	23	17	2	0	191	180	8	58	81	11.3	2.54	186	.249	.305	9	.134	-1	44	46	-3	3.7
1940 Bos-A	7	6	.538	22	21	9	1	0	153¹	159	20	50	62	12.3	3.99	113	.269	.328	8	.151	-1	7	9	0	0.5
1941 Bos-A	7	7	.500	21	21	10	0	0	134	155	8	42	54	13.4	4.37	95	.287	.340	5	.111	-1	-3	-3	-2	-0.6
Total 17	300	141	.680	616	457	298	35	55	3940²	3849	162	1187	2266	11.6	3.06	148	.255	.311	202	.148	-37	595	643	-15	61.2

● **CHARLIE GROVER** Grover, Charles Bert "Bugs" (Born Charles Byrd Grover) b: 6/20/1890, Huntington Township, Ohio d: 5/24/71, Emmett, Mich. BL/TR, 6'1.5", 185 lbs. Deb: 9/9/13

| 1913 Det-A | 0 | 0 | — | 2 | 1 | 0 | 0 | 0 | 10² | 9 | 0 | 7 | 2 | 13.5 | 3.38 | 86 | .265 | .390 | 0 | .000 | -1 | -1 | -1 | -0 | 0.0 |

● **TOM GRUBBS** Grubbs, Thomas Dillard "Judge" b: 2/22/1894, Mt.Sterling, Ky. d: 1/28/86, Lexington, Ky. BR/TR, 6'2", 165 lbs. Deb: 10/3/20

| 1920 NY-N | 0 | 1 | .000 | 1 | 1 | 0 | 0 | 0 | 5 | 9 | 0 | 5 | 0 | 16.2 | 7.20 | 42 | .409 | .409 | 0 | — | -0 | -2 | -2 | -0 | -0.4 |

● **HENRY GRUBER** Gruber, Henry John b: 12/14/1863, Hamden, Conn. d: 9/26/32, New Haven, Conn. BR/TR, 5'9", 155 lbs. Deb: 7/28/1887

1887 Det-N	4	3	.571	7	7	7	0	0	62¹	63	3	21	12	12.1	2.74	148	.262	.322	4	.167	1	9	9	-1	0.7
1888 Det-N	11	14	.440	27	25	25	3	0	240	196	8	41	71	9.0	2.29	121	.213	.249	13	.141	-1	15	13	1	1.1
1889 Cle-N	7	16	.304	25	23	23	0	1	205	198	6	94	74	13.2	3.64	111	.246	.331	7	.101	-1	8	9	-0	0.7
1890 Cle-P	22	23	.489	48	44	39	1	0	383¹	464	15	204	110	16.0	4.27	93	.286	.371	36	.221	6	-2	-13	1	-0.5
1891 Cle-N	17	22	.436	44	40	35	1	0	348²	407	10	119	79	13.8	4.13	84	.281	.338	23	.163	1	-30	-26	2	-2.0
Total 5	61	78	.439	151	139	129	5	1	1239¹	1328	42	479	346	13.4	3.67	99	.264	.332	83	.170	5	1	-7	3	0.0

● **KEN GRUNDT** Grundt, Kenneth Allan b: 8/26/69, Melrose Park, Ill. BL/TL, 6'4", 195 lbs. Deb: 8/8/96

| 1996 Bos-A | 0 | 0 | — | 4 | 0 | 0 | 0 | 0 | 3 | 4 | 1 | 1 | 2 | 15.0 | 0.00 | — | .308 | .357 | 0 | — | 0 | 1 | 1 | -0 | 0.0 |

| 1996 Bos-A | 0 | 0 | — | 4 | 0 | 0 | 0 | 0 | 3 | 4 | 0 | 1 | 2 | 27.0 | 27.00 | 19 | .500 | .500 | 0 | — | 0 | -1 | -1 | -0 | -0.2 |

● **AL GRUNWALD** Grunwald, Alfred Henry "Stretch" b: 2/13/30, Los Angeles, Cal. BL/TL, 6'4", 210 lbs. Deb: 4/18/55

1955 Pit-N	0	0	—	3	0	0	0	0	7²	7	1	7	2	16.4	4.70	88	.241	.389	2	.500	1	-1	-0	-0	0.1
1959 KC-A	0	1	.000	6	1	0	0	1	11¹	18	1	11	9	23.0	7.94	50	.360	.475	0	.000	-1	-5	-5	-0	-0.5
Total 2	0	1	.000	9	1	0	0	1	19	25	2	18	11	20.4	6.63	61	.316	.443	2	.250	0	-6	-5	-0	-0.4

● **JOE GRZENDA** Grzenda, Joseph Charles b: 6/8/37, Scranton, Pa. BR/TL, 6'2", 180 lbs. Deb: 4/26/61

1961 Det-A	1	0	1.000	4	0	0	0	0	5²	9	2	2	2	17.5	7.94	52	.375	.423	1	1.000	-0	-2	-2	-0	-0.3
1964 KC-A	0	2	.000	20	0	0	0	0	25	34	2	13	17	17.3	5.40	71	.324	.403	0	.000	-0	-5	-4	1	-0.2
1966 KC-A	0	2	.000	21	0	0	0	0	22	28	1	12	14	16.4	3.27	104	.337	.421	0	.000	-0	0	0	-1	0.1
1967 NY-N	0	0	—	11	0	0	0	0	16²	14	0	8	9	12.4	2.16	157	.237	.338	0	.000	-0	2	2	-1	-0.1
1969 *Min-A	4	1	.800	38	0	0	0	3	48²	52	4	17	24	12.9	3.88	94	.281	.345	0	.000	-0	-1	-1	0	0.0
1970 Was-A	3	6	.333	49	5	0	0	2	84²	86	8	34	38	13.1	5.00	71	.267	.343	0	.000	-1	-12	-14	0	-1.6
1971 Was-A	5	2	.714	46	0	0	0	5	70¹	54	2	17	56	9.2	1.92	172	.217	.270	1	.143	-0	12	11	0	1.2
1972 StL-N	1	0	1.000	30	0	0	0	0	35	46	1	17	15	17.0	5.66	60	.326	.410	0	.000	-0	-9	-9	-0	-0.2
Total 8	14	13	.519	219	3	0	0	14	308	323	20	120	173	13.2	4.00	88	.277	.349	2	.067	-2	-15	-17	3	-1.1

● **CECILIO GUANTE** Guante, Cecilio (Magallane) b: 2/1/60, Villa Mella, D.R. BR/TR, 6'3", 205 lbs. Deb: 5/1/82

1982 Pit-N	0	0	—	10	0	0	0	0	27	28	1	5	26	11.7	3.33	111	.264	.310	0	.000	-1	1	1	-0	-0.1
1983 Pit-N	2	6	.250	49	0	0	0	9	100¹	90	5	46	82	12.4	3.32	112	.241	.327	2	.091	-1	3	4	-1	0.2
1984 Pit-N	2	3	.400	27	0	0	0	0	41¹	32	3	16	30	10.9	2.61	138	.224	.311	0	.000	-0	4	5	-1	0.5
1985 Pit-N	4	6	.400	63	0	0	0	0	109	84	5	40	92	10.7	2.72	131	.214	.295	1	.059	-1	10	10	-1	0.8
1986 Pit-N	5	2	.714	52	0	0	0	0	78	65	11	29	63	11.2	3.35	115	.225	.302	0	.000	-0	3	4	-2	0.2
1987 NY-A	2	3	.600	23	0	0	0	0	44	42	8	20	46	12.9	5.73	77	.247	.330	0	—	-0	-6	-7	-1	-0.7
1988 NY-A	5	6	.455	56	0	0	0	11	79¹	66	9	24	61	10.3	2.88	137	.225	.283	0	—	0	9	9	-2	1.3
Tex-A	0	0	—	7	0	0	0	1	4²	8	1	4	4	23.1	1.93	212	.400	.500	0	—	0	1	1	-0	-0.1
Yr	5	6	.455	63	0	0	0	12	79²	67	11	26	65	10.5	2.82	140	.221	.283	0	—	0	10	10	-2	1.2

YEAR	TM/L	W	L	PCT	G	GS	CG	SH	SV	IP	H	HR	BB	SO	RAT	ERA	ERA+	OAV	OOB	BH	AVG	PB	PR	/A	PD	TPI
1989	Tex-A	6	6	.500	50	0	0	0	2	69	66	7	36	69	13.8	3.91	101	.249	.348	0	—	0	-0	0	-1	-0.1
1990	Cle-A	2	3	.400	26	1	0	0	0	46²	38	10	18	30	11.4	5.01	78	.220	.304	0	—	0	-6	-6	-0	-0.5
Total	9	29	34	.460	363	1	0	0	35	595	512	61	236	503	11.7	3.48	110	.232	.313	3	.061	-3	20	23	-8	1.5

● EDDIE GUARDADO　Guardado, Edward Adrain　b: 10/2/70, Stockton, Cal.　BR/TL, 6', 190 lbs.　Deb: 6/13/93

YEAR	TM/L	W	L	PCT	G	GS	CG	SH	SV	IP	H	HR	BB	SO	RAT	ERA	ERA+	OAV	OOB	BH	AVG	PB	PR	/A	PD	TPI
1993	Min-A	3	8	.273	19	16	0	0	0	94²	123	13	36	46	15.2	6.18	70	.319	.379	0	—	0	-20	-19	-1	-1.9
1994	Min-A	0	2	.000	4	4	0	0	0	17	26	3	4	8	15.9	8.47	57	.351	.385	0	—	0	-7	-7	-1	-0.7
1995	Min-A	4	9	.308	51	5	0	0	2	91¹	99	13	45	71	14.2	5.12	93	.280	.361	0	—	0	-4	-4	-1	-0.6
1996	Min-A	6	5	.545	83	0	0	0	4	73²	61	12	33	74	11.9	5.25	98	.228	.320	0	—	0	-2	-1	-0	-0.3
Total	4	13	24	.351	157	25	0	0	6	276²	309	41	118	199	14.0	5.73	83	.286	.359	0	—	0	-33	-31	-3	-3.5

● MARK GUBICZA　Gubicza, Mark Steven　b: 8/14/62, Philadelphia, Pa.　BR/TR, 6'6", 215 lbs.　Deb: 4/6/84

YEAR	TM/L	W	L	PCT	G	GS	CG	SH	SV	IP	H	HR	BB	SO	RAT	ERA	ERA+	OAV	OOB	BH	AVG	PB	PR	/A	PD	TPI
1984	KC-A	10	14	.417	29	29	4	2	0	189	172	13	75	111	12.0	4.05	99	.243	.320	0	—	0	-1	-0	2	0.1
1985	*KC-A	14	10	.583	29	28	0	0	0	177¹	160	14	77	99	12.3	4.06	102	.238	.321	0	—	0	2	2	2	0.4
1986	KC-A	12	6	.667	35	24	3	2	0	180²	155	8	84	118	12.2	3.64	117	.233	.324	0	—	0	11	12	3	1.3
1987	KC-A	13	18	.419	35	35	10	2	0	241²	231	18	120	166	13.3	3.98	114	.259	.350	0	—	0	13	15	4	2.0
1988	KC-A★	20	8	.714	35	35	8	4	0	269²	237	11	83	183	10.9	2.70	147	.234	.296	0	—	0	38	38	3	4.2
1989	KC-A★	15	11	.577	36	36	8	1	0	255	252	10	63	173	11.3	3.04	127	.259	.307	0	—	0	24	23	2	2.5
1990	KC-A	4	7	.364	16	16	2	0	0	94	101	5	38	71	13.7	4.50	85	.283	.358	0	—	0	-6	-7	-0	-0.6
1991	KC-A	9	12	.429	26	26	0	0	0	133	168	10	42	89	14.6	5.68	72	.308	.364	0	—	0	-23	-23	2	-2.9
1992	KC-A	7	6	.538	18	18	2	1	0	111¹	110	8	36	81	11.9	3.72	109	.259	.319	0	—	0	3	4	0	0.3
1993	KC-A	5	8	.385	49	6	0	0	2	104¹	128	4	43	80	14.9	4.66	98	.307	.374	0	—	0	-4	-1	-1	-0.2
1994	KC-A	7	9	.438	22	22	0	0	0	130	158	11	26	59	12.7	4.50	111	.301	.334	0	—	0	4	7	1	0.6
1995	KC-A	12	14	.462	33	33	3	2	0	213¹	222	21	62	81	12.2	3.75	127	.272	.328	0	—	0	23	24	2	2.8
1996	KC-A	4	12	.250	19	19	2	1	0	119¹	132	22	34	55	13.0	5.13	95	.284	.343	0	—	0	-2	-3	-0	-0.1
Total	13	132	135	.494	382	327	42	16	2	2218²	2226	153	783	1366	12.4	3.91	109	.263	.329	0	—	0	80	92	21	10.4

● MARV GUDAT　Gudat, Marvin John　b: 8/27/05, Goliad, Tex.　d: 3/1/54, Los Angeles, Cal.　BL/TL, 5'11", 162 lbs.　Deb: 5/21/29 ♦

YEAR	TM/L	W	L	PCT	G	GS	CG	SH	SV	IP	H	HR	BB	SO	RAT	ERA	ERA+	OAV	OOB	BH	AVG	PB	PR	/A	PD	TPI
1929	Cin-N	1	1	.500	7	2	2	0	0	26²	29	0	4	0	11.1	3.38	135	.282	.308	2	.200	-0	4	4	-1	0.1
1932	*Chi-N	0	0	—	1	0	0	0	0	1	1	0	2	0	9.0	0.00	—	.250	.250	24	.255	0	0	0	0	0.0
Total	2	1	1	.500	8	2	2	0	0	27²	30	0	6	0	11.1	3.25	139	.280	.306	26	.250	-0	4	4	-1	0.1

● WHITEY GUESE　Guese, Theodore　b: 1/24/1872, New Bremen, Ohio　d: 4/8/51, Wapakoneta, Ohio　BR/TR, 6'0.5", 200 lbs.　Deb: 7/13/01

YEAR	TM/L	W	L	PCT	G	GS	CG	SH	SV	IP	H	HR	BB	SO	RAT	ERA	ERA+	OAV	OOB	BH	AVG	PB	PR	/A	PD	TPI
1901	Cin-N	1	4	.200	6	5	4	0	0	44¹	62	5	14	11	16.0	6.09	53	.328	.383	3	.200	1	-14	-14	-2	-1.3

● LEE GUETTERMAN　Guetterman, Arthur Lee　b: 11/22/58, Chattanooga, Tenn.　BL/TL, 6'8", 225 lbs.　Deb: 9/12/84

YEAR	TM/L	W	L	PCT	G	GS	CG	SH	SV	IP	H	HR	BB	SO	RAT	ERA	ERA+	OAV	OOB	BH	AVG	PB	PR	/A	PD	TPI
1984	Sea-A	0	0	—	3	0	0	0	0	4¹	9	0	2	1	22.8	4.15	96	.450	.500	0	—	0	-0	-0	0	0.0
1986	Sea-A	0	4	.000	41	4	1	0	0	76	108	7	30	38	16.8	7.34	58	.347	.412	0	—	0	-27	-26	0	-1.2
1987	Sea-A	11	4	.733	25	17	2	1	0	113¹	117	13	35	42	12.2	3.81	124	.267	.324	0	—	0	8	11	1	1.2
1988	NY-A	1	2	.333	20	2	0	0	0	40²	49	2	14	15	14.2	4.65	85	.306	.366	0	—	0	-3	-3	-0	-0.2
1989	NY-A	5	5	.500	70	0	0	0	13	103	98	6	26	51	10.8	2.45	158	.250	.305	0	—	0	16	16	2	2.1
1990	NY-A	11	7	.611	64	0	0	0	2	93	80	6	26	48	10.3	3.39	117	.236	.290	0	—	0	5	6	1	1.2
1991	NY-A	3	4	.429	64	0	0	0	6	88	91	6	25	35	12.2	3.68	112	.268	.323	0	—	0	4	4	0	0.4
1992	NY-A	1	1	.500	15	0	0	0	2	22²	35	5	13	5	19.1	9.53	44	.354	.429	0	—	0	-14	-14	0	-1.0
	NY-N	3	4	.429	43	0	0	0	2	43¹	57	5	14	15	15.0	5.82	60	.324	.377	0	.000	-0	-11	-11	-1	-1.9
1993	StL-N	3	3	.500	40	0	0	0	1	46	41	1	16	19	11.5	2.93	135	.240	.312	1	.500	1	6	5	-1	0.6
1995	Sea-A	0	0	—	23	0	0	0	1	17	21	1	11	11	18.5	6.88	69	.300	.417	0	—	0	-4	-4	1	0.0
1996	Sea-A	0	2	.000	17	0	0	0	0	11	11	0	10	6	17.2	4.09	120	.275	.420	0	—	0	1	1	0	0.2
Total	11	38	36	.514	425	23	3	1	25	658¹	717	52	222	287	13.1	4.33	95	.282	.343	1	.250	0	-19	-15	4	1.4

● RON GUIDRY　Guidry, Ronald Ames　b: 8/28/50, Lafayette, La.　BL/TL, 5'11", 162 lbs.　Deb: 7/27/75

YEAR	TM/L	W	L	PCT	G	GS	CG	SH	SV	IP	H	HR	BB	SO	RAT	ERA	ERA+	OAV	OOB	BH	AVG	PB	PR	/A	PD	TPI
1975	NY-A	0	1	.000	10	1	0	0	0	15²	15	0	9	15	14.4	3.45	107	.259	.368	0	—	0	1	0	-1	0.0
1976	*NY-A	0	0	—	7	0	0	0	0	16	20	1	4	12	13.5	5.63	61	.294	.333	0	—	0	-4	-4	0	-0.1
1977	*NY-A	16	7	.696	31	25	9	5	1	210²	174	12	65	176	10.2	2.82	140	.224	.284	0	—	0	29	26	-1	2.6
1978	*NY-A★	25	3	.893	35	35	16	9	0	273²	187	13	72	248	8.6	1.74	208	.193	.250	0	—	0	61	57	2	6.2
1979	NY-A★	18	8	.692	33	30	15	2	2	236¹	203	20	71	201	10.4	2.78	146	.236	.294	0	—	0	38	34	-0	3.5
1980	*NY-A	17	10	.630	37	29	5	3	1	219²	215	19	80	166	12.1	3.56	110	.260	.326	0	—	0	11	9	2	1.3
1981	*NY-A	11	5	.688	23	21	0	0	0	127	100	12	26	104	9.0	2.76	129	.214	.257	0	—	0	13	11	1	1.5
1982	NY-A☆	14	8	.636	34	33	6	1	0	222	216	22	69	162	11.6	3.81	105	.254	.311	0	—	0	6	3	0	0.2
1983	NY-A†	21	9	.700	31	31	21	3	0	250¹	232	26	60	156	10.6	3.42	114	.244	.291	0	—	0	18	13	0	1.4
1984	NY-A	10	11	.476	29	28	5	1	0	195²	223	24	44	127	12.4	4.51	84	.287	.327	0	—	0	-11	-16	-0	-1.5
1985	NY-A	22	6	.786	34	33	11	2	0	259	243	28	42	143	9.9	3.27	122	.248	.279	0	—	0	25	21	-1	2.2
1986	NY-A	9	12	.429	30	30	5	0	0	192¹	202	18	38	140	11.3	3.98	103	.265	.301	0	—	0	4	2	-1	0.1
1987	NY-A	5	8	.385	22	17	2	0	0	117²	111	14	38	96	11.5	3.67	119	.250	.308	0	—	0	10	9	-0	0.9
1988	NY-A	2	3	.400	12	10	0	0	0	56	57	7	15	32	11.9	4.18	94	.259	.312	0	—	0	-1	-1	-1	-0.1
Total	14	170	91	.651	368	323	95	26	4	2392	2198	226	633	1778	10.7	3.29	119	.244	.294	0	—	0	201	167	-3	18.2

● SKIP GUINN　Guinn, Drannon Eugene　b: 10/25/44, St.Charles, Mo.　BR/TL, 5'10", 180 lbs.　Deb: 5/7/68

YEAR	TM/L	W	L	PCT	G	GS	CG	SH	SV	IP	H	HR	BB	SO	RAT	ERA	ERA+	OAV	OOB	BH	AVG	PB	PR	/A	PD	TPI
1968	Atl-N	0	0	—	3	0	0	0	0	5	3	0	3	4	10.8	3.60	83	.167	.286	0	—	0	-0	-0	-0	0.0
1969	Hou-N	1	2	.333	28	0	0	0	0	27	34	3	21	33	18.7	6.67	53	.304	.418	0	.000	0	-9	-9	-0	-1.0
1971	Hou-N	0	0	—	4	0	0	0	1	4²	1	0	3	3	7.7	0.00	—	.067	.222	0	—	0	2	2	0	0.1
Total	3	1	2	.333	35	0	0	0	1	36²	38	3	27	40	16.2	5.40	64	.262	.382	0	.000	-0	-8	-8	-0	-0.9

● LEFTY GUISE　Guise, Witt Orison　b: 9/18/09, Driggs, Ark.　d: 8/13/68, Little Rock, Ark.　BL/TL, 6'2", 172 lbs.　Deb: 9/13/40

YEAR	TM/L	W	L	PCT	G	GS	CG	SH	SV	IP	H	HR	BB	SO	RAT	ERA	ERA+	OAV	OOB	BH	AVG	PB	PR	/A	PD	TPI
1940	Cin-N	0	0	—	2	0	0	0	0	7²	8	0	5	1	16.4	1.17	323	.296	.424	1	.333	0	2	2	0	0.0

● DON GULLETT　Gullett, Donald Edward　b: 1/6/51, Lynn, Ky.　BR/TL, 6', 190 lbs.　Deb: 4/10/70　C

YEAR	TM/L	W	L	PCT	G	GS	CG	SH	SV	IP	H	HR	BB	SO	RAT	ERA	ERA+	OAV	OOB	BH	AVG	PB	PR	/A	PD	TPI
1970	*Cin-N	5	2	.714	44	2	0	0	6	77²	54	4	76	11.4	2.43	166	.196	.306	4	.211	1	14	14	-1	1.4
1971	*Cin-N	16	6	.727	35	31	4	3	0	217²	196	14	64	107	10.8	2.65	127	.242	.299	9	.120	-2	20	17	-2	1.2
1972	*Cin-N	9	10	.474	31	16	2	0	2	134²	127	15	43	96	11.4	3.94	81	.250	.309	8	.211	2	-7	-11	-2	-1.5
1973	*Cin-N	18	8	.692	45	30	7	4	2	228¹	198	24	69	153	10.6	3.51	97	.232	.292	12	.188	3	-4	-3	-0	0.4
1974	Cin-N	17	11	.607	36	35	10	3	0	243	201	22	88	183	10.8	3.04	115	.222	.292	19	.237	4	16	12	-0	1.7
1975	*Cin-N	15	4	.789	22	22	8	3	0	159²	127	11	56	98	10.4	2.42	148	.218	.289	14	.226	3	21	21	-1	2.6
1976	*Cin-N	11	3	.786	23	20	4	0	1	126	119	8	48	64	11.9	3.00	117	.253	.322	8	.182	-0	7	6	-0	0.5
1977	*NY-A	14	4	.778	22	22	7	1	0	158¹	137	14	69	116	11.8	3.58	110	.232	.314	0	—	0	8	6	-2	0.5
1978	NY-A	4	2	.667	8	8	1	0	0	44²	46	7	20	28	13.5	3.63	100	.269	.349	0	—	0	-1	-0	-0	0.0
Total	9	109	50	.686	266	186	44	14	11	1390	1205	115	501	921	11.1	3.11	113	.233	.302	74	.194	10	83	63	-8	6.7

● BILL GULLICKSON　Gullickson, William Lee　b: 2/20/59, Marshall, Minn.　BR/TR, 6'3", 215 lbs.　Deb: 9/26/79

YEAR	TM/L	W	L	PCT	G	GS	CG	SH	SV	IP	H	HR	BB	SO	RAT	ERA	ERA+	OAV	OOB	BH	AVG	PB	PR	/A	PD	TPI
1979	Mon-N	0	0	—	1	0	0	0	0	1	2	0	0	1	18.0	0.00	—	.500	.500	0	—	0	0	0	0	0.0
1980	Mon-N	10	5	.667	24	19	5	2	0	141	127	6	50	120	11.4	3.00	119	.238	.305	7	.175	0	9	9	0	1.0
1981	*Mon-N	7	9	.438	22	22	3	2	0	157¹	142	13	34	115	10.3	2.80	125	.239	.284	7	.152	0	12	12	-1	1.1
1982	Mon-N	12	14	.462	34	34	6	0	0	236²	231	25	61	155	11.3	3.57	102	.254	.304	10	.122	-2	1	2	-4	-0.4
1983	Mon-N	17	12	.586	34	34	10	1	0	242¹	230	19	59	120	10.9	3.75	96	.251	.299	11	.134	1	-3	-4	-1	-0.5
1984	Mon-N	12	9	.571	32	32	2	1	0	226²	230	27	37	100	10.6	3.61	95	.264	.295	8	.110	-2	-1	-5	-4	-1.1
1985	Mon-N	14	12	.538	29	29	4	1	0	181¹	187	8	47	68	11.7	3.52	96	.271	.318	12	.188	2	-1	-1	-2	-0.8
1986	Cin-N	15	12	.556	37	37	6	0	0	244²	245	24	60	121	11.3	3.38	114	.264	.310	6	.076	-4	9	13	-2	0.7
1987	Cin-N	10	11	.476	27	27	3	1	0	165	172	33	39	89	11.6	4.85	87	.267	.313	11	.208	-1	-14	-11	-2	-1.2
	NY-A	4	2	.667	8	8	1	0	0	48	46	7	11	28	11.0	4.88	90	.253	.299	0	—	0	-2	-3	-0	-0.4
1990	Hou-N	10	14	.417	32	32	2	1	0	193¹	221	20	61	73	13.2	3.82	97	.287	.341	9	.158	0	-1	-2	-3	-0.4
1991	Det-A	20	9	.690	35	35	4	0	0	226¹	256	22	44	91	12.1	3.90	107	.288	.324	0	—	0	5	6	-3	0.5
1992	Det-A	14	13	.519	34	34	4	0	0	221²	228	35	50	64	11.3	4.34	91	.267	.308	0	—	0	-10	-10	-0	-1.1

YEAR TM/L	W	L	PCT	G	GS	CG	SH	SV	IP	H	HR	BB	SO	RAT	ERA	ERA+	OAV	OOB	BH	AVG	PB	PR	/A	PD	TPI
1993 Det-A	13	9	.591	28	28	2	0	0	159¹	186	28	44	70	13.2	5.37	80	.291	.340	0	—	0	-19	-19	0	-2.1
1994 Det-A	4	5	.444	21	19	1	0	0	115¹	156	24	25	65	14.4	5.93	82	.322	.361	0	—	0	-14	-14	1	-0.9
Total 14	162	136	.544	398	390	54	11	0	2560	2659	282	622	1279	11.7	3.93	97	.268	.314	81	.141	-1	-26	-29	-20	-4.9

● AD GUMBERT
Gumbert, Addison Courtney b: 10/10/1868, Pittsburgh, Pa. d: 4/23/25, Pittsburgh, Pa. BR/TR, 5'10", 200 lbs. Deb: 9/15/1888 F

YEAR TM/L	W	L	PCT	G	GS	CG	SH	SV	IP	H	HR	BB	SO	RAT	ERA	ERA+	OAV	OOB	BH	AVG	PB	PR	/A	PD	TPI
1888 Chi-N	3	3	.500	6	6	5	0	0	48²	44	0	10	16	10.9	3.14	96	.234	.291	8	.333	2	-2	-1	-1	0.0
1889 Chi-N	16	13	.552	31	28	25	2	0	246¹	258	16	76	91	12.7	3.62	115	.261	.323	44	.288	11	11	15	-1	2.2
1890 Bos-P	23	12	.657	39	33	27	1	0	277¹	338	18	86	81	14.1	3.96	111	.288	.342	35	.241	5	8	14	2	1.7
1891 Chi-N	17	11	.607	32	31	24	1	0	256¹	282	5	90	73	13.4	3.58	93	.269	.332	32	.305	12	-7	-7	1	0.6
1892 Chi-N	22	19	.537	46	45	39	0	0	382²	399	11	107	118	12.2	3.41	97	.258	.312	42	.236	4	-5	-4	1	0.1
1893 Pit-N	11	7	.611	22	20	16	2	0	162²	207	5	78	40	16.0	5.15	88	.301	.376	21	.221	1	-9	-11	-2	-0.9
1894 Pit-N	15	14	.517	37	31	26	0	0	269	372	13	84	65	15.5	6.02	87	.324	.373	33	.292	5	-21	-23	1	-1.3
1895 Bro-N	11	16	.407	33	26	20	1	0	234	288	11	69	45	14.2	5.08	87	.298	.352	35	.361	11	-8	-18	-1	-0.7
1896 Bro-N	0	4	.000	5	4	2	0	0	31	34	2	11	3	13.1	3.77	109	.276	.336	2	.182	-0	2	1	1	0.2
Phi-N	5	3	.625	11	10	7	1	0	77¹	99	0	23	14	14.7	4.54	95	.308	.362	9	.265	1	-2	-2	-1	-0.1
Yr	5	7	.417	16	14	9	1	0	108¹	133	2	34	17	14.2	4.32	97	.300	.355	11	.244	1	1	-1	0	0.1
Total 9	123	102	.547	262	234	191	7	0	1985¹	2321	81	634	546	13.8	4.27	97	.283	.341	261	.273	52	-31	-33	1	1.8

● HARRY GUMBERT
Gumbert, Harry Edward "Gunboat" b: 11/5/09, Elizabeth, Pa. d: 1/4/95, Wimberley, Tex. BR/TR, 6'2", 185 lbs. Deb: 9/12/35

YEAR TM/L	W	L	PCT	G	GS	CG	SH	SV	IP	H	HR	BB	SO	RAT	ERA	ERA+	OAV	OOB	BH	AVG	PB	PR	/A	PD	TPI
1935 NY-N	1	2	.333	6	3	1	0	0	23²	35	1	10	11	17.1	6.08	63	.330	.388	0	.000	-1	-5	-6	-0	-0.7
1936 *NY-N	11	3	.786	39	15	3	0	0	140²	157	7	54	52	13.6	3.90	100	.281	.346	11	.250	2	2	-0	3	0.5
1937 *NY-N	10	11	.476	34	24	10	1	1	200¹	194	11	62	65	11.7	3.68	106	.257	.317	13	.181	-1	5	5	8	1.1
1938 NY-N	15	13	.536	38	33	14	1	0	235²	238	13	84	84	12.6	4.01	94	.261	.328	13	.155	-3	-6	-6	8	-0.2
1939 NY-N	18	11	.621	36	34	14	2	0	243²	257	21	81	81	12.5	4.32	91	.271	.329	18	.200	-0	-11	-11	6	-0.5
1940 NY-N	12	14	.462	35	30	14	2	2	237	230	17	81	77	11.9	3.76	103	.252	.316	17	.195	2	2	3	4	0.9
1941 NY-N	1	1	.500	5	5	1	0	0	32¹	34	3	18	9	14.5	4.45	83	.266	.356	2	.167	-0	-3	-3	1	-0.1
StL-N	11	5	.688	33	17	8	3	1	144¹	139	7	30	53	10.6	2.74	137	.251	.291	17	.321	6	14	16	4	2.7
Yr	12	6	.667	38	22	9	3	1	176²	173	10	48	62	11.3	3.06	123	.254	.304	19	.292	5	11	14	4	2.6
1942 *StL-N	9	5	.643	38	19	5	0	5	163	156	3	59	52	11.9	3.26	105	.250	.315	6	.111	-2	1	3	5	0.5
1943 StL-N	10	5	.667	21	19	7	3	0	133	115	4	32	40	9.9	2.84	118	.237	.284	7	.156	-2	8	8	2	0.8
1944 StL-N	4	2	.667	10	7	3	0	1	61¹	60	1	19	16	11.6	2.49	141	.258	.313	4	.190	-0	8	7	1	0.8
Cin-N	10	8	.556	24	19	11	2	2	155¹	157	7	40	40	11.5	3.30	106	.262	.310	5	.096	-2	5	3	2	0.4
Yr	14	10	.583	34	26	14	2	3	216²	217	8	59	56	11.5	3.07	114	.261	.311	9	.123	-2	13	10	3	1.2
1946 Cin-N	6	8	.429	36	10	5	0	4	119	112	8	42	44	11.7	3.25	103	.248	.314	5	.250	1	2	1	1	0.4
1947 Cin-N	10	10	.500	46	0	0	0	10	90¹	88	3	47	43	13.5	3.89	106	.260	.351	6	.273	1	2	2	0	0.6
1948 Cin-N	10	8	.556	**61**	0	0	0	17	106¹	123	5	34	25	13.3	3.47	113	.291	.344	1	.040	-1	6	5	4	1.2
1949 Cin-N	4	3	.571	29	0	0	0	2	40²	58	5	8	12	14.8	5.53	76	.341	.374	0	.000	-0	-7	-6	1	-0.9
Pit-N	1	4	.200	16	0	0	0	3	27²	30	5	18	5	15.6	5.86	72	.270	.372	1	.250	-0	-6	-5	1	-0.8
Yr	5	7	.417	45	0	0	0	5	68¹	88	10	26	17	15.0	5.66	74	.312	.370	1	.167	-0	-12	-11	2	-1.7
1950 Pit-N	0	0	—	1	0	0	0	0	1²	3	0	2	0	27.0	5.40	81	.333	.455	1	1.000	-0	0	0	0	0.1
Total 15	143	113	.559	508	235	96	14	48	2156	2186	121	721	709	12.2	3.68	102	.263	.323	130	.184	-2	18	17	50	6.8

● BILLY GUMBERT
Gumbert, William Skeen b: 8/8/1865, Pittsburgh, Pa. d: 4/13/46, Pittsburgh, Pa. BR/TR, 6'1.5", 200 lbs. Deb: 6/19/1890 F

YEAR TM/L	W	L	PCT	G	GS	CG	SH	SV	IP	H	HR	BB	SO	RAT	ERA	ERA+	OAV	OOB	BH	AVG	PB	PR	/A	PD	TPI
1890 Pit-N	4	6	.400	10	10	8	0	0	79¹	96	0	31	18	15.3	5.22	63	.290	.365	9	.243	3	-15	-17	1	-1.3
1892 Pit-N	3	2	.600	6	3	2	0	0	39²	30	0	23	3	12.3	1.36	242	.201	.312	2	.111	-1	8	9	-1	0.8
1893 Lou-N	0	0	—	1	1	0	0	0	0²	2	0	5	0	94.5	27.00	16	.500	.778	1	1.000	-1	-2	-2	-0	0.1
Total 3	7	8	.467	17	14	10	0	0	119²	128	0	59	21	14.7	4.06	81	.264	.355	12	.214	3	-8	-10	-1	-0.4

● DAVE GUMPERT
Gumpert, David Lawrence b: 5/5/58, South Haven, Mich. BR/TR, 6'1", 190 lbs. Deb: 7/25/82

YEAR TM/L	W	L	PCT	G	GS	CG	SH	SV	IP	H	HR	BB	SO	RAT	ERA	ERA+	OAV	OOB	BH	AVG	PB	PR	/A	PD	TPI
1982 Det-A	0	0	—	5	1	0	0	1	2	7	1	2	0	40.5	27.00	15	.700	.750	0	—	0	-5	-5	-0	-0.5
1983 Det-A	0	2	.000	26	0	0	0	2	44¹	41	4	7	14	10.2	2.64	148	.257	.287	0	—	0	7	6	-1	0.2
1985 Chi-N	1	0	1.000	9	0	0	0	0	10¹	12	0	7	4	16.5	3.48	115	.279	.380	0	.000	-0	0	1	-0	0.0
1986 Chi-N	2	0	1.000	38	0	0	0	2	59²	60	4	28	45	13.4	4.37	92	.267	.350	0	.000	-1	-4	-2	-1	-0.2
1987 KC-A	0	0	—	8	0	0	0	0	19¹	27	3	6	13	15.4	6.05	75	.333	.379	0	—	0	-3	-3	0	-0.1
Total 5	3	2	.600	86	1	0	0	5	135²	149	9	50	76	13.3	4.31	95	.283	.347	0	.000	-1	-6	-4	-2	-0.6

● RANDY GUMPERT
Gumpert, Randall Pennington b: 1/23/18, Monocacy, Pa. BR/TR, 6'3", 205 lbs. Deb: 6/13/36

YEAR TM/L	W	L	PCT	G	GS	CG	SH	SV	IP	H	HR	BB	SO	RAT	ERA	ERA+	OAV	OOB	BH	AVG	PB	PR	/A	PD	TPI
1936 Phi-A	1	2	.333	22	3	2	0	2	62¹	74	2	32	9	15.3	4.76	107	.295	.375	6	.273	0	2	**2**	-1	0.1
1937 Phi-A	0	0	—	10	1	0	0	0	12	16	1	9	5	24.0	12.00	39	.333	.500	1	.333	0	-10	-10	0	0.0
1938 Phi-A	0	2	.000	4	2	0	0	0	12¹	24	1	10	1	24.8	10.95	44	.393	.479	1	.250	0	-8	-8	1	-0.9
1946 NY-A	11	3	.786	33	12	4	0	1	132²	113	8	32	63	9.8	2.31	150	.229	.276	6	.128	-2	18	17	-1	1.4
1947 NY-A	4	1	.800	24	6	2	0	0	56¹	71	4	28	25	15.8	5.43	65	.311	.387	1	.071	-1	-11	-12	-1	-1.1
1948 NY-A	1	0	1.000	15	0	0	0	0	25	27	0	6	12	12.2	2.88	142	.267	.315	0	—	0	4	3	0	0.1
Chi-A	2	6	.250	16	11	6	1	0	97¹	103	6	13	31	10.9	3.79	112	.275	.303	4	.138	-2	5	5	-1	0.1
Yr	3	6	.333	31	11	6	1	0	122¹	130	6	19	43	11.1	3.60	117	.273	.303	4	.138	-2	9	8	-1	0.2
1949 Chi-A	13	16	.448	34	32	18	3	1	234	223	22	83	78	11.8	3.81	110	.253	.318	16	.190	-1	10	9	1	1.0
1950 Chi-A	5	12	.294	40	17	6	1	0	155¹	165	15	58	48	13.2	4.75	94	.275	.343	3	.071	-4	-3	-5	-0	-0.8
1951 Chi-A☆	9	8	.529	33	16	7	1	2	141²	156	20	34	45	12.1	4.32	93	.272	.314	15	.333	3	-3	-4	-3	-0.5
1952 Bos-A	1	0	1.000	10	1	0	0	1	19²	15	1	5	6	9.6	4.12	96	.205	.266	0	.000	-1	-0	-0	-1	-0.1
Was-A	4	9	.308	20	12	2	0	0	104	112	12	30	29	12.7	4.24	84	.273	.330	7	.206	-0	-7	-8	-1	-0.9
Yr	5	9	.357	30	13	2	0	1	123²	127	13	35	35	12.2	4.22	88	.262	.318	7	.179	-0	-8	-8	-1	-1.0
Total 10	51	59	.464	261	113	47	6	7	1052²	1099	92	346	352	12.5	4.17	98	.268	.328	60	.182	-5	-4	-10	-5	-1.6

● ERIC GUNDERSON
Gunderson, Eric Andrew b: 3/29/66, Portland, Ore. BR/TL, 6', 175 lbs. Deb: 4/11/90

YEAR TM/L	W	L	PCT	G	GS	CG	SH	SV	IP	H	HR	BB	SO	RAT	ERA	ERA+	OAV	OOB	BH	AVG	PB	PR	/A	PD	TPI
1990 SF-N	1	2	.333	7	4	0	0	0	19²	24	3	11	14	16.0	5.49	66	.293	.376	0	.000	-1	-4	-4	0	-0.6
1991 SF-N	0	0	—	2	0	0	0	1	3¹	6	1	2	2	18.9	5.40	66	.353	.389	0	—	0	-1	-1	0	0.0
1992 Sea-A	2	1	.667	9	0	0	0	0	9¹	12	1	5	2	17.4	8.68	46	.324	.419	0	—	0	-5	-5	0	-1.3
1994 NY-N	0	0	—	14	0	0	0	0	9	5	0	4	4	9.0	0.00	—	.185	.290	0	—	0	4	4	-0	0.6
1995 NY-N	1	1	.500	30	0	0	0	0	24¹	25	2	8	19	12.6	3.70	109	.269	.333	0	—	0	1	1	1	0.1
Bos-A	2	1	.667	19	0	0	0	0	12¹	13	0	9	9	17.5	5.11	95	.295	.436	0	—	0	-0	-1	-0	-0.2
1996 Bos-A	0	1	.000	28	0	0	0	0	17¹	21	3	6	7	16.1	8.31	62	.300	.387	0	—	0	-6	-6	-1	-0.6
Total 6	6	6	.500	109	4	0	0	1	95¹	106	10	46	57	14.9	5.29	80	.286	.374	0	.000	-0	-11	-11	0	-2.6

● RED GUNKEL
Gunkel, Woodward William b: 4/15/1894, Sheffield, Ill. d: 4/19/54, Chicago, Ill. BB/TR, 5'8", 158 lbs. Deb: 6/18/16

YEAR TM/L	W	L	PCT	G	GS	CG	SH	SV	IP	H	HR	BB	SO	RAT	ERA	ERA+	OAV	OOB	BH	AVG	PB	PR	/A	PD	TPI
1916 Cle-A	0	0	—	1	0	0	0	0	1	0	0	1	1	18.0	0.00	—	.000	.500	0	—	0	0	0	-0	0.0

● LARRY GURA
Gura, Lawrence Cyril b: 11/26/47, Joliet, Ill. BB/TL, 6'1", 185 lbs. Deb: 4/30/70

YEAR TM/L	W	L	PCT	G	GS	CG	SH	SV	IP	H	HR	BB	SO	RAT	ERA	ERA+	OAV	OOB	BH	AVG	PB	PR	/A	PD	TPI
1970 Chi-N	1	3	.250	20	3	1	0	1	38	35	6	23	21	14.0	3.79	119	.254	.364	0	—	-1	1	3	0	0.2
1971 Chi-N	0	0	—	6	0	0	0	0	3	6	0	1	2	21.0	6.00	66	.400	.438	0	.000	-0	-1	-1	-0	-0.1
1972 Chi-N	0	0	—	7	0	0	0	0	12¹	11	3	4	13	10.2	3.65	104	.250	.298	0	.000	-0	-0	0	-0	0.0
1973 Chi-N	2	4	.333	21	7	0	0	0	64²	79	10	11	43	12.7	4.87	81	.296	.326	3	.200	-2	-9	-7	1	-0.4
1974 NY-A	5	1	.833	8	8	4	2	0	56	54	2	12	17	10.6	2.41	146	.248	.287	0	—	0	8	7	-0	0.8
1975 NY-A	7	8	.467	26	20	5	0	0	151¹	173	13	41	65	12.9	3.51	105	.295	.344	0	—	0	5	3	-0	0.3
1976 *KC-A	4	0	1.000	20	2	1	1	1	62²	64	4	20	22	9.8	2.30	152	.213	.281	0	—	0	11	11	0	0.6
1977 *KC-A	8	5	.615	52	6	1	1	10	106¹	108	8	28	46	11.6	3.13	129	.265	.314	0	—	0	11	11	0	1.4
1978 *KC-A	16	4	.800	35	26	8	2	0	221²	183	13	60	81	10.0	2.72	141	.229	.286	0	—	0	26	27	2	2.6
1979 KC-A	13	12	.520	39	33	7	1	0	233²	226	29	73	66	11.9	4.47	95	.253	.315	0	—	0	-7	-5	1	-0.5
1980 *KC-A☆	18	10	.643	36	36	16	4	0	283¹	272	20	76	113	11.2	2.95	137	.255	.307	0	—	0	34	35	1	3.3
1981 *KC-A	11	8	.579	23	23	12	2	0	172¹	139	11	39	61	9.3	2.72	133	.223	.269	0	—	0	18	17	0	1.9
1982 KC-A	18	12	.600	37	37	8	3	0	248	251	31	64	98	11.6	4.03	101	.261	.311	0	—	0	1	-1	0	0.4
1983 KC-A	11	18	.379	34	31	5	0	0	200¹	220	23	76	57	13.7	4.90	83	.284	.354	0	—	0	-19	-18	3	-2.0

YEAR	TM/L	W	L	PCT	G	GS	CG	SH	SV	IP	H	HR	BB	SO	RAT	ERA	ERA+	OAV	OOB	BH	AVG	PB	PR	/A	PD	TPI
1984	KC-A	12	9	.571	31	25	3	0	0	168²	175	26	67	68	13.1	5.18	78	.269	.341	0	—	0	-22	-22	1	-2.3
1985	KC-A	0	0	—	3	0	0	0	1	4¹	7	1	4	2	22.8	12.46	33	.368	.478	0	—	0	-4	-4	0	-0.2
	Chi-N	0	3	.000	5	4	0	0	0	20¹	34	4	6	7	18.1	8.41	47	.370	.414	0	.000	-0	-11	-10	-1	-1.2
Total	16	126	97	.565	403	261	71	16	14	2047	2020	204	600	801	11.7	3.76	105	.260	.317	3	.091	-2	39	46	11	4.8

● CHARLIE GUTH
Guth, Charles J. b: 1856, Chicago, Ill. d: 7/5/1883, Cambridge, Mass. Deb: 9/30/1880

YEAR	TM/L	W	L	PCT	G	GS	CG	SH	SV	IP	H	HR	BB	SO	RAT	ERA	ERA+	OAV	OOB	BH	AVG	PB	PR	/A	PD	TPI
1880	Chi-N	1	0	1.000	1	1	1	0	0	9	12	0	1	7	13.0	5.00	48	.293	.310	1	.250	0	-3	-3	-0	-0.2

● MARK GUTHRIE
Guthrie, Mark Andrew b: 9/22/65, Buffalo, N.Y. BB/TR, 6'4", 195 lbs. Deb: 7/25/89

YEAR	TM/L	W	L	PCT	G	GS	CG	SH	SV	IP	H	HR	BB	SO	RAT	ERA	ERA+	OAV	OOB	BH	AVG	PB	PR	/A	PD	TPI
1989	Min-A	2	4	.333	13	8	0	0	0	57¹	66	7	21	38	13.8	4.55	91	.292	.355	0	—	0	-4	-3	-0	-0.7
1990	Min-A	7	9	.438	24	21	3	1	0	144²	154	8	39	101	12.1	3.79	109	.276	.325	0	—	0	2	6	1	0.2
1991	*Min-A	7	5	.583	41	12	0	0	2	98	116	11	41	72	14.5	4.32	99	.303	.372	0	—	0	-2	-1	-1	-0.1
1992	Min-A	2	3	.400	54	0	0	0	5	75	59	7	23	76	9.8	2.88	141	.215	.276	0	—	0	9	10	-0	0.7
1993	Min-A	2	1	.667	22	0	0	0	0	21	20	2	16	15	15.4	4.71	92	.267	.396	0	—	0	-1	-1	0	-0.1
1994	Min-A	4	2	.667	50	0	0	0	1	51¹	65	8	18	38	14.9	6.14	79	.316	.376	0	—	0	-8	-7	0	-0.7
1995	Min-A	5	3	.625	36	0	0	0	0	42¹	47	5	16	48	13.6	4.46	107	.290	.358	0	—	0	1	1	-1	0.1
	*LA-N	0	2	.000	24	0	0	0	0	19²	19	1	9	19	13.3	3.66	104	.241	.326	0	.000	-0	1	0	0	0.0
1996	*LA-N	2	3	.400	66	0	0	0	0	73	65	3	22	56	10.8	2.22	173	.240	.299	0	.000	-0	16	13	0	0.8
Total	8	31	32	.492	330	43	3	1	9	582¹	611	52	205	463	12.7	3.93	108	.274	.337	0	.000	0	14	20	-1	0.2

● JOHNNY GUZMAN
Guzman, Dionini Ramon (Estrella) b: 1/21/71, Hatillo Palma, D.R. BR/TL, 5'10", 155 lbs. Deb: 6/8/91

YEAR	TM/L	W	L	PCT	G	GS	CG	SH	SV	IP	H	HR	BB	SO	RAT	ERA	ERA+	OAV	OOB	BH	AVG	PB	PR	/A	PD	TPI
1991	Oak-A	1	0	1.000	5	0	0	0	0	5	11	0	2	3	23.4	9.00	43	.500	.542	0	—	0	-3	-3	0	-0.5
1992	Oak-A	0	0	—	2	0	0	0	0	3	8	0	1	0	27.0	12.00	31	.471	.500	0	—	0	-3	-3	-0	0.0
Total	2	1	0	1.000	7	0	0	0	0	8	19	0	3	3	24.8	10.13	38	.487	.524	0	—	0	-5	-6	0	-0.5

● JOSE GUZMAN
Guzman, Jose Alberto (Mirabal) b: 4/9/63, Santa Isabel, P.R. BR/TR, 6'2", 195 lbs. Deb: 9/10/85

YEAR	TM/L	W	L	PCT	G	GS	CG	SH	SV	IP	H	HR	BB	SO	RAT	ERA	ERA+	OAV	OOB	BH	AVG	PB	PR	/A	PD	TPI
1985	Tex-A	3	2	.600	5	5	0	0	0	32²	27	3	14	24	11.3	2.76	153	.214	.293	0	—	0	5	5	0	0.7
1986	Tex-A	9	15	.375	29	29	2	0	0	172¹	199	23	60	87	13.8	4.54	95	.293	.355	0	—	0	-7	-5	0	-0.6
1987	Tex-A	14	14	.500	37	30	6	0	0	208¹	196	30	82	143	12.1	4.67	96	.251	.324	0	—	0	-5	-4	1	-0.4
1988	Tex-A	11	13	.458	30	30	6	2	0	206²	180	20	82	157	11.6	3.70	110	.231	.308	0	—	0	6	9	-0	0.7
1991	Tex-A	13	7	.650	25	25	5	1	0	169²	152	10	84	125	12.7	3.08	131	.239	.331	0	—	0	19	18	2	2.2
1992	Tex-A	16	11	.593	33	33	5	0	0	224	229	17	73	179	12.3	3.66	104	.268	.329	0	—	0	7	3	-0	0.4
1993	Chi-N	12	10	.545	30	30	2	1	0	191	188	25	74	163	12.5	4.34	92	.258	.329	7	.111	-3	-6	-7	0	-1.0
1994	Chi-N	2	2	.500	4	4	0	0	0	19²	22	1	13	11	16.5	9.15	45	.289	.400	0	.000	-1	-11	-11	0	-1.7
Total	8	80	74	.519	193	186	26	4	0	1224¹	1193	129	482	889	12.5	4.05	101	.256	.329	7	.099	-3	8	8	3	0.3

● JUAN GUZMAN
Guzman, Juan Andres (Correa) b: 10/28/66, Santo Domingo, D.R. BR/TR, 5'11", 190 lbs. Deb: 6/7/91

YEAR	TM/L	W	L	PCT	G	GS	CG	SH	SV	IP	H	HR	BB	SO	RAT	ERA	ERA+	OAV	OOB	BH	AVG	PB	PR	/A	PD	TPI
1991	*Tor-A	10	3	.769	23	23	1	0	0	138²	98	6	66	123	10.9	2.99	141	.197	.296	0	—	0	17	19	-2	1.4
1992	*Tor-A★	16	5	.762	28	28	1	0	0	180²	135	6	72	165	10.4	2.64	155	.207	.287	0	—	0	26	29	-2	3.1
1993	*Tor-A	14	3	.824	33	33	2	1	0	221	211	17	110	194	13.2	3.99	108	.252	.341	0	—	0	8	8	-2	0.3
1994	Tor-A	12	11	.522	25	25	2	0	0	147¹	165	20	76	124	14.9	5.68	85	.282	.367	0	—	0	-14	-14	-2	-1.9
1995	Tor-A	4	14	.222	24	24	3	0	0	135¹	151	13	73	94	15.1	6.32	75	.281	.370	0	—	0	-24	-24	-2	-2.7
1996	Tor-A	11	8	.579	27	27	4	1	0	187²	158	20	53	165	**10.5**	**2.93**	**173**	**.228**	**.290**	0	—	0	43	44	-1	3.9
Total	6	67	44	.604	160	160	13	2	0	1010²	918	82	450	865	12.4	3.97	114	.242	.325	0	—	0	56	62	-10	4.1

● SANTIAGO GUZMAN
Guzman, Santiago Donovan (b: Santiago Donovan (Guzman))
b: 7/25/49, San Pedro De Macoris, D.R. BR/TR, 6'2", 180 lbs. Deb: 9/30/69

YEAR	TM/L	W	L	PCT	G	GS	CG	SH	SV	IP	H	HR	BB	SO	RAT	ERA	ERA+	OAV	OOB	BH	AVG	PB	PR	/A	PD	TPI
1969	StL-N	0	1	.000	1	1	0	0	0	7¹	9	2	3	7	14.7	4.91	73	.321	.387	1	.333	0	-1	-1	-0	-0.1
1970	StL-N	1	1	.500	8	3	1	0	0	13²	14	1	13	9	17.8	7.24	57	.275	.422	1	.200	-0	-5	-5	-0	-0.6
1971	StL-N	0	0	—	2	1	0	0	0	10	6	0	2	13	7.2	0.00	—	.162	.205	0	.000	-0	4	4	-0	0.1
1972	StL-N	0	0	—	1	0	0	0	0	1	1	1	0	0	9.0	9.00	38	.250	.250	0	—	0	-1	-1	0	0.0
Total	4	1	2	.333	12	5	1	0	0	32	30	4	18	29	13.5	4.50	85	.250	.348	2	.222	-0	-3	-2	-1	-0.7

● BRUNO HAAS
Haas, Bruno Philip "Boon" b: 5/5/1891, Worcester, Mass. d: 6/5/52, Sarasota, Fla. BB/TL, 5'10", 180 lbs. Deb: 6/23/15 ♦

YEAR	TM/L	W	L	PCT	G	GS	CG	SH	SV	IP	H	HR	BB	SO	RAT	ERA	ERA+	OAV	OOB	BH	AVG	PB	PR	/A	PD	TPI
1915	Phi-A	0	1	.000	6	2	1	0	0	14¹	23	0	28	7	32.0	11.93	25	.404	.600	1	.056	-1	-14	-14	0	-0.9

● MOOSE HAAS
Haas, Bryan Edmund b: 4/22/56, Baltimore, Md. BR/TR, 6', 180 lbs. Deb: 9/8/76

YEAR	TM/L	W	L	PCT	G	GS	CG	SH	SV	IP	H	HR	BB	SO	RAT	ERA	ERA+	OAV	OOB	BH	AVG	PB	PR	/A	PD	TPI
1976	Mil-A	0	1	.000	5	2	0	0	0	16	12	0	12	9	13.5	3.94	89	.207	.343	0	—	0	-1	-1	1	0.1
1977	Mil-A	10	12	.455	32	32	6	0	0	197²	195	21	84	113	12.8	4.33	94	.261	.338	0	—	0	-6	-6	-2	-0.8
1978	Mil-A	2	3	.400	7	6	2	0	0	30²	33	6	8	32	12.0	6.16	61	.273	.318	0	—	0	-8	-8	-0	-1.2
1979	Mil-A	11	11	.500	29	28	8	1	0	184²	198	26	59	95	12.5	4.78	87	.275	.330	0	—	0	-12	-13	-1	-1.4
1980	Mil-A	16	15	.516	33	33	14	3	0	252¹	246	25	56	146	10.8	3.10	125	.258	.300	0	—	0	26	21	-0	2.4
1981	*Mil-A	11	7	.611	24	22	5	0	0	137¹	146	10	40	64	12.3	4.46	77	.275	.327	0	—	0	-12	-16	-1	-1.9
1982	*Mil-A	11	8	.579	32	27	3	0	1	193²	232	15	39	104	12.8	4.47	85	.302	.339	0	—	0	-8	-15	-2	-1.3
1983	Mil-A	13	3	.813	25	25	7	3	0	179	170	12	42	75	10.7	3.27	114	.251	.296	0	—	0	16	9	-1	0.7
1984	Mil-A	9	11	.450	31	30	4	0	0	189	205	15	43	84	11.8	3.99	96	.279	.318	0	—	0	-0	-3	3	0.2
1985	Mil-A	8	8	.500	27	26	6	1	0	161²	165	21	25	78	10.6	3.84	108	.260	.289	0	—	0	5	6	-1	0.4
1986	Oak-A	7	2	.778	12	12	1	0	0	72¹	58	4	19	40	9.7	2.74	141	.218	.273	0	—	0	12	9	-0	1.2
1987	Oak-A	2	2	.500	9	9	0	0	0	40²	57	7	9	13	14.6	5.75	72	.335	.369	0	—	0	-6	-7	-0	-0.6
Total	12	100	83	.546	266	252	56	8	2	1655	1717	162	436	853	11.8	4.01	97	.269	.317	0	—	0	6	-23	-5	-2.2

● DAVE HAAS
Haas, Robert David b: 10/19/65, Independence, Mo. BR/TR, 6'1", 200 lbs. Deb: 9/8/91

YEAR	TM/L	W	L	PCT	G	GS	CG	SH	SV	IP	H	HR	BB	SO	RAT	ERA	ERA+	OAV	OOB	BH	AVG	PB	PR	/A	PD	TPI
1991	Det-A	1	0	1.000	11	0	0	0	0	10²	8	1	12	6	17.7	6.75	62	.242	.457	0	—	0	-3	-3	-0	-0.3
1992	Det-A	5	3	.625	12	11	1	1	0	61²	68	8	16	29	12.4	3.94	100	.276	.323	0	—	0	-0	0	0	0.2
1993	Det-A	1	2	.333	20	0	0	0	0	28	45	9	8	17	17.0	6.11	70	.351	.414	0	—	0	-6	-6	-0	-0.5
Total	3	7	5	.583	43	11	1	1	0	100¹	121	18	36	52	14.3	4.84	84	.303	.364	0	—	0	-9	-9	-0	-0.6

● BOB HABENICHT
Habenicht, Robert Julius "Hobby" b: 2/13/26, St.Louis, Mo. d: 12/24/80, Richmond, Va. BR/TR, 6'2", 185 lbs. Deb: 4/17/51

YEAR	TM/L	W	L	PCT	G	GS	CG	SH	SV	IP	H	HR	BB	SO	RAT	ERA	ERA+	OAV	OOB	BH	AVG	PB	PR	/A	PD	TPI
1951	StL-N	0	0	—	3	0	0	0	0	5	5	0	1	2	25.2	7.20	55	.278	.519	0	.000	—	-2	-2	0	0.0
1953	StL-A	0	0	—	1	0	0	0	0	1²	1	0	1	1	16.2	5.40	78	.167	.375	0	—	0	-0	-0	-0	0.0
Total	2	0	0	—	4	0	0	0	0	6²	6	0	2	3	23.0	6.75	60	.250	.486	0	.000	—	-2	-2	0	0.0

● JOHN HABYAN
Habyan, John Gabriel b: 1/29/64, Bay Shore, N.Y. BR/TR, 6'1", 195 lbs. Deb: 9/29/85

YEAR	TM/L	W	L	PCT	G	GS	CG	SH	SV	IP	H	HR	BB	SO	RAT	ERA	ERA+	OAV	OOB	BH	AVG	PB	PR	/A	PD	TPI
1985	Bal-A	1	0	1.000	2	0	0	0	0	2²	3	0	0	2	10.1	0.00	—	.250	.250	0	—	0	1	1	0	0.6
1986	Bal-A	1	3	.250	6	5	0	0	0	26¹	24	3	18	14	14.4	4.44	93	.250	.368	0	—	0	-1	-1	-0	-0.1
1987	Bal-A	6	7	.462	27	13	0	0	1	116¹	110	20	40	64	11.8	4.80	92	.248	.313	0	—	0	-4	-5	-1	-0.4
1988	Bal-A	1	0	—	7	0	0	0	0	14²	22	2	4	4	16.0	4.30	91	.355	.394	0	—	0	-1	-1	-0	0.0
1990	NY-A	0	0	—	6	0	0	0	0	8²	10	0	2	4	13.5	2.08	191	.294	.351	0	—	0	2	2	-0	0.2
1991	NY-A	4	2	.667	66	0	0	0	2	90	73	2	20	70	9.5	2.30	180	.225	.275	0	—	0	18	18	0	1.2
1992	NY-A	5	6	.455	56	0	0	0	7	72²	84	6	21	44	13.3	3.84	102	.295	.347	0	—	0	1	1	1	0.2
1993	NY-A	2	1	.667	36	0	0	0	0	42¹	45	5	16	29	13.0	4.04	103	.276	.341	0	—	0	0	0	0	0.2
	KC-A	0	0	—	12	0	0	0	0	14	14	1	4	10	11.6	4.50	102	.259	.310	0	—	0	1	0	0	0.0
	Yr	2	1	.667	48	0	0	0	0	56¹	59	6	20	39	12.6	4.15	103	.269	.331	0	—	0	1	1	0	0.2
1994	StL-N	1	0	1.000	52	0	0	0	1	47¹	52	3	20	38	13.3	3.23	128	.275	.347	0	—	0	5	5	1	0.2
1995	StL-N	3	2	.600	31	0	0	0	0	40²	32	0	15	35	10.6	2.88	146	.222	.300	0	.000	-0	6	6	1	0.5
	Cal-A	1	2	.333	28	0	0	0	0	32²	36	2	14	25	13.5	4.13	114	.279	.345	0	.000	-0	-1	-1	0	0.1
1996	Col-N	1	1	.500	19	0	0	0	0	24	34	4	14	25	18.4	7.13	76	.347	.434	0	.000	-0	-8	-5	-0	-0.4
Total	11	26	24	.520	348	18	0	0	11	532¹	537	47	208	372	12.4	4.35	111	.265	.330	0	.000	-0	22	24	2	2.3

● WARREN HACKER
Hacker, Warren Louis b: 11/21/24, Marissa, Ill. BR/TR, 6'1", 185 lbs. Deb: 9/24/48

YEAR	TM/L	W	L	PCT	G	GS	CG	SH	SV	IP	H	HR	BB	SO	RAT	ERA	ERA+	OAV	OOB	BH	AVG	PB	PR	/A	PD	TPI
1948	Chi-N	0	0	1.000	3	0	0	0	0	3	7	0	3	0	30.0	21.00	19	.438	.526	0	—	0	-6	-6	0	-1.3
1949	Chi-N	5	8	.385	30	12	3	0	0	125²	141	7	53	40	14.2	4.23	95	.283	.356	7	.184	-1	-3	-3	1	-0.3

YEAR TM/L	W	L	PCT	G	GS	CG	SH	SV	IP	H	HR	BB	SO	RAT	ERA	ERA+	OAV	OOB	BH	AVG	PB	PR	/A	PD	TPI
1950 Chi-N	0	1	.000	5	3	1	0	1	15^1	20	3	8	5	16.4	5.28	80	.313	.389	0	.000	-1	-2	-2	1	-0.1
1951 Chi-N	0	0	—	2	0	0	0	0	1^1	3	0	0	2	27.0	13.50	30	.500	.571	0	—	0	-1	-1	0	0.0
1952 Chi-N	15	9	.625	33	20	12	5	1	185	144	17	31	84	**8.6**	2.58	149	**.212**	**.247**	7	.121	-2	24	26	-4	2.8
1953 Chi-N	12	19	.387	39	32	9	0	2	221^2	225	35	54	106	11.4	4.38	101	.254	.299	17	.218	0	-2	2	-3	0.0
1954 Chi-N	6	13	.316	39	18	4	1	2	158^2	157	28	37	80	11.2	4.25	99	.257	.304	13	.236	-1	-3	-1	-1	-0.1
1955 Chi-N	11	15	.423	35	30	13	0	3	213	202	38	43	80	10.4	4.27	96	.245	.285	18	.250	2	-5	-4	-4	-0.6
1956 Chi-N	3	13	.188	34	24	4	0	0	168	190	28	44	65	12.6	4.66	81	.285	.330	8	.148	-2	-17	-17	-3	-1.9
1957 Cin-N	3	2	.600	15	6	0	0	0	43^1	50	5	13	18	13.7	5.19	79	.294	.355	1	.125	-0	-6	-5	-0	-0.6
Phi-N	4	4	.500	20	10	1	0	0	74	72	10	18	33	11.1	4.50	85	.257	.304	6	.261	1	-5	-6	-1	-0.5
Yr	7	6	.538	35	16	1	0	0	117^1	122	15	31	51	11.8	4.76	82	.267	.315	7	.226	1	-11	-11	-1	-1.1
1958 Phi-N	1	0	1.000	9	1	0	0	0	17	24	2	8	4	16.9	7.41	53	.329	.395	0	.000	-0	-7	-7	-0	-0.4
1961 Chi-A	3	3	.500	42	0	0	0	8	57^1	62	8	8	40	11.1	3.77	104	.272	.300	1	.111	-1	2	1	-1	-0.1
Total 12	62	89	.411	306	157	47	6	17	1283^1	1297	181	320	557	11.5	4.21	96	.259	.307	78	.195	-2	-32	-22	-15	-3.1

● **JIM HACKETT**   Hackett, James Joseph "Sunny Jim" b: 10/1/1877, Jacksonville, Ill. d: 3/28/61, Douglas, Mich. BR/TR, 6'2", 185 lbs. Deb: 9/14/02 ◆

YEAR TM/L	W	L	PCT	G	GS	CG	SH	SV	IP	H	HR	BB	SO	RAT	ERA	ERA+	OAV	OOB	BH	AVG	PB	PR	/A	PD	TPI
1902 StL-N	0	3	.000	4	3	3	0	0	30^1	46	0	16	7	18.7	6.23	44	.348	.423	6	.286	1	-12	-12	-0	-0.9
1903 StL-N	1	3	.250	7	6	5	0	1	48^1	47	0	18	21	12.7	3.72	88	.249	.324	80	.228	1	-2	-2	-0	-0.1
Total 2	1	6	.143	11	9	8	0	1	78^2	93	0	34	28	15.0	4.69	65	.290	.365	86	.231	2	-14	-14	-0	-1.0

● **HARVEY HADDIX**   Haddix, Harvey "The Kitten" b: 9/18/25, Medway, Ohio d: 1/8/94, Springfield, Ohio BL/TL, 5'9.5", 170 lbs. Deb: 8/20/52 C

YEAR TM/L	W	L	PCT	G	GS	CG	SH	SV	IP	H	HR	BB	SO	RAT	ERA	ERA+	OAV	OOB	BH	AVG	PB	PR	/A	PD	TPI
1952 StL-N	2	2	.500	7	6	3	0	0	42	31	4	10	31	9.2	2.79	133	.201	.259	3	.214	0	4	4	-1	0.4
1953 StL-N☆	20	9	.690	36	33	19	**6**	1	253	220	24	69	163	10.4	3.06	139	.232	.287	28	.289	10	35	34	1	4.7
1954 StL-N†	18	13	.581	43	35	13	3	4	259^2	247	26	77	184	11.3	3.57	115	.249	.305	18	.194	3	14	16	-0	2.0
1955 StL-N★	12	16	.429	37	30	9	2	1	208	216	27	62	150	12.2	4.46	91	.268	.325	12	.164	0	-10	-9	1	-0.9
1956 StL-N	1	0	1.000	4	4	1	1	0	23^2	28	3	10	16	14.5	5.32	71	.298	.365	2	.222	1	-4	-4	-0	-0.1
Phi-N	12	8	.600	31	26	11	2	2	206^2	196	23	55	154	11.2	3.48	107	.247	.301	22	.237	4	7	5	-1	0.9
Yr	13	8	.619	35	30	12	3	2	230^1	224	26	65	170	11.5	3.67	102	.253	.308	24	.235	5	3	1	-1	0.8
1957 Phi-N	10	13	.435	27	25	8	1	0	170^2	176	18	39	136	11.4	4.06	94	.264	.306	21	.309	7	-3	-5	-2	-0.1
1958 Cin-N	8	7	.533	29	26	8	1	0	184	191	28	43	110	11.8	3.52	118	.268	.315	11	.180	3	9	13	-1	1.2
1959 Pit-N	12	12	.500	31	29	14	2	0	224^1	189	26	49	149	**9.6**	3.13	124	.228	**.273**	12	.145	-0	20	18	-0	1.8
1960 *Pit-N	11	10	.524	29	28	4	0	1	172^1	189	13	38	101	11.9	3.97	94	.277	.316	17	.254	4	-4	-4	3	0.3
1961 Pit-N	10	6	.625	29	22	5	2	0	156	159	15	41	99	11.7	4.10	97	.266	.316	8	.143	0	-1	-2	-0	-0.1
1962 Pit-N	9	6	.600	28	20	4	0	0	141^1	146	17	42	101	12.1	4.20	94	.264	.319	13	.250	4	-4	-4	-1	0.0
1963 Pit-N	3	4	.429	49	1	0	0	1	70	67	7	20	70	11.7	3.34	99	.256	.318	2	.182	1	-0	-0	0	0.0
1964 Bal-A	5	5	.500	49	0	0	0	10	89^2	68	4	23	90	9.3	2.31	155	.211	.268	0	.000	-2	13	13	1	1.5
1965 Bal-A	3	2	.600	24	0	0	0	0	33^2	31	5	23	21	15.0	3.48	100	.248	.373	0	.000	-0	-0	-0	-0	0.0
Total 14	136	113	.546	453	285	99	20	21	2235	2154	240	601	1575	11.3	3.63	108	.252	.305	169	.212	35	75	74	1	11.6

● **GEORGE HADDOCK**   Haddock, George Silas "Gentleman George" b: 12/25/1866, Portsmouth, N.H. d: 4/18/26, Boston, Mass. BR/TR, 5'11", 155 lbs. Deb: 9/27/1888

YEAR TM/L	W	L	PCT	G	GS	CG	SH	SV	IP	H	HR	BB	SO	RAT	ERA	ERA+	OAV	OOB	BH	AVG	PB	PR	/A	PD	TPI
1888 Was-N	0	2	.000	2	2	2	0	0	16	9	2	9	3	18.0	2.25	125	.148	.188	1	.200	0	1	1	1	0.2
1889 Was-N	11	19	.367	33	31	30	0	0	276^1	299	13	123	106	14.0	4.20	94	.268	.345	25	.223	7	-6	-8	0	0.0
1890 Buf-P	9	26	.257	35	34	31	0	0	290^2	366	15	149	123	16.4	5.76	71	.295	.377	36	.247	7	-49	-54	4	-3.4
1891 Bos-a	34	11	.756	51	47	37	**5**	1	379^2	330	8	137	169	11.4	2.49	140	.226	.299	45	.243	9	**52**	42	6	5.3
1892 Bro-N	29	13	.690	46	44	39	3	1	381^1	340	11	163	132	12.2	3.14	101	.229	.311	28	.177	-1	6	1	2	0.2
1893 Bro-N	8	9	.471	23	20	12	0	0	151	193	10	89	37	17.2	5.60	79	.302	.393	24	.282	4	-16	-20	-3	-1.5
1894 Phi-N	4	3	.571	10	7	5	0	0	56	63	0	34	7	15.8	5.79	88	.281	.378	5	.172	-1	-3	-4	1	-0.4
Was-N	0	4	.000	4	4	4	0	0	29	50	2	17	1	21.1	8.69	61	.373	.447	3	.188	-1	-11	-11	-0	-1.0
Yr	4	7	.364	14	11	9	0	0	85	113	2	51	8	17.5	6.78	76	.315	.401	8	.178	-1	-14	-15	1	-1.4
Total 7	95	87	.522	204	189	160	8	2	1580	1650	56	714	599	13.8	4.07	93	.259	.340	167	.227	25	-25	-53	11	-0.6

● **BUMP HADLEY**   Hadley, Irving Darius b: 7/5/04, Lynn, Mass. d: 2/15/63, Lynn, Mass. BR/TR, 5'11", 190 lbs. Deb: 4/20/26

YEAR TM/L	W	L	PCT	G	GS	CG	SH	SV	IP	H	HR	BB	SO	RAT	ERA	ERA+	OAV	OOB	BH	AVG	PB	PR	/A	PD	TPI
1926 Was-A	0	0	—	1	0	0	0	0	3	6	0	2	0	24.0	12.00	32	.429	.500	0	—	0	-3	-3	-0	0.0
1927 Was-A	14	6	.700	30	27	13	0	0	198^2	177	2	86	60	12.3	2.85	142	.244	.332	19	.271	2	28	27	0	2.6
1928 Was-A	12	13	.480	33	31	16	3	0	231^2	236	4	100	80	13.4	3.54	113	.268	.348	17	.210	1	13	12	-0	1.3
1929 Was-A	6	16	.273	37	27	7	1	0	195^1	196	10	85	98	13.2	5.62	75	.263	.342	6	.097	-4	-30	-30	1	-3.1
1930 Was-A	15	11	.577	42	34	15	1	2	260^1	242	6	105	162	12.2	3.73	123	.247	.323	21	.226	1	27	25	-1	2.2
1931 Was-A	11	10	.524	**55**	11	2	1	8	179^2	145	4	92	124	11.9	3.06	140	**.218**	.314	9	.167	-1	26	25	2	2.7
1932 Chi-A	1	1	.500	2	1	0	0	1	18^2	21	3	13	12	13.1	3.86	112	.262	.342	1	.167	-0	1	1	0	0.1
StL-A	13	20	.394	40	33	12	1	1	229^2	244	20	163	132	16.3	5.53	88	.274	.391	22	.282	4	-27	-17	-3	-1.9
Yr	14	21	.400	43	35	13	1	2	248^1	261	23	171	145	15.9	5.40	89	.273	.388	23	.274	4	-25	-16	-3	-1.8
1933 StL-A	15	20	.429	45	36	19	2	3	**316^1**	309	17	141	149	12.9	3.92	119	.256	.335	17	.156	-4	13	26	-3	1.9
1934 StL-A	10	16	.385	39	32	7	2	0	213	212	14	127	79	14.6	4.35	115	.257	.361	13	.203	-1	3	5	-0	1.5
1935 Was-A	10	15	.400	35	32	13	0	0	230^1	268	18	102	77	14.6	4.92	88	.292	.366	15	.195	1	-12	-15	1	-1.2
1936 *NY-A	14	4	.778	31	24	8	1	1	173^2	194	12	89	74	14.7	4.35	107	.283	.366	16	.235	2	13	6	1	0.7
1937 *NY-A	11	8	.579	29	25	6	0	0	178^1	199	16	83	70	14.4	5.30	84	.281	.358	11	.169	1	-13	-17	-1	-1.4
1938 NY-A	9	8	.529	29	17	8	1	0	167^1	165	13	66	61	12.6	3.60	126	.254	.325	5	.093	-1	22	17	3	1.6
1939 *NY-A	12	6	.667	26	18	7	1	2	154	132	10	85	65	12.9	2.98	146	.237	.342	11	.177	-1	28	24	2	2.6
1940 NY-N	3	5	.375	25	2	0	0	2	80	88	4	52	39	15.9	5.74	70	.276	.379	3	.111	-1	-12	-15	-0	-1.4
1941 NY-N	1	0	1.000	3	2	0	0	0	13	19	1	9	4	19.4	6.23	59	.345	.438	0	.000	-0	-4	-4	-0	-0.3
Phi-A	4	6	.400	22	5	1	0	2	102^1	131	4	41	37	15.8	5.01	84	.310	.381	4	.129	-1	-10	-9	-1	-0.9
Total 16	161	165	.494	528	355	135	14	25	2945^2	2980	167	1442	1318	13.7	4.24	105	.263	.350	190	.189	-1	65	69	2	7.0

● **MICKEY HAEFNER**   Haefner, Milton Arnold b: 10/9/12, Lenzburg, Ill. d: 1/3/95, New Athens, Ill. BL/TL, 5'8", 160 lbs. Deb: 4/22/43

YEAR TM/L	W	L	PCT	G	GS	CG	SH	SV	IP	H	HR	BB	SO	RAT	ERA	ERA+	OAV	OOB	BH	AVG	PB	PR	/A	PD	TPI
1943 Was-A	11	5	.688	36	13	8	1	6	165^1	126	4	60	65	10.3	2.29	140	.208	.283	6	.133	0	19	17	-0	1.8
1944 Was-A	12	15	.444	31	28	18	3	1	228	221	7	71	86	11.7	3.04	107	.251	.310	11	.157	-1	10	5	1	0.6
1945 Was-A	16	14	.533	37	28	19	1	3	238^1	226	10	69	83	11.4	3.47	89	.247	.305	20	.244	4	-3	-10	1	-0.7
1946 Was-A	14	11	.560	33	27	17	2	1	227^2	220	10	80	85	12.1	2.85	118	.251	.317	15	.203	4	17	13	-1	1.7
1947 Was-A	10	14	.417	31	28	14	4	1	193	195	8	85	77	13.2	3.64	102	.264	.343	8	.136	-1	1	2	-1	0.0
1948 Was-A	5	13	.278	28	20	4	0	0	147^2	151	7	61	45	13.3	4.02	108	.265	.342	7	.163	-1	4	5	2	0.7
1949 Was-A	5	5	.500	19	12	4	1	0	91^2	85	9	53	23	13.7	4.42	96	.249	.353	5	.200	-1	-2	-1	-0	0.0
Chi-A	4	6	.400	14	4	4	1	1	80^1	84	9	41	17	14.6	4.37	95	.275	.370	6	.261	2	-2	-0	-0	0.0
Yr	9	11	.450	33	24	8	2	1	172	169	16	94	40	14.0	4.40	96	.260	.358	11	.229	2	-4	-2	-1	0.0
1950 Chi-A	1	6	.143	24	9	2	0	0	70^2	83	11	45	10	16.6	5.73	78	.299	.400	9	.200	1	-9	-10	-1	-0.8
Bos-N	0	2	.000	24	2	0	0	0	24	23	4	12	10	13.1	5.63	68	.247	.333	2	.286	1	-4	-5	-0	-0.3
Total 8	78	91	.462	261	179	91	13	13	1466^2	1414	76	577	508	12.5	3.50	102	.252	.326	84	.188	8	31	13	1	3.0

● **BUD HAFEY**   Hafey, Daniel Albert b: 8/6/12, Berkeley, Cal. d: 7/27/86, Sacramento, Cal. BR/TR, 6', 185 lbs. Deb: 4/21/35 F◆

YEAR TM/L	W	L	PCT	G	GS	CG	SH	SV	IP	H	HR	BB	SO	RAT	ERA	ERA+	OAV	OOB	BH	AVG	PB	PR	/A	PD	TPI
1939 Phi-N	0	0	—	2	0	0	0	0	1^1	7	0	1	1	54.0	33.75	12	.700	.727	9	.176	-0	-4	-4	0	-0.6

● **LEO HAFFORD**   Hafford, Leo Edgar b: 9/17/1883, Somerville, Mass. d: 10/2/11, Willimantic, Conn. TR, 6', 170 lbs. Deb: 4/15/06

YEAR TM/L	W	L	PCT	G	GS	CG	SH	SV	IP	H	HR	BB	SO	RAT	ERA	ERA+	OAV	OOB	BH	AVG	PB	PR	/A	PD	TPI
1906 Cin-N	1	1	.500	3	1	1	0	0	19	13	0	11	9	11.8	0.95	291	.191	.313	2	.222	-0	4	4	-1	0.3

● **FRANK HAFNER**   Hafner, Francis R. b: 8/14/1867, Hannibal, Mo. d: 3/2/57, Hannibal, Mo. TR, Deb: 5/5/1888

YEAR TM/L	W	L	PCT	G	GS	CG	SH	SV	IP	H	HR	BB	SO	RAT	ERA	ERA+	OAV	OOB	BH	AVG	PB	PR	/A	PD	TPI
1888 KC-a	0	2	.000	2	2	2	0	0	18	24	2	16	5	20.5	7.00	49	.308	.432	0	.000	-1	-8	-7	-0	-0.6

● **ART HAGAN**   Hagan, Arthur Charles b: 3/17/1863, Providence, R.I. d: 3/25/36, Providence, R.I. TR, Deb: 6/30/1883

YEAR TM/L	W	L	PCT	G	GS	CG	SH	SV	IP	H	HR	BB	SO	RAT	ERA	ERA+	OAV	OOB	BH	AVG	PB	PR	/A	PD	TPI
1883 Phi-N	1	14	.067	17	16	15	0	0	137	207	2	33	39	15.8	5.45	57	.342	.376	6	.102	-5	-35	-36	-1	-3.3
Buf-N	0	2	.000	2	2	1	0	0	15	17	0	6	7	13.8	3.60	88	.270	.333	0	.000	-1	-1	-1	0	-0.2
Yr	1	16	.059	19	18	16	0	0	152	224	2	39	46	15.6	5.27	59	.335	.371	6	.091	-7	-36	-37	-1	-3.5

YEAR	TM/L	W	L	PCT	G	GS	CG	SH	SV	IP	H	HR	BB	SO	RAT	ERA	ERA+	OAV	OOB	BH	AVG	PB	PR	/A	PD	TPI
1884	Buf-N	1	2	.333	3	3	3	0	0	26	53	1	4	4	19.7	5.88	54	.384	.401	4	.308	0	-8	-8	-1	-0.7
Total	2	2	18	.100	22	21	19	0	0	178	277	3	43	50	16.2	5.36	58	.343	.376	10	.127	-6	-44	-45	-2	-4.2

● CASEY HAGEMAN
Hageman, Kurt Moritz   b: 5/12/1887, Mt.Oliver, Pa.   d: 4/1/64, New Bedford, Pa.   BR/TR, 5'10.5", 186 lbs.   Deb: 9/18/11

YEAR	TM/L	W	L	PCT	G	GS	CG	SH	SV	IP	H	HR	BB	SO	RAT	ERA	ERA+	OAV	OOB	BH	AVG	PB	PR	/A	PD	TPI
1911	Bos-A	0	2	.000	2	2	2	0	0	17	16	2	5	8	11.6	2.12	155	.262	.328	0	.000	-0	2	2	-1	0.1
1912	Bos-A	0	0	—	2	1	0	0	0	1¹	5	0	3	1	54.0	27.00	13	.500	.615	0	—	-0	-4	-3	-0	0.0
1914	StL-N	2	4	.333	12	7	2	0	0	55¹	43	0	20	21	11.1	2.44	115	.215	.302	2	.125	-1	2	2	1	0.3
	Chi-N	1	1	.500	16	1	0	0	1	46²	44	0	12	17	11.4	3.47	80	.254	.314	7	.467	3	-4	-4	-0	0.0
	Yr	3	5	.375	28	8	2	0	1	102	87	0	32	38	10.8	2.91	96	.230	.295	9	.290	2	-1	-1	-0	0.3
Total	3	3	7	.300	32	11	4	0	1	120¹	108	2	40	47	11.7	3.07	93	.243	.318	9	.257	2	-3	-3	-1	0.4

● KEVIN HAGEN
Hagen, Kevin Eugene   b: 3/8/60, Renton, Wash.   BR/TR, 6'2", 185 lbs.   Deb: 6/4/83

YEAR	TM/L	W	L	PCT	G	GS	CG	SH	SV	IP	H	HR	BB	SO	RAT	ERA	ERA+	OAV	OOB	BH	AVG	PB	PR	/A	PD	TPI
1983	StL-N	2	2	.500	9	4	0	0	0	22¹	34	0	7	7	16.5	4.84	75	.362	.406	0	.000	-1	-3	-3	0	-0.5
1984	StL-N	1	0	1.000	4	0	0	0	0	7¹	9	0	1	2	12.3	2.45	141	.300	.323	0	—	0	1	1	-0	0.1
Total	2	3	2	.600	13	4	0	0	0	29²	43	0	8	9	15.5	4.25	84	.347	.386	0	.000	-1	-2	-2	-0	-0.4

● RIP HAGERMAN
Hagerman, Zeriah Zequiel   b: 6/20/1888, Lyndon, Kan.   d: 1/30/30, Albuquerque, N.Mex   BR/TR, 6'2", 200 lbs.   Deb: 4/16/09

YEAR	TM/L	W	L	PCT	G	GS	CG	SH	SV	IP	H	HR	BB	SO	RAT	ERA	ERA+	OAV	OOB	BH	AVG	PB	PR	/A	PD	TPI
1909	Chi-N	4	4	.500	13	7	4	1	0	79	64	0	28	32	10.7	1.82	139	.225	.298	3	.130	-0	7	6	-0	0.3
1914	Cle-A	9	15	.375	37	26	12	3	0	198	189	3	118	112	14.2	3.09	93	.265	.374	1	.016	-5	-8	-4	-3	-1.4
1915	Cle-A	6	14	.300	29	22	7	0	0	151	156	4	77	69	14.2	3.52	87	.277	.370	4	.105	-2	-10	-8	-3	-1.5
1916	Cle-A	0	0	—	2	0	0	0	0	3²	5	1	2	1	22.1	12.27	25	.333	.474	0	—	-0	-4	-4	-0	0.0
Total	4	19	33	.365	81	55	23	4	0	431²	414	8	225	214	13.6	3.09	93	.263	.360	8	.065	-9	-14	-10	-6	-2.4

● NOODLES HAHN
Hahn, Frank George   b: 4/29/1879, Nashville, Tenn.   d: 2/6/60, Candler, N.C.   BL/TL, 5'9", 160 lbs.   Deb: 4/18/1899

YEAR	TM/L	W	L	PCT	G	GS	CG	SH	SV	IP	H	HR	BB	SO	RAT	ERA	ERA+	OAV	OOB	BH	AVG	PB	PR	/A	PD	TPI
1899	Cin-N	23	8	.742	38	34	32	4	0	309	280	3	68	**145**	10.4	2.68	146	.242	.289	16	.147	-4	40	43	-4	2.8
1900	Cin-N	16	20	.444	39	37	29	4	0	311¹	306	4	89	**132**	11.6	3.27	112	.256	.312	24	.209	0	15	14	-0	1.4
1901	Cin-N	22	19	.537	42	42	**41**	2	0	**375**	370	12	69	**239**	10.7	2.71	118	.256	.294	24	.170	-1	26	20	-0	1.9
1902	Cin-N	23	12	.657	36	36	35	6	0	321	282	7	58	142	9.7	1.77	170	.236	.275	22	.185	0	36	44	-2	4.6
1903	Cin-N	22	12	.647	34	34	34	5	0	296	297	3	47	127	10.7	2.52	141	.262	.297	18	.161	-2	25	34	-1	3.2
1904	Cin-N	16	18	.471	35	34	33	2	0	297²	258	3	35	98	9.1	2.06	143	.234	.262	17	.172	1	23	29	-0	3.3
1905	Cin-N	5	3	.625	13	8	5	1	0	77	85	0	9	17	11.2	2.81	118	.272	.297	4	.167	-4	2	4	-2	0.1
1906	NY-A	3	2	.600	6	6	3	1	0	42	38	0	6	17	10.1	3.86	77	.245	.287	4	.333	1	-5	-4	-1	-0.4
Total	8	130	94	.580	243	231	212	25	0	2029¹	1916	27	381	917	10.4	2.55	133	.249	.289	129	.176	-5	161	187	-11	16.9

● FRED HAHN
Hahn, Frederick Aloys   b: 2/16/29, Nyack, N.Y.   d: 8/16/84, Valhalla, N.Y.   BR/TL, 6'3", 174 lbs.   Deb: 4/19/52

YEAR	TM/L	W	L	PCT	G	GS	CG	SH	SV	IP	H	HR	BB	SO	RAT	ERA	ERA+	OAV	OOB	BH	AVG	PB	PR	/A	PD	TPI
1952	StL-N	0	0	—	1	0	0	0	0	2	2	0	1	0	13.5	0.00	∞	.250	.333	0	—	0	1	1	0	0.0

● HAL HAID
Haid, Harold Augustine   b: 12/21/1897, Barberton, Ohio   d: 8/13/52, Los Angeles, Cal.   BR/TR, 5'10.5", 150 lbs.   Deb: 9/5/19

YEAR	TM/L	W	L	PCT	G	GS	CG	SH	SV	IP	H	HR	BB	SO	RAT	ERA	ERA+	OAV	OOB	BH	AVG	PB	PR	/A	PD	TPI
1919	StL-A	0	0	—	1	0	0	0	0	2	5	0	3	1	36.0	18.00	18	.556	.667	0	—	0	-3	-3	0	0.0
1928	StL-N	2	2	.500	27	0	0	0	5	47	39	1	11	21	9.8	2.30	174	.218	.267	3	.375	1	9	9	0	1.0
1929	StL-N	9	9	.500	38	12	8	0	4	154²	171	8	66	41	14.1	4.07	115	.284	.360	4	.082	-4	11	10	-1	0.6
1930	StL-N	3	2	.600	20	0	0	0	2	33	38	1	14	13	15.0	4.09	123	.297	.379	-0	3	3	1	0.5
1931	Bos-N	0	2	.000	27	0	0	0	1	56	59	3	16	20	12.5	4.50	84	.263	.321	1	.125	-1	-4	-4	0	0.0
1933	Chi-A	0	0	—	6	0	0	0	0	14²	18	2	13	7	20.3	7.98	53	.310	.452	1	.250	-0	-6	-6	0	0.0
Total	6	14	15	.483	119	12	8	0	12	307¹	330	15	123	103	13.7	4.16	106	.275	.349	9	.125	-3	10	9	2	2.1

● JESSE HAINES
Haines, Jesse Joseph "Pop"   b: 7/22/1893, Clayton, Ohio   d: 8/5/78, Dayton, Ohio   BR/TR, 6', 190 lbs.   Deb: 7/20/18   CH

YEAR	TM/L	W	L	PCT	G	GS	CG	SH	SV	IP	H	HR	BB	SO	RAT	ERA	ERA+	OAV	OOB	BH	AVG	PB	PR	/A	PD	TPI
1918	Cin-N	0	0	—	1	0	0	0	0	5	5	0	1	2	10.8	1.80	148	.294	.333	1	1.000	0	1	0	0	0.1
1920	StL-N	13	20	.394	**47**	37	19	4	2	301²	303	9	80	120	11.7	2.98	100	.270	.324	19	.176	-1	5	0	-5	-0.7
1921	StL-N	18	12	.600	37	29	13	**3**	0	244¹	261	15	56	84	12.0	3.50	105	.286	.333	17	.181	-3	8	5	2	0.4
1922	StL-N	11	9	.550	29	26	11	2	0	183	207	10	45	62	12.6	3.84	101	.284	.329	12	.167	-2	5	1	1	0.0
1923	StL-N	20	13	.606	37	36	23	1	0	266	283	7	75	73	12.3	3.11	125	.275	.328	20	.202	-2	26	23	-0	2.4
1924	StL-N	8	19	.296	35	31	16	1	0	222²	275	14	66	69	14.0	4.41	86	.309	.360	14	.189	-2	-13	-15	-1	-1.9
1925	StL-N	13	14	.481	29	25	15	0	0	207²	234	11	52	63	12.5	4.57	95	.290	.334	13	.176	-4	-7	-6	-1	-0.9
1926	*StL-N	13	4	.765	33	21	14	3	1	183	186	10	48	46	11.6	3.25	120	.265	.314	13	.213	-1	12	13	-3	0.7
1927	StL-N	24	10	.706	38	36	**25**	**6**	1	300²	273	11	77	89	10.6	2.72	145	.245	.297	23	.202	-1	40	41	1	4.3
1928	*StL-N	20	8	.714	33	28	20	1	0	240¹	238	14	72	77	11.8	3.18	126	.266	.324	16	.184	-1	22	22	-3	1.9
1929	StL-N	13	10	.565	28	25	12	0	0	179²	230	21	73	59	15.3	5.71	82	.313	.376	11	.159	-3	-20	-21	-4	-2.7
1930	*StL-N	13	8	.619	29	24	14	0	1	182	215	15	54	68	13.4	4.30	117	.298	.348	16	.246	1	14	14	-3	1.0
1931	StL-N	12	3	.800	19	17	8	2	0	122¹	134	8	28	27	11.9	3.02	131	.278	.318	6	.133	-2	12	13	-1	1.0
1932	StL-N	3	5	.375	20	10	4	1	0	85¹	116	4	16	27	14.0	4.75	83	.326	.357	5	.185	-0	-8	-8	-1	-0.7
1933	StL-N	9	6	.600	32	10	5	0	1	115¹	113	3	37	37	11.8	2.50	139	.252	.311	2	.067	-3	11	13	-2	1.2
1934	*StL-N	4	4	.500	37	6	0	0	0	90	86	6	19	17	10.9	3.50	121	.262	.311	3	.158	-1	**6**	**7**	2	0.7
1935	StL-N	6	5	.545	30	12	3	0	2	115¹	110	4	24	28	10.8	3.59	114	.252	.299	9	.273	1	6	7	-2	0.5
1936	StL-N	7	5	.583	25	9	4	0	1	99¹	110	4	21	19	12.0	3.90	101	.284	.323	5	.167	-1	1	1	-0	0.0
1937	StL-N	3	3	.500	16	6	2	0	0	65²	81	5	22	18	14.4	4.52	88	.303	.361	4	.182	-0	-4	-4	-1	-0.5
Total	19	210	158	.571	555	388	208	24	10	3208²	3460	165	871	981	12.3	3.64	108	.280	.330	209	.186	-22	114	104	-21	7.0

● JIM HAISLIP
Haislip, James Clifton "Slim"   b: 8/4/1891, Farmersville, Tex.   d: 1/22/70, Dallas, Tex.   BR/TR, 6'1", 186 lbs.   Deb: 8/27/13

YEAR	TM/L	W	L	PCT	G	GS	CG	SH	SV	IP	H	HR	BB	SO	RAT	ERA	ERA+	OAV	OOB	BH	AVG	PB	PR	/A	PD	TPI
1913	Phi-N	0	0	—	1	0	0	0	0	3	4	0	3	0	21.0	21.00	56	.400	.538	0	.000	-0	-1	-1	0	0.0

● ED HALBRITER
Halbriter, Edward L.   b: 2/2/1860, Auburn, N.Y.   d: 8/9/36, Los Angeles, Cal.   Deb: 5/23/1882

YEAR	TM/L	W	L	PCT	G	GS	CG	SH	SV	IP	H	HR	BB	SO	RAT	ERA	ERA+	OAV	OOB	BH	AVG	PB	PR	/A	PD	TPI
1882	Phi-a	0	1	.000	1	1	1	0	0	8	17	1	4	2	23.6	7.88	38	.405	.457	0	.000	-0	-5	-4	-0	-0.4

● DAD HALE
Hale, Ray Luther   b: 2/18/1880, Allegan, Mich.   d: 2/1/46, Allegan, Mich.   BR/TR, 5'10", 180 lbs.   Deb: 4/21/02

YEAR	TM/L	W	L	PCT	G	GS	CG	SH	SV	IP	H	HR	BB	SO	RAT	ERA	ERA+	OAV	OOB	BH	AVG	PB	PR	/A	PD	TPI
1902	Bos-N	1	3	.250	8	5	3	0	0	40	57	1	16	11	16.6	6.07	46	.333	.394	0	.000	-0	-15	-14	-0	-1.4
	Bal-A	0	1	.000	3	2	1	0	0	14	21	0	6	6	18.0	4.50	84	.344	.412	0	.000	-0	-1	-1	-0	-0.2
Total	1	1	4	.200	11	7	4	0	0	54	78	1	22	17	17.0	5.67	54	.336	.398	0	.000	-2	-16	-16	-1	-1.6

● ED HALICKI
Halicki, Edward Louis   b: 10/4/50, Newark, N.J.   BR/TR, 6'7", 220 lbs.   Deb: 7/8/74

YEAR	TM/L	W	L	PCT	G	GS	CG	SH	SV	IP	H	HR	BB	SO	RAT	ERA	ERA+	OAV	OOB	BH	AVG	PB	PR	/A	PD	TPI
1974	SF-N	1	8	.111	16	11	2	0	0	74¹	84	6	31	40	14.2	4.24	90	.275	.345	6	.240	1	-5	-4	-1	-0.3
1975	SF-N	9	13	.409	24	23	7	2	0	159²	143	6	59	153	11.6	3.49	109	.240	.312	6	.113	-2	2	5	-1	0.5
1976	SF-N	12	14	.462	32	31	8	4	0	186¹	171	10	61	130	11.3	3.62	100	.246	.309	9	.130	-3	0	0	-0	0.1
1977	SF-N	16	12	.571	37	37	7	2	0	257²	241	27	70	168	11.1	3.32	118	.244	.298	15	.176	3	17	17	-3	1.7
1978	SF-N	9	10	.474	29	28	9	4	1	199	166	11	45	105	9.9	2.85	121	.221	**.271**	9	.136	-1	16	13	0	0.8
1979	SF-N	5	8	.385	33	19	3	1	0	125²	134	12	47	81	13.2	4.58	76	.266	.333	7	.206	1	-12	-15	-1	-1.3
1980	SF-N	0	0	—	11	2	0	0	0	25	29	5	10	14	14.0	5.40	65	.293	.358	1	.167	-0	-5	-5	-0	0.0
	Cal-A	3	1	.750	10	6	0	0	0	35¹	39	5	11	16	12.7	4.84	81	.279	.331	0	—	-0	-3	-4	-1	-0.4
Total	7	55	66	.455	192	157	36	13	1	1063	1007	82	334	707	11.6	3.62	102	.247	.308	53	.165	-1	8	8	-7	1.1

● DREW HALL
Hall, Andrew Clark   b: 3/27/63, Louisville, Ky.   BL/TL, 6'4", 205 lbs.   Deb: 9/14/86

YEAR	TM/L	W	L	PCT	G	GS	CG	SH	SV	IP	H	HR	BB	SO	RAT	ERA	ERA+	OAV	OOB	BH	AVG	PB	PR	/A	PD	TPI
1986	Chi-N	1	2	.333	5	4	1	0	1	23²	24	3	10	21	12.9	4.56	89	.267	.340	1	.143	-0	-2	-1	-0	-0.2
1987	Chi-N	1	1	.500	21	6	0	0	0	32²	40	4	14	20	14.9	6.89	62	.308	.375	0	.000	-0	-10	-9	-0	-0.6
1988	Chi-N	1	1	.500	19	0	0	0	0	22¹	26	4	9	22	14.5	7.66	47	.295	.367	0	.000	-0	-10	-10	-0	-0.9
1989	Tex-A	2	1	.667	38	0	0	0	0	58¹	43	3	33	45	12.5	3.70	107	.207	.326	0	—	0	1	2	0	0.1
1990	Mon-N	4	7	.364	42	0	0	0	3	58¹	52	6	29	40	12.6	5.09	72	.242	.332	0	.000	-0	-8	-9	1	-1.7
Total	5	9	12	.429	125	4	1	0	4	195¹	184	20	95	148	13.0	5.21	75	.253	.343	1	.063	-1	-30	-29	-0	-3.3

● CHARLEY HALL
Hall, Charles Louis "Sea Lion" (b: Carlos Clolo)   b: 7/27/1885, Ventura, Cal.   d: 12/6/43, Ventura, Cal.   BL/TR, 6'1", 187 lbs.   Deb: 7/12/06

YEAR	TM/L	W	L	PCT	G	GS	CG	SH	SV	IP	H	HR	BB	SO	RAT	ERA	ERA+	OAV	OOB	BH	AVG	PB	PR	/A	PD	TPI
1906	Cin-N	4	8	.333	14	9	9	1	0	95	86	1	50	49	13.6	3.32	83	.258	.368	6	.128	-1	-7	-6	-0	-0.9
1907	Cin-N	4	2	.667	11	9	5	0	0	68	51	0	43	25	13.0	2.51	103	.226	.359	7	.269	1	-0	1	-0	0.1

YEAR	TM/L	W	L	PCT	G	GS	CG	SH	SV	IP	H	HR	BB	SO	RAT	ERA	ERA+	OAV	OOB	BH	AVG	PB	PR	/A	PD	TPI
1909	Bos-A	6	4	.600	11	7	3	0	0	59²	59	0	17	27	11.9	2.56	98	.271	.332	3	.158	-1	-1	-0	-0	-0.2
1910	Bos-A	12	9	.571	35	16	13	0	2	188²	142	6	73	95	10.7	1.91	134	.207	.292	17	.207	13	13	14	0	2.0
1911	Bos-A	8	7	.533	32	10	6	0	4	146¹	149	3	72	83	13.9	3.75	87	.279	.370	9	.141	-1	-7	-8	-2	-1.0
1912	*Bos-A	15	8	.652	34	20	9	2	2	191	178	3	70	83	11.9	3.02	113	.257	.329	20	.267	5	6	8	1	1.6
1913	Bos-A	5	4	.556	35	4	2	0	2	105	97	1	46	48	12.7	3.43	86	.235	.319	9	.214	1	-6	-6	-1	-0.5
1916	StL-N	0	4	.000	10	5	2	0	1	42²	45	1	14	15	12.4	5.48	48	.280	.337	2	.143	-1	-14	-13	-0	-1.3
1918	Det-A	0	1	.000	6	1	0	0	0	13¹	14	1	6	2	13.5	6.75	39	.269	.345	0	.000	-0	-6	-6	-0	-0.5
Total 9		54	47	.535	188	80	49	3	12	909²	821	16	391	427	12.4	3.09	95	.248	.334	73	.197	7	-21	-17	-2	-0.7

● **BERT HALL**   Hall, Herbert Ernest b: 10/15/1888, Portland, Ore. d: 7/18/48, Seattle, Wash. BR/TR, 5'10", 178 lbs. Deb: 8/21/11

YEAR	TM/L	W	L	PCT	G	GS	CG	SH	SV	IP	H	HR	BB	SO	RAT	ERA	ERA+	OAV	OOB	BH	AVG	PB	PR	/A	PD	TPI
1911	Phi-N	0	1	.000	7	1	0	0	0	19	19	0	13	8	16.5	4.00	86	.297	.423	1	.333	0	-1	-1	-1	-0.1

● **HERB HALL**   Hall, Herbert Silas "Iron Duke" b: 6/5/1893, Steeleville, Ill. d: 7/1/70, Fresno, Cal. BB/TR, 6'4", 220 lbs. Deb: 4/28/18

YEAR	TM/L	W	L	PCT	G	GS	CG	SH	SV	IP	H	HR	BB	SO	RAT	ERA	ERA+	OAV	OOB	BH	AVG	PB	PR	/A	PD	TPI
1918	Det-A	0	0		3	0	0	0	0	6	12	0	7	1	31.5	15.00	18	.500	.636	0	.000	-0	-8	-8	0	0.0

● **JOHN HALL**   Hall, John Sylvester b: 1/9/24, Muskogee, Okla. d: 1/17/95, Midwest City, Okla. BR/TR, 6'2.5", 170 lbs. Deb: 4/21/48

YEAR	TM/L	W	L	PCT	G	GS	CG	SH	SV	IP	H	HR	BB	SO	RAT	ERA	ERA+	OAV	OOB	BH	AVG	PB	PR	/A	PD	TPI
1948	Bro-N	0	0		3	0	0	0	0	4¹	4	1	2	2	12.5	6.23	64	.267	.353	0	—	0	-1	-1	0	0.0

● **MARC HALL**   Hall, Marcus b: 8/12/1887, Joplin, Mo. d: 2/24/15, Joplin, Mo. BR/TR, 6'1.5", 190 lbs. Deb: 8/20/10

YEAR	TM/L	W	L	PCT	G	GS	CG	SH	SV	IP	H	HR	BB	SO	RAT	ERA	ERA+	OAV	OOB	BH	AVG	PB	PR	/A	PD	TPI
1910	StL-A	1	7	.125	8	7	5	0	0	46¹	50	0	31	25	16.3	4.27	58	.289	.406	1	.067	-2	-9	-9	1	-1.5
1913	Det-A	10	12	.455	30	21	8	1	0	165	154	1	79	69	12.8	3.27	89	.255	.344	4	.089	-3	-6	-6	0	-1.1
1914	Det-A	4	6	.400	25	8	1	0	0	90¹	88	1	27	18	11.5	2.69	104	.267	.322	1	.043	-2	1	0	-0	-0.1
Total 3		15	25	.375	63	36	14	1	0	301²	292	2	137	112	12.9	3.25	87	.264	.348	6	.072	-7	-15	-15	1	-2.7

● **DARREN HALL**   Hall, Michael Darren b: 7/14/64, Marysville, Ohio BR/TR, 6'3", 205 lbs. Deb: 4/30/94

YEAR	TM/L	W	L	PCT	G	GS	CG	SH	SV	IP	H	HR	BB	SO	RAT	ERA	ERA+	OAV	OOB	BH	AVG	PB	PR	/A	PD	TPI
1994	Tor-A	2	3	.400	30	0	0	0	17	31²	26	3	14	28	11.7	3.41	141	.226	.315	0	—	0	5	5	1	1.2
1995	Tor-A	0	2	.000	17	0	0	0	3	16¹	21	2	9	11	16.5	4.41	107	.309	.390	0	—	0	1	1	-0	0.1
1996	LA-N	0	2	.000	9	0	0	0	0	12	13	2	5	12	13.5	6.00	64	.271	.340	0	—	0	-2	-3	-0	-0.4
Total 3		2	7	.222	56	0	0	0	20	60	60	7	28	51	13.4	4.20	109	.260	.342	0	—	0	3	3	0	0.9

● **DICK HALL**   Hall, Richard Wallace b: 9/27/30, St.Louis, Mo. BR/TR, 6'6", 200 lbs. Deb: 4/15/52 ♦

YEAR	TM/L	W	L	PCT	G	GS	CG	SH	SV	IP	H	HR	BB	SO	RAT	ERA	ERA+	OAV	OOB	BH	AVG	PB	PR	/A	PD	TPI
1955	Pit-N	6	6	.500	15	13	4	0	1	94¹	92	8	28	46	11.6	3.91	105	.253	.310	7	.175	1	1	2	-2	0.2
1956	Pit-N	0	7	.000	19	9	1	0	1	62¹	64	8	21	27	12.3	4.76	79	.270	.329	10	.345	2	-7	-7	-1	-0.5
1957	Pit-N	0	0	—	8	0	0	0	0	10	17	4	5	7	20.7	10.80	35	.362	.434	0	.000	-0	-8	-8	-0	-0.1
1959	Pit-N	0	1	.000	2	1	0	0	0	8²	12	1	1	3	13.5	3.12	124	.333	.351	0	.000	0	1	1	-0	0.0
1960	KC-A	8	13	.381	29	28	9	1	0	182¹	183	28	38	79	11.1	4.05	98	.261	.301	6	.107	-2	-4	-1	-1	-0.4
1961	Bal-A	7	5	.583	29	13	4	2	4	122¹	102	10	30	92	9.7	3.09	124	.227	.275	5	.139	-0	13	10	1	1.1
1962	Bal-A	6	6	.500	43	6	1	0	6	118¹	99	9	19	71	9.2	2.28	162	.230	.262	4	.167	1	22	19	-0	2.1
1963	Bal-A	5	5	.500	47	3	0	0	12	111²	91	12	16	74	8.9	2.98	116	.224	.260	13	.464	6	8	6	1	1.4
1964	Bal-A	9	1	.900	45	0	0	0	7	87²	58	8	16	52	7.6	1.85	193	.188	.228	2	.125	-0	17	17	-0	2.1
1965	Bal-A	11	8	.579	48	0	0	0	12	93²	84	8	11	79	9.1	3.07	113	.243	.266	5	.333	3	4	4	-1	1.0
1966	Bal-A	6	2	.750	32	0	0	0	7	66	59	8	8	44	9.5	3.95	84	.233	.265	2	.167	-0	-4	-5	-0	-0.6
1967	Phi-N	10	8	.556	48	1	1	0	8	86	83	5	12	49	10.2	2.20	155	.255	.286	1	.071	-1	11	12	1	2.7
1968	Phi-N	4	1	.800	32	0	0	0	0	46	53	6	5	31	11.5	4.89	61	.296	.319	1	.333	-1	-10	-10	-1	-1.1
1969	*Bal-A	5	2	.714	39	0	0	0	6	65²	49	3	9	31	8.1	1.92	186	.213	.246	2	.286	1	12	12	-1	1.5
1970	*Bal-A	10	5	.667	32	0	0	0	3	61¹	51	6	6	30	8.4	3.08	118	.229	.249	1	.083	-0	4	4	-1	0.7
1971	*Bal-A	6	6	.500	27	0	0	1	6	43¹	52	4	11	26	13.3	4.98	67	.302	.348	2	.400	1	-7	-8	-1	-2.1
Total 16		93	75	.554	495	74	20	3	68	1259²	1152	130	236	741	10.0	3.32	110	.244	.283	150	.210	10	55	48	-7	8.0

● **BOB HALL**   Hall, Robert Lewis b: 12/22/23, Swissvale, Pa. d: 3/12/83, St.Petersburg, Fla BR/TR, 6'2", 195 lbs. Deb: 4/23/49

YEAR	TM/L	W	L	PCT	G	GS	CG	SH	SV	IP	H	HR	BB	SO	RAT	ERA	ERA+	OAV	OOB	BH	AVG	PB	PR	/A	PD	TPI
1949	Bos-N	6	4	.600	31	6	2	0	0	74¹	77	7	41	43	14.4	4.36	87	.272	.366	8	.364	3	-3	-5	-2	-0.5
1950	Bos-N	0	2	.000	21	4	0	0	0	50¹	58	8	33	22	16.6	6.97	55	.293	.399	1	.083	-1	-16	-17	-0	-0.7
1953	Pit-N	3	12	.200	37	17	6	1	1	152	172	17	72	68	14.5	5.39	83	.286	.364	6	.158	0	-19	-15	-1	-1.4
Total 3		9	18	.333	89	27	8	1	1	276²	307	32	146	133	14.9	5.40	77	.284	.371	15	.208	2	-37	-38	-3	-2.6

● **TOM HALL**   Hall, Tom Edward b: 11/23/47, Thomasville, N.C. BL/TL, 6', 155 lbs. Deb: 6/9/68

YEAR	TM/L	W	L	PCT	G	GS	CG	SH	SV	IP	H	HR	BB	SO	RAT	ERA	ERA+	OAV	OOB	BH	AVG	PB	PR	/A	PD	TPI
1968	Min-A	2	1	.667	8	4	0	0	0	29²	27	1	12	18	12.1	2.43	127	.239	.317	0	.000	-1	2	2	-0	0.1
1969	*Min-A	8	7	.533	31	18	5	2	0	140²	129	12	50	92	11.5	3.33	110	.243	.308	8	.186	1	5	5	-2	0.4
1970	*Min-A	11	6	.647	52	11	1	0	4	155²	94	11	66	184	9.4	2.55	146	.173	.265	8	.182	-0	20	20	-2	1.9
1971	Min-A	4	7	.364	48	11	0	0	9	129²	104	13	58	137	11.2	3.33	107	.216	.300	9	.265	2	2	3	1	0.6
1972	*Cin-N	10	1	.909	47	7	1	1	8	124¹	77	13	56	134	9.8	2.61	123	.173	.269	3	.100	-1	12	8	-2	0.6
1973	*Cin-N	8	5	.615	54	7	0	0	8	103²	74	13	48	96	10.6	3.47	98	.202	.295	1	.045	-2	2	-1	-2	-0.3
1974	Cin-N	3	1	.750	40	1	0	0	0	64	54	9	30	48	11.8	4.08	86	.232	.319	0	.000	-1	-3	-4	-0	-0.3
1975	Cin-N	0	0	—	2	0	0	0	0	2	2	0	2	3	18.0	0.00	—	.250	.400	0	—	0	1	1	0	0.0
	NY-N	4	3	.571	34	4	0	0	1	60²	58	10	31	48	13.6	4.75	73	.254	.351	2	.400	1	-8	-9	-0	-0.9
	Yr	4	3	.571	36	4	0	0	1	62²	60	10	33	51	13.8	4.60	75	.254	.353	2	.400	1	-7	-8	-0	-0.9
1976	NY-N	1	1	.500	5	0	0	0	0	4²	5	0	5	2	19.3	5.79	57	.250	.400	0	—	0	-1	-1	0	-0.5
	*KC-A	1	1	.500	31	0	0	0	2	30¹	28	4	18	25	13.6	4.45	79	.246	.348	0	—	0	-3	-3	1	-0.2
1977	KC-A	0	0	—	6	0	0	0	0	7²	4	2	6	10	11.7	3.52	115	.154	.313	0	—	0	0	0	0	0.0
Total 10		52	33	.612	358	63	7	3	32	852²	656	88	382	797	11.0	3.27	107	.211	.299	31	.161	-4	28	22	-8	1.2

● **BILL HALL**   Hall, William Bernard "Beanie" b: 2/22/1894, Charleston, W.Va. d: 8/15/47, Newport, Ky. BR/TR, 6'2", 250 lbs. Deb: 7/4/13

YEAR	TM/L	W	L	PCT	G	GS	CG	SH	SV	IP	H	HR	BB	SO	RAT	ERA	ERA+	OAV	OOB	BH	AVG	PB	PR	/A	PD	TPI
1913	Bro-N	0	0		3	0	0	0	0	4²	4	1	3	2	15.9	5.79	57	.267	.476	0	.000	-1	-1	-1	1	0.0

● **JOHN HALLA**   Halla, John Arthur b: 5/13/1884, St.Louis, Mo. d: 9/30/47, ElSegundo, Cal. BL/TL, 5'11", 175 lbs. Deb: 8/18/05

YEAR	TM/L	W	L	PCT	G	GS	CG	SH	SV	IP	H	HR	BB	SO	RAT	ERA	ERA+	OAV	OOB	BH	AVG	PB	PR	/A	PD	TPI
1905	Cle-A	0	0	—	3	0	0	0	0	12²	12	0	4	4	9.2	2.84	92	.250	.265	1	.200	-0	-0	-0	-0	0.0

● **BILL HALLAHAN**   Hallahan, William Anthony "Wild Bill" b: 8/4/02, Binghamton, N.Y. d: 7/8/81, Binghamton, N.Y. BR/TL, 5'10.5", 170 lbs. Deb: 4/16/25

YEAR	TM/L	W	L	PCT	G	GS	CG	SH	SV	IP	H	HR	BB	SO	RAT	ERA	ERA+	OAV	OOB	BH	AVG	PB	PR	/A	PD	TPI
1925	StL-N	1	0	1.000	6	0	0	0	0	15¹	14	0	11	8	14.7	3.52	123	.259	.385	1	.333	0	1	1	0	0.1
1926	*StL-N	1	4	.200	19	3	0	0	0	56²	45	1	32	28	12.4	3.65	107	.260	.379	4	.250	-1	**1**	**2**	-1	0.1
1929	StL-N	4	4	.500	20	12	5	0	0	93²	94	6	60	52	14.8	4.42	106	.269	.376	4	.154	-1	3	3	-1	0.2
1930	*StL-N	15	9	.625	35	32	13	2	2	237¹	233	15	126	**177**	13.6	4.66	108	.260	.351	10	.123	-6	8	9	-0	0.2
1931	*StL-N	**19**	9	.679	37	30	16	3	4	248²	242	10	112	**159**	12.8	3.29	120	.259	.339	8	.099	-4	16	18	-2	1.2
1932	StL-N	12	7	.632	25	22	13	1	1	176¹	169	10	69	108	12.1	3.11	129	.253	.323	12	.214	-2	15	16	-1	1.7
1933	StL-N★	16	13	.552	36	32	16	2	0	244¹	245	8	89	93	12.6	3.50	99	.260	.330	12	.150	-0	-4	-1	-3	-0.5
1934	*StL-N	8	12	.400	32	26	10	2	0	162²	195	2	66	70	14.4	4.26	99	.294	.358	10	.182	-1	-4	-1	-0	-0.2
1935	StL-N	15	8	.652	40	23	8	2	1	181¹	196	7	57	73	12.6	3.42	120	.275	.329	8	.143	-2	12	14	-1	1.3
1936	StL-N	2	2	.500	9	6	1	0	0	37	58	4	17	16	18.2	6.32	62	.360	.421	5	.556	3	-9	-10	0	-0.6
	Cin-N	5	9	.357	23	19	5	2	0	135	150	3	57	32	13.9	4.33	88	.287	.359	9	.191	1	-5	-8	1	-0.5
	Yr	7	11	.389	32	25	6	2	0	172	208	7	74	48	14.8	4.76	81	.305	.373	14	.250	3	-14	-17	1	-1.1
1937	Cin-N	3	9	.250	21	9	2	0	0	63	90	3	29	18	17.3	6.14	61	.345	.414	2	.095	-1	-16	-17	0	-2.7
1938	Phi-N	1	8	.111	21	10	1	0	0	89	107	4	45	22	15.6	5.46	71	.295	.376	3	.192	-0	-17	-16	-1	-1.4
Total 12		102	94	.520	324	224	90	14	8	1740¹	1838	71	779	856	13.6	4.03	102	.274	.351	90	.162	-9	12	17	-6	-1.1

● **JACK HALLETT**   Hallett, Jack Price b: 11/13/14, Toledo, Ohio d: 6/11/82, Toledo, Ohio BR/TR, 6'4", 215 lbs. Deb: 9/13/40

YEAR	TM/L	W	L	PCT	G	GS	CG	SH	SV	IP	H	HR	BB	SO	RAT	ERA	ERA+	OAV	OOB	BH	AVG	PB	PR	/A	PD	TPI
1940	Chi-A	1	1	.500	2	1	1	0	0	14	15	1	9	4	14.1	6.43	69	.273	.355	2	.400	0	-3	-3	0	-0.3
1941	Chi-A	5	5	.500	22	6	3	0	0	74²	96	7	38	25	16.5	6.03	68	.306	.386	4	.154	0	-16	-16	0	-1.8
1942	Pit-N	0	0		3	2	0	0	0	22¹	22	2	6	5	12.5	4.84	70	.274	.337	2	.375	2	-4	-4	0	0.0
1943	Pit-N	1	2	.333	9	4	2	1	0	47²	36	0	11	11	9.1	1.70	205	.212	.264	4	.286	2	9	9	-1	0.7
1946	Pit-N	5	7	.417	35	9	3	1	0	115	107	6	39	64	11.4	3.29	107	.267	.332	6	.231	0	2	3	0	0.4
1948	NY-N	0	0	—	2	0	0	0	0	4²	4	1	3	4	15.8	4.50	87	.214	.389	0	.000	-0	-0	-0	-0	0.0
Total 6		12	16	.429	73	24	11	2	0	277²	280	8	106	128	12.7	4.05	92	.270	.340	19	.237	4	-12	-10	-1	-1.0

YEAR TM/L	W	L	PCT	G	GS	CG	SH	SV	IP	H	HR	BB	SO	RAT	ERA	ERA+	OAV	OOB	BH	AVG	PB	PR	/A	PD	TPI
● BILL HALLMAN Hallman, William Wilson b: 3/31/1867, Pittsburgh, Pa. d: 9/11/20, Philadelphia, Pa. BR/TR, 5'8", 160 lbs. Deb: 4/23/1888 M♦																								
1896 Phi-N	0	0	—	1	0	0	0	0	2	4	0	2	0	27.0	18.00	24	.400	.500	150	.320	0	-3	-3	-0	0.0
● CHARLIE HALLSTROM Hallstrom, Charles E. "Swedish Wonder" b: 1/22/1864, Jonkoping, Sweden d: 5/6/49, Chicago, Ill. Deb: 9/23/1885																								
1885 Pro-N	0	1	.000	1	1	1	0	0	9	18	3	6	0	24.0	11.00	24	.409	.480	0	.000	-1	-8	-8	-0	-0.6
● DOC HAMANN Hamann, Elmer Joseph b: 12/21/1900, New Ulm, Minn. d: 1/11/73, Milwaukee, Wis. BR/TR, 6'1", 180 lbs. Deb: 9/21/22																								
1922 Cle-A	0	0	—	1	0	0	0	0	0	3	0	3	0	∞	∞	—	1.000	1.000	0	—	0	-6	-6	-0	-0.5
● ROGER HAMBRIGHT Hambright, Roger Dee b: 3/26/49, Sunnyside, Wash. BR/TR, 5'10", 180 lbs. Deb: 7/19/71																								
1971 NY-A	3	1	.750	18	0	0	0	2	26²	22	5	10	14	10.8	4.39	74	.224	.296	1	.500	0	-3	-3	-0	-0.5
● JOHN HAMILL Hamill, John Alexander Charles b: 12/18/1860, New York, N.Y. d: 12/6/11, Bristol, R.I. BR/TR, 5'8", 158 lbs. Deb: 5/1/1884																								
1884 Was-a	2	17	.105	19	19	18	1	0	156²	197	8	43	50	14.1	4.48	68	.287	.333	7	.099	-3	-21	-25	-1	-2.6
● DAVE HAMILTON Hamilton, David Edward b: 12/13/47, Seattle, Wash. BL/TL, 6', 190 lbs. Deb: 5/29/72																								
1972 *Oak-A	6	6	.500	25	14	1	0	0	101²	94	7	31	55	11.2	2.93	97	.249	.307	4	.154	2	1	-1	-0	0.1
1973 Oak-A	6	4	.600	16	11	1	0	0	69²	74	8	24	34	12.8	4.39	81	.274	.336	0	—	0	-4	-7	-1	-0.8
1974 Oak-A	7	4	.636	29	18	1	1	0	117	104	10	48	69	12.1	3.15	105	.241	.324	0	—	0	6	2	-0	0.1
1975 Oak-A	1	2	.333	11	4	0	0	0	35²	42	4	18	20	15.1	4.04	90	.290	.368	0	—	0	-1	-2	-0	-0.1
Chi-A	6	5	.545	30	1	0	0	6	69²	63	4	29	51	11.9	2.84	136	.246	.323	1	—	0	7	8	0	1.3
Yr	7	7	.500	41	5	0	0	6	105¹	105	8	47	71	13.0	3.25	117	.261	.339	1	—	0	6	6	0	1.2
1976 Chi-A	6	6	.500	45	1	0	0	10	90¹	81	8	45	62	13.0	3.59	99	.243	.340	0	—	-1	-0	-1	0	-0.1
1977 Chi-A	4	5	.444	55	0	0	0	9	67¹	71	6	33	45	13.9	3.61	113	.267	.351	0	—	0	3	4	0	0.5
1978 StL-N	0	0	—	13	0	0	0	0	14	16	5	6	8	14.1	6.43	55	.296	.367	0	.000	-0	-4	-5	0	0.0
Pit-N	0	2	.000	16	0	0	0	1	26¹	23	2	12	15	12.0	3.42	108	.221	.302	0	.000	-1	0	1	-0	0.0
Yr	0	2	.000	29	0	0	0	1	40¹	39	7	18	23	12.7	4.46	81	.247	.324	0	.000	-1	-4	-4	-0	0.0
1979 Oak-A	3	4	.429	40	7	1	0	5	82²	80	5	43	52	13.5	3.70	109	.261	.353	0	—	0	5	3	1	0.4
1980 Oak-A	0	3	.000	21	1	0	0	0	30	44	6	28	23	22.5	11.40	33	.344	.472	0	—	0	-25	-25	-0	-2.2
Total 9	39	41	.488	301	57	4	1	31	704	692	61	317	434	13.1	3.85	93	.259	.341	4	.121	1	-12	-22	-2	-0.7
● EARL HAMILTON Hamilton, Earl Andrew b: 7/19/1891, Gibson City, Ill. d: 11/17/68, Anaheim, Cal. BL/TL, 5'8", 160 lbs. Deb: 4/14/11																								
1911 StL-A	5	12	.294	32	17	10	1	0	177	191	4	69	55	13.4	3.97	85	.284	.354	6	.107	-1	-12	-12	1	-1.0
1912 StL-A	11	14	.440	41	26	17	1	2	249²	228	3	86	139	11.6	3.24	102	.248	.319	13	.178	-0	2	2	-2	0.1
1913 StL-A	13	12	.520	31	24	19	3	1	217¹	197	3	83	101	12.0	2.57	114	.241	.318	10	.135	-2	9	9	-1	0.7
1914 StL-A	17	18	.486	44	35	20	5	2	302¹	265	5	100	111	11.2	2.50	108	.239	.307	15	.176	4	8	7	-4	0.8
1915 StL-A	9	17	.346	35	27	13	1	0	204	203	4	69	63	12.5	2.87	100	.274	.346	7	.113	-1	2	-0	-2	-0.4
1916 StL-A	0	0	—	1	0	0	0	0	4	4	0	4	0	18.0	9.00	31	.250	.400	0	—	0	-3	-3	-0	-0.3
Det-A	1	2	.333	5	5	3	0	0	37¹	34	0	22	7	14.5	2.65	108	.254	.375	1	.077	-1	1	1	0	0.1
StL-A	5	7	.417	22	12	3	0	0	91¹	97	2	26	25	12.3	3.05	90	.284	.339	0	.000	-1	-2	-3	-1	-0.7
Yr	6	9	.400	28	17	6	0	0	132²	135	2	52	32	12.8	3.12	89	.273	.344	1	.027	-2	-4	-5	-1	-0.6
1917 StL-A	0	9	.000	27	8	2	0	1	83	86	1	41	19	14.0	3.14	83	.274	.361	7	.368	3	-4	-5	-1	-0.3
1918 Pit-N	6	0	1.000	6	6	6	1	0	54	47	0	13	20	10.0	0.83	345	.242	.290	6	.286	1	12	12	-0	1.7
1919 Pit-N	8	11	.421	28	19	9	1	1	160¹	167	3	49	39	12.4	3.31	91	.280	.340	7	.135	-2	-7	-5	2	-0.7
1920 Pit-N	10	13	.435	39	23	12	0	3	230¹	223	2	69	74	11.5	3.24	99	.258	.314	10	.149	-3	-1	-0	-0	-0.4
1921 Pit-N	13	15	.464	35	30	12	2	0	225	237	5	58	59	12.1	3.36	114	.272	.323	12	.160	-0	11	12	4	1.6
1922 Pit-N	11	7	.611	33	14	9	1	2	160	183	6	40	34	12.6	3.99	102	.296	.339	9	.155	-2	2	1	-1	-0.1
1923 Pit-N	7	9	.438	28	15	5	0	1	141	148	6	42	42	12.2	3.77	106	.271	.324	9	.173	-2	4	4	2	0.5
1924 Phi-N	0	1	.000	3	0	0	0	0	6	9	0	2	2	18.0	10.50	42	.391	.462	0	.000	-0	-4	-4	0	-0.6
Total 14	116	147	.441	410	261	140	16	13	2342²	2319	43	773	790	12.1	3.16	102	.264	.329	112	.153	-9	13	15	-4	1.3
● JACK HAMILTON Hamilton, Jack Edwin b: 12/25/38, Burlington, Iowa BR/TR, 6', 200 lbs. Deb: 4/13/62																								
1962 Phi-N	9	12	.429	41	26	4	1	2	182	185	18	107	101	14.7	5.09	76	.264	.370	3	.056	-4	-23	-25	2	-2.7
1963 Phi-N	2	1	.667	19	1	0	0	1	30	22	3	17	23	11.7	5.40	60	.200	.307	0	.000	-0	-7	-7	1	-0.7
1964 Det-A	0	1	.000	5	1	0	0	0	15	24	2	8	5	19.8	8.40	44	.364	.440	0	.000	-0	-8	-8	1	-0.5
1965 Det-A	1	1	.500	4	1	0	0	0	4¹	6	1	4	3	20.8	14.54	24	.316	.435	0	—	0	-5	-5	0	-1.8
1966 NY-N	6	13	.316	57	13	3	1	13	148²	138	13	88	93	14.0	3.93	92	.248	.356	5	.132	-1	-5	-5	1	-0.7
1967 NY-N	2	0	1.000	17	1	0	0	1	31¹	24	2	16	22	11.8	3.73	91	.205	.306	1	.200	1	-1	-1	0	-0.2
Cal-A	9	6	.600	26	20	0	0	1	119¹	104	6	63	74	12.7	3.24	97	.239	.337	6	.158	-0	4	3	0	-0.2
1968 Cal-A	3	1	.750	21	2	1	0	2	38	34	0	15	18	11.6	3.32	88	.246	.320	1	.143	0	1	0	0	-0.2
1969 Cle-A	0	2	.000	20	0	0	0	1	30²	37	3	23	13	17.6	4.40	86	.316	.429	0	.000	-0	-3	-2	0	-0.2
Chi-A	0	3	.000	8	0	0	0	0	12¹	23	1	7	5	21.9	11.68	33	.411	.476	0	—	0	-11	-11	-0	-2.1
Yr	0	5	.000	28	0	0	0	1	43	60	4	30	18	18.8	6.49	56	.345	.441	0	.000	-0	-14	-13	-0	-2.3
Total 8	32	40	.444	218	65	8	2	20	611²	597	48	348	357	14.1	4.53	78	.259	.359	16	.107	-6	-66	-67	4	-9.1
● JEFF HAMILTON Hamilton, Jeffrey Robert b: 3/19/64, Flint, Mich. BR/TR, 6'3", 207 lbs. Deb: 6/28/86 ♦																								
1989 LA-N	0	1	.000	1	0	0	0	0	1²	2	0	1	2	16.2	5.40	63	.286	.375	134	.245	0	-0	-0	0	-0.2
● JOEY HAMILTON Hamilton, Johns Joseph b: 9/9/70, Statesboro, Ga. BR/TR, 6'4", 220 lbs. Deb: 5/24/94																								
1994 SD-N	9	6	.600	16	16	1	1	0	108²	98	7	29	61	11.0	2.98	138	.241	.302	0	.000	-4	15	14	0	1.4
1995 SD-N	6	9	.400	31	30	2	2	0	204¹	189	17	56	123	11.3	3.08	131	.246	.307	7	.108	-2	25	21	-1	1.2
1996 *SD-N	15	9	.625	34	33	3	1	0	211²	206	19	83	184	12.7	4.17	96	.256	.332	11	.162	1	1	-4	-0	-0.3
Total 3	30	24	.556	81	79	6	4	0	524²	493	43	168	368	11.8	3.50	115	.249	.316	18	.104	-4	41	31	-0	2.3
● STEVE HAMILTON Hamilton, Steve Absher b: 11/30/35, Columbia, Ky. BL/TL, 6'7", 195 lbs. Deb: 4/23/61 C																								
1961 Cle-A	0	0	—	2	0	0	0	0	3	2	0	3	4	15.0	3.00	137	.200	.385	1	1.000	0	0	0	0	0.1
1962 Was-A	3	8	.273	41	10	1	0	1	107¹	103	10	39	83	12.2	3.77	107	.248	.317	2	.077	-1	2	3	1	0.3
1963 Was-A	0	1	.000	3	0	0	0	0	2	5	0	2	1	31.5	13.50	27	.556	.636	0	—	0	-2	-2	0	-0.9
*NY-A	5	1	.833	34	0	0	0	0	62¹	49	3	24	63	10.7	2.60	135	.220	.298	4	.286	1	7	6	1	0.9
Yr	5	2	.714	37	0	0	0	0	64¹	54	3	26	64	11.3	2.94	120	.232	.312	4	.286	1	5	4	1	0.4
1964 *NY-A	7	2	.778	30	3	1	0	3	60¹	55	6	15	49	10.4	3.28	110	.246	.293	4	.200	1	2	2	0	0.4
1965 NY-A	3	1	.750	46	1	0	0	5	58¹	47	2	16	51	9.7	1.39	136	.214	.267	1	.167	0	13	13	-2	1.0
1966 NY-A	8	3	.727	44	0	0	1	3	90	69	8	22	57	9.4	3.00	111	.218	.276	1	.053	-2	4	3	-1	0.1
1967 NY-A	2	4	.333	44	0	0	0	5	62	57	7	23	54	11.8	3.48	90	.250	.321	1	.111	-0	-2	-2	-0	-0.3
1968 NY-A	2	2	.500	40	0	0	0	11	50²	37	0	13	42	9.1	2.13	136	.211	.270	0	.000	-0	5	5	0	0.7
1969 NY-A	3	4	.429	38	0	0	0	2	57	39	7	21	39	9.5	3.32	105	.194	.270	1	.000	-1	2	1	-0	-0.1
1970 NY-A	4	3	.571	35	0	0	0	3	45¹	36	3	16	33	10.5	2.78	126	.222	.296	0	.000	-1	5	4	0	0.5
Chi-A	0	0	—	3	0	0	0	0	3	4	0	1	3	15.0	6.00	55	.333	.385	0	—	0	-1	-1	0	0.0
Yr	4	3	.571	38	0	0	0	3	48¹	40	3	17	36	10.6	2.98	119	.227	.295	0	.000	-1	4	3	0	0.5
1971 *SF-N	2	2	.500	39	0	0	0	4	44²	29	4	11	38	8.3	3.02	112	.186	.244	0	—	0	2	2	-0	0.1
1972 Chi-N	1	0	1.000	22	0	0	0	2	17	24	1	8	13	17.5	4.76	80	.333	.407	0	—	0	-2	-2	-0	-0.1
Total 12	40	31	.563	421	17	3	1	42	663	556	51	214	531	10.6	3.05	114	.229	.295	14	.125	-2	36	32	-1	2.7
● LUKE HAMLIN Hamlin, Luke Daniel "Hot Potato" b: 7/3/04, Ferris Center, Mich. d: 2/18/78, Clare, Mich. BL/TR, 6'2", 168 lbs. Deb: 9/18/33																								
1933 Det-A	1	0	1.000	3	3	0	0	0	16²	20	3	10	10	16.2	4.86	89	.294	.385	2	.400	1	-1	-1	-1	0.0
1934 Det-A	2	3	.400	20	5	1	0	1	75¹	87	11	44	30	15.7	5.38	82	.289	.380	6	.231	-0	-7	-8	-0	-0.5
1937 Bro-N	11	13	.458	39	25	11	1	1	185²	183	6	48	93	11.2	3.59	113	.252	.298	11	.186	-1	7	9	-3	0.7
1938 Bro-N	12	15	.444	44	30	10	3	6	237¹	243	6	65	97	11.8	3.68	106	.263	.313	11	.141	-3	3	6	-4	0.0
1939 Bro-N	20	13	.606	40	35	20	3	1	269²	255	27	54	88	10.3	3.64	111	.248	.285	13	.126	-5	8	12	-5	0.4
1940 Bro-N	9	8	.529	33	25	9	2	0	182¹	186	17	34	91	10.8	3.06	131	.256	.292	5	.086	-4	16	19	-4	0.8
1941 Bro-N	8	8	.500	30	20	5	1	1	136	139	14	41	58	12.0	4.24	87	.261	.316	6	.146	-1	-9	-9	-2	-1.2

YEAR TM/L	W	L	PCT	G	GS	CG	SH	SV	IP	H	HR	BB	SO	RAT	ERA	ERA+	OAV	OOB	BH	AVG	PB	PR	/A	PD	TPI
1942 Pit-N	4	4	.500	23	14	6	1	0	112	128	3	19	38	11.9	3.94	86	.281	.312	9	.243	1	-8	-7	-2	-0.6
1944 Phi-A	6	12	.333	29	23	9	0	0	190	204	13	38	58	11.6	3.74	93	.271	.309	13	.232	3	-7	-6	-5	-0.7
Total 9	73	76	.490	261	181	70	12	9	1405	1442	106	353	563	11.6	3.77	103	.262	.308	76	.164	-8	2	16	-25	-1.1

● **PETE HAMM**   Hamm, Peter Whitfield b: 9/20/47, Buffalo, N.Y. BR/TR, 6'5", 210 lbs. Deb: 7/29/70

YEAR TM/L	W	L	PCT	G	GS	CG	SH	SV	IP	H	HR	BB	SO	RAT	ERA	ERA+	OAV	OOB	BH	AVG	PB	PR	/A	PD	TPI
1970 Min-A	0	2	.000	10	0	0	0	0	16¹	17	3	7	3	13.2	5.51	68	.262	.333	0	.000	-0	-3	-3	-1	-0.4
1971 Min-A	2	4	.333	13	8	1	0	0	44	55	7	18	16	15.1	6.75	53	.309	.376	3	.273	1	-16	-16	0	-1.8
Total 2	2	6	.250	23	8	1	0	0	60¹	72	10	25	19	14.6	6.41	56	.296	.364	3	.250	1	-19	-19	-0	-2.2

● **ATLEE HAMMAKER**   Hammaker, Charlton Atlee b: 1/24/58, Carmel, Cal. BB/TL, 6'3", 200 lbs. Deb: 8/13/81

YEAR TM/L	W	L	PCT	G	GS	CG	SH	SV	IP	H	HR	BB	SO	RAT	ERA	ERA+	OAV	OOB	BH	AVG	PB	PR	/A	PD	TPI
1981 KC-A	1	3	.250	10	6	0	0	0	39	44	2	12	11	12.9	5.54	65	.286	.337	0	—	-0	-8	-8	-1	-0.8
1982 SF-N	12	8	.600	29	27	4	1	0	175	189	16	28	102	11.3	4.11	87	.278	.309	4	.068	-4	-10	-10	1	-1.4
1983 SF-N★	10	9	.526	23	23	8	3	0	172¹	147	9	32	127	**9.5**	**2.25**	**157**	**.228**	**.267**	6	.102	-1	26	25	1	2.7
1984 SF-N	2	0	1.000	6	6	0	0	0	33	32	2	9	24	11.2	2.18	161	.256	.306	2	.182	1	5	5	0	0.4
1985 SF-N	5	12	.294	29	29	1	1	0	170²	161	17	47	100	11.0	3.74	92	.247	.298	4	.085	-3	-3	-6	1	-0.7
1987 *SF-N	10	10	.500	31	27	2	0	0	168¹	159	22	57	107	11.7	3.58	107	.248	.313	7	.123	-1	9	5	-1	0.3
1988 SF-N	9	9	.500	43	17	3	1	5	144²	136	11	41	65	11.2	3.73	87	.248	.304	4	.121	-1	-5	-8	2	-0.3
1989 *SF-N	6	6	.500	28	9	0	0	0	76²	78	5	23	30	12.0	3.76	90	.271	.327	7	.368	2	-2	-5	1	-0.3
1990	4	5	.444	25	6	0	0	0	67¹	69	7	21	28	12.0	4.28	85	.273	.328	1	.059	-1	-4	-5	-1	-0.7
SD-N	0	4	.000	9	1	0	0	0	19¹	16	1	6	16	10.2	4.66	82	.213	.272	1	.500	-0	-2	-2	-0	-0.3
Yr	4	9	.308	34	7	0	0	0	86²	85	8	27	44	11.6	4.36	84	.256	.312	2	.105	-1	-5	-7	-1	-1.0
1991 SD-N	0	1	.000	1	1	0	0	0	4²	8	0	3	1	21.2	5.79	66	.364	.440	0	.000	-1	-1	0	0	-0.2
1994 Chi-A	0	0	—	2	0	0	0	0	1¹	1	0	0	1	6.8	0.00	—	.200	.200	0	—	-0	1	1	0	0.3
1995 Chi-A	0	0	—	13	0	0	0	0	6¹	11	2	8	3	28.4	12.79	35	.393	.541	0	—	-0	-6	-6	0	0.3
Total 12	59	67	.468	249	152	18	6	5	1078²	1051	94	287	615	11.3	3.66	97	.255	.306	36	.118	-7	1	-13	1	-1.5

● **CHRIS HAMMOND**   Hammond, Christopher Andrew b: 1/21/66, Atlanta, Ga. BL/TL, 6'1", 190 lbs. Deb: 7/16/90

YEAR TM/L	W	L	PCT	G	GS	CG	SH	SV	IP	H	HR	BB	SO	RAT	ERA	ERA+	OAV	OOB	BH	AVG	PB	PR	/A	PD	TPI
1990 Cin-N	0	2	.000	3	3	0	0	0	11¹	13	2	12	4	19.9	6.35	62	.302	.455	0	.000	-0	-3	-3	0	-0.5
1991 Cin-N	7	7	.500	20	18	0	0	0	99²	92	4	48	50	12.8	4.06	94	.250	.340	12	.353	5	-4	-3	0	0.1
1992 Cin-N	7	10	.412	28	26	0	0	0	147¹	149	13	55	79	12.6	4.21	85	.266	.334	6	.136	2	-12	-10	-0	-0.9
1993 Fla-N	11	12	.478	32	32	1	0	0	191	207	18	66	108	12.9	4.66	93	.277	.337	12	.190	4	-13	-7	-0	-0.3
1994 Fla-N	4	4	.500	13	13	1	1	0	73¹	79	5	23	40	12.6	3.07	142	.281	.338	3	.136	0	9	11	-2	0.9
1995 Fla-N	9	6	.600	25	24	3	2	0	161	157	17	47	126	11.9	3.80	111	.256	.318	13	.271	6	7	7	-0	1.2
1996 Fla-N	5	8	.385	38	9	0	0	0	81	104	14	27	50	15.0	6.56	62	.315	.374	1	.067	-1	-21	-23	-0	-3.1
Total 7	43	49	.467	159	125	5	3	0	764²	801	73	278	457	12.9	4.39	93	.272	.339	47	.205	16	-37	-28	-1	-2.6

● **GRANNY HAMNER**   Hamner, Granville Wilbur b: 4/26/27, Richmond, Va. d: 9/12/93, Philadelphia, Pa. BR/TR, 5'10", 163 lbs. Deb: 9/14/44 F◆

YEAR TM/L	W	L	PCT	G	GS	CG	SH	SV	IP	H	HR	BB	SO	RAT	ERA	ERA+	OAV	OOB	BH	AVG	PB	PR	/A	PD	TPI
1956 Phi-N	0	1	.000	3	1	0	0	0	8¹	10	2	4	4	13.0	4.32	86	.294	.333	90	.224	1	-1	-1	-0	0.0
1957 Phi-N	0	0	—	1	0	0	0	0	1	1	0	0	1	9.0	0.00	—	.250	.250	114	.227	0	0	0	0	0.0
1962 KC-A	0	1	.000	3	0	0	0	0	4	10	0	6	0	36.0	9.00	47	.476	.593	0	—	0	-2	-2	0	-0.4
Total 3	0	2	.000	7	1	0	0	0	13¹	21	2	10	5	19.6	5.40	72	.356	.433	1529	.262	1	-2	-2	-0	-0.4

● **RALPH HAMNER**   Hamner, Ralph Conant "Bruz" b: 9/12/16, Gibsland, La. BR/TR, 6'3", 165 lbs. Deb: 4/28/46

YEAR TM/L	W	L	PCT	G	GS	CG	SH	SV	IP	H	HR	BB	SO	RAT	ERA	ERA+	OAV	OOB	BH	AVG	PB	PR	/A	PD	TPI
1946 Chi-A	2	7	.222	25	7	1	0	1	71¹	80	2	39	29	15.6	4.42	77	.276	.371	3	.167	-0	-7	-8	-1	-1.0
1947 Chi-N	1	2	.333	3	3	2	0	0	25	24	0	16	14	14.4	2.52	157	.267	.377	1	.125	-0	4	4	-1	0.4
1948 Chi-N	5	9	.357	27	17	5	0	0	111¹	110	12	69	53	14.9	4.69	83	.259	.369	6	.182	1	-9	-10	2	-0.8
1949 Chi-N	0	2	.000	6	1	0	0	0	12¹	22	1	8	3	22.6	8.76	46	.407	.492	0	.000	-0	-6	-6	1	-0.8
Total 4	8	20	.286	61	28	8	0	1	220	236	15	132	99	15.5	4.58	82	.275	.378	10	.164	-0	-18	-20	1	-2.2

● **MIKE HAMPTON**   Hampton, Michael William b: 9/9/72, Brooksville, Fla. BR/TL, 5'10", 180 lbs. Deb: 4/17/93

YEAR TM/L	W	L	PCT	G	GS	CG	SH	SV	IP	H	HR	BB	SO	RAT	ERA	ERA+	OAV	OOB	BH	AVG	PB	PR	/A	PD	TPI
1993 Sea-A	1	3	.250	13	3	0	0	0	17	28	3	17	8	23.8	9.53	46	.368	.484	0	—	0	-10	-10	-0	-2.0
1994 Hou-N	2	1	.667	44	0	0	0	0	41¹	46	4	16	24	13.9	3.70	107	.282	.354	0	.000	-0	2	1	2	0.2
1995 Hou-N	9	8	.529	24	24	0	0	0	150²	141	13	49	115	11.6	3.35	116	.247	.310	7	.146	1	14	9	0	1.0
1996 Hou-N	10	10	.500	27	27	2	1	0	160¹	175	12	49	101	12.7	3.59	106	.280	.335	10	.238	4	11	4	2	1.1
Total 4	22	22	.500	108	54	2	1	0	369¹	390	32	131	248	12.9	3.78	103	.271	.336	17	.187	4	18	4	4	0.3

● **LEE HANCOCK**   Hancock, Leland David b: 6/27/67, N.Hollywood, Cal. BL/TL, 6'4", 215 lbs. Deb: 9/3/95

YEAR TM/L	W	L	PCT	G	GS	CG	SH	SV	IP	H	HR	BB	SO	RAT	ERA	ERA+	OAV	OOB	BH	AVG	PB	PR	/A	PD	TPI
1995 Pit-N	0	0	—	11	0	0	0	0	14	10	0	2	6	7.7	1.93	223	.192	.222	0	—	0	4	4	-0	0.0
1996 Pit-N	0	0	—	13	0	0	0	0	18¹	21	5	10	13	16.2	6.38	69	.276	.375	0	—	0	-4	-4	1	0.1
Total 2	0	0	—	24	0	0	0	0	32¹	31	5	12	19	12.5	4.45	98	.242	.317	0	—	0	-1	-0	1	0.1

● **GARRY HANCOCK**   Hancock, Ronald Garry b: 1/23/54, Tampa, Fla. BL/TL, 6', 175 lbs. Deb: 7/16/78 ◆

YEAR TM/L	W	L	PCT	G	GS	CG	SH	SV	IP	H	HR	BB	SO	RAT	ERA	ERA+	OAV	OOB	BH	AVG	PB	PR	/A	PD	TPI
1984 Oak-A	0	0	—	1	0	0	0	0	1¹	1	0	0	0	0.0	0.00	—	.000	.000	13	.217	0	1	1	0	0.0

● **RYAN HANCOCK**   Hancock, Ryan Lee b: 11/11/71, Santa Clara, Cal. BR/TR, 6'2", 220 lbs. Deb: 6/8/96

YEAR TM/L	W	L	PCT	G	GS	CG	SH	SV	IP	H	HR	BB	SO	RAT	ERA	ERA+	OAV	OOB	BH	AVG	PB	PR	/A	PD	TPI
1996 Cal-A	4	1	.800	11	4	0	0	0	27²	34	2	17	19	17.2	7.48	65	.306	.408	1	1.000	0	-8	-8	0	-1.1

● **RICH HAND**   Hand, Richard Allen b: 7/10/48, Bellevue, Wash. BR/TR, 6'1", 195 lbs. Deb: 4/9/70

YEAR TM/L	W	L	PCT	G	GS	CG	SH	SV	IP	H	HR	BB	SO	RAT	ERA	ERA+	OAV	OOB	BH	AVG	PB	PR	/A	PD	TPI
1970 Cle-A	6	13	.316	35	25	3	1	3	159²	132	27	69	110	11.6	3.83	103	.228	.314	6	.146	-1	-2	2	0	0.1
1971 Cle-A	2	6	.250	15	12	0	0	0	60²	74	6	38	26	17.2	5.79	66	.311	.414	2	.125	-0	-16	-13	-1	-1.7
1972 Tex-A	10	14	.417	30	28	2	1	0	170²	139	12	103	109	12.9	3.32	91	.226	.340	8	.154	1	-5	-6	-0	-0.7
1973 Tex-A	2	3	.400	8	7	1	0	0	41²	49	2	19	14	15.1	5.40	69	.290	.368	0	—	-1	-7	-8	-1	-0.8
Cal-A	4	3	.571	16	6	0	0	0	54²	58	5	21	19	13.2	3.62	98	.274	.342	0	—	-0	1	-0	1	0.2
Yr	6	6	.500	24	13	1	0	0	96¹	107	7	40	33	13.8	4.39	82	.277	.347	0	—	-0	-6	-9	-0	-0.6
Total 4	24	39	.381	104	78	6	2	3	487¹	452	52	250	278	13.2	4.01	89	.249	.345	16	.147	-0	-29	-25	-1	-2.9

● **JIM HANDIBOE**   Handiboe, James Edward "Nick" b: 7/17/1866, Columbus, Ohio d: 11/8/42, Columbus, Ohio BR/TR, 5'11", 160 lbs. Deb: 5/28/1886

YEAR TM/L	W	L	PCT	G	GS	CG	SH	SV	IP	H	HR	BB	SO	RAT	ERA	ERA+	OAV	OOB	BH	AVG	PB	PR	/A	PD	TPI
1886 Pit-a	7	7	.500	14	14	12	1	0	114	82	1	33	83	10.0	3.32	102	.195	.273	5	.114	-2	2	1	-0	-0.2

● **VERN HANDRAHAN**   Handrahan, James Vernon b: 11/27/38, Charlottetown, P.E.I., Canada BL/TR, 6'2", 185 lbs. Deb: 4/14/64

YEAR TM/L	W	L	PCT	G	GS	CG	SH	SV	IP	H	HR	BB	SO	RAT	ERA	ERA+	OAV	OOB	BH	AVG	PB	PR	/A	PD	TPI
1964 KC-A	0	1	.000	18	1	0	0	0	35²	33	9	25	18	15.1	6.06	63	.252	.380	2	.222	0	-10	-9	0	-0.2
1966 KC-A	0	1	.000	16	1	0	0	1	25¹	20	5	15	18	12.8	4.26	80	.227	.346	0	.000	-0	-2	-2	0	-0.1
Total 2	0	2	.000	34	2	0	0	1	61	53	14	40	36	14.2	5.31	69	.242	.366	2	.167	-0	-12	-11	0	-0.3

● **BILL HANDS**   Hands, William Alfred b: 5/6/40, Hackensack, N.J. BR/TR, 6'2", 185 lbs. Deb: 6/3/65

YEAR TM/L	W	L	PCT	G	GS	CG	SH	SV	IP	H	HR	BB	SO	RAT	ERA	ERA+	OAV	OOB	BH	AVG	PB	PR	/A	PD	TPI
1965 SF-N	0	2	.000	4	2	0	0	0	13	16	3	6	5	28.5	16.50	22	.433	.528	0	.000	-0	-9	-9	-0	-2.0
1966 Chi-N	8	13	.381	41	26	4	0	0	159	168	17	59	93	13.1	4.58	80	.272	.340	2	.041	-3	-17	-16	1	-2.2
1967 Chi-N	7	8	.467	49	11	3	1	6	150	134	9	48	84	11.0	2.46	144	.239	.301	4	.105	-1	15	18	-0	1.9
1968 Chi-N	16	10	.615	38	34	11	4	0	258²	221	26	36	148	9.2	2.89	109	.231	.264	5	.061	-5	3	8	-0	0.2
1969 Chi-N	20	14	.588	41	41	18	3	0	300	268	21	73	181	10.4	2.49	162	.237	.287	9	.092	-5	37	**51**	1	5.5
1970 Chi-N	18	15	.545	39	38	12	2	1	265	278	36	56	170	12.2	3.70	114	.269	.322	10	.133	1	10	24	1	3.0
1971 Chi-N	12	18	.400	36	35	14	0	0	242¹	248	27	50	128	11.1	3.42	115	.260	.298	6	.083	-3	1	14	-0	1.3
1972 Chi-N	11	8	.579	32	28	6	3	0	189	168	12	47	96	10.3	3.00	127	.237	.286	1	.018	-4	10	17	-2	1.0
1973 Min-A	7	10	.412	39	15	3	0	0	142	138	14	41	78	11.5	3.49	114	.252	.307	0	—	0	5	7	-1	0.7
1974 Min-A	4	5	.444	35	10	0	0	0	115¹	130	9	25	74	12.4	4.45	84	.284	.327	0	—	0	-11	-9	-1	-0.9
Tex-A	2	0	1.000	2	2	1	0	0	14	11	0	3	4	9.0	1.93	185	.208	.250	0	—	0	3	3	0	0.4
Yr	6	5	.545	37	12	1	0	0	129¹	141	9	28	78	11.8	4.18	89	.274	.311	0	—	0	-8	-7	-1	-0.5
1975 Tex-A	6	7	.462	18	16	1	0	0	109²	118	12	28	70	11.8	4.02	93	.271	.319	0	—	0	-4	-3	0	-0.3
Total 11	111	110	.502	374	260	72	17	14	1951	1895	167	492	1128	11.2	3.35	114	.253	.302	37	.078	-20	44	104	-0	8.6

● **CHRIS HANEY**   Haney, Christopher Deane b: 11/16/68, Baltimore, Md. BL/TL, 6'3", 185 lbs. Deb: 6/21/91 F

YEAR TM/L	W	L	PCT	G	GS	CG	SH	SV	IP	H	HR	BB	SO	RAT	ERA	ERA+	OAV	OOB	BH	AVG	PB	PR	/A	PD	TPI
1991 Mon-N	3	7	.300	16	16	0	0	0	84²	94	6	43	51	14.7	4.04	90	.280	.363	2	.074	-2	-3	-4	1	-0.5

YEAR	TM/L	W	L	PCT	G	GS	CG	SH	SV	IP	H	HR	BB	SO	RAT	ERA	ERA+	OAV	OOB	BH	AVG	PB	PR	/A	PD	TPI
1992	Mon-N	2	3	.400	9	6	1	1	0	38	40	6	10	27	12.8	5.45	64	.270	.333	2	.222	0	-8	-8	-0	-1.0
	KC-A	2	3	.400	7	7	1	1	0	42	35	5	16	27	10.9	3.86	105	.226	.298	0	—	0	0	1	-1	-0.2
1993	KC-A	9	9	.500	23	23	1	1	0	124	141	13	53	65	14.3	6.02	76	.286	.359	0	—	0	-23	-20	0	-2.4
1994	KC-A	2	2	.500	6	6	0	0	0	28¹	36	2	11	18	15.2	7.31	68	.333	.400	0	—	0	-8	-7	1	-0.9
1995	KC-A	3	4	.429	16	13	1	0	0	81¹	78	7	33	31	12.5	3.65	131	.262	.339	0	—	0	10	10	0	0.7
1996	KC-A	10	14	.417	35	35	4	1	0	228	267	29	51	115	12.8	4.70	104	.291	.332	0	—	0	7	5	-2	0.3
Total 6		31	42	.425	112	106	8	4	0	626¹	691	68	217	334	13.3	4.84	93	.281	.344	4	.111	-1	-25	-23	-1	-4.0

● **DON HANKINS**   Hankins, Donald Wayne   b: 2/9/02, Pendleton, Ind.   d: 5/16/63, Winston-Salem, N.C   BR/TR, 6′3″, 183 lbs.   Deb: 4/23/27

YEAR	TM/L	W	L	PCT	G	GS	CG	SH	SV	IP	H	HR	BB	SO	RAT	ERA	ERA+	OAV	OOB	BH	AVG	PB	PR	/A	PD	TPI
1927	Det-A	2	1	.667	20	1	0	0	2	42²	67	1	13	10	16.9	6.33	67	.383	.426	1	.143	-1	-10	-10	0	-0.7

● **FRANK HANKINSON**   Hankinson, Frank Edward   b: 4/29/1856, New York, N.Y.   d: 4/5/11, Palisades Park, N.J   BR/TR, 5′11″, 168 lbs.   Deb: 5/1/1878 ♦

YEAR	TM/L	W	L	PCT	G	GS	CG	SH	SV	IP	H	HR	BB	SO	RAT	ERA	ERA+	OAV	OOB	BH	AVG	PB	PR	/A	PD	TPI
1878	Chi-N	0	1	.000	1	1	1	0	0	9	11	0	0	4	11.0	6.00	40	.282	.282	64	.267	0	-4	-4	-0	-0.3
1879	Chi-N	15	10	.600	26	25	25	2	0	230²	248	6	27	69	10.7	2.50	103	.255	.275	31	.181	-4	0	2	4	0.2
1880	Cle-N	1	1	.500	4	2	2	0	1	25	20	0	3	8	8.3	1.08	218	.215	.240	55	.209	-0	4	4	1	0.4
1885	NY-a	0	0	—	1	0	0	0	0	2	2	1	1	0	13.5	4.50	66	.500	.600	81	.224	0	-0	-0	-0	0.3
Total 4		16	12	.571	32	28	28	2	1	266²	281	1	31	81	10.5	2.50	102	.253	.274	747	.228	-4	-0	1	5	0.3

● **JIM HANLEY**   Hanley, James Patrick   b: 10/13/1885, Providence, R.I.   d: 5/1/61, Elmhurst, N.Y.   BR/TL, 5′11″, 165 lbs.   Deb: 7/3/13

YEAR	TM/L	W	L	PCT	G	GS	CG	SH	SV	IP	H	HR	BB	SO	RAT	ERA	ERA+	OAV	OOB	BH	AVG	PB	PR	/A	PD	TPI
1913	NY-A	0	0	—	1	0	0	0	0	4	5	0	4	2	20.3	6.75	44	.313	.450	0	.000	-0	-2	-2	0	0.0

● **PRESTON HANNA**   Hanna, Preston Lee   b: 9/10/54, Pensacola, Fla.   BR/TR, 6′1″, 195 lbs.   Deb: 9/13/75

YEAR	TM/L	W	L	PCT	G	GS	CG	SH	SV	IP	H	HR	BB	SO	RAT	ERA	ERA+	OAV	OOB	BH	AVG	PB	PR	/A	PD	TPI
1975	Atl-N	0	0	—	4	0	0	0	0	5²	7	0	5	2	22.2	1.59	238	.304	.467	0	—	0	1	1	-0	0.0
1976	Atl-N	0	0	—	5	0	0	0	0	8	11	0	4	3	16.9	4.50	84	.333	.405	0	.000	-0	-1	-1	-0	0.0
1977	Atl-N	2	6	.250	17	9	1	0	1	60	69	6	34	37	15.8	4.95	90	.285	.378	1	.071	-0	-7	-3	1	-0.3
1978	Atl-N	7	13	.350	29	28	0	0	0	140¹	132	10	93	90	14.6	5.13	79	.251	.367	9	.184	1	-24	-17	-0	-2.1
1979	Atl-N	1	1	.500	6	4	0	0	0	24¹	27	1	15	15	15.5	2.96	137	.284	.382	0	.000	-0	2	3	1	0.3
1980	Atl-N	2	0	1.000	32	0	0	0	0	79¹	63	3	44	35	12.5	3.18	118	.224	.335	2	.143	-0	4	5	-1	0.3
1981	Atl-N	2	1	.667	20	1	0	0	0	35¹	45	2	23	22	17.3	6.37	56	.341	.439	1	.250	-0	-11	-11	2	-0.7
1982	Atl-N	3	0	1.000	20	1	0	0	0	36	36	3	28	17	16.0	3.75	90	.277	.405	2	.400	1	-1	-0	-1	0.0
	Oak-A	0	4	.000	23	2	1	0	0	48¹	54	3	33	32	16.4	5.59	70	.287	.396	0	—	0	-8	-9	-0	-0.7
Total 8		17	25	.405	156	47	2	0	1	437¹	444	28	279	253	15.1	4.61	86	.269	.378	15	.161	1	-45	-31	1	-3.5

● **GERRY HANNAHS**   Hannahs, Gerald Ellis   b: 3/6/53, Binghamton, N.Y.   BL/TL, 6′3″, 210 lbs.   Deb: 9/8/76

YEAR	TM/L	W	L	PCT	G	GS	CG	SH	SV	IP	H	HR	BB	SO	RAT	ERA	ERA+	OAV	OOB	BH	AVG	PB	PR	/A	PD	TPI
1976	Mon-N	2	0	1.000	3	3	0	0	0	16	20	2	12	10	18.0	6.75	55	.323	.432	3	.375	1	-6	-5	-0	-0.5
1977	Mon-N	1	5	.167	8	7	0	0	0	37	43	7	17	21	14.6	4.86	78	.291	.364	0	.000	-0	-4	-4	-0	-0.7
1978	LA-N	0	0	—	1	0	0	0	0	2	3	0	0	5	13.5	9.00	39	.333	.333	1	.000	-0	-1	-1	0	0.0
1979	LA-N	0	2	.000	4	2	0	0	0	16	10	2	13	6	12.9	3.38	108	.175	.329	1	.250	1	0	0	0	0.1
Total 4		3	7	.300	16	12	0	0	0	71	76	11	42	42	15.0	5.07	74	.275	.371	4	.211	1	-10	-10	-1	-1.1

● **JIM HANNAN**   Hannan, James John   b: 1/7/40, Jersey City, N.J.   BR/TR, 6′3″, 205 lbs.   Deb: 4/17/62

YEAR	TM/L	W	L	PCT	G	GS	CG	SH	SV	IP	H	HR	BB	SO	RAT	ERA	ERA+	OAV	OOB	BH	AVG	PB	PR	/A	PD	TPI
1962	Was-A	2	4	.333	42	3	0	0	4	68	56	4	49	39	13.9	3.31	122	.230	.360	1	.091	-1	5	5	0	0.5
1963	Was-A	2	2	.500	13	2	0	0	0	27²	23	2	17	14	13.0	4.88	76	.228	.339	0	.000	-0	-4	-4	0	-0.5
1964	Was-A	4	7	.364	49	7	0	0	3	106	108	13	45	67	13.0	4.16	89	.266	.339	3	.150	-1	-6	-5	-1	-0.4
1965	Was-A	1	1	.500	4	1	1	1	0	14²	18	0	16	6	15.3	4.91	71	.340	.417	0	.000	-0	-2	-2	-1	-0.4
1966	Was-A	3	9	.250	30	18	2	0	0	114	125	9	59	68	14.8	4.26	81	.288	.377	2	.067	-2	-10	-10	-0	-1.2
1967	Was-A	1	1	.500	8	2	0	0	0	21²	28	3	7	14	15.0	5.40	59	.315	.371	0	.000	-0	-5	-5	-0	-0.5
1968	Was-A	10	6	.625	25	22	4	1	0	140¹	147	4	50	75	12.9	3.01	97	.272	.338	3	.064	-2	-1	-1	-0	-0.5
1969	Was-A	7	6	.538	35	28	1	0	0	158¹	138	17	91	72	13.1	3.64	95	.238	.343	6	.115	-2	-0	-3	-1	-0.5
1970	Was-A	9	11	.450	42	17	1	1	0	128	119	17	54	61	12.2	4.01	89	.250	.328	4	.129	-0	-4	-6	-1	-0.9
1971	Det-A	1	0	1.000	7	0	0	0	0	11	7	1	7	6	12.3	3.27	110	.189	.333	0	.000	-0	0	0	0	0.1
	Mil-A	1	1	.500	21	1	0	0	0	32¹	38	7	21	17	16.7	5.01	69	.295	.397	0	.000	-0	-6	-6	-0	-0.4
	Yr	2	1	.667	28	1	0	0	0	43¹	45	8	28	23	15.4	4.57	77	.269	.378	0	.000	-1	-5	-5	-0	-0.3
Total 10		41	48	.461	276	101	9	4	7	822	807	79	406	438	13.4	3.88	89	.261	.350	19	.091	-9	-34	-38	-1	-5.0

● **LOY HANNING**   Hanning, Loy Vernon   b: 10/18/17, Bunker, Mo.   d: 6/24/86, Anaconda, Mo.   BR/TR, 6′2″, 175 lbs.   Deb: 9/20/39

YEAR	TM/L	W	L	PCT	G	GS	CG	SH	SV	IP	H	HR	BB	SO	RAT	ERA	ERA+	OAV	OOB	BH	AVG	PB	PR	/A	PD	TPI
1939	StL-A	0	1	.000	4	1	0	0	0	10	6	1	4	8	9.0	3.60	135	.158	.238	0	.000	-0	1	1	0	0.1
1942	StL-A	1	1	.500	11	0	0	0	0	17¹	26	2	12	9	20.3	7.79	48	.356	.453	1	.250	0	-8	-8	1	-0.7
Total 2		1	2	.333	15	1	0	0	0	27¹	32	3	16	17	16.1	6.26	66	.288	.383	1	.200	-0	-7	-6	1	-0.7

● **GREG HANSELL**   Hansell, Gregory Michael   b: 3/12/71, Bellflower, Cal.   BR/TR, 6′5″, 215 lbs.   Deb: 4/28/95

YEAR	TM/L	W	L	PCT	G	GS	CG	SH	SV	IP	H	HR	BB	SO	RAT	ERA	ERA+	OAV	OOB	BH	AVG	PB	PR	/A	PD	TPI
1995	LA-N	0	1	.000	20	0	0	0	0	19¹	29	5	6	13	17.2	7.45	51	.349	.407	0	—	0	-7	-8	-1	-0.4
1996	Min-A	3	0	1.000	50	0	0	0	3	74¹	83	14	31	46	14.0	5.69	90	.285	.358	0	—	0	-6	-5	-1	-0.3
Total 2		3	1	.750	70	0	0	0	3	93²	112	19	37	59	14.7	6.05	80	.299	.369	0	—	0	-13	-13	-1	-0.7

● **ANDY HANSEN**   Hansen, Andrew Viggo "Swede"   b: 11/12/24, Lake Worth, Fla.   BR/TR, 6′3″, 190 lbs.   Deb: 6/30/44

YEAR	TM/L	W	L	PCT	G	GS	CG	SH	SV	IP	H	HR	BB	SO	RAT	ERA	ERA+	OAV	OOB	BH	AVG	PB	PR	/A	PD	TPI
1944	NY-N	3	3	.500	23	4	0	0	1	52²	63	3	32	15	16.7	6.49	56	.301	.402	2	.167	0	-17	-17	1	-1.6
1945	NY-N	4	3	.571	23	13	4	0	3	92²	98	7	28	37	12.4	4.66	84	.273	.329	0	.000	-3	-9	-8	2	-0.7
1947	NY-N	1	5	.167	27	9	1	0	0	82¹	78	8	38	18	12.7	4.37	93	.248	.330	4	.190	-0	-3	-3	-1	-0.1
1948	NY-N	5	3	.625	36	9	3	0	0	100	96	4	36	27	11.9	2.97	133	.255	.320	1	.050	-0	11	11	-0	0.7
1949	NY-N	2	6	.250	33	2	0	0	0	66¹	69	5	28	26	11.7	4.61	86	.234	.312	0	.000	-1	-4	-5	0	-0.5
1950	NY-N	0	1	.000	31	0	0	0	0	57	64	8	26	19	14.4	5.53	74	.279	.355	0	.000	-1	-9	-9	-0	-0.4
1951	Phi-N	3	1	.750	24	0	0	0	0	39	34	4	7	11	9.7	2.54	152	.228	.268	1	.333	1	6	6	1	0.7
1952	Phi-N	5	6	.455	43	0	0	0	4	77¹	76	6	27	18	12.3	3.26	112	.259	.328	3	.182	1	4	4	1	0.7
1953	Phi-N	0	2	.000	30	1	0	0	0	51¹	60	6	24	17	14.9	4.03	104	.296	.373	2	.286	1	1	1	1	0.1
Total 9		23	30	.434	270	39	8	0	16	627	627	52	246	188	12.9	4.22	93	.265	.339	12	.102	-3	-19	-20	5	-1.1

● **SNIPE HANSEN**   Hansen, Roy Emil Frederick   b: 2/21/07, Chicago, Ill.   d: 9/11/78, Chicago, Ill.   BB/TL, 6′3″, 195 lbs.   Deb: 7/5/30

YEAR	TM/L	W	L	PCT	G	GS	CG	SH	SV	IP	H	HR	BB	SO	RAT	ERA	ERA+	OAV	OOB	BH	AVG	PB	PR	/A	PD	TPI
1930	Phi-N	0	7	.000	22	9	1	0	0	84¹	123	8	38	25	17.4	6.72	81	.364	.431	3	.111	-2	-16	-12	-1	-1.0
1932	Phi-N	10	10	.500	39	23	5	0	2	191	215	13	51	56	12.8	3.72	118	.278	.328	8	.127	-4	3	15	-2	0.9
1933	Phi-N	6	14	.300	32	22	8	0	1	168¹	199	12	30	47	12.5	4.44	86	.284	.328	9	.155	-3	-21	-12	-1	-1.7
1934	Phi-N	6	12	.333	50	16	5	1	0	151	194	15	61	40	15.4	5.42	87	.307	.371	10	.233	-0	-23	-17	1	-1.1
1935	Phi-N	0	1	.000	2	1	0	0	0	4¹	8	0	5	0	27.0	12.46	36	.421	.542	0	.000	-0	-4	-4	0	-0.7
	StL-A	0	1	.000	10	0	0	0	0	8	16	2	9	8	18.2	8.78	55	.364	.412	1	.143	-0	-13	-12	-1	-0.5
Total 5		22	45	.328	155	71	19	2	6	625²	783	50	194	176	14.3	5.01	90	.306	.358	31	.155	-10	-73	-36	-3	-4.1

● **ROY HANSEN**   Hansen, Roy Inglof "Ing"   b: 3/6/1898, Beloit, Wis.   d: 2/9/77, Beloit, Wis.   BR/TR, 6′, 165 lbs.   Deb: 5/28/18

YEAR	TM/L	W	L	PCT	G	GS	CG	SH	SV	IP	H	HR	BB	SO	RAT	ERA	ERA+	OAV	OOB	BH	AVG	PB	PR	/A	PD	TPI
1918	Was-A	1	0	1.000	5	0	0	0	0	9	10	1	3	2	14.0	3.00	91	.278	.350	0	—	0	-0	-0	0	0.0

● **F. C. HANSFORD**   Hansford, F. C.   TL , 6′, 180 lbs.   Deb: 6/9/1898

YEAR	TM/L	W	L	PCT	G	GS	CG	SH	SV	IP	H	HR	BB	SO	RAT	ERA	ERA+	OAV	OOB	BH	AVG	PB	PR	/A	PD	TPI
1898	Bro-N	0	0	—	1	0	0	0	0	7	10	0	5	2	19.3	3.86	93	.333	.429	0	.000	-1	-0	-0	-0	-0.1

● **DON HANSKI**   Hanski, Donald Thomas (b: Donald Thomas Hanyzewski)   b: 2/27/16, LaPorte, Ind.   d: 9/2/57, Worth, Ill.   BL/TL, 5′11″, 180 lbs.   Deb: 5/6/43 ♦

YEAR	TM/L	W	L	PCT	G	GS	CG	SH	SV	IP	H	HR	BB	SO	RAT	ERA	ERA+	OAV	OOB	BH	AVG	PB	PR	/A	PD	TPI
1943	Chi-A	0	0	—	1	0	0	0	0	1	0	0	2	0	18.0	0.00	—	.333	.500	5	.238	0	0	-0	-0	0.0
1944	Chi-A	0	0	—	2	0	0	0	0	3	6	0	3	0	21.0	12.00	29	.357	.438	0	.000	-3	-3	-0		0.0
Total 2		0	0	—	3	0	0	0	0	4	6	0	5	0	20.3	9.00	38	.353	.450	5	.227	-2	-2	-0		0.0

● **OLLIE HANSON**   Hanson, Earl Sylvester   b: 1/19/1896, Holbrook, Mass.   d: 8/19/51, Clifton, N.J.   BR/TR, 5′11″, 178 lbs.   Deb: 4/27/21

YEAR	TM/L	W	L	PCT	G	GS	CG	SH	SV	IP	H	HR	BB	SO	RAT	ERA	ERA+	OAV	OOB	BH	AVG	PB	PR	/A	PD	TPI
1921	Chi-N	0	2	.000	2	2	1	0	0	9	16	0	6	2	16.0	7.00	55	.265	.390	0	.000	-0	-3	-3	0	-0.6

● **ERIK HANSON**   Hanson, Erik Brian   b: 5/18/65, Kinnelon, N.J.   BR/TR, 6′6″, 210 lbs.   Deb: 9/5/88

YEAR	TM/L	W	L	PCT	G	GS	CG	SH	SV	IP	H	HR	BB	SO	RAT	ERA	ERA+	OAV	OOB	BH	AVG	PB	PR	/A	PD	TPI
1988	Sea-A	2	3	.400	6	6	0	0	0	41²	35	4	12	36	10.4	3.24	128	.230	.291	0	—	0	3	4	-0	0.4
1989	Sea-A	9	5	.643	17	17	1	0	0	113¹	103	7	32	75	11.1	3.18	127	.243	.304	0	—	0	9	11	0	1.1

YEAR	TM/L	W	L	PCT	G	GS	CG	SH	SV	IP	H	HR	BB	SO	RAT	ERA	ERA+	OAV	OOB	BH	AVG	PB	PR	/A	PD	TPI
1990	Sea-A	18	9	.667	33	33	5	1	0	236	205	15	68	211	10.5	3.24	122	.232	.289	0	—	0	17	19	-0	2.0
1991	Sea-A	8	8	.500	27	27	2	1	0	174²	182	16	56	143	12.4	3.81	108	.269	.327	0	—	0	5	6	-1	0.4
1992	Sea-A	8	17	.320	31	30	6	1	0	186²	209	14	57	112	13.2	4.82	82	.287	.345	0	—	0	-18	-18	-0	-2.1
1993	Sea-A	11	12	.478	31	30	7	0	0	215	215	17	60	163	11.7	3.47	127	.263	.317	0	—	0	20	22	1	2.2
1994	Cin-N	5	5	.500	22	21	0	0	0	122²	137	10	23	101	12.0	4.11	101	.283	.320	6	.154	-1	0	1	0	0.0
1995	*Bos-A☆	15	5	.750	29	29	1	1	0	186²	187	17	59	139	11.9	4.24	115	.258	.314	0	—	0	10	13	-0	1.1
1996	Tor-A	13	17	.433	35	35	4	1	0	214²	243	26	102	156	14.5	5.41	93	.289	.367	0	—	0	-10	-9	-3	-1.2
Total	9	89	81	.524	231	228	26	5	0	1491¹	1516	126	469	1161	12.4	4.07	107	.264	.323	6	.154	-1	38	49	-3	3.9

● ED HANYZEWSKI
Hanyzewski, Edward Michael b: 9/18/20, Union Mills, Ind. d: 10/8/91, Fargo, N.D. BR/TR, 6'1", 200 lbs. Deb: 5/12/42

YEAR	TM/L	W	L	PCT	G	GS	CG	SH	SV	IP	H	HR	BB	SO	RAT	ERA	ERA+	OAV	OOB	BH	AVG	PB	PR	/A	PD	TPI
1942	Chi-N	1	1	.500	6	1	0	0	0	19	17	2	8	6	11.8	3.79	84	.254	.333	1	.200	-0	-1	-1	0	-0.1
1943	Chi-N	8	7	.533	33	16	3	0	0	130	120	2	45	55	11.6	2.56	130	.243	.309	2	.049	-4	12	11	2	1.0
1944	Chi-N	2	5	.286	14	7	3	0	0	58¹	61	6	20	19	12.7	4.47	79	.261	.322	1	.059	-1	-6	-6	3	-0.4
1945	Chi-N	0	0	—	2	1	0	0	0	4²	7	1	1	0	15.4	5.79	63	.350	.381	0	.000	-0	-1	-1	0	-0.1
1946	Chi-N	1	0	1.000	3	0	0	0	0	6	8	0	5	1	21.0	4.50	74	.348	.483	0	.000	-0	-1	-1	0	-0.1
Total	5	12	13	.480	58	25	6	0	0	218	213	11	79	81	12.2	3.30	102	.254	.321	4	.062	-5	4	2	5	0.4

● MEL HARDER
Harder, Melvin Leroy "Chief" b: 10/15/09, Beemer, Neb. BR/TR, 6'1", 195 lbs. Deb: 4/24/28 MC

YEAR	TM/L	W	L	PCT	G	GS	CG	SH	SV	IP	H	HR	BB	SO	RAT	ERA	ERA+	OAV	OOB	BH	AVG	PB	PR	/A	PD	TPI
1928	Cle-A	0	2	.000	23	1	0	0	1	49	64	4	32	15	17.6	6.61	63	.335	.430	0	.000	-1	-14	-13	-1	-0.7
1929	Cle-A	1	0	1.000	11	0	0	0	0	17²	24	2	5	4	16.3	5.60	79	.333	.400	0	.000	-0	-3	-2	-0	-0.2
1930	Cle-A	11	10	.524	36	19	7	0	2	175¹	205	9	68	45	14.2	4.21	115	.295	.361	9	.143	-4	9	12	-1	0.8
1931	Cle-A	13	14	.481	40	24	9	0	1	194	229	8	72	63	14.2	4.36	106	.289	.352	19	.253	-1	0	6	0	0.8
1932	Cle-A	15	13	.536	39	32	17	1	0	254²	277	9	68	90	12.3	3.75	127	.272	.319	17	.181	-0	21	28	3	2.9
1933	Cle-A	15	17	.469	43	31	14	2	4	253	254	10	67	81	11.5	2.95	**151**	.259	.309	16	.190	-1	**37**	**42**	8	**5.7**
1934	Cle-A★	20	12	.625	44	29	17	**6**	4	255¹	246	6	81	91	11.8	2.61	**174**	.254	.316	14	.161	-4	54	**55**	2	**6.4**
1935	Cle-A★	22	11	.667	42	35	17	4	2	287³	313	6	53	95	11.5	3.29	137	.275	.307	21	.206	-1	37	39	5	4.4
1936	Cle-A★	15	15	.500	36	30	13	0	1	224²	294	13	71	84	14.9	5.17	97	.313	.365	11	.138	-4	-3	-3	0	-0.7
1937	Cle-A★	15	12	.556	38	30	13	0	2	233²	269	9	86	95	13.8	4.28	108	.288	.350	15	.174	-1	9	9	2	0.9
1938	Cle-A	17	10	.630	38	29	15	2	4	240	257	16	62	102	12.2	3.83	121	.271	.319	10	.114	-5	26	22	2	1.8
1939	Cle-A	15	9	.625	29	26	12	1	1	208	213	15	64	67	12.1	3.50	126	.269	.326	10	.139	-2	26	21	-2	1.8
1940	Cle-A	12	11	.522	31	25	5	0	0	186¹	200	16	59	76	12.8	4.06	104	.278	.337	11	.177	-1	7	3	1	0.4
1941	Cle-A	5	4	.556	15	10	1	0	1	68²	76	8	37	21	15.1	5.24	75	.279	.370	2	.080	-2	-8	-10	-1	-1.2
1942	Cle-A	13	14	.481	29	29	13	4	0	198²	179	8	82	74	12.0	3.44	100	.240	.317	8	.119	-3	5	0	1	-0.2
1943	Cle-A	8	7	.533	19	18	6	1	0	135¹	126	7	61	40	12.5	3.06	102	.254	.337	10	.213	2	4	1	-0	0.2
1944	Cle-A	12	10	.545	30	27	12	2	0	196¹	211	5	69	64	13.0	3.71	89	.278	.341	16	.216	1	-6	-9	-1	-0.9
1945	Cle-A	3	7	.300	11	11	2	0	0	76	93	3	23	16	13.7	3.67	88	.303	.352	2	.080	-2	-3	-4	1	-0.6
1946	Cle-A	5	4	.556	13	12	4	1	0	92¹	85	4	31	21	11.3	3.41	97	.249	.311	3	.086	-2	1	-1	-2	-0.5
1947	Cle-A	6	4	.600	15	15	4	1	0	80	91	4	27	17	13.4	4.50	77	.289	.347	5	.179	-0	-7	-9	-1	-1.1
Total	20	223	186	.545	582	433	181	25	23	3426¹	3706	161	1118	1161	12.8	3.80	113	.276	.334	199	.165	-27	190	182	18	20.0

● JIM HARDIN
Hardin, James Warren b: 8/6/43, Morris Chapel, Tenn. d: 3/9/91, Key West, Fla. BR/TR, 6', 175 lbs. Deb: 6/23/67

YEAR	TM/L	W	L	PCT	G	GS	CG	SH	SV	IP	H	HR	BB	SO	RAT	ERA	ERA+	OAV	OOB	BH	AVG	PB	PR	/A	PD	TPI
1967	Bal-A	8	3	.727	19	14	5	2	0	111	85	5	27	64	9.3	2.27	139	.211	.266	5	.135	-4	12	11	-1	1.0
1968	Bal-A	18	13	.581	35	35	16	2	0	244	188	20	70	160	9.9	2.51	117	.212	.277	-3	.085	-3	13	11	-0	1.1
1969	Bal-A	6	7	.462	30	20	3	1	1	137²	128	18	43	64	11.6	3.60	99	.248	.313	7	.156	2	0	-0	-1	0.0
1970	Bal-A	6	5	.545	36	19	3	2	1	145¹	150	13	26	78	11.0	3.53	103	.267	.301	3	.067	-1	3	2	-2	-0.2
1971	Bal-A	0	0	—	6	0	0	0	0	5²	12	0	3	3	23.8	4.76	70	.480	.536	0	—	-0	-1	-1	0	0.0
	NY-A	0	2	.000	12	3	0	0	0	28¹	35	3	9	14	14.3	5.08	64	.313	.369	0	.000	-0	-5	-6	-0	-0.5
	Yr	0	2	.000	18	3	0	0	0	34	47	3	12	17	15.9	5.03	65	.343	.400	0	.000	-0	-6	-7	-0	-0.5
1972	Atl-N	5	2	.714	26	9	1	0	2	79²	93	11	24	25	13.4	4.41	86	.287	.340	2	.095	1	-8	-5	-1	-0.5
Total	6	43	32	.573	164	100	28	7	4	751²	691	70	202	408	11.0	3.18	104	.244	.300	24	.103	-3	14	11	-5	0.9

● CHARLIE HARDING
Harding, Charles Harold "Slim" b: 1/3/1891, Nashville, Tenn. d: 10/30/71, Bold Spring, Tenn BR/TR, 6'2.5", 172 lbs. Deb: 9/18/13

YEAR	TM/L	W	L	PCT	G	GS	CG	SH	SV	IP	H	HR	BB	SO	RAT	ERA	ERA+	OAV	OOB	BH	AVG	PB	PR	/A	PD	TPI
1913	Det-A	0	0	—	1	0	0	0	0	2	3	0	1	0	18.0	4.50	65	.375	.444	0	—	0	-0	-0	0	0.0

● ALEX HARDY
Hardy, David Alexander "Dooney" b: 1877, Toronto, Ont., Canada d: 4/22/40, Toronto, Ont., Can. TL, Deb: 9/4/02

YEAR	TM/L	W	L	PCT	G	GS	CG	SH	SV	IP	H	HR	BB	SO	RAT	ERA	ERA+	OAV	OOB	BH	AVG	PB	PR	/A	PD	TPI
1902	Chi-N	2	2	.500	4	4	4	1	0	35	29	0	12	12	10.5	3.60	75	.227	.293	3	.214	-0	-3	-3	-1	-0.4
1903	Chi-N	1	1	.500	3	3	1	0	0	12²	21	0	7	4	20.6	6.39	49	.375	.453	1	.167	-0	-4	-5	0	-0.5
Total	2	3	3	.500	7	7	5	1	0	47²	50	0	19	16	13.2	4.34	65	.272	.343	4	.200	1	-8	-8	-0	-0.9

● RED HARDY
Hardy, Francis Joseph b: 1/6/23, Marmarth, N.Dak. BR/TR, 5'11", 175 lbs. Deb: 6/20/51

YEAR	TM/L	W	L	PCT	G	GS	CG	SH	SV	IP	H	HR	BB	SO	RAT	ERA	ERA+	OAV	OOB	BH	AVG	PB	PR	/A	PD	TPI
1951	NY-N	0	0	—	2	0	0	0	0	1¹	4	0	1	0	40.5	6.75	58	.571	.667	0	—	0	-0	-0	0	0.0

● HARRY HARDY
Hardy, Harry b: 11/5/1875, Steubenville, Ohio d: 9/4/43, Steubenville, Ohio BL/TL, 5'6", 155 lbs. Deb: 9/26/05

YEAR	TM/L	W	L	PCT	G	GS	CG	SH	SV	IP	H	HR	BB	SO	RAT	ERA	ERA+	OAV	OOB	BH	AVG	PB	PR	/A	PD	TPI
1905	Was-A	1	1	.500	3	2	2	0	0	24	20	0	6	10	9.8	1.88	141	.227	.277	1	.111	-1	2	2	-1	-0.1
1906	Was-A	0	3	.000	5	3	2	0	0	20	35	0	12	4	21.1	9.00	29	.385	.456	0	.000	-1	-14	-14	0	-1.7
Total	2	1	4	.200	8	5	4	0	0	44	55	0	18	14	14.9	5.11	52	.307	.371	1	.067	-2	-12	-12	-0	-1.8

● LARRY HARDY
Hardy, Howard Lawrence b: 1/10/48, Goose Creek, Tex. BR/TR, 5'10", 180 lbs. Deb: 4/28/74

YEAR	TM/L	W	L	PCT	G	GS	CG	SH	SV	IP	H	HR	BB	SO	RAT	ERA	ERA+	OAV	OOB	BH	AVG	PB	PR	/A	PD	TPI
1974	SD-N	9	4	.692	76	1	0	0	2	101²	129	9	44	57	15.3	4.69	76	.317	.384	0	.000	-1	-12	-13	1	-1.5
1975	SD-N	0	0	—	3	0	0	0	0	2²	6	3	2	3	33.8	13.50	26	.500	.556	0	—	-0	-3	-3	-0	0.0
1976	Hou-N	0	0	—	15	0	0	0	3	21²	34	2	10	10	18.3	7.06	45	.362	.423	0	.000	-0	-9	-9	-0	-0.3
Total	3	9	4	.692	94	1	0	0	5	126	171	14	56	70	16.2	5.29	66	.331	.396	0	.000	-1	-24	-25	1	-1.8

● JACK HARDY
Hardy, John Graydon b: 10/8/59, St.Petersburg, Fla. BR/TR, 6'2", 175 lbs. Deb: 5/23/89

YEAR	TM/L	W	L	PCT	G	GS	CG	SH	SV	IP	H	HR	BB	SO	RAT	ERA	ERA+	OAV	OOB	BH	AVG	PB	PR	/A	PD	TPI
1989	Chi-A	0	0	—	5	0	0	0	0	12¹	14	1	5	4	14.6	6.57	58	.286	.364	0	—	0	-4	-4	1	0.2

● STEVE HARGAN
Hargan, Steven Lowell b: 9/8/42, Ft.Wayne, Ind. BR/TR, 6'3", 180 lbs. Deb: 8/3/65

YEAR	TM/L	W	L	PCT	G	GS	CG	SH	SV	IP	H	HR	BB	SO	RAT	ERA	ERA+	OAV	OOB	BH	AVG	PB	PR	/A	PD	TPI
1965	Cle-A	4	3	.571	17	8	1	0	2	60¹	55	2	28	37	12.5	3.43	101	.246	.332	1	.053	-1	0	0	0	-0.1
1966	Cle-A	13	10	.565	38	21	7	3	0	192	173	9	45	132	10.3	2.48	138	.241	.286	7	.121	-2	20	20	0	2.3
1967	Cle-A☆	14	13	.519	30	29	15	**6**	0	223	180	9	72	141	10.3	2.62	125	.224	.290	11	.164	1	15	16	1	2.3
1968	Cle-A	8	15	.348	32	27	4	2	0	158¹	139	11	81	78	12.8	4.15	71	.241	.340	9	.176	1	-21	-21	-2	-3.1
1969	Cle-A	5	14	.263	32	23	1	1	0	143²	145	14	81	76	14.3	5.70	66	.265	.363	7	.159	-1	-33	-31	0	-3.6
1970	Cle-A	11	3	.786	23	19	8	1	0	142²	101	14	53	72	9.9	2.90	136	.201	.281	5	.111	-2	13	17	3	1.5
1971	Cle-A	1	13	.071	37	16	1	0	1	113¹	138	18	56	52	15.9	6.19	62	.304	.388	2	.063	-3	-34	-30	-1	-3.8
1972	Cle-A	0	3	.000	12	1	0	0	0	20	23	1	15	10	17.1	5.85	55	.291	.404	0	.000	-0	-6	-6	1	-0.8
1974	Tex-A	12	9	.571	37	27	8	2	0	186²	202	15	48	98	12.3	3.95	96	.275	.324	0	—	0	-7	-8	2	-0.7
1975	Tex-A	9	10	.474	33	26	5	1	0	189¹	203	17	62	93	12.9	3.80	99	.275	.336	0	—	0	-1	-1	2	0.1
1976	Tex-A	8	8	.500	35	8	2	1	1	124¹	127	8	38	63	12.2	3.62	99	.261	.318	0	—	0	-1	-0	-0	-0.1
1977	Tor-A	1	3	.250	9	5	1	0	0	29¹	36	2	14	11	15.3	5.22	80	.308	.382	0	—	0	-4	-3	0	-0.4
	Tex-A	1	0	1.000	7	0	0	0	0	12¹	22	2	5	10	19.7	8.76	47	.393	.443	0	—	0	-6	-6	-0	-0.5
	Yr	2	3	.400	16	5	1	0	0	41²	58	4	19	21	16.6	6.26	66	.335	.401	0	—	0	-10	-10	0	-0.9
	Atl-N	0	3	.000	16	5	0	0	0	36²	49	3	16	18	16.0	6.87	65	.325	.389	0	.000	-1	-12	-10	1	-0.7
Total	12	87	107	.448	354	215	56	11	5	1632	1593	125	614	891	12.4	3.92	91	.257	.328	42	.129	-7	-77	-64	6	-7.6

● ALAN HARGESHEIMER
Hargesheimer, Alan Robert b: 11/21/56, Chicago, Ill. BR/TR, 6'3", 195 lbs. Deb: 7/14/80

YEAR	TM/L	W	L	PCT	G	GS	CG	SH	SV	IP	H	HR	BB	SO	RAT	ERA	ERA+	OAV	OOB	BH	AVG	PB	PR	/A	PD	TPI
1980	SF-N	4	6	.400	15	13	0	0	0	75	72	3	32	40	13.7	4.32	82	.285	.356	4	.182	1	-6	-7	-1	-0.8
1981	SF-N	1	2	.333	6	3	0	0	0	18²	20	1	9	6	14.5	4.34	79	.299	.390	1	.200	0	-2	-2	0	-0.2
1983	Chi-N	0	0	—	5	0	0	0	0	4	6	0	2	4	18.0	9.00	42	.375	.444	0	—	0	-2	-2	-0	0.0
1986	KC-A	0	1	.000	5	1	0	0	0	13	18	1	7	4	18.0	6.23	68	.340	.426	0	—	0	-3	-3	-0	-0.3
Total	4	5	9	.357	31	17	0	0	0	110²	126	5	50	55	14.5	4.72	77	.297	.374	5	.185	1	-13	-14	-1	-1.3

YEAR	TM/L	W	L	PCT	G	GS	CG	SH	SV	IP	H	HR	BB	SO	RAT	ERA	ERA+	OAV	OOB	BH	AVG	PB	PR	/A	PD	TPI

● TIM HARIKKALA   Harikkala, Timothy Allan b: 7/15/71, W.Palm Beach, Fla.   BR/TR, 6'2", 185 lbs.   Deb: 5/27/95

1995	Sea-A	0	0	—	1	0	0	0	0	3¹	7	1	1	1	21.6	16.20	29	.412	.444	0	—	0	-4	-4	-0	0.0
1996	Sea-A	0	1	.000	1	1	0	0	0	4¹	4	1	2	1	14.5	12.46	40	.250	.368	0	—	0	-4	-4	-0	-0.5
Total	2	0	1	.000	2	1	0	0	0	7²	11	2	3	2	17.6	14.09	34	.333	.405	0	—	0	-8	-8	-0	-0.5

● MIKE HARKEY   Harkey, Michael Anthony b: 10/25/66, San Diego, Cal.   BR/TR, 6'5", 220 lbs.   Deb: 9/5/88

1988	Chi-N	0	3	.000	5	5	0	0	0	34²	33	0	15	18	13.0	2.60	139	.248	.333	1	.091	-1	3	4	-1	0.2
1990	Chi-N	12	6	.667	27	27	2	1	0	173²	153	14	59	94	11.3	3.26	125	.234	.305	14	.250	3	10	16	-1	1.8
1991	Chi-N	0	2	.000	4	4	0	0	0	18²	21	3	6	15	13.0	5.30	73	.273	.325	2	.400	1	-3	-3	-0	-0.2
1992	Chi-N	4	0	1.000	7	7	0	0	0	38	34	4	15	21	11.8	1.89	190	.243	.321	4	.267	1	7	7	-0	0.9
1993	Chi-N	10	10	.500	28	28	1	0	0	157¹	187	17	43	67	13.3	5.26	76	.305	.353	5	.093	-2	-21	-22	-1	-2.8
1994	Col-N	1	6	.143	24	13	0	0	0	91²	125	10	35	39	15.8	5.79	86	.336	.395	4	.182	-1	-16	-8	1	-0.5
1995	Oak-A	4	6	.400	14	12	0	0	0	66	75	12	31	28	14.9	6.27	71	.292	.375	0	—	0	-11	-13	1	-1.5
	Cal-A	4	3	.571	12	8	1	0	0	61¹	80	12	16	28	14.2	4.55	103	.311	.354	0	—	0	1	1	-2	0.0
	Yr	8	9	.471	26	20	1	0	0	127¹	155	24	47	56	14.3	5.44	84	.299	.358	0	—	0	-10	-12	-1	-1.5
Total	7	35	36	.493	121	104	4	1	0	641¹	708	72	220	310	13.3	4.49	94	.283	.345	30	.184	1	-31	-19	-3	-2.1

● JOHN HARKINS   Harkins, John Joseph "Pa" b: 4/12/1859, New Brunswick, N.J d: 11/20/40, New Brunswick, N.J   BR/TR, 6'1", 205 lbs.   Deb: 5/2/1884

1884	Cle-N	12	32	.273	46	45	42	3	0	391	399	7	108	192	11.7	3.68	86	.249	.297	47	.205	-4	-30	-23	-1	-2.4
1885	Bro-a	14	20	.412	34	34	33	1	0	293	303	7	56	141	11.2	3.75	88	.250	.287	42	.264	5	-16	-15	4	-0.5
1886	Bro-a	15	16	.484	34	33	33	0	0	292¹	286	6	114	118	12.5	3.60	97	.244	.313	32	.225	1	-5	-4	2	-0.3
1887	Bro-a	10	14	.417	24	24	22	0	0	199	262	6	77	36	15.6	6.02	72	.309	.369	23	.235	-4	-38	-38	-1	-3.2
1888	Bal-a	0	1	.000	1	1	1	0	0	8	12	0	3	2	16.9	6.75	44	.333	.385	0	.000	-0	-3	-3	-0	-0.3
Total	5	51	83	.381	139	137	131	4	0	1183¹	1262	26	358	489	12.5	4.09	85	.259	.312	144	.228	4	-93	-81	5	-6.2

● SPEC HARKNESS   Harkness, Frederick Harvey b: 12/13/1887, Los Angeles, Cal. d: 5/16/52, Compton, Cal.   BR/TR, 5'11", 180 lbs.   Deb: 6/13/10

1910	Cle-A	10	7	.588	26	16	6	1	1	136¹	132	2	55	60	12.5	3.04	85	.268	.345	7	.140	-1	-8	-7	-1	-1.1
1911	Cle-A	2	2	.500	12	6	3	0	0	53¹	62	1	21	25	14.0	4.22	81	.310	.376	6	.316	1	-5	-5	-2	-0.4
Total	2	12	9	.571	38	22	9	1	1	189²	194	3	76	85	13.0	3.37	84	.280	.354	13	.188	-0	-13	-12	-3	-1.5

● DICK HARLEY   Harley, Henry Risk b: 8/18/1874, Springfield, Ohio d: 5/16/61, Springfield, Ohio   BR/TR,   Deb: 4/15/05

| 1905 | Bos-N | 2 | 5 | .286 | 9 | 4 | 4 | 1 | 0 | 65² | 72 | 5 | 19 | 19 | 12.6 | 4.66 | 67 | .286 | .338 | 1 | .045 | -2 | -12 | -11 | 2 | -1.1 |

● LARRY HARLOW   Harlow, Larry Duane b: 11/13/51, Colorado Springs, Colo.   BL/TL, 6'2", 185 lbs.   Deb: 9/20/75 ♦

| 1978 | Bal-A | 0 | 0 | — | 1 | 0 | 0 | 0 | 0 | 0² | 2 | 1 | 4 | 2 | 81.0 | 67.50 | 5 | .500 | .750 | 112 | .243 | 1 | -5 | -5 | 0 | 0.0 |

● BILL HARMAN   Harman, William Bell b: 1/2/19, Bridgewater, Va.   BR/TR, 6'4", 200 lbs.   Deb: 6/17/41 ♦

| 1941 | Phi-N | 0 | 0 | — | 5 | 0 | 0 | 0 | 0 | 13¹ | 15 | 0 | 8 | 3 | 15.9 | 4.85 | 76 | .319 | .418 | 1 | .071 | -0 | -2 | -2 | -0 | -0.1 |

● BOB HARMON   Harmon, Robert Green "Hickory Bob" b: 10/15/1887, Liberal, Mo. d: 11/27/61, Monroe, La.   BB/TR, 6', 187 lbs.   Deb: 6/23/09

1909	StL-N	6	11	.353	21	17	10	0	0	159	155	6	65	48	12.7	3.68	69	.265	.342	13	.255	4	-19	-20	-1	-1.7
1910	StL-N	13	15	.464	43	33	15	0	2	236	227	11	133	87	14.0	4.46	67	.258	.360	14	.184	2	-37	-39	2	-3.8
1911	StL-N	23	16	.590	51	41	28	2	4	348	290	10	181	144	12.4	3.13	108	.235	.336	17	.153	0	11	10	1	1.1
1912	StL-N	18	18	.500	43	34	15	3	0	268	284	4	116	73	13.5	3.93	87	.281	.357	23	.232	1	-15	-15	4	-1.3
1913	StL-N	8	21	.276	42	27	16	1	2	273¹	291	6	99	66	13.0	3.92	83	.286	.353	24	.261	5	-22	-21	2	-1.4
1914	Pit-N	13	17	.433	37	30	19	2	3	245	226	3	55	61	10.6	2.53	105	.252	.300	12	.140	-1	7	3	-1	0.1
1915	Pit-N	16	17	.485	37	32	25	5	1	269²	242	6	62	86	10.2	2.50	109	.247	.294	14	.147	1	7	7	4	1.4
1916	Pit-N	8	11	.421	31	17	10	2	0	172²	175	4	39	62	11.2	2.81	95	.267	.309	6	.109	-3	-4	-2	3	-0.2
1918	Pit-N	2	7	.222	16	9	5	0	0	82¹	76	3	12	7	9.6	2.62	110	.254	.283	4	.148	-1	1	2	0	0.2
Total	9	107	133	.446	321	240	143	15	12	2054	1966	43	762	634	12.1	3.33	90	.260	.331	127	.184	7	-71	-76	14	-5.6

● PETE HARNISCH   Harnisch, Peter Thomas b: 9/23/66, Commack, N.Y.   BB/TR, 6'1", 195 lbs.   Deb: 9/13/88

1988	Bal-A	0	2	.000	2	2	0	0	0	13	13	1	9	10	15.2	5.54	70	.260	.373	0	—	0	-2	-2	-0	-0.3
1989	Bal-A	5	9	.357	18	17	2	0	0	103¹	97	10	64	70	14.5	4.62	82	.249	.362	0	—	0	-8	-9	-1	-1.1
1990	Bal-A	11	11	.500	31	31	3	0	0	188²	189	17	86	122	13.2	4.34	87	.261	.341	0	—	0	-9	-11	-2	-1.4
1991	Hou-N★	12	9	.571	33	33	4	2	0	216²	169	14	83	172	10.7	2.70	130	**.212**	.291	6	.097	-1	24	19	-3	1.3
1992	Hou-N	9	10	.474	34	34	0	0	0	206²	182	18	64	164	10.9	3.70	91	.233	.296	11	.164	2	-5	-3	-6	-0.8
1993	Hou-N	16	9	.640	33	33	5	**4**	0	217²	171	20	79	185	10.6	2.98	130	**.214**	.290	7	.104	-1	26	22	-4	1.8
1994	Hou-N	8	5	.615	17	17	1	0	0	95	100	13	39	62	13.5	5.40	73	.269	.343	6	.171	1	-13	-15	-1	-1.7
1995	NY-N	2	8	.200	18	18	0	0	0	110	111	13	24	82	11.3	3.68	110	.261	.305	2	.091	-0	6	4	-1	0.1
1996	NY-N	8	12	.400	31	31	2	0	0	194²	195	30	61	114	12.2	4.21	93	.260	.322	6	.091	-0	-6	-3	-3	-1.0
Total	9	71	75	.486	217	216	17	7	0	1345²	1227	134	509	981	11.8	3.79	99	.241	.315	38	.119	-4	19	-7	-16	-3.1

● JACK HARPER   Harper, Charles William b: 4/2/1878, Galloway, Pa. d: 9/30/50, Jamestown, N.Y.   BR/TR, 6', 178 lbs.   Deb: 9/18/1899

1899	Cle-N	1	4	.200	5	5	5	0	0	37	44	3	12	14	14.4	3.89	94	.295	.360	2	.182	1	-0	-1	-0	0.0
1900	StL-N	0	1	.000	1	1	0	0	0	3	4	0	2	0	18.0	12.00	30	.308	.400	0	.000	-0	-3	-3	0	-0.6
1901	StL-N	23	13	.639	39	37	28	1	0	308²	294	7	99	128	11.9	3.62	88	.249	.316	20	.172	1	-10	-15	1	-1.3
1902	StL-A	15	11	.577	29	26	20	2	0	222¹	224	8	81	74	12.7	4.13	85	.262	.332	17	.205	-0	-14	-15	1	-1.4
1903	Cin-N	8	9	.471	17	15	13	0	0	135	143	2	70	45	14.9	4.33	82	.271	.367	14	.250	2	-16	-12	1	-1.0
1904	Cin-N	23	9	.719	35	35	31	6	0	293²	262	2	85	125	10.9	2.30	128	.234	.293	18	.159	-2	14	21	-5	1.4
1905	Cin-N	9	13	.409	26	23	15	1	1	179¹	189	7	69	70	13.3	3.86	86	.271	.344	10	.167	-1	-17	-11	-0	-1.3
1906	Cin-N	1	4	.200	5	5	3	0	0	36²	38	1	20	10	14.7	4.17	66	.286	.387	3	.273	1	-6	-6	-1	-0.7
	Chi-N	0	0	—	1	1	0	0	0	1	0	0	0	0	0.00	0.00	—	.000	.000	0	—	0	0	0	0	0.0
	Yr	1	4	.200	6	6	3	0	0	37²	38	1	20	10	13.9	4.06	68	.275	.367	3	.273	1	-6	-6	-1	-0.7
Total	8	80	64	.556	158	148	115	10	1	1216²	1198	29	438	466	12.5	3.55	92	.256	.327	84	.186	2	-51	-39	-3	-4.9

● GEORGE HARPER   Harper, George B. b: 8/17/1866, Milwaukee, Wis. d: 12/11/31, Stockton, Cal.   BR/TR, 5'10", 165 lbs.   Deb: 7/11/1894

1894	Phi-N	6	6	.500	12	9	7	0	0	86¹	128	3	49	24	18.7	5.32	96	.340	.418	6	.150	-4	0	-2	-1	-0.5
1896	Bro-N	4	8	.333	16	11	7	0	0	86	106	4	39	22	15.5	5.55	74	.300	.375	6	.162	0	-11	-14	1	-1.3
Total	2	10	14	.417	28	20	14	0	0	172¹	234	7	88	46	17.1	5.43	85	.321	.397	12	.156	-4	-11	-16	0	-1.8

● HARRY HARPER   Harper, Harry Clayton b: 4/24/1895, Hackensack, N.J. d: 4/23/63, New York, N.Y.   BL/TL, 6'2", 165 lbs.   Deb: 6/27/13

1913	Was-A	0	0	—	4	0	0	0	0	12²	10	1	5	9	11.4	3.55	83	.204	.291	1	.250	0	-1	-1	0	0.0
1914	Was-A	2	1	.667	23	3	1	0	2	57	45	1	35	35	13.4	3.47	81	.211	.336	3	.250	0	-5	-4	-1	-0.4
1915	Was-A	4	4	.500	19	10	5	2	2	86¹	66	1	40	54	11.2	1.77	168	.222	.317	0	.000	-0	11	11	-2	0.5
1916	Was-A	14	10	.583	36	34	13	2	0	249²	209	4	101	149	11.5	2.45	114	.235	.319	18	.207	1	10	9	-4	0.5
1917	Was-A	11	12	.478	31	31	10	4	0	179¹	145	1	106	99	12.8	3.01	87	.230	.345	7	.117	-3	-8	-3	-3	-1.6
1918	Was-A	11	10	.524	35	32	14	3	1	244	182	1	104	78	10.8	2.18	125	.212	.303	11	.134	-4	16	15	-5	0.3
1919	Was-A	6	21	.222	35	31	9	0	0	208	220	3	97	87	14.1	3.72	86	.284	.370	11	.169	-1	-11	-12	-1	-1.8
1920	Bos-A	5	14	.263	27	22	11	1	0	162²	163	9	66	71	12.8	3.04	120	.275	.349	6	.120	-3	14	11	-3	0.5
1921	*NY-A	4	3	.571	9	7	4	0	0	52²	52	3	25	22	13.5	3.76	113	.263	.351	2	.125	-1	3	3	-2	0.0
1923	Bro-N	0	1	.000	1	1	0	0	0	3²	8	2	3	1	27.0	14.73	26	.421	.500	0	.000	-0	-4	-4	-0	-0.7
Total	10	57	76	.429	219	171	66	12	5	1256	1100	26	582	623	12.3	2.87	105	.243	.335	59	.147	-16	26	21	-21	-2.7

● JACK HARPER   Harper, John Wesley b: 8/5/1893, Hendricks, W.Va. d: 6/18/27, Halstead, Kan.   BR/TR, 5'11", 180 lbs.   Deb: 4/17/15

| 1915 | Phi-A | 0 | 0 | — | 3 | 0 | 0 | 0 | 0 | 8² | 5 | 0 | 1 | 3 | 6.2 | 3.12 | 94 | .161 | .188 | 0 | — | 0 | 0 | -0 | 0 | 0.0 |

● BILL HARPER   Harper, William Homer "Blue Sleeve" b: 6/14/1889, Bertrand, Mo. d: 6/17/51, Somerville, Tenn.   BB/TR, 6'1", 180 lbs.   Deb: 6/10/11

| 1911 | StL-A | 0 | 0 | — | 2 | 0 | 0 | 0 | 0 | 4 | 6 | 1 | 3 | 3 | 20.2 | 6.75 | 50 | .300 | .400 | 0 | — | 0 | -3 | -3 | 0 | 0.0 |

● SLIM HARRELL   Harrell, Oscar Martin b: 7/31/1890, Grandview, Tex. d: 4/30/71, Hillsboro, Tex.   BR/TR, 6'3", 180 lbs.   Deb: 6/21/12

| 1912 | Phi-A | 0 | 0 | — | 1 | 0 | 0 | 0 | 0 | 3 | 4 | 0 | 0 | 1 | 12.0 | 0.00 | — | .364 | .364 | 0 | .000 | -0 | 1 | 1 | -0 | 0.0 |

YEAR	TM/L	W	L	PCT	G	GS	CG	SH	SV	IP	H	HR	BB	SO	RAT	ERA	ERA+	OAV	OOB	BH	AVG	PB	PR	/A	PD	TPI

● RAY HARRELL Harrell, Raymond James "Cowboy" b: 2/16/12, Petrolia, Tex. d: 1/28/84, Alexandria, La. BR/TR, 6'1", 185 lbs. Deb: 4/16/35

YEAR	TM/L	W	L	PCT	G	GS	CG	SH	SV	IP	H	HR	BB	SO	RAT	ERA	ERA+	OAV	OOB	BH	AVG	PB	PR	/A	PD	TPI
1935	StL-N	1	1	.500	11	1	0	0	0	29²	39	4	11	13	15.2	6.67	61	.320	.376	0	.000	-1	-9	-8	-0	-0.6
1937	StL-N	3	7	.300	35	15	1	1	1	96²	99	7	59	41	14.9	5.87	68	.263	.366	1	.045	-2	-21	-20	-1	-2.1
1938	StL-N	2	3	.400	32	3	1	0	2	63	78	6	29	32	15.7	4.86	81	.308	.386	0	.000	-1	-7	-6	-0	-0.6
1939	Chi-N	0	2	.000	4	2	0	0	0	17¹	29	2	6	5	18.2	8.31	47	.387	.432	0	.000	-1	-8	-8	0	-0.8
	Phi-N	3	7	.300	22	10	4	0	0	94²	101	6	56	35	15.3	5.42	74	.270	.371	3	.115	-1	-16	-15	-3	-1.7
	Yr	3	9	.250	26	12	4	0	0	112	130	8	62	40	15.8	5.87	68	.290	.381	3	.097	-2	-24	-23	-3	-2.5
1940	Pit-N	0	0	—	3	0	0	0	0	3¹	5	0	2	3	18.9	8.10	47	.333	.412	0	—	0	-2	-2	-0	0.0
1945	NY-N	0	0	—	12	0	0	0	0	25¹	34	1	14	7	17.4	4.97	79	.343	.430	1	.200	1	-3	-3	0	0.1
Total	6	9	20	.310	119	31	6	1	3	330	385	26	177	136	15.6	5.70	70	.293	.381	5	.069	-5	-66	-63	-3	-5.7

● BILL HARRELSON Harrelson, William Charles b: 11/17/45, Tahlequah, Okla. BB/TR, 6'5", 215 lbs. Deb: 7/31/68

YEAR	TM/L	W	L	PCT	G	GS	CG	SH	SV	IP	H	HR	BB	SO	RAT	ERA	ERA+	OAV	OOB	BH	AVG	PB	PR	/A	PD	TPI
1968	Cal-A	1	6	.143	10	5	1	0	0	33²	28	4	26	22	14.7	5.08	57	.226	.364	1	.100	-0	-8	-8	-0	-1.7

● ANDY HARRINGTON Harrington, Andrew Francis b: 11/13/1888, Wakefield, Mass. d: 11/12/38, Malden, Mass. BR/TR, 6', 193 lbs. Deb: 9/8/13

YEAR	TM/L	W	L	PCT	G	GS	CG	SH	SV	IP	H	HR	BB	SO	RAT	ERA	ERA+	OAV	OOB	BH	AVG	PB	PR	/A	PD	TPI
1913	Cin-N	0	0	—	1	0	0	0	0	4	6	0	1	1	15.8	9.00	36	.353	.389	1	.500	0	-3	-3	-0	0.0

● BILL HARRINGTON Harrington, William Womble b: 10/3/27, Sanford, N.C. BR/TR, 5'11", 160 lbs. Deb: 4/16/53

YEAR	TM/L	W	L	PCT	G	GS	CG	SH	SV	IP	H	HR	BB	SO	RAT	ERA	ERA+	OAV	OOB	BH	AVG	PB	PR	/A	PD	TPI
1953	Phi-A	0	0	—	1	0	0	0	0	2	5	0	0	0	22.5	13.50	32	.500	.500	0	—	-0	-2	-2	-0	0.0
1955	KC-A	3	3	.500	34	1	0	0	2	76²	69	6	41	26	13.1	4.11	102	.246	.347	2	.118	-1	-1	1	-1	-0.1
1956	KC-A	2	2	.500	23	1	0	0	1	37²	40	3	26	14	15.8	6.45	67	.274	.384	0	.000	-1	-10	-9	-0	-0.9
Total	3	5	5	.500	58	2	0	0	3	116¹	114	9	67	40	14.2	5.03	84	.261	.362	2	.083	-1	-13	-10	-1	-1.0

● BEN HARRIS Harris, Ben Franklin b: 12/17/1889, Donelson, Tenn. d: 4/29/27, St.Louis, Mo. BR/TR, 6', 220 lbs. Deb: 4/19/14

YEAR	TM/L	W	L	PCT	G	GS	CG	SH	SV	IP	H	HR	BB	SO	RAT	ERA	ERA+	OAV	OOB	BH	AVG	PB	PR	/A	PD	TPI
1914	KC-F	7	7	.500	31	14	5	0	1	154	179	7	41	40	13.2	4.09	68	.303	.354	9	.200	1	-21	-22	1	-1.7
1915	KC-F	0	0	—	1	0	0	0	0	2	1	0	0	0	4.5	0.00	—	.143	.143	0	—	0	1	1	0	0.0
Total	2	7	7	.500	32	14	5	0	1	156	180	7	41	40	13.1	4.04	69	.301	.352	9	.200	1	-20	-22	1	-1.7

● LUM HARRIS Harris, Chalmer Luman b: 1/17/15, New Castle, Ala. BR/TR, 6'1", 180 lbs. Deb: 4/19/41 MC

YEAR	TM/L	W	L	PCT	G	GS	CG	SH	SV	IP	H	HR	BB	SO	RAT	ERA	ERA+	OAV	OOB	BH	AVG	PB	PR	/A	PD	TPI
1941	Phi-A	4	4	.500	33	10	5	0	2	131²	134	16	51	49	12.8	4.78	88	.260	.329	11	.275	2	-9	-9	-1	-0.4
1942	Phi-A	11	15	.423	26	20	10	1	0	166	146	14	70	60	11.8	3.74	101	.234	.313	10	.161	-2	2	-1	-1	-0.1
1943	Phi-A	7	21	.250	32	27	15	1	1	216¹	241	17	63	55	12.8	4.20	81	.279	.330	12	.171	-1	-22	-19	-0	-2.4
1944	Phi-A	10	9	.526	23	22	12	2	0	174¹	193	8	26	33	11.3	3.30	105	.281	.308	10	.169	-1	2	3	-1	0.2
1946	Phi-A	3	14	.176	34	12	4	0	0	125¹	153	11	48	33	14.4	5.24	68	.308	.369	8	.222	1	-24	-24	3	-2.4
1947	Was-A	0	0	—	3	0	0	0	0	6¹	7	0	7	2	19.9	2.84	131	.318	.483	0	.000	-0	1	1	1	0.0
Total	6	35	63	.357	151	91	46	4	3	820	874	66	265	232	12.6	4.16	88	.273	.329	51	.190	-0	-54	-47	1	-5.1

● BUBBA HARRIS Harris, Charles b: 2/15/26, Sulligent, Ala. BR/TR, 6'4", 204 lbs. Deb: 4/29/48

YEAR	TM/L	W	L	PCT	G	GS	CG	SH	SV	IP	H	HR	BB	SO	RAT	ERA	ERA+	OAV	OOB	BH	AVG	PB	PR	/A	PD	TPI
1948	Phi-A	5	2	.714	45	0	0	0	5	93²	89	2	35	32	12.0	4.13	104	.249	.317	3	.125	-1	2	2	-0	0.0
1949	Phi-A	1	1	.500	37	0	0	0	3	84¹	92	12	42	18	14.4	5.44	75	.286	.370	3	.125	-2	-12	-12	2	-0.3
1951	Phi-A	0	0	—	3	0	0	0	0	4	4	0	5	2	22.5	9.00	48	.250	.455	0	—	-0	-2	-2	0	0.0
	Cle-A	0	0	—	2	0	0	0	0	4	5	0	4	1	20.3	4.50	84	.333	.474	0	—	-0	-0	-0	0	0.0
	Yr	0	0	—	5	0	0	0	0	8	9	0	9	3	20.3	6.75	60	.281	.439	0	—	-0	-2	-2	0	0.0
Total	3	6	3	.667	87	0	0	0	8	186	190	14	86	53	13.5	4.84	87	.267	.349	6	.125	-3	-12	-13	2	-0.3

● GREG HARRIS Harris, Greg Allen b: 11/2/55, Lynwood, Cal. BB/TR, 6', 175 lbs. Deb: 5/20/81

YEAR	TM/L	W	L	PCT	G	GS	CG	SH	SV	IP	H	HR	BB	SO	RAT	ERA	ERA+	OAV	OOB	BH	AVG	PB	PR	/A	PD	TPI
1981	NY-N	3	5	.375	16	14	0	0	1	68²	65	8	28	54	12.5	4.46	78	.245	.322	4	.182	-0	-7	-7	-1	-0.9
1982	Cin-N	2	6	.250	34	10	1	0	1	91¹	96	12	37	67	13.3	4.83	77	.274	.346	3	.167	-0	-12	-11	0	-0.9
1983	Cin-N	0	0	—	1	0	0	0	0	1	2	0	3	1	54.0	27.00	14	.500	.750	0	.000	-0	-3	-3	0	0.0
1984	Mon-N	0	1	.000	15	0	0	0	2	17²	10	7	15	9	9.7	2.04	168	.172	.284	0	—	0	3	3	0	0.2
	*SD-N	2	1	.667	19	1	0	0	1	36²	28	3	18	30	11.8	2.70	132	.209	.312	3	.375	1	4	4	-0	0.4
	Yr	2	2	.500	34	1	0	0	3	54¹	38	3	25	45	10.8	2.48	142	.196	.294	3	.333	1	7	6	-0	0.6
1985	Tex-A	5	4	.556	58	0	0	0	11	113	74	7	43	111	9.7	2.47	171	.186	.274	0	—	0	21	22	1	2.1
1986	Tex-A	10	8	.556	73	0	0	0	20	111¹	103	12	42	95	11.8	2.83	152	.251	.322	0	—	0	17	18	1	3.3
1987	Tex-A	5	10	.333	42	19	0	0	0	140²	157	18	56	106	13.9	4.86	92	.281	.351	0	—	0	-6	-6	0	-0.5
1988	Phi-N	4	6	.400	66	1	0	0	1	107	80	7	52	71	11.4	2.36	151	.209	.311	3	.333	1	13	14	0	1.5
1989	Phi-N	2	2	.500	44	0	0	0	0	75¹	64	7	43	51	13.0	3.58	99	.234	.342	1	.167	1	-1	-0	1	0.1
	Bos-A	2	2	.500	15	0	0	0	0	28	21	1	15	25	11.6	2.57	159	.208	.310	0	—	0	4	5	0	0.3
1990	*Bos-A	13	9	.591	34	30	1	0	0	184¹	186	13	77	117	13.0	4.00	102	.265	.342	0	—	0	-2	1	3	0.2
1991	Bos-A	11	12	.478	53	21	0	0	2	173	157	13	69	127	12.0	3.85	112	.243	.321	0	—	0	5	9	2	1.2
1992	Bos-A	4	9	.308	70	2	1	0	4	107²	82	6	60	73	12.2	2.51	168	.215	.327	0	—	0	17	20	1	2.4
1993	Bos-A	6	7	.462	**80**	0	0	0	8	112¹	95	7	60	103	13.2	3.77	123	.232	.344	0	—	0	7	11	-0	1.1
1994	Bos-A	3	4	.429	35	0	0	0	0	45²	60	8	23	44	16.6	8.28	61	.321	.398	0	—	0	-18	-16	0	-2.3
	NY-A	0	1	.000	3	0	0	0	0	5	4	1	3	4	16.2	5.40	85	.222	.391	0	—	0	-0	-0	-0	-0.0
	Yr	3	5	.375	38	0	0	0	0	50²	64	9	26	48	16.3	7.99	62	.309	.391	0	—	0	-18	-17	0	-2.3
1995	Mon-N	2	3	.400	45	0	0	0	2	48¹	45	6	16	47	11.5	2.61	165	.245	.308	1	.333	1	8	9	-0	0.9
Total	15	74	90	.451	703	98	4	0	54	1467	1329	129	652	1141	12.5	3.69	112	.243	.330	15	.221	3	49	71	7	9.1

● GREG HARRIS Harris, Gregory Wade b: 12/1/63, Greensboro, N.C. BR/TR, 6'3", 190 lbs. Deb: 9/14/88

YEAR	TM/L	W	L	PCT	G	GS	CG	SH	SV	IP	H	HR	BB	SO	RAT	ERA	ERA+	OAV	OOB	BH	AVG	PB	PR	/A	PD	TPI
1988	SD-N	2	0	1.000	3	1	1	0	0	18	13	0	3	15	8.0	1.50	226	.200	.235	0	.000	-1	4	4	-0	0.3
1989	SD-N	8	9	.471	56	6	0	0	6	135	106	8	52	106	10.7	2.60	134	.215	.293	1	.053	-1	13	13	1	1.8
1990	SD-N	8	8	.500	73	0	0	0	9	117¹	92	6	49	97	11.1	2.30	166	.220	.307	1	.083	-0	19	20	0	2.9
1991	SD-N	9	5	.643	20	20	3	2	0	133	116	16	27	95	9.7	2.23	170	.233	.274	3	.083	-1	21	23	-1	2.2
1992	SD-N	4	8	.333	20	20	1	0	0	118	113	13	35	66	11.4	4.12	87	.252	.309	4	.129	-1	-8	-7	0	-0.6
1993	SD-N	10	8	.526	22	22	4	0	0	152	151	18	39	83	11.4	3.67	113	.257	.307	9	.170	1	6	8	1	1.1
	Col-N	1	8	.111	13	13	0	0	0	73¹	88	15	30	40	15.0	6.50	73	.299	.372	1	.050	-2	-20	-14	0	-1.6
	Yr	11	17	.393	35	35	4	0	0	225¹	239	33	69	123	12.5	4.59	94	.270	.328	10	.137	-0	-14	-6	1	-0.5
1994	Col-N	3	12	.200	29	19	1	0	1	130	154	22	52	82	14.6	6.65	75	.300	.370	7	.175	-0	-35	-24	1	-2.4
1995	Min-A	0	5	.000	7	6	0	0	0	32²	50	5	16	21	18.2	8.82	54	.355	.420	0	—	0	-15	-15	0	-1.7
Total	8	45	64	.413	243	109	10	2	16	909¹	883	103	303	605	11.9	3.98	102	.255	.319	26	.119	-3	-14	7	3	2.0

● HERB HARRIS Harris, Herbert Benjamin "Hub" or "Lefty" b: 4/24/13, Chicago, Ill. d: 1/18/91, Crystal Lake, Ill. BL/TL, 6'1", 175 lbs. Deb: 7/21/36

YEAR	TM/L	W	L	PCT	G	GS	CG	SH	SV	IP	H	HR	BB	SO	RAT	ERA	ERA+	OAV	OOB	BH	AVG	PB	PR	/A	PD	TPI
1936	Phi-N	0	0	—	4	0	0	0	0	11	19	2	9	1	25.7	10.29	44	.380	.526	0	.000	-0	-5	-4	0	0.0

● PEP HARRIS Harris, Hernando Petrocelli b: 9/23/72, Lancaster, S.C. BR/TR, 6'2", 185 lbs. Deb: 8/14/96

YEAR	TM/L	W	L	PCT	G	GS	CG	SH	SV	IP	H	HR	BB	SO	RAT	ERA	ERA+	OAV	OOB	BH	AVG	PB	PR	/A	PD	TPI
1996	Cal-A	2	0	1.000	11	0	0	0	0	32¹	31	4	17	20	14.2	3.90	126	.254	.359	0	—	0	4	4	0	0.2

● JOE HARRIS Harris, Joseph White b: 2/1/1882, Melrose, Mass. d: 4/12/66, Melrose, Mass. BR/TR, 6'1", 198 lbs. Deb: 9/22/05

YEAR	TM/L	W	L	PCT	G	GS	CG	SH	SV	IP	H	HR	BB	SO	RAT	ERA	ERA+	OAV	OOB	BH	AVG	PB	PR	/A	PD	TPI
1905	Bos-A	1	2	.333	3	3	3	0	0	23	16	0	8	14	9.4	2.35	115	.198	.270	1	.111	-1	1	1	-0	0.0
1906	Bos-A	2	21	.087	30	24	20	1	2	235	211	5	67	99	10.9	3.52	78	.243	.303	13	.160	-2	-22	-20	6	-1.5
1907	Bos-A	0	7	.000	12	5	3	0	0	59	57	0	13	24	10.8	3.05	84	.256	.300	4	.190	-0	-3	-3	-0	-0.4
Total	3	3	30	.091	45	32	26	1	2	317	284	5	88	137	10.8	3.35	81	.242	.300	18	.162	-3	-24	-22	6	-1.9

● MICKEY HARRIS Harris, Maurice Charles b: 1/30/17, New York, N.Y. d: 4/15/71, Farmington, Mich. BL/TL, 6', 195 lbs. Deb: 4/23/40

YEAR	TM/L	W	L	PCT	G	GS	CG	SH	SV	IP	H	HR	BB	SO	RAT	ERA	ERA+	OAV	OOB	BH	AVG	PB	PR	/A	PD	TPI
1940	Bos-A	4	2	.667	13	9	3	0	0	68¹	83	8	26	36	14.6	5.00	90	.292	.356	6	.273	2	-5	-4	0	-0.1
1941	Bos-A	8	14	.364	35	22	11	1	1	194	189	6	86	111	12.9	3.25	128	.250	.328	6	.109	2	19	20	-1	2.2
1946	*Bos-A☆	17	9	.654	34	30	15	0	0	222²	236	18	76	131	12.7	3.64	101	.268	.329	18	.231	4	-3	-1	-1	0.3
1947	Bos-A	5	4	.556	15	6	1	0	0	51²	42	3	23	35	11.3	2.44	159	.225	.310	5	.417	3	7	8	0	1.7
1948	Bos-A	7	10	.412	20	17	6	0	0	113²	120	10	59	42	14.3	5.30	83	.271	.360	2	.063	-1	-13	-12	-2	-1.7
1949	Bos-A	2	3	.400	7	6	2	0	0	37²	53	2	20	14	17.7	5.02	87	.323	.400	1	.083	-1	-3	-3	-0	-0.4
	Was-A	2	12	.143	23	19	4	0	1	129	151	8	55	54	14.4	5.16	82	.292	.360	4	.205	-1	-14	/13	-2	-1.2
	Yr	4	15	.211	30	25	6	0	1	166²	204	10	75	68	15.1	5.13	83	.299	.368	9	.176	1	-17	-16	-2	-1.6

YEAR	TM/L	W	L	PCT	G	GS	CG	SH	SV	IP	H	HR	BB	SO	RAT	ERA	ERA+	OAV	OOB	BH	AVG	PB	PR	/A	PD	TPI
1950	Was-A	5	9	.357	53	0	0	0	15	98	93	10	46	41	12.9	4.78	94	.247	.330	4	.235	1	-2	-3	-1	-0.5
1951	Was-A	6	8	.429	41	0	0	0	4	87¹	87	6	43	47	13.5	3.81	107	.260	.347	3	.188	1	3	3	-1	0.4
1952	Was-A	0	0	—	1	0	0	0	0	1	1	1	0	0	9.0	9.00	40	.250	.250	0	—	0	-1	-1	-0	0.0
	Cle-A	3	0	1.000	29	0	0	0	1	46²	42	6	21	23	12.3	4.63	72	.249	.335	1	.200	-0	-5	-7	0	-0.4
	Yr	3	0	1.000	30	0	0	0	1	47²	43	7	21	23	12.3	4.72	71	.249	.333	1	.200	-0	-6	-7	-0	-0.4
Total	9	59	71	.454	271	109	42	2	21	1050	1097	79	455	534	13.4	4.18	98	.267	.342	54	.188	11	-16	-9	-7	0.3

● REGGIE HARRIS   Harris, Reginald Allen b: 8/12/68, Waynesboro, Va. BR/TR, 6'1", 180 lbs. Deb: 7/4/90

YEAR	TM/L	W	L	PCT	G	GS	CG	SH	SV	IP	H	HR	BB	SO	RAT	ERA	ERA+	OAV	OOB	BH	AVG	PB	PR	/A	PD	TPI
1990	Oak-A	1	0	1.000	16	1	0	0	0	41¹	25	5	21	31	10.5	3.48	107	.176	.291	0	—	0	2	1	-0	0.2
1991	Oak-A	0	0	—	2	0	0	0	0	3	5	0	3	2	24.0	12.00	32	.455	.571	0	—	0	-3	-3	-0	0.0
1996	Bos-A	0	0	—	4	0	0	0	0	4¹	7	2	5	4	27.0	12.46	41	.389	.542	0	—	0	-4	-4	-0	0.0
Total	3	1	0	1.000	22	1	0	0	0	48²	37	7	29	37	12.8	4.81	80	.216	.340	0	—	0	-4	-5	-1	0.2

● BOB HARRIS   Harris, Robert Arthur b: 5/1/17, Gillette, Wyo. d: 8/8/89, North Platte, Neb. BR/TR, 6', 185 lbs. Deb: 9/19/38

YEAR	TM/L	W	L	PCT	G	GS	CG	SH	SV	IP	H	HR	BB	SO	RAT	ERA	ERA+	OAV	OOB	BH	AVG	PB	PR	/A	PD	TPI
1938	Det-A	1	0	1.000	3	1	1	0	0	10	14	0	4	7	16.2	7.20	69	.318	.375	1	.333	0	-3	-2	0	-0.1
1939	Det-A	1	1	.500	5	1	0	0	0	18	18	4	8	9	13.0	4.00	122	.269	.347	2	.400	0	1	2	0	0.2
	StL-A	3	12	.200	28	16	6	0	0	126	162	5	71	48	16.6	5.71	85	.321	.405	7	.189	-0	-15	-12	3	-0.9
	Yr	4	13	.235	33	17	6	0	0	144	180	9	79	57	16.2	5.50	89	.315	.398	9	.214	-0	-14	-10	3	-0.7
1940	StL-A	11	15	.423	35	28	8	1	1	193²	225	24	85	49	14.5	4.93	93	.290	.362	15	.250	3	-12	-7	-0	-0.6
1941	StL-A	12	14	.462	34	29	9	2	1	186²	237	18	85	57	15.6	5.21	83	.312	.383	7	.115	-3	-22	-19	-2	-2.6
1942	StL-A	1	5	.167	6	6	0	0	0	33²	37	2	17	9	14.4	5.61	66	.268	.348	0	.000	-1	-7	-7	-1	-1.2
	Phi-A	1	5	.167	16	8	2	1	0	78	77	5	24	26	11.7	2.88	131	.253	.308	7	.269	1	7	8	2	0.9
	Yr	2	10	.167	22	14	2	1	0	111²	114	7	41	35	12.5	3.71	101	.258	.321	7	.194	-0	-1	1	2	-0.3
Total	5	30	52	.366	127	89	26	4	2	646	770	58	294	205	14.9	4.96	89	.297	.370	39	.193	1	-51	-38	3	-4.3

● GENE HARRIS   Harris, Tyrone Eugene b: 12/5/64, Sebring, Fla. BR/TR, 5'11", 190 lbs. Deb: 4/5/89

YEAR	TM/L	W	L	PCT	G	GS	CG	SH	SV	IP	H	HR	BB	SO	RAT	ERA	ERA+	OAV	OOB	BH	AVG	PB	PR	/A	PD	TPI
1989	Mon-N	1	1	.500	11	0	0	0	0	20	16	1	10	11	11.7	4.95	71	.242	.342	0	.000	-0	-3	-3	2	-0.2
	Sea-A	1	4	.200	10	6	0	0	1	33¹	47	3	15	14	17.0	6.48	62	.353	.423	0	—	0	-10	-9	-1	-1.4
1990	Sea-A	1	2	.333	25	0	0	0	1	38	31	5	30	43	14.7	4.74	84	.217	.356	0	—	0	-4	-3	-0	-0.3
1991	Sea-A	0	0	—	8	0	0	0	1	13¹	15	1	10	6	16.9	4.05	102	.273	.385	0	—	0	0	0	0	0.0
1992	Sea-A	0	0	—	9	0	0	0	0	9	8	3	6	6	14.0	7.00	57	.235	.350	0	—	0	-3	-3	-0	-0.2
	SD-N	0	2	.000	14	0	0	0	0	21¹	15	0	9	19	10.5	2.95	121	.195	.287	1	.333	-0	1	1	0	0.2
1993	SD-N	6	6	.500	59	0	0	0	23	59¹	57	3	37	39	14.4	3.03	136	.254	.363	0	.000	-0	7	7	1	1.9
1994	SD-N	1	1	.500	13	0	0	0	0	12¹	21	2	8	9	21.2	8.03	51	.389	.468	0	—	0	-5	-5	-0	-0.8
	Det-A	0	0	—	11	0	0	0	1	11¹	13	1	4	10	14.3	7.15	68	.271	.340	0	—	0	-3	-3	-0	-0.1
1995	Phi-N	2	2	.500	21	0	0	0	0	19	19	2	8	9	12.8	4.26	99	.260	.333	0	—	0	0	0	0	0.0
	Bal-A	0	0	—	3	0	0	0	0	4	4	0	1	4	11.3	4.50	106	.267	.313	0	—	0	0	0	0	0.0
Total	7	12	18	.400	183	7	0	0	26	241	246	21	138	170	14.5	4.71	86	.267	.365	1	.167	-0	-20	-18	1	-0.7

● BUDDY HARRIS   Harris, Walter Francis b: 12/5/48, Philadelphia, Pa. BR/TR, 6'7", 245 lbs. Deb: 9/10/70

YEAR	TM/L	W	L	PCT	G	GS	CG	SH	SV	IP	H	HR	BB	SO	RAT	ERA	ERA+	OAV	OOB	BH	AVG	PB	PR	/A	PD	TPI
1970	Hou-N	0	0	—	2	0	0	0	0	6¹	6	3	0	2	8.5	5.68	68	.240	.240	0	.000	-0	-1	-1	-0	0.0
1971	Hou-N	1	1	.500	20	0	0	0	0	30²	33	3	16	21	14.4	6.46	52	.275	.360	0	.000	-0	-10	-11	-1	-0.7
Total	2	1	1	.500	22	0	0	0	0	37	39	6	16	23	13.4	6.32	55	.269	.342	0	.000	-0	-11	-12	-1	-0.7

● BILL HARRIS   Harris, William Milton b: 6/23/1900, Wylie, Tex. d: 8/21/65, Indian Trail, N.C. BR/TR, 6'1", 180 lbs. Deb: 4/22/23

YEAR	TM/L	W	L	PCT	G	GS	CG	SH	SV	IP	H	HR	BB	SO	RAT	ERA	ERA+	OAV	OOB	BH	AVG	PB	PR	/A	PD	TPI
1923	Cin-N	3	2	.600	22	3	0	0	0	69²	79	3	18	18	12.9	5.17	75	.292	.342	6	.353	1	-9	-10	0	-0.5
1924	Cin-N	0	0	—	3	0	0	0	0	7	10	0	2	5	15.4	9.00	42	.323	.364	1	1.000	0	-4	-4	0	0.1
1931	Pit-N	2	2	.500	4	4	3	1	0	31	21	0	9	10	8.7	0.87	442	.194	.256	1	.091	-1	10	10	0	1.3
1932	Pit-N	10	9	.526	37	17	4	0	2	168	178	6	38	63	11.9	3.64	105	.271	.317	10	.182	-1	4	3	-2	0.1
1933	Pit-N	4	4	.500	31	0	0	0	5	58²	68	1	14	19	12.7	3.22	103	.289	.332	0	.000	-1	1	-1	-1	-0.1
1934	Pit-N	0	0	—	11	2	0	0	0	19	29	2	7	8	17.1	6.63	62	.350	.409	1	.500	0	-5	-5	-0	-0.3
1938	Bos-A	5	5	.500	13	11	5	1	1	80¹	83	5	21	26	11.8	4.03	122	.268	.316	6	.214	-0	7	8	-0	0.8
Total	7	24	22	.522	121	37	13	2	8	433²	467	17	109	149	12.2	3.92	101	.276	.324	25	.203	-1	4	2	-2	1.8

● BILL HARRIS   Harris, William Thomas b: 12/3/31, Duguayville, N.B., Canada BL/TR, 5'8", 187 lbs. Deb: 9/27/57

YEAR	TM/L	W	L	PCT	G	GS	CG	SH	SV	IP	H	HR	BB	SO	RAT	ERA	ERA+	OAV	OOB	BH	AVG	PB	PR	/A	PD	TPI
1957	Bro-N	0	1	.000	1	1	0	0	0	7	9	1	1	3	12.9	3.86	108	.321	.345	1	.500	0	0	0	0	0.1
1959	LA-N	0	0	—	1	0	0	0	0	1²	0	0	3	0	16.2	0.00	—	.000	.375	0	—	0	1	1	0	0.1
Total	2	0	1	.000	2	1	0	0	0	8²	9	1	4	3	13.5	3.12	134	.273	.351	1	.500	0	1	1	0	0.1

● BOB HARRISON   Harrison, Robert Lee b: 9/22/30, St.Louis, Mo. BL/TR, 5'11", 178 lbs. Deb: 9/23/55

YEAR	TM/L	W	L	PCT	G	GS	CG	SH	SV	IP	H	HR	BB	SO	RAT	ERA	ERA+	OAV	OOB	BH	AVG	PB	PR	/A	PD	TPI
1955	Bal-A	0	0	—	1	0	0	0	0	2	3	0	4	0	31.5	9.00	42	.500	.700	0	—	0	-1	-1	-0	0.0
1956	Bal-A	0	0	—	1	1	0	0	0	1²	3	0	5	0	43.2	16.20	24	.375	.615	0	—	0	-2	-2	-0	0.0
Total	2	0	0	—	2	1	0	0	0	3²	6	0	9	0	36.8	12.27	31	.429	.652	0	—	0	-3	-3	-0	0.0

● RORIC HARRISON   Harrison, Roric Edward b: 9/20/46, Los Angeles, Cal. BR/TR, 6'3", 195 lbs. Deb: 4/18/72

YEAR	TM/L	W	L	PCT	G	GS	CG	SH	SV	IP	H	HR	BB	SO	RAT	ERA	ERA+	OAV	OOB	BH	AVG	PB	PR	/A	PD	TPI
1972	Bal-A	3	4	.429	39	2	0	0	4	94	68	2	34	62	10.1	2.30	134	.209	.292	2	.118	1	8	8	-1	0.7
1973	Atl-N	11	8	.579	38	22	3	0	5	177¹	161	15	98	130	13.3	4.16	94	.242	.342	3	.056	-2	-10	-5	-1	-0.8
1974	Atl-N	6	11	.353	20	20	3	0	0	126	148	12	49	46	14.3	4.71	80	.294	.360	7	.184	2	-15	-13	-2	-1.6
1975	Atl-N	3	4	.429	15	7	2	0	1	54²	58	7	19	22	12.7	4.77	79	.266	.325	3	.200	1	-7	-6	0	-0.7
	Cle-A	7	7	.500	19	19	4	0	0	126	137	9	46	52	13.4	4.79	79	.275	.341	0	—	0	-14	-14	-1	-1.5
1978	Min-A	0	1	.000	9	0	0	0	0	12	18	0	11	7	21.8	7.50	51	.346	.460	0	—	0	-5	-5	-0	-0.5
Total	5	30	35	.462	140	70	12	0	10	590	590	45	257	319	13.1	4.24	87	.261	.340	15	.121	2	-43	-35	-5	-4.4

● TOM HARRISON   Harrison, Thomas James b: 1/18/45, Trail, B.C., Canada BR/TR, 6'3", 200 lbs. Deb: 5/7/65 ♦

YEAR	TM/L	W	L	PCT	G	GS	CG	SH	SV	IP	H	HR	BB	SO	RAT	ERA	ERA+	OAV	OOB	BH	AVG	PB	PR	/A	PD	TPI
1965	KC-A	0	0	—	1	0	0	0	0	1	2	0	1	0	27.0	9.00	39	.667	.750	0	—	0	-1	-1	-0	0.0

● SLIM HARRISS   Harriss, William Jennings Bryan b: 12/11/1896, Brownwood, Tex. d: 9/19/63, Temple, Tex. BR/TR, 6'6", 180 lbs. Deb: 4/19/20

YEAR	TM/L	W	L	PCT	G	GS	CG	SH	SV	IP	H	HR	BB	SO	RAT	ERA	ERA+	OAV	OOB	BH	AVG	PB	PR	/A	PD	TPI
1920	Phi-A	9	14	.391	31	25	11	1	0	192	226	5	57	60	13.5	4.08	99	.305	.359	7	.106	-7	-6	-1	3	-0.5
1921	Phi-A	11	16	.407	39	28	14	0	2	227²	258	16	73	92	13.4	4.27	104	.290	.350	12	.148	-7	0	5	-1	-0.2
1922	Phi-A	9	20	.310	47	32	13	0	3	229²	262	19	94	102	14.1	5.02	85	.290	.359	13	.176	-4	-25	-19	1	-2.5
1923	Phi-A	10	16	.385	46	28	9	0	6	209¹	221	9	95	89	13.7	4.00	103	.280	.359	4	.066	-8	0	3	5	0.0
1924	Phi-A	6	10	.375	36	12	4	1	2	123	138	5	62	45	14.9	4.68	92	.291	.377	7	.167	-3	-6	-5	4	-0.5
1925	Phi-A	19	12	.613	46	33	15	2	1	252²	263	8	95	95	13.0	3.49	133	.268	.336	18	.205	-3	25	33	4	3.6
1926	Phi-A	3	5	.375	12	10	2	0	0	57	66	0	22	13	13.9	4.11	102	.289	.352	1	.059	-2	-1	0	0	-0.1
	Bos-A	6	10	.375	21	18	6	1	0	113	135	0	34	34	13.5	4.46	91	.311	.362	7	.206	-0	-6	-5	1	-0.5
	Yr	9	15	.375	33	28	8	1	0	170	201	0	55	47	13.7	4.34	95	.304	.359	8	.157	-2	-6	-4	1	-0.6
1927	Bos-A	14	21	.400	44	27	11	1	1	217²	253	8	66	77	13.6	4.18	101	.298	.355	8	.121	-5	1	1	1	-0.2
1928	Bos-A	8	11	.421	27	15	4	1	1	128¹	141	5	33	37	12.3	4.63	89	.287	.335	5	.139	-3	-8	-7	-2	-1.3
Total	9	95	135	.413	349	228	89	7	16	1750¹	1963	75	630	644	13.5	4.25	100	.290	.354	82	.145	-40	-27	3	15	-2.2

● EARL HARRIST   Harrist, Earl "Irish" b: 8/20/19, Dubach, La. BR/TR, 6', 178 lbs. Deb: 8/18/45

YEAR	TM/L	W	L	PCT	G	GS	CG	SH	SV	IP	H	HR	BB	SO	RAT	ERA	ERA+	OAV	OOB	BH	AVG	PB	PR	/A	PD	TPI
1945	Cin-N	2	4	.333	14	5	1	0	0	62¹	60	2	27	15	12.7	3.61	104	.249	.327	0	.000	-2	1	1	-1	-0.2
1947	Chi-A	3	8	.273	33	4	0	0	5	93²	85	3	49	55	13.2	3.56	103	.248	.347	5	.208	-0	1	1	0	0.0
1948	Chi-A	1	3	.250	11	1	0	0	0	23	23	4	13	14	15.3	5.87	73	.267	.382	0	.000	-1	-4	-4	0	-0.7
	Was-A	3	3	.500	23	4	0	0	0	60²	70	1	37	21	16.3	4.60	94	.297	.394	3	.167	-1	-2	-2	-1	-0.3
	Yr	4	6	.400	34	5	0	0	0	83²	93	5	50	35	15.7	4.95	87	.284	.383	3	.136	-2	-6	-6	-1	-1.0
1952	StL-A	2	8	.200	36	9	1	0	5	116²	119	7	47	49	13.6	4.01	98	.269	.352	3	.097	-2	-4	-4	-1	-0.3
1953	Chi-A	1	0	1.000	7	0	0	0	0	8¹	9	1	5	1	15.1	7.56	53	.290	.389	0	.000	-0	-3	-3	-0	-0.4
	Det-A	0	2	.000	8	1	0	0	0	18²	25	7	8	6	19.3	8.68	47	.333	.444	0	.000	-0	-10	-10	1	-0.8
	Yr	1	2	.333	15	1	0	0	0	27	34	8	13	7	18.0	8.33	49	.321	.429	0	.000	-0	-13	-13	1	-1.2
Total	5	12	28	.300	132	24	2	0	10	383¹	391	20	193	162	14.2	4.34	90	.268	.361	11	.115	-7	-21	-18	-0	-2.5

YEAR	TM/L	W	L	PCT	G	GS	CG	SH	SV	IP	H	HR	BB	SO	RAT	ERA	ERA+	OAV	OOB	BH	AVG	PB	PR	/A	PD	TPI

● JACK HARSHMAN Harshman, John Elvin b: 7/12/27, San Diego, Cal. BL/TL, 6'2", 185 lbs. Deb: 9/16/48 ♦

1952	NY-N	0	2	.000	2	2	0	0	0	6¹	12	2	6	6	25.6	14.21	26	.429	.529	0	.000	-0	-7	-7	0	-1.5
1954	Chi-A	14	8	.636	35	21	9	4	1	177	157	7	96	134	13.1	2.95	127	.238	.339	8	.143	3	15	15	-1	2.1
1955	Chi-A	11	7	.611	32	23	9	0	0	179¹	144	16	97	116	12.3	3.36	117	.224	.330	11	.183	4	12	12	-0	1.4
1956	Chi-A	15	11	.577	34	30	15	4	0	226²	183	14	102	143	11.4	3.10	132	.221	.308	12	.169	6	27	25	-2	3.0
1957	Chi-A	8	8	.500	30	26	6	0	1	151¹	142	16	62	83	13.6	4.10	91	.250	.349	10	.222	5	-5	-6	-3	-0.3
1958	Bal-A	12	15	.444	34	29	17	3	4	236¹	204	20	75	161	10.7	2.89	124	.231	.294	16	.195	8	23	18	1	3.4
1959	Bal-A	0	6	.000	14	8	0	0	0	47¹	58	6	28	24	16.7	6.85	55	.319	.415	2	.200	1	-16	-16	1	-1.5
	Bos-A	2	3	.400	8	2	0	0	0	24²	29	2	10	14	14.2	6.57	62	.284	.348	1	.143	0	-7	-7	-1	-1.2
	Cle-A	5	1	.833	13	6	5	1	1	66	46	6	13	35	8.0	2.59	142	.179	.219	7	.206	2	9	8	-0	0.9
	Yr	7	10	.412	35	16	5	1	1	138	133	14	51	73	12.0	4.76	79	.244	.308	10	.196	3	-14	-15	1	-1.8
1960	Cle-A	2	4	.333	15	8	0	0	0	54¹	50	7	30	25	13.3	3.98	94	.243	.339	3	.176	-0	-1	-1	-0	-0.2
Total	8	69	65	.515	217	155	61	12	7	1169¹	1025	96	539	741	12.2	3.50	109	.235	.323	76	.179	29	50	41	-5	6.1

● OSCAR HARSTAD Harstad, Oscar Theander b: 5/24/1892, Parkland, Wash. d: 11/14/85, Corvallis, Ore. BR/TR, 6', 174 lbs. Deb: 4/23/15

| 1915 | Cle-A | 3 | 5 | .375 | 32 | 7 | 4 | 0 | 1 | 82 | 81 | 1 | 35 | 35 | 12.8 | 3.40 | 90 | .270 | .348 | 2 | .125 | -1 | -4 | -3 | 2 | -0.2 |

● BILLY HART Hart, Robert Lee b: 5/16/1866, Palmyra, Mo. d: 5/14/44, Hannibal, Mo. 5'8" Deb: 7/13/1890

| 1890 | StL-a | 12 | 8 | .600 | 26 | 24 | 20 | 0 | 0 | 201¹ | 188 | 6 | 66 | 95 | 12.1 | 3.67 | 118 | .240 | .312 | 15 | .192 | -1 | 5 | 15 | -3 | 0.8 |

● BILL HART Hart, William Franklin b: 7/19/1865, Louisville, Ky. d: 9/19/36, Cincinnati, Ohio TR, 5'10", 163 lbs. Deb: 7/26/1886 U

1886	Phi-a	9	13	.409	22	22	22	2	0	186	183	7	66	78	12.4	3.19	110	.244	.299	10	.137	-5	5	6	1	0.3
1887	Phi-a	1	2	.333	3	3	3	0	0	26	28	1	17	14	15.9	4.50	95	.272	.380	1	.077	-2	-1	-1	0	-0.2
1892	Bro-N	9	12	.429	28	23	16	2	1	195	188	3	96	65	13.4	3.28	97	.243	.332	24	.192	3	0	-2	3	0.3
1895	Pit-N	14	17	.452	36	29	24	0	1	261²	293	4	135	85	15.2	4.75	95	.279	.369	25	.236	-2	1	-7	6	-0.3
1896	StL-N	12	29	.293	42	41	37	0	0	336	411	11	141	65	15.2	5.12	85	.299	.370	30	.186	-5	-28	-29	6	-2.5
1897	StL-N	9	27	.250	39	38	31	0	0	294²	395	10	148	67	17.1	6.26	70	.318	.398	39	.250	-1	-64	-61	3	-5.2
1898	Pit-N	5	9	.357	16	15	13	1	1	125	141	4	44	19	13.8	4.82	74	.282	.348	12	.240	-1	-17	-18	0	-1.6
1901	Cle-A	7	11	.389	20	19	16	0	0	157²	180	3	57	48	14.1	3.77	94	.283	.352	14	.219	-1	-2	-4	2	-0.3
Total	8	66	120	.355	206	190	162	5	3	1582	1819	43	704	431	14.8	4.65	86	.281	.359	155	.207	-14	-105	-114	22	-9.5

● CHUCK HARTENSTEIN Hartenstein, Charles Oscar "Twiggy" b: 5/26/42, Seguin, Tex. BR/TR, 5'11", 165 lbs. Deb: 9/11/65 C♦

1966	Chi-N	0	0	—	5	0	0	0	0	9¹	8	0	3	4	11.6	1.93	191	.222	.300	0	—	0	2	2	0	0.0
1967	Chi-N	9	5	.643	45	0	0	0	10	73	74	4	17	20	11.3	3.08	115	.278	.324	1	.063	-1	2	4	-0	0.7
1968	Chi-N	2	4	.333	28	0	0	0	1	35²	41	3	11	17	13.4	4.54	70	.291	.346	0	.000	0	-6	-5	-0	-1.0
1969	Pit-N	5	4	.556	56	0	0	0	10	95²	84	9	27	44	10.8	3.95	88	.241	.303	1	.071	-1	-4	-5	1	-0.5
1970	Pit-N	1	1	.500	17	0	0	0	1	23²	25	3	8	14	12.5	4.56	85	.278	.337	0	.000	0	-1	-2	1	-0.1
	StL-N	0	0	—	6	0	0	0	0	13¹	24	1	5	9	19.6	8.78	47	.375	.420	0	.000	0	-7	-7	0	-0.2
	Yr	1	1	.500	23	0	0	0	1	37	49	4	13	23	15.1	6.08	65	.316	.369	0	.000	0	-8	-9	1	-0.1
	Bos-A	0	3	.000	17	0	0	0	1	19	21	6	12	12	16.1	8.05	49	.288	.395	0	—	0	-9	-9	-1	-1.3
1977	Tor-A	0	2	.000	13	0	0	0	0	27¹	40	8	6	15	15.5	6.59	64	.348	.385	0	—	0	-8	-7	-0	-0.5
Total	6	17	19	.472	187	0	0	0	23	297	317	34	89	135	12.6	4.52	80	.280	.337	2	.054	-2	-31	-29	2	-2.7

● FRANK HARTER Harter, Franklin Pierce "Chief" b: 9/19/1886, Keyesport, Ill. d: 4/14/59, Breese, Ill. BR/TR, 5'11", 165 lbs. Deb: 8/31/12

1912	Cin-N	1	2	.333	6	3	1	0	0	29¹	25	1	11	12	11.0	3.07	110	.234	.305	1	.091	-1	1	1	-1	-0.1
1913	Cin-N	1	1	.500	17	2	0	0	0	46²	47	3	19	10	12.7	3.86	84	.272	.344	2	.143	-1	-3	-3	-1	-0.3
1914	Ind-F	1	2	.333	6	1	1	0	0	24²	33	0	7	8	14.6	4.01	78	.330	.374	0	.000	-1	-3	-2	-0	-0.4
Total	3	3	5	.375	29	6	2	0	0	100²	105	4	37	30	12.7	3.67	89	.276	.341	3	.091	-3	-5	-5	-2	-0.8

● DEAN HARTGRAVES Hartgraves, Dean Charles b: 8/12/66, Bakersfield, Cal. BR/TL, 6', 185 lbs. Deb: 5/3/95

1995	Hou-N	2	0	1.000	40	0	0	0	0	36¹	30	2	16	24	11.4	3.22	120	.227	.311	0	.000	-0	4	3	0	0.1
1996	Hou-N	0	0	—	19	0	0	0	0	19	18	1	16	16	16.6	5.21	73	.257	.402	0	—	0	-2	-3	0	0.0
	Atl-N	1	0	1.000	20	0	0	0	0	18²	16	3	7	14	11.6	4.34	101	.232	.312	0	—	0	-0	-0	0	0.0
	Yr	1	0	1.000	39	0	0	0	0	37²	34	4	23	30	13.9	4.78	86	.241	.352	0	—	0	-2	-3	0	0.0
Total	2	3	0	1.000	79	0	0	0	0	74	64	6	39	54	12.8	4.01	99	.236	.337	0	.000	-0	2	-0	0	0.1

● MIKE HARTLEY Hartley, Michael Edward b: 8/31/61, Hawthorne, Cal. BR/TR, 6'1", 192 lbs. Deb: 9/10/89

1989	LA-N	0	1	.000	5	0	0	0	0	6	2	0	4	4	3.0	1.50	228	.100	.100	0	.000	-0	1	1	0	0.2
1990	LA-N	6	3	.667	32	6	1	1	1	79¹	58	7	30	76	10.2	2.95	124	.200	.280	1	.077	-1	7	6	-0	0.6
1991	LA-N	2	0	1.000	57	0	0	0	0	57	53	7	37	44	14.7	4.42	81	.245	.363	0	.000	-0	-5	-5	-0	-0.2
	Phi-N	2	1	.667	18	0	0	0	0	26¹	21	4	10	19	11.6	3.76	98	.219	.312	0	.000	-0	-0	-1	-1	-0.1
	Yr	4	1	.800	58	0	0	0	0	83¹	74	11	47	63	13.4	4.21	86	.234	.339	0	.000	-0	-5	-6	-1	-0.3
1992	Phi-N	7	6	.538	46	0	0	0	0	55	54	5	23	53	12.9	3.44	102	.255	.333	0	.000	-0	3	2	-0	0.0
1993	Min-A	1	2	.333	53	0	0	0	0	81	86	4	36	57	14.3	4.00	109	.281	.370	0	—	0	3	-3	2	0.0
1995	Bos-A	0	0	—	5	0	0	0	0	7	8	1	2	2	15.4	9.00	54	.308	.400	0	—	0	-3	-0	0	0.0
	Bal-A	1	0	1.000	3	0	0	0	0	7	5	0	1	4	7.7	1.29	369	.217	.250	0	—	0	3	3	0	0.4
	Yr	1	0	1.000	8	0	0	0	0	14	13	1	3	6	10.3	5.14	94	.245	.286	0	—	0	-1	-1	0	0.4
Total	6	19	13	.594	202	6	1	1	4	318²	287	28	139	259	12.6	3.70	104	.241	.330	1	.043	-2	6	5	-3	0.9

● CHARLIE HARTMAN Hartman, Charles Otto b: 8/10/1888, Los Angeles, Cal. d: 10/22/60, Los Angeles, Cal. Deb: 6/24/08

| 1908 | Bos-A | 0 | 0 | — | 1 | 0 | 0 | 0 | 0 | 2 | 1 | 0 | 2 | 1 | 13.5 | 4.50 | 55 | .143 | .333 | 0 | — | 0 | -0 | -0 | 0 | 0.0 |

● BOB HARTMAN Hartman, Robert Louis b: 8/28/37, Kenosha, Wis. BR/TL, 5'11", 185 lbs. Deb: 4/26/59

1959	Mil-N	0	0	—	3	0	0	0	0	1²	6	0	2	1	43.2	27.00	13	.545	.615	0	—	0	-4	-4	-0	0.0
1962	Cle-A	0	1	.000	8	2	0	0	0	17¹	14	1	8	11	11.4	3.12	124	.209	.293	0	.000	-1	2	1	-0	-0.2
Total	2	0	1	.000	11	2	0	0	0	19	20	1	10	12	14.2	5.21	74	.256	.341	0	.000	-1	-3	-3	-0	-0.2

● RAY HARTRANFT Hartranft, Raymond Joseph b: 9/19/1890, Quakertown, Pa. d: 2/10/55, Spring City, Pa. BL/TL, 6'1", 195 lbs. Deb: 6/16/13

| 1913 | Phi-N | 0 | 0 | — | 1 | 0 | 0 | 0 | 0 | 1 | 3 | 0 | 1 | 1 | 36.0 | 9.00 | 37 | .500 | .571 | 0 | — | 0 | -1 | -1 | 0 | 0.0 |

● JEFF HARTSOCK Hartsock, Jeffrey Roger b: 11/19/66, Fairfield, Ohio BR/TR, 6', 190 lbs. Deb: 9/12/92

| 1992 | Chi-N | 0 | 0 | — | 4 | 0 | 0 | 0 | 0 | 9 | 15 | 2 | 4 | 6 | 18.3 | 6.75 | 53 | .375 | .432 | 0 | .000 | -0 | -3 | -3 | 0 | 0.2 |

● CLINT HARTUNG Hartung, Clinton Clarence "Floppy" or "The Hondo Hurricane" b: 8/10/22, Hondo, Tex. BR/TR, 6'4", 215 lbs. Deb: 4/15/47 ♦

1947	NY-N	9	7	.563	23	20	8	1	0	138	140	15	69	54	13.8	4.57	89	.263	.350	29	.309	9	-8	-8	-1	0.1
1948	NY-N	8	8	.500	36	19	6	2	1	153¹	146	15	72	42	13.1	4.75	83	.258	.347	10	.179	2	-14	-14	-0	-1.2
1949	NY-N	9	11	.450	33	25	8	0	0	154²	156	16	86	48	14.3	5.00	80	.260	.357	12	.190	4	-17	-18	2	-1.5
1950	NY-N	3	3	.500	20	8	1	0	0	65¹	87	10	44	23	18.3	6.61	62	.326	.425	13	.302	4	-18	-18	2	-0.8
Total	4	29	29	.500	112	72	23	3	1	511¹	529	56	271	167	14.3	5.02	80	.269	.361	90	.238	19	-56	-57	3	-3.4

● PAUL HARTZELL Hartzell, Paul Franklin b: 11/2/53, Bloomsburg, Pa. BR/TR, 6'5", 200 lbs. Deb: 4/10/76

1976	Cal-A	7	4	.636	37	15	7	2	2	166	166	6	43	51	11.9	2.77	120	.266	.323	0	—	0	14	10	1	1.3
1977	Cal-A	8	12	.400	41	23	6	0	4	189¹	200	14	38	79	11.5	3.57	110	.274	.313	0	—	0	10	7	0	0.8
1978	Cal-A	6	10	.375	54	12	1	0	6	157	168	8	41	55	12.3	3.44	105	.278	.329	0	—	0	6	3	1	0.7
1979	Min-A	6	10	.375	28	26	4	0	0	163	193	18	44	44	13.3	5.36	82	.301	.350	0	—	0	-21	-18	1	-1.4
1980	Bal-A	0	2	.000	9	4	1	0	0	17²	22	3	9	5	15.8	6.62	60	.310	.387	0	—	0	-5	-5	-1	-0.6
1984	Mil-A	0	1	.000	4	1	0	0	0	10¹	17	0	6	3	20.0	7.84	49	.370	.442	0	—	0	-4	-5	0	-0.2
Total	6	27	39	.409	170	77	22	2	12	703¹	766	49	181	237	12.4	3.90	98	.282	.332	0	—	0	-0	-7	3	0.4

● BRYAN HARVEY Harvey, Bryan Stanley b: 6/2/63, Soddy-Daisy, Tenn. BR/TR, 6'2", 215 lbs. Deb: 5/16/87

| 1987 | Cal-A | 0 | 0 | — | 3 | 0 | 0 | 0 | 0 | 5 | 6 | 0 | 2 | 3 | 14.4 | 0.00 | — | .300 | .364 | 0 | — | 0 | 2 | 2 | -0 | 0.1 |
| 1988 | Cal-A | 7 | 5 | .583 | 50 | 0 | 0 | 0 | 17 | 76 | 59 | 4 | 20 | 67 | 9.5 | 2.13 | 181 | .214 | .269 | 0 | — | 0 | 15 | 15 | -2 | 2.7 |

YEAR	TM/L	W	L	PCT	G	GS	CG	SH	SV	IP	H	HR	BB	SO	RAT	ERA	ERA+	OAV	OOB	BH	AVG	PB	PR	/A	PD	TPI
1989	Cal-A	3	3	.500	51	0	0	0	25	55	36	6	41	78	12.6	3.44	111	.183	.324	0	—	0	3	2	0	0.5
1990	Cal-A	4	4	.500	54	0	0	0	25	64¹	45	4	35	82	11.2	3.22	119	.201	.309	0	—	0	5	4	-0	0.9
1991	Cal-A☆	2	4	.333	67	0	0	0	**46**	78²	51	6	17	101	7.9	1.60	256	.178	.227	0	—	0	22	22	-0	3.7
1992	Cal-A	0	4	.000	25	0	0	0	13	28²	22	4	11	34	10.4	2.83	141	.208	.282	0	—	0	4	4	-1	0.7
1993	Fla-N★	1	5	.167	59	0	0	0	45	69	45	4	13	73	7.6	1.70	255	.186	.227	0	—	0	18	20	-1	3.9
1994	Fla-N	0	0	—	12	0	0	0	6	10¹	12	1	4	10	13.9	5.23	84	.279	.340	0	—	0	-1	-1	0	-0.1
1995	Fla-N	0	0	—	1	0	0	0	0	0	2	1	1	0	—	∞	—	1.000	1.000	0	—	0	-3	-3	0	-0.3
Total	9	17	25	.405	322	0	0	0	177	387	278	30	144	448	9.9	2.49	161	.199	.275	0	—	0	65	65	-3	12.0

● **ZAZA HARVEY**   Harvey, Ervin King b: 1/5/1879, Saratoga, Cal. d: 6/3/54, Santa Monica, Cal. BL/TL, 6′, 190 lbs. Deb: 5/3/00 ◆

YEAR	TM/L	W	L	PCT	G	GS	CG	SH	SV	IP	H	HR	BB	SO	RAT	ERA	ERA+	OAV	OOB	BH	AVG	PB	PR	/A	PD	TPI
1900	Chi-A	0	0	—	1	0	0	0	0	4	3	0	1	0	9.0	0.00	—	.214	.267	0	—	-1	2	2	-0	-0.1
1901	Chi-A	3	6	.333	16	9	5	0	1	92	91	2	34	27	12.7	3.62	96	.255	.328	10	.250	2	0	-1	2	0.3
Total	2	3	6	.333	17	9	5	0	1	96	94	2	35	27	12.6	3.47	101	.253	.326	86	.332	2	2	0	2	0.2

● **HERB HASH**   Hash, Herbert Howard b: 2/13/11, Woolwine, Va. BR/TR, 6′1″, 180 lbs. Deb: 4/19/40

YEAR	TM/L	W	L	PCT	G	GS	CG	SH	SV	IP	H	HR	BB	SO	RAT	ERA	ERA+	OAV	OOB	BH	AVG	PB	PR	/A	PD	TPI
1940	Bos-A	7	7	.500	34	12	3	1	3	120	123	11	84	36	15.9	4.95	91	.266	.385	7	.175	-0	-8	-6	1	-0.6
1941	Bos-A	1	0	1.000	4	0	0	0	0	8¹	7	1	7	3	15.1	5.40	77	.226	.368	0	.000	-0	-1	-1	0	-0.2
Total	2	8	7	.533	38	12	3	1	3	128¹	130	12	91	39	15.8	4.98	90	.264	.384	7	.167	-1	-9	-7	1	-0.8

● **ANDY HASSLER**   Hassler, Andrew Earl b: 10/18/51, Texas City, Tex. BL/TL, 6′5″, 220 lbs. Deb: 5/30/71

YEAR	TM/L	W	L	PCT	G	GS	CG	SH	SV	IP	H	HR	BB	SO	RAT	ERA	ERA+	OAV	OOB	BH	AVG	PB	PR	/A	PD	TPI
1971	Cal-A	0	3	.000	6	4	0	0	0	18²	25	0	15	13	19.8	3.86	84	.333	.451	0	.000	-1	-1	-1	-0	-0.2
1973	Cal-A	0	4	.000	7	4	1	0	0	31²	33	0	19	19	15.6	3.69	96	.262	.372	0	—	0	-1	-0	-0	0.3
1974	Cal-A	7	11	.389	23	22	10	2	1	162	132	10	79	76	12.2	2.61	132	.225	.326	0	—	0	18	15	0	1.7
1975	Cal-A	3	12	.200	30	18	6	1	0	133¹	158	12	53	82	14.6	5.94	60	.303	.373	0	—	0	-32	-35	1	-2.9
1976	Cal-A	0	6	.000	14	4	0	0	0	47¹	50	7	17	16	12.7	5.13	65	.284	.347	0	—	0	-8	-10	-0	-0.7
	*KC-A	5	6	.455	19	14	4	1	0	99²	89	7	39	45	11.6	2.89	121	.242	.314	0	—	0	7	7	1	0.7
	Yr	5	12	.294	33	18	4	1	0	147	139	5	56	61	11.9	3.61	95	.254	.323	0	—	0	-2	-3	1	0.0
1977	*KC-A	9	6	.600	29	27	3	1	0	156¹	166	7	75	83	14.2	4.20	96	.270	.354	0	—	0	-2	-3	0	-0.2
1978	KC-A	1	4	.200	11	9	1	0	0	58¹	76	1	24	26	15.7	4.32	88	.317	.383	0	—	0	-4	-3	-1	-0.3
	Bos-A	2	1	.667	13	2	0	0	1	30	38	0	13	23	15.3	3.00	137	.302	.367	0	—	0	3	4	-0	0.3
	Yr	3	5	.375	24	11	1	0	1	88¹	114	1	37	49	15.4	3.87	101	.308	.371	0	—	0	-1	0	-0	0.0
1979	Bos-A	1	2	.333	8	0	0	0	0	15¹	23	1	0	7	18.2	8.80	50	.365	.437	0	—	0	-8	-7	-0	-1.4
	NY-N	4	5	.444	29	8	1	0	0	80¹	74	5	42	53	13.0	3.70	98	.252	.345	0	.000	-2	-0	-1	1	-0.2
1980	Pit-N	0	0	—	6	0	0	0	0	11²	12	1	4	10	10.0	3.86	94	.243	.317	0	.000	-0	-0	-1	0	0.0
	Cal-A	5	1	.833	41	0	0	0	10	83	67	8	37	75	11.4	2.49	158	.214	.299	0	—	0	14	13	-1	1.3
1981	Cal-A	4	3	.571	42	0	0	0	5	75²	72	4	26	33	11.9	3.21	114	.262	.341	0	—	0	4	5	1	0.4
1982	*Cal-A	2	1	.667	54	0	0	0	4	71¹	58	5	40	38	12.9	2.78	146	.232	.347	0	—	0	10	10	2	1.0
1983	Cal-A	0	5	.000	42	0	0	0	4	36¹	42	2	17	20	14.6	5.45	74	.302	.378	0	—	0	-6	-6	-1	-0.7
1984	StL-N	1	0	1.000	3	0	0	0	0	2¹	4	2	2	1	23.1	11.57	30	.364	.462	0	—	0	-2	-2	-0	-0.7
1985	StL-N	0	1	.000	10	0	0	0	0	10	9	2	6	3	11.7	1.80	196	.225	.295	0	—	0	2	2	-0	0.2
Total	14	44	71	.383	387	112	26	5	29	1123¹	1125	67	520	630	13.4	3.83	97	.264	.349	0	.000	-3	-5	-15	4	-1.7

● **CHARLIE HASTINGS**   Hastings, Charles Morton b: 11/11/1870, Ironton, Ohio d: 8/3/34, Parkersburg, W.Va. 5′11″, 179 lbs. Deb: 5/3/1893

YEAR	TM/L	W	L	PCT	G	GS	CG	SH	SV	IP	H	HR	BB	SO	RAT	ERA	ERA+	OAV	OOB	BH	AVG	PB	PR	/A	PD	TPI
1893	Cle-N	4	5	.444	15	9	6	0	1	92	128	5	33	14	16.2	4.70	104	.320	.379	7	.179	0	-0	2	-2	0.0
1896	Pit-N	5	10	.333	17	13	9	0	1	104	126	1	44	19	15.3	5.88	71	.296	.372	8	.216	-0	-18	-19	1	-2.0
1897	Pit-N	5	4	.556	16	10	9	0	0	118	138	3	47	42	14.6	4.58	91	.289	.362	10	.233	3	-3	-5	-1	-0.1
1898	Pit-N	4	10	.286	19	13	12	0	0	137¹	142	2	52	40	13.4	3.41	104	.265	.341	10	.233	3	2	1	1	0.5
Total	4	18	29	.383	67	45	36	0	2	451¹	534	11	176	115	14.7	4.55	91	.291	.362	35	.216	5	-18	-21	-1	-1.6

● **BOB HASTY**   Hasty, Robert Keller b: 5/3/1896, Canton, Ga. d: 5/28/72, Dallas, Ga. BR/TR, 6′3″, 210 lbs. Deb: 9/11/19

YEAR	TM/L	W	L	PCT	G	GS	CG	SH	SV	IP	H	HR	BB	SO	RAT	ERA	ERA+	OAV	OOB	BH	AVG	PB	PR	/A	PD	TPI
1919	Phi-A	0	2	.000	2	2	1	0	0	12	15	1	9	5	14.3	5.25	65	.306	.358	1	.333	0	-3	-2	1	-0.4
1920	Phi-A	1	3	.250	19	4	1	0	0	71²	91	5	28	12	14.9	5.02	80	.323	.384	6	.250	0	-10	-8	2	-0.2
1921	Phi-A	5	16	.238	35	22	9	0	0	179¹	238	8	40	46	14.1	4.87	92	.331	.388	20	.294	2	-12	-8	0	-0.5
1922	Phi-A	9	14	.391	28	26	14	1	0	191²	225	20	41	33	12.6	4.26	100	.298	.336	15	.200	-2	-5	-0	-2	-0.4
1923	Phi-A	13	15	.464	44	36	10	1	1	243¹	274	11	72	56	13.1	4.44	93	.291	.347	17	.193	-3	-12	-9	-1	-1.2
1924	Phi-A	1	3	.250	18	4	0	0	0	52²	57	4	30	15	15.0	5.64	76	.282	.378	1	.077	-1	-8	-8	2	-0.5
Total	6	29	53	.354	146	94	35	2	1	751¹	900	49	215	167	13.5	4.65	91	.305	.355	60	.221	-3	-49	-35	-0	-3.2

● **MICKEY HATCHER**   Hatcher, Michael Vaughn b: 3/15/55, Cleveland, Ohio BR/TR, 6′2″, 200 lbs. Deb: 8/3/79 C◆

YEAR	TM/L	W	L	PCT	G	GS	CG	SH	SV	IP	H	HR	BB	SO	RAT	ERA	ERA+	OAV	OOB	BH	AVG	PB	PR	/A	PD	TPI
1989	LA-N	0	0	—	1	0	0	0	0	1	0	0	3	0	36.0	9.00	38	.000	.667	66	.295	0	-1	-1	0	0.0

● **GIL HATFIELD**   Hatfield, Gilbert "Colonel" b: 1/27/1855, Hoboken, N.J. d: 5/27/21, Hoboken, N.J. TR, 5′9.5″, 168 lbs. Deb: 9/24/1885 F◆

YEAR	TM/L	W	L	PCT	G	GS	CG	SH	SV	IP	H	HR	BB	SO	RAT	ERA	ERA+	OAV	OOB	BH	AVG	PB	PR	/A	PD	TPI
1889	NY-N	2	4	.333	6	5	5	0	0	52	53	2	25	28	13.7	3.98	99	.256	.339	23	.184	-0	0	-0	-0	0.2
1890	NY-P	1	1	.500	3	0	0	0	1	7²	8	1	4	3	15.3	3.52	129	.258	.361	80	.279	0	1	1	-0	0.2
1891	Was-a	0	0	—	4	0	0	0	0	18	29	1	14	3	21.5	11.00	34	.349	.443	128	.256	1	-15	-15	-0	0.2
Total	3	3	5	.375	13	5	5	0	1	77²	90	4	43	34	15.6	5.56	71	.280	.369	295	.248	1	-14	-14	-0	0.2

● **JOHN HATFIELD**   Hatfield, John Van Buskirk b: 7/20/1847, New Jersey d: 2/20/09, Long Island City, N.Y. 5′10″, 165 lbs. Deb: 5/18/1871 FM◆

YEAR	TM/L	W	L	PCT	G	GS	CG	SH	SV	IP	H	HR	BB	SO	RAT	ERA	ERA+	OAV	OOB	BH	AVG	PB	PR	/A	PD	TPI
1874	Mut-n	0	1	.000	3	0	0	0	0	8	11	0	0	0	12.4	2.25	99	.314	.314	66	.226	-0	-0	-0		0.1

● **HILLY HATHAWAY**   Hathaway, Hillary Houston b: 9/12/69, Jacksonville, Fla. BL/TL, 6′4″, 195 lbs. Deb: 9/8/92

YEAR	TM/L	W	L	PCT	G	GS	CG	SH	SV	IP	H	HR	BB	SO	RAT	ERA	ERA+	OAV	OOB	BH	AVG	PB	PR	/A	PD	TPI
1992	Cal-A	0	0	—	2	1	0	0	0	5²	8	1	3	1	17.5	7.94	50	.333	.407	0	—	0	-3	-2	-0	-0.5
1993	Cal-A	4	3	.571	11	11	0	0	0	57¹	71	6	26	11	16.0	5.02	90	.326	.410	0	—	0	-4	-3	1	-0.5
Total	2	4	3	.571	13	12	0	0	0	63	79	7	29	12	16.1	5.29	84	.326	.409	0	—	0	-7	-6	0	-0.5

● **RAY HATHAWAY**   Hathaway, Ray Wilson b: 10/13/16, Greenville, Ohio BR/TR, 6′, 165 lbs. Deb: 4/20/45

YEAR	TM/L	W	L	PCT	G	GS	CG	SH	SV	IP	H	HR	BB	SO	RAT	ERA	ERA+	OAV	OOB	BH	AVG	PB	PR	/A	PD	TPI
1945	Bro-N	0	1	.000	4	1	0	0	0	9	11	1	6	3	17.0	4.00	94	.297	.395	0	.000	-0	-0	-0	-0	0.0

● **JOE HATTEN**   Hatten, Joseph Hilarian b: 11/17/16, Bancroft, Iowa d: 12/16/88, Redding, Cal. BR/TL, 6′, 176 lbs. Deb: 4/21/46

YEAR	TM/L	W	L	PCT	G	GS	CG	SH	SV	IP	H	HR	BB	SO	RAT	ERA	ERA+	OAV	OOB	BH	AVG	PB	PR	/A	PD	TPI
1946	Bro-N	14	11	.560	42	30	13	1	2	222	207	10	110	85	13.1	2.84	119	.253	.347	6	.076	-6	14	13	-2	0.6
1947	*Bro-N	17	8	.680	42	32	11	3	0	225¹	211	9	105	76	12.8	3.63	114	.252	.339	17	.205	0	11	12	3	1.5
1948	Bro-N	13	10	.565	42	30	11	1	0	208²	228	9	94	73	14.0	3.58	112	.283	.360	13	.206	1	9	10	4	1.5
1949	*Bro-N	12	8	.600	37	29	11	2	2	187¹	194	15	69	58	12.7	4.18	98	.271	.337	12	.179	-1	-3	-2	-0	-0.3
1950	Bro-N	2	2	.500	23	8	2	1	0	68²	82	10	31	29	14.8	4.59	89	.294	.365	2	.111	-1	-3	-3	1	-0.4
1951	Bro-N	1	0	1.000	11	6	1	0	0	49¹	55	5	21	22	13.9	4.56	86	.281	.350	1	.133	-1	-3	-3	1	-0.1
	Chi-N	2	6	.250	23	6	0	0	0	75¹	82	6	37	23	14.3	5.14	80	.281	.364	4	.235	0	-10	-9	-0	-0.8
	Yr	3	6	.333	34	12	1	0	0	124²	137	11	58	45	14.1	4.91	82	.281	.358	6	.188	-1	-13	-12	1	-0.9
1952	Chi-N	4	4	.500	13	8	2	0	0	50¹	65	6	25	15	16.3	6.08	63	.314	.391	1	.067	-1	-13	-12	1	-1.7
Total	7	65	49	.570	233	149	51	8	4	1087	1124	70	492	381	13.5	3.87	101	.271	.351	57	.160	-8	1	5	6	0.3

● **CLYDE HATTER**   Hatter, Clyde Melno b: 8/7/08, Poplar Hills, Ky. d: 10/16/37, Yosemite, Ky. BR/TL, 5′11″, 170 lbs. Deb: 4/23/35

YEAR	TM/L	W	L	PCT	G	GS	CG	SH	SV	IP	H	HR	BB	SO	RAT	ERA	ERA+	OAV	OOB	BH	AVG	PB	PR	/A	PD	TPI
1935	Det-A	0	0	—	8	2	0	0	0	33¹	44	2	30	15	20.3	7.56	55	.319	.444	3	.300	1	-12	-13	-1	-0.1
1937	Det-A	1	0	1.000	3	0	0	0	0	9¹	17	0	11	4	28.0	11.57	40	.415	.547	0	—	-0	-7	-7	-0	-0.6
Total	2	1	0	1.000	11	2	0	0	0	42²	61	2	41	19	21.9	8.44	51	.341	.468	3	.231	0	-19	-20	-1	-0.7

● **CHRIS HAUGHEY**   Haughey, Christopher Francis "Bud" b: 10/3/25, Astoria, N.Y. BR/TR, 6′1″, 180 lbs. Deb: 10/3/43

YEAR	TM/L	W	L	PCT	G	GS	CG	SH	SV	IP	H	HR	BB	SO	RAT	ERA	ERA+	OAV	OOB	BH	AVG	PB	PR	/A	PD	TPI
1943	Bro-N	0	1	.000	1	1	0	0	0	7	5	0	10	0	19.3	3.86	87	.238	.484	0	.000	-0	-0	-0	-0	-0.1

● **PHIL HAUGSTAD**   Haugstad, Philip Donald b: 2/23/24, Black River Falls, Wis. BR/TR, 6′2″, 165 lbs. Deb: 9/1/47

YEAR	TM/L	W	L	PCT	G	GS	CG	SH	SV	IP	H	HR	BB	SO	RAT	ERA	ERA+	OAV	OOB	BH	AVG	PB	PR	/A	PD	TPI
1947	Bro-N	1	0	1.000	6	1	0	0	0	12²	14	1	4	4	12.8	2.84	145	.298	.353	0	—	0	2	2	-0	0.1
1948	Bro-N	0	0	—	1	0	0	0	0	1	1	0	0	0	9.0	0.00	—	.333	.333	0	—	0	-0	-0	0	0.0
1951	Bro-N	0	1	.000	21	1	0	0	0	30²	28	4	24	22	16.1	6.46	61	.233	.374	0	.000	0	-9	-9	0	-0.2

YEAR	TM/L	W	L	PCT	G	GS	CG	SH	SV	IP	H	HR	BB	SO	RAT	ERA	ERA+	OAV	OOB	BH	AVG	PB	PR	/A	PD	TPI
1952	Cin-N	0	0	—	9	0	0	0	0	12	8	1	13	2	16.5	6.75	56	.190	.393	0	.000	-0	-4	-4	0	0.0
Total	4	1	1	.500	37	2	0	0	0	56¹	51	6	41	28	15.3	5.59	70	.241	.374	0	.000	-0	-10	-10	1	-0.1

● TOM HAUSMAN   Hausman, Thomas Matthew   b: 3/31/53, Mobridge, S.D.   BR/TR, 6'5", 200 lbs.   Deb: 4/26/75

YEAR	TM/L	W	L	PCT	G	GS	CG	SH	SV	IP	H	HR	BB	SO	RAT	ERA	ERA+	OAV	OOB	BH	AVG	PB	PR	/A	PD	TPI
1975	Mil-A	3	6	.333	29	9	1	0	0	112	110	7	47	46	13.1	4.10	93	.258	.340	0	—	0	-4	-3	1	-0.2
1976	Mil-A	0	0	—	3	0	0	0	0	3¹	3	0	3	1	16.2	5.40	65	.250	.400	0	—	0	-1	-1	0	0.2
1978	NY-N	3	3	.500	10	10	0	0	0	51²	58	6	9	16	11.8	4.70	74	.287	.321	3	.176	1	-6	-7	0	-0.7
1979	NY-N	2	6	.250	19	10	1	0	2	78²	65	6	19	33	10.1	2.75	133	.226	.284	3	.115	-1	9	8	0	0.7
1980	NY-N	6	5	.545	55	4	0	0	1	122	125	12	26	53	11.4	3.98	89	.266	.309	1	.063	-1	-5	-6	1	-0.5
1981	NY-N	0	1	.000	20	0	0	0	0	33	28	2	7	13	9.5	2.18	160	.235	.278	0	.000	0	5	5	0	0.2
1982	NY-N	1	2	.333	21	0	0	0	0	36²	44	4	6	16	12.8	4.42	82	.295	.331	0	.000	0	-3	-3	-1	-0.3
	Atl-N	0	0	—	3	0	0	0	0	3²	6	0	4	2	24.5	4.91	76	.500	.625	0	—	0	-1	-0	0	-0.3
	Yr	1	2	.333	24	0	0	0	0	40¹	50	4	10	18	13.4	4.46	82	.299	.339	0	.000	0	-4	-4	-0	-0.3
Total	7	15	23	.395	160	33	2	0	3	441	439	37	121	180	11.8	3.80	96	.262	.317	7	.111	-2	-7	-8	2	-0.6

● CLEM HAUSMANN   Hausmann, Clemens Raymond   b: 8/17/19, Houston, Tex.   d: 8/29/72, Baytown, Tex.   BR/TR, 5'9", 165 lbs.   Deb: 4/28/44

YEAR	TM/L	W	L	PCT	G	GS	CG	SH	SV	IP	H	HR	BB	SO	RAT	ERA	ERA+	OAV	OOB	BH	AVG	PB	PR	/A	PD	TPI
1944	Bos-A	4	7	.364	32	12	3	0	2	137	139	6	69	43	13.9	3.42	99	.266	.355	3	.079	-3	0	-0	-0	-0.3
1945	Bos-A	5	7	.417	31	13	4	2	2	125	131	5	60	30	13.9	5.04	68	.270	.352	4	.103	-3	-23	-23	2	-2.2
1949	Phi-A	0	0	—	1	0	0	0	0	1	0	0	2	0	18.0	9.00	46	.000	.500	0	—	-1	-1	-0	0	0.0
Total	3	9	14	.391	64	25	7	2	4	263	270	11	131	73	13.9	4.21	81	.267	.354	7	.091	-5	-24	-23	2	-2.5

● BRAD HAVENS   Havens, Bradley David   b: 11/17/59, Highland Park, Mich   BL/TL, 6'1", 196 lbs.   Deb: 6/5/81

YEAR	TM/L	W	L	PCT	G	GS	CG	SH	SV	IP	H	HR	BB	SO	RAT	ERA	ERA+	OAV	OOB	BH	AVG	PB	PR	/A	PD	TPI
1981	Min-A	3	6	.333	14	12	1	1	0	78	76	6	24	43	11.7	3.58	110	.257	.315	0	—	0	1	3	-1	0.0
1982	Min-A	10	14	.417	33	32	4	1	0	208²	201	32	80	129	12.1	4.31	98	.250	.318	0	—	0	-6	-2	-3	-0.5
1983	Min-A	5	8	.385	16	14	1	0	0	80¹	110	11	38	40	16.6	8.18	52	.333	.402	0	—	0	-37	-35	-2	-4.7
1985	Bal-A	0	1	.000	8	1	0	0	0	14¹	20	4	10	19	18.8	8.79	46	.333	.429	0	—	0	-7	-8	-0	-0.3
1986	Bal-A	3	3	.500	46	0	0	0	1	71	64	7	29	57	11.8	4.56	91	.248	.324	0	—	0	-3	-3	1	-0.1
1987	LA-N	0	0	—	31	1	0	0	1	35¹	30	2	23	23	13.8	4.33	92	.227	.346	0	.000	-0	-1	-1	-1	-0.1
1988	LA-N	0	0	—	9	0	0	0	0	9²	15	1	4	8	17.7	4.66	72	.357	.413	0	.000	-0	-1	-1	1	0.1
	Cle-A	2	3	.400	28	0	0	0	1	57¹	62	7	17	30	12.4	3.14	131	.273	.324	0	—	0	5	6	-0	0.4
1989	Cle-A	0	0	—	7	0	0	0	0	13¹	13	3	7	6	16.9	4.05	98	.353	.431	0	—	0	-0	-0	-0	-0.0
	Det-A	1	2	.333	13	1	0	0	0	22²	28	3	14	15	17.9	5.56	69	.308	.417	0	—	0	-4	-4	-0	-0.4
	Yr	1	2	.333	20	1	0	0	0	36	46	6	21	21	17.5	5.00	77	.319	.417	0	—	0	-4	-5	-1	-0.4
Total	8	24	37	.393	205	61	6	2	3	590²	624	76	246	370	13.3	4.81	86	.272	.344	0	.000	-0	-54	-46	-4	-5.6

● RYAN HAWBLITZEL   Hawblitzel, Ryan Wade   b: 4/30/71, West Palm Beach, Fla.   BR/TR, 6'2", 170 lbs.   Deb: 6/9/96

YEAR	TM/L	W	L	PCT	G	GS	CG	SH	SV	IP	H	HR	BB	SO	RAT	ERA	ERA+	OAV	OOB	BH	AVG	PB	PR	/A	PD	TPI
1996	Col-N	0	1	.000	8	0	0	0	0	15	18	2	6	7	14.4	6.00	91	.290	.353	0	.000	-0	-3	-1	0	-0.1

● ED HAWK   Hawk, Edward   b: 5/11/1890, Neosho, Mo.   d: 3/26/36, Neosho, Mo.   BL/TR, 5'11", 175 lbs.   Deb: 9/7/11

YEAR	TM/L	W	L	PCT	G	GS	CG	SH	SV	IP	H	HR	BB	SO	RAT	ERA	ERA+	OAV	OOB	BH	AVG	PB	PR	/A	PD	TPI
1911	StL-A	0	4	.000	5	4	0	0	0	37²	38	1	8	14	11.9	3.35	101	.253	.309	2	.154	-1	-0	0	0	-0.1

● BILL HAWKE   Hawke, William Victor "Dick"   b: 4/28/1870, Elsmere, Del.   d: 12/11/02, Wilmington, Del.   BR/TR, 5'8.5", 169 lbs.   Deb: 7/28/1892

YEAR	TM/L	W	L	PCT	G	GS	CG	SH	SV	IP	H	HR	BB	SO	RAT	ERA	ERA+	OAV	OOB	BH	AVG	PB	PR	/A	PD	TPI
1892	StL-N	5	5	.500	14	11	10	1	0	97¹	108	2	45	55	14.9	3.70	86	.270	.355	4	.089	-4	-4	-5	0	-0.9
1893	StL-N	0	1	.000	1	1	0	0	0	5¹	9	0	3	1	20.3	5.06	93	.360	.429	1	.333	0	-0	-0	-0	0.0
	Bal-N	11	16	.407	29	29	22	1	0	225	248	8	108	69	14.6	4.76	100	.271	.354	16	.172	-4	-2	-0	0	-0.4
	Yr	11	17	.393	30	30	22	1	0	230¹	257	8	111	70	14.7	4.77	100	.274	.356	17	.177	-4	-3	-1	0	-0.4
1894	*Bal-N	16	9	.640	32	25	17	0	3	206	264	9	78	68	15.5	5.81	94	.308	.374	28	.304	2	-11	-8	1	-0.5
Total	3	32	31	.508	76	66	49	2	3	533²	629	19	234	193	15.0	4.98	95	.286	.363	49	.210	-7	-18	-15	1	-1.8

● LA TROY HAWKINS   Hawkins, La Troy   b: 12/21/72, Gary, Ind.   BR/TR, 6'5", 195 lbs.   Deb: 4/29/95

YEAR	TM/L	W	L	PCT	G	GS	CG	SH	SV	IP	H	HR	BB	SO	RAT	ERA	ERA+	OAV	OOB	BH	AVG	PB	PR	/A	PD	TPI
1995	Min-A	2	3	.400	6	6	1	0	0	27	39	3	12	9	17.3	8.67	55	.339	.406	0	—	0	-12	-12	0	-1.6
1996	Min-A	1	1	.500	7	6	0	0	0	26¹	42	8	9	24	17.4	8.20	63	.372	.418	0	—	0	-9	-9	0	-0.5
Total	2	3	4	.429	13	12	1	0	0	53¹	81	11	21	33	17.4	8.44	59	.355	.412	0	—	0	-21	-21	0	-2.1

● ANDY HAWKINS   Hawkins, Melton Andrew   b: 1/21/60, Waco, Tex.   BR/TR, 6'3", 223 lbs.   Deb: 7/17/82

YEAR	TM/L	W	L	PCT	G	GS	CG	SH	SV	IP	H	HR	BB	SO	RAT	ERA	ERA+	OAV	OOB	BH	AVG	PB	PR	/A	PD	TPI
1982	SD-N	2	5	.286	15	10	1	0	0	63²	66	4	27	25	13.4	4.10	84	.274	.352	0	.000	-2	-4	-5	-1	-0.7
1983	SD-N	5	7	.417	21	19	4	1	0	119²	106	8	48	59	12.0	2.93	119	.244	.326	2	.065	-1	9	7	1	0.7
1984	*SD-N	8	9	.471	36	22	2	1	0	146	143	13	72	77	13.4	4.68	76	.254	.341	8	.195	-4	-18	-18	-1	-2.0
1985	SD-N	18	8	.692	33	33	5	2	0	228²	229	18	65	69	11.7	3.15	112	.267	.321	6	.078	-4	11	10	-1	0.6
1986	SD-N	10	8	.556	37	35	3	1	0	209¹	218	24	75	117	12.8	4.30	85	.268	.334	10	.149	-1	-14	-15	-2	-1.4
1987	SD-N	3	10	.231	24	20	0	0	0	117²	131	16	49	51	13.9	5.05	78	.287	.358	5	.156	-0	-13	-14	0	-1.4
1988	SD-N	14	11	.560	33	33	4	2	0	217²	196	16	76	91	11.5	3.35	101	.244	.314	7	.113	-2	2	1	-3	-0.3
1989	NY-A	15	15	.500	34	34	5	2	0	208¹	238	23	76	98	13.8	4.80	81	.290	.355	0	—	0	-21	-21	-3	-2.9
1990	NY-A	5	12	.294	28	26	2	1	0	157²	156	20	82	74	13.7	5.37	74	.260	.351	0	—	0	-26	-24	-2	-2.5
1991	NY-A	0	2	.000	4	3	0	0	0	12²	23	5	6	5	20.6	9.95	42	.383	.439	0	—	0	-8	-8	1	-0.9
	Oak-A	4	4	.500	15	14	1	0	0	77	68	5	36	40	12.7	4.79	80	.237	.332	0	—	0	-6	-8	0	-0.7
	Yr	4	6	.400	19	17	1	0	0	89²	91	10	42	45	13.9	5.52	70	.262	.350	0	—	0	-14	-16	1	-1.6
Total	10	84	91	.480	280	249	27	10	0	1558¹	1574	152	612	706	12.9	4.22	87	.265	.338	38	.117	-8	-86	-96	-11	-11.5

● WYNN HAWKINS   Hawkins, Wynn Firth "Hawk"   b: 2/20/36, E.Palestine, Ohio   BR/TR, 6'3", 195 lbs.   Deb: 4/22/60

YEAR	TM/L	W	L	PCT	G	GS	CG	SH	SV	IP	H	HR	BB	SO	RAT	ERA	ERA+	OAV	OOB	BH	AVG	PB	PR	/A	PD	TPI
1960	Cle-A	4	4	.500	15	9	1	0	0	66	68	10	39	39	14.7	4.23	88	.269	.369	2	.100	-1	-3	-4	1	-0.4
1961	Cle-A	7	9	.438	30	21	3	1	1	133	139	16	59	51	13.5	4.06	97	.270	.347	4	.108	-2	-1	-2	-1	-0.5
1962	Cle-A	1	0	1.000	3	0	0	0	0	3²	9	1	1	0	24.5	7.36	53	.429	.455	0	—	0	-1	-1	-0	-0.3
Total	3	12	13	.480	48	30	4	1	1	202²	216	27	99	90	14.1	4.17	93	.274	.357	6	.105	-2	-5	-7	-1	-1.2

● PINK HAWLEY   Hawley, Emerson P.   b: 12/5/1872, Beaver Dam, Wis.   d: 9/19/38, Beaver Dam, Wis.   BL/TR, 5'10", 185 lbs.   Deb: 8/13/1892

YEAR	TM/L	W	L	PCT	G	GS	CG	SH	SV	IP	H	HR	BB	SO	RAT	ERA	ERA+	OAV	OOB	BH	AVG	PB	PR	/A	PD	TPI
1892	StL-N	6	14	.300	20	20	18	0	0	166¹	160	4	63	63	12.7	3.19	100	.243	.319	12	.169	-2	2	0	-2	-0.4
1893	StL-N	5	17	.227	31	24	21	0	1	227	249	6	103	73	14.7	4.60	103	.270	.356	26	.286	7	2	3	-3	0.6
1894	StL-N	19	27	.413	53	41	36	0	0	392²	481	14	149	120	14.9	4.90	110	.298	.365	43	.264	2	18	22	2	2.1
1895	Pit-N	31	22	.585	**56**	50	44	**4**	1	**444**¹	449	7	122	142	12.2	3.18	142	.258	.319	57	.308	14	**79**	66	2	**7.4**
1896	Pit-N	22	21	.512	49	43	37	2	0	378	382	2	157	137	13.5	3.57	118	.260	.343	39	.239	2	33	26	3	2.8
1897	Pit-N	18	18	.500	40	39	33	0	0	311²	362	7	94	88	13.9	4.80	87	.288	.350	30	.231	-4	-17	-22	0	-2.0
1898	Cin-N	27	11	.711	43	37	32	3	0	331	357	5	91	69	12.8	3.37	114	.273	.331	24	.185	-4	9	17	-5	0.7
1899	Cin-N	14	17	.452	34	29	25	0	1	250¹	289	7	65	46	13.4	4.24	92	.289	.344	22	.218	-1	-11	-9	-2	-1.2
1900	NY-N	18	18	.500	41	38	**34**	2	0	329¹	377	7	89	80	13.3	3.53	103	.287	.341	25	.203	-2	6	3	4	0.5
1901	Mil-A	7	14	.333	26	23	17	0	0	182¹	228	3	41	50	13.7	4.59	78	.302	.346	19	.260	2	-19	-20	1	-1.5
Total	10	167	179	.483	393	344	297	11	3	3012²	3334	62	974	868	13.5	3.96	107	.277	.342	297	.241	15	103	89	-0	9.0

● SCOTT HAWLEY   Hawley, Marvin Hiram   b: Painesville, Ohio   d: 4/28/04, Alliance, Ohio   Deb: 9/22/1894

YEAR	TM/L	W	L	PCT	G	GS	CG	SH	SV	IP	H	HR	BB	SO	RAT	ERA	ERA+	OAV	OOB	BH	AVG	PB	PR	/A	PD	TPI
1894	Bos-N	0	1	.000	1	1	1	0	0	7	9	1	7	2	24.4	7.71	74	.333	.487	0	.000	-1	-2	-2	0	-0.2

● HAL HAYDEL   Haydel, John Harold   b: 7/9/44, Houma, La.   BR/TR, 6', 190 lbs.   Deb: 9/7/70

YEAR	TM/L	W	L	PCT	G	GS	CG	SH	SV	IP	H	HR	BB	SO	RAT	ERA	ERA+	OAV	OOB	BH	AVG	PB	PR	/A	PD	TPI
1970	Min-A	2	0	1.000	4	0	0	0	0	9	7	2	4	4	11.0	3.00	124	.226	.314	2	.667	2	1	1	-0	0.4
1971	Min-A	4	2	.667	31	0	0	0	0	40	33	3	20	29	12.4	4.27	83	.243	.348	1	.333	0	-4	-3	-0	-0.5
Total	2	6	2	.750	35	0	0	0	0	49	40	5	24	33	12.1	4.04	89	.240	.342	3	.500	2	-3	-2	-0	-0.1

● LEFTY HAYDEN   Hayden, Eugene Franklin   b: 4/14/35, San Francisco, Cal   BL/TL, 6'2", 175 lbs.   Deb: 6/26/58

YEAR	TM/L	W	L	PCT	G	GS	CG	SH	SV	IP	H	HR	BB	SO	RAT	ERA	ERA+	OAV	OOB	BH	AVG	PB	PR	/A	PD	TPI
1958	Cin-N	0	0	—	3	0	0	0	0	3²	3	1	3	3	14.7	4.91	84	.313	.353	0	—	0	-0	-0	0	-0.0

● BEN HAYES   Hayes, Ben Joseph   b: 8/4/57, Niagara Falls, N.Y.   BR/TR, 6'1", 180 lbs.   Deb: 6/25/82

YEAR	TM/L	W	L	PCT	G	GS	CG	SH	SV	IP	H	HR	BB	SO	RAT	ERA	ERA+	OAV	OOB	BH	AVG	PB	PR	/A	PD	TPI
1982	Cin-N	5	0	1.000	26	0	0	0	2	45²	37	3	22	30	11.6	1.97	188	.219	.309	0	.000	-0	8	9	-1	0.3

YEAR	TM/L	W	L	PCT	G	GS	CG	SH	SV	IP	H	HR	BB	SO	RAT	ERA	ERA+	OAV	OOB	BH	AVG	PB	PR	/A	PD	TPI
1983	Cin-N	4	6	.400	60	0	0	0	7	69¹	82	8	37	44	15.6	6.49	59	.301	.387	0	.000	-1	-22	-21	0	-3.2
Total	2	6	6	.500	86	0	0	0	9	115	119	11	59	82	14.0	4.70	80	.270	.357	0	.000	-1	-14	-12	-1	-2.9

● JIM HAYES
Hayes, James Millard "Whitey" b: 2/25/12, Montevallo, Ala. d: 11/27/93, Decatur, Ga. BL/TR, 6'1", 168 lbs. Deb: 7/13/35

YEAR	TM/L	W	L	PCT	G	GS	CG	SH	SV	IP	H	HR	BB	SO	RAT	ERA	ERA+	OAV	OOB	BH	AVG	PB	PR	/A	PD	TPI
1935	Was-A	2	4	.333	7	4	1	0	0	28	38	0	23	4	19.6	8.36	52	.322	.433	2	.250	-0	-12	-13	-1	-2.0

● HEATH HAYNES
Haynes, Heath Burnett b: 11/30/68, Wheeling, W.Va. BR/TR, 6', 175 lbs. Deb: 6/1/94

YEAR	TM/L	W	L	PCT	G	GS	CG	SH	SV	IP	H	HR	BB	SO	RAT	ERA	ERA+	OAV	OOB	BH	AVG	PB	PR	/A	PD	TPI
1994	Mon-N	0	0	—	4	0	0	0	0	3²	3	0	3	1	14.7	0.00	—	.231	.375	0	—	0	2	2	-0	0.00

● JIMMY HAYNES
Haynes, Jimmy Wayne b: 9/5/72, LaGrange, Ga. BR/TR, 6'4", 185 lbs. Deb: 9/13/95

YEAR	TM/L	W	L	PCT	G	GS	CG	SH	SV	IP	H	HR	BB	SO	RAT	ERA	ERA+	OAV	OOB	BH	AVG	PB	PR	/A	PD	TPI
1995	Bal-A	2	1	.667	4	3	0	0	0	24	11	2	12	22	8.6	2.25	211	.136	.247	0	—	0	7	7	-0	0.8
1996	Bal-A	3	6	.333	26	11	0	0	1	89	122	14	58	65	18.4	8.29	59	.333	.427	0	—	0	-33	-34	0	-2.7
Total	2	5	7	.417	30	14	0	0	1	113	133	16	70	87	16.3	7.01	69	.298	.395	0	—	0	-26	-27	0	-1.9

● JOE HAYNES
Haynes, Joseph Walton b: 9/21/17, Lincolnton, Ga. d: 1/6/67, Hopkins, Minn. BR/TR, 6'2.5", 190 lbs. Deb: 4/24/39 C

YEAR	TM/L	W	L	PCT	G	GS	CG	SH	SV	IP	H	HR	BB	SO	RAT	ERA	ERA+	OAV	OOB	BH	AVG	PB	PR	/A	PD	TPI
1939	Was-A	8	12	.400	27	20	10	1	0	173	186	10	78	64	13.8	5.36	81	.276	.352	14	.209	0	-14	-19	-1	-1.9
1940	Was-A	3	6	.333	22	7	1	0	0	63¹	85	4	34	23	17.1	6.54	64	.327	.407	2	.105	-2	-15	-17	-1	-2.1
1941	Chi-A	0	0	—	8	0	0	0	0	28	30	0	11	18	13.2	3.86	106	.280	.347	1	.273	1	1	-0	0.0
1942	Chi-A	8	5	.615	**40**	1	1	0	6	103	88	6	47	35	12.1	2.62	137	.234	.324	5	.179	0	12	11	0	1.5
1943	Chi-A	7	2	.778	35	2	1	0	3	109¹	114	2	32	37	12.2	2.96	113	.263	.316	9	.265	2	4	5	-1	0.5
1944	Chi-A	5	6	.455	33	12	8	0	2	154¹	145	5	43	44	11.1	2.57	134	.254	.306	10	.200	1	15	15	0	1.3
1945	Chi-A	5	5	.500	14	13	8	1	1	104	92	5	29	34	10.6	3.55	94	.237	.291	7	.175	-2	-2	-3	-1	-0.4
1946	Chi-A	7	9	.438	32	23	9	0	0	177¹	203	14	60	60	13.6	3.76	91	.289	.349	14	.246	3	-5	-7	-1	-0.2
1947	Chi-A	14	6	.700	29	22	7	2	0	182	174	5	61	50	11.7	**2.42**	151	.250	.312	17	.262	2	26	25	0	2.9
1948	Chi-A☆	9	10	.474	27	22	6	0	0	149²	167	13	52	52	13.4	3.97	107	.284	.344	8	.160	-1	5	5	-2	0.2
1949	Was-A	2	9	.182	37	10	6	0	0	96¹	106	6	55	19	15.3	6.26	68	.283	.380	6	.240	1	-22	-21	1	-2.0
1950	Was-A	7	5	.583	26	10	1	1	0	101²	124	14	46	15	15.5	5.84	77	.305	.382	7	.200	-1	-14	-15	-1	-1.3
1951	Was-A	1	4	.200	26	3	1	0	2	73	85	9	37	18	15.2	4.56	90	.290	.372	2	.333	2	-4	-4	-1	-0.1
1952	Was-A	0	3	.000	22	2	0	0	3	66	70	2	35	18	14.5	4.50	79	.275	.364	2	.105	-1	-6	-7	-1	-0.5
Total	14	76	82	.481	379	147	53	5	21	1581	1672	95	620	475	13.2	4.01	96	.272	.342	111	.213	7	-20	-31	-2	-2.1

● RAY HAYWARD
Hayward, Raymond Alton b: 4/27/61, Enid, Okla. BL/TL, 6'1", 190 lbs. Deb: 9/20/86

YEAR	TM/L	W	L	PCT	G	GS	CG	SH	SV	IP	H	HR	BB	SO	RAT	ERA	ERA+	OAV	OOB	BH	AVG	PB	PR	/A	PD	TPI
1986	SD-N	0	2	.000	3	3	0	0	0	10	16	1	4	6	18.0	9.00	41	.340	.392	0	.000	-0	-6	-6	-0	-1.0
1987	SD-N	0	0	—	4	0	0	0	0	6	12	3	3	2	22.5	16.50	24	.444	.500	0	.000	-0	-8	-8	1	-1.0
1988	Tex-A	4	6	.400	12	12	1	1	0	62²	63	6	35	37	14.1	5.46	75	.276	.373	0	—	0	-10	-10	1	-1.3
Total	3	4	8	.333	19	15	1	1	0	78²	91	10	42	45	15.2	6.75	60	.301	.387	0	.000	-1	-25	-24	1	-2.3

● BILL HAYWOOD
Haywood, William Kiernan b: 4/21/37, Colon, Panama BR/TR, 6'3", 205 lbs. Deb: 7/28/68

YEAR	TM/L	W	L	PCT	G	GS	CG	SH	SV	IP	H	HR	BB	SO	RAT	ERA	ERA+	OAV	OOB	BH	AVG	PB	PR	/A	PD	TPI
1968	Was-A	0	0	—	14	0	0	0	0	23	27	1	12	10	16.0	4.70	62	.314	.410	0	—	0	-4	-5	-0	-0.4

● ED HEAD
Head, Edward Marvin b: 1/25/18, Selma, La. d: 1/31/80, Bastrop, La. BR/TR, 6'1", 175 lbs. Deb: 7/27/40

YEAR	TM/L	W	L	PCT	G	GS	CG	SH	SV	IP	H	HR	BB	SO	RAT	ERA	ERA+	OAV	OOB	BH	AVG	PB	PR	/A	PD	TPI
1940	Bro-N	1	2	.333	13	5	2	0	0	39¹	40	0	18	13	13.3	4.12	97	.260	.337	2	.182	-0	-1	-1	-1	-0.2
1942	Bro-N	10	6	.625	36	15	5	1	4	136²	118	11	47	78	11.1	3.56	92	.231	.300	13	.333	4	-4	-4	0	-0.1
1943	Bro-N	9	10	.474	47	18	7	3	6	169²	166	8	66	83	12.3	3.66	92	.250	.318	7	.152	-2	-5	-6	1	-0.7
1944	Bro-N	4	3	.571	12	9	2	1	0	63¹	54	2	19	17	10.4	2.70	132	.232	.290	5	.263	1	6	6	-1	0.6
1946	Bro-N	3	2	.600	13	7	3	1	1	56	56	3	24	17	12.9	3.21	105	.267	.342	5	.313	1	-0	1	0	0.2
Total	5	27	23	.540	118	53	22	6	11	465	434	24	174	208	11.8	3.48	98	.245	.314	32	.244	5	-4	-4	-1	-0.2

● RALPH HEAD
Head, Ralph b: 8/30/1893, Tallapoosa, Ga. d: 10/8/62, Muscadine, Ala. BR/TR, 5'10", 175 lbs. Deb: 4/18/23

YEAR	TM/L	W	L	PCT	G	GS	CG	SH	SV	IP	H	HR	BB	SO	RAT	ERA	ERA+	OAV	OOB	BH	AVG	PB	PR	/A	PD	TPI
1923	Phi-N	2	9	.182	35	13	6	0	0	132¹	185	13	57	24	16.5	6.66	69	.341	.404	3	.071	-5	-39	-30	-1	-2.6

● TOM HEALEY
Healey, Thomas F. b: 1853, Cranston, R.I. d: 2/6/1891, Lewiston, Maine TR, Deb: 6/13/1878

YEAR	TM/L	W	L	PCT	G	GS	CG	SH	SV	IP	H	HR	BB	SO	RAT	ERA	ERA+	OAV	OOB	BH	AVG	PB	PR	/A	PD	TPI
1878	Pro-N	0	3	.000	3	3	3	0	0	24	27	1	7	2	12.8	3.00	74	.278	.327	2	.222	0	-2	-2	-0	-0.2
	Ind-N	6	4	.600	11	10	9	0	1	89	98	1	13	18	11.2	2.22	91	.270	.295	8	.178	-1	1	-2	-0	-0.3
	Yr	6	7	.462	14	13	12	0	**1**	113	125	2	20	20	11.5	2.39	87	.272	.302	10	.185	-1	-1	-4	-0	-0.5

● JOHN HEALY
Healy, John J. "Egyptian" or "Long John" b: 10/27/1866, Cairo, Ill. d: 3/16/1899, St.Louis, Mo. BR/TR, 6'2", 158 lbs. Deb: 9/11/1885

YEAR	TM/L	W	L	PCT	G	GS	CG	SH	SV	IP	H	HR	BB	SO	RAT	ERA	ERA+	OAV	OOB	BH	AVG	PB	PR	/A	PD	TPI
1885	StL-N	1	7	.125	8	8	7	0	0	66	54	0	20	32	10.1	3.00	92	.210	.267	1	.042	-3	-1	-2	1	-0.4
1886	StL-N	17	23	.425	43	41	39	3	0	353²	315	5	118	213	11.0	2.88	112	.230	.291	14	.097	-12	17	14	-2	0.0
1887	Ind-N	12	29	.293	41	41	40	3	0	341	415	24	108	75	14.2	5.17	80	.294	.350	24	.174	-42	-39	-39	-4	-4.0
1888	Ind-N	12	24	.333	37	37	36	1	0	321²	347	13	87	124	12.6	3.89	76	.267	.320	30	.229	-4	-37	-33	1	-2.8
1889	Was-N	1	11	.083	13	12	10	0	0	101	139	4	38	49	16.2	6.24	63	.317	.378	10	.222	1	-25	-26	2	-2.0
	Chi-N	1	4	.200	5	5	5	0	0	46	48	4	18	22	13.7	4.50	92	.261	.340	2	.100	-2	-2	-1	-0	-0.3
	Yr	2	15	.118	18	17	15	0	0	147	187	8	56	71	15.1	5.69	70	.298	.360	12	.185	-1	-27	-27	1	-2.3
1890	Tol-a	22	21	.512	46	46	44	2	0	389	326	5	127	225	11.0	2.89	137	.221	.293	34	.218	7	42	46	-2	4.7
1891	Bal-a	8	10	.444	23	22	19	0	0	170¹	179	6	57	54	12.7	3.75	100	.261	.322	9	.141	-2	1	-0	-5	-0.6
1892	Bal-N	3	6	.333	9	8	5	0	0	68¹	82	4	21	24	13.8	4.74	72	.286	.339	6	.222	0	-11	-10	-0	-1.0
	Lou-N	1	1	.500	2	2	2	0	0	18¹	15	0	5	2	9.8	1.96	156	.214	.267	2	.286	1	3	2	-1	0.3
	Yr	4	7	.364	11	10	7	0	0	86²	97	4	26	26	12.8	4.15	81	.270	.319	8	.235	1	-8	-8	-1	-0.7
Total	8	78	136	.364	227	222	208	9	0	1875	1920	63	599	822	12.4	3.84	94	.257	.318	132	.174	-9	-57	-50	-10	-6.1

● CHARLIE HEARD
Heard, Charles b: 1/30/1872, Philadelphia, Pa. d: 2/20/45, Philadelphia, Pa. BR/TR, 6'2", 190 lbs. Deb: 7/14/1890 ♦

YEAR	TM/L	W	L	PCT	G	GS	CG	SH	SV	IP	H	HR	BB	SO	RAT	ERA	ERA+	OAV	OOB	BH	AVG	PB	PR	/A	PD	TPI
1890	Pit-N	0	6	.000	6	6	5	0	0	44	75	5	32	13	22.3	8.39	39	.366	.456	3	.186	-1	-24	-25	-1	-2.3

● JAY HEARD
Heard, Jehosie b: 1/17/20, Atlanta, Ga. BL/TL, 5'7", 155 lbs. Deb: 4/24/54

YEAR	TM/L	W	L	PCT	G	GS	CG	SH	SV	IP	H	HR	BB	SO	RAT	ERA	ERA+	OAV	OOB	BH	AVG	PB	PR	/A	PD	TPI
1954	Bal-A	0	0	—	2	0	0	0	0	3¹	6	1	3	2	24.3	13.50	27	.375	.474	0	—	0	-4	-4	0	0.0

● BUNNY HEARN
Hearn, Bunn b: 5/21/1891, Chapel Hill, N.C. d: 10/10/59, Wilson, N.C. BL/TL, 5'11", 190 lbs. Deb: 9/17/10

YEAR	TM/L	W	L	PCT	G	GS	CG	SH	SV	IP	H	HR	BB	SO	RAT	ERA	ERA+	OAV	OOB	BH	AVG	PB	PR	/A	PD	TPI
1910	StL-N	1	3	.250	5	5	4	0	0	39	49	2	16	14	15.2	5.08	59	.322	.391	2	.133	-0	-9	-9	-1	-0.9
1911	StL-N	0	0	—	2	0	0	0	0	2²	5	0	1	1	23.6	13.50	25	.538	.538	0	.000	-0	-3	-3	-0	0.0
1913	NY-N	1	1	.500	2	1	1	0	0	13	13	0	7	3	13.8	2.77	113	.277	.370	2	.400	1	1	1	-0	0.1
1915	Pit-F	6	11	.353	29	17	8	1	0	175²	187	6	37	49	11.6	3.38	80	.285	.326	10	.189	-0	-13	-13	-1	-1.3
1918	Bos-N	5	6	.455	17	12	9	1	0	126¹	119	2	29	30	10.5	2.49	108	.256	.300	8	.178	-1	4	3	1	0.2
1920	Bos-N	0	3	.000	11	4	2	0	0	43	54	4	11	13	13.8	5.65	54	.329	.375	2	.143	-0	-12	-12	-0	-0.9
Total	6	13	24	.351	66	40	24	2	0	399²	429	14	100	111	12.0	3.56	78	.287	.333	24	.180	-2	-32	-34	-2	-2.8

● BUNNY HEARN
Hearn, Elmer Lafayette b: 1/13/04, Brooklyn, N.Y. d: 3/31/74, Venice, Fla. BL/TL, 5'8", 160 lbs. Deb: 4/13/26

YEAR	TM/L	W	L	PCT	G	GS	CG	SH	SV	IP	H	HR	BB	SO	RAT	ERA	ERA+	OAV	OOB	BH	AVG	PB	PR	/A	PD	TPI
1926	Bos-N	4	9	.308	34	12	3	0	2	117¹	121	2	56	40	13.6	4.22	84	.276	.358	3	.100	-2	-5	-9	2	-0.9
1927	Bos-N	2	2	.500	15	1	0	0	0	12²	16	0	9	5	17.8	4.26	87	.327	.431	2	.400	-1	-1	-0	-0	-0.3
1928	Bos-N	1	0	1.000	7	0	0	0	0	10	6	0	2	3	13.5	6.30	62	.167	.333	0	.000	-0	-3	-3	-0	-0.3
1929	Bos-N	2	0	1.000	9	0	0	0	0	18¹	18	2	3	11	13.3	4.42	106	.277	.365	0	.000	0	1	1	-0	0.1
Total	4	7	11	.389	59	13	3	0	2	158¹	161	4	82	65	13.9	4.38	85	.273	.363	5	.132	-2	-8	-12	2	-1.1

● JIM HEARN
Hearn, James Tolbert b: 4/11/21, Atlanta, Ga. BR/TR, 6'3", 205 lbs. Deb: 4/17/47

YEAR	TM/L	W	L	PCT	G	GS	CG	SH	SV	IP	H	HR	BB	SO	RAT	ERA	ERA+	OAV	OOB	BH	AVG	PB	PR	/A	PD	TPI
1947	StL-N	12	7	.632	37	21	4	1	0	162	151	9	63	57	11.9	3.22	128	.248	.319	8	.145	-1	15	16	-1	1.5
1948	StL-N	8	6	.571	34	13	3	0	1	89²	92	9	35	27	12.9	4.22	97	.271	.342	5	.200	1	-3	-1	-2	-0.4
1949	StL-N	1	3	.250	17	4	0	0	0	42	43	3	23	18	15.6	5.14	81	.294	.388	1	.000	-0	-5	-5	-0	-0.5
1950	StL-N	0	1	.000	9	1	0	0	0	9	12	1	6	4	18.0	10.00	43	.333	.429	1	1.000	-0	-6	-6	-0	-0.5
	NY-N	11	3	.786	16	16	11	5	0	125	72	8	38	54	7.9	1.94	211	.169	.237	6	.136	-5	31	30	1	3.3
	Yr	11	4	.733	22	16	11	**5**	0	134	84	9	44	58	8.6	**2.49**	165	.182	.253	7	.175	-5	25	24	0	2.8
1951	*NY-N	17	9	.654	34	34	11	0	0	211¹	204	21	82	66	12.3	3.62	108	.251	.321	12	.162	-1	8	7	5	1.3
1952	NY-N☆	14	7	.667	37	34	11	0	0	223²	208	16	97	89	12.5	3.78	98	.245	.326	14	.182	P8	-1	-2	4	0.6
1953	NY-N	9	12	.429	36	32	6	0	0	196²	206	22	84	77	13.4	4.53	95	.266	.341	9	.136	1	-5	-5	2	-0.3

YEAR	TM/L	W	L	PCT	G	GS	CG	SH	SV	IP	H	HR	BB	SO	RAT	ERA	ERA+	OAV	OOB	BH	AVG	PB	PR	/A	PD	TPI
1954	NY-N	8	8	.500	29	18	3	2	1	130	137	10	66	45	14.2	4.15	97	.272	.359	5	.111	-1	-1	-2	1	-0.1
1955	NY-N	14	16	.467	39	33	11	1	0	226²	225	27	66	86	11.7	3.73	108	.260	.314	12	.156	1	8	7	2	1.2
1956	NY-N	5	11	.313	30	19	2	0	1	129¹	124	17	44	66	11.9	3.97	95	.254	.319	4	.098	-3	-3	-3	-0	-0.6
1957	Phi-N	5	1	.833	36	4	1	0	3	74	79	6	18	46	12.0	3.65	104	.274	.321	0	.000	-2	2	1	1	0.0
1958	Phi-N	5	3	.625	39	1	0	0	0	73¹	88	6	27	33	14.1	4.17	95	.292	.351	0	.000	-1	-2	-2	-1	-0.4
1959	Phi-N	0	2	.000	6	0	0	0	0	11	15	2	6	1	17.2	5.73	72	.333	.412	0	.000	-2	-2	-2	-0	-0.3
Total 13		109	89	.551	396	229	63	10	8	1703²	1661	157	655	669	12.4	3.81	105	.255	.326	77	.141	-3	35	35	11	4.9

● **SPENCER HEATH** Heath, Spencer Paul b: 11/5/1894, Chicago, Ill. d: 1/25/30, Chicago, Ill. BR/TR, 6', 170 lbs. Deb: 5/4/20

YEAR	TM/L	W	L	PCT	G	GS	CG	SH	SV	IP	H	HR	BB	SO	RAT	ERA	ERA+	OAV	OOB	BH	AVG	PB	PR	/A	PD	TPI
1920	Chi-A	0	0	—	4	0	0	0	0	7	19	1	2	0	27.0	15.43	24	.475	.500	0	.000	-1	-9	-9	-0	-0.1

● **JEFF HEATHCOCK** Heathcock, Ronald Jeffrey b: 11/18/59, Covina, Cal. BR/TR, 6'4", 205 lbs. Deb: 9/3/83

YEAR	TM/L	W	L	PCT	G	GS	CG	SH	SV	IP	H	HR	BB	SO	RAT	ERA	ERA+	OAV	OOB	BH	AVG	PB	PR	/A	PD	TPI
1983	Hou-N	2	1	.667	6	3	0	0	1	28	19	1	4	12	7.7	3.21	106	.181	.218	0	.000	-1	1	1	0	0.0
1985	Hou-N	3	1	.750	14	7	1	0	1	56¹	50	9	13	25	10.2	3.36	103	.239	.287	1	.063	0	1	1	0	0.1
1987	Hou-N	4	2	.667	19	2	0	0	1	42²	44	4	9	15	11.4	3.16	124	.277	.320	0	.000	-1	4	4	-0	0.4
1988	Hou-N	0	5	.000	17	1	0	0	0	31	33	2	16	12	14.5	5.81	57	.275	.365	0	.000	-0	-8	-9	-0	-1.3
Total 4		9	9	.500	56	13	1	0	3	158	146	16	42	64	10.9	3.76	94	.246	.300	1	.029	-2	-1	-4	-0	-0.8

● **NEAL HEATON** Heaton, Neal b: 3/3/60, Holtsville, N.Y. BL/TL, 6'1", 205 lbs. Deb: 9/3/82

YEAR	TM/L	W	L	PCT	G	GS	CG	SH	SV	IP	H	HR	BB	SO	RAT	ERA	ERA+	OAV	OOB	BH	AVG	PB	PR	/A	PD	TPI
1982	Cle-A	0	2	.000	8	4	0	0	0	31	32	1	16	14	13.9	5.23	78	.260	.345	0	—	0	-4	-4	-0	-0.2
1983	Cle-A	11	7	.611	39	16	4	3	7	149¹	157	11	44	75	12.2	4.16	102	.269	.321	0	—	0	-2	1	-2	-0.2
1984	Cle-A	12	15	.444	38	34	4	1	0	198²	231	21	75	75	13.9	5.21	78	.269	.293	0	—	0	-27	-25	-3	-3.3
1985	Cle-A	9	17	.346	36	33	5	1	0	207²	244	19	80	82	14.3	4.90	84	.298	.365	0	—	0	-17	-18	-3	-2.1
1986	Cle-A	3	6	.333	12	12	0	0	0	74¹	73	8	34	34	13.1	4.24	98	.254	.335	0	—	0	-1	-1	-0	-0.1
	Min-A	4	9	.308	21	17	3	0	1	124¹	128	18	47	66	12.7	3.98	108	.273	.340	0	—	0	3	4	-1	0.3
	Yr	7	15	.318	33	29	5	0	1	198²	201	26	81	90	12.8	4.08	104	.266	.337	0	—	0	2	4	-1	0.2
1987	Mon-N	13	10	.565	32	32	3	1	0	193¹	207	25	37	105	11.5	4.52	93	.271	.354	14	.209	2	-9	-7	-1	-0.7
1988	Mon-N	3	10	.231	32	11	0	0	2	97¹	98	14	43	43	13.3	4.99	72	.271	.354	3	.143	-0	-17	-15	-0	-2.0
1989	Pit-N	6	7	.462	42	18	1	0	0	147¹	127	12	55	67	11.5	3.05	110	.233	.311	9	.214	1	7	5	1	0.5
1990	Pit-N☆	12	9	.571	30	24	0	0	0	146	143	17	38	68	11.3	3.45	105	.263	.314	2	.047	-2	6	3	-0	0.1
1991	Pit-N	3	3	.500	42	1	0	0	0	68²	72	6	21	34	12.7	4.33	83	.275	.338	4	.286	0	-5	-6	-1	-0.4
1992	KC-A	3	1	.750	31	0	0	0	0	41	43	5	22	29	14.5	4.17	97	.274	.367	0	—	0	-1	-1	-0	-0.2
	Mil-A	0	0	—	1	0	0	0	0	1	0	1	2	9.0		0.00	—	.000	.250	0	—	0	0	0	0	0.1
	Yr	3	1	.750	32	0	0	0	0	42	43	5	23	31	14.1	4.07	99	.262	.353	0	—	0	-1	-0	-0	-0.1
1993	NY-A	1	0	1.000	18	0	0	0	0	27	34	6	11	15	16.0	6.00	69	.301	.378	0	—	0	-5	-6	-0	-0.5
Total 12		80	96	.455	382	202	22	6	10	1507	1589	163	524	699	12.8	4.37	91	.273	.337	32	.171	2	-72	-68	-11	-8.1

● **DAVE HEAVERLO** Heaverlo, David Wallace b: 8/25/50, Ellensburg, Wash. BR/TR, 6'1", 210 lbs. Deb: 4/14/75

YEAR	TM/L	W	L	PCT	G	GS	CG	SH	SV	IP	H	HR	BB	SO	RAT	ERA	ERA+	OAV	OOB	BH	AVG	PB	PR	/A	PD	TPI
1975	SF-N	3	1	.750	42	0	0	0	1	64	62	2	31	35	13.2	2.39	159	.262	.349	2	.500	1	9	10	1	0.7
1976	SF-N	4	4	.500	61	0	0	0	1	75	85	2	15	40	12.2	4.44	82	.289	.328	1	.333	1	-8	-7	1	-0.6
1977	SF-N	5	1	.833	56	0	0	0	1	98²	92	10	21	58	10.6	2.55	153	.251	.297	0	.000	-0	15	15	2	1.0
1978	Oak-A	3	6	.333	69	0	0	0	10	130	141	11	41	71	12.8	3.25	112	.281	.339	0	—	0	7	6	3	0.8
1979	Oak-A	4	11	.267	62	0	0	0	9	85²	97	7	42	40	15.0	4.20	96	.294	.380	0	.000	0	-0	-2	-0	-0.2
1980	Sea-A	6	3	.667	60	0	0	0	4	78²	75	9	35	42	13.2	3.89	106	.253	.342	0	—	0	1	2	-2	0.1
1981	Oak-A	1	0	1.000	6	0	0	0	0	5²	7	0	3	2	15.9	1.59	219	.292	.370	0	—	0	1	1	-0	0.4
Total 7		26	26	.500	356	0	0	0	26	537²	559	41	188	288	12.8	3.41	113	.273	.339	3	.231	1	26	26	4	2.2

● **WALLY HEBERT** Hebert, Wallace Andrew "Preacher" b: 8/21/07, Lake Charles, La. BL/TL, 6'1", 195 lbs. Deb: 5/1/31

YEAR	TM/L	W	L	PCT	G	GS	CG	SH	SV	IP	H	HR	BB	SO	RAT	ERA	ERA+	OAV	OOB	BH	AVG	PB	PR	/A	PD	TPI
1931	StL-A	6	7	.462	23	13	5	0	0	103	128	11	43	26	15.2	5.07	91	.306	.375	9	.209	-1	-8	-5	-2	-0.8
1932	StL-A	1	12	.077	35	15	2	0	1	108¹	145	6	45	29	16.0	6.48	75	.322	.353	12	.353	2	-24	-20	0	-1.7
1933	StL-A	4	6	.400	33	10	3	0	0	88¹	114	4	35	19	15.3	5.30	88	.308	.369	9	.391	3	-10	-6	-1	-0.4
1943	Pit-N	10	11	.476	34	23	12	1	0	184	197	3	45	41	11.9	2.98	117	.272	.316	13	.220	1	8	10	1	1.4
Total 4		21	36	.368	125	61	22	1	1	483²	584	24	168	115	14.1	4.63	91	.298	.355	43	.270	5	-34	-21	-1	-1.5

● **GUY HECKER** Hecker, Guy Jackson b: 4/3/1856, Youngsville, Pa. d: 12/3/38, Wooster, Ohio BR/TR, 6', 190 lbs. Deb: 5/2/1882 MU♦

YEAR	TM/L	W	L	PCT	G	GS	CG	SH	SV	IP	H	HR	BB	SO	RAT	ERA	ERA+	OAV	OOB	BH	AVG	PB	PR	/A	PD	TPI
1882	Lou-a	6	6	.500	13	11	10	0	0	104	75	0	5	33	**6.9**	1.30	191	**.188**	**.199**	94	.276	4	16	14	3	2.1
1883	Lou-a	28	23	.549	53	51	50	3	0	469	526	4	35	164	11.5	3.34	90	.266	.292	90	.271	12	-2	-18	4	-0.2
1884	Lou-a	**52**	20	.722	**75**	73	**72**	6	0	**670²**	526	4	56	**385**	8.0	**1.80**	172	.204	**.226**	94	.297	28	108	**96**	7	**12.6**
1885	Lou-a	30	23	.566	53	53	51	2	0	480	454	6	54	209	9.4	2.18	148	.237	.265	81	.273	9	57	56	5	**6.6**
1886	Lou-a	26	23	.531	49	48	45	2	0	420²	390	6	118	133	11.1	2.87	127	.231	.285	117	.341	18	27	36	1	5.2
1887	Lou-a	18	12	.600	34	32	32	2	1	285¹	325	9	50	58	12.1	4.16	105	.272	.307	118	.319	11	4	7	5	1.8
1888	Lou-a	8	17	.320	26	25	25	0	0	223¹	215	5	43	63	12.3	3.39	91	.274	.313	48	.227	2	-8	-1	-0	-0.4
1889	Lou-a	5	13	.278	19	16	15	0	0	151¹	215	7	47	33	15.9	5.59	69	.324	.373	93	.284	4	-29	-29	1	-2.2
1890	Pit-N	2	9	.182	14	12	11	0	0	119²	160	9	44	32	15.6	5.11	64	.311	.369	77	.226	2	-21	-24	-1	-1.6
Total 9		175	146	.545	336	322	312	15	1	2924	2922	50	492	1110	10.7	2.93	113	.247	.281	812	.282	90	153	127	25	23.9

● **HARRY HEDGPETH** Hedgpeth, Harry Malcolm b: 9/4/1888, Fayetteville, N.C. d: 7/30/66, Richmond, Va. BL/TL, 6'1.5", 194 lbs. Deb: 10/3/13

YEAR	TM/L	W	L	PCT	G	GS	CG	SH	SV	IP	H	HR	BB	SO	RAT	ERA	ERA+	OAV	OOB	BH	AVG	PB	PR	/A	PD	TPI
1913	Was-A	0	0	—	1	0	0	0	0						9.0	0.00	—	.250	.250	0	—	0	0	0	0	0.1

● **MIKE HEDLUND** Hedlund, Michael David "Red" b: 8/11/46, Dallas, Tex. BR/TR, 6'1", 190 lbs. Deb: 5/8/65

YEAR	TM/L	W	L	PCT	G	GS	CG	SH	SV	IP	H	HR	BB	SO	RAT	ERA	ERA+	OAV	OOB	BH	AVG	PB	PR	/A	PD	TPI
1965	Cle-A	0	0	—	6	0	0	0	0	5¹	6	0	5	4	18.6	5.06	69	.286	.423	0	.000	-0	-1	-1	-0	0.0
1968	Cle-A	0	0	—	3	0	0	0	0	1²	6	0	2	0	48.6	10.80	27	.545	.643	0	—	0	-1	-1	0	0.0
1969	KC-A	3	6	.333	34	16	1	0	2	125	123	8	40	74	11.8	3.24	114	.259	.318	5	.152	-1	5	6	1	0.6
1970	KC-A	2	3	.400	9	0	0	0	0	15	18	6	7	5	15.0	7.20	52	.300	.373	0	.000	0	-6	-6	-0	-1.7
1971	KC-A	15	8	.652	32	30	7	1	0	205²	168	15	72	76	10.5	2.71	126	.227	.296	6	.088	-4	17	16	3	1.8
1972	KC-A	5	7	.417	29	16	1	0	0	113	119	10	41	52	13.1	4.78	63	.275	.343	6	.188	-0	-22	-22	1	-2.2
Total 6		25	24	.510	113	62	9	1	2	465²	440	39	167	211	11.9	3.56	96	.253	.321	17	.123	-7	-7	-8	5	-1.5

● **DANNY HEEP** Heep, Daniel William b: 7/3/57, San Antonio, Tex. BL/TL, 5'11", 185 lbs. Deb: 8/31/79 ♦

YEAR	TM/L	W	L	PCT	G	GS	CG	SH	SV	IP	H	HR	BB	SO	RAT	ERA	ERA+	OAV	OOB	BH	AVG	PB	PR	/A	PD	TPI
1988	*LA-N	0	0	—	1	0	0	0	0	2	2	1	0	0		9.00	37	.222	.222	36	.242	0	-1	-1	-0	0.0
1990	*Bos-A	0	0	—	1	0	0	0	0	1	4	0	0	0	36.0	9.00	45	.667	.667	12	.174	0	-1	-1	0	0.0
Total 2		0	0	—	2	0	0	0	0	3	6	1	0	0	18.0	9.00	40	.400	.400	503	.257	0	-2	-2	-0	0.0

● **BOB HEFFNER** Heffner, Robert Frederic b: 9/13/38, Allentown, Pa. BR/TR, 6'4", 205 lbs. Deb: 6/19/63

YEAR	TM/L	W	L	PCT	G	GS	CG	SH	SV	IP	H	HR	BB	SO	RAT	ERA	ERA+	OAV	OOB	BH	AVG	PB	PR	/A	PD	TPI
1963	Bos-A	4	9	.308	20	19	3	1	0	124²	131	15	36	77	12.2	4.26	89	.267	.319	5	.116	-1	-9	-7	-0	-0.8
1964	Bos-A	7	9	.438	55	10	1	1	6	158²	152	20	44	112	11.3	4.08	94	.251	.305	7	.159	1	-8	-4	-1	-0.5
1965	Bos-A	0	2	.000	27	1	0	0	0	49	59	9	18	42	14.3	7.16	52	.304	.366	0	.000	-1	-20	-19	-1	-0.9
1966	Cle-A	0	1	.000	5	1	0	0	0	13	12	1	3	7	10.4	3.46	99	.240	.283	0	.000	0	1	0	0	0.0
1968	Cal-A	0	0	—	7	0	0	0	0	8	6	0	6	3	13.5	2.25	129	.240	.387	0	—	0	1	1	0	0.0
Total 5		11	21	.344	114	31	4	2	6	353¹	360	45	107	241	12.0	4.51	84	.264	.320	12	.128	-1	-36	-29	-2	-2.2

● **BRONSON HEFLIN** Heflin, Bronson Wayne b: 8/29/71, Clarksville, Tenn. BR/TR, 6'3", 195 lbs. Deb: 8/1/96

YEAR	TM/L	W	L	PCT	G	GS	CG	SH	SV	IP	H	HR	BB	SO	RAT	ERA	ERA+	OAV	OOB	BH	AVG	PB	PR	/A	PD	TPI
1996	Phi-N	0	0	—	3	0	0	0	0	4	5	1	1	2	13.5	6.75	68	.367	.424	0	—	0	-2	-2	-0	0.0

● **RANDY HEFLIN** Heflin, Randolph Rutherford b: 9/11/18, Fredericksburg, Va. BL/TR, 6', 185 lbs. Deb: 6/9/45

YEAR	TM/L	W	L	PCT	G	GS	CG	SH	SV	IP	H	HR	BB	SO	RAT	ERA	ERA+	OAV	OOB	BH	AVG	PB	PR	/A	PD	TPI
1945	Bos-A	4	10	.286	20	14	6	0	0	102	102	3	61	39	14.7	4.06	84	.272	.380	3	.086	-3	-8	-7	1	-1.1
1946	Bos-A	0	1	.000	5	1	0	0	0	14²	16	0	12	6	17.8	2.45	149	.296	.433	2	.667	1	2	2	1	0.3
Total 2		4	11	.267	25	15	6	0	0	116²	118	3	73	45	15.1	3.86	89	.275	.387	5	.132	-2	-6	-5	2	-0.8

● **JAKE HEHL** Hehl, Herman Jacob b: 12/8/1899, Brooklyn, N.Y. d: 7/4/61, Brooklyn, N.Y. BR/TR, 5'11", 180 lbs. Deb: 6/20/18

YEAR	TM/L	W	L	PCT	G	GS	CG	SH	SV	IP	H	HR	BB	SO	RAT	ERA	ERA+	OAV	OOB	BH	AVG	PB	PR	/A	PD	TPI
1918	Bro-N	0	0	—	1	0	0	0	0	1	0	0	0	0	9.0	0.00	—	.000	.250	0	—	0	0	0	0	0.0

YEAR TM/L	W	L	PCT	G	GS	CG	SH	SV	IP	H	HR	BB	SO	RAT	ERA	ERA+	OAV	OOB	BH	AVG	PB	PR	/A	PD	TPI
● **EMMET HEIDRICK** Heidrick, R. Emmet "Snags" b: 7/9/1876, Queenstown, Pa. d: 1/20/16, Clarion, Pa. BL/TR, 6′, 185 lbs. Deb: 9/14/1898 ♦																									
1902 StL-A	0	0	—	1	0	0	0	0	1	0	0	0	0	0.0	0.00	—	.000	.000	129	.289	0	0	0	-0	0.0
● **FRANK HEIFER** Heifer, Franklin "Heck" b: 1/18/1854, Reading, Pa. d: 8/29/1893, Reading, Pa. 5′10.5″, 175 lbs. Deb: 6/4/1875 ♦																									
1875 Bos-n	0	0	—	2	0	0	0	1	2¹	6	0	0	0	23.1	15.43	14	.462	.462	14	.280	1	-3	-3		-0.3
● **FRED HEIMACH** Heimach, Frederick Amos "Lefty" b: 1/27/01, Camden, N.J. d: 6/1/73, Ft.Myers, Fla. BL/TL, 6′, 175 lbs. Deb: 10/1/20																									
1920 Phi-A	0	1	.000	1	1	0	0	0	5	13	0	1	0	25.2	14.40	28	.542	.560	0	.000	-0	-6	-6	1	-0.7
1921 Phi-A	1	0	1.000	1	1	1	1	0	9	7	0	1	0	8.0	0.00	—	.226	.250	1	.250	-0	4	4	1	0.6
1922 Phi-A	7	11	.389	37	19	7	0	1	171²	220	18	63	47	15.0	5.03	85	.316	.375	15	.250	2	-19	-15	1	-1.0
1923 Phi-A	6	12	.333	40	19	10	0	0	208¹	238	14	69	63	13.5	4.32	95	.292	.352	30	.254	-8	-5	0		-0.1
1924 Phi-A	14	12	.538	40	26	10	0	0	198	243	6	60	60	14.0	4.73	91	.306	.357	29	.322	6	-11	-10	2	-0.3
1925 Phi-A	0	1	.000	10	0	0	0	0	20¹	24	2	9	6	15.0	3.98	117	.312	.391	1	.167	-0	1	2	0	0.1
1926 Phi-A	1	0	1.000	13	1	0	0	0	31²	28	1	5	8	9.4	2.84	147	.239	.270	1	.100	-1	4	5	2	0.2
Bos-A	2	9	.182	20	13	6	0	0	102	119	5	42	17	14.2	5.65	72	.303	.370	13	.295	-18	-18	3		-1.1
Yr	3	9	.250	33	14	6	0	0	133²	147	6	47	25	13.1	4.98	82	.288	.348	14	.259	2	-14	-13	5	-0.9
1928 NY-A	2	3	.400	13	9	5	0	0	68	66	3	16	25	11.0	3.31	114	.250	.295	5	.167	-1	6	3	0	0.1
1929 NY-A	11	6	.647	35	10	3	3	4	134²	141	4	29	26	11.6	4.01	96	.272	.314	9	.184	-1	4	2	2	-0.1
1930 Bro-N	0	2	.000	9	0	0	0	1	7¹	14	0	3	1	20.9	4.91	100	.424	.472	1	.250	-0	0	0	0	0.0
1931 Bro-N	9	7	.563	31	10	7	1	1	135¹	145	6	23	43	11.2	3.46	110	.274	.306	12	.197	-1	6	5	4	1.0
1932 Bro-N	9	4	.692	36	15	7	0	0	167²	203	6	28	30	12.7	3.97	96	.299	.333	9	.164	-1	-2	-3	1	0.0
1933 Bro-N	0	1	.000	10	3	0	0	0	29²	49	7	2	11	18.8	10.01	32	.374	.431	2	.200	-1	-22	-22	-0	-0.7
Total 13	62	69	.473	296	127	56	5	7	1288²	1510	64	360	310	13.1	4.46	90	.296	.346	128	.236	12	-61	-61	16	-2.0
● **GORMAN HEIMUELLER** Heimueller, Gorman John b: 9/24/55, Los Angeles, Cal. BL/TL, 6′4″, 195 lbs. Deb: 7/12/83																									
1983 Oak-A	3	5	.375	16	14	2	1	0	83²	93	8	29	31	13.2	4.41	87	.286	.346	0	—		-3	-5	2	0.0
1984 Oak-A	0	1	.000	6	0	0	0	0	14²	21	2	7	3	17.2	6.14	61	.344	.412	0	—		-3	-4	0	0.2
Total 2	3	6	.333	22	14	2	1	0	98¹	114	10	36	34	13.8	4.67	82	.295	.357	0	—	0	-7	-9	3	0.2
● **DON HEINKEL** Heinkel, Donald Elliott b: 10/20/59, Racine, Wis. BL/TR, 6′, 185 lbs. Deb: 4/7/88																									
1988 Det-A	0	0	—	21	0	0	0	0	36¹	30	4	12	30	10.7	3.96	96	.219	.287	0		-0	0	-1	0	0.1
1989 StL-N	1	1	.500	7	5	0	0	0	26¹	40	2	7	16	16.1	5.81	62	.348	.385	0	.000	-0	-7	-6	0	-0.4
Total 2	1	1	.500	28	5	0	0	1	62²	70	6	19	46	12.9	4.74	79	.278	.331	0	.000	-0	-7	-7	0	-0.3
● **KEN HEINTZELMAN** Heintzelman, Kenneth Alphonse b: 10/14/15, Peruque, Mo. BR/TL, 5′11.5″, 185 lbs. Deb: 10/3/37 F																									
1937 Pit-N	1	0	1.000	1	1	1	0	0	9	6	0	3	4	10.0	2.00	193	.207	.303	0	.000	-1	2	2	-1	0.1
1938 Pit-N	0	0	—	1	0	0	0	0	2	1	0	3	1	18.0	9.00	42	.167	.444	0	—	-1	-1	0	0	0.0
1939 Pit-N	1	1	.500	17	2	1	1	0	35²	36	2	18	18	13.4	5.05	76	.250	.335	2	.222	-1	-4	-5	0	-0.2
1940 Pit-N	8	8	.500	39	16	5	2	3	165	193	7	65	71	14.3	4.47	85	.292	.359	9	.167	-1	-11	-12	3	-1.0
1941 Pit-N	11	11	.500	35	24	13	2	0	196	206	8	83	81	13.3	3.44	105	.272	.345	8	.127	-2	4	4	1	0.3
1942 Pit-N	8	11	.421	27	18	5	3	0	130	143	9	63	39	14.3	4.57	74	.281	.361	3	.086	-2	-18	-17	-2	-2.6
1946 Pit-N	8	12	.400	32	24	6	1	1	157²	165	7	86	57	14.3	3.77	94	.271	.362	6	.136	-1	-6	-4	2	-0.4
1947 Pit-N	0	0	—	2	1	0	0	0	4	9	2	6	2	33.8	20.25	21	.409	.536	0	—	-0	-7	-7	0	-0.0
Phi-N	7	10	.412	24	19	8	0	1	136	144	12	46	55	12.7	4.04	99	.277	.338	5	.116	-2	0	0	-3	-0.5
Yr	7	10	.412	26	20	8	0	1	140	153	14	52	57	13.3	4.50	89	.283	.351	5	.116	-2	-7	-8	-3	-0.5
1948 Phi-N	6	11	.353	27	16	5	2	2	130	117	10	45	57	11.3	4.29	92	.241	.307	5	.135	-1	-5	-5	-1	-0.8
1949 Phi-N	17	10	.630	33	32	15	**5**	0	250	239	19	93	65	12.0	3.02	130	.255	.323	13	.157	-1	28	26	-3	2.2
1950 *Phi-N	3	9	.250	23	17	4	1	0	125¹	122	10	54	39	12.6	4.09	99	.250	.325	2	.053	-3	1	-1	-2	-0.6
1951 Phi-N	6	12	.333	35	12	3	0	2	118¹	119	13	53	55	13.4	4.18	92	.267	.350	3	.107	-1	-3	-4	-1	0.1
1952 Phi-N	1	3	.250	23	1	0	0	1	42²	41	1	12	20	11.2	3.16	115	.266	.319	0	.000	-0	3	2	-1	0.1
Total 13	77	98	.440	319	183	66	18	10	1501²	1540	100	630	564	13.1	3.93	96	.267	.341	56	.127	-16	-18	-23	-7	-4.2
● **CLARENCE HEISE** Heise, Clarence Edward "Lefty" b: 8/7/07, Topeka, Kan. BL/TL, 5′10″, 172 lbs. Deb: 4/22/34																									
1934 StL-N	0	0	—	1	0	0	0	0	2	3	1	1	0	13.5	4.50	94	.300	.300	0	—	0	-0	-0	-0	0.0
● **JIM HEISE** Heise, James Edward b: 10/2/32, Scottdale, Pa. BR/TR, 6′1″, 185 lbs. Deb: 6/29/57																									
1957 Was-A	0	3	.000	8	2	0	0	0	19	25	2	16	8	19.4	8.05	48	.329	.446	0	.000	-0	-9	-9	-1	-1.2
● **ROY HEISER** Heiser, Le Roy Barton b: 6/22/42, Baltimore, Md. BR/TR, 6′4″, 190 lbs. Deb: 9/2/61																									
1961 Was-A	0	0	—	3	0	0	0	0	5²	6	1	9	1	25.4	6.35	63	.261	.485	0	.000	-0	-1	-1	0	-0.1
● **CRESE HEISMANN** Heismann, Christian Ernest b: 4/16/1880, Cincinnati, Ohio d: 11/19/51, Cincinnati, Ohio BR/TL, 6′2″, 175 lbs. Deb: 9/25/01																									
1901 Cin-N	0	1	.000	3	2	1	0	0	13²	18	1	6	6	17.8	5.93	54	.316	.409	2	.400	1	-4	-4	-1	-0.2
1902 Cin-N	2	1	.667	5	3	2	0	0	33	33	1	10	15	13.1	2.45	122	.260	.338	3	.214	-1	1	2	0	0.2
Bal-A	0	3	.000	3	3	2	0	0	16	20	1	12	2	19.1	8.44	45	.308	.430	1	.143	-1	-9	-8	-0	-1.2
Total 2	2	5	.286	11	8	5	0	0	62²	71	3	28	23	15.7	4.74	69	.285	.380	6	.231	-1	-11	-10	-1	-1.2
● **HARRY HEITMANN** Heitmann, Henry Anton b: 10/6/1896, Albany, N.Y. d: 12/15/58, Brooklyn, N.Y. BR/TR, 6′, 175 lbs. Deb: 7/27/18																									
1918 Bro-N	0	1	.000	1	1	0	0	0	0¹	4	0	0	0	108.0	108.00	3	1.000	1.000	0	—	0	-4	-4	0	-3.0
● **MEL HELD** Held, Melvin Nicholas "Country" b: 4/12/29, Edon, Ohio BR/TR, 6′1″, 178 lbs. Deb: 4/27/56																									
1956 Bal-A	0	0	—	4	0	0	0	0	7	7	1	3	4	12.9	5.14	76	.318	.400	0		0	-1	-1	0	0.0
● **RICK HELLING** Helling, Ricky Allen b: 12/15/70, Devils Lake, N.D. BR/TR, 6′3″, 215 lbs. Deb: 4/10/94																									
1994 Tex-A	3	2	.600	9	9	1	1	0	52	62	14	18	25	13.8	5.88	82	.295	.351	0		-6	-6	-1		-0.6
1995 Tex-A	0	2	.000	3	3	0	0	0	12¹	17	2	8	5	19.7	6.57	73	.340	.450	0		-0	-3	-2	0	-0.4
1996 Tex-A	1	2	.333	6	2	0	0	0	20¹	23	7	9	16	14.2	7.52	71	.280	.352	0		-0	-6	-5	-0	-0.6
Fla-N	2	1	.667	5	4	0	0	0	27²	14	2	7	26	6.8	1.95	207	.143	.200	1	.111	-0	7	6	-1	0.6
Total 3	6	7	.462	23	18	1	1	0	112¹	116	25	42	72	12.6	5.29	89	.264	.331	1	.111	-0	-8	-7	-2	-1.0
● **HORACE HELMBOLD** Helmbold, Horace b: Philadelphia, Pa. Deb: 10/11/1890																									
1890 Phi-a	0	1	.000	1	1	1	0	0	7	17	0	6	3	29.6	14.14	27	.447	.523	0	.000	-1	-8	-8	0	-0.7
● **RUSS HEMAN** Heman, Russell Fredrick b: 2/10/33, Olive, Cal. BR/TR, 6′4″, 200 lbs. Deb: 4/20/61																									
1961 Cle-A	0	0	—	6	0	0	0	1	10	8	0	4	6	15.3	3.60	109	.216	.370	0	.000	-0	0	0	0	0.0
LA-A	0	0	—	6	0	0	0	0	10	4	1	6	4	9.0	1.80	251	.125	.200	0	.000	-0	2	3	0	0.0
Yr	0	0	—	12	0	0	0	1	20	12	1	10	10	10.3	2.70	156	.171	.284	0	.000	-0	3	3	0	0.0
● **GEORGE HEMMING** Hemming, George Earl "Old Wax Figger" b: 12/15/1868, Carrollton, Ohio d: 6/3/30, Springfield, Mass. BR/TR, 5′11″, 170 lbs. Deb: 4/21/1890																									
1890 Cle-P	0	1	.000	3	1	1	0	0	21	25	1	19	3	19.7	6.86	58	.284	.422	2	.182	-1	-6	-7	1	-0.2
Bro-P	8	4	.667	19	11	11	0	3	123	117	3	59	32	13.1	3.98	117	.240	.325	9	.158	-4	6	9	0	0.3
Yr	8	5	.615	22	12	12	0	**3**	144	142	4	78	35	13.9	4.25	103	.246	.338	11	.162	-5	-0	2	1	0.1
1891 Bro-N	8	15	.348	27	22	19	1	1	199²	231	11	84	83	14.7	4.96	87	.279	.353	13	.159	-1	-36	-37	1	-3.3
1892 Cin-N	0	1	.000	1	0	0	0	0	6	10	1	2	0	18.0	7.50	44	.357	.400	1	.333	-1	-3	-3	0	-0.3
Lou-N	2	2	.500	4	4	4	0	0	35	36	1	17	12	13.6	4.63	66	.255	.335	1	.077	-1	-5	-6	0	-0.6
Yr	2	3	.400	5	4	4	0	0	41	46	2	19	12	14.3	5.05	61	.272	.346	2	.125	-1	-8	-9	0	-0.9
1893 Lou-N	18	17	.514	41	32	32	1	1	332	369	7	176	79	15.2	5.10	86	.273	.363	32	.203	-2	-16	-26	2	1.9
1894 Lou-N	13	19	.406	35	32	31	1	0	294¹	358	7	133	66	15.3	4.37	117	.297	.371	33	.252	2	31	24	-1	1.9
*Bal-N	4	0	1.000	6	6	5	0	0	45¹	48	0	26	13	15.1	3.57	153	.268	.367	6	.286	1	9	9	-0	0.7
Yr	17	19	.472	41	38	36	1	0	339²	406	7	159	79	15.0	4.27	121	.291	.365	39	.257	3	40	33	-1	2.6
1895 Bal-N	20	13	.606	34	31	26	1	0	262¹	288	10	96	43	13.4	4.05	118	.275	.339	33	.282	3	21	21	-1	1.9

YEAR	TM/L	W	L	PCT	G	GS	CG	SH	SV	IP	H	HR	BB	SO	RAT	ERA	ERA+	OAV	OOB	BH	AVG	PB	PR	/A	PD	TPI
1896	Bal-N	15	6	.714	25	21	20	3	0	202	233	9	54	33	12.9	4.19	102	.287	.333	25	.258	4	4	2	-3	0.2
1897	Lou-N	3	4	.429	9	8	7	0	0	67	80	5	25	7	14.2	5.10	83	.294	.356	5	.179	-1	-6	-6	1	-0.5
Total	8	91	82	.526	204	168	156	7	6	1587²	1795	55	691	362	14.4	4.53	98	.279	.353	160	.223	-0	-1	-19	-2	-1.9

● **BERNIE HENDERSON**   Henderson, Bernard "Barnyard"   b: 4/12/1899, Douglassville, Tex   d: 6/6/66, Linden, Tex.   BR/TR, 5'9", 175 lbs.   Deb: 9/5/21

YEAR	TM/L	W	L	PCT	G	GS	CG	SH	SV	IP	H	HR	BB	SO	RAT	ERA	ERA+	OAV	OOB	BH	AVG	PB	PR	/A	PD	TPI
1921	Cle-A	0	1	.000	2	1	0	0	0	3	5	0	0	1	15.0	9.00	47	.333	.333	0	.000	-0	-2	-2	-0	-0.4

● **ED HENDERSON**   Henderson, Edward J. (b: Eugene J. Ball)   b: 12/25/1884, Newark, N.J.   d: 1/15/64, New York, N.Y.   BL/TL, 5'9", 168 lbs.   Deb: 5/15/14

YEAR	TM/L	W	L	PCT	G	GS	CG	SH	SV	IP	H	HR	BB	SO	RAT	ERA	ERA+	OAV	OOB	BH	AVG	PB	PR	/A	PD	TPI
1914	Pit-F	0	1	.000	6	1	1	0	0	16	14	2	8	4	12.4	3.94	73	.241	.333	0	.000	-0	-2	-2	-1	-0.2
	Ind-F	1	0	1.000	2	1	1	0	0	10	8	0	4	1	13.5	4.50	69	.229	.357	0	.000	-1	-2	-2	-0	-0.2
	Yr	1	1	.500	8	2	2	0	0	26	22	2	12	5	12.8	4.15	71	.237	.343	0	.000	-1	-4	-3	-1	-0.4

● **HARDIE HENDERSON**   Henderson, James Harding   b: 10/31/1862, Philadelphia, Pa.   d: 2/6/03, Philadelphia, Pa.   BR/TR,   Deb: 5/2/1883   U

YEAR	TM/L	W	L	PCT	G	GS	CG	SH	SV	IP	H	HR	BB	SO	RAT	ERA	ERA+	OAV	OOB	BH	AVG	PB	PR	/A	PD	TPI
1883	Phi-N	0	1	.000	1	1	1	0	0	9	26	0	2	2	28.0	19.00	16	.481	.500	2	.250		-16	-16	-0	-0.9
	Bal-a	10	32	.238	45	42	38	0	0	358¹	383	4	87	145	11.8	4.02	87	.256	.297	31	.162	-6	-28	-21	-2	-2.6
1884	Bal-a	27	23	.540	52	52	50	4	0	439¹	382	9	116	346	10.5	2.62	132	.216	.271	46	.227	2	31	41	1	4.4
1885	Bal-a	25	35	.417	61	61	59	0	0	539¹	539	6	117	263	11.3	3.19	102	.253	.298	51	.223	3	4	4	0	0.7
1886	Bal-a	3	15	.167	19	19	19	0	0	171¹	188	0	66	88	13.8	4.62	74	.252	.320	16	.235	2	-22	-23	2	-1.4
	Bro-a	10	4	.714	14	14	14	0	0	124	112	2	51	49	11.8	2.90	120	.232	.306	9	.180	-1	8	8	0	0.6
	Yr	13	19	.406	33	33	33	0	0	295¹	300	2	117	137	12.7	3.90	88	.242	.308	25	.212	1	-15	-15	0	-0.8
1887	Bro-a	5	8	.385	13	12	12	0	0	111²	127	3	63	28	15.7	3.95	109	.281	.375	5	.122	-3	4	4	1	0.2
1888	Pit-N	1	3	.250	5	5	4	0	0	35¹	47	0	20	9	16.6	5.35	50	.289	.380	1	.278	-1	-10	-11	0	-0.9
Total	6	81	121	.401	210	206	197	4	0	1788¹	1800	25	522	930	11.9	3.50	98	.247	.302	165	.204	-2	-30	-13	2	0.1

● **JOE HENDERSON**   Henderson, Joseph Lee   b: 7/4/46, Lake Cormorant, Miss.   BL/TR, 6'2", 195 lbs.   Deb: 6/7/74

YEAR	TM/L	W	L	PCT	G	GS	CG	SH	SV	IP	H	HR	BB	SO	RAT	ERA	ERA+	OAV	OOB	BH	AVG	PB	PR	/A	PD	TPI
1974	Chi-A	1	0	1.000	5	3	0	0	0	15	21	2	11	12	19.2	8.40	44	.328	.427	0	.000	-0	-8	-8	-0	-0.5
1976	Cin-N	2	0	1.000	4	0	0	0	0	11	9	0	7	6	13.9	0.00	—	.225	.354	0	—	0	4	4	0	0.9
1977	Cin-N	0	2	.000	7	0	0	0	0	9	17	2	6	8	23.0	12.00	33	.386	.460	0	—	0	-8	-8	-0	-1.5
Total	3	3	2	.600	16	3	0	0	0	35	47	4	25	27	18.5	6.69	55	.318	.416	0	.000	-0	-12	-12	-0	-1.1

● **ROD HENDERSON**   Henderson, Rodney Wood   b: 3/11/71, Greensburg, Ky.   BR/TR, 6'4", 195 lbs.   Deb: 4/19/94

YEAR	TM/L	W	L	PCT	G	GS	CG	SH	SV	IP	H	HR	BB	SO	RAT	ERA	ERA+	OAV	OOB	BH	AVG	PB	PR	/A	PD	TPI
1994	Mon-N	0	1	.000	3	2	0	0	0	6²	9	1	7	3	21.6	9.45	45	.333	.471	0	.000	-0	-4	-4	0	-0.5

● **BILL HENDERSON**   Henderson, William Maxwell   b: 11/4/01, Pensacola, Fla.   d: 10/6/66, Pensacola, Fla.   BR/TR, 6', 190 lbs.   Deb: 6/20/30

YEAR	TM/L	W	L	PCT	G	GS	CG	SH	SV	IP	H	HR	BB	SO	RAT	ERA	ERA+	OAV	OOB	BH	AVG	PB	PR	/A	PD	TPI
1930	NY-A	0	0	—	3	0	0	0	0	8	7	1	4	2	12.4	4.50	96	.250	.344	1	.500	0	0	-0	0	0.0

● **BOB HENDLEY**   Hendley, Charles Robert   b: 4/30/39, Macon, Ga.   BR/TL, 6'2", 190 lbs.   Deb: 6/23/61

YEAR	TM/L	W	L	PCT	G	GS	CG	SH	SV	IP	H	HR	BB	SO	RAT	ERA	ERA+	OAV	OOB	BH	AVG	PB	PR	/A	PD	TPI
1961	Mil-N	5	7	.417	19	13	3	0	0	97	96	8	39	44	12.5	3.90	96	.262	.333	1	.032	-3	1	-2	1	-0.4
1962	Mil-N	11	13	.458	35	29	7	2	1	200	188	17	59	112	11.1	3.60	105	.247	.301	7	.119	1	8	4	1	0.6
1963	Mil-N	9	9	.500	41	24	7	3	3	169¹	153	16	64	105	11.6	3.93	82	.244	.315	5	.106	-1	-12	-13	1	-1.4
1964	SF-N	10	11	.476	30	29	4	1	0	163¹	161	18	59	104	12.2	3.64	98	.258	.325	5	.106	-1	-2	-1	-2	-0.5
1965	SF-N	0	0	—	8	2	0	0	0	15	27	6	13	8	24.6	12.60	29	.397	.500	0	.000	-0	-15	-15	0	0.0
	Chi-N	4	4	.500	18	10	2	0	0	62	59	9	25	38	12.3	4.35	85	.244	.317	0	.000	-1	-6	-5	1	-0.7
	Yr	4	4	.500	26	12	2	0	0	77	86	15	38	46	14.6	5.96	62	.277	.357	0	.000	-2	-21	-20	1	-0.7
1966	Chi-N	4	5	.444	43	6	0	0	7	89²	98	10	39	65	13.8	3.91	94	.285	.358	3	.167	-1	-3	-2	-1	-0.1
1967	Chi-N	2	0	1.000	7	0	0	0	0	12¹	17	4	3	10	14.6	6.57	54	.315	.351	0	.000	-1	-4	-4	-0	-0.8
	NY-N	3	3	.500	15	13	2	0	0	70²	71	11	28	36	12.0	3.44	99	.241	.314	2	.111	-1	-0	-2	-2	-0.2
	Yr	5	3	.625	22	13	2	0	1	83	82	15	31	46	12.4	3.90	87	.253	.320	2	.083	-1	-5	-5	-2	-1.0
Total	7	48	52	.480	216	126	25	6	12	879¹	864	99	329	522	12.3	3.97	90	.257	.325	23	.095	-6	-34	-38	0	-3.5

● **ED HENDRICKS**   Hendricks, Edward "Big Ed"   b: 6/20/1885, Zeeland, Mich.   d: 11/28/30, Jackson, Mich.   BL/TL, 6'3", 200 lbs.   Deb: 9/15/10

YEAR	TM/L	W	L	PCT	G	GS	CG	SH	SV	IP	H	HR	BB	SO	RAT	ERA	ERA+	OAV	OOB	BH	AVG	PB	PR	/A	PD	TPI
1910	NY-N	0	1	.000	4	1	1	0	1	12	12	0	4	2	12.0	3.75	79	.261	.320	0	.000	-1	-1	-1	-1	-0.2

● **ELLIE HENDRICKS**   Hendricks, Elrod Jerome   b: 12/22/40, Charlotte Amalie, V.I.   BL/TR, 6'1", 175 lbs.   Deb: 4/13/68   C◆

YEAR	TM/L	W	L	PCT	G	GS	CG	SH	SV	IP	H	HR	BB	SO	RAT	ERA	ERA+	OAV	OOB	BH	AVG	PB	PR	/A	PD	TPI
1978	Bal-A	0	0	—	1	0	0	0	0	2¹	1	0	1	0	7.7	0.00	—	.125	.222	6	.333	1	1	1	-0	0.0

● **DON HENDRICKSON**   Hendrickson, Donald William   b: 7/14/15, Kewanna, Ind.   d: 1/19/77, Norfolk, Va.   BR/TR, 6'2", 204 lbs.   Deb: 7/4/45

YEAR	TM/L	W	L	PCT	G	GS	CG	SH	SV	IP	H	HR	BB	SO	RAT	ERA	ERA+	OAV	OOB	BH	AVG	PB	PR	/A	PD	TPI
1945	Bos-N	4	8	.333	37	2	1	0	5	73¹	74	8	39	14	14.0	4.91	78	.261	.353	3	.167	-0	-9	-9	-1	-1.5
1946	Bos-N	0	1	.000	2	0	0	0	0	2	4	0	2	2	27.0	4.50	76	.364	.462	0	.000	-0	-0	-0	-0	-0.1
Total	2	4	9	.308	39	2	1	0	5	75¹	78	8	41	16	14.3	4.90	78	.265	.357	3	.158	-0	-9	-9	-1	-1.6

● **CLAUDE HENDRIX**   Hendrix, Claude Raymond   b: 4/13/1889, Olathe, Kan.   d: 3/22/44, Allentown, Pa.   BR/TR, 6', 195 lbs.   Deb: 6/7/11

YEAR	TM/L	W	L	PCT	G	GS	CG	SH	SV	IP	H	HR	BB	SO	RAT	ERA	ERA+	OAV	OOB	BH	AVG	PB	PR	/A	PD	TPI
1911	Pit-N	4	6	.400	22	12	6	1	1	118²	85	1	57	50	10.5	2.73	126	.204	.295	4	.098	-1	9	9	4	1.0
1912	Pit-N	24	9	.727	39	32	25	4	1	288²	256	6	105	176	11.5	2.59	126	.246	.320	39	.322	16	26	22	5	4.3
1913	Pit-N	14	15	.483	42	25	17	2	3	241	216	3	89	138	11.6	2.84	106	.248	.321	27	.273	10	10	5	2	1.7
1914	Chi-F	29	10	.744	49	37	34	6	5	362	262	6	77	189	8.6	1.69	157	.203	.251	30	.231	4	48	39	6	5.4
1915	Chi-F	16	15	.516	40	31	26	5	4	285	256	7	84	107	10.8	3.00	84	.241	.298	11	.265	11	-9	-15	-4	-1.0
1916	Chi-N	8	16	.333	36	24	15	3	2	218	193	4	67	117	11.0	2.68	108	.242	.306	16	.200	2	-2	5	2	1.1
1917	Chi-N	10	12	.455	40	21	13	1	1	215	202	3	72	81	11.6	2.60	112	.257	.322	22	.256	3	3	7	-2	1.0
1918	*Chi-N	20	7	.741	32	27	21	3	0	233	229	2	54	86	11.1	2.78	100	.259	.305	24	.264	9	-0	0	1	1.1
1919	Chi-N	10	14	.417	33	25	15	2	0	206¹	208	3	42	69	11.3	2.62	110	.266	.311	15	.192	-0	7	6	1	0.8
1920	Chi-N	9	12	.429	27	23	12	0	0	203²	216	7	54	79	12.1	3.58	90	.273	.322	15	.181	-2	-10	-8	-1	-1.0
Total	10	144	116	.554	360	257	184	27	17	2371¹	2123	41	697	1092	10.9	2.65	110	.243	.303	222	.241	50	82	71	14	14.4

● **LAFAYETTE HENION**   Henion, Lafayette Marion   b: 6/7/1899, Eureka, Cal.   d: 7/22/55, San Luis Obispo, Cal.   BR/TR, 5'11", 154 lbs.   Deb: 9/10/19

YEAR	TM/L	W	L	PCT	G	GS	CG	SH	SV	IP	H	HR	BB	SO	RAT	ERA	ERA+	OAV	OOB	BH	AVG	PB	PR	/A	PD	TPI
1919	Bro-N	0	0	—	1	0	0	0	0	3	2	0	2	2	12.0	6.00	50	.200	.333	0	—	-1	-1	-1	-0	0.0

● **TOM HENKE**   Henke, Thomas Anthony   b: 12/21/57, Kansas City, Mo.   BR/TR, 6'5", 215 lbs.   Deb: 9/10/82

YEAR	TM/L	W	L	PCT	G	GS	CG	SH	SV	IP	H	HR	BB	SO	RAT	ERA	ERA+	OAV	OOB	BH	AVG	PB	PR	/A	PD	TPI
1982	Tex-A	1	0	1.000	8	0	0	0	0	15²	14	0	8	9	13.2	1.15	337	.246	.348	0	—	0	5	5	0	0.7
1983	Tex-A	1	0	1.000	8	0	0	0	1	16	16	1	4	17	11.3	3.38	119	.262	.308	0	—	0	1	1	0	0.2
1984	Tex-A	1	1	.500	25	0	0	0	2	28¹	36	4	20	25	18.1	6.35	65	.313	.419	0	—	0	-7	-7	-0	-0.7
1985	*Tor-A	3	3	.500	28	0	0	0	13	40	29	4	8	42	8.3	2.02	208	.206	.248	0	—	0	9	10	-0	1.9
1986	Tor-A	9	5	.643	63	0	0	0	27	91¹	63	6	32	118	9.5	3.35	126	.191	.265	0	—	0	8	9	-2	1.5
1987	Tor-A★	0	6	.000	72	0	0	0	34	94	62	10	25	128	8.3	2.49	180	.188	.245	0	—	0	21	21	1	2.9
1988	Tor-A	4	4	.500	52	0	0	0	25	68	60	6	24	66	11.4	2.91	135	.237	.308	0	—	0	8	8	1	1.4
1989	*Tor-A	8	3	.727	64	0	0	0	20	89	66	5	25	116	9.4	1.92	196	.205	.266	0	—	0	19	18	0	2.9
1990	Tor-A	2	4	.333	61	0	0	0	32	74²	58	8	19	75	9.4	2.17	182	.213	.267	0	—	0	14	15	-1	2.0
1991	*Tor-A	0	2	.000	49	0	0	0	32	50¹	33	4	11	53	7.9	2.32	181	.184	.232	0	—	0	10	11	-1	1.1
1992	*Tor-A	3	2	.600	57	0	0	0	34	55²	40	5	22	46	10.2	2.26	180	.197	.276	0	—	0	10	11	-1	1.7
1993	Tex-A	5	5	.500	66	0	0	0	40	74¹	55	7	27	79	10.0	2.91	143	.205	.280	0	—	0	12	10	1	2.3
1994	Tex-A	3	6	.333	37	0	0	0	15	38	33	6	12	39	10.7	3.79	127	.232	.292	0	—	0	4	4	-0	1.2
1995	StL-N★	1	1	.500	52	0	0	0	36	54²	42	4	18	48	9.9	1.82	230	.209	.274	0	.000	-0	14	14	-2	2.1
Total	14	41	42	.494	642	0	0	0	311	789²	607	64	255	861	9.9	2.67	155	.211	.278	0	.000	-0	129	130	-3	21.2

● **WELDON HENLEY**   Henley, Weldon   b: 10/25/1880, Jasper, Ga.   d: 11/16/60, Palatka, Fla.   BR/TR, 6', 175 lbs.   Deb: 4/23/03

YEAR	TM/L	W	L	PCT	G	GS	CG	SH	SV	IP	H	HR	BB	SO	RAT	ERA	ERA+	OAV	OOB	BH	AVG	PB	PR	/A	PD	TPI
1903	Phi-A	12	10	.545	29	21	13	1	0	186¹	186	3	67	86	12.8	3.91	78	.259	.333	9	.132	-3	-20	-18	-1	-2.3
1904	Phi-A	15	17	.469	36	34	31	5	0	295²	245	3	76	130	10.3	2.53	106	.226	.289	24	.222	2	2	5	4	1.2
1905	Phi-A	4	11	.267	25	19	13	1	0	183²	155	4	49	93	10.3	2.60	102	.231	.309	11	.169	-1	1	1	4	0.4
1907	Bro-N	1	5	.167	7	7	5	0	0	56	54	1	21	11	12.2	3.05	77	.273	.345	4	.200	-1	-4	-4	2	-0.2
Total	4	32	43	.427	97	81	62	7	0	721²	640	11	213	309	11.4	2.94	93	.240	.310	48	.184	-2	-20	-16	9	-0.9

● **MIKE HENNEMAN**   Henneman, Michael Alan   b: 12/11/61, St.Charles, Mo.   BR/TR, 6'4", 205 lbs.   Deb: 5/11/87

YEAR	TM/L	W	L	PCT	G	GS	CG	SH	SV	IP	H	HR	BB	SO	RAT	ERA	ERA+	OAV	OOB	BH	AVG	PB	PR	/A	PD	TPI
1987	*Det-A	11	3	.786	55	0	0	0	7	96²	86	8	30	75	11.1	2.98	142	.238	.301	0	.000	0	16	13	0	1.9

YEAR TM/L	W	L	PCT	G	GS	CG	SH	SV	IP	H	HR	BB	SO	RAT	ERA	ERA+	OAV	OOB	BH	AVG	PB	PR	/A	PD	TPI
1988 Det-A	9	6	.600	65	0	0	0	22	91^1	72	7	24	58	9.7	1.87	204	.218	.275	0	—	0	**21**	**20**	-1	3.9
1989 Det-A☆	11	4	.733	60	0	0	0	8	90	84	4	51	69	14.0	3.70	103	.251	.358	0	—	0	2	1	0	0.2
1990 Det-A	8	6	.571	69	0	0	0	22	94^1	90	4	33	50	13.0	3.05	130	.253	.321	0	—	0	9	9	1	0.7
1991 Det-A	10	2	.833	60	0	0	0	21	84^1	81	2	34	61	12.3	2.88	144	.258	.330	0	—	0	11	12	-0	1.9
1992 Det-A	2	6	.250	60	0	0	0	24	77^1	75	6	20	58	11.1	3.96	100	.256	.304	0	—	0	-0	-0	-1	0.4
1993 Det-A	5	3	.625	63	0	0	0	24	71^2	69	4	32	58	12.9	2.64	162	.251	.333	0	—	0	13	13	0	2.0
1994 Det-A	1	3	.250	30	0	0	0	8	34^2	43	5	17	27	16.1	5.19	93	.297	.378	0	—	0	-2	-1	0	-0.2
1995 Det-A	0	1	.000	29	0	0	0	18	29^1	24	0	9	24	10.1	1.53	310	.222	.282	0	—	0	10	10	-1	1.4
Hou-N	0	1	.000	21	0	0	0	8	21	21	1	4	19	11.6	3.00	129	.266	.318	0	—	0	3	2	-0	0.2
1996 *Tex-A	0	7	.000	49	0	0	0	31	42	41	6	17	34	12.4	5.79	92	.258	.330	0	—	0	-4	-2	-0	-0.7
Total 10	57	42	.576	561	0	0	0	193	732^2	686	47	271	533	12.0	3.21	130	.249	.320	0	.000	0	80	77	-1	12.3

● **GEORGE HENNESSEY** Hennessey, George "Three Star" b: 10/28/07, Slatington, Pa. d: 1/15/88, Princeton, N.J. BR/TR, 5'10", 168 lbs. Deb: 9/2/37

YEAR TM/L	W	L	PCT	G	GS	CG	SH	SV	IP	H	HR	BB	SO	RAT	ERA	ERA+	OAV	OOB	BH	AVG	PB	PR	/A	PD	TPI
1937 StL-A	0	1	.000	5	0	0	0	0	7	15	2	6	4	27.0	10.29	47	.500	.583	0	—		-4	-4	0	-0.5
1942 Phi-N	1	1	.500	5	1	0	0	0	17	11	1	10	2	11.1	2.65	125	.180	.296	0	.000	-1	1	1	0	0.0
1945 Chi-N	0	0	—	2	0	0	0	0	3^2	5	0	1	2	19.6	7.36	50	.438	.471	0	—		-1	-2	0	-0.2
Total 3	1	2	.333	12	1	0	0	0	27^2	33	3	17	8	16.3	5.20	72	.308	.403	0	.000	-1	-5	-5	-0	-0.5

● **PHIL HENNIGAN** Hennigan, Phillip Winston b: 4/10/46, Jasper, Tex. BR/TR, 5'11.5", 185 lbs. Deb: 9/2/69

YEAR TM/L	W	L	PCT	G	GS	CG	SH	SV	IP	H	HR	BB	SO	RAT	ERA	ERA+	OAV	OOB	BH	AVG	PB	PR	/A	PD	TPI
1969 Cle-A	2	1	.667	9	0	0	0	0	16^1	14	0	4	10	10.5	3.31	114	.241	.302	0	.000	-0	1	1	-1	0.1
1970 Cle-A	6	3	.667	42	1	0	0	3	71^2	69	7	44	43	14.7	4.02	99	.263	.377	1	.143	1	-2	-0	1	0.1
1971 Cle-A	4	3	.571	57	0	0	0	14	82	80	13	51	69	14.7	4.94	77	.281	.371	0	.000	-0	-13	-10	-1	-1.3
1972 Cle-A	5	3	.625	38	1	0	0	5	67^1	54	8	18	44	9.9	2.67	120	.226	.286	1	.083	-0	3	4	-1	0.4
1973 NY-N	0	4	.000	30	0	0	0	3	43^1	50	6	16	22	13.9	6.23	58	.289	.353	1	.333	0	-12	-13	-1	-1.3
Total 5	17	14	.548	176	2	0	0	25	280^2	267	34	133	188	13.2	4.26	86	.257	.347	3	.100	1	-25	-18	-2	-2.0

● **PETE HENNING** Henning, Ernest Herman b: 12/28/1887, Crown Point, Ind. d: 11/4/39, Dyer, Ind. BR/TR, 5'11", 185 lbs. Deb: 4/17/14

YEAR TM/L	W	L	PCT	G	GS	CG	SH	SV	IP	H	HR	BB	SO	RAT	ERA	ERA+	OAV	OOB	BH	AVG	PB	PR	/A	PD	TPI
1914 KC-F	5	10	.333	28	14	7	0	2	138	153	6	58	45	14.2	4.83	58	.291	.369	8	.182		-30	-31	0	-3.1
1915 KC-F	9	15	.375	40	20	15	1	2	207	181	5	76	73	11.3	3.17	83	.235	.307	14	.206	-1	-10	-13	4	-1.2
Total 2	14	25	.359	68	34	22	1	4	345	334	11	134	118	12.5	3.83	70	.258	.332	22	.196	-1	-40	-44	4	-4.3

● **RICK HENNINGER** Henninger, Richard Lee b: 1/11/48, Hastings, Neb. BR/TR, 6'6", 225 lbs. Deb: 9/3/73

YEAR TM/L	W	L	PCT	G	GS	CG	SH	SV	IP	H	HR	BB	SO	RAT	ERA	ERA+	OAV	OOB	BH	AVG	PB	PR	/A	PD	TPI
1973 Tex-A	1	0	1.000	6	2	0	0	0	23	23	1	11	6	13.3	2.74	136	.261	.343	0	—	0	3	3	-1	0.1

● **RANDY HENNIS** Hennis, Randall Philip b: 12/16/65, Clearlake, Cal. BR/TR, 6'6", 220 lbs. Deb: 9/17/90

YEAR TM/L	W	L	PCT	G	GS	CG	SH	SV	IP	H	HR	BB	SO	RAT	ERA	ERA+	OAV	OOB	BH	AVG	PB	PR	/A	PD	TPI
1990 Hou-N	0	0	—	3	1	0	0	0	9^2	1	0	3	4	4.7	0.00	—	.033	.147	0	.000	-0	4	4	0	0.0

● **DWAYNE HENRY** Henry, Dwayne Allen b: 2/16/62, Elkton, Md. BR/TR, 6'3", 205 lbs. Deb: 9/7/84

YEAR TM/L	W	L	PCT	G	GS	CG	SH	SV	IP	H	HR	BB	SO	RAT	ERA	ERA+	OAV	OOB	BH	AVG	PB	PR	/A	PD	TPI
1984 Tex-A	0	1	.000	3	0	0	0	0	4^1	5	0	7	2	24.9	8.31	50	.294	.500	0	—	0	-2	-2	-0	-0.5
1985 Tex-A	2	2	.500	16	0	0	0	3	21	16	0	7	20	9.9	2.57	164	.211	.277	0	—	0	4	4	0	0.8
1986 Tex-A	1	0	1.000	19	0	0	0	0	19^1	14	1	22	17	17.2	4.66	92	.209	.411	0	—	0	-1	-1	0	0.2
1987 Tex-A	0	0	—	5	0	0	0	0	10	12	2	9	7	18.9	9.00	50	.293	.420	0	—	0	-5	-5	0	-0.6
1988 Tex-A	0	1	.000	11	0	0	0	1	10^1	15	1	9	10	23.5	8.71	47	.326	.466	0	—	0	-5	-5	-0	-0.6
1989 Atl-N	0	2	.000	12	0	0	0	0	12^2	12	2	5	16	12.1	4.26	86	.250	.321	0	—	0	-1	-1	-0	-0.2
1990 Atl-N	2	2	.500	34	0	0	0	0	38^1	41	3	25	34	15.5	5.63	72	.273	.377	0	—	0	-8	-7	-1	-0.7
1991 Hou-N	3	2	.600	52	0	0	0	2	67^2	51	7	39	51	12.2	3.19	110	.219	.336	0	.000	-0	4	2	-1	0.1
1992 Cin-N	3	3	.500	60	0	0	0	0	83^2	59	4	44	72	11.2	3.33	108	.199	.304	1	.250	0	2	2	0	0.2
1993 Cin-N	0	1	.000	3	0	0	0	0	4^2	6	0	4	2	19.3	3.86	104	.273	.385	0	—	0	0	0	-0	0.0
Sea-A	2	1	.667	31	0	0	0	0	54	56	6	35	35	15.5	6.67	66	.273	.384	0	—	0	-14	-14	-2	-0.9
1995 Det-A	1	0	1.000	10	0	0	0	5	8^2	11	0	10	9	21.8	6.23	76	.306	.457	0	—	0	-1	-1	-0	-0.3
Total 11	14	15	.483	256	1	0	0	14	334^2	298	26	216	275	14.1	4.65	84	.241	.357	1	.167	-0	-29	-27	-3	-2.1

● **EARL HENRY** Henry, Earl Clifford "Hook" b: 6/10/17, Roseville, Ohio BL/TL, 5'11", 172 lbs. Deb: 9/23/44

YEAR TM/L	W	L	PCT	G	GS	CG	SH	SV	IP	H	HR	BB	SO	RAT	ERA	ERA+	OAV	OOB	BH	AVG	PB	PR	/A	PD	TPI
1944 Cle-A	1	1	.500	2	2	1	0	0	17^2	18	0	3	10	10.7	4.58	72	.269	.300	0	.000	-0	-2	-3	0	-0.3
1945 Cle-A	0	3	.000	15	1	0	0	0	21^2	20	0	20	5	17.0	5.40	60	.253	.410	2	.500	1	-5	-5	1	-0.5
Total 2	1	4	.200	17	3	1	0	0	39^1	38	0	23	15	14.2	5.03	65	.260	.365	2	.222	1	-7	-8	1	-0.7

● **BUTCH HENRY** Henry, Floyd Bluford b: 10/7/68, ElPaso, Tex. BL/TL, 6'1", 195 lbs. Deb: 4/9/92

YEAR TM/L	W	L	PCT	G	GS	CG	SH	SV	IP	H	HR	BB	SO	RAT	ERA	ERA+	OAV	OOB	BH	AVG	PB	PR	/A	PD	TPI
1992 Hou-N	6	9	.400	28	28	2	1	0	165^2	185	16	41	96	12.3	4.02	84	.285	.329	8	.148	1	-10	-12	1	-0.9
1993 Col-N	2	8	.200	20	15	1	0	0	84^2	117	14	24	39	15.1	6.59	72	.331	.375	2	.091	-1	-24	-17	-0	-1.9
Mon-N	1	1	.500	10	1	0	0	0	18^1	18	1	4	8	10.8	3.93	106	.289	.289	0	.000	-0	0	-0	-1	0.0
Yr	3	9	.250	30	16	1	0	0	103	135	15	28	47	14.2	6.12	76	.313	.354	2	.083	-2	-24	-17	-1	-1.9
1994 Mon-N	8	3	.727	24	15	0	0	1	107^1	97	10	20	70	10.0	2.43	174	.241	.280	9	.290	3	21	21	0	2.4
1995 Mon-N	7	9	.438	21	21	1	1	0	126^2	133	11	28	60	11.6	2.84	151	.275	.317	2	.048	-4	19	20	2	2.2
Total 4	24	30	.444	103	80	4	2	1	502^2	550	52	117	273	12.0	3.81	106	.280	.323	21	.139	-2	7	12	2	1.8

● **DUTCH HENRY** Henry, Frank John b: 5/12/02, Cleveland, Ohio d: 8/23/68, Cleveland, Ohio BL/TL, 6'1", 175 lbs. Deb: 9/16/21

YEAR TM/L	W	L	PCT	G	GS	CG	SH	SV	IP	H	HR	BB	SO	RAT	ERA	ERA+	OAV	OOB	BH	AVG	PB	PR	/A	PD	TPI
1921 StL-A	0	0	—	1	0	0	0	0	2	3	0	1	0	9.0	4.50	100	.250	.250	1	1.000	0	-0	-0	0	0.0
1922 StL-A	0	0	—	4	0	0	0	0	5	7	0	5	2	21.6	5.40	77	.280	.400	0	—	-1	-1	-1	0	0.0
1923 Bro-N	4	6	.400	17	9	5	2	0	94^1	105	9	28	28	12.9	3.91	99	.281	.334	8	.229	1	1	1	-0	0.0
1924 Bro-N	1	2	.333	16	4	0	0	0	46	69	0	15	11	16.4	5.67	66	.352	.398	5	.250	1	-9	-10	1	-0.5
1927 NY-N	11	6	.647	45	15	7	1	4	163^2	184	6	31	40	11.8	4.23	91	.278	.311	13	.236	1	-6	-7	-2	-0.7
1928 NY-N	3	6	.333	17	8	4	0	1	64	82	4	25	23	15.2	3.80	103	.325	.388	3	.158	-1	1	1	1	0.1
1929 NY-N	5	6	.455	27	9	4	0	1	101^1	129	10	31	27	14.3	3.82	120	.316	.366	7	.250	1	10	9	-1	0.8
Chi-A	1	0	1.000	2	1	0	0	0	15	20	1	7	2	16.2	6.00	71	.308	.375	1	.143	0	-3	-3	-1	-0.2
1930 Chi-A	2	17	.105	35	16	4	0	0	155	211	12	48	35	15.3	4.88	95	.331	.381	12	.235	1	-4	-4	3	-0.1
Total 8	27	43	.386	164	62	25	3	6	646^1	809	42	190	170	14.0	4.39	95	.308	.356	50	.231	6	-10	-16	-0	-0.6

● **JIM HENRY** Henry, James Francis b: 6/26/10, Danville, Pa. d: 8/15/76, Memphis, Tenn. BR/TR, 6'2", 175 lbs. Deb: 4/23/36

YEAR TM/L	W	L	PCT	G	GS	CG	SH	SV	IP	H	HR	BB	SO	RAT	ERA	ERA+	OAV	OOB	BH	AVG	PB	PR	/A	PD	TPI
1936 Bos-A	5	1	.833	21	8	2	0	0	76^1	75	10	40	36	13.8	4.60	116	.255	.348	3	.115	-1	4	6	0	0.3
1937 Bos-A	1	0	1.000	3	2	1	0	0	15^1	15	2	11	8	15.3	5.28	90	.263	.382	0	.000	-0	-1	-1	-0	-0.1
1939 Phi-N	0	1	.000	9	1	0	0	1	23	24	3	8	7	12.9	5.09	79	.276	.344	0	.000	-1	-3	-3	-0	-0.3
Total 3	6	2	.750	33	11	3	0	1	114^2	114	15	59	51	13.8	4.79	104	.260	.352	3	.083	-2	0	2	-1	-0.1

● **JOHN HENRY** Henry, John Michael b: 9/2/1863, Springfield, Mass. d: 6/11/39, Hartford, Conn. TL, Deb: 8/13/1884 ♦

YEAR TM/L	W	L	PCT	G	GS	CG	SH	SV	IP	H	HR	BB	SO	RAT	ERA	ERA+	OAV	OOB	BH	AVG	PB	PR	/A	PD	TPI
1884 Cle-N	1	4	.200	5	5	5	1	0	42	46	2	26	23	15.4	3.64	87	.257	.351	4	.154	-1	-3	-2	1	-0.3
1885 Bal-a	2	7	.222	9	9	9	0	0	71	71	0	13	31	10.9	4.31	76	.247	.284	9	.265	1	-8	-8	2	-0.5
1886 Was-N	1	3	.250	4	4	4	0	0	27^2	35	1	15	19	16.3	4.23	78	.285	.362	5	.357	1	-3	-3	-0	-0.3
Total 3	4	14	.222	18	18	18	1	0	140^2	152	3	54	73	13.3	4.09	79	.258	.322	53	.243	1	-14	-13	2	-1.1

● **DOUG HENRY** Henry, Richard Douglas b: 12/10/63, Sacramento, Cal. BR/TR, 6'4", 185 lbs. Deb: 7/15/91

YEAR TM/L	W	L	PCT	G	GS	CG	SH	SV	IP	H	HR	BB	SO	RAT	ERA	ERA+	OAV	OOB	BH	AVG	PB	PR	/A	PD	TPI
1991 Mil-A	2	1	.667	32	0	0	0	15	36	16	1	14	28	7.5	1.00	397	.133	.224	0	—	0	12	12	1	1.9
1992 Mil-A	1	4	.200	68	0	0	0	29	65	64	6	24	52	12.2	4.02	96	.256	.321	0	—	0	-1	-1	-0	-0.1
1993 Mil-A	4	4	.500	54	0	0	0	17	55	67	7	25	38	15.5	5.56	76	.300	.378	0	—	0	-8	-8	0	-1.4
1994 Mil-A	2	3	.400	25	0	0	0	0	31^1	32	7	23	20	16.1	4.60	109	.271	.394	0	—	0	-2	-2	0	-0.4
1995 NY-N	3	6	.333	51	0	0	0	4	67	48	7	25	62	9.9	2.96	137	.198	.276	1	1.000	0	9	8	0	1.1
1996 NY-N	2	8	.200	58	0	0	0	9	75	82	7	36	58	14.3	4.68	84	.273	.353	0	.000	-1	-4	-6	-1	-1.0
Total 6	14	26	.350	288	0	0	0	74	329^1	309	35	147	258	12.6	3.94	104	.247	.329	1	.143	-0	10	6	-1	0.7

● **BILL HENRY** Henry, William Francis b: 2/15/42, Long Beach, Cal. BL/TL, 6'3", 195 lbs. Deb: 9/13/66

YEAR TM/L	W	L	PCT	G	GS	CG	SH	SV	IP	H	HR	BB	SO	RAT	ERA	ERA+	OAV	OOB	BH	AVG	PB	PR	/A	PD	TPI
1966 NY-A	0	0	—	2	0	0	0	0	3	0	0	2	3	6.0	0.00	—	.000	.200	0	—	0	1	1	0	0.0

YEAR	TM/L	W	L	PCT	G	GS	CG	SH	SV	IP	H	HR	BB	SO	RAT	ERA	ERA+	OAV	OOB	BH	AVG	PB	PR	/A	PD	TPI

● **BILL HENRY**   Henry, William Rodman   b: 10/15/27, Alice, Tex.   BL/TL, 6'2", 180 lbs.   Deb: 4/17/52

YEAR	TM/L	W	L	PCT	G	GS	CG	SH	SV	IP	H	HR	BB	SO	RAT	ERA	ERA+	OAV	OOB	BH	AVG	PB	PR	/A	PD	TPI
1952	Bos-A	5	4	.556	13	10	5	0	0	76²	75	7	36	23	13.3	3.87	102	.254	.339	8	.258	2	-2	1	-1	0.1
1953	Bos-A	5	5	.500	21	12	4	1	1	85²	86	4	33	56	12.9	3.26	129	.260	.334	6	.188	-0	7	9	-1	0.9
1954	Bos-A	3	7	.300	24	13	3	1	0	95²	104	9	49	38	14.5	4.52	91	.270	.354	4	.118	-1	-8	-4	-1	-0.7
1955	Bos-A	2	4	.333	17	7	0	0	0	59²	56	7	21	23	11.6	3.32	129	.247	.310	2	.105	-1	4	6	0	0.5
1958	Chi-N	5	4	.556	44	0	0	0	6	81¹	63	8	17	58	9.0	2.88	136	.214	.259	4	.235	1	10	9	-1	1.1
1959	Chi-N	9	8	.529	**65**	0	0	0	12	134¹	111	19	26	115	9.2	2.68	147	.227	.267	6	.194	0	19	**19**	-1	2.5
1960	Cin-N★	1	5	.167	51	0	0	0	17	67²	62	8	20	58	11.4	3.19	120	.247	.313	0	.000	-1	4	5	1	0.6
1961	*Cin-N	2	1	.667	47	0	0	0	16	53¹	50	8	15	53	11.0	2.19	185	.244	.295	0	.000	-1	11	11	0	1.2
1962	Cin-N	4	2	.667	40	0	0	0	11	37¹	40	5	20	35	14.7	4.58	88	.280	.372	1	.333	0	-3	-2	-1	-0.5
1963	Cin-N	1	3	.250	47	0	0	0	14	52	55	4	11	45	11.6	4.15	81	.279	.321	1	.167	-1	-5	-5	-0	-0.7
1964	Cin-N	2	2	.500	37	0	0	0	6	52	31	2	12	28	8.0	0.87	418	.170	.234	3	.500	1	15	16	-0	1.7
1965	Cin-N	2	0	1.000	3	0	0	0	0	5	3	0	1	5	7.2	0.00	—	.176	.222	0	—	0	2	2	-0	0.9
	SF-N	2	2	.500	35	0	0	0	4	42	40	2	8	35	10.5	3.64	99	.248	.288	1	.200	-0	-0	-0	-0	-0.1
	Yr	4	2	.667	38	0	0	0	4	47	43	2	9	40	10.1	3.26	111	.242	.282	1	.200	-0	1	2	-1	0.8
1966	SF-N	1	1	.500	35	0	0	0	1	22	15	3	10	15	10.6	2.45	149	.190	.289	0	.000	-0	3	3	-0	0.2
1967	SF-N	2	0	1.000	28	1	0	0	2	21²	16	1	9	23	11.2	2.08	158	.198	.293	0	.000	-0	3	3	-0	0.3
1968	SF-N	0	2	.000	7	1	0	0	0	5	4	0	3	0	14.4	5.40	55	.250	.400	0	—	0	-1	-1	0	-0.5
	Pit-N	0	0	—	10	0	0	0	0	16²	29	2	3	9	18.4	8.10	36	.382	.420	0	.000	-0	-9	-10	-1	-0.1
	Yr	0	2	.000	17	1	0	0	0	21²	33	2	6	9	17.0	7.48	39	.355	.406	0	.000	-0	-11	-11	-1	-0.6
1969	Hou-N	0	0	—	3	0	0	0	0	5	2	0	2	2	7.2	0.00	—	.111	.200	0	—	0	2	2	-0	0.0
Total	16	46	50	.479	527	44	12	2	90	913	842	89	296	621	11.5	3.26	119	.244	.308	36	.177	-0	51	63	-6	7.4

● **ROY HENSHAW**   Henshaw, Roy Knikelbine   b: 7/29/11, Chicago, Ill.   d: 6/8/93, LaGrange, Ill.   BR/TL, 5'8", 155 lbs.   Deb: 4/15/33

YEAR	TM/L	W	L	PCT	G	GS	CG	SH	SV	IP	H	HR	BB	SO	RAT	ERA	ERA+	OAV	OOB	BH	AVG	PB	PR	/A	PD	TPI
1933	Chi-N	2	1	.667	21	0	0	0	0	38²	32	0	20	16	12.6	4.19	78	.230	.335	2	.200	-0	-4	-4	-1	-0.4
1935	*Chi-N	13	5	.722	31	18	7	3	1	142²	135	6	68	53	13.1	3.28	120	.249	.337	13	.255	-2	12	10	-3	1.0
1936	Chi-N	6	5	.545	39	14	6	2	1	129¹	152	8	56	69	14.8	3.97	100	.296	.370	6	.136	-2	1	0	-2	-0.4
1937	Bro-N	5	12	.294	42	16	5	0	2	156¹	176	14	69	98	14.3	5.07	80	.278	.352	8	.167	-2	-20	-18	0	-1.9
1938	StL-N	5	11	.313	27	15	4	0	0	130	132	7	48	34	12.5	4.02	99	.266	.332	9	.220	-0	-3	-1	-1	-0.2
1942	Det-A	2	4	.333	23	2	0	0	1	61²	63	3	27	24	13.3	4.09	97	.269	.347	1	.083	-1	-3	-1	-1	-0.2
1943	Det-A	0	2	.000	26	3	0	0	1	71¹	75	2	33	33	14.0	3.79	93	.276	.360	2	.111	-1	-4	-2	-0	-0.2
1944	Det-A	0	0	—	7	1	0	0	0	12¹	17	0	4	10	16.8	8.76	41	.315	.383	0	.000	-1	-7	-7	0	0.0
Total	8	33	40	.452	216	69	22	5	7	742¹	782	40	327	337	13.7	4.16	94	.271	.349	41	.179	-5	-29	-22	-8	-2.3

● **PHIL HENSIEK**   Hensiek, Philip Frank "Sid"   b: 10/13/01, St.Louis, Mo.   d: 2/21/72, St.Louis, Mo.   BR/TR, 6', 160 lbs.   Deb: 8/15/35

YEAR	TM/L	W	L	PCT	G	GS	CG	SH	SV	IP	H	HR	BB	SO	RAT	ERA	ERA+	OAV	OOB	BH	AVG	PB	PR	/A	PD	TPI
1935	Was-A	0	3	.000	6	1	0	0	0	13	21	2	9	6	20.8	9.69	45	.356	.441	2	.667	1	-8	-8	-0	-1.4

● **CHUCK HENSLEY**   Hensley, Charles Floyd   b: 3/11/59, Tulare, Cal.   BL/TL, 6'3", 190 lbs.   Deb: 5/10/86

YEAR	TM/L	W	L	PCT	G	GS	CG	SH	SV	IP	H	HR	BB	SO	RAT	ERA	ERA+	OAV	OOB	BH	AVG	PB	PR	/A	PD	TPI
1986	SF-N	0	0	—	11	0	0	0	1	7¹	5	2	2	6	8.6	2.45	143	.179	.233	0	—	0	1	1	0	0.0

● **PAT HENTGEN**   Hentgen, Patrick George   b: 11/13/68, Detroit, Mich.   BR/TR, 6'2", 200 lbs.   Deb: 9/3/91

YEAR	TM/L	W	L	PCT	G	GS	CG	SH	SV	IP	H	HR	BB	SO	RAT	ERA	ERA+	OAV	OOB	BH	AVG	PB	PR	/A	PD	TPI
1991	Tor-A	0	0	—	3	1	0	0	0	7¹	5	1	3	3	12.3	2.45	171	.208	.345		0	—	0	1	1	-0	-0.2
1992	Tor-A	5	2	.714	28	2	0	0	0	50¹	49	7	32	39	14.5	5.36	76	.254	.360		0	—	0	-8	-7	-1	-1.2
1993	*Tor-A☆	19	9	.679	34	32	3	0	0	216¹	215	27	74	122	12.3	3.87	112	.258	.323		0	—	0	11	11	-2	1.1
1994	Tor-A★	13	8	.619	24	24	6	3	0	174²	158	21	59	147	11.3	3.40	142	.240	.306		0	—	0	27	28	0	2.9
1995	Tor-A	10	14	.417	30	30	2	0	0	200²	236	24	90	135	14.8	5.11	92	.290	.364		0	—	0	-9	-9	-2	-1.0
1996	Tor-A	20	10	.667	35	35	**10**	3	0	**265²**	238	20	94	177	11.4	3.22	157	.241	.310		0	—	0	**52**	**54**	-1	**5.3**
Total	6	67	43	.609	154	124	21	6	0	915	901	100	352	623	12.5	3.93	119	.257	.328		0	—	0	75	78	-5	6.9

● **BILL HEPLER**   Hepler, William Lewis   b: 9/25/45, Covington, Va.   BL/TL, 6', 160 lbs.   Deb: 4/23/66

YEAR	TM/L	W	L	PCT	G	GS	CG	SH	SV	IP	H	HR	BB	SO	RAT	ERA	ERA+	OAV	OOB	BH	AVG	PB	PR	/A	PD	TPI
1966	NY-N	3	3	.500	37	3	0	0	0	69	71	3	51	25	16.3	3.52	103	.274	.399	3	.214	-1	1	1	-1	0.0

● **RON HERBEL**   Herbel, Ronald Samuel   b: 1/16/38, Denver, Colo.   BR/TR, 6'1", 195 lbs.   Deb: 9/10/63

YEAR	TM/L	W	L	PCT	G	GS	CG	SH	SV	IP	H	HR	BB	SO	RAT	ERA	ERA+	OAV	OOB	BH	AVG	PB	PR	/A	PD	TPI
1963	SF-N	0	0	—	2	0	0	0	0	1¹	1	0	1	1	13.5	6.75	47	.200	.333	0	—	0	-1	-1	-0	0
1964	SF-N	9	9	.500	40	22	7	2	1	161	162	7	61	98	12.6	3.07	116	.259	.328	0	.000	-4	8	9	2	0.7
1965	SF-N	12	9	.571	47	21	1	0	1	170²	172	16	47	106	11.7	3.85	94	.261	.313	1	.020	-4	-6	-5	2	-0.8
1966	SF-N	4	5	.444	32	18	0	0	1	129²	149	15	39	55	13.2	4.16	88	.291	.344	1	.026	-4	-8	-7	-1	-0.9
1967	SF-N	4	5	.444	42	11	1	1	1	125²	125	10	35	52	11.6	3.08	107	.268	.322	3	.107	0	4	3	4	0.6
1968	SF-N	0	0	—	28	2	0	0	0	42²	51	5	8	29	13.0	3.38	87	.309	.366	0	.000	-1	1	0	0	0.0
1969	SF-N	4	1	.800	39	4	2	0	1	87¹	92	7	23	34	12.0	4.02	87	.275	.323	0	.000	-2	-4	-5	0	-0.4
1970	SD-N	7	5	.583	64	1	0	0	9	111	114	14	39	53	12.7	4.95	80	.266	.333	0	.000	-1	-11	-12	-0	-1.5
	NY-N	2	2	.500	12	0	0	0	1	13	14	1	2	8	11.1	1.38	291	.275	.302	0	—	0	4	4	-0	1.1
	Yr	9	7	.563	**76**	1	0	0	10	124	128	15	41	61	12.3	4.57	87	.262	.319	0	.000	-1	-7	-8	-1	-0.4
1971	Atl-N	0	1	.000	25	0	0	0	1	51²	61	6	23	22	15.3	5.23	71	.300	.383	1	.091	-1	-10	-9	0	-0.3
Total	9	42	37	.532	331	79	11	3	16	894	945	81	285	447	12.6	3.83	94	.273	.332	6	.029	-15	-25	-25	7	-1.5

● **ERNIE HERBERT**   Herbert, Ernie Albert "Tex"   b: 1/30/1887, Hale, Mo.   d: 1/13/68, Dallas, Tex.   BR/TR, 5'10", 165 lbs.   Deb: 7/27/13

YEAR	TM/L	W	L	PCT	G	GS	CG	SH	SV	IP	H	HR	BB	SO	RAT	ERA	ERA+	OAV	OOB	BH	AVG	PB	PR	/A	PD	TPI
1913	Cin-N	0	0	—	6	0	0	0	0	17¹	12	0	5	9	9.3	2.08	156	.179	.247	1	.250	0	2	2	-1	-0.1
1914	StL-F	1	1	.500	18	2	0	0	1	50¹	56	2	27	34	15.6	3.75	81	.293	.392	7	.538	2	-5	-4	-2	-0.2
1915	StL-F	1	0	1.000	11	1	1	1	0	48	48	1	18	23	12.9	3.38	85	.253	.327	5	.278	1	-3	-3	-1	0.0
Total	3	2	1	.667	35	3	1	1	1	115²	116	3	50	66	13.3	3.42	84	.259	.344	13	.371	3	-6	-4	-4	-0.3

● **FRED HERBERT**   Herbert, Frederick (b: Herbert Frederick Kemman)   b: 3/4/1887, LaGrange, Ill.   d: 5/29/63, Tice, Fla.   BR/TR, 6', 185 lbs.   Deb: 9/25/15

YEAR	TM/L	W	L	PCT	G	GS	CG	SH	SV	IP	H	HR	BB	SO	RAT	ERA	ERA+	OAV	OOB	BH	AVG	PB	PR	/A	PD	TPI
1915	NY-N	1	1	.500	2	1	1	0	0	17	12	4	4	6	8.5	1.06	242	.197	.246	1	.167	-0	3	3	0	0.4

● **RAY HERBERT**   Herbert, Raymond Ernest   b: 12/15/29, Detroit, Mich.   BR/TR, 5'11", 185 lbs.   Deb: 8/27/50

YEAR	TM/L	W	L	PCT	G	GS	CG	SH	SV	IP	H	HR	BB	SO	RAT	ERA	ERA+	OAV	OOB	BH	AVG	PB	PR	/A	PD	TPI
1950	Det-A	1	2	.333	8	3	1	0	1	22¹	20	1	15	12	12.9	3.63	129	.244	.340	2	.286	1	2	3	1	0.4
1951	Det-A	4	0	1.000	5	0	0	0	0	12²	8	0	9	9	12.1	1.42	294	.190	.333	0	.000	-0	4	4	-0	1.1
1953	Det-A	4	6	.400	43	3	0	0	6	87²	109	5	46	37	15.9	5.24	78	.308	.387	3	.158	-0	-12	-11	3	-1.0
1954	Det-A	3	6	.333	42	4	0	0	0	84¹	114	6	50	44	17.7	5.87	63	.334	.422	3	.176	2	-20	-20	2	-1.6
1955	KC-A	1	8	.111	23	11	2	0	0	87²	99	10	40	30	14.4	6.26	67	.292	.368	4	.190	0	-22	-20	2	-1.6
1958	KC-A	8	8	.500	42	16	5	0	3	175	161	20	55	108	11.3	3.50	112	.248	.311	10	.192	1	5	8	2	1.1
1959	KC-A	11	11	.500	37	26	10	2	1	183²	196	24	62	99	12.7	4.85	83	.275	.334	12	.211	-2	-20	-17	-1	-1.8
1960	KC-A	14	15	.483	37	33	14	0	1	252²	256	17	72	122	11.9	3.28	121	.267	.323	13	.171	1	17	20	3	2.5
1961	KC-A	3	6	.333	13	12	1	1	0	83²	103	10	30	34	14.5	5.38	78	.303	.363	3	.107	-1	-13	-11	0	-1.1
	Chi-A	9	6	.600	21	20	4	0	0	137²	142	15	36	50	11.6	4.05	97	.265	.311	12	.226	4	-0	-2	1	0.3
	Yr	12	12	.500	34	32	5	1	0	221¹	245	25	66	84	12.6	4.55	88	.278	.328	15	.185	3	-13	-13	1	-0.8
1962	Chi-A★	20	9	**.690**	35	35	12	2	0	236²	228	13	74	115	11.5	3.27	119	.255	.312	16	.195	5	18	17	3	2.8
1963	Chi-A	13	10	.565	33	33	14	**7**	0	224²	230	16	35	105	10.7	3.24	108	.265	.295	14	.222	6	10	7	2	1.5
1964	Chi-A	6	7	.462	20	19	1	0	0	111²	117	14	17	40	11.0	3.47	100	.275	.306	5	.139	-1	2	-0	-1	-0.2
1965	Phi-N	5	8	.385	25	19	4	1	1	130²	162	13	19	51	12.5	3.86	90	.309	.334	11	.268	3	-5	-6	-0	-0.2
1966	Phi-N	2	5	.286	23	2	0	0	0	50¹	55	7	14	13	12.5	4.29	84	.293	.345	1	.077	-1	-4	-4	-0	-0.6
Total	14	104	107	.493	407	236	68	13	15	1881¹	2000	167	571	864	12.4	4.01	96	.276	.331	109	.192	20	-38	-35	18	1.6

● **FELIX HEREDIA**   Heredia, Felix (Perez)   b: 6/18/76, Barahona, D.R.   BL/TL, 6', 160 lbs.   Deb: 8/9/96

YEAR	TM/L	W	L	PCT	G	GS	CG	SH	SV	IP	H	HR	BB	SO	RAT	ERA	ERA+	OAV	OOB	BH	AVG	PB	PR	/A	PD	TPI
1996	Fla-N	1	1	.500	21	0	0	0	0	16²	21	1	10	10	16.7	4.32	94	.313	.403	0	—	0	-0	-1	-1	-0.1

● **GIL HEREDIA**   Heredia, Gilbert   b: 10/26/65, Nogales, Ariz.   BR/TR, 6'1", 190 lbs.   Deb: 9/1/91

YEAR	TM/L	W	L	PCT	G	GS	CG	SH	SV	IP	H	HR	BB	SO	RAT	ERA	ERA+	OAV	OOB	BH	AVG	PB	PR	/A	PD	TPI
1991	SF-N	0	2	.000	7	4	0	0	0	33	27	4	7	13	9.3	3.82	94	.233	.276	3	.429	1	-0	-1	-1	0.0
1992	SF-N	2	3	.400	13	4	0	0	0	30	32	3	16	15	14.7	5.40	61	.278	.371	1	.167	0	-6	-7	-1	-1.2
	Mon-N	0	0	—	7	1	0	0	0	14²	12	1	4	7	9.8	1.84	188	.250	.308	0	.000	-0	3	3	0	0.0

YEAR	TM/L	W	L	PCT	G	GS	CG	SH	SV	IP	H	HR	BB	SO	RAT	ERA	ERA+	OAV	OOB	BH	AVG	PB	PR	/A	PD	TPI
	Yr	2	3	.400	20	5	0	0	0	44²	44	4	20	22	12.9	4.23	79	.268	.348	1	.111	-0	-4	-4	-1	-1.2
1993	Mon-N	4	2	.667	20	9	1	0	2	57¹	66	4	14	40	12.9	3.92	106	.293	.340	2	.154	-0	1	2	1	0.2
1994	Mon-N	6	3	.667	39	3	0	0	0	75¹	85	7	13	62	11.9	3.46	122	.281	.314	5	.313	1	6	6	0	0.8
1995	Mon-N	5	6	.455	40	18	0	0	1	119	137	7	21	74	12.3	4.31	100	.291	.329	6	.182	-0	-2	-0	1	0.0
1996	Tex-A	2	5	.286	44	0	0	0	0	73¹	91	12	14	43	13.0	5.89	90	.301	.334	0	—	0	-7	-5	-0	-0.5
Total	6	19	21	.475	170	39	1	0	4	402²	450	38	89	254	12.3	4.34	99	.285	.328	17	.218	2	-6	-3	0	-0.7

● UBALDO HEREDIA
Heredia, Ubaldo Jose (Martinez) b: 5/4/56, Ciudad Bolivar, Ven. BR/TR, 6'2", 180 lbs. Deb: 5/12/87

YEAR	TM/L	W	L	PCT	G	GS	CG	SH	SV	IP	H	HR	BB	SO	RAT	ERA	ERA+	OAV	OOB	BH	AVG	PB	PR	/A	PD	TPI
1987	Mon-N	0	1	.000	2	2	0	0	0	10	10	2	3	6	12.6	5.40	78	.263	.333	0	.000	-0	-1	-1	0	-0.1

● WILSON HEREDIA
Heredia, Wilson b: 3/30/72, LaRomana, D.R. BR/TR, 6', 175 lbs. Deb: 4/27/95

YEAR	TM/L	W	L	PCT	G	GS	CG	SH	SV	IP	H	HR	BB	SO	RAT	ERA	ERA+	OAV	OOB	BH	AVG	PB	PR	/A	PD	TPI
1995	Tex-A	0	1	.000	6	0	0	0	0	12	9	2	15	6	18.0	3.75	129	.225	.436	0	—	0	1	1	-0	-0.1

● ART HERMAN
Herman, Arthur b: 5/11/1871, Louisville, Ky. d: 9/20/55, Los Angeles, Cal. Deb: 6/29/1896

YEAR	TM/L	W	L	PCT	G	GS	CG	SH	SV	IP	H	HR	BB	SO	RAT	ERA	ERA+	OAV	OOB	BH	AVG	PB	PR	/A	PD	TPI
1896	Lou-N	4	6	.400	14	12	9	0	0	94¹	122	4	36	13	15.3	5.63	77	.310	.371	5	.139	-4	-13	-14	-1	-1.5
1897	Lou-N	0	1	.000	3	2	1	0	0	18	23	1	5	4	14.0	4.00	107	.307	.350	2	.333	1	1	1	0	0.2
Total	2	4	7	.364	17	14	10	0	0	112¹	145	5	41	17	15.1	5.37	80	.310	.368	7	.167	-2	-13	-13	-1	-1.3

● DUSTIN HERMANSON
Hermanson, Dustin Michael b: 12/21/72, Springfield, Ohio BR/TR, 6'3", 195 lbs. Deb: 5/8/95

YEAR	TM/L	W	L	PCT	G	GS	CG	SH	SV	IP	H	HR	BB	SO	RAT	ERA	ERA+	OAV	OOB	BH	AVG	PB	PR	/A	PD	TPI
1995	SD-N	3	1	.750	26	0	0	0	0	31²	35	8	22	19	16.5	6.82	59	.280	.392	0	—	0	-9	-10	-0	-1.1
1996	SD-N	1	0	1.000	8	0	0	0	0	13²	18	3	4	11	14.5	8.56	47	.340	.386	0	—	0	-7	-7	0	-0.4
Total	2	4	1	.800	34	0	0	0	0	45¹	53	11	26	30	15.9	7.35	55	.298	.390	0	—	0	-16	-17	0	-1.5

● JESUS HERNAIZ
Hernaiz, Jesus Rafael (Rodriguez) b: 1/8/45, Santurce, P.R. BR/TR, 6'2", 175 lbs. Deb: 6/14/74

YEAR	TM/L	W	L	PCT	G	GS	CG	SH	SV	IP	H	HR	BB	SO	RAT	ERA	ERA+	OAV	OOB	BH	AVG	PB	PR	/A	PD	TPI
1974	Phi-N	2	3	.400	27	0	0	0	1	41¹	53	6	25	16	17.0	5.88	64	.323	.413	0	.000	-0	-10	-10	-0	-1.2

● LIVAN HERNANDEZ
Hernandez, Eisler Livan b: 2/20/75, Villa Clara, Cuba BR/TR, 6'2", 220 lbs. Deb: 9/24/96

YEAR	TM/L	W	L	PCT	G	GS	CG	SH	SV	IP	H	HR	BB	SO	RAT	ERA	ERA+	OAV	OOB	BH	AVG	PB	PR	/A	PD	TPI
1996	Fla-N	0	0	—	1	0	0	0	0	3	3	0	2	2	15.0	0.00	—	.273	.385	1	1.000	0	1	1	-0	0.0

● XAVIER HERNANDEZ
Hernandez, Francis Xavier b: 8/16/65, Port Arthur, Tex. BL/TR, 6'2", 185 lbs. Deb: 6/4/89

YEAR	TM/L	W	L	PCT	G	GS	CG	SH	SV	IP	H	HR	BB	SO	RAT	ERA	ERA+	OAV	OOB	BH	AVG	PB	PR	/A	PD	TPI
1989	Tor-A	1	0	1.000	7	0	0	0	0	22²	25	2	8	7	13.5	4.76	79	.278	.343	0	—	0	-2	-3	-1	-0.1
1990	Hou-N	2	1	.667	34	1	0	0	0	62¹	60	8	24	24	12.7	4.62	80	.256	.336	1	.333	0	-6	-6	-1	-0.4
1991	Hou-N	2	7	.222	32	6	0	0	3	63	66	6	32	55	14.0	4.71	74	.263	.346	0	.000	0	-7	-8	0	-1.2
1992	Hou-N	9	1	.900	77	0	0	0	7	111	81	5	42	96	10.2	2.11	159	.200	.281	0	.000	-1	17	15	-2	1.3
1993	Hou-N	4	5	.444	72	0	0	0	9	96²	75	6	28	101	9.7	2.61	149	.212	.272	0	.000	-1	15	14	-1	1.2
1994	NY-A	4	4	.500	31	0	0	0	6	40	48	7	21	37	16.0	5.85	78	.300	.388	0	—	0	-5	-6	1	-1.0
1995	*Cin-N	7	2	.778	59	0	0	0	3	90	95	8	31	84	13.0	4.60	89	.273	.339	0	.000	-0	-4	-5	-0	-0.6
1996	Cin-N	0	0	—	3	0	0	0	0	3²	8	2	2	3	27.0	13.50	31	.471	.526	0	—	0	-3	-3	-0	-0.0
	Hou-N	5	5	.500	58	0	0	0	6	74²	69	11	26	78	11.7	4.22	91	.245	.313	0	.000	-0	-0	-3	-0	-0.5
	Yr	5	5	.500	61	0	0	0	6	78	77	13	28	81	12.3	4.62	83	.258	.325	0	.000	-0	-3	-7	-0	-0.5
Total	8	34	25	.576	373	7	0	0	34	563²	527	55	214	485	12.1	3.88	98	.246	.320	1	.027	-3	5	-5	-3	-1.3

● EVELIO HERNANDEZ
Hernandez, Gregorio Evelio (Lopez) b: 12/24/30, Guanabacoa, Havana, Cuba BR/TR, 6'1", 195 lbs. Deb: 9/12/56

YEAR	TM/L	W	L	PCT	G	GS	CG	SH	SV	IP	H	HR	BB	SO	RAT	ERA	ERA+	OAV	OOB	BH	AVG	PB	PR	/A	PD	TPI
1956	Was-A	1	1	.500	4	4	1	0	0	22²	24	2	8	9	12.7	4.76	91	.276	.337	2	.182	-0	-1	-2	-1	-0.1
1957	Was-A	0	0	—	14	2	0	0	0	36	38	2	20	15	14.5	4.25	92	.268	.358	0	.000	-1	-2	-1	-1	-0.1
Total	2	1	1	.500	18	6	1	0	0	58²	62	4	28	24	13.8	4.45	91	.271	.350	2	.118	-1	-3	-3	-1	-0.2

● WILLIE HERNANDEZ
Hernandez, Guillermo (Villanueva) b: 11/14/54, Aguada, P.R. BL/TL, 6'3", 180 lbs. Deb: 4/9/77

YEAR	TM/L	W	L	PCT	G	GS	CG	SH	SV	IP	H	HR	BB	SO	RAT	ERA	ERA+	OAV	OOB	BH	AVG	PB	PR	/A	PD	TPI
1977	Chi-N	8	7	.533	67	1	0	0	4	110	94	11	28	78	10.1	3.03	145	.234	.285	1	.063	-1	11	17	3	2.3
1978	Chi-N	8	2	.800	54	0	0	0	3	59²	57	6	35	38	14.0	3.77	107	.263	.368	0	.000	-0	-1	2	1	0.3
1979	Chi-N	4	4	.500	51	2	0	0	0	79	85	8	39	53	14.6	5.01	82	.281	.370	2	.250	0	-11	-8	-0	-0.7
1980	Chi-N	1	9	.100	53	7	0	0	0	108¹	115	8	45	75	13.5	4.40	89	.276	.349	4	.211	0	-10	-6	2	-0.3
1981	Chi-N	0	0	—	12	0	0	0	0	13²	14	0	8	13	14.5	3.95	94	.280	.379	0	—	-0	-1	-0	0	0.0
1982	Chi-N	4	6	.400	75	0	0	0	10	75	74	3	24	54	11.9	3.00	124	.268	.329	0	.000	-0	5	6	2	1.2
1983	Chi-N	1	0	1.000	11	1	0	0	1	19²	16	0	6	18	10.1	3.20	118	.222	.282	1	.500	0	1	1	0	0.1
	*Phi-N	8	4	.667	63	0	0	0	7	95²	93	9	26	75	11.3	3.29	108	.254	.305	5	.385	2	4	3	-0	0.5
	Yr	9	4	.692	74	1	0	0	8	115¹	109	9	32	93	11.1	3.28	110	.249	.301	6	.400	2	4	4	0	0.6
1984	*Det-A★	9	3	.750	**80**	0	0	0	32	140¹	96	6	36	112	8.7	1.92	204	.194	.254	0	—	0	**32**	**31**	-1	3.9
1985	Det-A★	8	10	.444	74	0	0	0	31	106²	82	13	14	76	8.2	2.70	151	.210	.239	0	.000	-0	17	16	-2	3.3
1986	Det-A☆	8	7	.533	64	0	0	0	24	88²	87	13	21	77	11.5	3.55	116	.251	.304	0	—	0	6	6	1	1.2
1987	*Det-A	3	4	.429	45	0	0	0	8	49	53	8	20	30	13.4	3.67	115	.276	.344	0	—	0	4	3	-1	0.4
1988	Det-A	6	5	.545	63	0	0	0	10	67²	50	8	31	59	11.3	3.06	125	.208	.309	0	—	0	7	6	1	1.2
1989	Det-A	2	2	.500	32	0	0	0	15	31¹	36	4	16	30	15.2	5.74	66	.293	.379	0	—	0	-6	-7	-0	-1.3
Total	13	70	63	.526	744	11	0	0	147	1044²	952	97	349	788	11.4	3.38	118	.245	.311	13	.206	1	57	70	6	12.1

● JEREMY HERNANDEZ
Hernandez, Jeremy Stuart b: 7/6/66, Burbank, Cal. BR/TR, 6'5", 195 lbs. Deb: 9/2/91

YEAR	TM/L	W	L	PCT	G	GS	CG	SH	SV	IP	H	HR	BB	SO	RAT	ERA	ERA+	OAV	OOB	BH	AVG	PB	PR	/A	PD	TPI
1991	SD-N	0	0	—	9	0	0	0	2	14¹	8	0	5	9	8.2	0.00	—	.157	.232	0	.000	-0	6	6	0	0.2
1992	SD-N	1	4	.200	26	0	0	0	1	36²	39	4	11	25	12.5	4.17	86	.291	.349	0	.000	-0	-3	-2	0	-0.3
1993	SD-N	0	2	.000	21	0	0	0	0	34¹	41	2	7	26	12.6	4.72	88	.301	.336	0	.000	-0	-3	-2	0	-0.1
	Cle-A	6	5	.545	49	0	0	0	8	77¹	75	12	27	44	11.9	3.14	138	.261	.325	0	—	0	10	10	-0	1.5
1994	Fla-N	3	3	.500	21	0	0	0	9	23¹	16	0	14	13	12.3	2.70	162	.205	.340	0	.000	-0	4	4	-0	1.3
1995	Fla-N	0	0	—	7	0	0	0	0	7	12	2	3	5	20.6	11.57	36	.400	.471	0	.000	-0	-6	-6	-0	0.0
Total	5	10	14	.417	133	0	0	0	20	193	191	20	67	122	12.2	3.64	113	.267	.333	0	.000	-1	9	10	-0	2.6

● MANNY HERNANDEZ
Hernandez, Manuel Antonio (Montas) b: 5/7/61, LaRomana, D.R. BR/TR, 6', 150 lbs. Deb: 6/5/86

YEAR	TM/L	W	L	PCT	G	GS	CG	SH	SV	IP	H	HR	BB	SO	RAT	ERA	ERA+	OAV	OOB	BH	AVG	PB	PR	/A	PD	TPI
1986	Hou-N	2	3	.400	9	4	0	0	0	27²	33	2	12	14	14.6	3.90	92	.306	.375	0	.000	-1	-1	-1	-0	-0.2
1987	Hou-N	0	4	.000	6	3	0	0	0	21²	25	1	5	12	12.9	5.40	73	.301	.348	0	.000	-1	-3	-4	-0	-0.6
1989	NY-N	0	0	—	1	0	0	0	0	1	0	0	0	1	0.0	0.00	—	.000	.000	0	0	0	0	0	0	0.0
Total	3	2	7	.222	16	7	0	0	0	50¹	58	3	17	22	13.6	4.47	83	.299	.358	0	.000	-1	-3	-4	-0	-0.8

● RAMON HERNANDEZ
Hernandez, Ramon (Gonzalez) b: 8/31/40, Carolina, P.R. BB/TL, 5'9", 170 lbs. Deb: 4/11/67

YEAR	TM/L	W	L	PCT	G	GS	CG	SH	SV	IP	H	HR	BB	SO	RAT	ERA	ERA+	OAV	OOB	BH	AVG	PB	PR	/A	PD	TPI
1967	Atl-N	0	2	.000	46	0	0	0	5	51²	60	5	14	28	13.2	4.18	79	.296	.347	0	.000	-0	-5	-5	1	-0.3
1968	Chi-N	0	0	—	8	0	0	0	0	9	14	1	0	3	15.0	9.00	35	.350	.366	0	—	0	-6	-6	0	0.0
1971	Pit-N	0	1	.000	10	0	0	0	4	12¹	5	0	2	7	5.1	0.73	463	.122	.163	1	.500	0	4	4	0	0.6
1972	*Pit-N	5	0	1.000	53	0	0	0	14	70	50	3	22	47	9.6	1.67	199	.194	.265	2	.167	0	14	13	1	1.6
1973	Pit-N	4	5	.444	59	0	0	0	11	89²	71	5	25	64	10.0	2.41	146	.218	.282	1	.125	0	12	11	1	1.4
1974	*Pit-N	5	2	.714	58	0	0	0	2	68²	68	3	18	33	11.5	2.75	125	.258	.310	1	.250	1	7	5	-0	0.6
1975	*Pit-N	7	2	.778	46	0	0	0	5	64	62	6	28	43	12.7	2.95	120	.252	.328	1	.000	0	5	4	1	0.7
1976	Pit-N	2	2	.500	37	0	0	0	6	43	42	3	16	17	12.3	3.56	98	.262	.333	0	—	0	-0	-0	-1	-0.1
	Chi-N	0	0	—	2	0	0	0	0	1²	2	0	0	1	10.8	0.00	—	.333	.333	0	—	0	1	1	0	0.0
	Yr	2	2	.500	39	0	0	0	6	44²	44	3	16	18	12.1	3.43	102	.257	.321	0	—	0	1	1	-0	-0.1
1977	Chi-N	0	0	—	12	0	0	0	0	7²	11	1	3	4	16.4	8.22	53	.324	.408	0	—	0	-4	-3	-0	-0.1
	Bos-A	0	1	.000	12	0	0	0	0	12²	14	2	7	8	15.6	5.68	79	.280	.379	0	—	0	-2	-2	-0	-0.2
Total	9	23	15	.605	337	0	0	0	46	430¹	399	23	135	255	11.5	3.03	115	.245	.308	5	.125	1	25	22	1	4.2

● ROBERTO HERNANDEZ
Hernandez, Roberto Manuel (Rodriguez) b: 11/11/64, Santurce, P.R. BR/TR, 6'4", 220 lbs. Deb: 9/2/91

YEAR	TM/L	W	L	PCT	G	GS	CG	SH	SV	IP	H	HR	BB	SO	RAT	ERA	ERA+	OAV	OOB	BH	AVG	PB	PR	/A	PD	TPI
1991	Chi-A	1	0	1.000	9	3	0	0	0	15	18	1	7	6	15.0	7.80	51	.290	.362	0	—	0	-6	-6	-0	-0.4
1992	Chi-A	7	3	.700	43	0	0	0	12	71	45	4	20	68	8.7	1.65	234	.180	.252	0	—	0	18	17	-0	2.8
1993	*Chi-A	3	4	.429	70	0	0	0	38	78²	66	6	20	71	9.8	2.29	183	.228	.277	0	—	0	18	17	0	2.7
1994	Chi-A	4	4	.500	45	0	0	0	14	47²	44	5	19	50	12.1	4.91	95	.238	.312	0	—	-1	-1	-1	-1	-0.3
1995	Chi-A	3	7	.300	60	0	0	0	32	59²	63	8	28	84	14.2	3.92	114	.266	.351	0	—	0	5	4	0	1.1

YEAR TM/L	W	L	PCT	G	GS	CG	SH	SV	IP	H	HR	BB	SO	RAT	ERA	ERA+	OAV	OOB	BH	AVG	PB	PR	/A	PD	TPI
1996 Chi-A★	6	5	.545	72	0	0	0	38	84²	65	2	38	85	10.9	1.91	246	.208	.293	0	—	0	29	26	-1	4.9
Total 6	24	23	.511	299	3	0	0	134	356²	301	27	132	364	11.1	2.93	148	.225	.299	0	—	0	63	56	-3	10.8

● **RUDY HERNANDEZ** Hernandez, Rudolph Albert (Fuentes) b: 12/10/31, Santiago, D.R. BR/TR, 6'3", 185 lbs. Deb: 7/3/60

YEAR TM/L	W	L	PCT	G	GS	CG	SH	SV	IP	H	HR	BB	SO	RAT	ERA	ERA+	OAV	OOB	BH	AVG	PB	PR	/A	PD	TPI
1960 Was-A	4	1	.800	21	0	0	0	0	34²	34	2	21	22	14.5	4.41	88	.262	.368	1	.167	-0	-2	-2	-0	-0.3
1961 Was-A	0	1	.000	7	0	0	0	0	9	8	0	3	4	11.0	3.00	134	.250	.314	0	—	-0	1	1	0	0.1
Total 2	4	2	.667	28	0	0	0	0	43²	42	2	24	26	13.8	4.12	95	.259	.358	1	.167	-0	-1	-1	-0	-0.2

● **WALT HERRELL** Herrell, Walter William "Reds" b: 2/19/1889, Rockville, Md. d: 1/23/49, Front Royal, Va. Deb: 6/10/11

YEAR TM/L	W	L	PCT	G	GS	CG	SH	SV	IP	H	HR	BB	SO	RAT	ERA	ERA+	OAV	OOB	BH	AVG	PB	PR	/A	PD	TPI
1911 Was-A	0	0	—	1	0	0	0	0	2	5	0	2	0	31.5	18.00	18	.556	.636	0	.000	-0	-3	-3	0	0.0

● **BOBBY HERRERA** Herrera, Procopio Rodriguez "Tito" (b: Procopio Rodriguez (Herrera)) b: 7/26/26, Nuevo Laredo, Mex BR/TR, 6', 184 lbs. Deb: 4/19/51

YEAR TM/L	W	L	PCT	G	GS	CG	SH	SV	IP	H	HR	BB	SO	RAT	ERA	ERA+	OAV	OOB	BH	AVG	PB	PR	/A	PD	TPI
1951 StL-A	0	0	—	3	0	0	0	0	2¹	6	2	4	2	42.4	27.00	16	.462	.611	0	—	-0	-6	-6	-0	-0.8

● **TROY HERRIAGE** Herriage, William Troy "Dutch" b: 12/20/30, Tipton, Okla. BR/TR, 6'1", 170 lbs. Deb: 4/25/56

YEAR TM/L	W	L	PCT	G	GS	CG	SH	SV	IP	H	HR	BB	SO	RAT	ERA	ERA+	OAV	OOB	BH	AVG	PB	PR	/A	PD	TPI
1956 KC-A	1	13	.071	31	16	1	0	0	103	135	16	64	59	17.9	6.64	65	.321	.418	3	.120	-1	-28	-26	-2	-3.3

● **TOM HERRIN** Herrin, Thomas Edward b: 9/12/29, Shreveport, La. BR/TR, 6'3", 190 lbs. Deb: 4/13/54

YEAR TM/L	W	L	PCT	G	GS	CG	SH	SV	IP	H	HR	BB	SO	RAT	ERA	ERA+	OAV	OOB	BH	AVG	PB	PR	/A	PD	TPI
1954 Bos-A	1	2	.333	14	1	0	0	0	28¹	34	3	22	8	17.8	7.31	56	.315	.431	1	.125	-0	-11	-10	1	-0.9

● **ART HERRING** Herring, Arthur L "Red" or "Sandy" b: 3/10/07, Altus, Okla. BR/TR, 5'7", 168 lbs. Deb: 9/12/29

YEAR TM/L	W	L	PCT	G	GS	CG	SH	SV	IP	H	HR	BB	SO	RAT	ERA	ERA+	OAV	OOB	BH	AVG	PB	PR	/A	PD	TPI
1929 Det-A	2	1	.667	4	4	2	0	0	32	38	0	19	15	16.3	4.78	90	.302	.397	3	.214	1	-2	-2	0	0.0
1930 Det-A	3	3	.500	23	6	1	0	0	77²	97	2	36	16	15.8	5.33	90	.315	.392	3	.130	-2	-6	-5	-0	-0.5
1931 Det-A	7	13	.350	35	16	9	0	1	165	186	8	67	64	14.2	4.31	106	.281	.355	11	.200	-1	1	5	2	0.6
1932 Det-A	1	2	.333	12	0	0	0	2	22¹	25	2	15	12	16.5	5.24	90	.284	.394	0	.000	-0	-2	-1	0	-0.2
1933 Det-A	1	2	.333	24	3	1	0	0	61	61	6	20	20	12.1	3.84	112	.264	.325	1	.077	-1	3	3	-1	0.0
1934 Bro-N	2	4	.333	14	4	2	0	0	49¹	63	3	29	15	16.8	6.20	63	.307	.393	2	.143	-1	-12	-13	-0	-1.3
1939 Chi-N	0	0	—	7	0	0	0	0	14¹	13	2	5	8	11.9	5.65	84	.250	.328	0	.000	-0	-2	-1	0	0.0
1944 Bro-N	3	4	.429	12	6	3	1	0	55¹	59	3	17	19	11.5	3.42	104	.277	.333	3	.200	0	1	1	0	0.2
1945 Bro-N	7	4	.636	22	15	7	2	2	124	103	11	43	34	10.8	3.48	108	.222	.292	4	.095	-2	4	4	1	0.2
1946 Bro-N	7	2	.778	35	2	0	0	5	86	91	2	29	34	12.7	3.35	101	.277	.338	4	.182	0	1	0	2	0.2
1947 Pit-N	1	3	.250	11	0	0	0	2	10²	18	3	4	6	18.6	8.44	50	.360	.407	-0	—	-0	-5	-5	-0	-1.8
Total 11	34	38	.472	199	56	25	3	13	697²	754	41	284	243	13.6	4.32	96	.276	.349	31	.149	-4	-18	-14	4	-2.6

● **HERB HERRING** Herring, Herbert Lee b: 7/22/1891, Danville, Ark. d: 4/22/64, Tucson, Ariz. BR/TR, 5'11", 178 lbs. Deb: 9/4/12

YEAR TM/L	W	L	PCT	G	GS	CG	SH	SV	IP	H	HR	BB	SO	RAT	ERA	ERA+	OAV	OOB	BH	AVG	PB	PR	/A	PD	TPI
1912 Was-A	0	0	—	1	0	0	0	0	1	1	0	1	0	18.0	0.00	—	.250	.400	0	—	0	0	0	-0	0.0

● **LEFTY HERRING** Herring, Silas Clarke b: 3/4/1880, Philadelphia, Pa. d: 2/11/65, Massapequa, N.Y. BL/TL, 5'11", 160 lbs. Deb: 5/16/1899 ◆

YEAR TM/L	W	L	PCT	G	GS	CG	SH	SV	IP	H	HR	BB	SO	RAT	ERA	ERA+	OAV	OOB	BH	AVG	PB	PR	/A	PD	TPI
1899 Was-N	0	0	—	2	0	0	0	0	2	0	0	2	0	9.0	0.00	—	.000	.250	1	1.000	1	1	1	0	0.1

● **BILL HERRING** Herring, William Francis "Smoke" b: 10/31/1893, New York, N.Y. d: 9/10/62, Honesdale, Pa. BR/TR, 6'3", 185 lbs. Deb: 6/26/15

YEAR TM/L	W	L	PCT	G	GS	CG	SH	SV	IP	H	HR	BB	SO	RAT	ERA	ERA+	OAV	OOB	BH	AVG	PB	PR	/A	PD	TPI
1915 Bro-F	0	0	—	3	0	0	0	0	3	5	1	2	3	24.0	15.00	18	.385	.500	1	—	0	-4	-4	-0	0.0

● **LEROY HERRMANN** Herrmann, Leroy George b: 2/27/06, Steward, Ill. d: 7/3/72, Livermore, Cal. BR/TR, 5'10", 185 lbs. Deb: 7/30/32

YEAR TM/L	W	L	PCT	G	GS	CG	SH	SV	IP	H	HR	BB	SO	RAT	ERA	ERA+	OAV	OOB	BH	AVG	PB	PR	/A	PD	TPI
1932 Chi-N	2	1	.667	7	0	0	0	0	12²	18	0	9	5	19.2	6.39	59	.346	.443	1	.500	1	-4	-4	-0	-0.7
1933 Chi-N	0	1	.000	9	1	0	0	1	21	26	3	8	4	16.3	5.57	59	.299	.384	1	.167	-0	-5	-5	-1	-0.4
1935 Cin-N	3	5	.375	29	8	2	0	1	108	124	9	31	30	13.6	3.58	111	.297	.357	8	.267	1	5	5	-0	0.4
Total 3	5	7	.417	45	9	2	0	1	141²	168	12	48	39	14.5	4.13	93	.302	.370	10	.263	1	-4	-4	-1	-0.7

● **MARTY HERRMANN** Herrmann, Martin John "Lefty" b: 1/10/1893, Oldenburg, Ind. d: 9/11/56, Cincinnati, Ohio BL/TL, 5'10", 150 lbs. Deb: 7/10/18 F

YEAR TM/L	W	L	PCT	G	GS	CG	SH	SV	IP	H	HR	BB	SO	RAT	ERA	ERA+	OAV	OOB	BH	AVG	PB	PR	/A	PD	TPI
1918 Bro-N	0	0	—	1	0	0	0	0	1	0	0	1	0	9.0	0.00	—	.000	.250	0	—	-0	0	0	-0	0.0

● **FRANK HERSHEY** Hershey, Frank b: 12/13/1877, Gorham, N.Y. d: 12/15/49, Canandaigua, N.Y. TR, 175 lbs. Deb: 4/20/05

YEAR TM/L	W	L	PCT	G	GS	CG	SH	SV	IP	H	HR	BB	SO	RAT	ERA	ERA+	OAV	OOB	BH	AVG	PB	PR	/A	PD	TPI
1905 Bos-N	0	1	.000	1	1	0	0	0	4	5	0	2	1	15.8	6.75	46	.313	.389	0	.000	-0	-2	-2	-0	-0.3

● **OREL HERSHISER** Hershiser, Orel Leonard Quinton b: 9/16/58, Buffalo, N.Y. BR/TR, 6'3", 192 lbs. Deb: 9/1/83

YEAR TM/L	W	L	PCT	G	GS	CG	SH	SV	IP	H	HR	BB	SO	RAT	ERA	ERA+	OAV	OOB	BH	AVG	PB	PR	/A	PD	TPI
1983 LA-N	0	0	—	8	0	0	0	1	8	7	1	6	5	14.6	3.38	106	.233	.361	0	—	0	0	0	0	0.0
1984 LA-N	11	8	.579	45	20	8	4	2	189²	160	9	50	150	10.2	2.66	133	.225	.279	10	.200	2	20	18	1	2.1
1985 *LA-N	19	3	**.864**	36	34	9	5	0	239²	179	8	68	157	9.5	2.03	171	.206	.268	15	.197	3	42	39	2	4.2
1986 LA-N	14	14	.500	35	35	8	1	0	231¹	213	13	86	153	11.8	3.85	90	.243	.314	17	.239	4	-3	-10	1	-0.6
1987 LA-N★	16	16	.500	37	35	10	1	1	264²	247	17	74	190	11.2	3.06	130	.247	.305	19	.211	4	30	27	1	**3.6**
1988 *LA-N★	**23**	8	.742	35	34	**15**	**8**	1	267	208	18	73	178	9.6	2.26	147	.213	.271	11	.129	-0	**35**	**32**	6	4.5
1989 LA-N☆	15	15	.500	35	33	8	4	0	256²	226	9	77	178	10.7	2.31	148	.240	.299	14	.182	3	**34**	**31**	4	**4.6**
1990 LA-N	1	1	.500	4	4	0	0	0	25¹	26	1	4	16	11.0	4.26	86	.260	.295	-1	.000	-1	-1	-2	0	-0.2
1991 LA-N	7	2	.778	21	21	0	0	0	112	112	3	32	73	12.0	3.46	104	.259	.317	8	.258	3	3	1	1	0.6
1992 LA-N	10	15	.400	33	33	1	0	0	210²	209	15	69	130	12.2	3.67	94	.257	.322	5	.221	4	-4	-5	3	0.2
1993 LA-N	12	14	.462	33	33	5	1	0	215²	201	17	72	141	11.7	3.59	106	.246	.312	26	.356	10	11	5	3	1.9
1994 LA-N	6	6	.500	21	21	1	0	0	135¹	146	15	42	72	12.6	3.79	103	.279	.335	9	.205	2	6	4	1	0.6
1995 *Cle-A	16	6	.727	26	26	1	1	0	167¹	151	21	51	111	11.1	3.87	121	.244	.306	0	—	0	16	15	2	2.0
1996 *Cle-A	15	9	.625	33	33	1	0	0	206	238	21	58	125	13.5	4.24	115	.287	.343	0	—	0	17	15	4	1.9
Total 14	165	117	.585	402	362	67	25	5	2529¹	2323	168	762	1679	11.2	3.16	119	.243	.304	144	.214	34	205	169	30	25.4

● **JOE HESKETH** Hesketh, Joseph Thomas b: 2/15/59, Lackawanna, N.Y. BR/TL, 6'2", 170 lbs. Deb: 8/7/84

YEAR TM/L	W	L	PCT	G	GS	CG	SH	SV	IP	H	HR	BB	SO	RAT	ERA	ERA+	OAV	OOB	BH	AVG	PB	PR	/A	PD	TPI
1984 Mon-N	2	2	.500	11	5	1	1	1	45	38	2	15	32	10.6	1.80	190	.233	.298	1	.100	0	9	8	-0	0.8
1985 Mon-N	10	5	.667	25	25	2	1	0	155¹	125	10	45	113	9.8	2.49	136	.222	.280	4	.091	-1	19	16	-1	1.3
1986 Mon-N	6	5	.545	15	15	0	0	0	82²	92	11	31	67	13.6	5.01	74	.283	.349	0	.000	-2	-12	-12	-1	-1.7
1987 Mon-N	0	0	—	18	0	0	0	1	28²	23	2	15	31	12.6	3.14	134	.211	.317	0	.000	-0	3	3	-1	-0.1
1988 Mon-N	4	3	.571	60	0	0	0	9	72²	63	1	35	64	12.1	2.85	126	.242	.332	0	.000	0	5	6	1	0.9
1989 Mon-N	6	4	.600	43	0	0	0	0	48¹	54	5	26	44	14.9	5.77	61	.292	.379	1	.500	-0	-12	-12	0	-2.3
1990 Mon-N	1	0	1.000	2	0	0	0	0	3	2	0	2	2	12.0	0.00	—	.200	.333	0	—	-0	1	1	0	0.4
Atl-N	0	2	.000	31	0	0	0	5	31	30	5	12	21	12.5	5.81	69	.248	.321	0	.000	-0	-7	-6	0	-0.6
Yr	1	2	.333	33	0	0	0	5	34	32	5	14	24	12.4	5.29	76	.244	.322	0	.000	-0	-6	-5	0	-0.2
Bos-A	0	4	.000	12	2	0	0	0	25²	37	2	11	26	16.8	3.51	116	.333	.393	—	—	0	1	2	-0	0.1
1991 Bos-A	12	4	.750	39	17	0	0	0	153¹	142	19	53	104	11.4	3.29	131	.250	.314	0	—	0	14	17	0	1.6
1992 Bos-A	8	9	.471	30	25	1	0	0	148²	162	15	58	104	13.4	4.36	97	.276	.343	0	—	0	-7	-2	-0	-0.2
1993 Bos-A	3	4	.429	28	5	0	0	1	53¹	52	4	29	34	15.4	5.06	91	.291	.379	0	—	-0	-4	-3	-0	-0.5
1994 Bos-A	8	5	.615	25	20	0	0	0	114	117	9	46	83	13.0	4.26	118	.267	.340	0	—	0	7	10	-2	0.8
Total 11	60	47	.561	339	114	4	2	21	961²	947	85	378	726	12.5	3.78	107	.259	.330	6	.070	-2	16	26	-2	0.5

● **OTTO HESS** Hess, Otto C. b: 10/10/1878, Bern, Switzerland d: 2/25/26, Tucson, Ariz. BL/TL, 6'1", 170 lbs. Deb: 8/3/02 ◆

YEAR TM/L	W	L	PCT	G	GS	CG	SH	SV	IP	H	HR	BB	SO	RAT	ERA	ERA+	OAV	OOB	BH	AVG	PB	PR	/A	PD	TPI
1902 Cle-A	2	4	.333	7	4	4	0	0	43²	47	0	23	13	18.8	5.98	58	.351	.423	1	.071	-1	-12	-12	1	-1.3
1904 Cle-A	8	7	.533	21	16	15	4	0	151¹	134	2	31	64	10.1	1.67	152	.238	.284	12	.120	-3	16	15	-0	1.1
1905 Cle-A	10	15	.400	26	25	22	4	0	213²	179	1	72	109	11.0	3.16	83	.229	.302	44	.254	5	-12	-13	1	-0.9
1906 Cle-A	20	17	.541	43	36	33	7	**3**	333²	274	4	85	167	10.3	1.83	143	.227	.291	31	.201	1	32	**29**	-2	3.3
1907 Cle-A	6	6	.500	17	14	7	0	1	93¹	84	1	37	36	12.8	2.89	87	.243	.337	4	.133	-0	-4	-4	-1	-0.6
1908 Cle-A	0	0	—	4	0	0	0	0	7	11	0	1	2	15.4	5.14	46	.407	.429	0	.000	-1	-2	-2	0	-0.3
1912 Bos-N	12	17	.414	33	31	21	0	0	254	270	3	90	83	13.3	3.76	95	.283	.354	23	.245	-3	-10	-5	-4	-0.6
1913 Bos-N	7	17	.292	29	27	19	2	0	218¹	231	4	70	80	12.7	3.83	86	.279	.340	26	.313	4	-15	-13	1	-0.5
1914 Bos-N	5	6	.455	14	11	7	1	1	89	89	2	33	24	12.8	3.03	91	.271	.347	11	.234	1	-2	-3	2	0.0
1915 Bos-N	0	1	.000	4	1	1	0	1	14²	6	0	6	2	15.4	3.86	67	.286	.375	2	.400	1	-2	-2	-0	-0.1
Total 10	70	90	.438	198	165	129	18	5	1418	1355	25	448	580	12.0	2.98	98	.257	.324	154	.216	14	-11	-12	-2	0.4

● **GEORGE HESSELBACHER** Hesselbacher, George Edward b: 1/18/1895, Philadelphia, Pa. d: 2/18/80, Rydal, Pa. BR/TR, 6'2", 175 lbs. Deb: 6/29/16

YEAR TM/L	W	L	PCT	G	GS	CG	SH	SV	IP	H	HR	BB	SO	RAT	ERA	ERA+	OAV	OOB	BH	AVG	PB	PR	/A	PD	TPI
1916 Phi-A	0	4	.000	6	4	2	0	0	26	37	3	22	6	20.4	7.27	39	.349	.461	1	.125	-0	-13	-13	1	-1.6

YEAR	TM/L	W	L	PCT	G	GS	CG	SH	SV	IP	H	HR	BB	SO	RAT	ERA	ERA+	OAV	OOB	BH	AVG	PB	PR	/A	PD	TPI

● **LARRY HESTERFER** Hesterfer, Lawrence b: 6/9/1878, Newark, N.J. d: 9/22/43, Cedar Grove, N.J. BR/TL, 5'8", 145 lbs. Deb: 9/5/01

| 1901 | NY-N | 0 | 1 | .000 | 1 | 1 | 1 | 0 | 0 | 6 | 15 | 0 | 3 | 2 | 27.0 | 7.50 | 44 | .469 | .514 | 0 | .000 | 0 | -3 | -3 | -0 | -0.3 |

● **JOHNNY HETKI** Hetki, John Edward b: 5/12/22, Leavenworth, Kan. BR/TR, 6'1", 205 lbs. Deb: 9/14/45

1945	Cin-N	1	2	.333	5	2	2	0	0	32²	28	1	11	9	10.7	3.58	105	.235	.300	1	.091	-1	1	1	1	0.0
1946	Cin-N	6	6	.500	32	11	4	0	1	126¹	121	3	31	41	10.9	2.99	112	.253	.300	11	.333	3	6	5	-1	0.7
1947	Cin-N	3	4	.429	37	5	2	0	0	96	110	7	48	33	14.9	5.81	71	.287	.368	6	.222	1	-19	-18	0	-1.1
1948	Cin-N	0	1	.000	3	0	0	0	0	6²	8	0	3	3	14.9	9.45	41	.286	.355	0	.000	-0	-4	-4	-0	-0.5
1950	Cin-N	1	2	.333	22	0	0	0	0	53	53	9	27	21	14.1	5.09	83	.265	.361	2	.222	0	-6	-5	-0	-0.3
1952	StL-A	0	1	.000	3	1	0	0	0	9¹	15	2	2	4	16.4	3.86	101	.357	.386	0	.000	-0	-0	-0	0	0.0
1953	Pit-N	3	6	.333	54	2	0	0	3	118¹	120	7	33	38	11.7	3.95	113	.266	.318	5	.208	1	4	7	0	0.7
1954	Pit-N	4	4	.500	58	1	0	0	9	83	102	11	30	27	14.3	4.99	84	.297	.353	2	.222	-0	-8	-7	-1	-0.9
Total	8	18	26	.409	214	23	8	0	13	525¹	557	42	185	175	12.8	4.39	91	.272	.335	27	.235	5	-26	-23	-2	-1.4

● **ERIC HETZEL** Hetzel, Eric Paul b: 9/25/63, Crowley, La. BR/TR, 6'3", 175 lbs. Deb: 7/1/89

1989	Bos-A	2	3	.400	12	11	0	0	0	50¹	61	7	28	33	16.3	6.26	66	.296	.386	0	—	0	-13	-12	-1	-1.2
1990	Bos-A	1	4	.200	9	8	0	0	0	35	39	3	21	20	15.7	5.91	69	.281	.379	0	—	0	-8	-7	-0	-1.0
Total	2	3	7	.300	21	19	0	0	0	85¹	100	10	49	53	16.0	6.12	67	.290	.383	0	—	0	-21	-19	-2	-2.2

● **ED HEUSSER** Heusser, Edward Burlton "The Wild Elk Of The Wasatch" b: 5/7/09, Salt Lake County, Utah d: 3/1/56, Aurora, Cal. BB/TR, 6'0.5", 187 lbs. Deb: 4/25/35

1935	StL-N	5	5	.500	33	11	2	0	2	123¹	125	5	27	39	11.2	2.92	140	.263	.305	4	.118	-1	15	16	-1	1.0
1936	StL-N	7	3	.700	42	3	0	0	3	104¹	130	6	38	26	14.8	5.43	73	.310	.373	7	.269	3	-16	-17	-0	-1.3
1938	Phi-N	0	0	—	1	0	0	0	0	1	2	1	1	0	27.0	27.00	14	.400	.500	0	—	0	-3	-3	-0	0.0
1940	Phi-A	6	13	.316	41	6	2	0	5	110	144	11	42	39	15.4	4.99	89	.308	.368	5	.167	1	-7	-7	-1	-0.9
1943	Cin-N	4	3	.571	26	10	3	1	0	91	97	4	23	28	11.9	3.46	96	.275	.319	5	.185	-1	-1	-1	-1	-0.3
1944	Cin-N	13	11	.542	30	23	17	4	2	192²	165	9	42	42	9.7	**2.38**	**146**	.231	.275	15	.217	1	26	24	-1	2.9
1945	Cin-N	11	16	.407	31	30	18	4	1	223	248	10	60	56	12.6	3.71	101	.280	.328	19	.247	4	1	0	0	0.2
1946	Cin-N	7	14	.333	29	21	9	1	2	167²	167	11	39	47	11.1	3.22	104	.260	.304	11	.208	2	4	2	-2	0.2
1948	Phi-N	3	2	.600	33	0	0	0	0	74	89	7	28	22	14.2	4.99	79	.299	.359	3	.158	-1	-8	-9	-0	-0.6
Total	9	56	67	.455	266	104	50	10	15	1087	1167	64	300	299	12.3	3.69	101	.274	.328	69	.206	8	11	6	-5	1.6

● **JOE HEVING** Heving, Joseph William b: 9/2/1900, Covington, Ky. d: 4/11/70, Covington, Ky. BR/TR, 6'1", 185 lbs. Deb: 4/29/30 F

1930	NY-N	7	5	.583	41	6	0	0	6	89²	109	7	37	37	13.8	5.22	91	.309	.360	5	.227	-0	-2	-5	4	-0.3
1931	NY-N	1	6	.143	22	0	0	0	3	42¹	48	4	11	26	13.0	4.89	76	.277	.328	1	.125	-0	-5	-6	1	-0.9
1933	Chi-A	7	5	.583	40	6	3	1	6	118	113	6	17	47	10.8	2.67	159	.249	.295	8	.211	0	21	21	0	2.1
1934	Chi-A	1	7	.125	33	2	0	0	4	88	94	12	48	40	18.8	7.26	65	.343	.419	5	.185	-1	-27	-25	1	-1.9
1937	Cle-A	8	4	.667	40	0	0	0	5	72²	92	6	30	35	15.4	4.83	95	.311	.378	5	.263	-1	-2	-3	1	-0.1
1938	Cle-A	1	1	.500	3	0	0	0	0	6	10	0	5	0	22.5	9.00	52	.370	.469	0	—	-0	-3	-3	-0	-0.7
	Bos-A	8	1	.889	16	11	7	1	2	82	94	5	27	34	13.5	3.73	132	.283	.330	4	.133	-1	10	11	2	1.1
	Yr	9	2	.818	19	11	7	1	2	88	104	5	27	34	13.5	4.09	120	.290	.341	4	.129	-2	7	8	2	0.4
1939	Bos-A	11	3	.786	46	5	1	0	7	107	124	8	34	43	13.5	3.70	128	.295	.350	6	.188	-1	**11**	**12**	0	1.4
1940	Bos-A	12	7	.632	39	7	4	0	3	119	129	7	42	55	13.2	4.01	112	.272	.335	8	.200	0	6	9	2	0.9
1941	Cle-A	5	2	.714	27	3	1	0	5	70²	63	2	31	18	12.1	2.29	172	.240	.323	0	.000	-1	15	13	2	1.5
1942	Cle-A	5	3	.625	27	2	0	0	9	46¹	52	4	25	13	15.3	4.86	71	.278	.369	0	.000	-0	-6	-7	-1	-1.3
1943	Cle-A	1	1	.500	30	1	0	0	9	72	54	1	34	34	11.8	2.75	113	.230	.326	1	.071	-0	4	3	2	0.3
1944	Cle-A	8	3	.727	**63**	1	0	0	10	119²	106	2	41	46	11.2	1.96	169	.239	.307	4	.182	-0	**20**	18	1	2.0
1945	Bos-N	1	0	1.000	5	1	0	0	0	5¹	9	0	3	1	15.2	3.38	114	.294	.429	0	.000	0	0	1	0	0.1
Total	13	76	48	.613	430	40	17	3	63	1038²	1136	64	380	429	13.3	3.90	108	.279	.344	47	.170	-4	40	36	14	4.2

● **JAKE HEWITT** Hewitt, Charles Jacob b: 6/6/1870, Maidsville, W.Va. d: 5/18/59, Morgantown, W.Va. BL/TL, 5'7", 150 lbs. Deb: 8/6/1895

| 1895 | Pit-N | 1 | 0 | 1.000 | 4 | 2 | 1 | 0 | 2 | 13 | 13 | 0 | 2 | 4 | 11.1 | 4.15 | 109 | .255 | .296 | 1 | .167 | -1 | 1 | 1 | 0 | 0.0 |

● **GREG HEYDEMAN** Heydeman, Gregory George b: 1/2/52, Carmel, Cal. BR/TR, 6', 180 lbs. Deb: 9/2/73

| 1973 | LA-N | 0 | 0 | — | 1 | 0 | 0 | 0 | 0 | 2 | 2 | 0 | 1 | 0 | 18.0 | 4.50 | 76 | .222 | .364 | 0 | — | 0 | -0 | -0 | -0 | 0.0 |

● **JOHN HEYNER** Heyner, John b: Hyde Park, Ill. Deb: 8/19/1890

| 1890 | Pit-N | 0 | 0 | — | 1 | 0 | 0 | 0 | 0 | 4 | 7 | 2 | 5 | 1 | 27.0 | 13.50 | 24 | .368 | .500 | 0 | .000 | -0 | -4 | -5 | 0 | 0.0 |

● **GREG HIBBARD** Hibbard, James Gregory b: 9/13/64, New Orleans, La. BL/TL, 6', 180 lbs. Deb: 5/31/89

1989	Chi-A	6	7	.462	23	23	2	0	0	137¹	142	5	41	55	12.1	3.21	118	.268	.323	0	—	0	10	9	1	0.9
1990	Chi-A	14	9	.609	33	33	3	1	0	211	202	11	55	92	11.2	3.16	121	.255	.308	0	—	0	18	16	-1	1.6
1991	Chi-A	11	11	.500	32	29	5	0	0	194	196	23	57	71	11.8	4.31	92	.266	.320	0	—	0	-5	-7	-1	-0.8
1992	Chi-A	10	7	.588	31	28	0	0	1	176	187	17	57	69	12.8	4.40	88	.277	.340	0	—	0	-9	-11	-2	-0.7
1993	Chi-N	15	11	.577	31	31	1	0	0	191	209	19	47	82	12.2	3.96	101	.286	.332	6	.092	-3	2	1	-3	0.0
1994	Sea-A	1	5	.167	15	14	0	0	0	80²	115	11	31	39	16.5	6.69	73	.328	.385	0	—	0	-17	-16	-1	-0.9
Total	6	57	50	.533	165	158	11	1	1	990	1051	86	288	408	12.4	4.05	98	.275	.330	6	.092	-3	-1	-9	-1	-0.2

● **JOHN HIBBARD** Hibbard, John Denison b: 12/2/1864, Chicago, Ill. d: 11/17/37, Hollywood, Cal. TL, Deb: 7/31/1884

| 1884 | Chi-N | 1 | 1 | .500 | 2 | 2 | 2 | 1 | 0 | 17 | 18 | 1 | 9 | 4 | 14.3 | 2.65 | 118 | .300 | .391 | 1 | .143 | -0 | 1 | 1 | 0 | 0.0 |

● **BRYAN HICKERSON** Hickerson, Bryan David b: 10/13/63, Bemidji, Minn. BL/TL, 6'2", 195 lbs. Deb: 7/25/91

1991	SF-N	2	2	.500	17	6	0	0	0	50	53	3	17	43	12.6	3.60	94	.275	.333	0	.000	-0	0	-0	-1	-0.3
1992	SF-N	5	3	.625	61	6	0	0	0	87¹	74	7	21	68	9.9	3.09	107	.236	.286	0	.000	-0	4	2	-2	-0.1
1993	SF-N	7	5	.583	47	15	0	0	0	120¹	137	14	39	69	13.8	4.26	92	.291	.347	3	.143	-0	-3	-5	-2	-0.6
1994	SF-N	4	8	.333	28	14	0	0	1	98¹	118	20	38	59	14.4	5.40	74	.301	.364	5	.185	-1	-13	-15	-2	-1.7
1995	Chi-N	2	3	.400	38	0	0	0	0	31²	36	3	19	28	14.5	6.82	60	.283	.359	1	.500	1	-9	-10	-1	-1.3
	Col-N	1	0	1.000	18	0	0	0	0	16²	33	5	13	12	25.4	11.88	45	.407	.495	1	1.000	1	-14	-12	-1	-0.6
	Yr	3	3	.500	56	0	0	0	0	48¹	69	8	32	40	18.2	8.57	53	.332	.414	2	.667	1	-24	-22	-1	-1.9
Total	5	21	21	.500	209	36	0	0	2	404¹	451	52	143	279	13.3	4.72	81	.286	.347	11	.149	-1	-35	-40	-7	-4.6

● **JIM HICKEY** Hickey, James Robert "Sid" b: 10/22/20, N.Abington, Mass. BR/TR, 6'1", 204 lbs. Deb: 4/25/42

1942	Bos-N	0	1	.000	1	1	0	0	0	1¹	4	1	2	0	40.5	20.25	16	.500	.600	0	.000	-0	-3	-3	-0	-1.0
1944	Bos-N	0	0	—	8	0	0	0	0	9¹	15	0	5	3	20.3	4.82	79	.366	.447	0	.000	-0	-1	-0	0	0.0
Total	2	0	1	.000	9	1	0	0	0	10²	19	1	7	3	22.8	6.75	56	.388	.474	0	.000	-0	-4	-4	-0	-1.0

● **JOHN HICKEY** Hickey, John William b: 11/3/1881, Minneapolis, Minn. d: 12/28/41, Seattle, Wash. BR/TL, 5'10", 170 lbs. Deb: 4/16/04

| 1904 | Cle-A | 0 | 1 | .000 | 2 | 1 | 0 | 0 | 0 | 12¹ | 14 | 0 | 11 | 5 | 18.2 | 7.30 | 35 | .286 | .417 | 0 | .000 | -1 | -6 | -7 | 0 | -0.5 |

● **KEVIN HICKEY** Hickey, Kevin John b: 2/25/57, Chicago, Ill. BL/TL, 6'1", 200 lbs. Deb: 4/14/81

1981	Chi-A	0	2	.000	41	0	0	0	3	44¹	38	3	18	17	11.6	3.65	98	.232	.311	0	—	0	0	-0	1	0.2
1982	Chi-A	4	4	.500	60	0	0	0	6	78	73	4	30	38	12.1	3.00	134	.256	.331	0	—	0	9	9	2	1.2
1983	Chi-A	1	2	.333	23	0	0	0	0	20²	23	5	11	8	14.8	5.23	80	.264	.347	0	—	0	-3	-2	-0	-0.7
1989	Bal-A	2	3	.400	51	0	0	0	2	49¹	38	6	23	28	11.3	2.92	130	.220	.315	0	—	0	5	5	0	0.5
1990	Bal-A	1	3	.250	37	0	0	0	6	26¹	26	3	14	16	13.3	5.13	74	.265	.351	0	—	0	-4	-4	0	-0.5
1991	Bal-A	1	0	1.000	19	0	0	0	0	14	15	0	6	10	13.5	9.00	44	.278	.350	0	—	0	-8	-8	-0	-0.5
Total	6	9	14	.391	231	0	0	0	17	232²	213	21	101	118	12.3	3.91	99	.247	.329	0	—	0	-1	-2	0	0.2

● **CHARLIE HICKMAN** Hickman, Charles Taylor "Cheerful Charlie" or "Piano Legs" b: 3/4/1876, Taylortown, Dunkard Township, Pa. d: 4/19/34, Morgantown, W.Va. BR/TR, 5'11.5", 215 lbs. Deb: 9/8/1897 ♦

| 1897 | *Bos-N | 0 | 0 | — | 2 | 0 | 0 | 0 | 0 | 7² | 10 | 0 | 5 | 0 | 17.6 | 5.87 | 76 | .313 | .405 | 2 | .667 | 2 | -1 | -1 | 0 | 0.1 |

YEAR	TM/L	W	L	PCT	G	GS	CG	SH	SV	IP	H	HR	BB	SO	RAT	ERA	ERA+	OAV	OOB	BH	AVG	PB	PR	/A	PD	TPI
1898	Bos-N	1	2	.333	6	3	3	1	2	33	22	0	13	9	9.5	2.18	169	.188	.269	15	.259	0	5	6	-1	0.4
1899	Bos-N	6	0	1.000	11	9	5	2	1	66¹	52	3	40	14	13.6	4.48	93	.216	.346	25	.397	6	-5	-2	-1	0.2
1901	NY-N	3	5	.375	9	9	6	0	0	65	76	1	26	11	14.5	4.57	72	.290	.361	113	.278	2	-9	-9	1	-0.7
1902	Cle-A	0	1	.000	1	1	1	0	0	8	11	0	5	1	19.1	7.88	44	.324	.425	161	.378	1	-4	-4	-0	-0.3
1907	Was-A	0	0	—	1	0	0	0	0	5	4	0	5	2	16.2	3.60	67	.222	.391	55	.278	0	-1	-1	1	0.1
Total	6	10	8	.556	30	22	15	3	4	185	175	4	94	37	13.7	4.28	86	.249	.347	1176	.295	11	-14	-12	-1	-0.2

● **ERNIE HICKMAN**   Hickman, Ernest P. b: 1856, E.St.Louis, Ill. d: 11/19/1891, E.St.Louis, Ill Deb: 6/7/1884

| 1884 | KC-U | 4 | 13 | .235 | 17 | 17 | 15 | 0 | 0 | 137¹ | 172 | 5 | 36 | 68 | 13.6 | 4.52 | 49 | .287 | .328 | 12 | .167 | -7 | -32 | -35 | -1 | -3.6 |

● **JIM HICKMAN**   Hickman, James Lucius b: 5/10/37, Henning, Tenn. BR/TR, 6'4", 205 lbs. Deb: 4/14/62 ♦

| 1967 | LA-N | 0 | 0 | — | 1 | 0 | 0 | 0 | 0 | 2 | 2 | 1 | 0 | 0 | 9.0 | 4.50 | 69 | .286 | .286 | 16 | .163 | 0 | -0 | -0 | -0 | 0.0 |

● **JESSE HICKMAN**   Hickman, Jesse Owens b: 2/18/39, Lecompte, La. BR/TR, 6'2", 186 lbs. Deb: 6/5/65

1965	KC-A	0	1	.000	12	0	0	0	0	15¹	9	3	6	16	10.0	5.87	59	.184	.298	0	—	0	-4	-4	-0	-0.3
1966	KC-A	0	0	—	1	0	0	0	0	1	0	0	1	0	9.0	0.00	—	.000	.333	0	—	0	0	0	-0	0.0
Total	2	0	1	.000	13	0	0	0	0	16¹	9	3	9	16	9.9	5.51	63	.176	.300	0	—	0	-4	-4	-0	-0.3

● **KIRBY HIGBE**   Higbe, Walter Kirby b: 4/8/15, Columbia, S.C. d: 5/6/85, Columbia, S.C. BR/TR, 5'11", 190 lbs. Deb: 10/3/37

1937	Chi-N	1	0	1.000	1	0	0	0	0	5	4	1	1	2	9.0	5.40	74	.182	.217	0	.000	-0	-1	-1	-0	-0.2
1938	Chi-N	0	0	—	2	0	0	0	0	10	10	1	6	4	14.4	5.40	71	.263	.364	0	.000	-0	-2	-2	1	0.0
1939	Chi-N	2	1	.667	9	2	0	0	0	22²	12	0	22	16	13.5	3.18	124	.158	.347	2	.286	1	2	2	-0	0.3
	Phi-N	10	14	.417	34	26	14	1	2	187¹	208	10	101	79	15.3	4.85	83	.283	.378	11	.167	-2	-19	-18	-4	-2.6
	Yr	12	15	.444	43	28	14	1	2	210	220	10	123	95	15.1	4.67	86	.272	.374	13	.178	-2	-18	-16	-4	-2.3
1940	Phi-N☆	14	19	.424	41	36	20	1	1	283	242	12	121	**137**	11.6	3.72	105	.232	.313	17	.165	-2	4	6	-1	0.4
1941	*Bro-N	**22**	9	.710	**48**	39	19	2	3	298	244	17	132	121	11.5	3.14	117	.220	.306	21	.188	1	16	17	-5	1.3
1942	Bro-N	16	11	.593	38	32	13	2	0	221¹	180	17	106	115	11.7	3.25	100	.223	.315	8	.104	-4	2	0	-1	-0.6
1943	Bro-N	13	10	.565	35	27	8	1	0	185	189	4	95	108	14.1	3.70	91	.264	.354	9	.138	-2	-6	-7	-1	-1.1
1946	Bro-N★	17	8	.680	42	29	11	3	1	210²	178	6	107	134	12.2	3.03	111	.229	.323	10	.130	-4	9	8	1	0.6
1947	Bro-N	2	0	1.000	4	3	0	0	0	15²	18	0	12	10	17.8	5.17	80	.295	.419	1	.200	0	-2	-2	0	-0.2
	Pit-N	11	17	.393	46	30	10	1	5	225	204	22	110	99	12.7	3.72	113	.240	.329	10	.139	-1	8	13	-4	0.9
	Yr	13	17	.433	50	33	10	1	5	240²	222	22	122	109	13.0	3.81	111	.243	.334	11	.143	-1	7	11	-4	0.7
1948	Pit-N	8	7	.533	56	8	3	0	10	158	140	11	83	86	12.9	3.36	121	.240	.337	10	.208	-1	10	12	-1	1.2
1949	Pit-N	0	2	.000	7	1	0	0	0	15¹	25	2	12	5	21.7	13.50	31	.379	.474	0	.000	-0	-16	-16	0	-1.6
	NY-N	2	0	1.000	37	2	0	0	2	80¹	72	12	41	38	12.8	3.47	115	.242	.335	1	.067	-0	5	5	-1	0.0
	Yr	2	2	.500	44	3	0	0	2	95²	97	14	53	43	14.2	5.08	79	.266	.361	1	.056	-1	-11	-11	-1	-1.6
1950	NY-N	0	3	.000	18	1	0	0	0	34²	37	2	30	17	17.4	4.93	83	.285	.419	1	.250	-0	-3	-3	1	-0.1
Total	12	118	101	.539	418	238	98	11	24	1952¹	1763	117	979	971	12.8	3.69	102	.241	.333	101	.153	-14	7	14	-16	-1.7

● **IRV HIGGINBOTHAM**   Higginbotham, Irving Clinton b: 4/26/1882, Homer, Neb. d: 6/12/59, Seattle, Wash. BR/TR, 6'1", 196 lbs. Deb: 8/11/06

1906	StL-N	1	4	.200	7	6	4	0	0	47¹	50	1	11	14	11.8	3.23	81	.266	.310	4	.222	0	-3	-3	1	-0.2
1908	StL-N	3	8	.273	19	11	7	1	0	107	113	0	33	38	12.5	3.20	74	.270	.328	5	.132	-1	-10	-10	-1	-1.3
1909	StL-N	1	0	1.000	3	1	1	0	0	11¹	5	0	2	5	5.6	1.59	159	.143	.189	0	.000	-0	1	1	-1	0.0
	Chi-N	5	2	.714	19	6	4	0	1	78	64	0	20	32	10.0	2.19	116	.213	.269	6	.231	1	4	3	-1	0.2
	Yr	6	2	.750	22	7	5	0	1	89¹	69	0	22	34	9.5	2.12	120	.205	.260	6	.207	0	5	4	-2	0.2
Total	3	10	14	.417	48	24	16	1	1	243²	232	1	66	86	11.3	2.81	88	.246	.300	15	.176	-1	-8	-9	-2	-1.3

● **DENNIS HIGGINS**   Higgins, Dennis Dean b: 8/4/39, Jefferson City, Mo. BR/TR, 6'4", 190 lbs. Deb: 4/12/66

1966	Chi-A	1	0	1.000	42	1	0	0	5	93	66	9	33	86	10.1	2.52	126	.202	.286	3	.176	0	9	7	1	0.2
1967	Chi-A	1	2	.333	9	0	0	0	0	12¹	10	1	8	19	19.0	5.84	53	.271	.426	0	.000	-0	-4	-4	0	-0.9
1968	Was-A	4	4	.500	59	0	0	0	13	99²	81	8	46	66	11.7	3.25	90	.226	.319	2	.133	-0	-3	-4	-1	-0.6
1969	Was-A	10	9	.526	55	0	0	0	16	85¹	79	7	56	71	14.6	3.48	100	.252	.371	1	.091	-1	1	-0	-1	-0.2
1970	Cle-A	4	6	.400	58	0	0	0	11	90¹	82	8	54	82	13.7	3.99	99	.248	.358	3	.250	1	-3	-0	1	0.1
1971	StL-N	1	0	1.000	3	0	0	0	0	7	6	0	2	6	10.3	3.86	93	.240	.296	0	.000	-0	-0	-0	0	0.0
1972	StL-N	1	2	.333	15	1	0	0	1	22²	19	0	22	20	16.3	3.97	86	.226	.387	0	.000	-0	-1	-1	-0	-0.2
Total	7	22	23	.489	241	2	0	0	46	410¹	346	32	223	339	12.8	3.42	98	.233	.340	9	.155	-0	-0	-1	-1	-1.6

● **EDDIE HIGGINS**   Higgins, Thomas Edward "Doc" or "Irish" b: 3/18/1888, Nevada, Ill. d: 2/14/59, Elgin, Ill. BR/TR, 6'0.5", 174 lbs. Deb: 5/14/09

1909	StL-N	3	3	.500	16	5	5	0	0	66	68	4	17	15	11.7	4.50	56	.273	.322	4	.190	-0	-14	-14	0	-1.2
1910	StL-N	0	1	.000	2	0	0	0	0	10¹	15	0	7	1	19.2	4.35	68	.349	.440	2	.400	1	-2	-2	1	0.0
Total	2	3	4	.429	18	5	5	0	0	76¹	83	4	24	16	12.7	4.48	58	.284	.341	6	.231	1	-15	-16	1	-1.2

● **ED HIGH**   High, Edward T. "Lefty" b: 12/26/1876, Baltimore, Md. d: 2/10/26, Baltimore, Md. TL. Deb: 7/4/01

| 1901 | Det-A | 1 | 0 | 1.000 | 4 | 1 | 1 | 0 | 0 | 18 | 21 | 0 | 6 | 4 | 14.0 | 3.50 | 110 | .288 | .350 | 0 | .000 | -1 | 0 | 1 | -0 | 0.0 |

● **TEDDY HIGUERA**   Higuera, Teodoro Valenzuela (Valenzuela) b: 11/9/58, Los Mochis, Mexico BB/TL, 5'10", 178 lbs. Deb: 4/23/85

1985	Mil-A	15	8	.652	32	30	7	2	0	212¹	186	22	63	127	10.7	3.90	107	.235	.293	0	—	0	6	6	-3	0.4
1986	Mil-A★	20	11	.645	34	34	15	4	0	248¹	226	26	74	207	11.0	2.79	155	.241	.299	0	—	0	38	42	-1	4.8
1987	Mil-A	18	10	.643	35	35	14	3	0	261²	236	24	87	240	11.2	3.85	119	.241	.304	0	—	0	18	21	-2	1.6
1988	Mil-A	16	9	.640	31	31	8	1	0	227¹	168	15	59	192	**9.2**	2.45	162	.207	**.265**	0	—	0	**38**	38	-1	4.3
1989	Mil-A	9	6	.600	22	22	2	1	0	135¹	125	9	48	91	11.6	3.46	111	.248	.318	0	—	0	6	6	-2	0.4
1990	Mil-A	11	10	.524	27	27	4	1	0	170	167	16	50	129	11.6	3.76	103	.256	.312	0	—	0	3	2	-1	0.2
1991	Mil-A	3	2	.600	7	6	0	0	0	36¹	37	2	10	33	11.9	4.46	89	.262	.316	0	—	0	-1	-2	0	-0.2
1993	Mil-A	1	3	.250	8	8	0	0	0	30	43	4	16	27	18.0	7.20	59	.333	.411	0	—	0	-10	-10	-1	-1.1
1994	Mil-A	1	5	.167	17	12	0	0	0	58²	74	13	36	35	17.2	7.06	71	.311	.406	0	—	0	-15	-13	0	-1.1
Total	9	94	64	.595	213	205	50	12	0	1380	1262	131	443	1081	11.3	3.61	116	.243	.306	0	—	0	83	90	-9	9.3

● **WHITEY HILCHER**   Hilcher, Walter Frank b: 2/28/09, Chicago, Ill. d: 11/21/62, Minneapolis, Minn. BR/TR, 6', 174 lbs. Deb: 9/17/31

1931	Cin-N	0	1	.000	7	2	1	0	0	12	16	0	4	5	15.8	3.00	125	.320	.382	0	.000	-1	1	1	-0	0.0
1932	Cin-N	0	3	.000	11	2	0	0	0	18²	24	3	10	6	16.4	7.71	50	.316	.395	1	.333	1	-8	-8	0	-1.0
1935	Cin-N	2	0	1.000	4	2	1	1	0	19¹	19	0	5	9	11.2	2.79	142	.264	.312	1	.167	-0	3	3	1	0.3
1936	Cin-N	1	2	.333	14	1	0	0	0	35	44	3	14	10	15.2	6.17	62	.299	.364	0	.000	-2	-8	-9	-1	-0.8
Total	4	3	6	.333	31	6	1	1	0	85	103	6	33	28	14.6	5.29	73	.299	.363	2	.095	-2	-13	-14	-0	-1.5

● **ORAL HILDEBRAND**   Hildebrand, Oral Clyde b: 4/7/07, Indianapolis, Ind. d: 9/8/77, Southport, Ind. BR/TR, 6'3", 175 lbs. Deb: 9/8/31

1931	Cle-A	2	1	.667	5	2	2	0	0	26²	25	0	13	6	13.8	4.39	105	.243	.345	2	.182	-1	-0	-1	-0	0.0
1932	Cle-A	8	6	.571	27	15	7	0	0	129¹	124	7	62	49	12.9	3.69	129	.249	.333	7	.146	-3	11	15	-2	0.9
1933	Cle-A☆	16	11	.593	36	31	15	**6**	0	220¹	205	8	88	90	12.0	3.76	118	.245	.318	16	.190	-1	13	17	-0	1.6
1934	Cle-A	11	9	.550	33	28	10	1	1	198	225	14	99	72	14.9	4.50	112	.282	.364	13	.171	-1	-0	1	1	0.2
1935	Cle-A	9	8	.529	34	20	8	0	4	171¹	171	12	63	49	12.4	3.94	114	.263	.331	9	.164	-2	10	11	-0	0.8
1936	Cle-A	10	11	.476	36	21	9	0	4	174²	197	10	83	65	14.6	4.90	103	.283	.362	12	.190	-0	3	3	-1	0.2
1937	StL-A	8	17	.320	30	27	12	1	1	201¹	228	18	87	75	14.2	5.14	94	.284	.356	14	.200	-1	-12	-7	-1	-0.8
1938	StL-A	10	14	.444	23	23	10	0	0	163	194	18	73	66	14.9	5.69	87	.297	.370	15	.254	-1	-16	-13	-1	-1.3
1939	*NY-A	10	4	.714	21	15	7	1	2	126²	102	11	41	50	10.2	3.06	143	.219	.284	8	.182	-1	22	18	-1	1.6
1940	NY-A	1	1	.500	13	0	0	0	1	19¹	19	1	14	5	15.8	1.86	217	.268	.395	0	.000	-0	5	5	-0	0.4
Total	10	83	78	.516	258	182	80	9	13	1430²	1490	99	623	527	13.4	4.35	107	.267	.343	96	.187	-9	36	50	-8	3.4

● **TOM HILGENDORF**   Hilgendorf, Thomas Eugene b: 3/10/42, Clinton, Iowa BB/TL, 6'1", 190 lbs. Deb: 8/15/69

1969	StL-N	0	0	—	6	0	0	0	0	6¹	2	0	3	2	7.1	1.42	251	.150	.227	1	1.000	1	2	2	-0	0.2
1970	StL-N	0	4	.000	23	0	0	0	3	20²	22	0	13	16	15.2	3.92	105	.272	.372	0	—	-0	0	0	0	0.1
1972	Cle-A	3	1	.750	19	5	0	0	0	47	51	4	21	25	14.2	2.68	120	.283	.365	1	.077	-1	2	3	0	0.2

YEAR	TM/L	W	L	PCT	G	GS	CG	SH	SV	IP	H	HR	BB	SO	RAT	ERA	ERA+	OAV	OOB	BH	AVG	PB	PR	/A	PD	TPI
1973	Cle-A	5	3	.625	48	1	1	0	6	94²	87	9	36	58	12.0	3.14	125	.242	.316	0	—	0	7	8	1	0.8
1974	Cle-A	4	3	.571	35	0	0	0	3	48¹	58	6	17	23	14.2	4.84	75	.302	.362	0	—	0	-7	-7	-0	-0.9
1975	Phi-N	7	3	.700	53	0	0	0	0	96²	81	6	38	52	11.2	2.14	174	.230	.307	3	.250	-1	16	17	1	1.9
Total	6	19	14	.576	184	6	2	0	14	313²	302	25	127	173	12.5	3.04	122	.255	.331	5	.185	1	20	24	2	2.3

● **CARMEN HILL**   Hill, Carmen Proctor "Specs" or "Bunker" b: 10/1/1895, Royalton, Minn. d: 1/1/90, Indianapolis, Ind. BR/TR, 6'1", 180 lbs. Deb: 8/24/15

YEAR	TM/L	W	L	PCT	G	GS	CG	SH	SV	IP	H	HR	BB	SO	RAT	ERA	ERA+	OAV	OOB	BH	AVG	PB	PR	/A	PD	TPI
1915	Pit-N	2	1	.667	8	3	2	1	0	47	42	0	13	24	10.9	1.15	238	.255	.317	2	.154	0	8	8	1	0.7
1916	Pit-N	0	0	—	2	0	0	0	0	6¹	11	0	5	5	24.2	8.53	31	.611	.708	0	—	0	-4	-4	-0	-0.5
1918	Pit-N	2	3	.400	6	4	3	0	0	43²	24	0	17	15	8.5	1.24	232	.160	.246	2	.167	0	7	8	0	1.1
1919	Pit-N	0	0	—	4	0	0	0	0	5	12	0	1	1	23.4	9.00	34	.480	.500	0	—	0	-3	-3	-0	0.0
1922	NY-N	2	1	.667	8	4	0	0	0	28¹	33	0	5	6	12.1	4.76	84	.295	.325	2	.182	-0	-2	-2	1	-0.2
1926	Pit-N	3	3	.500	6	6	4	1	0	39²	42	2	9	8	12.0	3.40	116	.288	.338	3	.176	-1	2	2	1	0.4
1927	*Pit-N	22	11	.667	43	31	22	2	3	277²	260	12	80	95	11.2	3.24	127	.249	.305	22	.212	2	21	27	1	3.2
1928	Pit-N	16	10	.615	36	31	16	1	2	237	229	16	81	73	11.9	3.53	115	.259	.324	20	.233	1	12	14	-3	1.3
1929	Pit-N	2	3	.400	27	3	0	0	3	79	94	4	35	28	14.7	3.99	120	.297	.366	1	.036	-3	6	7	0	0.1
	StL-N	0	0	—	3	1	0	0	0	8²	10	2	8	1	19.7	8.31	56	.303	.452	0	.000	-0	-3	-4	0	0.0
	Yr	2	3	.400	30	4	0	0	3	87²	104	6	43	29	15.2	4.41	108	.297	.376	1	.032	-4	3	3	0	0.1
1930	StL-N	0	1	.000	4	2	0	0	0	14²	12	2	13	8	15.3	7.36	68	.240	.397	1	.333	-0	-4	-4	-0	-0.2
Total	10	49	33	.598	147	85	47	5	8	787	769	38	267	264	12.0	3.44	116	.261	.326	53	.191	-0	40	49	1	6.4

● **RED HILL**   Hill, Clifford Joseph b: 1/20/1893, Marshall, Tex. d: 8/11/38, ElPaso, Tex. BB/TL Deb: 4/21/17

YEAR	TM/L	W	L	PCT	G	GS	CG	SH	SV	IP	H	HR	BB	SO	RAT	ERA	ERA+	OAV	OOB	BH	AVG	PB	PR	/A	PD	TPI
1917	Phi-A	0	0	—	1	0	0	0	0	2²	5	0	1	0	20.3	6.75	41	.385	.429	0	—	0	-1	-1	0	0.0

● **DAVE HILL**   Hill, David Burnham b: 11/11/37, New Orleans, La. BR/TL, 6'2", 170 lbs. Deb: 8/22/57

YEAR	TM/L	W	L	PCT	G	GS	CG	SH	SV	IP	H	HR	BB	SO	RAT	ERA	ERA+	OAV	OOB	BH	AVG	PB	PR	/A	PD	TPI
1957	KC-A	0	0	—	2	0	0	0	0	2¹	6	3	3	1	34.7	27.00	15	.462	.563	0	—	0	-6	-6	-0	0.0

● **DONNIE HILL**   Hill, Donald Earl b: 11/12/60, Pomona, Cal. BB/TR, 5'10", 160 lbs. Deb: 7/25/83 ♦

YEAR	TM/L	W	L	PCT	G	GS	CG	SH	SV	IP	H	HR	BB	SO	RAT	ERA	ERA+	OAV	OOB	BH	AVG	PB	PR	/A	PD	TPI
1990	Cal-A	0	0	—	1	0	0	0	0	1	0	0	1	1	9.0		—	.000	.250	93	.264	1	0	0		0.0

● **GARRY HILL**   Hill, Garry Alton b: 11/3/46, Rutherfordton, N.C. BR/TR, 6'2", 195 lbs. Deb: 6/12/69

YEAR	TM/L	W	L	PCT	G	GS	CG	SH	SV	IP	H	HR	BB	SO	RAT	ERA	ERA+	OAV	OOB	BH	AVG	PB	PR	/A	PD	TPI
1969	Atl-N	0	1	.000	1	1	0	0	0	2¹	6	1	1	2	27.0	15.43	23	.462	.500	0	—	0	-3	-3	0	-0.8

● **HERBERT HILL**   Hill, Herbert Lee b: 8/19/1891, Hutchins, Tex. d: 9/2/70, Farmers Branch, Tex. BR/TR, 5'11.5", 175 lbs. Deb: 7/17/15

YEAR	TM/L	W	L	PCT	G	GS	CG	SH	SV	IP	H	HR	BB	SO	RAT	ERA	ERA+	OAV	OOB	BH	AVG	PB	PR	/A	PD	TPI
1915	Cle-A	0	0	—	1	0	0	0	0	2	0	0	2	0	13.5	0.00	—	.250	.500	0	—	0	1	1	-0	0.0

● **KEN HILL**   Hill, Kenneth Wade b: 12/14/65, Lynn, Mass. BR/TR, 6'2", 175 lbs. Deb: 9/3/88

YEAR	TM/L	W	L	PCT	G	GS	CG	SH	SV	IP	H	HR	BB	SO	RAT	ERA	ERA+	OAV	OOB	BH	AVG	PB	PR	/A	PD	TPI
1988	StL-N	0	1	.000	4	1	0	0	0	14	16	0	6	6	14.1	5.14	68	.286	.355	0	.000	-0	-3	-3	0	-0.2
1989	StL-N	7	15	.318	33	33	2	1	0	196²	186	9	99	112	13.3	3.80	96	.252	.344	9	.153	-0	-7	-4	0	-0.4
1990	StL-N	5	6	.455	17	14	1	0	0	78²	79	7	33	58	12.9	5.49	69	.264	.339	4	.211	1	-15	-15	0	-1.7
1991	StL-N	11	10	.524	30	30	0	0	0	181¹	147	15	67	121	10.9	3.57	104	.224	.302	5	.100	-1	2	3	0	0.2
1992	Mon-N	16	9	.640	33	33	3	3	0	218	187	13	75	150	10.9	2.68	129	.230	.298	11	.177	5	20	19	1	3.0
1993	Mon-N	9	7	.563	28	28	2	0	0	183²	163	7	74	90	11.9	3.23	129	.238	.318	6	.115	-1	16	19	3	1.8
1994	Mon-N★	16	5	.762	23	23	1	1	0	154²	145	12	44	85	11.3	3.32	127	.248	.307	7	.146	-0	15	16	2	2.1
1995	StL-N	6	7	.462	18	18	0	0	0	110¹	125	16	45	50	13.9	5.06	83	.286	.353	6	.194	-1	-11	-11	1	-0.9
	*Cle-A	4	1	.800	12	11	1	0	0	74²	77	5	32	48	13.3	3.98	118	.268	.344	0		0	6	6	2	0.4
1996	*Tex-A	16	10	.615	35	35	7	3	0	250²	250	19	95	170	12.6	3.63	146	.263	.334	0		0	38	47	2	3.9
Total	9	90	71	.559	233	226	18	8	0	1462²	1375	103	570	890	12.2	3.66	113	.250	.324	48	.148	4	63	76	12	8.2

● **MILT HILL**   Hill, Milton Giles b: 8/22/65, Atlanta, Ga. BR/TR, 6', 180 lbs. Deb: 8/1/91

YEAR	TM/L	W	L	PCT	G	GS	CG	SH	SV	IP	H	HR	BB	SO	RAT	ERA	ERA+	OAV	OOB	BH	AVG	PB	PR	/A	PD	TPI
1991	Cin-N	1	1	.500	22	0	0	0	0	33¹	36	1	8	20	11.9	3.78	101	.295	.338	0	.000	-0	-0	-0	-1	-0.1
1992	Cin-N	0	0	—	14	0	0	0	1	20	15	1	5	10	9.4	3.15	114	.211	.273	0		0	1	1	-0	0.0
1993	Cin-N	3	0	1.000	19	0	0	0	0	28²	34	5	9	23	13.5	5.65	71	.301	.352	0	.000	-0	-5	-5	-1	-0.6
1994	Atl-N	0	0	—	10	0	0	0	0	11¹	18	3	6	10	19.1	7.94	53	.367	.436	0		0	-5	-5	-0	-0.2
	Sea-A	1	0	1.000	13	0	0	0	0	23²	30	4	11	16	15.6	6.46	76	.306	.376	0		0	-4	-4	-0	-0.2
Total	4	5	1	.833	78	0	0	0	2	117	133	14	39	79	13.5	5.08	80	.294	.351	0		0	-14	-13	-2	-0.9

● **BILL HILL**   Hill, William Cicero "Still Bill" b: 8/2/1874, Chattanooga, Tenn. d: 1/28/38, Cincinnati, Ohio BL/TL, 6'1", 201 lbs. Deb: 4/18/1896 F

YEAR	TM/L	W	L	PCT	G	GS	CG	SH	SV	IP	H	HR	BB	SO	RAT	ERA	ERA+	OAV	OOB	BH	AVG	PB	PR	/A	PD	TPI
1896	Lou-N	9	28	.243	43	39	32	0	2	319²	353	14	155	104	14.8	4.31	100	.278	.364	24	.207	-5	2	1	4	-0.1
1897	Lou-N	7	17	.292	27	26	20	1	0	199	209	6	69	55	13.3	3.62	118	.268	.341	7	.095	-8	15	14	2	0.8
1898	Cin-N	13	14	.481	33	32	26	2	0	262	261	8	119	75	13.6	3.98	96	.258	.346	13	.133	-7	-1	-1	-0	-0.9
1899	Cle-N	3	6	.333	11	10	7	0	0	72¹	96	0	19	29	17.3	6.97	53	.318	.403	4	.129	-2	-25	-26	0	-2.6
	Bal-N	3	4	.429	8	7	6	0	0	61	64	1	18	17	12.5	3.25	122	.269	.328	7	.292	1	4	5	2	0.4
	Bro-N	1	0	1.000	2	1	1	0	1	11	11	0	6	3	13.9	0.82	478	.262	.354	3	.600	2	4	4	0	0.6
	Yr	7	10	.412	21	18	14	0	1	144¹	171	1	63	46	14.6	4.93	78	.290	.359	14	.233	0	-17	-18	1	-1.4
Total	4	36	69	.343	124	115	92	3	3	925	994	24	406	280	14.2	4.16	99	.273	.355	58	.167	-20	-11	-6	7	-1.6

● **HOMER HILLEBRAND**   Hillebrand, Homer Hiller Henry b: 10/10/1879, Freeport, Ill. d: 1/20/74, Elsinore, Cal. BR/TL, 5'8", 165 lbs. Deb: 4/24/05 ♦

YEAR	TM/L	W	L	PCT	G	GS	CG	SH	SV	IP	H	HR	BB	SO	RAT	ERA	ERA+	OAV	OOB	BH	AVG	PB	PR	/A	PD	TPI
1905	Pit-N	5	2	.714	10	6	4	0	1	60²	43	0	19	37	9.5	2.82	107	.198	.269	26	.236	1	1	1	-1	0.2
1906	Pit-N	3	2	.600	7	5	4	1	0	53	42	1	21	32	10.9	2.21	121	.220	.300	5	.238	1	3	3	-0	0.5
1908	Pit-N	0	0	—	1	0	0	0	0	1	1	0	0	1	9.0	0.00	—	.333	.333	0	—	0	0	0	-0	0.0
Total	3	8	4	.667	18	11	8	1	1	114²	86	1	40	70	10.1	2.51	113	.209	.284	31	.237	2	4	4	-1	0.7

● **SHAWN HILLEGAS**   Hillegas, Shawn Patrick b: 8/21/64, Dos Palos, Cal. BR/TR, 6'2", 208 lbs. Deb: 8/9/87

YEAR	TM/L	W	L	PCT	G	GS	CG	SH	SV	IP	H	HR	BB	SO	RAT	ERA	ERA+	OAV	OOB	BH	AVG	PB	PR	/A	PD	TPI
1987	LA-N	4	3	.571	12	10	1	0	0	58	52	5	31	51	12.9	3.57	111	.241	.336	0	.000	-1	3	3	-1	0.1
1988	LA-N	3	4	.429	11	10	0	0	0	56²	54	5	17	30	11.8	4.13	81	.250	.314	2	.133	-0	-4	-5	-1	-0.7
	Chi-A	3	2	.600	6	6	0	0	0	40	30	4	18	26	11.0	3.15	126	.207	.299	0		0	4	4	-0	0.4
1989	Chi-A	7	11	.389	50	13	0	0	3	119²	132	12	51	76	14.0	4.74	80	.279	.353	0		0	-11	-12	-1	-1.8
1990	Chi-A	0	0	—	7	0	0	0	0	11¹	4	0	5	7	7.1	0.79	481	.111	.220	0		0	4	4	0	0.1
1991	Cle-A	3	4	.429	51	1	0	0	7	83	67	7	46	66	12.5	4.34	96	.223	.330	0		0	-2	-2	-0	-0.3
1992	NY-A	1	8	.111	21	4	1	0	0	78¹	96	14	33	46	14.8	5.51	71	.306	.372	0		0	-14	-14	-1	-1.5
	Oak-A	0	0	—	5	0	0	0	0	7²	8	1	4	3	14.1	2.35	159	.276	.364	0		0	2	2	-0	0.2
	Yr	1	8	.111	26	4	1	0	0	86	104	15	37	49	14.8	5.23	75	.301	.368	0		0	-12	-13	-1	-1.3
1993	Oak-A	3	6	.333	18	11	0	0	0	60²	78	8	33	29	17.1	6.97	58	.321	.406	0		0	-18	-20	-1	-2.3
Total	7	24	38	.387	181	62	1	1	10	515¹	521	54	238	332	13.5	4.61	84	.264	.347	2	.069	-1	-37	-41	-6	-5.7

● **FRANK HILLER**   Hiller, Frank Walter "Dutch" b: 7/13/20, Newark, N.J. d: 1/8/87, West Chester, Pa. BR/TR, 6', 200 lbs. Deb: 5/25/46

YEAR	TM/L	W	L	PCT	G	GS	CG	SH	SV	IP	H	HR	BB	SO	RAT	ERA	ERA+	OAV	OOB	BH	AVG	PB	PR	/A	PD	TPI
1946	NY-A	0	2	.000	3	1	0	0	0	11¹	13	2	6	4	15.1	4.76	72	.295	.380	1	.250	0	-2	-2	-0	-0.3
1948	NY-A	5	2	.714	22	5	1	0	0	62¹	59	8	30	25	13.0	4.04	101	.244	.330	6	.375	2	2	0	-0	0.2
1949	NY-A	0	2	.000	4	0	0	0	0	7²	9	1	7	2	18.8	5.87	69	.290	.421	1	.500	1	-2	-2	-0	-0.3
1950	Chi-N	12	5	.706	38	17	9	2	1	153	153	16	32	55	11.1	3.53	119	.258	.300	5	.114	-3	10	11	1	1.0
1951	Chi-N	6	12	.333	24	21	6	2	1	141¹	147	17	31	50	11.9	4.84	85	.268	.317	6	.125	-2	-14	-12	1	-1.4
1952	Cin-N	5	8	.385	28	15	6	1	1	124¹	129	7	37	50	12.5	4.63	81	.271	.331	5	.167	1	-12	-12	0	-1.1
1953	NY-N	2	1	.667	19	1	0	0	0	33²	43	6	15	10	16.6	6.15	70	.303	.385	2	.500	1	-7	-7	-0	-0.4
Total	7	30	32	.484	138	60	22	5	4	533²	553	56	158	197	12.4	4.42	92	.266	.325	26	.176	-1	-24	-22	3	-2.4

● **JOHN HILLER**   Hiller, John Frederick b: 4/8/43, Toronto, Ont., Canada BR/TL, 6', 195 lbs. Deb: 9/6/65

YEAR	TM/L	W	L	PCT	G	GS	CG	SH	SV	IP	H	HR	BB	SO	RAT	ERA	ERA+	OAV	OOB	BH	AVG	PB	PR	/A	PD	TPI
1965	Det-A	0	0	—	5	0	0	0	1	6	5	0	1	4	9.0	0.00	—	.227	.261	0		0	2	2	-0	0.1
1966	Det-A	0	0	—	2	0	0	0	0	2	2	0	2	1	18.0	9.00	39	.286	.444	0		0	-1	-1	-0	0.0
1967	Det-A	4	3	.571	23	6	2	2	3	65	57	4	9	49	9.1	2.63	124	.233	.260	2	.133	-0	4	5	0	0.5
1968	*Det-A	9	6	.600	39	12	4	2	2	128	92	9	51	78	10.1	2.39	126	.200	.280	3	.081	0	8	9	-0	0.8
1969	Det-A	4	4	.500	40	8	1	1	4	99¹	97	13	44	74	12.9	3.99	94	.257	.336	4	.286	-2	-4	-3	-0	-0.2
1970	Det-A	6	6	.500	47	5	1	1	3	104	82	12	46	89	11.3	3.03	123	.219	.307	0	.000	-2	8	8	-1	0.6

YEAR TM/L	W	L	PCT	G	GS	CG	SH	SV	IP	H	HR	BB	SO	RAT	ERA	ERA+	OAV	OOB	BH	AVG	PB	PR	/A	PD	TPI
1972 *Det-A	1	2	.333	24	3	1	0	3	44¹	39	4	13	26	11.2	2.03	155	.232	.299	0	.000	-0	5	5	1	0.5
1973 Det-A	10	5	.667	65	0	0	0	38	125¹	89	7	39	124	9.2	1.44	285	.198	.262	0	—	0	33	37	0	6.7
1974 Det-A☆	17	14	.548	59	0	0	0	13	150	127	10	62	134	11.5	2.64	144	.231	.312	0	—	0	16	19	-2	3.9
1975 Det-A	2	3	.400	36	0	0	0	14	70²	52	6	36	87	11.2	2.17	185	.205	.303	0	.000	-0	13	15	-0	1.5
1976 Det-A	12	8	.600	56	1	1	1	13	121	93	7	67	117	12.0	2.38	156	.219	.329	0	.000	-0	15	18	-1	3.3
1977 Det-A	8	14	.364	45	8	3	0	7	124	120	15	61	115	13.2	3.56	121	.258	.345	0	—	-1	7	10	-1	1.6
1978 Det-A	9	4	.692	51	0	0	0	15	92¹	64	6	30	74	9.6	2.34	165	.202	.281	0	—	-0	15	16	-1	2.6
1979 Det-A	4	7	.364	43	0	0	0	9	79¹	83	14	55	46	15.7	5.22	83	.274	.385	0	—	-0	-9	-8	-0	-1.2
1980 Det-A	1	0	1.000	11	0	0	0	0	30²	38	3	14	18	15.3	4.40	93	.309	.380	0	—	-0	-1	-1	-0	-0.1
Total 15	87	76	.534	545	43	13	6	125	1242	1040	110	535	1036	11.5	2.83	133	.229	.312	11	.109	-3	112	130	-8	20.6

● DAVE HILLMAN
Hillman, Darius Dutton   b: 9/14/27, Dungannon, Va.   BR/TR, 5'11", 168 lbs.   Deb: 4/30/55

YEAR TM/L	W	L	PCT	G	GS	CG	SH	SV	IP	H	HR	BB	SO	RAT	ERA	ERA+	OAV	OOB	BH	AVG	PB	PR	/A	PD	TPI
1955 Chi-N	0	0	—	25	3	0	0	0	57²	63	10	25	23	13.9	5.31	77	.283	.357	1	.100	-0	-8	-8	0	0.0
1956 Chi-N	0	2	.000	2	2	0	0	0	12¹	10	0	5	6	11.7	2.19	172	.216	.286	0	.000	-1	2	2	0	0.3
1957 Chi-N	6	11	.353	32	14	1	0	1	103¹	115	13	37	53	13.2	4.35	89	.280	.340	0	.000	-2	-5	-6	-0	-1.1
1958 Chi-N	4	8	.333	31	16	3	0	1	125²	132	12	31	65	11.7	3.15	124	.265	.308	6	.146	-1	11	11	-0	0.8
1959 Chi-N	8	11	.421	39	24	4	1	0	191	178	17	43	88	10.5	3.53	112	.248	.292	9	.150	1	9	9	1	1.0
1960 Bos-A	0	3	.000	16	3	0	0	0	36²	41	6	12	14	13.0	5.65	72	.281	.335	0	.000	-0	-7	-7	0	-0.5
1961 Bos-A	3	2	.600	28	1	0	0	0	78	70	8	23	39	10.7	2.77	151	.242	.298	0	.000	-2	11	12	0	0.5
1962 Cin-N	0	0	—	2	0	0	0	0	3²	8	0	1	2	22.1	9.82	41	.421	.450	0	—	0	-2	-2	-0	0.0
NY-N	0	0	—	13	1	0	0	1	15²	21	5	8	7	17.2	6.32	66	.333	.417	0	.000	-0	-4	-4	0	-0.1
Yr	0	0	—	15	1	0	0	1	19¹	29	5	9	8	18.2	6.98	59	.354	.424	0	.000	-0	-7	-6	-0	-0.1
Total 8	21	37	.362	188	64	8	1	3	624	639	71	185	296	11.9	3.87	103	.264	.317	16	.098	-5	6	8	1	0.9

● ERIC HILLMAN
Hillman, John Eric   b: 4/27/66, Gary, Ind.   BL/TL, 6'10", 225 lbs.   Deb: 5/18/92

YEAR TM/L	W	L	PCT	G	GS	CG	SH	SV	IP	H	HR	BB	SO	RAT	ERA	ERA+	OAV	OOB	BH	AVG	PB	PR	/A	PD	TPI
1992 NY-N	2	2	.500	11	8	0	0	0	52¹	67	9	10	16	13.6	5.33	65	.318	.354	1	.077	-1	-11	-11	-1	-0.9
1993 NY-N	2	9	.182	27	22	3	1	0	145	173	12	24	60	12.5	3.97	101	.299	.331	7	.159	-0	1	1	-1	0.0
1994 NY-N	0	3	.000	11	6	0	0	0	34²	45	9	11	20	15.1	7.79	54	.321	.379	0	.000	-0	-14	-14	-0	-1.1
Total 3	4	14	.222	49	36	3	1	0	232	285	30	45	96	13.1	4.85	81	.306	.344	8	.123	-2	-23	-24	-1	-2.0

● CHARLIE HILSEY
Hilsey, Charles T.   b: 3/23/1864, Philadelphia, Pa.   d: 10/31/18, Philadelphia, Pa.   5'7", 180 lbs.   Deb: 9/27/1883 ♦

YEAR TM/L	W	L	PCT	G	GS	CG	SH	SV	IP	H	HR	BB	SO	RAT	ERA	ERA+	OAV	OOB	BH	AVG	PB	PR	/A	PD	TPI
1883 Phi-N	0	3	.000	3	3	3	0	0	26	36	1	4	8	13.8	5.54	56	.305	.328	1	.100	-1	-7	-7	-0	-0.7
1884 Phi-a	2	1	.667	3	3	3	0	0	27	29	0	5	10	11.3	4.67	73	.257	.288	5	.208	0	-4	-4	1	-0.3
Total 2	2	4	.333	6	6	6	0	0	53	65	1	9	18	12.6	5.09	64	.281	.308	6	.176	-1	-11	-11	0	-1.0

● HOWARD HILTON
Hilton, Howard James   b: 1/3/64, Oxnard, Cal.   BR/TR, 6'3", 230 lbs.   Deb: 4/9/90

YEAR TM/L	W	L	PCT	G	GS	CG	SH	SV	IP	H	HR	BB	SO	RAT	ERA	ERA+	OAV	OOB	BH	AVG	PB	PR	/A	PD	TPI
1990 StL-N	0	0	—	2	0	0	0	0	3	2	0	3	2	15.0	0.00	—	.182	.357	0	—	0	1	1	-0	0.0

● SAM HINDS
Hinds, Samuel Russell   b: 7/11/53, Frederick, Md.   BR/TR, 6'6", 215 lbs.   Deb: 5/21/77

YEAR TM/L	W	L	PCT	G	GS	CG	SH	SV	IP	H	HR	BB	SO	RAT	ERA	ERA+	OAV	OOB	BH	AVG	PB	PR	/A	PD	TPI
1977 Mil-A	0	3	.000	29	1	0	0	2	72¹	72	5	40	46	14.2	4.73	86	.266	.364	0	—	0	-5	-5	-0	-0.3

● PAUL HINES
Hines, Paul A.   b: 3/1/1852, Washington, D.C.   d: 7/10/35, Hyattsville, Md.   BR/TR, 5'9.5", 173 lbs.   Deb: 4/20/1872 ♦

YEAR TM/L	W	L	PCT	G	GS	CG	SH	SV	IP	H	HR	BB	SO	RAT	ERA	ERA+	OAV	OOB	BH	AVG	PB	PR	/A	PD	TPI
1884 *Pro-N	0	0	—	1	0	0	0	0	1	3	0	0	0	27.0	0.00	—	.500	.500	148	.302	0	0	0	-0	0.0

● PAUL HINRICHS
Hinrichs, Paul Edwin "Herky"   b: 8/31/25, Marengo, Iowa   BR/TR, 6', 180 lbs.   Deb: 5/16/51

YEAR TM/L	W	L	PCT	G	GS	CG	SH	SV	IP	H	HR	BB	SO	RAT	ERA	ERA+	OAV	OOB	BH	AVG	PB	PR	/A	PD	TPI
1951 Bos-A	0	0	—	4	0	0	0	0	3¹	7	1	4	1	29.7	21.60	21	.412	.524	0	—	0	-6	-6	0	0.0

● DUTCH HINRICHS
Hinrichs, William Louis   b: 4/27/1889, Orange, Cal.   d: 8/18/72, Kingsburg, Cal.   BR/TR, 6'3", 195 lbs.   Deb: 6/25/10

YEAR TM/L	W	L	PCT	G	GS	CG	SH	SV	IP	H	HR	BB	SO	RAT	ERA	ERA+	OAV	OOB	BH	AVG	PB	PR	/A	PD	TPI
1910 Was-A	0	1	.000	3	0	0	0	1	7	10	0	3	5	16.7	2.57	97	.357	.419	0	.000	-1	-0	-0	-0	-0.1

● JERRY HINSLEY
Hinsley, Jerry Dean   b: 4/9/44, Hugo, Okla.   BR/TR, 5'11", 165 lbs.   Deb: 4/18/64

YEAR TM/L	W	L	PCT	G	GS	CG	SH	SV	IP	H	HR	BB	SO	RAT	ERA	ERA+	OAV	OOB	BH	AVG	PB	PR	/A	PD	TPI
1964 NY-N	0	2	.000	9	2	0	0	0	15¹	21	0	7	11	16.4	8.22	44	.313	.378	0	.000	-0	-8	-8	-1	-1.0
1967 NY-N	0	0	—	2	0	0	0	0	5	6	0	4	3	16.2	3.60	94	.316	.435	0	—	0	-0	-0	-0	-0.0
Total 2	0	2	.000	11	2	0	0	0	20¹	27	0	11	14	16.8	7.08	50	.314	.392	0	.000	-0	-8	-8	-1	-1.0

● RICH HINTON
Hinton, Richard Michael   b: 5/22/47, Tucson, Ariz.   BL/TL, 6'2", 185 lbs.   Deb: 7/17/71

YEAR TM/L	W	L	PCT	G	GS	CG	SH	SV	IP	H	HR	BB	SO	RAT	ERA	ERA+	OAV	OOB	BH	AVG	PB	PR	/A	PD	TPI
1971 Chi-A	3	4	.429	18	2	0	0	0	24¹	27	1	6	15	12.6	4.44	81	.310	.362	0	.000	-0	-3	-3	1	-0.5
1972 NY-A	1	0	1.000	7	3	0	0	0	16²	20	2	8	13	15.1	4.86	61	.299	.373	0	—	-0	-3	-4	-0	-0.3
Tex-A	0	1	.000	5	0	0	0	0	11¹	7	1	10	4	13.5	2.38	126	.171	.333	1	.500	1	1	1	0	0.2
Yr	1	1	.500	12	3	0	0	0	28	27	3	18	17	14.5	3.86	77	.245	.352	1	.200	1	-2	-3	-0	-0.1
1975 Chi-A	1	0	1.000	15	0	0	0	0	37¹	41	3	15	30	13.5	4.82	80	.270	.335	0	—	0	-4	-4	1	-0.3
1976 Cin-N	1	2	.333	12	1	0	0	0	17²	30	4	8	8	20.9	7.64	46	.380	.456	0	.000	-0	-8	-8	-0	-1.3
1978 Chi-A	2	6	.250	29	4	2	0	0	80²	78	5	28	48	12.0	4.02	95	.261	.328	0	—	-0	-2	-2	1	-0.3
1979 Chi-A	1	2	.333	16	2	0	0	0	41²	57	4	8	27	14.5	6.05	70	.331	.368	0	—	0	-8	-8	1	-0.6
Sea-A	0	2	.000	14	1	0	0	0	20	23	4	5	7	13.5	5.40	81	.284	.341	0	—	0	-3	-2	0	-0.2
Yr	1	4	.200	30	3	0	0	0	61²	80	8	13	34	13.9	5.84	73	.310	.348	0	—	0	-11	-11	0	-0.8
Total 6	9	17	.346	116	13	2	0	3	249²	283	24	91	152	13.7	4.87	78	.289	.354	1	.143	0	-31	-30	0	-3.0

● HERB HIPPAUF
Hippauf, Herbert August   b: 5/9/39, New York, N.Y.   d: 7/17/95, Santa Clara, Cal.   BR/TL, 6', 180 lbs.   Deb: 4/27/66

YEAR TM/L	W	L	PCT	G	GS	CG	SH	SV	IP	H	HR	BB	SO	RAT	ERA	ERA+	OAV	OOB	BH	AVG	PB	PR	/A	PD	TPI
1966 Atl-N	0	1	.000	3	0	0	0	0	2²	6	0	1	2	23.6	13.50	27	.462	.500	0	—	0	-3	-3	-0	-0.9

● HARLEY HISNER
Hisner, Harley Parnell   b: 11/6/26, Maples, Ind.   BR/TR, 6'1", 185 lbs.   Deb: 9/30/51

YEAR TM/L	W	L	PCT	G	GS	CG	SH	SV	IP	H	HR	BB	SO	RAT	ERA	ERA+	OAV	OOB	BH	AVG	PB	PR	/A	PD	TPI
1951 Bos-A	0	1	.000	1	1	0	0	0	6	7	0	4	3	16.5	4.50	99	.292	.393	1	.500	0	-0	-0	0	0.0

● STERLING HITCHCOCK
Hitchcock, Sterling Alex   b: 4/29/71, Fayetteville, N.C.   BL/TL, 6'1", 200 lbs.   Deb: 9/11/92

YEAR TM/L	W	L	PCT	G	GS	CG	SH	SV	IP	H	HR	BB	SO	RAT	ERA	ERA+	OAV	OOB	BH	AVG	PB	PR	/A	PD	TPI
1992 NY-A	0	2	.000	3	3	0	0	0	13	23	1	6	6	20.8	8.31	47	.377	.441	0	—	0	-6	-6	-0	-0.7
1993 NY-A	1	2	.333	6	6	0	0	0	31	32	4	14	26	13.6	4.65	89	.271	.353	0	—	-0	-1	-2	-0	-0.1
1994 NY-A	4	1	.800	23	5	1	0	2	49¹	48	3	29	37	14.0	4.20	109	.265	.367	0	—	0	3	2	-0	0.2
1995 *NY-A	11	10	.524	27	27	4	1	0	168¹	155	22	68	121	12.2	4.70	98	.245	.323	0	—	0	0	-2	-3	-0.3
1996 Sea-A	13	9	.591	35	35	0	0	0	196²	245	27	73	132	14.9	5.35	92	.309	.372	0	—	0	-8	-9	-1	-0.9
Total 5	29	24	.547	94	76	5	1	2	458¹	503	58	190	322	13.9	5.03	93	.282	.355	0	—	0	-12	-17	-4	-1.8

● BRUCE HITT
Hitt, Bruce Smith   b: 3/14/1897, Comanche, Tex.   d: 11/10/73, Portland, Ore.   BR/TR, 6'1", 190 lbs.   Deb: 9/23/17

YEAR TM/L	W	L	PCT	G	GS	CG	SH	SV	IP	H	HR	BB	SO	RAT	ERA	ERA+	OAV	OOB	BH	AVG	PB	PR	/A	PD	TPI
1917 StL-N	0	0	—	2	0	0	0	0	4	7	1	1	1	18.0	9.00	30	.368	.400	0	.000	-0	-3	-3	0	0.0

● ROY HITT
Hitt, Roy Wesley "Rhino"   b: 6/22/1887, Carleton, Neb.   d: 2/8/56, Pomona, Cal.   BL/TL, 5'10", 200 lbs.   Deb: 4/27/07

YEAR TM/L	W	L	PCT	G	GS	CG	SH	SV	IP	H	HR	BB	SO	RAT	ERA	ERA+	OAV	OOB	BH	AVG	PB	PR	/A	PD	TPI
1907 Cin-N	6	10	.375	21	18	14	2	0	153¹	143	2	56	63	12.4	3.40	76	.258	.339	10	.179	-0	-16	-14	-1	-1.5

● LLOYD HITTLE
Hittle, Lloyd Eldon "Red"   b: 2/21/24, Lodi, Cal.   BR/TL, 5'10.5", 164 lbs.   Deb: 6/12/49

YEAR TM/L	W	L	PCT	G	GS	CG	SH	SV	IP	H	HR	BB	SO	RAT	ERA	ERA+	OAV	OOB	BH	AVG	PB	PR	/A	PD	TPI
1949 Was-A	5	7	.417	36	9	3	2	0	109	123	2	57	32	14.9	4.21	101	.285	.369	4	.143	-2	-0	1	-1	-0.2
1950 Was-A	2	4	.333	11	4	1	0	0	43¹	60	1	17	9	16.0	4.98	90	.326	.383	1	.077	-1	-2	-2	1	-0.3
Total 2	7	11	.389	47	13	4	2	0	152¹	183	3	74	41	15.2	4.43	98	.298	.373	5	.122	-3	-2	-1	-0	-0.5

● MYRIL HOAG
Hoag, Myril Oliver   b: 3/9/08, Davis, Cal.   d: 7/28/71, High Springs, Fla   BR/TR, 5'11", 180 lbs.   Deb: 4/15/31 ♦

YEAR TM/L	W	L	PCT	G	GS	CG	SH	SV	IP	H	HR	BB	SO	RAT	ERA	ERA+	OAV	OOB	BH	AVG	PB	PR	/A	PD	TPI
1939 StL-A★	0	0	—	1	0	0	0	0	1	0	0	0	0	0.00	—	.000	.000	142	.295	0	1	1	0	0.0
1945 Cle-A	0	0	—	2	0	0	0	0	3	3	1	1	0	12.0	0.00	—	.300	.364	27	.211	0	1	1	0	0.0
Total 2	0	0	—	3	0	0	0	0	4	3	1	1	0	9.0	0.00	—	.214	.267	854	.271	1	2	2	0	0.0

● ED HOBAUGH
Hobaugh, Edward Russell   b: 6/27/34, Kittanning, Pa.   BR/TR, 6', 176 lbs.   Deb: 4/19/61

YEAR TM/L	W	L	PCT	G	GS	CG	SH	SV	IP	H	HR	BB	SO	RAT	ERA	ERA+	OAV	OOB	BH	AVG	PB	PR	/A	PD	TPI
1961 Was-A	7	9	.438	26	18	3	0	0	126¹	142	12	64	67	14.7	4.42	91	.281	.363	4	.098	-2	-6	-6	0	-0.8
1962 Was-A	2	1	.667	26	2	0	0	1	69¹	66	9	25	43	11.8	3.76	107	.258	.324	2	.167	0	2	2	-1	0.0
1963 Was-A	0	0	—	9	1	0	0	0	16	20	3	6	11	15.8	6.19	60	.308	.384	1	.500	-0	-5	-4	-0	0.2
Total 3	9	10	.474	61	21	3	0	1	211²	228	24	95	115	13.9	4.34	92	.276	.352	7	.127	-1	-8	-8	-0	-0.6

YEAR	TM/L	W	L	PCT	G	GS	CG	SH	SV	IP	H	HR	BB	SO	RAT	ERA	ERA+	OAV	OOB	BH	AVG	PB	PR	/A	PD	TPI
● **GLEN HOBBIE**				Hobbie, Glen Frederick		b: 4/24/36, Witt, Ill.		BR/TR, 6'2", 195 lbs.		Deb: 9/20/57																
1957	Chi-N	0	0	—	2	0	0	0	0	4¹	6	0	5	3	22.8	10.38	37	.333	.478	0	.000	-0	-3	-3	0	0.0
1958	Chi-N	10	6	.625	55	16	2	1	2	168¹	163	13	93	91	14.1	3.74	105	.252	.353	7	.146	-2	4	3	4	0.5
1959	Chi-N	16	13	.552	46	33	10	3	0	234	204	15	106	138	12.2	3.69	107	.236	.324	9	.114	-3	7	7	1	0.5
1960	Chi-N	16	20	.444	46	36	16	4	1	258²	253	27	101	134	12.6	3.97	95	.256	.330	13	.151	1	-6	-5	4	-0.2
1961	Chi-N	7	13	.350	36	29	7	2	2	198²	207	26	54	103	12.1	4.26	98	.268	.321	11	.167	2	-5	-2	3	0.4
1962	Chi-N	5	14	.263	42	23	5	0	0	162	198	19	62	87	14.6	5.22	79	.304	.367	6	.122	-1	-23	-19	1	-2.1
1963	Chi-N	7	10	.412	36	24	4	1	0	165¹	172	17	49	94	12.4	3.92	90	.270	.328	4	.080	-2	-12	-8	-1	-1.1
1964	Chi-N	0	3	.000	8	4	0	0	0	27¹	39	4	10	14	16.5	7.90	47	.325	.382	0	.000	0	-13	-12	0	-1.2
	StL-N	1	2	.333	13	5	1	0	1	44¹	41	4	15	18	11.6	4.26	89	.241	.306	2	.154	-1	-4	-2	1	0.0
	Yr	1	5	.167	21	9	1	0	1	71²	80	8	25	32	13.3	5.65	67	.275	.334	2	.111	-1	-17	-15	1	-1.2
Total	8	62	81	.434	284	170	45	11	6	1263	1283	125	495	682	12.9	4.20	93	.264	.337	52	.131	-5	-55	-42	13	-3.2
● **JOHN HOBBS**				Hobbs, John Douglas		b: 11/11/56, Philadelphia, Pa.		BR/TL, 6'3", 190 lbs.		Deb: 8/31/81																
1981	Min-A	0	0	—	4	0	0	0	0	5²	5	0	6	1	20.6	3.18	124	.238	.448	0	—	0	0	-0	-0	-0.1
● **HARRY HOCH**				Hoch, Harry Keller		b: 1/9/1887, Woodside, Del.		d: 10/26/81, Lewes, Del.		BR/TR, 5'10.5", 165 lbs.		Deb: 4/16/08													
1908	Phi-N	2	1	.667	3	3	1	0	0	26	20	1	13	4	12.1	2.77	88	.211	.318	1	.200	1	-1	-1	0	0.0
1914	StL-A	0	2	.000	15	2	1	0	0	54	55	1	27	13	14.0	3.00	90	.284	.377	1	.056	-2	-2	-2	2	-0.1
1915	StL-A	0	4	.000	12	3	1	0	0	40	52	2	26	9	18.2	7.20	40	.311	.413	2	.200	-0	-19	-19	-0	-1.7
Total	3	2	7	.222	30	8	4	0	0	120	127	4	66	26	15.0	4.35	62	.279	.378	4	.121	-1	-22	-22	2	-1.8
● **CHUCK HOCKENBERY**				Hockenbery, Charles Marion		b: 12/15/50, LaCrosse, Wis.		BB/TR, 6'1", 195 lbs.		Deb: 7/4/75															
1975	Cal-A	0	5	.000	16	4	0	0	1	41	48	3	19	15	15.4	5.27	67	.296	.380	0	—	0	-7	-8	-0	-0.9
● **GEORGE HOCKETTE**				Hockette, George Edward "Lefty"		b: 4/7/08, Perth, Miss.		d: 1/20/74, Plantation, Fla.		BL/TL, 6', 174 lbs.		Deb: 9/17/34												
1934	Bos-A	2	1	.667	3	3	3	2	0	27¹	22	3	6	14	9.2	1.65	292	.218	.262	3	.273	0	9	10	-0	1.1
1935	Bos-A	2	3	.400	23	4	0	0	0	61	83	6	12	11	14.2	5.16	92	.329	.362	2	.143	-1	-5	-3	3	0.1
Total	2	4	4	.500	26	7	3	2	0	88¹	105	9	18	25	12.6	4.08	117	.297	.333	5	.200	-0	4	7	3	1.1
● **SHOVEL HODGE**				Hodge, Clarence Clemet		b: 7/6/1893, Mount Andrew, Ala.		d: 12/31/67, Ft.Walton Beach, Fla.		BL/TR, 6'4", 190 lbs.		Deb: 9/6/20											
1920	Chi-A	1	1	.500	4	2	1	0	0	19²	15	0	12	5	12.4	2.29	165	.224	.342	0	.000	-0	3	3	-1	0.1
1921	Chi-A	6	8	.429	36	10	5	0	2	142²	191	7	54	25	15.8	6.56	65	.335	.397	17	.327	3	-36	-37	3	-2.5
1922	Chi-A	7	6	.538	35	8	2	0	1	139	154	3	65	37	14.3	4.14	98	.300	.381	12	.207	-1	-2	-1	2	-0.1
Total	3	14	15	.483	75	20	8	0	3	301¹	360	10	131	67	14.9	5.17	80	.313	.387	29	.250	1	-34	-35	4	-2.5
● **ED HODGE**				Hodge, Ed Oliver		b: 4/19/58, Bellflower, Cal.		BL/TL, 6'2", 192 lbs.		Deb: 5/1/84														
1984	Min-A	4	3	.571	25	15	0	0	0	100	116	13	29	59	13.1	4.77	88	.291	.340	0	—	0	-9	-6	-2	-0.7
● **ELI HODKEY**				Hodkey, Aloysius Joseph		b: 11/3/17, Lorain, Ohio		BL/TL, 6'4", 185 lbs.		Deb: 9/12/46														
1946	Phi-N	0	1	.000	2	1	0	0	0	4¹	9	0	5	0	29.1	12.46	28	.391	.500	0	.000	-0	-4	-4	-0	-0.8
● **CHARLIE HODNETT**				Hodnett, Charles		b: 1861, Iowa		Deb: 5/3/1883																	
1883	StL-a	2	2	.500	4	4	3	0	0	32	28	1	7	6	9.8	1.41	248	.220	.261	2	.182	-0	7	7	-0	0.8
1884	StL-U	12	2	.857	14	14	12	1	0	121	121	0	16	41	10.2	2.01	119	.243	.267	12	.207	-1	6	5	-2	0.1
Total	2	14	4	.778	18	18	15	1	0	153	149	1	23	47	10.1	1.88	139	.239	.266	14	.203	-1	13	12	-2	0.9
● **GEORGE HODSON**				Hodson, George S.		b: 6/1870, Pennsylvania		TR		Deb: 8/9/1894															
1894	Bos-N	4	4	.500	12	11	8	0	0	74	103	4	35	12	17.4	5.84	97	.326	.402	3	.100	-4	-4	-1	-1	-0.5
1895	Phi-N	1	2	.333	4	2	1	0	0	17	27	4	9	6	19.1	9.53	50	.355	.424	0	.000	-1	-9	-9	-1	-1.1
Total	2	5	6	.455	16	13	9	0	0	91	130	8	44	18	17.7	6.53	84	.332	.406	3	.086	-5	-13	-10	-2	-1.6
● **BILLY HOEFT**				Hoeft, William Frederick		b: 5/17/32, Oshkosh, Wis.		BL/TL, 6'3", 205 lbs.		Deb: 4/18/52													
1952	Det-A	2	7	.222	34	10	1	0	0	125	123	14	63	67	13.8	4.32	88	.260	.353	6	.150	-0	-9	-7	1	-0.5
1953	Det-A	9	14	.391	29	27	9	0	2	197²	223	24	58	90	13.0	4.83	84	.283	.335	11	.172	0	-18	-17	-2	-1.8
1954	Det-A	7	15	.318	34	25	10	4	1	175	180	22	59	114	12.5	4.58	81	.266	.328	10	.192	4	-17	-17	-2	-1.7
1955	Det-A☆	16	7	.696	32	29	17	**7**	0	220	187	17	75	133	11.0	2.99	129	.229	.298	17	.207	3	24	21	-3	2.1
1956	Det-A	20	14	.588	38	34	18	4	0	248	276	29	104	172	14.0	4.06	101	.280	.360	20	.250	6	3	1	-3	0.5
1957	Det-A	9	11	.450	34	28	10	1	1	207	188	15	69	111	11.4	3.48	111	.244	.310	10	.149	2	7	9	-2	0.0
1958	Det-A	10	9	.526	36	21	6	0	3	143	148	16	49	94	12.5	4.15	97	.268	.328	12	.273	3	-6	-4	-2	-0.1
1959	Det-A	1	1	.500	2	2	0	0	0	9	8	1	5	7	13.0	5.00	81	.188	.297	1	.333	-0	-1	-0	-0	-0.2
	Bos-A	0	3	.000	5	3	0	0	0	17²	22	1	8	8	15.8	5.60	72	.319	.397	0	.000	-0	-3	-3	-0	-0.5
	Bal-A	1	1	.500	16	3	0	0	0	41	50	6	19	30	15.1	5.71	66	.307	.379	3	.250	-1	-8	-9	-0	-0.3
	Yr	2	5	.286	23	8	0	0	0	67²	78	7	31	40	14.5	5.59	70	.301	.363	4	.222	-1	-13	-13	-0	-1.0
1960	Bal-A	2	1	.667	19	0	0	0	0	18²	18	2	14	14	15.4	4.34	88	.240	.360	0	.000	-0	-1	-1	-1	-0.1
1961	Bal-A	7	4	.636	35	12	3	1	3	138	106	7	55	100	10.6	2.02	190	.216	.296	7	.179	1	**31**	28	1	2.4
1962	Bal-A	4	8	.333	57	4	0	0	7	113²	103	7	43	73	11.6	4.59	81	.243	.315	3	.158	-0	-8	-11	-0	-1.0
1963	SF-N	2	0	1.000	23	0	0	0	4	24¹	26	5	10	18	13.3	4.44	72	.271	.340	1	1.000	0	-3	-3	-0	-0.4
1964	Mil-N	4	0	1.000	42	0	0	0	4	73¹	76	9	18	47	11.7	3.80	93	.271	.318	2	.222	-1	-2	-3	0	-0.4
1965	Chi-N	2	2	.500	29	2	1	0	1	51¹	41	3	20	44	10.7	2.81	131	.215	.289	3	.273	1	4	5	-1	0.4
1966	Chi-N	1	2	.333	36	0	0	0	3	41	43	4	14	30	12.7	4.61	80	.264	.326	1	.250	0	-5	-4	1	-0.3
	SF-N	0	2	.000	4	0	0	0	0	3²	4	0	3	3	17.2	7.36	50	.250	.368	0	—	0	-2	-2	-0	-0.7
	Yr	1	4	.200	40	0	0	0	3	44²	47	4	17	33	12.9	4.84	76	.263	.325	1	.250	0	-6	-6	0	-1.0
Total	15	97	101	.490	505	200	75	17	33	1847¹	1820	173	685	1140	12.4	3.94	98	.259	.327	107	.202	24	-15	-15	-11	-1.4
● **ART HOELSKOETTER**				Hoelskoetter, Arthur "Holley" or "Hoss" (a.k.a. Arthur H. Hostetter)																						
				b: 9/30/1882, St.Louis, Mo.		d: 8/3/54, St.Louis, Mo.		BR/TR, 6'2",		Deb: 9/10/05 ◆															
1905	StL-N	0	1	.000	1	1	1	0	0	6	6	1	5	4	16.5	1.50	199	.273	.407	20	.241	0	1	0	-0	0.2
1906	StL-N	1	4	.200	12	3	2	0	0	58¹	53	1	34	20	13.6	4.63	57	.240	.344	71	.224	1	-13	-13	-1	-1.1
1907	StL-N	0	0	—	2	0	0	0	0	11	9	0	10	8	17.2	5.73	44	.209	.382	98	.247	0	-4	-4	-0	-0.1
Total	3	1	5	.167	15	4	3	0	0	75¹	68	2	49	32	14.3	4.54	58	.238	.355	225	.236	1	-16	-16	-1	-0.9
● **JOE HOERNER**				Hoerner, Joseph Walter		b: 11/12/36, Dubuque, Iowa		d: 10/4/96, Hermann, Mo.		BR/TL, 6'1", 200 lbs.		Deb: 9/27/63											
1963	Hou-N	0	0	—	1	0	0	0	0	3	2	0	2	4	6.0	0.00	—	.182	.182	0	.000	-0	1	1	0	0.0
1964	Hou-N	0	0	—	7	0	0	0	0	11	13	3	6	4	15.5	4.91	70	.310	.396	0	.000	-0	-2	-2	0	-0.2
1966	StL-N	5	1	.833	57	0	0	0	13	76	57	5	21	63	9.7	1.54	233	.212	.279	1	.125	1	17	17	-1	2.0
1967	*StL-N	4	4	.500	57	0	0	0	15	66	51	5	20	50	10.0	2.59	127	.225	.290	2	.182	-0	6	5	-0	0.9
1968	*StL-N	8	2	.800	47	0	0	0	17	48²	34	2	12	42	8.5	1.48	196	.192	.243	0	.000	-0	8	8	-0	2.3
1969	StL-N	2	3	.400	45	0	0	0	15	53¹	44	5	13	46	9.1	2.87	125	.230	.269	0	.000	-0	4	4	0	0.6
1970	Phi-N☆	9	5	.643	44	0	0	0	9	57²	53	5	20	39	11.5	2.65	150	.247	.314	2	.200	-1	9	9	-0	1.3
1971	Phi-N	4	5	.444	49	0	0	0	9	73	57	6	21	57	9.7	1.97	179	.215	.275	1	.100	1	12	13	-1	1.8
1972	Phi-N	0	2	.000	15	0	0	0	3	21²	21	2	5	12	11.2	2.08	173	.259	.310	0	.000	-0	3	4	-1	0.4
	Atl-N	1	3	.250	25	0	0	0	2	23¹	34	4	8	19	16.6	6.56	58	.351	.406	-0	.000	-0	-8	-7	-0	-1.4
	Yr	1	5	.167	40	0	0	0	5	45	55	6	13	31	13.6	4.40	84	.301	.350	0	—	-0	-5	-4	-1	-1.0
1973	Atl-N	2	2	.500	20	0	0	0	2	12²	17	1	4	10	14.9	6.39	61	.333	.382	-0	—	0	-4	-3	-0	-1.1
	KC-A	2	0	1.000	22	0	0	0	2	19¹	28	0	13	15	19.1	5.12	80	.329	.418	-0	—	-0	-6	-5	-0	-0.8
1974	KC-A	2	3	.400	30	0	0	0	1	35¹	32	3	12	24	12.2	3.82	100	.244	.327	-0	—	0	-1	-0	-0	-0.5
1975	Phi-N	0	0	—	25	0	0	0	2	21	25	3	8	20	14.6	2.57	145	.298	.366	0	.000	-0	2	4	0	-0.1
1976	Tex-A	0	4	.000	25	0	0	0	2	35	41	3	9	20	13.1	3.60	115	.310	.370	0	—	-0	-5	-4	-0	-1.1
1977	Cin-N	0	0	—	8	0	0	0	0	5²	9	0	4	3	23.8	12.71	31	.375	.500	-0	—	-0	-6	-6	-0	-1.1
Total	14	39	34	.534	493	0	0	0	99	562²	519	50	181	412	11.5	2.99	119	.249	.314	6	.102	-1	35	36	-7	5.0

YEAR	TM/L	W	L	PCT	G	GS	CG	SH	SV	IP	H	HR	BB	SO	RAT	ERA	ERA+	OAV	OOB	BH	AVG	PB	PR	/A	PD	TPI

● LEFTY HOERST Hoerst, Frank Joseph b: 8/11/17, Philadelphia, Pa. BL/TL, 6'3", 192 lbs. Deb: 4/26/40

1940	Phi-N	1	0	1.000	6	0	0	0	0	12	12	1	8	3	15.0	5.25	74	.250	.357	0	.000	-0	-2	-2	1	-0.1
1941	Phi-N	3	10	.231	37	11	1	0	0	105²	111	7	50	33	13.8	5.20	71	.275	.357	4	.182	-0	-18	-18	2	-1.7
1942	Phi-N	4	16	.200	33	22	5	0	1	150²	162	11	78	52	14.4	5.20	64	.271	.357	7	.152	-0	-32	-32	2	-3.7
1946	Phi-N	1	6	.143	18	7	2	0	0	68¹	77	4	36	17	15.0	4.61	74	.288	.375	1	.059	-1	-9	-9	-1	-1.1
1947	Phi-N	1	1	.500	4	1	0	0	0	11¹	19	1	3	0	17.5	7.94	50	.358	.393	2	.500	1	-5	-5	0	-0.6
Total	5	10	33	.233	98	41	8	0	1	348	381	24	175	105	14.5	5.17	68	.279	.362	14	.154	-1	-66	-65	4	-7.2

● RED HOFF Hoff, Chester Cornelius b: 5/8/1891, Ossining, N.Y. BL/TL, 5'9", 162 lbs. Deb: 9/6/11

1911	NY-A	0	1	.000	5	1	0	0	0	20²	21	0	7	10	12.2	2.18	165	.262	.322	2	.286	0	3	3	1	0.2
1912	NY-A	0	1	.000	5	1	0	0	0	15²	20	0	6	14	14.9	6.89	52	.303	.361	1	.200	-0	-6	-6	-0	-0.3
1913	NY-A	0	0	—	2	0	0	0	0	3	0	0	1	2	3.0	0.00	—	.000	.111	0	.000	-0	1	1	-0	0.1
1915	StL-A	2	2	.500	11	3	2	0	0	43²	26	0	24	23	10.5	1.24	232	.169	.285	3	.176	-1	8	8	1	0.7
Total	4	2	4	.333	23	5	2	0	0	83	67	0	38	49	11.5	2.49	127	.218	.305	6	.200	-1	6	6	1	0.6

● BILL HOFFER Hoffer, William Leopold "Chick" or "Wizard"
b: 11/8/1870, Cedar Rapids, Iowa d: 7/21/59, Cedar Rapids, Ia. BR/TR, 5'9", 155 lbs. Deb: 4/26/1895

1895	*Bal-N	31	6	.838	41	38	32	4	0	314	296	9	124	80	12.6	3.21	148	.245	.325	27	.214	-3	55	54	-2	4.3
1896	*Bal-N	25	7	.781	35	35	32	3	0	309	317	1	95	93	12.3	3.38	127	.263	.323	38	.304	11	34	31	2	3.6
1897	*Bal-N	22	11	.667	38	33	29	1	0	303¹	350	5	104	62	14.0	4.30	97	.287	.351	33	.237	2	-0	-4	-0	-0.3
1898	Bal-N	0	4	.000	4	4	4	0	0	34¹	62	0	16	5	20.7	7.34	49	.387	.446	5	.208	0	-14	-14	-0	-1.2
	Pit-N	3	0	1.000	4	3	3	0	0	31	26	0	15	11	11.9	1.74	204	.226	.315	1	.091	-1	6	6	-0	0.5
	Yr	3	4	.429	8	7	7	0	0	65¹	88	0	31	16	16.4	4.68	76	.319	.388	6	.171	-1	-8	-8	-0	-0.7
1899	Pit-N	8	10	.444	23	19	15	2	0	163²	169	5	64	44	13.4	3.63	105	.266	.343	18	.198	-1	4	3	-0	0.2
1901	Cle-A	3	8	.273	16	10	10	0	3	99	113	2	35	19	13.5	4.55	78	.283	.343	6	.136	-1	-10	-11	-0	-1.1
Total	6	92	46	.667	161	142	125	10	3	1254¹	1333	22	453	314	13.2	3.75	112	.270	.339	128	.229	6	76	65	-1	6.0

● DANNY HOFFMAN Hoffman, Daniel John b: 3/2/1880, Canton, Conn. d: 3/14/22, Manchester, Conn. BL/TL, 5'9", 175 lbs. Deb: 4/20/03 ♦

| 1903 | Phi-A | 0 | 0 | — | 1 | 0 | 0 | 0 | 0 | 3 | 2 | 0 | 2 | 0 | 12.0 | 3.00 | 102 | .182 | .308 | 61 | .246 | 0 | -0 | 0 | -0 | 0.0 |

● FRANK HOFFMAN Hoffman, Frank J. "The Texas Wonder" b: Houston, Tex. TR Deb: 8/13/1888

| 1888 | KC-a | 3 | 9 | .250 | 12 | 12 | 12 | 0 | 0 | 104 | 102 | 3 | 42 | 38 | 13.0 | 2.77 | 124 | .248 | .326 | 6 | .154 | -1 | 3 | 8 | 0 | 0.7 |

● GUY HOFFMAN Hoffman, Guy Alan b: 7/9/56, Ottawa, Ill. BL/TL, 5'9", 185 lbs. Deb: 7/4/79

1979	Chi-A	0	5	.000	24	0	0	0	2	30¹	30	1	23	18	16.0	5.34	80	.261	.388	0	—	0	-4	-4	0	-0.6
1980	Chi-A	1	0	1.000	23	1	0	0	1	37²	38	1	17	24	13.1	2.63	153	.268	.346	0	—	0	6	6	-1	0.1
1983	Chi-A	1	0	1.000	11	0	0	0	0	6	14	1	2	4	24.0	7.50	56	.483	.516	0	—	0	-2	-2	0	-0.6
1986	Chi-N	6	2	.750	32	8	1	0	0	84	92	6	29	47	13.2	3.86	105	.288	.351	1	.067	-1	-1	2	-1	-0.1
1987	Cin-N	9	10	.474	36	22	0	0	0	158²	160	20	49	87	12.1	4.37	97	.265	.325	5	.111	-2	-5	-2	-2	-0.6
1988	Tex-A	0	0	—	11	0	0	0	0	22¹	22	5	8	9	12.5	5.24	78	.247	.316	0	—	0	-3	-3	0	-0.1
Total	6	17	17	.500	137	31	1	0	3	339	356	33	128	187	13.1	4.25	98	.274	.343	6	.100	-2	-10	-3	-4	-1.9

● TREVOR HOFFMAN Hoffman, Trevor William b: 10/13/67, Bellflower, Cal. BR/TR, 6'1", 200 lbs. Deb: 4/6/93 F

1993	Fla-N	2	2	.500	28	0	0	0	2	35²	24	5	19	26	10.9	3.28	132	.185	.289	0	.000	-0	3	4	0	0.5
	SD-N	2	4	.333	39	0	0	0	3	54¹	56	5	20	53	12.4	4.31	96	.264	.330	1	.200	-0	-2	-1	-0	-0.2
	Yr	4	6	.400	67	0	0	0	5	90	80	10	39	79	12.0	3.90	108	.233	.313	1	.143	-0	1	3	-0	0.3
1994	SD-N	4	4	.500	47	0	0	0	20	56	39	4	20	68	9.5	2.57	160	.193	.266	0	.000	-0	10	10	0	1.8
1995	SD-N	7	4	.636	55	0	0	0	31	53¹	48	10	14	52	10.5	3.88	104	.235	.284	1	.500	1	2	1	-1	0.2
1996	*SD-N	9	5	.643	70	0	0	0	42	88	50	6	31	111	8.5	2.25	177	.161	.241	0	.000	-1	19	17	-0	3.8
Total	4	24	19	.558	239	0	0	0	98	287¹	217	30	104	310	10.1	3.13	131	.205	.278	2	.100	-1	33	31	-1	6.1

● BILL HOFFMAN Hoffman, William Joseph b: 3/3/18, Philadelphia, Pa. BL/TL, 5'9", 170 lbs. Deb: 8/13/39

| 1939 | Phi-N | 0 | 0 | — | 3 | 0 | 0 | 0 | 0 | 6 | 8 | 2 | 7 | 1 | 27.0 | 13.50 | 30 | .333 | .529 | 0 | .000 | -0 | -6 | -6 | -0 | 0.0 |

● JOHN HOFFORD Hofford, John William b: 5/25/1863, Philadelphia, Pa. d: 12/16/15, Philadelphia, Pa. Deb: 9/26/1885

1885	Pit-a	0	3	.000	3	3	3	0	0	25	28	1	9	21	13.3	3.60	89	.275	.333	1	.125	-1	-1	-1	0	-0.1
1886	Pit-a	3	6	.333	9	9	9	0	0	81	88	1	40	25	14.4	4.33	78	.261	.343	10	.294	3	-8	-9	1	-0.4
Total	2	3	9	.250	12	12	12	0	0	106	116	2	49	46	14.2	4.16	80	.264	.341	11	.262	2	-9	-10	1	-0.5

● GEORGE HOGAN Hogan, George A. b: 9/25/1885, Marion, Ohio d: 2/22/22, Bartlesville, Okla BR/TR, 6', 160 lbs. Deb: 4/18/14 F

| 1914 | KC-F | 0 | 1 | .000 | 4 | 1 | 0 | 0 | 0 | 13 | 12 | 1 | 7 | 7 | 13.8 | 4.15 | 67 | .255 | .364 | 0 | .000 | -1 | -2 | -2 | -0 | -0.2 |

● EDDIE HOGAN Hogan, Robert Edward b: 4/1860, St.Louis, Mo. BR, 5'7", 153 lbs. Deb: 7/5/1882 ♦

| 1882 | StL-a | 0 | 1 | .000 | 1 | 0 | 0 | 0 | 0 | 4 | 11 | 0 | 4 | 11.3 | 1.13 | 249 | .286 | .286 | 1 | .333 | 0 | 1 | 1 | -1 | 0.1 |

● BRAD HOGG Hogg, Carter Bradley b: 3/26/1888, Buena Vista, Ga. d: 4/2/35, Buena Vista, Ga. BR/TR, 6', 185 lbs. Deb: 9/1/11

1911	Bos-N	0	3	.000	8	3	2	0	1	25²	33	0	14	8	16.8	6.66	57	.337	.425	4	.444	1	-9	-8	0	-0.7
1912	Bos-N	1	1	.500	10	1	0	0	1	31	37	2	16	12	16.0	6.97	51	.308	.399	1	.091	-1	-12	-12	-1	-0.8
1915	Chi-N	1	0	1.000	2	1	1	0	0	13	12	1	6	0	13.2	2.08	134	.245	.339	0	.000	-0	1	1	0	0.1
1918	Phi-N	13	13	.500	29	25	17	3	1	228	201	3	61	81	10.6	2.53	119	.245	.302	18	.228	3	6	12	2	2.0
1919	Phi-N	5	12	.294	22	19	13	0	0	150¹	163	7	55	48	13.4	4.43	73	.292	.360	17	.283	3	-25	-20	-2	-2.1
Total	5	20	29	.408	71	50	33	4	3	448	446	13	152	149	12.3	3.70	85	.271	.338	40	.247	5	-40	-27	-0	-1.5

● BILL HOGG Hogg, William Johnston "Buffalo Bill" b: 9/11/1881, Port Huron, Mich. d: 12/8/09, New Orleans, La. BR/TR, 6', 200 lbs. Deb: 4/25/05

1905	NY-A	9	13	.409	39	22	9	3	1	205	178	1	101	125	12.8	3.20	92	.236	.336	4	.060	-1	-13	-6	-5	-1.8
1906	NY-A	14	13	.519	28	25	15	3	0	206	171	5	72	107	11.1	2.93	101	.229	.307	5	.125	-5	-5	1	-5	-0.9
1907	NY-A	10	8	.556	25	21	13	0	0	166²	173	3	83	64	14.1	3.08	91	.270	.359	11	.183	-0	-10	-5	-2	-0.8
1908	NY-A	4	16	.200	24	21	6	0	0	152¹	155	4	63	72	13.1	3.01	82	.262	.337	4	.093	-3	-10	-9	-2	-1.7
Total	4	37	50	.425	116	89	43	6	1	730	677	13	319	368	12.7	3.06	92	.248	.334	28	.116	-14	-38	-20	-13	-5.2

● CHIEF HOGSETT Hogsett, Elon Chester b: 11/2/03, Brownell, Kan. BL/TL, 6', 190 lbs. Deb: 9/18/29

1929	Det-A	1	2	.333	4	4	2	1	0	28²	34	0	9	9	13.8	2.83	152	.312	.370	2	.200	-0	5	5	0	0.4
1930	Det-A	9	8	.529	33	17	4	0	1	146	174	9	63	54	15.2	5.42	88	.300	.377	17	.293	-3	-13	-10	2	-0.6
1931	Det-A	3	9	.250	22	12	5	0	2	112¹	150	8	33	47	15.1	5.93	77	.324	.375	11	.234	-0	-19	-17	0	-1.5
1932	Det-A	11	9	.550	47	15	7	0	7	178	201	8	66	56	13.8	3.54	133	.286	.351	14	.246	3	19	23	2	2.9
1933	Det-A	6	10	.375	45	2	0	0	9	116	137	7	56	39	15.3	4.50	96	.296	.377	8	.211	-0	-3	-2	1	-0.3
1934	*Det-A	3	2	.600	26	0	0	0	1	50¹	61	6	19	23	14.5	4.29	102	.303	.367	3	.231	-0	1	1	0	0.1
1935	*Det-A	6	6	.500	40	6	1	0	5	96²	109	8	49	39	15.2	3.54	118	.288	.377	6	.261	2	10	7	3	1.2
1936	Det-A	0	1	.000	3	0	0	0	0	4	8	1	2	1	20.3	9.00	55	.400	.429	0	—	-0	-2	-2	-0	-0.3
	StL-A	13	15	.464	39	29	10	0	1	215¹	278	15	90	67	16.0	5.52	97	.310	.383	10	.143	-2	-11	-3	-1	-0.5
	Yr	13	16	.448	42	29	10	0	1	219¹	286	16	91	68	16.1	5.58	96	.312	.384	10	.143	-2	-13	-5	-1	-0.8
1937	StL-A	6	19	.240	37	26	8	1	2	177¹	245	16	75	68	16.5	6.29	77	.328	.393	13	.210	-0	-33	-29	-1	-3.3
1938	Was-A	5	6	.455	31	9	1	0	3	91	107	12	36	33	14.9	6.03	75	.292	.368	7	.304	1	-13	-15	0	-1.3
1944	Det-A	0	0	—	3	0	0	0	0	6¹	7	1	4	5	18.5	0.00	—	.250	.382	0	.000	-0	2	3	-0	0.0
Total	11	63	87	.420	330	114	37	2	33	1222	1511	85	501	441	15.3	5.02	94	.305	.376	91	.226	8	-57	-42	9	-3.2

● CAL HOGUE Hogue, Calvin Grey b: 10/24/27, Dayton, Ohio BR/TR, 6', 185 lbs. Deb: 7/15/52

1952	Pit-N	1	8	.111	19	12	3	0	0	83²	77	7	68	34	16.2	4.84	82	.258	.399	6	.250	1	-10	-8	-2	-0.8
1953	Pit-N	1	1	.500	3	2	2	0	0	19	19	4	16	10	17.1	5.21	86	.250	.387	0	.000	-1	-2	-2	0	-0.2
1954	Pit-N	0	1	.000	3	2	0	0	0	11	13	1	12	7	18.8	4.91	85	.282	.451	0	.000	-0	-1	-1	0	-0.1
Total	3	2	10	.167	25	16	5	0	0	113²	109	12	96	51	16.6	4.91	84	.259	.402	6	.188	-0	-13	-10	-1	-1.1

YEAR	TM/L	W	L	PCT	G	GS	CG	SH	SV	IP	H	HR	BB	SO	RAT	ERA	ERA+	OAV	OOB	BH	AVG	PB	PR	/A	PD	TPI
● **BOBBY HOGUE**					Hogue, Robert Clinton b: 4/5/21, Miami, Fla. d: 12/22/87, Miami, Fla. BR/TR, 5'10", 195 lbs. Deb: 4/24/48																				
1948	Bos-N	8	2	.800	40	1	0	0	2	86¹	88	4	19	43	11.4	3.23	119	.265	.309	2	.095	-1	7	6	-1	0.4
1949	Bos-N	2	2	.500	33	0	0	0	3	72	78	4	25	23	13.1	3.13	121	.280	.343	6	.286	1	7	5	2	0.6
1950	Bos-N	3	5	.375	36	1	0	0	7	62²	69	8	31	15	14.9	5.03	77	.280	.370	3	.231	1	-6	-8	1	-1.0
1951	Bos-N	0	0	—	3	0	0	0	0	5	4	1	3	0	12.6	5.40	68	.235	.350	1	.500	0	-1	-1	-0	0.0
	StL-A	1	1	.500	18	0	0	0	1	29²	31	1	23	11	16.4	5.16	85	.279	.403	2	.667	-1	-3	-3	1	0.0
	*NY-A	1	0	1.000	7	0	0	0	0	7¹	4	0	3	2	8.6	0.00	—	.174	.269	0	—	0	3	3	0	0.4
	Yr	2	1	.667	25	0	0	0	1	37	35	1	26	13	14.8	4.14	104	.261	.381	2	.667	-1	-0	1	1	0.4
1952	NY-A	3	5	.375	27	0	0	0	4	47¹	52	6	25	12	14.8	5.32	62	.294	.384	3	.273	0	-9	-11	-1	-1.9
	StL-A	0	1	.000	8	1	0	0	0	16¹	10	1	13	2	12.7	2.76	142	.179	.333	0	.000	-0	2	2	0	0.1
	Yr	3	6	.333	35	1	0	0	4	63²	62	7	38	14	14.1	4.66	74	.265	.368	3	.231	0	-7	-8	-1	-1.8
Total	5	18	16	.529	172	3	0	0	17	326²	336	25	142	108	13.4	3.97	96	.271	.350	17	.233	3	-0	-6	1	-1.4
● **WALLY HOLBOROW**					Holborow, Walter Albert b: 11/30/13, New York, N.Y. d: 7/14/86, Ft.Lauderdale, Fla. BR/TR, 5'11", 187 lbs. Deb: 9/27/44																				
1944	Was-A	0	0	—	1	0	0	0	0	3	0	0	2	1	6.0	0.00	—	.000	.182	0	—	0	1	1	0	0.0
1945	Was-A	1	1	.500	15	1	1	1	0	31¹	20	0	16	14	10.3	2.30	135	.189	.295	0	.000	-0	4	3	-1	0.1
1948	Phi-N	1	2	.333	5	1	1	0	0	17¹	32	1	7	3	20.3	5.71	75	.421	.470	2	.500	1	-3	-3	1	-0.2
Total	3	2	3	.400	21	2	2	1	0	51²	52	1	25	18	13.4	3.31	106	.272	.356	2	.333	1	2	1	-0	-0.1
● **KEN HOLCOMBE**					Holcombe, Kenneth Edward b: 8/23/18, Burnsville, N.C. BR/TR, 5'11.5", 169 lbs. Deb: 4/27/45																				
1945	NY-A	3	3	.500	23	6	0	0	0	55¹	43	3	27	20	11.4	1.79	194	.226	.323	2	.133	-1	10	10	-0	1.0
1948	Cin-N	0	0	—	2	0	0	0	0	2¹	3	0	0	2	11.6	7.71	51	.300	.300	0	—	0	-1	-1	-0	0.0
1950	Chi-A	3	10	.231	24	15	5	0	1	96	122	10	45	37	15.7	4.59	98	.307	.378	5	.156	-2	-0	-1	-0	-0.3
1951	Chi-A	11	12	.478	28	23	12	2	0	159¹	142	9	68	39	11.9	3.78	107	.241	.321	11	.250	1	6	4	2	0.9
1952	Chi-A	0	5	.000	7	7	1	0	0	35	38	3	18	12	14.9	6.17	59	.286	.379	0	.000	-1	-10	-10	0	-1.3
	StL-A	0	2	.000	12	1	0	0	0	21	20	1	9	7	12.4	3.86	101	.263	.341	1	.333	-0	-0	-0	1	0.1
	Yr	0	7	.000	19	8	1	0	0	56	58	4	27	19	13.7	5.30	71	.275	.357	1	.077	-1	-10	-10	1	-1.2
1953	Bos-A	1	0	1.000	3	0	0	1	0	3	9	0	3	1	18.0	6.00	70	.333	.400	0	.000	-0	-1	-1	-0	0.2
Total	6	18	32	.360	99	48	18	2	2	375	377	25	170	118	13.2	3.98	101	.265	.345	19	.179	-3	3	2	3	0.2
● **FRED HOLDSWORTH**					Holdsworth, Fredrick William b: 5/29/52, Detroit, Mich. BR/TR, 6'1", 190 lbs. Deb: 7/27/72																				
1972	Det-A	0	1	.000	2	2	0	0	0	7	13	0	2	5	19.3	12.86	24	.419	.455	1	.333	0	-8	-8	-0	-0.8
1973	Det-A	0	0	—	5	2	0	0	0	14²	13	3	6	9	11.7	6.75	61	.236	.311	0	—	0	-5	-4	-0	-0.7
1974	Det-A	0	3	.000	8	5	0	0	0	35²	40	4	14	16	13.9	4.29	89	.286	.351	0	—	0	-3	-2	-1	-0.5
1976	Bal-A	4	1	.800	16	0	0	0	2	39²	24	0	13	24	8.4	2.04	160	.179	.252	0	—	0	7	5	-0	0.8
1977	Bal-A	0	1	.000	12	0	0	0	0	14¹	17	0	16	4	21.3	6.28	60	.333	.500	0	—	0	-4	-4	0	0.2
	Mon-N	3	3	.500	14	6	1	0	0	42¹	35	6	18	21	11.3	3.19	119	.230	.312	0	.000	-1	3	3	0	0.3
1978	Mon-N	0	0	—	6	0	0	0	0	8²	16	3	8	3	24.9	7.27	48	.381	.480	0	—	0	-4	-4	-0	0.0
1980	Mil-A	0	0	—	9	0	0	0	0	19²	24	2	9	12	15.1	4.58	85	.286	.355	0	—	0	-1	-2	0	0.2
Total	7	7	10	.412	72	15	0	0	2	182	182	18	86	94	13.4	4.64	84	.264	.347	1	.077	-1	-13	-15	-2	-0.4
● **WALTER HOLKE**					Holke, Walter Henry "Union Man" b: 12/25/1892, St.Louis, Mo. d: 10/12/54, St.Louis, Mo. BB/TL, 6'1.5", 185 lbs. Deb: 10/6/14 C♦																				
1923	Phi-N	0	0	—	1	0	0	0	0	0¹	1	0	0	0	27.0	0.00	—	.500	.500	175	.311	0	0	0	0	0.0
● **AL HOLLAND**					Holland, Alfred Willis b: 8/16/52, Roanoke, Va. BR/TL, 5'11", 207 lbs. Deb: 9/5/77																				
1977	Pit-N	0	0	—	2	0	0	0	0	2¹	4	0	5	2	15.4	7.71	52	.400	.400	0	—	0	-1	-1	-0	0.0
1979	SF-N	0	0	—	3	0	0	0	0	7	3	0	5	7	10.3	0.00	—	.125	.276	0	—	0	3	3	-0	0.4
1980	SF-N	5	3	.625	54	0	0	0	7	82¹	71	2	34	65	11.6	1.75	202	.233	.312	1	.200	1	17	16	0	2.0
1981	SF-N	7	5	.583	47	3	0	0	7	100²	87	4	44	78	11.9	2.41	142	.233	.317	1	.063	-1	12	11	1	1.3
1982	SF-N	7	3	.700	58	7	0	0	5	129²	115	12	40	97	10.8	3.33	108	.231	.289	2	.059	-3	4	4	0	0.3
1983	*Phi-N	8	4	.667	68	0	0	0	25	91²	63	8	30	100	9.1	2.26	158	.188	.255	0	.000	-1	14	13	-2	2.1
1984	Phi-N☆	5	10	.333	68	0	0	0	29	98¹	82	14	30	61	10.3	3.39	107	.225	.286	0	.000	-1	2	3	-2	0.3
1985	Phi-N	0	1	.000	3	0	0	0	1	4	5	0	4	1	20.3	4.50	82	.333	.474	—	—	0	-0	-0	-0	-0.1
	Pit-N	1	3	.250	38	0	0	0	4	58²	48	5	17	47	10.0	3.38	106	.227	.285	2	.400	2	1	1	-1	0.1
	Yr	1	4	.200	41	0	0	0	5	62²	53	5	21	48	10.6	3.45	104	.233	.298	2	.400	2	1	1	-1	0.1
	Cal-A	0	1	.000	15	0	0	0	0	24¹	17	4	10	14	10.0	1.48	278	.193	.276	0	—	0	7	7	-0	0.3
1986	NY-A	1	0	1.000	25	1	0	0	0	40²	44	5	9	37	11.7	5.09	80	.268	.306	0	—	0	-4	-5	-1	-0.2
1987	NY-A	0	0	—	3	0	0	0	0	6¹	9	1	9	5	25.6	14.21	31	.321	.486	0	—	0	-7	-7	-0	0.0
Total	10	34	30	.531	384	11	0	0	78	646	548	55	232	513	10.9	2.98	121	.227	.296	6	.083	-2	48	46	-6	5.9
● **MUL HOLLAND**					Holland, Howard Arthur b: 1/6/03, Franklin, Va. d: 2/16/69, Winchester, Va. BR/TR, 6'4", 185 lbs. Deb: 5/25/26																				
1926	Cin-N	0	0	—	3	0	0	0	0	6²	3	0	5	0	10.8	1.35	273	.136	.296	1	.500	1	2	1	0	0.1
1927	NY-N	1	0	1.000	2	0	0	0	0	2	0	0	3	0	13.5	0.00	—	.000	.333	0	—	0	1	1	-0	0.4
1929	StL-N	0	1	.000	8	0	0	0	0	14¹	13	3	7	5	13.2	9.42	50	.232	.328	1	.250	0	-7	-8	-0	-0.4
Total	3	1	1	.500	13	0	0	0	0	23	16	3	15	5	12.5	6.26	69	.190	.320	2	.333	1	-5	-5	0	0.1
● **BILL HOLLAND**					Holland, William David "Dutch" b: 6/4/15, Varina, N.C. BL/TL, 6'1", 190 lbs. Deb: 9/17/39																				
1939	Was-A	0	1	.000	4	6	1	5	2	4	6	1	5	2	24.8	11.25	39	.400	.550	0	—	0	-3	-3	0	-0.6
● **ED HOLLEY**					Holley, Edward Edgar b: 7/23/1899, Benton, Ky. d: 10/26/86, Paducah, Ky. BR/TR, 6'1.5", 195 lbs. Deb: 5/24/28																				
1928	Chi-N	0	0	—	13	1	0	0	0	31	31	1	16	10	14.2	3.77	102	.265	.363	0	.000	-0	1	0	-1	-0.1
1932	Phi-N	11	14	.440	34	30	16	2	0	228	247	15	55	87	12.2	3.95	112	.273	.319	12	.132	-6	-2	12	-2	0.4
1933	Phi-N	13	15	.464	30	28	12	3	0	206²	219	18	62	56	12.8	3.53	108	.273	.335	12	.162	-2	-4	7	-3	0.4
1934	Phi-N	1	8	.111	15	13	2	0	0	72²	85	10	31	14	14.9	7.18	66	.294	.370	5	.208	-1	-25	-20	-2	-2.2
	Pit-N	0	3	.000	5	4	0	0	0	9¹	20	1	6	2	27.0	15.43	27	.426	.509	2	1.000	-1	-12	-12	-0	-2.4
	Yr	1	11	.083	20	17	2	0	0	82	105	11	37	16	15.8	8.12	57	.309	.380	7	.269	-1	-37	-32	-1	-4.6
Total	4	25	40	.385	97	76	30	5	0	547²	602	45	170	169	13.1	4.40	95	.279	.339	31	.158	-8	-42	-13	-6	-3.9
● **BUG HOLLIDAY**					Holliday, James Wear b: 2/8/1867, St.Louis, Mo. d: 2/15/10, Cincinnati, Ohio BR/TR, 5'11", 151 lbs. Deb: 4/17/1889 U♦																				
1892	Cin-N	0	0	—	1	0	0	0	0	4	13	0	4	0	31.5	11.25	29	.520	.538	176	.292	0	-4	-4	0	0.0
1896	Cin-N	0	0	—	1	0	0	0	0	1	4	0	2	0	63.0	0.00	—	.571	.700	27	.321	0	0	-1	-0	0.0
Total	2	0	0	—	2	0	0	0	0	5	17	0	3	0	37.8	9.00	39	.531	.583	1134	.311	1	-3	-5	0	0.0
● **CARL HOLLING**					Holling, Carl b: 7/9/1896, Dana, Cal. d: 7/18/62, Santa Rosa, Cal. BR/TR, 6'1", 172 lbs. Deb: 4/19/21																				
1921	Det-A	3	7	.300	35	11	4	0	4	136	162	8	58	38	14.8	4.30	99	.305	.378	13	.271	1	-0	-0	2	0.2
1922	Det-A	1	1	.500	5	1	0	0	0	9¹	21	1	5	2	27.0	15.43	25	.525	.596	0	.000	-0	-12	-12	0	-1.9
Total	2	4	8	.333	40	12	4	0	4	145¹	183	9	63	40	15.6	5.02	85	.320	.394	13	.260	1	-12	-12	2	-1.7
● **AL HOLLINGSWORTH**					Hollingsworth, Albert Wayne "Boots" b: 2/25/08, St.Louis, Mo. d: 4/28/96, Austin, Tex. BL/TL, 6', 174 lbs. Deb: 4/16/35 C																				
1935	Cin-N	6	13	.316	38	22	8	0	0	173¹	165	5	79	89	12.6	3.89	102	.243	.321	8	.148	-2	2	-1	2	0.0
1936	Cin-N	9	10	.474	29	25	9	0	0	184	204	4	66	76	13.5	4.16	92	.281	.345	23	.315	3	-3	-7	-2	-0.1
1937	Cin-N	9	15	.375	43	24	11	1	5	202¹	224	8	73	74	13.3	3.91	95	.278	.339	19	.250	3	0	-4	1	-0.1
1938	Cin-N	2	2	.500	9	4	1	0	0	34	43	2	12	13	14.6	7.15	51	.307	.362	3	.250	-1	-13	-13	-0	-1.2
	Phi-N	5	16	.238	24	21	11	1	0	174¹	177	4	77	80	13.1	3.82	102	.264	.340	15	.224	-0	-1	1	-1	-0.1
	Yr	7	18	.280	33	25	12	1	0	208¹	220	6	89	93	13.3	4.36	88	.272	.344	18	.228	-1	-13	-12	-2	-1.3
1939	Phi-N	1	9	.100	15	10	3	0	0	60	78	2	27	24	15.6	6.90	57	.317	.385	2	.100	-1	-13	-12	-1	-1.9
	Bro-N	1	2	.333	8	5	1	0	0	27¹	33	1	11	11	14.8	5.27	76	.311	.381	1	.125	-1	-4	-4	-1	-0.3
	Yr	2	11	.154	23	15	4	0	0	87¹	111	3	38	35	15.5	6.39	64	.315	.384	3	.107	-2	-17	-16	-2	-2.2
1940	Was-A	1	1	.500	9	2	1	0	0	17	15	1	7	14	14.5	5.50	76	.261	.363	1	.167	0	-1	1	0	0.0
1942	StL-A	10	6	.625	33	18	7	1	4	161	173	4	52	60	12.7	2.96	125	.272	.329	10	.179	1	12	13	0	1.4
1943	StL-A	6	13	.316	35	20	9	1	3	154	169	7	51	63	13.0	4.21	79	.281	.339	7	.140	-1	-16	-15	-1	-2.0

YEAR	TM/L	W	L	PCT	G	GS	CG	SH	SV	IP	H	HR	BB	SO	RAT	ERA	ERA+	OAV	OOB	BH	AVG	PB	PR	/A	PD	TPI
1944	*StL-A	5	7	.417	26	10	3	2	1	92^2	108	3	37	22	14.2	4.47	81	.291	.357	2	.071	-2	-11	-9	-1	-1.4
1945	StL-A	12	9	.571	26	22	15	1	1	173^1	164	4	68	64	12.0	2.70	130	.251	.322	12	.197	1	13	16	2	2.2
1946	StL-A	0	0	—	5	0	0	0	0	11	23	1	4	3	22.1	6.55	57	.411	.450	0	.000	-0	-4	-3	-1	-0.1
	Chi-A	3	2	.600	21	2	0	0	1	55	63	2	22	22	13.9	4.58	74	.288	.353	0	.000	-1	-7	-7	-0	-0.8
	Yr	3	2	.600	26	2	0	0	1	66	86	3	26	25	15.3	4.91	71	.313	.372	0	.000	-1	-10	-11	-1	-0.9
Total 11		70	104	.402	315	185	78	7	15	1520^1	1642	47	587	608	13.3	3.99	93	.275	.341	103	.196	3	-44	-44	-2	-4.4

● **BONNIE HOLLINGSWORTH** Hollingsworth, John Burnette b: 12/26/1895, Jacksboro, Tenn. d: 1/4/90, Knoxville, Tenn. BR/TR, 5'10", 170 lbs. Deb: 5/30/22

YEAR	TM/L	W	L	PCT	G	GS	CG	SH	SV	IP	H	HR	BB	SO	RAT	ERA	ERA+	OAV	OOB	BH	AVG	PB	PR	/A	PD	TPI
1922	Pit-N	0	0	—	9	0	0	0	0	13^2	17	0	8	7	17.1	7.90	52	.315	.413	0	—	0	-6	-6	-0	0.0
1923	Was-A	3	7	.300	17	8	1	0	0	72^2	72	3	50	26	15.5	4.09	92	.272	.393	2	.091	-1	-1	-3	-1	-0.5
1924	Bro-N	1	0	1.000	3	1	1	0	0	8^2	8	0	10	7	18.7	6.23	60	.267	.450	0	.000	-1	-2	-2	0	-0.3
1928	Bos-N	0	2	.000	7	2	0	0	0	22^1	30	2	13	10	17.3	5.24	75	.341	.426	1	.167	-0	-3	-3	0	-0.2
Total 4		4	9	.308	36	11	2	0	0	117^1	127	5	81	50	16.3	4.91	78	.291	.406	3	.097	-2	-12	-14	-1	-1.0

● **JESSIE HOLLINS** Hollins, Jessie Edward b: 1/27/70, Conroe, Tex. BR/TR, 6'3", 190 lbs. Deb: 9/19/92

YEAR	TM/L	W	L	PCT	G	GS	CG	SH	SV	IP	H	HR	BB	SO	RAT	ERA	ERA+	OAV	OOB	BH	AVG	PB	PR	/A	PD	TPI
1992	Chi-N	0	0	—	4	0	0	0	0	4^2	8	1	5	0	25.1	13.50	27	.400	.520	0	—	0	-5	-5	-0	0.0

● **JOHN HOLLISON** Hollison, John Henry "Swede" b: 5/3/1870, Chicago, Ill. d: 8/19/69, Chicago, Ill. BR/TL, 5'8", 162 lbs. Deb: 8/13/1892

YEAR	TM/L	W	L	PCT	G	GS	CG	SH	SV	IP	H	HR	BB	SO	RAT	ERA	ERA+	OAV	OOB	BH	AVG	PB	PR	/A	PD	TPI
1892	Chi-N	0	0	—	1	0	0	0	0	4	1	1	0	2	2.3	2.25	148	.077	.077		.000	-0	0	0	0	0.0

● **BOBO HOLLOMAN** Holloman, Alva Lee b: 3/7/25, Thomaston, Ga. d: 5/1/87, Athens, Ga. BR/TR, 6'2", 207 lbs. Deb: 4/18/53

YEAR	TM/L	W	L	PCT	G	GS	CG	SH	SV	IP	H	HR	BB	SO	RAT	ERA	ERA+	OAV	OOB	BH	AVG	PB	PR	/A	PD	TPI
1953	StL-A	3	7	.300	22	10	1	1	0	65^1	69	2	50	25	16.5	5.23	80	.275	.397	2	.105	-2	-9	-8	-0	-1.2

● **JIM HOLLOWAY** Holloway, James Madison b: 9/22/08, Plaquemine, La. BR/TR, 6'1", 165 lbs. Deb: 5/17/29

YEAR	TM/L	W	L	PCT	G	GS	CG	SH	SV	IP	H	HR	BB	SO	RAT	ERA	ERA+	OAV	OOB	BH	AVG	PB	PR	/A	PD	TPI
1929	Phi-N	0	0	—	3	0	0	0	0	4^2	10	2	5	1	28.9	13.50	38	.455	.556	1	1.000	0	-5	-4	-0	0.0

● **KEN HOLLOWAY** Holloway, Kenneth Eugene (b: Kenneth Eugene Hollaway) b: 8/8/1897, Thomas County, Ga. d: 9/25/68, Thomasville, Ga. BR/TR, 6', 185 lbs. Deb: 8/27/22

YEAR	TM/L	W	L	PCT	G	GS	CG	SH	SV	IP	H	HR	BB	SO	RAT	ERA	ERA+	OAV	OOB	BH	AVG	PB	PR	/A	PD	TPI
1922	Det-A	0	0	—	1	0	0	0	0	1	0	0	0	1	9.0	0.00	—	.250	.250	0	—	0	0	0	0	0.0
1923	Det-A	11	10	.524	42	24	7	1	1	194	232	12	75	55	14.7	4.45	87	.302	.372	8	.123	-5	-10	-13	1	-1.5
1924	Det-A	14	6	.700	49	13	5	0	3	181^1	209	6	61	46	13.7	4.07	101	.299	.361	11	.190	-1	3	1	2	0.2
1925	Det-A	13	4	.765	38	14	6	0	2	157^2	170	8	67	29	13.6	4.62	93	.282	.356	11	.229	-0	-4	-6	-2	-0.8
1926	Det-A	4	6	.400	36	12	3	0	2	139	192	2	42	43	15.7	5.12	79	.343	.397	11	.239	0	-17	-16	0	-1.0
1927	Det-A	11	12	.478	36	23	11	1	6	183^1	210	10	61	36	13.5	4.07	103	.299	.359	8	.129	-5	1	3	2	0.0
1928	Det-A	4	8	.333	30	11	5	0	2	120^1	137	2	32	32	13.0	4.34	95	.291	.343	4	.121	-2	-4	-3	1	-0.4
1929	Cle-A	6	5	.545	25	11	6	0	2	119	118	2	37	32	11.9	3.03	147	.264	.323	7	.171	-2	16	19	-2	1.2
1930	Cle-A	1	1	.500	12	2	0	0	2	30	49	5	14	8	18.9	8.40	57	.374	.434	0	.000	-2	-13	-12	1	-0.9
	NY-A	0	0	—	16	0	0	0	0	34^1	52	3	8	11	15.7	5.24	82	.374	.408	3	.231	-0	-2	-4	-0	-0.9
	Yr	1	1	.500	28	2	0	0	2	64^1	101	8	22	19	17.2	6.72	68	.374	.421	3	.120	-1	-15	-16	1	-0.9
Total 9		64	52	.552	285	110	43	4	18	1160	1370	50	397	293	14.0	4.40	95	.303	.364	63	.167	-18	-29	-30	-1	-3.2

● **JEFF HOLLY** Holly, Jeffrey Owen b: 3/1/53, San Pedro, Cal. BL/TL, 6'5", 210 lbs. Deb: 5/1/77

YEAR	TM/L	W	L	PCT	G	GS	CG	SH	SV	IP	H	HR	BB	SO	RAT	ERA	ERA+	OAV	OOB	BH	AVG	PB	PR	/A	PD	TPI
1977	Min-A	2	3	.400	18	5	0	0	0	48^1	57	8	12	32	13.0	6.89	58	.300	.345	0	—	0	-15	-16	-1	-1.3
1978	Min-A	1	1	.500	15	1	0	0	0	35^1	28	1	18	12	11.7	3.57	107	.222	.319	0	—	0	1	1	0	0.0
1979	Min-A	0	0	—	6	0	0	0	0	6^1	10	0	3	5	18.5	7.11	62	.385	.448	0	—	0	-2	-2	0	0.0
Total 3		3	4	.429	39	6	0	0	0	90	95	9	33	49	12.9	5.60	70	.278	.343	0	—	0	-16	-17	-0	-1.3

● **BRAD HOLMAN** Holman, Bradly Thomas b: 2/9/68, Kansas City, Mo. BR/TR, 6'5", 200 lbs. Deb: 7/4/93 F

YEAR	TM/L	W	L	PCT	G	GS	CG	SH	SV	IP	H	HR	BB	SO	RAT	ERA	ERA+	OAV	OOB	BH	AVG	PB	PR	/A	PD	TPI
1993	Sea-A	1	3	.250	19	0	0	0	3	36^1	27	1	16	17	11.9	3.72	118	.208	.318	0	—	0	2	3	-1	0.2

● **BRIAN HOLMAN** Holman, Brian Scott b: 1/25/65, Denver, Colo. BR/TR, 6'4", 185 lbs. Deb: 6/25/88 F

YEAR	TM/L	W	L	PCT	G	GS	CG	SH	SV	IP	H	HR	BB	SO	RAT	ERA	ERA+	OAV	OOB	BH	AVG	PB	PR	/A	PD	TPI
1988	Mon-N	4	8	.333	18	16	1	1	0	100^1	101	3	34	58	12.1	3.23	111	.264	.324	3	.107	-1	2	4	-1	0.2
1989	Mon-N	1	2	.333	10	3	0	0	0	31^2	34	2	15	23	14.2	4.83	73	.270	.352	1	.125	-0	-5	-5	-0	-0.5
	Sea-A	8	10	.444	23	22	6	2	0	159^2	160	9	62	82	12.9	3.44	117	.261	.335	0	—	0	8	10	1	1.2
1990	Sea-A	11	11	.500	28	28	3	0	0	189^2	188	17	66	121	12.3	4.03	98	.260	.327	0	.000	-0	-3	-2	-1	-0.3
1991	Sea-A	13	14	.481	30	30	5	0	0	195^1	199	16	77	108	13.2	3.69	112	.268	.345	0	—	0	9	9	2	1.4
Total 4		37	45	.451	109	99	15	6	0	676^2	682	47	254	392	12.8	3.71	106	.263	.335	4	.108	-1	12	18	-0	2.0

● **SCOTT HOLMAN** Holman, Randy Scott b: 9/18/58, Santa Paula, Cal. BR/TR, 6'1", 190 lbs. Deb: 9/20/80

YEAR	TM/L	W	L	PCT	G	GS	CG	SH	SV	IP	H	HR	BB	SO	RAT	ERA	ERA+	OAV	OOB	BH	AVG	PB	PR	/A	PD	TPI
1980	NY-N	0	0	—	4	0	0	0	0	7	6	0	1	6	9.0	1.29	276	.250	.280	0	—	0	2	2	-0	0.0
1982	NY-N	2	1	.667	4	4	1	0	0	26^2	24	1	9	10	10.1	2.36	154	.232	.283	2	.222	0	4	4	1	0.5
1983	NY-N	1	7	.125	35	10	0	0	0	101	90	7	52	44	12.7	3.74	97	.242	.336	5	.217	0	-1	-1	2	0.2
Total 3		3	8	.273	43	14	1	0	0	134^2	119	9	60	58	12.0	3.34	108	.240	.324	7	.219	1	4	4	2	0.7

● **SHAWN HOLMAN** Holman, Shawn Leroy b: 11/10/64, Sewickley, Pa. BR/TR, 6'2", 185 lbs. Deb: 9/5/89

YEAR	TM/L	W	L	PCT	G	GS	CG	SH	SV	IP	H	HR	BB	SO	RAT	ERA	ERA+	OAV	OOB	BH	AVG	PB	PR	/A	PD	TPI
1989	Det-A	0	0	—	5	0	0	0	0	10	8	0	11	9	17.1	1.80	212	.211	.388	0	—	0	2	2	-0	0.0

● **DARREN HOLMES** Holmes, Darren Lee b: 4/25/66, Asheville, N.C. BR/TR, 6', 199 lbs. Deb: 9/1/90

YEAR	TM/L	W	L	PCT	G	GS	CG	SH	SV	IP	H	HR	BB	SO	RAT	ERA	ERA+	OAV	OOB	BH	AVG	PB	PR	/A	PD	TPI
1990	LA-N	0	1	.000	14	0	0	0	0	17^1	15	1	11	19	13.5	5.19	70	.238	.351	0	—	0	-3	-3	-0	-0.2
1991	Mil-A	1	4	.200	40	0	0	0	3	76^1	90	6	27	59	13.9	4.72	84	.295	.354	0	—	0	-5	-6	1	-0.2
1992	Mil-A	4	4	.500	41	0	0	0	6	42^1	35	1	11	31	10.2	2.55	150	.224	.284	0	—	0	7	6	0	1.3
1993	Col-N	3	3	.500	62	0	0	0	25	66^2	56	6	20	60	10.5	4.05	118	.222	.285	0	—	0	-0	5	0	0.8
1994	Col-N	0	3	.000	29	0	0	0	3	28^1	35	5	24	33	19.1	6.35	78	.313	.438	0	.000	-0	-7	-4	-0	-0.5
1995	*Col-N	6	1	.857	68	0	0	0	14	66^2	59	3	28	61	11.9	3.24	166	.237	.317	0	.000	-0	7	16	1	2.2
1996	Col-N	4	9	.556	62	0	0	0	1	77	78	8	28	73	12.5	3.97	137	.259	.324	0	.000	-0	2	12	-1	1.3
Total 7		19	25	.487	316	0	0	0	52	374^2	368	30	149	336	12.6	4.08	115	.256	.329	0	.000	-0	4	26	1	4.7

● **CHICK HOLMES** Holmes, Elwood Marter b: 3/22/1896, Beverly, N.J. d: 4/15/54, Camden, N.J. TR, Deb: 6/27/18

YEAR	TM/L	W	L	PCT	G	GS	CG	SH	SV	IP	H	HR	BB	SO	RAT	ERA	ERA+	OAV	OOB	BH	AVG	PB	PR	/A	PD	TPI
1918	Phi-A	0	0	—	2	0	0	0	0	2	4	0	1	0	27.0	13.50	22	.400	.500	0	—	0	-2	-2	-0	0.0

● **JIM HOLMES** Holmes, James Scott b: 8/2/1882, Lawrenceburg, Ky. d: 3/10/60, Jacksonville, Fla. Deb: 9/8/06

YEAR	TM/L	W	L	PCT	G	GS	CG	SH	SV	IP	H	HR	BB	SO	RAT	ERA	ERA+	OAV	OOB	BH	AVG	PB	PR	/A	PD	TPI
1906	Phi-A	0	1	.000	3	1	0	0	0	9	10	0	4	1	19.0	4.00	68	.286	.432	3	.600	1	-1	-1	0	0.0
1908	Bro-N	1	4	.200	13	1	1	0	0	40	37	0	20	10	13.5	3.37	69	.270	.375	4	.077	-1	-4	-5	-2	-0.9
Total 2		1	5	.167	16	2	1	0	0	49	47	0	24	11	14.3	3.53	69	.273	.387	4	.222	-2	-6	-6	-2	-0.9

● **DUCKY HOLMES** Holmes, James William b: 1/28/1869, Des Moines, Iowa d: 8/6/32, Truro, Iowa BL/TR, 5'6", 170 lbs. Deb: 8/8/1895 ♦

YEAR	TM/L	W	L	PCT	G	GS	CG	SH	SV	IP	H	HR	BB	SO	RAT	ERA	ERA+	OAV	OOB	BH	AVG	PB	PR	/A	PD	TPI
1895	Lou-N	1	0	1.000	2	1	0	0	0	14	16	1	4	0	13.5	5.79	80	.281	.339	60	.373	1	-2	-2	0	-0.2
1896	Lou-N	0	1	.000	2	1	0	0	0	12	26	0	8	3	25.5	7.50	58	.433	.500	38	.270	0	-4	-4	0	-0.2
Total 2		1	1	.500	4	2	1	0	0	26	42	1	12	3	19.0	6.58	68	.359	.423	1014	.282	1	-6	-6	0	-0.2

● **HERM HOLSHOUSER** Holshouser, Herman Alexander b: 1/20/07, Rockwell, N.C. d: 7/26/94, Concord, N.C. BR/TR, 6', 170 lbs. Deb: 4/15/30

YEAR	TM/L	W	L	PCT	G	GS	CG	SH	SV	IP	H	HR	BB	SO	RAT	ERA	ERA+	OAV	OOB	BH	AVG	PB	PR	/A	PD	TPI
1930	StL-A	0	1	.000	25	1	0	0	0	62^1	103	8	28	37	19.3	7.80	63	.376	.439	2	.125	-1	-22	-20	-0	-0.4

● **CHRIS HOLT** Holt, Christopher Michael b: 9/18/71, Dallas, Tex. BR/TR, 6'4", 205 lbs. Deb: 9/1/96

YEAR	TM/L	W	L	PCT	G	GS	CG	SH	SV	IP	H	HR	BB	SO	RAT	ERA	ERA+	OAV	OOB	BH	AVG	PB	PR	/A	PD	TPI
1996	Hou-N	0	1	.000	4	0	0	0	0	5	10	0	3	6	15.4	5.79	66	.263	.364	0	.000	-0	-1	-1	0	-0.2

● **VERN HOLTGRAVE** Holtgrave, Lavern George "Woody" b: 10/18/42, Aviston, Ill. BR/TR, 6'1", 183 lbs. Deb: 9/26/65

YEAR	TM/L	W	L	PCT	G	GS	CG	SH	SV	IP	H	HR	BB	SO	RAT	ERA	ERA+	OAV	OOB	BH	AVG	PB	PR	/A	PD	TPI
1965	Det-A	0	0	—	1	0	0	0	0	3	4	0	2	2	18.0	6.00	58	.308	.400	0	—	0	-1	-1	-0	0.0

● **BRIAN HOLTON** Holton, Brian John b: 11/29/59, McKeesport, Pa. BR/TR, 6', 193 lbs. Deb: 9/9/85

YEAR	TM/L	W	L	PCT	G	GS	CG	SH	SV	IP	H	HR	BB	SO	RAT	ERA	ERA+	OAV	OOB	BH	AVG	PB	PR	/A	PD	TPI
1985	LA-N	1	1	.500	3	0	0	0	0	4	9	0	1	1	22.5	9.00	39	.450	.476	0	—	0	-2	-2	0	-1.0
1986	LA-N	2	3	.400	12	3	0	0	0	24^1	28	1	6	24	12.9	4.44	78	.292	.340	0	.000	-1	-2	-3	0	-0.5
1987	LA-N	3	2	.600	53	1	0	0	2	83^1	87	11	32	58	12.9	3.89	102	.269	.335	1	.200	0	2	1	1	0.1

YEAR	TM/L	W	L	PCT	G	GS	CG	SH	SV	IP	H	HR	BB	SO	RAT	ERA	ERA+	OAV	OOB	BH	AVG	PB	PR	/A	PD	TPI
1988	*LA-N	7	3	.700	45	0	0	0	1	84²	69	1	26	49	10.2	1.70	196	.228	.292	0	.000	-1	16	15	-0	1.7
1989	Bal-A	5	7	.417	39	12	0	0	0	116¹	140	11	39	51	13.9	4.02	94	.300	.355	0	—	0	-2	-3	-0	-0.3
1990	Bal-A	2	3	.400	33	0	0	0	0	58	68	7	21	27	13.8	4.50	84	.292	.350	0	—	0	-4	-5	1	-0.3
Total	6	20	19	.513	185	16	0	0	3	370²	401	31	125	210	12.8	3.62	102	.278	.337	1	.050	-1	8	3	1	-0.3

● MIKE HOLTZ
Holtz, Michael James b: 10/10/72, Arlington, Va. BL/TL, 5′9″, 172 lbs. Deb: 7/11/96

YEAR	TM/L	W	L	PCT	G	GS	CG	SH	SV	IP	H	HR	BB	SO	RAT	ERA	ERA+	OAV	OOB	BH	AVG	PB	PR	/A	PD	TPI
1996	Cal-A	3	3	.500	30	0	0	0	0	29¹	21	1	19	31	13.2	2.45	199	.204	.344	0		0	8	8	0	1.4

● KEN HOLTZMAN
Holtzman, Kenneth Dale b: 11/3/45, St.Louis, Mo. BR/TL, 6′2″, 175 lbs. Deb: 9/4/65

YEAR	TM/L	W	L	PCT	G	GS	CG	SH	SV	IP	H	HR	BB	SO	RAT	ERA	ERA+	OAV	OOB	BH	AVG	PB	PR	/A	PD	TPI
1965	Chi-N	0	0	—	3	0	0	0	0	4	2	1	3	3	11.3	2.25	164	.143	.294	0	—	0	1	1	0	0.0
1966	Chi-N	11	16	.407	34	33	9	0	0	220²	194	27	68	171	11.3	3.79	97	.235	.296	9	.123	-3	-5	-3	-2	-0.8
1967	Chi-N	9	0	1.000	12	12	3	0	0	92²	76	11	44	62	11.8	2.53	140	.222	.314	7	.200	1	9	10	0	1.1
1968	Chi-N	11	14	.440	34	32	6	3	1	215	201	17	76	151	11.8	3.35	94	.248	.317	10	.125	-2	-9	-4	-1	-0.7
1969	Chi-N	17	13	.567	39	39	12	6	0	261¹	248	18	93	176	11.9	3.58	112	.247	.314	15	.150	-1	0	13	-1	1.2
1970	Chi-N	17	11	.607	39	38	15	1	0	287²	271	30	94	202	11.5	3.38	133	.248	.309	21	.200	1	21	36	0	3.4
1971	Chi-N	9	15	.375	30	29	9	3	0	195	213	18	64	143	12.9	4.48	88	.276	.333	9	.130	-1	-22	-12	-1	-1.5
1972	*Oak-A☆	19	11	.633	39	37	16	4	0	265¹	232	23	52	134	9.8	2.51	113	.236	.278	16	.178	2	16	10	0	1.4
1973	*Oak-A★	21	13	.618	40	40	16	4	0	297¹	275	22	66	157	10.4	2.97	120	.243	.287	0	—	0	28	19	-1	2.0
1974	*Oak-A	19	17	.528	39	38	9	3	0	255¹	273	14	51	117	11.5	3.07	108	.272	.309	0	—	0	16	7	0	1.0
1975	*Oak-A	18	14	.563	39	38	13	2	0	266¹	217	16	108	122	11.2	3.14	115	.222	.303	0	.000	0	19	14	3	1.9
1976	Bal-A	5	4	.556	13	13	6	1	0	97²	100	4	35	22	12.5	2.86	115	.271	.336	0	—	0	7	5	1	0.5
	NY-A	9	7	.563	21	21	10	2	0	149	165	14	35	41	12.1	4.17	82	.283	.323	0	—	0	-11	-12	-1	-1.3
	Yr	14	11	.560	34	34	16	3	0	246²	265	18	70	66	12.2	3.65	92	.277	.326	0	—	0	-4	-8	1	-0.8
1977	NY-A	2	3	.400	18	11	0	0	0	71²	105	7	24	14	16.3	5.78	68	.362	.413	0	—	0	-14	-15	2	-0.6
1978	NY-A	1	0	1.000	5	3	0	0	0	17²	21	2	9	3	15.3	4.08	89	.313	.395	0	—	0	-1	-1	1	0.2
	Chi-N	0	3	.000	23	6	0	0	2	53	61	0	35	36	16.5	6.11	66	.286	.390	2	.200	0	-15	-12	-0	-0.8
1979	Chi-N	6	9	.400	23	20	3	2	0	117²	133	16	53	44	14.7	4.59	90	.287	.368	10	.233	0	-11	-6	-2	-0.7
Total	15	174	150	.537	451	410	127	31	3	2867¹	2787	249	740	1601	11.8	3.49	104	.255	.315	99	.163	-1	31	48	1	6.3

● MARK HOLZEMER
Holzemer, Mark Harold b: 8/20/69, Littleton, Colo. BL/TL, 6′, 165 lbs. Deb: 8/21/93

YEAR	TM/L	W	L	PCT	G	GS	CG	SH	SV	IP	H	HR	BB	SO	RAT	ERA	ERA+	OAV	OOB	BH	AVG	PB	PR	/A	PD	TPI
1993	Cal-A	0	3	.000	5	4	0	0	0	23¹	34	2	13	10	19.3	8.87	51	.340	.431	0	—	0	-12	-11	0	-1.3
1995	Cal-A	0	1	.000	12	0	0	0	0	8¹	11	1	7	5	20.5	5.40	87	.306	.432	0	—	0	-1	-1	-1	-0.1
1996	Cal-A	1	0	1.000	25	0	0	0	0	24²	35	7	8	20	16.8	8.76	56	.327	.390	0	—	0	-10	-11	1	-0.3
Total	3	1	4	.200	42	4	0	0	0	56¹	80	10	28	35	18.4	8.31	57	.329	.414	0	—	0	-23	-23	-0	-1.7

● RICK HONEYCUTT
Honeycutt, Frederick Wayne b: 6/29/54, Chattanooga, Tenn. BL/TL, 5′11″, 190 lbs. Deb: 8/24/77

YEAR	TM/L	W	L	PCT	G	GS	CG	SH	SV	IP	H	HR	BB	SO	RAT	ERA	ERA+	OAV	OOB	BH	AVG	PB	PR	/A	PD	TPI
1977	Sea-A	0	1	.000	10	3	0	0	0	29	26	7	11	17	12.4	4.34	95	.239	.325	0	—	0	-1	-1	1	0.0
1978	Sea-A	5	11	.313	26	24	4	1	0	134¹	150	12	49	50	13.5	4.89	78	.285	.349	0	—	0	-17	-16	1	-1.5
1979	Sea-A	11	12	.478	33	28	8	1	0	194	201	22	67	83	12.7	4.04	108	.268	.333	0	—	0	4	7	-1	0.6
1980	Sea-A☆	10	17	.370	30	30	9	1	0	203¹	221	22	60	79	12.5	3.94	105	.280	.333	0	—	0	2	4	-0	0.5
1981	Tex-A	11	6	.647	20	20	8	2	0	127²	120	12	17	40	9.7	3.31	105	.246	.272	0	—	0	5	2	1	0.5
1982	Tex-A	5	17	.227	30	26	4	1	0	164	201	20	54	64	14.2	5.27	73	.305	.360	0	—	0	-22	-25	1	-2.5
1983	Tex-A★	14	8	.636	25	25	5	2	0	174²	168	9	37	56	10.9	**2.42**	**165**	.262	.308	0	—	0	**32**	**31**	3	**4.3**
	*LA-N	2	3	.400	9	7	1	0	0	39	46	6	13	18	14.1	5.77	62	.297	.359	1	.083	-1	-9	-9	2	-1.0
1984	LA-N	10	9	.526	29	28	6	2	0	183²	180	11	51	75	11.4	2.84	124	.258	.310	8	.143	-0	15	14	2	1.6
1985	LA-N	8	12	.400	31	25	1	0	1	142	141	9	49	67	12.1	3.42	102	.261	.323	5	.132	-1	3	1	3	0.4
1986	LA-N	11	9	.550	32	28	0	0	0	171	164	9	45	100	11.2	3.32	104	.249	.300	3	.070	0	8	3	2	0.5
1987	LA-N	2	12	.143	27	20	1	1	0	115²	133	10	45	92	14.0	4.59	86	.278	.343	7	.233	2	-7	-8	-0	-0.7
	Oak-A	1	4	.200	7	4	0	0	0	23²	25	3	9	10	13.7	5.32	77	.275	.353	0	—	0	-2	-3	-0	-0.5
1988	*Oak-A	3	2	.600	55	0	0	0	7	79²	74	6	25	47	11.5	3.50	108	.253	.318	0	—	0	4	2	1	0.4
1989	*Oak-A	2	2	.500	64	0	0	0	12	76²	56	5	26	52	9.7	2.35	157	.207	.279	0	—	0	13	11	1	1.0
1990	*Oak-A	2	2	.500	63	0	0	0	7	63¹	46	2	22	38	9.8	2.70	138	.204	.278	0	.000	0	8	7	1	0.6
1991	*Oak-A	2	4	.333	43	0	0	0	0	37²	37	3	20	26	14.1	3.58	107	.261	.360	0	—	0	2	2	1	0.4
1992	*Oak-A	1	4	.200	54	0	0	0	3	39	41	2	10	32	12.5	3.69	101	.272	.329	0	—	0	1	0	-1	0.2
1993	Oak-A	1	4	.200	52	0	0	0	1	41²	30	2	20	21	11.0	2.81	145	.211	.313	0	—	0	7	6	0	1.0
1994	Tex-A	1	2	.333	42	0	0	0	1	25	37	4	9	18	17.3	7.20	67	.349	.410	0	—	0	-7	-7	1	-0.6
1995	Oak-A	5	1	.833	49	0	0	0	2	44²	37	5	9	21	9.5	2.42	185	.231	.276	0	—	0	11	10	-0	1.2
	NY-A	0	0	—	3	0	0	0	0	1	2	1	1	0	27.0	27.00	17	.400	.500	0	—	0	-2	-2	0	0.0
	Yr	5	1	.833	52	0	0	0	2	45²	39	6	10	21	9.7	2.96	151	.234	.277	0	—	0	9	8	-1	1.2
1996	*StL-N	2	1	.667	61	0	0	0	4	47¹	42	3	7	30	9.7	2.85	149	.240	.269	0	.000	1	7	7	1	0.6
Total	20	109	143	.433	795	268	47	11	38	2158	2178	185	656	1036	12.0	3.71	104	.264	.322	24	.132	2	56	35	16	7.0

● DON HOOD
Hood, Donald Harris b: 10/16/49, Florence, S.C. BL/TL, 6′2″, 180 lbs. Deb: 7/16/73

YEAR	TM/L	W	L	PCT	G	GS	CG	SH	SV	IP	H	HR	BB	SO	RAT	ERA	ERA+	OAV	OOB	BH	AVG	PB	PR	/A	PD	TPI
1973	*Bal-A	3	2	.600	8	4	1	1	0	32¹	31	1	6	18	10.6	3.90	96	.256	.297	0	—	0	-0	-1	-1	-0.1
1974	Bal-A	1	1	.500	20	2	0	0	1	57¹	47	1	20	26	10.5	3.45	100	.223	.290	0	—	0	1	-0	-0	0.0
1975	Cle-A	6	10	.375	29	19	2	0	0	135¹	136	16	57	51	12.8	4.39	86	.268	.342	0	—	0	-9	-9	-2	-1.1
1976	Cle-A	3	5	.375	33	6	0	0	1	77²	89	5	41	32	15.5	4.87	72	.296	.387	0	—	0	-12	-12	0	-1.1
1977	Cle-A	2	1	.667	41	5	1	0	0	105	87	3	49	62	12.0	3.00	131	.224	.317	0	—	0	12	11	-2	0.4
1978	Cle-A	5	6	.455	36	19	1	0	0	154²	166	11	77	73	14.2	4.48	83	.278	.361	0	—	0	-12	-13	0	-0.7
1979	Cle-A	1	0	1.000	13	0	0	0	1	22	13	1	14	7	11.5	3.68	116	.169	.304	0	—	0	1	1	0	0.1
	NY-A	3	1	.750	27	6	0	0	1	67¹	62	3	30	22	12.6	3.07	132	.252	.338	0	—	0	9	7	1	0.5
	Yr	4	1	.800	40	6	0	0	2	89¹	75	4	44	29	12.2	3.22	128	.231	.327	0	—	0	10	9	1	0.6
1980	StL-N	4	6	.400	33	8	1	0	0	82¹	90	2	34	35	13.8	3.39	109	.288	.362	4	.200	-0	2	3	1	0.4
1982	KC-A	4	0	1.000	30	3	0	0	0	66²	71	7	22	21	12.8	3.51	116	.276	.338	0	—	0	4	3	0	0.3
1983	KC-A	2	3	.400	27	0	0	0	0	47²	48	5	14	21	12.1	2.27	180	.273	.333	0	—	0	10	10	1	1.1
Total	10	34	35	.493	297	72	6	1	6	848¹	840	57	364	374	13.0	3.79	101	.263	.342	4	.200	-0	5	2	-0	-0.2

● WALLY HOOD
Hood, Wallace James Jr. b: 9/24/25, Los Angeles, Cal. BR/TR, 6′1″, 190 lbs. Deb: 9/23/49 F

YEAR	TM/L	W	L	PCT	G	GS	CG	SH	SV	IP	H	HR	BB	SO	RAT	ERA	ERA+	OAV	OOB	BH	AVG	PB	PR	/A	PD	TPI
1949	NY-A	0	0	—	2	0	0	0	0	2¹	0	0	1	2	3.9	0.00	—	.000	.143	0	—	0	1	1	-0	0.0

● CHRIS HOOK
Hook, Christopher Wayne b: 8/4/68, San Diego, Cal. BR/TR, 6′5″, 230 lbs. Deb: 4/30/95

YEAR	TM/L	W	L	PCT	G	GS	CG	SH	SV	IP	H	HR	BB	SO	RAT	ERA	ERA+	OAV	OOB	BH	AVG	PB	PR	/A	PD	TPI
1995	SF-N	5	1	.833	45	0	0	0	0	52¹	55	7	29	40	15.0	5.50	74	.274	.373	0	—	0	-8	-8	-0	-0.9
1996	SF-N	0	1	.000	10	0	0	0	0	13¹	16	3	14	4	21.6	7.43	55	.308	.471	1	.500	-0	-5	-5	0	-0.2
Total	2	5	2	.714	55	0	0	0	0	65²	71	10	43	44	16.3	5.89	69	.281	.395	1	.200	0	-12	-13	0	-1.1

● JAY HOOK
Hook, James Wesley b: 11/18/36, Waukegan, Ill. BL/TR, 6′2″, 182 lbs. Deb: 9/3/57

YEAR	TM/L	W	L	PCT	G	GS	CG	SH	SV	IP	H	HR	BB	SO	RAT	ERA	ERA+	OAV	OOB	BH	AVG	PB	PR	/A	PD	TPI
1957	Cin-N	0	1	.000	3	2	0	0	0	10	6	0	8	6	12.6	4.50	91	.176	.333	0	.000	-0	-1	-0	0	-0.1
1958	Cin-N	0	1	.000	1	1	0	0	0	3	3	2	2	5	15.0	12.00	35	.250	.357	0	—	0	-3	-3	-0	-0.6
1959	Cin-N	5	5	.500	17	15	4	0	0	79	79	11	39	37	13.8	5.13	79	.266	.357	3	.125	-1	-10	-9	-1	-1.2
1960	Cin-N	11	18	.379	36	33	10	2	0	222	222	31	73	103	12.2	4.50	85	.263	.325	6	.083	-3	-18	-17	-1	-2.4
1961	Cin-N	1	3	.250	22	5	0	0	0	62²	83	14	22	36	15.8	7.76	52	.322	.386	2	.133	-1	-26	-26	-1	-1.6
1962	NY-N	8	19	.296	37	34	13	0	0	213²	230	31	71	113	13.0	4.84	86	.273	.335	14	.203	2	-21	-16	-1	-1.5
1963	NY-N	4	14	.222	41	20	3	0	1	152²	168	21	53	89	13.6	5.48	64	.281	.348	9	.237	2	-37	-34	-1	-3.7
1964	NY-N	0	1	.000	3	2	0	0	0	9²	17	2	7	5	22.3	9.31	38	.395	.480	0	.000	-0	-6	-6	-0	-0.5
Total	8	29	62	.319	160	112	30	2	1	752²	808	112	275	394	13.3	5.23	75	.276	.344	34	.151	-2	-123	-110	-4	-11.6

● BUCK HOOKER
Hooker, William Edward b: 8/28/1880, Richmond, Va. d: 7/2/29, Richmond, Va. TR, 5′6″ Deb: 9/5/02

YEAR	TM/L	W	L	PCT	G	GS	CG	SH	SV	IP	H	HR	BB	SO	RAT	ERA	ERA+	OAV	OOB	BH	AVG	PB	PR	/A	PD	TPI
1902	Cin-N	0	1	.000	1	1	1	0	0	8	11	1	0	2	12.4	4.50	67	.324	.324	0	.000	-0	-2	-1	-0	-0.2
1903	Cin-N	0	0	—	1	0	0	0	0	2¹	2	0	2	0	15.4	0.00	—	.250	.400	0	—	0	1	1	-0	0.0
Total	2	0	1	.000	2	1	1	0	0	10¹	13	1	2	2	13.1	3.48	90	.310	.341	0	—	-1	-1	-0	-0	-0.2

YEAR	TM/L	W	L	PCT	G	GS	CG	SH	SV	IP	H	HR	BB	SO	RAT	ERA	ERA+	OAV	OOB	BH	AVG	PB	PR	/A	PD	TPI

● **HARRY HOOPER** Hooper, Harry Bartholomew b: 8/24/1887, Bell Station, Cal. d: 12/18/74, Santa Cruz, Cal. BL/TR, 5′10″, 168 lbs. Deb: 4/16/09 H◆

| 1913 | Bos-A | 0 | 0 | — | 1 | 0 | 0 | 0 | 0 | 2 | 2 | 0 | 1 | 0 | 13.5 | 0.00 | — | .333 | .429 | 169 | .288 | 0 | 1 | 1 | -0 | 0.0 |

● **BOB HOOPER** Hooper, Robert Nelson b: 5/30/22, Leamington, Ont., Canada d: 3/17/80, New Brunswick, N.J BR/TR, 5′11″, 195 lbs. Deb: 4/19/50

1950	Phi-A	15	10	.600	45	20	3	0	5	170¹	181	15	91	58	14.4	5.02	91	.272	.361	7	.125	-2	-8	-9	3	-1.0
1951	Phi-A	12	10	.545	38	23	9	0	5	189	192	13	61	64	12.2	4.38	98	.267	.327	15	.208	-1	-5	-2	1	-0.2
1952	Phi-A	8	15	.348	43	14	4	0	6	144¹	158	13	68	40	14.3	5.18	76	.279	.361	8	.195	1	-24	-20	3	-2.6
1953	Cle-A	5	4	.556	43	0	0	0	7	69¹	50	4	38	16	11.7	4.02	93	.206	.318	1	.083	-0	-2	-1	0	-0.3
1954	Cle-A	0	0	—	17	0	0	0	2	34²	39	3	16	12	14.5	4.93	74	.289	.368	0	.000	-1	-5	-5	-0	-0.1
1955	Cin-N	0	2	.000	8	0	0	0	0	13	20	2	6	6	18.0	7.62	56	.357	.419	0	.000	-0	-5	-5	0	-0.6
Total	6	40	41	.494	194	57	16	0	25	620²	640	50	280	196	13.5	4.80	87	.268	.348	31	.166	-4	-48	-42	8	-4.8

● **LEON HOOTEN** Hooten, Michael Leon b: 4/4/48, Downey, Cal. BR/TR, 5′11″, 180 lbs. Deb: 4/13/74

| 1974 | Oak-A | 0 | 0 | — | 6 | 0 | 0 | 0 | 0 | 8¹ | 6 | 1 | 4 | 1 | 11.9 | 3.24 | 102 | .207 | .324 | 0 | — | 0 | 0 | 0 | 0 | 0.0 |

● **BURT HOOTON** Hooton, Burt Carlton b: 2/7/50, Greenville, Tex. BR/TR, 6′1″, 210 lbs. Deb: 6/17/71

1971	Chi-N	2	0	1.000	3	3	2	1	0	21¹	8	2	10	22	7.6	2.11	186	.111	.220	0	.000	-1	3	4	-0	0.3
1972	Chi-N	11	14	.440	33	31	9	3	0	218¹	201	13	81	132	11.7	2.80	136	.246	.315	9	.125	-1	16	24	1	2.8
1973	Chi-N	14	17	.452	42	34	9	2	0	239²	248	16	73	134	12.2	3.68	107	.270	.327	9	.129	-0	1	7	-1	0.7
1974	Chi-N	7	11	.389	48	21	3	1	1	176¹	214	16	51	94	13.7	4.80	79	.299	.348	1	.060	-4	-23	-19	3	-1.9
1975	Chi-N	0	2	.000	3	3	0	0	0	11	18	2	4	5	18.0	8.18	47	.383	.431	0	.000	-0	-6	-5	1	-0.7
	LA-N	18	7	.720	31	30	12	4	0	223²	172	16	64	148	9.5	2.82	121	.210	.267	9	.129	1	20	14	-2	1.4
	Yr	18	9	.667	34	33	12	4	0	234²	190	18	68	153	9.9	3.07	111	.219	.276	9	.123	1	14	9	-1	0.7
1976	LA-N	11	15	.423	33	33	8	4	0	226²	203	16	60	116	10.5	3.26	104	.241	.292	6	.097	-2	6	3	-2	0.0
1977	*LA-N	12	7	.632	32	31	6	2	1	223¹	184	14	60	153	10.0	2.62	146	.225	.281	11	.164	-0	32	30	0	2.4
1978	*LA-N	19	10	.655	32	32	10	3	0	236	196	17	61	104	9.8	2.71	130	.226	.277	10	.149	1	23	21	-1	2.6
1979	LA-N	11	10	.524	29	29	12	1	0	212	191	11	63	129	10.9	2.97	122	.244	.302	11	.147	-1	18	16	-0	1.4
1980	LA-N	14	8	.636	34	33	4	2	1	206²	194	22	64	118	11.2	3.66	96	.249	.306	4	.063	-3	-1	-4	-0	-0.7
1981	*LA-N★	11	6	.647	23	23	5	4	0	142¹	124	3	33	74	10.1	2.28	146	.237	.285	8	.190	-1	19	16	-1	2.1
1982	LA-N	4	7	.364	21	21	2	2	0	120²	130	5	37	51	12.3	4.03	86	.275	.325	3	.086	-1	-6	-8	0	-0.7
1983	LA-N	9	8	.529	33	27	2	0	0	160	156	21	59	87	12.2	4.22	85	.254	.321	8	.160	1	-11	-11	-0	-1.1
1984	LA-N	3	6	.333	54	6	0	0	4	110	109	5	43	62	12.4	3.44	103	.263	.333	1	.071	-1	2	1	-0	0.0
1985	Tex-A	5	8	.385	29	20	2	0	0	124	133	18	40	62	13.7	5.23	81	.297	.349	0	—	-0	-15	-14	-1	-1.4
Total	15	151	136	.526	480	377	86	29	7	2652	2497	193	799	1491	11.3	3.38	108	.250	.306	92	.123	-9	77	77	-4	7.2

● **JOHN HOOVER** Hoover, John Nicklaus b: 11/22/62, Fresno, Cal. BR/TR, 6′2″, 190 lbs. Deb: 5/23/90

| 1990 | Tex-A | 0 | 0 | — | 2 | 0 | 0 | 0 | 0 | 4² | 8 | 0 | 3 | 0 | 21.2 | 11.57 | 34 | .364 | .440 | 0 | — | 0 | -4 | -4 | -0 | 0.0 |

● **DICK HOOVER** Hoover, Richard Lloyd b: 12/11/25, Columbus, Ohio d: 4/12/81, Lake Placid, Fla. BL/TL, 6′, 170 lbs. Deb: 4/16/52

| 1952 | Bos-N | 0 | 0 | — | 2 | 0 | 0 | 0 | 0 | 4² | 8 | 1 | 3 | 0 | 21.2 | 7.71 | 47 | .348 | .423 | 0 | — | 0 | -2 | -2 | -0 | 0.0 |

● **JOHN HOPE** Hope, John Alan b: 12/21/70, Ft.Lauderdale, Fla. BR/TR, 6′3″, 195 lbs. Deb: 8/29/93

1993	Pit-N	0	2	.000	7	7	0	0	0	38	47	3	8	8	13.5	4.03	101	.313	.356	1	.077	-1	0	0	0	0.0
1994	Pit-N	0	0	—	9	0	0	0	0	14	18	1	6	6	15.4	5.79	75	.310	.375	1	.333	0	-2	-2	0	0.0
1995	Pit-N	0	0	—	3	0	0	0	0	2¹	8	0	4	2	57.9	30.86	14	.615	.750	0	—	0	-7	-7	-0	0.0
1996	Pit-N	1	3	.250	5	4	0	0	0	19¹	17	5	11	13	14.0	6.98	63	.243	.361	1	.200	-0	-6	-6	0	-0.9
Total	4	1	5	.167	24	11	0	0	0	73²	90	8	27	29	15.4	5.99	70	.309	.385	3	.143	-1	-15	-15	1	-0.9

● **SAM HOPE** Hope, Samuel b: 12/4/1878, Brooklyn, N.Y. d: 6/30/46, Greenport, N.Y. BR/TR, 5′10″, Deb: 8/5/07

| 1907 | Phi-A | 0 | 0 | — | 1 | 0 | 0 | 0 | 0 | 0¹ | 1 | 0 | 0 | 0 | 81.0 | 81.00 | — | .750 | .750 | 0 | — | 0 | -2 | -2 | 0 | 0.0 |

● **PAUL HOPKINS** Hopkins, Paul Henry b: 9/25/04, Chester, Conn. BR/TR, 6′, 175 lbs. Deb: 9/29/27

1927	Was-A	1	0	1.000	2	1	0	0	0	9	13	1	4	5	17.0	5.00	81	.361	.425	2	.667	1	-1	-1	-0	0.0
1929	Was-A	0	1	.000	7	1	0	0	0	16¹	15	1	9	5	13.2	2.20	192	.250	.348	0	.000	-1	4	4	-0	0.1
	StL-A	0	0	—	2	0	0	0	0	2	0	0	2	1	9.0	0.00	—	.000	.286	0	—	0	1	1	-0	0.0
	Yr	0	1	.000	9	1	0	0	0	18¹	15	1	11	6	12.8	1.96	217	.231	.342	0	.000	-1	5	5	-0	0.1
Total	2	1	1	.500	11	1	0	0	0	27¹	28	2	15	11	14.2	2.96	142	.277	.371	2	.333	1	4	4	-0	0.1

● **LEFTY HOPPER** Hopper, Clarence F. b: 5/27/1874, Jersey City, N.J. TL, Deb: 10/10/1898

| 1898 | Bro-N | 0 | 2 | .000 | 2 | 2 | 2 | 0 | 0 | 11 | 14 | 0 | 5 | 5 | 15.5 | 4.91 | 73 | .304 | .373 | 0 | .000 | -1 | -2 | -2 | 0 | -0.3 |

● **JIM HOPPER** Hopper, James McDaniel b: 9/1/19, Charlotte, N.C. d: 1/23/82, Charlotte, N.C. BR/TR, 6′1″, 175 lbs. Deb: 4/21/46

| 1946 | Pit-N | 0 | 1 | .000 | 2 | 1 | 0 | 0 | 0 | 4 | 6 | 1 | 3 | 1 | 20.3 | 11.25 | 31 | .316 | .409 | 0 | — | 0 | -3 | -3 | 0 | -0.7 |

● **BILL HOPPER** Hopper, William Booth "Bird Dog" b: 10/26/1890, Jackson, Tenn. d: 1/14/65, Allen Park, Mich. BR/TR, 6′, 175 lbs. Deb: 9/11/13

1913	StL-N	0	3	.000	3	3	2	0	0	24	20	2	8	3	11.6	3.75	86	.230	.316	3	.375	1	-1	-1	-0	0.0
1914	StL-N	0	0	—	3	0	0	0	0	5	6	0	5	1	19.8	3.60	78	.286	.423	0	—	0	-0	-0	-0	0.0
1915	Was-A	0	1	.000	13	0	0	0	1	31¹	39	0	16	8	16.1	4.60	65	.348	.434	1	.200	0	-6	-6	1	-0.1
Total	3	0	4	.000	19	3	2	0	1	60¹	65	2	29	12	14.6	4.18	73	.295	.387	4	.308	1	-8	-7	1	-0.1

● **JOHN HORAN** Horan, Patrick J. b: 1863, Ireland 5′10.5″, 160 lbs. Deb: 5/17/1884

| 1884 | CP-U | 3 | 6 | .333 | 13 | 10 | 9 | 0 | 0 | 98 | 94 | 2 | 24 | 55 | 10.8 | 3.49 | 70 | .236 | .279 | 6 | .088 | -8 | -11 | -11 | -1 | -1.4 |

● **JOE HORLEN** Horlen, Joel Edward b: 8/14/37, San Antonio, Tex. BR/TR, 6′, 175 lbs. Deb: 9/4/61

1961	Chi-A	1	3	.250	5	4	0	0	0	17²	25	2	13	11	19.4	6.62	59	.338	.437	0	.000	-1	-5	-5	0	-1.0
1962	Chi-A	7	6	.538	20	19	5	1	0	108²	108	10	43	63	12.7	4.89	80	.262	.335	2	.053	-3	-11	-12	2	-1.3
1963	Chi-A	11	7	.611	33	21	3	0	0	124	122	10	55	61	13.0	3.27	107	.261	.341	9	.225	-1	5	3	1	0.7
1964	Chi-A	13	9	.591	32	28	9	2	0	210²	142	11	55	138	8.6	1.88	184	**.190**	**.250**	11	.159	-1	41	37	3	4.2
1965	Chi-A	13	13	.500	34	34	7	4	0	219	203	16	39	125	10.1	2.88	111	.245	.281	9	.132	0	14	8	-0	0.9
1966	Chi-A	10	13	.435	37	29	4	1	2	211	185	14	53	124	10.3	2.43	130	.233	.286	4	.067	-4	24	17	6	2.2
1967	Chi-A☆	19	7	**.731**	35	35	13	**6**	0	258	188	13	58	103	8.7	2.06	151	.203	**.253**	14	.169	1	**34**	30	3	3.5
1968	Chi-A	12	14	.462	35	35	4	1	0	223²	197	16	70	102	11.3	2.37	127	.238	.308	7	.104	-1	15	16	2	2.1
1969	Chi-A	13	16	.448	36	35	7	2	0	235²	237	20	77	121	12.2	3.78	102	.261	.323	14	.182	-1	-4	2	-1	0.0
1970	Chi-A	6	16	.273	28	26	4	0	0	172¹	198	18	41	77	12.7	4.86	80	.287	.331	6	.115	-2	-22	-18	4	-1.9
1971	Chi-A	8	9	.471	34	18	3	0	2	137¹	150	7	30	82	12.1	4.26	84	.284	.329	4	.100	-2	-12	-10	1	-1.4
1972	*Oak-A	3	4	.429	32	6	0	0	0	84	74	3	20	58	10.5	3.00	95	.236	.291	3	.176	-1	1	-1	1	-0.1
Total	12	116	117	.498	361	290	59	18	4	2002	1829	145	554	1065	11.0	3.11	109	.243	.300	83	.134	-12	78	66	22	7.9

● **TRADER HORNE** Horne, Berlyn Dale "Sonny" b: 4/12/1899, Bachman, Ohio d: 2/3/83, Franklin, Ohio BB/TR, 5′9″, 155 lbs. Deb: 4/24/29

| 1929 | Chi-N | 1 | 1 | .500 | 11 | 1 | 0 | 0 | 0 | 23 | 24 | 3 | 21 | 6 | 17.6 | 5.09 | 91 | .273 | .413 | 2 | .400 | 0 | -1 | -1 | 0 | 0.0 |

● **JACK HORNER** Horner, William Frank b: 9/21/1863, Baltimore, Md. d: 7/14/10, New Orleans, La. BR, Deb: 5/7/1894

| 1894 | Bal-N | 0 | 1 | .000 | 2 | 1 | 1 | 0 | 0 | 11 | 15 | 0 | 7 | 2 | 18.8 | 9.00 | 61 | .319 | .418 | 1 | .167 | -0 | -4 | -4 | 0 | -0.3 |

● **JOE HORNUNG** Hornung, Michael Joseph "Ubbo Ubbo" b: 6/12/1857, Carthage, N.Y. d: 10/30/31, Howard Beach, N.Y. BR/TR, 5′8.5″, 164 lbs. Deb: 5/1/1879 U◆

| 1880 | Buf-N | 0 | 0 | — | 1 | 0 | 0 | 0 | 0 | 3 | 2 | 0 | 1 | 0 | 9.0 | 6.00 | 41 | .167 | .231 | 91 | .266 | 0 | -1 | -0 | 1 | 0.0 |

● **HANSON HORSEY** Horsey, Hanson b: 11/26/1889, Galena, Md. d: 12/1/49, Millington, Md. BR/TR, 5′11″, 165 lbs. Deb: 4/27/12

| 1912 | Cin-N | 0 | 0 | — | 1 | 0 | 0 | 0 | 0 | 4 | 14 | 0 | 3 | 0 | 38.3 | 22.50 | 15 | .609 | .654 | 0 | .000 | -0 | -8 | -9 | -0 | -0.1 |

● **VINCE HORSMAN** Horsman, Vincent Stanley Joseph b: 3/9/67, Halifax, N.S., Can. BR/TR, 6′2″, 175 lbs. Deb: 9/5/91

| 1991 | Tor-A | 0 | 0 | — | 4 | 0 | 0 | 0 | 0 | 4 | 2 | 0 | 3 | 2 | 11.3 | 0.00 | — | .167 | .333 | 0 | — | 0 | 2 | 2 | -0 | -0.2 |
| 1992 | Oak-A | 2 | 1 | .667 | 58 | 0 | 0 | 0 | 1 | 43¹ | 39 | 3 | 21 | 18 | 12.5 | 2.49 | 150 | .252 | .341 | 0 | — | 0 | 7 | 6 | -0 | 0.5 |

YEAR	TM/L	W	L	PCT	G	GS	CG	SH	SV	IP	H	HR	BB	SO	RAT	ERA	ERA+	OAV	OOB	BH	AVG	PB	PR	/A	PD	TPI
1993	Oak-A	2	0	1.000	40	0	0	0	0	25	25	2	15	17	15.5	5.40	75	.255	.371	0	—	0	-3	-4	-0	-0.3
1994	Oak-A	0	1	.000	33	0	0	0	0	29¹	29	2	11	20	12.6	4.91	90	.266	.339	0	—	-0	-2	1	0.4	
1995	Min-A	0	0	—	6	0	0	0	0	9	12	2	4	4	16.0	7.00	68	.333	.400	0	—	0	-2	-0	0.0	
Total	5	4	2	.667	141	0	0	0	1	110²	107	9	54	61	13.4	4.07	101	.261	.353	0	—	0	3	0	-1	0.4

● OSCAR HORSTMANN
Horstmann, Oscar Theodore b: 6/2/1891, Alma, Mo. d: 5/11/77, Salina, Kan. BR/TR, 5'11", 165 lbs. Deb: 4/18/17

YEAR	TM/L	W	L	PCT	G	GS	CG	SH	SV	IP	H	HR	BB	SO	RAT	ERA	ERA+	OAV	OOB	BH	AVG	PB	PR	/A	PD	TPI
1917	StL-N	9	4	.692	35	11	4	1	1	138²	111	5	54	50	11.0	3.44	78	.225	.307	9	.196	-1	-11	-12	1	-1.1
1918	StL-N	0	2	.000	9	2	0	0	0	23	29	0	14	6	16.8	5.48	49	.349	.443	0	.000	-0	-7	-7	1	-0.5
1919	StL-N	0	1	.000	6	2	0	0	0	15	14	0	12	5	15.6	3.00	93	.264	.400	1	.500	0	-0	-0	0	0.0
Total	3	9	7	.563	50	15	4	1	1	176²	154	5	80	61	12.1	3.67	74	.245	.334	10	.192	1	-18	-19	1	-1.6

● ELMER HORTON
Horton, Elmer E. "Herky Jerky" b: 9/4/1869, Hamilton, Ohio d: 8/12/20, Vienna, N.Y. Deb: 9/24/1896

YEAR	TM/L	W	L	PCT	G	GS	CG	SH	SV	IP	H	HR	BB	SO	RAT	ERA	ERA+	OAV	OOB	BH	AVG	PB	PR	/A	PD	TPI
1896	Pit-N	0	2	.000	2	2	2	0	0	15	22	0	9	3	19.2	9.60	44	.338	.427	0	.000	-1	-9	-9	-1	-0.9
1898	Bro-N	0	1	.000	1	1	1	0	0	9	16	0	6	0	22.0	10.00	36	.381	.458	1	.250	-0	-6	-6	-0	-0.5
Total	2	0	3	.000	3	3	3	0	0	24	38	0	15	3	20.3	9.75	41	.355	.439	1	.091	-1	-15	-15	-1	-1.4

● RICKY HORTON
Horton, Ricky Neal b: 7/30/59, Poughkeepsie, N.Y. BL/TL, 6'2", 195 lbs. Deb: 4/7/84

YEAR	TM/L	W	L	PCT	G	GS	CG	SH	SV	IP	H	HR	BB	SO	RAT	ERA	ERA+	OAV	OOB	BH	AVG	PB	PR	/A	PD	TPI
1984	StL-N	9	4	.692	37	18	1	1	1	125²	140	14	39	76	12.9	3.44	101	.285	.339	2	.065	-2	2	0	3	0.2
1985	*StL-N	3	2	.600	49	3	0	0	1	89²	84	5	34	59	12.1	2.91	121	.251	.326	1	.063	-0	7	6	2	0.5
1986	StL-N	4	3	.571	42	9	1	0	3	100¹	77	7	26	49	9.3	2.24	162	.218	.273	1	.056	0	16	16	2	1.3
1987	*StL-N	8	3	.727	67	6	0	0	7	125	127	15	42	55	12.2	3.82	109	.263	.323	5	.172	0	4	5	2	0.7
1988	Chi-A	6	10	.375	52	9	1	0	0	109¹	106	9	36	28	13.3	4.86	82	.291	.355	0	—	-1	-11	-11	1	-1.3
	*LA-N	1	1	.500	12	0	0	0	0	9	11	2	2	8	13.0	5.00	67	.306	.342	0	—	0	-2	-2	1	-0.3
1989	LA-N	0	0	—	23	0	0	0	0	26²	35	1	11	12	15.9	5.06	69	.343	.412	0	.000	0	-5	-5	-0	-0.0
	StL-N	0	3	.000	11	8	0	0	0	45²	50	2	10	14	12.4	4.73	77	.282	.332	3	.273	1	-6	-6	-0	-0.2
	Yr	0	3	.000	34	8	0	0	0	72¹	85	3	21	26	13.6	4.85	73	.301	.356	3	.250	1	-11	-10	-0	-0.2
1990	StL-N	1	1	.500	32	0	0	0	0	42	52	3	22	18	16.1	4.93	77	.315	.399	0	—	-1	-5	-5	-2	-0.1
Total	7	32	27	.542	325	53	3	1	15	673¹	696	55	222	319	12.5	3.76	100	.273	.334	12	.109	-1	-0	-1	12	0.8

● DAVE HOSKINS
Hoskins, David Taylor b: 8/3/25, Greenwood, Miss. d: 4/2/70, Flint, Mich. BL/TR, 6'1", 180 lbs. Deb: 4/18/53

YEAR	TM/L	W	L	PCT	G	GS	CG	SH	SV	IP	H	HR	BB	SO	RAT	ERA	ERA+	OAV	OOB	BH	AVG	PB	PR	/A	PD	TPI
1953	Cle-A	9	3	.750	26	7	3	0	1	112²	102	9	38	55	11.5	3.99	94	.243	.312	15	.259	4	0	-3	0	0.1
1954	Cle-A	0	1	.000	14	1	0	0	0	26²	29	3	10	9	13.2	3.04	121	.284	.348	0	.000	-1	2	2	-0	0.0
Total	2	9	4	.692	40	8	3	0	1	139¹	131	12	48	64	11.8	3.81	98	.251	.319	15	.227	3	2	-1	0	0.1

● GENE HOST
Host, Eugene Earl "Twinkles" or "Slick" b: 1/1/33, Leeper, Pa. BB/TL, 5'11", 190 lbs. Deb: 9/16/56

YEAR	TM/L	W	L	PCT	G	GS	CG	SH	SV	IP	H	HR	BB	SO	RAT	ERA	ERA+	OAV	OOB	BH	AVG	PB	PR	/A	PD	TPI
1956	Det-A	0	0	—	1	1	0	0	0	4²	9	2	5	5	21.2	7.71	53	.409	.458	0	.000	-0	-2	-2	0	0.0
1957	KC-A	0	2	.000	11	2	0	0	0	23²	29	5	14	9	16.4	7.23	55	.315	.406	0	.000	-1	-9	-9	0	-0.7
Total	2	0	2	.000	12	3	0	0	0	28¹	38	7	16	14	17.2	7.31	55	.333	.415	0	.000	-1	-11	-10	0	-0.7

● BYRON HOUCK
Houck, Byron Simon "Duke" b: 8/28/1891, Prosper, Minn. d: 6/17/69, Santa Cruz, Cal. BR/TR, 6', 175 lbs. Deb: 5/15/12

YEAR	TM/L	W	L	PCT	G	GS	CG	SH	SV	IP	H	HR	BB	SO	RAT	ERA	ERA+	OAV	OOB	BH	AVG	PB	PR	/A	PD	TPI
1912	Phi-A	8	8	.500	30	17	10	0	1	180²	148	1	74	75	11.7	2.94	105	.234	.326	4	.065	-7	8	3	-1	-0.5
1913	Phi-A	14	6	.700	41	19	4	1	0	176	147	3	122	71	14.1	4.14	67	.214	.337	5	.083	-4	-24	-27	-2	-3.4
1914	Phi-A	0	0	—	3	3	0	0	0	11	14	0	6	4	16.4	3.27	80	.318	.400	1	.333	0	-1	-1	-0	0.0
	Bro-F	2	6	.250	17	9	3	0	0	92	96	4	45	43	13.7	3.13	92	.272	.355	7	.233	-2	-3	-3	-3	-0.3
1918	StL-A	2	4	.333	27	2	0	0	2	71²	58	0	29	29	10.9	2.39	115	.225	.303	1	.150	-1	3	3	-1	0.1
Total	4	26	24	.520	118	50	17	1	3	531¹	462	8	274	224	12.8	3.30	87	.234	.334	20	.114	-9	-16	-24	-6	-4.1

● CHARLIE HOUGH
Hough, Charles Oliver b: 1/5/48, Honolulu, Hawaii BR/TR, 6'2", 190 lbs. Deb: 8/12/70

YEAR	TM/L	W	L	PCT	G	GS	CG	SH	SV	IP	H	HR	BB	SO	RAT	ERA	ERA+	OAV	OOB	BH	AVG	PB	PR	/A	PD	TPI
1970	LA-N	0	0	—	8	0	0	0	2	17	18	7	11	8	15.4	5.29	72	.265	.367	1	.333	0	-2	-3	0	0.0
1971	LA-N	0	0	—	4	0	0	0	0	4¹	3	1	4	2	14.5	4.15	78	.200	.333	0	—	0	-0	-0	0	0.0
1972	LA-N	0	0	—	2	0	0	0	0	2²	2	0	2	4	16.9	3.38	99	.200	.385	0	—	0	-0	-0	0	0.0
1973	LA-N	4	2	.667	37	0	0	0	5	71²	52	3	45	70	12.9	2.76	124	.207	.341	3	.214	0	7	5	0	0.6
1974	*LA-N	9	4	.692	49	0	0	0	1	96	65	12	40	63	10.0	3.75	91	.196	.291	0	.000	-1	-1	-4	0	-0.6
1975	LA-N	3	7	.300	38	0	0	0	4	61	43	3	34	34	12.5	2.95	115	.195	.323	2	.333	1	5	3	-1	0.5
1976	LA-N	12	8	.600	77	0	0	0	18	142²	102	6	77	81	11.8	2.21	153	.200	.314	6	.286	2	**20**	**19**	-1	**3.3**
1977	*LA-N	6	12	.333	70	1	0	0	22	127¹	98	10	70	105	12.4	3.32	115	.213	.326	4	.182	1	2	1	2	1.2
1978	*LA-N	5	5	.500	55	0	0	0	7	93¹	69	6	48	66	11.8	3.28	107	.205	.313	4	.333	1	3	2	-0	0.4
1979	LA-N	7	5	.583	42	14	0	0	0	151¹	152	16	66	76	13.4	4.76	76	.264	.348	6	.158	-0	-17	-19	-1	-1.4
1980	LA-N	1	3	.250	19	1	0	0	1	32¹	37	4	21	25	16.7	5.57	63	.291	.400	1	.500	1	-7	-7	-1	-0.9
	Tex-A	2	2	.500	16	2	2	1	0	61¹	54	2	37	43	13.8	3.96	98	.240	.355	0	—	-0	-0	-0	0	0.1
1981	Tex-A	4	1	.800	21	5	2	1	0	82	61	4	31	69	10.4	2.96	117	.207	.290	0	—	0	6	5	-1	0.2
1982	Tex-A	16	13	.552	34	34	12	2	0	228	217	21	72	128	11.7	3.95	98	.251	.314	0	—	0	3	-2	1	0.2
1983	Tex-A	15	13	.536	34	33	11	3	0	252	219	22	95	152	11.3	3.18	126	.238	.311	0	—	0	25	23	4	2.9
1984	Tex-A	16	14	.533	36	36	**17**	1	0	266	260	26	94	164	12.3	3.76	110	.255	.324	0	—	0	7	12	3	1.5
1985	Tex-A	14	16	.467	34	34	14	1	0	250¹	198	23	83	141	10.4	3.31	128	.215	.285	0	—	0	23	26	1	2.9
1986	Tex-A★	17	10	.630	33	33	7	2	0	230¹	188	20	89	146	11.2	3.79	113	.221	.302	0	—	0	10	13	1	1.5
1987	Tex-A	18	13	.581	40	40	13	0	0	285¹	238	36	124	223	12.0	3.79	118	.223	.314	0	—	0	21	22	3	2.4
1988	Tex-A	15	16	.484	34	34	10	0	0	252	202	20	126	174	12.1	3.32	123	.221	.324	0	—	0	18	21	4	2.9
1989	Tex-A	10	13	.435	30	30	1	0	0	182	168	20	95	94	13.3	4.35	91	.245	.342	0	—	0	-9	-8	-2	-1.0
1990	Tex-A	12	12	.500	32	32	5	0	0	218²	190	24	119	114	13.2	4.07	96	.235	.342	0	—	0	-4	-4	-0	-0.4
1991	Chi-A	9	10	.474	31	29	4	1	0	199¹	167	21	94	107	12.3	4.02	99	.229	.326	0	—	0	2	-1	0	0.1
1992	Chi-A	7	12	.368	27	27	4	1	0	176¹	160	19	66	76	11.9	3.93	98	.239	.314	0	—	0	-0	-1	-1	-0.2
1993	Fla-N	9	16	.360	34	34	0	0	0	204¹	202	21	71	126	12.4	4.27	101	.259	.328	2	.032	-0	-5	-1	2	-0.2
1994	Fla-N	5	9	.357	21	21	1	1	0	113²	118	17	52	65	14.3	5.15	85	.274	.366	4	.121	-1	-12	-10	0	-1.1
Total	25	216	216	.500	858	440	107	13	61	3801¹	3283	383	1665	2362	12.1	3.75	106	.233	.322	33	.146	-2	101	98	13	14.9

● PAT HOUSE
House, Patrick Lory b: 9/1/40, Boise, Idaho BL/TL, 6'3", 185 lbs. Deb: 9/6/67

YEAR	TM/L	W	L	PCT	G	GS	CG	SH	SV	IP	H	HR	BB	SO	RAT	ERA	ERA+	OAV	OOB	BH	AVG	PB	PR	/A	PD	TPI
1967	Hou-N	1	0	1.000	6	0	0	0	1	4	3	0	2	9	9.0	4.50	78	.214	.267	0	—	-1	-1	-0	-0.1	
1968	Hou-N	1	1	.500	18	0	0	0	0	16¹	21	0	6	16	16.0	7.71	38	.323	.397	0	—	0	-9	-9	-0	-1.1
Total	2	2	1	.667	24	0	0	0	1	20¹	24	0	8	14	14.6	7.08	43	.304	.375	0	—	-0	-9	-9	-0	-1.2

● TOM HOUSE
House, Thomas Ross b: 4/29/47, Seattle, Wash. BL/TL, 5'11", 190 lbs. Deb: 6/23/71 C

YEAR	TM/L	W	L	PCT	G	GS	CG	SH	SV	IP	H	HR	BB	SO	RAT	ERA	ERA+	OAV	OOB	BH	AVG	PB	PR	/A	PD	TPI
1971	Atl-N	1	0	1.000	11	1	0	0	0	20²	20	2	3	11	10.5	3.05	122	.263	.300	2	.400	1	1	2	0	0.1
1972	Atl-N	0	0	—	8	0	0	0	0	9¹	7	1	6	7	13.5	2.89	131	.226	.368	0	.000	0	1	1	0	0.0
1973	Atl-N	4	2	.667	52	0	0	0	4	67¹	58	13	31	42	12.2	4.68	84	.243	.335	2	.200	0	-8	-6	-0	-0.5
1974	Atl-N	6	2	.750	56	0	0	0	11	102²	74	5	27	64	9.1	1.93	196	.203	.264	4	.400	1	19	21	1	2.4
1975	Atl-N	7	7	.500	58	0	0	0	11	79¹	79	2	36	36	13.3	3.18	119	.262	.344	1	.111	0	4	5	1	1.1
1976	Bos-A	1	3	.250	36	0	0	0	4	43²	39	4	19	27	12.4	4.33	90	.241	.328	0	—	0	-4	-2	1	-0.2
1977	Bos-A	1	0	1.000	8	0	0	0	0	7²	15	0	6	6	24.7	12.91	35	.405	.488	0	—	0	-8	-7	-0	-0.9
	Sea-A	4	5	.444	26	11	1	0	1	89¹	94	12	19	39	11.8	3.93	105	.268	.313	0	—	1	2	-1	0	0.1
	Yr	5	5	.500	34	11	1	0	1	97	109	12	25	45	12.8	4.64	89	.281	.331	0	—	1	-6	-5	-0	-0.8
1978	Sea-A	5	4	.556	34	9	0	0	0	116	130	10	35	29	13.2	4.66	82	.289	.347	0	—	-1	-12	-11	-0	-0.8
Total	8	29	23	.558	289	21	1	0	33	536	516	49	182	261	12.1	3.79	102	.256	.324	9	.257	1	6	5	1	1.3

● FRED HOUSE
House, Willard Edwin b: 10/3/1890, Cabool, Mo. d: 11/16/23, Kansas City, Mo. BR/TR, 6'3", 190 lbs. Deb: 4/22/13

YEAR	TM/L	W	L	PCT	G	GS	CG	SH	SV	IP	H	HR	BB	SO	RAT	ERA	ERA+	OAV	OOB	BH	AVG	PB	PR	/A	PD	TPI
1913	Det-A	1	2	.333	19	2	0	0	0	53²	64	3	24	14	15.7	5.20	56	.325	.384	1	.091	-0	-14	-14	1	-0.7

● CHARLIE HOUSEHOLDER
Householder, Charles F. b: 1856, Harrisburg, Pa. BR/TR, 5'7", 150 lbs. Deb: 4/20/1884 ◆

YEAR	TM/L	W	L	PCT	G	GS	CG	SH	SV	IP	H	HR	BB	SO	RAT	ERA	ERA+	OAV	OOB	BH	AVG	PB	PR	/A	PD	TPI
1884	CP-U	0	0	—	2	0	0	0	0	3	4	0	3	2	12.0	3.00	81	.308	.308	74	.239	-0	-0	-0	-1	0.00

● FRANK HOUSEMAN
Houseman, Frank b: Holland Deb: 9/2/1886

YEAR	TM/L	W	L	PCT	G	GS	CG	SH	SV	IP	H	HR	BB	SO	RAT	ERA	ERA+	OAV	OOB	BH	AVG	PB	PR	/A	PD	TPI
1886	Bal-a	0	1	.000	1	1	1	0	0	8	6	0	1	5	9.0	3.38	101	.182	.229	1	.250	-0	0	0	0	0.0

YEAR TM/L	W	L	PCT	G	GS	CG	SH	SV	IP	H	HR	BB	SO	RAT	ERA	ERA+	OAV	OOB	BH	AVG	PB	PR	/A	PD	TPI
● JOE HOUSER　Houser, Joseph William　b: 7/3/1891, Steubenville, Ohio　d: 1/3/53, Orlando, Fla.　BL/TL, 5'9.5", 160 lbs.　Deb: 4/24/14																									
1914 Buf-F	0	1	.000	7	2	0	0	0	23	21	1	20	6	16.0	5.48	54	.250	.394	1	.143	-0	-7	-6	1	-0.2
● ART HOUTTEMAN　Houtteman, Arthur Joseph　b: 8/7/27, Detroit, Mich.　BR/TR, 6'2", 188 lbs.　Deb: 4/29/45																									
1945 Det-A	0	2	.000	13	0	0	0	0	25¹	27	1	11	9	13.9	5.33	66	.270	.348	0	.000	-1	-6	-5	1	-0.4
1946 Det-A	0	1	.000	1	1	0	0	0	8	15	1	0	2	16.9	9.00	41	.385	.385	1	.500	0	-5	-5	-0	-0.4
1947 Det-A	7	2	.778	23	9	7	2	0	110²	106	6	36	58	11.6	3.42	110	.247	.306	12	.300	2	4	4	0	0.5
1948 Det-A	2	16	.111	43	20	4	0	10	164¹	186	11	52	74	13.1	4.66	94	.287	.342	11	.196	-2	-7	-5	4	-0.4
1949 Det-A	15	10	.600	34	25	13	2	0	203²	227	19	59	85	12.9	3.71	112	.282	.335	19	.244	1	11	10	5	1.7
1950 Det-A★	19	12	.613	41	34	21	**4**	4	274²	257	29	99	88	11.9	3.54	132	.251	.322	14	.151	-3	32	35	3	3.5
1952 Det-A	8	20	.286	35	28	10	2	1	221	218	19	65	109	11.7	4.36	87	.253	.309	7	.101	-4	-17	-14	1	-1.9
1953 Det-A	2	6	.250	16	9	3	1	1	68²	87	11	29	28	15.7	5.90	69	.309	.381	3	.158	-0	-15	-14	-0	-1.4
Cle-A	7	7	.500	22	13	6	1	3	109	113	4	25	40	11.8	3.80	99	.269	.318	5	.147	-1	2	-1	0	-0.2
Yr	9	13	.409	38	22	9	2	4	177²	200	15	54	68	13.1	4.61	84	.283	.339	8	.151	-1	-12	-15	-0	-1.6
1954 *Cle-A	15	7	.682	32	25	11	1	0	188	198	14	59	64	12.4	3.35	110	.273	.330	18	.277	5	8	7	2	1.4
1955 Cle-A	10	6	.625	35	12	3	1	0	124¹	126	15	44	53	12.5	3.98	100	.265	.330	6	.158	-1	-0	0	2	0.2
1956 Cle-A	2	2	.500	22	4	0	0	1	46²	60	5	31	19	18.3	6.56	64	.317	.424	2	.167	-1	-12	-12	0	-1.0
1957 Cle-A	0	0	—	3	0	0	0	0	4	6	1	3	3	20.3	6.75	55	.353	.450	0	—	-0	-1	-1	-0	0.0
Bal-A	0	0	—	5	1	0	0	0	6²	20	0	3	3	31.1	17.55	20	.513	.548	1	.500	0	-10	-10	-0	0.1
Yr	0	0	—	8	1	0	0	0	11	26	1	6	6	27.0	13.50	27	.464	.516	1	.500	-0	-12	-12	0	0.1
Total　12	87	91	.489	325	181	78	14	20	1555	1646	136	516	639	12.7	4.14	99	.272	.333	99	.193	-4	-16	-11	17	1.7
● ED HOVLIK　Hovlik, Edward Charles　b: 8/20/1891, Cleveland, Ohio　d: 3/19/55, Painesville, Ohio　BR/TR, 6', 180 lbs.　Deb: 7/14/18　F																									
1918 Was-A	2	1	.667	8	2	1	0	0	28	25	0	10	10	11.3	1.29	212	.272	.343	1	.125	-1	5	4	-1	0.4
1919 Was-A	0	0	—	3	0	0	0	0	5²	12	0	9	3	33.4	12.71	25	.480	.618	0	.000	-0	-6	-6	0	0.0
Total　2	2	1	.667	11	2	1	0	0	33²	37	0	19	13	15.0	3.21	88	.316	.412	1	.100	-1	-1	-1	-0	0.4
● JOE HOVLIK　Hovlik, Joseph　b: 8/16/1884, Czechoslovakia　d: 11/3/51, Oxford Junction, Ia　BR/TR, 5'10.5", 194 lbs.　Deb: 7/10/09　F																									
1909 Was-A	0	0	—	3	0	0	0	0	6	13	0	1	3	25.5	4.50	54	.419	.486	0	.000	-0	-1	-1	0	0.1
1910 Was-A	0	0	—	1	0	0	0	0	1²	6	0	0	2	37.8	16.20	15	.500	.538	0	—	0	-3	-3	-0	0.0
1911 Chi-A	2	0	1.000	12	3	1	1	0	47	47	1	20	24	12.8	3.06	105	.257	.330	1	.077	-0	1	1	1	0.1
Total　3	2	0	1.000	16	3	1	1	0	54²	66	1	23	25	15.0	3.62	86	.292	.363	1	.067	-0	-2	-3	1	0.2
● BRUCE HOWARD　Howard, Bruce Ernest　b: 3/23/43, Salisbury, Md.　BB/TR, 6'2", 180 lbs.　Deb: 9/4/63　F																									
1963 Chi-A	2	1	.667	7	0	0	0	1	17	12	0	14	9	13.8	2.65	132	.207	.361	1	.250	0	2	2	-0	0.3
1964 Chi-A	2	1	.667	3	3	1	1	0	22¹	10	0	8	17	7.7	0.81	429	.139	.235	0	.000	-1	7	7	-0	0.9
1965 Chi-A	9	8	.529	30	22	1	0	0	148	123	13	72	120	11.9	3.47	92	.224	.316	6	.146	2	-0	-4	-1	-0.4
1966 Chi-A	9	5	.643	27	21	4	2	0	149	110	14	44	85	9.4	2.30	138	.202	.263	3	.070	-1	19	14	0	1.3
1967 Chi-A	3	10	.231	30	17	1	0	0	112²	102	9	52	76	12.5	3.43	90	.240	.327	5	.179	-1	-3	-4	1	-0.3
1968 Bal-A	2	0	1.000	10	5	0	0	0	31	30	2	26	19	16.8	3.77	78	.268	.414	2	.286	2	-3	-3	0	0.1
Was-A	1	4	.200	13	7	0	0	0	48²	62	7	23	23	15.7	5.36	54	.330	.403	0	.000	-2	-13	-13	-0	-1.4
Yr	3	4	.429	23	12	0	0	0	79²	92	9	49	42	15.9	4.74	62	.302	.398	2	.087	0	-16	-16	1	-1.3
Total　6	26	31	.456	120	75	7	4	1	528²	449	45	239	349	11.8	3.18	99	.231	.317	17	.116	2	9	-2	1	0.5
● CHRIS HOWARD　Howard, Christian　b: 11/18/65, Lynn, Mass.　BR/TL, 6', 185 lbs.　Deb: 9/21/93																									
1993 Chi-A	1	0	1.000	3	0	0	0	0	2¹	2	0	3	1	19.3	0.00	—	.286	.500	0	—	0	1	1	-0	0.4
1994 Bos-A	1	0	1.000	37	0	0	0	1	39²	35	5	12	22	10.7	3.63	139	.233	.290	0	—	0	5	6	-0	-0.1
1995 Tex-A	0	0	—	4	0	0	0	0	4	3	0	1	2	9.0	0.00	—	.231	.286	0	—	0	2	2	0	0.0
Total　3	2	0	1.000	44	0	0	0	1	46	40	5	16	25	11.0	3.13	159	.235	.301	0	—	0	8	9	-1	0.3
● DAVID HOWARD　Howard, David Wayne　b: 2/26/67, Sarasota, Fla.　BB/TR, 6', 165 lbs.　Deb: 4/14/91　♦																									
1994 KC-A	0	0	—	1	0	0	0	0	2	2	0	5	0	31.5	4.50	111	.286	.583	19	.229	0	0	0	-0	0.0
● EARL HOWARD　Howard, Earl Nycum　b: 6/25/1893, Everett, Pa.　d: 4/4/37, Everett, Pa.　BR/TR, 6'1", 160 lbs.　Deb: 4/18/18																									
1918 StL-N	0	0	—	1	0	0	0	0	2	2	0	2	0	9.0	0.00	—	.000	.286	0	—	0	1	1	1	0.1
● FRED HOWARD　Howard, Fred Irving　b: 9/2/56, Portland, Maine　BR/TR, 6'3", 190 lbs.　Deb: 5/26/79																									
1979 Chi-A	1	5	.167	28	6	0	0	0	68	73	5	32	36	14.0	3.57	119	.283	.364	0	—	0	5	5	-1	0.3
● DEL HOWARD　Howard, George Elmer　b: 12/24/1877, Kenney, Ill.　d: 12/24/56, Seattle, Wash.　BL/TR, 6', 180 lbs.　Deb: 4/15/05　F♦																									
1905 Pit-N	0	0	—	1	0	0	0	0	6	4	1	1	0	9.0	0.00	—	.200	.273	127	.292	0	2	2	0	0.1
● LEE HOWARD　Howard, Lee Vincent　b: 11/11/23, Staten Island, N.Y　BL/TL, 6'2", 175 lbs.　Deb: 9/22/46																									
1946 Pit-N	0	1	.000	3	2	1	0	0	13¹	14	0	9	6	15.5	2.03	174	.286	.397	0	.000	-1	2	2	-0	0.1
1947 Pit-N	0	0	—	2	0	0	0	0	2²	4	1	0	2	13.5	3.38	125	.333	.333	0	—	0	0	0	-0	0.0
Total　2	0	1	.000	5	2	1	0	0	16	18	1	9	8	15.2	2.25	162	.295	.386	0	.000	-1	2	2	-0	0.1
● CAL HOWE　Howe, Calvin Earl　b: 11/27/24, Rock Falls, Ill.　BL/TL, 6'3", 205 lbs.　Deb: 9/26/52																									
1952 Chi-N	0	0	—	2	0	0	0	0	2	0	0	1	2	4.5	0.00	—	.000	.143	0	—	0	1	1	-0	0.0
● LES HOWE　Howe, Lester Curtis "Lucky"　b: 8/24/1895, Brooklyn, N.Y.　d: 7/16/76, Woodmere, N.Y.　BR/TR, 5'11.5", 170 lbs.　Deb: 8/18/23																									
1923 Bos-A	1	0	1.000	12	2	0	0	0	30	23	0	7	9	9.3	2.40	171	.211	.265	0	.000	-1	5	6	0	0.1
1924 Bos-A	1	0	1.000	4	0	0	0	0	7¹	11	0	2	1	17.2	7.36	59	.423	.483	1	.500	0	-3	-2	0	-0.2
Total　2	2	0	1.000	16	2	0	0	0	37¹	34	0	9	10	10.8	3.38	123	.252	.308	1	.125	-1	3	3	0	-0.1
● STEVE HOWE　Howe, Steven Roy　b: 3/10/58, Pontiac, Mich.　BL/TL, 6'1", 180 lbs.　Deb: 4/11/80																									
1980 LA-N	7	9	.438	59	0	0	0	17	84²	83	1	22	39	11.4	2.66	132	.256	.307	1	.091	-0	9	8	1	1.8
1981 *LA-N	5	3	.625	41	0	0	0	8	54	51	2	18	32	11.5	2.50	133	.254	.315	0	.000	-0	6	5	-1	0.8
1982 LA-N★	7	5	.583	66	0	0	0	13	99¹	87	3	17	49	9.4	2.08	166	.240	.274	0	—	-1	17	15	-0	2.1
1983 LA-N	4	7	.364	46	0	0	0	18	68²	55	2	12	52	8.9	1.44	249	.217	.256	1	.125	-1	17	16	1	3.6
1985 LA-N	1	1	.500	19	0	0	0	1	22	30	2	5	11	14.7	4.91	71	.319	.360	0	—	0	-3	-4	0	-0.4
Min-A	2	3	.400	13	0	0	0	0	19	28	1	7	10	16.6	6.16	72	.333	.385	0	—	0	-4	-4	-0	-1.1
1987 Tex-A	3	3	.500	24	0	0	0	1	31¹	33	2	8	19	12.6	4.31	104	.280	.341	0	—	0	1	1	0	0.1
1991 NY-A	3	1	.750	37	0	0	0	3	48¹	39	1	7	34	9.1	1.68	247	.222	.263	0	—	0	13	13	0	1.1
1992 NY-A	3	0	1.000	20	0	0	0	6	22	9	1	3	12	4.9	2.45	160	.122	.156	0	—	0	4	4	1	0.7
1993 NY-A	3	5	.375	51	0	0	0	4	50²	58	7	10	19	12.6	4.97	83	.297	.341	0	—	0	-4	-5	-1	-0.5
1994 NY-A	3	0	1.000	40	0	0	0	15	40	28	2	7	18	7.9	1.80	254	.194	.232	0	—	0	13	12	0	1.6
1995 *NY-A	6	3	.667	56	0	0	0	2	49	66	5	17	28	16.0	4.96	93	.324	.387	0	—	-1	-2	-1	1	-0.2
1996 NY-A	0	1	1.000	25	0	0	0	1	19	19	1	6	5	13.8	6.35	80	.284	.351	0	—	0	-3	-2	0	-0.1
Total　12	47	41	.534	497	0	0	0	91	606	586	32	139	328	11.0	3.03	128	.255	.303	2	.074	-1	64	58	3	9.5
● HARRY HOWELL　Howell, Henry Harry　b: 11/14/1876, New Jersey　d: 5/22/56, Spokane, Wash.　BR/TR, 5'9"　Deb: 10/10/1898　U♦																									
1898 Bro-N	2	0	1.000	2	1	1	0	0	18	15	0	11	2	13.5	5.00	72	.224	.342	2	.250	0	-3	-3	0	-0.2
1899 Bal-N	13	8	.619	28	25	21	0	0	209¹	248	1	69	58	14.1	3.91	101	.294	.355	12	.146	-3	-1	1	1	-0.2
1900 *Bro-N	6	5	.545	21	10	7	2	0	110¹	131	4	36	26	13.9	3.75	102	.294	.351	12	.286	4	-1	1	1	0.5
1901 Bal-A	14	21	.400	37	34	32	1	0	294²	333	5	79	142	12.8	3.67	106	.281	.330	41	.218	1	0	7	-1	0.6
1902 Bal-A	9	15	.375	26	23	19	1	0	199	243	5	48	33	13.5	4.12	92	.301	.346	93	.268	5	-12	-8	4	0.1
1903 NY-A	9	6	.600	25	15	13	0	0	155²	140	4	44	62	11.0	3.53	89	.240	.300	23	.217	2	-10	-7	3	-0.1
1904 StL-A	13	21	.382	34	33	32	2	0	299²	254	0	60	122	9.8	2.19	113	.230	.278	25	.221	5	14	10	9	2.9
1905 StL-A	15	22	.405	38	37	**35**	4	0	323	252	0	101	198	10.2	1.98	129	.217	.286	26	.193	3	24	20	18	**4.9**
1906 StL-A	15	14	.517	35	33	26	6	1	276²	233	1	61	140	9.9	2.11	122	.231	.282	13	.126	-3	18	14	8	2.1
1907 StL-A	16	15	.516	42	35	26	2	3	316¹	258	3	88	118	10.1	1.93	130	.225	.285	27	.237	6	21	20	8	3.7

YEAR	TM/L	W	L	PCT	G	GS	CG	SH	SV	IP	H	HR	BB	SO	RAT	ERA	ERA+	OAV	OOB	BH	AVG	PB	PR	/A	PD	TPI
1908	StL-A	18	18	.500	41	32	27	2	1	324¹	279	1	70	117	10.2	1.89	127	.240	.293	22	.183	1	18	18	0	2.3
1909	StL-A	1	1	.500	10	3	0	0	0	37¹	42	0	8	16	12.8	3.13	77	.294	.344	6	.176	0	-3	-3	-0	-0.2
1910	StL-A	0	0		1	0	0	0	0	3¹	7	0	2	1	24.3	10.80	23	.467	.529	0	.000	-0	-3	-3	0	0.0
Total	13	131	146	.473	340	282	244	20	6	2567²	2435	27	677	986	11.2	2.74	108	.252	.307	302	.217	21	63	64	51	16.4

● **JAY HOWELL** Howell, Jay Canfield b: 11/26/55, Miami, Fla. BR/TR, 6'3", 205 lbs. Deb: 8/10/80

YEAR	TM/L	W	L	PCT	G	GS	CG	SH	SV	IP	H	HR	BB	SO	RAT	ERA	ERA+	OAV	OOB	BH	AVG	PB	PR	/A	PD	TPI
1980	Cin-N	0	0		5	0	0	0	0	3¹	8	0	1	2	24.3	13.50	26	.471	.500	0			-4	-4	-0	0.0
1981	Chi-N	2	0	1.000	10	2	0	0	0	22¹	23	3	10	10	14.1	4.84	76	.277	.368	0	.000	0	-3	-3	1	-0.1
1982	NY-A	2	3	.400	6	6	0	0	0	28	42	1	13	21	17.7	7.71	52	.341	.404	0	—	0	-11	-12	-0	-1.6
1983	NY-A	1	5	.167	19	12	2	0	0	82	89	7	35	61	13.9	5.38	72	.275	.351	0	—	0	-12	-14	-0	-0.7
1984	NY-A	9	4	.692	61	1	0	0	7	103²	86	9	34	109	10.4	2.69	141	.223	.286	0	—	0	15	13	2	1.9
1985	Oak-A☆	9	8	.529	63	0	0	0	29	98	98	5	31	68	11.9	2.85	135	.261	.319	0	—	0	14	11	0	2.5
1986	Oak-A	3	6	.333	38	0	0	0	16	53¹	53	3	23	42	13.0	3.38	115	.262	.341	0	—	0	5	3	-0	0.7
1987	Oak-A★	3	4	.429	36	0	0	0	16	44¹	48	6	21	35	14.2	5.89	70	.277	.359	0	—	0	-7	-9	-0	-1.4
1988	*LA-N	5	3	.625	50	0	0	0	21	65	44	1	21	70	9.1	2.08	160	.188	.258	0	.000	0	10	9	0	1.6
1989	LA-N★	5	3	.625	56	0	0	0	28	79²	60	3	22	55	9.3	1.58	216	.211	.268	0	.000	0	17	16	-0	2.7
1990	LA-N	5	5	.500	45	0	0	0	16	66	59	5	20	59	11.6	2.18	168	.242	.315	0	.000	0	12	11	-0	2.0
1991	LA-N	6	5	.545	44	0	0	0	16	51	39	3	11	40	9.0	3.18	113	.213	.262	0	—	0	3	2	0	0.6
1992	LA-N	1	3	.250	41	0	0	0	4	46²	41	2	18	36	11.6	1.54	223	.230	.305	0	—	0	10	10	1	1.0
1993	Atl-N	3	3	.500	54	0	0	0	0	58¹	48	3	16	37	9.9	2.31	173	.229	.283	0	—	0	11	11	0	1.0
1994	Tex-A	4	1	.800	40	0	0	0	2	43	44	1	16	22	12.8	5.44	89	.262	.330	0	—	0	-3	-3	-0	-0.3
Total	15	58	53	.523	568	21	2	0	155	844²	782	57	291	666	11.6	3.34	114	.246	.313	0	.000	-1	56	43	2	9.9

● **KEN HOWELL** Howell, Kenneth b: 11/28/60, Detroit, Mich. BR/TR, 6'3", 228 lbs. Deb: 6/25/84

YEAR	TM/L	W	L	PCT	G	GS	CG	SH	SV	IP	H	HR	BB	SO	RAT	ERA	ERA+	OAV	OOB	BH	AVG	PB	PR	/A	PD	TPI
1984	LA-N	5	5	.500	32	1	0	0	6	51¹	51	1	9	54	10.7	3.33	106	.267	.303	0	.000	-1	1	1	0	0.2
1985	*LA-N	4	7	.364	56	0	0	0	12	86	66	8	35	85	10.6	3.77	92	.208	.287	0	.000	-0	-2	-3	0	-0.4
1986	LA-N	6	12	.333	62	0	0	0	12	97²	86	7	63	104	14.0	3.87	89	.239	.357	0	.000	-1	-2	-5	-1	-1.1
1987	LA-N	3	4	.429	40	2	0	0	1	55	54	7	29	60	13.6	4.91	81	.265	.356	1	.250	-0	-5	-6	-0	-0.7
1988	LA-N	0	1	.000	4	1	0	0	0	12²	16	0	4	12	14.2	6.39	52	.320	.370	0	.000	-0	-4	-4	0	-0.3
1989	Phi-N	12	12	.500	33	32	1	1	0	204	155	11	86	164	10.7	3.44	103	.215	.300	6	.092	-2	1	-2	-1	-0.1
1990	Phi-N	8	7	.533	18	18	2	0	0	106²	106	12	49	70	13.3	4.64	82	.260	.343	2	.067	-1	-10	-10	-1	-1.4
Total	7	38	48	.442	245	54	3	1	31	613¹	534	46	275	549	12.0	3.95	91	.237	.323	9	.079	-5	-20	-24	-3	-3.8

● **DIXIE HOWELL** Howell, Millard b: 1/7/20, Bowman, Ky. d: 3/18/60, Hollywood, Fla. BL/TR, 6'2", 210 lbs. Deb: 9/14/40

YEAR	TM/L	W	L	PCT	G	GS	CG	SH	SV	IP	H	HR	BB	SO	RAT	ERA	ERA+	OAV	OOB	BH	AVG	PB	PR	/A	PD	TPI
1940	Cle-A	0	0		3	0	0	0	0	5	4	0	2	2	10.8	1.80	234	.143	.333	0			1	1	0	0.0
1949	Cin-N	0	1	.000	5	1	0	0	0	13¹	21	3	8	7	19.6	8.10	52	.362	.439	1	.111	-0	-6	-6	-0	-0.4
1955	Chi-A	8	3	.727	35	0	0	0	9	73²	70	1	25	25	11.6	2.93	135	.250	.311	8	.381	-2	8	8	1	1.7
1956	Chi-A	5	6	.455	34	1	0	0	4	64¹	79	3	36	28	16.4	4.62	89	.309	.398	4	.235	-2	-3	-4	-0	-0.4
1957	Chi-A	6	5	.545	37	0	0	0	6	68¹	64	6	30	37	12.4	3.29	113	.255	.335	5	.185	4	4	3	1	1.0
1958	Chi-A	0	0		1	0	0	0	0	1²	1	0	0	0		0.00		.000	.000	0	—	0	1	0	0	0.0
Total	6	19	15	.559	115	2	0	0	19	226¹	236	13	103	99	13.6	3.78	104	.273	.352	18	.243	8	5	4	2	1.9

● **ROLAND HOWELL** Howell, Roland Boatner "Billiken" b: 1/3/1892, Napoleonville, La. d: 3/31/73, Baton Rouge, La. BR/TR, 6'4", 210 lbs. Deb: 6/14/12

YEAR	TM/L	W	L	PCT	G	GS	CG	SH	SV	IP	H	HR	BB	SO	RAT	ERA	ERA+	OAV	OOB	BH	AVG	PB	PR	/A	PD	TPI
1912	StL-N	0	0		3	0	0	0	0	1²	5	0	5	0	54.0	27.00	13	.556	.714	0	—	0	-4	-4	-0	0.0

● **PETER HOY** Hoy, Peter Alexander b: 6/29/66, Brockville, Ont., Canada BL/TR, 6'7", 220 lbs. Deb: 4/11/92

YEAR	TM/L	W	L	PCT	G	GS	CG	SH	SV	IP	H	HR	BB	SO	RAT	ERA	ERA+	OAV	OOB	BH	AVG	PB	PR	/A	PD	TPI
1992	Bos-A	0	0		5	0	0	0	0	3²	8	0	2	2	24.5	7.36	57	.471	.526	0	—	0	-1	-1	0	0.0

● **TEX HOYLE** Hoyle, Roland Edison b: 7/17/21, Carbondale, Pa. d: 7/4/94, Carbondale, Pa. BR/TR, 6'4", 170 lbs. Deb: 4/18/52

YEAR	TM/L	W	L	PCT	G	GS	CG	SH	SV	IP	H	HR	BB	SO	RAT	ERA	ERA+	OAV	OOB	BH	AVG	PB	PR	/A	PD	TPI
1952	Phi-A	0	0		3	0	0	0	0	2¹	9	2	1	0	38.6	27.00	15	.563	.588	0	—	0	-6	-6	-0	0.0

● **LA MARR HOYT** Hoyt, Dewey La Marr b: 1/1/55, Columbia, S.C. BR/TR, 6'1", 222 lbs. Deb: 9/14/79

YEAR	TM/L	W	L	PCT	G	GS	CG	SH	SV	IP	H	HR	BB	SO	RAT	ERA	ERA+	OAV	OOB	BH	AVG	PB	PR	/A	PD	TPI
1979	Chi-A	0	0		2	0	0	0	0	3	2	0	0	0	6.0	0.00	—	.200	.200	0	—	0	1	1	-0	0.0
1980	Chi-A	9	3	.750	24	13	3	1	0	112¹	123	8	41	55	13.3	4.57	88	.281	.345	0	—	0	-7	-7	-2	-0.8
1981	Chi-A	9	3	.750	43	1	0	0	10	90²	80	10	28	60	11.0	3.57	100	.240	.305	0	—	0	1	0	-1	0.0
1982	Chi-A	**19**	15	.559	39	32	14	2	0	239²	248	17	48	124	11.2	3.53	114	.266	.303	0	—	0	14	13	-1	1.6
1983	*Chi-A	**24**	10	.706	36	36	11	1	0	260²	236	27	31	148	**9.3**	3.66	114	.238	**.262**	0	—	0	12	15	5	2.3
1984	Chi-A	13	18	.419	34	34	11	1	0	235²	244	31	43	126	11.2	4.47	93	.266	.302	0	—	0	-13	-8	1	-0.9
1985	SD-N★	16	8	.667	31	31	8	3	0	210¹	210	20	20	83	9.9	3.47	102	.261	.281	4	.063	-4	3	3	1	-0.1
1986	SD-N	8	11	.421	35	25	1	0	0	159	170	27	68	85	13.6	5.15	71	.276	.351	6	.130	-5	-25	-26	-2	-3.1
Total	8	98	68	.590	244	172	48	8	10	1311¹	1313	140	279	681	11.0	3.99	98	.260	.302	10	.091	-5	-13	-10	1	-1.0

● **WAITE HOYT** Hoyt, Waite Charles "Schoolboy" b: 9/9/1899, Brooklyn, N.Y. d: 8/25/84, Cincinnati, Ohio BR/TR, 6', 180 lbs. Deb: 7/24/18 H

YEAR	TM/L	W	L	PCT	G	GS	CG	SH	SV	IP	H	HR	BB	SO	RAT	ERA	ERA+	OAV	OOB	BH	AVG	PB	PR	/A	PD	TPI
1918	NY-N	0	0	—	1	0	0	0	0	1	1	0	0	2	0.0	0.00	—	.000	.000	0	—	-0	0	0	-0	0.0
1919	Bos-A	4	6	.400	13	11	6	1	0	105¹	99	1	22	28	10.3	3.25	93	.262	.303	5	.132	-3	-0	-3	1	-0.4
1920	Bos-A	6	6	.500	22	11	6	2	1	121¹	123	2	47	45	12.7	4.38	83	.270	.339	5	.116	-3	-8	-10	1	-1.1
1921	*NY-A	19	13	.594	43	32	21	1	3	282²	301	3	81	102	12.3	3.09	137	.276	.329	22	.222	-2	37	36	-1	3.3
1922	*NY-A	19	12	.613	37	31	16	3	0	265	271	13	76	95	12.1	3.43	117	.269	.326	20	.217	1	18	17	-2	1.7
1923	*NY-A	17	9	.654	37	28	19	1	1	238²	227	9	66	60	11.2	3.02	131	.253	.307	16	.190	-2	26	24	-1	2.1
1924	NY-A	18	13	.581	46	32	14	2	4	247	295	6	76	71	13.6	3.79	110	.300	.352	10	.133	-5	12	10	-0	1.3
1925	NY-A	11	14	.440	46	30	11	1	6	243	283	14	78	86	13.4	4.00	107	.292	.346	24	.304	6	11	7	3	1.3
1926	*NY-A	16	12	.571	40	28	12	1	4	217²	224	4	62	79	11.9	3.85	100	.264	.316	16	.211	-0	4	0	-3	-0.3
1927	*NY-A	**22**	7	**.759**	36	32	23	3	1	256¹	242	10	54	86	10.5	2.63	146	.251	.294	22	.222	2	43	35	-0	3.5
1928	*NY-A	23	7	.767	42	31	19	3	**8**	273	279	16	60	67	11.2	3.36	112	.272	.313	28	.257	2	21	12	-1	1.2
1929	NY-A	10	9	.526	30	25	12	0	1	201²	219	9	57	57	13.0	4.24	91	.279	.339	17	.224	1	-9	-2	-0	-0.3
1930	NY-A	2	2	.500	8	7	2	0	0	47²	64	7	9	10	13.8	4.53	95	.317	.346	1	.063	-2	-1	-0	-3	-0.3
	Det-A	9	8	.529	26	20	8	1	4	135²	176	7	47	25	14.9	4.78	100	.313	.368	9	.196	-2	-2	-0	-3	-0.5
	Yr	11	10	.524	34	27	10	1	4	183¹	240	14	56	35	14.6	4.71	99	.313	.363	10	.161	-4	-1	-1	-3	-0.8
1931	Det-A	3	8	.273	16	12	5	0	0	92	124	2	32	10	15.5	5.87	78	.319	.374	4	.133	-2	-15	-13	-0	-1.5
	*Phi-A	10	5	.667	16	14	9	2	0	111	130	9	37	30	13.5	4.22	107	.298	.353	13	.302	3	2	3	1	0.7
	Yr	13	13	.500	32	26	14	2	0	203	254	11	69	40	14.5	4.97	91	.307	.360	17	.233	0	-13	-10	0	-0.8
1932	Bro-N	1	3	.250	8	4	0	1	0	26²	38	3	12	7	16.9	7.76	49	.342	.407	0	.000	-1	-12	-12	-1	-1.5
	NY-N	5	7	.417	18	12	3	0	0	97¹	103	5	25	29	12.3	3.42	109	.275	.328	3	.097	-2	5	3	1	0.2
	Yr	6	10	.375	26	16	3	1	0	124	141	8	37	36	13.3	4.35	86	.290	.347	3	.081	-3	-7	-9	2	-1.3
1933	Pit-N	5	7	.417	36	8	4	1	4	117	118	3	19	44	10.6	2.92	114	.262	.293	6	.156	-1	5	5	1	0.5
1934	Pit-N	15	6	.714	48	15	8	3	5	190²	184	6	43	105	10.8	2.93	141	.252	.296	10	.179	-1	24	25	1	2.5
1935	Pit-N	7	11	.389	39	11	5	0	6	164	187	8	27	63	11.8	3.40	121	.285	.315	14	.259	2	11	13	-0	1.6
1936	Pit-N	7	5	.583	22	9	6	0	1	116²	115	5	20	37	10.6	2.70	150	.255	.291	6	.154	-1	17	18	1	1.6
1937	Pit-N	1	2	.333	11	0	0	0	2	28	31	3	6	21	11.9	4.50	86	.270	.306	1	.083	-1	-2	-1	-0	-0.4
	Bro-N	7	7	.500	27	19	10	1	0	167	180	5	30	44	11.3	3.23	125	.270	.301	4	.083	-2	13	14	1	0.8
	Yr	8	9	.471	38	19	10	1	2	195	211	8	36	65	11.4	3.42	117	.270	.302	5	.083	-3	11	13	2	0.4
1938	Bro-N	0	3	.000	6	1	0	0	0	16¹	24	1	4	3	16.0	4.96	79	.333	.377	0	.000	0	-2	-2	-0	-0.4
Total	21	237	182	.566	674	423	226	26	52	3762¹	4037	154	1003	1206	12.2	3.59	112	.276	.325	255	.198	-17	210	173	-7	14.4

● **AL HRABOSKY** Hrabosky, Alan Thomas b: 7/21/49, Oakland, Cal. BR/TL, 5'11", 185 lbs. Deb: 6/16/70

YEAR	TM/L	W	L	PCT	G	GS	CG	SH	SV	IP	H	HR	BB	SO	RAT	ERA	ERA+	OAV	OOB	BH	AVG	PB	PR	/A	PD	TPI
1970	StL-N	2	1	.667	16	1	0	0	0	19	22	2	7	12	13.7	4.74	87	.286	.345	0	.000	-0	-1	-1	-1	-0.3
1971	StL-N	0	0		1	0	0	0	0	2	1	0	1	2	9.0	0.00	—	.250	.250	0	—	1	1	1	0	0.3
1972	StL-N	1	0	1.000	5	0	0	0	0	7	3	0	3	9	6.4	0.00	—	.087	.192	0	—	0	3	3	-0	0.3
1973	StL-N	2	4	.333	44	0	0	0	5	56	45	2	21	56	10.9	2.09	174	.220	.298	0	.000	-0	10	10	1	1.9
1974	StL-N	8	1	.889	65	0	0	0	9	88¹	71	3	38	82	11.2	2.95	121	.221	.306	4	.308	-1	7	6	-1	0.7
1975	StL-N	13	3	.813	65	0	0	0	**22**	97¹	72	3	33	82	9.8	1.66	226	.205	.275	3	.200	1	**21**	**23**	-2	4.8

YEAR TM/L	W	L	PCT	G	GS	CG	SH	SV	IP	H	HR	BB	SO	RAT	ERA	ERA+	OAV	OOB	BH	AVG	PB	PR	/A	PD	TPI
1976 StL-N	8	6	.571	68	0	0	0	13	95¹	89	5	39	73	12.5	3.30	107	.252	.333	0	.000	0	2	2	-0	0.4
1977 StL-N	6	5	.545	65	0	0	0	10	86¹	82	12	41	69	13.1	4.38	88	.256	.346	0	.000	-1	-5	-5	-1	-0.9
1978 *KC-A	8	7	.533	58	0	0	0	20	75	52	6	35	60	10.6	2.88	133	.200	.297	0	—	0	7	8	-0	1.8
1979 KC-A	9	4	.692	58	0	0	0	11	65	67	3	41	39	15.1	3.74	114	.272	.378	0	—	0	3	4	-2	0.5
1980 Atl-N	4	2	.667	45	0	0	0	3	59²	50	8	31	31	12.2	3.62	103	.223	.318	0	.000	-0	-0	1	-2	-0.1
1981 Atl-N	1	1	.500	24	0	0	0	1	33²	24	1	9	13	8.8	1.07	335	.207	.264	0	.000	-0	9	9	-1	0.5
1982 Atl-N	2	1	.667	31	0	0	0	3	37¹	41	5	17	20	14.0	5.54	67	.285	.360	1	.333	0	-8	-8	-1	-0.7
Total 13	64	35	.646	545	0	0	0	97	722	619	50	315	548	11.8	3.10	121	.234	.318	8	.143	0	49	52	-11	8.1

● **CARL HUBBELL** Hubbell, Carl Owen "King Carl" or "The Mealticket"
b: 6/22/03, Carthage, Mo. d: 11/21/88, Scottsdale, Ariz. BR/TL, 6', 170 lbs. Deb: 7/26/28 H

YEAR TM/L	W	L	PCT	G	GS	CG	SH	SV	IP	H	HR	BB	SO	RAT	ERA	ERA+	OAV	OOB	BH	AVG	PB	PR	/A	PD	TPI
1928 NY-N	10	6	.625	20	14	8	1	1	124	117	7	21	37	10.2	2.83	138	.248	.284	5	.106	-3	16	15	2	1.7
1929 NY-N	18	11	.621	39	35	19	1	1	268	273	17	67	106	11.6	3.69	124	.265	.313	12	.129	-6	30	26	5	2.3
1930 NY-N	17	12	.586	37	32	17	3	2	241²	263	11	58	117	12.4	3.87	122	.278	.327	13	.151	-5	29	23	-1	1.7
1931 NY-N	14	12	.538	36	30	21	4	3	248	211	14	67	155	**10.2**	2.65	139	**.227**	**.282**	20	.241	4	34	29	-2	3.1
1932 NY-N	18	11	.621	40	32	22	0	2	284	260	20	40	137	**9.6**	2.50	148	.238	**.268**	26	.241	4	43	38	6	**4.8**
1933 *NY-N★	**23**	12	.657	45	33	22	**10**	5	**308²**	256	6	47	156	**8.9**	**1.66**	**193**	.227	**.260**	20	.183	1	**58**	**53**	7	**7.5**
1934 NY-N★	21	12	.636	49	34	**25**	5	**8**	313	286	17	37	118	**9.3**	**2.30**	**168**	.239	**.263**	23	.197	-1	**61**	**54**	4	6.0
1935 NY-N☆	23	12	.657	42	35	24	1	0	302²	314	27	49	150	10.9	3.27	118	.263	.294	26	.239	4	25	20	4	2.9
1936 *NY-N★	**26**	6	**.813**	42	34	25	3	3	304	265	7	57	123	**9.7**	**2.31**	**169**	.236	**.276**	25	.227	1	**58**	**54**	1	**5.5**
1937 *NY-N★	22	8	**.733**	39	32	18	4	4	261²	261	18	55	**159**	11.0	3.20	122	.257	.298	21	.216	1	21	20	-1	2.1
1938 NY-N	13	10	.565	24	22	13	1	1	179	171	16	33	104	**10.4**	3.07	123	.249	**.285**	9	.155	-2	14	14	-1	1.3
1939 NY-N	11	9	.550	29	18	10	0	2	154	150	11	24	62	**10.3**	2.75	143	.249	**.280**	8	.151	-1	20	20	1	2.5
1940 NY-N★	11	12	.478	31	27	11	2	0	214¹	220	22	59	86	11.8	3.65	106	.259	.309	15	.185	-0	5	5	1	0.6
1941 NY-N	11	9	.550	26	22	11	1	1	164	169	10	53	75	12.3	3.57	104	.266	.325	8	.140	-2	1	2	-3	-0.2
1942 NY-N☆	11	8	.579	24	20	11	0	0	157¹	158	17	34	61	11.0	3.95	85	.259	.299	11	.183	-0	-11	-10	-1	-1.3
1943 NY-N	4	4	.500	12	11	3	0	0	66	87	7	24	31	15.1	4.91	70	.322	.378	4	.200	-0	-11	-11	-1	-1.3
Total 16	253	154	.622	535	431	260	36	33	3590¹	3461	227	725	1677	10.6	2.98	130	.251	.291	246	.191	-5	394	355	22	39.2

● **BILL HUBBELL** Hubbell, Wilbert William b: 6/17/1897, San Francisco, Cal. d: 8/3/80, Lakewood, Colo. BR/TR, 6'1.5", 195 lbs. Deb: 9/24/19

YEAR TM/L	W	L	PCT	G	GS	CG	SH	SV	IP	H	HR	BB	SO	RAT	ERA	ERA+	OAV	OOB	BH	AVG	PB	PR	/A	PD	TPI
1919 NY-N	1	1	.500	2	2	2	0	0	18¹	19	0	2	3	11.3	1.96	143	.260	.299	1	.125	-1	2	2	-0	0.1
1920 NY-N	0	1	.000	14	0	0	0	2	30	26	2	15	18	12.6	2.10	143	.239	.336	-0	.200	-0	3	3	1	0.2
Phi-N	9	9	.500	24	18	9	1	2	150	176	3	42	26	13.3	3.84	89	.301	.352	7	.132	-3	-12	-7	-2	-1.3
Yr	9	10	.474	38	18	9	1	4	180	202	5	57	34	13.1	3.55	94	.291	.348	8	.138	-3	-8	-4	-1	-1.1
1921 Phi-N	9	16	.360	36	30	15	1	2	220¹	269	18	38	43	12.7	4.33	98	.306	.337	12	.160	-2	-13	-2	-1	-0.4
1922 Phi-N	7	15	.318	35	26	11	1	1	189	257	14	41	33	14.4	5.00	93	.317	.353	12	.171	-2	-19	-7	0	-0.8
1923 Phi-N	1	6	.143	22	5	1	0	0	55	102	13	17	8	19.8	8.35	55	.235	.394	4	.235	0	-27	-23	0	-2.3
1924 Phi-N	10	9	.526	36	22	9	2	2	179	233	6	45	30	14.1	4.83	92	.324	.365	13	.220	-1	-19	-7	-0	-0.7
1925 Phi-N	0	0	—	2	0	0	0	0	2²	5	1	0	1	20.3	0.00	—	.385	.429	0	.000	-0	1	1	1	0.0
Bro-N	3	6	.333	33	5	3	0	1	86²	120	8	24	16	15.2	5.30	79	.337	.382	3	.150	0	-10	-11	-1	-0.8
Yr	3	6	.333	35	5	3	0	1	89¹	125	8	25	16	15.3	5.14	82	.339	.384	3	.143	0	-9	-9	2	-0.8
Total 7	40	63	.388	204	108	50	5	10	931	1207	67	225	167	14.0	4.68	89	.317	.359	53	.172	-8	-93	-52	0	-6.0

● **EARL HUCKLEBERRY** Huckleberry, Earl Eugene b: 5/23/10, Konawa, Okla. BR/TR, 5'11", 165 lbs. Deb: 9/13/35

YEAR TM/L	W	L	PCT	G	GS	CG	SH	SV	IP	H	HR	BB	SO	RAT	ERA	ERA+	OAV	OOB	BH	AVG	PB	PR	/A	PD	TPI
1935 Phi-A	1	0	1.000	1	1	0	0	0	6²	8	1	4	2	16.2	9.45	48	.296	.387	0	.000	-0	-4	-4	-0	-0.4

● **JOHN HUDEK** Hudek, John Raymond b: 8/8/66, Tampa, Fla. BB/TR, 6'1", 200 lbs. Deb: 4/23/94

YEAR TM/L	W	L	PCT	G	GS	CG	SH	SV	IP	H	HR	BB	SO	RAT	ERA	ERA+	OAV	OOB	BH	AVG	PB	PR	/A	PD	TPI
1994 Hou-N★	0	2	.000	42	0	0	0	16	39¹	24	5	18	39	9.8	2.97	133	.174	.274		—	0	5	4	0	0.5
1995 Hou-N	2	2	.500	19	0	0	0	7	20	19	3	5	29	10.8	5.40	72	.247	.293	1	1.000	1	-3	-3	1	-0.7
1996 Hou-N	2	0	1.000	15	0	0	0	2	16	12	2	5	14	9.6	2.81	136	.207	.270	0	—	0	2	2	1	0.3
Total 3	4	4	.500	76	0	0	0	25	75¹	55	10	28	82	10.0	3.58	109	.211	.278	1	1.000	1	5	3	1	0.1

● **WILLIS HUDLIN** Hudlin, George Willis "Ace" b: 5/23/06, Wagoner, Okla. BR/TR, 6', 190 lbs. Deb: 8/15/26 C

YEAR TM/L	W	L	PCT	G	GS	CG	SH	SV	IP	H	HR	BB	SO	RAT	ERA	ERA+	OAV	OOB	BH	AVG	PB	PR	/A	PD	TPI
1926 Cle-A	1	3	.250	8	2	1	0	0	32¹	25	1	13	6	11.1	2.78	146	.227	.320	1	.125	0	4	5	2	0.7
1927 Cle-A	18	12	.600	43	30	18	1	0	264²	291	3	83	65	13.1	4.01	105	.283	.343	24	.250	2	4	6	3	1.1
1928 Cle-A	14	14	.500	42	26	10	0	7	220¹	231	7	90	62	13.4	4.04	103	.279	.355	14	.194	-0	0	2	2	0.5
1929 Cle-A	17	15	.531	40	33	22	2	1	280¹	299	7	73	60	12.0	3.34	133	.272	.318	19	.196	-3	28	34	7	**3.9**
1930 Cle-A	13	16	.448	37	33	13	1	1	216²	255	12	76	60	13.8	4.57	106	.293	.351	16	.219	-1	2	6	5	1.0
1931 Cle-A	15	14	.517	44	34	15	1	4	254¹	313	14	83	63	13.1	4.60	100	.301	.356	20	.200	1	-6	1	4	0.5
1932 Cle-A	12	8	.600	33	21	12	0	2	181²	204	10	59	65	13.1	4.71	101	.278	.332	13	.203	1	-5	1	1	0.2
1933 Cle-A	5	13	.278	34	17	6	0	1	147¹	161	7	61	44	13.7	3.97	112	.275	.346	6	.146	-1	5	8	4	1.1
1934 Cle-A	15	10	.600	36	26	15	1	4	195	210	8	65	58	12.9	4.75	96	.277	.338	14	.206	-3	-6	-4	5	0.2
1935 Cle-A	15	11	.577	36	29	14	3	5	231²	252	8	61	45	12.3	3.69	122	.277	.324	24	.279	6	20	21	0	2.7
1936 Cle-A	1	5	.167	27	7	1	0	0	64	112	1	31	20	20.4	9.00	56	.397	.460	2	.111	-1	-28	-28	1	-2.0
1937 Cle-A	12	11	.522	35	23	10	2	2	175²	213	8	43	31	13.2	4.10	112	.295	.337	11	.169	-1	10	10	3	1.3
1938 Cle-A	8	8	.500	29	15	8	0	1	127	158	8	45	27	14.5	4.89	95	.303	.361	5	.116	-2	-1	-1	-1	-0.5
1939 Cle-A	9	10	.474	27	20	7	0	3	143	175	6	42	28	13.7	4.91	90	.303	.352	9	.188	1	-5	-8	5	-0.4
1940 Cle-A	1	2	.667	4	4	2	0	0	23²	31	3	2	8	12.5	4.94	85	.316	.330	1	.125	0	-1	-2	-0	-0.2
Was-A	1	2	.333	8	6	1	0	0	37¹	50	9	5	9	13.7	6.51	64	.314	.343	1	.100	-1	-9	-10	0	-0.7
StL-A	0	1	.000	6	1	0	0	0	11¹	19	1	6	4	21.4	11.12	41	.358	.443	1	.500	0	-8	-8	0	-0.6
Yr	3	4	.429	18	11	3	0	0	72¹	100	12	15	21	14.3	6.72	63	.321	.352	3	.150	-1	-19	-20	0	-1.5
NY-N	1	0	1.000	1	1	0	0	0	5	9	1	1	1	18.0	10.80	36	.409	.435	0	.000	-0	-4	-4	0	-0.5
1944 StL-A	0	1	.000	2	0	0	0	0	2	3	0	0	1	13.5	4.50	80	.300	.300	0	—	-0	-0	-0	-1	-0.1
Total 16	158	156	.503	491	328	155	11	31	2613¹	3011	118	846	677	13.4	4.41	102	.289	.345	180	.201	4	-0	26	42	8.2

● **CHARLIE HUDSON** Hudson, Charles b: 8/18/49, Ada, Okla. BL/TL, 6'3", 185 lbs. Deb: 5/21/72

YEAR TM/L	W	L	PCT	G	GS	CG	SH	SV	IP	H	HR	BB	SO	RAT	ERA	ERA+	OAV	OOB	BH	AVG	PB	PR	/A	PD	TPI
1972 StL-N	1	0	1.000	12	0	0	0	0	12¹	10	0	7	4	13.1	5.11	67	.233	.353	0	—	0	-2	-2	-0	-0.2
1973 Tex-A	4	2	.667	25	4	1	1	1	62¹	59	3	31	34	13.0	4.62	81	.254	.342	0	—	0	-6	-6	0	-0.5
1975 Cal-A	0	1	.000	3	1	0	0	0	5²	7	0	4	0	17.5	9.53	37	.304	.407	0	—	0	-4	-4	0	-0.2
Total 3	5	3	.625	40	5	1	1	1	80¹	76	3	42	38	13.5	5.04	73	.255	.349	0	—	0	-11	-12	0	-0.9

● **CHARLES HUDSON** Hudson, Charles Lynn b: 3/16/59, Ennis, Tex. BB/TR, 6'3", 185 lbs. Deb: 5/31/83

YEAR TM/L	W	L	PCT	G	GS	CG	SH	SV	IP	H	HR	BB	SO	RAT	ERA	ERA+	OAV	OOB	BH	AVG	PB	PR	/A	PD	TPI
1983 *Phi-N	8	8	.500	26	26	5	3	0	169¹	158	13	53	101	11.2	3.35	106	.248	.305	5	.093	-2	5	4	-1	0.1
1984 Phi-N	9	11	.450	30	30	1	1	0	173²	181	12	52	94	12.2	4.04	90	.265	.319	5	.089	-2	-9	-8	-2	-1.3
1985 Phi-N	8	13	.381	38	26	3	0	0	193	188	23	74	122	12.3	3.78	97	.252	.320	8	.140	-4	-4	-2	-0	-0.5
1986 Phi-N	7	10	.412	33	23	0	0	0	144	165	24	58	82	13.9	4.94	78	.291	.357	2	.047	-3	-20	-17	-0	-2.2
1987 NY-A	11	7	.611	35	16	6	2	0	154²	137	19	57	100	11.5	3.61	122	.239	.311	0	—	0	15	13	-2	1.3
1988 NY-A	6	6	.500	28	12	1	0	2	106¹	99	9	36	58	11.3	4.49	88	.235	.306	0	—	0	-6	-6	-0	-0.7
1989 Det-A	1	5	.167	18	7	0	0	0	66²	75	14	31	23	14.6	6.35	60	.288	.369	0	—	0	-18	-19	-1	-1.5
Total 7	50	60	.455	208	140	14	3	2	1007²	997	110	361	580	12.2	4.14	92	.258	.324	20	.095	-8	-37	-35	-8	-4.8

● **HAL HUDSON** Hudson, Hal Campbell "Bud" or "Lefty" b: 5/4/27, Grosse Pointe, Mich. BL/TL, 5'10", 175 lbs. Deb: 4/20/52

YEAR TM/L	W	L	PCT	G	GS	CG	SH	SV	IP	H	HR	BB	SO	RAT	ERA	ERA+	OAV	OOB	BH	AVG	PB	PR	/A	PD	TPI
1952 StL-A	0	0	—	3	0	0	0	0	5²	9	0	6	0	23.8	12.71	31	.360	.484	0	.000	-0	-6	-6	-0	0.0
Chi-A	0	0	—	2	0	0	0	0	4	7	0	4	4	18.0	2.25	162	.389	.421	0	.000	-0	1	1	-0	0.0
Yr	0	0	—	5	0	0	0	0	9²	16	0	7	4	21.4	8.38	45	.372	.460	0	.000	-0	-5	-5	-0	0.0
1953 Chi-A	0	0	—	1	0	0	0	0	0²	0	0	1	0		0.00	—	.000	.000	0	—	-0	0	0	-0	0.0
Total 2	0	0	—	6	0	0	0	0	9²	16	0	8	4	22.3	7.84	49	.364	.451	0	.000	-0	-5	-5	0	0.0

● **JESSE HUDSON** Hudson, Jesse James b: 7/22/48, Mansfield, La. BL/TL, 6'2", 165 lbs. Deb: 9/19/69

YEAR TM/L	W	L	PCT	G	GS	CG	SH	SV	IP	H	HR	BB	SO	RAT	ERA	ERA+	OAV	OOB	BH	AVG	PB	PR	/A	PD	TPI
1969 NY-N	0	0	—	1	0	0	0	0	2	2	0	2	3	18.0	4.50	81	.250	.400	0	—	0	-0	-0	0	0.0

YEAR TM/L	W	L	PCT	G	GS	CG	SH	SV	IP	H	HR	BB	SO	RAT	ERA	ERA+	OAV	OOB	BH	AVG	PB	PR	/A	PD	TPI
● JOE HUDSON				Hudson, Joseph Paul b: 9/29/70, Philadelphia, Pa. BR/TR, 6'1", 175 lbs. Deb: 6/10/95																					
1995 *Bos-A	0	1	.000	39	0	0	0	1	46	53	2	23	29	15.3	4.11	118	.301	.388	0	—	0	3	4	-0	0.0
1996 Bos-A	3	5	.375	36	0	0	0	1	45	57	4	32	19	17.8	5.40	95	.318	.422	0	—	0	-2	-1	-0	-0.3
Total 2	3	6	.333	75	0	0	0	2	91	110	6	55	48	16.5	4.75	105	.310	.405	0	—	0	1	3	-0	-0.3
● NAT HUDSON				Hudson, Nathaniel P. b: 1/12/1859, Chicago, Ill. d: 3/14/28, Chicago, Ill. BR/TR, Deb: 4/18/1886																					
1886 *StL-a	16	10	.615	29	27	25	0	1	234¹	224	3	62	100	11.1	3.03	113	.243	.293	35	.233	1	11	11	-1	0.9
1887 StL-a	4	4	.500	9	9	7	0	0	67	91	2	20	15	15.4	4.97	91	.305	.357	12	.250	0	-5	-3	-2	-0.4
1888 StL-a	25	10	.714	39	37	36	5	0	333	283	8	59	130	9.6	2.54	128	.222	.264	50	.255	5	19	27	-1	2.7
1889 StL-a	3	2	.600	9	5	4	0	0	60	71	2	15	13	13.5	4.20	101	.285	.336	13	.250	0	-2	0	-1	0.0
Total 4	48	26	.649	86	78	72	5	1	694¹	669	15	156	258	11.0	3.08	114	.244	.291	110	.247	6	23	34	-4	3.2
● REX HUDSON				Hudson, Rex Haughton b: 8/11/53, Tulsa, Okla. BB/TR, 5'11", 165 lbs. Deb: 7/27/74																					
1974 LA-N	0	0	—	1	0	0	0	0	2	6	2	0	0	27.0	22.50	15	.500	.500	0	—	0	-4	-4	-0	0.0
● SID HUDSON				Hudson, Sidney Charles b: 1/3/15, Coalfield, Tenn. BR/TR, 6'4", 180 lbs. Deb: 4/18/40 C																					
1940 Was-A	17	16	.515	38	31	19	3	1	252	272	20	81	96	12.7	4.57	91	.274	.330	22	.237	2	-5	-11	1	-1.0
1941 Was-A★	13	14	.481	33	33	17	3	0	249²	242	12	97	108	12.3	3.46	117	.253	.322	16	.186	-0	19	16	2	1.8
1942 Was-A☆	10	17	.370	35	31	19	1	2	239¹	266	9	70	72	12.8	4.36	84	.276	.328	19	.213	1	-19	-19	3	-1.5
1946 Was-A	8	11	.421	31	15	6	1	1	142¹	160	9	37	35	12.7	3.60	93	.280	.328	12	.279	3	-2	-4	2	0.0
1947 Was-A	6	9	.400	20	17	5	1	0	106	113	8	58	37	14.6	5.60	66	.272	.363	12	.237	2	-22	-22	1	-2.4
1948 Was-A	4	16	.200	39	29	4	0	1	182	217	11	107	53	16.3	5.88	74	.299	.394	14	.237	2	-32	-31	3	-2.4
1949 Was-A	8	17	.320	40	27	11	2	1	209	234	15	91	54	14.2	4.22	101	.283	.357	16	.239	2	-1	1	4	0.6
1950 Was-A	14	14	.500	30	30	17	0	0	237²	261	17	98	75	13.8	4.09	110	.286	.356	20	.215	-1	13	11	3	1.3
1951 Was-A	5	12	.294	23	19	8	0	0	138²	168	8	52	43	14.5	5.13	80	.302	.365	12	.273	2	-15	-16	3	-1.3
1952 Was-A	3	4	.429	7	7	6	0	0	62²	59	4	29	24	12.6	2.73	130	.257	.340	4	.167	-0	7	6	2	0.8
Bos-A	7	9	.438	21	18	7	0	0	134¹	145	9	36	50	12.6	3.62	109	.276	.330	8	.174	-1	1	5	4	0.8
Yr	10	13	.435	28	25	13	0	0	197	204	13	65	74	12.6	3.34	114	.270	.333	12	.171	-1	7	11	6	1.6
1953 Bos-A	6	9	.400	30	17	4	0	2	156	164	13	49	60	12.5	3.52	120	.269	.327	7	.140	-2	8	12	1	0.9
1954 Bos-A	3	4	.429	33	5	0	0	5	71¹	60	3	30	27	14.5	4.42	93	.296	.369	2	.154	-1	-5	-2	-0	-0.3
Total 12	104	152	.406	380	279	123	11	13	2181	2384	136	835	734	13.5	4.28	95	.278	.345	164	.220	9	-54	-55	28	-2.7
● AL HUENKE				Huenke, Albert A. b: 6/26/1891, New Bremen, Ohio d: 9/20/74, St.Marys, Ohio BR/TR, 6', 175 lbs. Deb: 10/6/14																					
1914 NY-N	0	0	—	1	0	0	0	0	2	2	0	2	0	9.0	4.50	59	.250	.250	0	.000	-0	-0	-0	-0	0.0
● PHIL HUFFMAN				Huffman, Phillip Lee b: 6/20/58, Freeport, Tex. BR/TR, 6'2", 180 lbs. Deb: 4/10/79																					
1979 Tor-A	6	18	.250	31	31	2	1	0	173	220	25	68	56	15.0	5.77	75	.304	.364	0	—	0	-30	-28	0	-3.2
1985 Bal-A	0	0	—	2	1	0	0	0	4²	7	1	5	2	23.1	15.43	26	.350	.480	0	—	0	-6	-6	0	0.0
Total 2	6	18	.250	33	32	2	1	0	177²	227	26	73	58	15.2	6.03	72	.305	.367	0	—	0	-36	-33	0	-3.2
● ED HUGHES				Hughes, Edward J. b: 10/5/1880, Chicago, Ill. d: 10/11/27, McHenry, Ill. BR/TR, 6'1", 180 lbs. Deb: 8/29/02 F♦																					
1905 Bos-A	3	2	.600	6	4	2	0	0	33¹	38	0	9	8	13.0	4.59	59	.288	.338	3	.214	-0	-7	-7	-2	-1.1
1906 Bos-A	0	0	—	2	0	0	0	0	10	15	0	3	3	16.2	5.40	51	.349	.391	0	.000	-0	-3	-3	-0	-0.1
Total 2	3	2	.600	8	4	2	0	0	43¹	53	0	12	11	13.7	4.78	57	.303	.351	4	.190	-1	-10	-10	-2	-1.2
● JAY HUGHES				Hughes, James Jay b: 1/22/1874, Sacramento, Cal. d: 6/2/24, Sacramento, Cal. BR/TR, 185 lbs. Deb: 4/18/1898 F																					
1898 Bal-N	23	12	.657	38	35	31	5	0	300²	268	4	100	81	11.6	3.20	112	.237	.309	37	.226	4	14	13	2	1.9
1899 Bro-N	28	6	.824	35	35	30	3	0	291²	250	6	119	99	11.8	2.68	146	.231	.316	27	.252	5	38	40	2	4.7
1901 Bro-N	17	12	.586	31	29	24	0	0	250²	265	3	102	96	13.6	3.27	103	.269	.345	16	.176	-1	2	2	1	0.2
1902 Bro-N	15	10	.600	30	29	26	0	0	245	223	3	51	92	10.4	2.87	96	.243	.289	19	.209	4	-2	-3	1	0.3
Total 4	83	40	.675	134	128	111	8	0	1088	1006	16	372	368	11.8	3.00	114	.245	.315	99	.219	13	51	52	7	7.1
● JIM HUGHES				Hughes, James Michael b: 7/2/51, Los Angeles, Cal. BR/TR, 6'3", 190 lbs. Deb: 9/14/74																					
1974 Min-A	0	2	.000	2	2	1	0	0	10¹	8	2	4	8	10.5	5.23	71	.216	.293	0	—	0	-2	-1	-0	-0.3
1975 Min-A	16	14	.533	37	34	12	2	0	249²	241	17	127	130	13.7	3.82	100	.256	.351	0	—	0	-1	0	1	0.0
1976 Min-A	9	14	.391	37	26	3	0	0	177	190	17	73	87	13.8	4.98	72	.281	.358	0	—	0	-29	-28	-1	-3.5
1977 Min-A	0	0	—	2	0	0	0	0	4¹	4	0	1	1	10.4	2.08	192	.250	.294	0	—	0	1	1	-0	0.1
Total 4	25	30	.455	78	62	16	2	0	441¹	443	36	205	226	13.6	4.30	87	.265	.352	0	—	0	-31	-28	-1	-3.7
● JIM HUGHES				Hughes, James Robert b: 3/21/23, Chicago, Ill. BR/TR, 6'1", 200 lbs. Deb: 9/13/52																					
1952 Bro-N	2	1	.667	6	0	0	0	0	18²	16	0	11	8	13.0	1.45	252	.235	.342	0	.000	-0	8	8	-1	0.6
1953 *Bro-N	4	3	.571	48	0	0	0	9	85²	80	6	41	49	13.0	3.47	123	.245	.332	4	.286	1	8	7	-3	0.7
1954 Bro-N	8	4	.667	60	0	0	0	24	86²	76	7	44	58	12.5	3.22	127	.239	.331	3	.188	-0	8	11	-4	1.4
1955 Bro-N	0	2	.000	24	0	0	0	6	42²	41	10	19	22	12.7	4.22	96	.256	.335	0	.000	-2	-1	-1	-0	-0.2
1956 Bro-N	0	0	—	5	0	0	0	0	12	10	3	4	8	10.5	5.25	76	.233	.298	0	.000	-0	-2	-2	-0	-0.1
Chi-N	1	3	.250	25	1	0	0	0	45¹	43	4	30	20	15.3	5.16	73	.259	.365	2	.286	1	-7	-7	-1	-0.5
Yr	1	3	.250	30	1	0	0	0	57¹	53	7	34	28	14.3	5.18	74	.254	.358	2	.222	1	-9	-9	-1	-0.6
1957 Chi-A	0	0	—	4	0	0	0	0	5	8	1	3	0	27.0	10.80	35	.462	.517	0	—	0	-4	-4	-0	-0.3
Total 6	15	13	.536	172	1	0	0	39	296	278	30	152	165	13.2	3.83	106	.251	.344	9	.170	-2	7	7	-3	1.9
● MICKEY HUGHES				Hughes, Michael J. b: 10/25/1866, New York, N.Y. d: 4/10/31, Jersey City, N.J. TR, 5'6", 165 lbs. Deb: 4/22/1888 F																					
1888 Bro-a	25	13	.658	40	40	40	2	0	363	281	9	98	159	9.5	2.13	140	.206	.262	19	.137	-7	38	34	-1	2.4
1889 *Bro-a	9	8	.529	20	17	13	0	0	153	172	6	86	54	15.6	4.35	86	.275	.369	12	.176	-3	-9	-11	-0	-1.2
1890 Bro-N	4	4	.500	9	8	6	0	0	66¹	77	1	30	22	15.1	5.16	67	.282	.362	1	.038	-4	-12	-13	0	-1.4
Phi-a	1	3	.250	6	5	4	0	0	41¹	64	2	21	15	19.6	5.44	70	.344	.425	2	.125	-1	-7	-7	-1	-0.7
Total 3	39	28	.582	75	70	63	2	0	623²	594	12	235	250	12.3	3.22	102	.243	.315	34	.137	-14	10	4	-1	-0.9
● DICK HUGHES				Hughes, Richard Henry b: 2/13/38, Stephens, Ark. BR/TR, 6'3", 195 lbs. Deb: 9/11/66																					
1966 StL-N	2	1	.667	6	2	1	1	1	21	12	0	7	20	9.0	1.71	209	.162	.253	2	.400	1	4	4	0	0.8
1967 *StL-N	16	6	.727	37	27	12	3	3	222¹	164	22	48	161	8.8	2.67	123	.203	.252	10	.128	-1	17	15	-2	1.2
1968 *StL-N	2	2	.500	25	5	0	0	4	64	45	7	21	49	9.3	3.52	82	.202	.270	0	.000	-1	-4	-4	1	-0.4
Total 3	20	9	.690	68	34	13	4	8	307¹	221	29	76	230	8.9	2.78	116	.200	.256	12	.122	-2	18	15	-1	1.6
● TOM HUGHES				Hughes, Thomas Edward b: 9/13/34, Ancon, C.Z. BL/TR, 6'2", 180 lbs. Deb: 9/13/59																					
1959 StL-N	0	2	.000	2	2	0	0	0	4	9	2	2	2	24.8	15.75	27	.409	.458	0	.000	-0	-5	-5	-0	-1.5
● TOM HUGHES				Hughes, Thomas James "Long Tom" b: 11/29/1878, Chicago, Ill. d: 2/8/56, Chicago, Ill. BR/TR, 6'1", 175 lbs. Deb: 9/7/00 F																					
1900 Chi-N	1	1	.500	3	3	3	0	0	21	31	0	7	12	16.7	5.14	70	.341	.394	0	.000	-0	-3	-4	0	-0.3
1901 Chi-N	10	23	.303	37	35	32	1	0	308¹	309	4	115	225	12.9	3.24	100	.259	.333	14	.119	-8	3	0	-2	-1.0
1902 Bal-A	7	5	.583	13	13	12	1	0	108¹	120	2	32	45	12.4	3.90	97	.281	.334	6	.140	-2	-4	-4	-1	-0.3
Bos-A	3	3	.500	9	8	4	0	0	49¹	51	0	24	15	13.9	3.28	109	.267	.352	11	.367	2	2	0	-0	0.4
Yr	10	8	.556	22	21	16	1	0	157²	171	2	56	60	13.0	3.71	100	.276	.337	17	.233	0	-2	0	-1	0.1
1903 *Bos-A	20	7	.741	33	31	25	5	0	244²	232	5	60	112	11.1	2.57	118	.249	.301	26	.280	7	11	13	-4	1.5
1904 NY-A	7	11	.389	19	18	12	1	0	136¹	141	4	48	75	12.8	3.70	73	.264	.334	13	.241	1	-17	-15	-3	-2.0
Was-A	2	13	.133	16	14	14	0	1	124¹	133	4	34	48	12.5	3.47	77	.274	.330	13	.228	3	-12	-11	-1	-1.1
Yr	9	24	.273	35	32	26	1	1	260²	274	7	82	123	12.5	3.59	75	.269	.328	26	.234	4	-29	-26	-3	-3.1
1905 Was-A	17	20	.459	39	35	26	6	0	291¹	239	3	79	149	10.1	2.35	113	.225	.285	22	.212	4	10	10	-4	1.3
1906 Was-A	7	17	.292	30	25	15	5	0	204	230	5	81	90	13.5	3.62	73	.287	.355	14	.212	3	-21	-22	-4	-2.6
1907 Was-A	7	14	.333	34	23	18	2	4	211	206	1	97	102	11.3	3.11	78	.258	.309	19	.237	3	-13	-16	-1	-1.3
1908 Was-A	18	15	.545	43	31	24	3	0	276¹	224	7	77	165	10.0	2.21	103	.227	.287	17	.195	-2	7	6	1	0.6
1909 Was-A	4	7	.364	22	13	7	2	0	120¹	113	0	33	77	11.3	2.69	90	.246	.303	3	.083	-3	-0	-0	1	-0.6
1911 Was-A	11	17	.393	34	27	17	2	0	223	251	7	77	86	13.4	3.47	95	.288	.348	15	.185	-1	-3	-5	0	-0.9

YEAR	TM/L	W	L	PCT	G	GS	CG	SH	SV	IP	H	HR	BB	SO	RAT	ERA	ERA+	OAV	OOB	BH	AVG	PB	PR	/A	PD	TPI
1912	Was-A	13	10	.565	31	26	11	1	0	196	201	8	78	108	13.1	2.94	113	.270	.344	13	.194	1	8	9	0	1.0
1913	Was-A	4	12	.250	36	12	4	0	6	129²	129	6	61	59	14.2	4.30	69	.253	.350	4	.111	-1	-20	-19	1	-2.4
Total	13	131	175	.428	399	313	227	25	16	2644	2610	52	853	1368	12.1	3.09	93	.259	.323	190	.198	12	-57	-64	-18	-7.7

● **TOM HUGHES**   Hughes, Thomas L. "Salida Tom" b: 1/28/1884, Coal Creek, Colo. d: 11/1/61, Los Angeles, Cal.   BR/TR, 6'2", 175 lbs.   Deb: 9/18/06

YEAR	TM/L	W	L	PCT	G	GS	CG	SH	SV	IP	H	HR	BB	SO	RAT	ERA	ERA+	OAV	OOB	BH	AVG	PB	PR	/A	PD	TPI
1906	NY-A	1	0	1.000	3	1	1	0	0	15	11	2	1	5	7.2	4.20	71	.208	.222	1	.200	0	-3	-2	-1	-0.2
1907	NY-A	2	0	1.000	4	3	2	0	0	27	16	0	11	10	9.7	2.67	95	.174	.276	1	.143	-0	-0	0	-1	-0.1
1909	NY-A	7	8	.467	24	15	9	2	2	118²	109	3	37	69	11.4	2.65	95	.249	.313	5	.128	0	-2	-2	-1	-0.2
1910	NY-A	7	9	.438	23	15	11	0	1	151²	153	2	37	64	11.5	3.50	76	.271	.320	9	.164	-1	-17	-14	1	-1.4
1914	Bos-N	2	0	1.000	2	1	1	0	0	17	14	0	4	9	9.5	2.65	104	.226	.273	0	.000	-1	0	0	1	0.0
1915	Bos-N	16	14	.533	**50**	25	17	4	**9**	280¹	208	4	58	171	8.9	2.12	122	.213	.265	9	.100	-3	20	15	-2	1.1
1916	Bos-N	16	3	**.842**	40	13	7	1	5	161	121	2	51	97	10.1	2.35	106	.215	.290	10	.192	2	5	2	-1	0.4
1917	Bos-N	5	3	.625	11	8	6	2	0	74	54	1	30	40	10.6	1.95	131	.216	.307	0	.000	-3	6	5	-0	0.2
1918	Bos-N	0	2	.000	3	3	1	0	0	18¹	17	0	6	11	11.3	3.44	78	.250	.311	2	.333	1	-1	-2	0	0.0
Total	9	56	39	.589	160	85	55	9	17	863	703	14	235	476	10.1	2.56	102	.229	.291	37	.130	-4	8	4	-4	-0.2

● **TOMMY HUGHES**   Hughes, Thomas Owen b: 10/7/19, Wilkes-Barre, Pa. d: 11/28/90, Wilkes-Barre, Pa.   BR/TR, 6'1", 190 lbs.   Deb: 4/19/41

YEAR	TM/L	W	L	PCT	G	GS	CG	SH	SV	IP	H	HR	BB	SO	RAT	ERA	ERA+	OAV	OOB	BH	AVG	PB	PR	/A	PD	TPI
1941	Phi-N	9	14	.391	34	24	5	2	0	170	187	12	82	59	14.5	4.45	83	.280	.362	11	.200	0	-15	-14	1	-1.6
1942	Phi-N	12	18	.400	40	31	19	0	1	253	224	8	99	77	11.5	3.06	108	.238	.310	8	.100	-5	7	7	3	0.5
1946	Phi-N	6	9	.400	29	13	3	2	1	111	123	5	44	34	13.6	4.38	78	.281	.349	3	.097	-1	-12	-12	-1	-1.7
1947	Phi-N	4	11	.267	29	15	4	1	1	127	121	6	59	44	12.8	3.47	115	.265	.350	2	.050	-4	8	8	0	0.5
1948	Cin-N	0	4	.000	12	4	0	0	0	27	43	3	24	7	22.3	9.00	43	.364	.472	1	.143	-0	-15	-15	-0	-1.9
Total	5	31	56	.356	144	87	31	5	3	688	698	33	308	221	13.2	3.92	91	.266	.344	25	.117	-10	-27	-26	2	-4.2

● **VERN HUGHES**   Hughes, Vernon Alexander "Lefty" b: 4/15/1893, Etna, Pa. d: 9/26/61, Sewickley, Pa.   BL/TL, 5'10", 155 lbs.   Deb: 7/6/14

YEAR	TM/L	W	L	PCT	G	GS	CG	SH	SV	IP	H	HR	BB	SO	RAT	ERA	ERA+	OAV	OOB	BH	AVG	PB	PR	/A	PD	TPI
1914	Bal-F	0	0	—	3	0	0	0	0	5²	5	0	3	0	12.7	3.18	95	.250	.348	0	.000	-0	-0	-0	-0	0.0

● **BILL HUGHES**   Hughes, William Nesbert b: 11/18/1896, Philadelphia, Pa. d: 2/25/63, Birmingham, Ala.   BR/TR, 5'10.5", 155 lbs.   Deb: 9/15/21

YEAR	TM/L	W	L	PCT	G	GS	CG	SH	SV	IP	H	HR	BB	SO	RAT	ERA	ERA+	OAV	OOB	BH	AVG	PB	PR	/A	PD	TPI
1921	Pit-N	0	0	—	1	0	0	0	0	2	3	0	1	2	22.5	4.50	85	.375	.500	0	—	0	-0	-0	0	0.0

● **BILL HUGHES**   Hughes, William R. b: 11/25/1866, Blandinsville, Ill. d: 8/25/43, Santa Ana, Cal.   BL/TL,   Deb: 9/28/1884   ♦

YEAR	TM/L	W	L	PCT	G	GS	CG	SH	SV	IP	H	HR	BB	SO	RAT	ERA	ERA+	OAV	OOB	BH	AVG	PB	PR	/A	PD	TPI
1885	Phi-a	0	2	.000	2	2	2	0	0	16²	18	0	10	4	16.2	4.86	71	.269	.380	3	.188	0	-3	-3	-0	-0.2

● **JIM HUGHEY**   Hughey, James Ulysses "Coldwater Jim" b: 3/8/1869, Wakeshma Twsp., Mich. d: 3/29/45, Coldwater, Mich.   TR, 6',   Deb: 9/29/1891

YEAR	TM/L	W	L	PCT	G	GS	CG	SH	SV	IP	H	HR	BB	SO	RAT	ERA	ERA+	OAV	OOB	BH	AVG	PB	PR	/A	PD	TPI
1891	Mil-a	1	0	1.000	2	1	1	0	0	15	14	0	3	9	12.6	3.00	146	.286	.318	1	.143	-1	1	2	0	0.1
1893	Chi-N	0	1	.000	2	2	1	0	0	9	14	0	3	4	18.0	11.00	42	.341	.400	0	.000	-0	-6	-6	0	-0.4
1896	Pit-N	6	8	.429	25	14	11	0	0	155	171	3	67	48	14.2	4.99	84	.278	.355	14	.215	-1	-11	-14	-3	-1.3
1897	Pit-N	6	10	.375	25	17	13	0	1	149¹	193	3	45	38	14.8	5.06	82	.310	.364	8	.127	-5	-12	-15	-2	-1.7
1898	StL-N	7	24	.226	35	33	31	0	0	283²	325	2	71	74	12.9	3.93	96	.285	.333	11	.113	-5	-10	-5	-1	-1.0
1899	Cle-N	4	30	.118	36	34	32	0	0	283	403	9	88	54	16.3	5.41	68	.334	.389	18	.162	-6	-49	-54	-4	-5.7
1900	StL-N	5	7	.417	20	12	11	0	0	112²	151	4	40	23	15.4	5.19	70	.314	.375	7	.171	0	-19	-19	-1	-1.8
Total	7	29	80	.266	145	113	100	0	1	1007²	1271	21	317	250	14.7	4.87	80	.306	.363	59	.153	-17	-106	-110	-11	-11.8

● **TEX HUGHSON**   Hughson, Cecil Carlton b: 2/9/16, Buda, Tex. d: 8/6/93, Austin, Tex.   BR/TR, 6'3", 198 lbs.   Deb: 4/16/41

YEAR	TM/L	W	L	PCT	G	GS	CG	SH	SV	IP	H	HR	BB	SO	RAT	ERA	ERA+	OAV	OOB	BH	AVG	PB	PR	/A	PD	TPI
1941	Bos-A	5	3	.625	12	8	4	0	0	61	70	3	13	22	12.4	4.13	101	.289	.328	1	.059	-1	0	0	0	-0.1
1942	Bos-A☆	**22**	6	.786	38	30	**22**	4	4	281	258	10	75	**113**	10.7	2.59	144	.245	.296	18	.176	1	33	**35**	1	3.8
1943	Bos-A★	12	15	.444	35	32	**20**	2	4	266	242	23	73	114	10.7	2.64	126	.247	.300	9	.105	-4	19	20	1	1.7
1944	Bos-A★	18	5	**.783**	28	23	19	2	5	203¹	172	4	41	112	**9.5**	2.26	151	.225	**.267**	10	.152	-1	26	26	-0	3.0
1946	*Bos-A	20	11	.645	39	35	21	6	3	278	252	15	51	172	9.9	2.75	133	.238	.274	12	.132	-2	23	28	-2	2.7
1947	Bos-A	12	11	.522	29	26	13	3	0	189¹	173	17	71	119	11.7	3.33	117	.244	.314	2	.033	-6	8	12	-0	0.7
1948	Bos-A	3	1	.750	15	0	0	0	0	19¹	21	0	7	6	13.0	5.12	86	.276	.337	0	.000	-0	-2	-2	-1	-0.4
1949	Bos-A	4	2	.667	29	2	0	0	1	77²	82	5	41	35	14.4	5.33	82	.268	.356	1	.045	-3	-10	-8	-2	-1.0
Total	8	96	54	.640	225	156	99	19	17	1375²	1270	77	372	693	10.8	2.94	125	.245	.297	53	.119	-15	99	111	-3	10.4

● **RICK HUISMAN**   Huisman, Richard Allen b: 5/17/69, Oak Park, Ill.   BR/TR, 6'3", 200 lbs.   Deb: 9/4/95

YEAR	TM/L	W	L	PCT	G	GS	CG	SH	SV	IP	H	HR	BB	SO	RAT	ERA	ERA+	OAV	OOB	BH	AVG	PB	PR	/A	PD	TPI
1995	KC-A	0	0	—	7	0	0	0	0	9²	14	2	1	12	14.0	7.45	64	.333	.349	0	—	0	-3	-3	-0	-0.3
1996	KC-A	2	1	.667	22	0	0	0	1	29¹	25	4	18	23	13.2	4.60	106	.231	.341	0	—	0	1	1	0	0.1
Total	2	2	1	.667	29	0	0	0	1	39	39	6	19	35	13.4	5.31	92	.260	.343	0	—	0	-2	-2	0	0.1

● **MARK HUISMANN**   Huismann, Mark Lawrence b: 5/11/58, Littleton, Colo.   BR/TR, 6'3", 195 lbs.   Deb: 8/16/83

YEAR	TM/L	W	L	PCT	G	GS	CG	SH	SV	IP	H	HR	BB	SO	RAT	ERA	ERA+	OAV	OOB	BH	AVG	PB	PR	/A	PD	TPI
1983	KC-A	2	1	.667	13	0	0	0	0	30²	29	1	17	20	13.5	5.58	73	.250	.346	0	—	0	-5	-5	-1	-0.5
1984	*KC-A	3	3	.500	38	0	0	0	3	75	84	7	21	54	12.7	4.20	96	.286	.335	0	—	0	-2	-1	-0	-0.1
1985	KC-A	1	0	1.000	9	0	0	0	0	18²	14	1	3	9	8.2	1.93	216	.219	.254	0	—	0	5	5	0	0.2
1986	KC-A	0	1	.000	10	0	0	0	1	17¹	18	1	6	13	12.5	4.15	102	.269	.329	0	—	0	0	0	0	0.0
	Sea-A	3	3	.500	36	1	0	0	4	80	80	18	19	59	11.2	3.71	114	.256	.301	0	—	0	4	5	0	0.4
	Yr	3	4	.429	46	1	0	0	5	97¹	98	19	25	72	11.5	3.79	112	.258	.305	0	—	0	4	5	0	0.4
1987	Sea-A	0	0	—	6	0	0	0	0	14²	10	1	4	15	9.8	4.91	96	.196	.281	0	—	-1	-0	0	0	-0.0
	Cle-A	2	3	.400	20	0	0	0	2	35¹	38	6	8	23	11.7	5.09	89	.271	.311	0	—	0	-3	-2	-0	-0.3
	Yr	2	3	.400	26	0	0	0	2	50	48	7	12	38	10.8	5.04	91	.247	.291	0	—	0	-3	-3	0	-0.3
1988	Det-A	1	0	1.000	5	0	0	0	0	5¹	6	0	2	4	13.5	5.06	76	.286	.348	0	—	0	-1	-1	1	0.1
1989	Bal-A	0	0	—	8	0	0	0	0	11¹	13	0	0	13	10.3	6.35	60	.277	.277	0	—	0	-3	-3	1	0.1
1990	Pit-N	1	0	1.000	2	0	0	0	0	2	6	1	2	4	24.0	9.00	40	.462	.533	0	—	0	-2	-2	-0	-0.2
1991	Pit-N	0	0	—	5	0	0	0	0	5	7	0	2	5	16.2	7.20	51	.304	.360	0	—	0	-2	-2	0	-0.0
Total	9	13	11	.542	152	1	0	0	11	296¹	305	37	83	219	11.9	4.40	95	.266	.318	0	—	0	-9	-7	1	-0.7

● **HARRY HULIHAN**   Hulihan, Harry Joseph b: 4/18/1899, Rutland, Vt. d: 9/11/80, Rutland, Vt.   BR/TL, 5'11", 170 lbs.   Deb: 8/16/22

YEAR	TM/L	W	L	PCT	G	GS	CG	SH	SV	IP	H	HR	BB	SO	RAT	ERA	ERA+	OAV	OOB	BH	AVG	PB	PR	/A	PD	TPI
1922	Bos-N	2	3	.400	7	6	2	0	0	40	40	0	26	16	15.7	3.15	127	.274	.398	2	.154	-0	4	4	-1	0.3

● **HANK HULVEY**   Hulvey, James Hensel b: 7/18/1897, Mount Sidney, Va. d: 4/9/82, Mount Sidney, Va.   BB/TR, 6', 180 lbs.   Deb: 9/5/23

YEAR	TM/L	W	L	PCT	G	GS	CG	SH	SV	IP	H	HR	BB	SO	RAT	ERA	ERA+	OAV	OOB	BH	AVG	PB	PR	/A	PD	TPI
1923	Phi-A	0	1	.000	1	1	0	0	0	7	10	1	2	2	15.4	7.71	53	.357	.400	1	.500	0	-3	-3	0	-0.3

● **TOM HUME**   Hume, Thomas Hubert b: 3/29/53, Cincinnati, Ohio   BR/TR, 6'1", 185 lbs.   Deb: 5/25/77

YEAR	TM/L	W	L	PCT	G	GS	CG	SH	SV	IP	H	HR	BB	SO	RAT	ERA	ERA+	OAV	OOB	BH	AVG	PB	PR	/A	PD	TPI
1977	Cin-N	3	3	.500	14	5	0	0	0	43	54	5	17	22	14.9	7.12	55	.305	.366	2	.200	1	-15	-15	-0	-1.7
1978	Cin-N	8	11	.421	42	23	5	0	1	174	198	12	50	90	13.0	4.14	86	.289	.341	3	.067	-3	-11	-11	0	-1.4
1979	*Cin-N	10	9	.526	57	12	2	0	17	163	162	12	33	80	10.8	2.76	**135**	.262	.300	8	.174	0	18	18	0	2.4
1980	Cin-N	9	10	.474	78	0	0	0	25	137	121	6	38	68	10.6	2.56	140	.240	.297	3	.188	-0	16	15	3	3.0
1981	Cin-N	9	4	.692	51	0	0	0	13	67²	63	7	31	27	12.6	3.46	103	.259	.345	0	.000	-0	0	1	-0	0.1
1982	Cin-N★	2	6	.250	46	0	0	0	17	63²	57	7	21	22	11.2	3.11	119	.245	.310	0	.000	-1	3	4	-1	0.6
1983	Cin-N	3	5	.375	48	0	0	0	9	66	66	8	31	34	15.0	4.77	80	.264	.374	0	.000	-1	-8	-7	1	-1.0
1984	Cin-N	4	13	.235	54	8	0	0	3	113¹	142	14	41	59	14.6	5.64	67	.309	.367	3	.136	-0	-26	-23	1	-3.3
1985	Cin-N	3	5	.375	56	0	0	0	3	80	65	7	35	50	11.6	3.26	116	.224	.314	0	.000	-1	3	5	-0	0.4
1986	Phi-N	4	1	.800	48	1	0	0	1	94¹	89	5	34	51	12.0	2.77	139	.252	.323	0	.000	-1	10	11	1	0.6
1987	Phi-N	1	4	.200	38	6	0	0	0	70²	75	10	41	29	15.3	5.60	76	.277	.380	3	.200	0	-12	-11	0	-0.6
	Cin-N	1	0	1.000	11	0	0	0	0	13¹	14	0	2	4	11.5	4.05	105	.292	.333	0	—	0	-0	0	0	0.0
	Yr	2	4	.333	49	6	0	0	0	84	89	10	43	33	14.3	5.36	79	.274	.360	3	.200	0	-12	-10	0	-0.6
Total	11	57	71	.445	543	55	5	0	92	1086	1106	88	384	536	12.5	3.85	97	.268	.334	22	.120	-5	-22	-14	5	-0.9

● **BILL HUMPHREY**   Humphrey, Byron William b: 6/17/11, Vienna, Mo. d: 2/13/92, Springfield, Mo.   BR/TR, 6', 180 lbs.   Deb: 4/24/38

YEAR	TM/L	W	L	PCT	G	GS	CG	SH	SV	IP	H	HR	BB	SO	RAT	ERA	ERA+	OAV	OOB	BH	AVG	PB	PR	/A	PD	TPI
1938	Bos-A	0	0	—	2	0	0	0	0	2	5	0	2	1	27.0	9.00	55	.500	.545	0	—	0	-1	-1	-0	0.0

● **BOB HUMPHREYS**   Humphreys, Robert William b: 8/18/35, Covington, Va.   BR/TR, 5'11", 170 lbs.   Deb: 9/8/62

YEAR	TM/L	W	L	PCT	G	GS	CG	SH	SV	IP	H	HR	BB	SO	RAT	ERA	ERA+	OAV	OOB	BH	AVG	PB	PR	/A	PD	TPI
1962	Det-A	0	1	.000	4	0	0	0	1	5	8	3	2	3	18.0	7.20	57	.381	.435	0	—	0	-2	-2	0	-0.4

(continued — Humphreys)

YEAR TM/L	W	L	PCT	G	GS	CG	SH	SV	IP	H	HR	BB	SO	RAT	ERA	ERA+	OAV	OOB	BH	AVG	PB	PR	/A	PD	TPI
1963 StL-N	0	1	.000	9	0	0	0	0	10²	11	4	7	8	16.0	5.06	70	.282	.404	0	—	0	-2	-2	0	-0.2
1964 *StL-N	2	0	1.000	28	0	0	0	2	42²	32	3	15	36	10.1	2.53	150	.213	.289	1	.250	1	5	6	-0	0.4
1965 Chi-N	2	0	1.000	41	0	0	0	0	65²	59	6	27	38	12.1	3.15	117	.244	.325	0	.000	-0	3	4	-1	0.0
1966 Was-A	7	3	.700	58	1	0	0	3	111²	91	6	28	88	9.9	2.82	123	.229	.287	2	.167	1	8	8	-0	0.8
1967 Was-A	6	2	.750	48	2	0	0	4	105²	93	13	41	54	11.6	4.17	76	.238	.314	2	.133	1	-11	-12	-1	-1.1
1968 Was-A	5	7	.417	56	0	0	0	2	92²	78	13	30	56	10.5	3.69	79	.233	.296	2	.400	1	-7	-8	1	-0.9
1969 Was-A	3	3	.500	47	0	0	0	5	79²	69	3	38	43	12.2	3.05	114	.233	.322	1	.077	-1	5	4	0	0.3
1970 Was-A	0	0	—	5	0	0	0	0	6²	4	1	9	6	17.6	1.35	263	.200	.448	0	—	0	2	2	0	0.0
Mil-A	2	4	.333	23	1	0	0	3	45²	37	3	22	32	12.0	3.15	120	.222	.319	0	.000	-1	3	3	-0	0.4
Yr	2	4	.333	28	1	0	0	3	52¹	41	4	31	38	12.7	2.92	129	.219	.336	0	.000	-1	5	5	0	0.4
Total 9	27	21	.563	319	4	0	0	20	566	482	55	219	364	11.4	3.36	101	.234	.234	8	.131	-1	3	3	-2	-0.7

● **BERT HUMPHRIES** Humphries, Albert b: 9/26/1880, California, Pa. d: 9/21/45, Orlando, Fla. BR/TR, 5'11.5", 182 lbs. Deb: 4/16/10

YEAR TM/L	W	L	PCT	G	GS	CG	SH	SV	IP	H	HR	BB	SO	RAT	ERA	ERA+	OAV	OOB	BH	AVG	PB	PR	/A	PD	TPI
1910 Phi-N	0	0	—	5	0	0	0	2	9²	13	0	3	3	15.8	4.66	67	.317	.378	0	.000	0	-2	-2	0	0.0
1911 Phi-N	3	1	.750	11	5	2	0	1	41	56	1	10	13	15.8	4.17	83	.339	.398	5	.333	3	-4	-3	-1	-0.1
Cin-N	4	3	.571	14	7	3	0	0	65	62	3	18	16	11.9	2.35	141	.266	.335	1	.063	-1	8	7	0	0.6
Yr	7	4	.636	25	12	5	0	1	106	118	4	28	29	12.9	3.06	110	.292	.347	6	.194	-2	4	4	-0	0.5
1912 Cin-N	9	11	.450	30	15	9	1	2	158²	162	6	36	58	11.7	3.23	104	.270	.319	7	.137	-2	3	2	-1	-0.1
1913 Chi-N	16	4	.800	28	20	13	2	1	181	169	10	24	61	9.7	2.69	118	.250	.277	12	.194	1	10	10	-2	0.9
1914 Chi-N	10	11	.476	34	22	8	2	0	171	162	5	37	62	10.6	2.68	104	.250	.293	13	.236	2	2	2	-2	0.9
1915 Chi-N	8	13	.381	31	22	10	4	3	171²	183	6	23	45	11.1	2.31	120	.280	.309	8	.174	0	8	9	-2	0.9
Total 6	50	43	.538	153	91	45	9	9	798	807	31	151	258	11.1	2.79	110	.267	.309	46	.186	3	26	25	-3	2.8

● **JOHNNY HUMPHRIES** Humphries, John William b: 6/23/15, Clifton Forge, Va d: 6/24/65, New Orleans, La. BR/TR, 6'1", 185 lbs. Deb: 5/8/38

YEAR TM/L	W	L	PCT	G	GS	CG	SH	SV	IP	H	HR	BB	SO	RAT	ERA	ERA+	OAV	OOB	BH	AVG	PB	PR	/A	PD	TPI
1938 Cle-A	9	8	.529	45	6	1	0	6	103¹	105	6	63	56	14.7	5.23	89	.264	.367	3	.103	-1	-5	-7	-1	-1.1
1939 Cle-A	2	4	.333	15	1	0	1	0	28¹	30	0	32	12	20.0	8.26	53	.294	.467			-1	-11	-12	-0	-2.2
1940 Cle-A	0	2	.000	19	1	1	0	1	33²	35	5	29	17	17.6	8.29	51	.269	.410	0	.000	-0	-15	-15	-1	-1.0
1941 Cle-A	4	2	.667	16	4	4	4	1	73¹	63	2	22	25	10.6	1.84	223	.230	.290	2	.087	-1	19	18	-1	1.2
1942 Chi-A	12	12	.500	28	28	17	2	0	228¹	227	9	59	71	11.5	2.68	134	.257	.309	18	.225	1	25	23	-2	2.7
1943 Chi-A	11	11	.500	28	27	8	0	1	188¹	198	7	54	51	12.3	3.30	101	.268	.322	20	.290	5	-0	1	-2	0.6
1944 Chi-A	8	10	.444	30	20	8	1	0	169	170	9	57	42	12.3	3.67	93	.267	.331	10	.189	0	-5	-5	-3	-0.8
1945 Chi-A	6	14	.300	22	21	10	1	1	153	172	11	48	33	13.1	4.24	78	.282	.337	8	.148	-3	-15	-16	-4	-2.5
1946 Phi-N	0	0	—	10	1	0	0	0	24²	24	1	9	10	12.4	4.01	85	.258	.330	2	.250	0	-2	-2	-1	-0.1
Total 9	52	63	.452	211	111	49	9	12	1002	1024	50	373	317	12.8	3.78	97	.265	.334	63	.191	-4	-9	-13	-14	-3.2

● **BEN HUNT** Hunt, Benjamin Franklin "High Pockets" b: 11/10/1888, Eufaula, Okla. d: 9/27/27, Greybull, Wyo. BL/TL, 6'5", 190 lbs. Deb: 8/24/10

YEAR TM/L	W	L	PCT	G	GS	CG	SH	SV	IP	H	HR	BB	SO	RAT	ERA	ERA+	OAV	OOB	BH	AVG	PB	PR	/A	PD	TPI
1910 Bos-A	2	3	.400	7	7	3	0	0	46²	45	4	20	19	12.5	4.05	63	.266	.344	1	.056	-2	-8	-8	-1	-1.0
1913 StL-N	0	1	.000	2	1	0	0	0	8	6	0	9	6	18.0	3.38	96	.240	.457			-0	-0	-0	1	0.0
Total 2	2	4	.333	9	8	3	0	0	54²	51	4	29	25	13.3	3.95	67	.263	.362	1	.050	-2	-8	-8	-0	-1.0

● **KEN HUNT** Hunt, Kenneth Raymond b: 12/14/38, Ogden, Utah BR/TR, 6'4", 200 lbs. Deb: 4/16/61

YEAR TM/L	W	L	PCT	G	GS	CG	SH	SV	IP	H	HR	BB	SO	RAT	ERA	ERA+	OAV	OOB	BH	AVG	PB	PR	/A	PD	TPI
1961 *Cin-N	9	10	.474	29	22	4	0	0	136¹	130	13	66	75	13.3	3.96	103	.257	.349	7	.179	0	1	2	-1	0.1

● **GEORGE HUNTER** Hunter, George Henry b: 7/8/1887, Buffalo, N.Y. d: 1/11/68, Harrisburg, Pa. BB/TL, 5'8.5", 165 lbs. Deb: 5/4/09 F♦

YEAR TM/L	W	L	PCT	G	GS	CG	SH	SV	IP	H	HR	BB	SO	RAT	ERA	ERA+	OAV	OOB	BH	AVG	PB	PR	/A	PD	TPI
1909 Bro-N	4	10	.286	16	13	10	0	0	113¹	105	0	44	43	11.5	2.46	105	.254	.322	28	.228	2	2	2	0	0.5

● **CATFISH HUNTER** Hunter, James Augustus "Jim" b: 4/8/46, Hertford, N.C. BR/TR, 6', 195 lbs. Deb: 5/13/65 H

YEAR TM/L	W	L	PCT	G	GS	CG	SH	SV	IP	H	HR	BB	SO	RAT	ERA	ERA+	OAV	OOB	BH	AVG	PB	PR	/A	PD	TPI
1965 KC-A	8	8	.500	32	20	3	2	0	133	124	21	46	82	11.6	4.26	82	.246	.311	6	.150	-1	-12	-11	-2	-1.5
1966 KC-A☆	9	11	.450	30	25	4	0	0	176²	158	17	64	103	11.4	4.02	84	.239	.308	9	.153	1	-12	-12	-3	-1.5
1967 KC-A★	13	17	.433	35	35	13	5	0	259²	209	16	84	196	10.2	2.81	113	.219	.284	18	.196	4	12	11	-5	1.2
1968 Oak-A	13	13	.500	36	34	11	2	1	234	210	29	69	172	10.9	3.35	84	.238	.296	19	.232	5	-10	-14	-3	-1.3
1969 Oak-A	12	15	.444	38	35	10	3	0	247	210	34	85	150	10.9	3.35	103	.234	.304	19	.224	7	7	2	-1	0.6
1970 Oak-A★	18	14	.563	40	40	9	1	0	262¹	253	32	74	178	11.5	3.81	93	.233	.307	18	.200	4	-3	-8	-2	-0.7
1971 *Oak-A	21	11	.656	37	37	16	4	0	273²	225	27	80	181	10.2	2.96	113	.223	.282	36	.350	13	15	11	-4	2.4
1972 *Oak-A☆	21	7	.750	38	37	16	5	0	295¹	200	21	70	191	8.3	2.04	139	.189	.242	23	.219	3	33	26	-3	2.7
1973 *Oak-A★	21	5	.808	36	36	11	3	0	256¹	222	39	69	124	10.3	3.34	106	.232	.284	1	1.000	1	14	6	-4	0.2
1974 *Oak-A★	25	12	.676	41	41	23	6	0	318¹	268	25	46	143	9.0	2.49	133	.229	.260				40	29	-4	3.0
1975 NY-A★	23	14	.622	39	39	30	7	0	328	248	25	83	177	9.2	2.58	143	.208	.263		—	0	44	40	-4	3.9
1976 *NY-A★	17	15	.531	36	36	21	2	0	298²	268	28	68	173	10.2	3.53	97	.286		0	.000	-0	-0	-4	-2	-0.6
1977 *NY-A	9	9	.500	22	22	8	0	0	143¹	137	29	47	52	11.7	4.71	84	.250	.313	0	—	0	-10	-12	-3	-1.6
1978 *NY-A	12	6	.667	21	20	5	0	0	118	98	16	35	56	10.2	3.58	101	.226	.286	0	—	0	-13	-14	-1	-1.4
1979 NY-A	2	9	.182	19	19	1	0	0	105	128	15	34	34	14.0	5.31	77	.312	.366	0	—	0	-13	-14	-1	-1.4
Total 15	224	166	.574	500	476	181	42	1	3449¹	2958	374	954	2012	10.3	3.26	104	.231	.287	149	.226	33	109	51	-40	5.4

● **JIM HUNTER** Hunter, James Mac Gregor b: 6/22/64, Jersey City, N.J. BR/TR, 6'3", 205 lbs. Deb: 5/17/91

YEAR TM/L	W	L	PCT	G	GS	CG	SH	SV	IP	H	HR	BB	SO	RAT	ERA	ERA+	OAV	OOB	BH	AVG	PB	PR	/A	PD	TPI
1991 Mil-A	0	5	.000	8	6	0	0	0	31	45	3	17	14	19.2	7.26	55	.349	.440		—	0	-11	-11	1	-1.4

● **RICH HUNTER** Hunter, Richard Thomas b: 9/25/74, Pasadena, Cal. BR/TR, 6'1", 185 lbs. Deb: 4/6/96

YEAR TM/L	W	L	PCT	G	GS	CG	SH	SV	IP	H	HR	BB	SO	RAT	ERA	ERA+	OAV	OOB	BH	AVG	PB	PR	/A	PD	TPI
1996 Phi-N	3	7	.300	14	14	0	0	0	69¹	84	10	33	32	15.8	6.49	67	.303	.387	3	.167	0	-18	-16	0	-1.9

● **LEM HUNTER** Hunter, Robert Lemuel b: 1/16/1863, Warren, Ohio d: 11/9/56, W.Lafayette, Ohio Deb: 9/1/1883 ♦

YEAR TM/L	W	L	PCT	G	GS	CG	SH	SV	IP	H	HR	BB	SO	RAT	ERA	ERA+	OAV	OOB	BH	AVG	PB	PR	/A	PD	TPI
1883 Cle-N	0	0	—	1	1	0	0	0	6¹	10	0	2	4	17.1	1.42	222	.370	.414	1	.250	-0	1	1	0	0.0

● **WILLARD HUNTER** Hunter, Willard Mitchell b: 3/8/34, Newark, N.J. BR/TL, 6'2", 180 lbs. Deb: 4/16/62

YEAR TM/L	W	L	PCT	G	GS	CG	SH	SV	IP	H	HR	BB	SO	RAT	ERA	ERA+	OAV	OOB	BH	AVG	PB	PR	/A	PD	TPI
1962 LA-N	0	0	—	1	0	0	0	0	2	6	1	4	1	45.0	40.50	9	.545	.667	0	—	0	-8	-8	0	-1.0
NY-N	1	6	.143	27	6	1	0	0	63	67	9	34	40	14.6	5.57	75	.270	.360	3	.231	-1	-11	-10	-1	-1.0
Yr	1	6	.143	28	6	1	0	0	65	73	10	38	41	15.5	6.65	63	.281	.375	3	.231	-1	-20	-18	-1	-1.0
1964 NY-N	3	3	.500	41	0	0	0	5	49	54	4	9	22	11.9	4.41	81	.284	.323	1	1.000	0	-5	-5	-0	-0.6
Total 2	4	9	.308	69	6	1	0	5	114	127	14	47	63	14.0	5.68	69	.283	.355	4	.286	-1	-24	-22	-1	-1.6

● **WALT HUNTZINGER** Huntzinger, Walter Henry "Shakes" b: 2/6/1899, Pottsville, Pa. d: 8/11/81, Upper Darby, Pa. BR/TR, 6', 150 lbs. Deb: 9/29/23

YEAR TM/L	W	L	PCT	G	GS	CG	SH	SV	IP	H	HR	BB	SO	RAT	ERA	ERA+	OAV	OOB	BH	AVG	PB	PR	/A	PD	TPI
1923 NY-N	0	1	.000	2	1	0	0	0	8	9	1	2	2	11.3	7.88	49	.290	.313	0	.000	-0	-3	-4	-0	-0.4
1924 NY-N	1	1	.500	12	1	0	0	0	32¹	41	3	9	6	13.9	4.45	82	.318	.362	4	.500	-1	-2	-3	-0	-0.1
1925 NY-N	5	1	.833	26	1	0	0	0	64¹	68	3	17	19	11.9	3.50	115	.281	.328	1	.091	-1	6	4	-1	0.1
1926 StL-N	0	4	.000	9	4	2	0	0	34	35	4	14	9	13.0	4.24	94	.267	.338	0	.000	-0	-1	-2	-0	-0.2
Chi-N	1	1	.500	11	0	0	0	0	28²	26	0	4	11	11.6	0.94	408	.260	.333	1	.143	-0	9	9	0	0.7
Yr	1	5	.167	20	4	2	0	0	62¹	61	4	18	20	12.4	2.73	142	.264	.336	1	.067	-2	8	6	-1	0.5
Total 4	7	8	.467	60	8	2	0	3	167¹	179	10	49	40	12.4	3.60	108	.283	.337	6	.167	-4	8	6	-1	0.1

● **TOM HURD** Hurd, Thomas Carr "Whitey" b: 5/27/24, Danville, Va. d: 9/5/82, Waterloo, Iowa BR/TR, 5'9", 155 lbs. Deb: 7/30/54

YEAR TM/L	W	L	PCT	G	GS	CG	SH	SV	IP	H	HR	BB	SO	RAT	ERA	ERA+	OAV	OOB	BH	AVG	PB	PR	/A	PD	TPI
1954 Bos-A	2	0	1.000	16	0	0	0	0	29²	24	2	12	14	10.0	3.03	135	.198	.280	1	.333	0	2	4	0	0.3
1955 Bos-A	8	6	.571	43	0	0	0	5	80²	72	7	38	48	12.4	3.01	142	.242	.330	1	.071	-1	8	11	-0	1.9
1956 Bos-A	3	4	.429	40	0	0	0	6	76	84	5	47	34	15.9	5.33	87	.289	.393	6	.500	2	-10	-6	-1	-0.5
Total 3	13	10	.565	99	0	0	0	11	186¹	177	14	97	96	13.4	3.96	111	.255	.350	8	.276	1	1	9	-1	1.7

● **BRUCE HURST** Hurst, Bruce Vee b: 3/24/58, St.George, Utah BL/TL, 6'3", 215 lbs. Deb: 4/12/80

YEAR TM/L	W	L	PCT	G	GS	CG	SH	SV	IP	H	HR	BB	SO	RAT	ERA	ERA+	OAV	OOB	BH	AVG	PB	PR	/A	PD	TPI
1980 Bos-A	2	2	.500	12	7	0	0	0	30²	39	4	16	16	16.7	9.10	46	.307	.393	0	—	0	-17	-17	-0	-2.0
1981 Bos-A	2	0	1.000	5	2	0	0	0	23	23	1	12	11	14.1	4.30	90	.258	.353	0	—	0	-1	-1	-0	-0.1
1982 Bos-A	3	7	.300	28	19	0	0	0	117	161	16	40	53	15.7	5.77	75	.333	.388	0	—	0	-22	-19	1	-1.7
1983 Bos-A	12	12	.500	33	32	6	2	0	211¹	241	16	62	115	13.0	4.09	106	.290	.342	0	—	0	-1	6	1	0.7
1984 Bos-A	12	12	.500	33	33	6	2	0	218	232	26	88	136	13.5	3.92	106	.271	.343	0	—	0	-1	6	0	0.6
1985 Bos-A	11	13	.458	35	31	6	1	0	229¹	243	31	70	189	12.4	4.51	95	.273	.328	0	—	0	-9	-6	0	-0.5

YEAR	TM/L	W	L	PCT	G	GS	CG	SH	SV	IP	H	HR	BB	SO	RAT	ERA	ERA+	OAV	OOB	BH	AVG	PB	PR	/A	PD	TPI
1986	*Bos-A	13	8	.619	25	25	11	4	0	174^1	169	18	50	167	11.5	2.99	139	.256	.311	0	—	0	23	23	-1	2.5
1987	Bos-A☆	15	13	.536	33	33	15	3	0	238^2	239	35	76	190	11.9	4.41	103	.262	.320	0	—	0	1	3	0	0.3
1988	*Bos-A	18	6	.750	33	32	7	1	0	216^2	222	21	65	166	12.0	3.66	113	.264	.318	0	—	0	7	11	0	1.1
1989	SD-N	15	11	.577	33	33	10	2	0	244^2	214	16	66	179	10.3	2.69	130	.237	.289	5	.071	-2	22	22	1	2.3
1990	SD-N	11	9	.550	33	33	9	4	0	223^2	188	21	63	162	10.1	3.14	122	.228	.284	6	.090	-2	16	17	0	1.2
1991	SD-N	15	8	.652	31	31	4	0	0	221^2	201	17	59	141	10.7	3.29	115	.241	.293	9	.134	0	10	13	-1	1.1
1992	SD-N	14	9	.609	32	32	6	4	0	217^1	223	22	51	131	11.3	3.85	93	.267	.309	11	.159	1	-8	-7	-1	-0.6
1993	SD-N	0	1	.000	2	2	0	0	0	4^1	9	0	3	3	24.9	12.46	33	.409	.480	0	—	0	-4	-4	0	-0.7
	Col-N	0	1	.000	3	3	0	0	0	8^2	6	1	3	6	9.3	5.19	92	.194	.265	0	.000	-0	-1	-0	0	
	Yr	0	2	.000	5	5	0	0	0	13	15	1	6	9	14.5	7.62	60	.283	.356	0	.000	-0	-5	-4	0	-0.7
1994	Tex-A	2	1	.667	8	8	0	0	0	38	53	8	16	24	16.3	7.11	68	.342	.404	0	—	0	-10	-10	-1	-0.7
Total	15	145	113	.562	379	359	83	23	0	2417^1	2463	258	740	1689	12.0	3.92	103	.265	.321	31	.113	-3	7	37	2	3.4

● JAMES HURST   Hurst, James Lavon   b: 6/1/67, Plantation, Fla.   BL/TL, 6', 160 lbs.   Deb: 4/4/94

YEAR	TM/L	W	L	PCT	G	GS	CG	SH	SV	IP	H	HR	BB	SO	RAT	ERA	ERA+	OAV	OOB	BH	AVG	PB	PR	/A	PD	TPI
1994	Tex-A	0	0	—	8	0	0	0	0	10^2	17	1	8	5	21.1	10.13	48	.362	.455	0	—	0	-6	-6	0	0.0

● JONATHAN HURST   Hurst, Jonathan   b: 10/20/66, New York, N.Y.   BR/TR, 6'3", 175 lbs.   Deb: 6/9/92

YEAR	TM/L	W	L	PCT	G	GS	CG	SH	SV	IP	H	HR	BB	SO	RAT	ERA	ERA+	OAV	OOB	BH	AVG	PB	PR	/A	PD	TPI
1992	Mon-N	1	1	.500	3	3	0	0	0	16^1	18	1	7	4	14.3	5.51	63	.281	.361	0	.000	-0	-4	-4	-0	-0.5
1994	NY-N	0	1	.000	7	0	0	0	0	10	15	5	5	6	18.0	12.60	36	.341	.408	0	—	-0	-9	-9	-0	-0.8
Total	2	1	2	.333	10	3	0	0	0	26^1	33	6	12	10	15.7	8.20	46	.306	.380	0	.000	-0	-13	-13	-0	-1.3

● BILL HURST   Hurst, William Hansel   b: 4/28/70, Miami Beach, Fla.   BR/TR, 6'7", 220 lbs.   Deb: 9/18/96

YEAR	TM/L	W	L	PCT	G	GS	CG	SH	SV	IP	H	HR	BB	SO	RAT	ERA	ERA+	OAV	OOB	BH	AVG	PB	PR	/A	PD	TPI
1996	Fla-N	0	0	—	2	0	0	0	0	2	3	0	1	1	18.0	0.00	—	.333	.400	0	—	0	1	1	-0	0.0

● EDWIN HURTADO   Hurtado, Edwin Amilgar   b: 2/1/70, Barquismeto, Venez.   BR/TR, 6'3", 215 lbs.   Deb: 5/22/95

YEAR	TM/L	W	L	PCT	G	GS	CG	SH	SV	IP	H	HR	BB	SO	RAT	ERA	ERA+	OAV	OOB	BH	AVG	PB	PR	/A	PD	TPI
1995	Tor-A	5	2	.714	14	10	1	0	0	77^2	81	11	40	33	14.6	5.45	86	.275	.371	0	—	0	-6	-6	-1	-0.5
1996	Sea-A	2	5	.286	16	4	0	0	2	47^2	61	10	30	36	17.2	7.74	64	.324	.417	0	—	0	-15	-15	1	-1.7
Total	2	7	7	.500	30	14	1	0	2	125^1	142	21	70	69	15.6	6.32	76	.294	.389	0	—	0	-21	-21	-0	-2.2

● BILL HUSTED   Husted, William J.   b: 10/11/1866, Gloucester, N.J.   d: 5/17/41, Gloucester, N.J.   Deb: 4/29/1890

YEAR	TM/L	W	L	PCT	G	GS	CG	SH	SV	IP	H	HR	BB	SO	RAT	ERA	ERA+	OAV	OOB	BH	AVG	PB	PR	/A	PD	TPI
1890	Phi-P	5	10	.333	18	17	12	0	0	129	148	4	67	33	15.3	4.88	88	.276	.361	6	.107	-6	-9	-9	-2	-1.3

● BERT HUSTING   Husting, Berthold Juneau "Pete"   b: 3/6/1878, Fond Du Lac, Wis.   d: 9/3/48, Milwaukee, Wis.   BR/TR,   Deb: 8/16/00

YEAR	TM/L	W	L	PCT	G	GS	CG	SH	SV	IP	H	HR	BB	SO	RAT	ERA	ERA+	OAV	OOB	BH	AVG	PB	PR	/A	PD	TPI
1900	Pit-N	0	0	—	2	0	0	0	0	8	10	2	5	7	18.0	5.63	65	.303	.410	0	.000	-1	-2	-2	1	0.0
1901	Mil-A	10	15	.400	34	26	19	0	1	217^1	234	5	95	67	14.2	4.27	84	.272	.353	19	.202	-1	-14	-16	5	-1.2
1902	Bos-A	0	1	.000	1	1	1	0	0	8	15	0	4	1	25.9	9.00	40	.395	.500	1	.250	-1	-5	-5	-0	-0.4
	Phi-A	14	5	.737	32	27	17	1	0	204	240	7	91	44	15.0	3.79	97	.293	.370	13	.159	-3	-5	-3	2	-0.3
	Yr	14	6	.700	33	28	18	1	0	212	255	7	99	48	15.4	3.99	92	.298	.377	14	.163	-3	-10	-8	3	-0.7
Total	3	24	21	.533	69	54	37	1	0	437^1	499	14	199	122	14.8	4.16	87	.285	.366	33	.180	-4	-26	-26	8	-1.9

● JOHNNY HUTCHINGS   Hutchings, John Richard Joseph   b: 4/14/16, Chicago, Ill.   d: 4/27/63, Indianapolis, Ind.   BB/TR, 6'2", 250 lbs.   Deb: 4/26/40

YEAR	TM/L	W	L	PCT	G	GS	CG	SH	SV	IP	H	HR	BB	SO	RAT	ERA	ERA+	OAV	OOB	BH	AVG	PB	PR	/A	PD	TPI
1940	*Cin-N	2	1	.667	19	4	0	0	0	54	53	3	18	18	12.0	3.50	108	.260	.323	2	.154		2	2	-1	0.0
1941	Cin-N	0	0	—	8	0	0	0	0	11	12	0	4	5	13.1	4.09	88	.279	.340	0	—	0	-1	-1	0	0.0
	Bos-N	1	6	.143	36	7	1	1	2	95^2	110	6	22	36	12.8	4.14	86	.287	.333	4	.148	0	-5	-6	-0	-0.4
	Yr	1	6	.143	44	7	1	1	2	106^2	122	6	26	41	12.8	4.13	86	.286	.333	4	.148	0	-6	-7	0	-0.4
1942	Bos-N	1	0	1.000	20	3	0	0	0	65^2	66	2	34	27	14.0	4.39	76	.260	.352	1	.050	-2	-8	-8	-1	-0.4
1944	Bos-N	1	4	.200	14	7	1	0	1	56^2	55	3	26	26	13.0	3.97	96	.252	.335	1	.067	-1	-2	-1	-1	-0.2
1945	Bos-N	7	6	.538	57	12	3	2	3	185	173	21	75	99	12.3	3.75	102	.244	.320	13	.241	-1	2	2	0	0.3
1946	Bos-N	0	1	.000	1	1	0	0	0	5	5	1	1	1	18.0	9.00	38	.357	.400	0	.000	-0	-2	-2	-0	-0.5
Total	6	12	18	.400	155	34	5	3	6	471	474	36	180	212	12.7	3.96	93	.260	.333	21	.162	-1	-15	-14	-2	-1.2

● FRED HUTCHINSON   Hutchinson, Frederick Charles   b: 8/12/19, Seattle, Wash.   d: 11/12/64, Bradenton, Fla.   BL/TR, 6'2", 200 lbs.   Deb: 5/2/39   M♦

YEAR	TM/L	W	L	PCT	G	GS	CG	SH	SV	IP	H	HR	BB	SO	RAT	ERA	ERA+	OAV	OOB	BH	AVG	PB	PR	/A	PD	TPI
1939	Det-A	3	6	.333	13	12	3	0	0	84^2	95	9	51	22	15.5	5.21	94	.287	.382	13	.382	3	-6	-3	0	-0.8
1940	*Det-A	3	7	.300	17	10	1	0	0	76	85	6	26	32	13.4	5.68	84	.281	.342	8	.267	-0	-11	-8	0	-0.8
1946	Det-A	14	11	.560	28	26	16	3	2	207	184	14	66	138	10.9	3.09	118	.236	.295	28	.315	8	10	13	3	2.8
1947	Det-A	18	10	.643	33	25	18	3	2	219^2	211	14	61	113	11.2	3.03	124	.251	.304	32	.302	11	16	18	2	3.7
1948	Det-A	13	11	.542	33	28	15	0	0	221	223	32	48	92	11.1	4.32	101	.258	.297	23	.205	4	-1	1	3	0.9
1949	Det-A	15	7	.682	33	21	9	4	1	188^2	167	18	52	54	10.5	2.96	141	.237	.290	18	.247	4	26	25	2	3.4
1950	Det-A	17	8	.680	39	26	10	1	0	231^2	269	18	48	71	12.5	3.96	118	.290	.329	31	.326	10	18	19	2	2.9
1951	Det-A★	10	10	.500	31	20	9	2	2	188^1	204	11	27	53	11.1	3.68	113	.275	.302	16	.188	-2	9	10	2	1.0
1952	Det-A	2	1	.667	12	1	0	0	0	37^1	44	2	9	12	12.1	3.38	132	.276	.323	1	.056	-1	1	2	2	0.2
1953	Det-A	0	0	—	3	0	0	0	0	9^2	9	0	4	5	8.4	2.79	146	.243	.243	1	.167	0	1	1	-0	0.2
Total	10	95	71	.572	242	169	81	13	7	1464	1487	126	388	591	11.6	3.73	113	.262	.311	171	.263	39	62	79	15	14.1

● IRA HUTCHINSON   Hutchinson, Ira Kendall   b: 8/31/10, Chicago, Ill.   d: 8/21/73, Chicago, Ill.   BR/TR, 5'10.5", 180 lbs.   Deb: 9/24/33

YEAR	TM/L	W	L	PCT	G	GS	CG	SH	SV	IP	H	HR	BB	SO	RAT	ERA	ERA+	OAV	OOB	BH	AVG	PB	PR	/A	PD	TPI
1933	Chi-A	0	0	—	1	1	0	0	0	4	7	1	3	2	22.5	13.50	31	.368	.455	1	.500	0	-4	-4	-0	0.0
1937	Bos-N	4	6	.400	31	8	1	0	0	91^2	99	4	35	29	13.3	3.73	96	.286	.353	1	.115	-1	2	1	-0	-0.2
1938	Bos-N	9	8	.529	36	12	4	1	4	151	150	8	61	38	12.8	2.74	125	.258	.332	9	.173	-1	18	12	1	1.3
1939	Bro-N	5	2	.714	41	1	0	0	1	105^2	103	9	46	52	13.2	4.34	93	.265	.352	1	.037	-3	-5	-4	1	-0.4
1940	StL-N	2	4	.667	20	2	1	0	1	63^1	68	3	19	19	12.4	3.13	128	.271	.322	4	.222	0	5	6	0	0.6
1941	StL-N	1	5	.167	29	0	0	0	5	46^2	32	3	19	19	10.2	3.86	98	.196	.288	2	.250	0	-1	-0	0	0.0
1944	Bos-N	9	7	.563	40	8	1	1	1	119^2	136	8	53	22	14.4	4.21	91	.296	.373	4	.138	-1	-8	-5	1	-0.7
1945	Bos-N	2	3	.400	11	0	0	0	1	28^2	32	2	8	4	13.2	5.02	76	.277	.328	0	.000	-1	-4	-4	1	-0.7
Total	8	34	33	.507	209	32	7	2	13	610^2	628	33	249	179	13.1	3.76	100	.270	.344	24	.140	-7	-2	-1	5	-0.1

● BILL HUTCHISON   Hutchison, William Forrest "Wild Bill"   b: 12/17/1859, New Haven, Conn.   d: 3/19/26, Kansas City, Mo.   BR/TR, 5'9", 175 lbs.   Deb: 6/10/1884

YEAR	TM/L	W	L	PCT	G	GS	CG	SH	SV	IP	H	HR	BB	SO	RAT	ERA	ERA+	OAV	OOB	BH	AVG	PB	PR	/A	PD	TPI
1884	KC-U	1	1	.500	2	2	2	0	0	17	14	0	1	5	7.9	2.65	84	.209	.221	2	.250	-0	-0	-1	2	0.0
1889	Chi-N	16	17	.485	37	36	33	3	0	318	306	11	117	136	12.2	3.54	118	.245	.314	21	.158	-5	17	22	5	1.8
1890	Chi-N	42	25	.627	71	66	65	5	2	603	505	20	199	289	10.7	2.70	135	.220	.286	53	.203	-4	58	64	5	5.9
1891	Chi-N	44	19	.698	66	58	56	4	1	561	508	26	178	261	11.1	2.81	119	.232	.292	45	.185	-1	34	33	-2	2.7
1892	Chi-N	36	36	.500	75	70	67	5	1	622	571	11	190	312	11.2	2.76	120	.234	.293	57	.217	-3	36	39	4	4.6
1893	Chi-N	16	24	.400	44	40	38	2	0	348^1	420	9	156	80	15.2	4.75	97	.289	.364	41	.253	1	-3	-5	-3	-0.5
1894	Chi-N	14	16	.467	36	34	28	0	0	277^2	373	9	140	59	17.2	6.06	93	.318	.398	42	.309	5	-23	-14	-2	-0.7
1895	Chi-N	13	21	.382	38	35	30	2	0	291	371	6	129	85	15.9	4.73	108	.305	.378	25	.198	-7	2	12	-0	0.4
1897	StL-N	1	4	.200	11	4	3	0	0	40	55	5	22	5	17.8	6.07	73	.324	.407	5	.278	1	-8	-7	-1	-0.7
Total	9	183	163	.529	375	346	321	21	4	3078	3123	104	1132	1232	12.7	3.59	111	.255	.323	291	.216	-7	112	139	7	13.5

● HERB HUTSON   Hutson, George Herbert   b: 7/17/49, Savannah, Ga.   BR/TR, 6'2", 205 lbs.   Deb: 4/10/74

YEAR	TM/L	W	L	PCT	G	GS	CG	SH	SV	IP	H	HR	BB	SO	RAT	ERA	ERA+	OAV	OOB	BH	AVG	PB	PR	/A	PD	TPI
1974	Chi-N	0	2	.000	20	0	0	0	0	28^2	24	3	15	22	12.6	3.45	110	.233	.336	0	.000	-0	1	1	-1	0.0

● MARK HUTTON   Hutton, Mark Steven   b: 2/6/70, South Adelaide, Australia   BR/TR, 6'6", 240 lbs.   Deb: 7/23/93

YEAR	TM/L	W	L	PCT	G	GS	CG	SH	SV	IP	H	HR	BB	SO	RAT	ERA	ERA+	OAV	OOB	BH	AVG	PB	PR	/A	PD	TPI
1993	NY-A	1	1	.500	7	4	0	0	0	22	24	2	17	12	17.2	5.73	72	.293	.420	0	—	0	-3	-4	-0	-0.3
1994	NY-A	0	0	—	2	0	0	0	0	3^2	4	0	1	1	9.8	4.91	93	.250	.250	0	—	0	-0	-0	-0	0.2
1996	NY-A	0	2	.000	12	2	0	0	0	30^1	32	3	18	25	15.1	5.04	100	.269	.370	0	—	0	-1	-1	-0	-0.1
	Fla-N	5	1	.833	13	9	0	0	0	56^1	47	6	18	31	10.9	3.67	110	.222	.292	6	.316	2	1	1	-0	0.4
Total	3	6	4	.600	34	15	0	0	0	112^1	107	11	53	69	13.2	4.49	97	.249	.339	6	.316	2	-2	-2	-0	0.2

● TOM HUTTON   Hutton, Thomas George   b: 4/20/46, Los Angeles, Cal.   BL/TL, 5'11", 180 lbs.   Deb: 9/16/66   ♦

YEAR	TM/L	W	L	PCT	G	GS	CG	SH	SV	IP	H	HR	BB	SO	RAT	ERA	ERA+	OAV	OOB	BH	AVG	PB	PR	/A	PD	TPI
1980	Mon-N	0	0	—	1	0	0	0	0	1	3	1	1	0	36.0	27.00	13	.500	.571	12	.218	0	-3	-3	0	0.0

● DICK HYDE   Hyde, Richard Elde   b: 8/3/28, Hindsboro, Ill.   BR/TR, 5'11", 170 lbs.   Deb: 4/23/55

YEAR	TM/L	W	L	PCT	G	GS	CG	SH	SV	IP	H	HR	BB	SO	RAT	ERA	ERA+	OAV	OOB	BH	AVG	PB	PR	/A	PD	TPI
1955	Was-A	0	0	—	3	0	0	0	0	2	2	0	1	1	13.5	4.50	85	.286	.375	0	—	0	-0	-0	-0	0.0

YEAR	TM/L	W	L	PCT	G	GS	CG	SH	SV	IP	H	HR	BB	SO	RAT	ERA	ERA+	OAV	OOB	BH	AVG	PB	PR	/A	PD	TPI
1957	Was-A	4	3	.571	52	2	0	0	1	109¹	104	4	56	46	13.7	4.12	95	.261	.361	3	.167	-0	-4	-3	1	-0.1
1958	Was-A	10	3	.769	53	0	0	0	18	103	82	1	35	49	10.4	1.75	218	.220	.291	0	.000	-2	23	24	2	3.9
1959	Was-A	2	5	.286	37	0	0	0	4	54¹	56	5	27	29	14.1	4.97	79	.269	.359	0	.000	-1	-7	-6	2	-0.7
1960	Was-A	0	1	.000	9	0	0	0	0	8²	11	2	5	4	17.7	4.15	94	.355	.459	0	—	0	-0	-0	-0	0.0
1961	Bal-A	1	2	.333	15	0	0	0	0	21	18	1	13	15	13.7	5.57	69	.228	.344	1	1.000	-0	-4	-4	1	-0.3
Total 6		17	14	.548	169	2	0	0	23	298¹	273	13	137	144	12.8	3.56	109	.249	.339	4	.093	-2	8	10	6	2.8

● **JIM HYNDMAN** Hyndman, James William b: 7/1865, Ontario, Canada Deb: 7/23/1886 ♦

YEAR	TM/L	W	L	PCT	G	GS	CG	SH	SV	IP	H	HR	BB	SO	RAT	ERA	ERA+	OAV	OOB	BH	AVG	PB	PR	/A	PD	TPI
1886	Phi-a	0	1	.000	1	1	0	0	0	2	5	1	5	1	49.5	27.00	13	.455	.647	0	.000	-1	-5	-5	0	-1.2

● **PAT HYNES** Hynes, Patrick J. b: 3/12/1884, St.Louis, Mo. d: 3/12/07, St.Louis, Mo. TL , Deb: 9/27/03 ♦

YEAR	TM/L	W	L	PCT	G	GS	CG	SH	SV	IP	H	HR	BB	SO	RAT	ERA	ERA+	OAV	OOB	BH	AVG	PB	PR	/A	PD	TPI
1903	StL-N	0	1	.000	1	1	1	0	0	9	10	0	6	1	16.0	4.00	82	.294	.400	0	.000	-0	-1	-1	-1	-0.2
1904	StL-A	1	0	1.000	5	2	1	0	0	26	35	1	7	6	14.5	6.23	40	.321	.362	60	.236	-0	-10	-11	-1	-0.5
Total 2		1	1	.500	6	3	2	0	0	35	45	1	13	7	14.9	5.66	47	.315	.372	60	.233	-0	-11	-12	-2	-0.7

● **HAM IBURG** Iburg, Herman Edward b: 10/29/1877, San Francisco, Cal d: 2/11/45, San Francisco, Cal BR/TR, 5'11", 165 lbs. Deb: 4/17/02

YEAR	TM/L	W	L	PCT	G	GS	CG	SH	SV	IP	H	HR	BB	SO	RAT	ERA	ERA+	OAV	OOB	BH	AVG	PB	PR	/A	PD	TPI
1902	Phi-N	11	18	.379	30	29	20	1	0	236	286	1	62	106	13.7	3.89	72	.299	.349	12	.138	-5	-29	-28	0	-3.5

● **GARY IGNASIAK** Ignasiak, Gary Raymond b: 9/1/49, Anchorville, Mich. BR/TL, 5'11", 185 lbs. Deb: 9/20/73 F

YEAR	TM/L	W	L	PCT	G	GS	CG	SH	SV	IP	H	HR	BB	SO	RAT	ERA	ERA+	OAV	OOB	BH	AVG	PB	PR	/A	PD	TPI
1973	Det-A	0	0	—	3	0	0	0	0	4²	5	0	3	4	15.4	3.86	106	.278	.381	0	—	0	-0	-0	0	0.0

● **MIKE IGNASIAK** Ignasiak, Michael James b: 3/12/66, Mt.Clemens, Mich. BB/TR, 5'11", 175 lbs. Deb: 8/22/91 F

YEAR	TM/L	W	L	PCT	G	GS	CG	SH	SV	IP	H	HR	BB	SO	RAT	ERA	ERA+	OAV	OOB	BH	AVG	PB	PR	/A	PD	TPI
1991	Mil-A	2	1	.667	4	1	0	0	0	12²	7	2	8	10	10.7	5.68	70	.163	.294	0	—	0	-2	-2	-0	-0.4
1993	Mil-A	1	1	.500	27	0	0	0	0	37	32	2	21	28	13.4	3.65	116	.241	.353	0	—	0	3	2	-1	0.1
1994	Mil-A	3	1	.750	23	5	0	0	0	47²	51	5	13	24	12.3	4.53	111	.276	.327	0	—	0	1	3	-1	-0.1
1995	Mil-A	4	1	.800	25	0	0	0	0	39²	51	5	23	26	17.2	5.90	84	.325	.418	0	—	0	-5	-4	-1	-0.6
Total 4		10	4	.714	79	6	0	0	0	137	141	14	65	88	13.9	4.80	98	.272	.359	0	—	0	-3	-1	-2	-1.0

● **BLAISE ILSLEY** Ilsley, Blaise Francis b: 4/9/64, Alpena, Mich. BL/TL, 6'1", 195 lbs. Deb: 4/4/94

YEAR	TM/L	W	L	PCT	G	GS	CG	SH	SV	IP	H	HR	BB	SO	RAT	ERA	ERA+	OAV	OOB	BH	AVG	PB	PR	/A	PD	TPI
1994	Chi-N	0	0	—	10	0	0	0	0	15	25	1	9	9	20.4	7.80	53	.385	.459	0	.000	-0	-6	-6	0	-1.0

● **DOC IMLAY** Imlay, Harry Miller b: 1/12/1889, Allentown, N.J. d: 10/7/48, Bordentown, N.J. BR/TR, 5'11", 168 lbs. Deb: 7/7/13

YEAR	TM/L	W	L	PCT	G	GS	CG	SH	SV	IP	H	HR	BB	SO	RAT	ERA	ERA+	OAV	OOB	BH	AVG	PB	PR	/A	PD	TPI
1913	Phi-N	0	0	—	9	0	0	0	0	13²	19	1	7	7	17.1	7.24	46	.358	.433	0	.000	-0	-6	-6	0	-1.0

● **BOB INGERSOLL** Ingersoll, Robert Randolph b: 1/8/1883, Rapid City, S.D. d: 1/13/27, Minneapolis, Minn. BR/TR, 5'11.5", 175 lbs. Deb: 4/23/14

YEAR	TM/L	W	L	PCT	G	GS	CG	SH	SV	IP	H	HR	BB	SO	RAT	ERA	ERA+	OAV	OOB	BH	AVG	PB	PR	/A	PD	TPI
1914	Cin-N	0	0	—	4	0	0	0	0	6	5	0	5	2	16.5	3.00	98	.250	.423	1	1.000	0	-0	-0	0	0.0

● **BERT INKS** Inks, Albert John b: 1/27/1871, Ligonier, Ind. d: 10/3/41, Ligonier, Ind. BL/TL, 6'3", 175 lbs. Deb: 9/2/1891

YEAR	TM/L	W	L	PCT	G	GS	CG	SH	SV	IP	H	HR	BB	SO	RAT	ERA	ERA+	OAV	OOB	BH	AVG	PB	PR	/A	PD	TPI
1891	Bro-N	3	10	.231	13	13	11	1	0	96¹	99	2	43	47	13.8	4.02	82	.256	.339	10	.286	2	-7	-8	-0	-0.7
1892	Bro-N	4	2	.667	9	8	4	1	0	58	48	0	33	25	13.2	3.88	82	.216	.328	10	.440	3	-4	-5	-0	-0.1
	Was-N	1	2	.333	3	3	3	0	0	21	29	0	10	11	17.6	5.14	63	.315	.394	3	.300	1	-4	-4	-0	-0.4
	Yr	5	4	.556	12	11	7	1	0	79	77	0	43	36	13.9	4.22	76	.242	.336	13	.371	4	-8	-9	-0	-0.5
1894	Bal-N	9	4	.692	22	14	10	0	1	133	181	4	54	30	16.6	5.55	98	.321	.391	18	.316	2	-3	-1	-1	-0.1
	Lou-N	2	6	.250	8	8	8	0	0	59²	87	2	34	8	18.4	6.49	79	.336	.415	12	.444	3	-8	-9	-0	-0.6
	Yr	11	10	.524	30	22	18	0	1	192²	268	6	88	38	16.7	5.84	92	.321	.387	30	.357	5	-11	-11	-1	-0.7
1895	Lou-N	7	20	.259	28	27	21	0	0	205¹	294	3	78	42	17.0	6.40	72	.331	.394	21	.250	-0	-37	-40	1	-3.6
1896	Phi-N	0	1	.000	3	1	1	0	0	10¹	21	1	5	2	23.5	7.84	55	.412	.474	1	.200	-0	-4	-4	-1	-0.5
	Cin-N	1	1	.500	3	3	2	0	0	20	21	0	9	2	13.9	4.50	102	.269	.352	0	.000	-1	-0	-0	-1	-0.1
	Yr	1	2	.333	6	4	2	0	0	30¹	42	1	14	4	16.9	5.64	80	.323	.393	1	.083	-1	-4	-4	-1	-0.5
Total 5		27	46	.370	89	77	59	2	1	603²	780	12	266	167	16.2	5.52	81	.307	.382	75	.300	9	-68	-72	-2	-6.0

● **JEFF INNIS** Innis, Jeffrey David b: 7/5/62, Decatur, Ill. BR/TR, 6'1", 170 lbs. Deb: 5/16/87

YEAR	TM/L	W	L	PCT	G	GS	CG	SH	SV	IP	H	HR	BB	SO	RAT	ERA	ERA+	OAV	OOB	BH	AVG	PB	PR	/A	PD	TPI
1987	NY-N	0	1	.000	17	1	0	0	0	25²	29	5	4	28	11.9	3.16	120	.279	.312	0	.000	-0	3	2	-0	0.0
1988	NY-N	1	1	.500	12	0	0	0	0	19	19	0	2	14	9.9	1.89	170	.250	.269	0	—	0	3	3	-1	0.2
1989	NY-N	0	1	.000	29	0	0	0	0	39²	38	2	8	16	10.7	3.18	103	.255	.297	0	.000	-0	1	0	1	0.1
1990	NY-N	1	3	.250	18	0	0	0	0	26¹	19	4	10	12	10.3	2.39	156	.209	.294	0	—	0	4	4	0	0.6
1991	NY-N	0	2	.000	69	0	0	0	0	84²	66	2	23	47	9.5	2.66	137	.219	.274	0	.000	-0	10	9	3	0.5
1992	NY-N	6	9	.400	76	0	0	0	1	88	85	4	36	39	13.0	2.86	121	.266	.351	0	.000	-0	6	6	2	1.2
1993	NY-N	2	3	.400	67	0	0	0	3	76²	81	5	38	36	14.7	4.11	98	.278	.373	0	—	0	-1	-1	1	0.0
Total 7		10	20	.333	288	1	0	0	5	360	337	22	121	192	11.8	3.05	119	.253	.322	0	—	0	27	23	6	2.6

● **DANE IORG** Iorg, Dane Charles b: 5/11/50, Eureka, Cal. BL/TR, 6', 180 lbs. Deb: 4/9/77 F♦

YEAR	TM/L	W	L	PCT	G	GS	CG	SH	SV	IP	H	HR	BB	SO	RAT	ERA	ERA+	OAV	OOB	BH	AVG	PB	PR	/A	PD	TPI
1986	SD-N	0	0	—	2	0	0	0	0	2	4	1	1	1	18.0	12.00	30	.357	.400	24	.226	-0	-3	-3	0	0.0

● **HOOKS IOTT** Iott, Clarence Eugene b: 12/3/19, Mountain Grove, Mo. d: 8/17/80, St.Petersburg, Fla BB/TL, 6'2", 200 lbs. Deb: 9/6/41

YEAR	TM/L	W	L	PCT	G	GS	CG	SH	SV	IP	H	HR	BB	SO	RAT	ERA	ERA+	OAV	OOB	BH	AVG	PB	PR	/A	PD	TPI
1941	StL-A	0	0	—	2	0	0	0	0	2	1	0	1	1	13.5	9.00	36	.250	.333		—	0	-1	-1	0	0.0
1947	StL-A	0	1	.000	4	0	0	0	0	8¹	15	4	14	6	31.3	16.20	24	.375	.537	0	.000	-0	-12	-11	0	-1.1
	NY-N	3	8	.273	20	9	2	1	0	71¹	67	3	52	46	15.1	5.93	69	.251	.375	3	.143	1	-15	-15	-0	-1.9
Total 2		3	9	.250	26	9	2	1	0	81²	84	7	67	53	16.8	7.05	58	.267	.397	3	.130	1	-27	-27	0	-3.0

● **DARYL IRVINE** Irvine, Daryl Keith b: 11/15/64, Harrisonburg, Va. BR/TR, 6'3", 195 lbs. Deb: 4/28/90

YEAR	TM/L	W	L	PCT	G	GS	CG	SH	SV	IP	H	HR	BB	SO	RAT	ERA	ERA+	OAV	OOB	BH	AVG	PB	PR	/A	PD	TPI
1990	Bos-A	1	1	.500	11	0	0	0	0	17¹	15	0	10	9	13.0	4.67	87	.246	.352	0	—	0	-1	-1	0	-0.4
1991	Bos-A	0	0	—	9	0	0	0	0	18	25	2	9	8	18.0	6.00	72	.321	.404	0	—	0	-4	-3	0	-0.2
1992	Bos-A	3	4	.429	21	0	0	0	0	28	31	1	14	10	15.1	6.11	69	.287	.379	0	—	0	-7	-6	0	-1.5
Total 3		4	5	.444	41	0	0	0	0	63¹	71	3	33	27	15.3	5.68	74	.287	.380	0	—	0	-12	-10	1	-2.1

● **ARTHUR IRWIN** Irwin, Arthur Albert "Doc" or "Sandy"
b: 2/14/1858, Toronto, Ont., Can. d: 7/16/21, At Sea Atlantic Ocean N.Y. To Boston BL/TR, 5'8.5", 158 lbs. Deb: 5/1/1880 FMU♦

YEAR	TM/L	W	L	PCT	G	GS	CG	SH	SV	IP	H	HR	BB	SO	RAT	ERA	ERA+	OAV	OOB	BH	AVG	PB	PR	/A	PD	TPI
1884	*Pro-N	0	0	—	1	0	0	0	0	3	5	0	1	0	18.0	3.00	94	.357	.400	97	.240	-0	-0	-0	0	0.0
1889	Was-N	0	0	—	1	0	0	0	0	1	1	0	0	0	9.0	0.00		.250	.250	73	.233	-0	-0	-0	0	0.0
Total 2		0	0	—	2	0	0	0	0	4	6	0	1	0	15.8	2.25	138	.333	.368	934	.241	-0	-0	-0	0	0.0

● **BILL IRWIN** Irwin, William Franklin "Phil" b: 9/16/1859, Neville, Ohio d: 8/7/33, Ft.Thomas, Ky. BR/TR, 6', 195 lbs. Deb: 8/30/1886

YEAR	TM/L	W	L	PCT	G	GS	CG	SH	SV	IP	H	HR	BB	SO	RAT	ERA	ERA+	OAV	OOB	BH	AVG	PB	PR	/A	PD	TPI
1886	Cin-a	0	2	.000	2	2	2	0	0	17	18	2	8	6	13.8	5.82	60	.247	.321	0	.000	-0	-4	-4	0	-0.4

● **FRANK ISBELL** Isbell, William Frank "Bald Eagle" b: 8/21/1875, Delevan, N.Y. d: 7/15/41, Wichita, Kan. BL/TR, 5'11", 190 lbs. Deb: 5/1/1898 ♦

YEAR	TM/L	W	L	PCT	G	GS	CG	SH	SV	IP	H	HR	BB	SO	RAT	ERA	ERA+	OAV	OOB	BH	AVG	PB	PR	/A	PD	TPI
1898	Chi-N	4	7	.364	13	9	7	0	0	81	86	0	42	16	15.0	3.56	101	.270	.368	37	.233	-0	0	0	0	0.1
1901	Chi-A	0	0	—	1	0	0	0	0	1	2	0	0	0	18.0	9.00	39	.400	.400	143	.257	0	-1	-1	0	0.1
1902	Chi-A	0	0	—	1	1	0	0	0	1	3	0	1	0	36.0	9.00	38	.500	.571	130	.252	0	-1	-1	0	0.1
1906	*Chi-A	0	0	—	1	0	0	0	0	2	1	0	0	2	4.5	0.00	—	.143	.143	153	.279	0	1	1	0	0.1
1907	Chi-A	0	0	—	1	0	0	0	0	0¹	0	0	0	1	0.0	0.00	—	.000	.000	118	.243	0	0	0	0	0.1
Total 5		4	7	.364	17	10	7	0	1	85¹	92	0	43	19	15.0	3.59	99	.273	.367	1056	.250	-0	-0	-1	0	0.2

● **JASON ISRINGHAUSEN** Isringhausen, Jason Derik b: 9/7/72, Brighton, Ill. BR/TR, 6'3", 195 lbs. Deb: 7/17/95

YEAR	TM/L	W	L	PCT	G	GS	CG	SH	SV	IP	H	HR	BB	SO	RAT	ERA	ERA+	OAV	OOB	BH	AVG	PB	PR	/A	PD	TPI
1995	NY-N	9	2	.818	14	14	1	0	0	93	88	6	31	55	11.7	2.81	144	.254	.319	4	.148	1	14	13	-1	1.4
1996	NY-N	6	14	.300	27	27	2	1	0	171²	190	13	73	114	14.2	4.77	82	.284	.361	13	.255	6	-11	-16	-0	-1.0
Total 2		15	16	.484	41	41	3	1	0	264²	278	19	104	169	13.3	4.08	97	.274	.347	17	.218	7	4	-3	-0	0.4

● **AL JACKSON** Jackson, Alvin Neil b: 12/25/35, Waco, Tex. BL/TL, 5'10", 169 lbs. Deb: 6/1/59 C

YEAR	TM/L	W	L	PCT	G	GS	CG	SH	SV	IP	H	HR	BB	SO	RAT	ERA	ERA+	OAV	OOB	BH	AVG	PB	PR	/A	PD	TPI
1959	Pit-N	0	0	—	8	3	0	0	0	18	30	1	8	13	19.0	6.50	60	.405	.463	1	.200	-5	-5	-5	-0	0.0
1961	Pit-N	1	0	1.000	3	1	0	0	0	23²	22	2	4	15	9.1	3.42	117	.233	.267	0	.000	-1	2	1	1	0.1
1962	NY-N	8	20	.286	36	33	12	4	0	231¹	244	16	78	118	12.7	4.40	95	.273	.335	5	.068	-5	-12	-5	4	-0.6
1963	NY-N	13	17	.433	37	34	11	0	1	227	237	25	84	142	13.2	3.96	88	.267	.338	16	.203	2	-17	-12	2	-1.2

YEAR	TM/L	W	L	PCT	G	GS	CG	SH	SV	IP	H	HR	BB	SO	RAT	ERA	ERA+	OAV	OOB	BH	AVG	PB	PR	/A	PD	TPI
1964	NY-N	11	16	.407	40	31	11	3	1	213¹	229	18	60	112	12.4	4.26	84	.272	.323	11	.153	2	-17	-16	0	-1.6
1965	NY-N	8	20	.286	37	31	7	3	1	205¹	217	17	61	120	12.5	4.34	81	.271	.329	7	.117	-1	-18	-18	2	-2.2
1966	StL-N	13	15	.464	36	30	11	3	0	232²	222	18	45	90	10.4	2.51	143	.250	.288	13	.176	2	28	28	4	4.2
1967	StL-N	9	4	.692	38	11	1	1	1	107	117	7	29	43	12.4	3.95	83	.279	.327	8	.258	2	-7	-8	2	-0.4
1968	NY-N	3	7	.300	25	9	0	0	3	92²	88	5	17	59	10.4	3.69	82	.249	.287	7	.250	1	-7	-7	1	-0.6
1969	NY-N	0	0	—	9	0	0	0	0	11	18	1	4	10	18.8	10.64	34	.353	.411	0	.000	-0	-9	-9	0	0.0
	Cin-N	1	0	1.000	33	0	0	0	3	27¹	27	5	17	16	15.5	5.27	71	.260	.379	1	.250	0	-5	-5	0	-0.3
	Yr	1	0	1.000	42	0	0	0	3	38¹	45	6	21	26	16.2	6.81	55	.285	.379	1	.200	0	-14	-13	0	-0.3
Total	10	67	99	.404	302	184	54	14	10	1389¹	1449	115	407	738	12.3	3.98	91	.268	.324	69	.159	3	-67	-56	16	-2.6

● **CHARLIE JACKSON**   Jackson, Charles Bernard b: 8/4/1876, Versailles, Ohio d: 11/23/57, Scottsbluff, Neb. TR, Deb: 8/11/05

YEAR	TM/L	W	L	PCT	G	GS	CG	SH	SV	IP	H	HR	BB	SO	RAT	ERA	ERA+	OAV	OOB	BH	AVG	PB	PR	/A	PD	TPI
1905	Det-A	0	2	.000	2	2	1	0	0	11	14	1	7	3	17.2	5.73	48	.311	.404	1	.250	0	-4	-4	-0	-0.6

● **DANNY JACKSON**   Jackson, Danny Lynn b: 1/5/62, San Antonio, Tex. BR/TL, 6', 205 lbs. Deb: 9/11/83

YEAR	TM/L	W	L	PCT	G	GS	CG	SH	SV	IP	H	HR	BB	SO	RAT	ERA	ERA+	OAV	OOB	BH	AVG	PB	PR	/A	PD	TPI
1983	KC-A	1	1	.500	4	3	0	0	0	19	26	1	6	9	15.2	5.21	78	.325	.372	0	—	0	-2	-2	0	-0.2
1984	KC-A	2	6	.250	15	11	1	0	0	76	84	4	35	40	14.7	4.26	94	.285	.370	0	—	0	-2	-2	-0	-0.3
1985	*KC-A	14	12	.538	32	32	4	3	0	208	209	7	76	114	12.6	3.42	122	.261	.329	0	—	0	17	17	-1	1.8
1986	KC-A	11	12	.478	32	27	4	1	1	185²	177	13	79	115	12.6	3.20	133	.256	.335	0	—	0	20	22	-1	2.3
1987	KC-A	9	18	.333	36	34	11	2	0	224	219	11	109	152	13.5	4.02	113	.258	.347	0	—	0	11	13	-2	1.2
1988	Cin-N☆	23	8	.742	35	35	**15**	6	0	260²	206	13	71	161	9.6	2.73	131	.218	.275	13	.144	-0	21	25	2	3.2
1989	Cin-N	6	11	.353	20	20	1	0	0	115²	122	10	57	70	14.0	5.60	64	.271	.354	8	.222	1	-27	-26	-1	-3.3
1990	*Cin-N	6	6	.500	22	21	0	0	0	117¹	119	11	40	76	12.3	3.61	109	.266	.329	2	.054	-2	2	4	-1	0.1
1991	Chi-N	1	5	.167	17	14	0	0	0	70²	89	8	48	31	17.6	6.75	58	.309	.409	2	.087	-1	-24	-23	-1	-1.9
1992	Chi-N	4	9	.308	19	19	0	0	0	113	117	5	48	51	13.4	4.22	85	.270	.346	3	.083	-2	-9	-8	-1	-1.2
	*Pit-N	4	4	.500	15	15	0	0	0	88¹	94	1	29	46	12.6	3.36	102	.276	.334	2	.083	-1	1	1	0	0.0
	Yr	8	13	.381	34	34	0	0	0	201¹	211	6	77	97	12.9	3.84	92	.269	.336	5	.083	-3	-8	-7	-1	-1.2
1993	*Phi-N	12	11	.522	32	32	2	1	0	210¹	214	12	80	120	12.8	3.77	105	.263	.332	5	.077	-2	6	5	-2	0.0
1994	Phi-N★	14	6	.700	25	25	4	1	0	179¹	183	13	46	129	11.6	3.26	131	.266	.314	9	.158	1	19	20	1	2.3
1995	StL-N	2	12	.143	19	19	2	1	0	100²	120	10	48	52	15.6	5.90	71	.303	.387	5	.161	-0	-19	-19	-1	-2.3
1996	*StL-N	1	1	.500	13	4	0	0	0	36¹	33	3	16	27	12.4	4.46	95	.243	.327	3	.333	1	-1	-1	0	0.1
Total	14	110	122	.474	336	311	44	15	1	2005	2012	122	788	1193	12.8	3.89	103	.263	.335	52	.127	-6	13	27	-7	1.8

● **DARRELL JACKSON**   Jackson, Darrell Preston b: 4/3/56, Los Angeles, Cal. BB/TL, 5'10", 150 lbs. Deb: 6/16/78

YEAR	TM/L	W	L	PCT	G	GS	CG	SH	SV	IP	H	HR	BB	SO	RAT	ERA	ERA+	OAV	OOB	BH	AVG	PB	PR	/A	PD	TPI
1978	Min-A	4	6	.400	19	15	1	1	0	92¹	89	9	48	54	13.5	4.48	85	.256	.350	0	—	0	-7	-7	-1	-0.8
1979	Min-A	4	4	.500	24	8	1	0	0	69¹	89	5	26	43	15.1	4.28	102	.319	.379	0	—	0	-1	1	1	0.0
1980	Min-A	9	9	.500	32	25	1	0	1	172	161	15	69	90	12.1	3.87	113	.250	.325	0	—	0	3	9	-0	0.9
1981	Min-A	3	3	.500	14	5	0	0	0	32²	35	1	19	26	15.2	4.41	90	.282	.382	0	—	0	-3	-2	-1	-0.4
1982	Min-A	0	5	.000	13	7	0	0	0	44²	51	6	24	16	15.3	6.25	68	.297	.386	0	—	0	-11	-10	-1	-1.1
Total	5	20	27	.426	102	60	3	1	1	411	425	36	186	229	13.5	4.38	96	.272	.352	0	—	0	-18	-8	-2	-1.4

● **DARRIN JACKSON**   Jackson, Darrin Jay b: 8/22/62, Los Angeles, Cal. BR/TR, 6'1", 170 lbs. Deb: 6/17/85 ♦

YEAR	TM/L	W	L	PCT	G	GS	CG	SH	SV	IP	H	HR	BB	SO	RAT	ERA	ERA+	OAV	OOB	BH	AVG	PB	PR	/A	PD	TPI
1991	SD-N	0	0	—	1	0	0	0	0	2	3	0	2	0	22.5	9.00	42	.375	.500	94	.262	0	-1	-1	-0	0.0

● **GRANT JACKSON**   Jackson, Grant Dwight "Buck" b: 9/28/42, Fostoria, Ohio BB/TL, 6', 190 lbs. Deb: 9/3/65 C

YEAR	TM/L	W	L	PCT	G	GS	CG	SH	SV	IP	H	HR	BB	SO	RAT	ERA	ERA+	OAV	OOB	BH	AVG	PB	PR	/A	PD	TPI
1965	Phi-N	1	1	.500	6	2	0	0	0	13²	17	4	5	15	14.5	7.24	48	.304	.361	0	.000	-0	-6	-6	0	-0.8
1966	Phi-N	0	0	—	2	0	0	0	0	1²	2	0	3	0	27.0	5.40	67	.333	.556	0	—	0	-0	-0	0	0.0
1967	Phi-N	2	3	.400	43	4	0	0	1	84¹	86	3	43	83	14.0	3.84	89	.267	.357	2	.133	-0	-4	-4	-2	-0.4
1968	Phi-N	1	6	.143	33	6	1	0	0	61	59	4	20	49	11.7	2.95	102	.248	.306	3	.300	1	0	0	0	0.2
1969	Phi-N☆	14	18	.438	38	35	13	4	1	253	237	16	92	180	11.9	3.34	106	.249	.318	12	.140	-1	7	6	-2	0.5
1970	Phi-N	5	15	.250	32	23	1	0	0	149²	170	17	61	104	14.0	5.29	75	.288	.356	4	.091	-2	-21	-22	0	-2.7
1971	*Bal-A	4	3	.571	29	9	0	0	0	77²	72	7	20	51	10.9	3.13	107	.249	.302	2	.091	0	3	2	-0	0.2
1972	*Bal-A	1	1	.500	32	0	0	0	8	41	33	1	9	34	9.2	2.63	117	.217	.261	0	.000	-0	2	2	0	0.2
1973	*Bal-A	8	0	1.000	45	0	0	0	9	80¹	54	5	24	47	8.7	1.90	196	.198	.263	0	—	0	17	16	-0	2.0
1974	Bal-A	6	4	.600	49	0	0	0	12	66²	48	7	22	56	9.6	2.57	135	.198	.268	0	—	0	8	7	-1	1.1
1975	Bal-A	4	3	.571	41	0	0	0	7	48¹	42	3	21	39	11.9	3.35	105	.241	.327	0	—	0	2	1	-0	0.1
1976	Bal-A	1	1	.500	13	0	0	0	2	19¹	19	1	9	14	14.0	5.12	64	.268	.366	0	—	0	-3	-4	-0	-0.5
	*NY-A	6	0	1.000	21	2	1	1	2	58²	38	1	16	25	8.4	1.69	202	.186	.249	0	—	0	12	11	-1	1.0
	Yr	7	1	.875	34	2	1	1	4	78	57	2	25	39	9.6	2.54	133	.205	.273	0	—	0	8	7	-2	0.5
1977	Pit-N	5	3	.625	49	2	0	0	4	91	81	11	39	41	12.0	3.86	103	.240	.321	6	.333	2	1	1	-1	0.2
1978	Pit-N	7	5	.583	60	0	0	0	5	77¹	89	5	32	46	14.2	3.26	114	.298	.367	3	.250	1	3	4	0	0.7
1979	*Pit-N	8	5	.615	72	0	0	0	14	82	67	9	35	39	11.4	2.96	131	.230	.317	0	.000	-1	7	8	-1	1.3
1980	Pit-N	8	4	.667	61	0	0	0	4	71	71	4	20	31	11.5	2.92	125	.275	.327	0	—	-1	5	6	-0	0.9
1981	Pit-N	1	2	.333	35	0	0	0	4	32¹	30	1	10	17	11.1	2.51	143	.248	.305	0	.000	-0	4	4	-1	0.3
	Mon-N	1	0	1.000	10	0	0	0	0	10²	14	2	9	4	19.4	7.59	46	.333	.451	0	—	0	-5	-5	-0	-0.4
	Yr	2	2	.500	45	0	0	0	4	43	44	3	19	21	13.2	3.77	95	.267	.342	0	.000	-0	-1	-1	-1	-0.1
1982	KC-A	3	1	.750	20	0	0	0	0	38¹	42	7	21	15	15.3	5.17	79	.271	.365	0	—	0	-5	-5	-0	-0.5
	Pit-N	0	0	—	1	0	0	0	0	0²	1	0	1	0	13.5	13.50	27	.333	.333	0	—	0	-1	-1	-0	-0.5
Total	18	86	75	.534	692	83	16	5	79	1358²	1272	109	511	889	11.9	3.46	104	.251	.322	32	.136	-2	26	22	-9	3.4

● **JOHN JACKSON**   Jackson, John Lewis b: 7/15/09, Wynnefield, Pa. d: 10/22/56, Somers Point, N.J. BR/TR, 6'2", 180 lbs. Deb: 6/20/33

YEAR	TM/L	W	L	PCT	G	GS	CG	SH	SV	IP	H	HR	BB	SO	RAT	ERA	ERA+	OAV	OOB	BH	AVG	PB	PR	/A	PD	TPI
1933	Phi-N	2	2	.500	10	7	1	0	0	54	74	3	35	11	19.0	6.00	64	.329	.430	3	.143	-1	-16	-13	-2	-1.2

● **LARRY JACKSON**   Jackson, Lawrence Curtis b: 6/2/31, Nampa, Idaho d: 8/28/90, Boise, Idaho BR/TR, 6'2", 190 lbs. Deb: 4/17/55

YEAR	TM/L	W	L	PCT	G	GS	CG	SH	SV	IP	H	HR	BB	SO	RAT	ERA	ERA+	OAV	OOB	BH	AVG	PB	PR	/A	PD	TPI
1955	StL-N	9	14	.391	37	25	4	1	2	177¹	189	25	72	88	13.7	4.31	94	.277	.353	-6	.053	-6	-5	-5	0	-1.1
1956	StL-N	2	2	.500	51	2	0	0	9	85¹	75	5	45	50	13.2	4.11	92	.240	.337	1	.091	-0	-3	-3	2	-0.1
1957	StL-N★	15	9	.625	41	22	6	2	1	210¹	196	21	57	96	11.0	3.47	114	.248	.302	13	.181	-0	10	12	4	1.7
1958	StL-N	13	13	.500	49	23	11	1	8	198	211	21	51	124	12.4	3.68	112	.272	.325	9	.150	-2	6	10	-2	0.8
1959	StL-N	14	13	.519	40	37	12	3	0	256	271	13	64	145	11.9	3.30	128	.270	.316	9	.112	-3	18	27	-0	2.2
1960	StL-N★	18	13	.581	43	38	14	3	0	**282**	277	22	70	171	11.2	3.48	118	.257	.304	20	.211	2	9	19	-2	2.0
1961	StL-N	14	11	.560	33	28	12	3	0	211	203	20	56	113	11.2	3.75	117	.252	.303	13	.176	0	7	15	2	1.8
1962	StL-N	16	11	.593	36	35	11	2	0	252¹	267	26	64	112	12.0	3.75	114	.269	.318	15	.169	2	6	15	1	1.7
1963	Chi-N★	14	18	.438	37	37	13	4	0	275	256	11	54	153	10.3	2.55	137	.245	.286	17	.195	2	22	29	2	4.1
1964	Chi-N	**24**	11	.686	40	38	19	3	0	297²	265	17	53	148	9.8	3.14	118	.235	.273	20	.175	1	13	19	7	3.0
1965	Chi-N	14	21	.400	39	39	12	4	0	257¹	268	28	57	131	11.5	3.85	96	.267	.310	11	.128	1	-9	-5	3	-0.2
1966	Chi-N	0	2	.000	3	2	0	0	0	8	14	3	4	5	20.3	13.50	27	.368	.429	0	.000	-0	-9	-9	0	-1.5
	Phi-N	15	13	.536	35	33	12	5	0	247	243	22	58	107	11.1	2.99	120	.259	.306	13	.146	-0	17	17	1	2.0
	Yr	15	15	.500	38	35	12	**5**	0	255	257	25	62	112	11.4	3.32	108	.264	.311	13	.141	-1	8	8	2	0.5
1967	Phi-N	13	15	.464	40	37	11	4	0	261²	247	25	62	139	10.4	3.10	110	.241	.284	14	.161	-0	8	9	4	1.5
1968	Phi-N	13	17	.433	34	34	12	2	0	243²	229	19	60	127	10.8	2.77	109	.248	.297	12	.141	-0	6	6	2	0.9
Total	14	194	183	.515	558	429	149	37	20	3262²	3206	259	824	1709	11.3	3.40	113	.256	.306	170	.156	-5	95	155	25	18.8

● **MIKE JACKSON**   Jackson, Michael Ray b: 12/22/64, Houston, Tex. BR/TR, 6'1", 185 lbs. Deb: 8/11/86

YEAR	TM/L	W	L	PCT	G	GS	CG	SH	SV	IP	H	HR	BB	SO	RAT	ERA	ERA+	OAV	OOB	BH	AVG	PB	PR	/A	PD	TPI
1986	Phi-N	0	0	—	9	0	0	0	0	13¹	12	2	4	3	12.2	3.38	114	.250	.333	0	—	0	1	1	-0	0.0
1987	Phi-N	3	10	.231	55	7	0	0	1	109¹	88	16	56	93	12.1	4.20	101	.219	.319	2	.118	-0	-1	-1	-1	-0.1
1988	Sea-A	6	5	.545	62	0	0	0	4	99¹	74	10	43	76	10.8	2.63	158	.209	.298	0	—	0	15	17	-0	1.8
1989	Sea-A	4	6	.400	65	0	0	0	7	99¹	81	8	54	94	12.8	3.17	127	.223	.333	0	—	0	8	9	-1	0.9
1990	Sea-A	5	7	.417	63	0	0	0	3	77¹	64	8	44	69	12.8	4.54	87	.229	.338	0	—	0	-5	-5	-0	-0.7
1991	Sea-A	7	7	.500	72	0	0	0	14	88²	64	5	34	74	10.6	3.25	127	.201	.290	0	—	0	8	9	-1	1.4
1992	SF-N	6	6	.500	67	0	0	0	2	82	76	4	33	80	12.4	3.73	89	.252	.333	0	.000	0	-2	-4	-0	-0.6
1993	SF-N	6	6	.500	**81**	0	0	0	1	77¹	58	7	24	70	9.9	3.03	129	.204	.273	2	.667	2	9	8	0	1.3
1994	SF-N	3	2	.600	36	0	0	0	4	42¹	23	4	11	51	7.7	1.49	269	.164	.235	0	.000	-0	**13**	12	0	1.5

YEAR TM/L	W	L	PCT	G	GS	CG	SH	SV	IP	H	HR	BB	SO	RAT	ERA	ERA+	OAV	OOB	BH	AVG	PB	PR	/A	PD	TPI
1995 *Cin-N	6	1	.857	40	0	0	0	2	49	38	5	19	41	10.7	2.39	172	.213	.293	1	.250	0	10	9	-1	1.2
1996 Sea-A	1	1	.500	73	0	0	0	6	72	61	11	24	70	11.4	3.63	136	.225	.302	0	—	0	11	10	1	0.5
Total 11	47	51	.480	623	7	0	0	44	810	639	83	346	721	11.4	3.33	122	.217	.308	5	.185	1	65	66	-1	7.2

● **MIKE JACKSON**   Jackson, Michael Warren b: 3/27/46, Paterson, N.J.   BL/TL, 6'3", 190 lbs. Deb: 5/10/70

YEAR TM/L	W	L	PCT	G	GS	CG	SH	SV	IP	H	HR	BB	SO	RAT	ERA	ERA+	OAV	OOB	BH	AVG	PB	PR	/A	PD	TPI
1970 Phi-N	1	1	.500	5	0	0	0	0	6¹	6	0	4	4	14.2	1.42	281	.286	.400	1	1.000	0	2	2	0	0.6
1971 StL-N	0	0	—	1	0	0	0	0	0²	1	0	1	0	27.0	0.00	—	.333	.500	0	—	0	0	0	0	0.0
1972 KC-A	1	2	.333	7	3	0	0	0	19²	24	0	14	15	17.4	6.41	47	.320	.427	0	.000	-1	-7	-7	1	-1.0
1973 KC-A	0	0	—	9	0	0	0	0	22¹	25	3	20	13	18.5	6.85	60	.301	.442	0	—	0	-8	-7	-0	0.0
Cle-A	0	0	—	1	0	0	0	0	0²	1	0	1	1	13.5	0.00	—	.333	.333	0	—	0	0	0	0	0.0
Yr	0	0	—	10	0	0	0	0	23	26	3	20	14	18.0	6.65	62	.295	.426	0	—	0	-7	-7	-0	0.0
Total 4	2	3	.400	23	3	0	0	0	49²	57	3	39	33	17.6	5.80	63	.308	.431	1	.143	-0	-12	-12	1	-0.4

● **ROY LEE JACKSON**   Jackson, Roy Lee b: 5/1/54, Opelika, Ala.   BR/TR, 6'2", 194 lbs. Deb: 9/13/77

YEAR TM/L	W	L	PCT	G	GS	CG	SH	SV	IP	H	HR	BB	SO	RAT	ERA	ERA+	OAV	OOB	BH	AVG	PB	PR	/A	PD	TPI
1977 NY-N	0	2	.000	4	4	0	0	0	24	25	2	15	13	16.1	6.00	62	.263	.381	0	.000	-1	-6	-6	-1	-0.6
1978 NY-N	0	0	—	4	2	0	0	0	12²	21	2	6	6	20.6	9.24	38	.429	.509	2	.667	1	-8	-8	0	0.1
1979 NY-N	1	0	1.000	8	0	0	0	0	16¹	11	1	5	10	9.4	2.20	165	.200	.279	1	1.000	0	3	3	0	0.2
1980 NY-N	1	7	.125	24	8	1	0	1	70²	78	4	20	58	12.5	4.20	84	.287	.336	3	.188	1	-5	-5	-1	-0.6
1981 Tor-A	1	2	.333	39	0	0	0	7	62	65	5	25	27	13.2	2.61	151	.275	.347	0	—	0	7	9	0	0.6
1982 Tor-A	8	8	.500	48	2	0	0	6	97	77	7	31	71	10.2	3.06	146	.218	.284	0	—	0	11	15	0	2.4
1983 Tor-A	8	3	.727	49	0	0	0	7	92	92	6	41	48	13.3	4.50	96	.267	.351	0	—	0	4	3	-0	-0.5
1984 Tor-A	7	8	.467	54	0	0	0	10	86	73	12	31	58	11.0	3.56	115	.230	.301	0	—	0	4	5	0	0.9
1985 SD-N	2	3	.400	22	0	0	0	2	40	32	4	13	28	10.3	2.70	131	.224	.293	0	.000	-1	4	4	0	0.4
1986 Min-A	0	1	.000	28	0	0	0	1	58¹	57	7	16	32	11.7	3.86	112	.256	.314	0	—	0	2	3	-1	-0.1
Total 10	28	34	.452	280	18	1	0	34	559	531	50	203	351	12.1	3.77	107	.254	.325	6	.194	1	8	17	-1	2.8

● **TONY JACOBS**   Jacobs, Anthony Robert b: 8/5/25, Dixmoor, Ill.   d: 12/21/80, Nashville, Tenn.   BB/TR, 5'9", 150 lbs. Deb: 9/19/48

YEAR TM/L	W	L	PCT	G	GS	CG	SH	SV	IP	H	HR	BB	SO	RAT	ERA	ERA+	OAV	OOB	BH	AVG	PB	PR	/A	PD	TPI
1948 Chi-N	0	0	—	1	0	0	0	0	2	3	1	2	2	13.5	4.50	87	.333	.333	0	—	0	-0	-0	0	0.0
1955 StL-N	0	0	—	1	0	0	0	0	2	6	1	1	1	31.5	18.00	23	.500	.538	0	.000	0	-3	-3	0	0.0
Total 2	0	0	—	2	0	0	0	0	4	9	2	3	3	22.5	11.25	35	.429	.455	0	.000	0	-3	-3	-0	0.0

● **ART JACOBS**   Jacobs, Arthur Edward b: 8/28/02, Luckey, Ohio   d: 6/8/67, Inglewood, Cal.   BL/TL, 5'10", 170 lbs. Deb: 6/18/39

YEAR TM/L	W	L	PCT	G	GS	CG	SH	SV	IP	H	HR	BB	SO	RAT	ERA	ERA+	OAV	OOB	BH	AVG	PB	PR	/A	PD	TPI
1939 Cin-N	0	0	—	1	0	0	0	0	2	1	0	2	0	27.0	9.00	43	.400	.500	0	—	0	-1	-1	-0	-0.1

● **BUCKY JACOBS**   Jacobs, Newton Smith b: 3/21/13, Altavista, Va.   d: 6/15/90, Richmond, Va.   BR/TR, 5'11", 155 lbs. Deb: 6/27/37

YEAR TM/L	W	L	PCT	G	GS	CG	SH	SV	IP	H	HR	BB	SO	RAT	ERA	ERA+	OAV	OOB	BH	AVG	PB	PR	/A	PD	TPI
1937 Was-A	1	1	.500	11	1	0	0	0	22¹	26	1	11	8	14.9	4.84	92	.295	.374	0	.000	-1	-1	-1	0	-0.1
1939 Was-A	0	0	—	2	0	0	0	0	3	1	0	3	1	3.0	0.00	—	.100	.100	0	—	0	2	1	-0	0.0
1940 Was-A	0	1	.000	9	0	0	0	0	15	16	1	9	6	16.2	6.00	80	.271	.386	0	.000	0	-3	-3	1	-0.1
Total 3	1	2	.333	22	1	0	0	0	40¹	43	1	20	15	14.5	4.91	88	.274	.363	0	.000	-1	-2	-3	2	-0.2

● **ELMER JACOBS**   Jacobs, William Elmer b: 8/10/1892, Salem, Mo.   d: 2/10/58, Salem, Mo.   BR/TR, 6', 165 lbs. Deb: 4/23/14

YEAR TM/L	W	L	PCT	G	GS	CG	SH	SV	IP	H	HR	BB	SO	RAT	ERA	ERA+	OAV	OOB	BH	AVG	PB	PR	/A	PD	TPI
1914 Phi-N	1	3	.250	14	7	1	0	0	50²	65	2	20	17	15.6	4.80	61	.342	.413	0	.000	-2	-11	-10	0	-0.9
1916 Pit-N	6	10	.375	34	17	8	0	0	153	151	2	38	46	11.4	2.94	91	.258	.308	3	.075	-2	-5	-4	-2	-0.8
1917 Pit-N	6	19	.240	38	25	10	1	2	227²	214	5	76	58	11.7	2.81	101	.262	.329	12	.179	-1	-2	-1	2	0.1
1918 Pit-N	0	1	.000	8	4	0	0	0	23¹	31	1	14	2	17.4	5.79	50	.344	.433	2	.286	0	-8	-8	1	-0.2
Phi-N	9	5	.643	18	14	12	4	1	123	91	3	42	33	10.0	2.41	124	.210	.285	6	.158	-1	5	8	-2	0.6
Yr	9	6	.600	26	18	12	4	1	146¹	122	4	56	35	11.2	2.95	101	.233	.312	8	.178	-1	-3	-0	-1	0.4
1919 Phi-N	6	10	.375	17	15	13	0	0	128²	150	5	44	37	14.0	3.85	84	.304	.368	8	.178	-1	-13	-9	1	-1.1
StL-N	3	6	.333	17	8	4	1	1	85¹	81	2	25	31	11.7	2.53	110	.264	.329	8	.348	3	4	2	-0	0.6
Yr	9	16	.360	34	23	17	1	1	214	231	7	69	68	12.8	3.32	92	.287	.347	16	.235	2	-10	-6	1	-0.5
1920 StL-N	4	8	.333	23	9	1	0	1	77²	91	2	33	21	14.9	5.21	57	.296	.374	6	.192	-0	-18	-19	1	-2.7
1924 Chi-N	11	12	.478	38	22	13	1	1	190¹	181	9	72	50	12.1	3.74	104	.258	.329	6	.111	-4	3	4	1	0.1
1925 Chi-N	2	3	.400	18	4	1	1	0	55²	63	2	22	19	13.9	5.17	84	.274	.340	3	.231	-0	-6	-5	0	-0.4
1927 Chi-A	2	4	.333	25	8	2	1	0	74¹	105	3	37	22	17.7	4.60	88	.354	.432	3	.150	-1	-4	-5	2	-0.3
Total 9	50	81	.382	250	133	65	9	7	1189¹	1223	40	423	336	12.8	3.55	91	.275	.343	56	.161	-8	-57	-44	5	-5.0

● **BEANY JACOBSON**   Jacobson, Albert L. (b: Albin L. Jacobson)
b: 6/5/1881, Port Washington, Wis.   d: 1/31/33, Decatur, Ill.   BL/TL, 6', 170 lbs. Deb: 4/30/04

YEAR TM/L	W	L	PCT	G	GS	CG	SH	SV	IP	H	HR	BB	SO	RAT	ERA	ERA+	OAV	OOB	BH	AVG	PB	PR	/A	PD	TPI
1904 Was-A	6	23	.207	33	30	21	1	0	253²	276	6	57	75	11.9	3.55	75	.278	.319	8	.091	-6	-27	-25	2	-3.1
1905 Was-A	7	8	.467	22	17	12	0	1	144¹	139	1	35	50	11.2	3.30	80	.255	.305	7	.159	1	-10	-11	-2	-1.1
1906 StL-A	9	9	.500	24	15	12	0	0	155	146	3	27	53	10.3	2.50	103	.252	.290	5	.091	-4	3	1	-0	-0.3
1907 StL-A	1	6	.143	7	6	6	0	0	57¹	55	1	26	16	12.7	2.98	84	.255	.335	4	.222	-0	-3	-3	-0	-0.4
Bos-A	0	0	—	2	1	0	0	0	2	2	0	3	1	22.5	9.00	29	.250	.455	0	—	0	-1	-1	0	0.0
Yr	1	6	.143	9	8	6	0	0	59¹	57	1	29	17	13.0	3.19	79	.254	.340	4	.222	-0	-4	-4	-0	-0.4
Total 4	23	46	.333	88	70	53	1	0	612¹	618	11	148	195	11.4	3.19	82	.264	.311	24	.117	-9	-38	-38	-1	-4.9

● **LARRY JACOBUS**   Jacobus, Stuart Louis b: 12/18/1893, Cincinnati, Ohio   d: 8/19/65, N.College Hill, O.   BB/TR, 6'2", 186 lbs. Deb: 7/15/18

YEAR TM/L	W	L	PCT	G	GS	CG	SH	SV	IP	H	HR	BB	SO	RAT	ERA	ERA+	OAV	OOB	BH	AVG	PB	PR	/A	PD	TPI
1918 Cin-N	0	1	.000	5	0	0	0	0	17¹	25	0	1	8	13.5	5.71	47	.368	.377	0	.000	-1	-6	-6	-0	-0.4

● **JASON JACOME**   Jacome, Jason James b: 11/24/70, Tulsa, Okla.   BL/TL, 6'1", 155 lbs. Deb: 7/2/94

YEAR TM/L	W	L	PCT	G	GS	CG	SH	SV	IP	H	HR	BB	SO	RAT	ERA	ERA+	OAV	OOB	BH	AVG	PB	PR	/A	PD	TPI
1994 NY-N	4	3	.571	8	8	1	1	0	54	54	3	17	30	11.8	2.67	157	.269	.326	1	.063	0	9	9	1	1.0
1995 NY-N	0	4	.000	5	5	0	0	0	21	33	3	15	11	21.0	10.29	39	.359	.454	0	.000	-1	-14	-15	-0	-2.0
KC-A	4	6	.400	15	14	1	0	0	84	101	15	21	39	13.2	5.36	89	.300	.343	0	—	0	-6	-5	2	-0.4
1996 KC-A	0	4	.000	49	2	0	0	1	47²	67	5	22	32	17.2	4.72	104	.337	.408	0	—	0	1	1	2	0.2
Total 3	8	17	.320	77	29	2	1	1	206²	255	26	75	112	14.5	5.01	91	.308	.368	1	.043	-2	-10	-10	4	-1.2

● **PAT JACQUEZ**   Jacquez, Patrick Thomas b: 4/23/47, Stockton, Cal.   BR/TR, 6', 200 lbs. Deb: 4/18/71

YEAR TM/L	W	L	PCT	G	GS	CG	SH	SV	IP	H	HR	BB	SO	RAT	ERA	ERA+	OAV	OOB	BH	AVG	PB	PR	/A	PD	TPI
1971 Chi-A	0	0	—	2	0	0	0	0	2	4	0	2	1	27.0	4.50	80	.444	.545	0	.000	-0	-0	-0	0	0.0

● **JAKE JAECKEL**   Jaeckel, Paul Henry b: 4/1/42, E.Los Angeles, Cal.   BR/TR, 5'10", 170 lbs. Deb: 9/19/64

YEAR TM/L	W	L	PCT	G	GS	CG	SH	SV	IP	H	HR	BB	SO	RAT	ERA	ERA+	OAV	OOB	BH	AVG	PB	PR	/A	PD	TPI
1964 Chi-N	1	0	1.000	4	0	0	0	1	8	4	0	3	2	7.9	0.00	—	.160	.250	0	.000	-0	3	3	-0	0.5

● **CHARLIE JAEGER**   Jaeger, Charles Thomas b: 4/17/1875, Ottawa, Ill.   d: 9/27/42, Ottawa, Ill.   BR/TR, Deb: 9/9/04

YEAR TM/L	W	L	PCT	G	GS	CG	SH	SV	IP	H	HR	BB	SO	RAT	ERA	ERA+	OAV	OOB	BH	AVG	PB	PR	/A	PD	TPI
1904 Det-A	3	3	.500	8	6	5	0	0	49	49	0	15	13	12.9	2.57	99	.261	.335	1	.059	-2	0	-0	-1	-0.3

● **JOE JAEGER**   Jaeger, Joseph Peter "Zip" b: 3/3/1895, St.Cloud, Minn.   d: 12/13/63, Hampton, Iowa   BR/TR, 6'1", 190 lbs. Deb: 7/28/20

YEAR TM/L	W	L	PCT	G	GS	CG	SH	SV	IP	H	HR	BB	SO	RAT	ERA	ERA+	OAV	OOB	BH	AVG	PB	PR	/A	PD	TPI
1920 Chi-N	0	0	—	2	0	0	0	0	3	6	0	4	0	30.0	12.00	27	.500	.625	0	.000	-0	-3	-3	0	0.0

● **SIG JAKUCKI**   Jakucki, Sigmund "Jack" b: 8/20/09, Camden, N.J.   d: 5/28/79, Galveston, Tex.   BR/TR, 6'2.5", 198 lbs. Deb: 8/30/36

YEAR TM/L	W	L	PCT	G	GS	CG	SH	SV	IP	H	HR	BB	SO	RAT	ERA	ERA+	OAV	OOB	BH	AVG	PB	PR	/A	PD	TPI
1936 StL-A	0	3	.000	7	2	0	0	0	20²	32	2	12	9	19.6	8.71	62	.348	.429	0	.000	-1	-8	-8	0	-0.9
1944 *StL-A	13	9	.591	35	24	12	4	3	198	211	17	54	67	12.2	3.55	101	.268	.318	11	.151	-2	-3	1	1	0.1
1945 StL-A	12	10	.545	30	24	15	1	2	192¹	188	9	65	55	11.9	3.51	100	.257	.318	13	.186	1	3	0	0	0.1
Total 3	25	22	.532	72	50	27	5	5	411	431	28	131	131	12.4	3.79	96	.268	.325	24	.161	-2	-14	-6	1	-0.7

● **LEFTY JAMERSON**   Jamerson, Charles Dewey "Charlie" b: 1/26/1900, Enfield, Ill.   d: 8/4/80, Mocksville, N.C.   BL/TL, 6'1", 195 lbs. Deb: 8/16/24

YEAR TM/L	W	L	PCT	G	GS	CG	SH	SV	IP	H	HR	BB	SO	RAT	ERA	ERA+	OAV	OOB	BH	AVG	PB	PR	/A	PD	TPI
1924 Bos-A	0	0	—	1	0	0	0	0	1	0	3	0	36.0	18.00	24	.250	.571	0	—	0	-2	-2	0	0.0

● **JEFF JAMES**   James, Jeffrey Lynn "Jesse" b: 9/29/41, Indianapolis, Ind.   BR/TR, 6'3", 195 lbs. Deb: 4/13/68

YEAR TM/L	W	L	PCT	G	GS	CG	SH	SV	IP	H	HR	BB	SO	RAT	ERA	ERA+	OAV	OOB	BH	AVG	PB	PR	/A	PD	TPI
1968 Phi-N	4	4	.500	29	13	1	1	0	116	112	8	46	83	12.6	4.27	70	.256	.332	4	.121	-1	-17	-16	0	-1.2
1969 Phi-N	2	2	.500	6	5	1	0	0	31²	36	5	14	21	14.2	5.40	66	.288	.360	2	.182	-0	-6	-7	-0	-0.8
Total 2	6	6	.500	35	18	2	1	0	147²	148	13	60	104	12.9	4.51	69	.263	.338	6	.136	-1	-23	-23	-0	-2.0

YEAR	TM/L	W	L	PCT	G	GS	CG	SH	SV	IP	H	HR	BB	SO	RAT	ERA	ERA+	OAV	OOB	BH	AVG	PB	PR	/A	PD	TPI
● **JOHNNY JAMES**					James, John Phillip			b: 7/23/33, Bonners Ferry, Idaho			BL/TR, 5'10", 160 lbs.		Deb: 9/6/58												
1958	NY-A	0	0	—	1	0	0	0	0	3	2	0	4	1	18.0	0.00	—	.250	.500	0	.000	-0	1	1	0	0.0
1960	NY-A	5	1	.833	28	0	0	0	2	43¹	38	3	26	29	13.9	4.36	82	.248	.368	0	.000	-0	-2	-4	0	-0.5
1961	NY-A	0	0	—	1	0	0	0	0	1¹	1	0	0	2	6.8	0.00	—	.250	.250	0	—	-0	1	1	0	0.0
	LA-A	0	2	.000	36	3	0	0	0	71¹	66	12	54	41	15.4	5.30	85	.246	.377	0	.000	-1	-10	-6	-0	-0.3
	Yr	0	2	.000	37	3	0	0	0	72²	67	12	54	43	15.2	5.20	86	.246	.375	0	.000	-1	-10	-6	-0	-0.3
Total	3	5	3	.625	66	3	0	0	2	119	107	15	84	73	14.8	4.76	87	.247	.375	0	.000	-2	-11	-8	0	-0.8
● **MIKE JAMES**					James, Michael Elmo			b: 8/15/67, Ft.Walton Beach, Fla.			BR/TR, 6'4", 215 lbs.		Deb: 4/29/95												
1995	Cal-A	3	0	1.000	46	0	0	0	1	55²	49	6	26	36	12.6	3.88	121	.238	.332	0	—	0	5	5	-0	0.2
1996	Cal-A	5	5	.500	69	0	0	0	1	81	62	7	42	65	12.7	2.67	183	.214	.333	0	—	0	21	20	1	2.2
Total	2	8	5	.615	115	0	0	0	2	136²	111	13	68	101	12.6	3.16	152	.224	.333	0	—	0	26	25	1	2.4
● **RICK JAMES**					James, Richard Lee			b: 10/11/47, Sheffield, Ala.			BR/TR, 6'2.5", 205 lbs.		Deb: 9/20/67												
1967	Chi-N	0	1	.000	3	1	0	0	0	4²	9	1	2	2	21.2	13.50	26	.529	.579	0	.000	-0	-5	-5	-0	-0.9
● **BOB JAMES**					James, Robert Harvey			b: 8/15/58, Glendale, Cal.			BR/TR, 6'4", 230 lbs.		Deb: 9/7/78												
1978	Mon-N	0	1	.000	4	1	0	0	0	4	4	1	4	3	18.0	9.00	39	.267	.421	0	—	0	-2	-2	0	-0.5
1979	Mon-N	0	0	—	2	0	0	0	0	2	2	0	3	1	22.5	13.50	27	.250	.455	0	—	0	-2	-2	-0	0.0
1982	Mon-N	0	0	—	7	0	0	0	0	9	10	0	8	11	18.0	6.00	61	.294	.429	0	—	0	-2	-2	-0	-0.2
	Det-A	0	2	.000	12	1	0	0	0	19²	22	4	8	20	13.7	5.03	81	.278	.345	0	—	0	-2	-2	-0	-0.2
1983	Det-A	0	0	—	4	0	0	0	0	4	5	2	3	4	11.25	35	.313	.421	0	—	0	-3	-3	-0	0.0
	Mon-N	1	0	1.000	27	0	0	0	7	50	37	3	26	56	11.3	2.88	125	.210	.312	2	.286	0	4	4	1	0.4
1984	Mon-N	6	6	.500	62	0	0	0	10	96	92	6	45	91	13.2	3.66	94	.251	.339	2	.143	-0	-1	-2	-1	-0.5
1985	Chi-A	8	7	.533	69	0	0	0	32	110	90	5	23	88	9.4	2.13	203	.226	.271	0	—	0	25	**27**	-1	4.8
1986	Chi-A	5	4	.556	49	0	0	0	14	58¹	61	8	23	32	13.6	5.25	82	.268	.345	0	—	0	-1	-1	0	-1.4
1987	Chi-A	4	6	.400	43	0	0	0	10	54	54	6	17	34	12.5	4.67	98	.256	.323	0	—	0	-1	-1	0	-0.3
Total	8	24	26	.480	279	2	0	0	73	407	377	39	157	340	12.2	3.80	105	.246	.323	4	.190	0	9	8	-2	2.3
● **LEFTY JAMES**					James, William A.			b: 7/1/1889, Glen Roy, Ohio			d: 5/3/33, Glen Roy, Ohio			BL/TL, 5'11.5", 175 lbs.		Deb: 4/13/12						
1912	Cle-A	0	1	.000	3	1	0	0	1	6	8	0	4	2	21.0	7.50	45	.348	.483	0	.000	-0	-3	-3	-0	-0.5
1913	Cle-A	2	2	.500	11	4	3	0	0	39	42	0	9	18	12.5	3.00	101	.273	.325	3	.231	-0	-0	0	-1	-0.1
1914	Cle-A	0	3	.000	17	6	1	0	0	50²	44	0	32	16	13.9	3.20	90	.251	.373	0	.000	-1	-3	-2	1	-0.1
Total	3	2	6	.250	31	11	4	0	1	95²	94	0	45	36	13.7	3.39	88	.267	.361	3	.107	-1	-6	-4	-0	-0.7
● **BILL JAMES**					James, William Henry "Big Bill"			b: 1/20/1887, Detroit, Mich.			d: 5/24/42, Venice, Cal.			BB/TR, 6'4", 195 lbs.		Deb: 6/12/11						
1911	Cle-A	2	4	.333	8	6	4	0	0	51²	58	1	32	21	16.0	4.88	70	.284	.387	1	.059	-1	-9	-8	-1	-1.0
1912	Cle-A	0	0	—	3	0	0	0	0	13²	15	0	9	5	15.8	4.61	74	.288	.393	0	.000	-0	-2	-2	-1	-0.1
1914	StL-A	15	14	.517	44	35	20	3	1	284	269	4	109	109	12.2	2.85	95	.257	.330	10	.112	-3	-3	-5	5	-0.4
1915	StL-A	7	10	.412	34	23	8	0	1	170¹	155	2	92	58	13.4	3.59	80	.255	.359	8	.190	-1	-12	-14	2	-1.1
	Det-A	7	3	.700	11	9	3	1	0	67	57	1	33	24	12.1	2.42	125	.243	.336	6	.286	2	4	5	1	1.0
	Yr	14	13	.519	45	32	11	1	1	237¹	212	3	125	82	12.8	3.26	89	.249	.345	14	.222	2	-9	-9	3	-0.1
1916	Det-A	8	12	.400	30	20	8	0	1	151²	141	6	79	61	13.7	3.68	78	.255	.360	-3	.068	-3	-14	-14	-0	-2.1
1917	Det-A	13	10	.565	34	23	10	2	1	198	163	2	96	62	12.3	2.09	127	.229	.330	12	.211	2	13	12	-0	1.7
1918	Det-A	6	11	.353	19	18	8	1	0	122	127	8	42	44	14.8	3.76	71	.279	.379	5	.109	-3	-13	-15	2	-2.1
1919	Det-A	1	0	1.000	2	1	0	0	0	9¹	12	0	7	3	18.3	5.79	55	.324	.432	1	.250	-0	-3	-3	-0	-0.3
	Bos-A	3	5	.375	13	7	4	0	0	72²	74	2	39	12	14.4	4.09	74	.280	.379	3	.143	-1	-7	-9	0	-0.9
	*Chi-A	3	2	.600	5	5	3	2	0	39¹	39	0	14	11	12.6	2.52	126	.281	.355	2	.143	-1	3	3	-1	0.2
	Yr	7	7	.500	20	13	7	2	0	121¹	125	2	60	26	13.9	3.71	83	.282	.370	6	.154	-2	-6	-8	-1	-1.0
Total	8	65	71	.478	203	147	68	9	4	1179²	1110	16	578	408	13.2	3.20	88	.258	.352	51	.142	-8	-44	-49	8	-5.1
● **BILL JAMES**					James, William Lawrence "Seattle Bill"			b: 3/12/1892, Iowa Hill, Cal.			d: 3/10/71, Oroville, Cal.			BR/TR, 6'3", 196 lbs.		Deb: 4/17/13						
1913	Bos-N	6	10	.375	24	14	10	1	0	135²	134	4	57	73	13.1	2.79	118	.264	.347	12	.255	1	6	8	0	1.0
1914	*Bos-N	26	7	**.788**	46	37	30	4	3	332¹	261	7	118	156	10.6	1.90	145	.225	.304	33	.256	4	**33**	**32**	-1	**3.6**
1915	Bos-N	5	4	.556	13	10	4	0	0	68¹	68	3	22	23	12.1	3.03	86	.269	.332	1	.048	-2	-2	-3	-1	-0.5
1919	Bos-N	0	0	—	1	0	0	0	0	5¹	6	0	2	1	13.5	3.38	85	.273	.333	0	.000	-0	-0	-0	0	0.0
Total	4	37	21	.638	84	61	44	5	3	541²	469	14	199	253	11.5	2.28	126	.242	.319	46	.231	4	37	35	1	4.1
● **CHARLIE JAMIESON**					Jamieson, Charles Devine "Cuckoo"			b: 2/7/1893, Paterson, N.J.			d: 10/27/69, Paterson, N.J.			BL/TL, 5'8.5", 165 lbs.		Deb: 9/20/15 ♦				
1916	Was-A	0	0	—	1	0	0	0	0	4	2	0	3	2	11.3	4.50	62	.143	.294	36	.248	0	0	0	-0	0.0
1917	Was-A	0	0	—	1	0	0	0	0	2¹	10	0	2	1	46.3	38.57	7	.625	.667	6	.171	0	-9	-9	-0	0.0
1918	Phi-A	2	1	.667	5	2	1	0	0	23	24	0	13	2	15.3	4.30	68	.261	.364	84	.202	0	-4	-4	-0	-0.5
1919	Cle-A	0	0	—	4	1	0	0	0	13	12	0	8	0	13.8	5.54	60	.250	.357	6	.353	0	-3	-3	-0	0.1
1922	Cle-A	0	0	—	2	0	0	0	0	5²	7	0	4	2	17.5	3.18	126	.318	.423	183	.323	1	1	1	-0	0.0
Total	5	2	1	.667	13	3	1	0	0	48	55	0	30	7	16.3	6.19	51	.286	.388	1990	.303	2	-17	-16	-1	-0.4
● **JERRY JANESKI**					Janeski, Gerard Joseph			b: 4/18/46, Pasadena, Cal.			BR/TR, 6'4", 205 lbs.		Deb: 4/10/70									
1970	Chi-A	10	17	.370	35	35	4	1	0	205²	247	22	63	79	13.8	4.77	82	.300	.353	5	.076	-1	-24	-20	1	-2.6
1971	Was-A	1	5	.167	23	10	0	0	1	61²	72	5	34	19	15.9	4.96	67	.304	.398	3	.214	-1	-10	-11	1	-1.0
1972	Tex-A	0	1	.000	4	1	0	0	0	12²	11	0	7	7	12.8	2.84	106	.229	.327	0	.000	-0	0	0	-0	0.0
Total	3	11	23	.324	62	46	4	1	1	280	330	27	104	105	14.2	4.72	79	.298	.362	8	.098	-4	-34	-31	2	-3.6
● **LARRY JANSEN**					Jansen, Lawrence Joseph			b: 7/16/20, Verboort, Ore.			BR/TR, 6'2", 190 lbs.		Deb: 4/17/47 C								
1947	NY-N	21	5	**.808**	42	30	20	1	1	248	241	23	57	104	10.9	3.16	129	.262	.306	16	.186	-0	25	25	-0	2.4
1948	NY-N	18	12	.600	42	36	15	4	2	277	283	25	54	126	11.0	3.61	109	.265	.303	13	.137	-2	11	10	2	1.0
1949	NY-N	15	16	.484	37	35	17	3	0	259²	271	36	62	113	11.6	3.85	104	.263	.306	16	.165	-0	6	4	3	0.6
1950	NY-N★	19	13	.594	40	35	21	**5**	3	275	238	31	55	161	**9.6**	3.01	136	.232	**.271**	16	.167	-0	35	33	2	3.8
1951	*NY-N☆	**23**	11	.676	39	34	18	3	0	278²	254	26	56	145	10.1	3.04	129	.239	.279	9	.094	-5	29	27	3	2.9
1952	NY-N	11	11	.500	34	27	8	1	2	167¹	183	16	47	74	12.7	4.09	91	.281	.335	8	.178	-3	-7	-7	2	-0.4
1953	NY-N	11	16	.407	36	26	6	0	1	184²	185	24	55	88	11.8	4.14	104	.256	.311	8	.133	-1	3	3	-1	0.2
1954	NY-N	2	2	.500	13	7	0	0	0	40²	57	5	15	15	16.2	5.98	68	.337	.395	4	.286	1	-9	-9	-1	-0.5
1956	Cin-N	2	3	.400	8	7	2	0	1	34²	39	5	9	16	12.7	5.19	77	.281	.329	0	.000	-1	-5	-5	-0	-0.8
Total	9	122	89	.578	291	237	107	17	10	1765²	1751	191	410	842	11.1	3.58	112	.258	.302	90	.150	-6	87	82	11	9.2
● **MARTY JANZEN**					Janzen, Martin Thomas			b: 5/31/73, Homestead, Fla.			BR/TR, 6'3", 197 lbs.		Deb: 5/12/96								
1996	Tor-A	4	6	.400	15	11	0	0	0	73²	95	16	38	47	16.5	7.33	69	.317	.397	0	—	0	-19	-19	-1	-2.0
● **KEVIN JARVIS**					Jarvis, Kevin Thomas			b: 8/1/69, Lexington, Ky.			BL/TR, 6'2", 200 lbs.		Deb: 4/6/94								
1994	Cin-N	1	1	.500	6	3	0	0	0	17²	22	4	5	10	13.8	7.13	58	.301	.346	1	.250	0	-6	-6	0	-0.5
1995	Cin-N	3	4	.429	19	11	1	1	0	79	91	13	32	33	14.4	5.70	72	.292	.363	3	.143	-0	-13	-14	0	-1.1
1996	Cin-N	8	9	.471	24	20	1	1	0	120¹	152	17	43	63	14.7	5.98	69	.305	.362	6	.167	-0	-24	-24	-1	-2.9
Total	3	12	14	.462	49	34	2	2	0	217	265	34	80	106	14.5	5.97	69	.300	.361	10	.164	-0	-43	-44	-1	-4.5
● **RAY JARVIS**					Jarvis, Raymond Arnold			b: 5/10/46, Providence, R.I.			BR/TR, 6'2", 198 lbs.		Deb: 4/15/69								
1969	Bos-A	5	6	.455	29	12	2	0	1	100¹	105	8	43	36	13.5	4.75	80	.274	.352	2	.069	-2	-13	-11	1	-1.2
1970	Bos-A	0	1	.000	15	0	0	0	0	16	17	1	14	8	18.6	3.94	101	.274	.423	0	—	0	-0	-0	0	0.0
Total	2	5	7	.417	44	12	2	0	1	116¹	122	9	57	44	14.2	4.64	82	.274	.363	2	.069	-2	-13	-11	1	-1.2
● **PAT JARVIS**					Jarvis, Robert Patrick			b: 3/18/41, Carlyle, Ill.			BR/TR, 5'10.5", 180 lbs.		Deb: 8/4/66								
1966	Atl-N	6	2	.750	10	9	3	1	0	62¹	46	9	12	41	8.5	2.31	157	.206	.250	0	.000	-2	9	9	-1	0.8
1967	Atl-N	15	10	.600	32	30	7	1	0	194	195	15	62	118	12.1	3.66	91	.260	.320	6	.085	-3	-6	-7	-2	-1.4
1968	Atl-N	16	12	.571	34	34	14	1	0	202	159	15	50	157	8.9	2.60	115	.214	.255	12	.141	0	11	11	-3	1.0

YEAR TM/L	W	L	PCT	G	GS	CG	SH	SV	IP	H	HR	BB	SO	RAT	ERA	ERA+	OAV	OOB	BH	AVG	PB	PR	/A	PD	TPI
1969 *Atl-N	13	11	.542	37	33	4	1	0	217¹	204	25	73	123	11.5	4.43	81	.246	.308	8	.113	-2	-20	-20	-0	-2.3
1970 Atl-N	16	16	.500	36	34	11	1	0	254	240	21	72	173	11.1	3.61	119	.247	.299	15	.183	-4	12	19	2	2.4
1971 Atl-N	6	14	.300	35	23	3	3	1	162¹	162	16	51	68	12.0	4.10	90	.261	.320	5	.106	-2	-12	-7	1	-1.0
1972 Atl-N	11	7	.611	37	6	0	0	2	98²	94	7	44	56	12.6	4.10	92	.260	.341	3	.125	-0	-7	-3	1	-0.1
1973 Mon-N	2	1	.667	28	0	0	0	0	39¹	37	6	16	19	12.4	3.20	119	.250	.327	0	.000	-0	2	3	-0	0.1
Total 8	85	73	.538	249	169	42	8	3	1284	1180	106	380	755	11.0	3.58	101	.243	.300	49	.121	-10	-11	3	-3	-0.9

● **HI JASPER**   Jasper, Henry W.   b: 11/15/1880, St.Louis, Mo.   d: 5/22/37, St.Louis, Mo.   BR/TR, 5'11", 180 lbs.   Deb: 4/19/14

YEAR TM/L	W	L	PCT	G	GS	CG	SH	SV	IP	H	HR	BB	SO	RAT	ERA	ERA+	OAV	OOB	BH	AVG	PB	PR	/A	PD	TPI
1914 Chi-A	1	0	1.000	16	0	0	0	0	32¹	22	0	20	19	12.0	3.34	80	.210	.341	0	.000	-1	-2	-2	1	0.0
1915 Chi-A	0	1	.000	3	2	1	0	0	15²	8	2	9	15	9.8	4.60	65	.157	.283	2	.286	-0	-3	-3	1	0.0
1916 StL-N	5	6	.455	21	9	2	0	1	107	97	0	42	37	12.3	3.28	81	.254	.339	7	.212	1	-8	-8	2	-0.5
1919 Cle-A	4	5	.444	12	10	5	0	0	82²	83	1	28	25	12.1	3.59	93	.269	.340	3	.103	-0	-3	-2	1	-0.4
Total 4	10	12	.455	52	21	8	0	1	237²	210	3	99	96	12.2	3.48	84	.248	.333	12	.162	-2	-16	-15	5	-0.9

● **LARRY JASTER**   Jaster, Larry Edward   b: 1/13/44, Midland, Mich.   BL/TL, 6'3.5", 205 lbs.   Deb: 9/17/65

YEAR TM/L	W	L	PCT	G	GS	CG	SH	SV	IP	H	HR	BB	SO	RAT	ERA	ERA+	OAV	OOB	BH	AVG	PB	PR	/A	PD	TPI
1965 StL-N	3	0	1.000	4	3	3	0	0	28	21	1	7	10	9.0	1.61	239	.206	.257	2	.200	0	6	7	-1	0.7
1966 StL-N	11	5	.688	26	21	6	**5**	0	151²	124	17	45	92	10.3	3.26	110	.227	.291	8	.178	1	6	5	-1	0.6
1967 *StL-N	9	7	.563	34	23	2	1	3	152¹	141	12	44	87	11.0	3.01	109	.244	.300	5	.100	-1	6	5	-2	0.1
1968 *StL-N	9	13	.409	31	21	3	1	0	154¹	153	13	38	70	11.5	3.50	83	.262	.313	6	.140	0	-9	-10	-2	-1.6
1969 Mon-N	1	6	.143	24	11	1	0	0	77	95	17	28	39	14.6	5.49	67	.302	.362	8	.421	3	-16	-16	-2	-1.2
1970 Atl-N	1	1	.500	14	0	0	0	0	22¹	33	5	9	16	16.5	6.85	50	.330	.410	0	.000	-0	-7	-6	1	-0.5
1972 Atl-N	1	1	.500	5	1	0	0	0	12¹	12	4	8	9	14.6	5.11	74	.267	.377	0	.000	-0	-2	-2	-0	-0.3
Total 7	35	33	.515	138	80	15	7	3	598	579	69	178	313	11.6	3.64	93	.256	.314	29	.170	3	-16	-17	-7	-2.2

● **AL JAVERY**   Javery, Alva William "Beartracks"   b: 6/5/18, Worcester, Mass.   d: 9/13/77, Woodstock, Conn.   BR/TR, 6'3", 183 lbs.   Deb: 4/23/40

YEAR TM/L	W	L	PCT	G	GS	CG	SH	SV	IP	H	HR	BB	SO	RAT	ERA	ERA+	OAV	OOB	BH	AVG	PB	PR	/A	PD	TPI
1940 Bos-N	2	4	.333	29	4	1	0	1	83¹	99	2	36	42	14.8	5.51	68	.293	.364	2	.087	-1	-15	-17	-2	-1.4
1941 Bos-N	10	11	.476	34	23	9	1	1	160²	181	5	65	54	14.1	4.31	83	.283	.355	6	.103	-4	-12	-13	1	-1.8
1942 Bos-N	12	16	.429	42	37	19	5	0	261	251	8	78	85	11.4	3.03	110	.251	.307	9	.105	-5	8	9	2	0.6
1943 Bos-N★	17	16	.515	41	35	19	5	0	**303**	288	13	99	134	11.6	3.21	106	.248	.309	17	.163	-3	6	7	2	0.7
1944 Bos-N☆	10	19	.345	40	33	11	3	3	254	248	12	118	137	13.0	3.54	108	.262	.345	12	.152	-3	2	8	-2	0.3
1945 Bos-N	2	7	.222	17	14	2	1	0	77¹	92	4	51	18	16.6	6.28	61	.295	.394	6	.207	-0	-21	-21	1	-2.0
1946 Bos-N	0	1	.000	2	1	0	0	0	3¹	5	0	5	0	27.0	13.50	25	.417	.588	0	.000	-0	-4	-4	0	-0.9
Total 7	53	74	.417	205	147	61	15	5	1142²	1164	44	452	470	13.0	3.80	94	.264	.335	52	.137	-15	-37	-31	2	-4.5

● **JOEY JAY**   Jay, Joseph Richard   b: 8/15/35, Middletown, Conn.   BB/TR, 6'4", 228 lbs.   Deb: 7/21/53

YEAR TM/L	W	L	PCT	G	GS	CG	SH	SV	IP	H	HR	BB	SO	RAT	ERA	ERA+	OAV	OOB	BH	AVG	PB	PR	/A	PD	TPI
1953 Mil-N	1	0	1.000	3	1	1	1	0	10	6	0	5	4	9.9	0.00	—	.188	.297	0	.000	-0	5	4	0	0.3
1954 Mil-N	1	0	1.000	15	1	0	0	1	18	21	2	16	13	19.0	6.50	57	.304	.442	0	—	0	-5	-6	-0	-0.3
1955 Mil-N	0	0	—	12	1	0	0	0	19	23	2	13	3	17.1	4.74	79	.324	.429	2	.667	1	-1	-2	-1	0.0
1957 Mil-N	0	0	—	1	0	0	0	1	0²	0	0	0	0	0.0	—	—	.000	.000	0	—	0	0	0	0	0.1
1958 Mil-N	7	5	.583	18	12	6	3	0	96²	60	8	43	74	9.7	2.14	164	.177	.272	3	.094	-1	19	15	0	1.7
1959 Mil-N	6	11	.353	34	19	4	1	0	136¹	130	11	64	88	13.1	4.09	87	.248	.336	3	.086	-1	-2	-8	2	-0.9
1960 Mil-N	9	8	.529	32	11	3	0	1	133¹	128	10	59	90	13.0	3.24	106	.254	.339	7	.156	0	8	3	-0	0.3
1961 *Cin-N☆	**21**	10	.677	34	34	14	**4**	0	247¹	217	25	92	157	11.4	3.53	115	.236	.309	8	.090	-5	14	15	-1	1.0
1962 Cin-N	21	14	.600	39	37	16	4	0	273	269	26	100	155	12.3	3.76	107	.260	.327	15	.167	3	6	8	-2	1.0
1963 Cin-N	7	18	.280	30	22	4	1	1	170	172	19	73	116	13.1	4.29	78	.266	.343	8	.160	-1	-19	-18	-0	-2.5
1964 Cin-N	11	11	.500	34	23	10	0	2	183	167	17	36	134	10.1	3.39	107	.245	.285	3	.057	-3	3	5	2	0.0
1965 Cin-N	9	8	.529	37	24	4	1	1	155²	150	21	63	102	12.5	4.22	89	.252	.328	2	.041	-3	-12	-8	-0	-1.2
1966 Cin-N	6	2	.750	12	10	1	1	0	73²	78	8	23	44	12.7	3.91	100	.275	.335	3	.115	-1	-2	-0	-1	-0.2
Atl-N	0	4	.000	9	8	0	1	0	29²	39	4	20	19	18.2	7.89	46	.315	.414	1	.125	-0	-14	-14	-0	-1.7
Yr	6	6	.500	21	18	1	1	0	103¹	117	12	43	63	14.0	5.05	76	.285	.354	4	.118	-1	-17	-14	-1	-1.9
Total 13	99	91	.521	310	203	63	16	7	1546¹	1460	153	607	999	12.2	3.77	99	.251	.325	55	.114	-10	-1	-5	-6	-2.4

● **DOMINGO JEAN**   Jean, Domingo (Luisa)   b: 1/9/69, San Pedro De Macoris, D.R.   BR/TR, 6'2", 175 lbs.   Deb: 8/8/93

YEAR TM/L	W	L	PCT	G	GS	CG	SH	SV	IP	H	HR	BB	SO	RAT	ERA	ERA+	OAV	OOB	BH	AVG	PB	PR	/A	PD	TPI
1993 NY-A	1	1	.500	10	6	0	0	0	40¹	37	7	19	20	12.5	4.46	93	.237	.320	0	—	0	-1	-1	-0	0.0

● **TEX JEANES**   Jeanes, Ernest Lee   b: 12/19/1900, Maypearl, Tex.   d: 4/5/73, Longview, Tex.   BR/TR, 6', 176 lbs.   Deb: 4/20/21 ♦

YEAR TM/L	W	L	PCT	G	GS	CG	SH	SV	IP	H	HR	BB	SO	RAT	ERA	ERA+	OAV	OOB	BH	AVG	PB	PR	/A	PD	TPI
1922 Cle-A	0	0	—	1	0	0	0	0	1	0	0	0	0	—	—	—	—	1.000	0	.000	0	0	0	0	0.0
1927 NY-N	0	0	—	1	0	0	0	0	1	2	0	3	0	36.0	9.00	43	.400	.571	6	.300	0	-1	-1	-0	0.0
Total 2	0	0	—	2	0	0	0	0	1	2	0	3	0	45.0	9.00	43	.400	.625	20	.274	0	-1	-1	-0	0.0

● **GEORGE JEFFCOAT**   Jeffcoat, George Edward   b: 12/24/13, New Brookland, S.C.   d: 10/13/78, Leesville, S.C.   BR/TR, 5'11.5", 175 lbs.   Deb: 4/20/36 F

YEAR TM/L	W	L	PCT	G	GS	CG	SH	SV	IP	H	HR	BB	SO	RAT	ERA	ERA+	OAV	OOB	BH	AVG	PB	PR	/A	PD	TPI
1936 Bro-N	5	6	.455	40	6	0	0	3	95²	84	7	63	46	14.6	4.52	92	.239	.366	3	.130	-1	-5	-4	1	-0.6
1937 Bro-N	1	3	.250	21	3	1	1	0	54¹	58	4	27	29	14.2	5.13	79	.274	.358	0	.000	0	-7	-7	-0	-0.6
1939 Bro-N	0	0	—	1	0	0	0	0	2	2	0	0	1	9.0	0.00	—	.286	.286	0	—	-0	1	1	-0	0.2
1943 Bos-N	1	2	.333	8	0	0	0	0	17²	15	1	10	10	12.7	3.06	112	.217	.316	2	.500	1	1	1	0	0.2
Total 4	7	11	.389	70	9	1	1	3	169²	159	12	100	86	14.2	4.51	89	.248	.358	5	.128	-2	-11	-9	-1	-1.0

● **HAL JEFFCOAT**   Jeffcoat, Harold Bentley   b: 9/6/24, W.Columbia, S.C.   BR/TR, 5'10.5", 185 lbs.   Deb: 4/20/48 F♦

YEAR TM/L	W	L	PCT	G	GS	CG	SH	SV	IP	H	HR	BB	SO	RAT	ERA	ERA+	OAV	OOB	BH	AVG	PB	PR	/A	PD	TPI
1954 Chi-N	5	6	.455	43	3	1	0	7	104	110	12	58	35	14.9	5.19	81	.276	.373	8	.258	2	-13	-11	1	-0.8
1955 Chi-N	8	6	.571	50	1	0	0	6	100²	107	5	53	32	14.7	2.95	139	.276	.369	4	.174	1	12	13	1	1.9
1956 Cin-N	8	2	.800	38	16	2	0	0	171	189	12	55	55	13.1	3.84	104	.281	.340	8	.148	-1	-1	3	3	0.3
1957 Cin-N	12	13	.480	37	31	10	1	0	207	236	29	46	63	12.6	4.52	91	.294	.338	14	.203	6	-15	-9	-1	-0.6
1958 Cin-N	6	8	.429	49	0	0	0	1	75	76	8	26	35	12.5	3.72	111	.268	.333	5	.556	2	2	4	2	1.1
1959 Cin-N	0	1	.000	17	0	0	0	1	21²	21	3	10	12	12.9	3.32	122	.253	.333	1	1.000	0	1	2	0	0.2
StL-N	0	1	.000	11	0	0	0	0	17²	33	4	9	7	21.4	9.17	46	.402	.462	0	—	-0	-10	-10	0	-0.5
Yr	0	2	.000	28	0	0	0	1	39¹	54	7	19	19	16.7	5.95	70	.327	.397	1	.250	-0	-9	-8	0	-0.3
Total 6	39	37	.513	245	51	13	1	25	697	772	73	257	239	13.6	4.22	97	.285	.352	487	.248	10	-24	-10	5	1.6

● **MIKE JEFFCOAT**   Jeffcoat, James Michael   b: 8/3/59, Pine Bluff, Ark.   BL/TL, 6'2", 187 lbs.   Deb: 8/21/83

YEAR TM/L	W	L	PCT	G	GS	CG	SH	SV	IP	H	HR	BB	SO	RAT	ERA	ERA+	OAV	OOB	BH	AVG	PB	PR	/A	PD	TPI
1983 Cle-A	1	3	.250	11	0	0	0	0	32²	32	1	13	9	12.7	3.31	128	.256	.331	0	—	0	3	3	-0	0.3
1984 Cle-A	5	2	.714	63	1	0	0	1	75¹	82	7	24	41	12.8	2.99	137	.281	.338	0	—	0	8	9	1	0.9
1985 Cle-A	0	0	—	9	0	0	0	0	9²	8	1	6	4	13.0	2.79	148	.235	.350	0	—	0	1	1	1	0.1
SF-N	0	2	.000	19	1	0	0	0	22	27	4	6	10	14.3	5.32	65	.307	.365	0	.000	-0	-4	-5	1	-0.3
1987 Tex-A	0	1	.000	2	2	0	0	0	7	11	4	4	5	19.3	12.86	35	.355	.429	0	—	-0	-7	-7	-0	-0.7
1988 Tex-A	0	2	.000	5	2	0	0	0	10	19	1	5	9	23.4	11.70	35	.432	.510	0	—	-0	-9	-8	-0	-1.4
1989 Tex-A	9	6	.600	22	22	0	0	0	130²	139	7	33	64	12.1	3.58	111	.270	.319	0	—	0	4	5	-0	0.5
1990 Tex-A	5	6	.455	44	12	1	0	5	110²	122	12	28	58	12.4	4.47	88	.283	.330	0	—	0	-7	-7	-1	-0.4
1991 Tex-A	5	3	.625	70	0	0	0	1	79²	104	8	25	43	15.0	4.63	87	.320	.376	1	1.000	1	-5	-5	0	-0.4
1992 Tex-A	0	1	.000	6	3	0	0	0	19²	28	2	5	6	15.1	7.32	52	.341	.388	0	—	0	-7	-8	-0	-0.3
1994 Fla-N	0	0	—	4	0	0	0	0	2²	4	1	0	4	13.5	10.13	43	.364	.364	0	—	-0	-2	-2	-0	-0.0
Total 10	25	26	.490	255	45	3	2	7	500	576	49	149	242	13.3	4.37	91	.292	.346	1	.500	1	-23	-22	1	-2.1

● **JESSE JEFFERSON**   Jefferson, Jesse Harrison   b: 3/3/49, Midlothian, Va.   BR/TR, 6'3", 195 lbs.   Deb: 6/23/73

YEAR TM/L	W	L	PCT	G	GS	CG	SH	SV	IP	H	HR	BB	SO	RAT	ERA	ERA+	OAV	OOB	BH	AVG	PB	PR	/A	PD	TPI
1973 Bal-A	6	5	.545	18	15	3	0	0	100²	104	15	46	52	13.4	4.11	91	.267	.345	0	—	0	-3	-4	1	-0.3
1974 Bal-A	1	0	1.000	20	2	0	0	0	57¹	55	2	38	31	14.6	4.40	79	.261	.373	0	—	0	-5	-6	0	0.1
1975 Bal-A	1	2	.333	7	0	0	0	0	7²	5	0	8	4	15.3	2.35	149	.227	.433	0	—	0	1	1	0	0.3
Chi-A	5	9	.357	22	21	4	0	0	107²	100	10	94	67	16.4	5.10	76	.249	.394	0	—	0	-16	-15	-1	-1.7
Yr	5	11	.313	26	21	1	0	0	115¹	105	10	102	71	16.3	4.92	78	.248	.397	0	—	0	-15	-14	1	-1.4
1976 Chi-A	2	5	.286	9	9	2	0	0	62¹	86	3	42	30	18.8	8.52	42	.339	.436	0	—	0	-35	-34	1	-3.3
1977 Tor-A	9	17	.346	33	33	8	0	0	217	224	23	83	114	12.8	4.31	97	.269	.336	0	—	0	-6	-3	-0	-0.3
1978 Tor-A	7	16	.304	31	30	9	2	0	211²	214	28	86	97	12.9	4.38	90	.267	.340	0	—	0	-15	-11	-0	-1.2
1979 Tor-A	2	10	.167	34	10	2	0	1	116	150	19	45	43	15.3	5.51	79	.328	.390	0	—	0	-17	-15	1	-1.4

YEAR	TM/L	W	L	PCT	G	GS	CG	SH	SV	IP	H	HR	BB	SO	RAT	ERA	ERA+	OAV	OOB	BH	AVG	PB	PR	/A	PD	TPI
1980	Tor-A	4	13	.235	29	18	2	2	0	121²	130	12	52	53	13.6	5.47	79	.281	.357	0	—	0	-19	-16	1	-2.1
	Pit-N	1	0	1.000	1	1	0	0	0	6²	3	0	2	4	6.8	1.35	270	.143	.217	0	.000	-0	2	2	0	0.3
1981	Cal-A	2	4	.333	26	5	0	0	0	77	80	4	24	27	12.4	3.62	101	.269	.328	0	—	-0	0	0	-1	-0.1
Total	9	39	81	.325	237	144	25	4	1	1085²	1151	116	520	522	14.0	4.81	83	.277	.360	0	.000	-0	-112	-101	3	-9.7

● **FERGIE JENKINS**   Jenkins, Ferguson Arthur b: 12/13/43, Chatham, Ont., Can.   BR/TR, 6'5", 210 lbs.   Deb: 9/10/65   H

YEAR	TM/L	W	L	PCT	G	GS	CG	SH	SV	IP	H	HR	BB	SO	RAT	ERA	ERA+	OAV	OOB	BH	AVG	PB	PR	/A	PD	TPI
1965	Phi-N	2	1	.667	7	0	0	0	1	12¹	7	2	2	10	6.6	2.19	158	.159	.196	0	.000	-0	2	2	-0	0.4
1966	Phi-N	0	0	—	1	0	0	0	0	2¹	3	0	1	2	15.4	3.86	93	.273	.333	0	—	-0	-0	-0	-0	0.0
	Chi-N	6	8	.429	60	12	2	1	5	182	147	24	51	148	9.9	3.31	111	.219	.277	7	.137	1	6	7	-2	0.5
	Yr	6	8	.429	61	12	2	1	5	184¹	150	24	52	150	10.0	3.32	111	.220	.278	7	.137	1	6	7	-2	0.5
1967	Chi-N★	20	13	.606	38	38	20	3	0	289¹	230	30	83	236	9.9	2.80	127	.217	.277	14	.151	1	19	24	2	3.1
1968	Chi-N	20	15	.571	40	40	20	3	0	308	255	26	65	260	9.4	2.63	120	.222	.266	16	.160	2	12	18	-1	2.3
1969	Chi-N	21	15	.583	43	42	23	7	1	311¹	284	27	71	273	10.5	3.21	125	.242	.290	15	.139	-1	13	28	0	3.2
1970	Chi-N	22	16	.579	40	39	24	3	0	313	265	30	60	274	9.5	3.39	133	.224	.265	23	.124	-3	23	39	-1	4.0
1971	Chi-N★	24	13	.649	39	39	30	3	0	325	304	29	37	263	9.6	2.77	142	.246	.271	28	.243	10	25	42	2	6.4
1972	Chi-N☆	20	12	.625	36	36	23	5	0	289¹	253	32	62	184	10.0	3.20	119	.234	.280	20	.183	1	8	19	3	2.7
1973	Chi-N	14	16	.467	38	38	7	2	0	271	267	35	57	170	10.9	3.89	101	.259	.301	10	.119	-1	-7	2	3	0.4
1974	Tex-A	25	12	.676	41	41	29	6	0	328¹	286	27	45	225	9.3	2.82	126	.232	.264	1	.500	1	29	27	-0	3.0
1975	Tex-A	17	18	.486	37	37	22	4	0	270	261	37	56	157	10.9	3.93	95	.251	.295	0	—	0	-5	-5	1	-0.6
1976	Bos-A	12	11	.522	30	29	12	2	0	209	201	20	43	142	10.7	3.27	119	.253	.296	0	—	0	6	15	-1	0.9
1977	Bos-A	10	10	.500	28	28	11	1	0	193	190	30	36	105	10.5	3.68	123	.257	.291	0	—	0	8	17	1	1.3
1978	Tex-A	18	8	.692	34	30	16	4	0	249	228	21	41	157	9.8	3.04	123	.245	.279	0	—	0	20	20	2	2.2
1979	Tex-A	16	14	.533	37	37	10	3	0	259	252	40	81	164	11.7	4.07	102	.256	.314	0	—	0	4	2	4	0.7
1980	Tex-A	12	12	.500	29	29	12	0	0	198	190	22	52	129	11.2	3.77	103	.250	.301	0	—	0	6	3	1	0.5
1981	Tex-A	5	8	.385	19	16	1	0	0	106	122	14	40	63	13.8	4.50	77	.290	.351	0	—	0	-10	-12	2	-1.1
1982	Chi-N	14	15	.483	34	34	4	1	0	217¹	221	16	68	134	12.2	3.15	119	.264	.323	10	.149	-1	11	14	-0	1.6
1983	Chi-N	6	9	.400	33	29	1	1	0	167¹	176	19	46	96	12.3	4.30	88	.275	.329	13	.245	3	-13	-10	-1	-0.6
Total	19	284	226	.557	664	594	267	49	7	4500²	4142	484	997	3192	10.4	3.34	115	.243	.289	148	.165	13	157	254	14	30.9

● **JACK JENKINS**   Jenkins, Warren Washington b: 12/22/42, Covington, Va.   BR/TR, 6'2", 195 lbs.   Deb: 9/13/62

YEAR	TM/L	W	L	PCT	G	GS	CG	SH	SV	IP	H	HR	BB	SO	RAT	ERA	ERA+	OAV	OOB	BH	AVG	PB	PR	/A	PD	TPI
1962	Was-A	0	1	.000	3	1	1	0	0	13¹	12	4	7	10	12.8	4.05	100	.245	.339	0	.000	-0	-0	-0	-0	-0.1
1963	Was-A	0	2	.000	4	2	0	0	0	12¹	16	2	12	5	20.4	5.84	64	.340	.475	1	.333	0	-3	-3	-0	-0.4
1969	LA-N	0	0	—	1	0	0	0	0	1	0	0	0	1	0.0	0.00	—	.000	.000	0	—	0	0	0	0	0.0
Total	3	0	3	.000	8	3	1	0	0	26²	28	6	19	16	15.9	4.73	82	.283	.398	1	.143	-0	-3	-3	-0	-0.5

● **WILLIE JENSEN**   Jensen, William Christian b: 11/17/1889, Philadelphia, Pa. d: 3/27/17, Philadelphia, Pa.   BL/TR, 5'11.5", 170 lbs.   Deb: 9/10/12

YEAR	TM/L	W	L	PCT	G	GS	CG	SH	SV	IP	H	HR	BB	SO	RAT	ERA	ERA+	OAV	OOB	BH	AVG	PB	PR	/A	PD	TPI
1912	Det-A	1	2	.333	5	4	1	0	0	33	43	1	18	8	17.2	4.91	66	.339	.429	0	.000	-2	-6	-6	-0	-0.7
1914	Phi-A	0	1	.000	1	1	1	0	0	9	7	1	2	1	9.0	2.00	131	.226	.273	0	.000	0	1	1	0	0.1
Total	2	1	3	.250	6	5	2	0	0	42	50	2	20	9	15.4	4.29	73	.316	.400	0	.000	-2	-5	-5	-0	-0.6

● **VIRGIL JESTER**   Jester, Virgil Milton b: 7/23/27, Denver, Colo.   BR/TR, 5'11", 188 lbs.   Deb: 6/18/52

YEAR	TM/L	W	L	PCT	G	GS	CG	SH	SV	IP	H	HR	BB	SO	RAT	ERA	ERA+	OAV	OOB	BH	AVG	PB	PR	/A	PD	TPI
1952	Bos-N	3	5	.375	19	8	4	1	0	73	80	5	23	25	12.8	3.33	108	.283	.339	4	.211	1	3	2	-1	0.2
1953	Mil-N	0	0	—	2	0	0	0	0	2	4	1	4	0	36.0	22.50	17	.400	.571	0	—	0	-4	-4	0	-0.0
Total	2	3	5	.375	21	8	4	1	0	75	84	6	27	25	13.4	3.84	94	.287	.349	4	.211	1	-1	-2	-1	0.2

● **GERMAN JIMENEZ**   Jimenez, German (Camarena) b: 12/5/62, Santiago, Mex.   BL/TL, 5'11", 200 lbs.   Deb: 6/28/88

YEAR	TM/L	W	L	PCT	G	GS	CG	SH	SV	IP	H	HR	BB	SO	RAT	ERA	ERA+	OAV	OOB	BH	AVG	PB	PR	/A	PD	TPI
1988	Atl-N	1	6	.143	15	9	0	0	0	55²	65	4	12	26	12.6	5.01	73	.294	.333	1	.059	-1	-10	-8	-1	-1.2

● **JUAN JIMENEZ**   Jimenez, Juan Antonio (Martes) b: 3/8/49, LaTorre, La Vega, D.R.   BR/TR, 6'1", 165 lbs.   Deb: 9/9/74

YEAR	TM/L	W	L	PCT	G	GS	CG	SH	SV	IP	H	HR	BB	SO	RAT	ERA	ERA+	OAV	OOB	BH	AVG	PB	PR	/A	PD	TPI
1974	Pit-N	0	0	—	4	0	0	0	0	4	6	0	2	2	18.0	6.75	51	.353	.421	0	—	0	-1	-1	-0	0.0

● **MIGUEL JIMENEZ**   Jimenez, Miguel Anthony b: 8/19/69, New York, N.Y.   BR/TR, 6'2", 205 lbs.   Deb: 9/12/93

YEAR	TM/L	W	L	PCT	G	GS	CG	SH	SV	IP	H	HR	BB	SO	RAT	ERA	ERA+	OAV	OOB	BH	AVG	PB	PR	/A	PD	TPI
1993	Oak-A	1	0	1.000	5	4	0	0	0	27	27	5	16	13	14.7	4.00	102	.262	.367	0	—	0	1	0	-1	0.2
1994	Oak-A	1	4	.200	8	7	0	0	0	34	38	9	32	22	18.8	7.41	60	.275	.415	0	—	0	-10	-11	0	-1.1
Total	2	2	4	.333	13	11	0	0	0	61	65	14	48	35	17.0	5.90	72	.270	.395	0	—	0	-9	-11	-1	-0.9

● **TOMMY JOHN**   John, Thomas Edward b: 5/22/43, Terre Haute, Ind.   BR/TL, 6'3", 185 lbs.   Deb: 9/6/63

YEAR	TM/L	W	L	PCT	G	GS	CG	SH	SV	IP	H	HR	BB	SO	RAT	ERA	ERA+	OAV	OOB	BH	AVG	PB	PR	/A	PD	TPI
1963	Cle-A	0	2	.000	6	3	0	0	0	20¹	23	1	6	9	12.8	2.21	164	.284	.333	0	.000	-1	3	3	-0	0.2
1964	Cle-A	2	9	.182	25	14	2	1	0	94¹	97	6	35	65	12.6	3.91	92	.262	.326	5	.208	-1	-3	-3	1	-0.3
1965	Chi-A	14	7	.667	39	27	6	1	3	183²	162	12	58	126	10.9	3.09	103	.237	.298	10	.169	2	8	2	3	0.8
1966	Chi-A	14	11	.560	34	33	10	5	0	223	195	13	57	138	10.5	2.62	121	.235	.290	10	.145	2	20	14	1	1.8
1967	Chi-A	10	13	.435	31	29	9	6	0	178¹	143	10	47	110	9.8	2.47	126	.219	.277	8	.157	-0	15	13	6	2.3
1968	Chi-A★	10	5	.667	25	25	5	1	0	177¹	135	10	49	117	9.9	1.98	153	.212	.280	12	.194	2	20	21	6	2.9
1969	Chi-A	9	11	.450	33	33	6	2	0	232¹	230	16	90	128	12.4	3.25	119	.261	.330	9	.114	-2	9	16	7	1.9
1970	Chi-A	12	17	.414	37	37	10	3	0	269¹	253	19	101	138	12.1	3.27	119	.251	.324	17	.202	1	13	19	4	2.5
1971	Chi-A	13	16	.448	38	35	10	3	0	229¹	244	17	58	131	12.0	3.61	99	.274	.321	10	.145	-1	-4	-1	-1	-0.3
1972	LA-N	11	5	.688	29	29	4	1	0	186²	172	14	40	117	10.4	2.89	115	.244	.287	10	.159	-1	12	9	4	1.1
1973	LA-N	16	7	.696	36	31	4	2	0	218	202	16	50	116	10.6	3.10	111	.246	.293	15	.203	2	14	8	7	1.8
1974	LA-N	13	3	.813	22	22	5	3	0	153	133	4	42	78	10.4	2.59	131	.235	.289	6	.118	-1	18	14	2	1.5
1976	LA-N	10	10	.500	31	31	6	2	0	207	207	7	61	91	11.7	3.09	110	.261	.314	7	.109	-2	10	7	-1	0.3
1977	*LA-N	20	7	.741	31	31	11	3	0	220¹	225	12	50	123	11.4	2.78	138	.267	.311	14	.177	1	28	26	2	3.4
1978	*LA-N☆	17	10	.630	33	30	7	0	1	213	230	11	53	124	12.2	3.30	106	.271	.318	8	.121	-1	7	5	2	0.7
1979	NY-A☆	21	9	.700	37	36	17	3	0	276¹	268	9	65	111	11.0	2.96	137	.260	.306	0	—	0	38	34	2	3.8
1980	*NY-A★	22	9	.710	36	36	16	6	0	265¹	270	15	56	78	11.3	3.43	114	.268	.311	0	—	0	18	15	1	1.7
1981	*NY-A	9	8	.529	20	20	7	0	0	140¹	135	10	39	50	11.4	2.63	136	.256	.311	0	—	0	16	15	1	1.9
1982	NY-A	10	10	.500	30	26	9	2	0	186²	190	11	34	54	10.9	3.66	109	.266	.302	0	—	0	8	7	2	0.8
	*Cal-A	4	2	.667	7	7	1	0	0	35	49	4	5	14	13.9	3.86	105	.336	.358	0	—	0	1	1	-0	0.2
	Yr	14	12	.538	37	33	10	2	0	221²	239	15	39	68	11.3	3.69	108	.274	.305	0	—	0	9	7	2	1.0
1983	Cal-A	11	13	.458	34	34	9	0	0	234²	287	20	49	65	13.0	4.33	93	.304	.340	0	—	0	-7	-8	1	-0.7
1984	Cal-A	7	13	.350	32	29	4	1	0	181¹	223	15	56	47	14.0	4.52	88	.306	.359	0	—	0	-11	-11	0	-1.0
1985	Cal-A	2	4	.333	12	6	0	0	0	38¹	51	3	15	17	15.7	4.70	87	.329	.392	0	—	0	-2	-3	1	-0.2
	Oak-A	2	6	.250	11	11	0	0	0	48	66	6	13	8	15.0	6.19	62	.332	.376	0	—	0	-11	-12	1	-1.6
	Yr	4	10	.286	23	17	0	0	0	86¹	117	9	28	25	15.2	5.53	72	.328	.378	0	—	0	-13	-15	2	-1.8
1986	NY-A	5	3	.625	13	10	1	0	0	70²	73	6	15	28	11.5	2.93	140	.275	.319	0	—	0	10	9	1	1.0
1987	NY-A	13	6	.684	33	33	3	1	0	187²	212	12	47	63	12.7	4.03	109	.288	.336	0	—	0	9	7	-1	0.6
1988	NY-A	9	8	.529	35	32	0	0	0	176¹	221	11	46	81	13.9	4.49	88	.308	.355	0	—	0	-10	-11	2	-0.7
1989	NY-A	2	7	.222	10	10	0	0	0	63²	87	6	22	18	15.8	5.80	67	.336	.394	0	—	0	-14	-14	2	-1.4
Total	26	288	231	.555	760	700	162	46	4	4710¹	4783	302	1259	2245	11.7	3.34	110	.265	.316	141	.157	1	214	179	55	25.0

● **AUGIE JOHNS**   Johns, Augustus Francis "Lefty" b: 9/10/1899, St.Louis, Mo. d: 9/12/75, San Antonio, Tex.   BL/TL, 5'8.5", 170 lbs.   Deb: 4/16/26

YEAR	TM/L	W	L	PCT	G	GS	CG	SH	SV	IP	H	HR	BB	SO	RAT	ERA	ERA+	OAV	OOB	BH	AVG	PB	PR	/A	PD	TPI
1926	Det-A	6	4	.600	35	14	3	1	1	112²	117	6	69	40	15.3	5.35	76	.271	.377	4	.143	-1	-17	-16	-2	-1.6
1927	Det-A	0	0	—	1	0	0	0	0	1	1	0	1	1	18.0	9.00	47	.333	.500	0	—	0	-1	-1	0	-0.0
Total	2	6	4	.600	36	14	3	1	1	113²	118	6	70	41	15.3	5.38	75	.271	.378	4	.143	-1	-17	-17	-2	-1.6

● **DOUG JOHNS**   Johns, Douglas Alan b: 12/19/67, South Bend, Ind.   BR/TL, 6'2", 185 lbs.   Deb: 7/8/95

YEAR	TM/L	W	L	PCT	G	GS	CG	SH	SV	IP	H	HR	BB	SO	RAT	ERA	ERA+	OAV	OOB	BH	AVG	PB	PR	/A	PD	TPI
1995	Oak-A	5	3	.625	11	9	1	1	0	54²	44	5	26	25	12.3	4.61	97	.226	.332	0	—	0	1	-1	1	0.0
1996	Oak-A	6	12	.333	40	23	0	0	0	158	187	21	69	71	14.9	5.98	80	.297	.372	0	—	0	-17	-21	2	-1.7
Total	2	11	15	.423	51	32	1	1	0	212²	231	26	95	96	14.3	5.63	84	.280	.362	0	—	0	-17	-21	3	-1.7

● **OLLIE JOHNS**   Johns, Oliver Tracy b: 8/21/1879, Trenton, Ohio d: 6/17/61, Hamilton, Ohio   BL/TL,   Deb: 9/24/05

YEAR	TM/L	W	L	PCT	G	GS	CG	SH	SV	IP	H	HR	BB	SO	RAT	ERA	ERA+	OAV	OOB	BH	AVG	PB	PR	/A	PD	TPI
1905	Cin-N	1	0	1.000	4	1	1	0	0	18	31	1	4	8	17.5	3.50	94	.369	.398	1	.200	-0	-1	-0	-0	-0.1

YEAR	TM/L	W	L	PCT	G	GS	CG	SH	SV	IP	H	HR	BB	SO	RAT	ERA	ERA+	OAV	OOB	BH	AVG	PB	PR	/A	PD	TPI

● ABE JOHNSON   Johnson, Abraham   b: Chicago, Ill.   Deb: 7/16/1893

| 1893 | Chi-N | 0 | 0 | — | 1 | 0 | 0 | 0 | 1 | 1 | 2 | 0 | 2 | 0 | 45.0 | 36.00 | 13 | .400 | .625 | 0 | — | 0 | -3 | -3 | -0 | -0.5 |

● RANKIN JOHNSON   Johnson, Adam Rankin Jr.   b: 3/1/17, Hayden, Ariz.   BR/TR, 6'3", 177 lbs.   Deb: 4/17/41   F

| 1941 | Phi-A | 1 | 0 | 1.000 | 7 | 0 | 0 | 0 | 0 | 10 | 14 | 0 | 3 | 0 | 15.3 | 3.60 | 116 | .326 | .370 | 0 | .000 | -0 | 1 | 1 | 0 | 0.1 |

● RANKIN JOHNSON   Johnson, Adam Rankin Sr. "Tex"   b: 2/4/1888, Burnet, Tex.   d: 7/2/72, Williamsport, Pa.   BR/TR, 6'1.5", 185 lbs.   Deb: 4/20/14   F

1914	Bos-A	4	9	.308	16	13	4	2	0	99¹	92	4	34	24	11.7	3.08	87	.265	.336	4	.133	-1	-4	-4	-2	-0.8
	Chi-F	9	5	.643	16	14	12	2	0	120	88	5	29	60	9.1	1.58	169	.209	.267	4	.108	-3	17	14	-1	1.1
1915	Chi-F	2	4	.333	11	6	3	0	1	57	58	2	23	19	12.9	4.42	57	.270	.343	1	.045	-3	-11	-12	-2	-1.7
	Bal-F	7	11	.389	23	19	12	2	1	150²	143	3	58	62	12.1	3.35	86	.255	.326	8	.157	-2	-10	-8	-3	-1.4
	Yr	9	15	.375	34	25	15	2	2	207²	201	5	81	81	12.3	3.64	76	.259	.330	9	.123	-5	-21	-20	-5	-3.1
1918	StL-N	1	1	.500	6	1	0	0	0	23	20	0	7	4	10.6	2.74	99	.250	.325	1	.250	-0	-0	-1	0	0.1
Total	3	23	30	.434	72	53	31	6	2	450	401	12	151	169	11.2	2.92	93	.248	.315	18	.125	-9	-7	-10	-7	-2.7

● ART JOHNSON   Johnson, Arthur Gilbert   b: 2/15/1897, Warren, Pa.   d: 6/7/82, Sarasota, Fla.   BB/TL, 6'1", 167 lbs.   Deb: 9/18/27

| 1927 | NY-N | 0 | 0 | — | 1 | 0 | 0 | 0 | 0 | 3 | 1 | 0 | 1 | 0 | 6.0 | 0.00 | — | .125 | .222 | 0 | — | 0 | 1 | 1 | -0 | 0.0 |

● ART JOHNSON   Johnson, Arthur Henry "Lefty"   b: 7/16/16, Winchester, Mass.   BL/TL, 6'2", 185 lbs.   Deb: 9/22/40

1940	Bos-N	0	1	.000	2	1	0	0	0	6	10	0	3	1	21.0	10.50	35	.345	.424	0	.000	-0	-4	-5	0	-0.6
1941	Bos-N	7	15	.318	43	18	6	0	1	183¹	189	7	71	70	13.0	3.53	101	.270	.342	8	.145	-2	2	1	-0	-0.1
1942	Bos-N	0	0	—	4	0	0	0	0	6¹	4	0	5	0	14.2	1.42	235	.190	.370	0	.000	-0	1	1	-0	0.0
Total	3	7	16	.304	49	19	6	0	1	195²	203	7	79	71	13.3	3.68	97	.271	.346	8	.140	-2	-1	-2	1	-0.7

● BEN JOHNSON   Johnson, Benjamin Franklin   b: 5/16/31, Greenwood, S.C.   BR/TR, 6'2", 190 lbs.   Deb: 9/6/59

1959	Chi-N	0	0	—	4	2	0	0	0	16²	17	1	4	6	11.3	2.16	183	.262	.304	0	.000	-0	3	3	-0	-0.1
1960	Chi-N	2	1	.667	17	0	0	0	1	29¹	39	3	11	9	15.6	4.91	77	.355	.418	0	.000	-0	-4	-4	1	-0.3
Total	2	2	1	.667	21	2	0	0	1	46	56	4	15	15	14.1	3.91	98	.320	.377	0	.000	-1	-0	-0	-0	-0.4

● CHET JOHNSON   Johnson, Chester Lillis "Chesty Chet"   b: 8/1/17, Redmond, Wash.   d: 4/10/83, Seattle, Wash.   BL/TL, 6', 175 lbs.   Deb: 9/12/46   F

| 1946 | StL-A | 0 | 0 | — | 5 | 3 | 0 | 0 | 0 | 18 | 20 | 0 | 13 | 8 | 16.5 | 5.00 | 75 | .286 | .398 | 0 | .000 | -1 | -3 | -3 | -1 | -0.2 |

● BART JOHNSON   Johnson, Clair Barth   b: 1/3/50, Torrance, Cal.   BR/TR, 6'5", 215 lbs.   Deb: 9/8/69

1969	Chi-A	1	3	.250	4	3	0	0	0	22¹	22	2	6	14	11.3	3.22	120	.259	.308	1	.167	0	1	2	-0	0.3
1970	Chi-A	4	7	.364	18	15	2	1	0	89²	92	11	46	71	14.1	4.82	81	.268	.358	8	.276	2	-11	-9	-0	-0.6
1971	Chi-A	12	10	.545	53	16	4	0	14	178	148	9	111	153	13.4	2.93	122	.227	.345	11	.193	0	10	13	-1	1.7
1972	Chi-A	0	3	.000	9	0	0	0	1	13²	18	2	13	9	21.1	9.22	34	.327	.464	0	.000	-0	-9	-9	-0	-2.0
1973	Chi-A	3	3	.500	22	9	0	0	0	80²	76	6	40	56	13.2	4.13	96	.252	.343	0	—	0	-3	-2	-0	-0.4
1974	Chi-A	10	4	.714	18	18	8	2	0	121²	105	6	32	76	10.2	2.74	136	.229	.281	0	—	0	12	13	-2	1.3
1976	Chi-A	9	16	.360	32	32	8	3	0	211¹	231	20	62	91	12.5	4.73	75	.282	.334	0	—	0	-28	-27	-0	-2.9
1977	Chi-A	4	5	.444	29	4	0	0	2	92	114	5	38	46	15.1	4.01	102	.302	.369	0	—	0	-4	-6	-0	-0.1
Total	8	43	51	.457	185	97	22	6	17	809¹	806	61	348	520	13.0	3.94	95	.261	.339	20	.215	3	-28	-19	-4	-2.7

● CONNIE JOHNSON   Johnson, Clifford   b: 12/27/22, Stone Mountain, Ga   BR/TR, 6'4", 200 lbs.   Deb: 4/17/53

1953	Chi-A	4	4	.500	14	10	2	1	0	60²	55	4	38	44	14.1	3.56	113	.238	.351	1	.050	-2	3	3	-1	0.1
1955	Chi-A	7	4	.636	17	16	5	2	0	99	95	5	52	72	13.5	3.45	114	.251	.343	5	.152	-1	6	5	-1	0.3
1956	Chi-A	0	1	.000	5	2	0	0	0	12¹	11	1	7	6	13.1	3.65	112	.234	.333	0	.000	-0	1	1	-0	0.0
	Bal-A	9	10	.474	26	25	9	2	0	183²	165	12	62	130	11.2	3.43	114	.239	.303	15	.259	-3	15	10	-3	1.0
	Yr	9	11	.450	31	27	9	2	0	196	176	13	69	136	11.3	3.44	114	.239	.305	15	.246	-3	16	11	-3	1.0
1957	Bal-A	14	11	.560	35	30	14	3	0	242	212	17	66	177	10.5	3.20	112	.235	.289	12	.135	-4	16	11	-4	0.2
1958	Bal-A	6	9	.400	26	17	4	0	1	118¹	116	13	42	68	11.3	3.88	93	.260	.310	7	.206	1	-1	-4	-2	-0.5
Total	5	40	39	.506	123	100	34	8	1	716	654	52	257	497	11.5	3.44	109	.243	.310	40	.169	-3	38	26	-10	1.1

● DANE JOHNSON   Johnson, Dane Edward   b: 2/10/63, Coral Gables, Fla.   BR/TR, 6'5", 205 lbs.   Deb: 5/30/94

1994	Chi-A	2	1	.667	15	0	0	0	0	12¹	16	2	11	7	19.7	6.57	71	.327	.450	0	—	0	-2	-3	-0	-0.5
1996	Tor-A	0	0	—	10	0	0	0	0	9	5	0	5	7	10.0	3.00	168	.161	.278	0	—	0	2	2	0	0.0
Total	2	2	1	.667	25	0	0	0	0	21¹	21	2	16	14	15.6	5.06	95	.262	.385	0	—	0	-0	-1	-0	-0.5

● DAVE JOHNSON   Johnson, David Charles   b: 10/4/48, Abilene, Tex.   BR/TR, 6'1", 183 lbs.   Deb: 7/2/74

1974	Bal-A	2	2	.500	11	0	0	0	2	15¹	17	1	5	6	12.9	2.93	118	.274	.328	0	—	0	1	-0	0	0.2
1975	Bal-A	0	1	.000	6	0	0	0	0	8²	8	0	7	4	15.6	4.15	84	.250	.385	0	—	0	-0	-1	-0	-0.0
1977	Min-A	2	5	.286	30	6	0	0	0	72²	86	7	23	33	14.1	4.58	87	.299	.361	0	—	0	-4	-5	-0	-0.4
1978	Min-A	0	2	.000	6	1	0	0	0	12¹	15	1	9	7	18.0	7.50	51	.313	.421	0	—	0	-5	-5	-0	-0.7
Total	4	4	10	.286	53	7	0	0	2	108²	126	9	44	50	14.5	4.64	83	.293	.365	0	—	0	-8	-10	-0	-0.9

● DAVE JOHNSON   Johnson, David Wayne   b: 10/24/59, Baltimore, Md.   BR/TR, 5'10", 180 lbs.   Deb: 5/29/87

1987	Pit-N	0	0	—	5	0	0	0	0	6¹	13	1	2	4	21.3	9.95	41	.448	.484	0	—	0	-4	-4	0	0.0
1989	Bal-A	4	7	.364	14	14	4	0	0	89¹	90	11	28	26	12.3	4.23	90	.265	.328	0	—	0	-3	-4	-2	-0.7
1990	Bal-A	13	9	.591	30	29	3	0	0	180	196	30	43	68	12.1	4.10	93	.280	.324	0	—	0	-4	-6	-3	-0.9
1991	Bal-A	4	8	.333	22	14	0	0	0	84	127	18	24	38	16.6	7.07	56	.349	.395	0	—	0	-28	-29	-1	-3.5
1993	Det-A	1	1	.500	6	0	0	0	0	8¹	13	3	5	7	21.6	12.96	33	.342	.444	0	—	0	-8	-8	-0	-1.5
Total	5	22	25	.468	77	57	7	0	0	368	439	63	102	143	13.5	5.11	75	.298	.349	0	—	0	-47	-52	-6	-6.6

● DON JOHNSON   Johnson, Donald Roy   b: 11/12/26, Portland, Ore.   BR/TR, 6'3", 200 lbs.   Deb: 4/20/47

1947	NY-A	4	3	.571	15	8	2	0	0	54¹	57	2	23	16	13.4	3.64	97	.270	.345	0	.000	-2	0	-1	-0	-0.3
1950	NY-A	1	0	1.000	8	0	0	0	0	18	35	2	12	9	23.5	10.00	43	.398	.470	0	.000	-0	-11	-11	-0	-0.6
	StL-A	5	6	.455	25	12	4	1	1	96	126	14	55	31	17.1	6.09	81	.321	.410	2	.069	-3	-16	-12	-1	-1.5
	Yr	6	6	.500	33	12	4	1	1	114	161	16	67	40	18.1	6.71	72	.338	.421	2	.063	-4	-27	-24	-1	-2.1
1951	StL-A	0	1	.000	6	3	0	0	0	15	27	4	18	8	27.6	12.60	35	.391	.523	1	.333	0	-14	-14	-0	-0.7
	Was-A	7	11	.389	21	20	8	1	0	143²	138	9	58	52	12.4	3.95	104	.255	.329	4	.085	-5	3	2	-0	-0.3
	Yr	7	12	.368	27	23	8	1	0	158²	165	13	76	60	13.8	4.76	87	.270	.352	5	.100	-5	-11	-11	-0	-1.0
1952	Was-A	0	5	.000	29	6	0	0	2	69	80	4	33	37	15.3	4.43	80	.287	.370	1	.077	-1	-6	-7	-0	-0.6
1954	Chi-A	8	7	.533	46	16	3	3	7	144	129	14	43	68	10.8	3.13	119	.243	.300	1	.029	-1	10	10	-0	0.7
1955	Bal-A	2	4	.333	31	5	0	0	0	68	89	4	35	27	16.4	5.82	65	.335	.411	0	.000	-0	-14	-15	-0	-1.3
1958	SF-N	0	1	.000	17	0	0	0	0	23	31	2	8	14	16.0	6.26	61	.323	.387	0	.000	-0	-6	-6	-0	-0.4
Total	7	27	38	.415	198	70	17	5	12	631	712	55	285	262	14.4	4.78	84	.288	.364	10	.058	-16	-54	-55	-2	-4.9

● EARL JOHNSON   Johnson, Earl Douglas "Lefty"   b: 4/2/19, Redmond, Wash.   d: 12/3/94, Seattle, Wash.   BL/TL, 6'3", 190 lbs.   Deb: 7/20/40   F

1940	Bos-A	6	2	.750	17	10	2	0	0	70¹	69	0	39	26	14.1	4.09	110	.260	.359	-3	.074	-3	2	3	1	0.1
1941	Bos-A	4	5	.444	17	12	4	0	0	93²	90	4	46	41	13.8	4.52	92	.247	.344	10	.294	-2	-4	-4	2	0.1
1946	*Bos-A	5	4	.556	29	5	0	0	3	80	78	5	39	40	13.4	3.71	99	.250	.337	5	.227	2	-0	-0	4	0.1
1947	Bos-A	12	11	.522	45	17	6	3	8	142¹	129	7	62	65	12.2	2.97	131	.246	.328	12	.273	1	12	14	2	2.8
1948	Bos-A	10	4	.714	35	3	1	0	5	91¹	98	7	42	45	13.8	4.53	97	.276	.353	3	.097	-3	-2	-1	2	-0.3
1949	Bos-A	3	6	.333	19	3	0	0	0	49¹	65	1	29	20	17.9	7.48	58	.327	.422	0	.000	-0	-18	-17	-1	-2.7
1950	Bos-A	0	0	—	11	0	0	0	0	13²	18	0	12	6	17.8	7.24	68	.333	.429	0	.000	-0	-4	-4	1	0.0
1951	Det-A	0	0	—	6	0	0	0	1	5²	9	0	2	2	17.5	6.35	66	.375	.423	0	—	0	-1	-0	0	0.0
Total	8	40	32	.556	179	50	13	3	17	546¹	556	24	272	250	13.9	4.30	96	.265	.353	32	.187	-2	-18	-10	7	0.1

● WALT JOHNSON   Johnson, Ellis Walter   b: 12/8/1892, Minneapolis, Minn.   d: 1/4/65, Minneapolis, Minn.   BR/TR, 6'0.5", 180 lbs.   Deb: 7/6/12

| 1912 | Chi-A | 0 | 0 | — | 3 | 0 | 0 | 0 | 0 | 11² | 11 | 0 | 7 | 7 | 14.7 | 3.86 | 83 | .262 | .380 | 0 | .000 | -0 | -1 | -0 | -0 | 0.0 |
| 1915 | Chi-A | 0 | 0 | — | 1 | 0 | 0 | 0 | 0 | 2 | 3 | 0 | 0 | 3 | 13.5 | 9.00 | 33 | .333 | .333 | 0 | — | 0 | -1 | -0 | -0 | 0.0 |

YEAR	TM/L	W	L	PCT	G	GS	CG	SH	SV	IP	H	HR	BB	SO	RAT	ERA	ERA+	OAV	OOB	BH	AVG	PB	PR	/A	PD	TPI
1917	Phi-A	0	2	.000	4	2	0	0	0	13²	15	0	5	8	13.2	7.24	38	.294	.357	0	.000	0	-7	-7	0	-0.8
Total 3		0	2	.000	8	2	0	0	0	27¹	29	0	12	18	13.8	5.93	50	.284	.365	0	.000	0	-9	-9	-0	-0.8

● ERNIE JOHNSON
Johnson, Ernest Thorwald b: 6/16/24, Brattleboro, Vt. BR/TR, 6'4", 195 lbs. Deb: 4/28/50

YEAR	TM/L	W	L	PCT	G	GS	CG	SH	SV	IP	H	HR	BB	SO	RAT	ERA	ERA+	OAV	OOB	BH	AVG	PB	PR	/A	PD	TPI
1950	Bos-N	2	0	1.000	16	1	0	0	0	20²	37	1	13	15	21.8	6.97	55	.394	.467	1	.500	-1	-6	-7	1	-0.4
1952	Bos-N	6	3	.667	29	10	2	1	1	92	100	7	31	45	13.0	4.11	88	.270	.329	2	.091	-0	-4	-5	1	-0.4
1953	Mil-N	4	3	.571	36	1	0	0	0	81	79	4	22	36	11.6	2.67	147	.263	.320	1	.071	-1	15	11	0	0.7
1954	Mil-N	5	2	.714	40	4	1	0	2	99¹	77	11	34	68	10.1	2.81	133	.219	.290	3	.231	0	14	10	1	0.8
1955	Mil-N	5	7	.417	40	2	0	0	4	92	81	5	55	43	13.5	3.42	110	.240	.349	2	.100	-1	6	3	-0	0.3
1956	Mil-N	4	3	.571	36	0	0	0	6	51	54	9	21	26	13.4	3.71	93	.270	.342	1	.250	0	-1	0	-0	-0.2
1957	*Mil-N	7	3	.700	30	0	0	0	4	65	67	9	26	44	13.0	3.88	90	.265	.336	6	.353	3	0	-3	1	0.0
1958	Mil-N	3	1	.750	15	0	0	0	1	23¹	35	4	10	13	17.7	8.10	43	.357	.422	0	.000	0	-11	-12	-0	-1.8
1959	Bal-A	4	1	.800	31	1	0	0	1	50¹	57	6	19	29	14.1	4.11	92	.286	.357	2	.333	1	-1	-2	0	-0.1
Total 9		40	23	.635	273	19	3	1	19	574²	587	56	231	319	13.0	3.77	98	.266	.340	18	.180	2	13	-5	5	-1.1

● FRED JOHNSON
Johnson, Frederick Edward "Deacon" or "Cactus" b: 3/10/1894, Tolar, Tex. d: 6/14/72, Kerrville, Tex. BR/TR, 6', 185 lbs. Deb: 9/27/22

YEAR	TM/L	W	L	PCT	G	GS	CG	SH	SV	IP	H	HR	BB	SO	RAT	ERA	ERA+	OAV	OOB	BH	AVG	PB	PR	/A	PD	TPI
1922	NY-N	0	2	.000	2	2	1	0	0	18	20	3	1	8	10.5	4.00	100	.294	.304	0	.000	-1	0	0	-0	-0.1
1923	NY-N	2	0	1.000	3	2	1	0	0	17	11	2	7	5	9.5	4.24	90	.177	.261	0	.000	-1	-0	-1	1	-0.1
1938	StL-A	3	7	.300	17	6	3	0	3	69	91	7	27	24	15.5	5.61	89	.316	.377	6	.240	-0	-6	-5	-2	-0.8
1939	StL-A	0	1	.000	5	2	1	0	0	14	23	0	9	2	20.6	6.43	76	.383	.464	0	.000	-1	-3	-2	1	-0.1
Total 4		5	10	.333	27	12	6	0	3	118	145	12	44	39	14.5	5.26	89	.303	.363	6	.154	-2	-9	-8	0	-1.1

● CHIEF JOHNSON
Johnson, George Howard "Murphy" or "Big Murph" b: 3/30/1886, Winnebago, Neb. d: 6/11/22, Des Moines, Iowa BR/TR, 5'11.5", 190 lbs. Deb: 4/16/13

YEAR	TM/L	W	L	PCT	G	GS	CG	SH	SV	IP	H	HR	BB	SO	RAT	ERA	ERA+	OAV	OOB	BH	AVG	PB	PR	/A	PD	TPI
1913	Cin-N	14	16	.467	44	31	13	3	0	269	251	8	86	107	11.5	3.01	108	.256	.320	10	.114	-3	6	7	0	0.5
1914	Cin-N	0	0	—	1	1	0	0	0	4	6	0	2	1	11.5	6.75	43	.333	.400	0	—	0	-2	-2	-0	0.0
	KC-F	9	10	.474	20	19	12	2	0	134	157	2	33	78	13.0	3.16	88	.298	.345	6	.122	-2	-4	-6	-3	-1.2
1915	KC-F	17	17	.500	46	34	19	4	2	281¹	253	5	71	118	10.6	2.75	96	.242	.295	11	.126	-4	-1	-4	2	-0.6
Total 3		40	43	.482	111	85	44	9	2	688¹	667	15	192	304	11.5	2.95	98	.259	.315	27	.121	-9	-1	-4	-1	-1.3

● HANK JOHNSON
Johnson, Henry Ward b: 5/21/06, Bradenton, Fla. d: 8/20/82, Bradenton, Fla. BR/TR, 5'11.5", 175 lbs. Deb: 4/17/25

YEAR	TM/L	W	L	PCT	G	GS	CG	SH	SV	IP	H	HR	BB	SO	RAT	ERA	ERA+	OAV	OOB	BH	AVG	PB	PR	/A	PD	TPI
1925	NY-A	1	3	.250	24	4	2	1	0	67	88	3	37	25	17.9	6.85	62	.319	.414	1	.059	-1	-18	-19	1	-1.0
1926	NY-A	0	0	—	1	0	0	0	1	1	2	0	2	0	36.0	18.00	21	.400	.571	0	—	0	-2	-2	-0	-0.3
1928	NY-A	14	9	.609	31	22	10	1	0	199	188	16	104	110	13.7	4.30	88	.250	.351	19	.241	2	-6	-12	0	-1.1
1929	NY-A	3	3	.500	12	8	2	0	0	42²	37	5	39	24	16.0	5.06	76	.237	.390	1	.071	-1	-4	-6	-1	-0.9
1930	NY-A	14	11	.560	44	15	7	1	2	175¹	177	12	104	115	14.5	4.67	92	.265	.366	17	.266	5	-0	-7	2	-0.3
1931	NY-A	13	8	.619	40	23	8	0	4	196¹	176	13	102	106	12.8	4.72	84	.234	.326	15	.195	2	-7	-16	-3	-1.7
1932	NY-A	2	2	.500	5	4	2	0	0	31¹	34	7	15	27	14.1	4.88	83	.266	.343	3	.231	0	-1	-3	0	-0.4
1933	Bos-A	8	6	.571	25	21	7	0	1	155¹	156	13	74	65	13.5	4.06	108	.263	.348	12	.231	2	3	6	-2	0.6
1934	Bos-A	6	8	.429	31	14	7	1	0	124¹	162	12	53	66	15.9	5.36	90	.316	.385	10	.233	1	-12	-8	-1	-0.8
1935	Bos-A	2	1	.667	13	2	0	0	1	31	41	3	14	14	16.0	5.52	86	.331	.399	0	.000	-1	-4	-3	-1	-0.4
1936	Phi-A	0	2	.000	3	3	0	0	0	11²	14	1	10	6	20.8	7.71	66	.296	.415	1	.250	-1	-3	-3	-0	-0.4
1939	Cin-N	0	3	.000	20	0	0	0	1	31¹	30	1	13	10	12.4	2.01	191	.268	.344	2	.400	1	7	6	-1	0.5
Total 12		63	56	.529	249	116	45	4	11	1066¹	1107	89	567	568	14.4	4.75	88	.268	.361	81	.215	9	-47	-67	-6	-6.1

● JIM JOHNSON
Johnson, James Brian b: 11/3/45, Muskegon, Mich. BL/TL, 5'11", 175 lbs. Deb: 4/13/70

YEAR	TM/L	W	L	PCT	G	GS	CG	SH	SV	IP	H	HR	BB	SO	RAT	ERA	ERA+	OAV	OOB	BH	AVG	PB	PR	/A	PD	TPI
1970	SF-N	1	0	1.000	3	0	0	0	0	6²	8	0	5	2	17.6	8.10	49	.320	.433	0	.000	0	-3	-3	0	-0.4

● JERRY JOHNSON
Johnson, Jerry Michael b: 12/3/43, Miami, Fla. BR/TR, 6'3", 200 lbs. Deb: 7/17/68

YEAR	TM/L	W	L	PCT	G	GS	CG	SH	SV	IP	H	HR	BB	SO	RAT	ERA	ERA+	OAV	OOB	BH	AVG	PB	PR	/A	PD	TPI
1968	Phi-N	4	4	.500	16	11	2	0	0	80²	82	5	29	40	12.6	3.24	93	.264	.330	2	.080	-0	-2	-2	1	-0.2
1969	Phi-N	6	13	.316	33	21	4	2	1	147¹	151	18	57	82	12.9	4.28	83	.268	.338	9	.209	2	-11	-12	-1	-1.4
1970	StL-N	2	0	1.000	7	0	0	0	1	11¹	6	1	3	5	7.1	3.18	130	.146	.205	0	.000	0	1	1	-0	0.2
	SF-N	3	4	.429	33	1	0	0	3	65¹	67	5	38	44	14.6	4.27	93	.266	.364	1	.067	-1	-2	-2	-0	-0.4
	Yr	5	4	.556	40	1	0	0	4	76²	73	6	41	49	13.5	4.11	97	.249	.343	1	.063	-1	-1	-1	-0	-0.2
1971	*SF-N	12	9	.571	67	0	0	0	18	109	93	9	48	85	11.7	2.97	114	.230	.313	2	.154	-0	6	5	0	1.2
1972	SF-N	8	6	.571	48	0	0	0	8	73¹	73	4	40	57	13.9	4.42	79	.261	.353	0	.000	-1	-8	-8	0	-1.6
1973	Cle-A	5	6	.455	39	1	0	0	0	59²	70	7	39	45	16.4	6.18	63	.299	.399	0	—	0	-16	-15	0	-2.8
1974	Hou-N	2	1	.667	34	0	0	0	0	45	47	2	24	32	14.2	4.80	72	.276	.366	0	.000	-0	-6	-7	-0	-0.4
1975	SD-N	3	1	.750	21	4	0	0	0	54	60	3	18	15	15.2	5.17	67	.282	.373	1	.083	-0	-9	-10	-1	-0.8
1976	SD-N	1	3	.250	24	1	0	0	0	39	39	0	26	27	15.0	5.31	62	.260	.369	0	.000	-0	-9	-9	-0	-0.9
1977	Tor-A	2	4	.333	43	0	0	0	5	86	91	8	54	54	15.2	4.60	91	.279	.382	0	—	0	-5	-4	-0	-0.4
Total 10		48	51	.485	365	39	6	2	41	770²	779	63	389	489	13.7	4.31	92	.265	.352	15	.123	-2	-60	-62	-1	-7.5

● JOHNNY JOHNSON
Johnson, John Clifford "Swede" b: 9/29/14, Belmore, Ohio d: 6/26/91, Iron Mountain, Mich. BL/TL, 6', 182 lbs. Deb: 4/19/44

YEAR	TM/L	W	L	PCT	G	GS	CG	SH	SV	IP	H	HR	BB	SO	RAT	ERA	ERA+	OAV	OOB	BH	AVG	PB	PR	/A	PD	TPI
1944	NY-A	0	2	.000	22	1	0	0	3	26²	25	0	24	11	16.9	4.05	86	.243	.391	3	.500	1	-2	-2	-1	-0.1
1945	Chi-A	3	0	1.000	29	0	0	0	4	69²	85	2	35	38	15.6	4.26	78	.306	.385	4	.286	2	-7	-7	-1	-0.4
Total 2		3	2	.600	51	1	0	0	7	96¹	110	2	59	49	16.0	4.20	80	.289	.387	7	.350	3	-9	-9	-2	-0.4

● YOUNGY JOHNSON
Johnson, John Godfred b: 7/22/1877, San Francisco, Cal. d: 8/28/36, Berkeley, Cal. TR, Deb: 4/29/1897

YEAR	TM/L	W	L	PCT	G	GS	CG	SH	SV	IP	H	HR	BB	SO	RAT	ERA	ERA+	OAV	OOB	BH	AVG	PB	PR	/A	PD	TPI
1897	Phi-N	1	2	.333	5	2	1	0	0	29	39	0	12	7	16.4	4.66	90	.320	.390	1	.077	-2	-1	-1	-0	-0.3
1899	NY-N	0	0	—	1	0	0	0	0	2	0	0	2	1	9.0	0.00	—	.000	.250	0	—	-0	1	0	0	0.0
Total 2		1	2	.333	6	2	1	0	0	31	39	0	14	8	16.0	4.35	96	.305	.382	1	.071	-2	-0	-1	-0	-0.3

● JOHN HENRY JOHNSON
Johnson, John Henry b: 8/21/56, Houston, Tex. BL/TL, 6'2", 190 lbs. Deb: 4/10/78

YEAR	TM/L	W	L	PCT	G	GS	CG	SH	SV	IP	H	HR	BB	SO	RAT	ERA	ERA+	OAV	OOB	BH	AVG	PB	PR	/A	PD	TPI
1978	Oak-A	11	10	.524	33	30	7	2	0	186	164	18	82	91	11.9	3.39	107	.238	.319	0	—	0	8	5	-3	0.4
1979	Oak-A	2	8	.200	14	13	1	0	0	84²	89	13	36	50	13.4	4.36	93	.269	.342	0	—	0	-1	-3	-1	-0.2
	Tex-A	2	6	.250	17	12	1	0	0	82¹	79	12	36	46	12.7	4.92	84	.255	.334	0	—	0	-6	-7	-1	-0.6
	Yr	4	14	.222	31	25	2	0	0	167	168	25	72	96	13.0	4.63	88	.261	.336	0	—	0	-8	-10	-1	-0.8
1980	Tex-A	2	2	.500	33	0	0	0	4	38²	27	2	15	44	10.0	2.33	167	.199	.283	0	—	0	7	7	0	0.9
1981	Tex-A	3	1	.750	24	0	0	0	1	23²	19	2	6	8	9.9	2.66	130	.232	.292	0	—	0	3	2	1	0.6
1983	Bos-A	3	2	.600	34	1	0	0	1	53¹	58	3	20	51	13.3	3.71	117	.283	.350	0	—	0	2	4	-0	0.2
1984	Bos-A	1	2	.333	30	3	0	0	1	63²	64	7	27	57	12.9	3.53	118	.260	.333	0	—	0	3	4	-0	0.3
1986	Mil-A	2	1	.667	19	0	0	0	1	44	43	2	10	42	10.8	2.66	163	.251	.293	0	—	0	7	8	-1	0.3
1987	Mil-A	0	1	.000	10	2	0	0	0	26¹	42	4	18	18	20.5	9.57	48	.365	.451	0	—	0	-15	-15	0	-0.5
Total 8		26	33	.441	214	61	9	2	8	602²	565	60	250	407	12.5	3.90	102	.256	.331	0	—	0	4	6	-5	1.1

● JOHN JOHNSON
Johnson, John Louis (b: John Louis Mercer) b: 11/18/1869, Pekin, Ill. d: 1/28/41, Kansas City, Mo. TL, 5'10", 165 lbs. Deb: 9/11/1894

YEAR	TM/L	W	L	PCT	G	GS	CG	SH	SV	IP	H	HR	BB	SO	RAT	ERA	ERA+	OAV	OOB	BH	AVG	PB	PR	/A	PD	TPI
1894	Phi-N	1	1	.500	4	3	2	0	0	32²	44	3	15	10	16.5	6.06	84	.319	.390	3	.188	-1	-3	-3	0	-0.2

● JOE JOHNSON
Johnson, Joseph Richard b: 10/30/61, Brookline, Mass. BR/TR, 6'2", 195 lbs. Deb: 7/25/85

YEAR	TM/L	W	L	PCT	G	GS	CG	SH	SV	IP	H	HR	BB	SO	RAT	ERA	ERA+	OAV	OOB	BH	AVG	PB	PR	/A	PD	TPI
1985	Atl-N	4	4	.500	15	14	1	0	0	85²	95	9	24	34	12.8	4.10	94	.285	.339	1	.043	-1	-5	-2	-2	-0.5
1986	Atl-N	6	7	.462	17	15	2	0	0	87	101	8	35	49	14.3	4.97	80	.289	.358	3	.115	-1	-12	-10	2	-1.2
	Tor-A	7	2	.778	16	15	0	0	0	88	94	3	22	39	12.2	3.89	109	.281	.331	0	—	0	3	3	-1	0.1
1987	Tor-A	3	5	.375	14	14	0	0	0	66²	77	10	18	27	13.1	5.13	88	.289	.339	0	—	0	-5	-5	-0	-0.5
Total 3		20	18	.526	62	58	3	0	0	327¹	367	30	99	149	13.1	4.48	92	.286	.342	4	.082	-2	-19	-13	-2	-2.1

● KEN JOHNSON
Johnson, Kenneth Travis b: 6/16/33, W.Palm Beach, Fla. BR/TR, 6'4", 210 lbs. Deb: 9/13/58

YEAR	TM/L	W	L	PCT	G	GS	CG	SH	SV	IP	H	HR	BB	SO	RAT	ERA	ERA+	OAV	OOB	BH	AVG	PB	PR	/A	PD	TPI
1958	KC-A	0	0	—	2	0	0	0	0	2¹	1	1	6	3	34.7	27.00	14	.429	.529	0	—	0	-6	-6	0	0.0
1959	KC-A	1	1	.500	2	2	0	0	0	11	11	2	5	7	13.1	4.09	98	.268	.348	0	—	0	0	-1	0	0.0
1960	KC-A	5	10	.333	42	16	2	0	3	120¹	120	16	40	65	12.9	4.26	93	.263	.338	5	.167	-1	-5	-4	2	-0.3
1961	KC-A	0	4	.000	6	6	1	0	0	9¹	11	2	7	4	17.4	10.61	39	.297	.409	0	.000	-0	-7	-7	1	-2.1
	*Cin-N	6	2	.750	15	11	3	1	0	83	71	11	22	42	10.3	3.25	125	.229	.284	6	.240	1	7	7	0	0.9

YEAR	TM/L	W	L	PCT	G	GS	CG	SH	SV	IP	H	HR	BB	SO	RAT	ERA	ERA+	OAV	OOB	BH	AVG	PB	PR	/A	PD	TPI
1962	Hou-N	7	16	.304	33	31	5	1	0	197	195	18	46	178	11.3	3.84	97	.257	.305	4	.077	-3	2	-2	1	-0.4
1963	Hou-N	11	17	.393	37	32	6	1	1	224	204	12	50	148	10.5	2.65	119	.242	.291	5	.068	-4	16	12	2	1.4
1964	Hou-N	11	16	.407	35	35	7	1	0	218	209	15	44	117	10.7	3.63	94	.250	.293	6	.079	-2	-2	-5	1	-0.6
1965	Hou-N	3	2	.600	8	8	1	0	0	51²	52	4	11	28	11.7	4.18	80	.267	.319	2	.111	-0	-4	-5	1	-0.3
	Mil-N	13	8	.619	29	26	8	1	2	179²	165	15	37	123	10.3	3.21	110	.240	.282	7	.115	-2	7	6	-3	0.2
	Yr	16	10	.615	37	34	9	1	2	231¹	217	19	48	151	10.4	3.42	102	.244	.285	9	.114	-2	3	2	-2	-0.1
1966	Atl-N	14	8	.636	32	31	11	2	0	215²	213	24	46	105	10.8	3.30	110	.262	.301	10	.143	-0	7	8	0	0.8
1967	Atl-N	13	9	.591	29	29	6	0	0	210¹	191	19	38	85	10.1	2.74	121	.244	.285	9	.127	-0	15	14	-2	1.2
1968	Atl-N	5	8	.385	31	16	1	0	0	135	145	10	25	57	11.9	3.47	86	.279	.324	7	.175	-0	-7	-7	-1	-0.8
1969	Atl-N	0	1	.000	9	2	0	0	1	29	32	4	9	20	12.7	4.97	73	.283	.336	0	.000	-0	-4	-4	0	-0.2
	NY-A	1	2	.333	12	0	0	0	0	26	19	1	11	21	10.4	3.46	100	.202	.286	0	.000	-0	0	0	1	0.1
	Chi-N	1	2	.333	9	1	0	0	1	19	17	2	13	18	14.2	2.84	142	.230	.345	0	.000	-0	2	2	0	0.3
1970	Mon-N	0	0	—	3	0	0	0	0	6	9	1	4	4	18.0	7.50	55	.321	.387	0	—	-2	-2	-0	0	-0.2
Total	13	91	106	.462	334	231	50	7	9	1737¹	1670	157	413	1042	11.1	3.46	101	.253	.302	61	.114	-12	18	8	5	0.2

● KEN JOHNSON
Johnson, Kenneth Wandersee "Hook"   b: 1/14/23, Topeka, Kan.   BL/TL, 6'1", 185 lbs.   Deb: 9/18/47

YEAR	TM/L	W	L	PCT	G	GS	CG	SH	SV	IP	H	HR	BB	SO	RAT	ERA	ERA+	OAV	OOB	BH	AVG	PB	PR	/A	PD	TPI
1947	StL-N	1	0	1.000	2	1	0	0	0	10	2	0	5	8	7.2	0.00	—	.063	.211	2	.500	1	5	5	0	0.5
1948	StL-N	2	4	.333	13	4	0	0	0	45¹	43	1	30	20	14.7	4.76	86	.250	.379	6	.300	2	-4	-3	-0	-0.3
1949	StL-N	0	1	.000	14	2	0	0	0	33²	29	1	35	18	17.9	6.42	65	.250	.435	2	.250	-0	-9	-8	1	-0.1
1950	StL-N	0	0	—	2	0	0	0	0	3	1	0	3	1	18.0	0.00	—	.167	.444	0	—	0	1	1	0	0.1
	*Phi-N	4	1	.800	14	8	3	1	0	60²	61	3	43	32	15.6	4.01	101	.260	.376	3	.158	-1	1	0	0	0.0
	Yr	4	1	.800	16	8	3	1	0	62²	62	3	46	33	15.7	3.88	105	.257	.378	3	.158	-0	2	1	0	0.0
1951	Phi-N	5	8	.385	20	18	4	3	0	106¹	103	8	68	58	14.7	4.57	84	.259	.371	5	.143	-1	-7	-9	-0	-1.0
1952	Det-A	0	0	—	9	1	0	0	0	11¹	12	1	11	10	18.3	6.35	60	.273	.418	1	.333	0	-3	-3	0	-0.1
Total	6	12	14	.462	74	34	8	4	0	269¹	251	14	195	147	15.2	4.58	87	.252	.379	19	.213	1	-17	-18	1	-0.9

● LLOYD JOHNSON
Johnson, Lloyd William "Eppa"   b: 12/24/10, Santa Rosa, Cal.   d: 10/8/80, Stockton, Cal.   BL/TL, 6'4", 204 lbs.   Deb: 4/21/34

YEAR	TM/L	W	L	PCT	G	GS	CG	SH	SV	IP	H	HR	BB	SO	RAT	ERA	ERA+	OAV	OOB	BH	AVG	PB	PR	/A	PD	TPI
1934	Pit-N	0	0	—	1	0	0	0	0	1	1	0	0	0	9.0	0.00	—	.333	.333	0	—	0	0	0	-0	0.0

● MIKE JOHNSON
Johnson, Michael Norton   b: 3/2/51, Slayton, Minn.   BR/TR, 6'1", 185 lbs.   Deb: 7/25/74

YEAR	TM/L	W	L	PCT	G	GS	CG	SH	SV	IP	H	HR	BB	SO	RAT	ERA	ERA+	OAV	OOB	BH	AVG	PB	PR	/A	PD	TPI
1974	SD-N	0	2	.000	18	0	0	0	0	21¹	29	1	15	15	19.0	4.64	77	.326	.429	0	—	0	-2	-3	-0	-0.2

● RANDY JOHNSON
Johnson, Randall David   b: 9/10/63, Walnut Creek, Cal.   BR/TL, 6'10", 225 lbs.   Deb: 9/15/88

YEAR	TM/L	W	L	PCT	G	GS	CG	SH	SV	IP	H	HR	BB	SO	RAT	ERA	ERA+	OAV	OOB	BH	AVG	PB	PR	/A	PD	TPI
1988	Mon-N	3	0	1.000	4	4	1	0	0	26	23	3	7	25	10.4	2.42	148	.225	.275	1	.111	-0	3	3	-1	0.3
1989	Mon-N	0	4	.000	7	6	0	0	0	29²	29	2	26	26	16.7	6.67	53	.264	.404	1	.143	-0	-10	-10	-1	-1.2
	Sea-A	7	9	.438	22	22	2	0	0	131	118	11	70	104	13.1	4.40	94	.244	.344	0	—	0	-7	-5	-0	-0.6
1990	Sea-A☆	14	11	.560	33	33	5	2	0	219²	174	26	120	194	12.3	3.65	109	.216	.321	0	—	0	6	8	-1	0.6
1991	Sea-A	13	10	.565	33	33	2	1	0	201¹	151	15	152	228	14.1	3.98	104	.213	.361	0	—	0	3	5	-1	0.4
1992	Sea-A	12	14	.462	31	31	6	2	0	210¹	154	13	144	**241**	13.5	3.77	105	**.206**	.347	0	—	0	4	5	-1	0.4
1993	Sea-A★	19	8	.704	35	34	10	3	1	255¹	185	22	99	**308**	10.6	3.24	136	**.203**	.292	0	—	0	31	33	1	3.1
1994	Sea-A★	13	6	.684	23	23	**9**	**4**	0	172	132	14	72	**204**	11.0	3.19	153	.216	.304	0	—	0	31	32	2	3.3
1995	*Sea-A★	18	2	**.900**	30	30	6	3	0	214¹	159	12	65	**294**	**9.7**	**2.48**	**191**	**.201**	**.267**	0	—	0	53	54	1	**4.6**
1996	Sea-A	5	0	1.000	14	8	0	0	1	61¹	48	8	25	85	11.0	3.67	134	.211	.294	0	—	0	9	9	0	0.6
Total	9	104	64	.619	232	224	41	15	2	1521	1173	126	780	1709	12.0	3.53	122	.213	.318	2	.125	-1	122	131	-0	11.3

● BOB JOHNSON
Johnson, Robert Dale   b: 4/25/43, Aurora, Ill.   BL/TR, 6'4", 220 lbs.   Deb: 9/19/69

YEAR	TM/L	W	L	PCT	G	GS	CG	SH	SV	IP	H	HR	BB	SO	RAT	ERA	ERA+	OAV	OOB	BH	AVG	PB	PR	/A	PD	TPI
1969	NY-N	0	0	—	2	0	0	0	1	1²	1	0	1	1	10.8	0.00	—	.167	.286	0	—	0	1	1	0	0.1
1970	KC-A	8	13	.381	40	26	10	1	4	214	178	18	82	206	11.4	3.07	122	.228	.310	6	.105	-1	15	16	-1	1.3
1971	*Pit-N	9	10	.474	31	27	7	1	0	174²	170	19	55	101	12.0	3.45	98	.259	.323	3	.063	-1	0	-1	-1	-0.4
1972	*Pit-N	4	4	.500	31	11	1	0	3	115²	98	14	46	79	11.5	2.96	112	.231	.312	5	.143	-0	6	5	-2	0.4
1973	Pit-N	4	2	.667	50	2	0	0	4	92	98	4	38	68	13.4	3.62	97	.276	.348	0	.000	0	0	-1	-2	-0.4
1974	Cle-A	3	4	.429	14	10	0	0	0	72	75	12	37	36	14.4	4.38	83	.273	.365	0	—	0	-6	-6	-0	-0.6
1977	Atl-N	0	1	.000	15	0	0	0	0	22¹	24	7	14	16	16.1	7.25	61	.270	.381	1	.333	0	-8	-7	-1	-0.3
Total	7	28	34	.452	183	76	18	2	12	692¹	644	82	269	507	12.3	3.48	102	.249	.327	15	.096	-4	9	6	-7	-0.2

● ROY JOHNSON
Johnson, Roy J "Hardrock"   b: 10/1/1895, Madill, Okla.   d: 1/10/86, Scottsdale, Ariz.   BR/TR, 6', 185 lbs.   Deb: 8/7/18   MC

YEAR	TM/L	W	L	PCT	G	GS	CG	SH	SV	IP	H	HR	BB	SO	RAT	ERA	ERA+	OAV	OOB	BH	AVG	PB	PR	/A	PD	TPI
1918	Phi-A	1	5	.167	10	8	4	0	0	50	47	0	34	12	14.9	3.42	86	.254	.376	1	.067	-2	-4	-3	-0	-0.5

● JING JOHNSON
Johnson, Russell Conwell   b: 10/9/1894, Parker Ford, Pa.   d: 12/6/50, Pottstown, Pa.   BR/TR, 5'9", 172 lbs.   Deb: 6/27/16

YEAR	TM/L	W	L	PCT	G	GS	CG	SH	SV	IP	H	HR	BB	SO	RAT	ERA	ERA+	OAV	OOB	BH	AVG	PB	PR	/A	PD	TPI
1916	Phi-A	2	8	.200	12	12	8	0	0	84¹	90	3	39	25	13.8	3.74	76	.288	.368	2	.074	-1	-8	-8	3	-0.7
1917	Phi-A	9	12	.429	34	23	13	0	0	191	184	3	56	55	11.5	2.78	99	.260	.319	12	.203	2	-2	-1	3	-0.2
1919	Phi-A	9	15	.375	34	25	12	0	0	202	222	8	62	67	12.8	3.61	95	.291	.346	14	.194	0	-9	-4	5	0.1
1927	Phi-A	4	2	.667	17	3	2	0	0	51²	42	2	16	16	10.8	3.48	122	.225	.312	2	.167	-0	4	4	1	0.2
1928	Phi-A	0	0	—	3	0	0	0	0	10²	13	1	5	3	15.2	5.06	79	.310	.383	2	.500	1	-1	-1	0	0.1
Total	5	24	37	.393	100	63	35	0	0	539²	551	17	178	166	12.4	3.35	95	.275	.338	32	.184	-8	-17	-10	10	0.4

● SI JOHNSON
Johnson, Silas Kenneth   b: 10/5/06, Danway, Ill.   d: 5/12/94, Sheridan, Ill.   BR/TR, 5'11.5", 185 lbs.   Deb: 5/2/28

YEAR	TM/L	W	L	PCT	G	GS	CG	SH	SV	IP	H	HR	BB	SO	RAT	ERA	ERA+	OAV	OOB	BH	AVG	PB	PR	/A	PD	TPI
1928	Cin-N	0	0	—	3	0	0	0	0	10¹	9	0	5	4	12.2	4.35	91	.250	.341	1	.250	0	-0	-0	0	0.0
1929	Cin-N	0	0	—	1	0	0	0	0	2	2	0	1	0	13.5	4.50	101	.250	.333	0	—	0	-0	-0	0	0.0
1930	Cin-N	3	1	.750	35	3	0	0	0	78¹	86	5	31	47	13.9	4.94	98	.286	.360	4	.235	-0	0	-1	-0	-0.1
1931	Cin-N	11	19	.367	42	33	14	0	0	262¹	273	5	74	95	12.1	3.77	99	.269	.323	13	.149	-3	3	-1	-5	-0.9
1932	Cin-N	13	15	.464	42	27	14	2	2	245	246	8	57	94	11.2	3.27	118	.263	.302	10	.125	-4	17	16	-0	1.3
1933	Cin-N	7	18	.280	34	28	14	4	1	211¹	212	7	54	51	11.5	3.49	97	.263	.312	3	.042	-7	-4	-2	-1	-1.1
1934	Cin-N	7	22	.241	46	31	9	0	3	215²	264	15	84	89	14.8	5.22	78	.297	.362	10	.139	-4	-28	-27	-3	-3.7
1935	Cin-N	5	11	.313	30	20	4	1	0	130	155	14	59	40	15.0	6.23	64	.293	.367	1	.024	-4	-32	-33	-1	-3.7
1936	Cin-N	0	0	—	2	0	0	0	0	4	7	1	0	2	15.8	13.50	28	.368	.368	0	—	0	-4	-4	-0	0.0
	StL-N	5	3	.625	12	5	1	0	1	61²	82	4	9	21	13.7	4.38	90	.314	.344	4	.190	-1	-2	-3	-1	-0.5
	Yr	5	3	.625	14	5	1	0	1	65²	89	5	11	23	13.8	4.93	80	.318	.346	4	.190	-0	-7	-7	-1	-0.5
1937	StL-N	12	12	.500	38	21	12	1	1	192¹	222	14	43	64	12.4	3.32	120	.292	.330	9	.138	5	13	14	-2	1.2
1938	StL-N	0	3	.000	6	3	0	0	0	15²	27	0	6	4	19.0	7.47	53	.380	.429	0	.000	-0	-6	-6	0	-1.0
1940	Phi-N	5	14	.263	42	14	5	0	1	138¹	145	13	42	58	12.3	4.88	80	.268	.323	6	.140	-4	-16	-15	-2	-2.3
1941	Phi-N	5	12	.294	39	21	6	1	2	163¹	207	8	54	80	14.4	4.52	82	.309	.362	7	.149	-4	-16	-15	-1	-1.7
1942	Phi-N	8	19	.296	39	26	10	1	0	195¹	198	6	72	78	12.5	3.69	90	.266	.332	6	.103	-4	-8	-8	-3	-1.7
1943	Phi-N	8	3	.727	21	14	9	1	2	113	110	4	25	46	10.8	3.27	103	.252	.292	6	.182	-0	1	0	-0	0.1
1946	Phi-N	0	0	—	1	0	0	0	0	3	7	1	0	2	21.0	3.00	114	.538	.538	1	1.000	0	0	0	-0	0.0
	Bos-N	6	5	.545	28	12	5	1	1	127	134	8	35	41	12.3	2.76	124	.272	.325	5	.135	-2	9	9	-1	0.5
	Yr	6	5	.545	29	12	5	1	1	130	141	9	35	43	12.5	2.77	124	.279	.330	6	.158	-1	9	10	-1	0.5
1947	Bos-N	6	8	.429	36	10	3	0	2	112²	124	7	34	27	12.7	4.23	92	.275	.327	1	.033	-3	-2	-4	-3	-0.5
Total	17	101	165	.380	492	272	108	13	15	2281¹	2510	120	687	840	12.8	4.09	92	.279	.333	87	.123	-37	-76	-79	-17	-14.1

● SYL JOHNSON
Johnson, Sylvester W (Born Sylvester Johnson)   b: 12/31/1900, Portland, Ore.   d: 2/20/85, Portland, Ore.   BR/TR, 5'11", 180 lbs.   Deb: 4/24/22   C

YEAR	TM/L	W	L	PCT	G	GS	CG	SH	SV	IP	H	HR	BB	SO	RAT	ERA	ERA+	OAV	OOB	BH	AVG	PB	PR	/A	PD	TPI
1922	Det-A	7	3	.700	29	8	3	0	1	97	99	7	30	29	12.3	3.71	105	.273	.336	8	.222	-0	4	2	-2	0.0
1923	Det-A	12	7	.632	37	18	7	0	0	176¹	181	12	47	93	11.8	3.98	97	.274	.325	10	.161	-1	0	-2	-5	-0.8
1924	Det-A	5	4	.556	29	9	2	0	3	104	117	8	42	55	14.2	4.93	83	.287	.360	7	.206	-0	-8	-9	-1	-0.9
1925	Det-A	0	2	.000	9	0	0	0	0	13	11	1	10	5	14.5	3.46	124	.250	.389	0	.000	-1	1	1	0	0.1
1926	StL-N	0	3	.000	19	6	1	0	0	49	54	3	15	10	13.0	4.22	92	.297	.357	0	.000	-2	-2	-1	-1	-0.4
1927	StL-N	0	0	—	3	1	0	0	0	3	2	0	3	2	15.0	6.00	66	.200	.333	0	—	0	-1	-1	0	0.0
1928	*StL-N	8	4	.667	34	6	2	0	3	120	117	13	32	66	11.6	3.90	103	.259	.315	6	.158	-0	1	1	0	0.0
1929	*StL-N	13	7	.650	42	19	12	3	3	182¹	186	11	56	80	12.3	3.60	129	.265	.325	7	.117	-2	23	21	-4	1.4
1930	*StL-N	12	10	.545	32	24	9	2	2	187²	215	13	38	92	12.3	4.65	108	.293	.332	15	.214	-0	7	8	-3	0.4

YEAR TM/L	W	L	PCT	G	GS	CG	SH	SV	IP	H	HR	BB	SO	RAT	ERA	ERA+	OAV	OOB	BH	AVG	PB	PR	/A	PD	TPI
1931 *StL-N	11	9	.550	32	24	12	2	2	186	186	9	29	82	10.5	3.00	131	.255	.286	14	.233	2	18	19	-3	1.8
1932 StL-N	5	14	.263	32	22	7	0	2	164^2	199	14	35	70	13.0	4.92	80	.299	.338	10	.196	-1	-19	-18	-1	-2.0
1933 StL-N	3	3	.500	35	1	0	0	3	84	89	7	16	28	11.6	4.29	81	.271	.311	5	.238	0	-9	-8	-2	-0.7
1934 Cin-N	0	0	—	2	0	0	0	0	6^2	9	2	0	1	12.2	2.70	151	.310	.310	1	.500	1	1	1	-0	0.1
Phi-N	5	9	.357	42	10	4	3	3	133^2	122	14	24	54	9.9	3.50	135	.242	.277	8	.195	-1	8	18	-4	1.4
Yr	5	9	.357	44	10	4	3	3	140^1	131	16	24	54	10.0	3.46	136	.245	.279	9	.209	-1	9	19	-4	1.5
1935 Phi-N	10	8	.556	37	18	8	1	6	174^2	182	15	31	89	11.1	3.56	128	.265	.299	14	.241	1	9	19	-3	1.7
1936 Phi-N	5	7	.417	39	8	1	0	7	111	129	10	29	48	13.1	4.30	106	.288	.335	9	.250	-1	-3	3	-2	0.1
1937 Phi-N	4	10	.286	32	15	4	0	3	138	155	20	22	46	11.7	5.02	86	.288	.318	7	.146	-3	-17	-11	-1	-1.3
1938 Phi-N	2	7	.222	22	6	2	0	0	83	87	4	11	21	10.6	4.23	92	.267	.291	1	.034	-3	-4	-3	-2	-0.8
1939 Phi-N	8	8	.500	22	13	6	0	2	111	112	10	15	37	10.4	3.81	105	.264	.291	5	.152	-1	1	2	-1	0.1
1940 Phi-N	2	2	.500	17	2	2	0	2	40^2	37	6	5	13	9.3	4.20	93	.236	.259		.000	-1	-2	-1	-0	-0.3
Total 19	112	117	.489	542	209	82	11	43	2165^2	2290	173	488	920	11.7	4.06	104	.273	.316	127	.181	-10	8	43	-36	-0.1

● **TOM JOHNSON**   Johnson, Thomas Raymond b: 4/2/51, St.Paul, Minn. BR/TR, 6'1", 185 lbs. Deb: 9/10/74

YEAR TM/L	W	L	PCT	G	GS	CG	SH	SV	IP	H	HR	BB	SO	RAT	ERA	ERA+	OAV	OOB	BH	AVG	PB	PR	/A	PD	TPI
1974 Min-A	2	0	1.000	4	0	0	0	1	7	4	0	4	4	5.1	0.00	—	.167	.167	0	—	0	3	3	-0	1.0
1975 Min-A	1	2	.333	18	0	0	0	3	38^2	40	4	21	17	14.7	4.19	91	.263	.360	0	—	0	-2	-2	0	-0.1
1976 Min-A	3	1	.750	18	1	0	0	0	48^1	44	7	8	37	9.7	2.61	137	.243	.275	0	—	0	5	5	0	0.4
1977 Min-A	16	7	.696	71	0	0	0	15	146^2	152	11	47	87	12.5	3.13	127	.272	.334	0	—	0	15	14	1	2.4
1978 Min-A	1	4	.200	18	0	0	0	3	32^2	42	1	17	21	16.8	5.51	69	.318	.404	0	—	0	-6	-6	0	-1.0
Total 5	23	14	.622	129	1	0	0	22	273^1	282	19	93	166	12.6	3.39	114	.269	.334	0	—	0	15	14	1	2.7

● **VIC JOHNSON**   Johnson, Victor Oscar b: 8/3/20, Eau Claire, Wis. BR/TL, 6', 160 lbs. Deb: 5/3/44

YEAR TM/L	W	L	PCT	G	GS	CG	SH	SV	IP	H	HR	BB	SO	RAT	ERA	ERA+	OAV	OOB	BH	AVG	PB	PR	/A	PD	TPI
1944 Bos-A	0	3	.000	7	5	0	0	0	27^1	42	0	15	7	18.8	6.26	54	.362	.435	0	.000	-1	-9	-9	1	-0.9
1945 Bos-A	6	4	.600	26	9	4	1	2	85^1	90	4	46	21	14.6	4.01	85	.276	.369	5	.167	-1	-6	-6	1	-0.7
1946 Cle-A	0	1	.000	9	1	0	0	0	13^2	20	1	8	3	18.4	9.22	36	.357	.438	0	.000	-0	-9	-9	1	-0.6
Total 3	6	8	.429	42	15	4	1	2	126^1	152	5	69	31	15.9	5.06	67	.305	.392	5	.119	-3	-23	-23	2	-2.2

● **WALTER JOHNSON**   Johnson, Walter Perry "Barney" or "The Big Train" b: 11/6/1887, Humboldt, Kan. d: 12/10/46, Washington, D.C. BR/TR, 6'1", 200 lbs. Deb: 8/2/07 MH♦

YEAR TM/L	W	L	PCT	G	GS	CG	SH	SV	IP	H	HR	BB	SO	RAT	ERA	ERA+	OAV	OOB	BH	AVG	PB	PR	/A	PD	TPI
1907 Was-A	5	9	.357	14	12	11	2	0	110^1	100	1	20	71	10.0	1.88	129	.244	.282	4	.111	-2	8	7	-2	0.4
1908 Was-A	14	14	.500	36	30	23	6	1	256^1	194	0	53	160	9.1	1.65	139	.211	.262	13	.165	3	21	18	-4	2.0
1909 Was-A	13	25	.342	40	36	27	4	1	296^1	247	1	84	164	10.5	2.22	110	.221	.284	13	.129	-3	9	7	-2	0.4
1910 Was-A	25	17	.595	45	42	38	8	1	370	262	1	76	313	8.5	1.36	183	.205	.257	24	.175	1	48	46	-1	5.8
1911 Was-A	25	13	.658	40	37	36	6	1	322^1	292	8	70	207	10.3	1.90	173	.238	.283	30	.234	3	52	50	4	6.4
1912 Was-A	33	12	.733	50	37	34	7	2	369	259	2	76	303	8.6	1.39	240	.196	.248	36	.264	9	79	80	1	11.2
1913 Was-A	36	7	.837	48	36	29	11	2	346	232	9	38	243	7.3	1.14	258	.187	.217	35	.261	10	69	70	0	10.9
1914 Was-A	28	18	.609	51	40	33	9	1	371^2	287	3	74	225	9.0	1.72	164	.217	.265	30	.221	8	42	45	2	7.3
1915 Was-A	27	13	.675	47	39	35	7	4	336^2	258	1	56	203	8.9	1.55	192	.214	.260	34	.231	6	52	53	2	7.7
1916 Was-A	25	20	.556	48	38	36	3	1	369^2	290	0	82	228	9.3	1.90	147	.220	.270	32	.225	8	38	37	-5	5.1
1917 Was-A	23	16	.590	47	34	30	8	3	326	248	3	68	188	9.1	2.21	119	.211	.263	33	.254	10	16	15	-1	3.0
1918 Was-A	23	13	.639	39	29	29	8	3	326	241	2	70	162	8.8	1.27	215	.210	.260	40	.267	6	55	53	-3	7.6
1919 Was-A	20	14	.588	39	29	27	7	2	290^1	235	0	51	147	9.1	1.49	216	.219	.259	24	.192	2	56	56	0	7.2
1920 Was-A	8	10	.444	21	15	12	4	3	143^2	135	1	27	78	10.5	3.13	119	.245	.286	17	.266	4	11	10	-1	1.4
1921 Was-A	17	14	.548	35	32	25	1	1	264	265	7	92	143	12.2	3.51	117	.263	.326	30	.270	4	23	18	-3	2.0
1922 Was-A	15	16	.484	41	31	23	4	4	280	283	8	99	105	12.5	2.99	129	.267	.334	22	.204	-1	33	27	1	2.8
1923 Was-A	17	12	.586	42	34	18	3	4	261	263	9	73	130	12.3	3.48	108	.269	.333	18	.194	1	15	8	-2	0.7
1924 *Was-A	23	7	.767	38	38	20	6	0	277^2	233	10	77	158	10.4	2.72	148	.224	.284	32	.283	7	47	41	-1	4.5
1925 *Was-A	20	7	.741	30	29	16	3	0	229	217	7	78	108	11.9	3.07	138	.250	.317	42	.433	17	34	30	-4	4.3
1926 Was-A	15	16	.484	33	33	22	2	0	260^2	259	13	73	125	11.6	3.63	107	.263	.317	20	.194	1	11	7	-5	0.3
1927 Was-A	5	6	.455	18	15	7	1	0	107^1	113	7	26	48	12.2	5.10	80	.278	.332	6	.348	6	-11	-12	-0	-0.5
Total 21	417	279	.599	802	666	531	110	34	5914^1	4913	97	1363	3509	9.9	2.17	147	.227	.279	547	.235	99	706	668	-23	90.5

● **BILL JOHNSON**   Johnson, William Charles b: 10/6/60, Wilmington, Del. BR/TR, 6'5", 205 lbs. Deb: 9/6/83

YEAR TM/L	W	L	PCT	G	GS	CG	SH	SV	IP	H	HR	BB	SO	RAT	ERA	ERA+	OAV	OOB	BH	AVG	PB	PR	/A	PD	TPI
1983 Chi-N	1	0	1.000	10	0	0	0	0	12^1	17	0	3	4	14.6	4.38	87	.347	.385	0	—	0	-1	-1	0	0.0
1984 Chi-N	0	0	—	4	0	0	0	0	5^1	4	0	1	3	8.4	1.69	232	.235	.278	0	—	0	1	1	0	0.0
Total 2	1	0	1.000	14	0	0	0	0	17^2	21	0	4	7	12.7	3.57	107	.318	.357	0	—	0	0	1	0	0.0

● **JEFF JOHNSON**   Johnson, William Jeffrey b: 8/4/66, Durham, N.C. BR/TL, 6'3", 200 lbs. Deb: 6/5/91

YEAR TM/L	W	L	PCT	G	GS	CG	SH	SV	IP	H	HR	BB	SO	RAT	ERA	ERA+	OAV	OOB	BH	AVG	PB	PR	/A	PD	TPI
1991 NY-A	6	11	.353	23	23	0	0	0	127	156	15	33	62	13.8	5.95	70	.305	.354	0	—	0	-26	-26	-0	-2.8
1992 NY-A	2	3	.400	13	8	0	0	0	52^2	74	4	23	14	16.4	6.66	59	.329	.398	0	—	0	-16	-16	-0	-1.3
1993 NY-A	0	2	.000	2	2	0	0	0	2^2	12	1	2	0	47.3	30.38	14	.600	.636	0	—	0	-8	-8	0	-2.6
Total 3	8	16	.333	38	33	0	0	0	182^1	239	20	58	76	15.1	6.52	63	.320	.375	0	—	0	-50	-49	-1	-6.7

● **JOEL JOHNSTON**   Johnston, Joel Raymond b: 3/8/67, West Chester, Pa. BR/TR, 6'4", 220 lbs. Deb: 9/5/91

YEAR TM/L	W	L	PCT	G	GS	CG	SH	SV	IP	H	HR	BB	SO	RAT	ERA	ERA+	OAV	OOB	BH	AVG	PB	PR	/A	PD	TPI
1991 KC-A	1	0	1.000	13	0	0	0	0	22^1	9	0	9	21	7.3	0.40	1022	.120	.214	0	—	0	9	9	-0	0.3
1992 KC-A	0	0	—	5	0	0	0	0	2^2	3	2	2	0	16.9	13.50	30	.273	.385	0	—	0	-3	-3	-0	-0.2
1993 Pit-N	2	4	.333	33	0	0	0	2	53^1	38	7	19	31	9.6	3.38	120	.203	.277	2	.333	1	4	4	-1	0.5
1994 Pit-N	0	0	—	4	0	0	0	0	3^1	14	0	4	5	54.0	29.70	15	.583	.667	0	—	0	-9	-9	-0	-0.8
1995 Bos-A	0	1	.000	4	0	0	0	0	4	2	1	3	4	13.5	11.25	43	.143	.333	0	—	0	-3	-3	-0	-0.8
Total 5	3	5	.375	59	0	0	0	2	85^2	66	10	37	61	11.1	4.31	96	.212	.302	2	.333	1	-2	-1	-2	-0.2

● **JOHN JOHNSTONE**   Johnstone, John William b: 11/25/68, Liverpool, N.Y. BR/TR, 6'3", 195 lbs. Deb: 9/3/93

YEAR TM/L	W	L	PCT	G	GS	CG	SH	SV	IP	H	HR	BB	SO	RAT	ERA	ERA+	OAV	OOB	BH	AVG	PB	PR	/A	PD	TPI
1993 Fla-N	0	2	.000	7	0	0	0	0	10^2	16	1	7	5	19.4	5.91	73	.340	.426	0	—	0	-2	-2	-0	-0.3
1994 Fla-N	1	2	.333	17	0	0	0	0	21^1	23	4	16	23	16.9	5.91	74	.264	.385	0	—	0	-4	-4	0	-0.4
1995 Fla-N	0	0	—	4	0	0	0	0	4^2	7	1	2	3	17.4	3.86	109	.333	.391	0	—	0	0	0	0	0.0
1996 Hou-N	1	0	1.000	9	0	0	0	0	13	17	2	5	5	15.2	5.54	69	.321	.379	0	—	0	-2	-2	-0	-0.2
Total 4	2	4	.333	37	0	0	0	0	49^2	63	8	30	36	17.0	5.62	75	.303	.393	0	—	0	-8	-8	-0	-0.9

● **ROY JOINER**   Joiner, Roy Merrill "Pop" b: 10/30/06, Red Bluff, Cal. d: 12/26/89, Red Bluff, Cal. BL/TL, 6', 170 lbs. Deb: 4/30/34

YEAR TM/L	W	L	PCT	G	GS	CG	SH	SV	IP	H	HR	BB	SO	RAT	ERA	ERA+	OAV	OOB	BH	AVG	PB	PR	/A	PD	TPI
1934 Chi-N	0	1	.000	20	2	0	0	0	34	61	3	9	9	18.3	8.21	47	.391	.421	2	.200	-0	-16	-16	-0	-0.5
1935 Chi-N	0	0	—	2	0	0	0	0	3^1	6	0	2	0	21.6	5.40	73	.429	.500	0	.000	-0	-1	-1	0	0.0
1940 NY-N	3	2	.600	30	2	0	0	1	53	66	8	17	25	14.9	3.40	114	.308	.373	3	.273	1	3	3	0	0.3
Total 3	3	3	.500	52	4	0	0	1	90^1	133	11	27	34	16.4	5.28	74	.346	.397	5	.227		-13	-14	0	-0.2

● **DAVE JOLLY**   Jolly, David "Gabby" b: 10/14/24, Stony Point, N.C. d: 5/27/63, Durham, N.C. BR/TR, 6', 165 lbs. Deb: 5/9/53

YEAR TM/L	W	L	PCT	G	GS	CG	SH	SV	IP	H	HR	BB	SO	RAT	ERA	ERA+	OAV	OOB	BH	AVG	PB	PR	/A	PD	TPI
1953 Mil-N	0	0	—	24	0	0	0	0	38^1	34	4	27	23	14.6	3.52	111	.239	.365	1	.500		3	2	0	0.1
1954 Mil-N	11	6	.647	47	1	0	0	10	111^1	87	6	64	62	12.4	2.43	154	.215	.326	9	.290	3	20	16	0	3.0
1955 Mil-N	2	3	.400	36	0	0	0	5	58^1	58	6	15	23	17.0	5.71	66	.258	.397	1	.167	0	-11	-13	1	-0.9
1956 Mil-N	2	3	.400	29	0	0	0	7	45^2	39	5	35	20	14.6	3.74	92	.238	.372	0	.000	-0	-1	-1	-1	-0.3
1957 Mil-N	1	1	.500	23	0	0	0	1	37^2	37	4	21	27	14.6	5.02	70	.264	.372	3	.600	1	-5	-6	-0	-0.2
Total 5	16	14	.533	159	1	0	0	19	291^1	255	27	198	155	14.2	3.77	98	.236	.357	14	.292	5	8	-3	0	1.7

● **COWBOY JONES**   Jones, Albert Edward "Bronco" b: 8/23/1874, Golden, Colo. d: 2/9/58, Inglewood, Cal. BL/TL, 5'11", 160 lbs. Deb: 6/24/1898

YEAR TM/L	W	L	PCT	G	GS	CG	SH	SV	IP	H	HR	BB	SO	RAT	ERA	ERA+	OAV	OOB	BH	AVG	PB	PR	/A	PD	TPI
1898 Cle-N	4	4	.500	9	9	7	0	0	72	74	0	29	26	13.6	3.00	121	.269	.345	2	.071	-3	5	5	-2	0.0
1899 StL-N	6	5	.545	12	12	9	0	0	85^1	111	1	22	28	14.7	3.59	111	.314	.384	5	.172	0	3	4	0	0.6
1900 StL-N	13	19	.406	39	36	29	3	0	292^2	334	10	82	68	13.4	3.57	102	.286	.343	21	.179	-3	4	2	5	0.4
1901 StL-N	2	6	.250	10	9	7	0	0	76^1	99	0	22	25	14.4	4.48	71	.307	.358	4	.148	0	-10	-11	2	-0.8
Total 4	25	34	.424	70	66	52	3	0	526^1	618	11	155	147	13.8	3.63	100	.292	.349	32	.159	0	2	-0	6	0.2

● **ALEX JONES**   Jones, Alexander b: 12/25/1869, Pittsburgh, Pa. d: 4/4/41, Woodville, Pa. BL/TL, 5'6", 135 lbs. Deb: 9/25/1889

YEAR TM/L	W	L	PCT	G	GS	CG	SH	SV	IP	H	HR	BB	SO	RAT	ERA	ERA+	OAV	OOB	BH	AVG	PB	PR	/A	PD	TPI
1889 Pit-N	1	0	1.000	1	1	1	0	0	9	7	0	1	10	8.0	3.00	125	.206	.229	1	.200	0	1	1	0	0.1

YEAR	TM/L	W	L	PCT	G	GS	CG	SH	SV	IP	H	HR	BB	SO	RAT	ERA	ERA+	OAV	OOB	BH	AVG	PB	PR	/A	PD	TPI
1892	Lou-N	5	11	.313	18	16	13	1	0	146²	130	3	56	44	12.0	3.31	93	.228	.307	8	.145	-1	-0	-4	2	-0.3
	Was-N	0	3	.000	4	4	3	0	0	27	33	0	14	7	16.3	4.00	81	.289	.377	3	.273	-0	-2	-2	-1	-0.2
	Yr	5	14	.263	22	20	16	1	0	173²	163	3	70	51	12.2	3.42	91	.235	.307	11	.167	-1	-3	-6	1	-0.5
1894	Phi-N	1	0	1.000	1	1	1	0	0	9	10	0	2	2	10.0	2.00	255	.278	.278	1	.250	-0	3	3	0	0.2
1903	Det-A	0	1	.000	2	2	0	0	0	8²	19	0	6	2	26.0	12.46	23	.432	.500	0	.000	-1	-9	-9	-0	-0.8
Total 4		7	15	.318	26	24	18	1	0	200¹	199	3	77	65	12.9	3.73	86	.249	.324	13	.165	-2	-7	-12	1	-1.0

● **AL JONES**   Jones, Alfornia   b: 2/10/59, Charleston, Miss.   BR/TR, 6'4", 210 lbs.   Deb: 8/6/83

YEAR	TM/L	W	L	PCT	G	GS	CG	SH	SV	IP	H	HR	BB	SO	RAT	ERA	ERA+	OAV	OOB	BH	AVG	PB	PR	/A	PD	TPI
1983	Chi-A	0	0	—	2	0	0	0	0	2¹	3	0	2	2	19.3	3.86	109	.375	.500	0	—	0	0	0	-0	0.0
1984	Chi-A	1	1	.500	20	0	0	0	5	20¹	23	3	11	15	15.5	4.43	94	.299	.393	0	—	0	-1	-1	0	-0.3
1985	Chi-A	1	0	1.000	5	0	0	0	0	6	3	0	3	2	9.0	1.50	288	.167	.286	0	—	0	2	2	0	0.3
Total 3		2	1	.667	27	0	0	0	5	28²	29	3	16	19	14.4	3.77	111	.282	.383	0	—	0	1	1	0	0.0

● **ART JONES**   Jones, Arthur Lennox   b: 2/7/06, Kershaw, S.C.   d: 11/25/80, Columbia, S.C.   BR/TR, 6', 165 lbs.   Deb: 4/23/32

YEAR	TM/L	W	L	PCT	G	GS	CG	SH	SV	IP	H	HR	BB	SO	RAT	ERA	ERA+	OAV	OOB	BH	AVG	PB	PR	/A	PD	TPI
1932	Bro-N	0	0	—	1	0	0	0	0	1	2	0	1	0	27.0	18.00	21	.667	.750	—	0	-2	-2	0	0.0

● **BARRY JONES**   Jones, Barry Louis   b: 2/15/63, Centerville, Ind.   BR/TR, 6'4", 225 lbs.   Deb: 7/18/86

YEAR	TM/L	W	L	PCT	G	GS	CG	SH	SV	IP	H	HR	BB	SO	RAT	ERA	ERA+	OAV	OOB	BH	AVG	PB	PR	/A	PD	TPI
1986	Pit-N	3	4	.429	26	0	0	0	3	37¹	29	3	21	29	12.1	2.89	132	.215	.321	1	.200		3	4	1	0.8
1987	Pit-N	2	4	.333	32	0	0	0	1	43¹	55	6	23	28	16.2	5.61	73	.314	.394	0	.000	-0	-7	-7	0	-0.9
1988	Pit-N	1	1	.500	42	0	0	0	2	56¹	57	3	21	31	12.6	3.04	112	.271	.341	0	.000		3	2	0	0.0
	Chi-A	2	2	.500	17	0	0	0	1	26	15	3	17	17	11.1	2.42	164	.170	.305	0	—		4	4	0	0.7
1989	Chi-A	3	2	.600	22	0	0	0	1	30¹	22	2	8	17	9.2	2.37	160	.208	.270	0	—		5	5	1	0.9
1990	Chi-A	11	4	.733	65	0	0	0	1	74	62	6	33	45	11.7	2.31	165	.235	.322	0	—		13	12	2	2.7
1991	Mon-N	4	9	.308	**77**	0	0	0	13	88²	76	8	33	46	11.2	3.35	108	.246	.321	0	.000		3	3	1	0.5
1992	Phi-N	5	6	.455	44	0	0	0	1	54¹	65	3	24	19	15.1	4.64	75	.305	.381	0	.000		-7	-7	-1	-1.3
	NY-N	2	0	1.000	17	0	0	0	1	15¹	20	0	11	11	18.2	9.39	37	.317	.419	0	—		-10	-10	-0	-1.3
	Yr	7	6	.538	61	0	0	0	2	69²	85	3	35	30	15.5	5.68	61	.304	.381	0	.000		-17	-17	-1	-2.6
1993	Chi-A	0	1	.000	6	0	0	0	0	7¹	14	2	3	7	20.9	8.59	49	.412	.459	0	—		-3	-4	-0	-0.3
Total 8		33	33	.500	348	0	0	0	23	433	415	32	194	250	12.8	3.66	102	.260	.342	1	.063	-1	4	3	5	1.8

● **CALVIN JONES**   Jones, Calvin Douglas   b: 9/26/63, Compton, Cal.   BR/TR, 6'3", 185 lbs.   Deb: 6/14/91

YEAR	TM/L	W	L	PCT	G	GS	CG	SH	SV	IP	H	HR	BB	SO	RAT	ERA	ERA+	OAV	OOB	BH	AVG	PB	PR	/A	PD	TPI
1991	Sea-A	2	2	.500	27	0	0	0	2	46¹	33	0	29	42	12.2	2.53	163	.209	.335	0	—	0	8	8	0	0.7
1992	Sea-A	3	5	.375	38	1	0	0	0	61²	50	8	47	49	14.4	5.69	70	.226	.367	0	—	0	-12	-12	-0	-1.4
Total 2		5	7	.417	65	1	0	0	2	108	83	8	76	91	13.5	4.33	93	.219	.354	0	—	0	-4	-4	0	-0.7

● **DEACON JONES**   Jones, Carroll Elmer   b: 12/20/1892, Arcadia, Kan.   d: 12/28/52, Pittsburg, Kan.   BR/TR, 6'1", 174 lbs.   Deb: 9/23/16

YEAR	TM/L	W	L	PCT	G	GS	CG	SH	SV	IP	H	HR	BB	SO	RAT	ERA	ERA+	OAV	OOB	BH	AVG	PB	PR	/A	PD	TPI
1916	Det-A	0	0	—	1	0	0	0	0	7	7	0	5	2	15.4	2.57	111	.269	.387	0	.000		0	0	-0	0.0
1917	Det-A	4	4	.500	24	6	2	0	0	77	69	0	26	28	11.8	2.92	91	.246	.334	0	.000	-1	-2	-2	1	-0.2
1918	Det-A	3	1	.750	21	4	1	0	0	67	60	0	38	15	13.3	3.09	86	.244	.347	5	.185	-1	-2	-3	1	-0.1
Total 3		7	5	.583	46	10	3	0	0	151	136	0	69	45	12.6	2.98	89	.251	.343	5	.114	-2	-4	-5	2	-0.3

● **BUMPUS JONES**   Jones, Charles Leander   b: 1/1/1870, Cedarville, Ohio   d: 6/25/38, Xenia, Ohio   BR/TR,   Deb: 10/15/1892

YEAR	TM/L	W	L	PCT	G	GS	CG	SH	SV	IP	H	HR	BB	SO	RAT	ERA	ERA+	OAV	OOB	BH	AVG	PB	PR	/A	PD	TPI
1892	Cin-N	1	0	1.000	1	1	1	0	0	9	0	0	4	3	4.0	0.00	—	.000	.129	0	.000	-0	3	3	-1	0.3
1893	Cin-N	1	3	.250	6	5	2	0	0	28²	37	1	23	6	20.4	10.05	48	.303	.433	4	.250	1	-17	-17	-1	-1.5
	NY-N	0	1	.000	1	1	0	0	0	4	5	0	10	1	36.0	11.25	41	.294	.571	0	—		-3	-3	1	-0.4
	Yr	1	4	.200	7	6	2	0	0	32²	42	1	33	7	20.9	10.19	47	.295	.427	4	.250	1	-20	-20	-0	-1.9
Total 2		2	4	.333	8	7	3	0	0	41²	42	1	37	10	18.4	7.99	56	.253	.407	4	.222	1	-17	-16	-1	-1.6

● **CHARLEY JONES**   Jones, Charles Wesley "Baby" (b: Benjamin Wesley Rippay)   b: 4/30/1850, Alamance Co., N.C.   BR/TR, 5'11.5", 202 lbs.   Deb: 5/4/1875   U♦

YEAR	TM/L	W	L	PCT	G	GS	CG	SH	SV	IP	H	HR	BB	SO	RAT	ERA	ERA+	OAV	OOB	BH	AVG	PB	PR	/A	PD	TPI
1887	NY-a	0	0	—	2	0	0	0	0	4	2	0	4	0	18.0	3.00	142	.286	.545	63	.255		0	0	-0	0.0

● **DALE JONES**   Jones, Dale Eldon "Nubs"   b: 12/17/18, Marquette, Neb.   d: 11/8/80, Orlando, Fla.   BR/TR, 6'1", 172 lbs.   Deb: 9/7/41

YEAR	TM/L	W	L	PCT	G	GS	CG	SH	SV	IP	H	HR	BB	SO	RAT	ERA	ERA+	OAV	OOB	BH	AVG	PB	PR	/A	PD	TPI
1941	Phi-N	0	1	.000	2	1	0	0	0	8¹	13	0	6	2	20.5	7.56	49	.342	.432	1	.333	0	-4	-4	-1	-0.4

● **JACK JONES**   Jones, Daniel Albion "Jumping Jack"   b: 10/23/1860, Litchfield, Conn.   d: 10/19/36, Wallingford, Conn.   TR,   Deb: 7/9/1883

YEAR	TM/L	W	L	PCT	G	GS	CG	SH	SV	IP	H	HR	BB	SO	RAT	ERA	ERA+	OAV	OOB	BH	AVG	PB	PR	/A	PD	TPI
1883	Det-N	6	5	.545	12	12	9	1	0	92²	103	0	19	33	11.8	3.50	89	.259	.293	8	.190	-2	-4	-4	-2	-0.6
	Phi-a	5	2	.714	7	7	7	0	0	65	58	1	6	28	8.9	2.63	132	.223	.241	6	.240	0	6	6	-0	0.5
Total 1		11	7	.611	19	19	16	1	0	157²	161	1	25	61	10.6	3.14	104	.245	.273	14	.209	-1	1	2	-2	-0.1

● **DICK JONES**   Jones, Decatur Poindexter   b: 5/22/02, Meadville, Miss.   d: 8/2/94, Burlingame, Cal.   BL/TR, 6', 184 lbs.   Deb: 9/11/26

YEAR	TM/L	W	L	PCT	G	GS	CG	SH	SV	IP	H	HR	BB	SO	RAT	ERA	ERA+	OAV	OOB	BH	AVG	PB	PR	/A	PD	TPI
1926	Was-A	2	1	.667	4	3	1	0	0	21	20	0	11	3	13.3	4.29	90	.263	.356	2	.200		-1	-1	0	-0.1
1927	Was-A	0	0	—	2	0	0	0	0	3¹	8	0	5	1	35.1	21.60	19	.444	.565	0	—		-6	-6	-0	0.0
Total 2		2	1	.667	6	3	1	0	0	24¹	28	0	16	4	16.6	6.66	58	.298	.400	2	.200		-7	-7	-0	-0.1

● **DOUG JONES**   Jones, Douglas Reid   b: 6/24/57, Lebanon, Ind.   BR/TR, 6'3", 195 lbs.   Deb: 4/9/82

YEAR	TM/L	W	L	PCT	G	GS	CG	SH	SV	IP	H	HR	BB	SO	RAT	ERA	ERA+	OAV	OOB	BH	AVG	PB	PR	/A	PD	TPI
1982	Mil-A	0	0	—	4	0	0	0	0	2²	5	1	1	1	20.3	10.13	37	.385	.429	0	—	0	-2	-2	0	0.0
1986	Cle-A	1	0	1.000	11	0	0	0	1	18	18	0	6	12	12.5	2.50	166	.257	.325	0	—	0	3	3	0	0.2
1987	Cle-A	6	5	.545	49	0	0	0	8	91¹	101	4	24	87	12.9	3.15	148	.281	.336	0	—	0	13	14	1	1.8
1988	Cle-A★	3	4	.429	51	0	0	0	37	83¹	69	1	16	72	9.4	2.27	181	.218	.260	0	—	0	16	17	0	2.8
1989	Cle-A★	7	10	.412	59	0	0	0	32	80²	76	4	13	65	10.0	2.34	169	.251	.284	0	—	0	14	14	1	4.0
1990	Cle-A☆	5	5	.500	66	0	0	0	43	84¹	66	5	22	55	9.6	2.56	153	.218	.275	0	—	0	13	13	1	4.0
1991	Cle-A	4	8	.333	36	4	0	0	7	63¹	87	7	17	48	14.8	5.54	75	.320	.360	0	—	0	-10	-10	-1	-1.8
1992	Hou-N★	11	8	.579	80	0	0	0	36	111²	96	5	17	93	9.5	1.85	181	.235	.274	0	.000	-0	20	19	1	4.2
1993	Hou-N	4	10	.286	71	0	0	0	26	85¹	102	7	21	66	13.5	4.54	85	.300	.348	0	—	0	-5	-6	-0	-1.3
1994	Phi-N★	2	4	.333	47	0	0	0	27	54	55	2	6	38	10.2	2.17	198	.255	.275	1	1.000	0	12	**13**	1	2.5
1995	Bal-A	0	4	.000	52	0	0	0	22	46²	55	6	16	42	14.1	5.01	95	.286	.348	0	—	0	-2	-1	0	-0.3
1996	Chi-N	2	2	.500	28	0	0	0	2	32¹	41	4	7	26	13.6	5.01	85	.306	.345	0	—	0	-3	-4	-0	-0.4
	Mil-A	5	0	1.000	24	0	0	0	1	31²	31	3	13	34	13.1	3.41	154	.254	.336	0	—	0	6	7	0	0.9
Total 12		50	60	.455	578	4	0	0	242	785¹	802	49	179	639	11.6	3.21	127	.263	.309	1	.200	-0	76	77	4	15.0

● **EARL JONES**   Jones, Earl Leslie "Lefty"   b: 6/11/19, Fresno, Cal.   d: 1/24/89, Fresno, Cal.   BL/TL, 5'10.5", 190 lbs.   Deb: 7/6/45

YEAR	TM/L	W	L	PCT	G	GS	CG	SH	SV	IP	H	HR	BB	SO	RAT	ERA	ERA+	OAV	OOB	BH	AVG	PB	PR	/A	PD	TPI
1945	StL-A	0	0	—	10	0	0	0	1	28¹	18	0	18	13	11.4	2.54	139	.184	.310	2	.200	1	3	3	-1	0.1

● **ELIJAH JONES**   Jones, Elijah Albert "Bumpus"   b: 1/27/1882, Oxford, Mich.   d: 4/29/43, Pontiac, Mich.   BR/TR, 5'11.5",   Deb: 4/13/07

YEAR	TM/L	W	L	PCT	G	GS	CG	SH	SV	IP	H	HR	BB	SO	RAT	ERA	ERA+	OAV	OOB	BH	AVG	PB	PR	/A	PD	TPI
1907	Det-A	0	1	.000	4	1	1	0	1	16	23	0	4	9	15.8	5.06	51	.359	.384	0	—	-1	-4	-4	-0	-0.4
1909	Det-A	1	1	.500	2	2	1	0	0	10	10	0	3	2	9.0	2.70	93	.278	.278	1	.250	-0	-0	-1	-1	-0.1
Total 2		1	2	.333	6	3	1	0	1	26	33	0	7	11	13.2	4.15	62	.317	.349	1	.125	-1	-5	-5	-1	-0.5

● **GARY JONES**   Jones, Gareth Howell   b: 6/12/45, Huntington Park, Cal.   BL/TL, 6', 191 lbs.   Deb: 9/25/70   F

YEAR	TM/L	W	L	PCT	G	GS	CG	SH	SV	IP	H	HR	BB	SO	RAT	ERA	ERA+	OAV	OOB	BH	AVG	PB	PR	/A	PD	TPI
1970	NY-A	0	0	—	2	0	0	0	0	2	3	0	1	2	18.0	0.00	—	.375	.444	0	—		1	1	-0	0.0
1971	NY-A	0	0	—	12	0	0	0	0	14	19	1	7	10	16.7	9.00	36	.317	.388	0	.000		-9	-9	-0	0.0
Total 2		0	0	—	14	0	0	0	0	16	22	1	8	12	16.9	7.88	41	.324	.395	0	.000		-8	-8	-0	0.0

● **GORDON JONES**   Jones, Gordon Bassett   b: 4/2/30, Portland, Ore.   d: 4/25/94, Lodi, Cal.   BR/TR, 6', 190 lbs.   Deb: 8/6/54   C

YEAR	TM/L	W	L	PCT	G	GS	CG	SH	SV	IP	H	HR	BB	SO	RAT	ERA	ERA+	OAV	OOB	BH	AVG	PB	PR	/A	PD	TPI
1954	StL-N	4	4	.500	11	10	4	2	0	81	78	3	19	48	10.9	2.00	206	.248	.293	3	.125	-1	19	19	-0	1.7
1955	StL-N	1	4	.200	15	9	0	0	0	57	66	10	28	46	15.0	5.84	70	.286	.365	1	.071	-1	-11	-11	-1	-1.1
1956	StL-N	2	0	1.000	11	1	0	0	0	11¹	14	2	5	5	15.1	5.56	68	.311	.380	0	—	-0	-2	-2	-0	-0.4
1957	NY-N	1	0	1.000	10	0	0	0	0	11²	16	1	4	5	15.4	6.17	64	.320	.370	1	.500	-0	-3	-3	-1	-0.2
1958	SF-N	3	1	.750	10	3	0	0	0	30¹	32	3	5	18	11.6	2.37	161	.284	.320	0	.000	-0	5	5	-1	0.6
1959	SF-N	2	3	.600	31	0	0	0	0	43²	42	5	19	29	13.4	4.33	88	.280	.359	0	.000	-0	-2	-3	-0	-0.1
1960	Bal-A	1	1	.500	29	0	0	0	2	55	49	3	13	30	11.9	4.42	86	.281	.326	2	.400	-0	-3	-4	-0	-0.1
1961	Bal-A	0	0	—	3	0	0	0	0	5	5	3	0	4	9.0	5.40	71	.250	.250	—	PB	-1	-1	-1	-0	-0.3
1962	KC-A	3	2	.600	21	0	0	0	6	32²	31	10	14	28	12.4	6.34	67	.252	.328	0	—	-0	-9	-8	-0	-1.4

YEAR	TM/L	W	L	PCT	G	GS	CG	SH	SV	IP	H	HR	BB	SO	RAT	ERA	ERA+	OAV	OOB	BH	AVG	PB	PR	/A	PD	TPI
1964	Hou-N	0	1	.000	34	0	0	0	0	50	58	3	14	28	13.0	4.14	83	.290	.336	1	.250	0	-3	-4	-0	-0.1
1965	Hou-N	0	0	—	1	0	0	0	0	1	0	0	0	0	0.0	0.00	—	.000	.000	0	—	0	0	-0	-0	0.0
Total	11	15	18	.455	171	21	4	2	12	378²	405	49	120	232	12.6	4.16	94	.275	.332	8	.119	-3	-10	-11	-2	-1.4

● **HENRY JONES** Jones, Henry b: Pittsburgh, Pa. Deb: 4/22/1890

YEAR	TM/L	W	L	PCT	G	GS	CG	SH	SV	IP	H	HR	BB	SO	RAT	ERA	ERA+	OAV	OOB	BH	AVG	PB	PR	/A	PD	TPI
1890	Pit-N	2	1	.667	5	4	2	0	0	31	35	1	14	13	14.2	3.48	95	.276	.348	2	.222	-0		-1	-1	-0.1

● **JIMMY JONES** Jones, James Condia b: 4/20/64, Dallas, Tex. BR/TR, 6'2", 190 lbs. Deb: 9/21/86

YEAR	TM/L	W	L	PCT	G	GS	CG	SH	SV	IP	H	HR	BB	SO	RAT	ERA	ERA+	OAV	OOB	BH	AVG	PB	PR	/A	PD	TPI
1986	SD-N	2	0	1.000	3	3	1	1	0	18	10	1	3	15	6.5	2.50	146	.164	.203	1	.167	-0	2	2	-0	0.2
1987	SD-N	9	7	.563	30	22	2	1	0	145²	154	14	54	51	13.2	4.14	96	.270	.339	8	.163	1	-1	-3	1	0.0
1988	SD-N	9	14	.391	29	29	3	0	0	179	192	14	44	82	12.0	4.12	82	.277	.323	9	.164	2	-13	-14	1	-1.4
1989	NY-A	2	1	.667	11	6	0	0	0	48	56	7	16	25	13.9	5.25	74	.293	.354	0	—	0	-7	-7	1	-0.3
1990	NY-A	1	2	.333	17	7	0	0	0	50	72	8	23	25	17.3	6.30	63	.344	.412	0	—	0	-13	-13	-1	-0.8
1991	Hou-N	6	8	.429	26	22	1	1	0	135¹	143	9	51	88	13.1	4.39	80	.270	.337	7	.184	2	-11	-13	-1	-1.0
1992	Hou-N	10	6	.625	25	23	0	0	0	139¹	135	13	39	69	11.6	4.07	83	.258	.315	6	.167	2	-9	-11	-1	-1.1
1993	Mon-N	4	1	.800	12	6	0	0	0	39²	47	6	9	21	12.7	6.35	66	.285	.322	1	.111	0	-10	-10	-0	-1.0
Total	8	43	39	.524	153	118	7	3	0	755	809	72	239	376	12.7	4.46	81	.275	.333	32	.166	7	-62	-69	3	-5.4

● **JIM JONES** Jones, James Tilford "Sheriff" b: 12/25/1876, London, Ky. d: 5/6/53, London, Ky. BR/TR, 5'10", 162 lbs. Deb: 6/29/1897 ♦

YEAR	TM/L	W	L	PCT	G	GS	CG	SH	SV	IP	H	HR	BB	SO	RAT	ERA	ERA+	OAV	OOB	BH	AVG	PB	PR	/A	PD	TPI
1897	Lou-N	0	0	—	1	0	0	0	0	6²	19	1	5	0	35.1	18.90	23	.500	.578	1	.250	1	-11	-11	-0	0.0
1901	NY-N	0	1	.000	1	1	0	0	0	5	6	0	2	3	14.4	10.80	31	.300	.364	19	.209	0	-4	-4	0	-0.5
Total	2	0	1	.000	2	1	0	0	0	11²	25	1	7	3	26.2	15.43	25	.431	.507	79	.230	1	-15	-15	-0	-0.5

● **JEFF JONES** Jones, Jeffrey Allen b: 7/29/56, Detroit, Mich. BR/TR, 6'3", 210 lbs. Deb: 4/10/80

YEAR	TM/L	W	L	PCT	G	GS	CG	SH	SV	IP	H	HR	BB	SO	RAT	ERA	ERA+	OAV	OOB	BH	AVG	PB	PR	/A	PD	TPI
1980	Oak-A	1	3	.250	35	0	0	0	5	44¹	32	4	26	34	12.0	2.84	133	.204	.321	0		0	6	5	1	0.6
1981	*Oak-A	4	1	.800	33	0	0	0	3	61	51	7	40	43	13.9	3.39	102	.233	.359	0		0	2	1	-1	0.4
1982	Oak-A	3	1	.750	18	2	0	0	0	37	44	6	26	18	17.3	5.11	76	.306	.415	0		0	-4	-5	-0	-0.5
1983	Oak-A	1	1	.500	13	1	0	0	0	29²	43	7	8	14	16.1	5.76	67	.339	.387	0		0	-6	-6	-0	-0.4
1984	Oak-A	0	3	.000	13	0	0	0	0	33	31	4	12	19	11.7	3.55	106	.258	.326	0		0	2	1	-0	0.4
Total	5	9	9	.500	112	3	0	0	8	205	201	26	112	128	14.2	3.95	94	.262	.361	0		0	-1	-5	-0	0.1

● **BROADWAY JONES** Jones, Jesse Frank b: 11/15/1898, Millsboro, Del. d: 9/7/77, Lewes, Del. BR/TR, 5'9", 154 lbs. Deb: 7/4/23

YEAR	TM/L	W	L	PCT	G	GS	CG	SH	SV	IP	H	HR	BB	SO	RAT	ERA	ERA+	OAV	OOB	BH	AVG	PB	PR	/A	PD	TPI
1923	Phi-N	0	0	—	3	0	0	0	0	8	5	0	7	1	13.5	9.00	51	.185	.353	1	.500		-4	-4	-0	-0.2

● **JOHNNY JONES** Jones, John Paul "Admiral" b: 8/25/1892, Arcadia, La. d: 6/5/80, Ruston, La. BR/TR, 6'1", 151 lbs. Deb: 4/24/19

YEAR	TM/L	W	L	PCT	G	GS	CG	SH	SV	IP	H	HR	BB	SO	RAT	ERA	ERA+	OAV	OOB	BH	AVG	PB	PR	/A	PD	TPI
1919	NY-N	0	0	—	2	0	0	0	0	6²	9	0	3	3	17.6	5.40	52	.310	.394	0	.000	-0	-2	-2	-0	-0.1
1920	Bos-N	1	0	1.000	3	1	0	0	0	9²	16	1	5	6	19.6	6.52	47	.372	.438	1	.250	1	-4	-4	0	-0.3
Total	2	1	0	1.000	5	1	0	0	0	16¹	25	1	8	9	18.7	6.06	49	.347	.420	1	.143	1	-5	-6	0	-0.4

● **STACY JONES** Jones, Joseph Stacy b: 5/26/67, Gadsden, Ala. BR/TR, 6'6", 225 lbs. Deb: 7/30/91

YEAR	TM/L	W	L	PCT	G	GS	CG	SH	SV	IP	H	HR	BB	SO	RAT	ERA	ERA+	OAV	OOB	BH	AVG	PB	PR	/A	PD	TPI
1991	Bal-A	0	0	—	4	1	0	0	0	11	11	1	5	10	13.1	4.09	97	.256	.333	0		0	1	1	-0	0.3
1996	Chi-A	0	0	—	2	0	0	0	0	2	0	0	1	1	4.5	0.00	—	.000	.143	0		0	1	1	-0	0.0
Total	2	0	0	—	6	1	0	0	0	13	11	1	6	11	11.8	3.46	118	.224	.309	0		0	1	1	0	0.3

● **KEN JONES** Jones, Kenneth Frederick "Broadway" b: 4/13/03, Dover, N.J. d: 5/15/91, Hartford, Conn. BR/TR, 6'3", 193 lbs. Deb: 5/19/24

YEAR	TM/L	W	L	PCT	G	GS	CG	SH	SV	IP	H	HR	BB	SO	RAT	ERA	ERA+	OAV	OOB	BH	AVG	PB	PR	/A	PD	TPI
1924	Det-A	0	0	—	1	0	0	0	0	2	1	0	1	0	9.0	0.00	—	.143	.250	0		0	1	1	-0	0.0
1930	Bos-N	0	1	.000	8	1	0	0	0	19²	28	1	4	4	14.6	5.95	83	.359	.390	1	.200	-0	-2	-2	-0	-0.1
Total	2	0	1	.000	9	1	0	0	0	21²	29	1	5	4	14.1	5.40	90	.341	.378	1	.200	-0	-1	-1	0	-0.1

● **MIKE JONES** Jones, Michael b: 7/6/1865, Hamilton, Ont., Canada d: 3/24/1894, Hamilton, Ont., Canada BL/TL, 5'11.5", 168 lbs. Deb: 8/12/1890

YEAR	TM/L	W	L	PCT	G	GS	CG	SH	SV	IP	H	HR	BB	SO	RAT	ERA	ERA+	OAV	OOB	BH	AVG	PB	PR	/A	PD	TPI
1890	Lou-a	2	0	1.000	3	3	2	0	0	22	21	2	9	6	12.3	3.27	118	.244	.316	4	.444	2	1	1	-0	0.2

● **MIKE JONES** Jones, Michael Carl b: 7/30/59, Penfield, N.Y. BL/TL, 6'6", 215 lbs. Deb: 9/6/80

YEAR	TM/L	W	L	PCT	G	GS	CG	SH	SV	IP	H	HR	BB	SO	RAT	ERA	ERA+	OAV	OOB	BH	AVG	PB	PR	/A	PD	TPI
1980	KC-A	0	1	.000	3	1	0	0	0	4²	6	0	5	2	21.2	11.57	35	.333	.478	0		0	-4	-4	-0	-0.7
1981	*KC-A	6	3	.667	12	11	0	0	0	75²	74	7	28	29	12.4	3.21	112	.256	.326	0		0	4	3	-0	0.4
1984	*KC-A	2	3	.400	23	12	0	0	0	81	86	10	36	43	13.7	4.89	82	.270	.346	0		0	-8	-8	-1	-0.5
1985	KC-A	3	3	.500	33	1	0	0	0	64	62	6	39	32	14.2	4.78	87	.257	.361	0		0	-5	-4	-0	-0.4
Total	4	11	10	.524	71	25	0	0	0	225¹	228	23	108	106	13.5	4.43	88	.263	.347	0		0	-13	-13	-1	-1.2

● **ODELL JONES** Jones, Odell b: 1/13/53, Tulare, Cal. BR/TR, 6'3", 175 lbs. Deb: 9/11/75

YEAR	TM/L	W	L	PCT	G	GS	CG	SH	SV	IP	H	HR	BB	SO	RAT	ERA	ERA+	OAV	OOB	BH	AVG	PB	PR	/A	PD	TPI
1975	Pit-N	0	0	—	3	0	0	0	0	6	0	0	0	2	3.0	0.00	—	.100	.100	0		0	1	1	-0	0.1
1977	Pit-N	3	7	.300	34	15	1	0	0	108	118	14	31	66	12.7	5.08	78	.278	.332	4	.143	-1	-14	-13	-2	-1.4
1978	Pit-N	2	0	1.000	3	1	0	0	0	9	7	0	4	10	11.0	2.00	185	.206	.289	0	.000	-0	2	2	-0	0.4
1979	Sea-A	3	11	.214	25	19	3	0	0	118²	151	16	58	72	16.1	6.07	72	.317	.395	0	—	-0	-24	-23	-2	-2.4
1981	Pit-N	4	5	.444	13	8	0	0	0	54¹	51	3	20	36	12.3	3.31	108	.250	.326	2	.200	-0	1	0	-0	0.3
1983	Tex-A	3	6	.333	42	6	0	0	10	67	56	4	22	50	10.7	3.09	130	.223	.313	0		0	7	7	-1	1.0
1984	Tex-A	2	4	.333	33	4	0	0	2	59¹	62	6	23	28	13.2	3.64	114	.281	.354	0		0	2	3	1	0.3
1986	Bal-A	2	2	.500	21	0	0	0	0	49¹	58	4	23	32	14.8	3.83	108	.305	.380	0		0	2	2	0	0.1
1988	Mil-A	5	0	1.000	28	2	0	0	1	80²	75	8	29	48	11.7	4.35	91	.251	.319	0		0	-3	-3	-1	-0.3
Total	9	24	35	.407	201	45	4	0	13	549¹	579	56	213	338	13.2	4.42	92	.275	.344	6	.154	-1	-27	-23	-5	-2.0

● **OSCAR JONES** Jones, Oscar Winfield "Flip Flap" b: 1/21/1879, London Grove, Pa. d: 10/8/46, Perkasie, Pa. BR/TR, 5'7", 163 lbs. Deb: 4/20/03

YEAR	TM/L	W	L	PCT	G	GS	CG	SH	SV	IP	H	HR	BB	SO	RAT	ERA	ERA+	OAV	OOB	BH	AVG	PB	PR	/A	PD	TPI
1903	Bro-N	19	14	.576	38	36	31	4	0	324¹	320	4	77	95	11.5	2.94	109	.260	.313	32	.256	3	12	9	-3	0.7
1904	Bro-N	17	25	.405	46	41	38	0	0	377	387	7	92	96	11.8	2.75	100	.270	.321	24	.175	-1	0	-0	-7	-0.8
1905	Bro-N	8	15	.348	29	20	14	0	1	174	197	6	56	66	13.6	4.66	62	.285	.347	13	.200	0	-32	-34	-4	-4.3
Total	3	44	54	.449	113	97	83	4	1	875¹	904	17	225	257	12.1	3.20	92	.269	.324	69	.211	2	-20	-25	-14	-4.4

● **PERCY JONES** Jones, Percy Lee b: 10/28/1899, Harwood, Tex. d: 3/18/79, Dallas, Tex. BR/TL, 5'11.5", 175 lbs. Deb: 8/6/20

YEAR	TM/L	W	L	PCT	G	GS	CG	SH	SV	IP	H	HR	BB	SO	RAT	ERA	ERA+	OAV	OOB	BH	AVG	PB	PR	/A	PD	TPI
1920	Chi-N	0	0	—	4	0	0	0	0	7	15	1	3	0	24.4	11.57	28	.455	.514	0	.000	-0	-7	-7	-0	0.0
1921	Chi-N	3	5	.375	32	3	1	0	0	98²	116	2	39	46	14.5	4.56	84	.295	.365	6	.222	-0	-8	-2	-0	-0.8
1922	Chi-N	8	9	.471	44	24	7	2	1	162	197	10	68	45	15.0	4.78	88	.310	.381	4	.085	-4	-12	-10	-1	-1.3
1925	Chi-N	6	6	.500	28	13	6	1	0	124	123	12	71	60	14.4	4.65	93	.263	.366	6	.154	-3	-5	-4	2	-0.4
1926	Chi-N	12	7	.632	30	20	10	2	2	160¹	151	9	90	80	13.8	3.09	125	.250	.359	13	.260	3	13	13	-1	1.6
1927	Chi-N	7	8	.467	30	11	5	1	0	112²	123	7	72	37	16.1	4.07	95	.285	.394	14	.350	3	-2	-3	-1	0.1
1928	Chi-N	10	6	.625	39	18	9	1	5	154	167	4	56	46	13.4	4.03	95	.288	.358	11	.196	0	-1	-3	-0	-0.4
1929	Bos-N	7	15	.318	35	22	11	1	0	188¹	219	15	84	69	14.7	4.64	101	.298	.373	9	.148	-3	2	1	-3	-0.1
1930	Pit-N	0	1	.000	9	2	0	0	0	19	26	3	11	3	18.9	6.63	70	.329	.430	0	.000	-0	-4	-3	-1	-0.2
Total	9	53	57	.482	251	113	49	8	6	1026	1137	53	494	381	14.7	4.34	95	.288	.373	63	.194	-5	-24	-24	-1	-1.5

● **RANDY JONES** Jones, Randall Leo b: 1/12/50, Fullerton, Cal. BR/TL, 6', 178 lbs. Deb: 6/16/73

YEAR	TM/L	W	L	PCT	G	GS	CG	SH	SV	IP	H	HR	BB	SO	RAT	ERA	ERA+	OAV	OOB	BH	AVG	PB	PR	/A	PD	TPI
1973	SD-N	7	6	.538	20	19	6	1	0	139²	129	13	37	77	10.8	3.16	110	.241	.291	8	.167	0	8	5	0	0.4
1974	SD-N	8	22	.267	40	34	6	1	2	208¹	217	16	78	124	13.0	4.45	80	.270	.339	10	.154	-1	-19	-21	2	-2.6
1975	SD-N★	20	12	.625	37	36	18	6	0	285	242	17	56	103	**9.4**	**2.24**	**155**	.232	.271	11	.133	-1	44	39	5	**4.9**
1976	SD-N★	**22**	14	.611	40	40	**25**	5	0	315¹	274	15	50	93	**9.4**	2.74	119	.234	**.267**	6	.058	-6	27	19	8	2.3
1977	SD-N	6	12	.333	27	25	1	0	0	147¹	173	12	36	44	12.8	4.58	77	.291	.330	5	.116	-1	-11	-17	4	-1.6
1978	SD-N	13	14	.481	37	36	7	2	0	253	263	6	64	71	11.6	2.88	115	.272	.317	15	.183	1	20	12	2	1.6
1979	SD-N	11	12	.478	39	36	5	1	0	263	257	17	64	112	11.1	3.63	97	.259	.306	3	.174	0	-3	-4	2	-0.5
1980	SD-N	5	13	.278	24	24	4	3	0	154¹	165	14	29	53	11.3	3.91	88	.276	.310	3	.067	-3	-5	-8	0	-0.9
1981	NY-N	1	8	.111	13	12	0	0	0	59¹	65	8	34	14	15.8	4.85	72	.274	.377	2	.118	-1	-9	-9	-2	-1.2
1982	NY-N	7	10	.412	28	20	1	0	0	107²	116	11	51	44	15.5	4.60	79	.304	.384	4	-13	-0	-12	-12	3	-1.4
Total	10	100	123	.448	305	285	73	19	2	1933	1915	129	503	735	11.3	3.42	95	.260	.309	79	.132	-12	44	6	32	1.7

YEAR TM/L	W	L	PCT	G	GS	CG	SH	SV	IP	H	HR	BB	SO	RAT	ERA	ERA+	OAV	OOB	BH	AVG	PB	PR	/A	PD	TPI
● **BOBBY JONES** Jones, Robert Joseph b: 2/10/70, Fresno, Cal. BR/TR, 6'4", 210 lbs. Deb: 8/14/93
1993 NY-N	2	4	.333	9	9	0	0	0	61²	61	6	22	35	12.4	3.65	110	.262	.331	1	.050	-2	3	2	-0	0.0
1994 NY-N	12	7	.632	24	24	1	1	0	160	157	10	56	80	12.4	3.15	133	.257	.324	5	.109	-2	19	18	2	2.0
1995 NY-N	10	10	.500	30	30	3	1	0	195²	209	20	53	127	12.4	4.19	97	.274	.327	9	.161	-1	-0	-3	-0	-0.4
1996 NY-N	12	8	.600	31	31	3	1	0	195²	219	26	46	116	12.3	4.42	89	.288	.331	7	.117	-1	-4	-11	0	-1.0
Total 4	36	29	.554	94	94	7	3	0	613	646	62	177	358	12.3	3.93	103	.273	.328	22	.121	-5	17	7	2	0.6
● **SAM JONES** Jones, Samuel "Toothpick Sam" b: 12/14/25, Stewartsville, Ohio d: 11/5/71, Morgantown, W.Va. BR/TR, 6'4", 200 lbs. Deb: 9/22/51
1951 Cle-A	0	1	.000	2	1	0	0	0	8²	4	0	5	4	9.3	2.08	182	.143	.273	0	.000	-0	2	2	-0	0.1
1952 Cle-A	2	3	.400	14	4	0	0	1	36	38	6	37	28	19.8	7.25	46	.270	.434	1	.100	-1	-14	-16	-1	-2.1
1955 Chi-N★	14	20	.412	36	34	12	4	0	241²	175	22	185	**198**	13.9	4.10	100	**.206**	.357	14	.182	-2	-2	-0	-0	-0.4
1956 Chi-N	9	14	.391	33	28	8	2	0	188²	155	21	115	**176**	13.3	3.91	96	.221	.338	10	.175	-0	-3	-3	-1	-0.4
1957 StL-N	12	9	.571	28	27	10	2	0	182²	164	17	71	154	11.9	3.60	110	.239	.316	10	.159	-1	6	7	0	0.7
1958 StL-N	14	13	.519	35	35	14	2	0	250	204	23	107	**225**	11.4	2.88	143	.223	.309	9	.100	-6	30	**35**	-1	2.9
1959 SF-N★	**21**	15	.583	50	35	16	**4**	4	270²	232	18	109	209	11.6	**2.83**	135	**.228**	.307	11	.129	-2	**34**	30	-2	3.4
1960 SF-N	18	14	.563	39	35	13	3	0	234	200	18	91	190	11.3	3.19	109	.230	.306	16	.200	1	15	7	-2	0.9
1961 SF-N	8	8	.500	37	17	2	0	1	128¹	134	12	57	105	14.0	4.49	85	.264	.348	5	.139	-1	-7	-10	-2	-1.3
1962 Det-A	2	4	.333	30	6	1	0	1	81¹	77	13	35	73	12.6	3.65	111	.254	.335	2	.095	-1	3	4	-0	0.2
1963 StL-N	2	0	1.000	11	0	0	0	2	11	15	0	5	8	16.4	9.00	54	.319	.385	0	—	0	-7	-7	-0	-1.4
1964 Bal-A	0	0	—	7	0	0	0	0	10¹	5	1	5	6	8.7	2.61	137	.152	.263	0	—	0	1	1	-0	0.0
Total 12	102	101	.502	322	222	76	17	9	1643¹	1403	151	822	1376	12.5	3.59	108	.230	.328	78	.149	-11	58	50	-8	2.8
● **SAM JONES** Jones, Samuel Pond "Sad Sam" b: 7/26/1892, Woodsfield, Ohio d: 7/6/66, Barnesville, Ohio BR/TR, 6', 170 lbs. Deb: 6/13/14
1914 Cle-A	0	0	—	1	0	0	0	0	3¹	2	0	2	0	10.8	2.70	107	.200	.333	1	.500	-0	0	0	0	0.0
1915 Cle-A	4	9	.308	48	9	2	0	4	145²	131	0	63	42	12.0	3.65	84	.252	.334	5	.156	-0	-11	-10	-1	-0.9
1916 Bos-A	0	1	.000	12	0	0	0	1	27	25	0	10	7	11.7	3.67	76	.272	.343	2	.333	0	-3	-3	-0	-0.1
1917 Bos-A	0	1	.000	9	1	0	0	1	16¹	15	1	6	5	11.6	4.41	59	.259	.328	0	.000	-1	-3	-3	1	-0.3
1918 *Bos-A	16	5	**.762**	24	21	16	5	0	184	151	1	70	44	11.2	2.25	119	.230	.312	10	.175	2	11	9	-1	1.1
1919 Bos-A	12	20	.375	35	31	21	5	1	245	258	4	95	67	13.2	3.75	81	.278	.350	11	.136	-0	-14	-20	3	-2.2
1920 Bos-A	13	16	.448	37	33	21	3	0	274	302	9	79	86	12.6	3.94	93	.288	.340	20	.217	1	-4	-9	-1	-0.8
1921 Bos-A	23	16	.590	40	38	25	**5**	1	298²	318	16	78	98	12.1	3.22	131	.279	.329	24	.240	5	35	33	-3	4.0
1922 *NY-A	13	13	.500	45	28	20	0	**8**	260	270	16	76	81	12.1	3.67	109	.275	.329	23	.264	8	11	10	-1	1.6
1923 *NY-A	21	8	.724	39	27	18	3	4	243	239	11	69	68	11.6	3.63	109	.257	.312	19	.224	2	10	8	1	1.1
1924 NY-A	9	6	.600	36	21	8	3	3	178²	187	6	76	53	13.3	3.63	115	.276	.350	9	.176	-0	12	11	-1	0.7
1925 NY-A	15	21	.417	43	31	14	1	2	246²	267	14	104	92	13.6	4.63	92	.281	.354	13	.162	-3	-7	-10	-1	-1.5
1926 *NY-A	9	8	.529	39	23	6	1	5	161	186	6	80	65	15.1	4.98	77	.288	.381	10	.204	1	-17	-20	-1	-2.3
1927 StL-A	8	14	.364	30	26	11	0	0	189²	211	13	102	72	15.0	4.32	101	.282	.371	6	.109	-2	-4	-2	-2	-0.3
1928 Was-A	17	7	.708	30	27	19	4	0	224²	209	5	78	63	11.6	2.84	141	.252	.319	20	.253	6	30	29	1	3.5
1929 Was-A	9	9	.500	24	24	8	1	0	153²	156	5	49	36	12.2	3.92	108	.264	.324	8	.157	0	5	5	-1	0.4
1930 Was-A	15	7	.682	25	25	14	1	0	183¹	195	4	61	60	12.7	4.07	113	.277	.337	9	.148	-1	12	11	-1	0.8
1931 Was-A	9	10	.474	25	24	8	1	1	148	185	10	47	58	14.4	4.32	99	.304	.358	15	.313	4	1	-0	0	0.3
1932 Chi-A	10	15	.400	30	28	10	0	0	200¹	217	9	75	64	13.3	4.22	102	.270	.335	11	.193	2	6	2	3	0.7
1933 Chi-A	10	12	.455	27	25	11	2	0	176²	181	13	65	60	12.7	3.36	126	.265	.333	9	.155	-0	18	17	-1	1.8
1934 Chi-A	8	12	.400	27	26	11	1	0	183¹	217	16	60	60	13.7	5.11	93	.289	.343	12	.200	-1	-12	-8	-2	-0.7
1935 Chi-A	3	7	.533	21	19	7	0	0	140	162	8	51	38	13.8	4.05	114	.284	.343	8	.167	6	9	9	0	0.9
Total 22	229	217	.513	647	487	250	36	31	3883	4084	152	1396	1223	12.9	3.84	104	.274	.339	245	.197	25	81	61	-8	8.1
● **SHELDON JONES** Jones, Sheldon Leslie "Available" b: 2/2/22, Tecumseh, Neb. d: 4/18/91, Greenville, N.C. BR/TR, 6', 180 lbs. Deb: 9/9/46
1946 NY-N	1	2	.333	6	4	1	0	0	28	21	4	17	24	12.5	3.21	107	.208	.328	2	.250	0	1	1	-0	0.1
1947 NY-N	2	2	.500	15	6	0	0	0	55²	51	2	29	24	13.4	3.88	105	.250	.352	2	.125	-1	1	1	-1	-0.1
1948 NY-N	16	8	.667	55	21	8	1	5	201¹	204	16	90	82	13.4	3.35	117	.263	.344	13	.203	-1	14	13	0	1.6
1949 NY-N	15	12	.556	42	29	11	0	0	207¹	198	19	88	79	12.8	3.34	119	.248	.331	8	.121	-3	16	15	-0	1.4
1950 NY-N	13	16	.448	40	28	11	2	2	199	188	26	90	97	12.9	4.61	89	.249	.335	6	.105	-2	-10	-11	-2	-1.9
1951 *NY-N	6	11	.353	41	12	2	0	4	120¹	119	12	52	58	13.1	4.26	92	.260	.340	3	.097	-0	-4	-5	-0	-0.7
1952 Bos-N	1	4	.200	39	1	0	0	1	70	81	8	31	40	14.5	4.76	76	.286	.359	1	.125	-0	-8	-9	-0	-0.6
1953 Chi-N	0	2	.000	22	0	0	0	0	38¹	47	3	16	9	16.0	5.40	82	.299	.382	0	.000	-0	-5	-4	-0	-0.3
Total 8	54	57	.486	260	101	33	4	12	918	909	90	413	413	13.5	3.96	100	.258	.342	35	.136	-7	4	1	-3	-0.5
● **SHERMAN JONES** Jones, Sherman Jarvis "Roadblock" b: 2/10/35, Winton, N.C. BL/TR, 6'4", 205 lbs. Deb: 8/2/60
1960 SF-N	1	1	.500	16	0	0	0	1	32	37	3	11	10	13.8	3.09	112	.291	.353	2	.286	-0	2	1	-1	0.1
1961 *Cin-N	1	1	.500	24	2	0	0	0	55	51	6	32	32	13.1	4.42	92	.256	.351	2	.182	-0	-2	-2	-0	-0.1
1962 NY-N	0	4	.000	8	3	0	0	0	23¹	31	3	8	11	15.8	7.71	54	.326	.390	3	.429	1	-10	-9	-0	-1.2
Total 3	2	6	.250	48	5	0	0	3	110¹	119	12	46	53	13.9	4.73	83	.283	.360	7	.280	1	-10	-10	-1	-1.2
● **STEVE JONES** Jones, Steven Howell b: 4/22/41, Huntington Park, Cal. BL/TL, 5'10", 175 lbs. Deb: 8/15/67 F
1967 Chi-A	2	2	.500	11	3	0	0	0	25²	21	1	12	17	11.6	4.21	74	.223	.311	1	.250	-0	-3	-3	-0	-0.5
1968 Was-A	1	2	.333	7	0	0	0	0	10²	8	3	7	11	12.7	5.91	49	.205	.326	0	.000	-0	-3	-4	-0	-1.0
1969 KC-A	2	3	.400	20	4	0	0	0	44²	45	3	24	31	14.5	4.23	87	.260	.360	1	.125	-0	-3	-3	-0	-0.2
Total 3	5	7	.417	38	7	0	0	0	81	74	7	43	59	13.3	4.44	76	.242	.341	2	.154	-0	-9	-9	-1	-1.7
● **RICK JONES** Jones, Thomas Fredrick b: 4/16/55, Jacksonville, Fla. BL/TL, 6'5", 190 lbs. Deb: 4/18/76
1976 Bos-A	5	3	.625	24	14	1	0	0	104¹	133	6	26	45	13.8	3.36	116	.311	.352	0	—	0	2	6	-0	0.4
1977 Sea-A	1	4	.200	10	10	0	0	0	42¹	47	10	37	16	17.9	5.10	81	.283	.414	0	—	0	-5	-5	-0	-0.4
1978 Sea-A	0	2	.000	3	2	0	0	0	12¹	17	1	7	11	17.5	5.84	65	.315	.393	0	—	0	-3	-0	-0	-0.4
Total 3	6	9	.400	37	26	1	0	0	159	197	17	70	72	15.2	4.02	99	.304	.373	0	—	0	-6	-1	-0	-0.4
● **TIM JONES** Jones, Timothy Byron b: 1/24/54, Sacramento, Cal. BB/TR, 6'5", 220 lbs. Deb: 9/4/77
1977 Pit-N	1	0	1.000	3	1	0	0	0	10	4	0	3	5	6.3	0.00	—	.118	.189	0	.000	-0	4	4	-0	0.4
● **TODD JONES** Jones, Todd Barton Givin b: 4/24/68, Marietta, Ga. BL/TR, 6'3", 200 lbs. Deb: 7/7/93
1993 Hou-N	1	2	.333	27	0	0	0	2	37¹	28	4	15	25	10.6	3.13	124	.214	.299	0	—	0	4	3	-0	0.2
1994 Hou-N	5	2	.714	48	0	0	0	5	72²	52	3	26	63	9.8	2.72	145	.202	.278	2	.400	1	12	10	-1	0.9
1995 Hou-N	6	5	.545	68	0	0	0	15	99²	89	8	52	96	13.3	3.07	126	.237	.339	1	.200	0	12	9	-1	1.1
1996 Hou-N	6	3	.667	51	0	0	0	17	57¹	61	5	32	44	15.4	4.40	87	.274	.377	0	.000	-0	-1	-4	-0	-0.7
Total 4	18	12	.600	194	0	0	0	39	267	230	20	125	228	12.4	3.27	119	.233	.327	3	.273	1	27	18	-3	1.5
● **TIM JONES** Jones, William Timothy b: 12/1/62, Sumter, S.C. BL/TR, 5'10", 172 lbs. Deb: 7/26/88 ♦
1990 StL-N	0	0	—	1	0	0	0	0	1¹	1	0	2	0	20.3	6.75	57	.167	.375	28	.219	0	-0	-0	-0	0.0
● **CLAUDE JONNARD** Jonnard, Claude Alfred b: 11/23/1897, Nashville, Tenn. d: 8/27/59, Nashville, Tenn. BR/TR, 6'1", 165 lbs. Deb: 10/1/21 F
1921 NY-N	0	0	—	1	0	0	0	1	4	4	0	0	7	9.0	0.00	—	.267	.267	0	.000	-0	2	2	-0	0.1
1922 NY-N	6	1	.857	33	0	0	0	**5**	96	96	7	28	44	11.9	3.84	104	.272	.331	1	.042	-3	3	2	-2	-0.1
1923 *NY-N	4	3	.571	**45**	1	1	0	**5**	96	105	6	35	45	13.1	3.28	116	.279	.340	1	.038	-3	8	6	-1	0.4
1924 *NY-N	4	5	.444	34	3	0	0	3	89²	80	2	24	40	10.6	2.41	152	.229	.282	1	.045	-3	**15**	**13**	-0	1.0
1926 StL-A	0	2	.000	12	0	0	0	1	36	46	1	24	13	17.5	6.00	71	.313	.409	0	—	0	-8	-7	-1	-0.3
1929 Chi-N	0	0	—	12	2	0	0	0	27²	41	4	11	11	17.2	7.48	62	.320	.379	2	.200	-1	-9	-9	-0	-0.2
Total 6	14	12	.538	137	6	2	0	17	349¹	372	20	122	160	12.9	3.79	104	.272	.334	5	.056	-9	10	6	-1	0.4
● **CHARLIE JORDAN** Jordan, Charles T. "Kid" b: 10/4/1871, Baltimore, Md. d: 6/1/28, Hazleton, Pa. Deb: 7/31/1896
1896 Phi-N	0	0	—	2	2	0	0	0	4²	9	0	2	3	21.2	7.71	56	.409	.458	1	.500	0	-2	-2	0	0.0

YEAR	TM/L	W	L	PCT	G	GS	CG	SH	SV	IP	H	HR	BB	SO	RAT	ERA	ERA+	OAV	OOB	BH	AVG	PB	PR	/A	PD	TPI

● HARRY JORDAN   Jordan, Harry J.   b: 2/14/1873, Pittsburgh, Pa.   d: 3/1/20, Pittsburgh, Pa.   Deb: 9/25/1894

1894	Pit-N	1	0	1.000	1	1	1	0	0	9	10	0	2	1	13.0	4.00	131	.278	.333	0	.000	-0	1	1	-0	0.1
1895	Pit-N	0	2	.000	2	2	2	0	0	17	24	0	6	4	16.4	4.24	107	.329	.387	2	.286	-0	1	1	-0	0.0
Total	2	1	2	.333	3	3	3	0	0	26	34	0	8	5	15.2	4.15	115	.312	.370	2	.200	-0	2	2	-1	0.1

● MILT JORDAN   Jordan, Milton Mignot   b: 5/24/27, Mineral Springs, Pa.   d: 5/13/93, Ithaca, N.Y.   BR/TR, 6'2.5", 207 lbs.   Deb: 4/16/53

| 1953 | Det-A | 0 | 1 | .000 | 8 | 1 | 0 | 0 | 0 | 17 | 26 | 3 | 5 | 4 | 16.4 | 5.82 | 70 | .366 | .408 | 1 | .500 | 0 | -3 | -3 | 0 | -0.1 |

● NILES JORDAN   Jordan, Niles Chapman   b: 12/1/25, Lyman, Wash.   BL/TL, 5'11", 180 lbs.   Deb: 8/26/51

1951	Phi-N	2	3	.400	5	5	2	1	0	36²	35	4	8	11	10.6	3.19	121	.250	.291	1	.077	-1	3	3	-1	0.2
1952	Cin-N	0	1	.000	3	1	0	0	0	6¹	14	1	3	2	24.2	9.95	38	.452	.500	0	.000	-0	-4	-4	0	-0.6
Total	2	2	4	.333	8	6	2	1	0	43	49	5	11	13	12.6	4.19	92	.287	.330	1	.071	-1	-1	-2	-1	-0.4

● RIP JORDAN   Jordan, Raymond Willis "Lanky"   b: 9/28/1889, Portland, Me.   d: 6/5/60, Meriden, Conn.   BL/TR, 6', 172 lbs.   Deb: 6/25/12

1912	Chi-A	0	0	—	4	0	0	0	0	12¹	13	2	3	1	12.4	5.11	63	.289	.347	0	.000	-1	-2	-3	-0	-0.1
1919	Was-A	0	0	—	1	1	0	0	0	4	6	1	2	2	18.0	11.25	29	.353	.421	0	.000	-0	-4	-4	-0	0.0
Total	2	0	0	—	5	1	0	0	0	16¹	19	3	5	3	13.8	6.61	48	.306	.368	0	.000	-1	-6	-6	-1	-0.1

● RICARDO JORDAN   Jordan, Ricardo   b: 6/27/70, Boynton Beach, Fla   BL/TL, 5'11", 165 lbs.   Deb: 6/23/95

1995	Tor-A	1	0	1.000	15	0	0	0	1	15	18	3	13	10	19.8	6.60	71	.305	.446	0	—	0	-3	-3	0	-0.2
1996	Phi-N	2	2	.500	26	0	0	0	0	25	18	2	12	17	11.2	1.80	242	.202	.297	0	.000	-0	7	7	-0	1.0
Total	2	3	2	.600	41	0	0	0	1	40	36	3	25	27	14.2	3.60	125	.243	.360	0	.000	-0	4	3	-0	0.8

● ORVILLE JORGENS   Jorgens, Orville Edward   b: 6/4/08, Rockford, Ill.   d: 1/11/92, Colorado Springs, Colo.   BR/TR, 6'1", 180 lbs.   Deb: 4/19/35   F

1935	Phi-N	10	15	.400	53	24	6	0	2	188¹	216	12	96	57	15.3	4.83	94	.283	.370	6	.097	-5	-17	-6	-3	-0.9
1936	Phi-N	8	8	.500	39	21	4	0	0	167¹	196	16	69	58	14.6	4.79	95	.290	.361	12	.200	-1	-14	-5	1	-0.4
1937	Phi-N	3	4	.429	52	9	1	0	3	140²	172	12	68	34	14.8	4.41	98	.298	.383	5	.143	-1	-8	-1	2	0.0
Total	3	21	27	.438	144	54	11	0	5	496¹	571	40	233	149	14.9	4.70	95	.290	.370	23	.146	-7	-39	-12	5	-1.3

● ADDIE JOSS   Joss, Adrian   b: 4/12/1880, Woodland, Wis.   d: 4/14/11, Toledo, Ohio   BR/TR, 6'3", 185 lbs.   Deb: 4/26/02   H

1902	Cle-A	17	13	.567	32	29	28	**5**	0	269¹	225	2	75	106	10.5	2.77	124	.228	.291	12	.117	-5	24	20	6	2.0
1903	Cle-A	18	13	.581	32	31	31	3	0	283²	232	3	37	120	**8.8**	2.19	130	.223	**.256**	22	.193	0	24	21	4	2.7
1904	Cle-A	14	10	.583	25	24	20	5	0	192¹	160	0	30	83	9.2	**1.59**	159	.227	.266	10	.132	-4	22	20	0	2.2
1905	Cle-A	20	12	.625	33	32	31	3	0	286	246	4	46	132	9.5	2.01	131	.234	.273	13	.134	0	20	20	5	2.7
1906	Cle-A	21	9	.700	34	31	28	9	1	282	220	3	43	106	8.5	1.72	152	.218	.252	21	.210	2	30	28	2	3.7
1907	Cle-A	**27**	11	.711	42	38	34	6	2	338²	279	3	54	127	9.0	1.83	137	.227	.263	13	.114	-5	27	25	9	3.4
1908	Cle-A	24	11	.686	42	35	29	9	2	325	232	3	30	130	**7.3**	**1.16**	205	**.197**	**.218**	15	.155	-3	44	44	7	5.9
1909	Cle-A	14	13	.519	33	28	24	4	0	242²	198	0	31	67	8.6	1.71	150	.226	.255	8	.100	-3	21	23	0	2.4
1910	Cle-A	5	5	.500	13	12	9	1	0	107¹	96	1	18	49	9.7	2.26	114	.245	.282	4	.111	-1	3	4	2	0.4
Total	9	160	97	.623	286	260	234	45	5	2327	1888	19	364	920	8.9	1.89	142	.223	.260	118	.144	-14	216	206	30	25.4

● MIKE JOYCE   Joyce, Michael Lewis   b: 2/12/41, Detroit, Mich.   BR/TR, 6'2", 193 lbs.   Deb: 7/2/62

1962	Chi-A	2	1	.667	25	1	0	0	0	43¹	40	2	14	9	11.2	3.32	118	.247	.307	3	.429	1	3	3	0	0.3
1963	Chi-A	0	0	—	6	0	0	0	0	10²	13	1	8	7	17.7	8.44	42	.289	.396	0	—	0	-6	-6	-0	0.0
Total	2	2	1	.667	31	1	0	0	0	54	53	3	22	16	12.5	4.33	88	.256	.328	3	.429	1	-3	-3	0	0.3

● DICK JOYCE   Joyce, Richard Edward   b: 11/18/43, Portland, Me.   BL/TL, 6'5", 225 lbs.   Deb: 9/3/65

| 1965 | KC-A | 0 | 1 | .000 | 5 | 3 | 0 | 0 | 0 | 13 | 12 | 0 | 4 | 7 | 11.1 | 2.77 | 126 | .240 | .296 | 0 | .000 | -0 | 1 | 1 | -0 | 0.0 |

● BOB JOYCE   Joyce, Robert Emmett   b: 1/14/15, Stockton, Cal.   d: 12/10/81, San Francisco, Cal   BR/TR, 6'1", 180 lbs.   Deb: 5/4/39

1939	Phi-A	3	5	.375	30	6	1	0	0	107²	156	13	37	25	16.2	6.69	70	.337	.387	3	.086	-3	-25	-24	1	-1.6
1946	NY-N	3	4	.429	14	7	2	0	0	60²	79	3	20	24	14.7	5.34	64	.315	.365	3	.158	0	-13	-13	1	-1.2
Total	2	6	9	.400	44	13	3	0	0	168¹	235	16	57	49	15.7	6.20	69	.329	.380	6	.111	-3	-38	-37	2	-2.8

● RALPH JUDD   Judd, Ralph Wesley   b: 12/7/01, Perrysburg, Ohio   d: 5/6/57, Lapeer, Mich.   BL/TR, 5'10", 170 lbs.   Deb: 10/2/27

1927	Was-A	0	0	—	1	0	0	0	0	4	8	0	2	2	22.5	6.75	60	.400	.455	0	.000	-0	-1	-1	-0	-0.1
1929	NY-N	3	0	1.000	18	0	0	0	0	50²	49	4	11	21	10.7	2.66	172	.261	.302	0	.000	-2	12	11	0	0.4
1930	NY-N	0	0	—	2	0	0	0	1	7²	13	0	3	0	18.8	5.87	81	.394	.444	0	.000	-1	-1	-1	-0	-0.1
Total	3	3	0	1.000	21	0	0	0	1	62¹	70	4	16	23	12.4	3.32	138	.290	.335	0	.000	-3	10	9	0	0.2

● OSCAR JUDD   Judd, Thomas William Oscar "Ossie"   b: 2/14/08, London, Ont., Can.   d: 12/27/95, Ingersoll, Ont., Can.   BL/TL, 6'0.5", 180 lbs.   Deb: 4/16/41

1941	Bos-A	0	0	—	7	0	0	0	0	12¹	15	1	10	5	18.2	8.76	48	.300	.417	2	.500	-0	-6	-6	0	0.1
1942	Bos-A	8	10	.444	31	19	11	0	2	150¹	135	3	90	70	13.6	3.89	96	.239	.346	18	.269	6	-4	-3	-0	0.3
1943	Bos-A☆	11	6	.647	23	20	8	1	0	155¹	131	2	69	53	11.8	2.90	114	.230	.317	14	.259	4	7	7	2	1.4
1944	Bos-A	1	1	.500	9	6	1	0	0	30	30	1	15	9	13.5	3.60	94	.261	.346	2	.182	-1	-1	-0	0	0.0
1945	Bos-A	0	1	.000	2	1	0	0	0	6¹	14	0	5	3	18.5	8.53	40	.333	.394	1	.500	0	-4	-4	-0	-0.4
	Phi-N	5	4	.556	23	9	3	1	2	82²	80	7	40	36	13.2	3.81	101	.254	.340	8	.267	3	-0	-1	4	0.4
1946	Phi-N	11	12	.478	30	24	12	1	2	173¹	169	6	90	65	13.5	3.53	97	.260	.350	25	.316	8	-2	-2	4	1.1
1947	Phi-N	4	15	.211	32	19	8	1	0	146²	155	6	69	54	13.9	4.60	87	.279	.361	12	.188	2	-9	-10	1	-0.7
1948	Phi-N	0	2	.000	4	1	0	0	0	14¹	19	1	11	7	18.8	6.91	57	.317	.423	1	.167	-0	-5	-5	-0	-0.5
Total	8	40	51	.440	161	99	43	4	7	771¹	744	24	397	304	13.4	3.90	93	.256	.347	83	.262	26	-23	-22	8	1.7

● JEFF JUDEN   Juden, Jeffrey Daniel   b: 1/19/71, Salem, Mass.   BR/TR, 6'7", 245 lbs.   Deb: 9/15/91

1991	Hou-N	0	2	.000	4	3	0	0	0	18	19	3	7	11	13.0	6.00	58	.275	.342	0	.000	-1	-5	-5	-1	-0.6
1993	Hou-N	0	1	.000	2	0	0	0	0	5	4	1	3	2	14.4	5.40	72	.222	.342	0	—	-1	-1	-0	-0	-0.2
1994	Phi-N	1	4	.200	6	5	0	0	0	27²	29	4	12	22	13.7	6.18	69	.276	.356	1	.111	-0	-6	-6	-0	-0.9
1995	Phi-N	2	4	.333	13	10	1	0	0	62²	53	6	31	47	12.8	4.02	105	.235	.340	1	.056	-1	1	1	-0	-0.1
1996	SF-N	4	0	1.000	36	0	0	0	0	41²	39	7	20	35	13.0	4.10	100	.250	.339	0	.000	-0	1	0	-0	-0.1
	Mon-N	1	0	1.000	22	18	1	0	0	32²	22	1	14	26	11.0	2.20	196	.188	.296	0	.000	0	7	8	-1	0.2
	Yr	5	0	1.000	58	0	0	0	0	74¹	61	8	34	61	12.0	3.27	128	.221	.315	0	.000	-0	8	8	-1	0.1
Total	5	8	11	.421	83	18	1	0	0	187²	166	22	88	148	12.7	4.27	97	.240	.335	2	.057	-2	-3	-3	-2	-1.6

● HOWIE JUDSON   Judson, Howard Kolls   b: 2/16/26, Hebron, Ill.   BR/TR, 6'1", 195 lbs.   Deb: 4/22/48

1948	Chi-A	4	5	.444	40	5	1	0	8	107¹	102	7	56	38	13.5	4.78	89	.255	.351	3	.103	-2	-6	-6	0	-0.7
1949	Chi-A	1	14	.067	26	12	3	0	1	108	114	13	70	36	15.4	4.58	91	.274	.380	2	.065	-3	-5	-5	0	-0.8
1950	Chi-A	2	3	.400	46	3	1	0	0	112	105	10	63	34	13.7	3.94	114	.252	.353	2	.100	-1	8	7	-2	0.1
1951	Chi-A	5	6	.455	27	14	3	0	1	121²	124	9	55	43	13.4	3.77	107	.264	.343	4	.121	-2	5	4	-0	0.1
1952	Chi-A	0	1	.000	21	0	0	0	1	34	30	4	22	15	13.8	4.24	86	.244	.359	0	.000	-0	-2	-2	-0	-0.1
1953	Cin-N	0	1	.000	10	6	0	0	0	38²	58	8	11	16	16.1	5.59	78	.341	.381	1	.111	-4	-6	-5	0	0.0
1954	Cin-N	5	7	.417	37	8	0	0	3	93¹	86	9	42	27	12.6	3.95	106	.251	.338	2	.083	-2	3	2	-0	0.1
Total	7	17	37	.315	207	48	8	0	14	615	619	60	319	204	13.9	4.29	98	.265	.356	14	.093	-9	-4	-6	-3	-1.4

● KEN JUNGELS   Jungels, Kenneth Peter "Curly"   b: 6/23/16, Aurora, Ill.   d: 9/9/75, West Bend, Wis.   BR/TR, 6'1", 180 lbs.   Deb: 9/15/37

1937	Cle-A	0	0	—	2	0	0	0	0	9	9	1	3	0	12.0	0.00	—	.273	.333	0	—	0	2	2	0	0.0
1938	Cle-A	1	0	1.000	9	0	0	0	0	15¹	21	1	18	7	24.1	8.80	53	.339	.500	0	.000	-1	-7	-7	-0	-0.4
1940	Cle-A	0	0	—	2	0	0	0	0	3¹	3	0	1	1	10.8	2.70	156	.273	.333	0	.000	-0	0	0	0	0.0
1941	Cle-A	0	0	—	6	0	0	0	0	13²	17	4	8	6	17.1	7.24	54	.293	.388	0	.000	-0	-5	-5	-0	-0.1
1942	Pit-N	0	0	—	6	0	0	0	0	13²	6	0	2	7	6.59	6.59	51	.235	.291	1	.100	-0	-5	-5	-0	-0.0
Total	5	1	0	1.000	25	0	0	0	0	49	56	6	32	21	16.7	6.80	60	.290	.399	1	.100	-2	-14	-15	-0	-0.5

● MIKE JUREWICZ   Jurewicz, Michael Allen   b: 9/20/45, Buffalo, N.Y.   BB/TL, 6'3", 205 lbs.   Deb: 9/7/65

| 1965 | NY-A | 0 | 0 | — | 2 | 0 | 0 | 0 | 0 | 2¹ | 5 | 0 | 1 | 2 | 23.1 | 7.71 | 44 | .417 | .462 | 0 | — | 0 | -1 | -1 | -0 | 0.0 |

YEAR TM/L	W	L	PCT	G	GS	CG	SH	SV	IP	H	HR	BB	SO	RAT	ERA	ERA+	OAV	OOB	BH	AVG	PB	PR	/A	PD	TPI
● **AL JURISICH**	Jurisich, Alvin Joseph b: 8/25/21, New Orleans, La. d: 11/3/81, New Orleans, La. BR/TR, 6'2", 193 lbs. Deb: 4/26/44																								
1944 *StL-N	7	9	.438	30	14	5	2	1	130	102	7	65	53	11.9	3.39	104	.221	.323	8	.178	-1	3	2	-1	0.0
1945 StL-N	3	3	.500	27	6	1	0	0	71²	61	7	41	42	12.9	5.15	73	.232	.338	2	.087	-2	-11	-11	-1	-1.1
1946 Phi-N	4	3	.571	13	10	2	1	1	68¹	71	9	31	34	13.6	3.69	93	.263	.341	3	.130	-0	-2	-2	-1	-0.4
1947 Phi-N	1	7	.125	34	12	5	0	3	118¹	110	15	52	48	12.4	4.94	81	.258	.340	1	.032	-3	-12	-12	-2	-1.2
Total 4	15	22	.405	104	42	13	3	5	388¹	344	38	189	177	12.5	4.24	87	.242	.334	14	.115	-6	-21	-24	-5	-2.7
● **WALT JUSTIS**	Justis, Walter Newton "Smoke" b: 8/17/1883, Moores Hill, Ind. d: 10/4/41, Lawrenceburg, Ind. BR/TR, 5'11.5", 195 lbs. Deb: 8/1/05																								
1905 Det-A	0	0	—	2	0	0	0	0	3¹	4	0	6	0	29.7	8.10	34	.308	.550	0	—	0	-2	-2	-0	0.0
● **HEROLD JUUL**	Juul, Earl Herold b: 5/21/1893, Chicago, Ill. d: 1/4/42, Chicago, Ill. BR/TR, 5'9.5", 150 lbs. Deb: 4/24/14																								
1914 Bro-F	0	3	.000	9	3	0	0	0	29	26	0	31	16	18.0	6.21	46	.248	.423	2	.222	-0	-11	-11	-0	-1.0
● **HERB JUUL**	Juul, Herbert Victor b: 2/2/1886, Chicago, Ill. d: 11/14/28, Chicago, Ill. BL/TL, 5'11", 150 lbs. Deb: 7/11/11 ♦																								
1911 Cin-N	0	0	—	1	0	0	0	0	4	3	0	4	2	15.8	4.50	74	.231	.412	0	.000	-0	-0	-1	-0	0.0
● **JIM KAAT**	Kaat, James Lee b: 11/7/38, Zeeland, Mich. BL/TL, 6'4", 217 lbs. Deb: 8/2/59 C♦																								
1959 Was-A	0	2	.000	3	2	0	0	0	5	7	1	4	2	23.4	12.60	31	.350	.500	0	.000	-0	-5	-5	0	-1.4
1960 Was-A	1	5	.167	13	9	0	0	0	50	48	8	31	25	15.1	5.58	70	.255	.375	2	.143	-1	-9	-9	0	-1.0
1961 Min-A	9	17	.346	36	29	8	1	0	200²	188	12	82	122	12.6	3.90	109	.248	.331	15	.238	3	3	8	3	1.6
1962 Min-A☆	18	14	.563	39	35	16	5	1	269	243	23	75	173	11.2	3.14	130	.243	.307	18	.180	3	25	28	6	**4.2**
1963 Min-A	10	10	.500	31	27	7	1	1	178¹	195	24	38	105	12.2	4.19	87	.274	.319	8	.131	-0	-11	-11	4	-0.7
1964 Min-A	17	11	.607	36	34	13	0	1	243	231	23	60	171	11.1	3.22	111	.251	.304	14	.169	5	11	10	3	1.9
1965 *Min-A	18	11	.621	45	42	7	2	2	264¹	267	25	63	154	11.4	2.83	126	.258	.304	23	.247	6	19	21	3	3.5
1966 Min-A★	**25**	13	.658	41	41	**19**	3	0	304²	271	29	55	205	9.7	2.75	131	.235	.271	23	.195	4	23	**29**	0	4.1
1967 Min-A	16	13	.552	42	38	13	2	0	263¹	269	21	42	211	10.9	3.04	114	.260	.295	17	.172	3	6	12	1	1.8
1968 Min-A	14	12	.538	30	29	9	2	0	208	192	16	40	130	10.2	2.94	105	.243	.282	12	.156	0	1	3	-0	0.4
1969 Min-A	14	13	.519	40	32	10	0	1	242¹	252	23	75	139	12.5	3.49	105	.265	.325	18	.207	6	3	4	-3	0.8
1970 *Min-A	14	10	.583	45	34	4	1	0	230¹	244	26	58	120	11.9	3.56	105	.273	.319	15	.197	3	4	4	2	0.9
1971 Min-A	13	14	.481	39	38	15	4	0	260¹	275	16	47	137	11.3	3.32	107	.268	.304	15	.161	-0	2	2	-1	0.2
1972 Min-A	10	2	.833	15	15	5	0	0	113¹	94	6	20	64	9.1	2.06	155	.227	.263	13	.289	5	13	14	0	2.3
1973 Min-A	11	12	.478	29	28	7	2	0	181²	206	26	39	93	12.3	4.41	90	.282	.322	0	—	0	-12	-9	-1	-1.2
Chi-A	4	1	.800	7	7	3	1	0	42²	44	4	4	16	10.1	4.22	94	.260	.277	0	—	0	-2	-1	-0	-0.2
Yr	15	13	.536	36	35	10	3	0	224¹	250	30	43	109	11.8	4.37	90	.276	.309	0	—	0	-14	-10	-1	-1.4
1974 Chi-A	21	13	.618	42	39	15	3	0	277¹	263	18	63	142	10.8	2.92	128	.250	.296	0	.000	0	21	25	-2	2.8
1975 Chi-A★	20	14	.588	43	41	12	1	0	303²	321	20	77	142	12.1	3.11	124	.274	.324	0	—	0	22	26	-2	2.5
1976 *Phi-N	12	14	.462	38	35	7	1	0	227²	241	21	32	83	10.8	3.48	102	.274	.300	4	.177	2	1	2	-3	0.1
1977 Phi-N	6	11	.353	35	27	2	0	0	160¹	211	20	40	55	14.2	5.39	74	.320	.361	10	.189	1	-26	-25	-2	-2.4
1978 Phi-N	8	5	.615	26	24	2	1	0	140¹	150	9	32	48	12.0	4.10	87	.280	.326	7	.146	-1	-8	-8	-2	-1.0
1979 Phi-N	1	0	1.000	3	1	0	0	0	8¹	9	1	5	2	15.1	4.32	89	.281	.378	0	.000	-0	-1	-0	-0	0.0
NY-A	2	3	.400	40	1	0	0	2	58¹	64	4	14	23	12.3	3.86	106	.287	.335	0	—	0	-2	1	-1	0.0
1980 NY-A	0	1	.000	8	0	0	0	0	9	8	0	4	1	21.6	7.20	54	.381	.480	0	—	0	-3	-3	-0	-0.3
StL-N	8	7	.533	49	14	6	1	4	129²	140	6	33	36	12.0	3.82	97	.281	.325	5	.143	1	-3	-2	-2	-0.3
1981 StL-N	6	6	.500	41	1	0	0	4	53	60	2	17	13	13.1	3.40	105	.299	.353	2	.375	1	1	1	0	0.4
1982 *StL-N	5	3	.625	62	2	0	0	3	75	79	6	23	35	12.5	4.08	89	.276	.334	0	.000	-1	-4	-4	-1	-0.5
1983 StL-N	0	0	—	24	0	0	0	0	34²	48	5	10	19	15.1	3.89	93	.327	.369	0	.000	-0	-1	-1	-0	0.0
Total 25	283	237	.544	898	625	180	31	18	4530¹	4620	395	1083	2461	11.6	3.45	107	.264	.311	232	.185	41	74	119	6	19.0
● **GEORGE KAHLER**	Kahler, George Runnells "Krum" b: 9/6/1889, Athens, Ohio d: 2/7/24, Battle Creek, Va. BR/TR, 6', 183 lbs. Deb: 8/13/10																								
1910 Cle-A	6	4	.600	12	12	8	2	0	95¹	80	0	46	38	12.3	1.60	161	.237	.335	5	.143	-2	10	10	-1	0.8
1911 Cle-A	9	8	.529	30	17	10	0	1	154¹	153	1	66	97	13.5	3.27	104	.270	.360	9	.167	-2	1	3	-1	-0.1
1912 Cle-A	12	19	.387	41	32	17	3	1	246¹	263	1	121	104	14.4	3.69	92	.291	.382	9	.112	-5	-10	-8	-4	-1.7
1913 Cle-A	5	11	.313	24	15	5	0	0	117²	118	1	32	43	11.8	3.14	97	.266	.322	2	.061	-3	-3	-1	-4	-0.9
1914 Cle-A	0	1	.000	2	1	1	0	0	14	17	0	7	3	15.4	3.86	75	.309	.387	0	.000	-0	-2	-2	-0	-0.2
Total 5	32	43	.427	109	77	41	5	2	627²	631	3	272	285	13.4	3.17	101	.274	.358	25	.121	-13	-4	2	-9	-2.1
● **DON KAINER**	Kainer, Donald Wayne b: 9/3/55, Houston, Tex. BR/TR, 6'3", 205 lbs. Deb: 9/6/80																								
1980 Tex-A	0	0	—	4	3	0	0	0	19²	22	0	9	10	15.6	1.83	213	.289	.386	0	—	0	5	5	1	0.1
● **DON KAISER**	Kaiser, Clyde Donald "Tiger" b: 2/3/35, Byng, Okla. BR/TR, 6'5", 195 lbs. Deb: 7/20/55																								
1955 Chi-N	0	0	—	11	0	0	0	0	18¹	20	2	5	11	12.8	5.40	76	.274	.329	0	—	0	-3	-3	-0	-0.1
1956 Chi-N	4	9	.308	27	22	5	1	0	150¹	144	15	52	74	11.8	3.59	105	.247	.310	2	.043	-5	3	3	-3	-0.3
1957 Chi-N	2	6	.250	20	13	1	0	0	72	91	4	28	23	14.9	5.00	77	.316	.377	2	.105	-1	-9	-9	2	-0.8
Total 3	6	15	.286	58	35	6	1	0	240²	255	21	85	108	12.8	4.15	92	.270	.332	4	.059	-6	-9	-9	-1	-1.2
● **JEFF KAISER**	Kaiser, Jeffrey Patrick b: 7/24/60, Wyandotte, Mich. BR/TL, 6'3", 195 lbs. Deb: 4/11/85																								
1985 Oak-A	0	0	—	15	0	0	0	0	16²	25	6	20	10	24.8	14.58	26	.342	.489	0	—	0	-19	-20	1	0.1
1987 Cle-A	0	0	—	2	0	0	0	0	3¹	4	1	3	2	21.6	16.20	28	.286	.444	0	—	0	-4	-4	0	0.0
1988 Cle-A	0	0	—	3	0	0	0	0	2²	2	0	1	0	10.1	0.00	—	.286	.375	0	—	0	1	1	0	0.0
1989 Cle-A	0	1	.000	3	0	0	0	0	3²	5	4	3	4	24.5	7.36	54	.313	.476	0	—	0	-1	-1	-0	-0.5
1990 Cle-A	0	0	—	5	0	0	0	0	12²	16	2	7	9	16.3	3.55	110	.308	.390	0	—	0	2	1	0	0.2
1991 Det-A	0	1	.000	10	0	0	0	2	5	6	1	6	4	19.8	9.00	46	.286	.423	0	—	0	-3	-3	-0	-0.7
1993 Cin-N	0	0	—	3	0	0	0	0	3¹	4	2	4	5	16.2	2.70	149	.286	.375	0	—	0	1	1	0	0.2
NY-N	0	0	—	6	0	0	0	0	4²	6	1	3	5	17.4	11.57	35	.353	.450	0	—	0	-4	-4	0	-0.5
Yr	0	0	—	9	0	0	0	0	8	10	1	7	10	16.9	7.88	51	.323	.417	0	—	0	-3	-3	0	-0.3
Total 7	0	2	.000	50	0	0	0	2	52	68	12	48	38	20.1	9.17	45	.318	.443	0	—	0	-30	-30	1	-1.1
● **BOB KAISER**	Kaiser, Robert Thomas b: 4/29/50, Cincinnati, Ohio BB/TL, 5'10", 175 lbs. Deb: 9/3/71																								
1971 Cle-A	0	0	—	5	0	0	0	0	3	2	0	4	3	19.5	4.50	85	.333	.448	0	—	0	-1	-0	-0	0.0
● **GEORGE KAISERLING**	Kaiserling, George b: 5/12/1893, Steubenville, Ohio d: 3/2/18, Steubenville, Ohio BR/TR, 6', 175 lbs. Deb: 4/20/14																								
1914 Ind-F	17	10	.630	37	33	20	1	0	275¹	288	8	72	75	12.3	3.11	100	.274	.330	11	.112	-7	-7	0	-3	-1.0
1915 New-F	15	15	.500	41	29	16	5	2	261¹	246	1	73	75	11.3	2.24	114	.257	.316	12	.152	-3	14	9	-1	0.6
Total 2	32	25	.561	78	62	36	6	2	536²	534	9	145	150	11.8	2.68	106	.266	.323	23	.130	-10	8	9	-5	-0.4
● **BILL KALFASS**	Kalfass, William Philip "Lefty" b: 3/3/16, New York, N.Y. d: 9/8/68, Brooklyn, N.Y. BR/TL, 6'3.5", 190 lbs. Deb: 9/15/37																								
1937 Phi-A	1	0	1.000	4	1	0	0	0	9	9	1	6	5	15.0	3.00	157	.233	.377	0	.000	-1	2	2	-0	0.1
● **RUDY KALLIO**	Kallio, Rudolph b: 12/14/1892, Portland, Ore. d: 4/6/79, Newport, Ore. BR/TR, 5'10", 160 lbs. Deb: 4/25/18																								
1918 Det-A	8	14	.364	30	22	11	0	2	181¹	178	0	76	70	12.7	3.62	73	.261	.336	9	.161	-1	-17	-19	-0	-2.4
1919 Det-A	0	0	—	12	1	0	0	1	22¹	28	0	8	3	14.9	5.64	57	.326	.389	0	.000	-1	-6	-6	-0	-0.2
1925 Bos-A	1	4	.200	7	4	1	0	0	18²	28	0	9	2	18.3	7.71	59	.364	.437	2	.333	0	-7	-7	-0	-1.3
Total 3	9	18	.333	49	27	12	0	2	222¹	234	0	93	75	13.4	4.17	69	.277	.351	11	.167	-1	-30	-32	-1	-3.9
● **SCOTT KAMIENIECKI**	Kamieniecki, Scott Andrew b: 4/19/64, Mt.Clemens, Mich. BR/TR, 6', 195 lbs. Deb: 6/18/91																								
1991 NY-A	4	4	.500	9	9	1	0	0	55¹	54	9	22	34	12.8	3.90	106	.256	.335	0	—	0	1	1	1	0.2
1992 NY-A	6	14	.300	28	28	4	0	0	188	193	13	74	88	13.0	4.36	90	.269	.342	0	—	0	-9	-9	-1	-0.9
1993 NY-A	10	7	.588	30	20	2	0	0	154¹	163	17	59	72	13.1	4.08	102	.277	.346	0	—	0	4	1	3	0.4
1994 NY-A	8	6	.571	22	16	1	0	0	117¹	115	9	59	71	13.6	3.76	122	.261	.353	0	—	0	14	11	0	1.3
1995 *NY-A	7	6	.538	17	16	1	0	0	89²	83	8	49	43	13.6	4.01	115	.246	.346	0	—	0	7	6	1	0.8
1996 NY-A	1	2	.333	7	5	0	0	0	22²	36	6	19	15	22.6	11.12	45	.364	.475	0	—	0	-15	-15	0	-1.5
Total 6	36	39	.480	113	94	8	0	1	627¹	644	65	282	323	13.6	4.33	98	.269	.351	0	—	0	2	-5	1	0.3

YEAR TM/L	W	L	PCT	G	GS	CG	SH	SV	IP	H	HR	BB	SO	RAT	ERA	ERA+	OAV	OOB	BH	AVG	PB	PR	/A	PD	TPI
● **BOB KAMMEYER**			Kammeyer, Robert Lynn b: 12/2/50, Kansas City, Kan. BR/TR, 6'4", 210 lbs. Deb: 7/3/78																					
1978 NY-A	0	0	—	7	0	0	0	0	21²	24	1	6	11	13.3	5.82	62	.276	.337	0	—	0	-5	-5	1	0.1
1979 NY-A	0	0	—	1	0	0	0	0	0	7	2	0	0	∞	∞		1.000	1.000	0	—	0	-8	-8	0	-0.6
Total 2	0	0	—	8	0	0	0	0	21²	31	3	6	11	16.6	9.14	40	.330	.388	0	—	0	-13	-13	1	-0.5
● **IKE KAMP**			Kamp, Alphonse Francis b: 9/5/1900, Roxbury, Mass. d: 2/25/55, Boston, Mass. BB/TL, 6', 170 lbs. Deb: 9/16/24																					
1924 Bos-N	0	1	.000	1	1	0	0	0	7	9	0	5	4	18.0	5.14	74	.360	.467	0	.000	-0	-1	-1	0	-0.1
1925 Bos-N	2	4	.333	24	4	1	0	0	58¹	68	0	35	20	15.9	5.09	79	.301	.395	2	.167	-0	-5	-7	0	-0.6
Total 2	2	5	.286	25	5	1	0	0	65¹	77	0	40	24	16.1	5.10	78	.307	.402	2	.154	-0	-6	-8	1	-0.7
● **HARRY KANE**			Kane, Harry "Klondike" (b: Harry Cohen) b: 7/27/1883, Hamburg, Ark. d: 9/15/32, Portland, Ore. BL/TL Deb: 8/8/02																					
1902 StL-A	0	1	.000	4	1	0	0	0	23	34	2	16	7	19.6	5.48	64	.343	.435	1	.111	-1	-5	-5	-0	-0.3
1903 Det-A	0	2	.000	3	3	2	0	0	18	26	0	8	10	17.5	8.50	34	.338	.407	1	.143	-0	-11	-11	-1	-1.0
1905 Phi-N	1	1	.500	2	2	1	0	0	17	12	0	8	12	10.6	1.59	184	.203	.299	1	.167	-0	3	3	-0	0.2
1906 Phi-N	1	3	.250	6	3	2	0	0	28	28	0	18	14	15.8	3.86	68	.255	.374	0	.000	-1	-4	-4	0	-0.6
Total 4	2	7	.222	15	9	5	0	0	86	100	2	50	43	16.1	4.81	62	.290	.386	3	.100	-2	-17	-17	-1	-1.7
● **ERV KANTLEHNER**			Kantlehner, Erving Leslie "Peanuts" b: 7/31/1892, San Jose, Cal. d: 2/3/90, Santa Barbara, Cal. BL/TL, 6', 190 lbs. Deb: 4/17/14																					
1914 Pit-N	3	2	.600	21	5	3	2	0	67	51	0	39	26	12.5	3.09	86	.218	.337	1	.067	-0	-2	-3	-0	-0.3
1915 Pit-N	5	12	.294	29	18	10	1	3	163	135	1	58	64	10.9	2.26	121	.230	.304	15	.288	3	9	8	1	1.4
1916 Pit-N	5	15	.250	34	21	7	2	2	165	151	1	57	49	11.6	3.16	85	.249	.317	8	.174	-0	-10	-9	1	-1.0
Phi-N				3	0	0	0	0	4	7	0	3	2	22.5	9.00	29	.500	.588	0	—	-0	-3	-3	0	0.0
Yr	5	15	.250	37	21	7	2	2	169	158	1	60	51	11.6	3.30	81	.253	.318	8	.174	-0	-13	-12	1	-1.0
Total 3	13	29	.310	87	44	20	5	5	399	344	2	157	141	11.5	2.84	95	.239	.318	24	.212	2	-6	-6	2	0.1
● **MATT KARCHNER**			Karchner, Matthew Dean b: 6/28/67, Berwick, Pa. BR/TR, 6'4", 245 lbs. Deb: 7/18/95																					
1995 Chi-A	4	2	.667	31	0	0	0	0	32	33	2	12	24	12.9	1.69	264	.275	.346	0	—	0	11	10	0	2.0
1996 Chi-A	7	4	.636	50	0	0	0	0	59¹	61	10	41	46	15.8	5.76	81	.266	.382	0	—	0	-5	-7	-1	-1.1
Total 2	11	6	.647	81	0	0	0	0	91¹	94	12	53	70	14.8	4.34	106	.269	.370	0	—	0	6	3	-1	0.9
● **PAUL KARDOW**			Kardow, Paul Otto "Tex" b: 9/19/15, Humble, Tex. d: 4/27/68, San Antonio, Tex. BR/TR, 6'6", 210 lbs. Deb: 7/1/36																					
1936 Cle-A	0	0	—	2	0	0	0	0	2	1	0	2	0	13.5	4.50	112	.167	.375			0	0	0	-0	0.0
● **ED KARGER**			Karger, Edwin "Loose" b: 5/6/1883, San Angelo, Tex. d: 9/9/57, Delta, Colo. BR/TL, 5'11", 185 lbs. Deb: 4/15/06																					
1906 Pit-N	2	3	.400	6	2	0	0	0	28	21	0	9	8	10.3	1.93	139	.204	.281	1	.091	-1	2	2	1	0.5
StL-N	5	16	.238	25	20	17	0	1	191²	193	0	43	73	11.4	2.72	97	.271	.319	17	.233	4	-2	-2	3	0.6
Yr	7	19	.269	31	22	17	0	1	219²	214	0	52	81	11.2	2.62	100	.262	.312	18	.214	3	0	0	4	1.1
1907 StL-N	15	19	.441	39	32	29	6	1	314	257	2	65	137	9.5	2.04	123	.223	.270	20	.179	1	15	16	4	2.6
1908 StL-N	4	9	.308	22	15	9	1	0	141⁴	148	1	50	34	12.7	3.06	77	.260	.322	13	.241	1	-11	-11	-1	-0.8
1909 Cin-N	1	3	.250	9	5	1	0	0	34¹	26	0	30	15	15.2	4.46	58	.217	.382	3	.273	2	-7	-7	-0	-0.6
Bos-A	5	2	.714	12	6	3	0	0	68	71	0	22	17	12.7	3.18	79	.273	.337	1	.125	-0	-5	-5	-0	-0.6
1910 Bos-A	11	7	.611	27	25	16	1	1	183¹	162	5	53	81	10.8	3.19	80	.230	.289	20	.294	6	-14	-13	-2	-0.9
1911 Bos-A	5	8	.385	25	18	6	1	0	131	134	4	42	57	12.4	3.37	97	.272	.334	11	.234	3	-0	-1	-0	0.2
Total 6	48	67	.417	165	123	81	9	3	1091²	1012	12	314	415	11.2	2.79	94	.246	.305	88	.220	18	-22	-20	5	1.0
● **ANDY KARL**			Karl, Anton Andrew b: 4/8/14, Mt.Vernon, N.Y. d: 4/8/89, LaJolla, Cal. BR/TR, 6'1.5", 175 lbs. Deb: 4/24/43																					
1943 Bos-A	1	1	.500	11	0	0	0	1	26	31	0	13	6	15.2	3.46	96	.310	.389	2	.286	0	-0	-0	1	0.1
Phi-N	1	2	.333	9	2	0	0	0	26²	44	0	11	4	18.6	7.09	48	.383	.437	2	.250	1	-11	-11	0	-1.0
1944 Phi-N	2	3	.600	38	0	0	0	2	89	76	1	26	29	9.9	2.33	155	.237	.287	3	.200	1	13	13	1	0.9
1945 Phi-N	8	8	.500	**67**	2	1	0	**15**	180²	175	7	50	51	11.4	2.99	128	.253	.306	7	.143	-2	**16**	**17**	1	1.6
1946 Phi-N	3	7	.300	39	0	0	0	5	65¹	84	6	22	15	14.7	4.96	69	.321	.375	1	.100	-0	-11	-11	1	-1.8
1947 Bos-N	2	3	.400	27	0	0	0	3	55	41	2	13	3	13.9	3.86	101	.318	.380	1	.167	-0	1	0	2	0.2
Total 5	18	23	.439	191	4	1	0	26	422²	451	16	130	107	12.5	3.51	104	.279	.334	16	.168	-0	7	7	6	0.0
● **SCOTT KARL**			Karl, Randall Scott b: 8/9/71, Fontana, Cal. BL/TL, 6'2", 195 lbs. Deb: 5/4/95																					
1995 Mil-A	6	7	.462	25	18	1	0	0	124	141	10	50	59	14.1	4.14	120	.288	.358	0	—	0	8	12	0	0.8
1996 Mil-A	13	9	.591	32	32	3	1	0	207¹	220	29	72	121	13.2	4.86	108	.271	.338	0	—	0	3	9	-1	0.5
Total 2	19	16	.543	57	50	4	1	0	331¹	361	39	122	180	13.5	4.59	112	.277	.346	0	—	0	11	21	-0	1.3
● **BILL KARNS**			Karns, William Arthur b: 12/28/1875, Richmond, Iowa d: 11/15/41, Seattle, Wash. BL/TL, Deb: 8/1/01																					
1901 Bal-A	1	0	1.000	3	1	0	0	0	17	30	0	9	5	20.6	6.35	61	.380	.443	1	.143	-0	-5	-5	-0	-0.3
● **RYAN KARP**			Karp, Ryan Jason b: 4/5/70, Los Angeles, Cal. BL/TL, 6'4", 220 lbs. Deb: 6/23/95																					
1995 Phi-N	0	0	—	1	0	0	0	0	2	1	0	3	2	18.0	4.50	94	.143	.400	0	—	0	-0	-0	-0	0.0
● **HERB KARPEL**			Karpel, Herbert "Lefty" b: 12/27/17, Brooklyn, N.Y. BL/TL, 5'9.5", 180 lbs. Deb: 4/19/46																					
1946 NY-A	0	0	—	2	0	0	0	0	1²	4	0	0	0	21.6	10.80	32	.500	.500	0	—	0	-1	-1	-0	0.0
● **BENN KARR**			Karr, Benjamin Joyce "Baldy" b: 11/28/1893, Mt.Pleasant, Miss. d: 12/8/68, Memphis, Tenn. BL/TR, 6', 175 lbs. Deb: 4/20/20																					
1920 Bos-A	3	8	.273	26	6	3	0	0	91²	109	3	24	21	13.2	4.81	76	.304	.349	21	.280	6	-10	-12	-1	-0.8
1921 Bos-A	8	7	.533	26	7	5	0	0	117²	123	8	38	37	12.4	3.67	115	.283	.342	16	.258	1	8	7	-0	0.9
1922 Bos-A	5	12	.294	41	13	7	0	1	183¹	212	10	45	41	12.9	4.47	92	.302	.348	21	.214	-1	-9	-7	-1	-0.7
1925 Cle-A	11	12	.478	32	24	12	1	0	197²	248	8	80	41	15.2	4.78	92	.317	.385	24	.261	4	-8	-8	2	-0.2
1926 Cle-A	5	6	.455	30	7	4	0	0	113¹	137	9	41	23	14.6	5.00	81	.291	.355	10	.222	2	-12	-12	1	-0.8
1927 Cle-A	3	3	.500	22	5	1	0	2	76²	92	5	32	17	14.7	5.05	83	.315	.385	4	.200	1	-8	-8	1	-0.3
Total 6	35	48	.422	177	58	29	1	5	780¹	921	43	260	180	13.9	4.60	90	.303	.362	96	.245	12	-40	-39	2	-1.9
● **STEVE KARSAY**			Karsay, Stefan Andrew b: 3/24/72, Flushing, N.Y. BR/TR, 6'3", 210 lbs. Deb: 8/17/93																					
1993 Oak-A	3	3	.500	8	8	0	0	0	49	49	4	16	33	12.3	4.04	101	.258	.322	0	—	0	2	0	-1	0.3
1994 Oak-A	1	1	.500	4	4	1	0	0	28	26	1	8	15	11.3	2.57	172	.252	.313	0	—	0	7	6	0	0.7
Total 2	4	4	.500	12	12	1	0	0	77	75	5	24	48	11.9	3.51	120	.256	.319	0	—	0	8	6	-1	1.0
● **JACK KATOLL**			Katoll, John "Big Jack" b: 6/24/1872, Germany d: 6/18/55, Hartland, Ill. BR/TR, 5'11", 195 lbs. Deb: 9/9/1898																					
1898 Chi-N	0	1	.000	2	1	1	0	0	11	8	0	1	3	7.4	0.82	438	.200	.220	0	.000	-1	3	3	-0	0.2
1899 Chi-N	1	1	.500	2	2	2	0	0	18	17	0	4	1	11.0	6.00	62	.250	.301	0	.000	-1	-4	-5	0	-0.4
1901 Chi-A	11	10	.524	27	25	19	0	0	208	231	3	53	59	12.8	2.81	124	.278	.330	10	.125	-4	20	15	2	1.1
1902 Chi-A	0	0	—	1	0	0	0	0	1	1	0	0	2	9.0	0.00		.250	.250	0	.000	-0	0	0	0	0.0
Bal-A	5	10	.333	15	13	13	0	0	123	175	5	32	25	15.3	4.02	94	.334	.375	10	.175	-0	-6	-3	4	0.0
Yr	5	10	.333	16	13	13	0	0	124	176	5	32	27	15.2	3.99	94	.333	.374	10	.172	-0	-6	-3	4	0.0
Total 4	17	22	.436	47	41	35	0	0	361	432	8	90	90	13.4	3.32	109	.294	.341	20	.134	-6	13	11	6	0.9
● **BOB KATZ**			Katz, Robert Clyde b: 1/30/11, Lancaster, Pa. d: 12/14/62, St.Joseph, Mich. BR/TR, 5'11.5", 190 lbs. Deb: 5/12/44																					
1944 Cin-N	0	1	.000	6	2	0	0	0	18¹	17	0	7	4	11.8	3.93	89	.254	.324	0	.000	-1	-1	-1	1	0.0
● **CURT KAUFMAN**			Kaufman, Curt Gerrard b: 7/19/57, Omaha, Neb. BR/TR, 6'2", 175 lbs. Deb: 9/10/82																					
1982 NY-A	1	0	1.000	7	0	0	0	0	8²	9	2	6	6	15.6	5.19	77	.265	.375	0	—	0	-1	-1	-0	-0.1
1983 NY-A	0	0	—	4	0	0	0	0	8²	10	0	4	3	14.5	3.12	125	.303	.378	0	—	0	1	0	-1	0.1
1984 Cal-A	2	3	.400	29	1	0	0	1	69	68	13	20	41	11.5	4.57	87	.254	.306	0	—	0	-4	-5	0	-0.3
Total 3	3	3	.500	40	1	0	0	1	86¹	87	15	30	50	12.2	4.48	88	.260	.321	0	—	0	-5	-5	-0	-0.3
● **TONY KAUFMANN**			Kaufmann, Anthony Charles b: 12/16/1900, Chicago, Ill. d: 6/4/82, Elgin, Ill. BR/TR, 5'11", 165 lbs. Deb: 9/23/21 C♦																					
1921 Chi-N	1	0	1.000	2	1	1	0	0	13	12	0	3	6	10.4	4.15	92	.240	.283	2	.400	1	-1	-0	-1	0.0
1922 Chi-N	7	13	.350	37	14	4	1	3	153	161	15	57	45	13.1	4.06	103	.273	.343	9	.200	1	1	2	-1	0.3

YEAR	TM/L	W	L	PCT	G	GS	CG	SH	SV	IP	H	HR	BB	SO	RAT	ERA	ERA+	OAV	OOB	BH	AVG	PB	PR	/A	PD	TPI
1923	Chi-N	14	10	.583	33	24	18	2	3	206	209	14	67	72	12.5	3.10	129	.264	.330	16	.216	3	21	21	-1	2.4
1924	Chi-N	16	11	.593	34	26	16	3	0	208¹	218	21	66	79	12.4	4.02	97	.272	.330	24	.316	6	-3	-3	-1	0.1
1925	Chi-N	13	13	.500	31	23	14	2	2	196	221	9	77	49	14.0	4.50	96	.292	.363	15	.192	1	-5	-4	-0	-0.3
1926	Chi-N	9	7	.563	26	21	14	1	2	169²	169	6	44	52	11.6	3.02	127	.262	.316	15	.250	2	15	15	-2	1.4
1927	Chi-N	3	3	.500	9	6	3	0	0	53¹	75	8	19	21	16.5	6.41	60	.338	.400	5	.313	3	-15	-15	2	-1.0
	Phi-N	0	3	.000	5	5	1	0	0	18²	37	2	8	4	21.7	10.61	39	.425	.474	1	.143	0	-14	-13	-0	-1.6
	StL-N	0	0	—	1	0	0	0	0	0¹	4	0	1	0	135.0	81.00	5	1.000	1.000	0	—	0	-3	-3	0	0.0
	Yr	3	6	.333	15	11	4	0	0	72¹	116	10	28	25	17.9	7.84	50	.366	.417	6	.261	3	-32	-31	1	-2.6
1928	StL-N	0	0	—	4	1	0	0	0	4²	8	1	4	2	25.1	9.64	41	.444	.565	0	—	0	-3	-3	-0	0.0
1930	StL-N	0	1	.000	2	1	0	0	0	10¹	15	2	4	2	16.5	7.84	64	.357	.413	1	.333	0	-3	-3	-0	-0.2
1931	StL-N	1	1	.500	15	1	0	0	0	49	65	3	17	13	15.2	6.06	65	.319	.374	2	.111	-1	-12	-12	0	-0.6
1935	StL-N	0	0	—	3	0	0	0	0	3²	4	0	1	0	12.3	2.45	167	.286	.333	0	—	0	1	1	0	0.0
Total	11	64	62	.508	202	123	71	9	12	1086¹	1198	81	368	345	13.3	4.18	97	.284	.347	91	.220	17	-22	-17	-5	0.5

● **GREG KEAGLE**   Keagle, Gregory Charles   b: 6/28/71, Corning, N.Y.   BR/TR, 6'1", 185 lbs.   Deb: 4/1/96

YEAR	TM/L	W	L	PCT	G	GS	CG	SH	SV	IP	H	HR	BB	SO	RAT	ERA	ERA+	OAV	OOB	BH	AVG	PB	PR	/A	PD	TPI
1996	Det-A	3	6	.333	26	6	0	0	0	87²	104	13	68	70	18.6	7.39	68	.298	.425	0	—	0	-23	-23	-0	-1.8

● **STEVE KEALEY**   Kealey, Steven William   b: 5/13/47, Torrance, Cal.   BR/TR, 6', 185 lbs.   Deb: 9/9/68

YEAR	TM/L	W	L	PCT	G	GS	CG	SH	SV	IP	H	HR	BB	SO	RAT	ERA	ERA+	OAV	OOB	BH	AVG	PB	PR	/A	PD	TPI
1968	Cal-A	0	1	.000	6	0	0	0	0	10	10	0	5	4	13.5	2.70	108	.256	.341	0	—	0	0	0	-1	0.0
1969	Cal-A	2	0	1.000	15	3	1	1	0	36²	48	4	13	17	15.2	3.93	89	.322	.380	0	.000	-1	-1	-2	-1	-0.3
1970	Cal-A	1	0	1.000	17	0	0	0	0	21²	19	2	6	14	10.4	4.15	87	.260	.316	1	.250	0	-1	-1	-1	-0.1
1971	Chi-A	2	2	.500	54	1	0	0	6	77¹	69	10	26	50	11.1	3.84	93	.239	.302	2	.200	1	-3	-2	-0	-0.1
1972	Chi-A	3	2	.600	40	0	0	0	4	57¹	50	4	12	37	9.7	3.30	95	.234	.274	0	.000	-0	-2	-1	-1	-0.2
1973	Chi-A	0	0	—	7	0	0	0	0	11¹	22	2	7	4	23.8	15.09	26	.418	.484	0	—	0	-14	-14	-0	-0.7
Total	6	8	5	.615	139	4	1	1	11	214¹	219	22	69	126	12.1	4.28	80	.267	.325	3	.115	-0	-21	-20	-3	-0.7

● **ED KEAS**   Keas, Edward James   b: 2/2/1863, Dubuque, Iowa   d: 1/12/40, Dubuque, Iowa   Deb: 8/25/1888

YEAR	TM/L	W	L	PCT	G	GS	CG	SH	SV	IP	H	HR	BB	SO	RAT	ERA	ERA+	OAV	OOB	BH	AVG	PB	PR	/A	PD	TPI
1888	Cle-a	3	3	.500	6	6	6	0	0	51	53	1	12	18	11.6	2.29	135	.259	.303	2	.087	-2	4	5	1	0.3

● **RAY KEATING**   Keating, Raymond Herbert   b: 7/21/1891, Bridgeport, Conn.   d: 12/28/63, Sacramento, Cal.   BR/TR, 5'11", 185 lbs.   Deb: 9/12/12

YEAR	TM/L	W	L	PCT	G	GS	CG	SH	SV	IP	H	HR	BB	SO	RAT	ERA	ERA+	OAV	OOB	BH	AVG	PB	PR	/A	PD	TPI
1912	NY-A	0	3	.000	6	5	3	0	0	35²	36	0	18	21	13.9	5.80	62	.265	.355	6	.375	1	-10	-9	0	-0.5
1913	NY-A	6	12	.333	28	21	9	2	0	151¹	147	3	51	83	11.9	3.21	93	.253	.316	3	.070	-3	-5	-4	-2	-0.9
1914	NY-A	7	11	.389	34	25	14	0	1	210	198	1	67	109	11.6	2.96	93	.253	.316	12	.169	-0	-5	-5	2	-0.1
1915	NY-A	3	6	.333	11	10	8	1	0	79¹	66	3	45	37	12.9	3.63	81	.228	.337	4	.154	-1	-6	-6	1	-0.6
1916	NY-A	5	6	.455	14	11	6	0	0	91	91	4	35	35	12.9	3.07	94	.271	.349	7	.241	1	-2	-2	1	-0.5
1918	NY-A	2	2	.500	15	6	1	0	0	48¹	39	0	30	16	13.2	3.91	72	.238	.362	3	.188	0	-6	-6	0	-0.5
1919	Bos-N	7	11	.389	22	14	9	1	0	136	129	2	45	48	11.6	2.98	96	.261	.325	7	.152	-1	-1	-2	-2	-0.2
Total	7	30	51	.370	130	92	50	4	1	751²	706	13	293	349	12.2	3.29	88	.254	.329	42	.170	-2	-35	-33	-2	-2.7

● **BOB KEATING**   Keating, Robert M.   b: 9/22/1862, Springfield, Mass   d: 1/19/22, Springfield, Mass.   BL/TL, 6'4", 190 lbs.   Deb: 8/27/1887

YEAR	TM/L	W	L	PCT	G	GS	CG	SH	SV	IP	H	HR	BB	SO	RAT	ERA	ERA+	OAV	OOB	BH	AVG	PB	PR	/A	PD	TPI
1887	Bal-a	0	1	.000	1	1	1	0	0	9	16	0	6	0	22.0	11.00	37	.372	.449	1	.250	-1	-7	-7	0	-0.4

● **CACTUS KECK**   Keck, Frank Joseph   b: 1/13/1899, St.Louis, Mo.   d: 2/6/81, Kirkwood, Mo.   BR/TR, 5'11", 170 lbs.   Deb: 5/26/22

YEAR	TM/L	W	L	PCT	G	GS	CG	SH	SV	IP	H	HR	BB	SO	RAT	ERA	ERA+	OAV	OOB	BH	AVG	PB	PR	/A	PD	TPI
1922	Cin-N	7	6	.538	27	15	5	1	1	131	138	4	29	27	11.8	3.37	119	.276	.322	7	.159	-1	11	9	-3	0.3
1923	Cin-N	3	6	.333	35	6	1	0	2	87	84	5	32	16	12.3	3.72	104	.254	.325	1	.059	-1	3	1	1	0.1
Total	2	10	12	.455	62	21	6	1	3	218	222	9	61	43	12.0	3.51	112	.267	.323	8	.131	-2	13	10	-3	0.4

● **DAVE KEEFE**   Keefe, David Edwin   b: 1/9/1897, Williston, Vt.   d: 2/4/78, Kansas City, Mo.   BL/TR, 5'9", 165 lbs.   Deb: 4/21/17   C

YEAR	TM/L	W	L	PCT	G	GS	CG	SH	SV	IP	H	HR	BB	SO	RAT	ERA	ERA+	OAV	OOB	BH	AVG	PB	PR	/A	PD	TPI
1917	Phi-A	1	0	1.000	3	0	0	0	0	5	5	0	4	1	16.2	1.80	153	.250	.409	0	.000	-0	0	1	0	0.1
1919	Phi-A	0	1	.000	1	1	1	0	0	9	8	0	3	5	11.0	4.00	86	.242	.306	0	.000	-0	-1	-1	0	-0.1
1920	Phi-A	6	7	.462	31	13	7	1	0	130¹	129	2	30	41	11.4	2.97	136	.262	.313	10	.250	-0	12	15	1	1.5
1921	Phi-A	2	9	.182	44	12	4	0	1	173	214	19	64	68	14.7	4.68	65	.311	.374	10	.175	-3	-8	-4	-2	-0.7
1922	Cle-A	0	0	—	18	1	0	0	0	36¹	47	2	12	11	14.6	6.19	65	.333	.386	2	.333	1	-9	-9	-0	-0.1
Total	5	9	17	.346	97	27	12	1	1	353²	403	23	113	126	13.4	4.15	101	.294	.352	22	.206	-3	-5	2	-1	0.8

● **GEORGE KEEFE**   Keefe, George W.   b: 1/7/1867, Washington, D.C.   d: 8/24/35, Washington, D.C.   BL/TL, 5'9", 168 lbs.   Deb: 7/30/1886

YEAR	TM/L	W	L	PCT	G	GS	CG	SH	SV	IP	H	HR	BB	SO	RAT	ERA	ERA+	OAV	OOB	BH	AVG	PB	PR	/A	PD	TPI
1886	Was-N	0	3	.000	4	4	4	0	0	31¹	28	0	15	5	12.4	5.17	64	.233	.319	0	.000	-2	-6	-7	-1	-0.7
1887	Was-N	0	1	.000	1	1	1	0	0	8	16	1	4	0	24.8	9.00	45	.364	.440	0	.000	-1	-4	-4	-0	-0.4
1888	Was-N	6	7	.462	13	13	13	1	0	114	87	2	43	52	10.6	2.84	99	.206	.286	9	.214	1	0	-0	1	0.2
1889	Was-N	8	18	.308	30	28	24	0	0	230	266	6	143	90	16.2	5.13	77	.281	.378	16	.163	-2	-28	-30	-2	-2.8
1890	Buf-P	6	16	.273	25	22	22	0	1	196	280	11	138	95	19.4	6.52	63	.321	.417	16	.203	1	-50	-53	-1	-3.9
1891	Was-a	0	3	.000	5	4	4	0	1	37	44	0	17	11	15.1	2.68	140	.286	.360	2	.143	-0	4	4	1	0.3
Total	6	20	48	.294	78	72	68	5	1	616¹	721	20	360	213	16.0	5.05	74	.282	.374	43	.172	-3	-85	-90	-4	-7.3

● **JOHN KEEFE**   Keefe, John Thomas   b: 5/5/1867, Fitchburg, Mass.   d: 8/9/37, Fitchburg, Mass.   TL ,   Deb: 4/28/1890

YEAR	TM/L	W	L	PCT	G	GS	CG	SH	SV	IP	H	HR	BB	SO	RAT	ERA	ERA+	OAV	OOB	BH	AVG	PB	PR	/A	PD	TPI
1890	Syr-a	17	24	.415	43	41	36	2	0	352¹	355	9	148	120	13.5	4.32	82	.254	.336	30	.191	-5	-17	-31	0	-3.1

● **BOBBY KEEFE**   Keefe, Robert Francis   b: 6/16/1882, Folsom, Cal.   d: 12/7/64, Sacramento, Cal.   BR/TR, 5'11", 155 lbs.   Deb: 4/15/07

YEAR	TM/L	W	L	PCT	G	GS	CG	SH	SV	IP	H	HR	BB	SO	RAT	ERA	ERA+	OAV	OOB	BH	AVG	PB	PR	/A	PD	TPI
1907	NY-A	3	5	.375	19	3	0	0	3	57²	60	1	20	20	12.6	2.50	112	.270	.333	1	.053	-2	0	2	0	0.1
1911	Cin-N	12	13	.480	39	26	15	0	3	234¹	196	7	76	105	10.6	2.69	123	.229	.294	6	.086	-2	19	16	-5	0.8
1912	Cin-N	1	3	.250	17	6	0	0	2	68²	78	0	33	29	15.1	5.24	64	.289	.375	3	.167	-1	-14	-14	0	-0.9
Total	3	16	21	.432	75	35	15	0	8	360²	334	8	129	154	11.8	3.14	103	.248	.317	10	.093	-5	5	4	-5	0.0

● **TIM KEEFE**   Keefe, Timothy John "Smiling Tim" or "Sir Timothy"   b: 1/1/1857, Cambridge, Mass.   d: 4/23/33, Cambridge, Mass.   BR/TR, 5'10.5", 185 lbs.   Deb: 8/6/1880   UH

YEAR	TM/L	W	L	PCT	G	GS	CG	SH	SV	IP	H	HR	BB	SO	RAT	ERA	ERA+	OAV	OOB	BH	AVG	PB	PR	/A	PD	TPI
1880	Tro-N	6	6	.500	12	12	12	0	0	105	68	0	16	39	**7.2**	**0.86**	**294**	**.178**	**.212**	10	.233	-0	18	19	1	2.2
1881	Tro-N	18	27	.400	45	45	45	4	0	402	442	4	81	103	11.7	3.25	91	.274	.309	35	.230	4	-21	-13	-0	-0.9
1882	Tro-N	17	26	.395	43	42	41	1	0	375	368	4	81	116	10.8	2.50	113	.244	.283	43	.228	5	17	14	5	2.2
1883	NY-a	41	27	.603	**68**	68	**68**	5	0	**619**	488	6	108	**359**	**8.7**	2.41	138	**.203**	**.237**	57	.220	4	61	64	6	6.6
1884	*NY-A	37	17	.685	58	58	56	4	0	483	380	5	71	334	8.7	2.25	138	**.204**	.239	50	.238	12	53	47	-0	5.5
1885	NY-N	32	13	.711	46	46	45	7	0	400	300	6	102	227	9.0	**1.58**	**169**	.203	.255	27	.163	-1	55	49	0	4.7
1886	NY-N	**42**	20	.677	**64**	64	**62**	2	0	**535**	479	9	102	297	9.8	2.56	126	.231	.267	35	.171	1	45	39	1	3.7
1887	NY-N	35	19	.648	56	56	54	2	0	476²	428	11	108	189	**10.3**	3.12	121	**.230**	**.276**	42	.220	8	51	35	3	3.8
1888	*NY-N	**35**	12	**.745**	51	51	48	**8**	0	434¹	317	5	90	**335**	**8.7**	**1.74**	**157**	**.196**	.243	23	.127	-6	**54**	48	1	4.2
1889	*NY-N	28	13	.683	47	45	39	1	0	364	319	9	151	225	12.1	3.31	119	**.228**	.312	23	.154	-4	28	25	2	2.1
1890	NY-P	17	11	.607	30	30	23	1	0	229	225	6	89	89	12.7	3.38	134	.246	.318	10	.109	-5	22	30	1	2.4
1891	NY-N	2	5	.286	8	7	4	0	0	55	70	1	27	30	16.5	5.24	61	.299	.381	2	.095	-1	-12	-12	0	-1.2
	Phi-N	3	6	.333	11	10	9	0	0	78¹	82	2	30	34	13.3	3.91	87	.259	.331	5	.172	-0	-5	-4	0	-0.4
	Yr	5	11	.313	19	17	13	0	0	133¹	152	3	57	64	14.4	4.45	75	.274	.346	7	.140	-1	-16	-17	1	-1.6
1892	Phi-N	19	16	.543	39	38	31	2	0	313¹	264	4	100	127	10.8	2.36	138	.219	.286	10	.085	-7	32	31	1	2.2
1893	Phi-N	10	7	.588	22	22	17	0	0	178	202	8	50	56	14.9	4.40	104	.277	.359	18	.228	0	5	4	-2	0.1
Total	14	342	225	.603	600	594	554	39	2	5047²	4432	75	1236	2560	10.3	2.62	125	.226	.275	390	.187	11	404	375	18	37.2

● **ED KEEGAN**   Keegan, Edward Charles   b: 7/8/39, Camden, N.J.   BR/TR, 6'3", 165 lbs.   Deb: 8/24/59

YEAR	TM/L	W	L	PCT	G	GS	CG	SH	SV	IP	H	HR	BB	SO	RAT	ERA	ERA+	OAV	OOB	BH	AVG	PB	PR	/A	PD	TPI
1959	Phi-N	0	3	.000	3	3	0	0	0	9	19	2	13	3	33.0	18.00	23	.432	.569	0	.000	-0	-14	-14	-0	-2.6
1961	KC-A	0	0	—	6	0	0	0	1	6	6	0	5	3	16.5	4.50	93	.261	.393	0	—	-0	-0	-0	-0	0.0
1962	Phi-N	0	0	—	4	0	0	0	0	8	6	1	5	5	13.5	2.25	172	.214	.353	0	—	-0	1	-0	-0	0.0
Total	3	0	3	.000	13	3	0	0	1	23	31	3	23	11	21.9	9.00	45	.326	.467	0	.000	-0	-13	-13	-1	-2.6

● **BOB KEEGAN**   Keegan, Robert Charles "Smiley"   b: 8/4/20, Rochester, N.Y.   BR/TR, 6'2.5", 207 lbs.   Deb: 5/24/53

YEAR	TM/L	W	L	PCT	G	GS	CG	SH	SV	IP	H	HR	BB	SO	RAT	ERA	ERA+	OAV	OOB	BH	AVG	PB	PR	/A	PD	TPI
1953	Chi-A	7	5	.583	22	11	4	2	1	98²	80	4	33	32	10.5	2.74	147	.223	.293	9	.321	2	14	14	1	1.9
1954	Chi-A★	16	9	.640	31	27	14	2	2	209²	211	16	82	61	12.6	3.09	121	.266	.336	9	.120	-2	15	15	-1	1.4

YEAR TM/L	W	L	PCT	G	GS	CG	SH	SV	IP	H	HR	BB	SO	RAT	ERA	ERA+	OAV	OOB	BH	AVG	PB	PR	/A	PD	TPI
1955 Chi-A	2	5	.286	18	11	1	0	0	58²	83	4	28	29	17.2	5.83	68	.336	.406	6	.333	2	-12	-12	0	-1.1
1956 Chi-A	5	7	.417	20	16	4	0	0	105¹	119	15	35	32	13.3	3.93	104	.286	.344	4	.125	-1	3	2	-0	0.1
1957 Chi-A	10	8	.556	30	20	6	2	2	142²	131	22	37	36	10.7	3.53	106	.243	.294	4	.103	-1	4	3	-1	0.1
1958 Chi-A	0	2	.000	14	2	0	0	0	29²	44	9	18	8	18.8	6.07	60	.358	.440	0	.000	-1	-8	-8	1	-0.5
Total 6	40	36	.526	135	87	29	6	5	644²	668	70	233	198	12.7	3.66	105	.270	.335	32	.163	-2	16	14	-1	1.9

● **BURT KEELEY**   Keeley, Burton Elwood "Speed"   b: 11/2/1879, Wilmington, Ill.   d: 5/3/52, Ely, Minn.   BR/TR, 5'9", 170 lbs.   Deb: 4/18/08

YEAR TM/L	W	L	PCT	G	GS	CG	SH	SV	IP	H	HR	BB	SO	RAT	ERA	ERA+	OAV	OOB	BH	AVG	PB	PR	/A	PD	TPI
1908 Was-A	6	11	.353	28	15	12	1	1	169	173	3	48	68	12.0	2.98	77	.259	.313	5	.102	-3	-11	-13	2	-1.5
1909 Was-A	0	0	—	2	0	0	0	0	7	12	0	1	0	18.0	11.57	21	.364	.400	1	.500	0	-7	-7	1	0.1
Total 2	6	11	.353	30	15	12	1	1	176	185	3	49	68	12.2	3.32	69	.264	.317	6	.118	-3	-18	-20	2	-1.4

● **VIC KEEN**   Keen, Howard Victor   b: 3/16/1899, Bel Air, Md.   d: 12/10/76, Salisbury, Md.   BR/TR, 5'9", 165 lbs.   Deb: 8/13/18

YEAR TM/L	W	L	PCT	G	GS	CG	SH	SV	IP	H	HR	BB	SO	RAT	ERA	ERA+	OAV	OOB	BH	AVG	PB	PR	/A	PD	TPI
1918 Phi-A	0	1	.000	1	1	0	0	0	8	9	1	1	1	11.3	3.38	87	.300	.323	0	.000	-0	-1	-0	-1	-0.1
1921 Chi-N	0	3	.000	5	4	1	0	0	25	29	0	9	9	14.0	4.68	82	.319	.386	0	.000	-0	-2	-2	0	-0.3
1922 Chi-N	1	2	.333	7	2	2	0	1	34²	36	4	10	11	12.2	3.89	108	.275	.331	4	.333	1	1	1	-0	0.2
1923 Chi-N	12	8	.600	35	17	10	0	1	177	169	8	57	46	11.7	3.00	133	.255	.319	3	.151	-3	20	20	-2	1.6
1924 Chi-N	15	14	.517	40	28	15	0	3	234²	242	17	80	75	12.5	3.80	103	.272	.335	12	.156	-4	2	3	-3	-0.5
1925 Chi-N	2	6	.250	30	8	1	0	1	83¹	125	8	41	19	17.9	6.26	69	.359	.427	6	.240	0	-18	-18	1	-1.4
1926 *StL-N	10	9	.526	26	21	12	1	0	152	179	15	42	29	13.1	4.56	86	.295	.342	3	.057	-6	-12	-11	-2	-2.0
1927 StL-N	2	1	.667	21	0	0	0	0	33²	39	3	8	12	13.1	4.81	82	.293	.343	1	.250	0	-3	-3	0	-0.2
Total 8	42	44	.488	165	81	41	1	6	748¹	828	56	248	202	13.1	4.11	97	.287	.346	34	.148	-12	-15	-11	-6	-2.7

● **KID KEENAN**   Keenan, Harry Leon   b: 1875, Louisville, Ky.   d: 6/11/03, Covington, Ky.   TR ,   Deb: 8/11/1891

YEAR TM/L	W	L	PCT	G	GS	CG	SH	SV	IP	H	HR	BB	SO	RAT	ERA	ERA+	OAV	OOB	BH	AVG	PB	PR	/A	PD	TPI
1891 Cin-a	0	1	.000	1	1	1	0	0	8	6	0	4	5	12.4	0.00	—	.200	.314	2	.500		3	4	-0	0.5

● **JIM KEENAN**   Keenan, James William   b: 2/10/1858, New Haven, Conn.   d: 9/21/26, Cincinnati, Ohio   BR/TR, 5'10", 186 lbs.   Deb: 5/17/1875   ◆

YEAR TM/L	W	L	PCT	G	GS	CG	SH	SV	IP	H	HR	BB	SO	RAT	ERA	ERA+	OAV	OOB	BH	AVG	PB	PR	/A	PD	TPI
1884 Ind-a	0	0	—	1	0	0	0	0	3	2	0	0	0	6.0	3.00	110	.182	.182	73	.293	0	0	0	-0	0.0
1885 Cin-a	0	0	—	1	0	0	0	0	8	7	0	1	0	9.0	1.13	290	.233	.258	35	.265	0	2	2	-0	0.0
1886 Cin-a	0	1	.000	2	0	0	0	0	8	8	0	3	2	12.4	3.38	104	.258	.324	40	.270	0	0	0	-0	0.0
Total 3	0	1	.000	4	0	0	0	0	19	17	0	4	2	9.9	2.37	142	.236	.276	452	.241	0	2	2	-0	0.0

● **JIMMIE KEENAN**   Keenan, James William "Sparkplug"   b: 5/25/1898, Avon, N.Y.   d: 6/5/80, Seminole, Fla.   BL/TL, 5'7", 155 lbs.   Deb: 9/9/20

YEAR TM/L	W	L	PCT	G	GS	CG	SH	SV	IP	H	HR	BB	SO	RAT	ERA	ERA+	OAV	OOB	BH	AVG	PB	PR	/A	PD	TPI
1920 Phi-N	0	0	—	1	0	0	0	0	3	3	1	2	0	12.0	3.00	114	.333	.400	0	.000	-0	0	-0	-0	0.0
1921 Phi-N	1	2	.333	15	2	0	0	0	32¹	48	3	15	7	17.8	6.68	63	.364	.432	0	.000	-1	-10	-9	-1	-0.9
Total 2	1	2	.333	16	2	0	0	0	35¹	51	3	17	7	17.3	6.37	65	.362	.430	0	.000	-2	-10	-9	-1	-0.9

● **JEFF KEENER**   Keener, Jeffrey Bruce   b: 1/14/59, Pana, Ill.   BL/TR, 6', 170 lbs.   Deb: 6/8/82

YEAR TM/L	W	L	PCT	G	GS	CG	SH	SV	IP	H	HR	BB	SO	RAT	ERA	ERA+	OAV	OOB	BH	AVG	PB	PR	/A	PD	TPI
1982 StL-N	1	1	.500	19	0	0	0	0	22¹	19	1	19	25	15.3	1.61	224	.235	.380	0	—	0	5	5	0	0.4
1983 StL-N	0	0	—	4	0	0	0	0	4¹	6	0	1	4	16.6	8.31	44	.333	.400	0	—	0	-2	-2	0	0.0
Total 2	1	1	.500	23	0	0	0	0	26²	25	1	20	29	15.5	2.70	134	.253	.383	0	—	0	3	3	0	0.4

● **JOE KEENER**   Keener, Joseph Donald   b: 4/21/53, San Pedro, Cal.   BR/TR, 6'4", 200 lbs.   Deb: 9/18/76

YEAR TM/L	W	L	PCT	G	GS	CG	SH	SV	IP	H	HR	BB	SO	RAT	ERA	ERA+	OAV	OOB	BH	AVG	PB	PR	/A	PD	TPI
1976 Mon-N	0	1	.000	2	2	0	0	0	4¹	7	0	8	1	33.2	10.38	36	.389	.593	0	.000	-0	-3	-3	0	-0.6

● **HARRY KEENER**   Keener, Joshua Harry "Beans"   b: 9/1869, Easton, Pa.   d: 3/5/12, Easton, Pa.   TR ,   Deb: 6/27/1896

YEAR TM/L	W	L	PCT	G	GS	CG	SH	SV	IP	H	HR	BB	SO	RAT	ERA	ERA+	OAV	OOB	BH	AVG	PB	PR	/A	PD	TPI
1896 Phi-N	3	11	.214	16	13	11	0	0	113¹	144	5	39	28	15.2	5.88	73	.307	.371	16	.314	2	-19	-20	0	-1.6

● **RICKEY KEETON**   Keeton, Rickey   b: 3/18/57, Cincinnati, Ohio   BR/TR, 6'2", 190 lbs.   Deb: 5/27/80

YEAR TM/L	W	L	PCT	G	GS	CG	SH	SV	IP	H	HR	BB	SO	RAT	ERA	ERA+	OAV	OOB	BH	AVG	PB	PR	/A	PD	TPI
1980 Mil-A	2	2	.500	5	5	0	0	0	28¹	26	3	9	8	14.0	4.76	81	.307	.358	0	—	0	-2	-3	0	-0.3
1981 Mil-A	1	0	1.000	17	0	0	0	0	35¹	47	4	11	9	14.8	5.09	67	.329	.377	0	—	0	-6	-7	0	-0.3
Total 2	3	2	.600	22	5	0	0	0	63²	82	8	20	17	14.4	4.95	73	.319	.368	0	—	0	-8	-9	0	-0.5

● **FRANK KEFFER**   Keffer, Frank   b: Harrisburg, Pa.   Deb: 4/19/1890

YEAR TM/L	W	L	PCT	G	GS	CG	SH	SV	IP	H	HR	BB	SO	RAT	ERA	ERA+	OAV	OOB	BH	AVG	PB	PR	/A	PD	TPI
1890 Syr-a	1	1	.500	2	1	1	0	0	16	15	0	4	9	13.5	5.63	63	.242	.338	1	.143	-1	-3	-4	0	-0.4

● **CHET KEHN**   Kehn, Chester Lawrence   b: 10/30/21, San Diego, Cal.   d: 4/5/84, San Diego, Cal.   BR/TR, 5'11", 168 lbs.   Deb: 4/30/42

YEAR TM/L	W	L	PCT	G	GS	CG	SH	SV	IP	H	HR	BB	SO	RAT	ERA	ERA+	OAV	OOB	BH	AVG	PB	PR	/A	PD	TPI
1942 Bro-N	0	0	—	3	1	0	0	0	7²	8	2	4	3	14.1	7.04	46	.267	.353	2	1.000	1	-3	-3	0	0.2

● **KATSY KEIFER**   Keifer, Sherman Carl   b: 9/3/1891, California, Pa.   d: 2/19/27, Outwood, Ky.   BB/TL,   Deb: 10/8/14

YEAR TM/L	W	L	PCT	G	GS	CG	SH	SV	IP	H	HR	BB	SO	RAT	ERA	ERA+	OAV	OOB	BH	AVG	PB	PR	/A	PD	TPI
1914 Ind-F	1	0	1.000	1	1	0	0	0	9	6	2	2	4	10.0	2.00	156	.194	.242	1	.333	0	1	0	0	0.1

● **MIKE KEKICH**   Kekich, Michael Dennis   b: 4/2/45, San Diego, Cal.   BR/TL, 6'1", 200 lbs.   Deb: 6/9/65

YEAR TM/L	W	L	PCT	G	GS	CG	SH	SV	IP	H	HR	BB	SO	RAT	ERA	ERA+	OAV	OOB	BH	AVG	PB	PR	/A	PD	TPI
1965 LA-N	0	1	.000	5	1	0	0	0	10¹	10	2	13	9	20.0	9.58	34	.263	.451	0	.000	-0	-7	-7	-0	-0.7
1968 LA-N	2	10	.167	25	20	1	1	0	115	116	9	46	84	12.8	3.91	71	.267	.339	3	.081	-2	-12	-15	-1	-1.8
1969 NY-A	4	6	.400	28	13	1	0	1	105	91	11	49	66	12.2	4.54	77	.236	.325	3	.111	-1	-11	-12	-1	-1.3
1970 NY-A	6	3	.667	26	14	1	0	0	98²	103	12	55	63	14.5	4.83	73	.267	.360	3	.094	-1	-12	-14	-1	-1.4
1971 NY-A	10	9	.526	37	24	3	0	0	170¹	167	13	82	93	13.4	4.07	79	.257	.344	8	.154	-0	-11	-16	1	-1.5
1972 NY-A	10	13	.435	29	28	2	0	0	175¹	172	13	76	78	12.9	3.70	80	.263	.344	8	.136	-1	-12	-15	-1	-2.1
1973 NY-A	1	1	.500	5	4	0	0	0	14²	20	1	14	4	22.1	9.20	40	.351	.493	0	—	0	-9	-9	-0	-1.0
Cle-A	1	4	.200	16	6	0	0	0	50	73	6	35	26	19.4	7.02	56	.349	.443	0	—	0	-18	-17	-1	-1.6
Yr	2	5	.286	21	10	0	0	0	64²	93	7	49	30	19.8	7.52	51	.346	.447	0	—	0	-27	-26	-2	-2.6
1975 Tex-A	0	0	—	23	0	0	0	0	31¹	33	2	21	19	15.5	3.73	101	.282	.391	0	—	0	1	1	0	0.1
1977 Sea-A	4	4	.556	41	2	0	0	3	90	90	11	51	55	14.4	5.60	73	.265	.365	0	—	0	-15	-15	-0	-1.4
Total 9	39	51	.433	235	112	8	1	6	860²	875	80	442	497	13.9	4.59	72	.268	.358	25	.120	-5	-108	-121	-4	-12.7

● **GEORGE KELB**   Kelb, George Francis "Pugger" or "Lefty"   b: 7/17/1870, Toledo, Ohio   d: 10/20/36, Toledo, Ohio   BL/TL,   Deb: 4/17/1898

YEAR TM/L	W	L	PCT	G	GS	CG	SH	SV	IP	H	HR	BB	SO	RAT	ERA	ERA+	OAV	OOB	BH	AVG	PB	PR	/A	PD	TPI
1898 Cle-N	0	1	.000	3	1	0	0	0	16¹	23	0	1	3	13.2	4.41	82	.329	.373	1	.200		-1	-1	0	-0.1

● **HAL KELLEHER**   Kelleher, Harold Joseph   b: 6/24/13, Philadelphia, Pa.   d: 8/27/89, Cape May Court House, N.J.   BR/TR, 6', 165 lbs.   Deb: 9/17/35

YEAR TM/L	W	L	PCT	G	GS	CG	SH	SV	IP	H	HR	BB	SO	RAT	ERA	ERA+	OAV	OOB	BH	AVG	PB	PR	/A	PD	TPI
1935 Phi-N	2	0	1.000	3	3	2	1	0	25	26	0	12	12	14.0	1.80	252	.260	.345	3	.375		6	8	0	0.7
1936 Phi-N	0	5	.000	14	4	1	0	0	44	60	2	29	13	18.8	5.32	85	.331	.432	2	.167	-0	-6	-4	0	-0.4
1937 Phi-N	2	4	.333	27	2	1	0	0	58¹	72	3	31	20	17.0	6.63	65	.308	.404	3	.176	-0	-18	-15	-0	-1.4
1938 Phi-N	0	0	—	6	0	0	0	0	7¹	16	0	9	4	30.7	18.41	21	.432	.543	1	.500		-12	-12	0	0.1
Total 4	4	9	.308	50	9	4	1	0	134²	174	5	81	49	17.8	5.95	74	.315	.413	9	.231	0	-30	-23	0	-1.0

● **RON KELLER**   Keller, Ronald Lee   b: 6/3/43, Indianapolis, Ind.   BR/TR, 6'2", 200 lbs.   Deb: 7/9/66

YEAR TM/L	W	L	PCT	G	GS	CG	SH	SV	IP	H	HR	BB	SO	RAT	ERA	ERA+	OAV	OOB	BH	AVG	PB	PR	/A	PD	TPI
1966 Min-A	0	0	—	2	0	0	0	0	5¹	7	0	1	3	13.5	5.06	71	.318	.348	0	.000	-0	-1	-1	0	0.0
1968 Min-A	0	1	.000	7	1	0	0	0	16	18	3	4	11	12.9	2.81	110	.305	.359	0	.000	-0	0	0	0	0.0
Total 2	0	1	.000	9	1	0	0	0	21¹	25	3	5	12	13.1	3.38	95	.309	.356	0	.000	-0	-1	-0	0	0.0

● **AL KELLETT**   Kellett, Alfred Henry   b: 10/30/01, Red Bank, N.J.   d: 7/14/60, New York, N.Y.   BR/TR, 6'3", 200 lbs.   Deb: 7/1/23

YEAR TM/L	W	L	PCT	G	GS	CG	SH	SV	IP	H	HR	BB	SO	RAT	ERA	ERA+	OAV	OOB	BH	AVG	PB	PR	/A	PD	TPI
1923 Phi-A	0	1	.000	5	0	0	0	0	10	11	0	8	1	17.1	6.30	65	.282	.404	1	.333	0	-3	-2	1	-0.1
1924 Bos-A	0	0	—	1	0	0	0	0	0	0	0	2	0	∞	∞			1.000	0	—	0	-2	-2	0	-0.2
Total 2	0	1	.000	6	0	0	0	0	10	11	0	10	1	18.9	8.10	51	.282	.429	1	.333	0	-5	-4	1	-0.3

● **HARRY KELLEY**   Kelley, Harry Leroy   b: 2/13/06, Parkin, Ark.   d: 3/23/58, Parkin, Ark.   BR/TR, 5'9.5", 170 lbs.   Deb: 4/16/25

YEAR TM/L	W	L	PCT	G	GS	CG	SH	SV	IP	H	HR	BB	SO	RAT	ERA	ERA+	OAV	OOB	BH	AVG	PB	PR	/A	PD	TPI
1925 Was-A	1	1	.500	6	1	0	0	0	16	30	0	12	7	23.6	9.00	47	.405	.488	0	.000	-1	-8	-8	1	-0.8
1926 Was-A	0	0	—	10	1	0	0	0	10	17	0	8	6	23.4	8.10	48	.405	.510	0	.000	-0	-5	-5	0	-0.5
1936 Phi-A	15	12	.556	35	27	20	1	3	235¹	250	21	75	82	12.5	3.86	132	.275	.332	18	.198	-1	31	32	-2	2.9
1937 Phi-A	13	21	.382	41	29	14	0	0	205	267	16	79	68	15.3	5.36	88	.306	.365	16	.225	-1	-17	-15	-1	-1.9
1938 Phi-A	2	0	.000	4	3	1	1	0	8	17	1	10	3	30.4	16.88	29	.436	.551	0	—	0	-11	-11	-0	-1.8
Was-A	9	8	.529	38	14	7	2	1	148¹	162	11	46	44	12.7	4.49	100	.276	.330	12	.250	-1	5	0	0	0.2
Yr	9	10	.474	42	17	7	2	1	156¹	179	12	56	47	13.6	5.12	88	.286	.346	12	.240	1	-6	-10	-0	-1.6

YEAR	TM/L	W	L	PCT	G	GS	CG	SH	SV	IP	H	HR	BB	SO	RAT	ERA	ERA+	OAV	OOB	BH	AVG	PB	PR	/A	PD	TPI
1939	Was-A	4	3	.571	15	3	2	0	1	53²	69	2	14	20	14.4	4.70	93	.314	.363	4	.267	1	-0	-2	-0	-0.2
Total	6	42	47	.472	146	78	43	3	5	676¹	812	51	244	230	14.2	4.86	98	.296	.356	50	.216	0	-5	-8	-2	-1.6

● DICK KELLEY
Kelley, Richard Anthony b: 1/8/40, Boston, Mass d: 12/12/91, Northridge, Cal. BR/TL, 6′, 175 lbs. Deb: 4/15/64

YEAR	TM/L	W	L	PCT	G	GS	CG	SH	SV	IP	H	HR	BB	SO	RAT	ERA	ERA+	OAV	OOB	BH	AVG	PB	PR	/A	PD	TPI
1964	Mil-N	0	0	—	2	0	0	0	0	2	2	0	3	2	22.5	18.00	20	.250	.455	0	—	0	-3	-3	-0	0.0
1965	Mil-N	1	1	.500	21	4	0	0	0	45	37	5	20	31	11.4	3.00	117	.226	.310	0	.000	-1	3	3	-0	0.0
1966	Atl-N	7	5	.583	20	13	2	2	0	81	75	6	21	50	11.0	3.22	113	.247	.302	1	.036	-3	3	3	-0	0.1
1967	Atl-N	2	9	.182	39	9	1	1	2	98	88	8	42	75	12.0	3.77	88	.247	.328	4	.250	1	-4	-5	1	-0.3
1968	Atl-N	2	4	.333	31	11	1	1	1	98	86	4	45	73	12.1	2.76	99	.238	.324	1	.043	-1	3	3	1	0.2
1969	SD-N	4	8	.333	27	23	1	1	0	136	113	11	61	96	11.8	3.57	99	.230	.321	5	.106	-2	0	-1	2	-0.1
1971	SD-N	2	3	.400	48	1	0	0	2	59²	52	5	23	42	11.9	3.47	95	.232	.315	1	.333	0	-0	-1	-0	-0.1
Total	7	18	30	.375	188	61	5	5	5	519²	453	39	215	369	11.8	3.39	100	.237	.319	12	.096	-5	1	-1	2	-0.3

● TOM KELLEY
Kelley, Thomas Henry b: 1/5/44, Manchester, Conn. BR/TR, 6′, 191 lbs. Deb: 5/5/64

YEAR	TM/L	W	L	PCT	G	GS	CG	SH	SV	IP	H	HR	BB	SO	RAT	ERA	ERA+	OAV	OOB	BH	AVG	PB	PR	/A	PD	TPI
1964	Cle-A	0	0	—	6	0	0	0	0	9²	9	1	9	7	17.7	5.59	64	.237	.396	0	—	-2	-2	-0	0.0
1965	Cle-A	2	1	.667	4	4	1	0	0	30	19	1	13	31	9.6	2.40	145	.186	.278	2	.222	0	4	4	-0	0.4
1966	Cle-A	4	8	.333	31	7	1	0	0	95¹	97	14	42	64	13.1	4.34	79	.264	.340	4	.143	-1	-10	-10	-1	-1.4
1967	Cle-A	0	0	—	1	0	0	0	0	1	0	0	2	0	18.0	0.00		.000	.500	0	—	0	0	0	0	0.0
1971	Atl-N	9	5	.643	28	20	5	0	0	143	140	8	69	68	13.2	2.96	125	.262	.347	2	.047	-4	8	12	-1	0.7
1972	Atl-N	5	7	.417	27	14	2	1	0	116¹	122	14	65	59	14.5	4.56	83	.272	.364	2	.088	-2	-14	-10	-3	-1.4
1973	Atl-N	0	1	.000	7	0	0	0	0	12²	13	0	7	5	14.2	2.84	138	.289	.385	0	—	1	2	-0	0.0
Total	7	20	22	.476	104	45	9	1	0	408	400	38	207	234	13.4	3.75	97	.260	.349	11	.095	-6	-13	-4	-5	-1.6

● ALEX KELLNER
Kellner, Alexander Raymond b: 8/26/24, Tucson, Ariz. d: 5/3/96, Tucson, Ariz. BR/TL, 6′, 200 lbs. Deb: 4/29/48 F

YEAR	TM/L	W	L	PCT	G	GS	CG	SH	SV	IP	H	HR	BB	SO	RAT	ERA	ERA+	OAV	OOB	BH	AVG	PB	PR	/A	PD	TPI
1948	Phi-A	0	0	—	13	6	1	0	0	23	21	4	16	14	15.3	7.83	55	.239	.368	0	.000	-1	-9	-9	-0	-0.1
1949	Phi-A☆	20	12	.625	38	27	19	0	1	245	243	18	129	94	13.7	3.75	110	.261	.352	20	.217	1	12	10	-0	1.3
1950	Phi-A	8	20	.286	36	29	15	0	2	225¹	253	28	112	85	14.7	5.47	83	.282	.363	16	.200	1	-22	-23	-2	-2.7
1951	Phi-A	11	14	.440	33	29	11	1	2	209²	218	20	93	94	13.5	4.46	96	.272	.350	18	.228	-1	-8	-4	-1	-0.6
1952	Phi-A	12	14	.462	34	33	14	2	0	231¹	223	21	86	105	12.2	4.36	91	.252	.321	17	.207	0	-18	-10	-2	-1.2
1953	Phi-A	11	12	.478	25	25	14	2	0	201²	210	8	51	81	11.8	3.93	109	.269	.317	15	.217	1	2	8	-2	0.8
1954	Phi-A	6	17	.261	27	27	8	1	0	173²	204	16	88	69	15.4	5.39	72	.301	.387	10	.182	-0	-32	-29	-0	-3.3
1955	KC-A	11	8	.579	30	24	6	3	0	162²	164	18	60	75	12.7	4.20	99	.265	.335	12	.214	2	-4	-1	-0	0.2
1956	KC-A	7	4	.636	20	17	5	0	0	91²	103	15	33	44	13.5	4.32	100	.289	.353	6	.200	0	-2	0	-0	0.0
1957	KC-A	6	5	.545	28	21	3	0	0	132²	141	18	41	72	12.5	4.27	93	.278	.335	11	.234	4	-7	-5	0	0.1
1958	KC-A	0	2	.000	7	6	0	0	0	33²	40	5	8	22	12.8	5.88	66	.315	.356	1	.091	-0	-8	-7	-0	-0.4
	Cin-N	7	3	.700	18	7	4	0	0	82	74	8	20	42	10.6	2.30	180	.243	.296	10	.357	3	15	17	2	2.1
1959	StL-N	2	1	.667	12	4	0	0	0	37	31	9	10	19	10.2	3.16	134	.220	.276	2	.222	0	3	4	-0	0.3
Total	12	101	112	.474	321	250	99	9	5	1849¹	1925	184	747	816	13.2	4.41	95	.270	.343	138	.215	7	-78	-47	-8	-3.5

● WALT KELLNER
Kellner, Walter Joseph b: 4/26/29, Tucson, Ariz. BR/TR, 6′, 200 lbs. Deb: 9/6/52 F

YEAR	TM/L	W	L	PCT	G	GS	CG	SH	SV	IP	H	HR	BB	SO	RAT	ERA	ERA+	OAV	OOB	BH	AVG	PB	PR	/A	PD	TPI
1952	Phi-A	0	0	—	1	0	0	0	1	4	4	0	3	2	15.8	6.75	59	.250	.368	0	.000	-0	-1	-1	-0	-0.1
1953	Phi-A	0	0	—	2	0	0	0	0	3¹	1	0	4	4	18.0	6.00	71	.111	.429	0	—	0	-1	-1	-0	0.0
Total	2	0	0	—	3	0	0	0	1	7	5	0	7	6	16.7	6.43	64	.200	.394	0	.000	-0	-2	-2	-0	-0.1

● AL KELLOGG
Kellogg, Albert C. b: 9/9/1886, Providence, R.I. d: 7/21/53, Portland, Ore. TL, 6′3″, 208 lbs. Deb: 9/25/08

YEAR	TM/L	W	L	PCT	G	GS	CG	SH	SV	IP	H	HR	BB	SO	RAT	ERA	ERA+	OAV	OOB	BH	AVG	PB	PR	/A	PD	TPI
1908	Phi-A	0	2	.000	3	3	2	0	0	17	20	1	9	8	15.9	5.82	44	.294	.385	1	.125	-0	-6	-6	0	-0.7

● WIN KELLUM
Kellum, Winford Ansley b: 4/11/1876, Waterford, Ont., Canada d: 8/10/51, Big Rapids, Mich. BB/TL, 5′10″, 190 lbs. Deb: 4/26/01

YEAR	TM/L	W	L	PCT	G	GS	CG	SH	SV	IP	H	HR	BB	SO	RAT	ERA	ERA+	OAV	OOB	BH	AVG	PB	PR	/A	PD	TPI
1901	Bos-A	2	3	.400	6	6	5	0	0	48	61	3	7	8	13.3	6.38	55	.305	.338	3	.167	-1	-14	-15	1	-1.2
1904	Cin-N	15	10	.600	31	24	22	1	2	224²	206	1	46	70	10.5	2.60	113	.244	.291	13	.159	2	3	8	1	1.1
1905	StL-N	3	3	.500	11	7	5	1	0	74	70	1	10	19	9.9	2.92	102	.255	.283	5	.200	1	1	0	1	0.2
Total	3	20	16	.556	48	37	32	2	2	346²	337	5	63	97	10.7	3.19	95	.255	.297	21	.168	2	-10	-6	3	0.1

● BRYAN KELLY
Kelly, Bryan Keith b: 2/24/59, Silver Spring, Md. BR/TR, 6′2″, 195 lbs. Deb: 9/2/86

YEAR	TM/L	W	L	PCT	G	GS	CG	SH	SV	IP	H	HR	BB	SO	RAT	ERA	ERA+	OAV	OOB	BH	AVG	PB	PR	/A	PD	TPI
1986	Det-A	1	2	.333	6	4	0	0	0	20	21	4	10	18	13.9	4.50	92	.269	.352	0	—	0	-1	-1	0	-0.1
1987	Det-A	0	1	.000	5	0	0	0	0	10²	12	2	7	10	16.0	5.06	83	.286	.388	0	—	0	-1	-1	-0	-0.1
Total	2	1	3	.250	11	4	0	0	0	30²	33	6	17	28	14.7	4.70	89	.275	.365	0	—	0	-2	-2	0	-0.2

● ED KELLY
Kelly, Edward Leo b: 12/10/1888, Pawtucket, R.I. d: 11/4/28, Red Lodge, Mont. BR/TR, 5′11.5″, 173 lbs. Deb: 4/14/14

YEAR	TM/L	W	L	PCT	G	GS	CG	SH	SV	IP	H	HR	BB	SO	RAT	ERA	ERA+	OAV	OOB	BH	AVG	PB	PR	/A	PD	TPI
1914	Bos-A	0	0	—	3	0	0	0	0	2¹	1	0	1	4	7.7	0.00		.100	.182	0	.000	-0	1	1	0	0.0

● GEORGE KELLY
Kelly, George Lange "Highpockets" b: 9/10/1895, San Francisco, Cal. d: 10/13/84, Burlingame, Cal. BR/TR, 6′4″, 190 lbs. Deb: 8/18/15 FCH♦

YEAR	TM/L	W	L	PCT	G	GS	CG	SH	SV	IP	H	HR	BB	SO	RAT	ERA	ERA+	OAV	OOB	BH	AVG	PB	PR	/A	PD	TPI
1917	NY-N	1	0	1.000	4	0	0	0	0	5	4	0	1	2	9.0	0.00		.211	.250	0	.000	-0	1	1	-0	0.3

● HERB KELLY
Kelly, Herbert Barrett "Moke" b: 6/4/1892, Mobile, Ala. d: 5/18/73, Torrance, Cal. BL/TL, 5′9″, 160 lbs. Deb: 9/25/14

YEAR	TM/L	W	L	PCT	G	GS	CG	SH	SV	IP	H	HR	BB	SO	RAT	ERA	ERA+	OAV	OOB	BH	AVG	PB	PR	/A	PD	TPI
1914	Pit-N	0	2	.000	5	2	2	0	0	25²	24	1	4	6	10.9	2.45	108	.253	.304	2	.222	1	-2	-1	1	-0.1
1915	Pit-N	1	1	.500	5	1	0	0	0	11	10	1	7	6	12.3	4.09	67	.250	.333	1	.500	1	-2	-2	1	-0.1
Total	2	1	3	.250	10	3	2	0	0	36²	34	2	11	12	11.3	2.95	91	.252	.313	3	.273	1	-1	-1	1	-0.1

● MIKE KELLY
Kelly, Michael J. b: 11/9/02, St.Louis, Mo. BR/TR, 6′1″, 178 lbs. Deb: 9/3/26

YEAR	TM/L	W	L	PCT	G	GS	CG	SH	SV	IP	H	HR	BB	SO	RAT	ERA	ERA+	OAV	OOB	BH	AVG	PB	PR	/A	PD	TPI
1926	Phi-N	0	0	—	4	0	0	0	0	4	8	0	3	2	18.9	9.45	44	.346	.452	0	.000	-0	-4	-4	0	-0.1

● KING KELLY
Kelly, Michael Joseph b: 12/31/1857, Troy, N.Y. d: 11/8/1894, Boston, Mass. BR/TR, 5′10″, 170 lbs. Deb: 5/1/1878 MH♦

YEAR	TM/L	W	L	PCT	G	GS	CG	SH	SV	IP	H	HR	BB	SO	RAT	ERA	ERA+	OAV	OOB	BH	AVG	PB	PR	/A	PD	TPI
1880	Chi-N	0	0	—	1	0	0	0	0	3	3	1	1	0	12.0	0.00		.250	.308	100	.291	0	1	1	0	0.0
1883	Chi-N	0	0	—	1	0	0	0	0	1	1	0	0	0	9.0	0.00	—	.333	.333	109	.255	0	0	0	0	0.0
1884	Chi-N	0	1	.000	2	0	0	0	0	5¹	12	2	2	2	23.6	8.44	37	.400	.438	160	.354	1	-3	-3	-0	-0.4
1887	Bos-N	1	0	1.000	1	1	1	0	0	8	13	1	14	0	21.5	3.46	117	.298	.437	156	.322	1	1	1	0	0.1
1890	Bos-P	1	0	1.000	1	0	0	0	0	2	1	0	2	2	13.5	4.50	98	.143	.333	111	.326	0	0	0	0	0.0
1891	Cin-a	0	1	.000	3	0	1	0	0	15¹	21	2	7	0	17.0	5.28	78	.313	.387	84	.297	1	-2	-0	0	0.0
1892	*Bos-N	0	0	—	3	0	0	0	0	6	8	0	4	0	22.5	1.50	234	.308	.455	53	.189	0	1	1	-0	0.0
Total	7	2	2	.500	12	1	0	0	0	45²	63	5	30	4	19.1	4.14	92	.312	.411	1813	.308	4	-3	-2	-0	-0.3

● REN KELLY
Kelly, Reynolds Joseph b: 11/18/1899, San Francisco, Cal d: 8/24/63, Millbrae, Cal. BR/TR, 6′, 183 lbs. Deb: 9/18/23 F

YEAR	TM/L	W	L	PCT	G	GS	CG	SH	SV	IP	H	HR	BB	SO	RAT	ERA	ERA+	OAV	OOB	BH	AVG	PB	PR	/A	PD	TPI
1923	Phi-A	0	0	—	1	0	0	0	0	7	7	0	4	1	14.1	2.57	160	.259	.355	0	.000	-0	1	1	-0	-0.1

● BOB KELLY
Kelly, Robert Edward b: 10/4/27, Cleveland, Ohio BR/TR, 6′, 180 lbs. Deb: 5/4/51

YEAR	TM/L	W	L	PCT	G	GS	CG	SH	SV	IP	H	HR	BB	SO	RAT	ERA	ERA+	OAV	OOB	BH	AVG	PB	PR	/A	PD	TPI
1951	Chi-N	7	4	.636	35	11	4	0	0	123²	130	8	55	48	13.5	4.66	88	.275	.352	5	.161	-1	-10	-8	-0	-0.7
1952	Chi-N	4	9	.308	31	15	3	2	0	125¹	114	7	46	50	11.7	3.59	107	.236	.306	8	.216	0	2	4	1	0.5
1953	Chi-N	0	1	.000	14	0	0	0	0	17	27	2	9	6	19.6	9.53	47	.375	.451	0	.000	-0	-10	-10	0	-0.5
	Cin-N	1	2	.333	28	5	0	0	2	66¹	71	7	26	35	13.2	4.34	100	.276	.343	2	.118	-0	-1	-0	-0	-0.1
	Yr	1	3	.250	42	5	0	0	2	83¹	98	9	35	41	14.4	5.40	81	.297	.364	2	.111	-0	-10	-9	-1	-0.6
1958	Cin-N	0	0	—	2	0	0	0	0	2	3	0	1	0	27.0	4.50	92	.500	.667	0	—	0	0	0	0	0.0
	Cle-A	0	2	.000	13	0	0	0	0	27²	29	4	13	12	14.0	5.20	70	.282	.368	1	.250	-0	-4	-5	0	-0.3
Total	4	12	18	.400	123	35	7	2	2	362	374	28	152	146	13.2	4.50	90	.268	.343	16	.178	-1	-22	-18	1	-1.1

● BILL KELSO
Kelso, William Eugene b: 2/19/40, Kansas City, Mo. BR/TR, 6′4″, 215 lbs. Deb: 7/31/64

YEAR	TM/L	W	L	PCT	G	GS	CG	SH	SV	IP	H	HR	BB	SO	RAT	ERA	ERA+	OAV	OOB	BH	AVG	PB	PR	/A	PD	TPI
1964	LA-A	2	0	1.000	10	1	0	0	0	23²	19	3	9	21	11.0	2.28	144	.218	.299	0	.000	-0	4	3	0	0.2
1966	Cal-A	1	1	.500	5	0	0	0	0	11¹	11	1	6	11	14.3	2.38	141	.244	.346	0	—	0	1	1	0	0.2
1967	Cal-A	5	3	.625	69	1	0	0	11	112	85	6	63	91	12.2	2.97	106	.219	.333	2	.105	-1	3	2	1	0.2
1968	Cin-N	4	1	.800	35	0	0	0	1	54	56	6	15	39	12.3	4.00	79	.277	.336	0	.000	-1	-6	-5	-1	-0.7
Total	4	12	5	.706	119	2	0	0	12	201	171	16	93	162	12.2	3.13	102	.237	.331	2	.059	-2	2	1	-0	-0.1

YEAR	TM/L	W	L	PCT	G	GS	CG	SH	SV	IP	H	HR	BB	SO	RAT	ERA	ERA+	OAV	OOB	BH	AVG	PB	PR	/A	PD	TPI

● RUSS KEMMERER
Kemmerer, Russell Paul "Rusty" or "Dutch" b: 11/1/31, Pittsburgh, Pa. BR/TR, 6'3", 200 lbs. Deb: 6/27/54

YEAR	TM/L	W	L	PCT	G	GS	CG	SH	SV	IP	H	HR	BB	SO	RAT	ERA	ERA+	OAV	OOB	BH	AVG	PB	PR	/A	PD	TPI
1954	Bos-A	5	3	.625	19	9	2	1	0	75¹	71	4	41	37	13.6	3.82	108	.257	.357	3	.143	-0	-1	2	0	0.2
1955	Bos-A	1	1	.500	7	2	0	0	0	17¹	18	3	15	11	17.1	7.27	59	.269	.402	0	.000	-0	-6	-6	-0	-0.6
1957	Bos-A	0	0	—	1	0	0	0	0	4	5	0	2	1	15.8	4.50	89	.333	.412	0	.000	-0	-0	-0	-0	0.0
	Was-A	7	11	.389	39	26	6	0	0	172¹	214	20	71	81	15.0	4.96	79	.309	.375	3	.067	-1	-22	-20	-3	-2.3
	Yr	7	11	.389	40	26	6	0	0	176¹	219	20	73	82	15.0	4.95	79	.309	.375	3	.065	-1	-23	-21	-3	-2.3
1958	Was-A	6	15	.286	40	30	6	0	0	224¹	234	25	74	111	12.5	4.61	83	.270	.330	11	.159	-2	-21	-20	0	-1.9
1959	Was-A	8	17	.320	37	28	8	0	0	206	221	20	71	89	12.9	4.50	87	.276	.338	8	.133	-1	-15	-13	0	-1.5
1960	Was-A	0	2	.000	3	3	0	0	0	17¹	18	2	10	10	15.1	7.79	50	.269	.372	0	.000	-0	-8	-8	1	-0.6
	Chi-A	6	3	.667	36	7	2	1	2	120²	111	5	45	76	11.7	2.98	127	.248	.318	0	.000	-3	12	11	0	0.5
	Yr	6	5	.545	39	10	2	1	2	138	129	7	55	86	12.1	3.59	106	.250	.323	0	.000	-3	4	3	1	-0.1
1961	Chi-A	3	3	.500	47	2	0	0	2	96²	102	10	26	35	11.9	4.38	89	.278	.326	3	.200	-1	-4	-5	1	-0.1
1962	Chi-A	2	1	.667	20	0	0	0	0	28	30	3	11	17	13.2	3.86	101	.270	.336	1	.500	1	0	0	1	0.2
	Hou-N	5	3	.625	36	2	0	0	3	68	72	10	15	23	11.9	4.10	91	.272	.318	3	.333	1	-1	-3	0	-0.2
1963	Hou-N	0	0	—	17	0	0	0	1	36²	48	1	8	12	13.7	5.65	56	.320	.354	2	.286	0	-10	-10	1	-0.2
Total 9		43	59	.422	302	109	24	2	8	1066²	1144	103	389	505	13.1	4.46	86	.277	.342	34	.128	-5	-76	-72	1	-6.3

● DUTCH KEMNER
Kemner, Herman John b: 3/4/1899, Quincy, Ill. d: 1/16/88, Quincy, Ill. BR/TR, 5'10.5", 175 lbs. Deb: 4/19/29

YEAR	TM/L	W	L	PCT	G	GS	CG	SH	SV	IP	H	HR	BB	SO	RAT	ERA	ERA+	OAV	OOB	BH	AVG	PB	PR	/A	PD	TPI
1929	Cin-N	0	0	—	9	0	0	0	1	15¹	19	0	8	10	15.8	7.63	60	.328	.409	1	.250	0	-5	-5	0	-0.1

● ED KENNA
Kenna, Edward Benninghaus "The Pitching Poet" b: 10/17/1877, Charleston, W.Va. d: 3/22/12, Grant, Fla. TR, 6', 180 lbs. Deb: 5/5/02

YEAR	TM/L	W	L	PCT	G	GS	CG	SH	SV	IP	H	HR	BB	SO	RAT	ERA	ERA+	OAV	OOB	BH	AVG	PB	PR	/A	PD	TPI
1902	Phi-A	1	1	.500	2	1	1	0	0	17	19	1	11	5	16.4	5.29	69	.284	.392	1	.125	-0	-3	-3	0	-0.3

● VERN KENNEDY
Kennedy, Lloyd Vernon b: 3/20/07, Kansas City, Mo. d: 1/28/93, Mendon, Mo. BL/TR, 6', 175 lbs. Deb: 9/18/34

YEAR	TM/L	W	L	PCT	G	GS	CG	SH	SV	IP	H	HR	BB	SO	RAT	ERA	ERA+	OAV	OOB	BH	AVG	PB	PR	/A	PD	TPI
1934	Chi-A	0	2	.000	3	3	1	0	0	19¹	21	1	9	7	14.0	3.72	127	.300	.380	2	.286	0	2	2	1	0.3
1935	Chi-A	11	11	.500	31	25	16	2	1	211²	211	17	95	65	13.2	3.91	118	.262	.343	18	.247	1	13	17	2	1.8
1936	Chi-A☆	21	9	.700	35	34	20	1	0	274¹	282	13	147	99	14.2	4.63	112	.268	.360	32	.283	5	13	17	1	2.0
1937	Chi-A	14	13	.519	32	30	15	1	0	221	238	16	124	114	14.9	5.09	90	.273	.366	20	.230	-2	-12	-12	0	-1.0
1938	Det-A☆	12	9	.571	33	26	11	0	2	190¹	215	13	113	53	15.6	5.06	99	.287	.381	23	.291	3	-6	-1	2	0.3
1939	Det-A	0	3	.000	4	4	1	0	0	21	25	4	9	9	15.0	6.43	76	.301	.376	2	.286	0	-4	-4	1	-0.3
	StL-A	9	17	.346	33	27	12	1	0	191²	229	18	115	55	16.2	5.73	85	.297	.389	10	.149	-2	-24	-18	-1	-2.3
	Yr	9	20	.310	37	31	13	1	0	212²	254	22	124	64	16.0	5.80	84	.297	.387	12	.162	-2	-28	-22	0	-2.6
1940	StL-A	12	17	.414	34	32	18	0	0	222¹	263	18	122	70	15.7	5.59	82	.298	.385	25	.298	6	-30	-25	2	-1.8
1941	StL-A	2	4	.333	6	6	2	0	0	45	44	5	27	6	14.2	4.40	98	.259	.360	6	.400	2	-1	-1	0	0.2
	Was-A	1	7	.125	17	7	2	0	0	66¹	77	5	39	22	16.0	5.70	71	.297	.393	3	.143	-1	-11	-12	0	-1.3
	Yr	3	11	.214	23	13	4	0	0	111¹	121	10	66	28	15.3	5.17	80	.282	.380	9	.250	2	-13	-13	0	-1.1
1942	Cle-A	4	8	.333	28	12	4	0	0	108	99	1	50	37	12.5	4.08	84	.244	.328	6	.200	1	-5	-8	0	-0.6
1943	Cle-A	10	7	.588	28	17	8	1	0	146²	130	4	59	63	11.7	2.45	127	.242	.319	12	.231	1	14	11	1	1.5
1944	Cle-A	2	5	.286	12	10	2	0	0	59	66	0	37	17	15.7	5.03	66	.289	.389	2	.087	-2	-11	-11	1	-1.3
	Phi-N	1	5	.167	12	7	3	0	0	55¹	60	3	20	23	13.0	4.23	85	.269	.329	6	.286	1	-4	-4	0	-0.3
1945	Phi-N	0	3	.000	12	3	0	0	0	36	43	2	14	13	14.3	5.50	70	.297	.358	2	.182	0	-7	-7	1	-0.4
	Cin-N	5	12	.294	24	20	11	1	1	157²	170	10	69	38	13.8	4.00	94	.280	.356	12	.226	2	-3	-4	1	-0.1
	Yr	5	15	.250	36	23	11	1	1	193²	213	12	83	51	13.9	4.28	88	.283	.356	14	.219	2	-10	-11	2	-0.5
Total 12		104	132	.441	344	263	126	7	5	2025²	2173	130	1049	691	14.4	4.67	94	.277	.363	181	.244	19	-77	-63	13	-3.3

● MONTE KENNEDY
Kennedy, Montia Calvin b: 5/11/22, Amelia, Va. BR/TL, 6'2", 185 lbs. Deb: 4/18/46

YEAR	TM/L	W	L	PCT	G	GS	CG	SH	SV	IP	H	HR	BB	SO	RAT	ERA	ERA+	OAV	OOB	BH	AVG	PB	PR	/A	PD	TPI
1946	NY-N	9	10	.474	38	27	10	1	1	186²	153	14	116	71	13.2	3.42	101	.224	.340	15	.234	2	-0	0	-0	0.2
1947	NY-N	9	12	.429	34	24	9	0	0	148¹	158	8	88	60	15.2	4.85	84	.272	.372	8	.167	-1	-13	-13	-0	-1.6
1948	NY-N	3	9	.250	25	16	7	1	0	114¹	118	10	57	63	14.0	4.01	98	.264	.351	4	.129	-1	-1	-1	-0	-0.3
1949	NY-N	12	14	.462	38	32	14	4	1	223¹	208	13	100	95	12.5	3.43	116	.242	.323	12	.145	-1	15	14	-2	1.1
1950	NY-N	5	4	.556	36	17	5	0	2	114¹	120	14	53	41	13.9	4.72	87	.269	.351	2	.056	-3	-7	-8	-0	-0.9
1951	*NY-N	1	2	.333	29	5	1	0	0	68	68	0	31	22	13.1	2.25	174	.270	.350	3	.200	-1	13	13	-0	0.5
1952	NY-N	3	4	.429	31	6	2	1	0	83¹	73	6	31	48	11.4	3.02	122	.230	.303	2	.091	-1	7	6	1	0.4
1953	NY-N	0	0	—	18	0	0	0	0	22²	30	2	19	11	19.9	7.15	60	.337	.459	0	.000	-0	-7	-7	0	0.0
Total 8		42	55	.433	249	127	48	7	4	961	928	67	495	411	13.5	3.84	101	.253	.344	46	.153	-5	6	4	-4	-0.6

● TED KENNEDY
Kennedy, Theodore A. b: 2/1865, Henry, Ill. d: 10/31/07, St.Louis, Mo. BL , Deb: 6/12/1885

YEAR	TM/L	W	L	PCT	G	GS	CG	SH	SV	IP	H	HR	BB	SO	RAT	ERA	ERA+	OAV	OOB	BH	AVG	PB	PR	/A	PD	TPI
1885	Chi-N	7	2	.778	9	9	8	0	0	78²	91	5	28	36	13.6	3.43	88	.288	.346	3	.083	-4	-5	-3	-0	-0.7
1886	Phi-a	5	15	.250	20	19	19	0	0	172²	196	4	65	68	14.0	4.53	77	.271	.338	3	.044	-9	-21	-20	1	-2.4
	Lou-a	0	4	.000	4	4	4	0	0	32	53	1	16	14	19.7	5.34	68	.351	.417	1	.077	-1	-7	-6	-1	-0.7
	Yr	5	19	.208	24	23	23	0	0	204²	249	5	81	82	14.6	4.66	76	.282	.343	4	.049	-10	-28	-26	0	-3.1
Total 2		12	21	.364	33	32	31	0	0	283¹	340	10	109	118	14.5	4.32	79	.286	.350	7	.060	-14	-33	-29	0	-3.8

● BILL KENNEDY
Kennedy, William Aulton "Lefty" b: 3/14/21, Carnesville, Ga. d: 4/9/83, Seattle, Wash. BL/TL, 6'2", 195 lbs. Deb: 4/26/48

YEAR	TM/L	W	L	PCT	G	GS	CG	SH	SV	IP	H	HR	BB	SO	RAT	ERA	ERA+	OAV	OOB	BH	AVG	PB	PR	/A	PD	TPI
1948	Cle-A	1	0	1.000	6	3	0	0	0	11¹	16	0	13	12	23.0	11.12	37	.333	.475	2	.667	1	-9	-9	0	-0.5
	StL-A	7	8	.467	26	20	3	0	0	132	132	10	104	77	16.4	4.70	97	.259	.389	11	.250	1	-6	-2	-1	-0.2
	Yr	8	8	.500	32	23	3	0	0	143¹	148	10	117	89	17.0	5.21	87	.265	.397	13	.277	2	-15	-11	-1	-0.7
1949	StL-A	4	11	.267	48	16	2	0	1	153²	172	12	73	69	14.5	4.69	97	.285	.365	6	.150	-2	-8	-3	-2	-0.5
1950	StL-A	0	0	—	1	0	0	0	0	2	1	0	2	1	13.5	0.00	—	.143	.333	0	—	0	1	1	-0	0.0
1951	StL-A	1	5	.167	19	5	1	0	0	56	76	4	37	29	18.3	5.79	76	.332	.427	2	.125	-2	-10	-9	1	-0.8
1952	Chi-A	2	2	.500	47	1	0	0	5	70²	54	4	38	46	11.8	2.80	130	.213	.318	3	.231	0	7	7	1	0.4
1953	Bos-A	0	0	—	16	0	0	0	0	24¹	24	2	17	14	15.5	3.70	114	.255	.375	1	.500	1	-0	-0	-0	0.0
1956	Cin-N	0	0	—	1	0	0	0	0	2	6	1	0	0	27.0	18.00	22	.667	.667	0	—	0	-3	-3	-0	0.0
1957	Cin-N	0	2	.000	8	0	0	0	0	12²	16	1	5	1	16.3	6.39	64	.314	.386	0	.000	-0	-4	-3	-0	-0.6
Total 8		15	28	.349	172	45	6	0	11	464²	497	34	289	256	15.5	4.73	92	.275	.379	25	.208	-1	-31	-24	-2	-2.2

● BILL KENNEDY
Kennedy, William Gorman b: 12/22/18, Alexandria, Va. d: 8/20/95, Alexandria, Va. BL/TL, 6'1", 175 lbs. Deb: 5/1/42

YEAR	TM/L	W	L	PCT	G	GS	CG	SH	SV	IP	H	HR	BB	SO	RAT	ERA	ERA+	OAV	OOB	BH	AVG	PB	PR	/A	PD	TPI
1942	Was-A	0	1	.000	8	2	1	0	0	18	21	1	10	4	15.5	8.00	46	.296	.383	0	.000	-1	-9	-9	1	-0.6
1946	Was-A	1	2	.333	21	2	0	0	3	39	40	1	29	18	15.9	6.00	56	.270	.390	1	.125	-0	-11	-11	-0	-1.1
1947	Was-A	0	0	—	2	0	0	0	0	6²	10	1	5	1	20.3	8.10	46	.370	.400	0	.000	-0	-3	-3	0	0.0
Total 3		1	3	.250	31	4	1	0	5	63²	71	3	44	23	16.3	6.79	51	.289	.397	1	.071	-1	-23	-23	0	-1.7

● BRICKYARD KENNEDY
Kennedy, William P. b: 10/7/1867, Bellaire, Ohio d: 9/23/15, Bellaire, Ohio BR/TR, 5'11", 160 lbs. Deb: 4/26/1892

YEAR	TM/L	W	L	PCT	G	GS	CG	SH	SV	IP	H	HR	BB	SO	RAT	ERA	ERA+	OAV	OOB	BH	AVG	PB	PR	/A	PD	TPI
1892	Bro-N	13	8	.619	26	21	18	0	1	191	189	3	95	108	13.6	3.86	82	.248	.334	14	.165	-1	-12	-15	-0	-1.5
1893	Bro-N	25	20	.556	46	44	40	2	1	382²	376	15	168	107	13.0	3.72	119	.249	.327	39	.248	2	40	30	5	3.2
1894	Bro-N	24	20	.545	48	41	34	0	2	360²	445	15	149	107	15.1	4.92	101	.300	.368	49	.304	4	16	1	3	0.6
1895	Bro-N	19	12	.613	39	33	26	2	1	279²	335	13	93	39	14.0	5.12	86	.292	.349	39	.307	4	-10	-22	-1	-1.6
1896	Bro-N	17	20	.459	42	38	28	1	1	305²	334	12	130	76	14.0	4.42	93	.276	.352	23	.189	-7	-2	-10	3	-1.3
1897	Bro-N	18	20	.474	44	40	36	2	1	343¹	370	6	149	81	13.8	3.91	105	.272	.348	40	.272	4	16	8	2	1.2
1898	Bro-N	16	22	.421	40	39	38	0	0	339¹	360	12	123	73	12.9	3.37	107	.270	.334	34	.252	3	9	8	6	1.6
1899	Bro-N	22	9	.710	40	33	27	2	2	277¹	297	11	86	55	12.5	2.79	140	.273	.329	27	.248	4	33	35	3	3.7
1900	Bro-N	20	13	.606	42	35	26	2	0	292	316	5	111	75	13.4	3.91	98	.276	.344	37	.301	7	-2	1	3	0.5
1901	Bro-N	3	5	.375	14	8	6	0	0	85¹	80	1	24	28	11.1	3.06	110	.246	.300	6	.167	-1	3	3	-0	0.5
1902	NY-N	1	4	.200	6	6	4	1	0	38²	44	0	16	19	14.0	3.96	71	.286	.353	4	.267	1	-5	-5	-1	-0.6
1903	*Pit-N	9	6	.600	18	15	10	1	0	125¹	130	0	57	39	13.6	3.45	94	.277	.357	21	.362	8	-3	-3	-1	-0.6
Total 12		187	159	.540	405	353	293	13	9	3021	3276	93	1201	797	13.5	3.96	102	.273	.343	333	.261	27	78	33	15	6.1

● ART KENNEY
Kenney, Arthur Joseph b: 4/29/16, Milford, Mass. BL/TL, 6', 175 lbs. Deb: 7/1/38

YEAR	TM/L	W	L	PCT	G	GS	CG	SH	SV	IP	H	HR	BB	SO	RAT	ERA	ERA+	OAV	OOB	BH	AVG	PB	PR	/A	PD	TPI
1938	Bos-N	0	0	—	2	0	0	0	0	2¹	3	0	8	2	42.4	15.43	22	.300	.611	0	—	0	-3	-3	0	0.0

YEAR	TM/L	W	L	PCT	G	GS	CG	SH	SV	IP	H	HR	BB	SO	RAT	ERA	ERA+	OAV	OOB	BH	AVG	PB	PR	/A	PD	TPI

● ED KENT   Kent, Edward C.   b: 1859, New York   BR/TR, 5'6.5", 152 lbs.   Deb: 8/14/1884

| 1884 | Tol-a | 0 | 1 | .000 | 1 | 1 | 1 | 0 | 0 | 9 | 14 | 0 | 3 | 4 | 18.0 | 6.00 | 57 | .298 | .353 | 0 | .000 | -1 | -3 | -3 | 0 | -0.2 |

● MAURY KENT   Kent, Maurice Allen   b: 9/17/1885, Marshalltown, la.   d: 4/19/66, Iowa City, Iowa   BR/TR, 6', 168 lbs.   Deb: 4/15/12

1912	Bro-N	5	5	.500	20	9	2	1	0	93	107	3	46	24	14.9	4.84	69	.296	.377	8	.229	1	-15	-15	1	-1.3
1913	Bro-N	0	0	—	3	0	0	0	0	7¹	5	0	3	1	9.8	2.45	134	.192	.276	0	.000	-0	1	1	-0	-0.1
Total	2	5	5	.500	23	9	2	1	0	100¹	112	3	49	25	14.5	4.66	72	.289	.371	8	.211	1	-14	-15	1	-1.4

● MATT KEOUGH   Keough, Matthew Lon   b: 7/3/55, Pomona, Cal.   BR/TR, 6'3", 190 lbs.   Deb: 9/3/77   F

1977	Oak-A	1	3	.250	7	6	0	0	0	42²	39	4	22	23	13.1	4.85	83	.247	.343	0	—	0	-4	-4	-1	-0.3
1978	Oak-A★	8	15	.348	32	32	6	0	0	197¹	178	9	85	108	12.2	3.24	112	.241	.323	0	—	0	11	9	2	1.1
1979	Oak-A	2	17	.105	30	28	7	0	0	176²	220	18	78	95	15.5	5.04	80	.315	.389	0	—	0	-16	-20	2	-1.3
1980	Oak-A	16	13	.552	34	32	20	2	0	250	218	24	94	121	11.4	2.92	129	.236	.310	0	—	0	31	24	-1	3.0
1981	*Oak-A	10	6	.625	19	19	1	0	0	140¹	125	11	45	60	11.0	3.40	102	.239	.299	0	—	0	4	1	-2	0.2
1982	Oak-A	11	18	.379	34	34	10	2	0	209¹	233	38	101	75	14.6	5.72	68	.284	.366	0	—	0	-38	-42	-3	-4.8
1983	Oak-A	2	3	.400	14	4	0	0	0	44	50	7	31	28	16.6	5.52	70	.284	.391	0	—	0	-7	-8	-0	-0.6
	NY-A	3	4	.429	12	12	0	0	0	55²	59	12	20	26	13.1	5.17	75	.266	.332	0	—	0	-7	-8	-0	-0.7
	Yr	5	7	.417	26	16	0	0	0	99²	109	19	51	54	14.6	5.33	73	.273	.358	0	—	0	-14	-16	-1	-1.3
1985	StL-N	0	1	.000	4	1	0	0	0	10	10	0	4	10	13.5	4.50	79	.278	.366	0	.000	-0	-1	-1	-0	-0.1
1986	Chi-N	2	2	.500	19	2	0	0	0	29	36	4	12	19	15.2	4.97	81	.316	.386	2	.400	-1	-4	-3	-1	-0.3
	Hou-N	3	2	.600	10	5	0	0	0	35	22	5	8	25	10.5	3.09	117	.180	.291	4	.364	1	2	1	0	0.4
	Yr	5	4	.556	29	7	0	0	0	64	58	9	20	44	12.5	3.94	94	.245	.332	6	.375	-2	-2	-1	-1	0.1
Total	9	58	84	.408	215	175	53	7	0	1190	1190	132	510	590	13.1	4.17	91	.262	.341	6	.333	2	-28	-50	-5	-3.4

● KURT KEPSHIRE   Kepshire, Kurt David   b: 7/3/59, Bridgeport, Conn.   BL/TR, 6'1", 180 lbs.   Deb: 7/4/84

1984	StL-N	6	5	.545	17	16	2	0	0	109	100	7	44	71	11.9	3.30	105	.249	.323	2	.056	-2	3	2	-2	-0.2
1985	StL-N	10	9	.526	32	29	0	0	0	153¹	155	16	71	67	13.3	4.75	74	.264	.343	6	.118	-1	-20	-21	-2	-2.6
1986	StL-N	0	1	.000	2	1	0	0	0	8	8	2	4	6	13.5	4.50	81	.258	.343	0	.000	-0	-1	-1	0	-0.1
Total	3	16	15	.516	51	46	2	2	0	270¹	263	25	119	144	12.7	4.16	84	.258	.335	8	.091	-3	-17	-20	-3	-2.9

● CHARLIE KERFELD   Kerfeld, Charles Patrick   b: 9/28/63, Knob Noster, Mo.   BR/TR, 6'6", 225 lbs.   Deb: 7/27/85

1985	Hou-N	4	2	.667	11	6	0	0	0	44¹	44	2	25	30	14.0	4.06	85	.268	.365	0	.000	-1	-2	-3	-1	-0.6
1986	*Hou-N	11	2	.846	61	0	0	0	7	93²	71	5	42	77	11.0	2.59	139	.213	.305	1	.111	-0	12	10	-1	1.5
1987	Hou-N	0	2	.000	21	0	0	0	0	29²	34	3	21	17	17.0	6.67	59	.309	.424	0	.000	-0	-9	-9	-0	-0.6
1990	Hou-N	0	2	.000	5	0	0	0	0	3¹	9	0	6	4	40.5	16.20	23	.529	.652	0	—	-0	-5	-5	-0	-2.1
	Atl-N	3	1	.750	25	0	0	0	2	30²	31	2	23	27	15.8	5.58	72	.270	.391	0	—	-0	-6	-5	-0	-0.7
	Yr	3	3	.500	30	0	0	0	2	34	40	2	29	31	18.3	6.62	60	.303	.429	0	—	-1	-11	-10	-0	-2.8
Total	4	18	9	.667	123	6	0	0	9	201²	189	12	117	155	13.8	4.20	88	.256	.360	1	.038	-2	-10	-11	-2	-2.5

● GUS KERIAZAKOS   Keriazakos, Constantine Nicholas   b: 7/28/31, W.Orange, N.J.   d: 5/4/96, Hilton Head, S.C.   BR/TR, 6'3", 187 lbs.   Deb: 10/1/50

1950	Chi-A	0	1	.000	1	1	0	0	0	2¹	7	0	5	1	46.3	19.29	23	.500	.632	1	1.000	0	-4	-4	-0	-0.9
1954	Was-A	2	3	.400	22	3	2	0	0	59²	59	4	30	33	13.4	3.77	94	.262	.349	1	.067	-1	-0	-1	-1	-0.2
1955	KC-A	0	1	.000	5	1	0	0	0	11²	15	4	7	8	17.0	12.34	34	.333	.423	0	.000	-0	-11	-11	-0	-0.8
Total	3	2	5	.286	28	5	2	0	0	73²	81	8	42	42	15.0	5.62	65	.285	.377	2	.105	-1	-15	-16	-1	-1.9

● BILL KERKSIECK   Kerksieck, Wayman William   b: 12/6/13, Ulm, Ark.   d: 3/11/70, Stuttgart, Ark.   BR/TR, 6'1", 183 lbs.   Deb: 6/21/39

| 1939 | Phi-N | 0 | 2 | .000 | 23 | 2 | 1 | 0 | 0 | 62² | 81 | 13 | 32 | 13 | 16.2 | 7.18 | 56 | .328 | .405 | 1 | .083 | -0 | -23 | -22 | -1 | -0.7 |

● JIM KERN   Kern, James Lester   b: 3/15/49, Gladwin, Mich.   BR/TR, 6'5", 205 lbs.   Deb: 9/6/74

1974	Cle-A	0	1	.000	4	3	1	0	0	15¹	16	1	14	11	17.6	4.70	77	.262	.400	0	—	-0	-2	-2	-0	-0.1
1975	Cle-A	1	1	.333	13	7	0	0	0	71⁴	60	5	45	55	13.8	3.77	100	.233	.357	0	—	0	0	0	0	0.0
1976	Cle-A	10	7	.588	50	2	0	0	15	117²	91	2	50	111	11.2	2.37	147	.222	.314	0	—	0	15	15	-0	2.6
1977	Cle-A★	8	10	.444	60	0	0	0	18	92	85	3	47	91	13.5	3.42	115	.260	.363	0	—	0	6	5	0	1.3
1978	Cle-A★	10	10	.500	58	0	0	0	13	99¹	77	4	58	95	12.5	3.08	121	.224	.342	0	.000	0	8	7	1	1.7
1979	Tex-A★	13	5	.722	71	0	0	0	29	143	99	5	62	136	10.3	1.57	264	.199	.290	0	—	0	42	41	-1	6.7
1980	Tex-A	3	11	.214	38	1	0	0	0	63¹	65	4	45	40	15.9	4.83	81	.279	.400	0	—	-0	-6	-7	-0	-1.1
1981	Tex-A	1	2	.333	23	0	0	0	6	30	21	0	22	20	13.2	2.70	128	.204	.349	0	—	0	3	3	-0	0.6
1982	Cin-N	3	5	.375	50	0	0	0	2	76	61	3	48	43	13.1	2.84	130	.222	.342	0	.000	0	6	7	1	0.8
	Chi-A	2	1	.667	13	1	0	0	2	28	20	3	12	23	10.3	5.14	78	.204	.291	0	—	-0	-3	-3	-0	-0.4
1983	Chi-A	0	0	—	1	0	0	0	0	0²		0	1	0	13.5	0.00	—	.333	.333	0	—	0	0	0	0	0.0
1984	Phi-N	0	1	.000	13	1	0	0	2	13¹	20	0	3	10	20.3	10.13	36	.339	.435	0	—	-0	-10	-10	-0	-0.7
	Mil-A	1	0	1.000	6	0	0	0	0	4²	6	0	3	4	17.4	0.00	—	.300	.391	0	—	-0	2	2	-0	0.2
1985	Mil-A	0	1	.000	5	0	0	0	0	11	14	1	4	3	15.5	6.55	64	.318	.388	0	—	-0	-3	-3	-1	-0.2
1986	Cle-A	1	1	.500	16	0	0	0	0	27¹	14	4	15	16	19.8	7.90	52	.298	.429	0	.000	-0	-11	-11	-0	-0.8
Total	13	53	57	.482	416	14	1	0	88	793¹	670	35	444	651	13.0	3.32	115	.235	.344	0	.000	-0	48	45	1	11.0

● DICKIE KERR   Kerr, Richard Henry   b: 7/3/1893, St.Louis, Mo.   d: 5/4/63, Houston, Tex.   BL/TL, 5'7", 155 lbs.   Deb: 4/25/19

1919	*Chi-A	13	7	.650	39	17	10	1	0	212¹	208	2	64	79	11.6	2.88	110	.259	.316	17	.250	5	8	7	1	1.2
1920	Chi-A	21	9	.700	45	27	19	3	**5**	253²	266	7	72	72	12.1	3.37	112	.278	.331	14	.156	-4	12	11	3	1.1
1921	Chi-A	19	17	.528	44	37	25	3	1	308²	357	12	96	80	13.5	4.72	90	.295	.352	25	.238	5	-15	-17	-2	-1.2
1925	Chi-A	0	1	.000	12	2	0	0	0	36²	45	3	18	4	15.7	5.15	81	.304	.383	4	.333	1	-3	-4	-0	-0.1
Total	4	53	34	.609	140	83	54	7	6	811¹	876	24	250	235	12.7	3.84	99	.281	.338	60	.218	7	2	-2	1	1.1

● JOE KERRIGAN   Kerrigan, Joseph Thomas   b: 11/30/54, Philadelphia, Pa.   BR/TR, 6'5", 205 lbs.   Deb: 7/9/76   C

1976	Mon-N	2	6	.250	38	0	0	0	1	56²	63	3	23	22	14.0	3.81	98	.289	.362	0	—	-1	-2	-1	1	-0.1
1977	Mon-N	3	5	.375	66	0	0	0	11	89¹	80	4	33	43	11.7	3.22	118	.241	.315	0	.000	-1	7	6	1	0.6
1978	Bal-A	3	1	.750	26	2	0	0	3	71²	75	10	36	41	14.2	4.77	73	.273	.361	0	—	-0	-8	-10	-2	-0.5
1980	Bal-A	0	0	—	1	0	0	0	0	2¹	3	0	1	1	11.6	3.86	103	.273	.273	0	—	-0	-0	-0	-0	0.1
Total	4	8	12	.400	131	2	0	0	15	220	221	17	92	107	13.1	3.89	95	.264	.342	0	.000	-1	-3	-5	-3	0.1

● RICK KESTER   Kester, Richard Lee   b: 7/7/46, Iola, Kan.   BR/TR, 6', 190 lbs.   Deb: 8/18/68

1968	Atl-N	0	0	—	5	0	0	0	0	6¹	8	0	3	9	15.6	5.68	53	.308	.379	0	—	-0	-2	-2	-0	0.0
1969	Atl-N	0	0	—	1	0	0	0	0	2	5	0	1	0	22.5	13.50	27	.455	.455	0	—	-0	-3	-3	-0	-0.2
1970	Atl-N	0	0	—	15	0	0	0	0	32¹	34	4	19	22	15.1	5.57	77	.283	.377	0	.000	-1	-5	-5	-1	-0.2
Total	3	0	0	—	21	0	0	0	0	40²	47	4	23	31	15.7	5.98	68	.299	.382	0	.000	-1	-10	-9	-1	-0.2

● GUS KETCHUM   Ketchum, Augustus Franklin   b: 3/21/1897, Royse City, Tex.   d: 9/6/80, Oklahoma City, Okla.   BR/TR, 5'9.5", 170 lbs.   Deb: 8/7/22

| 1922 | Phi-A | 0 | 1 | .000 | 6 | 0 | 0 | 0 | 0 | 16 | 19 | 2 | 8 | 4 | 15.8 | 5.63 | 76 | .302 | .389 | 0 | .000 | -1 | -3 | -2 | -1 | -0.3 |

● HENRY KEUPPER   Keupper, Henry J.   b: 6/24/1887, Staunton, Ill.   d: 8/14/60, Marion, Ill.   BL/TL, 6'1", 185 lbs.   Deb: 4/19/14

| 1914 | StL-F | 8 | 20 | .286 | 42 | 25 | 12 | 1 | 0 | 213 | 256 | 3 | 49 | 70 | 13.1 | 4.27 | 71 | .291 | .332 | 17 | .250 | 1 | -33 | -29 | 2 | -3.1 |

● JIMMY KEY   Key, James Edward   b: 4/22/61, Huntsville, Ala.   BR/TL, 6'1", 190 lbs.   Deb: 4/6/84

1984	Tor-A	4	5	.444	63	0	0	0	10	62	70	8	32	44	15.0	4.65	88	.286	.371	0	—	-0	-5	-4	1	-0.7
1985	*Tor-A★	14	6	.700	35	32	3	0	0	212²	188	22	50	85	10.2	3.00	140	.237	.284	0	—	0	27	28	4	2.9
1986	Tor-A	14	11	.560	36	35	4	2	0	232	222	24	74	141	11.6	3.57	118	.256	.317	0	—	0	16	17	3	1.8
1987	Tor-A	17	8	.680	36	36	8	1	0	261	210	24	66	161	**9.6**	**2.76**	**163**	**.221**	**.273**	0	—	0	**49**	**50**	2	4.4
1988	Tor-A	12	5	.706	21	21	2	1	0	131¹	127	13	30	65	11.0	3.29	119	.250	.298	0	—	0	10	9	-0	1.1
1989	*Tor-A	13	14	.481	33	33	5	1	0	216	226	18	27	118	10.0	3.88	97	.270	.295	0	—	0	-0	-3	2	0.0
1990	Tor-A	13	7	.650	27	27	0	0	0	154²	169	20	22	88	11.2	4.25	93	.281	.307	0	—	0	-6	-5	-0	-0.1
1991	*Tor-A★	16	12	.571	33	33	2	0	0	209¹	207	12	44	125	10.9	3.05	138	.254	.295	0	—	0	24	27	3	3.5
1992	*Tor-A	13	13	.500	33	33	4	2	0	216²	205	24	59	117	11.1	3.53	116	.248	.301	0	—	0	10	13	0	1.4

YEAR	TM/L	W	L	PCT	G	GS	CG	SH	SV	IP	H	HR	BB	SO	RAT	ERA	ERA+	OAV	OOB	BH	AVG	PB	PR	/A	PD	TPI
1993	NY-A★	18	6	.750	34	34	4	2	0	236²	219	26	43	173	10.0	3.00	138	.246	.282	0	—	0	35	30	0	3.0
1994	NY-A★	17	4	.810	25	25	1	0	0	168	177	10	52	112	12.4	3.27	140	.273	.330	0	—	0	29	24	3	3.2
1995	NY-A	1	2	.333	5	5	0	0	0	30¹	40	3	6	14	13.6	5.64	82	.323	.354	0	—	0	-3	-3	0	-0.2
1996	*NY-A	12	11	.522	30	30	0	0	0	169¹	171	21	58	116	12.3	4.68	108	.266	.329	0	—	0	6	7	1	0.9
Total	13	164	104	.612	411	344	33	12	10	2300	2231	225	563	1344	11.1	3.49	122	.255	.302				192	192	19	20.6

● **BRIAN KEYSER**   Keyser, Brian Lee b: 10/31/66, Castro Valley, Cal. BR/TR, 6'1", 180 lbs. Deb: 6/2/95

1995	Chi-A	5	6	.455	23	10	0	0	0	92¹	114	10	27	48	13.9	4.97	90	.306	.356	0	—	0	-3	-5	1	-0.3
1996	Chi-A	1	2	.333	28	0	0	0	1	59²	78	3	28	19	16.0	4.98	94	.328	.398	0	—	0	0	-2	2	0.2
Total	2	6	8	.429	51	10	0	0	1	152	192	13	55	67	14.7	4.97	91	.314	.373	0	—	0	-3	-7	3	-0.1

● **DANA KIECKER**   Kiecker, Dana Ervin b: 2/25/61, Sleepy Eye, Minn. BR/TR, 6'3", 180 lbs. Deb: 4/12/90

1990	*Bos-A	8	9	.471	32	25	0	0	0	152	145	7	54	93	12.3	3.97	103	.253	.328	0	—	0	-1	2	2	0.0
1991	Bos-A	2	3	.400	18	5	0	0	0	40¹	56	6	23	21	18.1	7.36	58	.344	.431	0	—	0	-15	-14	1	-1.6
Total	2	10	12	.455	50	30	0	0	0	192¹	201	13	77	114	13.5	4.68	88	.273	.351	0	—	0	-16	-12	3	-1.6

● **JOE KIEFER**   Kiefer, Joseph William "Harlem Joe" or "Smoke" b: 7/19/1899, W.Leyden, N.Y. d: 7/5/75, Utica, N.Y. BR/TR, 5'11", 190 lbs. Deb: 10/1/20

1920	Chi-A	0	1	.000	2	1	0	0	0	4²	7	0	5	1	25.1	15.43	24	.333	.481	0	.000	-0	-6	-6	-0	-0.9
1925	Bos-A	0	2	.000	2	2	0	0	0	15	20	0	9	4	18.0	6.00	76	.351	.448	0	.000	-1	-3	-2	1	-0.3
1926	Bos-A	0	2	.000	11	1	0	0	0	30	29	2	16	4	14.1	4.80	85	.266	.370	1	.143	-0	-3	-2	0	-0.1
Total	3	0	5	.000	15	4	0	0	0	49²	56	2	30	9	16.3	6.16	68	.299	.407	1	.077	-1	-11	-11	1	-1.3

● **MARK KIEFER**   Kiefer, Mark Andrew b: 11/13/68, Orange, Cal. BR/TR, 6'4", 175 lbs. Deb: 9/20/93 F

1993	Mil-A	0	0	—	6	0	0	0	1	9¹	3	0	5	7	8.7	0.00	—	.097	.243	0	—	0	4	4	0	0.2
1994	Mil-A	1	0	1.000	7	0	0	0	0	10²	15	4	8	10	19.4	8.44	60	.357	.460	0	—	0	-4	-4	-0	-0.5
1995	Mil-A	4	1	.800	24	0	0	0	0	49²	37	6	27	41	11.6	3.44	145	.203	.306	0	—	0	7	8	-1	0.4
1996	Mil-A	0	0	—	7	0	0	0	0	10	15	1	5	3	18.0	8.10	65	.366	.435	0	—	0	-3	-3	-0	-0.1
Total	4	5	1	.833	44	0	0	0	1	79²	70	11	45	61	13.1	4.29	115	.236	.339	0	—	0	4	6	-2	-0.0

● **JOHN KIELY**   Kiely, John Francis b: 10/4/64, Boston, Mass. BR/TR, 6'3", 210 lbs. Deb: 7/26/91

1991	Det-A	0	1	.000	7	0	0	0	0	6²	13	0	9	1	31.1	14.85	28	.448	.590	0	—	0	-8	-8	-0	-1.1
1992	Det-A	4	2	.667	39	0	0	0	0	55	44	2	28	18	11.8	2.13	186	.224	.321	0	—	0	11	11	2	1.4
1993	Det-A	0	2	.000	8	0	0	0	0	11²	13	2	13	5	20.8	7.71	56	.295	.466	0	—	0	-4	-4	1	-0.5
Total	3	4	5	.444	54	0	0	0	0	73¹	70	4	50	24	15.0	4.17	96	.260	.380	0	—	0	-1	-1	3	-0.2

● **LEO KIELY**   Kiely, Leo Patrick "Kiki" b: 11/30/29, Hoboken, N.J. d: 1/18/84, Montclair, N.J. BL/TL, 6'2", 180 lbs. Deb: 6/27/51

1951	Bos-A	7	7	.500	17	16	4	0	0	113¹	106	9	39	46	11.7	3.34	134	.251	.317	5	.143	-1	10	14	1	1.7
1954	Bos-A	5	8	.385	28	19	4	1	0	131	153	12	58	59	14.6	3.50	117	.295	.367	9	.180	-3	3	9	-1	0.7
1955	Bos-A	3	3	.500	33	4	0	0	6	90	91	5	37	36	12.8	2.80	153	.269	.341	5	.192	-0	12	15	1	1.3
1956	Bos-A	2	2	.500	23	0	0	0	3	31¹	47	1	14	9	18.1	5.17	89	.362	.432	1	.167	-0	-4	-2	0	-0.3
1958	Bos-A	5	2	.714	47	0	0	0	12	81	77	3	18	26	10.8	3.00	134	.254	.300	0	.000	-2	7	9	1	1.0
1959	Bos-A	3	3	.500	41	0	0	0	7	55²	67	8	18	30	13.9	4.20	97	.299	.354	0	.000	-1	-2	-1	-1	-0.1
1960	KC-A	1	2	.333	20	0	0	0	1	20²	21	1	5	6	11.8	1.74	229	.266	.318	0	.000	0	5	5	1	0.9
Total	7	26	27	.491	209	39	8	1	29	523	562	39	189	212	13.1	3.37	125	.279	.343	20	.144	-4	31	49	5	5.2

● **DARRYL KILE**   Kile, Darryl Andrew b: 12/2/68, Garden Grove, Cal. BR/TR, 6'5", 185 lbs. Deb: 4/8/91

1991	Hou-N	7	11	.389	37	22	0	0	0	153²	144	16	84	100	13.7	3.69	95	.246	.347	0	.000	-1	-0	-3	-2	-0.8
1992	Hou-N	5	10	.333	22	22	2	0	0	125¹	124	8	63	90	13.7	3.95	85	.261	.352	5	.156	1	-6	-8	-2	-1.1
1993	Hou-N☆	15	8	.652	32	26	4	2	0	171²	152	12	69	141	12.4	3.51	110	.239	.327	5	.094	-1	10	7	-2	0.6
1994	Hou-N	9	6	.600	24	24	0	0	0	147²	153	13	82	105	14.9	4.57	86	.275	.377	7	.149	1	-6	-10	-1	-0.9
1995	Hou-N	4	12	.250	25	21	0	0	0	127	114	5	73	113	14.1	4.96	78	.240	.355	4	.111	0	-11	-15	2	-1.5
1996	Hou-N	12	11	.522	35	33	4	0	0	219	233	16	97	219	14.2	4.19	91	.276	.362	10	.137	1	1	-9	1	-0.7
Total	6	52	58	.473	175	148	10	2	0	944¹	920	70	468	768	13.8	4.12	91	.257	.353	31	.111	-4	-13	-39	-4	-4.4

● **JOHN KILEY**   Kiley, John Frederick b: 7/1/1859, Dedham, Mass. d: 12/18/40, Norwood, Mass. BL/TL, 5'7", 147 lbs. Deb: 5/1/1884 ♦

1891	Bos-N	0	1	.000	1	1	1	0	0	8	13	3	5	1	20.3	6.75	54	.351	.429	0	.000	0	-3	-3	0	-0.2

● **PAUL KILGUS**   Kilgus, Paul Nelson b: 2/2/62, Bowling Green, Ky. BL/TL, 6'1", 185 lbs. Deb: 6/7/87

1987	Tex-A	2	7	.222	25	12	0	0	0	89¹	95	14	31	42	12.9	4.13	108	.271	.334	0	—	0	3	3	-1	0.2
1988	Tex-A	12	15	.444	32	32	5	3	0	203¹	190	18	71	88	11.6	4.16	98	.243	.314	0	—	0	-4	-2	1	-0.1
1989	*Chi-N	6	10	.375	35	23	0	0	0	145²	164	9	49	61	13.5	4.39	86	.283	.344	3	.073	-1	-14	-10	0	-1.3
1990	Tor-A	0	0	—	11	0	0	0	0	16¹	19	2	7	7	14.9	6.06	65	.306	.386	0	—	0	-4	-4	0	-0.1
1991	Bal-A	0	2	.000	38	0	0	0	1	62	60	8	24	32	12.6	5.08	78	.256	.333	0	—	0	-7	-8	2	-0.1
1993	StL-N	1	0	1.000	22	1	0	0	0	28²	18	1	8	21	8.5	0.63	631	.180	.248	1	.200	0	11	11	0	0.4
Total	6	21	34	.382	163	68	5	3	4	545¹	546	52	190	251	12.5	4.19	96	.259	.327	4	.087	-2	-15	-9	2	-0.7

● **MIKE KILKENNY**   Kilkenny, Michael David b: 4/11/45, Bradford, Ont., Can. BR/TL, 6'3.5", 175 lbs. Deb: 4/11/69

1969	Det-A	8	6	.571	39	15	6	4	2	128¹	99	13	63	97	11.6	3.37	111	.211	.310	2	.054	-2	4	5	-0	0.3
1970	Det-A	7	6	.538	36	21	3	0	0	129	141	10	70	105	14.9	5.16	72	.279	.369	3	.077	-3	-21	-21	0	-2.1
1971	Det-A	4	5	.444	30	11	2	0	1	86¹	83	8	44	47	13.4	5.00	72	.247	.338	2	.083	-2	-15	-14	-0	-1.6
1972	Det-A	0	0	—	1	0	0	0	0	1	1	0	1	0	9.0	9.00	35	.250	.250	0	—	0	-1	-1	0	0.0
	Oak-A	0	0	—	1	0	0	0	0	1	0	0	0	0	0.00	0.00	—	.000	.000	0	—	0	0	0	0	0.0
	SD-N	0	0	—	5	0	0	0	0	4¹	7	1	3	5	20.8	8.31	40	.350	.435	0	—	0	-2	-2	0	0.0
	Cle-A	4	1	.800	22	7	1	0	0	58	51	5	39	44	14.0	3.41	94	.237	.354	1	.071	-1	-2	-1	1	-0.2
	Yr	4	1	.800	24	7	1	0	1	60	52	6	39	44	13.6	3.45	95	.234	.349	1	.071	-1	-4	-3	1	-0.3
1973	Cle-A	0	0	—	5	0	0	0	0	2	5	1	9	3	49.5	22.50	17	.455	.647	0	—	0	-4	-4	0	0.0
Total	5	23	18	.561	139	54	12	4	4	410	387	39	224	301	13.6	4.43	82	.248	.345	8	.070	-8	-41	-37	1	-3.6

● **EVANS KILLEEN**   Killeen, Evans Henry b: 2/27/36, Brooklyn, N.Y. BR/TR, 6', 190 lbs. Deb: 9/7/59

1959	KC-A	0	0	—	4	0	0	0	0	5²	4	0	4	1	12.7	4.76	84	.211	.348	0	—	0	-1	-0	-0	0.0

● **HENRY KILLEEN**   Killeen, Henry b: 1871, Troy, N.Y. 5'9", 150 lbs. Deb: 9/11/1891

1891	Cle-N	0	1	.000	1	1	0	0	0	8²	11	1	3	8	19.7	6.23	56	.297	.422	0	.000	-0	-3	-3	0	-0.2

● **FRANK KILLEN**   Killen, Frank Bissell "Lefty" b: 11/30/1870, Pittsburgh, Pa. d: 12/3/39, Pittsburgh, Pa. BL/TL, 6'1", 200 lbs. Deb: 8/27/1891

1891	Mil-a	7	4	.636	11	11	11	2	0	96²	73	1	51	38	11.8	1.68	262	.202	.306	8	.229	1	22	29	-0	3.0
1892	Was-N	29	26	.527	60	52	46	2	0	459²	448	15	182	147	12.3	3.31	98	.245	.320	37	.199	10	-1	-3	3	1.0
1893	Pit-N	36	14	.720	55	48	38	2	0	415	401	12	140	99	12.1	3.64	125	.246	.312	47	.275	14	47	42	1	5.2
1894	Pit-N	14	11	.560	28	28	20	1	0	204	261	3	86	62	15.5	4.50	116	.308	.375	21	.262	0	19	17	1	1.5
1895	Pit-N	5	5	.500	13	11	6	0	0	95	113	3	57	25	16.2	5.49	82	.291	.383	13	.342	-1	-8	-10	1	-0.4
1896	Pit-N	30	18	.625	52	50	44	5	0	432¹	476	7	119	134	12.7	3.41	123	.277	.329	40	.231	9	46	38	2	4.2
1897	Pit-N	17	23	.425	42	41	38	1	0	337¹	417	4	76	99	13.4	4.46	94	.301	.341	32	.248	4	-5	-10	-1	-0.6
1898	Pit-N	10	11	.476	23	23	17	0	0	177²	201	3	41	48	12.8	3.75	95	.283	.332	17	.262	2	-3	-4	0	-0.2
	Was-N	6	9	.400	17	16	15	0	0	128¹	149	4	29	43	12.6	3.58	102	.288	.328	15	.273	3	0	1	0	0.5
	Yr	16	20	.444	40	39	32	0	0	306	350	7	70	91	12.6	3.68	98	.282	.322	32	.267	5	-2	-3	0	0.3
1899	Was-N	0	2	.000	2	2	1	0	0	12	18	0	4	3	17.3	6.00	65	.346	.404	1	.200	0	-3	-3	-1	-0.4
	Bos-N	7	5	.583	12	12	11	0	0	99¹	108	3	26	23	12.4	4.26	98	.276	.326	7	.171	-2	-4	-1	-0	-0.3
	Yr	7	7	.500	14	14	12	0	0	111¹	126	3	30	26	12.9	4.45	93	.284	.335	8	.174	-2	-7	-4	-1	-0.6
1900	Chi-N	3	3	.500	6	6	6	0	0	54	65	1	9	4	13.0	4.67	77	.297	.336	3	.150	-1	-6	-6	-0	-0.6
Total	10	164	131	.556	321	300	253	13	0	2511¹	2730	55	822	725	13.0	3.78	109	.272	.332	241	.241	44	104	92	5	12.9

YEAR TM/L	W	L	PCT	G	GS	CG	SH	SV	IP	H	HR	BB	SO	RAT	ERA	ERA+	OAV	OOB	BH	AVG	PB	PR	/A	PD	TPI
● ED KILLIAN				Killian, Edwin Henry "Twilight Ed"			b: 11/12/1876, Racine, Wis.		d: 7/18/28, Detroit, Mich.			BL/TL, 5'11", 170 lbs.		Deb: 8/25/03											
1903 Cle-A	3	4	.429	9	8	7	3	0	61²	61	1	13	18	11.4	2.48	115	.257	.307	5	.179	-1	3	3	-0	0.2
1904 Det-A	14	20	.412	40	34	32	4	1	331²	293	0	93	124	10.9	2.44	104	.238	.301	18	.143	-3	6	4	-5	-0.5
1905 Det-A	23	14	.622	39	37	33	8	0	313¹	263	0	102	110	10.9	2.27	120	.230	.300	32	.271	6	13	16	-4	2.3
1906 Det-A	10	6	.625	21	16	14	0	2	149²	165	0	54	47	13.5	3.43	81	.283	.348	-1	-12	-11	-2	-1.5		
1907 *Det-A	25	13	.658	42	34	29	3	1	314	286	2	91	96	11.1	1.78	147	.245	.306	39	.320	10	27	29	-2	4.7
1908 *Det-A	12	9	.571	27	23	15	0	1	180²	170	3	53	47	11.5	2.99	81	.252	.314	10	.137	-3	-12	-11	3	-1.4
1909 Det-A	11	9	.550	25	19	14	3	1	173¹	150	1	49	54	10.6	1.71	147	.236	.297	10	.161	-1	15	15	-1	1.6
1910 Det-A	4	3	.571	11	9	5	1	0	74	75	2	27	20	13.1	3.04	87	.268	.345	4	.148	-1	-4	-3	-1	-0.5
Total 8	102	78	.567	214	180	149	22	6	1598¹	1463	9	482	516	11.3	2.38	110	.246	.310	127	.209	6	35	41	-12	4.9
● JACK KILLILAY				Killilay, John William b: 5/24/1887, Leavenworth, Kan. d: 10/21/68, Tulsa, Okla. BR/TR, 5'11", 165 lbs. Deb: 5/13/11																					
1911 Bos-A	4	2	.667	14	7	1	0	0	61	65	0	36	28	16.4	3.54	93	.302	.425	1	.042	-2	-1	-2	0	-0.4
● MATT KILROY				Kilroy, Matthew Aloysius "Matches" b: 6/21/1866, Philadelphia, Pa. d: 3/2/40, Philadelphia, Pa. BL/TL, 5'9", 175 lbs. Deb: 4/17/1886 F																					
1886 Bal-a	29	34	.460	**68**	68	**66**	5	0	583	476	10	182	**513**	10.5	3.37	102	.210	.274	38	.174	-5	5	4	6	0.4
1887 Bal-a	**46**	19	.708	**69**	69	**66**	6	0	**589¹**	585	9	157	217	11.6	3.07	134	.253	.306	59	.247	6	**80**	67	10	**7.3**
1888 Bal-a	17	21	.447	40	40	35	2	0	321	347	5	79	135	12.6	4.04	74	.266	.319	26	.179	-0	-35	-38	-1	-3.7
1889 Bal-a	29	25	.537	59	56	**55**	5	0	480²	476	8	142	217	12.1	2.85	139	.250	.312	57	.274	10	54	59	8	**6.9**
1890 Bos-P	9	15	.375	30	27	18	0	1	217²	268	14	87	48	15.3	4.26	103	.290	.361	20	.215	-0	-1	-3	1	0.5
1891 Cin-a	1	4	.200	7	6	4	0	0	45¹	51	1	19	6	15.5	2.98	138	.274	.366	3	.150	-1	4	6	0	0.5
1892 Was-N	1	1	.500	4	3	2	0	0	26¹	20	0	15	1	12.0	2.39	136	.202	.319	2	.200	-0	3	3	2	0.3
1893 Lou-N	3	2	.600	5	5	5	1	0	35	57	2	23	4	21.6	9.00	49	.354	.447	7	.438	3	-17	-18	1	-1.4
1894 Lou-N	0	5	.000	8	7	3	0	0	37	46	2	20	11	16.5	3.89	131	.301	.389	2	.118	-2	6	5	1	0.4
1898 Chi-N	6	7	.462	13	11	10	0	0	100¹	119	2	30	18	14.4	4.31	83	.292	.357	22	.229	2	-8	-8	1	-0.4
Total 10	141	133	.515	303	292	264	19	1	2435²	2445	53	754	1170	12.3	3.47	109	.252	.314	236	.222	15	92	83	28	10.4
● MIKE KILROY				Kilroy, Michael Joseph b: 11/4/1872, Philadelphia, Pa. d: 10/2/60, Philadelphia, Pa. BR/TR, 5'11", 180 lbs. Deb: 9/1/1888 F																					
1888 Bal-a	0	1	.000	1	1	1	0	0	9	12	1	4	1	17.0	8.00	37	.308	.386	1	.000	-0	-5	-5	-0	-0.4
1891 Phi-N	0	2	.000	3	1	0	0	0	10	15	1	4	3	18.9	9.90	34	.333	.412	2	.400	1	-7	-7	-0	-0.9
Total 2	0	3	.000	4	2	1	0	0	19	27	2	8	4	18.0	9.00	36	.321	.400	2	.222	0	-12	-12	-0	-1.3
● NEWT KIMBALL				Kimball, Newell W. b: 3/27/15, Logan, Utah BR/TR, 6'2.5", 190 lbs. Deb: 5/7/37																					
1937 Chi-N	0	0	—	2	0	0	0	0	5	12	1	1	0	23.4	10.80	37	.444	.464	0	.000	-0	-4	-4	0	0.0
1938 Chi-N	0	0	—	1	0	0	0	0	1	3	0	1	0	27.0	9.00	43	.500	.500	0	—	-0	-1	-0	0	0.0
1940 Bro-N	3	1	.750	21	0	0	0	1	33²	29	2	15	21	11.8	3.21	129	.238	.321	0	.000	-1	2	3	-0	0.2
StL-N	1	0	1.000	2	1	0	0	0	14	11	1	6	6	10.9	2.57	155	.208	.288	2	.333	1	2	2	-0	0.2
Yr	4	1	.800	23	1	0	0	1	47²	40	3	21	27	11.5	3.02	132	.229	.311	2	.182	0	4	5	-1	0.4
1941 Bro-N	3	1	.750	15	1	0	0	0	52	43	0	29	17	12.5	3.63	101	.225	.327	3	.214	-0	-0	0	-0	-0.2
1942 Bro-N	2	0	1.000	14	1	0	0	0	29¹	27	0	19	8	14.4	3.68	89	.265	.385	1	.200	-0	-1	-1	-2	0.0
1943 Bro-N	1	1	.500	5	0	0	1	0	11	9	0	2	2	11.5	1.64	205	.214	.298	0	.000	-0	2	2	0	0.4
Phi-N	1	6	.143	34	6	2	0	2	89²	85	4	42	33	12.8	4.12	82	.253	.338	1	.188	1	-7	-7	-2	-0.3
Yr	2	7	.222	39	6	2	1	2	100²	94	4	44	35	12.7	3.84	94	.249	.333	1	.158	1	-5	-5	-2	0.0
Total 6	11	9	.550	94	13	4	0	5	235²	219	8	117	88	12.9	3.78	94	.249	.339	9	.180	1	-6	-6	-4	-0.1
● SAM KIMBER				Kimber, Samuel Jackson b: 10/29/1852, Philadelphia, Pa. d: 11/7/25, Philadelphia, Pa. BR/TR, 5'10.5", 165 lbs. Deb: 5/1/1884																					
1884 Bro-a	18	20	.474	41	41	41	4	0	361¹	364	6	72	122	11.2	3.81	87	.247	.289	21	.148	-5	-23	-20	-1	-2.2
1885 Pro-N	0	1	.000	1	1	1	0	0	8	15	1	5	4	22.5	11.25	40	.405	.476	0	.000	-0	-7	-8	-0	-0.6
Total 2	18	21	.462	42	42	42	4	0	369¹	379	7	77	126	11.5	3.97	83	.251	.294	21	.145	-6	-30	-27	-1	-2.8
● HARRY KIMBERLIN				Kimberlin, Harry Lydle "Murphy" or "Mule Trader" b: 3/13/09, Sullivan, Mo. BR/TR, 6'3", 175 lbs. Deb: 7/11/36																					
1936 StL-A	0	0	—	13	0	0	0	0	20	24	3	4	4	18.0	5.40	100	.296	.412	0	.000	-0	-1	-0	-0	-0.1
1937 StL-A	0	2	.000	3	2	1	0	0	15¹	16	2	9	5	14.7	2.35	206	.254	.347	1	.200	0	4	4	-0	0.5
1938 StL-A	0	0	—	1	1	0	0	0	8	8	1	3	2	12.4	3.38	147	.286	.355	0	.000	-0	1	1	-0	-0.1
1939 StL-A	1	2	.333	17	3	0	0	0	41	59	6	19	11	17.6	5.49	89	.326	.396	3	.333	-0	-4	-3	-0	-0.1
Total 4	1	4	.200	34	6	1	0	0	84¹	107	12	47	21	16.6	4.70	106	.303	.388	4	.250	0	0	3	-1	0.3
● HAL KIME				Kime, Harold Lee "Lefty" b: 3/15/1899, W.Salem, Ohio d: 5/16/39, Columbus, Ohio BL/TL, 5'9", 160 lbs. Deb: 6/19/20																					
1920 StL-N	0	0	—	4	0	0	0	0	9	7	2	9	1	15.4	2.57	116	.333	.400	0	.000	-0	0	0	0	0.0
● CHAD KIMSEY				Kimsey, Clyde Elias b: 8/6/06, Copperhill, Tenn. d: 12/3/42, Pryor, Okla. BL/TR, 6'2", 200 lbs. Deb: 4/21/29																					
1929 StL-A	3	6	.333	24	3	1	0	1	64¹	73	2	19	13	14.3	5.04	88	.340	.388	8	.267	3	-6	-4	3	0.0
1930 StL-A	6	10	.375	42	4	1	0	1	113¹	139	8	45	32	14.6	6.35	77	.312	.377	24	.343	7	-21	-19	1	-1.3
1931 StL-A	4	6	.400	42	1	0	0	7	94¹	121	1	27	27	14.3	4.39	106	.312	.360	10	.270	5	-0	3	2	0.1
1932 StL-A	4	2	.667	33	0	0	0	3	78¹	85	3	19	13	13.6	4.02	121	.281	.352	6	.333	1	4	7	1	0.7
Chi-A	1	1	.500	7	0	0	0	0	11	8	4	19	6	11.5	2.45	176	.211	.318	0	.000	-0	2	2	1	0.5
Yr	5	3	.625	40	0	0	0	3	89¹	93	7	38	19	13.3	3.83	125	.274	.348	6	.300	1	6	**10**	2	1.2
1933 Chi-A	4	1	.800	28	2	0	0	0	96	124	7	36	19	15.4	5.53	77	.318	.381	5	.152	-2	-13	-14	1	-0.7
1936 Det-A	2	3	.400	22	0	0	0	3	52	58	2	29	14	15.2	4.85	102	.284	.376	5	.313	2	1	1	2	0.4
Total 6	24	29	.453	198	10	2	0	17	509¹	618	23	194	121	14.5	5.07	92	.307	.371	58	.282	16	-33	-24	11	0.6
● ELLIS KINDER				Kinder, Ellis Raymond "Old Folks" b: 7/26/14, Atkins, Ark. d: 10/16/68, Jackson, Tenn. BR/TR, 6', 195 lbs. Deb: 4/30/46																					
1946 StL-A	3	3	.500	33	7	1	0	1	86²	78	8	36	59	11.8	3.32	112	.241	.318	1	.053	-1	2	4	-1	0.1
1947 StL-A	8	15	.348	34	26	10	2	1	194¹	201	11	82	110	13.1	4.49	86	.264	.336	8	.129	-4	-17	-13	-3	-2.1
1948 Bos-A	10	7	.588	28	22	10	1	0	178	183	10	64	53	12.5	3.74	117	.266	.330	6	.097	-4	11	13	-3	0.4
1949 Bos-A	23	6	**.793**	43	30	19	**6**	4	252	251	20	99	138	12.6	3.36	130	.260	.330	12	.130	-4	24	28	-4	2.1
1950 Bos-A	14	12	.538	48	23	11	1	9	207	212	23	79	95	12.7	4.26	115	.263	.328	13	.183	-1	7	15	-2	1.4
1951 Bos-A	11	2	.846	**63**	3	1	0	**14**	127	108	9	46	84	10.9	2.55	175	.230	.298	4	.118	-3	**22**	27	-2	2.7
1952 Bos-A	5	6	.455	23	10	4	0	1	97²	85	11	28	50	10.5	2.58	153	.234	.290	0	.000	-4	19	19	-1	1.3
1953 Bos-A	10	6	.625	**69**	0	0	0	**27**	107	84	9	38	39	10.4	1.85	227	.215	.288	11	.379	5	**26**	28	0	5.9
1954 Bos-A	8	8	.500	48	4	0	0	15	107	106	7	36	67	11.9	3.62	114	.260	.321	5	.185	0	1	6	-2	0.9
1955 Bos-A	5	5	.500	43	0	0	0	18	66²	57	5	19	41	9.9	2.84	151	.229	.275	3	.250	-1	8	11	-1	2.1
1956 StL-N	2	0	1.000	22	0	0	0	6	25²	23	7	9	11	11.2	3.51	108	.245	.311	0	.000	-0	1	1	-1	0.6
Chi-A	3	1	.750	29	0	0	0	3	29²	33	2	19	19	12.4	2.73	150	.277	.323	0	.000	-0	5	5	-1	0.6
1957 Chi-A	0	0	—	1	0	0	0	0	1	2	0	0	3	18.0	0.00	—	.000	.250	0	—	-0	0	0	-0	0.0
Total 12	102	71	.590	484	122	56	10	102	1479²	1421	118	539	749	12.0	3.43	125	.252	.318	63	.142	-19	101	139	-17	15.4
● SILVER KING				King, Charles Frederick (b: Charles Frederick Koenig)																					
				b: 1/11/1868, St.Louis, Mo. d: 5/21/38, St.Louis, Mo. BR/TR, 6', 170 lbs. Deb: 9/28/1886																					
1886 KC-N	1	3	.250	5	5	5	0	0	39	43	1	9	23	12.0	4.85	78	.243	.280	1	.045	-2	-5	-1	-3	-0.5
1887 *StL-a	32	12	.727	46	44	43	2	1	390	401	4	109	128	12.2	3.78	120	.260	.316	46	.207	-4	22	33	-3	2.0
1888 *StL-a	**45**	21	.682	**66**	65	**64**	**6**	0	**585²**	437	6	76	258	**8.3**	**1.64**	**198**	.200	**.237**	43	.208	-5	**92**	105	-1	**11.4**
1889 StL-a	35	16	.686	56	53	47	2	0	458	462	15	125	188	11.7	**2.69**	**161**	**.232**	.301	31	.168	-6	**79**	84	6	7.1
1890 Chi-P	30	22	.577	56	56	48	**4**	0	461	420	5	163	185	11.7	3.14	134	.250	.309	43	.209	-1	36	55	-3	4.5
1891 Pit-N	14	29	.326	48	44	40	1	0	384¹	382	7	144	160	12.7	3.11	105	.250	.321	25	.169	-1	10	7	-2	0.4
1892 NY-N	22	24	.478	51	47	45	1	0	410¹	392	15	171	170	12.0	3.29	98	.244	.322	34	.209	0	5	7	-5	0.1
1893 NY-N	3	4	.429	7	7	4	0	0	49	69	4	26	13	17.8	8.63	54	.322	.401	3	.176	-1	-22	-22	0	-2.0
Cin-N	5	6	.455	17	15	8	0	0	105	119	5	56	30	15.6	4.89	98	.277	.369	5	.162	-0	-3	-1	-3	-0.1
Yr	8	10	.444	24	22	12	0	0	154	188	9	82	43	16.2	6.08	78	.291	.377	8	.167	-1	-24	-23	-0	-2.1
1896 Was-N	10	7	.588	22	16	12	0	1	145¹	179	3	43	35	14.0	4.09	108	.300	.351	16	.276	3	4	5	-3	0.5

YEAR TM/L	W	L	PCT	G	GS	CG	SH	SV	IP	H	HR	BB	SO	RAT	ERA	ERA+	OAV	OOB	BH	AVG	PB	PR	/A	PD	TPI
1897 Was-N	6	9	.400	23	19	12	0	1	154	196	7	45	32	14.7	4.79	91	.307	.363	11	.193	0	-8	-8	1	-0.5
Total 10	203	153	.570	397	371	328	19	6	3181²	3100	69	967	1222	11.9	3.18	122	.247	.308	259	.198	7	204	251	-6	22.9

● **CLYDE KING**   King, Clyde Edward   b: 5/23/25, Goldsboro, N.C.   BB/TR, 6'1", 175 lbs.   Deb: 6/21/44   MC

YEAR TM/L	W	L	PCT	G	GS	CG	SH	SV	IP	H	HR	BB	SO	RAT	ERA	ERA+	OAV	OOB	BH	AVG	PB	PR	/A	PD	TPI
1944 Bro-N	2	1	.667	14	3	1	0	0	43²	42	1	12	14	11.3	3.09	115	.256	.311	2	.200	-0	3	2	-1	0.0
1945 Bro-N	5	5	.500	42	2	0	0	3	112¹	131	8	48	29	14.3	4.09	92	.295	.364	4	.125	-2	-4	-4	1	-0.5
1947 Bro-N	6	5	.545	29	9	2	0	0	87²	85	11	29	31	11.7	2.77	149	.252	.311	3	.115	-1	13	13	-1	1.3
1948 Bro-N	0	1	.000	9	0	0	0	0	12¹	14	3	6	5	15.3	8.03	50	.286	.375	0	.000	-0	-6	-6	0	-0.4
1951 Bro-N	14	7	.667	48	3	1	0	6	121¹	118	15	50	33	12.7	4.15	94	.263	.341	4	.138	-0	-3	-3	0	-0.5
1952 Bro-N	2	0	1.000	23	0	0	0	0	42²	56	5	12	17	14.6	5.06	72	.318	.365	0	.000	-1	-6	-7	1	-0.3
1953 Cin-N	3	6	.333	35	4	0	0	2	76	78	15	32	21	13.3	5.21	84	.271	.348	0	.000	-0	-8	-7	-0	-0.9
Total 7	32	25	.561	200	21	4	0	11	496	524	58	189	150	13.1	4.14	95	.275	.343	13	.114	-4	-11	-11	-0	-1.3

● **ERIC KING**   King, Eric Steven   b: 4/10/64, Oxnard, Cal.   BR/TR, 6'2", 215 lbs.   Deb: 5/15/86

YEAR TM/L	W	L	PCT	G	GS	CG	SH	SV	IP	H	HR	BB	SO	RAT	ERA	ERA+	OAV	OOB	BH	AVG	PB	PR	/A	PD	TPI
1986 Det-A	11	4	.733	33	16	3	1	3	138¹	108	11	63	79	11.6	3.51	117	.216	.313	0	—	0	10	9	0	1.0
1987 *Det-A	6	9	.400	55	4	0	0	9	116	111	15	60	89	13.6	4.89	86	.251	.345	0	—	0	-6	-9	-2	-0.8
1988 Det-A	4	1	.800	23	5	0	0	3	68²	60	7	34	45	13.0	3.41	112	.233	.334	0	—	0	4	3	-1	0.2
1989 Chi-A	9	10	.474	25	25	1	1	0	159¹	144	13	64	72	12.0	3.39	112	.244	.322	0	—	0	9	7	-0	0.8
1990 Chi-A	12	4	.750	25	25	2	2	0	151	135	10	40	70	10.8	3.28	117	.237	.294	0	—	0	11	9	-1	0.9
1991 Cle-A	6	11	.353	25	24	2	1	0	150²	166	14	44	59	12.7	4.60	90	.279	.332	0	—	0	-8	-7	-2	-1.0
1992 Det-A	4	6	.400	17	14	0	0	1	79¹	90	12	28	45	13.5	5.22	76	.285	.345	0	—	0	-11	-11	-1	-1.4
Total 7	52	45	.536	203	113	8	5	16	863¹	814	73	333	459	12.3	3.97	100	.249	.324	0	—	0	8	2	-3	-0.3

● **KEVIN KING**   King, Kevin Ray   b: 2/11/69, Atwater, Cal.   BL/TL, 6'4", 170 lbs.   Deb: 9/2/93

YEAR TM/L	W	L	PCT	G	GS	CG	SH	SV	IP	H	HR	BB	SO	RAT	ERA	ERA+	OAV	OOB	BH	AVG	PB	PR	/A	PD	TPI
1993 Sea-A	0	1	.000	13	0	0	0	0	11²	9	3	4	10	10.8	6.17	71	.231	.318	0	—	0	-2	-2	-0	-0.3
1994 Sea-A	0	2	.000	19	0	0	0	0	15¹	21	3	17	6	22.9	7.04	69	.333	.481	0	—	0	-4	-4	0	-0.5
1995 Sea-A	—	—	—	2	0	0	0	0	3²	7	0	1	3	22.1	12.27	39	.412	.474	0	—	0	-3	-3	-0	-0.1
Total 3	0	3	.000	34	0	0	0	0	30²	37	3	22	17	18.2	7.34	64	.311	.431	0	—	0	-9	-9	-0	-0.9

● **NELLIE KING**   King, Nelson Joseph   b: 3/15/28, Shenandoah, Pa.   BR/TR, 6'6", 185 lbs.   Deb: 4/15/54

YEAR TM/L	W	L	PCT	G	GS	CG	SH	SV	IP	H	HR	BB	SO	RAT	ERA	ERA+	OAV	OOB	BH	AVG	PB	PR	/A	PD	TPI
1954 Pit-N	0	0	—	4	0	0	0	0	7	10	1	6	3	14.1	5.14	81	.400	.423	0	—	0	-1	-1	-0	0.0
1955 Pit-N	1	3	.250	17	4	0	0	0	54¹	60	2	14	21	12.6	2.98	138	.286	.336	0	.000	-2	6	7	-0	0.3
1956 Pit-N	4	1	.800	38	0	0	0	5	60	54	8	19	25	11.1	3.15	120	.241	.303	0	.000	-1	4	4	-1	0.2
1957 Pit-N	2	1	.667	36	0	0	0	1	52	69	6	11	23	15.1	4.50	84	.337	.390	0	.000	-0	-4	-4	-0	-0.3
Total 4	7	5	.583	95	4	0	0	6	173¹	193	17	50	72	12.9	3.58	109	.291	.345	0	.000	-3	6	6	-1	0.2

● **BRIAN KINGMAN**   Kingman, Brian Paul   b: 7/27/54, Los Angeles, Cal.   BR/TR, 6'2", 200 lbs.   Deb: 6/28/79

YEAR TM/L	W	L	PCT	G	GS	CG	SH	SV	IP	H	HR	BB	SO	RAT	ERA	ERA+	OAV	OOB	BH	AVG	PB	PR	/A	PD	TPI
1979 Oak-A	8	7	.533	18	17	5	1	0	112²	113	10	33	58	11.9	4.31	94	.258	.314	0	—	0	-1	-3	-2	-0.5
1980 Oak-A	8	20	.286	32	30	10	1	0	211²	209	21	82	116	12.6	3.83	98	.256	.326	0	—	0	5	-2	-2	-0.2
1981 *Oak-A	3	6	.333	18	15	3	1	0	100¹	112	11	32	52	13.3	3.95	88	.286	.347	0	—	0	-3	-5	-2	-0.4
1982 Oak-A	4	12	.250	23	20	3	0	1	122²	131	11	57	46	14.3	4.48	87	.279	.365	0	—	0	-5	-8	-3	-0.8
1983 SF-N	0	0	—	3	0	0	0	0	4²	10	0	1	1	21.2	7.71	46	.417	.440	0	—	0	-2	-2	-0	0.0
Total 5	23	45	.338	94	82	21	3	1	551²	575	52	205	273	13.0	4.13	92	.269	.338	0	—	0	-7	-20	-9	-1.9

● **DAVE KINGMAN**   Kingman, David Arthur   b: 12/21/48, Pendleton, Ore.   BR/TR, 6'6", 210 lbs.   Deb: 7/30/71   ◆

YEAR TM/L	W	L	PCT	G	GS	CG	SH	SV	IP	H	HR	BB	SO	RAT	ERA	ERA+	OAV	OOB	BH	AVG	PB	PR	/A	PD	TPI
1973 SF-N	0	0	—	2	0	0	0	0	4	3	0	6	4	20.3	9.00	42	.200	.429	62	.203	1	-2	-2	-0	0.0

● **DENNIS KINNEY**   Kinney, Dennis Paul   b: 2/26/52, Toledo, Ohio   BL/TL, 6'1", 190 lbs.   Deb: 4/9/78

YEAR TM/L	W	L	PCT	G	GS	CG	SH	SV	IP	H	HR	BB	SO	RAT	ERA	ERA+	OAV	OOB	BH	AVG	PB	PR	/A	PD	TPI
1978 Cle-A	0	2	.000	18	0	0	0	5	38²	37	3	14	19	12.1	4.42	84	.259	.329	0	—	0	-3	-3	-0	-0.2
SD-N	0	1	.000	7	0	0	0	0	7	6	3	4	2	12.9	6.43	52	.222	.323	0	.000	-0	-2	-2	-0	-0.4
1979 SD-N	0	0	—	13	0	0	0	0	18	17	2	8	11	13.0	3.50	101	.250	.338	0	.000	-0	0	-0	-0	0.0
1980 SD-N	4	6	.400	50	0	0	0	1	82²	79	3	37	40	12.7	4.25	81	.252	.333	1	.083	-0	-6	-7	-0	-1.0
1981 Det-A	0	0	—	6	0	0	0	0	3²	5	0	4	3	22.1	9.82	38	.313	.450	0	—	0	-3	-2	-0	-0.2
1982 Oak-A	0	0	—	3	0	0	0	0	4¹	9	1	4	0	27.0	8.31	47	.474	.565	0	—	0	-2	-2	-0	0.4
Total 5	4	9	.308	97	0	0	0	6	154¹	153	12	71	75	13.2	4.55	78	.261	.344	1	.071	-1	-15	-17	-1	-1.4

● **WALT KINNEY**   Kinney, Walter William   b: 9/9/1893, Denison, Tex.   d: 7/1/71, Escondido, Cal.   BL/TL, 6'2", 186 lbs.   Deb: 7/26/18

YEAR TM/L	W	L	PCT	G	GS	CG	SH	SV	IP	H	HR	BB	SO	RAT	ERA	ERA+	OAV	OOB	BH	AVG	PB	PR	/A	PD	TPI
1918 Bos-A	0	0	—	5	0	0	0	0	15	5	0	8	4	9.0	1.80	149	.106	.263	0	—	-1	2	1	-0	-0.1
1919 Phi-A	9	15	.375	43	21	13	0	2	202²	199	7	91	97	13.2	3.64	94	.262	.347	25	.284	5	-9	-5	3	0.5
1920 Phi-A	2	4	.333	10	8	5	1	0	61	59	3	28	19	13.0	3.10	130	.261	.345	9	.346	2	5	6	0	0.3
1923 Phi-A	0	1	.000	5	1	0	0	0	12	11	0	9	9	15.0	7.50	55	.229	.351	1	.167	1	-5	-5	-0	-0.3
Total 4	11	20	.355	63	30	18	1	2	290²	274	10	136	129	13.0	3.59	100	.254	.343	35	.280	7	-8	-2	3	0.3

● **MIKE KINNUNEN**   Kinnunen, Michael John   b: 4/1/58, Seattle, Wash.   BL/TL, 6'1", 185 lbs.   Deb: 6/12/80

YEAR TM/L	W	L	PCT	G	GS	CG	SH	SV	IP	H	HR	BB	SO	RAT	ERA	ERA+	OAV	OOB	BH	AVG	PB	PR	/A	PD	TPI
1980 Min-A	0	0	—	21	0	0	0	0	24²	29	1	9	8	14.2	5.11	85	.290	.355	0	—	0	-3	-3	-0	-0.2
1986 Bal-A	0	0	—	9	0	0	0	0	7	8	1	5	1	16.7	6.43	64	.308	.419	0	—	0	-2	-2	-0	0.1
1987 Bal-A	0	0	—	18	0	0	0	0	20	27	3	16	14	19.3	4.95	89	.338	.448	0	—	0	-1	-0	-0	0.1
Total 3	0	0	—	48	0	0	0	0	51²	64	5	30	23	16.5	5.23	83	.311	.401	0	—	0	-6	-5	-0	0.0

● **ED KINSELLA**   Kinsella, Edward William "Rube"   b: 1/15/1882, Lexington, Ill.   d: 1/17/76, Bloomington, Ill.   BR/TR, 6'1.5", 175 lbs.   Deb: 9/16/05

YEAR TM/L	W	L	PCT	G	GS	CG	SH	SV	IP	H	HR	BB	SO	RAT	ERA	ERA+	OAV	OOB	BH	AVG	PB	PR	/A	PD	TPI
1905 Pit-N	0	1	.000	3	2	2	0	0	17	19	0	3	11	12.2	2.65	113	.292	.333	0	.000	-0	1	1	-1	-0.1
1910 StL-A	1	3	.250	10	5	2	0	0	50	62	0	16	10	14.4	3.78	65	.321	.379	3	.250	2	-7	-7	1	-0.3
Total 2	1	4	.200	13	7	4	0	0	67	81	0	19	21	13.8	3.49	75	.314	.368	3	.200	2	-6	-7	-0	-0.4

● **MATT KINZER**   Kinzer, Matthew Roy   b: 6/17/63, Indianapolis, Ind.   BR/TR, 6'2", 210 lbs.   Deb: 5/18/89

YEAR TM/L	W	L	PCT	G	GS	CG	SH	SV	IP	H	HR	BB	SO	RAT	ERA	ERA+	OAV	OOB	BH	AVG	PB	PR	/A	PD	TPI
1989 StL-N	0	2	.000	8	1	0	0	0	13¹	25	3	4	8	19.6	12.83	28	.403	.439	0	.000	-0	-14	-14	-0	-1.8
1990 Det-A	0	0	—	1	0	0	0	0	1²	3	0	1	1	32.4	16.20	24	.375	.545	0	—	0	-2	-2	-0	-0.1
Total 2	0	2	.000	9	1	0	0	0	15	28	3	5	9	21.0	13.20	28	.400	.455	0	.000	-0	-16	-16	-1	-1.9

● **HARRY KINZY**   Kinzy, Henry Hershel "Slim"   b: 7/19/10, Hallsville, Tex.   BR/TR, 6'4", 185 lbs.   Deb: 6/8/34

YEAR TM/L	W	L	PCT	G	GS	CG	SH	SV	IP	H	HR	BB	SO	RAT	ERA	ERA+	OAV	OOB	BH	AVG	PB	PR	/A	PD	TPI
1934 Chi-A	0	1	.000	13	2	1	0	0	34¹	38	1	31	12	19.1	4.98	95	.290	.440	3	.300	1	-2	-1	-0	0.0

● **FRED KIPP**   Kipp, Fred Leo   b: 10/1/31, Piqua, Kan.   BL/TL, 6'4", 200 lbs.   Deb: 9/10/57

YEAR TM/L	W	L	PCT	G	GS	CG	SH	SV	IP	H	HR	BB	SO	RAT	ERA	ERA+	OAV	OOB	BH	AVG	PB	PR	/A	PD	TPI
1957 Bro-N	0	0	—	1	0	0	0	0	4	6	2	0	2	13.5	9.00	46	.333	.333	0	—	0	-2	-2	-0	-0.3
1958 LA-N	6	6	.500	40	9	0	0	0	102¹	107	16	45	58	13.5	5.01	82	.273	.349	9	.250	1	-12	-10	1	-0.9
1959 LA-N	0	0	—	2	0	0	0	0	2²	2	0	3	1	16.9	0.00	—	.222	.417	0	—	0	1	1	-0	0.0
1960 NY-A	0	1	.000	4	0	0	0	0	4¹	4	0	0	2	8.3	6.23	57	.250	.250	0	—	0	-1	-1	-0	-0.3
Total 4	6	7	.462	47	9	0	0	0	113¹	119	18	48	64	13.3	5.08	80	.274	.347	9	.243	1	-14	-13	1	-1.2

● **BOB KIPPER**   Kipper, Robert Wayne   b: 7/8/64, Aurora, Ill.   BR/TL, 6'2", 200 lbs.   Deb: 4/12/85

YEAR TM/L	W	L	PCT	G	GS	CG	SH	SV	IP	H	HR	BB	SO	RAT	ERA	ERA+	OAV	OOB	BH	AVG	PB	PR	/A	PD	TPI
1985 Cal-A	0	1	.000	2	1	0	0	0	3¹	7	1	0	0	27.0	21.60	19	.467	.556	0	—	0	-6	-6	0	-1.2
Pit-N	1	2	.333	5	4	0	0	0	24²	21	4	7	13	10.2	5.11	70	.221	.275	2	.250	0	-4	-4	0	-0.4
1986 Pit-N	6	8	.429	20	19	0	0	0	114	123	17	34	81	12.6	4.03	95	.271	.324	1	.030	-3	-4	-2	-1	-0.7
1987 Pit-N	5	9	.357	24	20	1	1	0	110²	117	25	52	81	13.9	5.94	69	.271	.352	8	.242	2	-23	-22	-0	-2.3
1988 Pit-N	2	6	.250	50	0	0	0	0	65	54	7	26	39	11.4	3.74	91	.234	.317	0	.000	-0	4	2	-0	0.2
1989 Pit-N	3	4	.429	52	0	0	0	4	83	55	5	33	58	9.5	2.93	115	.188	.270	1	.111	-0	5	4	0	0.3
1990 Pit-N	5	2	.714	41	1	0	0	4	62²	44	7	26	35	10.5	3.02	120	.195	.286	1	.143	-0	5	4	0	0.5
1991 *Pit-N	2	2	.500	52	0	0	0	0	60	66	7	22	38	13.2	4.65	77	.276	.337	0	—	0	-3	-3	-0	-0.3
1992 Min-A	3	3	.500	25	0	0	0	0	38²	40	8	14	22	13.3	4.42	92	.268	.343	0	—	0	-2	-2	-0	-0.2
Total 8	27	37	.422	271	45	1	1	11	562	527	81	217	369	12.1	4.34	86	.247	.320	13	.137	-1	-37	-39	-2	-4.8

● **THORNTON KIPPER**   Kipper, Thornton John   b: 9/27/28, Bagley, Wis.   BR/TR, 6'3", 190 lbs.   Deb: 6/7/53

YEAR TM/L	W	L	PCT	G	GS	CG	SH	SV	IP	H	HR	BB	SO	RAT	ERA	ERA+	OAV	OOB	BH	AVG	PB	PR	/A	PD	TPI
1953 Phi-N	3	3	.500	20	3	0	0	0	45²	59	8	12	15	14.0	4.73	89	.319	.360	1	.091	-1	-2	-3	-0	-0.4

YEAR TM/L	W	L	PCT	G	GS	CG	SH	SV	IP	H	HR	BB	SO	RAT	ERA	ERA+	OAV	OOB	BH	AVG	PB	PR	/A	PD	TPI
1954 Phi-N	0	0	—	11	0	0	0	1	13²	22	0	12	5	23.0	7.90	51	.379	.493	0	.000	-0	-6	-6	0	-0.1
1955 Phi-N	0	1	.000	24	0	0	0	0	39²	47	4	22	15	15.9	4.99	80	.301	.391	1	.333	-4	-4	-5	-1	-0.1
Total 3	3	4	.429	55	3	0	0	1	99	128	12	46	35	16.0	5.27	78	.321	.394	2	.125	-1	-12	-13	-1	-0.6

● **CLAY KIRBY**   Kirby, Clayton Laws   b: 6/25/48, Washington, D.C.   d: 10/11/91, Arlington, Va.   BR/TR, 6'3", 185 lbs.   Deb: 4/11/69

YEAR TM/L	W	L	PCT	G	GS	CG	SH	SV	IP	H	HR	BB	SO	RAT	ERA	ERA+	OAV	OOB	BH	AVG	PB	PR	/A	PD	TPI
1969 SD-N	7	20	.259	35	35	2	0	0	215²	204	18	100	113	12.9	3.80	93	.252	.339	4	.061	-2	-5	-6	-2	-1.1
1970 SD-N	10	16	.385	36	34	6	1	0	214²	198	29	120	154	13.7	4.53	88	.248	.352	11	.149	-0	-11	-13	-2	-1.6
1971 SD-N	15	13	.536	38	36	13	2	0	267¹	213	20	103	231	10.7	2.83	117	.216	.292	8	.093	-3	19	14	-0	1.1
1972 SD-N	12	14	.462	34	34	9	2	0	238²	197	21	116	175	11.9	3.13	105	.226	.318	5	.068	-4	9	4	-1	-0.1
1973 SD-N	8	18	.308	34	31	4	2	0	191²	214	30	66	129	13.2	4.79	72	.282	.341	5	.093	-3	-24	-28	-2	-3.8
1974 Cin-N	12	9	.571	36	35	7	1	0	230²	210	15	91	160	11.8	3.28	106	.242	.316	7	.095	-3	9	5	-2	-0.1
1975 Cin-N	10	6	.625	26	19	1	0	0	110²	113	14	54	69	14.0	4.72	76	.263	.352	6	.188	1	-13	-14	-2	-1.9
1976 Mon-N	1	8	.111	22	15	0	0	0	78²	81	10	63	51	16.7	5.72	65	.273	.403	1	.056	-1	-19	-18	-1	-2.0
Total 8	75	104	.419	261	239	42	8	0	1548	1430	156	713	1061	12.6	3.84	92	.246	.331	47	.098	-15	-37	-56	-13	-9.5

● **JOHN KIRBY**   Kirby, John F.   b: 1/13/1865, St.Louis, Mo.   d: 10/6/31, St.Louis, Mo.   TR, 5'8", 172 lbs.   Deb: 8/1/1884

YEAR TM/L	W	L	PCT	G	GS	CG	SH	SV	IP	H	HR	BB	SO	RAT	ERA	ERA+	OAV	OOB	BH	AVG	PB	PR	/A	PD	TPI
1884 KC-U	0	1	.000	2	2	1	0	0	11	13	0	2	1	12.3	4.09	55	.277	.306	1	.143	-1	-2	-2	1	-0.2
1885 StL-N	5	8	.385	14	14	14	0	0	129¹	118	0	44	46	11.3	3.55	77	.241	.303	3	.060	-6	-10	-12	-2	-1.6
1886 StL-N	11	26	.297	41	41	38	1	0	325	329	9	134	129	12.8	3.30	98	.252	.322	6	.110	-9	1	-3	-1	-1.2
1887 Ind-N	1	6	.143	8	8	5	0	0	62	70	3	43	7	16.7	6.10	68	.272	.381	4	.138	-2	-14	-13	-1	-1.3
Cle-a	0	5	.000	5	5	5	0	0	41	62	1	28	6	20.2	9.00	48	.339	.432	3	.167	-1	-21	-21	-0	-1.7
1888 KC-a	4	4	.200	5	5	5	0	0	43	48	0	7	11	11.7	4.19	82	.273	.304	1	.063	-2	-5	-4	-0	-0.5
Total 5	18	50	.265	75	75	68	1	0	611¹	640	13	258	200	13.3	4.09	80	.260	.332	27	.105	-21	-53	-55	-3	-6.5

● **LA RUE KIRBY**   Kirby, La Rue   b: 12/30/1889, Eureka, Mich.   d: 6/10/61, Lansing, Mich.   BB/TR, 6', 185 lbs.   Deb: 8/7/12 ♦

YEAR TM/L	W	L	PCT	G	GS	CG	SH	SV	IP	H	HR	BB	SO	RAT	ERA	ERA+	OAV	OOB	BH	AVG	PB	PR	/A	PD	TPI
1912 NY-N	1	0	1.000	3	1	1	0	0	11	13	1	6	2	16.4	5.73	59	.295	.392	1	.200	0	-3	-3	0	-0.2
1915 StL-F	0	0	—	1	0	0	0	0	7	7	1	2	7	11.6	5.14	56	.269	.321	38	.213	0	-2	-2	-0	0.0
Total 2	1	0	1.000	4	1	1	0	0	18	20	2	8	9	14.5	5.50	58	.286	.367	87	.230	0	-5	-5	0	-0.2

● **MIKE KIRCHER**   Kircher, Michael Andrew (b: Wolfgang Andrew Kerscher)   b: 9/30/1897, Rochester, N.Y.   d: 6/26/72, Rochester, N.Y.   BB/TR, 6', 180 lbs.   Deb: 8/8/19

YEAR TM/L	W	L	PCT	G	GS	CG	SH	SV	IP	H	HR	BB	SO	RAT	ERA	ERA+	OAV	OOB	BH	AVG	PB	PR	/A	PD	TPI
1919 Phi-A	0	0	—	2	0	0	0	0	8	15	0	3	2	20.3	7.88	44	.429	.474	0	.000	-0	-4	-4	-1	-0.1
1920 StL-N	2	1	.667	9	3	1	0	0	36²	50	0	5	5	14.0	5.40	55	.333	.363	3	.273	0	-9	-10	-1	-0.9
1921 StL-N	0	1	.000	3	0	0	0	0	3¹	4	0	1	2	16.2	8.10	45	.364	.462	0	—	-0	-2	-2	-0	-0.4
Total 3	2	2	.500	14	3	1	0	0	48	69	0	9	9	15.2	6.00	52	.352	.389	3	.214	-0	-15	-15	-2	-1.4

● **BILL KIRK**   Kirk, William Partlemore   b: 7/19/35, Coatesville, Pa.   BL/TL, 6', 165 lbs.   Deb: 9/23/61

YEAR TM/L	W	L	PCT	G	GS	CG	SH	SV	IP	H	HR	BB	SO	RAT	ERA	ERA+	OAV	OOB	BH	AVG	PB	PR	/A	PD	TPI
1961 KC-A	0	0	—	1	1	0	0	0	3	6	2	1	3	21.0	12.00	35	.375	.412	0	—	0	-3	-3	-0	0.0

● **DON KIRKWOOD**   Kirkwood, Donald Paul   b: 9/24/49, Pontiac, Mich.   BR/TR, 6'3", 188 lbs.   Deb: 9/13/74

YEAR TM/L	W	L	PCT	G	GS	CG	SH	SV	IP	H	HR	BB	SO	RAT	ERA	ERA+	OAV	OOB	BH	AVG	PB	PR	/A	PD	TPI
1974 Cal-A	0	0	—	3	0	0	0	0	7¹	12	0	6	4	22.1	8.59	40	.375	.474	0	—	0	-4	-4	-0	0.2
1975 Cal-A	6	5	.545	44	2	0	0	7	84	85	6	28	49	12.1	3.11	114	.270	.329	0	—	0	6	4	-0	0.8
1976 Cal-A	6	12	.333	28	26	4	0	0	157²	167	12	57	78	12.8	4.62	72	.278	.341	0	—	0	-19	-23	1	-2.1
1977 Cal-A	1	0	1.000	13	0	0	0	1	17²	20	3	9	10	14.8	5.09	77	.290	.372	0	—	0	-2	-2	1	0.0
Chi-A	1	1	.500	16	0	0	0	1	40	49	3	10	24	13.5	5.17	79	.310	.355	0	—	0	-5	-5	0	-0.2
Yr	2	1	.667	29	0	0	0	1	57²	69	6	19	34	13.9	5.15	78	.304	.360	0	—	0	-7	-7	1	-0.2
1978 Tor-A	4	5	.444	16	9	3	0	0	68	76	6	25	29	13.4	4.24	93	.289	.351	0	—	0	-4	-2	-0	-0.4
Total 5	18	23	.439	120	37	7	0	8	374²	409	30	135	194	13.1	4.37	82	.284	.347	0	—	0	-28	-33	2	-1.7

● **HARRY KIRSCH**   Kirsch, Harry Louis "Casey"   b: 10/17/1887, Pittsburgh, Pa.   d: 12/25/25, Overbrook, Pa.   BR/TR, 5'11", 170 lbs.   Deb: 4/16/10

YEAR TM/L	W	L	PCT	G	GS	CG	SH	SV	IP	H	HR	BB	SO	RAT	ERA	ERA+	OAV	OOB	BH	AVG	PB	PR	/A	PD	TPI
1910 Cle-A	0	0	—	2	0	0	0	0	3	5	0	1	5	18.0	6.00	43	.385	.429	0	—	0	-1	-1	-0	0.0

● **GARLAND KISER**   Kiser, Garland Routhard   b: 7/8/68, Charlotte, N.C.   BL/TL, 6'3", 190 lbs.   Deb: 9/9/91

YEAR TM/L	W	L	PCT	G	GS	CG	SH	SV	IP	H	HR	BB	SO	RAT	ERA	ERA+	OAV	OOB	BH	AVG	PB	PR	/A	PD	TPI
1991 Cle-A	0	0	—	7	0	0	0	0	4²	7	0	4	3	23.1	9.64	43	.368	.500	0	—	0	-3	-3	-0	0.0

● **RUBE KISINGER**   Kisinger, Charles Samuel   b: 12/13/1876, Adrian, Mich.   d: 7/14/41, Huron, Ohio   BR/TR, 6', 190 lbs.   Deb: 9/10/02

YEAR TM/L	W	L	PCT	G	GS	CG	SH	SV	IP	H	HR	BB	SO	RAT	ERA	ERA+	OAV	OOB	BH	AVG	PB	PR	/A	PD	TPI
1902 Det-A	2	3	.400	5	5	5	0	0	43¹	48	0	14	7	13.5	3.12	117	.281	.346	3	.158	-1	2	3	-0	0.2
1903 Det-A	7	9	.438	16	14	13	2	0	118²	118	0	27	33	11.1	2.96	98	.259	.303	6	.128	-3	0	-1	-1	-0.3
Total 2	9	12	.429	21	19	18	2	0	162	166	0	41	40	11.8	3.00	103	.265	.315	9	.136	-4	2	2	1	-0.1

● **BRUCE KISON**   Kison, Bruce Eugene   b: 2/18/50, Pasco, Wash.   BR/TR, 6'4", 178 lbs.   Deb: 7/4/71 C

YEAR TM/L	W	L	PCT	G	GS	CG	SH	SV	IP	H	HR	BB	SO	RAT	ERA	ERA+	OAV	OOB	BH	AVG	PB	PR	/A	PD	TPI
1971 *Pit-N	6	5	.545	18	13	2	1	0	95¹	93	6	36	60	12.7	3.40	100	.259	.337	2	.065	-1	1	-0	1	0.0
1972 *Pit-N	9	7	.563	32	18	6	1	3	152	123	11	69	102	11.9	3.26	102	.220	.316	10	.189	2	3	1	-1	0.2
1973 Pit-N	3	0	1.000	7	7	0	0	0	43²	36	4	24	26	12.6	3.09	114	.232	.339	1	.083	0	3	2	0	0.2
1974 *Pit-N	9	8	.529	40	16	1	0	2	129	123	8	57	71	13.3	3.49	99	.247	.338	4	.108	-0	2	-1	1	0.0
1975 *Pit-N	12	11	.522	33	29	6	0	0	192	160	10	92	89	12.0	3.23	109	.227	.320	7	.119	-2	8	7	2	0.8
1976 Pit-N	14	9	.609	31	29	6	1	0	193	180	6	52	98	11.0	3.08	113	.247	.299	12	.203	4	9	9	1	1.5
1977 Pit-N	9	10	.474	33	32	3	1	0	193	209	25	54	122	12.6	4.90	81	.278	.333	18	.261	5	-21	-20	1	-1.3
1978 Pit-N	6	6	.500	28	11	0	0	0	96	81	9	39	62	11.7	3.19	116	.229	.314	4	.138	1	4	5	1	0.8
1979 *Pit-N	13	7	.650	33	25	3	1	0	172¹	157	13	45	105	10.8	3.19	122	.246	.300	8	.145	0	10	13	1	1.6
1980 Cal-A	3	6	.333	13	13	2	1	0	73¹	73	6	32	28	13.3	4.91	80	.264	.346	0	—	0	-7	-8	-1	-0.8
1981 Cal-A	1	1	.500	11	4	0	0	0	44	40	8	14	19	11.0	3.48	105	.241	.300	0	—	0	0	0	1	0.1
1982 *Cal-A	10	5	.667	33	16	3	1	1	142	120	15	44	86	10.7	3.17	128	.226	.292	0	—	0	14	14	2	1.6
1983 Cal-A	11	5	.688	26	17	4	1	2	126²	128	13	43	83	12.4	4.05	99	.264	.330	0	—	0	-1	-1	0	0.1
1984 Cal-A	4	5	.444	20	7	0	0	0	65¹	72	10	28	66	14.6	5.37	74	.280	.364	0	—	0	-10	-10	-1	-1.3
1985 Bos-A	5	3	.625	22	9	0	0	0	92	98	9	32	56	12.8	4.11	104	.274	.335	0	—	0	2	2	0	0.0
Total 15	115	88	.567	380	246	36	8	12	1809²	1693	150	662	1073	12.1	3.66	102	.248	.321	66	.163	8	18	14	11	3.5

● **BILL KISSINGER**   Kissinger, William Francis "Shang"   b: 8/15/1871, Dayton, Ky.   d: 4/20/29, Cincinnati, Ohio   BR/TR, 185 lbs.   Deb: 5/30/1895 ♦

YEAR TM/L	W	L	PCT	G	GS	CG	SH	SV	IP	H	HR	BB	SO	RAT	ERA	ERA+	OAV	OOB	BH	AVG	PB	PR	/A	PD	TPI
1895 Bal-N	1	0	1.000	2	2	1	0	0	11¹	18	0	2	3	15.9	3.97	120	.353	.377	1	.200	-0	1	-0	0	0.0
StL-N	4	12	.250	24	14	9	0	0	140²	222	8	51	31	18.0	6.72	72	.352	.408	24	.247	-2	-30	-29	0	-2.4
Yr	5	12	.294	26	16	10	0	0	152	240	8	53	34	17.8	6.51	74	.352	.406	25	.245	-2	-29	-28	0	-2.4
1896 StL-N	2	9	.182	20	12	11	0	1	136	209	5	55	22	18.0	6.49	67	.349	.411	22	.301	-1	-32	-32	2	-1.7
1897 StL-N	0	4	.000	7	4	2	0	0	31¹	51	2	15	5	21.3	11.49	38	.362	.451	11	.333	-2	-25	-25	0	-2.0
Total 3	7	25	.219	53	32	23	0	1	319¹	500	15	123	61	18.2	6.99	66	.352	.413	60	.280	1	-86	-85	2	-6.1

● **FRANK KITSON**   Kitson, Frank R.   b: 9/11/1869, Hopkins, Mich.   d: 4/14/30, Allegan, Mich.   BL/TR, 5'11", 165 lbs.   Deb: 5/19/1898

YEAR TM/L	W	L	PCT	G	GS	CG	SH	SV	IP	H	HR	BB	SO	RAT	ERA	ERA+	OAV	OOB	BH	AVG	PB	PR	/A	PD	TPI
1898 Bal-N	8	5	.615	17	13	13	1	0	119¹	123	0	35	32	12.5	3.24	110	.265	.327	27	.314	4	5	4	0	0.8
1899 Bal-N	22	16	.579	40	37	34	2	0	327²	329	6	65	75	11.2	2.77	143	.261	.303	27	.201	-2	39	43	-2	3.9
1900 *Bro-N	15	13	.536	40	30	21	0	4	253¹	283	12	56	55	12.4	4.19	92	.282	.326	32	.294	-5	-14	-10	-5	-0.9
1901 Bro-N	19	11	.633	38	32	26	5	2	280²	312	6	67	127	12.5	2.98	112	.279	.326	35	.263	5	11	12	-3	1.5
1902 Bro-N	13	13	.594	32	31	29	3	0	268²	256	4	52	109	10.6	2.85	97	.251	.292	32	.276	8	-2	-2	0	0.7
1903 Det-A	15	16	.484	31	28	28	2	0	257²	277	8	38	102	11.2	2.58	113	.274	.303	21	.181	-1	11	9	-2	0.7
1904 Det-A	8	13	.381	26	24	19	0	1	199²	211	9	38	69	11.5	3.07	83	.272	.312	15	.208	1	-10	-11	-0	-1.1
1905 Det-A	12	14	.462	33	27	21	5	1	225²	230	3	57	78	11.9	3.47	79	.266	.319	16	.204	-1	-20	-18	-2	-2.4
1906 Was-A	6	14	.300	30	21	15	1	0	197	196	2	57	59	11.8	3.65	72	.262	.320	22	.244	8	-21	-22	-0	-1.3
1907 Was-A	0	3	.000	5	3	2	0	0	32	41	1	9	11	14.6	3.94	61	.313	.366	1	.100	-0	-5	-5	-1	-0.6
NY-A	4	1	1.000	12	4	3	0	0	61	75	0	17	14	13.2	3.10	90	.305	.360	7	.280	1	-4	-2	-1	-0.2
Yr	4	4	.571	17	7	5	0	0	93	116	1	26	25	14.1	3.39	79	.306	.357	8	.229	0	-9	-7	-2	-0.8
Total 10	128	118	.520	304	250	211	19	8	2222²	2333	52	491	731	11.8	3.17	99	.270	.315	235	.240	27	-11	-5	-15	1.1

YEAR TM/L	W	L	PCT	G	GS	CG	SH	SV	IP	H	HR	BB	SO	RAT	ERA	ERA+	OAV	OOB	BH	AVG	PB	PR	/A	PD	TPI

● MALACHI KITTRIDGE   Kittridge, Malachi Jeddidah "Jeddidah"
b: 10/12/1869, Clinton, Mass.   d: 6/23/28, Gary, Ind.   BR/TR, 5'7", 170 lbs.   Deb: 4/19/1890 M♦

| 1896 Chi-N | 0 | 0 | — | 1 | 0 | 0 | 0 | 0 | 1² | 2 | 0 | 1 | 0 | 16.2 | 5.40 | 84 | .286 | .375 | 48 | .223 | -0 | -0 | -0 | -0 | 0.0 |

● HUGO KLAERNER   Klaerner, Hugo Emil "Dutch" b: 10/15/08, Fredericksburg, Tex.   d: 2/3/82, Fredericksburg, Tex.   BR/TR, 5'11", 190 lbs.   Deb: 9/10/34

| 1934 Chi-A | 0 | 2 | .000 | 3 | 3 | 1 | 0 | 0 | 17¹ | 24 | 4 | 16 | 9 | 20.8 | 10.90 | 43 | .329 | .449 | 2 | .333 | 1 | -12 | -12 | 1 | -0.8 |

● FRED KLAGES   Klages, Frederick Albert Antony b: 10/31/43, Ambridge, Pa.   BR/TR, 6'2", 185 lbs.   Deb: 9/11/66

1966 Chi-A	1	0	1.000	3	3	0	0	0	15²	9	0	7	6	9.2	1.72	184	.167	.262	3	.500	1	3	3	0	0.3
1967 Chi-A	4	4	.500	11	9	0	0	0	44²	43	6	16	17	12.1	3.83	81	.256	.324	0	.000	-1	-3	-4	-1	-0.8
Total 2	5	4	.556	14	12	0	0	0	60¹	52	6	23	23	11.3	3.28	95	.234	.309	3	.167	-0	0	-1	-1	-0.5

● AL KLAWITTER   Klawitter, Albert "Dutch" b: 4/12/1888, Wilkes-Barre, Pa.   d: 5/2/50, Milwaukee, Wis.   BR/TR, 5'11.5", 187 lbs.   Deb: 9/20/09

1909 NY-N	1	1	.500	6	3	2	0	1	27	24	1	13	6	12.3	2.00	128	.247	.336	3	.333	1	2	2	1	0.4
1910 NY-N	0	0	—	1	0	0	0	0	1	2	0	2	0	36.0	9.00	33	.400	.571	0	—	0	-1	-1	-0	0.0
1913 Det-A	1	2	.333	8	3	1	0	0	32	39	0	15	10	15.2	5.91	49	.305	.378	0	.000	-2	-11	-11	0	-1.0
Total 3	2	3	.400	15	6	3	0	1	60	65	1	30	16	14.3	4.20	66	.283	.365	3	.150	-0	-9	-10	1	-0.6

● TOM KLAWITTER   Klawitter, Thomas Carl b: 6/24/58, LaCrosse, Wis.   BR/TL, 6'2", 190 lbs.   Deb: 4/14/85

| 1985 Min-A | 0 | 0 | — | 7 | 2 | 0 | 0 | 0 | 9¹ | 7 | 2 | 13 | 5 | 19.3 | 6.75 | 65 | .226 | .455 | 0 | — | 0 | -3 | -2 | 0 | -0.3 |

● HAL KLEINE   Kleine, Harold John b: 6/8/23, St.Louis, Mo.   d: 12/10/57, St.Louis, Mo.   BL/TL, 6'2", 193 lbs.   Deb: 4/26/44

1944 Cle-A	1	2	.333	11	6	1	0	0	40²	38	0	36	13	16.4	5.75	57	.248	.392	2	.143	-1	-11	-11	-1	-0.9
1945 Cle-A	0	0	—	3	0	0	0	0	7	8	0	7	5	19.3	3.86	84	.286	.429	1	.333	-1	-0	-0	-0	0.0
Total 2	1	2	.333	14	6	1	0	0	47²	46	0	43	18	16.8	5.48	60	.254	.397	3	.176	-0	-11	-12	-1	-0.9

● TED KLEINHANS   Kleinhans, Theodore Otto b: 4/8/1899, Deer Park, Wis.   d: 7/24/85, Redington Beach, Fla.   BR/TL, 6', 170 lbs.   Deb: 4/20/34

1934 Phi-N	0	0	—	5	0	0	0	0	6	11	1	3	2	21.0	9.00	52	.379	.438	-0	—	-0	-3	-3	0	0.0
Cin-N	2	6	.250	24	9	0	0	0	80	107	2	38	23	16.4	5.74	71	.321	.392	3	.130	-1	-15	-15	1	-1.2
Yr	2	6	.250	29	9	0	0	0	86	118	3	41	25	16.7	5.97	69	.326	.396	3	.125	-1	-18	-18	2	-1.2
1936 NY-A	1	1	.500	19	0	0	0	1	29¹	36	0	23	10	18.1	5.83	80	.300	.413	1	.167	-0	-3	-4	-1	-0.3
1937 Cin-N	1	2	.333	7	3	1	0	0	27¹	29	1	12	13	13.8	2.30	162	.271	.350	2	.250	-1	5	4	-1	0.4
1938 Cin-N	0	0	—	1	0	0	0	0	1	2	0	2	0	18.0	9.00	41	.400	.400	0	—	0	-1	-0	-0	0.0
Total 4	4	9	.308	56	12	1	0	1	143²	185	4	76	48	16.5	5.26	79	.311	.391	6	.158	-1	-16	-17	1	-1.1

● NUB KLEINKE   Kleinke, Norbert George b: 5/19/11, Fond Du Lac, Wis.   d: 3/16/50, Off Marin Coast, Cal.   BR/TR, 6'1", 170 lbs.   Deb: 4/25/35

1935 StL-N	0	0	—	4	0	0	0	0	12²	19	1	3	5	15.6	4.97	82	.358	.393	0	.000	-0	-1	-1	-0	0.0
1937 StL-N	1	1	.500	5	2	1	0	0	20²	25	0	7	9	13.9	4.79	83	.321	.376	0	.000	-1	-2	-2	0	-0.2
Total 2	1	1	.500	9	4	1	0	0	33¹	44	1	10	14	14.6	4.86	83	.336	.383	0	.000	-1	-3	-3	-0	-0.2

● ED KLEPFER   Klepfer, Edward Lloyd "Big Ed" b: 3/17/1888, Summerville, Pa.   d: 8/9/50, Tulsa, Okla.   BR/TR, 6', 185 lbs.   Deb: 7/4/11

1911 NY-A	0	0	—	5	0	0	0	0	4	5	0	2	4	15.8	6.75	53	.250	.318	0	.000	-0	-1	-1	0	0.0
1913 NY-A	0	1	.000	8	1	0	0	0	24²	38	2	12	10	19.0	7.66	39	.373	.448	1	.167	-0	-13	-13	0	-0.4
1915 Chi-A	1	0	1.000	3	2	1	0	0	12²	11	0	5	3	11.4	2.84	105	.234	.308	0	.000	-0	0	0	-0	0.0
Cle-A	1	6	.143	8	7	2	0	0	43	47	0	11	13	12.1	2.09	146	.283	.328	2	.167	-0	4	5	1	0.8
Yr	2	6	.250	11	9	3	0	0	55²	58	0	16	16	12.0	2.26	134	.272	.323	2	.133	-0	4	5	0	0.8
1916 Cle-A	6	6	.500	31	13	4	1	2	143	136	4	46	62	11.7	2.52	119	.262	.327	1	.025	-4	5	4	0	0.2
1917 Cle-A	14	4	.778	41	27	9	0	1	213	208	0	55	66	11.1	2.37	120	.264	.312	2	.032	-6	7	11	-2	0.1
1919 Cle-A	0	0	—	5	0	0	0	0	7¹	12	1	6	7	22.1	7.36	45	.375	.474	0	.000	-0	-3	-3	0	0.0
Total 6	22	17	.564	98	50	16	1	3	447²	457	3	137	165	12.1	2.81	104	.269	.327	6	.048	-11	-0	2	-1	0.7

● ED KLIEMAN   Klieman, Edward Frederick "Specs" or "Babe" b: 3/21/18, Norwood, Ohio   d: 11/15/79, Homosassa, Fla.   BR/TR, 6'1", 190 lbs.   Deb: 9/24/43

1943 Cle-A	1	0	1.000	1	1	1	0	0	8	5	0	5	2	13.0	1.00	311	.286	.394	0	.000	-0	2	1	-1	0.2
1944 Cle-A	11	13	.458	47	19	5	1	5	178¹	185	4	70	44	13.2	3.38	98	.274	.348	6	.105	-3	1	-2	1	-0.5
1945 Cle-A	5	8	.385	38	12	4	1	4	126¹	123	3	49	33	12.5	3.85	84	.261	.336	8	.200	-1	-7	-8	-1	-0.5
1946 Cle-A	0	0	—	9	0	0	0	0	15	18	0	10	2	16.8	6.60	50	.290	.389	0	.000	-0	-5	-5	-1	-0.1
1947 Cle-A	5	4	.556	**58**	0	0	0	**17**	92	78	5	39	21	11.6	3.03	115	.231	.315	2	.105	-1	7	5	2	0.7
1948 *Cle-A	3	2	.600	44	0	0	0	4	79²	62	3	46	12	12.4	2.60	156	.224	.345	2	.143	-0	**15**	**13**	1	0.9
1949 Was-A	0	0	—	2	0	0	0	0	3	8	0	3	1	33.0	18.00	24	.500	.579	1	1.000	-0	-5	-0	0	0.4
Chi-A	2	0	1.000	18	0	0	0	3	33	33	2	15	9	13.1	4.09	139	.273	.353	0	.250	0	4	4	1	0.4
Yr	2	0	1.000	20	0	0	0	3	36	41	2	18	10	14.8	4.25	98	.299	.381	1	.333	-0	-0	-1	1	0.4
1950 Phi-A	0	0	—	5	0	0	0	0	5²	10	0	2	0	22.2	9.53	48	.357	.438	0	.000	-0	-3	-3	-0	0.0
Total 8	26	28	.481	222	32	10	2	33	542	525	17	239	130	13.0	3.49	100	.261	.345	21	.146	-3	10	1	6	1.1

● RON KLIMKOWSKI   Klimkowski, Ronald Bernard b: 3/1/44, Jersey City, N.J.   BR/TR, 6'2", 190 lbs.   Deb: 9/15/69

1969 NY-A	0	0	—	3	1	0	0	0	14	6	0	5	3	7.1	0.64	541	.130	.216	0	.000	-0	5	4	-0	-0.1
1970 NY-A	6	7	.462	45	3	1	1	1	98¹	80	7	33	40	10.6	2.65	132	.223	.294	1	.053	-2	12	9	1	1.1
1971 Oak-A	2	2	.500	26	0	0	0	2	45¹	37	3	23	25	12.1	3.38	99	.220	.318	2	.400	1	0	0	-1	0.2
1972 NY-A	0	3	.000	16	2	0	0	1	31¹	32	3	15	11	13.8	4.02	73	.271	.358	0	.000	-1	-3	-4	0	-0.5
Total 4	8	12	.400	90	6	1	1	4	189	155	13	76	79	11.2	2.90	116	.224	.306	3	.091	-2	13	10	1	0.7

● BOBBY KLINE   Kline, John Robert b: 1/27/29, St.Petersburg, Fla   BR/TR, 6', 179 lbs.   Deb: 4/11/55 ♦

| 1955 Was-A | 0 | 0 | — | 1 | 0 | 0 | 0 | 0 | 4 | 11 | 1 | 2 | 0 | 45.0 | 27.00 | 14 | .667 | .714 | 31 | .221 | 0 | -3 | -3 | 0 | 0.0 |

● BOB KLINE   Kline, Robert George "Junior" b: 12/9/09, Enterprise, Ohio   d: 3/16/87, Westerville, Ohio   BR/TR, 6'3", 200 lbs.   Deb: 9/17/30

1930 Bos-A	0	0	—	1	0	0	0	0	1	1	0	0	0	9.0	0.00	—	.333	.333	0	—	0	1	1	-0	0.0
1931 Bos-A	5	5	.500	28	10	3	0	0	98	110	3	35	25	13.6	4.41	98	.298	.364	9	.333	2	-0	-1	2	0.3
1932 Bos-A	11	13	.458	47	19	4	1	2	172	203	10	76	31	14.7	5.28	85	.294	.365	7	.130	-3	-15	-15	3	-1.8
1933 Bos-A	7	8	.467	46	8	1	0	4	127	127	6	67	16	14.2	4.54	97	.265	.362	6	.176	-1	-4	-2	3	0.0
1934 Phi-A	6	2	.750	20	0	0	0	0	39²	50	6	13	14	14.3	6.35	69	.314	.366	3	.333	1	-8	-9	-1	-1.3
Was-A	1	0	1.000	6	0	0	0	1	4	10	0	4	1	33.8	15.75	27	.500	.600	0	—	0	-5	-5	0	-1.0
Yr	7	2	.778	26	0	0	0	1	43²	60	6	17	15	16.1	7.21	61	.335	.396	3	.333	-1	-13	-14	-1	-2.3
Total 5	30	28	.517	148	37	8	1	7	441²	501	24	195	87	14.4	5.05	87	.291	.367	25	.202	-1	-32	-32	9	-3.8

● RON KLINE   Kline, Ronald Lee b: 3/9/32, Callery, Pa.   BR/TR, 6'3", 205 lbs.   Deb: 4/21/52

1952 Pit-N	0	7	.000	27	11	0	0	0	78²	74	3	66	27	16.7	5.49	73	.253	.401	0	.000	-2	-15	-13	-1	-1.4
1955 Pit-N	6	13	.316	36	19	2	1	2	136²	161	13	53	48	14.4	4.15	99	.298	.366	5	.132	-2	-2	-7	0	-0.2
1956 Pit-N	14	18	.438	44	39	9	2	2	264	263	26	81	125	11.9	3.38	112	.263	.321	10	.127	-3	12	12	-0	1.1
1957 Pit-N	9	16	.360	40	31	11	2	0	205	214	28	61	88	12.1	4.04	94	.268	.321	4	.061	-6	-4	-6	-1	-1.3
1958 Pit-N	13	16	.448	32	32	11	2	0	237²	220	25	92	109	11.8	3.53	110	.252	.323	2	.027	-6	11	9	-1	0.4
1959 Pit-N	11	13	.458	33	29	7	0	0	186	186	23	70	91	12.5	4.26	91	.263	.331	8	.136	-4	-6	-8	-1	-1.1
1960 StL-N	4	9	.308	34	17	1	0	0	117²	133	21	43	54	13.5	6.04	68	.294	.344	5	.143	-3	-30	-25	-2	-2.6
1961 LA-A	4	8	.333	26	12	0	0	0	104²	119	16	44	70	14.1	4.90	79	.288	.358	3	.097	-2	-10	-5	1	-0.5
Det-A	5	3	.625	10	3	2	0	1	56¹	53	7	17	27	11.2	2.72	151	.245	.300	0	.167	-0	8	9	1	1.1
Yr	8	9	.471	36	20	3	0	1	161	172	19	61	97	13.0	4.14	106	.272	.336	6	.122	-2	-2	4	0	0.6
1962 Det-A	4	6	.333	36	4	0	0	2	77¹	88	9	28	47	13.7	4.31	94	.284	.347	2	.125	-1	-7	-4	-0	-0.3
1963 Was-A	3	8	.273	62	0	0	0	17	93²	85	3	30	49	11.3	2.79	133	.249	.316	1	.091	-9	9	10	-1	1.4
1964 Was-A	10	7	.588	61	0	0	0	14	81¹	81	4	26	66	11.8	2.32	159	.262	.313	1	.167	-0	12	12	-0	3.0
1965 Was-A	7	6	.538	74	0	0	0	**29**	99¹	106	7	32	68	12.7	2.63	132	.275	.333	0	.000	-1	9	9	-2	1.6
1966 Was-A	6	4	.600	63	0	0	0	23	90¹	79	7	17	46	9.6	2.39	145	.237	.274	1	.167	-0	10	11	-2	1.6
1967 Min-A	7	1	.875	54	0	0	0	5	71²	71	10	15	36	10.9	3.77	92	.261	.302	0	.000	-1	-4	-2	-1	-0.4
1968 Pit-N	12	5	.706	56	0	0	0	7	112²	94	3	31	48	10.1	1.68	174	.234	.293	0	.000	-1	**16**	**16**	-1	2.4

YEAR	TM/L	W	L	PCT	G	GS	CG	SH	SV	IP	H	HR	BB	SO	RAT	ERA	ERA+	OAV	OOB	BH	AVG	PB	PR	/A	PD	TPI
1969	Pit-N	1	3	.250	20	0	0	0	3	31	37	3	5	15	12.5	5.81	60	.296	.328	0	.000	-1	-8	-8	-0	-1.2
	SF-N	0	2	.000	7	0	0	0	0	11	16	1	6	7	18.0	4.09	86	.364	.440	0	—	-1	-1	-1	-0	-0.1
	Yr	1	5	.167	27	0	0	0	3	42	53	4	11	22	13.7	5.36	65	.310	.352	0	.000	-1	-8	-9	-0	-1.3
	Bos-A	0	1	.000	16	0	0	0	1	17	24	4	17	7	21.7	4.76	80	.329	.456	0	—	0	-2	-2	0	-0.1
1970	Atl-N	0	0	—	5	0	0	0	1	6¹	6	2	2	3	15.6	7.11	60	.321	.367	0	—	0	-2	-2	-0	-0.1
Total	17	114	144	.442	736	203	44	8	108	2078	2113	218	731	989	12.5	3.75	101	.266	.331	45	.092	-28	1	13	-5	3.5

● STEVE KLINE
Kline, Steven Jack b: 10/6/47, Wenatchee, Wash.   BR/TR, 6'3", 205 lbs.   Deb: 7/10/70

YEAR	TM/L	W	L	PCT	G	GS	CG	SH	SV	IP	H	HR	BB	SO	RAT	ERA	ERA+	OAV	OOB	BH	AVG	PB	PR	/A	PD	TPI
1970	NY-A	6	6	.500	16	15	5	0	0	100¹	99	8	24	49	11.0	3.41	103	.254	.298	5	.179	-2	3	1	1	0.4
1971	NY-A	12	13	.480	31	30	15	1	0	222¹	206	21	37	81	9.8	2.96	109	.244	.276	3	.136	-0	13	7	3	1.1
1972	NY-A	16	9	.640	32	32	11	4	0	236¹	210	11	44	58	10.1	2.40	123	.237	.281	7	.092	-3	17	14	2	1.5
1973	NY-A	4	7	.364	14	13	2	1	0	74	76	5	31	19	13.1	4.01	91	.270	.344	0	—	0	-2	-3	-0	-0.2
1974	NY-A	2	2	.500	4	4	0	0	0	26	26	3	5	6	11.1	3.46	102	.263	.305	0	—	0	0	0	-0	0.1
	Cle-A	3	8	.273	16	11	1	0	0	71	70	9	31	17	13.3	5.07	71	.266	.352	0	—	0	-11	-11	1	-1.5
	Yr	5	10	.333	20	15	1	0	0	97	96	12	36	23	12.6	4.64	77	.264	.337	0	—	0	-11	-11	-1	-1.4
1977	Atl-N	0	0	—	16	0	0	0	0	20¹	21	4	12	10	14.6	6.64	67	.259	.355	0	—	0	-6	-5	-0	-0.1
Total	6	43	45	.489	129	105	34	6	1	750¹	708	61	184	240	10.9	3.26	101	.249	.298	21	.124	-1	14	3	5	1.3

● BILL KLING
Kling, William b: 1/14/1867, Kansas City, Mo.   d: 8/26/34, Kansas City, Mo.   BL/TR, 6', 190 lbs.   Deb: 8/13/1891   F

YEAR	TM/L	W	L	PCT	G	GS	CG	SH	SV	IP	H	HR	BB	SO	RAT	ERA	ERA+	OAV	OOB	BH	AVG	PB	PR	/A	PD	TPI
1891	Phi-N	4	2	.667	12	7	4	0	0	75	91	2	32	26	15.0	4.32	79	.289	.358	6	.194	1	-8	-8	-1	-0.5
1892	Bal-N	0	2	.000	2	2	0	0	0	11	17	1	7	7	21.3	11.45	30	.340	.441	1	.250	1	-10	-10	-0	-1.1
1895	Lou-N	0	0	—	1	0	0	0	0	1	0	0	1	0	9.0	0.00	—	.000	.250	0	—	-0	1	1	-0	0.0
Total	3	4	4	.500	15	9	4	0	0	87	108	3	40	33	15.7	5.17	66	.293	.369	7	.194	1	-18	-17	-1	-1.6

● SCOTT KLINGENBECK
Klingenbeck, Scott Edward b: 2/3/71, Cincinnati, Ohio   BR/TR, 6'2", 205 lbs.   Deb: 6/2/94

YEAR	TM/L	W	L	PCT	G	GS	CG	SH	SV	IP	H	HR	BB	SO	RAT	ERA	ERA+	OAV	OOB	BH	AVG	PB	PR	/A	PD	TPI
1994	Bal-A	1	0	1.000	1	1	0	0	0	7	4	5	6	14.1	3.86	130	.240	.367	0	—	0	1	1	-0	0.0
1995	Bal-A	2	2	.500	6	5	0	0	0	31¹	32	6	18	15	14.4	4.88	97	.269	.365	0	—	0	-1	-0	1	0.0
	Min-A	0	2	.000	18	4	0	0	0	48¹	69	16	24	27	18.1	8.57	56	.338	.418	0	—	0	-21	-20	-1	-0.8
	Yr	2	4	.333	24	9	0	0	0	79²	101	22	42	42	16.6	7.12	67	.313	.398	0	—	0	-21	-21	-0	-0.8
1996	Min-A	1	1	.500	10	3	0	0	0	28²	42	5	10	15	16.6	7.85	65	.339	.393	0	—	0	-9	-9	0	-0.5
Total	3	4	5	.444	35	13	0	0	0	115¹	149	28	56	62	16.5	7.10	69	.316	.395	0	—	0	-30	-29	0	-1.3

● BOB KLINGER
Klinger, Robert Harold b: 6/4/08, Allenton, Mo.   d: 8/19/77, Villa Ridge, Mo.   BR/TR, 6', 180 lbs.   Deb: 4/19/38

YEAR	TM/L	W	L	PCT	G	GS	CG	SH	SV	IP	H	HR	BB	SO	RAT	ERA	ERA+	OAV	OOB	BH	AVG	PB	PR	/A	PD	TPI
1938	Pit-N	12	5	.706	28	21	10	1	1	159¹	152	7	42	58	11.3	2.99	127	.253	.308	10	.167	-2	14	14	0	1.3
1939	Pit-N	14	17	.452	37	33	10	2	0	225	251	11	81	64	13.4	4.36	88	.284	.346	17	.202	0	-11	-13	3	-1.3
1940	Pit-N	8	13	.381	39	22	3	0	3	142	196	5	53	48	16.1	5.39	71	.329	.388	6	.143	-2	-24	-25	1	-3.4
1941	Pit-N	9	4	.692	35	9	3	0	4	116²	127	5	30	36	12.2	3.93	92	.276	.322	8	.250	2	-4	-4	-0	-0.3
1942	Pit-N	8	11	.421	37	19	8	1	1	152²	151	4	45	58	11.7	3.24	104	.252	.307	4	.200	1	1	2	1	0.5
1943	Pit-N	11	8	.579	33	25	14	3	0	195	185	6	58	65	11.2	2.72	128	.252	.307	16	.246	1	14	16	0	1.9
1946	*Bos-A	3	2	.600	28	1	0	0	9	57	49	1	25	16	11.8	2.37	155	.238	.323	1	.313	1	7	8	-0	1.1
1947	Bos-A	1	1	.500	28	0	0	0	5	42	42	5	24	12	14.4	3.86	101	.253	.351	1	.111	-1	-1	0	-0	-0.1
Total	8	66	61	.520	265	130	48	7	23	1089²	1153	44	358	357	12.6	3.68	100	.271	.331	71	.204	3	-3	-3	5	-0.3

● JOE KLINK
Klink, Joseph Charles b: 2/3/62, Johnstown, Pa.   BL/TL, 5'11", 170 lbs.   Deb: 4/9/87

YEAR	TM/L	W	L	PCT	G	GS	CG	SH	SV	IP	H	HR	BB	SO	RAT	ERA	ERA+	OAV	OOB	BH	AVG	PB	PR	/A	PD	TPI
1987	Min-A	0	1	.000	12	0	0	0	0	23	37	4	11	17	18.8	6.65	69	.359	.421	0	—	0	-6	-5	0	-0.3
1990	*Oak-A	0	0	—	40	0	0	0	1	39²	34	1	18	19	11.8	2.04	182	.233	.317	0	—	0	8	7	-1	-0.1
1991	Oak-A	10	3	.769	62	0	0	0	2	62	60	4	21	34	12.5	4.35	88	.259	.333	0	—	0	-2	-4	-0	-0.7
1993	Fla-N	0	2	.000	59	0	0	0	0	37²	37	0	24	22	14.6	5.02	86	.266	.374	0	.000	-0	-4	-3	-1	-0.2
1996	Sea-A	0	0	—	3	0	0	0	0	2¹	3	1	1	2	15.4	3.86	128	.300	.364	0	—	0	0	-0	0	0.0
Total	5	10	6	.625	176	0	0	0	3	164²	171	10	75	94	13.7	4.26	95	.271	.354	0	.000	-0	-3	-4	-2	-1.3

● JOHNNY KLIPPSTEIN
Klippstein, John Calvin b: 10/17/27, Washington, D.C.   BR/TR, 6'1", 185 lbs.   Deb: 5/3/50

YEAR	TM/L	W	L	PCT	G	GS	CG	SH	SV	IP	H	HR	BB	SO	RAT	ERA	ERA+	OAV	OOB	BH	AVG	PB	PR	/A	PD	TPI
1950	Chi-N	2	9	.182	33	11	3	0	1	104²	112	9	64	51	15.5	5.25	80	.279	.383	11	.333	4	-13	-12	-1	-0.8
1951	Chi-N	6	6	.500	35	11	1	0	1	123²	125	10	53	56	13.4	4.29	95	.263	.344	4	.108	-2	-5	-3	0	-0.4
1952	Chi-N	9	14	.391	41	25	7	2	3	202²	208	17	89	110	13.5	4.44	87	.265	.344	11	.175	1	-16	-13	1	-1.2
1953	Chi-N	10	11	.476	48	19	5	0	6	167²	169	15	107	113	15.2	4.83	92	.258	.369	9	.155	-1	-10	-7	-2	-1.0
1954	Chi-N	4	11	.267	36	21	4	0	1	148	155	13	96	69	15.5	5.29	79	.272	.381	6	.133	-2	-20	-18	-1	-1.7
1955	Cin-N	9	10	.474	39	14	3	2	0	138	120	13	60	68	12.0	3.39	115	.233	.318	2	.065	-2	10	13	-0	1.4
1956	Cin-N	12	11	.522	37	29	11	0	1	211	219	26	82	86	13.3	4.09	97	.275	.350	7	.099	-4	-8	-3	-1	-0.6
1957	Cin-N	8	11	.421	46	18	3	1	3	146	146	17	68	99	13.4	5.05	81	.261	.344	3	.073	-3	-19	-15	-1	-2.3
1958	Cin-N	3	2	.600	12	4	0	0	0	33	37	3	14	22	14.2	4.91	84	.285	.359	1	.125	-1	-4	-3	-1	-0.5
	LA-N	3	5	.375	45	0	0	0	0	90	81	12	44	73	12.7	3.80	108	.248	.341	1	.050	-2	2	3	-0	0.1
	Yr	6	7	.462	57	4	0	0	0	123	118	15	58	95	13.0	4.10	100	.258	.344	2	.071	-2	-2	-1	-0	-0.4
1959	*LA-N	4	0	1.000	28	0	0	0	2	45²	48	8	33	30	16.4	5.91	72	.276	.397	1	.143	-0	-10	-9	-0	-0.8
1960	Cle-A	5	5	.500	49	0	0	0	14	74¹	75	8	35	46	10.8	2.91	129	.205	.303	2	.143	-0	8	7	0	1.2
1961	Was-A	2	2	.500	42	1	0	0	0	71²	83	13	43	41	16.3	6.78	59	.297	.399	1	.143	-0	-22	-22	1	-1.1
1962	Cin-N	7	6	.538	40	2	0	0	4	108²	113	13	64	67	15.0	4.47	90	.278	.381	3	.125	-0	-6	-5	0	-0.5
1963	Phi-N	5	6	.455	49	1	0	0	5	112	90	8	46	86	10.4	1.93	168	.204	.293	1	.038	-2	16	16	-1	1.6
1964	Phi-N	2	1	.667	11	0	0	0	0	22¹	22	8	6	13	12.9	4.03	86	.250	.327	0	.000	-0	-1	-1	-0	-0.2
	Min-A	0	4	.000	33	0	0	0	0	45²	44	4	20	39	12.6	1.97	181	.260	.342	0	.000	-0	8	9	-0	0.9
1965	*Min-A	9	3	.750	56	0	0	0	5	76¹	66	9	31	59	11.0	2.24	159	.217	.304	0	.000	-1	10	11	-1	1.7
1966	Min-A	1	1	.500	26	0	0	0	0	39²	35	2	20	26	12.9	3.40	106	.238	.337	0	.000	-0	1	1	-0	0.1
1967	Det-A	0	0	—	6	0	0	0	0	6²	6	1	1	4	9.5	5.40	60	.250	.280	0	—	0	-2	-2	0	0.0
Total	18	101	118	.461	711	161	37	6	66	1967²	1915	203	997	1158	13.6	4.24	94	.258	.350	63	.125	-14	-80	-54	-5	-4.2

● FRED KLOBEDANZ
Klobedanz, Frederick Augustus "Duke"
b: 6/13/1871, Waterbury, Conn.   d: 4/12/40, Waterbury, Conn.   BL/TL, 5'11", 190 lbs.   Deb: 8/20/1896

YEAR	TM/L	W	L	PCT	G	GS	CG	SH	SV	IP	H	HR	BB	SO	RAT	ERA	ERA+	OAV	OOB	BH	AVG	PB	PR	/A	PD	TPI
1896	Bos-N	6	4	.600	10	9	9	0	0	80²	69	5	31	26	11.9	3.01	151	.229	.316	13	.317	2	12	14	-1	1.5
1897	*Bos-N	26	7	**.788**	38	37	30	2	0	309¹	344	13	125	92	14.3	4.60	97	.279	.357	48	.324	9	-10	-4	-4	0.1
1898	Bos-N	19	10	.655	35	33	25	0	0	270²	281	13	99	51	13.0	3.89	95	.266	.336	27	.213	4	-8	-6	-1	-0.6
1899	Bos-N	1	4	.200	5	5	4	0	0	33¹	39	2	9	8	13.5	4.86	86	.291	.345	2	.182	1	-4	-3	1	-0.2
1902	Bos-N	1	0	1.000	1	1	1	0	0	8	9	0	2	4	13.5	1.13	251	.281	.343	1	.500	1	2	2	0	0.3
Total	5	53	25	.679	89	85	69	2	0	702	742	33	266	181	13.5	4.12	101	.269	.343	91	.277	13	-8	2	-6	1.1

● STAN KLOPP
Klopp, Stanley Harold "Betz" b: 12/22/10, Womelsdorf, Pa.   d: 3/11/80, Robesonia, Pa.   BR/TR, 6'1.5", 180 lbs.   Deb: 4/30/44

YEAR	TM/L	W	L	PCT	G	GS	CG	SH	SV	IP	H	HR	BB	SO	RAT	ERA	ERA+	OAV	OOB	BH	AVG	PB	PR	/A	PD	TPI
1944	Bos-N	1	2	.333	24	0	0	0	0	46¹	47	1	33	17	15.5	4.27	89	.272	.388	2	.286	1	-3	-2	-1	-0.2

● BRENT KNACKERT
Knackert, Brent Bradley b: 8/1/69, Los Angeles, Cal.   BR/TR, 6'3", 185 lbs.   Deb: 4/10/90

YEAR	TM/L	W	L	PCT	G	GS	CG	SH	SV	IP	H	HR	BB	SO	RAT	ERA	ERA+	OAV	OOB	BH	AVG	PB	PR	/A	PD	TPI
1990	Sea-A	1	1	.500	24	0	0	0	0	37¹	50	5	21	28	17.6	6.51	61	.313	.399	0	—	0	-11	-11	-0	-0.5
1996	Bos-A	0	1	.000	8	0	0	0	0	10	16	1	5	5	20.7	9.00	57	.356	.442	0	—	0	-4	-4	1	-0.3
Total	2	1	2	.333	32	0	0	0	0	47¹	66	6	28	33	18.3	7.04	60	.322	.409	0	—	0	-15	-15	0	-0.8

● CHRIS KNAPP
Knapp, Robert Christian b: 9/16/53, Cherry Point, N.C.   BR/TR, 6'5", 195 lbs.   Deb: 9/4/75

YEAR	TM/L	W	L	PCT	G	GS	CG	SH	SV	IP	H	HR	BB	SO	RAT	ERA	ERA+	OAV	OOB	BH	AVG	PB	PR	/A	PD	TPI
1975	Chi-A	0	0	—	2	0	0	0	0	4	4	0	2	2	27.0	4.50	86	.250	.500	0	—	0	-0	-0	0	-0.1
1976	Chi-A	3	1	.750	11	6	1	0	0	52¹	54	5	32	41	15.0	4.82	74	.273	.377	0	—	0	-8	-7	-0	-0.6
1977	Chi-A	12	7	.632	27	26	4	0	0	146¹	166	16	61	103	14.4	4.80	85	.283	.357	0	—	0	-12	-15	-1	-1.4
1978	Cal-A	14	8	.636	30	29	6	0	0	188¹	178	25	67	126	11.8	4.21	86	.250	.317	0	—	0	-9	-13	-2	-1.5
1979	*Cal-A	5	5	.500	20	18	3	0	0	98	109	9	35	36	13.4	5.51	74	.275	.337	0	—	0	-14	-16	-0	-1.3
1980	Cal-A	2	11	.154	32	20	1	0	1	117¹	133	18	51	46	14.7	6.14	64	.289	.369	0	—	0	-27	-29	-1	-2.9
Total	6	36	32	.529	122	99	15	0	1	604¹	642	72	255	355	13.6	4.99	77	.272	.347	0	—	0	-70	-76	-5	-7.8

FRANK KNAUSS
Knauss, Frank H.　b: 1868, Cleveland, Ohio　BL/TL, 5'10", 170 lbs.　Deb: 6/25/1890

YEAR	TM/L	W	L	PCT	G	GS	CG	SH	SV	IP	H	HR	BB	SO	RAT	ERA	ERA+	OAV	OOB	BH	AVG	PB	PR	/A	PD	TPI
1890	Col-a	17	12	.586	37	34	28	3	2	275²	206	3	106	148	10.9	2.81	128	.202	.290	24	.226	5	33	24	-1	2.5
1891	Cle-N	0	3	.000	3	3	1	0	0	15	23	2	6	6	21.0	7.20	48	.338	.438	1	.167	-0	-6	-6	0	-0.9
1892	Cin-N	0	0	—	1	0	0	0	0	8	13	0	5	2	20.3	3.38	97	.351	.429	1	.333	0	-0	-0	0	0.1
1894	Cle-N	0	1	.000	2	2	1	0	0	11	7	0	14	2	19.6	5.73	95	.179	.429	0	.000	-1	-0	-0	0	0.0
1895	NY-N	0	0	—	1	1	0	0	0	3²	9	0	2	1	27.0	17.18	27	.450	.500	0	.000	-0	-5	-5	0	0.0
Total 5		17	16	.515	44	40	30	3	2	313¹	258	5	135	159	12.1	3.30	111	.218	.312	26	.217	4	20	12	-0	1.7

RUDY KNEISCH
Kneisch, Rudolph Frank　b: 4/10/1899, Baltimore, Md.　d: 4/6/65, Baltimore, Md.　BR/TL, 5'10.5", 175 lbs.　Deb: 9/21/26

YEAR	TM/L	W	L	PCT	G	GS	CG	SH	SV	IP	H	HR	BB	SO	RAT	ERA	ERA+	OAV	OOB	BH	AVG	PB	PR	/A	PD	TPI
1926	Det-A	0	1	.000	2	2	1	0	0	17	18	2	6	4	13.8	2.65	153	.273	.351	0	.000	-1	3	3	0	0.1

PHIL KNELL
Knell, Philip Louis　b: 3/12/1865, San Francisco, Cal　d: 6/5/44, Santa Monica, Cal.　BR/TL, 5'7.5", 154 lbs.　Deb: 7/6/1888

YEAR	TM/L	W	L	PCT	G	GS	CG	SH	SV	IP	H	HR	BB	SO	RAT	ERA	ERA+	OAV	OOB	BH	AVG	PB	PR	/A	PD	TPI
1888	Pit-N	1	2	.333	3	3	3	0	0	26¹	21	0	18	15	14.7	3.76	71	.217	.374	1	.091	-1	-3	-3	-0	-0.4
1890	Phi-P	22	11	.667	35	31	30	2	0	286²	287	10	166	99	15.1	3.83	71	.249	.358	29	.220	-1	13	14	0	1.1
1891	Col-a	28	27	.509	58	52	47	5	0	462	363	4	226	228	12.5	2.92	118	.209	.319	34	.158	-9	41	28	5	2.2
1892	Was-N	9	13	.409	22	21	17	1	0	170	156	4	76	74	12.9	3.65	89	.234	.323	8	.118	-5	-7	-8	-0	-1.2
	Phi-N	5	5	.500	11	9	7	0	0	80	87	0	35	43	15.0	4.05	80	.266	.357	3	.088	-3	-7	-7	-2	-1.1
	Yr	14	18	.438	33	30	24	1	0	250	243	4	111	117	13.1	3.78	86	.242	.324	11	.108	-7	-14	-15	-2	-2.3
1894	Pit-N	0	0	—	1	0	0	0	0	7	11	0	6	0	23.1	11.57	45	.355	.474	0	.000	-1	-5	-5	1	0.0
	Lou-N	7	21	.250	32	28	25	0	0	247	330	9	104	67	16.3	5.32	96	.317	.387	31	.274	-0	-6	-6	-2	-0.6
	Yr	7	21	.250	33	28	25	0	0	254	341	9	110	67	16.5	5.49	93	.318	.388	31	.267	-0	-5	-11	-2	-0.6
1895	Lou-N	0	6	.000	10	6	3	0	0	56²	75	3	21	19	16.2	6.51	71	.314	.388	3	.231	-0	-11	-12	1	-0.8
	Cle-N	7	5	.583	20	13	9	0	0	116²	149	7	53	30	16.0	5.40	92	.306	.381	11	.200	-3	-8	-5	0	-0.6
	Yr	7	11	.389	30	19	12	0	0	173¹	224	10	74	49	15.8	5.76	85	.306	.374	17	.210	-3	-19	-17	1	-1.4
Total 6		79	90	.467	192	163	141	8	0	1452¹	1478	38	705	575	14.4	4.05	99	.256	.351	123	.187	-21	14	-5	2	-1.4

CHARLIE KNEPPER
Knepper, Charles　b: 2/18/1871, Anderson, Ind.　d: 2/6/46, Muncie, Ind.　BR/TR, 6'4", 190 lbs.　Deb: 5/26/1899

YEAR	TM/L	W	L	PCT	G	GS	CG	SH	SV	IP	H	HR	BB	SO	RAT	ERA	ERA+	OAV	OOB	BH	AVG	PB	PR	/A	PD	TPI
1899	Cle-N	4	22	.154	27	26	26	0	0	219²	307	11	77	43	16.3	5.78	64	.329	.390	12	.135	-5	-47	-51	-1	-5.0

BOB KNEPPER
Knepper, Robert Wesley　b: 5/25/54, Akron, Ohio　BL/TL, 6'2", 200 lbs.　Deb: 9/10/76

YEAR	TM/L	W	L	PCT	G	GS	CG	SH	SV	IP	H	HR	BB	SO	RAT	ERA	ERA+	OAV	OOB	BH	AVG	PB	PR	/A	PD	TPI
1976	SF-N	1	2	.333	4	4	0	0	0	25	26	0	7	11	11.9	3.24	112	.277	.327	1	.111	-0	1	1	0	0.1
1977	SF-N	11	9	.550	27	27	6	2	0	166	151	14	72	100	12.3	3.36	116	.242	.323	10	.182	1	10	10	-1	1.2
1978	SF-N	17	11	.607	36	35	16	6	0	260	218	10	85	147	10.6	2.63	131	.229	.295	5	.063	-0	27	24	-2	1.9
1979	SF-N	9	12	.429	34	34	6	2	0	207¹	241	30	77	123	13.9	4.64	75	.289	.352	12	.182	3	-21	-27	-1	-2.2
1980	SF-N	9	16	.360	35	33	8	1	0	215¹	242	15	61	103	13.0	4.10	86	.281	.335	10	.152	0	-12	-13	2	-1.3
1981	*Hou-N★	9	5	.643	22	22	6	5	0	156²	128	5	38	75	9.8	2.18	151	.226	.280	7	.149	1	23	19	-1	1.8
1982	Hou-N	5	15	.250	33	29	4	0	1	180	193	14	60	108	12.8	4.45	75	.278	.338	3	.058	-2	-17	-23	1	-2.5
1983	Hou-N	6	13	.316	35	29	4	3	0	203	202	12	71	125	12.3	3.19	107	.261	.326	12	.182	3	10	5	1	0.6
1984	Hou-N	15	10	.600	35	34	11	3	0	233²	223	26	55	140	10.7	3.20	104	.251	.296	13	.171	4	10	3	-1	0.6
1985	Hou-N	15	13	.536	37	37	4	0	0	241	253	21	54	131	11.6	3.55	98	.271	.313	11	.141	0	1	-2	-3	-0.5
1986	*Hou-N	17	12	.586	40	38	8	5	0	258	232	19	62	143	10.4	3.14	115	.242	.290	9	.099	-3	17	13	2	1.3
1987	Hou-N	8	17	.320	33	31	1	0	0	177²	226	26	54	76	14.4	5.27	74	.302	.364	5	.098	-1	-23	-27	2	-3.2
1988	Hou-N★	14	5	.737	27	27	3	2	0	175	156	13	67	103	11.6	3.14	106	.243	.316	6	.125	-1	6	4	2	0.3
1989	Hou-N	4	10	.286	22	20	0	0	0	113	135	12	60	45	15.7	5.89	57	.303	.388	7	.226	5	-30	-31	1	-2.9
	SF-N	3	2	.600	13	6	1	1	0	52	55	4	15	19	12.3	3.46	97	.270	.323	1	.083	-1	0	-1	-0	-0.1
	Yr	7	12	.368	35	26	1	1	0	165	190	16	75	64	14.5	5.13	66	.290	.364	8	.186	6	-30	-32	0	-3.0
1990	SF-N	3	3	.500	12	7	0	0	0	44¹	56	7	19	24	15.4	5.68	64	.311	.380	3	.231	1	-9	-10	-1	-1.1
Total 15		146	155	.485	445	413	78	30	1	2708	2737	228	857	1473	12.1	3.68	95	.264	.323	115	.137	7	-8	-55	-1	-5.5

LOU KNERR
Knerr, Wallace Luther　b: 8/21/21, Strasburg, Pa.　d: 3/23/80, Denver, Pa.　BR/TR, 6'1", 210 lbs.　Deb: 4/17/45

YEAR	TM/L	W	L	PCT	G	GS	CG	SH	SV	IP	H	HR	BB	SO	RAT	ERA	ERA+	OAV	OOB	BH	AVG	PB	PR	/A	PD	TPI
1945	Phi-A	5	11	.313	27	17	5	0	0	130	142	6	74	41	15.0	4.22	81	.283	.376	9	.191	-1	-12	-11	0	-1.4
1946	Phi-A	3	16	.158	30	22	6	0	0	148¹	171	13	67	58	14.5	5.40	66	.288	.361	9	.180	0	-31	-31	-0	-3.5
1947	Was-A	0	0	—	6	0	0	0	0	9	17	1	8	5	25.0	11.00	34	.405	.500	1	1.000	1	-7	-7	0	0.1
Total 3		8	27	.229	63	39	11	0	0	287¹	330	20	149	104	15.1	5.04	69	.290	.373	19	.194	-1	-51	-49	0	-4.8

ELMER KNETZER
Knetzer, Elmer Ellsworth "Baron"　b: 7/22/1885, Carrick, Pa.　d: 10/3/75, Pittsburgh, Pa.　BR/TR, 5'10", 180 lbs.　Deb: 9/11/09

YEAR	TM/L	W	L	PCT	G	GS	CG	SH	SV	IP	H	HR	BB	SO	RAT	ERA	ERA+	OAV	OOB	BH	AVG	PB	PR	/A	PD	TPI
1909	Bro-N	1	3	.250	5	4	3	0	0	35²	33	2	22	17	13.9	3.03	86	.252	.359	0	.000	-2	-2	-2	1	-0.3
1910	Bro-N	7	5	.583	20	15	10	3	0	132²	122	1	60	56	12.4	3.19	95	.255	.339	2	.053	-3	-2	-2	-2	-0.6
1911	Bro-N	11	12	.478	35	20	11	3	0	204	202	1	93	66	13.1	3.49	96	.255	.359	6	.097	-4	-2	-3	-1	-0.8
1912	Bro-N	7	9	.438	33	16	4	1	0	140¹	135	6	70	61	13.4	4.55	74	.254	.345	1	.135	-1	-18	-19	-0	-2.0
1914	Pit-F	20	12	.625	37	30	20	3	0	272	257	9	88	146	11.5	2.88	100	.254	.315	9	.099	-9	0	-0	-0	-0.8
1915	Pit-F	18	14	.563	41	33	22	3	3	279	256	5	89	120	11.2	2.58	105	.251	.311	12	.132	-7	5	4	-0	-0.3
1916	Bos-N	0	2	.000	2	0	0	0	0	5	11	0	2	2	23.4	7.20	38	.524	.565	0	—	-0	-3	-3	1	-0.2
	Cin-N	5	12	.294	36	16	12	0	1	171¹	161	6	48	70	11.1	2.89	90	.252	.307	8	.154	-5	-6	-5	3	-0.4
	Yr	5	14	.263	38	16	12	0	1	176¹	172	6	50	72	11.5	3.01	86	.258	.316	8	.154	-5	-8	-8	3	-1.2
1917	Cin-N	0	0	—	11	0	0	0	1	27¹	29	0	12	7	14.2	2.96	88	.282	.368	0	.000	-0	-1	-1	0	-0.1
Total 8		69	69	.500	220	134	82	13	6	1267¹	1206	30	484	535	12.1	3.15	93	.258	.330	42	.109	-25	-27	-32	2	-6.0

LON KNIGHT
Knight, Alonzo P.　b: 6/16/1853, Philadelphia, Pa.　d: 4/23/32, Philadelphia, Pa.　BR/TR, 5'11.5", 165 lbs.　Deb: 9/4/1875　MU◆

YEAR	TM/L	W	L	PCT	G	GS	CG	SH	SV	IP	H	HR	BB	SO	RAT	ERA	ERA+	OAV	OOB	BH	AVG	PB	PR	/A	PD	TPI
1875	Ath-n	6	5	.545	13	13	12	0	0	107	114	0	12	15	10.6	2.27	105	.259	.278	6	.128	-3	-1	1	-0	-0.1
1876	Phi-N	10	22	.313	34	32	27	0	0	282	383	0	34	12	13.3	2.62	93	.297	.315	60	.250	-1	-10	-6	-1	-0.4
1884	Phi-a	0	1	.000	2	1	1	0	0	14	24	0	4	2	18.6	9.00	38	.348	.392	131	.271	-0	-9	-9	0	-0.4
1885	Phi-a	0	0	—	1	0	0	0	0	5	4	0	1	2	10.8	1.80	191	.103	.146	25	.210	-0	1	1	0	0.0
	Pro-N	0	0	—	1	0	0	0	0	2	0	0	0	0		6.75	39	.255	.381	13	.160	-2	-2	-0	0	0.0
Total 3		10	23	.303	38	33	28	0	0	305	415	1	44	16	13.6	2.95	84	.293	.315	549	.245	-1	-20	-16	-1	-1.0

JACK KNIGHT
Knight, Elma Russell　b: 1/12/1895, Pittsboro, Miss.　d: 7/30/76, San Antonio, Tex.　BL/TR, 6', 175 lbs.　Deb: 9/20/22

YEAR	TM/L	W	L	PCT	G	GS	CG	SH	SV	IP	H	HR	BB	SO	RAT	ERA	ERA+	OAV	OOB	BH	AVG	PB	PR	/A	PD	TPI
1922	StL-N	0	0	—	1	1	0	0	0	4	9	0	3	1	27.0	9.00	43	.474	.545	1	.500	0	-2	-2	0	0.0
1925	Phi-N	7	6	.538	33	11	4	0	3	105¹	161	14	36	19	16.9	6.84	70	.354	.402	9	.205	-1	-30	-24	-1	-2.7
1926	Phi-N	3	12	.200	35	15	6	0	2	142²	206	14	48	29	16.6	6.62	68	.347	.396	12	.214	-0	-44	-39	5	-3.1
1927	Bos-N	0	0	—	3	0	0	0	0	3	6	0	2	0	24.0	15.00	25	.429	.500	0	—	-0	-4	-4	1	0.1
Total 4		10	18	.357	72	27	10	0	5	255	382	28	89	49	16.7	6.85	64	.353	.403	22	.216	-1	-80	-70	4	-5.7

GEORGE KNIGHT
Knight, George Henry　b: 11/24/1855, Lakeville, Conn.　d: 10/4/12, Lakeville, Conn.　Deb: 9/28/1875

YEAR	TM/L	W	L	PCT	G	GS	CG	SH	SV	IP	H	HR	BB	SO	RAT	ERA	ERA+	OAV	OOB	BH	AVG	PB	PR	/A	PD	TPI
1875	NH-n	1	0	1.000	9						12	0	0	0	12.0	3.00	69	.293	.293	0	.000		-1	-1		-0.1

JOE KNIGHT
Knight, Joseph William "Quiet Joe"　b: 9/28/1859, Port Stanley, Ont., Canada　d: 10/16/38, Lynhurst, Ont., Canada　BL/TL, 5'11", 185 lbs.　Deb: 5/16/1884　◆

YEAR	TM/L	W	L	PCT	G	GS	CG	SH	SV	IP	H	HR	BB	SO	RAT	ERA	ERA+	OAV	OOB	BH	AVG	PB	PR	/A	PD	TPI
1884	Phi-N	2	4	.333	6	6	6	0	0	51	66	2	21	8	15.4	5.47	55	.293	.354	6	.250	1	-14	-14	-0	-1.2

HUB KNOLLS
Knolls, Oscar Edward　b: 12/18/1883, Valparaiso, Ind.　d: 7/1/46, Chicago, Ill.　TR, 6'2", 190 lbs.　Deb: 5/1/06

YEAR	TM/L	W	L	PCT	G	GS	CG	SH	SV	IP	H	HR	BB	SO	RAT	ERA	ERA+	OAV	OOB	BH	AVG	PB	PR	/A	PD	TPI
1906	Bro-N	0	0	—	2	0	0	0	0	6²	13	0	2	3	20.3	4.05	62	.382	.417	1	1.000	1	-1	-1	-1	0.0

JACK KNOTT
Knott, John Henry　b: 3/2/07, Dallas, Tex.　d: 10/13/81, Brownwood, Tex.　BR/TR, 6'2.5", 200 lbs.　Deb: 4/13/33

YEAR	TM/L	W	L	PCT	G	GS	CG	SH	SV	IP	H	HR	BB	SO	RAT	ERA	ERA+	OAV	OOB	BH	AVG	PB	PR	/A	PD	TPI
1933	StL-A	1	8	.111	20	9	0	0	0	82²	88	11	33	19	13.4	5.01	93	.269	.340	7	.304	-1	-7	-3	-1	-0.3
1934	StL-A	10	3	.769	45	9	2	0	4	138	149	11	67	56	14.2	4.96	101	.278	.359	4	.133	-1	-7	1	0	-0.1
1935	StL-A	11	8	.579	48	19	7	2	7	187²	219	8	78	45	14.3	4.60	104	.287	.353	7	.115	-5	-3	4	1	0.0
1936	StL-A	9	17	.346	47	23	9	0	0	192²	272	15	93	60	17.2	7.29	74	.330	.401	4	.070	-5	-42	-41	-1	-4.9
1937	StL-A	8	18	.308	38	23	6	1	0	191¹	226	15	91	74	14.9	4.89	99	.291	.370	8	.140	-4	-6	-1	-2	-0.5
1938	StL-A	1	2	.333	7	4	0	0	0	30	35	3	15	10	15.0	4.80	104	.285	.362	1	.100	-1	-0	-1	-0	-0.1
	Chi-A	5	10	.333	20	18	0	0	0	131	135	8	54	35	13.0	4.05	121	.271	.342	5	.125	-2	11	12	1	1.0
	Yr	6	12	.333	27	22	0	0	0	161	170	11	69	45	13.4	4.19	117	.273	.346	6	.120	-3	11	13	1	0.9

YEAR	TM/L	W	L	PCT	G	GS	CG	SH	SV	IP	H	HR	BB	SO	RAT	ERA	ERA+	OAV	OOB	BH	AVG	PB	PR	/A	PD	TPI
1939	Chi-A	11	6	.647	25	23	8	0	0	149²	157	13	41	56	12.0	4.15	114	.269	.318	8	.151	-3	8	10	-1	0.6
1940	Chi-A	11	9	.550	25	23	4	2	0	158	166	12	52	44	12.5	4.56	97	.265	.324	5	.088	-4	-3	-2	-1	-0.7
1941	Phi-A	13	11	.542	27	26	11	0	0	194¹	212	20	81	54	13.7	4.40	95	.279	.350	5	.077	-3	-5	-5	-3	-1.0
1942	Phi-A	2	10	.167	20	14	4	0	0	95¹	127	7	36	31	15.5	5.57	68	.310	.367	4	.138	-1	-20	-19	1	-2.0
1946	Phi-A	0	1	.000	3	1	0	0	0	6¹	7	1	1	2	12.8	5.68	62	.280	.333	-0	—	0	-1	-1	-0	-0.2
Total	11	82	103	.443	325	192	62	4	19	1557	1787	140	642	484	14.2	4.97	95	.287	.355	58	.120	-29	-83	-46	-5	-8.3

● **ED KNOUFF** Knouff, Edward "Fred" b: 6/1868, Philadelphia, Pa. d: 9/14/1900, Philadelphia, Pa. BR/TR, 210 lbs. Deb: 7/1/1885 ◆

YEAR	TM/L	W	L	PCT	G	GS	CG	SH	SV	IP	H	HR	BB	SO	RAT	ERA	ERA+	OAV	OOB	BH	AVG	PB	PR	/A	PD	TPI
1885	Phi-a	7	6	.538	14	13	12	0	0	106	103	0	44	43	13.2	3.65	94	.228	.309	9	.188	-2	-5	-2	1	-0.3
1886	Bal-a	0	1	.000	1	1	1	0	0	9	2	0	5	8	10.0	2.00	171	.067	.263	-0	.000	-0	1	1	1	0.2
1887	Bal-a	2	6	.250	9	9	6	0	0	63	79	0	41	27	19.0	7.57	54	.295	.413	9	.290	-0	-23	-24	-0	-2.0
	StL-a	4	2	.667	6	6	6	1	0	50	40	0	36	18	14.2	4.50	101	.225	.364	10	.179	-1	-1	0	-0	-0.1
	Yr	6	8	.429	15	15	12	1	0	113	119	0	77	45	15.8	6.21	69	.259	.369	19	.218	-1	-24	-24	-0	-2.1
1888	StL-a	5	4	.556	9	9	9	0	0	81	66	0	37	25	12.3	2.67	122	.214	.314	3	.097	-2	4	5	-2	0.1
	Cle-a	0	1	.000	2	2	1	0	0	9	8	0	3	2	12.0	1.00	309	.229	.308	1	.167	-0	2	2	1	0.3
	Yr	5	5	.500	11	11	10	0	0	90	74	0	40	27	11.5	2.50	130	.211	.293	4	.108	-2	6	7	-1	0.4
1889	Phi-a	2	0	1.000	3	3	2	0	0	25	37	2	9	5	16.9	3.96	96	.333	.388	3	.250	-0	-0	-1	-0	-0.1
Total	5	20	20	.500	44	43	37	1	0	343	335	2	175	128	14.4	4.17	89	.242	.344	35	.187	-4	-22	-18	0	-1.8

● **DAROLD KNOWLES** Knowles, Darold Duane b: 12/9/41, Brunswick, Mo. BL/TL, 6', 190 lbs. Deb: 4/18/65 C

YEAR	TM/L	W	L	PCT	G	GS	CG	SH	SV	IP	H	HR	BB	SO	RAT	ERA	ERA+	OAV	OOB	BH	AVG	PB	PR	/A	PD	TPI
1965	Bal-A	0	1	.000	5	1	0	0	0	14²	14	2	10	12	16.6	9.20	38	.250	.391	0	.000	-0	-9	-9	0	-0.6
1966	Phi-N	6	5	.545	69	0	0	0	13	100¹	98	4	46	88	13.5	3.05	118	.260	.351	4	.250	-0	6	6	2	1.1
1967	Was-A	6	8	.429	61	1	0	0	14	113¹	91	5	52	85	11.7	2.70	117	.228	.322	1	.063	-1	7	6	2	1.0
1968	Was-A	1	1	.500	32	0	0	0	4	41¹	38	0	12	37	11.1	2.18	134	.241	.298	1	.250	1	4	3	0	0.4
1969	Was-A★	9	2	.818	53	0	0	0	13	84¹	73	8	31	59	11.5	2.24	155	.236	.314	1	.077	0	13	11	0	1.9
1970	Was-A	2	14	.125	71	0	0	0	27	119¹	100	4	58	71	12.2	2.04	175	.231	.328	1	.050	-1	22	20	2	**3.5**
1971	Was-A	2	2	.500	12	0	0	0	2	15¹	17	2	6	16	13.5	3.52	94	.266	.329	0	.000	-0	-0	-0	-0	-0.1
	*Oak-A	5	2	.714	43	0	0	0	7	52²	40	3	16	40	10.1	3.59	93	.221	.295	1	.125	-0	-1	-1	1	-0.2
	Yr	7	4	.636	55	0	0	0	9	68	57	5	22	56	10.9	3.57	93	.233	.304	1	.100	-1	-1	-2	1	-0.3
1972	Oak-A	5	1	.833	54	0	0	0	11	65²	49	1	37	36	11.8	1.37	207	.212	.321	3	.250	1	12	11	3	1.9
1973	*Oak-A	6	8	.429	52	5	1	1	9	99	87	7	49	46	12.6	3.09	115	.246	.343	0	—	0	8	5	2	0.9
1974	Oak-A	3	3	.500	45	1	0	0	3	53¹	61	6	35	18	16.5	4.22	79	.296	.403	0	—	0	-4	-5	1	-0.3
1975	Chi-N	6	9	.400	58	0	0	0	15	88¹	107	3	36	63	14.9	5.81	66	.298	.367	1	.067	-1	-21	-19	3	-3.5
1976	Chi-N	5	7	.417	58	0	0	0	9	71²	61	6	22	39	10.7	2.89	134	.242	.308	1	.143	1	5	8	2	1.8
1977	Tex-A	5	2	.714	42	0	0	0	4	50¹	50	7	23	14	13.4	3.22	127	.272	.359	0	—	0	5	5	1	0.8
1978	Mon-N	3	3	.500	60	0	0	0	6	72	63	9	34	34	11.6	2.38	148	.250	.330	1	.167	-0	10	9	2	1.1
1979	StL-N	2	5	.286	48	0	0	0	6	48²	54	5	17	22	13.1	4.07	92	.277	.335	0	.000	-0	-2	-2	-1	-0.3
1980	StL-N	0	1	.000	2	0	0	0	0	1²	3	1	0	1	16.2	10.80	34	.375	.375	0	—	0	-1	-1	-0	-0.6
Total	16	66	74	.471	765	8	1	1	143	1092	1006	65	480	681	12.6	3.12	112	.250	.336	15	.120	-2	53	45	20	8.8

● **TOM KNOWLSON** Knowlson, Thomas Herbert "Doc" b: 4/23/1895, Pittsburgh, Pa. d: 4/11/43, Miami Shores, Fla. BB/TR, 5'11", 178 lbs. Deb: 7/3/15

YEAR	TM/L	W	L	PCT	G	GS	CG	SH	SV	IP	H	HR	BB	SO	RAT	ERA	ERA+	OAV	OOB	BH	AVG	PB	PR	/A	PD	TPI
1915	Phi-A	4	6	.400	18	9	8	0	0	100²	99	1	60	24	14.8	3.49	84	.273	.386	3	.083	-3	-6	-6	-0	-0.9

● **BILL KNOWLTON** Knowlton, William Young b: 8/18/1892, Philadelphia, Pa. d: 2/25/44, Philadelphia, Pa. BR/TR, Deb: 9/3/20

YEAR	TM/L	W	L	PCT	G	GS	CG	SH	SV	IP	H	HR	BB	SO	RAT	ERA	ERA+	OAV	OOB	BH	AVG	PB	PR	/A	PD	TPI
1920	Phi-A	0	1	.000	1	1	0	0	0	5²	9	0	3	5	23.8	4.76	84	.346	.469	0	.000	-0	-1	-0	-0	-0.1

● **KURT KNUDSEN** Knudsen, Kurt David b: 2/20/67, Arlington Heights, Ill. BR/TR, 6'3", 200 lbs. Deb: 5/16/92

YEAR	TM/L	W	L	PCT	G	GS	CG	SH	SV	IP	H	HR	BB	SO	RAT	ERA	ERA+	OAV	OOB	BH	AVG	PB	PR	/A	PD	TPI
1992	Det-A	2	3	.400	48	1	0	0	5	70²	70	9	41	51	14.3	4.58	86	.264	.365	0	—	0	-5	-5	-0	-0.4
1993	Det-A	3	2	.600	30	0	0	0	0	37²	41	9	16	29	14.6	4.78	90	.281	.367	0	—	0	-2	-2	-0	-0.3
1994	Det-A	1	0	1.000	4	0	0	0	0	5¹	7	2	11	1	30.4	13.50	36	.304	.529	0	—	0	-5	-5	-0	-0.7
Total	3	6	5	.545	82	1	0	0	5	113²	118	20	68	81	15.1	5.07	81	.272	.377	0	—	0	-12	-12	-0	-1.4

● **MARK KNUDSON** Knudson, Mark Richard b: 10/28/60, Denver, Colo. BR/TR, 6'5", 215 lbs. Deb: 7/8/85

YEAR	TM/L	W	L	PCT	G	GS	CG	SH	SV	IP	H	HR	BB	SO	RAT	ERA	ERA+	OAV	OOB	BH	AVG	PB	PR	/A	PD	TPI
1985	Hou-N	0	2	.000	2	2	0	0	0	11	21	0	3	4	19.6	9.00	38	.429	.462	0	.000	0	-7	-7	-0	-0.9
1986	Hou-N	1	5	.167	9	7	0	0	0	42²	48	5	15	20	13.5	4.22	85	.279	.340	0	.000	-1	-2	-3	-1	-0.5
	Mil-A	0	1	.000	4	1	0	0	0	17²	22	7	5	9	13.8	7.64	57	.286	.329	0	—	0	-7	-7	-0	-0.4
1987	Mil-A	4	4	.500	15	8	1	0	0	62	88	7	14	26	14.8	5.37	85	.331	.364	0	—	0	-6	-6	-1	-0.9
1988	Mil-A	0	0	—	5	0	0	0	0	16	17	1	2	7	10.7	1.13	354	.279	.302	0	—	0	5	5	0	0.0
1989	Mil-A	8	5	.615	40	7	1	0	0	123²	110	15	29	47	10.3	3.35	115	.237	.286	0	—	0	7	7	-1	0.5
1990	Mil-A	10	9	.526	30	27	4	2	0	168¹	187	14	40	56	12.3	4.12	94	.282	.332	0	—	0	-4	-5	-2	-0.5
1991	Mil-A	1	3	.250	12	7	0	0	0	35	54	6	8	15	18.0	7.97	50	.355	.417	0	—	0	-15	-16	-1	-1.5
1993	Col-N	0	0	—	4	0	0	0	0	5²	16	4	5	3	33.4	22.24	21	.471	.538	0	.000	-0	-11	-11	-0	-1.0
Total	8	24	29	.453	121	59	6	2	0	482	563	61	128	195	13.1	4.72	84	.290	.337	0	.000	-1	-40	-41	-5	-4.3

● **KEVIN KOBEL** Kobel, Kevin Richard b: 10/2/53, Buffalo, N.Y. BR/TL, 6'1", 195 lbs. Deb: 9/8/73

YEAR	TM/L	W	L	PCT	G	GS	CG	SH	SV	IP	H	HR	BB	SO	RAT	ERA	ERA+	OAV	OOB	BH	AVG	PB	PR	/A	PD	TPI
1973	Mil-A	0	1	.000	2	1	0	0	0	8¹	9	2	8	4	18.4	8.64	44	.273	.415	0	—	0	-4	-5	-0	-0.4
1974	Mil-A	6	14	.300	34	24	3	2	0	169¹	166	16	54	74	11.8	3.99	91	.258	.317	0	—	0	-7	-7	1	-0.7
1976	Mil-A	0	1	.000	3	0	0	0	0	3	6	3	1	1	22.5	11.25	31	.375	.500	0	—	0	-3	-3	-0	-0.7
1978	NY-N	5	6	.455	32	11	1	0	0	108¹	95	9	30	51	10.6	2.91	120	.239	.295	4	.160	-0	8	7	-1	0.6
1979	NY-N	6	8	.429	30	21	1	1	0	161²	169	14	46	67	12.1	3.51	104	.274	.328	9	.196	-0	4	2	0	0.3
1980	NY-N	1	4	.200	14	7	0	0	0	24¹	36	5	11	8	17.4	7.03	51	.353	.416	0	.000	-0	-9	-9	-0	-1.7
Total	6	18	34	.346	115	64	5	3	0	476	481	49	152	205	12.1	3.88	93	.266	.326	13	.178	0	-12	-15	0	-2.6

● **ALAN KOCH** Koch, Alan Goodman b: 3/25/38, Decatur, Ala. BR/TR, 6'4", 195 lbs. Deb: 7/26/63

YEAR	TM/L	W	L	PCT	G	GS	CG	SH	SV	IP	H	HR	BB	SO	RAT	ERA	ERA+	OAV	OOB	BH	AVG	PB	PR	/A	PD	TPI
1963	Det-A	1	1	.500	7	1	0	0	0	10	21	3	9	5	27.0	10.80	35	.467	.564	2	.667	1	-8	-8	0	-1.2
1964	Det-A	0	0	—	3	0	0	0	0	4	6	1	3	1	20.3	6.75	54	.375	.474	0	—	0	-1	-1	-0	0.0
	Was-A	3	10	.231	32	14	1	0	0	114	110	18	43	67	12.3	4.89	76	.253	.325	8	.250	2	-16	-15	-2	-1.6
	Yr	3	10	.231	35	14	1	0	0	118	116	19	46	68	12.6	4.96	75	.258	.331	8	.250	2	-17	-17	-2	-1.6
Total	2	4	11	.267	42	15	1	0	0	128	137	22	55	73	13.8	5.41	68	.277	.354	10	.286	3	-25	-24	-2	-2.8

● **DICK KOECHER** Koecher, Richard Finlay "Highpockets" b: 3/30/26, Philadelphia, Pa. BL/TL, 6'5", 196 lbs. Deb: 9/29/46

YEAR	TM/L	W	L	PCT	G	GS	CG	SH	SV	IP	H	HR	BB	SO	RAT	ERA	ERA+	OAV	OOB	BH	AVG	PB	PR	/A	PD	TPI
1946	Phi-N	0	1	.000	1	1	0	0	0	2²	7	0	1	2	27.0	10.13	34	.467	.500	0	.000	-0	-2	-2	-0	-0.5
1947	Phi-N	0	2	.000	3	2	1	0	0	17	20	1	10	4	16.4	4.76	84	.299	.397	0	.000	-1	-1	-1	-0	-0.2
1948	Phi-N	0	0	—	3	0	0	0	0	6	4	0	3	2	10.5	3.00	132	.235	.350	0	—	0	1	1	-0	0.1
Total	3	0	3	.000	7	3	1	0	0	25²	31	1	14	8	16.1	4.91	80	.313	.404	0	.000	-1	-3	-3	-0	-0.6

● **MARK KOENIG** Koenig, Mark Anthony b: 7/19/04, San Francisco, Cal. d: 4/22/93, Willows, Cal. BB/TR, 6', 180 lbs. Deb: 9/8/25 ◆

YEAR	TM/L	W	L	PCT	G	GS	CG	SH	SV	IP	H	HR	BB	SO	RAT	ERA	ERA+	OAV	OOB	BH	AVG	PB	PR	/A	PD	TPI
1930	Det-A	0	1	.000	2	1	0	0	0	9	11	0	8	6	20.0	10.00	48	.314	.455	64	.240	0	-5	-5	-0	-0.4
1931	Det-A	0	0	—	3	0	0	0	0	7	7	0	11	3	23.1	6.43	71	.280	.500	92	.253	0	-2	-1	0	0.0
Total	2	0	1	.000	5	1	0	0	0	16	18	0	19	9	21.4	8.44	56	.300	.475	1190	.279	0	-7	-7	-0	-0.4

● **WILL KOENIGSMARK** Koenigsmark, William Thomas b: 2/27/1896, Waterloo, Ill. d: 7/1/72, Waterloo, Ill. BR/TR, 6'4", 180 lbs. Deb: 9/10/19

YEAR	TM/L	W	L	PCT	G	GS	CG	SH	SV	IP	H	HR	BB	SO	RAT	ERA	ERA+	OAV	OOB	BH	AVG	PB	PR	/A	PD	TPI
1919	StL-N	0	0	—	1	0	0	0	0	1	1	0	2	0	27.0	∞		1.000	1.000	0	—	0	-2	-2	-0	-0.2

● **ELMER KOESTNER** Koestner, Elmer Joseph "Bob" b: 11/30/1885, Piper City, Ill. d: 10/27/59, Fairbury, Ill. BR/TR, 6'1.5", 175 lbs. Deb: 4/23/10

YEAR	TM/L	W	L	PCT	G	GS	CG	SH	SV	IP	H	HR	BB	SO	RAT	ERA	ERA+	OAV	OOB	BH	AVG	PB	PR	/A	PD	TPI
1910	Cle-A	5	10	.333	27	13	8	1	2	145	145	0	63	44	13.3	3.04	85	.282	.367	15	.313	-2	-8	-7	-2	-0.7
1914	Chi-N	0	0	—	4	0	0	0	0	6¹	6	0	4	6	14.2	2.84	98	.261	.370	0	.000	-0	-0	-0	-0	0.0
	Cin-N	0	0	—	5	1	0	0	0	18¹	18	0	9	6	13.3	4.42	66	.265	.351	2	.400	1	-3	-3	0	0.1
	Yr	0	0	—	9	1	0	0	0	24²	24	0	13	12	13.5	4.01	72	.264	.356	2	.333	1	-3	-3	0	0.1
Total	2	5	10	.333	36	14	8	1	2	169²	169	0	76	56	13.3	3.18	83	.279	.365	17	.315	3	-12	-10	-2	-0.6

YEAR	TM/L	W	L	PCT	G	GS	CG	SH	SV	IP	H	HR	BB	SO	RAT	ERA	ERA+	OAV	OOB	BH	AVG	PB	PR	/A	PD	TPI

● JOE KOHLMAN
Kohlman, Joseph James "Blackie" b: 1/28/13, Philadelphia, Pa. d: 3/16/74, Philadelphia, Pa. BR/TR, 6', 160 lbs. Deb: 9/26/37

YEAR	TM/L	W	L	PCT	G	GS	CG	SH	SV	IP	H	HR	BB	SO	RAT	ERA	ERA+	OAV	OOB	BH	AVG	PB	PR	/A	PD	TPI
1937	Was-A	1	0	1.000	2	1	0	0	0	13	15	0	3	3	12.5	4.15	107	.283	.321	1	.200	-0	1	0	-0	0.0
1938	Was-A	0	0	—	7	0	0	0	0	14¹	12	1	11	5	14.4	6.28	72	.240	.377	0	.000	-0	-2	-3	0	0.0
Total	2	1	0	1.000	9	1	1	0	0	27¹	27	1	14	8	13.5	5.27	85	.262	.350	1	.125	-1	-2	-2	0	0.0

● EDDIE KOLB
Kolb, Edward William b: 7/20/1880, Cincinnati, Ohio BR/TR, Deb: 10/15/1899

YEAR	TM/L	W	L	PCT	G	GS	CG	SH	SV	IP	H	HR	BB	SO	RAT	ERA	ERA+	OAV	OOB	BH	AVG	PB	PR	/A	PD	TPI
1899	Cle-N	0	1	.000	1	1	1	0	0	8	18	0	5	1	27.0	10.13	36	.439	.511	1	.250	-0	-6	-6	-1	-0.5

● RAY KOLP
Kolp, Raymond Carl "Jockey" b: 10/1/1894, New Berlin, Ohio d: 7/29/67, New Orleans, La. BR/TR, 5'10.5", 187 lbs. Deb: 4/16/21

YEAR	TM/L	W	L	PCT	G	GS	CG	SH	SV	IP	H	HR	BB	SO	RAT	ERA	ERA+	OAV	OOB	BH	AVG	PB	PR	/A	PD	TPI
1921	StL-A	8	7	.533	37	18	5	1	0	166²	208	13	51	43	14.0	4.97	90	.314	.363	7	.127	-5	-13	-9	1	-1.1
1922	StL-A	14	4	.778	32	18	9	1	0	169²	199	10	36	54	12.7	3.93	106	.292	.332	17	.298	5	2	4	-4	0.4
1923	StL-A	5	12	.294	34	17	11	1	1	171¹	178	11	54	44	12.5	3.89	107	.273	.335	6	.111	-4	2	5	-2	-0.1
1924	StL-A	5	7	.417	25	12	5	1	0	96²	131	4	25	29	14.9	5.68	79	.329	.375	6	.200	-0	-16	-13	-1	-1.4
1927	Cin-N	3	3	.500	24	5	2	1	3	82¹	86	5	29	28	12.7	3.06	124	.278	.342	6	.200	-0	8	7	0	0.5
1928	Cin-N	13	10	.565	44	24	12	1	3	209	219	9	55	61	12.0	3.19	124	.280	.330	15	.214	3	19	18	1	2.2
1929	Cin-N	8	10	.444	30	16	4	1	0	145¹	151	8	39	27	11.8	4.03	113	.278	.328	8	.163	-2	11	9	1	0.8
1930	Cin-N	7	12	.368	37	19	5	2	3	168¹	180	10	34	40	11.4	4.22	114	.278	.314	12	.245	-1	14	11	-1	1.1
1931	Cin-N	4	9	.308	30	10	2	0	1	107	144	8	39	24	15.7	4.96	75	.332	.392	4	.125	-1	-13	-15	-1	-1.8
1932	Cin-N	6	10	.375	32	19	7	2	1	159²	176	13	27	42	11.6	3.89	99	.280	.313	9	.184	-1	-0	-1	-2	-0.4
1933	Cin-N	6	9	.400	30	14	4	0	1	150¹	168	7	23	28	11.5	3.53	96	.290	.318	7	.156	-1	-3	-2	1	-0.1
1934	Cin-N	0	2	.000	28	2	0	0	3	61²	78	1	12	19	13.4	4.52	90	.312	.348	1	.083	-1	-3	-3	2	-0.1
Total	12	79	95	.454	383	174	66	11	18	1688	1918	98	424	439	12.7	4.08	102	.292	.338	98	.184	-7	8	13	-6	-0.1

● HAL KOLSTAD
Kolstad, Harold Everette b: 6/1/35, Rice Lake, Wis. BR/TR, 5'9", 190 lbs. Deb: 4/22/62

YEAR	TM/L	W	L	PCT	G	GS	CG	SH	SV	IP	H	HR	BB	SO	RAT	ERA	ERA+	OAV	OOB	BH	AVG	PB	PR	/A	PD	TPI
1962	Bos-A	0	2	.000	27	2	0	0	2	61¹	65	11	35	36	15.0	5.43	76	.269	.366	1	.056	-2	-10	-9	-0	-0.5
1963	Bos-A	0	2	.000	7	0	0	0	0	11	16	4	6	6	19.6	13.09	29	.340	.436	0	.000	-0	-12	-11	-0	-1.7
Total	2	0	4	.000	34	2	0	0	2	72¹	81	15	41	42	15.7	6.59	62	.280	.377	1	.053	-2	-22	-20	0	-2.2

● ED KONETCHY
Konetchy, Edward Joseph "Big Ed" b: 9/3/1885, LaCrosse, Wis. d: 5/27/47, Ft.Worth, Tex. BR/TR, 6'2.5", 195 lbs. Deb: 6/29/07 ◆

YEAR	TM/L	W	L	PCT	G	GS	CG	SH	SV	IP	H	HR	BB	SO	RAT	ERA	ERA+	OAV	OOB	BH	AVG	PB	PR	/A	PD	TPI
1910	StL-N	0	0	—	1	0	0	0	0	4	4	0	1	0	11.3	4.50	66	.267	.313	157	.302	0	-1	-1	-0	0.0
1913	StL-N	1	0	1.000	1	0	0	0	0	4²	1	0	3	6	9.6	—	.071	.278	139	.276	0	2	2	-0	0.4
1918	Bos-N	0	1	.000	1	1	1	0	0	8	14	1	3	3	18.0	6.75	40	.378	.410	103	.236	0	-4	-4	-1	-0.4
Total	3	1	1	.500	3	1	1	0	0	16²	19	1	7	6	14.0	4.32	67	.288	.356	2150	.281	1	-3	-3	-1	0.0

● DOUG KONIECZNY
Konieczny, Douglas James b: 9/27/51, Detroit, Mich. BR/TR, 6'4", 220 lbs. Deb: 9/11/73

YEAR	TM/L	W	L	PCT	G	GS	CG	SH	SV	IP	H	HR	BB	SO	RAT	ERA	ERA+	OAV	OOB	BH	AVG	PB	PR	/A	PD	TPI
1973	Hou-N	0	1	.000	2	2	0	0	0	13	12	0	4	6	11.1	5.54	66	.279	.340	0	.000	-0	-3	-3	-0	-0.2
1974	Hou-N	0	3	.000	6	3	0	0	0	16	18	0	12	8	18.0	7.88	44	.290	.421	0	.000	-1	-8	-8	-0	-1.3
1975	Hou-N	6	13	.316	32	29	4	1	0	171	184	15	87	89	14.3	4.47	75	.280	.365	8	.160	1	-16	-21	-2	-2.2
1977	Hou-N	1	1	.500	4	4	0	0	0	21	26	1	8	7	15.0	6.00	58	.302	.368	1	.143	-0	-5	-6	-0	-0.5
Total	4	7	18	.280	44	38	4	1	0	221	240	16	111	110	14.5	4.93	69	.283	.368	9	.138	-0	-31	-37	-2	-4.2

● ALEX KONIKOWSKI
Konikowski, Alexander James "Whitey" b: 6/8/28, Throop, Pa. BR/TR, 6'1", 187 lbs. Deb: 6/16/48

YEAR	TM/L	W	L	PCT	G	GS	CG	SH	SV	IP	H	HR	BB	SO	RAT	ERA	ERA+	OAV	OOB	BH	AVG	PB	PR	/A	PD	TPI
1948	NY-N	2	3	.400	22	1	0	0	1	33¹	46	7	17	9	17.0	7.56	52	.346	.420	0	.000	0	-13	-13	1	-1.7
1951	*NY-N	0	0	—	3	0	0	0	0	4	2	0	0	5	4.5	0.00	—	.154	.154	0	—	0	2	2	0	0.0
1954	NY-N	0	0	—	10	0	0	0	0	12	10	1	12	6	16.5	7.50	54	.244	.415	0	.000	0	-5	-5	-0	0.0
Total	3	2	3	.400	35	1	0	0	1	49¹	58	8	29	20	15.9	6.93	57	.310	.403	0	.000	0	-16	-16	0	-1.7

● JIM KONSTANTY
Konstanty, Casimir James b: 3/2/17, Strykersville, N.Y. d: 6/11/76, Oneonta, N.Y. BR/TR, 6'1.5", 202 lbs. Deb: 6/18/44

YEAR	TM/L	W	L	PCT	G	GS	CG	SH	SV	IP	H	HR	BB	SO	RAT	ERA	ERA+	OAV	OOB	BH	AVG	PB	PR	/A	PD	TPI
1944	Cin-N	6	4	.600	20	12	5	1	0	112²	113	11	33	19	11.7	2.80	125	.266	.320	10	.294	2	10	9	1	1.0
1946	Bos-N	0	1	.000	10	1	0	0	0	15¹	17	2	7	9	14.1	5.28	65	.283	.358	0	.000	-0	-3	-3	-1	-0.1
1948	Phi-N	1	0	1.000	6	0	0	0	2	9²	7	0	2	7	8.4	0.93	424	.233	.281	0	.000	-0	3	3	-0	0.4
1949	Phi-N	9	5	.643	53	0	0	0	7	97	98	9	29	43	11.9	3.25	121	.280	.337	3	.176	-0	9	8	1	1.2
1950	*Phi-N★	16	7	.696	74	0	0	0	22	152	108	11	50	56	9.4	2.66	152	.205	.274	4	.108	-2	25	23	-1	3.6
1951	Phi-N	4	11	.267	58	5	0	0	9	115²	127	9	31	27	12.3	4.05	95	.282	.328	3	.158	-0	-1	-0	-0	-1.5
1952	Phi-N	5	3	.625	42	2	2	1	6	80	87	9	21	16	12.1	3.94	93	.274	.319	1	.071	-0	-2	-3	-0	-0.3
1953	Phi-N	14	10	.583	48	19	7	0	5	170²	198	18	42	45	12.8	4.43	95	.290	.334	11	.220	-1	-3	-4	0	-0.5
1954	Phi-N	2	3	.400	33	1	0	0	3	50¹	62	7	12	11	13.2	3.75	108	.316	.356	0	.000	-2	2	2	0	0.0
	NY-A	1	1	.500	9	0	0	0	2	18¹	11	0	6	3	8.3	0.98	350	.183	.258	0	.000	-0	6	5	0	0.6
1955	NY-A	7	2	.778	45	0	0	0	11	73²	68	5	24	19	11.2	2.32	161	.247	.308	1	.125	-0	13	12	-0	1.7
1956	NY-A	0	0	—	8	0	0	0	2	11	15	3	6	6	17.2	4.91	79	.319	.396	0	.000	-0	-1	-1	-0	-0.1
	StL-N	1	1	.500	27	0	0	0	5	39¹	46	4	7	7	11.9	4.58	83	.301	.327	0	—	-0	-4	-3	-1	-0.3
Total	11	66	48	.579	433	36	14	2	74	945²	957	88	269	268	11.7	3.46	112	.268	.320	33	.163	-5	54	44	2	7.0

● DENNIS KONUSZEWSKI
Konuszewski, Dennis John b: 2/4/71, Bridgeport, Mich. BR/TR, 6'3", 210 lbs. Deb: 8/4/95

YEAR	TM/L	W	L	PCT	G	GS	CG	SH	SV	IP	H	HR	BB	SO	RAT	ERA	ERA+	OAV	OOB	BH	AVG	PB	PR	/A	PD	TPI
1995	Pit-N	0	0	—	1	0	0	0	0	0¹	3	0	1	0	108.0	54.00	9	1.000	1.000	0	—	0	-2	-2	0	0.0

● ERNIE KOOB
Koob, Ernest Gerald b: 9/11/1892, Keeler, Mich. d: 11/12/41, Lemay, Mo. BL/TL, 5'10", 160 lbs. Deb: 6/23/15

YEAR	TM/L	W	L	PCT	G	GS	CG	SH	SV	IP	H	HR	BB	SO	RAT	ERA	ERA+	OAV	OOB	BH	AVG	PB	PR	/A	PD	TPI
1915	StL-A	4	5	.444	28	13	6	0	1	133²	119	2	50	37	12.1	2.36	122	.254	.339	5	.135	-1	9	8	-2	0.2
1916	StL-A	11	8	.579	33	20	10	2	2	166²	153	1	56	26	11.6	2.54	108	.252	.321	0	.000	-1	5	4	-4	0.0
1917	StL-A	6	14	.300	39	18	3	1	1	133²	139	1	57	47	13.6	3.91	67	.280	.361	4	.114	-1	-18	-19	1	-2.9
1919	StL-A	2	3	.400	25	4	0	0	0	66	77	3	23	11	13.9	4.64	72	.296	.358	0	.000	-2	-10	-10	0	-0.9
Total	4	23	30	.434	125	55	19	3	4	500	488	7	186	121	12.6	3.13	90	.266	.342	9	.070	-5	-15	-18	-4	-3.6

● CAL KOONCE
Koonce, Calvin Lee b: 11/18/40, Fayetteville, N.C. d: 10/28/93, Winston-Salem, N.C. BR/TR, 6'1", 185 lbs. Deb: 4/14/62

YEAR	TM/L	W	L	PCT	G	GS	CG	SH	SV	IP	H	HR	BB	SO	RAT	ERA	ERA+	OAV	OOB	BH	AVG	PB	PR	/A	PD	TPI
1962	Chi-N	10	10	.500	35	30	3	1	0	190²	200	17	86	84	13.8	3.97	105	.271	.353	6	.094	-4	-0	4	-1	-0.1
1963	Chi-N	2	6	.250	21	13	0	0	0	72²	75	9	32	44	13.5	4.58	77	.273	.353	2	.105	-0	-10	-9	-1	-0.8
1964	Chi-N	3	0	1.000	6	2	0	0	0	31	30	1	7	17	10.7	2.03	183	.254	.296	0	.000	-1	5	6	2	0.6
1965	Chi-N	7	9	.438	38	23	1	1	0	173	181	17	52	88	12.4	3.69	100	.271	.329	5	.102	-0	-3	-0	-0	-0.1
1966	Chi-N	5	5	.500	45	5	0	0	2	108²	113	13	35	65	12.3	3.81	97	.268	.325	3	.130	0	-2	-1	0	-0.0
1967	Chi-N	2	2	.500	34	0	0	0	2	51	52	2	21	28	13.1	4.59	77	.268	.343	0	.000	-1	-7	-6	1	-0.5
	NY-N	3	3	.500	11	6	2	1	0	45	45	2	7	24	10.4	2.80	121	.259	.287	2	.154	-0	3	3	-1	0.5
	Yr	5	5	.500	45	6	2	1	2	96	97	4	28	52	11.7	3.75	94	.262	.314	2	.100	-1	-4	-3	-2	0.0
1968	NY-N	6	4	.600	55	2	0	0	11	97	80	4	32	50	10.5	2.41	125	.235	.303	1	.235	-0	6	7	-1	0.8
1969	*NY-N	6	3	.667	40	0	0	0	7	83	85	8	42	48	14.1	4.99	73	.269	.360	4	.235	-1	-13	-12	1	-1.3
1970	NY-N	0	3	.000	22	0	0	0	4	22	25	2	14	10	16.4	3.27	123	.301	.408	0	.000	-0	2	2	0	0.1
	Bos-A	3	4	.429	23	6	1	0	2	76¹	64	7	29	37	11.3	3.54	112	.231	.311	2	.095	-0	2	2	0	0.5
1971	Bos-A	0	1	.000	13	1	0	0	0	21	22	3	11	9	14.1	5.57	66	.278	.367	0	.000	-0	-5	-4	1	-0.1
Total	10	47	49	.490	334	90	9	3	24	971¹	972	85	368	504	12.6	3.78	98	.264	.335	24	.100	-6	-23	-9	-9	-0.2

● JERRY KOOSMAN
Koosman, Jerome Martin b: 12/23/42, Appleton, Minn. BR/TL, 6'2", 208 lbs. Deb: 4/14/67

YEAR	TM/L	W	L	PCT	G	GS	CG	SH	SV	IP	H	HR	BB	SO	RAT	ERA	ERA+	OAV	OOB	BH	AVG	PB	PR	/A	PD	TPI
1967	NY-N	0	2	.000	9	3	0	0	0	22¹	22	3	19	11	16.5	6.04	56	.259	.394	0	.000	0	-7	-7	-0	-0.5
1968	NY-N★	19	12	.613	35	34	17	7	0	263²	221	16	69	178	10.2	2.08	145	.228	.285	7	.077	-3	26	27	-1	3.0
1969	*NY-N★	17	9	.654	32	32	16	6	0	241	187	14	68	180	9.7	2.28	160	.216	.277	4	.048	-7	35	37	-1	3.1
1970	NY-N	12	7	.632	30	29	5	1	0	212	189	22	71	118	11.1	3.14	128	.237	.300	6	.086	-2	21	23	-3	1.2
1971	NY-N	6	11	.353	26	24	4	0	0	165²	160	12	51	96	11.5	3.04	112	.256	.313	8	.160	-0	8	7	-1	0.6
1972	NY-N	11	12	.478	34	34	4	1	0	163	155	12	52	147	11.8	4.14	81	.250	.314	4	.085	-3	-12	-14	0	-2.2
1973	*NY-N	14	15	.483	35	35	12	3	0	263	234	18	76	156	10.7	2.84	127	.242	.300	4	.103	-3	24	23	-1	2.7
1974	NY-N	15	11	.577	35	35	6	2	0	265	258	16	85	188	11.9	3.36	106	.257	.320	16	.186	2	8	6	-0	0.8
1975	NY-N	14	13	.519	36	34	11	4	2	239²	234	19	98	173	12.6	3.42	101	.261	.333	14	.261	3	7	5	-1	0.5
1976	NY-N	21	10	.677	34	32	17	3	0	247¹	205	19	66	200	9.9	2.69	122	.226	.279	17	.215	3	22	17	0	2.4
1977	NY-N	8	20	.286	32	32	6	1	0	226²	195	17	81	192	11.1	3.49	107	.232	.302	8	.111	-0	10	6	-1	0.2

YEAR	TM/L	W	L	PCT	G	GS	CG	SH	SV	IP	H	HR	BB	SO	RAT	ERA	ERA+	OAV	OOB	BH	AVG	PB	PR	/A	PD	TPI
1978	NY-N	3	15	.167	38	32	3	0	2	235¹	221	17	84	160	12.0	3.75	93	.255	.327	6	.086	-3	-4	-7	2	-0.7
1979	Min-A	20	13	.606	37	36	10	2	0	263²	268	19	83	157	12.1	3.38	130	.268	.326	0	—	0	24	29	2	3.6
1980	Min-A	16	13	.552	38	34	8	0	2	243¹	252	24	69	149	12.1	4.03	108	.272	.326	0	—	0	0	9	1	0.8
1981	Min-A	3	9	.250	19	13	2	1	5	94¹	98	8	34	55	12.6	4.20	94	.272	.335	0	—	0	-6	-3	0	-0.4
	Chi-A	1	4	.200	8	3	1	0	0	27	27	2	7	21	11.3	3.33	107	.260	.306	0	—	0	1	1	-0	0.1
	Yr	4	13	.235	27	16	3	1	5	121¹	125	10	41	76	12.3	4.01	96	.267	.325	0	—	0	-5	-2	-0	-0.3
1982	Chi-A	11	7	.611	42	19	3	1	3	173¹	194	9	38	88	12.1	3.84	105	.287	.327	0	—	0	4	4	0	0.4
1983	*Chi-A	11	7	.611	37	24	2	1	2	169²	176	19	53	90	12.5	4.77	88	.266	.326	0	—	0	-13	-11	0	-1.1
1984	Phi-N	14	15	.483	36	34	3	1	0	224	232	8	60	137	11.9	3.25	112	.267	.317	8	.108	-3	8	9	-1	0.8
1985	Phi-N	6	4	.600	19	18	3	1	0	99¹	107	14	34	60	13.0	4.62	80	.276	.340	3	.088	-7	-11	-10	-0	-1.2
Total	19	222	209	.515	612	527	140	33	17	3839¹	3635	290	1198	2556	11.5	3.36	110	.252	.313	109	.119	-22	145	143	-6	13.1

● HOWIE KOPLITZ
Koplitz, Howard Dean b: 5/4/38, Oshkosh, Wis. BR/TR, 5'11", 195 lbs. Deb: 9/8/61

YEAR	TM/L	W	L	PCT	G	GS	CG	SH	SV	IP	H	HR	BB	SO	RAT	ERA	ERA+	OAV	OOB	BH	AVG	PB	PR	/A	PD	TPI
1961	Det-A	2	0	1.000	4	1	0	0	0	12	16	0	8	9	18.0	2.25	182	.327	.421	0	.000	-1	2	2	-0	0.3
1962	Det-A	3	0	1.000	10	6	1	0	0	37²	54	5	10	10	15.3	5.26	77	.342	.381	3	.231	1	-5	-5	-0	-0.3
1964	Was-A	0	0	—	6	1	0	0	0	17	20	3	13	9	17.5	4.76	78	.290	.402	0	.000	-0	-2	-2	0	-0.0
1965	Was-A	4	7	.364	33	11	0	0	1	106²	97	11	48	59	12.5	4.05	86	.249	.336	3	.100	-1	-7	-7	1	-0.7
1966	Was-A	0	0	—	1	0	0	0	0	2	0	0	1	4	4.5	0.00	—	.000	.200	0	—	0	1	1	0	0.1
Total	5	9	7	.563	54	19	2	0	1	175¹	187	19	80	87	13.4	4.27	87	.280	.359	6	.118	-1	-11	-11	1	-0.7

● GEORGE KORINCE
Korince, George Eugene "Moose" b: 1/10/46, Ottawa, Ont., Canada BR/TR, 6'3", 210 lbs. Deb: 9/10/66

YEAR	TM/L	W	L	PCT	G	GS	CG	SH	SV	IP	H	HR	BB	SO	RAT	ERA	ERA+	OAV	OOB	BH	AVG	PB	PR	/A	PD	TPI
1966	Det-A	0	0	—	2	0	0	0	0	3	1	0	3	2	15.0	0.00	—	.091	.333	0	—	0	1	1	-0	0.0
1967	Det-A	1	0	1.000	9	0	0	0	0	14	10	1	11	11	13.5	5.14	63	.204	.350	0	.000	-0	-3	-3	0	-0.2
Total	2	1	0	1.000	11	0	0	0	0	17	11	1	14	13	13.8	4.24	78	.183	.347	0	.000	-0	-2	-2	-0	-0.2

● JIM KORWAN
Korwan, James "Long Jim" b: 3/4/1874, Brooklyn, N.Y. d: 7/24/1899, Brooklyn, N.Y. BR/TR, 6'1", 181 lbs. Deb: 4/24/1894

YEAR	TM/L	W	L	PCT	G	GS	CG	SH	SV	IP	H	HR	BB	SO	RAT	ERA	ERA+	OAV	OOB	BH	AVG	PB	PR	/A	PD	TPI
1894	Bro-N	0	0	—	1	0	0	0	0	5	9	1	5	2	25.2	14.40	34	.391	.500	1	.000	-0	-5	-5	0	-0.1
1897	Chi-N	1	2	.333	5	4	3	0	0	34	47	1	28	12	20.1	5.82	77	.324	.437	0	.000	-2	-6	-5	2	-0.4
Total	2	1	2	.333	6	4	3	0	0	39	56	2	33	14	20.8	6.92	66	.333	.446	1	.000	-2	-11	-10	2	-0.4

● BILL KOSKI
Koski, William John "T-Bone" b: 2/6/32, Madera, Cal. BR/TR, 6'4", 185 lbs. Deb: 4/28/51

YEAR	TM/L	W	L	PCT	G	GS	CG	SH	SV	IP	H	HR	BB	SO	RAT	ERA	ERA+	OAV	OOB	BH	AVG	PB	PR	/A	PD	TPI
1951	Pit-N	0	1	.000	13	1	0	0	0	27	26	1	28	6	18.0	6.67	63	.257	.419	0	.000	-1	-8	-7	-1	-0.4

● DAVE KOSLO
Koslo, George Bernard (b: George Bernard Koslowski) b: 3/31/20, Menasha, Wis. d: 12/1/75, Menasha, Wis. BL/TL, 5'11", 180 lbs. Deb: 9/12/41

YEAR	TM/L	W	L	PCT	G	GS	CG	SH	SV	IP	H	HR	BB	SO	RAT	ERA	ERA+	OAV	OOB	BH	AVG	PB	PR	/A	PD	TPI
1941	NY-N	1	2	.333	4	3	2	0	0	23²	17	0	12	10	10.3	1.90	194	.202	.287	1	.111	-1	5	5	-1	0.5
1942	NY-N	3	6	.333	19	11	3	1	0	78	79	7	32	42	12.9	5.08	66	.261	.333	1	.120	-3	-15	-15	-1	-1.7
1946	NY-N	14	19	.424	40	35	17	3	1	265¹	251	15	101	121	12.1	3.63	95	.249	.320	11	.125	-3	-6	-6	2	-0.8
1947	NY-N	15	10	.600	39	31	10	3	0	217¹	223	23	82	86	12.8	4.39	93	.259	.326	10	.128	-1	-8	-8	-1	-1.0
1948	NY-N	8	10	.444	35	18	5	3	3	149	168	7	62	58	14.0	3.87	102	.290	.359	5	.114	-1	2	1	-1	-0.1
1949	NY-N	11	14	.440	38	23	15	0	4	212	193	13	43	64	**10.0**	**2.50**	159	.239	**.278**	10	.145	1	**36**	35	0	4.2
1950	NY-N	13	15	.464	40	22	7	1	3	186²	190	18	68	56	12.7	3.91	105	.268	.337	8	.123	-1	5	4	-0	0.4
1951	*NY-N	10	9	.526	39	16	5	2	3	149²	153	18	45	54	12.0	3.31	118	.258	.313	5	.100	1	11	10	2	1.3
1952	NY-N	10	7	.588	41	17	8	2	5	166¹	154	17	47	67	11.0	3.19	116	.242	.296	2	.037	-4	10	9	1	0.7
1953	NY-N	6	12	.333	37	12	2	0	2	111²	135	8	36	36	13.9	4.76	90	.296	.349	1	.033	-3	-6	-6	1	-1.1
1954	Bal-A	0	1	.000	3	1	0	0	0	14¹	20	1	3	3	14.4	3.14	114	.333	.365	0	.000	0	1	1	-0	0.0
	Mil-N	1	1	.500	12	0	0	0	0	17¹	13	0	9	7	11.4	3.12	120	.228	.333	0	.000	-1	1	1	-0	0.1
1955	Mil-N	0	1	.000	1	0	0	0	0	1	1	0	0	0	—	∞	—	1.000	1.000	0	—	-1	-0	-0	-0	-0.1
Total	12	92	107	.462	348	189	74	15	22	1591¹	1597	121	538	606	12.2	3.68	105	.260	.321	56	.109	-15	34	32	2	2.4

● JOE KOSTAL
Kostal, Joseph William "Cudgey" b: 3/17/1876, Chicago, Ill. d: 10/17/33, Guelph, Ont., Can. BR/TR, 5'6", 130 lbs. Deb: 7/14/1896

YEAR	TM/L	W	L	PCT	G	GS	CG	SH	SV	IP	H	HR	BB	SO	RAT	ERA	ERA+	OAV	OOB	BH	AVG	PB	PR	/A	PD	TPI
1896	Lou-N	0	0	—	2	0	0	0	0	2	4	0	4	0	18.0	0.00	—	.400	.400	0	—	0	1	1	-0	0.0

● SANDY KOUFAX
Koufax, Sanford (b: Sanford Braun) b: 12/30/35, Brooklyn, N.Y. BR/TL, 6'2", 210 lbs. Deb: 6/24/55 H

YEAR	TM/L	W	L	PCT	G	GS	CG	SH	SV	IP	H	HR	BB	SO	RAT	ERA	ERA+	OAV	OOB	BH	AVG	PB	PR	/A	PD	TPI
1955	Bro-N	2	2	.500	12	5	2	2	0	41²	33	2	28	30	13.4	3.02	134	.216	.341	0	.000	-2	5	5	-0	0.2
1956	Bro-N	2	4	.333	16	10	0	0	0	58²	66	10	29	30	14.6	4.91	81	.286	.365	2	.118	-0	-7	-6	-1	-0.7
1957	Bro-N	5	4	.556	34	13	2	0	0	104¹	83	14	51	122	11.7	3.88	107	.216	.311	0	.000	-0	3	3	-2	-0.3
1958	LA-N	11	11	.500	40	26	5	0	1	158²	132	19	105	131	13.5	4.48	91	**.220**	.337	6	.122	-2	-9	-7	-0	-1.1
1959	*LA-N	8	6	.571	35	23	6	1	2	153¹	136	23	92	173	13.4	4.05	104	.235	.340	6	.111	-1	-2	-3	-1	-0.2
1960	LA-N	8	13	.381	37	26	7	2	1	175	133	20	100	197	12.0	3.91	102	**.207**	.315	7	.123	-1	-3	-1	-1	-0.2
1961	LA-N★	18	13	.581	42	35	15	2	1	255²	212	27	96	**269**	10.9	3.52	123	**.222**	.295	5	.065	-5	15	23	-3	1.8
1962	LA-N☆	14	7	.667	28	26	11	2	1	184¹	134	13	57	216	**9.4**	**2.54**	143	**.197**	**.261**	6	.083	-3	29	22	-2	1.9
1963	*LA-N☆	**25**	5	.833	40	40	20	**11**	0	311	214	18	58	**306**	**8.0**	**1.88**	161	**.189**	**.230**	7	.064	-4	**49**	39	-4	3.0
1964	LA-N☆	19	5	**.792**	29	28	15	**7**	1	223	154	13	53	223	**8.4**	**1.74**	187	**.191**	**.241**	7	.095	-2	45	37	-4	3.5
1965	*LA-N★	**26**	8	**.765**	43	41	**27**	8	2	**335²**	216	26	71	**382**	**7.8**	**2.04**	160	**.179**	**.228**	20	.177	5	**56**	46	-2	5.0
1966	*LA-N★	**27**	9	.750	41	41	**27**	5	0	323	241	19	77	**317**	8.9	**1.73**	191	.205	.253	9	.076	-4	**67**	**56**	-4	5.4
Total	12	165	87	.655	397	314	137	40	9	2324¹	1754	204	817	2396	10.0	2.76	131	.205	.276	75	.097	-25	243	221	-25	18.5

● JOE KOUKALIK
Koukalik, Joseph b: 3/3/1880, Chicago, Ill. d: 12/27/45, Chicago, Ill. 5'8", 160 lbs. Deb: 9/1/04

YEAR	TM/L	W	L	PCT	G	GS	CG	SH	SV	IP	H	HR	BB	SO	RAT	ERA	ERA+	OAV	OOB	BH	AVG	PB	PR	/A	PD	TPI
1904	Bro-N	0	1	.000	1	1	1	0	0	8	10	1	4	1	15.8	1.13	244	.333	.412	0	.000	-0	1	1	-0	0.1

● LOU KOUPAL
Koupal, Louis Laddie b: 12/19/1898, Tabor, S.D. d: 12/8/61, San Gabriel, Cal. BR/TR, 5'11", 175 lbs. Deb: 4/17/25

YEAR	TM/L	W	L	PCT	G	GS	CG	SH	SV	IP	H	HR	BB	SO	RAT	ERA	ERA+	OAV	OOB	BH	AVG	PB	PR	/A	PD	TPI
1925	Pit-N	0	0	—	6	0	0	0	0	9	14	1	7	0	21.0	9.00	50	.378	.477	0	.000	-0	-5	-5	0	0.0
1926	Pit-N	0	2	.000	6	2	1	0	0	19²	22	0	8	7	14.2	3.20	123	.289	.365	1	.250	0	1	2	-0	0.2
1928	Bro-N	1	0	1.000	17	1	1	0	1	37¹	43	0	15	10	14.2	2.41	165	.303	.373	1	.111	-1	7	6	1	0.2
1929	Bro-N	0	1	.000	18	3	0	0	4	40¹	49	3	25	17	16.5	5.36	86	.308	.402	1	.071	-2	-3	-3	-1	-0.3
	Phi-N	5	5	.500	15	12	3	0	2	86²	106	5	29	18	14.2	4.78	109	.305	.362	4	.125	-2	-1	-1	-1	0.1
	Yr	5	6	.455	33	15	3	0	6	127	155	8	54	35	15.0	4.96	101	.306	.375	5	.109	-4	-3	-3	1	-0.2
1930	Phi-N	0	4	.000	13	4	1	0	0	36²	52	4	17	11	17.2	8.59	64	.344	.414	1	.083	-1	-15	-13	-1	-1.3
1937	StL-A	4	9	.308	26	13	6	0	0	105²	150	10	55	24	17.5	6.56	74	.339	.412	3	.094	-3	-23	-20	0	-2.3
Total	6	10	21	.323	101	35	12	0	7	335¹	436	23	156	87	16.0	5.58	86	.322	.394	11	.106	-9	-38	-29	-2	-3.4

● FABIAN KOWALIK
Kowalik, Fabian Lorenz b: 4/22/08, Falls City, Tex. d: 8/14/54, Karnes City, Tex. BR/TR, 5'11", 185 lbs. Deb: 9/4/32

YEAR	TM/L	W	L	PCT	G	GS	CG	SH	SV	IP	H	HR	BB	SO	RAT	ERA	ERA+	OAV	OOB	BH	AVG	PB	PR	/A	PD	TPI
1932	Chi-A	0	1	.000	2	1	0	0	0	10¹	16	2	4	2	18.3	6.97	62	.340	.404	5	.385	1	-3	-3	-0	-0.1
1935	*Chi-N	2	2	.500	20	2	1	0	1	55	60	2	19	20	12.9	4.42	89	.280	.339	3	.200	-0	-1	-1	0	-0.2
1936	Chi-N	0	2	.000	6	0	0	0	0	16	24	1	7	1	17.4	6.75	59	.358	.419	0	.000	-1	-5	-5	-0	-0.6
	Phi-N	1	5	.167	22	8	2	0	0	77	100	5	31	19	15.5	5.38	84	.308	.372	13	.228	-0	-12	-7	-2	-0.7
	Bos-N	0	1	.000	1	1	0	0	0	9	18	0	2	0	20.0	8.00	48	.419	.444	2	.400	1	-4	-4	-0	-0.3
	Yr	1	8	.111	29	9	2	0	0	102	142	6	40	20	16.1	5.82	75	.325	.382	15	.224	-0	-20	-16	-2	-1.6
Total	3	3	11	.214	51	12	4	0	1	167¹	218	10	63	42	15.3	5.43	78	.313	.373	23	.242	-1	-26	-22	-1	-1.9

● JOE KRAEMER
Kraemer, Joseph Wayne b: 9/10/64, Olympia, Wash. BL/TL, 6'2", 185 lbs. Deb: 8/22/89

YEAR	TM/L	W	L	PCT	G	GS	CG	SH	SV	IP	H	HR	BB	SO	RAT	ERA	ERA+	OAV	OOB	BH	AVG	PB	PR	/A	PD	TPI
1989	Chi-N	0	1	.000	1	1	0	0	0	3²	7	2	5	2	22.1	4.91	77	.368	.429	0	—	-1	-1	-0	-0	-0.1
1990	Chi-N	0	0	—	18	0	0	0	0	25	31	2	14	16	16.9	7.20	57	.310	.405	0	—	-0	-9	-9	0	-0.1
Total	2	0	1	.000	19	1	0	0	0	28²	38	2	16	21	17.6	6.91	58	.319	.409	0	.000	-1	-10	-9	0	-0.1

● JOE KRAKAUSKAS
Krakauskas, Joseph Victor Lawrence b: 3/28/15, Montreal, Que., Can d: 7/8/60, Hamilton, Ont., Can BL/TL, 6'1", 203 lbs. Deb: 9/9/37

YEAR	TM/L	W	L	PCT	G	GS	CG	SH	SV	IP	H	HR	BB	SO	RAT	ERA	ERA+	OAV	OOB	BH	AVG	PB	PR	/A	PD	TPI
1937	Was-A	4	1	.800	5	4	3	0	0	40	33	0	22	18	12.4	2.70	164	.226	.327	2	.125	-0	9	8	-1	0.7
1938	Was-A	7	5	.583	29	10	5	1	0	121¹	99	4	88	104	14.1	3.12	145	.220	.362	6	.182	1	23	19	-1	1.6
1939	Was-A	11	17	.393	39	29	12	0	1	217¹	230	13	114	110	14.3	4.60	95	.276	.364	16	.208	3	-1	-6	-2	-0.6
1940	Was-A	1	6	.143	32	10	2	0	0	109	137	7	73	68	17.3	6.44	65	.309	.406	8	.250	1	-25	-28	1	-1.4
1941	Cle-A	1	2	.333	12	5	0	0	0	41²	39	3	29	25	14.7	4.10	96	.245	.362	1	.077	-1	0	-1	0	-0.1
1942	Cle-A	0	0	—	3	0	0	0	0	7	7	1	4	2	14.1	3.86	89	.259	.355	0	.000	-0	-0	-1	0	0.0

YEAR	TM/L	W	L	PCT	G	GS	CG	SH	SV	IP	H	HR	BB	SO	RAT	ERA	ERA+	OAV	OOB	BH	AVG	PB	PR	/A	PD	TPI
1946	Cle-A	2	5	.286	29	5	0	0	1	47¹	60	2	25	20	16.2	5.51	60	.314	.394	0	.000	-1	-11	-12	1	-1.7
Total	7	26	36	.419	149	63	22	1	4	583²	605	30	355	347	14.9	4.53	93	.269	.369	33	.180	2	-4	-20	-1	-1.5

● JACK KRALICK
Kralick, John Francis b: 6/1/35, Youngstown, Ohio BL/TL, 6'2", 180 lbs. Deb: 4/15/59

YEAR	TM/L	W	L	PCT	G	GS	CG	SH	SV	IP	H	HR	BB	SO	RAT	ERA	ERA+	OAV	OOB	BH	AVG	PB	PR	/A	PD	TPI
1959	Was-A	0	0	—	6	0	0	0	0	12¹	13	5	6	7	13.9	6.57	60	.289	.373	0	.000	-0	-4	-4	1	0.1
1960	Was-A	8	6	.571	35	18	7	2	1	151	139	12	45	71	11.2	3.04	128	.245	.305	5	.122	-1	14	14	-1	1.1
1961	Min-A	13	11	.542	33	33	11	2	0	242	257	21	64	137	12.0	3.61	118	.274	.323	11	.151	-2	11	17	2	1.5
1962	Min-A	12	11	.522	39	37	7	1	0	242²	239	30	61	139	11.2	3.86	106	.258	.305	18	.202	3	3	6	1	0.9
1963	Min-A	1	4	.200	5	5	1	1	0	25²	28	2	8	13	13.0	3.86	94	.280	.339	1	.167	1	-1	-1	0	0.0
	Cle-A	13	9	.591	28	27	10	3	0	197¹	187	19	41	116	10.4	2.92	124	.249	.288	11	.183	1	16	15	-1	1.7
	Yr	14	13	.519	33	32	11	4	0	223	215	21	49	129	10.7	3.03	120	.252	.293	12	.182	2	15	15	-1	1.7
1964	Cle-A☆	12	7	.632	30	29	8	3	0	190²	196	17	51	119	12.1	3.21	112	.267	.322	10	.156	-1	9	8	0	0.7
1965	Cle-A	5	11	.313	30	16	1	0	0	86	106	9	21	34	13.5	4.92	71	.298	.340	1	.143	-1	-14	-14	-1	-2.5
1966	Cle-A	3	4	.429	27	4	0	0	0	68¹	69	9	20	31	11.9	3.82	90	.268	.324	1	.077	-1	-3	-3	1	-0.3
1967	Cle-A	0	2	.000	2	0	0	0	0	2	4	0	1	1	22.5	9.00	36	.444	.500	0	—	0	-1	-1	1	-0.9
Total	9	67	65	.508	235	169	45	12	1	1218	1238	124	318	668	11.7	3.56	108	.264	.314	62	.162	0	30	38	3	2.3

● STEVE KRALY
Kraly, Steve Charles "Lefty" b: 4/18/29, Whiting, Ind. BL/TL, 5'10", 152 lbs. Deb: 8/9/53

YEAR	TM/L	W	L	PCT	G	GS	CG	SH	SV	IP	H	HR	BB	SO	RAT	ERA	ERA+	OAV	OOB	BH	AVG	PB	PR	/A	PD	TPI
1953	NY-A	0	2	.000	5	3	0	1	0	25	19	3	18	13	13.3	3.24	114	.209	.339	0	.000	-1	2	1	0	0.0

● JACK KRAMER
Kramer, John Henry b: 1/5/18, New Orleans, La. d: 5/18/95, Metairie, La. BR/TR, 6'2", 190 lbs. Deb: 4/25/39

YEAR	TM/L	W	L	PCT	G	GS	CG	SH	SV	IP	H	HR	BB	SO	RAT	ERA	ERA+	OAV	OOB	BH	AVG	PB	PR	/A	PD	TPI
1939	StL-A	9	16	.360	40	31	10	2	0	211²	269	18	127	68	17.0	5.83	84	.318	.409	9	.136	-1	-28	-23	2	-2.3
1940	StL-A	3	7	.300	16	9	1	0	0	64²	86	4	26	12	15.6	6.26	73	.327	.388	1	.050	-1	-14	-12	0	-1.6
1941	StL-A	4	3	.571	29	3	0	0	2	59¹	69	5	40	20	16.5	5.16	83	.289	.391	0	.000	1	-7	-6	0	-0.5
1943	StL-A	0	0	—	3	0	0	0	0	9	11	0	8	4	20.0	8.00	42	.297	.435	1	.500	1	-5	-5	-0	0.1
1944	*StL-A	17	13	.567	33	31	18	1	0	257	233	3	75	124	10.8	2.49	145	.241	.297	14	.165	1	27	32	3	4.3
1945	StL-A†	10	15	.400	29	25	15	3	2	193	190	13	73	69	12.9	3.36	105	.254	.320	9	.148	-0	0	4	1	0.5
1946	StL-A★	13	11	.542	31	28	13	3	0	194²	190	6	68	69	11.9	3.19	117	.257	.319	8	.136	-1	7	12	-0	1.2
1947	StL-A☆	11	16	.407	33	28	9	1	1	199¹	206	16	89	77	13.4	4.97	78	.270	.348	7	.113	-2	-28	-24	1	-3.0
1948	Bos-A	18	5	.783	29	29	14	2	0	205	233	12	64	72	13.0	4.35	101	.284	.336	11	.151	-1	-1	-3	-2	-0.2
1949	Bos-A	6	8	.429	21	18	7	2	1	111²	126	8	49	24	14.2	5.16	85	.286	.358	9	.257	3	-12	-10	-1	-0.9
1950	NY-N	3	6	.333	35	9	1	0	1	86²	91	6	39	27	13.7	3.53	116	.268	.346	2	.100	1	6	5	0	0.6
1951	NY-N	0	0	—	4	1	0	0	0	4²	11	0	3	2	27.0	15.43	25	.524	.583	0	—	-0	-6	-6	0	0.0
	NY-A	1	3	.250	19	3	0	0	0	40²	46	1	21	15	14.8	4.65	82	.280	.362	1	.100	-0	-2	-4	-1	-0.5
Total	12	95	103	.480	322	215	88	14	7	1637¹	1761	92	682	613	13.5	4.24	96	.276	.347	72	.144	0	-63	-35	0	-2.3

● RANDY KRAMER
Kramer, Randall John b: 9/20/60, Palo Alto, Cal. BR/TR, 6'2", 170 lbs. Deb: 9/11/88

YEAR	TM/L	W	L	PCT	G	GS	CG	SH	SV	IP	H	HR	BB	SO	RAT	ERA	ERA+	OAV	OOB	BH	AVG	PB	PR	/A	PD	TPI
1988	Pit-N	1	2	.333	5	1	0	0	0	10	12	1	1	7	12.6	5.40	63	.316	.350	0	.000	-0	-2	-2	-0	-0.6
1989	Pit-N	5	9	.357	35	15	1	1	2	111¹	90	10	61	52	12.8	3.96	85	.224	.337	5	.152	-0	-6	-7	-1	-1.0
1990	Pit-N	0	1	.000	12	2	0	0	0	25²	27	3	9	15	13.3	4.91	74	.273	.345	0	.000	-1	-3	-4	1	-0.1
	Chi-N	0	2	.000	10	2	0	0	0	20¹	20	3	12	12	14.6	3.98	102	.253	.359	0	.000	-0	-0	-0	0	0.0
	Yr	0	3	.000	22	4	0	0	0	46	47	6	21	27	13.5	4.50	85	.261	.342	0	.000	-1	-4	-3	0	-0.1
1992	Sea-A	0	1	.000	4	4	0	0	0	16¹	30	2	7	6	20.9	7.71	51	.400	.458	0	—	-0	-7	-7	-0	-0.4
Total	4	6	15	.286	66	24	1	1	2	183²	179	19	90	92	13.8	4.51	78	.259	.354	5	.122	-1	-18	-20	-2	-2.1

● TOM KRAMER
Kramer, Thomas Joseph b: 1/9/68, Cincinnati, Ohio BB/TR, 6', 185 lbs. Deb: 9/12/91

YEAR	TM/L	W	L	PCT	G	GS	CG	SH	SV	IP	H	HR	BB	SO	RAT	ERA	ERA+	OAV	OOB	BH	AVG	PB	PR	/A	PD	TPI
1991	Cle-A	0	0	—	4	0	0	0	0	4²	10	1	6	4	30.9	17.36	24	.476	.593	0	—	0	-7	-7	-0	0.0
1993	Cle-A	7	3	.700	39	16	1	0	0	121	126	19	59	71	13.9	4.02	108	.269	.353	0	—	0	4	4	-1	0.2
Total	2	7	3	.700	43	16	1	0	0	125²	136	20	65	75	14.5	4.51	96	.278	.364	0	—	0	-3	-3	-1	0.2

● GENE KRAPP
Krapp, Eugene Hamlet "Rubber Arm" b: 5/12/1887, Rochester, N.Y. d: 4/13/23, Detroit, Mich. BR/TR, 5'5", 165 lbs. Deb: 4/14/11

YEAR	TM/L	W	L	PCT	G	GS	CG	SH	SV	IP	H	HR	BB	SO	RAT	ERA	ERA+	OAV	OOB	BH	AVG	PB	PR	/A	PD	TPI
1911	Cle-A	13	9	.591	35	26	14	1	1	222	188	1	138	132	13.7	3.41	100	.232	.353	17	.230	4	-1	0	4	0.8
1912	Cle-A	2	5	.286	9	7	4	0	0	58²	57	0	42	22	15.8	4.60	74	.273	.404	7	.318	-1	-8	-8	2	-0.5
1914	Buf-F	16	14	.533	36	29	18	1	0	252²	198	4	115	106	11.6	2.49	119	.210	.304	11	.143	-2	11	13	5	1.8
1915	Buf-F	9	19	.321	38	30	14	1	0	231	188	6	123	93	12.3	3.51	80	.230	.333	9	.129	-3	-20	-18	7	-1.7
Total	4	40	47	.460	118	92	50	3	1	764¹	631	11	418	353	12.7	3.23	95	.227	.343	44	.181	-1	-19	-13	19	0.4

● JACK KRAUS
Kraus, John William "Tex" or "Texas Jack" b: 4/26/18, San Antonio, Tex. d: 1/2/76, San Antonio, Tex. BR/TL, 6'4", 190 lbs. Deb: 4/25/43

YEAR	TM/L	W	L	PCT	G	GS	CG	SH	SV	IP	H	HR	BB	SO	RAT	ERA	ERA+	OAV	OOB	BH	AVG	PB	PR	/A	PD	TPI
1943	Phi-N	9	15	.375	34	25	10	1	2	199²	197	7	78	48	12.4	3.16	107	.259	.328	4	.067	-5	5	5	1	0.2
1945	Phi-N	4	9	.308	19	13	0	0	0	81²	96	3	40	28	15.4	5.40	71	.293	.376	3	.120	-1	-15	-14	0	-2.0
1946	NY-N	2	1	.667	17	1	0	0	0	25	25	4	15	7	14.8	6.12	56	.260	.366	0	.000	-0	-8	-7	1	-0.8
Total	3	15	25	.375	70	39	10	1	2	306¹	318	14	133	83	13.4	4.00	88	.268	.345	7	.080	-6	-17	-17	2	-2.6

● HARRY KRAUSE
Krause, Harry William "Hal" b: 7/12/1887, San Francisco, Cal. d: 10/23/40, San Francisco, Cal BB/TL, 5'10", 165 lbs. Deb: 4/20/08

YEAR	TM/L	W	L	PCT	G	GS	CG	SH	SV	IP	H	HR	BB	SO	RAT	ERA	ERA+	OAV	OOB	BH	AVG	PB	PR	/A	PD	TPI
1908	Phi-A	1	1	.500	4	2	2	0	0	21	20	0	4	10	11.6	2.57	100	.247	.307	0	.000	-1	-0	-0	-1	-0.2
1909	Phi-A	18	8	.692	32	21	16	7	0	213	151	2	49	139	9.0	**1.39**	**173**	.204	.266	12	.156	-1	26	**24**	-3	2.6
1910	Phi-A	6	6	.500	16	11	9	2	0	112¹	99	4	42	60	11.9	2.88	82	.254	.298	8	.211	-1	-5	-6	-2	-0.8
1911	Phi-A	11	8	.579	27	19	12	1	2	169	155	2	47	85	11.2	3.04	104	.251	.313	15	.254	2	6	2	-3	0.1
1912	Phi-A	0	2	.000	4	2	0	0	0	5¹	10	0	2	3	21.9	13.50	23	.435	.500	1	.250	-0	-6	-6	-0	-1.6
	Cle-A	0	1	.000	2	2	0	0	0	4²	11	0	2	1	25.1	11.57	29	.500	.542	0	—	-0	-4	-4	-0	-0.7
	Yr	0	3	.000	6	4	0	0	0	10	21	0	4	4	22.5	12.60	26	.457	.500	1	.250	-0	-10	-10	-0	-2.3
Total	5	36	26	.581	85	57	39	10	2	525¹	446	8	146	298	10.7	2.50	107	.238	.305	36	.195	1	16	10	-9	-0.6

● LEW KRAUSSE
Krausse, Lewis Bernard Jr. b: 4/25/43, Media, Pa. BR/TR, 5'11", 186 lbs. Deb: 6/16/61 F

YEAR	TM/L	W	L	PCT	G	GS	CG	SH	SV	IP	H	HR	BB	SO	RAT	ERA	ERA+	OAV	OOB	BH	AVG	PB	PR	/A	PD	TPI
1961	KC-A	2	5	.286	12	8	2	1	0	55²	49	5	44	32	15.5	4.85	86	.243	.386	2	.118	-1	-5	-4	-1	-0.6
1964	KC-A	0	2	.000	5	4	0	0	0	14²	12	2	9	9	20.3	7.36	52	.349	.446	0	.000	-0	-6	-6	-0	-0.7
1965	KC-A	2	4	.333	7	5	0	0	0	25	29	1	8	22	13.3	5.04	69	.284	.336	0	.000	-1	-4	-4	-1	-1.0
1966	KC-A	14	9	.609	36	22	4	1	3	177²	144	8	63	87	10.8	2.99	114	.222	.297	8	.154	0	9	8	-3	0.8
1967	KC-A	7	17	.292	48	19	0	0	6	160	140	17	67	96	11.9	4.27	75	.236	.317	6	.146	1	-19	-19	-0	-2.9
1968	Oak-A	10	11	.476	36	25	2	0	4	185	147	16	62	105	10.3	3.11	91	.217	.286	9	.161	3	-3	-6	-2	-0.6
1969	Oak-A	7	7	.500	43	16	4	2	7	140	134	23	48	85	12.0	4.44	77	.256	.325	8	.167	4	-13	-16	-1	-1.3
1970	Mil-A	13	18	.419	37	35	8	1	0	216	235	33	67	130	12.8	4.75	80	.275	.330	9	.138	1	-25	-23	-0	-3.0
1971	Mil-A	8	12	.400	43	22	1	0	0	180¹	164	23	62	92	11.5	2.94	118	.239	.307	1	.023	-3	10	11	-1	0.7
1972	Bos-A	1	3	.250	24	7	0	0	1	60²	74	7	28	35	15.6	6.38	50	.308	.387	2	.125	-0	-22	-21	1	-1.5
1973	StL-N	0	0	—	2	0	0	0	0	2	2	0	1	1	13.5	0.00	—	.250	.333	0	—	-0	1	1	0	0.1
1974	Atl-N	4	3	.571	29	4	0	0	2	66²	65	3	27	22	13.4	4.18	90	.258	.346	2	.333	2	-4	-3	-1	-0.2
Total	12	68	91	.428	321	167	21	5	21	1283²	1205	137	493	721	12.2	4.00	85	.248	.322	47	.133	6	-81	-84	-9	-10.3

● LEW KRAUSSE
Krausse, Lewis Bernard Sr. b: 6/8/12, Media, Pa. d: 9/6/88, Sarasota, Fla. BR/TR, 6'0.5", 167 lbs. Deb: 6/11/31 F

YEAR	TM/L	W	L	PCT	G	GS	CG	SH	SV	IP	H	HR	BB	SO	RAT	ERA	ERA+	OAV	OOB	BH	AVG	PB	PR	/A	PD	TPI
1931	Phi-A	1	0	1.000	3	1	1	0	0	11	6	2	6	1	9.8	4.09	110	.150	.261	0	.000	-0	0	0	0	0.1
1932	Phi-A	4	1	.800	20	3	2	1	0	57	64	3	24	16	13.9	4.58	99	.281	.349	2	.133	-0	-1	-0	1	0.0
Total	2	5	1	.833	23	4	3	1	0	68	70	5	30	17	13.2	4.50	100	.261	.336	2	.118	-0	-0	-1	0	0.1

● KEN KRAVEC
Kravec, Kenneth Peter b: 7/29/51, Cleveland, Ohio BL/TL, 6'2", 185 lbs. Deb: 9/4/75

YEAR	TM/L	W	L	PCT	G	GS	CG	SH	SV	IP	H	HR	BB	SO	RAT	ERA	ERA+	OAV	OOB	BH	AVG	PB	PR	/A	PD	TPI
1975	Chi-A	1	0	1.000	2	1	0	0	0	4¹	1	0	8	1	18.7	6.23	62	.071	.409	0	—	-1	-1	-1	1	-0.2
1976	Chi-A	1	5	.167	9	8	1	0	0	49²	49	3	32	38	14.9	4.89	73	.257	.366	0	—	-0	-8	-7	-0	-0.8
1977	Chi-A	11	8	.579	26	25	6	1	0	166²	161	12	57	125	12.1	4.10	99	.250	.317	0	—	-1	-0	-0	0	-0.1
1978	Chi-A	11	16	.407	30	30	7	2	0	203	188	22	95	154	12.7	4.08	93	.245	.336	0	—	-0	7	6	-0	-0.8
1979	Chi-A	15	13	.536	36	35	10	3	1	250	208	20	111	132	12.0	3.74	113	.233	.327	0	—	0	13	14	-1	1.3
1980	Chi-A	3	6	.333	20	15	0	0	0	81²	100	13	44	37	16.4	6.94	58	.298	.387	0	—	-1	-26	-26	0	-2.4
1981	Chi-N	1	6	.143	24	12	0	0	0	78¹	80	5	39	50	14.1	5.06	73	.268	.361	0	.000	-1	-14	-12	1	-1.1

YEAR	TM/L	W	L	PCT	G	GS	CG	SH	SV	IP	H	HR	BB	SO	RAT	ERA	ERA+	OAV	OOB	BH	AVG	PB	PR	/A	PD	TPI
1982	Chi-N	1	1	.500	13	2	0	0	0	25	27	3	18	20	16.2	6.12	61	.267	.378	0	.000	-0	-7	-7	-0	-0.5
Total	8	43	56	.434	160	128	24	6	1	858²	814	78	404	557	13.2	4.47	89	.251	.341	0	.000	-1	-51	-46	-0	-4.5

● **RAY KRAWCZYK**   Krawczyk, Raymond Allen b: 10/9/59, Pittsburgh, Pa.   BR/TR, 6'1", 186 lbs.   Deb: 6/29/84

1984	Pit-N	0	0	—	4	0	0	0	0	5¹	7	0	4	3	18.6	3.38	107	.350	.458	0	—	0	0	0	-0	0.0
1985	Pit-N	0	2	.000	8	0	0	0	0	8¹	20	1	6	9	29.2	14.04	25	.455	.529	0	—	0	-10	-10	-0	-1.9
1986	Pit-N	0	1	.000	12	0	0	0	0	12¹	17	3	10	7	19.7	7.30	53	.321	.429	0	—	0	-5	-5	-0	-0.4
1988	Cal-A	0	1	.000	14	1	0	0	1	24¹	29	2	8	17	14.4	4.81	80	.299	.364	0	—	0	-2	-3	1	0.1
1989	Mil-A	0	0	—	1	0	0	0	0	2	4	0	1	6	22.5	13.50	28	.400	.455	0	—	0	-2	-2	0	0.0
Total	5	0	4	.000	39	1	0	0	1	52¹	77	6	29	42	18.7	7.05	54	.344	.426	0	—	0	-19	-19	0	-2.2

● **RAY KREMER**   Kremer, Remy Peter "Wiz" b: 3/23/1893, Oakland, Cal. d: 2/8/65, Pinole, Cal.   BR/TR, 6'1", 190 lbs.   Deb: 4/18/24

1924	Pit-N	18	10	.643	**41**	30	17	**4**	1	259¹	262	7	51	64	11.0	3.19	120	.265	.304	13	.151	-4	19	19	-2	1.3
1925	*Pit-N	17	8	.680	40	27	14	0	2	214²	232	19	47	62	12.1	3.69	121	.278	.323	14	.197	1	14	18	-3	1.6
1926	Pit-N	**20**	6	.769	37	26	18	3	5	231¹	221	9	51	74	10.7	**2.61**	151	.252	.296	21	.253	2	**31**	**34**	-3	**3.7**
1927	*Pit-N	19	8	.704	35	28	18	3	2	226	205	9	53	63	10.3	**2.47**	166	.244	.289	14	.169	-1	36	41	-3	4.3
1928	Pit-N	15	13	.536	34	31	17	1	0	219	253	15	68	61	13.4	4.64	87	.297	.352	14	.179	0	-16	-14	-4	-1.9
1929	Pit-N	18	10	.643	34	27	14	0	0	221²	226	21	60	66	11.7	4.26	112	.271	.320	11	.128	-2	11	13	-3	0.8
1930	Pit-N	**20**	12	.625	39	38	15	0	0	**276**	366	29	63	58	14.0	5.02	99	.322	.359	16	.157	0	-2	-1	-4	-0.9
1931	Pit-N	11	15	.423	30	30	15	1	0	230	246	6	65	58	12.4	3.33	116	.271	.323	17	.227	4	14	13	-6	1.2
1932	Pit-N	4	3	.571	11	10	3	1	0	56²	61	5	16	6	12.4	4.29	89	.270	.321	2	.105	-1	-3	-3	-2	-0.6
1933	Pit-N	1	0	1.000	7	0	0	0	0	20	36	2	9	4	20.2	10.35	32	.387	.441	0	.000	-1	-16	-16	1	-0.7
Total	10	143	85	.627	308	247	134	14	10	1954²	2108	122	483	516	12.1	3.76	113	.278	.323	122	.178	-7	90	104	-27	8.8

● **JIM KREMMEL**   Kremmel, James Louis b: 2/28/48, Belleville, Ill.   BL/TL, 6', 175 lbs.   Deb: 7/4/73

1973	Tex-A	0	2	.000	4	2	0	0	0	9	15	1	6	6	23.0	9.00	41	.366	.469	0	.000	0	-5	-5	-0	-0.9
1974	Chi-N	0	2	.000	23	2	0	0	0	31	37	3	18	22	16.3	5.23	73	.303	.397	0	.000	-0	-6	-5	-0	-0.3
Total	2	0	4	.000	27	4	0	0	0	40	52	4	24	28	17.8	6.07	62	.319	.416	0	.000	-0	-11	-10	-0	-1.2

● **RED KRESS**   Kress, Ralph b: 1/2/07, Columbia, Cal. d: 11/29/62, Los Angeles, Cal.   BR/TR, 5'11.5", 165 lbs.   Deb: 9/24/27 C♦

1935	Was-A	0	0	—	3	0	0	0	0	5²	8	0	5	3	20.6	12.71	34	.333	.448	75	.298	1	-5	-5	0	0.1
1946	NY-N	0	0	—	1	0	0	0	0	3²	5	1	1	1	17.2	12.27	28	.333	.412	0	.000	0	-4	-4	1	0.1
Total	2	0	0	—	4	0	0	0	0	9¹	13	1	6	4	19.3	12.54	32	.333	.435	1454	.286	1	-9	-9	1	0.2

● **LOU KRETLOW**   Kretlow, Louis Henry "Lena" b: 6/27/21, Apache, Okla.   BR/TR, 6'2", 185 lbs.   Deb: 9/26/46

1946	Det-A	1	0	1.000	1	1	1	0	0	9	4	1	6	4	9.0	3.00	122	.206	.250	2	.500	1	1	1	-0	0.2
1948	Det-A	2	1	.667	5	2	1	0	0	23¹	21	1	11	9	12.3	4.63	94	.233	.317	4	.500	1	-1	-1	0	0.0
1949	Det-A	3	2	.600	25	10	1	0	0	76	85	5	69	40	18.4	6.16	68	.290	.427	0	.000	-4	-17	-17	2	-1.1
1950	StL-A	0	2	.000	9	2	0	0	0	14¹	25	2	18	10	28.3	11.93	41	.403	.549	0	.000	-1	-12	-11	-0	-1.3
	Chi-A	0	0	—	11	1	0	0	0	21¹	17	1	27	14	18.6	3.80	118	.221	.423	0	.000	0	2	-1	-1	-0.1
	Yr	0	2	.000	20	3	0	0	0	35²	42	3	45	24	22.0	7.07	66	.298	.468	0	.000	-1	-10	-9	-1	-1.4
1951	Chi-A	6	9	.400	26	18	7	1	0	137	129	7	74	89	13.5	4.20	96	.250	.347	4	.083	-5	-1	-3	-0	-0.8
1952	Chi-A	4	4	.500	19	11	4	2	1	79	52	5	56	63	12.4	2.96	123	.186	.323	1	.050	-1	6	6	-1	0.4
1953	Chi-A	0	0	—	9	3	0	0	0	20²	12	2	30	15	18.1	3.48	116	.171	.426	0	.000	-0	1	1	1	0.0
	StL-A	1	5	.167	22	11	0	0	0	81	93	5	52	37	16.1	5.11	82	.286	.385	5	.200	-1	-10	-8	-2	-0.8
	Yr	1	5	.167	31	14	0	0	0	101²	105	7	82	52	16.6	4.78	87	.265	.391	5	.172	-1	-9	-7	-1	-0.7
1954	Bal-A	6	11	.353	32	24	5	0	0	166²	169	12	82	82	13.6	4.37	82	.269	.354	8	.157	-0	-12	-15	0	-1.3
1955	Bal-A	0	4	.000	15	5	0	0	0	38¹	50	3	27	26	18.3	8.22	46	.316	.419	1	.091	-1	-18	-19	1	-1.6
1956	KC-A	4	9	.308	25	20	5	0	1	118²	121	11	74	61	14.8	5.31	82	.262	.364	2	.061	-3	-15	-13	-1	-1.5
Total	10	27	47	.365	199	104	22	3	1	785¹	781	62	522	450	15.0	4.87	82	.261	.372	27	.114	-13	-76	-77	-1	-7.8

● **RICK KREUGER**   Kreuger, Richard Allen b: 11/3/48, Grand Rapids, Mich.   BR/TL, 6'2", 185 lbs.   Deb: 9/6/75

1975	Bos-A	0	0	—	2	0	0	0	0	4	3	0	1	9	9.0	4.50	90	.200	.250	0	—	0	-0	0	-0	-0.1
1976	Bos-A	2	1	.667	8	4	1	0	0	31	31	3	16	12	13.6	4.06	96	.272	.362	0	—	0	-2	-1	0	0.0
1977	Bos-A	0	1	.000	1	0	0	0	0	0	2	0	0	0	—	∞	—	1.000	1.000	0	—	0	-2	-2	0	-0.2
1978	Cle-A	0	0	—	6	0	0	0	0	9¹	6	1	3	7	8.7	3.86	97	.194	.265	0	—	0	-0	-0	1	-0.0
Total	4	2	2	.500	17	4	1	0	0	44¹	42	4	20	20	12.6	4.47	87	.259	.341	0	—	0	-4	-3	1	-0.3

● **FRANK KREUTZER**   Kreutzer, Franklin James b: 2/7/39, Buffalo, N.Y.   BR/TL, 6'1", 190 lbs.   Deb: 9/20/62

1962	Chi-A	0	0	—	1	0	0	0	0	1¹	1	0	2	1	6.8	0.00	—	.200	.200	0	—	0	1	1	-0	0.0
1963	Chi-A	1	0	1.000	2	1	0	0	0	5	3	1	0	7	7.2	1.80	195	.188	.235	0	.000	-0	1	1	0	0.2
1964	Chi-A	3	1	.750	17	2	0	0	0	40¹	37	1	18	32	12.3	3.35	103	.239	.318	1	.125	-0	1	0	-1	0.1
	Was-A	2	6	.250	13	9	0	0	0	45¹	48	6	23	27	14.3	4.76	78	.267	.353	0	.000	-0	-6	-5	-1	-1.0
	Yr	5	7	.417	30	11	0	0	0	85²	85	7	41	59	13.3	4.10	87	.253	.336	1	.053	-1	-5	-5	-2	-0.9
1965	Was-A	2	6	.250	33	14	2	1	0	85¹	73	7	54	65	13.6	4.32	80	.232	.348	1	.045	-1	-8	-8	-1	-1.0
1966	Was-A	0	5	.000	9	6	0	0	0	31¹	30	9	10	24	11.8	6.03	57	.236	.297	2	.250	-0	-9	-9	1	-1.2
1969	Was-A	0	0	—	4	0	0	0	0	2	2	0	2	2	22.5	4.50	77	.333	.455	0	—	0	-0	-0	-0	-0.0
Total	6	8	18	.308	78	32	2	1	1	210²	194	24	109	151	13.1	4.40	80	.241	.334	4	.078	-2	-20	-21	-1	-2.9

● **KRIEGER**   Krieger Deb: 7/28/1884 ♦

1884	KC-U	0	1	.000	1	1	0	0	0	7	9	0	5	3	18.0	0.00	—	.290	.389	0	.000	-1	2	2	0	0.1

● **KURT KRIEGER**   Krieger, Kurt Ferdinand "Dutch" b: 9/16/26, Traisen, Austria d: 8/16/70, St.Louis, Mo.   BR/TR, 6'3", 212 lbs.   Deb: 4/21/49

1949	StL-N	0	0	—	1	0	0	0	0	1	1	0	1	0	9.0	9.00	—	.000	.250	0	—	0	-0	-0	-0	0.0
1951	StL-N	0	0	—	2	0	0	0	0	4	6	1	5	3	24.8	15.75	25	.353	.500	0	—	0	-5	-5	0	-0.5
Total	2	0	0	—	3	0	0	0	0	5	7	1	6	3	21.6	12.60	32	.300	.462	0	—	0	-5	-5	0	-0.5

● **HOWIE KRIST**   Krist, Howard Wilbur "Spud" b: 2/28/16, W.Henrietta, N.Y. d: 4/23/89, Buffalo, N.Y.   BL/TR, 6'1", 175 lbs.   Deb: 9/12/37

1937	StL-N	3	1	.750	6	4	1	0	0	27²	34	0	10	6	14.3	4.23	94	.304	.361	0	.000	-1	-1	-1	-1	-0.3
1938	StL-N	0	0	—	2	0	0	0	0	1¹	1	0	1	4	6.8	0.00	—	.250	.250	0	—	-1	1	1	-0	0.1
1941	StL-N	10	0	1.000	37	8	2	0	2	114	107	10	35	36	11.3	4.03	93	.246	.304	9	.237	-0	-5	-3	-0	-0.3
1942	StL-N	13	3	.813	34	8	2	0	1	118¹	103	2	43	47	11.3	2.51	136	.233	.304	6	.143	-1	11	12	-2	1.2
1943	*StL-N	11	5	.688	34	17	9	2	3	164¹	141	5	62	57	11.3	2.90	116	.233	.309	10	.167	-2	9	8	-5	0.1
1946	StL-N	0	2	.000	15	0	0	0	0	18²	22	3	8	0	14.9	6.75	51	.306	.383	0	—	-0	-7	-7	-0	-0.7
Total	6	37	11	.771	128	37	15	2	6	444¹	408	20	158	150	11.6	3.32	106	.244	.313	25	.168	-3	7	10	-9	0.0

● **RICK KRIVDA**   Krivda, Rick Michael b: 1/19/70, McKeesport, Pa.   BR/TL, 6'1", 180 lbs.   Deb: 7/7/95

1995	Bal-A	2	7	.222	13	13	0	0	0	75¹	76	9	25	53	12.5	4.54	105	.266	.333	0	—	0	1	2	-1	0.1
1996	Bal-A	3	5	.375	22	11	0	0	0	81²	89	14	39	54	14.2	4.96	99	.283	.363	0	—	0	-0	-0	-1	-0.1
Total	2	5	12	.294	35	24	0	0	0	157	165	23	64	107	13.4	4.76	101	.275	.349	0	—	0	2	2	-1	-0.1

● **GUS KROCK**   Krock, August H. b: 5/9/1866, Milwaukee, Wis. d: 3/22/05, Pasadena, Cal.   TL, 6', 196 lbs.   Deb: 4/24/1888

1888	Chi-N	25	14	.641	39	39	39	4	0	339²	295	20	45	161	9.2	2.44	124	.227	.258	22	.164	-3	16	22	-3	1.6
1889	Chi-N	3	3	.500	7	7	5	0	0	60²	86	10	14	16	15.1	4.90	85	.323	.362	4	.167	-1	-6	-5	-0	-0.5
	Ind-N	2	2	.500	6	6	4	0	0	32	48	2	14	10	17.4	7.31	57	.336	.395	5	.357	-1	-12	-11	-1	-0.8
	Was-N	2	4	.333	6	6	4	1	0	48	65	1	22	17	16.5	5.25	75	.314	.383	2	.087	-2	-7	-7	-0	-0.8
	Yr	7	9	.438	17	17	14	0	0	140²	199	13	50	43	16.0	5.57	73	.322	.374	11	.180	-2	-24	-23	-1	-2.2
1890	Buf-P	0	3	.000	4	3	3	0	0	25	43	1	15	5	20.9	6.12	67	.364	.436	1	.083	-1	-5	-6	-0	-0.5
Total	3	32	26	.552	60	59	56	4	0	505¹	537	34	110	209	11.7	3.49	97	.264	.306	34	.164	-7	-14	-6	-4	-1.1

● **RUBE KROH**   Kroh, Floyd Myron b: 8/25/1886, Friendship, N.Y. d: 3/17/44, New Orleans, La.   BL/TL, 6'2", 186 lbs.   Deb: 9/30/06

1906	Bos-A	1	0	1.000	1	1	1	1	0	9	2	0	4	5	6.0	0.00	—	.074	.194	0	.000	-0	3	3	0	0.4

YEAR	TM/L	W	L	PCT	G	GS	CG	SH	SV	IP	H	HR	BB	SO	RAT	ERA	ERA+	OAV	OOB	BH	AVG	PB	PR	/A	PD	TPI
1907	Bos-A	1	4	.200	7	5	1	0	0	34¹	33	0	8	8	11.3	2.62	98	.256	.309	3	.273	0	-0	-0	-0	0.0
1908	Chi-N	0	0	—	2	1	0	0	0	12	9	0	4	11	9.8	1.50	157	.200	.265	0	.000	-0	1	1	0	0.3
1909	Chi-N	9	4	.692	17	13	10	2	0	120¹	97	2	30	51	9.6	1.65	154	.224	.276	6	.150	-0	13	12	1	1.4
1910	Chi-N	3	1	.750	6	4	1	0	0	34¹	33	1	15	16	13.1	4.46	65	.254	.340	3	.250	0	-5	-6	1	-0.6
1912	Bos-N	0	0	—	3	1	0	0	0	6¹	10	0	6	1	19.9	5.68	63	.364	.500	1	.500	0	-2	-1	0	0.1
Total	6	14	9	.609	36	25	13	3	0	216¹	182	3	67	92	10.6	2.29	115	.232	.296	13	.181	-0	9	8	2	1.3

● **GARY KROLL** Kroll, Gary Melvin b: 7/8/41, Culver City, Cal. BR/TR, 6'6", 220 lbs. Deb: 7/26/64

YEAR	TM/L	W	L	PCT	G	GS	CG	SH	SV	IP	H	HR	BB	SO	RAT	ERA	ERA+	OAV	OOB	BH	AVG	PB	PR	/A	PD	TPI
1964	Phi-N	0	0	—	2	0	0	0	0	3	3	0	2	2	15.0	3.00	116	.250	.357	0	—	0	0	0	-0	0.0
	NY-N	0	1	.000	8	2	0	0	0	21²	19	1	15	24	14.5	4.15	86	.241	.368	1	.333	0	-1	-1	1	0.1
	Yr	0	1	.000	10	2	0	0	0	24²	22	1	17	26	14.6	4.01	89	.242	.367	1	.333	0	-1	-1	1	0.1
1965	NY-N	6	6	.500	32	11	1	0	1	87	83	12	41	62	13.4	4.45	79	.249	.342	3	.115	-1	-9	-9	-0	-1.2
1966	Hou-N	0	0	—	10	0	0	0	0	23²	26	2	11	22	14.1	3.80	90	.280	.356	0	.000	-0	-1	-1	0	0.0
1969	Cle-A	0	0	—	19	0	0	0	0	24	16	3	22	28	14.3	4.13	91	.188	.355	0	—	0	-1	-1	-0	0.0
Total	4	6	7	.462	71	13	1	0	1	159¹	147	18	91	138	13.8	4.24	84	.244	.350	4	.125	-1	-12	-12	1	-1.1

● **MARC KROON** Kroon, Marc Jason b: 4/2/73, Bronx, N.Y. BB/TR, 6'2", 195 lbs. Deb: 7/7/95

YEAR	TM/L	W	L	PCT	G	GS	CG	SH	SV	IP	H	HR	BB	SO	RAT	ERA	ERA+	OAV	OOB	BH	AVG	PB	PR	/A	PD	TPI
1995	SD-N	0	1	.000	2	0	0	0	0	1²	1	0	2	2	16.2	10.80	37	.200	.429	0	—	0	-1	-1	-0	-0.6

● **BILL KRUEGER** Krueger, William Culp b: 4/24/58, Waukegan, Ill. BL/TL, 6'5", 210 lbs. Deb: 4/10/83

YEAR	TM/L	W	L	PCT	G	GS	CG	SH	SV	IP	H	HR	BB	SO	RAT	ERA	ERA+	OAV	OOB	BH	AVG	PB	PR	/A	PD	TPI
1983	Oak-A	7	6	.538	17	16	2	0	0	109²	104	7	53	58	13.0	3.61	107	.252	.340	0	—	0	5	3	-2	0.2
1984	Oak-A	10	10	.500	26	24	1	0	0	142	156	9	85	61	15.4	4.75	79	.285	.383	0	—	0	-12	-16	-2	-1.7
1985	Oak-A	9	10	.474	32	23	2	0	0	151¹	165	13	69	56	14.0	4.52	85	.276	.353	0	—	0	-6	-11	-1	-1.0
1986	Oak-A	1	2	.333	11	3	0	0	1	34¹	40	4	13	10	13.9	6.03	64	.301	.363	0	—	0	-7	-8	1	-0.5
1987	Oak-A	0	3	.000	9	0	0	0	0	5²	9	0	8	2	27.0	9.53	43	.360	.515	0	—	0	-3	-3	-0	-1.4
	LA-N	0	0	—	2	0	0	0	0	2¹	3	0	1	2	15.4	0.00	—	.250	.308	0	—	0	1	1	-0	0.0
1988	LA-N	0	0	—	1	1	0	0	0	2¹	4	0	2	1	27.0	11.57	29	.364	.500	0	—	0	-2	-2	0	0.0
1989	Mil-A	3	2	.600	34	5	0	0	3	93²	96	9	33	72	12.4	3.84	100	.264	.325	0	—	0	0	-0	-0	0.0
1990	Mil-A	6	8	.429	30	17	0	0	0	129	137	10	54	64	13.5	3.98	97	.276	.351	0	—	0	-1	-2	-1	-0.2
1991	Sea-A	11	8	.579	35	25	1	0	0	175	194	15	60	91	13.3	3.60	114	.289	.351	0	—	0	10	10	1	1.1
1992	Min-A	10	6	.625	27	27	2	2	0	161¹	166	18	46	86	12.0	4.30	94	.263	.317	0	—	0	-6	-4	-3	-0.8
	Mon-N	0	2	.000	9	2	0	0	0	17¹	23	2	7	13	16.1	6.75	51	.315	.383	0	.000	-0	-6	-6	-0	-0.7
1993	Det-A	6	4	.600	32	7	0	0	0	82	90	6	30	60	13.6	3.40	126	.285	.354	0	—	0	8	8	-0	0.9
1994	Det-A	2	0	.000	16	2	0	0	0	19²	26	3	17	17	20.1	9.61	50	.321	.444	0	—	0	-11	-10	-0	-0.8
	SD-N	3	2	.600	8	7	1	0	0	41	42	5	7	30	11.0	4.83	85	.259	.294	6	.500	3	-3	-3	-0	-0.1
1995	SD-N	0	0	—	6	0	0	0	0	7²	12	1	6	4	20.0	7.04	57	.371	.436	0	—	0	-2	-3	-0	0.0
	Sea-A	2	1	.667	6	5	0	0	0	20	37	4	4	10	18.4	5.85	81	.407	.432	0	—	0	-3	-2	-0	-0.3
Total	13	68	66	.507	301	164	9	2	4	1194¹	1305	104	493	639	13.7	4.35	91	.280	.352	6	.400	2	-38	-50	-8	-5.3

● **ABE KRUGER** Kruger, Abraham b: 2/14/1885, Morris Run, Pa. d: 7/4/62, Elmira, N.Y. BR/TR, 6'2", 190 lbs. Deb: 10/6/08

YEAR	TM/L	W	L	PCT	G	GS	CG	SH	SV	IP	H	HR	BB	SO	RAT	ERA	ERA+	OAV	OOB	BH	AVG	PB	PR	/A	PD	TPI
1908	Bro-N	0	1	.000	2	1	0	0	0	6¹	5	0	3	2	15.6	4.26	55	.238	.407	0	.000	-0	-1	-1	1	-0.1

● **MIKE KRUKOW** Krukow, Michael Edward b: 1/21/52, Long Beach, Cal. BR/TR, 6'5", 205 lbs. Deb: 9/6/76

YEAR	TM/L	W	L	PCT	G	GS	CG	SH	SV	IP	H	HR	BB	SO	RAT	ERA	ERA+	OAV	OOB	BH	AVG	PB	PR	/A	PD	TPI
1976	Chi-N	0	0	—	2	0	0	0	0	4¹	6	0	2	1	16.6	8.31	46	.333	.400	0	—	0	-2	-2	-0	0.0
1977	Chi-N	8	14	.364	34	33	1	1	0	172	195	16	61	106	13.6	4.40	100	.281	.341	11	.200	-0	-9	-0	1	0.0
1978	Chi-N	9	3	.750	27	20	3	1	0	138	125	11	53	81	11.9	3.91	103	.243	.320	11	.244	3	-5	2	-0	0.4
1979	Chi-N	9	9	.500	28	28	0	0	0	164²	172	13	81	119	14.0	4.21	98	.275	.361	16	.314	5	-9	-2	-2	0.1
1980	Chi-N	10	15	.400	34	34	3	0	0	205	200	13	80	130	12.6	4.39	89	.258	.334	16	.246	2	-18	-11	-3	-1.3
1981	Chi-N	9	9	.500	25	25	2	1	0	144¹	146	11	55	101	12.7	3.68	100	.264	.333	9	.180	-0	-3	0	0	0.1
1982	Phi-N	13	11	.542	33	33	7	2	0	208	211	8	82	138	12.8	3.12	118	.268	.339	13	.181	-0	11	13	2	1.5
1983	SF-N	11	11	.500	31	31	2	1	0	184¹	189	17	76	136	13.1	3.95	89	.261	.333	16	.254	5	-7	-9	-2	-0.6
1984	SF-N	11	12	.478	35	33	3	1	1	199¹	234	22	78	141	14.3	4.56	77	.290	.356	10	.139	-1	-22	-23	-2	-2.7
1985	SF-N	8	11	.421	28	28	6	1	0	194²	176	19	49	150	10.5	3.38	102	.238	.288	12	.218	5	5	1	-0	0.6
1986	SF-N★	20	9	.690	34	34	10	2	0	245	204	24	55	178	9.7	3.05	115	.223	.271	12	.146	0	18	13	-1	1.4
1987	*SF-N	5	6	.455	30	28	3	0	0	163	182	24	46	104	12.7	4.80	80	.288	.338	9	.167	1	-13	-17	1	-0.8
1988	SF-N	7	4	.636	20	20	1	0	0	124²	111	13	31	75	10.6	3.54	92	.236	.291	3	.073	-0	-1	-4	-0	-0.4
1989	SF-N	4	3	.571	8	8	0	0	0	43	37	5	18	18	11.7	3.98	85	.236	.318	1	.063	-1	-2	-3	0	-0.5
Total	14	124	117	.515	369	355	41	10	1	2190¹	2188	196	767	1478	12.3	3.90	96	.260	.325	139	.193	17	-57	-42	-5	-2.2

● **AL KRUMM** Krumm, Albert b: 1/1865, Pennsylvania TR, Deb: 5/17/1889

YEAR	TM/L	W	L	PCT	G	GS	CG	SH	SV	IP	H	HR	BB	SO	RAT	ERA	ERA+	OAV	OOB	BH	AVG	PB	PR	/A	PD	TPI
1889	Pit-N	0	1	.000	1	1	1	0	0	9	8	0	10	4	18.0	10.00	37	.229	.400	0	.000	-1	-6	-6	-0	-0.5

● **JOHNNY KUCAB** Kucab, John Albert b: 12/17/19, Olyphant, Pa. d: 5/26/77, Youngstown, Ohio BR/TR, 6'2", 185 lbs. Deb: 9/14/50

YEAR	TM/L	W	L	PCT	G	GS	CG	SH	SV	IP	H	HR	BB	SO	RAT	ERA	ERA+	OAV	OOB	BH	AVG	PB	PR	/A	PD	TPI
1950	Phi-A	1	1	.500	4	2	2	0	0	26	29	4	8	8	12.8	3.46	131	.282	.333	1	.111	-0	3	3	-1	0.1
1951	Phi-A	4	3	.571	30	1	0	0	4	74²	76	9	23	23	12.1	4.22	101	.265	.322	0	.000	-2	-1	-0	-2	-0.3
1952	Phi-A	0	1	.000	25	0	0	0	2	51¹	64	5	20	17	14.9	5.26	75	.312	.376	2	.200	-0	-9	-7	-0	-0.2
Total	3	5	5	.500	59	3	2	0	6	152	169	18	51	48	13.1	4.44	95	.284	.343	3	.086	-2	-7	-4	-2	-0.4

● **JACK KUCEK** Kucek, John Andrew Charles b: 6/8/53, Warren, Ohio BR/TR, 6'2", 200 lbs. Deb: 8/8/74

YEAR	TM/L	W	L	PCT	G	GS	CG	SH	SV	IP	H	HR	BB	SO	RAT	ERA	ERA+	OAV	OOB	BH	AVG	PB	PR	/A	PD	TPI
1974	Chi-A	1	4	.200	9	7	0	0	0	37²	48	3	21	25	16.7	5.26	71	.320	.407	0	—	0	-7	-6	1	-0.8
1975	Chi-A	0	0	—	2	0	0	0	0	3²	9	0	4	1	31.9	4.91	79	.500	.591	0	—	0	-0	-0	-0	0.0
1976	Chi-A	0	0	—	2	0	0	0	0	4²	9	2	4	2	25.1	9.64	37	.429	.520	0	—	0	-3	-3	-0	0.0
1977	Chi-A	8	3	.000	8	3	0	0	0	34²	35	4	10	25	12.2	3.63	112	.267	.329	0	—	0	2	1	1	0.1
1978	Chi-A	2	3	.400	10	5	3	0	1	52	42	3	27	30	11.9	3.29	116	.220	.317	0	—	0	3	3	-0	0.2
1979	Chi-A	0	0	—	1	0	0	0	0	2	3	0	2	0	40.5	0.00	—	.000	.500	0	—	0	0	0	0	0.0
	Phi-N	0	1	0	1.000	4	0	0	0	0	4¹	6	2	1	2	14.5	8.31	46	.333	.368	0	—	0	-2	-2	-0	-0.4
1980	Tor-A	3	8	.273	23	12	0	0	1	68	83	9	41	35	16.5	6.75	64	.300	.392	0	—	0	-21	-19	-1	-2.7
Total	7	7	16	.304	59	27	3	0	2	205²	232	25	111	121	15.2	5.12	78	.287	.376	0	—	0	-29	-26	0	-3.6

● **JOHNNY KUCKS** Kucks, John Charles b: 7/27/33, Hoboken, N.J. BR/TR, 6'3", 184 lbs. Deb: 4/17/55

YEAR	TM/L	W	L	PCT	G	GS	CG	SH	SV	IP	H	HR	BB	SO	RAT	ERA	ERA+	OAV	OOB	BH	AVG	PB	PR	/A	PD	TPI
1955	*NY-A	8	7	.533	29	13	3	1	0	126²	122	8	44	49	11.9	3.41	110	.252	.317	2	.050	-4	8	5	0	0.1
1956	*NY-A☆	18	9	.667	34	31	12	3	0	224¹	223	19	72	67	12.2	3.85	100	.261	.326	11	.143	-2	8	0	0	-0.1
1957	*NY-A	8	10	.444	37	23	4	1	2	179¹	169	13	59	78	11.8	3.56	101	.251	.319	6	.109	-2	4	0	3	0.2
1958	*NY-A	8	8	.500	34	15	4	1	4	126	132	14	39	64	12.6	3.93	90	.269	.331	5	.125	-1	-2	-6	1	-0.7
1959	NY-A	0	1	.000	9	1	0	0	0	16²	21	5	9	9	16.2	8.64	42	.323	.405	0	—	0	-9	-9	-0	-0.5
	KC-A	8	11	.421	33	23	6	1	1	151¹	163	10	42	51	12.9	3.87	104	.278	.339	4	.085	-3	-0	3	1	0.2
	Yr	8	12	.400	42	24	6	1	1	168	184	15	51	60	13.2	4.34	91	.282	.345	4	.083	-3	-9	-7	2	-0.4
1960	KC-A	4	10	.286	31	17	1	0	0	114	140	22	43	38	14.5	6.00	66	.306	.367	4	.133	-1	-27	-26	-0	-2.8
Total	6	54	56	.491	207	123	30	7	7	938¹	970	91	308	338	12.6	4.10	92	.269	.333	32	.110	-12	-18	-32	5	-3.7

● **BERT KUCZYNSKI** Kuczynski, Bernard Carl b: 1/8/20, Philadelphia, Pa. BR/TR, 6', 195 lbs. Deb: 6/2/43

YEAR	TM/L	W	L	PCT	G	GS	CG	SH	SV	IP	H	HR	BB	SO	RAT	ERA	ERA+	OAV	OOB	BH	AVG	PB	PR	/A	PD	TPI
1943	Phi-A	0	1	.000	6	1	0	0	0	24²	36	2	9	8	17.1	4.01	85	.336	.398	0	.000	-0	-2	-2	-0	-0.1

● **FRED KUHAULUA** Kuhaulua, Fred Mahele b: 2/23/53, Honolulu, Hawaii BL/TL, 5'11", 175 lbs. Deb: 8/2/77

YEAR	TM/L	W	L	PCT	G	GS	CG	SH	SV	IP	H	HR	BB	SO	RAT	ERA	ERA+	OAV	OOB	BH	AVG	PB	PR	/A	PD	TPI
1977	Cal-A	0	0	—	3	1	0	0	0	6¹	15	1	7	3	31.3	15.63	25	.455	.550	0	—	0	-8	-8	-0	0.0
1981	SD-N	1	0	1.000	5	4	0	0	0	29¹	28	1	9	16	11.4	2.45	133	.257	.314	1	.111	-0	3	3	-1	-0.1
Total	2	1	0	1.000	8	5	0	0	0	35²	43	2	16	19	14.9	4.79	70	.303	.373	1	.111	-0	-5	-6	-1	-0.1

● **BUB KUHN** Kuhn, Bernard Daniel b: 10/12/1899, Vicksburg, Mich. d: 11/20/56, Detroit, Mich. BL/TR, 6'1.5", 182 lbs. Deb: 9/1/24

YEAR	TM/L	W	L	PCT	G	GS	CG	SH	SV	IP	H	HR	BB	SO	RAT	ERA	ERA+	OAV	OOB	BH	AVG	PB	PR	/A	PD	TPI
1924	Cle-A	0	1	.000	1	0	0	0	0	1	4	1	0	0	36.0	27.00	16	.667	.667	0	—	0	-3	-3	0	-1.2

YEAR TM/L	W	L	PCT	G	GS	CG	SH	SV	IP	H	HR	BB	SO	RAT	ERA	ERA+	OAV	OOB	BH	AVG	PB	PR	/A	PD	TPI
● **JOHN KULL** Kull, John A. (b: John A Kolonauski) b: 6/24/1882, Shenandoah, Pa. d: 3/30/36, Schuylkill Haven, Pa. BL/TL, 6'2", 190 lbs. Deb: 10/2/09																									
1909 Phi-A	1	0	1.000	1	0	0	0	0	3	3	0	5	4	27.0	3.00	80	.250	.500	1	1.000	0	-0	-0	0	0.0
● **MIKE KUME** Kume, John Michael b: 5/19/26, Premier, W.Va. BR/TR, 6'1", 195 lbs. Deb: 8/26/55																									
1955 KC-A	0	2	.000	6	4	0	0	0	23²	35	1	15	7	20.2	7.99	52	.354	.453	1	.125	-0	-11	-10	-0	-0.8
● **JEFF KUNKEL** Kunkel, Jeffrey William b: 3/25/62, W.Palm Beach, Fla. BR/TR, 6'2", 180 lbs. Deb: 7/23/84 F♦																									
1988 Tex-A	0	0	—	1	0	0	0	0	1	0	0	0	1	0.0	0.00	—	.000	.000	35	.227	1	0	0	0	0.0
1989 Tex-A	0	0	—	1	0	0	0	0	1²	4	1	3	0	37.8	21.60	18	.444	.583	79	.270	1	-3	-3	0	0.0
Total 2	0	0	—	2	0	0	0	0	2²	4	1	3	1	23.6	13.50	30	.333	.467	192	.267	2	-3	-3	0	0.0
● **BILL KUNKEL** Kunkel, William Gustave James b: 7/7/36, Hoboken, N.J. d: 5/4/85, Red Bank, N.J. BR/TR, 6'1", 187 lbs. Deb: 4/15/61 FU																									
1961 KC-A	3	4	.429	58	2	0	0	4	88²	103	11	32	46	13.7	5.18	81	.289	.348	1	.125	-0	-11	-10	-1	-0.8
1962 KC-A	0	0	—	9	0	0	0	0	7²	8	3	4	6	14.1	3.52	120	.258	.343	0	—	0	0	1	-0	0.0
1963 NY-A	3	2	.600	22	0	0	0	0	46¹	42	3	13	31	10.7	2.72	129	.239	.291	2	.333	1	5	4	-1	0.4
Total 3	6	6	.500	89	2	0	0	4	142¹	153	17	49	83	12.7	4.29	92	.272	.330	4	.214	1	-6	-5	-1	-0.4
● **EARL KUNZ** Kunz, Earl Dewey "Pinches" b: 12/25/1899, Sacramento, Cal. d: 4/14/63, Sacramento, Cal. BR/TR, 5'10", 170 lbs. Deb: 4/19/23																									
1923 Pit-N	1	2	.333	21	2	1	0	1	45²	48	2	24	12	14.2	5.52	73	.293	.383	1	.083	-1	-8	-8	-1	-0.7
● **RYAN KUROSAKI** Kurosaki, Ryan Yoshitomo b: 7/3/52, Honolulu, Hawaii BR/TR, 5'10", 160 lbs. Deb: 5/20/75																									
1975 StL-N	0	0	—	7	0	0	0	0	13	15	3	7	6	15.2	7.62	49	.283	.367	0	.000	-0	-6	-6	0	0.0
● **HAL KURTZ** Kurtz, Harold James "Bud" b: 8/20/43, Washington, D.C. BR/TR, 6'3", 205 lbs. Deb: 4/18/68																									
1968 Cle-A	1	0	1.000	28	0	0	0	1	38	37	3	15	16	13.5	5.21	57	.255	.345	0	.000	-0	-9	-10	-1	-0.4
● **ED KUSEL** Kusel, Edward D. b: 2/15/1886, Cleveland, Ohio d: 10/20/48, Cleveland, Ohio TR, 6', 165 lbs. Deb: 9/18/09																									
1909 StL-A	0	3	.000	3	3	3	0	0	24	43	1	1	2	16.5	7.13	34	.384	.389	3	.300	1	-12	-13	-1	-1.2
● **EMIL KUSH** Kush, Emil Benedict b: 11/4/16, Chicago, Ill. d: 11/26/69, River Grove, Ill. BR/TR, 5'11", 185 lbs. Deb: 9/21/41																									
1941 Chi-N	0	0	—	2	0	0	0	0	4	2	0	0	2	4.5	2.25	156	.143	.143	0	.000	-0	1	1	-0	0.0
1942 Chi-N	0	0	—	1	0	0	0	0	2	1	0	1	1	9.0	0.00	—	.167	.286	0	.000	-0	1	1	-0	0.0
1946 Chi-N	9	2	.818	40	6	1	1	2	129²	120	4	43	50	11.5	3.05	109	.253	.319	8	.211	0	5	4	2	0.6
1947 Chi-N	8	3	.727	47	1	1	0	5	91	80	8	53	44	13.5	3.36	117	.247	.358	5	.250	1	7	6	1	0.9
1948 Chi-N	1	4	.200	34	1	0	0	3	72	70	5	37	31	13.6	4.38	89	.253	.345	-3	.154	-0	-3	-4	1	-0.2
1949 Chi-N	3	3	.500	26	0	0	0	2	47²	51	7	24	22	14.5	3.78	107	.283	.374	3	.333	1	1	1	1	0.4
Total 6	21	12	.636	150	8	2	1	12	346¹	324	24	158	150	12.8	3.48	106	.254	.341	18	.220	1	12	9	5	1.7
● **CRAIG KUSICK** Kusick, Craig Robert b: 9/30/48, Milwaukee, Wis. BR/TR, 6'3", 232 lbs. Deb: 9/8/73 ♦																									
1979 Tor-A	0	0	—	1	0	0	0	0	3²	1	0	0	0	7.4	4.91	88	.214	.214	11	.204	0	-0	-0	-0	0.0
● **MARTY KUTYNA** Kutyna, Marion John b: 11/14/32, Philadelphia, Pa. BR/TR, 6', 190 lbs. Deb: 9/19/59																									
1959 KC-A	0	0	—	4	0	0	0	1	7¹	7	0	1	1	9.8	0.00	—	.250	.276	0	—	0	3	3	0	0.1
1960 KC-A	3	2	.600	51	0	0	0	4	61²	64	7	32	20	14.0	3.94	101	.274	.361	1	.200	-0	-0	0	0	0.0
1961 Was-A	6	8	.429	50	6	0	0	3	143	147	12	48	64	12.4	3.97	101	.271	.332	7	.206	-0	1	1	3	0.4
1962 Was-A	5	6	.455	54	0	0	0	0	78	83	9	27	25	12.7	4.04	100	.275	.334	1	.125	-0	0	0	1	0.1
Total 4	14	16	.467	159	6	0	0	8	290	301	28	108	110	12.8	3.88	103	.272	.338	9	.191	-0	3	4	4	0.6
● **JERRY KUTZLER** Kutzler, Jerry Scott b: 3/25/65, Waukegan, Ill. BL/TR, 6'1", 175 lbs. Deb: 4/28/90																									
1990 Chi-A	2	1	.667	7	7	0	0	0	31¹	38	2	14	21	14.9	6.03	63	.304	.374	0	—	0	-7	-8	-0	-0.7
● **BOB KUZAVA** Kuzava, Robert Leroy "Sarge" b: 5/28/23, Wyandotte, Mich. BB/TL, 6'2", 204 lbs. Deb: 9/21/46																									
1946 Cle-A	1	0	1.000	2	2	0	0	0	12	9	0	11	4	15.8	3.00	110	.191	.356	1	.200	-0	1	0	-0	0.1
1947 Cle-A	1	1	.500	4	4	1	1	0	21²	22	1	9	9	13.3	4.15	84	.265	.344	1	.111	-1	-1	-2	1	-0.1
1949 Chi-A	10	6	.625	29	18	9	1	0	156²	139	6	91	83	13.3	4.02	104	.240	.344	2	.036	-6	3	3	-2	-0.6
1950 Chi-A	1	3	.250	10	7	1	0	0	44¹	43	5	27	21	14.2	5.68	79	.257	.361	1	.083	-5	-6	-0	-0.5
Was-A	8	7	.533	22	22	8	1	0	155	156	8	75	84	13.5	3.95	114	.263	.346	5	.100	-2	11	9	-1	0.5
Yr	9	10	.474	32	29	9	1	0	199¹	199	13	102	105	13.6	4.33	104	.261	.350	6	.097	-2	5	3	-1	0.0
1951 Was-A	3	3	.500	8	8	3	0	0	52¹	57	5	28	22	15.0	5.50	74	.284	.377	3	.176	-0	-8	-8	-0	-0.8
*NY-A	8	4	.667	23	8	4	1	5	82¹	76	5	27	50	11.4	2.40	159	.241	.303	3	.136	0	16	13	-1	1.8
Yr	11	7	.611	31	16	7	1	5	134²	133	10	55	72	12.6	3.61	109	.257	.329	6	.154	0	8	5	-1	0.4
1952 *NY-A	8	8	.500	28	12	6	1	3	133	115	7	63	67	12.1	3.45	96	.240	.329	4	.093	-1	3	2	-2	-0.5
1953 *NY-A	6	5	.545	33	6	2	1	0	92³	92	9	34	48	12.3	3.31	111	.264	.330	1	.048	-1	7	4	-2	0.2
1954 NY-A	1	3	.250	20	3	0	0	1	39²	46	3	18	22	14.5	5.45	63	.297	.370	0	.000	-0	-8	-9	-1	-1.0
Bal-A	1	3	.250	4	4	0	0	0	23²	30	0	11	15	15.6	4.18	86	.323	.394	0	.000	-1	-2	-1	-0	-0.4
Yr	2	6	.250	24	7	0	0	1	63¹	76	3	29	37	14.9	4.97	70	.304	.376	0	.000	-1	-9	-10	-1	-1.4
1955 Bal-A	0	1	.000	6	1	0	0	0	12¹	10	0	4	5	10.2	3.65	105	.222	.286	0	.000	-0	0	0	-0	0.0
Phi-N	1	0	1.000	17	4	0	0	0	32¹	47	5	12	13	16.4	7.24	55	.333	.386	1	.143	-0	-11	-12	-0	-0.3
1957 Pit-N	0	0	—	4	0	0	0	0	2	3	0	3	1	27.0	9.00	42	.333	.500	0	—	-0	-1	-0	-0	0.0
StL-N	0	0	—	3	0	0	0	0	2¹	4	0	2	2	23.1	3.86	103	.364	.462	0	—	-0	0	0	-0	0.0
Yr	0	0	—	7	0	0	0	0	4¹	7	0	5	3	24.9	6.23	62	.350	.480	0	—	-0	-1	-0	-0	0.0
Total 10	49	44	.527	213	99	34	7	13	862	849	54	415	446	13.3	4.05	97	.260	.345	22	.086	-14	5	-12	-8	-1.6
● **CLEM LABINE** Labine, Clement Walter b: 8/6/26, Lincoln, R.I. BR/TR, 6', 180 lbs. Deb: 4/18/50																									
1950 Bro-N	0	0	—	1	0	0	0	0	2	2	0	1	0	13.5	4.50	91	.286	.375	0	—	0	-0	-0	-1	0.0
1951 Bro-N	5	1	.833	14	6	5	2	0	65¹	52	4	20	39	9.9	2.20	178	.223	.285	3	.143	-1	13	12	-1	0.9
1952 Bro-N	8	4	.667	25	9	0	0	0	77	76	3	47	43	14.5	5.14	71	.259	.364	1	.045	-2	-12	-13	1	-1.9
1953 *Bro-N	11	6	.647	37	7	0	0	7	110¹	92	9	30	44	10.2	2.77	154	.225	.278	2	.071	-1	19	18	0	2.7
1954 Bro-N	7	6	.538	47	2	0	0	6	108¹	101	7	56	43	13.1	4.15	98	.247	.339	1	.033	-2	-1	-1	0	-0.2
1955 *Bro-N	13	5	.722	**60**	1	0	0	11	144¹	121	12	55	67	11.0	3.24	120	.229	.301	3	.097	-1	13	13	2	2.1
1956 *Bro-N☆	10	6	.625	62	3	1	0	**19**	115²	111	11	39	75	11.9	3.35	119	.253	.318	2	.087	-1	5	5	1	1.3
1957 Bro-N★	5	7	.417	58	0	0	0	**17**	104²	104	8	27	67	11.4	3.44	121	.259	.307	2	.100	-1	5	8	2	1.3
1958 LA-N	6	6	.500	52	2	0	0	14	104	112	8	33	43	12.6	4.15	99	.283	.340	1	.056	-1	-0	-0	-0	-0.2
1959 *LA-N	5	10	.333	56	0	0	0	9	84²	91	11	25	37	12.4	3.93	108	.282	.335	0	.000	-2	0	3	1	0.5
1960 LA-N	0	1	.000	13	0	0	0	1	17	26	1	8	15	18.0	5.82	68	.351	.420	1	.500	1	-4	-4	-0	-0.2
Det-A	0	3	.000	14	0	0	0	2	19¹	19	2	12	6	14.4	5.12	77	.257	.360	0	.000	-0	-1	-0	-0	-0.4
*Pit-N	3	0	1.000	15	0	0	0	3	30¹	29	0	11	21	12.2	1.48	253	.254	.325	0	—	0	8	8	0	0.9
1961 Pit-N	4	1	.800	56	1	0	0	8	92²	102	8	31	49	13.1	3.69	108	.284	.344	1	.100	-0	4	3	-1	0.1
1962 NY-N	0	0	—	3	0	0	0	0	4	5	1	2	3	16.2	11.25	37	.278	.316	0	—	0	-3	-3	0	0.0
Total 13	77	56	.579	513	38	7	2	96	1079²	1043	81	396	551	12.1	3.63	112	.256	.323	17	.075	-11	41	50	8	6.9
● **BOB LACEY** Lacey, Robert Joseph b: 8/25/53, Fredericksburg, Va. BR/TL, 6'5", 210 lbs. Deb: 5/13/77																									
1977 Oak-A	6	8	.429	64	0	0	0	7	121²	100	13	43	69	10.6	3.03	133	.234	.304	0	—	0	14	13	3	2.0
1978 Oak-A	8	9	.471	**74**	0	0	0	5	119²	126	10	35	60	12.2	3.01	121	.270	.323	0	—	0	10	8	2	1.4
1979 Oak-A	1	5	.167	42	0	0	0	4	47²	66	7	24	33	17.2	5.85	69	.327	.401	0	—	0	-9	-10	-2	-1.2
1980 Oak-A	3	2	.600	47	1	1	0	6	79²	68	7	21	46	10.2	2.94	128	.234	.288	0	—	0	10	7	-0	0.6
1981 Cle-A	0	0	—	14	0	0	0	0	21¹	36	5	11	16.5	7.59	48	.371	.390	0	—	0	-9	-9	-0	0.0	
Tex-A	0	0	—	1	0	0	0	0	1	1	1	0	0	9.0	9.00	39	.250	.250	0	—	0	-1	-1	0	0.0
Yr	0	0	—	15	0	0	0	0	22¹	37	6	11	16.1	7.66	47	.356	.374	0	—	0	-10	-10	-0	0.0	
1983 Cal-A	2	2	.333	9	0	0	0	0	8²	12	1	9	5	21.8	5.19	77	.343	.343	0	—	0	-1	-1	-0	-0.3
1984 SF-N	1	3	.250	34	0	0	0	0	51	55	5	13	26	12.0	3.88	90	.276	.321	2	.333	-1	-2	-2	-0	-0.1
Total 7	20	29	.408	284	2	1	1	22	450²	464	49	139	251	12.1	3.67	103	.269	.325	2	.333	1	12	6	5	2.4

YEAR	TM/L	W	L	PCT	G	GS	CG	SH	SV	IP	H	HR	BB	SO	RAT	ERA	ERA+	OAV	OOB	BH	AVG	PB	PR	/A	PD	TPI

● MARCEL LACHEMANN
Lachemann, Marcel Ernest b: 6/13/41, Los Angeles, Cal. BR/TR, 6′, 185 lbs. Deb: 6/4/69 FMC

YEAR	TM/L	W	L	PCT	G	GS	CG	SH	SV	IP	H	HR	BB	SO	RAT	ERA	ERA+	OAV	OOB	BH	AVG	PB	PR	/A	PD	TPI
1969	Oak-A	4	1	.800	28	0	0	0	2	43¹	43	1	19	16	13.3	3.95	87	.261	.344	0	.000	-0	-2	-2	1	-0.3
1970	Oak-A	3	3	.500	41	0	0	0	3	58¹	58	6	18	39	12.0	2.78	127	.266	.328	0	.000	-1	6	5	1	0.6
1971	Oak-A	0	0	—	1	0	0	0	0	0¹	2	0	1	0	81.0	54.00	6	1.000	1.000	0	—	0	-2	-2	0	0.0
Total	3	7	4	.636	70	0	0	0	5	102	103	7	38	55	12.8	3.44	102	.268	.340	0	.000	-1	3	1	2	0.3

● AL LACHOWICZ
Lachowicz, Allen Robert b: 9/6/60, Pittsburgh, Pa. BR/TR, 6′3″, 198 lbs. Deb: 9/13/83

YEAR	TM/L	W	L	PCT	G	GS	CG	SH	SV	IP	H	HR	BB	SO	RAT	ERA	ERA+	OAV	OOB	BH	AVG	PB	PR	/A	PD	TPI
1983	Tex-A	0	1	.000	2	1	0	0	0	8	9	0	2	8	12.4	2.25	178	.281	.324	0	—	0	2	2	0	0.2

● LACKEY
Lackey b: Columbus, Ohio Deb: 10/2/1890

YEAR	TM/L	W	L	PCT	G	GS	CG	SH	SV	IP	H	HR	BB	SO	RAT	ERA	ERA+	OAV	OOB	BH	AVG	PB	PR	/A	PD	TPI
1890	Phi-a	0	0	—	1	0	0	0	0	2	1	0	3	1	18.0	9.00	43	.143	.400	0	.000	-0	-1	-1	-0	0.0

● GEORGE LaCLAIRE
LaClaire, George Lewis "Frenchy" b: 10/18/1886, Milton, Vt. d: 10/10/18, Farnham, Que., Can. BR/TR, 5′9″, 170 lbs. Deb: 6/5/14

YEAR	TM/L	W	L	PCT	G	GS	CG	SH	SV	IP	H	HR	BB	SO	RAT	ERA	ERA+	OAV	OOB	BH	AVG	PB	PR	/A	PD	TPI
1914	Pit-F	5	2	.714	22	7	5	1	0	103¹	99	0	25	49	10.9	4.01	72	.262	.309	5	.147	-2	-13	-13	0	-1.0
1915	Pit-F	1	2	.333	14	3	1	0	1	45²	43	1	13	10	11.0	3.35	81	.253	.306	2	.154	-1	-3	-3	1	-0.3
	Buf-F	0	0	—	1	0	0	0	0	3	4	0	1	2	15.0	6.00	47	.333	.385	0	—	-0	-1	-1	-0	0.0
	Bal-F	1	8	.111	18	9	6	1	0	84	76	2	22	30	10.5	2.46	116	.246	.296	2	.083	-2	2	4	0	0.2
	Yr	2	10	.167	33	12	7	1	2	132²	123	3	36	42	10.8	2.85	99	.251	.302	4	.108	-3	-2	-1	1	-0.1
Total	2	7	12	.368	55	19	12	2	2	236	222	3	61	91	10.8	3.36	85	.255	.305	9	.127	-5	-15	-14	1	-1.1

● FRANK LaCORTE
LaCorte, Frank Joseph b: 10/13/51, San Jose, Cal. BR/TR, 6′1″, 180 lbs. Deb: 9/8/75

YEAR	TM/L	W	L	PCT	G	GS	CG	SH	SV	IP	H	HR	BB	SO	RAT	ERA	ERA+	OAV	OOB	BH	AVG	PB	PR	/A	PD	TPI
1975	Atl-N	0	3	.000	3	2	0	0	0	13²	13	1	6	10	12.5	5.27	72	.245	.322	0	.000	-1	-3	-2	0	-0.5
1976	Atl-N	3	12	.200	19	17	1	0	0	105¹	97	6	53	79	13.3	4.70	81	.249	.348	3	.091	-2	-14	-11	-0	-1.6
1977	Atl-N	1	8	.111	14	7	0	0	0	37	67	10	29	28	23.8	11.68	38	.394	.488	2	.200	-0	-32	-30	-0	-5.3
1978	Atl-N	0	1	.000	2	2	0	0	0	14²	9	0	4	7	8.0	3.68	110	.180	.241	0	.000	-0	-1	-0	0	-0.1
1979	Atl-N	0	0	—	6	0	0	0	0	8¹	9	2	5	6	15.1	7.56	54	.273	.368	0	.000	-0	-4	-3	-0	-0.5
	Hou-N	1	2	.333	12	3	0	0	0	27	21	3	10	24	10.3	5.00	70	.208	.279	0	.000	-0	-4	-4	-1	-0.5
	Yr	1	2	.333	18	3	0	0	0	35¹	30	5	15	30	11.5	5.60	65	.224	.302	0	.000	-0	-7	-8	-1	-0.5
1980	*Hou-N	8	5	.615	55	0	0	0	11	83	61	4	43	66	11.3	2.82	117	.210	.311	1	.167	0	7	4	-2	0.6
1981	*Hou-N	4	2	.667	37	0	0	0	5	42	41	1	21	40	13.3	3.64	90	.258	.344	1	.333	-0	-1	-2	-0	-0.3
1982	Hou-N	1	5	.167	55	0	0	0	7	76¹	71	5	46	51	13.8	4.48	74	.247	.350	0	.000	-1	-7	-10	-2	-1.2
1983	Hou-N	4	4	.500	37	0	0	0	3	53¹	35	3	28	48	11.0	5.06	67	.190	.304	1	.200	0	-9	-10	-1	-1.5
1984	Cal-A	1	2	.333	13	1	0	0	0	29	33	9	13	14	14.1	7.06	56	.282	.354	0	—	0	-10	-10	-0	-0.9
Total	10	23	44	.343	253	32	1	0	26	490	457	49	258	372	13.3	5.01	72	.249	.345	8	.104	-4	-75	-77	-7	-11.2

● MIKE LaCOSS
LaCoss, Michael James (b: Michael James Marks) b: 5/30/56, Glendale, Cal. BR/TR, 6′4″, 190 lbs. Deb: 7/18/78

YEAR	TM/L	W	L	PCT	G	GS	CG	SH	SV	IP	H	HR	BB	SO	RAT	ERA	ERA+	OAV	OOB	BH	AVG	PB	PR	/A	PD	TPI
1978	Cin-N	4	8	.333	16	15	2	1	0	96	104	5	46	31	14.2	4.50	79	.288	.370	2	.067	-2	-10	-10	-1	-1.4
1979	*Cin-N★	14	8	.636	35	32	6	1	0	205²	202	13	79	73	12.4	3.50	107	.263	.333	9	.129	-1	5	5	1	0.5
1980	Cin-N	10	12	.455	34	29	4	2	0	169¹	207	9	68	59	14.7	4.62	77	.303	.367	5	.091	-3	-19	-20	1	-2.5
1981	Cin-N	4	7	.364	20	13	1	1	1	78	97	7	30	22	15.3	6.12	58	.325	.386	0	.000	-2	-23	-22	0	-3.0
1982	Hou-N	6	6	.500	41	8	0	0	0	115	107	3	54	51	12.9	2.90	115	.252	.342	6	.250	2	9	5	-1	0.7
1983	Hou-N	5	7	.417	38	17	2	0	1	138	142	10	56	53	13.0	4.43	77	.273	.346	3	.086	-2	-12	-16	1	-1.4
1984	Hou-N	7	5	.583	39	18	2	1	3	132	132	3	55	86	12.8	4.02	83	.261	.334	4	.129	-1	-6	-10	1	-0.9
1985	KC-A	1	1	.500	21	0	0	0	1	40²	49	2	29	26	17.3	5.09	82	.304	.411	0	—	0	-4	-4	-0	-0.2
1986	SF-N	10	13	.435	37	31	4	1	0	204¹	179	14	70	86	11.2	3.57	99	.240	.310	14	.230	6	3	-1	0	0.5
1987	*SF-N	13	10	.565	39	26	2	1	0	171	184	16	63	79	13.1	3.68	104	.283	.348	3	.060	-2	8	3	4	0.5
1988	SF-N	7	7	.500	19	19	1	1	0	114¹	99	5	47	70	11.6	3.62	90	.234	.312	8	.242	3	-2	-5	3	0.1
1989	*SF-N	10	10	.500	45	18	1	0	6	150¹	143	5	65	78	12.9	3.17	106	.255	.340	3	.073	-1	5	3	-1	0.3
1990	SF-N	6	4	.600	13	12	1	0	0	77²	75	5	39	39	13.2	3.94	92	.259	.347	1	.043	-1	-1	-3	-1	-0.5
1991	SF-N	1	5	.167	18	5	0	0	0	47¹	61	4	24	30	16.5	7.23	50	.314	.395	2	.222	1	-19	-19	-0	-2.1
Total	14	98	103	.488	415	243	26	9	12	1739²	1786	99	725	783	13.1	4.02	88	.270	.345	60	.125	-4	-66	-93	8	-9.4

● KERRY LACY
Lacy, Kerry Ardeen b: 8/7/72, Chattanooga, Tenn. BR/TR, 6′2″, 195 lbs. Deb: 8/16/96

YEAR	TM/L	W	L	PCT	G	GS	CG	SH	SV	IP	H	HR	BB	SO	RAT	ERA	ERA+	OAV	OOB	BH	AVG	PB	PR	/A	PD	TPI
1996	Bos-A	2	0	1.000	11	0	0	0	0	10²	15	2	8	9	20.3	3.38	152	.333	.444	0	—	0	2	2	-0	0.3

● PETE LADD
Ladd, Peter Linwood b: 7/17/56, Portland, Maine BR/TR, 6′3″, 240 lbs. Deb: 8/17/79

YEAR	TM/L	W	L	PCT	G	GS	CG	SH	SV	IP	H	HR	BB	SO	RAT	ERA	ERA+	OAV	OOB	BH	AVG	PB	PR	/A	PD	TPI
1979	Hou-N	1	1	.500	10	0	0	0	0	12¹	8	1	8	6	13.1	2.92	120	.178	.327	0	.000	-0	1	1	0	0.1
1982	*Mil-A	1	3	.250	16	0	0	0	3	18	16	5	6	12	11.0	4.00	95	.239	.301	0	—	-0	-1	-0	1	-0.1
1983	Mil-A	3	4	.429	44	0	0	0	25	49¹	30	3	16	41	8.6	2.55	146	.172	.246	0	—	0	8	6	-0	1.6
1984	Mil-A	4	9	.308	54	0	0	0	3	91	94	8	38	75	13.2	5.24	73	.266	.339	0	—	-0	-13	-14	-2	-1.9
1985	Mil-A	0	0	—	29	0	0	0	2	45²	58	5	10	22	13.8	4.53	92	.315	.357	0	—	-0	-2	-2	-0	-0.0
1986	Sea-A	8	6	.571	52	0	0	0	6	70²	69	10	18	53	11.5	3.82	111	.258	.313	0	—	0	3	3	-1	0.5
Total	6	17	23	.425	205	1	0	0	39	287	275	40	96	209	11.9	4.14	96	.252	.318	0	.000	-0	-2	-6	-4	0.2

● DOYLE LADE
Lade, Doyle Marion "Porky" b: 2/17/21, Fairbury, Neb. BR/TR, 5′10″, 183 lbs. Deb: 9/18/46

YEAR	TM/L	W	L	PCT	G	GS	CG	SH	SV	IP	H	HR	BB	SO	RAT	ERA	ERA+	OAV	OOB	BH	AVG	PB	PR	/A	PD	TPI
1946	Chi-N	0	2	.000	3	2	0	0	0	15¹	15	0	3	8	11.2	4.11	81	.238	.284	1	.200	-0	-1	-1	0	-0.2
1947	Chi-N	11	10	.524	34	25	7	1	0	187¹	202	15	79	62	13.5	3.94	100	.276	.347	13	.217	2	2	0	2	0.5
1948	Chi-N	5	6	.455	19	12	6	0	0	87¹	99	4	31	29	13.5	4.02	97	.283	.343	5	.156	-1	-1	-1	-0	-0.1
1949	Chi-N	4	5	.444	36	13	5	1	1	129²	141	14	58	43	14.0	5.00	81	.274	.350	7	.219	2	-14	-14	0	-0.7
1950	Chi-N	5	6	.455	34	12	2	0	2	117²	126	14	50	36	13.6	4.74	89	.275	.349	10	.286	3	-8	-7	3	-0.0
Total	5	25	29	.463	126	64	20	2	3	537¹	583	47	221	178	13.6	4.39	91	.275	.346	36	.220	6	-21	-23	7	-0.5

● STEVE LADEW
Ladew, Stephen b: St.Louis, Mo. Deb: 9/27/1889 ♦

YEAR	TM/L	W	L	PCT	G	GS	CG	SH	SV	IP	H	HR	BB	SO	RAT	ERA	ERA+	OAV	OOB	BH	AVG	PB	PR	/A	PD	TPI
1889	KC-a	0	0	—	1	0	0	0	0	2	3	0	3	0	18.0	4.50	93	.143	.400	0	.000	-0	-0	-0	0	0.0

● FLIP LAFFERTY
Lafferty, Frank Bernard b: 5/4/1854, Scranton, Pa. d: 2/8/10, Wilmington, Del. TR, Deb: 9/15/1876 ♦

YEAR	TM/L	W	L	PCT	G	GS	CG	SH	SV	IP	H	HR	BB	SO	RAT	ERA	ERA+	OAV	OOB	BH	AVG	PB	PR	/A	PD	TPI
1876	Phi-N	0	1	.000	1	1	1	0	0	9	5	0	0	0	5.0	0.00	—	.152	.152	0	.000	-1	2	1	0	0.2

● ED LAFITTE
Lafitte, Edward Francis "Doc" b: 4/7/1886, New Orleans, La. d: 4/12/71, Jenkintown, Pa. BR/TR, 6′2″, 188 lbs. Deb: 4/16/09

YEAR	TM/L	W	L	PCT	G	GS	CG	SH	SV	IP	H	HR	BB	SO	RAT	ERA	ERA+	OAV	OOB	BH	AVG	PB	PR	/A	PD	TPI
1909	Det-A	0	0	.000	3	1	0	0	1	14	22	2	2	11	16.1	3.86	65	.344	.373	1	.250	0	-2	-2	0	-0.2
1911	Det-A	11	8	.579	29	20	15	0	1	172¹	205	2	52	63	13.7	3.92	88	.302	.356	11	.157	-2	-11	-9	-2	-1.3
1912	Det-A	0	0	—	1	0	0	0	0	1²	2	0	2	0	21.6	16.20	20	.333	.500	0	—	-0	-2	-0	0	0.0
1914	Bro-F	18	15	.545	42	33	23	6	1	290²	260	7	127	137	12.5	2.63	109	.248	.338	26	.257	3	8	8	3	1.5
1915	Bro-F	6	9	.400	17	16	7	0	0	117²	126	6	57	34	14.1	3.98	68	.288	.371	14	.264	2	-16	-16	-2	-1.9
	Buf-F	2	2	.500	14	5	1	0	1	50¹	53	1	22	17	13.8	3.40	82	.286	.368	2	.118	-1	-4	-3	-0	-0.4
	Yr	8	11	.421	31	21	8	0	1	168	179	7	79	51	13.9	3.80	74	.287	.369	16	.229	1	-20	-20	-2	-2.3
Total	5	37	35	.514	106	75	47	1	5	646²	668	18	262	262	13.3	3.34	89	.284	.353	54	.220	1	-27	-25	-2	-2.3

● ED LAGGER
Lagger, Edwin Joseph b: 7/14/12, Joliet, Ill. d: 11/10/81, Joliet, Ill. BR/TR, 6′3″, 200 lbs. Deb: 6/15/34

YEAR	TM/L	W	L	PCT	G	GS	CG	SH	SV	IP	H	HR	BB	SO	RAT	ERA	ERA+	OAV	OOB	BH	AVG	PB	PR	/A	PD	TPI
1934	Phi-A	0	0	—	8	0	0	0	0	18	27	1	14	2	21.0	11.00	40	.342	.447	0	.000	-1	-13	-13	1	0.0

● LERRIN LaGROW
LaGrow, Lerrin Harris b: 7/8/48, Phoenix, Ariz. BR/TR, 6′5″, 220 lbs. Deb: 7/28/70

YEAR	TM/L	W	L	PCT	G	GS	CG	SH	SV	IP	H	HR	BB	SO	RAT	ERA	ERA+	OAV	OOB	BH	AVG	PB	PR	/A	PD	TPI
1970	Det-A	1	0	.000	10	0	0	0	0	12¹	16	2	6	7	16.1	7.30	51	.308	.379	0	.000	-0	-5	-5	-0	-0.4
1972	*Det-A	0	1	.000	16	0	0	0	2	27¹	22	0	6	9	9.2	1.32	239	.222	.267	0	—	0	5	6	-0	0.3
1973	Det-A	1	5	.167	21	3	0	0	0	54	54	8	23	33	13.0	4.33	94	.263	.341	0	—	0	-3	-1	1	-0.2
1974	Det-A	8	19	.296	37	34	11	0	0	216¹	245	21	80	85	13.6	4.66	83	.287	.350	0	—	0	-25	-21	3	-2.2
1975	Det-A	7	14	.333	32	26	7	0	0	164¹	183	15	66	75	13.7	4.38	92	.280	.348	0	—	0	-11	-7	-2	-1.1
1976	StL-N	1	1	.500	9	0	0	0	0	24¹	11	0	13	16	11.1	1.48	239	.241	.305	0	—	0	5	5	0	0.5
1977	Chi-A	7	3	.700	66	0	0	0	25	98²	81	9	35	63	10.7	2.46	166	.230	.302	0	—	0	17	18	1	2.7
1978	Chi-A	6	5	.545	46	0	0	0	16	88	85	9	38	41	12.9	4.40	86	.260	.342	0	—	0	-6	-6	2	-0.8
1979	Chi-A	0	3	.000	11	2	0	0	1	17²	27	1	8	9	22.4	9.17	46	.346	.463	0	—	0	-10	-10	-0	-1.5
	LA-N	5	1	.833	31	0	0	0	4	37	38	2	18	22	13.6	3.41	107	.270	.358	1	.333	0	1	1	-0	0.2

YEAR TM/L	W	L	PCT	G	GS	CG	SH	SV	IP	H	HR	BB	SO	RAT	ERA	ERA+	OAV	OOB	BH	AVG	PB	PR	/A	PD	TPI
1980 Phi-N	0	2	.000	25	0	0	0	3	39	42	5	17	21	13.6	4.15	91	.276	.349	1	.250	0	-2	-2	-0	-0.1
Total 10	34	55	.382	309	67	19	2	54	779	814	74	312	375	13.1	4.11	94	.271	.342	2	.154	-0	-33	-21	2	-2.9

● **JEFF LAHTI**   Lahti, Jeffrey Allen b: 10/8/56, Oregon City, Ore.   BR/TR, 6', 180 lbs.   Deb: 6/27/82

YEAR TM/L	W	L	PCT	G	GS	CG	SH	SV	IP	H	HR	BB	SO	RAT	ERA	ERA+	OAV	OOB	BH	AVG	PB	PR	/A	PD	TPI
1982 *StL-N	5	4	.556	33	1	0	0	0	56²	53	3	21	22	12.1	3.81	95	.245	.318	1	.077	-1	-1	-1	2	-0.2
1983 StL-N	3	3	.500	53	0	0	0	0	74	64	2	29	26	11.4	3.16	114	.240	.316	0	.000	-1	4	4	1	0.3
1984 StL-N	4	2	.667	63	0	0	0	1	84²	69	6	34	45	11.2	3.72	93	.225	.306	1	.167	-1	-1	-2	0	-0.1
1985 *StL-N	5	2	.714	52	0	0	0	19	68¹	63	3	26	41	11.7	1.84	192	.251	.321	0	.000	-1	13	13	-0	1.9
1986 StL-N	0	0	—	4	0	0	0	0	2¹	3	0	1	3	15.4	0.00	—	.333	.400	—	0	1	1	-0	0.0
Total 5	17	11	.607	205	1	0	0	20	286	252	14	111	137	11.6	3.12	114	.240	.316	2	.053	-3	15	14	2	1.9

● **EDDIE LAKE**   Lake, Edward Erving "Sparky" b: 3/18/16, Antioch, Cal.   d: 6/7/95, Castro Valley, Cal.   BR/TR, 5'7", 160 lbs.   Deb: 9/26/39 ◆

YEAR TM/L	W	L	PCT	G	GS	CG	SH	SV	IP	H	HR	BB	SO	RAT	ERA	ERA+	OAV	OOB	BH	AVG	PB	PR	/A	PD	TPI
1944 Bos-A	0	0	—	6	0	0	0	0	19¹	20	2	11	7	15.8	4.19	81	.278	.395	26	.206	-1	-2	-2	0	0.1

● **JOE LAKE**   Lake, Joseph Henry b: 1/6/1881, Brooklyn, N.Y.   d: 6/30/50, Brooklyn, N.Y.   BR/TR, 6', 185 lbs.   Deb: 4/21/08

YEAR TM/L	W	L	PCT	G	GS	CG	SH	SV	IP	H	HR	BB	SO	RAT	ERA	ERA+	OAV	OOB	BH	AVG	PB	PR	/A	PD	TPI
1908 NY-A	9	22	.290	38	27	19	2	0	269¹	252	6	77	118	11.2	3.17	78	.242	.298	21	.188	0	-23	-21	-4	-2.8
1909 NY-A	14	11	.560	31	26	17	3	1	215¹	180	2	59	117	10.2	1.88	135	.225	.283	14	.173	1	14	16	5	2.7
1910 StL-A	11	17	.393	35	29	24	1	2	261¹	243	2	77	141	11.1	2.20	112	.248	.304	21	.231	2	9	8	1	1.2
1911 StL-A	10	15	.400	30	25	14	2	0	215¹	245	3	40	69	12.1	3.30	102	.282	.316	21	.262	2	1	2	6	1.0
1912 StL-A	1	7	.125	11	6	4	0	0	57	70	4	16	28	13.7	4.42	75	.314	.363	3	.150	-1	-7	-7	2	-0.8
Det-A	9	11	.450	26	14	11	0	1	162²	190	3	39	86	12.8	3.10	105	.296	.340	9	.145	-3	4	3	0	0.1
Yr	10	18	.357	37	20	15	0	1	219²	260	3	55	114	13.0	3.44	95	.301	.345	12	.146	-5	-3	-4	2	-0.7
1913 Det-A	8	7	.533	28	12	6	0	1	137	149	3	24	35	11.4	3.28	89	.278	.309	12	.267	4	-5	-6	3	0.2
Total 6	62	90	.408	199	139	95	8	5	1318	1329	19	332	594	11.5	2.85	99	.261	.309	101	.206	4	-7	-5	12	1.6

● **AL LAKEMAN**   Lakeman, Albert Wesley "Moose" b: 12/31/18, Cincinnati, Ohio   d: 5/25/76, Spartanburg, S.C.   BR/TR, 6'2", 195 lbs.   Deb: 4/19/42 C◆

YEAR TM/L	W	L	PCT	G	GS	CG	SH	SV	IP	H	HR	BB	SO	RAT	ERA	ERA+	OAV	OOB	BH	AVG	PB	PR	/A	PD	TPI
1948 Phi-N	0	0	—	1	0	0	0	0	0²	1	1	0	0	13.5	13.50	29	.333	.333	11	.162	0	-1	-1	-0	0.0

● **JACK LAMABE**   Lamabe, John Alexander b: 10/3/36, Farmingdale, N.Y.   BR/TR, 6'1", 198 lbs.   Deb: 4/17/62

YEAR TM/L	W	L	PCT	G	GS	CG	SH	SV	IP	H	HR	BB	SO	RAT	ERA	ERA+	OAV	OOB	BH	AVG	PB	PR	/A	PD	TPI
1962 Pit-N	3	1	.750	46	0	0	0	2	78	70	4	40	56	12.7	2.88	136	.238	.329	0	.000	-1	9	9	1	0.5
1963 Bos-A	7	4	.636	65	2	0	0	6	151¹	139	8	46	93	11.2	3.15	120	.247	.308	3	.094	-1	8	11	1	0.8
1964 Bos-A	9	13	.409	39	25	3	0	1	177¹	235	25	57	109	14.9	5.89	65	.318	.369	6	.115	-1	-45	-40	-0	-4.6
1965 Bos-A	0	3	.000	14	0	0	0	0	25¹	34	5	14	17	18.1	8.17	46	.340	.436	0	.000	-0	-13	-13	0	-1.4
Hou-N	0	2	.000	3	2	0	0	0	12²	17	3	3	6	14.2	4.26	79	.315	.351	1	.250	-0	-1	-1	-0	-0.2
1966 Chi-A	7	9	.438	34	17	3	2	0	121¹	116	9	35	67	11.3	3.93	81	.251	.305	2	.057	-2	-7	-10	-0	-1.5
1967 Chi-A	1	0	1.000	3	0	0	0	0	5	7	1	2	6	14.4	1.80	172	.318	.348	0	1	1	1	0	0.1
NY-N	0	3	.000	16	2	0	1	0	31²	24	4	8	23	9.1	3.98	85	.200	.250	0	-2	-2	-0	-0.2
*StL-N	3	4	.429	23	1	1	1	4	47²	43	2	10	30	10.0	2.83	116	.244	.285	1	.200	0	4	3	0	0.4
Yr	3	7	.300	39	3	1	1	5	79¹	67	6	18	53	9.6	3.29	101	.226	.270	1	.133	0	1	0	0	0.2
1968 Chi-N	3	2	.600	42	0	0	0	1	61¹	68	7	24	30	13.6	4.26	74	.289	.358	1	.200	-1	-9	-7	-1	-0.6
Total 7	33	41	.446	285	49	7	3	15	711²	753	67	238	434	12.7	4.24	85	.272	.333	15	.096	-6	-55	-51	0	-6.7

● **AL LaMACCHIA**   LaMacchia, Alfred Anthony b: 7/22/21, St.Louis, Mo.   BR/TR, 5'10.5", 190 lbs.   Deb: 9/27/43

YEAR TM/L	W	L	PCT	G	GS	CG	SH	SV	IP	H	HR	BB	SO	RAT	ERA	ERA+	OAV	OOB	BH	AVG	PB	PR	/A	PD	TPI
1943 StL-A	0	1	.000	1	1	0	0	0	4	9	0	2	2	24.8	11.25	30	.450	.500	0	.000	-0	-4	-4	-0	-0.6
1945 StL-A	2	0	1.000	5	0	0	0	0	9	6	3	2	2	9.2	2.00	176	.207	.281	0	.000	-0	1	2	0	0.3
1946 StL-A	0	1	.000	8	0	0	0	0	15	17	2	7	3	14.4	6.00	62	.279	.353	0	.000	-0	-4	-4	-0	-1.1
Was-A	0	1	.000	2	0	0	0	0	2²	6	1	2	0	27.0	16.88	20	.462	.533	—	0	-4	-4	-0	-1.1
Yr	0	2	.000	10	0	0	0	0	17²	23	3	9	3	16.3	7.64	48	.311	.386	0	.000	-0	-8	-8	-0	-1.1
Total 3	2	2	.500	16	1	0	0	0	30²	38	3	14	7	15.3	6.46	55	.309	.380	0	.000	-1	-10	-10	-1	-1.4

● **FRANK LaMANNA**   LaManna, Frank "Hank" b: 8/22/19, Waterton, Pa.   d: 9/1/80, Syracuse, N.Y.   BR/TR, 6'2.5", 195 lbs.   Deb: 4/16/40

YEAR TM/L	W	L	PCT	G	GS	CG	SH	SV	IP	H	HR	BB	SO	RAT	ERA	ERA+	OAV	OOB	BH	AVG	PB	PR	/A	PD	TPI
1940 Bos-N	1	0	1.000	5	1	0	0	0	13¹	13	1	8	3	14.2	4.73	79	.271	.375	1	.200	0	-1	-1	0	-0.1
1941 Bos-N	5	4	.556	35	4	0	0	1	72²	77	5	56	23	16.6	5.33	67	.285	.410	9	.281	-1	-14	-14	1	-1.4
1942 Bos-N	0	1	.000	5	0	0	0	0	6²	5	1	3	2	10.8	5.40	62	.208	.296	0	.000	-0	-2	-2	-0	-0.3
Total 3	6	5	.545	45	5	1	0	1	92²	95	7	67	28	15.8	5.24	68	.278	.398	10	.256	1	-17	-17	1	-1.8

● **FRANK LAMANSKE**   Lamanske, Frank James "Lefty" b: 9/30/06, Oglesby, Ill.   d: 8/4/71, Olney, Ill.   BL/TL, 5'11", 170 lbs.   Deb: 4/27/35

YEAR TM/L	W	L	PCT	G	GS	CG	SH	SV	IP	H	HR	BB	SO	RAT	ERA	ERA+	OAV	OOB	BH	AVG	PB	PR	/A	PD	TPI
1935 Bro-N	0	0	—	2	0	0	0	0	3²	5	0	1	1	14.7	7.36	54	.313	.353	0	.000	-0	-1	-1	0	0.0

● **WAYNE LaMASTER**   LaMaster, Noble Wayne b: 2/13/07, Speed, Ind.   d: 8/4/89, New Albany, Ind.   BL/TL, 5'8", 170 lbs.   Deb: 4/19/37

YEAR TM/L	W	L	PCT	G	GS	CG	SH	SV	IP	H	HR	BB	SO	RAT	ERA	ERA+	OAV	OOB	BH	AVG	PB	PR	/A	PD	TPI
1937 Phi-N	15	19	.441	50	30	10	1	4	220	255	24	82	135	13.8	5.31	82	.290	.352	15	.190	-2	-34	-24	-4	-3.9
1938 Phi-N	4	7	.364	18	12	1	1	0	63²	80	8	31	35	16.1	7.77	50	.301	.380	9	.409	4	-28	-27	1	-3.4
Bro-N	0	1	.000	3	0	0	0	0	11¹	17	0	3	3	15.9	4.76	82	.340	.377	1	.167	-0	-1	-1	-0	-0.1
Yr	4	8	.333	21	12	1	1	0	75	97	8	34	38	15.7	7.32	53	.304	.371	10	.357	4	-29	-29	1	-3.5
Total 2	19	27	.413	71	42	11	2	4	295¹	352	32	116	173	14.4	5.82	72	.295	.360	25	.234	1	-64	-53	-4	-7.4

● **JOHN LAMB**   Lamb, John Andrew b: 7/20/46, Sharon, Conn.   BR/TR, 6'3", 180 lbs.   Deb: 8/12/70

YEAR TM/L	W	L	PCT	G	GS	CG	SH	SV	IP	H	HR	BB	SO	RAT	ERA	ERA+	OAV	OOB	BH	AVG	PB	PR	/A	PD	TPI
1970 Pit-N	0	1	.000	23	0	0	0	0	32¹	23	2	13	24	10.6	2.78	140	.209	.304	0	.000	-0	5	4	-1	0.1
1971 Pit-N	0	0	—	2	0	0	0	0	4¹	3	0	1	1	8.3	0.00	—	.188	.235	0	2	2	0	0.0
1973 Pit-N	0	1	.000	22	0	0	0	5	29²	37	3	10	11	14.3	6.07	58	.308	.362	0	.000	-0	-8	-8	0	-0.4
Total 3	0	2	.000	47	0	0	0	5	66¹	63	5	24	36	12.1	4.07	91	.256	.327	0	.000	-1	-2	-3	-1	-0.3

● **RAY LAMB**   Lamb, Raymond Richard b: 12/28/44, Glendale, Cal.   BR/TR, 6'1", 175 lbs.   Deb: 8/1/69

YEAR TM/L	W	L	PCT	G	GS	CG	SH	SV	IP	H	HR	BB	SO	RAT	ERA	ERA+	OAV	OOB	BH	AVG	PB	PR	/A	PD	TPI
1969 LA-N	0	1	.000	10	0	0	0	0	15	12	2	7	11	11.4	1.80	185	.235	.328	0	.000	-0	3	3	0	0.2
1970 LA-N	5	1	.857	35	0	0	0	0	57	59	4	27	32	14.2	3.79	101	.277	.369	0	.000	-0	-1	-1	-0	-0.1
1971 Cle-A	6	12	.333	43	21	3	1	1	158¹	147	11	69	91	12.3	3.35	114	.247	.326	4	.093	-2	2	8	-2	0.5
1972 Cle-A	5	6	.455	34	9	0	0	1	107²	101	5	29	64	11.0	3.09	104	.248	.299	0	.000	-1	-0	1	-1	-0.1
1973 Cle-A	4	3	.500	32	1	0	0	2	86	98	7	42	60	14.6	4.60	85	.291	.373	0	-0	-8	-7	-0	-0.5
Total 5	20	23	.465	154	31	3	1	4	424	417	29	174	258	12.7	3.54	104	.260	.335	4	.058	-4	-1	7	-4	0.0

● **CLAYTON LAMBERT**   Lambert, Clayton Patrick b: 3/26/17, Summit, Ill.   d: 4/3/81, Ogden, Utah   BR/TR, 6'2", 185 lbs.   Deb: 4/22/46

YEAR TM/L	W	L	PCT	G	GS	CG	SH	SV	IP	H	HR	BB	SO	RAT	ERA	ERA+	OAV	OOB	BH	AVG	PB	PR	/A	PD	TPI
1946 Cin-N	2	2	.500	23	4	2	0	1	52²	48	3	20	21	11.8	4.27	78	.251	.325	2	.154	-1	-5	-5	-1	-0.6
1947 Cin-N	0	0	—	3	0	0	0	0	5²	12	3	6	1	28.6	15.88	26	.444	.545	0	.000	-0	-7	-7	0	-0.7
Total 2	2	2	.500	26	4	2	0	1	58¹	60	6	26	22	13.4	5.40	63	.273	.355	2	.143	-1	-12	-13	-1	-1.4

● **GENE LAMBERT**   Lambert, Eugene Marion b: 4/26/21, Crenshaw, Miss.   BR/TR, 5'11", 175 lbs.   Deb: 9/14/41

YEAR TM/L	W	L	PCT	G	GS	CG	SH	SV	IP	H	HR	BB	SO	RAT	ERA	ERA+	OAV	OOB	BH	AVG	PB	PR	/A	PD	TPI
1941 Phi-N	0	1	.000	2	1	0	0	0	9	11	0	2	3	13.0	2.00	185	.297	.333	0	.000	-0	2	2	-0	0.1
1942 Phi-N	0	0	—	1	0	0	0	0	1	3	0	0	1	27.0	9.00	37	.500	.500	—	0	-1	-1	0	0.0
Total 2	0	1	.000	3	1	0	0	0	10	14	0	2	4	14.4	2.70	136	.326	.356	0	.000	-0	2	2	0	0.1

● **OTIS LAMBETH**   Lambeth, Otis Samuel b: 5/13/1890, Berlin, Kan.   d: 6/5/76, Moran, Kan.   BR/TR, 6', 175 lbs.   Deb: 7/16/16

YEAR TM/L	W	L	PCT	G	GS	CG	SH	SV	IP	H	HR	BB	SO	RAT	ERA	ERA+	OAV	OOB	BH	AVG	PB	PR	/A	PD	TPI
1916 Cle-A	4	3	.571	15	9	3	0	1	74	69	1	38	28	13.4	2.92	103	.256	.354	3	.111	-1	1	1	-2	-0.3
1917 Cle-A	7	6	.538	26	10	2	0	1	97¹	97	2	30	27	12.8	3.14	90	.274	.349	6	.188	-0	-5	-3	-1	-0.6
1918 Cle-A	0	0	—	2	0	0	0	0	7	10	0	6	3	20.6	6.43	47	.370	.485	1	1.000	-0	-3	-3	0	0.0
Total 3	11	9	.550	43	19	5	0	3	178¹	176	3	74	58	13.3	3.18	92	.270	.357	10	.167	-1	-9	-5	-3	-0.9

● **FRED LAMLINE**   Lamline, Frederick Arthur "Dutch" (b: Frederick Arthur Lamlein)
   b: 8/14/1887, Port Huron, Mich.   d: 9/20/70, Port Huron, Mich.   BR/TR, 5'11", 171 lbs.   Deb: 9/18/12

YEAR TM/L	W	L	PCT	G	GS	CG	SH	SV	IP	H	HR	BB	SO	RAT	ERA	ERA+	OAV	OOB	BH	AVG	PB	PR	/A	PD	TPI
1912 Chi-A	0	0	—	2	0	0	0	0	2	7	0	2	1	40.5	31.50	10	.583	.643	0	—	0	-6	-6	0	0.0
1915 StL-N	0	0	—	4	0	0	0	0	19	21	0	3	11	12.3	1.42	196	.300	.347	1	.125	-0	3	3	0	0.0
Total 2	0	0	—	6	0	0	0	0	21	28	0	5	12	15.0	4.29	64	.329	.393	1	.125	-0	-3	-3	0	0.0

YEAR	TM/L	W	L	PCT	G	GS	CG	SH	SV	IP	H	HR	BB	SO	RAT	ERA	ERA+	OAV	OOB	BH	AVG	PB	PR	/A	PD	TPI

● **DENNIS LAMP**   Lamp, Dennis Patrick   b: 9/23/52, Los Angeles, Cal.   BR/TR, 6'3", 210 lbs.   Deb: 8/21/77

YEAR	TM/L	W	L	PCT	G	GS	CG	SH	SV	IP	H	HR	BB	SO	RAT	ERA	ERA+	OAV	OOB	BH	AVG	PB	PR	/A	PD	TPI
1977	Chi-N	0	2	.000	11	3	0	0	0	30	43	3	8	12	15.9	6.30	70	.344	.393	3	.375	1	-8	-6	0	-0.3
1978	Chi-N	7	15	.318	37	36	6	3	0	223²	221	16	56	73	11.3	3.30	122	.258	.307	15	.205	0	7	18	3	2.1
1979	Chi-N	11	10	.524	38	32	6	1	0	200¹	223	14	46	86	12.3	3.50	117	.287	.331	9	.155	0	5	14	4	1.6
1980	Chi-N	10	14	.417	41	37	2	1	0	202²	259	16	82	83	15.2	5.20	75	.317	.380	6	.098	-3	-36	-29	2	-3.2
1981	Chi-A	7	6	.538	27	10	3	0	0	127	103	4	43	71	10.4	2.41	148	.222	.289	0	—	0	18	16	1	1.7
1982	Chi-A	11	8	.579	44	27	3	2	5	189²	206	9	59	78	12.9	3.99	101	.279	.337	0	—	0	2	1	2	0.2
1983	*Chi-A	7	7	.500	49	5	1	0	15	116¹	123	6	29	44	12.1	3.71	113	.275	.325	0	—	0	5	6	0	0.8
1984	Tor-A	8	8	.500	56	4	0	0	9	85	97	9	38	45	14.4	4.55	90	.285	.359	0	—	0	-5	-4	1	-0.7
1985	*Tor-A	11	0	1.000	53	1	0	0	2	105²	96	7	27	68	10.5	3.32	127	.247	.296	0	—	0	10	10	2	1.2
1986	Tor-A	2	6	.250	40	2	0	0	2	73	96	5	23	30	15.0	5.05	83	.309	.358	0	—	0	-7	-7	0	-0.7
1987	Oak-A	1	3	.250	36	5	0	0	0	56²	76	5	22	36	15.7	5.08	81	.326	.387	0	—	0	-4	-6	-0	-0.1
1988	Bos-A	7	6	.538	46	0	0	0	0	82²	92	3	19	49	12.3	3.48	118	.284	.328	0	—	0	4	6	1	1.0
1989	Bos-A	4	2	.667	42	0	0	0	0	112¹	96	4	27	61	9.9	2.32	176	.235	.283	0	—	0	19	22	2	1.2
1990	*Bos-A	3	5	.375	47	1	0	0	0	105¹	114	10	30	49	12.3	4.68	87	.279	.333	0	—	0	-9	-7	0	-0.5
1991	Bos-A	6	3	.667	51	0	0	0	0	92	100	8	31	57	13.1	4.70	92	.275	.337	0	—	0	-6	-4	0	-0.4
1992	Pit-N	1	1	.500	21	0	0	0	0	28	33	3	9	15	14.1	5.14	67	.292	.355	0	.000	0	-5	-5	0	-0.4
Total	16	96	96	.500	639	163	21	7	35	1830²	1975	122	549	857	12.6	3.93	103	.278	.333	33	.164	-3	-11	26	18	3.5

● **HENRY LAMPE**   Lampe, Henry Joseph   b: 9/19/1872, Boston, Mass.   d: 9/16/36, Dorchester, Mass.   BR/TL, 5'11.5", 175 lbs.   Deb: 5/14/1894

YEAR	TM/L	W	L	PCT	G	GS	CG	SH	SV	IP	H	HR	BB	SO	RAT	ERA	ERA+	OAV	OOB	BH	AVG	PB	PR	/A	PD	TPI
1894	Bos-N	0	1	.000	2	1	0	0	0	5¹	17	5	7	1	40.5	11.81	48	.531	.615	0	.000	—	-4	-4	0	-0.4
1895	Phi-N	0	2	.000	7	3	2	0	0	44	68	3	33	18	20.9	7.57	63	.347	.443	2	.125	-1	-14	-14	-0	-0.5
Total	2	0	3	.000	9	4	2	0	0	49¹	85	8	40	19	23.0	8.03	61	.373	.468	2	.111	-1	-17	-17	0	-0.9

● **DICK LANAHAN**   Lanahan, Richard Anthony   b: 9/27/11, Washington, D.C.   d: 3/12/75, Rochester, Minn.   BL/TL, 6', 186 lbs.   Deb: 9/15/35

YEAR	TM/L	W	L	PCT	G	GS	CG	SH	SV	IP	H	HR	BB	SO	RAT	ERA	ERA+	OAV	OOB	BH	AVG	PB	PR	/A	PD	TPI
1935	Was-A	0	3	.000	3	3	0	0	0	20²	27	2	17	10	20.0	5.66	76	.314	.438	1	.167	-0	-3	-3	-0	-0.4
1937	Was-A	0	1	.000	6	2	0	0	0	11¹	16	2	13	2	23.8	12.71	35	.320	.469	0	.000	-0	-10	-10	-0	-0.6
1940	Pit-N	6	8	.429	40	8	4	0	2	108	121	8	42	45	13.7	4.25	90	.279	.345	4	.118	-2	-5	-5	-0	-0.8
1941	Pit-N	0	1	.000	7	0	0	0	0	12	13	1	3	5	13.5	5.25	69	.283	.353	0	.000	-0	-2	-2	-0	-0.2
Total	4	6	13	.316	56	13	4	0	2	152	177	13	75	62	15.3	5.15	76	.288	.371	-2	.119	-2	-20	-21	0	-2.0

● **LES LANCASTER**   Lancaster, Lester Wayne   b: 4/21/62, Dallas, Tex.   BR/TR, 6'2", 205 lbs.   Deb: 4/7/87

YEAR	TM/L	W	L	PCT	G	GS	CG	SH	SV	IP	H	HR	BB	SO	RAT	ERA	ERA+	OAV	OOB	BH	AVG	PB	PR	/A	PD	TPI
1987	Chi-N	8	3	.727	27	18	0	0	0	132¹	138	14	51	78	12.9	4.90	87	.268	.335	4	.082	-2	-12	-9	-1	-1.0
1988	Chi-N	4	6	.400	44	3	1	0	5	85²	89	4	34	36	13.0	3.78	95	.273	.343	1	.050	-1	-3	-2	1	-0.3
1989	*Chi-N	4	2	.667	42	0	0	0	8	72²	60	7	15	56	9.3	1.36	276	.226	.267	2	.182	0	17	19	-1	2.0
1990	Chi-N	9	5	.643	55	6	1	1	6	109	121	9	40	65	13.4	4.62	88	.283	.346	1	.050	-1	-10	-7	-1	-0.8
1991	Chi-N	9	7	.563	64	11	1	0	3	156	150	13	49	102	11.7	3.52	110	.256	.317	5	.179	-1	3	6	-1	0.5
1992	Det-A	3	4	.429	41	1	0	0	0	86²	101	11	51	35	16.1	6.33	62	.294	.389	0	—	0	-23	-23	-1	-1.7
1993	StL-N	4	1	.800	50	0	0	0	0	61¹	56	5	21	36	11.4	2.93	135	.242	.308	0	.000	-0	8	7	-1	0.4
Total	7	41	28	.594	323	39	3	1	22	703²	715	60	261	408	12.6	4.05	98	.265	.333	13	.098	-4	-21	-7	-2	-0.9

● **GARY LANCE**   Lance, Gary Dean   b: 9/21/48, Greenville, S.C.   BB/TR, 6'3", 195 lbs.   Deb: 9/28/77

YEAR	TM/L	W	L	PCT	G	GS	CG	SH	SV	IP	H	HR	BB	SO	RAT	ERA	ERA+	OAV	OOB	BH	AVG	PB	PR	/A	PD	TPI
1977	KC-A	0	1	.000	1	0	0	0	0	2	2	0	2	2	18.0	4.50	90	.286	.444	0	—	0	-0	-0	-0	-0.1

● **DOC LANDIS**   Landis, Samuel H.   b: 8/16/1854, Philadelphia, Pa.   BR, 5'11", 172 lbs.   Deb: 5/2/1882

YEAR	TM/L	W	L	PCT	G	GS	CG	SH	SV	IP	H	HR	BB	SO	RAT	ERA	ERA+	OAV	OOB	BH	AVG	PB	PR	/A	PD	TPI
1882	Phi-a	1	1	.500	2	2	2	0	0	17	16	1	1	13	9.0	3.18	94	.232	.243	2	.167	-0	-1	-0	-0	-0.1
	Bal-a	11	27	.289	42	39	35	0	0	341	409	7	46	62	12.0	3.33	83	.278	.300	29	.166	-6	-24	-22	-2	-2.6
	Yr	12	28	.300	44	41	37	0	0	358	425	8	47	75	11.9	3.32	83	.276	.298	31	.166	-7	-25	-22	-3	-2.7

● **BILL LANDIS**   Landis, William Henry   b: 10/8/42, Hanford, Cal.   BL/TL, 6'2", 178 lbs.   Deb: 9/28/63

YEAR	TM/L	W	L	PCT	G	GS	CG	SH	SV	IP	H	HR	BB	SO	RAT	ERA	ERA+	OAV	OOB	BH	AVG	PB	PR	/A	PD	TPI
1963	KC-A	0	0	—	1	0	0	0	0	1²	0	0	1	3	5.4	0.00	—	.000	.167	0	—	0	1	1	-0	0.0
1967	Bos-A	1	0	1.000	18	1	0	0	0	25²	24	6	11	23	12.3	5.26	66	.253	.330	0	.000	-0	-6	-5	-1	-0.3
1968	Bos-A	3	3	.500	38	1	0	0	3	60	48	4	30	59	12.0	3.15	100	.223	.324	0	.000	-1	-1	0	-1	-0.2
1969	Bos-A	5	5	.500	45	5	0	0	1	82¹	82	7	49	50	14.6	5.25	72	.269	.375	0	.000	-0	-15	-13	-0	-1.5
Total	4	9	8	.529	102	7	0	0	4	169²	154	17	91	135	13.3	4.46	79	.248	.349	-1	.000	-1	-21	-17	-2	-2.0

● **LARRY LANDRETH**   Landreth, Larry Robert   b: 3/11/55, Stratford, Ont., Can   BR/TR, 6'1", 175 lbs.   Deb: 9/16/76

YEAR	TM/L	W	L	PCT	G	GS	CG	SH	SV	IP	H	HR	BB	SO	RAT	ERA	ERA+	OAV	OOB	BH	AVG	PB	PR	/A	PD	TPI
1976	Mon-N	1	2	.333	3	3	0	0	0	11	13	1	3	10	18.8	4.09	91	.310	.442	0	.000	-0	-1	-0	-0	-0.2
1977	Mon-N	0	2	.000	4	1	0	0	0	9¹	16	0	8	5	23.1	9.64	39	.381	.480	0	.000	-0	-6	-6	-0	-1.1
Total	2	1	4	.200	7	4	0	0	0	20¹	29	1	18	12	20.8	6.64	57	.345	.461	0	.000	-0	-7	-6	-1	-1.3

● **JOE LANDRUM**   Landrum, Joseph Butler   b: 12/13/28, Columbia, S.C.   BR/TR, 5'11", 180 lbs.   Deb: 7/13/50   F

YEAR	TM/L	W	L	PCT	G	GS	CG	SH	SV	IP	H	HR	BB	SO	RAT	ERA	ERA+	OAV	OOB	BH	AVG	PB	PR	/A	PD	TPI
1950	Bro-N	0	0	—	7	0	0	0	0	6²	12	2	1	6	18.9	8.10	51	.414	.452	0	—	0	-3	-3	0	-0.1
1952	Bro-N	1	3	.250	9	5	2	0	0	38	46	3	10	17	13.5	5.21	70	.301	.348	1	.125	-0	-6	-7	-0	-0.7
Total	2	1	3	.250	16	5	2	0	1	44²	58	5	11	22	14.3	5.64	66	.319	.364	1	.125	-0	-9	-10	-0	-0.8

● **BILL LANDRUM**   Landrum, Thomas William   b: 8/17/57, Columbia, S.C.   BR/TR, 6'2", 200 lbs.   Deb: 8/31/86   F

YEAR	TM/L	W	L	PCT	G	GS	CG	SH	SV	IP	H	HR	BB	SO	RAT	ERA	ERA+	OAV	OOB	BH	AVG	PB	PR	/A	PD	TPI
1986	Cin-N	0	0	—	10	0	0	0	0	13¹	23	0	4	14	18.2	6.75	57	.390	.429	0	.000	-0	-4	-4	-0	0.0
1987	Cin-N	3	2	.600	44	2	0	0	0	65	68	3	34	42	14.1	4.71	90	.292	.382	1	.200	0	-5	-3	1	-0.2
1988	Chi-N	1	0	1.000	7	0	0	0	0	12¹	16	1	3	6	16.1	5.84	62	.365	.400	0	.000	-0	-3	-3	-0	-0.3
1989	Pit-N	2	3	.400	56	0	0	0	26	81	60	2	28	51	9.8	1.67	201	.205	.275	0	.000	-0	16	15	-0	1.8
1990	*Pit-N	7	3	.700	54	0	0	0	13	71²	69	4	21	39	11.3	2.13	169	.262	.317	1	.111	-0	13	12	-0	2.0
1991	*Pit-N	4	4	.500	61	0	0	0	17	76¹	76	4	19	45	11.2	3.18	112	.262	.297	0	.000	-0	3	3	-1	0.3
1992	Mon-N	1	1	.500	10	0	0	0	0	20	27	3	9	7	17.1	7.20	48	.325	.404	0	—	0	-8	-8	-0	-0.8
1993	Cin-N	0	2	.000	18	0	0	0	0	21²	18	1	6	14	10.0	3.74	108	.231	.286	0	.000	-0	1	1	1	0.1
Total	8	18	15	.545	268	2	0	0	58	361¹	360	18	124	218	12.1	3.39	109	.265	.327	2	.080	-1	12	12	-0	2.9

● **JERRY LANE**   Lane, Jerald Hal   b: 2/7/26, Ashland, N.Y.   d: 7/24/88, Chattanooga, Tenn   BR/TR, 6'0.5", 205 lbs.   Deb: 7/7/53

YEAR	TM/L	W	L	PCT	G	GS	CG	SH	SV	IP	H	HR	BB	SO	RAT	ERA	ERA+	OAV	OOB	BH	AVG	PB	PR	/A	PD	TPI
1953	Was-A	1	4	.200	20	2	0	0	0	56²	64	3	16	26	12.9	4.92	79	.288	.339	1	.111	-0	-6	-6	-0	-0.5
1954	Cin-N	1	0	1.000	3	0	0	0	0	10²	9	0	3	2	10.1	1.69	248	.237	.293	0	.000	-0	3	3	-1	0.2
1955	Cin-N	0	2	.000	8	0	0	0	0	11	11	2	6	5	13.9	4.91	86	.289	.386	0	—	0	-1	-1	-0	-0.1
Total	3	2	6	.250	31	2	0	0	0	78¹	84	5	25	33	12.6	4.48	89	.282	.340	1	.077	-0	-4	-4	-1	-0.4

● **SAM LANFORD**   Lanford, Lewis Grover   b: 1/8/1886, Woodruff, S.C.   d: 9/14/70, Woodruff, S.C.   BR/TR, 5'9", 155 lbs.   Deb: 8/19/07

YEAR	TM/L	W	L	PCT	G	GS	CG	SH	SV	IP	H	HR	BB	SO	RAT	ERA	ERA+	OAV	OOB	BH	AVG	PB	PR	/A	PD	TPI
1907	Was-A	0	1	.000	3	2	1	0	0	14	9	0	3	2	23.1	5.14	47	.333	.474	1	.333	0	-2	-2	-0	-0.3

● **WALT LANFRANCONI**   Lanfranconi, Walter Oswald   b: 11/9/16, Barre, Vt.   d: 8/18/86, Barre, Vt.   BR/TR, 5'7.5", 155 lbs.   Deb: 9/12/41

YEAR	TM/L	W	L	PCT	G	GS	CG	SH	SV	IP	H	HR	BB	SO	RAT	ERA	ERA+	OAV	OOB	BH	AVG	PB	PR	/A	PD	TPI
1941	Chi-N	0	1	.000	2	1	0	0	0	6	7	0	2	1	13.5	3.00	117	.280	.333	0	.000	-0	0	0	-0	0.0
1947	Bos-N	4	4	.500	36	4	1	0	1	64	65	2	27	18	12.9	2.95	132	.272	.346	0	.000	-1	8	7	1	0.8
Total	2	4	5	.444	38	5	1	0	1	70	72	2	29	19	13.0	2.96	131	.273	.345	0	.000	-1	8	7	1	0.8

● **MARTY LANG**   Lang, Martin John   b: 9/27/05, Hooper, Neb.   d: 1/13/68, Lakewood, Colo.   BR/TL, 5'11", 160 lbs.   Deb: 7/4/30

YEAR	TM/L	W	L	PCT	G	GS	CG	SH	SV	IP	H	HR	BB	SO	RAT	ERA	ERA+	OAV	OOB	BH	AVG	PB	PR	/A	PD	TPI
1930	Pit-N	0	0	—	2	0	0	0	0	1²	3	0	3	2	64.8	54.00	9	.692	.750	0	—	0	-9	-9	-0	-0.4

● **CHIP LANG**   Lang, Robert David   b: 8/21/52, Pittsburgh, Pa.   BR/TR, 6'4", 205 lbs.   Deb: 9/8/75

YEAR	TM/L	W	L	PCT	G	GS	CG	SH	SV	IP	H	HR	BB	SO	RAT	ERA	ERA+	OAV	OOB	BH	AVG	PB	PR	/A	PD	TPI
1975	Mon-N	0	0	—	1	1	0	0	0	1²	2	0	3	2	27.0	10.80	35	.333	.556	0	—	0	-1	-1	-0	0.0
1976	Mon-N	1	3	.250	29	2	0	0	0	62¹	56	3	34	30	13.4	4.19	89	.242	.347	1	.167	-0	-5	-3	-0	-0.2
Total	2	1	3	.250	30	3	0	0	0	64	58	3	37	32	13.8	4.36	85	.245	.354	1	.167	-0	-6	-5	-0	-0.2

● **ERV LANGE**   Lange, Erwin Henry   b: 8/12/1887, Forest Park, Ill.   d: 4/24/71, Maywood, Ill.   BR/TR, 5'10", 170 lbs.   Deb: 4/19/14

YEAR	TM/L	W	L	PCT	G	GS	CG	SH	SV	IP	H	HR	BB	SO	RAT	ERA	ERA+	OAV	OOB	BH	AVG	PB	PR	/A	PD	TPI
1914	Chi-F	12	11	.522	36	22	10	2	2	190	162	3	55	87	10.4	2.23	119	.224	.282	9	.176	2	14	9	-3	0.9

YEAR TM/L	W	L	PCT	G	GS	CG	SH	SV	IP	H	HR	BB	SO	RAT	ERA	ERA+	OAV	OOB	BH	AVG	PB	PR	/A	PD	TPI

● FRANK LANGE   Lange, Frank Herman "Seagan" b: 10/28/1883, Columbia, Wis. d: 12/26/45, Madison, Wis. BR/TR, 5'11", 180 lbs. Deb: 5/16/10

YEAR TM/L	W	L	PCT	G	GS	CG	SH	SV	IP	H	HR	BB	SO	RAT	ERA	ERA+	OAV	OOB	BH	AVG	PB	PR	/A	PD	TPI
1910 Chi-A	9	4	.692	23	15	6	1	0	130²	93	2	54	98	10.7	1.65	145	.204	.301	13	.255	8	13	11	-2	1.2
1911 Chi-A	8	8	.500	29	22	8	1	0	161²	151	3	77	104	12.9	3.23	100	.251	.339	22	.289	8	2	-0	-1	0.7
1912 Chi-A	10	10	.500	31	20	11	2	3	165¹	165	4	68	96	12.9	3.27	98	.270	.347	14	.215	2	1	-1	-1	0.0
1913 Chi-A	1	3	.250	12	3	0	0	0	40²	46	0	20	20	14.8	4.87	60	.295	.379	3	.167	1	-9	-9	1	-0.6
Total 4	28	25	.528	95	60	25	4	3	498¹	455	9	219	318	12.5	2.96	100	.249	.335	52	.248	14	7	1	-2	1.3

● DICK LANGE   Lange, Richard Otto b: 9/1/48, Harbor Beach, Mich. BR/TR, 5'10", 185 lbs. Deb: 9/9/72

YEAR TM/L	W	L	PCT	G	GS	CG	SH	SV	IP	H	HR	BB	SO	RAT	ERA	ERA+	OAV	OOB	BH	AVG	PB	PR	/A	PD	TPI
1972 Cal-A	0	0	—	2	1	0	0	0	7²	7	0	4	8	10.6	4.70	62	.233	.281	0	.000	-0	-1	-2	0	0.0
1973 Cal-A	2	1	.667	17	4	1	0	0	52²	61	9	21	27	14.2	4.44	80	.292	.359	0	—	0	-4	-5	0	-0.3
1974 Cal-A	3	8	.273	21	18	1	0	0	113²	111	10	47	57	12.8	3.80	90	.248	.325	0	—	0	-2	-5	-1	-0.5
1975 Cal-A	4	6	.400	30	8	1	0	1	102	119	12	53	45	15.3	5.21	68	.292	.374	0	—	0	-16	-19	-1	-1.7
Total 4	9	15	.375	70	31	3	0	1	276	298	31	123	137	13.9	4.47	78	.272	.349	0	.000	-0	-24	-30	-1	-2.5

● RICK LANGFORD   Langford, James Rick b: 3/20/52, Farmville, Va. BR/TR, 6', 180 lbs. Deb: 6/13/76

YEAR TM/L	W	L	PCT	G	GS	CG	SH	SV	IP	H	HR	BB	SO	RAT	ERA	ERA+	OAV	OOB	BH	AVG	PB	PR	/A	PD	TPI
1976 Pit-N	1	0	1.000	12	1	0	0	0	23	27	2	14	17	16.0	6.26	56	.307	.402	1	.200	-0	-7	-7	0	-0.2
1977 Oak-A	8	19	.296	37	31	6	1	0	208¹	223	18	73	141	12.9	4.02	100	.273	.334	0	—	0	1	0	1	0.1
1978 Oak-A	7	13	.350	37	24	4	2	0	175²	169	15	56	92	11.7	3.43	106	.253	.314	0	—	0	6	4	1	0.6
1979 Oak-A	12	16	.429	34	29	14	1	0	218²	233	22	57	101	12.1	4.28	94	.273	.322	0	—	0	-2	-6	2	0.0
1980 Oak-A	19	12	.613	35	33	**28**	2	0	290	276	29	64	102	10.6	3.26	116	.255	.297	0	—	0	25	16	1	2.2
1981 *Oak-A	12	10	.545	24	24	**18**	2	0	195¹	190	14	58	84	11.6	2.99	116	.255	.311	0	—	0	14	10	-2	1.0
1982 Oak-A	11	16	.407	32	31	15	2	0	237¹	265	33	49	79	12.0	4.21	93	.281	.318	0	.000	-0	-4	-8	-1	-0.8
1983 Oak-A	0	4	.000	7	7	0	0	0	20	43	4	10	2	24.7	12.15	32	.448	.509	0	—	0	-18	-18	-0	-2.7
1984 Oak-A	0	0	—	3	2	0	0	0	8²	15	2	2	2	17.7	8.31	45	.366	.395	0	—	0	-4	-4	-0	-0.4
1985 Oak-A	3	5	.375	23	3	0	0	0	59	60	8	15	21	11.4	3.51	110	.261	.306	0	—	0	4	2	-0	0.3
1986 Oak-A	1	10	.091	16	11	0	0	0	55	69	13	18	30	14.4	7.36	53	.300	.353	0	—	0	-19	-21	-1	-3.5
Total 11	73	106	.408	260	196	85	10	0	1491	1570	160	416	671	12.1	4.01	95	.271	.322	1	.167	0	-3	-32	3	-3.0

● MARK LANGSTON   Langston, Mark Edward b: 8/20/60, San Diego, Cal. BR/TL, 6'2", 190 lbs. Deb: 4/7/84

YEAR TM/L	W	L	PCT	G	GS	CG	SH	SV	IP	H	HR	BB	SO	RAT	ERA	ERA+	OAV	OOB	BH	AVG	PB	PR	/A	PD	TPI
1984 Sea-A	17	10	.630	35	33	5	2	0	225	188	16	118	**204**	12.6	3.40	117	.230	.332	0	—	0	15	15	1	1.8
1985 Sea-A	7	14	.333	24	24	2	0	0	126²	122	22	91	72	15.3	5.47	77	.255	.376	0	—	0	-19	-18	-2	-2.3
1986 Sea-A	12	14	.462	37	36	9	0	0	239¹	234	30	123	**245**	13.6	4.85	87	.255	.346	0	—	0	-18	-16	-1	-1.6
1987 Sea-A★	19	13	.594	35	35	14	3	0	272	242	30	114	**262**	11.9	3.84	123	.238	.318	0	—	0	19	27	1	2.7
1988 Sea-A	15	11	.577	35	35	9	3	0	261¹	222	32	110	235	11.5	3.34	125	.233	.314	0	—	0	18	24	3	2.5
1989 Sea-A	4	5	.444	10	10	3	1	0	73¹	60	5	19	60	10.2	3.56	113	.221	.282	0	—	0	3	4	-0	0.3
Mon-N	12	9	.571	24	24	6	4	0	176²	138	9	93	175	11.8	2.39	147	.218	.318	11	.172	0	22	22	-0	2.7
1990 Cal-A	10	17	.370	33	33	5	1	0	223	215	13	104	195	13.1	4.40	87	.259	.345	0	—	0	-12	-14	-2	-1.3
1991 Cal-A☆	19	8	.704	34	34	7	0	0	246¹	190	30	96	183	10.5	3.00	137	.215	.293	0	—	0	30	30	1	3.2
1992 Cal-A★	13	14	.481	32	32	9	2	0	229	206	14	74	174	11.2	3.66	109	.242	.307	0	.000	0	7	8	1	1.1
1993 Cal-A★	16	11	.593	35	35	7	0	0	256¹	220	22	85	196	10.7	3.20	141	.234	.298	0	—	0	32	37	3	3.9
1994 Cal-A	7	8	.467	18	18	2	1	0	119¹	121	19	54	109	13.2	4.68	105	.268	.346	0	—	0	2	3	0	0.5
1995 Cal-A	15	7	.682	31	31	2	1	0	200¹	212	21	64	142	12.5	4.63	101	.272	.330	0	—	0	2	1	2	0.3
1996 Cal-A	6	5	.545	18	18	2	0	0	123¹	116	18	45	83	11.9	4.82	102	.247	.316	0	—	0	2	2	2	0.3
Total 13	172	146	.541	401	398	81	18	0	2772	2486	283	1190	2335	12.1	3.85	110	.241	.323	11	.167	0	102	124	20	14.2

● MAX LANIER   Lanier, Hubert Max b: 8/18/15, Denton, N.C. BR/TL, 5'10", 187 lbs. Deb: 4/20/38 F

YEAR TM/L	W	L	PCT	G	GS	CG	SH	SV	IP	H	HR	BB	SO	RAT	ERA	ERA+	OAV	OOB	BH	AVG	PB	PR	/A	PD	TPI
1938 StL-N	0	3	.000	18	3	1	0	0	45	57	1	28	14	17.4	4.20	94	.317	.414	1	.100	-0	-2	-1	-0	-0.1
1939 StL-N	2	1	.667	7	6	2	0	0	37²	29	0	13	14	10.3	2.39	172	.220	.295	4	.286	1	6	7	-0	0.6
1940 StL-N	9	6	.600	35	11	4	2	0	105	113	4	38	49	13.0	3.34	119	.276	.339	6	.200	1	6	8	1	1.1
1941 StL-N	10	8	.556	35	18	8	2	3	153	126	4	59	93	10.9	2.82	133	.225	.300	10	.192	-1	14	16	2	2.0
1942 *StL-N	13	8	.619	34	20	8	2	2	161	137	4	60	93	11.1	2.98	116	.234	.308	12	.255	2	6	8	1	1.4
1943 *StL-N☆	15	7	.682	32	25	14	2	3	213¹	195	4	75	123	11.5	1.90	**177**	.246	.312	12	.164	-2	**35**	**35**	-0	3.5
1944 *StL-N†	17	12	.586	33	30	16	3	0	224¹	192	5	71	141	10.7	2.65	133	.234	.297	14	.182	-0	24	22	-0	2.6
1945 StL-N	2	2	.500	4	3	3	0	0	26	22	0	8	16	10.4	1.73	216	.222	.280	2	.182	-0	6	6	-0	0.8
1946 StL-N	6	0	1.000	6	6	3	2	0	56	45	1	19	36	10.4	1.93	179	.228	.300	5	.200	-0	9	9	-0	1.0
1949 StL-N	5	4	.556	15	15	4	1	0	92	92	6	35	37	12.4	3.82	109	.261	.328	2	.074	-2	2	4	-1	0.1
1950 StL-N	11	9	.550	27	27	10	2	0	181	173	13	68	89	12.0	3.13	137	.249	.317	11	.162	-1	20	24	0	2.3
1951 StL-N	11	9	.550	31	23	6	0	0	160	149	14	50	59	11.2	3.26	122	.248	.306	8	.151	-2	12	12	0	1.3
1952 NY-N	7	12	.368	37	16	6	1	5	137	124	11	65	62	12.6	3.94	94	.244	.333	11	.268	3	-3	-4	3	0.5
1953 NY-N	0	0	—	3	0	0	0	0	5¹	8	1	3	2	18.9	6.75	64	.381	.458	0	.000	-0	-1	-1	0	-0.0
StL-A	0	1	.000	10	1	0	0	0	22¹	28	2	19	8	18.9	7.25	58	.322	.443	1	.167	-0	-8	-8	-0	-0.3
Total 14	108	82	.568	327	204	91	21	17	1619¹	1490	65	611	821	11.8	3.01	125	.247	.318	99	.185	-3	127	136	5	16.3

● JOHNNY LANNING   Lanning, John Young "Tobacco Chewin' Johnny" b: 9/6/10, Asheville, N.C. d: 11/8/89, Asheville, N.C. BR/TR, 6'1", 185 lbs. Deb: 4/17/36 F

YEAR TM/L	W	L	PCT	G	GS	CG	SH	SV	IP	H	HR	BB	SO	RAT	ERA	ERA+	OAV	OOB	BH	AVG	PB	PR	/A	PD	TPI
1936 Bos-N	7	11	.389	28	20	3	1	0	153	164	9	55	33	12.3	3.65	105	.263	.326	7	.135	-2	6	3	-2	0.0
1937 Bos-N	5	7	.417	32	11	4	1	0	116²	107	10	40	37	11.4	3.93	91	.236	.300	4	.121	-1	-0	-5	-0	-0.5
1938 Bos-N	8	7	.533	32	18	4	1	0	138	146	5	52	39	13.0	3.72	92	.267	.332	9	.188	-1	1	-4	-1	-0.6
1939 Bos-N	5	6	.455	37	6	3	0	4	129	120	6	53	45	12.2	3.42	108	.252	.329	6	.143	-1	7	4	0	0.2
1940 Pit-N	8	4	.667	38	7	2	0	2	115²	119	8	39	42	12.3	4.05	94	.268	.327	7	.200	1	-3	-3	-0	-0.2
1941 Pit-N	11	11	.500	34	23	9	0	1	175²	175	6	47	41	11.4	3.13	116	.256	.304	6	.107	-2	10	9	1	1.1
1942 Pit-N	6	8	.429	34	8	2	1	1	119¹	125	7	26	31	11.5	3.32	102	.274	.314	4	.138	-1	3	1	0	0.6
1943 Pit-N	4	1	.800	12	2	0	0	2	27	23	0	9	11	10.7	2.33	149	.223	.286	1	.167	-0	3	3	-1	0.6
1945 Pit-N	0	0	—	1	0	0	0	0	2	8	1	0	1	36.0	36.00	11	.571	.571	0	—	0	-5	-5	0	-0.6
1946 Pit-N	4	5	.444	27	6	3	0	1	91	97	3	31	16	12.8	3.07	115	.269	.329	3	.143	-0	7	7	1	0.6
1947 Bos-N	0	0	—	3	0	0	0	0	3²	4	0	6	0	24.5	9.82	40	.400	.625	0	—	0	-2	-2	0	-0.2
Total 11	58	60	.492	278	104	30	4	13	1071	1078	55	358	295	12.1	3.58	101	.261	.321	47	.146	-7	19	5	-1	1.1

● RED LANNING   Lanning, Lester Alfred b: 5/13/1895, Harvard, Ill. d: 6/13/62, Bristol, Conn. BL/TL, 5'9", 165 lbs. Deb: 6/20/16 ◆

YEAR TM/L	W	L	PCT	G	GS	CG	SH	SV	IP	H	HR	BB	SO	RAT	ERA	ERA+	OAV	OOB	BH	AVG	PB	PR	/A	PD	TPI
1916 Phi-A	0	3	.000	6	3	1	0	0	24¹	38	1	17	9	21.1	8.14	35	.362	.460	6	.182	1	-14	-14	0	-1.4

● TOM LANNING   Lanning, Thomas Newton b: 4/22/07, Asheville, N.C. d: 11/4/67, Marietta, Ga. BL/TL, 6'1", 165 lbs. Deb: 9/14/38 F

YEAR TM/L	W	L	PCT	G	GS	CG	SH	SV	IP	H	HR	BB	SO	RAT	ERA	ERA+	OAV	OOB	BH	AVG	PB	PR	/A	PD	TPI
1938 Phi-N	0	1	.000	3	1	0	0	0	7	8	1	4	4	16.7	6.43	60	.300	.344	1	1.000	0	-2	-2	-0	-0.2

● GENE LANSING   Lansing, Eugene Hewitt "Jigger" b: 1/11/1898, Albany, N.Y. d: 1/18/45, Rensselaer, N.Y. BR/TR, 6'1", 185 lbs. Deb: 4/27/22

YEAR TM/L	W	L	PCT	G	GS	CG	SH	SV	IP	H	HR	BB	SO	RAT	ERA	ERA+	OAV	OOB	BH	AVG	PB	PR	/A	PD	TPI
1922 Bos-N	0	1	.000	15	1	0	0	0	40²	46	1	22	14	15.0	5.98	67	.301	.389	0	.000	-1	-8	-9	-0	-0.3

● PAUL LaPALME   LaPalme, Paul Edmore "Lefty" b: 12/14/23, Springfield, Mass. BL/TL, 5'10", 184 lbs. Deb: 5/28/51

YEAR TM/L	W	L	PCT	G	GS	CG	SH	SV	IP	H	HR	BB	SO	RAT	ERA	ERA+	OAV	OOB	BH	AVG	PB	PR	/A	PD	TPI
1951 Pit-N	1	5	.167	22	8	1	0	0	54¹	79	6	31	24	18.4	6.29	67	.333	.413	1	.100	-0	-14	-12	-1	-1.3
1952 Pit-N	1	2	.333	31	2	0	0	0	59²	56	6	37	25	14.2	3.92	102	.253	.363	1	.100	-0	-1	-0	1	0.0
1953 Pit-N	8	16	.333	35	24	7	1	2	176¹	191	20	64	86	13.6	4.59	97	.272	.333	5	.085	-5	-6	-2	-2	-0.9
1954 Pit-N	4	10	.286	33	15	2	0	0	120¹	147	15	54	57	15.0	5.52	76	.302	.372	5	.143	-0	-19	-18	-2	-1.8
1955 StL-N	4	3	.571	56	0	0	0	7	91²	76	10	34	39	10.9	2.75	148	.228	.301	4	.211	0	13	13	1	1.1
1956 StL-N	0	0	—	1	0	0	0	0	0²	4	0	2	0	81.0	81.00	5	.667	.750	2	—	0	-6	-6	-0	0.0
Cin-N	2	4	.333	11	2	0	0	0	27	26	7	4	4	10.0	4.67	85	.257	.286	2	.500	1	-3	-2	-0	-0.3
Yr	2	4	.333	12	2	0	0	0	27²	30	7	6	4	11.7	6.51	61	.280	.319	2	.500	1	-8	-8	-0	-0.3
Chi-A	2	1	.750	29	0	0	0	2	45²	37	2	27	23	11.4	2.36	173	.195	.312	0	.000	-1	9	9	1	0.7
1957 Chi-A	1	4	.200	35	0	0	0	0	40¹	35	5	19	14	12.3	3.35	112	.235	.325	2	.500	1	2	1	0	0.5
Total 7	24	45	.348	253	51	10	2	14	616¹	645	71	272	277	13.4	4.42	95	.269	.345	20	.136	-4	-25	-16	-2	-2.0

YEAR TM/L	W	L	PCT	G	GS	CG	SH	SV	IP	H	HR	BB	SO	RAT	ERA	ERA+	OAV	OOB	BH	AVG	PB	PR	/A	PD	TPI
● **ANDY LAPIHUSKA** Lapihuska, Andrew "Apples" b: 11/1/22, Delmont, N.J. d: 2/17/96, Millville, R.I. BL/TR, 5'10.5", 175 lbs. Deb: 9/12/42																								
1942 Phi-N	0	2	.000	3	2	0	0	0	20²	17	0	13	8	13.9	5.23	63	.221	.348	2	.286	0	-4	-4	0	-0.3
1943 Phi-N	0	0	—	1	0	0	0	0	2¹	5	1	3	0	30.9	23.14	15	.417	.533	0	.000	-0	-5	-5	-0	0.0
Total 2	0	2	.000	4	2	0	0	0	23	22	1	16	8	15.7	7.04	47	.247	.374	2	.222	0	-10	-10	0	-0.3
● **DAVE LaPOINT** LaPoint, David Jeffrey b: 7/29/59, Glens Falls, N.Y. BL/TL, 6'3", 215 lbs. Deb: 9/10/80																								
1980 Mil-A	1	0	1.000	5	3	0	0	0	15	17	2	13	5	18.0	6.00	64	.293	.423	0	—	0	-3	-4	-1	-0.1
1981 StL-N	1	0	1.000	10²	3	2	0	0	10²	12	1	2	4	12.7	4.22	84	.293	.341	0	.000	-1	-1	-1	0	-0.1
1982 *StL-N	9	3	.750	42	21	0	0	0	152²	170	8	52	81	13.3	3.42	106	.290	.350	2	.053	-3	3	3	-3	-0.4
1983 StL-N	12	9	.571	37	29	1	0	0	191¹	191	12	84	113	13.1	3.95	92	.267	.347	9	.153	1	-7	-7	-1	-0.7
1984 StL-N	12	10	.545	33	33	2	1	0	193	205	14	77	130	13.2	3.96	88	.278	.347	4	.068	-3	-8	-11	-2	-1.6
1985 SF-N	7	17	.292	31	31	2	1	0	206²	215	18	74	122	12.6	3.57	96	.269	.331	10	.167	2	0	-3	-2	-0.4
1986 Det-A	3	6	.333	16	8	0	0	0	67²	85	11	32	36	15.6	5.72	72	.307	.379	0	—	0	-12	-12	-1	-1.4
SD-N	1	4	.200	24	4	0	0	0	61¹	67	8	24	41	13.5	4.26	86	.276	.343	0	.000	-1	-4	-4	-0	-0.4
1987 StL-N	1	1	.500	6	2	0	0	0	16	26	4	5	8	17.4	6.75	62	.351	.392	0	.000	0	-5	-5	-0	-0.5
Chi-A	6	3	.667	14	12	2	1	0	82²	69	7	31	43	11.0	2.94	156	.224	.297	0	—	0	14	15	2	1.5
1988 Chi-A	10	11	.476	25	25	1	1	0	161¹	151	10	47	79	11.2	3.40	117	.245	.300	0	—	0	10	10	-2	1.0
Pit-N	4	2	.667	8	8	1	0	0	52	54	4	10	19	11.1	2.77	123	.271	.306	1	.063	-1	4	4	0	0.3
1989 NY-A	6	9	.400	20	20	0	0	0	113²	146	12	45	51	15.3	5.62	69	.310	.373	0	—	0	-22	-22	-2	-2.6
1990 NY-A	7	10	.412	28	27	2	0	0	157²	180	11	57	67	13.6	4.11	97	.292	.353	0	—	0	-4	-2	-0	-0.3
1991 Phi-N	0	1	.000	2	2	0	0	0	5	10	1	6	3	30.6	16.20	23	.435	.567	0	.000	0	-7	-7	-0	-1.0
Total 12	80	86	.482	294	227	11	4	1	1486²	1598	117	559	802	13.2	4.02	93	.277	.343	26	.104	-6	-40	-46	-12	-6.7
● **ANDY LARKIN** Larkin, Andrew Dane b: 6/27/74, Chelan, Wash. BR/TR, 6'4", 180 lbs. Deb: 9/29/96																								
1996 Fla-N	0	0	—	1	1	0	0	0	5	3	0	4	2	14.4	1.80	225	.176	.364	0	.000	-0	1	1	-0	0.0
● **TERRY LARKIN** Larkin, Frank S. d: 9/16/1894, Brooklyn, N.Y. BR/TR, Deb: 5/20/1876 ◆																								
1876 NY-N	0	1	.000	1	1	1	0	0	9	9	0	0	0	9.0	3.00	71	.231	.231	0	.000	-1	-1	-1	-0	-0.1
1877 Har-N	29	25	.537	56	56	55	4	0	501	510	2	53	96	10.1	2.14	114	**.245**	.264	52	.228	6	37	16	-1	1.8
1878 Chi-N	29	26	.527	56	56	56	1	0	506	511	4	31	163	9.6	2.24	108	.246	.257	65	.288	13	4	10	-4	1.8
1879 Chi-N	31	23	.574	58	58	57	4	0	513¹	514	5	30	142	9.5	2.44	105	.240	**.250**	50	.219	1	3	7	-7	0.1
1880 Tro-N	0	5	.000	5	5	3	0	0	38	83	1	10	5	22.0	8.76	29	.421	.449	3	.150	4	-27	-26	0	-2.4
Total 5	89	80	.527	176	176	172	9	0	1567¹	1627	12	124	406	10.1	2.43	102	.249	.263	215	.235	19	17	9	-12	1.2
● **PAT LARKIN** Larkin, Patrick Clibborn b: 6/14/60, Arcadia, Cal. BL/TL, 6', 180 lbs. Deb: 7/16/83																								
1983 SF-N	0	0	—	5	0	0	0	0	10¹	13	1	6	3	15.7	4.35	81	.317	.391	0	.000	-0	-1	-1	-0	0.0
● **STEVE LARKIN** Larkin, Stephen Patrick b: 12/9/10, Cincinnati, Ohio d: 5/2/69, Norristown, Pa. BR/TR, 6'1", 195 lbs. Deb: 5/6/34																								
1934 Det-A	0	0	—	2	1	0	0	0	6	8	0	5	8	19.5	1.50	293	.296	.406	1	.333	1	2	2	0	0.1
● **DAVE LaROCHE** LaRoche, David Eugene b: 5/14/48, Colorado Springs, Colo. BL/TL, 6'2", 200 lbs. Deb: 5/11/70 C																								
1970 Cal-A	4	1	.800	38	0	0	0	4	49²	41	6	21	44	12.0	3.44	105	.224	.317	2	.250	1	1	0	0	0.2
1971 Cal-A	5	1	.833	56	0	0	0	9	72	55	3	27	63	10.4	2.50	129	.212	.289	1	.091	-0	8	6	-1	0.5
1972 Min-A	5	7	.417	62	0	0	0	10	95¹	72	9	39	79	11.0	2.83	113	.209	.300	1	.091	0	2	4	0	0.7
1973 Chi-N	4	1	.800	45	0	0	0	4	54¹	55	7	29	34	14.1	5.80	68	.274	.368	2	.500	1	-13	-11	1	-0.9
1974 Chi-N	5	6	.455	49	4	0	0	5	92	103	9	47	49	15.0	4.79	80	.286	.373	9	.333	4	-12	-10	-0	-1.0
1975 Cle-A	5	3	.625	61	0	0	0	17	82¹	61	5	57	94	13.1	2.19	173	.210	.344	0	—	0	15	15	1	2.1
1976 Cle-A☆	1	4	.200	61	0	0	0	21	96¹	57	2	49	104	10.0	2.24	156	.175	.285	0	—	0	14	13	-1	1.3
1977 Cle-A	2	2	.500	13	0	0	0	4	18²	15	3	7	18	10.6	5.30	74	.234	.310	0	—	0	-3	-3	-0	-0.6
Cal-A★	6	5	.545	46	0	0	0	13	81¹	64	8	37	61	11.4	3.10	126	.218	.310	0	—	0	9	7	-0	1.2
Yr	8	7	.533	59	0	0	0	17	100	79	11	44	79	11.3	3.51	112	.220	.309	0	—	0	6	5	-0	0.6
1978 Cal-A	10	9	.526	59	0	0	0	25	95²	73	7	48	70	11.6	2.82	128	.215	.316	0	—	0	10	8	-0	2.3
1979 *Cal-A	7	11	.389	53	1	0	0	10	85²	107	13	32	59	14.8	5.57	73	.314	.376	0	—	0	-13	-14	-1	-2.5
1980 Cal-A	3	5	.375	52	9	1	0	4	128	122	14	39	89	11.5	4.08	96	.256	.317	0	—	0	-1	-2	-1	-0.2
1981 *NY-A	4	1	.800	26	1	0	0	6	47	38	5	16	24	10.5	2.49	144	.229	.301	0	—	0	6	6	-1	0.6
1982 NY-A	4	2	.667	25	0	0	0	6	50	54	4	11	31	11.9	3.42	117	.273	.314	0	—	0	4	3	-1	0.3
1983 NY-A	0	0	—	1	0	0	0	0	1	2	1	0	0	18.0	18.00	22	.400	.400	0	—	0	-2	-2	0	-0.2
Total 14	65	58	.528	647	15	1	0	126	1049¹	919	94	459	819	12.1	3.53	105	.239	.325	15	.246	4	26	22	-1	4.2
● **JOHN LaROSE** LaRose, Henry John b: 10/25/51, Pawtucket, R.I. BL/TL, 6'1", 185 lbs. Deb: 9/20/78																								
1978 Bos-A	0	0	—	1	0	0	0	0	3	1	3	0	27.0	22.50	18	.375	.545	0	—	0	-4	-4	0	-0.5		
● **DON LARSEN** Larsen, Don James b: 8/7/29, Michigan City, Ind. BR/TR, 6'4", 227 lbs. Deb: 4/18/53																								
1953 StL-A	7	12	.368	38	22	7	2	2	192²	201	11	64	96	12.6	4.16	101	.267	.328	23	.284	5	-3	1	-1	0.8
1954 Bal-A	3	21	.125	29	28	12	1	0	201²	213	18	89	80	13.5	4.37	82	.274	.349	22	.250	8	-15	-18	-0	-1.0
1955 *NY-A	9	2	.818	19	13	5	1	2	97	81	9	51	44	12.2	3.06	122	.229	.329	6	.146	2	10	7	-1	0.9
1956 *NY-A	11	5	.688	38	20	6	1	1	179²	133	19	96	107	11.8	3.26	119	.204	.313	19	.241	6	18	12	-1	1.5
1957 *NY-A	10	4	.714	27	20	4	1	0	139²	113	12	87	81	12.9	3.74	96	.220	.333	14	.250	5	1	-2	-0	0.1
1958 *NY-A	9	6	.600	19	19	5	3	0	114¹	100	4	52	55	12.3	3.07	115	.233	.322	15	.306	4	9	6	-1	1.4
1959 NY-A	6	7	.462	25	18	3	1	3	124²	122	14	76	69	14.4	4.33	84	.260	.365	12	.255	4	-7	-10	-0	-0.6
1960 KC-A	1	10	.091	22	15	0	0	0	83²	97	11	42	43	15.0	5.38	74	.293	.373	6	.207	0	-14	-13	-1	-1.6
1961 KC-A	1	1	1.000	8	1	0	0	0	15	21	2	11	13	19.8	4.20	100	.344	.452	6	.300	1	-0	-0	-0	0.1
Chi-A	7	2	.778	25	2	0	0	2	74¹	64	5	29	53	11.4	4.12	95	.231	.306	8	.320	3	-1	-2	0	0.1
Yr	8	2	.800	33	4	0	0	2	89¹	85	7	40	66	13.0	4.13	96	.251	.332	14	.311	4	-1	-2	1	0.3
1962 *SF-N	5	4	.556	49	0	0	0	11	86¹	83	9	47	58	13.8	4.38	87	.256	.354	5	.200	1	-4	-6	-0	-0.6
1963 SF-N	7	7	.500	46	0	0	0	8	62	46	8	30	44	11.0	3.05	105	.203	.296	2	.182	0	2	1	0	0.3
1964 SF-N	0	1	.000	6	0	0	0	0	10¹	12	4	4	8	14.8	4.35	82	.286	.356	0	.000	-0	-1	-1	-0	-0.1
Hou-N	4	8	.333	30	10	4	0	1	103¹	92	4	20	58	9.8	2.26	151	.233	.272	3	.097	0	15	13	0	1.6
Yr	4	9	.308	36	10	4	0	1	113²	102	4	26	64	10.2	2.45	140	.235	.280	3	.094	0	14	12	0	1.5
1965 Hou-N	0	0	—	1	1	0	0	0	5¹	8	0	3	1	18.6	5.06	66	.348	.423	0	.000	-0	-1	-1	1	0.0
Bal-A	1	2	.333	27	1	0	0	4	54	53	4	20	40	12.3	2.67	130	.255	.323	1	.273	1	5	5	1	0.5
1967 Chi-N	0	0	—	3	0	0	0	0	4	5	1	2	1	15.8	9.00	39	.333	.412	0	—	0	-3	-2	0	0.0
Total 14	81	91	.471	412	171	44	11	26	1548	1442	130	725	849	12.8	3.78	99	.247	.332	144	.242	46	10	-9	-1	3.5
● **DAN LARSON** Larson, Daniel James b: 7/4/54, Los Angeles, Cal. BR/TR, 6', 180 lbs. Deb: 7/18/76																								
1976 Hou-N	5	8	.385	13	13	5	0	0	92¹	81	3	28	42	10.7	3.02	106	.236	.296	9	.290	4	0	2	0	0.7
1977 Hou-N	1	7	.125	32	10	1	0	1	97²	108	13	45	44	14.3	5.81	61	.280	.358	6	.214	1	-21	-24	0	-1.7
1978 Phi-N	0	0	—	1	0	0	0	0	1	1	1	2	0	18.0	9.00	40	.250	.400	0	—	-1	-1	-0	0	0.0
1979 Phi-N	1	1	.500	3	3	0	0	0	19	17	1	9	12	13.3	4.26	90	.250	.346	0	.000	-1	-1	-1	-0	-0.1
1980 Phi-N	0	5	.000	12	7	0	0	0	45²	46	4	24	17	13.8	3.15	120	.271	.361	2	.154	0	2	3	-1	0.3
1981 Phi-N	3	0	1.000	5	4	1	0	0	28	27	4	15	15	13.5	4.18	87	.260	.353	1	.111	0	-2	-2	-0	-0.2
1982 Chi-N	0	4	.000	12	6	0	0	0	39²	51	4	18	22	16.1	5.67	66	.327	.403	3	.273	0	-9	-9	1	-0.6
Total 7	10	25	.286	78	43	7	0	1	323¹	331	30	140	151	13.3	4.40	80	.269	.346	21	.216	4	-26	-31	1	-1.6
● **AL LARY** Lary, Alfred Allen b: 9/26/29, Northport, Ala. BR/TR, 6'3", 185 lbs. Deb: 9/6/54 F◆																								
1954 Chi-N	0	0	—	1	1	0	0	0	6	3	0	7	4	15.0	3.00	140	.150	.370	1	.500	1	1	1	0	0.0
1962 Chi-N	0	1	.000	15	3	0	0	0	34	42	5	15	18	15.1	7.15	58	.311	.380	1	.167	0	-12	-11	-0	-0.3
Total 2	0	1	.000	16	4	0	0	0	40	45	5	22	22	15.1	6.52	64	.290	.379	2	.250	1	-11	-11	-0	-0.3
● **FRANK LARY** Lary, Frank Strong "Mule" or "The Yankee Killer" b: 4/10/30, Northport, Ala. BR/TR, 5'11", 180 lbs. Deb: 9/14/54 F																								
1954 Det-A	0	0	—	3	0	0	0	0	3²	4	0	3	5	17.2	2.45	150	.286	.412	0	—	0	1	1	-0	0.0

YEAR TM/L	W	L	PCT	G	GS	CG	SH	SV	IP	H	HR	BB	SO	RAT	ERA	ERA+	OAV	OOB	BH	AVG	PB	PR	/A	PD	TPI
1955 Det-A	14	15	.483	36	31	16	2	1	235	232	10	89	98	12.5	3.10	124	.262	.334	16	.195	1	22	19	1	2.5
1956 Det-A	**21**	13	.618	41	38	20	3	1	**294**	289	20	116	165	12.8	3.15	131	.257	.333	19	.184	0	33	31	-0	3.4
1957 Det-A	11	16	.407	40	35	12	2	3	237²	250	23	72	107	12.6	3.98	97	.276	.337	9	.123	-3	-5	-3	-0	-0.6
1958 Det-A	16	15	.516	39	34	**19**	3	1	**260¹**	249	20	68	131	11.4	2.90	139	.251	.307	15	.170	-1	25	33	-0	3.6
1959 Det-A	17	10	.630	32	32	11	3	0	223	225	23	46	137	11.4	3.55	114	.261	.307	10	.125	0	8	13	-0	1.2
1960 Det-A★	15	15	.500	38	36	**15**	2	1	**274¹**	262	25	62	149	11.3	3.51	113	.249	.302	17	.183	4	11	14	-2	1.6
1961 Det-A★	23	9	.719	36	36	**22**	4	0	275¹	252	24	66	146	10.6	3.24	127	.243	.293	25	.231	4	24	26	4	3.7
1962 Det-A	2	6	.250	17	14	2	1	0	80	98	17	21	41	13.8	5.74	71	.297	.346	4	.167	1	-16	-15	-1	-1.3
1963 Det-A	4	9	.308	16	14	6	0	0	107¹	90	15	26	46	10.1	3.27	114	.226	.281	8	.229	1	4	6	1	0.9
1964 Det-A	0	2	.000	6	4	0	0	0	18	24	3	10	6	18.5	7.00	52	.316	.416	0	.000	-1	-7	-7	-1	-0.8
NY-N	2	3	.400	13	8	3	1	1	57¹	62	7	14	27	12.6	4.55	79	.279	.333	2	.118	1	-6	-6	-0	-0.5
Mil-N	1	0	1.000	5	2	0	0	0	12¹	15	4	0	4	10.9	4.38	80	.306	.306	0	.000	-0	-1	-1	1	0.0
Yr	3	3	.500	18	10	3	1	1	69²	77	11	14	31	11.8	4.52	79	.279	.314	2	.100	0	-8	-7	0	-0.5
1965 NY-N	1	3	.250	14	7	0	0	1	57¹	48	2	16	23	10.2	2.98	118	.233	.291	4	.211	0	4	3	0	0.3
Chi-A	1	0	1.000	14	1	0	0	2	26²	23	4	7	14	10.8	4.05	79	.230	.294	0	.500	0	-2	-3	0	-0.1
Total 12	128	116	.525	350	292	126	21	11	2162¹	2123	197	616	1099	11.8	3.49	113	.257	.316	130	.177	5	95	112	3	13.9

● **FRED LASHER** Lasher, Frederick Walter b: 8/19/41, Poughkeepsie, N.Y. BR/TR, 6'4", 210 lbs. Deb: 4/12/63

YEAR TM/L	W	L	PCT	G	GS	CG	SH	SV	IP	H	HR	BB	SO	RAT	ERA	ERA+	OAV	OOB	BH	AVG	PB	PR	/A	PD	TPI
1963 Min-A	0	0	—	11	0	0	0	0	11¹	12	1	11	10	18.3	4.76	76	.286	.434	0	.000	-0	-1	-1	0	0.0
1967 Det-A	2	1	.667	17	0	0	0	9	30	25	1	11	28	11.1	3.90	84	.221	.296	1	.111	-0	-2	-2	-0	-0.4
1968 *Det-A	5	1	.833	34	0	0	0	5	48²	37	5	22	32	10.9	3.33	90	.215	.304	1	.111	-0	-2	-2	1	-0.2
1969 Det-A	2	1	.667	32	0	0	0	6	44	34	5	22	26	11.9	3.07	122	.224	.330	0	.000	-0	3	3	0	0.2
1970 Det-A	1	3	.250	12	0	0	0	3	9	10	0	12	8	23.0	5.00	75	.278	.469	0	.000	-0	-1	-1	0	-0.6
Cle-A	1	7	.125	43	1	0	0	5	57²	57	6	30	44	14.0	4.06	98	.264	.361	0	.000	-1	-2	-1	-1	-0.3
Yr	2	10	.167	55	1	0	0	8	66²	67	6	42	52	15.1	4.18	94	.264	.375	0	.000	-1	-3	-2	-1	-0.9
1971 Cal-A	0	0	—	2	0	0	0	0	1¹	4	0	2	0	40.5	27.00	12	.667	.750	0	—	0	-3	-4	-0	0.0
Total 6	11	13	.458	151	1	0	0	22	202	179	18	110	148	13.2	3.88	91	.243	.347	2	.063	-2	-10	-8	-1	-1.3

● **BILL LASKEY** Laskey, William Alan b: 12/20/57, Toledo, Ohio BR/TR, 6'5", 190 lbs. Deb: 4/23/82

YEAR TM/L	W	L	PCT	G	GS	CG	SH	SV	IP	H	HR	BB	SO	RAT	ERA	ERA+	OAV	OOB	BH	AVG	PB	PR	/A	PD	TPI
1982 SF-N	13	12	.520	32	31	7	1	0	189¹	186	14	43	88	11.0	3.14	115	.261	.304	8	.129	-2	10	10	0	1.0
1983 SF-N	13	10	.565	25	25	1	0	0	148¹	151	18	45	81	12.1	4.19	84	.266	.323	5	.106	0	-9	-11	-1	-1.6
1984 SF-N	9	14	.391	35	34	2	0	0	207²	222	20	50	71	12.0	4.33	81	.273	.320	4	.063	-3	-17	-19	-3	-2.5
1985 SF-N	5	11	.313	19	19	0	0	0	114	110	10	39	42	11.8	3.55	97	.255	.317	4	.133	1	0	-1	0	-0.1
Mon-N	0	5	.000	11	7	0	0	0	34¹	55	9	14	18	18.6	9.44	36	.362	.423	1	.143	-0	-22	-23	1	-2.7
Yr	5	16	.238	30	26	0	0	0	148¹	165	19	53	60	13.3	4.91	70	.281	.343	5	.135	0	-22	-25	1	-2.8
1986 SF-N	1	1	.500	20	0	0	0	0	27¹	28	5	13	18	13.5	4.28	82	.275	.357	0	.000	-2	-2	-2	0	-0.1
1988 Cle-A	1	0	1.000	17	0	0	0	1	24¹	32	0	6	17	14.1	5.18	79	.320	.358	0	—	0	-3	-3	0	-0.3
Total 6	42	53	.442	159	116	10	1	2	745¹	784	76	210	325	12.2	4.14	85	.272	.325	22	.105	-4	-44	-50	-2	-6.3

● **BILL LASLEY** Lasley, Willard Almond b: 7/13/02, Gallipolis, Ohio d: 8/21/90, Seattle, Wash. BB/TR, 6', 175 lbs. Deb: 9/19/24

YEAR TM/L	W	L	PCT	G	GS	CG	SH	SV	IP	H	HR	BB	SO	RAT	ERA	ERA+	OAV	OOB	BH	AVG	PB	PR	/A	PD	TPI
1924 StL-A	0	0	—	2	0	0	0	0	4	7	0	2	4	20.3	6.75	67	.412	.474	0	.000	—	-1	-1	0	0.0

● **TOM LASORDA** Lasorda, Thomas Charles b: 9/22/27, Norristown, Pa. BL/TL, 5'10", 175 lbs. Deb: 8/5/54 MC

YEAR TM/L	W	L	PCT	G	GS	CG	SH	SV	IP	H	HR	BB	SO	RAT	ERA	ERA+	OAV	OOB	BH	AVG	PB	PR	/A	PD	TPI
1954 Bro-N	0	0	—	4	0	0	0	0	9	8	2	5	5	13.0	5.00	82	.242	.342	0	.000	-0	-1	-1	-0	0.0
1955 Bro-N	0	0	—	4	1	0	0	0	4	5	1	6	4	27.0	13.50	30	.313	.522	0	—	-0	-4	-4	-0	0.0
1956 KC-A	0	4	.000	18	5	0	0	1	45¹	40	6	45	28	17.5	6.15	70	.240	.409	1	.077	-1	-10	-9	0	-0.8
Total 3	0	4	.000	26	6	0	0	1	58¹	53	9	56	37	17.4	6.48	66	.245	.409	1	.071	-2	-15	-14	0	-0.8

● **BILL LATHAM** Latham, William Carol b: 8/29/60, Birmingham, Ala. BL/TL, 6'2", 190 lbs. Deb: 4/15/85

YEAR TM/L	W	L	PCT	G	GS	CG	SH	SV	IP	H	HR	BB	SO	RAT	ERA	ERA+	OAV	OOB	BH	AVG	PB	PR	/A	PD	TPI
1985 NY-N	1	3	.250	7	3	0	0	0	22²	21	1	7	10	11.1	3.97	87	.250	.308	1	.333	-1	-1	-1	1	-0.1
1986 Min-A	0	1	.000	7	2	0	0	0	16	24	1	6	8	17.4	7.31	59	.358	.419	0	—	0	-6	-5	-1	-0.5
Total 2	1	4	.200	14	5	0	0	0	38²	45	2	13	18	13.7	5.35	71	.298	.358	1	.333	1	-7	-7	0	-0.6

● **BILL LATHROP** Lathrop, William George b: 8/12/1891, Hanover, Wis. d: 11/20/58, Janesville, Wis. BR/TR, 6'2.5", 184 lbs. Deb: 7/29/13

YEAR TM/L	W	L	PCT	G	GS	CG	SH	SV	IP	H	HR	BB	SO	RAT	ERA	ERA+	OAV	OOB	BH	AVG	PB	PR	/A	PD	TPI
1913 Chi-A	0	1	.000	6	0	0	0	0	17	16	0	12	9	15.4	4.24	69	.262	.392	0	.000	-1	-2	-2	0	-0.2
1914 Chi-A	1	2	.333	19	1	0	0	0	47²	41	0	19	7	11.7	2.64	102	.241	.325	0	.000	-1	1	0	1	-0.1
Total 2	1	3	.250	25	1	0	0	0	64²	57	0	31	16	12.7	3.06	90	.247	.343	0	.000	-2	-2	-1	1	-0.3

● **BARRY LATMAN** Latman, Arnold Barry b: 5/21/36, Los Angeles, Cal. BR/TR, 6'3", 210 lbs. Deb: 9/10/57

YEAR TM/L	W	L	PCT	G	GS	CG	SH	SV	IP	H	HR	BB	SO	RAT	ERA	ERA+	OAV	OOB	BH	AVG	PB	PR	/A	PD	TPI
1957 Chi-A	1	2	.333	7	2	0	0	1	12¹	12	2	13	9	19.0	8.03	47	.267	.441	0	.000	-0	-6	-6	0	-1.3
1958 Chi-A	3	0	1.000	13	3	1	1	0	47²	27	1	17	28	8.5	0.76	481	.162	.243	1	.083	-1	16	15	-1	0.8
1959 Chi-A	8	5	.615	37	21	5	2	0	156	138	15	72	97	12.3	3.75	100	.235	.323	6	.128	-1	2	0	-3	-0.4
1960 Cle-A	7	7	.500	31	20	4	0	0	147¹	146	19	72	94	13.7	4.03	93	.258	.348	9	.220	1	-3	-5	-1	-0.4
1961 Cle-A☆	13	5	.722	45	18	4	2	5	176²	163	23	54	108	11.3	4.02	98	.244	.306	4	.073	-3	-0	-2	-3	-0.8
1962 Cle-A	8	13	.381	45	21	7	1	5	179¹	179	23	72	117	12.8	4.17	93	.261	.336	10	.189	2	-4	-6	-1	-0.5
1963 Cle-A	7	12	.368	38	21	4	0	0	149¹	146	23	52	133	12.3	4.94	73	.257	.325	8	.182	2	-22	-22	3	-2.1
1964 LA-A	6	10	.375	40	18	2	1	2	138	128	15	52	81	12.2	3.85	85	.244	.321	5	.125	-1	-3	-9	-1	-1.1
1965 Cal-A	1	1	.500	18	0	0	0	1	31²	30	3	16	18	13.1	2.84	120	.254	.343	0	.000	-0	2	2	-1	0.0
1966 Hou-N	2	7	.222	31	9	1	1	1	103	88	5	35	74	11.4	2.71	126	.233	.310	4	.154	0	10	8	-0	0.7
1967 Hou-N	3	6	.333	39	14	0	0	1	77²	73	13	34	70	13.1	4.52	73	.252	.342	1	.091	-1	-10	-10	0	-1.2
Total 11	59	68	.465	344	134	28	10	16	1219	1130	142	489	829	12.3	3.91	94	.246	.325	48	.145	-1	-17	-34	-8	-6.3

● **BILL LATTIMORE** Lattimore, William Hershel "Slothful Bill" b: 5/25/1884, Roxton, Tex. d: 10/30/19, Colorado Springs, Colo. BL/TL, 5'9", 165 lbs. Deb: 4/17/08

YEAR TM/L	W	L	PCT	G	GS	CG	SH	SV	IP	H	HR	BB	SO	RAT	ERA	ERA+	OAV	OOB	BH	AVG	PB	PR	/A	PD	TPI
1908 Cle-A	1	2	.333	4	4	1	1	0	24	24	0	7	5	11.6	4.50	53	.247	.298	4	.444	1	-6	-6	-1	-0.6

● **CHUCK LAUER** Lauer, John Charles b: 1865, Pittsburgh, Pa. TR, Deb: 7/17/1884 ♦

YEAR TM/L	W	L	PCT	G	GS	CG	SH	SV	IP	H	HR	BB	SO	RAT	ERA	ERA+	OAV	OOB	BH	AVG	PB	PR	/A	PD	TPI
1884 Pit-a	0	2	.000	3	3	2	0	0	19	23	0	9	8	16.6	7.58	44	.277	.368	5	.114	-1	-9	-9	-1	-0.8

● **GEORGE LAUZERIQUE** Lauzerique, George Albert b: 7/22/47, Havana, Cuba BR/TR, 6'1", 180 lbs. Deb: 9/17/67

YEAR TM/L	W	L	PCT	G	GS	CG	SH	SV	IP	H	HR	BB	SO	RAT	ERA	ERA+	OAV	OOB	BH	AVG	PB	PR	/A	PD	TPI
1967 KC-A	0	2	.000	3	2	0	0	0	16	11	2	6	10	10.1	2.25	142	.193	.281	0	.000	-0	2	2	0	0.2
1968 Oak-A	0	0	—	1	0	0	0	0	1	0	0	1	0	9.0	0.00	—	.000	.333	0	—	0	0	0	0	0.0
1969 Oak-A	3	4	.429	19	8	1	0	0	61¹	58	14	27	39	12.8	4.70	73	.250	.333	2	.100	-1	-7	-9	1	-0.9
1970 Mil-A	1	2	.333	11	4	1	0	0	35	41	7	14	24	14.4	6.94	55	.295	.364	2	.200	1	-13	-12	-0	-0.9
Total 4	4	8	.333	34	14	2	0	0	113¹	110	23	48	73	12.9	5.00	70	.256	.336	4	.121	-0	-18	-19	1	-1.6

● **GARY LAVELLE** Lavelle, Gary Robert b: 1/3/49, Scranton, Pa. BB/TL, 6'1", 200 lbs. Deb: 9/10/74

YEAR TM/L	W	L	PCT	G	GS	CG	SH	SV	IP	H	HR	BB	SO	RAT	ERA	ERA+	OAV	OOB	BH	AVG	PB	PR	/A	PD	TPI
1974 SF-N	0	3	.000	10	0	0	0	0	16²	14	1	10	13	13.0	2.16	176	.222	.329	0	.000	-0	3	3	-0	0.5
1975 SF-N	6	3	.667	65	0	0	0	0	82¹	80	3	48	51	14.3	2.95	129	.260	.365	1	.111	-0	6	8	0	1.0
1976 SF-N	10	6	.625	65	0	0	0	12	110¹	102	6	52	71	12.7	2.69	135	.246	.333	1	.077	-1	10	11	-2	1.7
1977 SF-N★	7	7	.500	73	0	0	0	20	118¹	106	4	37	93	10.9	2.05	190	.239	.298	1	.067	-2	24	24	1	3.5
1978 SF-N	13	10	.565	67	0	0	0	14	97²	96	3	44	63	13.1	3.32	104	.263	.345	1	.067	-1	3	1	0	0.3
1979 SF-N	9	7	.438	70	0	0	0	20	96²	96	5	42	80	12.1	2.51	139	.247	.332	1	.250	0	13	11	0	2.1
1980 SF-N	6	8	.429	62	0	0	0	0	100	106	4	36	64	12.8	3.42	103	.275	.336	0	.000	-1	2	1	0	0.1
1981 SF-N	2	6	.250	34	3	0	0	0	65¹	59	5	21	45	11.4	3.84	89	.244	.316	3	.273	1	-3	-3	-1	-0.2
1982 SF-N	10	7	.588	68	0	0	0	0	104²	97	6	29	76	10.9	2.67	135	.247	.300	2	.154	0	11	11	-2	2.1
1983 SF-N☆	7	4	.636	56	0	0	0	20	87	73	4	19	68	9.5	2.59	137	.229	.272	0	.000	-2	10	9	-2	1.5
1984 SF-N	5	4	.556	77	0	0	0	12	101	92	5	42	71	11.1	3.10	127	.246	.324	0	.000	-1	8	6	0	0.8
1985 *Tor-A	5	7	.417	69	0	0	0	8	72²	54	5	36	50	11.1	3.10	136	.214	.313	0	.000	-0	8	9	0	1.4
1987 Tor-A	2	3	.400	23	0	0	0	0	27²	36	2	19	17	17.9	5.53	81	.313	.410	0	—	0	-3	-3	0	-0.5
Oak-A	0	0	—	6	0	0	0	0	4¹	4	0	3	6	14.5	8.31	50	.267	.389	0	—	0	-2	-2	-0	0.3

YEAR	TM/L	W	L	PCT	G	GS	CG	SH	SV	IP	H	HR	BB	SO	RAT	ERA	ERA+	OAV	OOB	BH	AVG	PB	PR	/A	PD	TPI
	Yr	2	3	.400	29	0	0	0	1	32	40	2	22	23	17.4	5.91	75	.305	.405	0	—	0	-5	-5	0	-0.2
Total	13	80	77	.510	745	3	0	0	136	1085	1004	51	440	769	12.1	2.93	125	.249	.325	9	.081	-6	92	89	4	14.6

● **JIMMY LAVENDER** Lavender, James Sanford b: 3/25/1884, Barnesville, Ga. d: 1/12/60, Cartersville, Ga. BR/TR, 5'11", 165 lbs. Deb: 4/23/12

YEAR	TM/L	W	L	PCT	G	GS	CG	SH	SV	IP	H	HR	BB	SO	RAT	ERA	ERA+	OAV	OOB	BH	AVG	PB	PR	/A	PD	TPI
1912	Chi-N	16	13	.552	42	31	15	3	3	251²	240	11	89	109	12.1	3.04	110	.257	.328	13	.149	-3	10	8	1	0.6
1913	Chi-N	10	14	.417	40	20	10	0	2	204	206	6	98	91	14.0	3.66	87	.267	.359	8	.118	-4	-10	-11	-2	-1.8
1914	Chi-N	11	11	.500	37	28	11	2	0	214¹	191	11	87	87	12.1	3.07	91	.247	.331	11	.175	2	-7	-7	3	-0.1
1915	Chi-N	10	16	.385	41	24	13	1	4	220	178	5	67	117	10.4	2.58	108	.228	.298	9	.134	-2	4	5	3	0.7
1916	Chi-N	10	14	.417	36	25	9	4	2	188	163	3	62	91	11.2	2.82	103	.240	.312	8	.151	-2	-4	-3	-1	-0.1
1917	Phi-N	6	8	.429	28	14	7	0	1	129¹	119	5	44	52	11.6	3.55	79	.250	.317	5	.139	-1	-12	-11	-2	-1.5
Total	6	63	76	.453	224	142	65	10	12	1207¹	1097	38	447	547	11.9	3.09	97	.249	.325	54	.144	-9	-19	-12	2	-2.2

● **RON LAW** Law, Ronald David b: 3/14/46, Hamilton, Ont., Can. BR/TR, 6'2", 165 lbs. Deb: 6/29/69

YEAR	TM/L	W	L	PCT	G	GS	CG	SH	SV	IP	H	HR	BB	SO	RAT	ERA	ERA+	OAV	OOB	BH	AVG	PB	PR	/A	PD	TPI
1969	Cle-A	3	4	.429	35	1	0	0	1	52¹	68	2	34	29	17.9	4.99	76	.325	.424	1	.143	-0	-8	-7	0	-0.9

● **VANCE LAW** Law, Vance Aaron b: 10/1/56, Boise, Idaho BR/TR, 6'2", 190 lbs. Deb: 6/1/80 F♦

YEAR	TM/L	W	L	PCT	G	GS	CG	SH	SV	IP	H	HR	BB	SO	RAT	ERA	ERA+	OAV	OOB	BH	AVG	PB	PR	/A	PD	TPI
1986	Mon-N	0	0	—	3	0	0	0	0	4	3	0	2	0	11.3	2.25	164	.214	.313	81	.225	1	1	1	0	0.0
1987	Mon-N	0	0	—	3	0	0	0	0	3¹	5	0	0	2	13.5	5.40	78	.333	.333	119	.273	1	-0	-0	0	0.0
1991	Oak-A	0	0	—	1	0	0	0	0	0²	1	0	1	0	27.0	0.00	—	.333	.500	28	.209	1	0	0	0	0.0
Total	3	0	0	—	7	0	0	0	0	8	9	0	3	2	13.5	3.38	116	.281	.343	972	.256	3	0	0	0	0.0

● **VERN LAW** Law, Vernon Sanders "Deacon" b: 3/12/30, Meridian, Idaho BR/TR, 6'2", 195 lbs. Deb: 6/11/50 FC

YEAR	TM/L	W	L	PCT	G	GS	CG	SH	SV	IP	H	HR	BB	SO	RAT	ERA	ERA+	OAV	OOB	BH	AVG	PB	PR	/A	PD	TPI
1950	Pit-N	7	9	.438	27	17	5	1	0	128	137	11	49	57	13.4	4.92	89	.272	.341	3	.073	-2	-11	-8	-2	-1.2
1951	Pit-N	6	9	.400	28	14	2	1	2	114	109	9	51	41	13.1	4.50	94	.253	.341	11	.344	5	-7	-3	-1	0.0
1954	Pit-N	9	13	.409	39	18	7	0	3	161²	201	20	56	57	14.5	5.51	76	.311	.368	12	.231	3	-26	-24	-1	-2.5
1955	Pit-N	10	10	.500	43	24	8	1	1	200²	221	19	61	82	12.7	3.81	108	.280	.333	16	.254	3	5	7	0	1.0
1956	Pit-N	8	16	.333	39	32	6	0	2	195²	218	24	49	60	12.6	4.32	87	.281	.329	10	.175	1	-12	-12	-1	-1.3
1957	Pit-N	10	8	.556	31	25	9	3	1	172²	172	18	32	55	10.7	2.87	132	.256	.291	12	.190	1	19	18	-2	1.7
1958	Pit-N	14	12	.538	35	29	6	1	3	202¹	235	16	39	56	12.2	3.96	98	.297	.331	12	.194	6	-0	-2	-0	0.3
1959	Pit-N	18	9	.667	34	33	20	2	1	266	245	25	53	110	10.2	2.98	130	.243	.282	16	.167	1	29	26	1	2.8
1960	*Pit-N★	20	9	.690	35	35	**18**	3	0	271²	266	25	40	120	10.3	3.08	122	.257	.287	17	.181	3	21	20	1	2.6
1961	Pit-N	3	4	.429	11	10	1	0	0	59¹	72	10	18	20	13.8	4.70	85	.305	.357	5	.263	1	-4	-5	1	-0.3
1962	Pit-N	10	7	.588	23	20	7	2	0	139¹	156	21	27	78	11.9	3.94	100	.276	.310	14	.311	5	-0	-0	1	0.6
1963	Pit-N	4	5	.444	18	12	1	1	0	76²	91	11	13	31	12.2	4.93	67	.296	.325	5	.217	1	-14	-14	1	-1.3
1964	Pit-N	12	13	.480	35	29	7	5	0	192	203	18	32	93	11.1	3.61	97	.270	.300	19	.311	8	-2	-2	1	0.6
1965	Pit-N	17	9	.654	29	28	13	4	0	217¹	182	17	35	101	9.1	2.15	163	.229	.264	20	.244	4	33	33	1	4.6
1966	Pit-N	12	8	.600	31	28	8	4	0	177²	203	19	24	88	11.7	4.05	88	.292	.320	16	.242	9	-9	-9	2	-0.4
1967	Pit-N	2	6	.250	25	10	1	0	0	97	122	5	18	43	13.1	4.18	81	.308	.340	3	.111	-0	-9	-9	-0	-0.7
Total	16	162	147	.524	483	364	119	28	13	2672	2833	268	597	1092	11.7	3.77	101	.272	.314	191	.216	45	14	15	2	6.5

● **BROOKS LAWRENCE** Lawrence, Brooks Ulysses "Bull" b: 1/30/25, Springfield, Ohio BR/TR, 6', 205 lbs. Deb: 6/24/54

YEAR	TM/L	W	L	PCT	G	GS	CG	SH	SV	IP	H	HR	BB	SO	RAT	ERA	ERA+	OAV	OOB	BH	AVG	PB	PR	/A	PD	TPI
1954	StL-N	15	6	.714	35	18	8	0	1	158²	141	17	72	72	12.5	3.74	110	.243	.335	10	.189	0	6	6	0	0.8
1955	StL-N	3	8	.273	46	10	2	1	1	96	102	11	58	52	15.7	6.56	62	.278	.387	2	.095	-2	-27	-27	1	-2.8
1956	Cin-N☆	19	10	.655	49	30	11	1	0	218²	210	26	71	96	11.6	3.99	100	.256	.317	11	.157	-1	-5	-0	3	0.2
1957	Cin-N	16	13	.552	49	32	12	1	4	250¹	234	26	76	121	11.4	3.52	117	.247	.309	14	.171	-0	10	16	-0	1.8
1958	Cin-N	8	13	.381	46	23	6	2	5	181	194	12	55	74	12.6	4.13	100	.275	.331	6	.113	-2	-4	-0	-0	-0.2
1959	Cin-N	7	12	.368	43	14	3	0	10	128¹	144	17	45	64	13.5	4.77	85	.281	.344	6	.150	-1	-12	-10	-1	-1.6
1960	Cin-N	1	0	1.000	7	0	0	0	1	7²	9	1	8	2	20.0	10.57	36	.310	.459	0	—	0	-6	-6	0	-0.0
Total	7	69	62	.527	275	127	42	5	22	1040²	1034	110	385	481	12.6	4.25	96	.261	.332	49	.154	-5	-38	-20	4	-2.6

● **BOB LAWRENCE** Lawrence, Robert Andrew "Larry" b: 12/14/1899, Brooklyn, N.Y. d: 11/6/83, Jamaica, N.Y. BR/TR, 5'11", 180 lbs. Deb: 7/19/24

YEAR	TM/L	W	L	PCT	G	GS	CG	SH	SV	IP	H	HR	BB	SO	RAT	ERA	ERA+	OAV	OOB	BH	AVG	PB	PR	/A	PD	TPI
1924	Chi-A	0	0	—	1	0	0	0	0	1	1	0	1	1	18.0	9.00	46	.250	.400	0	—	0	-1	-1	0	0.0

● **ROXIE LAWSON** Lawson, Alfred Voyle b: 4/13/06, Donnellson, Iowa d: 4/9/77, Stockport, Iowa BR/TR, 6', 170 lbs. Deb: 8/3/30

YEAR	TM/L	W	L	PCT	G	GS	CG	SH	SV	IP	H	HR	BB	SO	RAT	ERA	ERA+	OAV	OOB	BH	AVG	PB	PR	/A	PD	TPI
1930	Cle-A	1	2	.333	7	4	2	0	0	33²	46	1	23	10	18.4	6.15	79	.324	.418	1	.091	-1	-6	-5	-0	-0.4
1931	Cle-A	0	2	.000	17	3	0	0	0	55²	72	5	36	20	17.5	7.60	61	.304	.396	2	.143	-0	-20	-18	-1	-0.6
1933	Det-A	0	1	.000	4	2	0	0	0	16	17	2	17	6	19.1	7.31	59	.270	.425	0	.000	-0	-5	-5	0	-0.3
1935	Det-A	3	1	.750	7	4	4	2	2	40	34	3	24	16	13.0	1.57	265	.233	.341	4	.308	1	13	12	-1	1.2
1936	Det-A	8	6	.571	41	8	3	0	3	128	139	13	71	34	15.0	5.48	90	.281	.376	10	.222	1	-6	-8	-1	-0.6
1937	Det-A	18	7	.720	37	29	15	0	1	217¹	236	15	115	68	14.6	5.26	89	.271	.357	21	.259	3	-15	-14	-1	-1.2
1938	Det-A	8	9	.471	27	16	5	0	1	127	154	10	82	39	16.7	5.46	92	.299	.395	2	.044	-5	-9	-6	1	-1.1
1939	Det-A	1	1	.500	2	1	0	0	0	11¹	7	1	7	4	11.1	4.76	103	.167	.286	0	.000	-1	-0	-0	0	0.0
	StL-A	3	7	.300	36	14	5	0	0	150²	181	10	83	43	15.9	5.32	92	.307	.394	8	.186	-1	-12	-8	-1	-0.5
	Yr	4	8	.333	38	15	5	0	0	162	188	11	90	47	15.6	5.28	92	.297	.387	8	.170	-2	-12	-7	-0	-0.5
1940	StL-A	5	5	.625	30	2	0	0	4	72	77	5	54	18	16.4	5.13	89	.278	.396	1	.045	-3	-6	-4	-0	-0.2
Total	9	47	39	.547	208	83	34	2	11	851²	963	70	512	258	15.7	5.37	89	.285	.380	49	.173	-6	-67	-57	-2	-4.2

● **AL LAWSON** Lawson, Alfred William b: 3/24/1869, London, England d: 11/29/54, San Antonio, Tex. BR/TR, 5'11", 161 lbs. Deb: 5/13/1890

YEAR	TM/L	W	L	PCT	G	GS	CG	SH	SV	IP	H	HR	BB	SO	RAT	ERA	ERA+	OAV	OOB	BH	AVG	PB	PR	/A	PD	TPI
1890	Bos-N	0	1	.000	1	1	1	0	0	9	12	0	4	1	16.0	4.00	94	.308	.372	0	.000	-0	-0	-0	0	0.0
	Pit-N	0	2	.000	2	2	1	0	0	10	15	0	10	2	22.5	9.00	37	.333	.455	0	.000	-1	-6	-6	0	-0.9
	Yr	0	3	.000	3	3	2	0	0	19	27	0	14	3	19.4	6.63	53	.321	.418	0	.000	-1	-6	-7	0	-0.9

● **BOB LAWSON** Lawson, Robert Baker b: 8/23/1876, Brookneal, Va. d: 10/28/52, Durham, N.C. BR/TR, 5'10", 170 lbs. Deb: 5/7/01

YEAR	TM/L	W	L	PCT	G	GS	CG	SH	SV	IP	H	HR	BB	SO	RAT	ERA	ERA+	OAV	OOB	BH	AVG	PB	PR	/A	PD	TPI
1901	Bos-N	2	2	.500	6	4	4	0	0	46	45	0	28	12	14.9	3.33	109	.254	.365	4	.148	-0	-2	-1	1	-0.2
1902	Bal-A	0	2	.000	3	2	1	0	0	13	21	0	3	5	18.0	4.85	78	.362	.413	1	.167	-0	-2	-2	1	-0.2
Total	2	2	4	.333	9	6	5	0	0	59	66	0	31	17	15.6	3.66	100	.281	.376	5	.152	-1	-4	-3	1	-0.4

● **STEVE LAWSON** Lawson, Steven George b: 12/28/50, Oakland, Cal. BR/TL, 6'1", 175 lbs. Deb: 8/3/72

YEAR	TM/L	W	L	PCT	G	GS	CG	SH	SV	IP	H	HR	BB	SO	RAT	ERA	ERA+	OAV	OOB	BH	AVG	PB	PR	/A	PD	TPI
1972	Tex-A	0	0	—	13	0	0	0	1	16	13	1	10	13	12.9	2.81	107	.213	.324	1	1.000	0	0	-0	0	0.0

● **BILL LAXTON** Laxton, William Harry b: 1/5/48, Camden, N.J. BL/TL, 6'1", 190 lbs. Deb: 9/15/70

YEAR	TM/L	W	L	PCT	G	GS	CG	SH	SV	IP	H	HR	BB	SO	RAT	ERA	ERA+	OAV	OOB	BH	AVG	PB	PR	/A	PD	TPI
1970	Phi-N	0	0	—	2	0	0	0	0	2	2	2	2	2	22.5	13.50	30	.250	.455	0	—	0	-2	-2	-0	0.0
1971	SD-N	0	2	.000	18	0	0	0	0	27²	32	5	26	23	19.2	6.83	48	.305	.447	0	—	0	-10	-11	0	-0.7
1974	SD-N	0	1	.000	30	1	0	0	0	44²	37	5	38	40	15.7	4.03	88	.226	.380	1	.200	0	-2	-2	-0	-0.1
1976	Det-A	0	5	.000	26	3	0	0	0	94²	77	13	51	74	12.7	4.09	91	.221	.331	0	—	0	-6	-4	0	-0.4
1977	Sea-A	3	2	.600	43	0	0	0	0	72²	62	10	39	49	13.0	4.95	83	.233	.340	0	—	0	-7	-7	-1	-0.6
	Cle-A	0	0	—	2	0	0	0	0	1²	2	0	2	1	21.6	5.40	73	.286	.444	0	—	0	-0	-0	0	0.0
	Yr	3	2	.600	45	0	0	0	0	74¹	64	10	41	50	13.2	4.96	83	.228	.326	0	—	0	-7	-7	-1	-0.6
Total	5	3	10	.231	121	4	0	0	5	243¹	212	34	158	189	14.2	4.73	79	.236	.359	1	.200	0	-28	-26	-3	-1.8

● **TIM LAYANA** Layana, Timothy Joseph b: 3/2/64, Inglewood, Cal. BR/TR, 6'2", 195 lbs. Deb: 4/9/90

YEAR	TM/L	W	L	PCT	G	GS	CG	SH	SV	IP	H	HR	BB	SO	RAT	ERA	ERA+	OAV	OOB	BH	AVG	PB	PR	/A	PD	TPI
1990	Cin-N	5	3	.625	55	0	0	0	2	80	71	7	44	53	13.2	3.49	113	.244	.347	0	.000	-1	3	4	0	0.4
1991	Cin-N	0	2	.000	22	0	0	0	0	20²	23	1	11	14	14.8	6.97	55	.277	.362	0	.000	-0	-8	-7	0	-0.6
1993	SF-N	0	0	—	1	0	0	0	0	2	7	1	1	1	36.0	22.50	17	.538	.571	0	.000	-0	-4	-4	0	-0.2
Total	3	5	5	.500	78	0	0	0	2	102²	101	9	56	68	13.9	4.56	86	.261	.357	0	.000	-1	-9	-7	1	-0.2

● **DANNY LAZAR** Lazar, John Daniel b: 11/14/43, East Chicago, Ind. BL/TL, 6'1", 190 lbs. Deb: 6/21/68

YEAR	TM/L	W	L	PCT	G	GS	CG	SH	SV	IP	H	HR	BB	SO	RAT	ERA	ERA+	OAV	OOB	BH	AVG	PB	PR	/A	PD	TPI
1968	Chi-A	0	1	.000	8	1	0	0	0	13¹	14	1	4	11	12.2	4.05	75	.269	.321	0	.000	0	-2	-2	0	-0.1
1969	Chi-A	0	0	—	9	3	0	0	0	20²	21	5	11	9	14.4	6.53	59	.280	.379	0	.000	-0	-7	-6	-0	-0.1
Total	2	0	1	.000	17	4	0	0	0	34	35	6	15	20	13.5	5.56	63	.276	.357	0	.000	-0	-8	-8	-0	-0.2

YEAR	TM/L	W	L	PCT	G	GS	CG	SH	SV	IP	H	HR	BB	SO	RAT	ERA	ERA+	OAV	OOB	BH	AVG	PB	PR	/A	PD	TPI

● JACK LAZORKO   Lazorko, Jack Thomas   b: 3/30/56, Hoboken, N.J.   BR/TR, 5'11", 200 lbs.   Deb: 6/4/84

1984	Mil-A	0	1	.000	15	1	0	0	1	39²	37	7	22	24	13.6	4.31	89	.245	.345	0	—	0	-1	-2	0	0.2
1985	Sea-A	0	0	—	15	0	0	0	1	20¹	23	1	8	7	15.0	3.54	119	.291	.378	0	—	0	1	2	1	0.0
1986	Det-A	0	0	—	3	0	0	0	0	6²	8	0	4	3	16.2	4.05	102	.296	.387	0	—	0	0	0	0	0.0
1987	Cal-A	5	6	.455	26	11	2	0	0	117²	108	20	44	55	11.8	4.59	94	.248	.320	0	—	0	-2	-4	2	0.0
1988	Cal-A	0	1	.000	10	3	0	0	0	37²	37	5	16	19	12.9	3.35	115	.255	.333	0	—	0	3	2	0	0.2
Total 5		5	8	.385	69	15	2	0	2	222	213	33	94	108	12.7	4.22	98	.254	.334	0	—	0	1	-2	3	0.4

● CHARLIE LEA   Lea, Charles William   b: 12/25/56, Orleans, France   BR/TR, 6'4", 197 lbs.   Deb: 6/12/80

1980	Mon-N	7	5	.583	21	19	0	0	0	104	103	5	55	56	13.8	3.72	96	.262	.356	3	.081	-2	-1	-2	-1	-0.5
1981	Mon-N	5	4	.556	16	11	2	2	0	64¹	63	4	26	31	12.6	4.62	76	.268	.344	2	.133	-0	-8	-8	-0	-1.1
1982	Mon-N	12	10	.545	27	27	4	2	0	177²	145	16	56	115	10.2	3.24	112	.222	.283	8	.123	-1	7	8	-1	0.7
1983	Mon-N	16	11	.593	33	33	8	4	0	222	195	15	84	137	11.4	3.12	115	.238	.309	2	.114	-2	12	11	-1	1.0
1984	Mon-N★	15	10	.600	30	30	8	0	0	224¹	198	19	68	123	10.8	2.89	119	.239	.299	8	.111	-3	17	13	0	1.2
1987	Mon-N	0	1	.000	1	1	0	0	0	1	4	1	2	0	54.0	36.00	12	.571	.667	0	—	0	-4	-4	0	-1.5
1988	Min-A	7	7	.500	24	23	0	0	0	130	156	19	50	72	14.6	4.85	84	.301	.368	0	—	0	-13	-11	-1	-1.3
Total 7		62	48	.564	152	144	22	8	0	923¹	864	79	341	535	11.9	3.54	102	.250	.320	29	.112	-7	11	8	-4	-1.5

● RICK LEACH   Leach, Richard Max   b: 5/4/57, Ann Arbor, Mich.   BL/TL, 6', 195 lbs.   Deb: 4/30/81   ♦

| 1984 | Tor-A | 0 | 0 | — | 1 | 0 | 0 | 0 | 0 | 1 | 2 | 1 | 2 | 0 | 36.0 | 27.00 | 15 | .400 | .571 | 23 | .261 | 0 | -3 | -3 | 0 | 0.0 |

● TERRY LEACH   Leach, Terry Hester   b: 3/13/54, Selma, Ala.   BR/TR, 6', 215 lbs.   Deb: 8/12/81

1981	NY-N	1	1	.500	21	1	0	0	0	35¹	26	2	12	16	9.7	2.55	137	.205	.273	0	.000	1	4	4	1	0.3
1982	NY-N	2	1	.667	21	1	1	1	3	45¹	46	2	18	30	12.7	4.17	87	.271	.340	1	.125	-0	-3	-3	-0	-0.2
1985	NY-N	3	4	.429	22	4	1	1	1	55²	48	3	14	30	10.2	2.91	119	.235	.288	2	.167	1	4	3	1	0.6
1986	NY-N	0	0	—	6	0	0	0	0	6²	9	0	3	4	12.2	2.70	131	.222	.300	0	—	1	1	1	0	0.0
1987	NY-N	11	1	.917	44	12	1	1	0	131¹	132	14	29	61	11.1	3.22	117	.262	.304	2	.061	-2	13	8	1	0.6
1988	*NY-N	7	2	.778	52	0	0	0	3	92	95	5	24	51	11.9	2.54	127	.268	.320	2	.143	-0	9	7	2	0.9
1989	NY-N	0	0	—	10	0	0	0	0	21¹	19	1	9	10	10.1	4.22	77	.244	.289	0	.000	-0	-2	-1	0	0.0
	KC-A	5	6	.455	30	3	0	0	0	73²	78	4	36	34	14.0	4.15	93	.278	.362	0	—	0	-2	-3	1	-0.2
1990	Min-A	2	5	.286	55	0	0	0	2	81²	84	2	21	46	11.7	3.20	130	.268	.316	0	—	0	6	9	1	0.8
1991	*Min-A	1	2	.333	50	0	0	0	0	67¹	82	3	14	32	12.8	3.61	118	.299	.333	0	—	0	4	5	1	0.2
1992	Chi-A	6	5	.545	51	0	0	0	0	73²	57	2	20	22	9.9	1.95	197	.215	.280	0	—	0	16	16	1	2.3
1993	Chi-A	0	0	—	14	0	0	0	0	16	15	0	3	4	10.1	2.81	149	.250	.286	0	—	0	2	1	0	0.0
Total 11		38	27	.585	376	21	3	3	10	700	688	38	197	331	11.5	3.15	119	.259	.313	7	.097	-1	53	47	8	5.3

● LUIS LEAL   Leal, Luis Enrique (Alvarado)   b: 3/21/57, Barquisimeto, Ven.   BR/TR, 6'3", 205 lbs.   Deb: 5/25/80

1980	Tor-A	3	4	.429	13	10	1	0	0	59²	72	6	31	26	15.7	4.53	95	.314	.398	0	—	0	-3	-1	-1	-0.2
1981	Tor-A	7	13	.350	29	19	3	0	1	129²	127	8	44	71	12.2	3.68	107	.254	.321	0	—	0	-0	-4	-1	0.4
1982	Tor-A	12	15	.444	38	38	10	0	0	249²	250	24	79	111	12.0	3.93	114	.262	.320	0	—	0	4	15	-1	1.2
1983	Tor-A	13	12	.520	35	35	7	1	0	217¹	216	23	65	116	11.9	4.31	100	.257	.315	0	—	0	-6	-0	-1	-0.3
1984	Tor-A	13	8	.619	35	35	6	2	0	222¹	221	27	77	134	12.2	3.89	105	.256	.323	0	—	0	3	5	0	0.4
1985	Tor-A	3	6	.333	15	14	0	0	0	67¹	82	13	24	33	14.6	5.75	73	.303	.366	0	—	0	-12	-12	0	-1.3
Total 6		51	58	.468	165	151	27	3	1	946	968	101	320	491	12.5	4.14	103	.265	.328	0	—	0	-15	11	-2	0.2

● KING LEAR   Lear, Charles Bernard   b: 1/23/1891, Greencastle, Pa.   d: 10/31/76, Greencastle, Pa.   BR/TR, 6', 175 lbs.   Deb: 5/2/14

1914	Cin-N	1	2	.333	17	4	3	1	1	55²	55	3	19	20	12.3	3.07	95	.271	.339	3	.188	1	-2	-1	-0	0.0
1915	Cin-N	6	10	.375	40	15	9	0	0	167²	169	7	45	46	11.8	3.01	95	.270	.324	8	.170	-1	-5	-3	-4	-0.8
Total 2		7	12	.368	57	19	12	1	1	223¹	224	10	64	66	11.9	3.02	95	.270	.328	11	.175	-0	-6	-4	-4	-0.8

● FRANK LEARY   Leary, Francis Patrick   b: 2/26/1881, Wayland, Mass.   d: 10/4/07, Natick, Mass.   TR ,   Deb: 4/30/07

| 1907 | Cin-N | 0 | 1 | .000 | 2 | 1 | 0 | 0 | 0 | 8 | 7 | 0 | 6 | 4 | 14.6 | 1.13 | 231 | .269 | .406 | 0 | .000 | -0 | 1 | 1 | 0 | 0.2 |

● JACK LEARY   Leary, John J.   b: 1858, New Haven, Conn.   TL , 5'11", 186 lbs.   Deb: 8/21/1880   ♦

1880	Bos-N	0	1	.000	1	1	0	0	0	3	8	0	0	1	24.0	15.00	15	.727	.727	0	.000	-0	-4	-4	0	-0.8
1881	Det-N	0	2	.000	2	2	1	0	0	13	13	0	2	2	14.0	4.15	70	.255	.283	3	.273	1	-2	-2	-0	-0.2
1882	Pit-a	1	0	1.000	3	1	0	0	0	18²	28	0	3	5	14.9	6.27	42	.326	.348	75	.292	1	-7	-8	0	-0.2
	Bal-a	2	1	.667	3	3	3	0	0	26	29	1	8	2	12.8	1.38	199	.264	.314	4	.222	0	4	4	-0	0.4
	Yr	3	1	.750	6	4	3	0	0	44²	57	1	11	7	13.7	3.43	79	.291	.329	79	.287	1	-4	-4	-0	0.2
1884	Alt-U	0	3	.000	3	3	2	0	0	24	31	0	2	7	12.4	5.25	51	.292	.306	3	.091	-2	-7	-7	-0	-0.7
	CP-U	0	2	.000	2	1	0	0	0	10	14	0	5	6	17.1	5.40	45	.311	.380	7	.175	-1	-3	-3	-0	-0.5
	Yr	0	5	.000	5	4	3	0	0	34	45	0	7	13	13.8	5.29	49	.298	.329	10	.137	-3	-11	-10	-0	-1.2
Total 4		3	9	.250	14	12	8	0	0	94²	123	1	20	23	13.6	4.56	59	.301	.333	125	.232	-2	-21	-20	-0	-2.0

● TIM LEARY   Leary, Timothy James   b: 12/23/58, Santa Monica, Cal.   BR/TR, 6'3", 205 lbs.   Deb: 4/12/81

1981	NY-N	0	0	—	1	1	0	0	0	2	0	0	1	3	4.5	0.00	—	.000	.143	0	.000	-0	1	1	0	0.0
1983	NY-N	1	1	.500	2	2	1	0	0	10²	15	0	4	9	16.0	3.38	107	.319	.373	1	.333	0	0	0	0	0.1
1984	NY-N	3	3	.500	20	7	0	0	0	53²	61	2	18	29	13.6	4.02	88	.285	.346	3	.300	2	-3	-3	-1	-0.9
1985	Mil-A	1	4	.200	5	5	0	0	0	33¹	40	5	9	29	13.2	4.05	103	.296	.340	0	—	0	0	0	1	0.1
1986	Mil-A	12	12	.500	33	30	3	2	0	188¹	216	20	53	110	13.2	4.21	103	.288	.342	0	—	0	3	1	-3	0.3
1987	LA-N	3	11	.214	39	12	0	0	1	107¹	121	15	36	61	13.3	4.76	83	.285	.344	7	.304	2	-8	-10	1	-0.9
1988	*LA-N	17	11	.607	35	34	9	6	0	228²	201	13	56	180	10.4	2.91	114	.234	.285	18	.269	6	14	11	2	2.0
1989	LA-N	6	7	.462	19	17	2	0	0	117¹	107	9	31	59	11.5	3.38	101	.247	.309	2	.061	-2	1	1	-0	-0.1
	Cin-N	2	7	.222	14	14	0	0	0	89²	98	8	31	64	12.0	3.71	97	.278	.342	5	.192	-2	-2	-0	-0	0.0
	Yr	8	14	.364	33	31	2	0	0	207	205	17	62	123	12.0	3.52	99	.259	.320	7	.119	-1	-1	-1	0	0.0
1990	NY-A	9	19	.321	31	31	6	1	0	208	202	18	78	138	12.4	4.11	97	.257	.330	0	—	0	-5	-3	-2	-0.2
1991	NY-A	4	10	.286	28	18	1	0	0	120²	150	20	57	83	15.7	6.49	64	.312	.389	0	—	0	-32	-31	-1	-3.1
1992	NY-A	5	6	.455	18	15	2	0	0	97	84	9	57	34	13.5	5.57	70	.245	.359	0	—	0	-18	-18	-1	-1.8
	Sea-A	3	4	.429	8	8	1	0	0	44	47	3	30	12	16.8	4.91	81	.280	.404	0	—	0	-5	-5	1	-0.6
	Yr	8	10	.444	26	23	3	0	0	141	131	12	87	46	14.2	5.36	73	.251	.364	0	—	0	-22	-22	-0	-2.4
1993	Sea-A	11	9	.550	33	27	0	0	0	169¹	202	21	58	68	14.2	5.05	87	.300	.362	0	—	0	-14	-12	1	-1.1
1994	Tex-A	1	1	.500	6	3	0	0	0	24	31	4	11	9	16.3	8.14	59	.306	.392	0	—	0	-8	-8	-0	-0.5
Total 13		78	105	.426	292	224	25	9	1	1491¹	1570	147	535	888	13.0	4.36	89	.273	.340	36	.221	9	-78	-76	7	-5.9

● RAZOR LEDBETTER   Ledbetter, Ralph Overton   b: 12/8/1894, Rutherford College, N.C.   d: 2/1/69, W.Palm Beach, Fla.   BR/TR, 6'3", 190 lbs.   Deb: 4/16/15

| 1915 | Det-A | 0 | 0 | — | 1 | 0 | 0 | 0 | 0 | 1 | 1 | 0 | 0 | 0 | 9.0 | — | — | .333 | .333 | 0 | — | 0 | 0 | 0 | 0 | 0.0 |

● DON LEE   Lee, Donald Edward   b: 2/26/34, Globe, Ariz.   BR/TR, 6'4", 210 lbs.   Deb: 4/23/57   F

1957	Det-A	1	3	.250	11	6	0	0	0	38²	48	6	18	19	15.6	4.66	83	.308	.383	2	.167	-0	-4	-3	-0	-0.4
1958	Det-A	0	0	—	1	0	0	0	0	2	1	1	0	4	13.5	9.00	45	.143	.333	0	—	0	-1	-0	0	0.0
1960	Was-A	8	7	.533	44	20	1	0	3	165	160	16	64	88	12.4	3.44	113	.258	.330	5	.116	-3	8	8	1	0.8
1961	Min-A	3	6	.333	37	10	4	0	1	115	93	12	35	65	10.3	3.52	120	.221	.288	2	.067	-3	6	9	2	0.6
1962	Min-A	3	3	.500	9	4	1	0	0	52	51	8	24	28	14.2	4.50	91	.256	.357	4	.211	0	-2	-0	-0	-0.2
	LA-A	8	8	.500	27	22	4	2	2	153¹	153	12	39	74	11.4	3.11	124	.256	.305	9	.184	-0	15	13	-2	1.1
	Yr	11	11	.500	36	31	5	2	2	205¹	204	20	63	102	11.8	3.46	113	.254	.310	13	.191	-0	12	10	-2	0.9
1963	LA-A	8	11	.421	40	22	3	2	1	154	148	12	51	89	12.2	3.68	93	.251	.320	7	.156	-1	-4	-1	-0	-0.0
1964	LA-A	5	4	.556	33	8	0	0	0	89¹	99	6	25	73	12.6	2.72	121	.279	.328	6	.261	2	9	6	-1	0.7
1965	Cal-A	0	1	.000	10	0	0	0	0	14	21	4	5	12	17.4	6.43	53	.350	.409	1	.333	1	-5	-5	-0	-0.3
	Hou-N	0	0	—	9	0	0	0	0	8	7	1	3	5	13.5	3.38	99	.267	.353	0	—	0	-0	-0	0	0.0
1966	Hou-N	2	0	1.000	9	0	0	0	0	18	17	1	4	9	10.5	2.50	137	.250	.292	1	1.000	0	1	2	1	0.3
	Chi-N	2	1	.667	16	0	0	0	0	19	28	3	12	7	18.9	7.11	52	.346	.430	0	—	0	-7	-7	-0	-1.0

YEAR	TM/L	W	L	PCT	G	GS	CG	SH	SV	IP	H	HR	BB	SO	RAT	ERA	ERA+	OAV	OOB	BH	AVG	PB	PR	/A	PD	TPI
	Yr	4	1	.800	25	0	0	0	0	37	45	4	16	16	14.8	4.86	73	.302	.370	1	1.000	1	-5	-5	1	-0.7
Total	9	40	44	.476	244	97	13	4	11	828¹	827	81	281	467	12.4	3.61	104	.260	.326	37	.164	-1	20	14	1	0.9

● **MARK LEE** — Lee, Mark Linden b: 6/14/53, Inglewood, Cal. BR/TR, 6'4", 225 lbs. Deb: 4/23/78

YEAR	TM/L	W	L	PCT	G	GS	CG	SH	SV	IP	H	HR	BB	SO	RAT	ERA	ERA+	OAV	OOB	BH	AVG	PB	PR	/A	PD	TPI
1978	SD-N	5	1	.833	56	0	0	0	2	85	74	2	36	31	11.9	3.28	101	.240	.324	0	.000	-1	3	0	2	0.1
1979	SD-N	2	4	.333	46	1	0	0	5	65	88	3	25	25	15.9	4.29	82	.332	.394	2	.333	1	-4	-6	1	-0.4
1980	Pit-N	0	1	.000	4	0	0	0	0	5²	3	1	2	2	12.7	4.76	76	.227	.307	0	—	0	-1	-1	0	0.0
1981	Pit-N	0	2	.000	12	0	0	0	2	19²	17	1	5	5	10.1	2.75	131	.233	.282	1	.500	0	2	2	1	0.4
Total	4	7	8	.467	118	1	0	0	9	175¹	184	6	69	63	13.2	3.64	94	.275	.347	3	.231	1	-0	-4	4	0.1

● **MARK LEE** — Lee, Mark Owen b: 7/20/64, Williston, N.Dak. BL/TL, 6'3", 198 lbs. Deb: 9/8/88

YEAR	TM/L	W	L	PCT	G	GS	CG	SH	SV	IP	H	HR	BB	SO	RAT	ERA	ERA+	OAV	OOB	BH	AVG	PB	PR	/A	PD	TPI
1988	KC-A	0	0	—	4	0	0	0	0	5	6	0	1	0	12.6	3.60	111	.300	.333	0	—	0	0	0	0	0.0
1990	Mil-A	1	0	1.000	11	0	0	0	0	21¹	20	1	4	14	10.1	2.11	184	.256	.293	0	—	0	4	4	-0	0.2
1991	Mil-A	2	5	.286	62	0	0	0	1	67²	72	10	31	43	13.8	3.86	103	.283	.364	0	—	0	2	1	1	0.3
1995	Bal-A	2	0	1.000	39	0	0	0	1	33¹	31	5	18	27	13.5	4.86	98	.246	.345	0	—	0	-1	-0	-1	-0.1
Total	4	5	5	.500	116	0	0	0	2	127¹	129	16	54	84	13.1	3.82	109	.270	.346	0	—	0	6	5	-1	0.4

● **MIKE LEE** — Lee, Michael Randall b: 5/19/41, Bell, Cal. BL/TL, 6'5", 220 lbs. Deb: 5/6/60

YEAR	TM/L	W	L	PCT	G	GS	CG	SH	SV	IP	H	HR	BB	SO	RAT	ERA	ERA+	OAV	OOB	BH	AVG	PB	PR	/A	PD	TPI
1960	Cle-A	0	0	—	7	0	0	0	0	9	6	1	11	6	18.0	2.00	187	.207	.439	0	—	0	2	2	-0	0.1
1963	LA-A	1	1	.500	6	4	0	0	0	26	30	3	14	11	15.6	3.81	90	.300	.391	0	.000	-1	-1	-1	1	-0.1
Total	2	1	1	.500	13	4	0	0	0	35	36	4	25	17	16.2	3.34	105	.279	.404	0	.000	-1	1	1	1	-0.1

● **BOB LEE** — Lee, Robert Dean "Moose" or "Horse" b: 11/26/37, Ottumwa, Iowa BR/TR, 6'3", 230 lbs. Deb: 4/15/64

YEAR	TM/L	W	L	PCT	G	GS	CG	SH	SV	IP	H	HR	BB	SO	RAT	ERA	ERA+	OAV	OOB	BH	AVG	PB	PR	/A	PD	TPI
1964	LA-A	6	5	.545	64	5	0	0	19	137	87	6	58	111	9.6	**1.51**	217	.182	.272	0	.000	-2	**32**	27	-2	2.5
1965	Cal-A☆	9	7	.563	69	0	0	0	23	131¹	95	11	42	89	9.5	1.92	194	.205	.272	3	.143	1	22	22	-1	3.4
1966	Cal-A	5	4	.556	61	0	0	0	16	101²	90	8	31	46	10.8	2.74	122	.237	.297	0	.000	-0	8	7	-1	0.7
1967	LA-N	0	0	—	4	0	0	0	0	6²	6	2	3	2	13.5	5.40	57	.222	.323	0	—	-1	-2	-2	-0	0.0
	Cin-N	3	3	.500	27	1	0	0	2	50²	51	0	25	33	13.5	4.44	84	.262	.345	3	.375	1	-6	-4	-1	-0.5
	Yr	3	3	.500	31	1	0	0	2	57¹	57	2	28	35	13.3	4.55	81	.254	.337	3	.375	1	-8	-6	-1	-0.5
1968	Cin-N	2	4	.333	44	1	0	0	2	65¹	73	4	37	34	15.3	5.10	62	.302	.396	1	.200	1	-15	-14	-1	-1.6
Total	5	25	23	.521	269	7	0	0	63	492²	402	31	196	315	11.0	2.70	125	.225	.304	7	.104	-1	40	36	-6	4.5

● **ROY LEE** — Lee, Roy Edwin b: 9/28/17, Elmira, N.Y. d: 11/11/85, St.Louis, Mo. BL/TL, 5'11.5", 175 lbs. Deb: 9/23/45

YEAR	TM/L	W	L	PCT	G	GS	CG	SH	SV	IP	H	HR	BB	SO	RAT	ERA	ERA+	OAV	OOB	BH	AVG	PB	PR	/A	PD	TPI
1945	NY-N	0	2	.000	3	1	0	0	0	7	8	3	3	0	14.1	11.57	34	.267	.333	0	.000	-0	-6	-6	-0	-1.3

● **TOM LEE** — Lee, Thomas Frank b: 6/8/1862, Philadelphia, Pa. d: 3/4/1886, Milwaukee, Wis. Deb: 6/14/1884

YEAR	TM/L	W	L	PCT	G	GS	CG	SH	SV	IP	H	HR	BB	SO	RAT	ERA	ERA+	OAV	OOB	BH	AVG	PB	PR	/A	PD	TPI
1884	Chi-N	1	4	.200	5	5	4	2	0	45¹	55	12	15	14	13.9	3.77	83	.272	.323	3	.125	-2	-4	-3	-0	-0.4
	Bal-U	5	8	.385	15	14	12	0	0	122	121	1	29	81	11.1	3.39	79	.242	.283	23	.280	-1	-13	-10	-0	-0.9
Total	1	6	12	.333	20	19	17	0	0	167¹	176	13	44	95	11.8	3.50	80	.250	.295	26	.245	-4	-17	-13	0	-1.3

● **THORNTON LEE** — Lee, Thornton Starr "Lefty" b: 9/13/06, Sonoma, Cal. BL/TL, 6'3", 205 lbs. Deb: 9/19/33 F

YEAR	TM/L	W	L	PCT	G	GS	CG	SH	SV	IP	H	HR	BB	SO	RAT	ERA	ERA+	OAV	OOB	BH	AVG	PB	PR	/A	PD	TPI
1933	Cle-A	1	1	.500	3	2	2	0	0	17¹	13	1	11	7	12.5	4.15	107	.203	.320	3	.375	1	0	1	-0	0.2
1934	Cle-A	1	1	.500	24	6	0	0	0	85²	105	8	44	41	16.0	5.04	90	.308	.392	2	.095	-1	-5	-5	0	-0.2
1935	Cle-A	7	10	.412	32	20	8	1	1	180²	179	6	71	81	12.7	4.04	112	.259	.331	12	.197	-1	8	9	2	0.8
1936	Cle-A	3	5	.375	43	8	2	0	3	127	138	2	67	49	14.7	4.89	103	.271	.358	5	.122	-2	**2**	2	2	0.1
1937	Chi-A	12	10	.545	30	25	13	2	0	204²	209	17	60	80	11.9	3.52	131	.260	.312	15	.211	1	25	25	-1	2.2
1938	Chi-A	13	12	.520	33	30	18	1	1	245¹	252	12	94	77	12.8	3.49	140	.263	.331	25	.258	6	36	**38**	-2	3.8
1939	Chi-A	15	11	.577	33	29	15	2	3	235	260	14	70	81	12.8	4.21	112	.285	.338	15	.165	-3	11	14	0	1.1
1940	Chi-A	12	13	.480	28	27	24	1	0	228	223	13	56	87	11.1	3.47	127	.254	.300	23	.274	4	23	24	-3	2.4
1941	Chi-A★	22	11	.667	35	34	**30**	3	1	300¹	258	18	92	130	**10.6**	**2.37**	173	.232	**.293**	29	.254		**59**	**58**	-2	**6.6**
1942	Chi-A	2	6	.250	11	8	6	1	0	76	82	4	31	25	13.0	3.32	109	.278	.351	6	.200		3	2	-0	0.4
1943	Chi-A	5	9	.357	19	19	7	1	0	127	129	8	50	35	13.0	4.18	80	.266	.340	3	.071	-4	-12	-12	-3	-1.9
1944	Chi-A	3	9	.250	15	14	6	0	0	113¹	105	3	25	39	10.4	3.02	114	.246	.290	4	.095	-3	5	5	2	0.4
1945	Chi-A†	15	12	.556	29	28	19	1	0	228¹	208	6	76	108	11.6	2.44	136	.245	.314	14	.179	-1	23	22	-1	2.4
1946	Chi-A	2	4	.333	7	7	2	0	0	43¹	31	9	23	23	13.1	3.53	97	.244	.342	4	.267	1	-0	-1	0	-0.1
1947	Chi-A	3	7	.300	21	11	2	1	0	86²	84	5	56	57	15.0	4.47	82	.261	.372	6	.207	0	-7	-8	0	-0.8
1948	NY-N	1	3	.250	11	4	1	0	0	32²	41	3	12	17	14.9	4.41	89	.304	.365	1	.091	-0	-2	-2	0	-0.2
Total	16	117	124	.485	374	272	155	14	10	2331¹	2327	121	838	937	12.4	3.56	119	.260	.326	167	.200	1	169	172	-7	16.9

● **BILL LEE** — Lee, William Crutcher "Big Bill" b: 10/21/09, Plaquemine, La. d: 6/15/77, Plaquemine, La. BR/TR, 6'3", 195 lbs. Deb: 4/29/34

YEAR	TM/L	W	L	PCT	G	GS	CG	SH	SV	IP	H	HR	BB	SO	RAT	ERA	ERA+	OAV	OOB	BH	AVG	PB	PR	/A	PD	TPI
1934	Chi-N	13	14	.481	35	29	16	4	1	214¹	218	9	74	104	12.3	3.40	114	.263	.325	10	.132	-2	16	11	2	1.2
1935	*Chi-N	20	6	**.769**	39	32	18	3	1	252	241	11	84	100	11.8	2.96	133	.251	.314	24	.235	2	30	27	-0	2.7
1936	Chi-N	18	11	.621	43	33	20	**4**	1	258²	238	14	93	102	11.6	3.31	121	.246	.314	12	.138	-3	21	19	1	1.7
1937	Chi-N	14	15	.483	42	34	17	2	3	272¹	289	14	73	108	12.0	3.54	113	.272	.320	15	.172	-1	11	13	3	1.1
1938	*Chi-N★	22	9	.710	44	37	19	**9**	2	291	281	18	74	121	11.0	**2.66**	**144**	.252	.299	20	.198	1	37	38	1	**4.0**
1939	Chi-N★	19	15	.559	37	36	20	1	0	282¹	295	18	85	105	12.1	3.44	114	.272	.325	13	.126	-4	15	16	5	1.7
1940	Chi-N	9	17	.346	37	30	9	1	0	211¹	226	12	70	70	13.5	5.03	75	.290	.350	10	.132	-2	-28	-30	-1	-3.5
1941	Chi-N	8	14	.364	28	22	12	0	1	167¹	179	6	43	62	12.0	3.76	93	.270	.316	11	.186	1	-2	-5	1	-0.3
1942	Chi-N	13	13	.500	32	30	18	1	0	219²	221	4	67	75	11.8	3.85	83	.258	.312	11	.159	1	-13	-16	1	-1.5
1943	Chi-N	3	7	.300	13	12	4	0	0	78¹	70	4	27	18	12.6	3.56	94	.273	.332	7	.269	1	-2	-1	-0	-0.2
	Phi-N	1	5	.167	13	7	2	0	3	60²	70	4	21	17	13.6	4.60	73	.298	.358	1	.059	-2	-8	-8	-1	-1.1
	Yr	4	12	.250	26	19	6	0	3	139	153	8	48	35	13.1	4.01	84	.284	.344	8	.186	-0	-10	-10	-2	-1.3
1944	Phi-N	10	11	.476	31	28	11	3	1	208¹	199	9	57	50	11.2	3.15	115	.248	.300	14	.194	-0	11	11	2	1.2
1945	Phi-N	3	6	.333	13	13	2	0	0	77¹	107	4	30	13	15.9	4.66	82	.318	.374	4	.167	-1	-7	-7	-0	-0.7
	Bos-N	6	3	.667	16	13	6	1	0	106¹	112	6	36	12	12.5	2.79	137	.279	.338	4	.129	-1	12	12	1	1.0
	Yr	9	9	.500	29	26	8	1	0	183²	219	6	66	25	14.0	3.58	107	.297	.354	8	.145	-1	5	5	0	0.3
1946	Bos-N	10	9	.526	25	21	8	0	0	140	148	7	45	32	12.5	4.18	82	.273	.330	8	.170	1	-12	-12	1	-1.4
1947	Chi-N	0	2	.000	14	2	0	0	0	24	26	2	14	9	15.4	4.50	88	.268	.366	1	.333	0	-1	-1	0	-0.1
Total	14	169	157	.518	462	379	182	29	13	2864	2953	138	893	998	12.2	3.54	106	.266	.322	165	.168	-10	78	66	14	6.2

● **BILL LEE** — Lee, William Francis "Spaceman" b: 12/28/46, Burbank, Cal. BL/TL, 6'3", 210 lbs. Deb: 6/25/69

YEAR	TM/L	W	L	PCT	G	GS	CG	SH	SV	IP	H	HR	BB	SO	RAT	ERA	ERA+	OAV	OOB	BH	AVG	PB	PR	/A	PD	TPI
1969	Bos-A	1	3	.250	20	1	0	0	0	52	56	9	28	45	14.9	4.50	84	.281	.376	0	.000	-0	-5	-4	-0	-0.4
1970	Bos-A	2	2	.500	11	5	0	0	1	37	48	3	14	19	15.1	4.62	86	.320	.378	0	.000	-1	-4	-3	1	-0.3
1971	Bos-A	9	2	.818	47	3	0	0	2	102	102	7	46	74	13.1	2.74	135	.256	.335	5	.217	-1	8	11	0	1.3
1972	Bos-A	7	4	.636	47	0	0	0	5	84¹	75	5	32	43	11.5	3.20	100	.248	.322	3	.188	1	-0	2	0	0.1
1973	Bos-A☆	17	11	.607	38	33	18	1	1	284²	275	20	76	120	11.3	2.75	146	.257	.309	0	—	0	34	40	4	4.0
1974	Bos-A	17	15	.531	38	37	16	1	0	282¹	320	25	67	95	12.5	3.51	110	.290	.333	0	—	0	3	11	4	1.3
1975	*Bos-A	17	9	.654	41	34	17	4	0	260	274	20	69	78	12.0	3.95	103	.273	.322	0	—	0	-5	4	2	0.5
1976	Bos-A	5	7	.417	24	14	3	0	0	96	124	13	28	29	14.5	5.63	70	.307	.356	0	—	0	-22	-18	1	-2.1
1977	Bos-A	9	5	.643	27	16	4	0	1	128	155	14	29	31	12.9	4.43	101	.306	.344	0	—	0	-5	1	2	0.1
1978	Bos-A	10	10	.500	28	24	8	1	0	177	198	20	56	43	13.6	3.46	119	.285	.343	0	—	0	6	13	0	0.8
1979	Mon-N	16	10	.615	33	33	6	3	0	222	230	20	46	59	11.2	3.04	121	.265	.303	16	.216	2	17	16	1	1.5
1980	Mon-N	4	6	.400	24	18	2	0	0	118	156	13	32	34	13.8	4.96	72	.319	.352	9	.220	-1	-18	-10	-1	-1.4
1981	*Mon-N	5	6	.455	31	7	0	0	6	88²	90	6	14	34	10.8	2.94	119	.265	.289	8	.364	3	5	5	3	1.4
1982	Mon-N	0	0	—	7	0	0	0	0	12¹	19	1	1	8	14.6	4.38	83	.352	.364	0	—	0	-1	-0	0	-0.1
Total	14	119	90	.569	416	225	72	10	19	1944¹	2122	176	531	713	12.4	3.62	107	.280	.329	41	.208	5	12	55	16	7.7

● **WATTY LEE** — Lee, Wyatt Arnold b: 8/12/1879, Lynch Station, Va. d: 3/6/36, Washington, D.C. BL/TL, 5'10.5", 171 lbs. Deb: 4/30/01 ♦

YEAR	TM/L	W	L	PCT	G	GS	CG	SH	SV	IP	H	HR	BB	SO	RAT	ERA	ERA+	OAV	OOB	BH	AVG	PB	PR	/A	PD	TPI
1901	Was-A	16	16	.500	36	33	25	2	0	262	328	14	45	63	13.2	4.40	83	.303	.337	33	.256	4	-21	-21	2	-1.5
1902	Was-A	5	7	.417	13	10	10	0	0	98	118	5	20	24	13.4	5.05	73	.298	.344	100	.256	3	-16	-15	1	-1.2
1903	Was-A	8	12	.400	22	20	15	2	0	166²	169	5	40	70	11.7	3.08	102	.262	.313	48	.208	1	-2	1	3	0.6

YEAR	TM/L	W	L	PCT	G	GS	CG	SH	SV	IP	H	HR	BB	SO	RAT	ERA	ERA+	OAV	OOB	BH	AVG	PB	PR	/A	PD	TPI
1904	Pit-N	1	2	.333	5	3	1	0	0	22²	34	0	9	5	18.3	8.74	31	.337	.407	4	.333	1	-15	-15	0	-1.5
Total	4	30	37	.448	76	66	51	4	0	549¹	649	24	114	162	13.0	4.29	81	.292	.334	185	.242	10	-55	-50	5	-3.6

● SAM LEEVER
Leever, Samuel "Deacon" or "The Goshen Schoolmaster"
b: 12/23/1871, Goshen, Ohio   d: 5/19/53, Goshen, Ohio   BR/TR, 5'10.5", 175 lbs.   Deb: 5/26/1898

YEAR	TM/L	W	L	PCT	G	GS	CG	SH	SV	IP	H	HR	BB	SO	RAT	ERA	ERA+	OAV	OOB	BH	AVG	PB	PR	/A	PD	TPI
1898	Pit-N	1	0	1.000	5	3	2	0	0	33	26	0	5	15	8.7	2.45	145	.215	.252	3	.250	0	4	4	-0	0.1
1899	Pit-N	21	23	.477	51	39	35	4	3	379	353	7	122	121	11.5	3.18	120	.247	.311	33	.226	3	28	27	1	3.0
1900	*Pit-N	15	13	.536	30	29	25	3	0	232²	236	2	48	84	11.3	2.71	134	.263	.306	18	.205	0	26	24	-1	2.4
1901	Pit-N	14	5	.737	21	20	18	2	0	176	182	2	39	82	11.7	2.86	114	.263	.311	13	.183	-0	9	8	2	0.8
1902	Pit-N	15	7	.682	28	26	23	4	2	222	203	2	31	86	9.8	2.39	114	.243	.277	16	.178	0	10	9	-4	0.3
1903	*Pit-N	25	7	.781	36	34	30	7	1	284¹	255	2	60	90	10.1	2.06	157	.238	.282	19	.165	-4	38	37	-0	3.4
1904	Pit-N	18	11	.621	34	32	26	1	0	253¹	224	2	54	63	10.1	2.17	127	.237	.282	26	.263	7	16	16	-1	2.4
1905	Pit-N	20	5	.800	33	29	20	3	1	229²	199	3	54	81	10.4	2.70	111	.231	.286	9	.102	-4	8	8	-0	0.4
1906	Pit-N	22	7	.759	36	31	25	6	0	260¹	232	3	48	76	9.9	2.32	115	.243	.284	20	.211	2	9	10	-5	0.7
1907	Pit-N	14	9	.609	31	24	17	5	0	216²	182	3	46	65	9.8	1.66	147	.229	.278	11	.151	-1	20	19	-5	1.3
1908	Pit-N	15	7	.682	38	20	14	4	2	192²	179	1	41	28	10.6	2.10	110	.249	.295	9	.148	0	6	4	-4	0.1
1909	Pit-N	8	1	.889	19	4	2	0	2	70	74	0	14	23	11.8	2.83	96	.276	.322	4	.167	0	-2	-1	-0	-0.1
1910	Pit-N	6	5	.545	26	8	4	0	2	111	104	2	25	33	10.9	2.76	112	.259	.313	2	.065	-3	3	4	1	0.2
Total	13	194	100	.660	388	299	241	39	13	2660²	2449	29	587	847	10.6	2.47	123	.245	.293	183	.184	1	175	169	-15	15.0

● BILL LEFEBVRE
Lefebvre, Wilfred Henry "Lefty"   b: 11/11/15, Natick, R.I.   BL/TL, 5'11.5", 180 lbs.   Deb: 6/10/38   ♦

YEAR	TM/L	W	L	PCT	G	GS	CG	SH	SV	IP	H	HR	BB	SO	RAT	ERA	ERA+	OAV	OOB	BH	AVG	PB	PR	/A	PD	TPI
1938	Bos-A	0	0	—	1	0	0	0	0	4	8	2	0	0	20.3	13.50	37	.400	.429	1	1.000	1	-4	-4	-0	0.1
1939	Bos-A	1	1	.500	5	3	0	0	0	26¹	35	2	14	8	16.7	5.81	81	.333	.412	3	.300	1	-3	-3	-1	-0.2
1943	Was-A	2	0	1.000	6	3	1	0	0	32¹	33	3	16	10	13.6	4.45	72	.268	.353	4	.286	2	-4	-4	-0	-0.1
1944	Was-A	2	4	.333	24	4	2	0	3	69²	86	3	21	18	14.0	4.52	72	.305	.355	16	.258	3	-8	-10	-0	-0.3
Total	4	5	5	.500	36	10	3	0	3	132¹	162	10	51	36	14.6	5.03	71	.306	.369	24	.276	7	-20	-21	-1	-0.5

● CRAIG LEFFERTS
Lefferts, Craig Lindsay   b: 9/29/57, Munich, W.Germany   BL/TL, 6'1", 210 lbs.   Deb: 4/7/83

YEAR	TM/L	W	L	PCT	G	GS	CG	SH	SV	IP	H	HR	BB	SO	RAT	ERA	ERA+	OAV	OOB	BH	AVG	PB	PR	/A	PD	TPI
1983	Chi-N	3	4	.429	56	5	0	0	1	89	80	13	29	60	11.2	3.13	121	.243	.308	2	.111	-1	5	6	0	0.5
1984	*SD-N	3	4	.429	62	0	0	0	10	105²	88	4	24	56	9.6	2.13	167	.229	.276	5	.294	1	17	17	-1	1.4
1985	SD-N	7	6	.538	60	0	0	0	2	83¹	75	7	30	48	11.3	3.35	106	.244	.312	1	.250	0	2	2	-0	0.2
1986	SD-N	9	8	.529	83	0	0	0	4	107²	98	7	44	72	12.0	3.09	118	.245	.331	1	.125	1	7	7	2	1.3
1987	SD-N	2	2	.500	33	0	0	0	2	51¹	56	9	15	39	12.8	4.38	90	.272	.327	1	.333	0	-2	-2	-1	-0.2
	*SF-N	3	3	.500	44	0	0	0	4	47¹	36	4	18	18	10.3	3.23	119	.216	.292	1	.250	0	4	3	-1	0.4
	Yr	5	5	.500	77	0	0	0	6	98²	92	13	33	57	11.4	3.83	102	.245	.306	2	.286	1	3	1	-2	0.2
1988	SF-N	3	8	.273	64	0	0	0	11	92¹	74	7	23	58	9.6	2.92	112	.225	.278	0	.000	-1	5	3	-1	0.5
1989	*SF-N	2	4	.333	70	0	0	0	20	107	93	11	22	71	9.8	2.69	125	.233	.275	0	.000	-1	10	8	1	0.5
1990	SD-N	7	5	.583	56	0	0	0	23	78²	68	10	22	60	10.4	2.52	152	.228	.283	1	.250	0	11	11	0	2.3
1991	SD-N	6	6	.143	54	0	0	0	23	69	74	5	14	48	11.6	3.91	97	.285	.324	0	.000	-0	-2	-1	-0	-0.2
1992	SD-N	13	9	.591	27	27	0	0	0	163¹	180	16	35	81	11.8	3.69	97	.285	.322	4	.077	-3	-3	-2	-1	-0.6
	Bal-A	1	3	.250	9	5	1	0	0	33	34	3	6	23	10.9	4.09	98	.268	.301	0	—	-1	-0	-1	-0	-0.2
1993	Tex-A	3	9	.250	52	8	0	0	0	83¹	102	17	28	58	14.1	6.05	69	.304	.360	0	—	-0	-16	-18	-0	-2.0
1994	Cal-A	1	1	.500	30	0	0	0	1	34²	50	7	14	27	16.1	4.67	105	.350	.400	0	—	0	0	1	-1	-0.1
Total	12	58	72	.446	696	45	1	0	101	1145²	1108	120	322	719	11.3	3.43	108	.257	.311	16	.121	-3	39	36	-4	3.6

● PHIL LEFTWICH
Leftwich, Philip Dale   b: 5/19/69, Lynchburg, Va.   BR/TR, 6'5", 205 lbs.   Deb: 7/29/93

YEAR	TM/L	W	L	PCT	G	GS	CG	SH	SV	IP	H	HR	BB	SO	RAT	ERA	ERA+	OAV	OOB	BH	AVG	PB	PR	/A	PD	TPI
1993	Cal-A	4	6	.400	12	12	1	0	0	80²	81	5	27	31	12.4	3.79	119	.262	.327	0	—	0	5	6	-0	0.6
1994	Cal-A	5	10	.333	20	20	1	0	0	114	127	16	42	67	13.6	5.68	86	.283	.349	0	—	0	-11	-10	-0	-1.2
1996	Cal-A	0	1	.000	2	2	0	0	0	7¹	12	1	3	4	18.4	7.36	66	.375	.429	0	—	0	-2	-2	-0	-0.1
Total	3	9	17	.346	34	34	2	0	0	202	220	22	72	102	13.3	4.99	95	.279	.344	0	—	0	-8	-6	-0	-0.7

● REGIS LEHENY
Leheny, Regis Francis   b: 1/5/08, Pittsburgh, Pa.   d: 11/2/76, Pittsburgh, Pa.   BL/TL, 6'0.5", 180 lbs.   Deb: 5/21/32

YEAR	TM/L	W	L	PCT	G	GS	CG	SH	SV	IP	H	HR	BB	SO	RAT	ERA	ERA+	OAV	OOB	BH	AVG	PB	PR	/A	PD	TPI
1932	Bos-A	0	0	—	2	0	0	0	0	2²	5	0	3	1	27.0	16.88	27	.417	.533	0	.000	-0	-4	-4	-0	0.0

● JIM LEHEW
Lehew, James Anthony   b: 8/19/37, Baltimore, Md.   BR/TR, 6', 185 lbs.   Deb: 9/13/61

YEAR	TM/L	W	L	PCT	G	GS	CG	SH	SV	IP	H	HR	BB	SO	RAT	ERA	ERA+	OAV	OOB	BH	AVG	PB	PR	/A	PD	TPI
1961	Bal-A	0	0	—	2	0	0	0	0	2	1	0	0	0	4.5	0.00	—	.167	.167	0	—	0	1	1	0	0.0
1962	Bal-A	0	0	—	6	0	0	0	0	9²	10	0	3	2	12.1	1.86	199	.303	.361	0	.000	-0	2	2	0	0.0
Total	2	0	0	—	8	0	0	0	0	11²	11	0	3	2	10.8	1.54	241	.282	.333	0	.000	-0	3	3	0	0.0

● KEN LEHMAN
Lehman, Kenneth Karl   b: 6/10/28, Seattle, Wash.   BL/TL, 6', 186 lbs.   Deb: 9/5/52

YEAR	TM/L	W	L	PCT	G	GS	CG	SH	SV	IP	H	HR	BB	SO	RAT	ERA	ERA+	OAV	OOB	BH	AVG	PB	PR	/A	PD	TPI
1952	*Bro-N	1	2	.333	4	3	0	0	0	15¹	19	1	6	7	14.7	5.28	69	.297	.357	0	.000	0	-4	-4	-0	-0.4
1956	Bro-N	2	3	.400	25	4	0	0	0	49¹	65	11	23	29	16.1	5.66	70	.325	.395	3	.300	1	-10	-9	1	-0.7
1957	Bro-N	0	0	—	3	0	0	0	0	7	7	0	1	3	10.3	0.00	—	.259	.286	1	.500	0	3	3	0	0.0
	Bal-A	8	3	.727	30	3	1	0	6	68	57	1	22	32	10.5	2.78	129	.232	.295	4	.200	1	8	6	-1	1.2
1958	Bal-A	2	1	.667	31	1	1	0	0	62	64	5	18	36	12.0	3.48	103	.276	.333	1	.071	-1	2	1	-0	-0.1
1961	Phi-N	1	1	.500	41	2	0	0	0	63¹	61	6	25	27	12.4	4.26	96	.260	.333	0	.000	-1	-2	-1	1	0.0
Total	5	14	10	.583	134	13	2	0	7	265	273	24	95	134	12.6	3.91	97	.272	.337	9	.161	1	-2	-3	2	0.0

● NORM LEHR
Lehr, Norman Carl Michael "King"   b: 5/28/01, Rochester, N.Y.   d: 7/17/68, Livonia, N.Y.   BR/TR, 6', 168 lbs.   Deb: 5/20/26

YEAR	TM/L	W	L	PCT	G	GS	CG	SH	SV	IP	H	HR	BB	SO	RAT	ERA	ERA+	OAV	OOB	BH	AVG	PB	PR	/A	PD	TPI
1926	Cle-A	0	0	—	4	0	0	0	0	14²	11	0	4	2	9.2	3.07	132	.216	.273	0	.000	-1	2	2	1	0.0

● HANK LEIBER
Leiber, Henry Edward   b: 1/17/11, Phoenix, Ariz.   d: 11/8/93, Tucson, Ariz.   BR/TR, 6'1.5", 205 lbs.   Deb: 4/16/33   ♦

YEAR	TM/L	W	L	PCT	G	GS	CG	SH	SV	IP	H	HR	BB	SO	RAT	ERA	ERA+	OAV	OOB	BH	AVG	PB	PR	/A	PD	TPI
1942	NY-N	0	1	.000	1	1	0	0	0	9	9	0	5	5	15.0	6.00	56	.290	.405	32	.218	0	-3	-3	0	-0.2

● CHARLIE LEIBRANDT
Leibrandt, Charles Louis   b: 10/4/56, Chicago, Ill.   BR/TL, 6'3", 200 lbs.   Deb: 9/17/79

YEAR	TM/L	W	L	PCT	G	GS	CG	SH	SV	IP	H	HR	BB	SO	RAT	ERA	ERA+	OAV	OOB	BH	AVG	PB	PR	/A	PD	TPI
1979	*Cin-N	0	0	—	3	0	0	0	0	4¹	2	0	2	1	8.3	0.00	—	.154	.267	0	—	0	2	2	0	0.0
1980	Cin-N	10	9	.526	36	27	5	2	0	173²	200	15	54	62	13.3	4.25	84	.294	.346	11	.196	1	-13	-13	-1	-1.1
1981	Cin-N	1	1	.500	7	4	1	1	0	30	28	0	15	9	12.9	3.60	99	.262	.352	0	.000	-0	-0	-0	-0	-0.1
1982	Cin-N	5	7	.417	36	11	0	0	2	107²	130	4	48	34	15.0	5.10	73	.308	.381	2	.080	-1	-18	-17	-0	-2.0
1984	*KC-A	11	7	.611	23	23	0	0	0	143²	158	11	38	53	12.5	3.63	111	.277	.326	0	—	0	6	6	-2	0.6
1985	*KC-A	17	9	.654	33	33	8	3	0	237²	223	17	68	108	11.1	2.69	155	.248	.302	0	—	0	38	39	4	4.5
1986	KC-A	14	11	.560	35	34	8	1	0	231¹	238	18	63	108	11.9	4.09	104	.268	.319	0	—	0	2	4	0	0.6
1987	KC-A	16	11	.593	35	35	8	3	0	240¹	235	23	74	151	11.6	3.41	134	.253	.308	0	—	0	28	31	4	3.5
1988	KC-A	13	12	.520	35	35	7	2	0	243	244	20	62	125	11.5	3.19	125	.264	.313	0	—	0	21	22	2	2.3
1989	KC-A	5	11	.313	33	27	3	1	0	161	196	13	54	73	14.1	5.14	75	.304	.360	0	—	0	-23	-23	-0	-2.1
1990	Atl-N	9	11	.450	24	24	5	2	0	162¹	164	9	35	76	11.3	3.16	128	.261	.304	9	.180	-1	16	16	1	2.1
1991	*Atl-N	15	13	.536	36	36	1	1	0	229²	212	18	56	128	10.7	3.49	111	.245	.294	3	.043	-4	5	10	4	1.2
1992	*Atl-N	15	7	.682	32	31	5	2	0	193	191	9	42	104	11.1	3.36	109	.258	.302	7	.121	-1	3	6	3	0.9
1993	Tex-A	9	10	.474	26	26	1	0	0	150¹	169	15	45	89	13.1	4.55	91	.284	.339	0	—	0	-7	-5	-3	-0.5
Total	14	140	119	.541	394	346	52	18	2	2308	2390	172	656	1121	12.0	3.71	108	.268	.321	32	.120	-5	60	77	25	10.4

● LEFTY LEIFIELD
Leifield, Albert Peter   b: 9/5/1883, Trenton, Ill.   d: 10/10/70, Alexandria, Va.   BL/TL, 6'1", 165 lbs.   Deb: 9/3/05   C

YEAR	TM/L	W	L	PCT	G	GS	CG	SH	SV	IP	H	HR	BB	SO	RAT	ERA	ERA+	OAV	OOB	BH	AVG	PB	PR	/A	PD	TPI
1905	Pit-N	5	2	.714	8	7	6	1	0	56	52	0	14	10	11.3	2.89	104	.248	.307	7	.350	3	1	1	1	0.5
1906	Pit-N	18	13	.581	37	31	24	8	1	255²	214	3	68	111	10.4	1.87	143	.231	.294	11	.125	-3	22	23	1	2.7
1907	Pit-N	20	16	.556	40	33	24	6	1	286	270	1	100	112	12.0	2.33	105	.256	.328	15	.147	0	5	3	4	0.8
1908	Pit-N	15	14	.517	34	26	18	5	2	218²	168	1	86	87	10.9	2.10	110	.212	.299	17	.227	4	6	5	-0	1.0
1909	*Pit-N	19	8	.704	32	26	13	3	0	201²	172	4	54	43	10.4	2.37	115	.229	.286	14	.192	1	5	8	-2	1.0
1910	Pit-N	15	13	.536	40	30	13	3	2	218¹	190	4	64	75	10.5	2.64	117	.235	.320	11	.183	0	10	13	0	1.1
1911	Pit-N	16	16	.500	42	37	26	2	1	318	301	7	61	111	11.3	2.63	130	.260	.318	24	.235	-8	27	28	-1	3.2
1912	Pit-N	1	2	.333	6	1	1	0	0	23²	29	1	9	8	15.6	4.18	78	.302	.380	1	.143	0	-2	-2	1	-0.1
	Chi-N	7	2	.778	13	9	4	1	0	70²	68	0	21	23	11.7	2.42	138	.258	.319	3	.115	-1	8	7	1	0.8
	Yr	8	4	.667	19	10	5	1	0	94¹	97	0	31	31	12.5	2.86	116	.268	.331	4	.121	-1	6	5	2	0.7

YEAR TM/L	W	L	PCT	G	GS	CG	SH	SV	IP	H	HR	BB	SO	RAT	ERA	ERA+	OAV	OOB	BH	AVG	PB	PR	/A	PD	TPI
1913 Chi-N	0	1	.000	6	1	0	0	0	21¹	28	0	5	4	13.9	5.48	58	.329	.367	0	.000	-1	-5	-5	1	-0.3
1918 StL-A	2	6	.250	15	6	3	1	0	67	61	1	19	22	11.0	2.55	107	.252	.312	1	.053	-2	2	1	1	0.1
1919 StL-A	6	4	.600	19	9	6	2	0	92	96	4	25	18	12.2	2.93	113	.270	.325	3	.100	-2	3	4	1	0.2
1920 StL-A	0	0	—	4	0	0	0	0	9	17	0	3	3	20.0	7.00	56	.405	.444	0	.000	-0	-3	-3	-0	-0.1
Total 12	124	97	.561	296	216	138	33	7	1838	1673	27	554	616	11.3	2.47	116	.248	.313	107	.175	6	77	81	10	11.5

● DAVE LEIPER
Leiper, David Paul b: 6/18/62, Whittier, Cal. BL/TL, 6'1", 160 lbs. Deb: 9/2/84

YEAR TM/L	W	L	PCT	G	GS	CG	SH	SV	IP	H	HR	BB	SO	RAT	ERA	ERA+	OAV	OOB	BH	AVG	PB	PR	/A	PD	TPI
1984 Oak-A	1	0	1.000	8	0	0	0	0	7	12	2	5	3	21.9	9.00	42	.353	.436	0	—	0	-4	-4	0	-0.5
1986 Oak-A	2	2	.500	33	0	0	0	1	31²	28	3	18	15	13.6	4.83	80	.252	.366	0	—	0	-2	-3	0	-0.3
1987 Oak-A	2	1	.667	45	0	0	0	1	52¹	49	6	18	33	11.7	3.78	109	.246	.312	0	—	0	4	2	1	0.3
SD-N	1	0	1.000	12	0	0	0	1	16	16	2	5	10	11.8	4.50	88	.267	.323	0	—	0	-1	-1	-0	-0.1
1988 SD-N	3	0	1.000	35	0	0	0	1	54	45	1	14	33	9.8	2.17	157	.231	.282	1	.500	0	8	7	0	0.5
1989 SD-N	0	1	.000	22	0	0	0	0	28²	40	2	20	7	19.5	5.02	70	.333	.437	0	.000	-0	-5	-5	1	-0.1
1994 Oak-A	0	0	—	26	0	0	0	0	18²	13	0	6	14	9.6	1.93	229	.206	.286	0	—	0	6	5	-0	0.4
1995 Oak-A	1	1	.500	24	0	0	0	0	22²	23	3	13	10	14.7	3.57	125	.258	.359	0	—	0	3	2	-0	0.2
Mon-N	0	2	.000	26	0	0	0	2	22	16	2	6	12	9.0	2.86	150	.200	.256	0	.000	-3	3	0	0	0.4
1996 Phi-N	2	0	1.000	26	0	0	0	0	21	31	4	7	10	16.3	6.43	68	.348	.396	0	—	0	-5	-5	-0	-0.4
Mon-N	0	1	.000	7	0	0	0	0	4	9	0	2	3	24.8	11.25	38	.474	.524	0	—	0	-3	-3	0	-0.6
Yr	2	1	.667	33	0	0	0	0	25	40	4	9	13	17.6	7.20	60	.370	.419	0	—	0	-8	-8	0	-1.0
Total 8	12	8	.600	264	0	0	0	7	278	282	25	114	150	13.0	3.98	99	.266	.342	1	.250	0	4	-1	2	-0.2

● JACK LEIPER
Leiper, John Henry Thomas b: 12/23/1867, Chester, Pa. d: 8/23/60, West Goshen, Pa. BL/TL, 5'11", Deb: 9/4/1891

YEAR TM/L	W	L	PCT	G	GS	CG	SH	SV	IP	H	HR	BB	SO	RAT	ERA	ERA+	OAV	OOB	BH	AVG	PB	PR	/A	PD	TPI
1891 Col-a	2	2	.500	6	5	4	0	0	45	41	3	39	19	16.8	5.40	64	.234	.385	3	.143	-2	-8	-10	-1	-0.8

● JOHN LEISTER
Leister, John William b: 1/3/61, San Antonio, Tex. BR/TR, 6'2", 200 lbs. Deb: 5/28/87

YEAR TM/L	W	L	PCT	G	GS	CG	SH	SV	IP	H	HR	BB	SO	RAT	ERA	ERA+	OAV	OOB	BH	AVG	PB	PR	/A	PD	TPI
1987 Bos-A	0	2	.000	8	6	0	0	0	30¹	49	9	12	16	18.1	9.20	49	.368	.421	0	—	0	-16	-16	-1	-0.9
1990 Bos-A	0	0	—	2	1	0	0	0	5²	7	0	4	3	17.5	4.76	86	.304	.407	0	—	0	-1	-0	-0	-0.2
Total 2	0	2	.000	10	7	0	0	0	36	56	9	16	19	18.0	8.50	53	.359	.419	0	—	0	-17	-16	-1	-1.1

● AL LEITER
Leiter, Alois Terry b: 10/23/65, Toms River, N.J. BL/TL, 6'3", 210 lbs. Deb: 9/15/87 F

YEAR TM/L	W	L	PCT	G	GS	CG	SH	SV	IP	H	HR	BB	SO	RAT	ERA	ERA+	OAV	OOB	BH	AVG	PB	PR	/A	PD	TPI
1987 NY-A	2	2	.500	4	4	0	0	0	22²	24	2	15	28	15.5	6.35	69	.273	.379	0	—	0	-5	-5	-0	-0.7
1988 NY-A	4	4	.500	14	14	0	0	0	57¹	49	7	33	60	13.7	3.92	100	.231	.348	0	—	0	0	0	1	0.1
1989 NY-A	1	2	.333	4	4	0	0	0	26²	23	1	21	22	15.5	6.08	64	.235	.380	0	—	0	-6	-7	-0	-0.6
Tor-A	0	0	—	1	1	0	0	0	6²	9	1	2	4	14.9	4.05	93	.310	.355	0	—	0	-0	-0	-0	-0.1
Yr	1	2	.333	5	5	0	0	0	33¹	32	2	23	26	14.9	5.67	68	.246	.359	0	—	0	-7	-7	-1	-0.6
1990 Tor-A	0	0	—	4	0	0	0	0	6¹	1	0	2	5	4.3	0.00	—	.050	.136	0	—	0	3	3	0	-0.1
1991 Tor-A	0	0	—	3	0	0	0	0	1²	3	0	5	1	43.2	27.00	16	.429	.667	0	—	0	-4	-4	0	-0.2
1992 Tor-A	0	0	—	1	0	0	0	0	1	1	0	2	0	27.0	9.00	45	.200	.429	0	—	0	-1	-1	0	-0.2
1993 *Tor-A	9	6	.600	34	12	1	1	2	105	93	8	56	66	13.1	4.11	105	.240	.342	0	—	0	2	2	-1	0.2
1994 Tor-A	6	7	.462	20	20	1	0	0	111²	125	6	65	100	15.5	5.08	95	.285	.380	0	—	0	-3	-3	-0	-0.3
1995 Tor-A	11	11	.500	28	28	2	1	0	183	162	15	108	153	13.6	3.64	129	.238	.347	0	—	0	22	22	-2	2.1
1996 Fla-N★	16	12	.571	33	33	2	1	0	215¹	153	14	119	200	11.8	2.93	138	**.202**	.319	7	.100	-2	31	27	-1	2.8
Total 10	49	44	.527	146	116	6	3	2	737¹	643	54	428	639	13.4	3.94	110	.236	.346	7	.100	-2	38	34	-4	3.1

● MARK LEITER
Leiter, Mark Edward b: 4/13/63, Joliet, Ill. BR/TR, 6'3", 200 lbs. Deb: 7/24/90 F

YEAR TM/L	W	L	PCT	G	GS	CG	SH	SV	IP	H	HR	BB	SO	RAT	ERA	ERA+	OAV	OOB	BH	AVG	PB	PR	/A	PD	TPI
1990 NY-A	1	1	.500	8	3	0	0	0	26¹	33	5	9	21	15.0	6.84	58	.314	.379	0	—	0	-9	-8	1	-0.5
1991 Det-A	9	7	.563	38	15	1	0	1	134²	125	16	50	103	12.1	4.21	99	.245	.319	0	—	0	-2	-1	-1	-0.2
1992 Det-A	8	5	.615	35	14	1	0	0	112	116	9	43	75	13.0	4.18	95	.277	.348	0	—	0	-3	-3	-0	-0.3
1993 Det-A	6	6	.500	27	13	1	0	0	106²	111	17	44	70	13.3	4.73	91	.267	.341	0	—	0	-5	-5	-1	-0.6
1994 Cal-A	4	7	.364	40	7	0	0	0	95¹	99	13	35	71	13.5	4.72	104	.265	.343	0	—	0	1	2	1	0.2
1995 SF-N	10	12	.455	30	29	7	1	0	195²	185	19	55	129	11.8	3.82	107	.254	.321	6	.098	-2	8	6	-3	0.1
1996 SF-N	4	10	.286	23	22	1	0	0	135¹	151	25	50	118	14.0	5.19	79	.283	.355	6	.143	-0	-15	-17	-2	-1.7
Mon-N	4	2	.667	12	12	1	0	0	69²	68	12	19	46	12.1	4.39	98	.254	.320	2	.080	-1	-1	-1	-1	-0.1
Yr	8	12	.400	35	34	2	0	0	205	219	37	69	164	13.0	4.92	85	.269	.332	8	.119	-1	-16	-17	-1	-1.8
Total 7	46	50	.479	213	115	12	1	3	875²	888	116	305	633	12.8	4.48	94	.265	.336	14	.109	-4	-25	-27	-3	-3.1

● BILL LEITH
Leith, William "Shady Bill" b: 5/31/1873, Matteawan, N.Y. d: 7/16/40, Beacon, N.Y. TL, Deb: 9/25/1899

YEAR TM/L	W	L	PCT	G	GS	CG	SH	SV	IP	H	HR	BB	SO	RAT	ERA	ERA+	OAV	OOB	BH	AVG	PB	PR	/A	PD	TPI
1899 Was-N	0	0	—	1	0	0	0	0	2	4	0	4	1	31.5	18.00	22	.400	.538	0	.000	-0	-3	-3	-0	0.0

● DOC LEITNER
Leitner, George Aloysius b: 9/14/1865, Piermont, N.Y. d: 5/18/37, New York, N.Y. BR/TR, 5'11.5", 185 lbs. Deb: 8/10/1887

YEAR TM/L	W	L	PCT	G	GS	CG	SH	SV	IP	H	HR	BB	SO	RAT	ERA	ERA+	OAV	OOB	BH	AVG	PB	PR	/A	PD	TPI
1887 Ind-N	2	6	.250	8	8	8	0	0	65	69	6	41	27	15.2	5.68	73	.259	.358	4	.148	-3	-12	-11	-2	-1.3

● DUMMY LEITNER
Leitner, George Michael b: 6/19/1871, Parkton, Md. d: 2/20/60, Baltimore, Md. BL/TR, 5'7", 120 lbs. Deb: 6/29/01

YEAR TM/L	W	L	PCT	G	GS	CG	SH	SV	IP	H	HR	BB	SO	RAT	ERA	ERA+	OAV	OOB	BH	AVG	PB	PR	/A	PD	TPI
1901 Phi-A	0	0	—	1	0	0	0	0	2	1	0	1	0	9.0	0.00	—	.143	.250	0	—	-0	1	1	-0	0.0
NY-N	0	2	.000	2	2	2	0	0	18	27	0	4	3	16.0	4.50	73	.342	.381	1	.143	-0	-2	-2	-0	-0.3
1902 Cle-A	0	0	—	1	1	0	0	0	8	11	0	1	0	13.5	4.50	77	.324	.343	1	.250	0	-1	-1	0	0.0
Chi-A	0	0	—	1	0	0	0	0	4	9	0	2	1	29.3	13.50	25	.450	.542	0	—	0	-4	-4	0	0.0
Yr	0	0	—	2	1	0	0	0	12	20	0	3	1	18.8	7.50	46	.370	.424	1	.143	-0	-5	-5	1	0.0
Total 2	0	2	.000	5	3	2	0	0	32	48	0	8	4	16.6	5.34	63	.343	.391	2	.133	-1	-7	-7	0	-0.3

● BILL LELIVELT
Lelivelt, William John b: 10/21/1884, Chicago, Ill. d: 2/14/68, Chicago, Ill. BR/TR, 6', 195 lbs. Deb: 7/19/09 F

YEAR TM/L	W	L	PCT	G	GS	CG	SH	SV	IP	H	HR	BB	SO	RAT	ERA	ERA+	OAV	OOB	BH	AVG	PB	PR	/A	PD	TPI
1909 Det-A	0	1	.000	4	2	1	0	1	20	27	0	2	4	13.0	4.50	56	.325	.341	2	.333	1	-4	-4	-0	-0.2
1910 Det-A	0	1	.000	1	1	1	0	0	9	6	0	3	2	9.0	1.00	263	.207	.281	1	.500	1	2	2	0	0.3
Total 2	0	2	.000	5	3	2	0	1	29	33	0	5	6	11.8	3.41	75	.295	.325	3	.375	2	-3	-3	0	0.1

● DAVE LEMANCZYK
Lemanczyk, David Lawrence b: 8/17/50, Syracuse, N.Y. BR/TR, 6'4", 235 lbs. Deb: 4/15/73

YEAR TM/L	W	L	PCT	G	GS	CG	SH	SV	IP	H	HR	BB	SO	RAT	ERA	ERA+	OAV	OOB	BH	AVG	PB	PR	/A	PD	TPI
1973 Det-A	0	0	—	1	0	0	0	0	2¹	4	0	0	0	15.4	11.57	35	.364	.364	0	—	0	-2	-2	-0	-0.1
1974 Det-A	2	1	.667	22	3	0	0	0	78²	79	12	44	52	14.3	4.00	95	.261	.358	0	—	0	-3	-2	1	-0.1
1975 Det-A	2	7	.222	26	6	4	0	0	109	120	8	46	67	14.0	4.46	90	.281	.355	0	—	0	-8	-5	0	-0.7
1976 Det-A	4	6	.400	20	10	1	0	0	81¹	86	7	34	51	13.3	5.09	73	.271	.342	0	—	0	-14	-12	1	-1.6
1977 Tor-A	13	16	.448	34	34	11	0	0	252	278	20	87	105	13.2	4.25	99	.282	.343	0	—	0	-5	-1	0	-0.2
1978 Tor-A	4	14	.222	29	20	3	0	0	136²	170	16	65	62	15.7	6.26	63	.313	.389	0	—	0	-38	-35	-1	-4.2
1979 Tor-A☆	8	10	.444	22	20	11	3	0	143	137	12	45	63	11.8	3.71	117	.258	.324	0	—	0	8	10	0	1.0
1980 Tor-A	1	5	.286	10	8	0	0	0	43¹	54	7	15	10	15.0	5.40	80	.322	.375	0	—	0	-7	-5	1	-0.8
Cal-A	2	4	.333	21	2	0	0	0	66²	81	7	27	19	14.9	4.32	91	.301	.369	0	—	0	-2	-3	-2	-0.3
Yr	4	9	.308	31	10	0	0	0	110	135	12	42	29	14.9	4.75	86	.308	.370	0	—	0	-9	-8	-1	-1.1
Total 8	37	63	.370	185	103	30	3	0	913	1012	87	363	429	13.8	4.62	88	.284	.354	0	—	0	-72	-56	0	-7.0

● DENNY LEMASTER
Lemaster, Denver Clayton b: 2/25/39, Corona, Cal. BR/TR, 6'1", 185 lbs. Deb: 7/15/62

YEAR TM/L	W	L	PCT	G	GS	CG	SH	SV	IP	H	HR	BB	SO	RAT	ERA	ERA+	OAV	OOB	BH	AVG	PB	PR	/A	PD	TPI
1962 Mil-N	3	4	.429	17	12	4	0	0	86²	75	11	32	69	11.4	3.01	126	.233	.308	4	.121	-1	9	8	-2	0.3
1963 Mil-N	11	14	.440	46	31	10	1	1	237	199	30	85	190	10.8	3.04	106	.227	.296	14	.189	3	7	5	-3	0.5
1964 Mil-N	17	11	.607	39	35	9	3	1	221	216	27	75	185	12.0	4.15	85	.252	.315	9	.134	0	-15	-15	-0	-1.8
1965 Mil-N	7	13	.350	32	23	4	1	0	146¹	140	12	58	111	12.4	4.43	80	.251	.325	4	.089	-1	-14	-15	0	-2.0
1966 Atl-N	11	8	.579	27	27	10	3	0	171	170	25	41	139	11.2	3.74	97	.258	.303	7	.119	-1	-2	-2	-2	-0.5
1967 Atl-N†	9	9	.500	31	31	8	2	0	215¹	184	20	72	148	10.8	3.34	99	.229	.295	7	.104	-2	1	-1	-0	-0.3
1968 Hou-N	10	15	.400	33	32	7	2	0	224	231	11	72	146	12.3	2.81	105	.262	.321	2	.031	-3	4	4	-3	-0.3
1969 Hou-N	13	17	.433	38	37	11	1	1	244²	232	20	72	173	11.2	3.16	112	.246	.300	15	.170	3	12	10	-1	1.4
1970 Hou-N	7	12	.368	39	21	3	0	3	162	169	22	65	120	13.0	4.56	85	.268	.338	8	.167	-0	-9	-12	-2	-1.2
1971 Hou-N	2	0	.000	42	0	0	0	2	60	59	4	20	22	12.3	3.45	98	.262	.331	1	.167	-0	-1	-1	-0	0.0
1972 Mon-N	2	0	1.000	13	0	0	0	0	19²	28	2	6	13	16.0	7.78	46	.329	.380	1	.333	1	-9	-9	-1	-0.9
Total 11	90	105	.462	357	249	66	14	8	1787²	1703	184	600	1305	11.7	3.58	96	.249	.312	72	.130	1	-18	-28	-13	-4.8

YEAR TM/L	W	L	PCT	G	GS	CG	SH	SV	IP	H	HR	BB	SO	RAT	ERA	ERA+	OAV	OOB	BH	AVG	PB	PR	/A	PD	TPI

● **DICK LeMAY** LeMay, Richard Paul b: 8/28/38, Cincinnati, Ohio BL/TL, 6'3", 190 lbs. Deb: 6/13/61

YEAR TM/L	W	L	PCT	G	GS	CG	SH	SV	IP	H	HR	BB	SO	RAT	ERA	ERA+	OAV	OOB	BH	AVG	PB	PR	/A	PD	TPI
1961 SF-N	3	6	.333	27	5	1	0	3	83¹	65	11	36	54	11.3	3.56	107	.217	.309	2	.077	-2	4	2	-0	0.1
1962 SF-N	0	1	.000	9	0	0	0	1	9¹	9	1	5	9	17.4	7.71	49	.265	.419	0	—	-0	-4	-4	-0	-0.4
1963 Chi-N	0	1	.000	9	1	0	0	0	15¹	26	1	4	10	17.6	5.28	66	.394	.429	0	.000	-0	-3	-3	-0	-0.2
Total 3	3	8	.273	45	6	1	0	4	108	100	14	49	69	12.8	4.17	91	.250	.338	2	.071	-1	-3	-5	-0	-0.5

● **BOB LEMON** Lemon, Robert Granville b: 9/22/20, San Bernardino, Cal. BL/TR, 6', 185 lbs. Deb: 9/9/41 MCH♦

YEAR TM/L	W	L	PCT	G	GS	CG	SH	SV	IP	H	HR	BB	SO	RAT	ERA	ERA+	OAV	OOB	BH	AVG	PB	PR	/A	PD	TPI
1946 Cle-A	4	5	.444	32	5	1	0	1	94	77	4	68	39	13.9	2.49	133	.229	.359	16	.180	2	11	9	4	1.3
1947 Cle-A	11	5	.688	37	15	6	1	3	167¹	150	7	97	65	13.5	3.44	101	.242	.348	18	.321	9	5	1	4	1.6
1948 *Cle-A☆	20	14	.588	43	37	20	10	2	293²	231	12	129	147	11.1	2.82	144	.216	.302	34	.286	14	48	40	8	6.8
1949 Cle-A☆	22	10	.688	37	33	22	2	1	279²	211	19	137	138	11.4	2.99	133	.211	.309	29	.269	16	37	31	6	5.7
1950 Cle-A★	23	11	.676	44	37	22	3	3	288	281	28	146	170	13.4	3.84	113	.257	.345	37	.272	17	23	16	5	3.7
1951 Cle-A★	17	14	.548	42	34	17	1	2	263¹	244	19	124	132	12.6	3.52	108	.244	.328	21	.206	5	18	8	4	1.7
1952 Cle-A★	22	11	.667	42	36	28	5	4	309²	236	15	105	131	10.1	2.50	134	.208	.279	28	.226	7	40	29	7	4.6
1953 Cle-A☆	21	15	.583	41	36	23	5	1	286²	283	16	110	98	12.7	3.36	112	.262	.336	26	.232	8	20	13	8	3.2
1954 *Cle-A★	23	7	.767	36	33	21	2	0	258¹	228	12	92	110	11.3	2.72	135	.237	.307	21	.214	6	29	27	4	4.1
1955 Cle-A	18	10	.643	35	31	5	0	2	211¹	218	17	74	100	12.8	3.88	103	.266	.330	19	.244	6	2	3	2	1.1
1956 Cle-A	20	14	.588	39	35	21	2	3	255¹	230	23	89	94	11.5	3.03	139	.239	.307	18	.194	5	32	33	4	5.2
1957 Cle-A	6	11	.353	21	17	2	0	0	117¹	129	14	64	45	15.3	4.60	81	.287	.385	3	.065	-3	-11	-12	3	-1.5
1958 Cle-A	0	1	.000	11	1	0	0	0	25¹	41	3	16	8	20.6	5.33	68	.376	.460	0	.231	-0	-4	-5	1	-0.1
Total 13	207	128	.618	460	350	188	31	22	2850	2559	181	1251	1277	12.2	3.23	119	.241	.324	274	.232	90	251	193	60	37.4

● **DAVE LEMONDS** Lemonds, David Lee b: 7/5/48, Charlotte, N.C. BL/TL, 6'1.5", 180 lbs. Deb: 6/30/69

YEAR TM/L	W	L	PCT	G	GS	CG	SH	SV	IP	H	HR	BB	SO	RAT	ERA	ERA+	OAV	OOB	BH	AVG	PB	PR	/A	PD	TPI
1969 Chi-N	0	1	.000	2	1	0	0	0	4²	5	0	5	0	19.3	3.86	104	.313	.476	0	.000	-0	-0	0	-0	0.0
1972 Chi-A	4	7	.364	31	18	0	0	0	94²	87	6	38	69	12.0	2.95	106	.247	.322	3	.120	-1	1	2	-0	0.1
Total 2	4	8	.333	33	19	0	0	0	99¹	92	6	43	69	12.3	2.99	106	.250	.330	3	.115	-1	1	2	-0	0.1

● **MARK LEMONGELLO** Lemongello, Mark b: 7/21/55, Jersey City, N.J. BR/TR, 6'1", 180 lbs. Deb: 9/14/76

YEAR TM/L	W	L	PCT	G	GS	CG	SH	SV	IP	H	HR	BB	SO	RAT	ERA	ERA+	OAV	OOB	BH	AVG	PB	PR	/A	PD	TPI
1976 Hou-N	3	1	.750	4	4	1	0	0	29	26	2	7	9	10.2	2.79	114	.236	.282	0	.000	-1	2	1	1	0.2
1977 Hou-N	9	14	.391	34	30	5	0	0	214²	237	20	52	83	12.2	3.48	102	.281	.325	6	.087	-4	10	2	-1	-0.2
1978 Hou-N	9	14	.391	33	30	9	1	0	210¹	204	20	66	77	11.9	3.94	84	.259	.323	11	.172	-1	-8	-15	0	-1.4
1979 Tor-A	1	9	.100	18	10	2	0	0	83	97	14	34	40	14.5	6.29	69	.299	.371	0	—	0	-19	-18	1	-1.8
Total 4	22	38	.367	89	74	17	1	1	537	564	56	159	209	12.4	4.06	88	.273	.329	17	.121	-3	-15	-30	1	-3.2

● **ED LENNON** Lennon, Edward Francis b: 8/17/1897, Philadelphia, Pa. d: 9/13/47, Philadelphia, Pa. BR/TR, 5'11", 170 lbs. Deb: 6/30/28

YEAR TM/L	W	L	PCT	G	GS	CG	SH	SV	IP	H	HR	BB	SO	RAT	ERA	ERA+	OAV	OOB	BH	AVG	PB	PR	/A	PD	TPI
1928 Phi-N	0	0	—	2	0	0	0	0	12¹	19	0	10	6	21.2	8.76	49	.373	.475	0	.000	-1	-7	-6	-0	-0.1

● **DANILO LEON** Leon, Danilo Enrique (Lineco) b: 4/3/67, LaConcepcion, Venez. BR/TR, 6'1", 170 lbs. Deb: 6/6/92

YEAR TM/L	W	L	PCT	G	GS	CG	SH	SV	IP	H	HR	BB	SO	RAT	ERA	ERA+	OAV	OOB	BH	AVG	PB	PR	/A	PD	TPI
1992 Tex-A	1	1	.500	15	0	0	0	0	18¹	18	5	10	15	15.2	5.89	64	.254	.369	0	—	0	-4	-4	-0	-0.4

● **IZZY LEON** Leon, Isidoro (Becerra) b: 1/4/11, Cruces, Las Villas, Cuba BR/TR, 5'10", 160 lbs. Deb: 6/21/45

YEAR TM/L	W	L	PCT	G	GS	CG	SH	SV	IP	H	HR	BB	SO	RAT	ERA	ERA+	OAV	OOB	BH	AVG	PB	PR	/A	PD	TPI
1945 Phi-N	0	4	.000	14	4	0	0	0	38²	49	3	19	11	15.8	5.35	72	.312	.386	1	.111	-0	-7	-7	0	-0.6

● **MAX LEON** Leon, Maximino (Molino) b: 2/4/50, Pozo Hondo, Aculo, Mexico BR/TR, 6', 170 lbs. Deb: 7/18/73

YEAR TM/L	W	L	PCT	G	GS	CG	SH	SV	IP	H	HR	BB	SO	RAT	ERA	ERA+	OAV	OOB	BH	AVG	PB	PR	/A	PD	TPI
1973 Atl-N	2	2	.500	12	1	1	0	0	27	30	4	9	18	14.0	5.33	74	.278	.350	2	.286	0	-5	-4	-0	-0.6
1974 Atl-N	4	7	.364	34	2	1	1	3	75	68	5	14	38	10.0	2.64	143	.242	.280	2	.133	-1	8	9	1	1.4
1975 Atl-N	2	1	.667	50	1	0	0	6	85	90	5	33	53	13.8	4.13	91	.274	.352	3	.333	-1	-5	-3	1	0.0
1976 Atl-N	2	4	.333	30	0	0	0	3	36	32	2	15	16	12.3	2.75	138	.234	.318	0	.000	-0	3	4	-1	0.7
1977 Atl-N	4	4	.500	31	9	0	0	1	81²	89	9	25	44	13.6	3.97	112	.280	.349	6	.316	1	-1	4	0	0.5
1978 Atl-N	0	0	—	5	0	0	0	0	5²	6	1	4	1	17.5	6.35	64	.273	.407	0	—	-0	-2	-1	-0	0.0
Total 6	14	18	.438	162	13	2	1	13	310¹	315	28	100	170	12.7	3.71	107	.264	.332	13	.250	-1	-1	9	1	2.0

● **DENNIS LEONARD** Leonard, Dennis Patrick b: 5/8/51, Brooklyn, N.Y. BR/TR, 6'1", 190 lbs. Deb: 9/4/74

YEAR TM/L	W	L	PCT	G	GS	CG	SH	SV	IP	H	HR	BB	SO	RAT	ERA	ERA+	OAV	OOB	BH	AVG	PB	PR	/A	PD	TPI
1974 KC-A	0	4	.000	5	4	0	0	0	22	28	0	12	8	17.6	5.32	72	.329	.430	0	—	0	-4	-4	1	-0.5
1975 KC-A	15	7	.682	32	30	8	0	0	212¹	212	18	90	146	13.2	3.77	102	.263	.344	0	—	0	0	0	0	0.2
1976 *KC-A	17	10	.630	35	34	16	2	0	259	247	16	70	150	11.4	3.51	100	.255	.313	0	—	0	-0	-4	0	-0.5
1977 *KC-A	20	12	.625	38	37	21	5	1	292²	246	18	79	244	10.2	3.04	133	.227	.285	0	—	0	33	32	-2	3.1
1978 *KC-A	21	17	.553	40	40	20	4	0	294²	283	27	78	183	11.3	3.33	115	.254	.308	0	—	0	14	16	0	1.9
1979 KC-A	14	12	.538	32	32	12	5	0	236	226	31	56	126	11.0	4.08	104	.253	.299	0	—	0	8	8	0	0.3
1980 *KC-A	20	11	.645	38	38	9	3	0	280¹	271	30	80	155	11.3	3.79	107	.253	.306	0	—	0	8	8	0	0.8
1981 *KC-A	13	11	.542	26	26	9	2	0	201²	202	15	41	107	11.0	2.99	121	.258	.298	0	—	0	15	14	0	1.7
1982 KC-A	10	6	.625	21	21	2	0	0	130²	145	20	46	58	13.3	5.10	80	.279	.340	0	—	0	-15	-15	-1	-1.5
1983 KC-A	6	3	.667	10	10	1	0	0	63	69	3	19	31	12.6	3.71	110	.277	.328	0	—	0	2	3	0	0.3
1985 KC-A	0	0	—	2	0	0	0	0	2	1	0	1	4	4.5	0.00	—	.143	.143	0	—	0	0	0	-0	0.0
1986 KC-A	8	13	.381	33	30	5	0	0	192²	207	22	51	114	12.2	4.44	96	.275	.324	0	—	0	-6	-4	0	-0.4
Total 12	144	106	.576	312	302	103	23	1	2187	2137	202	622	1323	11.6	3.70	106	.257	.312	0	—	0	52	58	-3	5.4

● **ELMER LEONARD** Leonard, Elmer Ellsworth "Tiny" b: 11/12/1888, Napa, Cal. d: 5/27/81, Napa, Cal. BR/TR, 6'3.5", 210 lbs. Deb: 6/22/11

YEAR TM/L	W	L	PCT	G	GS	CG	SH	SV	IP	H	HR	BB	SO	RAT	ERA	ERA+	OAV	OOB	BH	AVG	PB	PR	/A	PD	TPI
1911 Phi-A	2	2	.500	5	1	0	0	0	19	26	0	10	10	18.0	2.84	111	.329	.418	2	.286	1	1	1	-1	0.1

● **DUTCH LEONARD** Leonard, Emil John b: 3/25/09, Auburn, Ill. d: 4/17/83, Springfield, Ill. BR/TR, 6', 175 lbs. Deb: 8/31/33 C

YEAR TM/L	W	L	PCT	G	GS	CG	SH	SV	IP	H	HR	BB	SO	RAT	ERA	ERA+	OAV	OOB	BH	AVG	PB	PR	/A	PD	TPI
1933 Bro-N	2	3	.400	10	3	2	0	0	40	42	0	11	7	12.9	2.93	110	.261	.304	2	.000	-1	2	1	0	0.0
1934 Bro-N	14	11	.560	44	20	11	2	5	183²	210	12	33	58	12.1	3.28	119	.286	.320	12	.179	-1	16	13	1	1.7
1935 Bro-N	2	9	.182	43	11	4	0	8	137²	152	11	29	41	11.9	3.92	101	.280	.318	1	.026	-4	1	1	-1	-0.5
1936 Bro-N	0	0	—	16	0	0	0	1	32	34	2	5	11	13.6	3.66	113	.262	.289	2	.400	1	-0	0	0	0.1
1938 Was-A	12	15	.444	33	31	15	3	0	223¹	221	11	53	68	11.3	3.43	132	.256	.305	19	.232	1	34	27	0	3.1
1939 Was-A	20	8	.714	34	34	21	2	0	269¹	273	16	59	88	11.3	3.54	123	.262	.305	21	.221	1	32	24	2	2.4
1940 Was-A☆	14	19	.424	35	35	23	2	0	289	328	19	78	124	12.7	3.49	120	.286	.332	16	.158	-5	29	22	5	2.2
1941 Was-A	18	13	.581	34	33	19	6	0	256	271	6	54	91	11.5	3.45	117	.270	.309	9	.102	-5	20	17	-1	1.2
1942 Was-A	2	2	.500	6	5	1	1	0	35	28	1	5	15	8.5	4.11	89	.214	.243	1	.100	-1	-2	-2	-0	-0.2
1943 Was-A★	11	13	.458	31	30	15	2	0	219²	218	9	46	51	11.0	3.28	98	.257	.298	7	.104	-4	9	7	2	-0.5
1944 Was-A☆	14	14	.500	32	31	17	3	0	229¹	222	8	37	62	10.3	3.06	106	.252	.284	18	.228	1	9	5	1	0.9
1945 Was-A†	17	7	.708	31	29	12	4	0	216	208	5	35	96	10.2	2.13	146	.248	.279	18	.231	1	30	23	0	2.8
1946 Was-A	10	10	.500	26	23	7	2	0	161²	182	9	36	62	12.4	3.56	94	.281	.323	9	.170	-1	-1	-4	-3	-0.2
1947 Phi-N	17	12	.586	32	29	19	3	0	235	224	14	57	103	11.0	2.68	149	.258	.306	14	.175	-1	36	35	4	4.3
1948 Phi-N	12	17	.414	34	31	16	1	0	225²	226	16	54	102	11.3	2.51	157	.256	.312	12	.145	-3	36	36	4	4.6
1949 Chi-N	7	16	.304	33	28	10	1	0	180	198	17	43	83	12.4	4.15	97	.272	.319	12	.203	-0	-3	-3	-0	-0.1
1950 Chi-N	5	1	.833	35	1	0	0	3	74	70	7	27	28	12.0	3.77	111	.248	.318	1	.063	-2	3	4	0	0.2
1951 Chi-N☆	10	6	.625	41	1	0	0	7	81²	69	3	28	30	10.9	2.64	155	.234	.305	0	.000	-3	12	13	2	2.4
1952 Chi-N	2	2	.500	45	0	0	0	11	66²	56	3	24	37	11.2	2.16	178	.235	.313	2	.200	-2	12	13	2	1.4
1953 Chi-N	2	3	.400	45	0	0	0	8	62²	72	9	24	27	13.9	4.60	97	.289	.354	3	.300	-1	-2	-1	0	0.0
Total 20	191	181	.513	640	375	192	30	44	3218¹	3304	158	737	1170	11.5	3.25	119	.265	.309	177	.168	-21	267	224	24	25.8

● **DUTCH LEONARD** Leonard, Hubert Benjamin b: 4/16/1892, Birmingham, Ohio d: 7/11/52, Fresno, Cal. BL/TL, 5'10.5", 185 lbs. Deb: 4/12/13

YEAR TM/L	W	L	PCT	G	GS	CG	SH	SV	IP	H	HR	BB	SO	RAT	ERA	ERA+	OAV	OOB	BH	AVG	PB	PR	/A	PD	TPI
1913 Bos-A	14	16	.467	42	28	14	3	1	259¹	245	0	94	144	11.9	2.39	123	.253	.321	15	.181	-1	16	16	-2	1.7
1914 Bos-A	19	5	.792	36	25	17	7	3	224²	139	3	60	176	8.3	0.96	280	.180	.246	10	.147	-1	44	43	-3	4.6
1915 *Bos-A	15	7	.682	32	21	10	2	0	183¹	130	3	67	116	10.4	2.36	118	.208	.299	14	.264	5	12	9	-4	1.1
1916 *Bos-A	18	12	.600	48	34	17	6	6	274	244	6	66	144	10.4	2.36	117	.247	.300	12	.200	-1	17	13	-5	0.3
1917 Bos-A	16	17	.485	37	36	26	4	1	294¹	257	4	72	144	10.2	2.17	119	.236	.286	16	.087	-6	16	13	-6	0.3
1918 Bos-A	8	6	.571	16	16	12	1	0	125²	119	2	53	47	12.5	2.72	99	.254	.332	8	.186	-1	-1	-2	0	-0.2
1919 Det-A	14	13	.519	29	28	18	4	0	217¹	212	7	65	102	11.8	2.77	115	.254	.313	11	.155	-3	11	10	-4	0.5

YEAR	TM/L	W	L	PCT	G	GS	CG	SH	SV	IP	H	HR	BB	SO	RAT	ERA	ERA+	OAV	OOB	BH	AVG	PB	PR	/A	PD	TPI
1920	Det-A	10	17	.370	28	27	10	3	0	191¹	192	8	63	76	12.4	4.33	86	.271	.338	12	.211	2	-11	-13	-1	-1.5
1921	Det-A	11	13	.458	36	32	16	1	0	245	273	15	63	120	12.7	3.75	114	.286	.336	14	.171	-4	15	14	-3	0.6
1924	Det-A	3	2	.600	9	7	3	0	1	51¹	68	1	18	26	15.3	4.56	90	.327	.383	4	.211	-0	-2	-3	-0	-0.3
1925	Det-A	11	4	.733	18	18	9	0	0	125²	143	7	43	65	13.4	4.51	95	.289	.347	10	.200	-1	-2	-3	-0	-0.6
Total 11		139	112	.554	331	272	152	33	13	2192	2022	54	664	1160	11.3	2.76	115	.249	.311	124	.173	-5	114	98	-32	7.1

● DAVE LEONHARD
Leonhard, David Paul b: 1/22/41, Arlington, Va. BR/TR, 5'11", 165 lbs. Deb: 9/21/67

YEAR	TM/L	W	L	PCT	G	GS	CG	SH	SV	IP	H	HR	BB	SO	RAT	ERA	ERA+	OAV	OOB	BH	AVG	PB	PR	/A	PD	TPI
1967	Bal-A	0	0	—	3	2	0	1	0	14¹	11	1	6	9	11.3	3.14	100	.200	.290	0	.000	-1	0	0	0	0.0
1968	Bal-A	7	7	.500	28	18	5	2	1	126¹	95	10	57	61	11.0	3.13	93	.216	.309	4	.129	-1	-2	-3	1	-0.3
1969	*Bal-A	7	4	.636	37	3	1	1	1	94	78	8	38	37	11.1	2.49	143	.228	.305	2	.095	-0	12	11	-1	1.2
1970	Bal-A	0	0	—	23	0	0	0	0	28¹	32	5	18	14	15.9	5.08	72	.294	.394	0	.000	-0	-4	-5	1	0.1
1971	*Bal-A	2	3	.400	12	6	1	1	1	54	51	5	19	18	11.8	2.83	118	.252	.320	5	.278	1	4	3	1	0.5
1972	Bal-A	0	0	—	14	0	0	0	0	20	20	3	12	7	14.4	4.50	68	.260	.360	1	1.000	1	-3	-3	0	0.1
Total 6		16	14	.533	117	29	7	4	5	337	287	32	150	146	11.8	3.15	103	.234	.320	12	.156	1	6	4	3	1.6

● RUDY LEOPOLD
Leopold, Rudolph Matas b: 7/27/05, Grand Cane, La. d: 9/3/65, Baton Rouge, La. BL/TL, 6', 160 lbs. Deb: 7/4/28

YEAR	TM/L	W	L	PCT	G	GS	CG	SH	SV	IP	H	HR	BB	SO	RAT	ERA	ERA+	OAV	OOB	BH	AVG	PB	PR	/A	PD	TPI
1928	Chi-A	0	0	—	2	0	0	0	0	2¹	3	0	0	1	11.6	3.86	105	.273	.273	0	.000	-0	0	0	-0	0.0

● RANDY LERCH
Lerch, Randy Louis b: 10/9/54, Sacramento, Cal. BL/TL, 6'5", 190 lbs. Deb: 9/14/75

YEAR	TM/L	W	L	PCT	G	GS	CG	SH	SV	IP	H	HR	BB	SO	RAT	ERA	ERA+	OAV	OOB	BH	AVG	PB	PR	/A	PD	TPI
1975	Phi-N	0	0	—	3	0	0	0	0	7	6	1	1	8	9.0	6.43	58	.231	.259	0	—	0	-2	-2	-0	0.0
1976	Phi-N	0	0	—	1	0	0	0	1	3	3	0	0	0	9.0	3.00	118	.250	.250	1	1.000	0	1	0	-0	0.1
1977	Phi-N	10	6	.625	32	28	3	0	0	168²	207	20	75	81	15.1	5.07	79	.312	.383	9	.167	-0	-22	-20	2	-1.5
1978	*Phi-N	11	8	.579	33	28	5	0	0	184	183	15	70	96	12.4	3.96	90	.263	.332	15	.250	7	-8	-8	1	0.0
1979	Phi-N	10	13	.435	37	35	6	1	0	214	228	20	60	92	12.2	3.74	102	.281	.333	11	.153	1	-0	-2	2	0.4
1980	Phi-N	4	14	.222	30	22	2	0	0	150	178	15	55	57	14.0	5.16	73	.302	.362	12	.267	3	-26	-23	1	-2.1
1981	*Mil-A	7	9	.438	23	18	1	0	0	110²	134	8	43	53	14.4	4.31	79	.303	.365	0	—	0	-8	-11	0	-1.2
1982	Mil-A	8	7	.533	21	20	1	1	0	108²	123	12	51	33	14.7	4.97	76	.286	.366	0	—	0	-11	-14	-1	-1.5
	Mon-N	2	0	1.000	6	4	0	0	0	23²	26	0	8	4	12.9	3.42	106	.289	.347	2	.250	0	0	1	0	0.1
1983	Mon-N	1	3	.250	19	5	0	0	0	38²	45	6	18	24	14.9	6.75	53	.292	.370	2	.222	1	-13	-14	-0	-1.2
	SF-N	1	0	1.000	7	0	0	0	0	10²	9	1	8	6	14.3	3.38	105	.231	.362	0	—	0	0	0	0	0.0
	Yr	2	3	.400	26	5	0	0	0	49¹	54	7	26	30	14.6	6.02	59	.277	.362	2	.222	1	-13	-13	-0	-1.2
1984	SF-N	5	3	.625	37	4	0	0	2	72¹	80	3	36	48	14.6	4.23	83	.287	.370	2	.133	1	-5	-6	1	-0.5
1986	Phi-N	1	1	.500	4	0	0	0	0	6¹	8	1	5	7	19.1	7.88	49	.286	.405	1	.333	1	-4	-4	-0	-0.7
Total 11		60	64	.484	253	164	18	2	3	1099¹	1232	101	432	507	13.7	4.53	82	.289	.356	55	.206	15	-98	-98	4	-8.1

● LOUIS LeROY
LeRoy, Louis Paul "Chief" b: 2/18/1879, Omro, Wis. d: 10/10/44, Shawano, Wis. BR/TR, 5'10", 180 lbs. Deb: 9/22/05

YEAR	TM/L	W	L	PCT	G	GS	CG	SH	SV	IP	H	HR	BB	SO	RAT	ERA	ERA+	OAV	OOB	BH	AVG	PB	PR	/A	PD	TPI
1905	NY-A	1	1	.500	3	3	2	0	0	24	26	2	1	8	10.5	3.75	78	.277	.292	1	.125	-0	-3	-2	-0	-0.2
1906	NY-A	2	0	1.000	11	2	1	0	1	44²	33	0	12	28	9.5	2.22	134	.209	.273	2	.143	-1	2	4	1	0.2
1910	Bos-A	0	0	—	1	0	0	0	0	4	7	1	2	3	20.3	11.25	23	.389	.450	0	.000	-0	-4	-4	0	-0.0
Total 3		3	1	.750	15	5	3	0	1	72²	66	3	15	39	10.4	3.22	91	.244	.292	3	.130	-1	-4	-2	1	0.0

● BARRY LERSCH
Lersch, Barry Lee b: 9/7/44, Denver, Colo. BB/TR, 6', 180 lbs. Deb: 4/8/69

YEAR	TM/L	W	L	PCT	G	GS	CG	SH	SV	IP	H	HR	BB	SO	RAT	ERA	ERA+	OAV	OOB	BH	AVG	PB	PR	/A	PD	TPI
1969	Phi-N	0	3	.000	10	0	0	0	2	17²	20	6	10	13	15.8	7.13	50	.286	.383	0	.000	-0	-7	-7	1	-1.2
1970	Phi-N	6	3	.667	42	11	3	0	3	138	119	17	47	92	10.9	3.26	122	.232	.297	2	.065	-2	12	11	-1	0.5
1971	Phi-N	5	14	.263	38	30	3	0	0	214¹	203	28	50	113	10.7	3.78	93	.252	.298	10	.169	2	-7	-6	-1	-0.4
1972	Phi-N	4	6	.400	36	8	3	1	0	100²	86	9	33	48	10.9	3.04	118	.231	.299	0	.000	-2	5	6	-0	0.3
1973	Phi-N	3	6	.333	42	4	0	0	1	98¹	105	10	27	51	12.3	4.39	86	.279	.330	3	.176	0	-8	-7	-0	-0.6
1974	StL-N	0	0	—	1	0	0	0	0	1¹	3	1	5	0	54.0	40.50	9	.429	.667	0	—	0	-5	-5	0	-0.0
Total 6		18	32	.360	169	53	9	1	6	570¹	536	70	172	317	11.3	3.82	97	.250	.308	15	.113	-3	-11	-8	-1	-1.4

● DON LESHNOCK
Leshnock, Donald Lee b: 11/25/46, Youngstown, Ohio BR/TL, 6'3", 195 lbs. Deb: 6/7/72

YEAR	TM/L	W	L	PCT	G	GS	CG	SH	SV	IP	H	HR	BB	SO	RAT	ERA	ERA+	OAV	OOB	BH	AVG	PB	PR	/A	PD	TPI
1972	Det-A	0	0	—	1	0	0	0	0	1	2	0	0	2	18.0	0.00	—	.400	.400	0	—	0	0	0	0	0.0

● CURT LESKANIC
Leskanic, Curtis John b: 4/2/68, Homestead, Pa. BR/TR, 6', 180 lbs. Deb: 6/27/93

YEAR	TM/L	W	L	PCT	G	GS	CG	SH	SV	IP	H	HR	BB	SO	RAT	ERA	ERA+	OAV	OOB	BH	AVG	PB	PR	/A	PD	TPI
1993	Col-N	1	5	.167	18	8	0	0	0	57	59	7	27	30	13.9	5.37	89	.266	.351	2	.154	0	-8	-4	-0	-0.4
1994	Col-N	1	1	.500	8	3	0	0	0	22¹	27	2	10	17	14.9	5.64	88	.314	.385	1	.167	0	-4	-2	-0	-0.1
1995	*Col-N	6	3	.667	**76**	0	0	0	10	98	83	7	33	107	10.7	3.40	159	.226	.289	1	.143	-0	9	22	2	2.3
1996	Col-N	7	5	.583	70	0	0	0	6	73²	82	12	38	76	14.9	6.23	87	.285	.372	1	.333	0	-16	-7	-1	-1.0
Total 4		15	14	.517	172	11	0	0	16	251	251	28	108	230	13.0	4.88	107	.260	.337	5	.172	-0	-20	10	1	0.8

● BRAD LESLEY
Lesley, Bradley Jay b: 9/11/58, Turlock, Cal. BR/TR, 6'6", 230 lbs. Deb: 7/31/82

YEAR	TM/L	W	L	PCT	G	GS	CG	SH	SV	IP	H	HR	BB	SO	RAT	ERA	ERA+	OAV	OOB	BH	AVG	PB	PR	/A	PD	TPI
1982	Cin-N	0	2	.000	28	0	0	0	4	38¹	27	1	13	29	9.4	2.58	143	.197	.267	0	.000	-0	4	5	-0	0.3
1983	Cin-N	0	0	—	5	0	0	0	0	8¹	9	1	0	5	9.7	2.16	176	.290	.290	0	—	0	1	2	-0	0.0
1984	Cin-N	0	1	.000	16	0	0	0	2	19¹	17	3	14	7	14.4	5.12	74	.246	.373	1	.500	0	-3	-3	-0	-0.2
1985	Mil-A	1	0	1.000	5	0	0	0	0	6¹	8	2	2	5	14.2	9.95	42	.296	.345	0	—	0	-4	-4	-0	-0.5
Total 4		1	3	.250	54	0	0	0	6	72¹	61	7	29	46	11.2	3.86	98	.231	.307	1	.333	-0	-2	-1	-0	-0.4

● WALT LEVERENZ
Leverenz, Walter Fred "Tiny" b: 7/21/1887, Chicago, Ill. d: 3/19/73, Atascadero, Cal. BL/TL, 5'10", 175 lbs. Deb: 4/18/13

YEAR	TM/L	W	L	PCT	G	GS	CG	SH	SV	IP	H	HR	BB	SO	RAT	ERA	ERA+	OAV	OOB	BH	AVG	PB	PR	/A	PD	TPI
1913	StL-A	6	17	.261	30	27	13	2	1	202²	159	3	89	87	11.5	2.58	114	.222	.318	12	.176	-1	8	8	-1	0.6
1914	StL-A	1	12	.077	27	16	5	0	0	111¹	107	5	63	44	14.1	3.80	71	.264	.368	6	.182	-0	-13	-14	-1	-1.7
1915	StL-A	0	2	.000	5	1	0	0	1	9	11	0	8	3	20.0	8.00	36	.333	.476	0	.000	-0	-5	-5	0	-1.1
Total 3		7	31	.184	62	44	18	2	2	323	277	8	160	134	13.0	3.15	91	.240	.341	18	.176	-1	-10	-11	-3	-2.2

● DIXIE LEVERETT
Leverett, Gorham Vance b: 3/29/1894, Georgetown, Tex. d: 2/20/57, Beaverton, Ore. BR/TR, 5'11", 190 lbs. Deb: 5/6/22

YEAR	TM/L	W	L	PCT	G	GS	CG	SH	SV	IP	H	HR	BB	SO	RAT	ERA	ERA+	OAV	OOB	BH	AVG	PB	PR	/A	PD	TPI
1922	Chi-A	13	10	.565	33	27	16	4	2	223²	224	11	79	60	12.3	3.34	122	.264	.329	21	.253	3	18	18	-1	1.9
1923	Chi-A	10	13	.435	38	24	9	0	3	192²	212	6	64	64	13.2	4.06	97	.280	.341	16	.267	4	-2	-2	-1	0.1
1924	Chi-A	2	3	.400	21	11	4	0	0	99	123	2	41	29	15.2	5.82	71	.314	.383	6	.188	-1	-17	-19	-0	-0.8
1926	Chi-A	1	1	.500	6	3	1	0	0	24	31	1	7	12	14.3	6.00	64	.316	.362	1	.143	-0	-5	-6	0	-0.4
1929	Bos-N	3	7	.300	24	12	3	0	0	97²	135	5	30	28	15.7	6.36	74	.339	.393	6	.188	-0	-18	-18	-0	-1.6
Total 5		29	34	.460	122	77	33	4	6	637	725	25	221	193	13.6	4.51	92	.291	.353	50	.234	6	-25	-27	-1	-0.8

● HOD LEVERETTE
Leverette, Horace Wilbur "Levy" b: 2/4/1889, Shreveport, La. d: 4/10/58, St.Petersburg, Fla BR/TR, 6', 180 lbs. Deb: 4/22/20

YEAR	TM/L	W	L	PCT	G	GS	CG	SH	SV	IP	H	HR	BB	SO	RAT	ERA	ERA+	OAV	OOB	BH	AVG	PB	PR	/A	PD	TPI
1920	StL-A	0	2	.000	3	2	0	0	0	10¹	9	1	12	0	18.3	5.23	75	.250	.438	0	.000	-1	-2	-1	1	-0.2

● ALAN LEVINE
Levine, Alan Brian b: 5/22/68, Park Ridge, Ill. BL/TR, 6'3", 180 lbs. Deb: 6/22/96

YEAR	TM/L	W	L	PCT	G	GS	CG	SH	SV	IP	H	HR	BB	SO	RAT	ERA	ERA+	OAV	OOB	BH	AVG	PB	PR	/A	PD	TPI
1996	Chi-A	0	1	—	16	0	0	0	0	16	19	2	13	10	17.4	5.40	87	.289	.357	0	—	0	-1	-1	1	0.1

● DUTCH LEVSEN
Levsen, Emil Henry b: 4/29/1898, Wyoming, Iowa d: 3/12/72, St.Louis Park, Minn. BR/TR, 6', 180 lbs. Deb: 9/28/23

YEAR	TM/L	W	L	PCT	G	GS	CG	SH	SV	IP	H	HR	BB	SO	RAT	ERA	ERA+	OAV	OOB	BH	AVG	PB	PR	/A	PD	TPI
1923	Cle-A	0	0	—	3	0	0	0	0	4¹	4	0	4	1	8.3	0.00	—	.267	.267	0	.000	-0	2	2	1	0.1
1924	Cle-A	1	1	.500	4	1	0	0	0	16¹	22	0	4	3	14.3	4.41	97	.333	.371	0	.000	-1	-0	-0	0	-0.1
1925	Cle-A	2	3	.333	4	3	2	0	0	24¹	30	1	16	9	17.4	5.55	80	.313	.416	2	.250	0	-3	-3	-1	-0.3
1926	Cle-A	16	13	.552	33	31	18	2	0	237¹	235	11	85	59	12.4	3.41	119	.261	.330	17	.205	-0	16	17	-1	1.8
1927	Cle-A	3	7	.300	25	13	2	0	0	80¹	96	1	37	15	15.1	5.49	77	.303	.379	5	.200	-1	-12	-11	1	-1.2
1928	Cle-A	0	1	—	11	3	0	0	0	41¹	39	4	31	7	15.7	5.44	76	.258	.391	0	.000	-2	-6	-6	-0	-0.6
Total 6		21	26	.447	80	51	23	2	0	404	426	17	173	88	13.6	4.17	99	.276	.354	24	.178	-4	-4	-2	1	-0.3

● DENNIS LEWALLYN
Lewallyn, Dennis Dale b: 8/11/53, Pensacola, Fla. BR/TR, 6'4", 200 lbs. Deb: 9/21/75

YEAR	TM/L	W	L	PCT	G	GS	CG	SH	SV	IP	H	HR	BB	SO	RAT	ERA	ERA+	OAV	OOB	BH	AVG	PB	PR	/A	PD	TPI
1975	LA-N	0	0	—	2	0	0	0	0	3	1	0	0	3	3.0	0.00	—	.100	.100	0	—	0	1	1	0	0.0
1976	LA-N	1	1	.500	4	2	0	0	0	16²	12	1	6	4	9.7	2.16	157	.207	.281	0	—	0	2	2	0	0.2
1977	LA-N	3	1	.750	17	2	0	0	0	17	22	1	4	8	13.8	4.24	90	.306	.342	0	—	0	-1	-1	-0	-0.3
1978	LA-N	0	0	—	1	0	0	0	0	1	1	0	0	1	9.0	0.00	—	.250	.250	0	—	0	1	1	0	0.0
1979	LA-N	0	1	.000	7	0	0	0	0	12¹	19	0	5	1	18.2	5.11	71	.358	.424	1	.500	0	-2	-2	0	-0.1

YEAR TM/L	W	L	PCT	G	GS	CG	SH	SV	IP	H	HR	BB	SO	RAT	ERA	ERA+	OAV	OOB	BH	AVG	PB	PR	/A	PD	TPI
1980 Tex-A	0	0	—	4	0	0	0	0	5²	7	0	4	1	17.5	7.94	49	.304	.407	0	—	0	-2	-3	0	0.1
1981 Cle-A	0	0	—	7	0	0	0	0	13¹	16	1	2	11	12.2	5.40	67	.296	.321	0	—	0	-3	-3	-0	0.0
1982 Cle-A	0	1	.000	4	0	0	0	0	10¹	13	3	1	3	12.2	6.97	59	.310	.326	0	—	0	-3	-3	-0	-0.3
Total 8	4	4	.500	34	3	0	0	1	80¹	92	6	22	28	12.9	4.48	82	.287	.335	1	.077	-1	-6	-7	0	-0.4

● DAN LEWANDOWSKI
Lewandowski, Daniel William   b: 1/6/28, Buffalo, N.Y.   d: 7/19/96, Hamilton, Ohio   BR/TR, 6′, 180 lbs.   Deb: 9/22/51

YEAR TM/L	W	L	PCT	G	GS	CG	SH	SV	IP	H	HR	BB	SO	RAT	ERA	ERA+	OAV	OOB	BH	AVG	PB	PR	/A	PD	TPI
1951 StL-N	0	1	.000	2	0	0	0	0	1	3	0	1	1	36.0	9.00	44	.500	.571	0	—	0	-1	-1	0	-0.4

● LEWIS
Lewis   b: Brooklyn, N.Y.   Deb: 7/12/1890 ♦

YEAR TM/L	W	L	PCT	G	GS	CG	SH	SV	IP	H	HR	BB	SO	RAT	ERA	ERA+	OAV	OOB	BH	AVG	PB	PR	/A	PD	TPI
1890 Buf-P	0	1	.000	1	1	0	0	0	3	13	3	7	1	60.0	60.00	7	.591	.690	1	.200	-0	-19	-19	1	-2.0

● TED LEWIS
Lewis, Edward Morgan "Parson"   b: 12/25/1872, Machynlleth, Wales   d: 5/24/36, Durham, N.H.   BR/TR, 5′10.5″, 158 lbs.   Deb: 7/6/1896

YEAR TM/L	W	L	PCT	G	GS	CG	SH	SV	IP	H	HR	BB	SO	RAT	ERA	ERA+	OAV	OOB	BH	AVG	PB	PR	/A	PD	TPI
1896 Bos-N	1	4	.200	6	5	4	0	0	41²	37	2	27	12	13.8	3.24	140	.236	.348	1	.111	-4	5	6	1	0.4
1897 *Bos-N	21	12	.636	38	34	30	2	1	290	316	11	125	65	14.0	3.85	116	.275	.351	28	.248	-2	15	20	-5	1.2
1898 Bos-N	26	8	**.765**	41	33	29	1	2	313¹	267	9	109	72	11.1	2.90	127	.229	.300	37	.282	4	25	28	-1	2.9
1899 Bos-N	17	11	.607	29	25	23	2	0	234²	245	10	73	60	12.5	3.49	119	.269	.328	25	.260	-0	10	17	-4	1.4
1900 Bos-N	13	12	.520	30	22	19	1	0	209	215	11	86	66	13.1	4.13	100	.265	.339	10	.137	-4	-10	-0	-3	-0.6
1901 Bos-A	16	17	.485	39	34	31	1	1	316¹	299	14	91	103	11.3	3.53	113	.247	.304	21	.174	-2	5	0	-2	-0.4
Total 6	94	64	.595	183	153	136	7	4	1405	1379	57	511	378	12.4	3.53	113	.255	.324	122	.223	-5	49	71	-13	4.9

● DUFFY LEWIS
Lewis, George Edward   b: 4/18/1888, San Francisco, Cal   d: 6/17/79, Salem, N.H.   BL/TL, 5′10.5″, 165 lbs.   Deb: 4/16/10   C♦

YEAR TM/L	W	L	PCT	G	GS	CG	SH	SV	IP	H	HR	BB	SO	RAT	ERA	ERA+	OAV	OOB	BH	AVG	PB	PR	/A	PD	TPI
1913 Bos-A	0	0	—	1	0	0	0	0	1	3	0	1	0	27.0	18.00	16	.500	.500	164	.298		-2	-2	-0	0.0

● JIM LEWIS
Lewis, James Martin   b: 10/12/55, Miami, Fla.   BR/TR, 6′3″, 190 lbs.   Deb: 9/12/79

YEAR TM/L	W	L	PCT	G	GS	CG	SH	SV	IP	H	HR	BB	SO	RAT	ERA	ERA+	OAV	OOB	BH	AVG	PB	PR	/A	PD	TPI
1979 Sea-A	0	0	—	2	0	0	0	0	2¹	10	1	1	0	42.4	15.43	28	.625	.647	0	—	0	-3	-3	-0	-0.1
1982 NY-A	0	0	—	1	0	0	0	0	0²	3	0	3	0	81.0	54.00	7	.500	.667	0	—	0	-4	-4	0	0.1
1983 Min-A	0	0	—	6	0	0	0	0	18	24	5	7	8	16.0	6.50	65	.324	.390	0	—	0	-5	-5	-0	-0.2
1985 Sea-A	0	1	.000	2	1	0	0	0	4²	8	1	1	1	21.2	7.71	55	.421	.500	0	—	0	-2	-2	0	-0.4
Total 4	0	1	.000	11	1	0	0	0	25²	45	7	12	9	21.0	8.77	48	.391	.462	0	—	0	-13	-13	-0	-0.6

● JIM LEWIS
Lewis, James Steven   b: 7/20/64, Jackson, Mich.   BR/TR, 6′2″, 200 lbs.   Deb: 8/9/91

YEAR TM/L	W	L	PCT	G	GS	CG	SH	SV	IP	H	HR	BB	SO	RAT	ERA	ERA+	OAV	OOB	BH	AVG	PB	PR	/A	PD	TPI
1991 SD-N	0	0	—	12	0	0	0	0	13	14	2	11	10	17.3	4.15	91	.275	.403	0	.000	-0	-1	-1	1	0.0

● RICHIE LEWIS
Lewis, Richie Todd   b: 1/25/66, Muncie, Ind.   BR/TR, 5′10″, 170 lbs.   Deb: 7/31/92

YEAR TM/L	W	L	PCT	G	GS	CG	SH	SV	IP	H	HR	BB	SO	RAT	ERA	ERA+	OAV	OOB	BH	AVG	PB	PR	/A	PD	TPI
1992 Bal-A	1	1	.500	2	2	0	0	0	6²	13	1	7	4	27.0	10.80	37	.406	.513	0	—	0	-5	-5	0	-1.1
1993 Fla-N	6	3	.667	57	0	0	0	0	77¹	68	7	43	65	13.0	3.26	133	.239	.340	1	.500	0	7	9	1	1.0
1994 Fla-N	1	4	.200	45	0	0	0	0	54	62	7	38	45	16.8	5.67	77	.284	.393	0	.000	-0	-9	-8	-0	-0.7
1995 Fla-N	0	1	.000	21	1	0	0	0	36	30	9	15	32	11.5	3.75	112	.224	.307	0	.000	0	2	2	-0	0.0
1996 Det-A	4	6	.400	72	0	0	0	0	90¹	78	9	65	78	14.6	4.18	121	.238	.370	0	.000	0	8	9	-1	0.7
Total 5	12	15	.444	197	3	0	0	0	264¹	251	33	168	224	14.5	4.32	106	.252	.363	1	.111	0	3	7	-1	-0.1

● SCOTT LEWIS
Lewis, Scott Allen   b: 12/5/65, Grants Pass, Ore.   BR/TR, 6′3″, 190 lbs.   Deb: 9/25/90

YEAR TM/L	W	L	PCT	G	GS	CG	SH	SV	IP	H	HR	BB	SO	RAT	ERA	ERA+	OAV	OOB	BH	AVG	PB	PR	/A	PD	TPI
1990 Cal-A	1	1	.500	2	2	0	0	0	16¹	10	2	9	6	6.6	2.20	173	.172	.200	0	—	0	3	3	-0	0.3
1991 Cal-A	3	5	.375	16	11	0	0	0	60¹	81	9	21	37	15.5	6.27	65	.316	.373	0	—	0	-15	-14	0	-1.6
1992 Cal-A	4	0	1.000	21	2	0	0	0	38¹	36	3	14	18	12.2	3.99	100	.255	.331	0	—	0	-0	-0	1	0.1
1993 Cal-A	1	2	.333	15	4	0	0	0	32	37	3	12	14	14.3	4.22	107	.311	.383	0	—	0	1	-1	-0	0.0
1994 Cal-A	0	1	.000	20	0	0	0	0	31	46	5	10	14	16.8	6.10	70	.359	.414	0	—	0	-4	-4	0	-0.1
Total 5	9	9	.500	74	19	1	0	0	178	210	22	59	84	14.0	5.01	85	.299	.360	0	—	0	-16	-15	-0	-1.3

● BERT LEWIS
Lewis, William Burton   b: 10/3/1895, Tonawanda, N.Y.   d: 3/24/50, Tonawanda, N.Y.   BR/TR, 6′2″, 176 lbs.   Deb: 4/19/24

YEAR TM/L	W	L	PCT	G	GS	CG	SH	SV	IP	H	HR	BB	SO	RAT	ERA	ERA+	OAV	OOB	BH	AVG	PB	PR	/A	PD	TPI
1924 Phi-N	0	0	—	12	0	0	0	0	18	23	1	7	3	15.5	6.00	74	.315	.383	0	.000	-1	-4	-3	0	-0.1

● TERRY LEY
Ley, Terrence Richard   b: 2/21/47, Portland, Ore.   BL/TL, 6′, 190 lbs.   Deb: 8/20/71

YEAR TM/L	W	L	PCT	G	GS	CG	SH	SV	IP	H	HR	BB	SO	RAT	ERA	ERA+	OAV	OOB	BH	AVG	PB	PR	/A	PD	TPI
1971 NY-A	0	0	—	6	0	0	0	0	9	9	1	9	7	20.0	5.00	65	.257	.435	0	—	0	-2	-2	0	0.0

● AL LIBKE
Libke, Albert Walter   b: 9/12/18, Tacoma, Wash.   BL/TL, 6′4″, 215 lbs.   Deb: 4/19/45 ♦

YEAR TM/L	W	L	PCT	G	GS	CG	SH	SV	IP	H	HR	BB	SO	RAT	ERA	ERA+	OAV	OOB	BH	AVG	PB	PR	/A	PD	TPI
1945 Cin-N	0	0	—	4	0	0	0	0	4¹	3	0	3	2	12.5	—		.200	.333	127	.283	1	2	2	0	0.0
1946 Cin-N	0	0	—	1	1	0	0	0	5	4	0	3	2	12.6	3.60	93	.235	.350	109	.253	0	-0	-0	0	0.0
Total 2	0	0	—	5	1	0	0	0	9¹	7	0	6	4	12.5	1.93	183	.219	.342	236	.268	2	2	2	0	0.0

● DON LIDDLE
Liddle, Donald Eugene   b: 5/25/25, Mt.Carmel, Ill.   BL/TL, 5′10″, 165 lbs.   Deb: 4/17/53

YEAR TM/L	W	L	PCT	G	GS	CG	SH	SV	IP	H	HR	BB	SO	RAT	ERA	ERA+	OAV	OOB	BH	AVG	PB	PR	/A	PD	TPI
1953 Mil-N	7	6	.538	31	15	4	0	2	128²	119	6	55	68	12.3	3.08	127	.248	.328	3	.088	-2	17	12	-1	0.9
1954 *NY-N	9	4	.692	28	19	4	3	0	126²	100	6	55	44	11.2	3.06	132	.223	.312	7	.189	2	14	14	-1	1.4
1955 NY-N	10	4	.714	33	13	4	1	0	106¹	97	18	61	56	13.7	4.23	95	.246	.353	5	.185	1	-2	-2	-1	-0.2
1956 NY-N	1	2	.333	11	5	1	0	1	41¹	45	5	14	21	13.1	3.92	97	.278	.339	2	.167	-0	-1	-0	0	0.0
StL-N	1	2	.333	14	2	0	0	0	24²	36	8	18	14	19.7	8.39	45	.353	.450	0	.000	-0	-13	-13	-0	-1.4
Yr	2	4	.333	25	7	1	0	1	66	81	13	32	35	15.4	5.59	68	.302	.377	2	.143	-0	-13	-13	-0	-1.4
Total 4	28	18	.609	117	54	13	4	3	427²	397	42	203	198	12.8	3.75	106	.250	.339	17	.152	-1	16	10	-2	0.7

● DUTCH LIEBER
Lieber, Charles Edwin   b: 2/1/10, Alameda, Cal.   d: 12/31/61, Sawtelle, Cal.   BR/TR, 6′0.5″, 180 lbs.   Deb: 4/18/35

YEAR TM/L	W	L	PCT	G	GS	CG	SH	SV	IP	H	HR	BB	SO	RAT	ERA	ERA+	OAV	OOB	BH	AVG	PB	PR	/A	PD	TPI
1935 Phi-A	1	1	.500	18	1	0	0	2	46²	45	1	19	14	12.5	3.09	147	.263	.340	2	.143	-1	7	8	0	0.3
1936 Phi-A	0	1	.000	3	0	0	0	0	11²	17	0	6	1	17.7	7.71	66	.362	.434	0	.000	-0	-3	-3	1	-0.2
Total 2	1	2	.333	21	1	0	0	2	58¹	62	1	25	15	13.6	4.01	116	.284	.361	2	.118	-2	4	4	1	0.1

● JON LIEBER
Lieber, Jonathan Ray   b: 4/2/70, Council Bluffs, Iowa   BL/TR, 6′3″, 220 lbs.   Deb: 5/15/94

YEAR TM/L	W	L	PCT	G	GS	CG	SH	SV	IP	H	HR	BB	SO	RAT	ERA	ERA+	OAV	OOB	BH	AVG	PB	PR	/A	PD	TPI
1994 Pit-N	6	7	.462	17	17	1	0	0	108²	116	12	25	71	11.8	3.73	116	.271	.313	4	.103	-2	6	7	-1	0.5
1995 Pit-N	4	7	.364	21	12	0	0	0	72²	103	7	14	45	15.0	6.32	68	.346	.383	1	.048	-2	-17	-16	1	-2.2
1996 Pit-N	9	5	.643	51	15	0	0	1	142	156	19	28	94	11.9	3.99	110	.279	.316	7	.194	2	4	6	2	0.9
Total 3	19	19	.500	89	44	1	0	1	323¹	375	38	67	210	12.5	4.43	98	.292	.331	12	.125	-2	-8	-3	1	-0.8

● GLENN LIEBHARDT
Liebhardt, Glenn Ignatius "Sandy"
b: 7/31/10, Cleveland, Ohio   d: 3/14/92, Winston-Salem, N.C.   BR/TR, 5′10.5″, 170 lbs.   Deb: 4/22/30   F

YEAR TM/L	W	L	PCT	G	GS	CG	SH	SV	IP	H	HR	BB	SO	RAT	ERA	ERA+	OAV	OOB	BH	AVG	PB	PR	/A	PD	TPI
1930 Phi-A	0	1	.000	5	0	0	0	0	9	14	2	8	4	22.0	11.00	42	.359	.468	0	.000	-0	-6	-6	-0	-0.6
1936 StL-A	0	0	—	24	0	0	0	0	55¹	98	4	27	20	20.7	8.78	61	.375	.438	0	.000	-2	-23	-21	-2	-0.3
1938 StL-A	0	0	—	2	0	0	0	0	3	4	1	0	1	12.0	6.00	83	.308	.308	0	—	0	-0	-0	0	0.0
Total 3	0	1	.000	31	0	0	0	0	67¹	116	7	35	23	20.5	8.96	59	.371	.437	0	.000	-2	-30	-28	-2	-0.9

● GLENN LIEBHARDT
Liebhardt, Glenn John   b: 3/10/1883, Milton, Ind.   d: 7/13/56, Cleveland, Ohio   BR/TR, 5′10″, 175 lbs.   Deb: 10/2/06   F

YEAR TM/L	W	L	PCT	G	GS	CG	SH	SV	IP	H	HR	BB	SO	RAT	ERA	ERA+	OAV	OOB	BH	AVG	PB	PR	/A	PD	TPI
1906 Cle-A	2	0	1.000	2	2	2	0	0	18	13	0	4	6	7.0	1.50	175	.206	.219	0	.000	-1	2	2	0	0.2
1907 Cle-A	18	14	.563	38	34	27	4	1	280¹	254	1	85	110	11.2	2.05	122	.244	.307	14	.161	-1	15	14	1	1.6
1908 Cle-A	15	16	.484	38	26	19	3	0	262	222	2	81	146	10.5	2.20	109	.235	.297	14	.175	0	6	6	1	0.7
1909 Cle-A	1	5	.167	12	4	1	0	0	52¹	54	0	16	15	12.2	2.92	87	.314	.376	0	.000	-2	-3	-2	-2	-0.6
Total 4	36	35	.507	90	66	49	7	2	612²	543	3	183	280	10.9	2.17	113	.244	.306	28	.147	-4	21	20	0	1.9

● GENE LILLARD
Lillard, Robert Eugene   b: 11/12/13, Santa Barbara, Cal   d: 4/12/91, Goleta, Cal.   BR/TR, 5′10.5″, 178 lbs.   Deb: 5/8/36   F♦

YEAR TM/L	W	L	PCT	G	GS	CG	SH	SV	IP	H	HR	BB	SO	RAT	ERA	ERA+	OAV	OOB	BH	AVG	PB	PR	/A	PD	TPI
1939 Chi-N	3	5	.375	20	7	2	0	0	55	68	2	36	31	17.5	6.55	60	.309	.413	1	.100		-16	-16	0	-1.9
1940 StL-N	0	1	.000	2	1	0	0	0	4²	8	1	4	2	25.1	13.50	30	.364	.481	0	—	0	-5	-5	0	-0.8
Total 2	3	6	.333	22	8	2	0	0	59²	76	3	40	33	18.1	7.09	56	.314	.420	8	.182	1	-21	-21	0	-2.7

● JIM LILLIE
Lillie, James J. "Grasshopper" (b: James J. Lilly)   b: 7/27/1861, New Haven, Conn.   d: 11/9/1890, Kansas City, Mo.   Deb: 5/17/1883 ♦

YEAR TM/L	W	L	PCT	G	GS	CG	SH	SV	IP	H	HR	BB	SO	RAT	ERA	ERA+	OAV	OOB	BH	AVG	PB	PR	/A	PD	TPI
1883 Buf-N	0	1	.000	3	0	0	0	0	12	16	0	4	4	13.5	3.00	106	.302	.327	47	.234	0	0	0	0	0.0
1884 Buf-N	0	1	.000	3	1	0	0	0	13	22	0	6	4	18.7	6.23	64	.324	.370	105	.223	0	-5	-4	0	0.0

YEAR	TM/L	W	L	PCT	G	GS	CG	SH	SV	IP	H	HR	BB	SO	RAT	ERA	ERA+	OAV	OOB	BH	AVG	PB	PR	/A	PD	TPI
1886	KC-N	0	0	—	1	0	0	0	0	6	8	0	1	0	13.5	4.50	84	.348	.375	73	.175	-0	-1	-0	0	0.0
Total	3	0	2	.000	6	1	0	0	0	31	46	0	8	8	15.7	4.65	71	.319	.355	332	.219	-0	-5	-5	1	-0.2

● DEREK LILLIQUIST   Lilliquist, Derek Jansen b: 2/20/66, Winter Park, Fla. BL/TL, 6′, 200 lbs. Deb: 4/13/89

YEAR	TM/L	W	L	PCT	G	GS	CG	SH	SV	IP	H	HR	BB	SO	RAT	ERA	ERA+	OAV	OOB	BH	AVG	PB	PR	/A	PD	TPI
1989	Atl-N	8	10	.444	32	30	0	0	0	165²	202	16	34	79	12.9	3.97	92	.301	.337	12	.190	0	-9	-6	-1	-0.7
1990	Atl-N	2	8	.200	12	11	0	0	0	61²	75	10	19	34	13.9	6.28	64	.301	.353	8	.348	4	-17	-15	-1	-1.9
	SD-N	3	3	.500	16	7	1	1	0	60¹	61	6	23	29	12.8	4.33	88	.266	.339	3	.150	-0	-4	-3	-2	-0.5
	Yr	5	11	.313	28	18	1	1	0	122	136	16	42	63	13.3	5.31	74	.282	.342	11	.256	4	-21	-19	-3	-2.4
1991	SD-N	0	2	.000	6	2	0	0	0	14¹	25	3	4	7	18.2	8.79	43	.379	.414	0	.000	-0	-8	-8	0	-0.9
1992	Cle-A	5	3	.625	71	0	0	0	6	61²	39	5	18	47	8.6	1.75	223	.186	.257	0	—	0	15	15	0	2.1
1993	Cle-A	4	4	.500	56	2	0	0	10	64	64	5	19	40	11.6	2.25	192	.263	.319	0	—	0	15	15	-0	2.0
1994	Cle-A	1	3	.250	36	0	0	0	1	29¹	34	6	8	15	13.2	4.91	96	.304	.355	0	—	0	-0	-1	-1	-0.1
1995	Bos-A	2	1	.667	28	0	0	0	0	23	27	7	9	9	14.1	6.26	78	.303	.367	0	—	0	-4	-4	-0	-0.5
1996	Cin-N	0	0	—	5	0	0	0	0	3²	5	1	0	1	12.3	7.36	56	.357	.357	0	—	0	-1	-1	0	0.0
Total	8	25	34	.424	262	52	1	1	17	483²	532	59	134	261	12.6	4.13	96	.283	.333	23	.213	4	-13	-8	-4	-0.5

● JOSE LIMA   Lima, Jose Desiderio Rodriguez (b: Jose Desiderio Rodriguez (Lima)) b: 9/30/72, Santiago, D.R. BR/TR, 6′2″, 170 lbs. Deb: 4/20/94

YEAR	TM/L	W	L	PCT	G	GS	CG	SH	SV	IP	H	HR	BB	SO	RAT	ERA	ERA+	OAV	OOB	BH	AVG	PB	PR	/A	PD	TPI
1994	Det-A	0	1	.000	3	1	0	0	0	6²	11	2	4	7	18.9	13.50	36	.355	.412	0	—	0	-6	-6	-0	-0.7
1995	Det-A	3	9	.250	15	15	0	0	0	73²	85	10	18	37	13.1	6.11	78	.288	.338	0	—	0	-11	-11	-2	-1.6
1996	Det-A	5	6	.455	39	4	0	0	3	72²	87	13	22	59	14.1	5.70	89	.296	.355	0	—	0	-6	-5	2	-0.4
Total	3	8	16	.333	57	20	0	0	3	153	183	25	43	103	13.8	6.24	79	.295	.350	0	—	0	-24	-23	-0	-2.7

● EZRA LINCOLN   Lincoln, Ezra Perry b: 11/17/1868, Raynham, Mass. d: 5/7/51, Taunton, Mass. BL/TL, 5′11″, 160 lbs. Deb: 5/2/1890

YEAR	TM/L	W	L	PCT	G	GS	CG	SH	SV	IP	H	HR	BB	SO	RAT	ERA	ERA+	OAV	OOB	BH	AVG	PB	PR	/A	PD	TPI
1890	Cle-N	3	11	.214	15	15	13	0	0	118	157	1	53	22	16.1	4.42	81	.310	.376	8	.157	-3	-11	-11	0	-1.2
	Syr-a	0	3	.000	3	3	2	0	0	20	33	1	4	6	17.1	10.35	34	.359	.392	0	.000	-1	-14	-15	-0	-1.5
Total	1	3	14	.176	18	18	15	0	0	138	190	2	57	28	16.2	5.28	68	.317	.378	8	.136	-4	-26	-26	0	-2.7

● VIVE LINDAMAN   Lindaman, Vivan Alexander b: 10/28/1877, Charles City, Iowa d: 2/13/27, Charles City, Iowa BR/TR, 6′1″, 200 lbs. Deb: 4/14/06

YEAR	TM/L	W	L	PCT	G	GS	CG	SH	SV	IP	H	HR	BB	SO	RAT	ERA	ERA+	OAV	OOB	BH	AVG	PB	PR	/A	PD	TPI
1906	Bos-N	12	23	.343	39	36	32	2	0	307¹	303	4	90	115	11.8	2.43	111	.264	.324	14	.132	-2	7	9	-2	0.7
1907	Bos-N	11	15	.423	34	28	24	2	1	260	252	10	108	90	13.0	3.63	70	.265	.349	11	.122	-2	-34	-31	-2	-3.5
1908	Bos-N	12	16	.429	43	30	21	2	1	270²	246	7	70	68	10.8	2.36	102	.249	.306	15	.176	0	0	2	-3	-0.2
1909	Bos-N	1	6	.143	15	6	6	1	0	66	75	1	28	13	14.2	4.64	61	.299	.371	6	.273	1	-15	-13	-1	-1.4
Total	4	36	60	.375	131	100	83	7	2	904	876	22	296	286	12.0	2.92	88	.263	.329	46	.152	-3	-41	-34	-8	-4.4

● PAUL LINDBLAD   Lindblad, Paul Aaron b: 8/9/41, Chanute, Kan. BL/TL, 6′1″, 195 lbs. Deb: 9/15/65

YEAR	TM/L	W	L	PCT	G	GS	CG	SH	SV	IP	H	HR	BB	SO	RAT	ERA	ERA+	OAV	OOB	BH	AVG	PB	PR	/A	PD	TPI
1965	KC-A	0	1	.000	4	0	0	0	0	7¹	12	3	0	12	16.0	11.05	32	.353	.371	0	.000	-0	-6	-6	0	-0.7
1966	KC-A	5	10	.333	38	14	0	0	1	121	138	14	37	69	13.2	4.17	82	.292	.348	5	.147	0	-10	-10	-0	-1.2
1967	KC-A	5	8	.385	46	10	1	1	6	115²	106	15	35	83	11.4	3.58	89	.241	.306	7	.206	2	-4	-5	-0	-0.5
1968	Oak-A	4	3	.571	47	1	0	0	2	56¹	51	6	14	42	10.4	2.40	118	.237	.284	3	.375	1	4	3	0	0.6
1969	Oak-A	9	6	.600	60	0	0	0	9	78¹	72	8	33	64	12.3	4.14	83	.240	.319	4	.333	1	-4	-6	-0	-1.1
1970	Oak-A	8	2	.800	62	0	0	0	3	63¹	52	7	28	42	11.4	2.70	131	.222	.305	0	.000	-1	7	6	-0	0.9
1971	Oak-A	1	0	1.000	8	0	0	0	0	16	18	1	2	4	11.8	3.94	85	.295	.328	1	.333	0	-1	-1	0	0.0
	Was-A	4	4	.600	43	0	0	0	8	83²	58	6	29	50	9.6	2.58	128	.196	.272	4	.158	0	8	7	1	1.1
	Yr	5	4	.556	51	0	0	0	8	99²	76	7	31	54	9.8	2.80	118	.212	.279	4	.182	1	7	6	1	1.1
1972	Tex-A	5	8	.385	66	0	0	0	9	99²	95	7	29	51	11.2	2.62	115	.257	.311	3	.200	0	5	4	-1	0.6
1973	*Oak-A	1	5	.167	36	3	0	0	2	78	89	9	28	33	13.8	3.69	96	.292	.357	0	—	0	1	-1	-1	-0.2
1974	Oak-A	4	4	.500	45	2	0	0	6	100²	85	4	30	46	10.5	2.06	161	.231	.292	0	—	0	17	14	0	1.3
1975	*Oak-A	9	1	.900	68	0	0	0	7	122¹	105	6	43	58	10.9	2.72	133	.237	.305	0	.000	0	14	12	1	1.2
1976	Oak-A	6	5	.545	65	0	0	0	3	114²	111	5	24	37	10.8	3.06	110	.253	.296	0	—	0	6	4	1	0.7
1977	Tex-A	4	5	.444	42	1	0	0	4	98²	103	6	29	46	12.1	4.20	97	.270	.324	0	—	0	-2	-1	0	-0.2
1978	Tex-A	1	1	.500	18	0	0	0	2	39²	41	2	15	25	13.2	3.63	103	.279	.354	0	—	0	1	0	-0	0.0
	*NY-A	0	0	—	7	1	0	0	0	18¹	21	4	8	9	14.2	4.42	82	.284	.354	0	—	0	-1	-2	0	0.2
	Yr	1	1	.500	25	1	0	0	2	58	62	6	23	34	13.2	3.88	95	.276	.343	0	—	0	-1	-1	0	0.2
Total	14	68	63	.519	655	32	1	1	64	1213²	1157	112	384	671	11.6	3.29	104	.253	.314	26	.195	5	35	17	2	2.7

● LYMAN LINDE   Linde, Lyman Gilbert b: 9/20/20, Beaver Dam, Wis. BR/TR, 5′11″, 185 lbs. Deb: 9/11/47

YEAR	TM/L	W	L	PCT	G	GS	CG	SH	SV	IP	H	HR	BB	SO	RAT	ERA	ERA+	OAV	OOB	BH	AVG	PB	PR	/A	PD	TPI
1947	Cle-A	0	0	—	1	0	0	0	0	0²	3	0	1	0	54.0	27.00	13	.600	.667	0	—	0	-2	-2	0	0.0
1948	Cle-A	0	0	—	3	0	0	0	0	10	9	1	4	5	11.7	5.40	75	.243	.317	0	.000	-0	-1	-1	-0	-0.1
Total	2	0	0	—	4	0	0	0	0	10²	12	1	5	5	14.3	6.75	60	.286	.362	0	.000	-0	-3	-3	-0	-0.1

● JOHNNY LINDELL   Lindell, John Harlan b: 8/30/16, Greeley, Colo. d: 8/27/85, Newport Beach, Cal. BR/TR, 6′4.5″, 217 lbs. Deb: 4/18/41 ♦

YEAR	TM/L	W	L	PCT	G	GS	CG	SH	SV	IP	H	HR	BB	SO	RAT	ERA	ERA+	OAV	OOB	BH	AVG	PB	PR	/A	PD	TPI
1942	NY-A	2	1	.667	23	2	0	0	1	52²	52	3	22	28	12.8	3.76	92	.254	.329	6	.250	-1	-1	-2	-0	0.0
1953	Pit-N	5	16	.238	27	23	13	1	0	175²	173	17	116	102	15.1	4.71	95	.262	.377	26	.286	6	-8	-5	3	1.1
	Phi-N	1	1	.500	5	3	2	0	0	23¹	22	0	23	16	17.4	4.24	99	.259	.417	7	.389	2	-0	-0	-0	0.2
	Yr	6	17	.261	32	26	15	1	0	199	195	17	139	118	15.1	4.66	95	.259	.375	33	.303	8	-8	-5	2	1.3
Total	2	8	18	.308	55	28	15	1	1	251²	247	20	161	146	14.8	4.47	95	.260	.371	762	.273	9	-9	-7	2	1.3

● ERNIE LINDEMANN   Lindemann, Ernest b: 6/10/1883, New York, N.Y. d: 12/27/51, Brooklyn, N.Y. BR/TR, Deb: 6/28/07

YEAR	TM/L	W	L	PCT	G	GS	CG	SH	SV	IP	H	HR	BB	SO	RAT	ERA	ERA+	OAV	OOB	BH	AVG	PB	PR	/A	PD	TPI
1907	Bos-N	0	0	—	1	1	0	0	0	6¹	6	0	4	3	14.2	5.68	45	.286	.400	1	.500	0	-2	-2	0	0.1

● CARL LINDQUIST   Lindquist, Carl Emil b: 5/9/19, Morris Run, Pa. BR/TR, 6′2″, 185 lbs. Deb: 9/27/43

YEAR	TM/L	W	L	PCT	G	GS	CG	SH	SV	IP	H	HR	BB	SO	RAT	ERA	ERA+	OAV	OOB	BH	AVG	PB	PR	/A	PD	TPI
1943	Bos-N	0	2	.000	2	2	0	0	0	13	17	3	4	1	14.5	6.23	55	.315	.362	0	.000	-1	-4	-4	0	-0.5
1944	Bos-N	0	0	—	5	0	0	0	0	8²	8	1	2	4	10.4	3.12	123	.222	.263	0	.000	-0	0	1	-0	0.0
Total	2	0	2	.000	7	2	0	0	0	21²	25	4	6	5	12.9	4.98	72	.278	.323	0	.000	-1	-4	-3	-0	-0.5

● JIM LINDSEY   Lindsey, James Kendrick b: 1/24/1898, Greensburg, La. d: 10/25/63, Jackson, La. BR/TR, 6′1″, 175 lbs. Deb: 5/1/22

YEAR	TM/L	W	L	PCT	G	GS	CG	SH	SV	IP	H	HR	BB	SO	RAT	ERA	ERA+	OAV	OOB	BH	AVG	PB	PR	/A	PD	TPI
1922	Cle-A	4	5	.444	29	5	0	0	1	83²	105	4	24	29	14.2	6.02	67	.324	.376	4	.167	-1	-18	-19	-1	-1.9
1924	Cle-A	0	0	—	3	0	0	0	0	3	8	0	3	0	33.0	21.00	20	.500	.579	0	.000	-1	-6	-6	0	0.0
1929	StL-N	1	1	.500	2	2	1	0	0	16¹	20	1	2	8	12.7	5.51	85	.290	.319	1	.200	-0	-1	-2	0	-0.2
1930	*StL-N	7	5	.583	39	6	2	0	5	105²	131	6	46	50	15.4	4.43	113	.312	.385	8	.286	-1	6	7	-3	0.5
1931	*StL-N	6	4	.600	35	2	1	1	7	74²	77	2	45	32	14.7	2.77	142	.270	.370	1	.111	-0	**9**	**10**	-0	1.3
1932	StL-N	3	3	.500	33	5	0	0	3	89¹	96	6	38	31	13.7	4.94	80	.279	.354	3	.143	-1	-10	-10	-1	-0.9
1933	StL-N	0	0	—	4	0	0	0	0	4	4	0	2	1	13.5	4.50	77	.286	.375	-0	—	-0	-0	-0	-0	0.0
1934	Cin-N	0	0	—	4	0	0	0	0	4	4	0	2	1	15.8	4.50	91	.286	.412	0	—	0	-0	-0	0	0.0
	StL-N	0	1	.000	11	0	0	0	1	14	21	2	3	7	14.5	6.43	66	.328	.358	0	—	0	-4	-4	-0	-0.3
	Yr	0	1	.000	15	0	0	0	1	18	25	2	5	9	15.0	6.00	70	.316	.357	0	—	-0	-4	-4	-0	-0.3
1937	Bro-N	0	1	.000	20	0	0	0	2	38¹	43	4	12	15	13.1	3.52	115	.295	.352	1	.167	-0	2	2	-1	0.0
Total	9	21	20	.512	177	20	5	1	19	431	507	25	176	175	14.5	4.70	91	.300	.370	18	.186	-3	-23	-21	-6	-1.5

● AXEL LINDSTROM   Lindstrom, Axel Olaf b: 8/26/1895, Gustavsberg, Sweden d: 6/24/40, Asheville, N.C. BR/TR, 5′10″, 180 lbs. Deb: 10/3/16

YEAR	TM/L	W	L	PCT	G	GS	CG	SH	SV	IP	H	HR	BB	SO	RAT	ERA	ERA+	OAV	OOB	BH	AVG	PB	PR	/A	PD	TPI
1916	Phi-A	0	0	—	1	0	0	0	0	4	3	0	3	2	6.8	4.50	63	.182	.250	1	.500	0	-1	-1	0	

● DICK LINES   Lines, Richard George b: 8/17/38, Montreal, Que., Can. BR/TL, 6′1″, 175 lbs. Deb: 4/16/66

YEAR	TM/L	W	L	PCT	G	GS	CG	SH	SV	IP	H	HR	BB	SO	RAT	ERA	ERA+	OAV	OOB	BH	AVG	PB	PR	/A	PD	TPI
1966	Was-A	5	2	.714	53	0	0	0	5	83	63	9	24	49	9.5	2.28	152	.213	.274	0	.000	-1	11	11	1	
1967	Was-A	2	5	.286	54	0	0	0	2	85²	83	6	24	54	11.2	3.36	94	.245	.295	1	.111	1	-1	-2	0	-0.1
Total	2	7	7	.500	107	0	0	0	7	168²	146	10	48	103	10.4	2.83	117	.230	.285	1	.053	0	9	9	2	1.0

● FRED LINK   Link, Edward Theodore "Laddie" b: 3/11/1886, Columbus, Ohio d: 5/22/39, Houston, Tex. BL/TL, 6′, 170 lbs. Deb: 4/15/10

YEAR	TM/L	W	L	PCT	G	GS	CG	SH	SV	IP	H	HR	BB	SO	RAT	ERA	ERA+	OAV	OOB	BH	AVG	PB	PR	/A	PD	TPI
1910	Cle-A	5	6	.455	22	13	6	1	1	127²	121	0	50	55	12.5	3.17	82	.259	.340	7	.167	-1	-9	-8	-1	-1.0
	StL-A	0	1	.000	3	3	0	0	0	17	24	0	13	5	20.1	4.24	58	.375	.487	1	.167	-0	-3	-3	-0	-0.2
	Yr	5	7	.417	25	16	6	1	1	144²	145	0	63	60	13.0	3.30	78	.270	.347	8	.167	-1	-12	-12	-2	-1.2

YEAR	TM/L	W	L	PCT	G	GS	CG	SH	SV	IP	H	HR	BB	SO	RAT	ERA	ERA+	OAV	OOB	BH	AVG	PB	PR	/A	PD	TPI
● ED LINKE	Linke, Edward Karl "Babe" b: 11/9/11, Chicago, Ill. d: 6/21/88, Chicago, Ill. BR/TR, 5'11", 180 lbs. Deb: 4/27/33																									
1933	Was-A	1	0	1.000	3	2	0	0	0	16	15	0	11	6	14.6	5.06	83	.250	.366	1	.167	0	-1	-2	-0	-0.1
1934	Was-A	2	2	.500	7	4	2	0	0	34²	38	1	9	9	12.2	4.15	104	.277	.322	2	.182	0	1	1	0	0.1
1935	Was-A	11	7	.611	40	22	10	1	3	178	211	6	80	51	14.8	5.01	86	.296	.367	20	.294	6	-11	-14	-1	-0.8
1936	Was-A	1	5	.167	13	6	1	0	0	52	73	4	14	11	15.1	7.10	67	.330	.370	6	.400	5	-12	-13	1	-0.7
1937	Was-A	6	1	.857	36	7	0	0	3	128²	158	11	59	61	15.5	5.60	79	.304	.379	10	.217	1	-14	-17	-0	-0.8
1938	StL-A	1	7	.125	21	2	0	0	0	39²	60	6	33	18	21.1	7.94	63	.357	.463	2	.200	0	-14	-13	1	-2.0
Total	6	22	22	.500	120	43	13	1	6	449	555	28	206	156	15.4	5.61	79	.305	.377	41	.263	12	-51	-58	0	-4.3
● ROYCE LINT	Lint, Royce James b: 1/1/21, Birmingham, Ala. BL/TL, 6'1", 165 lbs. Deb: 4/13/54																									
1954	StL-N	2	3	.400	30	4	1	1	0	70¹	75	9	30	36	13.4	4.86	85	.273	.344	1	.100	1	-6	-6	1	-0.2
● DOUG LINTON	Linton, Douglas Warren b: 2/9/65, Santa Ana, Cal. BR/TR, 6'1", 185 lbs. Deb: 8/3/92																									
1992	Tor-A	1	3	.250	8	3	0	0	0	24	31	5	17	16	18.0	8.63	47	.323	.425	0	—	0	-12	-12	-0	-1.7
1993	Tor-A	0	1	.000	4	1	0	0	0	11	11	0	9	4	17.2	6.55	66	.256	.396	0	—	0	-3	-3	-0	-0.2
	Cal-A	2	0	1.000	19	0	0	0	0	25²	35	8	14	19	17.2	7.71	58	.324	.402	0	—	0	-10	-9	-0	-0.6
	Yr	2	1	.667	23	1	0	0	0	36²	46	8	23	23	16.9	7.36	60	.299	.390	0	—	0	-12	-12	-0	-0.8
1994	NY-N	6	2	.750	32	3	0	0	0	50¹	74	4	20	29	16.8	4.47	93	.341	.397	0	.000	-1	-1	-2	-1	-0.4
1995	KC-A	0	1	.000	7	2	0	0	0	22¹	12	0	10	13	13.7	7.25	66	.256	.347	0	—	0	-6	-6	-0	-0.2
1996	KC-A	7	9	.438	21	18	0	0	0	104	111	13	26	87	12.5	5.02	97	.271	.327	0	—	-1	-1	-1	-0	-0.1
Total	5	16	16	.500	91	27	0	0	0	237¹	284	34	96	168	14.8	5.84	78	.296	.366	0	—	-1	-33	-33	-2	-3.2
● FRANK LINZY	Linzy, Frank Alfred b: 9/15/40, Ft.Gibson, Okla BR/TR, 6'1", 190 lbs. Deb: 8/14/63																									
1963	SF-N	0	0	—	8	1	0	0	0	16²	22	0	10	14	17.8	4.86	66	.324	.418	0	.000	-0	-3	-3	0	0.0
1965	SF-N	9	3	.750	57	0	0	0	21	81²	76	2	23	35	11.2	1.43	251	.250	.309	4	.222	1	**19**	**20**	5	4.9
1966	SF-N	7	11	.389	51	0	0	0	16	100¹	107	4	34	57	12.8	2.96	124	.273	.334	3	.150	0	7	8	1	1.7
1967	SF-N	7	7	.500	57	0	0	0	17	95²	67	4	34	38	9.5	1.51	218	.203	.277	0	.000	-2	20	19	3	3.9
1968	SF-N	9	8	.529	57	0	0	0	12	94²	76	1	27	36	9.9	2.09	141	.218	.277	0	.000	-1	9	9	4	2.3
1969	SF-N	14	9	.609	58	0	0	0	11	116¹	129	5	38	62	13.2	3.64	96	.283	.342	8	.267	3	-1	-2	3	0.3
1970	SF-N	2	1	.667	20	0	0	0	1	25²	33	3	11	16	15.8	7.01	57	.327	.398	0	.000	-0	-8	-9	-0	-1.0
	StL-N	3	5	.375	47	0	0	0	2	61¹	66	3	23	19	13.1	3.67	112	.282	.346	0	.000	-1	3	3	1	0.4
	Yr	5	6	.455	67	0	0	0	3	87	99	6	34	35	13.8	4.66	88	.293	.358	0	.000	-1	-6	-6	1	-0.6
1971	StL-N	4	3	.571	50	0	0	0	6	59¹	49	2	27	24	11.5	2.12	170	.226	.311	2	.500	1	9	10	1	1.5
1972	Mil-A	2	2	.500	47	0	0	0	12	77¹	70	4	27	24	11.5	3.03	100	.248	.318	1	.111	0	0	0	1	0.1
1973	Mil-A	2	6	.250	42	1	0	0	13	63	68	7	21	21	12.9	3.57	105	.282	.342	0	—	0	2	1	0	0.2
1974	Phi-N	3	2	.600	22	0	0	0	1	24²	27	1	7	12	12.4	3.28	115	.284	.333	0	—	0	1	1	1	0.3
Total	11	62	57	.521	516	2	0	0	111	816²	790	35	282	358	12.0	2.85	122	.257	.323	18	.149	0	58	57	20	14.6
● ANGELO LiPETRI	LiPetri, Michael Angelo b: 7/6/30, Brooklyn, N.Y. BR/TR, 6'1.5", 180 lbs. Deb: 4/25/56																									
1956	Phi-N	0	0	—	6	0	0	0	0	11	7	2	3	8	9.0	3.27	114	.175	.250	0	.000	-0	1	1	0	0.0
1958	Phi-N	0	0	—	4	0	0	0	0	4	6	1	0	1	15.8	11.25	35	.353	.389	0	—	0	-3	-3	0	-0.1
Total	2	0	0	—	10	0	0	0	0	15	13	3	3	9	10.8	5.40	70	.228	.290	0	.000	-0	-3	-3	0	0.0
● TOM LIPP	Lipp, Thomas Charles (b: Thomas Charles Lieb) b: 6/4/1870, Baltimore, Md. d: 5/30/32, Baltimore, Md. 5'11.5", 170 lbs. Deb: 9/18/1897																									
1897	Phi-N	0	1	.000	1	1	0	0	0	3	8	0	2	1	30.0	15.00	28	.471	.526	1	1.000	0	-4	-4	-0	-0.7
● NIG LIPSCOMB	Lipscomb, Gerard b: 2/24/11, Rutherfordton, N.C d: 2/27/78, Huntersville, N.C. BR/TR, 6', 175 lbs. Deb: 4/23/37 ♦																									
1937	StL-A	—	—	—	3	0	0	0	0	3	5	3	5	1	16.8	6.52	74	.333	.409	31	.323	1	-2	-2	-0	-0.1
● FELIPE LIRA	Lira, Antonio Felipe b: 4/26/72, Santa Teresa, Venez. BR/TR, 6', 170 lbs. Deb: 4/27/95																									
1995	Det-A	9	13	.409	37	22	0	0	1	146¹	151	17	56	89	13.2	4.31	110	.271	.346	0	—	0	7	7	-1	0.9
1996	Det-A	6	14	.300	32	32	3	2	0	194²	204	30	66	113	12.9	5.22	97	.269	.336	0	—	0	-5	-4	2	-0.1
Total	2	15	27	.357	69	54	3	2	1	341	355	47	122	202	13.1	4.83	102	.270	.340	0	—	0	2	4	2	0.8
● HOD LISENBEE	Lisenbee, Horace Milton b: 9/23/1898, Clarksville, Tenn d: 11/14/87, Clarksville, Tenn. BR/TR, 5'11", 170 lbs. Deb: 4/23/27																									
1927	Was-A	18	9	.667	39	34	17	4	1	242	221	6	78	105	11.2	3.57	114	.245	.307	11	.133	-5	15	13	-2	0.6
1928	Was-A	2	6	.250	16	9	3	0	0	77	102	4	32	13	16.2	6.08	66	.326	.397	4	.174	-0	-17	-18	-1	-1.6
1929	Bos-A	0	0	—	5	0	0	0	0	8²	10	1	4	2	14.5	5.19	82	.294	.368	0	.000	-0	-1	-1	0	0.0
1930	Bos-A	10	17	.370	37	31	15	0	0	237³	254	20	86	47	13.1	4.40	105	.280	.346	20	.267	1	7	6	-4	0.3
1931	Bos-A	5	12	.294	41	17	6	0	1	164²	190	14	49	42	13.2	5.19	83	.281	.332	12	.226	1	-15	-16	-2	-1.5
1932	Bos-A	0	4	.000	19	6	3	0	0	73¹	87	9	25	13	13.9	5.65	80	.296	.353	1	.048	-2	-10	-9	-1	-0.7
1936	Phi-A	1	7	.125	19	7	4	0	0	85²	115	9	24	17	14.6	6.20	82	.322	.365	3	.120	-1	-11	-10	-1	-0.9
1945	Cin-N	1	3	.250	31	3	0	0	0	80¹	97	12	16	14	12.9	5.49	68	.294	.330	0	.000	-3	-15	-15	-0	-1.1
Total	8	37	58	.389	207	107	48	4	1	969	1076	74	314	253	13.1	4.81	90	.282	.340	51	.169	-10	-47	-51	-11	-4.9
● AD LISKA	Liska, Adolph James b: 7/10/06, Dwight, Neb. BR/TR, 5'11.5", 160 lbs. Deb: 4/17/29																									
1929	Was-A	3	9	.250	24	10	4	0	0	94¹	87	1	42	33	12.6	4.77	89	.249	.335	5	.172	-1	-6	-6	-3	-0.4
1930	Was-A	9	7	.563	32	16	7	1	1	150²	140	6	71	40	12.9	3.29	140	.250	.340	5	.096	-4	23	22	6	2.2
1931	Was-A	0	1	.000	2	1	0	0	0	4	9	1	1	2	22.5	6.75	64	.450	.476	0	.000	-0	-1	-1	0	-0.2
1932	Phi-N	2	0	1.000	8	0	0	0	1	26²	22	0	16	6	11.1	1.69	261	.239	.320	0	.000	-0	6	8	1	0.7
1933	Phi-N	3	1	.750	45	1	0	0	1	75²	96	5	26	23	14.5	4.52	84	.310	.363	1	.071	-1	-10	-6	4	-0.1
Total	5	17	18	.486	111	28	11	1	3	351¹	354	12	150	104	13.1	3.87	112	.266	.344	11	.107	-7	13	19	14	2.2
● MARK LITTELL	Littell, Mark Alan b: 1/17/53, Cape Girardeau, Mo. BL/TR, 6'3", 210 lbs. Deb: 6/14/73																									
1973	KC-A	1	3	.250	8	7	1	0	0	38	44	5	23	16	15.9	5.68	72	.288	.381	0	—	0	-8	-7	-0	-0.9
1975	KC-A	2	4	.333	7	3	1	0	0	24¹	19	1	15	19	12.6	3.70	104	.229	.347	0	—	0	1	0	1	0.1
1976	*KC-A	8	4	.667	60	1	0	0	16	104	68	0	60	92	11.1	2.08	169	.188	.304	0	.000	0	**17**	16	-1	2.4
1977	*KC-A	8	4	.667	48	5	0	0	12	104²	73	6	55	106	11.1	3.61	112	.198	.304	0	.000	-0	5	5	-1	0.5
1978	StL-N	4	8	.333	72	2	0	0	11	106¹	80	8	56	130	12.1	2.79	126	.213	.326	0	.000	-0	9	9	-1	1.0
1979	StL-N	9	4	.692	63	0	0	0	13	82¹	60	4	39	67	10.8	2.19	172	.203	.296	0	.000	-1	14	14	0	2.5
1980	StL-N	0	2	.000	14	0	0	0	2	10²	14	2	7	7	17.7	9.28	40	.318	.412	0	.000	-0	-7	-7	-0	-1.4
1981	StL-N	1	3	.250	28	1	0	0	2	41	36	2	31	22	14.7	4.39	81	.237	.366	2	.250	-1	-4	-4	-1	-0.4
1982	StL-N	0	1	.000	16	0	0	0	0	20²	22	1	15	7	16.1	5.23	69	.272	.385	0	.000	-0	-4	-4	-1	-0.2
Total	9	32	31	.508	316	19	2	0	56	532	416	28	304	466	12.3	3.32	112	.217	.326	2	.059	-2	23	24	-4	3.6
● JEFF LITTLE	Little, Donald Jeffrey b: 12/25/54, Fremont, Ohio BR/TL, 6'6", 220 lbs. Deb: 9/6/80																									
1980	StL-N	1	1	.500	7	2	0	0	0	18²	18	0	9	17	13.0	3.86	96	.250	.333	1	.167	-0	-1	-0	-0	-0.1
1982	Min-A	2	0	1.000	33	0	0	0	0	36¹	33	6	27	26	14.9	4.21	101	.244	.370	0	—	0	-1	-0	-0	-0.2
Total	2	3	1	.750	40	2	0	0	0	55	51	6	36	43	14.2	4.09	99	.246	.358	1	.167	-0	-1	-0	-1	-0.3
● JOHN LITTLEFIELD	Littlefield, John Andrew b: 1/5/54, Covina, Cal. BR/TR, 6'2", 200 lbs. Deb: 6/8/80																									
1980	StL-N	5	5	.500	52	0	0	0	9	66	71	3	20	22	12.5	3.14	118	.282	.337	0	—	-1	3	4	0	0.6
1981	SD-N	2	3	.400	42	0	0	0	2	64	53	6	28	21	11.5	3.66	89	.235	.322	0	—	-0	-1	-3	-0	-0.3
Total	2	7	8	.467	94	0	0	0	11	130	124	9	48	43	12.0	3.39	102	.259	.330	0	—	-1	2	1	-0	0.3
● DICK LITTLEFIELD	Littlefield, Richard Bernard b: 3/18/26, Detroit, Mich. BL/TL, 6', 180 lbs. Deb: 7/7/50																									
1950	Bos-A	2	2	.500	15	2	0	0	1	23¹	27	6	24	13	20.1	9.26	53	.297	.448	0	.000	-1	-12	-11	1	-1.6
1951	Chi-A	1	1	.500	4	2	0	0	0	8²	9	3	6	7	22.8	8.38	48	.243	.481	0	.000	-0	-5	-7	-0	-0.7
1952	Det-A	0	3	.000	28	1	0	0	1	47²	46	4	25	32	13.4	4.34	88	.257	.348	1	.143	-1	-4	-3	-1	-0.3
	StL-A	2	3	.400	7	5	3	0	0	46¹	35	4	17	34	10.1	2.72	144	.205	.277	1	.063	-2	5	6	-1	0.3
	Yr	2	6	.250	35	6	3	0	1	94	81	8	42	66	11.8	3.54	109	.231	.314	2	.087	-2	1	3	-2	0.0
1953	StL-A	7	12	.368	36	22	7	0	0	152¹	153	17	84	104	14.2	5.08	83	.264	.361	8	.190	-1	-18	-15	-1	-1.8

YEAR	TM/L	W	L	PCT	G	GS	CG	SH	SV	IP	H	HR	BB	SO	RAT	ERA	ERA+	OAV	OOB	BH	AVG	PB	PR	/A	PD	TPI
1954	Bal-A	0	0	—	3	0	0	0	0	6	8	0	6	5	22.5	10.50	34	.333	.484	0	.000	-0	-5	-5	-0	0.0
	Pit-N	10	11	.476	23	21	7	1	0	155	140	10	85	92	13.2	3.60	116	.239	.337	8	.163	0	8	10	-3	1.0
1955	Pit-N	5	12	.294	35	17	4	1	0	130	148	15	68	70	15.1	5.12	80	.290	.375	6	.176	-0	-16	-15	-2	-1.8
1956	Pit-N	0	0	—	6	2	0	0	0	12²	14	2	6	10	14.2	4.26	88	.286	.364	0	.000	-0	-1	-1	-0	-0.1
	StL-N	0	2	.000	3	2	0	0	0	9²	9	2	4	5	12.1	7.45	51	.237	.310	0	.000	-0	-4	-4	-0	-0.7
	NY-N	4	4	.500	31	7	0	0	2	97	78	16	39	65	10.9	4.08	93	.231	.310	2	.083	-2	-3	-3	0	-0.4
	Yr	4	6	.400	40	11	0	0	2	119¹	101	20	49	80	11.3	4.37	86	.238	.316	2	.071	-2	-8	-8	-1	-1.2
1957	Chi-A	2	3	.400	48	2	0	0	4	65²	76	12	37	51	15.6	5.35	72	.295	.385	2	.182	0	-11	-11	-1	-1.0
1958	Mil-N	0	1	.000	4	0	0	0	1	6¹	7	2	1	7	12.8	4.26	83	.280	.333	0	—	-0	-0	-1	-0	-0.1
Total	9	33	54	.379	243	83	16	2	9	761²	750	91	413	495	13.9	4.71	86	.260	.355	28	.145	-5	-65	-56	-9	-7.2

● CARLISLE LITTLEJOHN Littlejohn, Charles Carlisle b: 10/6/01, Irene, Tex. d: 10/27/77, Kansas City, Mo. BR/TR, 5'10", 175 lbs. Deb: 5/11/27

YEAR	TM/L	W	L	PCT	G	GS	CG	SH	SV	IP	H	HR	BB	SO	RAT	ERA	ERA+	OAV	OOB	BH	AVG	PB	PR	/A	PD	TPI
1927	StL-N	3	1	.750	14	2	1	0	0	42	47	4	14	16	13.1	4.50	88	.292	.349	5	.417	2	-3	-3	-1	-0.2
1928	StL-N	2	1	.667	12	2	1	0	0	32	36	2	14	6	14.1	3.66	109	.286	.357	0	.000	-2	1	1	-0	-0.1
Total	2	5	2	.714	26	4	2	0	0	74	83	6	28	22	13.5	4.14	96	.289	.352	5	.217	-0	-2	-1	-1	-0.3

● GREG LITTON Litton, Jon Gregory b: 7/13/64, New Orleans, La. BR/TR, 6', 175 lbs. Deb: 5/2/89 ◆

YEAR	TM/L	W	L	PCT	G	GS	CG	SH	SV	IP	H	HR	BB	SO	RAT	ERA	ERA+	OAV	OOB	BH	AVG	PB	PR	/A	PD	TPI
1991	SF-N	0	0	—	1	0	0	0	0	1	1	0	3	0	36.0	9.00	40	.250	.571	23	.181	0	-1	-1	0	0.0

● BUDDY LIVELY Lively, Everett Adrian "Red" b: 2/14/25, Birmingham, Ala. BR/TR, 6'0.5", 200 lbs. Deb: 4/17/47 F

YEAR	TM/L	W	L	PCT	G	GS	CG	SH	SV	IP	H	HR	BB	SO	RAT	ERA	ERA+	OAV	OOB	BH	AVG	PB	PR	/A	PD	TPI
1947	Cin-N	4	7	.364	38	17	3	1	0	123	126	16	63	52	13.8	4.68	88	.265	.351	6	.188	2	-9	-8	-0	-0.5
1948	Cin-N	0	0	—	10	0	0	0	0	22²	13	0	11	12	9.9	2.38	164	.165	.275	0	.000	-0	4	4	-1	0.1
1949	Cin-N	4	6	.400	31	10	3	1	1	103¹	91	11	53	30	12.5	3.92	107	.245	.339	4	.154	-1	1	3	-1	0.0
Total	3	8	13	.381	79	27	6	2	1	249	230	27	127	94	12.9	4.16	99	.248	.339	10	.167	1	-3	-1	-2	-0.4

● JACK LIVELY Lively, Henry Everett b: 5/29/1885, Joppa, Ala. d: 12/5/67, Arab, Ala. BR/TR, 5'9", 185 lbs. Deb: 4/16/11 F

YEAR	TM/L	W	L	PCT	G	GS	CG	SH	SV	IP	H	HR	BB	SO	RAT	ERA	ERA+	OAV	OOB	BH	AVG	PB	PR	/A	PD	TPI
1911	Det-A	7	5	.583	18	14	10	0	0	113²	143	1	34	45	14.6	4.59	75	.313	.369	11	.256	3	-16	-14	-1	-1.1

● WES LIVENGOOD Livengood, Wesley Amos b: 7/18/10, Salisbury, N.C. d: 9/2/96, Winston-Salem, N.C. BR/TR, 6'2", 172 lbs. Deb: 5/30/39

YEAR	TM/L	W	L	PCT	G	GS	CG	SH	SV	IP	H	HR	BB	SO	RAT	ERA	ERA+	OAV	OOB	BH	AVG	PB	PR	/A	PD	TPI
1939	Cin-N	0	0	—	5	0	0	0	0	9	11	2	9	4	19.6	9.53	40	.360	.429	0	—	-0	-4	-4	0	0.0

● JAKE LIVINGSTONE Livingstone, Jacob M. b: 1/1/1880, St.Petersburg, Russia d: 3/22/49, Wassaic, N.Y. Deb: 9/6/01

YEAR	TM/L	W	L	PCT	G	GS	CG	SH	SV	IP	H	HR	BB	SO	RAT	ERA	ERA+	OAV	OOB	BH	AVG	PB	PR	/A	PD	TPI
1901	NY-N	0	0	—	2	0	0	0	0	12	26	0	7	4	27.0	9.00	37	.433	.514	1	.167	0	-8	-8	-0	0.0

● CLEM LLEWELLYN Llewellyn, Clement Manly "Lew" b: 8/1/1895, Dobson, N.C. d: 11/26/69, Concord, N.C. BL/TR, 6'2", 195 lbs. Deb: 6/18/22

YEAR	TM/L	W	L	PCT	G	GS	CG	SH	SV	IP	H	HR	BB	SO	RAT	ERA	ERA+	OAV	OOB	BH	AVG	PB	PR	/A	PD	TPI
1922	NY-A	0	0	—	1	0	0	0	0	1	1	0	0	1	9.0	0.00	—	.250	.250	0	—	0	0	0	-0	0.0

● GRAEME LLOYD Lloyd, Graeme John b: 4/9/67, Victoria, Australia BL/TL, 6'7", 215 lbs. Deb: 4/11/93

YEAR	TM/L	W	L	PCT	G	GS	CG	SH	SV	IP	H	HR	BB	SO	RAT	ERA	ERA+	OAV	OOB	BH	AVG	PB	PR	/A	PD	TPI
1993	Mil-A	3	4	.429	55	0	0	0	0	63²	64	5	13	31	11.3	2.83	150	.256	.301	0	—	0	11	10	1	1.1
1994	Mil-A	2	3	.400	43	0	0	0	3	47	49	4	15	31	12.8	5.17	97	.269	.335	0	—	0	-2	-1	-0	-0.1
1995	Mil-A	0	5	.000	33	0	0	0	4	32	28	4	8	13	10.1	4.50	111	.246	.295	0	—	0	1	2	0	0.1
1996	Mil-A	2	4	.333	52	0	0	0	0	51	49	3	17	24	11.8	2.82	186	.254	.318	0	—	0	12	14	0	1.1
	*NY-A	0	2	.000	13	0	0	0	0	5²	12	1	5	6	27.0	17.47	29	.429	.515	0	—	0	-8	-8	-0	-2.2
	Yr	2	6	.250	65	0	0	0	0	56²	61	4	22	30	13.2	4.29	122	.274	.339	0	—	0	4	6	-0	-1.1
Total	4	7	18	.280	196	0	0	0	7	199¹	202	17	58	105	12.1	4.06	119	.263	.321	0	—	0	14	17	0	1.1

● ESTEBAN LOAIZA Loaiza, Esteban Antonio Veyna b: 12/31/71, Tijuana, Mexico BR/TR, 6'4", 190 lbs. Deb: 4/29/95

YEAR	TM/L	W	L	PCT	G	GS	CG	SH	SV	IP	H	HR	BB	SO	RAT	ERA	ERA+	OAV	OOB	BH	AVG	PB	PR	/A	PD	TPI
1995	Pit-N	8	9	.471	32	31	1	0	0	172²	205	21	55	85	13.8	5.16	83	.300	.357	10	.192	1	-19	-17	1	-1.3
1996	Pit-N	2	3	.400	10	10	1	1	0	52²	65	11	19	32	14.5	4.96	88	.308	.371	2	.118	-1	-4	-3	1	-0.3
Total	2	10	12	.455	42	41	2	1	0	225¹	270	32	74	117	14.0	5.11	84	.302	.360	12	.174	0	-23	-20	2	-1.6

● HARRY LOCHHEAD Lochhead, Robert Henry b: 3/29/1876, Stockton, Cal. d: 8/22/09, Stockton, Cal. BR/TR, 5'11", 172 lbs. Deb: 4/16/1899 ◆

YEAR	TM/L	W	L	PCT	G	GS	CG	SH	SV	IP	H	HR	BB	SO	RAT	ERA	ERA+	OAV	OOB	BH	AVG	PB	PR	/A	PD	TPI
1899	Cle-N	0	0	—	1	0	0	0	0	3²	4	0	2	0	14.7	0.00	—	.286	.375	129	.238	0	2	2	-0	0.0

● CHUCK LOCKE Locke, Charles Edward b: 5/5/32, Malden, Mo. BR/TR, 5'11", 185 lbs. Deb: 9/16/55

YEAR	TM/L	W	L	PCT	G	GS	CG	SH	SV	IP	H	HR	BB	SO	RAT	ERA	ERA+	OAV	OOB	BH	AVG	PB	PR	/A	PD	TPI
1955	Bal-A	0	0	—	2	0	0	0	0	3	0	0	1	1	3.0	0.00	—	.000	.100	0	—	0	1	1	0	0.0

● BOBBY LOCKE Locke, Lawrence Donald b: 3/3/34, Rowes Run, Pa. BR/TR, 5'11", 185 lbs. Deb: 6/18/59

YEAR	TM/L	W	L	PCT	G	GS	CG	SH	SV	IP	H	HR	BB	SO	RAT	ERA	ERA+	OAV	OOB	BH	AVG	PB	PR	/A	PD	TPI
1959	Cle-A	3	2	.600	24	7	0	0	2	77²	66	6	41	40	12.7	3.13	118	.233	.336	8	.333	3	6	5	0	0.7
1960	Cle-A	3	5	.375	32	11	2	2	2	123	121	10	37	53	11.7	3.37	111	.255	.311	9	.237	3	7	5	2	0.8
1961	Cle-A	4	4	.500	37	4	0	0	2	95¹	112	12	40	37	14.5	4.53	87	.300	.371	4	.211	0	-5	-6	1	-0.4
1962	StL-N	0	0	—	1	0	0	0	0	2	1	0	2	1	13.5	0.00	—	.143	.333	0	—	1	0	0	-0	0.0
	Phi-N	1	0	1.000	5	0	0	0	0	15²	16	4	10	9	14.9	5.74	67	.262	.366	2	.286	-0	-3	-3	1	-0.1
	Yr	1	0	1.000	6	0	0	0	0	17²	17	4	12	10	14.8	5.09	77	.250	.363	2	.286	0	-2	-2	1	-0.1
1963	Phi-N	0	0	—	9	0	0	0	0	10²	10	0	5	7	12.7	5.91	55	.244	.326	0	.000	-0	-3	-3	-0	-0.1
1964	Phi-N	0	0	—	8	0	0	0	0	19¹	21	2	6	11	12.6	2.79	124	.276	.329	0	.000	-0	2	1	0	0.0
1965	Cin-N	0	1	.000	11	0	0	0	0	17¹	20	3	6	14	14.5	5.71	66	.299	.373	0	.000	-0	-4	-4	-1	-0.1
1967	Cal-A	3	0	1.000	9	1	0	0	2	19¹	14	1	3	7	8.4	2.33	135	.203	.247	2	.667	1	2	2	0	0.5
1968	Cal-A	2	3	.400	29	0	0	0	0	36¹	51	3	13	21	16.1	6.44	45	.331	.387	0	.000	-0	-14	-14	-1	-2.2
Total	9	16	15	.516	165	23	2	2	10	416²	432	40	165	194	13.1	4.02	91	.269	.340	25	.255	8	-12	-17	4	-0.8

● RON LOCKE Locke, Ronald Thomas b: 4/4/42, Wakefield, R.I. BR/TL, 5'11", 168 lbs. Deb: 4/23/64

YEAR	TM/L	W	L	PCT	G	GS	CG	SH	SV	IP	H	HR	BB	SO	RAT	ERA	ERA+	OAV	OOB	BH	AVG	PB	PR	/A	PD	TPI
1964	NY-N	1	2	.333	25	3	0	0	0	41¹	46	3	22	17	15.0	3.48	103	.289	.379	0	.000	-0	0	0	-0	0.0

● BOB LOCKER Locker, Robert Awtry b: 3/15/38, George, Iowa BB/TR, 6'3", 200 lbs. Deb: 4/14/65

YEAR	TM/L	W	L	PCT	G	GS	CG	SH	SV	IP	H	HR	BB	SO	RAT	ERA	ERA+	OAV	OOB	BH	AVG	PB	PR	/A	PD	TPI
1965	Chi-A	5	2	.714	51	0	0	0	2	91¹	71	6	30	69	10.1	3.15	101	.216	.285	0	.000	-2	3	0	3	0.2
1966	Chi-A	9	8	.529	56	0	0	0	12	95	73	2	23	70	9.6	2.46	129	.206	.264	4	.250	1	10	7	3	2.0
1967	Chi-A	7	5	.583	77	0	0	0	20	124²	102	5	23	80	9.7	2.09	148	.222	.274	0	.000	-1	16	14	5	2.3
1968	Chi-A	5	4	.556	70	0	0	0	10	90¹	78	4	27	62	10.6	2.29	132	.234	.293	0	.000	-1	7	7	2	1.2
1969	Chi-A	2	3	.400	17	0	0	0	4	22	26	6	15	13	13.1	6.55	59	.292	.337	0	.000	-0	-7	-7	-0	-1.6
	Sea-A	3	3	.500	51	0	0	0	6	78¹	69	3	26	46	11.3	2.18	166	.234	.302	1	.083	-0	13	13	2	1.3
	Yr	5	6	.455	68	0	0	0	10	100¹	95	9	32	61	11.7	3.14	117	.247	.310	1	.077	-1	5	6	2	-0.3
1970	Mil-A	0	1	.000	28	0	0	0	6	31²	37	1	10	19	14.8	3.41	111	.306	.382	0	.000	-0	1	1	-0	0.0
	Oak-A	3	3	.500	38	0	0	0	4	56¹	49	1	19	33	11.0	2.88	123	.232	.299	1	.167	-0	5	4	1	0.5
	Yr	3	4	.429	66	0	0	0	10	88	86	2	29	52	11.9	3.07	118	.254	.315	1	.143	-0	6	5	0	0.5
1971	*Oak-A	7	2	.778	47	0	0	0	6	72¹	68	3	19	46	10.9	2.86	116	.249	.300	0	.000	-0	7	6	-1	0.2
1972	*Oak-A	6	1	.857	56	0	0	0	10	78	69	1	16	47	10.0	2.65	107	.235	.280	0	.000	-1	4	4	-1	0.2
1973	Chi-N	10	6	.625	63	0	0	0	18	106¹	96	6	42	76	12.0	2.54	155	.244	.323	1	.067	-0	13	17	2	3.1
1975	Chi-N	0	1	.000	22	0	0	0	0	32²	38	3	16	14	15.4	4.96	77	.306	.394	0	.000	-0	-4	-4	-1	-0.1
Total	10	57	39	.594	576	0	0	0	95	879	776	41	257	577	10.9	2.75	122	.237	.300	7	.074	-4	64	58	18	9.7

● SKIP LOCKWOOD Lockwood, Claude Edward b: 8/17/46, Boston, Mass. BR/TR, 6', 190 lbs. Deb: 4/23/65 ◆

YEAR	TM/L	W	L	PCT	G	GS	CG	SH	SV	IP	H	HR	BB	SO	RAT	ERA	ERA+	OAV	OOB	BH	AVG	PB	PR	/A	PD	TPI
1969	Sea-A	0	1	.000	6	3	0	0	0	23	24	3	6	10	11.7	3.52	103	.279	.326	0	.000	-1	0	0	0	0.0
1970	Mil-A	5	12	.294	27	26	3	1	0	173²	173	22	79	93	13.4	4.30	88	.266	.351	12	.226	2	-11	-10	-1	-0.8
1971	Mil-A	10	15	.400	33	32	9	1	0	208	191	19	91	115	12.4	3.33	104	.246	.329	5	.081	-1	3	-3	-0	-0.1
1972	Mil-A	8	15	.348	29	27	5	3	0	170	148	11	71	106	11.8	3.60	84	.232	.313	7	.132	-1	-10	-11	-3	-1.8
1973	Mil-A	5	12	.294	37	15	3	0	0	154²	164	10	59	87	13.3	3.90	96	.280	.352	0	—	-0	-1	-2	-3	-0.7
1974	Cal-A	2	5	.286	37	2	0	0	2	81¹	81	8	32	39	13.1	4.32	80	.264	.343	0	—	-0	-6	-8	-0	-0.7
1975	NY-N	1	3	.250	24	2	0	0	2	48¹	28	3	25	61	10.1	1.49	232	.174	.289	1	.167	-0	11	11	-1	0.9
1976	NY-N	10	7	.588	56	0	0	0	19	94	87	3	34	108	9.3	2.67	123	.186	.266	6	.333	3	9	7	0	1.7
1977	NY-N	4	8	.333	63	0	0	0	20	104	87	5	31	84	10.6	3.38	111	.227	.291	0	.000	-0	6	4	-2	0.4
1978	NY-N	7	13	.350	57	0	0	0	15	90²	78	10	48	73	10.8	3.57	98	.236	.302	2	.182	1	0	-1	-2	-0.3
1979	NY-N	2	5	.286	27	0	0	0	0	42¹	33	3	14	42	10.0	1.49	245	.224	.292	0	.000	-0	11	10	-1	2.0

YEAR	TM/L	W	L	PCT	G	GS	CG	SH	SV	IP	H	HR	BB	SO	RAT	ERA	ERA+	OAV	OOB	BH	AVG	PB	PR	/A	PD	TPI
1980	Bos-A	3	1	.750	24	1	0	0	2	45²	61	4	17	11	15.4	5.32	79	.321	.377	0	—	0	-7	-6	-1	-0.6
Total	12	57	97	.370	420	106	16	5	68	1236	1130	98	490	829	12.0	3.55	99	.246	.323	40	.154	3	4	-3	-13	0.5

● **MILO LOCKWOOD** Lockwood, Milo Hathaway b: 4/7/1858, Solon, Ohio d: 10/9/1897, Economy, Pa. 5'10", 160 lbs. Deb: 4/17/1884 ♦

| 1884 | Was-U | 1 | 9 | .100 | 11 | 10 | 6 | 0 | 0 | 67² | 99 | 4 | 15 | 48 | 15.2 | 7.45 | 32 | .319 | .351 | 14 | .209 | -2 | -38 | -38 | 1 | -3.8 |

● **BILLY LOES** Loes, William b: 12/13/29, Long Island City, N.Y. BR/TR, 6'1", 170 lbs. Deb: 5/18/50

1950	Bro-N	0	0	—	10	0	0	0	0	12²	16	5	5	2	14.9	7.82	52	.314	.375	0	.000	0	-5	-5	-0	0.0
1952	*Bro-N	13	8	.619	39	21	8	4	1	187¹	154	12	71	115	11.0	2.69	135	.224	.299	5	.093	-3	22	20	-0	1.8
1953	*Bro-N	14	8	.636	32	25	9	1	0	162²	165	21	53	75	12.2	4.54	84	.261	.322	7	.125	-2	-5	-5	3	-0.5
1954	Bro-N	13	5	.722	28	21	6	0	0	147²	154	14	60	97	13.1	4.14	99	.269	.339	6	.118	-2	-1	-1	-1	-0.4
1955	*Bro-N	10	4	.714	22	19	6	0	0	128	116	16	46	85	11.5	3.59	113	.240	.308	4	.091	-3	6	7	-0	0.4
1956	Bro-N	0	1	.000	1	1	0	0	0	1¹	5	1	1	2	40.5	40.50	10	.556	.600	0	—	0	-5	-5	-0	-1.6
	Bal-A	2	7	.222	21	6	1	0	3	56²	65	4	23	22	14.3	4.76	82	.291	.363	3	.176	-1	-4	-5	1	-0.8
1957	Bal-A★	12	7	.632	31	18	8	3	4	155¹	142	8	37	86	10.6	3.24	111	.245	.295	9	.080	-3	9	6	2	0.6
1958	Bal-A	3	9	.250	32	10	1	0	5	114	106	10	44	44	12.5	3.63	99	.252	.334	2	.067	-2	2	-0	-0	-0.3
1959	Bal-A	4	7	.364	37	0	0	0	14	64¹	58	5	25	34	12.0	4.06	93	.239	.317	1	.125	-0	-1	-2	1	-0.3
1960	SF-N	3	2	.600	37	0	0	0	5	45²	40	9	17	28	12.0	4.93	71	.247	.333	1	.250	-0	-6	-7	1	-0.8
1961	SF-N	6	5	.545	26	18	3	1	0	114²	114	13	39	55	12.4	4.24	90	.258	.325	5	.156	-0	-3	-5	-0	-0.5
Total	11	80	63	.559	316	139	42	9	32	1190¹	1135	118	421	645	12.0	3.89	99	.252	.321	38	.110	-17	9	-5	6	-2.4

● **FRANK LOFTUS** Loftus, Francis Patrick b: 3/10/1898, Scranton, Pa. d: 10/27/80, Belchertown, Mass. BR/TR, 5'9", 190 lbs. Deb: 9/26/26

| 1926 | Was-A | 0 | 0 | — | 1 | 0 | 0 | 0 | 0 | 1 | 3 | 0 | 2 | 0 | 45.0 | 9.00 | 43 | .600 | .714 | 0 | — | 0 | -1 | -1 | -0 | 0.0 |

● **BOB LOGAN** Logan, Robert Dean "Lefty" b: 2/10/10, Thompson, Neb. d: 5/20/78, Indianapolis, Ind. BR/TL, 5'10", 170 lbs. Deb: 4/18/35

1935	Bro-N	0	1	.000	2	0	0	0	0	2²	2	0	1	1	10.1	3.38	118	.182	.250		—	0	0	0	0	0.1
1937	Det-A	0	0	—	1	0	0	0	0	0²	1	0	1	0	27.0	0.00	—	.333	.500		—	0	0	0	0	0.0
	Chi-N	0	0	—	4	0	0	0	0	6¹	6	0	4	2	14.2	1.42	280	.261	.370	0	.000	-0	2	2	-0	0.0
1938	Chi-N	0	2	.000	14	0	0	0	2	22²	18	0	17	10	14.3	2.78	138	.222	.364	0	.000	-0	3	3	-0	0.2
1941	Cin-N	0	1	.000	3	0	0	0	0	3¹	5	0	5	0	27.0	8.10	44	.333	.500		—	0	-2	-2	-0	-0.4
1945	Bos-N	7	11	.389	34	25	5	1	1	187	213	9	53	53	12.9	3.18	121	.283	.331	13	.213	-1	13	14	0	1.4
Total	5	7	15	.318	57	25	5	1	4	222²	245	9	81	67	13.3	3.15	122	.277	.339	13	.200	1	16	17	0	1.3

● **BILL LOHRMAN** Lohrman, William Le Roy b: 5/22/13, Brooklyn, N.Y. BR/TR, 6'1", 185 lbs. Deb: 6/19/34

1934	Phi-N	0	1	.000	4	0	0	0	0	6	5	0	1	2	9.0	4.50	105	.217	.250	1	.500	0	-0	0	0	0.1
1937	NY-N	1	0	1.000	2	1	1	0	1	10	5	0	2	3	6.3	0.90	432	.152	.200	0	.000	-0	3	3	0	0.4
1938	NY-N	9	6	.600	31	14	3	0	0	152	152	9	33	52	11.1	3.32	114	.253	.294	4	.082	-4	8	8	2	0.5
1939	NY-N	12	13	.480	38	24	9	1	1	185²	200	15	45	70	12.0	4.07	96	.282	.327	14	.233	4	-3	-3	0	0.0
1940	NY-N	10	15	.400	31	28	11	4	1	195	200	19	43	73	11.4	3.78	103	.264	.306	8	.123	-2	1	2	2	0.2
1941	NY-N	9	10	.474	33	20	6	2	3	159	184	7	40	61	12.7	4.02	92	.286	.327	11	.229	4	-7	-6	-0	-0.3
1942	StL-N	1	1	.500	5	0	0	0	0	12²	11	0	2	6	9.2	1.42	241	.244	.277	2	.667	1	3	3	0	0.5
	NY-N	13	4	.765	26	19	12	2	0	158	143	11	33	41	10.1	2.56	131	.240	.282	7	.121	-3	13	14	1	1.1
	Yr	14	5	.737	31	19	12	2	0	170²	154	11	35	47	10.1	2.48	136	.240	.281	9	.148	-2	16	17	1	1.6
1943	NY-N	5	6	.455	17	12	3	0	1	80¹	110	7	25	16	15.3	5.15	67	.324	.374	1	.037	-3	-16	-15	-1	-2.3
	Bro-N	0	2	.000	6	2	2	0	0	27²	29	2	10	5	13.0	3.58	94	.274	.342	1	.143	0	-1	-1	-0	0.0
	Yr	5	8	.385	23	14	5	0	1	108	139	9	35	21	14.6	4.75	72	.311	.362	2	.059	-3	-16	-16	-1	-2.3
1944	Bro-N	0	0	—	3	0	0	0	0	2²	4	0	4	1	27.0	0.00	—	.500	.667	0	—	0	1	1	-0	0.0
	Cin-N	0	1	.000	2	1	0	0	0	1²	5	0	2	0	37.8	27.00	13	.500	.583	0	—	0	-4	-4	-0	-1.6
	Yr	0	1	.000	5	1	0	0	0	4¹	9	0	6	1	31.2	10.38	34	.500	.625	0	—	0	-3	-3	-0	-1.6
Total	9	60	59	.504	198	121	47	9	8	990²	1048	70	240	330	11.8	3.69	101	.271	.315	49	.153	-3	-1	2	3	-1.4

● **RICH LOISELLE** Loiselle, Richard Frank b: 1/12/72, Neenah, Wis. BR/TR, 6'5", 225 lbs. Deb: 9/7/96

| 1996 | Pit-N | 1 | 0 | 1.000 | 5 | 3 | 0 | 0 | 0 | 20² | 22 | 3 | 8 | 9 | 13.1 | 3.05 | 144 | .268 | .333 | 2 | .250 | 1 | 3 | 3 | 0 | 0.2 |

● **MICKEY LOLICH** Lolich, Michael Stephen b: 9/12/40, Portland, Ore. BB/TL, 6', 210 lbs. Deb: 5/12/63

1963	Det-A	5	9	.357	33	18	4	0	0	144¹	145	13	56	103	12.8	3.55	105	.265	.338	2	.056	-1	1	3	-1	0.2
1964	Det-A	18	9	.667	44	33	12	6	2	232	196	26	64	192	10.3	3.26	112	.225	.282	7	.109	1	9	10	-2	1.0
1965	Det-A	15	9	.625	43	37	7	3	3	243²	216	23	72	226	11.1	3.44	101	.236	.301	5	.058	-6	1	1	-2	-0.7
1966	Det-A	14	14	.500	40	33	5	1	3	203²	204	24	83	173	12.9	4.77	73	.257	.331	9	.141	1	-30	-29	-3	-4.0
1967	Det-A	14	13	.519	31	30	11	**6**	0	204	165	14	56	174	10.1	3.04	107	.221	.282	12	.197	3	4	5	-2	0.7
1968	*Det-A	17	9	.654	39	32	8	4	1	220	178	26	65	197	10.4	3.19	94	.219	.286	8	.114	-0	-5	-4	-2	-0.8
1969	Det-A☆	19	11	.633	37	36	15	1	1	280²	214	22	122	271	11.2	3.14	119	.210	.304	8	.088	-3	15	18	-0	1.6
1970	Det-A	14	19	.424	40	39	13	3	0	272²	272	27	109	230	12.7	3.80	98	.260	.333	11	.134	1	-2	-2	1	0.0
1971	Det-A★	**25**	14	.641	45	45	**29**	4	0	**376**	336	36	92	**308**	10.4	2.92	123	.237	.287	15	.130	1	23	28	-4	2.6
1972	*Det-A★	22	14	.611	41	41	23	4	0	327¹	282	29	74	250	10.1	2.50	126	.234	.284	6	.067	-0	20	23	-4	2.2
1973	Det-A	16	15	.516	42	42	17	3	0	308²	315	35	79	214	11.6	3.82	107	.266	.315	0	—	0	-9	-9	-1	0.7
1974	Det-A	16	21	.432	41	41	27	3	0	308	310	38	78	202	11.4	4.15	92	.268	.316	1	—	-2	-18	-12	-4	-1.7
1975	Det-A	12	18	.400	32	32	19	1	0	240²	260	19	64	139	12.1	3.78	106	.279	.325	0	—	-0	-6	2	-2	0.5
1976	NY-N	8	13	.381	31	30	5	2	0	192²	184	14	52	120	11.0	3.22	102	.252	.302	7	.130	2	-2	-1	0	0.1
1978	SD-N	2	1	.667	20	2	0	0	1	34²	30	0	11	13	10.9	1.56	214	.240	.307	0	.000	-0	8	7	-0	0.6
1979	SD-N	0	2	.000	20	0	0	0	0	42¹	47	1	19	14	13.8	4.74	74	.304	.375	0	.000	-0	-6	-7	-0	-0.3
Total	16	217	191	.532	586	496	195	41	11	3638¹	3366	347	1099	2832	11.3	3.44	104	.246	.306	90	.110	-4	25	58	-25	2.7

● **TIM LOLLAR** Lollar, William Timothy b: 3/17/56, Poplar Bluff, Mo. BL/TL, 6'3", 200 lbs. Deb: 6/28/80

1980	NY-A	1	0	1.000	14	1	0	0	2	32¹	33	3	20	13	14.8	3.34	117	.280	.384	0	—	0	2	2	0	0.1
1981	SD-N	2	8	.200	24	11	0	0	0	76²	87	4	51	38	16.6	6.10	53	.293	.402	3	.167	-1	-22	-24	2	-2.6
1982	SD-N	16	9	.640	34	34	4	2	0	232²	192	20	87	150	10.9	3.13	109	.224	.298	21	.247	9	12	8	0	1.8
1983	SD-N	7	12	.368	30	30	1	0	0	175²	170	22	85	135	13.3	4.61	76	.258	.347	14	.241	6	-19	-22	-2	-1.8
1984	*SD-N	11	13	.458	31	31	3	2	0	195²	168	18	105	131	12.6	3.91	91	.234	.333	15	.221	7	-7	-7	-2	-0.4
1985	Chi-N	5	3	.375	18	13	0	0	0	83	83	8	58	61	15.4	4.66	93	.266	.383	0	—	0	-5	-3	-0	-0.3
	Bos-A	5	5	.500	16	10	1	0	0	67	57	9	40	44	13.2	4.57	94	.230	.339	0	.000	0	-3	-2	-1	-0.4
	Yr	8	10	.444	34	23	1	0	1	150	140	19	98	105	14.3	4.62	93	.248	.360	0	.000	0	-8	-5	-1	-0.7
1986	Bos-A	2	0	1.000	32	1	0	0	0	43	51	7	34	28	18.4	6.91	60	.304	.429	1	1.000	0	-13	-13	1	-0.4
Total	7	47	52	.475	199	131	9	4	4	906	841	93	480	600	13.3	4.27	85	.249	.345	54	.234	24	-55	-63	-3	-4.0

● **VIC LOMBARDI** Lombardi, Victor Alvin b: 9/20/22, Reedley, Cal. BL/TL, 5'7", 158 lbs. Deb: 4/18/45

1945	Bro-N	10	11	.476	38	24	9	0	4	203²	195	11	86	64	12.6	3.31	113	.252	.331	13	.183	-1	11	10	-1	0.9
1946	Bro-N	13	10	.565	41	25	13	2	3	193	170	10	84	60	11.9	2.89	117	.235	.316	14	.230	2	11	10	0	1.4
1947	*Bro-N	12	11	.522	33	20	7	3	3	174²	156	12	65	72	11.5	2.99	138	.241	.312	16	.242	-2	21	22	1	3.0
1948	Pit-N	10	9	.526	38	17	9	0	4	163	156	14	67	64	12.4	3.70	110	.255	.330	10	.208	1	5	7	1	0.9
1949	Pit-N	5	5	.500	34	12	4	0	0	134	149	14	64	64	14.8	4.57	92	.286	.372	17	.347	5	-8	-5	1	0.3
1950	Pit-N	0	5	.000	39	2	0	0	2	76¹	93	14	48	26	16.9	6.60	66	.310	.409	4	.250	1	-21	-19	0	-1.0
Total	6	50	51	.495	223	100	42	5	16	944²	919	70	418	340	12.9	3.68	106	.257	.337	74	.238	10	19	25	3	5.5

● **LOU LOMBARDO** Lombardo, Louis b: 11/18/28, Carlstadt, N.J. BL/TL, 6'2", 210 lbs. Deb: 9/22/48

| 1948 | NY-N | 0 | 0 | — | 2 | 0 | 0 | 0 | 0 | 5¹ | 5 | 1 | 5 | 0 | 18.6 | 6.75 | 58 | .250 | .423 | 0 | .000 | -0 | -2 | -2 | 0 | 0.0 |

● **KEVIN LOMON** Lomon, Kevin Dale b: 11/20/71, Fort Smith, Ark. BR/TR, 6'1", 195 lbs. Deb: 4/27/95

1995	NY-N	0	1	.000	6	0	0	0	0	9¹	17	0	5	4	21.2	6.75	60	.405	.468		—	0	-1	-0	-0	-0.3
1996	Atl-N	0	0	—	6	0	0	0	0	7¹	7	0	3	3	13.5	4.91	90	.259	.355	0	—	0	-1	-0	1	0.0
Total	2	0	1	.000	12	0	0	0	0	16²	24	0	8	7	17.8	5.94	71	.348	.423	0	—	0	-3	-3	0	-0.3

YEAR	TM/L	W	L	PCT	G	GS	CG	SH	SV	IP	H	HR	BB	SO	RAT	ERA	ERA+	OAV	OOB	BH	AVG	PB	PR	/A	PD	TPI

● JIM LONBORG   Lonborg, James Reynold   b: 4/16/42, Santa Maria, Cal.   BR/TR, 6′5″, 210 lbs.   Deb: 4/23/65

1965	Bos-A	9	17	.346	32	31	7	1	0	185¹	193	20	65	113	12.7	4.47	83	.262	.324	8	.136	0	-21	-15	-2	-2.1
1966	Bos-A	10	10	.500	45	23	3	1	2	181²	173	16	55	131	11.6	3.86	98	.249	.310	5	.093	-2	-9	-1	-1	-0.4
1967	*Bos-A☆	**22**	9	.710	39	39	15	2	0	273¹	228	23	83	**246**	10.9	3.16	110	.225	.296	14	.141	-1	2	10	-2	0.7
1968	Bos-A	6	10	.375	23	17	4	1	0	113¹	89	11	59	73	12.6	4.29	74	.216	.330	11	.282	3	-16	-14	-2	-1.8
1969	Bos-A	7	11	.389	29	23	4	0	0	143²	148	15	65	100	13.8	4.51	84	.270	.355	4	.098	-1	-14	-11	-0	-1.4
1970	Bos-A	4	1	.800	9	4	0	0	0	34	33	3	9	21	11.1	3.18	125	.260	.309	4	.444	2	2	3	-0	0.7
1971	Bos-A	10	7	.588	27	26	5	1	0	167²	167	15	67	100	13.3	4.13	89	.259	.342	9	.170	0	-13	-8	1	-0.7
1972	Mil-A	14	12	.538	33	30	11	2	1	223	197	17	76	143	11.5	2.83	107	.238	.311	10	.145	-1	6	5	-2	0.3
1973	Phi-N	13	16	.448	38	30	6	0	0	191¹	218	25	80	106	13.9	4.88	78	.279	.353	8	.136	-1	-27	-24	-1	-3.2
1974	Phi-N	17	13	.567	39	39	16	3	0	283	280	22	70	121	11.3	3.21	118	.261	.310	9	.096	-4	13	18	-4	1.0
1975	Phi-N	8	6	.571	27	26	6	2	0	159¹	161	12	45	72	11.9	4.12	90	.257	.312	1	.023	-3	-9	-7	-0	-0.8
1976	*Phi-N	18	10	.643	33	32	8	1	1	222	210	18	50	118	10.7	3.08	115	.249	.294	11	.164	1	10	11	-3	1.2
1977	*Phi-N	11	4	.733	25	25	4	1	0	157²	157	15	50	76	12.1	4.11	97	.261	.323	5	.104	-2	-4	-2	-1	-0.5
1978	Phi-N	8	10	.444	22	22	1	0	0	113²	132	16	45	48	14.2	5.23	68	.293	.359	6	.176	1	-21	-21	-0	-2.9
1979	Phi-N	0	1	.000	4	1	0	0	0	7¹	14	3	4	7	23.3	11.05	35	.389	.463	0	.000	-0	-6	-6	-0	-0.7
Total	15	157	137	.534	425	368	90	15	4	2464¹	2400	233	823	1475	12.2	3.86	94	.255	.322	105	.136	-5	-106	-63	-18	-10.6

● LEP LONG   Long, Lester   b: 7/12/1888, Summit, N.J.   d: 10/21/58, Birmingham, Ala.   BR/TR, 5′10″, 153 lbs.   Deb: 6/29/11

1911	Phi-A	0	0	—	4	0	0	0	0	8	15	0	5	4	22.5	4.50	70	.405	.476	0	.000	-0	-1	-1	0	0.0

● RED LONG   Long, Nelson   b: 9/28/1876, Burlington, Ont., Canada   d: 8/11/29, Hamilton, Ont., Can   BR/TR, 6′1″, 190 lbs.   Deb: 9/11/02

1902	Bos-N	0	0	—	1	1	0	0	0	8	4	0	3	5	9.0	1.13	251	.148	.258	0	.000	-0	1	2	-0	0.0

● BOB LONG   Long, Robert Earl   b: 11/11/54, Jasper, Tenn.   BR/TR, 6′3″, 178 lbs.   Deb: 9/2/81

1981	Pit-N	1	2	.333	5	3	0	0	0	19²	23	2	10	8	15.1	5.95	60	.299	.379	0	.000	-0	-5	-5	-1	-0.8
1985	Sea-A	0	0	—	28	0	0	0	0	38¹	30	7	17	29	11.5	3.76	112	.210	.302	0	—	0	2	2	-0	0.0
Total	2	1	2	.333	33	3	0	0	0	58	53	9	27	37	12.7	4.50	89	.241	.329	0	.000	-0	-4	-3	-1	-0.8

● TOM LONG   Long, Thomas Francis "Little Hawk"   b: 4/22/1898, Memphis, Tenn.   d: 9/16/73, Louisville, Ky.   BL/TL, 5′9″, 154 lbs.   Deb: 4/26/24

1924	Bro-N	0	0	—	1	0	0	0	0	2	2	0	2	0	18.0	9.00	42	.333	.500	0	—	0	-1	-1	-0	0.0

● BILL LONG   Long, William Douglas   b: 2/29/60, Cincinnati, Ohio   BR/TR, 6′, 185 lbs.   Deb: 7/21/85

1985	Chi-A	0	1	.000	4	3	0	0	0	14	25	4	5	13	19.3	10.29	42	.391	.435	0	—	0	-10	-9	0	-0.5
1987	Chi-A	8	8	.500	29	23	5	2	1	169	179	20	28	72	11.2	4.37	105	.272	.304	0	—	0	2	4	0	0.2
1988	Chi-A	8	11	.421	47	18	3	0	2	174	187	14	43	77	12.1	4.03	98	.280	.327	0	—	0	-1	-1	-0	-0.1
1989	Chi-A	5	5	.500	30	8	0	0	1	98²	101	8	37	51	13.0	3.92	97	.265	.336	0	—	0	-0	-1	-0	-0.0
1990	Chi-A	0	1	.000	4	0	0	0	0	5²	6	2	2	2	12.7	6.35	60	.261	.320	0	—	0	-2	-2	-0	-0.2
	Chi-N	6	1	.857	42	0	0	0	5	55²	66	8	21	32	14.2	4.37	93	.301	.365	0	.000	-0	-4	-4	-0	-0.2
1991	Mon-N	0	0	—	3	0	0	0	0	1²	4	0	4	0	43.2	10.80	33	.500	.667	0	—	0	-1	-1	-0	0.0
Total	6	27	27	.500	159	52	8	2	9	518²	568	63	140	247	12.5	4.37	95	.281	.331	0	.000	-0	-16	-13	1	-0.8

● BRIAN LOONEY   Looney, Brian James   b: 9/26/69, New Haven, Conn.   BL/TL, 5′10″, 180 lbs.   Deb: 9/26/93

1993	Mon-N	0	0	—	3	1	0	0	0	6	8	0	2	7	15.0	3.00	139	.308	.357	0	.000	-0	1	1	0	0.0
1994	Mon-N	0	0	—	1	0	0	0	0	2	4	1	2	4	22.5	22.50	19	.400	.455	0	—	0	-4	-4	-0	0.0
1995	Bos-A	0	1	.000	3	1	0	0	0	4²	12	1	4	2	30.9	17.36	28	.545	.615	0	—	0	-7	-6	-0	-1.1
Total	3	0	1	.000	7	2	0	0	0	12²	24	2	6	11	22.0	11.37	39	.414	.477	0	.000	-0	-10	-10	-0	-1.1

● PETE LOOS   Loos, Ivan   b: 3/23/1878, Philadelphia, Pa.   d: 2/23/56, Darby, Pa.   TR,   Deb: 5/2/01

1901	Phi-A	0	1	.000	1	1	0	0	0	1	2	0	4	0	54.0	27.00	14	.400	.667	0	—	0	-3	-3	0	-1.2

● ED LOPAT   Lopat, Edmund Walter (b: Edmund Walter Lopatynski)   b: 6/21/18, New York, N.Y.   d: 6/15/92, Darien, Conn.   BL/TL, 5′10″, 185 lbs.   Deb: 4/30/44   MC

1944	Chi-A	11	10	.524	27	25	13	1	0	210	217	12	59	75	11.9	3.26	105	.265	.316	25	.309	6	4	4	1	1.2
1945	Chi-A	10	13	.435	26	24	17	1	1	199¹	226	8	56	74	13.0	4.11	81	.285	.336	24	.293	-3	-16	-17	-1	-1.4
1946	Chi-A	13	13	.500	29	29	20	2	0	231	216	18	48	89	10.3	2.73	125	.248	.288	22	.253	6	20	18	1	2.8
1947	Chi-A	16	13	.552	31	31	22	3	0	252²	241	17	73	109	11.3	2.81	130	.253	.307	19	.198	-0	25	24	-1	2.6
1948	NY-A	17	11	.607	33	31	13	3	0	226²	246	16	66	83	12.5	3.65	112	.284	.336	14	.173	-1	16	11	2	1.2
1949	*NY-A	15	10	.600	31	30	14	4	1	215¹	222	19	69	70	12.4	3.26	124	.269	.330	20	.263	7	22	19	0	2.7
1950	*NY-A	18	8	.692	35	32	15	3	1	236¹	244	19	65	70	12.3	3.47	124	.266	.317	19	.232	8	29	22	1	2.9
1951	*NY-A★	21	9	.700	31	31	20	4	0	234²	209	21	71	93	**10.9**	2.91	131	.239	**.298**	15	.179	1	31	24	2	3.0
1952	*NY-A	10	5	.667	20	19	10	2	0	149¹	127	11	53	56	11.1	2.53	131	.234	.307	9	.173	1	19	13	0	1.4
1953	*NY-A	16	4	**.800**	25	24	9	3	0	178¹	169	13	32	50	10.3	**2.42**	**152**	.250	.288	12	.190	1	31	25	1	2.9
1954	NY-A	12	4	.750	26	23	7	0	0	170	189	14	33	54	12.1	3.55	97	.288	.328	1	.018	-5	3	-2	-1	-0.8
1955	NY-A	4	8	.333	16	12	3	1	0	86²	101	12	16	24	12.3	3.74	100	.294	.328	4	.138	-1	2	0	-1	-0.2
	Bal-A	3	4	.429	10	7	1	0	0	49	57	8	9	10	12.7	4.22	90	.294	.335	3	.176	0	-1	-2	-1	-0.2
	Yr	7	12	.368	26	19	4	1	0	135²	158	20	25	34	12.3	3.91	96	.293	.328	7	.152	-1	1	-2	-1	-0.4
Total	12	166	112	.597	340	318	164	27	3	2439¹	2464	179	650	859	11.6	3.21	116	.264	.315	187	.211	29	186	138	4	18.1

● ART LOPATKA   Lopatka, Arthur Joseph   b: 5/28/19, Chicago, Ill.   BB/TL, 5′10″, 170 lbs.   Deb: 9/12/45

1945	StL-N	1	0	1.000	4	1	1	0	0	11²	7	0	3	5	8.5	1.54	243	.159	.229	1	.250	-0	3	3	-0	0.2
1946	Phi-N	0	1	.000	4	1	0	0	0	5¹	13	1	4	4	28.7	16.88	20	.448	.515	0	—	0	-8	-8	-0	-1.2
Total	2	1	1	.500	8	2	1	0	0	17	20	1	7	9	14.8	6.35	57	.274	.346	1	.250	0	-5	-5	-0	-1.0

● ALBIE LOPEZ   Lopez, Albert Anthony   b: 8/18/71, Mesa, Ariz.   BR/TR, 6′1″, 205 lbs.   Deb: 7/6/93

1993	Cle-A	3	1	.750	9	9	0	0	0	49²	49	7	32	25	14.9	5.98	72	.262	.373	0	—	0	-9	-9	-0	-0.6
1994	Cle-A	1	2	.333	4	4	1	1	0	17	20	3	6	18	14.3	4.24	111	.290	.355	0	—	0	1	1	-0	0.1
1995	Cle-A	0	0	—	6	2	0	0	0	23	17	4	7	22	9.8	3.13	150	.205	.275	0	—	0	4	4	-0	-0.1
1996	Cle-A	5	4	.556	13	10	0	0	0	62	80	14	22	45	15.1	6.39	77	.311	.370	0	—	0	-10	-10	-0	-1.2
Total	4	9	7	.563	32	25	1	1	0	151²	166	28	67	110	14.5	5.52	84	.279	.356	0	—	0	-14	-14	-0	-1.8

● AURELIO LOPEZ   Lopez, Aurelio Alejandro (Rios)   b: 9/21/48, Tecamachalco, Mexico   d: 9/22/92, Matehuala, Mex.   BR/TR, 6′, 220 lbs.   Deb: 9/1/74

1974	KC-A	0	0	—	16	0	0	0	0	16	21	0	10	5	17.4	5.63	68	.344	.437	0	—	0	-4	-3	-0	0.0
1978	StL-N	4	2	.667	25	4	0	0	0	65	52	4	32	46	11.8	4.29	82	.218	.313	3	.214	-0	-5	-6	-1	-0.6
1979	Det-A	10	5	.667	61	0	0	0	21	127	95	12	51	106	10.6	2.41	179	.210	.294	0	—	0	25	27	-0	3.7
1980	Det-A	13	6	.684	67	1	0	0	21	124	125	9	45	97	12.6	3.77	109	.263	.330	0	—	0	4	5	-1	0.7
1981	Det-A	5	2	.714	29	3	0	0	3	81²	70	8	31	53	11.4	3.64	104	.233	.309	0	—	0	3	4	-0	0.1
1982	Det-A	3	1	.750	19	0	0	0	3	41	41	8	19	26	13.2	5.27	77	.268	.349	0	—	0	-5	-5	-0	-0.6
1983	Det-A☆	9	8	.529	57	0	0	0	18	115¹	87	12	49	90	10.7	2.81	139	.210	.295	0	—	0	16	14	-1	2.5
1984	*Det-A	10	1	.909	71	0	0	0	14	137²	109	16	52	94	10.7	2.94	133	.221	.298	0	—	0	16	15	-2	1.3
1985	Det-A	3	7	.300	51	0	0	0	5	86¹	96	11	33	59	13.3	4.80	85	.285	.335	0	—	0	-6	-7	-0	-0.8
1986	*Hou-N	3	3	.500	45	0	0	0	7	78	64	6	25	44	10.3	3.46	104	.221	.283	0	.000	-1	-2	-2	-0	-0.2
1987	Hou-N	2	1	.667	26	0	0	0	2	38	39	6	20	21	12.6	4.50	87	.273	.338	0	.000	-0	-2	-2	-0	-0.2
Total	11	62	36	.633	459	9	0	0	93	910	785	102	367	635	11.5	3.56	111	.234	.313	3	.125	-1	41	39	-8	5.9

● RAMON LOPEZ   Lopez, Jose Ramon (Hevia)   b: 5/26/33, Las Villas, Cuba   d: 9/4/82, Miami, Fla.   BR/TR, 6′, 175 lbs.   Deb: 8/21/66

1966	Cal-A	0	0	—	4	1	0	0	0	7	4	1	4	5	10.3	3.86	85	.154	.267	0	—	0	-1	-1	-0	-0.2

● MARCELINO LOPEZ   Lopez, Marcelino Pons   b: 9/23/43, Havana, Cuba   BR/TL, 6′3″, 210 lbs.   Deb: 4/14/63

1963	Phi-N	1	0	1.000	4	2	0	0	0	9	7	2	9	7	22.5	6.00	54	.333	.484	0	.000	-0	-2	-2	-0	-0.3
1965	Cal-A	14	13	.519	35	32	8	1	1	215¹	185	12	82	122	11.3	2.93	116	.230	.305	14	.203	3	13	11	4	2.3
1966	Cal-A	7	14	.333	37	32	6	2	1	199	188	20	68	132	12.0	3.93	85	.251	.321	11	.190	2	-11	-13	2	-1.0
1967	Cal-A	0	2	.000	9	9	1	1	0	9	11	1	4	6	20.0	9.00	35	.324	.465	1	.500	0	-6	-6	-0	-1.1

YEAR	TM/L	W	L	PCT	G	GS	CG	SH	SV	IP	H	HR	BB	SO	RAT	ERA	ERA+	OAV	OOB	BH	AVG	PB	PR	/A	PD	TPI
	Bal-A	1	0	1.000	4	4	0	0	0	17²	15	1	10	15	12.7	2.55	124	.227	.329	0	.000	-0	1	1	-1	0.0
	Yr	1	2	.333	8	7	0	0	0	26²	26	2	19	21	15.2	4.73	67	.257	.375	1	.143	-0	-4	-5	-1	-1.1
1969	*Bal-A	5	3	.625	27	4	0	0	0	69¹	65	3	34	57	13.1	4.41	81	.252	.344	3	.214	1	-6	-7	-1	-0.7
1970	*Bal-A	1	1	.500	25	3	0	0	0	60²	47	2	37	49	12.5	2.08	176	.217	.331	1	.077	0	11	11	-1	0.2
1971	Mil-A	2	7	.222	31	11	0	0	0	67²	64	5	60	42	16.5	4.66	75	.251	.394	1	.059	-1	-9	-9	-1	-1.2
1972	Cle-A	0	0	—	4	2	0	0	0	8¹	8	0	10	1	19.4	5.40	60	.276	.462	0	.000	-0	-2	-2	0	0.0
Total 8		31	40	.437	171	93	14	3	2	653	591	44	317	426	12.7	3.62	94	.243	.334	31	.171	4	-11	-15	4	-1.8

● **BRIS LORD**   Lord, Bristol Robotham "The Human Eyeball" b: 9/21/1883, Upland, Pa. d: 11/13/64, Annapolis, Md. BR/TR, 5'9", 185 lbs. Deb: 4/21/05 ♦

YEAR	TM/L	W	L	PCT	G	GS	CG	SH	SV	IP	H	HR	BB	SO	RAT	ERA	ERA+	OAV	OOB	BH	AVG	PB	PR	/A	PD	TPI
1907	Phi-A	0	0	—	1	0	0	0	0	1	3	0	0	0	27.0	9.00	29	.500	.500	31	.182	0	-1	-1	-0	0.0

● **LEFTY LORENZEN**   Lorenzen, Adolph Andreas b: 1/12/1893, Davenport, Iowa d: 3/5/63, Davenport, Iowa BL/TL, 5'10", 164 lbs. Deb: 9/12/13

1913	Det-A	0	0	—	1	0	0	0	0	2	4	0	3	0	31.5	18.00	16	.667	.778	1	.500	0	-3	-3	1	0.1

● **ANDREW LORRAINE**   Lorraine, Andrew Jason b: 8/11/72, Los Angeles, Cal. BL/TL, 6'3", 195 lbs. Deb: 7/17/94

1994	Cal-A	0	2	.000	4	3	0	0	0	18²	30	7	11	10	19.8	10.61	46	.366	.441	0	—	0	-12	-12	0	-1.0
1995	Chi-A	0	0	—	5	0	0	0	0	8	3	0	2	5	9.8	3.38	132	.111	.200	0	—	0	1	1	-0	0.0
Total 2		0	2	.000	9	3	0	0	0	26²	33	7	13	15	15.9	8.44	56	.303	.382	0	—	0	-11	-11	0	-1.0

● **JOE LOTZ**   Lotz, Joseph Peter "Smokey" b: 1/2/1891, Remsen, Iowa d: 1/1/71, Castro Valley, Cal. BR/TR, 5'8.5", 175 lbs. Deb: 7/15/16

1916	StL-N	0	3	.000	12	3	1	0	0	40	31	1	17	18	11.0	4.27	62	.225	.314	4	.333	1	-7	-7	-1	-0.5

● **ART LOUDELL**   Loudell, Arthur (b: Arthur Laudel) b: 4/10/1882, Latham, Mo. d: 2/19/61, Kansas City, Mo. BR/TR, 5'11", 173 lbs. Deb: 8/13/10

1910	Det-A	1	1	.500	5	2	1	0	0	21¹	22	0	12	12	15.6	3.38	78	.284	.389	1	.143	-0	-2	-1	-1	-0.3

● **LARRY LOUGHLIN**   Loughlin, Larry John b: 8/16/41, Tacoma, Wash. BL/TL, 6'1", 190 lbs. Deb: 5/27/67

1967	Phi-N	0	0	—	3	0	0	0	0	5¹	9	1	4	5	21.9	15.19	22	.375	.464	1	1.000	1	-7	-7	-0	0.1

● **DON LOUN**   Loun, Donald Nelson b: 11/9/40, Frederick, Md. BR/TL, 6'2", 185 lbs. Deb: 9/23/64

1964	Was-A	1	1	.500	2	2	1	0	0	13	13	0	3	3	11.1	2.08	178	.250	.291	0	.000	-0	2	2	0	0.4

● **SLIM LOVE**   Love, Edward Haughton b: 8/1/1890, Love, Miss. d: 11/30/42, Memphis, Tenn. BL/TL, 6'7", 195 lbs. Deb: 9/8/13

1913	Was-A	1	0	1.000	5	1	0	0	1	16²	14	0	6	5	10.8	1.62	182	.226	.294	1	.200	0	2	2	-1	0.1
1916	NY-A	2	0	1.000	20	1	0	0	0	47²	46	2	23	21	13.0	4.91	59	.274	.361	0	—	-2	-11	-11	-0	-0.6
1917	NY-A	6	5	.545	33	9	2	0	1	130¹	115	0	57	82	11.9	2.35	114	.251	.335	6	.167	-1	5	5	-2	0.1
1918	NY-A	13	12	.520	38	29	13	1	1	228²	207	3	116	95	13.1	3.07	92	.253	.353	17	.230	2	-7	-6	-5	-0.9
1919	Det-A	6	4	.600	22	8	4	0	0	89²	92	3	40	46	13.9	3.01	106	.275	.363	6	.222	0	-2	-2	0	0.0
1920	Det-A	0	0	—	1	0	0	0	0	4¹	6	0	4	2	20.8	8.31	45	.375	.500	0	—	-0	-2	-2	0	0.0
Total 6		28	21	.571	119	48	19	1	4	517¹	480	8	246	251	12.9	3.04	94	.259	.351	30	.192	-0	-11	-10	-9	-1.3

● **VANCE LOVELACE**   Lovelace, Vance Odell b: 8/9/63, Tampa, Fla. BL/TL, 6'5", 205 lbs. Deb: 9/10/88

1988	Cal-A	0	0	—	3	0	0	0	0	1¹	2	1	3	0	33.8	13.50	29	.400	.625	0	—	0	-1	-1	0	0.1
1989	Cal-A	0	0	—	1	0	0	0	0	1	0	0	1	0	9.0	0.00	—	.000	.250	0	—	0	0	0	0	0.1
1990	Sea-A	0	0	—	5	0	0	0	0	2¹	3	0	6	1	38.6	3.86	103	.300	.588	0	—	0	0	0	-0	0.0
Total 3		0	0	—	9	0	0	0	0	4²	5	1	10	2	30.9	5.79	67	.278	.552	0	—	0	-1	-1	-0	0.2

● **LYNN LOVENGUTH**   Lovenguth, Lynn Richard b: 11/29/22, Camden, N.Y. BL/TR, 5'10.5", 170 lbs. Deb: 4/18/55

1955	Phi-N	0	1	.000	14	0	0	0	0	18	17	1	10	14	14.5	4.50	88	.258	.372	0	.000	-0	-1	-1	0	-0.1
1957	StL-N	0	1	.000	9	0	0	0	0	9	6	0	6	6	12.0	2.00	198	.182	.308	0	.000	0	2	2	-0	0.1
Total 2		0	2	.000	16	1	0	0	0	27	23	1	16	20	13.7	3.67	108	.232	.350	0	.000	-1	1	1	-1	0.0

● **JOHN LOVETT**   Lovett, John b: 5/6/1877, Monday, Ohio d: 12/5/37, Murray City, Ohio Deb: 5/22/03

1903	StL-N	0	0	—	3	1	0	0	0	5	6	0	5	3	21.6	5.40	60	.300	.462	1	.333	0	-1	-1	-0	0.0

● **LEN LOVETT**   Lovett, Leonard Walker b: 7/17/1852, Lancaster Co., Pa d: 11/18/22, Newark, Del. BR/TR, Deb: 8/4/1873 ♦

1873	Res-n	0	1	.000	1	1	1	0	0	9	22	0	1	1	23.0	7.00	48	.400	.411	2	.400	0	-4	-4		-0.2

● **TOM LOVETT**   Lovett, Thomas Joseph b: 12/7/1863, Providence, R.I. d: 3/19/28, Providence, R.I. BR, 5'8", 162 lbs. Deb: 6/4/1885

1885	Phi-a	7	8	.467	16	16	15	1	0	138²	130	3	38	56	11.2	3.70	93	.236	.291	19	.224	-0	-7	-4	-1	-0.5
1889	*Bro-a	17	10	.630	29	28	23	1	0	229	234	3	65	92	12.1	4.32	86	.256	.311	19	.190	-1	-12	-15	-0	-1.5
1890	*Bro-N	30	11	**.732**	44	41	39	4	0	372	327	14	141	124	11.7	2.78	124	.229	.306	33	.201	0	33	27	1	2.3
1891	Bro-N	23	19	.548	44	43	39	3	0	365²	361	14	129	129	12.6	3.69	90	.248	.306	25	.163	-5	-14	-16	-2	-2.0
1893	Bro-N	3	5	.375	14	8	6	0	0	96	134	2	35	15	16.4	6.56	67	.321	.381	9	.180	-2	-20	-23	-1	-1.6
1894	Bos-N	8	6	.571	15	13	10	0	0	104	155	12	36	23	16.8	5.97	95	.341	.394	7	.143	-5	-7	-3	-1	-0.8
Total 6		88	59	.599	162	149	132	9	1	1305¹	1341	48	444	439	12.7	3.94	94	.257	.322	106	.185	-13	-28	-34	-5	-4.1

● **PETE LOVRICH**   Lovrich, Peter b: 10/16/42, Blue Island, Ill. BR/TR, 6'4", 200 lbs. Deb: 4/26/63

1963	KC-A	1	1	.500	20	1	0	0	0	20²	25	5	10	16	15.7	7.84	50	.291	.371	0	—	0	-10	-9	-0	-0.9

● **GROVER LOWDERMILK**   Lowdermilk, Grover Cleveland "Slim" b: 1/15/1885, Sandborn, Ind. d: 3/31/68, Odin, Ill. BR/TR, 6'4", 190 lbs. Deb: 7/3/09 F

1909	StL-N	0	2	.000	7	1	0	0	0	29	28	0	30	14	18.9	6.21	41	.292	.473	1	.100	-0	-12	-12	0	-0.8
1911	StL-N	0	1	.000	11	2	1	1	0	33¹	37	3	33	15	19.4	7.29	46	.301	.456	1	.111	-1	-14	-14	0	-0.4
1912	Chi-N	0	1	.000	2	1	1	0	0	13	17	1	14	8	21.5	9.69	34	.304	.443	0	—	-1	-9	-9	-0	-0.6
1915	StL-A	9	17	.346	38	29	14	1	0	222²	183	0	133	130	13.4	3.12	92	.234	.357	9	.125	-3	-4	-6	-1	-1.0
	Det-A	4	1	.800	7	5	0	0	0	28	17	0	24	18	13.5	4.18	73	.185	.359	1	.125	0	-4	-4	-0	-0.6
	Yr	13	18	.419	45	34	14	1	0	250²	200	0	157	148	13.5	3.24	89	.225	.342	10	.125	-3	-8	-10	-1	-1.6
1916	Det-A	0	0	—	1	0	0	0	0	0¹	1	0	0	1	81.0	0.00	—	.000	.750	0	—	0	0	0	0	0.0
	Cle-A	1	5	.167	10	5	2	0	0	51¹	52	0	45	28	17.5	3.16	95	.277	.424	3	.167	-0	-2	-1	0	-0.1
	Yr	1	5	.167	11	5	2	0	0	51²	52	0	48	29	17.9	3.14	96	.257	.429	3	.167	-0	-2	-1	0	-0.1
1917	StL-A	2	1	.667	3	2	1	0	0	19	16	0	4	9	9.5	1.42	183	.225	.267	0	.000	-1	3	2	0	0.1
1918	StL-A	2	6	.250	13	11	4	0	0	80	74	0	38	25	12.9	3.15	87	.255	.347	7	.250	-1	-3	-4	2	0.1
1919	StL-A	0	0	—	7	0	0	0	0	12	6	0	4	6	11.3	0.75	442	.176	.349	0	.000	-0	3	3	0	0.2
	*Chi-A	5	5	.500	20	11	5	0	0	96²	95	0	43	43	13.2	2.79	114	.268	.353	3	.088	-3	5	4	1	0.2
	Yr	5	5	.500	27	11	5	0	0	108²	101	0	47	49	12.6	2.57	125	.256	.342	3	.086	-4	8	7	1	0.4
1920	Chi-A	0	0	—	3	0	0	0	0	5¹	5	0	4	5	23.6	6.75	56	.409	.519	0	—	0	-1	-1	0	0.0
Total 9		23	39	.371	122	73	30	3	0	590¹	534	4	376	296	14.4	3.58	82	.253	.375	25	.131	-8	-40	-41	5	-2.9

● **LOU LOWDERMILK**   Lowdermilk, Louis Bailey b: 2/23/1887, Sandborn, Ind. d: 12/27/75, Centralia, Ill. BR/TL, 6'1", 180 lbs. Deb: 4/20/11 F

1911	StL-N	3	4	.429	16	3	0	0	0	65	72	0	29	20	14.7	3.46	98	.304	.391	2	.111	-1	-0	-1	-2	-0.3
1912	StL-N	1	1	.500	4	1	0	0	1	15	14	0	9	2	15.0	3.00	114	.246	.348	1	.200	0	1	1	0	0.1
Total 2		4	5	.444	20	4	0	0	1	80	86	0	38	22	14.5	3.37	100	.293	.383	3	.136	-1	0	-0	-2	-0.2

● **GEORGE LOWE**   Lowe, George Wesley "Doc" b: 4/25/1895, Ridgefield Park, N.J. d: 9/2/81, Somers Point, N.J. BR/TR, 6'2", 180 lbs. Deb: 7/28/20

1920	Cin-N	0	0	—	1	0	0	0	0	2	1	0	0	0	9.0	0.00	—	.167	.286	0	—	0	1	1	0	0.0

● **BOBBY LOWE**   Lowe, Robert Lincoln "Link" b: 7/10/1868, Pittsburgh, Pa. d: 12/8/51, Detroit, Mich. BR/TR, 5'10", 150 lbs. Deb: 4/19/1890 M ♦

1891	Bos-N	0	0	—	1	0	0	0	0	1	3	0	1	0	36.0	9.00	41	.500	.571	129	.260	-0	-1	-1	-0	0.0

● **TURK LOWN**   Lown, Omar Joseph b: 5/30/24, Brooklyn, N.Y. BR/TR, 6'1", 185 lbs. Deb: 4/24/51

1951	Chi-N	4	9	.308	31	18	3	0	0	127	125	14	90	39	15.3	5.46	75	.260	.378	8	.205	1	-21	-19	0	-1.6
1952	Chi-N	4	11	.267	33	19	5	0	0	156²	154	13	93	73	14.4	4.37	88	.257	.370	1	.140	-1	-9	-1	0	-0.7
1953	Chi-N	8	7	.533	49	12	2	0	3	148¹	166	20	84	76	15.3	5.16	86	.282	.373	6	.125	-2	-14	-12	2	-1.0
1954	Chi-N	0	2	.000	15	0	0	0	0	22	23	1	15	16	15.5	6.14	68	.261	.369	0	—	0	-5	-5	1	-0.3

YEAR TM/L	W	L	PCT	G	GS	CG	SH	SV	IP	H	HR	BB	SO	RAT	ERA	ERA+	OAV	OOB	BH	AVG	PB	PR	/A	PD	TPI
1956 Chi-N	9	8	.529	61	0	0	0	13	110²	95	10	78	74	14.2	3.58	105	.240	.366	5	.217	2	2	2	-1	0.6
1957 Chi-N	5	7	.417	**67**	0	0	0	12	93	74	10	51	51	12.1	3.77	103	.221	.324	2	.200	0	1	1	2	0.3
1958 Chi-N	0	0	—	4	0	0	0	0	4	2	0	3	4	11.3	4.50	87	.154	.313	0	—	-0	-0	-0	-0	0.0
Cin-N	0	2	.000	11	0	0	0	0	11²	12	2	12	9	18.5	5.40	77	.273	.429	0	.000	-0	-2	-2	-0	-0.3
Yr	0	2	.000	15	0	0	0	0	15²	14	2	15	13	16.7	5.17	79	.246	.403	0	—	-2	-2	-0	-0	-0.3
Chi-A	3	3	.500	27	0	0	0	8	40²	49	1	28	40	17.0	3.98	91	.308	.412	3	.333	1	-1	-2	0	-0.2
1959 *Chi-A	9	2	.818	60	0	0	0	**15**	93¹	73	12	42	63	11.3	2.89	130	.215	.305	3	.250	1	10	9	1	1.4
1960 Chi-A	2	3	.400	45	0	0	0	5	67¹	60	6	34	39	12.6	3.88	98	.239	.330	1	.200	1	-0	-1	0	0.0
1961 Chi-A	7	5	.583	59	0	0	0	11	101	87	13	35	50	10.9	2.76	142	.238	.304	0	.000	-2	14	13	-1	1.5
1962 Chi-A	4	2	.667	42	0	0	0	6	56¹	58	3	25	40	13.4	3.04	129	.269	.347	0	.000	-0	6	5	1	0.8
Total 11	55	61	.474	504	49	10	1	73	1032	978	105	590	574	13.8	4.12	96	.252	.352	35	.164	1	-21	-18	7	0.5

● **SAM LOWRY**   Lowry, Samuel Joseph b: 3/25/20, Philadelphia, Pa. d: 12/1/92, Philadelphia, Pa. BR/TR, 5'11", 170 lbs. Deb: 9/19/42

YEAR TM/L	W	L	PCT	G	GS	CG	SH	SV	IP	H	HR	BB	SO	RAT	ERA	ERA+	OAV	OOB	BH	AVG	PB	PR	/A	PD	TPI
1942 Phi-A	0	0	—	1	0	0	0	0	3	3	0	1	0	12.0	6.00	63	.250	.308	0	.000	-0	-1	-1	0	0.0
1943 Phi-A	0	0	—	5	0	0	0	0	18	18	1	9	3	13.5	5.00	68	.269	.355	1	.167	-0	-3	-3	0	0.0
Total 2	0	0	—	6	0	0	0	0	21	21	1	10	3	13.3	5.14	67	.266	.348	1	.143	-0	-4	-4	0	0.0

● **MIKE LOYND**   Loynd, Michael Wallace b: 3/26/64, St.Louis, Mo. BR/TR, 6'4", 210 lbs. Deb: 7/24/86

YEAR TM/L	W	L	PCT	G	GS	CG	SH	SV	IP	H	HR	BB	SO	RAT	ERA	ERA+	OAV	OOB	BH	AVG	PB	PR	/A	PD	TPI
1986 Tex-A	2	2	.500	9	8	0	0	1	42	49	4	19	33	15.0	5.36	80	.290	.368	0	—	0	-6	-5	0	-0.5
1987 Tex-A	1	5	.167	26	8	0	0	1	69¹	82	14	38	48	15.7	6.10	73	.287	.372	0	—	0	-13	-13	-1	-1.0
Total 2	3	7	.300	35	16	0	0	2	111¹	131	18	57	81	15.4	5.82	76	.288	.371	0	—	0	-18	-17	-1	-1.5

● **PAT LUBY**   Luby, John Perkins b: 6/1869, Charleston, S.C. d: 4/24/1899, Charleston, S.C. TR, 6', 185 lbs. Deb: 6/16/1890

YEAR TM/L	W	L	PCT	G	GS	CG	SH	SV	IP	H	HR	BB	SO	RAT	ERA	ERA+	OAV	OOB	BH	AVG	PB	PR	/A	PD	TPI
1890 Chi-N	20	9	.690	34	31	26	0	1	267²	226	6	95	85	11.3	3.19	115	.222	.298	31	.267	8	11	14	-2	1.7
1891 Chi-N	8	11	.421	30	24	18	0	1	206	221	11	94	52	14.6	4.76	70	.264	.352	24	.245	7	-32	-33	-0	-1.8
1892 Chi-N	11	16	.407	31	27	24	1	0	252¹	248	10	103	68	12.9	3.07	108	.247	.323	31	.190	1	6	7	1	0.8
1895 Lou-N	1	5	.167	11	6	5	0	0	71¹	115	5	19	12	17.8	6.81	68	.357	.405	15	.283	3	-16	-17	1	-0.7
Total 4	40	41	.494	106	88	73	1	2	797¹	810	32	311	217	13.2	3.88	92	.254	.331	101	.235	18	-31	-29	-1	0.0

● **RED LUCAS**   Lucas, Charles Frederick "The Nashville Narcissus" b: 4/28/02, Columbia, Tenn. d: 7/9/86, Nashville, Tenn. BL/TR, 5'9.5", 170 lbs. Deb: 4/19/23 ♦

YEAR TM/L	W	L	PCT	G	GS	CG	SH	SV	IP	H	HR	BB	SO	RAT	ERA	ERA+	OAV	OOB	BH	AVG	PB	PR	/A	PD	TPI
1923 NY-N	0	0	—	3	0	0	0	1	5¹	9	0	4	3	21.9	0.00	—	.346	.433	0	.000	-0	2	2	1	0.1
1924 Bos-N	1	4	.200	27	4	1	0	0	83²	112	5	18	30	14.6	5.16	74	.332	.377	11	.333	2	-12	-12	1	-0.4
1926 Cin-N	8	5	.615	39	11	7	1	2	154	161	6	30	34	11.3	3.68	100	.277	.314	23	.303	6	-2	-0	-1	0.9
1927 Cin-N	18	11	.621	37	23	19	4	2	239²	231	6	39	51	10.1	3.38	112	.256	.287	47	.313	7	14	11	-1	2.3
1928 Cin-N	13	9	.591	27	19	13	**4**	1	167¹	164	9	42	35	11.1	3.39	117	.258	.304	23	.315	6	11	11	-0	1.9
1929 Cin-N	19	12	.613	32	32	**28**	2	0	270	267	14	58	72	**10.9**	3.60	127	**.257**	**.297**	41	.293	11	33	29	4	4.0
1930 Cin-N	14	16	.467	33	28	18	1	1	210²	270	15	44	53	13.5	5.38	90	.315	.349	38	.336	15	-10	-13	-3	-0.3
1931 Cin-N	14	13	.519	29	29	**24**	3	0	238	261	10	39	56	11.3	3.59	104	.280	.309	43	.281	11	7	4	1	1.6
1932 Cin-N	13	17	.433	31	31	**28**	0	0	269¹	261	10	35	63	9.9	2.94	131	.249	.274	43	.287	13	28	27	-0	4.4
1933 Cin-N	10	16	.385	29	29	21	3	0	219²	248	13	40	81	11.0	3.40	100	.289	.305	35	.287	12	-2	-0	0	1.4
1934 Pit-N	10	9	.526	29	21	12	1	0	172²	198	14	40	44	12.5	4.38	94	.283	.324	23	.219	3	-6	-5	-3	-0.5
1935 Pit-N	8	6	.571	20	19	8	2	0	125²	136	10	23	29	11.5	3.44	119	.272	.307	21	.318	8	8	9	-1	1.6
1936 Pit-N	15	4	.789	27	22	12	0	0	175²	178	7	26	53	10.6	3.18	128	.257	.287	26	.241	4	16	17	-1	2.0
1937 Pit-N	8	10	.444	20	20	9	1	0	126¹	150	12	23	20	12.4	4.27	90	.302	.322	22	.268	5	-5	-6	-2	-0.4
1938 Pit-N	6	3	.667	13	13	4	0	0	84	90	5	16	19	11.5	3.54	107	.283	.319	5	.109	-2	2	2	-1	-0.1
Total 15	157	135	.538	396	301	204	22	7	2542	2736	136	455	602	11.4	3.72	107	.275	.308	404	.281	98	92	77	-9	18.5

● **GARY LUCAS**   Lucas, Gary Paul b: 11/8/54, Riverside, Cal. BL/TL, 6'5", 200 lbs. Deb: 4/16/80

YEAR TM/L	W	L	PCT	G	GS	CG	SH	SV	IP	H	HR	BB	SO	RAT	ERA	ERA+	OAV	OOB	BH	AVG	PB	PR	/A	PD	TPI
1980 SD-N	5	8	.385	46	18	0	0	3	150	138	6	43	85	10.9	3.24	106	.250	.306	6	.171	-0	6	3	1	0.3
1981 SD-N	7	7	.500	**57**	0	0	0	13	90	78	1	36	53	11.7	2.00	163	.247	.330	1	.100	-1	**15**	13	0	2.3
1982 SD-N	1	10	.091	65	0	0	0	16	97¹	89	5	29	64	11.0	3.24	106	.245	.303	0	.000	-1	4	2	1	0.8
1983 SD-N	5	8	.385	62	0	0	0	17	91	85	9	34	60	11.8	2.87	122	.245	.312	0	.000	-1	8	6	-1	0.8
1984 Mon-N	0	3	.000	55	0	0	0	8	53	54	4	20	42	12.6	2.72	126	.267	.333	0	.000	-1	5	4	2	0.5
1985 Mon-N	6	2	.750	49	0	0	0	1	67²	63	6	24	31	11.6	3.19	106	.251	.316	0	.000	-1	3	1	-0	0.1
1986 *Cal-A	4	1	.800	27	0	0	0	2	45²	45	1	6	31	10.1	3.15	130	.253	.277	0	—	0	5	5	1	0.6
1987 Cal-A	1	5	.167	48	0	0	0	3	74¹	66	7	35	44	12.5	3.63	106	.241	.331	0	—	0	7	6	1	0.5
Total 8	29	44	.397	409	18	0	0	63	669	618	41	227	410	11.5	3.01	118	.249	.314	7	.087	-4	53	40	4	5.3

● **RAY LUCAS**   Lucas, Ray Wesley "Luke" b: 10/2/08, Springfield, Ohio d: 10/9/69, Harrison, Mich. BR/TR, 6'2", 175 lbs. Deb: 9/28/29

YEAR TM/L	W	L	PCT	G	GS	CG	SH	SV	IP	H	HR	BB	SO	RAT	ERA	ERA+	OAV	OOB	BH	AVG	PB	PR	/A	PD	TPI
1929 NY-N	0	0	—	3	0	0	0	1	8	3	0	1	1	6.8	0.00	—	.111	.200	1	.500	0	4	4	0	0.2
1930 NY-N	0	0	—	6	0	0	0	0	10¹	9	2	10	1	17.4	6.97	68	.265	.444	0	.000	-0	-2	-3	1	0.0
1931 NY-N	0	0	—	1	0	0	0	0	2	1	1	1	0		4.50	82	.143	.250		—	-0	-0	-0	0	0.0
1933 Bro-N	0	0	—	2	0	0	0	0	5	6	0	4	0	19.8	7.20	45	.316	.458	0	—	-0	-2	-2	0	0.0
1934 Bro-N	1	1	.500	10	2	0	0	0	30²	39	2	14	3	16.4	6.75	58	.328	.412	2	.333	1	-9	-10	1	-0.3
Total 5	1	1	.500	22	2	0	0	1	56	58	5	32	5	15.3	5.79	71	.282	.391	3	.333	1	-10	-11	2	-0.1

● **JOE LUCEY**   Lucey, Joseph Earl "Scootch" b: 3/27/1897, Holyoke, Mass. d: 7/30/80, Holyoke, Mass. BR/TR, 6', 168 lbs. Deb: 7/6/20 ♦

YEAR TM/L	W	L	PCT	G	GS	CG	SH	SV	IP	H	HR	BB	SO	RAT	ERA	ERA+	OAV	OOB	BH	AVG	PB	PR	/A	PD	TPI
1925 Bos-A	0	1	.000	7	2	0	0	0	11	18	0	14	2	26.2	9.00	50	.360	.500	2	.133	-1	-6	-5	1	-0.4

● **CON LUCID**   Lucid, Cornelius Cecil b: 2/24/1874, Dublin, Ireland d: 6/25/31, Houston, Tex. 5'7", 170 lbs. Deb: 5/1/1893

YEAR TM/L	W	L	PCT	G	GS	CG	SH	SV	IP	H	HR	BB	SO	RAT	ERA	ERA+	OAV	OOB	BH	AVG	PB	PR	/A	PD	TPI
1893 Lou-N	0	1	.000	2	1	0	0	0	6	10	0	10	0	31.5	15.00	29	.357	.538	1	.333	0	-7	-7	-0	-0.7
1894 Bro-N	5	3	.625	10	9	7	0	0	71¹	87	6	44	15	17.7	6.56	75	.298	.406	7	.212	-2	-10	-13	-2	-1.3
1895 Bro-N	10	7	.588	21	19	12	2	0	137	164	4	72	24	16.0	5.52	80	.292	.380	13	.245	2	-11	-17	-1	-1.4
Phi-N	6	3	.667	10	10	7	1	0	69²	80	3	35	19	16.0	5.94	81	.284	.380	10	.345	4	-9	-9	-2	-0.7
Yr	16	10	.615	31	29	19	3	0	206²	244	7	107	43	15.7	5.66	80	.287	.373	23	.280	6	-20	-26	-2	-2.1
1896 Phi-N	1	4	.200	5	5	5	0	0	42	75	2	17	3	20.1	8.36	52	.383	.437	2	.125	-2	-19	-19	-1	-1.7
1897 StL-N	1	5	.167	6	6	5	0	0	49	66	0	26	4	16.9	3.67	120	.319	.395	3	.176	-2	3	4	1	0.4
Total 5	23	23	.500	54	50	36	3	2	375	482	15	204	65	17.1	6.02	76	.308	.397	36	.238	-5	-52	-60	-5	-5.4

● **LOU LUCIER**   Lucier, Louis Joseph b: 3/23/18, Northbridge, Mass. BR/TR, 5'8", 160 lbs. Deb: 4/23/43

YEAR TM/L	W	L	PCT	G	GS	CG	SH	SV	IP	H	HR	BB	SO	RAT	ERA	ERA+	OAV	OOB	BH	AVG	PB	PR	/A	PD	TPI
1943 Bos-A	3	4	.429	16	9	3	0	0	74	94	1	33	23	15.7	3.89	85	.322	.394	4	.200	0	-5	-5	3	-0.1
1944 Bos-A	0	0	—	2	0	0	0	0	5¹	7	0	7	2	23.6	5.06	67	.292	.452	0	.000	-0	-1	-1	-0	0.0
Phi-N	0	0	—	1	0	0	0	0	2	3	0	2	1	22.5	13.50	27	.333	.455	0	—	0	-2	-2	-0	0.0
1945 Phi-N	0	1	.000	13	0	0	0	1	20¹	14	1	5	5	8.4	2.21	173	.194	.247	1	.250	0	1	1	1	0.3
Total 3	3	5	.375	33	9	3	0	1	101²	118	2	47	31	14.8	3.81	90	.297	.374	5	.200	0	-4	-4	4	0.3

● **WILLIE LUDOLPH**   Ludolph, William Francis "Wee Willie" b: 1/21/1900, San Francisco, Cal d: 4/8/52, Oakland, Cal. BR/TR, 6'1.5", 170 lbs. Deb: 5/28/24

YEAR TM/L	W	L	PCT	G	GS	CG	SH	SV	IP	H	HR	BB	SO	RAT	ERA	ERA+	OAV	OOB	BH	AVG	PB	PR	/A	PD	TPI
1924 Det-A	0	0	—	3	0	0	0	0	5²	5	0	2	1	12.7	4.76	86	.250	.348	0	.000	-0	-0	-0	0	0.0

● **ERIC LUDWICK**   Ludwick, Eric David b: 12/14/71, Whiteman Afb, Mo. BR/TR, 6'5", 210 lbs. Deb: 9/1/96

YEAR TM/L	W	L	PCT	G	GS	CG	SH	SV	IP	H	HR	BB	SO	RAT	ERA	ERA+	OAV	OOB	BH	AVG	PB	PR	/A	PD	TPI
1996 StL-N	0	1	.000	6	1	0	0	0	10	11	4	3	12	13.5	9.00	47	.275	.341	0	.000	-0	-5	-5	-0	-0.5

● **STEVE LUEBBER**   Luebber, Stephen Lee b: 7/9/49, Clinton, Mo. BR/TR, 6'3", 195 lbs. Deb: 6/27/71

YEAR TM/L	W	L	PCT	G	GS	CG	SH	SV	IP	H	HR	BB	SO	RAT	ERA	ERA+	OAV	OOB	BH	AVG	PB	PR	/A	PD	TPI
1971 Min-A	2	5	.286	18	12	0	0	1	68	73	7	37	35	15.1	5.03	71	.278	.375	1	.053	-2	-12	-11	0	-1.3
1972 Min-A	0	0	—	2	0	0	0	0	2¹	3	0	2	1	19.3	0.00	—	.333	.455	0	—	0	1	1	0	0.0
1976 Min-A	4	5	.444	38	12	2	1	2	119¹	109	9	62	45	13.0	4.00	89	.248	.342	0	—	0	-6	-6	-1	-0.6
1979 Tor-A	0	0	—	1	0	0	0	0	1	1	0	1	0	18.0	∞	—	1.000	1.000	0	—	-0	-1	-1	0	-0.1
1981 Bal-A	0	0	—	7	0	0	0	0	16²	26	3	4	12	16.7	7.56	48	.366	.408	0	—	-0	-7	-7	0	-0.3
Total 5	6	10	.375	66	24	2	1	3	206¹	213	19	106	93	14.2	4.62	77	.271	.362	1	.053	-2	-26	-24	-1	-2.0

YEAR	TM/L	W	L	PCT	G	GS	CG	SH	SV	IP	H	HR	BB	SO	RAT	ERA	ERA+	OAV	OOB	BH	AVG	PB	PR	/A	PD	TPI

● **LARRY LUEBBERS**   Luebbers, Larry Christopher   b: 10/11/69, Cincinnati, Ohio   BR/TR, 6'6", 190 lbs.   Deb: 7/3/93

1993	Cin-N	2	5	.286	14	14	0	0	0	77¹	74	7	38	38	13.2	4.54	89	.261	.350	6	.250	1	-4	-4	-1	-0.3

● **DICK LUEBKE**   Luebke, Richard Raymond   b: 4/8/35, Chicago, Ill.   d: 12/4/74, San Diego, Cal.   BR/TL, 6'4", 200 lbs.   Deb: 8/11/62

1962	Bal-A	1	0	1.000	10	0	0	0	0	13¹	12	0	6	12	12.2	2.70	137	.250	.333	0	—	0	2	1	-0	0.1

● **RICK LUECKEN**   Luecken, Richard Fred   b: 11/15/60, McAllen, Tex.   BR/TR, 6'6", 210 lbs.   Deb: 6/6/89

1989	KC-A	2	1	.667	19	0	0	0	1	23²	23	3	13	16	13.7	3.42	112	.258	.353	0	—	1	1	1	-0	0.1
1990	Atl-N	1	4	.200	36	0	0	0	1	53	73	5	30	35	18.0	5.77	70	.336	.424	1	.333	1	-12	-10	0	-0.9
	Tor-A	0	0	—	1	0	0	0	0	1	2	1	1	0	27.0	9.00	44	.500	.600	0	—	0	-1	-1	0	-0.0
Total	2	3	5	.375	56	0	0	0	2	77²	98	9	44	51	16.8	5.10	78	.316	.406	1	.333	1	-11	-10	0	-0.8

● **HENRY LUFF**   Luff, Henry T.   b: 9/14/1856, Philadelphia, Pa.   d: 10/11/16, Philadelphia, Pa.   5'11", 175 lbs.   Deb: 4/21/1875 ◆

1875	NH-n	1	6	.143	10	7	5	0	0	68²	98	2	3	5	13.2	3.28	63	.295	.301	45	.271	3	-8	-9		-0.5

● **URBANO LUGO**   Lugo, Rafael Urbano (Colina)   b: 8/12/62, Punto Fijo, Venez.   BR/TR, 6', 190 lbs.   Deb: 4/28/85

1985	Cal-A	3	4	.429	20	10	1	0	0	83	86	10	29	42	12.9	3.69	111	.274	.343	0	—	0	4	4	0	0.3
1986	Cal-A	1	1	.500	6	3	0	0	0	21¹	21	4	6	9	11.4	3.80	108	.266	.318	0	—	0	1	1	-0	0.1
1987	Cal-A	0	2	.000	7	5	0	0	0	28	42	8	18	24	19.3	9.32	46	.339	.423	0	—	0	-15	-16	-0	-0.9
1988	Cal-A	0	0	—	1	0	0	0	0	2	2	1	1	1	13.5	9.00	43	.250	.333	0	—	0	-1	-1	-0	-0.0
1989	Mon-N	0	0	—	3	0	0	0	0	4	4	1	0	3	9.0	6.75	52	.250	.250	0	—	0	-1	-1	0	-0.0
1990	Det-A	2	0	1.000	13	1	0	0	0	24¹	30	9	13	12	17.0	7.03	56	.313	.411	0	—	0	-8	-8	1	-0.6
Total	6	6	7	.462	50	19	1	0	0	162²	185	33	67	91	14.3	5.31	77	.290	.364	0	—	0	-21	-22	0	-1.1

● **WILD BILL LUHRSEN**   Luhrsen, William Ferdinand   b: 4/14/1884, Buckley, Ill.   d: 8/15/73, Little Rock, Ark.   BR/TR, 5'9", 165 lbs.   Deb: 8/23/13

1913	Pit-N	3	1	.750	5	3	2	0	0	29	25	3	16	11	13.3	2.48	121	.248	.361	0	.000	-1	2	2	1	0.2

● **AL LUKENS**   Lukens, Albert P.   b: 11/1868, Pennsylvania   5'9", 168 lbs.   Deb: 6/23/1894

1894	Phi-N	0	1	.000	3	2	1	0	0	15	26	1	10	6	23.4	10.20	50	.377	.476	0	.000	-2	-8	-8	-0	-0.5

● **RALPH LUMENTI**   Lumenti, Raphael Anthony   b: 12/21/36, Milford, Mass.   BL/TL, 6'3", 185 lbs.   Deb: 9/7/57

1957	Was-A	0	1	.000	3	2	0	0	0	9¹	9	1	5	8	14.5	6.75	58	.250	.357	0	.000	0	-3	-3	0	-0.3
1958	Was-A	1	2	.333	8	4	0	0	0	21	21	2	36	20	24.9	8.57	44	.266	.500	2	.250	0	-11	-11	0	-1.3
1959	Was-A	0	0	—	2	0	0	0	0	3	2	0	1	2	9.0	0.00	—	.200	.273	0	—	0	1	1	0	0.0
Total	3	1	3	.250	13	6	0	0	0	33¹	32	3	42	30	20.5	7.29	53	.256	.450	2	.200	0	-13	-13	0	-1.6

● **MEMO LUNA**   Luna, Guillermo Romero   b: 6/25/30, Tacubaya, Mexico   BL/TL, 6', 168 lbs.   Deb: 4/20/54

1954	StL-N	0	1	.000	1	1	0	0	0	0²	2	0	2	0	54.0	27.00	15	.667	.800	0	—	0	-2	-2	-0	-1.2

● **JACK LUNDBOM**   Lundbom, John Frederick   b: 3/10/1877, Manistee, Mich.   d: 10/31/49, Manistee, Mich.   BR/TR, 6'2", 187 lbs.   Deb: 5/9/02

1902	Cle-A	1	1	.500	8	3	1	0	0	34	48	1	16	7	17.2	6.62	52	.333	.404	4	.267	1	-11	-12	-0	-0.6

● **CARL LUNDGREN**   Lundgren, Carl Leonard   b: 2/16/1880, Marengo, Ill.   d: 8/21/34, Marengo, Ill.   BR/TR, 5'11", 175 lbs.   Deb: 6/19/02

1902	Chi-N	9	9	.500	18	18	17	1	0	160	158	2	45	68	11.8	1.97	137	.258	.315	7	.106	-4	14	13	-3	0.7
1903	Chi-N	11	9	.550	27	20	16	0	3	193	191	1	60	67	12.0	2.94	107	.262	.323	7	.115	-1	7	4	-2	0.4
1904	Chi-N	17	9	.654	31	27	25	2	1	242	203	2	77	106	10.6	2.60	102	.226	.290	20	.222	4	4	2	-1	0.4
1905	Chi-N	13	5	.722	23	19	16	3	0	169¹	132	3	53	69	10.3	2.23	134	.220	.293	11	.180	1	15	14	1	1.6
1906	Chi-N	17	6	.739	27	24	21	5	2	207²	160	3	89	103	11.1	2.21	119	.221	.313	12	.179	2	10	10	-1	1.2
1907	Chi-N	18	7	.720	28	25	21	7	0	207	130	4	92	84	9.7	1.17	212	**.185**	.282	7	.106	-3	**30**	30	-0	3.6
1908	Chi-N	6	9	.400	23	15	9	1	0	138²	149	5	56	38	13.3	4.22	56	.284	.353	7	.149	-1	-29	-29	-2	-3.3
1909	Chi-N	0	1	.000	2	1	0	0	0	4¹	6	0	4	0	20.8	4.15	61	.353	.476	1	.500	0	-1	-1	-0	-0.2
Total	8	91	55	.623	179	149	125	19	6	1322	1129	16	476	535	11.2	2.42	113	.235	.308	72	.157	-2	50	44	-8	4.0

● **DEL LUNDGREN**   Lundgren, Ebin Delmar   b: 9/21/1899, Lindsborg, Kan.   d: 10/19/84, Lindsborg, Kan.   BR/TR, 5'8", 160 lbs.   Deb: 4/27/24

1924	Pit-N	0	1	.000	8	1	0	0	0	16²	25	1	3	4	15.7	6.48	59	.403	.439			-1	-5	-5	0	-0.3
1926	Bos-A	0	2	.000	18	1	0	0	0	31	35	2	28	11	19.2	7.55	54	.307	.455	0	.000	-0	-12	-12	0	-0.7
1927	Bos-A	5	12	.294	30	17	5	2	0	136¹	160	7	87	39	16.6	6.27	67	.302	.405	7	.135	-2	-32	-31	-2	-3.5
Total	3	5	15	.250	56	19	5	2	0	184	220	9	118	54	16.9	6.51	64	.312	.416	7	.137	-3	-49	-48	-2	-4.5

● **DOLF LUQUE**   Luque, Adolfo Domingo De Guzman "The Pride Of Havana"   b: 8/4/1890, Havana, Cuba   d: 7/3/57, Havana, Cuba   BR/TR, 5'7", 160 lbs.   Deb: 5/20/14   C

1914	Bos-N	0	1	.000	2	1	1	0	0	8²	7	1	4	9	9.3	4.15	66	.167	.265	0	.000	-0	-1	-1	-1	-0.2
1915	Bos-N	0	0	—	2	1	0	0	0	5	6	0	4	3	18.0	3.60	72	.286	.400	0	—	-0	-1	-0	0	0.0
1918	Cin-N	6	3	.667	12	10	7	1	0	83	84	1	32	26	12.7	3.80	70	.277	.348	9	.321	5	-10	-10	-0	-0.6
1919	*Cin-N	10	3	.769	30	9	6	2	3	106	89	2	36	40	10.8	2.63	105	.237	.308	4	.125	-0	3	2	1	0.3
1920	Cin-N	13	9	.591	37	23	10	1	1	207²	168	5	60	72	10.1	2.51	121	**.225**	.286	17	.266	4	14	12	-2	1.5
1921	Cin-N	17	19	.472	41	36	25	**3**	3	304	318	13	64	102	11.3	3.38	106	.273	.312	30	.270	6	14	7	1	1.3
1922	Cin-N	13	23	.361	39	33	18	0	0	261	266	7	72	79	11.7	3.31	121	.268	.318	18	.209	2	23	20	0	2.6
1923	Cin-N	**27**	8	.771	41	37	28	**6**	2	322	279	2	88	151	10.4	**1.93**	**200**	**.235**	.282	21	.202	2	**74**	69	1	**7.4**
1924	Cin-N	10	15	.400	31	28	13	2	0	219¹	229	5	53	86	11.7	3.16	119	.271	.316	13	.178	-1	17	15	1	1.6
1925	Cin-N	16	18	.471	36	36	22	**4**	0	291	263	7	78	140	**10.6**	**2.63**	**156**	**.239**	.291	26	.255	-5	**53**	48	4	**6.1**
1926	Cin-N	13	16	.448	34	30	16	1	0	233²	231	7	77	83	11.9	3.43	108	.260	.321	27	.346	8	10	7	2	1.8
1927	Cin-N	13	12	.520	29	27	17	2	0	230²	225	10	56	76	11.0	3.20	118	.260	.305	18	.217	2	18	15	4	2.1
1928	Cin-N	11	10	.524	33	29	11	1	1	234¹	254	12	84	72	13.1	3.57	111	.284	.347	8	.119	-1	11	10	-2	0.5
1929	Cin-N	5	16	.238	32	22	8	1	0	176	213	7	56	43	13.9	4.50	101	.300	.364	15	.278	4	-1	-2	-1	-0.5
1930	Bro-N	14	8	.636	31	24	16	2	2	199	221	18	58	62	12.6	4.30	114	.287	.337	18	.240	1	15	14	1	1.5
1931	Bro-N	7	6	.538	19	15	5	0	0	102²	122	6	27	25	13.1	4.56	84	.297	.342	4	.133	-0	-8	-9	-1	-1.0
1932	NY-N	6	7	.462	38	5	1	0	5	110	128	4	32	32	13.1	4.01	93	.290	.338	1	.040	-2	-4	-4	-1	-0.5
1933	*NY-N	8	2	.800	35	0	0	0	5	80¹	75	4	19	23	10.5	2.69	119	.251	.296	5	.263	1	6	5	0	0.7
1934	NY-N	4	3	.571	26	0	0	0	7	42¹	54	3	17	12	15.3	3.83	101	.316	.381	2	.286	1	1	1	0	0.2
1935	NY-N	0	0	—	2	0	0	0	0	2	4	0	3	1	4.9	0.00	—	.077	.143	1	1.000	0	2	2	0	0.5
Total	20	194	179	.520	550	366	206	26	28	3220¹	3231	113	918	1130	11.7	3.24	117	.265	.318	237	.227	37	245	200	13	26.3

● **JOHNNY LUSH**   Lush, John Charles   b: 10/8/1885, Williamsport, Pa.   d: 11/18/46, Beverly Hills, Cal   BL/TL, 5'9.5", 165 lbs.   Deb: 4/22/04 ◆

1904	Phi-N	0	6	.000	7	6	3	0	0	42²	52	1	27	27	18.1	3.59	75	.301	.415	102	.276	2	-4	-4	1	-0.3
1905	Phi-N	2	0	1.000	2	1	1	0	0	17	12	0	8	8	11.1	1.59	184	.194	.296	5	.313	1	3	3	0	0.4
1906	Phi-N	18	15	.545	37	35	24	5	0	281	254	2	119	151	12.5	2.37	110	.236	.321	56	.264	7	8	8	3	2.1
1907	Phi-N	3	5	.375	8	8	5	2	0	57¹	48	0	21	20	11.3	2.98	81	.227	.306	8	.200	1	-3	-4	1	-0.4
	StL-N	7	10	.412	20	19	13	3	0	144	132	6	42	71	11.4	2.50	100	.246	.311	23	.280	5	-0	-0	0	0.8
	Yr	10	15	.400	28	27	20	5	0	201¹	180	2	63	91	11.2	2.64	94	.240	.306	31	.254	6	-4	-4	0	0.4
1908	StL-N	11	18	.379	38	32	23	3	1	250²	221	6	57	93	10.4	2.12	111	.231	.283	15	.169	1	7	7	0	1.0
1909	StL-N	11	18	.379	34	28	21	2	0	221¹	215	4	69	66	12.0	3.13	81	.260	.324	24	.239	4	-13	-15	-1	-1.4
1910	StL-N	14	13	.519	36	25	13	1	1	225¹	235	6	70	54	12.5	3.20	93	.276	.336	21	.226	4	-4	-5	-2	-0.4
Total	7	66	85	.437	182	155	105	16	2	1239¹	1169	17	413	490	11.9	2.68	97	.249	.318	252	.254	24	-7	-11	1	1.8

● **SPARKY LYLE**   Lyle, Albert Walter   b: 7/22/44, DuBois, Pa.   BL/TL, 6'1", 192 lbs.   Deb: 7/4/67

1967	Bos-A	1	2	.333	27	0	0	0	5	43¹	33	3	14	42	10.2	2.28	153	.213	.287	2	.250	1	5	6	-0	0.6
1968	Bos-A	6	1	.857	49	0	0	0	11	65²	67	6	14	52	11.5	2.74	115	.261	.299	1	.125	-1	2	3	-1	0.3
1969	Bos-A	8	3	.727	71	0	0	0	17	102²	91	8	48	93	12.3	2.54	150	.240	.327	2	.118	-1	12	14	1	2.1
1970	Bos-A	1	7	.125	63	0	0	0	20	67¹	62	5	34	51	13.0	3.88	102	.244	.336	0	.000	-1	-1	-1	-1	-0.1
1971	Bos-A	6	4	.600	50	0	0	0	16	52¹	41	5	24	37	11.0	2.75	134	.228	.315	3	1.000	1	4	4	-0	0.8
1972	NY-A	9	5	.643	59	0	0	0	**35**	107²	84	3	29	75	9.4	1.92	153	.216	.271	4	.190	1	**14**	**12**	-1	2.7
1973	NY-A★	5	9	.357	51	0	0	0	27	82¹	66	4	18	63	9.2	2.51	146	.216	.259	0			12	11	0	2.6

YEAR TM/L	W	L	PCT	G	GS	CG	SH	SV	IP	H	HR	BB	SO	RAT	ERA	ERA+	OAV	OOB	BH	AVG	PB	PR	/A	PD	TPI
1974 NY-A	9	3	.750	66	0	0	0	15	114	93	6	43	89	10.8	1.66	213	.226	.300	0	.000	0	25	24	-1	3.0
1975 NY-A	5	7	.417	49	0	0	0	6	89¹	94	1	36	65	13.3	3.12	118	.275	.347	0	—	0	6	6	0	0.8
1976 *NY-A☆	7	8	.467	64	0	0	0	23	103²	82	5	42	61	10.8	2.26	151	.225	.305	0	—	0	15	13	-1	2.5
1977 *NY-A★	13	5	.722	**72**	0	0	0	26	137	131	7	33	68	10.9	2.17	182	.257	.305	0	—	0	**29**	**27**	-1	**4.4**
1978 *NY-A	9	3	.750	59	0	0	0	9	111²	116	6	33	33	12.3	3.47	104	.278	.337	0	—	0	4	2	0	0.3
1979 Tex-A	5	8	.385	67	0	0	0	13	95	78	9	28	48	10.0	3.13	133	.226	.284	0	—	0	11	11	-1	1.6
1980 Tex-A	3	2	.600	49	0	0	0	8	80²	97	4	28	43	13.9	4.69	83	.306	.362	0	—	0	-6	-7	-0	-0.5
Phi-N	0	0	—	10	0	0	0	2	14	11	0	6	6	10.9	1.93	196	.220	.304	0	—	0	3	3	-0	0.7
1981 *Phi-N	9	6	.600	48	0	0	0	2	75	85	4	33	29	14.3	4.44	82	.301	.377	2	.400	1	-8	-7	1	-1.1
1982 Phi-N	3	3	.500	34	0	0	0	2	36²	50	3	12	12	15.2	5.15	71	.327	.376	1	.500	1	-6	-6	1	-0.8
Chi-A	0	0	—	12	0	0	0	0	11	11	0	7	6	13.5	3.00	134	.262	.367	0	—	0	1	1	-0	0.0
Total 16	99	76	.566	899	0	0	0	238	1390¹	1292	84	481	873	11.6	2.88	127	.251	.316	15	.192	2	121	119	-4	20.0

● **JIM LYLE**   Lyle, James Charles b: 7/24/1900, Lake, Miss. d: 10/10/77, Williamsport, Pa. BR/TR, 6'1", 180 lbs. Deb: 10/2/25

YEAR TM/L	W	L	PCT	G	GS	CG	SH	SV	IP	H	HR	BB	SO	RAT	ERA	ERA+	OAV	OOB	BH	AVG	PB	PR	/A	PD	TPI
1925 Was-A	0	0	—	1	0	0	0	0	3	5	0	1	3	18.0	6.00	70	.333	.375	0	—	0	-1	-1	-0	0.0

● **ADRIAN LYNCH**   Lynch, Adrian Ryan b: 2/9/1897, Laurens, Iowa d: 3/16/34, Davenport, Iowa BB/TR, 6'1.5", 185 lbs. Deb: 8/4/20

YEAR TM/L	W	L	PCT	G	GS	CG	SH	SV	IP	H	HR	BB	SO	RAT	ERA	ERA+	OAV	OOB	BH	AVG	PB	PR	/A	PD	TPI
1920 StL-A	2	0	1.000	5	3	1	0	0	22¹	23	1	17	8	16.5	5.24	75	.277	.406	2	.222	0	-4	-3	-1	-0.3

● **ED LYNCH**   Lynch, Edward Francis b: 2/25/56, Brooklyn, N.Y. BR/TR, 6'6", 230 lbs. Deb: 8/31/80

YEAR TM/L	W	L	PCT	G	GS	CG	SH	SV	IP	H	HR	BB	SO	RAT	ERA	ERA+	OAV	OOB	BH	AVG	PB	PR	/A	PD	TPI
1980 NY-N	1	1	.500	5	4	0	0	0	19¹	24	0	5	9	14.0	5.12	69	.304	.353	2	.333	0	-3	-3	-0	-0.3
1981 NY-N	4	5	.444	17	13	0	0	0	80¹	79	6	21	27	11.3	2.91	120	.254	.303	3	.143	1	5	5	-1	0.6
1982 NY-N	4	8	.333	43	12	0	0	2	139¹	145	6	40	51	12.0	3.55	102	.273	.325	0	.000	-3	1	1	-1	-0.4
1983 NY-N	10	10	.500	30	27	1	0	0	174²	208	17	41	44	13.0	4.28	85	.302	.344	8	.154	-1	-13	-13	-1	-1.5
1984 NY-N	9	8	.529	40	13	0	0	2	124	169	14	24	62	14.3	4.50	79	.324	.359	6	.222	1	-13	-13	-1	-1.8
1985 NY-N	10	8	.556	31	29	6	1	0	191	188	19	27	65	10.2	3.44	100	.256	.283	4	.077	-2	3	0	-4	-0.6
1986 NY-N	0	0	—	1	0	0	0	0	1²	2	0	1	0	10.8	0.00	—	.286	.286	0	—	-1	1	1	-0	0.0
Chi-N	7	5	.583	23	13	1	1	0	99²	105	10	23	57	11.6	3.79	107	.279	.322	1	.033	-2	-1	3	-1	0.0
Yr	7	5	.583	24	13	1	1	0	101¹	107	10	23	58	11.6	3.73	108	.279	.321	1	.033	-2	-0	3	-1	0.0
1987 Chi-N	2	9	.182	58	8	0	0	8	110¹	130	8	40	44	14.7	5.38	79	.295	.367	3	.188	-0	-16	-14	-1	-1.2
Total 8	47	54	.465	248	119	8	2	8	940¹	1050	89	229	396	12.4	4.00	92	.284	.329	27	.114	-6	-35	-33	-8	-5.2

● **JACK LYNCH**   Lynch, John H. b: 2/5/1857, New York, N.Y d: 4/20/23, Bronx, N.Y. BR/TR, 5'8", 185 lbs. Deb: 5/2/1881

YEAR TM/L	W	L	PCT	G	GS	CG	SH	SV	IP	H	HR	BB	SO	RAT	ERA	ERA+	OAV	OOB	BH	AVG	PB	PR	/A	PD	TPI
1881 Buf-N	10	9	.526	20	19	17	0	0	165²	203	2	29	32	12.6	3.59	77	.297	.325	13	.167	-3	-15	-15	1	-1.5
1883 NY-a	13	15	.464	29	29	29	1	0	255	263	6	119	122	10.2	4.09	82	.250	.267	20	.187	-3	-22	-21	-1	-2.1
1884 NY-a	37	15	.712	55	53	53	5	0	496	420	10	42	292	8.6	2.67	117	.215	.284	30	.152	-7	32	25	-5	1.0
1885 NY-a	23	21	.523	44	43	43	1	0	379	410	17	42	177	10.8	3.61	82	.263	.283	30	.196	-4	-15	-27	-5	-2.8
1886 NY-a	20	30	.400	51	50	50	0	0	432²	485	10	116	193	12.8	3.95	86	.271	.320	27	.160	-6	-24	-26	-3	-3.1
1887 NY-a	7	14	.333	21	21	21	0	0	187	245	6	36	45	13.1	5.10	83	.305	.338	14	.169	-4	-17	-18	-2	-1.5
1890 Bro-a	0	1	.000	1	1	1	0	0	9	22	1	5	1	27.0	12.00	32	.449	.500	3	.750	2	-8	-8	1	-0.4
Total 7	110	105	.512	221	216	214	8	0	1924¹	2048	54	295	859	11.1	3.69	89	.260	.289	137	.173	-18	-69	-91	-10	-10.4

● **MIKE LYNCH**   Lynch, Michael Joseph b: 6/28/1880, Holyoke, Mass. d: 4/2/27, Garrison, N.Y. BR/TR, 6'2", 170 lbs. Deb: 6/21/04

YEAR TM/L	W	L	PCT	G	GS	CG	SH	SV	IP	H	HR	BB	SO	RAT	ERA	ERA+	OAV	OOB	BH	AVG	PB	PR	/A	PD	TPI
1904 Pit-N	15	11	.577	27	24	24	1	0	222²	200	1	91	95	12.4	2.71	101	.243	.330	20	.230	4	1	1	-2	0.2
1905 Pit-N	17	8	.680	33	22	13	0	2	206¹	191	3	107	106	13.2	3.79	79	.254	.351	11	.136	-1	-18	-18	0	-2.2
1906 Pit-N	6	5	.545	18	12	7	0	0	119	101	2	31	48	10.6	2.42	110	.232	.295	8	.205	-0	3	3	-1	0.2
1907 Pit-N	2	2	.500	7	4	2	0	0	36	37	0	22	9	15.0	2.25	108	.282	.390	3	.250	1	1	1	1	0.3
NY-N	3	6	.333	12	10	7	0	1	72	68	3	30	34	12.3	3.38	73	.249	.323	8	.296	2	-7	-7	0	-0.6
Yr	5	8	.385	19	14	9	0	1	108	105	3	52	43	13.1	3.00	82	.259	.344	11	.282	3	-6	-6	2	-0.3
Total 4	43	32	.573	97	72	53	1	3	656	597	9	281	292	12.4	3.05	91	.248	.333	50	.203	5	-21	-20	-1	-2.1

● **TOM LYNCH**   Lynch, Thomas S. b: 1863, Peru, Ill. d: 5/13/03, Peru, Ill. BL, 5'11", 175 lbs. Deb: 8/5/1884

YEAR TM/L	W	L	PCT	G	GS	CG	SH	SV	IP	H	HR	BB	SO	RAT	ERA	ERA+	OAV	OOB	BH	AVG	PB	PR	/A	PD	TPI
1884 Chi-N	0	0	—	1	1	0	0	0	7	3	2	2	9	12.9	2.57	122	.241	.313	0	.000	-1	0	0	1	0.0

● **RED LYNN**   Lynn, Japhet Monroe b: 12/27/13, Kenney, Tex. d: 10/27/77, Bellville, Tex. BR/TR, 6', 162 lbs. Deb: 4/25/39

YEAR TM/L	W	L	PCT	G	GS	CG	SH	SV	IP	H	HR	BB	SO	RAT	ERA	ERA+	OAV	OOB	BH	AVG	PB	PR	/A	PD	TPI
1939 Det-A	0	1	.000	4	0	0	0	0	8¹	7	1	2	3	16.2	8.64	57	.324	.395	0	.000	-0	-4	-3	0	-0.4
NY-N	1	0	1.000	26	0	0	0	1	49²	44	3	21	22	12.1	3.08	127	.240	.325	0	.000	-1	5	5	-1	-0.1
1940 NY-N	4	3	.571	33	0	0	0	3	42¹	40	3	24	25	13.8	3.83	101	.247	.348	0	.000	-1	0	0	-1	-0.1
1944 Chi-N	5	4	.556	22	7	4	1	1	84¹	80	4	37	35	12.6	4.06	87	.251	.331	6	.207	0	-4	-5	1	-0.3
Total 3	10	8	.556	85	7	4	1	5	184²	175	12	85	85	12.9	3.95	96	.251	.336	6	.146	-1	-3	-4	-1	-0.9

● **AL LYONS**   Lyons, Albert Harold b: 7/18/18, St.Joseph, Mo. d: 12/20/65, Inglewood, Cal. BR/TR, 6'2", 195 lbs. Deb: 4/19/44

YEAR TM/L	W	L	PCT	G	GS	CG	SH	SV	IP	H	HR	BB	SO	RAT	ERA	ERA+	OAV	OOB	BH	AVG	PB	PR	/A	PD	TPI
1944 NY-A	0	0	—	11	0	0	0	0	39²	43	2	24	14	15.7	4.54	77	.291	.397	9	.346	2	-5	-5	0	0.2
1946 NY-A	0	1	.000	2	1	0	0	0	8¹	11	0	6	4	15.4	5.40	64	.314	.429	0	—	-1	-2	-2	-0	-0.2
1947 NY-A	1	0	1.000	6	0	0	0	0	11	18	2	9	7	22.1	9.00	39	.367	.466	4	.667	2	-6	-7	0	-0.3
Pit-N	1	2	.333	13	0	0	0	0	28¹	36	4	16	16	15.6	7.31	58	.300	.368	2	.200	1	-10	-10	1	-0.7
1948 Bos-N	1	0	1.000	7	0	0	0	0	12²	17	1	8	5	17.8	7.82	49	.309	.397	2	.167	0	-5	-6	1	-0.2
Total 4	3	3	.500	39	1	0	0	0	100	125	9	59	46	16.9	6.30	59	.307	.400	17	.293	5	-29	-28	2	-1.2

● **CURT LYONS**   Lyons, Curt Russell b: 10/17/74, Greencastle, Ind. BR/TR, 6'5", 230 lbs. Deb: 9/19/96

YEAR TM/L	W	L	PCT	G	GS	CG	SH	SV	IP	H	HR	BB	SO	RAT	ERA	ERA+	OAV	OOB	BH	AVG	PB	PR	/A	PD	TPI
1996 Cin-N	2	0	1.000	3	3	0	0	0	16	17	1	7	14	14.1	4.50	92	.274	.357	0	.000	-1	-1	-1	-0	-0.1

● **GEORGE LYONS**   Lyons, George Tony "Smooth" b: 1/25/1891, Bible Grove, Ill. d: 8/12/81, Nevada, Mo. BR/TR, 5'11", 180 lbs. Deb: 9/6/20

YEAR TM/L	W	L	PCT	G	GS	CG	SH	SV	IP	H	HR	BB	SO	RAT	ERA	ERA+	OAV	OOB	BH	AVG	PB	PR	/A	PD	TPI
1920 StL-N	2	1	.667	7	1	2	0	0	23¹	21	2	9	5	12.0	3.09	97	.262	.344	1	.143	-0	0	-0	1	0.0
1924 StL-A	3	2	.600	26	6	2	0	0	77²	97	2	45	25	15.7	5.21	87	.323	.420	5	.250	-0	-8	-6	1	-0.2
Total 2	5	3	.625	33	8	3	0	0	101	118	4	54	30	15.9	4.72	88	.311	.405	6	.222	-0	-8	-7	2	-0.2

● **HARRY LYONS**   Lyons, Harry P. b: 3/25/1866, Chester, Pa. d: 6/30/12, Mauricetown, N.J. BR/TR, 5'10.5", 157 lbs. Deb: 8/29/1887 ♦

YEAR TM/L	W	L	PCT	G	GS	CG	SH	SV	IP	H	HR	BB	SO	RAT	ERA	ERA+	OAV	OOB	BH	AVG	PB	PR	/A	PD	TPI
1890 Roc-a	0	0	—	1	0	0	0	0	3²	8	0	1	2	22.1	12.27	29	.421	.450	152	.260	0	-3	-4	0	0.0

● **HERSH LYONS**   Lyons, Herschel Englebert b: 7/23/15, Fresno, Cal. BR/TR, 5'11", 195 lbs. Deb: 4/17/41

YEAR TM/L	W	L	PCT	G	GS	CG	SH	SV	IP	H	HR	BB	SO	RAT	ERA	ERA+	OAV	OOB	BH	AVG	PB	PR	/A	PD	TPI
1941 StL-N	0	0	—	1	0	0	0	0	1¹	1	0	3	1	27.0	0.00	—	.200	.500	0	—	0	1	1	0	0.0

● **STEVE LYONS**   Lyons, Stephen John b: 6/3/60, Tacoma, Wash. BL/TR, 6'3", 192 lbs. Deb: 4/15/85 ♦

YEAR TM/L	W	L	PCT	G	GS	CG	SH	SV	IP	H	HR	BB	SO	RAT	ERA	ERA+	OAV	OOB	BH	AVG	PB	PR	/A	PD	TPI
1990 Chi-A	0	0	—	1	0	0	0	0	2	2	0	0	1	27.0	4.50	85	.250	.500	28	.192	0	-0	-0	0	0.0
1991 Bos-A	0	0	—	1	0	0	0	0	1	2	0	4	1	18.0	0.00	—	.400	.400	51	.241	0	0	0	0	0.0
Total 2	0	0	—	2	0	0	0	0	3	4	0	4	2	24.0	3.00	133	.308	.471	545	.252	0	0	0	0	0.0

● **TED LYONS**   Lyons, Theodore Amar b: 12/28/1900, Lake Charles, La. d: 7/25/86, Sulphur, La. BB/TR, 5'11", 200 lbs. Deb: 7/2/23 MCH♦

YEAR TM/L	W	L	PCT	G	GS	CG	SH	SV	IP	H	HR	BB	SO	RAT	ERA	ERA+	OAV	OOB	BH	AVG	PB	PR	/A	PD	TPI
1923 Chi-A	2	1	.667	9	2	1	0	0	22²	30	2	15	6	18.3	6.35	62	.323	.422	1	.200	0	-6	-6	1	-0.6
1924 Chi-A	12	11	.522	41	22	12	0	3	216¹	279	10	72	52	14.7	4.87	85	.322	.375	17	.221	0	-15	-18	-3	-1.9
1925 Chi-A	**21**	11	.656	43	32	19	**5**	3	262²	274	6	83	45	12.3	3.26	128	.278	.335	18	.186	-3	33	26	2	2.7
1926 Chi-A	18	16	.529	39	31	24	3	2	283²	268	6	106	51	11.9	3.01	128	.252	.320	22	.212	-0	32	27	4	3.3
1927 Chi-A	**22**	14	.611	39	34	**30**	2	2	307²	291	6	67	71	10.5	2.84	143	.255	.292	28	.255	5	**45**	**41**	5	**5.1**
1928 Chi-A	15	14	.517	39	27	21	0	6	240	276	11	68	60	13.0	3.98	102	.295	.344	23	.253	1	2	5	2	0.5
1929 Chi-A	14	20	.412	37	31	21	1	2	259¹	276	11	76	57	12.3	4.10	105	.278	.331	20	.220	1	4	5	3	0.9
1930 Chi-A	22	15	.595	42	36	**29**	1	1	297²	331	12	57	69	11.8	3.78	122	.285	.319	38	.311	8	29	28	3	4.1
1931 Chi-A	4	6	.400	22	12	7	0	0	101	117	6	33	16	13.4	4.01	106	.296	.350	5	.152	-1	-4	-3	1	0.2
1932 Chi-A	10	15	.400	33	26	19	1	2	230²	243	10	58	58	12.4	3.28	132	.272	.327	19	.260	5	31	27	-1	3.0
1933 Chi-A	10	21	.323	36	27	14	2	1	228	260	10	74	74	13.2	4.38	97	.280	.350	26	.286	6	-0	0	2	0.2
1934 Chi-A	11	13	.458	30	24	21	0	1	205¹	249	15	66	53	13.9	4.87	93	.293	.345	20	.206	1	-8	-3	2	0.0
1935 Chi-A	15	8	.652	23	22	19	3	0	190²	194	15	56	54	11.9	3.02	153	.262	.317	18	.220	-0	30	34	-1	3.6

YEAR	TM/L	W	L	PCT	G	GS	CG	SH	SV	IP	H	HR	BB	SO	RAT	ERA	ERA+	OAV	OOB	BH	AVG	PB	PR	/A	PD	TPI
1936	Chi-A	10	13	.435	26	24	15	1	0	182	227	21	45	48	13.6	5.14	101	.305	.347	11	.157	-3	-2	1	1	0.0
1937	Chi-A	12	7	.632	22	22	11	0	0	169¹	182	21	45	45	12.1	4.15	111	.278	.326	12	.211	1	9	9	0	1.0
1938	Chi-A	9	11	.450	23	23	17	1	0	194²	238	13	52	54	13.4	3.70	132	.299	.342	14	.194	-1	24	26	2	2.3
1939	Chi-A☆	14	6	.700	21	21	16	0	0	172²	162	7	26	65	**9.9**	2.76	171	.247	**.276**	18	.295	4	36	38	-1	4.3
1940	Chi-A	12	8	.600	22	22	17	**4**	0	186¹	188	17	37	72	10.9	3.24	137	.252	.287	18	.240	2	24	25	-2	2.3
1941	Chi-A	12	10	.545	22	22	19	2	0	187¹	199	9	37	63	11.5	3.70	111	.269	.308	20	.270	4	9	8	1	1.3
1942	Chi-A	14	6	.700	20	20	20	1	0	180¹	167	11	26	50	9.7	**2.10**	**172**	.245	.275	16	.239	4	31	30	1	**4.0**
1946	Chi-A	1	4	.200	5	5	5	0	0	42²	38	2	9	10	9.9	2.32	147	.235	.275	0	.000	-1	6	5	0	0.5
Total	21	260	230	.531	594	484	356	27	23	4161	4489	223	1121	1073	12.2	3.67	118	.276	.324	364	.233	32	313	302	12	36.7

● **TOBY LYONS**   Lyons, Thomas A. b: 3/27/1869, Cambridge, Mass. d: 8/27/20, Boston, Mass.   Deb: 4/18/1890

1890	Syr-a	0	2	.000	3	3	3	0	0	22¹	40	1	21	6	25.0	10.48	34	.377	.484	4	.333	1	-16	-17	0	-1.0

● **RICK LYSANDER**   Lysander, Richard Eugene b: 2/21/53, Huntington Park, Cal.   BR/TR, 6'2", 190 lbs.   Deb: 4/12/80

1980	Oak-A	0	0	—	5	0	0	0	0	13²	24	3	4	5	18.4	7.90	48	.381	.418	0	—	0	-6	-6	0	0.4
1983	Min-A	5	12	.294	61	4	1	1	3	125	132	8	43	58	12.7	3.38	126	.275	.337	0	—	0	9	12	1	1.4
1984	Min-A	4	3	.571	36	0	0	0	9	56²	62	4	27	22	14.1	3.49	120	.283	.362	0	—	0	3	4	0	0.3
1985	Min-A	0	2	.000	35	1	0	0	3	61	72	3	22	26	13.9	6.05	73	.305	.364	0	—	0	-13	-11	-1	-0.7
Total	4	9	17	.346	137	5	1	1	11	256¹	290	16	96	111	13.6	4.28	99	.291	.354	0	—	0	-6	-1	0	1.4

● **BILL LYSTON**   Lyston, William Edward b: 1863, Near Baltimore, Md. d: 8/4/44, Baltimore, Md.   TR ,   Deb: 8/29/1891

1891	Col-a	0	1	.000	1	1	1	0	0	6	10	0	6	1	25.5	10.50	33	.357	.486	0	.000	-0	-5	-5	-0	-0.5
1894	Cle-N	0	0	—	1	1	0	0	0	3²	5	1	4	0	22.1	9.82	56	.313	.450	0	.000	-0	-2	-2	-0	0.0
Total	2	0	1	.000	2	2	1	0	0	9²	15	1	10	1	24.2	10.24	41	.341	.473	0	.000	-0	-7	-7	-0	-0.5

● **DUKE MAAS**   Maas, Duane Fredrick b: 1/31/29, Utica, Mich. d: 12/7/76, Mt.Clemens, Mich.   BR/TR, 5'10", 170 lbs.   Deb: 4/21/55

1955	Det-A	5	6	.455	18	16	5	2	0	86²	91	7	50	42	14.8	4.88	79	.271	.369	5	.167	0	-9	-10	0	-1.1
1956	Det-A	0	7	.000	26	7	0	0	0	63¹	81	9	32	34	16.9	6.54	63	.313	.401	3	.188	0	-17	-17	0	-1.7
1957	Det-A	10	14	.417	45	26	8	2	6	219¹	210	23	65	116	11.4	3.28	118	.252	.309	6	.085	-4	12	14	0	1.2
1958	KC-A	4	5	.444	10	7	3	1	1	55¹	49	3	13	19	10.2	3.90	100	.241	.290	3	.176	0	-1	-0	0	0.1
	*NY-A	7	3	.700	22	13	2	1	0	101¹	93	9	36	50	11.6	3.82	92	.242	.310	3	.088	-2	-1	-3	-1	-0.6
	Yr	11	8	.579	32	20	5	2	1	156²	142	12	49	69	11.1	3.85	95	.241	.302	6	.118	-1	-1	-3	-1	-0.5
1959	NY-A	14	8	.636	38	21	3	1	4	138	149	14	53	67	13.3	4.43	82	.278	.345	5	.125	-1	-9	-12	1	-1.9
1960	*NY-A	5	1	.833	35	1	0	0	4	70¹	70	6	35	28	13.6	4.09	87	.265	.353	0	.000	-1	-2	-4	-1	-0.4
1961	NY-A	0	0	—	1	0	0	0	0	4	6	1	0	1	54.0	54.00	7	1.000	1.000	0	—	0	-2	-2	0	0.0
Total	7	45	44	.506	195	91	21	7	15	734²	745	71	284	356	12.8	4.19	90	.264	.326	25	.117	-7	-27	-34	0	-4.4

● **BOB MABE**   Mabe, Robert Lee b: 10/8/29, Danville, Va.   BR/TR, 5'11", 165 lbs.   Deb: 4/18/58

1958	StL-N	3	9	.250	31	13	4	0	0	111²	113	11	41	74	12.7	4.51	91	.260	.330	1	.042	-2	-7	-5	0	-0.6
1959	Cin-N	4	2	.667	18	1	0	0	3	29²	29	6	19	8	14.6	5.46	74	.254	.361	0	.000	-1	-5	-5	-0	-1.0
1960	Bal-A	0	0	—	2	0	0	0	0	2	4	0	1	0	67.5	27.00	9	.571	.625	0	—	0	-2	-2	-0	0.0
Total	3	7	11	.389	51	14	4	0	3	142	146	17	61	82	13.4	4.82	85	.263	.340	1	.032	-3	-14	-11	0	-1.6

● **MAC MacARTHUR**   MacArthur, Malcolm b: 1/19/1862, Glasgow, Scotland d: 10/18/32, Detroit, Mich.   TR , 5'9.5", 164 lbs.   Deb: 5/2/1884

1884	Ind-a	1	5	.167	6	6	6	0	0	52	57	1	21	19	13.8	5.02	66	.263	.333	2	.095	-2	-10	-10	0	-1.0

● **FRANK MacCORMACK**   MacCormack, Frank Louis b: 9/21/54, Jersey City, N.J.   BR/TR, 6'4", 210 lbs.   Deb: 6/14/76

1976	Det-A	0	5	.000	9	8	0	0	0	32²	35	1	34	14	19.3	5.79	64	.294	.455	0	.000	0	-8	-8	-0	-1.1
1977	Sea-A	0	0	—	3	3	0	0	0	7	4	0	12	4	24.4	3.86	107	.174	.500	0	—	0	0	0	0	0.1
Total	2	0	5	.000	12	11	0	0	0	39²	39	1	46	18	20.2	5.45	69	.275	.464	0	.000	0	-8	-7	-0	-1.1

● **ROB MacDONALD**   MacDonald, Robert Joseph b: 4/27/65, East Orange, N.J.   BL/TL, 6'3", 200 lbs.   Deb: 8/14/90

1990	Tor-A	0	0	—	4	0	0	0	0	2¹	0	0	0	0	7.7	0.00	—	.000	.250	0	—	0	1	1	0	-0.1
1991	*Tor-A	3	3	.500	45	0	0	0	0	53²	51	5	25	24	12.7	2.85	148	.252	.335	0	—	0	7	8	-1	0.5
1992	Tor-A	1	0	1.000	27	0	0	0	0	47¹	50	4	16	26	12.7	4.37	93	.270	.332	0	—	0	-2	-2	-1	-0.3
1993	Det-A	3	3	.500	68	0	0	0	0	65²	67	8	33	39	13.8	5.35	80	.268	.356	0	—	0	-7	-8	1	-0.6
1995	NY-A	1	1	.500	33	0	0	0	0	46¹	50	7	22	41	14.2	4.86	95	.282	.365	0	—	0	-1	-1	-0	-0.1
1996	NY-N	0	2	.000	20	0	0	0	0	19	16	2	9	12	11.8	4.26	92	.235	.325	0	—	0	-0	-1	-0	-0.1
Total	6	8	9	.471	197	0	0	0	0	234¹	234	26	107	142	13.2	4.34	98	.264	.345	0	—	0	-2	-2	-0	-0.7

● **BILL MACDONALD**   Macdonald, William Paul b: 3/28/29, Alameda, Cal. d: 5/4/91, Shasta Lake, Cal.   BR/TR, 5'10", 170 lbs.   Deb: 5/6/50

1950	Pit-N	8	10	.444	32	20	6	2	1	153	138	17	88	60	13.4	4.29	102	.243	.346	6	.122	-2	-3	2	-3	-0.3
1953	Pit-N	0	1	.000	4	1	0	0	0	7¹	12	0	8	4	25.8	12.27	36	.400	.538	0	—	0	-7	-6	-0	-0.7
Total	2	8	11	.421	36	21	6	2	1	160¹	150	17	96	64	13.9	4.66	94	.251	.356	6	.122	-2	-9	-5	-3	-1.0

● **JIMMY MACE**   Mace, Harry L. b: Washington, D.C.   5'11", 185 lbs.   Deb: 5/5/1891

1891	Was-a	0	1	.000	3	1	1	0	0	16	18	0	8	3	15.2	7.31	51	.273	.360	0	.000	-1	-6	-6	-0	-0.4

● **DANNY MacFAYDEN**   MacFayden, Daniel Knowles "Deacon Danny" b: 6/10/05, N.Truro, Mass. d: 8/26/72, Brunswick, Me.   BR/TR, 5'11", 170 lbs.   Deb: 8/25/26

1926	Bos-A	0	1	.000	3	1	0	0	0	13	10	0	7	1	11.8	4.85	84	.217	.321	1	.333	0	-1	-1	1	0.0
1927	Bos-A	5	8	.385	34	16	6	1	2	160¹	176	9	59	42	13.5	4.27	99	.294	.363	13	.283	4	-2	-1	-2	0.2
1928	Bos-A	9	15	.375	33	28	9	0	0	195	215	12	78	61	13.8	4.75	87	.289	.361	9	.143	-1	-15	-14	-1	-1.6
1929	Bos-A	10	18	.357	32	26	14	4	0	221	225	8	81	61	12.7	3.62	118	.271	.340	13	.176	-3	15	16	2	1.7
1930	Bos-A	11	14	.440	36	33	18	1	2	269¹	293	9	93	76	13.1	4.21	109	.281	.343	13	.141	-4	13	12	2	0.7
1931	Bos-A	16	12	.571	35	32	17	2	0	230²	263	4	79	74	13.6	4.02	107	.281	.341	10	.123	-5	9	7	2	0.5
1932	Bos-A	1	10	.091	12	11	6	0	0	77²	91	3	33	29	14.5	5.10	88	.289	.358	4	.120	-2	-5	-5	0	-0.7
	NY-A	7	5	.583	17	15	9	0	1	121¹	137	11	37	33	13.1	3.93	104	.281	.340	5	.102	-3	7	2	-2	-0.3
	Yr	8	15	.348	29	26	15	0	1	199	228	14	70	62	13.6	4.39	97	.284	.342	8	.108	-1	2	-3	-1	-1.0
1933	NY-A	3	2	.600	25	6	2	0	0	90¹	120	8	37	28	15.8	5.88	66	.319	.383	1	.029	-4	-16	-20	0	-1.3
1934	NY-A	4	3	.571	22	11	4	0	0	96	110	5	31	41	13.4	4.50	90	.288	.345	4	.103	-2	-4	-5	-1	-0.5
1935	Cin-N	1	2	.333	7	4	1	0	0	36	39	1	13	13	13.0	4.75	84	.281	.342	1	.091	-1	-3	-3	1	-0.2
	Bos-N	5	13	.278	28	20	7	1	0	151²	200	8	34	46	14.2	5.10	74	.314	.354	8	.157	-1	-18	-22	2	-2.1
	Yr	6	15	.286	35	24	8	1	0	187²	239	9	47	59	14.0	5.04	76	.308	.352	9	.145	-2	-21	-25	3	-2.3
1936	Bos-N	17	13	.567	37	31	21	2	0	266²	268	5	66	86	11.4	2.87	134	.259	.307	8	.096	-5	34	29	3	2.7
1937	Bos-N	14	14	.500	32	32	16	2	0	246	250	8	60	70	11.4	2.93	123	.268	.313	13	.157	-2	27	18	1	1.8
1938	Bos-N	14	9	.609	29	29	19	5	0	219²	208	6	64	58	11.3	2.95	116	.251	.304	9	.117	-4	20	12	-1	0.4
1939	Bos-N	8	14	.364	33	28	8	0	2	191²	221	11	59	46	13.3	3.90	95	.291	.345	12	.179	-0	0	-4	1	-0.4
1940	Pit-N	5	4	.556	35	8	0	0	0	91¹	112	5	27	24	14.1	3.55	107	.302	.356	5	.179	-0	3	3	1	0.3
1941	Was-N	0	1	.000	5	0	0	0	0	7	12	1	5	2	21.9	10.29	39	.375	.459	—	—	0	-5	-5	-0	-0.5
1943	Bos-N	2	1	.667	10	1	0	0	0	21¹	31	1	9	7	17.3	5.91	58	.344	.410	1	.250	1	-6	-6	-0	-0.8
Total	17	132	159	.454	465	332	158	18	9	2706	2981	112	872	797	13.0	3.96	101	.281	.340	129	.142	-34	58	11	10	0.1

● **JULIO MACHADO**   Machado, Julio Segundo (Rondon) b: 12/1/65, Zulia, Venezuela   BR/TR, 5'9", 165 lbs.   Deb: 9/7/89

1989	NY-N	0	1	.000	10	0	0	0	0	11	9	0	3	14	9.8	3.27	100	.214	.267	0	—	0	-0	-0	-0	0.0
1990	NY-N	4	1	.800	27	0	0	0	0	34¹	32	4	17	27	13.4	3.15	119	.248	.345	0	—	0	3	4	0	0.3
	Mil-A	0	0	—	10	0	0	0	0	13	9	0	12	11	11.8	0.69	559	.191	.309	0	—	0	5	5	-0	0.2
1991	Mil-A	3	3	.500	54	0	0	0	3	88²	65	12	55	98	12.5	3.45	115	.211	.336	0	—	0	6	5	-1	0.4
Total	3	7	5	.583	101	0	0	0	3	147	115	16	87	150	12.2	3.12	123	.219	.331	0	—	0	14	12	-1	0.9

● **CHUCK MACHEMEHL**   Machemehl, Charles Walter b: 4/20/47, Brenham, Tex.   BR/TR, 6'4", 200 lbs.   Deb: 4/6/71

1971	Cle-A	0	2	.000	14	0	0	0	3	18¹	16	2	15	9	15.2	6.38	60	.246	.387	1	.500	0	-6	-5	0	-0.7

YEAR TM/L	W	L	PCT	G	GS	CG	SH	SV	IP	H	HR	BB	SO	RAT	ERA	ERA+	OAV	OOB	BH	AVG	PB	PR	/A	PD	TPI
● **DENNY MACK** Mack, Dennis Joseph (b: Dennis Joseph McGee) b: 1851, Easton, Pa. d: 4/10/1888, Wilkes-Barre, Pa. BR/TR, 5'7", 164 lbs. Deb: 5/6/1871 MU♦																									
1871 Rok-n	0	1	.000	3	1	1	0	0	13	20	0	3	1	15.9	3.46	118	.299	.329	30	.246	-0	1	1		0.1
● **FRANK MACK** Mack, Frank George "Stubby" b: 2/2/1900, Oklahoma City, Okla. d: 7/2/71, Clearwater, Fla. BR/TR, 6'1.5", 180 lbs. Deb: 8/16/22																									
1922 Chi-A	2	2	.500	8	4	1	1	0	34¹	36	2	16	11	13.6	3.67	111	.281	.361	3	.250	1	1	2	-1	0.1
1923 Chi-A	0	1	.000	11	0	0	0	0	23¹	23	0	11	6	13.1	4.24	93	.284	.370	0	.000	-1	-1	-1	0	-0.1
1925 Chi-A	0	0	—	8	0	0	0	0	13¹	24	1	13	6	25.0	9.45	44	.444	.552	1	.333	0	-7	-8	-0	0.0
Total 3	2	3	.400	27	4	1	1	0	71	83	3	40	23	15.6	4.94	82	.316	.406	4	.190	-0	-7	-7	-1	0.0
● **TONY MACK** Mack, Tony Lynn b: 4/30/61, Lexington, Ky. BR/TR, 5'10", 177 lbs. Deb: 7/27/85																									
1985 Cal-n	0	1	.000	1	1	0	0	0	2¹	8	0	0	0	30.9	15.43	27	.571	.571	0	—	0	-3	-3	-0	-0.7
● **BILL MACK** Mack, William Francis b: 2/12/1885, Elmira, N.Y. d: 9/30/71, Elmira, N.Y. BL/TL, 6'1", 155 lbs. Deb: 7/14/08																									
1908 Chi-N	0	0	—	2	0	0	0	0	6	5	1	1	2	10.5	3.00	78	.263	.333	2	.667	1	-0	-0	-0	0.2
● **KEN MacKENZIE** MacKenzie, Kenneth Purvis b: 3/10/34, Gore Bay, Ont., Can. BR/TL, 6', 185 lbs. Deb: 5/2/60																									
1960 Mil-N	0	1	.000	9	0	0	0	0	8¹	9	2	3	9	13.0	6.48	53	.281	.343	0	.000	-0	-3	-3	-0	-0.3
1961 Mil-N	0	1	.000	5	0	0	0	0	7	8	1	2	5	14.1	5.14	73	.296	.367	0	.000	-0	-1	-1	-0	-0.1
1962 NY-N	5	4	.556	42	1	0	0	1	80	87	10	34	51	13.9	4.95	84	.280	.356	1	.083	-1	-9	-7	1	-0.7
1963 NY-N	3	1	.750	34	0	0	0	3	58	63	11	12	41	11.9	4.97	70	.267	.308	0	.000	-1	-11	-10	-1	-0.9
StL-N	0	0	—	8	0	0	0	0	9	9	1	3	7	12.0	4.00	89	.250	.308	0	—	0	-1	-0	-0	0.0
Yr	3	1	.750	42	0	0	0	3	67	72	12	15	48	11.7	4.84	72	.262	.300	0	.000	-1	-12	-10	-1	-0.9
1964 SF-N	0	0	—	10	0	0	0	0	9	9	1	3	3	12.0	5.00	71	.265	.324	0	—	0	-1	-1	-0	0.0
1965 Hou-N	0	3	.000	21	0	0	0	0	37	46	7	6	26	12.6	3.89	86	.299	.325	3	.273	1	-1	-2	-0	-0.1
Total 6	8	10	.444	129	1	0	0	5	208¹	231	33	63	142	13.0	4.80	78	.278	.334	4	.111	-2	-27	-24	-1	-2.1
● **JOHN MACKINSON** Mackinson, John Joseph b: 10/29/23, Orange, N.J. d: 10/17/89, Reseda, Cal. BR/TR, 5'10.5", 160 lbs. Deb: 4/16/53																									
1953 Phi-A	0	0	—	1	0	0	0	0	1¹	1	0	2	0	20.3	0.00	—	.200	.429	0	—	0	1	1	0	0.0
1955 StL-N	0	1	.000	8	1	0	0	0	20²	24	3	10	8	15.2	7.84	52	.296	.380	0	.000	-0	-9	-9	-0	-0.4
Total 2	0	1	.000	9	1	0	0	0	22	25	3	12	8	15.5	7.36	55	.291	.384	0	.000	-0	-8	-8	-0	-0.4
● **BILLY MacLEOD** MacLeod, William Daniel b: 5/13/42, Gloucester, Mass. BL/TL, 6'2", 190 lbs. Deb: 9/13/62																									
1962 Bos-A	0	1	.000	2	0	0	0	0	1²	4	0	1	2	27.0	5.40	76	.444	.500	0	—	0	-0	-0	-0	-0.1
● **MAX MACON** Macon, Max Cullen b: 10/14/15, Pensacola, Fla. d: 8/5/89, Jupiter, Fla. BL/TL, 6'3", 175 lbs. Deb: 4/21/38 ♦																									
1938 StL-N	4	11	.267	38	12	5	1	2	129¹	133	9	61	39	13.8	4.11	96	.268	.352	11	.306	2	-5	-2	1	0.0
1940 Bro-N	1	0	1.000	2	0	0	0	0	2	5	2	0	1	22.5	22.50	18	.455	.455	1	1.000	0	-4	-4	-0	-1.3
1942 Bro-N	5	3	.625	14	8	4	1	1	84	67	3	33	27	10.9	1.93	169	.220	.300	12	.279	4	13	12	0	1.6
1943 Bro-N	7	5	.583	25	9	0	0	0	77	91	4	32	21	14.8	5.96	56	.291	.364	9	.164	-1	-22	-22	1	-3.2
1944 Bos-N	0	0	—	1	0	0	0	0	3	10	1	1	1	33.0	21.00	18	.556	.579	100	.273	0	-6	-6	0	0.0
1947 Bos-N	0	0	—	1	0	0	0	0	2	1	1	1	1	9.0	0.00	—	.167	.286	0	—	0	1	1	0	0.0
Total 6	17	19	.472	81	29	9	2	3	297¹	307	20	128	90	13.5	4.24	85	.267	.345	133	.265	5	-23	-21	1	-2.9
● **HARRY MacPHERSON** MacPherson, Harry William b: 7/10/26, N.Andover, Mass. BR/TR, 5'10", 150 lbs. Deb: 8/14/44																									
1944 Bos-N	0	0	—	1	0	0	0	0	1	0	0	1	1	9.0	0.00	—	.000	.250	0	—	0	0	0	0	0.0
● **JIMMY MACULLAR** Macullar, James F. "Little Mac" b: 1/16/1855, Boston, Mass. d: 4/8/24, Baltimore, Md. BR/TL, 5'6", 155 lbs. Deb: 5/5/1879 MU♦																									
1885 Bal-a	0	0	—	1	0	0	0	0	1	0	0	0	0	0.0	0.00	—	.000	.000	61	.191	0	0	0	0	0.0
1886 Bal-a	0	0	—	1	0	0	0	0	2	4	0	1	0	18.0	9.00	38	.400	.400	55	.205	-1	-1	-1	-0	0.0
Total 2	0	0	—	2	0	0	0	0	3	4	0	1	0	12.0	6.00	56	.308	.308	319	.207	-1	-1	-1	-0	0.0
● **KEITH MacWHORTER** MacWhorter, Keith b: 12/30/55, Worcester, Mass. BR/TR, 6'4", 190 lbs. Deb: 5/10/80																									
1980 Bos-A	0	3	.000	14	2	0	0	0	42¹	46	3	18	21	14.0	5.53	76	.280	.359	0	—	0	-7	-6	0	-0.5
● **LEN MADDEN** Madden, Leonard Joseph "Lefty" b: 7/2/1890, Toledo, Ohio d: 9/9/49, Toledo, Ohio BL/TL, 6'2", 165 lbs. Deb: 8/31/12																									
1912 Chi-N	0	1	.000	6	2	0	0	0	12¹	16	1	9	5	19.0	2.92	114	.302	.413	1	.250	0	1	1	-0	0.0
● **MIKE MADDEN** Madden, Michael Anthony b: 1/13/58, Denver, Colo. BL/TL, 6'1", 190 lbs. Deb: 4/5/83																									
1983 Hou-N	9	5	.643	28	13	0	0	0	94²	76	4	45	44	11.6	3.14	108	.231	.325	1	.045	-1	5	3	0	0.3
1984 Hou-N	2	3	.400	17	7	0	0	0	40²	41	6	35	29	17.9	5.53	60	.297	.426	2	.333	1	-9	-10	-1	-1.1
1985 Hou-N	0	0	—	13	0	0	0	0	19	29	1	11	16	18.9	4.26	81	.363	.440	0	—	0	-1	-2	-0	-0.2
1986 Hou-N	1	2	.333	13	6	0	0	0	39²	47	3	22	30	15.7	4.08	88	.297	.383	0	.000	-1	-2	-2	-0	-0.2
Total 4	12	10	.545	71	26	0	0	0	194	198	9	113	119	14.5	3.94	87	.274	.373	3	.081	-1	-7	-11	-1	-1.0
● **KID MADDEN** Madden, Michael Joseph b: 10/22/1866, Portland, Me. d: 3/16/1896, Portland, Maine TL, 5'7.5", 130 lbs. Deb: 5/6/1887																									
1887 Bos-N	21	14	.600	37	37	36	3	0	321	317	20	122	81	12.9	3.79	107	.251	.327	32	.242	4	10	10	-2	0.9
1888 Bos-N	7	11	.389	20	18	17	1	0	165	142	6	24	53	9.9	2.95	97	.228	.273	11	.164	-2	-2	-1	1	-0.3
1889 Bos-N	10	10	.500	22	19	18	1	0	178	194	7	71	64	14.2	4.40	95	.269	.348	25	.291	-2	-8	-5	0	-0.2
1890 Bos-P	3	2	.600	10	7	5	1	0	62	85	2	25	24	17.1	4.79	92	.313	.387	7	.184	-1	-4	-3	1	-0.2
1891 Bos-a	0	1	.000	1	1	1	0	0	8	10	1	6	6	21.4	6.75	52	.294	.442	2	.667	1	-3	-3	-0	-0.2
Bal-a	13	12	.520	32	27	20	1	1	224	239	4	88	56	14.1	4.10	91	.264	.345	29	.271	5	-9	-9	4	-0.1
Yr	13	13	.500	33	28	21	1	1	232	249	5	94	62	14.2	4.19	89	.264	.346	31	.282	6	-12	-12	4	-0.3
Total 5	54	50	.519	122	109	97	7	3	958	987	41	336	284	13.2	3.92	97	.259	.332	106	.245	10	-15	-11	4	-0.1
● **MORRIS MADDEN** Madden, Morris De Wayne b: 8/31/60, Laurens, S.C. BL/TL, 6' ", 155 lbs. Deb: 6/11/87																									
1987 Det-A	0	0	—	2	0	0	0	0	1²	4	0	3	0	37.8	16.20	26	.444	.583	0	—	0	-2	-2	-0	0.0
1988 Pit-N	0	0	—	5	0	0	0	0	5²	5	0	7	3	19.1	0.00	—	.294	.500	0	—	0	2	2	0	0.0
1989 Pit-N	2	2	.500	9	3	0	0	0	14	17	0	13	6	19.3	7.07	47	.327	.462	0	.000	-0	-6	-6	-1	-1.5
Total 3	2	2	.500	16	3	0	0	0	21¹	26	0	23	9	20.7	5.91	58	.333	.485	0	.000	-0	-6	-6	-1	-1.5
● **NICK MADDOX** Maddox, Nicholas b: 11/9/1886, Govans, Md. d: 11/27/54, Pittsburgh, Pa. BL/TR, 6', 175 lbs. Deb: 9/13/07																									
1907 Pit-N	5	1	.833	6	6	6	1	0	54	32	0	13	38	8.2	0.83	292	.178	.249	5	.250	2	10	10	-0	1.5
1908 Pit-N	23	8	.742	36	32	22	6	1	260²	209	5	90	70	10.7	2.28	101	.223	.298	25	.266	8	2	1	-1	0.9
1909 *Pit-N	13	8	.619	31	27	17	4	0	203¹	173	2	39	56	10.0	2.21	123	.232	.283	15	.224	4	9	11	-1	1.4
1910 Pit-N	2	3	.400	20	7	2	0	0	87¹	73	0	28	29	10.9	3.40	90	.246	.321	6	.214	1	-4	-3	-0	-0.1
Total 4	43	20	.683	93	72	47	9	1	605¹	487	7	170	193	10.3	2.29	112	.225	.292	51	.244	15	17	19	-2	3.7
● **GREG MADDUX** Maddux, Gregory Alan b: 4/14/66, San Angelo, Tex. BR/TR, 6', 150 lbs. Deb: 9/3/86 F																									
1986 Chi-N	2	4	.333	6	5	1	0	0	31	44	3	11	20	16.3	5.52	73	.336	.392	4	.333	1	-6	-5	0	-0.8
1987 Chi-N	6	14	.300	30	27	1	1	0	155²	181	17	74	101	15.0	5.61	76	.294	.374	5	.119	-2	-26	-23	6	-2.2
1988 Chi-N☆	18	8	.692	34	34	9	3	0	249	230	13	81	140	11.6	3.18	113	.244	.309	19	.198	2	7	12	2	1.7
1989 *Chi-N	19	12	.613	35	35	7	1	0	238¹	222	13	82	135	11.7	2.95	128	.249	.317	17	.210	2	15	21	3	3.4
1990 Chi-N	15	15	.500	35	35	8	2	0	237	242	11	71	144	12.0	3.46	118	.265	.321	12	.145	-2	9	16	8	2.6
1991 Chi-N	15	11	.577	37	37	7	2	0	263	232	18	66	198	10.4	3.35	116	.237	.289	18	.205	3	10	15	5	2.4
1992 Chi-N★	**20**	11	.645	35	35	9	4	0	268	201	7	70	199	9.6	2.18	**165**	.210	.273	15	.170	2	**39**	**42**	6	6.2
1993 *Atl-N★	20	10	.667	36	36	**8**	1	0	267	228	14	52	197	**9.6**	2.36	**170**	.232	**.274**	15	.165	-1	**50**	**49**	7	6.1
1994 *Atl-N★	**16**	6	.727	25	25	**10**	**3**	0	**202**	150	4	31	156	**8.3**	**1.56**	**272**	**.207**	**.245**	14	.222	2	**60**	**60**	7	**7.3**
1995 *Atl-N☆	**19**	2	**.905**	28	28	**10**	**3**	0	**209²**	147	8	23	181	**7.5**	**1.63**	**261**	**.197**	**.225**	11	.153	-0	**59**	**61**	6	6.8
1996 *Atl-N☆	15	11	.577	35	35	5	1	0	245	225	11	28	172	9.4	2.72	162	.241	.265	15	.147	-1	41	46	10	5.6
Total 11	165	104	.613	336	332	75	21	0	2365²	2102	119	589	1643	10.5	2.86	139	.238	.291	140	.179	6	257	297	56	39.1
● **MIKE MADDUX** Maddux, Michael Ausley b: 8/27/61, Dayton, Ohio BL/TR, 6'2", 180 lbs. Deb: 6/3/86 F																									
1986 Phi-N	3	7	.300	16	16	0	0	0	78	88	6	34	44	14.4	5.42	71	.286	.362	1	.045	-1	-15	-14	-1	-1.7

YEAR TM/L	W	L	PCT	G	GS	CG	SH	SV	IP	H	HR	BB	SO	RAT	ERA	ERA+	OAV	OOB	BH	AVG	PB	PR	/A	PD	TPI
1987 Phi-N	2	0	1.000	7	2	0	0	0	17	17	0	5	15	11.6	2.65	160	.254	.306	0	.000	-0	3	3	-0	0.3
1988 Phi-N	4	3	.571	25	11	0	0	0	88²	91	6	34	59	13.2	3.76	95	.275	.351	3	.130	-0	-3	-2	1	0.0
1989 Phi-N	1	3	.250	16	4	0	1	1	43²	52	3	14	26	14.0	5.15	69	.304	.364	0	.000	-1	-8	-8	2	-0.6
1990 LA-N	0	1	.000	11	2	0	0	0	20²	24	3	4	11	12.6	6.53	56	.293	.333	0	.000	-0	-6	-7	0	-0.3
1991 SD-N	7	2	.778	64	1	0	0	5	98²	78	4	27	57	9.7	2.46	154	.221	.278	1	.077	-0	13	15	1	1.5
1992 SD-N	2	2	.500	50	1	0	0	5	79²	71	2	24	60	10.7	2.37	151	.236	.292	1	.111	-0	10	11	2	0.8
1993 NY-N	3	8	.273	58	0	0	0	5	75	67	3	27	57	11.8	3.60	111	.243	.319	0	.000	-0	4	3	1	0.6
1994 NY-N	2	1	.667	27	0	0	0	2	44	45	7	13	32	11.9	5.11	82	.263	.315	0	.000	-0	-4	-5	1	-0.2
1995 Pit-N	1	0	1.000	8	0	0	0	0	9	14	0	3	4	17.0	9.00	48	.359	.405	0	—	0	-5	-5	0	-0.5
*Bos-A	4	1	.800	36	4	0	0	1	89²	86	5	15	65	10.3	3.61	135	.247	.282	0	—	0	11	13	0	0.5
1996 Bos-A	3	2	.600	23	7	0	0	0	64¹	76	12	27	32	15.1	4.48	115	.295	.372	0	—	0	4	5	1	0.4
Total 11	32	30	.516	341	48	2	1	19	708¹	709	51	227	462	12.2	3.93	103	.262	.325	6	.068	-4	3	10	7	0.8

● **TONY MADIGAN** Madigan, William J. "Tice" b: 7/1868, Washington, D.C. d: 12/4/54, Washington, D.C. TR, 5'5.5", 126 lbs. Deb: 7/10/1886

YEAR TM/L	W	L	PCT	G	GS	CG	SH	SV	IP	H	HR	BB	SO	RAT	ERA	ERA+	OAV	OOB	BH	AVG	PB	PR	/A	PD	TPI
1886 Was-N	1	13	.071	14	13	13	0	0	114²	154	3	44	29	15.5	4.87	68	.310	.366	4	.083	-4	-20	-20	0	-2.2

● **DAVE MADISON** Madison, David Pledger b: 2/1/21, Brooksville, Miss. d: 12/6/85, Macon, Miss. BR/TR, 6'3", 190 lbs. Deb: 9/26/50

YEAR TM/L	W	L	PCT	G	GS	CG	SH	SV	IP	H	HR	BB	SO	RAT	ERA	ERA+	OAV	OOB	BH	AVG	PB	PR	/A	PD	TPI
1950 NY-A	0	0	—	1	0	0	0	0	3	3	1	1	1	12.0	6.00	72	.273	.333	0	—	0	-0	-1	-0	0.0
1952 StL-A	4	2	.667	31	4	0	0	0	78	78	7	48	35	15.0	4.38	89	.264	.374	2	.118	-1	-6	-4	0	-0.4
Det-A	1	1	.500	10	1	0	0	0	15	16	1	10	7	16.2	7.80	49	.291	.409	0	.000	-0	-7	-7	0	-0.8
Yr	5	3	.625	41	5	0	0	0	93	94	8	58	42	14.8	4.94	79	.265	.370	2	.105	-1	-13	-11	-0	-1.2
1953 Det-A	3	4	.429	32	1	0	0	0	62	76	7	44	27	17.9	6.82	60	.303	.413	1	.091	-0	-19	-19	0	-1.9
Total 3	8	7	.533	74	6	0	0	0	158	173	16	103	70	16.2	5.70	70	.282	.392	2	.100	-2	-33	-30	0	-3.1

● **ALEX MADRID** Madrid, Alexander b: 4/18/63, Springerville, Ariz BR/TR, 6'3", 200 lbs. Deb: 7/20/87

YEAR TM/L	W	L	PCT	G	GS	CG	SH	SV	IP	H	HR	BB	SO	RAT	ERA	ERA+	OAV	OOB	BH	AVG	PB	PR	/A	PD	TPI
1987 Mil-A	0	0	—	3	0	0	0	0	5¹	11	1	4	1	20.3	15.19	30	.440	.462	0	—	0	-6	-6	-0	-0.1
1988 Phi-N	1	1	.500	5	2	1	0	0	16¹	15	0	6	2	11.6	2.76	129	.246	.313	0	.000	-0	1	1	-0	0.1
1989 Phi-N	1	2	.333	6	3	0	0	0	24²	32	3	14	13	17.1	5.47	65	.314	.402	0	.000	-0	-5	-5	-0	-0.7
Total 3	2	3	.400	14	5	1	0	0	46¹	58	4	21	16	15.5	5.63	65	.309	.381	0	.000	-1	-11	-10	-1	-0.7

● **CALVIN MADURO** Maduro, Calvin Gregory b: 9/5/74, Santa Cruz, Aruba BR/TR, 6', 175 lbs. Deb: 9/8/96

YEAR TM/L	W	L	PCT	G	GS	CG	SH	SV	IP	H	HR	BB	SO	RAT	ERA	ERA+	OAV	OOB	BH	AVG	PB	PR	/A	PD	TPI
1996 Phi-N	0	1	.000	4	2	0	0	0	15¹	13	1	3	11	10.6	3.52	124	.232	.295	0	.000	-0	1	1	-0	0.0

● **HECTOR MAESTRI** Maestri, Hector Anibal (Garcia) b: 4/19/35, Havana, Cuba BR/TR, 5'10", 158 lbs. Deb: 9/24/60

YEAR TM/L	W	L	PCT	G	GS	CG	SH	SV	IP	H	HR	BB	SO	RAT	ERA	ERA+	OAV	OOB	BH	AVG	PB	PR	/A	PD	TPI
1960 Was-A	0	0	—	1	0	0	0	0	2	1	0	1	1	9.0	0.00	—	.167	.286	0	—	0	1	1	-0	0.0
1961 Was-A	0	1	.000	1	1	0	0	0	6	6	1	2	2	12.0	1.50	268	.250	.308	0	.000	-0	2	2	0	0.3
Total 2	0	1	.000	2	1	0	0	0	7¹	7	1	3	3	11.3	1.13	354	.233	.303	0	.000	-0	3	3	-0	0.3

● **BILL MAGEE** Magee, William J. b: 1875, Canada BR/TR, 5'10", 154 lbs. Deb: 5/18/1897

YEAR TM/L	W	L	PCT	G	GS	CG	SH	SV	IP	H	HR	BB	SO	RAT	ERA	ERA+	OAV	OOB	BH	AVG	PB	PR	/A	PD	TPI
1897 Lou-N	4	12	.250	22	16	13	1	0	155¹	186	6	99	44	17.1	5.39	79	.294	.398	13	.210	-2	-19	-19	1	-1.6
1898 Lou-N	16	15	.516	38	33	29	3	0	295¹	294	8	129	55	13.5	4.05	88	.258	.343	14	.126	-9	-15	-16	-2	-2.3
1899 Lou-N	3	7	.300	12	10	6	1	0	71	91	0	28	13	16.2	5.20	74	.311	.388	3	.111	-2	-11	-11	1	-1.2
Phi-N	3	5	.375	9	9	7	0	0	70	82	0	32	4	15.6	5.66	65	.292	.378	5	.161	-2	-14	-15	-1	-1.5
Was-N	1	4	.200	8	7	4	0	0	42	54	3	28	11	19.1	8.57	44	.312	.428	5	.333	-1	-22	-22	1	-1.7
Yr	7	16	.304	29	26	17	1	0	183	227	3	88	28	15.8	6.15	62	.298	.375	13	.178	-5	-47	-48	-1	-4.4
1901 StL-N	0	0	—	1	1	0	0	0	8	8	0	4	3	13.5	4.50	71	.258	.343	2	.500	1	-1	-1	-0	0.1
NY-N	0	4	.000	6	5	4	0	0	42¹	56	4	11	14	15.1	5.95	56	.316	.370	2	.143	-1	-12	-12	-0	-1.0
Yr	0	4	.000	7	6	4	0	0	50¹	64	4	15	17	14.8	5.72	57	.308	.366	4	.222	-1	-13	-14	-1	-0.9
1902 NY-N	0	0	—	2	1	0	0	0	5	5	0	1	2	10.8	3.60	78	.263	.300	0	.000	-0	-0	-0	-0	0.0
Phi-N	2	4	.333	8	7	6	0	0	53²	61	1	18	15	13.5	3.69	76	.285	.349	4	.211	-0	-5	-5	-0	-0.6
Yr	2	4	.333	10	8	6	0	0	58²	66	1	19	17	13.5	3.68	76	.283	.345	4	.200	-1	-6	-6	-0	-0.6
Total 5	29	51	.363	106	89	69	5	0	742²	837	23	350	161	15.1	4.93	75	.283	.370	48	.169	-13	-99	-102	-0	-9.8

● **SAL MAGLIE** Maglie, Salvatore Anthony "The Barber" b: 4/26/17, Niagara Falls, N.Y d: 12/28/92, Niagara Falls, N.Y BR/TR, 6'2", 180 lbs. Deb: 8/9/45 C

YEAR TM/L	W	L	PCT	G	GS	CG	SH	SV	IP	H	HR	BB	SO	RAT	ERA	ERA+	OAV	OOB	BH	AVG	PB	PR	/A	PD	TPI
1945 NY-N	5	4	.556	13	10	7	3	0	84¹	72	2	32	32	10.2	2.35	167	.231	.286	5	.167	-1	14	15	0	1.4
1950 NY-N	18	4	**.818**	47	16	12	**5**	1	206	169	14	86	96	11.6	2.71	**151**	.226	.314	8	.121	-1	33	32	3	3.3
1951 *NY-N★	**23**	6	.793	42	37	22	3	4	298	254	27	86	146	10.4	2.93	**134**	**.230**	.289	17	.152	-3	**34**	33	1	2.9
1952 NY-N☆	18	8	.692	35	31	12	5	1	216	194	19	66	112	11.7	2.92	127	.244	.312	5	.072	-3	20	19	1	1.9
1953 NY-N	8	9	.471	27	24	9	3	0	145¹	158	19	47	80	12.8	4.15	103	.278	.334	13	.271	2	2	2	-2	0.3
1954 *NY-N	14	6	.700	34	32	9	1	2	218¹	222	16	70	117	12.2	3.26	124	.262	.320	8	.127	-2	20	19	0	1.4
1955 NY-N	9	5	.643	23	21	6	0	0	129²	142	18	48	71	13.4	3.75	107	.278	.344	5	.125	-1	4	4	-2	0.0
Cle-A	0	2	.000	10	2	0	0	0	25²	26	0	7	11	11.9	3.86	103	.252	.306	0	—	0	-0	-0	-1	-0.1
1956 Cle-A	0	0	—	2	0	0	0	0	5	6	1	2	4	14.4	3.60	117	.300	.364	0	—	0	-0	-0	-0	0.0
*Bro-N	13	5	.722	28	26	9	3	0	191	154	21	52	108	9.9	2.87	**138**	.222	.281	9	.129	-3	19	23	-2	1.5
1957 Bro-N	6	6	.500	19	17	4	1	1	101¹	94	12	26	50	11.0	2.93	142	.245	.300	2	.034	-3	11	11	-1	1.2
NY-A	2	0	1.000	6	3	1	1	3	26	22	1	7	9	10.4	1.73	207	.227	.286	2	.250	-0	6	5	0	0.6
1958 NY-A	1	1	.500	7	3	0	0	0	23¹	27	3	9	7	13.9	4.63	76	.300	.364	1	.143	-1	-0	-0	-1	-0.1
StL-N	2	6	.250	10	10	2	0	0	53	46	14	25	21	12.4	4.75	87	.232	.324	2	.125	-1	-5	-4	-1	-0.6
Total 10	119	62	.657	303	232	93	25	14	1723	1591	169	562	862	11.5	3.15	127	.245	.309	76	.135	-16	156	160	-2	13.7

● **MIKE MAGNANTE** Magnante, Michael Anthony b: 6/17/65, Glendale, Cal. BL/TL, 6'1", 180 lbs. Deb: 4/22/91

YEAR TM/L	W	L	PCT	G	GS	CG	SH	SV	IP	H	HR	BB	SO	RAT	ERA	ERA+	OAV	OOB	BH	AVG	PB	PR	/A	PD	TPI
1991 KC-A	0	1	.000	38	0	0	0	0	55	55	3	23	42	12.8	2.45	168	.262	.335	0	—	0	10	10	-0	0.1
1992 KC-A	4	9	.308	44	12	0	0	0	89¹	115	5	35	31	15.3	4.94	82	.325	.389	0	—	0	-10	-9	2	-1.2
1993 KC-A	1	2	.333	7	6	0	0	0	35¹	37	3	11	16	12.5	4.08	112	.282	.343	0	—	0	1	2	0	0.1
1994 KC-A	2	3	.400	36	1	0	0	0	47	55	5	16	21	13.6	4.60	109	.289	.367	0	—	0	1	2	0	0.1
1995 KC-A	1	1	.500	28	0	0	0	0	44²	45	6	16	28	12.7	4.23	113	.268	.339	0	—	0	2	3	1	0.1
1996 KC-A	2	2	.500	38	0	0	0	0	54	58	5	24	32	14.3	5.67	86	.282	.368	0	—	0	-4	-5	2	-0.1
Total 6	10	18	.357	191	19	0	0	0	325¹	365	27	125	170	13.8	4.40	102	.290	.358	0	—	0	0	4	5	-1.1

● **JIM MAGNUSON** Magnuson, James Robert b: 8/18/46, Marinette, Wis. d: 5/30/91, Green Bay, Wis. BR/TL, 6'2", 190 lbs. Deb: 6/28/70

YEAR TM/L	W	L	PCT	G	GS	CG	SH	SV	IP	H	HR	BB	SO	RAT	ERA	ERA+	OAV	OOB	BH	AVG	PB	PR	/A	PD	TPI
1970 Chi-A	1	5	.167	13	6	0	0	0	44²	45	7	16	20	12.5	4.84	81	.263	.330	0	.000	-1	-6	-5	-0	-0.7
1971 Chi-A	1	1	.500	15	4	0	0	0	30	30	0	16	14	14.4	4.50	82	.265	.366	0	.000	-0	-3	-3	-0	-0.3
1973 NY-A	0	1	.000	8	0	0	0	0	27¹	38	2	9	6	15.5	4.28	86	.342	.392	0	—	0	-1	-2	0	-0.0
Total 3	2	7	.222	36	10	0	0	0	102	113	9	41	40	13.9	4.59	82	.286	.358	0	.000	-2	-10	-10	-0	-1.0

● **JOE MAGRANE** Magrane, Joseph David b: 7/2/64, Des Moines, Iowa BR/TL, 6'6", 225 lbs. Deb: 4/25/87

YEAR TM/L	W	L	PCT	G	GS	CG	SH	SV	IP	H	HR	BB	SO	RAT	ERA	ERA+	OAV	OOB	BH	AVG	PB	PR	/A	PD	TPI
1987 *StL-N	9	7	.563	27	26	4	2	0	170¹	157	9	60	101	12.0	3.54	117	.245	.320	7	.135	-1	10	12	0	1.1
1988 StL-N	5	9	.357	24	24	4	3	0	165¹	133	6	51	100	10.1	**2.18**	160	.217	.280	8	.167	1	23	24	2	2.5
1989 StL-N	18	9	.667	34	33	9	3	0	234²	219	5	72	127	11.4	2.91	124	.251	.313	11	.138	1	15	19	-1	2.1
1990 StL-N	10	17	.370	31	31	3	0	0	203¹	204	10	59	100	12.0	3.59	106	.264	.322	7	.127	-0	5	5	1	0.8
1992 StL-N	1	2	.333	5	5	0	0	0	31¹	34	2	15	20	14.6	4.02	84	.279	.367	2	.200	1	-2	-2	-0	-0.1
1993 StL-N	8	10	.444	22	20	0	0	0	116	127	15	37	38	13.1	4.97	80	.286	.348	4	.114	-1	-12	-13	0	-1.8
Cal-A	3	2	.600	8	8	0	0	0	48	44	3	21	24	12.9	3.94	114	.265	.342	0	—	0	2	3	2	0.4
1994 Cal-A	2	6	.250	20	11	1	0	0	74	89	4	51	33	17.8	7.30	67	.300	.412	0	—	0	-21	-20	-0	-1.8
1996 Chi-A	1	5	.167	19	8	0	0	0	53²	70	10	25	21	16.4	6.88	68	.318	.395	0	—	0	-11	-13	-0	-1.2
Total 8	57	67	.460	190	166	21	10	0	1096²	1081	79	391	564	12.4	3.81	103	.260	.330	39	.139	3	10	15	3	2.0

● **PETE MAGRINI** Magrini, Peter Alexander b: 6/8/42, San Francisco, Cal. BR/TR, 6', 195 lbs. Deb: 4/13/66

YEAR TM/L	W	L	PCT	G	GS	CG	SH	SV	IP	H	HR	BB	SO	RAT	ERA	ERA+	OAV	OOB	BH	AVG	PB	PR	/A	PD	TPI
1966 Bos-A	0	1	.000	3	1	0	0	0	7¹	7	1	9	3	20.9	9.82	39	.308	.486	0	—	0	-5	-5	-0	-0.6

● **ART MAHAFFEY** Mahaffey, Arthur b: 6/4/38, Cincinnati, Ohio BR/TR, 6'2", 200 lbs. Deb: 7/30/60

YEAR TM/L	W	L	PCT	G	GS	CG	SH	SV	IP	H	HR	BB	SO	RAT	ERA	ERA+	OAV	OOB	BH	AVG	PB	PR	/A	PD	TPI
1960 Phi-N	7	3	.700	14	12	5	1	0	93¹	78	9	34	56	10.9	2.31	168	.229	.301	3	.100	-2	15	16	-1	1.5

YEAR TM/L	W	L	PCT	G	GS	CG	SH	SV	IP	H	HR	BB	SO	RAT	ERA	ERA+	OAV	OOB	BH	AVG	PB	PR	/A	PD	TPI
1961 Phi-N★	11	19	.367	36	32	12	3	0	219¹	205	27	70	158	11.6	4.10	99	.249	.314	8	.127	-2	-2	-1	-2	-0.4
1962 Phi-N★	19	14	.576	41	39	20	2	0	274	253	36	81	177	11.4	3.94	98	.246	.309	13	.141	1	0	-2	-4	-0.6
1963 Phi-N	7	10	.412	26	22	6	1	0	149	143	18	48	97	11.8	3.99	81	.255	.319	10	.200	2	-12	-12	-1	-1.2
1964 Phi-N	12	9	.571	34	29	2	2	0	157¹	161	17	82	80	14.2	4.52	77	.269	.362	6	.120	0	-17	-18	-2	-2.4
1965 Phi-N	2	5	.286	22	9	1	0	0	71	82	11	32	52	15.3	6.21	56	.294	.381	2	.095	-1	-21	-22	-1	-2.1
1966 StL-N	1	4	.200	12	5	0	0	1	35	37	7	21	19	15.2	6.43	56	.276	.378	-1	.000	-1	-11	-11	-1	-1.6
Total 7	59	64	.480	185	148	46	9	1	999	959	125	368	639	12.3	4.17	89	.255	.328	42	.134	-2	-47	-50	-11	-6.8

● **ROY MAHAFFEY**   Mahaffey, Lee Roy "Popeye" b: 2/9/03, Belton, S.C. d: 7/23/69, Anderson, S.C. BR/TR, 6', 180 lbs. Deb: 8/31/26

YEAR TM/L	W	L	PCT	G	GS	CG	SH	SV	IP	H	HR	BB	SO	RAT	ERA	ERA+	OAV	OOB	BH	AVG	PB	PR	/A	PD	TPI
1926 Pit-N	0	0	—	4	0	0	0	0	4²	5	0	1	3	13.5	0.00	—	.294	.368	0	.000	-0	2	2	-0	-0.1
1927 Pit-N	1	0	1.000	2	1	0	0	0	9¹	9	0	9	2	20.3	7.71	53	.300	.500	2	.400	-0	-4	-4	-0	-0.3
1930 Phi-A	9	5	.643	33	16	6	0	0	152²	186	16	53	38	14.3	5.01	93	.298	.357	7	.119	-5	-6	-6	-1	-1.0
1931 *Phi-A	15	4	.789	30	20	8	0	2	162¹	161	9	82	59	13.6	4.21	107	.258	.347	12	.190	1	3	5	-3	0.3
1932 Phi-A	13	13	.500	37	28	13	0	0	222²	245	27	96	106	14.0	5.09	89	.274	.348	11	.172	-1	-15	-14	-2	-1.6
1933 Phi-A	13	10	.565	33	23	9	0	0	179¹	198	5	74	60	13.9	5.41	83	.275	.346	14	.215	-0	-18	-18	-2	-2.0
1934 Phi-A	6	7	.462	37	14	3	0	2	129	142	10	55	37	13.8	5.37	82	.276	.347	13	.271	2	-13	-14	-2	-1.1
1935 Phi-A	8	4	.667	27	17	5	0	0	136	153	11	42	39	13.2	3.90	116	.283	.341	9	.176	-2	8	10	-1	0.4
1936 StL-A	2	6	.250	21	9	1	0	1	60	82	6	40	13	18.5	8.10	66	.315	.409	-1	.063	-1	-20	-18	-2	-2.2
Total 9	67	49	.578	224	128	45	0	5	1056	1181	84	452	365	14.1	5.01	90	.280	.353	73	.184	-7	-63	-57	-13	-7.6

● **LOU MAHAFFEY**   Mahaffey, Louis Wood b: 1/3/1874, Kentucky d: 10/26/49, Torrance, Cal. BR, 5'9", 170 lbs. Deb: 4/26/1898

YEAR TM/L	W	L	PCT	G	GS	CG	SH	SV	IP	H	HR	BB	SO	RAT	ERA	ERA+	OAV	OOB	BH	AVG	PB	PR	/A	PD	TPI
1898 Lou-N	0	1	.000	1	1	1	0	0	9	10	0	5	1	15.0	3.00	119	.278	.366	0	.000	-0	1	1	-0	0.0

● **ART MAHAN**   Mahan, Arthur Leo b: 6/8/13, Somerville, Mass. BL/TL, 5'11", 178 lbs. Deb: 4/30/40 ♦

YEAR TM/L	W	L	PCT	G	GS	CG	SH	SV	IP	H	HR	BB	SO	RAT	ERA	ERA+	OAV	OOB	BH	AVG	PB	PR	/A	PD	TPI
1940 Phi-N	0	0	—	1	0	0	0	0	1	1	0	0	0	9.0	0.00	—	.333	.333	133	.244	0	0	0	-0	0.0

● **MICKEY MAHLER**   Mahler, Michael James b: 7/30/52, Montgomery, Ala. BB/TL, 6'3", 189 lbs. Deb: 9/13/77 F

YEAR TM/L	W	L	PCT	G	GS	CG	SH	SV	IP	H	HR	BB	SO	RAT	ERA	ERA+	OAV	OOB	BH	AVG	PB	PR	/A	PD	TPI
1977 Atl-N	1	2	.333	5	5	0	0	0	23	31	4	9	14	16.0	6.26	71	.326	.390	3	.500	2	-6	-5	-0	-0.4
1978 Atl-N	4	11	.267	34	21	1	0	0	134²	130	16	66	92	13.6	4.68	87	.255	.349	4	.098	-2	-16	-9	-1	-1.3
1979 Atl-N	5	11	.313	26	18	1	0	0	100	123	11	47	71	15.6	5.85	69	.304	.381	3	.111	-1	-24	-20	-0	-2.9
1980 Pit-N	0	0	—	2	0	0	0	0	1	4	1	3	1	63.0	63.00	6	.571	.700	0	—	0	-7	-7	0	0.0
1981 Cal-A	0	0	—	6	0	0	0	0	6¹	1	0	2	5	4.3	0.00	—	.056	.150	0	—	0	3	3	0	0.0
1982 Cal-A	2	0	1.000	6	0	0	0	0	8	9	0	5	6	16.9	1.13	360	.300	.417	0	—	0	3	3	-0	0.6
1985 Mon-N	1	4	.200	9	7	1	1	1	48¹	40	3	24	32	12.1	3.54	96	.229	.325	3	.188	1	0	-1	-1	-0.1
Det-A	1	2	.333	3	2	0	0	0	20²	19	2	4	14	10.0	1.74	234	.241	.277	0	—	0	6	5	-0	0.8
1986 Tex-A	0	2	.000	29	5	0	0	3	63	71	3	29	14	14.7	4.14	104	.295	.377	0	—	0	0	1	-0	0.0
Tor-A	0	0	—	2	0	0	0	0	1	1	0	0	0	18.0	18.00	—	.200	.333	0	—	0	-0	-0	0	0.0
Yr	0	2	.000	31	5	0	0	3	64	72	3	29	28	14.3	4.08	105	.285	.360	0	—	0	1	2	-0	0.0
Total 8	14	32	.304	122	58	3	1	4	406	429	40	190	262	14.1	4.68	86	.274	.359	13	.144	-1	-41	-29	-3	-3.3

● **RICK MAHLER**   Mahler, Richard Keith b: 8/5/53, Austin, Tex. BR/TR, 6'1", 202 lbs. Deb: 4/20/79 F

YEAR TM/L	W	L	PCT	G	GS	CG	SH	SV	IP	H	HR	BB	SO	RAT	ERA	ERA+	OAV	OOB	BH	AVG	PB	PR	/A	PD	TPI
1979 Atl-N	0	0	—	15	0	0	0	0	22	28	4	11	12	16.0	6.14	66	.311	.386	1	.500	0	-6	-5	-0	0.0
1980 Atl-N	0	0	—	2	0	0	0	0	3²	2	0	1	1	4.9	2.45	152	.154	.154	0	—	0	1	0	0	0.0
1981 Atl-N	8	6	.571	34	14	1	0	2	112¹	109	5	43	54	12.3	2.80	128	.258	.328	4	.148	-1	9	10	1	1.2
1982 *Atl-N	9	10	.474	39	33	5	2	0	205¹	213	18	62	105	12.1	4.21	89	.272	.327	11	.190	2	-14	-11	2	-0.6
1983 Atl-N	0	0	—	10	0	0	0	0	14¹	16	0	9	7	15.7	5.02	77	.296	.397	0	.000	-0	-2	-2	-0	0.0
1984 Atl-N	13	10	.565	38	29	9	1	0	222	209	13	62	106	11.1	3.12	123	.251	.305	21	.296	5	12	18	2	2.6
1985 Atl-N	17	15	.531	39	39	6	1	0	266²	272	24	79	107	11.9	3.48	111	.268	.322	16	.156	-1	3	11	1	1.3
1986 Atl-N	14	18	.438	39	39	7	1	0	237²	283	25	95	137	14.4	4.88	81	.301	.367	16	.193	-2	-31	-24	-2	-2.6
1987 Atl-N	8	13	.381	39	28	3	1	0	197	212	24	85	95	13.7	4.98	87	.283	.357	11	.169	1	-20	-14	2	-1.0
1988 Atl-N	9	16	.360	39	34	5	0	0	249	279	17	42	131	11.9	3.69	100	.282	.317	9	.125	-1	-7	-0	1	-0.1
1989 Cin-N	9	13	.409	40	31	5	2	0	220²	242	15	51	102	12.4	3.83	94	.282	.329	11	.177	2	-8	-6	-0	-0.4
1990 *Cin-N	7	6	.538	35	16	2	1	4	134²	134	16	39	68	11.8	4.28	92	.261	.317	4	.114	-1	-7	-5	-0	-0.6
1991 Mon-N	1	3	.250	10	6	0	0	0	37¹	37	2	15	17	12.5	3.62	100	.268	.340	1	.111	-0	0	0	1	0.0
Atl-N	1	1	.500	13	2	0	0	0	28²	33	2	13	10	15.1	5.65	69	.282	.364	1	.200	-0	-6	-6	-0	-0.3
Yr	2	4	.333	23	8	0	0	0	66	70	4	28	27	13.6	4.50	83	.273	.350	2	.143	-0	-6	-6	1	-0.3
Total 13	96	111	.464	392	271	43	9	6	1951²	2069	165	606	922	12.4	3.99	96	.275	.332	104	.179	7	-77	-33	10	-0.5

● **PAT MAHOMES**   Mahomes, Patrick Lavon b: 8/9/70, Bryan, Tex. BR/TR, 6'1", 175 lbs. Deb: 4/12/92

YEAR TM/L	W	L	PCT	G	GS	CG	SH	SV	IP	H	HR	BB	SO	RAT	ERA	ERA+	OAV	OOB	BH	AVG	PB	PR	/A	PD	TPI
1992 Min-A	3	4	.429	14	13	0	0	0	69²	73	5	37	44	14.2	5.04	80	.279	.368			0	-9	-8	-1	-1.0
1993 Min-A	1	5	.167	12	5	0	0	0	37¹	47	8	16	23	15.4	7.71	56	.309	.379			0	-14	-14	0	-1.8
1994 Min-A	9	5	.643	21	21	0	0	0	120	121	22	62	53	13.8	4.72	103	.269	.359			0	1	2	-1	0.1
1995 Min-A	4	10	.286	47	7	0	0	3	94²	100	22	47	67	14.2	6.37	75	.271	.356			0	-17	-17	-0	-2.1
1996 Min-A	1	4	.200	20	5	0	0	0	45	63	10	27	30	18.0	7.20	71	.330	.413			0	-11	-10	-0	-0.9
Bos-A	2	0	1.000	11	0	0	0	2	12¹	9	3	6	6	10.9	5.84	88	.209	.306			0	-1	-1	-0	-0.2
Yr	3	4	.429	31	5	0	0	2	57¹	72	13	33	36	16.5	6.91	74	.305	.390			0	-12	-11	-0	-1.1
Total 5	20	28	.417	125	51	0	0	5	379	413	70	195	223	14.5	5.82	81	.282	.368			0	-51	-48	-1	-5.9

● **AL MAHON**   Mahon, Alfred Gwinn "Lefty" b: 9/23/09, Albion, Neb. d: 12/26/77, New Haven, Conn. BL/TL, 5'11", 160 lbs. Deb: 4/22/30

YEAR TM/L	W	L	PCT	G	GS	CG	SH	SV	IP	H	HR	BB	SO	RAT	ERA	ERA+	OAV	OOB	BH	AVG	PB	PR	/A	PD	TPI
1930 Phi-A	0	0	—	3	0	0	0	0	4¹	11	0	7	0	37.4	22.85	20	.579	.692	0	.000	-0	-9	-9	0	0.0

● **CHRIS MAHONEY**   Mahoney, Christopher John b: 6/11/1885, Milton, Mass. d: 7/15/54, Visalia, Cal. BR/TR, 5'9", 160 lbs. Deb: 7/12/10

YEAR TM/L	W	L	PCT	G	GS	CG	SH	SV	IP	H	HR	BB	SO	RAT	ERA	ERA+	OAV	OOB	BH	AVG	PB	PR	/A	PD	TPI
1910 Bos-A	0	1	.000	2	1	0	0	1	11	16	1	5	6	17.2	3.27	78	.327	.389	1	.143	-0	-1	-1	1	-0.1

● **MIKE MAHONEY**   Mahoney, George W. "Big Mike" b: 12/5/1873, Boston, Mass. d: 1/3/40, Boston, Mass. BR, 6'4", 220 lbs. Deb: 5/18/1897 ♦

YEAR TM/L	W	L	PCT	G	GS	CG	SH	SV	IP	H	HR	BB	SO	RAT	ERA	ERA+	OAV	OOB	BH	AVG	PB	PR	/A	PD	TPI
1897 Bos-N	0	0	—	1	0	0	0	0	3	0	1	1	36.0	18.00	25	.500	.571	1	.500	-0	-2	-2	0	-0.1

● **BOB MAHONEY**   Mahoney, Robert Paul b: 6/20/28, LeRoy, Minn. BR/TR, 6'1", 185 lbs. Deb: 5/3/51

YEAR TM/L	W	L	PCT	G	GS	CG	SH	SV	IP	H	HR	BB	SO	RAT	ERA	ERA+	OAV	OOB	BH	AVG	PB	PR	/A	PD	TPI
1951 Chi-A	0	0	—	3	0	0	0	0	6²	5	1	5	3	13.5	5.40	75	.208	.345	0	—	0	-1	-1	-0	-0.1
StL-A	2	5	.286	30	4	0	0	0	81	86	7	41	30	14.1	4.44	99	.274	.358	4	.222	-0	-3	-0	-1	-0.1
Yr	2	5	.286	33	4	0	0	0	87²	91	8	46	33	14.1	4.52	97	.269	.357	4	.222	-0	-4	-1	-1	-0.1
1952 StL-A	0	0	—	3	0	0	0	0	3	8	0	4	1	36.0	18.00	22	.500	.600	-0		0	-5	-5	-0	0.0
Total 2	2	5	.286	36	4	0	0	0	90²	99	8	50	34	14.8	4.96	88	.280	.369	4	.222	-0	-9	-6	-1	-0.1

● **DUSTER MAILS**   Mails, John Walter "Walter" or "The Great" b: 10/1/1894, San Quentin, Cal. d: 7/5/74, San Francisco, Cal BL/TL, 6', 195 lbs. Deb: 9/28/15

YEAR TM/L	W	L	PCT	G	GS	CG	SH	SV	IP	H	HR	BB	SO	RAT	ERA	ERA+	OAV	OOB	BH	AVG	PB	PR	/A	PD	TPI
1915 Bro-N	0	1	.000	2	0	0	0	0	6	2	5	3	19.8	3.60	77	.333	.478	0	—	-0	-0	-0	-0	-0.1
1916 Bro-N	0	1	.000	11	0	0	0	0	17¹	15	1	9	13	12.5	3.63	74	.242	.338	1	.250	-0	-2	-2	-0	-0.1
1920 *Cle-A	7	0	1.000	9	8	6	2	0	63¹	54	1	18	25	10.2	1.85	206	.230	.285	4	.200	0	14	14	-1	1.3
1921 Cle-A	14	8	.636	34	24	10	2	2	194²	210	4	89	87	13.9	3.94	108	.283	.361	6	.094	-4	8	7	-3	0.0
1922 Cle-A	4	7	.364	26	13	4	0	0	104	122	8	40	54	14.4	5.28	76	.291	.359	5	.161	-0	-14	-15	-1	-1.3
1925 StL-N	7	7	.500	21	16	9	0	0	131	145	11	58	49	14.4	4.60	94	.279	.360	6	.133	-2	-5	-4	-1	-0.7
1926 StL-N	0	1	.000	1	0	0	0	0	1	1	0	0	1	27.0	0.00	—	.400	.500	0		0	0	0	0	0.5
Total 7	32	25	.561	104	61	29	5	2	516	554	27	220	232	13.7	4.10	100	.277	.352	22	.133	-7	0	0	-5	-0.4

● **WOODY MAIN**   Main, Forrest Harry b: 2/12/22, Delano, Cal. d: 6/27/92, Whittier, Cal. BR/TR, 6'3.5", 195 lbs. Deb: 4/21/48

YEAR TM/L	W	L	PCT	G	GS	CG	SH	SV	IP	H	HR	BB	SO	RAT	ERA	ERA+	OAV	OOB	BH	AVG	PB	PR	/A	PD	TPI
1948 Pit-N	1	1	.500	17	0	0	0	0	27	35	4	19	12	18.0	8.33	49	.324	.425	0	.000	-0	-13	-13	0	-0.8
1950 Pit-N	1	0	1.000	12	0	0	0	1	20¹	19	1	10	14	14.6	4.87	90	.256	.351	2	.400	-0	-2	-1	-0	0.0
1952 Pit-N	2	12	.143	48	11	2	0	2	153¹	149	14	52	79	11.8	4.46	90	.253	.314	-3	.054	-3	-12	-8	-3	-1.3
1953 Pit-N	0	0	—	2	0	0	0	0	4	5	1	2	4	15.8	11.25	40	.294	.368	0		0	-3	-3	-0	0.0
Total 4	4	13	.235	79	11	2	0	3	204²	210	21	84	107	13.0	5.14	89	.264	.335	-4	.091	-3	-30	-25	-3	-2.1

YEAR	TM/L	W	L	PCT	G	GS	CG	SH	SV	IP	H	HR	BB	SO	RAT	ERA	ERA+	OAV	OOB	BH	AVG	PB	PR	/A	PD	TPI

● **ALEX MAIN**   Main, Miles Grant b: 5/13/1884, Montrose, Mich. d: 12/29/65, Royal Oak, Mich. BL/TR, 6'5", 195 lbs. Deb: 4/18/14

1914	Det-A	6	6	.500	32	12	5	1	3	138¹	131	2	59	55	12.6	2.67	105	.259	.340	4	.100	-2	1	2	4	0.4
1915	KC-F	13	14	.481	35	28	18	2	3	230	181	4	75	91	10.2	2.54	103	.222	.291	15	.197	-0	5	2	3	0.6
1918	Phi-N	2	2	.500	8	4	1	1	0	35	30	1	16	14	13.1	4.63	65	.240	.349	1	.091	-1	-7	-6	0	-0.8
Total	3	21	22	.488	75	44	24	4	6	403¹	342	7	150	160	11.3	2.77	98	.236	.313	20	.157	-3	-1	-2	7	0.2

● **JIM MAINS**   Mains, James Royal b: 6/12/22, Bridgton, Maine d: 3/17/69, Bridgton, Maine BR/TR, 6'2", 190 lbs. Deb: 8/22/43

1943	Phi-A	0	1	.000	1	1	0	0	0	8	9	3	4	3	13.5	5.63	60	.281	.343	0	.000		-2	-2	-0	-0.2

● **WILLARD MAINS**   Mains, Willard Eben "Grasshopper" b: 7/7/1868, N.Windham, Maine d: 5/23/23, Bridgton, Maine TR, 6'2", 190 lbs. Deb: 8/3/1888

1888	Chi-N	1	1	.500	2	2	1	0	0	11	8	0	6	5	12.3	4.91	62	.211	.333	1	.143		-3	-2	-0	-0.4
1891	Cin-a	12	12	.500	30	23	19	0	0	204	196	3	107	76	13.9	2.69	153	.244	.342	22	.244	1	23	32	3	3.5
	Mil-a	0	2	.000	2	2	1	0	0	10	14	1	10	2	21.6	10.80	41	.318	.444	3	.600	-1	-8	-7	-0	-0.9
	Yr	12	14	.462	32	25	20	0	0	214	210	4	117	78	13.8	3.07	135	.244	.335	25	.263	2	16	25	3	2.6
1896	Bos-N	3	2	.600	8	5	3	0	1	42²	43	1	31	13	16.0	5.48	83	.261	.384	6	.273	-0	-5	-4	-0	-0.4
Total	3	16	17	.485	42	32	24	0	1	267²	261	5	154	96	14.5	3.53	118	.249	.353	32	.258	1	8	19	3	1.8

● **FRANK MAKOSKY**   Makosky, Frank b: 1/20/10, Boonton, N.J. d: 1/10/87, Stroudsburg, Pa. BR/TR, 6'1", 185 lbs. Deb: 4/30/37

1937	NY-A	5	2	.714	26	1	0	3		58	64	6	24	27	13.7	4.97	90	.277	.345	5	.313	1	-2	-3	2	-0.1

● **TOM MAKOWSKI**   Makowski, Thomas Anthony b: 12/22/50, Buffalo, N.Y. BR/TL, 5'11", 185 lbs. Deb: 5/1/75

1975	Det-A	0	0	—	3	0	0	0	0	9¹	10	2	9	4	18.3	4.82	83	.278	.422	0	—	0	-1	-1	0	-0.1

● **JOHN MALARKEY**   Malarkey, John S. "Liz" b: 5/4/1872, Springfield, Ohio d: 10/29/49, Cincinnati, Ohio TR, 5'11", 155 lbs. Deb: 9/21/1894

1894	Was-N	2	1	.667	3	3	3	0	0	26	42	1	5	4	16.3	4.15	127	.359	.385	1	.071	-2	3	3	-1	0.0
1895	Was-N	0	8	.000	22	8	5	0	0	100²	135	3	60	32	18.1	5.99	80	.316	.410	5	.135	-4	-14	-13	-1	-1.2
1896	Was-N	0	1	.000	1	1	0	0	0	7	9	1	3	0	15.4	1.29	343	.310	.375	1	.500	1	2	2	0	0.4
1899	Chi-N	0	1	.000	1	1	1	0	0	9	19	0	5	7	25.0	13.00	29	.422	.490	1	.200	-0	-9	-9	-0	-0.6
1902	Bos-N	8	10	.444	21	19	17	1	1	170¹	158	0	58	39	11.4	2.59	109	.246	.309	13	.210	2	4	4	2	0.9
1903	Bos-N	11	16	.407	32	27	25	2	0	253	266	5	96	98	13.3	3.94	96	.274	.344	14	.161	1	5	3	2	0.6
Total	6	21	37	.362	80	59	51	3	3	566	629	10	227	179	13.9	3.64	96	.281	.353	35	.169	-2	-8	-9	2	0.1

● **BILL MALARKEY**   Malarkey, William John b: 11/26/1878, Port Byron, Ill. d: 12/12/56, Phoenix, Ariz. BR/TR, 5'10", 185 lbs. Deb: 4/16/08

1908	NY-N	0	2	.000	15	0	0	0	2	35	31	1	10	12	10.8	2.57	94	.242	.302	0	.000	-1	-1	-1	-0	-0.2

● **CARLOS MALDONADO**   Maldonado, Carlos Cesar (Delgado) b: 10/18/66, Chepo, Panama BB/TR, 6'2", 210 lbs. Deb: 9/16/90

1990	KC-A	0	0	—	4	0	0	0	0	6	9	0	4	9	19.5	9.00	43	.346	.433		0	-3	-3	-0	0.1
1991	KC-A	0	0	—	5	0	0	0	0	7²	11	0	9	1	23.5	8.22	50	.333	.476		0	-4	-3	-0	-0.1
1993	Mil-A	2	2	.500	29	0	0	0	0	37¹	40	2	17	18	13.7	4.58	93	.282	.358	0	—	-1	-1	-0	-0.1
Total	3	2	2	.500	38	0	0	0	0	51	60	2	30	28	15.9	5.65	74	.299	.390		0	-8	-8	-1	-0.1

● **CY MALIS**   Malis, Cyrus Sol b: 2/26/07, Philadelphia, Pa. d: 1/12/71, N.Hollywood, Cal. BR/TR, 5'11", 175 lbs. Deb: 8/17/34

1934	Phi-N	0	0	—	1	0	0	0	0	3²	4	0	2	1	14.7	4.91	96	.267	.353	0		0	-0	-0	-0	0.0

● **MAL MALLETTE**   Mallette, Malcolm Francis b: 1/30/22, Syracuse, N.Y. BL/TL, 6'2", 200 lbs. Deb: 9/25/50

1950	Bro-N	0	0	—	2	0	0	0	0	1¹	2	0	1	2	20.3	0.00	—	.333	.429		0	1	1	0	0.0

● **ROB MALLICOAT**   Mallicoat, Robbin Dale b: 11/16/64, St.Helens, Ore. BL/TL, 6'3", 180 lbs. Deb: 9/11/87

1987	Hou-N	0	0	—	4	1	0	0	0	6²	8	0	6	4	18.9	6.75	58	.320	.452		0	-2	-2	-0	-0.2
1991	Hou-N	0	2	.000	24	0	0	0	1	23¹	22	2	13	18	14.3	3.86	91	.259	.370	0	.000	-0	-0	-1	-1	-0.2
1992	Hou-N	0	0	—	23	0	0	0	0	23²	26	2	19	20	19.0	7.23	47	.283	.431	0	.000	-0	-10	-10	-0	0.0
Total	3	0	2	.000	51	1	0	0	1	53²	56	4	38	42	16.9	5.70	61	.277	.409	0	.000	-0	-12	-13	-1	-0.2

● **ALEX MALLOY**   Malloy, Archibald Alexander "Lick" b: 10/31/1886, Laurinburg, N.C. d: 3/1/61, Ferris, Tex. BR/TR, 6'2", 180 lbs. Deb: 9/10/10

1910	StL-A	0	6	.000	7	6	4	0	0	52²	47	0	17	24	11.3	2.56	97	.261	.332	1	.063	-0	-0	-1	-0	-0.2

● **HERM MALLOY**   Malloy, Herman "Tug" b: 6/1/1885, Massillon, Ohio d: 5/9/42, Nimishillen Twsp., Ohio BR/TR, 6', Deb: 10/6/07

1907	Det-A	0	1	.000	1	1	1	0	0	8	13	1	6	6	20.3	5.63	46	.371	.450	1	.250		-3	-3	-0	-0.3
1908	Det-A	0	2	.000	3	2	2	0	0	17	20	1	4	8	13.8	3.71	65	.278	.333	3	.333	1	-2	-2	1	-0.1
Total	2	0	3	.000	4	3	3	0	0	25	33	2	10	14	15.8	4.32	57	.308	.373	4	.308	1	-5	-5	1	-0.4

● **BOB MALLOY**   Malloy, Robert Paul b: 5/28/18, Canonsburg, Pa. BR/TR, 5'11", 185 lbs. Deb: 5/4/43

1943	Cin-N	0	0	—	6	0	0	0	0	10	14	1	4	4	19.8	6.30	53	.778	.846	2	.667		-3	-3	-0	0.1
1944	Cin-N	1	1	.500	9	0	0	0	0	23¹	22	1	6	11	12.7	3.09	113	.265	.351	0	.000	-1	1	1	0	0.4
1946	Cin-N	2	5	.286	27	3	1	0	2	72	71	2	26	24	12.4	2.75	122	.265	.334	5	.278	1	5	5	-1	0.5
1947	Cin-N	0	0	—	1	0	0	0	0	1	3	1	4	0	27.0	18.00	23	.600	.600		0	-2	-2	-0	0.0
1949	StL-A	1	1	.500	5	0	0	0	0	9²	6	0	7	2	12.1	2.79	162	.200	.351	0	.000	-0	2	2	0	0.3
Total	5	4	7	.364	48	3	1	0	2	116	116	4	52	35	13.2	3.26	106	.287	.371	7	.226	1	3	3	-1	0.9

● **BOB MALLOY**   Malloy, Robert William b: 11/24/64, Arlington, Va. BR/TR, 6'5", 200 lbs. Deb: 5/26/87

1987	Tex-A	0	0	—	2	2	0	0	0	11	13	6	3	8	13.1	6.55	68	.271	.314		0	-3	-3	-0	-0.3
1990	Mon-N	0	0	—	1	0	0	0	0	1	1	0	1	1	9.0	0.00	—	.143	.250		0	1	1	0	0.1
Total	2	0	0	—	3	2	0	0	0	13	14	6	4	9	12.5	5.54	78	.255	.305		0	-2	-2	-0	-0.1

● **CHUCK MALONE**   Malone, Charles Ray b: 7/8/65, Harrisburg, Ark. BR/TR, 6'7", 250 lbs. Deb: 9/6/90

1990	Phi-N	1	0	1.000	7	0	0	0	0	7¹	3	1	11	7	17.2	3.68	104	.130	.412		0	-0	-0	-0	0.1

● **MARTIN MALONE**   Malone, Martin Deb: 6/20/1872

1872	Eck-n	0	3	.000	3	3	3	0	0	27	85	1	0	0	28.3	10.33	33	.445	.445	5	.313	1	-20	-21		-1.3

● **PAT MALONE**   Malone, Perce Leigh b: 9/25/02, Altoona, Pa. d: 5/13/43, Altoona, Pa. BL/TR, 6', 200 lbs. Deb: 4/12/28

1928	Chi-N	18	13	.581	42	25	16	2	2	250²	218	15	99	155	11.6	2.84	136	.236	.314	18	.189	1	32	28	0	3.3
1929	*Chi-N	**22**	10	.688	40	30	19	**5**	2	267	283	12	102	**166**	13.2	3.57	129	.276	.345	22	.210	2	34	31	-3	3.0
1930	Chi-N	**20**	9	.690	45	35	**22**	1	4	271²	290	14	96	142	13.0	3.94	124	.271	.334	26	.248	5	31	28	-2	2.8
1931	Chi-N	16	9	.640	36	30	12	0	0	228¹	229	9	88	112	12.7	3.90	99	.258	.328	17	.215	2	-1	-1	0	0.0
1932	*Chi-N	15	17	.469	37	33	17	2	0	237	222	14	78	120	11.6	3.38	111	.244	.308	14	.179	0	13	10	-3	0.9
1933	Chi-N	10	14	.417	31	26	13	2	0	186¹	186	10	59	72	12.1	3.91	84	.258	.318	10	.159	-2	-12	-13	-1	-1.9
1934	Chi-N	14	7	.667	34	21	8	1	0	191	200	14	55	111	12.2	3.53	110	.270	.322	11	.172	-2	11	7	-1	0.4
1935	NY-A	3	5	.375	29	2	1	0	3	56¹	53	7	33	25	13.9	5.43	75	.252	.357	0	.000	-3	-6	-9	-0	-1.4
1936	*NY-A	12	4	.750	35	9	5	0	**9**	134²	124	6	40	72	13.9	3.81	122	.273	.352	10	.196	-1	18	13	-2	1.2
1937	NY-A	4	4	.500	28	9	3	0	6	92	109	5	35	49	14.5	5.48	81	.291	.357	1	.030	-5	-9	-11	-2	-1.5
Total	10	134	92	.593	357	220	115	15	26	1915	1934	103	705	1024	12.6	3.74	111	.262	.330	129	.188	-2	112	85	-14	6.8

● **CHARLIE MALONEY**   Maloney, Charles Michael b: 5/22/1886, Cambridge, Mass. d: 1/17/67, Arlington, Mass. BR/TR, 5'8", 155 lbs. Deb: 8/10/08

1908	Bos-N	0	0	—	1	0	0	0	0	2	3	0	1	0	18.0	4.50	54	.429	.500	0		0	-0	-0	0	0.0

● **JIM MALONEY**   Maloney, James William b: 6/2/40, Fresno, Cal. BL/TR, 6'2", 207 lbs. Deb: 7/27/60

1960	Cin-N	2	6	.250	11	11	2	1	0	63²	61	5	37	48	14.1	4.66	82	.255	.360	2	.111	-0	-6	-6	-0	-0.7
1961	*Cin-N	6	7	.462	27	11	3	0	2	94²	86	16	59	57	13.9	4.37	93	.242	.352	11	.379	4	-4	-3	-1	-0.1
1962	Cin-N	9	7	.563	22	17	3	0	1	115¹	90	11	66	105	12.3	3.51	115	.214	.323	8	.186	0	6	7	-1	0.7
1963	Cin-N	23	7	.767	33	33	13	6	0	250¹	183	17	88	265	10.0	2.77	121	.202	.276	15	.169	1	14	16	-2	1.8
1964	Cin-N	15	10	.600	31	31	11	2	0	216	175	16	83	214	10.8	2.71	133	.222	.297	13	.151	1	20	22	-2	2.4
1965	Cin-N★	20	9	.690	33	33	14	5	0	255¹	189	13	110	244	10.7	2.54	148	.206	.295	20	.225	7	28	34	-1	4.6

YEAR	TM/L	W	L	PCT	G	GS	CG	SH	SV	IP	H	HR	BB	SO	RAT	ERA	ERA+	OAV	OOB	BH	AVG	PB	PR	/A	PD	TPI
1966	Cin-N	16	8	.667	32	32	10	**5**	0	224²	174	18	90	216	11.0	2.80	139	.214	.300	18	.222	3	20	27	-0	3.2
1967	Cin-N	15	11	.577	30	29	6	3	0	196¹	181	8	72	153	11.7	3.25	115	.247	.317	11	.159	-0	3	11	-1	1.3
1968	Cin-N	16	10	.615	33	32	8	5	0	207	183	11	80	181	11.5	3.61	88	.239	.313	18	.243	6	-14	-10	-2	-0.8
1969	Cin-N	12	5	.706	30	27	6	3	0	178²	135	11	86	102	11.2	2.77	136	.208	.302	11	.200	6	16	20	-1	2.4
1970	Cin-N	0	1	.000	7	3	0	0	1	16²	26	3	15	7	23.2	11.34	36	.366	.489	0	.000	-0	-14	-14	-0	-0.8
1971	Cal-A	0	3	.000	13	4	0	0	0	30¹	35	3	24	13	17.8	5.04	64	.294	.417	1	.200	-0	-5	-6	-0	-0.6
Total	12	134	84	.615	302	262	74	30	4	1849	1518	138	810	1605	11.5	3.19	115	.224	.310	126	.201	26	64	98	-10	13.4

● **PAUL MALOY**   Maloy, Paul Augustus "Biff" b: 6/4/1892, Bascom, Ohio   d: 3/18/76, Sandusky, Ohio   BR/TR, 5'11", 185 lbs.   Deb: 7/11/13

YEAR	TM/L	W	L	PCT	G	GS	CG	SH	SV	IP	H	HR	BB	SO	RAT	ERA	ERA+	OAV	OOB	BH	AVG	PB	PR	/A	PD	TPI
1913	Bos-A	0	0	—	2	0	0	0	0	2	2	0	1	0	22.5	9.00	33	.286	.500	0	—	0	-1	-1	-0	0.0

● **GORDON MALTZBERGER**   Maltzberger, Gordon Ralph "Maltzy" b: 9/4/12, Utopia, Tex.   d: 12/11/74, Rialto, Cal.   BR/TR, 6', 170 lbs.   Deb: 4/27/43   C

YEAR	TM/L	W	L	PCT	G	GS	CG	SH	SV	IP	H	HR	BB	SO	RAT	ERA	ERA+	OAV	OOB	BH	AVG	PB	PR	/A	PD	TPI
1943	Chi-A	7	4	.636	37	0	0	0	**14**	98²	86	8	24	48	10.2	2.46	136	.236	.287	3	.120	0	9	10	0	1.5
1944	Chi-A	10	5	.667	46	0	0	0	**12**	91¹	81	2	19	49	10.2	2.96	116	.235	.277	3	.136	-1	5	5	-1	0.8
1946	Chi-A	2	0	1.000	19	0	0	0	2	39²	30	3	6	17	8.4	1.59	215	.205	.242	0	.000	-0	8	8	-1	0.4
1947	Chi-A	1	4	.200	33	0	0	0	5	63²	61	4	25	22	12.3	3.39	108	.257	.331	1	.143	1	2	2	1	0.3
Total	4	20	13	.606	135	0	0	0	33	293¹	258	17	74	136	10.3	2.70	128	.236	.288	7	.117	0	25	24	0	3.0

● **AL MAMAUX**   Mamaux, Albert Leon b: 5/30/1894, Pittsburgh, Pa.   d: 1/2/63, Santa Monica, Cal.   BR/TR, 6'0.5", 168 lbs.   Deb: 9/23/13

YEAR	TM/L	W	L	PCT	G	GS	CG	SH	SV	IP	H	HR	BB	SO	RAT	ERA	ERA+	OAV	OOB	BH	AVG	PB	PR	/A	PD	TPI
1913	Pit-N	0	0	—	1	0	0	0	0	3	2	0	2	2	12.0	3.00	100	.167	.286	0	.000	-0	0	0	0	0.0
1914	Pit-N	5	2	.714	13	6	4	2	0	63	41	1	24	30	9.6	1.71	155	.186	.272	5	.250	1	8	7	1	1.0
1915	Pit-N	21	8	.724	38	31	17	8	0	251²	182	3	96	152	10.3	2.04	134	.208	.293	15	.163	-2	20	19	-3	1.5
1916	Pit-N	21	15	.583	45	37	26	1	2	310	264	3	136	163	11.9	2.53	106	.239	.327	21	.191	1	3	5	0	0.9
1917	Pit-N	2	11	.154	16	13	5	0	0	85²	92	1	50	22	15.2	5.25	54	.278	.378	7	.226	0	-24	-23	-1	-3.2
1918	Bro-N	0	1	.000	2	1	0	0	0	8	14	0	2	2	18.0	6.75	41	.438	.471	0	.000	-0	-4	-4	-1	-0.4
1919	Bro-N	10	12	.455	30	22	16	2	0	199¹	174	2	66	80	11.0	2.66	112	.245	.312	11	.175	0	6	7	-1	0.7
1920	*Bro-N	12	8	.600	41	17	9	2	4	190²	172	2	63	101	11.3	2.69	119	.255	.322	10	.167	0	9	11	-1	1.0
1921	Bro-N	3	3	.500	12	1	0	0	1	43	36	1	13	21	10.5	3.14	124	.240	.305	2	.182	0	3	4	1	0.5
1922	Bro-N	1	4	.200	37	7	1	0	3	87²	97	7	33	35	13.6	3.70	110	.290	.358	4	.235	3	4	4	0	0.5
1923	Bro-N	0	2	.000	5	1	0	0	0	13	20	0	6	5	18.0	8.31	47	.385	.448	1	.500	1	-6	-6	0	-0.8
1924	NY-A	1	1	.500	14	2	0	0	0	38	44	2	20	12	15.4	5.68	73	.308	.396	1	.077	-1	-6	-6	-0	-0.5
Total	12	76	67	.531	254	138	78	15	10	1293	1138	22	511	625	11.7	2.90	104	.245	.325	77	.182	2	13	17	-3	1.2

● **HAL MANDERS**   Manders, Harold Carl b: 6/14/17, Waukee, Iowa   BR/TR, 6', 187 lbs.   Deb: 8/12/41

YEAR	TM/L	W	L	PCT	G	GS	CG	SH	SV	IP	H	HR	BB	SO	RAT	ERA	ERA+	OAV	OOB	BH	AVG	PB	PR	/A	PD	TPI
1941	Det-A	1	0	1.000	8	0	0	0	0	15¹	13	0	8	7	12.9	2.35	194	.236	.344	0	.000	-1	3	4	-0	0.1
1942	Det-A	2	0	1.000	18	0	0	0	0	33	39	4	15	14	15.0	4.09	97	.307	.385	1	.250	0	-1	-1	-0	0.0
1946	Det-A	0	0	—	2	0	0	0	0	6	8	1	2	3	16.5	10.50	35	.364	.440	1	.500	0	-5	-5	-0	-0.1
	Chi-N	0	1	.000	2	0	0	0	0	6	11	1	3	4	22.5	9.00	37	.423	.500	0	.000	-0	-4	-4	-0	-0.6
Total	3	3	1	.750	30	1	0	0	0	60¹	71	6	28	28	15.4	4.77	84	.309	.403	2	.167	-0	-7	-5	-1	-0.5

● **LEO MANGUM**   Mangum, Leo Allan "Blackie" b: 5/24/1896, Durham, N.C.   d: 7/9/74, Lima, Ohio   BR/TR, 6'1", 187 lbs.   Deb: 7/11/24

YEAR	TM/L	W	L	PCT	G	GS	CG	SH	SV	IP	H	HR	BB	SO	RAT	ERA	ERA+	OAV	OOB	BH	AVG	PB	PR	/A	PD	TPI
1924	Chi-A	1	4	.200	13	7	1	0	0	47	69	3	25	12	18.2	7.09	58	.359	.436	1	.071	-1	-15	-15	-0	-1.4
1925	Chi-A	1	0	1.000	7	0	0	0	0	15	25	0	6	6	18.6	7.80	53	.373	.425	1	.500	1	-6	-6	-0	-0.3
1928	NY-N	0	0	—	1	1	0	0	0	3	6	0	5	1	33.0	15.00	36	.500	.647	1	1.000	0	-4	-4	-0	0.1
1932	Bos-N	0	0	—	7	0	0	0	0	10¹	17	1	0	3	14.8	5.23	72	.333	.333	0	.000	-0	-2	-1	0	-0.1
1933	Bos-N	4	3	.571	25	5	2	1	0	84	93	4	11	28	11.1	3.32	92	.280	.303	2	.091	-2	0	-2	2	-0.2
1934	Bos-N	5	3	.625	29	3	1	0	1	94¹	127	9	23	28	14.3	5.72	67	.315	.352	9	.281	2	-17	-20	1	-1.2
1935	Bos-N	0	0	—	3	0	0	0	0	4²	6	0	2	0	15.4	3.86	98	.300	.364	0	—	0	-0	-0	0	-0.0
Total	7	11	10	.524	85	16	4	1	1	258¹	343	15	72	78	14.5	5.37	68	.318	.362	15	.200	-0	-43	-49	4	-2.9

● **ERNIE MANNING**   Manning, Ernest Devon "Ed" b: 10/9/1890, Florala, Ala.   d: 4/28/73, Pensacola, Fla.   BL/TR, 6', 175 lbs.   Deb: 5/3/14

YEAR	TM/L	W	L	PCT	G	GS	CG	SH	SV	IP	H	HR	BB	SO	RAT	ERA	ERA+	OAV	OOB	BH	AVG	PB	PR	/A	PD	TPI
1914	StL-A	0	0	—	4	0	0	0	0	10	11	0	3	3	12.6	3.60	75	.297	.350	0	.000	-0	-1	-1	0	0.0

● **JIM MANNING**   Manning, James Benjamin b: 7/21/43, L'Anse, Mich.   BR/TR, 6'1", 185 lbs.   Deb: 4/15/62

YEAR	TM/L	W	L	PCT	G	GS	CG	SH	SV	IP	H	HR	BB	SO	RAT	ERA	ERA+	OAV	OOB	BH	AVG	PB	PR	/A	PD	TPI
1962	Min-A	0	0	—	5	1	0	0	0	7	14	0	1	3	20.6	5.14	79	.389	.421	0	.000	-0	-1	-1	0	0.0

● **JACK MANNING**   Manning, John E. b: 12/20/1853, Braintree, Mass.   d: 8/15/29, Boston, Mass.   BR/TR, 5'8.5", 158 lbs.   Deb: 4/23/1873   M♦

YEAR	TM/L	W	L	PCT	G	GS	CG	SH	SV	IP	H	HR	BB	SO	RAT	ERA	ERA+	OAV	OOB	BH	AVG	PB	PR	/A	PD	TPI
1874	Bal-n	4	16	.200	22	20	17	0	0	176²	222	2	11	11	11.9	2.04	109	.267	.276	61	.351	7	3	6		0.9
1875	Bos-n	16	2	.889	27	18	8	1	6	144	152	1	14	34	10.4	2.38	90	.247	.263	94	.270	4	-2	-4		-0.3
1876	Bos-N	18	5	.783	34	20	13	0	**5**	197¹	213	1	32	21	11.2	2.14	105	.252	.279	76	.264	3	4	2	0	0.4
1877	Cin-N	0	4	.000	10	4	2	0	1	44	83	1	7	6	18.4	6.95	38	.379	.398	4	.317	4	-20	-21	0	-1.3
1878	Bos-N	1	0	1.000	3	1	0	0	0	11¹	24	1	5	2	23.0	14.29	17	.393	.439	63	.254	0	-15	-15	-0	-0.9
Total	2 n	20	18	.526	49	38	25	1	6	320²	374	3	25	45	11.2	2.19	100	.258	.271	199	.290	11	-0	-0		0.6
Total	3	19	9	.679	47	25	16	0	6	252²	320	3	44	29	11.3	3.53	66	.284	.311	725	.257	7	-32	-34	1	-1.8

● **RUBE MANNING**   Manning, Walter S. b: 4/29/1883, Chambersburg, Pa.   d: 4/23/30, Williamsport, Pa.   BR/TR, 6', 180 lbs.   Deb: 9/25/07

YEAR	TM/L	W	L	PCT	G	GS	CG	SH	SV	IP	H	HR	BB	SO	RAT	ERA	ERA+	OAV	OOB	BH	AVG	PB	PR	/A	PD	TPI
1907	NY-A	0	1	.000	4	1	1	0	0	9	8	0	3	3	12.0	3.00	93	.242	.324	0	.000	-0	-0	-0	-1	-0.1
1908	NY-A	13	16	.448	41	26	19	2	1	245	228	4	86	113	12.2	2.94	84	.256	.334	17	.187	0	-15	-13	-1	-1.6
1909	NY-A	7	11	.389	26	21	11	2	1	173	167	2	48	71	11.7	3.17	80	.265	.326	11	.183	-0	-13	-12	-1	-1.4
1910	NY-A	2	4	.333	16	9	4	0	0	75	80	4	25	25	13.1	3.72	71	.283	.349	5	.192	-0	-10	-9	-1	-0.7
Total	4	22	32	.407	84	57	35	4	2	502	483	10	162	212	12.1	3.14	81	.263	.333	33	.183	-0	-39	-34	-3	-3.8

● **RAMON MANON**   Manon, Ramon (Reyes) b: 1/20/68, Santo Domingo, D.R.   BR/TR, 6', 150 lbs.   Deb: 4/19/90

YEAR	TM/L	W	L	PCT	G	GS	CG	SH	SV	IP	H	HR	BB	SO	RAT	ERA	ERA+	OAV	OOB	BH	AVG	PB	PR	/A	PD	TPI
1990	Tex-A	0	0	—	1	0	0	0	0	2	3	0	3	3	27.0	13.50	29	.333	.500	0	—	0	-2	-2	0	0.0

● **TOM MANSELL**   Mansell, Thomas E. "Brick" b: 1/1/1855, Auburn, N.Y.   d: 10/6/34, Auburn, N.Y.   BL/TR, 5'8", 160 lbs.   Deb: 5/1/1879   F♦

YEAR	TM/L	W	L	PCT	G	GS	CG	SH	SV	IP	H	HR	BB	SO	RAT	ERA	ERA+	OAV	OOB	BH	AVG	PB	PR	/A	PD	TPI
1883	Det-N	0	0	—	1	0	0	0	0	6²	21	2	5	2	35.1	18.90	16	.553	.605	29	.221	0	-12	-12	-0	0.0

● **LOU MANSKE**   Manske, Louis Hugo b: 7/4/1884, Milwaukee, Wis.   d: 4/27/63, Milwaukee, Wis.   BL/TL, 6',   Deb: 8/31/06

YEAR	TM/L	W	L	PCT	G	GS	CG	SH	SV	IP	H	HR	BB	SO	RAT	ERA	ERA+	OAV	OOB	BH	AVG	PB	PR	/A	PD	TPI
1906	Pit-N	0	0	—	2	1	0	0	0	8	12	0	5	6	19.1	5.63	48	.387	.472	0	.000	-1	-3	-3	-0	-0.1

● **MATT MANTEI**   Mantei, Matthew Bruce b: 7/7/73, Tampa, Fla.   BR/TR, 6'1", 180 lbs.   Deb: 6/18/95

YEAR	TM/L	W	L	PCT	G	GS	CG	SH	SV	IP	H	HR	BB	SO	RAT	ERA	ERA+	OAV	OOB	BH	AVG	PB	PR	/A	PD	TPI
1995	Fla-N	0	1	.000	12	0	0	0	0	13¹	12	1	15	16	16.9	4.73	89	.245	.403	0	—	-1	-1	-0	0	0.0
1996	Fla-N	1	0	1.000	14	0	0	0	0	18¹	13	2	21	24	17.2	6.38	63	.197	.398	0	—	-0	-4	-5	1	-0.2
Total	2	1	1	.500	26	0	0	0	0	31²	25	3	34	40	17.1	5.68	72	.217	.400	0	.000	-0	-5	-6	1	-0.2

● **BARRY MANUEL**   Manuel, Barry Paul b: 8/12/65, Mamou, La.   BR/TR, 5'11", 180 lbs.   Deb: 9/6/91

YEAR	TM/L	W	L	PCT	G	GS	CG	SH	SV	IP	H	HR	BB	SO	RAT	ERA	ERA+	OAV	OOB	BH	AVG	PB	PR	/A	PD	TPI
1991	Tex-A	1	0	1.000	8	0	0	0	0	16	7	0	6	5	7.3	1.13	358	.143	.236	0	—	0	5	5	1	0.4
1992	Tex-A	1	0	1.000	3	0	0	0	0	5²	6	2	1	2	12.7	4.76	80	.261	.320	0	—	0	-1	-1	-0	0.1
1996	Mon-N	4	1	.800	53	0	0	0	0	86	70	10	26	62	10.8	3.24	133	.219	.293	0	—	-0	9	10	-1	0.4
Total	3	6	1	.857	64	0	0	0	0	107²	83	12	33	76	10.4	3.01	141	.212	.287	0	.000	-0	14	15	-0	0.9

● **MOXIE MANUEL**   Manuel, Mark Garfield b: 10/16/1881, Metropolis, Ill.   d: 4/26/24, Memphis, Tenn.   BR/TR, 5'11", 170 lbs.   Deb: 9/25/05

YEAR	TM/L	W	L	PCT	G	GS	CG	SH	SV	IP	H	HR	BB	SO	RAT	ERA	ERA+	OAV	OOB	BH	AVG	PB	PR	/A	PD	TPI
1905	Was-A	0	0	—	3	1	0	0	0	10	9	0	3	3	11.7	5.40	49	.243	.317	1	.250	1	-3	-3	-0	-0.1
1908	Chi-A	3	4	.429	18	6	3	0	0	60¹	52	0	25	25	11.8	3.28	71	.243	.328	1	.063	-1	-6	-6	-0	-0.9
Total	2	3	4	.429	21	7	4	0	0	70¹	61	0	28	28	11.8	3.58	66	.243	.326	2	.100	-1	-9	-10	-0	-0.9

● **DICK MANVILLE**   Manville, Richard Wesley b: 12/25/26, Des Moines, Iowa   BR/TR, 6'4", 192 lbs.   Deb: 4/30/50

YEAR	TM/L	W	L	PCT	G	GS	CG	SH	SV	IP	H	HR	BB	SO	RAT	ERA	ERA+	OAV	OOB	BH	AVG	PB	PR	/A	PD	TPI
1950	Bos-N	0	0	—	1	0	0	0	0	2	0	0	3	0	13.5	0.00	—	.000	.300	0	—	0	0	0	0	0.0
1952	Chi-N	0	0	—	11	0	0	0	0	17	25	2	12	6	19.6	7.94	48	.362	.457	1	.500	0	-8	-8	0	-0.1
Total	2	0	0	—	12	0	0	0	0	19	25	2	15	6	18.9	7.11	54	.329	.440	1	.500	0	-7	-7	0	0.1

YEAR	TM/L	W	L	PCT	G	GS	CG	SH	SV	IP	H	HR	BB	SO	RAT	ERA	ERA+	OAV	OOB	BH	AVG	PB	PR	/A	PD	TPI

● JOSIAS MANZANILLO   Manzanillo, Josias (Adams) b: 10/16/67, San Pedro De Macoris, D.R.   BR/TR, 6', 190 lbs.   Deb: 10/5/91   F

1991	Bos-A	0	0	—	1	0	0	0	0	1	2	0	3	1	45.0	18.00	24	.400	.625	0	—	0	-2	-2	0	-0.1
1993	Mil-A	1	1	.500	10	1	0	0	1	17	22	1	10	10	18.0	9.53	45	.314	.415	0	—	0	-10	-10	1	-1.0
	NY-N	0	0	—	6	0	0	0	0	12	8	1	9	11	12.8	3.00	134	.186	.327	0	.000	-0	1	1	-0	0.1
1994	NY-N	3	2	.600	37	0	0	0	2	47¹	34	4	13	48	9.5	2.66	157	.200	.269	0	.000	-0	8	8	-0	0.7
1995	NY-N	1	2	.333	12	0	0	0	0	16	18	3	6	14	13.5	7.88	51	.273	.333	0	—	-0	-7	-7	-0	-1.1
	NY-A	0	0	—	11	0	0	0	0	17¹	19	1	9	11	15.6	2.08	222	.279	.380	0	—	0	5	5	0	0.1
Total	4	5	5	.500	77	1	0	0	3	110²	103	10	50	95	13.0	4.55	93	.244	.334	0	.000	-1	-3	-4	-0	-1.4

● RAVELO MANZANILLO   Manzanillo, Ravelo (Adams) b: 10/17/63, San Pedro De Macoris, D.R.   BL/TL, 6', 210 lbs.   Deb: 9/25/88   F

1988	Chi-A	0	1	.000	2	2	0	0	0	9¹	7	1	12	10	19.3	5.79	69	.212	.435	0	—	-0	-2	-2	0	-0.2
1994	Pit-N	4	2	.667	46	0	0	0	1	50	45	4	42	39	16.2	4.14	104	.245	.393	2	.667	1	0	1	0	0.2
1995	Pit-N	0	0	—	5	0	0	0	0	3²	3	0	2	1	14.7	4.91	88	.231	.375	0	.000	-0	-0	-0	0	0.0
Total	3	4	3	.571	53	2	0	0	1	63	55	5	56	50	16.6	4.43	96	.239	.399	2	.500	1	-2	-1	0	0.0

● ROLLA MAPEL   Mapel, Rolla Hamilton "Lefty" b: 3/9/1890, Lees Summit, Mo.   d: 4/6/66, San Diego, Cal.   BL/TL, 5'11.5", 165 lbs.   Deb: 8/31/19

| 1919 | StL-A | 0 | 3 | .000 | 4 | 3 | 2 | 0 | 0 | 24 | 19 | 2 | 12 | 4 | 16.6 | 4.50 | 74 | .262 | .435 | 1 | .167 | -0 | -3 | -3 | 1 | -0.3 |

● PAUL MARAK   Marak, Paul Patrick b: 8/2/65, Lakenheath, England   BR/TR, 6'2", 175 lbs.   Deb: 9/1/90

| 1990 | Atl-N | 1 | 2 | .333 | 7 | 7 | 1 | 0 | 0 | 39 | 39 | 2 | 19 | 15 | 14.1 | 3.69 | 109 | .267 | .363 | 1 | .091 | -0 | 0 | 1 | 1 | 0.2 |

● GEORGES MARANDA   Maranda, Georges Henri b: 1/15/32, Levis, Que., Can.   BR/TR, 6'2", 195 lbs.   Deb: 4/26/60

1960	SF-N	1	4	.200	17	4	0	0	0	50²	50	6	30	28	14.2	4.62	75	.254	.352	2	.167	-0	-5	-6	2	-0.4
1962	Min-A	1	3	.250	32	4	0	0	0	72²	69	11	35	36	13.4	4.46	92	.252	.345	4	.250	1	-4	-3	1	0.0
Total	2	2	7	.222	49	8	0	0	0	123¹	119	17	65	64	13.7	4.52	85	.253	.348	6	.214	1	-9	-10	2	-0.4

● FIRPO MARBERRY   Marberry, Fredrick b: 11/30/1898, Streetman, Tex.   d: 6/30/76, Mexia, Tex.   BR/TR, 6'1", 190 lbs.   Deb: 8/11/23   U

1923	Was-A	4	0	1.000	11	4	2	0	0	44²	42	1	17	18	12.5	2.82	133	.258	.339	-1	.143	-1	6	5	-0	0.3
1924	*Was-A	11	12	.478	**50**	14	6	0	**15**	195¹	190	3	70	68	12.4	3.09	131	.262	.335	8	.136	-4	25	21	-1	2.0
1925	*Was-A	9	5	.643	**55**	0	0	0	**15**	93¹	84	4	45	53	12.8	3.47	122	.246	.341	5	.263	1	**10**	**8**	-1	1.5
1926	Was-A	12	7	.632	**64**	5	3	0	**22**	138	120	4	66	43	12.3	3.00	129	.243	.336	6	.176	-1	16	13	-1	1.9
1927	Was-A	10	7	.588	56	10	2	0	9	155¹	177	4	68	74	14.4	4.64	88	.296	.371	5	.122	-3	-9	-10	-1	-1.5
1928	Was-A	13	13	.500	**48**	11	7	1	3	161¹	160	4	42	76	11.4	3.85	104	.268	.319	5	.109	-4	3	3	-1	-0.1
1929	Was-A	19	12	.613	**49**	26	16	0	**11**	250¹	233	6	69	121	**11.1**	3.06	139	.252	**.308**	19	.235	-4	33	33	-2	3.8
1930	Was-A	15	5	.750	33	22	9	2	1	185	190	15	53	56	11.8	4.09	113	.270	.321	24	.329	5	12	11	-1	1.3
1931	Was-A	16	4	.800	45	25	11	1	7	219	211	13	63	88	11.4	3.45	124	.252	.307	19	.232	1	23	20	-2	1.7
1932	Was-A	8	4	.667	**54**	15	8	1	**13**	197²	202	13	72	66	12.6	4.01	108	.268	.333	11	.167	-2	10	7	1	0.4
1933	Det-A	16	11	.593	37	32	15	1	2	238¹	232	13	61	84	**11.1**	3.29	131	.254	**.302**	11	.122	-5	26	27	-3	2.0
1934	*Det-A	15	5	.750	38	19	6	1	3	155²	174	12	48	64	12.8	4.57	96	.276	.327	12	.218	2	-1	-3	-2	-0.3
1935	Det-A	0	1	.000	5	2	1	0	0	19	22	2	9	7	14.7	4.26	98	.289	.365	1	.200	-0	-0	-0	0	0.0
1936	NY-N	0	0	—	1	0	0	0	0	0¹	1	0	0	0	27.0	0.00	—	.500	.500	0	.000	-0	0	0	-0	0.0
	Was-A	0	2	.000	1	1	0	0	0	6	10	0	2	0	16.5	3.86	124	.208	.263	0	.000	-0	2	1	-0	0.1
Total	14	148	88	.627	551	186	86	7	101	2067¹	2049	96	686	822	12.1	3.63	116	.262	.325	128	.192	-8	156	136	-12	13.1

● WALT MARBET   Marbet, Walter William b: 9/13/1890, Plymouth Co., Ia.   d: 9/24/56, Hohenwald, Tenn.   BR/TR, 6'1", 175 lbs.   Deb: 6/17/13

| 1913 | StL-N | 0 | 1 | .000 | 3 | 1 | 0 | 0 | 0 | 3¹ | 9 | 0 | 4 | 1 | 35.1 | 16.20 | 20 | .500 | .591 | 0 | — | 0 | -5 | -5 | -0 | -1.1 |

● PHIL MARCHILDON   Marchildon, Philip Joseph "Babe" b: 10/25/13, Penetanguishene, Ont., Canada   BR/TR, 5'11", 175 lbs.   Deb: 9/22/40

1940	Phi-A	0	2	.000	2	2	1	0	0	10	12	1	8	4	18.0	7.20	62	.286	.400	0	.000	-0	-3	-3	0	-0.5
1941	Phi-A	10	15	.400	30	27	14	1	0	204¹	188	15	118	74	13.6	3.57	117	.245	.348	11	.167	1	13	14	-3	1.3
1942	Phi-A	17	14	.548	38	31	18	1	1	244	215	14	140	110	13.2	4.20	90	.235	.339	20	.238	3	-15	-12	-3	-1.3
1945	Phi-A	0	1	.000	3	2	0	0	0	9	5	0	11	2	16.0	4.00	86	.179	.410	1	.500	1	-1	-1	0	0.0
1946	Phi-A	13	16	.448	36	29	16	1	1	226²	197	14	114	95	12.5	3.49	101	.237	.332	5	.067	-6	0	-1	-2	-0.6
1947	Phi-A	19	9	.679	35	35	21	2	0	276²	228	15	141	128	12.2	3.22	118	.224	.323	15	.153	-2	15	18	-3	1.3
1948	Phi-A	9	15	.375	33	30	12	1	0	226¹	214	19	131	66	13.9	4.53	95	.251	.353	5	.069	-5	-6	-6	-1	-1.2
1949	Phi-A	0	3	.000	7	6	0	0	0	16	24	3	19	2	24.8	11.81	35	.358	.506	1	.167	-0	-14	-14	-0	-2.0
1950	Bos-A	0	0	—	1	0	0	0	0	1¹	1	0	2	0	20.3	6.75	73	.200	.429	0	—	-0	-0	-0	-0	0.0
Total	9	68	75	.476	185	162	82	6	2	1214¹	1084	81	684	481	13.3	3.93	100	.240	.342	58	.143	-10	-10	-1	-11	-3.0

● JOHNNY MARCUM   Marcum, John Alfred "Footsie" b: 9/9/09, Campbellsburg, Ky.   d: 9/10/84, Louisville, Ky.   BL/TR, 5'11", 197 lbs.   Deb: 9/7/33   ♦

1933	Phi-A	3	2	.600	5	5	4	2	0	37	28	0	20	14	11.7	1.95	220	.200	.300	2	.167	0	10	10	0	1.3
1934	Phi-A	14	11	.560	37	31	17	2	0	232	257	13	88	92	13.5	4.50	97	.280	.346	30	.268	6	-0	-3	-0	0.2
1935	Phi-A	17	12	.586	39	27	19	2	3	242²	256	16	83	99	12.6	4.08	111	.268	.328	37	.311	8	10	13	-3	1.9
1936	Bos-A	8	13	.381	31	23	14	0	0	174	194	6	52	57	12.7	4.81	110	.281	.332	18	.205	1	4	10	0	1.0
1937	Bos-A	13	11	.542	37	23	9	1	3	183²	230	17	47	59	13.7	4.85	98	.306	.348	23	.267	5	-5	-2	1	0.3
1938	Bos-A	5	6	.455	15	11	7	0	0	92¹	113	11	25	25	13.5	4.09	120	.298	.342	5	.135	-1	7	9	-1	0.7
1939	StL-A	2	5	.286	12	6	2	0	0	47²	66	12	10	14	14.5	7.74	63	.332	.367	10	.455	3	-17	-15	-0	-1.5
	Chi-A	3	3	.500	19	6	2	0	0	90	125	15	19	32	14.4	6.00	79	.326	.357	16	.281	2	-14	-13	-1	-0.5
	Yr	5	8	.385	31	12	4	0	0	137²	191	27	29	46	14.4	6.60	72	.327	.359	26	.329	6	-30	-28	-1	-2.0
Total	7	65	63	.508	195	132	69	8	7	1099¹	1269	91	344	392	13.3	4.66	101	.287	.340	141	.265	25	-4	7	-4	3.4

● LEO MARENTETTE   Marentette, Leo John b: 2/18/41, Detroit, Mich.   BR/TR, 6'2", 200 lbs.   Deb: 9/26/65

1965	Det-A	0	0	—	2	0	0	0	0	3	1	0	1	3	6.0	0.00	—	.111	.200	0	—	-0	1	1	0	0.0
1969	Mon-N	0	0	—	3	0	0	0	0	5¹	9	1	1	4	16.9	6.75	54	.391	.417	0	.000	-0	-2	-2	0	0.0
Total	2	0	0	—	5	0	0	0	0	8¹	10	1	2	7	13.0	4.32	83	.313	.353	0	.000	-0	-1	-1	0	0.0

● JOE MARGONERI   Margoneri, Joseph Emanuel b: 1/13/30, Somerset, Pa.   BL/TL, 6', 185 lbs.   Deb: 4/25/56

1956	NY-N	6	6	.500	23	13	2	0	0	91²	88	12	49	49	13.5	3.93	96	.254	.346	3	.103	-1	-2	-1	-0	-0.3
1957	NY-N	1	1	.500	13	2	1	0	0	34¹	44	1	21	18	17.3	5.24	75	.314	.407	0	.000	-1	-5	-5	-0	-0.4
Total	2	7	7	.500	36	15	3	0	0	126	132	13	70	67	14.5	4.29	89	.271	.364	3	.081	-2	-7	-6	-1	-0.7

● JUAN MARICHAL   Marichal, Juan Antonio (Sanchez) "Manito" b: 10/20/37, Laguna Verde, D.R.   BR/TR, 6', 185 lbs.   Deb: 7/19/60   H

1960	SF-N	6	2	.750	11	11	6	0	0	81¹	59	5	28	58	9.6	2.66	131	.200	.269	4	.129	0	10	7	0	0.7
1961	SF-N	13	10	.565	29	27	9	3	0	185	183	24	48	124	11.3	3.89	98	.257	.306	7	.119	-2	-3	-1	-1	-0.5
1962	*SF-N	18	11	.621	37	36	18	3	1	262²	233	34	90	153	11.2	3.36	113	.234	.300	21	.236	4	17	13	-1	1.6
1963	SF-N☆	**25**	8	.758	41	40	18	5	0	**321¹**	259	27	61	248	9.0	2.41	133	.216	.256	20	.179	3	31	28	-3	2.8
1964	SF-N★	21	8	.724	33	33	**22**	4	0	269	241	18	52	206	9.8	2.48	144	.236	.273	14	.144	-1	32	33	1	3.4
1965	SF-N★	22	13	.629	39	37	24	**10**	1	295¹	224	27	46	240	8.3	2.13	**169**	.205	.240	17	.173	1	46	**48**	-0	**6.0**
1966	SF-N★	25	6	**.806**	37	36	25	4	0	307¹	228	32	36	222	**7.9**	2.23	165	**.202**	**.230**	28	.250	6	47	49	0	5.8
1967	SF-N★	14	10	.583	26	26	18	2	0	202¹	195	20	42	166	10.6	2.76	119	.249	.288	14	.177	3	14	12	-2	1.5
1968	SF-N★	**26**	9	.743	38	38	**30**	5	0	**326**	295	21	46	218	9.6	2.43	121	.238	.269	20	.163	1	20	19	3	2.7
1969	SF-N☆	21	11	.656	37	36	27	**8**	0	299²	244	16	54	205	**9.1**	**2.10**	167	.222	.263	15	.138	-1	**50**	47	4	5.4
1970	SF-N	12	10	.545	34	33	14	1	0	242²	269	28	48	123	11.8	4.12	97	.277	.312	5	.059	-6	-2	-4	-2	-0.7
1971	*SF-N★	18	11	.621	37	37	18	4	0	279	244	27	56	159	9.8	2.94	116	.233	.274	14	.133	0	16	14	3	1.8
1972	SF-N	6	16	.273	25	24	6	0	0	165	176	16	46	72	12.3	3.71	94	.277	.329	10	.196	-5	-4	-4	-0	-0.4
1973	SF-N	11	15	.423	34	32	9	2	0	207¹	231	22	37	87	11.7	3.82	100	.277	.309	13	.188	-1	-0	-1	0	-0.5
1974	Bos-A	5	1	.833	11	9	0	0	0	57¹	61	3	14	21	12.1	4.87	79	.270	.318	0	—	-0	-8	-7	-0	-0.9
1975	LA-N	0	1	.000	2	1	0	0	0	6	11	2	5	1	24.0	13.50	25	.407	.500	0	.000	-0	-7	-7	-0	-0.8
Total	16	243	142	.631	471	457	244	52	2	3507¹	3153	320	709	2303	10.0	2.89	122	.237	.278	202	.165	10	262	247	9	28.9

● DAN MARION   Marion, Donald G. "Rube" b: 7/31/1890, Cleveland, Ohio   d: 1/18/33, Milwaukee, Wis.   BR/TR, 6'1", 187 lbs.   Deb: 4/23/14

| 1914 | Bro-F | 3 | 2 | .600 | 17 | 9 | 4 | 0 | 0 | 89¹ | 97 | 1 | 38 | 41 | 14.2 | 3.93 | 73 | .281 | .362 | 7 | .194 | -2 | -10 | -10 | -1 | -0.8 |

YEAR	TM/L	W	L	PCT	G	GS	CG	SH	SV	IP	H	HR	BB	SO	RAT	ERA	ERA+	OAV	OOB	BH	AVG	PB	PR	/A	PD	TPI
1915	Bro-F	12	9	.571	35	25	15	2	0	208¹	193	1	64	46	11.2	3.20	85	.248	.308	13	.176	-2	-11	-11	-1	-1.3
Total	2	15	11	.577	52	34	19	2	0	297²	290	2	102	87	12.1	3.42	81	.258	.325	20	.182	-3	-21	-22	-2	-2.1

● **DUKE MARKELL**   Markell, Harry Duquesne (b: Harry Duquesne Makowsky)
b: 8/17/23, Paris, France   d: 6/14/84, Ft.Lauderdale, Fla.   BR/TR, 6'1.5", 209 lbs.   Deb: 9/6/51

YEAR	TM/L	W	L	PCT	G	GS	CG	SH	SV	IP	H	HR	BB	SO	RAT	ERA	ERA+	OAV	OOB	BH	AVG	PB	PR	/A	PD	TPI
1951	StL-A	1	1	.500	5	2	1	0	0	21¹	25	3	20	10	19.0	6.33	69	.298	.433	1	.167	-0	-5	-5	-1	-0.4

● **CLIFF MARKLE**   Markle, Clifford Monroe   b: 5/3/1894, Dravosburg, Pa.   d: 5/24/74, Temple City, Cal.   BR/TR, 5'9", 163 lbs.   Deb: 9/18/15

YEAR	TM/L	W	L	PCT	G	GS	CG	SH	SV	IP	H	HR	BB	SO	RAT	ERA	ERA+	OAV	OOB	BH	AVG	PB	PR	/A	PD	TPI
1915	NY-A	2	0	1.000	3	2	2	0	0	23	15	1	6	12	8.2	0.39	750	.185	.241	0	.000	-0	7	6	+1	0.5
1916	NY-A	4	3	.571	11	7	3	1	0	45²	41	0	31	14	15.0	4.53	64	.256	.390	0	.000	-1	-9	-8	-0	-1.4
1921	Cin-N	2	6	.250	10	6	5	0	0	67	75	0	20	23	12.8	3.76	95	.291	.342	3	.125	-2	0	-1	-1	-0.4
1922	Cin-N	4	5	.444	25	3	2	1	0	75²	75	3	33	34	12.8	3.81	105	.268	.345	3	.150	-2	2	2	-0	0.1
1924	NY-A	0	3	.000	7	3	0	0	0	23¹	29	5	20	7	18.9	8.87	47	.333	.458	0	.000	-1	-12	-12	-1	-1.4
Total	5	12	17	.414	56	21	12	2	0	234²	235	9	110	90	13.4	4.10	87	.271	.356	6	.087	-5	-12	-14	-3	-2.6

● **DICK MARLOWE**   Marlowe, Richard Burton   b: 6/27/29, Hickory, N.C.   d: 12/30/68, Toledo, Ohio   BR/TR, 6'2", 170 lbs.   Deb: 9/19/51

YEAR	TM/L	W	L	PCT	G	GS	CG	SH	SV	IP	H	HR	BB	SO	RAT	ERA	ERA+	OAV	OOB	BH	AVG	PB	PR	/A	PD	TPI
1951	Det-A	0	1	.000	2	1	0	0	0	1²	5	0	2	1	37.8	32.40	13	.500	.583	0	—	0	-5	-5	-0	-1.8
1952	Det-A	0	2	.000	4	1	0	0	0	11	21	1	3	8	19.6	7.36	52	.420	.453	0	.000	-0	-5	-4	-0	-0.7
1953	Det-A	6	7	.462	42	11	2	0	0	119²	152	13	42	52	14.7	5.26	77	.319	.377	7	.219	-0	-17	-16	-1	-1.6
1954	Det-A	5	4	.556	38	2	0	0	2	84	76	11	40	39	12.4	4.18	88	.244	.330	3	.167	0	-4	-5	-1	-0.5
1955	Det-A	1	0	1.000	4	1	1	0	1	15	12	1	9	6	9.6	1.80	213	.218	.271	0	.000	-0	4	3	-0	0.2
1956	Det-A	1	1	.500	7	1	0	0	0	11	12	1	9	4	17.2	5.73	72	.279	.404	0	.000	-0	-2	-2	-0	-0.3
	Chi-A	0	0	—	1	0	0	0	0	1	2	1	1	0	27.0	9.00	46	.500	.600	0	—	0	-1	-1	-0	0.0
	Yr	1	1	.500	8	1	0	0	0	12	14	2	10	4	18.0	6.00	69	.298	.421	0	.000	-0	-2	-3	-0	-0.3
Total	6	13	15	.464	98	17	3	0	3	243¹	280	28	101	108	14.2	4.99	78	.295	.364	10	.175	-1	-30	-29	-2	-4.7

● **LOU MARONE**   Marone, Louis Stephen   b: 12/3/45, San Diego, Cal.   BR/TL, 5'11", 185 lbs.   Deb: 5/30/69

YEAR	TM/L	W	L	PCT	G	GS	CG	SH	SV	IP	H	HR	BB	SO	RAT	ERA	ERA+	OAV	OOB	BH	AVG	PB	PR	/A	PD	TPI
1969	Pit-N	1	1	.500	29	0	0	0	1	35¹	24	2	13	25	9.9	2.55	137	.195	.283	0	—	0	4	4	-1	0.1
1970	Pit-N	0	0	—	1	0	0	0	0	2¹	2	1	0	0	7.7	3.86	101	.222	.222	0	—	0	-0	-0	-0	0.0
Total	2	1	1	.500	30	0	0	0	1	37²	26	3	13	25	9.8	2.63	134	.197	.279	0	—	0	4	4	-1	0.1

● **RUBE MARQUARD**   Marquard, Richard William   b: 10/9/1886, Cleveland, Ohio   d: 6/1/80, Baltimore, Md.   BB/TL, 6'3", 180 lbs.   Deb: 9/25/08   H

YEAR	TM/L	W	L	PCT	G	GS	CG	SH	SV	IP	H	HR	BB	SO	RAT	ERA	ERA+	OAV	OOB	BH	AVG	PB	PR	/A	PD	TPI
1908	NY-N	0	1	.000	1	1	0	0	0	5	6	0	2	2	16.2	3.60	67	.316	.409	0	.000	-0	-1	-1	-0	-0.2
1909	NY-N	5	13	.278	29	21	8	0	1	173	155	2	73	109	12.3	2.60	98	.248	.335	8	.148	-1	-0	-1	-0	-0.3
1910	NY-N	4	4	.500	13	8	2	0	0	70²	62	4	52	53	13.9	4.46	67	.254	.363	3	.111	-2	-11	-12	-0	-1.4
1911	*NY-N	24	7	**.774**	45	33	22	5	3	277²	221	9	106	**237**	10.7	2.50	135	.219	.296	17	.163	-1	28	27	-4	2.3
1912	*NY-N	**26**	11	.703	43	38	22	1	1	294²	286	9	80	175	11.3	2.57	132	.255	.306	21	.219	2	28	27	-3	2.9
1913	*NY-N	23	10	.697	42	33	20	4	3	288	248	10	49	151	9.4	2.50	125	.237	.273	23	.219	2	23	20	-6	1.8
1914	NY-N	12	22	.353	39	33	15	4	2	268	261	6	47	92	10.4	3.06	87	.262	.297	15	.179	-1	-8	-12	-1	-1.6
1915	NY-N	9	8	.529	27	20	10	2	2	169	178	6	33	79	11.3	3.73	69	.272	.308	6	.109	-3	-18	-22	-0	-2.4
	Bro-N	2	2	.500	6	3	0	0	1	24²	29	0	5	13	12.4	6.20	45	.276	.309	1	.125	-0	-9	-9	-0	-1.5
	Yr	11	10	.524	33	23	10	2	3	193²	207	6	38	92	11.4	4.04	64	.272	.307	7	.111	-3	-28	-31	-0	-3.9
1916	*Bro-N	13	6	.684	36	21	15	2	5	205	169	2	38	107	9.1	1.58	170	.229	.267	9	.143	-1	24	25	-4	2.1
1917	Bro-N	19	12	.613	37	29	14	0	0	232²	200	5	60	117	10.1	2.55	110	.232	.282	15	.200	0	4	6	-4	0.4
1918	Bro-N	9	18	.333	34	29	19	4	0	239	231	7	59	89	11.0	2.64	106	.260	.307	13	.171	-2	3	1	0	0.0
1919	Bro-N	3	3	.500	8	7	3	0	0	59	54	1	10	29	9.8	2.29	130	.244	.277	6	.261	1	4	4	-0	0.4
1920	*Bro-N	10	7	.588	28	26	10	1	0	189²	181	5	35	89	10.3	3.23	99	.251	.287	10	.169	-1	-2	-0	-4	-0.6
1921	Cin-N	17	14	.548	39	35	18	2	0	265²	291	8	50	88	11.8	3.39	106	.285	.323	19	.200	-1	12	6	-3	0.1
1922	Bos-N	11	15	.423	39	25	7	0	1	198	255	12	66	57	14.6	5.09	79	.322	.374	14	.222	-1	-22	-24	1	-2.6
1923	Bos-N	11	14	.440	38	29	11	3	0	239	265	10	66	78	12.5	3.73	107	.288	.337	12	.140	-6	7	7	0	0.4
1924	Bos-N	1	2	.333	6	6	3	1	0	36	33	3	13	10	11.8	3.00	127	.254	.326	3	.273	0	3	3	-0	0.3
1925	Bos-N	2	8	.200	26	8	0	0	0	72	105	5	27	19	16.5	5.75	70	.341	.394	3	.136	-1	-12	-14	-2	-1.9
Total	18	201	177	.532	536	405	197	30	19	3306²	3233	107	858	1593	11.2	3.08	103	.260	.310	198	.179	-17	53	36	-31	-2.2

● **ISIDRO MARQUEZ**   Marquez, Isidro (Espinoza)   b: 5/15/65, Navojoa, Mexico   BR/TR, 6'3", 190 lbs.   Deb: 4/26/95

YEAR	TM/L	W	L	PCT	G	GS	CG	SH	SV	IP	H	HR	BB	SO	RAT	ERA	ERA+	OAV	OOB	BH	AVG	PB	PR	/A	PD	TPI
1995	Chi-A	0	1	.000	7	0	0	0	0	6	9	3	2	8	14.9	6.75	66	.321	.367	0	—	0	-2	-2	-0	-0.1

● **JIM MARQUIS**   Marquis, James Milburn   b: 11/18/1900, Yoakum, Tex.   d: 8/5/92, Jackson, Cal.   BR/TR, 5'11", 174 lbs.   Deb: 8/8/25

YEAR	TM/L	W	L	PCT	G	GS	CG	SH	SV	IP	H	HR	BB	SO	RAT	ERA	ERA+	OAV	OOB	BH	AVG	PB	PR	/A	PD	TPI
1925	NY-A	0	0	—	2	0	0	0	0	7¹	12	1	6	0	22.1	9.82	43	.414	.514	0	.000	-0	-4	-5	-0	-0.4

● **CONNIE MARRERO**   Marrero, Conrado Eugenio (Ramos)   b: 4/25/11, Las Villas, Cuba   BR/TR, 5'7", 158 lbs.   Deb: 4/21/50

YEAR	TM/L	W	L	PCT	G	GS	CG	SH	SV	IP	H	HR	BB	SO	RAT	ERA	ERA+	OAV	OOB	BH	AVG	PB	PR	/A	PD	TPI
1950	Was-A	6	10	.375	27	19	8	1	1	152	159	17	55	63	12.9	4.50	100	.269	.335	6	.122	-1	1	-0	-3	-0.4
1951	Was-A☆	11	9	.550	25	25	16	2	0	187	198	8	71	66	13.1	3.90	105	.268	.335	10	.164	-2	5	4	-2	0.1
1952	Was-A	11	8	.579	22	22	16	2	0	184¹	175	9	53	77	11.3	2.88	123	.249	.305	5	.079	-5	16	14	-3	0.5
1953	Was-A	8	7	.533	22	20	10	2	0	145²	130	14	48	65	11.3	3.03	129	.241	.309	6	.125	-2	16	14	-1	1.1
1954	Was-A	3	6	.333	22	8	1	0	0	66¹	74	12	22	26	13.0	4.75	75	.287	.343	0	.000	-1	-8	-9	-1	-1.3
Total	5	39	40	.494	118	94	51	7	1	735¹	736	60	249	297	12.3	3.67	108	.260	.323	27	.114	-11	30	23	-10	0.0

● **BUCK MARROW**   Marrow, Charles Kennon   b: 8/29/09, Tarboro, N.C.   d: 11/21/82, Newport News, Va.   BR/TR, 6'4", 200 lbs.   Deb: 7/3/32

YEAR	TM/L	W	L	PCT	G	GS	CG	SH	SV	IP	H	HR	BB	SO	RAT	ERA	ERA+	OAV	OOB	BH	AVG	PB	PR	/A	PD	TPI
1932	Det-A	2	5	.286	18	7	2	0	1	63²	70	6	29	31	14.8	4.81	98	.278	.366	3	.158	-0	-2	-1	1	0.0
1937	Bro-N	1	2	.333	6	3	1	0	0	16¹	19	2	9	2	15.4	6.61	61	.284	.368	0	.000	-1	-5	-5	0	-0.8
1938	Bro-N	0	1	.000	15	0	0	0	0	19²	23	1	11	6	15.6	4.58	85	.291	.398	0	.000	-0	-2	-1	-0	-0.1
Total	3	3	8	.273	39	10	3	0	1	99²	112	9	49	39	15.4	5.06	88	.281	.373	3	.120	-1	-9	-7	1	-0.9

● **ED MARS**   Mars, Edward M.   b: 12/4/1866, Chicago, Ill.   d: 12/9/41, Chicago, Ill.   5'9", 166 lbs.   Deb: 8/12/1890

YEAR	TM/L	W	L	PCT	G	GS	CG	SH	SV	IP	H	HR	BB	SO	RAT	ERA	ERA+	OAV	OOB	BH	AVG	PB	PR	/A	PD	TPI
1890	Syr-a	9	5	.643	16	14	14	0	0	121¹	132	2	49	59	13.8	4.67	76	.269	.341	14	.275	4	-11	-15	1	-1.0

● **CUDDLES MARSHALL**   Marshall, Clarence Westly   b: 4/28/25, Bellingham, Wash.   BR/TR, 6'3", 200 lbs.   Deb: 4/24/46

YEAR	TM/L	W	L	PCT	G	GS	CG	SH	SV	IP	H	HR	BB	SO	RAT	ERA	ERA+	OAV	OOB	BH	AVG	PB	PR	/A	PD	TPI
1946	NY-A	3	4	.429	23	11	1	0	0	81	96	4	56	32	16.9	5.33	65	.308	.413	4	.143	-1	-16	-17	1	-1.3
1948	NY-A	0	0	—	1	0	0	0	0	1	0	0	3	0	27.0	0.00	—	.000	.500	0	—	0	0	-0	-0	0.0
1949	NY-A	3	0	1.000	21	2	0	0	3	49¹	48	3	48	13	17.9	5.11	79	.259	.417	1	.111	-0	-5	-6	1	-0.4
1950	StL-A	1	3	.250	28	2	0	0	1	53²	72	1	51	24	20.8	7.88	63	.321	.449	4	.333	0	-20	-17	-1	-1.2
Total	4	7	7	.500	73	15	1	0	4	185	216	8	158	69	18.3	5.98	67	.298	.426	9	.184	-1	-41	-40	0	-2.9

● **MIKE MARSHALL**   Marshall, Michael Grant   b: 1/15/43, Adrian, Mich.   BR/TR, 5'10", 180 lbs.   Deb: 5/31/67

YEAR	TM/L	W	L	PCT	G	GS	CG	SH	SV	IP	H	HR	BB	SO	RAT	ERA	ERA+	OAV	OOB	BH	AVG	PB	PR	/A	PD	TPI
1967	Det-A	1	3	.250	37	0	0	0	10	59	51	6	20	41	11.1	1.98	165	.233	.303	2	.222	0	8	8	1	1.0
1969	Sea-A	3	10	.231	20	14	3	1	0	87²	99	8	35	47	14.0	5.13	71	.281	.350	7	.259	3	-15	-15	3	-1.4
1970	Hou-N	0	1	.000	4	0	0	0	0	5¹	8	0	4	5	21.9	8.44	46	.400	.520	0	—	0	-3	-3	1	-0.4
	Mon-N	3	7	.300	24	5	0	0	3	64²	56	4	29	38	11.8	3.48	118	.225	.306	1	.091	0	4	5	2	0.9
	Yr	3	8	.273	28	5	0	0	3	70	64	4	33	43	12.5	3.86	106	.237	.320	1	.091	0	1	2	3	0.5
1971	Mon-N	5	8	.385	66	0	0	0	23	111¹	100	9	50	85	12.4	4.28	82	.247	.336	3	.188	-0	-10	-9	3	-1.1
1972	Mon-N	14	8	.636	**65**	0	0	0	18	116	82	3	47	95	10.2	1.78	199	.202	.289	3	.136	0	22	23	0	5.3
1973	Mon-N	14	11	.560	**92**	0	0	0	31	179	163	10	75	124	12.2	2.66	143	.252	.333	8	.242	1	20	23	1	4.4
1974	*LA-N★	15	12	.556	**106**	0	0	0	21	208	191	9	56	143	10.7	2.42	141	.247	.299	8	.235	1	28	23	1	3.5
1975	LA-N☆	9	14	.391	57	0	0	0	13	109¹	98	8	39	64	11.6	3.29	103	.242	.315	1	.067	-1	4	1	2	0.4
1976	LA-N	4	3	.571	30	0	0	0	0	62²	64	2	25	39	12.9	4.45	76	.270	.342	0	.000	-0	-7	-7	2	-0.8
	Atl-N	2	1	.667	24	0	0	0	0	36²	35	4	14	17	12.3	3.19	119	.254	.333	1	.167	0	1	2	0	0.4
	Yr	6	4	.600	54	0	0	0	0	99²	99	6	39	56	12.6	3.99	89	.264	.335	1	.091	-0	-5	-5	2	-0.4
1977	Atl-N	1	0	1.000	7	0	0	0	0	6	12	1	2	6	21.0	9.00	49	.400	.438	1	1.000	0	-3	-3	-0	-0.4
	Tex-A	2	2	.500	17	0	0	0	0	35²	42	4	13	18	14.4	4.04	101	.304	.373	0	—	0	0	-0	1	0.0
1978	Min-A	10	12	.455	54	0	0	0	21	99	90	3	37	56	10.7	2.45	156	.225	.300	0	—	0	14	15	1	4.0
1979	Min-A	10	15	.400	**90**	1	0	0	**32**	142²	132	8	48	81	11.6	2.65	165	.254	.322	0	—	0	25	27	3	5.7

YEAR	TM/L	W	L	PCT	G	GS	CG	SH	SV	IP	H	HR	BB	SO	RAT	ERA	ERA+	OAV	OOB	BH	AVG	PB	PR	/A	PD	TPI
1980	Min-A	1	3	.250	18	0	0	0	1	32¹	42	2	12	13	15.6	6.12	71	.323	.389	0	—	0	-8	-6	1	-1.1
1981	NY-N	3	2	.600	20	0	0	0	0	31	26	2	8	8	9.9	2.61	133	.224	.274	0	—	0	3	3	-0	0.5
Total	14	97	112	.464	723	24	3	1	188	1386²	1281	79	514	880	11.9	3.14	118	.249	.321	35	.196	6	84	87	20	20.9

● RUBE MARSHALL
Marshall, Roy De Verne "Cy"   b: 1/19/1890, Salineville, Ohio   d: 6/11/80, Dover, Ohio   BR/TR, 5'11", 170 lbs.   Deb: 9/28/12

YEAR	TM/L	W	L	PCT	G	GS	CG	SH	SV	IP	H	HR	BB	SO	RAT	ERA	ERA+	OAV	OOB	BH	AVG	PB	PR	/A	PD	TPI
1912	Phi-N	0	1	.000	2	1	0	0	0	3	12	0	1	2	39.0	21.00	17	.632	.650	0	—	0	-6	-6	0	-1.2
1913	Phi-N	0	1	.000	14	1	0	0	1	45¹	54	2	22	18	15.3	4.57	73	.297	.371	1	.091	-1	-7	-6	0	-0.2
1914	Phi-N	6	7	.462	27	19	7	0	1	134¹	144	2	50	49	13.3	3.75	78	.279	.349	6	.140	-2	-14	-12	1	-1.3
1915	Buf-F	2	1	.667	21	4	2	0	0	59¹	62	1	33	21	14.7	3.94	71	.281	.379	5	.294	1	-8	-8	-1	-0.4
Total	4	8	10	.444	64	25	9	0	2	242	272	5	106	90	14.4	4.17	72	.290	.367	12	.169	-2	-35	-32	-0	-3.1

● PHONNEY MARTIN
Martin, Alphonse Case   b: 8/4/1845, New York, N.Y.   d: 5/24/33, Hollis, N.Y.   5'7", 148 lbs.   Deb: 4/26/1872 ♦

YEAR	TM/L	W	L	PCT	G	GS	CG	SH	SV	IP	H	HR	BB	SO	RAT	ERA	ERA+	OAV	OOB	BH	AVG	PB	PR	/A	PD	TPI
1872	Tro-n	1	2	.333	8	3	0	0	0	37¹	70	0	2	1	17.4	4.82	75	.350	.356	36	.308	1	-5	-5		-0.4
	Eck-n	2	7	.222	10	9	9	0	0	85	144	1	4	2	15.7	4.24	80	.321	.327	12	.154	-3	-6	-8		-0.7
	Yr	3	9	.250	18	12	9	0	0	122¹	214	1	6	3	16.2	4.41	78	.330	.336	48	.246	-2	-11	-13		-1.1
1873	Mut-n	0	1	.000	6	1	1	0	0	34	50	0	7	1	15.1	3.44	92	.294	.322	31	.221	-0	-1	-1		-0.1
Total	2 n	3	10	.231	24	13	10	0	0	156¹	264	1	13	4	15.9	4.20	75	.322	.333	79	.236	-3	-17	-18		-1.2

● BARNEY MARTIN
Martin, Barnes Robertson   b: 3/3/23, Columbia, S.C.   BR/TR, 5'11", 170 lbs.   Deb: 4/22/53   F

YEAR	TM/L	W	L	PCT	G	GS	CG	SH	SV	IP	H	HR	BB	SO	RAT	ERA	ERA+	OAV	OOB	BH	AVG	PB	PR	/A	PD	TPI
1953	Cin-N	0	0	—	1	0	0	0	0	2	3	0	1	1	18.0	9.00	48	.333	.400	0	—	0	-1	-1	-0	0.0

● RENIE MARTIN
Martin, Donald Renie   b: 8/30/55, Dover, Del.   BR/TR, 6'4", 190 lbs.   Deb: 5/9/79

YEAR	TM/L	W	L	PCT	G	GS	CG	SH	SV	IP	H	HR	BB	SO	RAT	ERA	ERA+	OAV	OOB	BH	AVG	PB	PR	/A	PD	TPI
1979	KC-A	0	3	.000	25	0	0	0	5	34²	32	1	14	25	12.2	5.19	82	.248	.326	0	—	0	-4	-4	1	-0.4
1980	*KC-A	10	10	.500	32	20	2	0	2	137¹	133	18	70	68	13.4	4.39	92	.255	.345	0	—	0	-5	-5	-0	-0.8
1981	*KC-A	4	5	.444	21	9	1	0	4	61²	55	2	29	25	12.3	2.77	130	.244	.331	0	—	0	6	6	1	1.0
1982	SF-N	7	10	.412	29	25	1	0	0	141¹	148	14	64	63	13.5	4.65	77	.274	.350	13	.265	3	-16	-17	1	-1.4
1983	SF-N	2	4	.333	37	6	0	0	1	94¹	91	15	41	43	14.2	4.20	84	.268	.365	9	.346	4	-6	-7	1	0.2
1984	SF-N	1	1	.500	12	0	0	0	0	23¹	29	2	16	12	17.4	3.86	91	.305	.405	4	.500	1	-1	-1	1	0.1
	Phi-N	0	2	.000	9	0	0	0	0	15²	17	2	12	5	16.7	4.60	79	.274	.392	0	.000	-0	-2	-2	1	-0.1
	Yr	1	3	.250	21	0	0	0	0	39	46	4	28	13	17.1	4.15	86	.293	.400	3	.375	1	-2	-3	2	0.0
Total	6	24	35	.407	173	51	3	0	12	508¹	509	50	256	237	13.6	4.27	88	.264	.352	25	.301	8	-28	-29	5	-1.4

● SPEED MARTIN
Martin, Elwood Good   b: 9/15/1893, Wawawai, Wash.   d: 6/14/83, Lemon Grove, Cal.   BR/TR, 6', 165 lbs.   Deb: 7/5/17

YEAR	TM/L	W	L	PCT	G	GS	CG	SH	SV	IP	H	HR	BB	SO	RAT	ERA	ERA+	OAV	OOB	BH	AVG	PB	PR	/A	PD	TPI
1917	StL-A	0	2	.000	9	2	1	0	0	15²	20	1	5	5	14.4	5.74	45	.339	.391	0	.000	-0	-5	-5	1	-0.6
1918	Chi-N	5	2	.714	9	5	4	1	1	53²	47	0	14	16	10.4	1.84	151	.246	.301	3	.188	-0	5	6	1	0.9
1919	Chi-N	8	8	.500	35	14	7	2	2	163²	158	6	52	54	11.8	2.47	116	.259	.321	8	.182	-1	8	7	2	0.8
1920	Chi-N	4	15	.211	35	13	6	0	2	136	165	3	44	50	14.3	4.83	66	.305	.365	7	.159	-0	-26	-25	1	-3.1
1921	Chi-N	11	15	.423	37	28	13	1	1	217¹	245	12	68	86	13.0	4.35	88	.298	.353	17	.233	1	-14	-13	2	-1.0
1922	Chi-N	1	0	1.000	1	1	0	0	0	6	10	0	2	2	18.0	7.50	56	.385	.429	0	.000	-0	-2	-2	-0	-0.3
Total	6	29	42	.408	126	63	30	4	6	592¹	645	16	191	207	12.8	3.78	87	.287	.344	35	.194	-0	-33	-32	7	-3.3

● FRED MARTIN
Martin, Fred Turner   b: 6/27/15, Williams, Okla.   d: 6/11/79, Chicago, Ill.   BR/TR, 6'1", 185 lbs.   Deb: 4/21/46   C

YEAR	TM/L	W	L	PCT	G	GS	CG	SH	SV	IP	H	HR	BB	SO	RAT	ERA	ERA+	OAV	OOB	BH	AVG	PB	PR	/A	PD	TPI
1946	StL-N	2	1	.667	6	3	2	0	0	28²	29	0	8	19	11.6	4.08	85	.254	.303	3	.273	0	-2	-2	0	-0.1
1949	StL-N	6	0	1.000	21	5	3	0	0	70	65	3	20	30	10.9	2.44	170	.243	.295	6	.300	1	12	13	0	1.1
1950	StL-N	4	2	.667	30	2	0	0	0	63¹	87	4	30	19	16.8	5.12	84	.331	.401	4	.267	1	-7	-6	1	-0.3
Total	3	12	3	.800	57	10	5	0	0	162	181	7	58	68	13.3	3.78	108	.281	.341	13	.283	2	3	6	1	0.7

● DOC MARTIN
Martin, Harold Winthrop   b: 9/23/1887, Roxbury, Mass.   d: 4/14/35, Milton, Mass.   BR/TR, 5'11", 165 lbs.   Deb: 10/7/08

YEAR	TM/L	W	L	PCT	G	GS	CG	SH	SV	IP	H	HR	BB	SO	RAT	ERA	ERA+	OAV	OOB	BH	AVG	PB	PR	/A	PD	TPI
1908	Phi-A	0	1	.000	1	1	0	0	0	2	2	0	3	2	27.0	13.50	19	.286	.545	0	—	-0	-2	-2	-0	-0.8
1911	Phi-A	1	1	.500	11	3	1	0	0	38	40	1	17	21	14.7	4.50	70	.272	.367	3	.214	-0	-6	-6	-0	-0.2
1912	Phi-A	0	0	—	2	0	0	0	0	4¹	5	0	5	4	22.8	10.38	30	.333	.524	0	.000	-1	-3	-4	0	-0.1
Total	3	1	2	.333	14	4	1	0	0	44¹	47	1	25	27	16.0	5.48	57	.278	.393	3	.167	-0	-11	-12	1	-1.0

● PEPPER MARTIN
Martin, John Leonard Roosevelt "The Wild Horse Of The Osage"
b: 2/29/04, Temple, Okla.   d: 3/5/65, McAlester, Okla.   BR/TR, 5'8", 170 lbs.   Deb: 4/16/28   C ♦

YEAR	TM/L	W	L	PCT	G	GS	CG	SH	SV	IP	H	HR	BB	SO	RAT	ERA	ERA+	OAV	OOB	BH	AVG	PB	PR	/A	PD	TPI
1934	*StL-N★	0	0	—	1	0	0	0	0	2	1	0	0	0	4.5	4.50	94	.167	.167	131	.289	0	-0	-0	0	0.0
1936	StL-N	0	0	—	1	0	0	0	0	2	1	0	2	0	13.5	0.00	—	.200	.429	177	.309	1	1	1	-0	0.0
Total	2	0	0	—	2	0	0	0	0	4	2	0	2	0	9.0	2.25	181	.182	.308	1227	.298	1	1	1	-0	0.0

● JOHN MARTIN
Martin, John Robert   b: 4/11/56, Wyandotte, Mich.   BB/TL, 6', 190 lbs.   Deb: 8/27/80

YEAR	TM/L	W	L	PCT	G	GS	CG	SH	SV	IP	H	HR	BB	SO	RAT	ERA	ERA+	OAV	OOB	BH	AVG	PB	PR	/A	PD	TPI
1980	StL-N	2	3	.400	9	5	1	0	0	42	39	1	9	23	10.3	4.29	86	.247	.287	3	.273	1	-3	-3	-1	-0.3
1981	StL-N	8	5	.615	17	15	4	0	0	102²	85	10	26	36	9.9	3.42	104	.228	.283	7	.212	2	4	4	1	0.1
1982	StL-N	4	5	.444	24	7	0	0	0	66	56	6	30	21	11.7	4.23	86	.230	.314	1	.091	-0	-5	-4	-1	-0.7
1983	StL-N	3	1	.750	26	5	0	0	0	66¹	60	6	26	29	11.9	3.53	103	.242	.319	4	.222	1	1	1	0	0.2
	Det-A	0	0	—	15	0	0	0	1	13¹	15	2	4	11	12.8	7.43	53	.294	.345	0	—	0	-5	-5	-0	-0.1
Total	4	17	14	.548	91	32	5	0	1	290¹	255	25	95	120	11.0	3.94	92	.238	.302	15	.205	3	-11	-10	-1	-0.5

● MORRIE MARTIN
Martin, Morris Webster "Lefty"   b: 9/3/22, Dixon, Mo.   BL/TL, 6', 180 lbs.   Deb: 4/25/49

YEAR	TM/L	W	L	PCT	G	GS	CG	SH	SV	IP	H	HR	BB	SO	RAT	ERA	ERA+	OAV	OOB	BH	AVG	PB	PR	/A	PD	TPI
1949	Bro-N	1	3	.250	10	4	0	0	0	30²	39	5	15	15	16.4	7.04	58	.320	.403	2	.200	—	-10	-10	-1	-1.1
1951	Phi-A	11	4	.733	35	13	8	3	1	138	139	13	63	35	13.5	3.78	113	.259	.343	11	.220	-1	5	8	2	0.8
1952	Phi-A	0	2	.000	5	5	0	0	0	25¹	32	1	15	13	17.4	6.39	62	.302	.398	1	.111	-1	-8	-7	-0	-0.6
1953	Phi-A	10	12	.455	58	11	2	0	7	156¹	158	12	59	64	13.0	4.43	97	.262	.336	4	.095	-4	-3	-0	-0.7	
1954	Phi-A	2	4	.333	13	6	2	0	0	52²	57	9	19	24	13.3	5.47	71	.278	.345	4	.235	0	-10	-9	-0	-0.9
	Chi-A	5	4	.556	35	2	1	0	5	70	52	5	24	31	9.9	2.06	182	.210	.282	2	.133	-0	13	13	-1	1.7
	Yr	7	8	.467	48	8	3	0	5	122²	109	14	43	55	11.2	3.52	108	.237	.304	6	.188	-0	3	4	-1	0.8
1955	Chi-A	2	3	.400	37	0	0	0	0	52	50	4	20	22	12.5	3.63	109	.259	.335	3	.300	1	2	2	-0	0.3
1956	Chi-A	1	0	1.000	10	0	0	0	0	18¹	21	1	4	5	13.7	4.91	84	.292	.354	1	.200	-0	-2	-2	-0	-0.1
	Bal-A	1	1	.500	9	0	0	0	0	5	10	1	5	7	23.4	10.80	36	.400	.464	0	—	-1	-4	-4	-1	-1.3
	Yr	2	1	.667	19	0	0	0	0	23¹	31	2	9	12	15.8	6.17	66	.316	.380	1	.200	-1	-5	-5	-1	-1.4
1957	StL-N	0	0	—	4	1	0	0	0	10²	5	0	4	7	8.4	2.53	157	.143	.250	0	.000	—	2	2	-0	0.1
1958	StL-N	3	1	.750	39	0	0	0	0	24²	19	3	12	16	12.0	4.74	87	.211	.317	0	.000	-0	-3	-3	-0	-0.3
	Cle-A	2	0	1.000	14	0	0	0	0	18²	20	0	8	13	13.5	2.41	151	.294	.368	0	—	-1	2	2	0	0.3
1959	Chi-N	0	0	—	2	0	0	0	0	2¹	5	2	1	1	27.0	19.29	20	.455	.538	0	—	0	-4	-4	0	0.0
Total	10	38	34	.528	250	42	8	1	15	604²	607	56	249	245	13.1	4.03	95	.262	.341	28	.170	0	-23	-13	-2	-1.9

● PAT MARTIN
Martin, Patrick Francis   b: 4/13/1892, Brooklyn, N.Y.   d: 2/4/49, Brooklyn, N.Y.   BL/TL, 5'11.5", 170 lbs.   Deb: 9/20/19

YEAR	TM/L	W	L	PCT	G	GS	CG	SH	SV	IP	H	HR	BB	SO	RAT	ERA	ERA+	OAV	OOB	BH	AVG	PB	PR	/A	PD	TPI
1919	Phi-A	0	2	.000	2	2	1	0	0	11	11	0	8	6	15.5	4.09	84	.256	.373	0	.000	—	-1	-1	-0	-0.2
1920	Phi-A	1	4	.200	8	5	2	0	0	32¹	48	2	25	14	21.4	6.12	66	.364	.478	4	.400	1	-8	-8	-1	-0.9
Total	2	1	6	.143	10	7	3	0	0	43¹	59	2	33	20	19.9	5.61	69	.337	.453	4	.308	1	-9	-9	-1	-1.1

● PAUL MARTIN
Martin, Paul Charles   b: 3/10/32, Brownstown, Pa.   BR/TR, 6'6", 235 lbs.   Deb: 7/2/55

YEAR	TM/L	W	L	PCT	G	GS	CG	SH	SV	IP	H	HR	BB	SO	RAT	ERA	ERA+	OAV	OOB	BH	AVG	PB	PR	/A	PD	TPI
1955	Pit-N	0	1	.000	7	1	0	0	0	7	13	0	17	3	39.9	14.14	29	.464	.674	0	—	0	-8	-8	-0	-0.9

● RAY MARTIN
Martin, Raymond Joseph   b: 3/13/25, Norwood, Mass.   BR/TR, 6'2", 177 lbs.   Deb: 8/15/43

YEAR	TM/L	W	L	PCT	G	GS	CG	SH	SV	IP	H	HR	BB	SO	RAT	ERA	ERA+	OAV	OOB	BH	AVG	PB	PR	/A	PD	TPI
1943	Bos-N	0	0	—	2	0	0	0	0	3¹	1	0	2	1	10.8	8.10	42	.231	.286	0	—	0	-2	-2	0	0.0
1947	Bos-N	1	0	1.000	1	1	1	1	0	9	7	0	4	2	11.0	1.00	389	.212	.297	0	.000	-0	3	3	0	0.4
1948	Bos-N	0	0	—	2	0	0	0	0	2¹	2	0	0	3	3.9	0.00	—	.222	.125	0	—	0	1	1	0	0.0
Total	3	1	0	1.000	5	1	1	1	0	14²	10	0	6	3	9.8	2.45	154	.189	.271	0	.000	-0	2	2	0	0.4

● JOE MARTINA
Martina, Joseph John "Oyster Joe"   b: 7/8/1889, New Orleans, La.   d: 3/22/62, New Orleans, La.   BR/TR, 6', 183 lbs.   Deb: 4/19/24

YEAR	TM/L	W	L	PCT	G	GS	CG	SH	SV	IP	H	HR	BB	SO	RAT	ERA	ERA+	OAV	OOB	BH	AVG	PB	PR	/A	PD	TPI
1924	*Was-A	6	8	.429	24	14	6	0	0	125¹	129	7	56	57	13.7	4.67	86	.271	.355	14	.326	3	-6	-9	-2	-0.7

YEAR	TM/L	W	L	PCT	G	GS	CG	SH	SV	IP	H	HR	BB	SO	RAT	ERA	ERA+	OAV	OOB	BH	AVG	PB	PR	/A	PD	TPI
● ALFREDO MARTINEZ	Martinez, Alfredo b: 3/15/57, Los Angeles, Cal. BR/TR, 6'3", 185 lbs. Deb: 4/20/80																									
1980	Cal-A	7	9	.438	30	23	4	1	0	149¹	150	14	59	57	12.7	4.52	87	.259	.328	0	—	0	-8	-10	-2	-1.0
1981	Cal-A	0	0	—	2	0	0	0	0	6	5	1	3	4	12.0	3.00	122	.227	.320	0	—	0	0	0	0	0.0
Total	2	7	9	.438	32	23	4	1	0	155¹	155	15	62	61	12.6	4.46	88	.257	.328	0	—	0	-8	-9	-2	-1.0
● DAVE MARTINEZ	Martinez, David b: 9/26/64, New York, N.Y. BL/TL, 5'10", 150 lbs. Deb: 6/15/86 ♦																									
1990	Mon-N	0	0	—	1	0	0	0	0	0¹	2	0	2	0	108.0	54.00	7	.667	.800	109	.279	0	-2	-2	0	0.0
1995	Chi-A	0	0	—	1	0	0	0	0	1	0	0	2	0	18.0	0.00	—	.000	.400	93	.307	1	1	0	0	0.0
Total	2	0	0	—	2	0	0	0	0	1¹	2	0	4	0	40.5	13.50	32	.333	.600	1037	.275	1	-1	-1	0	0.0
● TIPPY MARTINEZ	Martinez, Felix Anthony b: 5/31/50, LaJunta, Colo. BL/TL, 5'10", 180 lbs. Deb: 8/9/74																									
1974	NY-A	0	0	—	10	0	0	0	0	12²	14	0	9	10	17.1	4.26	83	.286	.407	0	—	0	-1	-1	-0	0.1
1975	NY-A	1	2	.333	23	2	0	0	8	37	27	2	32	20	14.6	2.68	137	.208	.368	0	—	0	5	4	-1	0.4
1976	NY-A	2	0	1.000	11	0	0	0	2	28	18	1	14	14	10.3	1.93	177	.191	.296	0	—	0	5	5	1	0.5
	Bal-A	3	1	.750	28	0	0	0	8	41²	32	0	24	31	13.2	2.59	126	.222	.353	0	—	0	4	3	1	0.6
	Yr	5	1	.833	39	0	0	0	10	69²	50	1	42	45	12.0	2.33	143	.210	.331	0	—	0	9	8	2	1.1
1977	Bal-A	5	1	.833	41	0	0	0	9	50	47	2	27	29	13.3	2.70	140	.266	.363	0	—	0	8	6	1	1.2
1978	Bal-A	3	3	.500	42	0	0	0	5	69	77	4	40	57	15.4	4.83	72	.281	.375	0	—	0	-8	-10	-1	-0.4
1979	*Bal-A	10	3	.769	39	0	0	0	3	78	59	0	31	61	10.5	2.88	139	.210	.291	0	—	0	12	10	1	1.9
1980	Bal-A	4	4	.500	53	0	0	0	10	80²	69	5	34	68	11.6	3.01	131	.240	.322	0	—	0	9	8	2	1.1
1981	Bal-A	3	3	.500	37	0	0	0	11	59	48	4	32	50	12.2	2.90	125	.231	.333	0	—	0	5	5	1	0.7
1982	Bal-A	8	8	.500	76	0	0	0	16	95	81	6	37	78	11.3	3.41	118	.240	.317	0	—	0	7	7	-0	1.3
1983	*Bal-A☆	9	3	.750	65	0	0	0	21	103¹	76	10	37	81	9.8	2.35	168	.211	.284	0	—	0	20	18	2	3.0
1984	Bal-A	4	9	.308	55	0	0	0	17	89²	88	9	51	72	14.0	3.91	99	.260	.356	0	—	0	1	-0	-0	-0.1
1985	Bal-A	3	3	.500	49	0	0	0	4	70	70	8	37	47	13.8	5.40	75	.261	.351	0	—	0	-10	-11	1	-0.8
1986	Bal-A	0	2	.000	14	0	0	0	1	16	18	1	12	11	16.9	5.63	73	.295	.411	0	—	0	-3	-3	-0	-0.3
1988	Min-A	0	0	—	3	0	0	0	0	4	8	1	4	3	29.3	18.00	23	.471	.591	0	—	0	-6	-6	-0	0.0
Total	14	55	42	.567	546	2	0	0	115	834	732	53	425	632	12.6	3.45	111	.242	.337	0	—	0	47	35	9	9.2
● BUCK MARTINEZ	Martinez, John Albert b: 11/7/48, Redding, Cal. BR/TR, 5'10", 190 lbs. Deb: 6/18/69 ♦																									
1979	Mil-A	0	0	—	1	0	0	0	0	1	1	0	1	0	18.0	9.00	46	.250	.400	53	.270	1	-1	-1	0	0.0
● DENNIS MARTINEZ	Martinez, Jose Dennis (Emilia) b: 5/14/55, Granada, Nicaragua BR/TR, 6'1", 185 lbs. Deb: 9/14/76																									
1976	Bal-A	1	2	.333	4	2	1	0	0	27²	23	1	8	18	10.1	2.60	126	.237	.295	0	—	0	3	2	0	0.5
1977	Bal-A	14	7	.667	42	13	5	0	4	166²	157	10	64	107	12.4	4.10	92	.253	.330	0	—	0	-1	-6	0	-0.6
1978	Bal-A	16	11	.593	40	38	15	2	0	276¹	257	20	93	142	11.5	3.52	99	.250	.314	0	—	0	8	-1	4	0.5
1979	*Bal-A	15	16	.484	40	39	18	3	0	292¹	279	28	78	132	11.6	3.66	109	.253	.303	0	—	0	18	11	3	1.5
1980	Bal-A	6	4	.600	25	12	2	0	0	99²	103	12	44	42	13.5	3.97	100	.272	.351	0	—	0	1	-0	0	0.0
1981	Bal-A	14	5	.737	25	24	9	2	0	179	173	10	62	88	11.9	3.32	109	.254	.318	0	—	0	7	6	4	1.1
1982	Bal-A	16	12	.571	40	39	10	2	0	252	262	30	87	111	12.7	4.21	96	.267	.331	0	—	0	-4	-5	0	-0.5
1983	Bal-A	7	16	.304	32	25	4	0	0	153	209	21	45	71	15.1	5.53	71	.330	.376	0	—	0	-25	-27	5	-2.9
1984	Bal-A	6	9	.400	34	20	2	0	0	141²	145	26	37	77	11.9	5.02	77	.263	.315	0	—	0	-16	-18	1	-1.5
1985	Bal-A	13	11	.542	33	31	3	1	0	180	203	29	63	68	13.8	5.15	78	.288	.353	0	—	0	-20	-22	0	-2.5
1986	Bal-A	0	0	—	4	0	0	0	0	6²	11	0	2	2	17.6	6.75	61	.367	.406	0	—	0	-2	-2	0	0.1
	Mon-N	3	6	.333	19	15	1	1	0	98	103	11	28	63	12.3	4.59	80	.274	.329	3	.100	-0	-10	-10	1	-0.8
1987	Mon-N	11	4	.733	22	22	2	1	0	144²	133	9	40	84	11.1	3.30	127	.244	.302	3	.065	-2	13	15	0	1.2
1988	Mon-N	15	13	.536	34	34	9	2	0	235¹	215	21	55	120	10.6	2.72	132	.239	.287	15	.192	2	19	23	0	3.0
1989	Mon-N	16	7	.696	34	33	5	2	0	232	227	21	49	142	11.0	3.18	111	.257	.301	9	.125	-1	8	9	3	1.1
1990	Mon-N★	10	11	.476	32	32	7	2	0	226	191	16	49	156	9.8	2.95	124	.228	.275	7	.103	-2	21	18	1	1.5
1991	Mon-N★	14	11	.560	31	31	9	5	0	222	187	9	62	123	10.3	2.39	151	.226	.283	11	.153	1	32	30	4	3.9
1992	Mon-N★	16	11	.593	32	32	6	0	0	226¹	172	12	60	147	9.6	2.47	141	.211	.273	14	.189	1	26	25	3	3.5
1993	Mon-N	15	9	.625	35	34	2	0	1	224²	211	27	64	138	11.5	3.85	108	.246	.307	11	.159	-0	5	8	3	1.1
1994	Cle-A	11	6	.647	24	24	7	3	0	176²	166	14	44	92	11.1	3.52	134	.247	.301	0	—	0	25	24	2	2.1
1995	*Cle-A★	12	5	.706	28	28	3	2	0	187	174	17	46	99	11.2	3.08	152	.247	.304	0	—	0	34	34	4	3.0
1996	Cle-A	9	6	.600	20	20	1	1	0	112	122	12	37	48	12.9	4.50	109	.278	.337	0	—	0	6	5	2	0.7
Total	21	240	182	.569	630	548	121	29	6	3859²	3723	356	1117	2070	11.5	3.63	108	.254	.311	73	.143	-3	147	119	42	16.0
● JOSE MARTINEZ	Martinez, Jose Miguel (Martinez) b: 4/1/71, Guayubin, D.R. BR/TR, 6'2", 180 lbs. Deb: 5/10/94																									
1994	SD-N	0	2	.000	4	1	0	0	0	12	18	2	5	7	17.3	6.75	61	.375	.434	0	.000	-0	-3	-4	0	-0.5
● MARTY MARTINEZ	Martinez, Orlando (Oliva) b: 8/23/41, Havana, Cuba BB/TR, 6'1", 175 lbs. Deb: 5/2/62 MC♦																									
1969	Hou-N	0	0	—	1	0	0	0	0	0²	1	1	0	0	13.5	13.50	26	.333	.333	61	.308	0	-1	-1	-0	0.0
● PEDRO MARTINEZ	Martinez, Pedro (Aquino) b: 11/29/68, Villa Mella, D.R. BL/TL, 6'2", 155 lbs. Deb: 6/29/93																									
1993	SD-N	3	1	.750	32	0	0	0	0	37	23	4	13	32	9.0	2.43	170	.172	.250	0	.000	-0	7	7	-0	0.6
1994	SD-N	3	2	.600	48	1	0	0	3	68¹	52	4	49	52	13.4	2.90	142	.210	.342	0	.000	-1	10	9	1	0.7
1995	Hou-N	0	0	—	25	0	0	0	0	20²	29	3	16	17	20.5	7.40	52	.330	.443	0	—	0	-7	-8	0	0.0
1996	NY-N	0	0	—	5	0	0	0	0	7	8	1	7	6	19.3	6.43	61	.296	.441	0	—	0	-2	-2	0	0.0
	Cin-N	0	0	—	4	0	0	0	0	3	5	1	1	3	18.0	6.00	69	.357	.400	0	—	0	-1	-1	0	0.0
	Yr	0	0	—	9	0	0	0	0	10	13	2	8	9	18.9	6.30	63	.310	.420	0	—	0	-2	-3	0	0.0
Total	4	6	3	.667	114	1	0	0	3	136	117	13	86	110	13.7	3.71	110	.229	.344	0	.000	-1	7	6	1	1.3
● PEDRO MARTINEZ	Martinez, Pedro Jaime (b: Pedro Jaime (Martinez)) b: 7/25/71, Manoguayabo, D.R. BR/TR, 5'11", 150 lbs. Deb: 9/24/92 F																									
1992	LA-N	0	1	.000	2	1	0	0	0	8	6	0	1	8	7.9	2.25	153	.200	.226	0	.000	-0	1	1	-0	0.1
1993	LA-N	10	5	.667	65	2	0	0	2	107	76	5	57	119	11.6	2.61	146	.201	.312	0	.000	-0	17	14	-2	1.7
1994	Mon-N	11	5	.688	24	23	1	1	1	144²	115	11	45	142	10.6	3.42	123	.220	.295	4	.091	-1	13	13	-1	1.1
1995	Mon-N	14	10	.583	30	30	2	2	0	194²	158	21	66	174	10.9	3.51	122	.227	.304	7	.111	-3	14	17	-0	1.6
1996	Mon-N★	13	10	.565	33	33	4	1	0	216²	189	19	70	222	10.9	3.70	117	.232	.296	6	.094	-2	12	15	-2	1.0
Total	5	48	31	.608	154	89	7	4	3	671	544	56	239	665	10.9	3.39	124	.223	.300	17	.096	-6	58	60	-6	5.5
● RAMON MARTINEZ	Martinez, Ramon Jaime (b: Ramon Jaime (Martinez)) b: 3/22/68, Santo Domingo, D.R. BR/TR, 6'4", 165 lbs. Deb: 8/13/88 F																									
1988	LA-N	1	3	.250	9	6	0	0	0	35²	27	0	22	23	12.4	3.79	88	.216	.333	0	.000	-1	-1	-2	-0	-0.3
1989	LA-N	6	4	.600	15	15	2	2	0	98²	79	11	41	89	11.4	3.19	107	.219	.308	6	.162	0	3	2	1	0.4
1990	LA-N★	20	6	.769	33	33	12	3	0	234¹	191	22	67	223	10.1	2.92	125	.220	.279	10	.125	-2	23	19	0	1.9
1991	LA-N	17	13	.567	33	33	6	4	0	220¹	190	18	69	150	10.9	3.27	110	.229	.294	9	.117	-1	10	8	-1	0.8
1992	LA-N	8	11	.421	25	25	1	1	0	150²	141	11	69	101	12.8	4.00	86	.245	.331	6	.120	-1	-8	-9	-1	-1.4
1993	LA-N	10	12	.455	32	32	4	3	0	211²	202	15	104	127	13.2	3.44	111	.255	.344	9	.129	-2	14	9	2	0.8
1994	LA-N	12	7	.632	24	24	4	3	0	170	160	18	56	119	11.8	3.97	99	.249	.315	18	.253	5	5	-1	-1	0.2
1995	*LA-N	17	7	.708	30	30	4	2	0	206¹	176	19	81	138	11.4	3.66	103	.231	.309	11	.172	1	12	3	-0	0.8
1996	LA-N	15	6	.714	28	27	2	2	0	168²	153	12	86	134	13.2	3.42	113	.248	.348	7	.119	0	15	8	1	0.8
Total	9	106	69	.606	229	225	35	20	0	1496¹	1319	126	595	1104	11.8	3.47	107	.237	.316	76	.149	-1	72	38	0	3.6
● ROGELIO MARTINEZ	Martinez, Rogelio (Ulloa) "Limonar" b: 11/5/18, Cidra, Cuba BR/TR, 6', 180 lbs. Deb: 7/13/50																									
1950	Was-A	0	1	.000	2	1	0	0	0	1¹	1	0	3	0	40.5	27.00	17	.500	.600	0	—	0	-3	-3	0	-1.5
● SILVIO MARTINEZ	Martinez, Silvio Ramon (Cabrera) b: 8/19/55, Santiago, D.R. BR/TR, 5'10", 170 lbs. Deb: 4/9/77																									
1977	Chi-A	0	1	.000	10	0	0	0	1	21	28	4	12	10	17.1	5.57	73	.337	.421	0	—	0	-4	-3	0	-0.2
1978	StL-N	9	8	.529	22	22	5	2	0	138¹	114	11	71	45	12.2	3.64	96	.228	.326	8	.170	1	-1	-2	-1	-0.4
1979	StL-N	15	8	.652	32	29	7	2	0	206²	204	14	67	102	11.8	3.27	115	.259	.317	8	.129	-2	11	11	-3	0.7
1980	StL-N	5	10	.333	25	20	2	0	0	119²	127	8	88	39	13.3	4.81	99	.273	.343	3	.086	-2	-16	-15	-2	-2.1

YEAR	TM/L	W	L	PCT	G	GS	CG	SH	SV	IP	H	HR	BB	SO	RAT	ERA	ERA+	OAV	OOB	BH	AVG	PB	PR	/A	PD	TPI
1981	StL-N	2	5	.286	18	16	0	1	0	97	95	4	39	34	12.5	3.99	89	.260	.333	7	.200	1	-5	-5	-1	-0.3
Total	5	31	32	.492	107	87	14	4	1	582²	568	41	237	230	12.5	3.88	95	.258	.331	26	.145	-3	-15	-14	-7	-2.3

● **WEDO MARTINI**   Martini, Guido Joe "Southern" b: 7/1/13, Birmingham, Ala. d: 10/28/70, Philadelphia, Pa. BR/TR, 5'10", 165 lbs. Deb: 7/28/35

1935	Phi-A	0	2	.000	3	2	0	0	0	6¹	8	0	11	1	27.0	17.05	27	.333	.543	0	.000	-0	-9	-9	-1	-1.7

● **JOE MARTY**   Marty, Joseph Anton b: 9/1/13, Sacramento, Cal. d: 10/4/84, Sacramento, Cal. BR/TR, 6', 182 lbs. Deb: 4/22/37 ◆

1939	Phi-N	0	0	—	1	0	0	0	0	4	2	0	3	1	11.3	4.50	89	.154	.313	76	.254	0	-0	-0	-0	0.0

● **RANDY MARTZ**   Martz, Randy Carl b: 5/28/56, Harrisburg, Pa. BL/TR, 6'4", 210 lbs. Deb: 9/6/80

1980	Chi-N	1	2	.333	6	6	0	0	0	30¹	28	1	11	5	11.6	2.08	188	.241	.307	1	.111	-1	5	6	1	0.6
1981	Chi-N	5	7	.417	33	14	1	0	6	107²	103	6	49	32	12.8	3.68	100	.256	.338	6	.214	1	-2	0	0	0.1
1982	Chi-N	11	10	.524	28	24	1	0	1	147²	157	17	36	40	11.9	4.21	89	.272	.318	6	.143	1	-10	-8	-1	-0.8
1983	Chi-A	0	0	—	1	1	0	0	0	5	4	0	4	1	14.4	3.60	116	.211	.348	0	—	0	0	0	-0	-0.1
Total	4	17	19	.472	68	45	2	0	7	290²	292	24	100	78	12.3	3.78	99	.262	.325	13	.165	1	-7	-1	1	-0.2

● **DEL MASON**   Mason, Adelbert William b: 10/29/1883, Newfane, N.Y. d: 12/31/62, Winter Park, Fla. BR/TR, 6', 160 lbs. Deb: 4/23/04

1904	Was-A	0	3	.000	5	3	2	0	0	33	45	1	13	16	16.4	6.00	44	.326	.392	0	.000	-2	-12	-12	-1	-1.2
1906	Cin-N	0	1	.000	2	1	1	0	0	12	10	1	6	4	12.8	4.50	61	.250	.362	0	.000	-1	-2	-2	-0	-0.3
1907	Cin-N	5	12	.294	25	17	13	1	0	146	144	6	55	45	12.6	3.14	86	.277	.353	8	.182	-0	-11	-9	1	-1.0
Total	3	5	16	.238	32	21	16	1	0	191	199	8	74	65	13.3	3.72	70	.286	.362	8	.125	-3	-26	-23	0	-2.5

● **CHARLIE MASON**   Mason, Charles E. b: 6/25/1853, New Orleans, La. d: 10/21/36, Philadelphia, Pa. BR/TR, 175 lbs. Deb: 4/26/1875 M◆

1875	Was-n	0	0	—	1	0	0	0	0	2	3	0	1	0	18.0	4.50	53	.300	.364	3	.091	-0	-1	-0		0.0

● **ERNIE MASON**   Mason, Ernest b: New Orleans, La. d: 7/30/04, Covington, La. Deb: 7/17/1894

1894	StL-N	0	3	.000	4	2	2	0	0	22²	34	1	10	3	17.5	7.15	76	.343	.404	3	.250	-0	-5	-4	-1	-0.4

● **HANK MASON**   Mason, Henry b: 6/19/31, Marshall, Mo. BR/TR, 6', 185 lbs. Deb: 9/12/58

1958	Phi-N	0	0	—	1	0	0	0	0	5	7	0	3	2	18.0	10.80	37	.368	.455	0	.000	-1	-4	-4	-0	0.0
1960	Phi-N	0	0	—	3	0	0	0	0	5²	9	1	5	3	22.2	9.53	41	.375	.483	0	.000	-0	-4	-4	-0	0.0
Total	2	0	0	—	4	0	0	0	0	10²	16	1	7	6	20.3	10.13	39	.372	.471	0	.000	-1	-7	-7	-0	0.0

● **MIKE MASON**   Mason, Michael Paul b: 11/21/58, Faribault, Minn. BL/TL, 6'2", 205 lbs. Deb: 9/13/82

1982	Tex-A	1	2	.333	4	4	0	0	0	23	21	3	9	8	11.7	5.09	76	.244	.316	0	—	0	-3	-3	0	-0.2
1983	Tex-A	0	2	.000	5	0	0	0	0	10²	10	0	6	4	14.3	5.91	68	.244	.354	0	—	0	-2	-2	0	-0.3
1984	Tex-A	9	13	.409	36	24	4	0	0	184¹	159	18	51	113	10.4	3.61	115	.233	.288	0	—	0	8	11	-1	1.0
1985	Tex-A	8	15	.348	38	30	1	1	0	179	212	22	73	92	14.5	4.83	88	.299	.366	0	—	0	-14	-12	0	-1.4
1986	Tex-A	7	3	.700	27	22	2	1	0	135	135	11	56	85	12.7	4.33	99	.257	.329	0	—	0	-2	-0	0	-0.1
1987	Tex-A	0	2	.000	8	6	0	0	0	29	37	6	22	21	19.6	5.59	80	.322	.447	0	—	0	-4	-4	-0	-0.2
	Chi-N	4	1	.800	17	4	0	0	0	38	43	4	23	28	15.9	5.68	75	.303	.404	2	.222	0	-7	-6	0	-0.7
1988	Min-A	0	1	.000	6	0	0	0	0	6²	8	1	9	7	23.0	10.80	38	.286	.459	0	—	0	-5	-5	-0	-0.7
Total	7	29	39	.426	140	90	7	2	0	605²	625	65	249	363	13.2	4.53	93	.268	.342	2	.222	0	-28	-21	-1	-2.6

● **ROGER MASON**   Mason, Roger Le Roy b: 9/18/58, Bellaire, Mich. BR/TR, 6'6", 215 lbs. Deb: 9/4/84

1984	Det-A	1	1	.500	5	2	0	0	1	22	23	1	10	15	13.5	4.50	87	.271	.347	0	—	0	-1	-1	0	-0.1
1985	SF-N	1	3	.250	5	5	1	1	0	29²	28	1	11	26	11.8	2.12	162	.243	.310	1	.091	-0	5	4	-0	0.5
1986	SF-N	3	4	.429	11	11	1	0	0	60	56	5	30	43	13.4	4.80	73	.250	.346	1	.048	-2	-7	-9	-1	-1.1
1987	SF-N	1	1	.500	5	5	0	0	0	26	30	4	10	18	13.8	4.50	85	.303	.367	1	.125	-1	-2	-2	0	-0.1
1989	Hou-N	0	0	—	2	0	0	0	0	1¹	2	0	2	3	27.0	20.25	17	.333	.500	0	—	0	-2	-2	-0	0.0
1991	*Pit-N	3	2	.600	24	0	0	0	0	29²	21	2	6	21	8.5	3.03	118	.200	.250	0	—	0	2	2	0	0.4
1992	*Pit-N	5	7	.417	65	0	0	0	8	88	80	11	33	56	12.0	4.09	84	.246	.323	0	.000	-1	-6	-6	-1	-1.2
1993	SD-N	0	7	.000	34	0	0	0	0	50	43	1	18	39	11.3	3.24	128	.242	.318	0	.000	-0	4	5	0	0.6
	*Phi-N	5	5	.500	34	0	0	0	0	49²	47	9	16	32	11.4	4.89	81	.246	.304	1	.333	1	-5	-5	-1	-1.0
	Yr	5	12	.294	68	0	0	0	0	99²	90	10	34	71	11.2	4.06	100	.241	.304	1	.167	1	-0	-0	-2	-0.4
1994	Phi-N	1	1	.500	6	0	0	0	0	8²	11	2	5	7	16.6	5.19	83	.306	.390	0	—	0	-1	-1	-0	-0.1
	NY-N	2	4	.333	41	0	0	0	1	51¹	44	6	20	26	11.6	3.51	119	.232	.311	0	—	0	4	4	-1	0.3
	Yr	3	5	.375	47	0	0	0	1	60	55	8	25	33	12.3	3.75	112	.243	.324	0	—	0	3	3	-1	0.1
Total	9	22	35	.386	232	23	2	1	13	416¹	385	42	161	286	12.1	4.02	94	.248	.323	4	.071	-2	-8	-12	-5	-1.9

● **WALT MASTERS**   Masters, Walter Thomas b: 3/28/07, Pen Argyl, Pa. d: 7/10/92, Ottawa, Ont., Can. BR/TR, 5'10.5", 180 lbs. Deb: 7/9/31

1931	Was-A	0	0	—	3	0	0	0	1	9	7	0	4	1	11.0	2.00	215	.226	.314	0	.000	-0	2	2	1	0.1
1937	Phi-N	0	0	—	1	0	0	0	0	1	5	0	1	0	54.0	36.00	12	.714	.750	0	—	0	-4	-4	-0	0.0
1939	Phi-A	0	0	—	4	0	0	0	0	11	15	0	8	2	18.8	6.55	72	.306	.404	0	.000	-0	-2	-0	0	0.0
Total	3	0	0	—	8	0	0	0	1	21	27	0	13	3	17.1	6.00	75	.310	.400	0	.000	-0	-4	-3	1	0.1

● **PAUL MASTERSON**   Masterson, Paul Nickalis "Lefty" b: 10/16/15, Chicago, Ill. BL/TL, 5'11", 165 lbs. Deb: 9/15/40

1940	Phi-N	0	0	—	2	0	0	0	0	5	5	0	2	3	12.6	7.20	54	.263	.333	0	.000	-0	-2	-2	-0	0.0
1941	Phi-N	1	0	1.000	2	1	1	0	0	11¹	11	0	6	8	13.5	4.76	78	.250	.340	0	.000	-1	-3	-3	-0	-0.2
1942	Phi-N	0	0	—	4	0	0	0	0	8¹	10	1	5	3	16.2	6.48	51	.303	.395	0	—	0	-3	-3	0	-0.2
Total	3	1	0	1.000	8	1	1	0	0	24²	26	1	13	14	14.2	5.84	62	.271	.358	0	.000	-1	-6	-6	0	-0.2

● **WALT MASTERSON**   Masterson, Walter Edward b: 6/22/20, Philadelphia, Pa. BR/TR, 6'2", 189 lbs. Deb: 5/8/39

1939	Was-A	2	2	.500	24	5	1	0	0	58¹	66	2	48	12	17.9	5.55	78	.293	.422	2	.154	-0	-6	-8	-1	-0.5
1940	Was-A	3	13	.188	31	19	3	0	2	130¹	128	6	88	68	15.1	4.90	85	.257	.371	7	.184	-1	-8	-11	-1	-1.2
1941	Was-A	4	3	.571	34	11	3	0	3	78¹	101	3	53	40	17.8	5.97	68	.321	.420	2	.105	-1	-16	-17	-1	-1.5
1942	Was-A	5	9	.357	25	15	8	4	2	142²	138	6	54	63	12.2	3.34	109	.251	.321	7	.156	-5	-2	-5	-2	0.2
1945	Was-A	1	3	.333	4	2	1	1	0	25	21	1	10	14	11.2	1.08	287	.228	.304	1	.111	-4	6	6	1	0.6
1946	Was-A	5	6	.455	29	9	2	0	1	91¹	105	8	67	61	17.2	6.01	56	.295	.411	2	.080	-1	-25	-27	0	-3.1
1947	Was-A★	12	16	.429	35	31	14	4	1	253	215	11	97	135	11.2	3.13	119	.234	.309	11	.133	-3	16	17	3	1.8
1948	Was-A★	8	15	.348	33	27	8	4	2	188	171	12	122	72	14.2	3.83	113	.247	.363	11	.193	-1	10	11	-2	1.0
1949	Was-A	3	2	.600	10	7	3	0	2	53	42	4	21	17	11.2	3.23	132	.216	.303	1	.056	-1	6	6	1	0.5
	Bos-A	3	4	.429	18	5	1	0	2	55	58	2	35	19	15.2	4.25	102	.283	.387	2	.118	-0	-1	1	-1	-0.1
	Yr	6	6	.500	28	12	4	0	4	108	100	6	56	36	13.0	3.75	115	.249	.341	3	.086	-2	5	7	0	0.4
1950	Bos-A	8	6	.571	33	15	4	0	1	129¹	145	15	82	60	15.9	5.64	87	.287	.387	6	.136	-3	-15	-11	-1	-1.1
1951	Bos-A	3	0	1.000	30	1	0	0	2	59¹	53	1	32	39	12.9	3.34	134	.244	.322	2	.182	-1	7	6	0	0.4
1952	Bos-A	1	1	.500	2	1	0	0	0	9¹	18	1	11	3	28.0	11.57	34	.400	.518	0	.000	-0	-8	-8	-0	-1.4
	Was-A	9	8	.529	24	21	11	0	0	160²	153	11	72	89	12.8	3.70	96	.253	.336	6	.120	-1	-0	-2	-1	-0.3
	Yr	10	9	.526	26	22	11	0	0	170	171	12	83	92	13.6	4.13	87	.263	.350	6	.115	-1	-9	-10	-1	-1.7
1953	Was-A	10	12	.455	29	20	10	4	0	166¹	145	16	62	95	11.4	3.63	107	.232	.304	7	.137	-1	7	7	-2	0.5
1956	Det-A	1	1	.500	35	0	0	0	0	49²	54	7	32	28	15.8	4.17	99	.289	.395	1	.250	-0	-0	-0	-1	-0.1
Total	14	78	100	.438	399	184	70	15	20	1649²	1613	101	886	815	13.8	4.15	96	.258	.353	68	.140	-14	-24	-27	0	-4.4

● **LEN MATARAZZO**   Matarazzo, Leonard b: 9/12/28, New Castle, Pa. BR/TR, 6'4", 195 lbs. Deb: 9/6/52

1952	Phi-A	0	0	—	1	0	0	0	0	1	1	0	0	0	18.0	0.00	—	.250	.400	0	—	0	0	0	-0	0.0

● **GREG MATHEWS**   Mathews, Gregory Inman b: 5/17/62, Harbor City, Cal. BR/TL, 6'2", 180 lbs. Deb: 6/3/86

1986	StL-N	11	8	.579	23	22	1	0	0	145¹	139	15	44	67	11.5	3.65	100	.259	.317	2	.047	-3	1	-0	-2	-0.5
1987	*StL-N	11	11	.500	32	32	2	1	0	197²	184	17	71	108	11.6	3.73	111	.249	.314	13	.191	1	8	9	-1	0.9
1988	StL-N	4	6	.400	13	13	1	0	0	68	61	4	33	31	12.7	4.24	82	.247	.340	4	.174	0	-6	-6	0	-0.8
1990	StL-N	0	5	.000	11	10	0	0	0	50²	53	2	30	18	15.1	5.33	72	.277	.381	3	.214	1	-9	-9	1	-0.5

YEAR	TM/L	W	L	PCT	G	GS	CG	SH	SV	IP	H	HR	BB	SO	RAT	ERA	ERA+	OAV	OOB	BH	AVG	PB	PR	/A	PD	TPI
1992	Phi-N	2	3	.400	14	7	0	0	0	52¹	54	7	24	27	13.6	5.16	68	.270	.351	0	.000	-1	-10	-10	-1	-1.0
Total	5	28	33	.459	93	84	4	1	0	514	491	45	202	251	12.3	4.08	94	.256	.330	22	.136	-1	-16	-15	-3	-1.9

● BOBBY MATHEWS

Mathews, Robert T.   b: 11/21/1851, Baltimore, Md.   d: 4/17/1898, Baltimore, Md.   BR/TR, 5'5.5", 140 lbs.   Deb: 5/4/1871   U♦

YEAR	TM/L	W	L	PCT	G	GS	CG	SH	SV	IP	H	HR	BB	SO	RAT	ERA	ERA+	OAV	OOB	BH	AVG	PB	PR	/A	PD	TPI
1871	Kek-n	6	11	.353	19	19	19	**1**	0	169	261	5	21	17	15.0	5.17	88	.305	.322	24	.270	-3	-18	-11		-0.8
1872	Bal-n	25	18	.581	49	47	39	0	0	406	480	3	52	**55**	11.8	3.19	115	.257	.277	50	.224	-8	20	21		1.2
1873	Mut-n	29	23	.558	52	52	47	2	0	443	489	5	42	**75**	11.2	2.56	124	.251	.274	43	.193	-2	34	30		1.8
1874	Mut-n	42	22	.656	65	65	62	**4**	0	578	652	3	41	**100**	10.8	1.88	119	.261	.273	72	.242	-2	19	23		1.5
1875	Mut-n	29	38	.433	70	70	**69**	3	0	**625²**	711	4	20	75	10.5	2.49	94	.260	.265	48	.182	-10	-18	-11		-2.3
1876	NY-N	21	34	.382	56	56	55	2	0	516	693	8	24	37	12.5	2.86	75	.301	.308	40	.183	-10	-32	-41	-3	-4.3
1877	Cin-N	3	12	.200	15	15	13	0	0	129¹	208	0	17	9	15.7	4.04	66	.339	.357	10	.169	-3	-18	-20	-1	-2.1
1879	Pro-N	12	6	.667	27	25	15	1	**1**	189	194	4	26	90	10.5	2.29	103	.258	.282	35	.202	-0	4	1	0	0.1
1881	Pro-N	4	8	.333	14	14	10	1	0	102¹	121	2	21	28	12.5	3.17	84	.268	.300	11	.193	-2	-4	-6	-1	-0.7
	Bos-N	1	0	1.000	5	1	1	0	2	23	22	0	11	5	12.9	2.35	113	.239	.320	12	.169	-1	1	1	-0	0.0
	Yr	5	8	.385	19	15	11	1	**2**	125¹	143	2	32	33	12.6	3.02	88	.263	.304	23	.180	-3	-3	-5	-2	-0.7
1882	Bos-N	19	15	.559	34	32	31	0	0	285	278	5	22	153	9.5	2.87	100	.232	.246	38	.225	-2	1	-0	-4	-0.6
1883	Phi-a	30	13	.698	44	44	41	1	0	381	396	11	31	203	10.1	2.46	141	.251	.265	31	.186	-7	36	43	-1	3.2
1884	Phi-a	30	18	.625	49	49	48	3	0	430²	401	10	49	286	9.7	3.32	102	.232	.258	34	.185	-5	-4	3	-2	-0.4
1885	Phi-a	30	17	.638	48	48	46	2	0	422¹	394	3	57	286	10.0	2.43	142	.233	.267	30	.168	-7	38	47	0	3.8
1886	Phi-a	13	9	.591	24	24	22	0	0	197²	226	3	53	93	13.3	3.96	88	.267	.320	21	.239	-0	-11	-10	-0	-0.9
1887	Phi-a	3	4	.429	7	7	7	0	0	58	75	4	25	14	16.0	6.67	64	.298	.368	5	.200	-0	-15	-15	-1	-1.3
Total	5 n	131	112	.539	255	253	236	10	0	2221²	2603	19	196	322	11.3	2.68	108	.261	.276	237	.216	-25	37	53		1.4
Total	10	166	136	.550	323	315	289	10	3	2734¹	3008	50	336	1199	11.2	3.00	100	.261	.285	267	.192	-37	-3	-3	-11	-3.2

● TERRY MATHEWS

Mathews, Terry Alan   b: 10/5/64, Alexandria, La.   BL/TR, 6'2", 200 lbs.   Deb: 6/21/91

YEAR	TM/L	W	L	PCT	G	GS	CG	SH	SV	IP	H	HR	BB	SO	RAT	ERA	ERA+	OAV	OOB	BH	AVG	PB	PR	/A	PD	TPI
1991	Tex-A	4	0	1.000	34	2	0	0	1	57¹	54	5	18	51	11.5	3.61	112	.251	.312	0	—	0	3	3	0	0.2
1992	Tex-A	2	4	.333	40	0	0	0	0	42¹	48	4	31	26	17.0	5.95	64	.294	.410	0	—	0	-9	-10	-1	-1.3
1994	Fla-N	2	1	.667	24	2	0	0	0	43	45	4	9	21	11.5	3.35	130	.268	.309	3	.500	1	4	5	0	0.5
1995	Fla-N	4	4	.500	57	0	0	0	3	82²	70	9	27	72	10.7	3.38	125	.235	.301	6	.462	3	7	8	-0	0.9
1996	Fla-N	2	4	.333	57	0	0	0	4	55	59	7	27	49	14.2	4.91	82	.273	.357	0	.000	-0	-4	-5	-0	-0.6
	*Bal-A	2	2	.500	14	0	0	0	0	18²	20	3	7	13	13.0	3.38	145	.282	.346	0	—	0	3	3	0	0.3
Total	5	16	15	.516	226	4	0	0	8	299	296	32	119	232	12.6	4.06	102	.262	.335	9	.391	3	4	3	0	0.3

● T. J. MATHEWS

Mathews, Timothy Jay   b: 1/9/70, Belleville, Ill.   BR/TR, 6'2", 200 lbs.   Deb: 7/28/95   F

YEAR	TM/L	W	L	PCT	G	GS	CG	SH	SV	IP	H	HR	BB	SO	RAT	ERA	ERA+	OAV	OOB	BH	AVG	PB	PR	/A	PD	TPI
1995	StL-N	1	1	.500	23	0	0	0	0	29²	21	1	11	28	9.7	1.52	276	.200	.276	0	.000	-0	9	9	1	0.7
1996	*StL-N	2	6	.250	67	0	0	0	6	83²	62	8	32	80	10.3	3.01	141	.203	.282	0	.000	-0	11	11	-2	0.9
Total	2	3	7	.300	90	0	0	0	8	113¹	83	9	43	108	10.2	2.62	161	.202	.281	0	.000	-1	20	20	-1	1.6

● CHRISTY MATHEWSON

Mathewson, Christopher "Matty" or "Big Six"
b: 8/12/1880, Factoryville, Pa.   d: 10/7/25, Saranac Lake, N.Y.   BR/TR, 6'1.5", 195 lbs.   Deb: 7/17/00   FMCH

YEAR	TM/L	W	L	PCT	G	GS	CG	SH	SV	IP	H	HR	BB	SO	RAT	ERA	ERA+	OAV	OOB	BH	AVG	PB	PR	/A	PD	TPI
1900	NY-N	0	3	.000	6	1	1	0	0	33²	37	1	20	15	16.3	5.08	71	.278	.389	2	.182	0	-5	-5	-0	-0.3
1901	NY-N	20	17	.541	40	38	36	5	0	336	288	3	97	221	10.7	2.41	137	.230	.292	28	.215	-1	34	33	8	4.1
1902	NY-N	14	17	.452	34	32	29	**8**	0	276²	241	3	73	159	10.5	2.11	133	.234	.292	26	.205	2	20	21	4	3.0
1903	NY-N	30	13	.698	45	42	37	3	2	366¹	321	4	100	**267**	10.6	2.26	148	.231	.287	28	.226	3	**41**	44	2	**5.3**
1904	NY-N	33	12	.733	48	46	33	4	1	367²	306	7	78	**212**	9.5	2.03	134	.226	.270	30	.226	6	29	28	6	4.7
1905	*NY-N	**31**	9	.775	43	37	32	**8**	2	338²	252	4	64	**206**	8.4	**1.28**	230	.205	**.245**	30	.236	10	**65**	**62**	6	**9.6**
1906	NY-N	22	12	.647	38	35	22	6	1	266²	262	3	77	128	11.5	2.97	88	.259	.313	24	.264	7	-10	-11	4	-0.2
1907	NY-N	**24**	12	.667	41	36	31	**8**	2	315	250	6	53	**178**	8.7	2.00	124	.212	**.247**	20	.187	3	17	17	1	2.5
1908	NY-N	**37**	11	.771	**56**	44	**34**	**11**	**5**	**390²**	285	5	42	**259**	7.6	**1.43**	169	.200	**.225**	20	.155	1	**41**	**43**	10	7.3
1909	NY-N	25	6	**.806**	37	33	26	**8**	2	275¹	192	2	36	149	7.5	**1.14**	223	**.228**	.228	25	.263	7	44	43	6	**7.0**
1910	NY-N	**27**	9	.750	38	35	**27**	2	0	318¹	292	6	60	184	10.0	1.89	157	.248	.286	25	.234	7	**40**	38	7	6.0
1911	*NY-N	26	13	.667	45	37	29	5	3	307	303	5	38	141	10.0	**1.99**	169	.259	.283	22	.196	0	**48**	**47**	7	6.7
1912	NY-N	23	12	.657	43	34	27	0	4	310	311	6	34	134	10.1	2.12	159	.260	**.281**	29	.264	5	44	43	0	5.2
1913	*NY-N	25	11	.694	40	35	25	4	2	306	291	8	21	93	9.2	2.06	152	.252	**.266**	19	.184	6	**39**	**36**	4	4.6
1914	NY-N	24	13	.649	41	35	29	5	2	312	314	16	23	80	9.8	3.00	88	.263	.278	23	.219	6	-7	-12	2	-0.6
1915	NY-N	8	14	.364	27	24	11	1	0	186	199	9	20	57	10.6	3.58	72	.277	.298	8	.157	3	-17	-21	1	-2.1
1916	NY-N	3	4	.429	12	6	4	1	2	65²	59	3	7	16	9.0	2.33	104	.243	.264	0	.000	-1	2	1	0	0.2
	Cin-N	1	0	1.000	1	1	1	0	0	9	15	1	1	3	16.0	8.00	32	.366	.381	3	.600	1	-5	-5	0	-0.3
	Yr	4	4	.500	13	7	5	1	2	74²	74	4	8	19	9.9	3.01	81	.261	.281	3	.136	1	-3	-3	0	-0.1
Total	17	373	188	.665	635	551	434	79	28	4780²	4218	91	844	2502	9.6	2.13	136	.236	.273	362	.215	59	420	403	68	62.7

● HENRY MATHEWSON

Mathewson, Henry   b: 12/24/1886, Factoryville, Pa.   d: 7/1/17, Factoryville, Pa.   BR/TR, 6'3", 175 lbs.   Deb: 9/28/06   F

YEAR	TM/L	W	L	PCT	G	GS	CG	SH	SV	IP	H	HR	BB	SO	RAT	ERA	ERA+	OAV	OOB	BH	AVG	PB	PR	/A	PD	TPI
1906	NY-N	0	1	.000	2	1	1	0	1	10	7	0	14	2	19.8	5.40	48	.194	.431	0	.000	-0	-3	-3	-0	-0.3
1907	NY-N	0	0	—	1	0	0	0	1	1	1	0	0	0	9.0	0.00	—	.250	.250	0	—	0	0	0	0	0.1
Total	2	0	1	.000	3	1	1	0	2	11	8	0	14	2	18.8	4.91	53	.200	.418	0	.000	-0	-3	-3	-0	-0.2

● CARL MATHIAS

Mathias, Carl Lynwood "Stubby"   b: 6/13/36, Bechtelsville, Pa   BB/TL, 5'11", 195 lbs.   Deb: 7/31/60

YEAR	TM/L	W	L	PCT	G	GS	CG	SH	SV	IP	H	HR	BB	SO	RAT	ERA	ERA+	OAV	OOB	BH	AVG	PB	PR	/A	PD	TPI
1960	Cle-A	0	1	.000	7	0	0	0	0	15¹	14	2	8	13	12.9	3.52	106	.233	.324	0	.000	-0	1	0	-0	0.0
1961	Was-A	0	1	.000	4	3	0	0	0	13²	22	3	4	7	17.8	11.20	36	.361	.409	1	.200	-0	-11	-11	-0	-0.7
Total	2	0	2	.000	11	3	0	0	0	29	36	5	12	20	15.2	7.14	54	.298	.366	1	.167	-0	-10	-11	0	-0.7

● RON MATHIS

Mathis, Ronald Vance   b: 9/25/58, Kansas City, Mo.   BR/TR, 6', 175 lbs.   Deb: 4/13/85

YEAR	TM/L	W	L	PCT	G	GS	CG	SH	SV	IP	H	HR	BB	SO	RAT	ERA	ERA+	OAV	OOB	BH	AVG	PB	PR	/A	PD	TPI
1985	Hou-N	3	5	.375	23	8	0	0	1	70	83	7	27	34	14.3	6.04	57	.293	.357	1	.071	-1	-19	-20	-0	-2.2
1987	Hou-N	0	1	.000	8	0	0	0	0	12	10	2	11	8	15.8	5.25	75	.233	.389	0	.000	-0	-2	-2	-0	-0.1
Total	2	3	6	.333	31	8	0	0	1	82	93	9	38	42	14.5	5.93	60	.285	.362	1	.063	-1	-21	-22	-0	-2.3

● JON MATLACK

Matlack, Jonathan Trumpbour   b: 1/19/50, West Chester, Pa.   BL/TL, 6'3", 205 lbs.   Deb: 7/11/71   C

YEAR	TM/L	W	L	PCT	G	GS	CG	SH	SV	IP	H	HR	BB	SO	RAT	ERA	ERA+	OAV	OOB	BH	AVG	PB	PR	/A	PD	TPI
1971	NY-N	0	3	.000	7	6	0	0	0	37	31	2	15	24	11.2	4.14	82	.228	.305	3	.273	1	-3	-3	-1	-0.2
1972	NY-N	15	10	.600	34	32	8	4	0	244	215	14	71	169	10.6	2.32	145	.234	.291	10	.128	1	31	28	-1	2.9
1973	*NY-N	14	16	.467	34	34	14	3	0	242	210	16	99	205	11.6	3.20	113	.236	.314	9	.138	2	12	11	1	1.6
1974	NY-N★	13	15	.464	34	34	14	**7**	0	265¹	221	8	76	195	10.2	2.41	148	.226	.285	8	.101	-4	36	34	-0	3.1
1975	NY-N★	16	12	.571	33	32	8	3	0	228²	224	15	58	154	11.1	3.38	102	.254	.300	7	.100	0	6	2	-0	0.4
1976	NY-N☆	17	10	.630	35	35	16	**6**	0	262	236	18	57	153	10.2	2.95	112	.242	.286	17	.193	4	16	10	-1	1.3
1977	NY-N	7	15	.318	26	26	5	3	0	169	175	14	43	79	11.7	4.21	89	.273	.321	3	.060	-2	-6	-9	-0	-1.2
1978	Tex-A	15	13	.536	35	33	18	2	1	270	252	14	59	157	10.2	2.27	165	.245	.284	0	—	0	45	44	0	4.7
1979	Tex-A	5	4	.556	13	13	2	0	0	85	98	9	15	35	12.1	4.13	100	.293	.325	0	—	0	1	0	0	0.1
1980	Tex-A	10	10	.500	35	34	8	1	0	234²	265	17	48	142	12.0	3.68	106	.287	.323	0	—	0	6	6	-3	-0.1
1981	Tex-A	4	7	.364	17	16	1	1	0	104¹	101	8	41	43	12.3	4.14	84	.258	.330	0	—	0	-6	-8	-0	-0.7
1982	Tex-A	7	7	.500	33	14	1	0	0	147²	158	14	37	78	12.0	3.53	109	.275	.321	0	—	0	9	6	0	0.7
1983	Tex-A	4	4	.333	12	9	2	0	0	73¹	74	2	19	30	14.7	4.66	86	.307	.372	0	—	0	-5	-5	-1	-0.3
Total	13	125	126	.498	361	318	97	30	3	2363	2276	161	638	1516	11.2	3.18	114	.254	.305	57	.129	2	145	115	-5	12.1

● AL MATTERN

Mattern, Alonzo Albert   b: 6/16/1883, W.Rush, N.Y.   d: 11/6/58, West Rush, N.Y.   BL/TR, 5'10", 165 lbs.   Deb: 9/16/08

YEAR	TM/L	W	L	PCT	G	GS	CG	SH	SV	IP	H	HR	BB	SO	RAT	ERA	ERA+	OAV	OOB	BH	AVG	PB	PR	/A	PD	TPI
1908	Bos-N	1	2	.333	5	3	1	1	0	30¹	30	1	8	10	10.7	2.08	116	.265	.303	1	.125	-0	1	1	-0	0.0
1909	Bos-N	15	21	.417	47	32	24	2	3	316¹	322	4	108	98	12.3	2.85	99	.268	.330	17	.168	-1	-9	-1	3	0.1
1910	Bos-N	16	19	.457	**51**	37	17	**6**	1	305	288	5	121	94	12.2	2.98	112	.257	.332	16	.163	-4	2	12	1	0.9
1911	Bos-N	4	15	.211	33	21	11	0	0	186¹	228	13	63	51	14.1	4.97	77	.320	.376	11	.175	-2	-33	-24	2	-2.1
1912	Bos-N	0	1	.000	2	1	0	0	0	6¹	10	0	1	1	15.6	7.11	50	.313	.333	0	.000	-0	-3	-2	0	-0.3
Total	5	36	58	.383	138	94	53	9	4	844¹	878	23	299	254	12.7	3.37	95	.276	.340	45	.165	-8	-41	-15	5	-1.4

● C. V. MATTERSON

Matterson, C.V.   b: Ohio   Deb: 6/13/1884   ♦

YEAR	TM/L	W	L	PCT	G	GS	CG	SH	SV	IP	H	HR	BB	SO	RAT	ERA	ERA+	OAV	OOB	BH	AVG	PB	PR	/A	PD	TPI
1884	StL-U	1	0	1.000	1	1	1	0	0	6	9	1	3	3	18.0	9.00	27	.321	.387	0	.000	-1	-4	-4	-0	-0.5

YEAR	TM/L	W	L	PCT	G	GS	CG	SH	SV	IP	H	HR	BB	SO	RAT	ERA	ERA+	OAV	OOB	BH	AVG	PB	PR	/A	PD	TPI

● **EDDIE MATTESON**   Matteson, Henry Edson "Matty" b: 9/7/1884, Guys Mills, Pa. d: 9/1/43, Westfield, N.Y.   BR/TR, 5'10.5", 160 lbs. Deb: 5/30/14

1914	Phi-N	3	2	.600	15	3	2	0	0	58	58	1	23	28	12.7	3.10	95	.278	.352	4	.182	-0	-2	-1	-2	-0.3
1918	Was-A	5	3	.625	14	6	2	0	0	67²	57	2	15	17	9.7	1.73	158	.238	.286	2	.105	-2	8	8	-1	0.6
Total	2	8	5	.615	29	9	4	0	0	125²	115	3	38	45	11.1	2.36	120	.257	.318	6	.146	-2	6	6	-3	0.3

● **JOE MATTHEWS**   Matthews, John Joseph "Lefty" b: 9/29/1898, Baltimore, Md. d: 2/8/68, Hagerstown, Md. BB/TL, 6', 170 lbs. Deb: 9/18/22

| 1922 | Bos-N | 0 | 1 | .000 | 3 | 1 | 0 | 0 | 0 | 10 | 5 | 1 | 6 | 0 | 10.8 | 3.60 | 111 | .143 | .286 | 0 | .000 | -0 | 1 | 0 | -0 | 0.0 |

● **WILLIAM MATTHEWS**   Matthews, William Calvin b: 1/12/1878, Mahanoy City, Pa. d: 1/23/46, Mahanoy City, Pa. TR , Deb: 8/28/09

| 1909 | Bos-A | 0 | 0 | — | 5 | 1 | 0 | 0 | 0 | 16² | 16 | 1 | 10 | 6 | 14.0 | 3.24 | 77 | .271 | .377 | 0 | .000 | -1 | -1 | -1 | -0 | -0.2 |

● **DALE MATTHEWSON**   Matthewson, Dale Wesley b: 5/15/23, Catasauqua, Pa. d: 2/20/84, Blairsville, Ga. BR/TR, 5'11.5", 145 lbs. Deb: 7/3/43

1943	Phi-N	0	3	.000	11	1	0	0	0	26	26	1	8	8	11.8	4.85	70	.271	.327	0	.000	-0	-4	-4	-0	-0.5
1944	Phi-N	0	0	—	17	1	0	0	0	32	27	1	16	8	12.1	3.94	92	.237	.331	1	.333	-0	-1	-1	-0	-0.0
Total	2	0	3	.000	28	2	0	0	0	58	53	2	24	16	11.9	4.34	81	.252	.329	1	.200	-0	-5	-5	-0	-0.5

● **MIKE MATTIMORE**   Mattimore, Michael Joseph b: 1859, Renovo, Pa. d: 4/28/31, Butte, Mont. BL/TL, 5'8.5", 160 lbs. Deb: 5/3/1887 ♦

1887	NY-N	3	3	.500	7	7	6	1	0	57¹	47	2	28	12	12.4	2.35	160	.218	.319	8	.250	-0	11	9	-1	0.6
1888	Phi-a	15	10	.600	26	24	24	4	0	221	221	6	65	80	12.2	3.38	88	.251	.312	38	.268	7	-8	-10	4	0.3
1889	Phi-a	2	1	.667	5	1	1	0	1	31	43	0	13	6	16.5	5.81	65	.319	.383	17	.233	1	-7	-7	-0	-0.5
	KC-a	0	0	—	1	0	0	0	0	3	3	1	2	1	15.0	3.00	139	.250	.357	12	.160	0	0	0	-0	0.0
	Yr	2	1	.667	6	1	1	0	1	34	46	1	15	7	16.1	5.56	69	.311	.374	29	.196	1	-6	-7	-0	-0.5
1890	Bro-a	6	13	.316	19	19	19	0	0	178¹	201	3	76	33	14.6	4.54	86	.276	.355	17	.132	-3	-13	-13	-0	-1.3
Total	4	26	27	.491	58	51	50	5	1	490²	515	12	184	132	13.4	3.83	90	.261	.334	92	.204	5	-17	-20	2	-1.2

● **EARL MATTINGLY**   Mattingly, Laurence Earl b: 11/4/04, Newport, Md. d: 9/8/93, Brookeville, Md. BR/TR, 5'10.5", 164 lbs. Deb: 4/15/31

| 1931 | Bro-N | 0 | 1 | .000 | 14 | 1 | 0 | 0 | 0 | 14¹ | 15 | 0 | 10 | 6 | 17.0 | 2.51 | 152 | .268 | .397 | 0 | .000 | -0 | 2 | 2 | 1 | 0.1 |

● **RICK MATULA**   Matula, Richard Carlton b: 11/22/53, Wharton, Tex. BR/TR, 6', 190 lbs. Deb: 4/8/79

1979	Atl-N	8	10	.444	28	28	1	0	0	171¹	193	14	64	67	13.7	4.11	98	.286	.350	5	.094	-3	-8	-2	1	-0.4
1980	Atl-N	11	13	.458	33	30	3	1	0	176²	195	17	60	62	13.0	4.58	82	.286	.343	6	.105	-3	-19	-17	1	-2.2
1981	Atl-N	0	0	—	5	0	0	0	0	7	8	1	2	0	12.9	6.43	56	.286	.333	0	.000	-0	-2	-2	0	-0.0
Total	3	19	23	.452	66	58	4	1	0	355	396	32	126	129	13.3	4.41	88	.286	.347	11	.099	-6	-30	-21	2	-2.6

● **HARRY MATUZAK**   Matuzak, Harry George "Matty" b: 1/27/10, Omer, Mich. d: 11/16/78, Fairhope, Ala. BR/TR, 5'11.5", 185 lbs. Deb: 4/19/34

1934	Phi-A	0	3	.000	11	0	0	0	0	24	28	2	10	9	14.6	4.88	90	.292	.364	1	.167	-0	-1	-1	0	-0.1
1936	Phi-A	0	1	.000	6	1	0	0	0	15	21	0	4	8	15.0	7.20	71	.318	.357	0	.000	-0	-4	-3	-0	-0.2
Total	2	0	4	.000	17	1	0	0	0	39	49	2	14	17	14.8	5.77	81	.302	.362	1	.111	-0	-5	-5	-0	-0.3

● **HAL MAUCK**   Mauck, Alfred Maris b: 3/6/1869, Princeton, Ind. d: 4/27/21, Princeton, Ind. BR/TR, 5'11", 185 lbs. Deb: 4/29/1893

| 1893 | Chi-N | 8 | 10 | .444 | 23 | 18 | 12 | 1 | 0 | 143 | 168 | 2 | 60 | 23 | 14.7 | 4.41 | 105 | .284 | .359 | 9 | .148 | -5 | 4 | 4 | -1 | -0.2 |

● **AL MAUL**   Maul, Albert Joseph "Smiling Al" b: 10/9/1865, Philadelphia, Pa. d: 5/3/58, Philadelphia, Pa. BR/TR, 6', 175 lbs. Deb: 6/20/1884 ♦

1884	Phi-U	0	1	.000	1	1	1	0	0	8	10	0	1	7	12.4	4.50	52	.286	.306	0	.000	-1	-2	-2	-0	-0.3
1887	Phi-N	4	2	.667	7	5	4	0	0	50¹	72	2	15	18	15.9	5.54	76	.326	.374	17	.304	3	-8	-7	0	-0.5
1888	Pit-N	0	2	.000	3	1	1	0	0	17	26	0	5	12	16.4	6.35	42	.342	.383	54	.208	1	-7	-7	-0	-0.6
1889	Pit-N	1	4	.200	6	4	4	0	0	42	64	3	28	11	19.9	9.86	38	.340	.429	71	.276	2	-27	-29	1	-2.0
1890	Pit-P	16	12	.571	30	28	26	2	0	246²	258	13	104	81	13.6	3.79	103	.257	.335	42	.259	7	12	3	5	1.2
1891	Pit-N	1	2	.333	8	3	3	0	1	39	44	0	16	13	14.5	2.31	142	.273	.350	28	.188	1	5	4	-0	0.2
1893	Was-N	12	21	.364	37	33	29	1	0	297	355	17	144	72	15.7	5.30	88	.288	.370	34	.254	10	-21	-22	0	-1.0
1894	Was-N	11	15	.423	28	26	21	0	0	201²	272	12	73	34	15.8	5.98	88	.319	.379	30	.242	3	-15	-16	2	-1.1
1895	Was-N	10	5	.667	16	16	14	0	0	135²	136	5	37	34	11.7	**2.45**	**196**	.257	.309	18	.250	1	35	35	1	3.3
1896	Was-N	5	2	.714	8	8	7	0	0	62	75	0	20	18	14.4	3.63	121	.296	.357	8	.286	2	5	5	-1	0.4
1897	Was-N	0	1	.000	1	1	0	0	0	2	4	0	1	0	22.5	9.00	48	.400	.455	0	.000	-0	-1	-1	-0	-0.3
	Bal-N	0	0	—	2	2	0	0	0	7²	9	0	8	2	24.7	7.04	59	.290	.488	1	.333	0	-2	-2	-0	-0.0
	Yr	0	1	.000	3	3	0	0	0	9²	13	0	9	2	24.2	7.45	56	.317	.481	1	.250	-0	-3	-3	-0	-0.3
1898	Bal-N	20	7	.741	28	28	26	1	0	239²	207	3	49	31	9.8	2.10	170	.231	.274	19	.204	4	40	39	-5	3.9
1899	Bro-N	2	0	1.000	5	4	2	0	0	26	35	1	6	2	14.4	4.50	87	.321	.368	3	.273	-0	-2	-2	-0	-0.1
1900	Phi-N	2	3	.400	5	4	3	0	0	38	53	2	3	6	13.7	6.16	59	.329	.349	2	.200	-0	-10	-11	-0	-1.0
1901	NY-N	0	3	.000	3	3	2	0	0	19	39	1	4	5	23.2	11.37	29	.419	.476	3	.375	-1	-17	-17	-0	-1.7
Total	15	84	80	.512	187	167	143	4	1	1431²	1659	59	518	346	14.1	4.43	96	.284	.349	331	.241	32	-15	-29	4	0.6

● **ERNIE MAUN**   Maun, Ernest Gerald b: 2/3/01, Clearwater, Kan. d: 1/1/87, Corpus Christi, Tex. BR/TR, 6', 165 lbs. Deb: 5/16/24

1924	NY-N	1	1	.500	22	0	0	0	1	35	46	2	10	5	14.7	5.91	62	.326	.375	2	.667	1	-8	-9	-1	-0.5
1926	Phi-N	1	4	.200	14	5	0	0	0	37²	57	4	18	9	18.2	6.45	64	.339	.406	3	.250	-0	-11	-10	-0	-1.1
Total	2	2	5	.286	36	5	0	0	1	72²	103	6	28	14	16.5	6.19	63	.333	.392	5	.333	1	-19	-18	-1	-1.6

● **DICK MAUNEY**   Mauney, Richard b: 1/26/20, Concord, N.C. d: 2/6/70, Albemarle, N.C. BR/TR, 5'11.5", 164 lbs. Deb: 6/13/45

1945	Phi-N	6	10	.375	20	16	6	2	1	122²	127	7	27	35	11.4	3.08	124	.268	.310	6	.146	-0	10	10	1	1.3
1946	Phi-N	6	4	.600	24	7	3	1	2	90	98	4	18	31	11.9	2.70	127	.279	.320	4	.167	-1	7	7	0	0.8
1947	Phi-N	0	0	—	9	1	0	0	1	16¹	15	1	7	6	12.7	3.86	104	.288	.383	0	.000	-0	0	0	1	0.1
Total	3	12	14	.462	53	24	9	3	4	229	240	12	52	72	11.7	2.99	123	.274	.319	10	.149	-1	17	18	2	2.2

● **HARRY MAUPIN**   Maupin, Harry Carr b: 7/11/1872, Wellsville, Mo. d: 8/25/52, Parsons, Kan. 5'7", 150 lbs. Deb: 10/5/1898

1898	StL-N	0	2	.000	2	2	2	0	0	18	22	0	3	6	14.0	5.00	69	.297	.350	3	.429	1	-4	-3	-1	-0.3
1899	Cle-N	0	3	.000	5	3	2	0	0	25	55	0	7	3	22.7	12.60	29	.437	.470	0	.000	-2	-24	-25	-1	-2.2
Total	2	0	5	.000	7	5	4	0	0	43	77	0	10	6	19.0	9.63	39	.385	.425	3	.176	-1	-28	-28	-1	-2.5

● **RALPH MAURIELLO**   Mauriello, Ralph "Tami" b: 8/25/34, Brooklyn, N.Y. BR/TR, 6'3", 195 lbs. Deb: 9/13/58

| 1958 | LA-N | 1 | 1 | .500 | 3 | 2 | 0 | 0 | 0 | 11² | 10 | 1 | 8 | 11 | 13.9 | 4.63 | 89 | .238 | .360 | 0 | .000 | -1 | -1 | -1 | -0 | -0.2 |

● **TIM MAUSER**   Mauser, Timothy Edward b: 10/4/66, Fort Worth, Tex. BR/TR, 6', 185 lbs. Deb: 7/7/91

1991	Phi-N	0	0	—	3	0	0	0	0	10²	18	3	3	6	17.7	7.59	48	.367	.404	0	.000	-0	-5	-5	-0	-0.1
1993	Phi-N	0	0	—	8	0	0	0	0	16¹	15	1	7	14	12.7	4.96	80	.238	.324	0	.000	-0	-2	-2	1	-0.0
	SD-N	0	1	.000	28	0	0	0	0	37²	36	5	17	32	12.7	3.58	115	.248	.327	0	—	-0	2	2	1	0.1
	Yr	0	1	.000	36	0	0	0	0	54	51	6	24	46	12.5	4.00	102	.244	.322	0	.000	-0	1	0	1	0.1
1994	SD-N	2	4	.333	35	0	0	0	0	49	50	3	19	32	12.9	3.49	118	.269	.340	1	.250	-0	4	3	-0	0.4
1995	SD-N	0	1	.000	2	0	0	0	0	5²	4	0	9	9	20.6	9.53	42	.190	.433	0	.000	-0	-3	-3	-0	-0.5
Total	4	2	6	.250	79	0	0	0	0	119¹	123	12	55	93	13.6	4.37	93	.265	.345	1	.071	-0	-4	-4	1	-0.1

● **BRIAN MAXCY**   Maxcy, David Brian b: 5/4/71, Amory, Miss. BR/TR, 6'1", 170 lbs. Deb: 5/27/95

1995	Det-A	4	5	.444	41	0	0	0	0	52¹	61	6	31	20	16.2	6.88	69	.293	.390	0	—	-0	-13	-12	1	-1.6
1996	Det-A	0	0	—	2	0	0	0	0	3¹	8	2	2	1	27.0	13.50	37	.471	.526	0	—	-0	-3	-3	0	0.1
Total	2	4	5	.444	43	0	0	0	0	55²	69	8	33	21	16.8	7.28	66	.307	.400	0	—	-0	-16	-15	2	-1.5

● **LARRY MAXIE**   Maxie, Larry Hans b: 10/10/40, Upland, Cal. BR/TR, 6'4", 220 lbs. Deb: 8/30/69

| 1969 | Atl-N | 0 | 0 | — | 2 | 0 | 0 | 0 | 0 | 3 | 1 | 0 | 2 | 1 | 9.0 | 3.00 | 120 | .111 | .273 | 0 | — | -0 | 0 | 0 | 0 | 0.0 |

● **BERT MAXWELL**   Maxwell, James Albert b: 10/17/1886, Texarkana, Ark. d: 12/10/61, Brady, Tex. BB/TR, 6', 180 lbs. Deb: 9/12/06

1906	Pit-N	0	1	.000	2	1	0	0	0	8	2	1	11.3	5.63	48	.286	.333	0	.000	-3	-3	0	-0.3
1908	Phi-A	0	0	—	4	0	0	0	0	13	23	0	9	7	23.5	11.08	23	.348	.442	0	.000	-1	-13	-12	-0	-0.1
1911	NY-N	1	2	.333	4	3	0	0	0	31	37	3	6	8	13.4	2.90	116	.311	.359	1	.111	-0	2	2	1	0.2

YEAR	TM/L	W	L	PCT	G	GS	CG	SH	SV	IP	H	HR	BB	SO	RAT	ERA	ERA+	OAV	OOB	BH	AVG	PB	PR	/A	PD	TPI
1914	Bro-F	3	4	.429	12	8	6	1	1	71¹	76	0	24	19	12.7	3.28	88	.276	.337	2	.087	-2	-3	-3	1	-0.5
Total	4	4	7	.364	21	12	9	1	5	123¹	144	0	42	35	13.9	4.16	71	.295	.357	3	.075	-3	-17	-16	1	-0.7

● DARRELL MAY   May, Darrell Kevin   b: 6/13/72, San Bernardino, Cal.   BL/TL, 6′2″, 170 lbs.   Deb: 9/10/95

YEAR	TM/L	W	L	PCT	G	GS	CG	SH	SV	IP	H	HR	BB	SO	RAT	ERA	ERA+	OAV	OOB	BH	AVG	PB	PR	/A	PD	TPI
1995	Atl-N	0	0	—	2	0	0	0	0	4	10	0	0	1	22.5	11.25	38	.500	.500	0	—	0	-3	-3	0	0.0
1996	Pit-N	0	1	.000	5	2	0	0	0	8²	15	5	4	5	20.8	9.35	47	.357	.426	1	.333	0	-5	-5	0	-0.4
	Cal-A	0	0	—	5	0	0	0	0	2²	3	1	2	1	16.9	10.13	48	.333	.455	0	—	0	-2	-2	-0	0.1
Total	2	0	1	.000	12	2	0	0	0	15¹	28	6	6	7	20.5	9.98	45	.394	.449	1	.333	0	-10	-9	0	-0.3

● JAKIE MAY   May, Frank Spruiell   b: 11/25/1895, Youngsville, N.C.   d: 6/3/70, Wendell, N.C.   BR/TL, 5′8″, 178 lbs.   Deb: 6/26/17

YEAR	TM/L	W	L	PCT	G	GS	CG	SH	SV	IP	H	HR	BB	SO	RAT	ERA	ERA+	OAV	OOB	BH	AVG	PB	PR	/A	PD	TPI
1917	StL-N	0	0	—	15	1	0	0	0	29¹	29	0	11	18	13.2	3.38	80	.302	.391	0	.000	-1	-2	-2	2	0.1
1918	StL-N	5	6	.455	29	15	6	0	0	152²	149	2	69	61	13.6	3.83	71	.264	.358	3	.067	-1	-18	-19	-2	-1.7
1919	StL-N	3	12	.200	28	19	8	1	0	125²	99	1	87	53	14.3	3.22	87	.230	.377	6	.162	-1	-4	-6	-1	-1.0
1920	StL-N	1	4	.200	16	5	3	0	0	70²	65	0	37	33	13.9	3.06	98	.251	.360	5	.227	-1	1	-1	-2	-0.1
1921	StL-N	1	3	.250	5	5	1	0	0	21	29	0	12	5	17.6	4.71	78	.333	.414	2	.333	1	-2	-2	-1	-0.4
1924	Cin-N	3	3	.500	38	3	2	0	6	99	104	2	29	59	12.6	3.00	126	.276	.337	1	.111	-2	10	8	-0	0.4
1925	Cin-N	8	9	.471	36	12	7	1	2	137¹	146	3	45	74	13.0	3.87	106	.272	.337	8	.186	-0	6	4	0	0.4
1926	Cin-N	13	9	.591	45	15	9	1	3	167²	175	4	44	103	12.1	3.22	115	.276	.329	7	.146	-1	11	9	-1	0.8
1927	Cin-N	15	12	.556	44	28	17	2	1	235²	242	4	70	121	12.4	3.51	108	.274	.337	14	.184	-0	11	7	1	0.8
1928	Cin-N	3	5	.375	21	11	1	1	1	79¹	99	4	35	39	15.3	4.42	89	.315	.386	8	.296	1	-4	-4	-1	-0.4
1929	Cin-N	10	14	.417	41	24	10	0	3	199	219	4	75	92	13.5	4.61	99	.285	.352	13	.203	-1	2	-1	0	-0.2
1930	Cin-N	3	11	.214	26	18	5	1	0	112¹	147	6	41	44	15.5	5.77	84	.320	.383	5	.128	-1	-10	-12	0	-1.2
1931	Chi-N	5	5	.500	31	4	1	0	2	79	81	2	43	38	14.5	3.87	100	.275	.372	5	.227	1	-0	-1	0	0.1
1932	*Chi-N	2	2	.500	35	0	0	0	1	53²	61	3	19	20	13.8	4.36	86	.281	.345	1	.125	-0	-3	-4	-0	-0.3
Total	14	72	95	.431	410	160	70	7	19	1562¹	1645	35	617	760	13.4	3.88	97	.278	.355	80	.171	-4	-2	-23	-6	-2.7

● RUDY MAY   May, Rudolph   b: 7/18/44, Coffeyville, Kan.   BL/TL, 6′3″, 207 lbs.   Deb: 4/18/65

YEAR	TM/L	W	L	PCT	G	GS	CG	SH	SV	IP	H	HR	BB	SO	RAT	ERA	ERA+	OAV	OOB	BH	AVG	PB	PR	/A	PD	TPI
1965	Cal-A	4	9	.308	30	19	2	1	0	124	111	7	78	76	14.0	3.92	87	.245	.361	6	.200	3	-6	-7	-2	-0.6
1969	Cal-A	10	13	.435	43	25	4	0	2	180¹	142	20	66	133	10.5	3.44	101	.220	.296	4	.082	-2	4	1	-1	-0.1
1970	Cal-A	7	13	.350	38	34	2	2	0	208²	190	20	81	164	11.8	4.01	90	.245	.319	6	.087	-2	-7	-9	0	-1.1
1971	Cal-A	11	12	.478	32	31	7	2	0	208¹	160	12	87	156	10.8	3.02	107	.213	.297	10	.147	0	10	5	-1	0.5
1972	Cal-A	12	11	.522	35	30	10	3	1	205¹	162	15	82	169	10.7	2.94	99	.215	.293	7	.113	-1	3	-1	-2	-0.4
1973	Cal-A	7	17	.292	34	28	10	4	0	185	177	20	80	134	12.6	4.38	81	.254	.333	0	—	0	-12	-17	2	-1.8
1974	Cal-A	0	1	.000	18	3	0	0	2	27	29	2	10	12	13.3	7.00	49	.274	.342	0	—	0	-10	-11	1	-0.1
	NY-A	8	4	.667	17	15	8	2	0	114¹	75	5	48	90	10.0	2.28	154	.188	.282	0	—	0	17	16	-2	1.6
	Yr	8	5	.615	35	18	8	2	2	141¹	104	7	58	102	10.6	3.18	110	.204	.293	0	—	0	7	5	-0	1.5
1975	NY-A	14	12	.538	32	31	13	1	0	212	179	9	99	145	11.9	3.06	120	.231	.320	0	—	0	17	15	-1	1.7
1976	NY-A	4	3	.571	11	11	2	1	0	68	49	5	28	38	10.3	3.57	96	.206	.292	0	—	0	-0	-1	0	-0.1
	Bal-A	11	7	.611	24	21	5	1	0	152¹	156	11	42	71	11.7	3.78	87	.267	.316	0	—	0	-4	-9	-1	-1.0
	Yr	15	10	.600	35	32	7	2	0	220¹	205	16	70	109	11.2	3.72	89	.249	.308	0	—	0	-5	-10	-1	-1.1
1977	Bal-A	18	14	.563	37	37	11	4	0	251²	243	25	78	105	11.7	3.61	105	.255	.315	0	—	0	13	5	-3	0.6
1978	Mon-N	8	10	.444	27	23	4	1	0	144	141	15	42	87	11.8	3.88	91	.255	.315	6	.143	0	-5	-6	-2	-0.8
1979	Mon-N	10	3	.769	33	7	2	1	0	93²	88	4	31	67	11.8	2.31	159	.255	.324	3	.143	-0	15	14	1	1.9
1980	*NY-A	15	5	.750	41	17	3	1	3	175¹	144	14	39	133	**9.4**	**2.46**	**159**	.224	**.268**	0	—	0	31	28	0	3.2
1981	*NY-A	6	11	.353	27	22	4	0	1	147²	137	10	41	79	11.0	4.14	86	.246	.300	0	—	0	-8	-9	1	-0.9
1982	NY-A	6	6	.500	41	6	0	0	3	106	109	4	14	85	10.5	2.89	138	.267	.292	0	—	0	14	13	1	1.5
1983	NY-A	1	5	.167	15	0	0	0	0	18¹	22	1	12	16	17.2	6.87	57	.293	.398	0	—	0	-6	-6	0	-1.6
Total	16	152	156	.494	535	360	87	24	12	2622	2314	199	958	1760	11.4	3.46	102	.238	.310	42	.123	-2	64	21	-7	2.5

● SCOTT MAY   May, Scott Francis   b: 11/11/61, West Bend, Wis.   BR/TR, 6′1″, 185 lbs.   Deb: 9/2/88

YEAR	TM/L	W	L	PCT	G	GS	CG	SH	SV	IP	H	HR	BB	SO	RAT	ERA	ERA+	OAV	OOB	BH	AVG	PB	PR	/A	PD	TPI
1988	Tex-A	0	0	—	3	1	0	0	0	7¹	8	3	4	4	14.7	8.59	48	.296	.387	0	—	0	-4	-4	0	-0.2
1991	Chi-N	0	0	—	2	0	0	0	0	2	6	1	1	1	31.5	18.00	22	.545	.583	0	—	0	-3	-3	-0	-0.2
Total	2	0	0	—	5	1	0	0	0	9¹	14	3	5	5	18.3	10.61	38	.368	.442	0	—	0	-7	-7	-0	-0.2

● BUCKSHOT MAY   May, William Herbert   b: 12/13/1899, Bakersfield, Cal.   d: 3/15/84, Bakersfield, Cal.   BR/TR, 6′2″, 169 lbs.   Deb: 5/9/24

YEAR	TM/L	W	L	PCT	G	GS	CG	SH	SV	IP	H	HR	BB	SO	RAT	ERA	ERA+	OAV	OOB	BH	AVG	PB	PR	/A	PD	TPI
1924	Pit-N	0	0	—	1	0	0	0	0	1	2	0	0	1	18.0	0.00	—	.500	.500	0	—	0	0	0	0	0.0

● ED MAYER   Mayer, Edwin David   b: 11/30/31, San Francisco, Cal   BL/TL, 6′2″, 185 lbs.   Deb: 9/15/57

YEAR	TM/L	W	L	PCT	G	GS	CG	SH	SV	IP	H	HR	BB	SO	RAT	ERA	ERA+	OAV	OOB	BH	AVG	PB	PR	/A	PD	TPI
1957	Chi-N	0	0	—	3	1	0	0	0	7²	8	2	2	3	12.9	5.87	66	.258	.324	1	.500	-0	-2	-2	0	0.1
1958	Chi-N	2	2	.500	19	0	0	0	1	23²	15	0	16	14	12.9	3.80	103	.190	.347	1	.200	-0	0	0	-0	0.0
Total	2	2	2	.500	22	1	0	0	1	31¹	23	2	18	17	12.9	4.31	91	.209	.341	2	.286	0	-1	-1	0	0.1

● ERSKINE MAYER   Mayer, Erskine John (b: James Erskine)   b: 1/16/1889, Atlanta, Ga.   d: 3/10/57, Los Angeles, Cal.   BR/TR, 6′, 168 lbs.   Deb: 9/4/12   F

YEAR	TM/L	W	L	PCT	G	GS	CG	SH	SV	IP	H	HR	BB	SO	RAT	ERA	ERA+	OAV	OOB	BH	AVG	PB	PR	/A	PD	TPI
1912	Phi-N	0	1	.000	7	1	0	0	0	21¹	27	1	7	5	14.8	6.33	57	.318	.376	0	.000	-0	-7	-6	0	-0.3
1913	Phi-N	9	9	.500	39	19	7	2	1	170²	172	6	46	51	12.0	3.11	107	.272	.330	6	.120	-2	2	4	0	0.2
1914	Phi-N	21	19	.525	48	39	24	4	2	321	308	8	91	116	11.6	2.58	114	.256	.315	21	.194	2	8	13	4	2.3
1915	*Phi-N	21	15	.583	43	33	20	2	2	274²	240	9	59	114	10.3	2.36	116	.243	.295	21	.239	5	12	12	1	2.2
1916	Phi-N	7	7	.500	28	16	7	2	0	140	148	7	33	62	11.9	3.15	84	.281	.328	5	.132	-1	-8	-8	3	-0.5
1917	Phi-N	11	6	.647	28	18	11	1	0	160	160	6	33	64	11.1	2.76	102	.268	.310	10	.196	-0	-1	1	-0	0.0
1918	Phi-N	7	4	.636	13	13	7	1	0	104	108	2	26	16	11.9	3.12	96	.276	.328	8	.216	1	-4	-1	-0	-0.1
	Pit-N	9	3	.750	15	14	11	1	0	123¹	122	1	27	25	11.2	2.26	127	.268	.314	7	.167	2	7	8	-2	0.8
	Yr	16	7	.696	28	27	18	1	0	227¹	230	3	53	41	11.4	2.65	110	.270	.316	15	.190	3	3	7	-2	0.7
1919	Pit-N	5	3	.625	18	10	6	0	1	88¹	100	2	12	20	11.6	4.48	67	.267	.294	6	.207	-0	-15	-14	-1	-1.4
	*Chi-A	1	3	.250	6	2	0	0	0	23²	30	1	11	9	15.6	8.37	38	.316	.387	0	—	-1	-14	-14	0	-1.9
Total	8	91	70	.565	245	165	93	12	6	1427	1415	43	345	482	11.4	2.96	99	.264	.316	84	.185	5	-21	-5	4	1.3

● SAM MAYER   Mayer, Samuel Frankel (b: Samuel Frankel Erskine)   b: 2/28/1893, Atlanta, Ga.   d: 7/1/62, Atlanta, Ga.   BR/TL, 5′10″, 164 lbs.   Deb: 9/14/15   F♦

YEAR	TM/L	W	L	PCT	G	GS	CG	SH	SV	IP	H	HR	BB	SO	RAT	ERA	ERA+	OAV	OOB	BH	AVG	PB	PR	/A	PD	TPI
1915	Was-A	0	0	—	1	0	0	0	0	0	0	0	2	0	—	—	—	—	1.000	7	.241	0	0	0	0	0.0

● AL MAYS   Mays, Albert C.   b: 5/17/1865, Canal Dover, Ohio   d: 5/7/05, Parkersburg, W.Va.   BR ,   Deb: 5/10/1885

YEAR	TM/L	W	L	PCT	G	GS	CG	SH	SV	IP	H	HR	BB	SO	RAT	ERA	ERA+	OAV	OOB	BH	AVG	PB	PR	/A	PD	TPI
1885	Lou-a	6	11	.353	17	17	17	0	0	150	129	3	43	61	10.8	2.76	117	.219	.282	13	.213	0	8	8	-0	0.7
1886	NY-a	11	27	.289	41	40	39	1	0	350	330	7	140	163	12.4	3.39	101	.240	.317	16	.119	-9	2	1	-1	-0.8
1887	NY-a	17	34	.333	52	52	50	0	0	441¹	551	11	136	124	14.4	4.73	90	.298	.353	45	.204	-1	-21	-24	6	-1.5
1888	Bro-a	9	9	.500	18	18	17	1	0	160²	150	1	32	67	10.8	2.80	107	.238	.287	5	.079	-4	5	3	2	0.1
1889	Col-a	10	7	.588	21	19	13	1	0	140	167	4	56	52	14.6	4.82	75	.287	.354	7	.130	-1	-15	-19	1	-1.7
1890	Col-a	0	1	.000	1	1	1	0	0	9	14	0	8	2	23.0	8.00	45	.341	.460	0	.000	-0	-4	-4	-1	-0.4
Total	6	53	89	.373	150	147	137	3	0	1251	1341	26	415	469	13.1	3.91	94	.265	.328	86	.160	-16	-26	-35	7	-3.6

● CARL MAYS   Mays, Carl William "Sub"   b: 11/12/1891, Liberty, Ky.   d: 4/4/71, ElCajon, Cal.   BL/TR, 5′11.5″, 195 lbs.   Deb: 4/15/15

YEAR	TM/L	W	L	PCT	G	GS	CG	SH	SV	IP	H	HR	BB	SO	RAT	ERA	ERA+	OAV	OOB	BH	AVG	PB	PR	/A	PD	TPI
1915	Bos-A	6	5	.545	38	6	2	0	7	131²	119	0	65	21	9.9	2.60	107	.244	.282	9	.237	-2	5	3	2	0.6
1916	*Bos-A	18	13	.581	44	24	14	2	5	245	208	1	74	76	10.7	2.39	116	.234	.299	18	.234	7	12	10	9	3.2
1917	Bos-A	22	9	.710	35	33	27	2	0	289	230	1	74	91	9.9	1.74	148	.221	.282	27	.252	6	30	27	8	4.8
1918	*Bos-A	21	13	.618	35	33	**30**	8	0	293¹	230	2	81	114	9.9	2.21	121	.221	.284	30	.288	10	19	15	9	4.1
1919	Bos-A	5	11	.313	21	16	14	2	2	146	131	3	40	53	10.8	2.47	123	.247	.306	8	.151	-2	12	9	3	1.1
	NY-A	9	3	.750	13	13	12	1	0	120	96	7	37	54	10.4	1.65	193	.216	.283	14	.311	3	21	21	1	2.7
	Yr	14	14	.500	34	29	26	3	2	266	227	5	77	107	10.5	2.10	148	.231	.291	22	.231	1	33	30	4	3.8
1920	NY-A	26	11	.703	45	37	26	**6**	2	312	310	13	84	92	11.6	3.06	125	.263	.316	26	.239	2	26	26	6	3.7
1921	*NY-A	**27**	9	**.750**	**49**	38	30	1	**7**	**336²**	332	11	76	70	11.1	3.05	139	.257	.303	49	.343	12	46	44	3	5.8
1922	*NY-A	13	14	.481	34	29	21	1	2	240	257	12	50	41	11.8	3.60	111	.285	.327	23	.250	1	12	11	6	1.9
1923	NY-A	5	2	.714	23	7	2	0	2	81¹	119	8	32	16	17.2	6.20	64	.357	.420	4	.148	1	-20	-20	3	-1.2
1924	Cin-N	20	9	.690	37	27	15	2	0	226	238	2	36	63	11.1	3.15	120	.270	.302	24	.289	7	18	16	8	3.4
1925	Cin-N	3	5	.375	12	5	3	0	2	51²	60	0	13	10	13.1	3.31	124	.294	.342	4	.250	1	6	5	1	0.8

YEAR	TM/L	W	L	PCT	G	GS	CG	SH	SV	IP	H	HR	BB	SO	RAT	ERA	ERA+	OAV	OOB	BH	AVG	PB	PR	/A	PD	TPI
1926	Cin-N	19	12	.613	39	33	**24**	3	1	281	286	3	53	58	11.0	3.14	118	.269	.306	22	.224	2	21	17	10	3.1
1927	Cin-N	3	7	.300	14	9	6	0	0	82	89	1	10	17	11.0	3.51	108	.276	.300	13	.406	5	4	2	4	1.3
1928	Cin-N	4	1	.800	14	7	4	1	1	62²	67	3	22	10	12.8	3.88	102	.275	.335	8	.296	1	1	1	0	0.2
1929	NY-N	7	2	.778	37	8	1	0	4	123	140	8	31	32	12.7	4.32	106	.287	.333	12	.353	4	5	4	2	0.8
Total	15	208	126	.623	490	325	231	29	31	3021¹	2912	73	734	862	11.1	2.92	119	.257	.307	291	.268	64	217	189	74	36.2

● **MATT MAYSEY**   Maysey, Matthew Samuel b: 1/8/67, Hamilton, Ont., Canada BR/TR, 6'4", 225 lbs. Deb: 7/8/92

YEAR	TM/L	W	L	PCT	G	GS	CG	SH	SV	IP	H	HR	BB	SO	RAT	ERA	ERA+	OAV	OOB	BH	AVG	PB	PR	/A	PD	TPI
1992	Mon-N	0	0	—	2	0	0	0	0	2¹	4	1	0	4	19.3	3.86	90	.364	.417	0	—	0	-0	-0	-0	0.0
1993	Mil-A	1	2	.333	23	0	0	0	1	22	28	4	13	10	17.2	5.73	74	.322	.416	1	1.000	0	-3	-4	-1	-0.5
Total	2	1	2	.333	25	0	0	0	1	24¹	32	5	13	11	17.4	5.55	75	.327	.416	1	1.000	0	-4	-4	-1	-0.5

● **JACK McADAMS**   McAdams, George D. b: 12/17/1886, Benton, Ark. d: 5/21/37, San Francisco, Cal BR/TR, 6'1.5", 170 lbs. Deb: 7/22/11

YEAR	TM/L	W	L	PCT	G	GS	CG	SH	SV	IP	H	HR	BB	SO	RAT	ERA	ERA+	OAV	OOB	BH	AVG	PB	PR	/A	PD	TPI
1911	StL-N	0	0	—	6	0	0	0	0	9²	7	0	5	4	13.0	3.72	91	.226	.368	0	—	-0	-0	-0	0	0.0

● **BILL McAFEE**   McAfee, William Fort b: 9/7/07, Smithville, Ga. d: 7/8/58, Culpeper, Va. BR/TR, 6'2", 186 lbs. Deb: 5/12/30

YEAR	TM/L	W	L	PCT	G	GS	CG	SH	SV	IP	H	HR	BB	SO	RAT	ERA	ERA+	OAV	OOB	BH	AVG	PB	PR	/A	PD	TPI
1930	Chi-N	0	0	—	2	0	0	0	0	1	3	0	2	0	45.0	0.00	—	.375	.500			0	1	1	-0	0.0
1931	Bos-N	0	1	.000	18	1	0	0	0	29²	39	2	10	9	14.9	6.37	59	.333	.386	0	.000	-1	-8	-9	0	-0.3
1932	Was-A	3	1	.857	8	5	2	0	0	41¹	47	3	22	10	15.0	3.92	110	.287	.371	2	.111	-2	3	2	1	0.2
1933	Was-A	3	2	.600	27	1	0	0	5	53	64	3	21	14	14.6	6.62	63	.296	.361	4	.267	2	-14	-14	-0	-1.2
1934	StL-A	1	0	1.000	28	0	0	0	0	61²	84	4	26	11	16.5	5.84	86	.332	.401	3	.188	-0	-9	-6	-1	-0.2
Total	5	10	4	.714	83	7	2	0	5	186²	237	12	81	44	15.5	5.69	78	.313	.382	9	.173	0	-28	-26	1	-1.5

● **JIMMY McALEER**   McAleer, James Robert "Loafer" b: 7/10/1864, Youngstown, Ohio d: 4/29/31, Youngstown, Ohio BR/TR, 6', 175 lbs. Deb: 4/24/1889 M♦

YEAR	TM/L	W	L	PCT	G	GS	CG	SH	SV	IP	H	HR	BB	SO	RAT	ERA	ERA+	OAV	OOB	BH	AVG	PB	PR	/A	PD	TPI
1901	Cle-A	0	0	—	1	0	0	0	0	0¹	2	0	3	0	135.0	0.00	—	.667	.833	1	.143	-0	0	0	0	0.0

● **JACK McALEESE**   McAleese, John James b: 1877, Sharon, Pa. d: 11/15/50, New York, N.Y. BR/TR, 5'8", Deb: 8/10/01 ♦

YEAR	TM/L	W	L	PCT	G	GS	CG	SH	SV	IP	H	HR	BB	SO	RAT	ERA	ERA+	OAV	OOB	BH	AVG	PB	PR	/A	PD	TPI
1901	Chi-A	0	0	—	1	0	0	0	0	3	7	0	1	1	24.0	9.00	39	.438	.471	0	.000	-0	-2	-2	0	0.0

● **SPORT McALLISTER**   McAllister, Lewis William b: 7/23/1874, Austin, Miss. d: 7/17/62, Wyandotte, Mich. BB/TR, 5'11", 180 lbs. Deb: 8/7/1896 ♦

YEAR	TM/L	W	L	PCT	G	GS	CG	SH	SV	IP	H	HR	BB	SO	RAT	ERA	ERA+	OAV	OOB	BH	AVG	PB	PR	/A	PD	TPI
1896	Cle-N	0	0	—	1	0	0	0	0	4	9	0	2	0	24.8	6.75	67	.450	.500	6	.222	-0	-1	-1	0	0.0
1897	Cle-N	1	2	.333	4	3	3	0	0	28	29	3	9	10	12.2	4.50	100	.266	.322	30	.219	-0	-1	-0	1	0.0
1898	Cle-N	3	4	.429	9	7	6	0	0	65¹	73	2	23	9	13.6	4.55	80	.281	.346	13	.228	1	-7	-7	-1	-0.6
1899	Cle-N	0	1	.000	3	1	1	0	0	16	29	0	10	2	24.2	9.56	39	.387	.483	99	.237	0	-10	-10	-0	-0.5
Total	4	4	7	.364	17	11	10	0	0	113¹	140	5	44	21	15.2	5.32	73	.302	.371	358	.247	1	-19	-18	0	-1.1

● **ERNIE McANALLY**   McAnally, Ernest Lee b: 8/15/46, Pittsburg, Tex. BR/TR, 6'1", 190 lbs. Deb: 4/11/71

YEAR	TM/L	W	L	PCT	G	GS	CG	SH	SV	IP	H	HR	BB	SO	RAT	ERA	ERA+	OAV	OOB	BH	AVG	PB	PR	/A	PD	TPI
1971	Mon-N	11	12	.478	31	25	8	2	0	177²	150	9	87	98	12.4	3.90	90	.228	.326	7	.117	-2	-9	-7	0	-1.1
1972	Mon-N	6	15	.286	29	27	4	0	0	170	159	13	71	102	12.7	3.81	93	.259	.337	6	.113	-2	-7	-5	3	-0.5
1973	Mon-N	7	9	.438	27	24	4	0	0	147	158	13	54	72	13.2	4.04	94	.274	.340	9	.184	-1	-6	-4	-0	-0.5
1974	Mon-N	6	13	.316	25	21	5	2	0	128²	126	10	56	79	13.3	4.48	86	.256	.336	5	.119	-2	-12	-9	1	-1.4
Total	4	30	49	.380	112	97	21	6	0	623¹	599	45	268	351	12.8	4.03	91	.253	.334	27	.132	-6	-34	-25	3	-3.5

● **JAMIE McANDREW**   McAndrew, James Brian b: 9/2/67, Williamsport, Pa. BR/TR, 6'2", 190 lbs. Deb: 7/17/95

YEAR	TM/L	W	L	PCT	G	GS	CG	SH	SV	IP	H	HR	BB	SO	RAT	ERA	ERA+	OAV	OOB	BH	AVG	PB	PR	/A	PD	TPI
1995	Mil-A	2	3	.400	10	4	0	0	0	36¹	37	2	12	19	12.4	4.71	106	.266	.329	0	—	0	0	1	-1	-0.2

● **JIM McANDREW**   McAndrew, James Clement b: 1/11/44, Lost Nation, Iowa BR/TR, 6'2", 185 lbs. Deb: 7/21/68 F

YEAR	TM/L	W	L	PCT	G	GS	CG	SH	SV	IP	H	HR	BB	SO	RAT	ERA	ERA+	OAV	OOB	BH	AVG	PB	PR	/A	PD	TPI
1968	NY-N	4	7	.364	12	12	2	1	0	79	66	5	17	46	9.9	2.28	133	.230	.282	1	.045	-1	6	7	-1	0.8
1969	NY-N	6	7	.462	27	21	4	2	0	135	112	12	44	90	10.5	3.47	105	.225	.291	5	.135	0	2	3	-1	0.1
1970	NY-N	10	14	.417	32	27	9	3	0	184¹	166	18	38	111	10.1	3.56	113	.239	.281	8	.148	1	10	9	-2	1.0
1971	NY-N	2	5	.286	24	10	0	0	1	90¹	78	10	32	42	11.1	4.38	78	.227	.294	1	.043	-1	-9	-10	1	-0.8
1972	NY-N	11	8	.579	28	23	4	0	1	160²	133	12	38	81	9.9	2.80	120	.225	.278	2	.047	-2	12	10	-1	0.8
1973	NY-N	3	8	.273	23	12	0	0	1	80¹	109	9	31	38	16.0	5.38	67	.330	.393	2	.133	-2	-15	-16	-1	-1.9
1974	SD-N	1	4	.200	15	5	1	0	1	41²	48	7	13	16	13.2	5.62	63	.284	.335	1	.143	-0	-9	-10	-1	-1.1
Total	7	37	53	.411	161	110	20	6	4	771¹	712	73	213	424	11.0	3.65	98	.245	.300	20	.100	-3	-4	-6	-6	-1.1

● **DIXIE McARTHUR**   McArthur, Oland Alexander b: 2/1/1892, Vernon, Ala. d: 5/31/86, West Point, Miss. BR/TR, 6'1", 185 lbs. Deb: 7/10/14

YEAR	TM/L	W	L	PCT	G	GS	CG	SH	SV	IP	H	HR	BB	SO	RAT	ERA	ERA+	OAV	OOB	BH	AVG	PB	PR	/A	PD	TPI
1914	Pit-N	0	0	—	1	0	0	0	0	1	1	0	1	0	18.0	.250	.250					0	0	0	0	0.0

● **WICKEY McAVOY**   McAvoy, James Eugene b: 10/22/1894, Rochester, N.Y. d: 7/6/73, Rochester, N.Y. BR/TR, 5'11", 172 lbs. Deb: 9/29/13 ♦

YEAR	TM/L	W	L	PCT	G	GS	CG	SH	SV	IP	H	HR	BB	SO	RAT	ERA	ERA+	OAV	OOB	BH	AVG	PB	PR	/A	PD	TPI
1918	Phi-A	0	0	—	1	0	0	0	0	0	1	0	0	3	13.5	13.50	22	.500	.500	66	.244	-1	-1	0	0.0

● **TOM McAVOY**   McAvoy, Thomas John b: 8/12/36, Brooklyn, N.Y. BL/TL, 6'3", 200 lbs. Deb: 9/27/59

YEAR	TM/L	W	L	PCT	G	GS	CG	SH	SV	IP	H	HR	BB	SO	RAT	ERA	ERA+	OAV	OOB	BH	AVG	PB	PR	/A	PD	TPI
1959	Was-A	0	0	—	1	0	0	0	0	2²	1	0	2	0	10.1	0.00	—	.125	.300	0	.000	-0	1	1	0	0.0

● **AL McBEAN**   McBean, Alvin O'Neal b: 5/15/38, Charlotte Amalie, V.I. BR/TR, 6', 180 lbs. Deb: 7/2/61

YEAR	TM/L	W	L	PCT	G	GS	CG	SH	SV	IP	H	HR	BB	SO	RAT	ERA	ERA+	OAV	OOB	BH	AVG	PB	PR	/A	PD	TPI
1961	Pit-N	3	2	.600	27	2	0	0	0	74¹	72	4	42	49	14.3	3.75	106	.263	.369	4	.267	1	2	2	2	0.5
1962	Pit-N	15	10	.600	33	29	6	2	0	189²	212	11	65	119	13.5	3.70	106	.285	.348	14	.209	2	5	5	0	0.8
1963	Pit-N	13	3	.813	55	7	2	1	11	121¹	100	5	39	74	10.4	2.57	128	.222	.287	6	.194	0	10	10	2	1.8
1964	Pit-N	8	3	.727	58	0	0	0	22	89²	76	4	17	41	9.7	1.91	184	.234	.280	1	.083	-1	**16**	**16**	4	3.3
1965	Pit-N	6	6	.500	62	1	0	0	18	114	111	5	42	54	12.3	2.29	153	.260	.331	6	.222	1	16	15	1	2.4
1966	Pit-N	4	3	.571	47	0	0	0	9	86²	95	9	24	54	12.6	3.22	111	.280	.332	1	.100	-1	4	3	1	0.3
1967	Pit-N	7	4	.636	51	8	5	0	4	131	118	6	43	54	11.1	2.54	132	.248	.312	6	.207	2	12	12	0	1.4
1968	Pit-N	9	12	.429	36	28	9	2	0	198¹	204	10	63	100	12.3	3.58	82	.269	.330	13	.194	2	-13	-15	4	-0.9
1969	SD-N	0	1	.000	1	1	0	0	0	7	10	1	2	1	15.4	5.14	69	.345	.387	1	.500	0	-1	-1	-0	-0.1
	LA-N	2	6	.250	31	0	0	0	0	48¹	46	6	21	26	12.8	3.91	85	.258	.343	0	.000	-0	-2	-3	-1	-0.7
	Yr	2	7	.222	32	1	0	0	0	55¹	56	7	23	27	13.2	4.07	82	.271	.349	1	.250	-0	-3	-4	-1	-0.8
1970	LA-N	0	0	—	1	0	0	0	0	1	1	0	0	0	9.0	0.00	—	.333	.333			0	0	0	0	0.0
	Pit-N	0	0	—	7	0	0	0	0	10	13	2	7	3	18.0	8.10	48	.317	.417	0	.000	-0	-5	-5	0	-0.1
	Yr	0	0	—	8	0	0	0	0	11	14	2	7	3	17.2	7.36	53	.318	.412	0	.000	-0	-4	-4	0	-0.1
Total	10	67	50	.573	409	76	22	5	63	1072¹	1058	63	365	575	12.2	3.13	111	.262	.327	52	.197	9	45	40	13	8.7

● **PRYOR McBEE**   McBee, Pryor Edward "Lefty" b: 6/20/01, Blanco, Okla. d: 4/19/63, Roseville, Cal. BR/TL, 6'1", 190 lbs. Deb: 5/22/26

YEAR	TM/L	W	L	PCT	G	GS	CG	SH	SV	IP	H	HR	BB	SO	RAT	ERA	ERA+	OAV	OOB	BH	AVG	PB	PR	/A	PD	TPI
1926	Chi-A	0	0	—	1	0	0	0	0	1	1	0	3	1	27.0	6.75	57	.250	.571			0	-0	-0	0	0.0

● **DICK McBRIDE**   McBride, James Dickson b: 1845, Philadelphia, Pa. d: 10/10/16, Philadelphia, Pa. TR, 5'9", 150 lbs. Deb: 5/20/1871 M

YEAR	TM/L	W	L	PCT	G	GS	CG	SH	SV	IP	H	HR	BB	SO	RAT	ERA	ERA+	OAV	OOB	BH	AVG	PB	PR	/A	PD	TPI
1871	Ath-n	18	5	**.783**	25	25	25	0	0	222	285	3	40	15	13.2	4.58	88	.280	.307	31	.235	-4	-9	-14		-1.1
1872	Ath-n	30	14	.682	47	47	47	1	0	419¹	508	3	26	44	11.5	2.85	124	.265	.275	74	.287	5	37	32		2.1
1873	Ath-n	24	19	.558	46	46	38	**3**	0	382²	453	3	47	25	11.8	3.32	103	.263	.282	71	.281	3	-3	4		0.4
1874	Ath-n	33	22	.600	55	55	55	0	0	487	514	6	32	36	**10.1**	**1.64**	**140**	**.240**	**.251**	57	.217	-7	**29**	**36**		1.8
1875	Ath-n	44	14	.759	60	60	59	6	0	538	607	4	24	27	10.6	2.33	103	.267	.275	73	.270	3	-6	4		-0.2
1876	Bos-N	0	0	—	4	4	0	0	0	33	53	1	0	0	15.8	2.73	83	.353	.374	-1	3	.188	-2	-2	-0		-0.3
Total	5 n	149	74	.668	233	233	224	10	0	2049	2367	19	169	147	11.1	2.70	111	.261	.274	306	.260	-0	48	69		3.0

● **KEN McBRIDE**   McBride, Kenneth Faye b: 8/12/35, Huntsville, Ala. BR/TR, 6', 195 lbs. Deb: 8/4/59 C

YEAR	TM/L	W	L	PCT	G	GS	CG	SH	SV	IP	H	HR	BB	SO	RAT	ERA	ERA+	OAV	OOB	BH	AVG	PB	PR	/A	PD	TPI
1959	Chi-A	0	1	.000	11	2	0	0	0	22²	20	1	17	12	14.7	3.18	118	.230	.356	1	.167	-0	2	1	1	0.1
1960	Chi-A	0	0	—	5	0	0	0	0	4²	7	0	4	3	19.3	3.86	98	.333	.455			0	-0	-0	0	0.0
1961	LA-A☆	12	15	.444	38	36	11	1	1	241²	229	28	102	180	12.6	3.65	124	.252	.332	7	.084	-5	10	23	4	2.3
1962	LA-A†	11	5	.688	24	23	6	4	0	149	136	9	70	83	13.0	3.50	110	.249	.344	9	.164	0	8	6	5	1.1
1963	LA-A★	13	12	.520	36	36	11	2	0	251	198	22	92	147	10.5	3.26	105	.218	.293	15	.172	2	10	5	3	0.9
1964	LA-A	4	13	.235	29	21	0	0	0	116¹	104	14	75	66	15.1	5.26	62	.239	.340	3	.214	3	-21	-26	-3	-2.8
1965	Cal-A	0	3	.000	8	4	0	0	0	22	24	1	14	11	16.4	6.14	55	.270	.381	0	.000	-0	-7	-0	-0	-0.9
Total	7	40	50	.444	151	122	28	7	3	807²	717	75	363	503	12.6	3.79	101	.240	.332	38	.144	-0	2	15	0.7

YEAR	TM/L	W	L	PCT	G	GS	CG	SH	SV	IP	H	HR	BB	SO	RAT	ERA	ERA+	OAV	OOB	BH	AVG	PB	PR	/A	PD	TPI

● **PETE McBRIDE** — McBride, Peter William b: 7/9/1875, Adams, Mass. d: 7/3/44, N.Adams, Mass. BR/TR, 5'10", 170 lbs. Deb: 9/20/1898

YEAR	TM/L	W	L	PCT	G	GS	CG	SH	SV	IP	H	HR	BB	SO	RAT	ERA	ERA+	OAV	OOB	BH	AVG	PB	PR	/A	PD	TPI
1898	Cle-N	0	1	.000	1	1	1	0	0	7	9	0	4	6	18.0	6.43	56	.310	.412	2	1.000	2	-2	-2	-0	-0.1
1899	StL-N	2	4	.333	11	6	4	0	0	64	65	4	40	26	15.3	4.08	98	.263	.375	5	.185	0	-2	-1	-1	-0.1
Total 2		2	5	.286	12	7	5	0	0	71	74	4	44	32	15.6	4.31	92	.268	.378	7	.241	2	-4	-3	-1	-0.2

● **RALPH McCABE** — McCabe, Ralph Herbert "Mack" b: 10/21/18, Napanee, Ont., Can. d: 5/3/74, Windsor, Ont., Can. BR/TR, 6'4", 195 lbs. Deb: 9/18/46

YEAR	TM/L	W	L	PCT	G	GS	CG	SH	SV	IP	H	HR	BB	SO	RAT	ERA	ERA+	OAV	OOB	BH	AVG	PB	PR	/A	PD	TPI
1946	Cle-A	0	1	.000	1	1	0	0	0	4	5	3	2	3	18.0	11.25	29	.313	.421	0	.000	-0	-3	-4	0	-0.6

● **DICK McCABE** — McCabe, Richard James b: 2/21/1896, Mamaroneck, N.Y. d: 4/11/50, Buffalo, N.Y. BR/TR, 5'10.5", 159 lbs. Deb: 5/30/18

YEAR	TM/L	W	L	PCT	G	GS	CG	SH	SV	IP	H	HR	BB	SO	RAT	ERA	ERA+	OAV	OOB	BH	AVG	PB	PR	/A	PD	TPI
1918	Bos-A	0	1	.000	3	1	0	0	0	9²	13	0	2	3	14.0	2.79	96	.351	.385	0	.000	-0	-0	0		0.0
1922	Chi-A	1	0	1.000	3	0	0	0	0	3¹	4	0	1	1	10.8	5.40	75	.308	.308	0	—	-1	-0	-0		-0.1
Total 2		1	1	.500	6	1	0	0	0	13	17	0	2	4	13.2	3.46	88	.340	.365	0	.000	-0	-1	-1	-0	-0.1

● **TIM McCABE** — McCabe, Timothy J. b: 10/19/1894, Ironton, Mo. d: 4/12/77, Ironton, Mo. BR/TR, 6', 190 lbs. Deb: 8/16/15

YEAR	TM/L	W	L	PCT	G	GS	CG	SH	SV	IP	H	HR	BB	SO	RAT	ERA	ERA+	OAV	OOB	BH	AVG	PB	PR	/A	PD	TPI
1915	StL-A	3	1	.750	7	4	4	1	0	41²	25	1	9	17	7.6	1.30	221	.177	.232	1	.067	-1	8	7	-1	0.5
1916	StL-A	2	0	1.000	13	0	0	0	0	25²	29	0	7	7	13.3	3.16	87	.282	.339	0	.000	-0	-1	-1	1	0.0
1917	StL-A	0	0	—	1	0	0	0	0	2¹	4	1	4	2	30.9	23.14	11	.400	.571	0	—	-5	-5	-0		0.0
1918	StL-A	0	0	—	1	0	0	0	0	1¹	2	0	1	0	20.3	13.50	20	.333	.429	0		0	-2	-2	-0	0.0
Total 4		5	1	.833	22	4	4	1	0	71	60	2	21	26	10.6	2.92	96	.231	.296	1	.053	-1	-0	-1	1	0.5

● **HARRY McCAFFERY** — McCaffery, Harry Charles b: 11/25/1858, St.Louis, Mo. d: 4/19/28, St.Louis, Mo. BR/TR, 5'10.5", 185 lbs. Deb: 6/15/1882 U♦

YEAR	TM/L	W	L	PCT	G	GS	CG	SH	SV	IP	H	HR	BB	SO	RAT	ERA	ERA+	OAV	OOB	BH	AVG	PB	PR	/A	PD	TPI
1885	Cin-a	1	0	1.000	3	1	1	0	0	17	17	0	5	4	17.0	6.00	54	.342	.405	0	.000	-1	-3	-3	-0	-0.3

● **BILL McCAHAN** — McCahan, William Glenn b: 6/7/21, Philadelphia, Pa. d: 7/3/86, Fort Worth, Tex. BR/TR, 5'11", 200 lbs. Deb: 9/15/46

YEAR	TM/L	W	L	PCT	G	GS	CG	SH	SV	IP	H	HR	BB	SO	RAT	ERA	ERA+	OAV	OOB	BH	AVG	PB	PR	/A	PD	TPI
1946	Phi-A	1	1	.500	4	2	2	1	0	18	16	0	9	6	12.5	1.00	355	.246	.338	2	.400	1	5	5	0	0.7
1947	Phi-A	10	5	.667	29	19	10	1	0	165¹	160	7	62	47	12.1	3.32	115	.252	.318	9	.164	-1	7	9	1	0.8
1948	Phi-A	4	7	.364	17	15	5	0	0	86²	98	8	65	20	16.9	5.71	75	.284	.398	8	.258	1	-14	-14	-1	-1.5
1949	Phi-A	1	1	.500	7	4	0	0	0	20²	23	0	9	3	13.9	2.61	157	.291	.364	1	.200	-0	4	3	0	0.2
Total 4		16	14	.533	57	40	17	2	0	290²	297	15	145	76	13.7	3.84	103	.264	.348	20	.208	1	2	4	-1	0.2

● **WINDY McCALL** — McCall, John William b: 7/18/25, San Francisco, Cal. BL/TL, 6', 180 lbs. Deb: 4/25/48

YEAR	TM/L	W	L	PCT	G	GS	CG	SH	SV	IP	H	HR	BB	SO	RAT	ERA	ERA+	OAV	OOB	BH	AVG	PB	PR	/A	PD	TPI
1948	Bos-A	0	1	.000	1	1	0	0	0	1¹	6	1	1	0	47.3	20.25	22	.600	.636	0	—	0	-2	-2	-0	-0.9
1949	Bos-A	0	0	—	5	0	0	0	0	9¹	13	2	10	8	22.2	11.57	38	.333	.469	2	.667	1	-8	-7	-0	0.0
1950	Pit-N	0	0	—	2	0	0	0	0	6²	12	2	4	5	21.6	9.45	46	.387	.457	0	.000	-0	-4	-4	0	0.0
1954	NY-N	2	5	.286	33	4	0	0	2	61	50	5	29	38	12.1	3.25	124	.219	.315	0	.000	-1	6	5	-1	0.3
1955	NY-N	6	5	.545	42	6	4	0	3	95	86	9	37	50	12.2	3.69	109	.244	.326	2	.118	-1	4	3	1	0.4
1956	NY-N	3	4	.429	46	6	0	0	5	77¹	74	7	20	41	11.1	3.61	105	.252	.302	3	.200	0	1	1	-2	0.2
1957	NY-N	0	0	—	5	0	0	0	0	3	8	1	2	2	33.0	15.00	26	.533	.611	0	—	0	-4	-4	-0	0.0
Total 7		11	15	.423	134	15	4	0	12	253²	249	26	103	144	12.9	4.22	94	.257	.335	7	.146	-1	-7	-7	-3	-0.2

● **LARRY McCALL** — McCall, Larry Stephen b: 9/8/52, Asheville, N.C. BL/TR, 6'2", 195 lbs. Deb: 9/10/77

YEAR	TM/L	W	L	PCT	G	GS	CG	SH	SV	IP	H	HR	BB	SO	RAT	ERA	ERA+	OAV	OOB	BH	AVG	PB	PR	/A	PD	TPI
1977	NY-A	0	1	.000	2	0	0	0	0	6	12	1	1	0	19.5	7.50	53	.375	.394	0	—	0	-2	-2	-0	-0.3
1978	NY-A	1	1	.500	5	1	0	0	0	16	20	2	6	7	15.2	5.63	64	.323	.391	0	—	0	-3	-4	0	-0.2
1979	Tex-A	1	0	1.000	2	1	0	0	0	8¹	7	0	3	3	10.8	2.16	192	.226	.294	0	—	0	2	2	0	0.3
Total 3		2	2	.500	9	2	0	0	0	30¹	39	3	10	10	14.8	5.04	76	.312	.368	0	—	0	-4	-4	0	-0.2

● **DUTCH McCALL** — McCall, Robert Leonard b: 12/27/20, Columbia, Tenn. d: 1/7/96, Little Rock, Ark. BL/TL, 6'1", 184 lbs. Deb: 4/27/48

YEAR	TM/L	W	L	PCT	G	GS	CG	SH	SV	IP	H	HR	BB	SO	RAT	ERA	ERA+	OAV	OOB	BH	AVG	PB	PR	/A	PD	TPI
1948	Chi-N	4	13	.235	30	20	5	0	0	151¹	158	14	85	89	14.5	4.82	81	.268	.361	9	.170	1	-14	-15	1	-1.3

● **RANDY McCAMENT** — McCament, Larry Randall b: 7/29/62, Albuquerque, N.Mex. BR/TR, 6'3", 195 lbs. Deb: 6/28/89

YEAR	TM/L	W	L	PCT	G	GS	CG	SH	SV	IP	H	HR	BB	SO	RAT	ERA	ERA+	OAV	OOB	BH	AVG	PB	PR	/A	PD	TPI
1989	SF-N	1	1	.500	25	0	0	0	0	36²	32	4	23	12	13.7	3.93	86	.241	.357	1	.333	0	-2	-2	0	0.0
1990	SF-N	0	0	—	3	0	0	0	0	6	8	0	5	5	19.5	3.00	121	.333	.448	0	.000	-0	1	0	-0	0.0
Total 2		1	1	.500	28	0	0	0	0	42²	40	4	28	17	14.6	3.80	90	.255	.371	1	.250	0	-1	-2	0	0.0

● **GENE McCANN** — McCann, Henry Eugene "Mike" b: 6/13/1876, Baltimore, Md. d: 4/26/43, New York, N.Y. TR, 5'10", Deb: 4/19/01

YEAR	TM/L	W	L	PCT	G	GS	CG	SH	SV	IP	H	HR	BB	SO	RAT	ERA	ERA+	OAV	OOB	BH	AVG	PB	PR	/A	PD	TPI
1901	Bro-N	2	3	.400	6	5	3	0	0	34	34	1	16	9	14.3	3.44	97	.260	.358	0	.000	-1	-0	-0	0	-0.1
1902	Bro-N	1	2	.333	3	3	3	0	0	30	32	0	12	9	13.2	2.40	115	.274	.341	1	.083	-1	1	1	1	0.1
Total 2		3	5	.375	9	8	6	0	0	64	66	1	28	18	13.8	2.95	104	.266	.350	1	.045	-2	1	1	1	0.1

● **GREG McCARTHY** — McCarthy, Gregory O'Neil b: 10/30/68, Norwalk, Conn. BL/TL, 6'2", 195 lbs. Deb: 8/28/96

YEAR	TM/L	W	L	PCT	G	GS	CG	SH	SV	IP	H	HR	BB	SO	RAT	ERA	ERA+	OAV	OOB	BH	AVG	PB	PR	/A	PD	TPI
1996	Sea-A	0	0	—	10	0	0	0	0	9	8	0	4	7	19.0	1.86	265	.229	.372	0	—	0	3	3	0	0.1

● **ARCH McCARTHY** — McCarthy, Archibald Joseph b: Ypsilanti, Mich. TR, 6', 160 lbs. Deb: 8/14/02

YEAR	TM/L	W	L	PCT	G	GS	CG	SH	SV	IP	H	HR	BB	SO	RAT	ERA	ERA+	OAV	OOB	BH	AVG	PB	PR	/A	PD	TPI
1902	Det-A	2	7	.222	10	8	8	0	0	72	90	2	31	10	15.6	6.13	60	.306	.380	2	.071	-3	-20	-20	-2	-2.3

● **JOHNNY McCARTHY** — McCarthy, John Joseph b: 1/7/10, Chicago, Ill. d: 9/13/73, Mundelein, Ill. BL/TL, 6'1.5", 185 lbs. Deb: 9/2/34 ♦

YEAR	TM/L	W	L	PCT	G	GS	CG	SH	SV	IP	H	HR	BB	SO	RAT	ERA	ERA+	OAV	OOB	BH	AVG	PB	PR	/A	PD	TPI
1939	NY-N	0	0	—	1	0	0	0	0	5	8	1	2	0	18.0	7.20	55	.364	.417	21	.262	0	-2	-2	0	0.0

● **TOMMY McCARTHY** — McCarthy, Thomas Francis Michael b: 7/24/1863, Boston, Mass. d: 8/5/22, Boston, Mass. BR/TR, 5'7", 170 lbs. Deb: 7/10/1884 MH♦

YEAR	TM/L	W	L	PCT	G	GS	CG	SH	SV	IP	H	HR	BB	SO	RAT	ERA	ERA+	OAV	OOB	BH	AVG	PB	PR	/A	PD	TPI
1884	Bos-U	0	7	.000	7	6	5	0	0	56	73	2	14	18	14.0	4.82	49	.296	.333	45	.215	-2	-15	-15	1	-1.4
1886	Phi-N	0	0	—	1	0	0	0	0	1	0	0	1	1	9.0	0.00	—	.000	.250	5	.185	0	0	0	0	0.0
1888	*StL-a	0	0	—	2	0	0	0	0	4¹	3	1	2	1	10.4	4.15	79	.188	.278	140	.274	0	-1	-0	-0	0.0
1889	StL-a	0	0	—	1	0	0	0	0	5	4	0	6	1	18.0	7.20	59	.211	.400	176	.291	0	-2	-2	-0	0.0
1891	StL-a	0	0	—	1	0	0	0	0	2	1	0	3	0	18.0	9.00	47	.400	.400	188	.310	-1	-1	-0	-0	0.0
1894	Bos-N	0	0	—	1	0	0	0	0	2	1	0	3	0	18.0	4.50	126	.143	.400	188	.349	0	-0	-0	-0	0.0
Total 6		0	7	.000	13	6	5	0	0	69¹	83	3	26	21	14.1	4.93	54	.279	.337	1496	.292	-1	-17	-17	1	-1.4

● **TOM McCARTHY** — McCarthy, Thomas Michael b: 6/18/61, Lundstahl, W.Ger. BR/TR, 6', 180 lbs. Deb: 7/5/85

YEAR	TM/L	W	L	PCT	G	GS	CG	SH	SV	IP	H	HR	BB	SO	RAT	ERA	ERA+	OAV	OOB	BH	AVG	PB	PR	/A	PD	TPI
1985	Bos-A	0	0	—	3	0	0	0	0	5	7	1	4	2	19.8	10.80	40	.350	.458	0	—	0	-4	-4	-0	-0.1
1988	Chi-A	2	0	1.000	6	0	0	0	0	13	9	0	2	5	9.0	1.38	287	.191	.255	0	—	0	4	4	0	0.7
1989	Chi-A	1	2	.333	31	0	0	0	0	66²	72	8	20	27	12.7	3.51	108	.280	.337	0	—	0	3	2	1	0.2
Total 3		3	2	.600	40	0	0	0	0	84²	88	9	26	34	12.5	3.61	107	.272	.333	0	—	0	3	2	1	0.8

● **TOM McCARTHY** — McCarthy, Thomas Patrick b: 5/22/1884, Ft.Wayne, Ind. d: 3/28/33, Mishawaka, Ind. TR, 5'7", 170 lbs. Deb: 5/10/08

YEAR	TM/L	W	L	PCT	G	GS	CG	SH	SV	IP	H	HR	BB	SO	RAT	ERA	ERA+	OAV	OOB	BH	AVG	PB	PR	/A	PD	TPI
1908	Cin-N	0	1	.000	1	1	0	0	0	3²	8	0	3	2	22.1	9.82	23	.300	.391	0	.000	-0	-3	-3	0	-0.6
	Pit-N	0	0	—	2	1	0	0	0	6	3	0	6	1	13.5	0.00		.176	.391	0	.000	-0	2	2	1	0.0
	Bos-N	7	3	.700	14	11	7	2	0	94	77	0	28	27	10.1	1.63	148	.235	.298	6	.171	0	8	8	1	1.0
	Yr	7	4	.636	17	13	7	2	0	103²	86	0	37	31	10.8	1.82	132	.236	.308	6	.146	-1	6	7	1	0.4
1909	Bos-N	0	5	.000	8	7	3	0	0	46¹	47	3	28	11	15.0	3.50	81	.272	.379	2	.125	-0	-5	-3	-0	-0.4
Total 2		7	9	.438	25	20	10	2	0	150	133	3	65	42	12.1	2.34	108	.248	.332	8	.140	-1	2	3	1	-0.0

● **BILL McCARTHY** — McCarthy, William Thomas b: 4/11/1882, Ashland, Mass. d: 5/29/39, Boston, Mass. BR/TR, 5'11", 180 lbs. Deb: 4/21/06

YEAR	TM/L	W	L	PCT	G	GS	CG	SH	SV	IP	H	HR	BB	SO	RAT	ERA	ERA+	OAV	OOB	BH	AVG	PB	PR	/A	PD	TPI
1906	Bos-N	0	0	—	1	0	0	0	0	2	2	0	3	0	22.5	9.00	30	.182	.357	0	.000	-0	-1	-1	-0	0.0

● **JOHN McCARTY** — McCarty, John A. b: St.Louis, Mo. TR, Deb: 4/18/1889

YEAR	TM/L	W	L	PCT	G	GS	CG	SH	SV	IP	H	HR	BB	SO	RAT	ERA	ERA+	OAV	OOB	BH	AVG	PB	PR	/A	PD	TPI
1889	KC-a	8	6	.571	15	14	13	0	0	119²	147	4	61	36	16.1	3.91	107	.293	.376	18	.228	-2	-1	4	-0	0.2

● **KIRK McCASKILL** — McCaskill, Kirk Edward b: 4/9/61, Kapuskasing, Ont., Canada BR/TR, 6'1", 200 lbs. Deb: 5/1/85

YEAR	TM/L	W	L	PCT	G	GS	CG	SH	SV	IP	H	HR	BB	SO	RAT	ERA	ERA+	OAV	OOB	BH	AVG	PB	PR	/A	PD	TPI
1985	Cal-A	12	12	.500	30	29	6	1	0	189²	189	23	64	102	12.5	4.70	87	.258	.321	0	—	0	-12	-12	0	-1.4
1986	*Cal-A	17	10	.630	34	33	10	2	0	246¹	207	19	92	202	11.1	3.36	122	.229	.303	0	—	0	22	20	-0	2.2
1987	Cal-A	4	6	.400	14	13	1	1	0	74²	84	14	34	56	14.5	5.67	76	.286	.364	0	—	0	-10	-11	1	-1.2
1988	Cal-A	8	6	.571	23	23	4	2	0	146¹	155	9	61	98	13.3	4.31	90	.274	.346	0	—	0	-6	-7	0	-0.4
1989	Cal-A	15	10	.600	32	32	4	0	0	212	202	16	59	107	11.2	2.93	130	.254	.308	0	—	0	22	21	2	2.6

YEAR TM/L	W	L	PCT	G	GS	CG	SH	SV	IP	H	HR	BB	SO	RAT	ERA	ERA+	OAV	OOB	BH	AVG	PB	PR	/A	PD	TPI
1990 Cal-A	12	11	.522	29	29	2	1	0	174¹	161	9	72	78	12.1	3.25	117	.244	.320	0	—	0	13	11	2	1.5
1991 Cal-A	10	19	.345	30	30	1	0	0	177²	193	19	66	71	13.3	4.26	96	.283	.349	0	—	0	-3	-3	1	-0.4
1992 Chi-A	12	13	.480	34	34	0	0	0	209	193	11	95	109	12.7	4.18	92	.242	.328	0	—	0	-6	-7	2	-0.6
1993 *Chi-A	4	8	.333	30	14	0	0	2	113²	144	12	36	65	14.3	5.23	80	.313	.364	0	—	0	-11	-13	2	-1.0
1994 Chi-A	1	4	.200	40	0	0	0	3	52²	51	6	22	37	12.5	3.42	137	.252	.326	0	—	0	8	7	0	0.7
1995 Chi-A	6	4	.600	55	1	0	0	2	81	97	10	33	50	15.0	4.89	91	.302	.376	0	—	0	-2	-4	0	-0.4
1996 Chi-A	5	5	.500	29	4	0	0	0	51²	72	6	31	28	18.3	6.97	67	.344	.434	0	—	0	-11	-13	1	-1.7
Total 12	106	108	.495	380	242	30	11	7	1729	1748	154	665	1003	12.7	4.12	99	.264	.334	0	—	0	5	-12	9	-0.1

● STEVE McCATTY   McCatty, Steven Earl b: 3/20/54, Detroit, Mich.   BR/TR, 6'3", 205 lbs. Deb: 9/17/77

YEAR TM/L	W	L	PCT	G	GS	CG	SH	SV	IP	H	HR	BB	SO	RAT	ERA	ERA+	OAV	OOB	BH	AVG	PB	PR	/A	PD	TPI
1977 Oak-A	0	0	—	4	2	0	0	0	14¹	16	1	7	9	15.1	5.02	80	.276	.364	0	—	0	-2	-2	-1	0.0
1978 Oak-A	0	0	—	9	0	0	0	0	20	26	1	9	10	15.7	4.50	81	.310	.376	0	—	0	-2	-2	-0	0.3
1979 Oak-A	11	12	.478	31	23	8	0	0	185²	207	17	80	87	14.4	4.22	96	.284	.363	0	—	0	-0	-4	-2	-0.2
1980 Oak-A	14	14	.500	33	31	11	1	0	221²	202	27	99	114	12.5	3.86	98	.240	.325	0	—	0	4	-2	-1	0.1
1981 *Oak-A	14	7	.667	22	22	16	4	0	185²	140	12	61	91	9.8	2.33	149	.211	.279	0	—	0	27	24	-1	2.8
1982 Oak-A	6	3	.667	21	20	2	0	0	128²	124	16	70	66	13.8	3.99	98	.255	.354	0	—	0	1	-1	-1	-0.1
1983 Oak-A	6	9	.400	38	24	3	2	5	167	156	16	82	65	12.9	3.99	97	.247	.334	0	—	0	1	-2	-2	-0.4
1984 Oak-A	8	14	.364	33	30	4	0	0	179²	206	24	71	63	13.9	4.76	79	.289	.355	0	—	0	-15	-20	-2	-1.9
1985 Oak-A	4	4	.500	30	9	1	0	0	85²	95	10	41	36	14.7	5.57	69	.286	.371	0	—	0	-14	-16	0	-1.2
Total 9	63	63	.500	221	161	45	7	5	1188¹	1172	124	520	541	13.0	3.99	95	.258	.339	0	—	0	2	-26	-9	-0.6

● AL McCAULEY   McCauley, Allen A. b: 3/4/1863, Indianapolis, Ind. d: 8/24/17, Wayne Twnshp., Ind BL/TL, 6', 180 lbs. Deb: 6/21/1884 ♦

YEAR TM/L	W	L	PCT	G	GS	CG	SH	SV	IP	H	HR	BB	SO	RAT	ERA	ERA+	OAV	OOB	BH	AVG	PB	PR	/A	PD	TPI
1884 Ind-a	2	7	.222	10	9	9	0	0	76	87	2	25	34	13.3	5.09	65	.261	.313	10	.189	2	-16	-15	2	-1.1

● JOE McCLAIN   McClain, Joseph Fred b: 5/5/33, Johnson City, Tenn.   BR/TR, 6', 183 lbs. Deb: 4/14/61

YEAR TM/L	W	L	PCT	G	GS	CG	SH	SV	IP	H	HR	BB	SO	RAT	ERA	ERA+	OAV	OOB	BH	AVG	PB	PR	/A	PD	TPI
1961 Was-A	8	18	.308	33	29	7	2	1	212	221	22	48	76	11.6	3.86	104	.270	.313	14	.206	1	4	4	-3	0.3
1962 Was-A	0	4	.000	10	4	0	0	0	24	33	8	11	6	17.3	9.38	43	.327	.404	1	.143	-0	-14	-14	0	-1.9
Total 2	8	22	.267	43	33	7	2	1	236	254	30	59	82	12.2	4.42	91	.276	.324	15	.200	1	-11	-11	-3	-1.6

● PAUL McCLELLAN   McClellan, Paul William b: 2/3/66, San Mateo, Cal.   BR/TR, 6'2", 180 lbs. Deb: 9/2/90

YEAR TM/L	W	L	PCT	G	GS	CG	SH	SV	IP	H	HR	BB	SO	RAT	ERA	ERA+	OAV	OOB	BH	AVG	PB	PR	/A	PD	TPI
1990 SF-N	0	1	.000	4	1	0	0	0	7	14	3	6	2	24.7	11.74	31	.389	.488	1	.500	0	-7	-7	0	-0.7
1991 SF-N	3	6	.333	13	12	1	0	0	71	68	12	25	44	11.9	4.56	78	.252	.318	3	.143	-0	-7	-8	-1	-1.0
Total 2	3	7	.300	17	13	1	0	0	78²	82	15	31	46	13.5	5.26	68	.268	.333	4	.174	0	-14	-15	-1	-1.7

● JIM McCLOSKEY   McCloskey, James Ellwood "Irish" b: 5/26/10, Danville, Pa. d: 8/18/71, Jersey City, N.J. BL/TL, 5'9.5", 180 lbs. Deb: 4/21/36

YEAR TM/L	W	L	PCT	G	GS	CG	SH	SV	IP	H	HR	BB	SO	RAT	ERA	ERA+	OAV	OOB	BH	AVG	PB	PR	/A	PD	TPI
1936 Bos-N	0	0	—	4	1	0	0	0	8	14	1	3	2	20.3	11.25	34	.378	.439	0	.000	0	-6	-7	0	-0.5

● JOHN McCLOSKEY   McCloskey, James John b: 8/20/1882, Wyoming, Pa. d: 6/5/19, Wilkes-Barre, Pa. Deb: 5/3/06

YEAR TM/L	W	L	PCT	G	GS	CG	SH	SV	IP	H	HR	BB	SO	RAT	ERA	ERA+	OAV	OOB	BH	AVG	PB	PR	/A	PD	TPI
1906 Phi-N	3	2	.600	9	4	3	0	0	41	46	2	9	6	12.3	2.85	92	.280	.322	3	.200	-1	-1	-1	-1	-0.2
1907 Phi-N	0	0	—	3	0	0	0	0	9	15	0	6	3	22.0	7.00	35	.417	.512	0	.000	-0	-5	-5	0	0.0
Total 2	3	2	.600	12	4	3	0	0	50	61	2	15	9	14.0	3.60	72	.305	.359	3	.158	-0	-6	-6	-1	-0.2

● BOB McCLURE   McClure, Robert Craig b: 4/29/52, Oakland, Cal.   BR/TL, 5'11", 170 lbs. Deb: 8/13/75   C

YEAR TM/L	W	L	PCT	G	GS	CG	SH	SV	IP	H	HR	BB	SO	RAT	ERA	ERA+	OAV	OOB	BH	AVG	PB	PR	/A	PD	TPI
1975 KC-A	1	0	1.000	12	0	0	0	1	15¹	7	0	14	15	10.6	0.00	—	.077	.273	0	—	0	6	7	-0	0.5
1976 KC-A	0	0	—	8	0	0	0	0	4	3	0	4	3	24.8	9.00	39	.214	.500	0	—	0	-2	-2	-0	-0.1
1977 Mil-A	2	1	.667	68	0	0	0	6	71¹	64	2	34	57	12.5	2.52	161	.249	.339	0	—	0	12	12	2	0.9
1978 Mil-A	2	6	.250	44	0	0	0	9	65	53	8	30	47	12.3	3.74	101	.223	.325	0	—	0	0	0	-1	0.0
1979 Mil-A	5	2	.714	36	0	0	0	5	51	53	6	24	37	14.1	3.88	107	.269	.357	0	—	0	2	2	-0	0.2
1980 Mil-A	5	8	.385	52	5	2	1	10	90²	83	6	37	47	12.1	3.08	126	.241	.318	0	—	0	10	8	-1	1.4
1981 *Mil-A	0	0	—	4	0	0	0	0	7²	7	1	4	6	12.9	3.52	97	.233	.324	0	—	0	-0	-0	-2	0.2
1982 *Mil-A	12	7	.632	34	26	5	0	0	172²	160	21	74	99	12.4	4.22	90	.248	.329	0	—	0	-3	-8	-1	-0.8
1983 Mil-A	9	9	.500	24	23	4	0	0	142	152	11	68	68	14.3	4.50	83	.277	.362	0	—	0	-7	-12	-1	-1.4
1984 Mil-A	4	8	.333	39	18	1	0	1	139²	154	9	52	68	13.4	4.38	88	.282	.347	0	—	0	-6	-8	-0	-0.4
1985 Mil-A	4	1	.800	38	1	0	0	0	85²	91	10	30	57	13.0	4.31	97	.274	.340	0	—	0	-2	-1	-0	-0.1
1986 Mil-A	1	1	.667	13	0	0	0	0	16¹	18	2	10	11	15.4	3.86	112	.286	.384	0	—	0	1	1	-0	-0.2
Mon-N	2	5	.286	52	0	0	0	0	62²	53	2	23	42	11.1	3.02	122	.232	.306	1	.250	0	5	5	0	0.6
1987 Mon-N	6	1	.857	52	0	0	0	5	52¹	47	8	20	33	11.5	3.44	122	.241	.312	0	.000	-0	4	4	0	0.6
1988 Mon-N	1	3	.250	19	0	0	0	0	19	23	3	6	12	14.2	6.16	58	.307	.366	0	.000	-0	-6	-5	0	-1.2
NY-N	1	0	1.000	14	0	0	0	0	11	12	1	2	7	12.3	4.09	79	.279	.326	0	—	0	-1	-1	-0	-0.1
Yr	2	3	.400	33	0	0	0	0	30	35	4	8	19	13.2	5.40	64	.289	.338	0	.000	-0	-7	-6	-1	-1.3
1989 Cal-A	6	1	.857	48	0	0	0	3	52¹	39	2	15	36	9.5	1.55	246	.212	.275	0	—	0	14	13	-1	1.7
1990 Cal-A	2	0	1.000	11	0	0	0	0	7	7	0	3	6	12.9	6.43	59	.269	.345	0	—	0	-2	-2	0	-0.5
1991 Cal-A	0	0	—	13	0	0	0	0	9²	13	3	5	10	17.7	9.31	44	.317	.404	0	—	0	-6	-6	0	-0.7
StL-N	1	1	.500	32	0	0	0	0	23	14	1	8	15	12.9	3.13	119	.282	.351	1	1.000	0	1	1	-0	0.2
1992 StL-N	2	2	.500	71	0	0	0	0	54	52	1	25	24	13.2	3.17	107	.261	.350	0	.000	-0	2	1	0	0.1
1993 Fla-N	1	1	.500	14	0	0	0	0	6¹	13	1	2	5	25.6	7.11	61	.419	.500	0	—	0	-2	-2	0	-0.5
Total 19	68	57	.544	698	73	12	1	52	1158²	1125	104	497	701	12.9	3.81	101	.257	.338	2	.222	0	21	6	-4	1.1

● HARRY McCLUSKEY   McCluskey, Harry Robert b: 3/29/1892, Clay Center, Ohio d: 6/7/62, Toledo, Ohio BL/TL, 5'11.5", 173 lbs. Deb: 7/29/15

YEAR TM/L	W	L	PCT	G	GS	CG	SH	SV	IP	H	HR	BB	SO	RAT	ERA	ERA+	OAV	OOB	BH	AVG	PB	PR	/A	PD	TPI
1915 Cin-N	0	0	—	3	0	0	0	0	5	4	0	2	4	7.2	5.40	53	.182	.182	0	—	0	-1	-1	-0	-0.1

● ALEX McCOLL   McColl, Alexander Boyd "Red" b: 3/29/1894, Eagleville, Ohio d: 2/6/91, Kingsville, Ohio BB/TR, 6'1", 178 lbs. Deb: 8/27/33

YEAR TM/L	W	L	PCT	G	GS	CG	SH	SV	IP	H	HR	BB	SO	RAT	ERA	ERA+	OAV	OOB	BH	AVG	PB	PR	/A	PD	TPI
1933 *Was-A	1	0	1.000	4	1	1	0	0	17	13	0	7	5	10.6	2.65	158	.210	.290	2	.333	1	3	3	-0	0.2
1934 Was-A	3	4	.429	42	2	1	0	1	112	129	6	36	29	13.3	3.86	112	.291	.345	3	.097	-2	8	6	2	0.3
Total 2	4	4	.500	46	3	2	0	1	129	142	6	43	34	13.0	3.70	116	.281	.338	5	.135	-1	11	9	2	0.5

● RALPH McCONNAUGHEY   McConnaughey, Ralph James b: 8/5/1889, Vandergrift, Pa. d: 6/4/66, Detroit, Mich. BR/TR, 5'8.5", 166 lbs. Deb: 7/8/14

YEAR TM/L	W	L	PCT	G	GS	CG	SH	SV	IP	H	HR	BB	SO	RAT	ERA	ERA+	OAV	OOB	BH	AVG	PB	PR	/A	PD	TPI
1914 Ind-F	0	2	.000	7	2	1	0	0	26	23	3	16	7	13.8	4.85	64	.245	.360	1	.125	-0	-6	-5	-0	-0.4

● GEORGE McCONNELL   McConnell, George Neely "Slats"
b: 9/16/1877, Shelbyville, Tenn d: 5/10/64, Chattanooga, Tenn.   BR/TR, 6'3", 190 lbs. Deb: 4/13/09 ♦

YEAR TM/L	W	L	PCT	G	GS	CG	SH	SV	IP	H	HR	BB	SO	RAT	ERA	ERA+	OAV	OOB	BH	AVG	PB	PR	/A	PD	TPI
1909 NY-A	0	1	.000	2	1	1	0	0	8	4	0	3	3	13.5	2.25	112	.231	.375	9	.209	0	0	0	1	0.1
1912 NY-A	8	12	.400	23	20	19	0	0	176²	172	3	52	91	11.6	2.75	131	.269	.328	27	.297	3	11	17	5	2.9
1913 NY-A	4	15	.211	35	20	8	0	0	180	162	2	60	72	11.4	3.20	94	.245	.314	12	.179	-1	-5	-4	5	-0.1
1914 Chi-N	0	1	.000	1	1	0	0	0	7	3	0	3	2	7.7	1.29	216	.125	.222	0	.000	-0	1	1	0	0.2
1915 Chi-F	25	10	.714	44	35	23	4	1	303	262	8	89	151	10.7	2.20	114	.232	.292	31	.248	4	18	11	3	2.0
1916 Chi-N	4	12	.250	28	21	8	1	0	171²	137	8	35	84	9.3	2.57	113	.223	.271	9	.158	-2	1	6	2	0.6
Total 6	41	51	.446	133	98	58	5	4	842	739	21	242	403	10.7	2.60	112	.240	.300	88	.229	4	26	30	15	5.7

● BILLY McCOOL   McCool, William John b: 7/14/44, Batesville, Ind.   BR/TL, 6'2", 203 lbs. Deb: 4/24/64

YEAR TM/L	W	L	PCT	G	GS	CG	SH	SV	IP	H	HR	BB	SO	RAT	ERA	ERA+	OAV	OOB	BH	AVG	PB	PR	/A	PD	TPI
1964 Cin-N	6	5	.545	40	3	0	0	7	89¹	66	3	29	87	9.7	2.42	150	.206	.274	0	.000	-2	11	12	-2	1.3
1965 Cin-N	9	10	.474	62	2	0	0	21	105¹	93	9	47	120	12.3	4.27	88	.237	.324	1	.037	-0	-9	-6	-0	-1.5
1966 Cin-N☆	8	8	.500	57	0	0	0	18	105¹	76	6	41	104	10.3	2.48	157	.205	.290	3	.167	-0	13	17	2	3.4
1967 Cin-N	3	7	.300	31	11	0	0	7	97¹	92	6	53	87	14.1	3.42	110	.246	.352	2	.077	-1	-1	4	-1	0.2
1968 Cin-N	3	4	.429	30	4	0	0	2	50²	59	4	41	30	17.8	4.97	64	.294	.413	1	.125	-0	-11	-10	-1	-1.6
1969 SD-N	3	5	.375	54	0	0	0	7	58²	59	2	42	35	16.4	4.30	82	.266	.396	0	.000	-0	-5	-5	-0	-0.8
1970 StL-N	0	3	.000	18	0	0	0	0	21²	20	0	16	12	15.0	6.23	66	.250	.375	0	.000	-0	-5	-5	-0	-0.7
Total 7	32	42	.432	292	20	0	0	58	528¹	465	31	272	471	12.9	3.59	103	.236	.338	7	.069	-6	-6	6	-3	0.3

● JIM McCORMICK   McCormick, James b: 11/3/1856, Glasgow, Scotland d: 3/10/18, Paterson, N.J. BR/TR, 5'10.5", 215 lbs. Deb: 5/20/1878   M

YEAR TM/L	W	L	PCT	G	GS	CG	SH	SV	IP	H	HR	BB	SO	RAT	ERA	ERA+	OAV	OOB	BH	AVG	PB	PR	/A	PD	TPI
1878 Ind-N	5	8	.385	14	14	12	1	0	117	128	4	15	36	11.0	1.69	120	.269	.292	8	.143	-3	8	4	2	0.3
1879 Cle-N	20	40	.333	62	60	59	3	0	546¹	582	4	74	197	10.8	2.42	103	.259	.282	62	.220	-1	4	5	4	0.7

YEAR	TM/L	W	L	PCT	G	GS	CG	SH	SV	IP	H	HR	BB	SO	RAT	ERA	ERA+	OAV	OOB	BH	AVG	PB	PR	/A	PD	TPI
1880	Cle-N	45	28	.616	74	74	72	7	0	657²	585	2	75	260	9.0	1.85	127	.226	.247	71	.246	1	38	37	1	4.0
1881	Cle-N	26	30	.464	59	58	57	2	0	526	484	4	84	178	9.7	2.45	107	.235	.265	79	.256	6	19	10	-3	1.2
1882	Cle-N	36	30	.545	68	67	65	4	0	595²	550	14	103	200	9.9	2.37	118	.238	.271	57	.218	-4	35	28	-2	2.0
1883	Cle-N	28	12	.700	43	41	36	1	1	342	316	1	65	145	10.0	1.84	171	.233	.268	37	.236	-1	49	50	7	5.4
1884	Cle-N	19	22	.463	42	41	39	3	0	359	357	17	75	182	10.8	2.86	110	.247	.285	50	.263	2	5	12	0	1.3
	Cin-U	21	3	.875	24	24	24	7	0	210	151	3	14	161	7.1	1.54	166	.188	.202	27	.245	-6	21	24	2	1.8
1885	Pro-N	1	3	.250	4	4	4	0	0	37	34	1	20	8	13.1	2.43	109	.234	.327	3	.214	0	2	1	3	0.4
	*Chi-N	20	4	.833	24	24	24	3	0	215	187	8	40	88	9.5	2.43	125	.224	.260	23	.223	0	9	15	3	1.6
	Yr	21	7	.750	28	28	28	3	0	252	221	9	60	96	10.0	2.43	123	.226	.271	26	.222	1	11	15	5	2.0
1886	*Chi-N	31	11	.738	42	42	38	2	0	347²	341	18	100	172	11.4	2.82	129	.253	.304	41	.236	2	19	32	2	3.4
1887	Pit-N	13	23	.361	36	36	36	0	0	322¹	377	12	84	77	13.2	4.30	90	.285	.334	33	.243	-0	-8	-15	-5	0.9
Total 10		265	214	.553	492	485	466	33	1	4275²	4092	84	749	1704	10.2	2.43	117	.242	.274	491	.236	-4	202	201	22	21.2

● JERRY McCORMICK
McCormick, John b: Philadelphia, Pa. d: 9/19/05, Philadelphia, Pa. Deb: 5/1/1883 ♦

YEAR	TM/L	W	L	PCT	G	GS	CG	SH	SV	IP	H	HR	BB	SO	RAT	ERA	ERA+	OAV	OOB	BH	AVG	PB	PR	/A	PD	TPI
1884	Phi-U	0	0	—	1	0	0	0	0	2	5	1	0	3	22.5	9.00	26	.455	.455	84	.285	-0	-1	-1	-0	0.0

● MIKE McCORMICK
McCormick, Michael Francis b: 9/29/38, Pasadena, Cal. BL/TL, 6'2", 195 lbs. Deb: 9/3/56

YEAR	TM/L	W	L	PCT	G	GS	CG	SH	SV	IP	H	HR	BB	SO	RAT	ERA	ERA+	OAV	OOB	BH	AVG	PB	PR	/A	PD	TPI
1956	NY-N	0	1	.000	3	2	0	0	0	7	1	10	4	23.0		9.45	40	.269	.472	0	.000	-0	-4	-4	-0	-0.5
1957	NY-N	3	1	.750	24	5	1	0	0	74²	79	7	32	50	13.7	4.10	96	.280	.360	6	.273	1	-2	-1	-1	0.0
1958	SF-N	11	8	.579	42	28	8	2	1	178¹	192	19	60	82	12.9	4.59	83	.276	.336	12	.222	1	-13	-15	2	-1.2
1959	SF-N	12	16	.429	47	31	7	3	4	225²	213	24	86	151	12.0	3.99	96	.248	.317	7	.106	-2	-1	-4	1	-0.6
1960	SF-N★	15	12	.556	40	34	15	4	3	253	228	15	65	154	10.5	2.70	129	.241	.291	16	.182	1	30	22	3	2.7
1961	SF-N★	13	16	.448	40	35	13	3	0	250	235	33	75	163	11.2	3.20	119	.249	.306	15	.188	1	23	17	-2	1.7
1962	SF-N	5	5	.500	28	15	1	0	0	98²	112	18	45	42	14.4	5.38	71	.286	.361	3	.107	0	-16	-17	-1	-1.6
1963	Bal-A	6	8	.429	25	21	2	0	0	136	132	18	66	75	13.1	4.30	81	.256	.340	8	.174	1	-10	-13	-0	-1.2
1964	Bal-A	0	2	.000	4	2	0	0	0	17¹	21	1	8	13	15.1	5.19	69	.288	.358	1	.167	-0	-3	-3	-0	-0.3
1965	Was-A	8	8	.500	44	21	3	1	1	158	158	17	36	88	11.1	3.36	103	.260	.301	3	.073	-1	2	2	-1	0.0
1966	Was-A	11	14	.440	41	32	8	3	0	216	193	23	51	101	10.3	3.46	100	.236	.282	14	.212	3	-1	0	-1	0.3
1967	SF-N	22	10	.688	40	35	14	5	0	262¹	220	25	81	150	10.5	2.85	115	.226	.289	10	.119	0	15	13	-2	1.3
1968	SF-N	12	14	.462	38	28	4	0	0	198¹	196	17	49	121	11.2	3.58	82	.254	.300	6	.103	1	-13	-14	-2	-2.0
1969	SF-N	11	9	.550	32	28	9	0	0	196²	175	20	77	76	11.6	3.34	105	.237	.310	9	.136	1	6	3	-1	0.3
1970	SF-N	3	4	.429	23	11	1	0	2	78¹	80	15	36	37	13.7	6.20	64	.262	.346	4	.160	0	-19	-19	1	-1.5
	NY-A	2	0	1.000	9	4	0	0	0	20²	26	2	13	12	17.0	6.10	58	.295	.386	1	.200	-0	-5	-6	-1	-0.6
1971	KC-A	0	0	—	4	1	0	0	0	9²	14	0	5	2	17.7	9.31	37	.350	.422	0	.000	-0	-6	-6	1	0.1
Total 16		134	128	.511	484	333	91	23	12	2380¹	2281	255	795	1321	11.7	3.73	95	.251	.313	115	.156	9	-18	-46	-5	-3.1

● HARRY McCORMICK
McCormick, Patrick Henry b: 10/25/1855, Syracuse, N.Y. d: 8/8/1889, Syracuse, N.Y. BR/TR, 5'9", 155 lbs. Deb: 5/1/1879

YEAR	TM/L	W	L	PCT	G	GS	CG	SH	SV	IP	H	HR	BB	SO	RAT	ERA	ERA+	OAV	OOB	BH	AVG	PB	PR	/A	PD	TPI
1879	Syr-N	18	33	.353	54	54	49	5	0	457¹	517	3	31	96	10.8	2.99	79	.266	.277	51	.222	1	-25	-32	-7	-3.4
1881	Wor-N	1	8	.111	9	9	9	1	0	78¹	89	1	15	7	11.9	3.56	85	.275	.307	6	.133	-2	-7	-5	-1	-0.7
1882	Cin-a	14	11	.560	25	25	24	3	0	219²	177	4	42	33	9.0	1.52	174	.206	.243	12	.129	-5	29	27	0	2.1
1883	Cin-a	8	6	.571	15	15	14	1	0	128²	139	1	27	21	11.6	2.87	113	.258	.294	17	.309	4	6	5	1	0.8
Total 4		41	58	.414	103	103	96	10	0	884	922	9	115	157	10.6	2.66	98	.252	.274	86	.203	-4	3	-4	-7	-1.2

● BILL McCORRY
McCorry, William Charles b: 7/9/1887, Saranac Lake, N.Y. d: 3/22/73, Augusta, Ga. BL/TR, 5'9", 157 lbs. Deb: 9/17/09

YEAR	TM/L	W	L	PCT	G	GS	CG	SH	SV	IP	H	HR	BB	SO	RAT	ERA	ERA+	OAV	OOB	BH	AVG	PB	PR	/A	PD	TPI
1909	StL-A	0	2	.000	2	2	0	0	0	15	29	1	6	10	21.0	9.00	27	.397	.443	0	.000	-0	-11	-11	-1	-1.1

● LES McCRABB
McCrabb, Lester William "Buster" b: 11/4/14, Wakefield, Pa. BR/TR, 5'11", 175 lbs. Deb: 9/7/39 C

YEAR	TM/L	W	L	PCT	G	GS	CG	SH	SV	IP	H	HR	BB	SO	RAT	ERA	ERA+	OAV	OOB	BH	AVG	PB	PR	/A	PD	TPI
1939	Phi-A	1	2	.333	5	4	2	0	0	35²	42	4	10	11	13.4	4.04	117	.290	.340	0	.000	-2	2	3	-0	0.0
1940	Phi-A	0	0	—	4	0	0	0	0	11²	19	2	2	4	17.0	6.94	64	.365	.400	1	.250	0	-3	-3	0	0.0
1941	Phi-A	9	13	.409	26	23	11	1	2	157¹	188	16	49	40	13.7	5.49	76	.293	.346	8	.143	-2	-24	-23	-2	-3.0
1942	Phi-A	0	0	—	1	0	0	0	0	2	14	2	2	0	38.3	31.50	17	.560	.607	0	.000	-0	-12	-12	0	0.0
1950	Phi-A	0	0	—	2	0	0	0	0	1¹	7	0	0	2	47.3	27.00	17	.636	.636	0	—	0	-3	-3	0	0.0
Total 5		10	15	.400	38	27	13	1	2	210	270	24	63	57	14.5	5.96	72	.309	.359	9	.122	-4	-40	-39	-3	-3.0

● ED McCREERY
McCreery, Esley Porterfield "Big Ed" b: 12/24/1889, Cripple Creek, Colo. d: 10/19/60, Sacramento, Cal. BR/TR, 6', 190 lbs. Deb: 8/16/14

YEAR	TM/L	W	L	PCT	G	GS	CG	SH	SV	IP	H	HR	BB	SO	RAT	ERA	ERA+	OAV	OOB	BH	AVG	PB	PR	/A	PD	TPI
1914	Det-A	1	0	1.000	3	1	0	0	0	4	6	0	3	4	20.3	11.25	25	.316	.409	0	.000	-0	-4	-4	0	-0.8

● TOM McCREERY
McCreery, Thomas Livingston b: 10/19/1874, Beaver, Pa. d: 7/3/41, Beaver, Pa. BB/TR, 5'11", 180 lbs. Deb: 6/8/1895 ♦

YEAR	TM/L	W	L	PCT	G	GS	CG	SH	SV	IP	H	HR	BB	SO	RAT	ERA	ERA+	OAV	OOB	BH	AVG	PB	PR	/A	PD	TPI
1895	Lou-N	3	1	.750	8	4	3	1	1	48²	51	0	38	14	17.4	5.36	86	.266	.400	35	.324	1	-3	-4	1	0.0
1896	Lou-N	0	1	.000	1	1	0	0	0	9	4	1	5	0	81.0	36.00	12	.571	.750	155	.351	0	-4	-4	0	-1.4
1900	Pit-N	0	0	—	1	0	0	0	0	3	3	2	1	0	12.0	12.00	30	.250	.308	29	.220	0	-3	-3	0	0.0
Total 3		3	2	.600	10	5	3	1	1	52²	58	3	44	14	18.3	6.32	72	.275	.412	855	.290	2	-9	-10	1	-1.4

● LANCE McCULLERS
McCullers, Lance Graye b: 3/8/64, Tampa, Fla. BB/TR, 6'1", 218 lbs. Deb: 8/12/85

YEAR	TM/L	W	L	PCT	G	GS	CG	SH	SV	IP	H	HR	BB	SO	RAT	ERA	ERA+	OAV	OOB	BH	AVG	PB	PR	/A	PD	TPI
1985	SD-N	0	2	.000	21	0	0	0	0	35	23	3	16	27	10.3	2.31	153	.195	.296	0	.000	-0	5	5	0	0.4
1986	SD-N	10	10	.500	70	7	0	0	5	136	103	12	58	92	10.9	2.78	131	.216	.306	2	.091	0	14	13	-1	1.9
1987	SD-N	8	10	.444	78	0	0	0	16	123¹	115	11	59	126	12.8	3.72	106	.244	.331	1	.071	-1	5	3	1	1.2
1988	SD-N	3	6	.333	60	0	0	0	10	97²	70	8	55	81	11.5	2.49	136	.205	.315	2	.250	-1	10	10	0	1.2
1989	NY-A	4	3	.571	52	1	0	0	3	84²	83	9	37	82	13.1	4.57	85	.255	.337	0	—	0	-6	-7	-0	-0.5
1990	NY-A	1	0	1.000	11	0	0	0	0	15	14	2	6	11	12.0	3.60	110	.241	.313	0	—	0	1	1	0	0.1
	Det-A	1	0	1.000	9	1	0	0	0	29²	18	2	13	20	9.4	2.73	145	.170	.261	0	—	0	4	4	-1	0.1
	Yr	2	0	1.000	20	1	0	0	0	44²	32	4	19	31	10.3	3.02	131	.194	.277	0	—	0	4	5	-1	0.1
1992	Tex-A	1	0	1.000	5	1	0	0	1	8¹	5	0	3	16	16.2	5.40	70	.067	.391	0	—	0	-1	-1	0	0.0
Total 7		28	31	.475	306	10	0	0	39	526¹	427	47	252	442	11.8	3.25	115	.223	.317	5	.104	0	32	28	-1	3.6

● CHARLIE McCULLOUGH
McCullough, Charles F. b: 1867, Dublin, Ireland Deb: 4/23/1890

YEAR	TM/L	W	L	PCT	G	GS	CG	SH	SV	IP	H	HR	BB	SO	RAT	ERA	ERA+	OAV	OOB	BH	AVG	PB	PR	/A	PD	TPI
1890	Bro-a	4	21	.160	26	25	24	0	0	215²	247	5	102	61	15.2	4.59	85	.279	.364	2	.023	-12	-17	-17	-2	-2.7
	Syr-a	1	2	.333	3	3	3	0	0	26	29	1	14	8	14.9	7.27	49	.274	.358	1	.111	0	-10	-11	-0	-0.9
	Yr	5	23	.179	29	28	27	0	0	241²	276	6	116	69	14.6	4.88	79	.274	.349	3	.032	-12	-27	-27	-3	-3.6

● PAUL McCULLOUGH
McCullough, Paul Willard b: 7/28/1898, New Castle, Pa. d: 11/7/70, New Castle, Pa. BR/TR, 5'9.5", 190 lbs. Deb: 7/2/29

YEAR	TM/L	W	L	PCT	G	GS	CG	SH	SV	IP	H	HR	BB	SO	RAT	ERA	ERA+	OAV	OOB	BH	AVG	PB	PR	/A	PD	TPI
1929	Was-A	0	0	—	3	0	0	0	0	7¹	7	1	2	3	11.0	8.59	49	.250	.300	0	.000	-0	-4	-4	0	0.0

● PHIL McCULLOUGH
McCullough, Pinson Lamar b: 7/22/17, Stockbridge, Ga. BR/TR, 6'4", 204 lbs. Deb: 4/22/42

YEAR	TM/L	W	L	PCT	G	GS	CG	SH	SV	IP	H	HR	BB	SO	RAT	ERA	ERA+	OAV	OOB	BH	AVG	PB	PR	/A	PD	TPI
1942	Was-A	0	0	—	1	0	0	0	0	3	5	0	3	2	21.0	6.00	61	.333	.412	0	.000	-0	-1	-1	0	0.0

● JEFF McCURRY
McCurry, Jeffrey Dee b: 1/21/70, Tokyo, Japan BR/TR, 6'7", 210 lbs. Deb: 5/6/95

YEAR	TM/L	W	L	PCT	G	GS	CG	SH	SV	IP	H	HR	BB	SO	RAT	ERA	ERA+	OAV	OOB	BH	AVG	PB	PR	/A	PD	TPI
1995	Pit-N	1	4	.200	55	0	0	0	1	61	82	9	30	27	17.3	5.02	86	.337	.421	0	.000	-0	-6	-5	0	-0.4
1996	Det-A	0	0	—	2	0	0	0	0	3¹	9	3	2	0	29.7	24.30	21	.474	.524	0	—	0	-7	-7	1	0.1
Total 2		1	4	.200	57	0	0	0	1	64¹	91	12	32	27	17.9	6.02	72	.347	.428	0	.000	-0	-13	-12	1	-0.3

● LINDY McDANIEL
McDaniel, Lyndall Dale b: 12/13/35, Hollis, Okla. BR/TR, 6'3", 195 lbs. Deb: 9/2/55 F

YEAR	TM/L	W	L	PCT	G	GS	CG	SH	SV	IP	H	HR	BB	SO	RAT	ERA	ERA+	OAV	OOB	BH	AVG	PB	PR	/A	PD	TPI
1955	StL-N	0	0	—	4	2	0	0	0	19	22	4	7	7	13.7	4.74	86	.293	.354	1	.200	-0	-1	-1	-0	0.0
1956	StL-N	7	6	.538	39	7	1	0	0	116¹	121	7	42	59	12.6	3.40	111	.273	.335	7	.219	2	5	5	1	0.8
1957	StL-N	15	9	.625	30	26	10	1	0	191	196	13	53	75	11.9	3.49	114	.266	.317	19	.257	4	8	10	0	1.6
1958	StL-N	5	7	.417	26	17	2	1	0	108²	139	17	31	47	14.2	5.80	71	.305	.352	2	.067	-3	-22	-20	1	-2.1
1959	StL-N	14	12	.538	62	7	1	0	0	132	144	11	41	86	12.7	3.82	111	.283	.338	1	.034	-2	2	6	2	1.3
1960	StL-N★	12	4	.750	65	2	1	0	26	116¹	85	8	24	105	8.5	2.09	196	.207	.253	6	.231	1	22	26	1	5.0
1961	StL-N	10	6	.625	55	0	0	0	0	94¹	117	11	31	65	14.3	4.87	90	.305	.361	4	.235	-0	-9	-5	1	0.1
1962	StL-N	3	10	.231	55	2	0	0	14	107	96	12	29	75	10.6	4.12	104	.239	.292	2	.095	-1	-2	2	0	0.4
1963	Chi-N	13	7	.650	57	0	0	0	22	88	82	9	27	75	11.1	2.86	123	.251	.308	2	.091	-0	4	6	0	1.8
1964	Chi-N	1	7	.125	63	0	0	0	15	95	104	4	23	71	12.1	3.88	96	.276	.319	2	.125	-1	-4	-2	0	-0.3

YEAR	TM/L	W	L	PCT	G	GS	CG	SH	SV	IP	H	HR	BB	SO	RAT	ERA	ERA+	OAV	OOB	BH	AVG	PB	PR	/A	PD	TPI
1965	Chi-N	5	6	.455	71	0	0	0	2	128²	115	12	47	92	11.3	2.59	142	.241	.309	0	.000	-1	14	16	2	1.5
1966	SF-N	10	5	.667	64	0	0	0	6	121²	103	5	35	93	10.2	2.66	138	.228	.284	2	.091	-1	13	14	1	1.7
1967	SF-N	2	6	.250	41	3	0	0	3	72²	69	5	24	48	11.8	3.72	88	.248	.313	1	.091	-1	-3	-3	2	-0.3
1968	SF-N	0	0	—	12	0	0	0	0	19¹	30	2	5	9	16.3	7.45	40	.357	.393	0	.000	-0	-10	-10	0	0.0
	NY-A	4	1	.800	24	0	0	0	10	51¹	30	5	12	43	7.5	1.75	165	.166	.222	0	.000	-1	7	7	2	1.1
1969	NY-A	5	6	.455	51	0	0	0	5	83²	84	5	23	60	11.5	3.55	98	.261	.310	0	.000	-1	1	-1	1	0.0
1970	NY-A	9	5	.643	62	0	0	0	29	111²	88	7	23	81	8.9	2.01	174	.217	.259	4	.167	0	21	19	1	3.3
1971	NY-A	5	10	.333	44	0	0	0	4	69²	82	12	24	39	13.7	5.04	64	.296	.352	1	.111	-0	-12	-14	0	-3.0
1972	NY-A	3	1	.750	37	0	0	0	0	68	54	4	25	47	10.5	2.25	131	.217	.288	2	.286	1	6	5	1	0.6
1973	NY-A	12	6	.667	47	3	1	0	10	160¹	148	11	49	93	11.1	2.86	128	.250	.309	0	.000	0	17	14	3	2.0
1974	KC-A	1	4	.200	38	5	2	0	1	106²	109	6	24	47	11.2	3.46	110	.265	.306	0	—	0	2	4	1	0.2
1975	KC-A	5	1	.833	40	0	0	0	1	78	81	9	3	24	40	12.1	4.15	93	.273	.327	0	—	0	-3	-3	-0	-0.3
Total	21	141	119	.542	987	74	18	2	172	2139¹	2099	172	623	1361	11.5	3.45	109	.258	.312	56	.148	-3	55	74	23	14.6

● **VON McDANIEL**   McDaniel, Max Von b: 4/18/39, Hollis, Okla. d: 8/20/95, Lawton, Okla. BR/TR, 6'2.5", 180 lbs. Deb: 6/13/57 F

YEAR	TM/L	W	L	PCT	G	GS	CG	SH	SV	IP	H	HR	BB	SO	RAT	ERA	ERA+	OAV	OOB	BH	AVG	PB	PR	/A	PD	TPI
1957	StL-N	7	5	.583	17	13	4	2	0	86²	71	7	31	45	10.7	3.22	123	.225	.296	0	.000	-3	6	7	-1	0.5
1958	StL-N	0	0	—	2	1	0	0	0	2	5	0	5	0	45.0	13.50	31	.500	.667	0	—	0	-2	-2	-0	0.0
Total	2	7	5	.583	19	14	4	2	0	88²	76	7	36	45	11.5	3.45	115	.233	.311	0	.000	-3	4	5	-1	0.5

● **JOE McDERMOTT**   McDermott, Joseph Deb: 5/4/1871 ♦

YEAR	TM/L	W	L	PCT	G	GS	CG	SH	SV	IP	H	HR	BB	SO	RAT	ERA	ERA+	OAV	OOB	BH	AVG	PB	PR	/A	PD	TPI
1872	Eck-n	0	7	.000	7	7	7	0	0	63	143	3	12	1	22.1	8.14	42	.377	.396	9	.281	2	-32	-33		-2.0

● **MICKEY McDERMOTT**   McDermott, Maurice Joseph "Maury" b: 8/29/28, Poughkeepsie, N.Y. BL/TL, 6'2", 170 lbs. Deb: 4/24/48 C♦

YEAR	TM/L	W	L	PCT	G	GS	CG	SH	SV	IP	H	HR	BB	SO	RAT	ERA	ERA+	OAV	OOB	BH	AVG	PB	PR	/A	PD	TPI
1948	Bos-A	0	0	—	7	0	0	0	0	23¹	16	2	35	17	20.1	6.17	71	.208	.460	3	.375	1	-5	-5	1	0.2
1949	Bos-A	5	4	.556	12	12	6	2	0	80	63	5	52	50	13.3	4.05	108	.220	.345	7	.212	1	1	3	-0	0.3
1950	Bos-A	7	3	.700	38	15	4	0	5	130	119	8	124	96	17.0	5.19	94	.249	.406	16	.364	6	-9	-4	1	0.3
1951	Bos-A	8	8	.500	34	19	9	1	3	172	141	10	92	127	12.5	3.35	140	.226	.330	18	.273	2	15	21	1	2.2
1952	Bos-A	10	9	.526	30	21	7	2	0	162	139	14	92	117	13.0	3.72	106	.234	.340	14	.226	3	-1	-4	-0	0.7
1953	Bos-A	18	10	.643	32	30	8	4	0	206¹	169	10	109	92	12.2	3.01	140	.224	.323	28	.301	7	23	27	1	4.4
1954	Was-A	7	15	.318	30	26	11	1	1	196¹	172	8	110	95	13.1	3.44	103	.239	.342	19	.200	3	6	3	1	0.6
1955	Was-A	10	10	.500	31	20	8	1	1	156	140	9	100	78	14.4	3.75	102	.243	.364	25	.263	7	4	1	0	1.0
1956	*NY-A	2	6	.250	23	9	1	0	0	87	85	10	47	38	13.7	4.24	91	.261	.354	11	.212	1	-1	-4	-0	-0.1
1957	KC-A	1	4	.200	29	4	0	0	0	69	68	9	50	29	15.4	5.48	72	.266	.386	12	.245	3	-13	-12	1	0.0
1958	Det-A	0	0	—	2	0	0	0	0	2	6	0	2	0	36.0	9.00	45	.500	.571	1	.333	0	-1	-1	-0	0.0
1961	StL-N	1	0	1.000	19	0	0	0	0	27	29	3	15	15	14.7	3.67	120	.271	.361	1	.071	-1	1	2	-0	0.0
	KC-A	0	0	—	4	0	0	0	0	5²	14	0	10	3	38.1	14.29	29	.452	.585	1	.200	1	-6	-6	-0	-0.0
Total	12	69	69	.500	291	156	54	11	14	1316²	1161	88	838	757	13.9	3.91	105	.240	.355	156	.252	36	14	29	4	9.6

● **MIKE McDERMOTT**   McDermott, Michael H. b: 5/6/1864, Fall River, Mass. d: 5/7/47, Fall River, Mass. 5'10", 152 lbs. Deb: 9/2/1889

YEAR	TM/L	W	L	PCT	G	GS	CG	SH	SV	IP	H	HR	BB	SO	RAT	ERA	ERA+	OAV	OOB	BH	AVG	PB	PR	/A	PD	TPI
1889	Lou-a	1	8	.111	9	9	9	0	0	84¹	108	4	34	12	15.4	4.16	92	.302	.365	6	.182	-1	-3	-3	-0	-0.3

● **MIKE McDERMOTT**   McDermott, Michael Joseph b: 9/7/1862, St.Louis, Mo. d: 6/30/43, St.Louis, Mo. TR, 5'8", 145 lbs. Deb: 4/20/1895

YEAR	TM/L	W	L	PCT	G	GS	CG	SH	SV	IP	H	HR	BB	SO	RAT	ERA	ERA+	OAV	OOB	BH	AVG	PB	PR	/A	PD	TPI
1895	Lou-N	4	19	.174	33	26	18	0	0	207¹	258	8	103	42	16.1	5.99	77	.300	.382	13	.159	-2	-28	-31	1	-2.5
1896	Lou-N	2	7	.222	12	10	4	1	0	65	87	4	44	12	19.0	7.34	59	.318	.423	8	.296	1	-21	-22	1	-2.0
1897	Cle-N	4	5	.444	9	7	4	0	0	62	75	2	25	12	15.0	4.50	100	.296	.367	8	.320	1	-1	-0	1	0.2
	StL-N	1	2	.333	4	4	1	0	0	21¹	23	2	19	3	17.7	9.28	47	.274	.408	2	.222	-0	-12	-12	1	-1.1
	Yr	5	7	.417	13	11	5	0	0	83¹	98	4	44	15	15.3	5.72	78	.288	.370	10	.294	1	-13	-12	2	-0.9
Total	3	11	33	.250	58	47	27	1	0	355²	443	16	191	69	16.5	6.17	74	.301	.389	31	.217	0	-62	-64	4	-5.4

● **DANNY McDEVITT**   McDevitt, Daniel Eugene b: 11/18/32, New York, N.Y. BL/TL, 5'10", 175 lbs. Deb: 6/17/57

YEAR	TM/L	W	L	PCT	G	GS	CG	SH	SV	IP	H	HR	BB	SO	RAT	ERA	ERA+	OAV	OOB	BH	AVG	PB	PR	/A	PD	TPI
1957	Bro-N	7	4	.636	22	17	5	2	0	119	105	5	72	90	13.8	3.25	128	.238	.353	6	.154	-0	8	12	2	1.2
1958	LA-N	2	6	.250	13	10	2	0	0	48¹	71	6	31	26	19.0	7.45	55	.355	.442	2	.133	-0	-19	-18	-1	-2.5
1959	LA-N	10	8	.556	39	22	6	2	4	145	149	16	51	106	13.3	3.97	106	.263	.339	5	.109	-2	-0	4	-0	0.3
1960	LA-N	0	4	.000	24	7	0	0	0	53	51	7	42	30	16.8	4.25	93	.260	.406	2	.200	-0	-3	-2	-0	-0.1
1961	NY-A	1	2	.333	8	2	0	0	1	13	18	2	8	9	18.7	7.62	49	.353	.450	0	.000	-0	-5	-6	0	-1.1
	Min-A	1	0	1.000	16	1	0	0	0	26²	20	1	19	15	14.5	2.36	179	.213	.368	0	.000	-0	5	6	0	0.2
	Yr	2	2	.500	24	3	0	0	1	39²	38	3	27	23	15.7	4.08	100	.259	.388	0	.000	-0	-0	-0	0	-0.9
1962	KC-A	0	3	.000	33	1	0	0	0	51	47	5	41	28	15.7	5.82	73	.250	.387	2	.222	0	-11	-9	1	-0.5
Total	6	21	27	.438	155	60	13	4	7	456	461	42	264	303	14.9	4.40	94	.265	.372	17	.138	-3	-25	-13	2	-2.5

● **HANK McDONALD**   McDonald, Henry Monroe b: 1/16/11, Santa Monica, Cal. d: 10/17/82, Hemet, Cal. BR/TR, 6'3", 200 lbs. Deb: 4/16/31

YEAR	TM/L	W	L	PCT	G	GS	CG	SH	SV	IP	H	HR	BB	SO	RAT	ERA	ERA+	OAV	OOB	BH	AVG	PB	PR	/A	PD	TPI
1931	Phi-A	2	4	.333	19	10	1	1	0	70¹	72	6	3	41	23	13.3	3.71	121	.239	.346	2	.095	-1	5	6	-1	0.3
1933	Phi-A	1	1	.500	4	1	0	0	0	12¹	14	0	4	1	13.1	5.11	84	.264	.316	0	.000	-0	-1	-1	-0	-0.2
	StL-A	0	4	.000	25	5	0	0	0	58¹	83	6	34	22	18.5	8.64	54	.332	.418	2	.143	-1	-28	-26	-0	-1.6
	Yr	1	5	.167	29	6	0	0	0	70²	97	6	38	23	17.6	8.02	57	.320	.401	2	.111	-1	-29	-27	-0	-1.8
Total	2	3	9	.250	48	16	1	1	0	141	159	12	79	46	15.4	5.87	77	.283	.375	4	.103	-2	-24	-21	-1	-1.5

● **JIM McDONALD**   McDonald, Jimmie Le Roy "Hot Rod" b: 5/17/27, Grants Pass, Ore. BR/TR, 5'10.5", 185 lbs. Deb: 7/27/50

YEAR	TM/L	W	L	PCT	G	GS	CG	SH	SV	IP	H	HR	BB	SO	RAT	ERA	ERA+	OAV	OOB	BH	AVG	PB	PR	/A	PD	TPI
1950	Bos-A	1	0	1.000	9	0	0	0	0	19	23	1	10	5	16.1	3.79	129	.329	.420	1	.333	1	2	2	1	0.3
1951	StL-A	4	7	.364	16	11	5	0	1	84	84	5	46	28	14.1	4.07	108	.260	.356	6	.207	-0	0	3	1	0.4
1952	NY-A	3	4	.429	26	5	1	0	0	69¹	71	4	40	20	14.7	3.50	95	.268	.368	6	.316	3	-1	-3	3	0.5
1953	*NY-A	9	7	.563	27	18	6	2	0	129²	128	4	39	43	11.7	3.82	97	.260	.316	4	.098	-3	3	-2	2	-0.3
1954	NY-A	4	1	.800	16	10	3	1	0	71	54	3	45	20	12.7	3.17	108	.213	.334	4	.211	2	4	2	1	0.4
1955	Bal-A	3	5	.375	21	8	0	0	0	51²	76	5	30	20	18.5	7.14	53	.345	.424	2	.182	-1	-18	-19	1	-2.3
1956	Chi-A	0	2	.000	8	3	0	0	0	18²	29	4	7	10	17.8	8.68	47	.377	.435	0	.000	-0	-9	-9	-0	-0.9
1957	Chi-A	0	0	—	10	0	0	0	0	22¹	18	0	12	11	11.3	2.01	185	.234	.322	0	.000	0	4	4	-0	0.2
1958	Chi-A	0	0	—	3	0	0	0	0	2¹	6	1	4	0	38.6	19.29	19	.429	.556	0	—	0	-4	-4	0	0.0
Total	9	24	27	.471	136	55	15	3	1	468	489	24	231	158	14.0	4.27	89	.273	.359	23	.180	4	-17	-25	8	-1.7

● **JOHN McDONALD**   McDonald, John Joseph (b: John Joseph McDonnell) b: 1/27/1883, Throop, Pa. d: 4/9/50, Roselle, N.J. BR/TR, 6'1", 170 lbs. Deb: 9/3/07

YEAR	TM/L	W	L	PCT	G	GS	CG	SH	SV	IP	H	HR	BB	SO	RAT	ERA	ERA+	OAV	OOB	BH	AVG	PB	PR	/A	PD	TPI
1907	Was-A	0	0	—	1	0	0	0	0	6	12	0	2	3	21.0	9.00	27	.414	.452	1	.333	1	-4	-4	-0	0.1

● **BEN McDONALD**   McDonald, Larry Benard b: 11/24/67, Baton Rouge, La. BR/TR, 6'7", 212 lbs. Deb: 9/6/89

YEAR	TM/L	W	L	PCT	G	GS	CG	SH	SV	IP	H	HR	BB	SO	RAT	ERA	ERA+	OAV	OOB	BH	AVG	PB	PR	/A	PD	TPI
1989	Bal-A	1	0	1.000	6	0	0	0	0	7¹	7	2	4	3	14.7	8.59	44	.286	.375	0	—	0	-4	-4	-0	-0.4
1990	Bal-A	8	5	.615	21	15	3	2	0	118²	88	9	35	65	9.3	2.43	156	.205	.265	0	—	0	20	18	0	1.9
1991	Bal-A	6	8	.429	21	21	1	0	0	126¹	126	16	43	85	12.1	4.84	82	.261	.323	0	—	0	-11	-13	-1	-1.3
1992	Bal-A	13	13	.500	35	35	4	2	0	227	213	32	74	158	11.7	4.24	95	.247	.313	0	—	0	-8	-6	1	-0.5
1993	Bal-A	13	14	.481	34	34	7	1	0	220¹	185	17	86	171	11.3	3.39	132	.228	.306	0	—	0	23	26	3	3.1
1994	Bal-A	14	7	.667	24	24	5	1	0	157¹	151	14	54	94	11.8	4.06	123	.255	.319	0	—	0	13	17	1	1.9
1995	Bal-A	3	6	.333	14	13	1	0	0	80	67	13	38	62	12.1	4.16	114	.224	.318	0	—	0	5	5	1	0.5
1996	Mil-A	12	10	.545	35	35	2	0	0	221¹	228	25	67	146	12.2	3.90	135	.264	.322	0	—	0	27	33	-0	2.5
Total	8	70	63	.526	190	177	23	6	0	1158¹	1066	125	401	784	11.6	3.89	115	.244	.311	0	—	0	65	76	4	7.7

● **McDOOLAN**   McDoolan Deb: 4/14/1873

YEAR	TM/L	W	L	PCT	G	GS	CG	SH	SV	IP	H	HR	BB	SO	RAT	ERA	ERA+	OAV	OOB	BH	AVG	PB	PR	/A	PD	TPI
1873	Mar-n	0	1	.000	1	1	1	0	0	9	18	0	0	0	18.0	3.00	108	.305	.305	0	.000	-1	0	0		0.0

● **SANDY McDOUGAL**   McDougal, John Auchanbolt b: 5/21/1874, Buffalo, N.Y. d: 10/2/10, Buffalo, N.Y. BR/TR, 5'10", 155 lbs. Deb: 6/12/1895

YEAR	TM/L	W	L	PCT	G	GS	CG	SH	SV	IP	H	HR	BB	SO	RAT	ERA	ERA+	OAV	OOB	BH	AVG	PB	PR	/A	PD	TPI
1895	Bro-N	0	0	—	1	0	0	0	1	3	5	0	5	2	24.0	12.00	37	.250	.471	0	—	0	-2	-5	-0	-0.2
1905	StL-N	1	4	.200	5	5	5	0	0	44²	50	5	12	10	12.5	3.43	87	.301	.348	2	.133	-0	-2	-2	3	0.0
Total	2	1	4	.200	6	5	5	0	1	47²	53	7	17	12	13.2	3.97	78	.298	.359	2	.125	-0	-5	-5	3	-0.2

YEAR TM/L	W	L	PCT	G	GS	CG	SH	SV	IP	H	HR	BB	SO	RAT	ERA	ERA+	OAV	OOB	BH	AVG	PB	PR	/A	PD	TPI
● DEWEY McDOUGAL	McDougal, John H.				b: 9/19/1871, Aledo, Ill.			d: 4/28/36, Galesburg, Ill.		TR, 170 lbs.		Deb: 4/24/1895													
1895 StL-N	3	10	.231	18	14	10	0	0	114²	187	11	46	23	19.1	8.32	58	.360	.423	6	.146	-2	-45	-44	-1	-3.6
1896 StL-N	0	1	.000	3	1	0	0	0	10	13	2	4	0	16.2	8.10	54	.310	.383	0	.000	-1	-4	-4	1	-0.3
Total 2	3	11	.214	21	15	10	0	0	124²	200	13	50	23	18.8	8.30	58	.357	.420	6	.136	-3	-49	-49	-1	-3.9
● JACK McDOWELL	McDowell, Jack Burns				b: 1/16/66, Van Nuys, Cal.			BR/TR, 6'5", 180 lbs.		Deb: 9/15/87															
1987 Chi-A	3	0	1.000	4	4	0	0	0	28	16	1	6	15	7.7	1.93	237	.168	.233	0	—	0	8	8	0	0.9
1988 Chi-A	5	10	.333	26	26	1	0	0	158²	147	12	68	84	12.6	3.97	100	.245	.329	0	—	0	-0	-0	-1	-0.1
1990 Chi-A	14	9	.609	33	33	4	0	0	205	189	20	77	165	12.6	3.82	100	.244	.317	0	—	0	2	0	-0	0.3
1991 Chi-A★	17	10	.630	35	35	**15**	3	0	253²	212	19	82	191	10.6	3.41	117	.228	.293	0	—	0	19	16	0	1.6
1992 Chi-A★	20	10	.667	34	34	**13**	1	0	260²	247	21	75	178	11.4	3.18	122	.251	.309	0	—	0	22	20	-1	2.1
1993 *Chi-A★	**22**	10	.688	34	34	10	**4**	0	256²	261	20	69	158	11.7	3.37	124	.266	.316	0	—	0	27	23	2	3.0
1994 Chi-A	10	9	.526	25	25	6	2	0	181	186	12	42	127	11.6	3.73	125	.266	.312	0	—	0	22	19	-0	1.7
1995 *NY-A	15	10	.600	30	30	**8**	2	0	217²	211	25	78	157	12.2	3.93	117	.254	.322	0	—	0	19	17	0	1.7
1996 *Cle-A	13	9	.591	30	30	5	1	0	192	214	22	67	141	13.4	5.11	96	.282	.343	0	—	0	-3	-5	1	-0.3
Total 9	119	77	.607	251	251	62	13	0	1753¹	1683	152	564	1216	11.8	3.73	114	.253	.315	0	—	0	116	98	1	10.6
● ROGER McDOWELL	McDowell, Roger Alan				b: 12/21/60, Cincinnati, Ohio			BR/TR, 6'1", 175 lbs.		Deb: 4/11/85															
1985 NY-N	6	5	.545	62	0	0	0	17	127¹	108	9	37	70	10.3	2.83	122	.230	.287	3	.158	0	11	9	2	1.2
1986 *NY-N	14	9	.609	75	0	0	0	22	128	107	4	42	65	10.7	3.02	117	.228	.296	5	.278	1	10	7	3	1.9
1987 NY-N	7	5	.583	56	0	0	0	25	88²	95	7	28	32	12.7	4.16	91	.276	.334	3	.231	1	-4	-1	-4	-0.4
1988 *NY-N	5	5	.500	62	0	0	0	16	89	80	1	31	46	11.5	2.63	122	.238	.308	3	.333	2	8	6	2	1.2
1989 NY-N	1	5	.167	25	0	0	0	4	35¹	34	1	16	15	13.2	3.31	99	.254	.342	1	.500	0	1	-0	2	0.2
Phi-N	3	3	.500	44	0	0	0	19	56²	45	2	22	32	10.8	1.11	319	.220	.298	0	.000	-0	15	15	1	2.8
Yr	4	8	.333	69	0	0	0	23	92	79	3	38	47	11.5	1.96	176	.231	.310	1	.333	0	16	15	3	3.0
1990 Phi-N	6	8	.429	72	0	0	0	22	86¹	92	3	35	39	13.4	3.86	99	.266	.359	0	.000	-0	-1	-0	1	0.0
1991 Phi-N	3	6	.333	38	0	0	0	3	59	61	1	32	28	14.5	3.20	114	.266	.361	0	.000	0	3	3	2	0.6
LA-N	6	3	.667	33	0	0	0	7	42¹	39	3	16	22	11.7	2.55	141	.257	.327	0	—	0	5	5	1	1.1
Yr	9	9	.500	71	0	0	0	10	101¹	100	4	48	50	13.1	2.93	124	.260	.343	0	.000	0	8	8	2	1.7
1992 LA-N	6	10	.375	65	0	0	0	14	83²	103	3	42	50	15.7	4.09	84	.306	.384	1	.000	1	-5	-6	2	-1.0
1993 LA-N	5	3	.625	54	0	0	0	2	68	76	2	30	27	14.3	2.25	170	.288	.365	1	.500	1	14	12	3	1.7
1994 LA-N	0	3	.000	32	0	0	0	0	41¹	50	3	22	29	15.9	5.23	75	.303	.388	0	.000	-0	-5	-6	-0	-0.4
1995 Tex-A	7	4	.636	64	0	0	0	4	85	86	5	34	49	13.3	4.02	120	.277	.359	0	—	0	7	8	2	1.1
1996 Bal-A	1	1	.500	41	0	0	0	0	59¹	69	7	23	20	14.3	4.25	115	.296	.364	0	—	0	5	4	2	0.4
Total 12	70	70	.500	723	2	0	0	159	1050	1045	50	410	524	12.7	3.30	114	.263	.337	16	.222	6	66	52	23	10.4
● SAM McDOWELL	McDowell, Samuel Edward Thomas "Sudden Sam"			b: 9/21/42, Pittsburgh, Pa.			BL/TL, 6'5", 218 lbs.		Deb: 9/15/61																
1961 Cle-A	0	0	—	1	1	0	0	0	6¹	3	0	5	5	11.4	0.00	—	.136	.296	0	.000	-0	3	3	0	0.0
1962 Cle-A	3	7	.300	25	13	0	0	1	87²	81	9	70	70	15.9	6.06	64	.243	.381	4	.154	-1	-20	-21	-0	-2.2
1963 Cle-A	3	5	.375	14	12	3	1	0	65	63	6	44	63	14.8	4.85	75	.256	.369	4	.211	0	-9	-9	-0	-1.0
1964 Cle-A	11	6	.647	31	24	6	2	1	173¹	148	8	100	177	13.0	2.70	133	.229	.336	8	.143	0	18	17	-1	1.6
1965 Cle-A★	17	11	.607	42	35	14	3	4	273	178	9	132	**325**	10.4	**2.18**	**160**	**.185**	.287	12	.126	-3	**39**	**40**	1	4.1
1966 Cle-A†	9	8	.529	35	28	8	**5**	3	194¹	130	12	102	**225**	11.0	2.87	120	**.188**	.298	12	.200	1	12	12	1	1.4
1967 Cle-A	13	15	.464	37	37	10	1	0	236¹	201	21	123	236	12.6	3.85	85	.233	.333	15	.183	-1	-16	-15	-1	-1.7
1968 Cle-A★	15	14	.517	38	37	11	3	0	269	181	13	110	**283**	10.1	1.81	164	.189	.279	13	.153	0	35	34	-1	4.0
1969 Cle-A★	18	14	.563	39	38	18	4	1	285	222	13	102	**279**	10.5	2.94	128	.213	.288	16	.174	-1	22	26	-0	2.8
1970 Cle-A★	20	12	.625	39	39	19	1	0	**305**	236	25	131	**304**	11.0	2.92	136	.213	.300	13	.124	-2	27	**35**	-2	3.0
1971 Cle-A†	13	17	.433	35	31	8	2	1	214²	160	22	153	192	13.2	3.40	113	.207	.340	13	.178	-1	2	10	-2	1.1
1972 SF-N	10	8	.556	28	25	4	0	0	164¹	155	12	86	122	13.5	4.33	81	.253	.350	7	.119	-1	-16	-15	-0	-1.7
1973 SF-N	1	2	.333	18	3	0	0	3	40	45	4	29	35	16.6	4.50	85	.285	.396	2	.167	-0	-4	-3	0	-0.3
NY-A	5	8	.385	16	15	2	1	0	95²	73	4	64	75	12.9	3.95	93	.212	.335	0	—	0	-1	-3	-0	-0.3
1974 NY-A	1	6	.143	13	7	0	0	0	48	42	6	41	33	15.6	4.69	75	.236	.379	0	—	0	-6	-6	-1	-0.9
1975 Pit-N	2	1	.667	14	1	0	0	0	34²	30	7	20	29	13.0	2.86	124	.242	.347	0	.000	-1	3	3	0	0.1
Total 15	141	134	.513	425	346	103	23	14	2492¹	1948	164	1312	2453	12.0	3.17	112	.215	.318	119	.154	-8	88	107	-5	10.0
● CHUCK McELROY	McElroy, Charles Dwayne				b: 10/1/67, Port Arthur, Tex.			BL/TL, 6', 160 lbs.		Deb: 9/4/89															
1989 Phi-N	0	0	—	11	0	0	0	0	10¹	12	1	4	8	13.9	1.74	203	.286	.348	0	—	0	2	2	-0	0.0
1990 Phi-N	0	1	.000	16	0	0	0	0	14	24	0	10	16	21.9	7.71	50	.369	.453	0	—	0	-6	-6	-0	-0.4
1991 Chi-N	6	2	.750	71	0	0	0	3	101¹	73	7	57	92	11.5	1.95	199	.210	.322	3	.300	1	**19**	**22**	1	1.8
1992 Chi-N	4	7	.364	72	0	0	0	6	83²	73	5	51	83	13.3	3.55	101	.237	.345	4	.667	3	-0	0	-1	0.3
1993 Chi-N	2	2	.500	49	0	0	0	0	47¹	51	4	25	31	14.6	4.56	87	.280	.370	0	.000	-1	-3	-3	-0	-0.3
1994 Cin-N	1	2	.333	52	0	0	0	5	57²	52	3	15	38	10.5	2.34	177	.244	.294	1	.167	0	12	11	-0	0.6
1995 Cin-N	3	4	.429	44	0	0	0	0	40¹	46	5	15	27	13.8	6.02	68	.291	.356	0	.000	0	-8	-9	-0	-1.4
1996 Cin-N	2	0	1.000	12	0	0	0	0	12¹	13	2	10	13	16.8	6.57	63	.265	.390	0	.000	-0	-3	-3	-0	-0.5
Cal-A	5	1	.833	40	0	0	0	0	36²	32	2	13	32	11.5	2.95	166	.239	.315	0	—	0	8	8	1	1.3
Total 8	23	19	.548	367	0	0	0	14	403²	376	29	200	340	12.9	3.48	115	.251	.341	8	.242	2	21	23	-1	1.4
● JIM McELROY	McElroy, James D.			b: 1863, San Francisco, Cal.			d: 7/24/1889, Needles, Cal.		5'10", 170 lbs.		Deb: 5/26/1884														
1884 Phi-N	1	12	.077	13	13	13	0	0	111	115	1	54	45	13.7	4.86	61	.254	.333	7	.146	-3	-23	-23	-0	-2.3
Wil-U	0	1	.000	1	1	0	0	0	5	10	0	3	3	18.0	10.80	25	.385	.385	0	.000	-0	-5	-5	-0	-0.6
Total 1	1	13	.071	14	14	13	0	0	116	125	1	54	48	13.9	5.12	58	.261	.336	7	.140	-4	-28	-28	-0	-2.9
● WILL McENANEY	McEnaney, William Henry			b: 2/14/52, Springfield, Ohio			BL/TL, 6', 180 lbs.		Deb: 7/3/74															
1974 Cin-N	2	1	.667	24	0	0	0	2	27	24	4	9	13	11.0	4.33	80	.250	.314	0	—	0	-2	-3	-1	-0.4
1975 *Cin-N	5	2	.714	70	0	0	0	15	91	92	6	23	48	11.6	2.47	145	.264	.314	0	.000	-2	12	11	-1	1.0
1976 *Cin-N	2	6	.250	55	0	0	0	7	72¹	97	3	23	28	15.1	4.85	72	.323	.373	1	.167	0	-11	-11	-0	-1.3
1977 Mon-N	3	5	.375	69	0	0	0	5	86²	92	6	22	38	12.0	3.95	96	.271	.319	0	.000	-1	-0	-1	-0	-0.2
1978 Pit-N	0	0	—	6	0	0	0	0	8²	15	3	2	6	18.7	10.38	36	.395	.439	0	—	0	-7	-6	0	-0.6
1979 StL-N	0	3	.000	45	0	0	0	0	64	60	3	16	15	11.0	2.95	127	.251	.304	0	.000	-0	6	6	2	0.4
Total 6	12	17	.414	269	0	0	0	29	349²	380	25	95	148	12.4	3.76	97	.279	.330	1	.032	-2	-3	-4	-1	-0.5
● LOU McEVOY	McEvoy, Louis Anthony		b: 5/30/02, Williamsburg, Kan.			d: 12/17/53, Webster Groves, Mo			BR/TR, 6'2.5", 203 lbs.		Deb: 4/28/30												
1930 NY-A	1	3	.250	28	1	0	0	3	52¹	64	4	29	14	16.3	6.71	64	.288	.375	2	.125	-1	-12	-14	-1	-1.2
1931 NY-A	0	0	—	6	0	0	0	1	12¹	19	1	12	3	23.4	12.41	32	.358	.485	0	.000	-1	-11	-12	-0	-0.2
Total 2	1	3	.250	34	1	0	0	4	64²	83	5	41	17	17.7	7.79	54	.302	.398	2	.100	-2	-23	-26	-1	-1.4
● BARNEY McFADDEN	McFadden, Bernard Joseph			b: 2/22/1874, Eckley, Pa.			d: 4/28/24, Mauch Chunk, Pa.			BR/TR, 6'1", 195 lbs.		Deb: 4/24/01												
1901 Cin-N	3	4	.429	8	5	4	0	0	46	54	2	40	11	19.6	6.07	53	.290	.431	3	.150	-1	-14	-15	-2	-1.8
1902 Phi-N	0	1	.000	1	1	0	0	0	9	14	0	7	3	21.0	8.00	35	.350	.447	0	.000	-0	-5	-5	-0	-0.5
Total 2	3	5	.375	9	6	4	0	0	55	68	2	47	14	19.8	6.38	49	.301	.434	3	.130	-2	-19	-20	-2	-2.3
● DAN McFARLAN	McFarlan, Anderson Daniel			b: 11/1/1873, Gainesville, Tex.			d: 9/23/24, Louisville, Ky.			Deb: 9/2/1895 F													
1895 Lou-N	0	7	.000	7	5	4	1	0	46	80	4	15	10	19.6	6.65	70	.376	.429	5	.238	-1	-10	-10	1	-1.1
1899 Bro-N	0	0	—	1	0	0	0	0	6	6	1	3	0	13.5	1.50	261	.261	.346	0	.000	-0	2	2	0	0.0
Was-N	8	18	.308	32	28	22	1	0	211²	268	6	64	41	14.6	4.76	83	.308	.363	16	.186	-0	-21	-20	-1	-2.0
Yr	8	18	.308	33	28	22	1	0	217²	274	6	67	41	14.6	4.67	84	.307	.363	16	.182	-1	-20	-18	-2	-2.0
Total 2	8	25	.242	40	35	28	1	0	263²	354	10	82	51	15.4	5.02	81	.320	.375	21	.193	-1	-29	-29	-1	-3.1
● CHAPPIE McFARLAND	McFarland, Charles A.			b: 3/13/1875, White Hall, Ill.			d: 12/14/24, Houston, Tex.		TR, 6'1"		Deb: 9/15/02 F											
1902 StL-N	0	1	.000	2	1	1	0	0	11	11	1	3	3	11.5	5.73	48	.262	.311	0	.000	-1	-4	-4	0	-0.3
1903 StL-N	9	19	.321	38	26	25	1	0	229	253	2	48	76	12.1	3.07	106	.284	.325	8	.108	-4	5	5	2	0.4

YEAR	TM/L	W	L	PCT	G	GS	CG	SH	SV	IP	H	HR	BB	SO	RAT	ERA	ERA+	OAV	OOB	BH	AVG	PB	PR	/A	PD	TPI
1904	StL-N	14	18	.438	32	31	28	1	0	269¹	266	7	56	111	10.9	3.21	84	.248	.288	13	.131	-2	-14	-15	7	-1.3
1905	StL-N	8	18	.308	31	28	22	3	1	250¹	281	3	65	85	12.7	3.81	78	.284	.332	14	.165	1	-22	-23	1	-2.0
1906	StL-N	2	1	.667	6	4	2	0	1	37¹	33	1	8	16	9.9	1.93	136	.219	.258	2	.133	-1	3	3	1	0.3
	Pit-N	1	3	.250	6	5	2	1	0	35¹	39	0	7	11	12.2	2.55	105	.298	.343	5	.385	-1	0	0	0	0.2
	Bro-N	0	1	.000	1	1	1	0	0	9	10	1	5	5	15.0	8.00	32	.286	.375	0	.000	-0	-5	-5	-0	-0.5
	Yr	3	5	.375	13	10	5	1	1	81²	82	2	20	32	11.2	2.87	92	.257	.301	7	.226	-2	-2	-2	1	0.0
Total 5		34	61	.358	106	96	81	6	2	841¹	893	15	192	307	11.8	3.35	87	.270	.313	42	.143	-6	-37	-39	11	-3.2

● **CHRIS McFARLAND** McFarland, Christopher b: 8/17/1861, Fall River, Mass. d: 5/24/18, New Bedford, Mass. 5'9", 170 lbs. Deb: 4/19/1884 ◆

YEAR	TM/L	W	L	PCT	G	GS	CG	SH	SV	IP	H	HR	BB	SO	RAT	ERA	ERA+	OAV	OOB	BH	AVG	PB	PR	/A	PD	TPI
1884	Bal-U	0	1	.000	1	1	0	0	0	3	9	1	1	3	30.0	15.00	18	.500	.526	3	.214	-0	-4	-4	-0	-0.8

● **MONTE McFARLAND** McFarland, Lamont Amos b: 11/7/1872, White Hall, Ill. d: 11/15/13, Peoria, Ill. Deb: 9/14/1895 F

YEAR	TM/L	W	L	PCT	G	GS	CG	SH	SV	IP	H	HR	BB	SO	RAT	ERA	ERA+	OAV	OOB	BH	AVG	PB	PR	/A	PD	TPI
1895	Chi-N	2	0	1.000	2	2	2	0	0	14	21	0	5	5	16.7	5.14	99	.339	.388	1	.143	-1	-1	-0	0	-0.1
1896	Chi-N	0	4	.000	4	3	2	0	0	25	32	0	21	3	19.8	7.20	63	.308	.433	0	.000	-2	-8	-7	0	-1.0
Total 2		2	4	.333	6	5	4	0	0	39	53	0	26	8	18.7	6.46	73	.319	.418	1	.053	-3	-8	-7	1	-1.1

● **JACK McFETRIDGE** McFetridge, John Reed b: 8/25/1869, Philadelphia, Pa. d: 1/10/17, Philadelphia, Pa. 6', 175 lbs. Deb: 6/7/1890

YEAR	TM/L	W	L	PCT	G	GS	CG	SH	SV	IP	H	HR	BB	SO	RAT	ERA	ERA+	OAV	OOB	BH	AVG	PB	PR	/A	PD	TPI
1890	Phi-N	1	0	1.000	1	1	1	0	0	9	5	0	2	4	7.0	1.00	366	.156	.206	3	.750	1	3	3	-0	0.4
1903	Phi-N	1	11	.083	14	13	11	0	0	103	120	2	49	31	15.0	4.89	67	.299	.379	6	.176	0	-19	-19	-1	-1.8
Total 2		2	11	.154	15	14	12	0	0	112	125	2	51	35	14.4	4.58	72	.288	.367	9	.237	2	-16	-16	-1	-1.4

● **ANDY McGAFFIGAN** McGaffigan, Andrew Joseph b: 10/25/56, W.Palm Beach, Fla. BR/TR, 6'3", 195 lbs. Deb: 9/22/81

YEAR	TM/L	W	L	PCT	G	GS	CG	SH	SV	IP	H	HR	BB	SO	RAT	ERA	ERA+	OAV	OOB	BH	AVG	PB	PR	/A	PD	TPI
1981	NY-A	0	0	—	2	0	0	0	0	7	5	1	3	2	10.3	2.57	139	.200	.286	0	—	0	1	1	-0	0.0
1982	SF-N	1	0	1.000	4	0	0	0	0	8	5	0	1	4	7.9	0.00	—	.179	.233	0	.000	-0	3	3	-0	0.4
1983	SF-N	3	9	.250	43	16	0	0	2	134¹	131	17	39	93	11.5	4.29	82	.255	.309	2	.067	-1	-10	-11	-3	-1.5
1984	Mon-N	3	4	.429	21	3	0	0	1	46	37	2	15	39	10.2	2.54	135	.220	.284	0	.000	-1	5	4	0	0.6
	Cin-N	0	2	.000	9	3	0	0	0	23	23	2	8	18	12.1	5.48	69	.261	.323	0	.000	-0	-5	-4	-1	-0.4
	Yr	3	6	.333	30	6	0	0	1	69	60	4	23	57	10.8	3.52	101	.233	.296	0	.000	-1	1	0	-1	0.2
1985	Cin-N	3	3	.500	15	15	0	0	0	94¹	88	4	30	83	11.4	3.72	102	.247	.309	1	.034	-2	-1	1	0	-0.1
1986	Mon-N	10	5	.667	48	14	1	1	2	142²	114	9	55	104	10.8	2.65	139	.223	.301	2	.061	-2	17	17	-2	1.3
1987	Mon-N	5	2	.714	69	0	0	0	12	120¹	105	5	42	100	11.2	2.39	176	.235	.305	0	.000	-1	23	24	0	1.6
1988	Mon-N	6	0	1.000	63	0	0	0	4	91¹	81	4	37	71	11.8	2.76	130	.233	.311	0	.000	-0	7	8	-1	0.5
1989	Mon-N	3	5	.375	57	0	0	0	1	75	85	3	30	40	14.2	4.68	75	.293	.365	1	1.000	-1	-10	-10	-1	-1.1
1990	SF-N	0	0	—	4	0	0	0	0	4²	10	2	4	4	27.0	17.36	21	.455	.538	0	—	0	-7	-7	-0	0.0
	KC-A	4	3	.571	24	11	0	0	1	78²	75	6	28	49	12.0	3.09	124	.248	.315	0	—	0	7	6	-1	0.5
1991	KC-A	0	0	—	4	0	0	0	0	8	14	0	2	3	18.0	4.50	92	.389	.421	0	—	0	-3	-3	-0	-0.1
Total 11		38	33	.535	363	62	3	1	24	833¹	773	65	294	610	11.7	3.38	110	.247	.314	6	.048	-7	30	32	-10	1.8

● **JACK McGEACHY** McGeachy, John Charles b: 5/23/1864, Clinton, Mass. d: 4/5/30, Cambridge, Mass. BR/TR, 5'8", 165 lbs. Deb: 6/17/1886 ◆

YEAR	TM/L	W	L	PCT	G	GS	CG	SH	SV	IP	H	HR	BB	SO	RAT	ERA	ERA+	OAV	OOB	BH	AVG	PB	PR	/A	PD	TPI
1887	Ind-N	0	1	.000	1	0	0	0	0	6¹	13	2	4	3	24.2	11.37	36	.351	.415	109	.269	-4	-5	-5	0	-0.5
1888	Ind-N	0	0	—	1	0	0	0	0	5	5	1	3	0	14.4	7.20	41	.238	.333	99	.219	0	-2	-2	0	0.0
1889	Ind-N	0	0	—	3	0	0	0	0	4²	7	2	6	3	25.1	11.57	36	.333	.481	142	.267	0	-4	-4	0	0.0
Total 3		0	1	.000	5	0	0	0	0	16	25	5	13	6	21.4	10.13	37	.316	.413	604	.245	-4	-11	-11	0	-0.5

● **BILL McGEE** McGee, William Henry "Fiddler Bill" b: 11/16/09, Batchtown, Ill. d: 2/11/87, St.Louis, Mo. BR/TR, 6'1", 215 lbs. Deb: 9/29/35

YEAR	TM/L	W	L	PCT	G	GS	CG	SH	SV	IP	H	HR	BB	SO	RAT	ERA	ERA+	OAV	OOB	BH	AVG	PB	PR	/A	PD	TPI
1935	StL-N	1	0	1.000	1	1	1	0	0	9	4	0	2	4	6.0	1.00	410	.103	.133	1	.333	0	3	3	-0	0.3
1936	StL-N	1	1	.500	7	2	0	0	0	16	23	3	4	8	15.2	7.88	50	.359	.397	1	.250	0	-7	-7	-0	-0.7
1937	StL-N	1	0	1.000	4	1	1	0	0	14	13	1	4	9	11.6	2.57	155	.255	.321	1	.200	-0	2	2	0	0.2
1938	StL-N	7	12	.368	47	25	10	1	5	216	216	4	78	104	12.3	3.21	123	.257	.321	14	.209	1	14	18	-0	1.6
1939	StL-N	12	5	.706	43	17	5	4	0	156	155	14	59	56	12.3	3.81	108	.261	.328	8	.145	-2	5	2	0	0.3
1940	StL-N	16	10	.615	38	31	11	3	0	218	222	4	96	78	13.2	3.80	105	.263	.340	13	.178	-1	1	5	-3	0.1
1941	StL-N	0	1	.000	4	3	0	0	0	14	17	1	13	2	19.9	5.14	73	.298	.437	0	.000	-1	-2	-2	-0	-0.2
	NY-N	2	9	.182	22	14	7	0	0	106	117	9	54	41	14.5	4.92	75	.285	.368	5	.161	-1	-15	-14	-2	-1.6
	Yr	2	10	.167	26	17	1	0	0	120	134	10	67	43	15.1	4.95	75	.286	.375	5	.143	-2	-18	-17	-2	-1.8
1942	NY-N	6	3	.667	31	8	2	1	1	104	95	8	46	40	12.3	2.94	114	.244	.326	3	.103	-2	4	5	-1	0.1
Total 8		46	41	.529	197	102	31	9	6	853	861	53	355	340	12.9	3.74	104	.263	.336	46	.170	-6	2	14	-5	0.1

● **CONNY McGEEHAN** McGeehan, Cornelius Bernard b: 8/25/1882, Drifton, Pa. d: 7/4/07, Hazleton, Pa. Deb: 7/15/03 F

YEAR	TM/L	W	L	PCT	G	GS	CG	SH	SV	IP	H	HR	BB	SO	RAT	ERA	ERA+	OAV	OOB	BH	AVG	PB	PR	/A	PD	TPI
1903	Phi-A	1	0	1.000	3	0	0	0	0	10	9	1	4	9	9.9	4.50	68	.237	.275	0	.000	-1	-2	-2	-0	-0.2

● **KEVIN McGEHEE** McGehee, George Kevin b: 1/18/69, Alexandria, La. BR/TR, 6', 190 lbs. Deb: 8/23/93

YEAR	TM/L	W	L	PCT	G	GS	CG	SH	SV	IP	H	HR	BB	SO	RAT	ERA	ERA+	OAV	OOB	BH	AVG	PB	PR	/A	PD	TPI
1993	Bal-A	0	0	—	5	0	0	0	0	16²	18	5	7	7	14.6	5.94	75	.281	.370	0	—	0	-3	-3	0	-0.2

● **PAT McGEHEE** McGehee, Patrick Henry b: 7/2/1888, Meadville, Miss. d: 12/30/46, Paducah, Ky. BL/TR, 6'2.5", 180 lbs. Deb: 8/23/12

YEAR	TM/L	W	L	PCT	G	GS	CG	SH	SV	IP	H	HR	BB	SO	RAT	ERA	ERA+	OAV	OOB	BH	AVG	PB	PR	/A	PD	TPI
1912	Det-A	0	0	—	1	1	0	0	0	2	0	1	0	1	9.0	0.00	—	.000	1.000	0	—	0	0	0	0	0.0

● **RANDY McGILBERRY** McGilberry, Randall Kent b: 10/29/53, Mobile, Ala. BB/TR, 6'1", 195 lbs. Deb: 9/6/77

YEAR	TM/L	W	L	PCT	G	GS	CG	SH	SV	IP	H	HR	BB	SO	RAT	ERA	ERA+	OAV	OOB	BH	AVG	PB	PR	/A	PD	TPI
1977	KC-A	0	0	.000	3	0	0	0	0	7	7	1	1	1	10.3	5.14	78	.280	.308	0	—	0	-1	-1	0	-0.1
1978	KC-A	0	1	.000	18	0	0	0	0	25²	27	2	18	12	15.8	4.21	91	.276	.388	0	—	0	-1	-1	0	-0.2
Total 2		0	1	.000	21	0	0	0	0	32²	34	3	19	13	14.6	4.41	88	.276	.373	0	—	0	-2	-2	0	-0.3

● **BILL McGILL** McGill, William John "Parson" b: 6/29/1880, Galva, Kan. d: 8/7/59, Alva, Okla. BR/TR, 6'2", Deb: 9/16/07

YEAR	TM/L	W	L	PCT	G	GS	CG	SH	SV	IP	H	HR	BB	SO	RAT	ERA	ERA+	OAV	OOB	BH	AVG	PB	PR	/A	PD	TPI
1907	StL-A	1	0	1.000	2	2	1	0	0	18¹	22	0	2	8	11.8	3.44	73	.301	.320	0	.000	-1	-2	-2	-0	-0.2

● **WILLIE McGILL** McGill, William Vaness "Kid" b: 11/10/1873, Atlanta, Ga. d: 8/29/44, Indianapolis, Ind. TL, 5'6.5", 170 lbs. Deb: 5/8/1890

YEAR	TM/L	W	L	PCT	G	GS	CG	SH	SV	IP	H	HR	BB	SO	RAT	ERA	ERA+	OAV	OOB	BH	AVG	PB	PR	/A	PD	TPI
1890	Cle-P	11	9	.550	24	20	19	0	0	183²	222	4	96	82	16.2	4.12	97	.286	.373	10	.147	2	2	-3	1	0.1
1891	Cin-a	2	5	.286	8	8	6	0	0	65	69	1	37	19	15.1	4.98	83	.263	.361	2	.100	-0	-9	-6	-1	-0.6
	StL-a	19	10	.655	35	31	22	1	1	249	225	10	131	154	13.4	2.93	144	.233	.333	14	.161	1	22	35	-4	3.0
	Yr	21	15	.583	43	39	28	1	1	314	294	11	168	173	13.6	3.35	125	.239	.337	16	.150	1	13	29	-5	2.4
1892	Cin-N	1	1	.500	3	3	1	0	0	17	18	0	5	7	12.2	5.29	62	.261	.311	2	.286	0	-4	-4	0	-0.3
1893	Chi-N	17	18	.486	39	34	26	1	0	302²	311	6	181	91	15.0	4.61	101	.258	.361	29	.234	-2	2	1	-5	-0.1
1894	Chi-N	7	19	.269	27	23	22	0	0	208	272	4	117	58	17.3	5.84	96	.312	.400	12	.244	0	-12	-5	-2	-0.6
1895	Phi-N	10	8	.556	20	20	13	0	0	146	177	2	81	70	16.2	5.55	86	.295	.382	14	.222	-0	-12	-12	0	-1.1
1896	Phi-N	5	4	.556	12	11	7	0	0	79²	87	0	53	29	16.3	5.31	88	.281	.386	6	.207	-0	-8	-9	0	-0.7
Total 7		72	74	.493	168	150	116	2	1	1251	1381	26	701	510	15.4	4.59	100	.273	.368	97	.202	5	-19	-19	-11	-0.3

● **JOHN McGILLEN** McGillen, John Joseph b: 8/6/17, Eddystone, Pa. d: 8/11/87, Upland, Pa. BL/TL, 6'1", 175 lbs. Deb: 4/20/44

YEAR	TM/L	W	L	PCT	G	GS	CG	SH	SV	IP	H	HR	BB	SO	RAT	ERA	ERA+	OAV	OOB	BH	AVG	PB	PR	/A	PD	TPI
1944	Phi-A	0	0	—	2	0	0	0	0	1	1	0	2	0	27.0	18.00	19	.333	.600	0	—	0	-2	-2	-0	0.0

● **JIM McGINLEY** McGinley, James William b: 10/2/1878, Groveland, Mass. d: 9/20/61, Haverhill, Mass. BR/TR, 5'9.5", 165 lbs. Deb: 9/22/04

YEAR	TM/L	W	L	PCT	G	GS	CG	SH	SV	IP	H	HR	BB	SO	RAT	ERA	ERA+	OAV	OOB	BH	AVG	PB	PR	/A	PD	TPI
1904	StL-N	2	1	.667	3	3	3	0	0	27	28	0	6	6	12.3	2.00	135	.267	.325	1	.091	-1	2	2	-1	0.0
1905	StL-N	0	1	.000	1	1	0	0	0	3	5	1	2	0	21.0	15.00	10	.333	.412	1	1.000	-0	-4	-4	0	-0.8
Total 2		2	2	.500	4	4	3	0	0	30	33	1	8	6	13.2	3.30	83	.275	.336	2	.167	-0	-2	-2	-2	-0.8

● **DAN McGINN** McGinn, Daniel Michael b: 11/29/43, Omaha, Neb. BL/TL, 6', 190 lbs. Deb: 9/3/68

YEAR	TM/L	W	L	PCT	G	GS	CG	SH	SV	IP	H	HR	BB	SO	RAT	ERA	ERA+	OAV	OOB	BH	AVG	PB	PR	/A	PD	TPI
1968	Cin-N	0	0	.000	14	0	0	0	0	12	13	1	11	16	18.8	5.25	60	.271	.417	0	.000	-0	-3	-3	0	-0.2
1969	Mon-N	7	10	.412	74	1	0	0	2	132¹	123	8	65	112	13.1	3.94	93	.245	.337	5	.172	1	-5	-4	-0	-0.3
1970	Mon-N	7	10	.412	52	19	3	2	1	130²	154	13	78	83	16.5	5.44	76	.296	.395	4	.114	-2	-20	-19	2	-2.2
1971	Mon-N	1	4	.200	28	6	1	0	0	71	74	7	42	40	14.8	5.96	59	.274	.374	4	.235	0	-20	-19	1	-1.1
1972	Chi-N	0	5	.000	42	6	0	0	0	62²	78	5	29	42	15.9	5.89	65	.301	.380	4	.250	-1	-17	-14	-1	-1.3
Total 5		15	30	.333	210	28	4	2	10	408²	442	34	225	293	15.1	5.11	70	.276	.372	16	.165	-0	-65	-59	3	-5.1

YEAR	TM/L	W	L	PCT	G	GS	CG	SH	SV	IP	H	HR	BB	SO	RAT	ERA	ERA+	OAV	OOB	BH	AVG	PB	PR	/A	PD	TPI
● GUS McGINNIS	McGinnis, August b: 1870, Painesville, Ohio TL , 5'11", 168 lbs. Deb: 4/27/1893																									
1893	Chi-N	2	5	.286	13	5	3	0	0	67¹	85	2	31	13	15.9	5.35	87	.299	.374	6	.240	2	-5	-5	0	-0.2
	Phi-N	1	3	.250	5	4	4	1	0	37¹	39	0	17	12	14.0	4.34	105	.262	.345	3	.200	-1	1	1	0	0.1
	Yr	3	8	.273	18	9	7	1	0	104²	124	2	48	25	15.0	4.99	92	.284	.358	9	.225	1	-4	-4	1	-0.1
● JUMBO McGINNIS	McGinnis, George Washington b: 2/22/1864, Alton, Mo. d: 5/18/34, St.Louis, Mo. 5'10", 197 lbs. Deb: 5/2/1882																									
1882	StL-a	25	18	.581	45	45	43	3	0	388¹	391	2	53	134	10.3	2.60	108	.245	.269	44	.217	1	4	9	-5	0.5
1883	StL-a	28	16	.636	45	45	41	6	0	382²	325	3	69	128	9.3	2.33	150	.215	.249	36	.200	-6	41	49	1	4.2
1884	StL-a	24	16	.600	40	40	39	5	0	354¹	331	4	35	141	9.6	2.84	115	.233	.258	34	.233	3	16	16	-1	1.6
1885	StL-a	6	6	.500	13	13	12	3	0	112	98	1	19	41	9.9	3.38	97	.225	.267	11	.220	0	-2	-1	-1	-0.3
1886	StL-a	5	5	.500	10	10	10	1	0	87²	107	4	27	30	14.5	3.80	91	.288	.347	7	.189	-1	-3	-3	0	-0.4
	Bal-a	11	13	.458	26	25	24	0	0	209¹	235	6	48	70	12.8	3.48	98	.280	.329	11	.188	-1	-1	-1	-0	-0.2
	Yr	16	18	.471	36	35	34	1	0	297	342	8	75	100	13.1	3.58	96	.281	.330	23	.189	-2	-4	-5	-0	-0.6
1887	Cin-a	3	5	.375	8	8	8	0	0	69¹	85	3	43	18	17.7	5.45	80	.296	.402	6	.194	-0	-9	-9	-0	-0.7
Total	6	102	79	.564	187	186	177	18	0	1603²	1572	21	294	562	10.7	2.95	112	.243	.281	154	.210	-5	47	61	-7	4.7
● JOE McGINNITY	McGinnity, Joseph Jerome "Iron Man" (b: Joseph Jerome McGinty)																									
	b: 3/19/1871, Rock Island, Ill. d: 11/14/29, Brooklyn, N.Y. BR/TR, 5'11", 206 lbs. Deb: 4/18/1899 CH																									
1899	Bal-N	28	16	.636	48	41	38	4	2	366¹	358	3	93	74	11.7	2.68	148	.256	.314	28	.193	-5	48	52	1	5.0
1900	*Bro-N	28	8	.778	44	37	32	1	0	343	350	5	113	93	13.2	2.94	131	.264	.340	28	.193	-5	29	34	-2	2.3
1901	Bal-A	26	20	.565	48	43	39	1	1	382	412	7	96	75	12.5	3.56	109	.272	.324	31	.209	-4	5	13	-1	0.8
1902	Bal-A	13	10	.565	25	23	19	0	0	198²	219	3	46	39	12.4	3.44	110	.280	.327	25	.287	4	3	7	-2	1.0
	NY-N	8	8	.500	19	16	16	1	0	153	122	1	32	67	9.6	2.06	136	.219	.273	8	.121	-4	12	13	1	0.9
1903	NY-N	31	20	.608	55	48	44	3	2	434	391	4	109	171	10.8	2.43	138	.236	.291	34	.206	-2	41	44	-4	4.0
1904	NY-N	35	8	.814	51	44	38	9	5	408	307	8	86	144	9.0	**1.61**	**169**	.206	.256	25	.176	-1	51	51	3	**5.6**
1905	*NY-N	21	15	.583	46	38	26	2	3	320¹	289	6	71	125	10.5	2.87	102	.240	.290	28	.233	6	5	2	2	1.0
1906	NY-N	27	12	.692	45	37	32	3	2	339²	316	1	71	105	10.4	2.25	116	.246	.289	15	.130	-3	14	14	1	1.3
1907	NY-N	18	18	.500	47	34	23	3	4	310¹	320	6	58	120	11.4	3.16	78	.266	.308	18	.175	0	-24	-24	2	-2.6
1908	NY-N	11	7	.611	37	20	7	5	5	186	192	8	37	55	11.4	2.27	106	.267	.310	11	.180	-0	2	3	-1	0.2
Total	10	246	142	.634	465	381	314	32	24	3441¹	3276	52	812	1068	11.2	2.66	120	.249	.302	251	.194	-14	186	207	-0	19.5
● LYNN McGLOTHEN	McGlothen, Lynn Everatt b: 3/27/50, Monroe, La. d: 8/14/84, Dubach, La. BL/TR, 6'2", 195 lbs. Deb: 6/25/72																									
1972	Bos-A	8	7	.533	22	22	4	1	0	145	135	9	59	112	12.5	3.41	94	.247	.328	10	.189	1	-6	-3	3	0.1
1973	Bos-A	1	2	.333	6	3	0	0	0	23	39	6	8	16	18.8	8.22	49	.386	.436	0	—	0	-11	-11	-0	-1.2
1974	StL-N★	16	12	.571	31	31	8	3	0	237¹	212	12	89	142	11.5	2.69	133	.241	.312	15	.181	-1	24	23	1	2.7
1975	StL-N	15	13	.536	35	34	9	2	0	239	231	21	97	146	12.5	3.92	96	.254	.329	7	.087	-5	-8	-4	-2	-1.2
1976	StL-N	13	15	.464	33	32	10	4	0	205	209	10	68	106	12.3	3.91	90	.268	.330	15	.211	2	-9	-8	-1	-1.0
1977	SF-N	2	9	.182	21	15	2	0	0	80	94	9	52	42	16.5	5.62	69	.299	.401	2	.105	-1	-15	-15	-2	-2.0
1978	SF-N	0	0	—	5	1	0	0	0	12²	15	0	4	9	13.5	4.97	69	.313	.365	0	.000	-0	-2	-2	-0	0.0
	Chi-N	5	3	.625	49	1	0	0	0	80	77	7	39	60	13.0	3.04	133	.257	.342	3	.231	1	5	9	-2	0.7
	Yr	5	3	.625	54	2	0	0	0	92²	92	7	43	69	13.1	3.30	120	.264	.344	3	.188	0	3	7	-2	0.7
1979	Chi-N	13	14	.481	42	29	6	1	2	212	236	27	55	147	12.5	4.12	100	.283	.330	16	.225	1	-9	-0	-2	-0.1
1980	Chi-N	12	14	.462	39	27	2	0	0	182¹	211	24	64	119	13.6	4.79	82	.293	.352	10	.196	2	-24	-18	-2	-2.4
1981	Chi-N	1	4	.200	20	6	0	0	0	54²	71	1	28	26	16.5	4.77	77	.317	.395	1	.083	-1	-8	-7	1	-0.6
	Chi-A	0	0	—	11	0	0	0	0	21²	14	0	7	12	9.1	4.15	86	.189	.268	0	—	0	-1	-1	-0	0.0
1982	NY-A	0	0	—	4	0	0	0	0	6	9	1	2	2	19.8	10.80	37	.375	.423	0	—	-1	-4	-4	0	0.0
Total	11	86	93	.480	318	201	41	13	2	1497²	1553	127	572	939	12.9	3.98	94	.270	.339	79	.173	-1	-68	-42	-7	-5.0
● PAT McGLOTHIN	McGlothin, Ezra Mac b: 10/20/20, Coalfield, Tenn. BL/TR, 6'3.5", 180 lbs. Deb: 4/25/49																									
1949	Bro-N	1	1	.500	7	0	0	0	0	15²	13	1	6	5	11.0	4.60	89	.224	.286	0	.000	-0	-1	-1	1	-0.1
1950	Bro-N	0	0	—	1	0	0	0	0	2	5	0	1	2	27.0	13.50	30	.455	.500	0	0	-0	-2	-2	-0	0.0
Total	2	1	1	.500	8	0	0	0	0	17²	18	1	7	7	13.3	5.60	73	.261	.320	0	.000	-0	-3	-3	1	-0.1
● JIM McGLOTHLIN	McGlothlin, James Milton "Red" b: 10/6/43, Los Angeles, Cal. d: 12/23/75, Union, Ky. BR/TR, 6'1", 185 lbs. Deb: 9/20/65																									
1965	Cal-A	0	3	.000	3	3	1	0	0	18	18	1	7	9	13.5	3.50	97	.261	.329	-0	—	-0	-0	-0	-0	-0.1
1966	Cal-A	3	1	.750	19	11	0	0	0	67²	79	8	19	41	13.2	4.52	74	.292	.340	1	.059	-0	-8	-9	-0	-0.5
1967	Cal-A★	12	8	.600	32	29	9	6	0	197¹	163	13	56	137	10.2	2.96	106	.226	.286	8	.140	-0	6	4	1	0.5
1968	Cal-A	10	15	.400	40	32	8	0	3	208¹	187	19	60	135	11.0	3.54	82	.244	.305	7	.111	-1	-13	-15	2	-1.8
1969	Cal-A	8	16	.333	37	35	4	1	0	201	188	19	58	96	11.2	3.18	110	.249	.307	7	.121	-1	10	7	2	0.9
1970	*Cin-N	14	10	.583	35	34	5	3	0	210²	192	19	60	97	12.0	3.59	112	.245	.322	8	.121	1	11	10	5	1.7
1971	Cin-N	8	12	.400	30	26	4	1	0	170²	151	15	47	93	10.7	3.22	104	.243	.301	7	.137	1	5	3	1	0.5
1972	*Cin-N	9	8	.529	31	21	3	1	0	145	165	15	49	69	13.3	3.91	82	.287	.343	8	.174	3	-7	-11	-0	-1.0
1973	Cin-N	3	3	.500	24	9	0	0	0	63¹	91	13	23	18	16.2	6.68	51	.340	.392	2	.125	0	-21	-23	1	-1.8
	Chi-A	0	1	.000	5	1	0	0	0	18¹	13	2	13	14	12.8	3.93	101	.203	.338	0	—	0	0	0	0	0.0
Total	9	67	77	.465	256	201	36	11	3	1300¹	1247	125	418	709	11.7	3.61	93	.255	.317	48	.126	2	-19	-34	11	-1.6
● STONEY McGLYNN	McGlynn, Ulysses Simpson Grant b: 5/26/1872, Lancaster, Pa. d: 8/26/41, Manitowoc, Wis. BR/TR, 5'11", 185 lbs. Deb: 9/20/06																									
1906	StL-N	2	2	.500	6	6	6	0	0	48	43	0	15	25	11.1	2.44	108	.249	.312	1	.059	-1	1	1	2	0.2
1907	StL-N	14	25	.359	45	39	33	3	1	352¹	329	6	112	109	11.4	2.91	86	.251	.312	25	.200	3	-17	-16	-1	-1.6
1908	StL-N	1	6	.143	16	6	4	0	0	75²	76	0	17	23	11.3	3.45	68	.256	.301	2	.077	-1	-9	-9	1	-0.9
Total	3	17	33	.340	67	51	43	3	2	476	448	6	144	157	11.3	2.95	85	.252	.310	28	.167	0	-25	-24	2	-2.3
● MICKEY McGOWAN	McGowan, Tullis Earl b: 11/26/21, Dothan, Ala. BL/TL, 6'2", 200 lbs. Deb: 4/22/48																									
1948	NY-N	0	0	—	3	0	0	0	0	3²	3	1	4	2	17.2	7.36	53	.231	.412	0	.000	-0	-1	-1	0	0.0
● HOWARD McGRANER	McGraner, Howard "Muck" b: 9/11/1889, Hamley Run, Ohio d: 10/22/52, Zaleski, Ohio BL/TL, 5'7", 155 lbs. Deb: 9/12/12																									
1912	Cin-N	1	0	1.000	4	2	0	0	0	19	22	2	5	11	14.2	7.11	47	.293	.361	2	.250	1	-8	-8	1	-0.2
● TUG McGRAW	McGraw, Frank Edwin b: 8/30/44, Martinez, Cal. BR/TL, 6', 185 lbs. Deb: 4/18/65																									
1965	NY-N	2	7	.222	37	9	2	0	1	97²	88	8	48	57	12.8	3.32	106	.249	.344	3	.130	-1	2	2	-1	0.1
1966	NY-N	2	9	.182	15	12	1	0	0	62¹	72	11	25	34	14.0	5.34	68	.294	.359	4	.235	1	-12	-12	-0	-1.8
1967	NY-N	0	3	.000	4	4	0	0	0	17¹	13	3	13	18	13.5	7.79	44	.206	.342	1	.250	0	-9	-8	0	-1.1
1969	*NY-N	9	3	.750	42	4	1	0	12	100¹	89	6	47	92	12.2	2.24	163	.243	.329	4	.167	0	15	16	1	2.4
1970	NY-N	4	6	.400	57	0	0	0	10	90²	77	6	49	81	12.6	3.28	123	.231	.332	4	.308	1	8	8	1	1.2
1971	NY-N	11	4	.733	51	1	0	0	8	111	73	4	41	109	9.5	1.70	200	.189	.271	4	.222	2	22	21	-1	3.4
1972	NY-N★	8	6	.571	54	0	0	0	27	106	71	3	40	92	9.7	1.70	198	.197	.282	2	.100	-0	21	20	-0	3.8
1973	*NY-N	5	6	.455	60	2	0	0	25	118²	106	11	55	81	12.4	3.87	93	.243	.331	4	.167	1	-3	-3	0	-0.3
1974	NY-N	6	11	.353	41	4	1	1	3	88²	96	12	32	54	13.0	4.16	86	.279	.340	1	.071	-0	-5	-6	-1	-1.2
1975	Phi-N☆	9	6	.600	56	0	0	0	14	102²	84	7	36	55	10.8	2.98	125	.226	.299	2	.154	-0	7	9	-0	1.4
1976	*Phi-N	7	6	.538	58	0	0	0	11	97¹	81	4	42	76	11.4	2.50	142	.226	.307	1	.143	-0	11	11	-1	1.7
1977	*Phi-N	7	3	.700	45	0	0	0	9	79	62	6	24	58	9.9	2.62	153	.221	.284	2	.400	1	11	12	0	1.9
1978	*Phi-N	8	7	.533	55	1	0	0	9	89²	82	6	23	63	10.5	3.21	111	.245	.293	0	.000	-0	4	4	-0	0.6
1979	Phi-N	4	3	.571	65	0	0	0	16	83²	83	9	29	57	12.3	5.16	74	.259	.324	1	.167	-0	-13	-12	-1	-1.6
1980	*Phi-N	5	4	.556	57	0	0	0	20	92¹	62	3	23	75	8.5	1.46	259	.194	.253	2	.250	-0	22	24	0	3.5
1981	*Phi-N	2	4	.333	34	0	0	0	10	44	35	2	14	26	10.0	2.66	136	.219	.282	0	.000	-0	4	5	-1	0.8
1982	Phi-N	3	3	.500	34	0	0	0	5	39²	50	3	12	25	14.3	4.31	85	.305	.356	-0	.000	-0	-3	-3	-0	-0.4
1983	Phi-N	1	2	.667	34	1	0	0	0	55²	58	6	19	30	12.4	3.56	100	.271	.330	1	.333	0	0	0	0	0.0
1984	Phi-N	2	0	1.000	25	0	0	0	3	38	36	1	10	26	10.9	3.79	94	.245	.293	1	.333	0	0	0	0	0.0
Total	19	96	92	.511	824	39	5	1	180	1514²	1318	108	582	1109	11.4	3.14	116	.237	.312	39	.182	5	81	85	-1	14.4

YEAR	TM/L	W	L	PCT	G	GS	CG	SH	SV	IP	H	HR	BB	SO	RAT	ERA	ERA+	OAV	OOB	BH	AVG	PB	PR	/A	PD	TPI
● **JOHN McGRAW**		McGraw, John (b: Roy Elmer Hoar) b: 12/8/1890, Intercourse, Pa. d: 4/27/67, Torrance, Cal. BR/TR, 5′9″, 160 lbs. Deb: 7/29/14																									
1914	Bro-F	0	0	—	1	0	0	0	0	2	0	0	0	2	4.5	0.00	—	.000	.143	0	—	0	1	1	-0	0.0
● **BOB McGRAW**		McGraw, Robert Emmett b: 4/10/1895, LaVeta, Colo. d: 6/2/78, Boise, Idaho BR/TR, 6′2″, 160 lbs. Deb: 9/25/17																									
1917	NY-A	0	1	.000	2	2	1	0	0	11	9	0	3	3	9.8	0.82	328	.257	.316	0	.000	-0	2	2	-0	0.1
1918	NY-A	0	1	.000	1	1	0	0	0	0	0	0	4	0	∞	∞	—	1.000	0	—	0	-4	-4	0	-0.4
1919	NY-A	1	0	1.000	6	0	0	0	0	16¹	11	1	10	3	12.1	3.31	97	.216	.355	0	.000	-0	-0	-0	0	0.0
	Bos-A	0	2	.000	10	1	0	0	0	26²	33	0	17	6	17.9	6.75	45	.347	.461	1	.100	-1	-10	-11	-1	-0.9
	Yr	1	2	.333	16	1	0	0	0	43	44	1	27	9	15.5	5.44	57	.299	.418	1	.077	-1	-11	-11	-1	-0.9
1920	NY-A	0	0	—	15	0	0	0	0	27	24	1	20	11	15.0	4.67	82	.240	.372	0	.000	-1	-3	-3	-1	-0.2
1925	Bro-N	0	2	.000	2	2	2	0	0	19²	14	0	13	3	12.4	3.20	130	.222	.355	1	.167	-0	2	2	-1	0.1
1926	Bro-N	9	13	.409	33	21	10	0	1	174¹	197	4	67	49	13.7	4.59	83	.292	.358	8	.145	-2	-15	-15	-1	-1.9
1927	Bro-N	0	1	.000	1	1	0	0	0	4	5	1	2	2	15.8	9.00	44	.313	.389	0	.000	-0	-2	-2	0	-0.4
	StL-N	4	5	.444	18	12	4	1	0	94	121	3	30	37	14.5	5.07	78	.323	.373	6	.182	1	-12	-12	1	-0.8
	Yr	4	6	.400	19	13	4	1	0	98	126	4	32	39	14.5	5.23	75	.322	.374	6	.176	1	-14	-14	1	-1.2
1928	Phi-N	7	8	.467	39	3	0	0	1	120	148	7	56	28	15.5	5.18	83	.317	.392	4	.111	-2	-16	-12	-1	-1.6
1929	Phi-N	5	5	.500	41	4	0	0	2	86¹	113	6	43	22	16.5	5.73	91	.324	.401	4	.200	-0	-10	-5	-1	-0.4
Total	9	26	38	.406	168	47	17	1	6	579¹	675	31	265	164	14.8	5.00	81	.303	.380	24	.138	-6	-67	-60	-2	-6.4
● **SCOTT McGREGOR**		McGregor, Scott Houston b: 1/18/54, Inglewood, Cal. BB/TL, 6′1″, 190 lbs. Deb: 9/19/76																									
1976	Bal-A	0	1	.000	3	2	0	0	0	14²	17	0	5	6	13.5	3.68	89	.293	.349	0	—	0	-0	-1	0	0.0
1977	Bal-A	3	5	.375	29	5	1	0	4	114	119	8	30	55	12.3	4.42	86	.275	.333	0	—	0	-5	-8	-1	-0.7
1978	Bal-A	15	13	.536	35	32	13	4	1	233	217	19	47	94	10.2	3.32	105	.248	.287	0	—	0	11	4	0	1.0
1979	*Bal-A	13	6	.684	27	23	7	2	0	174²	165	19	23	81	**9.8**	3.35	120	.248	**.275**	0	—	0	17	13	-1	1.4
1980	Bal-A	20	8	.714	36	36	12	4	0	252	254	16	58	119	11.2	3.32	119	.265	.308	0	—	0	20	18	-3	1.5
1981	Bal-A☆	13	5	.722	24	22	8	3	0	160	167	13	40	82	11.6	3.26	111	.273	.318	0	—	0	7	6	1	0.8
1982	Bal-A	14	12	.538	37	37	7	1	0	226¹	238	31	52	84	11.6	4.61	87	.267	.308	0	—	0	-14	-15	-1	-1.6
1983	*Bal-A	18	7	.720	36	36	12	2	0	260	271	24	45	86	11.0	3.18	124	.269	.301	0	—	0	25	22	-1	1.9
1984	Bal-A	15	12	.556	30	30	10	3	0	196¹	216	18	54	67	12.6	3.94	98	.280	.331	0	—	0	1	-2	2	0.1
1985	Bal-A	14	14	.500	35	34	8	1	0	204	226	24	65	86	12.9	4.81	84	.283	.337	0	—	0	-15	-18	-1	-2.0
1986	Bal-A	11	15	.423	34	33	4	2	0	203	216	35	57	95	12.2	4.52	91	.270	.321	0	—	0	-8	-9	-1	-0.9
1987	Bal-A	2	7	.222	26	15	1	1	0	85¹	112	15	35	39	15.8	6.64	66	.326	.393	0	—	0	-21	-21	3	-1.5
1988	Bal-A	0	3	.000	4	4	0	0	0	17¹	27	3	7	10	17.7	8.83	44	.370	.425	0	—	0	-9	-9	1	-1.1
Total	13	138	108	.561	356	309	83	23	5	2140²	2245	235	518	904	11.7	3.99	98	.271	.316	0	—	0	10	-19	-2	-1.1
● **SLIM McGREW**		McGrew, Walter Howard b: 8/5/1899, Yoakum, Tex. d: 8/21/67, Houston, Tex. BR/TR, 6′7.5″, 235 lbs. Deb: 4/18/22																									
1922	Was-A	0	0	—	1	0	0	0	0	1²	4	0	2	1	32.4	10.80	36	.500	.600	0	.000	-0	-1	-1	0	0.0
1923	Was-A	0	0	—	3	0	0	0	0	5	11	0	3	1	25.2	12.60	39	.440	.500	0	.000	-1	-5	-5	0	-0.3
1924	Was-A	0	1	.000	6	2	0	0	0	23¹	25	1	12	8	14.3	5.01	80	.281	.366	0	.000	-1	-2	-3	-1	-0.3
Total	3	0	1	.000	10	2	0	0	0	30	40	1	17	10	17.1	6.60	60	.328	.410	0	.000	-2	-8	-9	0	-0.3
● **McGUIRE**		McGuire Deb: 6/16/1894																									
1894	Cin-N	0	0	—	1	0	0	0	0	6	15	0	5	1	30.0	10.50	53	.469	.541	1	.250	-0	-3	-3	0	-0.1
● **DEACON McGUIRE**		McGuire, James Thomas b: 11/18/1863, Youngstown, Ohio d: 10/31/36, Duck Lake, Mich. BR/TR, 6′1″, 185 lbs. Deb: 6/21/1884 MC♦																									
1890	Roc-a	0	0	—	1	0	0	0	0	4	10	0	1	0	24.8	6.75	53	.455	.478	99	.299	—	-3	-3	1	0.0
● **TOM McGUIRE**		McGuire, Thomas Patrick "Elmer" b: 2/1/1892, Chicago, Ill. d: 12/7/59, Phoenix, Ariz. BR/TR, 6′, 175 lbs. Deb: 4/18/14																									
1914	Chi-F	5	6	.455	24	12	7	0	0	131¹	143	7	57	37	14.0	3.70	72	.288	.366	19	.271	4	-12	-15	0	-0.6
1919	Chi-A	0	0	—	1	0	0	0	0	3	5	0	3	0	24.0	9.00	35	.500	.615	0	.000	-0	-2	-2	0	-0.0
Total	2	5	6	.455	25	12	7	0	0	134¹	148	7	60	37	14.2	3.82	70	.292	.371	19	.268	3	-14	-17	1	-0.6
● **BILL McGUNNIGLE**		McGunnigle, William Henry "Gunner" b: 1/1/1855, Boston, Mass. d: 3/9/1899, Brockton, Mass. BR/TR, 5′9″, 155 lbs. Deb: 5/2/1879 M♦																									
1879	Buf-N	9	5	.643	14	13	13	2	0	120	113	0	16	62	9.7	2.63	99	**.235**	.260	30	.175	-2	-1	0	-1	-0.1
1880	Buf-N	2	3	.400	5	5	4	1	0	37	43	0	8	3	12.4	3.41	72	.279	.315	4	.182	-1	-4	-4	-1	-0.6
Total	2	11	8	.579	19	18	17	3	0	157	156	0	24	65	10.3	2.81	92	.246	.274	35	.173	-3	-6	-4	0	-0.7
● **MARTY McHALE**		McHale, Martin Joseph b: 10/30/1888, Stoneham, Mass. d: 5/7/79, Hempstead, N.Y. BR/TR, 5′11.5″, 174 lbs. Deb: 9/28/10																									
1910	Bos-A	0	2	.000	2	2	1	0	0	13²	15	0	6	14	14.5	4.61	55	.259	.338	0	—	0	-3	-3	-0	-0.5
1911	Bos-A	0	0	—	4	1	0	0	0	9¹	19	1	3	3	22.2	9.64	34	.475	.523	0	—	0	-7	-7	0	-0.7
1913	NY-A	2	4	.333	7	6	4	1	0	48²	49	1	10	11	11.1	2.96	101	.266	.308	0	—	0	2	1	0	-0.2
1914	NY-A	7	16	.304	31	23	12	0	1	191	195	4	33	75	10.9	2.97	94	.268	.303	12	.200	-1	-5	-4	0	-0.7
1915	NY-A	3	7	.300	13	11	6	0	0	78¹	86	1	19	25	12.1	4.25	69	.277	.318	3	.143	1	-11	-11	0	-1.3
1916	Bos-A	0	1	.000	2	1	0	0	0	6	7	0	4	2	18.0	3.00	92	.280	.400	0	—	0	-0	-0	0	0.1
	Cle-A				5	0	0	0	0	11¹	10	1	6	2	12.7	5.56	54	.270	.372	0	—	0	-3	-3	0	-0.1
	Yr	0	1	.000	7	1	0	0	0	17¹	17	1	10	4	14.0	4.67	63	.270	.370	0	—	0	-4	-3	0	0.0
Total	6	12	30	.286	64	44	23	1	1	358¹	381	6	81	131	11.8	3.57	80	.275	.319	15	.140	-0	-30	-29	-4	-2.7
● **VANCE McILREE**		McIlree, Vance Elmer b: 10/14/1897, Riverside, Iowa d: 5/6/59, Kansas City, Mo. BR/TR, 6′, 160 lbs. Deb: 9/13/21																									
1921	Was-A	0	0	—	1	0	0	0	0	1	1	0	0	0	9.00	9.00	46	.200	.200	0	—	-1	-1	-1	-0	-0.1
● **IRISH McILVEEN**		McIlveen, Henry Cooke b: 7/27/1880, Belfast, Ireland d: 10/18/60, Lorain, Ohio BL/TL, 5′11.5″, 180 lbs. Deb: 7/10/06 ♦																									
1906	Pit-N	0	0	—	2	1	0	0	0	7	10	1	2	3	15.4	7.71	35	.357	.400	2	.400	-1	-4	-4	0	-0.4
● **STOVER McILWAIN**		McIlwain, Stover William "Smokey" b: 9/22/39, Savannah, Ga. d: 1/15/66, Buffalo, N.Y. BR/TR, 6′2″, 195 lbs. Deb: 9/25/57																									
1957	Chi-A	0	0	—	1	0	0	0	0	1	2	0	1	0	27.0	∞	—	.500	.600	0	—	0	-0	-0	0	0.0
1958	Chi-A	0	0	—	1	1	0	0	0	4	2	0	1	4	9.0	2.25	162	.250	.250	0	—	-0	1	0	0	0.1
Total	2	0	0	—	2	1	0	0	0	5	4	0	2	4	12.6	1.80	203	.300	.333	0	—	0	1	0	0	0.1
● **HARRY McINTIRE**		McIntire, John Reid b: 1/11/1879, Dayton, Ohio d: 1/9/49, Daytona Beach, Fla. BR/TR, 5′11″, 180 lbs. Deb: 4/14/05																									
1905	Bro-N	8	25	.242	40	35	29	1	1	308²	340	6	101	135	13.4	3.70	78	.285	.351	34	.246	7	-24	-28	-3	-2.3
1906	Bro-N	13	21	.382	39	31	25	4	3	276	254	2	89	121	11.6	2.97	85	.247	.316	18	.175	1	-10	-14	-1	-1.6
1907	Bro-N	7	15	.318	28	22	19	3	0	199²	178	6	79	49	11.9	2.39	104	.248	.329	15	.217	5	2	-1	0	0.4
1908	Bro-N	11	20	.355	40	35	26	4	2	288	250	5	90	108	11.5	2.69	87	.252	.324	20	.200	2	-10	-11	-2	-1.2
1909	Bro-N	7	17	.292	32	26	20	2	1	228	200	5	91	84	12.3	3.63	71	.246	.337	13	.171	1	-26	-26	-0	-2.6
1910	*Chi-N	13	9	.591	28	19	10	2	0	176	150	5	50	65	10.8	3.07	94	.240	.305	17	.258	3	-1	-4	-1	-0.1
1911	Chi-N	11	7	.611	25	17	9	1	0	149	147	5	33	56	11.1	4.11	81	.257	.302	14	.264	4	-12	-13	-0	-1.0
1912	Chi-N	1	2	.333	4	3	2	0	0	23²	22	0	6	8	10.6	3.80	88	.256	.304	3	.300	1	-1	-1	-0	-0.1
1913	Cin-N	0	1	.000	1	1	0	0	0	2	5	0	3	0	27.0	27.00	12	.600	.600	0	—	0	-3	-3	-0	-1.3
Total	9	71	117	.378	237	188	140	17	7	1650	1555	34	539	626	11.9	3.22	83	.252	.326	134	.218	24	-85	-100	-7	-9.7
● **JOE McINTOSH**		McIntosh, Joseph Anthony b: 8/4/51, Billings, Mont. BB/TR, 6′2″, 185 lbs. Deb: 4/5/74																									
1974	SD-N	0	4	.000	10	5	0	0	0	37¹	36	3	17	22	13.0	3.62	98	.250	.333	0	.000	-1	0	-0	0	-0.2
1975	SD-N	8	15	.348	37	28	4	1	0	183	195	14	60	71	12.6	3.69	94	.273	.332	9	.188	2	-1	-4	-0	-0.3
Total	2	8	19	.296	47	33	4	1	0	220¹	231	17	77	93	12.7	3.68	95	.270	.332	9	.155	1	-1	-5	-1	-0.5
● **FRANK McINTYRE**		McIntyre, Frank W. b: 7/12/1859, Walled Lake, Mich. d: 7/8/1887, Detroit, Mich. Deb: 5/16/1883																									
1883	Det-N	1	0	1.000	1	1	1	0	0	11	11	1	0	8	9.8	0.82	380	.234	.250	0	.000	-0	3	3	0	0.2
	Col-a				2	2	2	0	0	19	20	0	7	6	12.8	5.21	59	.253	.314	0	.000	-0	-4	-5	-1	-0.4
Total	1	2	1	.667	3	3	3	0	0	30	31	0	8	6	11.7	3.60	86	.246	.291	0	.000	-1	-1	-2	-1	-0.2

YEAR TM/L	W	L	PCT	G	GS	CG	SH	SV	IP	H	HR	BB	SO	RAT	ERA	ERA+	OAV	OOB	BH	AVG	PB	PR	/A	PD	TPI

● **DOC McJAMES** McJames, James McCutchen (b: James Mc Cutchen James) b: 8/27/1873, Williamsburg, S.C. d: 9/23/01, Charleston, S.C. TR , Deb: 9/24/1895

1895	Was-N	1	1	.500	2	2	2	0	0	17	17	0	16	9	17.5	1.59	302	.258	.402	1	.143	-1	6	6	0	0.5
1896	Was-N	12	20	.375	37	33	29	0	1	280¹	310	2	135	103	14.5	4.27	103	.278	.359	18	.162	-9	3	4	-0	-0.4
1897	Was-N	15	23	.395	44	39	33	3	2	323²	361	7	137	156	14.4	3.61	120	.280	.358	21	.169	-7	25	26	0	1.8
1898	Bal-N	27	15	.643	45	42	40	2	0	374	327	5	113	178	10.9	2.36	152	.234	.296	27	.181	-4	52	51	-3	4.3
1899	Bro-N	19	15	.559	37	34	27	1	1	275¹	295	4	122	105	14.0	3.50	112	.274	.353	19	.170	-5	11	13	3	1.1
1901	Bro-N	5	6	.455	13	12	6	0	0	91	104	1	40	42	14.9	4.75	71	.285	.367	1	.029	-4	-14	-14	-2	-1.9
Total	6	79	80	.497	178	162	137	6	4	1361¹	1414	19	563	593	13.4	3.43	117	.266	.343	87	.162	-30	83	86	-1	5.4

● **ARCHIE McKAIN** McKain, Archie Richard "Happy" b: 5/12/11, Delphos, Kan. d: 5/21/85, Salina, Kan. BB/TL, 5'10", 175 lbs. Deb: 4/25/37

1937	Bos-A	8	8	.500	36	18	3	0	2	137	152	7	64	66	14.2	4.66	102	.273	.348	13	.265	3	-1	1	0	0.4
1938	Bos-A	5	4	.556	37	5	1	0	6	99²	119	6	44	27	14.9	4.52	109	.297	.369	2	.065	-2	3	5	2	0.3
1939	Det-A	5	6	.455	32	11	4	1	4	129²	120	6	54	49	12.1	3.68	133	.247	.322	9	.220	4	14	17	-2	1.6
1940	*Det-A	5	0	1.000	27	0	0	0	3	51	48	2	25	24	12.9	2.82	168	.247	.333	1	.143	9	9	11	1	1.2
1941	Det-A	2	1	.667	15	0	0	0	0	43	58	3	11	14	14.4	5.02	90	.330	.369	0	.000	-1	-4	-2	2	0.0
	StL-A	0	1	.000	8	0	0	0	1	10	16	2	4	2	18.9	8.10	53	.364	.429	0	.000	-0	-4	-4	1	-0.4
	Yr	2	2	.500	23	0	0	0	1	53	74	5	15	16	15.3	5.60	80	.336	.381	0	.000	-1	-9	-7	3	-0.4
1943	StL-A	1	1	.500	10	0	0	0	0	16	16	0	6	6	12.4	3.94	84	.242	.306	0	.000	-0	-1	-1	0	-0.1
Total	6	26	21	.553	165	34	8	1	16	486¹	529	26	208	188	13.7	4.26	112	.275	.347	25	.176	3	15	27	4	3.0

● **HAL McKAIN** McKain, Harold Le Roy b: 7/10/06, Logan, Iowa d: 1/24/70, Sacramento, Cal. BL/TR, 5'11", 185 lbs. Deb: 9/22/27

1927	Cle-A	0	1	.000	2	1	0	0	0	11	18	0	4	5	18.0	4.09	103	.391	.440	0	.000	-1	0	0	0	0.0
1929	Chi-A	6	9	.400	34	10	4	1	1	158	158	10	85	33	14.4	3.65	117	.275	.378	10	.227	2	11	11	4	1.5
1930	Chi-A	6	4	.600	32	5	0	0	5	89	108	0	42	52	15.5	5.56	83	.299	.377	13	.419	7	-9	-9	1	-0.2
1931	Chi-A	6	9	.400	27	8	3	0	0	112	134	10	57	39	15.6	5.71	75	.295	.377	5	.119	-1	-16	-18	2	-1.9
1932	Chi-A	0	0	—	8	0	0	0	0	11¹	17	1	5	7	17.5	11.12	39	.340	.400	0	.000	-0	-8	-9	0	0.0
Total	5	18	23	.439	103	24	7	1	6	381¹	435	21	193	136	15.2	4.93	88	.293	.380	28	.230	8	-23	-24	7	-0.6

● **REEVE McKAY** McKay, Reeve Stewart "Rip" b: 11/16/1881, Morgan, Tex. d: 1/18/46, Dallas, Tex. TR , 6'1.5", 168 lbs. Deb: 10/2/15

| 1915 | StL-A | 0 | 0 | — | 1 | 0 | 0 | 0 | 0 | 1 | 1 | 0 | 0 | 0 | 9.0 | 9.00 | 32 | .500 | .500 | 0 | — | 0 | -1 | -1 | 0 | 0.0 |

● **JIM McKEE** McKee, James Marion b: 2/1/47, Columbus, Ohio BR/TR, 6'7", 215 lbs. Deb: 9/15/72

1972	Pit-N	1	0	1.000	2	0	0	0	0	5	2	0	1	4	5.4	0.00	—	.125	.176	0	—	0	2	2	-0	0.4
1973	Pit-N	0	1	.000	15	1	0	0	0	27	31	2	17	13	16.3	5.67	62	.287	.389	0	.000	-0	-6	-6	-0	-0.3
Total	2	1	1	.500	17	1	0	0	0	32	33	2	18	17	14.6	4.78	73	.266	.364	0	.000	-0	-4	-5	-1	0.1

● **ROGERS McKEE** McKee, Rogers Hornsby b: 9/16/26, Shelby, N.C. BL/TL, 6'1", 160 lbs. Deb: 8/18/43

1943	Phi-N	1	0	1.000	4	1	1	0	0	13¹	12	0	5	1	11.5	6.08	56	.226	.293	1	.200	0	-4	-4	0	-0.2
1944	Phi-N	0	0	—	1	0	0	0	0	2	2	1	1	0	13.5	4.50	80	.250	.333	0	—	0	-0	-0	0	0.0
Total	2	1	0	1.000	5	1	1	0	0	15¹	14	1	6	1	11.7	5.87	58	.230	.299	1	.200	0	-4	-4	0	-0.2

● **TIM McKEITHAN** McKeithan, Emmett James b: 11/2/06, Lawndale, N.C. d: 8/20/69, Forest City, N.C. BR/TR, 6'2", 182 lbs. Deb: 7/21/32

1932	Phi-A	0	1	.000	4	2	0	0	0	12²	18	0	5	0	16.3	7.11	64	.340	.397	0	.000	0	-4	-4	0	-0.2
1933	Phi-A	1	0	1.000	3	1	0	0	0	9	10	0	4	3	14.0	4.00	107	.278	.350	1	.333	0	0	1	0	0.1
1934	Phi-A	0	0	—	3	0	0	0	0	4	7	2	5	0	27.0	15.75	28	.389	.522	0	.000	-0	-5	-5	-0	0.0
Total	3	1	1	.500	10	3	0	0	0	25²	35	2	14	3	17.2	7.36	60	.327	.405	1	.143	0	-8	-8	0	-0.1

● **RUSS McKELVY** McKelvy, Russell Errett b: 9/8/1854, Swissvale, Pa. d: 10/19/15, Omaha, Neb. BR/TR, Deb: 5/1/1878 ♦

| 1878 | Ind-N | 0 | 2 | .000 | 4 | 1 | 1 | 0 | 0 | 25 | 38 | 1 | 3 | 3 | 14.8 | 2.16 | 94 | .322 | .339 | 57 | .225 | 0 | 0 | -0 | 1 | 0.1 |

● **KIT McKENNA** McKenna, James William b: 2/10/1873, Lynchburg, Va. d: 3/31/41, Lynchburg, Va. Deb: 7/7/1898

1898	Bro-N	2	6	.250	14	9	7	0	0	100²	118	4	57	27	17.2	5.63	64	.290	.399	9	.225	0	-23	-23	2	-1.3
1899	Bal-N	2	3	.400	8	4	4	0	1	45	66	1	19	7	17.6	4.60	86	.340	.407	1	.059	-1	-4	-3	-0	-0.4
Total	2	4	9	.308	22	13	11	0	1	145²	184	5	76	34	17.3	5.31	70	.306	.402	10	.175	-0	-26	-26	1	-1.7

● **LIMB McKENRY** McKenry, Frank Gordon "Big Pete" b: 8/13/1888, Piney Flats, Tenn. d: 11/1/56, Fresno, Cal. BR/TR, 6'4", 205 lbs. Deb: 8/27/15

1915	Cin-N	5	5	.500	21	11	5	0	0	110¹	94	2	39	37	11.1	2.94	97	.238	.311	5	.152	0	-2	-1	1	0.1
1916	Cin-N	1	1	.500	6	1	0	0	0	14²	14	0	8	2	14.7	4.30	60	.259	.375	2	.400	2	-3	-3	-0	-0.2
Total	2	6	6	.500	27	12	5	0	0	125	108	2	47	39	11.5	3.10	91	.241	.319	7	.184	2	-5	-4	1	-0.1

● **JOEL McKEON** McKeon, Joel Jacob b: 2/25/63, Covington, Ky. BL/TL, 6', 185 lbs. Deb: 5/6/86

1986	Chi-A	3	1	.750	30	0	0	0	1	33	18	2	17	18	9.5	2.45	176	.165	.278	0	—	0	6	7	-1	0.7
1987	Chi-A	1	2	.333	13	0	0	0	0	21	27	8	15	14	18.0	9.43	49	.318	.420	0	—	0	-12	-11	-0	-1.5
Total	2	4	3	.571	43	0	0	0	1	54	45	10	32	32	12.8	5.17	85	.232	.341	0	—	0	-5	-5	-1	-0.8

● **LARRY McKEON** McKeon, Lawrence G. b: 3/25/1866, New York d: 7/18/15, Indianapolis, Ind 5'10", 168 lbs. Deb: 5/1/1884

1884	Ind-a	18	41	.305	61	60	59	0	0	512	488	20	94	308	10.5	3.50	94	.235	.275	53	.212	-3	-14	-12	8	-0.7
1885	Cin-a	20	13	.606	33	33	32	0	0	290	273	5	50	117	10.4	2.86	114	.241	.281	20	.165	-5	13	13	-0	0.7
1886	Cin-a	8	8	.500	19	19	16	0	0	156	174	6	54	46	13.3	5.08	69	.276	.336	19	.253	1	-28	-27	1	-1.9
	KC-N	0	2	.000	3	3	3	0	0	21	44	0	8	3	22.3	10.71	35	.411	.452	0	.000	-0	-17	-16	0	-1.1
Total	3	46	64	.418	116	115	110	4	0	979	979	31	206	474	11.2	3.71	90	.248	.291	92	.202	-9	-47	-42	8	-3.0

● **DENNY McLAIN** McLain, Dennis Dale b: 3/29/44, Chicago, Ill. BR/TR, 6'1", 185 lbs. Deb: 9/21/63

1963	Det-A	2	1	.667	3	3	2	0	0	21	20	2	16	22	15.4	4.29	87	.253	.379	1	.200	-1	-2	-1	1	0.0
1964	Det-A	4	5	.444	19	16	3	0	0	100	84	16	37	70	11.0	4.05	90	.225	.297	5	.135	-1	-5	-4	-2	-0.7
1965	Det-A	16	6	.727	33	29	13	4	1	220¹	174	25	62	192	9.7	2.61	133	.216	.273	4	.054	-4	21	21	-0	1.7
1966	Det-A★	20	14	.588	38	38	14	3	0	264¹	205	42	104	192	10.6	3.92	89	.214	.294	17	.183	2	-14	-13	-1	-1.5
1967	Det-A	17	16	.515	37	37	10	3	0	235	209	35	73	161	10.9	3.79	86	.237	.297	10	.118	-3	-15	-14	-2	-2.4
1968	*Det-A★	31	6	.838	41	41	28	6	0	336	241	31	63	280	8.3	1.96	154	.200	.243	18	.162	-0	38	39	1	4.9
1969	Det-A★	24	9	.727	42	41	23	9	0	325	288	25	67	181	9.8	2.80	133	.237	.279	17	.160	-1	30	34	-5	2.7
1970	Det-A	3	5	.375	14	14	1	0	0	91¹	100	19	28	52	12.9	4.63	80	.273	.330	2	.065	-2	-9	-9	-0	-0.9
1971	Was-A	10	22	.313	33	32	9	1	0	216²	233	31	72	103	12.8	4.28	77	.281	.341	6	.103	-1	-20	-23	-1	-3.3
1972	Oak-A	1	2	.333	5	5	0	0	0	22¹	32	4	8	16	16.1	6.04	47	.323	.374	0	.000	-0	-7	-8	0	-1.0
	Atl-N	3	5	.375	15	8	2	0	0	54	60	12	18	21	13.2	6.50	58	.279	.338	2	.167	0	-18	-16	-1	-2.3
Total	10	131	91	.590	280	264	105	29	2	1886	1646	242	548	1282	10.6	3.39	101	.234	.292	82	.133	-9	-1	5	-10	-2.8

● **BARNEY McLAUGHLIN** McLaughlin, Bernard b: 1857, Ireland d: 2/13/21, Lowell, Mass. BR/TR, Deb: 8/2/1884 F♦

| 1884 | KC-U | 1 | 3 | .250 | 7 | 4 | 4 | 0 | 0 | 48² | 62 | 2 | 15 | 14 | 14.2 | 5.36 | 42 | .291 | .338 | 37 | .228 | -1 | -16 | -17 | 0 | -1.0 |

● **BYRON McLAUGHLIN** McLaughlin, Byron Scott b: 9/29/55, Van Nuys, Cal. BR/TR, 6'1", 185 lbs. Deb: 9/18/77

1977	Sea-A	0	0	—	1	0	0	0	0	1¹	5	1	0	1	33.8	27.00	15	.625	.625	0	—	0	-3	-3	0	0.0
1978	Sea-A	4	8	.333	20	17	4	0	0	107	90	15	39	87	11.9	4.37	87	.238	.314	0	—	0	-7	-7	-2	-0.8
1979	Sea-A	7	7	.500	47	7	1	0	14	123²	114	13	60	74	12.8	4.22	103	.251	.340	0	—	0	-0	2	-2	0.0
1980	Sea-A	3	6	.333	45	4	0	0	2	90²	124	15	50	41	17.5	6.85	60	.331	.412	0	—	0	-28	-27	-2	-2.7
1983	Cal-A	2	4	.333	16	7	0	0	0	55²	70	3	22	45	14.1	5.17	78	.286	.357	0	—	0	-7	-7	-0	-0.7
Total	5	16	25	.390	129	35	5	0	16	378¹	403	47	171	248	13.9	5.11	80	.275	.356	0	—	0	-46	-43	-5	-4.2

● **FRANK McLAUGHLIN** McLaughlin, Francis Edward b: 6/19/1856, Lowell, Mass. d: 4/5/17, Lowell, Mass. BR/TR, 5'9", 160 lbs. Deb: 8/9/1882 F♦

1883	Pit-a	0	0	—	2	0	0	0	0	9	14	0	3	1	17.0	13.00	25	.333	.378	25	.219	0	-10	-10	-0	0.0
1884	KC-U	0	0	—	2	1	0	0	0	10	15	0	2	3	15.3	5.40	41	.326	.354	28	.228	-0	-3	-4	-1	0.0
Total	2	0	0	—	4	1	0	0	0	19	29	0	5	4	16.1	9.00	30	.330	.366	37	.228	-0	-13	-13	-0	0.0

YEAR TM/L	W	L	PCT	G	GS	CG	SH	SV	IP	H	HR	BB	SO	RAT	ERA	ERA+	OAV	OOB	BH	AVG	PB	PR	/A	PD	TPI

● **JIM McLAUGHLIN** McLaughlin, James Thomas b: 11/18/1860, Cleveland, Ohio d: 11/16/1895, Cleveland, Ohio BL/TL, 157 lbs. Deb: 5/30/1884

YEAR TM/L	W	L	PCT	G	GS	CG	SH	SV	IP	H	HR	BB	SO	RAT	ERA	ERA+	OAV	OOB	BH	AVG	PB	PR	/A	PD	TPI
1884 Bal-a	1	2	.333	3	2	2	0	0	22	27	2	11	8	15.5	3.68	94	.300	.376	5	.227	0	-1	-1	0	0.0

● **JOEY McLAUGHLIN** McLaughlin, Joey Richard b: 7/11/56, Tulsa, Okla. BR/TR, 6'2", 205 lbs. Deb: 6/11/77

YEAR TM/L	W	L	PCT	G	GS	CG	SH	SV	IP	H	HR	BB	SO	RAT	ERA	ERA+	OAV	OOB	BH	AVG	PB	PR	/A	PD	TPI
1977 Atl-N	0	0	—	3	0	0	0	0	6	10	3	3	0	19.5	15.00	30	.385	.448	0	.000	-0	-7	-7	0	0.0
1979 Atl-N	5	3	.625	37	0	0	0	5	69	54	3	34	40	11.6	2.48	163	.224	.322	2	.182	0	10	12	-1	1.5
1980 Tor-A	6	9	.400	55	10	0	0	4	135^2	159	16	53	70	14.3	4.51	95	.302	.370	0	—	0	-7	-3	-0	-0.6
1981 Tor-A	1	5	.167	40	0	0	0	10	60	55	2	21	38	11.4	2.85	138	.249	.314	0	—	0	5	7	-0	0.8
1982 Tor-A	8	6	.571	44	0	0	0	8	70	54	7	30	49	10.9	3.21	139	.212	.297	0	—	0	7	10	1	1.9
1983 Tor-A	7	4	.636	50	0	0	0	9	64^2	63	11	37	47	13.9	4.45	97	.259	.357	0	—	0	-3	-1	-0	-0.2
1984 Tor-A	0	0	—	6	0	0	0	0	10^2	12	0	7	3	16.0	2.53	162	.286	.388	0	—	0	2	2	0	-0.2
Tex-A	2	1	.667	15	0	0	0	0	32^2	33	4	13	21	12.7	4.41	94	.260	.329	0	—	0	-2	-1	-1	-0.4
Yr	2	1	.667	21	0	0	0	0	43^1	45	4	20	24	13.5	3.95	105	.265	.342	0	—	0	0	1	-0	-0.6
Total 7	29	28	.509	250	12	0	0	36	448^2	440	46	198	268	12.9	3.85	110	.262	.341	2	.167	-0	5	19	-0	2.8

● **JUD McLAUGHLIN** McLaughlin, Justin Theodore b: 3/24/12, Brighton, Mass. d: 9/27/64, Cambridge, Mass. BL/TL, 5'11", 155 lbs. Deb: 6/23/31

YEAR TM/L	W	L	PCT	G	GS	CG	SH	SV	IP	H	HR	BB	SO	RAT	ERA	ERA+	OAV	OOB	BH	AVG	PB	PR	/A	PD	TPI
1931 Bos-A	0	0	—	9	0	0	0	0	12	23	1	8	3	23.3	11.00	36	.397	.470	0	—	0	-10	-10	0	0.0
1932 Bos-A	0	0	—	1	0	0	0	0	3	5	0	4	0	27.0	15.00	30	.385	.529	0	.000	-0	-4	-4	0	0.0
1933 Bos-A	0	0	—	6	0	0	0	0	8^2	14	1	5	1	19.7	6.23	70	.359	.432	0	.000	-0	-2	-2	0	0.0
Total 3	0	0	—	16	0	0	0	0	23^2	42	2	17	4	22.4	10.27	42	.382	.465	0	.000	-0	-16	-16	0	0.0

● **BO McLAUGHLIN** McLaughlin, Michael Duane b: 10/23/53, Oakland, Cal. BR/TR, 6'5", 210 lbs. Deb: 7/20/76

YEAR TM/L	W	L	PCT	G	GS	CG	SH	SV	IP	H	HR	BB	SO	RAT	ERA	ERA+	OAV	OOB	BH	AVG	PB	PR	/A	PD	TPI
1976 Hou-N	4	5	.444	17	11	4	2	1	79	71	6	17	32	10.3	2.85	112	.244	.290	0	.000	-1	6	3	0	0.2
1977 Hou-N	4	7	.364	46	6	0	0	5	84^2	81	6	34	59	12.9	4.25	84	.260	.344	0	—	-1	-3	-6	1	-0.8
1978 Hou-N	0	1	.000	12	1	0	0	2	23^1	30	2	16	10	18.5	5.01	66	.313	.421	0	.000	-0	-4	-4	-0	-0.3
1979 Hou-N	1	2	.333	12	0	0	0	0	16^1	22	2	4	12	14.3	5.51	64	.314	.351	0	.000	-0	-4	-3	-0	-0.6
Atl-N	1	1	.500	37	1	0	0	0	49^2	63	4	16	45	14.7	4.89	83	.303	.358	0	.000	-0	-6	-5	-1	-0.3
Yr	2	3	.400	49	1	0	0	0	66	85	4	20	57	14.6	5.05	78	.305	.355	0	.000	-0	-10	-8	-1	-0.9
1981 Oak-A	0	0	—	11	0	0	0	0	11^2	17	1	9	3	20.8	11.57	30	.333	.443	0	—	0	-10	-10	-0	-0.1
1982 Oak-A	0	4	.000	21	2	0	0	0	48^1	51	3	27	27	14.7	4.84	81	.267	.361	0	—	0	-4	-5	-0	-0.2
Total 6	10	20	.333	156	21	4	2	8	313	335	22	123	188	13.6	4.49	80	.275	.348	0	.000	-3	-25	-32	0	-2.1

● **PAT McLAUGHLIN** McLaughlin, Patrick Elmer b: 8/17/10, Taylor, Tex. BR/TR, 6'2", 175 lbs. Deb: 4/25/37

YEAR TM/L	W	L	PCT	G	GS	CG	SH	SV	IP	H	HR	BB	SO	RAT	ERA	ERA+	OAV	OOB	BH	AVG	PB	PR	/A	PD	TPI
1937 Det-A	0	2	.000	10	3	0	0	0	32^2	39	3	16	8	15.2	6.34	74	.291	.367	1	.100	-1	-6	-6	0	-0.4
1940 Phi-A	0	0	—	1	0	0	0	0	1^2	4	1	1	0	27.0	16.20	27	.444	.500	0	—	0	-2	-2	0	0.0
1945 Det-A	0	0	—	1	0	0	0	0	1	2	0	0	0	18.0	9.00	39	.400	.400	0	—	0	-1	-1	0	0.0
Total 3	0	2	.000	12	3	0	0	0	35^1	45	4	17	8	15.8	6.88	67	.304	.376	1	.100	-1	-9	-9	-1	-0.4

● **WARREN McLAUGHLIN** McLaughlin, Warren A. b: 1/22/1876, N.Plainfield, N.J. d: 10/22/23, Plainfield, N.J. TL, Deb: 7/7/00

YEAR TM/L	W	L	PCT	G	GS	CG	SH	SV	IP	H	HR	BB	SO	RAT	ERA	ERA+	OAV	OOB	BH	AVG	PB	PR	/A	PD	TPI
1900 Phi-N	0	0	—	1	0	0	0	0	6	6	1	9	1	15.0	4.50	80	.190	.370	1	.500	1	-1	-1	0	0.1
1902 Pit-N	3	0	1.000	3	3	3	0	0	26	27	0	9	13	12.8	2.77	99	.267	.333	4	.364	1	-0	-1	0	0.0
1903 Pit-N	0	3	.000	3	2	2	0	0	23	38	0	11	3	19.6	7.04	46	.376	.442	2	.200	1	-10	-10	-1	-1.0
Total 3	3	3	.500	7	5	5	0	0	55	69	0	26	17	15.9	4.75	64	.309	.386	2	.304	2	-10	-10	-2	-0.9

● **AL McLEAN** McLean, Albert Eldon "Elrod" b: 9/20/12, Chicago, Ill. d: 9/29/90, Asheboro, N.C. BR/TR, 6', 175 lbs. Deb: 7/16/35

YEAR TM/L	W	L	PCT	G	GS	CG	SH	SV	IP	H	HR	BB	SO	RAT	ERA	ERA+	OAV	OOB	BH	AVG	PB	PR	/A	PD	TPI
1935 Was-A	0	0	—	4	0	0	0	0	8^2	12	0	5	3	17.7	7.27	59	.324	.405	0	.000	-0	-3	-3	0	-0.1

● **WAYNE McLELAND** McLeland, Wayne Gaffney "Nubbin" b: 8/29/24, Milton, Iowa BR/TR, 6', 180 lbs. Deb: 4/20/51

YEAR TM/L	W	L	PCT	G	GS	CG	SH	SV	IP	H	HR	BB	SO	RAT	ERA	ERA+	OAV	OOB	BH	AVG	PB	PR	/A	PD	TPI
1951 Det-A	0	1	.000	6	1	0	0	0	11	20	1	4	0	20.5	8.18	51	.400	.455	0	.000	-0	-5	-5	0	-0.4
1952 Det-A	0	0	—	4	0	0	0	0	2^2	4	0	6	0	33.8	10.13	38	.444	.667	0	—	-0	-2	-2	0	0.0
Total 2	0	1	.000	10	1	0	0	0	13^2	24	1	10	0	23.0	8.56	48	.407	.500	0	.000	-0	-7	-7	0	-0.4

● **CAL McLISH** McLish, Calvin Coolidge Julius Caesar Tuskahoma "Buster" b: 12/1/25, Anadarko, Okla. BB/TR, 6'1", 200 lbs. Deb: 5/13/44 C

YEAR TM/L	W	L	PCT	G	GS	CG	SH	SV	IP	H	HR	BB	SO	RAT	ERA	ERA+	OAV	OOB	BH	AVG	PB	PR	/A	PD	TPI
1944 Bro-N	3	10	.231	23	13	3	0	0	84	110	10	48	24	17.0	7.82	45	.321	.406	7	.219	-0	-39	-40	-2	-5.1
1946 Bro-N	0	0	—	1	0	0	0	0	0	1	0	0	0	—	∞	—	1.000	1.000	0	—	0	-2	-2	0	-0.2
1947 Pit-N	0	0	—	1	0	0	0	0	1	2	0	0	0	27.0	18.00	22	.400	.500	0	—	0	-2	-2	0	0.0
1948 Pit-N	0	0	—	2	1	0	0	0	5	8	0	2	1	18.0	9.00	45	.400	.455	0	.000	-0	-3	-3	0	-0.2
1949 Chi-N	1	1	.500	8	2	0	0	0	23	31	5	12	6	16.8	5.87	69	.341	.417	3	.333	2	-5	-5	1	-0.2
1951 Chi-N	4	10	.286	30	15	1	1	0	145^2	159	16	52	46	13.2	4.45	92	.283	.347	5	.119	-1	-6	-5	0	-0.6
1956 Cle-A	2	4	.333	37	2	0	0	0	61^2	67	5	32	27	14.4	4.96	85	.282	.367	1	.111	-1	-6	-5	-1	-0.2
1957 Cle-A	9	7	.563	42	7	2	0	1	144^1	118	11	67	88	11.7	2.74	135	.220	.309	8	.186	3	17	16	1	2.1
1958 Cle-A	16	8	.667	39	30	13	0	1	225^2	214	25	70	97	11.4	2.99	122	.251	.309	6	.094	-1	19	16	0	1.6
1959 Cle-A★	19	8	.704	35	32	13	0	1	235^1	253	26	72	113	12.6	3.63	101	.270	.326	14	.189	1	6	1	-0	0.6
1960 Cin-N	4	14	.222	37	21	2	0	0	151^1	170	16	48	56	13.4	4.16	92	.287	.348	2	.049	-3	-7	-6	-1	-0.9
1961 Chi-A	10	13	.435	31	27	4	0	1	162^1	178	21	47	80	12.5	4.38	89	.280	.330	9	.167	-1	-6	-8	-2	-1.0
1962 Phi-N	11	5	.688	32	24	5	1	1	154^2	184	15	45	71	13.4	4.25	91	.293	.343	4	.078	-2	-5	-6	-1	-0.8
1963 Phi-N	13	11	.542	32	32	10	2	0	209^2	184	14	56	98	10.5	3.26	99	.239	.294	14	.203	4	-1	-2	0	0.5
1964 Phi-N	0	1	.000	2	1	0	0	0	5^1	6	0	1	6	13.5	3.38	103	.261	.292	0	.000	-0	0	0	0	0.0
Total 15	92	92	.500	352	209	57	5	6	1609	1685	164	552	713	12.7	4.01	93	.270	.332	73	.149	4	-39	-50	9	-4.2

● **SAM McMACKIN** McMackin, Samuel b: 1872, Cleveland, Ohio d: 2/11/03, Columbus, Ohio BR/TL, Deb: 9/4/02

YEAR TM/L	W	L	PCT	G	GS	CG	SH	SV	IP	H	HR	BB	SO	RAT	ERA	ERA+	OAV	OOB	BH	AVG	PB	PR	/A	PD	TPI
1902 Chi-A	0	0	—	1	0	0	0	0	3	1	0	2	0	3.0	0.00	—	.100	.100	0	.000	-0	1	1	0	0.0
Det-A	0	1	.000	1	1	1	0	0	8^1	9	0	4	2	15.1	3.24	68	.273	.368	2	.500	1	0	0	0	0.1
Yr	0	1	.000	2	1	1	0	0	11^1	10	0	6	2	11.9	2.38	150	.233	.313	2	.400	1	1	1	0	0.1

● **JACK McMAHAN** McMahan, Jack Wally b: 7/22/32, Hot Springs, Ark. BR/TL, 6', 175 lbs. Deb: 4/18/56

YEAR TM/L	W	L	PCT	G	GS	CG	SH	SV	IP	H	HR	BB	SO	RAT	ERA	ERA+	OAV	OOB	BH	AVG	PB	PR	/A	PD	TPI
1956 Pit-N	0	0	—	11	0	0	0	0	13^1	18	1	9	9	18.2	6.08	62	.340	.435	0	.000	-0	-3	-3	0	0.0
KC-A	0	5	.000	23	9	0	0	0	61^2	69	7	31	13	14.9	4.82	90	.290	.376	0	.000	-2	-5	-3	0	-0.5
Total 1	0	5	.000	34	9	0	0	0	75	87	8	40	22	15.6	5.04	84	.299	.387	0	.000	-2	-8	-7	-0	-0.5

● **DON McMAHON** McMahon, Donald John b: 1/4/30, Brooklyn, N.Y. d: 7/22/87, Los Angeles, Cal. BR/TR, 6'2", 222 lbs. Deb: 6/30/57 C

YEAR TM/L	W	L	PCT	G	GS	CG	SH	SV	IP	H	HR	BB	SO	RAT	ERA	ERA+	OAV	OOB	BH	AVG	PB	PR	/A	PD	TPI
1957 *Mil-N	2	3	.400	32	0	0	0	9	46^2	33	0	29	46	12.0	1.54	227	.196	.315	2	.250	-1	12	10	-0	1.6
1958 *Mil-N☆	7	2	.778	38	0	0	0	8	58^2	50	4	29	37	12.4	3.68	96	.235	.332	1	.111	0	-2	-1	-0	-0.2
1959 Mil-N	5	3	.625	60	0	0	0	15	80^2	81	5	37	55	13.3	2.57	138	.259	.339	2	.222	1	12	9	-1	1.1
1960 Mil-N	3	6	.333	48	0	0	0	10	63^2	66	9	32	50	14.1	5.94	58	.263	.351	0	—	-1	-15	-18	-0	-3.0
1961 Mil-N	6	4	.600	53	0	0	0	8	92	84	4	51	53	13.4	2.84	132	.249	.351	3	.188	0	12	9	1	1.2
1962 Mil-N	0	1	.000	2	0	0	0	0	3	3	0	3	0	18.0	6.00	63	.250	.250	0	—	-0	-1	-1	-0	-0.2
Hou-N	5	5	.500	51	0	0	0	8	76^2	53	4	33	69	10.2	1.53	245	.201	.292	1	.083	-1	21	19	1	2.6
Yr	5	6	.455	53	0	0	0	8	79^2	56	4	33	72	10.2	1.69	221	.203	.290	1	.083	-1	20	18	1	2.4
1963 Hou-N	1	5	.167	49	2	0	0	5	87^2	80	8	26	70	11.3	4.05	78	.270	.327	1	.083	-0	-4	-4	-0	-0.7
1964 Cle-A	6	4	.600	70	0	0	0	16	101	67	7	52	92	10.8	2.41	150	.189	.297	2	.143	-0	14	13	-1	1.6
1965 Cle-A	3	3	.500	58	0	0	0	11	85	79	8	37	81	12.4	3.28	106	.248	.329	2	.222	0	2	2	1	0.3
1966 Cle-A	1	1	.500	12	0	0	0	1	12^1	14	1	8	11	16.1	2.92	118	.280	.392	0	.000	-0	0	0	0	0.1
Bos-A	8	7	.533	49	0	0	0	9	78	65	7	38	57	12.2	2.65	143	.232	.330	1	.091	-0	7	10	-1	2.1
Yr	9	8	.529	61	0	0	0	10	90^1	73	8	44	62	12.0	2.69	140	.226	.324	1	.077	-0	7	11	-1	2.2
1967 Bos-A	1	2	.333	11	0	0	0	2	17^2	14	3	13	13	13.8	3.57	98	.215	.346	0	.000	-0	0	0	0	0.0
Chi-A	5	0	1.000	52	0	0	0	3	91^2	54	5	27	74	8.5	1.67	186	.173	.252	2	.182	-0	16	15	0	0.9
Yr	6	2	.750	63	0	0	0	5	109^1	68	8	40	87	9.4	1.98	160	.180	.270	2	.154	-0	15	14	0	0.9
1968 Chi-A	2	1	.667	25	0	0	0	1	46	31	2	20	32	9.8	1.96	155	.190	.290	1	.333	-0	5	4	-0	0.3
*Det-A	3	1	.750	20	0	0	0	0	35^2	22	8	10	33	8.1	2.02	149	.180	.242	0	.000	-0	4	4	0	0.4
Yr	5	2	.714	45	0	0	0	1	81^2	53	10	30	65	9.1	1.98	152	.183	.259	1	.143	-0	9	9	-1	0.7

YEAR	TM/L	W	L	PCT	G	GS	CG	SH	SV	IP	H	HR	BB	SO	RAT	ERA	ERA+	OAV	OOB	BH	AVG	PB	PR	/A	PD	TPI
1969	Det-A	3	5	.375	34	0	0	0	11	37	25	2	18	38	10.7	3.89	96	.192	.295	0	.000	-1	-1	-1	0	-0.2
	SF-N	3	1	.750	13	0	0	0	2	23²	13	1	9	21	8.4	3.04	115	.157	.239	1	.333	0	1	1	0	0.3
1970	SF-N	9	5	.643	61	0	0	0	19	94¹	70	9	45	74	11.2	2.96	134	.202	.297	2	.143	0	11	11	-1	1.9
1971	*SF-N	10	6	.625	61	0	0	0	4	82	73	9	37	71	12.8	4.06	84	.242	.338	0	.000	-1	-5	-6	1	-1.2
1972	SF-N	3	3	.500	44	0	0	0	5	63	46	8	21	45	9.7	3.71	94	.206	.278	1	.250	0	-2	-2	-0	-0.2
1973	SF-N	4	0	1.000	22	0	0	0	0	30¹	21	1	7	20	8.3	1.48	257	.189	.237	1	1.000	0	7	8	0	1.4
1974	SF-N	0	0	—	9	0	0	0	0	11²	13	2	2	5	11.6	3.09	123	.283	.313	0	—	0	1	1	0	0.0
Total	18	90	68	.570	874	2	0	0	153	1310¹	1054	105	579	1003	11.4	2.96	119	.221	.310	23	.137	-1	96	83	-1	10.1

● DOC McMAHON   McMahon, Henry John b: 12/19/1886, Woburn, Mass. d: 12/11/29, Woburn, Mass. Deb: 10/6/08

YEAR	TM/L	W	L	PCT	G	GS	CG	SH	SV	IP	H	HR	BB	SO	RAT	ERA	ERA+	OAV	OOB	BH	AVG	PB	PR	/A	PD	TPI
1908	Bos-A	1	0	1.000	1	1	0	0	0	9	3	0	3	14.0		3.00	82	.350	.350	2	.400	1	-1	-1	-0	0.0

● SADIE McMAHON   McMahon, John Joseph b: 9/19/1867, Wilmington, Del. d: 2/20/54, Wilmington, Del BR/TR, 5'9.5", 165 lbs. Deb: 7/5/1889

YEAR	TM/L	W	L	PCT	G	GS	CG	SH	SV	IP	H	HR	BB	SO	RAT	ERA	ERA+	OAV	OOB	BH	AVG	PB	PR	/A	PD	TPI
1889	Phi-a	14	12	.538	28	27	27	2	0	242	230	5	102	117	12.9	3.53	107	.243	.325	16	.154	-6	8	7	4	0.4
1890	Phi-a	29	18	.617	48	46	44	0	1	410	414	5	133	225	12.4	3.34	115	.254	.318	40	.229	3	24	23	9	3.2
	Bal-a	7	3	.700	12	11	11	1	0	99	84	1	33	66	11.2	3.00	135	.223	.296	4	.103	-4	10	12	2	0.8
	Yr	36	21	.632	60	57	55	1	1	509	498	6	166	291	11.8	3.27	118	.246	.305	44	.206	-1	34	34	11	4.0
1891	Bal-a	35	24	.593	61	58	53	5	1	503	493	13	149	219	11.8	2.81	133	.248	.306	43	.205	-3	51	52	5	5.0
1892	Bal-N	19	25	.432	48	46	44	2	1	397	430	9	145	118	13.2	3.24	106	.265	.329	25	.141	-9	2	8	0	0.0
1893	Bal-N	23	18	.561	43	40	35	0	1	346¹	378	6	156	79	14.1	4.37	109	.269	.346	36	.243	-3	12	15	-1	1.0
1894	Bal-N	25	8	.758	35	33	26	0	1	275²	317	7	111	60	14.3	4.21	130	.285	.355	36	.286	0	34	38	3	3.5
1895	*Bal-N	10	4	.714	15	15	15	4	0	122¹	110	1	32	37	10.5	2.94	162	.237	.291	16	.314	1	25	25	-1	2.2
1896	Bal-N	11	9	.550	22	22	19	0	0	175²	195	4	55	33	13.0	3.48	123	.279	.334	9	.123	-7	17	16	0	0.7
1897	Bro-N	0	6	.000	9	7	5	0	0	63	75	1	29	13	15.3	5.86	70	.293	.372	5	.200	-1	-11	-12	0	-0.9
Total	9	173	127	.577	321	305	279	14	4	2634	2726	52	945	967	12.9	3.51	118	.260	.326	230	.204	-28	172	182	21	15.9

● JOHN McMAKIN   McMakin, John Weaver "Spartanburg John" b: 3/6/1878, Spartanburg, S.C. d: 9/25/56, Lyman, S.C. BR/TR, 5'11", 165 lbs. Deb: 4/19/02

YEAR	TM/L	W	L	PCT	G	GS	CG	SH	SV	IP	H	HR	BB	SO	RAT	ERA	ERA+	OAV	OOB	BH	AVG	PB	PR	/A	PD	TPI
1902	Bro-N	2	2	.500	4	4	4	0	0	32	34	0	11	6	13.2	3.09	89	.272	.341	2	.182	1	-1	-1	-0	-0.1

● JOE McMANUS   McManus, Joab Logan b: 9/7/1887, Palmyra, Ill. d: 12/23/55, Beckley, W.Va. BR/TR, 5'11", 180 lbs. Deb: 4/12/13

YEAR	TM/L	W	L	PCT	G	GS	CG	SH	SV	IP	H	HR	BB	SO	RAT	ERA	ERA+	OAV	OOB	BH	AVG	PB	PR	/A	PD	TPI
1913	Cin-N	0	0	—	1	0	0	0	0	2	3	0	4	1	31.5	18.00	18	.375	.583	0	—	0	-3	-3	0	0.0

● PAT McMANUS   McManus, Patrick b: Ireland d: 10/6/17, Brooklyn, N.Y. Deb: 5/22/1879

YEAR	TM/L	W	L	PCT	G	GS	CG	SH	SV	IP	H	HR	BB	SO	RAT	ERA	ERA+	OAV	OOB	BH	AVG	PB	PR	/A	PD	TPI
1879	Tro-N	0	2	.000	2	2	2	0	0	21	24	1	1	6	10.7	3.00	83	.258	.266	1	.125	-1	-1	-1	0	-0.1

● GREG McMICHAEL   McMichael, Gregory Winston b: 12/1/66, Knoxville, Tenn. BR/TR, 6'3", 215 lbs. Deb: 4/12/93

YEAR	TM/L	W	L	PCT	G	GS	CG	SH	SV	IP	H	HR	BB	SO	RAT	ERA	ERA+	OAV	OOB	BH	AVG	PB	PR	/A	PD	TPI
1993	*Atl-N	2	3	.400	74	0	0	0	19	91²	68	3	29	89	9.5	2.06	195	.206	.270	0	.000	-0	20	20	2	1.8
1994	Atl-N	4	6	.400	51	0	0	0	21	58²	66	1	19	47	13.0	3.84	111	.280	.333	0	.000	-0	2	3	-1	0.5
1995	*Atl-N	7	2	.778	67	0	0	0	2	80²	64	8	32	74	10.7	2.79	153	.213	.289	0	.000	-0	12	13	-1	1.2
1996	*Atl-N	5	3	.625	73	0	0	0	2	86²	84	4	27	78	11.6	3.22	137	.253	.311	0	—	0	10	11	1	1.1
Total	4	18	14	.563	265	0	0	0	44	317²	282	16	107	288	11.0	2.89	146	.235	.299	0	.000	-1	45	47	1	4.6

● GEORGE McMULLEN   McMullen, George b: California Deb: 7/2/1887

YEAR	TM/L	W	L	PCT	G	GS	CG	SH	SV	IP	H	HR	BB	SO	RAT	ERA	ERA+	OAV	OOB	BH	AVG	PB	PR	/A	PD	TPI
1887	NY-a	2	1	.667	3	3	2	0	0	21	25	2	19	2	18.9	7.71	55	.269	.393	1	.083	-2	-8	-8	0	-0.8

● JOHN McMULLIN   McMullin, John F. "Lefty" b: 1848, Philadelphia, Pa. d: 4/11/1881, Philadelphia, Pa. BR/TL, 5'9", 160 lbs. Deb: 5/9/1871 ◆

YEAR	TM/L	W	L	PCT	G	GS	CG	SH	SV	IP	H	HR	BB	SO	RAT	ERA	ERA+	OAV	OOB	BH	AVG	PB	PR	/A	PD	TPI
1871	Tro-n	12	15	.444	29	29	28	0	0	249	430	4	75	12	18.3	5.53	76	.342	.379	38	.279	1	-36	-36		-2.0
1872	Mut-n	1	0	1.000	3	1	1	0	0	15	18	0	2	1	12.0	3.60	94	.247	.267	61	.257	0	0	-0		0.1
1873	Ath-n	1	0	1.000	1	1	1	0	0	8	10	0	1	2	12.4	2.25	152	.303	.324	62	.273	0	1	1		0.1
1875	Phi-n	0	0	—	4	0	0	0	0	11¹	32	0	1	0	26.2	7.94	29	.464	.471	57	.257	1	-7	-7	0	-0.2
Total	4 n	14	15	.483	37	31	30	0	1	283¹	490	4	79	15	18.1	5.43	42	.342	.376	308	.285	2	-101	-99		-1.9

● CRAIG McMURTRY   McMurtry, Joe Craig b: 11/5/59, Troy, Tex. BR/TR, 6'5", 195 lbs. Deb: 4/10/83

YEAR	TM/L	W	L	PCT	G	GS	CG	SH	SV	IP	H	HR	BB	SO	RAT	ERA	ERA+	OAV	OOB	BH	AVG	PB	PR	/A	PD	TPI
1983	Atl-N	15	9	.625	36	35	6	3	0	224²	204	13	88	105	11.7	3.08	126	.243	.315	6	.086	-4	14	20	3	2.0
1984	Atl-N	9	17	.346	37	30	0	0	0	183¹	184	16	102	99	14.1	4.32	89	.268	.363	6	.115	-1	-15	-10	4	-1.0
1985	Atl-N	0	3	.000	17	6	0	0	0	45	56	6	27	28	16.8	6.60	58	.306	.398	1	.071	-1	-15	-14	1	-0.9
1986	Atl-N	1	6	.143	37	5	0	0	0	79²	82	7	43	50	14.3	4.74	84	.265	.359	2	.125	-0	-9	-7	0	-0.6
1988	Tex-A	3	3	.500	32	0	0	0	3	60	37	5	24	35	9.3	2.25	181	.180	.270	0	—	0	11	12	1	1.3
1989	Tex-A	0	0	—	19	0	0	0	0	23	29	3	13	14	17.2	7.43	53	.312	.407	0	—	0	-9	-9	0	-0.4
1990	Tex-A	0	3	.000	23	3	0	0	0	41²	43	4	30	14	16.0	4.32	91	.281	.402	0	—	0	-2	-2	1	-0.1
1995	Hou-N	0	1	.000	11	0	0	0	1	10	15	0	9	4	21.8	7.84	49	.357	.481	0	.000	-0	-4	-5	0	-0.4
Total	8	28	42	.400	212	79	6	3	4	667²	650	54	336	349	13.4	4.08	96	.259	.348	15	.098	-6	-29	-13	10	0.3

● EDGAR McNABB   McNabb, Edgar J. "Texas" b: 10/24/1865, Coshocton, Ohio d: 2/28/1894, Pittsburgh, Pa. BR/TR, 5'11.5", 170 lbs. Deb: 5/12/1893

YEAR	TM/L	W	L	PCT	G	GS	CG	SH	SV	IP	H	HR	BB	SO	RAT	ERA	ERA+	OAV	OOB	BH	AVG	PB	PR	/A	PD	TPI
1893	Bal-N	8	7	.533	21	14	12	0	0	142	167	6	53	18	14.5	4.12	115	.284	.352	13	.194	-2	9	10	0	0.6

● DAVE McNALLY   McNally, David Arthur b: 10/31/42, Billings, Mont. BR/TL, 5'11", 190 lbs. Deb: 9/26/62

YEAR	TM/L	W	L	PCT	G	GS	CG	SH	SV	IP	H	HR	BB	SO	RAT	ERA	ERA+	OAV	OOB	BH	AVG	PB	PR	/A	PD	TPI
1962	Bal-A	1	0	1.000	1	1	1	1	0	9	2	0	3	4	5.0	0.00	—	.071	.161	0	.000	-0	4	4	0	0.4
1963	Bal-A	7	8	.467	29	20	2	0	1	125²	133	9	55	78	13.8	4.58	76	.276	.356	2	.053	-2	-13	-15	-1	-2.0
1964	Bal-A	9	11	.450	30	23	5	3	0	159¹	157	15	51	86	12.3	3.67	97	.260	.327	7	.137	0	-1	-2	0	-0.2
1965	Bal-A	11	6	.647	35	29	6	2	0	198²	163	15	73	116	11.0	2.85	122	.222	.298	6	.092	-3	13	14	0	0.9
1966	*Bal-A	13	6	.684	34	33	5	1	0	213	212	22	64	158	11.8	3.17	105	.256	.313	15	.195	3	6	4	0	0.6
1967	Bal-A	7	7	.500	24	22	3	1	0	119	134	8	39	70	13.2	4.54	69	.295	.354	6	.158	-0	-17	-18	-2	-2.2
1968	Bal-A	22	10	.688	35	35	18	5	0	273	175	24	55	202	7.9	1.95	150	.182	.234	11	.128	4	31	30	-3	3.9
1969	*Bal-A★	20	7	.741	41	40	11	4	0	268²	232	21	84	166	10.8	3.22	111	.234	.297	8	.085	-2	12	10	-4	0.4
1970	*Bal-A☆	24	9	.727	40	40	16	1	0	296	277	29	78	185	11.0	3.22	113	.250	.304	14	.133	4	16	14	-2	1.6
1971	*Bal-A★	21	5	.808	30	30	11	1	0	224¹	188	24	58	91	10.1	2.89	116	.229	.284	12	.162	3	14	12	-0	1.6
1972	*Bal-A★	13	17	.433	36	36	12	6	0	241	220	15	68	120	10.8	2.95	104	.247	.302	12	.152	2	3	3	1	0.7
1973	Bal-A	17	17	.500	38	38	17	4	0	266	247	16	81	87	11.3	3.21	116	.251	.312	0	—	0	18	15	1	2.0
1974	*Bal-A	16	10	.615	39	37	13	4	0	259	260	19	81	111	12.1	3.58	96	.270	.331	0	—	0	1	-4	2	-0.1
1975	Mon-N	3	6	.333	12	12	0	0	0	77¹	88	8	36	36	14.9	5.24	73	.280	.362	4	.190	12	-14	-12	-1	-1.1
Total	14	184	119	.607	424	396	120	33	2	2730	2488	230	826	1512	11.2	3.24	106	.245	.306	97	.133	10	74	54	-8	6.5

● TIM McNAMARA   McNamara, Timothy Augustine b: 11/20/1898, Millville, Mass. d: 11/5/94, N.Smithfield, R.I. BR/TR, 5'11", 170 lbs. Deb: 4/27/22

YEAR	TM/L	W	L	PCT	G	GS	CG	SH	SV	IP	H	HR	BB	SO	RAT	ERA	ERA+	OAV	OOB	BH	AVG	PB	PR	/A	PD	TPI
1922	Bos-N	3	4	.429	24	5	4	2	0	70²	55	2	26	16	10.4	2.42	165	.225	.303	2	.118	-1	13	12	-0	1.0
1923	Bos-N	3	13	.188	32	16	3	0	0	139¹	185	8	29	32	14.1	4.91	81	.320	.357	7	.179	1	-14	-14	-2	-1.5
1924	Bos-N	8	12	.400	35	21	6	2	0	179	242	9	31	35	13.9	5.18	74	.334	.364	6	.140	-0	-26	-27	1	-2.6
1925	Bos-N	0	0	—	1	0	0	0	0	0²	6	0	2	1	108.0	81.00	5	.857	.889	0	—	0	-6	-6	0	0.0
1926	NY-N	0	0	—	6	0	0	0	0	6	7	0	4	8	16.5	9.00	42	.304	.407	0	—	0	-3	-3	0	0.0
Total	5	14	29	.326	98	42	13	4	0	395²	495	19	92	88	13.6	4.78	82	.314	.355	15	.152	-1	-36	-38	-3	-3.1

● GORDON McNAUGHTON   McNaughton, Gordon Joseph b: 7/31/10, Chicago, Ill. d: 8/6/42, Chicago, Ill. BR/TR, 6'1", 190 lbs. Deb: 8/13/32

YEAR	TM/L	W	L	PCT	G	GS	CG	SH	SV	IP	H	HR	BB	SO	RAT	ERA	ERA+	OAV	OOB	BH	AVG	PB	PR	/A	PD	TPI
1932	Bos-A	0	1	.000	6	2	0	0	0	21	21	1	22	10	19.7	6.43	70	.259	.434	2	.250	-1	-5	-5	1	-0.1

● HARRY McNEAL   McNeal, John Harley b: 8/11/1877, Iberia, Ohio d: 1/11/45, Cleveland, Ohio BR/TR, 6'3", 175 lbs. Deb: 8/5/01

YEAR	TM/L	W	L	PCT	G	GS	CG	SH	SV	IP	H	HR	BB	SO	RAT	ERA	ERA+	OAV	OOB	BH	AVG	PB	PR	/A	PD	TPI
1901	Cle-A	5	5	.500	12	10	9	0	0	85¹	120	4	30	15	16.7	4.43	80	.328	.391	6	.162	-2	-7	-8	-2	-1.1

● ED McNICHOL   McNichol, Edwin Briggs b: 1/10/1879, Martins Ferry, O. d: 11/1/52, Salineville, O. BR/TR, 5'5", 170 lbs. Deb: 7/9/04

YEAR	TM/L	W	L	PCT	G	GS	CG	SH	SV	IP	H	HR	BB	SO	RAT	ERA	ERA+	OAV	OOB	BH	AVG	PB	PR	/A	PD	TPI
1904	Bos-N	2	12	.143	17	15	12	1	0	122	120	3	74	39	14.7	4.28	64	.262	.371	4	.093	-4	-21	-21	-2	-2.6

● FRANK McPARTLIN   McPartlin, Frank b: 2/16/1872, Hoosick Falls, N.Y. d: 11/13/43, New York, N.Y. TR, 6', 180 lbs. Deb: 8/22/1899

YEAR	TM/L	W	L	PCT	G	GS	CG	SH	SV	IP	H	HR	BB	SO	RAT	ERA	ERA+	OAV	OOB	BH	AVG	PB	PR	/A	PD	TPI
1899	NY-N	0	0	—	1	0	0	0	0	4	4	0	3	2	20.3	4.50	83	.267	.450	0	.000	-0	-0	-0	0	0.0

YEAR	TM/L	W	L	PCT	G	GS	CG	SH	SV	IP	H	HR	BB	SO	RAT	ERA	ERA+	OAV	OOB	BH	AVG	PB	PR	/A	PD	TPI

● **JOHN McPHERSON** McPherson, John Jacob b: 3/9/1869, Easton, Pa. d: 9/30/41, Easton, Pa. Deb: 7/12/01

1901	Phi-A	0	1	.000	1	1	0	0	0	4	7	0	4	0	27.0	11.25	34	.368	.500	0	.000	-0	-3	-3	0	-0.5
1904	Phi-N	1	12	.077	15	12	11	1	0	128	130	1	46	32	12.8	3.66	73	.264	.334	3	.064	-4	-13	-14	0	-1.6
Total	2	1	13	.071	16	13	11	1	0	132	137	1	50	32	13.2	3.89	70	.268	.341	3	.063	-4	-16	-17	1	-2.1

● **HERB McQUAID** McQuaid, Herbert George b: 3/29/1899, San Francisco, Cal d: 4/4/66, Richmond, Cal. BR/TR, 6'2", 185 lbs. Deb: 6/22/23

1923	Cin-N	1	0	1.000	12	1	0	0	0	34¹	31	0	9	11	11.5	2.36	164	.238	.308	0	.000	-1	6	6	1	0.1
1926	NY-A	1	0	1.000	17	1	0	0	0	38¹	48	5	13	6	14.8	6.10	63	.329	.391	0	.000	-1	-9	-10	1	-0.3
Total	2	2	0	1.000	29	2	0	0	0	72²	79	5	23	15	13.3	4.33	89	.286	.352	0	.000	-2	-3	-4	1	-0.2

● **MIKE McQUEEN** McQueen, Michael Robert b: 8/30/50, Oklahoma City, Okla BL/TL, 5'11", 190 lbs. Deb: 10/2/69

1969	Atl-N	0	0	—	1	1	0	0	0	3	2	0	3	3	15.0	3.00	120	.182	.357	0	—	-0	-0	-0	0	0.0
1970	Atl-N	1	5	.167	22	8	1	0	1	66	67	10	31	54	13.5	5.59	77	.266	.349	6	.300	2	-11	-10	-1	-0.7
1971	Atl-N	4	1	.800	17	3	0	0	1	56	47	7	23	38	11.6	3.54	105	.228	.312	4	.211	-0	-1	1	-1	-0.0
1972	Atl-N	0	5	.000	23	7	1	0	1	78¹	79	11	44	42	14.2	4.60	82	.260	.355	2	.087	-2	-10	-7	-1	-0.7
1974	Cin-N	0	0	—	10	0	0	0	0	15	17	4	11	5	15.6	5.40	65	.288	.400	1	1.000	0	-3	-3	-1	0.0
Total	5	5	11	.313	73	19	2	0	3	218¹	212	32	112	140	13.5	4.66	84	.255	.346	13	.206	1	-24	-18	-4	-1.4

● **GEORGE McQUILLAN** McQuillan, George Watt b: 5/1/1885, Brooklyn, N.Y. d: 3/30/40, Columbus, Ohio BR/TR, 5'11.5", 175 lbs. Deb: 5/8/07

1907	Phi-N	4	0	1.000	6	5	5	3	0	41	21	0	11	28	7.2	0.66	368	.158	.228	4	.364	3	8	8	-2	1.1
1908	Phi-N	23	17	.575	48	42	32	7	2	359²	263	1	91	114	9.0	1.53	159	.207	.263	18	.151	-1	33	36	-3	3.9
1909	Phi-N	13	16	.448	41	28	16	4	2	247²	229	5	54	96	9.3	2.14	121	.226	.271	4	.118	-3	12	12	-2	0.8
1910	Phi-N	9	6	.600	24	17	13	3	1	152¹	109	2	50	71	9.6	**1.60**	196	.204	.276	7	.149	-1	24	26	-0	2.4
1911	Cin-N	2	6	.250	19	5	2	0	0	77	92	2	31	28	14.8	4.68	71	.308	.380	2	.091	-1	-11	-12	-1	-1.3
1913	Pit-N	8	6	.571	25	16	7	0	1	141²	144	1	35	59	11.4	3.43	88	.273	.319	4	.103	-1	-4	-7	-1	-0.8
1914	Pit-N	13	17	.433	45	28	15	4	0	259¹	248	8	60	96	11.0	2.98	89	.261	.310	5	.068	-4	-6	-10	0	-1.5
1915	Pit-N	8	10	.444	30	20	9	0	1	149	160	1	39	56	12.1	2.84	96	.284	.332	4	.091	-3	-1	-2	0	-0.5
	Phi-N	4	3	.571	9	8	5	1	0	63²	60	1	11	13	10.2	2.12	129	.247	.282	1	.043	-2	4	4	-1	0.2
	Yr	12	13	.480	39	28	14	1	1	212²	220	2	50	69	11.5	2.62	104	.272	.315	5	.075	-5	3	3	-1	-0.3
1916	Phi-N	1	7	.125	21	3	1	0	2	62	58	2	15	22	11.0	2.76	96	.251	.305	1	.091	-1	-1	-0	-0	-0.2
1918	Cle-A	0	1	.000	5	1	0	0	1	23	25	0	4	7	11.3	2.35	128	.284	.315	0	.000	-0	1	2	0	0.1
Total	10	85	89	.489	273	173	105	17	14	1576¹	1382	23	401	590	10.4	2.38	114	.241	.294	55	.117	-14	62	59	-9	4.2

● **HUGH McQUILLAN** McQuillan, Hugh A. "Handsome Hugh" b: 9/15/1897, New York, N.Y. d: 8/26/47, New York, N.Y. BR/TR, 6', 170 lbs. Deb: 7/26/18

1918	Bos-N	1	0	1.000	1	1	0	0	0	9	7	0	5	1	12.0	3.00	90	.219	.324	1	.250	0	-0	-0	0	0.0
1919	Bos-N	2	3	.400	16	7	2	0	1	60	66	3	14	13	12.2	3.45	83	.288	.332	4	.222	0	-4	-4	-1	-0.4
1920	Bos-N	11	15	.423	38	26	17	1	5	225²	230	4	70	53	12.0	3.55	86	.273	.330	19	.257	6	-10	-13	2	-0.6
1921	Bos-N	13	17	.433	45	31	13	2	5	250	284	9	90	94	13.5	4.00	91	.291	.352	18	.205	1	-6	-10	0	-0.9
1922	Bos-N	5	10	.333	28	17	7	0	0	136	154	3	56	33	14.0	4.24	94	.299	.369	7	.167	-1	-2	-4	-1	-0.4
	*NY-N	6	5	.545	15	13	5	0	1	94¹	111	7	34	24	13.9	3.82	105	.301	.360	7	.189	-1	3	2	-1	0.0
	Yr	11	15	.423	43	30	12	0	1	230¹	265	10	90	57	13.9	4.06	98	.299	.364	14	.177	-2	1	-2	-1	-0.4
1923	*NY-N	15	14	.517	38	32	15	5	0	229²	224	12	66	75	11.6	3.41	112	.259	.315	14	.171	-1	15	11	-1	0.8
1924	*NY-N	14	8	.636	27	23	14	1	3	184	179	8	43	49	11.0	2.69	136	.259	.304	14	.209	-1	24	20	-2	2.0
1925	NY-N	2	3	.400	14	11	2	0	1	70	95	9	23	23	15.3	6.04	67	.343	.395	3	.143	-1	-14	-16	1	-0.9
1926	NY-N	11	10	.524	33	22	12	1	0	167	171	7	42	47	11.5	3.72	101	.271	.318	7	.132	-3	2	1	-2	0.0
1927	NY-N	5	4	.556	11	9	5	0	0	58	73	4	22	17	14.9	4.50	86	.309	.371	4	.211	-1	-4	-4	0	-0.5
	Bos-N	3	5	.375	13	11	2	0	0	78	109	2	24	17	15.6	5.54	67	.332	.381	5	.227	0	-14	-16	0	-1.3
	Yr	8	9	.471	24	20	7	0	0	136	182	6	46	34	15.2	5.10	74	.322	.375	9	.220	-1	-18	-20	1	-1.8
Total	10	88	94	.484	279	203	95	10	16	1561²	1703	67	489	446	12.7	3.83	95	.284	.340	103	.195	0	-10	-32	1	-2.2

● **NORM McRAE** McRae, Norman b: 9/26/47, Elizabeth, N.J. BR/TR, 6'1", 195 lbs. Deb: 9/13/69

1969	Det-A	0	0	—	3	0	0	0	0	3	2	0	1	3	9.0	6.00	62	.200	.273	0	—	0	-1	-1	-0	0.0
1970	Det-A	0	0	—	19	0	0	0	0	31¹	26	1	25	16	14.9	2.87	130	.226	.369	0	.000	-0	3	3	1	0.0
Total	2	0	0	—	22	0	0	0	0	34¹	28	1	26	19	14.4	3.15	118	.224	.362	0	.000	-0	2	2	0	0.0

● **TRICK McSORLEY** McSorley, John Bernard b: 12/6/1852, St.Louis, Mo. d: 2/9/36, St.Louis, Mo. BR/TR, 5'4", 142 lbs. Deb: 5/6/1875 ♦

1884	Tol-a	0	0	—	1	0	0	0	0	2	5	0	0	1	22.5	4.50	76	.556	.556	17	.250	0	-0	-0	-0	0.0

● **BILL McTIGUE** McTigue, William Patrick "Rebel" b: 1/3/1891, Nashville, Tenn. d: 5/8/20, Nashville, Tenn. BL/TL, 6'1.5", 175 lbs. Deb: 5/2/11 ♦

1911	Bos-N	0	5	.000	14	8	0	0	0	37	37	4	49	23	21.4	7.05	54	.280	.481	1	.083	-1	-15	-13	-1	-1.7
1912	Bos-N	2	0	1.000	10	1	0	0	0	34²	39	0	18	17	14.8	5.45	66	.289	.373	1	.077	-0	-8	-7	1	-0.4
1916	Det-A	0	0	—	3	0	0	0	0	5¹	5	0	5	1	16.9	5.06	57	.278	.435	0	.000	-0	-1	-1	0	0.0
Total	3	2	5	.286	27	9	0	0	0	77	81	4	72	41	18.1	6.19	59	.284	.432	2	.077	-2	-24	-22	0	-2.1

● **CAL McVEY** McVey, Calvin Alexander b: 8/30/1850, Montrose, Iowa d: 8/20/26, San Francisco, Cal BR/TR, 5'9", 170 lbs. Deb: 5/5/1871 M♦

1875	Bos-n	1	0	1.000	3	2	0	0	1	15	15	0	2	1	13.1	4.91	44	.294	.308	138	.355	2	-3	-3		-0.2
1876	Chi-N	5	2	.714	11	6	5	2	0	59¹	57	0	2	9	8.9	1.52	161	.235	.241	107	.347	3	5	6	0	0.8
1877	Chi-N	4	8	.333	17	10	6	0	2	92	129	2	11	20	13.7	4.50	66	.301	.319	98	.368	6	-17	-16	-1	-1.4
1879	Cin-N	0	2	.000	3	1	0	0	0	14	34	1	2	7	23.1	8.36	28	.453	.468	105	.297	1	-9	-9	0	-0.9
Total	3	9	12	.429	31	17	12	0	5	165¹	210	3	15	36	12.8	5.10	71	.295	.309	393	.328	12	-21	-19	-1	-1.5

● **DOUG McWEENY** McWeeny, Douglas Lawrence "Buzz" b: 8/17/1896, Chicago, Ill. d: 1/1/53, Melrose Park, Ill. BR/TR, 6'2", 190 lbs. Deb: 4/24/21

1921	Chi-A	3	6	.333	27	8	3	0	2	97²	127	7	45	46	15.9	6.08	70	.325	.394	1	.032	-4	-20	-20	-1	-2.0
1922	Chi-A	0	1	.000	4	1	0	0	0	10²	13	0	7	5	16.9	5.91	69	.325	.426	0	.000	-0	-2	-2	-0	-0.2
1924	Chi-A	1	3	.250	13	5	2	0	0	43¹	47	2	17	18	13.7	4.57	90	.294	.369	0	.000	-0	-2	-2	3	0.1
1926	Bro-N	11	13	.458	42	24	10	1	1	216¹	213	6	84	96	12.7	3.04	126	.258	.333	7	.109	-1	19	19	1	1.4
1927	Bro-N	4	8	.333	34	22	6	0	1	164¹	167	13	70	73	13.4	3.56	111	.266	.347	2	.043	-4	7	7	0	0.2
1928	Bro-N	14	14	.500	42	32	12	**4**	1	244	218	11	114	79	12.4	3.17	125	.235	.322	14	.173	-1	22	22	3	2.5
1929	Bro-N	4	10	.286	36	24	4	0	1	146	167	17	39	59	16.2	6.10	76	.288	.390	5	.104	-2	-22	-24	-2	-2.2
1930	Cin-N	0	2	.000	8	2	0	0	0	25²	28	0	20	10	16.8	7.36	66	.283	.403	1	.143	-0	-7	-7	0	-0.4
Total	8	37	57	.394	206	118	37	5	6	948	980	56	450	386	13.8	4.17	98	.269	.353	30	.104	-16	-5	-7	2	-0.6

● **LARRY McWILLIAMS** McWilliams, Larry Dean b: 2/10/54, Wichita, Kan. BL/TL, 6'5", 180 lbs. Deb: 7/17/78

1978	Atl-N	9	3	.750	15	15	3	1	0	99¹	84	11	35	42	11.0	2.81	144	.224	.294	2	.063	-2	8	14	1	1.6
1979	Atl-N	3	2	.600	13	13	4	1	0	66¹	69	4	22	32	12.9	5.56	73	.272	.339	5	.208	1	-13	-11	1	-0.5
1980	Atl-N	9	14	.391	30	30	4	1	0	163²	188	27	39	77	12.9	4.95	76	.285	.332	8	.157	-0	-25	-22	-0	-2.8
1981	Atl-N	2	1	.667	6	5	2	1	0	37²	31	2	8	23	9.3	3.11	115	.230	.273	1	.100	-0	2	2	1	0.2
1982	Atl-N	2	3	.400	27	2	0	0	0	37²	37	3	20	24	17.7	6.21	60	.327	.409	1	.167	0	-11	-10	2	-1.1
	Pit-N	6	5	.545	19	18	2	1	0	121²	106	9	24	94	9.9	3.11	119	.232	.276	6	.188	-0	7	8	2	0.9
	Yr	8	8	.500	46	20	2	1	0	159¹	143	12	44	118	11.6	3.84	95	.255	.309	7	.184	-0	-4	-2	0	-0.2
1983	Pit-N	15	8	.652	35	35	8	4	0	238	205	19	87	199	11.2	3.25	114	.230	.300	9	.114	-4	10	12	1	0.9
1984	Pit-N	12	11	.522	34	32	7	1	0	227¹	226	18	78	149	12.1	2.93	123	.263	.326	9	.122	-3	17	17	1	1.3
1985	Pit-N	7	9	.438	30	19	2	0	0	126¹	139	9	52	54	13.8	4.70	76	.283	.371	5	.125	-1	-16	-16	-1	-1.9
1986	Pit-N	3	11	.214	49	15	0	0	0	122¹	129	16	49	80	13.6	5.15	74	.268	.345	4	.138	-5	-19	-18	-0	-1.9
1987	Atl-N	0	1	.000	9	2	0	0	0	20¹	25	2	7	13	15.0	5.75	76	.301	.370	1	.200	-0	-4	-3	-1	-0.1
1988	StL-N	6	9	.400	42	17	1	0	0	136	130	10	45	70	11.8	3.90	89	.253	.319	6	.162	1	-4	-4	-1	-0.6
1989	Phi-N	2	11	.154	40	16	2	1	0	120²	123	9	49	54	13.1	4.10	86	.265	.340	3	.111	-1	-8	-7	1	-0.8
	KC-A	2	2	.500	8	5	1	0	0	32²	31	2	8	21	11.6	4.13	93	.254	.316	0	.000	-1	-1	-0	0	-0.1
1990	KC-A	0	0	—	8	0	0	0	0	8¹	19	1	3	4	21.6	9.72	39	.452	.476	0	—	-1	-5	-5	0	0.1
Total	13	78	90	.464	370	224	34	13	3	1558¹	1548	137	542	940	12.4	3.99	93	.259	.326	60	.135	-8	-66	-48	0	-4.8

YEAR	TM/L	W	L	PCT	G	GS	CG	SH	SV	IP	H	HR	BB	SO	RAT	ERA	ERA+	OAV	OOB	BH	AVG	PB	PR	/A	PD	TPI

● RUSTY MEACHAM Meacham, Russell Loren b: 1/27/68, Stuart, Fla. BR/TR, 6'2", 166 lbs. Deb: 6/29/91

1991	Det-A	2	1	.667	10	4	0	0	0	27²	35	4	11	14	15.0	5.20	80	.315	.377	0	—	0	-3	-3	0	-0.4
1992	KC-A	10	4	.714	64	0	0	0	2	101¹	88	5	21	64	9.7	2.74	148	.233	.275	0	—	0	13	15	2	2.0
1993	KC-A	2	2	.500	15	0	0	0	0	21	31	5	5	13	16.7	5.57	82	.326	.379	0	—	0	-3	-2	0	-0.6
1994	KC-A	3	3	.500	36	0	0	0	4	50²	51	7	12	36	11.5	3.73	134	.263	.313	0	—	0	6	7	0	0.6
1995	KC-A	4	3	.571	49	0	0	0	0	59²	72	6	19	30	13.9	4.98	96	.304	.358	0	—	0	-2	-1	0	-0.2
1996	Sea-A	1	1	.500	15	5	0	0	1	42¹	57	9	13	25	15.7	5.53	89	.328	.387	0	—	0	-3	-3	-1	-0.1
Total	6	22	14	.611	189	9	0	0	9	303	334	33	81	182	12.7	4.16	109	.281	.333	0	—	0	9	12	3	1.3

● JOHNNY MEADOR Meador, John Davis b: 12/4/1892, Madison, N.C. d: 4/11/70, Winston-Salem, N.C BR/TR, 5'10.5", 165 lbs. Deb: 4/24/20

| 1920 | Pit-N | 0 | 2 | .000 | 12 | 8 | 0 | 0 | 0 | 36¹ | 48 | 1 | 7 | 5 | 13.4 | 4.21 | 76 | .340 | .372 | 1 | .167 | -0 | -4 | -4 | 1 | -0.2 |

● LEE MEADOWS Meadows, Henry Lee "Specs" b: 7/12/1894, Oxford, N.C. d: 1/29/63, Daytona Beach, Fla. BR/TR, 6', 190 lbs. Deb: 4/19/15

1915	StL-N	13	11	.542	39	26	14	1	0	244	232	5	88	104	12.0	2.99	93	.259	.329	8	.096	-4	-6	-5	-3	-1.2
1916	StL-N	12	23	.343	51	36	11	1	2	289	261	3	119	120	12.3	2.58	102	.247	.332	15	.158	-1	1	2	1	0.2
1917	StL-N	15	9	.625	43	37	18	4	2	265²	253	5	90	100	11.8	3.08	87	.262	.328	9	.101	-6	-11	-12	-3	-2.0
1918	StL-N	8	14	.364	30	23	12	0	1	165¹	176	1	56	49	13.2	3.59	75	.280	.348	7	.127	-2	-15	-16	-2	-2.5
1919	StL-N	4	10	.286	22	12	3	1	0	92	100	3	30	28	12.9	3.03	92	.292	.352	3	.103	-2	-1	-2	3	-0.3
	Phi-N	8	10	.444	18	17	15	3	0	158¹	128	2	49	88	10.5	2.33	138	.229	.300	6	.118	-3	10	16	-1	1.4
	Yr	12	20	.375	40	29	18	4	0	250¹	228	5	79	116	11.3	2.59	118	.252	.317	9	.112	-5	9	13	2	1.1
1920	Phi-N	16	14	.533	35	33	19	3	0	247	249	6	90	105	12.6	2.84	120	.270	.341	14	.171	-3	8	16	0	1.6
1921	Phi-N	11	16	.407	28	27	15	2	0	194¹	226	10	62	52	13.5	4.31	98	.288	.343	13	.210	-2	-11	-2	4	0.4
1922	Phi-N	12	18	.400	33	33	19	2	0	237	264	8	71	62	13.1	4.03	116	.288	.346	27	.314	3	2	17	3	2.6
1923	Phi-N	1	3	.250	8	5	0	0	1	19²	40	0	15	10	25.2	13.27	35	.430	.509	4	.400	2	-20	-19	0	-2.8
	Pit-N	16	10	.615	31	25	17	1	0	227	250	3	44	66	11.7	3.01	133	.284	.319	22	.250	3	25	25	2	3.1
	Yr	17	13	.567	39	30	17	1	1	246²	290	3	59	76	12.8	3.83	106	.298	.339	26	.265	5	5	6	2	0.3
1924	Pit-N	13	12	.520	36	30	15	3	0	229¹	240	7	51	61	11.6	3.26	118	.278	.322	16	.195	-1	16	15	-1	1.2
1925	*Pit-N	19	10	.655	35	31	20	1	1	255¹	272	11	67	87	12.2	3.67	122	.273	.323	17	.175	-1	17	23	1	2.2
1926	Pit-N	20	9	.690	36	31	15	1	0	226²	254	10	52	54	12.3	3.97	99	.287	.329	20	.227	-1	-4	-3	3	0.1
1927	*Pit-N	19	10	.655	40	38	25	2	0	299¹	315	11	66	84	11.7	3.40	121	.273	.317	18	.157	-5	17	24	-1	1.5
1928	Pit-N	1	1	.500	4	2	1	0	0	10	18	0	5	3	20.7	8.10	50	.383	.442	2	.500	1	-5	-4	-0	-0.7
1929	Pit-N	0	0	—	1	0	0	0	0	0²	2	0	1	0	40.5	13.50	35	.500	.600	0	.000	-0	-1	-1	0	-0.0
Total	15	188	180	.511	490	406	219	25	7	3160²	3280	84	956	1063	12.3	3.37	106	.274	.332	201	.180	-19	22	71	6	4.8

● RUFUS MEADOWS Meadows, Rufus Rivers b: 8/25/07, Chase City, Va. d: 5/10/70, Wichita, Kan. BL/TL, 5'11", 175 lbs. Deb: 4/23/26

| 1926 | Cin-N | 0 | 0 | — | 1 | 0 | 0 | 0 | 0 | 0¹ | 0 | 0 | 0 | 0 | 0.0 | 0.00 | — | .000 | .000 | 0 | .000 | -0 | 0 | 0 | 0 | 0.0 |

● DAVE MEADS Meads, David Donald b: 1/7/64, Montclair, N.J. BL/TL, 6'", 175 lbs. Deb: 4/13/87

1987	Hou-N	5	3	.625	45	0	0	0	0	48²	60	8	16	32	14.2	5.55	71	.321	.377	1	.333	1	-8	-9	-1	-1.3
1988	Hou-N	3	1	.750	22	2	0	0	0	39²	37	4	14	27	11.6	3.18	105	.240	.304	1	.250	1	1	1	-0	0.1
Total	2	8	4	.667	67	2	0	0	0	88¹	97	12	30	59	13.0	4.48	81	.284	.344	2	.286	1	-7	-8	-1	-1.2

● GEORGE MEAKIM Meakim, George Clinton b: 7/11/1865, Brooklyn, N.Y. d: 2/17/23, Queens, N.Y. BR/TR, 5'7.5", 154 lbs. Deb: 5/2/1890

1890	*Lou-a	12	7	.632	28	21	16	3	1	192	173	4	63	123	11.3	2.91	132	.233	.298	11	.153	-2	21	20	-1	1.4
1891	Phi-a	1	4	.200	6	6	4	0	0	35	51	1	22	13	19.0	6.94	55	.329	.416	3	.200	0	-13	-12	2	-1.1
1892	Chi-N	0	1	.000	1	1	1	0	0	9	18	0	2	0	20.0	11.00	30	.400	.426	2	.400	-1	-8	-8	-0	-0.5
	Cin-N	1	1	.500	3	3	1	0	0	13²	19	1	9	4	19.8	8.56	38	.317	.423	0	.000	-1	-8	-8	0	-0.9
	Yr	1	2	.333	4	4	2	0	0	22²	37	1	11	4	19.9	9.53	35	.352	.424	2	.200	-0	-16	-16	-0	-1.4
1895	Lou-N	1	0	1.000	1	1	1	0	0	7	7	0	4	2	14.1	2.57	180	.259	.355	1	.333	0	2	2	0	0.2
Total	4	15	13	.536	39	32	23	3	1	256²	268	6	100	142	13.2	4.03	95	.260	.331	17	.170	-2	-6	-6	1	-0.9

● JIM MECIR Mecir, James Jason b: 5/16/70, Bayside, N.Y. BB/TR, 6'1", 195 lbs. Deb: 9/4/95

1995	Sea-A	0	0	—	2	0	0	0	0	4²	5	0	2	3	13.5	0.00	—	.263	.333	0	—	0	2	2	-0	-0.1
1996	NY-A	1	1	.500	26	0	0	0	0	40¹	42	6	23	38	14.5	5.13	98	.275	.369	0	—	0	-1	-0	2	0.0
Total	2	1	1	.500	28	0	0	0	0	45	47	6	25	41	14.4	4.60	109	.273	.365	0	—	0	2	2	1	-0.1

● DOC MEDICH Medich, George Francis b: 12/9/48, Aliquippa, Pa. BR/TR, 6'5", 227 lbs. Deb: 9/5/72

1972	NY-A	0	0	—	1	1	0	0	0	2	2	0	2	0	—	∞	—	1.000	1.000	0	—	0	-2	-2	0	-0.2
1973	NY-A	14	9	.609	34	32	11	3	0	235	217	20	74	145	11.3	2.95	124	.241	.300	0	—	0	23	19	-2	1.7
1974	NY-A	19	15	.559	38	38	17	4	0	279²	275	24	91	154	12.0	3.60	98	.259	.323	0	—	0	0	-2	-1	-0.3
1975	NY-A	16	16	.500	38	37	15	2	0	272¹	271	25	72	132	11.4	3.50	105	.264	.313	0	—	0	8	5	-3	0.4
1976	Pit-N	8	11	.421	29	26	3	0	0	179	193	10	48	86	12.2	3.52	99	.281	.330	5	.096	-2	-0	-1	1	-0.1
1977	Oak-A	10	6	.625	26	25	1	0	0	147²	155	19	49	74	12.6	4.69	86	.265	.325	0	—	0	-10	-11	-1	-1.0
	Sea-A	2	0	1.000	3	3	1	0	0	22¹	26	1	4	3	12.9	3.63	113	.286	.330	0	—	0	1	1	-1	0.1
	Yr	12	6	.667	29	28	2	0	0	170	181	20	53	77	12.5	4.55	89	.265	.319	0	—	0	-9	-10	-2	-0.9
	NY-N	0	1	.000	1	1	0	0	0	7	6	0	1	3	9.0	3.86	97	.261	.292	0	.000	-0	0	0	-0	-0.1
1978	Tex-A	9	8	.529	28	22	6	2	2	171	166	10	52	71	11.6	3.74	100	.255	.313	0	—	0	0	0	1	0.1
1979	Tex-A	10	7	.588	29	19	4	1	0	149	156	9	49	58	12.6	4.17	100	.269	.330	0	—	0	1	0	1	0.2
1980	Tex-A	14	11	.560	34	32	6	0	0	204¹	230	13	56	91	12.7	3.92	99	.285	.334	0	—	0	3	-1	-1	-0.2
1981	Tex-A	10	6	.625	20	20	4	4	0	143¹	136	8	33	65	10.7	3.08	113	.252	.297	0	—	0	9	6	1	1.1
1982	Tex-A	7	11	.389	21	21	2	0	0	122²	146	8	61	37	15.4	5.06	76	.307	.390	0	—	0	-13	-16	0	-1.7
	*Mil-A	5	4	.556	10	10	1	0	0	63	57	4	32	36	12.9	5.00	76	.242	.335	0	—	0	-6	-9	-1	-0.6
	Yr	12	15	.444	31	31	3	0	0	185²	203	12	93	73	14.4	5.04	76	.281	.364	0	—	0	-20	-25	-0	-2.3
Total	11	124	105	.541	312	287	71	16	2	1996²	2036	151	624	955	12.1	3.78	99	.266	.324	5	.093	-2	13	-10	-5	-0.6

● IRV MEDLINGER Medlinger, Irving John b: 6/18/27, Chicago, Ill. d: 9/3/75, Wheeling, Ill. BL/TL, 5'11", 185 lbs. Deb: 4/20/49

1949	StL-A	0	0	—	3	0	0	0	0	4	11	1	3	4	31.5	27.00	17	.478	.538	0	—	0	-10	-10	-0	0.0
1951	StL-A	0	0	—	6	0	0	0	0	9²	10	1	12	5	20.5	8.38	52	.270	.449	0	—	0	-5	-4	-0	0.0
Total	2	0	0	—	9	0	0	0	0	13²	21	2	15	9	23.7	13.83	32	.350	.480	0	—	0	-15	-14	-0	0.0

● SCOTT MEDVIN Medvin, Scott Howard b: 9/16/61, North Olmsted, O. BR/TR, 6'1", 195 lbs. Deb: 5/11/88

1988	Pit-N	3	0	1.000	17	0	0	0	0	27²	23	1	9	16	10.7	4.88	70	.230	.300	0	.000	-0	-4	-5	0	-0.5
1989	Pit-N	0	1	.000	6	0	0	0	0	6¹	6	0	5	4	15.6	5.68	59	.240	.367	0	—	0	-2	-2	0	-0.2
1990	Sea-A	0	1	.000	5	0	0	0	0	4¹	7	0	2	1	20.8	6.23	64	.368	.455	0	—	0	-1	-1	0	-0.2
Total	3	3	2	.600	28	0	0	0	0	38¹	36	1	16	21	12.7	5.17	67	.250	.333	0	.000	-0	-7	-7	1	-0.9

● PETE MEEGAN Meegan, Peter J. "Steady Pete" b: 11/13/1863, San Francisco, Cal d: 3/15/05, San Francisco, Cal Deb: 8/12/1884

1884	Ric-a	7	12	.368	22	22	22	1	0	179	177	7	29	106	11.1	4.32	77	.246	.288	12	.160	-2	-21	-20	2	-1.7
1885	Pit-a	7	8	.467	18	16	14	1	0	146	146	1	38	58	12.0	3.39	95	.247	.303	13	.194	-1	-2	-3	-1	-0.4
Total	2	14	20	.412	40	38	36	2	0	325	323	8	67	164	11.5	3.90	84	.246	.295	25	.176	-3	-24	-23	1	-2.1

● BILL MEEHAN Meehan, William Thomas b: 9/4/1889, Osceola Mills, Pa. d: 10/8/82, Douglas, Wyo. BR/TR, 5'9", 155 lbs. Deb: 9/17/15

| 1915 | Phi-a | 0 | 1 | .000 | 1 | 1 | 0 | 0 | 0 | 4 | 7 | 0 | 3 | 4 | 22.5 | 11.25 | 26 | .389 | .476 | 1 | 1.000 | -1 | -4 | -4 | 0 | -0.6 |

● ROY MEEKER Meeker, Charles Roy b: 9/15/1900, Lead Mine, Mo. d: 3/25/29, Orlando, Fla. BL/TL, 5'9", 175 lbs. Deb: 9/22/23

1923	Phi-A	1	0	1.000	5	2	2	0	0	25	24	0	13	12	13.3	3.60	114	.253	.343	1	.111	-1	1	1	-0	0.1
1924	Phi-A	5	12	.294	30	14	5	1	0	146	166	7	81	55	15.5	4.68	91	.288	.381	11	.229	-0	-7	-6	-1	-0.8
1926	Cin-N	0	2	.000	7	1	0	0	0	21	24	1	9	5	14.1	6.43	57	.324	.398	0	.000	-1	-6	-6	0	-0.6
Total	3	6	14	.364	42	17	8	1	0	192	214	8	103	54	15.1	4.73	89	.289	.377	12	.194	-2	-12	-11	-1	-1.3

● JOUETT MEEKIN Meekin, George Jouett b: 2/21/1867, New Albany, Ind. d: 12/14/44, New Albany, Ind. BR/TR, 6'1", 180 lbs. Deb: 6/13/1891

| 1891 | Lou-a | 10 | 16 | .385 | 29 | 26 | 25 | 2 | 0 | 228 | 227 | 2 | 113 | 144 | 13.7 | 4.30 | 85 | .251 | .338 | 21 | .216 | 4 | -15 | -16 | -2 | -1.2 |

YEAR	TM/L	W	L	PCT	G	GS	CG	SH	SV	IP	H	HR	BB	SO	RAT	ERA	ERA+	OAV	OOB	BH	AVG	PB	PR	/A	PD	TPI
1892	Lou-N	7	10	.412	19	18	17	0	0	156¹	168	3	78	67	14.5	4.03	76	.264	.350	5	.078	-5	-13	-17	0	-1.9
	Was-N	3	10	.231	14	14	13	1	0	112	112	2	48	58	13.2	3.46	94	.250	.328	6	.133	-1	-2	-3	0	-0.3
	Yr	10	20	.333	33	32	30	1	0	268¹	280	5	126	125	13.8	3.79	83	.257	.336	11	.101	-5	-15	-19	0	-2.2
1893	Was-N	10	15	.400	31	28	24	1	0	245	289	6	140	91	16.0	4.96	93	.285	.376	28	.282	7	-8	-9	-1	-0.4
1894	*NY-N	33	9	.786	52	48	40	1	2	409	404	8	171	133	12.9	3.70	142	.255	.332	48	.282	7	74	70	-3	5.5
1895	NY-N	16	11	.593	29	29	24	1	0	225²	296	10	73	76	15.1	5.30	88	.312	.366	28	.292	4	-13	-17	-1	-1.2
1896	NY-N	26	14	.650	42	41	34	0	0	334¹	378	8	127	110	14.0	3.82	110	.283	.351	43	.299	12	20	14	-3	2.1
1897	NY-N	20	11	.645	37	34	30	2	0	303²	328	9	99	83	12.9	3.76	110	.273	.333	41	.299	6	19	13	-3	1.3
1898	NY-N	16	18	.471	38	37	34	1	0	320	329	9	108	82	12.6	3.77	92	.264	.328	27	.209	1	-6	-10	-5	-1.3
1899	NY-N	5	11	.313	18	18	16	0	0	148¹	169	4	70	30	15.0	4.37	86	.286	.369	12	.207	1	-8	-10	-3	-1.1
	Bos-N	7	6	.538	13	13	12	0	0	108	111	0	23	23	11.3	2.83	147	.266	.307	7	.171	-1	12	16	-2	1.3
	Yr	12	17	.414	31	31	28	0	0	256¹	280	4	93	53	13.2	3.72	105	.275	.337	19	.192	-1	4	6	-5	0.2
1900	Pit-N	0	2	.000	2	2	1	0	0	13	20	1	8	3	20.1	6.92	52	.351	.439	0	.000	-0	-5	-5	-1	-0.6
Total	10	153	133	.535	324	308	270	9	2	2603¹	2831	67	1058	900	13.8	4.07	102	.273	.345	267	.243	29	55	27	-22	2.2

● **PHIL MEELER**   Meeler, Charles Phillip b: 7/3/48, South Boston, Va.   BR/TR, 6′5″, 215 lbs.   Deb: 5/10/72

		W	L	PCT	G	GS	CG	SH	SV	IP	H	HR	BB	SO	RAT	ERA	ERA+	OAV	OOB	BH	AVG	PB	PR	/A	PD	TPI
1972	Det-A	0	1	.000	7	0	0	0	0	8¹	10	1	0	7	5	18.4	4.32	73	.303	.425	0	.000	-0	-1	-1	0	-0.2

● **RUSS MEERS**   Meers, Russell Harlan "Babe" b: 11/28/18, Tilton, Ill.   d: 11/16/94, Lancaster, Pa.   BL/TL, 5′10″, 170 lbs.   Deb: 9/28/41

		W	L	PCT	G	GS	CG	SH	SV	IP	H	HR	BB	SO	RAT	ERA	ERA+	OAV	OOB	BH	AVG	PB	PR	/A	PD	TPI
1941	Chi-N	0	1	.000	1	1	0	0	0	8	5	0	0	6	6.8	1.13	312	.172	.200	0	.000	-0	2	2	-0	0.2
1946	Chi-N	1	2	.333	7	2	0	0	0	11¹	10	0	10	12	15.9	3.18	104	.238	.385	1	1.000	-0	0	0	-0	0.1
1947	Chi-N	2	0	1.000	35	1	0	0	0	64¹	61	5	38	38	14.1	4.48	88	.263	.371	2	.143	-1	-3	-4	-0	-0.2
Total	3	3	3	.500	43	4	0	0	0	83²	76	5	48	35	13.7	3.98	96	.251	.359	3	.176	-1	-0	-1	-0	0.1

● **HEINIE MEINE**   Meine, Henry William "The Count Of Luxemburg" b: 5/1/1896, St.Louis, Mo.   d: 3/18/68, St.Louis, Mo.   BR/TR, 5′11″, 180 lbs.   Deb: 8/16/22

		W	L	PCT	G	GS	CG	SH	SV	IP	H	HR	BB	SO	RAT	ERA	ERA+	OAV	OOB	BH	AVG	PB	PR	/A	PD	TPI
1922	StL-A	0	0	—	1	0	0	0	0	4	5	1	2	0	15.8	4.50	92	.313	.389	0	.000	-0	-0	0	0	0.0
1929	Pit-N	7	6	.538	22	13	7	1	1	108	120	4	34	19	13.4	4.50	106	.291	.355	4	.103	-3	2	3	-2	0.0
1930	Pit-N	6	8	.429	20	16	4	0	1	117¹	168	6	44	18	16.6	6.14	81	.346	.406	5	.122	-3	-15	-15	3	-1.4
1931	Pit-N	**19**	13	.594	36	35	22	3	0	**284**	278	8	87	58	11.8	2.98	129	.254	.313	14	.146	-2	28	27	6	2.6
1932	Pit-N	12	9	.571	28	25	13	1	1	172¹	193	6	45	32	12.6	3.86	99	.278	.324	10	.164	-2	0	-1	-1	-0.4
1933	Pit-N	15	8	.652	32	29	12	0	2	207¹	227	10	50	50	12.1	3.65	91	.278	.321	13	.173	-1	-7	-8	-3	-1.2
1934	Pit-N	7	6	.538	26	14	2	0	0	106¹	134	12	25	22	13.5	4.32	95	.306	.345	3	.107	-1	-3	-2	-1	-0.9
Total	7	66	50	.569	165	132	60	7	3	999¹	1125	47	287	199	12.9	4.06	101	.291	.344	49	.144	-12	5	4	-4	-0.9

● **FRANK MEINKE**   Meinke, Frank Louis b: 10/18/1863, Chicago, Ill.   d: 11/8/31, Chicago, Ill.   BR, 5′10.5″, 172 lbs.   Deb: 5/1/1884   F♦

		W	L	PCT	G	GS	CG	SH	SV	IP	H	HR	BB	SO	RAT	ERA	ERA+	OAV	OOB	BH	AVG	PB	PR	/A	PD	TPI
1884	Det-N	8	23	.258	35	31	31	1	0	289	341	10	63	124	12.6	3.18	91	.275	.310	56	.164	-3	-6	-9	-2	-1.1
1885	Det-N	0	1	.000	1	1	0	0	0	5	13	0	4	0	30.6	3.60	79	.433	.500	0	.000	-0	-0	-0	-1	-0.1
Total	2	8	24	.250	36	32	31	1	0	294	354	10	67	124	12.9	3.18	91	.279	.315	56	.163	-3	-7	-9	-2	-1.2

● **SAM MEJIAS**   Mejias, Samuel Elias b: 5/9/52, Santiago, D.R.   BR/TR, 6′, 170 lbs.   Deb: 9/6/76   C♦

		W	L	PCT	G	GS	CG	SH	SV	IP	H	HR	BB	SO	RAT	ERA	ERA+	OAV	OOB	BH	AVG	PB	PR	/A	PD	TPI
1978	Mon-N	0	0	—	1	0	0	0	0	1	0	0	0	0	9.0	0.00	—	.000	.250	13	.232					

● **JOSE MELENDEZ**   Melendez, Jose Luis (Garcia) b: 9/2/65, Naguabo, P.R.   BR/TR, 6′2″, 175 lbs.   Deb: 9/11/90

		W	L	PCT	G	GS	CG	SH	SV	IP	H	HR	BB	SO	RAT	ERA	ERA+	OAV	OOB	BH	AVG	PB	PR	/A	PD	TPI
1990	Sea-A	0	0	—	3	0	0	0	0	5¹	8	2	3	7	20.3	11.81	33	.333	.429	0	—	0	-5	-5	-0	-0.6
1991	SD-N	8	5	.615	31	9	0	0	3	93²	77	11	24	60	9.8	3.27	116	.221	.273	2	.100	-0	4	6	-1	0.6
1992	SD-N	6	7	.462	56	3	0	0	0	89¹	82	9	20	82	10.6	2.92	122	.249	.298	0	.000	-0	6	7	-1	0.8
1993	Bos-A	2	1	.667	9	0	0	0	0	16	10	2	5	14	8.4	2.25	205	.179	.246	0	—	0	4	4	-0	0.5
1994	Bos-A	0	1	.000	10	0	0	0	0	16¹	20	3	8	9	16.5	6.06	83	.323	.417	0	—	0	-2	-2	-0	-0.2
Total	5	16	14	.533	109	12	0	0	3	220²	197	27	60	172	10.8	3.47	111	.241	.298	2	.080	-1	7	10	-2	1.7

● **STEVE MELTER**   Melter, Stephen Blazius b: 1/2/1886, Cherokee, Iowa   d: 1/28/62, Mishawaka, Ind.   BR/TR, 6′2″, 180 lbs.   Deb: 6/27/09

		W	L	PCT	G	GS	CG	SH	SV	IP	H	HR	BB	SO	RAT	ERA	ERA+	OAV	OOB	BH	AVG	PB	PR	/A	PD	TPI
1909	StL-N	0	1	.000	23	1	0	0	3	64¹	79	1	20	24	14.1	3.50	72	.322	.378	2	.133	-1	-6	-7	1	-0.1

● **CLIFF MELTON**   Melton, Clifford George "Mickey Mouse" or "Mountain Music" b: 1/3/12, Brevard, N.C.   d: 7/28/86, Baltimore, Md.   BL/TL, 6′5.5″, 203 lbs.   Deb: 4/25/37

		W	L	PCT	G	GS	CG	SH	SV	IP	H	HR	BB	SO	RAT	ERA	ERA+	OAV	OOB	BH	AVG	PB	PR	/A	PD	TPI
1937	*NY-N	20	9	.690	46	27	14	2	**7**	248	216	9	55	142	10.1	2.61	149	.233	.280	10	.122	-5	36	**35**	4	3.9
1938	NY-N	14	14	.500	36	31	10	1	0	243	266	19	61	101	12.1	3.89	97	.276	.319	14	.175	-1	-3	-3	2	-0.3
1939	NY-N	12	15	.444	41	23	9	2	5	207¹	214	7	65	95	12.3	3.56	110	.269	.327	12	.182	-1	8	8	1	1.0
1940	NY-N	10	11	.476	37	21	4	1	2	166²	185	9	68	91	13.8	4.91	79	.285	.355	12	.222	2	-20	-19	2	-1.9
1941	NY-N	8	11	.421	42	22	9	3	1	194¹	181	14	33	91	10.3	3.01	123	.246	.305	7	.115	-3	13	15	4	1.4
1942	NY-N†	4	5	.688	23	17	12	2	1	143²	122	9	33	61	9.8	2.63	128	.229	.276	11	.234	2	11	12	3	1.8
1943	NY-N	9	13	.409	34	28	6	2	0	186¹	184	7	69	55	12.4	3.19	108	.257	.325	8	.148	0	4	5	3	1.0
1944	NY-N	2	2	.500	13	10	1	0	0	64¹	78	5	19	15	13.7	4.06	90	.294	.344	3	.120	-1	-3	-3	1	-0.2
Total	8	86	80	.518	272	179	65	13	16	1453²	1446	79	431	660	11.8	3.42	109	.259	.314	77	.164	-9	47	50	20	6.7

● **RUBE MELTON**   Melton, Reuben Franklin b: 2/27/17, Cramerton, N.C.   d: 9/11/71, Greer, S.C.   BR/TR, 6′5″, 205 lbs.   Deb: 4/17/41

		W	L	PCT	G	GS	CG	SH	SV	IP	H	HR	BB	SO	RAT	ERA	ERA+	OAV	OOB	BH	AVG	PB	PR	/A	PD	TPI
1941	Phi-N	1	5	.167	25	5	2	0	0	83²	81	4	47	57	13.8	4.73	78	.258	.355	2	.105	-1	-10	-10	-1	-0.9
1942	Phi-N	9	20	.310	42	29	10	1	4	209¹	180	7	114	107	12.8	3.70	89	.234	.335	8	.123	-1	-9	-9	-2	-1.5
1943	Bro-N	5	8	.385	30	17	4	2	0	119¹	106	3	79	63	14.3	3.92	86	.243	.365	4	.105	-2	-7	-7	-1	-1.2
1944	Bro-N	9	13	.409	37	23	6	1	0	187¹	178	6	96	91	13.3	3.46	103	.254	.345	7	.123	-3	3	2	-0	0.0
1946	Bro-N	6	3	.667	24	12	3	2	1	99²	72	4	52	44	11.5	1.99	170	.206	.314	3	.107	-2	16	15	-0	1.2
1947	Bro-N	0	1	.000	4	1	0	0	0	4²	7	1	7	1	27.0	13.50	31	.350	.519	1	1.000	-0	-5	-5	-0	-0.8
Total	6	30	50	.375	162	87	25	6	5	704	624	22	395	363	13.2	3.62	95	.241	.344	25	.120	-9	-12	-14	-5	-3.2

● **MARIO MENDOZA**   Mendoza, Mario (Aizpuru) b: 12/26/50, Chihuahua, Mex.   BR/TR, 5′11″, 187 lbs.   Deb: 4/26/74   ♦

		W	L	PCT	G	GS	CG	SH	SV	IP	H	HR	BB	SO	RAT	ERA	ERA+	OAV	OOB	BH	AVG	PB	PR	/A	PD	TPI
1977	Pit-N	0	0	—	1	0	0	0	0	2	3	1	2	0	22.5	13.50	30	.375	.500	16	.198	0	-2	-2	0	-0.2

● **MIKE MENDOZA**   Mendoza, Michael Joseph b: 11/26/55, Inglewood, Cal.   BR/TR, 6′5″, 215 lbs.   Deb: 9/7/79   ♦

		W	L	PCT	G	GS	CG	SH	SV	IP	H	HR	BB	SO	RAT	ERA	ERA+	OAV	OOB	BH	AVG	PB	PR	/A	PD	TPI
1979	Hou-N	0	0	—	1	0	0	0	0	1	0	0	0	0	0.0	0.00	—	.000	.000	0	—	0	0	0	0	0.0

● **RAMIRO MENDOZA**   Mendoza, Ramiro b: 6/15/72, Los Santos, Panama   BR/TR, 6′2″, 154 lbs.   Deb: 5/25/96

		W	L	PCT	G	GS	CG	SH	SV	IP	H	HR	BB	SO	RAT	ERA	ERA+	OAV	OOB	BH	AVG	PB	PR	/A	PD	TPI
1996	NY-A	4	5	.444	12	11	0	0	0	53	80	5	10	34	16.0	6.79	74	.343	.381	0	—	0	-11	-10	1	-1.4

● **JOCK MENEFEE**   Menefee, John b: 1/15/1868, Rowlesburg, W.Va.   d: 3/11/53, Belle Vernon, Pa.   BR/TR, 6′, 165 lbs.   Deb: 8/17/1892   ♦

		W	L	PCT	G	GS	CG	SH	SV	IP	H	HR	BB	SO	RAT	ERA	ERA+	OAV	OOB	BH	AVG	PB	PR	/A	PD	TPI
1892	Pit-N	0	0	—	1	0	0	0	0	4	10	0	2	1	27.0	11.25	29	.455	.500	2	.274	-0	-4	-4	0	-0.2
1893	Lou-N	8	7	.533	15	15	14	1	0	129¹	150	3	40	30	13.4	4.24	104	.281	.335	20	.274	4	6	2	2	0.7
1894	Lou-N	8	17	.320	28	24	20	1	0	211²	258	3	50	43	13.5	4.29	119	.297	.342	13	.165	-6	24	19	2	1.3
	Pit-N	5	8	.385	13	13	13	0	0	111²	159	4	39	33	16.1	5.40	97	.331	.383	12	.255	-0	-1	-2	2	0.0
	Yr	13	25	.342	41	37	33	1	0	323¹	417	7	89	76	14.1	4.68	110	.307	.351	25	.198	-5	23	17	4	1.3
1895	Pit-N	0	1	.000	2	1	0	0	0	1²	2	0	2	0	54.0	16.20	28	.286	.667	0	—	-0	-2	-2	-0	-0.8
1898	NY-N	0	1	.000	1	1	0	0	0	9¹	11	0	2	3	14.5	4.82	72	.289	.357	0	—	-0	-1	-1	-0	-0.2
1900	Chi-N	9	4	.692	16	13	11	0	0	117	140	1	35	31	14.2	3.85	94	.296	.357	5	.109	-3	-2	-3	-2	-0.7
1901	Chi-N	8	12	.400	21	20	19	0	0	182¹	201	4	34	55	11.9	3.80	85	.278	.315	39	.257	4	-10	-11	-1	-0.7
1902	Chi-N	12	10	.545	22	21	20	2	0	197¹	202	2	26	60	10.7	2.42	112	.265	.294	50	.231	3	8	4	1	0.9
1903	Chi-N	8	10	.444	20	17	13	1	0	147	157	3	38	39	12.3	3.00	105	.275	.327	13	.203	1	2	2	-2	0.6
Total	9	58	70	.453	139	125	111	7	0	1111¹	1290	20	273	293	13.0	3.81	101	.288	.335	152	.222	2	23	6	6	1.2

● **TONY MENENDEZ**   Menendez, Antonio Gustavo (Remon) b: 2/20/65, Havana, Cuba   BR/TR, 6′2″, 190 lbs.   Deb: 6/22/92

		W	L	PCT	G	GS	CG	SH	SV	IP	H	HR	BB	SO	RAT	ERA	ERA+	OAV	OOB	BH	AVG	PB	PR	/A	PD	TPI
1992	Cin-N	1	0	1.000	3	0	0	0	0	4²	1	1	0	5	1.9	1.93	187	.067	.067	0	—	0	1	1	-0	0.2
1993	Pit-N	2	0	1.000	14	0	0	0	0	21	20	4	2	9	10.7	3.00	135	.256	.301	0	—	0	2	2	-0	0.2
1994	SF-N	0	1	.000	6	0	0	0	0	3¹	8	2	4	6	27.0	21.60	19	.471	.526	0	—	0	-6	-7	-0	-1.5
Total	3	3	1	.750	23	0	0	0	0	29	29	7	6	20	11.2	4.97	80	.264	.308	0	.000	-0	-3	-3	-1	-1.1

YEAR	TM/L	W	L	PCT	G	GS	CG	SH	SV	IP	H	HR	BB	SO	RAT	ERA	ERA+	OAV	OOB	BH	AVG	PB	PR	/A	PD	TPI
● PAUL MENHART	Menhart, Paul Gerard b: 3/25/69, St.Louis, Mo. BR/TR, 6'2", 190 lbs. Deb: 4/27/95																									
1995	Tor-A	1	4	.200	21	9	1	0	0	78²	72	9	47	50	14.3	4.92	96	.248	.364	0	—	0	-2	-2	-0	-0.1
1996	Sea-A	2	2	.500	11	6	0	0	0	42	55	9	25	18	17.6	7.29	68	.327	.421	0	—	0	-11	-11	1	-0.8
Total	2	3	6	.333	32	15	1	0	0	120²	127	18	72	68	15.4	5.74	83	.277	.385	0	—	0	-13	-13	0	-0.9
● MIKE MEOLA	Meola, Emile Michael b: 10/19/05, New York, N.Y. d: 9/1/76, Fair Lawn, N.J. BR/TR, 5'11", 175 lbs. Deb: 4/24/33																									
1933	Bos-A	0	0	—	3	0	0	0	0	2¹	5	0	2	1	27.0	23.14	19	.417	.500	0	—	0	-5	-5	-0	0.0
1936	StL-A	0	1	.000	9	0	0	0	0	19¹	29	0	13	6	20.0	9.31	58	.358	.453	1	.500	1	-9	-8	-0	-0.3
	Bos-A	0	2	.000	6	3	1	0	1	21¹	29	0	10	8	16.9	5.48	97	.326	.400	1	.143	-0	-1	-0	1	0.0
	Yr	0	3	.000	15	3	1	0	1	40²	58	0	23	14	18.1	7.30	73	.339	.421	2	.222	0	-10	-9	1	-0.3
Total	2	0	3	.000	18	3	1	0	1	43	63	0	25	15	18.8	8.16	65	.346	.431	2	.222	0	-15	-14	0	-0.3
● JOSE MERCEDES	Mercedes, Jose Miguel (Santana) b: 3/5/71, ElSeibo, D.R. BR/TR, 6'1", 180 lbs. Deb: 5/31/94																									
1994	Mil-A	2	0	1.000	19	0	0	0	0	31	22	4	16	11	11.6	2.32	217	.216	.333	0	—	0	9	9	-1	0.4
1995	Mil-A	0	1	.000	5	0	0	0	0	7¹	12	1	8	6	24.5	9.82	51	.375	.500	0	—	0	-4	-4	-0	-0.5
1996	Mil-A	0	2	.000	11	0	0	0	0	16²	20	6	5	6	13.5	9.18	57	.294	.342	0	—	0	-8	-7	-0	-0.7
Total	3	2	3	.400	35	0	0	0	0	55	54	11	29	23	13.9	5.40	94	.267	.365	0	—	0	-3	-3	-1	-0.8
● WIN MERCER	Mercer, George Barclay b: 6/20/1874, Chester, W.Va. d: 1/12/03, San Francisco, Cal BR/TR, 5'7", 140 lbs. Deb: 4/21/1894 ◆																									
1894	Was-N	17	23	.425	50	39	30	0	3	339¹	445	9	126	72	15.5	3.85	137	.313	.375	48	.291	3	56	54	2	5.0
1895	Was-N	13	23	.361	43	38	32	0	2	311	430	17	96	84	15.7	4.46	108	.323	.376	50	.255	6	11	12	-1	1.0
1896	Was-N	25	18	.581	46	45	38	2	0	366¹	456	10	117	94	14.6	4.13	107	.302	.360	38	.244	0	10	11	1	1.1
1897	Was-N	21	20	.512	47	43	35	3	3	342	403	6	104	91	14.1	3.18	136	.291	.353	44	.317	4	43	44	1	5.0
1898	Was-N	12	18	.400	33	30	24	0	0	233²	309	3	71	52	15.3	4.81	76	.316	.373	80	.321	8	-31	-30	-1	-2.5
1899	Was-N	7	14	.333	23	21	21	0	0	186	234	2	53	28	14.2	4.60	85	.307	.356	112	.299	5	-15	-14	3	-0.5
1900	NY-N	13	17	.433	33	29	26	1	0	242²	303	5	58	39	14.1	3.86	94	.305	.355	73	.294	7	-4	-7	2	0.1
1901	Was-A	9	13	.409	24	22	19	1	1	179²	217	8	50	31	13.9	4.56	80	.295	.348	42	.300	6	-18	-18	1	-1.1
1902	Det-A	15	18	.455	35	33	28	4	1	281²	282	5	80	40	11.9	3.04	120	.261	.318	18	.180	-2	17	19	4	2.1
Total	9	132	164	.446	334	300	253	11	10	2482¹	3079	64	755	531	14.4	3.98	107	.302	.358	505	.286	35	68	72	9	10.2
● JACK MERCER	Mercer, Harry Vernon b: 3/10/1889, Zanesville, Ohio d: 6/25/45, Dayton, Ohio Deb: 8/2/10																									
1910	Pit-N	0	0	—	1	0	0	0	0	1	0	0	2	1	18.0	0.00	—	.000	.500	0	—	0	0	0	0	0.0
● MARK MERCER	Mercer, Mark Kenneth b: 5/22/54, Fort Bragg, N.C. BL/TL, 6'5", 220 lbs. Deb: 9/1/81																									
1981	Tex-A	0	1	.000	7	0	0	0	2	7²	7	1	7	8	16.4	4.70	74	.241	.389	0	—	0	-1	-1	0	0.0
● KENT MERCKER	Mercker, Kent Franklin b: 2/1/68, Indianapolis, Ind. BL/TL, 6'1", 175 lbs. Deb: 9/22/89																									
1989	Atl-N	0	0	—	2	1	0	0	0	4¹	8	0	6	4	29.1	12.46	29	.400	.538	0	.000	-0	-4	-4	-0	0.0
1990	Atl-N	4	7	.364	36	0	0	0	7	48¹	43	6	24	39	12.8	3.17	127	.236	.332	0	.000	-0	3	5	-1	1.0
1991	*Atl-N	5	3	.625	50	4	0	0	6	73¹	56	5	35	62	11.3	2.58	151	.211	.305	1	.100	-0	9	11	-1	1.2
1992	*Atl-N	3	2	.600	53	0	0	0	6	68¹	51	4	35	49	11.7	3.42	107	.207	.313	0	.000	-0	1	2	-2	-0.1
1993	*Atl-N	3	1	.750	43	6	0	0	0	66	52	7	36	59	12.3	2.86	140	.212	.318	0	.000	-1	9	8	-1	0.2
1994	Atl-N	9	4	.692	20	17	2	1	0	112¹	90	16	45	111	10.8	3.45	123	.220	.297	2	.054	-2	10	10	-0	0.8
1995	*Atl-N	7	8	.467	29	26	0	0	0	143	140	16	61	102	12.8	4.15	103	.258	.336	5	.104	-2	0	2	0	0.0
1996	Bal-A	3	6	.333	14	12	0	0	0	58	73	12	35	22	17.2	7.76	63	.307	.402	0	—	0	-18	-18	-1	-2.2
	Cle-A	1	0	1.000	10	0	0	0	0	11²	10	1	3	7	10.0	3.09	159	.244	.295	0	—	0	2	2	-0	0.2
	Yr	4	6	.400	24	12	0	0	0	69²	83	13	38	29	15.6	6.98	70	.290	.373	0	—	0	-15	-16	-1	-2.0
Total	8	35	31	.530	257	66	2	1	19	585¹	523	62	280	455	12.6	3.91	107	.239	.329	8	.068	-7	12	17	-6	1.1
● SPIKE MERENA	Merena, John Joseph b: 11/18/09, Paterson, N.J. d: 3/9/77, Bridgeport, Conn. BL/TL, 6', 185 lbs. Deb: 9/16/34																									
1934	Bos-A	1	2	.333	4	3	2	1	0	24²	20	2	16	7	13.5	2.92	165	.222	.346	1	.143	-0	4	5	-1	0.5
● RON MERIDITH	Meridith, Ronald Knox b: 11/26/56, San Pedro, Cal. BL/TL, 6', 175 lbs. Deb: 9/16/84																									
1984	Chi-N	0	0	—	3	0	0	0	0	5¹	6	1	2	4	13.5	3.38	116	.273	.333	0	—	0	0	0	-0	0.0
1985	Chi-N	3	2	.600	32	0	0	0	1	46¹	53	3	24	23	15.2	4.47	89	.301	.388	1	.250	0	-5	-2	0	-0.2
1986	Tex-A	1	0	1.000	5	0	0	0	0	3	2	1	2	9	9.0	3.00	143	.286	.375	0	—	0	0	0	0	0.1
1987	Tex-A	1	0	1.000	11	0	0	0	0	20²	25	7	12	17	16.1	6.10	73	.298	.385	0	—	0	-4	-4	0	-0.1
Total	4	5	2	.714	51	0	0	0	1	75¹	86	11	39	46	15.1	4.78	87	.298	.383	1	.250	0	-8	-5	1	-0.2
● BRETT MERRIMAN	Merriman, Brett Alan b: 7/15/66, Jacksonville, Ill. BR/TR, 6'2", 180 lbs. Deb: 4/8/93																									
1993	Min-A	1	1	.500	19	0	0	0	0	27	36	3	23	14	20.7	9.67	45	.343	.473	0	—	0	-16	-16	0	-1.0
1994	Min-A	0	1	.000	15	0	0	0	0	17	18	0	14	10	19.1	6.35	77	.269	.424	0	—	0	-3	-3	-0	-0.2
Total	2	1	2	.333	34	0	0	0	0	44	54	3	37	24	20.0	8.39	54	.314	.454	0	—	0	-19	-19	-0	-1.2
● GEORGE MERRITT	Merritt, George Washington b: 4/14/1880, Paterson, N.J. d: 2/21/38, Memphis, Tenn. TR, 6', 160 lbs. Deb: 9/6/01 ◆																									
1901	Pit-N	3	0	1.000	3	3	3	0	0	24	28	0	5	5	13.1	4.88	67	.289	.337	3	.273	1	-4	-4	-0	-0.3
1903	Pit-N	0	0	—	1	0	0	0	0	4	4	0	1	2	11.3	2.25	144	.267	.313	4	.148	0	0	0	-0	0.0
Total	2	3	0	1.000	4	3	3	0	0	28	32	0	6	7	12.9	4.50	73	.286	.333	10	.213	1	-4	-4	-0	-0.3
● JIM MERRITT	Merritt, James Joseph b: 12/9/43, Altadena, Cal. BL/TL, 6'2", 180 lbs. Deb: 8/2/65																									
1965	*Min-A	5	4	.556	16	9	1	0	2	76²	68	11	20	61	10.3	3.17	112	.239	.289	3	.136	0	2	3	-0	0.4
1966	Min-A	7	14	.333	31	18	5	1	3	144	112	17	33	124	9.1	3.38	107	.212	.258	4	.103	-1	1	4	-0	0.4
1967	Min-A	13	7	.650	37	28	11	4	0	227²	196	21	30	161	9.2	2.53	137	.230	.262	10	.135	0	18	24	-2	2.0
1968	Min-A	12	16	.429	38	34	11	1	1	238¹	207	21	52	181	10.0	3.25	95	.232	.279	10	.141	0	-7	-4	-1	-0.5
1969	Cin-N	17	9	.654	42	36	8	1	0	251	269	33	61	144	12.0	4.37	86	.273	.318	11	.143	0	-22	-17	-3	-1.9
1970	*Cin-N★	20	12	.625	35	35	12	1	0	234	248	21	53	136	11.6	4.08	99	.270	.311	14	.169	3	-1	-1	-2	-0.1
1971	Cin-N	1	11	.083	28	11	0	0	0	107	115	14	31	44	12.5	4.37	77	.279	.334	4	.138	0	-11	-12	-2	-1.4
1972	Cin-N	1	0	1.000	4	1	0	0	0	8	13	1	2	4	16.9	4.50	71	.361	.395	0	.000	0	-1	-0	-0	-0.2
1973	Tex-A	5	13	.278	35	19	8	1	1	160	191	18	34	65	12.7	4.05	92	.296	.332	0	—	0	-4	-6	-1	-0.5
1974	Tex-A	0	0	—	26	1	0	0	0	32²	46	3	4	18	14.3	4.13	86	.329	.356	0	—	0	-2	-2	-1	0.0
1975	Tex-A	0	0	—	5	0	0	0	0	3	3	0	0	0	9.8	0.00	—	.214	.267	0	—	0	2	2	-0	0.0
Total	11	81	86	.485	297	192	56	9	7	1483	1468	160	322	932	11.0	3.65	98	.257	.300	56	.141	3	-25	-11	-10	-1.8
● LLOYD MERRITT	Merritt, Lloyd Wesley b: 4/8/33, St.Louis, Mo. BR/TR, 6', 189 lbs. Deb: 4/22/57																									
1957	StL-N	1	2	.333	44	0	0	0	0	65¹	60	7	28	35	12.7	3.31	120	.251	.339	0	.000	-0	4	5	0	0.3
● SAM MERTES	Mertes, Samuel Blair "Sandow" b: 8/6/1872, San Francisco, Cal. d: 3/11/45, San Francisco, Cal BR/TR, 5'10", 185 lbs. Deb: 6/30/1896 ◆																									
1902	Chi-A	1	0	1.000	1	0	0	0	0	8	6	0	0	0	6.8	1.13	301	.207	.207	140	.282	0	2	2	-1	0.2
● JIM MERTZ	Mertz, James Verlin b: 8/10/16, Lima, Ohio BR/TR, 5'10.5", 170 lbs. Deb: 5/1/43																									
1943	Was-A	5	7	.417	33	10	2	0	3	116²	109	7	58	53	12.9	4.63	69	.251	.339	7	.184	0	-17	-18	0	-1.8
● JOSE MESA	Mesa, Jose Ramon Nova (b: Jose Ramon Nova (Mesa)) b: 5/22/66, Pueblo Viejo, D.R. BR/TR, 6'3", 220 lbs. Deb: 9/10/87																									
1987	Bal-A	1	3	.250	6	5	0	0	0	31¹	38	5	15	17	15.2	6.03	73	.297	.371	0	—	0	-5	-6	-1	-0.7
1990	Bal-A	3	2	.600	7	7	0	0	0	46²	37	2	27	24	12.5	3.86	98	.218	.328	0	—	0	0	-0	0	0.1
1991	Bal-A	6	11	.353	23	23	1	0	0	123²	151	11	62	64	15.7	5.97	66	.307	.388	0	—	0	-26	-28	1	-3.1
1992	Bal-A	3	8	.273	13	12	0	0	0	67²	77	9	27	22	14.1	5.19	78	.287	.357	0	—	0	-9	-9	-0	-1.2
	Cle-A	4	4	.500	15	15	1	0	0	93	92	5	43	40	13.3	4.16	94	.262	.346	0	—	0	-2	-3	-1	-0.2
	Yr	7	12	.368	28	27	1	0	0	160²	169	14	70	62	13.5	4.59	86	.271	.346	0	—	0	-12	-11	-0	-1.4
1993	Cle-A	10	12	.455	34	33	3	0	0	208²	232	23	62	118	13.0	4.92	88	.286	.345	0	—	0	-14	-14	-0	-1.3
1994	Cle-A	7	5	.583	51	0	0	0	2	73	71	3	26	63	12.3	3.82	123	.254	.325	0	—	0	8	7	0	1.1
1995	*Cle-A★	3	0	1.000	62	0	0	0	46	64	49	3	17	58	9.3	1.13	417	.216	.270	0	—	0	26	25	1	4.3

YEAR TM/L	W	L	PCT	G	GS	CG	SH	SV	IP	H	HR	BB	SO	RAT	ERA	ERA+	OAV	OOB	BH	AVG	PB	PR	/A	PD	TPI
1996 *Cle-A☆	2	7	.222	69	0	0	0	39	72¹	69	6	28	64	12.4	3.73	131	.257	.333	0	—	0	10	9	-1	1.7
Total 8	39	52	.429	280	95	6	2	87	780¹	816	67	307	470	13.2	4.48	96	.273	.344	0	—		-13	-17	-1	0.7

● BUD MESSENGER
Messenger, Andrew Warren   b: 2/1/1898, Grand Blanc, Mich.   d: 11/4/71, Lansing, Mich.   BR/TR, 6′, 175 lbs.   Deb: 7/31/24

YEAR TM/L	W	L	PCT	G	GS	CG	SH	SV	IP	H	HR	BB	SO	RAT	ERA	ERA+	OAV	OOB	BH	AVG	PB	PR	/A	PD	TPI
1924 Cle-A	2	0	1.000	5	2	1	0	0	25	28	4	14	4	15.1	4.32	99	.283	.372	1	.125	-0	-0	-0	-0	-0.1

● ANDY MESSERSMITH
Messersmith, John Alexander   b: 8/6/45, Toms River, N.J.   BR/TR, 6′1″, 200 lbs.   Deb: 7/4/68

YEAR TM/L	W	L	PCT	G	GS	CG	SH	SV	IP	H	HR	BB	SO	RAT	ERA	ERA+	OAV	OOB	BH	AVG	PB	PR	/A	PD	TPI
1968 Cal-A	4	2	.667	28	5	2	1	4	81¹	44	3	35	74	8.9	2.21	132	.157	.253	2	.100	-1	7	6	0	0.5
1969 Cal-A	16	11	.593	40	33	10	2	2	250	169	17	100	211	9.9	2.52	138	.190	.276	12	.156	2	31	27	-1	3.0
1970 Cal-A	11	10	.524	37	26	6	1	5	194²	144	21	78	162	10.5	3.01	120	.205	.290	11	.157	0	15	13	-1	1.4
1971 Cal-A☆	20	13	.606	38	38	14	4	0	276²	224	16	121	179	11.5	2.99	108	.218	.304	16	.172	4	14	8	1	1.4
1972 Cal-A	8	11	.421	25	21	10	3	2	169²	150	5	68	142	10.3	2.81	104	.207	.290	10	.189	2	5	2	-0	0.5
1973 LA-N	14	10	.583	33	33	10	3	0	249²	196	24	77	177	10.1	2.70	127	.214	.279	15	.169	2	27	20	-0	2.0
1974 *LA-N★	20	6	.769	39	39	13	3	0	292¹	227	24	94	221	10.0	2.59	132	.212	.278	23	.240	9	34	26	0	3.4
1975 LA-N☆	19	14	.576	42	40	19	7	1	321²	244	22	96	213	9.7	2.29	148	.213	.276	17	.157	2	47	40	-2	4.1
1976 Atl-N†	11	11	.500	29	28	12	3	1	207¹	166	14	74	135	10.5	3.04	125	.219	.290	4	.118	-0	-6	1	-0	2.0
1977 Atl-N	5	4	.556	16	16	1	0	0	102¹	101	12	39	69	12.5	4.40	101	.256	.326	4	.118	-0	-6	1	-0	-0.4
1978 NY-A	0	3	.000	6	5	0	0	0	22¹	24	7	15	16	16.1	5.64	64	.267	.377	0	—	-0	-5	-5	-0	-0.4
1979 LA-N	2	4	.333	11	11	1	0	0	62¹	55	9	34	26	12.9	4.91	74	.244	.344	2	.091	-1	-8	-9	-0	-0.8
Total 12	130	99	.568	344	295	98	27	15	2230¹	1719	174	831	1625	10.5	2.86	121	.212	.289	124	.170	20	172	145	-1	17.1

● TOM METCALF
Metcalf, Thomas John   b: 7/16/40, Amherst, Wis.   BR/TR, 6′2.5″, 174 lbs.   Deb: 8/4/63

YEAR TM/L	W	L	PCT	G	GS	CG	SH	SV	IP	H	HR	BB	SO	RAT	ERA	ERA+	OAV	OOB	BH	AVG	PB	PR	/A	PD	TPI
1963 NY-A	1	0	1.000	8	0	0	0	0	13	12	1	3	10	10.4	2.77	127	.250	.294	0	—	0	1	1	-0	0.1

● DEWEY METIVIER
Metivier, George Dewey   b: 5/6/1898, Cambridge, Mass.   d: 3/2/47, Cambridge, Mass.   BL/TR, 5′11″, 175 lbs.   Deb: 9/15/22

YEAR TM/L	W	L	PCT	G	GS	CG	SH	SV	IP	H	HR	BB	SO	RAT	ERA	ERA+	OAV	OOB	BH	AVG	PB	PR	/A	PD	TPI
1922 Cle-A	2	0	1.000	2	2	2	0	0	18	18	1	3	1	11.0	4.50	89	.265	.306	1	.167	-0	-1	-1	-0	-0.1
1923 Cle-A	4	2	.667	26	5	1	0	1	73¹	111	1	38	9	19.0	6.50	61	.368	.448	3	.150	-0	-21	-21	0	-1.5
1924 Cle-A	1	5	.167	26	6	1	0	3	76¹	110	3	34	14	17.0	5.31	81	.358	.422	3	.125	-2	-9	-9	-1	-0.9
Total 3	7	7	.500	54	13	4	0	4	167²	239	5	75	24	17.2	5.74	72	.353	.423	7	.140	-2	-31	-30	-1	-2.5

● BUTCH METZGER
Metzger, Clarence Edward   b: 5/23/52, Lafayette, Ind.   BR/TR, 6′1″, 185 lbs.   Deb: 9/8/74

YEAR TM/L	W	L	PCT	G	GS	CG	SH	SV	IP	H	HR	BB	SO	RAT	ERA	ERA+	OAV	OOB	BH	AVG	PB	PR	/A	PD	TPI
1974 SF-N	1	0	1.000	10	0	0	0	0	12¹	11	0	12	5	16.3	3.55	107	.239	.397	0	—	-0	-0	-0		0.0
1975 SD-N	1	0	1.000	4	0	0	0	0	4²	6	1	4	6	19.3	7.71	45	.316	.435	0	—	-0	-2	-2	-0	-0.4
1976 SD-N	11	4	.733	77	0	0	0	16	123¹	119	5	52	89	12.7	2.92	112	.258	.337	0	.000	-0	8	5	-0	0.9
1977 SD-N	0	0	—	17	1	0	0	0	22²	26	1	16	9	15.9	5.56	64	.307	.396	0	.000	-0	-4	-5	-0	-0.1
StL-N	4	2	.667	58	0	0	0	7	92²	78	5	38	48	11.4	3.11	124	.228	.307	0	.000	-1	8	8	-1	0.4
Yr	4	2	.667	75	1	0	0	7	115¹	105	5	54	57	12.2	3.59	105	.242	.322	0	.000	-1	4	3	-1	0.3
1978 NY-N	1	3	.250	21	0	0	0	0	37¹	44	4	22	21	17.1	6.51	54	.324	.415	0	—	-1	-12	-13	-1	-1.3
Total 5	18	9	.667	191	1	0	0	23	293¹	289	23	140	175	13.3	3.74	94	.262	.348	0	.000	-1	-2	-7	-2	-0.7

● BRIAN MEYER
Meyer, Brian Scott   b: 1/29/63, Camden, N.J.   BR/TR, 6′, 190 lbs.   Deb: 9/3/88

YEAR TM/L	W	L	PCT	G	GS	CG	SH	SV	IP	H	HR	BB	SO	RAT	ERA	ERA+	OAV	OOB	BH	AVG	PB	PR	/A	PD	TPI
1988 Hou-N	0	0	—	8	0	0	0	1	12¹	9	2	4	10	9.5	1.46	227	.225	.295	0	—	0	3	3	1	0.1
1989 Hou-N	0	1	.000	12	0	0	0	1	18	16	0	13	13	15.0	4.50	75	.239	.370	0	—	-0	-2	-2	0	-0.1
1990 Hou-N	0	4	.000	14	0	0	0	0	20¹	16	3	6	6	9.7	2.21	168	.211	.268	0	.000	-0	4	3	1	0.7
Total 3	0	5	.000	34	0	0	0	2	50²	41	5	23	29	11.5	2.84	123	.224	.314	0	.000	-0	4	4	1	0.7

● JACK MEYER
Meyer, John Robert   b: 3/23/32, Philadelphia, Pa.   d: 3/9/67, Philadelphia, Pa.   BR/TR, 6′1″, 175 lbs.   Deb: 4/16/55

YEAR TM/L	W	L	PCT	G	GS	CG	SH	SV	IP	H	HR	BB	SO	RAT	ERA	ERA+	OAV	OOB	BH	AVG	PB	PR	/A	PD	TPI
1955 Phi-N	6	11	.353	50	5	0	0	16	110¹	75	14	66	97	11.7	3.43	116	.190	.310	2	.100	0	8	7	-1	1.1
1956 Phi-N	7	11	.389	41	7	2	0	2	96	86	8	51	66	13.2	4.41	84	.242	.343	4	.200	1	-7	-7	-0	-1.1
1957 Phi-N	0	2	.000	19	2	0	0	0	37²	44	7	28	34	17.4	5.73	66	.297	.412	1	.167	-0	-8	-8	0	-0.3
1958 Phi-N	3	6	.333	37	5	1	0	2	90¹	77	8	33	87	11.1	3.59	110	.232	.303	5	.278	1	4	4	-1	0.3
1959 Phi-N	5	3	.625	47	1	1	0	1	93²	76	9	53	71	12.5	3.36	122	.222	.328	1	.071	-0	6	8	0	0.5
1960 Phi-N	3	1	.750	7	4	0	0	2	25	25	2	11	18	13.0	4.32	90	.272	.350	1	.125	-0	-2	-1	-0	-0.2
1961 Phi-N	0	0	—	1	0	0	0	0	2	2	1	2	2	18.0	9.00	45	.286	.444	0	—	-0	-1	-1	-1	-0.1
Total 7	24	34	.414	202	24	4	0	21	455	385	49	244	375	12.6	3.92	100	.230	.332	14	.163	1	-0	-0	-1	0.1

● BOB MEYER
Meyer, Robert Bernard   b: 8/4/39, Toledo, Ohio   BR/TL, 6′2″, 185 lbs.   Deb: 4/20/64

YEAR TM/L	W	L	PCT	G	GS	CG	SH	SV	IP	H	HR	BB	SO	RAT	ERA	ERA+	OAV	OOB	BH	AVG	PB	PR	/A	PD	TPI
1964 NY-A	0	3	.000	7	1	0	0	0	18¹	16	1	12	12	13.7	4.91	74	.235	.350	0	.000	-0	-3	-3	0	-0.4
LA-A	1	1	.500	6	5	0	0	0	18	25	2	13	13	19.5	5.00	66	.333	.438	0	.000	-1	-3	-3	0	-0.4
KC-A	1	4	.200	9	7	2	0	0	42	37	2	33	30	15.0	3.86	99	.248	.385	0	.000	-1	-0	-1	-2	-0.2
Yr	2	8	.200	22	13	2	0	0	78¹	78	5	58	55	15.6	4.37	84	.266	.387	0	.000	-2	-6	-6	-0	-1.0
1969 Sea-A	0	3	.000	6	5	1	0	0	32²	30	4	10	17	11.6	3.31	110	.252	.321	1	.091	-1	1	1	-1	0.1
1970 Mil-A	0	1	.000	10	0	0	0	0	18¹	24	3	12	20	17.7	6.38	59	.329	.424	1	.333	-0	-5	-5	-0	-0.2
Total 3	2	12	.143	38	18	3	0	0	129¹	132	12	80	92	15.0	4.38	84	.273	.379	2	.057	-3	-11	-10	-1	-1.3

● RUSS MEYER
Meyer, Russell Charles "Rowdy" or "The Mad Monk"   b: 10/25/23, Peru, Ill.   BB/TR, 6′1″, 185 lbs.   Deb: 9/13/46   C

YEAR TM/L	W	L	PCT	G	GS	CG	SH	SV	IP	H	HR	BB	SO	RAT	ERA	ERA+	OAV	OOB	BH	AVG	PB	PR	/A	PD	TPI
1946 Chi-N	0	0	—	4	1	0	0	1	17	21	2	10	10	16.4	3.18	104	.309	.397	1	.200	0	0	0	0	0.0
1947 Chi-N	3	2	.600	23	2	1	0	0	45	43	4	14	22	11.6	3.40	116	.257	.319	3	.250	0	3	3	-0	0.2
1948 Chi-N	10	10	.500	29	26	8	3	0	164²	157	8	77	89	12.8	3.66	107	.254	.338	6	.107	-3	6	5	-0	0.2
1949 Phi-N	17	8	.680	37	28	14	2	1	213	199	14	70	78	11.4	3.08	128	.250	.311	10	.143	-1	23	20	-2	1.9
1950 *Phi-N	9	11	.450	32	25	3	0	1	159²	193	21	67	74	14.8	5.30	76	.304	.373	7	.140	-1	-21	-22	1	-2.4
1951 Phi-N	8	9	.471	28	24	7	2	0	168	172	13	55	65	12.3	3.48	111	.263	.322	5	.104	-1	9	7	-3	0.2
1952 Phi-N	13	14	.481	37	32	14	1	0	232¹	235	6	65	92	11.7	3.14	116	.260	.311	7	.089	-2	15	13	-2	1.0
1953 *Bro-N	15	5	.750	34	32	10	2	0	191¹	201	25	63	106	12.5	4.56	93	.269	.327	11	.147	-1	-6	-6	-0	-0.8
1954 Bro-N	11	6	.647	36	28	6	2	0	180¹	193	17	49	70	12.2	3.99	102	.275	.324	2	.043	-3	2	2	-2	-0.4
1955 *Bro-N	6	2	.750	18	11	2	1	0	73	86	8	31	26	14.4	5.42	75	.300	.368	1	.037	-3	-11	-11	1	-1.2
1956 Chi-N	1	6	.143	20	9	0	0	0	57	71	14	26	28	15.6	6.32	60	.313	.388	1	.083	-1	-16	-16	2	-1.6
Cin-N	0	0	—	1	0	0	0	0	1	1	0	0	1	18.0	0.00	—	.250	.250	0	—	-0	1	0	0	0.0
Yr	1	6	.143	21	9	0	0	0	58	72	14	26	29	15.2	6.21	61	.305	.374	1	.083	-1	-16	-16	2	-1.6
1957 Bos-A	0	0	—	2	1	0	0	0	5	10	1	3	1	23.4	5.40	74	.417	.481	1	1.000	0	-1	-1	1	0.1
1959 KC-A	1	0	1.000	2	1	0	0	0	12¹	14	3	11	10	13.5	4.50	89	.261	.346	0	.000	-2	-1	-1	-0	-0.1
Total 13	94	73	.563	319	219	65	13	5	1531¹	1606	136	541	672	12.7	3.99	99	.271	.334	55	.114	-18	2	-8	-5	-2.8

● LEVI MEYERLE
Meyerle, Levi Samuel "Long Levi"   b: 7/1845, Philadelphia, Pa.   d: 11/4/21, Philadelphia, Pa.   BR/TR, 6′1″, 177 lbs.   Deb: 5/20/1871   ♦

YEAR TM/L	W	L	PCT	G	GS	CG	SH	SV	IP	H	HR	BB	SO	RAT	ERA	ERA+	OAV	OOB	BH	AVG	PB	PR	/A	PD	TPI
1871 Ath-n	0	0	—	1	0	0	0	0	1	2	0	2	0	27.0	9.00	45	.250	.500	64	.492		-1	-1		0.0
1876 Phi-N	0	2	.000	2	2	2	0	0	18	28	1	4	0	14.5	5.00	48	.337	.345	87	.340		-5	-5	-0	-0.4

● DAN MICELI
Miceli, Daniel   b: 9/9/70, Newark, N.J.   BR/TR, 6′1″, 185 lbs.   Deb: 9/9/93

YEAR TM/L	W	L	PCT	G	GS	CG	SH	SV	IP	H	HR	BB	SO	RAT	ERA	ERA+	OAV	OOB	BH	AVG	PB	PR	/A	PD	TPI
1993 Pit-N	0	0	—	9	0	0	0	0	5¹	5	1	4	4	15.2	5.06	80	.273	.360		—	0	-1	-1	-0	-0.1
1994 Pit-N	2	1	.667	28	0	0	0	2	27¹	28	5	11	27	13.5	5.93	73	.267	.347	0	.000	-0	-5	-5	0	-0.5
1995 Pit-N	4	4	.500	58	0	0	0	21	58	61	7	28	56	14.4	4.66	92	.270	.360	0	.000	-0	-3	-2	-1	-0.5
1996 Pit-N	2	10	.167	44	9	0	0	1	85²	99	15	45	66	15.6	5.78	76	.291	.379	0	.000	-1	-15	-13	-2	-2.0
Total 4	8	15	.348	139	9	0	0	24	176¹	194	27	87	153	14.8	5.41	80	.280	.368	0	.000	-2	-24	-21	-3	-3.0

● GENE MICHAEL
Michael, Eugene Richard "Stick"   b: 6/2/38, Kent, Ohio   BB/TR, 6′2″, 183 lbs.   Deb: 7/15/66   MC♦

YEAR TM/L	W	L	PCT	G	GS	CG	SH	SV	IP	H	HR	BB	SO	RAT	ERA	ERA+	OAV	OOB	BH	AVG	PB	PR	/A	PD	TPI
1968 NY-A	0	0	—	1	0	0	0	0	3	5	0	2	3	18.0		—	.357	.400	23	.198	0	1	1	0	0.0

● JOHN MICHAELS
Michaels, John Joseph   b: 7/10/07, Bridgeport, Conn.   BL/TL, 5′10.5″, 154 lbs.   Deb: 4/16/32

YEAR TM/L	W	L	PCT	G	GS	CG	SH	SV	IP	H	HR	BB	SO	RAT	ERA	ERA+	OAV	OOB	BH	AVG	PB	PR	/A	PD	TPI
1932 Bos-A	1	6	.143	28	8	2	0	0	80²	101	4	27	16	14.6	5.13	88	.304	.362	3	.143	-1	-6	-6	1	-0.4

● JOHN MICHAELSON
Michaelson, John August "Mike"   b: 8/12/1893, Tivalkoski, Finland   d: 4/16/68, Woodruff, Wis.   BR/TR, 5′9″, 165 lbs.   Deb: 8/28/21

YEAR TM/L	W	L	PCT	G	GS	CG	SH	SV	IP	H	HR	BB	SO	RAT	ERA	ERA+	OAV	OOB	BH	AVG	PB	PR	/A	PD	TPI
1921 Chi-A	0	0	—	2	0	0	0	0	2²	4	0	1	1	16.9	10.13	42	.400	.455	0	—	0	-2	-2	-0	0.0

YEAR TM/L	W	L	PCT	G	GS	CG	SH	SV	IP	H	HR	BB	SO	RAT	ERA	ERA+	OAV	OOB	BH	AVG	PB	PR	/A	PD	TPI
● **GLENN MICKENS**				Mickens, Glenn Roger b: 7/26/30, Wilmar, Cal. BR/TR, 6′, 175 lbs. Deb: 7/19/53																				
1953 Bro-N	0	1	.000	4	2	0	0	0	6¹	11	2	4	5	21.3	11.37	37	.393	.469	0	.000	-0	-5	-5	0	-0.6
● **JIM MIDDLETON**				Middleton, James Blaine "Rifle Jim" b: 5/28/1889, Argos, Ind. d: 1/12/74, Argos, Ind. BR/TR, 5′11.5″, 165 lbs. Deb: 4/18/17																				
1917 NY-N	1	1	.500	13	0	0	0	1	36	35	1	8	9	11.0	2.75	93	.255	.301	0	.000	-1	-0	-1	1	-0.1
1921 Det-A	6	11	.353	38	10	2	0	**7**	121²	149	5	44	31	14.4	5.03	85	.302	.361	5	.147	-2	-10	-10	1	-1.4
Total 2	7	12	.368	51	10	2	0	8	157²	184	6	52	40	13.6	4.51	86	.292	.348	5	.119	-3	-10	-11	2	-1.5
● **JOHN MIDDLETON**				Middleton, John Wayne "Lefty" b: 4/11/1900, Mt.Calm, Tex. d: 11/3/86, Amarillo, Tex. BL/TL, 6′1″, 185 lbs. Deb: 9/6/22																				
1922 Cle-A	0	1	.000	2	1	0	0	0	7¹	8	1	6	2	17.2	7.36	54	.286	.412	1	.333	0	-3	-3	0	-0.3
● **DICK MIDKIFF**				Midkiff, Richard b: 9/28/14, Gonzales, Tex. d: 10/30/56, Temple, Tex. BR/TR, 6′2″, 185 lbs. Deb: 4/24/38																				
1938 Bos-A	1	1	.500	13	2	0	0	0	35¹	43	5	21	10	16.3	5.09	97	.305	.395	2	.200	-1	-1	-1	0	0.0
● **GARY MIELKE**				Mielke, Gary Roger b: 1/28/63, St.James, Minn. BR/TR, 6′3″, 185 lbs. Deb: 8/19/87																				
1987 Tex-A	0	0	—	3	0	0	0	3	3	2	1	3	2	12.0	6.00	75	.250	.308		0	-0	-1	-1	-0	0.0
1989 Tex-A	1	0	1.000	43	0	0	0	1	49²	52	4	25	26	14.3	3.26	122	.280	.371		0	-0	3	4	-0	0.0
1990 Tex-A	0	3	.000	33	0	0	0	0	41	42	4	15	13	13.0	3.73	105	.271	.343		0	-0	1	1	-0	0.1
Total 3	1	3	.250	79	0	0	0	4	93²	96	9	43	41	13.6	3.56	111	.275	.357		0	-0	4	4	-0	0.1
● **PETE MIKKELSEN**				Mikkelsen, Peter James b: 10/25/39, Staten Island, N.Y. BR/TR, 6′2″, 220 lbs. Deb: 4/17/64																				
1964 *NY-A	7	4	.636	50	0	0	0	12	86	79	3	41	63	13.0	3.56	102	.247	.340	1	.063	-1	1	1	1	0.1
1965 NY-A	4	9	.308	41	3	0	0	1	82¹	78	10	36	69	12.8	3.28	104	.249	.332	1	.100	-0	2	1	1	0.3
1966 Pit-N	9	8	.529	71	0	0	0	14	126	106	8	51	76	11.6	3.07	116	.234	.318	3	.150	-3	7	7	-0	1.0
1967 Pit-N	1	2	.333	32	0	0	0	1	56¹	50	7	19	30	11.5	4.31	78	.237	.309	0	.000	-0	-6	-6	-1	-0.5
Chi-N	0	0	—	7	0	0	0	0	7	9	1	5	0	19.3	6.43	55	.333	.455	0	—	0	-2	-2	-0	-0.1
Yr	1	2	.333	39	0	0	0	1	63¹	59	8	24	30	11.9	4.55	74	.244	.315	0	.000	-0	-8	-8	-1	-0.5
1968 Chi-N	0	0	—	5	0	0	0	0	4²	7	1	3	1	15.4	7.71	41	.350	.381	1	1.000	0	-2	-2	0	-0.1
StL-N	0	0	—	5	0	0	0	0	16	10	0	7	8	9.6	1.13	257	.179	.270	0	.000	-0	3	3	-1	0.1
Yr	0	0	—	8	0	0	0	0	20²	17	3	8	13	10.9	2.61	113	.224	.298	1	.250	1	1	1	-0	0.0
1969 LA-N	7	5	.583	48	0	0	0	4	81¹	57	9	30	51	10.1	2.77	120	.193	.277	1	.167	-0	7	5	1	0.8
1970 LA-N	4	2	.667	33	0	0	0	6	62	48	5	20	47	10.5	2.76	139	.211	.287	2	.333	1	9	7	0	0.9
1971 LA-N	8	5	.615	41	0	0	0	5	74	67	10	17	46	10.3	3.65	89	.242	.288	2	.200	-2	-3	-1	-0	-0.5
1972 LA-N	5	5	.500	33	0	0	0	5	57²	65	5	23	41	14.5	4.06	82	.283	.360	0	.000	-0	-4	-5	-0	-0.9
Total 9	45	40	.529	364	3	0	0	49	653¹	576	59	250	436	11.8	3.38	102	.237	.316	11	.133	-2	13	6	2	1.2
● **HANK MIKLOS**				Miklos, John Joseph b: 11/27/10, Chicago, Ill. BL/TL, 5′11″, 175 lbs. Deb: 4/23/44																				
1944 Chi-N	0	0	—	2	0	0	0	0	7	9	1	3	0	15.4	7.71	46	.333	.400	0	.000	-0	-3	-3	1	0.0
● **BOB MILACKI**				Milacki, Robert b: 7/28/64, Trenton, N.J. BR/TR, 6′4″, 220 lbs. Deb: 9/18/88																				
1988 Bal-A	2	0	1.000	3	3	1	1	0	25	9	1	9	18	6.5	0.72	542	.110	.198	0	—	0	9	9	0	0.9
1989 Bal-A	14	12	.538	37	36	3	2	0	243	233	21	88	113	12.0	3.74	101	.254	.320	0	—	0	4	1	-0	0.2
1990 Bal-A	5	8	.385	27	24	1	1	0	135¹	143	18	61	60	13.6	4.46	85	.273	.349	0	—	0	-8	-10	1	-0.8
1991 Bal-A	10	9	.526	31	26	3	1	0	184	175	17	53	108	11.2	4.01	99	.253	.307	0	—	0	-2	-1	-1	0.1
1992 Bal-A	6	8	.429	23	20	0	0	1	115²	140	16	44	51	14.5	5.84	69	.296	.358	0	—	0	-24	-23	-1	-2.5
1993 Cle-A	1	1	.500	5	2	0	0	0	16	19	3	11	7	16.9	3.38	128	.302	.405	0	—	0	2	2	0	0.2
1994 KC-A	0	5	.000	10	10	0	0	0	55²	68	6	20	17	14.4	6.14	81	.298	.357	0	—	0	-8	-7	1	-0.5
1996 Sea-A	1	4	.200	7	4	0	0	0	21	30	3	15	13	19.3	6.86	72	.330	.425	0	—	0	-4	-5	-0	-0.4
Total 8	39	47	.453	143	125	8	5	1	795²	817	85	301	387	12.7	4.38	91	.266	.333	0	—	0	-29	-34	2	-3.2
● **MIKE MILCHIN**				Milchin, Michael Wayne b: 2/28/68, Knoxville, Tenn. BL/TL, 6′3″, 190 lbs. Deb: 5/14/96																				
1996 Min-A	2	1	.667	26	0	0	0	0	21²	31	6	12	19	17.9	8.31	62	.341	.417	0	—	0	-8	-8	0	-0.9
Bal-A	1	0	1.000	13	0	0	0	0	11	13	0	5	10	14.7	5.73	86	.325	.400	0	—	0	-1	-1	0	-0.0
Yr	3	1	.750	39	0	0	0	0	32²	44	6	17	29	16.8	7.44	68	.336	.412	0	—	0	-9	-9	0	-0.9
● **CARL MILES**				Miles, Carl Thomas b: 3/22/18, Trenton, Mo. BB/TL, 5′11″, 178 lbs. Deb: 6/8/40																				
1940 Phi-A	0	0	—	2	0	0	0	0	8	9	2	8	6	19.1	13.50	33	.281	.425	3	.750	2	-8	-8	-0	0.2
● **JIM MILES**				Miles, James Charlie b: 8/8/43, Grenada, Miss. BR/TR, 6′2″, 210 lbs. Deb: 9/7/68																				
1968 Was-A	0	0	—	3	0	0	0	0	4¹	2	0	2	5	20.8	12.46	23	.421	.476		0	-0	-5	-5	-0	0.0
1969 Was-A	0	1	.000	10	1	0	0	0	20¹	19	2	15	15	16.8	6.20	56	.257	.409	1	.333	-0	-6	-6	1	-0.2
Total 2	0	1	.000	13	1	0	0	0	24²	27	2	17	20	17.5	7.30	46	.290	.421	1	.333	-0	-10	-11	1	-0.2
● **SAM MILITELLO**				Militello, Sam Salvatore b: 11/26/69, Tampa, Fla. BR/TR, 6′3″, 200 lbs. Deb: 8/9/92																				
1992 NY-A	3	3	.500	9	9	0	0	0	60	43	6	32	42	11.6	3.45	113	.195	.302	0	—	0	3	3	-1	0.2
1993 NY-A	1	1	.500	3	2	0	0	0	9¹	10	1	7	5	18.3	6.75	62	.270	.413	0	—	0	-3	-3	0	-0.4
Total 2	4	4	.500	12	11	0	0	0	69¹	53	7	39	47	12.5	3.89	101	.205	.319	0	—	0	1	-0	-1	-0.2
● **JOHNNY MILJUS**				Miljus, John Kenneth "Jovo" or "Big Serb"																				
				b: 6/30/1895, Pittsburgh, Pa. d: 2/11/76, Fort Harrison, Mont. BR/TR, 6′1″, 178 lbs. Deb: 10/2/15																				
1915 Pit-F	0	0	—	1	0	0	0	0	1	0	0	0	0	9.0	0.00	—	.250	.250		0	-0	0	0	0	0.0
1917 Bro-N	0	1	.000	4	1	1	0	0	15	14	0	8	9	15.0	0.60	466	.250	.373	0	.000	-1	4	4	-0	0.2
1920 Bro-N	1	0	1.000	9	0	0	0	0	23¹	24	2	4	9	10.8	3.09	104	.267	.298	2	.333	1	0	1	0	0.2
1921 Bro-N	6	3	.667	28	9	3	0	1	93²	115	3	27	37	13.8	4.23	92	.312	.362	5	.167	-2	-5	-4	2	-0.3
1927 *Pit-N	8	3	.727	19	6	3	2	0	75²	62	0	17	24	9.4	1.90	216	.228	.273	5	.179	-1	17	19	2	2.6
1928 Pit-N	5	7	.417	21	10	3	0	0	69²	90	2	33	26	16.3	5.30	77	.313	.389	8	.308	1	-10	-10	-1	-1.3
Cle-A	1	4	.200	11	4	1	0	1	50²	46	1	20	19	11.7	2.66	156	.243	.316	3	.200	0	8	8	0	0.7
1929 Cle-A	8	8	.500	34	13	4	0	2	128¹	174	10	64	42	16.9	5.19	86	.331	.406	11	.256	1	-13	-11	0	-0.7
Total 7	29	26	.527	127	45	15	2	5	457¹	526	16	173	166	14.0	3.92	104	.293	.359	34	.222	-0	7	4	1	1.0
● **DYAR MILLER**				Miller, Dyar K b: 5/29/46, Batesville, Ind. BR/TR, 6′1″, 195 lbs. Deb: 6/9/75 C																				
1975 Bal-A	6	3	.667	30	0	0	0	8	46¹	32	3	16	33	9.3	2.72	129	.199	.271	0	—	0	5	4	0	1.1
1976 Bal-A	2	4	.333	49	0	0	0	7	88²	79	5	36	37	11.8	2.94	111	.246	.324	0	—	0	6	3	-1	0.2
1977 Bal-A	2	2	.500	12	0	0	0	1	22¹	25	6	10	9	14.1	5.64	67	.278	.350	0	—	0	-4	-5	-0	-0.6
Cal-A	4	4	.500	41	0	0	0	4	92¹	81	10	30	49	10.8	3.02	129	.242	.304	0	—	0	11	9	-1	0.8
Yr	6	6	.500	53	0	0	0	5	114²	106	16	40	58	11.5	3.53	110	.249	.314	0	—	0	7	5	-1	0.2
1978 Cal-A	6	2	.750	41	0	0	0	1	84²	85	3	41	34	13.9	2.66	136	.264	.356	0	—	0	10	9	-2	0.7
1979 Cal-A	1	0	1.000	14	0	0	0	1	35¹	44	2	13	16	15.0	3.31	123	.319	.386	0	—	0	4	3	-1	0.1
Tor-A	0	0	—	10	0	0	0	0	15¹	27	3	5	7	18.8	10.57	41	.391	.432	1	.000	-0	-11	-11	-0	-0.1
Yr	1	0	1.000	24	0	0	0	1	50²	71	5	18	23	15.8	5.51	75	.333	.385	1	—	0	-7	-8	-1	0.1
1980 NY-N	1	2	.333	31	0	0	0	0	42	37	1	11	28	10.3	1.93	184	.242	.293	0	.000	-0	8	8	-1	0.5
1981 NY-N	1	0	1.000	31	0	0	0	0	42	34	2	15	22	15.3	3.29	106	.327	.392	1	.333	1	1	1	0	0.1
Total 7	23	17	.575	251	0	0	0	22	465¹	459	35	177	235	12.5	3.23	113	.264	.335	1	.250	0	30	22	-2	2.8
● **ELMER MILLER**				Miller, Elmer Joseph "Lefty" b: 4/17/03, Detroit, Mich. d: 1/8/87, Corona, Cal. BL/TL, 5′11″, 189 lbs. Deb: 6/21/29																				
1929 Phi-N	0	1	.000	8	0	0	0	0	11¹	12	1	21	10	28.6	11.12	47	.279	.537	9	.237	-8	-8	-7	-0	-0.5
● **FRANK MILLER**				Miller, Frank Lee "Bullet" b: 5/13/1886, Allegan, Mich. d: 2/19/74, Allegan, Mich. BR/TR, 6′, 188 lbs. Deb: 7/12/13																				
1913 Chi-A	0	1	.000	1	1	0	0	0	1²	4	0	3	2	37.8	27.00	11	.571	.700	0	—	0	-4	-4	-0	-1.3
1916 Pit-N	7	10	.412	30	20	16	4	1	173	135	4	49	88	9.9	2.29	117	.226	.292	7	.137	-1	6	8	-1	0.6
1917 Pit-N	10	19	.345	38	28	14	5	1	224	216	1	60	92	11.3	3.13	91	.251	.304	9	.118	-4	-11	-7	1	-1.4
1918 Pit-N	11	8	.579	23	23	14	2	0	170¹	152	1	37	47	10.4	2.38	121	.250	.301	6	.105	-3	7	9	-0	0.7

YEAR	TM/L	W	L	PCT	G	GS	CG	SH	SV	IP	H	HR	BB	SO	RAT	ERA	ERA+	OAV	OOB	BH	AVG	PB	PR	/A	PD	TPI
1919	Pit-N	13	12	.520	32	26	16	3	0	201²	170	6	34	59	9.3	3.03	100	.234	.272	7	.106	-5	-3	-0	1	-0.5
1922	Bos-N	11	13	.458	31	23	14	2	1	200	213	7	60	65	12.4	3.51	114	.279	.333	8	.118	-5	13	11	1	0.8
1923	Bos-N	0	3	.000	8	6	0	0	0	39¹	54	2	11	6	15.6	4.58	87	.335	.389	-0	.143	-0	-3	-3	-1	-0.3
Total 7		52	66	.441	163	127	68	14	4	1010	944	21	254	359	10.9	3.01	104	.253	.306	38	.117	-19	7	15	1	-1.4

● **FRED MILLER**   Miller, Frederick Holman "Speedy"   b: 6/28/1886, Fairfield, Ind.   d: 5/2/53, Brookville, Ind.   BL/TL, 6'2", 190 lbs.   Deb: 7/8/10

YEAR	TM/L	W	L	PCT	G	GS	CG	SH	SV	IP	H	HR	BB	SO	RAT	ERA	ERA+	OAV	OOB	BH	AVG	PB	PR	/A	PD	TPI
1910	Bro-N	1	1	.500	6	2	0	0	0	21	25	1	13	2	17.6	4.71	64	.309	.423	2	.250	0	-4	-4	0	-0.3

● **BERT MILLER**   Miller, Herbert A.   b: 10/26/1875, Riley, Mich.   d: 6/14/37, Flint, Mich.   Deb: 7/15/1897

YEAR	TM/L	W	L	PCT	G	GS	CG	SH	SV	IP	H	HR	BB	SO	RAT	ERA	ERA+	OAV	OOB	BH	AVG	PB	PR	/A	PD	TPI
1897	Lou-N	0	1	.000	4	1	1	0	0	17	32	0	3	3	18.5	7.94	54	.395	.417	1	.167	-1	-7	-7	0	-0.3

● **OX MILLER**   Miller, John Anthony   b: 5/4/15, Gause, Tex.   BR/TR, 6'1", 190 lbs.   Deb: 8/7/43

YEAR	TM/L	W	L	PCT	G	GS	CG	SH	SV	IP	H	HR	BB	SO	RAT	ERA	ERA+	OAV	OOB	BH	AVG	PB	PR	/A	PD	TPI
1943	Was-A	0	0	—	3	0	0	0	0	6	10	1	5	1	22.5	10.50	31	.370	.469	0	.000	-0	-5	-5	1	0.0
	StL-A	0	0	—	2	0	0	0	0	6	7	2	3	3	18.0	12.00	28	.304	.429	0	.000	-0	-6	-6	1	0.0
	Yr	0	0	—	5	0	0	0	0	12	17	3	8	4	20.3	11.25	29	.340	.450	0	.000	-0	-11	-11	1	0.0
1945	StL-A	2	1	.667	4	3	3	0	0	28¹	23	2	5	4	8.9	1.59	222	.219	.255	2	.182	-0	6	6	-1	0.5
1946	StL-A	1	3	.250	11	3	0	0	1	35¹	52	5	15	12	17.1	6.88	54	.338	.396	2	.286	1	-13	-12	1	-1.2
1947	Chi-N	1	2	.333	4	4	1	0	0	16	31	2	5	7	20.3	10.13	39	.397	.434	3	.429	2	-11	-11	-0	-1.4
Total 4		4	6	.400	24	10	4	0	1	91²	123	12	33	27	15.5	6.38	57	.318	.374	7	.259	2	-29	-28	0	-2.1

● **JOHN MILLER**   Miller, John Ernest   b: 5/30/41, Baltimore, Md.   BR/TR, 6'2", 210 lbs.   Deb: 9/22/62

YEAR	TM/L	W	L	PCT	G	GS	CG	SH	SV	IP	H	HR	BB	SO	RAT	ERA	ERA+	OAV	OOB	BH	AVG	PB	PR	/A	PD	TPI
1962	Bal-A	1	1	.500	2	1	0	0	0	10	2	0	5	4	6.3	0.90	411	.065	.194	0	.000	-0	3	3	0	0.7
1963	Bal-A	1	1	.500	3	2	0	0	0	17	12	0	14	16	13.8	3.18	109	.194	.342	0	.000	-1	1	1	-0	0.0
1965	Bal-A	6	4	.600	16	16	1	0	0	93¹	75	4	58	71	12.9	3.18	109	.223	.338	3	.100	-1	3	3	0	0.3
1966	Bal-A	4	8	.333	23	16	0	0	0	100²	92	15	58	81	13.4	4.74	70	.241	.342	4	.118	-1	-15	-16	1	-1.8
1967	Bal-A	0	0	—	2	0	0	0	0	6	7	1	3	6	18.0	7.50	42	.304	.429	0		0	-3	-3	0	0.0
Total 5		12	14	.462	46	35	1	0	0	227	188	20	138	178	13.0	3.89	88	.225	.337	7	.096	-3	-10	-12	1	-0.8

● **CYCLONE MILLER**   Miller, Joseph H.   b: 9/24/1859, Springfield, Mass   d: 10/13/16, New London, Conn.   TL, 5'9.5", 165 lbs.   Deb: 7/11/1884

YEAR	TM/L	W	L	PCT	G	GS	CG	SH	SV	IP	H	HR	BB	SO	RAT	ERA	ERA+	OAV	OOB	BH	AVG	PB	PR	/A	PD	TPI
1884	CP-U	1	0	1.000	1	1	1	0	0	9	4	0	3	13	4.0	1.00	244	.125	.125	1	.250	-0	1	1	1	0.2
	Pro-N	3	2	.600	6	5	2	0	0	34²	36	0	11	12	12.2	2.08	136	.259	.313	1	.043	-3	3	3	-1	0.1
	Phi-N	0	1	.000	1	1	1	0	0	9	17	5	6	1	23.0	10.00	30	.386	.460	0	.000	-1	-7	-7	0	-0.5
	Yr	3	3	.500	7	6	3	0	0	43²	53	5	17	13	14.4	3.71	77	.290	.350	1	.037	-4	-4	-4	-1	-0.4
1886	Phi-a	10	8	.556	19	19	19	1	0	169²	158	6	59	99	11.7	2.97	118	.239	.305	9	.136	-1	9	10	1	0.9
Total 2		14	11	.560	27	26	23	1	0	222¹	215	11	76	125	11.9	3.04	110	.245	.308	11	.113	-5	7	7	1	0.7

● **WHITEY MILLER**   Miller, Kenneth Albert   b: 5/2/15, St.Louis, Mo.   d: 4/3/91, St.Louis, Mo.   BR/TR, 6'1", 195 lbs.   Deb: 9/15/44

YEAR	TM/L	W	L	PCT	G	GS	CG	SH	SV	IP	H	HR	BB	SO	RAT	ERA	ERA+	OAV	OOB	BH	AVG	PB	PR	/A	PD	TPI
1944	NY-N	0	1	.000	4	0	0	0	0	5	1	0	4	2	9.0	0.00	—	.059	.238			0	2	2	0	0.4

● **KURT MILLER**   Miller, Kurt Everett   b: 8/24/72, Tucson, Ariz.   BR/TR, 6'5", 205 lbs.   Deb: 6/11/94

YEAR	TM/L	W	L	PCT	G	GS	CG	SH	SV	IP	H	HR	BB	SO	RAT	ERA	ERA+	OAV	OOB	BH	AVG	PB	PR	/A	PD	TPI
1994	Fla-N	1	3	.250	4	4	0	0	0	20	26	3	7	11	15.7	8.10	54	.317	.385	1	.167	-0	-9	-8	1	-1.2
1996	Fla-N	1	3	.250	26	5	0	0	0	46¹	57	5	33	30	17.9	6.80	60	.313	.424	3	.375	1	-13	-14	0	-1.0
Total 2		2	6	.250	30	9	0	0	0	66¹	83	8	40	41	17.2	7.19	58	.314	.412	4	.286	1	-22	-22	1	-2.2

● **LARRY MILLER**   Miller, Larry Don   b: 6/19/37, Topeka, Kan.   BL/TL, 6', 195 lbs.   Deb: 6/21/64

YEAR	TM/L	W	L	PCT	G	GS	CG	SH	SV	IP	H	HR	BB	SO	RAT	ERA	ERA+	OAV	OOB	BH	AVG	PB	PR	/A	PD	TPI
1964	LA-N	4	8	.333	16	14	1	0	0	79²	87	1	28	50	13.2	4.18	78	.275	.338	7	.269	2	-6	-7	-1	-1.0
1965	NY-N	1	4	.200	28	5	0	0	0	57¹	66	6	25	36	14.4	5.02	70	.289	.362	2	.182	0	-9	-10	-0	-0.8
1966	NY-N	0	2	.000	4	1	0	0	0	8¹	9	3	4	7	14.0	7.56	48	.273	.351	1	.500	0	-4	-4	-0	-0.7
Total 3		5	14	.263	48	20	1	0	0	145¹	162	10	57	93	13.7	4.71	72	.281	.349	10	.256	2	-19	-21	-1	-2.5

● **RED MILLER**   Miller, Leo Alphonso   b: 2/11/1897, Philadelphia, Pa.   d: 10/20/73, Orlando, Fla.   BR/TR, 5'11", 195 lbs.   Deb: 4/13/23

YEAR	TM/L	W	L	PCT	G	GS	CG	SH	SV	IP	H	HR	BB	SO	RAT	ERA	ERA+	OAV	OOB	BH	AVG	PB	PR	/A	PD	TPI
1923	Phi-N	0	0	—	1	0	0	0	0	1²	7	0	2	0	37.8	32.40	14	.545	.583	0	.000	-0	-5	-5	0	0.0

● **PAUL MILLER**   Miller, Paul Robert   b: 4/27/65, Burlington, Wis.   BR/TR, 6'5", 215 lbs.   Deb: 7/30/91

YEAR	TM/L	W	L	PCT	G	GS	CG	SH	SV	IP	H	HR	BB	SO	RAT	ERA	ERA+	OAV	OOB	BH	AVG	PB	PR	/A	PD	TPI
1991	Pit-N	0	0	—	1	1	0	0	0	5	4	0	3	2	12.6	5.40	66	.222	.333	0	.000	-0	-1	-1	-0	-0.1
1992	Pit-N	1	0	1.000	6	0	0	0	0	11¹	11	0	1	5	9.5	2.38	144	.256	.273	0	.000	-0	1	1	-0	0.1
1993	Pit-N	0	0	—	3	2	0	0	0	10	15	2	2	2	15.3	5.40	75	.349	.378	0	.000	-0	-2	-2	-0	-0.1
Total 3		1	0	1.000	10	3	0	0	0	26¹	30	2	6	9	12.3	4.10	90	.288	.327	0	.000	-1	-1	-1	-0	-0.1

● **RALPH MILLER**   Miller, Ralph Darwin   b: 3/15/1873, Cincinnati, Ohio   d: 5/8/73, Cincinnati, Ohio   BR/TR, 5'11", 170 lbs.   Deb: 5/4/1898

YEAR	TM/L	W	L	PCT	G	GS	CG	SH	SV	IP	H	HR	BB	SO	RAT	ERA	ERA+	OAV	OOB	BH	AVG	PB	PR	/A	PD	TPI
1898	Bro-N	4	14	.222	23	21	16	0	0	151²	161	4	86	43	15.4	5.34	67	.270	.374	12	.194	-1	-29	-30	3	-2.6
1899	Bal-N	1	3	.250	6	4	3	0	0	36	42	0	14	3	15.0	4.50	88	.292	.370	2	.182	1	-3	-2	-1	-0.1
Total 2		5	17	.227	29	25	19	0	0	187²	203	4	100	46	15.3	5.18	71	.274	.373	14	.192	1	-32	-32	2	-2.7

● **RALPH MILLER**   Miller, Ralph Henry "Moose" or "Lefty"
b: 1/14/1899, Vinton, Iowa   d: 2/18/67, White Bear Lake, Minn.   BR/TL, 6'1.5", 190 lbs.   Deb: 9/16/21   F

YEAR	TM/L	W	L	PCT	G	GS	CG	SH	SV	IP	H	HR	BB	SO	RAT	ERA	ERA+	OAV	OOB	BH	AVG	PB	PR	/A	PD	TPI
1921	Was-A	0	0	—	1	0	0	0	0	1	0	0	0	0	0.0	0.00	—	.000	.000			0	0	0	-0	0.0

● **RANDY MILLER**   Miller, Randall Scott   b: 3/18/53, Oxnard, Cal.   BR/TR, 6'1", 180 lbs.   Deb: 9/7/77

YEAR	TM/L	W	L	PCT	G	GS	CG	SH	SV	IP	H	HR	BB	SO	RAT	ERA	ERA+	OAV	OOB	BH	AVG	PB	PR	/A	PD	TPI
1977	Bal-A	0	0	—	1	0	0	0	0	0²	4	0	0	0	54.0	40.50	9	.800	.800			-0	-3	-3	0	0.0
1978	Mon-N	0	1	.000	5	0	0	0	0	7	11	1	3	6	18.0	10.29	34	.393	.452	0	.000	-0	-5	-5	0	-0.7
Total 2		0	1	.000	6	0	0	0	0	7²	15	1	3	6	21.1	12.91	27	.455	.500	0	.000	-0	-8	-8	0	-0.7

● **BOB MILLER**   Miller, Robert Gerald   b: 7/15/35, Berwyn, Ill.   BR/TL, 6'1", 185 lbs.   Deb: 6/25/53

YEAR	TM/L	W	L	PCT	G	GS	CG	SH	SV	IP	H	HR	BB	SO	RAT	ERA	ERA+	OAV	OOB	BH	AVG	PB	PR	/A	PD	TPI
1953	Det-A	1	2	.333	13	1	0	0	0	36¹	43	2	21	9	16.1	5.94	68	.289	.380	1	.125	-1	-8	-8	0	-0.6
1954	Det-A	1	1	.500	32	1	0	0	1	69²	62	1	26	27	11.4	2.45	150	.244	.314	2	.133	-0	10	10	-1	0.2
1955	Det-A	2	1	.667	7	3	1	0	0	25¹	26	4	12	11	13.5	2.49	154	.263	.342	2	.222	0	4	4	-0	0.4
1956	Det-A	0	2	.000	11	3	0	0	0	31²	37	5	22	16	16.8	5.68	72	.308	.415	1	.143	-0	-5	-6	-1	-0.3
1962	Cin-N	0	0	—	6	0	0	0	0	5¹	14	1	3	4	32.1	21.94	18	.538	.613	0	.000	-0	-11	-11	0	0.0
	NY-N	2	2	.500	17	0	0	0	1	20¹	24	2	8	8	14.6	7.08	59	.312	.384	0	.000	-0	-7	-7	0	-1.2
	Yr	2	2	.500	23	0	0	0	1	25²	38	3	11	12	17.5	10.17	41	.355	.420	0	.000	-0	-18	-17	0	-1.2
Total 5		6	8	.429	86	8	1	0	2	188²	206	15	92	75	14.4	4.72	83	.284	.368	6	.146	-1	-17	-17	-1	-1.5

● **BOB MILLER**   Miller, Robert John   b: 6/16/26, Detroit, Mich.   BR/TR, 6'3", 190 lbs.   Deb: 9/16/49

YEAR	TM/L	W	L	PCT	G	GS	CG	SH	SV	IP	H	HR	BB	SO	RAT	ERA	ERA+	OAV	OOB	BH	AVG	PB	PR	/A	PD	TPI
1949	Phi-N	0	0	—	3	0	0	0	0	2²	4	0	2	1	13.5	0.00	—	.200	.333			-0	1	1	0	0.0
1950	*Phi-N	11	6	.647	35	22	7	2	1	174	190	9	57	44	13.0	3.57	113	.277	.337	11	.180	-1	11	9	2	0.9
1951	Phi-N	2	1	.667	17	3	0	0	0	34¹	47	2	18	10	17.3	6.82	56	.331	.410	3	.429	1	-11	-11	-0	-0.9
1952	Phi-N	0	1	.000	9	0	0	0	0	9	13	2	1	4	16.0	6.00	61	.351	.368	0	.000	-0	-2	-2	0	-0.2
1953	Phi-N	8	9	.471	35	20	3	2	2	157¹	169	14	42	63	12.2	4.00	105	.271	.319	10	.182	-1	5	4	1	0.2
1954	Phi-N	7	9	.438	30	16	5	0	0	150	176	14	39	42	13.1	4.56	89	.300	.347	8	.160	0	-8	-9	1	-0.2
1955	Phi-N	8	4	.667	40	0	0	0	7	89²	80	6	28	28	10.9	2.41	165	.242	.304	5	.278	-1	16	16	0	2.0
1956	Phi-N	3	6	.333	49	6	1	0	5	122¹	115	14	34	53	11.2	3.24	115	.248	.303	4	.091	-1	7	7	0	0.4
1957	Phi-N	2	5	.286	32	1	0	0	6	60¹	61	4	17	12	11.8	2.69	142	.265	.319	2	.250	2	8	8	1	1.1
1958	Phi-N	1	1	.500	21	1	0	0	0	22¹	36	7	9	9	18.1	11.69	34	.360	.413	0	.000	-0	-19	-19	0	-1.5
Total 10		42	42	.500	261	69	23	6	15	822	889	72	247	263	12.6	3.96	101	.277	.332	41	.184	1	8	2	1	1.3

● **BOB MILLER**   Miller, Robert Lane (b: Robert Lane Gemeinweiser)
b: 2/18/39, St.Louis, Mo.   d: 8/6/93, Rancho Bernardo, Cal.   BR/TR, 6'1", 182 lbs.   Deb: 6/26/57   C

YEAR	TM/L	W	L	PCT	G	GS	CG	SH	SV	IP	H	HR	BB	SO	RAT	ERA	ERA+	OAV	OOB	BH	AVG	PB	PR	/A	PD	TPI
1957	StL-N	0	0	—	5	0	0	0	0	9	13	2	5	4	18.0	7.00	57	.325	.400	0	—	0	-3	-3	0	0.0
1959	StL-N	4	3	.571	11	10	3	0	0	70²	66	2	21	43	11.2	3.31	128	.248	.306	5	.208	0	5	7	1	0.8
1960	StL-N	4	3	.571	15	7	0	0	0	52²	53	2	17	33	12.1	3.42	120	.262	.323	2	.143	-1	2	4	0	0.5
1961	StL-N	1	3	.250	34	5	1	0	3	74¹	82	6	46	39	15.5	4.24	104	.287	.389	5	.357	2	-1	1	1	0.3
1962	NY-N	1	12	.077	33	21	1	0	0	143²	146	20	62	91	13.4	4.89	86	.259	.339	5	.122	-0	-15	-11	2	-0.8

YEAR	TM/L	W	L	PCT	G	GS	CG	SH	SV	IP	H	HR	BB	SO	RAT	ERA	ERA+	OAV	OOB	BH	AVG	PB	PR	/A	PD	TPI
1963	LA-N	10	8	.556	42	23	2	0	1	187	171	7	65	125	11.5	2.89	105	.244	.311	4	.070	-3	8	3	5	0.5
1964	LA-N	7	7	.500	**74**	2	0	0	9	137²	115	1	63	94	11.8	2.62	124	.226	.314	3	.158	1	14	10	2	1.4
1965	*LA-N	6	7	.462	61	1	0	0	9	103	82	9	26	77	9.7	2.97	110	.225	.282	0	.000	-1	7	3	2	0.5
1966	*LA-N	4	2	.667	46	0	0	0	5	84¹	70	5	29	58	10.7	2.77	119	.230	.299	1	.077	-1	8	5	-1	0.2
1967	LA-N	2	9	.182	52	4	0	0	0	85²	88	9	27	32	12.4	4.31	72	.273	.335	1	.125	-0	-9	-12	1	-1.4
1968	Min-A	0	3	.000	45	0	0	0	0	72¹	65	1	24	41	11.7	2.74	113	.239	.312	1	.143	-0	8	8	1	0.2
1969	*Min-A	5	5	.500	48	11	1	0	3	119¹	118	9	32	57	11.3	3.02	121	.264	.313	0	.000	-3	8	8	1	0.5
1970	Cle-A	2	2	.500	15	2	0	0	1	28	35	1	15	15	16.1	4.18	95	.310	.391	1	.200	0	-1	-1	-1	-0.2
	Chi-A	4	6	.400	15	12	0	0	1	70	88	11	33	36	16.1	5.01	78	.315	.396	4	.174	0	-10	-9	2	-0.9
	Yr	6	8	.429	30	14	0	0	1	98	123	12	48	51	16.1	4.78	82	.313	.393	5	.179	1	-12	-9	-1	-1.1
	Chi-N	0	0	—	7	1	0	0	2	9	6	3	6	4	12.0	5.00	90	.194	.324	0	—	-0	-1	-0	0	0.0
1971	Chi-N	0	0	—	2	0	0	0	0	7	10	1	0	1	14.1	5.14	76	.357	.379	0	.000	-0	-1	-1	0	0.0
	SD-N	7	3	.700	38	0	0	0	7	63²	53	0	26	36	11.3	1.41	233	.227	.308	0	.000	-1	15	13	1	2.4
	*Pit-N	1	2	.333	16	0	0	0	3	28	20	1	13	13	10.6	1.29	263	.200	.292	0	.000	-0	7	7	0	0.9
	Yr	8	5	.615	56	0	0	0	10	98²	83	1	40	51	11.2	1.64	205	.229	.305	0	.000	-1	20	19	2	3.3
1972	*Pit-N	5	2	.714	36	0	0	0	3	54¹	54	3	24	18	13.1	2.65	125	.263	.343	0	.000	-0	5	4	-0	0.5
1973	SD-N	0	0	—	18	0	0	0	0	30²	29	4	12	15	12.0	4.11	84	.244	.313	0	.000	-0	-2	-2	-1	-0.1
	NY-N	0	0	—	1	0	0	0	0	1	0	0	0	1	0.0	0.00	—	.000	.000	0	—	-0	0	0	0	0.0
	Yr	0	0	—	19	0	0	0	0	31²	29	4	12	16	11.7	3.98	87	.236	.304	0	.000	-0	-1	-2	-1	-0.1
	Det-A	4	2	.667	22	0	0	0	1	42	34	3	22	23	12.0	3.43	119	.230	.329	0	—	-0	2	3	0	0.0
1974	NY-N	2	2	.500	58	0	0	0	2	78	89	4	39	35	14.9	3.58	100	.296	.378	1	.111	-0	0	0	0	0.0
Total 17		69	81	.460	694	99	7	0	51	1551¹	1487	101	608	895	12.3	3.37	105	.255	.328	33	.110	-8	38	31	18	5.3

● **BOB MILLER** Miller, Robert W. b: 1862, Deb: 8/30/1890

YEAR	TM/L	W	L	PCT	G	GS	CG	SH	SV	IP	H	HR	BB	SO	RAT	ERA	ERA+	OAV	OOB	BH	AVG	PB	PR	/A	PD	TPI
1890	Roc-a	3	7	.300	13	12	11	0	1	92¹	89	2	26	20	11.5	4.29	83	.246	.302	6	.150	-1	-4	-7	0	-0.7
1891	Was-a	2	5	.286	7	7	3	0	0	42	53	3	24	13	17.8	4.29	87	.298	.399	2	.111	-2	-3	-3	1	-0.4
Total 2		5	12	.294	20	19	14	0	1	134¹	142	5	50	33	13.5	4.29	84	.263	.336	8	.138	-3	-7	-10	1	-1.1

● **ROGER MILLER** Miller, Roger Wesley b: 8/1/54, Connellsville, Pa. d: 4/26/93, Mill Run, Pa. BR/TR, 6'3", 200 lbs. Deb: 9/8/74

YEAR	TM/L	W	L	PCT	G	GS	CG	SH	SV	IP	H	HR	BB	SO	RAT	ERA	ERA+	OAV	OOB	BH	AVG	PB	PR	/A	PD	TPI
1974	Mil-A	0	0	—	2	0	0	0	0	2¹	3	1	0	2	15.4	11.57	31	.300	.364	0	—	0	-2	-2	-0	0.0

● **RONNIE MILLER** Miller, Roland Arthur b: 8/28/18, Mason City, Iowa BB/TR, 5'11", 167 lbs. Deb: 9/10/41

YEAR	TM/L	W	L	PCT	G	GS	CG	SH	SV	IP	H	HR	BB	SO	RAT	ERA	ERA+	OAV	OOB	BH	AVG	PB	PR	/A	PD	TPI
1941	Was-A	0	0	—	1	0	0	0	0	2	2	0	1	0	13.5	4.50	90	.333	.429	0	—	0	-0	-0	-0	0.0

● **ROSCOE MILLER** Miller, Roscoe Clyde "Roxy" or "Rubberlegs"
  b: 12/2/1876, Greenville, Ind. d: 4/18/13, Corydon, Ind. BR/TR, 6'2", 190 lbs. Deb: 4/25/01

YEAR	TM/L	W	L	PCT	G	GS	CG	SH	SV	IP	H	HR	BB	SO	RAT	ERA	ERA+	OAV	OOB	BH	AVG	PB	PR	/A	PD	TPI
1901	Det-A	23	13	.639	38	36	35	3	1	332	339	1	98	79	12.2	2.95	130	.261	.320	27	.208	0	26	33	4	3.5
1902	Det-A	6	12	.333	20	18	15	1	1	148²	158	3	57	39	13.6	3.69	99	.273	.347	11	.183	-2	-2	-1	1	-0.2
	NY-N	1	8	.111	10	9	7	0	0	72²	77	1	11	15	11.5	4.58	61	.271	.310	1	.048	-2	-15	-14	-1	-1.8
1903	NY-N	2	5	.286	15	8	6	0	**3**	85	101	1	24	30	13.3	4.13	81	.302	.351	5	.161	-1	-8	-7	-1	-0.7
1904	Pit-N	7	7	.500	19	17	11	2	0	134¹	133	4	39	35	11.8	3.35	82	.256	.313	2	.043	-4	-9	-9	-1	-1.4
Total 4		39	45	.464	102	88	74	6	5	772²	808	10	229	198	12.5	3.45	100	.268	.326	46	.160	-8	-7	1	2	-0.6

● **RUSS MILLER** Miller, Russell Lewis b: 3/25/1900, Etna, Ohio d: 4/30/62, Bucyrus, Ohio BR/TR, 5'11", 165 lbs. Deb: 9/24/27 F

YEAR	TM/L	W	L	PCT	G	GS	CG	SH	SV	IP	H	HR	BB	SO	RAT	ERA	ERA+	OAV	OOB	BH	AVG	PB	PR	/A	PD	TPI
1927	Phi-N	1	1	.500	5	1	1	0	0	15¹	21	2	3	4	14.7	5.28	78	.339	.379	1	.333	0	-2	-2	-0	-0.2
1928	Phi-N	0	12	.000	33	12	1	0	1	108	137	14	34	19	14.3	5.42	79	.315	.365	4	.148	-1	-17	-14	0	-1.4
Total 2		1	13	.071	35	14	2	0	1	123¹	158	16	37	23	14.3	5.40	79	.318	.366	5	.167	-1	-19	-16	0	-1.6

● **STU MILLER** Miller, Stuart Leonard b: 12/26/27, Northampton, Mass. BR/TR, 5'11.5", 165 lbs. Deb: 8/12/52

YEAR	TM/L	W	L	PCT	G	GS	CG	SH	SV	IP	H	HR	BB	SO	RAT	ERA	ERA+	OAV	OOB	BH	AVG	PB	PR	/A	PD	TPI
1952	StL-N	6	3	.667	12	11	6	2	0	88	63	3	26	64	9.3	2.05	182	.197	.262	3	.120	-1	16	16	3	1.8
1953	StL-N	7	8	.467	40	18	8	2	4	137²	161	19	47	79	13.7	5.56	77	.293	.351	8	.186	1	-19	-20	5	-1.5
1954	StL-N	2	3	.400	19	4	0	0	2	46²	55	5	29	22	16.8	5.79	71	.307	.412	4	.308	1	-9	-9	2	-0.6
1956	StL-N	0	1	.000	3	0	0	0	1	7¹	12	3	5	5	20.9	4.91	77	.387	.472	0	.000	-0	-1	-1	0	-0.1
	Phi-N	5	8	.385	24	15	2	0	0	106²	109	16	51	55	13.8	4.47	83	.263	.349	4	.160	2	-8	-9	0	-0.7
	Yr	5	9	.357	27	15	2	0	1	114	121	19	56	60	14.3	4.50	83	.271	.357	4	.154	2	-9	-10	0	-0.8
1957	NY-N	7	9	.438	38	13	0	0	1	124	110	15	45	60	11.5	3.63	108	.242	.315	2	.057	-3	4	3	0	0.3
1958	SF-N	6	9	.400	41	20	4	1	0	182	160	16	49	119	10.4	**2.47**	**154**	.233	**.286**	6	.120	-0	30	27	1	2.2
1959	SF-N	8	7	.533	59	9	2	0	8	167²	164	15	57	95	12.1	2.84	134	.260	.326	2	.044	-3	**21**	18	3	1.7
1960	SF-N	7	6	.538	47	3	2	0	2	101²	100	9	31	65	11.9	3.90	89	.256	.315	5	.200	-1	-2	-5	2	-0.3
1961	SF-N★	14	5	.737	63	0	0	0	**17**	122	95	4	37	89	9.8	2.66	143	.215	.277	4	.200	2	**19**	16	2	3.1
1962	*SF-N	5	8	.385	59	0	0	0	19	107	108	8	42	78	12.7	4.12	92	.268	.341	2	.125	-0	-4	-0	0	-0.6
1963	Bal-A	5	8	.385	**71**	0	0	0	**27**	112¹	93	5	53	114	11.9	2.24	155	.232	.326	5	.313	2	17	15	2	3.0
1964	Bal-A	7	7	.500	66	0	0	0	0	97	77	7	34	87	10.6	3.06	117	.222	.297	1	.111	-0	6	5	1	1.1
1965	Bal-A	14	7	.667	67	0	0	0	24	119¹	87	5	32	104	9.1	1.89	184	.207	.265	1	.063	-1	21	21	1	**4.7**
1966	Bal-A	9	4	.692	51	0	0	0	18	92	65	5	26	59	8.9	2.25	148	.201	.260	2	.105	-1	12	11	-1	1.8
1967	Bal-A	3	10	.231	42	0	0	0	0	81¹	63	5	36	60	11.1	2.55	124	.220	.309	0	.000	-1	6	5	-0	0.8
1968	Atl-N	0	0	—	2	0	0	0	0	1¹	1	0	4	1	33.8	27.00	11	.500	.833	0	—	0	-4	-4	0	0.0
Total 16		105	103	.505	704	93	24	5	154	1694	1522	140	600	1164	11.5	3.24	115	.242	.312	49	.133	-2	107	89	22	16.7

● **TRAVIS MILLER** Miller, Travis Eugene b: 11/2/72, Dayton, Ohio BR/TL, 6'3", 205 lbs. Deb: 8/25/96

YEAR	TM/L	W	L	PCT	G	GS	CG	SH	SV	IP	H	HR	BB	SO	RAT	ERA	ERA+	OAV	OOB	BH	AVG	PB	PR	/A	PD	TPI
1996	Min-A	1	2	.333	7	7	0	0	0	26¹	45	7	9	13	18.5	9.23	56	.388	.432	0	—	0	-12	-12	-1	-1.2

● **TREVER MILLER** Miller, Trever Douglas b: 5/29/73, Louisville, Ky. BR/TL, 6'3", 175 lbs. Deb: 9/4/96

YEAR	TM/L	W	L	PCT	G	GS	CG	SH	SV	IP	H	HR	BB	SO	RAT	ERA	ERA+	OAV	OOB	BH	AVG	PB	PR	/A	PD	TPI
1996	Det-A	0	4	.000	5	4	0	0	0	16²	28	3	9	8	21.1	9.18	55	.384	.464	0	—	0	-8	-8	-1	-1.3

● **JAKE MILLER** Miller, Walter b: 2/28/1898, Wagram, Ohio d: 8/20/75, Venice, Fla. BL/TL, 6'2", 170 lbs. Deb: 9/11/24 F

YEAR	TM/L	W	L	PCT	G	GS	CG	SH	SV	IP	H	HR	BB	SO	RAT	ERA	ERA+	OAV	OOB	BH	AVG	PB	PR	/A	PD	TPI
1924	Cle-A	0	1	.000	2	1	1	0	0	12	13	0	5	4	13.5	3.00	142	.265	.333	0	.000	-1	2	2	0	0.0
1925	Cle-A	10	13	.435	32	22	13	0	2	190¹	207	4	62	51	13.1	3.31	133	.279	.340	13	.183	-3	23	23	0	2.2
1926	Cle-A	7	4	.636	18	11	5	3	1	82²	88	9	18	24	13.0	3.27	124	.307	.348	2	.083	-2	7	7	-1	0.6
1927	Cle-A	10	8	.556	34	23	11	0	0	185¹	189	4	48	53	11.8	3.21	131	.271	.324	8	.138	-4	19	21	1	1.4
1928	Cle-A	8	9	.471	25	24	8	0	0	158	203	6	43	37	14.3	4.44	93	.332	.381	7	.135	-4	-7	-5	1	-0.8
1929	Cle-A	14	12	.538	29	29	14	2	0	206	227	7	60	58	12.8	3.58	124	.279	.334	15	.200	-3	15	20	1	2.0
1930	Cle-A	4	4	.500	24	9	1	0	0	88¹	147	6	38	31	19.3	7.13	68	.373	.433	10	.303	1	-24	-23	2	-1.4
1931	Cle-A	1	2	.667	10	5	1	1	0	41¹	45	2	19	13	13.9	4.35	106	.273	.348	1	.077	-1	0	1	1	0.0
1933	Chi-A	5	6	.455	26	14	4	2	0	105²	130	3	47	30	15.6	5.62	75	.297	.373	7	.189	-1	-16	-16	1	-1.4
Total 9		60	58	.508	200	139	58	8	3	1069²	1260	33	340	305	13.8	4.09	106	.294	.355	63	.171	-19	19	30	6	2.6

● **WALT MILLER** Miller, Walter W. b: 10/19/1884, Spiceland, Ind. d: 3/1/56, Marion, Ind. BR/TR, 5'11.5", 180 lbs. Deb: 9/20/11

YEAR	TM/L	W	L	PCT	G	GS	CG	SH	SV	IP	H	HR	BB	SO	RAT	ERA	ERA+	OAV	OOB	BH	AVG	PB	PR	/A	PD	TPI
1911	Bro-N	0	1	.000	3	2	0	0	0	11	16	0	6	6	18.8	6.55	51	.356	.442	0	.000	-1	-4	-4	-0	-0.4

● **BILL MILLER** Miller, William Francis "Wild Bill" b: 4/12/10, Hannibal, Mo. d: 2/26/82, Hannibal, Mo. BR/TR, 6', 180 lbs. Deb: 10/2/37

YEAR	TM/L	W	L	PCT	G	GS	CG	SH	SV	IP	H	HR	BB	SO	RAT	ERA	ERA+	OAV	OOB	BH	AVG	PB	PR	/A	PD	TPI
1937	StL-A	0	1	.000	1	1	0	0	0	4	7	1	4	1	27.0	13.50	36	.389	.522	0	.000	-0	-4	-4	0	-0.6

● **BILL MILLER** Miller, William Paul "Lefty" or "Hooks" b: 7/26/27, Minersville, Pa. BL/TL, 6', 175 lbs. Deb: 4/20/52

YEAR	TM/L	W	L	PCT	G	GS	CG	SH	SV	IP	H	HR	BB	SO	RAT	ERA	ERA+	OAV	OOB	BH	AVG	PB	PR	/A	PD	TPI
1952	NY-A	4	6	.400	21	13	5	2	0	88	78	4	49	45	13.2	3.48	96	.241	.345	6	.214	1	2	-2	-0	-0.1
1953	NY-A	2	1	.667	13	3	0	0	0	34	46	3	19	17	17.5	4.76	77	.324	.407	2	.200	1	-3	-4	1	-0.3
1954	NY-A	0	1	.000	2	1	0	0	0	5²	9	0	1	6	15.9	6.35	54	.375	.400	0	.000	-0	-2	-1	0	-0.3
1955	Bal-A	0	1	.000	5	1	0	0	0	4	3	0	6	4	29.3	13.50	28	.200	.520	1	1.000	0	-4	-4	0	-0.8
Total 4		6	9	.400	41	18	5	2	1	131²	136	7	79	72	14.9	4.24	81	.270	.372	9	.225	1	-7	-12	0	-1.5

● **JOHN MILLIGAN** Milligan, John Alexander b: 1/22/04, Schuylerville, N.Y. d: 5/15/72, Fort Pierce, Fla. BR/TL, 5'10", 172 lbs. Deb: 8/11/28

YEAR	TM/L	W	L	PCT	G	GS	CG	SH	SV	IP	H	HR	BB	SO	RAT	ERA	ERA+	OAV	OOB	BH	AVG	PB	PR	/A	PD	TPI
1928	Phi-N	2	5	.286	13	7	3	0	0	68	69	2	32	22	13.5	4.37	98	.274	.358	1	.050	-2	-3	-1	1	-0.2

YEAR	TM/L	W	L	PCT	G	GS	CG	SH	SV	IP	H	HR	BB	SO	RAT	ERA	ERA+	OAV	OOB	BH	AVG	PB	PR	/A	PD	TPI
1929	Phi-N	0	1	.000	8	3	0	0	0	9²	29	0	10	2	38.2	16.76	31	.527	.612	1	.333	0	-13	-12	0	-1.0
1930	Phi-N	1	2	.333	9	2	1	0	0	28¹	26	0	21	7	15.6	3.18	172	.255	.392	1	.111	-1	6	7	1	0.7
1931	Phi-N	0	0	—	3	0	0	0	0	8	11	0	4	6	18.0	3.38	126	.324	.410	0	.000	-0	0	1	0	-0.1
1934	Was-A	0	0	—	2	0	0	0	0	2²	6	0	1	2	20.3	10.13	43	.500	.500	0	—	0	-2	-2	0	0.0
Total	5	3	8	.273	35	12	4	0	0	116²	141	2	67	38	16.5	5.17	90	.310	.405	3	.088	-3	-11	-7	2	-0.6

● **BILLY MILLIGAN**   Milligan, William Joseph b: 8/19/1878, Buffalo, N.Y. d: 10/14/28, Buffalo, N.Y.   BR/TL, 5'7", Deb: 4/30/01

YEAR	TM/L	W	L	PCT	G	GS	CG	SH	SV	IP	H	HR	BB	SO	RAT	ERA	ERA+	OAV	OOB	BH	AVG	PB	PR	/A	PD	TPI
1901	Phi-A	0	3	.000	6	3	2	0	0	33	43	1	14	5	16.1	4.36	86	.312	.383	5	.333	2	-3	-2	-0	0.0
1904	NY-N	0	1	.000	5	1	1	0	2	25	36	2	4	6	14.8	5.40	51	.310	.339	1	.111	0	-7	-7	-0	-0.4
Total	2	0	4	.000	11	4	3	0	2	58	79	3	18	11	15.5	4.81	69	.311	.364	6	.250	2	-10	-10	-1	-0.4

● **BOB MILLIKEN**   Milliken, Robert Fogle "Bobo" b: 8/25/26, Majorsville, W.Va. BR/TR, 6', 195 lbs. Deb: 4/22/53 C

YEAR	TM/L	W	L	PCT	G	GS	CG	SH	SV	IP	H	HR	BB	SO	RAT	ERA	ERA+	OAV	OOB	BH	AVG	PB	PR	/A	PD	TPI
1953	*Bro-N	8	4	.667	37	10	3	0	2	117²	94	13	42	65	10.4	3.37	127	.214	.283	4	.118	-1	12	12	-2	0.8
1954	Bro-N	5	2	.714	24	3	0	0	2	62²	58	12	18	25	11.2	4.02	102	.246	.305	3	.176	-0	0	0	-1	-0.1
Total	2	13	6	.684	61	13	3	0	4	180¹	152	25	60	90	10.7	3.59	117	.225	.290	7	.137	-2	12	12	-3	0.7

● **ALAN MILLS**   Mills, Alan Bernard b: 10/18/66, Lakeland, Fla. BR/TR, 6'1", 190 lbs. Deb: 4/14/90

YEAR	TM/L	W	L	PCT	G	GS	CG	SH	SV	IP	H	HR	BB	SO	RAT	ERA	ERA+	OAV	OOB	BH	AVG	PB	PR	/A	PD	TPI
1990	NY-A	1	5	.167	36	0	0	0	0	41²	48	4	33	24	17.7	4.10	97	.298	.421	0	—	0	-1	-1	1	0.0
1991	NY-A	1	1	.500	6	2	0	0	0	16¹	16	1	8	11	13.2	4.41	94	.254	.338	0	—	0	-1	-0	1	0.0
1992	Bal-A	10	4	.714	35	3	0	0	2	103¹	78	5	54	60	11.6	2.61	154	.215	.319	0	—	0	15	16	1	2.1
1993	Bal-A	5	4	.556	45	0	0	0	4	100¹	80	14	51	68	12.1	3.23	138	.225	.328	0	—	0	12	14	0	1.1
1994	Bal-A	3	3	.500	47	0	0	0	2	45¹	43	7	24	44	13.7	5.16	97	.251	.350	0	—	0	-2	-1	-1	-0.2
1995	Bal-A	3	0	1.000	21	0	0	0	0	23	30	4	18	16	19.6	7.43	64	.309	.427	0	—	0	-7	-7	-1	-0.8
1996	*Bal-A	3	2	.600	49	0	0	0	3	54²	40	10	35	50	12.5	4.28	114	.208	.333	0	—	0	4	4	0	0.4
Total	7	26	19	.578	239	5	0	0	11	384²	335	45	223	273	13.3	3.84	115	.239	.348	0	—	0	21	25	1	2.6

● **ART MILLS**   Mills, Arthur Grant b: 3/2/03, Utica, N.Y. d: 7/23/75, Utica, N.Y. BR/TR, 5'10", 155 lbs. Deb: 4/16/27 FC

YEAR	TM/L	W	L	PCT	G	GS	CG	SH	SV	IP	H	HR	BB	SO	RAT	ERA	ERA+	OAV	OOB	BH	AVG	PB	PR	/A	PD	TPI
1927	Bos-N	0	1	.000	15	1	0	0	0	37²	41	1	18	7	14.8	3.82	97	.287	.378	0	.000	-1	-0	-0	1	0.0
1928	Bos-N	0	0	—	4	0	0	0	0	7²	17	3	8	0	31.7	12.91	30	.472	.587	0	.000	-0	-8	-8	-0	0.0
Total	2	0	1	.000	19	1	0	0	0	45¹	58	4	26	7	17.7	5.36	70	.324	.424	0	.000	-1	-7	-8	1	0.0

● **LEFTY MILLS**   Mills, Howard Robinson b: 5/12/10, Dedham, Mass. d: 9/23/82, Riverside, Cal. BL/TL, 6'1", 187 lbs. Deb: 6/10/34

YEAR	TM/L	W	L	PCT	G	GS	CG	SH	SV	IP	H	HR	BB	SO	RAT	ERA	ERA+	OAV	OOB	BH	AVG	PB	PR	/A	PD	TPI
1934	StL-A	0	0	—	4	0	0	0	0	8²	10	0	11	2	21.8	4.15	120	.303	.477	1	.333	0	0	1	-0	0.0
1937	StL-A	1	1	.500	2	1	1	0	0	12²	16	1	10	10	18.5	6.39	75	.286	.394	0	.000	-1	-2	-2	0	-0.3
1938	StL-A	10	12	.455	30	27	15	1	0	210¹	216	16	116	134	14.5	5.31	94	.262	.358	6	.091	-3	-12	-8	-2	-1.1
1939	StL-A	4	11	.267	34	14	4	0	2	144¹	147	16	113	103	16.7	6.55	74	.264	.395	11	.234	-3	-31	-27	-2	-2.3
1940	StL-A	0	6	.000	26	5	1	0	0	59	64	7	52	18	18.2	7.78	59	.275	.413	2	.154	-0	-22	-21	0	-1.7
Total	5	15	30	.333	96	48	21	1	2	435	453	40	302	267	16.0	6.06	81	.266	.382	20	.149	-3	-67	-57	-3	-5.4

● **DICK MILLS**   Mills, Richard Alan b: 1/29/45, Boston, Mass. BR/TR, 6'3", 195 lbs. Deb: 9/7/70

YEAR	TM/L	W	L	PCT	G	GS	CG	SH	SV	IP	H	HR	BB	SO	RAT	ERA	ERA+	OAV	OOB	BH	AVG	PB	PR	/A	PD	TPI
1970	Bos-A	0	0	—	2	0	0	0	0	3²	6	0	3	3	24.5	2.45	161	.353	.476	0	—	0	1	1	0	0.0

● **WILLIE MILLS**   Mills, William Grant "Wee Willie" b: 8/15/1877, Schenevus, N.Y. d: 7/5/14, Norwood, N.Y. BR/TR, 5'7", 150 lbs. Deb: 7/13/01 F

YEAR	TM/L	W	L	PCT	G	GS	CG	SH	SV	IP	H	HR	BB	SO	RAT	ERA	ERA+	OAV	OOB	BH	AVG	PB	PR	/A	PD	TPI
1901	NY-N	0	2	.000	2	2	2	0	0	16	21	2	4	3	14.6	8.44	39	.313	.361	1	.167	0	-9	-9	-0	-0.8

● **AL MILNAR**   Milnar, Albert Joseph "Happy" (b: Albert Joseph Milnar) b: 12/26/13, Cleveland, Ohio BL/TL, 6'2", 195 lbs. Deb: 4/30/36

YEAR	TM/L	W	L	PCT	G	GS	CG	SH	SV	IP	H	HR	BB	SO	RAT	ERA	ERA+	OAV	OOB	BH	AVG	PB	PR	/A	PD	TPI
1936	Cle-A	1	2	.333	4	3	1	0	0	22	26	0	18	9	18.0	7.36	68	.286	.404	3	.300	0	-6	-6	0	-0.5
1938	Cle-A	3	1	.750	23	5	2	0	1	68¹	90	5	26	29	15.3	5.00	93	.320	.378	4	.154	-0	-2	-3	0	-0.1
1939	Cle-A	14	12	.538	37	26	12	2	3	209	212	11	99	76	13.4	3.79	116	.264	.345	20	.253	4	19	14	0	1.9
1940	Cle-A☆	18	10	.643	37	33	15	4	3	242¹	242	14	99	99	12.7	3.27	129	.257	.328	17	.181	-1	30	26	-5	2.1
1941	Cle-A	12	19	.387	35	30	9	1	0	229¹	236	9	116	82	13.9	4.36	90	.266	.352	14	.171	2	-5	-11	-3	-1.3
1942	Cle-A	6	8	.429	28	19	8	2	0	157	139	3	85	35	13.5	4.13	84	.251	.350	12	.171	2	-8	-12	-1	-0.7
1943	Cle-A	1	3	.250	16	6	0	0	0	39	51	0	35	12	20.1	8.08	38	.329	.455	4	.211	0	-21	-22	0	-2.0
	StL-A	1	2	.333	3	2	1	0	0	14²	23	0	9	7	19.6	5.52	60	.354	.432	2	.333	1	-4	-4	0	-0.5
	Yr	2	5	.286	19	8	1	0	0	53²	74	0	44	19	19.8	7.38	43	.335	.445	6	.240	1	-24	-25	0	-2.5
1946	StL-A	1	1	.500	4	2	1	0	0	14²	15	1	6	1	12.9	2.45	152	.278	.350	3	.750	1	2	2	-0	0.4
	Phi-N	0	0	—	1	0	0	0	0	2	2	0	2	0	—	∞	—	1.000	1.000	0	—	0	-4	-4	-0	-0.3
Total	8	57	58	.496	188	127	49	10	7	996¹	1043	43	495	350	14.0	4.22	96	.270	.354	79	.203	9	2	-18	-6	-1.0

● **GEORGE MILSTEAD**   Milstead, George Earl "Cowboy" b: 6/26/03, Cleburne, Tex. d: 8/9/77, Cleburne, Tex. BL/TL, 5'10", 144 lbs. Deb: 6/27/24

YEAR	TM/L	W	L	PCT	G	GS	CG	SH	SV	IP	H	HR	BB	SO	RAT	ERA	ERA+	OAV	OOB	BH	AVG	PB	PR	/A	PD	TPI
1924	Chi-N	1	1	.500	13	2	1	0	0	29²	41	3	13	6	16.7	6.07	64	.328	.396	1	.167	0	-7	-7	0	-0.4
1925	Chi-N	1	1	.500	5	3	1	0	0	21	26	0	8	7	14.6	3.00	144	.310	.370	0	.000	-1	3	3	0	0.2
1926	Chi-N	1	5	.167	18	4	0	0	2	55¹	63	0	24	14	14.3	3.58	107	.309	.384	1	.053	-2	2	2	2	0.2
Total	3	3	7	.300	36	9	2	0	2	106	130	3	45	27	15.0	4.16	95	.315	.385	2	.063	-3	-3	-2	3	0.0

● **LARRY MILTON**   Milton, Samuel Lawrence "Tug" b: 5/4/1879, Owensboro, Ky. d: 5/16/42, Hannibal, Mo. TR , Deb: 5/7/03

YEAR	TM/L	W	L	PCT	G	GS	CG	SH	SV	IP	H	HR	BB	SO	RAT	ERA	ERA+	OAV	OOB	BH	AVG	PB	PR	/A	PD	TPI
1903	StL-N	0	0	—	1	0	0	0	0	4	3	0	1	0	9.0	2.25	145	.200	.250	1	.500	0	0	0	0	0.1

● **MIKE MIMBS**   Mimbs, Michael Randall b: 2/13/69, Macon, Ga. BL/TL, 6'2", 180 lbs. Deb: 5/6/95

YEAR	TM/L	W	L	PCT	G	GS	CG	SH	SV	IP	H	HR	BB	SO	RAT	ERA	ERA+	OAV	OOB	BH	AVG	PB	PR	/A	PD	TPI
1995	Phi-N	9	7	.563	35	19	2	1	1	136²	127	10	75	93	13.7	4.15	102	.250	.353	5	.143	-1	0	1	1	0.1
1996	Phi-N	3	9	.250	21	17	0	0	0	99¹	116	13	41	56	14.4	5.53	79	.294	.364	4	.121	-1	-14	-13	-1	-1.5
Total	2	12	16	.429	56	36	2	1	1	236	243	23	116	149	14.0	4.73	91	.269	.358	9	.132	-2	-14	-12	0	-1.4

● **COTTON MINAHAN**   Minahan, Edmund Joseph b: 12/10/1882, Springfield, Ohio d: 5/20/58, E.Orange, N.J. BR/TR, 6', 190 lbs. Deb: 4/21/07

YEAR	TM/L	W	L	PCT	G	GS	CG	SH	SV	IP	H	HR	BB	SO	RAT	ERA	ERA+	OAV	OOB	BH	AVG	PB	PR	/A	PD	TPI
1907	Cin-N	0	2	.000	2	2	1	0	0	14	12	0	13	4	16.7	1.29	202	.261	.433	0	.000	-1	2	2	-1	0.2

● **RUDY MINARCIN**   Minarcin, Rudy Anthony "Buster" b: 3/25/30, N.Vandergrift, Pa. BR/TR, 6', 195 lbs. Deb: 4/11/55

YEAR	TM/L	W	L	PCT	G	GS	CG	SH	SV	IP	H	HR	BB	SO	RAT	ERA	ERA+	OAV	OOB	BH	AVG	PB	PR	/A	PD	TPI
1955	Cin-N	5	9	.357	41	12	3	1	1	115²	116	17	51	45	13.2	4.90	86	.261	.341	5	.179	-1	-11	-9	2	-0.8
1956	Bos-A	1	0	1.000	3	1	0	0	0	9²	9	2	5	5	16.8	2.79	165	.250	.400	1	.500	1	1	1	0	0.3
1957	Bos-A	0	0	—	26	0	0	0	2	44²	44	5	30	20	15.1	4.43	90	.267	.383	0	.000	0	-3	-2	-0	0.0
Total	3	6	9	.400	70	13	3	1	3	170	169	24	89	70	13.9	4.66	90	.262	.356	6	.188	0	-13	-9	2	-0.5

● **NATE MINCHEY**   Minchey, Nathan Derek b: 8/31/69, Austin, Tex. BR/TR, 6'8", 225 lbs. Deb: 9/12/93

YEAR	TM/L	W	L	PCT	G	GS	CG	SH	SV	IP	H	HR	BB	SO	RAT	ERA	ERA+	OAV	OOB	BH	AVG	PB	PR	/A	PD	TPI
1993	Bos-A	1	2	.333	5	5	1	0	0	33	35	5	8	18	11.7	3.55	130	.265	.307	0	—	0	3	4	-1	0.2
1994	Bos-A	2	3	.400	6	5	0	0	0	23	44	1	14	15	22.7	8.61	58	.427	.496	0	—	0	-10	-9	0	-1.5
1996	Bos-A	0	2	.000	2	2	0	0	0	6	16	1	5	4	31.5	15.00	34	.533	.600	0	—	0	-7	-7	0	-1.4
Total	3	3	7	.300	13	12	1	0	0	62	95	7	27	37	17.7	6.53	74	.358	.418	0	—	0	-14	-12	-1	-2.7

● **RAY MINER**   Miner, Raymond Theodore "Lefty" b: 4/4/1897, Glens Falls, N.Y. d: 9/15/63, Glenridge, N.Y. BR/TL, 5'11", 160 lbs. Deb: 9/15/21

YEAR	TM/L	W	L	PCT	G	GS	CG	SH	SV	IP	H	HR	BB	SO	RAT	ERA	ERA+	OAV	OOB	BH	AVG	PB	PR	/A	PD	TPI
1921	Phi-A	0	0	—	1	0	0	0	0	1	2	0	3	0	45.0	36.00	12	.400	.625	0	—	0	-4	-4	0	-0.3

● **CRAIG MINETTO**   Minetto, Craig Stephen b: 4/25/54, Stockton, Cal. BL/TL, 6', 185 lbs. Deb: 7/4/78

YEAR	TM/L	W	L	PCT	G	GS	CG	SH	SV	IP	H	HR	BB	SO	RAT	ERA	ERA+	OAV	OOB	BH	AVG	PB	PR	/A	PD	TPI
1978	Oak-A	0	0	—	4	2	0	0	0	13	7	3	7	5	16.5	3.75	97	.283	.400	0	—	0	0	-0	-0	0.0
1979	Oak-A	1	5	.167	36	13	0	0	0	118¹	131	16	58	64	14.6	5.55	73	.282	.365	0	—	0	-18	-20	-2	-0.7
1980	Oak-A	0	2	.000	7	1	0	0	0	8	11	2	3	5	15.8	7.88	48	.324	.378	0	—	0	-3	-4	0	-0.5
1981	Oak-A	0	0	—	8	0	0	0	1	6²	7	0	4	2	16.2	2.70	129	.280	.400	0	—	0	1	1	0	0.2
Total	4	1	7	.125	55	15	0	0	1	145	162	19	72	76	14.9	5.40	73	.284	.370	0	—	0	-20	-23	-2	-1.0

● **STEVE MINGORI**   Mingori, Stephen Bernard b: 2/29/44, Kansas City, Mo. BL/TL, 5'10", 170 lbs. Deb: 8/5/70

YEAR	TM/L	W	L	PCT	G	GS	CG	SH	SV	IP	H	HR	BB	SO	RAT	ERA	ERA+	OAV	OOB	BH	AVG	PB	PR	/A	PD	TPI
1970	Cle-A	1	0	1.000	21	0	0	0	1	20¹	12	2	16	13.3	2.66	149	.227	.341	0	.000	-0	2	3	0	0.2
1971	Cle-A	1	2	.333	54	0	0	0	7	56²	31	2	24	45	9.8	1.43	268	.166	.264	1	.500	0	13	15	1	1.2
1972	Cle-A	0	6	.333	41	0	0	0	10	57	67	4	36	47	16.6	3.95	81	.293	.393	1	.125	0	-6	-5	1	-0.7
1973	Cle-A	0	0	—	5	0	0	0	0	11²	10	3	10	4	15.4	6.17	64	.233	.377	0	—	0	-3	-3	1	0.0

YEAR	TM/L	W	L	PCT	G	GS	CG	SH	SV	IP	H	HR	BB	SO	RAT	ERA	ERA+	OAV	OOB	BH	AVG	PB	PR	/A	PD	TPI
	KC-A	3	3	.500	19	1	0	0	1	56¹	59	6	23	46	13.6	3.04	135	.267	.344	0	—	0	5	7	-0	0.2
	Yr	3	3	.500	24	1	0	0	1	68	69	9	33	50	13.9	3.57	114	.261	.350	0	—	0	2	4	1	0.2
1974	KC-A	2	3	.400	36	0	0	0	1	67¹	53	4	23	43	10.4	2.81	136	.212	.284	0	—	0	6	8	2	0.6
1975	KC-A	0	3	.000	36	0	0	0	2	50¹	42	2	20	25	11.3	2.50	154	.226	.304	0	.000	0	7	8	0	0.5
1976	*KC-A	5	5	.500	55	0	0	0	10	85¹	73	3	25	38	10.7	2.32	151	.238	.301	0	—	0	11	11	3	1.9
1977	*KC-A	2	4	.333	43	0	0	0	4	64	59	4	19	19	11.1	3.09	130	.254	.313	0	—	0	7	7	1	0.7
1978	*KC-A	1	4	.200	45	0	0	0	7	69	64	5	16	28	10.8	2.74	140	.242	.292	0	—	0	8	8	0	0.8
1979	KC-A	3	3	.500	30	1	0	0	1	46²	69	10	17	18	16.8	5.79	74	.348	.403	0	—	0	-8	-8	-1	-1.1
Total	10	18	33	.353	385	2	0	0	42	584²	544	45	225	329	12.1	3.03	126	.248	.323	2	.167	0	43	51	7	4.3

● **PAUL MINNER**   Minner, Paul Edison "Lefty"   b: 7/30/23, New Wilmington, Pa.   BL/TL, 6'5", 210 lbs.   Deb: 9/12/46

YEAR	TM/L	W	L	PCT	G	GS	CG	SH	SV	IP	H	HR	BB	SO	RAT	ERA	ERA+	OAV	OOB	BH	AVG	PB	PR	/A	PD	TPI
1946	Bro-N	0	1	.000	3	0	0	0	0	4	6	1	3	3	20.3	6.75	50	.333	.429	0	—	0	-1	-1	-0	-0.4
1948	Bro-N	4	3	.571	28	2	0	0	1	62²	61	5	26	23	12.5	2.44	164	.257	.331	4	.190	1	11	11	0	1.3
1949	*Bro-N	3	1	.750	27	1	0	0	2	47¹	49	7	18	17	12.9	3.80	108	.272	.342	3	.214	-0	1	2	0	0.2
1950	Chi-N	8	13	.381	39	24	9	1	4	190¹	217	18	72	99	13.7	4.11	102	.287	.350	14	.215	2	1	2	3	0.7
1951	Chi-N	6	17	.261	33	28	14	3	1	201²	219	20	64	68	12.6	3.79	108	.277	.331	18	.254	5	4	7	3	1.6
1952	Chi-N	14	9	.609	28	27	12	2	0	180²	180	13	54	64	11.7	3.74	103	.258	.312	15	.234	6	-0	2	2	1.1
1953	Chi-N	12	15	.444	31	27	9	2	1	201	227	15	40	64	12.1	4.21	106	.283	.320	15	.221	2	2	5	4	1.2
1954	Chi-N	11	11	.500	32	29	12	0	1	218	236	19	50	79	11.8	3.96	106	.280	.321	13	.171	3	3	6	1	1.0
1955	Chi-N	9	9	.500	22	22	7	1	0	157²	173	15	47	53	12.6	3.48	117	.283	.335	13	.232	2	10	11	2	1.5
1956	Chi-N	2	5	.286	10	9	1	0	0	47	60	9	19	14	15.5	6.89	55	.324	.393	3	.250	2	-16	-16	0	-1.8
Total	10	69	84	.451	253	169	64	9	10	1310¹	1428	122	393	481	12.6	3.94	105	.279	.332	98	.219	22	12	27	15	6.4

● **DON MINNICK**   Minnick, Donald Athey   b: 4/14/31, Lynchburg, Va.   BR/TR, 6'3", 195 lbs.   Deb: 9/23/57

YEAR	TM/L	W	L	PCT	G	GS	CG	SH	SV	IP	H	HR	BB	SO	RAT	ERA	ERA+	OAV	OOB	BH	AVG	PB	PR	/A	PD	TPI
1957	Was-A	0	1	.000	2	1	0	0	0	9¹	14	1	2	7	15.4	4.82	81	.341	.372	0	.000	-0	-1	-1	-0	-0.1

● **BLAS MINOR**   Minor, Blas   b: 3/20/66, Merced, Cal.   BR/TR, 6'3", 195 lbs.   Deb: 7/28/92

YEAR	TM/L	W	L	PCT	G	GS	CG	SH	SV	IP	H	HR	BB	SO	RAT	ERA	ERA+	OAV	OOB	BH	AVG	PB	PR	/A	PD	TPI
1992	Pit-N	0	0		1	0	0	0	0	2	3	0	0	0	13.5	4.50	76	.333	.333	0		0	-0	-0	0	0.0
1993	Pit-N	8	6	.571	65	0	0	0	2	94¹	94	8	26	84	11.8	4.10	99	.263	.320	2	.200	1	-1	-1	1	0.1
1994	Pit-N	0	1	.000	17	0	0	0	1	19	27	4	9	17	17.5	8.05	54	.351	.425	0	—	0	-8	-8	-0	-0.4
1995	NY-N	4	2	.667	35	0	0	0	1	46²	44	6	13	43	11.2	3.66	110	.253	.309	0	.000	-0	3	2	0	0.2
1996	NY-N	0	0	—	17	0	0	0	0	25²	23	4	6	20	10.2	3.51	112	.237	.282	0	.000	-0	2	1	0	0.2
	Sea-A	0	1	.000	11	0	0	0	0	25¹	27	6	11	14	13.5	4.97	99	.276	.349	0		0	0	-0	0	-0.1
Total	5	12	10	.545	146	0	0	0	4	213	218	28	65	178	12.2	4.39	95	.268	.327	2	.154	0	-4	-6	1	-0.1

● **JIM MINSHALL**   Minshall, James Edward   b: 7/4/47, Covington, Ky.   BR/TR, 6'6", 215 lbs.   Deb: 9/14/74

YEAR	TM/L	W	L	PCT	G	GS	CG	SH	SV	IP	H	HR	BB	SO	RAT	ERA	ERA+	OAV	OOB	BH	AVG	PB	PR	/A	PD	TPI
1974	Pit-N	0	1	.000	5	0	0	0	0	4¹	1	0	2	3	6.2	0.00	—	.083	.214	0	—	0	2	2	-0	0.4
1975	Pit-N	0	0	—	1	0	0	0	0	1	0	1	2	2	18.0	0.00	—	.000	.400	0	—	0	0	-0	-0	-0
Total	2	0	1	.000	6	0	0	0	0	5¹	1	0	4	5	8.4	0.00	—	.067	.263	0		0	2	2	-0	0.4

● **GREG MINTON**   Minton, Gregory Brian   b: 7/29/51, Lubbock, Tex.   BB/TR, 6'2", 190 lbs.   Deb: 9/7/75

YEAR	TM/L	W	L	PCT	G	GS	CG	SH	SV	IP	H	HR	BB	SO	RAT	ERA	ERA+	OAV	OOB	BH	AVG	PB	PR	/A	PD	TPI
1975	SF-N	1	1	.500	4	2	0	0	0	17	19	1	11	6	16.4	6.88	55	.288	.397	0	.000	-1	-6	-6	1	-0.6
1976	SF-N	0	3	.000	10	2	0	0	0	25²	32	0	12	7	15.8	4.91	74	.317	.395	1	.200	-0	-4	-4	0	-0.4
1977	SF-N	1	1	.500	2	2	0	0	0	14	14	0	4	5	11.6	4.50	87	.264	.316	1	.333	1	-1	-1	0	0.0
1978	SF-N	0	1	.000	11	0	0	0	0	15²	22	3	8	6	17.8	8.04	43	.338	.419	0	—	-0	-8	-8	0	-0.5
1979	SF-N	4	3	.571	46	0	0	0	4	79²	59	0	27	33	9.9	1.81	193	.215	.289	0	.000	-0	17	15	2	1.6
1980	SF-N	4	6	.400	68	0	0	0	19	91¹	81	0	34	42	11.3	2.46	144	.243	.313	1	.125	-0	12	11	2	1.8
1981	SF-N	4	5	.444	55	0	0	0	21	84¹	84	4	36	29	12.8	2.88	119	.267	.342	0	.000	-1	6	5	3	1.0
1982	SF-N★	10	4	.714	78	0	0	0	30	123	108	5	42	58	11.1	1.83	196	.244	.313	3	.176	0	**24**	**24**	1	**3.9**
1983	SF-N	7	11	.389	73	0	0	0	22	106²	117	6	47	38	13.8	3.54	100	.283	.356	6	.545	4	1	-0	-0	0.4
1984	SF-N	4	9	.308	74	1	0	0	19	124¹	130	6	57	48	13.5	3.76	93	.267	.344	1	.048	-1	-2	-4	2	-0.4
1985	SF-N	5	4	.556	68	0	0	0	4	96²	98	6	54	37	14.2	3.54	97	.272	.367	0	.000	-1	1	-1	2	0.1
1986	SF-N	4	4	.500	48	0	0	0	5	68²	63	4	34	34	12.8	3.93	90	.251	.343	2	.400	2	-2	-3	2	0.0
1987	SF-N	1	0	1.000	15	0	0	0	0	23¹	30	2	10	9	15.8	3.47	111	.323	.394	0	.000	-0	2	1	0	0.0
	Cal-A	5	4	.556	41	0	0	0	10	76	71	4	29	35	12.0	3.08	140	.257	.330	0		0	12	10	2	1.6
1988	Cal-A	4	5	.444	44	0	0	0	7	79²	67	1	34	46	11.8	2.85	135	.233	.320	0		0	10	9	2	1.3
1989	Cal-A	4	3	.571	62	0	0	0	8	90	76	4	37	42	11.5	2.20	173	.230	.311	0		0	17	16	2	1.7
1990	Cal-A	1	1	.500	11	0	0	0	0	15¹	11	1	7	4	11.2	2.35	163	.212	.317	0		0	3	3	0	0.4
Total	16	59	65	.476	710	7	0	0	150	1082	1082	43	483	479	12.6	3.10	117	.257	.336	15	.146	0	80	68	19	11.9

● **STEVE MINTZ**   Mintz, Stephen Wayne   b: 11/24/68, Wilmington, N.C.   BL/TR, 5'11", 190 lbs.   Deb: 5/18/95

YEAR	TM/L	W	L	PCT	G	GS	CG	SH	SV	IP	H	HR	BB	SO	RAT	ERA	ERA+	OAV	OOB	BH	AVG	PB	PR	/A	PD	TPI
1995	SF-N	1	2	.333	14	0	0	0	0	19¹	26	4	12	7	18.6	7.45	55	.329	.430	0	—	-0	-7	-7	-0	-1.0

● **GINO MINUTELLI**   Minutelli, Gino Michael   b: 5/23/64, Wilmington, Del.   BL/TL, 6', 180 lbs.   Deb: 9/18/90

YEAR	TM/L	W	L	PCT	G	GS	CG	SH	SV	IP	H	HR	BB	SO	RAT	ERA	ERA+	OAV	OOB	BH	AVG	PB	PR	/A	PD	TPI
1990	Cin-N	0	0	—	2	0	0	0	0	1	0	0	2	0	27.0	9.00	44	.000	.500	0		0	-1	-1	0	-0.1
1991	Cin-N	0	2	.000	16	3	0	0	0	25¹	30	5	18	21	17.1	6.04	63	.288	.393	0	.000	-0	-7	-6	0	-0.5
1993	SF-N	0	1	.000	9	0	0	0	0	14¹	7	2	15	10	13.8	3.77	104	.152	.361	0	.000	-0	0	-0	-0	-0.1
Total	3	0	3	.000	27	3	0	0	0	40²	37	7	35	31	16.2	5.31	72	.242	.386	0	.000	-1	-7	-7	0	-0.6

● **PAUL MIRABELLA**   Mirabella, Paul Thomas   b: 3/20/54, Belleville, N.J.   BL/TL, 6'2", 196 lbs.   Deb: 7/28/78

YEAR	TM/L	W	L	PCT	G	GS	CG	SH	SV	IP	H	HR	BB	SO	RAT	ERA	ERA+	OAV	OOB	BH	AVG	PB	PR	/A	PD	TPI
1978	Tex-A	3	2	.600	10	4	0	0	1	28	30	2	17	23	15.1	5.79	65	.286	.385	0	—	0	-6	-6	-0	-1.1
1979	NY-A	0	4	.000	10	1	0	0	0	14¹	16	3	10	4	17.0	8.79	46	.276	.391	0	—	0	-7	-8	-0	-1.6
1980	Tor-A	5	12	.294	33	22	3	1	0	130²	151	11	66	53	15.2	4.34	99	.294	.378	0	—	0	-4	-1	0	-0.1
1981	Tor-A	0	0	—	8	1	0	0	0	14²	20	2	7	9	17.2	7.36	53	.313	.389	0	—	0	-6	-6	-0	-0.3
1982	Tex-A	1	1	.500	40	0	0	0	3	50²	46	4	22	29	12.4	4.80	81	.241	.326	0	—	0	-4	-5	0	-0.2
1983	Bal-A	0	0	—	3	2	0	0	0	14	9	1	4	5	14.9	5.59	71	.243	.364	0	—	0	-2	-2	-0	-0.0
1984	Sea-A	2	5	.286	52	1	0	0	3	68	74	6	32	41	14.2	4.37	91	.282	.363	0	—	0	-3	-3	1	-0.2
1985	Sea-A	0	0	—	10	0	0	0	0	13²	9	2	6	8	9.9	1.32	320	.188	.278	0	—	0	4	4	-0	0.4
1986	Sea-A	0	0	—	8	0	0	0	0	6¹	13	1	3	6	22.7	8.53	50	.419	.471	0	—	0	-3	-3	-0	-0.0
1987	Mil-A	2	1	.667	29	0	0	0	2	29¹	30	0	16	14	14.1	4.91	93	.268	.359	0	—	0	-1	-1	1	-0.1
1988	Mil-A	2	2	.500	38	0	0	0	4	60	44	3	21	33	9.8	1.65	241	.204	.274	0	—	0	15	16	1	1.2
1989	Mil-A	0	0	—	13	0	0	0	0	15¹	18	1	7	6	15.3	7.63	50	.290	.371	0	—	0	-6	-6	0	-0.6
1990	Mil-A	4	2	.667	44	0	0	0	2	59	66	9	27	28	14.5	3.97	98	.281	.360	0	—	0	-0	-1	-0	-0.0
Total	13	19	29	.396	298	33	3	1	13	499²	526	43	239	258	14.0	4.45	91	.272	.356	0	—	0	-24	-21	-0	-2.1

● **ANGEL MIRANDA**   Miranda, Angel Luis (Andujar)   b: 11/9/69, Arecibo, P.R.   BL/TL, 6'1", 160 lbs.   Deb: 6/5/93

YEAR	TM/L	W	L	PCT	G	GS	CG	SH	SV	IP	H	HR	BB	SO	RAT	ERA	ERA+	OAV	OOB	BH	AVG	PB	PR	/A	PD	TPI
1993	Mil-A	4	5	.444	22	17	2	0	0	120	100	12	52	88	11.6	3.30	129	.226	.310	0	—	-0	14	13	-1	0.8
1994	Mil-A	2	5	.286	8	8	1	0	0	46	39	4	27	24	12.9	5.28	95	.234	.340	0	—	-0	-2	-2	-1	-0.2
1995	Mil-A	4	5	.444	30	10	0	0	1	74	83	8	49	45	16.1	5.23	95	.291	.395	0	—	-0	-4	-2	-0	-0.2
1996	Mil-A	7	6	.538	46	12	0	0	1	109¹	116	12	69	78	15.4	4.94	107	.277	.382	0	—	0	1	4	-1	0.1
Total	4	17	21	.447	106	47	3	0	2	349¹	338	40	197	235	13.9	4.48	107	.257	.356	0	—	-0	8	13	-3	0.5

● **ROY MITCHELL**   Mitchell, Albert Roy   b: 4/19/1885, Belton, Tex.   d: 9/8/59, Temple, Tex.   BR/TR, 5'9.5", 170 lbs.   Deb: 9/10/10

YEAR	TM/L	W	L	PCT	G	GS	CG	SH	SV	IP	H	HR	BB	SO	RAT	ERA	ERA+	OAV	OOB	BH	AVG	PB	PR	/A	PD	TPI
1910	StL-A	4	2	.667	8	6	6	0	0	52	43	0	12	23	9.9	2.60	95	.244	.300	4	.211	0	-0	-1	1	0.0
1911	StL-A	4	8	.333	28	12	8	1	0	133¹	134	4	45	40	12.5	3.85	88	.273	.341	11	.224	1	-7	-7	-0	-0.4
1912	StL-A	3	4	.429	13	7	5	0	0	62	81	2	17	22	14.8	4.65	71	.323	.375	6	.316	3	-9	-9	-1	-0.7
1913	StL-A	13	16	.448	33	27	21	4	1	245¹	265	6	47	59	11.6	3.01	97	.280	.318	13	.148	-1	-2	-1	0	-0.5
1914	StL-A	5	4	.444	28	9	4	0	**4**	103¹	101	1	38	38	15.5	4.35	62	.320	.384	7	.206	1	-19	-19	-0	-1.6
1918	Chi-N	0	1	.000	3	2	1	0	0	12	18	1	3	6	16.5	7.50	36	.346	.393	0	.000	-0	-6	-6	0	-0.5
	Cin-N	4	0	1.000	5	3	2	0	0	36¹	27	0	9	6	7.9	0.74	359	.208	.237	3	.214	0	8	8	-0	1.0
1919	Cin-N	0	1	.000	7	1	0	0	0	31	32	0	6	10	11.9	2.32	119	.276	.328	0	.000	-2	2	1	0	0.0
Total	7	32	37	.464	122	67	47	7	5	675¹	734	14	177	204	12.4	3.42	86	.284	.336	44	.187	3	-34	-35	-1	-2.7

YEAR TM/L	W	L	PCT	G	GS	CG	SH	SV	IP	H	HR	BB	SO	RAT	ERA	ERA+	OAV	OOB	BH	AVG	PB	PR	/A	PD	TPI

● CHARLIE MITCHELL   Mitchell, Charles Ross b: 6/24/62, Dickson, Tenn.   BR/TR, 6'3", 170 lbs.   Deb: 8/9/84 F

1984 Bos-A	0	0	—	10	0	0	0	0	16¹	14	1	6	7	12.1	2.76	151	.226	.314	0	—	0	2	3	0	-0.1
1985 Bos-A	0	0	—	2	0	0	0	0	1²	5	1	0	2	27.0	16.20	26	.500	.500	0	—	0	-2	-2	0	0.0
Total 2	0	0	—	12	0	0	0	0	18	19	2	6	9	13.5	4.00	104	.264	.338	0	—	0	0	0	0	-0.1

● CLARENCE MITCHELL   Mitchell, Clarence Elmer b: 2/22/1891, Franklin, Neb.   d: 11/6/63, Grand Island, Neb.   BL/TL, 5'11.5", 190 lbs.   Deb: 6/2/11 C◆

1911 Det-A	1	0	1.000	5	1	0	0	0	14¹	20	1	7	4	17.0	8.16	42	.351	.422	2	.500	1	-8	-7	-1	-0.4
1916 Cin-N	11	10	.524	29	24	17	1	0	194²	211	4	45	52	12.3	3.14	83	.285	.334	28	.239	2	-11	-12	1	-0.8
1917 Cin-N	9	15	.375	32	20	10	2	1	159¹	166	4	34	37	11.4	3.22	81	.268	.308	25	.278	4	-9	-11	0	-1.2
1918 Bro-N	0	1	.000	1	1	0	0	0	0¹	4	0	0	0	108.0	108.00	3	1.000	1.000	6	.250	0	-4	-4	0	-3.0
1919 Bro-N	7	5	.583	23	11	9	0	0	108²	123	0	23	43	12.1	3.06	97	.297	.334	6	.183	6	-2	-1	1	0.7
1920 *Bro-N	5	2	.714	19	7	3	1	1	78²	85	1	23	18	12.4	3.09	104	.288	.340	25	.234	1	0	1	1	0.4
1921 Bro-N	11	9	.550	37	18	13	**3**	2	190	206	7	46	39	12.2	2.89	135	.280	.327	24	.264	3	19	21	3	2.8
1922 Bro-N	0	3	.000	5	3	0	0	0	12²	28	0	7	1	25.6	14.21	29	.467	.529	45	.290	2	-14	-14	1	-2.2
1923 Phi-N	9	10	.474	29	19	8	1	0	139¹	170	8	46	41	14.3	4.72	98	.299	.355	21	.269	3	-11	-2	-3	-0.2
1924 Phi-N	6	13	.316	30	26	9	1	1	165	223	10	58	36	15.7	5.62	79	.321	.379	26	.255	-1	-32	-21	3	-1.9
1925 Phi-N	10	17	.370	32	26	12	1	1	199¹	245	23	51	46	13.6	5.28	90	.302	.347	18	.196	-2	-22	-11	4	-1.0
1926 Phi-N	9	14	.391	28	25	12	0	1	178²	232	7	55	52	14.7	4.58	90	.318	.369	19	.244	1	-15	-9	4	-0.4
1927 Phi-N	6	3	.667	13	12	8	1	0	94²	99	7	28	17	12.3	4.09	101	.271	.327	10	.238	2	-2	0	1	0.3
1928 Phi-N	0	0	—	3	0	0	0	0	5²	13	0	2	0	23.8	9.53	45	.542	.577	1	.250	0	-3	-3	0	0.0
*StL-N	8	9	.471	19	18	9	1	0	150	149	8	38	31	11.4	3.30	121	.265	.315	7	.125	-3	12	12	1	1.1
Yr	8	9	.471	22	18	9	1	0	155²	162	8	40	31	11.9	3.53	114	.268	.326	8	.133	-3	8	8	1	1.1
1929 StL-N	8	11	.421	25	22	16	0	0	173	221	13	60	39	14.9	4.27	109	.320	.379	18	.273	4	9	8	-1	0.9
1930 StL-N	1	0	1.000	1	1	0	0	0	3	5	0	2	1	21.0	6.00	84	.357	.438	1	.500	0	-0	-0	0	-0.1
NY-N	10	3	.769	24	16	5	0	0	129	151	10	36	40	13.1	3.98	119	.298	.346	12	.255	0	14	11	2	1.1
Yr	11	3	.786	25	17	5	0	0	132	156	10	38	41	13.3	4.02	118	.300	.349	13	.265	1	14	11	2	1.0
1931 NY-N	13	11	.542	27	25	13	0	0	190¹	221	12	52	39	13.1	4.07	91	.285	.332	16	.219	5	-4	-8	-2	-0.9
1932 NY-N	1	3	.250	8	3	1	0	2	30¹	41	1	11	7	15.7	4.15	89	.325	.384	2	.200	0	-1	-1	-1	-0.3
Total 18	125	139	.473	390	278	145	12	9	2217	2613	116	624	543	13.4	4.12	95	.297	.347	324	.252	26	-86	-54	17	-5.1

● CRAIG MITCHELL   Mitchell, Craig Seton b: 4/14/54, Santa Rosa, Cal.   BR/TR, 6'3", 180 lbs.   Deb: 9/25/75

1975 Oak-A	0	1	.000	1	1	0	0	0	3²	6	0	2	2	19.6	12.27	30	.375	.444	0	—	0	-3	-4	0	-0.6
1976 Oak-A	0	0	—	1	0	0	0	0	3¹	3	0	0	0	8.1	2.70	124	.231	.231	0	—	0	0	0	0	0.0
1977 Oak-A	0	1	.000	3	1	0	0	0	5²	9	1	2	1	17.5	7.94	51	.346	.393	0	—	0	-2	-2	0	-0.3
Total 3	0	2	.000	5	2	0	0	0	12²	18	1	4	3	15.6	7.82	48	.340	.373	0	—	0	-6	-6	0	-0.9

● FRED MITCHELL   Mitchell, Frederick Francis (b: Frederick Francis Yapp)
b: 6/5/1878, Cambridge, Mass.   d: 10/13/70, Newton, Mass.   BR/TR, 5'9.5", 185 lbs.   Deb: 4/27/01 MC◆

1901 Bos-A	6	6	.500	17	13	10	0	0	108²	115	2	51	34	14.7	3.81	93	.268	.360	7	.159	-1	-2	-3	0	-0.4
1902 Bos-A	0	1	.000	1	0	0	0	0	4	8	1	5	2	29.3	11.25	32	.421	.542	-0	-3	-3	0	-0.5
Phi-A	5	7	.417	18	14	9	0	1	107²	120	4	59	22	15.6	3.59	102	.282	.380	9	.188	-1	-0	1	2	0.2
Yr	5	8	.385	19	14	9	0	1	111²	128	5	64	24	16.1	3.87	95	.284	.388	9	.184	-1	-4	-3	3	-0.3
1903 Phi-N	11	16	.407	28	28	24	1	0	227	250	4	102	69	14.7	4.48	73	.284	.370	19	.200	-1	-31	-30	-3	-3.3
1904 Phi-N	4	7	.364	13	13	11	0	0	108²	133	6	25	29	13.7	3.40	79	.306	.353	17	.207	1	-8	-9	3	-0.4
Bro-N	2	5	.286	8	8	8	0	0	66	73	0	23	16	13.5	3.82	72	.291	.357	7	.292	2	-8	-8	1	-0.4
Yr	6	12	.333	21	21	19	1	0	174²	206	6	48	45	13.2	3.56	76	.297	.345	24	.226	4	-16	-17	4	-0.8
1905 Bro-N	3	7	.300	12	10	9	0	0	96¹	107	2	38	44	14.0	4.76	61	.285	.358	15	.190	0	-19	-20	1	-1.7
Total 5	31	49	.387	97	86	71	2	1	718¹	806	16	303	216	14.6	4.10	78	.286	.366	120	.210	1	-71	-73	5	-6.5

● JOHN MITCHELL   Mitchell, John Kyle b: 8/11/65, Dickson, Tenn.   BR/TR, 6'2", 195 lbs.   Deb: 9/8/86 F

1986 NY-N	0	1	.000	4	1	0	0	0	10	10	1	4	2	12.6	3.60	98	.278	.350	0	.000	-0	-0	-0	0	-0.0
1987 NY-N	3	6	.333	20	19	1	0	0	111²	124	6	36	57	13.1	4.11	92	.279	.336	4	.114	-1	-0	-4	1	-0.3
1988 NY-N	0	0	—	1	0	0	0	0	1	2	0	1	1	27.0	0.00	—	.500	.600	0	.000	-0	0	0	0	0.0
1989 NY-N	0	1	.000	2	0	0	0	0	3	3	0	4	4	21.0	6.00	54	.231	.412	0	—	-0	-1	-1	-0	-0.3
1990 Bal-A	6	6	.500	24	17	0	0	0	114¹	133	7	48	43	14.5	4.64	82	.300	.372	0	—	0	-9	-11	1	-0.8
Total 5	9	14	.391	51	37	1	0	0	240	272	14	93	107	13.9	4.35	87	.289	.356	4	.105	-1	-10	-16	2	-1.4

● LARRY MITCHELL   Mitchell, Larry Paul b: 10/16/71, Flint, Mich.   BR/TR, 6'1", 200 lbs.   Deb: 8/11/96

| 1996 Phi-N | 0 | 0 | — | 7 | 0 | 0 | 0 | 0 | 12 | 14 | 1 | 5 | 7 | 14.3 | 4.50 | 97 | .311 | .380 | 0 | .000 | -0 | -0 | -0 | -0 | -0.1 |

● MONROE MITCHELL   Mitchell, Monroe Barr b: 9/11/01, Starkville, Miss.   d: 9/4/76, Valdosta, Ga.   BR/TL, 6'1.5", 170 lbs.   Deb: 7/11/23

| 1923 Was-A | 2 | 4 | .333 | 10 | 6 | 3 | 1 | 2 | 41² | 57 | 0 | 22 | 8 | 17.3 | 6.48 | 58 | .350 | .430 | 3 | .250 | 1 | -12 | -13 | -1 | -1.6 |

● PAUL MITCHELL   Mitchell, Paul Michael b: 8/19/49, Worcester, Mass.   BR/TR, 6'1", 195 lbs.   Deb: 7/1/75

1975 Bal-A	3	0	1.000	11	4	1	0	0	57	41	8	19	31	9.5	3.63	97	.204	.273	0	—	0	1	-1	-1	-0.1
1976 Oak-A	9	7	.563	26	26	4	1	0	142	169	15	30	67	12.7	4.25	79	.294	.331	0	—	0	-11	-14	1	-1.6
1977 Oak-A	0	3	.000	5	3	0	0	0	13²	21	3	7	5	18.4	10.54	38	.339	.406	0	—	0	-10	-10	0	-1.6
Sea-A	3	3	.500	9	9	0	0	0	39²	50	7	16	20	15.2	4.99	82	.311	.376	0	—	0	-4	-4	0	-0.4
Yr	3	6	.333	14	12	0	0	0	53¹	71	10	23	25	16.0	6.41	64	.318	.385	0	—	0	-14	-14	1	-2.0
1978 Sea-A	8	14	.364	29	29	4	2	0	168	173	21	79	75	13.6	4.18	91	.270	.352	0	—	0	-8	-7	-1	-0.9
1979 Sea-A	1	4	.200	10	6	1	0	0	36²	46	4	15	18	15.0	4.42	99	.309	.372	0	—	0	-1	-0	-0	-0.1
Mil-A	3	3	.500	18	8	0	1	0	75	81	11	10	32	11.3	5.76	72	.276	.307	0	—	0	-13	-13	-1	-1.0
Yr	4	7	.364	28	14	1	1	0	111²	127	15	25	50	12.5	5.32	79	.287	.329	0	—	0	-14	-14	-1	-1.1
1980 Mil-A	5	3	.500	17	11	1	1	1	89¹	92	7	15	29	10.9	3.53	110	.267	.300	0	—	0	5	3	0	0.4
Total 6	32	39	.451	125	96	11	4	1	621¹	673	76	191	277	12.6	4.45	85	.278	.332	0	—	0	-41	-46	-3	-5.3

● BOBBY MITCHELL   Mitchell, Robert McKasha b: 2/6/1856, Cincinnati, Ohio d: 5/1/33, Springfield, Ohio   BL/TL, 5'5", 135 lbs.   Deb: 9/6/1877 ◆

1877 Cin-N	6	5	.545	12	12	11	0	0	100	123	0	11	41	12.1	3.51	75	.281	.299	10	.204	-0	-8	-10	-0	-0.8
1878 Cin-N	7	2	.778	9	9	9	1	0	80	69	1	18	51	9.8	2.14	100	**.223**	.265	12	.245	1	2	-0	0	0.1
1879 Cle-N	7	15	.318	23	22	20	0	0	194²	236	0	42	90	12.9	3.28	74	.286	.317	16	.147	-4	-17	-17	-4	-2.2
1882 StL-a	0	1	.000	1	1	0	0	0	7	12	0	2	2	18.0	7.71	36	.353	.389	0	.000	-1	-4	-4	-0	-0.4
Total 4	20	23	.465	45	44	40	2	0	381²	440	1	73	184	12.1	3.18	77	.285	.311	38	.180	-5	-27	-30	-4	-3.3

● WILLIE MITCHELL   Mitchell, William b: 12/1/1889, Pleasant Grove, Miss.   d: 11/23/73, Sardis, Miss.   BR/TL, 6', 176 lbs.   Deb: 9/22/09

1909 Cle-A	1	2	.333	3	3	3	0	0	18³	18	0	10	8	12.5	1.57	163	.225	.340	2	.286	1	2	3	0	0.5
1910 Cle-A	12	8	.600	35	18	11	1	0	183²	155	2	55	102	11.0	2.60	100	.236	.310	10	.159	-3	-2	-0	-2	-0.6
1911 Cle-A	7	14	.333	30	22	9	0	0	177¹	190	1	60	78	13.3	3.76	91	.284	.354	7	.109	-5	-8	-7	-1	-1.3
1912 Cle-A	5	8	.385	29	15	8	0	1	163²	149	0	56	94	11.7	2.80	121	.240	.309	6	.113	-4	9	11	-3	0.1
1913 Cle-A	14	8	.636	35	22	14	4	0	217	153	1	88	141	10.3	1.91	159	.199	.288	10	.143	1	25	27	1	2.2
1914 Cle-A	12	17	.414	39	32	16	3	1	257	228	3	124	179	12.6	3.19	91	.238	.330	7	.086	-3	-13	-9	-5	-1.9
1915 Cle-A	11	14	.440	36	30	12	1	1	236	210	1	94	149	11.3	2.82	104	.241	.309	10	.127	-5	3	6	-4	-0.3
1916 Cle-A	2	5	.286	12	6	1	0	1	43²	55	1	19	24	15.3	5.15	58	.309	.376	0	.000	-1	-11	-10	-1	-1.8
Det-A	7	5	.583	23	17	7	2	0	127²	119	1	48	60	12.1	3.31	86	.253	.329	4	.250	2	-7	-6	-3	-0.7
Yr	9	10	.474	35	23	8	2	1	171¹	174	2	67	84	12.9	3.78	77	.269	.342	4	.191	-1	-18	-17	-4	-2.5
1917 Det-A	12	8	.600	30	22	12	5	0	185¹	172	2	46	80	11.2	2.19	121	.250	.309	7	.119	3	10	9	-2	0.4
1918 Det-A	0	1	.000	4	1	0	0	0	4	6	0	6	0	27.0	9.00	30	.400	.400	0	—	0	-3	-3	-0	-0.6
1919 Det-A	1	2	.333	3	2	1	0	0	13²	12	2	10	4	15.1	5.27	61	.255	.397	1	.200	0	-3	-3	0	-0.6
Total 11	84	92	.477	276	190	93	16	4	1632	1464	14	605	921	11.8	2.88	103	.243	.320	69	.130	-24	3	18	-23	-4.5

● VINEGAR BEND MIZELL   Mizell, Wilmer David b: 8/13/30, Leakesville, Miss.   BR/TL, 6'3.5", 205 lbs.   Deb: 4/22/52

| 1952 StL-N | 10 | 8 | .556 | 30 | 30 | 7 | 2 | 0 | 190 | 171 | 12 | 103 | 146 | 13.0 | 3.65 | 102 | .237 | .333 | 3 | .044 | -5 | 2 | 1 | -2 | -0.6 |

YEAR TM/L	W	L	PCT	G	GS	CG	SH	SV	IP	H	HR	BB	SO	RAT	ERA	ERA+	OAV	OOB	BH	AVG	PB	PR	/A	PD	TPI
1953 StL-N	13	11	.542	33	33	10	1	0	224¹	193	12	114	173	12.5	3.49	122	.227	.321	7	.084	-4	20	19	-0	1.4
1956 StL-N	14	14	.500	33	33	11	3	0	208²	172	20	92	153	11.7	3.62	104	.222	.310	8	.107	-3	3	4	0	0.2
1957 StL-N	8	10	.444	33	21	7	2	0	149¹	136	18	51	87	11.3	3.74	106	.241	.305	4	.089	-2	2	4	1	0.3
1958 StL-N	10	14	.417	30	29	8	2	0	189²	178	17	91	80	12.9	3.42	121	.252	.339	7	.115	-3	11	15	-1	1.4
1959 StL-N†	13	10	.565	31	30	8	1	0	201¹	196	21	89	108	13.1	4.20	101	.252	.334	14	.187	1	-6	1	-2	-0.1
1960 StL-N	1	3	.250	9	9	0	0	0	55¹	64	7	28	42	15.0	4.55	90	.291	.371	2	.111	-1	-5	-3	-0	-0.2
*Pit-N	13	5	.722	23	23	8	3	0	155²	141	7	46	71	11.0	3.12	120	.247	.306	7	.137	-1	11	11	-3	0.8
Yr	14	8	.636	32	32	8	3	0	211	205	14	74	113	12.0	3.50	110	.259	.325	9	.130	-1	6	8	-2	0.6
1961 Pit-N	7	10	.412	25	17	2	1	0	100	120	16	31	42	13.6	5.04	79	.299	.350	3	.130	-1	-11	-12	-3	-2.0
1962 Pit-N	1	1	.500	4	3	0	0	0	16¹	15	3	10	6	14.3	4.96	79	.254	.371	0	.000	-0	-2	-2	0	-0.2
NY-N	0	2	.000	17	2	0	0	0	38	48	10	25	15	17.5	7.34	57	.324	.425	2	.250	-1	-14	-13	-1	-0.7
Yr	1	3	.250	21	5	0	0	0	54¹	63	13	35	21	16.4	6.63	62	.301	.404	2	.143	-0	-16	-15	-0	-0.9
Total 9	90	88	.506	268	230	61	15	0	1528²	1434	143	680	918	12.6	3.85	104	.247	.329	57	.111	-19	12	25	-9	0.3

● **DAVE MLICKI** Mlicki, David John b: 6/8/68, Cleveland, Ohio BR/TR, 6'4", 185 lbs. Deb: 9/12/92

YEAR TM/L	W	L	PCT	G	GS	CG	SH	SV	IP	H	HR	BB	SO	RAT	ERA	ERA+	OAV	OOB	BH	AVG	PB	PR	/A	PD	TPI
1992 Cle-A	0	2	.000	4	4	0	0	0	21²	23	3	16	16	16.6	4.98	78	.280	.404	0	—	0	-3	-3	1	-0.1
1993 Cle-A	0	0	—	3	3	0	0	0	13¹	11	2	6	7	12.8	3.38	128	.220	.328	0	—	0	1	1	-0	0.0
1995 NY-N	9	7	.563	29	25	0	0	0	160²	160	23	54	123	12.2	4.26	95	.256	.319	2	.051	-1	-1	-4	-1	-0.5
1996 NY-N	6	7	.462	51	2	0	0	1	90	95	9	33	83	13.4	3.30	119	.277	.351	1	.100	-0	9	6	-1	0.7
Total 4	15	16	.484	87	34	0	0	1	285²	289	37	109	229	12.9	3.97	101	.263	.336	3	.061	-1	7	1	-2	0.1

● **KEVIN MMAHAT** Mmahat, Kevin Paul b: 11/9/64, Memphis, Tenn. BL/TL, 6'5", 220 lbs. Deb: 9/9/89

YEAR TM/L	W	L	PCT	G	GS	CG	SH	SV	IP	H	HR	BB	SO	RAT	ERA	ERA+	OAV	OOB	BH	AVG	PB	PR	/A	PD	TPI
1989 NY-A	0	2	.000	4	2	0	0	0	7²	13	2	8	3	25.8	12.91	30	.406	.537	0	—	0	-8	-8	-0	-1.5

● **MIKE MODAK** Modak, Michael b: 5/18/22, Campbell, Ohio BR/TR, 5'10.5", 195 lbs. Deb: 7/4/45

YEAR TM/L	W	L	PCT	G	GS	CG	SH	SV	IP	H	HR	BB	SO	RAT	ERA	ERA+	OAV	OOB	BH	AVG	PB	PR	/A	PD	TPI
1945 Cin-N	1	2	.333	20	3	1	1	0	42¹	52	0	23	7	15.9	5.74	65	.308	.391	1	.100	-1	-9	-9	-1	-0.8

● **BRIAN MOEHLER** Moehler, Brian Merritt b: 12/31/71, Rockingham, N.C. BR/TR, 6'3", 195 lbs. Deb: 9/22/96

YEAR TM/L	W	L	PCT	G	GS	CG	SH	SV	IP	H	HR	BB	SO	RAT	ERA	ERA+	OAV	OOB	BH	AVG	PB	PR	/A	PD	TPI
1996 Det-A	0	1	.000	2	2	0	0	0	10¹	11	1	8	2	16.5	4.35	116	.262	.380	0	—	0	1	1	-0	0.0

● **DENNIS MOELLER** Moeller, Dennis Michael b: 9/15/67, Tarzana, Cal. BR/TL, 6'2", 195 lbs. Deb: 7/28/92

YEAR TM/L	W	L	PCT	G	GS	CG	SH	SV	IP	H	HR	BB	SO	RAT	ERA	ERA+	OAV	OOB	BH	AVG	PB	PR	/A	PD	TPI
1992 KC-A	0	3	.000	5	4	0	0	0	18²	24	5	11	6	17.5	7.00	58	.333	.422	0	—	0	-6	-6	0	-0.9
1993 Pit-N	1	0	1.000	10	0	0	0	0	16¹	26	2	7	13	18.7	9.92	48	.356	.420	0	—	0	-11	-11	0	-0.6
Total 2	1	3	.250	15	4	0	0	0	34¹	50	7	18	19	18.1	8.39	48	.345	.421	0	—	0	-17	-17	1	-1.5

● **JOE MOELLER** Moeller, Joseph Douglas b: 2/15/43, Blue Island, Ill. BR/TR, 6'5", 208 lbs. Deb: 4/12/62

YEAR TM/L	W	L	PCT	G	GS	CG	SH	SV	IP	H	HR	BB	SO	RAT	ERA	ERA+	OAV	OOB	BH	AVG	PB	PR	/A	PD	TPI
1962 LA-N	6	5	.545	19	15	1	0	1	85²	87	10	58	46	15.2	5.25	69	.266	.377	7	.212	1	-12	-15	1	-1.6
1964 LA-N	7	13	.350	27	24	1	0	0	145¹	153	14	31	97	11.6	4.21	77	.265	.307	3	.067	-2	-11	-16	-0	-2.2
1966 *LA-N	2	4	.333	29	8	0	0	0	78²	73	4	14	31	10.3	2.52	131	.244	.285	2	.167	1	10	7	1	0.7
1967 LA-N	0	0	—	6	0	0	0	0	5	9	1	3	2	21.6	9.00	34	.409	.480	0	—	-0	-3	-3	0	-0.1
1968 LA-N	1	1	.500	3	3	0	0	0	16	17	1	2	11	11.3	5.06	55	.270	.303	0	.000	-1	-4	-4	0	-0.5
1969 LA-N	1	0	1.000	23	4	0	0	1	51¹	54	4	13	25	11.7	3.33	100	.278	.324	2	.200	0	1	0	1	0.1
1970 LA-N	7	9	.438	31	19	2	1	4	135¹	131	16	43	63	11.6	3.92	98	.248	.306	6	.154	0	-2	-1	-2	-0.3
1971 LA-N	2	4	.333	28	1	0	0	0	66¹	72	5	12	32	11.4	3.80	85	.279	.311	0	.000	-0	-2	-4	1	-0.4
Total 8	26	36	.419	166	74	4	1	7	583²	596	55	176	307	12.0	4.01	86	.266	.318	20	.129	-2	-20	-37	2	-4.2

● **RON MOELLER** Moeller, Ronald Ralph "The Kid" b: 10/13/38, Cincinnati, Ohio BL/TL, 6', 180 lbs. Deb: 9/8/56

YEAR TM/L	W	L	PCT	G	GS	CG	SH	SV	IP	H	HR	BB	SO	RAT	ERA	ERA+	OAV	OOB	BH	AVG	PB	PR	/A	PD	TPI
1956 Bal-A	0	1	.000	4	1	0	0	0	8²	10	3	4	2	13.5	4.15	94	.286	.342	0	.000	-0	-0	-0	-0	-0.1
1958 Bal-A	0	0	—	4	0	0	0	0	4¹	6	0	3	3	18.7	4.15	87	.333	.429	0	—	0	-0	-0	0	0.0
1961 LA-A	4	8	.333	33	18	1	1	0	112²	122	15	83	87	16.5	5.83	77	.275	.392	6	.207	2	-23	-17	1	-1.3
1963 LA-A	0	0	—	3	0	0	0	0	2²	5	1	1	2	20.3	6.75	51	.385	.429	0	—	0	-1	-1	0	0.0
Was-A	2	1	1.000	8	3	0	0	0	24¹	31	4	10	10	15.5	6.29	59	.316	.385	2	.222	0	-7	-7	-1	-0.6
Yr	2	1	1.000	11	3	0	0	0	27	36	5	11	12	16.0	6.33	58	.324	.390	2	.222	0	-8	-8	-1	-0.6
Total 4	6	9	.400	52	22	1	1	0	152²	174	20	100	104	16.3	5.78	74	.287	.390	8	.205	2	-31	-25	0	-2.0

● **SAM MOFFETT** Moffett, Samuel R. b: 3/14/1857, Wheeling, W.Va. d: 5/5/07, Butte, Mont. BR/TR, 6', 175 lbs. Deb: 5/15/1884 F♦

YEAR TM/L	W	L	PCT	G	GS	CG	SH	SV	IP	H	HR	BB	SO	RAT	ERA	ERA+	OAV	OOB	BH	AVG	PB	PR	/A	PD	TPI
1884 Cle-N	3	19	.136	24	22	21	0	0	197²	236	9	58	84	13.4	3.87	81	.284	.330	47	.184	-3	-20	-16	2	-1.4
1887 Ind-N	1	5	.167	6	6	6	0	0	50	47	1	23	3	13.3	3.78	110	.242	.335	5	.122	-2	2	2	-0	-0.1
1888 Ind-N	2	5	.286	7	7	6	1	0	56	62	3	17	7	13.0	4.66	64	.278	.335	4	.114	-1	-11	-11	-2	-1.3
Total 3	6	29	.171	37	35	33	1	0	303²	345	13	98	94	13.3	4.00	82	.276	.332	56	.169	-6	-29	-24	-0	-2.8

● **RANDY MOFFITT** Moffitt, Randall James b: 10/13/48, Long Beach, Cal. BR/TR, 6'3", 190 lbs. Deb: 6/11/72

YEAR TM/L	W	L	PCT	G	GS	CG	SH	SV	IP	H	HR	BB	SO	RAT	ERA	ERA+	OAV	OOB	BH	AVG	PB	PR	/A	PD	TPI
1972 SF-N	1	5	.167	40	0	0	0	4	70²	72	5	30	37	13.2	3.69	94	.266	.343	0	.000	-1	-2	-2	0	-0.2
1973 SF-N	4	4	.500	60	0	0	0	14	100¹	86	9	31	65	10.6	2.42	158	.225	.285	1	.059	-1	14	16	-1	1.4
1974 SF-N	5	7	.417	61	1	0	0	15	102	99	9	29	49	11.5	4.50	84	.256	.311	5	.313	2	-10	-8	1	-0.9
1975 SF-N	4	5	.444	55	0	0	0	11	74	73	6	32	39	13.1	3.89	98	.257	.339	3	.214	1	-2	-1	-0	-0.1
1976 SF-N	6	6	.500	58	0	0	0	14	103	92	6	35	50	11.2	2.27	160	.238	.303	2	.143	-0	14	16	-0	2.2
1977 SF-N	4	9	.308	64	0	0	0	11	87²	91	4	39	68	13.7	3.59	109	.273	.355	0	.000	-0	3	3	1	0.5
1978 SF-N	8	4	.667	70	0	0	0	12	81²	79	5	33	52	12.7	3.31	104	.258	.336	1	.143	0	2	1	-1	0.1
1979 SF-N	2	5	.286	28	0	0	0	1	35	34	5	24	16	17.7	7.71	45	.356	.418	0	.000	0	-15	-16	-0	-3.1
1980 SF-N	1	1	.500	13	0	0	0	0	16²	18	2	4	10	12.4	4.86	73	.281	.333	0	.000	-0	-2	-2	-0	-0.3
1981 SF-N	0	0	—	10	0	0	0	0	11¹	15	2	2	11	13.5	7.94	43	.313	.340	0	—	0	-6	-6	-0	-0.3
1982 Hou-N	2	4	.333	30	0	0	0	0	41²	36	3	13	20	11.7	3.02	110	.234	.307	0	.000	-0	3	1	1	0.1
1983 Tor-A	6	2	.750	45	0	0	0	10	57¹	52	5	24	38	12.1	3.77	114	.243	.322	0	—	0	5	3	1	0.1
Total 12	43	52	.453	534	1	0	0	96	781¹	766	61	286	455	12.4	3.65	102	.257	.327	12	.140	-1	0	5	-3	0.1

● **HERB MOFORD** Moford, Herbert b: 8/6/28, Brooksville, Ky. BR/TR, 6'1", 175 lbs. Deb: 4/12/55

YEAR TM/L	W	L	PCT	G	GS	CG	SH	SV	IP	H	HR	BB	SO	RAT	ERA	ERA+	OAV	OOB	BH	AVG	PB	PR	/A	PD	TPI
1955 StL-N	1	1	.500	14	1	0	0	2	24	29	5	15	8	16.9	7.88	52	.299	.398	0	.000	-0	-10	-10	1	-0.9
1958 Det-A	4	9	.308	25	11	6	0	0	109²	83	10	42	58	11.0	3.61	112	.214	.305	1	.027	-4	2	5	1	0.3
1959 Bos-A	0	2	.000	4	0	0	0	0	8²	10	3	6	7	16.6	11.42	36	.286	.390	0	.000	-0	-7	-7	0	-1.3
1962 NY-N	0	1	.000	7	0	0	0	0	15	21	3	1	5	13.2	7.20	58	.318	.328	1	.250	0	-5	-5	0	-0.3
Total 4	5	13	.278	50	14	6	0	3	157¹	143	21	64	78	12.4	5.03	81	.244	.329	2	.045	-4	-21	-17	2	-2.2

● **GEORGE MOGRIDGE** Mogridge, George Anthony b: 2/18/1889, Rochester, N.Y. d: 3/4/62, Rochester, N.Y. BL/TL, 6'2", 165 lbs. Deb: 8/17/11

YEAR TM/L	W	L	PCT	G	GS	CG	SH	SV	IP	H	HR	BB	SO	RAT	ERA	ERA+	OAV	OOB	BH	AVG	PB	PR	/A	PD	TPI
1911 Chi-A	0	2	.000	4	1	0	0	0	12²	12	1	1	5	9.2	4.97	65	.255	.271	2	.400	-0	-2	-2	-0	-0.3
1912 Chi-A	3	4	.429	17	8	2	0	3	64²	69	2	15	31	11.8	4.04	79	.264	.307	2	.125	-0	-5	-6	-1	-0.7
1915 NY-A	2	3	.400	6	5	3	1	0	41	33	0	11	11	10.3	1.76	167	.219	.285	1	.083	-1	5	5	-1	0.6
1916 NY-A	6	12	.333	30	21	10	2	0	194²	174	3	45	66	10.4	2.31	125	.252	.305	14	.212	-1	11	13	1	1.4
1917 NY-A	9	11	.450	29	25	15	1	0	196¹	185	5	39	46	10.7	2.98	90	.255	.301	11	.159	-1	-7	-6	-1	-0.7
1918 NY-A	16	13	.552	**45**	19	13	1	7	239¹	232	6	43	62	10.8	2.18	130	.255	.301	15	.190	-0	16	17	3	2.5
1919 NY-A	10	7	.588	35	18	13	3	0	169	159	6	46	58	11.3	2.77	115	.250	.307	6	.125	-1	9	8	1	0.8
1920 NY-A	9	5	.357	26	15	7	0	0	125¹	146	4	36	35	13.3	4.31	89	.287	.338	7	.167	-1	-7	-7	-1	-0.7
1921 Was-A	18	14	.563	38	36	21	4	0	288	301	12	66	100	11.7	3.00	137	.269	.313	15	.153	-5	41	36	2	3.0
1922 Was-A	18	13	.581	34	32	18	3	0	251²	300	12	72	61	13.7	3.58	108	.304	.358	21	.244	-1	13	8	-1	1.2
1923 Was-A	13	13	.500	33	30	17	3	1	211	228	10	56	62	12.2	3.11	121	.285	.334	17	.227	1	20	15	1	2.0
1924 *Was-A	16	11	.593	30	30	13	2	0	213	217	2	61	48	12.0	3.76	107	.291	.354	11	.176	-0	7	7	0	0.5
1925 Was-A	3	4	.429	10	8	3	0	0	53	58	2	18	12	13.6	4.08	104	.291	.362	2	.105	-2	-3	-2	1	-0.2
StL-A	1	1	.500	3	2	1	0	0	15¹	17	2	7	6	13.5	5.87	80	.279	.343	0	.000	-0	-3	-2	0	-0.2
Yr	4	5	.444	13	10	4	0	0	68¹	75	4	25	18	13.0	4.48	97	.284	.344	2	.087	-2	-6	-4	1	-0.4
1926 Bos-N	6	10	.375	39	10	2	0	3	142	173	6	46	46	13.4	4.50	79	.311	.356	8	.174	-1	-11	-15	2	-1.4
1927 Bos-N	6	4	.600	20	1	0	0	5	48²	48	4	15	26	12.0	3.70	100	.257	.319	3	.200	-1	1	-1	-0	0.1
Total 15	132	131	.502	398	261	138	20	20	2265²	2352	77	565	678	11.9	3.23	109	.273	.323	137	.182	-8	95	75	11	8.0

YEAR	TM/L	W	L	PCT	G	GS	CG	SH	SV	IP	H	HR	BB	SO	RAT	ERA	ERA+	OAV	OOB	BH	AVG	PB	PR	/A	PD	TPI

● GEORGE MOHART   Mohart, George Benjamin   b: 3/6/1892, Buffalo, N.Y.   d: 10/2/70, Silver Creek, N.Y.   BR/TR, 5'9", 165 lbs.   Deb: 4/15/20

YEAR	TM/L	W	L	PCT	G	GS	CG	SH	SV	IP	H	HR	BB	SO	RAT	ERA	ERA+	OAV	OOB	BH	AVG	PB	PR	/A	PD	TPI
1920	Bro-N	0	1	.000	13	1	0	0	0	35²	33	0	7	13	10.9	1.77	181	.250	.303	1	.125	-0	5	6	1	0.2
1921	Bro-N	0	0	—	2	0	0	0	0	7	8	0	1	1	12.9	3.86	101	.296	.345	1	.500	0	-0	0	-0	0.0
Total	2	0	1	.000	15	1	0	0	0	42²	41	0	8	14	11.2	2.11	157	.258	.310	2	.200	0	5	6	1	0.2

● MIKE MOHLER   Mohler, Michael Ross   b: 7/26/68, Dayton, Ohio   BR/TL, 6'2", 195 lbs.   Deb: 4/7/93

YEAR	TM/L	W	L	PCT	G	GS	CG	SH	SV	IP	H	HR	BB	SO	RAT	ERA	ERA+	OAV	OOB	BH	AVG	PB	PR	/A	PD	TPI
1993	Oak-A	1	6	.143	42	9	0	0	0	64¹	57	10	44	42	14.4	5.60	73	.241	.364	0	—	0	-9	-11	0	-1.0
1994	Oak-A	0	1	.000	1	1	0	0	0	2¹	1	2	2	4	15.4	7.71	57	.167	.286	0	—	0	-1	-1	0	-0.1
1995	Oak-A	1	1	.500	28	0	0	0	1	23²	16	0	18	15	12.9	3.04	147	.198	.343	0	—	0	4	4	-0	0.3
1996	Oak-A	6	3	.667	72	0	0	0	7	81	79	9	41	64	13.6	3.67	131	.263	.354	0	—	0	12	10	1	1.2
Total	4	8	11	.421	143	10	0	0	8	171¹	154	20	105	125	13.8	4.36	103	.244	.355	0	—	0	6	2	1	0.4

● DALE MOHORCIC   Mohorcic, Dale Robert   b: 1/25/56, Cleveland, Ohio   BR/TR, 6'3", 220 lbs.   Deb: 5/31/86

YEAR	TM/L	W	L	PCT	G	GS	CG	SH	SV	IP	H	HR	BB	SO	RAT	ERA	ERA+	OAV	OOB	BH	AVG	PB	PR	/A	PD	TPI
1986	Tex-A	2	4	.333	58	0	0	0	7	79	86	5	15	29	11.6	2.51	172	.279	.315	0	—	0	15	16	0	1.4
1987	Tex-A	7	6	.538	74	0	0	0	16	99¹	88	11	19	48	9.9	2.99	150	.244	.286	0	—	0	16	16	2	2.6
1988	Tex-A	2	6	.250	43	0	0	0	5	52	62	6	20	25	15.1	4.85	84	.295	.370	0	—	0	-5	-4	0	-0.7
	NY-A	2	2	.500	13	0	0	0	1	22²	21	1	9	19	13.1	2.78	142	.239	.330	0	—	0	3	3	-1	0.5
	Yr	4	8	.333	56	0	0	0	6	74²	83	7	29	44	13.9	4.22	96	.269	.338	0	—	0	-2	-0	-0	-0.2
1989	NY-A	2	1	.667	32	0	0	0	2	57²	65	8	18	24	13.9	4.99	77	.286	.355	0	—	0	-7	-7	1	-0.3
1990	Mon-N	1	2	.333	34	0	0	0	2	53	56	6	18	29	13.2	3.23	113	.286	.358	1	.125	-0	3	2	0	0.2
Total	5	16	21	.432	254	0	0	0	33	363²	378	34	97	174	12.3	3.49	118	.272	.330	1	.125	-0	25	26	3	3.7

● BILL MOISAN   Moisan, William Joseph   b: 7/30/25, Bradford, Mass.   BL/TR, 6'1", 170 lbs.   Deb: 9/17/53

YEAR	TM/L	W	L	PCT	G	GS	CG	SH	SV	IP	H	HR	BB	SO	RAT	ERA	ERA+	OAV	OOB	BH	AVG	PB	PR	/A	PD	TPI
1953	Chi-N	0	0	—	3	0	0	0	0	5	5	0	2	1	14.4	5.40	82	.278	.381	0	—	0	-1	-1	0	0.0

● CARLTON MOLESWORTH   Molesworth, Carlton   b: 2/15/1876, Frederick, Md.   d: 7/25/61, Frederick, Md.   BL/TL, 5'6", 200 lbs.   Deb: 9/14/1895

YEAR	TM/L	W	L	PCT	G	GS	CG	SH	SV	IP	H	HR	BB	SO	RAT	ERA	ERA+	OAV	OOB	BH	AVG	PB	PR	/A	PD	TPI
1895	Was-N	0	2	.000	4	3	1	0	0	16	33	1	15	7	29.3	14.63	33	.418	.531	1	.143	-1	-17	-17	-0	-1.4

● RICHIE MOLONEY   Moloney, Richard Henry   b: 6/7/50, Brookline, Mass.   BR/TR, 6'3", 185 lbs.   Deb: 9/20/70

YEAR	TM/L	W	L	PCT	G	GS	CG	SH	SV	IP	H	HR	BB	SO	RAT	ERA	ERA+	OAV	OOB	BH	AVG	PB	PR	/A	PD	TPI
1970	Chi-A	0	0	—	1	0	0	0	0	1	2	0	1	0	18.0	0.00	—	.400	.400	0	—	0	0	0	0	0.0

● VINCE MOLYNEAUX   Molyneaux, Vincent Leo   b: 8/17/1888, Lewiston, N.Y.   d: 5/4/50, Stamford, Conn.   BR/TR, 6', 180 lbs.   Deb: 7/5/17

YEAR	TM/L	W	L	PCT	G	GS	CG	SH	SV	IP	H	HR	BB	SO	RAT	ERA	ERA+	OAV	OOB	BH	AVG	PB	PR	/A	PD	TPI
1917	StL-A	0	0	—	7	0	0	0	0	22	18	0	20	4	15.5	4.91	53	.237	.396	0	.000	-1	-5	-6	0	0.0
1918	Bos-A	1	0	1.000	6	0	0	0	0	10²	3	0	8	1	9.3	3.38	80	.086	.256	0	.000	-0	-1	-1	0	-0.1
Total	2	1	0	1.000	13	0	0	0	0	32²	21	0	28	5	13.5	4.41	60	.189	.354	0	.000	-1	-6	-6	1	-0.1

● RINTY MONAHAN   Monahan, Edward Francis   b: 4/28/28, Brooklyn, N.Y.   BR/TR, 6'1.5", 195 lbs.   Deb: 8/9/53

YEAR	TM/L	W	L	PCT	G	GS	CG	SH	SV	IP	H	HR	BB	SO	RAT	ERA	ERA+	OAV	OOB	BH	AVG	PB	PR	/A	PD	TPI
1953	Phi-A	0	0	—	4	0	0	0	0	10²	11	0	7	2	15.2	4.22	102	.275	.383	0	.000	-0	-0	0	-0	-0.1

● BILL MONBOUQUETTE   Monbouquette, William Charles   b: 8/11/36, Medford, Mass.   BR/TR, 5'11", 195 lbs.   Deb: 7/18/58   C

YEAR	TM/L	W	L	PCT	G	GS	CG	SH	SV	IP	H	HR	BB	SO	RAT	ERA	ERA+	OAV	OOB	BH	AVG	PB	PR	/A	PD	TPI
1958	Bos-A	3	4	.429	10	8	3	0	0	54¹	52	4	20	30	11.9	3.31	121	.251	.317	3	.176	-1	3	4	-1	0.4
1959	Bos-A	7	7	.500	34	17	4	0	0	151²	165	15	33	87	11.9	4.15	98	.285	.327	3	.065	-4	-5	-2	-0	-0.5
1960	Bos-A★	14	11	.560	35	30	12	3	0	215	217	18	68	134	12.0	3.64	111	.263	.320	6	.092	-3	6	10	0	0.7
1961	Bos-A	14	14	.500	32	32	12	1	0	236¹	233	24	100	161	12.7	3.39	123	.254	.327	9	.130	-1	17	20	-1	2.1
1962	Bos-A☆	15	13	.536	35	35	11	4	0	235¹	227	24	65	153	11.3	3.33	124	.251	.303	7	.096	-3	17	21	-4	1.6
1963	Bos-A☆	20	10	.667	37	36	13	1	0	266²	258	31	42	174	10.1	3.81	99	.250	.280	10	.114	-3	-5	-1	0	-0.4
1964	Bos-A	13	14	.481	36	35	7	5	1	234	258	34	40	120	11.5	4.04	95	.277	.308	6	.083	-2	-11	-5	0	-0.7
1965	Bos-A	10	18	.357	35	35	10	2	0	228²	239	32	40	110	11.0	3.70	101	.269	.301	4	.059	-3	-6	1	0	-0.2
1966	Det-A	7	8	.467	30	14	2	1	0	102¹	120	14	22	61	12.7	4.73	74	.293	.333	4	.154	-1	-15	-14	-1	-2.0
1967	Det-A	0	0	—	2	0	0	0	0	2	1	0	0	2	4.5	0.00	—	.143	.143	0	—	0	1	1	0	0.0
	NY-A	6	5	.545	33	10	2	1	1	133¹	122	6	17	53	9.7	2.36	132	.246	.277	5	.156	-0	13	11	-1	0.9
	Yr	6	5	.545	35	10	2	1	1	135¹	123	6	17	55	9.6	2.33	134	.245	.275	5	.156	-0	14	12	-1	0.9
1968	NY-A	5	7	.417	17	11	2	0	0	89¹	92	7	13	32	10.9	4.43	65	.264	.296	3	.115	-0	-14	-15	1	-1.9
	SF-N	0	1	.000	7	0	0	0	0	12¹	11	4	2	5	13.9	3.65	88	.239	.271	-0	—	0	-2	-1	0	-0.1
Total	11	114	112	.504	343	263	78	18	3	1961²	1995	211	462	1122	11.4	3.68	104	.263	.307	60	.103	-20	-2	29	-6	-0.1

● SID MONGE   Monge, Isidro Pedroza   b: 4/11/51, Agua Prieta, Mexico   BB/TL, 6'2", 195 lbs.   Deb: 9/12/75

YEAR	TM/L	W	L	PCT	G	GS	CG	SH	SV	IP	H	HR	BB	SO	RAT	ERA	ERA+	OAV	OOB	BH	AVG	PB	PR	/A	PD	TPI
1975	Cal-A	0	2	.000	4	2	2	0	0	23²	22	3	10	17	12.5	4.18	85	.242	.324	0	—	0	-1	-2	-0	0.2
1976	Cal-A	6	7	.462	32	13	2	0	0	117²	108	10	49	53	12.1	3.37	99	.248	.326	0	—	0	2	-1	-1	0.2
1977	Cal-A	0	1	.000	4	0	0	0	1	12¹	14	2	6	4	14.6	2.92	134	.304	.385	0	—	0	1	0	0	0.5
	Cle-A	1	2	.333	33	0	0	0	3	39	47	6	27	25	17.1	6.23	63	.309	.413	0	—	0	-9	-10	-1	-0.7
	Yr	1	3	.250	37	0	0	0	4	51¹	61	8	33	29	16.5	5.44	72	.307	.405	0	—	0	-8	-9	-1	-0.2
1978	Cle-A	4	3	.571	48	2	0	0	6	84²	71	4	51	54	13.0	2.76	135	.225	.332	0	—	0	9	9	-0	0.9
1979	Cle-A☆	12	10	.545	76	0	0	0	19	131	96	9	64	108	11.1	2.40	177	.209	.307	0	—	0	26	27	-0	5.0
1980	Cle-A	3	5	.375	67	0	0	0	14	94¹	80	12	40	61	11.7	3.53	115	.227	.311	0	—	0	5	6	-2	0.5
1981	Cle-A	3	5	.375	31	0	0	0	1	58	58	9	21	41	12.3	4.34	83	.266	.331	0	—	0	-4	-5	-1	-0.7
1982	Phi-N	7	1	.875	47	0	0	0	2	72	70	8	22	43	11.8	3.75	98	.256	.316	1	.111	-0	-1	-1	1	-1.0
1983	Phi-N	3	0	1.000	14	0	0	0	0	11²	20	4	6	7	20.1	6.94	51	.377	.441	0	.000	-0	-4	-4	-0	-1.0
	SD-N	7	1	.875	47	0	0	0	7	68²	65	4	31	32	12.7	3.15	111	.257	.340	1	.100	-1	4	3	-0	0.3
	Yr	10	1	.909	61	0	0	0	7	80¹	85	8	37	39	13.8	3.70	95	.277	.357	1	.091	-1	-1	-1	-0	-0.7
1984	SD-N	2	1	.667	13	0	0	0	0	15	17	3	17	7	20.4	4.80	74	.293	.453	0	—	0	-2	-2	0	-0.4
	Det-A	1	1	.500	19	0	0	0	0	36	40	5	12	19	13.5	4.25	92	.282	.346	0	—	0	-1	-1	-0	-0.1
Total	10	49	40	.551	435	17	4	0	56	764	708	79	356	471	12.7	3.53	107	.248	.334	2	.095	-1	25	20	-6	4.7

● ED MONROE   Monroe, Edward Oliver "Peck"   b: 2/22/1895, Louisville, Ky.   d: 4/29/69, Louisville, Ky.   BR/TR, 6'5", 187 lbs.   Deb: 5/29/17

YEAR	TM/L	W	L	PCT	G	GS	CG	SH	SV	IP	H	HR	BB	SO	RAT	ERA	ERA+	OAV	OOB	BH	AVG	PB	PR	/A	PD	TPI
1917	NY-A	1	0	1.000	9	1	1	0	1	28²	35	6	12	13	13.5	3.45	78	.310	.355	2	.167	-0	-3	-2	-0	-0.1
1918	NY-A	0	0	—	1	0	0	0	0	2	1	0	2	0	13.5	4.50	63	.143	.333	0	—	0	-0	-0	0	0.0
Total	2	1	0	1.000	10	1	1	0	1	30²	36	1	8	13	13.5	3.52	77	.300	.354	2	.167	-0	-3	-3	0	-0.1

● LARRY MONROE   Monroe, Lawrence James   b: 6/20/56, Detroit, Mich.   BR/TR, 6'4", 200 lbs.   Deb: 8/23/76

YEAR	TM/L	W	L	PCT	G	GS	CG	SH	SV	IP	H	HR	BB	SO	RAT	ERA	ERA+	OAV	OOB	BH	AVG	PB	PR	/A	PD	TPI
1976	Chi-A	0	1	.000	8	2	0	0	0	21²	23	0	13	9	15.0	4.15	86	.284	.383	0	—	0	-2	-1	-0	-0.1

● ZACH MONROE   Monroe, Zachary Charles   b: 7/8/31, Peoria, Ill.   BR/TR, 6', 198 lbs.   Deb: 6/27/58

YEAR	TM/L	W	L	PCT	G	GS	CG	SH	SV	IP	H	HR	BB	SO	RAT	ERA	ERA+	OAV	OOB	BH	AVG	PB	PR	/A	PD	TPI
1958	*NY-A	4	2	.667	21	6	1	0	1	58	57	8	27	18	13.0	3.26	108	.263	.344	2	.118	-1	3	2	0	0.1
1959	NY-A	0	0	—	3	0	0	0	0	3¹	7	0	2	1	13.5	5.40	67	.231	.333	0	—	0	-1	-0	0	0.0
Total	2	4	2	.667	24	6	1	0	1	61¹	64	8	29	19	13.1	3.38	105	.261	.344	2	.118	-1	3	1	0	0.1

● JOHN MONTAGUE   Montague, John Evans   b: 9/12/47, Newport News, Va.   BR/TR, 6'2", 213 lbs.   Deb: 9/9/73

YEAR	TM/L	W	L	PCT	G	GS	CG	SH	SV	IP	H	HR	BB	SO	RAT	ERA	ERA+	OAV	OOB	BH	AVG	PB	PR	/A	PD	TPI
1973	Mon-N	0	0	—	4	0	0	0	0	7²	8	0	2	7	12.9	3.52	108	.286	.355	0	.000	-0	0	0	-0	0.0
1974	Mon-N	3	4	.429	46	1	0	0	3	82²	73	9	38	43	12.5	3.16	122	.241	.333	1	.100	-0	4	6	-2	0.4
1975	Mon-N	0	1	.000	12	0	0	0	0	17²	23	4	6	9	15.8	5.60	68	.324	.392	0	.000	-0	-4	-3	-0	-0.3
	Phi-N	0	0	—	3	0	0	0	0	5	8	1	4	1	21.6	9.00	41	.400	.500	0	—	0	-3	-3	0	-0.1
	Yr	0	1	.000	15	0	0	0	0	22²	31	5	10	10	16.3	6.35	60	.326	.390	0	.000	-0	-7	-6	0	-0.3
1977	Sea-A	8	12	.400	47	15	2	0	4	182¹	193	20	75	98	13.4	4.29	96	.272	.345	0	—	0	-5	-4	-1	-0.2
1978	Sea-A	1	3	.250	19	0	0	0	1	43²	52	2	24	14	15.7	6.18	62	.308	.394	0	—	0	-12	-12	-1	-1.1
1979	Sea-A	6	4	.600	41	0	0	0	1	116¹	125	14	47	60	13.5	5.57	78	.284	.356	0	—	0	-18	-16	1	-1.2
	*Cal-A	2	0	1.000	14	0	0	0	6	17²	16	3	9	6	13.2	5.09	80	.242	.333	0	—	0	-2	-2	0	-0.3
	Yr	8	4	.667	55	0	0	0	7	134	141	17	56	66	13.2	5.51	78	.273	.344	0	—	0	-19	-18	-1	-1.5
1980	Cal-A	4	2	.667	37	0	0	0	6	73²	97	8	21	22	14.5	5.13	77	.324	.371	0	—	0	-9	-10	-0	-0.7
Total	7	24	26	.480	223	17	2	0	21	546²	595	57	226	260	13.7	4.76	89	.283	.356	1	.083	-0	-47	-42	-1	-3.4

YEAR TM/L	W	L	PCT	G	GS	CG	SH	SV	IP	H	HR	BB	SO	RAT	ERA	ERA+	OAV	OOB	BH	AVG	PB	PR	/A	PD	TPI

● **RAFAEL MONTALVO**   Montalvo, Rafael Edgardo (Torres) b: 3/31/64, Rio Piedras, P.R.   BR/TR, 6', 185 lbs.   Deb: 4/13/86

| 1986 Hou-N | 0 | 0 | — | 1 | 0 | 0 | 0 | 0 | 1 | 1 | 0 | 2 | 0 | 27.0 | 9.00 | 40 | .250 | .500 | 0 | — | 0 | -1 | -1 | 0 | 0.0 |

● **AURELIO MONTEAGUDO**   Monteagudo, Aurelio Faustino (Cintra)
b: 11/19/43, Caibarien, Cuba d: 11/10/90, Saltillo, Mexico   BR/TR, 5'11", 185 lbs.   Deb: 9/1/63 F

1963 KC-A	0	0	—	4	0	0	0	0	7	4	0	3	3	9.0	2.57	152	.182	.280	0	—	0	1	1	0	0.0
1964 KC-A	0	4	.000	11	6	0	0	0	31¹	40	11	10	14	14.6	8.90	43	.317	.372	2	.286	1	-18	-18	-0	-1.9
1965 KC-A	0	0	—	4	0	0	0	0	7	5	1	4	5	11.6	3.86	90	.185	.290	0	—	0	-0	-0	-0	0.0
1966 KC-A	0	0	—	6	0	0	0	0	12²	12	0	7	3	13.5	2.84	120	.261	.358	0	—	0	1	1	0	0.0
Hou-N	0	0	—	10	0	0	0	1	15¹	14	1	11	7	14.7	4.70	73	.241	.362	0	.000	-0	-2	-2	-0	-0.1
1967 Chi-A	0	1	.000	1	1	0	0	0	1¹	4	1	2	0	40.5	20.25	15	.500	.600	0	—	0	-3	-3	-0	-1.0
1970 KC-A	1	1	.500	21	0	0	0	0	27¹	20	2	9	9	9.9	2.96	126	.200	.273	0	.000	-0	2	2	-1	0.1
1973 Cal-A	2	1	.667	15	0	0	0	3	30	23	2	16	8	12.9	4.20	84	.215	.339	0	—	0	-1	-2	0	0.3
Total 7	3	7	.300	72	7	0	0	4	132	122	18	62	58	13.0	5.05	72	.247	.338	2	.200	1	-20	-21	-1	-2.6

● **RENE MONTEAGUDO**   Monteagudo, Rene (Miranda) b: 3/12/16, Havana, Cuba d: 9/14/73, Hialeah, Fla.   BL/TL, 5'7", 165 lbs.   Deb: 9/6/38 F♦

1938 Was-A	1	1	.500	5	3	2	0	0	22	26	3	15	13	16.8	5.73	79	.286	.387	3	.500	1	-2	-3	-1	-0.2
1940 Was-A	2	6	.250	27	8	3	0	2	100²	128	7	52	64	16.4	6.08	69	.316	.398	6	.182	0	-19	-21	-1	-1.6
1945 Phi-N	0	0	—	14	0	0	0	0	45²	67	1	28	16	19.1	7.49	51	.347	.435	2	.301	2	-19	-19	-1	0.2
Total 3	3	7	.300	46	11	5	0	2	168¹	221	11	95	93	17.2	6.42	64	.321	.407	78	.289	4	-40	-43	-3	-1.6

● **JOHN MONTEFUSCO**   Montefusco, John Joseph "Count" b: 5/25/50, Long Branch, N.J.   BR/TR, 6'1", 180 lbs.   Deb: 9/3/74

1974 SF-N	3	2	.600	7	5	1	1	0	39¹	41	3	19	34	13.7	4.81	79	.256	.335	4	.286	3	-5	-4	-0	-0.3
1975 SF-N	15	9	.625	35	34	10	4	0	243²	210	11	86	215	11.2	2.88	132	.233	.305	7	.087	-2	20	25	-1	2.0
1976 SF-N★	16	14	.533	37	36	11	**6**	0	253¹	224	11	74	172	10.7	2.84	128	.238	.296	8	.103	-2	19	22	-4	2.0
1977 SF-N	7	12	.368	26	25	4	0	0	157¹	170	10	46	110	12.5	3.49	112	.273	.326	6	.122	-1	7	7	-2	0.5
1978 SF-N	11	9	.550	36	36	3	0	0	238²	233	25	68	177	11.5	3.81	91	.255	.310	4	.057	-3	-6	-10	-2	-1.2
1979 SF-N	3	8	.273	22	22	0	0	0	137	145	15	51	76	13.0	3.94	89	.279	.346	7	.167	-2	-3	-7	-0	-0.4
1980 SF-N	4	8	.333	22	17	1	0	0	113¹	120	15	39	85	12.8	4.37	81	.265	.327	1	.033	-2	-10	-10	-1	-1.4
1981 Atl-N	2	3	.400	26	9	0	0	1	77¹	75	9	27	34	11.9	3.49	103	.260	.324	1	.067	-1	-0	1	0	0.0
1982 SD-N	10	11	.476	32	32	1	0	0	184¹	177	17	41	83	10.8	4.00	86	.251	.295	5	.086	-2	-8	-12	-1	-1.5
1983 SD-N	9	4	.692	31	10	1	0	4	95¹	94	6	32	52	12.0	3.30	105	.265	.327	1	.053	-1	3	2	-1	0.1
NY-A	5	0	1.000	6	6	0	0	0	38	39	3	10	15	11.8	3.32	117	.271	.323	0	—	0	3	2	-1	0.3
1984 NY-A	5	3	.625	11	11	0	0	0	55¹	55	5	13	23	11.2	3.58	106	.253	.299	0	—	0	3	1	0	0.1
1985 NY-A	0	0	—	3	1	0	0	0	7	12	3	2	2	18.0	10.29	39	.387	.424	0	—	0	-5	-5	0	0.2
1986 NY-A	0	0	—	2	2	0	0	0	9¹	9	3	3	3	10.2	2.19	187	.200	.280	0	—	0	3	3	0	0.1
Total 13	90	83	.520	298	244	32	11	5	1652¹	1604	135	513	1081	11.7	3.54	102	.255	.314	44	.097	-10	20	16	-12	0.5

● **MANNY MONTEJO**   Montejo, Manuel (Bofill) b: 10/16/35, Caibarien, Cuba   BR/TR, 5'11", 150 lbs.   Deb: 7/25/61

| 1961 Det-A | 0 | 0 | — | 12 | 0 | 0 | 0 | 0 | 16¹ | 13 | 2 | 6 | 15 | 11.6 | 3.86 | 106 | .217 | .309 | 0 | — | 0 | -0 | -1 | 0 | -0.1 |

● **RICH MONTELEONE**   Monteleone, Richard b: 3/22/63, Tampa, Fla.   BR/TR, 6'2", 220 lbs.   Deb: 4/15/87

1987 Sea-A	0	0	—	3	0	0	0	0	7	10	4	3	4	19.3	6.43	73	.345	.441	0	—	0	-2	-1	0	-0.3
1988 Cal-A	0	0	—	3	0	0	0	0	4¹	4	0	1	3	12.5	0.00	—	.222	.300	0	—	0	2	2	0	0.2
1989 Cal-A	2	2	.500	24	0	0	0	0	39²	39	3	13	27	12.0	3.18	120	.255	.317	0	—	0	3	3	1	0.5
1990 NY-A	0	1	.000	5	0	0	0	0	7¹	8	0	2	8	12.3	6.14	65	.276	.323	0	—	0	-2	-2	0	-0.2
1991 NY-A	3	1	.750	26	0	0	0	0	47	42	5	19	34	11.7	3.64	114	.236	.310	0	—	0	2	3	1	0.2
1992 NY-A	7	3	.700	47	0	0	0	0	92²	82	7	27	62	10.6	3.30	119	.235	.290	0	—	0	7	6	-1	0.6
1993 NY-A	7	4	.636	42	0	0	0	0	85²	85	14	35	50	12.6	4.94	84	.262	.333	0	—	0	-6	-7	0	-0.5
1994 SF-N	4	3	.571	39	0	0	0	0	45¹	43	6	13	16	11.1	3.18	126	.253	.306	0	.000	-0	5	4	-1	0.4
1995 Cal-A	1	0	1.000	9	0	0	0	0	9	8	1	3	5	11.0	2.00	235	.267	.333	0	—	0	3	3	-0	0.3
1996 Cal-A	0	3	.000	12	0	0	0	0	15¹	23	5	2	5	15.3	5.87	83	.348	.377	0	—	0	-1	-2	-1	-0.1
Total 10	24	17	.585	210	0	0	0	0	353¹	344	43	119	212	11.9	3.87	105	.255	.318	0	.000	-0	11	8	-1	1.1

● **JEFF MONTGOMERY**   Montgomery, Jeffrey Thomas b: 1/7/62, Wellston, Ohio   BR/TR, 5'11", 180 lbs.   Deb: 8/1/87

1987 Cin-N	2	2	.500	14	1	0	0	0	19¹	25	2	9	13	15.8	6.52	65	.313	.382	0	.000	-0	-5	-5	0	-0.9
1988 KC-A	7	2	.778	45	0	0	0	1	62²	54	6	30	47	12.4	3.45	116	.231	.323	0	—	0	4	4	0	0.5
1989 KC-A	7	3	.700	63	0	0	0	18	92	66	3	25	94	9.1	1.37	281	.198	.258	0	—	0	**26**	**25**	-1	3.5
1990 KC-A	6	5	.545	73	0	0	0	24	94¹	81	6	34	94	11.4	2.39	161	.227	.303	0	—	0	16	15	0	2.4
1991 KC-A	4	4	.500	67	0	0	0	33	90	83	6	28	77	11.3	2.90	142	.246	.307	0	—	0	12	12	-0	1.7
1992 KC-A★	1	6	.143	65	0	0	0	39	82²	61	5	27	69	9.9	2.18	186	.205	.278	0	—	0	16	17	2	2.7
1993 KC-A★	7	5	.583	69	0	0	0	**45**	87¹	65	3	23	66	9.3	2.27	202	.206	.264	0	—	0	**20**	**22**	1	4.3
1994 KC-A	2	3	.400	42	0	0	0	27	44²	48	5	15	50	12.9	4.03	124	.276	.337	0	—	0	4	5	-1	0.7
1995 KC-A	2	3	.400	54	0	0	0	31	65²	60	7	25	49	11.9	3.43	140	.252	.328	0	—	0	9	10	1	1.4
1996 KC-A☆	4	6	.400	48	0	0	0	24	63¹	59	14	19	45	11.5	4.26	115	.251	.315	0	—	0	-1	-2	-1	-0.1
Total 10	42	39	.519	540	1	0	0	242	702	602	57	235	604	11.0	2.86	149	.231	.300	0	.000	-0	106	110	3	17.5

● **MONTY MONTGOMERY**   Montgomery, Monty Bryson b: 9/1/46, Albemarle, N.C.   BR/TR, 6'3", 200 lbs.   Deb: 9/14/71

1971 KC-A	3	0	1.000	3	2	0	0	0	21¹	16	0	3	12	8.0	2.11	163	.205	.235	0	.000	-0	3	3	0	0.4
1972 KC-A	3	3	.500	9	8	1	1	0	56¹	55	2	17	24	11.5	3.04	100	.263	.319	3	.176	1	-0	-0	-0	0.0
Total 2	6	3	.667	12	10	1	1	0	77²	71	2	20	36	10.5	2.78	113	.247	.296	3	.125	1	3	3	0	0.4

● **STEVE MONTGOMERY**   Montgomery, Steven Lewis b: 12/25/70, Westminster, Cal.   BR/TR, 6'4", 210 lbs.   Deb: 4/3/96

| 1996 Oak-A | 1 | 0 | 1.000 | 8 | 0 | 0 | 0 | 0 | 13² | 18 | 5 | 13 | 8 | 20.4 | 9.22 | 52 | .310 | .437 | 0 | — | 0 | -6 | -7 | -1 | -0.1 |

● **RAMON MONZANT**   Monzant, Ramon Segundo (Espina) b: 1/4/33, Maracaibo, Venez.   BR/TR, 6', 165 lbs.   Deb: 7/2/54

1954 NY-N	0	0	—	6	1	0	0	0	7²	8	0	11	5	22.3	4.70	86	.276	.475	0	.000	-0	-1	-1	-0	-0.1
1955 NY-N	4	8	.333	28	12	3	0	0	94²	98	11	43	54	13.7	3.99	101	.278	.361	3	.125	-1	0	-0	-1	-0.2
1956 NY-N	1	0	1.000	4	1	1	0	0	13	8	4	7	11	10.4	4.15	91	.170	.278	0	.000	-1	-1	-1	-0	-0.1
1957 NY-N	3	2	.600	24	2	0	0	0	49²	55	6	16	37	13.2	3.99	99	.286	.348	3	.300	1	-1	-0	-1	-0.1
1958 SF-N	8	11	.421	43	16	4	1	1	150²	160	21	57	93	13.3	4.72	81	.273	.344	8	.163	-1	-13	-15	1	-1.7
1960 SF-N	0	0	—	1	0	0	0	0	1	1	1	0	1	18.0	9.00	39	.250	.250	0	—	0	-1	-1	0	0.0
Total 6	16	21	.432	106	32	8	1	1	316²	330	43	134	201	13.5	4.38	89	.273	.350	14	.157	-2	-15	-17	-1	-2.2

● **LEO MOON**   Moon, Leo "Lefty" b: 6/22/1899, Belmont, N.C. d: 8/25/70, New Orleans, La.   BR/TR, 5'11", 165 lbs.   Deb: 7/9/32

| 1932 Cle-A | 0 | 0 | — | 1 | 0 | 0 | 0 | 0 | 5² | 11 | 0 | 7 | 1 | 28.6 | 11.12 | 43 | .379 | .500 | 1 | .500 | 0 | -4 | -4 | 0 | 0.0 |

● **JIM MOONEY**   Mooney, Jim Irving b: 9/4/06, Mooresburg, Tenn. d: 4/27/79, Johnson City, Tenn   BR/TL, 5'11", 168 lbs.   Deb: 8/14/31

1931 NY-N	7	1	.875	10	8	6	2	0	71²	71	3	38	11	11.1	2.01	184	.262	.306	4	.160	-1	15	13	-1	1.2
1932 NY-N	6	10	.375	29	18	4	1	0	124²	154	18	42	37	14.1	5.05	73	.299	.352	5	.122	-2	-16	-19	-2	-2.3
1933 StL-N	2	5	.286	21	8	2	0	1	77¹	87	1	26	14	13.2	3.72	93	.296	.353	1	.050	-2	-3	-2	1	-0.3
1934 *StL-N	2	4	.333	32	7	1	0	1	82¹	114	3	49	27	18.3	5.47	76	.326	.414	1	.053	-2	-13	-11	-1	-1.1
Total 4	17	20	.459	92	41	13	3	2	356	426	23	133	116	14.3	4.25	89	.298	.360	11	.105	-7	-18	-19	-3	-2.5

● **BILL MOONEYHAM**   Mooneyham, William Craig b: 8/16/60, Livermore, Cal.   BR/TR, 6', 175 lbs.   Deb: 4/19/86

| 1986 Oak-A | 4 | 5 | .444 | 45 | 6 | 0 | 0 | 2 | 99² | 103 | 4 | 67 | 75 | 15.6 | 4.52 | 86 | .270 | .384 | 0 | — | 0 | -4 | -7 | 1 | -0.1 |

● **BALOR MOORE**   Moore, Balor Lilbon b: 1/25/51, Smithville, Tex.   BL/TL, 6'2", 184 lbs.   Deb: 5/21/70

1970 Mon-N	0	2	.000	6	2	0	0	0	9²	14	0	8	6	20.5	7.45	55	.368	.478	1	.333	0	-4	-4	0	-0.6
1972 Mon-N	9	9	.500	22	22	6	3	0	147²	122	15	59	161	11.3	3.47	102	.226	.307	8	.145	-0	-0	1	0	0.1
1973 Mon-N	7	16	.304	35	32	3	0	0	176¹	151	18	109	151	13.4	4.49	85	.233	.346	3	.057	-3	-16	-13	-1	-2.0
1974 Mon-N	0	2	.000	8	2	0	0	0	13²	13	1	15	16	18.4	3.95	97	.245	.412	0	—	0	-1	-2	0	-0.1

YEAR TM/L	W	L	PCT	G	GS	CG	SH	SV	IP	H	HR	BB	SO	RAT	ERA	ERA+	OAV	OOB	BH	AVG	PB	PR	/A	PD	TPI
1977 Cal-A	0	2	.000	7	3	0	0	0	22²	28	7	10	14	16.3	3.97	99	.298	.383	0	—	0	0	0	-1	0.0
1978 Tor-A	6	9	.400	37	18	2	0	0	144¹	165	16	54	51	14.1	4.93	80	.294	.363	0	—	0	-19	-16	1	-1.4
1979 Tor-A	5	7	.417	34	16	5	0	0	139¹	135	17	79	51	14.3	4.84	90	.262	.369	0	—	0	-10	-8	-1	-0.7
1980 Tor-A	1	1	.500	31	3	0	0	0	64²	76	6	31	22	15.4	5.29	81	.309	.395	0	—	0	-9	-7	-0	-0.3
Total 8	28	48	.368	180	98	16	4	1	718¹	704	80	365	496	13.8	4.52	87	.261	.355	12	.106	-3	-58	-47	-1	-5.0

● **BRAD MOORE** — Moore, Bradley Alan b: 6/21/64, Loveland, Colo. BR/TR, 6'1", 185 lbs. Deb: 6/14/88

YEAR TM/L	W	L	PCT	G	GS	CG	SH	SV	IP	H	HR	BB	SO	RAT	ERA	ERA+	OAV	OOB	BH	AVG	PB	PR	/A	PD	TPI
1988 Phi-N	0	0	—	5	0	0	0	0	5²	4	0	4	2	12.7	0.00	—	.267	.421	0	—	0	2	2	0	0.0
1990 Phi-N	0	0	—	3	0	0	0	0	2²	4	0	2	1	20.3	3.38	113	.400	.500	0	—	0	0	0	0	0.0
Total 2	0	0	—	8	0	0	0	0	8¹	8	0	6	3	15.1	1.08	338	.320	.452	0	—	0	2	2	0	0.0

● **CARLOS MOORE** — Moore, Carlos Whitman b: 8/13/06, Clinton, Tenn. d: 7/2/58, New Orleans, La. BR/TR, 6'1.5", 180 lbs. Deb: 5/4/30

YEAR TM/L	W	L	PCT	G	GS	CG	SH	SV	IP	H	HR	BB	SO	RAT	ERA	ERA+	OAV	OOB	BH	AVG	PB	PR	/A	PD	TPI
1930 Was-A	0	0	—	4	0	0	0	0	11²	9	0	4	2	10.0	2.31	199	.225	.295	0	.000	-1	3	3	-0	-0.1

● **DEE MOORE** — Moore, D C b: 4/6/14, Hedley, Tex. BR/TR, 5'11", 190 lbs. Deb: 9/12/36 ♦

YEAR TM/L	W	L	PCT	G	GS	CG	SH	SV	IP	H	HR	BB	SO	RAT	ERA	ERA+	OAV	OOB	BH	AVG	PB	PR	/A	PD	TPI
1936 Cin-N	0	0	—	2	1	0	0	0	7	3	0	2	3	6.4	0.00	—	.120	.185	4	.400	1	3	3	0	0.1

● **DONNIE MOORE** — Moore, Donnie Ray b: 2/13/54, Lubbock, Tex. d: 7/18/89, Anaheim, Cal. BL/TR, 6', 185 lbs. Deb: 9/14/75

YEAR TM/L	W	L	PCT	G	GS	CG	SH	SV	IP	H	HR	BB	SO	RAT	ERA	ERA+	OAV	OOB	BH	AVG	PB	PR	/A	PD	TPI
1975 Chi-N	0	0	—	4	1	0	0	0	8²	12	1	4	8	16.6	4.15	92	.316	.381	0	.000	-0	-1	-0	-0	0.0
1977 Chi-N	4	2	.667	27	1	0	0	0	48²	51	1	18	34	12.8	4.07	108	.285	.350	3	.300	1	-1	2	1	0.4
1978 Chi-N	9	7	.563	71	1	0	0	4	103	117	7	31	50	13.1	4.11	98	.287	.340	4	.267	1	-6	-1	-0	0.0
1979 Chi-N	1	4	.200	39	1	0	0	0	73	95	8	25	43	15.0	5.18	79	.321	.378	2	.154	0	-12	-9	1	-0.5
1980 StL-N	1	1	.500	11	0	0	0	0	21²	25	1	5	10	12.9	6.23	59	.298	.344	3	.750	2	-6	-6	-1	-0.4
1981 Mil-A	0	0	—	3	0	0	0	0	4	4	0	4	2	18.0	6.75	51	.286	.444	0	—	-0	-1	-1	0	0.1
1982 *Atl-N	3	1	.750	16	0	0	0	0	27²	32	1	7	17	13.3	4.23	88	.294	.347	0	.000	-0	-2	-2	0	-0.2
1983 Atl-N	2	3	.400	43	0	0	0	0	68²	72	6	10	41	10.7	3.67	106	.279	.306	4	.500	1	-0	-2	-1	0.2
1984 Atl-N	4	5	.444	47	0	0	0	16	64¹	63	3	18	47	11.5	2.94	131	.258	.312	0	.000	-0	5	7	0	1.2
1985 Cal-A★	8	8	.500	65	0	0	0	31	103	91	9	21	72	9.8	1.92	214	.237	.277	0	—	0	**25**	25	-1	5.1
1986 *Cal-A	4	5	.444	49	0	0	0	21	72²	60	10	22	53	10.2	2.97	138	.228	.288	0	—	0	10	9	-1	1.5
1987 Cal-A	2	2	.500	14	0	0	0	5	26²	28	2	13	17	13.8	2.70	159	.259	.339	0	—	0	5	5	-1	0.8
1988 Cal-A	5	2	.714	27	0	0	0	4	33	48	4	8	22	15.3	4.91	79	.343	.378	0	—	0	-3	-4	0	-0.6
Total 13	43	40	.518	416	4	0	0	89	655	698	53	186	416	12.3	3.67	110	.276	.328	16	.281	5	12	27	-1	7.6

● **EARL MOORE** — Moore, Earl Alonzo "Big Ebbie" or "Crossfire" b: 7/29/1879, Pickerington, O. d: 11/28/61, Columbus, Ohio BR/TR, 6', 195 lbs. Deb: 4/25/01

YEAR TM/L	W	L	PCT	G	GS	CG	SH	SV	IP	H	HR	BB	SO	RAT	ERA	ERA+	OAV	OOB	BH	AVG	PB	PR	/A	PD	TPI
1901 Cle-A	16	14	.533	31	30	28	4	0	251¹	234	4	107	99	12.5	2.90	122	.244	.325	16	.162	-5	21	18	-4	0.9
1902 Cle-A	17	17	.500	36	34	29	4	0	293	304	8	101	84	12.7	2.95	117	.268	.331	24	.212	-4	20	16	-1	1.5
1903 Cle-A	19	9	.679	29	27	27	3	1	247²	196	6	62	148	9.6	**1.74**	**164**	**.217**	.271	8	.092	-5	**34**	31	-3	2.6
1904 Cle-A	12	11	.522	26	24	22	1	0	227²	186	2	61	139	10.2	2.25	113	.224	.285	12	.140	-2	9	7	-7	-0.3
1905 Cle-A	15	15	.500	31	30	28	3	0	269	232	6	92	131	11.4	2.64	99	.234	.311	10	.104	-4	0	-0	-2	-0.8
1906 Cle-A	1	1	.500	5	4	2	0	0	29²	27	1	18	8	14.3	3.94	66	.245	.362	0	.000	-1	-4	-4	-1	-0.5
1907 Cle-A	1	1	.500	3	2	1	0	0	19¹	18	0	8	7	12.6	4.66	54	.250	.333	0	.000	-0	-5	-5	-0	-0.5
NY-A	2	6	.250	12	9	3	0	1	64	72	1	30	28	14.9	3.94	71	.286	.371	6	.273	1	-10	-8	-0	-0.9
Yr	3	7	.300	15	11	4	0	1	83¹	90	1	38	35	14.3	4.10	66	.277	.360	6	.207	0	-14	-13	-0	-1.4
1908 Phi-N	2	1	.667	3	3	3	1	0	26	20	0	16	10	14.6	0.00	—	.217	.294	2	.222	0	7	7	1	1.0
1909 Phi-N	18	12	.600	38	34	24	4	0	299²	238	7	108	173	10.7	2.10	124	.210	.283	9	.094	-4	17	17	-5	0.6
1910 Phi-N	22	15	.595	46	35	18	**6**	0	283	228	5	121	185	11.4	2.58	121	.228	.318	20	.230	2	14	17	-4	2.0
1911 Phi-N	15	19	.441	42	36	21	5	1	308¹	265	11	164	174	12.9	2.63	131	.240	.345	11	.109	-6	27	28	-3	2.0
1912 Phi-N	9	14	.391	31	24	10	1	0	182¹	186	3	77	79	13.3	3.31	110	.275	.355	6	.107	-4	2	7	-2	0.1
1913 Phi-N	1	3	.250	12	5	0	0	1	52	50	3	40	24	15.8	5.02	66	.254	.382	0	.000	-2	-10	-10	1	-0.9
Chi-N	1	1	.500	7	2	0	0	0	28¹	34	3	12	12	14.6	4.45	72	.321	.390	1	.125	-0	-4	-4	1	-0.2
Yr	2	4	.333	19	7	0	0	1	80¹	84	6	52	36	15.2	4.82	68	.276	.382	1	.042	-2	-14	-14	2	-1.1
1914 Buf-F	11	15	.423	36	27	14	2	2	194²	184	3	99	96	13.5	4.30	69	.263	.362	9	.161	-2	-31	-29	-2	-3.9
Total 14	162	154	.513	388	326	230	34	7	2776	2474	57	1108	1403	12.0	2.78	110	.241	.321	134	.141	-34	87	88	-33	2.7

● **EUEL MOORE** — Moore, Euel Walton "Chief" b: 5/27/08, Reagan, Okla. d: 2/12/89, Tishomingo, Okla. BR/TR, 6'2", 185 lbs. Deb: 7/8/34

YEAR TM/L	W	L	PCT	G	GS	CG	SH	SV	IP	H	HR	BB	SO	RAT	ERA	ERA+	OAV	OOB	BH	AVG	PB	PR	/A	PD	TPI
1934 Phi-N	5	7	.417	20	16	3	0	1	122¹	145	9	41	38	13.7	4.05	117	.288	.342	5	.109	-4	0	9	-1	0.3
1935 Phi-N	1	6	.143	15	8	1	0	0	40¹	63	5	20	15	19.0	7.81	58	.354	.425	6	.400	1	-17	-15	0	-2.0
NY-N	1	0	1.000	6	0	0	0	0	8	9	0	4	3	14.6	5.63	69	.281	.361	0	.000	-1	-2	-0	0	-0.2
Yr	2	6	.250	21	8	1	0	0	48¹	72	5	24	18	17.9	7.45	59	.340	.407	6	.353	1	-18	-16	0	-2.2
1936 Phi-N	2	3	.400	20	5	1	0	1	54¹	76	4	12	19	14.7	6.96	65	.311	.346	4	.222	-0	-18	-15	-1	-1.3
Total 3	9	16	.360	61	29	5	0	2	225	293	18	77	75	14.9	5.48	84	.306	.360	15	.185	-3	-36	-22	-3	-3.2

● **GENE MOORE** — Moore, Eugene Sr. "Blue Goose" b: 11/9/1885, Lancaster, Tex. d: 8/31/38, Dallas, Tex. BL/TL, 6'2", 185 lbs. Deb: 9/28/09 F

YEAR TM/L	W	L	PCT	G	GS	CG	SH	SV	IP	H	HR	BB	SO	RAT	ERA	ERA+	OAV	OOB	BH	AVG	PB	PR	/A	PD	TPI
1909 Pit-N	0	0	—	1	0	0	0	0	2	4	0	3	2	31.5	18.00	15	.364	.500	0	.000	-1	-3	-3	-0	-0.1
1910 Pit-N	2	1	.667	4	1	0	0	0	17¹	19	1	7	9	13.5	3.12	99	.268	.333	0	.000	-1	-0	-0	-0	-0.1
1912 Cin-N	0	1	.000	5	2	0	0	0	14²	17	0	11	6	18.4	4.91	68	.304	.435	0	.000	-2	-2	-3	-0	-0.3
Total 3	2	2	.500	10	3	0	0	0	34	40	1	21	17	16.7	4.76	67	.291	.391	0	.000	-2	-6	-6	-0	-0.5

● **GEORGE MOORE** — Moore, George Raymond b: 11/25/1872, Cambridge, Mass. d: 11/17/48, Barnstable, Mass. BB/TR, 5'10", 165 lbs. Deb: 6/14/05

YEAR TM/L	W	L	PCT	G	GS	CG	SH	SV	IP	H	HR	BB	SO	RAT	ERA	ERA+	OAV	OOB	BH	AVG	PB	PR	/A	PD	TPI
1905 Pit-N	0	0	—	1	0	0	0	0	3	2	0	1	0	6.0	0.00	—	.200	.200	0	.000	-0	1	1	-0	0.0

● **JIM MOORE** — Moore, James Stanford b: 12/14/03, Prescott, Ark. d: 5/19/73, Seattle, Wash. BR/TR, 6', 165 lbs. Deb: 9/21/28

YEAR TM/L	W	L	PCT	G	GS	CG	SH	SV	IP	H	HR	BB	SO	RAT	ERA	ERA+	OAV	OOB	BH	AVG	PB	PR	/A	PD	TPI
1928 Cle-A	0	1	.000	1	1	1	0	0	9	5	1	5	1	10.0	2.00	207	.161	.278	0	.000	-0	2	2	-0	0.1
1929 Cle-A	0	0	—	2	0	0	0	0	5²	6	1	4	0	15.9	9.53	47	.273	.385	0	—	-0	-3	-3	0	0.0
1930 Chi-A	2	1	.667	9	5	2	0	0	40	42	4	9	5	13.1	3.60	128	.268	.320	3	.231	-0	5	5	-0	0.3
1931 Chi-A	0	2	.000	33	4	0	0	0	83²	93	3	27	15	13.0	4.95	86	.282	.338	1	.063	-1	-5	-6	-1	-0.2
1932 Chi-A	0	0	—	1	0	0	0	0	1	1	0	1	2	18.0	0.00	—	.250	.400	0	—	-0	-0	-0	0	0.0
Total 5	2	4	.333	46	10	3	0	1	139¹	147	9	49	29	12.7	4.52	97	.270	.332	4	.114	-2	-1	-2	1	0.2

● **WHITEY MOORE** — Moore, Lloyd Albert b: 6/10/12, Tuscarawas, Ohio d: 12/10/87, Uhrichsville, O. BR/TR, 6'1", 195 lbs. Deb: 9/27/36

YEAR TM/L	W	L	PCT	G	GS	CG	SH	SV	IP	H	HR	BB	SO	RAT	ERA	ERA+	OAV	OOB	BH	AVG	PB	PR	/A	PD	TPI
1936 Cin-N	1	0	1.000	1	0	0	0	0	5	3	0	3	4	10.8	5.40	71	.167	.286	0	.000	-0	-1	-1	-0	-0.2
1937 Cin-N	0	3	.000	13	6	0	0	0	38²	32	1	39	27	17.5	4.89	76	.239	.424	0	.000	-1	-4	-5	-0	-0.5
1938 Cin-N	6	4	.600	19	11	3	1	0	90¹	66	4	42	38	11.1	3.49	105	.205	.302	2	.077	-2	3	2	-1	-0.2
1939 *Cin-N	13	12	.520	42	24	9	2	3	187²	177	10	95	81	13.3	3.45	111	.254	.348	6	.098	-4	10	8	-1	0.5
1940 *Cin-N	8	8	.500	25	15	5	1	0	116²	100	8	56	60	12.6	3.63	104	.231	.329	5	.128	-1	3	2	-3	-0.3
1941 Cin-N	2	1	.667	23	4	1	0	0	61²	62	6	45	17	16.1	4.38	82	.256	.379	3	.167	-1	-5	-5	-1	-0.4
1942 Cin-N	0	0	—	1	0	0	0	0	1	1	0	1	0	16.1	0.00	—	.000	.250	0	—	-0	0	0	0	0.0
StL-N	0	1	.000	9	0	0	0	0	12¹	10	0	11	5	16.1	4.38	78	.217	.379	0	.000	-0	-1	-1	-1	-0.1
Yr	0	1	.000	10	0	0	0	0	13¹	11	0	12	5	15.5	4.05	84	.204	.371	0	.000	-0	-1	-1	-1	-0.1
Total 7	30	29	.508	133	60	18	4	3	513¹	450	25	292	228	13.4	3.75	100	.237	.346	16	.103	-10	4	-0	-7	-1.2

● **MARCUS MOORE** — Moore, Marcus Braymont b: 11/2/70, Oakland, Cal. BB/TR, 6'5", 195 lbs. Deb: 7/8/93

YEAR TM/L	W	L	PCT	G	GS	CG	SH	SV	IP	H	HR	BB	SO	RAT	ERA	ERA+	OAV	OOB	BH	AVG	PB	PR	/A	PD	TPI
1993 Col-N	3	1	.750	27	0	0	0	0	26¹	30	4	20	13	17.4	6.84	70	.291	.411	0	.000	-0	-8	-6	-1	-0.9
1994 Col-N	1	1	.500	29	0	0	0	0	33²	33	4	21	33	15.8	6.15	81	.252	.376	0	.000	-0	-7	-4	-0	-0.3
1996 Col-N	3	5	.500	23	0	0	0	0	26¹	26	3	22	27	17.1	5.81	71	.263	.407	1	.333	0	-5	-5	-1	-1.0
Total 3	7	5	.583	79	0	0	0	0	86¹	89	11	63	73	16.7	6.25	75	.267	.396	1	.200	0	-20	-15	-2	-2.2

● **MIKE MOORE** — Moore, Michael Wayne b: 11/26/59, Eakly, Okla. BR/TR, 6'4", 205 lbs. Deb: 4/11/82

YEAR TM/L	W	L	PCT	G	GS	CG	SH	SV	IP	H	HR	BB	SO	RAT	ERA	ERA+	OAV	OOB	BH	AVG	PB	PR	/A	PD	TPI
1982 Sea-A	7	14	.333	28	27	1	0	0	144¹	159	21	79	73	15.0	5.36	79	.285	.376	0	—	0	-21	-18	1	-2.2
1983 Sea-A	6	8	.429	22	21	3	2	0	128	130	10	60	108	13.6	4.71	90	.256	.352	0	—	0	-9	-6	2	-0.5
1984 Sea-A	7	17	.292	34	33	6	0	0	212	236	16	85	158	13.6	4.97	80	.282	.352	0	—	0	-23	-23	3	-2.0
1985 Sea-A	17	10	.630	35	34	14	2	0	247	230	18	70	155	11.1	3.46	122	.247	.302	0	—	0	19	21	2	2.3

YEAR TM/L	W	L	PCT	G	GS	CG	SH	SV	IP	H	HR	BB	SO	RAT	ERA	ERA+	OAV	OOB	BH	AVG	PB	PR	/A	PD	TPI
1986 Sea-A	11	13	.458	38	37	11	1	1	266	279	28	94	146	13.0	4.30	99	.273	.341	0	—	0	-4	-2	-1	-0.2
1987 Sea-A	9	19	.321	33	33	12	0	0	231	268	29	84	115	13.7	4.71	100	.292	.351	0	.000	0	-7	0	1	0.1
1988 Sea-A	9	15	.375	37	32	9	3	1	228²	196	24	63	182	10.3	3.78	110	.232	.287	0	—	0	5	10	1	0.7
1989 *Oak-A★	19	11	.633	35	35	6	3	0	241²	193	14	83	172	10.4	2.61	141	.219	.288	0	—	0	34	29	2	4.0
1990 *Oak-A	13	15	.464	33	33	3	0	0	199¹	204	14	84	73	13.1	4.65	80	.267	.342	0	—	0	-16	-21	1	-2.2
1991 Oak-A	17	8	.680	33	33	3	1	0	210	176	11	105	153	12.3	2.96	130	.229	.326	0	—	0	27	27	2	2.5
1992 *Oak-A	17	12	.586	36	36	2	0	0	223	229	20	103	117	13.7	4.12	91	.268	.353	0	—	0	-4	-9	-1	-0.8
1993 Det-A	13	9	.591	36	36	4	3	0	213²	227	35	89	89	13.4	5.22	82	.271	.343	0	—	0	-21	-22	4	-1.5
1994 Det-A	11	10	.524	25	25	4	0	0	154¹	152	27	89	62	14.2	5.42	89	.263	.364	0	—	0	-11	-10	3	-0.9
1995 Det-A	5	15	.250	25	25	1	0	0	132²	179	24	68	64	16.9	7.53	63	.323	.399	0	—	0	-42	-41	1	-4.6
Total 14	161	176	.478	450	440	79	16	2	2831²	2858	291	1156	1667	12.9	4.39	95	.264	.338	0	.000	0	-73	-74	22	-5.3

● RAY MOORE
Moore, Raymond Leroy "Farmer" b: 6/1/26, Meadows, Md. d: 3/2/95, Clinton, Md. BR/TR, 6'1", 205 lbs. Deb: 8/1/52

YEAR TM/L	W	L	PCT	G	GS	CG	SH	SV	IP	H	HR	BB	SO	RAT	ERA	ERA+	OAV	OOB	BH	AVG	PB	PR	/A	PD	TPI
1952 Bro-N	1	2	.333	14	2	0	0	0	28¹	29	3	26	11	18.1	4.76	76	.274	.425	0	.000	-0	-3	-4	-0	-0.4
1953 Bro-N	0	1	.000	1	1	1	0	0	8	6	1	4	4	11.3	3.38	126	.214	.313	0	.000	-0	1	1	-0	0.1
1955 Bal-A	10	10	.500	46	14	3	1	6	151²	128	14	80	80	12.6	3.92	97	.229	.329	6	.136	-2	1	-2	-2	-0.5
1956 Bal-A	12	7	.632	32	27	9	1	0	185	161	12	99	105	12.7	4.18	94	.238	.336	19	.271	6	-1	-5	-2	-0.1
1957 Bal-A	11	13	.458	34	32	7	1	0	227¹	196	17	112	117	12.3	3.72	97	.236	.328	18	.214	4	2	-3	-2	-0.2
1958 Chi-A	9	7	.563	32	20	4	2	2	136²	107	10	70	73	11.7	3.82	95	.220	.318	9	.205	2	-1	-3	-1	-0.2
1959 *Chi-A	3	6	.333	29	8	0	0	0	89²	86	10	46	49	13.3	4.12	91	.261	.354	2	.087	-1	-3	-4	-1	-0.5
1960 Chi-A	1	1	.500	14	0	0	0	0	20²	19	5	11	3	13.1	5.66	67	.253	.349	0	.000	-0	-4	-4	-0	-0.4
Was-A	3	2	.600	37	0	0	0	13	65²	49	5	27	29	10.6	2.88	135	.213	.298	1	.071	-1	7	7	-2	0.6
Yr	4	3	.571	51	0	0	0	13	86¹	68	10	38	32	11.2	3.54	109	.222	.310	1	.063	-1	3	3	-2	0.2
1961 Min-A	4	4	.500	46	0	0	0	14	56¹	49	8	38	45	14.1	3.67	115	.233	.353	0	.000	-1	2	4	-0	0.6
1962 Min-A	8	3	.727	49	0	0	0	9	64²	55	8	30	58	12.1	4.73	86	.231	.322	0	.000	-1	-5	-5	-1	-1.0
1963 Min-A	1	3	.250	31	1	0	0	2	38²	50	8	17	38	15.8	6.98	52	.309	.378	1	.333	-1	-14	-14	-0	-1.5
Total 11	63	59	.516	365	105	24	5	46	1072²	935	101	560	612	12.7	4.06	93	.238	.335	56	.187	6	-18	-32	-10	-3.6

● BARRY MOORE
Moore, Robert Barry b: 4/3/43, Statesville, N.C. BL/TL, 6'1", 190 lbs. Deb: 5/29/65

YEAR TM/L	W	L	PCT	G	GS	CG	SH	SV	IP	H	HR	BB	SO	RAT	ERA	ERA+	OAV	OOB	BH	AVG	PB	PR	/A	PD	TPI
1965 Was-A	0	0	—	1	0	0	0	0	1	1	0	1	0	18.0	0.00	—	.333	.500	0	—	0	0	0	-0	0.0
1966 Was-A	3	3	.500	12	11	1	0	0	62¹	55	3	39	28	13.7	3.75	92	.240	.353	2	.105	-1	-2	-2	-0	-0.3
1967 Was-A	7	11	.389	27	26	3	1	0	143²	127	15	71	74	12.6	3.76	84	.240	.333	6	.130	-0	-8	-10	-1	-1.1
1968 Was-A	4	6	.400	32	18	0	0	3	117²	116	8	42	56	12.2	3.37	87	.261	.327	3	.097	-1	-5	-6	-1	-0.6
1969 Was-A	9	8	.529	31	25	4	0	0	134	123	12	67	51	12.9	4.30	81	.246	.338	9	.209	2	-10	-12	-2	-1.5
1970 Cle-A	3	5	.375	13	12	0	0	0	70¹	70	6	46	35	15.0	4.22	94	.262	.373	1	.095	-1	-4	-2	1	-0.8
Chi-A	0	4	.000	24	7	0	0	0	70²	85	12	34	34	16.2	6.37	61	.302	.393	5	.263	1	-21	-19	1	-0.8
Yr	3	9	.250	37	19	0	0	0	141	155	20	80	69	15.5	5.30	74	.281	.380	7	.175	-0	-25	-21	1	-1.5
Total 6	26	37	.413	140	99	8	1	3	599²	577	58	300	278	13.4	4.16	82	.256	.348	27	.151	-1	-50	-51	-2	-4.6

● BOBBY MOORE
Moore, Robert Devell b: 11/8/58, Sweetwater, La. BR/TR, 6'4", 200 lbs. Deb: 9/11/85

YEAR TM/L	W	L	PCT	G	GS	CG	SH	SV	IP	H	HR	BB	SO	RAT	ERA	ERA+	OAV	OOB	BH	AVG	PB	PR	/A	PD	TPI
1985 SF-N	0	0	—	11	0	0	0	0	16²	18	1	10	10	15.1	3.24	106	.269	.364	0	.000	-0	1	0	-1	-0.1

● ROY MOORE
Moore, Roy Daniel b: 10/26/1898, Austin, Tex. d: 4/5/51, Seattle, Wash. BB/TR, 6', 185 lbs. Deb: 4/15/20

YEAR TM/L	W	L	PCT	G	GS	CG	SH	SV	IP	H	HR	BB	SO	RAT	ERA	ERA+	OAV	OOB	BH	AVG	PB	PR	/A	PD	TPI
1920 Phi-A	1	13	.071	24	14	5	0	0	132²	161	6	64	45	15.5	4.68	86	.314	.393	10	.200	-1	-13	-10	2	-0.9
1921 Phi-A	10	10	.500	29	26	12	0	0	191²	206	4	122	64	15.6	4.51	99	.280	.385	19	.257	3	-5	-1	2	0.5
1922 Phi-A	0	3	.000	15	6	0	0	0	50²	65	1	32	29	17.8	7.64	56	.319	.418	5	.263	-1	-20	-19	-0	-0.9
Det-A	0	0	—	9	0	0	0	2	19²	29	0	10	9	20.1	5.95	65	.367	.468	3	.429	1	-4	-5	-0	-0.9
Yr	0	3	.000	24	6	0	0	2	70¹	94	1	42	38	18.0	7.17	58	.329	.423	8	.308	2	-24	-24	-0	-0.9
1923 Det-A	0	0	—	3	0	0	0	1	12	15	0	11	7	19.5	3.00	129	.288	.413	0	.000	-0	1	1	1	0.0
Total 4	11	26	.297	80	46	17	0	3	406²	476	11	239	154	16.2	4.98	85	.300	.397	37	.239	4	-41	-33	4	-1.3

● TERRY MOORE
Moore, Terry Bluford b: 5/27/12, Vernon, Ala. d: 3/29/95, Collinsville, Ill. BR/TR, 5'11", 195 lbs. Deb: 4/16/35 MC◆

YEAR TM/L	W	L	PCT	G	GS	CG	SH	SV	IP	H	HR	BB	SO	RAT	ERA	ERA+	OAV	OOB	BH	AVG	PB	PR	/A	PD	TPI
1939 StL-N★	0	0	—	1	0	0	0	0	1	0	0	1	1	0.0	0.00	—	.000	.000	123	.295	0	0	0	0	0.0

● TOMMY MOORE
Moore, Tommy Joe b: 7/7/48, Lynwood, Cal. BR/TR, 5'11", 175 lbs. Deb: 9/15/72

YEAR TM/L	W	L	PCT	G	GS	CG	SH	SV	IP	H	HR	BB	SO	RAT	ERA	ERA+	OAV	OOB	BH	AVG	PB	PR	/A	PD	TPI
1972 NY-N	0	0	—	3	1	0	0	0	12¹	12	1	6	5	9.5	2.92	115	.273	.289	1	.333	0	1	1	-0	0.1
1973 NY-N	0	1	.000	3	1	0	0	0	3¹	6	1	3	2	24.3	10.80	33	.400	.500	0	—	0	-3	-3	-0	-0.7
1975 StL-N	0	0	—	10	0	0	0	0	18²	15	2	12	6	13.0	3.86	97	.203	.314	1	.500	0	-0	-0	-0	0.1
Tex-A	0	2	.000	12	0	0	0	0	21	31	1	12	15	18.9	8.14	46	.352	.436	0	—	0	-10	-10	-0	-0.8
1977 Sea-A	2	1	.667	14	1	0	0	0	33	36	1	21	13	16.4	4.91	84	.281	.395	0	—	0	-3	-3	-1	-0.3
Total 4	2	4	.333	42	3	0	0	0	88¹	100	6	49	30	15.6	5.40	71	.287	.381	2	.400	1	-16	-15	-0	-1.7

● CY MOORE
Moore, William Austin b: 2/7/05, Elberton, Ga. d: 3/28/72, Augusta, Ga. BR/TR, 6'1", 178 lbs. Deb: 6/7/29

YEAR TM/L	W	L	PCT	G	GS	CG	SH	SV	IP	H	HR	BB	SO	RAT	ERA	ERA+	OAV	OOB	BH	AVG	PB	PR	/A	PD	TPI
1929 Bro-N	3	3	.500	32	4	0	0	2	68	87	3	31	17	15.6	5.56	83	.320	.389	3	.188	-0	-6	-7	-1	-0.7
1930 Bro-N	0	0	—	1	0	0	0	0	2	2	0	0	0	—	—	—	1.000	1.000	0	—	0	0	0	-0	0.0
1931 Bro-N	1	2	.333	23	1	1	0	0	61²	62	5	13	35	11.5	3.79	100	.262	.311	2	.154	-1	0	0	-0	-0.1
1932 Bro-N	0	3	.000	20	2	0	0	0	48²	56	3	17	21	13.7	4.81	79	.293	.354	3	.214	-0	-5	-5	-0	-0.2
1933 Phi-N	8	9	.471	36	18	9	3	1	161¹	177	7	42	53	12.4	3.74	102	.279	.326	7	.063	-4	-7	-1	-1	-0.5
1934 Phi-N	4	9	.308	35	15	3	0	0	126²	163	11	65	55	16.3	6.47	73	.309	.387	6	.143	-3	-34	-25	-1	-2.5
Total 6	16	26	.381	147	40	13	3	3	466¹	547	29	168	181	14.0	4.86	86	.293	.355	17	.128	-8	-52	-34	-2	-3.8

● BILL MOORE
Moore, William Christopher b: 9/3/02, Corning, N.Y. d: 1/24/84, Corning, N.Y. BR/TR, 6'3", 195 lbs. Deb: 4/15/25

YEAR TM/L	W	L	PCT	G	GS	CG	SH	SV	IP	H	HR	BB	SO	RAT	ERA	ERA+	OAV	OOB	BH	AVG	PB	PR	/A	PD	TPI
1925 Det-A	0	0	—	1	0	0	0	0	0	3	0	3	0	∞	—	—	1.000	0	—	0	-2	-2	0	-0.2

● WILCY MOORE
Moore, William Wilcy "Cy" b: 5/20/1897, Bonita, Tex. d: 3/29/63, Hollis, Okla. BR/TR, 6', 195 lbs. Deb: 4/14/27

YEAR TM/L	W	L	PCT	G	GS	CG	SH	SV	IP	H	HR	BB	SO	RAT	ERA	ERA+	OAV	OOB	BH	AVG	PB	PR	/A	PD	TPI
1927 *NY-A	19	7	.731	50	12	6	1	13	213	185	3	59	75	10.4	2.28	169	.234	.289	6	.080	-7	44	37	8	4.8
1928 NY-A	4	4	.500	35	2	0	0	0	60¹	71	4	31	16	15.2	4.18	90	.286	.366	2	.143	-1	-1	-3	1	-0.3
1929 NY-A	6	4	.600	41	0	0	0	8	61	64	4	19	21	12.2	4.13	93	.268	.322	1	.067	-2	1	-2	2	-0.3
1931 Bos-A	11	13	.458	53	15	8	1	10	185¹	195	7	55	37	12.2	3.88	111	.269	.322	9	.161	-3	10	9	6	1.3
1932 Bos-A	4	10	.286	37	2	0	0	4	84¹	98	5	42	28	15.0	5.23	86	.284	.363	2	.045	-2	-7	-7	-3	-1.0
*NY-A	2	0	1.000	10	1	0	0	2	25	27	1	6	8	11.9	2.52	162	.273	.314	0	.000	-1	5	4	-0	0.3
Yr	6	10	.375	47	3	0	0	6	109¹	125	6	48	36	14.2	4.61	95	.281	.351	2	.033	-4	-2	-3	-3	-0.7
1933 NY-A	5	6	.455	35	0	0	0	8	62	92	1	20	17	16.3	5.52	70	.333	.378	2	.133	-1	-9	-11	-2	-2.0
Total 6	51	44	.537	261	32	14	2	49	691	732	25	232	204	12.6	3.70	110	.269	.327	21	.102	-17	44	27	20	2.8

● BOB MOORHEAD
Moorhead, Charles Robert b: 1/23/38, Chambersburg, Pa. d: 12/3/86, Lemoyne, Pa. BR/TR, 6'1", 208 lbs. Deb: 4/11/62

YEAR TM/L	W	L	PCT	G	GS	CG	SH	SV	IP	H	HR	BB	SO	RAT	ERA	ERA+	OAV	OOB	BH	AVG	PB	PR	/A	PD	TPI
1962 NY-N	0	2	.000	38	7	0	0	0	105¹	118	13	42	63	14.0	4.53	92	.289	.361	1	.045	-1	-7	-4	2	0.1
1965 NY-N	0	1	.000	9	0	0	0	0	14¹	16	0	5	5	13.2	4.40	80	.271	.328	0	—	-0	-1	-0	-0	-0.1
Total 2	0	3	.000	47	7	0	0	0	119²	134	13	47	68	13.9	4.51	91	.287	.357	1	.045	-1	-8	-5	3	0.0

● BOB MOOSE
Moose, Robert Ralph b: 10/9/47, Export, Pa. d: 10/9/76, Martins Ferry, Ohio BR/TR, 6', 200 lbs. Deb: 9/19/67

YEAR TM/L	W	L	PCT	G	GS	CG	SH	SV	IP	H	HR	BB	SO	RAT	ERA	ERA+	OAV	OOB	BH	AVG	PB	PR	/A	PD	TPI
1967 Pit-N	1	0	1.000	2	2	1	0	0	14²	14	1	4	7	11.7	3.68	91	.259	.322	2	.333	1	-1	-1	-0	0.1
1968 Pit-N	8	12	.400	38	22	3	3	1	171¹	136	14	47	76	9.5	2.73	107	.218	.269	5	.093	-2	5	4	2	0.5
1969 Pit-N	14	3	.824	44	19	6	1	4	170	149	9	62	105	11.4	2.91	120	.231	.303	4	.075	-1	13	11	1	1.0
1970 *Pit-N	11	10	.524	28	27	9	2	0	189²	186	14	64	119	12.0	3.99	98	.262	.326	12	.182	3	1	-2	-1	-0.1
1971 *Pit-N	11	7	.611	30	18	3	1	1	140	169	12	35	68	13.2	4.11	82	.301	.344	4	.103	-1	-10	-10	-1	-1.4
1972 *Pit-N	13	10	.565	31	30	6	3	0	226	213	11	47	144	10.5	2.91	114	.248	.290	12	.169	3	14	10	1	1.4
1973 Pit-N	12	13	.480	39	29	6	0	0	201¹	219	11	70	111	13.1	3.53	96	.280	.342	9	.134	-0	3	0	1	0.1
1974 Pit-N	1	5	.167	7	6	0	0	0	35²	76	3	14	12	7.57	45	.386	.420	2	.200	-0	-16	-16	2	-2.0
1975 Pit-N	2	2	.500	23	5	1	0	0	67²	63	4	25	34	12.0	3.72	95	.246	.318	3	.167	-1	-1	-2	0	0.1
1976 Pit-N	3	9	.250	53	2	0	0	10	88	100	4	32	38	13.9	3.68	95	.294	.362	3	.250	2	-2	-0	-0	-0.1
Total 10	76	71	.517	289	160	35	13	19	1304¹	1308	75	387	827	11.9	3.50	98	.262	.319	56	.141	4	7	-9	8	-0.4

Pitcher Register

YEAR TM/L	W	L	PCT	G	GS	CG	SH	SV	IP	H	HR	BB	SO	RAT	ERA	ERA+	OA

● JAKE MOOTY Mooty, J T b: 4/13/13, Bennett, Tex. d: 4/20/70, Fort Worth, Tex. BR/TR, 5'10.5", 170 lbs. Deb: 9/

1936 Cin-N	0	0	—	8	0	0	0	1	13²	10	0	4	11	9.2	3.95	97	
1937 Cin-N	0	3	.000	14	2	0	0	1	39	54	2	22	11	17.5	8.31	45	
1940 Chi-N	6	6	.500	20	12	6	0	1	114	101	11	49	42	11.9	2.92	1	
1941 Chi-N	8	9	.471	33	14	7	1	4	153¹	143	9	56	45	11.8	3.35		
1942 Chi-N	2	5	.286	19	10	1	0	1	84¹	89	11	44	28	14.2	4.70		
1943 Chi-N	0	0	—	2	0	0	0	0	1	2	0	1	1	27.0			
1944 Det-A	0	0	—	15	0	0	0	0	28¹	35	0	18	7	17.2			
Total 7	16	23	.410	111	38	14	1	8	433²	434	33	194	145	13.1			

● HIKER MORAN Moran, Albert Thomas b: 1/1/12, Rochester, N.Y. BR/TR, 6'4.5", 185 lbs.

1938 Bos-N	0	0	—	1	0	0	0	0	3	1	0	1	0				
1939 Bos-N	1	1	.500	6	2	1	0	0	20	21	3	11	4	14.4			
Total 2	1	1	.500	7	2	1	0	0	23	22	3	12	4	13.3			

● BILL MORAN Moran, Carl William "Bugs" b: 9/26/50, Portsmouth, Va. BR/TR, 6'4", 210 lbs. Deb: 4/12/

| 1974 Chi-A | 1 | 3 | .250 | 15 | 0 | 0 | 0 | 0 | 46¹ | 57 | 5 | 23 | 17 | 16.7 | 4.66 | | |

● CHARLIE MORAN Moran, Charles Barthell "Uncle Charlie" b: 2/22/1878, Nashville, Tenn. d: 6/14/49, Horse Cave,

| 1903 StL-N | 0 | 1 | .000 | 3 | 2 | 2 | 0 | 0 | 24 | 30 | 0 | 19 | 7 | 18.8 | 5.25 | 62 | .2 |

● HARRY MORAN Moran, Harry Edwin b: 4/2/1889, Slater, W.Va. d: 11/28/62, Beckley, W.Va. BL/TL, 6'1", 165 lbs. Deb: 6/

1912 Det-A	0	1	.000	5	2	1	0	0	14²	19	1	12	3	20.3	4.91	66	.339	.471
1914 Buf-F	10	7	.588	34	16	7	2	2	154	159	7	53	73	13.0	4.27	69	.276	.348
1915 New-F	13	9	.591	34	23	13	2	2	205²	193	2	66	87	12.1	2.54	101	.262	.337
Total 3	23	17	.575	73	41	21	4	2	374¹	371	10	131	163	12.8	3.34	82	.271	.348

● SAM MORAN Moran, Samuel b: 9/16/1870, Rochester, N.Y. d: 8/29/1897, Rochester, N.Y. TL, 160 lbs. Deb: 8/28/1895

| 1895 Pit-N | 2 | 4 | .333 | 10 | 6 | 6 | 0 | 0 | 62² | 78 | 2 | 51 | 19 | 19.0 | 7.47 | 61 | .300 | .420 |

● FORREST MORE More, Forrest b: 9/30/1883, Hayden, Ind. d: 8/17/68, Columbus, Ind. BR/TR, 6', 180 lbs. Deb: 4/15/09

1909 StL-N	1	5	.167	15	2	1	0	0	50	48	0	20	17	12.8	5.04	50	.258	.340
Bos-N	1	5	.167	10	4	3	0	0	48²	47	0	20	10	13.1	4.44	64	.270	.359
Yr	2	10	.167	25	6	4	0	0	98²	95	0	40	27	12.7	4.74	56	.262	.342

● DAVE MOREHEAD Morehead, David Michael "Moe" b: 9/5/42, San Diego, Cal. BR/TR, 6'1", 185 lbs. Deb: 4/13/63

1963 Bos-A	10	13	.435	29	29	6	1	0	174²	137	20	99	136	12.2	3.81	99	.211	.316	6	.105	-3	-4	-1	1	-0.3
1964 Bos-A	8	15	.348	32	30	3	1	0	166²	156	14	112	139	14.7	4.97	78	.248	.365	5	.093	-2	-25	-21	-1	-2.9
1965 Bos-A	10	18	.357	34	33	5	2	0	192²	157	18	113	163	12.8	4.06	92	.217	.326	8	.131	-0	-13	-7	-2	-1.2
1966 Bos-A	1	2	.333	12	5	0	0	0	28	31	7	7	20	12.2	5.46	70	.274	.317	3	.500	1	-6	-5	-0	-0.5
1967 *Bos-A	5	4	.556	10	9	1	1	0	47²	48	0	22	40	13.6	4.34	80	.264	.350	1	.083	-0	-6	-5	-1	-0.9
1968 Bos-A	1	4	.200	11	9	3	1	0	55	52	3	20	28	12.1	2.45	129	.249	.320	2	.125	-0	3	4	-1	0.2
1969 KC-A	2	3	.400	21	2	0	0	0	33	28	7	28	32	15.3	5.73	64	.239	.386	0	.000	-0	-8	-7	-1	-1.1
1970 KC-A	3	5	.375	28	17	1	0	1	121²	121	19	62	69	13.6	3.62	103	.261	.349	6	.167	-1	1	2	-2	-0.1
Total 8	40	64	.385	177	134	19	6	1	819¹	730	78	463	627	13.2	4.15	90	.237	.338	31	.127	-5	-57	-39	-7	-6.8

● SETH MOREHEAD Morehead, Seth Marvin "Moe" b: 8/15/34, Houston, Tex. BL/TL, 6'0.5", 195 lbs. Deb: 4/27/57

1957 Phi-N	1	1	.500	34	1	1	0	0	58²	57	1	20	36	12.1	3.68	103	.254	.321	0	.000	-1	1	1	-1	-0.1
1958 Phi-N	1	6	.143	27	11	0	0	0	92¹	121	8	26	54	14.4	5.85	68	.319	.365	4	.182	0	-19	-19	-2	-1.4
1959 Phi-N	0	2	.000	3	3	0	0	0	10	15	3	3	8	17.1	9.90	41	.333	.388	0	.000	-0	-7	-6	-0	-1.0
Chi-N	0	1	.000	11	2	0	0	0	18²	25	1	8	9	15.9	4.82	82	.313	.375	1	.500	1	-2	-1	-0	-0.1
Yr	0	3	.000	14	5	0	0	0	28²	40	4	11	17	16.0	6.59	61	.317	.372	1	.200	0	-8	-8	-1	-1.1
1960 Chi-N	2	9	.182	45	7	2	0	4	123¹	123	17	46	64	12.5	3.94	96	.258	.326	4	.138	-1	-2	-2	-0	-0.3
1961 Mil-N	1	0	1.000	12	0	0	0	0	15¹	16	4	7	13	14.1	6.46	58	.271	.358	0	—	0	-4	-5	-0	-0.3
Total 5	5	19	.208	132	24	3	0	5	318¹	357	34	110	184	13.4	4.81	80	.282	.343	9	.145	-1	-33	-34	-4	-3.2

● RAMON MOREL Morel, Ramon Rafael b: 8/15/74, Villa Gonzalez, D.R. BR/TR, 6'2", 175 lbs. Deb: 7/6/95

1995 Pit-N	0	1	.000	5	0	0	0	0	6¹	6	0	2	3	11.4	2.84	151	.300	.364	0	—	0	1	1	0	0.2
1996 Pit-N	2	1	.667	29	0	0	0	0	42	57	4	19	22	16.5	5.36	82	.324	.393	0	.000	-0	-5	-5	-1	-0.4
Total 2	2	2	.500	34	0	0	0	0	48¹	63	4	21	25	15.8	5.03	87	.321	.390	0	.000	-0	-4	-4	-0	-0.2

● LEW MOREN Moren, Lewis Howard "Hicks" b: 8/4/1883, Pittsburgh, Pa. d: 11/2/66, Pittsburgh, Pa. BR/TR, 5'11", 150 lbs. Deb: 9/21/03

1903 Pit-N	0	1	.000	1	1	1	0	0	6	9	0	2	1	18.0	9.00	36	.346	.414	0	.000	-0	-4	-4	-0	-0.5
1904 Pit-N	0	0	—	1	0	0	0	0	4	7	1	4	0	27.0	9.00	30	.412	.545	0	.000	-0	-3	-3	-0	0.0
1907 Phi-N	11	18	.379	37	31	21	3	1	255	202	3	101	98	11.0	2.54	95	.226	.311	6	.081	-2	-2	-3	-0	-0.7
1908 Phi-N	8	9	.471	28	16	9	4	0	154	146	1	49	72	11.5	2.92	83	.258	.320	12	.245	2	-10	-8	-0	-0.8
1909 Phi-N	16	15	.516	40	31	19	2	1	257²	226	6	93	110	11.3	2.65	98	.239	.309	10	.111	-3	-2	-2	-5	-1.1
1910 Phi-N	13	14	.481	34	26	12	1	1	205¹	207	6	82	74	13.1	3.55	88	.269	.347	11	.149	-1	-12	-10	-0	-1.4
Total 6	48	57	.457	141	105	62	10	3	882	797	17	331	356	11.8	2.95	90	.248	.323	39	.134	-5	-32	-30	-5	-4.5

● ANGEL MORENO Moreno, Angel (Veneroso) b: 6/6/55, LaMendosa Soledad, Mex. BL/TL, 5'9", 165 lbs. Deb: 8/15/81

1981 Cal-A	1	3	.250	8	4	1	0	0	31¹	27	2	14	12	11.8	2.87	127	.233	.315	0	—	0	3	3	-0	0.3
1982 Cal-A	3	7	.300	13	8	2	0	1	49¹	55	7	23	22	14.4	4.74	85	.288	.367	0	—	0	-4	-4	-0	-0.7
Total 2	4	10	.286	21	12	3	0	1	80²	82	9	37	34	13.4	4.02	97	.267	.348	0	—	0	-1	-1	-0	-0.4

● JULIO MORENO Moreno, Julio (Gonzalez) b: 1/28/21, Guines, Cuba d: 1/2/87, Miami, Fla. BR/TR, 5'8", 165 lbs. Deb: 9/8/50

1950 Was-A	1	1	.500	4	3	1	0	0	21¹	22	1	12	7	14.8	4.64	97	.268	.368	1	.125	-1	-0	-0	-0	-0.1
1951 Was-A	5	11	.313	31	18	5	0	2	132²	132	18	80	37	14.4	4.88	84	.256	.397	7	.175	-1	-11	-12	-0	-1.4
1952 Was-A	9	9	.500	26	22	7	0	0	147¹	154	10	52	62	12.9	3.97	90	.270	.337	6	.122	-2	-5	-7	-1	-1.1
1953 Was-A	3	1	.750	12	2	1	0	0	35¹	41	2	13	13	13.8	2.80	139	.291	.351	0	.000	-1	5	4	-0	0.3
Total 4	18	22	.450	73	45	14	0	2	336²	349	31	157	119	13.7	4.25	91	.267	.349	14	.132	-5	-12	-15	-0	-2.3

● ROGER MORET Moret, Rogelio (Torres) b: 9/16/49, Guayama, P.R. BB/TL, 6'4", 175 lbs. Deb: 9/13/70

1970 Bos-A	1	0	1.000	3	1	0	0	0	8¹	4	1	4	4	3.24	122	.226	.314	0	.000	-0	0	1	-0	0.0
1971 Bos-A	4	3	.571	13	7	4	1	0	71	50	5	40	47	11.7	2.92	127	.205	.322	2	.087	-1	4	6	-0	0.5
1972 Bos-A	0	0	—	3	0	0	0	0	5	5	0	4	4	19.8	3.60	89	.263	.440	0	.000	-0	-0	-0	-0	0.0
1973 Bos-A	13	2	.867	30	15	5	2	3	156¹	138	19	67	90	12.0	3.17	126	.238	.320	0	—	0	11	15	-0	1.4
1974 Bos-A	9	10	.474	31	21	10	1	2	173¹	158	15	79	111	12.4	3.74	103	.243	.327	0	—	0	-2	2	-2	-0.2
1975 *Bos-A	14	3	.824	36	16	4	1	1	145	132	8	76	80	13.0	3.60	113	.248	.344	0	—	0	3	8	-1	0.7
1976 Atl-N	3	5	.375	27	12	1	0	1	77¹	84	7	27	30	13.0	5.00	76	.280	.341	3	.130	-1	-13	-10	-0	-1.2
1977 Tex-A	3	3	.500	18	8	0	0	4	72¹	59	8	39	37	12.1	3.73	109	.220	.317	0	—	0	3	3	-1	0.4
1978 Tex-A	0	1	.000	9	2	0	0	1	14²	12	5	3	5	16.0	4.91	76	.390	.419	0	—	0	-2	-2	-0	-0.2
Total 9	47	27	.635	168	82	24	5	12	723¹	656	61	339	408	12.5	3.66	107	.245	.332	5	.100	-2	4	22	-6	1.1

● DAVE MOREY Morey, David Beale b: 2/25/1889, Malden, Mass. d: 1/4/86, Oak Bluffs, Mass. BL/TR, 6', 185 lbs. Deb: 7/4/13

| 1913 Phi-A | 0 | 0 | — | 2 | 0 | 0 | 0 | 0 | 4 | 2 | 0 | 1 | 2 | 11.3 | 4.50 | 61 | .182 | .357 | 0 | .000 | -0 | -1 | -1 | 0 | 0.0 |

● CY MORGAN Morgan, Cyril Arlon b: 11/11/1895, Lakeville, Mass. d: 9/11/46, Lakeville, Mass. BR/TR, 6', 170 lbs. Deb: 6/8/21

1921 Bos-N	1	1	.500	17	0	0	0	1	30¹	37	0	17	8	16.3	6.53	56	.314	.404	0	.000	-1	-9	-10	1	-0.6
1922 Bos-N	0	0	—	2	0	0	0	0	1¹	8	0	2	0	67.5	27.00	15	.667	.714	0	—	0	-3	-3	-0	0.0
Total 2	1	1	.500	19	0	0	0	1	31²	45	0	19	8	18.5	7.39	50	.346	.433	0	.000	-1	-13	-13	1	-0.6

Harry Richard Morgan — Morgan, Harry Richard   b: 11/10/1878, Pomeroy, Ohio   d: 6/28/62, Wheeling, W.Va.   BR/TR, 6', 175 lbs.   Deb: 9/18/03

Yr Tm	W	L	PCT	G	GS	CG	SH	SV	IP	H	HR	BB	SO	RAT	ERA	ERA+	OAV	OOB	BH	AVG	PB	PR	/A	PD	TPI
			.000	2	1	1	0	0	13	12	0	6	6	13.8	4.15	70	.245	.351	1	.250	0	-2	-2	-0	-0.3
			.000	8	3	2	0	0	51	51	3	10	24	11.1	3.71	67	.262	.304	1	.056	-2	-6	-7	1	-0.4
			.286	13	8	5	1	0	77¹	82	1	37	44	14.9	3.61	71	.273	.370	8	.258	2	-8	-9	2	-0.4
			.286	10	6	4	0	0	55	77	3	17	14	15.7	6.05	42	.333	.384	2	.100	-1	-21	-22	1	-2.4
		6	.500	16	13	9	2	0	114¹	77	1	34	50	9.0	1.97	131	.193	.262	2	.057	-4	7	8	-1	0.3
		11	.421	26	19	13	2	0	169¹	154	4	51	64	11.1	3.30	78	.244	.304	4	.073	-5	-14	-14	1	-2.1
		13	.519	30	26	17	2	1	205	166	7	90	99	11.7	2.46	100	.226	.319	8	.127	-3	-1	0	1	-0.3
		6	.250	12	10	5	0	1	64²	52	0	31	30	12.4	2.37	106	.240	.350	1	.050	-2	1	1	2	0.2
	16	11	.593	28	26	21	5	0	228²	152	3	71	81	9.4	1.65	146	.191	.271	8	.108	-3	21	19	-2	1.8
	18	17	.514	40	36	26	5	1	293¹	204	3	102	111	9.9	1.81	134	**.200**	.283	9	.096	-4	22	20	1	2.0
	18	12	.600	36	34	23	3	0	290²	214	0	117	134	10.8	1.55	153	.216	.310	14	.141	-4	31	32	1	2.5
	15	7	.682	38	30	15	2	1	249²	217	0	113	136	12.7	2.70	117	.243	.341	15	.160	-5	18	13	3	0.8
	3	8	.273	16	14	5	0	0	93²	75	0	51	47	12.6	3.75	82	.243	.338	1	.033	-3	-4	-7	2	-0.8
	0	1	.000	1	1	0	0	0	2¹	5	0	1	2	27.0	15.43	21	.500	.583	0	.000	-0	-3	-3	0	-0.8
	78	78	.500	210	172	107	15	3	1445¹	1180	18	578	667	11.5	2.51	105	.229	.318	61	.125	-25	32	19	12	0.2

L MORGAN — Morgan, Henry William   b: 10/1857, Washington, D.C.   Deb: 5/4/1875 ◆

Yr Tm	W	L	PCT	G	GS	CG	SH	SV	IP	H	HR	BB	SO	RAT	ERA	ERA+	OAV	OOB	BH	AVG	PB	PR	/A	PD	TPI
RS-n	1	3	.250	7	4	4	1	0	42	40	0	1	7	8.8	1.29	170	.212	.216	18	.261	1	4	4		0.4

MIKE MORGAN — Morgan, Michael Thomas   b: 10/8/59, Tulare, Cal.   BR/TR, 6'3", 195 lbs.   Deb: 6/11/78

Yr	Tm	W	L	PCT	G	GS	CG	SH	SV	IP	H	HR	BB	SO	RAT	ERA	ERA+	OAV	OOB	BH	AVG	PB	PR	/A	PD	TPI
78	Oak-A	0	3	.000	3	3	1	0	0	12¹	19	1	8	0	19.7	7.30	50	.373	.458	0	—	0	-5	-5	1	-0.8
79	Oak-A	2	10	.167	13	13	2	1	0	77¹	102	9	50	17	18.0	5.94	68	.332	.431	0	—	0	-15	-16	1	-1.7
82	NY-A	7	11	.389	30	23	2	0	0	150¹	167	15	67	71	14.1	4.37	91	.285	.360	0	—	0	-5	-6	1	-0.6
83	Tor-A	0	3	.000	16	4	0	0	0	45¹	48	6	21	22	13.7	5.16	83	.273	.350	0	—	0	-6	-4	1	-0.3
85	Sea-A	1	1	.500	2	2	0	0	0	6	11	2	5	2	24.0	12.00	35	.393	.485	0	—	0	-5	-5	0	-1.1
86	Sea-A	11	17	.393	37	33	9	1	1	216¹	243	24	86	116	13.9	4.53	94	.286	.354	0	—	0	-9	-7	0	-0.9
87	Sea-A	12	17	.414	34	31	8	2	0	207	245	25	53	85	13.2	4.65	101	.296	.342	0	—	0	-5	-5	1	0.3
88	Bal-A	1	6	.143	22	10	0	0	0	71¹	70	6	23	29	11.9	5.43	72	.255	.315	0	—	0	-12	-12	0	-0.8
89	LA-N	8	11	.421	40	19	0	0	0	152²	130	6	33	72	9.7	2.53	135	.234	.280	3	.083	-2	16	15	4	2.1
90	LA-N	11	15	.423	33	33	6	4	0	211	216	19	60	106	12.0	3.75	97	.266	.321	8	.113	-2	1	-2	3	-0.1
91	LA-N★	14	10	.583	34	33	5	1	0	236¹	197	12	61	140	9.9	2.78	129	.226	.279	7	.092	-3	24	21	2	2.0
92	Chi-N	16	8	.667	34	34	6	1	0	240	203	14	79	123	10.7	2.55	141	.234	.300	8	.108	-2	25	28	2	2.8
93	Chi-N	10	15	.400	32	32	1	1	0	207²	206	15	74	111	12.4	4.03	99	.262	.331	4	.061	-0	-1	0	-0	-0.4
94	Chi-N	2	10	.167	15	15	1	0	0	80²	111	12	35	57	16.7	6.69	62	.338	.409	3	.125	-1	-22	-23	-1	-2.9
95	Chi-N	2	1	.667	4	4	0	0	0	24²	19	2	9	15	10.6	2.19	187	.216	.296	1	.143	-0	5	5	1	0.7
	StL-N	5	6	.455	17	17	1	0	0	106²	114	10	25	46	12.2	3.88	108	.281	.333	1	.032	-2	4	4	2	0.3
	Yr	7	7	.500	21	21	1	0	0	131¹	133	12	34	61	11.8	3.56	117	.270	.324	2	.053	-2	9	9	2	1.0
96	StL-N	4	8	.333	18	18	0	0	0	103	118	14	40	55	13.8	5.24	81	.294	.358	2	.061	-3	-12	-12	-1	-1.5
	Cin-N	2	3	.400	5	5	0	0	0	27¹	28	2	7	19	11.9	2.30	180	.267	.319	0	.000	-1	6	6	-0	0.9
	Yr	6	11	.353	23	23	0	0	0	130¹	146	16	47	74	13.4	4.63	91	.285	.346	2	.050	-3	-6	-6	-1	-0.6
Total 16		108	155	.411	389	329	44	10	3	2176	2247	192	736	1086	12.5	4.02	99	.270	.333	37	.087	-19	-13	-14	15	-2.0

● TOM MORGAN — Morgan, Tom Stephen "Plowboy"   b: 5/20/30, ElMonte, Cal.   d: 1/13/87, Anaheim, Cal.   BR/TR, 6'2", 195 lbs.   Deb: 4/20/51 C

Yr	Tm	W	L	PCT	G	GS	CG	SH	SV	IP	H	HR	BB	SO	RAT	ERA	ERA+	OAV	OOB	BH	AVG	PB	PR	/A	PD	TPI
1951	*NY-A	9	3	.750	27	16	4	2	2	124²	119	11	36	57	11.4	3.68	104	.253	.310	12	.273	2	6	2	2	0.5
1952	NY-A	5	4	.556	16	12	2	1	2	93²	86	8	33	35	11.8	3.07	108	.252	.325	6	.182	1	6	3	3	0.6
1954	NY-A	11	5	.688	32	17	7	4	1	143	149	8	40	34	12.2	3.34	103	.274	.330	7	.143	0	6	4	2	0.4
1955	*NY-A	7	3	.700	40	1	0	0	10	72	72	3	24	17	12.6	3.25	115	.267	.338	4	.222	0	6	4	2	0.9
1956	*NY-A	6	7	.462	41	0	0	0	11	71¹	74	2	27	20	13.1	4.16	93	.284	.357	2	.154	-0	-2	1	-0	0.4
1957	KC-A	9	7	.563	46	13	5	0	7	143²	160	19	61	32	14.0	4.64	85	.299	.373	3	.091	-2	-14	-11	4	-1.1
1958	Det-A	2	5	.286	39	1	0	0	1	62²	70	7	44	32	10.8	3.16	128	.286	.300	2	.200	-0	4	6	-0	0.6
1959	Det-A	1	4	.200	46	1	0	0	9	92²	94	11	18	39	11.5	3.98	102	.265	.311	9	.391	-1	1	1	-0	0.4
1960	Det-A	3	2	.600	22	0	0	0	9	29	33	6	10	12	13.3	4.66	85	.295	.352	0	.000	-0	-3	-2	0	-0.3
	Was-A	1	3	.250	14	0	0	0	0	24	36	6	5	11	15.8	3.75	104	.343	.378	0	.000	-1	0	0	-0	0.0
	Yr	4	5	.444	36	0	0	0	1	53	69	12	15	23	14.4	4.25	92	.315	.362	0	.000	-1	-2	-2	0	-0.3
1961	LA-A	8	2	.800	59	0	0	0	10	91²	74	7	17	39	9.4	2.36	191	.224	.272	1	.083	-1	17	**22**	1	2.7
1962	LA-A	5	2	.714	48	0	0	0	9	58²	53	6	19	29	11.2	2.91	132	.247	.311	0	.000	-1	7	6	-1	0.7
1963	LA-A	0	0	—	13	0	0	0	1	16¹	21	0	6	7	16.0	5.51	62	.313	.397	0	.000	-0	-3	-4	-0	-0.1
Total 12		67	47	.588	443	61	18	7	64	1023¹	1040	95	300	364	12.1	3.61	106	.270	.329	46	.186	3	32	26	13	4.9

● GENE MORIARITY — Moriarity, Eugene John   b: 1/5/1865, Holyoke, Mass.   BL/TL, 5'8", 130 lbs.   Deb: 6/18/1884 ◆

Yr	Tm	W	L	PCT	G	GS	CG	SH	SV	IP	H	HR	BB	SO	RAT	ERA	ERA+	OAV	OOB	BH	AVG	PB	PR	/A	PD	TPI
1884	Ind-a	0	2	.000	2	2	2	0	0	13²	16	0	7	4	15.8	5.27	62	.267	.353	8	.216	0	-3	-3	0	-0.3
1885	Det-N	0	0	—	1	0	0	0	0	2	3	0	1	1	18.0	9.00	32	.300	.364	1	.026	-0	-1	-1	-0	0.0
Total 2		0	2	.000	3	2	2	0	0	15²	19	0	8	5	16.1	5.74	56	.271	.354	41	.152	-0	-4	-4	0	-0.3

● JOHN MORLAN — Morlan, John Glen   b: 11/22/47, Columbus, Ohio   BR/TR, 6', 178 lbs.   Deb: 7/20/73

Yr	Tm	W	L	PCT	G	GS	CG	SH	SV	IP	H	HR	BB	SO	RAT	ERA	ERA+	OAV	OOB	BH	AVG	PB	PR	/A	PD	TPI
1973	Pit-N	2	2	.500	10	7	1	0	0	41	42	4	23	23	14.3	3.95	89	.276	.371	2	.182	1	-1	-2	-1	-0.2
1974	Pit-N	0	3	.000	39	0	0	0	0	65	54	2	48	38	14.5	4.29	80	.227	.363	0	.000	-1	-5	-6	-1	-0.4
Total 2		2	5	.286	49	7	1	0	0	106	96	6	71	61	14.4	4.16	83	.246	.366	2	.111	0	-6	-8	-1	-0.6

● ALVIN MORMAN — Morman, Alvin   b: 1/6/69, Rockingham, N.C.   BL/TL, 6'3", 210 lbs.   Deb: 4/2/96

Yr	Tm	W	L	PCT	G	GS	CG	SH	SV	IP	H	HR	BB	SO	RAT	ERA	ERA+	OAV	OOB	BH	AVG	PB	PR	/A	PD	TPI
1996	Hou-N	4	1	.800	53	0	0	0	0	42	43	8	24	31	14.4	4.93	78	.261	.354	0	—	0	-3	-5	0	-0.5

● DAN MOROGIELLO — Morogiello, Daniel Joseph   b: 3/26/55, Brooklyn, N.Y.   BL/TL, 6'1", 200 lbs.   Deb: 5/20/83

Yr	Tm	W	L	PCT	G	GS	CG	SH	SV	IP	H	HR	BB	SO	RAT	ERA	ERA+	OAV	OOB	BH	AVG	PB	PR	/A	PD	TPI
1983	Bal-A	0	1	.000	22	0	0	0	1	37²	39	1	10	15	11.9	2.39	165	.265	.316	0	—	0	7	7	-1	0.1

● JIM MORONEY — Moroney, James Francis   b: 12/4/1883, Boston, Mass.   d: 2/26/29, Philadelphia, Pa.   BL/TL, 6'1", 175 lbs.   Deb: 4/24/06

Yr	Tm	W	L	PCT	G	GS	CG	SH	SV	IP	H	HR	BB	SO	RAT	ERA	ERA+	OAV	OOB	BH	AVG	PB	PR	/A	PD	TPI
1906	Bos-N	0	3	.000	3	3	3	0	0	27	28	1	12	11	15.3	5.33	50	.259	.365	1	.100	-1	-8	-8	0	-0.8
1910	Phi-N	1	2	.333	12	2	1	0	1	42	42	1	11	13	12.4	2.14	146	.295	.360	0	.000	-1	4	5	-0	0.2
1912	Chi-N	1	1	.500	10	3	1	0	1	23²	25	0	17	5	17.5	4.56	73	.316	.460	3	.500	-1	-3	-3	-0	-0.2
Total 3		2	6	.250	25	8	5	0	2	92²	96	2	40	29	14.6	3.69	83	.288	.388	4	.154	-1	-7	-7	-1	-0.8

● BILL MORRELL — Morrell, Willard Blackmer   b: 4/9/1893, Hyde Park, Mass.   d: 8/5/75, Birmingham, Ala.   BR/TR, 6', 172 lbs.   Deb: 4/20/26

Yr	Tm	W	L	PCT	G	GS	CG	SH	SV	IP	H	HR	BB	SO	RAT	ERA	ERA+	OAV	OOB	BH	AVG	PB	PR	/A	PD	TPI
1926	Was-A	3	3	.500	26	2	1	0	1	69²	83	5	29	16	14.7	5.30	73	.311	.383	4	.235	1	-10	-11	-1	-0.9
1930	NY-N	0	0	—	2	0	0	0	0	8	6	0	1	3	7.9	1.13	421	.214	.241	0	.000	-0	3	3	0	0.2
1931	NY-N	5	3	.625	20	7	2	0	1	66	83	4	27	16	15.0	4.36	85	.306	.369	2	.111	-0	-4	-5	0	-0.6
Total 3		8	6	.571	48	9	3	0	2	143²	172	9	57	35	14.5	4.64	83	.304	.370	6	.162	-0	-10	-13	-1	-1.5

● JOHN MORRILL — Morrill, John Francis "Honest John"   b: 2/19/1855, Boston, Mass.   d: 4/2/32, Boston, Mass.   BR/TR, 5'10.5", 155 lbs.   Deb: 4/24/1876 M◆

Yr	Tm	W	L	PCT	G	GS	CG	SH	SV	IP	H	HR	BB	SO	RAT	ERA	ERA+	OAV	OOB	BH	AVG	PB	PR	/A	PD	TPI
1880	Bos-N	0	0	—	1	0	0	0	0	10²	9	0	1	0	8.4	0.84	269	.273	.294	81	.237	0	2	2	0	0.0
1881	Bos-N	0	1	.000	3	0	0	0	1	5²	9	0	1	0	15.9	6.35	42	.333	.357	90	.289	1	-2	-2	-0	-0.4
1882	Bos-N	0	0	—	1	0	0	0	0	2	3	0	0	2	13.5	0.00	—	.375	.375	101	.289	0	1	1	0	0.0
1883	Bos-N	1	0	1.000	2	1	1	0	0	13	15	0	4	5	13.2	2.77	112	.268	.317	129	.319	1	1	0	0	0.1
1884	Bos-N	0	1	.000	7	1	1	0	**2**	23	34	0	6	13	15.7	7.43	39	.315	.351	114	.260	1	-11	-12	0	-0.5
1886	Bos-N	0	0	—	1	0	0	0	0	4	5	0	0	2	11.3	0.00	—	.313	.313	106	.247	0	1	1	0	0.0
1889	Was-N	0	0	—	3	0	0	0	0	0¹	0	0	0	0		0.00	—	.000	.000	27	.185	0	0	0	0	0.0
Total 7		1	2	.333	18	2	2	0	3	58²	75	0	12	22	13.3	4.30	66	.301	.333	1275	.260	4	-9	-10	-1	-0.8

● DANNY MORRIS — Morris, Danny Walker   b: 6/11/46, Greenville, Ky.   BR/TR, 6'1", 200 lbs.   Deb: 9/10/68

Yr	Tm	W	L	PCT	G	GS	CG	SH	SV	IP	H	HR	BB	SO	RAT	ERA	ERA+	OAV	OOB	BH	AVG	PB	PR	/A	PD	TPI
1968	Min-A	0	1	.000	3	2	0	0	0	10²	11	0	4	6	12.7	1.69	183	.262	.326	0	.000	-0	2	2	0	0.1

YEAR TM/L	W	L	PCT	G	GS	CG	SH	SV	IP	H	HR	BB	SO	RAT	ERA	ERA+	OAV	OOB	BH	AVG	PB	PR	/A	PD	TPI
1969 Min-A	0	2	.000	3	1	0	0	0	5¹	5	1	4	1	15.2	5.06	72	.238	.360	0	—	0	-1	-1	-0	-0.1
Total 2	0	2	.000	6	3	0	0	0	16	16	1	8	7	13.5	2.81	117	.254	.338	0	.000	-0	1	1	0	0.0

● **E. MORRIS**   Morris, E. b: Trenton, N.J.   Deb: 9/11/1884 ♦

YEAR TM/L	W	L	PCT	G	GS	CG	SH	SV	IP	H	HR	BB	SO	RAT	ERA	ERA+	OAV	OOB	BH	AVG	PB	PR	/A	PD	TPI
1884 Bal-U	0	0	—	1	1	0	0	0	1	2	0	2	0	36.0	9.00	30	.400	.571	0	.000	-1	-1	-1	-0	0.0

● **ED MORRIS**   Morris, Edward "Cannonball" b: 9/29/1862, Brooklyn, N.Y. d: 4/12/37, Pittsburgh, Pa. BR/TL, 5'7", 165 lbs. Deb: 5/1/1884

YEAR TM/L	W	L	PCT	G	GS	CG	SH	SV	IP	H	HR	BB	SO	RAT	ERA	ERA+	OAV	OOB	BH	AVG	PB	PR	/A	PD	TPI
1884 Col-a	34	13	**.723**	52	52	47	3	0	429²	335	3	51	302	8.4	2.18	139	.204	.234	37	.186	2	51	41	2	4.2
1885 Pit-a	39	24	.619	**63**	63	**63**	7	0	581	459	5	101	**298**	8.9	2.35	137	**.208**	**.247**	44	.186	-5	58	56	-1	4.5
1886 Pit-a	**41**	20	.672	64	63	63	**12**	1	555¹	455	5	118	326	9.4	2.45	138	.214	.258	38	.167	-7	62	58	-1	4.4
1887 Pit-N	14	22	.389	38	38	37	1	0	317²	375	13	71	91	12.9	4.31	90	.286	.326	25	.198	-4	-8	-15	-2	-1.8
1888 Pit-N	29	23	.558	**55**	55	**54**	5	0	480	470	7	74	135	10.4	2.31	116	.245	.276	19	.101	-11	29	19	1	0.7
1889 Pit-N	6	13	.316	21	21	18	0	0	170	196	4	48	40	13.2	4.13	91	.280	.332	7	.097	-5	-2	-7	-2	-1.2
1890 Pit-P	8	7	.533	18	15	15	1	0	144¹	178	5	35	25	13.5	4.86	80	.290	.332	9	.143	-4	-10	-15	-3	-1.6
Total 7	171	122	.584	311	307	297	29	1	2678	2468	42	498	1217	10.2	2.82	116	.235	.273	179	.161	-35	179	137	-5	9.2

● **JACK MORRIS**   Morris, John Scott b: 5/16/55, St.Paul, Minn. BR/TR, 6'3", 200 lbs. Deb: 7/26/77

YEAR TM/L	W	L	PCT	G	GS	CG	SH	SV	IP	H	HR	BB	SO	RAT	ERA	ERA+	OAV	OOB	BH	AVG	PB	PR	/A	PD	TPI
1977 Det-A	1	1	.500	7	6	1	0	0	45²	38	4	23	28	12.0	3.74	114	.235	.330	0	—	0	2	3	0	0.0
1978 Det-A	3	5	.375	28	7	0	0	0	106	107	8	49	48	13.5	4.33	89	.268	.352	0	—	0	-7	-5	-0	-0.5
1979 Det-A	17	7	.708	27	27	9	1	0	197²	179	19	59	113	11.0	3.28	132	.244	.304	0	—	0	21	23	-1	2.5
1980 Det-A	16	15	.516	36	36	11	2	0	250	252	20	87	112	12.3	4.18	98	.262	.326	0	—	0	-4	-2	3	0.1
1981 Det-A★	**14**	7	.667	25	25	15	1	0	198	153	14	78	97	10.6	3.05	124	.218	.298	0	—	0	13	16	-1	1.6
1982 Det-A	17	16	.515	37	37	17	3	0	266¹	247	37	96	135	11.6	4.06	100	.247	.312	0	—	0	1	0	-0	0.0
1983 Det-A	20	13	.606	37	37	20	1	0	**293¹**	257	30	83	**232**	10.5	3.34	117	.233	.289	0	—	0	24	19	-1	1.8
1984 *Det-A★	19	11	.633	35	35	9	1	0	240¹	221	20	87	148	11.6	3.60	109	.241	.308	0	—	0	11	9	2	1.2
1985 Det-A★	16	11	.593	35	35	13	4	0	257	212	21	110	191	11.5	3.33	122	.225	.309	0	—	0	23	21	-1	2.0
1986 Det-A	21	8	.724	35	35	15	**6**	0	267	229	40	82	223	10.5	3.27	126	.229	.287	0	—	0	27	25	0	2.6
1987 *Det-A★	18	11	.621	34	34	13	0	0	266	227	39	93	208	10.9	3.38	125	.228	.294	0	.000	0	32	25	-2	2.2
1988 Det-A	15	13	.536	34	34	10	2	0	235	225	20	83	168	11.9	3.94	97	.251	.318	0	—	0	1	-3	0	-2.0
1989 Det-A	6	14	.300	24	24	10	0	0	170¹	189	23	59	115	13.2	4.86	79	.283	.342	0	—	0	-19	-20	1	-2.0
1990 Det-A	15	18	.455	36	36	**11**	3	0	249²	231	26	97	162	12.0	4.51	88	.242	.316	0	—	0	-17	-15	-1	-1.9
1991 *Min-A★	18	12	.600	35	35	10	2	0	246²	226	18	92	163	11.8	3.43	124	.245	.317	0	—	0	18	23	-1	2.5
1992 *Tor-A	**21**	6	.778	34	34	6	1	0	240²	222	18	80	132	11.7	4.04	101	.246	.314	0	—	0	-3	1	-1	0.0
1993 Tor-A	7	12	.368	27	27	4	1	0	152²	189	18	65	103	15.2	6.19	70	.302	.371	0	—	0	-32	-32	-2	-3.5
1994 Cle-A	10	6	.625	23	23	1	0	0	141¹	163	14	67	100	14.9	5.60	84	.292	.371	0	—	0	-13	-14	0	-1.3
Total 18	254	186	.577	549	527	175	28	0	3824	3567	389	1390	2478	11.8	3.90	104	.247	.316	0	.000	0	78	74	-4	7.0

● **JOHN MORRIS**   Morris, John Wallace b: 8/23/41, Lewes, Del. BR/TL, 6'1", 198 lbs. Deb: 7/19/66

YEAR TM/L	W	L	PCT	G	GS	CG	SH	SV	IP	H	HR	BB	SO	RAT	ERA	ERA+	OAV	OOB	BH	AVG	PB	PR	/A	PD	TPI
1966 Phi-N	1	1	.500	13	0	0	0	0	13²	15	2	3	8	12.5	5.27	68	.278	.328	0	—	0	-3	-3	0	-0.3
1968 Bal-A	2	0	1.000	19	0	0	0	0	31²	19	4	17	22	11.4	2.56	114	.173	.305	0	.000	-1	1	1	0	0.0
1969 Sea-A	0	0	—	6	0	0	0	0	12²	16	2	8	8	17.1	6.39	57	.308	.400	1	1.000	1	-4	-4	1	0.2
1970 Mil-A	4	3	.571	20	9	1	0	0	73¹	70	4	22	40	11.5	3.93	96	.253	.312	3	.176	0	-2	-1	1	0.0
1971 Mil-A	2	2	.500	43	1	0	0	0	67²	69	4	27	42	12.9	3.72	93	.270	.342	1	.200	0	-2	-2	1	0.0
1972 SF-N	0	0	—	7	0	0	0	0	6¹	9	2	2	5	15.6	4.26	82	.310	.355	0	—	0	-1	-1	0	0.0
1973 SF-N	1	0	1.000	7	0	0	0	0	6¹	12	0	3	3	21.3	8.53	45	.429	.484	0	.000	-0	-3	-3	0	-0.5
1974 SF-N	1	1	.500	17	0	0	0	0	20²	17	1	4	9	9.1	3.05	125	.215	.253	1	1.000	1	1	2	-1	0.2
Total 8	11	7	.611	132	10	2	0	2	232¹	227	19	86	137	12.4	3.95	90	.256	.328	6	.194	0	-11	-10	3	-0.4

● **BUGS MORRIS**   Morris, Joseph Harley (a.k.a. Joseph Harley Bennett in 1918) b: 4/19/1892, Kansas City, Mo. d: 11/21/57, Noel, Mo. BR/TR, 5'9.5", 163 lbs. Deb: 7/20/18

YEAR TM/L	W	L	PCT	G	GS	CG	SH	SV	IP	H	HR	BB	SO	RAT	ERA	ERA+	OAV	OOB	BH	AVG	PB	PR	/A	PD	TPI
1918 StL-A	0	2	.000	4	2	0	0	0	10¹	12	1	7	0	16.5	3.48	79	.308	.413	1	.250	0	-1	-1	0	-0.1
1921 Chi-A	0	3	.000	3	2	1	0	0	17²	19	1	16	2	17.8	6.11	69	.297	.438	2	.333	0	-4	-4	1	-0.4
StL-A				3	1	0	0	0	5²	11	1	6	3	30.2	14.29	31	.407	.543	1	1.000	0	-6	-6	-0	-0.4
Yr	0	3	.000	6	3	1	0	0	23¹	30	2	22	5	20.8	8.10	53	.330	.470	3	.429	1	-10	-10	-0	-0.4
Total 2	0	5	.000	10	5	1	0	0	33²	42	3	29	5	19.5	6.68	57	.323	.453	4	.364	1	-11	-11	-0	-0.5

● **ED MORRIS**   Morris, Walter Edward "Big Ed" b: 12/7/1899, Foshee, Ala. d: 3/3/32, Century, Fla. BR/TR, 6'2", 185 lbs. Deb: 8/5/22

YEAR TM/L	W	L	PCT	G	GS	CG	SH	SV	IP	H	HR	BB	SO	RAT	ERA	ERA+	OAV	OOB	BH	AVG	PB	PR	/A	PD	TPI
1922 Chi-N	0	0	—	5	0	0	0	0	12	22	1	6	5	21.0	8.25	51	.386	.444	1	.250	-0	-6	-5	-0	0.0
1928 Bos-A	19	15	.559	47	29	20	0	5	257²	255	7	80	104	11.9	3.53	117	.264	.323	14	.154	-4	15	17	-2	1.5
1929 Bos-A	14	14	.500	33	26	17	2	1	208¹	227	7	95	73	14.0	4.45	96	.282	.360	16	.232	2	-5	-4	-2	-0.4
1930 Bos-A	4	9	.308	16	9	3	0	0	65¹	67	1	38	28	14.5	4.13	112	.260	.355	6	.316	2	4	3	-0	0.2
1931 Bos-A	5	7	.417	37	14	3	0	0	130²	131	4	74	46	14.5	4.75	91	.260	.361	6	.158	-2	-5	-6	-0	-0.6
Total 5	42	45	.483	140	78	43	2	6	674	702	20	293	256	13.4	4.19	101	.271	.348	43	.195	-1	3	4	-4	1.2

● **BILL MORRISETTE**   Morrisette, William Lee b: 1/17/1893, Baltimore, Md. d: 3/25/66, Virginia Beach, Va BR/TR, 6', 176 lbs. Deb: 9/19/15

YEAR TM/L	W	L	PCT	G	GS	CG	SH	SV	IP	H	HR	BB	SO	RAT	ERA	ERA+	OAV	OOB	BH	AVG	PB	PR	/A	PD	TPI
1915 Phi-A	2	0	1.000	4	1	1	0	0	20	15	0	5	11	9.0	1.35	217	.195	.244	2	.286	0	4	4	0	0.4
1916 Phi-A	0	0	—	1	0	0	0	0	4	6	0	5	2	24.8	6.75	42	.429	.579	0	—	0	-2	-2	1	-0.2
1920 Det-A	1	1	.500	8	3	1	0	0	27	25	0	19	15	15.7	4.33	86	.245	.379	0	.000	-1	-2	-2	0	-0.3
Total 3	3	1	.750	13	4	2	0	0	51	46	0	29	28	13.8	3.35	100	.238	.347	2	.125	-1	-0	-0	1	0.2

● **JIM MORRISON**   Morrison, James Forrest b: 9/23/52, Pensacola, Fla. BR/TR, 5'11", 182 lbs. Deb: 9/18/77 ♦

YEAR TM/L	W	L	PCT	G	GS	CG	SH	SV	IP	H	HR	BB	SO	RAT	ERA	ERA+	OAV	OOB	BH	AVG	PB	PR	/A	PD	TPI
1988 Atl-N	0	0	—	3	0	0	0	0	3	3	0	2	1	12.3	0.00	—	.214	.313	14	.152	0	1	1	0	0.0

● **JOHNNY MORRISON**   Morrison, John Dewey "Jughandle Johnny" b: 10/22/1895, Pellville, Ky. d: 3/20/66, Louisville, Ky. BR/TR, 5'11", 188 lbs. Deb: 9/28/20 F

YEAR TM/L	W	L	PCT	G	GS	CG	SH	SV	IP	H	HR	BB	SO	RAT	ERA	ERA+	OAV	OOB	BH	AVG	PB	PR	/A	PD	TPI
1920 Pit-N	1	0	1.000	2	1	1	0	0	7	4	0	1	3	6.4	0.00	—	.167	.200	0	.000	0	2	3	0	0.3
1921 Pit-N	9	7	.563	21	17	11	**3**	0	144	133	3	33	52	10.3	2.88	133	.258	.305	5	.119	-1	15	15	-0	1.4
1922 Pit-N	17	11	.607	45	33	20	**5**	1	286¹	315	10	87	104	12.8	3.43	119	.286	.341	20	.198	-2	21	21	0	1.5
1923 Pit-N	25	13	.658	42	37	27	2	2	301²	287	6	110	114	12.0	3.49	115	.253	.321	21	.183	-3	17	17	-0	1.6
1924 Pit-N	11	16	.407	**41**	25	10	0	2	237²	213	7	73	85	11.0	3.75	102	.245	.307	13	.169	-2	9	14	-2	-0.2
1925 *Pit-N	17	14	.548	**44**	26	10	0	**4**	211	245	12	60	60	13.3	3.88	115	.291	.343	13	.178	-3	9	14	2	1.3
1926 Pit-N	6	8	.429	26	13	6	2	2	122¹	119	2	44	39	12.1	3.38	116	.267	.335	3	.077	-4	6	7	-2	0.2
1927 Pit-N	3	2	.600	21	0	1	0	3	53²	63	2	21	21	14.1	4.19	98	.304	.368	2	.154	-0	-1	-2	-0	-0.2
1929 Bro-N	13	7	.650	39	10	4	0	**8**	136²	150	11	61	57	14.1	4.48	103	.279	.355	7	.163	-2	4	2	-3	-0.2
1930 Bro-N	1	2	.333	16	0	0	0	0	34²	47	4	16	11	16.4	5.45	90	.346	.414	0	.000	0	-2	-2	0	-0.2
Total 10	103	80	.563	297	164	90	13	23	1535	1574	57	506	546	12.4	3.85	113	.271	.332	84	.164	-18	74	79	-12	5.5

● **MIKE MORRISON**   Morrison, Michael b: 2/6/1867, Erie, Pa. d: 6/16/55, Erie, Pa. BR/TR, 5'8.5", 156 lbs. Deb: 4/19/1887

YEAR TM/L	W	L	PCT	G	GS	CG	SH	SV	IP	H	HR	BB	SO	RAT	ERA	ERA+	OAV	OOB	BH	AVG	PB	PR	/A	PD	TPI
1887 Cle-a	12	25	.324	40	40	35	0	0	316²	385	13	205	158	17.4	4.92	88	.294	.398	27	.191	-4	-22	-20	10	-1.2
1888 Cle-a	1	3	.250	4	4	4	0	0	35	40	1	19	14	15.4	5.40	57	.278	.366	4	.235	0	-9	-9	0	-0.8
1890 Syr-a	6	9	.400	17	14	13	1	0	127	131	4	81	69	15.9	5.88	60	.258	.374	29	.242	3	-28	-33	2	-2.5
Bal-a	1	2	.333	4	4	3	0	0	26	16	0	20	13	12.8	3.81	107	.163	.325	1	.111	-1	0	1	0	0.1
Yr	7	11	.389	21	18	16	1	0	153	146	4	101	82	14.6	5.53	66	.239	.348	30	.233	3	-28	-32	3	-2.4
Total 3	20	39	.339	65	62	55	1	0	504²	571	18	325	254	16.7	5.14	78	.278	.387	61	.213	-4	-59	-62	12	-4.4

● **PHIL MORRISON**   Morrison, Philip Melvin b: 10/18/1894, Rockport, Ind. d: 1/18/55, Lexington, Ky. BB/TR, 6'2", 190 lbs. Deb: 9/30/21 F

YEAR TM/L	W	L	PCT	G	GS	CG	SH	SV	IP	H	HR	BB	SO	RAT	ERA	ERA+	OAV	OOB	BH	AVG	PB	PR	/A	PD	TPI
1921 Pit-N	0	0	—	1	0	0	0	0	1	1	0	1	0	13.5	—	—	.333	.333	0	—	0	-0	0	0	0.0

● **HANK MORRISON**   Morrison, Stephen Henry b: 5/22/1866, Olneyville, R.I. d: 9/30/27, Attleboro, Mass. BR/TR, 5'10", 180 lbs. Deb: 5/28/1887

YEAR TM/L	W	L	PCT	G	GS	CG	SH	SV	IP	H	HR	BB	SO	RAT	ERA	ERA+	OAV	OOB	BH	AVG	PB	PR	/A	PD	TPI
1887 Ind-N	3	4	.429	7	7	5	0	0	57	79	2	27	13	16.9	7.58	55	.307	.375	3	.115	-2	-22	-22	-1	-2.0

YEAR TM/L	W	L	PCT	G	GS	CG	SH	SV	IP	H	HR	BB	SO	RAT	ERA	ERA+	OAV	OOB	BH	AVG	PB	PR	/A	PD	TPI
● **GUY MORRISON**				Morrison, Walter Guy b: 8/29/1895, Hinton, W.Va. d: 8/14/34, Grand Rapids, Mich BR/TR, 5'11", 185 lbs. Deb: 8/31/27																					
1927 Bos-N	1	2	.333	11	3	1	0	0	34¹	40	1	15	6	14.4	4.46	83	.296	.367	1	.125	1	-2	-3	1	0.0
1928 Bos-N	0	0	—	1	0	0	0	0	3	4	1	3	0	21.0	12.00	33	.308	.438	0	—	0	-3	-3	0	0.0
Total 2	1	2	.333	12	3	1	0	0	37¹	44	2	18	6	14.9	5.06	74	.297	.373	1	.125	1	-5	-6	1	0.0
● **FRANK MORRISSEY**				Morrissey, Michael Joseph "Deacon" b: 5/5/1876, Baltimore, Md. d: 2/22/39, Baltimore, Md. TR , 5'4", 140 lbs. Deb: 7/13/01																					
1901 Bos-A	0	0	—	1	0	0	0	0	4¹	5	0	2	1	18.7	2.08	170	.278	.409	0	.000	-1	1	1	0	0.0
1902 Chi-N	1	3	.250	5	5	5	0	0	40	40	0	8	13	11.2	2.25	120	.260	.305	2	.091	-1	2	2	0	0.1
Total 2	1	3	.250	6	5	5	0	0	44¹	45	0	10	14	12.0	2.23	125	.262	.317	2	.080	-1	3	3	1	0.1
● **CARL MORTON**				Morton, Carl Wendle b: 1/18/44, Kansas City, Mo. d: 4/12/83, Tulsa, Okla. BR/TR, 6', 200 lbs. Deb: 4/11/69																					
1969 Mon-N	0	3	.000	8	5	0	0	0	29¹	29	2	18	16	15.0	4.60	80	.264	.377	0	.000	-0	-3	-3	1	-0.3
1970 Mon-N	18	11	.621	43	37	10	4	0	284²	281	27	125	154	13.0	3.60	114	.262	.341	15	.161	2	14	16	1	1.8
1971 Mon-N	10	18	.357	36	35	9	0	1	213²	252	26	83	84	14.3	4.80	73	.295	.360	14	.182	2	-32	-30	2	-3.2
1972 Mon-N	7	13	.350	27	27	3	1	0	172	170	16	53	51	11.8	3.92	90	.258	.316	7	.135	1	-9	-7	1	-0.6
1973 Atl-N	15	10	.600	38	37	10	4	0	256¹	254	18	70	112	11.5	3.41	115	.259	.311	17	.181	4	7	15	0	1.8
1974 Atl-N	16	12	.571	38	38	7	1	0	274²	293	10	89	113	12.6	3.15	120	.277	.334	10	.112	-4	14	19	-1	1.4
1975 Atl-N	17	16	.515	39	39	11	2	0	277²	302	19	82	78	12.5	3.50	108	.278	.330	15	.160	-1	4	8	0	0.9
1976 Atl-N	4	9	.308	26	24	1	1	0	140¹	172	6	45	42	14.2	4.17	91	.306	.362	8	.178	-0	-10	-6	2	-0.3
Total 8	87	92	.486	255	242	51	13	1	1648²	1753	120	565	650	12.8	3.73	102	.275	.336	86	.157	3	-15	13	6	1.5
● **CHARLIE MORTON**				Morton, Charles Hazen b: 10/12/1854, Kingsville, Ohio d: 12/9/21, Massillon, Ohio BR/TR, 150 lbs. Deb: 5/2/1882 MU♦																					
1884 Tol-a	0	1	.000	3	1	1	0	0	23¹	18	0	5	7	9.3	3.09	111	.209	.261	18	.162	-0	0	1	-1	-0.1
● **GUY MORTON**				Morton, Guy Sr. "The Alabama Blossom" b: 6/1/1893, Vernon, Ala. d: 10/18/34, Sheffield, Ala. BR/TR, 6'1", 175 lbs. Deb: 6/20/14 F																					
1914 Cle-A	1	13	.071	25	13	6	1	0	128	116	1	55	80	12.2	3.02	95	.257	.341	1	.029	-4	-4	-2	-1	-0.8
1915 Cle-A	16	15	.516	34	27	15	6	1	240	189	5	60	134	9.4	2.14	143	.216	.268	12	.146	-4	21	24	-0	2.6
1916 Cle-A	12	8	.600	27	18	9	0	0	149²	139	1	42	88	11.1	2.89	104	.246	.302	12	.211	-1	-1	2	-1	0.1
1917 Cle-A	10	10	.500	35	18	6	1	2	161	158	3	59	62	12.2	2.74	103	.266	.335	4	.085	-4	-1	2	-2	-0.5
1918 Cle-A	14	8	.636	30	28	13	1	0	214²	189	1	77	123	11.3	2.64	114	.240	.310	12	.156	-1	3	9	-1	0.6
1919 Cle-A	9	9	.500	26	20	9	3	0	147¹	128	3	47	64	10.7	2.81	119	.233	.293	9	.161	-2	7	9	-1	0.7
1920 Cle-A	8	6	.571	29	17	6	1	1	137	140	2	57	72	13.0	4.47	85	.270	.344	10	.217	-1	-10	-10	-2	-1.3
1921 Cle-A	8	3	.727	30	7	3	0	0	107²	98	1	45	45	11.0	2.76	155	.244	.303	6	.171	-2	18	18	-2	1.2
1922 Cle-A	14	9	.609	38	23	13	3	0	202²	218	7	85	102	13.6	4.00	100	.277	.351	13	.191	-2	1	0	3	0.2
1923 Cle-A	6	6	.500	33	14	3	2	1	129¹	133	3	56	54	13.3	4.24	93	.276	.354	7	.159	-2	-4	-4	-1	-0.6
1924 Cle-A	0	1	.000	12	1	0	0	0	12¹	12	0	13	6	18.2	6.57	65	.250	.410	0	.000	-0	-3	-3	-0	-0.3
Total 11	98	88	.527	317	185	82	19	6	1629²	1520	27	583	830	11.7	3.13	108	.251	.319	86	.157	-24	27	48	-7	1.9
● **KEVIN MORTON**				Morton, Kevin Joseph b: 8/3/68, Norwalk, Conn. BR/TL, 6'2", 185 lbs. Deb: 7/5/91																					
1991 Bos-A	6	5	.545	16	15	1	0	0	86¹	93	9	40	45	14.0	4.59	94	.284	.363	0	—	0	-5	-3	1	-0.2
● **SPARROW MORTON**				Morton, William P. TL , Deb: 7/15/1884																					
1884 Phi-N	0	2	.000	2	2	2	0	0	17	16	0	11	5	14.3	5.29	56	.222	.325	3	.375	1	-4	-4	-0	-0.3
● **EARL MOSELEY**				Moseley, Earl Victor "Vic" b: 9/7/1884, Middleburg, Ohio d: 7/1/63, Alliance, Ohio BR/TR, 5'9.5", 168 lbs. Deb: 6/17/13																					
1913 Bos-A	8	5	.615	24	15	7	3	0	120²	105	1	49	62	11.5	3.13	94	.245	.322	3	.081	-2	-3	-3	1	-0.4
1914 Ind-F	19	18	.514	43	38	29	4	1	316²	303	5	123	205	12.2	3.47	90	.258	.330	12	.110	-8	-20	-12	-0	-2.2
1915 New-F	15	15	.500	38	32	22	5	1	268	222	4	99	142	10.8	1.91	134	.229	.302	13	.148	-4	24	19	-4	1.3
1916 Cin-N	7	10	.412	31	15	7	0	1	150¹	145	3	69	60	12.8	3.89	67	.257	.338	4	.087	-2	-21	-22	-2	-2.8
Total 4	49	48	.505	136	100	65	12	3	855²	775	13	340	469	11.8	3.01	94	.247	.322	32	.114	-17	-20	-18	-5	-4.1
● **WALTER MOSER**				Moser, Walter Fredrick b: 2/27/1881, Concord, N.C. d: 12/10/46, Philadelphia, Pa. BR/TR, 5'9", 170 lbs. Deb: 9/3/06																					
1906 Phi-N	0	4	.000	6	4	4	0	0	42²	49	0	15	17	13.7	3.59	73	.295	.357	0	.000	-2	-5	-5	-1	-0.7
1911 Bos-A	0	1	.000	6	3	1	0	0	24²	37	0	11	11	17.9	4.01	82	.366	.434	0	.000	-1	-2	-2	0	-0.2
StL-A	0	2	.000	2	2	0	0	0	3¹	11	0	4	2	40.5	21.60	16	.478	.556	1	1.000	0	-7	-7	0	-2.1
Yr	0	3	.000	8	5	1	0	0	28	48	0	15	13	20.3	6.11	54	.384	.450	1	.125	-1	-9	-9	0	-2.3
Total 2	0	7	.000	14	9	5	0	0	70²	97	0	30	30	16.4	4.58	63	.334	.401	1	.045	-3	-13	-13	-1	-3.0
● **JOHN MOSES**				Moses, John William b: 8/9/57, Los Angeles, Cal. BB/TL, 5'10", 170 lbs. Deb: 8/23/82 ♦																					
1989 Min-A	0	0	—	1	0	0	0	0	1	0	0	1	0	9.0	0.00	—	.000	.333	68	.281	0	0	0	0	0.0
1990 Min-A	0	0	—	2	0	0	0	0	2	5	0	2	3	31.5	13.50	31	.455	.538	38	.221	1	-2	-2	-0	0.0
Total 2	0	0	—	3	0	0	0	0	3	5	0	3	3	24.0	9.00	46	.385	.500	438	.254	1	-2	-2	-0	0.0
● **PAUL MOSKAU**				Moskau, Paul Richard b: 12/20/53, St.Joseph, Mo. BR/TR, 6'2", 210 lbs. Deb: 6/21/77																					
1977 Cin-N	6	6	.500	20	19	2	2	0	108	116	10	40	71	13.1	4.00	98	.278	.342	7	.184	2	-1	-1	1	0.1
1978 Cin-N	6	4	.600	26	25	2	1	1	145	139	17	57	88	12.4	3.97	89	.255	.329	10	.204	4	-6	-7	-2	-0.3
1979 Cin-N	5	4	.556	21	15	1	0	0	106¹	107	9	51	58	13.4	3.89	96	.263	.345	3	.081	-2	-2	-2	1	-0.3
1980 Cin-N	9	7	.563	33	19	1	0	2	152²	147	13	41	94	11.1	4.01	89	.257	.308	7	.159	-0	-7	-7	0	-0.8
1981 Cin-N	2	1	.667	27	1	0	0	0	54²	54	4	32	32	14.3	4.94	72	.258	.360	0	.000	-0	-9	-8	1	-0.5
1982 Pit-N	1	3	.250	13	5	0	0	0	35	43	7	8	15	13.1	4.37	85	.303	.340	1	.091	-1	-3	-3	-0	-0.4
1983 Chi-N	3	2	.600	8	8	0	0	0	32	44	7	14	16	16.3	6.75	56	.331	.395	2	.182	-0	-11	-11	-0	-1.4
Total 7	32	27	.542	148	92	7	4	5	633²	650	67	243	374	12.8	4.22	87	.268	.336	30	.153	2	-39	-39	-0	-3.6
● **JIM MOSOLF**				Mosolf, James Frederick b: 8/21/05, Puyallup, Wash. d: 12/28/79, Dallas, Ore. BL/TR, 5'10", 186 lbs. Deb: 9/9/29 ♦																					
1930 Pit-N	0	0	—	1	0	0	0	0	0¹	1	0	0	0	27.0	27.00	18	.500	.500	17	.333	0	-1	-1	0	0.0
● **MAL MOSS**				Moss, Charles Malcolm b: 4/18/05, Sullivan, Ind. d: 2/5/83, Savannah, Ga. BR/TL, 6', 175 lbs. Deb: 4/29/30																					
1930 Chi-N	0	0	—	12	1	0	0	0	18²	18	0	14	4	15.4	6.27	78	.254	.376	3	.273	0	-3	-3	0	-0.4
● **RAY MOSS**				Moss, Raymond Earl b: 12/5/01, Chattanooga, Tenn. BR/TR, 6'1", 185 lbs. Deb: 4/17/26																					
1926 Bro-N	0	0	—	1	0	0	0	0	1	3	0	0	0	27.0	9.00	42	.600	.600	0	.000	-0	-1	-1	-0	0.0
1927 Bro-N	1	0	1.000	1	1	0	0	0	8¹	11	0	1	1	13.0	3.24	122	.333	.353	1	.333	1	1	1	-0	0.1
1928 Bro-N	0	3	.000	22	5	1	1	1	60¹	62	5	35	5	14.5	4.92	81	.279	.377	8	.320	2	-6	-6	-0	-0.1
1929 Bro-N	11	6	.647	39	20	7	2	0	182	214	9	81	59	14.9	5.04	92	.296	.373	5	.076	-5	-9	-2	-3	-1.3
1930 Bro-N	9	6	.600	36	11	5	0	1	118¹	127	11	55	30	14.1	5.10	96	.275	.352	6	.154	-2	-7	-2	-2	-0.6
1931 Bro-N	0	0	—	1	0	0	0	0	1	1	0	1	0	18.0	0.00	—	.333	.500	0	0	0	0	0	0	0.0
Bos-N	1	3	.250	12	5	0	0	0	45	56	2	16	14	14.4	4.60	82	.306	.362	2	.133	-1	-4	-4	-0	-0.4
Yr	1	3	.250	13	5	0	0	0	46	57	2	17	14	14.5	4.50	84	.306	.365	2	.133	-1	-3	-4	0	-0.4
Total 6	22	18	.550	112	42	13	4	3	416	474	29	189	109	14.6	4.95	91	.289	.367	22	.148	-5	-18	-21	-4	-2.3
● **DON MOSSI**				Mossi, Donald Louis "The Sphinx" b: 1/11/29, St.Helena, Cal. BL/TL, 6'1", 195 lbs. Deb: 4/17/54																					
1954 *Cle-A	6	1	.857	40	5	2	0	7	93	56	5	39	55	9.3	1.94	190	.176	.268	3	.158	0	**18**	**18**	-1	1.5
1955 Cle-A	4	3	.571	57	1	0	0	9	81²	81	4	18	69	11.0	2.42	164	.253	.295	1	.111	0	14	14	2	1.7
1956 Cle-A	3	5	.545	48	3	0	0	11	87²	79	6	33	59	11.6	3.59	117	.240	.311	3	.150	0	6	6	0	0.8
1957 Cle-A★	11	10	.524	36	22	6	1	2	159	165	16	57	97	12.7	4.13	90	.265	.329	12	.218	2	-6	-7	-1	-0.8
1958 Cle-A	7	8	.467	43	5	0	0	2	101²	106	9	30	55	12.4	3.90	94	.269	.327	4	.115	-2	-1	-3	0	-0.5
1959 Det-A	17	9	.654	34	30	15	3	0	228	210	20	49	125	10.3	3.36	121	.243	.286	13	.169	0	13	18	0	2.0
1960 Det-A	8	8	.529	23	22	9	2	0	158¹	158	17	32	69	10.9	3.47	114	.258	.296	5	.192	1	0	2	0	0.8
1961 Det-A	15	7	.682	35	34	12	1	0	240¹	237	29	47	137	10.6	2.96	139	.258	.294	13	.165	1	28	**30**	0	2.7
1962 Det-A	11	13	.458	35	27	8	1	1	180¹	195	24	36	121	11.6	4.19	97	.270	.305	9	.164	-2	-4	-2	-2	-0.3
1963 Det-A	7	7	.500	24	16	3	0	0	122²	110	20	17	68	9.6	3.74	100	.236	.269	8	.205	2	-2	-0	0	0.2
1964 Chi-A	3	1	.750	34	0	0	0	7	40	37	9	7	36	10.1	2.93	118	.240	.278	1	.167	-0	3	2	-0	0.3

YEAR TM/L	W	L	PCT	G	GS	CG	SH	SV	IP	H	HR	BB	SO	RAT	ERA	ERA+	OAV	OOB	BH	AVG	PB	PR	/A	PD	TPI
1965 KC-A	5	8	.385	51	0	0	0	7	55¹	59	0	20	41	12.8	3.74	93	.278	.341	0	.000	-1	-2	-2	-0	-0.5
Total 12	101	80	.558	460	165	55	8	50	1548	1493	156	385	932	11.0	3.43	114	.252	.299	71	.163	4	74	83	-2	7.9

● EARL MOSSOR
Mossor, Earl Dalton b: 7/21/25, Forbus, Tenn. d: 12/29/88, Batavia, Ohio BL/TR, 6'1", 175 lbs. Deb: 4/30/51

YEAR TM/L	W	L	PCT	G	GS	CG	SH	SV	IP	H	HR	BB	SO	RAT	ERA	ERA+	OAV	OOB	BH	AVG	PB	PR	/A	PD	TPI
1951 Bro-N	0	0	—	3	0	0	0	0	1²	2	1	7	1	48.6	32.40	12	.333	.692	1	1.000	0	-5	-5	-0	0.0

● GLEN MOULDER
Moulder, Glen Hubert b: 9/28/17, Cleveland, Okla. d: 11/27/94, Decatur, Ga. BR/TR, 6', 180 lbs. Deb: 4/28/46

YEAR TM/L	W	L	PCT	G	GS	CG	SH	SV	IP	H	HR	BB	SO	RAT	ERA	ERA+	OAV	OOB	BH	AVG	PB	PR	/A	PD	TPI
1946 Bro-N	0	0	—	1	0	0	0	0	2	1	1	1	1	13.5	4.50	75	.286	.375	0	—	0	-0	-0	-0	0.0
1947 StL-A	4	2	.667	32	2	0	0	2	73	78	4	43	23	14.9	3.82	101	.283	.379	4	.235	-0	-1	0	1	0.1
1948 Chi-A	3	6	.333	33	9	0	0	2	85²	108	8	54	26	17.1	6.41	66	.316	.411	6	.300	1	-20	-20	-0	-1.8
Total 3	7	8	.467	66	11	0	0	4	160²	188	13	98	50	16.1	5.21	78	.301	.396	10	.270	1	-21	-20	1	-1.7

● FRANK MOUNTAIN
Mountain, Frank Henry b: 5/17/1860, Ft.Edward, N.Y. d: 11/19/39, Schenectady, N.Y. BR/TR, 5'11", 185 lbs. Deb: 7/19/1880 ♦

YEAR TM/L	W	L	PCT	G	GS	CG	SH	SV	IP	H	HR	BB	SO	RAT	ERA	ERA+	OAV	OOB	BH	AVG	PB	PR	/A	PD	TPI
1880 Tro-N	1	1	.500	2	2	2	0	0	17	23	0	6	2	15.4	5.29	48	.307	.358	2	.222	-0	-6	-5	0	-0.5
1881 Det-N	3	4	.429	7	7	7	0	0	60	80	2	18	13	14.7	5.25	56	.292	.336	4	.160	-0	-17	-15	-1	-1.5
1882 Wor-N	0	5	.000	5	5	5	0	0	42	47	0	11	5	12.4	3.00	104	.255	.297	1	.063	-2	-0	1	-1	-0.2
Phi-a	2	6	.250	8	8	8	0	0	69	72	1	11	15	10.8	3.91	76	.251	.279	12	.333	2	-9	-7	1	-0.3
Wor-N	2	11	.154	13	13	11	0	0	102	138	4	24	24	14.3	3.97	78	.299	.334	12	.271	-2	-12	-10	-1	-0.9
1883 Col-a	26	33	.441	59	59	57	4	0	503	546	8	123	159	12.0	3.60	86	.259	.300	60	.217	7	-16	-29	1	-1.9
1884 Col-a	23	17	.575	42	41	40	5	1	360²	289	7	78	156	9.4	2.45	124	.209	.257	50	.238	9	32	23	4	3.5
1885 Pit-a	1	4	.200	5	5	5	0	0	46	56	1	24	7	16.0	4.30	75	.320	.408	2	.100	-1	-5	-6	0	-0.5
1886 Pit-a	0	2	.000	2	2	2	0	0	16	22	0	14	2	23.1	7.88	43	.319	.466	1	.145	-0	-8	-8	-0	-0.7
Total 7	58	83	.411	143	142	137	9	1	1215²	1273	23	309	383	11.8	3.47	88	.254	.299	158	.220	16	-41	-54	4	-3.0

● BILL MOUNTJOY
Mountjoy, William Henry "Medicine Bill" b: 12/11/1858, London, Ontario, Canada d: 5/19/1894, London, Ont. Can. BL/TR, 5'6", 150 lbs. Deb: 9/29/1883

YEAR TM/L	W	L	PCT	G	GS	CG	SH	SV	IP	H	HR	BB	SO	RAT	ERA	ERA+	OAV	OOB	BH	AVG	PB	PR	/A	PD	TPI
1883 Cin-a	0	1	.000	1	1	1	0	0	8	9	0	2	3	12.4	2.25	144	.265	.306	0	.000	-1	1	1	-0	0.0
1884 Cin-a	19	12	.613	33	33	32	3	0	289	274	5	43	96	10.4	2.93	114	.238	.275	18	.151	-3	10	13	-0	0.8
1885 Cin-a	10	7	.588	17	17	17	1	0	153²	149	5	52	50	12.2	3.16	103	.247	.314	10	.167	0	1	1	-0	0.1
Bal-a	2	4	.333	6	6	6	1	0	53	72	1	13	15	15.1	5.43	60	.316	.363	1	.056	-0	-13	-13	1	-1.0
Yr	12	11	.522	23	23	23	2	0	206²	221	6	65	65	12.6	3.75	87	.264	.320	11	.141	0	-11	-11	-0	-0.9
Total 3	31	24	.564	57	57	56	5	0	503²	504	11	110	164	11.5	3.25	102	.250	.297	29	.145	-4	0	3	-1	-0.1

● ED MOYER
Moyer, Charles Edward b: 8/15/1885, Andover, Ohio d: 11/18/62, Jacksonville, Fla. Deb: 7/20/10

YEAR TM/L	W	L	PCT	G	GS	CG	SH	SV	IP	H	HR	BB	SO	RAT	ERA	ERA+	OAV	OOB	BH	AVG	PB	PR	/A	PD	TPI
1910 Was-A	0	3	.000	6	2	2	0	0	33⅓	21	1	13	3	13.7	3.24	77	.253	.369	1	.125	-1	-2	-1	1	-0.2

● JAMIE MOYER
Moyer, Jamie b: 11/18/62, Sellersville, Pa. BL/TL, 6', 170 lbs. Deb: 6/16/86

YEAR TM/L	W	L	PCT	G	GS	CG	SH	SV	IP	H	HR	BB	SO	RAT	ERA	ERA+	OAV	OOB	BH	AVG	PB	PR	/A	PD	TPI
1986 Chi-N	7	4	.636	16	16	1	0	0	87¹	107	10	42	45	15.7	5.05	80	.311	.391	2	.091	-0	-13	-10	1	-1.0
1987 Chi-N	12	15	.444	35	33	1	0	0	201	210	28	97	147	14.0	5.10	84	.271	.355	14	.230	3	-23	-19	2	-1.7
1988 Chi-N	9	15	.375	34	30	3	1	0	202	212	20	55	121	12.1	3.48	104	.272	.324	5	.083	-2	-1	3	3	0.4
1989 Tex-A	4	9	.308	15	15	1	0	0	76	84	10	33	44	14.1	4.86	82	.283	.358	0	—	0	-8	-8	1	-1.1
1990 Tex-A	2	6	.250	33	10	1	0	0	102¹	115	6	39	58	13.9	4.66	84	.290	.360	0	—	0	-9	-8	0	-0.6
1991 StL-N	0	5	.000	8	7	0	0	0	31¹	38	5	16	20	15.8	5.74	65	.319	.404	0	.000	-1	-7	-7	-0	-1.0
1993 Bal-A	12	9	.571	25	25	3	1	0	152	154	11	38	90	11.7	3.43	130	.265	.316	0	—	0	15	18	1	2.0
1994 Bal-A	5	7	.417	23	23	0	0	0	149	158	23	38	87	12.0	4.77	105	.271	.317	0	—	0	4	4	-0	-0.1
1995 Bal-A	8	6	.571	27	18	0	0	0	115²	117	18	30	65	11.7	5.21	91	.265	.316	0	—	0	-6	-6	1	-0.5
1996 Bos-A	7	1	.875	23	10	0	0	0	90	111	14	27	50	13.9	4.50	114	.300	.349	0	—	0	5	6	0	0.4
Sea-A	6	2	.750	11	11	0	0	0	70²	66	9	19	29	11.0	3.31	149	.243	.295	0	—	0	13	13	-1	1.2
Yr	13	3	.813	34	21	0	0	0	160²	177	23	46	79	12.5	3.98	127	.274	.323	0	—	0	18	19	-0	1.6
Total 10	72	79	.477	250	198	10	3	0	1277¹	1372	154	434	756	13.0	4.44	98	.277	.339	21	.139	1	-33	-13	9	-2.0

● RON MROZINSKI
Mrozinski, Ronald Frank b: 9/16/30, White Haven, Pa. BR/TL, 5'11", 160 lbs. Deb: 6/20/54

YEAR TM/L	W	L	PCT	G	GS	CG	SH	SV	IP	H	HR	BB	SO	RAT	ERA	ERA+	OAV	OOB	BH	AVG	PB	PR	/A	PD	TPI
1954 Phi-N	1	1	.500	15	4	1	0	0	48	49	10	25	26	13.9	4.50	90	.261	.347	1	.083	-1	-2	-2	-1	-0.3
1955 Phi-N	0	2	.000	22	1	0	0	1	34¹	38	2	19	18	16.0	6.55	61	.299	.407	0	.000	-1	-10	-10	-0	-0.6
Total 2	1	3	.250	37	5	1	0	1	82¹	87	12	44	44	14.8	5.36	75	.276	.372	1	.063	-2	-12	-12	-1	-0.9

● PHIL MUDROCK
Mudrock, Philip Ray b: 6/12/37, Louisville, Colo. BR/TR, 6'1", 190 lbs. Deb: 4/19/63

YEAR TM/L	W	L	PCT	G	GS	CG	SH	SV	IP	H	HR	BB	SO	RAT	ERA	ERA+	OAV	OOB	BH	AVG	PB	PR	/A	PD	TPI
1963 Chi-N	0	0	—	1	0	0	0	0	1	2	0	0	0	18.0	9.00	39	.400	.400	0	—	0	-1	-1	-0	0.0

● GORDIE MUELLER
Mueller, Joseph Gordon b: 12/10/22, Baltimore, Md. BR/TR, 6'4", 200 lbs. Deb: 4/19/50

YEAR TM/L	W	L	PCT	G	GS	CG	SH	SV	IP	H	HR	BB	SO	RAT	ERA	ERA+	OAV	OOB	BH	AVG	PB	PR	/A	PD	TPI
1950 Bos-A	0	0	—	8	0	0	0	0	7	11	1	13	1	30.9	10.29	48	.344	.533	0	.000	-0	-4	-4	-0	0.0

● LES MUELLER
Mueller, Leslie Clyde b: 3/4/19, Belleville, Ill. BR/TR, 6'3", 190 lbs. Deb: 8/15/41

YEAR TM/L	W	L	PCT	G	GS	CG	SH	SV	IP	H	HR	BB	SO	RAT	ERA	ERA+	OAV	OOB	BH	AVG	PB	PR	/A	PD	TPI
1941 Det-A	0	0	—	4	0	0	0	0	13	9	1	10	8	13.2	4.85	94	.205	.352	0	.000	-0	-1	-0	0	0.0
1945 *Det-A	6	8	.429	26	18	6	2	1	134²	117	9	58	42	11.8	3.68	96	.234	.316	8	.182	-0	-5	-2	-2	-0.4
Total 2	6	8	.429	30	18	6	2	1	147²	126	9	68	50	11.9	3.78	95	.231	.319	8	.170	-0	-6	-3	-2	-0.4

● WILLIE MUELLER
Mueller, Willard Lawrence b: 8/30/56, West Bend, Wis. BR/TR, 6'4", 220 lbs. Deb: 8/12/78

YEAR TM/L	W	L	PCT	G	GS	CG	SH	SV	IP	H	HR	BB	SO	RAT	ERA	ERA+	OAV	OOB	BH	AVG	PB	PR	/A	PD	TPI
1978 Mil-A	1	0	1.000	5	0	0	0	0	12²	16	1	6	6	15.6	6.39	59	.291	.361	0	—	0	-4	-4	0	-0.3
1981 Mil-A	0	0	—	1	0	0	0	0	2	4	0	1	1	18.0	4.50	76	.400	.400	0	—	0	-0	-0	-0	0.1
Total 2	1	0	1.000	6	0	0	0	0	14²	20	1	7	7	16.0	6.14	60	.308	.366	0	—	0	-4	-4	-0	-0.2

● BILLY MUFFETT
Muffett, Billy Arnold "Muff" b: 9/21/30, Hammond, Ind. BR/TR, 6'1", 198 lbs. Deb: 8/3/57 C

YEAR TM/L	W	L	PCT	G	GS	CG	SH	SV	IP	H	HR	BB	SO	RAT	ERA	ERA+	OAV	OOB	BH	AVG	PB	PR	/A	PD	TPI
1957 StL-N	3	2	.600	23	0	0	0	8	44	35	1	13	21	9.8	2.25	176	.222	.281	0	.000	-1	8	8	-1	1.1
1958 StL-N	4	6	.400	35	6	1	0	5	84	107	11	42	41	16.5	4.93	84	.316	.399	4	.200	-1	-9	-7	-1	-0.9
1959 SF-N	0	0	—	5	0	0	0	0	6²	11	2	3	3	18.9	5.40	71	.407	.467	0	—	0	-1	-1	-0	0.0
1960 Bos-A	6	4	.600	23	14	4	1	0	125	116	9	36	75	11.3	3.24	125	.242	.301	11	.268	2	9	11	0	1.1
1961 Bos-A	3	11	.214	38	11	2	0	2	112²	130	18	36	47	13.4	5.67	73	.291	.346	5	.217	2	-21	-19	0	-2.0
1962 Bos-A	0	0	—	1	1	0	0	0	4	8	2	2	1	22.5	9.00	46	.471	.526	0	.000	-0	-2	-2	-0	-0.1
Total 6	16	23	.410	125	32	7	1	15	376¹	407	38	132	188	13.2	4.33	94	.277	.342	20	.217	3	-16	-10	-2	-0.7

● JOE MUICH
Muich, Ignatius Andrew b: 11/23/03, St.Louis, Mo. d: 7/2/93, St.Louis, Mo. BR/TR, 6'2", 175 lbs. Deb: 9/4/24

YEAR TM/L	W	L	PCT	G	GS	CG	SH	SV	IP	H	HR	BB	SO	RAT	ERA	ERA+	OAV	OOB	BH	AVG	PB	PR	/A	PD	TPI
1924 Bos-N	0	0	—	3	0	0	0	0	9	19	1	5	2	24.0	11.00	35	.432	.490	0	.000	-1	-7	-7	-0	-0.1

● JOE MUIR
Muir, Joseph Allen b: 11/26/22, Oriole, Md. d: 6/25/80, Baltimore, Md. BL/TL, 6'1", 172 lbs. Deb: 4/21/51

YEAR TM/L	W	L	PCT	G	GS	CG	SH	SV	IP	H	HR	BB	SO	RAT	ERA	ERA+	OAV	OOB	BH	AVG	PB	PR	/A	PD	TPI
1951 Pit-N	0	2	.000	9	1	0	0	0	16¹	11	2	7	7	9.9	2.76	153	.180	.265	0	.000	-0	2	3	1	0.4
1952 Pit-N	2	3	.400	12	5	1	0	0	35²	42	3	18	15	15.1	6.31	63	.288	.366	1	.111	-0	-10	-9	-0	-1.2
Total 2	2	5	.286	21	6	1	0	0	52	53	5	25	22	13.5	5.19	78	.256	.336	1	.100	-0	-8	-7	1	-0.8

● HUGH MULCAHY
Mulcahy, Hugh Noyes "Losing Pitcher" b: 9/9/13, Brighton, Mass. BR/TR, 6'2", 190 lbs. Deb: 7/24/35 C

YEAR TM/L	W	L	PCT	G	GS	CG	SH	SV	IP	H	HR	BB	SO	RAT	ERA	ERA+	OAV	OOB	BH	AVG	PB	PR	/A	PD	TPI
1935 Phi-N	1	5	.167	18	5	0	0	1	52²	62	2	25	11	15.7	4.78	95	.295	.383	0	.000	-2	-4	-4	-1	-0.3
1936 Phi-N	1	1	.500	3	2	0	0	0	22²	20	0	12	2	13.5	3.18	143	.238	.347	2	.250	0	2	3	0	0.3
1937 Phi-N	8	18	.308	56	26	9	1	3	215²	256	17	97	54	15.0	5.13	84	.296	.372	11	.151	-3	-29	-19	3	-2.0
1938 Phi-N	10	20	.333	46	34	15	0	1	267¹	294	14	120	90	14.1	4.61	84	.278	.354	16	.170	-4	-24	-22	1	-2.3
1939 Phi-N	9	16	.360	38	32	14	1	0	225²	246	9	93	59	14.0	4.99	80	.282	.359	12	.158	-3	-27	-25	0	-2.7
1940 Phi-N☆	13	22	.371	36	36	21	3	0	280	283	12	91	82	12.1	3.60	108	.261	.320	19	.202	1	8	8	3	1.5
1945 Phi-N	1	3	.250	5	4	1	0	0	28¹	33	1	14	3	13.3	3.81	101	.295	.347	0	—	0	1	0	1	0.1
1946 Phi-N	2	4	.333	16	5	0	0	0	62²	69	3	33	12	15.4	4.45	77	.295	.393	1	.188	1	-7	-7	1	-0.4
1947 Pit-N	0	0	—	2	1	0	0	0	7	4	1	2	1	20.3	4.05	104	.333	.333	0	—	0	1	0	0	0.0
Total 9	45	89	.336	220	145	63	5	9	1161²	1271	69	487	314	13.9	4.49	89	.280	.355	64	.165	-9	-82	-61	11	-5.8

● TERRY MULHOLLAND
Mulholland, Terence John b: 3/9/63, Uniontown, Pa. BR/TL, 6'3", 200 lbs. Deb: 6/8/86

YEAR TM/L	W	L	PCT	G	GS	CG	SH	SV	IP	H	HR	BB	SO	RAT	ERA	ERA+	OAV	OOB	BH	AVG	PB	PR	/A	PD	TPI
1986 SF-N	1	7	.125	15	10	0	0	0	54²	51	3	35	27	14.3	4.94	71	.251	.364	1	.053	-1	-7	-9	-1	-1.3

YEAR	TM/L	W	L	PCT	G	GS	CG	SH	SV	IP	H	HR	BB	SO	RAT	ERA	ERA+	OAV	OOB	BH	AVG	PB	PR	/A	PD	TPI
1988	SF-N	2	1	.667	9	6	2	1	0	46	50	3	7	18	11.3	3.72	88	.281	.312	0	.000	-1	-1	-2	0	-0.2
1989	SF-N	0	0	—	5	1	0	0	0	11	15	0	4	6	15.5	4.09	82	.319	.373	0	.000	-0	-1	-1	0	0.0
	Phi-N	4	7	.364	20	17	2	1	0	104¹	122	8	32	60	13.6	5.00	71	.292	.348	2	.059	-2	-17	-17	1	-1.8
	Yr	4	7	.364	25	18	2	1	0	115¹	137	8	36	66	13.8	4.92	72	.295	.350	2	.056	-2	-18	-18	1	-1.8
1990	Phi-N	9	10	.474	33	26	6	1	0	180²	172	15	42	75	10.8	3.34	105	.252	.297	6	.097	-2	9	10	-3	0.4
1991	Phi-N	16	13	.552	34	34	8	3	0	232	231	15	49	142	11.0	3.61	102	.260	.301	7	.087	-4	2	1	-2	-0.4
1992	Phi-N	13	11	.542	32	32	12	2	0	229	227	14	46	125	10.8	3.81	92	.261	.300	8	.096	-2	-8	-8	1	-1.0
1993	*Phi-N★	12	9	.571	29	28	7	2	0	191	177	20	40	116	10.4	3.25	122	.241	.283	4	.065	-4	17	15	-1	1.0
1994	NY-A	6	7	.462	24	19	2	0	0	120²	150	24	37	72	14.2	6.49	70	.303	.355	0	—	-0	-23	-26	1	-2.0
1995	SF-N	5	13	.278	29	24	2	0	0	149	190	25	38	65	14.0	5.80	70	.313	.357	5	.102	-0	-27	-28	-1	-3.0
1996	Phi-N	8	7	.533	21	21	8	1	0	133¹	157	17	21	52	12.2	4.66	94	.293	.323	8	.178	1	-7	-4	-2	-0.5
	Sea-A	5	4	.556	12	12	0	0	0	69¹	75	5	28	34	13.6	4.67	105	.286	.360	0	—	0	2	2	-1	0.2
Total 10		81	89	.476	263	230	44	10	0	1521	1617	149	379	792	12.0	4.30	91	.273	.320	41	.091	-17	-61	-67	-8	-8.6

● TONY MULLANE

Mullane, Anthony John "Count" or "The Apollo Of The Box"   b: 1/20/1859, Cork, Ireland   d: 4/25/44, Chicago, Ill.   BB/TR, 5'10.5", 165 lbs.   Deb: 8/27/1881   ♦

YEAR	TM/L	W	L	PCT	G	GS	CG	SH	SV	IP	H	HR	BB	SO	RAT	ERA	ERA+	OAV	OOB	BH	AVG	PB	PR	/A	PD	TPI
1881	Det-N	1	4	.200	5	5	5	0	0	44	55	2	17	7	14.7	4.91	59	.302	.362	5	.263	-0	-10	-10	0	-0.9
1882	Lou-a	30	24	.556	55	55	51	5	0	460¹	418	4	78	170	9.7	1.88	132	.226	.257	78	.257	11	41	31	11	5.1
1883	StL-a	35	15	.700	53	49	49	3	1	460²	372	3	74	191	8.7	2.19	159	.207	.238	69	.225	1	57	66	1	6.2
1884	Tol-a	36	26	.581	67	65	64	7	0	567	481	6	89	325	9.6	2.52	135	.214	.255	97	.276	15	46	56	10	7.7
1886	Cin-a	33	27	.550	63	56	55	1	0	529²	501	11	166	250	11.6	3.70	95	.242	.303	73	.225	2	-15	-11	2	-0.6
1887	Cin-a	31	17	.646	48	48	47	6	0	416¹	414	11	121	97	12.3	3.24	134	.257	.322	44	.221	2	49	51	-1	4.5
1888	Cin-a	26	16	.619	44	42	41	4	1	380¹	341	9	75	186	10.5	2.84	112	.231	.282	44	.251	5	9	14	-0	1.8
1889	Cin-a	11	9	.550	33	24	17	0	5	220	218	4	89	112	13.1	2.99	131	.251	.329	58	.296	9	21	22	-1	2.2
1890	Cin-N	12	10	.545	25	21	21	0	1	209	175	7	96	91	12.0	2.24	159	.220	.311	79	.276	7	31	31	0	3.4
1891	Cin-N	23	26	.469	51	47	42	1	0	426¹	390	15	187	124	12.6	3.23	104	.234	.318	31	.148	-5	6	7	1	0.3
1892	Cin-N	21	13	.618	37	34	30	3	1	295	222	12	127	109	11.0	2.59	126	.201	.290	20	.169	-1	23	22	6	2.7
1893	Cin-N	6	6	.500	15	13	11	0	1	122¹	130	4	65	24	15.0	4.41	108	.264	.360	15	.288	3	3	5	0	0.6
	Bal-N	12	16	.429	34	26	23	0	1	244²	277	4	124	71	15.0	4.45	107	.277	.360	26	.228	-3	6	8	3	0.7
	Yr	18	22	.450	49	39	34	0	2	367	407	8	189	95	14.8	4.44	107	.271	.355	41	.247	-0	9	13	3	1.3
1894	Bal-N	6	9	.400	21	15	9	0	4	122²	155	4	90	43	18.5	6.31	87	.305	.417	21	.396	5	-13	-12	-1	-0.7
	Cle-N	1	2	.333	4	4	3	0	0	33	46	3	10	3	15.3	7.64	72	.326	.371	1	.077	-1	-8	-8	2	-0.4
	Yr	7	11	.389	25	19	12	0	4	155²	201	7	100	46	17.4	6.59	83	.306	.398	22	.333	4	-22	-20	1	-1.1
Total 13		284	220	.563	555	504	468	30	15	4531¹	4195	98	1408	1803	11.5	3.05	118	.236	.298	661	.243	50	245	270	33	32.6

● JOE MULLIGAN

Mulligan, Joseph Ignatius "Big Joe"   b: 7/31/13, Weymouth, Mass.   d: 6/5/86, W.Roxbury, Mass.   BR/TR, 6'4", 210 lbs.   Deb: 6/28/34

YEAR	TM/L	W	L	PCT	G	GS	CG	SH	SV	IP	H	HR	BB	SO	RAT	ERA	ERA+	OAV	OOB	BH	AVG	PB	PR	/A	PD	TPI
1934	Bos-A	1	0	1.000	14	2	1	0	0	44²	46	1	27	13	15.1	3.63	132	.279	.387	0	.000	-1	4	6	0	0.0

● DICK MULLIGAN

Mulligan, Richard Charles   b: 3/18/18, Swoyersville, Pa.   d: 12/15/92, Victoria, Tex.   BL/TL, 6', 167 lbs.   Deb: 9/24/41

YEAR	TM/L	W	L	PCT	G	GS	CG	SH	SV	IP	H	HR	BB	SO	RAT	ERA	ERA+	OAV	OOB	BH	AVG	PB	PR	/A	PD	TPI
1941	Was-A	0	1	.000	1	1	0	0	0	9	11	0	2	3	13.0	5.00	81	.306	.342	0	.000	-0	-1	-1	0	-0.1
1946	Phi-N	2	2	.500	19	5	1	0	1	54²	61	0	27	16	15.1	4.77	72	.289	.380	0	.000	-1	-8	-8	0	-0.7
	Bos-N	1	0	1.000	4	0	0	0	0	15¹	6	1	9	4	8.8	2.35	146	.122	.259	0	.000	0	2	2	-0	0.1
	Yr	3	2	.600	23	5	1	0	1	70	67	1	36	20	13.2	4.24	81	.254	.343	0	.000	-1	-6	-6	0	-0.6
1947	Bos-N	0	0	—	1	0	0	0	0	2	4	1	1	1	22.5	9.00	43	.400	.455	0	—	0	-1	-1	-0	0.0
Total 3		3	3	.500	25	6	2	0	1	81	82	1	39	23	13.6	4.44	79	.268	.358	0	.000	-1	-8	-8	-0	-0.7

● GEORGE MULLIN

Mullin, George Joseph "Wabash George"   b: 7/4/1880, Toledo, Ohio   d: 1/7/44, Wabash, Ind.   BR/TR, 5'11", 188 lbs.   Deb: 5/4/02   ♦

YEAR	TM/L	W	L	PCT	G	GS	CG	SH	SV	IP	H	HR	BB	SO	RAT	ERA	ERA+	OAV	OOB	BH	AVG	PB	PR	/A	PD	TPI
1902	Det-A	13	16	.448	35	30	25	0	0	260	282	4	95	78	13.3	3.67	99	.277	.343	39	.325	9	-3	-1	2	1.1
1903	Det-A	19	15	.559	41	36	31	6	2	320²	284	4	106	170	11.2	2.25	130	.237	.303	35	.278	8	26	24	5	4.1
1904	Det-A	17	23	.425	45	44	42	7	0	382¹	345	1	131	161	11.4	2.40	106	.242	.310	45	.290	11	8	6	8	3.2
1905	Det-A	21	21	.500	44	41	35	1	0	347²	303	4	138	168	11.6	2.51	109	.236	.314	35	.259	6	9	7		2.6
1906	Det-A	21	18	.538	40	40	35	2	0	330	315	1	108	123	11.9	2.78	99	.254	.322	32	.225	3	-3	-1	3	0.7
1907	*Det-A	20	20	.500	46	42	35	5	3	357¹	346	1	106	146	11.8	2.59	100	.256	.318	34	.217	3	-2	0	4	1.0
1908	*Det-A	17	13	.567	39	30	26	1	0	290²	301	1	71	121	11.7	3.10	78	.271	.319	32	.256	8	-23	-22	3	-1.1
1909	*Det-A	29	8	.784	40	35	29	3	1	303²	258	1	78	124	10.2	2.22	113	.234	.289	27	.214	5	9	10	1	2.0
1910	Det-A	21	12	.636	38	32	27	5	0	289	260	7	102	98	11.7	2.87	92	.254	.330	33	.256	6	-11	-8	1	-0.1
1911	Det-A	18	10	.643	30	29	25	2	0	234¹	245	7	61	87	12.2	3.07	113	.276	.331	28	.286	8	7	10	-2	1.6
1912	Det-A	12	17	.414	30	29	22	2	0	226	214	2	92	88	12.5	3.54	92	.255	.335	25	.278	9	-6	-7	0	0.2
1913	Det-A	1	6	.143	7	7	4	0	0	52¹	53	1	18	16	12.6	2.75	106	.268	.335	7	.350	3	1	1	1	0.5
	Was-A	3	5	.375	11	9	3	0	0	57¹	69	1	25	14	15.5	5.02	59	.283	.361	4	.190	-0	-13	-13	1	-1.5
	Yr	4	11	.267	18	16	7	0	0	109²	122	2	43	30	14.0	3.94	75	.275	.346	11	.268	3	-12	-12	1	-1.0
1914	Ind-F	14	10	.583	36	20	11	1	2	203	202	4	91	74	13.4	2.70	115	.261	.346	24	.312	8	4	9	-4	1.5
1915	New-F	2	2	.500	5	4	3	0	0	32¹	41	0	16	14	15.9	5.85	44	.318	.393	1	.100	-0	-11	-12	-1	-1.3
Total 14		228	196	.538	487	428	353	35	8	3686²	3518	42	1238	1482	11.9	2.82	101	.255	.322	401	.262	87	-12	7	28	14.5

● DOMINIC MULRENAN

Mulrenan, Dominic Joseph   b: 12/18/1893, Woburn, Mass.   d: 7/27/64, Melrose, Mass.   BR/TR, 5'11", 170 lbs.   Deb: 4/24/21

YEAR	TM/L	W	L	PCT	G	GS	CG	SH	SV	IP	H	HR	BB	SO	RAT	ERA	ERA+	OAV	OOB	BH	AVG	PB	PR	/A	PD	TPI
1921	Chi-A	2	8	.200	12	10	3	0	0	56	84	2	36	10	19.6	7.23	59	.359	.449	3	.150	-1	-18	-19	0	-2.6

● FRANK MULRONEY

Mulroney, Francis Joseph   b: 4/8/03, Mallard, Iowa   d: 11/11/85, Aberdeen, Wash.   BR/TR, 6', 170 lbs.   Deb: 4/15/30

YEAR	TM/L	W	L	PCT	G	GS	CG	SH	SV	IP	H	HR	BB	SO	RAT	ERA	ERA+	OAV	OOB	BH	AVG	PB	PR	/A	PD	TPI
1930	Bos-A	0	1	.000	2	0	0	0	0	3	3	0	0	2	9.0	3.00	154	.273	.273	0	—	0	1	1	0	0.2

● BOB MUNCRIEF

Muncrief, Robert Cleveland   b: 1/28/16, Madill, Okla.   d: 2/6/96, Duncanville, Tex.   BR/TR, 6'2", 190 lbs.   Deb: 9/30/37

YEAR	TM/L	W	L	PCT	G	GS	CG	SH	SV	IP	H	HR	BB	SO	RAT	ERA	ERA+	OAV	OOB	BH	AVG	PB	PR	/A	PD	TPI
1937	StL-A	0	0	—	1	1	0	0	0	2	3	1	2	0	22.5	4.50	107	.300	.417	0	—	0	0	0	-0	0.0
1939	StL-A	0	0	—	2	0	0	0	0	3	7	1	3	1	30.0	15.00	32	.500	.588	0	—	0	-3	-3	-0	-0.3
1941	StL-A	13	9	.591	36	24	12	2	1	214¹	221	18	53	67	11.7	3.65	118	.266	.314	18	.237	2	12	15	-1	1.5
1942	StL-A	6	8	.429	24	18	7	1	0	134¹	149	11	31	39	12.1	3.89	95	.280	.319	5	.111	-1	-3	-3	-0	-0.4
1943	StL-A	13	12	.520	35	27	12	3	0	205	211	13	48	80	11.5	2.81	118	.264	.307	10	.152	-2	11	12	-3	0.9
1944	*StL-A★	13	8	.619	33	27	12	3	1	219¹	216	11	50	88	11.0	3.08	127	.258	.302	18	.231	1	9	13	-1	1.3
1945	StL-A	13	4	.765	27	15	10	0	1	145²	132	8	44	54	11.0	2.72	130	.239	.297	3	.067	-4	10	13	-1	0.9
1946	StL-A	3	12	.200	29	14	4	1	0	115¹	149	6	31	49	14.0	4.99	75	.314	.356	1	.031	-3	-19	-16	-1	-2.4
1947	StL-A	8	14	.364	31	23	7	0	0	176¹	210	14	51	74	13.4	4.90	79	.299	.348	6	.105	-3	-23	-20	0	-2.5
1948	*Cle-A	5	4	.556	21	9	1	1	0	72¹	76	8	31	24	13.3	3.98	102	.289	.353	2	.111	-1	2	1	-0	-0.1
1949	Pit-N	1	5	.167	13	4	1	0	0	35²	44	2	13	11	14.4	6.31	67	.310	.368	2	.143	-0	-9	-8	1	-1.3
	Chi-N	5	6	.455	34	3	1	0	0	75	80	5	31	36	13.4	4.56	88	.276	.348	4	.286	-1	-4	-4	-0	-0.5
	Yr	6	11	.353	47	7	2	0	0	110²	124	7	44	47	13.7	5.12	80	.287	.354	5	.238	1	-13	-13	1	-1.8
1951	NY-A	0	0	—	2	0	0	0	0	3	5	0	4	2	27.0	9.00	43	.417	.563	0	—	0	-2	-2	0	-0.3
Total 12		80	82	.494	288	165	67	11	9	1401²	1503	108	392	525	12.3	3.80	91	.275	.325	68	.155	-10	-20	-3	-7	-2.6

● RED MUNGER

Munger, George David   b: 10/4/18, Houston, Tex.   d: 7/23/96, Houston, Tex.   BR/TR, 6'2", 200 lbs.   Deb: 5/1/43

YEAR	TM/L	W	L	PCT	G	GS	CG	SH	SV	IP	H	HR	BB	SO	RAT	ERA	ERA+	OAV	OOB	BH	AVG	PB	PR	/A	PD	TPI
1943	StL-N	9	5	.643	32	9	5	0	2	93¹	101	2	42	45	13.8	3.95	85	.281	.357	6	.214	1	-6	-6	1	-0.7
1944	StL-N†	11	3	.786	21	12	7	2	2	121	92	4	41	55	10.0	1.34	263	.212	.284	5	.114	-3	31	29	3	3.6
1946	*StL-N☆	2	2	.500	10	7	2	0	1	48²	47	0	12	28	10.9	3.33	104	.255	.301	4	.250	1	4	4	0	0.3
1947	StL-N☆	16	5	.762	40	31	13	6	3	224¹	218	12	76	123	11.9	3.37	123	.255	.318	15	.185	1	17	19	3	2.0
1948	StL-N	10	11	.476	39	25	7	2	0	166	179	13	74	72	13.8	4.50	91	.272	.347	8	.160	-0	-10	-8	2	-0.7
1949	StL-N★	15	8	.652	35	28	12	2	0	188¹	179	13	87	82	12.8	3.87	108	.255	.339	17	.258	4	4	6	1	1.1
1950	StL-N	8	8	.467	32	16	7	0	0	154²	158	15	70	61	13.4	3.90	110	.262	.342	7	.137	-2	4	7	0	0.4
1951	StL-N	4	6	.400	23	11	3	0	0	94²	106	13	46	44	14.5	5.32	74	.286	.365	5	.172	-0	-14	-14	2	-1.2
1952	StL-N	0	1	.000						4¹	7	1	4	1	18.7	12.46	30	.389	.450	0	.000	-0	-4	-4	2	-0.6
	Pit-N	0	3	.000						26¹	30	7	7	8	13.7	7.18	56	.283	.345	0	.000	-1	-10	-9	1	-0.9
	Yr	0	4	.000	6	5	0	0	0	30²	37	8	11	9	14.1	7.92	50	.296	.353	0	.000	-1	-14	-11	1	-1.5

YEAR	TM/L	W	L	PCT	G	GS	CG	SH	SV	IP	H	HR	BB	SO	RAT	ERA	ERA+	OAV	OOB	BH	AVG	PB	PR	/A	PD	TPI
1956	Pit-N	3	4	.429	35	13	0	0	2	107	126	8	41	45	14.0	4.04	93	.299	.361	3	.107	-0	-3	-3	-1	-0.3
Total	10	77	56	.579	273	161	54	13	12	1228²	1243	86	500	564	12.8	3.83	103	.264	.336	70	.174	-0	8	17	13	3.0

● **VAN MUNGO**   Mungo, Van Lingle b: 6/8/11, Pageland, S.C. d: 2/12/85, Pageland, S.C.   BR/TR, 6'2", 185 lbs.   Deb: 9/7/31 C

YEAR	TM/L	W	L	PCT	G	GS	CG	SH	SV	IP	H	HR	BB	SO	RAT	ERA	ERA+	OAV	OOB	BH	AVG	PB	PR	/A	PD	TPI
1931	Bro-N	3	1	.750	5	4	2	1	0	31	27	0	13	12	11.9	2.32	164	.241	.325	3	.250	1	5	5	-1	0.7
1932	Bro-N	13	11	.542	39	33	11	1	2	223¹	224	9	115	107	13.9	4.43	86	.260	.351	16	.203	-0	-14	-15	2	-1.3
1933	Bro-N	16	15	.516	41	28	18	3	0	248	223	7	84	110	11.1	2.72	118	.236	.298	15	.179	-0	17	14	1	1.8
1934	Bro-N★	18	16	.529	45	38	22	3	3	315¹	300	15	104	184	11.6	3.37	116	.249	.310	30	.248	4	24	19	2	2.5
1935	Bro-N	16	10	.615	37	26	18	**4**	2	214¹	205	13	90	143	12.5	3.65	109	.252	.328	26	.289	5	9	8	1	1.4
1936	Bro-N☆	18	19	.486	45	37	22	2	3	311²	275	8	118	**238**	11.4	3.35	123	**.234**	.305	22	.179	-4	23	27	2	2.8
1937	Bro-N★	9	11	.450	25	21	14	0	3	161	136	3	56	122	10.9	2.91	139	**.229**	.298	16	.250	-2	18	20	3	3.0
1938	Bro-N	4	11	.267	24	18	6	2	0	133¹	133	11	72	72	14.0	3.92	100	.259	.353	9	.191	-1	-0	-2	-0	0.2
1939	Bro-N	4	5	.444	14	10	1	0	0	77¹	70	7	33	34	12.3	3.26	124	.239	.322	10	.345	2	6	7	-1	1.0
1940	Bro-N	1	0	1.000	7	0	0	0	1	22	24	1	10	9	13.9	2.45	163	.282	.358	0	.000	-1	3	4	-0	0.1
1941	Bro-N	0	0	—	2	0	0	0	0	2	1	0	2	0	13.5	4.50	81	.143	.333	0	—	-0	-0	-0	-0	0.0
1942	NY-N	1	2	.333	9	5	0	0	0	36¹	38	4	21	27	14.6	5.94	57	.273	.369	3	.214	-0	-11	-10	-0	-0.8
1943	NY-N	3	7	.300	45	13	2	2	2	154¹	140	7	79	83	13.1	3.91	88	.243	.341	7	.159	-1	-9	-8	1	-0.5
1945	NY-N†	14	7	.667	26	26	7	2	0	183	161	4	71	101	11.6	3.20	122	.238	.314	17	.233	4	12	15	-0	1.9
Total	14	120	115	.511	364	259	123	20	16	2113	1957	89	868	1242	12.2	3.47	110	.245	.321	174	.221	13	83	83	11	12.8

● **MANNY MUNIZ**   Muniz, Manuel (Rodriguez) b: 12/31/47, Caguas, P.R.   BR/TR, 5'11", 190 lbs.   Deb: 9/3/71

YEAR	TM/L	W	L	PCT	G	GS	CG	SH	SV	IP	H	HR	BB	SO	RAT	ERA	ERA+	OAV	OOB	BH	AVG	PB	PR	/A	PD	TPI
1971	Phi-N	0	1	.000	5	0	0	0	0	10¹	9	2	8	6	14.8	6.97	51	.225	.354	0	.000	-0	-4	-4	-0	-0.4

● **SCOTT MUNNINGHOFF**   Munninghoff, Scott Andrew b: 12/5/58, Cincinnati, Ohio   BR/TR, 6', 175 lbs.   Deb: 4/13/80

YEAR	TM/L	W	L	PCT	G	GS	CG	SH	SV	IP	H	HR	BB	SO	RAT	ERA	ERA+	OAV	OOB	BH	AVG	PB	PR	/A	PD	TPI
1980	Phi-N	0	0	—	4	0	0	0	0	6	8	0	2	2	19.5	4.50	84	.320	.433	1	1.000	1	-1	-0	0	0.1

● **LES MUNNS**   Munns, Leslie Ernest "Big Ed" or "Nemo" b: 12/1/08, Fort Bragg, Cal.   BR/TR, 6'5", 212 lbs.   Deb: 4/22/34

YEAR	TM/L	W	L	PCT	G	GS	CG	SH	SV	IP	H	HR	BB	SO	RAT	ERA	ERA+	OAV	OOB	BH	AVG	PB	PR	/A	PD	TPI
1934	Bro-N	3	7	.300	33	9	4	0	1	99¹	106	7	60	41	15.0	4.71	83	.280	.378	7	.241	2	-7	-9	2	-0.4
1935	Bro-N	1	3	.250	21	5	0	0	1	58¹	74	5	33	13	17.1	5.55	72	.319	.413	3	.188	-0	-10	-10	-2	-0.8
1936	StL-N	0	3	.000	7	1	0	0	1	24	23	2	12	4	13.1	3.00	131	.240	.324	1	.111	-1	3	3	1	0.3
Total	3	4	13	.235	61	15	4	0	3	181²	203	14	105	58	15.5	4.76	83	.287	.382	11	.204	1	-14	-17	1	-0.9

● **OSCAR MUNOZ**   Munoz, Juan Oscar b: 9/25/69, Hialeah, Fla.   BR/TR, 6'3", 222 lbs.   Deb: 8/6/95

YEAR	TM/L	W	L	PCT	G	GS	CG	SH	SV	IP	H	HR	BB	SO	RAT	ERA	ERA+	OAV	OOB	BH	AVG	PB	PR	/A	PD	TPI
1995	Min-A	2	1	.667	10	3	0	0	0	35¹	40	6	17	25	14.8	5.60	85	.276	.356	0	—	0	-3	-3	-0	-0.3

● **MIKE MUNOZ**   Munoz, Michael Anthony b: 7/12/65, Baldwin Park, Cal.   BL/TL, 6'2", 190 lbs.   Deb: 9/6/89

YEAR	TM/L	W	L	PCT	G	GS	CG	SH	SV	IP	H	HR	BB	SO	RAT	ERA	ERA+	OAV	OOB	BH	AVG	PB	PR	/A	PD	TPI
1989	LA-N	0	0	—	3	0	0	0	0	2²	5	1	2	3	23.6	16.88	20	.417	.500	0	—	0	-4	-4	0	0.0
1990	LA-N	0	1	.000	8	0	0	0	0	5²	6	0	3	2	14.3	3.18	115	.300	.391	0	.000	-0	0	0	-0	0.0
1991	Det-A	0	0	—	6	0	0	0	0	9¹	14	0	5	3	18.3	9.64	43	.350	.422	0	—	0	-6	-6	0	-0.1
1992	Det-A	1	2	.333	65	0	0	0	0	48	44	3	25	23	12.9	3.00	132	.246	.338	0	—	0	5	5	2	0.5
1993	Det-A	0	1	.000	8	0	0	0	0	9	4	1	6	1	30.0	6.00	71	.308	.526	0	—	0	-1	-1	0	-0.1
	Col-N	2	1	.667	21	0	0	0	0	18	21	7	9	16	15.0	4.50	106	.309	.390	0	—	0	-1	-0	0	0.1
1994	Col-N	4	2	.667	57	0	0	0	1	45²	37	3	31	32	13.4	3.74	133	.223	.345	0	—	0	2	6	2	0.9
1995	*Col-N	2	4	.333	64	0	0	0	2	43²	54	9	27	37	16.9	7.42	73	.307	.402	1	.500	1	-16	-10	1	-1.1
1996	Col-N	2	2	.500	54	0	0	0	0	44²	55	4	16	45	14.5	6.65	82	.302	.362	1	.250	-0	-12	-6	1	-0.4
Total	8	11	13	.458	286	0	0	0	5	220²	240	22	124	162	14.9	5.38	89	.280	.373	1	.250	1	-31	-14	6	-0.1

● **BOBBY MUNOZ**   Munoz, Roberto (Sbert) b: 3/3/68, Rio Piedras, P.R.   BR/TR, 6'7", 237 lbs.   Deb: 5/29/93

YEAR	TM/L	W	L	PCT	G	GS	CG	SH	SV	IP	H	HR	BB	SO	RAT	ERA	ERA+	OAV	OOB	BH	AVG	PB	PR	/A	PD	TPI
1993	NY-A	3	3	.500	38	0	0	0	0	45²	48	1	26	33	14.6	5.32	78	.270	.363	0	—	0	-5	-6	-0	-0.5
1994	Phi-N	7	5	.583	21	14	1	0	1	104¹	101	8	35	59	11.8	2.67	160	.252	.314	7	.206	1	18	19	1	2.3
1995	Phi-N	2	2	.000	3	3	0	0	0	15²	15	2	9	6	15.5	5.74	74	.268	.397	0	.000	-1	-3	-3	-0	-0.3
1996	Phi-N	0	3	.000	6	6	0	0	1	25¹	42	5	7	8	17.8	7.82	56	.375	.417	1	.143	-0	-10	-10	-0	-1.0
Total	4	10	13	.435	68	23	1	0	1	191	206	16	77	106	13.6	4.24	100	.276	.347	8	.174	1	-0	-0	1	0.5

● **STEVE MURA**   Mura, Stephen Andrew b: 2/12/55, New Orleans, La.   BR/TR, 6'2", 190 lbs.   Deb: 9/5/78

YEAR	TM/L	W	L	PCT	G	GS	CG	SH	SV	IP	H	HR	BB	SO	RAT	ERA	ERA+	OAV	OOB	BH	AVG	PB	PR	/A	PD	TPI
1978	SD-N	2	0	.000	5	2	0	0	0	7²	15	1	5	5	23.5	11.74	28	.441	.513	0	.000	-0	-7	-7	-0	-1.5
1979	SD-N	4	4	.500	38	5	0	0	1	73	57	6	37	59	11.7	3.08	114	.217	.316	0	.000	-1	5	4	-0	0.2
1980	SD-N	8	7	.533	37	23	3	1	2	168²	149	9	86	109	12.7	3.68	93	.246	.343	7	.137	-0	-2	-5	0	-0.4
1981	SD-N	5	14	.263	23	22	2	0	0	138²	156	10	50	70	13.4	4.28	76	.285	.344	6	.136	-0	-12	-16	1	-1.9
1982	StL-N	12	11	.522	35	30	7	1	0	184¹	196	16	80	84	13.5	4.05	81	.284	.352	3	.057	-4	-9	-9	-1	-1.5
1983	Chi-A	0	0	—	6	0	0	0	0	12¹	13	1	6	4	13.9	4.38	96	.260	.339	0	—	0	-0	-0	-0	-0.2
1985	Oak-A	1	1	.500	23	1	0	0	2	48	41	3	25	29	12.4	4.13	93	.225	.319	0	—	0	-0	-1	0	0.3
Total	7	30	39	.435	167	83	12	2	5	632²	627	46	289	360	13.1	4.00	88	.263	.343	16	.101	-5	-25	-35	-1	-5.0

● **MASANORI MURAKAMI**   Murakami, Masanori b: 5/6/44, Otsuki, Japan   BL/TL, 6', 180 lbs.   Deb: 9/1/64

YEAR	TM/L	W	L	PCT	G	GS	CG	SH	SV	IP	H	HR	BB	SO	RAT	ERA	ERA+	OAV	OOB	BH	AVG	PB	PR	/A	PD	TPI
1964	SF-N	1	0	1.000	9	0	0	0	1	15	11	1	1	15	5.4	1.80	198	.163	.180	0	.000	-0	3	3	-1	0.1
1965	SF-N	4	1	.800	45	1	0	0	8	74¹	57	9	22	85	9.9	3.75	96	.205	.271	2	.154	-0	-2	-1	-2	-0.3
Total	2	5	1	.833	54	1	0	0	9	89¹	65	10	23	100	9.2	3.43	105	.199	.258	2	.125	-1	1	2	-2	-0.2

● **TIM MURCHISON**   Murchison, Thomas Malcolm b: 10/8/1896, Liberty, N.C. d: 10/20/62, Liberty, N.C.   BR/TL, 6', 185 lbs.   Deb: 6/21/17

YEAR	TM/L	W	L	PCT	G	GS	CG	SH	SV	IP	H	HR	BB	SO	RAT	ERA	ERA+	OAV	OOB	BH	AVG	PB	PR	/A	PD	TPI
1917	StL-N	0	0	—	1	0	0	0	0	1	0	0	2	1	18.0	0.00	—	.000	.400	0	—	0	2	1	0	0.0
1920	Cle-A	0	0	—	2	0	0	0	0	5	3	0	4	2	12.6	0.00	—	.200	.368	0	—	0	2	1	0	0.0
Total	2	0	0	—	3	0	0	0	0	6	3	0	6	3	13.5	0.00	—	.167	.375	0	—	-0	2	1	0	0.0

● **RED MURFF**   Murff, John Robert b: 4/1/21, Burlington, Tex.   BR/TR, 6'3", 195 lbs.   Deb: 4/21/56

YEAR	TM/L	W	L	PCT	G	GS	CG	SH	SV	IP	H	HR	BB	SO	RAT	ERA	ERA+	OAV	OOB	BH	AVG	PB	PR	/A	PD	TPI
1956	Mil-N	0	0	—	14	1	0	0	0	24¹	25	3	7	18	11.8	4.44	78	.272	.323	1	.200	-0	-2	-3	0	0.0
1957	Mil-N	2	2	.500	12	1	0	0	3	26	31	3	11	13	14.5	4.85	72	.301	.368	0	.000	-1	-3	-4	0	-0.6
Total	2	2	2	.500	26	2	0	0	3	50¹	56	6	18	31	13.2	4.65	75	.287	.347	1	.091	-1	-5	-7	1	-0.6

● **CON MURPHY**   Murphy, Cornelius B. "Monk" or "Razzle Dazzle"
   b: 10/15/1863, Worcester, Mass. d: 8/1/14, Worcester, Mass.   TR, 5'9", 130 lbs.   Deb: 9/11/1884

YEAR	TM/L	W	L	PCT	G	GS	CG	SH	SV	IP	H	HR	BB	SO	RAT	ERA	ERA+	OAV	OOB	BH	AVG	PB	PR	/A	PD	TPI
1884	Phi-N	0	3	.000	3	3	3	0	0	26	37	1	6	10	14.9	6.58	45	.319	.352	0	.000	-1	-10	-10	-0	-0.9
1890	Bro-P	4	10	.286	20	14	11	0	2	139	168	2	82	29	16.6	4.79	93	.286	.379	15	.217	-1	-9	-5	-1	-0.5
Total	2	4	13	.235	23	17	14	0	2	165	205	3	88	39	16.3	5.07	83	.292	.375	15	.190	-3	-19	-16	-0	-1.4

● **DANNY MURPHY**   Murphy, Daniel Francis b: 8/23/42, Beverly, Mass.   BL/TR, 5'11", 185 lbs.   Deb: 6/18/60 ♦

YEAR	TM/L	W	L	PCT	G	GS	CG	SH	SV	IP	H	HR	BB	SO	RAT	ERA	ERA+	OAV	OOB	BH	AVG	PB	PR	/A	PD	TPI
1969	Chi-A	2	1	.667	17	0	0	0	4	31¹	28	2	10	16	11.5	2.01	192	.252	.325	0	.000	0	6	6	-0	0.8
1970	Chi-A	2	3	.400	51	0	0	0	5	80²	82	11	49	42	15.1	5.69	68	.273	.382	4	.333	2	-18	-16	-1	-1.0
Total	2	4	4	.500	68	0	0	0	9	112	110	13	59	58	14.1	4.66	83	.268	.368	23	.177	2	-12	-10	-1	-0.2

● **DAN MURPHY**   Murphy, Daniel Lee b: 9/18/64, Artesia, Cal.   BR/TR, 6'2", 195 lbs.   Deb: 8/10/89

YEAR	TM/L	W	L	PCT	G	GS	CG	SH	SV	IP	H	HR	BB	SO	RAT	ERA	ERA+	OAV	OOB	BH	AVG	PB	PR	/A	PD	TPI
1989	SD-N	0	0	—	7	0	0	0	0	6¹	6	1	4	1	14.2	5.68	61	.231	.333	0	—	0	-2	-2	-0	0.0

● **ED MURPHY**   Murphy, Edward J. b: 1/22/1877, Auburn, N.Y. d: 1/29/35, Weedsport, N.Y.   TR, 6'1", 186 lbs.   Deb: 4/23/1898

YEAR	TM/L	W	L	PCT	G	GS	CG	SH	SV	IP	H	HR	BB	SO	RAT	ERA	ERA+	OAV	OOB	BH	AVG	PB	PR	/A	PD	TPI
1898	Phi-N	1	2	.333	7	3	2	0	1	30	41	3	10	11	15.6	5.10	67	.323	.377	5	.357	1	-5	-6	1	-0.3
1901	StL-N	10	9	.526	23	21	16	0	0	165	201	5	32	42	12.8	4.20	78	.298	.331	16	.250	3	-16	-19	2	-1.4
1902	StL-N	10	6	.625	23	17	12	1	0	164	187	7	31	37	12.1	3.02	91	.286	.321	16	.262	1	-4	-5	2	-0.2
1903	StL-N	4	8	.333	15	12	9	0	1	106	108	2	38	16	12.9	3.31	99	.262	.333	13	.203	-1	-0	-0	-1	-0.1
Total	4	25	25	.500	68	53	39	1	1	465	537	17	111	103	12.7	3.64	84	.288	.331	50	.246	4	-26	-30	4	-2.0

● **JOHN MURPHY**   Murphy, John Henry b: 3/8/1867, Fitchburg, Mass. d: 9/12/30, Hartford, Conn.   5'11", 165 lbs.   Deb: 4/17/1884

YEAR	TM/L	W	L	PCT	G	GS	CG	SH	SV	IP	H	HR	BB	SO	RAT	ERA	ERA+	OAV	OOB	BH	AVG	PB	PR	/A	PD	TPI
1884	Wil-U	0	6	.000	7	6	5	0	0	48	52	3	2	27	10.1	3.00	89	.259	.266	2	.065	-4	-3	-2	-1	-0.5

YEAR	TM/L	W	L	PCT	G	GS	CG	SH	SV	IP	H	HR	BB	SO	RAT	ERA	ERA+	OAV	OOB	BH	AVG	PB	PR	/A	PD	TPI
	Alt-U	5	6	.455	14	10	10	0	0	111²	141	3	9	46	12.1	3.87	69	.289	.302	14	.149	-7	-18	-15	1	-1.5
	Yr	5	12	.294	21	16	15	0	0	159²	193	6	11	73	11.5	3.61	74	.280	.291	16	.128	-11	-21	-17	0	-2.0

● JOHNNY MURPHY

Murphy, John Joseph "Grandma" "Fireman" Or "Fordham Johnny"
b: 7/14/08, New York, N.Y.   d: 1/14/70, New York, N.Y.   BR/TR, 6'2", 190 lbs.   Deb: 5/19/32

YEAR	TM/L	W	L	PCT	G	GS	CG	SH	SV	IP	H	HR	BB	SO	RAT	ERA	ERA+	OAV	OOB	BH	AVG	PB	PR	/A	PD	TPI
1932	NY-A	0	0	—	2	0	0	0	0	3¹	7	0	3	2	27.0	16.20	25	.438	.526	1	1.000	1	-4	-4	0	0.1
1934	NY-A	14	10	.583	40	20	10	0	4	207²	193	11	76	70	11.7	3.12	130	.250	.317	7	.099	-3	32	22	1	2.1
1935	NY-A	10	5	.667	40	8	4	0	5	117	110	7	55	28	12.7	4.08	99	.243	.325	5	.156	2	5	-0	-1	0.1
1936	*NY-A	9	3	.750	27	5	2	0	5	88	90	5	36	34	13.0	3.38	138	.262	.334	13	.361	4	16	13	1	2.0
1937	*NY-A☆	13	4	.765	39	4	0	0	10	110	121	7	50	36	14.1	4.17	107	.277	.352	8	.229	2	5	3	4	1.0
1938	*NY-A☆	8	2	.800	32	2	1	0	11	91¹	90	5	41	43	13.0	4.24	107	.256	.336	2	.063	-3	6	3	1	0.2
1939	*NY-A☆	3	6	.333	38	0	0	0	19	61¹	57	2	28	19	12.5	4.40	99	.252	.335	2	.182	1	1	-0	1	0.0
1940	NY-A	8	4	.667	35	1	0	0	9	63¹	58	5	15	23	10.4	3.69	109	.247	.292	1	.077	0	5	2	1	0.5
1941	*NY-A	8	3	.727	35	0	0	0	15	77¹	68	1	40	29	12.6	1.98	199	.237	.330	1	.056	-1	19	17	-1	2.7
1942	*NY-A	4	10	.286	31	0	0	0	11	58	66	2	23	24	14.1	3.41	101	.293	.364	2	.154	0	2	0	0	0.1
1943	*NY-A	12	4	.750	37	0	0	0	8	68	44	2	30	31	9.8	2.51	128	.183	.273	1	.053	-2	6	5	-0	1.1
1946	NY-A	4	2	.667	27	0	0	0	8	45	40	4	19	19	11.8	3.40	102	.240	.317	0	.000	-0	1	0	1	0.1
1947	Bos-A	0	0	—	32	0	0	0	3	54²	41	1	28	9	11.4	2.80	139	.206	.304	3	.273	1	6	7	0	0.2
Total 13		93	53	.637	415	40	17	0	107	1045	985	52	444	378	12.4	3.50	117	.249	.326	46	.154	-0	98	68	8	10.2

● JOE MURPHY

Murphy, Joseph Akin   b: 9/7/1866, St.Louis, Mo.   d: 3/28/51, Coral Gables, Fla.   5'11", 160 lbs.   Deb: 4/28/1886

YEAR	TM/L	W	L	PCT	G	GS	CG	SH	SV	IP	H	HR	BB	SO	RAT	ERA	ERA+	OAV	OOB	BH	AVG	PB	PR	/A	PD	TPI
1886	Cin-a	2	3	.400	5	5	5	0	0	46	50	0	21	11	14.1	4.89	72	.256	.332	0	.000	-3	-7	-7	-1	-0.9
	StL-N	0	4	.000	4	4	3	0	0	33	45	3	16	11	16.6	8.18	39	.319	.389	3	.214	0	-18	-18	-0	-1.5
	StL-a	1	0	1.000	1	1	1	0	0	7	5	0	3	3	10.3	3.86	89	.179	.258	0	.000	-1	-0	-0	-0	-0.1
1887	StL-a	1	0	1.000	1	1	1	0	0	9	13	0	4	5	17.0	5.00	91	.317	.378	1	.167	-1	-1	-0	-0	-0.1
Total 2		4	7	.364	11	11	10	0	0	95	113	3	44	30	15.0	5.97	59	.279	.351	4	.098	-4	-26	-26	-2	-2.6

● ROB MURPHY

Murphy, Robert Albert   b: 5/26/60, Miami, Fla.   BL/TL, 6'2", 205 lbs.   Deb: 9/13/85

YEAR	TM/L	W	L	PCT	G	GS	CG	SH	SV	IP	H	HR	BB	SO	RAT	ERA	ERA+	OAV	OOB	BH	AVG	PB	PR	/A	PD	TPI
1985	Cin-N	0	0	—	2	0	0	0	0	3	2	1	2	1	12.0	6.00	63	.200	.333	0	—	0	-1	-1	-0	0.0
1986	Cin-N	6	0	1.000	34	0	0	0	0	50¹	26	0	21	36	8.4	0.72	541	.155	.249	0	.000	-0	17	18	0	2.1
1987	Cin-N	8	5	.615	87	0	0	0	3	100²	91	7	32	99	11.0	3.04	140	.239	.299	0	1.200	0	12	13	0	1.7
1988	Cin-N	0	6	.000	76	0	0	0	3	84²	69	3	38	74	11.5	3.08	116	.229	.318	0	—	0	3	5	1	0.4
1989	Bos-A	5	7	.417	74	0	0	0	9	105	97	7	41	107	11.9	2.74	149	.251	.325	0	—	0	13	16	1	1.8
1990	*Bos-A	0	6	.000	68	0	0	0	7	57	85	10	32	54	18.6	6.32	65	.348	.426	0	—	0	-15	-14	0	-1.6
1991	Sea-A	0	1	.000	57	0	0	0	4	48	47	4	19	34	12.6	3.00	137	.250	.322	0	—	0	6	6	0	0.2
1992	Hou-N	3	1	.750	59	0	0	0	0	55²	56	2	21	42	12.4	4.04	83	.260	.326	0	.000	-0	-3	-4	1	-0.2
1993	StL-N	5	7	.417	73	0	0	0	1	64²	73	8	20	41	13.1	4.87	81	.290	.344	1	.500	0	-6	-7	-0	-1.1
1994	StL-N	4	3	.571	50	0	0	0	2	40¹	35	7	13	25	10.7	3.79	109	.230	.291	0	—	0	2	2	0	0.3
	NY-A	0	0	—	3	0	0	0	0	1²	3	2	0	0	16.2	16.20	28	.375	.375	0	—	0	-2	-2	0	0.1
1995	LA-N	0	1	.000	6	0	0	0	0	5	6	2	3	2	16.2	12.60	30	.300	.391	1	1.000	1	-5	-5	0	-0.8
	Fla-N	1	1	.500	8	0	0	0	0	7¹	8	1	5	5	16.0	9.82	43	.286	.394	0	—	0	-5	-5	0	-1.0
	Yr	1	2	.333	14	0	0	0	0	12¹	14	3	8	7	16.1	10.95	37	.292	.393	1	1.000	1	-9	-9	0	-1.8
Total 11		32	38	.457	597	0	0	0	30	623¹	598	54	247	520	12.3	3.64	109	.254	.326	3	.250	1	16	22	2	1.9

● BOB MURPHY

Murphy, Robert J.   b: 12/26/1866, Dutchess Co., N.Y.   Deb: 5/27/1890

YEAR	TM/L	W	L	PCT	G	GS	CG	SH	SV	IP	H	HR	BB	SO	RAT	ERA	ERA+	OAV	OOB	BH	AVG	PB	PR	/A	PD	TPI
1890	NY-N	1	0	1.000	3	2	1	0	0	18	23	1	10	8	16.5	5.50	64	.303	.384	1	.111	-1	-4	-4	-0	-0.3
	Bro-a	3	9	.250	12	12	10	0	0	96	121	6	46	26	16.1	5.72	68	.299	.377	9	.180	0	-20	-19	2	-1.6
Total 1		4	9	.308	15	14	11	0	0	114	144	6	56	34	16.2	5.68	67	.299	.378	10	.169	-1	-24	-23	2	-1.9

● TOM MURPHY

Murphy, Thomas Andrew   b: 12/30/45, Cleveland, Ohio   BR/TR, 6'3", 185 lbs.   Deb: 6/13/68

YEAR	TM/L	W	L	PCT	G	GS	CG	SH	SV	IP	H	HR	BB	SO	RAT	ERA	ERA+	OAV	OOB	BH	AVG	PB	PR	/A	PD	TPI
1968	Cal-A	5	6	.455	15	15	3	0	0	99¹	67	5	28	56	9.1	2.17	134	.191	.261	0	.000	-3	9	8	-1	0.5
1969	Cal-A	10	16	.385	36	35	4	0	0	215²	213	12	69	100	12.6	4.21	83	.260	.333	10	.141	-0	-14	-18	1	-1.9
1970	Cal-A	16	13	.552	39	38	9	5	0	227	223	32	81	99	12.3	4.24	85	.261	.330	14	.184	3	-13	-16	-1	-1.7
1971	Cal-A	6	17	.261	37	36	7	0	0	243¹	228	24	82	89	11.8	3.77	86	.256	.325	13	.173	1	-8	-14	1	-1.0
1972	Cal-A	0	0	—	6	0	0	0	0	10	13	1	0	8	18.9	5.40	54	.342	.457	0	.000	-0	-3	-3	1	0.1
	KC-A	4	4	.500	18	9	1	1	1	70¹	77	3	16	34	12.7	3.07	99	.287	.341	0	.000	-1	-0	-0	1	-0.1
	Yr	4	4	.500	24	9	1	1	1	80¹	90	3	24	36	13.4	3.36	90	.293	.356	0	—	-1	-3	-3	1	0.0
1973	StL-N	3	7	.300	19	13	2	0	0	88²	89	5	22	42	11.6	3.76	97	.269	.320	4	.174	0	-1	-1	1	0.0
1974	Mil-A	10	10	.500	70	0	0	0	20	123	97	6	51	47	11.0	1.90	190	.224	.309	1	.500	1	23	23	2	**4.9**
1975	Mil-A	1	9	.100	52	0	0	0	20	72¹	85	5	27	32	14.6	4.60	83	.295	.366	0	—	0	-7	-6	0	-1.2
1976	Mil-A	0	1	.000	15	0	0	0	0	18¹	25	2	9	7	17.7	7.36	47	.313	.396	0	—	0	-8	-6	0	-0.3
	Bos-A	4	5	.444	37	0	0	0	9	81	91	5	25	32	13.1	3.44	114	.290	.346	0	—	0	1	4	-0	-0.4
	Yr	4	6	.400	52	0	0	0	9	99¹	116	7	34	39	13.8	4.17	92	.293	.352	0	—	0	-7	-4	0	-0.7
1977	Bos-A	0	1	.000	16	0	0	0	0	30²	44	6	12	13	16.4	6.75	67	.338	.394	0	—	0	-9	-8	0	-1.0
	Tor-A	2	1	.667	19	1	0	0	0	52	52	6	18	26	14.2	3.63	115	.304	.363	0	—	0	2	3	0	0.1
	Yr	2	2	.500	35	1	0	0	0	82²	107	12	30	39	15.0	4.79	90	.317	.374	0	—	0	-7	-4	0	-0.9
1978	Tor-A	6	9	.400	50	0	0	0	7	94	87	11	37	36	11.9	3.93	100	.256	.329	0	—	0	-2	-0	2	-0.2
1979	Tor-A	1	2	.333	10	0	0	0	0	18¹	23	1	6	8	15.2	5.40	80	.311	.378	0	—	0	-2	-2	1	-0.3
Total 12		68	101	.402	439	147	22	3	59	1444	1425	123	493	621	12.3	3.78	94	.263	.332	42	.145	0	-32	-38	7	-2.1

● WALTER MURPHY

Murphy, Walter Joseph   b: 9/27/07, New York, N.Y.   d: 3/23/76, Houston, Tex.   BR/TR, 6'1.5", 180 lbs.   Deb: 4/19/31

YEAR	TM/L	W	L	PCT	G	GS	CG	SH	SV	IP	H	HR	BB	SO	RAT	ERA	ERA+	OAV	OOB	BH	AVG	PB	PR	/A	PD	TPI
1931	Bos-A	0	0	—	2	0	0	0	0	2	4	0	1	0	22.5	9.00	48	.444	.500			0	-1	-1	-0	0.0

● DALE MURRAY

Murray, Dale Albert   b: 2/2/50, Cuero, Tex.   BR/TR, 6'4", 205 lbs.   Deb: 7/7/74

YEAR	TM/L	W	L	PCT	G	GS	CG	SH	SV	IP	H	HR	BB	SO	RAT	ERA	ERA+	OAV	OOB	BH	AVG	PB	PR	/A	PD	TPI
1974	Mon-N	1	1	.500	32	0	0	0	10	69²	46	1	23	31	8.9	1.03	371	.187	.257	0	.000	-1	20	22	0	1.3
1975	Mon-N	15	8	.652	63	0	0	0	9	111¹	134	6	39	43	14.2	3.96	97	.305	.365	3	.214	-1	-4	-2	3	0.0
1976	Mon-N	4	9	.308	81	0	0	0	13	113¹	117	6	37	35	12.2	3.26	114	.277	.336	0	.000	-1	3	6	4	1.2
1977	Cin-N	7	2	.778	61	1	0	0	4	102	125	13	46	42	15.3	4.94	80	.314	.388	2	.167	-0	-12	-11	0	-1.0
1978	Cin-N	1	1	.500	15	0	0	0	0	32²	34	1	17	25	14.3	4.13	86	.272	.364	0	.000	-0	-2	-2	1	-0.1
	NY-N	8	5	.615	53	0	0	0	5	86¹	85	4	36	37	12.8	3.65	96	.266	.345	0	.000	-1	-3	-4	2	-0.1
	Yr	9	6	.600	68	0	0	0	7	119	119	5	53	62	13.2	3.78	93	.266	.346	0	.000	-1	-2	-2	2	-0.1
1979	NY-N	4	8	.333	58	0	0	0	4	97	105	6	52	37	14.6	4.82	75	.287	.376	0	.000	-1	-12	-13	1	-1.5
	Mon-N	1	2	.333	9	0	0	0	1	13¹	14	1	3	4	11.5	2.70	136	.292	.333	0	.000	-0	2	2	-1	0.3
	Yr	5	10	.333	67	0	0	0	5	110¹	119	7	55	41	14.2	4.57	80	.285	.369	0	.000	-1	-10	-11	0	-1.2
1980	Mon-N	1	0	1.000	16	0	0	0	0	29¹	36	3	12	16	15.6	6.14	58	.315	.375	0	.000	-0	-8	-8	-1	-0.4
1981	Tor-A	1	0	1.000	11	0	0	0	0	15¹	12	0	5	12	10.0	1.17	336	.211	.274	0	—	0	4	5	1	0.4
1982	Tor-A	8	7	.533	56	0	0	0	11	111	115	3	32	60	12.2	3.16	142	.268	.323	0	—	0	11	16	3	2.0
1983	NY-A	2	4	.333	40	0	0	0	0	94¹	115	7	32	42	13.0	4.48	87	.297	.337	0	—	0	-4	-6	0	-0.1
1984	NY-A	1	2	.333	19	0	0	0	0	23²	30	2	5	13	14.1	4.94	77	.306	.352	0	—	0	-3	-3	0	-0.1
1985	NY-A	0	0	—	3	0	0	0	0	2	4	0	0	0	18.0	13.50	30	.400	.400	0	—	0	-2	-2	-0	-0.1
	Tex-A	0	0	—	1	0	0	0	0	1	3	0	3	0	27.0	18.00	23	.750	.750	0	—	0	-2	-2	-0	-0.1
	Yr	0	0	—	4	0	0	0	0	3	7	0	3	0	21.0	15.00	27	.500	.500	0	—	0	-4	-4	-0	-0.1
Total 12		53	50	.515	518	2	0	0	60	902¹	976	40	329	400	13.2	3.85	100	.282	.346	5	.077	-3	-9	-1	13	1.6

● GEORGE MURRAY

Murray, George King "Smiler"   b: 9/23/1898, Charlotte, N.C.   d: 10/18/55, Memphis, Tenn.   BR/TR, 6'2", 200 lbs.   Deb: 5/8/22

YEAR	TM/L	W	L	PCT	G	GS	CG	SH	SV	IP	H	HR	BB	SO	RAT	ERA	ERA+	OAV	OOB	BH	AVG	PB	PR	/A	PD	TPI
1922	NY-A	3	2	.600	22	6	2	0	0	56²	53	0	26	14	12.7	3.97	101	.255	.340	5	.278	2	**0**	**0**	-0	0.2
1923	Bos-A	7	11	.389	39	18	5	0	0	177²	190	6	87	40	14.4	4.91	84	.291	.380	8	.164	-3	-18	-16	-2	-1.8
1924	Bos-A	2	9	.182	28	7	0	0	0	80¹	97	6	32	27	15.2	6.72	65	.307	.383	4	.182	-1	-22	-21	-0	-2.4
1926	Was-A	6	3	.667	12	12	5	0	0	81¹	89	1	37	28	14.6	5.64	69	.287	.374	5	.139	-2	-15	-16	-1	-1.7
1927	Was-A	1	1	.500	7	3	0	0	0	18	18	1	15	5	17.5	7.00	58	.265	.412	1	.167	-0	-6	-6	-1	-0.6

YEAR TM/L	W	L	PCT	G	GS	CG	SH	SV	IP	H	HR	BB	SO	RAT	ERA	ERA+	OAV	OOB	BH	AVG	PB	PR	/A	PD	TPI
1933 Chi-A	0	0	—	2	0	0	0	0	2¹	3	0	2	0	19.3	7.71	55	.375	.500	0		0	-1	-1	0	0.0
Total 6	19	26	.422	110	42	10	0	0	416¹	450	17	199	114	14.5	5.38	76	.288	.376	24	.175	-4	-61	-59	-3	-6.3

● **JIM MURRAY** Murray, James Francis "Big Jim" b: 12/31/1900, Scranton, Pa. d: 7/15/73, New York, N.Y. BB/TL, 6'2", 210 lbs. Deb: 7/3/22

YEAR TM/L	W	L	PCT	G	GS	CG	SH	SV	IP	H	HR	BB	SO	RAT	ERA	ERA+	OAV	OOB	BH	AVG	PB	PR	/A	PD	TPI
1922 Bro-N	0	0	—	4	0	0	0	1	6	8	0	3	3	16.5	4.50	90	.320	.393	1	.500	0	-0	-0	-0	0.0

● **AMBY MURRAY** Murray, Joseph Ambrose b: 6/4/13, Fall River, Mass. BL/TL, 5'7", 150 lbs. Deb: 7/5/36

YEAR TM/L	W	L	PCT	G	GS	CG	SH	SV	IP	H	HR	BB	SO	RAT	ERA	ERA+	OAV	OOB	BH	AVG	PB	PR	/A	PD	TPI
1936 Bos-N	0	0	—	4	1	0	0	0	11	15	1	3	2	14.7	4.09	94	.319	.360	1	.250	0	-0	-0	-0	0.0

● **JOE MURRAY** Murray, Joseph Ambrose b: 11/11/20, Wilkes-Barre, Pa. BL/TL, 6', 165 lbs. Deb: 8/17/50

YEAR TM/L	W	L	PCT	G	GS	CG	SH	SV	IP	H	HR	BB	SO	RAT	ERA	ERA+	OAV	OOB	BH	AVG	PB	PR	/A	PD	TPI
1950 Phi-A	0	3	.000	8	2	0	0	0	30	34	1	21	8	16.5	5.70	80	.283	.390	0	.000	-2	-4	-4	1	-0.4

● **MATT MURRAY** Murray, Matthew Michael b: 9/26/70, Boston, Mass. BL/TR, 6'6", 240 lbs. Deb: 8/12/95

YEAR TM/L	W	L	PCT	G	GS	CG	SH	SV	IP	H	HR	BB	SO	RAT	ERA	ERA+	OAV	OOB	BH	AVG	PB	PR	/A	PD	TPI
1995 Atl-N	0	2	.000	4	1	0	0	0	10²	10	3	5	3	13.5	6.75	63	.256	.356	1	.500	0	-3	-3	0	-0.4
Bos-A	0	1	.000	2	1	0	0	0	3¹	11	1	3	1	37.8	18.90	26	.524	.583	0	—	0	-5	-5	0	-1.1
Total 1	0	3	.000	6	2	0	0	0	14	21	4	8	4	19.3	9.64	46	.350	.435	1	.500	0	-8	-8	1	-1.5

● **PAT MURRAY** Murray, Patrick Joseph b: 7/18/1897, Scottsville, N.Y. d: 11/5/83, Rochester, N.Y. BR/TR, 6', 175 lbs. Deb: 7/1/19

YEAR TM/L	W	L	PCT	G	GS	CG	SH	SV	IP	H	HR	BB	SO	RAT	ERA	ERA+	OAV	OOB	BH	AVG	PB	PR	/A	PD	TPI
1919 Phi-N	0	2	.000	8	2	1	0	0	34¹	50	0	12	11	17.3	6.29	51	.347	.412	0	.000	-1	-13	-12	-0	-0.8

● **DENNIS MUSGRAVES** Musgraves, Dennis Eugene b: 12/25/43, Indianapolis, Ind. BR/TR, 6'4", 188 lbs. Deb: 7/9/65

YEAR TM/L	W	L	PCT	G	GS	CG	SH	SV	IP	H	HR	BB	SO	RAT	ERA	ERA+	OAV	OOB	BH	AVG	PB	PR	/A	PD	TPI
1965 NY-N	0	0	—	5	1	0	0	0	16	11	0	7	11	11.3	0.56	627	.200	.313	0		-0	5	5	-0	0.0

● **STAN MUSIAL** Musial, Stanley Frank "Stan The Man" b: 11/21/20, Donora, Pa. BL/TL, 6', 175 lbs. Deb: 9/17/41 H♦

YEAR TM/L	W	L	PCT	G	GS	CG	SH	SV	IP	H	HR	BB	SO	RAT	ERA	ERA+	OAV	OOB	BH	AVG	PB	PR	/A	PD	TPI
1952 StL-N★	0	0	—	1	0	0	0	0	0	0	0	0	0	—		.000	.000		194	.336	1	0	0	0	0.0

● **JEFF MUSSELMAN** Musselman, Jeffrey Joseph b: 6/21/63, Doylestown, Pa. BL/TL, 6', 180 lbs. Deb: 9/2/86

YEAR TM/L	W	L	PCT	G	GS	CG	SH	SV	IP	H	HR	BB	SO	RAT	ERA	ERA+	OAV	OOB	BH	AVG	PB	PR	/A	PD	TPI
1986 Tor-A	0	0	—	6	0	0	0	0	5¹	8	1	5	4	21.9	10.13	42	.333	.448	0		0	-4	-4	0	-0.1
1987 Tor-A	12	5	.706	68	1	0	0	3	89	75	7	54	54	13.3	4.15	108	.237	.354	0		0	3	3	1	0.5
1988 Tor-A	8	5	.615	15	15	0	0	0	85	80	4	30	39	12.0	3.18	124	.252	.322	0		0	7	7	-1	0.9
1989 Tor-A	0	1	.000	5	3	0	0	0	11	19	2	9	3	22.9	10.64	35	.404	.500	0		0	-8	-8	-0	-0.6
NY-N	3	2	.600	20	0	0	0	0	26¹	27	1	14	11	14.0	3.08	106	.267	.357	0		0	1	1	2	0.3
1990 NY-N	0	2	.000	28	0	0	0	0	32	40	3	11	14	14.6	5.63	67	.310	.369	0	.000	-0	-7	-7	0	-0.4
Total 5	23	15	.605	142	19	0	0	3	248²	249	18	123	125	13.7	4.31	94	.266	.356	0	.000	-7	-8	2	0.6

● **RON MUSSELMAN** Musselman, Ralph Ronald b: 11/11/54, Wilmington, N.C. BR/TR, 6'2", 185 lbs. Deb: 8/18/82

YEAR TM/L	W	L	PCT	G	GS	CG	SH	SV	IP	H	HR	BB	SO	RAT	ERA	ERA+	OAV	OOB	BH	AVG	PB	PR	/A	PD	TPI
1982 Sea-A	1	0	1.000	12	0	0	0	0	15²	18	2	14	14	14.4	3.45	123	.300	.373	0		0	1	1	0	-0.1
1984 Tor-A	0	2	.000	11	0	0	0	1	21¹	18	2	10	9	11.8	2.11	194	.225	.311	0		0	4	5	-0	0.1
1985 Tor-A	3	0	1.000	25	4	0	0	0	52¹	59	2	24	29	14.3	4.47	94	.284	.358	0		0	-2	-2	-1	-0.4
Total 3	4	2	.667	48	4	0	0	1	89¹	95	6	40	47	13.7	3.73	112	.273	.350	0		0	4	5	-1	-0.4

● **PAUL MUSSER** Musser, Paul b: 6/24/1889, Millheim, Pa. d: 7/7/73, State College, Pa. BR/TR, 6', 175 lbs. Deb: 6/6/12

YEAR TM/L	W	L	PCT	G	GS	CG	SH	SV	IP	H	HR	BB	SO	RAT	ERA	ERA+	OAV	OOB	BH	AVG	PB	PR	/A	PD	TPI
1912 Was-A	0	0	—	7	2	0	0	0	20²	16	0	16	10	14.8	2.61	128	.225	.382	0	.000	-1	2	2	-0	-0.1
1919 Bos-A	0	2	.000	5	4	1	0	0	19²	26	0	8	14	15.6	4.12	73	.342	.405	0	.000	-1	-2	-2	-0	-0.4
Total 2	0	2	.000	12	6	1	0	0	40¹	42	0	24	24	15.2	3.35	95	.286	.393	0	.000	-2	-0	-1	0	-0.5

● **BARNEY MUSSILL** Mussill, Bernard James b: 10/1/19, Bower Hill, Pa. BR/TL, 6'1", 200 lbs. Deb: 4/20/44

YEAR TM/L	W	L	PCT	G	GS	CG	SH	SV	IP	H	HR	BB	SO	RAT	ERA	ERA+	OAV	OOB	BH	AVG	PB	PR	/A	PD	TPI
1944 Phi-N	0	1	.000	16	0	0	0	0	19¹	20	1	13	13	15.4	6.05	60	.267	.375	0	.000	-0	-5	-5	-0	-0.3

● **MIKE MUSSINA** Mussina, Michael Cole b: 12/8/68, Williamsport, Pa. BR/TR, 6'2", 185 lbs. Deb: 8/4/91

YEAR TM/L	W	L	PCT	G	GS	CG	SH	SV	IP	H	HR	BB	SO	RAT	ERA	ERA+	OAV	OOB	BH	AVG	PB	PR	/A	PD	TPI
1991 Bal-A	4	5	.444	12	12	2	0	0	87²	77	7	21	52	10.2	2.87	137	.239	.288	0	—	0	12	10	-0	1.1
1992 Bal-A★	18	5	**.783**	32	32	8	4	0	241	212	16	48	130	**9.8**	2.54	158	.239	**.279**	0	—	0	37	40	-0	3.5
1993 Bal-A☆	14	6	.700	25	25	3	0	0	167²	163	20	44	117	11.3	4.46	100	.256	.307	0	—	0	-3	0	-0	-0.2
1994 Bal-A★	16	5	.762	24	24	3	0	0	176¹	163	19	42	99	10.5	3.06	163	.248	.294	0	—	0	34	36	1	3.9
1995 Bal-A	**19**	9	.679	32	32	7	**4**	0	221²	187	24	50	158	9.7	3.29	144	.226	.271	0	—	0	35	36	1	3.9
1996 *Bal-A	19	11	.633	36	36	4	1	0	243¹	264	31	69	204	12.4	4.81	102	.275	.326	0	—	0	5	2	1	0.4
Total 6	90	41	.687	161	161	27	11	0	1137²	1066	117	274	760	10.7	3.56	128	.249	.295	0	—	0	121	127	0	12.6

● **ALEX MUSTAIKIS** Mustaikis, Alexander Dominick b: 3/26/09, Chelsea, Mass. d: 1/17/70, Scranton, Pa. BR/TR, 6'3", 180 lbs. Deb: 7/7/40

YEAR TM/L	W	L	PCT	G	GS	CG	SH	SV	IP	H	HR	BB	SO	RAT	ERA	ERA+	OAV	OOB	BH	AVG	PB	PR	/A	PD	TPI
1940 Bos-A	0	1	.000	6	1	0	0	0	15	15	1	15	6	18.0	9.00	50	.254	.405	2	.333	-3	-8	-8	1	-0.3

● **JEFF MUTIS** Mutis, Jeffrey Thomas b: 12/20/66, Allentown, Pa. BL/TL, 6'2", 185 lbs. Deb: 6/15/91

YEAR TM/L	W	L	PCT	G	GS	CG	SH	SV	IP	H	HR	BB	SO	RAT	ERA	ERA+	OAV	OOB	BH	AVG	PB	PR	/A	PD	TPI
1991 Cle-A	0	3	.000	3	3	0	0	0	12¹	23	1	7	6	21.9	11.68	36	.397	.462	0		0	-10	-10	-0	-1.7
1992 Cle-A	0	2	.000	3	2	0	0	0	11¹	24	4	6	6	23.8	9.53	41	.429	.484	0		0	-7	-7	0	-0.9
1993 Cle-A	3	6	.333	17	13	1	1	0	81	93	14	33	29	14.8	5.78	75	.289	.367	0		0	-13	-13	1	-1.1
1994 Fla-N	1	0	1.000	35	0	0	0	0	38¹	61	6	15	30	15.7	5.40	81	.331	.394	0	.000	-0	-5	-4	0	-0.1
Total 4	4	11	.267	58	18	1	1	0	143	191	25	61	73	16.4	6.48	66	.324	.395	0	.000	-0	-36	-35	1	-3.8

● **ELMER MYERS** Myers, Elmer Glenn b: 3/2/1894, York Springs, Pa. d: 7/29/76, Collingswood, N.J. BR/TR, 6'2", 185 lbs. Deb: 10/6/15

YEAR TM/L	W	L	PCT	G	GS	CG	SH	SV	IP	H	HR	BB	SO	RAT	ERA	ERA+	OAV	OOB	BH	AVG	PB	PR	/A	PD	TPI
1915 Phi-A	1	0	1.000	1	1	1	1	0	9	2	0	5	12	7.0	0.00	—	.074	.219	0	.000	-0	3	3	-0	0.2
1916 Phi-A	14	23	.378	44	35	31	2	1	315	280	7	168	182	13.2	3.66	78	.248	.353	27	.214	2	-29	-28	5	-2.3
1917 Phi-A	9	16	.360	38	23	13	2	3	201²	221	2	79	88	13.6	4.42	62	.283	.353	18	.247	3	-39	-37	-4	-4.1
1918 Phi-A	4	8	.333	18	15	7	1	0	95¹	101	4	42	17	13.9	4.63	63	.283	.365	5	.143	-2	-20	-18	2	-2.2
1919 Cle-A	8	7	.533	23	15	6	1	1	134²	134	3	43	38	12.5	3.74	89	.264	.334	11	.239	2	-8	-6	1	-0.3
1920 Cle-A	2	4	.333	16	7	2	1	0	71²	91	1	23	16	15.1	4.77	80	.316	.374	6	.240	0	-8	-8	0	-0.6
Bos-A	9	1	.900	12	10	9	1	0	97	90	1	24	24	10.8	2.13	171	.249	.299	12	.316	3	18	16	-1	1.8
Yr	11	5	.688	28	17	11	1	0	168²	183	2	47	50	12.4	3.25	114	.277	.327	18	.286	3	10	9	-1	1.2
1921 Bos-A	8	12	.400	30	20	11	0	0	172	217	11	53	40	14.7	4.87	87	.315	.373	14	.215	-2	-11	-12	-0	-1.3
1922 Bos-A	0	1	.000	3	1	0	0	0	5²	10	1	3	1	23.8	17.47	24	.370	.469	0	.000	-0	-8	-8	-0	-1.1
Total 8	55	72	.433	185	127	78	8	2	1102	1148	30	440	428	13.4	4.06	80	.275	.352	93	.226	4	-102	-97	8	-9.9

● **HENRY MYERS** Myers, Henry C. b: 5/1858, Philadelphia, Pa. d: 4/18/1895, Philadelphia, Pa. BR/TR, 5'9", 159 lbs. Deb: 8/20/1881 M♦

YEAR TM/L	W	L	PCT	G	GS	CG	SH	SV	IP	H	HR	BB	SO	RAT	ERA	ERA+	OAV	OOB	BH	AVG	PB	PR	/A	PD	TPI
1882 Bal-a	0	2	.000	6	2	1	0	0	26	30	2	4	7	11.8	6.58	42	.270	.296	53	.180	-1	-11	-11	-0	-0.7

● **JIMMY MYERS** Myers, James Xavier b: 4/28/69, Oklahoma City, Okla. BR/TR, 6'1", 190 lbs. Deb: 4/6/96

YEAR TM/L	W	L	PCT	G	GS	CG	SH	SV	IP	H	HR	BB	SO	RAT	ERA	ERA+	OAV	OOB	BH	AVG	PB	PR	/A	PD	TPI
1996 Bal-A	0	0	—	11	0	0	0	0	14	18	4	3	6	13.5	7.07	69	.305	.339	0	—	0	-3	-3	-0	0.1

● **JOSEPH MYERS** Myers, Joseph William b: 3/18/1882, Wilmington, Del. d: 2/11/56, Delaware City, Del. BR/TR, 5'10.5", 205 lbs. Deb: 10/7/05

YEAR TM/L	W	L	PCT	G	GS	CG	SH	SV	IP	H	HR	BB	SO	RAT	ERA	ERA+	OAV	OOB	BH	AVG	PB	PR	/A	PD	TPI
1905 Phi-A	0	0	—	1	1	0	0	0	9	5	0	3	5	12.6	3.60	74	.176	.333	0	—	0	-1	-1	-0	0.0

● **MIKE MYERS** Myers, Michael Stanley b: 6/26/69, Cook County, Ill. BL/TL, 6'3", 200 lbs. Deb: 4/25/95

YEAR TM/L	W	L	PCT	G	GS	CG	SH	SV	IP	H	HR	BB	SO	RAT	ERA	ERA+	OAV	OOB	BH	AVG	PB	PR	/A	PD	TPI
1995 Fla-N	0	0	—	2	0	0	0	0	2	2	0	0	3	18.0	0.00		.167	.444	0		0	1	1	-0	0.0
Det-A	1	0	1.000	11	0	0	0	0	6¹	10	1	4	4	22.7	9.95	48	.385	.500	0		0	-4	-4	0	-0.4
1996 Det-A	1	5	.167	83	0	0	0	6	64²	70	6	34	69	15.0	5.01	101	.272	.366	0		0	-3	-2	2	0.2
Total 2	2	5	.286	96	0	0	0	6	73	81	7	41	73	15.8	5.30	95	.280	.381	0		0	-3	-2	2	-0.2

● **RANDY MYERS** Myers, Randall Kirk b: 9/19/62, Vancouver, Wash. BL/TL, 6'1", 190 lbs. Deb: 10/6/85

YEAR TM/L	W	L	PCT	G	GS	CG	SH	SV	IP	H	HR	BB	SO	RAT	ERA	ERA+	OAV	OOB	BH	AVG	PB	PR	/A	PD	TPI
1985 NY-N	0	0	—	1	0	0	0	0	2	0	0	1	2	4.5	0.00		.000	.143	0		0	1	1	0	0.0
1986 NY-N	0	0	—	10	0	0	0	0	10²	9	1	9	13	17.7	4.22	84	.256	.396	0		0	-1	-1	0	0.0
1987 NY-N	3	6	.333	54	0	0	0	6	75	61	9	30	92	10.9	3.96	95	.225	.302	2	.286	1	-2	0	-1	-0.1
1988 *NY-N	7	3	.700	55	0	0	0	26	68	45	9	17	69	8.5	1.72	187	.190	.250	1	.250	1	13	11	-1	2.5
1989 NY-N	7	4	.636	65	0	0	0	24	84¹	62	4	40	88	10.9	2.35	139	.206	.299	0	.000	-1	11	9	0	1.5
1990 *Cin-N★	4	6	.400	66	0	0	0	31	86²	59	6	38	98	10.4	2.08	190	.193	.288	1	.250	0	17	18	0	3.3
1991 Cin-N	6	13	.316	58	12	1	0	6	132	116	8	80	108	13.4	3.55	107	.242	.351	5	.172	0	2	4	-1	0.4

YEAR TM/L	W	L	PCT	G	GS	CG	SH	SV	IP	H	HR	BB	SO	RAT	ERA	ERA+	OAV	OOB	BH	AVG	PB	PR	/A	PD	TPI
1992 SD-N	3	6	.333	66	0	0	0	38	79^2	84	7	34	66	13.4	4.29	83	.279	.354	1	.143	0	-7	-6	-0	-1.3
1993 Chi-N	2	4	.333	73	0	0	0	**53**	75^1	65	7	26	86	11.0	3.11	128	.230	.297	1	.500	1	8	7	-1	1.5
1994 Chi-N★	1	5	.167	38	0	0	0	21	40^1	40	3	16	32	12.5	3.79	109	.260	.329	0	.000	-0	2	2	-1	0.3
1995 Chi-N★	1	2	.333	57	0	0	0	**38**	55^2	49	7	28	59	12.4	3.88	106	.237	.328	0	—	0	2	1	0	0.3
1996 *Bal-A	4	4	.500	62	0	0	0	31	58^2	60	7	29	74	13.8	3.53	139	.265	.352	0	—	0	10	9	-1	1.9
Total 12	38	53	.418	605	12	1	0	274	768^1	652	61	348	787	11.8	3.20	119	.232	.318	11	.186	2	58	53	-3	10.3

● **RODNEY MYERS**   Myers, Rodney Luther b: 6/26/69, Rockford, Ill.   BR/TR, 6'1", 200 lbs.   Deb: 4/3/96

YEAR TM/L	W	L	PCT	G	GS	CG	SH	SV	IP	H	HR	BB	SO	RAT	ERA	ERA+	OAV	OOB	BH	AVG	PB	PR	/A	PD	TPI
1996 Chi-N	2	1	.667	45	0	0	0	0	67^1	61	6	38	50	13.6	4.68	91	.243	.349	0	.000	-1	-3	-3	-1	-0.2

● **BOB MYRICK**   Myrick, Robert Howard b: 10/1/52, Hattiesburg, Miss.   BR/TL, 6'1", 195 lbs.   Deb: 5/28/76

YEAR TM/L	W	L	PCT	G	GS	CG	SH	SV	IP	H	HR	BB	SO	RAT	ERA	ERA+	OAV	OOB	BH	AVG	PB	PR	/A	PD	TPI
1976 NY-N	1	1	.500	21	1	0	0	0	27^2	34	2	13	11	15.3	3.25	101	.306	.379	0	.000	-0	1	0	0	0.0
1977 NY-N	2	2	.500	44	4	0	0	1	87^1	86	5	33	49	12.4	3.61	104	.265	.334	2	.182	-0	3	1	0	0.1
1978 NY-N	0	3	.000	17	0	0	0	0	24^2	18	3	13	13	11.3	3.28	106	.207	.310	0	.000	-0	1	1	0	0.1
Total 3	3	6	.333	82	5	0	0	2	139^2	138	10	59	73	12.8	3.48	104	.264	.340	2	.125	-1	4	2	1	0.2

● **CHRIS NABHOLZ**   Nabholz, Christopher William b: 1/5/67, Harrisburg, Pa.   BL/TL, 6'5", 210 lbs.   Deb: 6/11/90

YEAR TM/L	W	L	PCT	G	GS	CG	SH	SV	IP	H	HR	BB	SO	RAT	ERA	ERA+	OAV	OOB	BH	AVG	PB	PR	/A	PD	TPI
1990 Mon-N	6	2	.750	11	11	1	1	0	70	43	6	32	53	9.9	2.83	129	.176	.276	0	.000	-2	7	6	-0	0.5
1991 Mon-N	8	7	.533	24	24	1	0	0	153^2	134	5	57	99	11.3	3.63	100	.237	.309	6	.115	-1	1	-0	1	0.0
1992 Mon-N	11	12	.478	32	32	1	1	0	195	176	11	74	130	11.8	3.32	104	.244	.318	8	.123	-1	4	3	3	0.6
1993 Mon-N	9	8	.529	26	21	1	0	0	116^2	100	9	63	74	13.2	4.09	102	.236	.346	5	.128	-1	-1	1	0	0.0
1994 Cle-A	0	1	.000	6	4	0	0	0	11	23	1	9	5	27.0	11.45	41	.418	.508	0	—	0	-8	-8	0	-0.6
Bos-A	3	4	.429	8	8	0	0	0	42	44	5	29	23	16.1	6.64	76	.282	.401	0	—	0	-9	-8	0	-1.0
Yr	3	5	.375	14	12	0	0	0	53	67	6	38	28	18.2	7.64	65	.315	.423	0	—	0	-17	-16	0	-1.6
1995 Chi-N	0	1	.000	34	0	0	0	0	23^1	22	4	14	21	13.9	5.40	76	.253	.356	0	.000	-0	-3	-3	0	-0.1
Total 6	37	35	.514	141	100	4	2	0	611^2	542	41	278	405	12.4	3.94	97	.240	.329	19	.107	-5	-8	-9	4	-0.6

● **JACK NABORS**   Nabors, Herman John b: 11/19/1887, Montevallo, Ala. d: 11/20/23, Wilton, Ala.   BR/TR, 6'3", 185 lbs.   Deb: 8/9/15

YEAR TM/L	W	L	PCT	G	GS	CG	SH	SV	IP	H	HR	BB	SO	RAT	ERA	ERA+	OAV	OOB	BH	AVG	PB	PR	/A	PD	TPI
1915 Phi-A	0	5	.000	10	7	2	0	0	54	58	1	35	18	16.3	5.50	53	.304	.424	2	.125	-1	-15	-15	-0	-1.4
1916 Phi-A	1	20	.048	40	30	11	0	1	212^2	206	2	95	74	12.9	3.47	82	.266	.349	7	.101	-4	-15	-14	-2	-2.1
1917 Phi-A	0	0	—	2	0	0	0	0	3	2	0	1	2	9.0	3.00	92	.200	.273	0	—	0	-0	-0	0	0.0
Total 3	1	25	.038	52	37	13	0	1	269^2	266	3	131	94	13.5	3.87	74	.273	.364	9	.106	-6	-31	-30	-2	-3.5

● **BILL NAGEL**   Nagel, William Taylor b: 8/19/15, Memphis, Tenn. d: 10/8/81, Freehold, N.J.   BR/TR, 6'1", 190 lbs.   Deb: 4/20/39

YEAR TM/L	W	L	PCT	G	GS	CG	SH	SV	IP	H	HR	BB	SO	RAT	ERA	ERA+	OAV	OOB	BH	AVG	PB	PR	/A	PD	TPI
1939 Phi-A	0	0	—	1	0	0	0	0	3	7	1	1	0	24.0	12.00	39	.438	.471	86	.252	0	-2	-2	-0	0.0

● **JUDGE NAGLE**   Nagle, Walter Harold "Lucky" b: 3/10/1880, Santa Rosa, Cal. d: 5/26/71, Santa Rosa, Cal.   BR/TR, 6', 176 lbs.   Deb: 4/26/11

YEAR TM/L	W	L	PCT	G	GS	CG	SH	SV	IP	H	HR	BB	SO	RAT	ERA	ERA+	OAV	OOB	BH	AVG	PB	PR	/A	PD	TPI
1911 Pit-N	4	2	.667	8	3	1	0	1	27^1	33	3	6	11	13.2	3.62	95	.324	.367	1	.143	-0	-1	-1	0	-0.1
Bos-A	1	1	.500	5	1	0	0	0	27	27	2	6	12	11.0	3.33	98	.262	.303	1	.100	-1	0	-0	-1	-0.2
Total 1	5	3	.625	13	4	1	0	1	54^1	60	5	12	23	12.1	3.48	96	.293	.335	2	.118	-1	-1	-1	-1	-0.3

● **CHARLES NAGY**   Nagy, Charles Harrison b: 5/5/67, Bridgeport, Conn.   BL/TR, 6'3", 200 lbs.   Deb: 6/29/90

YEAR TM/L	W	L	PCT	G	GS	CG	SH	SV	IP	H	HR	BB	SO	RAT	ERA	ERA+	OAV	OOB	BH	AVG	PB	PR	/A	PD	TPI
1990 Cle-A	2	4	.333	9	8	0	0	0	45^2	58	7	21	26	15.8	5.91	66	.315	.388	0	—	0	-10	-10	1	-1.1
1991 Cle-A	10	15	.400	33	33	6	1	0	211^1	228	15	66	109	12.8	4.13	101	.275	.333	0	—	0	-1	1	-1	-0.1
1992 Cle-A★	17	10	.630	33	33	10	3	0	252	245	11	57	169	10.9	2.96	132	.260	.303	0	—	0	27	26	3	3.1
1993 Cle-A	2	6	.250	9	9	1	0	0	48^2	66	6	13	30	15.0	6.29	69	.322	.368	0	—	0	-11	-11	2	-1.2
1994 Cle-A	10	8	.556	23	23	3	0	0	169^1	175	14	48	108	12.1	3.45	137	.265	.320	0	—	0	25	24	1	2.2
1995 *Cle-A	16	6	.727	29	29	2	1	0	178	194	20	61	139	13.2	4.55	103	.278	.342	0	—	0	3	3	3	0.5
1996 *Cle-A★	17	5	**.773**	32	32	5	0	0	222	217	21	61	167	11.4	3.41	144	.255	.307	0	—	0	39	37	3	3.4 ♦
Total 7	74	54	.578	168	167	27	5	0	1127	1183	95	327	748	12.3	3.86	114	.271	.325	0	—	0	73	70	11	6.8

● **MIKE NAGY**   Nagy, Michael Timothy b: 3/25/48, Bronx, N.Y.   BR/TR, 6'3", 200 lbs.   Deb: 4/21/69

YEAR TM/L	W	L	PCT	G	GS	CG	SH	SV	IP	H	HR	BB	SO	RAT	ERA	ERA+	OAV	OOB	BH	AVG	PB	PR	/A	PD	TPI
1969 Bos-A	12	2	.857	33	28	7	1	0	196^2	183	10	106	84	13.7	3.11	122	.245	.347	5	.077	-2	11	15	0	0.8
1970 Bos-A	6	5	.545	23	20	4	0	0	128^2	138	16	64	56	14.3	4.48	88	.275	.359	11	.250	-2	-11	-7	-1	-0.5
1971 Bos-A	1	3	.250	12	7	0	0	0	38	46	4	20	9	15.6	6.63	56	.315	.398	1	.083	-1	-13	-12	-1	-1.3
1972 Bos-A	0	0	—	1	0	0	0	0	2	3	0	2	2	18.0	9.00	36	.375	.444	0	—	0	-1	-1	-0	0.0
1973 StL-N	0	2	.000	9	7	0	0	0	40^2	44	4	15	14	13.3	4.20	87	.282	.349	1	.091	-0	-2	-3	-0	-0.2
1974 Hou-N	1	1	.500	9	0	0	0	0	12^2	17	3	5	5	16.3	8.53	41	.309	.377	0	.000	-0	-7	-7	-0	-1.0
Total 6	20	13	.606	87	62	11	1	0	418^2	431	37	210	170	14.1	4.15	92	.267	.357	18	.135	-2	-24	-16	-1	-2.2

● **STEVE NAGY**   Nagy, Stephen b: 5/28/19, Franklin, N.J.   BL/TL, 5'9", 174 lbs.   Deb: 4/20/47

YEAR TM/L	W	L	PCT	G	GS	CG	SH	SV	IP	H	HR	BB	SO	RAT	ERA	ERA+	OAV	OOB	BH	AVG	PB	PR	/A	PD	TPI
1947 Pit-N	1	3	.250	6	1	0	0	0	14	18	1	9	4	17.4	5.79	73	.310	.403	1	.250	-0	-3	-2	-0	-0.6
1950 Was-A	2	5	.286	9	9	2	0	0	53^1	69	5	29	17	16.5	6.58	68	.307	.386	5	.227	2	-12	-12	-0	-1.1
Total 2	3	8	.273	15	10	2	0	0	67^1	87	6	38	21	16.7	6.42	69	.307	.389	6	.231	2	-15	-15	-0	-1.7

● **SAM NAHEM**   Nahem, Samuel Ralph "Subway Sam" b: 10/19/15, New York, N.Y.   BR/TR, 6'1.5", 190 lbs.   Deb: 10/2/38

YEAR TM/L	W	L	PCT	G	GS	CG	SH	SV	IP	H	HR	BB	SO	RAT	ERA	ERA+	OAV	OOB	BH	AVG	PB	PR	/A	PD	TPI
1938 Bro-N	1	0	1.000	1	1	1	0	0	9	6	0	4	2	10.0	3.00	130	.194	.286	2	.400	0	1	1	-0	0.1
1941 StL-N	5	2	.714	26	8	2	0	1	81^2	76	2	38	31	12.8	2.98	126	.243	.329	4	.174	-1	6	7	1	0.6
1942 Phi-N	1	3	.250	35	2	0	0	1	74^2	72	2	40	38	13.7	4.94	67	.254	.350	2	.100	-1	-13	-14	1	-0.7
1948 Phi-N	3	3	.500	28	1	0	0	0	59	68	4	45	30	17.7	7.02	56	.288	.408	2	.154	-0	-20	-20	-1	-1.9
Total 4	10	8	.556	90	12	3	0	1	224^1	222	8	127	101	14.3	4.69	78	.257	.357	10	.164	-2	-27	-26	1	-1.9

● **PETE NAKTENIS**   Naktenis, Peter Ernest b: 6/12/14, Aberdeen, Wash.   BL/TL, 6'1", 185 lbs.   Deb: 6/13/36

YEAR TM/L	W	L	PCT	G	GS	CG	SH	SV	IP	H	HR	BB	SO	RAT	ERA	ERA+	OAV	OOB	BH	AVG	PB	PR	/A	PD	TPI
1936 Phi-A	0	1	.000	7	1	0	0	0	18^2	24	2	27	18	25.6	12.54	41	.324	.515	1	.200	-0	-16	-15	-1	-0.7
1939 Cin-N	0	0	—	3	0	0	0	0	4	2	0	0	1	9.0	2.25	170	.154	.267	0	—	0	1	1	0	0.0
Total 2	0	1	.000	10	1	0	0	0	22^2	26	2	27	19	22.6	10.72	45	.299	.483	1	.200	-0	-15	-15	-0	-0.7

● **BUDDY NAPIER**   Napier, Skelton Le Roy b: 12/18/1889, Byromville, Ga. d: 3/29/68, Hutchins, Tex.   BR/TR, 5'11", 165 lbs.   Deb: 8/14/12

YEAR TM/L	W	L	PCT	G	GS	CG	SH	SV	IP	H	HR	BB	SO	RAT	ERA	ERA+	OAV	OOB	BH	AVG	PB	PR	/A	PD	TPI
1912 StL-A	1	2	.333	7	2	0	0	0	25^1	33	0	5	10	14.6	4.97	67	.317	.366	0	.000	-1	-5	-5	-0	-0.6
1918 Chi-N	0	0	—	1	0	0	0	0	6^2	10	0	4	2	18.9	5.40	52	.357	.438	1	.333	0	-2	-2	-0	-0.2
1920 Cin-N	4	2	.667	9	5	5	1	0	49	47	0	7	17	10.1	1.29	236	.254	.285	3	.214	1	10	10	0	1.3
1921 Cin-N	0	2	.000	22	6	1	0	0	56^2	72	2	13	14	13.5	5.56	64	.329	.366	2	.143	1	-11	-12	1	-0.2
Total 4	5	6	.455	39	13	6	1	0	137^2	162	2	29	43	12.7	3.92	84	.302	.343	6	.158	1	-8	-9	1	0.2

● **CHOLLY NARANJO**   Naranjo, Lazaro Ramon Gonzalo "Gonzalo" b: 11/25/34, Havana, Cuba   BL/TR, 5'11.5", 165 lbs.   Deb: 7/8/56

YEAR TM/L	W	L	PCT	G	GS	CG	SH	SV	IP	H	HR	BB	SO	RAT	ERA	ERA+	OAV	OOB	BH	AVG	PB	PR	/A	PD	TPI
1956 Pit-N	1	2	.333	17	3	0	0	0	34^1	37	7	17	26	14.4	4.46	85	.282	.369	1	.143	0	-3	-3	1	-0.1

● **RAY NARLESKI**   Narleski, Raymond Edmond b: 11/25/28, Camden, N.J.   BR/TR, 6'1", 175 lbs.   Deb: 4/17/54   F

YEAR TM/L	W	L	PCT	G	GS	CG	SH	SV	IP	H	HR	BB	SO	RAT	ERA	ERA+	OAV	OOB	BH	AVG	PB	PR	/A	PD	TPI
1954 *Cle-A	3	3	.500	42	2	1	0	13	89	59	8	44	52	10.6	2.22	165	.189	.293	0	.000	-2	15	14	-1	1.1
1955 Cle-A	9	1	.900	**60**	1	1	0	**19**	111^2	91	11	52	94	11.5	3.71	108	.220	.308	7	.292	1	3	3	-2	0.3
1956 Cle-A†	3	2	.600	32	0	0	0	4	59^1	36	5	19	42	8.5	1.52	277	.170	.241	2	.250	0	**17**	**18**	-1	1.6
1957 Cle-A	11	5	.688	46	15	7	1	16	154^1	136	14	70	93	12.2	3.09	120	.235	.322	4	.093	-1	12	11	-4	0.7
1958 Cle-A★	13	10	.565	44	24	7	0	1	183^1	179	21	91	102	13.4	4.07	90	.255	.343	11	.204	1	-6	-9	-3	-1.2
1959 Det-A	4	12	.250	42	10	1	0	5	104^1	105	21	59	71	14.2	5.78	70	.254	.348	2	.095	-1	-22	-20	-2	-3.2
Total 6	43	33	.566	266	52	17	1	58	702	606	80	335	454	12.2	3.60	106	.230	.320	26	.157	-2	19	18	-12	-0.7

● **BUSTER NARUM**   Narum, Leslie Ferdinand b: 11/16/40, Philadelphia, Pa.   BR/TR, 6'1", 200 lbs.   Deb: 4/14/63

YEAR TM/L	W	L	PCT	G	GS	CG	SH	SV	IP	H	HR	BB	SO	RAT	ERA	ERA+	OAV	OOB	BH	AVG	PB	PR	/A	PD	TPI
1963 Bal-A	0	0	—	7	0	0	0	0	9	8		5	5	13.0	3.00	116	.242	.342	1	1.000	-1	1	0	-0	0.2
1964 Was-A	9	15	.375	38	32	7	2	0	199	195	31	73	121	12.3	4.30	86	.255	.342	4	.061	-5	-15	-12	-2	-0.6
1965 Was-A	4	12	.250	46	24	2	0	0	173^2	176	16	91	86	14.2	4.46	78	.267	.361	2	.043	-2	-19	-19	2	-1.6
1966 Was-A	0	0	—	3	0	0	0	0	3^1	11	2	4	0	40.5	21.60	16	.579	.652	0	—	0	-7	-7	0	0.0
1967 Was-A	1	0	1.000	9	2	0	0	0	11^2	8		4	8	9.3	3.09	103	.195	.267	0	—	0	0	0	-0	-0.1
Total 5	14	27	.341	96	58	9	2	0	396^2	398	50	177	220	13.3	4.45	80	.264	.346	7	.059	-6	-40	-38	0	-3.7

YEAR TM/L	W	L	PCT	G	GS	CG	SH	SV	IP	H	HR	BB	SO	RAT	ERA	ERA+	OAV	OOB	BH	AVG	PB	PR	/A	PD	TPI
● JIM NASH Nash, James Edwin b: 2/9/45, Hawthorne, Nev. BR/TR, 6'5", 230 lbs. Deb: 7/3/66																									
1966 KC-A	12	1	.923	18	17	5	0	1	127	95	6	47	98	10.1	2.06	165	.204	.277	5	.102	-2	19	19	-3	1.5
1967 KC-A	12	17	.414	37	34	8	2	0	222¹	200	21	87	186	11.8	3.76	85	.242	.317	7	.100	-2	-13	-14	-2	-2.2
1968 Oak-A	13	13	.500	34	33	12	6	0	228²	185	18	55	169	9.6	2.28	123	.219	.270	5	.068	-2	18	14	-3	1.1
1969 Oak-A	8	8	.500	26	19	3	1	0	115¹	112	17	30	75	11.2	3.67	94	.247	.296	4	.111	-1	-1	-3	-1	-0.5
1970 Atl-N	13	9	.591	34	33	6	2	0	212¹	211	22	90	153	13.0	4.07	105	.257	.334	7	.087	-3	-1	5	0	0.2
1971 Atl-N	9	7	.563	32	19	2	0	2	133	166	17	50	65	14.6	4.94	75	.314	.374	1	.149	-1	-22	-18	-1	-2.3
1972 Atl-N	1	1	.500	11	4	0	0	1	31¹	35	2	25	10	17.2	5.46	69	.307	.432	2	.222	-0	-7	-6	-0	-0.4
Phi-N	0	8	.000	9	8	0	0	1	37¹	46	5	17	15	15.9	6.27	57	.311	.393	1	.100	-0	-12	-11	0	-2.0
Yr	1	9	.100	20	12	0	0	1	68²	81	7	42	25	16.5	5.90	62	.305	.405	3	.158	-0	-19	-17	-0	-2.4
Total 7	68	64	.515	201	167	36	11	4	1107¹	1050	108	401	771	11.9	3.58	96	.250	.318	38	.101	-11	-18	-16	-10	-4.6
● BILLY NASH Nash, William Mitchell b: 6/24/1865, Richmond, Va. d: 11/15/29, E.Orange, N.J. BR/TR, 5'8.5", 167 lbs. Deb: 8/5/1884 MU♦																									
1889 Bos-N	0	0	—	1	0	0	0	0	1	1	0	0	0	9.0	0.00	—	.000	.250	132	.274	0	0	0	-0	0.0
1890 Bos-P	0	0	—	1	0	0	0	0	0¹	1	0	0	0	27.0	0.00	—	.500	.500	130	.266	1	0	0	-0	0.0
Total 2	0	0	—	2	0	0	0	0	1¹	2	0	0	0	13.5	0.00	—	.200	.333	1606	.275	1	1	1	-0	0.0
● PHILIP NASTU Nastu, Philip b: 3/8/55, Bridgeport, Conn. BL/TL, 6'2", 180 lbs. Deb: 9/15/78																									
1978 SF-N	0	1	.000	3	1	0	0	0	8	8	1	2	5	11.3	5.63	61	.258	.303	0	.000	-0	-2	-2	-0	-0.2
1979 SF-N	3	4	.429	25	14	1	0	0	100	105	14	41	47	13.3	4.32	81	.272	.345	1	.042	-1	-7	-9	-0	-0.7
1980 SF-N	0	0	—	6	0	0	0	0	6	10	1	5	1	22.5	6.00	57	.357	.455	0	—	-0	-2	-2	-0	0.0
Total 3	3	5	.375	34	15	1	0	0	114	123	16	48	53	13.7	4.50	79	.276	.349	1	.040	-1	-10	-13	-0	-0.9
● DAN NAULTY Naulty, Daniel Donovan b: 1/6/70, Los Angeles, Cal. BR/TR, 6'6", 210 lbs. Deb: 4/2/96																									
1996 Min-A	3	2	.600	49	0	0	0	4	57	43	5	35	56	12.3	3.79	136	.207	.321	0	—	0	8	9	0	0.6
● JAIME NAVARRO Navarro, Jaime (Citron) b: 3/27/67, Bayamon, P.R. BR/TR, 6'4", 210 lbs. Deb: 6/20/89 F																									
1989 Mil-A	7	8	.467	19	17	1	0	0	109²	119	6	32	56	12.5	3.12	123	.277	.328	0	—	0	9	9	-0	1.1
1990 Mil-A	8	7	.533	32	22	3	0	1	149¹	176	11	41	75	13.3	4.46	87	.293	.343	0	—	0	-9	-10	-0	-0.9
1991 Mil-A	15	12	.556	34	34	10	2	0	234	237	16	73	114	12.2	3.92	101	.261	.320	0	—	0	4	1	-1	0.2
1992 Mil-A	17	11	.607	34	34	5	3	0	246	224	14	64	100	10.8	3.33	115	.246	.299	0	—	0	17	14	-3	1.2
1993 Mil-A	11	12	.478	35	34	5	1	0	214¹	254	21	73	114	14.2	5.33	80	.300	.363	0	—	0	-24	-26	-2	-2.5
1994 Mil-A	4	9	.308	29	10	0	0	0	89²	115	10	35	65	15.5	6.62	76	.314	.380	0	—	0	-18	-16	-1	-2.1
1995 Chi-N	14	6	.700	29	29	1	1	0	200¹	194	19	56	128	11.4	3.28	125	.251	.304	12	.185	2	20	18	-3	1.5
1996 Chi-N	15	12	.556	35	35	4	1	0	236²	244	25	72	158	12.4	3.92	109	.269	.329	10	.130	-3	7	-1	3	0.4
Total 8	91	77	.542	247	215	29	8	1	1480	1563	120	446	810	12.5	4.10	100	.272	.329	22	.155	-1	7	-1	-14	-1.3
● JULIO NAVARRO Navarro, Julio (Ventura) "Whiplash" b: 1/9/36, Vieques, P.R. BR/TR, 5'11", 190 lbs. Deb: 9/3/62 F																									
1962 LA-A	1	1	.500	9	0	0	0	0	15¹	20	2	4	11	14.1	4.70	82	.317	.358	1	.500	0	-1	-1	-0	-0.1
1963 LA-A	4	5	.444	57	0	0	0	12	90¹	75	7	32	53	10.9	2.89	119	.228	.300	3	.200	1	7	5	1	0.9
1964 LA-A	0	0	—	5	0	0	0	1	9¹	5	0	5	8	11.6	1.93	170	.167	.324	0	.000	-0	2	1	0	0.2
Det-A	2	1	.667	26	0	0	0	1	41	40	9	16	36	12.7	3.95	93	.250	.326	0	.000	-1	0	0	-0	-0.2
Yr	2	1	.667	31	0	0	0	3	50¹	45	9	21	44	12.2	3.58	100	.234	.316	0	.000	-1	0	0	-0	-0.2
1965 Det-A	0	2	.000	15	1	0	0	1	30	25	5	12	22	11.1	4.20	83	.238	.316	0	.000	-0	-2	-2	-0	-0.3
1966 Det-A	0	0	—	1	0	0	0	0	0	2	2	0	0	∞	—	1.000	1.000	0	—	0	-3	-3	-0	-0.3
1970 Atl-N	0	0	—	17	0	0	0	1	26¹	24	7	1	21	8.9	4.10	105	.233	.248	1	.167	-0	-1	1	0	0.0
Total 6	7	9	.438	130	1	0	0	17	212¹	191	32	70	151	11.4	3.65	99	.241	.309	5	.147	-0	1	-1	1	0.1
● EARL NAYLOR Naylor, Earl Eugene b: 5/19/19, Kansas City, Mo. d: 1/16/90, Winter Haven, Fla. BR/TR, 6', 190 lbs. Deb: 4/15/42 ♦																									
1942 Phi-N	0	5	.000	20	4	1	0	0	60¹	68	5	29	19	14.5	6.12	54	.286	.363	33	.196	1	-19	-19	-0	-1.4
● ROLLIE NAYLOR Naylor, Roleine Cecil b: 2/4/1892, Crum, Tex. d: 6/18/66, Fort Worth, Tex. BR/TR, 6'1.5", 180 lbs. Deb: 9/14/17																									
1917 Phi-A	2	2	.500	5	5	3	0	0	33	30	1	11	11	11.5	1.64	168	.265	.336	1	.091	-1	4	4	1	0.6
1919 Phi-A	5	18	.217	31	23	17	0	0	204²	210	6	64	68	12.2	3.34	103	.280	.339	12	.169	-2	-3	-2	-0	-0.1
1920 Phi-A	10	23	.303	42	36	20	0	0	251¹	306	7	86	90	14.3	3.47	116	.312	.371	14	.163	-6	9	15	2	1.4
1921 Phi-A	3	13	.188	32	19	6	0	0	169¹	214	10	55	39	14.5	4.84	92	.315	.369	6	.115	-4	-10	-7	-2	-1.1
1922 Phi-A	10	15	.400	35	26	11	0	0	171¹	212	7	51	37	14.0	4.73	90	.309	.359	11	.200	1	-13	-9	1	-1.0
1923 Phi-A	12	7	.632	26	20	9	2	0	143	149	5	59	27	13.1	3.46	119	.273	.344	11	.244	-1	8	10	2	1.2
1924 Phi-A	0	5	.000	10	7	1	0	0	38¹	53	2	20	10	17.1	6.34	68	.333	.408	3	.375	1	-9	-9	0	-0.8
Total 7	42	83	.336	181	136	67	2	0	1011	1174	34	346	282	13.7	3.93	102	.300	.359	58	.177	-11	-14	7	1	0.2
● MIKE NAYMICK Naymick, Michael John b: 9/6/17, Berlin, Pa. BR/TR, 6'8", 225 lbs. Deb: 9/24/39																									
1939 Cle-A	0	1	.000	2	1	1	0	0	4²	3	0	5	3	15.4	1.93	228	.188	.381	0	—	0	1	1	0	0.2
1940 Cle-A	1	2	.333	13	4	0	0	0	30	36	1	17	15	16.8	5.10	83	.290	.389	1	.167	0	-2	-3	1	-0.2
1943 Cle-A	4	4	.500	29	4	0	0	2	62²	32	3	47	41	11.8	2.30	135	.160	.328	3	.188	-0	7	6	1	0.8
1944 Cle-A	0	0	—	7	0	0	0	0	13	16	1	9	4	18.0	9.69	46	.314	.426	0	.000	-0	-9	-9	-0	0.0
StL-N	0	0	—	1	0	0	0	0	2	2	0	1	1	13.5	4.50	78	.333	.429	0	—	0	-0	-0	-0	0.0
Total 4	5	7	.417	52	9	1	0	2	112¹	89	5	80	64	14.0	3.93	89	.224	.362	4	.154	-1	-3	-6	1	0.8
● DENNY NEAGLE Neagle, Dennis Edward b: 9/13/68, Gambrills, Md. BL/TL, 6'4", 200 lbs. Deb: 7/27/91																									
1991 Min-A	0	1	.000	7	3	0	0	0	20	28	3	7	14	15.7	4.05	105	.329	.380	0	—	0	0	0	-0	-0.1
1992 *Pit-N	4	6	.400	55	6	0	0	2	86¹	81	9	43	77	13.1	4.48	77	.247	.338	0	—	-1	-9	-10	-1	-1.4
1993 Pit-N	3	5	.375	50	7	0	0	1	81¹	82	10	37	73	13.5	5.31	76	.258	.341	0	.000	-2	-11	-11	-1	-1.3
1994 Pit-N	9	10	.474	24	24	2	0	0	137	135	14	49	122	12.3	5.12	84	.259	.326	8	.190	1	-14	-14	-1	-1.4
1995 Pit-N★	13	8	.619	31	31	5	1	0	**209²**	221	20	45	150	11.5	3.43	125	.273	.314	9	.122	-0	17	20	1	1.9
1996 Pit-N	14	6	.700	27	27	1	0	0	182²	186	21	34	131	11.0	3.05	143	.267	.304	10	.182	-0	24	27	2	2.7
*Atl-N	2	3	.400	6	6	0	0	0	38²	40	5	14	18	12.6	5.59	79	.268	.331	2	.143	-0	-6	-5	-1	-0.6
Yr	16	9	.640	33	33	2	0	0	221¹	226	26	48	149	11.1	3.50	125	.266	.305	12	.174	-0	18	22	-1	2.1
Total 6	45	39	.536	200	104	9	1	3	755²	773	86	229	585	12.1	4.10	102	.266	.323	29	.138	-3	0	8	-2	-0.2
● JACK NEAGLE Neagle, John Henry b: 1/2/1858, Syracuse, N.Y. d: 9/20/04, Syracuse, N.Y. BR/TR, 5'6", 155 lbs. Deb: 7/8/1879 ♦																									
1879 Cin-N	0	1	.000	2	2	1	0	0	13	13	0	5	4	12.5	3.46	67	.241	.305	2	.167	-0	-1	-2	-0	-0.2
1883 Phi-N	1	7	.125	8	7	6	0	0	61¹	81	0	21	13	16.0	6.90	48	.315	.363	12	.164	-2	-26	-26	-1	-2.5
Bal-a	2	4	.200	6	5	4	0	0	46	48	1	20	16	13.3	4.89	71	.251	.322	10	.286	1	-8	-7	-0	-0.5
Pit-a	3	12	.200	16	16	12	0	0	114	156	4	25	41	14.3	5.84	55	.306	.338	19	.188	-1	-32	-33	-1	-3.3
Yr	4	16	.200	22	21	16	0	0	160	204	5	45	50	14.0	5.57	59	.291	.334	29	.213	-0	-40	-41	-1	-3.8
1884 Pit-a	11	26	.297	38	38	37	2	0	326	354	6	70	85	12.2	3.73	90	.255	.300	22	.149	-6	-17	-13	-3	-1.9
Total 3	16	50	.242	70	68	60	2	0	560¹	659	16	141	152	13.1	4.59	72	.272	.317	65	.176	-8	-85	-81	-5	-8.4
● JOE NEALE Neale, Joseph Hunt b: 5/7/1866, Wadsworth, Ohio d: 12/30/13, Akron, Ohio BR/TR, 5'8", 153 lbs. Deb: 6/21/1886 ♦																									
1886 Lou-a	0	1	.000	1	1	0	0	0	7	11	0	7	0	24.4	7.71	47	.393	.528	0	.000	-0	-3	-3	1	-0.3
1887 Lou-a	1	4	.200	5	4	4	0	0	41¹	60	4	15	11	16.6	6.97	63	.326	.383	1	.053	-2	-12	-12	0	-1.1
1890 StL-a	3	5	.625	10	9	8	0	0	69	53	4	15	23	9.4	3.39	127	.206	.261	2	.067	-3	4	7	-2	0.3
1891 StL-a	6	4	.600	15	11	9	1	0	110¹	109	4	36	24	12.4	4.24	99	.249	.317	6	.118	-3	-6	-2	-0	-0.2
Total 4	12	12	.500	31	25	21	1	1	227²	233	12	73	58	12.7	4.59	93	.257	.322	9	.086	-9	-18	-8	1	-1.3
● RON NECCIAI Necciai, Ronald Andrew b: 6/18/32, Gallatin, Pa. BR/TR, 6'5", 185 lbs. Deb: 8/10/52																									
1952 Pit-N	1	6	.143	12	9	1	0	0	54²	63	5	32	31	15.8	7.08	56	.296	.390	1	.059	-1	-20	-19	-0	-2.2
● RON NEGRAY Negray, Ronald Alvin b: 2/26/30, Akron, Ohio BR/TR, 6'1", 185 lbs. Deb: 9/14/52																									
1952 Bro-N	0	0	—	4	1	0	0	0	13	15	0	5	5	13.8	3.46	105	.294	.357	0	.000	-0	0	0	-0	0.0
1955 Phi-N	4	3	.571	19	10	2	0	0	71²	71	13	21	30	11.6	3.52	113	.257	.310	0	.000	-3	4	4	-0	0.0

YEAR	TM/L	W	L	PCT	G	GS	CG	SH	SV	IP	H	HR	BB	SO	RAT	ERA	ERA+	OAV	OOB	BH	AVG	PB	PR	/A	PD	TPI
1956	Phi-N	2	3	.400	39	4	0	0	3	66²	72	6	24	44	13.1	4.18	89	.280	.344	3	.429	1	-3	-3	0	-0.1
1958	LA-N	0	0	—	4	0	0	0	0	11¹	12	4	11	9	15.1	7.15	57	.279	.380	0	.000	-0	-4	-4	-0	0.0
Total	4	6	6	.500	66	15	2	0	3	162²	170	23	57	81	12.6	4.04	95	.271	.333	3	.086	-3	-3	-3	-1	-0.1

● **JIM NEHER** Neher, James Gilmore b: 2/5/1889, Rochester, N.Y. d: 11/11/51, Buffalo, N.Y. BR/TR, 5'11", 185 lbs. Deb: 9/10/12

YEAR	TM/L	W	L	PCT	G	GS	CG	SH	SV	IP	H	HR	BB	SO	RAT	ERA	ERA+	OAV	OOB	BH	AVG	PB	PR	/A	PD	TPI
1912	Cle-A	0	0	—	1	0	0	0	0	1	1	0	0	0	0.0	0.00	—	.000	.000	0		0	0	0	-0	0.0

● **ART NEHF** Nehf, Arthur Neukom b: 7/31/1892, Terre Haute, Ind. d: 12/18/60, Phoenix, Ariz. BL/TL, 5'9.5", 176 lbs. Deb: 8/13/15

YEAR	TM/L	W	L	PCT	G	GS	CG	SH	SV	IP	H	HR	BB	SO	RAT	ERA	ERA+	OAV	OOB	BH	AVG	PB	PR	/A	PD	TPI
1915	Bos-N	5	4	.556	12	10	6	4	0	78¹	60	0	21	39	9.7	2.53	103	.214	.276	4	.143	-1	2	1	0	0.0
1916	Bos-N	7	5	.583	22	13	6	1	0	121	110	0	20	36	9.9	2.01	124	.244	.281	5	.125	-0	8	6	-1	0.5
1917	Bos-N	17	8	.680	38	23	17	5	0	233¹	197	4	39	101	9.3	2.16	118	.231	.268	12	.171	5	14	10	-0	1.7
1918	Bos-N	15	15	.500	32	31	**28**	2	0	284¹	274	2	76	96	11.3	2.69	100	.259	.312	16	.168	1	2	-0	3	0.6
1919	Bos-N	8	9	.471	22	19	13	1	0	168²	151	6	40	53	10.5	3.09	92	.242	.294	13	.206	2	-3	-4	1	-0.1
	NY-N	9	2	.818	13	12	9	2	0	102	70	2	19	24	8.0	1.50	187	.196	.240	8	.229	3	16	15	-1	2.0
	Yr	17	11	.607	35	31	22	3	0	270²	221	8	59	77	9.4	2.49	114	.224	.269	21	.214	5	13	10	0	1.9
1920	NY-N	21	12	.636	40	33	22	4	0	280²	273	6	45	79	10.2	3.08	97	.260	.291	26	.268	5	2	-3	3	0.5
1921	*NY-N	20	10	.667	41	34	18	2	1	260²	266	18	55	67	11.2	3.63	101	.271	.311	18	.202	5	0	5	3	0.4
1922	*NY-N	19	13	.594	37	35	20	2	1	268¹	286	15	64	60	11.9	3.29	122	.276	.321	25	.255	4	24	21	1	2.5
1923	*NY-N	13	10	.565	34	27	7	1	2	196	219	14	49	50	12.4	4.50	85	.281	.326	12	.190	1	-11	-15	1	-1.3
1924	*NY-N	14	4	.778	30	20	11	0	2	171²	167	14	42	72	11.1	3.62	101	.254	.301	13	.228	6	5	1	2	0.9
1925	NY-N	11	9	.550	29	20	8	1	1	155	193	7	50	63	14.2	3.77	107	.308	.308	11	.216	1	9	5	2	0.8
1926	NY-N	0	0	—	2	0	0	0	0	1²	3	0	1	0	16.2	10.80	35	.286	.375	0	.000	-0	-1	-1	0	0.0
	Cin-N	0	1	.000	7	0	0	0	0	17	25	0	5	4	16.4	3.71	100	.379	.431	1	.200	0	0	-1	1	0.0
	Yr	0	1	.000	9	0	0	0	0	18²	27	0	6	4	16.4	4.34	85	.370	.425	1	.167	-1	-1	-1	1	0.0
1927	Cin-N	3	5	.375	21	5	1	0	4	45¹	59	2	14	21	14.5	5.56	68	.319	.367	3	.077	-1	-8	-9	1	-1.5
	Chi-N	1	1	.500	8	2	1	1	1	26¹	25	0	9	12	11.6	1.37	283	.260	.324	3	.429	1	7	7	-0	0.7
	Yr	4	6	.400	29	7	2	1	5	71²	84	2	23	33	13.4	4.02	95	.299	.352	4	.200	0	-1	-2	1	-0.8
1928	Chi-N	13	7	.650	31	21	10	2	0	176²	190	3	52	40	12.4	2.65	145	.281	.334	11	.190	2	26	24	1	2.8
1929	*Chi-N	8	5	.615	32	15	4	0	1	120²	148	11	39	27	14.1	5.59	83	.310	.365	13	.289	4	-12	-13	1	-0.8
Total	15	184	120	.605	451	320	182	28	13	2707²	2715	107	640	844	11.3	3.20	105	.265	.310	192	.210	34	85	45	17	9.7

● **GARY NEIBAUER** Neibauer, Gary Wayne b: 10/29/44, Billings, Mont. BR/TR, 6'3", 200 lbs. Deb: 4/12/69

YEAR	TM/L	W	L	PCT	G	GS	CG	SH	SV	IP	H	HR	BB	SO	RAT	ERA	ERA+	OAV	OOB	BH	AVG	PB	PR	/A	PD	TPI
1969	*Atl-N	1	2	.333	29	0	0	0	0	57²	42	9	31	42	11.5	3.90	92	.204	.311	0	.000	-1	-2	-2	-0	-0.2
1970	Atl-N	0	3	.000	7	0	0	0	0	11	8	9	8	9	13.5	4.97	86	.239	.352	0	.000	-1	-1	-1	-0	-0.1
1971	Atl-N	1	0	1.000	6	1	0	0	0	21	14	3	9	6	10.3	2.14	173	.187	.282	0	.000	-1	3	4	0	0.2
1972	Atl-N	0	0	—	8	1	0	0	0	17¹	27	6	6	8	17.7	7.27	52	.360	.415	0	.000	-0	-7	-7	-0	-0.1
	Phi-N	0	2	.000	9	2	0	0	0	18²	17	1	14	7	15.4	5.30	68	.239	.372	1	.250	-4	-4	-4	-0	-0.4
	Yr	0	2	.000	17	2	0	0	0	36	44	7	20	15	16.3	6.25	59	.297	.385	1	.125	0	-11	-10	-1	-0.5
1973	Atl-N	2	1	.667	16	1	0	0	1	21¹	24	3	19	9	19.0	7.17	55	.282	.425	1	.250	1	-8	-8	-1	-0.9
Total	5	4	8	.333	75	4	0	0	1	148²	135	22	87	81	13.8	4.78	78	.242	.350	2	.069	-1	-20	-17	-2	-1.6

● **JIM NEIDLINGER** Neidlinger, James Llewellyn b: 9/24/64, Vallejo, Cal. BB/TR, 6'4", 180 lbs. Deb: 8/1/90

YEAR	TM/L	W	L	PCT	G	GS	CG	SH	SV	IP	H	HR	BB	SO	RAT	ERA	ERA+	OAV	OOB	BH	AVG	PB	PR	/A	PD	TPI
1990	LA-N	5	3	.625	12	12	0	0	0	74	67	4	15	46	10.1	3.28	111	.241	.282	3	.120	-0	4	3	-1	0.2

● **AL NEIGER** Neiger, Alvin Edward b: 3/26/39, Wilmington, Del. BL/TL, 6', 195 lbs. Deb: 7/30/60

YEAR	TM/L	W	L	PCT	G	GS	CG	SH	SV	IP	H	HR	BB	SO	RAT	ERA	ERA+	OAV	OOB	BH	AVG	PB	PR	/A	PD	TPI
1960	Phi-N	0	0	—	6	0	0	0	0	12²	16	2	4	3	15.6	5.68	68	.340	.415	1	.500	0	-3	-3	-0	0.0

● **ERNIE NEITZKE** Neitzke, Ernest Fredrich b: 11/13/1894, Toledo, Ohio d: 4/27/77, Sylvania, Ohio BR/TR, 5'10", 180 lbs. Deb: 6/2/21 ♦

YEAR	TM/L	W	L	PCT	G	GS	CG	SH	SV	IP	H	HR	BB	SO	RAT	ERA	ERA+	OAV	OOB	BH	AVG	PB	PR	/A	PD	TPI
1921	Bos-A	0	0	—	2	0	0	0	0	7¹	8	0	4	1	14.7	6.14	69	.333	.429	6	.240	0	-2	-2	0	0.0

● **BOTS NEKOLA** Nekola, Francis Joseph b: 12/10/06, New York, N.Y. d: 3/11/87, Rockville, Md. BL/TL, 5'11.5", 175 lbs. Deb: 7/19/29

YEAR	TM/L	W	L	PCT	G	GS	CG	SH	SV	IP	H	HR	BB	SO	RAT	ERA	ERA+	OAV	OOB	BH	AVG	PB	PR	/A	PD	TPI
1929	NY-A	0	0	—	9	1	0	0	0	18²	21	0	15	2	17.4	4.34	89	.296	.419	2	.500	1	-0	-1	1	0.2
1933	Det-A	0	0	—	2	0	0	0	0	1¹	4	1	1	0	33.8	27.00	16	.500	.556	0	—	-0	-3	-3	-0	0.0
Total	2	0	0	—	11	1	0	0	0	20	25	1	16	2	18.4	5.85	66	.316	.432	2	.500	1	-4	-4	1	0.2

● **RED NELSON** Nelson, Albert Francis (b: Albert W. Horazdovsky) b: 5/19/1886, Cleveland, Ohio d: 10/26/56, St.Petersburg, Fla BR/TR, 5'11", 190 lbs. Deb: 9/9/10

YEAR	TM/L	W	L	PCT	G	GS	CG	SH	SV	IP	H	HR	BB	SO	RAT	ERA	ERA+	OAV	OOB	BH	AVG	PB	PR	/A	PD	TPI
1910	StL-A	5	1	.833	9	6	6	0	0	60	57	0	14	30	11.3	2.55	103	.261	.318	6	.261	-2	-0	-1	4	0.6
1911	StL-A	3	9	.250	16	13	6	0	0	81	103	1	44	24	17.1	5.22	65	.324	.417	3	.111	-2	-17	-17	-1	-2.3
1912	StL-A	0	2	.000	8	3	0	0	0	12	9	0	13	9	17.0	7.00	47	.318	.430	1	.333	1	-7	-7	-1	-0.8
	Phi-N	2	0	1.000	4	2	1	0	0	19¹	25	2	6	5	15.4	3.72	97	.305	.367	1	.100	-1	-0	-0	1	-0.1
1913	Phi-N	0	0	—	2	0	0	0	0	8¹	9	0	4	3	14.0	2.16	154	.290	.371	1	.333	1	1	1	-0	0.1
	Cin-N	0	0	—	2	0	0	0	0	1²	6	1	4	0	59.4	37.80	9	.667	.786	0	—	-0	-6	-6	-0	0.0
	Yr	0	0	—	4	0	0	0	0	10	15	1	8	3	21.6	8.10	41	.375	.490	1	.333	1	-5	-5	0	0.1
Total	4	10	12	.455	39	24	13	1	1	188¹	221	4	85	68	15.3	4.54	68	.305	.389	12	.182	0	-31	-30	2	-2.5

● **ANDY NELSON** Nelson, Andrew "Peaches" TL , Deb: 5/26/08

YEAR	TM/L	W	L	PCT	G	GS	CG	SH	SV	IP	H	HR	BB	SO	RAT	ERA	ERA+	OAV	OOB	BH	AVG	PB	PR	/A	PD	TPI
1908	Chi-A	0	0	—	2	1	0	0	0	9	11	0	4	1	16.0	2.00	116	.282	.364	0	.000	0	0	0	-1	-0.1

● **EMMETT NELSON** Nelson, George Emmett "Ramrod" b: 2/26/05, Viborg, S.Dak. d: 8/25/67, Sioux Falls, S.D. BR/TR, 6'3", 180 lbs. Deb: 6/24/35

YEAR	TM/L	W	L	PCT	G	GS	CG	SH	SV	IP	H	HR	BB	SO	RAT	ERA	ERA+	OAV	OOB	BH	AVG	PB	PR	/A	PD	TPI
1935	Cin-N	4	4	.500	19	7	3	1	1	60¹	70	2	23	14	14.2	4.33	92	.295	.363	2	.133	-1	-2	-2	1	-0.3
1936	Cin-N	1	0	1.000	6	1	0	0	0	17	24	1	4	3	15.4	3.18	120	.333	.377	1	.167	-0	2	1	0	0.0
Total	2	5	4	.556	25	8	3	1	1	77¹	94	3	27	17	14.4	4.07	97	.304	.366	3	.143	-1	-0	-1	1	-0.3

● **JIM NELSON** Nelson, James Lorin b: 7/4/47, Birmingham, Ala. BR/TR, 6', 180 lbs. Deb: 5/30/70

YEAR	TM/L	W	L	PCT	G	GS	CG	SH	SV	IP	H	HR	BB	SO	RAT	ERA	ERA+	OAV	OOB	BH	AVG	PB	PR	/A	PD	TPI
1970	Pit-N	4	2	.667	15	10	1	1	0	68¹	64	5	38	42	13.8	3.42	114	.255	.360	4	.200	0	5	4	-1	0.2
1971	Pit-N	2	2	.500	17	2	0	0	0	34²	27	0	26	11	15.1	2.34	145	.225	.384	3	.500	2	4	4	-0	0.6
Total	2	6	4	.600	32	12	1	1	0	103	91	5	64	53	14.2	3.06	122	.245	.368	7	.269	2	9	8	-1	0.8

● **JEFF NELSON** Nelson, Jeffrey Allan b: 11/17/66, Baltimore, Md. BR/TR, 6'8", 225 lbs. Deb: 4/16/92

YEAR	TM/L	W	L	PCT	G	GS	CG	SH	SV	IP	H	HR	BB	SO	RAT	ERA	ERA+	OAV	OOB	BH	AVG	PB	PR	/A	PD	TPI
1992	Sea-A	1	7	.125	66	0	0	0	6	81	71	7	44	46	13.4	3.44	115	.245	.356	0	—	0	4	5	0	0.5
1993	Sea-A	5	3	.625	71	0	0	0	1	60	57	5	34	61	14.9	4.35	101	.258	.376	0	—	0	-0	1	0	0.1
1994	Sea-A	0	0	—	28	0	0	0	0	42¹	35	3	20	44	13.4	2.76	177	.226	.344	0	—	0	10	10	-0	-0.1
1995	*Sea-A	7	3	.700	62	0	0	0	2	78²	58	4	27	96	10.4	2.17	218	.209	.294	0	—	0	22	22	0	2.5
1996	*NY-A	4	4	.500	73	0	0	0	2	74¹	75	6	36	91	13.7	4.36	116	.262	.349	0	—	0	5	6	2	0.6
Total	5	17	17	.500	300	0	0	0	11	336¹	296	25	161	338	13.0	3.43	134	.241	.343	0	—	0	41	43	3	3.6

● **LUKE NELSON** Nelson, Luther Martin b: 12/4/1893, Cable, Ill. d: 11/14/85, Moline, Ill. BR/TR, 6', 180 lbs. Deb: 5/25/19

YEAR	TM/L	W	L	PCT	G	GS	CG	SH	SV	IP	H	HR	BB	SO	RAT	ERA	ERA+	OAV	OOB	BH	AVG	PB	PR	/A	PD	TPI
1919	NY-A	3	0	1.000	9	1	0	0	0	24¹	22	1	11	11	12.6	2.96	108	.244	.333	1	.143	-0	1	1	-0	0.0

● **LYNN NELSON** Nelson, Lynn Bernard "Line Drive" b: 2/24/05, Sheldon, N.Dak. d: 2/15/55, Kansas City, Mo. BL/TR, 5'10.5", 170 lbs. Deb: 4/18/30 ♦

YEAR	TM/L	W	L	PCT	G	GS	CG	SH	SV	IP	H	HR	BB	SO	RAT	ERA	ERA+	OAV	OOB	BH	AVG	PB	PR	/A	PD	TPI
1930	Chi-N	3	2	.600	37	3	0	0	0	81¹	97	10	28	29	14.5	5.09	96	.300	.367	4	.222	-1	-1	-2	1	0.1
1933	Chi-N	5	5	.500	24	3	3	0	1	75²	65	2	30	20	11.3	3.21	102	.232	.306	5	.238	2	1	1	1	0.3
1934	Chi-N	0	1	.000	2	1	0	0	0	1	4	1	1	0	45.0	36.00	11	.667	.714	0	—	-0	-4	-4	-0	-1.9
1937	Phi-A	4	9	.308	30	4	1	0	2	116	140	4	51	49	15.0	5.90	80	.300	.371	40	.354	6	-16	-15	-2	-0.5
1938	Phi-A	10	11	.476	32	23	13	0	2	191	215	29	79	75	14.1	5.65	85	.277	.347	31	.277	4	-18	-17	-0	-1.1
1939	Phi-A	10	13	.435	35	24	12	2	0	197²	233	27	64	75	13.7	4.78	98	.292	.347	15	.188	-2	-0	-1	-0	-0.4
1940	Det-A	1	1	.500	6	2	0	0	0	14	23	3	9	7	20.6	10.93	44	.371	.451	8	.348	2	-10	-10	-0	-0.9
Total	7	33	42	.440	166	60	29	2	6	676²	777	86	262	255	14.0	5.25	88	.287	.353	103	.281	13	-52	-49	-1	-4.4

● **MEL NELSON** Nelson, Melvin Frederick b: 5/30/36, San Diego, Cal. BR/TL, 6', 185 lbs. Deb: 9/27/60

YEAR	TM/L	W	L	PCT	G	GS	CG	SH	SV	IP	H	HR	BB	SO	RAT	ERA	ERA+	OAV	OOB	BH	AVG	PB	PR	/A	PD	TPI
1960	StL-N	0	1	.000	7	1	0	0	0	8	7	1	2	7	10.1	3.38	121	.226	.273	1	.500	0	0	-0	-0	0.1
1963	LA-A	2	3	.400	36	3	0	0	1	52²	55	7	32	41	15.2	5.30	69	.263	.366	1	.091	-1	-10	-11	1	-1.0

YEAR	TM/L	W	L	PCT	G	GS	CG	SH	SV	IP	H	HR	BB	SO	RAT	ERA	ERA+	OAV	OOB	BH	AVG	PB	PR	/A	PD	TPI
1965	Min-A	0	4	.000	28	3	0	0	3	54²	57	7	23	31	13.5	4.12	86	.261	.337	1	.111	-0	-4	-3	-0	-0.4
1967	Min-A	0	0	—	1	0	0	0	0	0¹	3	1	0	0	81.0	54.00	6	.750	.750	0	—	-0	-2	-2	-0	-0.4
1968	*StL-N	2	1	.667	18	4	1	0	1	52²	49	3	9	16	9.9	2.91	100	.254	.287	2	.167	0	0	-0	-0	0.0
1969	StL-N	0	1	.000	8	0	0	0	0	5¹	13	0	3	3	27.0	11.81	38	.520	.571	0	—	-0	-5	-5	-0	-0.8
Total 6		4	10	.286	93	11	1	0	5	173²	184	19	69	98	13.3	4.40	76	.271	.341	5	.147	-1	-20	-21	0	-2.1

● **ROGER NELSON**   Nelson, Roger Eugene "Spider"   b: 6/7/44, Altadena, Cal.   BR/TR, 6'3", 205 lbs.   Deb: 9/9/67

YEAR	TM/L	W	L	PCT	G	GS	CG	SH	SV	IP	H	HR	BB	SO	RAT	ERA	ERA+	OAV	OOB	BH	AVG	PB	PR	/A	PD	TPI
1967	Chi-A	0	1	.000	5	0	0	0	0	7	4	1	0	4	7.7	1.29	241	.182	.250	0	—	0	2	1	0	0.2
1968	Bal-A	4	3	.571	19	6	0	0	1	71	49	3	26	70	9.6	2.41	121	.192	.270	1	.063	-0	5	4	-0	0.4
1969	KC-A	7	13	.350	29	29	8	1	0	193¹	170	12	65	82	11.2	3.31	112	.243	.313	8	.138	-1	7	8	-1	0.6
1970	KC-A	0	2	.000	4	2	0	0	0	9	18	3	0	3	19.0	10.00	37	.419	.432	0	—	0	-6	-6	0	-1.1
1971	KC-A	0	1	.000	13	1	0	0	0	34	35	1	5	20	10.6	5.29	65	.269	.296	2	.333	1	-7	-7	1	0.0
1972	KC-A	11	6	.647	34	19	10	6	3	173¹	120	13	31	120	7.9	2.08	146	.196	.236	5	.093	-2	19	18	1	1.9
1973	*Cin-N	3	2	.600	14	8	1	0	0	54²	49	4	24	17	12.5	3.46	98	.246	.336	2	.111	-1	1	-0	1	0.0
1974	Cin-N	4	4	.500	14	12	1	0	0	85¹	67	7	35	42	10.9	3.38	103	.213	.293	5	.179	0	2	1	-1	0.0
1976	KC-A	0	0	—	3	0	0	0	0	8²	4	0	4	4	10.4	2.08	169	.138	.286	0	—	0	1	1	0	0.0
Total 9		29	32	.475	135	77	20	7	5	636¹	516	44	190	371	10.2	3.06	110	.224	.288	23	.128	-3	23	21	2	2.0

● **GENE NELSON**   Nelson, Wayland Eugene   b: 12/3/60, Tampa, Fla.   BR/TR, 6', 174 lbs.   Deb: 5/4/81

YEAR	TM/L	W	L	PCT	G	GS	CG	SH	SV	IP	H	HR	BB	SO	RAT	ERA	ERA+	OAV	OOB	BH	AVG	PB	PR	/A	PD	TPI
1981	NY-A	3	1	.750	8	7	0	0	0	39¹	40	5	23	16	14.6	4.81	74	.261	.362	0		0	-5	-5	-0	-0.5
1982	Sea-A	6	9	.400	22	19	2	1	0	122²	133	16	60	71	14.3	4.62	92	.279	.362	0		0	-7	-5	1	-0.5
1983	Sea-A	0	3	.000	10	5	1	0	0	32	38	6	21	16	16.9	7.88	54	.295	.397	0		0	-14	-13	1	-1.1
1984	Chi-A	3	5	.375	20	9	2	0	1	74²	72	9	17	36	10.8	4.46	93	.254	.299	0		0	-4	-3	0	-0.2
1985	Chi-A	10	10	.500	46	18	1	0	2	145¹	144	23	67	101	13.5	4.26	101	.258	.345	0	.000	0	-2	1	0	0.1
1986	Chi-A	6	6	.500	54	1	0	0	0	114²	118	7	41	70	12.7	3.85	112	.271	.338	0		0	4	6	1	0.7
1987	Oak-A	6	5	.545	54	6	0	0	0	123²	120	11	35	94	11.6	3.93	105	.249	.307	0		0	7	3	-1	0.1
1988	*Oak-A	9	6	.600	54	1	0	0	3	111²	93	9	38	67	10.8	3.06	123	.228	.298	0		0	11	9	-1	1.1
1989	Oak-A	3	5	.375	50	0	0	0	0	80	60	5	30	70	10.3	3.26	113	.203	.280	0		0	6	4	-1	0.2
1990	*Oak-A	3	3	.500	51	0	0	0	5	74²	55	5	17	38	9.0	1.57	237	.208	.263	0		0	19	18	-1	1.5
1991	Oak-A	1	5	.167	44	0	0	0	0	48²	60	12	23	23	15.9	6.84	56	.306	.387	0		0	-15	-16	-1	-1.8
1992	Oak-A	3	1	.750	28	2	0	0	0	51²	68	5	22	23	15.7	6.45	58	.335	.400	0		0	-14	-16	-1	-1.1
1993	Cal-A	0	5	.000	46	0	0	0	4	52²	50	5	23	31	12.8	3.08	146	.251	.335	0		0	7	8	0	0.6
	Tex-A	0	0	—	6	0	0	0	1	8	10	0	1	4	12.4	3.38	123	.303	.324	0		0	1	1	-0	0.2
	Yr	0	5	.000	52	0	0	0	5	60²	60	5	24	35	12.5	3.12	143	.252	.331	0	.000	0	8	9	0	0.8
Total 13		53	64	.453	493	68	6	1	28	1080	1061	117	418	655	12.6	4.13	98	.258	.331	0	.000	0	-5	-9	-3	-0.7

● **BILL NELSON**   Nelson, William F.   b: 9/28/1863, Terre Haute, Ind.   d: 6/23/41, Terre Haute, Ind.   TR ,   Deb: 9/3/1884

YEAR	TM/L	W	L	PCT	G	GS	CG	SH	SV	IP	H	HR	BB	SO	RAT	ERA	ERA+	OAV	OOB	BH	AVG	PB	PR	/A	PD	TPI
1884	Pit-a	1	2	.333	3	3	3	0	0	26	26	1	8	6	13.2	4.50	75	.252	.330	2	.167	-1	-4	-3	-0	-0.4

● **ROBB NEN**   Nen, Robert Allen   b: 11/28/69, San Pedro, Cal.   BR/TR, 6'4", 200 lbs.   Deb: 4/10/93   F

YEAR	TM/L	W	L	PCT	G	GS	CG	SH	SV	IP	H	HR	BB	SO	RAT	ERA	ERA+	OAV	OOB	BH	AVG	PB	PR	/A	PD	TPI
1993	Tex-A	1	1	.500	9	3	0	0	0	22²	28	1	26	12	21.4	6.35	65	.326	.482	0		0	-5	-6	0	-0.2
	Fla-N	0	1	.000	15	1	0	0	0	33¹	35	5	20	27	14.9	7.02	62	.255	.350	0	.000	-0	-11	-10	0	-0.3
1994	Fla-N	5	5	.500	44	0	0	0	15	58	46	6	17	60	9.8	2.95	148	.222	.281	0	.000	-0	8	9	-0	1.8
1995	Fla-N	0	7	.000	62	0	0	0	23	65²	62	6	23	68	11.8	3.29	128	.244	.309	0		0	6	7	0	1.1
1996	Fla-N	5	1	.833	75	0	0	0	35	83	67	2	21	92	9.7	1.95	207	.225	.278	0	.000	-0	21	19	-0	2.6
Total 4		12	14	.462	205	4	0	0	73	262²	238	20	107	259	11.9	3.53	119	.242	.318	0	.000	-1	19	20	-0	5.0

● **HAL NEUBAUER**   Neubauer, Harold Charles   b: 5/13/02, Hoboken, N.J.   d: 9/9/49, Barrington, R.I.   BR/TR, 6'0.5", 185 lbs.   Deb: 6/12/25

YEAR	TM/L	W	L	PCT	G	GS	CG	SH	SV	IP	H	HR	BB	SO	RAT	ERA	ERA+	OAV	OOB	BH	AVG	PB	PR	/A	PD	TPI
1925	Bos-A	1	0	1.000	7	0	0	0	0	10¹	17	2	11	4	24.4	12.19	37	.378	.500	0		0	-9	-9	0	-0.7

● **TEX NEUER**   Neuer, John S.   b: 6/8/1877, Fremont, Ohio   d: 1/14/66, Northumberland, Pa   TL ,   Deb: 8/28/07

YEAR	TM/L	W	L	PCT	G	GS	CG	SH	SV	IP	H	HR	BB	SO	RAT	ERA	ERA+	OAV	OOB	BH	AVG	PB	PR	/A	PD	TPI
1907	NY-A	4	2	.667	7	6	6	3	0	54	40	1	19	22	9.8	2.17	129	.208	.280	2	.095	-2	2	4	-1	0.1

● **DAN NEUMEIER**   Neumeier, Daniel George   b: 3/9/48, Shawano, Wis.   BR/TR, 6'5", 205 lbs.   Deb: 9/8/72

YEAR	TM/L	W	L	PCT	G	GS	CG	SH	SV	IP	H	HR	BB	SO	RAT	ERA	ERA+	OAV	OOB	BH	AVG	PB	PR	/A	PD	TPI
1972	Chi-A	0	0	—	3	0	0	0	0	3	2	0	4	1	15.0	9.00	35	.200	.385	0		-0	-2	-2	-0	-0.2

● **ERNIE NEVEL**   Nevel, Ernie Wyre   b: 8/17/19, Charleston, Mo.   d: 7/10/88, Springfield, Mo.   BR/TR, 5'11", 190 lbs.   Deb: 9/26/50

YEAR	TM/L	W	L	PCT	G	GS	CG	SH	SV	IP	H	HR	BB	SO	RAT	ERA	ERA+	OAV	OOB	BH	AVG	PB	PR	/A	PD	TPI
1950	NY-A	0	1	.000	3	1	0	0	0	6¹	10	4	6	3	22.7	9.95	43	.345	.457	0	.000	-0	-4	-4	-0	-0.5
1951	NY-A	0	0	—	1	0	0	0	0	4	1	0	1	1	4.5	0.00	—	.083	.154	0	.000	-0	2	2	-0	0.1
1953	Cin-N	0	0	—	10	0	0	0	0	10¹	16	4	1	5	14.8	6.10	71	.390	.405	0	—	-0	-2	-2	-0	-0.1
Total 3		0	1	.000	14	1	0	0	1	20²	27	8	8	9	15.2	6.10	69	.329	.389	0	.000	-0	-4	-4	-0	-0.4

● **ERNIE NEVERS**   Nevers, Ernest Alonzo   b: 6/11/02, Willow River, Minn.   d: 5/3/76, San Rafael, Cal.   BR/TR, 6', 205 lbs.   Deb: 4/26/26

YEAR	TM/L	W	L	PCT	G	GS	CG	SH	SV	IP	H	HR	BB	SO	RAT	ERA	ERA+	OAV	OOB	BH	AVG	PB	PR	/A	PD	TPI
1926	StL-A	2	4	.333	11	7	4	0	0	74²	82	4	24	16	12.9	4.46	96	.290	.347	5	.185	-1	-4	-1	2	0.0
1927	StL-A	3	8	.273	27	5	2	0	2	94²	105	8	35	22	13.5	4.94	88	.311	.379	7	.219	-1	-8	-6	1	-0.6
1928	StL-A	1	0	1.000	6	0	0	0	0	9	9	1	2	1	11.0	3.00	140	.281	.324	0	—	-0	1	1	0	0.1
Total 3		6	12	.333	44	12	6	0	2	178¹	196	13	61	39	13.1	4.64	93	.300	.363	12	.200	-2	-11	-6	3	-0.5

● **DON NEWCOMBE**   Newcombe, Donald "Newk"   b: 6/14/26, Madison, N.J.   BL/TR, 6'4", 225 lbs.   Deb: 5/20/49   ◆

YEAR	TM/L	W	L	PCT	G	GS	CG	SH	SV	IP	H	HR	BB	SO	RAT	ERA	ERA+	OAV	OOB	BH	AVG	PB	PR	/A	PD	TPI
1949	*Bro-N★	17	8	.680	38	31	19	**5**	1	244¹	223	17	73	149	11.0	3.17	129	.243	.301	22	.229	3	24	25	1	2.8
1950	Bro-N★	19	11	.633	40	35	20	4	3	267¹	258	22	75	130	11.3	3.70	111	.254	.306	24	.247	1	13	12	-0	1.8
1951	Bro-N★	20	9	.690	40	36	18	3	0	272	235	19	91	**164**	11.0	3.28	120	.230	.297	23	.223	5	21	20	1	2.5
1954	Bro-N	9	8	.529	29	25	6	0	0	144¹	158	24	49	82	13.2	4.55	90	.274	.337	15	.319	4	-8	-8	-1	-0.5
1955	*Bro-N★	20	5	**.800**	34	31	17	1	0	233²	222	35	38	143	**10.1**	3.20	127	.249	.280	42	.359	20	22	22	-2	**4.2**
1956	*Bro-N	27	7	**.794**	38	36	18	5	0	268	219	30	46	139	**9.0**	3.06	130	**.221**	.257	26	.234	8	21	**27**	-2	**4.3**
1957	Bro-N	11	12	.478	28	28	12	4	0	198²	199	28	33	90	10.6	3.49	119	.258	.290	17	.230	5	9	15	1	2.2
1958	LA-N	0	6	.000	11	8	1	0	0	34¹	53	11	8	16	16.0	7.86	52	.346	.379	5	.417	-1	-15	-14	0	-1.9
	Cin-N	7	7	.500	20	18	7	0	0	133¹	159	20	28	53	12.7	3.85	108	.298	.335	21	.350	8	2	4	-2	1.1
	Yr	7	13	.350	31	26	8	0	0	167²	212	31	36	69	13.4	4.67	89	.309	.344	26	.361	10	-13	-10	-2	-0.8
1959	Cin-N	13	8	.619	30	29	17	2	1	222	216	25	27	100	10.1	3.16	128	.253	.280	32	.305	15	19	22	-1	**3.5**
1960	Cin-N	4	6	.400	16	15	1	0	0	82²	99	12	14	36	12.6	4.57	84	.304	.338	6	.139	-0	-7	-7	-1	-0.2
	Cle-A	2	3	.400	20	2	0	0	1	54	61	6	8	27	11.5	4.33	86	.289	.315	6	.300	2	-3	-4	-1	-0.2
Total 10		149	90	.623	344	294	136	24	7	2154²	2102	252	490	1129	11.0	3.56	114	.254	.299	238	.271	79	97	116	-6	18.9

● **TOM NEWELL**   Newell, Thomas Dean   b: 5/17/63, Monrovia, Cal.   BR/TR, 6'1", 185 lbs.   Deb: 9/9/87

YEAR	TM/L	W	L	PCT	G	GS	CG	SH	SV	IP	H	HR	BB	SO	RAT	ERA	ERA+	OAV	OOB	BH	AVG	PB	PR	/A	PD	TPI
1987	Phi-N	0	0	—	2	0	0	0	0	1	4	1	3	1	63.0	36.00	12	.571	.700	0	—	-0	-4	-4	0	0.0

● **DON NEWHAUSER**   Newhauser, Donald Louis   b: 11/7/47, Miami, Fla.   BR/TR, 6'4", 200 lbs.   Deb: 6/15/72

YEAR	TM/L	W	L	PCT	G	GS	CG	SH	SV	IP	H	HR	BB	SO	RAT	ERA	ERA+	OAV	OOB	BH	AVG	PB	PR	/A	PD	TPI
1972	Bos-A	4	2	.667	31	0	0	0	4	37	30	2	25	27	13.9	2.43	132	.226	.356	0	.000	-0	3	3	-0	0.6
1973	Bos-A	0	0	—	9	0	0	0	0	12	9	0	13	8	17.3	0.00	—	.205	.397	0	—	-0	5	5	-0	0.4
1974	Bos-A	0	1	.000	2	0	0	0	0	3²	5	0	4	2	22.1	9.82	39	.357	.500	0	—	-0	-3	-2	-0	-0.6
Total 3		4	3	.571	42	0	0	0	4	52²	44	2	42	37	15.2	2.39	144	.230	.377	0	.000	-0	6	6	-0	-0.4

● **HAL NEWHOUSER**   Newhouser, Harold   b: 5/20/21, Detroit, Mich.   BL/TL, 6'2", 192 lbs.   Deb: 9/29/39   H

YEAR	TM/L	W	L	PCT	G	GS	CG	SH	SV	IP	H	HR	BB	SO	RAT	ERA	ERA+	OAV	OOB	BH	AVG	PB	PR	/A	PD	TPI
1939	Det-A	0	1	.000	1	1	1	0	0	5	3	0	4	4	12.6	5.40	91	.188	.350	0	.000	-0	-0	-0	0	-0.1
1940	Det-A	9	9	.500	28	20	7	0	0	133¹	149	12	76	89	15.3	4.86	88	.282	.374	8	.200	-1	-7	-2	-2	-0.1
1941	Det-A	9	11	.450	33	27	5	1	0	173	166	6	137	106	15.8	4.79	95	.249	.378	6	.150	-2	-12	-5	-2	-0.5
1942	Det-A☆	8	14	.364	38	23	11	1	0	183²	137	8	114	103	12.4	2.45	161	**.207**	.325	8	.154	-1	25	31	2	4.0
1943	Det-A★	8	17	.320	37	25	10	1	1	195²	163	11	111	144	12.6	3.04	116	.226	.341	11	.183	-1	6	11	3	1.6
1944	Det-A★	**29**	9	**.763**	47	34	25	6	2	312¹	264	6	102	**187**	10.6	2.22	161	.230	.293	29	.242	-4	42	47	1	6.5
1945	*Det-A†	25	9	**.735**	40	36	**29**	8	2	313¹	239	6	110	212	10.0	1.81	194	**.211**	.281	28	.257	4	**54**	59	3	7.8
1946	Det-A★	26	9	.743	37	34	29	6	1	292²	215	10	98	275	**9.7**	1.94	189	**.201**	**.269**	13	.126	-1	51	56	2	7.1

YEAR TM/L	W	L	PCT	G	GS	CG	SH	SV	IP	H	HR	BB	SO	RAT	ERA	ERA+	OAV	OOB	BH	AVG	PB	PR	/A	PD	TPI
1947 Det-A★	17	17	.500	40	36	24	3	2	285	268	9	110	176	12.0	2.87	131	.249	.320	19	.198	2	26	28	3	3.9
1948 Det-A★	21	12	.636	39	35	19	2	1	272¹	249	10	99	143	11.5	3.01	145	.242	.309	19	.207	1	39	41	2	4.9
1949 Det-A	18	11	.621	38	35	22	3	1	292	277	19	111	144	12.0	3.36	124	.251	.319	18	.198	2	27	26	3	2.7
1950 Det-A	15	13	.536	35	30	15	1	3	213²	232	23	81	87	13.4	4.34	108	.279	.346	13	.176	-2	6	8	-0	0.8
1951 Det-A	6	6	.500	15	14	7	1	0	96¹	98	10	19	37	11.2	3.92	106	.268	.310	9	.310	2	2	3	1	0.6
1952 Det-A	9	9	.500	25	19	8	0	0	154	148	13	47	57	11.4	3.74	102	.254	.310	10	.217	3	-1	1	1	0.5
1953 Det-A	0	1	.000	7	4	0	0	1	21²	31	4	8	6	17.0	7.06	58	.348	.414	4	.500	2	-7	-7	-0	-0.2
1954 *Cle-A	7	2	.778	26	1	0	0	7	46²	34	3	18	25	10.0	2.51	147	.209	.287	2	.154	-0	6	6	-0	1.3
1955 Cle-A	0	0	—	2	0	0	0	0	2¹	1	0	4	1	19.3	0.00	—	.125	.417	0	—	0	1	1	-0	0.0
Total 17	207	150	.580	488	374	212	33	26	2993	2674	137	1249	1796	11.9	3.06	130	.239	.316	201	.201	12	257	305	22	40.8

● **FLOYD NEWKIRK** — Newkirk, Floyd Elmo "Three-Finger" b: 7/16/08, Norris City, Ill. d: 4/15/76, Clayton, Mo. BR/TR, 5'11", 178 lbs. Deb: 8/21/34 F

YEAR TM/L	W	L	PCT	G	GS	CG	SH	SV	IP	H	HR	BB	SO	RAT	ERA	ERA+	OAV	OOB	BH	AVG	PB	PR	/A	PD	TPI
1934 NY-A	0	0	—	1	0	0	0	0	1	1	0	1	0	18.0	0.00	—	.333	.500	0	—	0	0	0	0	0.0

● **JOEL NEWKIRK** — Newkirk, Joel Inez "Sailor" b: 5/1/1896, Kyana, Ind. d: 1/22/66, Eldorado, Ill. BR/TR, 6', 180 lbs. Deb: 8/20/19 F

YEAR TM/L	W	L	PCT	G	GS	CG	SH	SV	IP	H	HR	BB	SO	RAT	ERA	ERA+	OAV	OOB	BH	AVG	PB	PR	/A	PD	TPI
1919 Chi-N	0	0	—	1	0	0	0	0	2	3	0	3	1	27.0	13.50	21	.286	.545	0	.000	-0	-2	-2	0	0.0
1920 Chi-N	0	1	.000	2	1	0	0	0	6²	8	1	6	2	18.9	5.40	59	.333	.467	0	.000	-0	-2	-2	-1	-0.3
Total 2	0	1	.000	3	1	0	0	0	8²	10	1	9	3	20.8	7.27	43	.323	.488	0	.000	-1	-4	-4	-0	-0.3

● **MAURY NEWLIN** — Newlin, Maurice Milton b: 6/22/14, Bloomingdale, Ind d: 8/14/78, Houston, Tex. BR/TR, 6', 176 lbs. Deb: 9/20/40

YEAR TM/L	W	L	PCT	G	GS	CG	SH	SV	IP	H	HR	BB	SO	RAT	ERA	ERA+	OAV	OOB	BH	AVG	PB	PR	/A	PD	TPI
1940 StL-A	1	0	1.000	1	1	0	0	0	6	4	1	2	3	9.0	6.00	76	.190	.261	1	.500	0	-1	-1	-0	-0.1
1941 StL-A	0	2	.000	14	0	0	0	1	27²	43	4	12	10	17.9	6.51	66	.361	.420	0	.000	-1	-7	-7	1	-0.5
Total 2	1	2	.333	15	1	0	0	1	33²	47	5	14	13	16.3	6.42	68	.336	.396	1	.125	-1	-8	-8	0	-0.6

● **FRED NEWMAN** — Newman, Frederick William b: 2/21/42, Boston, Mass. d: 6/24/87, Framingham, Mass. BR/TR, 6'3", 190 lbs. Deb: 9/16/62

YEAR TM/L	W	L	PCT	G	GS	CG	SH	SV	IP	H	HR	BB	SO	RAT	ERA	ERA+	OAV	OOB	BH	AVG	PB	PR	/A	PD	TPI
1962 LA-A	0	1	.000	4	0	0	0	0	6¹	11	0	3	4	19.9	9.95	39	.393	.452	0	.000	-0	-4	-4	-0	-0.6
1963 LA-A	1	5	.167	12	8	0	0	0	44	56	6	15	16	14.9	5.32	64	.316	.376	4	.250	1	-8	-9	-0	-1.1
1964 LA-A	13	10	.565	32	28	7	2	0	190	177	9	39	83	10.6	2.75	120	.246	.291	11	.180	-0	19	11	4	2.1
1965 Cal-A	14	16	.467	36	36	10	2	0	260²	225	15	64	109	10.0	2.93	116	.234	.282	7	.095	-0	15	13	8	2.4
1966 Cal-A	4	7	.364	21	19	1	0	0	102²	112	7	31	42	13.1	4.73	71	.289	.351	6	.200	1	-15	-16	1	-1.4
1967 Cal-A	1	0	1.000	3	1	0	0	0	6¹	8	1	2	0	15.6	1.42	221	.320	.393	0	.000	-0	1	1	-0	0.2
Total 6	33	39	.458	108	93	18	4	0	610	589	38	154	254	11.2	3.41	99	.256	.308	28	.153	3	8	-3	12	1.6

● **JEFF NEWMAN** — Newman, Jeffrey Lynn b: 9/11/48, Fort Worth, Tex. BR/TR, 6'2", 218 lbs. Deb: 6/30/76 MC◆

YEAR TM/L	W	L	PCT	G	GS	CG	SH	SV	IP	H	HR	BB	SO	RAT	ERA	ERA+	OAV	OOB	BH	AVG	PB	PR	/A	PD	TPI
1977 Oak-A	0	0	—	1	0	0	0	0	1	1	0	0	0	18.0	0.00	—	.250	.400	36	.222		0	0	0	0.0

● **RAY NEWMAN** — Newman, Raymond Francis b: 6/20/45, Evansville, Ind. BL/TL, 6'5", 205 lbs. Deb: 5/16/71

YEAR TM/L	W	L	PCT	G	GS	CG	SH	SV	IP	H	HR	BB	SO	RAT	ERA	ERA+	OAV	OOB	BH	AVG	PB	PR	/A	PD	TPI
1971 Chi-N	1	2	.333	30	0	0	0	2	38¹	30	4	17	35	11.0	3.52	112	.219	.305	0	.000	-1	-0	-0	0	0.1
1972 Mil-A	0	0	—	4	0	0	0	1	7	4	0	2	1	7.7	0.00	—	.182	.250	1	1.000	0	2	2	0	0.2
1973 Mil-A	2	1	.667	11	0	0	0	1	18¹	19	2	5	10	11.8	2.95	128	.260	.308	0	—	0	2	2	1	0.5
Total 3	3	3	.500	45	0	0	0	4	63²	53	6	24	46	10.9	2.97	128	.228	.301	1	.143	-1	4	6	1	0.8

● **BOBO NEWSOM** — Newsom, Louis Norman "Buck" b: 8/11/07, Hartsville, S.C. d: 12/7/62, Orlando, Fla. BR/TR, 6'3", 200 lbs. Deb: 9/11/29

YEAR TM/L	W	L	PCT	G	GS	CG	SH	SV	IP	H	HR	BB	SO	RAT	ERA	ERA+	OAV	OOB	BH	AVG	PB	PR	/A	PD	TPI
1929 Bro-N	0	3	.000	3	2	0	0	0	9¹	15	0	5	9	19.3	10.61	44	.375	.444	0	.000	-0	-6	-6	0	-1.3
1930 Bro-N	0	0	—	2	0	0	0	0	3	2	0	2	1	12.0	0.00	—	.167	.286	0	.000	-0	2	2	-0	0.0
1932 Chi-N	0	0	—	1	0	0	0	0	1	0	0	0	0	9.0	0.00	—	.333	.333	0	—	0	0	0	0	0.0
1934 StL-A	16	20	.444	47	32	15	2	5	262¹	259	15	149	135	14.0	4.01	124	.261	.358	17	.183	-3	14	29	0	3.2
1935 StL-A	0	6	.000	7	6	1	0	1	42²	54	2	13	22	14.1	4.85	99	.303	.351	1	.091	-1	-2	-0	0	-0.1
Was-A	11	12	.478	28	23	17	2	2	198¹	222	9	84	65	14.1	4.45	97	.288	.361	22	.301	4	0	-3	-3	-0.1
Yr	11	18	.379	35	29	18	2	3	241	276	11	97	87	14.1	4.52	97	.291	.359	23	.274	3	-2	-3	-2	-0.2
1936 Was-A	17	15	.531	43	38	24	4	2	285²	294	13	146	156	14.0	4.32	111	.268	.355	23	.213	0	23	15	1	1.4
1937 Was-A	3	4	.429	11	10	3	0	0	67²	76	4	48	39	16.9	5.85	76	.287	.402	3	.120	-1	-9	-11	-0	-0.9
Bos-A	13	10	.565	30	27	14	1	0	207¹	193	14	119	127	13.7	4.46	106	.243	.344	19	.253	2	-6	-2	0	0.6
Yr	16	14	.533	41	37	17	1	0	275¹	269	18	167	166	14.3	4.81	97	.253	.356	22	.220	1	-6	-4	-1	-0.3
1938 StL-A☆	20	16	.556	44	40	31	0	1	329	334	30	192	226	14.5	5.08	98	.265	.364	31	.250	1	-11	-4	-3	-0.4
1939 StL-A	3	1	.750	6	6	3	0	0	45²	50	2	25	28	14.4	4.73	103	.266	.346	4	.222	-0	-1	1	0	0.0
Det-A☆	17	10	.630	35	31	21	3	2	246	222	14	104	164	12.0	3.37	145	.238	.316	18	.186	-4	34	42	-1	3.6
Yr	20	11	.645	41	37	24	3	2	291²	272	16	129	192	12.3	3.58	136	.243	.320	22	.191	-4	34	42	-1	3.6
1940 *Det-A★	21	5	.808	36	34	20	3	0	264	235	19	100	164	11.5	2.83	168	.238	.310	23	.215	-1	46	56	-3	4.6
1941 Det-A	12	20	.375	43	36	19	2	2	250¹	265	15	118	175	13.9	4.60	99	.264	.343	9	.102	-6	-13	-27	-2	-0.9
1942 Was-A	11	17	.393	30	29	15	2	0	213²	236	5	92	113	13.0	4.93	97	.280	.353	12	.160	-2	-30	-30	-3	-3.8
Bro-N	2	2	.500	6	5	2	1	0	32	28	1	14	21	12.1	3.38	97	.235	.321	0	.000	-1	-0	-0	-1	-0.0
1943 Bro-N	9	4	.692	22	12	6	1	1	125	113	6	57	75	12.4	3.02	111	.244	.329	11	.250	-1	5	5	0	0.6
StL-A	1	6	.143	10	9	6	0	0	52¹	69	7	35	37	18.1	7.39	45	.318	.415	5	.333	1	-24	-24	-1	-2.6
Was-A	3	3	.500	6	6	2	0	0	40	38	1	21	11	13.7	3.82	84	.247	.345	2	.133	-1	-2	-3	-1	-0.6
Yr	4	9	.308	16	15	2	0	0	92¹	107	8	56	48	16.1	5.85	56	.288	.384	7	.233	0	-26	-26	-2	-3.2
1944 Phi-A★	13	15	.464	37	33	18	2	1	265	243	11	82	142	11.2	2.82	124	.244	.304	10	.114	-6	18	19	-1	1.3
1945 Phi-A	8	20	.286	36	34	16	3	0	257¹	255	12	103	127	12.6	3.29	104	.260	.332	14	.163	-4	2	4	-4	-0.4
1946 Phi-A	3	5	.375	10	9	3	1	0	58²	61	6	30	32	14.7	3.38	105	.266	.364	2	.105	-1	-1	-1	-1	-0.1
Was-A	11	8	.579	24	22	14	2	1	178	163	5	60	82	11.4	2.78	120	.242	.306	10	.161	-2	14	13	-3	0.6
Yr	14	13	.519	34	31	17	3	1	236²	224	11	90	114	12.0	2.93	116	.247	.316	12	.148	-3	15	12	-4	0.6
1947 Was-A	4	6	.400	14	13	1	0	0	83²	99	7	37	40	14.7	4.09	91	.296	.368	7	.241	1	-4	-3	-2	-0.5
*NY-A	7	5	.583	17	15	6	2	0	115²	109	8	30	42	11.0	2.80	126	.250	.301	4	.095	-3	12	9	-2	0.4
Yr	11	11	.500	31	28	7	2	0	199¹	208	10	67	82	12.5	3.34	108	.270	.330	11	.155	-3	8	6	-3	0.4
1948 NY-N	0	4	.000	11	4	0	0	0	25²	35	1	13	19	16.8	4.21	94	.330	.403	3	.429	1	-1	-1	-0	-0.1
1952 Was-A	1	1	.500	10	0	0	0	2	12²	16	2	9	5	17.8	4.97	72	.302	.403	0	.000	-0	-2	-2	0	-0.4
Phi-A	3	3	.500	14	5	1	0	1	47²	38	2	23	22	11.9	3.59	110	.220	.318	2	.133	-1	2	2	0	0.2
Yr	4	4	.500	24	5	1	0	3	60¹	54	4	32	27	13.1	3.88	100	.239	.338	2	.118	-1	-1	-0	-1	-0.2
1953 Phi-A	2	1	.667	17	2	1	0	0	38²	44	3	24	11	16.3	4.89	88	.282	.395	1	.100	-1	-1	-0	0	-0.2
Total 20	211	222	.487	600	483	246	31	21	3759¹	3769	206	1732	2082	13.3	3.98	107	.261	.342	253	.189	-26	67	109	-29	3.9

● **DICK NEWSOME** — Newsome, Heber Hampton b: 12/13/09, Ahoskie, N.C. d: 12/15/65, Ahoskie, N.C. BR/TR, 6', 185 lbs. Deb: 4/25/41

YEAR TM/L	W	L	PCT	G	GS	CG	SH	SV	IP	H	HR	BB	SO	RAT	ERA	ERA+	OAV	OOB	BH	AVG	PB	PR	/A	PD	TPI
1941 Bos-A	19	10	.655	36	29	17	2	0	213²	235	13	79	58	13.5	4.13	101	.277	.344	19	.244	3	0	1	3	0.7
1942 Bos-A	8	10	.444	24	23	11	0	0	158	174	11	67	40	13.7	5.01	74	.278	.348	13	.236	2	-24	-23	1	-2.0
1943 Bos-A	8	13	.381	25	22	8	2	0	154¹	166	8	68	40	13.9	4.49	74	.274	.352	7	.146	-1	-20	-20	-2	-2.8
Total 3	35	33	.515	85	74	36	4	0	526	575	32	214	138	13.7	4.50	84	.276	.347	39	.215	3	-44	-42	2	-4.1

● **DOC NEWTON** — Newton, Eustace James b: 10/26/1877, Indianapolis, Ind. d: 5/14/31, Memphis, Tenn. BL/TL, 6', 185 lbs. Deb: 4/27/00

YEAR TM/L	W	L	PCT	G	GS	CG	SH	SV	IP	H	HR	BB	SO	RAT	ERA	ERA+	OAV	OOB	BH	AVG	PB	PR	/A	PD	TPI
1900 Cin-N	9	15	.375	35	27	22	1	0	234²	255	4	100	88	14.1	4.14	89	.276	.355	17	.198	-1	-12	-12	-2	-1.3
1901 Cin-N	4	13	.235	20	18	17	0	0	168¹	190	6	59	65	14.1	4.12	78	.282	.353	9	.130	-4	-15	-17	1	-1.8
Bro-N	6	5	.545	13	12	9	0	0	105	110	1	30	45	12.6	2.83	119	.268	.328	9	.220	1	6	6	-0	0.6
Yr	10	18	.357	33	30	26	0	0	273¹	300	7	89	110	13.0	3.62	90	.273	.332	18	.164	-4	-9	-11	1	-1.2
1902 Bro-N	15	14	.517	31	28	26	4	2	264¹	208	2	87	107	10.4	2.42	114	.217	.289	19	.174	-1	11	10	-2	0.8
1905 NY-A	2	2	.500	11	7	2	0	0	59²	61	1	24	15	13.1	2.11	139	.266	.341	3	.136	-1	4	5	-1	0.8
1906 NY-A	7	5	.583	21	15	6	3	0	125	118	4	33	52	11.4	3.17	94	.252	.311	9	.220	-0	-7	-3	2	-0.1
1907 NY-A	7	10	.412	19	15	10	0	0	133	132	0	31	70	11.5	3.18	88	.261	.313	4	.108	-1	-9	-6	1	-0.8
1908 NY-A	4	5	.444	23	13	6	1	0	88¹	78	0	41	49	12.8	2.95	84	.242	.341	4	.160	-0	-6	-5	-0	-0.5
1909 NY-A	0	3	.000	4	2	1	0	0	22¹	27	0	11	11	16.5	2.82	90	.300	.394	1	.167	-0	-1	-1	1	-0.3
Total 8	54	72	.429	177	137	99	9	2	1200²	1179	17	416	502	13.2	3.22	95	.257	.329	75	.172	-9	-29	-20	-2	-3.0

● **KID NICHOLS** — Nichols, Charles Augustus b: 9/14/1869, Madison, Wis. d: 4/11/53, Kansas City, Mo. BB/TR, 5'10.5", 175 lbs. Deb: 4/23/1890 MH

YEAR TM/L	W	L	PCT	G	GS	CG	SH	SV	IP	H	HR	BB	SO	RAT	ERA	ERA+	OAV	OOB	BH	AVG	PB	PR	/A	PD	TPI
1890 Bos-N	27	19	.587	48	47	47	7	0	424	374	8	112	222	10.5	2.23	168	.229	.284	43	.247	1	63	72	0	6.7

YEAR	TM/L	W	L	PCT	G	GS	CG	SH	SV	IP	H	HR	BB	SO	RAT	ERA	ERA+	OAV	OOB	BH	AVG	PB	PR	/A	PD	TPI
1891	Bos-N	30	17	.638	52	48	45	5	3	425¹	413	15	103	240	11.3	2.39	153	.245	.295	36	.197	-3	45	60	6	5.8
1892	*Bos-N	35	16	.686	53	51	49	5	0	453	404	15	121	192	10.6	2.84	124	.229	.282	39	.198	1	22	34	-1	3.2
1893	Bos-N	34	14	.708	52	44	43	1	1	425	426	15	118	94	11.8	3.52	140	.253	.308	39	.220	-2	54	67	-2	5.5
1894	Bos-N	32	13	.711	50	46	40	3	0	407	488	23	121	113	13.7	4.75	120	.294	.345	26	.294	3	26	42	0	3.5
1895	Bos-N	26	16	.619	47	42	42	1	3	379²	417	15	86	140	12.0	3.41	149	.275	.316	37	.236	-4	58	71	-0	5.7
1896	Bos-N	30	14	.682	49	43	37	3	1	372¹	387	14	101	102	12.0	2.83	161	.266	.316	28	.190	-3	63	71	2	6.6
1897	*Bos-N	31	11	.738	46	40	37	2	3	368	362	9	68	127	10.6	2.64	169	.255	.291	68	.265	4	69	75	-2	7.3
1898	Bos-N	31	12	.721	50	42	40	5	4	388	316	7	85	138	9.6	2.13	173	.221	.272	38	.241	3	64	67	-2	6.9
1899	Bos-N	21	19	.525	42	37	37	1	0	343¹	326	11	82	108	10.9	2.99	139	.250	.298	26	.191	-5	33	45	-1	3.9
1900	Bos-N	13	16	.448	29	27	25	4	0	231¹	215	11	72	53	11.6	3.07	134	.246	.311	22	.200	-2	16	27	-1	2.6
1901	Bos-N	19	16	.543	38	34	33	4	0	321	306	8	90	143	11.4	3.22	112	.250	.306	46	.282	9	4	14	-1	2.3
1904	StL-N	21	13	.618	36	35	35	3	1	317	268	3	50	134	9.2	2.02	134	.222	.256	17	.156	-1	25	24	-1	2.4
1905	StL-N	1	5	.167	7	7	5	0	0	51²	64	1	18	16	14.3	5.40	105	.296	.350	2	.227	0	-14	-14	-1	-1.4
	Phi-N	10	6	.625	17	16	15	1	0	138²	129	1	28	50	10.4	2.27	129	.250	.294	10	.189	0	11	10	-4	0.7
	Yr	11	11	.500	24	23	20	1	0	190¹	193	2	46	66	11.5	3.12	94	.264	.311	15	.200	-0	-2	-4	-5	-0.7
1906	Phi-N	0	0	—	4	2	1	0	0	11	17	0	13	1	26.2	9.82	57	.386	.542	0	.000	-0	-9	-9	-1	-0.8
Total	15	361	208	.634	620	561	531	48	17	5056¹	4912	156	1268	1873	11.2	2.95	139	.250	.300	471	.226	-0	531	653	-9	60.9

● **CHET NICHOLS**   Nichols, Chester Raymond Jr.   b: 2/22/31, Pawtucket, R.I.   d: 3/27/95, Lincoln, R.I.   BB/TL, 6'1.5", 195 lbs.   Deb: 4/19/51   F

YEAR	TM/L	W	L	PCT	G	GS	CG	SH	SV	IP	H	HR	BB	SO	RAT	ERA	ERA+	OAV	OOB	BH	AVG	PB	PR	/A	PD	TPI
1951	Bos-N	11	8	.579	33	19	12	3	2	156	142	4	69	71	12.2	2.88	127	.246	.327	7	.137	-2	19	14	2	1.5
1954	Mil-N	9	11	.450	35	20	5	1	1	122¹	132	5	65	55	14.8	4.41	84	.286	.379	3	.086	-3	-5	-9	1	-1.5
1955	Mil-N	9	8	.529	34	21	6	0	1	144	139	6	47	44	12.9	4.00	94	.253	.335	8	.154	-2	1	-4	2	-0.5
1956	Mil-N	0	1	.000	2	0	0	0	0	4	9	1	3	2	27.0	6.75	51	.563	.632	0	.000	-0	-1	-0	0	-0.3
1960	Bos-A	0	2	.000	6	1	0	0	0	12²	12	0	4	11	11.4	4.26	95	.240	.296	0	.000	-0	-1	-0	0	0.0
1961	Bos-A	3	2	.600	26	2	0	0	3	51²	40	3	26	20	11.5	2.09	199	.221	.319	1	.111	-0	11	12	3	1.5
1962	Bos-A	1	1	.500	29	1	0	0	0	57	61	4	22	33	13.1	3.00	138	.276	.342	0	.000	-1	6	7	1	0.4
1963	Bos-A	1	3	.250	21	7	0	0	0	52²	61	4	24	27	14.5	4.78	79	.298	.371	3	.231	0	-7	-6	-0	-0.4
1964	Cin-N	0	0	—	3	0	0	0	0	3	3	1	1	3	12.0	6.00	60	.308	.308	0	—	-1	-1	-0	0	0.0
Total	9	34	36	.486	189	71	23	4	10	603¹	600	45	280	266	13.2	3.64	105	.264	.346	22	.127	-8	22	11	8	0.7

● **CHET NICHOLS**   Nichols, Chester Raymond Sr. "Nick"   b: 7/3/1897, Woonsocket, R.I.   d: 7/11/82, Pawtucket, R.I.   BR/TR, 5'11", 160 lbs.   Deb: 7/30/26   F

YEAR	TM/L	W	L	PCT	G	GS	CG	SH	SV	IP	H	HR	BB	SO	RAT	ERA	ERA+	OAV	OOB	BH	AVG	PB	PR	/A	PD	TPI
1926	Pit-N	0	0	—	3	0	0	0	0	7²	13	0	5	2	21.1	8.22	48	.342	.419	1	.333	0	-4	-4	0	0.0
1927	Pit-N	0	3	.000	8	0	0	0	0	27²	34	1	17	9	16.9	5.86	70	.309	.406	1	.111	-0	-6	-5	-0	-0.6
1928	NY-N	0	0	—	3	0	0	0	0	2²	11	0	3	1	50.6	23.63	17	.611	.682	0	—	-6	-6	-0	0	-0.6
1930	Phi-N	1	2	.333	16	5	1	0	0	59²	76	8	16	15	14.2	6.79	80	.306	.353	6	.300	0	-12	-9	1	-0.2
1931	Phi-N	0	1	.000	3	0	0	0	0	5²	10	0	1	1	17.5	9.53	45	.435	.458	0	.000	-0	-4	-4	0	-0.6
1932	Phi-N	0	2	.000	11	0	0	0	0	19¹	23	2	14	5	17.2	6.98	63	.299	.407	1	.000	-1	-7	-6	-0	-0.6
Total	6	1	8	.111	44	5	2	0	0	122²	167	11	56	33	16.7	7.19	67	.325	.395	8	.211	-1	-38	-33	1	-1.9

● **DOLAN NICHOLS**   Nichols, Dolan Levon "Nick"   b: 2/28/30, Tishomingo, Miss.   d: 11/20/89, Tupelo, Miss.   BR/TR, 6', 195 lbs.   Deb: 4/15/58

YEAR	TM/L	W	L	PCT	G	GS	CG	SH	SV	IP	H	HR	BB	SO	RAT	ERA	ERA+	OAV	OOB	BH	AVG	PB	PR	/A	PD	TPI
1958	Chi-N	0	4	.000	24	0	0	0	1	41¹	46	1	16	9	13.7	5.01	78	.295	.364	0	.000	-0	-5	-5	1	-0.4

● **TRICKY NICHOLS**   Nichols, Frederick C.   b: 7/26/1850, Bridgeport, Conn.   d: 8/22/1897, Bridgeport, Conn.   BR/TR, 5'7.5", 150 lbs.   Deb: 4/21/1875

YEAR	TM/L	W	L	PCT	G	GS	CG	SH	SV	IP	H	HR	BB	SO	RAT	ERA	ERA+	OAV	OOB	BH	AVG	PB	PR	/A	PD	TPI
1875	NH-n	4	29	.121	34	33	30	0	0	288	321	2	9	48	10.3	2.38	87	.242	.248	23	.193	-2	-5	-10	0	-0.2
1876	Bos-N	1	0	1.000	1	1	1	0	0	9	7	0	0	0	7.0	1.00	226	.200	.200	0	.000	-1	1	1	0	0.1
1877	StL-N	18	23	.439	42	39	35	1	0	350	376	4	53	80	11.0	2.60	100	.263	.289	31	.167	-6	8	-0	-0	-0.6
1878	Pro-N	4	7	.364	11	10	10	0	0	98	157	0	8	21	15.2	4.22	52	.344	.356	9	.184	-0	-21	-22	2	-1.8
1880	Wor-N	0	2	.000	2	2	2	0	0	17²	29	0	4	4	16.8	4.08	64	.358	.388	0	—	-1	-3	-3	1	-0.4
1882	Bal-a	1	12	.077	16	13	12	0	0	118¹	155	2	17	21	13.1	5.02	55	.296	.319	15	.158	-2	-31	-30	-2	-2.7
Total	5	24	44	.353	72	65	60	1	0	593	724	4	82	126	12.2	3.37	76	.287	.309	55	.161	-10	-45	-53	-1	-5.4

● **ROD NICHOLS**   Nichols, Rodney Lea   b: 12/29/64, Burlington, Iowa   BR/TR, 6'2", 190 lbs.   Deb: 7/30/88

YEAR	TM/L	W	L	PCT	G	GS	CG	SH	SV	IP	H	HR	BB	SO	RAT	ERA	ERA+	OAV	OOB	BH	AVG	PB	PR	/A	PD	TPI
1988	Cle-A	1	7	.125	11	10	3	0	0	69¹	73	5	23	31	12.7	5.06	81	.272	.334	0	—	0	-8	-7	-0	-0.8
1989	Cle-A	4	6	.400	15	11	0	0	0	71²	81	9	24	42	13.4	4.40	90	.285	.345	0	—	0	-4	-3	-0	-0.6
1990	Cle-A	0	3	.000	4	2	0	0	0	16	24	5	6	3	18.0	7.88	50	.343	.410	0	—	0	-7	-7	-0	-1.0
1991	Cle-A	2	11	.154	31	16	3	1	0	137¹	145	6	30	76	11.9	3.54	117	.273	.319	0	—	0	8	9	-1	0.7
1992	Cle-A	4	3	.571	30	9	0	0	0	105¹	114	13	31	56	12.6	4.53	86	.273	.327	0	—	0	-7	-7	-0	-0.4
1993	LA-N	0	1	.000	4	0	0	0	0	6¹	9	1	2	3	15.6	5.68	67	.360	.407	0	—	0	-1	-1	-0	-0.1
1995	Atl-N	0	0	—	5	0	0	0	0	6²	14	3	5	3	25.7	5.40	79	.424	.500	0	—	0	-1	-1	-0	-0.1
Total	7	11	31	.262	100	48	9	1	0	412²	460	42	121	214	13.0	4.43	91	.282	.337	0	—	-0	-20	-18	-1	-2.2

● **FRANK NICHOLSON**   Nicholson, Frank Collins   b: 8/29/1889, Berlin, Pa.   d: 11/10/72, Jersey Shore, Pa.   BR/TR, 6'2", 175 lbs.   Deb: 9/6/12

YEAR	TM/L	W	L	PCT	G	GS	CG	SH	SV	IP	H	HR	BB	SO	RAT	ERA	ERA+	OAV	OOB	BH	AVG	PB	PR	/A	PD	TPI
1912	Phi-N	0	0	—	2	0	0	0	0	4	8	1	2	1	22.5	6.75	54	.471	.526	0	—	0	-1	-1	-0	0.0

● **CHRIS NICHTING**   Nichting, Christopher Thomas   b: 5/13/66, Cincinnati, Ohio   BR/TR, 6'1", 205 lbs.   Deb: 5/15/95

YEAR	TM/L	W	L	PCT	G	GS	CG	SH	SV	IP	H	HR	BB	SO	RAT	ERA	ERA+	OAV	OOB	BH	AVG	PB	PR	/A	PD	TPI
1995	Tex-A	0	0	—	13	0	0	0	0	24¹	36	1	13	6	18.5	7.03	69	.343	.420	0	—	-0	-6	-6	1	0.1

● **GEORGE NICOL**   Nicol, George Edward   b: 10/17/1870, Barry, Ill.   d: 8/10/24, Milwaukee, Wis.   TL, 5'7", 155 lbs.   Deb: 9/23/1890   ◆

YEAR	TM/L	W	L	PCT	G	GS	CG	SH	SV	IP	H	HR	BB	SO	RAT	ERA	ERA+	OAV	OOB	BH	AVG	PB	PR	/A	PD	TPI
1890	StL-a	2	1	.667	3	3	2	0	0	17	11	1	19	16	16.9	4.76	91	.180	.390	2	.286	1	-2	-1	-0	0.0
1891	Chi-N	0	1	.000	3	2	0	0	0	11	14	0	10	12	20.5	4.91	68	.298	.431	2	.333	-2	-2	-1	0	-0.1
1894	Pit-N	3	4	.429	8	5	3	0	0	44¹	57	2	33	11	19.3	6.50	81	.308	.426	9	.450	2	-6	-6	-1	-0.6
	Lou-N	0	1	.000	1	1	1	0	0	9	19	2	5	3	25.0	15.00	34	.422	.490	38	.352	0	-10	-10	0	-0.6
	Yr	3	5	.375	9	6	4	0	0	53¹	76	4	38	14	19.4	7.93	66	.323	.420	47	.367	2	-15	-16	-1	-1.2
Total	3	5	7	.417	15	11	6	0	0	81¹	101	5	67	42	19.6	6.86	70	.299	.428	51	.362	5	-19	-19	-2	-1.3

● **DAVID NIED**   Nied, David Glen   b: 12/22/68, Dallas, Texas   BR/TR, 6'2", 175 lbs.   Deb: 9/1/92

YEAR	TM/L	W	L	PCT	G	GS	CG	SH	SV	IP	H	HR	BB	SO	RAT	ERA	ERA+	OAV	OOB	BH	AVG	PB	PR	/A	PD	TPI
1992	Atl-N	3	0	1.000	6	2	0	0	0	23	10	0	5	19	5.9	1.17	312	.130	.183	2	.286	0	6	6	0	0.9
1993	Col-N	5	9	.357	16	16	1	0	0	87	99	8	42	46	14.7	5.17	92	.296	.376	4	.174	0	-11	-4	1	-0.5
1994	Col-N	9	7	.563	22	22	4	1	0	122	137	15	47	74	13.9	4.80	104	.287	.356	4	.100	-2	-8	2	-2	-0.1
1995	Col-N	0	0	—	2	0	0	0	0	4¹	11	2	3	3	29.1	20.77	26	.458	.519	0	.000	-0	-8	-0	0	-1.4
1996	Col-N	0	2	.000	6	1	0	0	0	11	11	1	8	4	21.9	13.50	40	.250	.464	0	.000	-0	-6	-5	-0	-1.4
Total	5	17	18	.486	52	41	3	1	0	241²	262	26	105	146	13.9	5.06	94	.281	.357	10	.141	-0	-26	-8	-2	-1.1

● **TOM NIEDENFUER**   Niedenfuer, Thomas Edward   b: 8/13/59, St.Louis Park, Minn.   BR/TR, 6'5", 225 lbs.   Deb: 8/15/81

YEAR	TM/L	W	L	PCT	G	GS	CG	SH	SV	IP	H	HR	BB	SO	RAT	ERA	ERA+	OAV	OOB	BH	AVG	PB	PR	/A	PD	TPI
1981	*LA-N	3	1	.750	17	0	0	0	2	26	25	1	6	12	11.1	3.81	87	.258	.308	0	—	0	-1	-1	-0	-0.3
1982	LA-N	3	4	.429	55	0	0	0	9	69²	71	3	25	60	12.7	2.71	128	.269	.337	0	.000	-0	7	6	-1	0.6
1983	*LA-N	8	3	.727	66	0	0	0	11	94²	55	6	29	66	8.1	1.90	189	.170	.240	0	.000	-0	18	18	-1	2.2
1984	LA-N	2	5	.286	33	0	0	0	11	47¹	39	3	23	45	12.2	2.47	143	.227	.325	0	.000	-0	6	6	-0	1.0
1985	*LA-N	7	9	.438	64	0	0	0	19	106¹	86	6	24	102	9.4	2.71	149	.223	.270	1	.111	-0	9	9	-1	1.5
1986	LA-N	6	6	.500	60	0	0	0	11	80	86	11	29	55	13.0	3.71	93	.280	.344	2	.500	1	0	-2	0	-0.3
1987	LA-N	1	0	1.000	15	0	0	0	1	16¹	13	1	9	10	12.7	2.76	144	.220	.333	0	—	-0	2	2	0	0.2
	Bal-A	3	5	.375	45	0	0	0	13	52¹	55	11	22	37	13.4	4.99	88	.266	.339	0	—	-1	-9	-8	-0	-0.7
1988	Bal-A	3	4	.429	59	0	0	0	18	59	59	8	19	40	12.2	3.51	111	.259	.321	0	—	-0	3	3	-1	0.4
1989	Sea-A	0	3	.000	25	0	0	0	0	36¹	46	7	15	14	15.4	6.69	60	.309	.376	0	—	-0	-11	-11	-0	-1.0
1990	StL-N	0	6	.000	25	0	0	0	2	65	66	3	20	30	12.6	3.46	110	.266	.337	0	.000	-0	3	5	0	0.5
Total	10	36	46	.439	484	0	0	0	97	653	601	60	226	474	11.6	3.29	112	.247	.314	3	.115	-1	34	28	-5	3.7

● **DICK NIEHAUS**   Niehaus, Richard J.   b: 10/24/1892, Covington, Ky.   d: 3/12/57, Atlanta, Ga.   BL/TL, 5'11", 165 lbs.   Deb: 9/9/13

YEAR	TM/L	W	L	PCT	G	GS	CG	SH	SV	IP	H	HR	BB	SO	RAT	ERA	ERA+	OAV	OOB	BH	AVG	PB	PR	/A	PD	TPI
1913	StL-N	0	2	.000	3	3	2	0	0	24	21	1	13	4	12.4	4.13	78	.241	.344	2	.286	1	-2	-2	0	-0.1
1914	StL-N	1	0	1.000	8	1	1	0	0	17¹	18	1	8	6	13.5	3.12	90	.269	.347	1	.250	1	-1	-1	-1	0.0
1915	StL-N	2	1	.667	15	5	2	0	0	45¹	48	2	22	21	14.1	3.97	70	.281	.366	1	.071	-1	-6	-6	-0	-0.4

YEAR TM/L	W	L	PCT	G	GS	CG	SH	SV	IP	H	HR	BB	SO	RAT	ERA	ERA+	OAV	OOB	BH	AVG	PB	PR	/A	PD	TPI
1920 Cle-A	1	2	.333	19	3	0	0	2	40	42	0	16	12	13.3	3.60	106	.269	.341	4	.444	2	1	1	-1	0.1
Total 4	4	5	.444	45	9	3	0	2	126²	128	4	59	43	13.4	3.77	85	.268	.351	8	.235	2	-8	-8	-1	-0.4

● **JOE NIEKRO** Niekro, Joseph Franklin b: 11/7/44, Martins Ferry, Ohio   BR/TR, 6'1", 190 lbs.   Deb: 4/16/67 F

YEAR TM/L	W	L	PCT	G	GS	CG	SH	SV	IP	H	HR	BB	SO	RAT	ERA	ERA+	OAV	OOB	BH	AVG	PB	PR	/A	PD	TPI
1967 Chi-N	10	7	.588	36	22	7	2	0	169²	171	15	32	77	10.9	3.34	106	.257	.293	9	.196	1	1	4	-1	0.4
1968 Chi-N	14	10	.583	34	29	2	1	2	177	204	18	59	65	13.5	4.32	73	.294	.351	6	.100	-2	-26	-23	0	-3.2
1969 Chi-N	0	1	.000	4	3	0	0	0	19¹	24	3	6	7	14.0	3.72	108	.304	.353	1	.200	0	-0	1	1	0.1
SD-N	8	17	.320	37	31	8	3	0	202	213	15	45	55	11.5	3.70	96	.273	.312	6	.118	0	-2	-4	-1	-0.5
Yr	8	18	.308	41	34	8	3	0	221¹	237	18	51	62	11.7	3.70	97	.275	.316	7	.125	0	-3	-3	-1	-0.4
1970 Det-A	12	13	.480	38	34	6	2	0	213	221	28	72	101	12.3	4.06	92	.266	.327	13	.197	4	-8	-8	1	-0.4
1971 Det-A	6	7	.462	31	15	0	0	1	122¹	136	13	49	43	13.8	4.49	80	.283	.352	4	.133	-0	-14	-12	1	-1.2
1972 *Det-A	3	2	.600	18	7	1	0	1	47	62	3	8	24	13.6	3.83	82	.330	.360	1	.250	1	-4	-4	-0	-0.3
1973 Atl-N	2	4	.333	20	0	0	0	3	24	23	2	11	12	12.8	4.13	95	.277	.362	1	.333	0	-1	-1	-1	-0.1
1974 Atl-N	3	2	.600	27	2	0	0	0	43	36	5	18	31	11.7	3.56	106	.237	.326	0	.000	-1	0	1	1	0.1
1975 Hou-N	6	4	.600	40	4	1	1	4	88	79	3	39	54	12.3	3.07	110	.240	.324	3	.214	1	5	3	0	0.5
1976 Hou-N	4	8	.333	36	13	0	0	0	118	107	8	56	77	12.5	3.36	95	.238	.324	5	.185	2	-2	-2	-1	0.0
1977 Hou-N	13	8	.619	44	14	9	2	5	180²	155	16	64	101	11.0	3.04	117	.237	.306	7	.140	-1	17	11	1	1.2
1978 Hou-N	14	14	.500	35	29	10	1	0	202²	190	13	73	97	12.1	3.86	86	.248	.321	9	.138	-1	-6	-13	-1	-1.8
1979 Hou-N☆	**21**	11	.656	38	38	11	**5**	0	263²	221	17	107	119	11.4	3.00	117	.228	.309	10	.120	-2	21	15	0	1.5
1980 *Hou-N	20	12	.625	37	36	11	2	0	256	268	12	79	127	12.3	3.55	93	.270	.326	22	.275	8	1	-8	-1	-0.1
1981 *Hou-N	9	9	.500	24	24	5	2	0	166	150	8	47	77	10.7	2.82	117	.243	.297	9	.176	1	12	9	1	0.9
1982 Hou-N	17	12	.586	35	35	16	5	0	270	224	12	64	130	9.8	2.47	134	.229	.279	8	.090	-4	34	25	0	2.3
1983 Hou-N	15	14	.517	38	38	9	1	0	263²	238	15	101	152	11.7	3.48	98	.241	.313	8	.094	-3	-4	-2	-2	-0.8
1984 Hou-N	16	12	.571	38	38	6	1	0	248²	223	16	89	127	11.5	3.04	109	.241	.310	11	.133	-2	15	8	1	0.7
1985 Hou-N	9	12	.429	32	32	4	1	0	213	197	21	99	117	12.7	3.72	93	.247	.333	17	.250	4	-3	-6	-0	-0.2
NY-A	2	1	.667	3	3	0	0	0	12¹	14	3	8	4	16.1	5.84	69	.280	.379	0	—	0	-2	-3	-0	-0.5
1986 NY-A	9	10	.474	25	25	0	0	0	125²	139	15	63	59	14.5	4.87	84	.275	.356	0	—	0	-10	-11	-1	-1.5
1987 NY-A	3	4	.429	8	8	1	0	0	50²	40	4	19	30	11.2	3.55	123	.215	.301	0	—	0	5	5	-0	0.5
*Min-A	4	9	.308	19	18	0	0	0	96¹	115	11	45	54	15.5	6.26	74	.296	.378	0	—	0	-19	-18	-1	-2.0
Yr	7	13	.350	27	26	1	0	0	147	155	15	64	84	13.8	5.33	85	.268	.347	0	—	0	-14	-13	-1	-1.5
1988 Min-A	1	1	.500	5	2	0	0	0	12¹	14	4	9	1	19.3	10.03	41	.320	.424	0	—	0	-8	-8	1	-1.0
Total 22	221	204	.520	702	500	107	29	16	3584	3466	276	1262	1747	12.0	3.59	94	.255	.321	152	.156	6	14	-38	-3	-5.4

● **PHIL NIEKRO** Niekro, Philip Henry b: 4/1/39, Blaine, Ohio   BR/TR, 6'1", 180 lbs.   Deb: 4/15/64 F

YEAR TM/L	W	L	PCT	G	GS	CG	SH	SV	IP	H	HR	BB	SO	RAT	ERA	ERA+	OAV	OOB	BH	AVG	PB	PR	/A	PD	TPI
1964 Mil-N	0	0	—	10	0	0	0	0	15	15	1	7	8	13.8	4.80	73	.273	.365	0	—	0	-2	-2	-0	0.0
1965 Mil-N	2	3	.400	41	1	0	0	6	74²	73	5	26	49	12.3	2.89	122	.258	.327	1	.100	-0	5	5	1	0.5
1966 Atl-N	4	3	.571	28	0	0	0	2	50¹	48	4	23	17	13.1	4.11	88	.249	.335	0	.000	-1	-3	-3	2	-0.3
1967 Atl-N	11	9	.550	46	20	10	1	9	207	164	9	55	129	9.8	**1.87**	178	.218	.277	7	.123	-0	35	33	1	3.8
1968 Atl-N	14	12	.538	37	34	15	5	2	257	228	16	45	140	9.7	2.59	116	.239	.277	8	.104	-1	11	11	3	1.5
1969 *Atl-N★	23	13	.639	40	35	21	4	1	284¹	235	21	57	193	9.4	2.56	141	.221	.264	20	.211	-3	33	33	2	4.8
1970 Atl-N	12	18	.400	34	32	10	3	0	229²	222	40	68	168	11.6	4.27	100	.248	.305	12	.152	-1	-6	-0	1	0.1
1971 Atl-N	15	14	.517	42	36	18	4	2	268²	248	27	70	173	10.8	2.98	124	.245	.296	14	.152	-2	14	22	2	2.3
1972 Atl-N	16	12	.571	38	36	17	1	0	282¹	254	22	53	164	9.9	3.06	124	.236	.275	18	.194	1	12	23	1	2.5
1973 Atl-N	13	10	.565	42	30	9	1	4	245	214	21	89	131	11.3	3.31	119	.234	.306	10	.122	-1	10	17	2	1.7
1974 Atl-N	20	13	.606	41	39	**18**	6	1	302¹	249	19	88	195	10.2	2.38	159	.225	.286	20	.192	-0	**42**	47	0	5.2
1975 Atl-N☆	15	15	.500	39	37	13	1	0	275²	285	29	72	144	12.0	3.20	118	.269	.322	17	.172	-0	13	18	1	1.9
1976 Atl-N	17	11	.607	38	37	10	2	0	270²	249	18	101	173	11.9	3.29	115	.242	.315	18	.191	1	6	15	1	1.7
1977 Atl-N	16	20	.444	44	43	**20**	2	0	330¹	315	26	164	**262**	13.3	4.03	110	.255	.346	19	.174	-3	-5	15	2	1.4
1978 Atl-N★	19	18	.514	44	42	**22**	4	1	334¹	295	16	102	248	11.0	2.88	141	.235	.299	27	.225	2	26	**43**	4	5.7
1979 Atl-N	**21**	20	.512	44	44	**23**	1	0	342	311	41	113	208	11.4	3.39	119	.241	.307	24	.195	1	13	25	3	3.4
1980 Atl-N	15	18	.455	40	38	11	3	1	275	256	30	85	176	11.3	3.63	103	.249	.308	12	.133	-2	-1	3	1	0.2
1981 Atl-N	7	7	.500	22	22	3	2	0	139¹	120	6	56	62	11.4	3.10	115	.233	.310	4	.077	-4	6	7	0	0.3
1982 *Atl-N☆	17	4	**.810**	35	35	4	2	0	234¹	225	23	73	144	11.6	3.61	103	.255	.314	17	.195	2	-0	3	1	0.6
1983 Atl-N	11	10	.524	34	33	2	0	0	201²	212	18	105	128	14.2	3.97	98	.276	.364	12	.185	0	-8	-2	0	-0.2
1984 NY-A☆	16	8	.667	32	31	5	1	0	215²	219	15	76	136	12.4	3.09	123	.267	.331	0	—	0	22	17	2	2.0
1985 NY-A	16	12	.571	33	33	7	1	0	220	203	29	120	149	13.3	4.09	98	.245	.342	0	—	0	-2	-2	-2	-0.4
1986 Cle-A	11	11	.500	34	32	5	0	0	210¹	241	24	95	81	14.6	4.32	96	.287	.363	0	—	0	-3	-4	-1	-0.4
1987 Tor-A	0	2	.000	3	3	0	0	0	12	15	4	7	7	16.5	8.25	54	.306	.393	0	—	0	-5	-5	-0	-0.7
Cle-A	7	11	.389	22	22	2	0	0	123²	142	18	53	57	14.5	5.89	77	.286	.359	0	—	0	-20	-19	0	-2.2
Yr	7	13	.350	25	25	2	0	0	135²	157	22	60	64	14.7	6.10	74	.288	.362	0	—	0	-25	-24	-0	-2.9
Atl-N	0	0	—	1	1	0	0	0	3	6	0	4	3	36.0	15.00	29	.429	.600	0	.000	-0	-4	-4	-0	0.0
Total 24	318	274	.537	864	716	245	45	29	5404¹	5044	482	1809	3342	11.6	3.35	115	.247	.312	260	.169	-6	192	299	28	35.4

● **JERRY NIELSEN** Nielsen, Gerald Arthur b: 8/5/66, Sacramento, Cal.   BL/TL, 6'3", 185 lbs.   Deb: 7/12/92

YEAR TM/L	W	L	PCT	G	GS	CG	SH	SV	IP	H	HR	BB	SO	RAT	ERA	ERA+	OAV	OOB	BH	AVG	PB	PR	/A	PD	TPI
1992 NY-A	1	0	1.000	20	0	0	0	0	19²	17	1	18	12	16.0	4.58	86	.243	.398	0	—	0	-1	-1	-0	0.0
1993 Cal-A	0	0	—	10	0	0	0	0	12¹	18	1	4	8	16.8	8.03	56	.340	.397	0	—	0	-5	-5	-0	0.0
Total 2	1	0	1.000	30	0	0	0	0	32	35	2	22	20	16.3	5.91	70	.285	.397	0	—	0	-6	-6	-0	0.0

● **SCOTT NIELSEN** Nielsen, Jeffrey Scott b: 12/18/58, Salt Lake City, Ut.   BR/TR, 6'1", 190 lbs.   Deb: 7/7/86

YEAR TM/L	W	L	PCT	G	GS	CG	SH	SV	IP	H	HR	BB	SO	RAT	ERA	ERA+	OAV	OOB	BH	AVG	PB	PR	/A	PD	TPI
1986 NY-A	4	4	.500	10	9	2	2	0	56	66	12	12	20	12.9	4.02	102	.299	.340	0	—	0	-0	-1	-0	0.0
1987 Chi-A	3	5	.375	19	7	1	1	2	66¹	83	9	25	23	14.8	6.24	73	.307	.368	0	—	0	-13	-12	-1	-1.3
1988 NY-A	2	1	.333	7	2	0	0	0	19²	27	5	13	4	18.3	6.86	57	.333	.426	0	—	0	-6	-6	0	-0.8
1989 NY-A	1	0	1.000	2	0	0	0	0	0²	2	0	1	0	40.5	13.50	29	.500	.600	0	—	0	-1	-1	0	-0.7
Total 4	9	11	.450	38	18	3	3	2	142²	178	26	51	47	14.6	5.49	78	.309	.368	0	—	0	-19	-19	-1	-2.8

● **RANDY NIEMANN** Niemann, Randal Harold b: 11/15/55, Scotia, Cal.   BL/TL, 6'4", 200 lbs.   Deb: 5/20/79

YEAR TM/L	W	L	PCT	G	GS	CG	SH	SV	IP	H	HR	BB	SO	RAT	ERA	ERA+	OAV	OOB	BH	AVG	PB	PR	/A	PD	TPI
1979 Hou-N	3	2	.600	26	7	3	2	1	67	68	1	22	24	12.2	3.76	93	.272	.333	2	.133	-0	-0	-2	-1	-0.2
1980 Hou-N	0	1	.000	22	1	0	0	0	33	40	2	12	18	14.2	5.45	60	.299	.356	2	.333	1	-7	-8	1	-0.1
1982 Pit-N	1	1	.500	20	0	0	0	0	35¹	34	1	17	26	13.5	5.09	73	.254	.346	2	1.000	1	-6	-5	1	-0.2
1983 Pit-N	0	1	1.000	8	1	0	0	0	13²	20	2	7	8	18.4	9.22	40	.357	.438	0	.000	-0	-8	-8	0	-0.5
1984 Chi-A	0	0	—	5	0	0	0	0	5¹	7	0	5	5	16.9	1.69	246	.263	.417	0	—	0	1	1	0	0.0
1985 NY-N	0	0	—	4	0	0	0	0	4²	5	0	0	2	9.6	0.00	—	.278	.278	0	—	0	2	2	0	0.0
1986 NY-N	2	3	.400	31	1	0	0	0	35²	44	2	12	18	14.1	3.79	93	.308	.361	2	.333	1	-0	-1	1	0.0
1987 Min-A	1	0	1.000	6	0	0	0	0	5¹	3	0	7	1	20.3	8.44	55	.158	.429	0	—	0	-2	-2	0	-0.2
Total 8	7	8	.467	122	10	3	2	3	200	219	8	82	102	13.8	4.64	83	.283	.357	8	.267	2	-21	-24	2	-1.4

● **JACK NIEMES** Niemes, Jacob Leland b: 10/19/19, Cincinnati, Ohio   d: 3/4/66, Hamilton, Ohio   BR/TL, 6'1", 180 lbs.   Deb: 5/30/43

YEAR TM/L	W	L	PCT	G	GS	CG	SH	SV	IP	H	HR	BB	SO	RAT	ERA	ERA+	OAV	OOB	BH	AVG	PB	PR	/A	PD	TPI
1943 Cin-N	0	0	—	3	0	0	0	0	3	5	0	2	1	21.0	6.00	55	.385	.467	0	—	0	-1	-1	-0	0.0

● **CHUCK NIESON** Nieson, Charles Bassett b: 9/24/42, Hanford, Cal.   BR/TR, 6'2", 185 lbs.   Deb: 9/18/64

YEAR TM/L	W	L	PCT	G	GS	CG	SH	SV	IP	H	HR	BB	SO	RAT	ERA	ERA+	OAV	OOB	BH	AVG	PB	PR	/A	PD	TPI
1964 Min-A	0	0	—	2	0	0	0	0	2	1	1	1	5	9.0	4.50	79	.143	.250	0	—	0	-0	-0	0	0.0

● **JUAN NIEVES** Nieves, Juan Manuel (Cruz) b: 1/5/65, Las Lomas, P.R.   BL/TL, 6'3", 175 lbs.   Deb: 4/10/86

YEAR TM/L	W	L	PCT	G	GS	CG	SH	SV	IP	H	HR	BB	SO	RAT	ERA	ERA+	OAV	OOB	BH	AVG	PB	PR	/A	PD	TPI
1986 Mil-A	11	12	.478	35	33	4	3	0	184²	224	17	77	116	14.7	4.92	88	.299	.366	0	—	0	-15	-12	-2	-1.6
1987 Mil-A	14	8	.636	34	33	3	1	0	195²	199	24	100	163	13.8	4.88	94	.264	.351	0	—	0	-9	-7	-1	-0.8
1988 Mil-A	7	5	.583	25	15	1	0	0	110¹	84	13	50	73	11.0	4.08	98	.208	.297	0	—	0	-1	-1	-0	-0.2
Total 3	32	25	.561	94	81	8	4	0	490²	507	54	227	352	13.5	4.71	92	.266	.345	0	—	0	-26	-20	-4	-2.6

● **JOHNNY NIGGELING** Niggeling, John Arnold b: 7/10/03, Remsen, Iowa   d: 9/16/63, LeMars, Iowa   BR/TR, 6', 170 lbs.   Deb: 4/30/38

YEAR TM/L	W	L	PCT	G	GS	CG	SH	SV	IP	H	HR	BB	SO	RAT	ERA	ERA+	OAV	OOB	BH	AVG	PB	PR	/A	PD	TPI
1938 Bos-N	1	0	1.000	2	0	0	0	0	4	4	0	1	2	22.5	9.00	38	.400	.455	0	—	0	-1	-1	-0	-0.5
1939 Cin-N	2	1	.667	10	5	2	1	0	40¹	51	3	13	20	14.7	5.80	66	.309	.367	2	.154	-0	-8	-9	-0	-0.6

YEAR TM/L	W	L	PCT	G	GS	CG	SH	SV	IP	H	HR	BB	SO	RAT	ERA	ERA+	OAV	OOB	BH	AVG	PB	PR	/A	PD	TPI
1940 StL-A	7	11	.389	28	20	10	0	0	153²	148	9	69	82	13.0	4.45	103	.250	.333	9	.176	-1	-1	2	-0	0.1
1941 StL-A	7	9	.438	24	20	13	1	0	168¹	168	17	63	68	12.4	3.80	113	.255	.320	10	.167	-1	7	9	-1	0.5
1942 StL-A	15	11	.577	28	27	16	3	0	206¹	173	10	93	107	12.1	2.66	139	.226	.319	10	.139	-2	23	24	-2	2.5
1943 StL-A	6	8	.429	20	20	7	0	0	150¹	122	7	57	73	11.1	3.17	105	.220	.299	3	.061	-4	2	3	-0	-0.3
Was-A	4	2	.667	6	6	5	3	0	51	27	0	17	24	7.8	0.88	363	.153	.227	5	.278	1	14	13	0	2.0
Yr	10	10	.500	26	26	12	3	0	201¹	149	7	74	97	10.0	2.59	127	.202	.275	8	.119	-3	16	16	0	1.7
1944 Was-A	10	8	.556	24	24	14	2	0	206	164	5	88	121	11.2	2.32	141	.221	.307	9	.130	-2	25	21	-1	1.5
1945 Was-A	7	12	.368	26	25	8	2	0	176²	161	7	73	90	12.1	3.16	98	.240	.318	7	.119	-4	4	-1	-2	-0.7
1946 Was-A	3	2	.600	8	6	3	0	0	38	39	1	21	10	14.4	4.03	83	.265	.361	2	.182	0	-2	-3	-0	-0.3
Bos-N	2	5	.286	8	8	3	0	0	58	54	2	21	24	11.8	3.26	105	.243	.311	2	.111	-1	1	1	0	0.0
Total 9	64	69	.481	184	161	81	12	0	1250²	1111	60	516	620	12.0	3.22	113	.236	.316	59	.140	-14	63	58	-7	4.2

● AL NIPPER
Nipper, Albert Samuel b: 4/2/59, San Diego, Cal. BR/TR, 6', 194 lbs. Deb: 9/6/83 C

YEAR TM/L	W	L	PCT	G	GS	CG	SH	SV	IP	H	HR	BB	SO	RAT	ERA	ERA+	OAV	OOB	BH	AVG	PB	PR	/A	PD	TPI
1983 Bos-A	1	1	.500	3	2	1	0	0	16	17	0	7	5	14.1	2.25	193	.293	.379	0	—	0	3	4	-0	0.2
1984 Bos-A	11	6	.647	29	24	6	0	0	182²	183	18	52	84	11.9	3.89	107	.257	.313	0	—	0	2	5	3	0.7
1985 Bos-A	9	12	.429	25	25	5	0	0	162	157	14	82	85	13.8	4.06	106	.256	.352	0	—	0	2	4	2	0.7
1986 *Bos-A	10	12	.455	26	26	0	0	0	159	186	24	47	79	13.4	5.38	77	.290	.342	0	—	0	-21	-21	3	-2.2
1987 Bos-A	11	12	.478	30	30	6	0	0	174	196	30	62	89	13.7	5.43	84	.284	.349	0	—	0	-19	-17	1	-1.8
1988 Chi-N	2	4	.333	22	12	0	0	0	80	72	9	34	27	12.3	3.04	119	.238	.322	2	.087	-1	4	5	-2	0.1
1990 Cle-A	2	3	.400	9	5	0	0	0	24	35	2	19	12	21.0	6.75	58	.354	.467	0	—	0	-8	-8	-0	-1.3
Total 7	46	50	.479	144	124	21	0	1	797²	846	97	303	381	13.3	4.52	93	.271	.342	2	.087	-1	-37	-28	7	-3.6

● MERLIN NIPPERT
Nippert, Merlin Lee b: 9/1/38, Mangum, Okla. BR/TR, 6'1", 175 lbs. Deb: 9/12/62

YEAR TM/L	W	L	PCT	G	GS	CG	SH	SV	IP	H	HR	BB	SO	RAT	ERA	ERA+	OAV	OOB	BH	AVG	PB	PR	/A	PD	TPI
1962 Bos-A	0	0	—	4	0	0	0	0	6	4	1	4	3	12.0	4.50	92	.200	.333	0	—	0	-0	-0	-0	0.0

● RON NISCHWITZ
Nischwitz, Ronald Lee b: 7/1/37, Dayton, Ohio BB/TL, 6'3", 205 lbs. Deb: 9/4/61

YEAR TM/L	W	L	PCT	G	GS	CG	SH	SV	IP	H	HR	BB	SO	RAT	ERA	ERA+	OAV	OOB	BH	AVG	PB	PR	/A	PD	TPI
1961 Det-A	0	1	.000	6	1	0	0	0	11¹	13	2	8	8	16.7	5.56	74	.295	.404	0	.000	-0	-2	-2	-0	-0.2
1962 Det-A	4	5	.444	48	0	0	0	4	64²	73	5	26	28	13.9	3.90	104	.285	.353	5	.417	2	1	1	-0	0.4
1963 Cle-A	0	2	.000	14	0	0	0	1	16²	17	3	6	10	13.5	6.48	56	.262	.342	0	.000	-0	-5	-5	-0	-0.7
1965 Det-A	1	0	1.000	20	0	0	0	1	22²	21	2	6	12	10.7	2.78	125	.259	.310	0	.000	-0	2	2	-0	0.0
Total 4	5	8	.385	88	1	0	0	6	115¹	124	12	48	58	13.5	4.21	92	.278	.349	5	.278	1	-5	-4	-0	-0.5

● OTHO NITCHOLAS
Nitchholas, Otho James b: 9/13/08, McKinney, Tex. d: 9/11/86, McKinney, Tex. BR/TR, 6', 190 lbs. Deb: 4/18/45

YEAR TM/L	W	L	PCT	G	GS	CG	SH	SV	IP	H	HR	BB	SO	RAT	ERA	ERA+	OAV	OOB	BH	AVG	PB	PR	/A	PD	TPI
1945 Bro-N	1	0	1.000	7	0	0	0	0	18²	19	4	1	4	9.6	5.30	71	.257	.267	1	.250	0	-3	-3	-0	-0.2

● C. J. NITKOWSKI
Nitkowski, Christopher John b: 3/9/73, Suffern, N.Y. BL/TL, 6'2", 185 lbs. Deb: 6/3/95

YEAR TM/L	W	L	PCT	G	GS	CG	SH	SV	IP	H	HR	BB	SO	RAT	ERA	ERA+	OAV	OOB	BH	AVG	PB	PR	/A	PD	TPI
1995 Cin-N	1	3	.250	9	7	0	0	0	32¹	41	4	15	18	16.1	6.12	67	.306	.384	2	.200	0	-7	-7	-1	-0.8
Det-A	1	4	.200	11	11	0	0	0	39¹	53	7	20	13	17.4	7.09	67	.335	.420	0	—	0	-10	-10	-0	-1.0
1996 Det-A	2	3	.400	11	8	0	0	0	45²	62	7	38	36	21.1	8.08	63	.332	.461	0	—	0	-16	-15	-0	-1.3
Total 2	4	10	.286	31	26	0	0	0	117¹	156	18	73	67	18.5	7.21	65	.326	.427	2	.200	0	-33	-33	-1	-3.1

● WILLARD NIXON
Nixon, Willard Lee b: 6/17/28, Taylorsville, Ga. BL/TR, 6'2", 195 lbs. Deb: 7/7/50

YEAR TM/L	W	L	PCT	G	GS	CG	SH	SV	IP	H	HR	BB	SO	RAT	ERA	ERA+	OAV	OOB	BH	AVG	PB	PR	/A	PD	TPI
1950 Bos-A	8	6	.571	22	15	2	0	2	101¹	126	8	58	57	16.5	6.04	81	.310	.398	5	.139	-1	-16	-13	-0	-1.6
1951 Bos-A	7	4	.636	33	14	2	1	1	125	136	12	56	70	14.3	4.90	91	.285	.368	13	.289	3	-11	-6	-0	-0.2
1952 Bos-A	5	4	.556	23	13	5	0	0	103²	115	12	61	50	15.6	4.86	81	.290	.390	11	.208	1	-14	-11	-1	-0.7
1953 Bos-A	4	8	.333	23	15	5	1	0	116²	114	6	59	57	13.4	3.93	107	.254	.343	8	.190	0	4	1	0	0.3
1954 Bos-A	11	12	.478	31	30	8	2	0	199²	182	16	87	102	12.5	4.06	101	.248	.335	18	.265	5	-7	1	1	0.4
1955 Bos-A	12	10	.545	31	31	7	3	0	208	207	10	85	95	12.8	4.07	105	.259	.333	18	.261	5	-2	5	2	1.2
1956 Bos-A	9	8	.529	23	22	9	1	0	145¹	142	9	57	74	12.8	4.21	110	.255	.333	11	.204	-1	-1	7	2	0.8
1957 Bos-A	12	13	.480	29	29	11	1	0	191	207	10	56	96	12.7	3.68	108	.280	.337	22	.293	-2	5	7	-1	1.2
1958 Bos-A	1	7	.125	10	8	2	0	0	43¹	48	7	11	15	12.3	6.02	67	.281	.324	5	.294	1	-11	-10	-1	-1.5
Total 9	69	72	.489	225	177	51	9	3	1234	1277	90	530	616	13.5	4.39	97	.270	.349	111	.242	17	-59	-16	5	0.3

● JUNIOR NOBOA
Noboa, Milciades Arturo (Diaz) b: 11/10/64, Azua, D.R. BR/TR, 5'10", 160 lbs. Deb: 8/22/84 ♦

YEAR TM/L	W	L	PCT	G	GS	CG	SH	SV	IP	H	HR	BB	SO	RAT	ERA	ERA+	OAV	OOB	BH	AVG	PB	PR	/A	PD	TPI
1990 Mon-N	0	0	—	1	0	0	0	0	2	4	0	0	3	13.5	0.00	—	.000	.500	42	.266	0	0	0	0	0.0

● THE ONLY NOLAN
Nolan, Edward Sylvester b: 11/7/1857, Paterson, N.J. d: 5/18/13, Paterson, N.J. BL/TR, 5'8", 171 lbs. Deb: 5/1/1878

YEAR TM/L	W	L	PCT	G	GS	CG	SH	SV	IP	H	HR	BB	SO	RAT	ERA	ERA+	OAV	OOB	BH	AVG	PB	PR	/A	PD	TPI
1878 Ind-N	13	22	.371	38	38	37	1	0	347	357	1	56	125	10.7	2.57	79	.253	.281	37	.243	6	-10	-21	2	-1.0
1881 Cle-N	8	14	.364	22	21	20	0	0	180	183	3	38	54	11.1	3.05	86	.251	.288	41	.244	1	-6	-9	-1	-0.9
1883 Pit-a	0	7	.000	7	7	6	0	0	55	81	0	13	23	14.9	4.25	75	.321	.347	8	.308	2	-6	-6	-0	-0.5
1884 Wil-U	1	4	.200	7	5	4	0	0	40	44	1	7	52	11.5	2.93	91	.262	.291	9	.273	-0	-2	-1	1	-0.3
1885 Phi-N	1	5	.167	7	7	6	0	0	54	55	1	24	20	13.2	4.17	91	.256	.331	2	.077	-2	-8	-8	-1	-0.9
Total 5	23	52	.307	79	78	74	1	0	676	720	6	135	274	11.4	2.98	80	.259	.294	97	.240	7	-32	-46	7	-3.3

● GARY NOLAN
Nolan, Gary Lynn b: 5/27/48, Herlong, Cal. BR/TR, 6'2.5", 197 lbs. Deb: 4/15/67

YEAR TM/L	W	L	PCT	G	GS	CG	SH	SV	IP	H	HR	BB	SO	RAT	ERA	ERA+	OAV	OOB	BH	AVG	PB	PR	/A	PD	TPI
1967 Cin-N	14	8	.636	33	32	8	5	0	226²	193	18	62	206	10.3	2.58	145	.228	.284	7	.104	-1	20	29	-1	2.6
1968 Cin-N	9	4	.692	23	22	4	2	0	150	105	10	49	111	9.4	2.40	132	.196	.267	6	.130	2	10	13	-2	1.2
1969 Cin-N	8	8	.500	16	15	2	1	0	108²	102	11	40	83	11.8	3.56	106	.240	.313	8	.229	3	-7	-0	-2	0.5
1970 *Cin-N	18	7	.720	37	37	4	2	0	250²	226	25	96	181	11.6	3.27	123	.240	.311	13	.159	1	22	21	-1	1.9
1971 *Cin-N	12	15	.444	35	35	9	0	0	244²	208	12	59	146	9.9	3.16	106	.227	.275	11	.147	-1	8	5	1	0.5
1972 *Cin-N†	15	5	**.750**	25	25	6	2	0	176	147	13	30	90	9.1	1.99	161	.227	.262	7	.117	-1	29	24	-1	2.6
1973 Cin-N	0	1	.000	2	2	0	0	0	10¹	6	1	7	3	11.3	3.48	98	.167	.302	0	.000	-0	-0	-0	-0	0.0
1975 *Cin-N	15	9	.625	32	32	5	1	0	210²	202	18	29	74	9.9	3.16	114	.251	.278	12	.176	2	11	10	-2	1.1
1976 *Cin-N	15	9	.625	34	34	7	1	0	239¹	232	28	57	113	9.8	3.46	101	.254	.276	8	.101	-1	1	1	-4	-0.6
1977 Cin-N	4	1	.800	9	8	2	0	0	39¹	53	5	12	28	14.9	4.81	82	.321	.367	1	.067	-0	-4	-4	-0	-0.6
Cal-A	0	3	.000	5	5	0	0	0	18¹	31	5	2	4	16.2	8.84	44	.365	.379	0	—	0	-10	-10	-0	-1.3
Total 10	110	70	.611	250	247	45	14	0	1674²	1505	146	413	1039	10.4	3.08	116	.239	.287	73	.138	0	87	93	-12	7.9

● DICK NOLD
Nold, Richard Louis b: 5/4/43, San Francisco, Cal. BR/TR, 6'2", 190 lbs. Deb: 8/19/67

YEAR TM/L	W	L	PCT	G	GS	CG	SH	SV	IP	H	HR	BB	SO	RAT	ERA	ERA+	OAV	OOB	BH	AVG	PB	PR	/A	PD	TPI
1967 Was-A	0	2	.000	7	3	0	0	0	20¹	19	1	13	10	14.2	4.87	65	.241	.348	0	.000	-0	-4	-4	-0	-0.4

● DICKIE NOLES
Noles, Dickie Ray b: 11/19/56, Charlotte, N.C. BR/TR, 6'2", 190 lbs. Deb: 7/5/79

YEAR TM/L	W	L	PCT	G	GS	CG	SH	SV	IP	H	HR	BB	SO	RAT	ERA	ERA+	OAV	OOB	BH	AVG	PB	PR	/A	PD	TPI
1979 Phi-N	3	4	.429	14	14	0	0	0	90	80	6	38	42	12.0	3.80	101	.246	.329	3	.100	-1	-1	0	1	0.0
1980 *Phi-N	1	4	.200	48	3	0	0	6	81	80	5	42	57	13.7	3.89	97	.254	.344	4	.308	1	-3	-4	-0	0.0
1981 *Phi-N	2	2	.500	13	6	0	0	0	58¹	57	2	23	34	12.8	4.17	87	.260	.339	2	.105	-1	-4	-4	-1	-0.5
1982 Chi-N	10	13	.435	31	30	2	2	0	171	180	11	61	85	12.9	4.42	84	.274	.340	6	.107	-2	-16	-13	0	-1.8
1983 Chi-N	5	10	.333	24	18	1	1	0	116¹	133	9	37	59	13.2	4.72	80	.287	.341	9	.237	1	-14	-12	-1	-1.3
1984 Chi-N	2	2	.500	21	1	0	0	0	50²	60	4	16	14	13.7	5.15	76	.305	.360	0	.000	-0	-9	-7	-1	-0.7
Tex-A	2	3	.400	18	6	0	0	0	57²	60	6	30	39	14.8	5.15	80	.262	.360	0	—	0	-7	-6	-1	-0.7
1985 Tex-A	4	8	.333	28	13	0	0	0	110¹	129	11	38	59	13.7	5.06	84	.289	.346	0	—	0	-11	-10	-1	-0.9
1986 Cle-A	3	2	.600	32	0	0	0	0	54²	56	9	30	32	15.0	5.10	81	.269	.351	0	—	0	4	5	1	0.5
1987 Chi-N	4	2	.667	41	1	0	0	2	64¹	59	1	27	33	12.7	3.50	122	.239	.326	0	.000	-0	6	6	0	0.3
Det-A	0	0	—	2	0	0	0	0	2	2	1	0	1	13.5	4.50	94	.250	.333		—	0	-0	-0	0	0.3
1988 Bal-A	0	2	.000	2	2	0	0	0	3¹	11	2	1	1	32.4	24.30	16	.500	.522		—	-0	-1	-1	0	-2.2
1990 Phi-N	0	0	—	2	0	0	0	0	2	0	0	2	0	54.0	27.00	14	.667	.667		—	-0	-1	-1	0	-1.2
Total 11	36	53	.404	277	96	3	3	11	860	909	66	338	455	13.4	4.56	86	.272	.345	24	.136	-3	-75	-61	-2	-8.9

● ERIC NOLTE
Nolte, Eric Carl b: 4/28/64, Canoga Park, Cal. BL/TL, 6'3", 205 lbs. Deb: 8/1/87

YEAR TM/L	W	L	PCT	G	GS	CG	SH	SV	IP	H	HR	BB	SO	RAT	ERA	ERA+	OAV	OOB	BH	AVG	PB	PR	/A	PD	TPI
1987 SD-N	2	6	.250	12	12	0	0	0	67¹	57	6	36	44	12.7	3.21	123	.226	.328	2	.095	-1	7	6	-1	0.5
1988 SD-N	0	0	—	2	0	0	0	0	3	3	1	2	1	15.0	6.00	57	.273	.385	0	—	0	-1	-1	0	-0.1
1989 SD-N	0	0	—	3	1	0	0	0	9	15	1	7	8	22.0	11.00	32	.375	.468	0	.000	-0	-8	-8	-0	-1.0
1991 SD-N	3	2	.600	6	6	0	0	0	22	37	6	10	15	19.2	11.05	34	.378	.435	1	.111	-0	-18	-18	-0	-2.9

YEAR	TM/L	W	L	PCT	G	GS	CG	SH	SV	IP	H	HR	BB	SO	RAT	ERA	ERA+	OAV	OOB	BH	AVG	PB	PR	/A	PD	TPI
	Tex-A	0	0	—	3	0	0	0	0	2²	3	0	3	1	20.3	3.38	119	.273	.429	0	—	0	0	0	-0	0.1
Total	4	5	8	.385	26	19	1	0	0	104	115	14	58	69	15.2	5.63	69	.279	.371	3	.094	-1	-20	-20	-1	-2.3

● **HIDEO NOMO**   Nomo, Hideo b: 8/31/68, Osaka, Japan BR/TR, 6'2", 210 lbs. Deb: 5/2/95

YEAR	TM/L	W	L	PCT	G	GS	CG	SH	SV	IP	H	HR	BB	SO	RAT	ERA	ERA+	OAV	OOB	BH	AVG	PB	PR	/A	PD	TPI
1995	*LA-N★	13	6	.684	28	28	4	**3**	0	191¹	124	14	78	**236**	9.7	2.54	149	**.182**	.271	6	.091	-4	35	27	-2	1.8
1996	*LA-N	16	11	.593	33	33	3	2	0	228¹	180	23	85	234	10.5	3.19	121	.218	.292	10	.133	-0	26	17	-1	1.6
Total	2	29	17	.630	61	61	7	5	0	419²	304	37	163	470	10.2	2.90	132	.201	.282	16	.113	-4	61	43	-4	3.4

● **JERRY NOPS**   Nops, Jeremiah H. b: 6/23/1875, Toledo, Ohio d: 3/26/37, Camden, N.J. BL/TL, 5'8.5", 168 lbs. Deb: 9/7/1896

YEAR	TM/L	W	L	PCT	G	GS	CG	SH	SV	IP	H	HR	BB	SO	RAT	ERA	ERA+	OAV	OOB	BH	AVG	PB	PR	/A	PD	TPI
1896	Phi-N	1	0	1.000	1	1	1	0	0	7	11	0	1	1	15.4	5.14	84	.355	.375	0	.000	-1	-1	-1	-0	-0.2
	Bal-N	2	1	.667	3	3	3	0	0	22	29	0	2	8	12.7	6.14	70	.315	.330	1	.111	-1	-4	-5	-0	-0.5
	Yr	3	1	.750	4	4	4	0	0	29	40	0	3	9	13.3	5.90	73	.325	.341	1	.077	-2	-5	-5	-0	-0.7
1897	*Bal-N	20	6	.769	30	25	23	1	0	220²	235	5	52	69	12.1	2.81	148	.271	.319	18	.196	-3	37	33	-2	2.7
1898	Bal-N	16	9	.640	33	29	23	2	0	235	241	5	78	91	12.8	3.56	101	.263	.332	20	.220	2	1	-0	-4	-0.2
1899	Bal-N	17	11	.607	33	33	26	2	0	259	296	1	71	60	13.1	4.03	98	.287	.339	29	.276	1	-5	-2	-3	-0.3
1900	Bro-N	4	4	.500	9	8	6	1	0	68	79	1	18	22	13.1	3.84	100	.289	.338	4	.160	-1	-1	-0	-1	-0.2
1901	Bal-A	12	10	.545	27	23	17	1	1	176²	192	5	59	43	13.4	4.08	95	.274	.341	13	.220	-0	-8	-4	-4	-0.8
Total	6	72	41	.637	136	122	99	7	1	988¹	1083	17	281	294	12.9	3.70	106	.277	.333	85	.221	-2	19	23	-15	0.5

● **WAYNE NORDHAGEN**   Nordhagen, Wayne Oren b: 7/4/48, Thief River Falls, Minn. BR/TR, 6'2", 205 lbs. Deb: 7/16/76 ◆

YEAR	TM/L	W	L	PCT	G	GS	CG	SH	SV	IP	H	HR	BB	SO	RAT	ERA	ERA+	OAV	OOB	BH	AVG	PB	PR	/A	PD	TPI
1979	Chi-A	0	0	—	2	0	0	0	0	2	3	0	2	1	13.5	9.00	47	.286	.375	54	.280	2	-1	-1	-0	0.0

● **JOHN NORIEGA**   Noriega, John Alan b: 12/20/43, Ogden, Utah BR/TR, 6'4", 185 lbs. Deb: 5/1/69

YEAR	TM/L	W	L	PCT	G	GS	CG	SH	SV	IP	H	HR	BB	SO	RAT	ERA	ERA+	OAV	OOB	BH	AVG	PB	PR	/A	PD	TPI
1969	Cin-N	0	0	—	5	0	0	0	0	7²	12	1	3	4	17.6	5.87	64	.400	.455	0	—	0	-2	-2	-0	0.0
1970	Cin-N	0	0	—	8	0	0	0	0	18	25	0	10	6	18.5	8.00	50	.333	.425	1	.250	0	-8	-8	1	0.1
Total	2	0	0	—	13	0	0	0	0	25²	37	1	13	10	18.2	7.36	54	.352	.433	1	.250	0	-10	-10	1	0.1

● **FRED NORMAN**   Norman, Fredie Hubert b: 8/20/42, San Antonio, Tex. BB/TL, 5'8", 160 lbs. Deb: 9/21/62

YEAR	TM/L	W	L	PCT	G	GS	CG	SH	SV	IP	H	HR	BB	SO	RAT	ERA	ERA+	OAV	OOB	BH	AVG	PB	PR	/A	PD	TPI
1962	KC-A	0	0	—	2	0	0	0	0	4	4	0	1	2	11.3	2.25	188	.250	.294	0	—	0	1	1	-0	0.0
1963	KC-A	0	1	.000	2	2	0	0	0	6¹	9	1	7	6	22.7	11.37	34	.346	.485	0	.000	-0	-5	-5	-0	-0.7
1964	Chi-N	0	4	.000	8	5	0	0	0	31²	34	9	21	20	15.9	6.54	57	.279	.389	1	.091	-1	-11	-10	-0	-1.2
1966	Chi-N	0	0	—	2	0	0	0	0	4	5	0	2	6	15.8	4.50	82	.313	.389	0	—	0	-0	-0	-0	0.0
1967	Chi-N	0	0	—	1	0	0	0	0	1	0	0	0	3	0.0	0.00	—	.000	.000	0	—	0	0	0	-0	0.0
1970	LA-N	2	0	1.000	30	0	0	0	1	62	65	9	33	47	14.5	5.23	73	.273	.366	1	.143	-0	-8	-10	-1	-0.3
	StL-N	0	0	—	1	0	0	0	0	1	1	0	0	0	9.0	0.00	—	.333	.333	0	—	0	0	0	-0	0.0
	Yr	2	0	1.000	31	0	0	0	1	63	66	9	33	47	14.1	5.14	75	.269	.356	1	.143	-0	-8	-9	-1	-0.3
1971	StL-N	0	0	—	4	0	0	0	0	3²	7	1	7	4	34.4	12.27	29	.438	.609	0	—	0	-4	-4	-0	-0.3
	SD-N	3	12	.200	20	18	5	0	0	127¹	114	7	56	77	12.2	3.32	99	.240	.323	9	.237	2	2	-0	-1	0.1
	Yr	3	12	.200	24	18	5	0	0	131	121	8	63	81	12.8	3.57	92	.246	.334	9	.237	2	-2	-4	-1	0.1
1972	SD-N	9	11	.450	42	28	10	6	2	211²	195	18	88	167	12.1	3.44	95	.244	.321	8	.125	1	0	-4	-1	-0.3
1973	SD-N	1	7	.125	12	11	1	0	0	74	72	9	29	49	12.4	4.26	82	.262	.334	1	.136	-0	-5	-6	-1	-0.6
	*Cin-N	12	6	.667	24	24	7	3	0	166¹	136	18	72	112	11.3	3.30	103	.224	.307	3	.052	-4	7	2	-1	-0.3
	Yr	13	13	.500	36	35	8	3	0	240¹	208	27	101	161	11.6	3.60	95	.235	.314	6	.075	-4	2	-5	-0	-0.9
1974	Cin-N	13	12	.520	35	26	8	2	0	186¹	170	15	68	141	11.6	3.14	111	.241	.309	8	.131	-2	10	7	-3	0.4
1975	Cin-N	12	4	.750	34	26	2	0	0	188	163	23	84	119	11.8	3.73	96	.235	.318	7	.117	-2	-2	-3	-2	-0.6
1976	*Cin-N	12	7	.632	33	24	8	3	0	180¹	153	10	70	126	11.3	3.09	113	.231	.308	7	.140	-1	8	8	-3	0.4
1977	Cin-N	14	13	.519	35	34	8	1	0	221²	200	28	98	160	12.2	3.38	116	.241	.324	8	.110	-2	13	14	-0	1.2
1978	Cin-N	11	9	.550	36	31	0	0	1	177¹	173	19	82	111	13.1	3.70	96	.255	.338	7	.140	-1	-3	-3	-1	-0.5
1979	*Cin-N	11	13	.458	34	31	5	0	0	195¹	193	14	57	95	11.5	3.64	103	.258	.311	9	.153	0	2	2	-2	0.1
1980	Mon-N	4	4	.500	48	8	2	0	0	95²	96	8	40	58	12.8	4.13	86	.259	.337	1	.050	-2	-6	-6	-1	-0.9
Total	16	104	103	.502	403	268	56	15	8	1939²	1790	188	815	1303	12.2	3.64	98	.246	.324	72	.125	-11	-0	-17	-15	-3.2

● **MIKE NORRIS**   Norris, Michael Kelvin b: 3/19/55, San Francisco, Cal. BR/TR, 6'2", 175 lbs. Deb: 4/10/75

YEAR	TM/L	W	L	PCT	G	GS	CG	SH	SV	IP	H	HR	BB	SO	RAT	ERA	ERA+	OAV	OOB	BH	AVG	PB	PR	/A	PD	TPI
1975	Oak-A	1	0	1.000	4	3	1	1	0	16²	6	0	8	5	7.6	—	.107	.219	0	—	0	7	7	0	0.4
1976	Oak-A	4	5	.444	24	19	1	1	0	96	91	10	56	44	14.0	4.78	70	.250	.353	0	—	0	-13	-15	3	-1.0
1977	Oak-A	2	7	.222	16	12	1	1	0	77¹	77	14	31	35	13.0	4.77	84	.260	.338	0	.000	0	-6	-6	1	-0.6
1978	Oak-A	0	5	.000	14	5	1	0	0	49	46	2	35	36	15.4	5.51	66	.249	.377	0	—	0	-10	-10	-0	-0.8
1979	Oak-A	5	8	.385	29	18	3	0	0	146¹	146	11	94	96	15.3	4.80	84	.265	.381	0	—	0	-9	-12	-1	-0.8
1980	Oak-A	22	9	.710	33	33	24	1	0	284¹	215	18	83	180	9.6	2.53	149	**.209**	.272	0	—	0	47	39	3	**4.7**
1981	*Oak-A★	12	9	.571	23	23	12	2	0	172²	145	17	63	78	11.4	3.75	93	.228	.308	0	—	0	1	-0	1	-0.6
1982	Oak-A	7	11	.389	28	28	7	1	0	166¹	154	25	84	83	13.2	4.76	82	.242	.336	0	—	0	-13	-16	1	-1.4
1983	Oak-A	4	5	.444	16	16	2	0	0	88²	68	11	36	63	10.9	3.76	91	.213	.299	0	—	0	3	1	-2	0.1
1990	Oak-A	1	0	1.000	14	0	0	0	0	27	24	0	9	16	11.7	3.00	124	.242	.318	0	—	0	3	2	0	0.2
Total	10	58	59	.496	201	157	52	7	0	1124¹	972	108	499	636	12.1	3.89	97	.233	.322	0	.000	0	7	-16	5	-0.7

● **LOU NORTH**   North, Louis Alexander b: 6/15/1891, Elgin, Ill. d: 5/16/74, Shelton, Conn. BR/TR, 5'11", 175 lbs. Deb: 8/22/13

YEAR	TM/L	W	L	PCT	G	GS	CG	SH	SV	IP	H	HR	BB	SO	RAT	ERA	ERA+	OAV	OOB	BH	AVG	PB	PR	/A	PD	TPI
1913	Det-A	0	1	.000	1	1	0	0	0	6	10	0	9	3	28.5	15.00	19	.357	.514	0	.000	-0	-8	-8	0	-0.8
1917	StL-N	0	0	—	5	0	0	0	0	11¹	14	1	4	4	14.3	3.97	68	.350	.409	0	.000	-0	-2	-2	0	-0.2
1920	StL-N	3	2	.600	24	6	3	0	1	88	90	3	32	37	12.7	3.27	91	.278	.346	7	.226	0	-1	-3	-1	-0.3
1921	StL-N	4	4	.500	40	0	0	0	7	86¹	81	5	32	28	11.9	3.54	103	.256	.327	3	.158	-1	2	1	-2	-0.2
1922	StL-N	10	3	.769	**53**	10	4	0	4	149²	164	4	64	84	14.1	4.45	87	.283	.361	11	.234	2	-6	-10	4	-0.2
1923	StL-N	3	4	.429	34	3	0	0	1	71²	90	8	31	24	15.6	5.15	76	.308	.380	4	.182	-1	-9	-10	1	-0.9
1924	StL-N	0	0	—	6	1	0	0	0	14²	15	1	9	8	14.7	6.75	56	.273	.375	1	.000	-0	-5	-5	-0	0.0
	Bos-N	1	2	.333	9	4	1	0	0	35¹	45	1	19	11	16.3	5.35	71	.321	.403	1	.111	-1	-6	-6	-1	-0.6
	Yr	1	2	.333	15	5	1	0	0	50	60	2	28	19	15.8	5.76	66	.308	.395	2	.154	-1	-11	-11	-1	-0.6
Total	7	21	16	.568	172	25	11	0	13	463	509	24	200	199	14.0	4.43	82	.287	.363	27	.197	-1	-34	-42	0	-3.0

● **JAKE NORTHROP**   Northrop, George Howard "Jerky" b: 3/5/1888, Monroeton, Pa. d: 11/16/45, Monroeton, Pa. BL/TR, 5'11", 170 lbs. Deb: 7/29/18

YEAR	TM/L	W	L	PCT	G	GS	CG	SH	SV	IP	H	HR	BB	SO	RAT	ERA	ERA+	OAV	OOB	BH	AVG	PB	PR	/A	PD	TPI
1918	Bos-N	5	1	.833	7	4	1	0	0	40	26	0	3	4	6.5	1.35	199	.183	.200	2	.154	-1	6	6	0	0.9
1919	Bos-N	1	5	.167	11	3	2	0	1	37¹	43	2	10	9	13.0	4.58	62	.301	.351	4	.500	3	-7	-7	1	-0.7
Total	2	6	6	.500	18	7	6	0	1	77¹	69	2	13	13	9.7	2.91	95	.242	.278	6	.286	2	-1	-1	1	0.2

● **EFFIE NORTON**   Norton, Elisha Strong "Leiter" b: 8/17/1873, Conneaut, Ohio d: 3/5/50, Aspinwall, Pa. BR/TR, Deb: 8/8/1896

YEAR	TM/L	W	L	PCT	G	GS	CG	SH	SV	IP	H	HR	BB	SO	RAT	ERA	ERA+	OAV	OOB	BH	AVG	PB	PR	/A	PD	TPI
1896	Was-N	3	1	.750	8	5	2	0	0	44	49	2	14	13	14.1	3.07	144	.280	.354	4	.211	-0	6	7	-0	0.4
1897	Was-N	2	1	.667	4	2	1	0	0	17	31	0	11	3	22.2	6.88	63	.387	.462	5	.278	1	-5	-5	-0	-0.6
Total	2	5	2	.714	12	7	3	0	0	61	80	2	25	16	16.4	4.13	106	.314	.388	9	.243	0	1	2	-1	-0.2

● **TOM NORTON**   Norton, Thomas John b: 4/26/50, Elyria, Ohio BR/TR, 6'1", 200 lbs. Deb: 4/18/72

YEAR	TM/L	W	L	PCT	G	GS	CG	SH	SV	IP	H	HR	BB	SO	RAT	ERA	ERA+	OAV	OOB	BH	AVG	PB	PR	/A	PD	TPI
1972	Min-A	0	1	.000	21	0	0	0	0	32¹	31	1	14	22	12.8	2.78	115	.252	.333	0	—	0	1	2	1	0.2

● **RANDY NOSEK**   Nosek, Randall William b: 1/8/67, Omaha, Neb. BR/TR, 6'4", 215 lbs. Deb: 5/27/89

YEAR	TM/L	W	L	PCT	G	GS	CG	SH	SV	IP	H	HR	BB	SO	RAT	ERA	ERA+	OAV	OOB	BH	AVG	PB	PR	/A	PD	TPI
1989	Det-A	0	2	.000	2	2	0	0	0	5¹	7	2	10	4	28.7	13.50	28	.333	.548	0	—	0	-6	-6	-0	-1.3
1990	Det-A	1	1	.500	3	2	0	0	0	7	7	1	9	3	20.6	7.71	51	.280	.471	0	—	0	-3	-3	-0	-0.7
Total	2	1	3	.250	5	4	0	0	0	12¹	14	3	19	7	24.1	10.22	38	.304	.508	0	—	0	-9	-9	-0	-2.0

● **DON NOTTEBART**   Nottebart, Donald Edward b: 1/23/36, West Newton, Mass. BR/TR, 6'1", 190 lbs. Deb: 7/1/60

YEAR	TM/L	W	L	PCT	G	GS	CG	SH	SV	IP	H	HR	BB	SO	RAT	ERA	ERA+	OAV	OOB	BH	AVG	PB	PR	/A	PD	TPI
1960	Mil-N	1	0	1.000	5	1	0	0	0	15¹	14	0	15	8	17.0	4.11	83	.233	.387	0	.000	-1	-1	-1	-0	-0.1
1961	Mil-N	6	7	.462	38	11	2	0	3	126¹	117	11	48	66	11.9	4.06	92	.251	.325	5	.184	-0	5	5	-2	0.2
1962	Mil-N	2	2	.500	39	0	0	0	2	64	64	4	20	36	12.4	3.23	117	.258	.324	2	.333	-1	5	4	2	0.5
1963	Hou-N	11	8	.579	31	27	9	2	0	193	170	20	39	118	9.8	3.17	99	.234	.275	11	.167	-0	3	-0	-0	0.0
1964	Hou-N	6	11	.353	28	24	6	0	0	157	165	12	37	90	11.6	3.90	88	.275	.319	3	.064	-2	-6	-8	4	-0.7
1965	Hou-N	4	15	.211	29	25	3	0	0	158	166	14	55	77	12.9	4.67	72	.273	.338	5	.104	-1	-20	-23	2	-2.4

YEAR	TM/L	W	L	PCT	G	GS	CG	SH	SV	IP	H	HR	BB	SO	RAT	ERA	ERA+	OAV	OOB	BH	AVG	PB	PR	/A	PD	TPI
1966	Cin-N	5	4	.556	59	1	0	0	11	111¹	97	11	43	69	11.5	3.07	127	.235	.311	4	.167	-0	7	10	1	1.1
1967	Cin-N	0	3	.000	47	0	0	0	4	79¹	75	4	19	48	10.9	1.93	194	.253	.303		.000	-0	13	16	1	0.8
1969	NY-A	0	0	—	4	0	0	0	0	6	6	1	0	5	10.5	4.50	77	.261	.292			0	-1	-1	0	0.0
	Chi-N	1	1	.500	16	0	0	0	0	18	20	2	6	8	17.5	7.00	58	.350	.402	0	.000	0	-7	-6	-0	-0.6
Total	9	36	51	.414	296	89	16	2	21	928¹	902	69	283	525	11.7	3.65	96	.256	.315	32	.134	-3	-8	-13	11	-1.6

● **CHET NOURSE**   Nourse, Chester Linwood b: 8/7/1887, Ipswich, Mass. d: 4/20/58, Clearwater, Fla. BR/TR, 6'3", 185 lbs. Deb: 7/27/09

YEAR	TM/L	W	L	PCT	G	GS	CG	SH	SV	IP	H	HR	BB	SO	RAT	ERA	ERA+	OAV	OOB	BH	AVG	PB	PR	/A	PD	TPI
1909	Bos-A	0	0	—	3	0	0	0	0	5	5	0	5	3	18.0	7.20	35	.263	.417		.000	-0	-3	-3	0	0.0

● **RAFAEL NOVOA**   Novoa, Rafael Angel b: 10/26/67, New York, N.Y. BL/TL, 6', 180 lbs. Deb: 7/31/90

YEAR	TM/L	W	L	PCT	G	GS	CG	SH	SV	IP	H	HR	BB	SO	RAT	ERA	ERA+	OAV	OOB	BH	AVG	PB	PR	/A	PD	TPI
1990	SF-N	0	1	.000	7	2	0	0	1	18²	21	3	13	14	16.4	6.75	54	.284	.391	1	.200	0	-6	-6	-1	-0.4
1993	Mil-A	0	3	.000	15	7	2	0	0	56	58	7	22	17	13.5	4.50	94	.267	.346			0	-1	-2	-1	-0.1
Total	2	0	4	.000	22	9	2	0	1	74²	79	10	35	31	14.2	5.06	81	.271	.358	1	.200	0	-7	-8	-1	-0.5

● **WIN NOYES**   Noyes, Winfield Charles b: 6/16/1889, Pleasanton, Neb. d: 4/8/69, Cashmere, Wash. BR/TR, 6', 180 lbs. Deb: 5/19/13

YEAR	TM/L	W	L	PCT	G	GS	CG	SH	SV	IP	H	HR	BB	SO	RAT	ERA	ERA+	OAV	OOB	BH	AVG	PB	PR	/A	PD	TPI
1913	Bos-N	0	0	—	11	0	0	0	0	20²	22	1	14	6	13.9	4.79	69	.289	.372	1	.250	0	-4	-3	0	0.0
1917	Phi-A	10	10	.500	27	22	11	1	1	171	156	5	77	64	12.5	2.95	93	.258	.345	6	.115	-2	-5	-4	-1	-0.8
1919	Phi-A	1	5	.167	10	6	3	0	0	49	66	1	15	20	15.1	5.69	60	.332	.381	2	.125	-1	-13	-12	-0	-1.4
	Chi-A	0	0	—	1	0	0	0	0	6	10	0	4	0	15.0	7.50	42	.385	.385	1	.500	0	-3	-3	-0	0.0
	Yr	1	5	.167	11	7	3	0	0	55	76	1	15	24	14.9	5.89	58	.336	.378	3	.167	-1	-16	-15	-1	-1.4
Total	3	11	15	.423	49	29	14	1	2	246²	254	7	98	93	13.2	3.76	78	.280	.356	10	.135	-3	-25	-22	-1	-2.2

● **EDWIN NUNEZ**   Nunez, Edwin (Martinez) b: 5/27/63, Humacao, P.R. BR/TR, 6'5", 237 lbs. Deb: 4/7/82

YEAR	TM/L	W	L	PCT	G	GS	CG	SH	SV	IP	H	HR	BB	SO	RAT	ERA	ERA+	OAV	OOB	BH	AVG	PB	PR	/A	PD	TPI
1982	Sea-A	1	2	.333	8	5	0	0	0	35¹	36	7	16	27	13.2	4.58	92	.269	.347	0	—	0	-2	-1	0	-0.1
1983	Sea-A	0	4	.000	14	5	0	0	0	37	40	3	22	35	15.8	4.38	97	.278	.385	0	—	0	-1	-0	0	-0.1
1984	Sea-A	2	2	.500	37	0	0	0	7	67²	55	8	21	57	10.5	3.19	125	.218	.286	0	—	0	6	6	-1	0.4
1985	Sea-A	7	3	.700	70	0	0	0	16	90¹	79	13	34	58	11.3	3.09	136	.234	.305	0	—	0	11	11	0	1.5
1986	Sea-A	1	2	.333	14	1	0	0	0	21²	25	5	5	17	12.5	5.82	73	.284	.323	0	—	0	-4	-4	-0	-0.5
1987	Sea-A	3	4	.429	48	0	0	0	12	47¹	45	7	18	34	12.2	3.80	124	.262	.335	0	—	0	3	5	-0	0.5
1988	Sea-A	1	4	.200	14	3	0	0	0	29¹	44	4	14	19	18.7	7.98	52	.366	.439	0	—	0	-13	-12	1	-1.9
	NY-N	1	0	1.000	10	0	0	0	0	14	21	1	3	8	15.4	4.50	72	.339	.369	0	—	0	-2	-2	-0	-0.2
1989	Det-A	3	4	.429	27	0	0	0	0	54	49	6	36	41	14.2	4.17	92	.254	.371	0	—	0	-2	-2	1	-0.1
1990	Det-A	3	1	.750	42	0	0	0	6	80¹	65	4	37	66	11.7	2.24	177	.218	.309	0	—	0	15	15	-0	0.8
1991	Mil-A	2	1	.667	23	0	0	0	8	25¹	28	6	13	24	14.6	6.04	66	.277	.360	0	—	0	-5	-6	-0	-0.8
1992	Mil-A	1	1	.500	10	0	0	0	0	13²	12	1	6	10	11.9	2.63	146	.231	.310	0	—	0	2	2	0	0.3
	Tex-A	0	2	.000	39	0	0	0	3	45²	51	5	16	39	13.6	5.52	69	.279	.343	0	—	0	-8	-9	-1	-0.3
	Yr	1	3	.250	49	0	0	0	3	59¹	63	6	22	49	13.2	4.85	78	.268	.336	0	—	0	-6	-7	-1	0.0
1993	Oak-A	3	6	.333	56	0	0	0	2	75²	89	2	29	58	14.7	3.81	107	.298	.371	0	—	0	4	2	-0	0.4
1994	Oak-A	0	0	—	15	0	0	0	0	15	26	2	10	15	21.6	12.00	37	.382	.462	0	—	0	-12	-13	0	-0.4
Total	13	28	36	.438	427	14	0	0	54	652¹	666	74	280	508	13.3	4.19	97	.266	.344	0	—	0	-8	-8	-1	0.0

● **JOSE NUNEZ**   Nunez, Jose (Jimenez) b: 1/13/64, Jarabacoa, D.R. BR/TR, 6'3", 175 lbs. Deb: 4/9/87

YEAR	TM/L	W	L	PCT	G	GS	CG	SH	SV	IP	H	HR	BB	SO	RAT	ERA	ERA+	OAV	OOB	BH	AVG	PB	PR	/A	PD	TPI
1987	Tor-A	5	2	.714	37	9	0	0	0	97	91	12	58	99	13.8	5.01	90	.256	.360	0	—	0	-6	-6	-1	-0.4
1988	Tor-A	0	1	.000	13	2	0	0	0	29¹	28	3	17	18	14.1	3.07	128	.259	.365	0	—	0	3	3	0	0.1
1989	Tor-A	0	0	—	6	1	0	0	0	10²	9	2	14	8	8.4	2.53	149	.200	.238	0	—	0	2	1	0	0.1
1990	Chi-N	4	7	.364	21	10	0	0	0	60²	61	6	34	40	14.1	6.53	62	.270	.365	0	.000	-1	-18	-17	0	-2.6
Total	4	9	10	.474	77	22	0	0	0	197²	188	20	111	171	13.7	5.05	84	.258	.356	0	.000	-1	-20	-18	-1	-2.9

● **HOWIE NUNN**   Nunn, Howard Ralph b: 10/18/35, Westfield, N.C. BR/TR, 6', 173 lbs. Deb: 4/11/59

YEAR	TM/L	W	L	PCT	G	GS	CG	SH	SV	IP	H	HR	BB	SO	RAT	ERA	ERA+	OAV	OOB	BH	AVG	PB	PR	/A	PD	TPI
1959	StL-N	2	2	.500	16	0	0	0	0	21¹	23	3	15	20	16.0	7.59	56	.291	.404	0	.000	-0	-9	-8	1	-1.2
1961	Cin-N	2	1	.667	24	0	0	0	0	37²	35	7	0	24	26	14.3	3.58	113	.252	.366	2	.250	1	2	2	0	0.1
1962	Cin-N	0	0	—	6	0	0	0	0	9²	15	0	3	4	16.8	5.59	72	.375	.419	0	.000	0	-2	-2	0	0.0
Total	3	4	3	.571	46	0	0	0	0	68²	73	3	42	50	15.2	5.11	80	.283	.385	2	.200	1	-9	-8	1	-1.1

● **JOE NUXHALL**   Nuxhall, Joseph Henry b: 7/30/28, Hamilton, Ohio BL/TL, 6'3", 219 lbs. Deb: 6/10/44

YEAR	TM/L	W	L	PCT	G	GS	CG	SH	SV	IP	H	HR	BB	SO	RAT	ERA	ERA+	OAV	OOB	BH	AVG	PB	PR	/A	PD	TPI
1944	Cin-N	0	0	—	1	0	0	0	0	0²	2	0	5	0	94.5	67.50	7	.500	.778	0	—	0	-5	-5	-0	0.0
1952	Cin-N	1	4	.200	37	5	2	0	1	92¹	83	4	42	52	12.5	3.22	117	.246	.334	2	.087	-1	5	6	2	0.3
1953	Cin-N	9	11	.450	30	17	5	1	2	141²	136	13	69	52	13.5	4.32	101	.252	.345	16	.327	7	-1	1	-2	0.6
1954	Cin-N	12	5	.706	35	14	5	1	0	166²	188	11	59	85	13.7	3.89	108	.292	.357	9	.173	4	3	6	0	0.8
1955	Cin-N★	17	12	.586	50	33	14	**5**	3	257	240	25	78	98	11.3	3.47	122	.249	.309	4	.186	4	16	22	-2	2.5
1956	Cin-N☆	13	11	.542	44	32	10	2	3	200²	196	18	87	120	13.0	3.72	107	.257	.338	11	.186	3	1	6	-1	0.9
1957	Cin-N	10	10	.500	39	28	6	2	1	174²	192	24	53	99	13.0	4.75	87	.275	.332	14	.237	8	-17	-12	-2	-1.2
1958	Cin-N	12	11	.522	36	26	8	0	1	175²	169	15	63	111	11.9	3.79	109	.257	.323	13	.210	0	3	7	-0	0.7
1959	Cin-N	9	9	.500	28	21	6	1	1	131²	155	10	35	75	13.1	4.24	96	.292	.337	11	.250	3	-4	-3	-1	-0.1
1960	Cin-N	1	8	.111	38	6	0	0	0	112	130	8	27	72	12.9	4.42	86	.297	.344	2	.077	-1	-8	-7	-2	-0.5
1961	KC-A	5	8	.385	37	13	4	0	0	128	135	14	65	81	14.3	5.34	78	.268	.355	19	.292	7	-19	-17	-1	-0.9
1962	LA-A	0	0	—	5	0	0	0	0	5¹	7	0	5	2	21.9	10.13	38	.304	.448	0	—	0	-4	-4	-0	0.0
	Cin-N	5	0	1.000	12	9	1	0	1	66	59	4	25	57	11.6	2.45	164	.240	.313	7	.269	0	11	12	0	1.1
1963	Cin-N	15	8	.652	35	29	14	2	2	217¹	194	14	39	169	9.9	2.61	128	.237	.277	12	.158	0	16	18	-1	1.8
1964	Cin-N	9	8	.529	32	27	4	2	2	154²	146	19	51	111	11.8	4.07	89	.250	.317	7	.130	-1	-9	-8	-3	-1.3
1965	Cin-N	11	4	.733	32	16	7	1	1	148²	142	18	31	117	10.7	3.45	109	.252	.295	8	.178	1	7	8	-1	0.3
1966	Cin-N	6	8	.429	35	16	2	0	0	130	136	14	42	71	12.9	4.50	87	.270	.338	4	.100	-2	-13	-9	-1	-1.2
Total	16	135	117	.536	526	287	83	20	19	2302²	2310	209	776	1372	12.3	3.90	102	.262	.327	152	.198	28	17	17	-17	4.1

● **RICH NYE**   Nye, Richard Raymond b: 8/4/44, Oakland, Cal. BL/TL, 6'4", 185 lbs. Deb: 9/16/66

YEAR	TM/L	W	L	PCT	G	GS	CG	SH	SV	IP	H	HR	BB	SO	RAT	ERA	ERA+	OAV	OOB	BH	AVG	PB	PR	/A	PD	TPI
1966	Chi-N	0	2	.000	4	3	2	0	0	17	16	1	7	9	12.2	2.12	174	.254	.329	1	.250		3	3	0	0.3
1967	Chi-N	13	10	.565	35	30	7	0	0	205	179	15	52	119	10.2	3.20	111	.234	.284	16	.213	3	4	8	0	1.2
1968	Chi-N	7	12	.368	27	20	6	1	1	132²	145	16	34	74	12.2	3.80	83	.271	.321	8	.182	-0	-12	-9	-0	-1.4
1969	Chi-N	3	5	.375	34	5	1	0	3	68²	72	13	21	39	12.3	5.11	79	.271	.326	1	.063	-1	-12	-11	-1	-1.2
1970	StL-N	0	0	—	6	0	0	0	0	8	13	2	6	5	21.4	4.50	91	.371	.463	1	.500	1	-0	-0	1	0.1
	Mon-N	3	2	.600	8	6	1	0	0	46¹	47	3	20	21	13.0	4.08	101	.260	.333	3	.176	0	-1	-1	0	0.1
	Yr	3	2	.600	14	6	1	0	0	54¹	60	5	26	26	14.2	4.14	99	.276	.354	4	.211	1	-1	-1	1	0.2
Total	5	26	31	.456	113	63	16	1	4	477²	472	50	140	267	11.6	3.71	96	.257	.311	30	.190	2	-17	-7	-2	-1.0

● **JERRY NYMAN**   Nyman, Gerald Smith b: 11/23/42, Logan, Utah BL/TL, 5'10", 165 lbs. Deb: 8/24/68

YEAR	TM/L	W	L	PCT	G	GS	CG	SH	SV	IP	H	HR	BB	SO	RAT	ERA	ERA+	OAV	OOB	BH	AVG	PB	PR	/A	PD	TPI
1968	Chi-A	2	1	.667	7	3	1	0	0	40¹	38	1	16	27	12.0	2.01	151	.247	.318	2	.154	-0	4	5	-0	0.3
1969	Chi-A	4	4	.500	20	10	2	1	0	64²	58	7	39	40	13.5	5.29	73	.244	.350	1	.050	-1	-12	-10	-1	-1.3
1970	SD-N	0	2	.000	3	2	0	0	0	5¹	8	1	2	2	16.9	15.19	26	.364	.417	0	.000	0	-7	-7	-0	-1.5
Total	3	6	7	.462	30	19	3	2	0	110¹	104	9	57	69	13.1	4.57	78	.251	.342	3	.091	-1	-14	-12	-1	-2.5

● **PRINCE OANA**   Oana, Henry Kauhane b: 1/22/08, Waipahu, Hawaii d: 6/19/76, Austin, Tex. BR/TR, 6'2", 193 lbs. Deb: 4/22/34 ◆

YEAR	TM/L	W	L	PCT	G	GS	CG	SH	SV	IP	H	HR	BB	SO	RAT	ERA	ERA+	OAV	OOB	BH	AVG	PB	PR	/A	PD	TPI
1943	Det-A	3	2	.600	10	0	0	0	1	34	34	4	19	15	14.6	4.50	78	.262	.364	10	.385	-2	-5	-4	-0	-0.1
1945	Det-A	0	0	—	3	0	0	0	0	11¹	3	0	7	3	7.9	1.59	221	.086	.238	1	.200	-0	2	1	-0	0.0
Total	2	3	2	.600	13	1	0	0	1	45¹	37	4	26	18	12.9	3.77	93	.224	.337	16	.308	4	-2	-1	-1	-0.1

● **HENRY OBERBECK**   Oberbeck, Henry A. b: 5/17/1858, Missouri d: 8/26/21, St.Louis, Mo. Deb: 5/7/1883 ◆

YEAR	TM/L	W	L	PCT	G	GS	CG	SH	SV	IP	H	HR	BB	SO	RAT	ERA	ERA+	OAV	OOB	BH	AVG	PB	PR	/A	PD	TPI
1884	Bal-U	0	0	—	1	0	0	0	0	6	6	0	2	1	16.5	3.00	89	.321	.367	23	.184	-1	-0	-0	-0	-0.1
	KC-U	0	5	.000	6	4	3	0	0	29²	27	2	9	6	11.2	5.76	39	.308	.352	17	.189	-1	-11	-12	-1	-1.5
	Yr	0	5	.000	8	5	0	0	0	35²	34	2	9	7	15.4	5.30	44	.335	.355	40	.186	-2	-11	-12	-1	-1.6

● **DOC OBERLANDER**   Oberlander, Hartman Louis b: 5/12/1864, Waukegan, Ill. d: 11/14/22, Pryor, Montana TL, Deb: 5/16/1888

YEAR	TM/L	W	L	PCT	G	GS	CG	SH	SV	IP	H	HR	BB	SO	RAT	ERA	ERA+	OAV	OOB	BH	AVG	PB	PR	/A	PD	TPI
1888	Cle-a	1	2	.333	3	3	3	0	0	25²	27	2	18	23	16.1	5.26	59	.260	.374	3	.214	0	-6	-6	-0	-0.5

YEAR TM/L	W	L	PCT	G	GS	CG	SH	SV	IP	H	HR	BB	SO	RAT	ERA	ERA+	OAV	OOB	BH	AVG	PB	PR	/A	PD	TPI

● FRANK OBERLIN Oberlin, Frank Rufus "Flossie" b: 3/29/1876, Elsie, Mich. d: 1/6/52, Ashley, Ind. BR/TR, 6'1", 165 lbs. Deb: 9/20/06

1906 Bos-A	1	3	.250	4	4	4	0	0	34	38	0	13	13	14.0	3.18	87	.286	.358	2	.154	-0	-2	-2	1	-0.1
1907 Bos-A	1	5	.167	12	4	2	0	0	46	48	2	24	18	14.5	4.30	60	.271	.365	2	.154	-0	-9	-9	-1	-1.1
Was-A	2	6	.250	11	8	3	0	0	48²	57	0	12	18	13.1	4.62	52	.294	.341	1	.056	-0	-11	-12	-1	-2.0
Yr	3	11	.214	23	12	5	0	0	94²	105	2	36	36	13.6	4.47	56	.282	.348	3	.097	-2	-20	-21	-2	-3.1
1909 Was-A	1	4	.200	9	4	1	0	0	41	41	1	16	13	13.8	3.73	65	.266	.358	2	.143	-1	-6	-6	-1	-0.9
1910 Was-A	0	6	.000	8	6	6	0	0	57¹	52	0	23	18	12.1	2.98	84	.259	.341	1	.053	-2	-3	-3	-0	-0.6
Total 4	5	24	.172	44	26	16	0	0	227	236	3	88	80	13.4	3.77	67	.275	.352	8	.104	-4	-31	-31	-3	-4.7

● DAN O'BRIEN O'Brien, Daniel Jogues b: 4/22/54, St.Petersburg, Fla. BR/TR, 6'4", 215 lbs. Deb: 9/4/78

1978 StL-N	0	2	.000	7	2	0	0	0	18	22	1	8	12	16.0	4.50	78	.301	.386	0	.000	-2	-2	-2	-0	-0.3
1979 StL-N	1	1	.500	6	0	0	0	0	11	21	0	3	5	19.6	8.18	46	.420	.453	0	.000	-0	-5	-5	-0	-0.9
Total 2	1	3	.250	13	2	0	0	0	29	43	1	11	17	17.4	5.90	61	.350	.412	0	.000	-1	-7	-7	-1	-1.2

● EDDIE O'BRIEN O'Brien, Edward Joseph b: 12/11/30, S.Amboy, N.J. BR/TR, 5'9", 165 lbs. Deb: 4/25/53 FC

1956 Pit-N	0	0	—	1	0	0	0	0	2	1	0	0	0	9.0	0.00	—	.167	.286	14	.264	0	1	1	-0	0.0
1957 Pit-N	1	0	1.000	3	1	1	0	0	12¹	11	2	3	10	10.2	2.19	173	.229	.275	0	.000	-1	2	2	0	0.1
1958 Pit-N	0	0	—	1	0	0	0	0	2	4	1	1	1	22.5	13.50	29	.444	.500	0	—	-0	-2	-2	-0	0.0
Total 3	1	0	1.000	5	1	1	0	0	16¹	16	3	4	11	11.6	3.31	115	.254	.309	131	.236	-0	1	1	-0	0.1

● DARBY O'BRIEN O'Brien, John F. b: 4/15/1867, Troy, N.Y. d: 3/11/1892, W.Troy, N.Y. BR/TR, 5'10", 165 lbs. Deb: 6/23/1888

1888 Cle-a	11	19	.367	30	30	30	1	0	259	245	5	99	135	12.4	3.30	94	.241	.315	20	.183	-3	-7	-6	2	-0.7
1889 Cle-N	22	17	.564	41	41	39	1	0	346²	345	9	167	122	13.9	4.15	97	.251	.343	35	.250	-4	-5	-5	2	-0.7
1890 Cle-P	8	16	.333	25	25	22	0	0	206¹	229	9	93	54	14.9	3.40	117	.269	.354	15	.156	-6	19	13	-1	0.5
1891 Bos-a	18	13	.581	40	30	22	0	2	268²	300	13	127	87	15.0	3.65	96	.273	.359	30	.234	-1	2	-5	-3	-0.7
Total 4	59	65	.476	136	126	113	2	2	1080²	1119	36	486	398	14.0	3.68	100	.258	.343	100	.211	-4	9	-2	-0	-0.8

● JOHNNY O'BRIEN O'Brien, John Thomas b: 12/11/30, S.Amboy, N.J. BR/TR, 5'9", 170 lbs. Deb: 4/19/53 F◆

1956 Pit-N	1	0	1.000	8	0	0	0	0	19	8	2	9	9	9.0	2.84	133	.133	.268	18	.173	-0	2	2	-1	0.0
1957 Pit-N	0	3	.000	16	1	0	0	0	40	46	7	24	19	16.0	6.07	62	.293	.390	11	.314	2	-10	-10	-1	-0.5
1958 StL-N	0	0	—	1	0	0	0	0	2	7	0	2	2	40.5	22.50	18	.538	.600	0	.000	0	-4	-4	-0	0.0
Total 3	1	3	.250	25	1	0	0	0	61	61	9	35	30	14.6	5.61	68	.265	.369	204	.250	0	-12	-12	-2	-0.5

● BOB O'BRIEN O'Brien, Robert Allen b: 4/23/49, Pittsburgh, Pa. BL/TL, 5'10", 170 lbs. Deb: 4/11/71

| 1971 LA-N | 2 | 2 | .500 | 14 | 4 | 1 | 1 | 0 | 42 | 42 | 4 | 13 | 15 | 12.0 | 3.00 | 108 | .262 | .322 | 1 | .111 | -0 | 2 | 1 | -1 | 0.0 |

● TOM O'BRIEN O'Brien, Thomas H. b: 6/22/1860, Salem, Mass. d: 4/21/21, Worcester, Mass. BR/TR, 6'1", 185 lbs. Deb: 6/14/1882 ◆

| 1887 NY-a | 0 | 0 | — | 1 | 0 | 0 | 0 | 0 | 3² | 4 | 0 | 5 | 0 | 22.1 | 7.36 | 58 | .211 | .375 | 25 | .194 | -0 | -1 | -1 | -0 | 0.0 |

● BUCK O'BRIEN O'Brien, Thomas Joseph b: 5/9/1882, Brockton, Mass. d: 7/25/59, Boston, Mass. BR/TR, 5'10", 188 lbs. Deb: 9/9/11

1911 Bos-A	5	1	.833	6	5	5	2	0	47²	30	0	21	31	9.8	0.38	868	.180	.275	2	.125	-1	16	15	1	2.0
1912 *Bos-A	20	13	.606	37	34	25	2	0	275²	237	6	90	115	11.0	2.58	132	.237	.306	13	.138	-5	23	25	0	2.4
1913 Bos-A	4	9	.308	15	12	6	0	0	90¹	103	0	35	54	13.7	3.69	80	.305	.370	5	.167	0	-8	-7	1	-0.9
Chi-A	0	2	.000	6	3	0	0	0	18¹	21	0	13	4	16.7	3.93	74	.318	.430	0	.000	-0	-2	-2	-0	-0.3
Yr	4	11	.267	21	15	6	0	0	108²	124	0	48	58	14.2	3.73	79	.307	.381	5	.152	-0	-10	-10	1	-1.2
Total 3	29	25	.537	64	54	36	4	0	432	391	3	159	204	11.7	2.63	125	.249	.322	20	.140	-6	29	31	3	3.2

● DARBY O'BRIEN O'Brien, William D. b: 9/1/1863, Peoria, Ill. d: 6/15/1893, Peoria, Ill. BR/TR, 6'1", 186 lbs. Deb: 4/16/1887 ◆

| 1887 NY-a | 0 | 0 | — | 1 | 0 | 0 | 0 | 0 | 1 | 1 | 0 | 1 | 0 | 18.0 | 0.00 | — | .333 | .500 | 157 | .301 | 0 | 0 | 0 | -0 | 0.0 |

● BILLY O'BRIEN O'Brien, William Smith b: 3/14/1860, Albany, N.Y. d: 5/26/11, Kansas City, Mo. BR, 6', 185 lbs. Deb: 9/27/1884 ◆

| 1884 StP-U | 1 | 0 | 1.000 | 1 | 1 | 1 | 0 | 0 | 10 | 8 | 0 | 3 | 7 | 9.9 | 1.80 | 74 | .205 | .262 | 7 | .233 | -0 | 1 | -1 | 0 | 0.0 |

● WALTER OCKEY Ockey, Walter Andrew "Footie" (b: Walter Andrew Okpych) b: 1/4/20, New York, N.Y. d: 12/4/71, Staten Island, N.Y. BR/TR, 6', 175 lbs. Deb: 5/3/44

| 1944 NY-N | 0 | 0 | — | 2 | 0 | 0 | 0 | 0 | 2² | 2 | 1 | 2 | 1 | 13.5 | 3.38 | 109 | .200 | .333 | 0 | — | 0 | 0 | 0 | -0 | 0.0 |

● PAT O'CONNELL O'Connell, Patrick H. b: 6/10/1861, Bangor, Me. d: 1/24/43, Lewiston, Maine BR/TR, 5'10", 175 lbs. Deb: 7/22/1886 ◆

| 1886 Bal-a | 0 | 0 | — | 1 | 0 | 0 | 0 | 0 | 3 | 4 | 0 | 2 | 1 | 18.0 | 6.00 | 57 | .333 | .429 | 30 | .181 | -0 | -1 | -1 | -0 | 0.0 |

● ANDY O'CONNOR O'Connor, Andrew James b: 9/14/1884, Roxbury, Mass. d: 9/26/80, Norwood, Mass. BR/TR, 6', 160 lbs. Deb: 10/6/08

| 1908 NY-A | 0 | 1 | .000 | 1 | 1 | 1 | 0 | 0 | 8 | 15 | 0 | 7 | 5 | 28.1 | 10.13 | 24 | .429 | .556 | 0 | .000 | -0 | -7 | -7 | -0 | -0.6 |

● FRANK O'CONNOR O'Connor, Frank Henry b: 9/15/1870, Keeseville, N.Y. d: 12/26/13, Brattleboro, Vt. BL/TL, 6', 185 lbs. Deb: 8/3/1893

| 1893 Phi-N | 0 | 0 | — | 3 | 1 | 0 | 0 | 1 | 4 | 2 | 0 | 9 | 0 | 24.8 | 11.25 | 41 | .143 | .478 | 2 | 1.000 | 2 | -3 | -3 | 0 | 0.0 |

● JACK O'CONNOR O'Connor, Jack William b: 6/2/58, Twentynine Palms, Cal. BL/TL, 6'3", 215 lbs. Deb: 4/9/81

1981 Min-A	3	2	.600	28	0	0	0	0	35¹	46	3	30	16	19.9	5.86	67	.336	.462		0	0	-9	-8	-1	-0.9
1982 Min-A	8	9	.471	23	19	6	0	0	126	122	8	57	56	12.9	4.29	99	.255	.337		0	0	-3	-1	-3	-0.4
1983 Min-A	2	3	.400	27	8	0	0	0	83	107	13	36	56	15.5	5.86	73	.315	.380		0	0	-17	-15	-1	-1.1
1984 Min-A	0	0	—	2	0	0	0	0	4²	1	1	4	9	9.6	1.93	218	.067	.263		0	0	1	1	-0	-0.3
1985 Mon-N	0	2	.000	20	1	0	0	0	23²	21	1	13	16	12.9	4.94	69	.239	.337		0	0	-4	-4	-1	-0.4
1987 Bal-A	1	1	.500	29	0	0	0	2	46	46	5	23	33	13.5	4.30	102	.263	.348		0	0	1	0	-1	0.2
Total 6	14	17	.452	129	28	6	0	2	318²	343	36	163	177	14.4	4.89	85	.278	.364		0	0	-30	-25	-5	-2.9

● HANK O'DAY O'Day, Henry Francis b: 7/8/1862, Chicago, Ill. d: 7/2/35, Chicago, Ill. TR, 6', 180 lbs. Deb: 5/2/1884 MU

1884 Tol-a	9	28	.243	41	40	35	2	1	326²	335	6	66	163	11.5	3.75	91	.252	.297	51	.211	-1	-18	-12	-4	-0.9
1885 Pit-a	5	7	.417	12	12	10	0	0	103	110	6	16	36	11.6	3.67	88	.258	.296	12	.245	1	-5	-5	0	-0.3
1886 Was-N	2	2	.500	6	6	6	0	0	49	41	1	17	47	10.7	1.65	199	.219	.284	1	.053	-2	9	9	1	0.5
1887 Was-N	8	20	.286	30	30	29	0	0	254²	255	15	109	86	13.2	4.17	97	.254	.332	23	.198	-3	-3	-1	1	-0.5
1888 Was-N	16	29	.356	46	46	46	3	0	403	359	19	117	186	11.0	3.10	90	.232	.293	23	.139	-7	-11	-13	-3	-2.2
1889 Was-N	2	10	.167	13	13	11	0	0	108	117	7	57	23	15.0	4.33	91	.268	.360	8	.182	-1	-4	-5	0	-0.4
*NY-N	9	1	.900	10	10	8	0	0	78	83	2	35	28	14.4	4.27	92	.264	.351	3	.097	-1	-2	-3	-1	-0.4
Yr	11	11	.500	23	23	19	0	0	186	200	9	92	51	14.5	4.31	92	.264	.349	11	.147	-2	-6	-8	-0	-0.8
1890 NY-P	22	13	.629	43	35	32	1	3	329	355	9	161	94	14.6	4.21	108	.264	.350	34	.227	-3	1	12	-4	0.0
Total 7	73	110	.399	201	192	177	5	4	1651¹	1655	65	578	663	12.6	3.74	97	.251	.319	155	.190	-17	-33	-22	-0	-3.8

● PAUL O'DEA O'Dea, Paul "Lefty" b: 7/3/20, Cleveland, Ohio d: 12/11/78, Cleveland, Ohio BL/TL, 6', 200 lbs. Deb: 4/19/44 ◆

1944 Cle-A	0	0	—	3	0	0	0	0	4¹	5	0	6	0	22.8	2.08	159	.333	.524	55	.318	1	1	1	-0	0.0
1945 Cle-A	0	0	—	1	0	0	0	0	2	4	0	2	0	27.0	13.50	24	.400	.500	52	.235	0	-2	-2	0	0.0
Total 2	0	0	—	4	0	0	0	0	6¹	9	0	8	0	24.2	5.68	58	.360	.515	107	.272	1	-2	-2	-0	0.0

● BILLY O'DELL O'Dell, William Oliver b: 2/10/33, Whitmire, S.C. BB/TL, 5'11", 170 lbs. Deb: 6/20/54

1954 Bal-A	1	1	.500	7	2	1	0	0	16¹	15	0	5	6	11.6	2.76	130	.242	.299	0	.000	-0	2	1	0	0.2
1956 Bal-A	0	0	—	4	1	0	0	0	8	6	0	6	6	13.5	1.13	349	.222	.364	0	.000	-0	2	3	-0	0.1
1957 Bal-A	4	10	.286	35	15	2	1	4	140¹	107	12	39	97	9.7	2.69	133	.212	.276	5	.147	-1	17	14	-2	1.1
1958 Bal-A★	14	11	.560	41	25	12	3	8	221¹	201	18	51	137	10.4	2.97	121	.241	.288	8	.111	-1	20	15	-0	1.7
1959 Bal-A★	10	12	.455	38	24	6	2	1	199¹	163	18	67	88	10.4	2.93	129	.220	.286	5	.083	-3	21	19	1	1.8
1960 SF-N	8	13	.381	44	24	6	1	2	202²	198	16	72	145	12.1	3.20	109	.252	.317	6	.107	1	13	6	-1	0.5
1961 SF-N	7	5	.583	46	14	4	1	2	130¹	132	10	33	110	11.5	3.59	106	.260	.306	4	.103	-2	8	5	-1	0.0
1962 *SF-N	19	14	.576	43	39	20	2	0	280²	282	26	66	195	11.4	3.53	108	.258	.304	12	.133	-1	13	8	-2	0.5
1963 SF-N	14	10	.583	36	33	10	3	1	221²	218	14	70	116	11.9	3.16	101	.253	.314	16	.205	4	3	1	-4	0.2
1964 SF-N	8	7	.533	37	6	0	0	1	85	90	10	35	54	12.8	5.40	66	.252	.332	0	.000	-2	-18	-17	-1	-3.2

YEAR	TM/L	W	L	PCT	G	GS	CG	SH	SV	IP	H	HR	BB	SO	RAT	ERA	ERA+	OAV	OOB	BH	AVG	PB	PR	/A	PD	TPI
1965	Mil-N	10	6	.625	62	1	0	0	18	111¹	87	10	30	78	9.6	2.18	161	.215	.272	4	.174	1	17	17	-0	3.0
1966	Atl-N	2	3	.400	24	0	0	0	6	41¹	44	3	18	20	13.9	2.40	152	.272	.352	2	.250	-0	6	6	-0	0.8
	Pit-N	3	2	.600	37	2	0	0	4	71¹	74	3	23	47	12.7	2.78	129	.275	.341	1	.063	-1	7	6	-1	0.3
	Yr	5	5	.500	61	2	0	0	10	112²	118	6	41	67	13.0	2.64	136	.273	.341	3	.125	-1	12	12	-1	1.1
1967	Pit-N	5	6	.455	27	11	1	0	0	86²	88	10	41	34	13.7	5.82	58	.265	.351	3	.115	-0	-24	-24	-1	-2.9
Total	13	105	100	.512	479	199	63	13	48	1817	1697	137	556	1133	11.4	3.29	109	.246	.306	66	.125	-7	85	59	-12	3.8

● **TED ODENWALD**   Odenwald, Theodore Joseph "Lefty"   b: 1/4/02, Hudson, Wis.   d: 10/23/65, Shakopee, Minn.   BR/TL, 5'10", 147 lbs.   Deb: 4/13/21

YEAR	TM/L	W	L	PCT	G	GS	CG	SH	SV	IP	H	HR	BB	SO	RAT	ERA	ERA+	OAV	OOB	BH	AVG	PB	PR	/A	PD	TPI
1921	Cle-A	1	0	1.000	10	0	0	0	0	17¹	16	0	6	4	11.9	1.56	274	.262	.338	0	.000	-1	5	5	0	0.2
1922	Cle-A	0	0	—	1	0	0	0	0	1¹	6	0	2	2	54.0	40.50	10	.600	.667	0	—	0	-5	-5	-0	0.0
Total	2	1	0	1.000	11	0	0	0	0	18²	22	0	8	6	14.9	4.34	98	.310	.387	0	.000	-1	-0	-0	-0	0.2

● **DAVE ODOM**   Odom, David Everett "Blimp" or "Porky"   b: 6/5/18, Dinuba, Cal.   d: 11/19/87, Myrtle Beach, S.C.   BR/TR, 6'1", 220 lbs.   Deb: 5/31/43

YEAR	TM/L	W	L	PCT	G	GS	CG	SH	SV	IP	H	HR	BB	SO	RAT	ERA	ERA+	OAV	OOB	BH	AVG	PB	PR	/A	PD	TPI
1943	Bos-N	0	3	.000	22	3	1	0	2	54²	54	3	30	17	14.5	5.27	65	.269	.374	0	.000	-2	-11	-11	-1	-1.0

● **BLUE MOON ODOM**   Odom, Johnny Lee   b: 5/29/45, Macon, Ga.   BR/TR, 6', 185 lbs.   Deb: 9/5/64 ◆

YEAR	TM/L	W	L	PCT	G	GS	CG	SH	SV	IP	H	HR	BB	SO	RAT	ERA	ERA+	OAV	OOB	BH	AVG	PB	PR	/A	PD	TPI
1964	KC-A	1	2	.333	5	5	1	1	0	17	29	5	11	10	21.2	10.06	38	.363	.440	0	.000	-0	-12	-12	0	-1.7
1965	KC-A	0	0	—	1	0	0	0	0	1	2	0	2	0	36.0	9.00	39	.400	.571	0	—	-1	-1	-1	0	0.0
1966	KC-A	5	5	.500	14	14	4	2	0	90¹	70	9	53	47	12.5	2.49	136	.215	.328	3	.097	-1	9	9	2	1.1
1967	KC-A	3	8	.273	29	17	0	0	0	103²	94	9	68	67	14.3	5.04	63	.243	.360	8	.286	2	-21	-21	-0	-1.9
1968	Oak-A★	16	10	.615	32	31	9	4	0	231¹	179	9	98	119	11.0	2.45	115	.216	.304	17	.218	-6	14	9	1	2.0
1969	Oak-A★	15	6	.714	32	32	10	3	0	231¹	179	15	112	150	11.6	2.92	118	.215	.312	21	.266	11	18	13	1	2.5
1970	Oak-A	9	8	.529	29	29	4	1	0	156¹	128	14	100	88	13.6	3.80	93	.227	.351	13	.241	6	-1	-5	2	0.5
1971	Oak-A	10	12	.455	25	25	3	1	0	140²	147	13	71	69	13.9	4.29	78	.271	.355	8	.160	-1	-13	-15	-1	-2.1
1972	*Oak-A	15	6	.714	31	30	4	1	0	194¹	164	10	87	86	11.8	2.50	114	.234	.321	12	.121	0	12	7	0	0.8
1973	*Oak-A	5	12	.294	30	24	3	0	0	150¹	153	14	67	83	13.3	4.49	79	.263	.341	0	.000	-1	-11	-16	-1	-1.8
1974	*Oak-A	1	5	.167	34	5	1	0	1	87¹	85	4	54	65	14.4	3.81	87	.267	.375	0	—	0	-2	-5	1	-0.3
1975	Oak-A	0	2	.000	7	2	0	0	0	11	19	1	11	4	25.4	12.27	30	.422	.544	0	—	0	-10	-11	0	-1.6
	Cle-A	1	0	1.000	3	1	1	0	0	10¹	4	1	8	10	10.5	2.61	145	.118	.286	0	—	0	1	1	-0	0.1
	Yr	1	2	.333	10	3	1	0	0	21¹	23	2	19	14	17.7	7.59	49	.284	.420	0	—	0	-9	-9	-0	-1.5
	Atl-N	1	7	.125	15	10	0	0	0	56	78	5	28	30	17.0	7.07	53	.342	.414	1	.077	-1	-21	-21	-0	-2.5
1976	Chi-A	2	2	.500	8	4	0	0	0	28	31	2	20	18	16.7	5.79	62	.282	.397	0	—	0	-7	-7	-1	-0.9
Total	13	84	85	.497	295	229	40	15	1	1509	1362	103	788	857	13.0	3.70	89	.244	.341	79	.195	26	-45	-71	5	-5.8

● **GEORGE O'DONNELL**   O'Donnell, George Dana   b: 5/27/29, Winchester, Ill.   BR/TR, 6'3", 175 lbs.   Deb: 4/18/54

YEAR	TM/L	W	L	PCT	G	GS	CG	SH	SV	IP	H	HR	BB	SO	RAT	ERA	ERA+	OAV	OOB	BH	AVG	PB	PR	/A	PD	TPI
1954	Pit-N	3	9	.250	21	10	3	1	1	87¹	105	4	21	8	13.2	4.53	72	.303	.350	2	.087	-1	-4	-3	1	-0.4

● **JOHN O'DONOGHUE**   O'Donoghue, John Eugene   b: 10/7/39, Kansas City, Mo.   BR/TL, 6'3", 210 lbs.   Deb: 9/29/63   F

YEAR	TM/L	W	L	PCT	G	GS	CG	SH	SV	IP	H	HR	BB	SO	RAT	ERA	ERA+	OAV	OOB	BH	AVG	PB	PR	/A	PD	TPI
1963	KC-A	0	1	.000	1	1	0	0	0	6	6	0	2	1	12.0	1.50	260	.286	.348	0	.000	-0	2	2	-0	0.2
1964	KC-A	10	14	.417	39	32	2	1	0	173²	202	24	65	79	14.0	4.92	78	.286	.349	13	.236	2	-25	-21	-1	-2.6
1965	KC-A☆	9	18	.333	34	30	4	1	0	177²	183	15	66	82	12.7	3.95	88	.267	.332	12	.218	3	-10	-9	0	-1.0
1966	Cle-A	6	8	.429	32	13	2	0	0	108	109	13	23	49	11.2	3.83	90	.264	.306	5	.152	-0	-5	-5	-1	-0.5
1967	Cle-A	8	9	.471	33	17	5	2	2	130²	120	10	33	81	10.7	3.24	101	.247	.298	4	.100	0	0	0	3	0.4
1968	Bal-A	0	0	—	16	0	0	0	0	22	34	2	7	16	16.8	6.14	48	.374	.418	0	.000	-0	-8	-8	-0	-0.2
1969	Sea-A	2	2	.500	55	0	0	0	6	70	58	5	37	48	12.6	2.96	123	.230	.336	1	.077	-1	5	5	-0	0.3
1970	Mil-A	2	0	1.000	25	0	0	0	0	23¹	29	4	19	13	14.7	5.01	76	.299	.358	0	.000	-0	-3	-3	-1	-0.2
	Mon-N	2	3	.400	30	0	0	0	4	22¹	20	2	11	6	13.3	5.24	78	.263	.371	0	.000	-0	-3	-3	-0	-0.6
1971	Mon-N	0	0	—	13	0	0	0	0	17¹	19	3	7	7	13.5	4.67	75	.271	.338	0	—	0	-2	-2	-0	-0.1
Total	9	39	55	.415	257	96	13	4	10	751	780	78	260	377	12.6	4.07	87	.269	.332	35	.170	2	-49	-44	4	-4.2

● **JOHN O'DONOGHUE**   O'Donoghue, John Preston   b: 5/26/69, Wilmington, Del.   BL/TL, 6'6", 198 lbs.   Deb: 6/27/93   F

YEAR	TM/L	W	L	PCT	G	GS	CG	SH	SV	IP	H	HR	BB	SO	RAT	ERA	ERA+	OAV	OOB	BH	AVG	PB	PR	/A	PD	TPI
1993	Bal-A	0	1	.000	11	1	0	0	0	19²	22	4	10	16	15.1	4.58	98	.278	.367	0	—	0	-1	-0	-0	-0.2

● **LEFTY O'DOUL**   O'Doul, Francis Joseph   b: 3/4/1897, San Francisco, Cal.   d: 12/7/69, San Francisco, Cal.   BL/TL, 6', 180 lbs.   Deb: 4/29/19 ◆

YEAR	TM/L	W	L	PCT	G	GS	CG	SH	SV	IP	H	HR	BB	SO	RAT	ERA	ERA+	OAV	OOB	BH	AVG	PB	PR	/A	PD	TPI
1919	NY-A	0	0	—	3	0	0	0	0	5	7	0	4	2	19.8	3.60	89	.304	.407	4	.250	-1	-0	-0	-0	0.0
1920	NY-A	0	0	—	3	0	0	0	0	3²	4	1	2	0	17.2	4.91	78	.286	.412	2	.167	-0	-0	-0	-0	0.0
1922	NY-A	0	0	—	6	0	0	0	0	16	24	0	12	5	20.3	3.38	119	.353	.450	3	.333	1	1	1	0	0.1
1923	Bos-A	1	1	.500	23	1	0	0	0	53	69	2	31	10	17.7	5.43	76	.337	.433	5	.143	-1	-9	-8	1	-0.3
Total	4	1	1	.500	34	1	0	0	0	77²	104	2	49	19	18.3	4.87	83	.335	.434	1140	.349	-1	-8	-7	1	-0.2

● **BRYAN OELKERS**   Oelkers, Bryan Alois   b: 3/11/61, Zaragoza, Spain   BL/TL, 6'3", 192 lbs.   Deb: 4/9/83

YEAR	TM/L	W	L	PCT	G	GS	CG	SH	SV	IP	H	HR	BB	SO	RAT	ERA	ERA+	OAV	OOB	BH	AVG	PB	PR	/A	PD	TPI
1983	Min-A	0	5	.000	10	8	0	0	0	34¹	56	7	17	13	19.1	8.65	49	.376	.440	0	—	0	-18	-17	-1	-2.2
1986	Cle-A	3	3	.500	35	4	0	0	0	69	70	13	40	33	15.1	4.70	88	.262	.371	0	—	0	-4	-4	-0	-0.3
Total	2	3	8	.273	45	12	0	0	0	103¹	126	20	57	46	16.5	6.01	70	.303	.395	0	—	0	-21	-21	-2	-2.5

● **JOE OESCHGER**   Oeschger, Joseph Carl   b: 5/24/1892, Chicago, Ill.   d: 7/28/86, Rohnert Park, Cal   BR/TR, 6' ", 190 lbs.   Deb: 4/21/14

YEAR	TM/L	W	L	PCT	G	GS	CG	SH	SV	IP	H	HR	BB	SO	RAT	ERA	ERA+	OAV	OOB	BH	AVG	PB	PR	/A	PD	TPI
1914	Phi-N	4	8	.333	32	10	5	0	1	124	129	5	54	47	14.0	3.77	78	.279	.366	3	.075	-4	-14	-11	-1	-1.6
1915	Phi-N	1	0	1.000	14	2	1	0	0	23²	21	1	9	12	11.4	3.42	80	.247	.319	0	.000	-1	-2	-2	-0	-0.2
1916	Phi-N	1	0	1.000	14	0	0	0	0	30¹	18	2	14	17	9.8	2.37	112	.184	.292	0	—	0	1	1	0	0.0
1917	Phi-N	15	14	.517	42	30	18	5	1	262	241	7	72	123	11.0	2.75	102	.249	.305	10	.114	-4	2	-2	-3	-0.6
1918	Phi-N	6	18	.250	30	23	13	2	**3**	184	159	3	83	60	12.2	3.03	99	.238	.328	5	.083	-4	-6	-1	-2	-0.7
1919	Phi-N	0	1	.000	5	4	2	0	0	38	52	1	16	5	16.6	5.92	54	.340	.409	0	.000	-2	-13	-11	-0	-0.5
	NY-N	0	1	.000	5	1	0	0	0	8	12	0	2	3	15.8	4.50	62	.400	.438	0	.000	-1	-2	-2	-1	-0.3
	Bos-N	4	2	.667	7	7	4	1	0	56²	63	0	21	16	13.5	2.54	112	.300	.366	2	.091	-1	2	2	-1	-0.1
	Yr	4	4	.500	17	12	6	1	0	102²	127	1	39	24	14.9	3.94	76	.322	.384	2	.053	-4	-12	-11	-2	-0.8
1920	Bos-N	15	13	.536	38	30	20	5	0	299	294	6	99	80	12.1	3.46	88	.265	.329	18	.178	-3	11	14	-3	-1.8
1921	Bos-N	20	14	.588	46	36	19	**3**	0	299	303	11	99	68	12.5	3.52	104	.274	.341	28	.255	2	9	4	-2	0.1
1922	Bos-N	6	21	.222	46	23	10	1	1	195²	234	8	81	51	14.9	5.06	79	.303	.353	12	.190	-0	-21	-23	1	-2.6
1923	Bos-N	5	15	.250	44	19	6	1	2	166¹	227	4	54	33	15.5	5.68	70	.330	.383	12	.231	-0	-31	-31	-0	-3.2
1924	NY-N	2	0	1.000	10	2	0	0	0	29	35	1	14	10	15.2	3.10	118	.287	.360	3	.429	1	2	1	-1	0.1
	Phi-N	2	7	.222	19	8	0	0	0	65¹	88	6	16	8	14.7	4.41	101	.333	.378	5	.250	-1	-0	-0	-0	0.1
	Yr	4	7	.364	29	10	0	0	0	94¹	123	7	30	18	14.9	4.01	105	.319	.372	8	.296	-1	1	0	-1	0.1
1925	Bro-N	1	2	.333	21	3	1	0	0	37	60	2	19	6	19.5	6.08	69	.382	.452	1	.125	-0	-7	-7	-0	-0.6
Total	12	82	116	.414	365	197	99	18	8	1818	1936	61	651	535	13.1	3.81	92	.281	.349	99	.165	-18	-96	-89	-8	-11.1

● **JACK OGDEN**   Ogden, John Mahlon   b: 11/5/1897, Ogden, Pa.   d: 11/9/77, Philadelphia, Pa.   BR/TR, 6', 190 lbs.   Deb: 6/22/18   F

YEAR	TM/L	W	L	PCT	G	GS	CG	SH	SV	IP	H	HR	BB	SO	RAT	ERA	ERA+	OAV	OOB	BH	AVG	PB	PR	/A	PD	TPI
1918	NY-N	0	0	—	5	0	0	0	0	8²	9	0	3	1	13.5	3.12	84	.296	.406	0	.000	-0	-0	-0	-0	-0.1
1928	StL-A	15	16	.484	38	31	18	1	2	242²	257	23	80	67	12.5	4.15	101	.274	.331	17	.200	-1	-3	1	-4	-0.3
1929	StL-A	4	8	.333	34	14	7	0	0	131¹	154	8	44	32	13.6	4.93	90	.301	.357	11	.244	0	-10	-7	-0	-0.5
1931	Cin-N	4	8	.333	29	13	6	1	1	89	79	3	32	24	11.2	2.93	127	.242	.310	4	.148	0	9	8	-1	0.8
1932	Cin-N	2	2	.500	24	3	1	0	0	57	72	5	22	20	14.8	5.21	74	.310	.370	2	.167	0	-8	-9	-1	-0.5
Total	5	25	34	.424	123	57	29	2	3	528²	570	39	181	144	12.8	4.24	97	.280	.340	34	.200	-1	-13	-8	-4	-0.6

● **CURLY OGDEN**   Ogden, Warren Harvey   b: 1/24/01, Ogden, Pa.   d: 8/6/64, Chester, Pa.   BR/TR, 6'1.5", 180 lbs.   Deb: 7/18/22   F

YEAR	TM/L	W	L	PCT	G	GS	CG	SH	SV	IP	H	HR	BB	SO	RAT	ERA	ERA+	OAV	OOB	BH	AVG	PB	PR	/A	PD	TPI
1922	Phi-A	1	4	.200	15	6	4	0	6	72¹	59	4	33	20	12.1	3.11	137	.237	.338	7	.241	-0	8	9	-0	0.5
1923	Phi-A	1	2	.333	18	2	0	0	0	46¹	63	2	32	14	19.0	5.63	73	.330	.434	5	.294	1	-8	-8	-0	-0.4
1924	Phi-A	0	3	.000	5	1	0	0	0	12²	14	1	7	4	15.6	4.97	86	.275	.373	0	.000	-1	-1	-1	-1	-0.3
	*Was-A	9	5	.643	16	16	9	3	0	108	83	3	51	23	11.3	2.58	156	.221	.317	13	.220	1	20	17	-0	2.2
	Yr	9	8	.529	21	17	9	3	0	120²	97	4	58	27	11.7	2.83	143	.227	.322	13	.260	1	19	16	-1	1.9
1925	Was-A	3	1	.750	17	4	2	1	0	42	45	1	14	6	13.9	4.50	94	.288	.369	3	.250	-0	-1	-0	-0	-0.1
1926	Was-A	4	4	.500	22	9	4	0	0	96¹	114	2	45	21	15.3	4.30	90	.305	.387	6	.185	PB	-3	-5	-0	-0.5
Total	5	18	19	.486	93	38	19	4	0	377²	378	13	186	88	13.9	3.79	108	.271	.364	33	.244	1	14	12	-2	1.4

YEAR	TM/L	W	L	PCT	G	GS	CG	SH	SV	IP	H	HR	BB	SO	RAT	ERA	ERA+	OAV	OOB	BH	AVG	PB	PR	/A	PD	TPI

● CHAD OGEA Ogea, Chad Wayne b: 11/9/70, Lake Charles, La. BR/TR, 6'2", 200 lbs. Deb: 5/3/94

1994	Cle-A	0	1	.000	4	1	0	0	0	16¹	21	2	10	11	17.6	6.06	78	.304	.400	0	—	0	-2	-2	-0	-0.1
1995	*Cle-A	8	3	.727	20	14	0	0	0	106¹	95	11	29	57	10.6	3.05	154	.233	.286	0	—	0	20	19	-1	1.7
1996	*Cle-A	10	6	.625	29	21	1	1	0	146²	151	22	42	101	12.1	4.79	102	.266	.322	0	—	0	3	2	-1	0.0
Total	3	18	10	.643	53	36	2	1	0	269¹	267	35	81	169	11.9	4.18	115	.256	.314	0	—	0	21	19	-2	1.6

● JOE OGRODOWSKI Ogrodowski, Joseph Anthony b: 11/20/06, Hoytville, Pa. d: 6/24/59, Elmira, N.Y. BR/TR, 5'11", 165 lbs. Deb: 4/27/25

| 1925 | Bos-N | 0 | 0 | — | 1 | 0 | 0 | 0 | 0 | 1 | 6 | 0 | 3 | 0 | 81.0 | 54.00 | 7 | .600 | .692 | 0 | — | 0 | -6 | -6 | -0 | 0.0 |

● BILL O'HARA O'Hara, William Alexander b: 8/14/1883, Toronto, Ont., Can. d: 6/15/31, Jersey City, N.J. BL/TR, 5'10", Deb: 4/15/09 ♦

| 1910 | StL-N | 0 | 0 | — | 1 | 0 | 0 | 0 | 0 | 1 | 0 | 0 | 0 | 0 | 0.0 | .000 | .000 | 3 | .150 | -0 | 0 | 0 | -0 | 0.0 |

● JOE OHL Ohl, Joseph Earl (b: Joseph Earl Von Ohl) b: 1/10/1888, Jobstown, N.J. d: 12/18/51, Camden, N.J. BL/TL, Deb: 7/29/09

| 1909 | Was-A | 0 | 0 | — | 4 | 0 | 0 | 0 | 0 | 8² | 7 | 0 | 1 | 2 | 9.3 | 2.08 | 117 | .194 | .237 | 0 | .000 | -0 | 0 | 0 | -0 | 0.0 |

● BOB OJEDA Ojeda, Robert Michael b: 12/17/57, Los Angeles, Cal. BL/TL, 6'1", 190 lbs. Deb: 7/13/80

1980	Bos-A	1	1	.500	7	7	0	0	0	26	39	2	14	12	18.3	6.92	61	.361	.434	0	—	0	-8	-8	-0	-0.9
1981	Bos-A	6	2	.750	10	10	2	0	0	66¹	50	6	25	28	10.4	3.12	124	.212	.293	0	—	0	4	6	-0	0.3
1982	Bos-A	4	6	.400	22	14	0	0	0	78¹	95	13	29	52	14.4	5.63	76	.296	.356	0	—	0	-14	-12	-1	-1.8
1983	Bos-A	12	7	.632	29	28	5	0	0	173²	173	15	73	94	12.9	4.04	108	.265	.342	0	—	0	0	6	-0	0.0
1984	Bos-A	12	12	.500	33	32	8	5	0	216²	211	17	96	137	12.8	3.99	104	.259	.338	0	—	0	4	11	-0	0.4
1985	Bos-A	9	11	.450	39	22	5	0	0	157²	166	11	48	102	12.3	4.00	107	.273	.328	0	—	0	3	5	-0	0.4
1986	*NY-N	18	5	**.783**	32	30	7	2	0	217¹	185	15	52	148	9.9	2.57	138	.230	.279	8	.113	-2	28	23	1	2.2
1987	NY-N	3	5	.375	10	7	0	0	0	46¹	45	5	10	21	10.7	3.88	97	.253	.293	1	.071	-0	1	-1	0	-0.1
1988	NY-N	10	13	.435	29	29	5	5	0	190¹	158	6	33	133	9.2	2.88	112	.225	.264	10	.164	1	12	7	2	1.1
1989	NY-N	13	11	.542	31	31	5	2	0	192	179	16	78	95	12.1	3.47	94	.245	.319	7	.106	-2	1	-4	2	-0.5
1990	NY-N	7	6	.538	38	12	0	0	0	118	123	10	40	62	12.6	3.66	102	.272	.334	4	.133	-0	2	1	3	0.3
1991	LA-N	12	9	.571	31	31	2	1	0	189¹	181	15	70	120	12.1	3.18	113	.257	.326	9	.161	1	11	9	1	1.2
1992	LA-N	6	9	.400	29	29	2	1	0	166¹	169	8	81	94	13.6	3.63	95	.268	.352	5	.102	-1	-2	-3	-2	-0.2
1993	Cle-A	2	1	.667	9	7	0	0	0	43	48	3	21	27	14.4	4.40	98	.289	.369	0	—	0	-0	-0	1	0.1
1994	NY-A	0	0	—	2	2	0	0	0	3	11	1	6	3	51.0	24.00	19	.611	.708	0	—	0	-6	-6	-0	0.1
Total	15	115	98	.540	351	291	41	16	1	1884¹	1833	145	676	1128	12.1	3.65	103	.257	.323	44	.127	-4	30	24	10	2.6

● FRANK OKRIE Okrie, Frank Anthony "Lefty" b: 10/28/1896, Detroit, Mich. d: 10/16/59, Detroit, Mich. BL/TL, 5'11", 175 lbs. Deb: 4/20/20 F

| 1920 | Det-A | 1 | 2 | .333 | 21 | 1 | 1 | 0 | 0 | 41 | 44 | 2 | 18 | 9 | 14.7 | 5.27 | 71 | .295 | .390 | 1 | .200 | -0 | -7 | -7 | 6 | 0.1 |

● RED OLDHAM Oldham, John Cyrus b: 7/15/1893, Zion, Md. d: 1/28/61, Costa Mesa, Cal. BB/TL, 6'", 176 lbs. Deb: 8/19/14

1914	Det-A	2	4	.333	9	7	3	0	0	45¹	42	1	8	23	10.5	3.38	83	.243	.288	4	.267	1	-3	-3	-1	-0.4
1915	Det-A	3	0	1.000	17	2	1	0	0	57²	52	1	17	17	11.4	2.81	108	.243	.311	2	.143	-0	1	1	-1	0.0
1920	Det-A	8	13	.381	39	22	10	1	1	215¹	248	6	91	62	14.4	3.85	97	.302	.376	12	.174	-1	-1	-3	4	0.0
1921	Det-A	11	14	.440	40	28	12	1	1	229¹	258	11	81	67	13.5	4.24	101	.288	.351	19	.224	2	1	1	1	0.4
1922	Det-A	10	13	.435	43	28	9	0	3	212	256	14	59	72	13.8	4.67	83	.305	.358	19	.260	4	-15	-19	1	-1.3
1925	*Pit-N	3	2	.600	11	4	0	0	1	53	66	2	18	10	14.6	3.91	114	.313	.372	6	.333	2	2	3	0	0.5
1926	Pit-N	2	2	.500	17	2	0	0	2	41²	56	1	18	16	16.2	5.62	70	.359	.429	2	.222	0	-8	-8	0	-0.7
Total	7	39	48	.448	176	93	38	2	12	854¹	978	35	292	267	13.7	4.15	93	.295	.358	64	.226	9	-23	-26	4	-1.5

● STEVE OLIN Olin, Steven Robert b: 10/4/65, Portland, Ore. d: 3/22/93, Little Lake Nellie, Fla. BR/TR, 6'3", 185 lbs. Deb: 7/29/89

1989	Cle-A	1	4	.200	25	0	0	0	1	36	35	1	14	24	12.3	3.75	106	.255	.325	0	—	0	1	1	0	0.1
1990	Cle-A	4	4	.500	50	1	0	0	1	92¹	96	3	26	64	12.5	3.41	115	.270	.331	0	—	0	5	5	2	0.7
1991	Cle-A	3	6	.333	48	0	0	0	17	56¹	61	2	23	38	13.6	3.36	124	.274	.344	0	—	0	5	5	0	1.0
1992	Cle-A	8	5	.615	72	0	0	0	29	88¹	80	8	27	47	11.3	2.34	167	.248	.314	0	—	0	16	15	1	3.2
Total	4	16	19	.457	195	1	0	0	48	273	272	14	90	173	12.3	3.10	128	.262	.328	0	—	0	26	26	3	5.0

● OMAR OLIVARES Olivares, Omar (Palqui) b: 7/6/67, Mayaguez, P.R. BR/TR, 6'1", 185 lbs. Deb: 8/18/90 F

1990	StL-N	1	1	.500	9	6	0	0	0	49¹	45	2	17	20	11.7	2.92	131	.249	.320	3	.176	1	5	5	1	0.4
1991	StL-N	11	7	.611	28	24	0	0	1	167¹	148	13	61	91	11.5	3.71	100	.243	.317	12	.226	3	-1	-0	2	0.5
1992	StL-N	9	9	.500	32	30	1	0	0	197	189	20	63	124	11.7	3.84	88	.257	.319	16	.235	4	-7	-10	3	-0.1
1993	StL-N	5	3	.625	58	9	0	0	1	118²	134	10	54	63	14.9	4.17	95	.288	.372	7	.269	2	-2	-3	4	0.4
1994	StL-N	3	4	.429	14	12	1	0	0	73²	84	10	37	26	15.3	5.74	72	.294	.382	6	.214	2	-13	-13	1	-0.9
1995	Col-N	1	3	.250	11	6	0	0	0	31²	44	4	21	16	19.0	7.39	73	.349	.450	1	.143	0	-11	-7	0	-0.7
	Phi-N	0	1	.000	5	0	0	0	0	10	11	1	2	7	12.6	5.40	78	.282	.333	1	.500	1	-2	-1	-0	-0.1
	Yr	1	4	.200	16	6	0	0	0	41²	55	5	23	22	17.1	6.91	74	.327	.411	2	.222	1	-13	-8	-1	-0.7
1996	Det-A	7	11	.389	25	25	4	0	0	160	169	16	75	81	14.2	4.89	103	.275	.362	0	—	0	2	3	0	0.3
Total	7	37	39	.487	182	112	6	0	3	807²	824	76	330	427	13.3	4.35	93	.269	.348	46	.229	13	-28	-27	10	-0.1

● DARREN OLIVER Oliver, Darren Christopher b: 10/6/70, Rio Linda, Cal. BR/TL, 6', 170 lbs. Deb: 9/1/93 F

1993	Tex-A	0	0	—	2	0	0	0	0	3¹	2	1	4	4	8.1	2.70	154	.154	.214	0	—	0	1	1	0	0.3
1994	Tex-A	4	0	1.000	43	0	0	0	2	50	40	4	35	50	14.6	3.42	141	.223	.368	0	—	0	8	8	2	0.8
1995	Tex-A	4	2	.667	17	7	0	0	0	49	47	3	32	39	14.7	4.22	114	.257	.370	0	—	0	3	3	1	0.2
1996	*Tex-A	14	6	.700	30	30	1	1	0	173²	190	20	76	112	14.3	4.66	114	.279	.359	0	—	0	6	12	-1	0.7
Total	4	22	8	.733	92	37	1	1	2	276	279	28	144	205	14.3	4.34	118	.264	.361	0	—	0	17	24	2	2.0

● FRANCISCO OLIVERAS Oliveras, Francisco Javier (Noa) b: 1/31/63, Santurce, P.R. BR/TR, 5'10", 170 lbs. Deb: 5/3/89

1989	Min-A	3	4	.429	12	8	0	0	0	55²	64	8	15	24	12.9	4.53	91	.288	.336	0	—	0	-4	-2	-1	-0.4
1990	SF-N	2	2	.500	33	2	0	0	2	55¹	45	5	21	41	11.4	2.77	132	.230	.308	0	.000	-1	6	5	-1	0.3
1991	SF-N	6	6	.500	55	1	0	0	2	79¹	69	12	22	48	10.4	3.86	93	.242	.299	2	.200	0	-2	-2	-0	-0.4
1992	SF-N	0	3	.000	16	7	0	0	0	44²	41	11	10	17	10.5	3.63	91	.250	.297	1	.143	0	-1	-1	-0	-0.1
Total	4	11	15	.423	116	18	1	0	5	235	221	36	68	130	11.3	3.71	99	.253	.310	3	.136	-0	-1	-1	-2	-0.6

● DIOMEDES OLIVO Olivo, Diomedes Antonio (Maldonado) b: 1/22/19, Guayubin, D.R. d: 2/15/77, Santo Domingo, D.R. BL/TL, 6'1", 195 lbs. Deb: 9/5/60 F

1960	Pit-N	0	0	—	4	0	0	0	0	9²	8	1	5	10	12.1	2.79	134	.216	.310	0	.000	-0	1	1	-0	0.0
1962	Pit-N	5	1	.833	62	1	0	0	0	84¹	88	5	25	66	12.1	2.77	142	.277	.329	3	.188	1	11	11	-0	0.9
1963	StL-N	0	5	.000	19	0	0	0	0	13¹	16	1	9	9	17.6	5.40	66	.296	.406	0	—	0	-3	-3	-0	-0.9
Total	3	5	6	.455	85	1	0	0	7	107¹	112	7	39	85	12.7	3.10	125	.274	.339	3	.176	0	9	9	-0	0.0

● CHI-CHI OLIVO Olivo, Federico Emilio (Maldonado) b: 3/18/28, Guayubin, D.R. d: 2/3/77, Guayubin, D.R. BR/TR, 6'2", 215 lbs. Deb: 6/5/61 F

1961	Mil-N	0	0	—	3	0	0	0	0	2	3	1	5	1	36.0	18.00	21	.500	.727	0	—	0	-3	-3	-0	0.0
1964	Mil-N	2	1	.667	38	0	0	0	5	60	55	7	21	45	11.4	3.75	94	.247	.311	1	.250	0	-1	-2	1	0.0
1965	Mil-N	0	1	.000	13	0	0	0	2	13	12	1	5	11	11.8	1.38	254	.267	.340	0	—	0	3	3	-0	0.2
1966	Atl-N	5	4	.556	47	0	0	0	5	66	59	4	19	41	11.1	4.23	86	.240	.297	1	.111	-0	-5	-4	-1	-0.8
Total	4	7	6	.538	96	0	0	0	12	141	129	13	50	98	11.5	3.96	90	.248	.315	2	.154	-0	-6	-6	-1	-0.6

● JIM OLLOM Ollom, James Donald b: 7/8/45, Snohomish, Wash. BR/TL, 6'4", 210 lbs. Deb: 9/3/66

1966	Min-A	0	0	—	3	1	0	0	0	10	6	1	9	7	9.2	3.60	100	.167	.211	0	.000	-0	-0	-0	-1	0.0
1967	Min-A	0	1	.000	21	2	0	0	0	35	33	4	11	17	12.3	5.40	64	.258	.336	1	.200	-0	-8	-8	-0	-0.2
Total	2	0	1	.000	24	3	0	0	0	45	39	5	12	28	11.2	5.00	70	.238	.309	1	.143	-0	-9	-9	-0	-0.2

● FRED OLMSTEAD Olmstead, Frederic William b: 7/3/1881, Grand Rapids, Mich. d: 10/22/36, Muskogee, Okla. BR/TR, 5'11", 170 lbs. Deb: 7/2/08

1908	Chi-A	0	0	—	1	0	0	0	0	2	6	1	3	1	31.5	13.50	17	.600	.636	0	.000	-0	-2	-2	-0	-0.1
1909	Chi-A	3	2	.600	8	6	5	0	0	54²	52	1	21	21	10.7	1.81	129	.277	.323	2	.095	-1	4	3	-0	0.2
1910	Chi-A	10	12	.455	32	20	14	6	0	184¹	174	1	50	68	11.1	1.95	123	.260	.316	10	.154	-2	12	9	-1	0.9

YEAR TM/L	W	L	PCT	G	GS	CG	SH	SV	IP	H	HR	BB	SO	RAT	ERA	ERA+	OAV	OOB	BH	AVG	PB	PR	/A	PD	TPI
1911 Chi-A	6	6	.500	25	11	7	1	2	117²	146	3	30	45	13.9	4.21	77	.309	.358	7	.189	-0	-11	-13	-1	-1.3
Total 4	19	20	.487	66	37	26	5	2	358²	378	6	93	135	12.1	2.74	97	.283	.334	19	.153	-3	2	-3	-0	-0.2

● **AL OLMSTED** Olmsted, Alan Ray b: 3/18/57, St.Louis, Mo. BR/TL, 6'2", 195 lbs. Deb: 9/12/80

YEAR TM/L	W	L	PCT	G	GS	CG	SH	SV	IP	H	HR	BB	SO	RAT	ERA	ERA+	OAV	OOB	BH	AVG	PB	PR	/A	PD	TPI
1980 StL-N	1	1	.500	5	5	0	0	0	34²	32	2	14	14	12.2	2.86	129	.244	.322	2	.182	-0	3	3	1	0.2

● **HANK OLMSTED** Olmsted, Henry Theodore b: 1/12/1879, Sac Bay, Mich. d: 1/6/69, Bradenton, Fla. BR/TR, 5'8.5", 147 lbs. Deb: 7/15/05

YEAR TM/L	W	L	PCT	G	GS	CG	SH	SV	IP	H	HR	BB	SO	RAT	ERA	ERA+	OAV	OOB	BH	AVG	PB	PR	/A	PD	TPI
1905 Bos-A	1	2	.333	3	3	3	0	0	25	18	0	12	6	10.8	3.24	83	.205	.300	1	.125	-0	-2	-2	-1	-0.3

● **OLE OLSEN** Olsen, Arthur b: 9/12/1894, S.Norwalk, Conn. d: 9/12/80, Norwalk, Conn. BR/TR, 5'10", 163 lbs. Deb: 4/12/22

YEAR TM/L	W	L	PCT	G	GS	CG	SH	SV	IP	H	HR	BB	SO	RAT	ERA	ERA+	OAV	OOB	BH	AVG	PB	PR	/A	PD	TPI
1922 Det-A	7	6	.538	37	15	5	0	3	137	147	8	40	52	13.2	4.53	86	.281	.348	7	.179	-1	-7	-10	1	-0.9
1923 Det-A	1	1	.500	17	2	1	0	0	41¹	42	1	17	12	13.9	6.31	61	.290	.383	1	.125	-1	-11	-11	-1	-0.6
Total 2	8	7	.533	54	17	6	0	3	178¹	189	9	57	64	13.4	4.95	78	.283	.356	8	.170	-2	-18	-21	-1	-1.5

● **VERN OLSEN** Olsen, Vern Jarl b: 3/16/18, Hillsboro, Ore. d: 7/13/89, Maywood, Ill. BR/TL, 6'0.5", 175 lbs. Deb: 9/8/39

YEAR TM/L	W	L	PCT	G	GS	CG	SH	SV	IP	H	HR	BB	SO	RAT	ERA	ERA+	OAV	OOB	BH	AVG	PB	PR	/A	PD	TPI
1939 Chi-N	1	0	1.000	4	0	0	0	0	7²	2	0	7	3	10.6	0.00	—	.087	.300	0	.000	0	3	3	-0	0.5
1940 Chi-N	13	9	.591	34	20	9	4	0	172²	172	5	62	71	12.3	2.97	126	.260	.325	15	.263	3	17	15	4	2.6
1941 Chi-N	10	8	.556	37	23	10	2	1	185²	202	7	59	73	12.7	3.15	111	.276	.331	15	.238	3	10	7	2	1.3
1942 Chi-N	6	9	.400	32	17	4	1	1	140¹	161	6	55	46	13.9	4.49	71	.283	.347	9	.188	1	-18	-20	-1	-1.8
1946 Chi-N	0	0	—	5	0	0	0	0	9²	10	0	9	8	17.7	2.79	119	.294	.442	0	—	0	1	1	0	0.0
Total 5	30	26	.536	112	60	23	7	2	516	547	18	192	201	13.0	3.40	103	.271	.335	39	.231	8	12	6	7	2.6

● **GREGG OLSON** Olson, Greggory William b: 10/11/66, Scribner, Neb. BR/TR, 6'4", 210 lbs. Deb: 9/2/88

YEAR TM/L	W	L	PCT	G	GS	CG	SH	SV	IP	H	HR	BB	SO	RAT	ERA	ERA+	OAV	OOB	BH	AVG	PB	PR	/A	PD	TPI
1988 Bal-A	1	1	.500	10	0	0	0	0	11	10	1	10	9	16.4	3.27	119	.244	.392	0	—	0	1	1	0	0.4
1989 Bal-A	5	2	.714	64	0	0	0	27	85	57	1	46	90	11.0	1.69	224	.188	.296	0	—	0	21	20	0	2.7
1990 Bal-A☆	6	5	.545	64	0	0	0	37	74¹	57	3	31	74	11.0	2.42	157	.213	.301	0	—	0	12	11	-1	2.6
1991 Bal-A	4	6	.400	72	0	0	0	31	73²	74	7	29	72	12.7	3.18	124	.261	.332	0	—	0	8	6	0	1.5
1992 Bal-A	1	5	.167	60	0	0	0	36	61¹	46	3	24	58	10.3	2.05	196	.211	.289	0	—	0	13	13	1	2.5
1993 Bal-A	0	2	.000	50	0	0	0	29	45	37	1	18	44	11.0	1.60	279	.223	.299	0	.000	0	14	14	0	2.2
1994 Atl-N	0	2	.000	16	0	0	0	1	14²	19	1	13	10	20.3	9.20	46	.317	.446	0	.000	-0	-8	-8	-1	-1.1
1995 Cle-A	0	0	—	3	0	0	0	0	2²	5	1	2	0	23.6	13.50	35	.417	.500	0	—	0	-3	-3	-0	-0.1
KC-A	3	3	.500	20	0	0	0	3	30¹	23	3	17	21	11.9	3.26	147	.215	.323	0	—	0	5	5	0	0.9
Yr	3	3	.500	23	0	0	0	3	33	28	4	19	21	12.8	4.09	117	.235	.341	0	—	0	2	3	0	0.8
1996 Det-A	3	0	1.000	43	0	0	0	8	43	43	6	28	29	15.1	5.02	101	.259	.369	0	—	0	-0	0	-1	0.0
Hou-N	1	0	1.000	9	0	0	0	0	9¹	12	1	7	8	18.3	4.82	79	.308	.413	0	—	0	-0	-0	-0	-0.1
Total 9	24	26	.480	411	0	0	0	172	450¹	383	22	225	415	12.3	2.94	140	.230	.324	0	.000	0	61	59	1	11.5

● **TED OLSON** Olson, Theodore Otto b: 8/27/12, Quincy, Mass. d: 12/9/80, Weymouth, Mass. BR/TR, 6'2.5", 185 lbs. Deb: 6/21/36

YEAR TM/L	W	L	PCT	G	GS	CG	SH	SV	IP	H	HR	BB	SO	RAT	ERA	ERA+	OAV	OOB	BH	AVG	PB	PR	/A	PD	TPI
1936 Bos-A	1	1	.500	5	3	1	0	0	18¹	24	3	8	5	15.7	7.36	72	.324	.390	1	.143	-0	-5	-4	-0	-0.4
1937 Bos-A	0	0	—	11	0	0	0	0	32¹	42	4	15	11	15.9	7.24	66	.318	.388	3	.300	1	-9	-9	1	0.2
1938 Bos-A	0	0	—	2	0	0	0	0	7	9	0	2	2	14.1	6.43	77	.310	.355	0	.000	-0	-1	-1	0	0.0
Total 3	1	1	.500	18	3	1	0	0	57²	75	7	25	18	15.6	7.18	69	.319	.385	4	.222	1	-15	-14	1	-0.2

● **ED OLWINE** Olwine, Edward R. b: 5/28/58, Greenville, Ohio BL/TL, 6'2", 165 lbs. Deb: 6/2/86

YEAR TM/L	W	L	PCT	G	GS	CG	SH	SV	IP	H	HR	BB	SO	RAT	ERA	ERA+	OAV	OOB	BH	AVG	PB	PR	/A	PD	TPI
1986 Atl-N	0	0	—	37	0	0	0	1	47²	35	5	17	37	10.0	3.40	117	.207	.283	1	.333	1	2	3	-0	0.0
1987 Atl-N	0	1	.000	27	0	0	0	1	23¹	25	4	8	12	13.1	5.01	87	.269	.333	0	—	0	-2	-2	-0	-0.1
1988 Atl-N	0	0	—	16	0	0	0	1	18²	22	4	4	5	13.0	6.75	54	.286	.329	0	—	0	-7	-6	-1	-0.1
Total 3	0	1	.000	80	0	0	0	3	89²	82	13	29	54	11.4	4.52	89	.242	.307	1	.333	1	-8	-5	-1	-0.2

● **SKINNY O'NEAL** O'Neal, Oran Herbert b: 5/2/1899, Gatewood, Mo. d: 6/2/81, Springfield, Mo. BR/TR, 5'11", 160 lbs. Deb: 4/18/25

YEAR TM/L	W	L	PCT	G	GS	CG	SH	SV	IP	H	HR	BB	SO	RAT	ERA	ERA+	OAV	OOB	BH	AVG	PB	PR	/A	PD	TPI
1925 Phi-N	0	0	—	11	1	0	0	0	20¹	35	2	12	6	20.8	9.30	51	.407	.480	1	.167	-0	-11	-10	-0	0.0
1927 Phi-N	0	0	—	2	0	0	0	0	5	9	0	2	2	19.8	9.00	46	.409	.458	0	.000	-0	-3	-3	1	0.0
Total 2	0	0	—	13	1	0	0	0	25¹	44	2	14	8	20.6	9.24	50	.407	.475	1	.143	-0	-14	-13	0	0.0

● **RANDY O'NEAL** O'Neal, Randall Jeffrey b: 8/30/60, Ashland, Ky. BR/TR, 6'2", 195 lbs. Deb: 9/12/84

YEAR TM/L	W	L	PCT	G	GS	CG	SH	SV	IP	H	HR	BB	SO	RAT	ERA	ERA+	OAV	OOB	BH	AVG	PB	PR	/A	PD	TPI
1984 Det-A	2	1	.667	4	3	0	0	0	18²	16	0	6	12	10.6	3.38	116	.222	.282	0	—	0	1	1	-0	0.1
1985 Det-A	5	5	.500	28	12	1	0	1	94¹	82	8	36	52	11.4	3.24	126	.240	.316	0	—	0	9	9	1	0.9
1986 Det-A	3	7	.300	37	11	1	0	2	122²	121	13	44	68	12.3	4.33	95	.260	.327	0	—	0	-2	-3	1	-0.1
1987 Atl-N	4	2	.667	16	10	0	0	0	61	79	12	24	33	15.5	5.61	78	.316	.380	2	.105	-1	-10	-9	1	-0.7
StL-N	0	0	—	1	1	0	0	0	5	2	0	2	4	7.2	1.80	231	.111	.200	1	1.000	0	1	1	0	0.1
Yr	4	2	.667	17	11	0	0	0	66	81	12	26	37	14.6	5.32	81	.298	.359	3	.150	-1	-9	-7	1	-0.6
1988 StL-N	2	3	.400	10	8	0	0	0	53	57	7	10	20	11.7	4.58	76	.274	.314	0	.000	-0	-7	-7	1	-0.3
1989 Phi-N	0	1	.000	20	1	0	0	0	39	46	5	9	29	12.7	6.23	57	.301	.340	0	—	0	-12	-12	1	-0.3
1990 SF-N	1	0	1.000	26	0	0	0	0	47	58	3	18	30	14.6	3.83	95	.314	.374	1	.167	-0	-0	-0	0	0.0
Total 7	17	19	.472	142	46	2	0	3	440²	461	48	149	248	12.6	4.35	91	.272	.334	4	.080	-3	-19	-19	5	-0.7

● **ED O'NEIL** O'Neil, Edward J. b: 3/11/1859, Fall River, Mass. d: 9/30/1892, Fall River, Mass. TR, 5'11", 180 lbs. Deb: 6/20/1890

YEAR TM/L	W	L	PCT	G	GS	CG	SH	SV	IP	H	HR	BB	SO	RAT	ERA	ERA+	OAV	OOB	BH	AVG	PB	PR	/A	PD	TPI
1890 Tol-a	0	2	.000	2	2	2	0	0	16	27	1	13	2	22.5	7.88	50	.365	.460	0	.000	-2	-7	-7	0	-0.7
Phi-a	0	6	.000	6	6	6	0	0	52	84	0	32	17	21.3	9.69	40	.353	.444	5	.161	-4	-34	-34	1	-2.5
Yr	0	8	.000	8	8	8	0	0	68	111	1	45	19	21.6	9.26	42	.356	.448	5	.125	-2	-41	-41	1	-3.2

● **J. O'NEILL** O'Neill, J. b: Brooklyn, N.Y. Deb: 8/20/1875

YEAR TM/L	W	L	PCT	G	GS	CG	SH	SV	IP	H	HR	BB	SO	RAT	ERA	ERA+	OAV	OOB	BH	AVG	PB	PR	/A	PD	TPI
1875 Atl-n	0	4	.000	5	4	3	0	0	34	59	1	0	0	15.6	5.03	41	.343	.343	2	.077	-2	-11	-11		-1.0

● **TIP O'NEILL** O'Neill, James Edward b: 5/25/1858, Woodstock, Ont., Canada d: 12/31/15, Montreal, Que., Can BR/TR, 6'1.5", 167 lbs. Deb: 5/5/1883 ♦

YEAR TM/L	W	L	PCT	G	GS	CG	SH	SV	IP	H	HR	BB	SO	RAT	ERA	ERA+	OAV	OOB	BH	AVG	PB	PR	/A	PD	TPI
1883 NY-N	5	12	.294	19	19	15	0	0	148	182	6	64	15	15.0	4.07	76	.289	.354	15	.197	-1	-15	-16	-1	-1.6
1884 StL-a	11	4	.733	17	14	14	0	0	141	125	3	51	36	11.5	2.68	122	.219	.288	82	.276	5	9	9	0	1.2
Total 2	16	16	.500	36	33	29	0	0	289	307	8	115	91	13.3	3.39	94	.256	.323	1386	.326	3	-6	-7	-1	-0.4

● **HARRY O'NEILL** O'Neill, Joseph Henry b: 2/20/1897, Ridgetown, Ont., Canada d: 9/5/69, Ridgetown, Ont., Can. BR/TR, 6', 180 lbs. Deb: 9/15/22

YEAR TM/L	W	L	PCT	G	GS	CG	SH	SV	IP	H	HR	BB	SO	RAT	ERA	ERA+	OAV	OOB	BH	AVG	PB	PR	/A	PD	TPI
1922 Phi-A	0	0	—	1	0	0	0	0	3	2	0	1	0	12.0	3.00	142	.200	.333	0	.000	-0	0	0	0	0.0
1923 Phi-A	0	0	—	3	0	0	0	0	2	1	0	3	2	18.0	0.00	—	.167	.444	0	—	0	1	1	-0	0.0
Total 2	0	0	—	4	0	0	0	0	5	3	0	4	2	14.4	1.80	233	.188	.381	0	.000	0	1	1	0	0.0

● **MIKE O'NEILL** O'Neill, Michael Joyce (a.k.a. Michael Joyce In 1901) b: 9/7/1877, Galway, Ireland d: 8/12/59, Scranton, Pa. BR/TR, 5'11", 185 lbs. Deb: 9/20/01 F♦

YEAR TM/L	W	L	PCT	G	GS	CG	SH	SV	IP	H	HR	BB	SO	RAT	ERA	ERA+	OAV	OOB	BH	AVG	PB	PR	/A	PD	TPI
1901 StL-N	2	2	.500	5	4	1	0	0	41	29	2	10	16	9.7	1.32	242	.197	.272	6	.400	3	9	8	-1	1.0
1902 StL-N	16	15	.516	36	32	29	2	2	288¹	297	3	66	105	11.7	2.90	94	.266	.314	43	.319	9	-4	-5	-0	0.8
1903 StL-N	4	13	.235	19	17	12	0	0	145	184	2	43	39	14.5	3.79	86	.304	.356	25	.227	-0	-8	-8	-0	-0.6
1904 StL-N	10	14	.417	25	24	23	1	0	220	229	1	50	68	11.5	2.09	129	.262	.304	21	.231	5	16	15	1	2.4
Total 4	32	44	.421	85	77	68	4	2	694¹	739	8	169	228	12.1	2.73	105	.269	.318	97	.255	9	13	10	3	3.6

● **PAUL O'NEILL** O'Neill, Paul Andrew b: 2/25/63, Columbus, Ohio BL/TL, 6'4", 205 lbs. Deb: 9/3/85 ♦

YEAR TM/L	W	L	PCT	G	GS	CG	SH	SV	IP	H	HR	BB	SO	RAT	ERA	ERA+	OAV	OOB	BH	AVG	PB	PR	/A	PD	TPI
1987 Cin-N	0	0	—	1	0	0	0	0	1	3	1	2	0	27.0	13.50	31	.286	.545	41	.256	0	-2	-2	-0	0.0

● **EMMETT O'NEILL** O'Neill, Robert Emmett "Pinky" b: 1/13/18, San Mateo, Cal. d: 10/11/93, Sparks, Nevada BR/TR, 6'3", 185 lbs. Deb: 8/3/43

YEAR TM/L	W	L	PCT	G	GS	CG	SH	SV	IP	H	HR	BB	SO	RAT	ERA	ERA+	OAV	OOB	BH	AVG	PB	PR	/A	PD	TPI
1943 Bos-A	1	4	.200	11	5	1	0	0	57²	56	3	46	20	16.1	4.53	73	.256	.387	3	.188	1	-8	-8	-0	-0.6
1944 Bos-A	6	11	.353	28	22	8	1	0	151²	154	6	89	68	14.5	4.63	73	.265	.365	10	.182	-0	-20	-21	-2	-2.3
1945 Bos-A	8	11	.421	24	22	10	1	0	141²	134	5	111	56	16.3	5.15	66	.258	.399	9	.188	-2	-28	-27	-1	-3.1
1946 Chi-N	0	0	—	1	0	0	0	0	1	0	0	9	0	27.0	0.00	—	.000	.500	0	—	0	1	0	-0	0.0
Chi-A	0	0	—	2	0	0	0	0	3²	4	0	5	0	22.1	0.00	—	.333	.529	0	.000	0	1	1	0	0.0
Total 4	15	26	.366	66	49	19	2	0	355²	348	14	260	144	15.6	4.76	71	.261	.385	22	.180	2	-54	-54	-2	-6.0

YEAR	TM/L	W	L	PCT	G	GS	CG	SH	SV	IP	H	HR	BB	SO	RAT	ERA	ERA+	OAV	OOB	BH	AVG	PB	PR	/A	PD	TPI

● STEVE ONTIVEROS   Ontiveros, Steven   b: 3/5/61, Tularosa, N.Mex.   BR/TR, 6', 180 lbs.   Deb: 6/14/85

1985	Oak-A	1	3	.250	39	0	0	0	8	74²	45	4	19	36	8.0	1.93	200	.174	.236	0	—	0	18	16	1	1.2
1986	Oak-A	2	2	.500	46	0	0	0	10	72²	72	4	10	25	12.1	4.71	82	.265	.329	0	—	0	-4	-7	0	-0.5
1987	Oak-A	10	8	.556	35	22	2	1	1	150²	141	19	50	97	11.6	4.00	103	.242	.306	0	—	2	8	2	-2	0.5
1988	Oak-A	3	4	.429	10	10	0	0	0	54²	57	4	21	30	12.8	4.61	82	.265	.331	0	—	0	-4	-5	1	-0.5
1989	Phi-N	2	1	.667	6	5	0	0	0	30²	34	2	15	14	14.4	3.82	93	.288	.368	1	.083	-0	-1	-1	1	0.0
1990	Phi-N	0	0	—	5	0	0	0	0	10	9	1	3	6	10.8	2.70	142	.225	.279	0	—	0	1	1	0	0.0
1993	Sea-A	0	2	.000	14	0	0	0	0	18	18	0	6	13	13.0	1.00	480	.277	.338	0	—	0	7	7	-0	0.6
1994	Oak-A	6	4	.600	27	13	2	0	0	115¹	93	7	26	56	**9.8**	**2.65**	167	.217	**.272**	0	—	0	28	23	2	2.4
1995	Oak-A★	9	6	.600	22	22	2	1	0	129²	144	12	38	77	12.9	4.37	102	.283	.338	0	—	0	5	1	3	0.8
Total	9	33	30	.524	204	72	6	2	19	656¹	613	59	203	381	11.4	3.62	114	.246	.308	1	.083	-0	57	38	11	4.5

● JOSE OQUENDO   Oquendo, Jose Manuel (Contreras)   b: 7/4/63, Rio Piedras, P.R.   BB/TR, 5'10", 160 lbs.   Deb: 5/2/83 ♦

1987	*StL-N	0	0	—	1	0	0	0	0	1	4	0	1	0	54.0	27.00	13	.571	.667	71	.286	0	-3	-3	-0	0.0
1988	StL-N	0	1	.000	1	0	0	0	0	4	4	0	6	1	22.5	4.50	77	.267	.476	125	.277	0	-0	-0	-0	-0.1
1991	StL-N	0	0	—	1	0	0	0	0	1	2	0	2	1	36.0	27.00	14	.400	.571	88	.240	0	-3	-3	-0	0.0
Total	3	0	1	.000	3	0	0	0	0	6	10	0	9	2	30.0	12.00	30	.370	.541	821	.256	1	-6	-6	-0	-0.1

● MIKE OQUIST   Oquist, Michael Lee   b: 5/30/68, LaJunta, Colo.   BR/TR, 6'2", 170 lbs.   Deb: 8/14/93

1993	Bal-A	0	0	—	5	0	0	0	0	11²	12	0	4	8	12.3	3.86	116	.261	.320	0	—	0	1	1	-0	-0.3
1994	Bal-A	3	3	.500	15	9	0	0	0	58¹	75	7	30	39	17.1	6.17	81	.319	.410	0	—	0	-9	-8	0	-0.9
1995	Bal-A	2	1	.667	27	0	0	0	0	54	51	6	41	27	15.7	4.17	114	.246	.376	0	—	0	3	4	-0	0.0
1996	SD-N	0	0	—	8	0	0	0	0	7²	6	0	4	4	11.7	2.35	170	.231	.333	0	—	0	2	1	-0	0.0
Total	4	5	4	.556	55	9	0	0	0	131²	144	13	79	78	15.8	4.92	97	.280	.384	0	—	0	-3	-2	-0	-1.2

● DON O'RILEY   O'Riley, Donald Lee   b: 3/12/45, Topeka, Kan.   BR/TR, 6'3", 205 lbs.   Deb: 6/20/69

1969	KC-A	1	1	.500	18	0	0	0	0	23¹	32	0	15	10	18.1	6.94	53	.311	.398	0	.000	-0	-9	-8	-0	-0.8
1970	KC-A	0	0	—	9	2	0	0	1	23¹	26	5	9	13	13.9	5.40	69	.277	.346	0	.000	-0	-4	-4	-0	-0.1
Total	2	1	1	.500	27	2	0	0	1	46²	58	5	24	23	16.0	6.17	60	.294	.374	0	.000	-1	-13	-13	-1	-0.9

● JESSE OROSCO   Orosco, Jesse Russell   b: 4/21/57, Santa Barbara, Cal.   BR/TL, 6'2", 185 lbs.   Deb: 4/5/79

1979	NY-N	1	2	.333	18	2	0	0	0	35	33	4	22	22	14.7	4.89	74	.260	.377	0	.000	-1	-4	-5	1	-0.4
1981	NY-N	0	1	.000	8	0	0	0	1	17¹	13	2	6	18	9.9	1.56	224	.213	.284	0	.000	0	4	4	0	0.2
1982	NY-N	4	10	.286	54	2	0	0	4	109¹	92	7	40	89	11.0	2.72	134	.230	.303	2	.143	-0	11	11	0	1.4
1983	NY-N★	13	7	.650	62	0	0	0	17	110	76	3	38	84	9.4	1.47	246	.197	.271	4	.333	1	**26**	**26**	1	**5.8**
1984	NY-N☆	10	6	.625	60	0	0	0	31	87	58	7	34	85	9.7	2.59	137	.185	.269	1	.250	1	10	9	-0	2.4
1985	NY-N	8	6	.571	54	0	0	0	17	79	66	6	34	68	11.4	2.73	126	.224	.304	3	.429	1	8	6	-1	1.4
1986	*NY-N	8	6	.571	58	0	0	0	21	81	64	6	35	62	11.3	2.33	151	.217	.306	0	.000	0	12	11	-1	2.3
1987	NY-N	3	9	.250	58	0	0	0	16	77	78	5	31	78	13.0	4.44	85	.266	.340	0	.000	-1	-3	-6	-0	-1.1
1988	*LA-N	3	2	.600	55	0	0	0	9	53	41	4	30	43	12.4	2.72	123	.215	.327	0	—	0	4	4	0	0.5
1989	Cle-A	3	4	.429	69	0	0	0	3	78	54	7	26	79	9.5	2.08	191	.198	.272	—	—	0	16	16	1	1.6
1990	Cle-A	5	4	.556	55	0	0	0	2	64²	58	9	38	55	13.4	3.90	101	.239	.342	0	—	0	0	0	1	0.1
1991	Cle-A	2	0	1.000	47	0	0	0	0	45²	52	4	15	36	13.4	3.74	111	.286	.343	0	—	0	2	2	-1	0.0
1992	Mil-A	3	1	.750	59	0	0	0	1	39	33	5	13	40	10.8	3.23	119	.232	.301	0	—	0	3	3	-0	0.4
1993	Mil-A	3	5	.375	57	0	0	0	8	56²	47	2	17	67	10.6	3.18	134	.224	.291	0	.000	0	7	7	3	1.2
1994	Mil-A	3	1	.750	40	0	0	0	0	39	32	4	26	36	13.8	5.08	99	.222	.349	0	—	0	-1	-0	-0	-0.3
1995	Bal-A	2	4	.333	**65**	0	0	0	3	49²	28	4	27	58	10.1	3.26	146	.169	.289	0	—	0	8	8	1	0.9
1996	*Bal-A	3	1	.750	66	0	0	0	0	55²	42	5	28	52	11.6	3.40	144	.207	.309	0	—	0	10	9	0	0.7
Total	17	74	69	.517	885	4	0	0	133	1077	867	84	460	972	11.3	2.98	130	.221	.307	10	.169	2	112	105	5	17.1

● O'ROURKE   O'Rourke   Deb: 7/9/1872

| 1872 | Eck-n | 0 | 1 | .000 | 1 | 1 | 1 | 0 | 0 | 9 | 16 | 0 | 2 | 0 | 18.0 | 8.00 | 42 | .327 | .353 | 0 | .000 | -1 | -4 | -5 | | -0.2 |

● JIM O'ROURKE   O'Rourke, James Henry "Orator Jim"   b: 9/1/1850, Bridgeport, Conn.   d: 1/8/19, Bridgeport, Conn.   BR/TR, 5'8", 185 lbs.   Deb: 4/26/1872   FMUH♦

1883	Buf-N	0	0	—	2	0	0	0	1	7	10	0	1	1	14.1	6.43	49	.357	.379	143	.328	1	-3	-3	-0	-0.1
1884	Buf-N	0	1	.000	4	0	0	0	1	12²	7	0	1	3	5.7	2.84	111	.175	.195	162	.347	2	0	0	-0	0.1
Total	2	0	1	.000	6	0	0	0	2	19²	17	0	2	4	8.7	4.12	77	.250	.271	2304	.310	2	-2	-2	-1	0.0

● MIKE O'ROURKE   O'Rourke, Michael J.   Deb: 9/1/1890

| 1890 | Bal-a | 1 | 2 | .333 | 5 | 5 | 5 | 0 | 0 | 41 | 45 | 4 | 10 | 8 | 12.7 | 3.95 | 103 | .271 | .324 | 3 | .115 | -1 | -0 | 0 | 1 | 0.00 |

● DAVE ORR   Orr, David L.   b: 9/29/1859, New York, N.Y.   d: 6/3/15, Brooklyn, N.Y.   BR/TR, 5'11", 250 lbs.   Deb: 5/17/1883   M♦

| 1885 | NY-a | 0 | 0 | — | 3 | 0 | 0 | 0 | 0 | 10 | 11 | 2 | 5 | 1 | 14.4 | 7.20 | 41 | .229 | .302 | 152 | .342 | 2 | -4 | -5 | -0 | 0.0 |

● JOE ORRELL   Orrell, Forrest Gordon   b: 10/6/17, National City, Cal.   d: 1/12/93, Chula Vista, Cal.   BR/TR, 6'4", 210 lbs.   Deb: 8/12/43

1943	Det-A	0	0	—	10	0	0	0	1	19¹	18	0	11	2	14.4	3.72	95	.257	.373	1	.250	0	-1	-0	-0	0.0
1944	Det-A	2	1	.667	10	2	0	0	0	22¹	26	0	11	10	15.3	2.42	147	.286	.369	1	.250	0	3	3	1	0.5
1945	Det-A	2	3	.400	12	5	1	0	0	48	46	1	24	14	13.5	3.00	117	.260	.355	2	.133	-1	2	3	-0	0.1
Total	3	4	4	.500	32	7	1	0	1	89²	90	1	46	26	14.2	3.01	117	.266	.362	4	.174	-1	4	5	0	0.6

● PHIL ORTEGA   Ortega, Filomeno Coronado "Kemo"   b: 10/7/39, Gilbert, Ariz.   BR/TR, 6'2", 175 lbs.   Deb: 9/10/60

1960	LA-N	0	0	—	3	1	0	0	0	6¹	12	1	5	4	24.2	17.05	23	.400	.486	0	.000	-0	-9	-9	-0	0.0
1961	LA-N	0	2	.000	4	2	1	0	0	13	10	6	2	15	8.3	5.54	78	.208	.240	1	.250	0	-2	-2	-0	-0.2
1962	LA-N	0	2	.000	24	3	0	0	1	53²	60	8	39	30	17.1	6.88	53	.276	.394	0	.000	-1	-17	-19	-1	-0.9
1963	LA-N	0	0	—	1	0	0	0	0	1	2	1	1	0	18.0	18.00	17	.400	.400		—		-2	-2	-0	0.0
1964	LA-N	7	9	.438	34	25	3	0	1	157¹	149	22	56	107	12.1	4.00	81	.249	.320	6	.136	-0	-8	-13	-2	-1.6
1965	Was-A	12	15	.444	35	29	4	2	0	179²	176	33	97	88	13.9	5.11	68	.262	.359	11	.208	4	-33	-33	-1	-4.1
1966	Was-A	12	12	.500	33	31	5	1	0	197¹	193	23	53	121	9.9	3.92	85	.218	.276	3	.056	-2	-11	-10	-1	-1.5
1967	Was-A	10	10	.500	34	34	5	0	0	219²	189	16	57	122	10.3	3.03	104	.231	.286	4	.061	-3	5	3	-1	-0.1
1968	Was-A	5	12	.294	31	16	1	1	0	115²	115	12	62	57	14.2	4.98	59	.263	.361	4	.167	1	-26	-27	-0	-3.6
1969	Cal-A	0	0	—	5	0	0	0	0	8	8	3	7	4	22.5	10.13	34	.333	.435	0	—	0	-6	-6	0	0.0
Total	10	46	62	.426	204	141	20	9	2	951²	884	131	378	549	12.2	4.43	75	.246	.323	29	.115	-6	-109	-117	-6	-12.0

● AL ORTH   Orth, Albert Lewis "Smiling Al" or "The Curveless Wonder"   b: 9/5/1872, Tipton, Ind.   d: 10/8/48, Lynchburg, Va.   BL/TR, 6', 200 lbs.   Deb: 8/15/1895   U♦

1895	Phi-N	8	1	.889	11	10	9	0	1	88	103	0	22	25	13.0	3.89	123	.288	.332	16	.356	4	9	9	-2	0.9
1896	Phi-N	15	10	.600	25	23	19	0	0	196	244	10	46	23	13.5	4.41	98	.302	.342	21	.256	3	-1	-2	1	0.1
1897	Phi-N	14	19	.424	36	34	29	2	0	282¹	349	12	82	64	13.9	4.62	91	.301	.350	50	.329	7	-10	-13	1	-0.4
1898	Phi-N	15	13	.536	32	28	25	1	0	250	290	2	53	52	12.6	3.02	114	.288	.329	36	.293	8	16	11	2	2.0
1899	Phi-N	14	3	.824	21	15	13	3	1	144²	149	16	19	35	10.6	**2.49**	148	.266	.294	13	.210	1	22	19	-4	1.6
1900	Phi-N	14	14	.500	33	30	24	2	1	262	302	4	60	68	12.9	3.78	96	.288	.335	40	.310	7	-2	-5	1	0.3
1901	Phi-N	20	12	.625	35	33	30	**6**	1	281²	250	3	32	92	**9.3**	2.27	150	.237	**.264**	36	.281	5	33	35	3	**4.8**
1902	Was-A	19	18	.514	38	37	36	1	0	324	367	10	40	76	11.6	3.97	93	.286	.312	38	.217	1	-14	-10	1	-0.6
1903	Was-A	10	22	.313	36	32	30	2	**2**	279²	326	8	62	88	12.7	4.34	72	.290	.331	49	.302	9	-43	-38	-0	-2.8
1904	Was-A	3	4	.429	10	7	7	0	0	73²	88	2	15	23	13.0	4.76	56	.297	.338	22	.216	0	-18	-17	-0	-1.4
	NY-A	11	6	.647	20	18	11	2	0	137²	122	0	19	47	9.4	2.68	101	.238	.270	19	.297	3	-1	-0	-0	0.0
	Yr	14	10	.583	30	25	18	2	0	211¹	210	2	34	70	10.5	3.41	79	.259	.291	41	.247	3	-19	-17	-1	-0.9
1905	NY-A	18	16	.529	40	37	26	6	0	305¹	273	6	61	121	10.1	2.86	103	.241	.284	24	.183	-1	-7	-5	0	0.1
1906	NY-A	**27**	17	.614	45	39	**36**	3	0	338²	371	2	66	133	10.2	2.34	127	.289	.289	37	.274	6	13	24	-1	**3.7**
1907	NY-A	14	21	.400	36	33	21	2	0	248²	244	6	53	78	11.0	2.61	107	.259	.303	34	.324	4	-2	-5	1	1.9
1908	NY-A	2	13	.133	21	17	8	1	0	139¹	134	4	30	22	10.9	3.42	72	.255	.300	20	.290	5	-16	-15	-1	-1.1

YEAR	TM/L	W	L	PCT	G	GS	CG	SH	SV	IP	H	HR	BB	SO	RAT	ERA	ERA+	OAV	OOB	BH	AVG	PB	PR	/A	PD	TPI
1909	NY-A	0	0	—	1	1	0	0	0	3	6	0	1	1	21.0	12.00	21	.429	.467	9	.265	0	-3	-3	-0	0.0
Total	15	204	189	.519	440	394	324	31	6	3354²	3564	75	661	948	11.6	3.37	101	.272	.311	464	.273	63	-24	15	2	9.6

● **BABY ORTIZ**   Ortiz, Oliverio (Nunez)   b: 12/5/19, Camaguey, Cuba   d: 3/27/84, Central Senado, Camaguey, Cuba   BR/TR, 6', 190 lbs.   Deb: 9/23/44   F

1944	Was-A	0	2	.000	2	2	1	0	0	13	13	6	4	13.2		6.23	52	.255	.333	1	.167	-0	-4	-4	-1	-0.6

● **OSSIE ORWOLL**   Orwoll, Oswald Christian   b: 11/17/1900, Portland, Ore.   d: 5/8/67, Decorah, Iowa   BL/TL, 6', 174 lbs.   Deb: 4/13/28   ◆

1928	Phi-A	6	5	.545	27	8	3	0	2	106	110	7	50	53	13.8	4.58	87	.274	.358	52	.306	7	-6	-7	-0	-0.3
1929	Phi-A	0	2	.000	12	0	0	0	1	30	32	6	6	12	11.4	4.80	88	.278	.314	13	.255	1	-2	-2	-0	-0.1
Total	2	6	7	.462	39	8	3	0	3	136	142	13	56	65	13.2	4.63	88	.275	.348	65	.294	7	-8	-9	-1	-0.4

● **OZZIE OSBORN**   Osborn, Danny Leon   b: 6/19/46, Springfield, Mo.   BR/TR, 6'2", 195 lbs.   Deb: 4/26/75

1975	Chi-A	3	0	1.000	24	0	0	0	0	58	57	2	37	38	14.9	4.50	86	.265	.378	0	—	0	-5	-4	-1	-0.4

● **BOB OSBORN**   Osborn, John Bode   b: 4/17/03, San Diego, Tex.   d: 4/19/60, Paris, Ark.   BR/TR, 6'1", 175 lbs.   Deb: 9/16/25

1925	Chi-N	0	0	—	1	0	0	0	0	2	6	0	0	0	27.0	0.00	—	.600	.600	0	—	0	1	1	0	0.0
1926	Chi-N	6	5	.545	31	15	6	0	1	136¹	157	3	58	43	14.2	3.63	106	.301	.371	6	.146	-3	3	3	2	0.2
1927	Chi-N	5	5	.500	24	12	2	0	0	107²	125	2	48	45	14.5	4.18	92	.294	.367	8	.205	-0	-3	-4	-1	-0.4
1929	Chi-N	0	0	—	3	1	0	0	0	9	8	0	2	1	10.0	3.00	154	.242	.286	1	.250	0	2	2	0	0.0
1930	Chi-N	10	6	.625	35	13	3	0	1	126²	147	9	53	42	14.3	4.97	98	.300	.369	4	.095	-5	-0	-1	2	-0.4
1931	Pit-N	6	1	.857	27	2	0	0	0	64²	85	3	20	9	14.8	5.01	77	.316	.366	3	.167	-0	-8	-8	-1	-0.9
Total	6	27	17	.614	121	43	11	0	2	446¹	528	17	181	140	14.4	4.32	97	.302	.368	22	.153	-8	-6	-7	2	-1.5

● **DONOVAN OSBORNE**   Osborne, Donovan Alan   b: 6/21/69, Roseville, Cal.   BB/TL, 6'2", 195 lbs.   Deb: 4/9/92

1992	StL-N	11	9	.550	34	29	0	0	0	179	193	14	38	104	11.7	3.77	90	.275	.314	7	.121	-1	-5	-8	-3	-1.2
1993	StL-N	10	7	.588	26	26	1	0	0	155²	153	18	47	83	12.0	3.76	105	.257	.319	10	.204	2	5	4	0	0.5
1995	StL-N	4	6	.400	19	19	0	0	0	113¹	112	17	34	82	11.8	3.81	110	.260	.318	5	.161	2	5	5	0	0.5
1996	*StL-N	13	9	.591	30	30	2	0	0	198²	191	22	57	134	11.3	3.53	120	.254	.307	13	.220	4	15	16	-2	1.7
Total	4	38	31	.551	109	104	3	0	0	646²	649	71	176	403	11.6	3.70	106	.262	.314	35	.178	6	19	16	-5	1.5

● **TINY OSBORNE**   Osborne, Earnest Preston   b: 4/9/1893, Porterdale, Ga.   d: 1/5/69, Atlanta, Ga.   BL/TR, 6'4.5", 215 lbs.   Deb: 4/15/22   F

1922	Chi-N	9	5	.643	41	14	7	1	3	184	183	7	95	81	14.2	4.50	93	.271	.370	9	.134	-4	-8	-6	-3	-1.0
1923	Chi-N	8	15	.348	37	25	8	1	1	179²	174	14	89	69	13.3	4.56	88	.255	.342	12	.200	-1	-11	-11	-1	-1.4
1924	Chi-N	0	0	—	2	0	0	0	1	3	3	0	2	2	15.0	3.00	130	.300	.417	0	—	0	0	0	0	0.0
	Bro-N	6	5	.545	21	13	6	0	0	104¹	123	1	54	52	15.6	5.09	74	.298	.384	9	.250	-1	-14	-16	-1	-1.4
	Yr	6	5	.545	23	13	6	0	1	107¹	126	1	56	54	15.6	5.03	75	.298	.385	9	.250	-1	-14	-15	-1	-1.4
1925	Bro-N	8	15	.348	41	22	10	0	1	175	210	16	75	54	14.9	4.94	85	.304	.375	14	.246	-1	-13	-15	-2	-1.6
Total	4	31	40	.437	142	74	31	2	6	646	693	31	315	263	14.3	4.72	86	.280	.367	44	.200	-3	-46	-47	-6	-5.4

● **FRED OSBORNE**   Osborne, Frederick W.   b: Hampton, Iowa   TL,   Deb: 7/14/1890   ◆

1890	Pit-N	0	5	.000	8	5	4	0	0	58	62	6	45	14	20.8	8.38	39	.323	.438	40	.238	1	-31	-33	-0	-2.0

● **WAYNE OSBORNE**   Osborne, Wayne Harold "Ossie" or "Fish Hook"
   b: 10/11/12, Watsonville, Cal.   d: 3/13/87, Vancouver, Wash.   BL/TR, 6'2.5", 172 lbs.   Deb: 4/18/35

1935	Pit-N	0	0	—	2	0	0	0	0	1¹	1	0	1	0	6.8	6.75	61	.250	.250	0	—	0	-0	-0	0	0.0
1936	Bos-N	1	1	.500	5	3	0	0	0	20	31	1	9	8	18.0	5.85	66	.352	.412	2	.250	0	-4	-4	0	-0.4
Total	2	1	1	.500	7	3	0	0	0	21¹	32	1	9	8	17.3	5.91	65	.348	.406	2	.250	-0	-4	-4	0	-0.4

● **PAT OSBURN**   Osburn, Larry Patrick   b: 5/4/49, Murray, Ky.   BL/TL, 6'4", 195 lbs.   Deb: 4/13/74

1974	Cin-N	0	0	—	6	0	0	0	0	9	11	2	4	1	15.0	8.00	44	.297	.366	0	.000	-0	-4	-5	0	-0.4
1975	Mil-A	0	1	.000	6	1	0	0	0	11²	19	2	9	1	23.1	5.40	71	.404	.517	0	—	-0	-2	-2	0	-0.2
Total	2	0	1	.000	12	1	0	0	0	20²	30	4	13	2	19.6	6.53	56	.357	.455	0	.000	-0	-6	-7	1	-0.2

● **CHARLIE OSGOOD**   Osgood, Charles Benjamin   b: 11/23/26, Somerville, Mass.   BR/TR, 5'10", 180 lbs.   Deb: 6/18/44

1944	Bro-N	0	0	—	1	0	0	0	0	3	2	0	3	0	18.0	3.00	118	.222	.462	0	—	0	0	0	0	0.0

● **DAN OSINSKI**   Osinski, Daniel   b: 11/17/33, Chicago, Ill.   BR/TR, 6'2", 195 lbs.   Deb: 4/11/62

1962	KC-A	0	0	—	4	0	0	0	0	4²	8	1	8	4	30.9	17.36	24	.381	.552	0	—	0	-7	-7	0	0.0
	LA-A	6	4	.600	33	0	0	0	4	54¹	45	3	30	44	12.4	2.82	137	.223	.323	0	.000	-1	7	6	0	1.1
	Yr	6	4	.600	37	0	0	0	4	59	53	4	38	48	13.9	3.97	98	.237	.347	0	.000	-1	0	-1	0	1.1
1963	LA-A	8	8	.500	47	16	4	1	0	159¹	145	16	80	104	12.5	3.28	105	.242	.333	5	.111	-2	6	3	-1	-0.1
1964	LA-A	3	3	.500	47	4	1	1	2	93	87	8	39	88	12.4	3.48	94	.244	.322	1	.056	-1	-2	-1	1	-0.1
1965	Mil-N	3	0	1.000	61	0	0	0	6	83	81	4	40	54	13.2	2.82	125	.261	.348	1	.167	-0	7	6	-0	0.3
1966	Bos-A	4	3	.571	44	1	0	0	2	67¹	68	9	28	44	13.0	3.61	105	.274	.350	2	.333	-1	1	1	-1	0.1
1967	*Bos-A	3	1	.750	34	0	0	0	2	63²	61	5	14	38	10.6	2.54	137	.243	.283	3	.333	1	5	7	-0	0.5
1969	Chi-A	5	5	.500	51	0	0	0	3	60²	56	3	23	27	11.7	3.56	108	.251	.321	0	—	0	2	2	2	0.5
1970	Hou-N	0	1	.000	3	0	0	0	0	3²	5	0	2	1	17.2	9.82	39	.357	.438	0	—	0	-2	-2	-0	-0.5
Total	8	29	28	.509	324	21	5	2	18	589²	556	47	264	400	12.6	3.34	107	.250	.331	12	.122	-3	16	15	1	1.8

● **CLAUDE OSTEEN**   Osteen, Claude Wilson   b: 8/9/39, Caney Spring, Tenn.   BL/TL, 5'11", 173 lbs.   Deb: 7/6/57   C

1957	Cin-N	0	0	—	3	0	0	0	0	4	4	0	3	3	15.8	2.25	183	.250	.368	0	.000	-0	1	1	-0	0.0
1959	Cin-N	0	0	—	2	0	0	0	0	7²	11	1	9	3	23.5	7.04	58	.333	.476	0	.000	-0	-3	-3	-0	0.0
1960	Cin-N	0	1	.000	20	3	0	0	0	48¹	53	5	30	15	15.6	5.03	76	.293	.396	1	.083	-1	-7	-6	-0	-0.2
1961	Cin-N	0	0	—	1	0	0	0	0	0¹	0	0	0	0	0.0	0.00	—	.000	.000	0	—	-0	0	0	-0	0.0
	Was-A	1	1	.500	3	3	0	0	0	18¹	14	3	9	14	11.8	4.91	82	.219	.324	1	.143	-0	-2	-2	-0	-0.2
1962	Was-A	8	13	.381	28	22	7	2	1	150¹	140	12	47	95	11.4	3.65	111	.246	.309	10	.208	-1	5	6	0	1.0
1963	Was-A	9	14	.391	40	29	8	2	0	212¹	222	20	60	109	12.0	3.35	111	.270	.320	12	.171	-1	9	7	0	0.8
1964	Was-A	15	13	.536	37	36	13	0	0	257	256	20	64	133	11.3	3.33	111	.259	.306	14	.156	1	8	11	2	1.5
1965	*LA-N	15	15	.500	40	40	9	1	0	287	253	19	78	162	10.5	2.79	117	.236	.290	12	.121	-1	24	15	6	2.0
1966	*LA-N	17	14	.548	39	38	8	3	0	240¹	238	6	65	137	11.4	2.85	116	.261	.312	16	.211	0	20	12	1	2.2
1967	LA-N☆	17	17	.500	39	39	14	5	0	288¹	298	19	52	152	11.0	3.22	96	.270	.304	8	.178	6	5	-4	0	0.2
1968	LA-N	12	18	.400	39	36	5	3	0	253²	267	14	54	119	11.6	3.09	90	.275	.316	15	.179	2	-3	-9	1	-0.7
1969	LA-N	20	15	.571	41	41	16	7	0	321	290	17	74	183	10.5	2.66	125	.245	.293	24	.216	6	33	24	3	3.5
1970	LA-N★	16	14	.533	37	37	11	4	0	258²	280	24	52	114	11.7	3.83	100	.276	.313	19	.204	5	6	-0	-1	0.4
1971	LA-N	14	11	.560	38	38	11	0	0	259	262	16	63	109	11.4	3.51	92	.266	.312	16	.186	2	-1	-8	6	0.1
1972	LA-N	20	11	.645	33	33	14	6	0	252	232	16	69	100	10.9	2.64	126	.245	.299	24	.273	10	23	19	2	3.5
1973	LA-N★	16	11	.593	33	33	12	3	0	236²	227	20	61	86	11.0	3.31	104	.258	.307	12	.154	-1	9	3	2	0.5
1974	Hou-N	9	9	.500	23	21	7	2	0	138¹	158	8	47	45	13.5	3.71	93	.292	.351	13	.283	3	-1	-4	-0	-0.1
	StL-N	0	2	.000	8	2	0	0	0	22²	26	1	11	6	14.7	4.37	82	.286	.363	0	.000	-0	-2	-2	-0	-0.2
	Yr	9	11	.450	31	23	7	2	0	161	184	9	58	51	13.5	3.80	92	.288	.347	13	.245	3	-3	-6	-0	-0.3
1975	Chi-A	7	16	.304	37	37	5	0	0	204¹	237	16	92	63	14.6	4.36	89	.294	.367	0	—	0	-13	-11	1	-1.1
Total	18	196	195	.501	541	488	140	40	1	3460¹	3471	249	940	1612	11.6	3.30	104	.263	.314	207	.188	38	110	50	20	13.2

● **DARRELL OSTEEN**   Osteen, Milton Darrell   b: 2/14/43, Oklahoma City, Okla.   BR/TR, 6'1", 170 lbs.   Deb: 9/2/65

1965	Cin-N	0	0	—	3	0	0	0	0	3	2	0	4	1	18.0	0.00	—	.200	.429	0	—	0	1	1	-0	0.0
1966	Cin-N	0	2	.000	13	1	0	0	1	15	26	3	9	17	21.0	12.00	33	.371	.443	1	.500	-0	-14	-13	-0	-1.8
1967	Cin-N	0	2	.000	10	0	0	0	0	14¹	10	1	13	13	16.3	6.28	60	.196	.388	0	.000	-0	-5	-4	0	-0.6
1970	Oak-A	1	0	1.000	3	0	0	0	0	5²	9	3	1	3	16.2	8.05	56	.346	.414	0	—	-0	-1	-2	-0	-0.2
Total	4	1	4	.200	29	1	0	0	1	38	47	4	27	34	18.7	8.05	47	.299	.418	1	.500	-0	-19	-18	-0	-2.7

● **FRED OSTENDORF**   Ostendorf, Frederick K.   b: 8/5/1890, Baltimore, Md.   d: 3/2/65, Kecoughtan, Va.   BL/TL, 6'0.5", 169 lbs.   Deb: 7/16/14

1914	Ind-F	0	0	—	1	0	0	0	0	2	5	0	2	0	36.0	22.50	14	.500	.615	0	.000	-0	-4	-4	0	0.0

● BILL OSTER Oster, William Charles b: 1/2/33, New York, N.Y. BL/TL, 6'3", 198 lbs. Deb: 8/23/54

YEAR TM/L	W	L	PCT	G	GS	CG	SH	SV	IP	H	HR	BB	SO	RAT	ERA	ERA+	OAV	OOB	BH	AVG	PB	PR	/A	PD	TPI
1954 Phi-A	0	1	.000	8	1	0	0	0	15²	19	2	12	5	17.8	6.32	62	.311	.425	1	.333	0	-5	-4	-0	-0.2

● FRITZ OSTERMUELLER Ostermueller, Frederick Raymond b: 9/15/07, Quincy, Ill. d: 12/17/57, Quincy, Ill. BL/TL, 5'11", 175 lbs. Deb: 4/21/34

YEAR TM/L	W	L	PCT	G	GS	CG	SH	SV	IP	H	HR	BB	SO	RAT	ERA	ERA+	OAV	OOB	BH	AVG	PB	PR	/A	PD	TPI
1934 Bos-A	10	13	.435	33	23	10	0	3	198²	200	7	99	75	13.6	3.49	138	.262	.348	13	.167	-2	22	29	3	3.1
1935 Bos-A	7	8	.467	22	19	10	0	1	137²	135	0	78	41	14.1	3.92	121	.257	.356	14	.286	1	8	13	-0	1.3
1936 Bos-A	10	16	.385	43	23	7	1	2	180²	210	8	84	90	14.8	4.88	109	.288	.364	15	.234	0	3	9	3	1.3
1937 Bos-A	3	7	.300	25	7	2	0	1	86²	101	2	44	29	15.2	4.98	95	.286	.367	11	.333	3	-4	-2	0	0.0
1938 Bos-A	13	5	.722	31	18	10	1	2	176²	199	15	58	46	13.2	4.58	108	.275	.331	16	.216	0	2	7	-0	0.7
1939 Bos-A	11	7	.611	34	20	8	0	4	159¹	173	6	58	61	13.2	4.24	112	.277	.341	9	.161	-2	7	9	-1	0.7
1940 Bos-A	5	9	.357	31	16	5	0	0	143²	166	7	70	80	14.8	4.95	91	.284	.361	17	.315	4	-9	-7	-1	-0.4
1941 StL-A	0	3	.000	15	2	0	0	0	46	45	3	23	20	13.3	4.50	96	.257	.343	3	.214	-0	-2	-1	0	0.0
1942 StL-A	3	1	.750	10	4	1	0	0	43²	46	4	17	21	13.0	3.71	100	.266	.332	3	.188	-0	-0	-0	-1	-0.1
1943 StL-A	0	2	.000	11	3	0	0	0	28²	36	1	13	4	15.4	5.02	66	.321	.392	2	.286	-0	-5	-5	-0	-0.3
Bro-N	1	1	.500	7	1	0	0	0	27¹	21	0	12	15	10.9	3.29	102	.212	.297	2	.000	-1	0	0	-0	-0.2
1944 Bro-N	2	1	.667	10	4	3	0	1	41²	46	3	12	17	12.5	3.24	110	.267	.315	2	.154	-0	2	1	-0	0.0
Pit-N	11	7	.611	28	24	14	1	1	204²	201	7	65	80	11.7	2.73	136	.260	.318	20	.250	2	20	23	-1	2.0
Yr	13	8	.619	38	28	17	1	2	246¹	247	10	77	97	11.9	2.81	131	.261	.317	22	.237	2	22	24	-1	2.0
1945 Pit-N	5	4	.556	14	11	4	1	0	80²	74	6	37	29	12.6	4.57	86	.236	.321	9	.321	2	-7	-6	0	-0.3
1946 Pit-N	13	10	.565	27	25	16	2	0	193¹	193	5	56	57	11.7	2.84	124	.263	.318	21	.328	6	12	15	-2	2.3
1947 Pit-N	12	10	.545	26	24	12	3	0	183	181	18	68	66	12.3	3.84	110	.254	.320	12	.188	-5	5	8	-1	0.7
1948 Pit-N	8	11	.421	23	22	10	2	0	134¹	143	13	41	43	12.4	4.42	92	.262	.315	8	.182	-0	-7	-5	-1	-0.8
Total 15	114	115	.498	390	246	113	11	15	2066²	2170	105	835	774	13.2	3.99	109	.262	.329	175	.234	16	49	85	-3	10.0

● JOE OSTROWSKI Ostrowski, Joseph Paul "Professor" or "Specs" b: 11/15/16, W.Wyoming, Pa. BL/TL, 6', 180 lbs. Deb: 7/18/48

YEAR TM/L	W	L	PCT	G	GS	CG	SH	SV	IP	H	HR	BB	SO	RAT	ERA	ERA+	OAV	OOB	BH	AVG	PB	PR	/A	PD	TPI
1948 StL-A	4	6	.400	26	9	3	0	3	78¹	108	6	17	20	14.4	5.97	76	.333	.367	4	.222	1	-15	-12	2	-1.2
1949 StL-A	8	8	.500	40	13	4	0	2	141	185	16	27	34	13.5	4.79	95	.307	.337	7	.189	2	-9	-4	-1	-0.3
1950 StL-A	2	4	.333	9	7	2	0	0	57¹	57	2	7	15	10.0	2.51	197	.251	.274	4	.222	1	13	16	-1	1.6
NY-A	1	1	.500	21	4	1	0	3	43²	50	11	15	15	13.4	5.15	83	.294	.351	1	.111	-0	-3	-4	-0	-0.2
Yr	3	5	.375	30	11	3	0	3	101	107	13	22	30	11.5	3.65	128	.270	.308	5	.185	1	10	11	-1	1.4
1951 *NY-A	6	4	.600	34	3	2	0	5	95¹	103	4	18	30	11.5	3.49	110	.279	.314	3	.107	-1	7	4	-1	0.1
1952 NY-A	2	2	.500	20	1	0	0	3	40	56	5	14	17	16.0	5.62	59	.327	.382	0	.000	-1	-9	-10	-1	-1.2
Total 5	23	25	.479	150	37	12	0	15	455²	559	44	98	131	13.0	4.54	95	.300	.336	19	.161	1	-16	-12	-1	-1.2

● AL OSUNA Osuna, Alfonso b: 8/10/65, Inglewood, Cal. BR/TL, 6'3", 200 lbs. Deb: 9/2/90

YEAR TM/L	W	L	PCT	G	GS	CG	SH	SV	IP	H	HR	BB	SO	RAT	ERA	ERA+	OAV	OOB	BH	AVG	PB	PR	/A	PD	TPI
1990 Hou-N	2	0	1.000	12	0	0	0	0	11¹	10	1	6	6	15.1	4.76	78	.270	.413	0	—	0	-1	-1	-0	-0.2
1991 Hou-N	7	6	.538	71	0	0	0	12	81²	59	5	46	68	11.9	3.42	103	.201	.316	0	.000	-0	2	1	-0	0.1
1992 Hou-N	6	3	.667	66	0	0	0	0	61²	52	8	38	37	13.3	4.23	79	.236	.351	0	—	0	-5	-6	-0	-0.8
1993 Hou-N	1	1	.500	44	0	0	0	0	25¹	17	3	13	21	11.0	3.20	121	.200	.313	0	—	0	2	2	-1	0.1
1994 LA-N	2	0	1.000	15	0	0	0	0	8²	13	0	4	7	17.7	6.23	63	.333	.395	0	—	0	-2	-2	-0	-0.5
1996 SD-N	0	0	—	10	0	0	0	0	4	5	0	2	4	18.0	2.25	177	.313	.421	0	.000	-0	1	1	0	0.0
Total 6	18	10	.643	218	0	0	0	14	192²	156	17	109	143	12.8	3.83	93	.226	.339	0	.000	-0	-2	-6	-1	-1.3

● ANTONIO OSUNA Osuna, Antonio Pedro b: 4/12/73, Sinaloa, Mexico BR/TR, 5'11", 160 lbs. Deb: 4/25/95

YEAR TM/L	W	L	PCT	G	GS	CG	SH	SV	IP	H	HR	BB	SO	RAT	ERA	ERA+	OAV	OOB	BH	AVG	PB	PR	/A	PD	TPI
1995 *LA-N	2	4	.333	39	0	0	0	0	44²	39	5	20	46	12.1	4.43	86	.241	.328	0	.000	-0	-1	-3	0	-0.4
1996 *LA-N	9	6	.600	73	0	0	0	4	84	65	6	32	85	10.6	3.00	128	.220	.300	0	.000	-0	11	8	0	1.3
Total 2	11	10	.524	112	0	0	0	4	128²	104	11	52	131	11.1	3.50	109	.227	.310	0	.000	-0	10	5	0	0.9

● BILL OTEY Otey, William Tilford "Steamboat Bill" b: 12/16/1886, Dayton, Ohio d: 4/23/31, Dayton, Ohio BL/TL, 6'2", 181 lbs. Deb: 9/27/07

YEAR TM/L	W	L	PCT	G	GS	CG	SH	SV	IP	H	HR	BB	SO	RAT	ERA	ERA+	OAV	OOB	BH	AVG	PB	PR	/A	PD	TPI
1907 Pit-N	0	1	.000	3	2	1	0	0	16¹	23	1	4	5	15.4	4.41	55	.319	.364	1	.250	0	-4	-4	-0	-0.3
1910 Was-A	0	1	.000	9	1	1	0	0	34²	40	1	6	12	12.2	3.38	74	.301	.336	5	.385	2	-3	-3	-1	0.0
1911 Was-A	1	3	.250	12	2	0	0	0	49²	68	2	15	16	15.6	6.34	52	.333	.387	1	.059	-2	-17	-17	1	-1.2
Total 3	1	5	.167	24	5	2	0	0	100²	131	4	25	33	14.4	5.01	57	.320	.367	7	.206	0	-23	-24	-1	-1.5

● HARRY OTIS Otis, Harry George "Cannonball" b: 10/5/1886, W.New York, N.J. d: 1/29/76, Teaneck, N.J. BR/TL, 6' ", 180 lbs. Deb: 9/5/09

YEAR TM/L	W	L	PCT	G	GS	CG	SH	SV	IP	H	HR	BB	SO	RAT	ERA	ERA+	OAV	OOB	BH	AVG	PB	PR	/A	PD	TPI
1909 Cle-A	2	2	.500	5	3	0	0	0	26¹	26	0	18	6	16.1	1.37	187	.283	.416	1	.111	-0	3	3	-0	0.5

● DENNIS O'TOOLE O'Toole, Dennis Joseph b: 3/13/49, Chicago, Ill. BR/TR, 6'3", 195 lbs. Deb: 9/8/69 F

YEAR TM/L	W	L	PCT	G	GS	CG	SH	SV	IP	H	HR	BB	SO	RAT	ERA	ERA+	OAV	OOB	BH	AVG	PB	PR	/A	PD	TPI
1969 Chi-A	0	0	—	2	0	0	0	0	4	5	1	2	4	15.8	6.75	57	.333	.412	0	—	0	-1	-1	-0	0.0
1970 Chi-A	0	0	—	3	0	0	0	0	3¹	2	0	3	1	18.9	2.70	144	.357	.438	0	—	0	1	1	-0	0.0
1971 Chi-A	0	0	—	1	0	0	0	0	2	0	0	1	2	4.5	0.00	—	.000	.143	0	—	0	1	1	0	0.0
1972 Chi-A	0	0	—	3	0	0	0	0	5	10	0	2	5	21.6	5.40	58	.417	.462	0	—	0	-1	-1	-0	0.0
1973 Chi-A	0	0	—	6	0	0	0	0	16	23	3	3	8	14.6	5.63	70	.329	.356	0	—	0	-3	-3	-0	-0.2
Total 5	0	0	—	15	0	0	0	0	30¹	43	3	10	22	15.7	5.04	75	.333	.381	0	—	0	-5	-4	-0	-0.2

● JIM O'TOOLE O'Toole, James Jerome b: 1/10/37, Chicago, Ill. BB/TL, 6', 198 lbs. Deb: 9/26/58 F

YEAR TM/L	W	L	PCT	G	GS	CG	SH	SV	IP	H	HR	BB	SO	RAT	ERA	ERA+	OAV	OOB	BH	AVG	PB	PR	/A	PD	TPI
1958 Cin-N	0	1	.000	1	1	0	0	0	7	4	0	5	4	11.6	1.29	322	.154	.290	0	.000	-0	2	2	-0	0.3
1959 Cin-N	5	8	.385	28	19	3	1	0	129¹	144	14	73	68	15.4	5.15	79	.287	.382	5	.135	-0	-17	-16	1	-1.4
1960 Cin-N	12	12	.500	34	31	7	2	1	196¹	198	14	66	124	12.3	3.80	100	.263	.325	7	.106	-3	-1	-0	-3	-0.6
1961 *Cin-N	19	9	.679	39	35	11	3	2	252²	229	16	93	178	11.6	3.10	131	.240	.310	16	.172	-1	26	27	-0	2.7
1962 Cin-N	16	13	.552	36	34	11	3	0	251²	222	20	87	170	11.2	3.50	115	.238	.307	10	.110	-5	12	15	-2	0.8
1963 Cin-N★	17	14	.548	33	32	12	5	0	234¹	208	13	57	146	10.3	2.88	116	.239	.288	11	.149	-1	11	12	-3	1.2
1964 Cin-N	17	7	.708	30	30	9	3	0	220	194	8	54	145	10.0	2.66	136	.235	.279	7	.100	-1	21	23	-2	2.2
1965 Cin-N	3	10	.231	29	22	2	0	1	127²	154	14	47	71	14.4	5.92	63	.294	.355	4	.089	-2	-34	-31	-2	-3.2
1966 Cin-N	5	7	.417	25	24	2	0	0	142	139	16	49	96	12.1	3.55	110	.254	.318	6	.128	-2	1	6	-1	0.1
1967 Chi-A	4	3	.571	15	10	1	1	0	54¹	53	4	18	37	11.9	2.82	110	.251	.313	1	.077	-1	3	2	-1	0.1
Total 10	98	84	.538	270	238	58	18	4	1615¹	1545	119	546	1039	11.8	3.57	106	.251	.315	67	.125	-15	24	40	-12	2.3

● MARTY O'TOOLE O'Toole, Martin James b: 11/27/1888, Wm.Penn, Pa. d: 2/18/49, Aberdeen, Wash. BR/TR, 5'11", 175 lbs. Deb: 9/21/08

YEAR TM/L	W	L	PCT	G	GS	CG	SH	SV	IP	H	HR	BB	SO	RAT	ERA	ERA+	OAV	OOB	BH	AVG	PB	PR	/A	PD	TPI
1908 Cin-N	1	0	1.000	3	2	1	0	0	15	15	0	7	5	13.2	2.40	96	.273	.355	1	.200	-0	-0	-0	-0	0.0
1911 Pit-N	3	2	.600	5	5	3	0	0	38	28	1	20	34	11.4	2.37	145	.215	.320	5	.357	2	4	4	0	0.8
1912 Pit-N	15	17	.469	37	36	17	5	0	275¹	237	4	159	150	13.0	2.71	120	.241	.348	22	.222	2	21	17	1	2.0
1913 Pit-N	6	8	.429	26	16	7	0	1	144²	148	3	55	58	12.8	3.30	91	.271	.341	7	.132	-2	-1	-5	-0	-0.7
1914 Pit-N	1	8	.111	19	9	1	0	1	92¹	92	4	37	36	13.5	4.68	57	.270	.358	8	.167	0	-19	-21	-1	-2.0
NY-N	1	1	.500	10	5	2	0	0	34	34	0	12	13	12.2	4.24	63	.262	.324	3	.300	1	-5	-6	-0	-0.3
Yr	2	9	.182	29	14	3	0	1	126¹	126	4	49	49	13.2	4.56	58	.268	.349	8	.200	1	-25	-27	-1	-2.3
Total 5	27	36	.429	100	73	31	5	2	599¹	554	11	300	296	12.9	3.21	95	.254	.345	43	.204	2	-1	-10	-1	-0.2

● JIM OTTEN Otten, James Edward b: 7/1/51, Lewistown, Mont. BR/TR, 6'2", 195 lbs. Deb: 7/31/74

YEAR TM/L	W	L	PCT	G	GS	CG	SH	SV	IP	H	HR	BB	SO	RAT	ERA	ERA+	OAV	OOB	BH	AVG	PB	PR	/A	PD	TPI
1974 Chi-A	0	1	.000	5	1	0	0	0	16¹	22	1	12	11	19.3	5.51	68	.324	.432	0	—	0	-3	-3	-0	-0.4
1975 Chi-A	0	0	—	2	0	0	0	0	5¹	4	1	7	3	18.6	6.75	57	.235	.458	0	—	0	-2	-2	-0	-0.1
1976 Chi-A	0	0	—	2	0	0	0	0	6	9	0	2	3	16.5	4.50	79	.333	.379	0	—	0	-1	-1	-0	-0.1
1980 StL-N	0	5	.000	31	4	0	0	0	55¹	71	3	26	38	16.1	5.53	67	.323	.399	1	.200	-0	-12	-11	-0	-0.9
1981 StL-N	1	0	1.000	24	0	0	0	0	35²	44	2	20	20	16.1	5.30	67	.321	.408	0	—	0	-7	-7	-1	-0.3
Total 5	1	6	.143	64	5	0	0	0	118²	150	7	67	75	16.7	5.46	67	.320	.408	1	.143	-0	-25	-24	-1	-1.8

● DAVE OTTO Otto, David Alan b: 11/12/64, Chicago, Ill. BL/TL, 6'7", 210 lbs. Deb: 9/8/87

YEAR TM/L	W	L	PCT	G	GS	CG	SH	SV	IP	H	HR	BB	SO	RAT	ERA	ERA+	OAV	OOB	BH	AVG	PB	PR	/A	PD	TPI
1987 Oak-A	0	0	—	3	0	0	0	0	6	7	1	1	3	12.0	9.00	46	.304	.333	0	—	0	-3	-3	-0	0.0
1988 Oak-A	0	0	—	3	2	0	0	0	10	7	1	3	5	13.5	1.80	210	.243	.349	0	—	0	2	2	0	0.2
1989 Oak-A	0	0	—	2	1	0	0	0	6²	6	0	2	4	10.8	2.70	136	.261	.320	0	—	0	1	1	-0	0.0
1990 Oak-A	0	0	—	2	0	0	0	0	2¹	3	0	3	2	23.1	7.71	48	.300	.462	0	—	0	-1	-1	-0	0.1

YEAR TM/L	W	L	PCT	G	GS	CG	SH	SV	IP	H	HR	BB	SO	RAT	ERA	ERA+	OAV	OOB	BH	AVG	PB	PR	/A	PD	TPI
1991 Cle-A	2	8	.200	18	14	1	0	0	100	108	7	27	47	12.5	4.23	98	.283	.337	0	—	0	-2	-1	-0	-0.1
1992 Cle-A	5	9	.357	18	16	0	0	0	80^1	110	12	33	32	16.1	7.06	55	.333	.396	0	—	0	-28	-28	-0	-3.9
1993 Pit-N	3	4	.429	28	8	0	0	0	68	85	9	28	30	15.4	5.03	81	.317	.388	4	.222	1	-7	-7	1	-0.5
1994 Chi-N	0	1	.000	36	0	0	0	0	45	49	4	22	19	14.4	3.80	109	.283	.367	0	.000	-0	2	2	-1	-0.1
Total 8	10	22	.313	109	41	1	0	0	318^1	377	33	122	144	14.4	5.06	80	.303	.367	4	.200	0	-35	-36	0	-4.3

● ORVAL OVERALL
Overall, Orval b: 2/2/1881, Farmersville, Cal. d: 7/14/47, Fresno, Cal. BB/TR, 6'2", 214 lbs. Deb: 4/16/05

YEAR TM/L	W	L	PCT	G	GS	CG	SH	SV	IP	H	HR	BB	SO	RAT	ERA	ERA+	OAV	OOB	BH	AVG	PB	PR	/A	PD	TPI
1905 Cin-N	18	23	.439	42	39	32	2	0	318	290	4	147	173	12.8	2.86	116	.252	.343	17	.145	-2	5	16	-1	1.5
1906 Cin-N	4	5	.444	13	10	6	0	0	82^1	77	1	46	33	13.9	4.26	65	.253	.359	6	.194	0	-15	-14	-1	-1.5
*Chi-N	12	3	.800	18	14	13	2	1	144	116	1	51	94	10.7	1.88	141	.217	.290	9	.170	-1	12	12	0	1.2
Yr	16	8	.667	31	24	19	2	1	226^2	193	2	97	127	11.7	2.74	98	.229	.311	15	.179	-1	-3	-2	-1	-0.3
1907 *Chi-N	23	7	.767	36	30	26	**8**	3	268^1	201	3	69	141	9.4	1.68	149	.208	.268	20	.213	3	24	24	2	3.5
1908 *Chi-N	15	11	.577	37	27	16	4	4	225	165	3	78	167	9.8	1.92	123	.208	.280	9	.129	-0	11	11	-1	1.1
1909 *Chi-N	20	11	.645	38	32	23	**9**	3	285	204	1	80	**205**	9.2	1.42	179	**.198**	.262	22	.229	8	37	35	0	5.1
1910 *Chi-N	12	6	.667	23	21	11	4	1	144^2	106	2	54	92	10.0	2.68	108	.212	.291	5	.122	-1	6	3	1	0.5
1913 Chi-N	1	1	.444	11	9	6	1	0	68	73	1	26	30	13.2	3.31	96	.284	.352	6	.250	-1	-1	-1	1	0.2
Total 7	108	71	.603	218	182	133	30	12	1535^1	1232	16	551	935	10.7	2.23	123	.223	.298	94	.179	9	79	86	1	11.6

● STUBBY OVERMIRE
Overmire, Frank W. b: 5/16/19, Moline, Mich. d: 3/3/77, Lakeland, Fla. BR/TL, 5'7", 170 lbs. Deb: 4/25/43 C

YEAR TM/L	W	L	PCT	G	GS	CG	SH	SV	IP	H	HR	BB	SO	RAT	ERA	ERA+	OAV	OOB	BH	AVG	PB	PR	/A	PD	TPI
1943 Det-A	7	6	.538	29	18	8	3	1	147	135	5	38	48	10.7	3.18	111	.243	.293	7	.167	0	2	6	-1	0.4
1944 Det-A	11	11	.500	32	28	11	3	1	199^2	214	4	41	57	11.6	3.07	116	.271	.309	11	.175	1	8	11	2	1.4
1945 *Det-A	9	9	.500	31	22	9	0	4	162^1	189	6	42	36	13.0	3.88	91	.294	.341	10	.189	0	-9	-7	0	-0.7
1946 Det-A	5	7	.417	24	13	3	0	1	97^1	106	6	29	34	12.5	4.62	79	.274	.325	5	.152	-1	-12	-10	1	-1.2
1947 Det-A	11	5	.688	28	17	7	3	0	140^2	142	9	44	33	12.0	3.77	100	.259	.315	7	.149	-1	-1	-0	-0	-0.1
1948 Det-A	3	4	.429	37	4	0	0	3	66^1	89	5	31	14	16.3	5.97	73	.326	.395	1	.071	-1	-12	-12	1	-1.2
1949 Det-A	1	3	.250	14	1	0	0	0	17^1	29	2	9	3	20.3	9.87	42	.377	.448	1	.333	0	-11	-11	0	-2.0
1950 StL-A	9	12	.429	31	19	8	2	0	161	200	14	45	39	13.8	4.19	118	.298	.343	8	.167	1	7	14	-2	1.4
1951 StL-A	1	6	.143	8	7	3	0	0	53^1	61	5	21	13	13.8	3.54	124	.281	.345	1	.071	-1	3	5	-1	0.4
NY-A	1	1	.500	15	4	1	0	0	44^2	50	2	18	14	14.1	4.63	83	.287	.361	1	.143	-1	-3	-4	0	-0.1
Yr	2	7	.222	23	11	4	0	0	98	111	7	39	27	14.0	4.04	102	.284	.352	2	.095	-0	1	1	-1	0.3
1952 StL-A	0	3	.000	17	4	0	0	0	41	44	3	7	10	11.2	3.73	105	.270	.300	2	.182	-0	-1	1	0	0.1
Total 10	58	67	.464	266	137	50	11	10	1130^2	1259	56	325	301	12.7	3.96	98	.280	.330	54	.161	-1	-28	-8	1	-1.6

● MIKE OVERY
Overy, Harry Michael b: 1/27/51, Clinton, Ill. BR/TR, 6'2", 190 lbs. Deb: 8/14/76

YEAR TM/L	W	L	PCT	G	GS	CG	SH	SV	IP	H	HR	BB	SO	RAT	ERA	ERA+	OAV	OOB	BH	AVG	PB	PR	/A	PD	TPI
1976 Cal-A	0	2	.000	5	0	0	0	0	7^1	6	1	3	6	12.3	6.14	54	.214	.313	0	—	0	-2	-2	0	-0.1

● ERNIE OVITZ
Ovitz, Ernest Gayhart b: 10/7/1885, Mineral Point, Wis. d: 9/11/80, Green Bay, Wis. BR/TL, 5'8.5", 156 lbs. Deb: 6/22/11

YEAR TM/L	W	L	PCT	G	GS	CG	SH	SV	IP	H	HR	BB	SO	RAT	ERA	ERA+	OAV	OOB	BH	AVG	PB	PR	/A	PD	TPI
1911 Chi-N	0	0	—	1	0	0	0	0	2	3	0	3	0	27.0	4.50	74	.375	.545	0	—	0	-0	-0	-0	0.0

● BOB OWCHINKO
Owchinko, Robert Dennis b: 1/1/55, Detroit, Mich. BL/TL, 6'2", 195 lbs. Deb: 9/25/76

YEAR TM/L	W	L	PCT	G	GS	CG	SH	SV	IP	H	HR	BB	SO	RAT	ERA	ERA+	OAV	OOB	BH	AVG	PB	PR	/A	PD	TPI
1976 SD-N	0	2	.000	2	2	0	0	0	4^1	11	0	3	4	29.1	16.62	20	.478	.538	0	.000	-0	-6	-6	0	-1.7
1977 SD-N	9	12	.429	30	28	3	2	0	170	191	20	67	101	13.7	4.45	80	.287	.352	4	.082	-2	-10	-17	-2	-2.2
1978 SD-N	10	13	.435	36	33	4	1	0	202^1	198	14	78	94	12.3	3.56	93	.263	.333	11	.175	1	0	-5	-1	-0.5
1979 SD-N	6	12	.333	42	20	2	0	0	149^1	144	16	55	66	12.1	3.74	94	.259	.328	4	.121	-0	-4	-3	-0	-0.5
1980 Cle-A	2	9	.182	29	14	1	1	0	114^1	138	13	47	66	14.7	5.27	77	.301	.368	0	—	0	-16	-15	-1	-1.3
1981 *Oak-A	4	3	.571	29	0	0	0	1	39^1	34	2	19	26	12.4	3.20	109	.245	.340	0	—	0	2	1	0	0.3
1982 Oak-A	2	4	.333	54	0	0	0	3	102	111	11	52	67	14.4	5.21	75	.275	.358	0	—	0	-13	-15	-1	-0.7
1983 Pit-N	0	0	—	1	0	0	0	0	0	2	1	0	0	—	∞	—	1.000	1.000	0	—	0	-1	-1	0	-0.1
1984 Cin-N	3	5	.375	49	4	0	0	2	94	91	10	39	60	12.4	4.12	92	.253	.327	2	.167	1	-6	-4	-1	-0.3
1986 Mon-N	1	0	1.000	15	0	0	0	0	15	17	1	3	6	12.0	3.60	103	.288	.323	1	.200	0	0	-0	-0	0.0
Total 10	37	60	.381	275	104	10	4	7	890^2	937	88	363	490	13.2	4.28	85	.274	.345	22	.135	-0	-49	-66	-5	-7.0

● FRANK OWEN
Owen, Frank Malcolm "Yip" b: 12/23/1879, Ypsilanti, Mich. d: 11/24/42, Dearborn, Mich. BB/TR, 5'11", 160 lbs. Deb: 4/29/01

YEAR TM/L	W	L	PCT	G	GS	CG	SH	SV	IP	H	HR	BB	SO	RAT	ERA	ERA+	OAV	OOB	BH	AVG	PB	PR	/A	PD	TPI
1901 Det-A	1	3	.250	8	5	3	0	1	56	70	1	30	17	16.7	4.34	89	.302	.391	1	.050	-2	-4	-3	2	-0.2
1903 Chi-A	8	12	.400	26	20	15	1	1	167^1	167	1	44	66	11.7	3.50	80	.259	.314	7	.123	-1	-10	-13	4	-1.2
1904 Chi-A	21	15	.583	37	36	34	4	1	315	243	2	61	103	9.0	1.94	126	.214	.261	23	.215	-5	23	18	6	3.5
1905 Chi-A	21	13	.618	42	38	32	3	0	334	276	6	56	125	9.2	2.10	117	.227	.266	18	.145	-4	21	14	3	1.3
1906 *Chi-A	22	13	.629	42	36	27	7	0	293	289	4	54	66	10.7	2.33	109	.261	.298	14	.136	-2	12	7	4	1.0
1907 Chi-A	2	3	.400	11	4	2	0	0	47	43	1	13	16	10.7	2.49	96	.246	.298	4	.250	-0	0	-2	-0	-0.2
1908 Chi-A	6	7	.462	25	14	5	1	0	140	142	2	37	48	11.7	3.41	68	.260	.310	9	.180	1	-16	-17	2	-1.3
1909 Chi-A	1	1	.500	3	2	1	0	0	16	19	0	3	2	13.5	4.50	52	.279	.319	1	.167	-0	-4	-4	1	-0.3
Total 8	82	67	.550	194	155	119	16	2	1368^1	1249	17	298	443	10.4	2.55	100	.244	.290	77	.159	-3	22	0	22	2.6

● JIM OWENS
Owens, James Philip "Bear" b: 1/16/34, Gifford, Pa. BR/TR, 5'11", 190 lbs. Deb: 4/19/55 C

YEAR TM/L	W	L	PCT	G	GS	CG	SH	SV	IP	H	HR	BB	SO	RAT	ERA	ERA+	OAV	OOB	BH	AVG	PB	PR	/A	PD	TPI
1955 Phi-N	0	2	.000	8	3	2	0	0	8^2	13	2	7	6	20.8	8.31	48	.382	.488	0	.000	-0	-4	-4	-0	-0.8
1956 Phi-N	0	4	.000	10	5	0	0	0	29^2	35	3	22	22	17.9	7.28	51	.313	.434	1	.167	-0	-12	-12	-0	-1.3
1958 Phi-N	1	0	1.000	1	1	0	0	0	7	4	1	5	3	11.6	2.57	154	.154	.290	0	.000	-0	1	1	-0	0.1
1959 Phi-N	12	12	.500	31	30	11	1	1	221^1	203	14	73	135	11.4	3.21	128	.244	.308	9	.120	-1	18	22	-0	2.1
1960 Phi-N	4	14	.222	31	22	6	0	0	150	182	21	64	83	14.8	5.04	77	.299	.367	3	.068	-3	-21	-19	-1	-2.5
1961 Phi-N	5	10	.333	20	17	3	0	0	106^2	119	8	32	38	12.7	4.47	91	.287	.339	2	.074	-1	-5	-5	-2	-0.9
1962 Phi-N	4	4	.333	23	12	1	0	0	69^2	90	7	33	21	15.9	6.33	61	.318	.389	2	.143	-1	-18	-19	-1	-1.6
1963 Cin-N	0	2	.000	19	3	0	0	4	42^1	42	6	24	29	14.0	5.31	63	.259	.355	1	.125	-0	-10	-9	-1	-0.6
1964 Hou-N	8	7	.533	48	11	0	0	6	118	116	7	32	88	11.2	3.28	104	.262	.312	3	.103	-1	2	1	-0	0.1
1965 Hou-N	6	5	.545	50	0	0	0	5	71^1	64	9	29	53	11.7	3.28	102	.238	.312	1	.125	-0	2	1	-0	0.0
1966 Hou-N	4	7	.364	40	0	0	0	0	50	53	5	17	32	12.8	4.68	73	.273	.335	0	.000	-0	-6	-7	-1	-1.5
1967 Hou-N	0	1	.000	5	0	0	0	0	10^2	12	1	5	6	11.8	4.22	78	.308	.341	0	—	0	-1	-0	-0	-0.1
Total 12	42	68	.382	286	103	21	1	21	885^1	932	84	340	516	13.0	4.31	88	.273	.340	22	.101	-7	-53	-51	-5	-7.1

● RICK OWNBEY
Ownbey, Richard Wayne b: 10/20/57, Corona, Cal. BR/TR, 6'3", 185 lbs. Deb: 8/17/82

YEAR TM/L	W	L	PCT	G	GS	CG	SH	SV	IP	H	HR	BB	SO	RAT	ERA	ERA+	OAV	OOB	BH	AVG	PB	PR	/A	PD	TPI
1982 NY-N	1	2	.333	8	8	1	0	0	50^1	44	3	43	28	15.6	3.75	97	.242	.387	3	.200	1	-1	-1	-1	0.0
1983 NY-N	1	3	.250	10	4	0	0	0	34^2	31	4	21	19	13.8	4.67	78	.240	.351	1	.111	-0	-4	-4	-0	-0.5
1984 StL-N	0	3	.000	4	4	0	0	0	19	23	1	8	11	14.7	4.74	73	.303	.369	0	.000	-0	-2	-3	-0	-0.5
1986 StL-N	1	3	.250	17	3	0	0	0	42^2	47	4	19	25	14.3	3.80	96	.294	.376	0	.000	-1	-1	-0	-1	-0.2
Total 4	3	11	.214	39	19	2	0	0	146^2	145	12	91	83	14.7	4.11	88	.265	.373	4	.114	-0	-8	-8	-2	-1.2

● DOC OZMER
Ozmer, Horace Robert b: 5/25/01, Atlanta, Ga. d: 12/28/70, Atlanta, Ga. BR/TR, 5'10.5", 185 lbs. Deb: 5/11/23

YEAR TM/L	W	L	PCT	G	GS	CG	SH	SV	IP	H	HR	BB	SO	RAT	ERA	ERA+	OAV	OOB	BH	AVG	PB	PR	/A	PD	TPI
1923 Phi-A	0	0	—	1	0	0	0	0	2	3	0	1	1	9.0	4.50	91	.167	.286	0	—	0	-0	-0	0	0.0

● CHARLIE PABOR
Pabor, Charles Henry b: 9/24/1846, New York, N.Y. d: 4/23/13, New Haven, Conn. BL/TL, 5'8", 155 lbs. Deb: 5/4/1871 M♦

YEAR TM/L	W	L	PCT	G	GS	CG	SH	SV	IP	H	HR	BB	SO	RAT	ERA	ERA+	OAV	OOB	BH	AVG	PB	PR	/A	PD	TPI
1871 Cle-n	0	2	.000	7	1	1	0	0	29^1	50	4	6	0	17.2	6.75	61	.325	.350	42	.296	-3	-8	-9		-0.3
1872 Cle-n	1	1	.500	2	2	2	0	0	18	20	0	3	0	11.5	4.00	89	.247	.274	19	.207	-0	-1	-1		0.1
1875 Atl-n	0	1	.000	1	1	1	0	0	4	11	0	1	0	27.0	9.00	23	.407	.429	36	.235	-0	-3	-3		-0.5
Total 3 n	1	4	.200	10	4	4	0	0	51^1	81	4	10	0	15.9	5.96	35	.309	.335	204	.285	-2	-21	-22		-0.7

● JOHN PACELLA
Pacella, John Lewis b: 9/15/56, Brooklyn, N.Y. BR/TR, 6'3", 195 lbs. Deb: 9/15/77

YEAR TM/L	W	L	PCT	G	GS	CG	SH	SV	IP	H	HR	BB	SO	RAT	ERA	ERA+	OAV	OOB	BH	AVG	PB	PR	/A	PD	TPI
1977 NY-N	0	0	—	2	0	0	0	0	4^2	2	0	2	1	9.0	0.00	—	.133	.235	0	—	0	2	2	-0	0.0
1979 NY-N	0	2	.000	4	3	0	0	0	16^1	16	0	4	12	11.0	4.41	83	.246	.290	0	.000	-1	-1	-1	-0	-0.2
1980 NY-N	3	4	.429	32	15	0	0	0	84	89	5	59	68	16.1	5.14	69	.280	.396	1	.250	0	-14	-15	-0	-1.3
1982 NY-N	0	1	.000	3	1	0	0	0	10	13	2	9	8	20.7	7.20	55	.342	.479	0	—	0	-4	-3	-0	-0.2
Min-A	1	2	.333	21	1	0	0	2	51^2	61	14	37	20	17.1	7.32	58	.299	.407	0	—	0	-19	-18	-1	-1.3
Yr	1	3	.250	24	2	0	0	2	61^2	74	16	46	22	17.5	7.30	58	.301	.411	0	—	0	-22	-21	-2	-1.5
1984 Bal-A	0	1	.000	6	1	0	0	0	14^2	15	2	9	8	14.7	6.75	57	.268	.369	0	—	0	-4	-0	-0	-0.2

YEAR	TM/L	W	L	PCT	G	GS	CG	SH	SV	IP	H	HR	BB	SO	RAT	ERA	ERA+	OAV	OOB	BH	AVG	PB	PR	/A	PD	TPI
1986	Det-A	0	0	—	5	0	0	0	1	11	10	0	13	5	18.8	4.09	101	.294	.489	0	—	0	0	0	1	0.1
Total 6		4	10	.286	74	21	0	0	1	191²	206	21	133	116	16.1	5.73	67	.282	.395	2	.083	-1	-40	-41	-2	-3.1

● **ALEX PACHECO**   Pacheco, Alexander Melchor (Lara) b: 7/19/73, Caracas, Venez.   BR/TR, 6'3", 200 lbs.   Deb: 4/17/96

YEAR	TM/L	W	L	PCT	G	GS	CG	SH	SV	IP	H	HR	BB	SO	RAT	ERA	ERA+	OAV	OOB	BH	AVG	PB	PR	/A	PD	TPI
1996	Mon-N	0	0	—	5	0	0	0	0	5²	8	2	1	7	14.3	11.12	39	.320	.346	0	—	0	-4	-4	-0	0.0

● **PAT PACILLO**   Pacillo, Patrick Michael b: 7/23/63, Jersey City, N.J.   BR/TR, 6'2", 205 lbs.   Deb: 5/23/87

YEAR	TM/L	W	L	PCT	G	GS	CG	SH	SV	IP	H	HR	BB	SO	RAT	ERA	ERA+	OAV	OOB	BH	AVG	PB	PR	/A	PD	TPI
1987	Cin-N	3	3	.500	12	7	0	0	0	39²	41	7	19	23	13.8	6.13	69	.270	.355	1	.091	-0	-9	-8	-1	-1.1
1988	Cin-N	1	0	1.000	6	0	0	0	0	10²	14	2	4	11	15.2	5.06	71	.318	.375	0	.000	-0	-2	-2	-0	-0.2
Total 2		4	3	.571	18	7	0	0	0	50¹	55	9	23	34	14.1	5.90	70	.281	.359	1	.083	-0	-11	-10	-1	-1.3

● **GENE PACKARD**   Packard, Eugene Milo b: 7/13/1887, Colorado Springs, Colorado   d: 5/19/59, Riverside, Cal.   BL/TL, 5'10", 155 lbs.   Deb: 9/27/12

YEAR	TM/L	W	L	PCT	G	GS	CG	SH	SV	IP	H	HR	BB	SO	RAT	ERA	ERA+	OAV	OOB	BH	AVG	PB	PR	/A	PD	TPI
1912	Cin-N	1	0	1.000	1	1	1	0	0	9	7	0	4	2	11.0	3.00	112	.206	.289	1	.250	1	0	0	0	0.1
1913	Cin-N	7	11	.389	39	21	9	2	0	190²	208	2	64	73	13.2	2.97	109	.286	.350	11	.180	-0	5	6	-1	0.4
1914	KC-F	20	14	.588	42	34	24	4	5	302	282	5	88	154	11.1	2.89	96	.246	.301	28	.241	2	-0	-4	9	0.7
1915	KC-F	20	12	.625	42	31	21	5	2	281²	250	3	74	108	10.6	2.68	98	.242	.298	22	.232	2	1	-2	7	0.7
1916	Chi-N	10	6	.625	37	16	5	2	5	155¹	154	4	38	36	11.3	2.78	105	.256	.304	7	.130	-1	-3	2	5	0.7
1917	Chi-N	0	0	—	2	0	0	0	0	1²	3	1	0	1	16.2	10.80	27	.375	.375	0	—	0	-1	-1	0	0.0
	StL-N	9	6	.600	34	11	6	0	2	153¹	138	4	25	44	9.7	2.47	109	.246	.281	15	.288	3	4	4	-1	0.7
	Yr	9	6	.600	36	11	6	0	2	155	141	5	25	45	9.8	2.55	105	.247	.283	15	.288	3	3	2	-0	0.7
1918	StL-N	12	12	.500	30	23	10	1	2	182¹	184	6	33	46	11.0	3.50	77	.266	.304	12	.174	-1	-15	-16	-1	-2.3
1919	Phi-N	6	8	.429	21	16	10	1	1	134¹	167	3	30	24	13.5	4.15	78	.321	.363	7	.137	-2	-19	-14	-0	-1.6
Total 8		85	69	.552	248	153	86	15	17	1410¹	1393	28	356	488	11.4	3.01	95	.262	.312	103	.205	4	-27	-25	17	-0.6

● **JOE PACTWA**   Pactwa, Joseph Martin b: 6/2/48, Hammond, Ind.   BL/TL, 5'11", 185 lbs.   Deb: 9/15/75

YEAR	TM/L	W	L	PCT	G	GS	CG	SH	SV	IP	H	HR	BB	SO	RAT	ERA	ERA+	OAV	OOB	BH	AVG	PB	PR	/A	PD	TPI
1975	Cal-A	1	0	1.000	4	3	0	0	0	16¹	23	1	10	3	18.2	3.86	92	.343	.429	0	—	0	-0	-1	-0	0.4

● **DAVE PAGAN**   Pagan, David Percy b: 9/15/49, Nipawin, Sask., Canada   BR/TR, 6'2", 175 lbs.   Deb: 7/1/73

YEAR	TM/L	W	L	PCT	G	GS	CG	SH	SV	IP	H	HR	BB	SO	RAT	ERA	ERA+	OAV	OOB	BH	AVG	PB	PR	/A	PD	TPI
1973	NY-A	0	0	—	4	1	0	0	0	12²	16	1	9	9	12.1	2.84	129	.320	.333	0	—	0	1	1	0	0.3
1974	NY-A	1	3	.250	16	6	1	0	0	49¹	49	1	28	39	14.0	5.11	69	.265	.362	0	—	0	-8	-9	-0	-0.7
1975	NY-A	0	0	—	13	0	0	0	0	31	30	2	13	18	13.1	4.06	91	.256	.341	0	—	0	-1	-1	-1	-0.1
1976	NY-A	1	1	.500	7	2	1	0	0	23²	18	0	4	13	8.4	2.28	150	.222	.259	0	—	0	3	3	-1	0.3
	Bal-A	1	4	.200	20	5	0	0	1	46²	54	2	23	34	15.0	5.98	55	.298	.380	0	—	0	-13	-14	-1	-1.1
	Yr	2	5	.286	27	7	1	0	1	70¹	72	2	27	47	12.8	4.73	70	.273	.342	0	—	0	-9	-11	-2	-0.8
1977	Sea-A	1	1	.500	24	4	1	1	2	66	86	3	26	30	15.5	6.14	67	.323	.388	0	—	0	-15	-15	-0	-0.5
	Pit-N	0	0	—	1	0	0	0	0	3	1	0	2	0	3.0	3.00		.100	.100	0	—	0	1	1	0	0.0
Total 5		4	9	.308	85	18	3	1	4	232¹	254	9	95	147	13.7	4.96	74	.285	.358	0	—	0	-31	-34	-2	-1.7

● **JOE PAGE**   Page, Joseph Francis "Fireman" b: 10/28/17, Cherry Valley, Pa.   d: 4/21/80, Latrobe, Pa.   BL/TL, 6'2", 205 lbs.   Deb: 4/19/44

YEAR	TM/L	W	L	PCT	G	GS	CG	SH	SV	IP	H	HR	BB	SO	RAT	ERA	ERA+	OAV	OOB	BH	AVG	PB	PR	/A	PD	TPI
1944	NY-A☆	5	7	.417	19	16	4	0	0	102²	100	3	52	63	13.6	4.56	76	.258	.351	5	.156	-0	-13	-12	-1	-1.4
1945	NY-A	6	3	.667	20	9	4	0	0	102	95	1	46	50	12.4	2.82	123	.246	.326	9	.250	1	6	7	-2	0.5
1946	NY-A	9	8	.529	31	17	6	1	3	136	126	7	72	77	13.4	3.57	97	.252	.351	7	.163	-0	-1	-2	-1	-0.3
1947	*NY-A★	14	8	.636	56	2	0	0	17	141¹	105	5	72	116	11.3	2.48	142	.208	.308	10	.217	1	**19**	**17**	-1	3.0
1948	NY-A☆	7	8	.467	**55**	1	0	0	16	107²	116	6	66	77	15.3	4.26	96	.275	.374	7	.292	3	-0	-1	0	-0.1
1949	*NY-A	13	8	.619	**60**	0	0	0	27	135¹	103	8	75	99	12.2	2.59	156	.215	.328	7	.175	-1	**24**	**22**	-2	3.8
1950	NY-A	3	7	.300	37	0	0	0	13	55¹	66	8	31	33	15.8	5.04	85	.295	.380	2	.250	1	-3	-5	-1	-0.9
1954	Pit-N	0	0	—	7	0	0	0	0	9²	16	4	7	4	22.3	11.17	37	.364	.462	0	—	0	-8	-8	0	-0.0
Total 8		57	49	.538	285	45	14	1	76	790	727	42	421	519	13.2	3.53	106	.247	.344	47	.205	5	25	18	-7	4.6

● **PHIL PAGE**   Page, Philippe Rausac b: 8/23/05, Springfield, Mass.   d: 7/27/58, Springfield, Mass   BR/TL, 6'2", 175 lbs.   Deb: 9/18/28   C

YEAR	TM/L	W	L	PCT	G	GS	CG	SH	SV	IP	H	HR	BB	SO	RAT	ERA	ERA+	OAV	OOB	BH	AVG	PB	PR	/A	PD	TPI
1928	Det-A	2	0	1.000	3	2	2	0	0	22	21	1	10	3	12.7	2.45	167	.256	.337	2	.222	-0	4	4	1	0.4
1929	Det-A	0	2	.000	10	4	1	0	0	25¹	29	1	19	6	17.4	8.17	53	.296	.415	1	.125	-1	-11	-11	-1	-0.8
1930	Det-A	0	1	.000	12	0	0	0	0	12	23	1	9	2	24.0	9.75	49	.434	.516	0	—	0	-7	-7	0	-0.4
1934	Bro-N	1	0	1.000	6	0	0	0	0	10	13	1	6	4	17.1	5.40	72	.342	.432	1	.000	-0	-1	-2	1	-0.1
Total 4		3	3	.500	31	6	3	0	0	69¹	86	4	44	15	17.0	6.23	68	.317	.415	3	.167	-1	-15	-15	1	-0.9

● **SAM PAGE**   Page, Samuel Walter b: 2/11/16, Woodruff, S.C.   BL/TR, 6', 172 lbs.   Deb: 9/11/39

YEAR	TM/L	W	L	PCT	G	GS	CG	SH	SV	IP	H	HR	BB	SO	RAT	ERA	ERA+	OAV	OOB	BH	AVG	PB	PR	/A	PD	TPI
1939	Phi-A	0	3	.000	4	3	1	0	0	22	34	1	15	11	20.0	6.95	68	.343	.430	3	.429	1	-6	-5	1	-0.4

● **VANCE PAGE**   Page, Vance Linwood b: 9/15/05, Elm City, N.C.   d: 7/14/51, Wilson, N.C.   BR/TR, 6', 180 lbs.   Deb: 8/6/38

YEAR	TM/L	W	L	PCT	G	GS	CG	SH	SV	IP	H	HR	BB	SO	RAT	ERA	ERA+	OAV	OOB	BH	AVG	PB	PR	/A	PD	TPI
1938	*Chi-N	5	4	.556	13	9	3	0	1	68	90	4	13	18	13.6	3.84	100	.323	.353	4	.154	-1	-0	-0	3	0.1
1939	Chi-N	7	7	.500	27	17	8	1	0	139¹	169	8	37	43	13.4	3.88	102	.298	.342	12	.255	3	1	1	1	0.4
1940	Chi-N	1	3	.250	30	1	0	0	2	59	65	1	26	22	13.9	4.42	85	.271	.342	4	.308	2	-4	-4	0	-0.1
1941	Chi-N	2	2	.500	25	3	1	0	1	48¹	48	2	30	17	14.9	4.28	82	.254	.362	2	.286	1	-3	-4	0	-0.2
Total 4		15	16	.484	95	30	12	1	5	314²	372	15	106	100	13.8	4.03	95	.292	.348	22	.237	4	-7	-8	4	0.2

● **PAT PAIGE**   Paige, George Lynn "Piggy" b: 5/5/1882, Paw Paw, Mich.   d: 6/8/39, Berlin, Wis.   BL/TR, 5'10", 175 lbs.   Deb: 5/20/11

YEAR	TM/L	W	L	PCT	G	GS	CG	SH	SV	IP	H	HR	BB	SO	RAT	ERA	ERA+	OAV	OOB	BH	AVG	PB	PR	/A	PD	TPI
1911	Cle-A	1	0	1.000	2	1	0	0	0	16	21	0	7	6	15.8	4.50	76	.339	.406	1	.143	-0	-2	-2	1	-0.1

● **SATCHEL PAIGE**   Paige, Leroy Robert b: 7/7/06, Mobile, Ala.   d: 6/8/82, Kansas City, Mo.   BR/TR, 6'3.5", 180 lbs.   Deb: 7/9/48   CH

YEAR	TM/L	W	L	PCT	G	GS	CG	SH	SV	IP	H	HR	BB	SO	RAT	ERA	ERA+	OAV	OOB	BH	AVG	PB	PR	/A	PD	TPI
1948	*Cle-A	6	1	.857	21	7	3	2	1	72²	61	2	22	43	10.4	2.48	164	.228	.290	2	.087	-2	15	13	-0	0.9
1949	Cle-A	4	7	.364	31	5	1	0	5	83	70	4	33	54	11.3	3.04	131	.230	.308	1	.063	-1	11	9	-1	1.0
1951	StL-A	3	4	.429	23	3	0	0	5	62	67	6	29	48	14.1	4.79	92	.276	.355	2	.125	-2	-5	-3	-1	-0.6
1952	StL-A☆	12	10	.545	46	6	3	2	10	138	116	7	57	91	11.5	3.07	128	.226	.307	5	.128	-2	9	13	0	2.0
1953	StL-A★	3	9	.250	57	4	0	0	11	117¹	114	12	39	51	11.8	3.53	116	.257	.319	2	.069	-3	6	9	-2	0.5
1965	KC-A	0	0	—	1	1	0	0	0	3	1	0	0	1	3.0	0.00	—	.100	.100	0	.000	-0	1	1	0	0.0
Total 6		28	31	.475	179	26	7	4	32	476	429	29	180	288	11.6	3.29	124	.241	.313	12	.097	-10	37	42	-3	3.8

● **PHIL PAINE**   Paine, Phillips Steere "Flip" b: 6/8/30, Chepachet, R.I.   d: 2/19/78, Lebanon, Pa.   BR/TR, 6'2", 181 lbs.   Deb: 7/14/51

YEAR	TM/L	W	L	PCT	G	GS	CG	SH	SV	IP	H	HR	BB	SO	RAT	ERA	ERA+	OAV	OOB	BH	AVG	PB	PR	/A	PD	TPI
1951	Bos-N	2	0	1.000	21	0	0	0	0	35¹	39	2	20	17	15.3	3.06	120	.271	.382	0	.000	-1	4	2	-0	0.0
1954	Mil-N	1	0	1.000	11	0	0	0	0	14	14	1	12	11	17.4	3.86	97	.292	.443	0	—	0	0	-0	-0	-0.1
1955	Mil-N	2	0	1.000	15	0	0	0	0	25¹	20	2	14	26	12.1	2.49	151	.225	.330	1	.333	0	4	4	0	0.3
1956	Mil-N	0	0	—	3	0	0	0	0	3	0	0	0	0	∞	—		1.000	1.000	0	—	0	-2	-2	0	-0.2
1957	Mil-N	0	0	—	1	0	0	0	0	2	1	0	3	2	18.0			.143	.400	0	—	0	1	1	0	0.0
1958	StL-N	5	1	.833	44	0	0	0	1	73¹	70	7	31	45	13.0	3.56	116	.256	.343	2	.286	-0	3	5	0	0.4
Total 6		10	1	.909	95	0	0	0	1	150	144	12	80	101	14.0	3.36	116	.260	.364	3	.214	-0	10	9	0	0.4

● **LANCE PAINTER**   Painter, Lance Telford b: 7/21/67, Bedford, England   BL/TL, 6'1", 195 lbs.   Deb: 5/19/93

YEAR	TM/L	W	L	PCT	G	GS	CG	SH	SV	IP	H	HR	BB	SO	RAT	ERA	ERA+	OAV	OOB	BH	AVG	PB	PR	/A	PD	TPI
1993	Col-N	2	2	.500	10	6	1	0	0	39	52	5	9	16	14.1	6.00	79	.333	.370	1	.300	1	-8	-5	0	-0.3
1994	Col-N	4	6	.400	15	14	0	0	0	73²	91	9	26	41	14.4	6.11	81	.302	.360	3	.143	-1	-16	-9	0	-1.1
1995	*Col-N	3	0	1.000	33	1	0	0	0	45¹	55	9	10	36	13.3	4.37	123	.296	.338	1	.111	-0	-1	5	0	0.3
1996	Col-N	4	2	.667	34	1	0	0	0	50²	56	12	25	48	14.9	5.86	93	.280	.368	4	.133	-1	-9	-2	-0	-0.4
Total 4		13	10	.565	92	22	1	0	0	208²	254	35	70	141	14.2	5.65	91	.301	.359	9	.164	-1	-34	-12	0	-1.5

● **VICENTE PALACIOS**   Palacios, Vicente (Diaz) b: 7/19/63, Veracruz, Mex.   BR/TR, 6'3", 165 lbs.   Deb: 9/4/87

YEAR	TM/L	W	L	PCT	G	GS	CG	SH	SV	IP	H	HR	BB	SO	RAT	ERA	ERA+	OAV	OOB	BH	AVG	PB	PR	/A	PD	TPI
1987	Pit-N	2	1	.667	6	4	0	0	0	29¹	27	1	9	13	11.4	4.30	96	.250	.314	1	.111	-0	-1	-1	-1	-0.2
1988	Pit-N	1	2	.333	7	3	0	0	0	24¹	28	5	15	15	15.9	6.66	51	.295	.391	0	.000	-0	-9	-9	-0	-1.0
1990	Pit-N	0	0	—	7	0	0	0	0	15	4	0	2	8	3.6	0.00	—	.083	.120	0	.000	-0	6	6	-0	0.2
1991	Pit-N	6	3	.667	33	7	1	1	3	81²	69	6	38	64	11.9	3.75	95	.228	.316	1	.071	-1	-2	-1	-3	-0.3
1992	Pit-N	3	2	.600	8	8	0	0	0	53	56	1	27	33	14.1	4.25	81	.280	.366	1	.071	-1	-4	-5	-0	-0.5
1994	StL-N	3	8	.273	31	17	1	0	0	117²	104	16	43	95	11.5	4.44	97	.245	.319	0	.000	-4	-3	-4	-0	-0.7

YEAR	TM/L	W	L	PCT	G	GS	CG	SH	SV	IP	H	HR	BB	SO	RAT	ERA	ERA+	OAV	OOB	BH	AVG	PB	PR	/A	PD	TPI
1995	StL-N	2	3	.400	20	5	0	0	0	40¹	48	7	19	34	15.4	5.80	72	.300	.381	1	.167	-0	-7	-7	-0	-0.8
Total	7	17	19	.472	127	44	2	2	7	361¹	336	40	153	262	12.4	4.36	88	.251	.331	4	.045	-6	-18	-21	-2	-3.3

● MIKE PALAGYI
Palagyi, Michael Raymond b: 7/4/17, Conneaut, Ohio BR/TR, 6'2", 185 lbs. Deb: 8/18/39

YEAR	TM/L	W	L	PCT	G	GS	CG	SH	SV	IP	H	HR	BB	SO	RAT	ERA	ERA+	OAV	OOB	BH	AVG	PB	PR	/A	PD	TPI
1939	Was-A	0	0	—	1	0	0	0	0	0	0	0	3	0	—	∞	—	—	1.000	0	—	0	-3	-3	-0	-0.2

● ERV PALICA
Palica, Ervin Martin (b: Ervin Martin Pavliecivich)
b: 2/9/28, Lomita, Cal. d: 5/29/82, Huntington Beach, Cal. BR/TR, 6'1.5", 180 lbs. Deb: 4/21/45 ♦

YEAR	TM/L	W	L	PCT	G	GS	CG	SH	SV	IP	H	HR	BB	SO	RAT	ERA	ERA+	OAV	OOB	BH	AVG	PB	PR	/A	PD	TPI
1947	Bro-N	0	1	.000	3	0	0	0	0	3	2	0	2	1	15.0	3.00	138	.182	.357	0	—	0	0	0	-0	0.1
1948	Bro-N	6	6	.500	41	10	3	0	3	125¹	111	13	58	74	12.4	4.45	90	.239	.327	5	.128	0	-7	-6	-1	-0.7
1949	*Bro-N	8	9	.471	49	1	0	0	6	97	93	6	49	44	13.3	3.62	113	.261	.352	3	.158	0	5	5	-0	0.3
1950	Bro-N	13	8	.619	43	19	10	2	1	201²	176	13	98	131	12.3	3.58	115	.237	.327	15	.221	2	13	12	-4	0.9
1951	Bro-N	2	6	.250	19	8	0	0	0	53	55	10	20	15	12.7	4.75	83	.259	.323	2	.154	0	-5	-5	1	-0.6
1953	Bro-N	0	0	—	4	0	0	0	0	6	10	1	8	3	27.0	12.00	36	.370	.514	1	1.000	0	-5	-5	0	0.1
1954	Bro-N	3	3	.500	25	3	0	0	0	67²	77	9	31	25	14.5	5.32	77	.285	.361	4	.250	1	-9	-9	-2	-0.8
1955	Bal-A	5	11	.313	33	25	5	1	0	169²	165	10	83	68	13.3	4.14	92	.260	.348	13	.236	2	-3	-6	-1	-0.3
1956	Bal-A	4	11	.267	29	14	2	0	0	116¹	117	10	50	62	13.0	4.49	87	.264	.339	5	.156	-2	-4	-7	-0	-1.0
Total	9	41	55	.427	246	80	20	3	10	839¹	806	72	399	423	13.0	4.22	94	.255	.340	48	.198	5	-16	-22	-7	-1.4

● DONN PALL
Pall, Donn Steven b: 1/11/62, Chicago, Ill. BR/TR, 6'2", 185 lbs. Deb: 8/1/88

YEAR	TM/L	W	L	PCT	G	GS	CG	SH	SV	IP	H	HR	BB	SO	RAT	ERA	ERA+	OAV	OOB	BH	AVG	PB	PR	/A	PD	TPI
1988	Chi-A	0	2	.000	17	0	0	0	0	28²	39	1	8	16	14.8	3.45	115	.328	.370	—	—	0	2	2	1	0.2
1989	Chi-A	5	4	.444	53	0	0	0	6	87	90	9	19	58	12.1	3.31	115	.270	.325	—	—	0	6	5	-1	0.4
1990	Chi-A	3	5	.375	56	0	0	0	2	76	63	7	24	39	10.8	3.32	115	.232	.303	—	—	0	5	4	-0	0.4
1991	Chi-A	7	2	.778	51	0	0	0	0	71	59	7	20	40	10.4	2.41	165	.231	.295	—	—	0	13	12	-1	1.5
1992	Chi-A	5	2	.714	39	0	0	0	1	73	79	9	27	27	13.3	4.93	78	.272	.339	—	—	0	-8	-9	-1	-0.8
1993	Chi-A	2	3	.400	39	0	0	0	1	58¹	62	5	11	29	11.5	3.22	130	.268	.307	—	—	0	7	6	0	0.6
	Phi-N	1	0	1.000	8	0	0	0	0	17²	15	1	3	11	9.2	2.55	156	.231	.265	—	—	0	3	3	-0	0.1
1994	NY-A	1	2	.333	26	0	0	0	0	35	43	3	9	21	13.6	3.60	127	.295	.340	—	—	0	5	4	0	0.4
	Chi-N	0	0	—	2	0	0	0	0	4	8	1	1	2	20.3	4.50	92	.444	.474	—	—	0	-0	-0	-0	0.0
1996	Fla-N	1	1	.500	12	0	0	0	0	18²	16	3	9	12	12.1	5.79	70	.232	.321	0	.000	0	-3	-4	-0	-0.4
Total	8	24	22	.522	303	0	0	0	10	469²	474	46	131	252	12.0	3.53	113	.264	.321	0	.000	0	29	23	-2	2.4

● MIKE PALM
Palm, Richard Paul b: 2/13/25, Boston, Mass. BR/TR, 6'3.5", 190 lbs. Deb: 7/11/48

YEAR	TM/L	W	L	PCT	G	GS	CG	SH	SV	IP	H	HR	BB	SO	RAT	ERA	ERA+	OAV	OOB	BH	AVG	PB	PR	/A	PD	TPI
1948	Bos-A	0	0	—	3	0	0	0	0	3	6	0	5	1	33.0	6.00	73	.400	.550	0	.000	-0	-1	-1	-0	-0.1

● PALMER
Palmer b: St.Louis, Mo. Deb: 5/28/1885

YEAR	TM/L	W	L	PCT	G	GS	CG	SH	SV	IP	H	HR	BB	SO	RAT	ERA	ERA+	OAV	OOB	BH	AVG	PB	PR	/A	PD	TPI
1885	StL-N	0	4	.000	4	4	4	0	0	34	46	2	20	9	17.5	3.44	80	.311	.393	1	.091	-0	-2	-3	-1	-0.4

● DAVID PALMER
Palmer, David William b: 10/19/57, Glens Falls, N.Y. BR/TR, 6'1", 205 lbs. Deb: 9/9/78

YEAR	TM/L	W	L	PCT	G	GS	CG	SH	SV	IP	H	HR	BB	SO	RAT	ERA	ERA+	OAV	OOB	BH	AVG	PB	PR	/A	PD	TPI
1978	Mon-N	0	1	.000	5	1	0	0	0	9²	9	1	2	7	10.2	2.79	126	.243	.282	0	.000	-0	1	1	1	0.1
1979	Mon-N	10	2	.833	36	11	2	1	2	122¹	110	10	30	72	10.4	2.64	139	.237	.286	1	.032	-3	15	14	-0	1.0
1980	Mon-N	8	6	.571	24	19	3	1	0	129²	124	11	30	73	10.8	2.98	119	.255	.301	9	.200	1	9	8	-1	1.1
1982	Mon-N	6	4	.600	13	13	1	0	0	73²	60	3	36	46	12.0	3.18	115	.224	.320	1	.042	-2	3	4	0	0.3
1984	Mon-N	7	3	.700	20	19	1	1	0	105¹	101	5	44	66	12.4	3.84	89	.256	.331	5	.152	1	-3	-5	1	-0.3
1985	Mon-N	7	10	.412	24	23	0	0	0	135²	128	9	67	106	13.1	3.71	91	.250	.341	4	.111	-1	-2	-5	-2	-0.5
1986	Atl-N	11	10	.524	35	35	2	0	0	209²	181	17	102	170	12.4	3.65	109	.234	.327	12	.182	1	2	8	2	1.1
1987	Atl-N	8	11	.421	28	28	0	0	0	152¹	169	17	64	111	14.2	4.90	89	.281	.357	4	.125	-0	-14	-9	1	-1.0
1988	Phi-N	7	9	.438	22	22	1	1	0	129	129	8	48	85	12.3	4.47	80	.261	.327	10	.256	5	-15	-13	-1	-1.1
1989	Det-A	0	3	.000	5	5	0	0	0	17¹	25	1	11	12	18.7	7.79	49	.342	.429	0	—	0	-8	-8	-0	-1.0
Total	10	64	59	.520	212	176	10	4	2	1085	1036	78	434	748	12.4	3.78	99	.252	.327	48	.149	2	-11	-6	5	-0.3

● JIM PALMER
Palmer, James Alvin b: 10/15/45, New York, N.Y. BR/TR, 6'3", 196 lbs. Deb: 4/17/65 H

YEAR	TM/L	W	L	PCT	G	GS	CG	SH	SV	IP	H	HR	BB	SO	RAT	ERA	ERA+	OAV	OOB	BH	AVG	PB	PR	/A	PD	TPI
1965	Bal-A	5	4	.556	27	6	0	0	1	92	75	6	56	75	13.0	3.72	93	.229	.345	5	.192	1	-3	-3	-0	-0.1
1966	*Bal-A	15	10	.600	30	30	6	0	0	208¹	176	21	91	147	11.5	3.46	96	.231	.313	7	.096	-2	-0	-3	-1	-0.6
1967	Bal-A	3	1	.750	9	9	2	1	0	49	34	6	20	23	9.9	2.94	107	.199	.283	1	.077	0	2	1	0	0.1
1969	*Bal-A	16	4	**.800**	26	23	11	6	0	181	131	16	64	123	10.7	2.34	152	.200	.272	13	.203	2	26	25	-4	2.6
1970	*Bal-A★	20	10	.667	39	39	17	**5**	0	305	263	21	100	199	10.7	2.71	134	.231	.294	17	.150	-1	**34**	32	-0	2.8
1971	*Bal-A★	20	9	.690	37	37	20	3	0	282	231	19	106	184	10.9	2.68	125	.221	.295	20	.196	2	24	21	0	2.4
1972	Bal-A★	21	10	.677	36	36	18	3	0	274¹	219	21	70	184	9.5	2.07	149	.217	.269	22	.224	4	30	31	-1	4.2
1973	*Bal-A	22	9	.710	38	37	19	6	1	296¹	225	16	113	158	10.4	**2.40**	156	.211	.289	0	—	0	47	44	-1	4.5
1974	Bal-A	7	12	.368	26	26	5	2	0	178²	176	12	69	84	12.5	3.27	105	.257	.328	0	—	0	4	5	2	0.5
1975	Bal-A☆	**23**	11	.676	39	38	25	**10**	1	323	253	20	80	193	9.3	**2.09**	168	.216	.267	0	—	0	**61**	51	2	**6.1**
1976	Bal-A	**22**	13	.629	40	40	23	6	0	315	255	20	84	159	9.9	2.51	130	.224	.282	0	—	0	35	27	1	3.6
1977	Bal-A★	**20**	11	.645	39	39	**22**	3	0	**319**	263	24	99	193	10.3	2.91	130	.229	.292	0	—	0	41	31	0	3.3
1978	Bal-A★	21	12	.636	38	38	19	6	0	**296**	246	19	97	138	10.5	2.46	142	.227	.291	0	—	0	43	34	1	4.3
1979	Bal-A	10	6	.625	23	22	7	0	0	155²	144	16	43	67	10.8	3.30	122	.246	.297	0	—	0	16	12	-0	1.4
1980	Bal-A	16	10	.615	34	33	4	0	0	224	238	26	74	109	12.7	3.98	99	.275	.334	0	—	0	1	-1	1	0.1
1981	Bal-A	7	8	.467	22	22	0	0	0	127¹	117	14	46	35	11.7	3.75	97	.247	.316	0	—	0	-1	-2	1	-0.1
1982	Bal-A	15	5	**.750**	36	32	8	2	0	227	195	22	63	103	10.4	3.13	129	.231	**.287**	0	—	0	24	23	1	2.0
1983	*Bal-A	5	4	.556	14	11	0	0	0	76²	86	11	19	34	12.3	4.23	94	.281	.323	0	—	0	-4	-4	-0	-0.3
1984	Bal-A	0	3	.000	5	3	0	0	0	17²	22	7	17	4	19.9	9.17	42	.319	.453	0	—	0	-10	-10	-0	-1.3
Total	19	268	152	.638	558	521	211	53	4	3948	3349	303	1311	2212	10.7	2.86	125	.230	.296	85	.174	7	374	315	3	35.5

● LOWELL PALMER
Palmer, Lowell Raymond b: 8/18/47, Sacramento, Cal. BR/TR, 6'1", 190 lbs. Deb: 6/21/69

YEAR	TM/L	W	L	PCT	G	GS	CG	SH	SV	IP	H	HR	BB	SO	RAT	ERA	ERA+	OAV	OOB	BH	AVG	PB	PR	/A	PD	TPI
1969	Phi-N	2	8	.200	26	9	1	1	0	90	91	12	47	68	14.4	5.20	68	.264	.362	3	.136	1	-16	-17	-0	-1.6
1970	Phi-N	1	2	.333	38	5	0	0	0	102	98	15	55	85	13.9	5.47	73	.255	.355	4	.148	1	-16	-17	-1	-0.4
1971	Phi-N	0	0	—	3	1	0	0	0	15	13	3	13	6	18.0	6.00	59	.236	.417	1	.200	-0	-4	-4	-0	-0.2
1972	StL-N	0	3	.000	16	2	0	0	0	34²	30	2	26	25	14.8	3.89	87	.244	.380	0	.000	-1	-2	-2	-0	-0.2
	Cle-A	0	0	—	1	0	0	0	0	2	2	0	3	2	18.0	4.50	71	.222	.364	0	—	0	-0	-0	-0	-0.0
1974	SD-N	2	5	.286	22	8	1	0	0	73	68	9	59	52	16.5	5.67	63	.256	.404	2	.087	-1	-17	-17	-1	-1.6
Total	5	5	18	.217	106	25	2	1	0	316²	302	41	202	239	15.0	5.29	69	.255	.374	10	.122	-0	-55	-57	-1	-3.8

● EMILIO PALMERO
Palmero, Emilio Antonio "Pal" b: 6/13/1895, Guanabacoa, Cuba d: 7/15/70, Toledo, Ohio BL/TL, 5'11", 157 lbs. Deb: 9/21/15

YEAR	TM/L	W	L	PCT	G	GS	CG	SH	SV	IP	H	HR	BB	SO	RAT	ERA	ERA+	OAV	OOB	BH	AVG	PB	PR	/A	PD	TPI
1915	NY-N	0	2	.000	3	2	1	0	0	11²	9	0	8	8	13.9	3.09	83	.233	.400	1	.250	-0	-0	-1	-0	-0.1
1916	NY-N	0	3	.000	4	2	0	0	0	15²	17	1	9	6	14.9	8.04	38	.288	.382	0	.000	-0	-9	-10	1	-1.5
1921	StL-A	4	7	.364	24	6	2	0	0	90	109	1	49	26	16.4	5.00	90	.319	.413	8	.216	1	-7	-5	1	-0.4
1926	Was-A	2	2	.500	7	3	0	0	0	17	22	1	15	6	20.1	4.76	81	.344	.475	1	.333	0	-1	-2	-0	-0.3
1928	Bos-N	0	1	.000	3	1	0	0	0	6²	14	0	2	2	21.6	5.40	72	.452	.485	0	.000	-0	-1	-1	-0	-0.2
Total	5	6	15	.286	41	17	5	0	0	141	172	4	83	48	17.0	5.17	77	.319	.420	10	.208	1	-19	-19	2	-2.5

● ED PALMQUIST
Palmquist, Edwin Lee b: 6/10/33, Los Angeles, Cal. BR/TR, 6'3", 195 lbs. Deb: 6/10/60

YEAR	TM/L	W	L	PCT	G	GS	CG	SH	SV	IP	H	HR	BB	SO	RAT	ERA	ERA+	OAV	OOB	BH	AVG	PB	PR	/A	PD	TPI
1960	LA-N	0	1	.000	22	0	0	0	0	39	34	6	16	23	11.8	2.54	156	.243	.325	0	.000	-1	5	6	0	0.1
1961	LA-N	0	1	.000	5	0	0	0	0	8²	10	0	7	5	19.7	6.23	70	.333	.487	—	—	0	-5	-6	-0	-0.2
	Min-A	1	1	.500	9	2	0	0	0	21	33	7	13	13	21.0	9.43	45	.359	.454	0	—	-0	-13	-12	-0	-1.0
Total	2	1	3	.250	36	2	0	0	0	68²	77	13	36	41	15.6	5.11	80	.294	.391	0	.000	-1	-9	-8	0	-1.1

● JOSE PANIAGUA
Paniagua, Jose Luis (Sanchez) b: 8/20/73, San Jose De Ocoa, D.R. BR/TR, 6'2", 185 lbs. Deb: 4/4/96

YEAR	TM/L	W	L	PCT	G	GS	CG	SH	SV	IP	H	HR	BB	SO	RAT	ERA	ERA+	OAV	OOB	BH	AVG	PB	PR	/A	PD	TPI
1996	Mon-N	2	4	.333	13	11	0	0	0	51	55	7	23	27	14.3	3.53	122	.282	.367	0	.000	-1	4	4	0	0.4

● JIM PANTHER
Panther, James Edward b: 3/1/45, Burlington, Iowa BR/TR, 6'1", 190 lbs. Deb: 4/5/71

YEAR	TM/L	W	L	PCT	G	GS	CG	SH	SV	IP	H	HR	BB	SO	RAT	ERA	ERA+	OAV	OOB	BH	AVG	PB	PR	/A	PD	TPI
1971	Oak-A	0	1	.000	3	0	0	0	0	5²	10	1	5	4	23.8	11.12	30	.385	.484	0	.000	-0	-5	-5	-0	-0.8
1972	Tex-A	5	9	.357	58	4	0	0	0	93²	101	8	46	44	14.6	4.13	73	.277	.365	1	.125	0	-11	-12	0	-1.7

YEAR	TM/L	W	L	PCT	G	GS	CG	SH	SV	IP	H	HR	BB	SO	RAT	ERA	ERA+	OAV	OOB	BH	AVG	PB	PR	/A	PD	TPI
1973	Atl-N	2	3	.400	23	0	0	0	0	30²	45	3	9	8	15.8	7.63	52	.363	.406	0	—	0	-14	-13	-1	-1.9
Total	3	7	13	.350	85	4	0	0	0	130	156	12	60	56	15.3	5.26	61	.303	.381	1	.111	-0	-30	-29	-1	-4.4

● JOHN PAPA
Papa, John Paul   b: 12/5/40, Bridgeport, Conn.   BR/TR, 5'11", 190 lbs.   Deb: 4/11/61

YEAR	TM/L	W	L	PCT	G	GS	CG	SH	SV	IP	H	HR	BB	SO	RAT	ERA	ERA+	OAV	OOB	BH	AVG	PB	PR	/A	PD	TPI
1961	Bal-A	0	0	—	2	0	0	0	0	1	2	1	3	3	45.0	18.00	21	.400	.625	0	—	0	-2	-2	-0	0.0
1962	Bal-A	0	0	—	1	0	0	0	0	1	3	0	1	0	36.0	27.00	14	.600	.667	0	—	0	-3	-3	-0	0.0
Total	2	0	0	—	3	0	0	0	0	2	5	1	4	3	40.5	22.50	17	.500	.643	0	—	0	-4	-4	-0	0.0

● AL PAPAI
Papai, Alfred Thomas   b: 5/7/17, Divernon, Ill.   d: 9/7/95, Springfield, Ill.   BR/TR, 6'3", 185 lbs.   Deb: 4/24/48

YEAR	TM/L	W	L	PCT	G	GS	CG	SH	SV	IP	H	HR	BB	SO	RAT	ERA	ERA+	OAV	OOB	BH	AVG	PB	PR	/A	PD	TPI
1948	StL-N	0	1	.000	10	0	0	0	0	16	14	3	7	8	11.8	5.06	81	.241	.323	0	.000	-0	-2	-2	0	-0.1
1949	StL-A	4	11	.267	42	15	6	0	2	142¹	175	8	81	31	16.3	5.06	90	.298	.384	3	.079	-2	-14	-8	3	-0.7
1950	Bos-A	4	2	.667	16	3	2	0	2	50²	61	5	28	19	15.8	6.75	73	.293	.377	3	.176	-0	-12	-10	-1	-1.1
	StL-N	1	0	1.000	13	0	0	0	0	19	21	0	14	7	16.6	5.21	82	.300	.417	0	.000	-0	-2	-2	0	-0.1
1955	Chi-A	0	0	—	7	0	0	0	0	11²	10	1	8	5	13.9	3.86	102	.244	.367	0	.000	-0	0	0	1	0.1
Total	4	9	14	.391	88	18	8	0	4	239²	281	17	138	70	15.8	5.37	84	.291	.381	6	.097	-3	-30	-22	4	-1.9

● LARRY PAPE
Pape, Laurence Albert   b: 7/21/1883, Norwood, Ohio   d: 7/21/18, Swissvale, Pa.   BR/TR, 5'11", 175 lbs.   Deb: 7/6/09

YEAR	TM/L	W	L	PCT	G	GS	CG	SH	SV	IP	H	HR	BB	SO	RAT	ERA	ERA+	OAV	OOB	BH	AVG	PB	PR	/A	PD	TPI
1909	Bos-A	2	0	1.000	11	3	2	1	2	58¹	46	0	12	18	9.7	2.01	125	.218	.276	3	.143	-1	3	3	-3	-0.2
1911	Bos-A	10	8	.556	27	19	10	1	0	176¹	167	3	63	49	11.9	2.45	134	.264	.335	13	.203	-1	18	16	5	1.8
1912	Bos-A	1	1	.500	13	2	1	0	1	48²	74	0	16	17	17.0	4.99	68	.366	.418	4	.235	1	-9	-9	-0	-0.3
Total	3	13	9	.591	51	24	13	2	3	283¹	287	3	91	84	12.4	2.80	112	.275	.339	20	.196	-1	12	11	2	1.3

● FRANK PAPISH
Papish, Frank Richard "Pap"   b: 10/21/17, Pueblo, Colo.   d: 8/30/65, Pueblo, Colo.   BR/TL, 6'2", 192 lbs.   Deb: 5/8/45

YEAR	TM/L	W	L	PCT	G	GS	CG	SH	SV	IP	H	HR	BB	SO	RAT	ERA	ERA+	OAV	OOB	BH	AVG	PB	PR	/A	PD	TPI
1945	Chi-A	4	4	.500	19	5	3	0	1	84¹	75	3	40	45	12.3	3.74	89	.241	.328	6	.231	1	-3	-4	1	-0.1
1946	Chi-A	7	5	.583	31	15	6	2	0	138	122	7	63	66	12.1	2.74	125	.243	.328	8	.186	-0	12	10	0	0.9
1947	Chi-A	12	12	.500	38	26	6	1	3	199	185	6	98	79	12.9	3.26	112	.245	.333	5	.086	-5	10	9	-1	0.4
1948	Chi-A	2	8	.200	32	14	2	0	4	95¹	97	7	75	41	16.5	5.00	85	.265	.394	1	.185	-1	-8	-8	-1	-0.9
1949	Cle-A	1	0	1.000	25	3	1	0	1	62	54	2	39	23	13.5	3.19	125	.240	.352	1	.125	1	7	5	0	0.1
1950	Pit-N	0	0	—	4	1	0	0	0	2¹	8	1	4	1	46.3	27.00	16	.533	.632	0	—	0	-6	-6	0	0.0
Total	6	26	29	.473	149	64	18	3	9	581	541	26	319	255	13.4	3.58	103	.249	.346	25	.154	-5	12	7	0	0.4

● JOHN PAPPALAU
Pappalau, John Joseph   b: 4/3/1875, Albany, N.Y.   d: 5/12/44, Albany, N.Y.   BR/TR, 6', 175 lbs.   Deb: 6/9/1897

YEAR	TM/L	W	L	PCT	G	GS	CG	SH	SV	IP	H	HR	BB	SO	RAT	ERA	ERA+	OAV	OOB	BH	AVG	PB	PR	/A	PD	TPI
1897	Cle-N	0	1	.000	2	1	1	0	0	12	22	0	3	3	22.5	10.50	43	.393	.469	0	.000	-0	-8	-8	0	-0.5

● MILT PAPPAS
Pappas, Milton Stephen "Gimpy" (b: Miltiades Stergios Papastegios)   b: 5/11/39, Detroit, Mich.   BR/TR, 6'3", 190 lbs.   Deb: 8/10/57

YEAR	TM/L	W	L	PCT	G	GS	CG	SH	SV	IP	H	HR	BB	SO	RAT	ERA	ERA+	OAV	OOB	BH	AVG	PB	PR	/A	PD	TPI
1957	Bal-A	0	0	—	4	0	0	0	0	9	6	3	3	9	9.0	1.00	359	.200	.273	0	—	-0	3	3	0	0.0
1958	Bal-A	10	10	.500	31	21	3	0	0	135¹	135	8	48	72	12.3	4.06	89	.262	.327	6	.143	-0	-4	-7	1	-0.8
1959	Bal-A	15	9	.625	33	27	15	4	3	209¹	175	8	75	120	10.9	3.27	116	.226	.298	11	.139	-3	14	12	-1	0.9
1960	Bal-A	15	11	.577	30	27	11	3	0	205²	184	15	83	126	11.9	3.37	113	.243	.323	3	.043	-5	12	10	1	0.7
1961	Bal-A	13	9	.591	26	23	11	4	1	177²	134	16	78	89	11.1	3.04	127	.208	.301	9	.136	1	19	16	2	2.2
1962	Bal-A★	12	10	.545	35	32	9	1	0	205	200	31	75	130	12.1	4.03	92	.257	.324	6	.087	-0	-1	-8	2	-0.6
1963	Bal-A	16	9	.640	34	32	11	4	0	216²	186	21	69	120	10.8	3.03	115	.233	.298	9	.127	-0	14	11	3	1.4
1964	Bal-A	16	7	.696	37	36	13	7	0	251²	225	21	48	157	10.0	2.97	120	.239	.281	12	.129	-2	18	17	-1	1.2
1965	Bal-A★	13	9	.591	34	34	9	3	0	221¹	192	22	52	127	10.0	2.60	133	.233	.281	5	.071	-3	21	21	-3	1.3
1966	Cin-N	12	11	.522	33	32	6	2	0	209²	224	23	39	133	11.4	4.29	91	.275	.310	8	.107	-2	-16	-9	-0	-1.1
1967	Cin-N	16	13	.552	34	32	5	3	0	217²	218	19	38	129	10.8	3.35	112	.259	.295	7	.097	-2	1	10	0	1.0
1968	Cin-N	2	5	.286	15	11	0	0	0	62²	70	9	10	43	11.8	5.60	56	.275	.307	1	.063	-0	-18	-17	-0	-1.9
	Atl-N	10	8	.556	22	19	3	1	0	121¹	111	8	22	75	10.1	2.37	126	.246	.285	6	.162	2	8	8	-1	1.5
	Yr	12	13	.480	37	30	3	1	0	184	181	17	32	118	10.6	3.47	88	.255	.290	7	.132	1	-10	-9	-1	-0.4
1969	*Atl-N	6	10	.375	26	24	1	0	0	144	149	14	44	72	12.3	3.63	99	.267	.325	7	.156	3	-0	-0	-0	0.2
1970	Atl-N	2	2	.500	11	3	1	0	0	35²	44	6	7	25	13.4	6.06	71	.293	.333	0	.000	-1	-8	-7	0	-0.8
	Chi-N	10	8	.556	21	20	6	2	0	144²	135	14	36	80	10.6	2.68	168	.248	.294	12	.240	4	22	29	-1	4.0
	Yr	12	10	.545	32	23	7	2	0	180¹	179	20	43	105	11.1	3.34	133	.256	.300	12	.200	3	14	22	-1	3.2
1971	Chi-N	17	14	.548	35	35	14	**5**	0	261¹	279	25	62	99	11.9	3.51	112	.274	.319	14	.154	-1	-1	12	-2	1.1
1972	Chi-N	17	7	.708	29	28	10	3	0	195	187	18	29	80	10.3	2.77	138	.251	.287	13	.191	1	15	23	0	3.1
1973	Chi-N	7	12	.368	30	29	1	1	0	162	192	20	40	48	13.1	4.28	92	.299	.344	3	.063	-3	-11	-6	-1	-1.0
Total	17	209	164	.560	520	465	129	43	4	3186	3046	298	858	1728	11.2	3.40	110	.252	.306	132	.123	-14	86	120	0	12.4

● CHAN HO PARK
Park, Chan Ho   b: 6/30/73, Kongju, South Korea   BR/TR, 6'2", 185 lbs.   Deb: 4/8/94

YEAR	TM/L	W	L	PCT	G	GS	CG	SH	SV	IP	H	HR	BB	SO	RAT	ERA	ERA+	OAV	OOB	BH	AVG	PB	PR	/A	PD	TPI
1994	LA-N	0	0	—	2	0	0	0	0	4	5	1	5	6	24.8	11.25	35	.294	.478	0	—	0	-3	-3	-0	0.0
1995	LA-N	0	0	—	2	1	0	0	0	4	2	1	2	7	9.0	4.50	84	.143	.250	0	.000	-0	-0	-0	-0	0.0
1996	LA-N	5	5	.500	48	10	0	0	0	108²	82	7	71	119	13.0	3.64	106	.209	.335	1	.053	-1	7	2	2	0.3
Total	3	5	5	.500	52	11	0	0	0	116²	89	9	78	132	13.3	3.93	98	.210	.339	1	.050	-1	4	-1	2	0.3

● JIM PARK
Park, James   b: 11/10/1892, Richmond, Ky.   d: 12/17/70, Lexington, Ky.   BR/TR, 6'2", 175 lbs.   Deb: 9/7/15

YEAR	TM/L	W	L	PCT	G	GS	CG	SH	SV	IP	H	HR	BB	SO	RAT	ERA	ERA+	OAV	OOB	BH	AVG	PB	PR	/A	PD	TPI
1915	StL-A	2	0	1.000	3	3	1	0	0	22²	18	1	9	5	10.7	1.19	240	.214	.290	4	.400	1	4	4	-1	0.5
1916	StL-A	1	4	.200	26	6	1	0	0	79	69	2	25	26	10.8	2.62	105	.244	.307	2	.100	-2	2	1	-2	-0.3
1917	StL-A	1	1	.500	13	0	0	0	0	20¹	27	1	12	9	17.3	6.64	39	.333	.419	0	.000	-0	-9	-9	-0	-0.7
Total	3	4	5	.444	42	9	2	0	0	122	114	4	46	40	11.9	3.02	91	.254	.325	6	.188	-0	-3	-4	-2	-0.7

● DOC PARKER
Parker, Harley Park   b: 6/14/1872, Theresa, N.Y.   d: 3/3/41, Chicago, Ill.   BR/TR, 6'2", 200 lbs.   Deb: 7/11/1893   F

YEAR	TM/L	W	L	PCT	G	GS	CG	SH	SV	IP	H	HR	BB	SO	RAT	ERA	ERA+	OAV	OOB	BH	AVG	PB	PR	/A	PD	TPI
1893	Chi-N	0	0	—	1	0	0	1	0	2	5	0	1	0	27.0	13.50	34	.455	.500	0	.000	-0	-2	-2	-0	-0.2
1895	Chi-N	4	2	.667	7	6	5	1	0	51¹	65	1	9	9	13.5	3.68	138	.304	.341	7	.318	1	6	8	0	0.8
1896	Chi-N	1	5	.167	9	7	7	0	0	73	100	3	27	15	16.0	6.16	74	.323	.382	10	.278	-0	-15	-13	1	-0.7
1901	Cin-N	0	1	.000	1	1	1	0	0	8	26	1	2	0	31.5	15.75	20	.531	.549	0	.000	-0	-11	-11	-0	-0.8
Total	4	5	8	.385	18	14	13	1	1	134¹	196	5	39	24	16.1	5.90	79	.336	.383	17	.274	-0	-21	-18	1	-0.9

● HARRY PARKER
Parker, Harry William   b: 9/14/47, Highland, Ill.   BR/TR, 6'3", 190 lbs.   Deb: 8/8/70

YEAR	TM/L	W	L	PCT	G	GS	CG	SH	SV	IP	H	HR	BB	SO	RAT	ERA	ERA+	OAV	OOB	BH	AVG	PB	PR	/A	PD	TPI
1970	StL-N	1	1	.500	7	4	0	0	0	22¹	24	0	15	9	15.7	3.22	128	.276	.382	2	.250	0	2	2	0	0.2
1971	StL-N	0	0	—	4	0	0	0	0	5	5	0	4	2	14.4	7.20	50	.286	.348	0	—	0	-2	-2	-0	0.0
1973	*NY-N	8	4	.667	38	9	0	0	5	96²	79	7	36	63	11.0	3.35	108	.217	.293	4	.174	-0	3	3	-0	0.3
1974	NY-N	4	12	.250	40	16	1	0	4	131	145	10	46	58	13.3	3.92	91	.281	.343	0	.000	-4	-4	-5	-2	-1.2
1975	NY-N	2	3	.400	18	1	0	0	0	34²	37	2	19	22	14.5	4.41	78	.272	.361	0	.000	1	-3	-4	-0	-0.5
	StL-N	0	1	.000	14	0	0	0	1	18²	21	3	10	7	14.9	6.27	60	.288	.373	0	.000	1	-5	-5	1	-0.2
	Yr	2	4	.333	32	1	0	0	1	53¹	58	5	29	29	14.7	5.06	70	.278	.366	0	.000	1	-9	-9	-0	-0.7
1976	Cle-A	0	0	—	3	0	0	0	0	7	3	0	5	0	3.9	—		.136	.136	0	—	0	3	3	0	0.0
Total	6	15	21	.417	124	30	1	0	12	315¹	315	24	128	172	12.8	3.85	94	.258	.332	6	.086	-3	-7	-8	-1	-1.4

● CLAY PARKER
Parker, James Clayton   b: 12/19/62, Columbia, La.   BR/TR, 6'1", 185 lbs.   Deb: 9/14/87

YEAR	TM/L	W	L	PCT	G	GS	CG	SH	SV	IP	H	HR	BB	SO	RAT	ERA	ERA+	OAV	OOB	BH	AVG	PB	PR	/A	PD	TPI
1987	Sea-A	0	0	—	3	1	0	0	0	7²	12	1	2	4	23.5	10.57	45	.405	.476	0	—	0	-5	-5	-0	-0.3
1989	NY-A	4	5	.444	22	17	2	0	0	120	123	12	31	53	11.7	3.68	105	.264	.313	0	.000	0	3	3	0	0.3
1990	NY-A	1	1	.500	5	2	0	0	0	22	19	5	7	20	10.6	4.50	88	.229	.289	0	—	0	-1	-1	-0	-0.2
	Det-A	2	2	.500	24	1	0	0	0	51	45	6	25	20	12.5	3.18	125	.242	.335	0	—	0	4	4	0	0.3
	Yr	3	3	.500	29	3	0	0	0	73	64	11	32	40	12.0	3.58	111	.237	.320	0	—	0	3	3	0	0.1
1992	Sea-A	0	2	.000	8	6	0	0	0	33¹	47	6	11	20	16.2	7.56	53	.338	.395	0	—	0	-13	-13	-0	-0.7
Total	4	7	10	.412	62	27	2	0	0	234	249	31	78	121	12.8	4.42	89	.273	.335	0	—	0	-13	-13	-0	-0.6

● JAY PARKER
Parker, Jay   b: 7/8/1874, Theresa, N.Y.   d: 6/8/35, Hartford, Mich.   BR/TR, 5'11", 185 lbs.   Deb: 9/27/1899   F

YEAR	TM/L	W	L	PCT	G	GS	CG	SH	SV	IP	H	HR	BB	SO	RAT	ERA	ERA+	OAV	OOB	BH	AVG	PB	PR	/A	PD	TPI
1899	Pit-N	0	0	—	1	0	0	0	0	1	1	0	2	1	∞	—			1.000	0	—	0	-2	-2	0	-0.2

● ROY PARKER
Parker, Roy William   b: 2/29/1896, Union, Mo.   d: 5/17/54, Tulsa, Okla.   BR/TR, 6'3", 200 lbs.   Deb: 9/10/19

YEAR	TM/L	W	L	PCT	G	GS	CG	SH	SV	IP	H	HR	BB	SO	RAT	ERA	ERA+	OAV	OOB	BH	AVG	PB	PR	/A	PD	TPI
1919	StL-N	0	0	—	2	0	0	0	0	2	6	0	1	0	36.0	31.50	9	.333	.400	0	—	0	-6	-6	0	0.0

YEAR	TM/L	W	L	PCT	G	GS	CG	SH	SV	IP	H	HR	BB	SO	RAT	ERA	ERA+	OAV	OOB	BH	AVG	PB	PR	/A	PD	TPI

● **SLICKER PARKS** Parks, Vernon Henry b: 11/10/1895, Dallas Twsp., Mich. d: 2/21/78, Royal Oak, Mich. BR/TR, 5'10", 158 lbs. Deb: 7/11/21

| 1921 | Det-A | 3 | 2 | .600 | 10 | 1 | 0 | 0 | 0 | 25¹ | 33 | 2 | 16 | 10 | 17.8 | 5.68 | 75 | .306 | .400 | 1 | .111 | -1 | -4 | -4 | -1 | -0.8 |

● **BILL PARKS** Parks, William Robert b: 6/4/1849, Easton, Pa. d: 10/10/11, Easton, Pa. BR/TR, 5'8", 150 lbs. Deb: 4/26/1875 M♦

1875	Was-n	4	8	.333	14	11	9	0	0	106²	144	3	5	3	12.6	3.29	72	.280	.287	20	.180	-3	-13	-11		-1.1
	Phi-n	0	0	—	2	0	0	0	0	5¹	13	0	1	0	23.6	8.44	27	.419	.438	1	.167	-0	-4	-4		0.0
	Yr	4	8	.333	16	11	9	0	0	112	157	3	6	3	13.1	3.54	67	.288	.295	21	.179	-3	-16	-15		-1.1

● **ROY PARMELEE** Parmelee, Le Roy Earl "Tarzan" b: 4/25/07, Lambertville, Mich. d: 8/31/81, Monroe, Mich. BR/TR, 6'1", 190 lbs. Deb: 9/28/29

1929	NY-N	1	0	1.000	2	1	0	0	0	7	13	1	3	1	21.9	9.00	51	.481	.548	1	.500		-3	-3	0	-0.3
1930	NY-N	0	1	.000	11	1	0	0	0	21	18	3	26	19	18.9	9.43	50	.228	.419	1	.250	1	-10	-11	0	-0.4
1931	NY-N	2	2	.500	13	5	4	0	0	58²	47	1	33	30	12.7	3.68	100	.223	.336	4	.200	-0	1	0	0	0.0
1932	NY-N	0	3	.000	8	3	0	0	0	25¹	25	0	14	23	14.6	3.91	95	.250	.353	2	.400	-0	-1	0	0	0.1
1933	NY-N	13	8	.619	32	32	14	3	0	218¹	191	9	77	132	11.6	3.17	101	.232	.309	19	.235	4	4	1	0	0.5
1934	NY-N	10	6	.625	22	20	7	2	0	152²	134	6	60	83	11.8	3.42	113	**.238**	.318	11	.200	2	11	8	2	1.1
1935	NY-N	14	10	.583	34	31	13	0	0	226	214	20	97	79	12.7	4.22	91	.249	.332	18	.209	3	-5	-9	2	-0.4
1936	StL-N	11	11	.500	37	28	9	0	0	221	226	13	107	79	14.0	4.56	86	.270	.360	15	.197	-0	-13	-15	-1	-1.4
1937	Chi-N	7	8	.467	33	18	8	0	0	145²	165	13	79	55	15.5	5.13	78	.286	.379	9	.173	0	-20	-19	1	-1.6
1939	Phi-A	1	6	.143	14	5	0	0	1	44²	42	2	35	13	16.1	6.45	73	.235	.369	2	.133	-1	-9	-9	0	-1.2
Total	10	59	55	.518	206	144	55	5	3	1120¹	1075	68	531	514	13.3	4.27	89	.253	.343	82	.207	9	-45	-58	5	-3.6

● **MEL PARNELL** Parnell, Melvin Lloyd "Dusty" b: 6/13/22, New Orleans, La. BL/TL, 6', 180 lbs. Deb: 4/20/47

1947	Bos-A	2	3	.400	15	5	1	0	0	50²	60	1	27	23	15.6	6.39	61	.296	.381	1	.056	-2	-15	-14	-1	-1.5
1948	Bos-A	15	8	.652	35	27	16	1	0	212	205	7	90	77	12.7	3.14	140	.252	.330	13	.162	-4	27	29	2	2.7
1949	Bos-A★	**25**	7	.781	39	33	**27**	4	2	295¹	258	8	134	122	12.1	2.77	157	.237	.324	29	.254	-2	**47**	**52**	-0	5.5
1950	Bos-A	18	10	.643	40	31	21	2	3	249	244	17	106	93	12.9	3.61	136	.259	.338	19	.194	-1	27	36	5	3.9
1951	Bos-A★	18	11	.621	36	29	11	3	2	221	229	11	77	77	12.5	3.26	137	.272	.333	25	.309	4	21	30	-0	**4.1**
1952	Bos-A	12	12	.500	33	29	15	3	2	214	207	13	89	107	12.7	3.62	109	.255	.332	8	.095	-1	1	8	1	0.6
1953	Bos-A	21	8	.724	38	34	12	5	2	241	217	15	116	136	12.6	3.06	137	.239	.328	21	.223	1	25	31	-2	3.4
1954	Bos-A	3	7	.300	19	15	4	1	0	92¹	104	7	35	38	13.6	3.70	111	.287	.352	3	.088	-2	0	4	0	0.2
1955	Bos-A	2	3	.400	13	9	0	1	0	46	62	12	25	18	17.2	7.83	55	.318	.398	6	.316	1	-20	-18	0	-1.6
1956	Bos-A	7	6	.538	21	20	6	1	0	131¹	129	13	59	41	12.9	3.77	123	.256	.335	7	.152	-2	6	12	-1	0.8
Total	10	123	75	.621	289	232	113	20	10	1752²	1715	104	758	732	12.8	3.50	125	.257	.336	132	.198	-7	119	170	3	18.1

● **RUBE PARNHAM** Parnham, James Arthur b: 2/1/1894, Heidelberg, Pa. d: 11/25/63, McKeesport, Pa. BR/TR, 6'3", 185 lbs. Deb: 9/20/16

1916	Phi-A	2	1	.667	4	3	2	0	0	24²	27	0	13	8	14.6	4.01	74	.300	.388	3	.273	-1	-3	-3	1	-0.2
1917	Phi-A	0	1	.000	2	2	0	0	0	11	12	1	9	4	17.2	4.09	67	.316	.447	0	.000	-0	-2	-2	0	-0.2
Total	2	2	2	.500	6	5	2	0	0	35²	39	1	22	12	15.4	4.04	70	.305	.407	3	.214	0	-5	-5	1	-0.4

● **JOSE PARRA** Parra, Jose Miguel b: 11/28/72, Jacaqua, D.R. BR/TR, 5'11", 160 lbs. Deb: 5/7/95

1995	LA-N	0	0	—	8	0	0	0	0	10¹	10	2	6	4	14.8	4.35	87	.256	.370	0	—	0	-0	-1	-0	0.0
	Min-A	1	5	.167	12	12	0	0	0	61²	83	11	22	29	15.6	7.59	63	.313	.370	0	—	0	-20	-19	-0	-1.5
1996	Min-A	5	5	.500	27	5	0	0	0	70	88	15	27	50	15.2	6.04	85	.308	.373	0	—	0	-8	-7	0	-0.8
Total	2	6	10	.375	47	17	0	0	0	142	181	28	55	86	15.3	6.59	74	.307	.372	0	—	0	-28	-27	-1	-2.3

● **JEFF PARRETT** Parrett, Jeffrey Dale b: 8/26/61, Indianapolis, Ind. BR/TR, 6'3", 200 lbs. Deb: 4/11/86

1986	Mon-N	0	1	.000	12	0	0	0	0	20¹	19	3	13	21	14.2	4.87	76	.247	.356	1	.500		-3	-3	0	-0.1
1987	Mon-N	7	6	.538	45	0	0	0	0	62	53	8	30	56	12.0	4.21	100	.229	.318	0	.000	-1	-1	-0	0	-0.1
1988	Mon-N	12	4	.750	61	0	0	0	6	91²	66	8	45	62	11.0	2.65	136	.214	.316	0	—	0	8	10	-1	1.7
1989	Phi-N	12	6	.667	72	0	0	0	6	105²	90	6	44	98	11.4	2.98	119	.232	.310	0	—	0	6	7	-1	1.0
1990	Phi-N	4	9	.308	47	5	0	0	1	81²	92	10	36	69	14.2	5.18	74	.293	.368	0	.000	-1	-13	-12	0	-1.9
	Atl-N	1	1	.500	20	0	0	0	1	27	27	1	19	17	15.7	3.00	134	.281	.405	1	1.000	0	2	3	0	0.3
	Yr	5	10	.333	67	5	0	0	2	108²	119	11	55	86	14.5	4.64	89	.289	.374	1	.091	-1	-10	-9	0	-1.6
1991	Atl-N	2	3	.333	18	0	0	0	0	21¹	31	2	12	14	18.1	6.33	61	.326	.402	0	—	0	-6	-6	1	-0.7
1992	*Oak-A	9	1	.900	66	0	0	0	0	98¹	81	7	42	78	11.4	3.02	124	.226	.311	0	—	0	10	8	-1	0.7
1993	Col-N	3	3	.500	40	6	0	0	1	73²	78	6	45	66	15.3	5.38	89	.274	.377	1	.091	-1	-11	-5	-0	-0.5
1995	StL-N	4	7	.364	59	0	0	0	0	76²	71	8	28	71	11.7	3.64	115	.243	.312	1	.500	1	5	5	-1	0.6
1996	StL-N	2	2	.500	33	0	0	0	1	42¹	40	7	20	42	13.0	4.25	100	.245	.332	0	.000	-1	-0	-1	-1	0.1
	Phi-N	1	1	.500	18	0	0	0	0	24	24	1	11	22	13.1	1.88	233	.270	.350	0	—	0	6	7	0	0.6
	Yr	3	3	.500	51	0	0	0	1	66¹	64	8	31	64	12.9	3.39	126	.252	.333	0	.000	-1	6	7	0	0.6
Total	10	56	43	.566	491	11	0	0	22	724²	672	61	345	616	12.7	3.80	104	.249	.336	4	.105	-1	4	13	-3	1.6

● **STEVE PARRIS** Parris, Steven Michael b: 12/17/67, Joliet, Ill. BR/TR, 6', 190 lbs. Deb: 6/21/95

1995	Pit-N	6	6	.500	15	15	1	1	0	82	89	14	33	61	14.2	5.38	80	.283	.363	7	.250	1	-11	-10	-0	-1.1
1996	Pit-N	0	3	.000	8	4	0	0	0	26¹	35	4	11	27	16.1	7.18	61	.321	.388	1	.167	0	-9	-8	-0	-0.7
Total	2	6	9	.400	23	19	1	1	0	108¹	124	16	44	88	14.6	5.82	74	.292	.370	8	.235	2	-20	-18	-0	-1.8

● **MIKE PARROTT** Parrott, Michael Everett Arch b: 12/6/54, Oxnard, Cal. BR/TR, 6'4", 210 lbs. Deb: 9/5/77

1977	Bal-A	0	0	—	3	0	0	0	0	4¹	4	0	2	2	12.5	2.08	183	.250	.333	0	—	0	1	1	-0	0.0
1978	Sea-A	1	5	.167	27	10	0	0	1	82¹	108	8	32	41	15.6	5.14	74	.316	.379	0	—	0	-13	-12	0	-0.8
1979	Sea-A	14	12	.538	38	30	13	2	0	229¹	231	17	86	127	12.7	3.77	116	.267	.338	0	—	0	11	15	3	1.7
1980	Sea-A	1	16	.059	27	16	1	0	0	94	136	16	42	53	17.1	7.28	57	.348	.412	0	—	0	-34	-33	4	-4.8
1981	Sea-A	3	6	.333	24	12	0	0	1	85	102	3	28	43	13.9	5.08	76	.299	.354	0	—	0	-13	-12	0	-1.3
Total	5	19	39	.328	119	68	14	2	5	495	581	44	190	266	14.2	4.87	85	.297	.363	0	—	0	-48	-41	6	-5.2

● **TOM PARROTT** Parrott, Thomas William "Tacky Tom" b: 4/10/1868, Portland, Ore. d: 1/1/32, Dundee, Ore. BR/TR, 5'10.5", 170 lbs. Deb: 6/18/1893 F♦

1893	Chi-N	0	3	.000	4	3	2	0	0	27	35	1	17	7	17.3	6.67	69	.304	.394	7	.259	-0	-6	-6	-1	-0.5
	Cin-N	10	7	.588	22	17	11	1	0	154	174	3	70	33	14.8	4.09	117	.276	.357	13	.191	-3	10	12	2	0.9
	Yr	10	10	.500	26	20	13	1	0	181	209	4	87	40	15.2	4.48	106	.281	.363	20	.211	-3	4	6	1	0.4
1894	Cin-N	17	19	.472	41	36	31	1	1	308²	402	19	126	61	15.7	5.60	99	.311	.377	74	.323	8	-9	-1	3	0.7
1895	Cin-N	11	18	.379	41	31	23	0	**3**	263¹	382	8	76	57	15.6	5.47	91	.334	.378	69	.343	10	-20	-14	3	-0.2
1896	StL-N	1	1	.500	7	2	2	0	0	42	62	4	18	8	17.8	6.21	77	.339	.407	138	.291	1	-9	-9	-0	-0.3
Total	4	39	48	.448	115	89	69	2	4	795	1055	33	307	166	15.7	5.33	96	.314	.376	301	.301	16	-34	-19	6	0.6

● **JIGGS PARSON** Parson, William Edwin b: 12/28/1885, Parker, S.Dak. d: 5/19/67, Los Angeles, Cal. BR/TR, 6'2", 180 lbs. Deb: 5/16/10

1910	Bos-N	0	2	.000	10	4	0	0	0	35¹	35	2	26	7	16.0	3.82	87	.278	.409	1	.083	-1	-3	-2	-0	-0.2
1911	Bos-N	0	1	.000	7	0	0	0	0	25	36	2	15	7	19.8	6.48	59	.375	.478	2	.200	-0	-9	-7	-1	-0.3
Total	2	0	3	.000	17	4	0	0	0	60¹	71	4	41	14	17.6	4.92	72	.320	.439	3	.136	-2	-12	-9	-1	-0.5

● **CHARLIE PARSONS** Parsons, Charles James b: 7/18/1863, Cherry Flats, Pa. d: 3/24/36, Mansfield, Pa. BL/TL, 5'10", 160 lbs. Deb: 5/29/1886

1886	Bos-N	0	2	.000	2	2	2	0	0	16	20	1	4	6	13.5	3.94	81	.308	.348	3	.375	-1	-1	-1	-1	-0.1
1887	NY-a	1	1	.500	4	4	4	0	0	34	51	0	6	5	15.4	4.50	94	.319	.347	3	.200	-1	-1	-1	-1	-0.1
1890	Cle-N	0	1	.000	2	1	0	0	0	9	12	1	6	2	22.0	6.00	60	.308	.449	3	.750	1	-2	-2	-0	-0.1
Total	3	1	4	.200	8	7	6	0	0	59	83	2	16	13	15.9	4.58	84	.314	.365	9	.333	-1	-4	-5	-1	-0.3

● **TOM PARSONS** Parsons, Thomas Anthony b: 9/13/39, Lakeville, Conn. BR/TR, 6'7", 210 lbs. Deb: 9/5/63

1963	Pit-N	0	1	.000	1	1	0	0	0	4¹	7	1	2	2	18.7	8.31	40	.368	.429	0	.000	-0	-2	-2	0	-0.4
1964	NY-N	1	2	.333	4	2	1	0	0	19¹	20	1	6	10	12.1	4.19	85	.274	.329	0	.000	-0	-2	-2	0	-0.3
1965	NY-N	1	10	.091	35	11	1	1	1	90²	108	17	17	58	12.4	4.67	76	.290	.321	1	.056	-2	-11	-11	1	-1.3
Total	3	2	13	.133	40	14	2	1	1	114¹	135	19	25	70	12.6	4.72	75	.291	.327	1	.037	-2	-15	-15	1	-2.0

YEAR	TM/L	W	L	PCT	G	GS	CG	SH	SV	IP	H	HR	BB	SO	RAT	ERA	ERA+	OAV	OOB	BH	AVG	PB	PR	/A	PD	TPI

● **BILL PARSONS** Parsons, William Raymond b: 8/17/48, Riverside, Cal. BR/TR, 6'6", 195 lbs. Deb: 4/13/71

YEAR	TM/L	W	L	PCT	G	GS	CG	SH	SV	IP	H	HR	BB	SO	RAT	ERA	ERA+	OAV	OOB	BH	AVG	PB	PR	/A	PD	TPI
1971	Mil-A	13	17	.433	36	35	12	4	0	244²	219	19	93	139	11.6	3.20	108	.241	.315	12	.167	3	7	7	0	1.3
1972	Mil-A	13	13	.500	33	30	10	2	0	214	194	27	68	111	11.1	3.91	77	.240	.301	11	.164	0	-20	-21	-3	-2.7
1973	Mil-A	3	6	.333	20	17	0	0	0	59²	59	6	67	30	19.0	6.79	55	.257	.424	0	—	0	-20	-20	-0	-2.6
1974	Oak-A	0	0	—	4	0	0	0	0	2	1	0	3	2	18.0	0.00		.143	.400	0	—	0	1	1	-0	0.0
Total	4	29	36	.446	93	82	22	6	0	520¹	473	52	231	282	12.3	3.89	85	.242	.325	23	.165	3	-32	-33	-3	-4.0

● **STAN PARTENHEIMER** Partenheimer, Stanwood Wendell "Party"
b: 10/21/22, Chicopee Falls, Mass. d: 1/28/89, Wilson, N.C. BR/TL, 5'11", 175 lbs. Deb: 5/27/44 F

YEAR	TM/L	W	L	PCT	G	GS	CG	SH	SV	IP	H	HR	BB	SO	RAT	ERA	ERA+	OAV	OOB	BH	AVG	PB	PR	/A	PD	TPI
1944	Bos-A	0	0	—	1	1	0	0	0	1	3	0	2	0	45.0	18.00	19	.500	.625	0	.000	-0	-2	-2	-0	0.0
1945	StL-N	0	0	—	8	2	0	0	0	13¹	12	2	16	6	18.9	6.08	62	.250	.438	0	.000	-0	-3	-3	-0	0.0
Total	2	0	0	—	9	3	0	0	0	14¹	15	2	18	6	20.7	6.91	54	.278	.458	0	.000	-1	-5	-5	0	0.0

● **BILL PASCHALL** Paschall, William Herbert b: 4/22/54, Norfolk, Va. BR/TR, 6', 175 lbs. Deb: 9/20/78

YEAR	TM/L	W	L	PCT	G	GS	CG	SH	SV	IP	H	HR	BB	SO	RAT	ERA	ERA+	OAV	OOB	BH	AVG	PB	PR	/A	PD	TPI
1978	KC-A	0	1	.000	2	0	0	0	1	8	6	0	0	5	7.9	3.38	113	.207	.233	0	—	0	0	0	-0	-0.1
1979	KC-A	0	1	.000	7	0	0	0	0	13²	18	2	5	3	16.5	6.59	65	.300	.373	0	—	0	-4	-4	-0	-0.4
1981	KC-A	0	0	—	2	0	0	0	0	2	2	0	0	1	9.0	4.50	80	.286	.286	0	—	0	-0	-0	-0	-0.0
Total	3	0	2	.000	11	0	0	0	1	23²	26	2	5	9	12.9	5.32	76	.271	.327	0	—	0	-3	-3	-1	-0.5

● **CAMILO PASCUAL** Pascual, Camilo Alberto (Lus) "Little Potato" b: 1/20/34, Havana, Cuba BR/TR, 5'11", 185 lbs. Deb: 4/15/54 FC

YEAR	TM/L	W	L	PCT	G	GS	CG	SH	SV	IP	H	HR	BB	SO	RAT	ERA	ERA+	OAV	OOB	BH	AVG	PB	PR	/A	PD	TPI
1954	Was-A	4	7	.364	48	4	1	0	3	119¹	126	7	61	60	14.6	4.22	84	.276	.368	4	.133	-0	-7	-9	3	-0.5
1955	Was-A	2	12	.143	43	16	1	0	3	129	158	15	70	82	16.3	6.14	62	.311	.401	7	.219	0	-31	-33	2	-3.0
1956	Was-A	6	18	.250	39	27	6	0	2	188²	194	33	89	162	13.8	5.87	74	.261	.345	8	.138	-2	-36	-32	1	-3.6
1957	Was-A	8	17	.320	29	26	8	2	0	175²	168	11	76	113	12.7	4.10	95	.258	.338	7	.140	-2	-6	-4	2	-0.5
1958	Was-A	8	12	.400	31	27	6	2	0	177¹	166	14	60	146	11.6	3.15	121	.248	.313	9	.158	-1	12	13	1	1.4
1959	Was-A†	17	10	.630	32	30	**17**	**6**	0	238²	202	10	69	185	10.3	2.64	148	.226	.284	26	.302	6	32	34	5	**5.0**
1960	Was-A†	12	8	.600	26	22	8	3	0	151²	139	11	53	143	11.5	3.03	128	.240	.306	9	.176	3	14	15	0	2.2
1961	Min-A★	15	16	.484	35	33	15	**8**	0	252¹	205	26	100	**221**	11.0	3.46	123	.217	.294	14	.165	0	16	22	1	2.5
1962	Min-A★	20	11	.645	34	33	**18**	**5**	0	257²	236	25	59	**206**	10.4	3.32	123	.241	.286	26	.268	8	19	22	0	3.4
1963	Min-A★	21	9	.700	31	31	**18**	3	0	248¹	205	21	81	**202**	10.5	2.46	148	.224	.289	23	.250	6	32	**33**	-1	4.6
1964	Min-A★	15	12	.556	36	36	14	1	0	267¹	245	30	98	213	11.6	3.30	108	.241	.309	17	.181	4	10	8	0	1.2
1965	*Min-A	9	3	.750	27	27	5	1	0	156	126	12	63	96	11.2	3.35	106	.217	.299	12	.200	3	2	4	2	0.7
1966	Min-A	8	6	.571	21	19	2	0	0	103	113	9	30	56	12.7	4.89	73	.278	.330	8	.216	1	-17	-15	2	-1.6
1967	Was-A	12	10	.545	28	27	5	1	0	164²	147	15	43	106	10.5	3.28	96	.237	.289	9	.176	1	-1	-2	-0	-0.1
1968	Was-A	13	12	.520	31	31	8	4	0	201	181	11	59	111	10.9	2.69	109	.239	.298	12	.185	1	7	5	1	0.9
1969	Was-A	2	5	.286	14	13	0	0	0	55¹	49	12	38	34	15.0	6.83	51	.239	.371	4	.235	0	-20	-21	-0	-2.2
	Cin-N	0	0	—	5	1	0	0	0	7¹	14	2	4	3	22.1	8.59	44	.424	.486	0	—	0	-4	-4	-0	0.0
1970	LA-N	0	0	—	10	0	0	0	0	14	12	5	8	11	11.6	2.57	149	.231	.310	0	—	0	2	5	0	0.0
1971	Cle-A	2	2	.500	9	1	0	0	0	23¹	17	7	10	20	11.2	3.09	124	.205	.305	3	.600	1	1	1	1	0.3
Total	18	174	170	.506	529	404	132	36	10	2930²	2703	256	1069	2167	11.8	3.63	103	.244	.314	198	.205	29	26	38	18	10.9

● **CARLOS PASCUAL** Pascual, Carlos Alberto (Lus) b: 3/13/31, Havana, Cuba BR/TR, 5'6", 165 lbs. Deb: 9/24/50 F

YEAR	TM/L	W	L	PCT	G	GS	CG	SH	SV	IP	H	HR	BB	SO	RAT	ERA	ERA+	OAV	OOB	BH	AVG	PB	PR	/A	PD	TPI
1950	Was-A	1	1	.500	2	2	2	0	0	17	12	0	8	3	11.1	2.12	212	.194	.296	1	.250	0	5	4	-1	0.4

● **LARRY PASHNICK** Pashnick, Larry John b: 4/25/56, Lincoln Park, Mich. BR/TR, 6'3", 205 lbs. Deb: 4/10/82

YEAR	TM/L	W	L	PCT	G	GS	CG	SH	SV	IP	H	HR	BB	SO	RAT	ERA	ERA+	OAV	OOB	BH	AVG	PB	PR	/A	PD	TPI
1982	Det-A	4	4	.500	28	13	1	0	0	94¹	110	17	25	19	13.0	4.01	101	.297	.343	0	—	0	1	1	-1	0.0
1983	Det-A	1	3	.250	12	6	0	0	0	37²	48	5	18	17	16.5	5.26	74	.308	.390	0	—	0	-5	-6	1	-0.5
1984	Min-A	2	1	.667	13	1	0	0	0	38¹	38	3	11	10	12.0	3.52	119	.260	.321	0	—	0	2	3	0	0.2
Total	3	7	8	.467	53	20	1	0	0	170¹	196	25	54	46	13.5	4.17	97	.292	.350	0	—	0	-2	-2	0	-0.3

● **CLAUDE PASSEAU** Passeau, Claude William b: 4/9/09, Waynesboro, Miss. BR/TR, 6'3", 198 lbs. Deb: 9/29/35

YEAR	TM/L	W	L	PCT	G	GS	CG	SH	SV	IP	H	HR	BB	SO	RAT	ERA	ERA+	OAV	OOB	BH	AVG	PB	PR	/A	PD	TPI
1935	Pit-N	0	1	.000	1	1	0	0	0	3	7	0	2	1	27.0	12.00	34	.500	.563	0	.000	-0	-3	-3	0	-0.6
1936	Phi-N	11	15	.423	49	21	8	2	3	217¹	247	7	55	85	12.7	3.48	130	.280	.325	22	.282	3	13	26	1	3.3
1937	Phi-N	14	18	.438	50	34	18	1	2	292¹	348	16	79	135	13.3	4.34	100	.296	.343	21	.196	-0	-14	-0	0	0.0
1938	Phi-N	11	18	.379	44	33	15	0	1	239	281	8	93	100	14.4	4.52	86	.287	.354	13	.162	-2	-19	-17	3	-1.7
1939	Phi-N	2	4	.333	8	8	4	1	0	53¹	54	1	25	29	13.5	4.22	95	.263	.346	4	.200	-2	-2	-1	0	-0.2
	Chi-N	13	9	.591	34	27	13	1	3	221	215	8	48	108	10.9	3.05	129	.254	.306	12	.156	-1	21	22	1	2.0
	Yr	15	13	.536	42	35	17	2	3	274¹	269	9	73	**137**	11.4	3.28		.255	.306	16	.165	-2	19	20	1	1.8
1940	Chi-N	20	13	.606	46	31	20	4	5	280²	259	8	59	124	10.3	2.50	150	.237	.278	20	.204	6	42	39	1	**5.3**
1941	Chi-N★	14	14	.500	34	30	20	3	0	231	262	16	57	80	12.3	3.35	105	.281	.320	19	.221	5	7	4	-1	0.9
1942	Chi-N★	19	14	.576	35	34	24	3	0	278²	284	13	74	89	11.7	2.68	119	.260	.309	19	.181	1	20	16	1	2.0
1943	Chi-N☆	15	12	.556	35	31	18	1	1	257	245	10	66	93	11.0	2.91	115	.249	.299	19	.198	1	14	12	1	1.5
1944	Chi-N	15	9	.625	34	27	18	2	1	227	234	5	50	89	11.3	2.89	122	.266	.306	13	.162	-1	18	16	1	1.6
1945	*Chi-N†	17	9	.654	34	27	19	**5**	1	227	205	4	59	98	10.5	2.46	149	.238	.289	17	.187	2	34	**30**	3	**3.8**
1946	Chi-N★	9	8	.529	21	21	10	1	2	129¹	118	5	42	47	11.2	3.13	106	.237	.298	10	.204	1	10	7	1	0.7
1947	Chi-N	2	6	.250	19	6	1	1	2	63¹	97	7	24	26	17.3	6.25	63	.353	.407	0	.000	-2	-15	-16	-1	-2.1
Total	13	162	150	.519	444	331	188	26	21	2719²	2856	105	728	1104	12.0	3.32	113	.267	.316	189	.192	13	120	128	11	16.5

● **FRANK PASTORE** Pastore, Frank Enrico b: 8/21/57, Alhambra, Cal. BR/TR, 6'3", 205 lbs. Deb: 4/4/79

YEAR	TM/L	W	L	PCT	G	GS	CG	SH	SV	IP	H	HR	BB	SO	RAT	ERA	ERA+	OAV	OOB	BH	AVG	PB	PR	/A	PD	TPI
1979	*Cin-N	6	7	.462	30	9	2	1	4	95¹	102	8	23	63	11.9	4.25	88	.271	.315	4	.160	-0	-5	-5	-0	-0.8
1980	Cin-N	13	7	.650	27	27	9	2	0	184²	161	13	42	110	9.9	3.27	109	.233	.277	10	.156	-1	7	6	-1	0.5
1981	Cin-N	4	9	.308	22	22	2	1	0	132	125	11	35	81	11.1	4.02	88	.247	.300	5	.114	-2	-8	-7	-2	-1.0
1982	Cin-N	8	13	.381	31	29	3	0	0	188¹	210	13	44	94	13.0	3.97	93	.286	.341	10	.172	1	-8	-6	-2	-0.7
1983	Cin-N	9	12	.429	36	29	4	1	0	184¹	207	20	64	93	13.3	4.88	78	.290	.349	11	.186	2	-26	-22	-1	-2.3
1984	Cin-N	3	8	.273	24	16	1	0	0	98¹	110	10	40	53	14.0	6.50	58	.285	.357	2	.071	-2	-32	-30	0	-3.1
1985	Cin-N	2	1	.667	17	6	1	0	0	54	54	1	16	29	12.8	3.83	99	.287	.341	2	.143	-0	-1	-0	0	0.0
1986	Min-A	3	1	.750	33	1	0	0	2	49¹	54	4	24	18	14.2	4.01	107	.283	.363	0	—	0	1	2	-1	0.0
Total	8	48	58	.453	220	139	22	7	6	986¹	1029	80	301	541	12.3	4.29	87	.270	.326	44	.151	-2	-72	-62	-5	-7.4

● **JIM PASTORIUS** Pastorius, James W. "Sunny Jim" b: 7/12/1881, Pittsburgh, Pa. d: 5/10/41, Pittsburgh, Pa. BL/TL, 5'9", 165 lbs. Deb: 4/15/06

YEAR	TM/L	W	L	PCT	G	GS	CG	SH	SV	IP	H	HR	BB	SO	RAT	ERA	ERA+	OAV	OOB	BH	AVG	PB	PR	/A	PD	TPI
1906	Bro-N	10	14	.417	29	24	16	3	0	211²	225	4	69	58	12.6	3.61	70	.274	.333	10	.141	-0	-23	-26	-1	-2.9
1907	Bro-N	16	12	.571	28	26	20	4	0	222	218	2	77	70	12.2	2.35	100	.264	.331	3	.205	3	3	-0	1	0.2
1908	Bro-N	4	20	.167	28	25	16	2	0	213²	171	5	74	54	10.6	2.44	96	.216	.288	8	.129	-0	-2	-2	0	-0.3
1909	Bro-N	1	9	.100	12	9	5	1	0	79²	91	4	58	23	16.9	5.76	45	.313	.429	2	.080	-1	-28	-28	1	-3.1
Total	4	31	55	.360	97	84	57	10	0	727	705	15	278	205	12.6	3.28	80	.263	.330	35	.152	1	-50	-56	-1	-6.1

● **JOE PATE** Pate, Joseph William b: 6/6/1892, Alice, Tex. d: 12/26/48, Fort Worth, Tex. BL/TL, 5'10", 184 lbs. Deb: 4/15/26

YEAR	TM/L	W	L	PCT	G	GS	CG	SH	SV	IP	H	HR	BB	SO	RAT	ERA	ERA+	OAV	OOB	BH	AVG	PB	PR	/A	PD	TPI
1926	Phi-A	9	0	1.000	47	2	0	0	6	113	109	3	51	24	12.9	2.71	154	.262	.345	4	.148	-0	**16**	**18**	3	1.8
1927	Phi-A	0	3	.000	32	0	0	0	6	53²	67	3	21	14	14.9	5.20	82	.318	.382	3	.300	1	-6	-6	0	-0.3
Total	2	9	3	.750	79	2	0	0	12	166²	176	6	72	38	13.6	3.51	120	.281	.358	7	.189	1	10	13	4	1.5

● **CASE PATTEN** Patten, Case Lyman "Casey" b: 5/7/1876, Westport, N.Y. d: 5/31/35, Rochester, N.Y. BB/TL, 6', 175 lbs. Deb: 5/4/01

YEAR	TM/L	W	L	PCT	G	GS	CG	SH	SV	IP	H	HR	BB	SO	RAT	ERA	ERA+	OAV	OOB	BH	AVG	PB	PR	/A	PD	TPI
1901	Was-A	18	10	.643	32	30	26	4	0	254¹	285	8	74	109	13.3	3.93	93	.280	.339	13	.135	-5	-7	-7	0	-1.1
1902	Was-A	17	16	.515	36	34	33	1	0	299²	331	11	89	92	12.9	4.05	91	.281	.337	12	.096	-10	-16	-12	-1	-2.1
1903	*Was-A	11	22	.333	36	34	32	0	1	300	313	11	80	133	11.9	3.60	87	.268	.317	14	.132	-6	-21	-16	-1	-2.1
1904	Was-A	14	23	.378	45	39	37	2	**3**	357²	367	3	79	150	11.7	3.07	87	.266	.315	16	.127	-5	-19	-16	-1	-2.1
1905	Was-A	14	22	.389	42	36	29	2	0	309²	300	3	86	113	11.5	3.14	84	.256	.312	16	.155	-2	-17	-17	-2	-2.3
1906	Was-A	19	16	.543	38	32	28	7	0	282²	253	3	99	96	10.8	2.17	122	.242	.299	11	.117	-4	17	15	-1	1.3
1907	Was-A	12	16	.429	36	29	20	1	0	237¹	272	3	63	58	12.9	3.56	68	.290	.331	11	.126	-3	-27	-30	-5	-4.1
1908	Was-A	0	2	.000	4	3	1	0	0	18	25	0	6	6	15.5	3.50	65	.333	.383	1	.200	-0	-2	-2	-0	-0.3
	Bos-A	0	1	.000	1	1	0	0	0	3	8	0	1	0	27.0	15.00	16	.533	.563	0	.000	-0	-4	-4	0	-0.9

YEAR TM/L	W	L	PCT	G	GS	CG	SH	SV	IP	H	HR	BB	SO	RAT	ERA	ERA+	OAV	OOB	BH	AVG	PB	PR	/A	PD	TPI
Yr	0	3	.000	5	4	1	0	0	21	33	0	7	6	17.1	5.14	45	.367	.412	1	.167	-0	-6	-7	-0	-1.2
Total 8	105	128	.451	270	238	206	17	5	2062^1	2154	40	557	757	12.2	3.36	88	.270	.323	94	.127	-35	-97	-91	-7	-13.7

● **DANNY PATTERSON**   Patterson, Danny Shane b: 2/17/71, San Gabriel, Cal. BR/TR, 6', 170 lbs. Deb: 7/26/96

YEAR TM/L	W	L	PCT	G	GS	CG	SH	SV	IP	H	HR	BB	SO	RAT	ERA	ERA+	OAV	OOB	BH	AVG	PB	PR	/A	PD	TPI
1996 *Tex-A	0	0	—	7	0	0	0	0	8^2	10	0	3	5	13.5	0.00	—	.286	.342	0	—	0	5	5	-0	0.0

● **DARYL PATTERSON**   Patterson, Daryl Alan b: 11/21/43, Coalinga, Cal. BL/TR, 6'4", 195 lbs. Deb: 4/10/68

YEAR TM/L	W	L	PCT	G	GS	CG	SH	SV	IP	H	HR	BB	SO	RAT	ERA	ERA+	OAV	OOB	BH	AVG	PB	PR	/A	PD	TPI
1968 *Det-A	2	3	.400	38	1	0	0	7	68	53	3	27	49	11.1	2.12	142	.213	.300	0	.000	-1	7	7	-0	0.5
1969 Det-A	0	2	.000	18	0	0	0	0	22^1	15	2	19	12	13.7	2.82	132	.205	.370	0	.000	-0	2	2	-1	0.1
1970 Det-A	7	1	.875	43	0	0	0	2	78	81	9	39	55	14.4	4.85	77	.269	.362	0	.000	-1	-10	-10	-1	-1.2
1971 Det-A	0	1	.000	12	0	0	0	0	9^1	14	1	6	5	20.3	4.82	74	.359	.457	0	—	-1	-1	-1	-0	-0.1
Oak-A	0	0	—	4	0	0	0	0	5^2	5	2	4	2	15.9	7.94	42	.238	.385	0	.000	-0	-3	-3	-0	0.0
Yr	0	1	.000	16	0	0	0	0	15	19	3	10	7	18.0	6.00	58	.311	.417	0	.000	-0	-4	-4	-0	-0.1
StL-N	0	1	.000	13	2	0	0	1	26^2	20	3	15	11	11.8	4.39	82	.211	.318	0	.000	-0	-3	-2	-1	-0.2
1974 Pit-N	2	1	.667	14	0	0	0	1	21	35	3	6	8	18.9	7.29	47	.376	.431	0	—	-1	-9	-9	0	-1.3
Total 5	11	9	.550	142	3	0	0	11	231	223	23	119	142	13.8	4.09	85	.256	.353	0	.000	-3	-17	-16	-3	-2.2

● **DAVE PATTERSON**   Patterson, David Glenn b: 7/25/56, Springfield, Mo. BR/TR, 6', 170 lbs. Deb: 6/9/79

YEAR TM/L	W	L	PCT	G	GS	CG	SH	SV	IP	H	HR	BB	SO	RAT	ERA	ERA+	OAV	OOB	BH	AVG	PB	PR	/A	PD	TPI
1979 LA-N	4	1	.800	36	0	0	0	6	53	62	5	22	34	14.3	5.26	79	.292	.359	1	.143	-0	-9	-10	-0	-1.1

● **GIL PATTERSON**   Patterson, Gilbert Thomas b: 9/5/55, Philadelphia, Pa. BR/TR, 6'1", 185 lbs. Deb: 4/19/77

YEAR TM/L	W	L	PCT	G	GS	CG	SH	SV	IP	H	HR	BB	SO	RAT	ERA	ERA+	OAV	OOB	BH	AVG	PB	PR	/A	PD	TPI
1977 NY-A	1	2	.333	10	6	0	0	1	33^1	38	3	20	29	16.5	5.40	73	.290	.396	0		0	-5	-5	1	-0.3

● **JEFF PATTERSON**   Patterson, Jeffrey Simmons b: 10/1/68, Anaheim, Cal. BR/TR, 6'2", 200 lbs. Deb: 4/30/95

YEAR TM/L	W	L	PCT	G	GS	CG	SH	SV	IP	H	HR	BB	SO	RAT	ERA	ERA+	OAV	OOB	BH	AVG	PB	PR	/A	PD	TPI
1995 NY-A	0	0	—	3	0	0	0	0	3^1	3	1	3	3	16.2	2.70	171	.231	.375	0	—	0	1	1	-0	0.0

● **KEN PATTERSON**   Patterson, Kenneth Brian b: 7/8/64, Costa Mesa, Cal. BL/TL, 6'4", 210 lbs. Deb: 7/9/88

YEAR TM/L	W	L	PCT	G	GS	CG	SH	SV	IP	H	HR	BB	SO	RAT	ERA	ERA+	OAV	OOB	BH	AVG	PB	PR	/A	PD	TPI
1988 Chi-A	0	2	.000	9	2	0	0	1	20^2	25	2	7	8	13.9	4.79	83	.294	.348	0	—	0	-2	-2	-0	-0.2
1989 Chi-A	6	1	.857	50	1	0	0	1	65^2	64	11	28	43	12.9	4.52	84	.257	.337	0	—	0	-5	-5	-1	-0.5
1990 Chi-A	2	1	.667	43	0	0	0	2	66^1	58	6	34	40	12.8	3.39	113	.242	.341	0	—	0	4	3	0	0.3
1991 Chi-A	3	0	1.000	43	0	0	0	1	63^2	48	5	35	32	11.9	2.83	140	.214	.323	0	—	0	9	8	-1	0.4
1992 Chi-N	2	3	.400	32	1	0	0	1	41^2	41	7	27	23	14.9	3.89	93	.268	.381	0	.000	-0	-2	-1	-0	-0.2
1993 Cal-A	1	1	.500	46	0	0	0	1	59	54	7	35	36	13.6	4.58	98	.249	.353	0	—	0	-2	-1	-0	-0.1
1994 Cal-A	0	0	—	1	0	0	0	0	0^2	0	0	0	1	0.0	0.00	—	.000	.000	0	—	0	0	0	0	0.0
Total 7	14	8	.636	224	4	0	0	7	317^2	290	38	166	183	13.1	3.88	102	.248	.344	0	.000	-0	3	3	-3	-0.3

● **REGGIE PATTERSON**   Patterson, Reginald Allen b: 11/7/58, Birmingham, Ala. BR/TR, 6'4", 180 lbs. Deb: 8/13/81

YEAR TM/L	W	L	PCT	G	GS	CG	SH	SV	IP	H	HR	BB	SO	RAT	ERA	ERA+	OAV	OOB	BH	AVG	PB	PR	/A	PD	TPI
1981 Chi-N	0	1	.000	6	1	0	0	0	7^1	14	1	6	2	24.5	13.50	26	.412	.500	0	—	0	-8	-8	-0	-0.9
1983 Chi-N	1	2	.333	5	2	0	0	0	18^2	17	3	6	10	12.1	4.82	79	.246	.325	0	.000	-1	-2	-2	-0	-0.4
1984 Chi-N	0	1	.000	3	1	0	0	0	6	10	1	2	5	18.0	10.50	37	.357	.400	0	—	0	-5	-4	-0	-0.6
1985 Chi-N	3	0	1.000	8	5	1	0	0	39	36	2	10	17	10.6	3.00	133	.250	.299	1	.100	-0	3	4	0	0.3
Total 4	4	4	.500	22	9	1	0	0	71	77	7	24	34	13.1	5.20	75	.280	.342	1	.056	-1	-13	-10	0	-1.6

● **BOB PATTERSON**   Patterson, Robert Chandler b: 5/16/59, Jacksonville, Fla. BR/TL, 6'2", 195 lbs. Deb: 9/2/85

YEAR TM/L	W	L	PCT	G	GS	CG	SH	SV	IP	H	HR	BB	SO	RAT	ERA	ERA+	OAV	OOB	BH	AVG	PB	PR	/A	PD	TPI
1985 SD-N	0	0	—	3	0	0	0	0	4	13	2	3	1	36.0	24.75	14	.565	.615	0	—	0	-9	-9	-0	0.0
1986 Pit-N	2	3	.400	11	5	0	0	0	36^1	49	0	5	20	13.4	4.95	77	.322	.344	1	.125	-0	-5	-5	1	-0.5
1987 Pit-N	1	4	.200	15	7	0	0	0	43	49	5	22	27	15.1	6.70	61	.290	.375	1	.083	-1	-13	-12	-0	-1.3
1989 Pit-N	4	3	.571	12	3	0	0	1	26^2	23	3	8	20	10.5	4.05	83	.232	.290	0	.000	-0	-2	-2	-0	-0.6
1990 *Pit-N	8	5	.615	55	5	0	0	5	94^2	88	9	21	70	10.6	2.95	123	.249	.296	1	.053	-1	9	7	-0	0.8
1991 *Pit-N	4	3	.571	54	1	0	0	2	65^2	67	7	15	57	11.2	4.11	87	.267	.308	1	.250	-0	-3	-4	0	-0.4
1992 *Pit-N	6	3	.667	60	0	0	0	9	64^2	59	7	23	43	11.4	2.92	118	.246	.312	2	.333	1	4	4	-1	0.7
1993 Tex-A	2	4	.333	52	0	0	0	1	52^2	59	8	11	46	12.1	4.78	87	.282	.321	0	—	0	-3	-4	-0	-0.3
1994 Cal-A	2	3	.400	47	0	0	0	0	42	35	6	15	30	11.1	4.07	120	.229	.306	0	—	0	3	-1	0	0.3
1995 Cal-A	5	2	.714	62	0	0	0	0	53^1	48	6	13	41	10.5	3.04	155	.246	.297	0	—	0	10	10	-1	1.0
1996 Chi-N	3	3	.500	79	0	0	0	0	54^2	46	6	22	53	11.4	3.13	136	.229	.308	1	.333	0	7	7	-1	0.8
Total 11	37	33	.529	450	21	0	0	27	537^2	536	59	158	408	11.8	4.03	98	.262	.318	7	.127	-1	-1	-5	-3	0.5

● **ROY PATTERSON**   Patterson, Roy Lewis "Boy Wonder" b: 12/17/1876, Stoddard, Wis. d: 4/14/53, St.Croix Falls, Wis. BR/TR, 6', 185 lbs. Deb: 4/24/01

YEAR TM/L	W	L	PCT	G	GS	CG	SH	SV	IP	H	HR	BB	SO	RAT	ERA	ERA+	OAV	OOB	BH	AVG	PB	PR	/A	PD	TPI
1901 Chi-A	20	16	.556	41	35	30	4	0	312^1	345	11	62	127	12.0	3.37	103	.277	.317	26	.222	1	10	4	0	0.4
1902 Chi-A	19	14	.576	34	30	26	2	0	268	262	5	67	61	11.1	3.06	111	.256	.304	20	.190	-2	15	10	1	1.0
1903 Chi-A	15	15	.500	34	30	26	3	0	293	275	5	69	89	10.9	2.70	104	.248	.298	11	.105	-6	8	3	2	-0.1
1904 Chi-A	9	9	.500	22	17	14	4	0	165	148	1	24	64	9.8	2.29	107	.241	.277	6	.103	-4	6	3	-1	-0.2
1905 Chi-A	4	6	.400	13	9	7	0	0	88^2	73	0	16	29	9.0	1.83	135	.226	.263	8	.267	2	8	6	1	1.0
1906 Chi-A	10	7	.588	21	18	12	3	1	142	119	1	17	45	8.9	2.09	121	.231	.261	3	.061	-5	9	7	0	0.4
1907 Chi-A	4	6	.400	19	13	4	1	0	96	105	0	18	27	11.7	2.63	91	.280	.316	3	.097	-3	-1	-2	1	-0.4
Total 7	81	73	.526	184	152	119	16	2	1365	1327	23	273	442	10.8	2.75	107	.255	.297	77	.156	-16	57	31	5	2.1

● **MARTY PATTIN**   Pattin, Martin William b: 4/6/43, Charleston, Ill. BR/TR, 5'11", 180 lbs. Deb: 5/14/68 C

YEAR TM/L	W	L	PCT	G	GS	CG	SH	SV	IP	H	HR	BB	SO	RAT	ERA	ERA+	OAV	OOB	BH	AVG	PB	PR	/A	PD	TPI
1968 Cal-A	4	4	.500	52	4	0	0	3	84	67	7	37	66	11.4	2.79	144	.221	.310	1	.083	-1	2	1	-1	-0.1
1969 Sea-A	7	12	.368	34	27	2	1	0	158^2	166	29	71	126	13.6	5.62	65	.268	.345	9	.155	-1	-35	-35	-1	-3.9
1970 Mil-A	14	12	.538	37	29	11	0	0	233^1	204	20	71	161	10.8	3.39	112	.235	.298	9	.129	-2	8	10	2	1.1
1971 Mil-A☆	14	14	.500	36	36	9	5	0	264^2	225	29	73	169	10.3	3.13	111	.235	.292	7	.084	-3	10	10	1	0.7
1972 Bos-A	17	13	.567	38	35	13	4	0	253	232	19	65	168	10.9	3.24	99	.243	.297	12	.140	1	-5	-1	1	0.0
1973 Bos-A	15	15	.500	34	30	11	2	1	219^1	238	31	69	119	12.9	4.31	93	.277	.337	0	—	0	-12	-7	1	-1.2
1974 KC-A	3	7	.300	25	11	2	0	0	117^1	121	10	28	50	11.6	3.99	96	.264	.309	0	—	0	-5	-2	-1	-0.7
1975 KC-A	10	10	.500	44	15	5	1	5	177	173	6	45	89	11.2	3.25	118	.253	.302	0	—	0	10	12	-1	1.1
1976 *KC-A	8	14	.364	44	15	4	1	5	141	114	9	38	65	9.9	2.49	141	.235	.273	0	—	0	16	16	0	2.5
1977 *KC-A	10	3	.769	31	10	4	0	0	128^1	120	16	37	55	10.8	3.58	113	.242	.300	0	—	0	7	7	-1	0.5
1978 *KC-A	3	5	.500	32	5	2	0	4	78^2	72	8	25	30	11.3	3.32	115	.248	.312	0	—	0	4	4	-2	-0.4
1979 KC-A	5	2	.714	31	7	1	0	3	94^1	109	11	21	41	12.5	4.58	93	.293	.332	0	—	0	-4	-3	-1	-0.4
1980 *KC-A	4	0	1.000	37	0	2	0	4	89	97	7	23	40	12.2	3.64	111	.277	.324	0	—	0	4	4	-1	0.1
Total 13	114	109	.511	475	224	64	14	25	2038^2	1933	209	603	1179	11.4	3.62	102	.250	.309	38	.123	-7	0	16	-6	-0.3

● **JIMMY PATTISON**   Pattison, James Wells b: 12/18/08, Bronx, N.Y. d: 2/22/91, Melbourne, Fla. BL/TL, 6', 185 lbs. Deb: 4/18/29

YEAR TM/L	W	L	PCT	G	GS	CG	SH	SV	IP	H	HR	BB	SO	RAT	ERA	ERA+	OAV	OOB	BH	AVG	PB	PR	/A	PD	TPI
1929 Bro-N	0	1	.000	6	0	0	0	0	11^2	9	1	4	5	10.0	4.63	100	.231	.302	1	.500	0	-0	-0	-0	0.0

● **HARRY PATTON**   Patton, Harry Claude b: 6/29/1884, Gillespie, Ill. d: 6/9/30, St.Louis, Mo. Deb: 8/22/10

YEAR TM/L	W	L	PCT	G	GS	CG	SH	SV	IP	H	HR	BB	SO	RAT	ERA	ERA+	OAV	OOB	BH	AVG	PB	PR	/A	PD	TPI
1910 StL-N	0	0	—	1	0	0	0	0	4	4	0	2	2	13.5	2.25	132	.267	.353	0	—	0	0	0	0	0.0

● **MIKE PAUL**   Paul, Michael George b: 4/18/45, Detroit, Mich. BL/TL, 6', 183 lbs. Deb: 5/27/68 C

YEAR TM/L	W	L	PCT	G	GS	CG	SH	SV	IP	H	HR	BB	SO	RAT	ERA	ERA+	OAV	OOB	BH	AVG	PB	PR	/A	PD	TPI
1968 Cle-A	5	8	.385	36	7	0	0	3	91^2	72	11	35	87	11.0	3.93	75	.213	.296	4	.167	-0	-10	-10	-1	-1.6
1969 Cle-A	5	10	.333	47	12	0	0	0	117^1	104	12	54	98	12.3	3.61	104	.241	.328	0	—	-3	-2	-3	-1	-1.1
1970 Cle-A	2	8	.200	30	15	1	0	0	88	91	13	45	70	13.9	4.81	82	.271	.357	4	.154	-1	-11	-8	-2	-1.1
1971 Cle-A	2	7	.222	17	12	1	0	0	62	58	8	14	33	14.1	5.95	64	.318	.367	1	.053	-1	-17	-16	-1	-2.1
1972 Tex-A	8	9	.471	49	20	2	1	0	161^2	149	4	52	108	11.3	2.17	139	.246	.308	8	.167	-1	16	15	1	1.7
1973 Tex-A	5	4	.556	36	10	1	0	2	87^1	104	4	36	49	14.9	4.95	75	.295	.368	0	—	0	-11	-12	1	-1.1
Chi-N	0	1	.000	11	0	0	0	0	18^1	17	2	9	6	12.8	3.44	115	.258	.347	0	.000	-0	-3	-3	0	-0.1
1974 Chi-N	0	0	—	2	0	0	0	0	1^1	4	1	1	1	33.8	27.00	14	.500	.556	0	—	0	-3	-3	-0	-1.6
Total 7	27	48	.360	228	77	5	1	8	627^2	619	60	246	452	12.7	3.91	89	.260	.334	17	.115	-4	-35	-30	-4	-5.9

● **GENE PAULETTE**   Paulette, Eugene Edward b: 5/26/1891, Centralia, Ill. d: 2/8/66, Little Rock, Ark. BR/TR, 6', 150 lbs. Deb: 6/16/11 ◆

YEAR TM/L	W	L	PCT	G	GS	CG	SH	SV	IP	H	HR	BB	SO	RAT	ERA	ERA+	OAV	OOB	BH	AVG	PB	PR	/A	PD	TPI
1918 StL-N	0	0	—	1	0	0	0	0	0^1	1	0	0	0	27.0	0.00	—	.500	.500	126	.273	0	0	0	0	0.0

YEAR TM/L	W	L	PCT	G	GS	CG	SH	SV	IP	H	HR	BB	SO	RAT	ERA	ERA+	OAV	OOB	BH	AVG	PB	PR	/A	PD	TPI
● **GIL PAULSEN** Paulsen, Guilford Paul Hans b: 11/14/02, Graettinger, Iowa d: 4/2/94, Harlan, Iowa BR/TR, 6'2.5", 190 lbs. Deb: 10/3/25																									
1925 StL-N	0	0	—	1	0	0	0	0	2	1	0	0	1	4.5	0.00	—	.125	.125	0	—	0	1	1	0	0.0
● **DAVE PAVLAS** Pavlas, David Lee b: 8/12/62, Frankfurt, W.Germany BR/TR, 6'7", 180 lbs. Deb: 8/21/90																									
1990 Chi-N	2	0	1.000	13	0	0	0	0	21¹	23	2	6	12	12.2	2.11	193	.271	.319	0	.000	0	4	5	-0	0.4
1991 Chi-N	0	0	—	1	0	0	0	0	1	3	1	0	0	27.0	18.00	22	.750	.750	0	—	0	-2	-2	-0	-0.3
1995 NY-A	0	0	—	4	0	0	0	0	5²	8	0	0	3	12.7	3.18	145	.333	.333	0	—	0	1	1	0	0.0
1996 NY-A	0	0	—	16	0	0	0	1	23	23	0	7	18	12.1	2.35	151	.264	.326	0	—	0	7	7	0	0.1
Total 4	2	0	1.000	34	0	0	0	1	51	57	3	13	33	12.5	2.65	173	.285	.332	0	.000	0	10	11	0	0.5
● **ROGER PAVLIK** Pavlik, Roger Allen b: 10/4/67, Houston, Tex. BB/TR, 6'3", 220 lbs. Deb: 5/2/92																									
1992 Tex-A	4	4	.500	13	12	1	0	0	62	66	3	34	45	15.0	4.21	90	.280	.377	0	—	0	-2	-3	-1	-0.3
1993 Tex-A	12	6	.667	26	26	2	0	0	166¹	151	18	80	131	12.8	3.41	122	.245	.336	0	—	0	17	14	1	1.6
1994 Tex-A	2	5	.286	11	11	0	0	0	50¹	61	8	30	31	17.0	7.69	63	.300	.401	0	—	0	-16	-16	0	-1.7
1995 Tex-A	10	10	.500	31	31	2	1	0	191²	174	19	90	149	12.6	4.37	111	.243	.331	0	—	0	7	10	3	1.1
1996 *Tex-A★	15	8	.652	34	34	7	0	0	201	216	28	81	127	13.5	5.19	102	.276	.347	0	—	0	-5	3	-3	-0.1
Total 5	43	33	.566	115	114	12	1	0	671¹	668	76	315	483	13.5	4.61	102	.261	.347	0	—	0	2	6	0	0.6
● **JOHN PAWLOWSKI** Pawlowski, John b: 9/6/63, Johnson City, N.Y. BR/TR, 6'2", 175 lbs. Deb: 9/19/87																									
1987 Chi-A	0	0	—	2	0	0	0	0	3²	7	0	3	2	24.5	4.91	93	.438	.526	0	—	0	-0	-0	-0	-0.1
1988 Chi-A	1	0	1.000	6	0	0	0	0	14	20	2	3	10	14.8	8.36	48	.328	.359	0	—	0	-7	-7	-0	-0.4
Total 2	1	0	1.000	8	0	0	0	0	17²	27	2	6	12	16.8	7.64	54	.351	.398	0	—	0	-7	-7	-0	-0.5
● **MIKE PAXTON** Paxton, Michael De Wayne b: 9/3/53, Memphis, Tenn. BR/TR, 5'11", 190 lbs. Deb: 5/25/77																									
1977 Bos-A	10	5	.667	29	12	2	1	0	108	134	7	58	58	13.5	3.83	117	.311	.353	0	—	0	3	8	0	0.2
1978 Cle-A	12	11	.522	33	27	5	2	0	191	179	13	63	96	11.8	3.86	97	.247	.314	0	—	0	-2	-3	-1	-0.3
1979 Cle-A	8	8	.500	33	24	3	0	0	159²	210	14	52	70	14.9	5.92	72	.315	.366	0	—	0	-30	-30	0	-2.5
1980 Cle-A	0	0	—	4	0	0	0	0	7²	13	4	6	6	22.3	12.91	32	.394	.487	0	—	0	-8	-8	-0	0.0
Total 4	30	24	.556	99	63	10	3	1	466¹	536	38	146	230	13.4	4.71	87	.289	.345	0	—	0	-37	-32	-2	-2.6
● **GEORGE PAYNE** Payne, George Washington b: 5/23/1890, Mt.Vernon, Ky. d: 1/24/59, Bellflower, Cal. BR/TR, 5'11", 172 lbs. Deb: 5/8/20																									
1920 Chi-A	1	1	.500	12	0	0	0	0	29²	39	2	9	7	14.6	5.46	69	.312	.358	1	.125	-0	-5	-6	-1	-0.5
● **HARLEY PAYNE** Payne, Harley Fenwick "Lady" b: 1/9/1868, Windsor, Ont., Can. d: 12/29/35, Orwell, Ohio BB/TL, 6', 160 lbs. Deb: 4/18/1896																									
1896 Bro-N	14	16	.467	34	28	24	2	0	241²	284	4	58	52	13.0	3.39	122	.290	.335	21	.214	-0	26	20	3	2.2
1897 Bro-N	14	17	.452	40	38	30	1	0	280	350	8	71	86	14.1	4.63	89	.303	.353	26	.236	-0	-10	-16	1	-1.3
1898 Bro-N	1	0	1.000	1	1	0	0	0	9	11	0	3	2	14.0	4.00	90	.297	.350	3	.750	1	-0	-0	0	0.1
1899 Pit-N	1	3	.250	5	5	2	0	0	26¹	33	2	4	8	13.3	3.76	101	.306	.342	1	.100	-1	0	0	2	0.1
Total 4	30	36	.455	80	72	57	3	0	557	678	14	136	148	13.6	4.04	101	.298	.345	51	.230	-0	16	3	7	1.1
● **MIKE PAYNE** Payne, Michael Earl b: 11/15/61, Woonsocket, R.I. BR/TR, 5'11", 165 lbs. Deb: 8/22/84																									
1984 Atl-N	0	1	.000	3	1	0	0	0	5²	7	0	3	3	15.9	6.35	61	.333	.417	0	.000	-0	-2	-2	0	-0.3
● **MIKE PAZIK** Pazik, Michael Joseph b: 1/26/50, Lynn, Mass. BL/TL, 6'2", 195 lbs. Deb: 5/11/75 C																									
1975 Min-A	0	4	.000	5	3	0	0	0	19²	28	5	10	9	17.4	8.24	46	.329	.400	0	—	0	-10	-10	-1	-1.6
1976 Min-A	0	0	—	5	0	0	0	0	9	13	0	4	6	18.0	7.00	51	.342	.419	0	—	0	-3	-3	-0	-0.1
1977 Min-A	1	0	1.000	3	3	0	0	0	18	18	1	6	12	12.0	2.50	159	.265	.324	0	—	0	3	3	0	0.3
Total 3	1	4	.200	13	6	0	0	0	46²	59	6	20	20	15.4	5.79	66	.309	.377	0	—	0	-10	-10	-1	-1.4
● **FRANK PEARCE** Pearce, Franklin Johnson b: 3/30/1860, Jefferson County, Ky. d: 11/13/26, Louisville, Ky. Deb: 10/4/1876																									
1876 Lou-N	0	0	—	1	0	0	0	0	4	5	0	1	1	13.5	4.50	60	.263	.300	0	.000	-0	-1	-1	-0	0.0
● **FRANK PEARCE** Pearce, Franklin Thomas b: 8/31/05, Middletown, Ky. d: 9/3/50, Van Buren, N.Y. BR/TR, 6', 170 lbs. Deb: 4/20/33																									
1933 Phi-N	5	4	.556	20	7	3	1	0	82	78	5	29	18	11.7	3.62	105	.251	.315	5	.192	-1	-3	2	0	0.1
1934 Phi-N	0	2	.000	7	1	0	0	0	20	25	4	5	4	13.5	7.20	66	.301	.341	2	.667	1	-7	-6	-1	-0.5
1935 Phi-N	0	0	—	5	0	0	0	0	13	22	0	6	7	19.4	8.31	55	.361	.418	2	.500	1	-6	-5	0	0.1
Total 3	5	6	.455	32	8	3	1	0	115	125	9	40	29	12.9	4.77	85	.275	.333	9	.273	1	-16	-9	-0	-0.3
● **GEORGE PEARCE** Pearce, George Thomas "Filbert" b: 1/10/1888, Aurora, Ill. d: 10/11/35, Joliet, Ill. BL/TL, 5'10.5", 175 lbs. Deb: 4/16/12																									
1912 Chi-N	0	0	—	3	2	0	0	0	14²	16	0	6	9	16.6	5.52	60	.185	.290	1	.167	-0	-3	-4	1	0.1
1913 Chi-N	13	5	.722	25	21	15	3	0	163²	137	4	59	73	11.0	2.31	137	.234	.308	4	.073	-3	16	16	0	1.3
1914 Chi-N	9	12	.429	30	16	4	0	1	141	122	3	65	78	12.1	3.51	79	.239	.327	4	.089	-3	-11	-11	2	-1.8
1915 Chi-N	13	9	.591	36	20	8	2	0	176	158	1	77	96	12.2	3.32	84	.244	.328	11	.196	1	-11	-11	-0	-1.2
1916 Chi-N	0	0	—	4	1	0	0	0	4¹	6	0	1	0	14.5	2.08	140	.300	.333	0	—	0	0	0	0	0.0
1917 StL-N	1	1	.500	5	0	0	0	0	10¹	7	0	4	4	9.6	3.48	77	.184	.262	0	.000	-1	-1	-1	0	-0.2
Total 6	36	27	.571	103	60	27	5	1	509²	445	8	217	260	11.9	3.11	94	.236	.318	20	.120	-6	-10	-10	2	-1.8
● **JIM PEARCE** Pearce, James Madison b: 6/9/25, Zebulon, N.C. BR/TR, 6'6", 180 lbs. Deb: 9/8/49																									
1949 Was-A	0	1	.000	2	1	0	0	0	5¹	9	1	5	1	23.6	8.44	50	.375	.483	0	.000	-0	-3	-2	1	-0.3
1950 Was-A	2	1	.667	20	3	1	0	0	56²	58	3	37	18	15.2	6.04	74	.270	.379	2	.154	-1	-9	-10	-0	-0.5
1953 Was-A	0	1	.000	4	1	0	0	0	9¹	15	3	6	0	20.3	7.71	51	.405	.488	0	.000	-0	-4	-4	-0	-0.4
1954 Cin-N	1	0	1.000	2	1	0	0	0	11	7	0	5	3	10.6	0.00	—	.194	.310	0	—	0	5	5	0	0.4
1955 Cin-N	0	1	.000	2	1	0	0	0	3¹	8	0	0	0	21.6	10.80	39	.471	.471	0	—	0	-3	-2	0	-0.6
Total 5	3	4	.429	30	7	2	0	0	85²	97	6	53	22	16.0	5.78	76	.295	.396	2	.105	-2	-13	-13	0	-1.4
● **DICKEY PEARCE** Pearce, Richard J. b: 2/29/1836, Brooklyn, N.Y. d: 10/12/08, Wareham, Mass. BR/TR, 5'3.5", 161 lbs. Deb: 5/18/1871 MU♦																									
1875 StL-n	0	0	—	2	0	0	0	0	5¹	10	0	0	0	16.9	3.38	60	.333	.333	77	.248	0	-1	-1		0.0
● **FRANK PEARS** Pears, Frank H. b: 8/30/1866, Kentucky d: 11/29/23, St.Louis, Mo. TR, 5'9", 145 lbs. Deb: 10/6/1889 U																									
1889 KC-a	0	2	.000	3	2	2	0	0	22	21	2	9	5	12.7	4.91	85	.244	.323	1	.091	—	-3	-2	-0	-0.2
1893 StL-N	0	0	—	1	0	0	0	0	4	9	0	2	0	27.0	13.50	35	.429	.500	0	.000	-0	-4	-4	0	0.0
Total 2	0	2	.000	4	2	2	0	0	26	30	2	11	5	14.9	6.23	69	.280	.358	1	.077	-2	-7	-6	-0	-0.2
● **ALEX PEARSON** Pearson, Alexander Franklin b: 3/9/1877, Greensboro, Pa. d: 10/30/66, Rochester, Pa. BR/TR, 5'10.5", 160 lbs. Deb: 8/1/02																									
1902 StL-N	2	6	.250	11	10	8	0	0	82	90	0	22	24	12.6	3.95	69	.279	.330	9	.265	-0	-11	-11	-0	-0.9
1903 Cle-A	1	2	.333	4	3	2	0	0	30¹	34	1	3	12	11.3	3.56	80	.281	.304	1	.083	-1	-2	-2	-0	-0.3
Total 2	3	8	.273	15	13	10	0	0	112¹	124	1	25	36	12.3	3.85	72	.279	.323	10	.217	-0	-13	-13	-0	-1.2
● **IKE PEARSON** Pearson, Issac Overton b: 3/1/17, Grenada, Miss. d: 3/17/85, Sarasota, Fla. BR/TR, 6'1", 180 lbs. Deb: 6/6/39																									
1939 Phi-N	2	13	.133	26	13	4	0	0	125	144	15	56	29	14.8	5.76	70	.296	.374	2	.054	-3	-26	-24	1	-2.7
1940 Phi-N	3	14	.176	29	20	5	1	1	145¹	160	13	70	43	13.6	5.45	72	.275	.343	9	.205	1	-26	-25	1	-2.4
1941 Phi-N	4	14	.222	46	10	0	0	6	136	139	8	70	38	14.4	3.57	104	.266	.361	5	.125	-2	1	2	0	0.0
1942 Phi-N	1	6	.143	35	7	0	0	0	85¹	87	4	50	21	14.9	4.54	73	.271	.376	1	.043	-2	-12	-12	-0	-1.2
1946 Phi-N	1	0	1.000	5	2	1	0	0	14¹	16	1	9	5	15.7	3.77	91	.271	.368	1	.200	1	-1	-0	0	0.1
1948 Chi-A	2	3	.400	23	2	0	0	1	53	62	8	27	12	15.5	4.92	87	.292	.378	2	.200	-1	-4	-4	1	-0.3
Total 6	13	50	.206	164	54	10	2	8	559	608	49	268	149	14.5	4.83	79	.279	.363	20	.126	-6	-66	-64	2	-6.5
● **MONTE PEARSON** Pearson, Montgomery Marcellus "Hoot" b: 9/2/09, Oakland, Cal. d: 1/27/78, Fresno, Cal. BR/TR, 6', 175 lbs. Deb: 4/22/32																									
1932 Cle-A	1	1	.500	4	3	1	0	0	26¹	24	1	6	3	23.6	10.13	47	.323	.500	0	—	0	-5	-5	1	-0.5
1933 Cle-A	10	5	.667	19	16	10	0	0	135¹	111	5	55	54	11.0	**2.33**	191	.221	.297	13	.260	1	29	32	-1	3.3
1934 Cle-A	18	13	.581	39	33	19	0	2	254²	257	16	130	140	13.7	4.52	101	.260	.346	25	.272	6	-1	-1	1	0.7
1935 Cle-A	8	13	.381	30	24	10	1	0	181²	199	9	103	90	15.0	4.90	92	.279	.371	11	.177	-0	-9	-8	0	-0.6
1936 *NY-A☆	19	7	**.731**	33	31	15	1	1	223	191	13	135	118	13.3	3.71	125	**.233**	.343	23	.253	6	33	23	1	2.9

YEAR TM/L	W	L	PCT	G	GS	CG	SH	SV	IP	H	HR	BB	SO	RAT	ERA	ERA+	OAV	OOB	BH	AVG	PB	PR	/A	PD	TPI
1937 *NY-A	9	3	.750	22	20	7	1	1	144²	145	6	64	71	13.1	3.17	140	.261	.339	11	.216	1	23	20	-1	1.5
1938 *NY-A	16	7	.696	28	27	17	1	0	202	198	12	113	98	13.9	3.97	114	.258	.354	1	.18	13	2	1.4		
1939 *NY-A	12	5	.706	22	20	8	0	0	146¹	151	9	70	76	13.7	4.49	97	.272	.354	17	.321	6	-2	-2	1	0.4
1940 NY-A☆	7	5	.583	16	16	7	1	0	109²	108	8	44	43	12.5	3.69	109	.262	.333	4	.121	-1	8	4	2	0.5
1941 Cin-N	1	3	.250	7	4	1	0	0	24¹	22	3	15	8	13.7	5.18	69	.242	.349	0	.000		-4	-4	-0	-0.7
Total 10	100	61	.621	224	191	94	5	4	1429²	1392	82	740	703	13.5	4.00	112	.256	.346	117	.228	19	95	75	8	9.5

● **MARV PEASLEY**   Peasley, Marvin Warren b: 7/16/1888, Jonesport, Me. d: 12/27/48, San Francisco, Cal   BL/TL, 6'1", 175 lbs. Deb: 9/27/10

YEAR TM/L	W	L	PCT	G	GS	CG	SH	SV	IP	H	HR	BB	SO	RAT	ERA	ERA+	OAV	OOB	BH	AVG	PB	PR	/A	PD	TPI
1910 Det-A	0	1	.000	2	1	0	0	0	10	13	0	11	4	22.5	8.10	32	.295	.446	0	.000	0	-6	-6	-0	-0.5

● **GEORGE PECHINEY**   Pechiney, George Adolphe "Pisch" b: 9/20/1861, Cincinnati, Ohio d: 7/14/43, Cincinnati, Ohio   BR/TR, 5'9", 184 lbs. Deb: 8/4/1885

YEAR TM/L	W	L	PCT	G	GS	CG	SH	SV	IP	H	HR	BB	SO	RAT	ERA	ERA+	OAV	OOB	BH	AVG	PB	PR	/A	PD	TPI
1885 Cin-a	7	4	.636	11	11	11	1	0	98	95	1	30	49	12.0	2.02	161	.247	.311	6	.150	-2	13	13	1	1.2
1886 Cin-a	15	21	.417	40	40	35	2	0	330¹	355	4	133	110	13.7	4.14	85	.266	.339	30	.208	-1	-25	-23	-3	-2.3
1887 Cle-a	1	9	.100	10	10	10	0	0	86	118	8	44	24	17.3	7.12	61	.303	.378	9	.250	-0	-27	-27	0	-2.1
Total 3	23	34	.404	61	61	56	3	0	514¹	568	13	207	183	14.0	4.23	85	.269	.341	45	.205	-3	-39	-36	-2	-3.2

● **BILL PECOTA**   Pecota, William Joseph b: 2/16/60, Redwood City, Cal.   BR/TR, 6'2", 195 lbs. Deb: 9/19/86 ◆

YEAR TM/L	W	L	PCT	G	GS	CG	SH	SV	IP	H	HR	BB	SO	RAT	ERA	ERA+	OAV	OOB	BH	AVG	PB	PR	/A	PD	TPI
1991 KC-A	0	0	—	1	0	0	0	0	2	4	0	0	0	18.0	4.50	92	.444	.444	114	.286	0	-0	-0	-0	0.0
1992 NY-N	0	0	—	1	0	0	0	0	1	1	0	0	0	9.00	9.00	39	.250	.250	61	.227	0	-1	-1	-0	0.0
Total 2	0	0	—	2	0	0	0	0	3	5	1	0	0	15.0	6.00	65	.385	.385	380	.249	0	-1	-1	-0	0.0

● **STEVE PEEK**   Peek, Stephen George b: 7/30/14, Springfield, Mass d: 9/20/91, Syracuse, N.Y.   BB/TR, 6'2", 195 lbs. Deb: 4/16/41

YEAR TM/L	W	L	PCT	G	GS	CG	SH	SV	IP	H	HR	BB	SO	RAT	ERA	ERA+	OAV	OOB	BH	AVG	PB	PR	/A	PD	TPI
1941 NY-A	4	2	.667	17	8	2	0	0	80	85	6	39	18	13.9	5.06	78	.276	.357	1	.036	-3	-8	-10	0	-0.9

● **RED PEERY**   Peery, George Allan b: 8/15/06, Payson, Utah d: 5/6/85, Salt Lake City, Ut.   BL/TL, 5'11", 160 lbs. Deb: 9/22/27

YEAR TM/L	W	L	PCT	G	GS	CG	SH	SV	IP	H	HR	BB	SO	RAT	ERA	ERA+	OAV	OOB	BH	AVG	PB	PR	/A	PD	TPI
1927 Pit-N	0	0	—	1	0	0	0	0	1	0	0	1	0	9.0	0.00	—	.000	.200	1		0	0	0	0	0.0
1929 Bos-N	0	1	.000	9	1	0	0	0	44	53	1	9	3	12.7	5.11	91	.305	.339	3	.214	1	-2	-2	-0	0.0
Total 2	0	1	.000	10	1	0	0	0	45	53	1	10	3	12.6	5.00	93	.298	.335	3	.214	1	-2	-2	0	0.0

● **HEINIE PEITZ**   Peitz, Henry Clement b: 11/28/1870, St.Louis, Mo. d: 10/23/43, Cincinnati, Ohio   BR/TR, 5'11", 165 lbs. Deb: 10/15/1892 FC ◆

YEAR TM/L	W	L	PCT	G	GS	CG	SH	SV	IP	H	HR	BB	SO	RAT	ERA	ERA+	OAV	OOB	BH	AVG	PB	PR	/A	PD	TPI
1894 StL-N	0	0	—	1	0	0	0	0	3	7	0	2	0	30.0	9.00	60	.438	.526	89	.263	0	-1	-1	-0	0.0
1897 Cin-N	0	1	.000	2	1	1	0	0	8	9	0	4	0	16.9	7.88	58	.281	.395	78	.293	0	-3	-3	1	-0.2
1899 Cin-N	0	0	—	1	0	0	0	0	5	6	0	1	2	12.6	5.40	73	.300	.333	79	.272	0	-1	-1	0	0.0
Total 3	0	1	.000	4	1	1	0	0	16	22	0	7	3	18.0	7.31	62	.324	.410	1117	.271	1	-5	-5	1	-0.2

● **BARNEY PELTY**   Pelty, Barney b: 9/10/1880, Farmington, Mo. d: 5/24/39, Farmington, Mo.   BR/TR, 5'9", 175 lbs. Deb: 8/20/03

YEAR TM/L	W	L	PCT	G	GS	CG	SH	SV	IP	H	HR	BB	SO	RAT	ERA	ERA+	OAV	OOB	BH	AVG	PB	PR	/A	PD	TPI
1903 StL-A	3	3	.500	7	6	5	0	1	48²	49	1	15	15	12.2	2.40	121	.261	.322	3	.150	-0	-8	3	-1	0.2
1904 StL-A	15	18	.455	39	35	31	2	0	301	270	7	77	126	11.0	2.84	87	.241	.301	15	.127	-6	-8	-12	-1	-2.1
1905 StL-A	14	14	.500	31	28	27	1	0	258²	222	3	68	114	10.5	2.75	93	.233	.293	15	.153	-3	-3	-6	3	-0.7
1906 StL-A	16	11	.593	34	30	25	4	2	260²	189	1	59	92	9.2	1.59	163	**.206**	.267	15	.165	-3	**32**	29	4	3.3
1907 StL-A	12	21	.364	36	31	29	5	1	273	234	1	64	85	10.4	2.57	98	.234	.292	16	.168	-2	-1	-2	-2	-0.2
1908 StL-A	7	4	.636	20	13	7	1	0	122	104	0	32	36	10.8	1.99	120	.241	.309	5	.119	-3	5	5	1	0.3
1909 StL-A	11	11	.500	27	23	17	5	0	199¹	158	2	53	88	9.8	2.30	105	.222	.281	15	.165	0	4	3	4	0.8
1910 StL-A	5	11	.313	27	19	13	3	0	165¹	157	3	70	48	12.8	3.48	71	.263	.348	15	.089	-4	-18	-19	4	-1.7
1911 StL-A	7	15	.318	28	22	18	1	0	197	197	4	69	59	12.3	2.97	114	.265	.331	9	.138	-3	8	9	1	0.7
1912 StL-A	1	5	.167	6	6	2	0	0	38²	43	1	9	10	14.2	5.59	59	.297	.374	0	.000	-2	-10	-10	0	-1.4
Was-A	1	4	.200	11	4	1	0	0	43²	40	0	10	15	11.1	3.30	101	.250	.310	2	.222	0	0	0	-1	0.0
Yr	2	9	.182	17	10	3	0	0	82¹	83	1	19	25	12.2	4.37	76	.269	.332	2	.095	-2	-10	-10	-1	-1.4
Total 10	92	117	.440	266	217	175	22	4	1908	1663	22	532	693	10.8	2.63	100	.239	.302	100	.143	-25	14	0	16	-0.8

● **ALEJANDRO PENA**   Pena, Alejandro (Vasquez) b: 6/25/59, Cambiaso, D.R.   BR/TR, 6'1", 205 lbs. Deb: 9/14/81

YEAR TM/L	W	L	PCT	G	GS	CG	SH	SV	IP	H	HR	BB	SO	RAT	ERA	ERA+	OAV	OOB	BH	AVG	PB	PR	/A	PD	TPI
1981 *LA-N	1	1	.500	14	0	0	0	2	25¹	18	2	11	14	10.3	2.84	117	.194	.279	0	.000	-1	2	1	-0	0.1
1982 LA-N	0	2	.000	29	0	0	0	0	35²	37	2	21	20	14.9	4.79	72	.272	.373	0	—	0	-5	-5	1	-0.2
1983 *LA-N	12	9	.571	34	26	4	3	1	177	152	7	51	120	10.4	2.75	131	.229	.285	6	.100	-2	17	17	2	1.9
1984 LA-N	12	6	.667	28	28	8	**4**	0	199¹	186	7	46	135	10.6	**2.48**	**142**	.246	.292	8	.121	-1	**24**	23	-1	1.8
1985 LA-N	0	1	.000	2	1	0	0	0	4¹	7	1	3	2	20.8	8.31	42	.350	.435	0	.000	-0	-2	-2	-0	-0.5
1986 LA-N	1	2	.333	24	10	0	0	1	70	74	6	30	46	13.5	4.89	71	.270	.344	3	.176	0	-9	-11	-1	-0.6
1987 LA-N	2	7	.222	37	7	0	0	11	87¹	82	9	37	76	12.5	3.50	113	.251	.331	1	.077	-1	6	4	-2	0.2
1988 *LA-N	6	7	.462	60	0	0	0	12	94¹	75	4	27	83	9.8	1.91	175	.218	.277	0	.000	-1	16	15	-0	2.3
1989 LA-N	4	3	.571	53	0	0	0	5	76	62	6	18	75	9.7	2.13	160	.220	.272	1	1.000	-0	12	11	-1	1.4
1990 NY-N	3	3	.500	52	0	0	0	5	76	71	4	22	76	11.1	3.20	117	.245	.300	1	.167	0	5	5	-1	0.3
1991 NY-N	6	1	.857	44	0	0	0	4	63	63	5	19	49	11.7	2.71	134	.267	.322	0	—	0	7	6	-0	0.7
*Atl-N	2	0	1.000	15	0	0	0	11	19¹	11	1	3	13	6.5	1.40	278	.167	.203	0	.000	-0	5	5	-0	1.1
Yr	8	1	.889	59	0	0	0	15	82¹	74	6	22	62	10.5	2.40	154	.242	.293	0	.000	-0	12	12	-0	1.8
1992 Atl-N	1	6	.143	41	0	0	0	15	42	40	7	13	34	11.4	4.07	90	.255	.312	0	.000	-0	-3	-2	-1	-0.6
1994 Pit-N	3	2	.600	22	0	0	0	7	28²	22	4	10	27	10.4	5.02	86	.206	.280	0	.000	-0	-3	-2	-1	-0.5
1995 Bos-A	1	1	.500	17	0	0	0	0	24¹	33	5	12	25	16.6	7.40	66	.314	.385	1	—	0	-7	-7	-0	-0.5
Fla-N	2	0	1.000	13	0	0	0	0	18	11	2	3	21	7.0	1.50	281	.169	.206	0	.000	-0	5	5	-0	0.5
*Atl-N	0	0	—	14	0	0	0	0	13	11	1	4	18	10.4	4.15	103	.224	.283	0	—	0	-0	-0	-0	-0.1
Yr	2	0	1.000	27	0	0	0	0	31	22	3	7	39	8.4	2.61	162	.193	.240	0	—	0	5	6	-0	0.5
1996 Fla-N	1	0	1.000	4	0	0	0	0	4	4	2	1	5	11.3	4.50	90	.235	.278	0	—	0	-0	-0	-0	-0.1
Total 15	56	52	.519	503	72	12	7	74	1057²	959	75	331	839	11.1	3.11	117	.240	.301	20	.110	-5	70	63	-8	6.9

● **HIPOLITO PENA**   Pena, Hipolito (Concepcion) b: 1/30/64, Fantino, D.R.   BL/TL, 6'3", 165 lbs. Deb: 9/1/86

YEAR TM/L	W	L	PCT	G	GS	CG	SH	SV	IP	H	HR	BB	SO	RAT	ERA	ERA+	OAV	OOB	BH	AVG	PB	PR	/A	PD	TPI
1986 Pit-N	0	3	.000	10	1	0	0	1	8¹	7	3	6	8	11.9	8.64	44	.206	.289	0	—	0	-5	-4	-0	-1.5
1987 Pit-N	0	3	.000	16	1	0	0	0	25²	26	2	26	16	14.7	4.56	90	.184	.372	1	.167	-0	-1	-1	-0	-0.2
1988 NY-A	1	1	.500	16	0	0	0	1	14¹	10	1	9	10	11.9	3.14	125	.192	.311	0	—	0	1	1	0	0.2
Total 3	1	7	.125	42	2	0	0	2	48¹	33	6	38	32	13.4	4.84	83	.191	.340	1	.167	-0	-5	-4	-0	-1.5

● **JIM PENA**   Pena, James Patrick b: 9/17/64, Los Angeles, Cal.   BL/TL, 6', 175 lbs. Deb: 7/7/92

YEAR TM/L	W	L	PCT	G	GS	CG	SH	SV	IP	H	HR	BB	SO	RAT	ERA	ERA+	OAV	OOB	BH	AVG	PB	PR	/A	PD	TPI
1992 SF-N	1	1	.500	25	2	0	0	0	44	49	4	20	32	14.3	3.48	95	.282	.359	1	.200	0	0	-1	1	0.0

● **JOSE PENA**   Pena, Jose (Gutierrez) b: 12/3/42, Ciudad Juarez, Mex.   BR/TR, 6'2", 190 lbs. Deb: 6/1/69

YEAR TM/L	W	L	PCT	G	GS	CG	SH	SV	IP	H	HR	BB	SO	RAT	ERA	ERA+	OAV	OOB	BH	AVG	PB	PR	/A	PD	TPI
1969 Cin-N	0	1	.500	6	0	0	0	0	5	10	0	5	3	27.0	18.00	21	.400	.500	0	—	0	-8	-8	0	-2.4
1970 LA-N	4	3	.571	29	0	0	0	4	57	51	8	29	31	13.1	4.42	87	.241	.340	1	.125	0	-2	-4	0	-0.4
1971 LA-N	2	0	1.000	21	0	0	0	0	43	32	7	18	44	10.7	3.56	91	.211	.298	2	.667	1	-0	-2	-0	0.0
1972 LA-N	1	0	—	5	0	0	0	1	7¹	13	1	6	4	23.3	8.59	39	.371	.463	0	—	0	-4	-4	-0	0.0
Total 4	7	4	.636	61	0	0	0	5	112¹	106	16	58	82	13.5	4.97	72	.250	.346	3	.273	1	-15	-18	0	-2.8

● **ORLANDO PENA**   Pena, Orlando Gregorio (Quevara) b: 11/17/33, Victoria De Las Tunas, Cuba   BR/TR, 5'11", 154 lbs. Deb: 8/24/58

YEAR TM/L	W	L	PCT	G	GS	CG	SH	SV	IP	H	HR	BB	SO	RAT	ERA	ERA+	OAV	OOB	BH	AVG	PB	PR	/A	PD	TPI
1958 Cin-N	1	0	1.000	9	0	0	0	0	15	11	0	4	11	8.4	0.60	691	.185	.241	0	—	0	6	6	-0	0.6
1959 Cin-N	5	9	.357	46	8	1	0	5	136	150	26	39	76	12.5	4.76	85	.280	.329	3	.088	-0	-12	-11	-1	-1.2
1960 Cin-N	0	0	—	4	0	0	0	0	9¹	11	3	0	9	10.6	2.89	132	.222	.282	0	.000	-0	1	1	-0	0.1
1962 KC-A	6	4	.600	13	12	6	1	0	89²	71	9	27	56	9.9	3.01	140	.213	.274	5	.161	-0	10	12	-1	1.1
1963 KC-A	12	20	.375	35	33	9	3	0	217	218	24	53	128	11.4	3.69	106	.260	.308	9	.145	-0	4	7	-3	0.5
1964 KC-A	12	14	.462	40	32	5	0	0	219¹	231	40	73	184	12.8	4.43	86	.268	.331	12	.160	-1	-20	-15	-2	-1.8
1965 KC-A	0	6	.000	12	5	0	0	0	35¹	42	4	13	24	14.5	6.88	51	.302	.370	1	.111	-0	-13	-13	0	-2.0
Det-A	4	6	.400	30	0	0	0	4	57¹	54	5	20	55	11.8	2.51	138	.252	.319	2	.250	-1	4	6	1	1.1
Yr	4	12	.250	42	5	0	0	4	92²	96	9	33	79	12.6	4.18	83	.270	.333	3	.176	1	-7	-7	-0	-0.9
1966 Det-A	4	2	.667	54	0	0	0	7	108	105	16	35	79	12.1	3.08	113	.252	.317	2	.111	-1	4	5	2	0.5
1967 Det-A	0	1	.000	2	0	0	0	0	2	5	0	0	2	27.0	13.50	24	.500	.545	0	—	0	-2	-2	-0	-0.9
Cle-A	0	3	.000	48	1	0	0	0	88¹	67	8	22	72	9.2	3.36	97	.208	.261	1	.000	-1	-1	-1	-0	-0.2

YEAR	TM/L	W	L	PCT	G	GS	CG	SH	SV	IP	H	HR	BB	SO	RAT	ERA	ERA+	OAV	OOB	BH	AVG	PB	PR	/A	PD	TPI
	Yr	0	4	.000	50	1	0	0	8	90¹	72	8	22	74	9.5	3.59	91	.216	.266	0	.000	-1	-4	-3	-1	-1.1
1970	Pit-N	2	1	.667	23	0	0	0	2	37²	38	6	7	25	11.0	4.78	82	.268	.307	0	.000	-1	-3	-4	1	-0.3
1971	Bal-A	0	1	.000	5	0	0	0	1	14²	16	0	5	4	12.9	3.07	109	.281	.339	-0		1	0	0	0	0.0
1973	Bal-A	1	1	.500	11	2	0	0	1	44²	36	10	8	23	9.3	4.03	93	.218	.263	0	—	-1	-1	-1	-0	-0.1
	StL-N	4	4	.500	42	0	0	0	6	62	60	3	14	38	10.7	2.18	167	.251	.292	1	.143	-0	10	10	0	1.5
1974	StL-N	5	2	.714	42	0	0	0	2	45	45	0	20	23	13.2	2.60	137	.269	.351	1	.500	-0	5	5	-0	0.8
	Cal-A	0	0	—	4	0	0	0	3	8	6	0	1	5	7.9	0.00	—	.214	.241	0		0	3	3	0	0.8
1975	Cal-A	0	2	.000	7	0	0	0	0	12²	13	0	8	4	14.9	2.13	166	.283	.389	0		0	2	2	-1	0.7
Total	14	56	77	.421	427	93	21	4	40	1202	1175	151	352	818	11.6	3.71	102	.255	.312	36	.136	-3	-7	8	-6	1.2

● **RAMON PENA**   Pena, Ramon Arturo (Padilla) b: 5/5/62, Santiago, D.R. BR/TR, 5'10", 155 lbs. Deb: 4/27/89 F

YEAR	TM/L	W	L	PCT	G	GS	CG	SH	SV	IP	H	HR	BB	SO	RAT	ERA	ERA+	OAV	OOB	BH	AVG	PB	PR	/A	PD	TPI
1989	Det-A	0	0	—	8	0	0	0	0	18	26	1	8	12	18.0	6.00	64	.338	.414	0	—	-0	-4	-4	1	0.1

● **RUSTY PENCE**   Pence, Russell William b: 3/11/1900, Marine, Ill. d: 8/11/71, Hot Springs, Ark. BR/TR, 6', 185 lbs. Deb: 5/13/21

YEAR	TM/L	W	L	PCT	G	GS	CG	SH	SV	IP	H	HR	BB	SO	RAT	ERA	ERA+	OAV	OOB	BH	AVG	PB	PR	/A	PD	TPI
1921	Chi-A	0	0	—	4	0	0	0	0	5¹	6	0	7	2	23.6	8.44	50	.286	.483	0	.000	-0	-2	-2	0	0.0

● **KEN PENNER**   Penner, Kenneth William b: 4/24/1896, Boonville, Ind. d: 5/28/59, Sacramento, Cal. BL/TR, 5'11.5", 170 lbs. Deb: 9/11/16

YEAR	TM/L	W	L	PCT	G	GS	CG	SH	SV	IP	H	HR	BB	SO	RAT	ERA	ERA+	OAV	OOB	BH	AVG	PB	PR	/A	PD	TPI
1916	Cle-A	1	0	1.000	4	0	0	0	0	12²	14	0	4	5	12.8	4.26	71	.304	.360	0	.000	-0	-2	-2	1	-0.1
1929	Chi-N	0	1	.000	5	0	0	0	0	12²	14	1	6	3	14.2	2.84	162	.280	.357	1	.250	0	3	2	-0	0.2
Total	2	1	1	.500	9	0	0	0	0	25¹	28	1	10	8	13.5	3.55	108	.292	.358	1	.167	-0	1	1	1	0.1

● **BRAD PENNINGTON**   Pennington, Brad Lee b: 4/14/69, Salem, Ind. BL/TL, 6'5", 205 lbs. Deb: 4/17/93

YEAR	TM/L	W	L	PCT	G	GS	CG	SH	SV	IP	H	HR	BB	SO	RAT	ERA	ERA+	OAV	OOB	BH	AVG	PB	PR	/A	PD	TPI
1993	Bal-A	3	2	.600	34	0	0	0	4	33	34	7	25	39	16.6	6.55	68	.266	.394	0	—	0	-8	-8	-0	-1.3
1994	Bal-A	0	1	.000	8	0	0	0	0	6	9	2	8	7	25.5	12.00	42	.346	.500	0	—	0	-5	-5	-0	-0.7
1995	Bal-A	0	1	.000	8	0	0	0	0	6²	3	1	11	10	18.9	8.10	59	.136	.424	0	—	0	-3	-2	-0	-0.3
	Cin-N	0	0	—	6	0	0	0	0	9²	9	0	11	7	19.6	5.59	74	.273	.467	0	.000	0	-2	-2	-0	-0.1
1996	Bos-A	0	0	—	14	0	0	0	0	13	6	1	15	13	14.5	2.77	186	.140	.362	0	—	0	3	3	0	0.4
	Cal-A	0	0	—	8	0	0	0	0	7¹	5	1	16	7	25.8	12.27	40	.185	.488	0	—	0	-6	-6	-0	-0.4
	Yr	0	2	.000	22	0	0	0	0	20¹	11	2	31	20	18.6	6.20	82	.155	.412	0	—	0	-3	-3	-0	0.4
Total	4	3	6	.333	78	0	0	0	4	75²	66	12	86	83	18.4	6.90	67	.237	.421	0	—	0	-20	-19	-1	-2.0

● **KEWPIE PENNINGTON**   Pennington, George Louis b: 9/24/1896, New York, N.Y. d: 5/3/53, Newark, N.J. BR/TR, 5'8.5", 168 lbs. Deb: 4/14/17

YEAR	TM/L	W	L	PCT	G	GS	CG	SH	SV	IP	H	HR	BB	SO	RAT	ERA	ERA+	OAV	OOB	BH	AVG	PB	PR	/A	PD	TPI
1917	StL-A	0	0	—	1	0	0	0	0	1	0	0	1	0	9.0	0.00	—	.250	.250	0	—	0	0	0	-0	0.0

● **HERB PENNOCK**   Pennock, Herbert Jefferis "The Knight Of Kennett Square"
    b: 2/10/1894, Kennett Square, Pa d: 1/30/48, New York, N.Y. BB/TL, 6', 160 lbs. Deb: 5/14/12 CH

YEAR	TM/L	W	L	PCT	G	GS	CG	SH	SV	IP	H	HR	BB	SO	RAT	ERA	ERA+	OAV	OOB	BH	AVG	PB	PR	/A	PD	TPI
1912	Phi-A	1	2	.333	17	2	1	0	2	50	48	1	30	38	14.6	4.50	68	.262	.375	2	.133	-1	-7	-8	1	-0.5
1913	Phi-A	2	1	.667	14	3	1	0	0	33¹	30	1	22	17	14.0	5.13	54	.221	.329	1	.111	-0	-8	-9	-0	-0.8
1914	*Phi-A	11	4	.733	28	14	8	3	3	151²	136	1	65	90	12.0	2.79	94	.248	.330	12	.214	-2	-1	-3	-1	-0.1
1915	Phi-A	3	6	.333	11	8	3	1	1	44	46	2	29	24	15.8	5.32	55	.266	.377	5	.278	1	-12	-12	-1	-2.0
	Bos-A	0	0	—	5	1	0	0	0	14	23	0	10	7	21.2	9.64	29	.390	.478	1	.167	-0	-10	-11	-1	-0.1
	Yr	3	6	.333	16	9	3	1	1	58	69	2	39	31	16.8	6.36	45	.295	.396	6	.250	1	-22	-22	-0	-2.1
1916	Bos-A	0	2	.000	9	4	1	0	1	26²	23	0	8	12	10.8	3.04	91	.245	.311	1	.125	-0	-1	-1	-0	-0.1
1917	Bos-A	5	5	.500	24	5	4	1	1	100²	90	2	25	35	10.4	3.31	78	.243	.292	4	.167	-2	-7	-8	-0	-0.7
1919	Bos-A	16	8	.667	32	26	16	5	0	219	223	2	48	70	11.3	2.71	111	.274	.316	13	.173	1	13	8	-2	0.6
1920	Bos-A	16	13	.552	37	31	19	4	2	242¹	244	8	68	68	11.5	3.68	99	.264	.312	20	.260	4	3	-1	-3	0.1
1921	Bos-A	13	14	.481	32	31	15	1	0	222²	268	7	59	91	13.3	4.04	105	.307	.352	18	.212	2	6	5	1	0.8
1922	Bos-A	10	17	.370	32	26	15	1	1	202	230	7	74	59	13.6	4.32	95	.297	.359	9	.138	-3	-6	-5	-1	-0.7
1923	*NY-A	19	6	**.760**	35	27	21	1	0	238	235	11	68	93	11.5	3.13	127	.261	.314	16	.193	-0	23	21	1	2.1
1924	NY-A	21	9	.700	40	34	25	4	3	286¹	302	13	64	101	11.5	2.83	147	.273	.314	16	.158	-2	45	**42**	-1	3.8
1925	NY-A	16	17	.485	47	31	21	2	2	277	267	11	71	88	**11.0**	2.96	144	.254	**.303**	20	.202	-3	**44**	40	-3	3.6
1926	*NY-A	23	11	.676	40	33	19	1	2	266¹	294	11	43	78	**11.5**	3.62	107	.282	**.313**	18	.212	3	12	7	1	1.1
1927	*NY-A	19	8	.704	34	26	18	1	2	209²	225	5	48	51	11.8	3.00	128	.283	.325	15	.217	-0	26	20	-2	2.1
1928	NY-A	17	6	.739	28	24	18	**5**	3	211	215	8	40	53	10.9	2.56	147	.267	.302	15	.203	-1	35	28	2	2.9
1929	NY-A	9	11	.450	27	23	8	1	2	157¹	205	11	28	49	13.5	4.92	78	.318	.349	9	.176	-1	-12	-19	-1	-2.1
1930	NY-A	11	7	.611	25	19	11	1	0	156¹	194	8	20	46	12.3	4.32	100	.301	.322	11	.183	-2	6	-0	-2	-0.4
1931	NY-A	11	6	.647	25	25	12	1	0	189¹	247	7	30	65	13.2	4.28	93	.315	.342	10	.152	1	2	-7	-1	-0.5
1932	*NY-A	9	5	.643	22	21	9	1	0	146²	191	8	38	54	14.1	4.60	89	.310	.350	8	.151	0	-2	-9	-1	-0.7
1933	NY-A	7	4	.636	23	5	2	1	4	65	96	4	21	22	16.2	5.54	70	.342	.387	5	.238	0	-9	-12	-0	-1.8
1934	Bos-A	2	0	1.000	30	2	1	0	1	62	68	3	16	12	12.2	3.05	158	.276	.321	3	.214	-0	**10**	**12**	-1	0.2
Total	22	241	162	.598	617	419	247	35	33	3571²	3900	128	916	1227	12.2	3.60	106	.281	.328	232	.191	3	150	81	-11	6.8

● **PAUL PENSON**   Penson, Paul Eugene b: 7/12/31, Kansas City, Kan. BR/TR, 6'1", 185 lbs. Deb: 4/21/54

YEAR	TM/L	W	L	PCT	G	GS	CG	SH	SV	IP	H	HR	BB	SO	RAT	ERA	ERA+	OAV	OOB	BH	AVG	PB	PR	/A	PD	TPI
1954	Phi-N	1	1	.500	5	3	0	0	0	16	14	1	14	3	15.8	4.50	90	.237	.384	0	.000	-1	-1	-1	-1	-0.2

● **GENE PENTZ**   Pentz, Eugene David b: 6/21/53, Johnstown, Pa. BR/TR, 6'1", 200 lbs. Deb: 7/29/75

YEAR	TM/L	W	L	PCT	G	GS	CG	SH	SV	IP	H	HR	BB	SO	RAT	ERA	ERA+	OAV	OOB	BH	AVG	PB	PR	/A	PD	TPI
1975	Det-A	0	4	.000	13	0	0	0	0	25¹	27	0	20	21	16.7	3.20	126	.293	.420	0	—	0	2	-2	-0	0.0
1976	Hou-N	3	3	.500	40	0	0	0	5	63²	62	5	31	36	13.3	2.97	108	.259	.347	1	.200	0	4	2	1	0.3
1977	Hou-N	5	2	.714	41	4	0	0	1	87	76	8	41	51	12.5	3.83	93	.236	.330	0	.000	-2	1	-3	0	-0.4
1978	Hou-N	0	0	—	10	0	0	0	1	15	12	1	13	8	15.6	6.00	55	.214	.371	0	.000	0	-4	-4	1	0.1
Total	4	8	9	.471	104	4	0	0	7	191	177	14	108	116	13.6	3.63	96	.250	.351	1	.053	-1	2	-3	1	0.0

● **JIMMY PEOPLES**   Peoples, James Elsworth b: 10/8/1863, Big Beaver, Mich. d: 8/29/20, Detroit, Mich. TR, 5'8", 200 lbs. Deb: 5/29/1884 U♦

YEAR	TM/L	W	L	PCT	G	GS	CG	SH	SV	IP	H	HR	BB	SO	RAT	ERA	ERA+	OAV	OOB	BH	AVG	PB	PR	/A	PD	TPI
1885	Cin-a	0	2	.000	2	2	1	0	0	15	30	0	2	4	21.0	12.00	27	.390	.427	4	.182	0	-15	-15	1	-1.2

● **LAURIN PEPPER**   Pepper, Hugh McLaurin b: 1/18/31, Vaughan, Miss. BR/TR, 5'11", 190 lbs. Deb: 7/4/54

YEAR	TM/L	W	L	PCT	G	GS	CG	SH	SV	IP	H	HR	BB	SO	RAT	ERA	ERA+	OAV	OOB	BH	AVG	PB	PR	/A	PD	TPI
1954	Pit-N	1	5	.167	14	8	0	0	0	50²	63	4	43	17	18.8	7.99	52	.315	.436	4	.235	0	-22	-21	1	-1.9
1955	Pit-N	0	1	.000	14	1	0	0	0	20	30	5	25	7	25.6	10.35	40	.370	.528	0	.000	-0	-14	-14	0	-0.7
1956	Pit-N	1	1	.500	11	7	0	0	0	30	30	1	25	12	16.5	3.00	126	.256	.387	0	.000	-0	3	3	-1	0.0
1957	Pit-N	0	1	.000	5	1	0	0	0	9	11	1	5	4	16.0	8.00	47	.297	.381	0	—	-0	-4	-4	-0	-0.4
Total	4	2	8	.200	44	17	0	0	0	109²	134	11	98	40	19.2	7.06	57	.308	.437	4	.160	-0	-38	-37	0	-3.0

● **BOB PEPPER**   Pepper, Robert Ernest b: 5/3/1895, Rosston, Pa. d: 4/8/68, Ford Cliff, Pa. BR/TR, 6'2", 178 lbs. Deb: 7/23/15

YEAR	TM/L	W	L	PCT	G	GS	CG	SH	SV	IP	H	HR	BB	SO	RAT	ERA	ERA+	OAV	OOB	BH	AVG	PB	PR	/A	PD	TPI
1915	Phi-A	0	0	—	1	0	0	0	0	5	6	0	4	0	19.8	1.80	163	.333	.478	0	.000	-0	1	1	0	0.0

● **HARRISON PEPPERS**   Peppers, Harrison (b: William Harrison Pepper) b: 9/1866, Kentucky d: 11/5/03, Webb City, Mo. BL, Deb: 6/30/1894

YEAR	TM/L	W	L	PCT	G	GS	CG	SH	SV	IP	H	HR	BB	SO	RAT	ERA	ERA+	OAV	OOB	BH	AVG	PB	PR	/A	PD	TPI
1894	Lou-N	0	1	.000	2	1	0	0	0	8	10	0	4	5	15.8	6.75	75	.303	.378	-1		-1	-1	-1	-0	-0.2

● **LUIS PERAZA**   Peraza, Luis (Rios) b: 6/17/42, Rio Piedras, P.R. BR/TR, 5'11", 185 lbs. Deb: 4/9/69

YEAR	TM/L	W	L	PCT	G	GS	CG	SH	SV	IP	H	HR	BB	SO	RAT	ERA	ERA+	OAV	OOB	BH	AVG	PB	PR	/A	PD	TPI
1969	Phi-N	0	0	—	8	0	0	0	0	9	12	1	2	4	14.0	6.00	59	.364	.400	0	.000	-0	-2	-2	-0	0.0

● **OSWALDO PERAZA**   Peraza, Oswald Jose b: 10/19/62, Puerto Cabello, Venez. BR/TR, 6'4", 172 lbs. Deb: 4/4/88

YEAR	TM/L	W	L	PCT	G	GS	CG	SH	SV	IP	H	HR	BB	SO	RAT	ERA	ERA+	OAV	OOB	BH	AVG	PB	PR	/A	PD	TPI
1988	Bal-A	5	7	.417	19	15	1	0	0	86	98	10	37	61	14.3	5.55	70	.282	.355	0	—	0	-15	-16	0	-1.8

● **TROY PERCIVAL**   Percival, Troy Eugene b: 8/9/69, Fontana, Cal. BR/TR, 6'3", 200 lbs. Deb: 4/26/95

YEAR	TM/L	W	L	PCT	G	GS	CG	SH	SV	IP	H	HR	BB	SO	RAT	ERA	ERA+	OAV	OOB	BH	AVG	PB	PR	/A	PD	TPI
1995	Cal-A	3	2	.600	62	0	0	0	3	74	37	6	26	94	7.8	1.95	241	.147	.229	0	—	0	23	23	-1	1.4
1996	Cal-A★	0	2	.000	62	0	0	0	36	74	38	8	31	100	8.6	2.31	212	.149	.247	0	.000	0	22	21	-1	2.2
Total	2	3	4	.429	124	0	0	0	39	148	75	14	57	194	8.2	2.13	225	.148	.238	0	.000	0	45	44	-2	3.6

● **HUB PERDUE**   Perdue, Herbert Rodney "The Gallatin Squash" b: 6/7/1882, Bethpage, Tenn. d: 10/31/68, Gallatin, Tex. BR/TR, 5'10.5", 192 lbs. Deb: 4/19/11

YEAR	TM/L	W	L	PCT	G	GS	CG	SH	SV	IP	H	HR	BB	SO	RAT	ERA	ERA+	OAV	OOB	BH	AVG	PB	PR	/A	PD	TPI
1911	Bos-N	6	10	.375	24	19	9	0	1	137¹	180	10	41	40	14.7	4.98	77	.321	.372	10	.208	-1	-24	-18	-0	-1.9
1912	Bos-N	13	16	.448	37	30	20	1	3	249	295	11	54	101	12.7	3.80	94	.303	.341	12	.138	-5	-11	-6	-4	-1.5
1913	Bos-N	16	13	.552	38	32	16	3	1	212¹	201	7	39	91	10.3	3.26	101	.249	.287	7	.104	-5	-1	0	-7	-1.1

YEAR	TM/L	W	L	PCT	G	GS	CG	SH	SV	IP	H	HR	BB	SO	RAT	ERA	ERA+	OAV	OOB	BH	AVG	PB	PR	/A	PD	TPI
1914	Bos-N	2	5	.286	9	9	2	0	0	51	60	5	11	13	13.1	5.82	47	.311	.357	1	.071	-0	-17	-17	0	-2.0
	StL-N	8	8	.500	22	19	12	0	1	153^1	160	3	35	43	11.7	2.82	99	.290	.338	8	.167	-1	-0	-0	-4	-0.6
	Yr	10	13	.435	31	28	14	0	1	204^1	220	8	46	56	11.9	3.57	78	.295	.340	9	.145	-1	-18	-18	-4	-2.6
1915	StL-N	6	12	.333	31	13	5	1	1	115^1	141	7	19	29	12.6	4.21	66	.311	.341	4	.111	-1	-19	-18	-0	-2.9
Total 5		51	64	.443	161	122	64	5	7	918^1	1037	43	199	317	12.3	3.85	85	.293	.334	42	.140	-13	-73	-60	-15	-10.0

● **CARLOS PEREZ**   Perez, Carlos Gross (b: Carlos Gross (Perez)) b: 4/14/71, Nigua, D.R.   BL/TL, 6'3", 195 lbs.   Deb: 4/27/95 F

YEAR	TM/L	W	L	PCT	G	GS	CG	SH	SV	IP	H	HR	BB	SO	RAT	ERA	ERA+	OAV	OOB	BH	AVG	PB	PR	/A	PD	TPI
1995	Mon-N★	10	8	.556	28	23	2	1	0	141^1	142	18	28	106	11.1	3.69	116	.257	.299	6	.133	1	8	9	0	1.2

● **GEORGE PEREZ**   Perez, George Thomas b: 12/29/37, San Fernando, Cal.   BR/TR, 6'2.5", 200 lbs.   Deb: 4/17/58

YEAR	TM/L	W	L	PCT	G	GS	CG	SH	SV	IP	H	HR	BB	SO	RAT	ERA	ERA+	OAV	OOB	BH	AVG	PB	PR	/A	PD	TPI
1958	Pit-N	0	1	.000	4	0	0	0	1	8^1	9	1	4	2	14.0	5.40	72	.300	.382	0	.000	-0	-1	-1	-0	-0.2

● **MELIDO PEREZ**   Perez, Melido Turpen Gross (b: Melido Turpen Gross (Perez)) b: 2/15/66, San Cristobal, D.R.   BR/TR, 6'4", 180 lbs.   Deb: 9/4/87 F

YEAR	TM/L	W	L	PCT	G	GS	CG	SH	SV	IP	H	HR	BB	SO	RAT	ERA	ERA+	OAV	OOB	BH	AVG	PB	PR	/A	PD	TPI
1987	KC-A	1	1	.500	3	3	0	0	0	10^1	18	2	5	5	20.0	7.84	58	.375	.434	0	—	0	-4	-4	-1	-0.6
1988	Chi-A	12	10	.545	32	32	3	1	0	197	186	26	72	138	11.9	3.79	105	.248	.316	0	—	0	4	4	-2	0.2
1989	Chi-A	11	14	.440	31	31	2	0	0	183^1	187	23	90	141	13.7	5.01	76	.264	.350	0	—	0	-23	-25	-1	-3.0
1990	Chi-A	13	14	.481	35	35	3	3	0	197	177	14	86	161	12.1	4.61	83	.241	.322	0	—	0	-16	-17	-2	-2.1
1991	Chi-A	8	7	.533	49	8	0	0	1	135^2	111	15	52	128	10.9	3.12	127	.224	.299	0	—	0	15	13	1	1.5
1992	NY-A	13	16	.448	33	33	10	1	0	247^2	212	16	93	218	11.3	2.87	136	.235	.310	0	—	0	29	29	-1	3.2
1993	NY-A	6	14	.300	25	25	0	0	0	163	173	22	64	148	13.1	5.19	80	.267	.334	0	—	0	-16	-19	-1	-1.9
1994	NY-A	9	4	.692	22	22	1	0	0	151^1	134	16	58	109	11.6	4.10	111	.238	.313	0	—	0	12	8	-0	0.6
1995	NY-A	5	5	.500	13	12	1	0	0	69^1	70	10	31	44	13.2	5.58	85	.261	.340	0	—	0	-7	-7	-1	-1.0
Total 9		78	85	.479	243	201	20	5	1	1354^2	1268	144	551	1092	12.2	4.17	97	.248	.323	0	—	0	-5	-18	-8	-3.1

● **MIKE PEREZ**   Perez, Michael Irvin (Ortega) b: 10/19/64, Yauco, P.R.   BR/TR, 6', 185 lbs.   Deb: 9/5/90

YEAR	TM/L	W	L	PCT	G	GS	CG	SH	SV	IP	H	HR	BB	SO	RAT	ERA	ERA+	OAV	OOB	BH	AVG	PB	PR	/A	PD	TPI
1990	StL-N	1	0	1.000	13	0	0	0	0	13^2	12	0	3	5	9.9	3.95	97	.240	.283	0	.000	-0	-0	-0	0	0.0
1991	StL-N	0	2	.000	14	0	0	0	0	17	19	1	7	7	14.3	5.82	64	.288	.365	0	—	0	-4	-4	-0	-0.5
1992	StL-N	9	3	.750	77	0	0	0	0	93	70	4	32	46	10.0	1.84	184	.210	.281	0	.000	-0	17	16	0	2.0
1993	StL-N	7	2	.778	65	0	0	0	7	72^2	65	4	20	58	10.7	2.48	160	.243	.299	0	.000	-0	13	12	1	1.6
1994	StL-N	2	3	.400	36	0	0	0	12	31	52	5	10	20	18.9	8.71	48	.391	.445	0	—	0	-15	-16	-0	-3.2
1995	Chi-N	2	6	.250	68	0	0	0	2	71^1	72	8	27	49	13.0	3.66	112	.268	.343	0	.000	-0	4	4	-1	0.3
1996	Chi-N	1	0	1.000	24	0	0	0	0	27	29	2	13	22	15.0	4.67	91	.264	.357	0	.000	-0	-1	-1	-0	-0.1
Total 7		22	16	.579	297	0	0	0	22	325^2	319	24	112	207	12.3	3.56	108	.260	.323	0	.000	-0	13	10	-0	0.1

● **PASCUAL PEREZ**   Perez, Pascual Gross (b: Pascual Gross (Perez)) b: 5/17/57, San Cristobal, D.R.   BR/TR, 6'2", 163 lbs.   Deb: 5/7/80 F

YEAR	TM/L	W	L	PCT	G	GS	CG	SH	SV	IP	H	HR	BB	SO	RAT	ERA	ERA+	OAV	OOB	BH	AVG	PB	PR	/A	PD	TPI
1980	Pit-N	0	1	.000	2	2	0	0	0	12	15	0	2	7	14.3	3.75	97	.341	.396	1	.250	-0	-0	-0	-0	0.0
1981	Pit-N	2	7	.222	17	13	2	0	0	86^1	92	5	34	46	13.4	3.96	91	.273	.345	3	.136	-0	-5	-4	-0	-0.4
1982	*Atl-N	4	4	.500	16	11	0	0	0	79^1	85	4	17	29	11.6	3.06	122	.276	.314	3	.167	1	5	6	0	0.7
1983	Atl-N★	15	8	.652	33	33	7	1	0	215^1	213	20	51	144	11.2	3.43	113	.260	.307	12	.160	-1	5	11	1	1.2
1984	Atl-N	14	8	.636	30	30	4	1	0	211^2	208	26	51	145	11.1	3.74	103	.260	.307	5	.076	-2	-4	3	3	0.4
1985	Atl-N	1	13	.071	22	22	0	0	0	95^1	115	10	57	57	16.3	6.14	63	.297	.389	3	.120	-2	-27	-24	-1	-3.2
1987	Mon-N	7	0	1.000	10	10	2	0	0	70^1	52	5	16	58	8.8	2.30	182	.206	.257	1	.042	-0	14	15	1	1.4
1988	Mon-N	12	8	.600	27	27	4	2	0	188	133	15	44	131	**8.8**	2.44	147	.196	**.253**	2	.037	-3	21	24	2	2.5
1989	Mon-N	9	13	.409	33	28	2	0	0	198^1	178	15	45	152	10.3	3.31	100	.237	.283	11	.204	2	4	5	0	0.8
1990	NY-A	1	2	.333	3	3	0	0	0	14	8	0	3	12	7.1	1.29	309	.163	.212	0	—	0	8	8	-0	0.5
1991	NY-A	2	4	.333	14	14	0	0	0	73^2	68	7	24	41	11.2	3.18	130	.250	.311	0	—	0	8	8	0	0.5
Total 11		67	68	.496	207	193	21	4	0	1244^1	1167	107	344	822	11.1	3.44	110	.249	.303	41	.120	-5	25	47	6	4.8

● **YORKIS PEREZ**   Perez, Yorkis Miguel Vargas (b: Yorkis Miguel Vargas (Perez)) b: 9/30/67, Bajos De Haina, D.R.   BL/TL, 6', 180 lbs.   Deb: 9/30/91

YEAR	TM/L	W	L	PCT	G	GS	CG	SH	SV	IP	H	HR	BB	SO	RAT	ERA	ERA+	OAV	OOB	BH	AVG	PB	PR	/A	PD	TPI
1991	Chi-N	1	0	1.000	3	0	0	0	0	4^1	2	0	2	3	8.3	2.08	187	.167	.286	0	—	0	1	1	0	0.2
1994	Fla-N	3	0	1.000	44	0	0	0	0	40^2	33	4	14	41	10.6	3.54	123	.220	.291	0	.000	-0	3	4	-1	0.2
1995	Fla-N	2	6	.250	69	0	0	0	1	46^2	35	6	28	47	12.5	5.21	81	.203	.322	0	.000	-0	-5	-5	-1	-0.9
1996	Fla-N	3	4	.429	64	0	0	0	0	47^2	51	3	21	47	15.7	5.29	77	.274	.381	0	.000	0	-6	-7	-0	-0.8
Total 4		9	10	.474	180	0	0	0	1	139^1	121	12	75	138	12.9	4.65	90	.233	.334	0	.000	-1	-7	-7	-1	-1.3

● **CECIL PERKINS**   Perkins, Cecil Boyce b: 12/1/40, Baltimore, Md.   BR/TR, 6', 175 lbs.   Deb: 7/5/67

YEAR	TM/L	W	L	PCT	G	GS	CG	SH	SV	IP	H	HR	BB	SO	RAT	ERA	ERA+	OAV	OOB	BH	AVG	PB	PR	/A	PD	TPI
1967	NY-A	0	1	.000	2	1	0	0	0	5	6	1	2	1	14.4	9.00	35	.316	.381	0	.000	-0	-3	-3	0	-0.6

● **CHARLIE PERKINS**   Perkins, Charles Sullivan "Lefty" b: 9/9/05, Ensley, Ala. d: 5/25/88, Salem, Ore.   BR/TL, 6'1", 175 lbs.   Deb: 5/1/30

YEAR	TM/L	W	L	PCT	G	GS	CG	SH	SV	IP	H	HR	BB	SO	RAT	ERA	ERA+	OAV	OOB	BH	AVG	PB	PR	/A	PD	TPI
1930	Phi-A	0	0	—	8	1	0	0	0	23^2	25	0	15	15	15.2	6.46	72	.313	.421	1	.125	-1	-5	-5	-0	-0.1
1934	Bro-N	0	3	.000	11	2	0	0	0	24^1	37	3	14	5	19.6	8.51	46	.336	.421	2	.286	-0	-12	-12	-1	-1.3
Total 2		0	3	.000	19	3	0	0	0	48	62	3	29	20	17.4	7.50	57	.326	.421	3	.207	-1	-17	-17	-1	-1.4

● **JOHN PERKOVICH**   Perkovich, John Joseph "Perky" b: 3/10/24, Chicago, Ill.   BR/TR, 5'11", 170 lbs.   Deb: 5/6/50

YEAR	TM/L	W	L	PCT	G	GS	CG	SH	SV	IP	H	HR	BB	SO	RAT	ERA	ERA+	OAV	OOB	BH	AVG	PB	PR	/A	PD	TPI
1950	Chi-A	0	0	—	1	0	0	0	0	3	3	1	4	1	14.4	7.20	62	.318	.348	0	.000	-0	-1	-2	-0	0.0

● **HARRY PERKOWSKI**   Perkowski, Harry Walter b: 9/6/22, Dante, Va.   BL/TL, 6'2.5", 196 lbs.   Deb: 9/13/47

YEAR	TM/L	W	L	PCT	G	GS	CG	SH	SV	IP	H	HR	BB	SO	RAT	ERA	ERA+	OAV	OOB	BH	AVG	PB	PR	/A	PD	TPI
1947	Cin-N	0	0	—	3	1	0	0	0	7^1	12	1	3	2	18.4	3.68	111	.375	.429	0	.000	0	0	0	-0	0.0
1949	Cin-N	1	1	.500	5	3	2	0	0	23^2	21	2	14	3	13.3	4.56	92	.236	.340	3	.333	1	-1	-1	-1	-0.1
1950	Cin-N	0	0	—	22	0	0	0	0	34^1	36	6	23	19	15.7	5.24	81	.286	.400	7	.318	2	-4	-4	1	0.3
1951	Cin-N	3	6	.333	35	7	1	0	1	102	96	2	46	56	12.6	2.82	144	.251	.333	1	.040	-3	13	14	1	1.0
1952	Cin-N	12	10	.545	33	24	11	1	0	194	197	9	89	86	13.4	3.80	99	.265	.347	12	.160	-0	-2	-1	1	0.0
1953	Cin-N	12	11	.522	33	25	7	2	2	193	204	26	62	70	12.5	4.52	96	.271	.327	14	.203	1	-5	-4	-0	-0.2
1954	Cin-N	2	8	.200	28	12	3	1	0	95^2	100	16	62	32	15.3	6.11	69	.276	.384	4	.160	-2	-22	-20	-1	-1.9
1955	Cin-N	3	4	.429	25	4	0	0	2	47^2	53	3	25	28	14.7	5.29	77	.283	.368	2	.154	-0	-7	-6	1	-0.8
Total 8		33	40	.452	184	76	24	4	5	697^2	719	65	324	296	13.5	4.37	94	.269	.350	43	.180	-1	-27	-21	2	-1.7

● **JON PERLMAN**   Perlman, Jonathan Samuel b: 12/13/56, Dallas, Tex.   BL/TR, 6'3", 185 lbs.   Deb: 9/6/85

YEAR	TM/L	W	L	PCT	G	GS	CG	SH	SV	IP	H	HR	BB	SO	RAT	ERA	ERA+	OAV	OOB	BH	AVG	PB	PR	/A	PD	TPI
1985	Chi-N	1	0	1.000	6	0	0	0	0	8^2	10	3	8	4	18.7	11.42	35	.313	.450	0	.000	-0	-8	-7	0	-0.7
1987	SF-N	0	0	—	10	0	0	0	0	11^1	11	1	4	3	12.7	3.97	97	.256	.333	0	—	0	-0	-0	-0	0.0
1988	Cle-A	0	2	.000	10	0	0	0	0	19^2	25	0	11	10	16.5	5.49	75	.309	.391	0	—	0	-3	-3	-1	-0.3
Total 3		1	2	.333	26	0	0	0	0	39^2	46	4	23	17	15.9	6.35	63	.295	.389	0	.000	-0	-11	-10	-1	-1.0

● **LEN PERME**   Perme, Leonard John b: 11/25/17, Cleveland, Ohio   BL/TL, 6', 170 lbs.   Deb: 9/8/42

YEAR	TM/L	W	L	PCT	G	GS	CG	SH	SV	IP	H	HR	BB	SO	RAT	ERA	ERA+	OAV	OOB	BH	AVG	PB	PR	/A	PD	TPI
1942	Chi-A	0	1	.000	4	1	0	0	0	13	5	0	4	6	6.9	1.38	260	.119	.213	1	.333	0	3	3	-0	0.2
1946	Chi-A	0	0	—	4	0	0	0	0	4^1	6	0	7	2	27.0	8.31	41	.316	.500	0	—	0	-2	-2	-0	0.0
Total 2		0	1	.000	8	1	0	0	0	17^1	11	0	11	6	11.9	3.12	114	.180	.315	1	.333	0	1	1	-0	0.2

● **HUB PERNOLL**   Pernoll, Henry Hubbard b: 3/14/1888, Grants Pass, Ore. d: 2/18/44, Grants Pass, Ore.   BR/TL, 5'8", 175 lbs.   Deb: 4/25/10

YEAR	TM/L	W	L	PCT	G	GS	CG	SH	SV	IP	H	HR	BB	SO	RAT	ERA	ERA+	OAV	OOB	BH	AVG	PB	PR	/A	PD	TPI
1910	Det-A	4	3	.571	11	5	4	0	0	54^2	54	1	14	25	12.0	2.96	89	.270	.333	1	.063	-2	-3	-2	3	-0.1
1912	Det-A	0	0	—	3	0	0	0	0	9	9	0	4	3	13.0	6.00	54	.265	.342	0	.000	-0	-3	-3	0	0.0
Total 2		4	3	.571	14	5	4	0	0	63^2	63	1	18	28	12.2	3.39	82	.270	.335	1	.053	-2	-5	-5	3	-0.1

● **RON PERRANOSKI**   Perranoski, Ronald Peter (b: Ronald Peter Perzanowski) b: 4/1/36, Paterson, N.J.   BL/TL, 6', 192 lbs.   Deb: 4/14/61 C

YEAR	TM/L	W	L	PCT	G	GS	CG	SH	SV	IP	H	HR	BB	SO	RAT	ERA	ERA+	OAV	OOB	BH	AVG	PB	PR	/A	PD	TPI
1961	LA-N	7	5	.583	53	1	0	0	6	91^2	82	5	41	56	12.5	2.65	164	.244	.333	1	.083		14	**17**		2.3
1962	LA-N	6	6	.500	**70**	0	0	0	20	107^1	103	1	36	68	11.7	2.85	127	.255	.316	1	.071	-1	13	9	-1	1.2
1963	*LA-N	16	3	**.842**	69	0	0	0	21	129	112	7	43	75	11.1	1.67	180	.231	.299	3	.125	0	**23**	19	0	3.7
1964	LA-N	5	7	.417	72	0	0	0	14	125^1	128	5	46	79	12.6	3.09	105	.263	.328	2	.105	-0	4	3	-0	0.6
1965	*LA-N	6	6	.500	59	0	0	0	17	104^2	85	2	40	59	11.0	2.24	146	.226	.305	3	.158	-0	15	12	-1	1.7
1966	*LA-N	6	7	.462	55	0	0	0	7	82	82	4	19	50	11.0	3.18	104	.269	.338	3	.250	-1	4	1	0	0.5
1967	LA-N	6	7	.462	**70**	0	0	0	16	110	97	4	45	51	11.9	2.45	126	.240	.320	1	.100	-1	11	8	1	1.3
1968	Min-A	8	7	.533	66	0	0	0	6	87	86	9	38	65	12.8	3.10	100	.252	.327	0	.000	-1	-1	-0	-0	-0.1

YEAR	TM/L	W	L	PCT	G	GS	CG	SH	SV	IP	H	HR	BB	SO	RAT	ERA	ERA+	OAV	OOB	BH	AVG	PB	PR	/A	PD	TPI
1969	*Min-A	9	10	.474	75	0	0	0	31	119²	85	4	52	62	10.4	2.11	173	.205	.295	2	.083	-1	20	21	1	4.4
1970	*Min-A	7	8	.467	67	0	0	0	34	111	108	7	42	55	12.2	2.43	153	.259	.328	1	.042	-2	16	16	-1	2.7
1971	Min-A	1	4	.200	36	0	0	0	5	42²	60	7	28	21	19.2	6.75	53	.337	.435	0	.000	-0	-16	-15	-0	-2.1
	Det-A	0	1	1.000	11	0	0	0	2	18	16	2	3	8	10.0	2.50	144	.254	.299	0	.000	-0	2	2	-0	0.1
	Yr	1	5	.167	47	0	0	0	7	60²	76	9	31	29	16.0	5.49	65	.309	.388	0	.000	-1	-14	-13	-1	-2.0
1972	Det-A	0	1	.000	17	0	0	0	0	18²	23	2	8	10	15.4	7.71	41	.307	.381	0	.000	-0	-10	-9	-1	-0.6
	LA-N	2	0	1.000	9	0	0	0	0	16²	19	0	8	6	14.6	2.70	123	.292	.370	0	—	0	1	1	-0	0.1
1973	Cal-A	0	2	.000	8	0	0	0	0	11	11	0	7	5	15.5	4.09	87	.282	.404	0	—	0	-1	-0	0	-0.1
Total	13	79	74	.516	737	1	0	0	179	1174²	1097	50	468	687	12.2	2.79	123	.250	.325	16	.096	-4	99	83	2	15.5

● **BILL PERRIN**   Perrin, William Joseph "Lefty" b: 6/23/10, New Orleans, La. d: 6/30/74, New Orleans, La. BR/TL, 5'11", 172 lbs. Deb: 9/30/34

YEAR	TM/L	W	L	PCT	G	GS	CG	SH	SV	IP	H	HR	BB	SO	RAT	ERA	ERA+	OAV	OOB	BH	AVG	PB	PR	/A	PD	TPI
1934	Cle-A	0	1	.000	1	1	0	0	0	5	13	0	2	3	28.8	14.40	32	.520	.571	0	.000	-0	-6	-5	0	-0.7

● **GEORGE PERRING**   Perring, George Wilson b: 8/13/1884, Sharon, Wis. d: 8/20/60, Beloit, Wis. BR/TR, 6', 190 lbs. Deb: 4/25/08 ♦

YEAR	TM/L	W	L	PCT	G	GS	CG	SH	SV	IP	H	HR	BB	SO	RAT	ERA	ERA+	OAV	OOB	BH	AVG	PB	PR	/A	PD	TPI
1914	KC-F	0	0	—	1	0	0	0	0	0²	2	0	1	0	40.5	13.50	21	1.000	1.000	138	.278	0	-1	-1	-0	0.0

● **POL PERRITT**   Perritt, William Dayton b: 8/30/1892, Arcadia, La. d: 10/15/47, Shreveport, La. BR/TR, 6'2", 168 lbs. Deb: 9/7/12

YEAR	TM/L	W	L	PCT	G	GS	CG	SH	SV	IP	H	HR	BB	SO	RAT	ERA	ERA+	OAV	OOB	BH	AVG	PB	PR	/A	PD	TPI
1912	StL-N	1	1	.500	6	3	1	0	0	31	25	0	10	13	10.2	3.19	107	.243	.310	2	.222	-0	1	1	0	0.0
1913	StL-N	6	14	.300	36	21	8	0	0	175	205	9	64	64	14.2	5.25	62	.300	.367	12	.203	-1	-40	-39	1	-4.0
1914	StL-N	16	13	.552	41	32	18	3	2	286	248	7	93	115	11.2	2.36	118	.245	.318	13	.141	-2	14	14	-3	0.8
1915	NY-N	12	18	.400	35	30	16	4	0	220	226	6	59	91	12.1	2.66	96	.266	.323	11	.162	-1	2	-2	-5	-1.0
1916	NY-N	18	11	.621	40	29	17	5	2	251	243	11	56	115	11.0	2.62	93	.257	.304	7	.084	-4	0	-5	-2	-1.3
1917	*NY-N	17	7	.708	35	26	14	5	1	215	186	3	45	72	10.0	1.88	135	.237	.284	11	.157	-2	20	16	1	1.7
1918	NY-N	18	13	.581	35	31	19	6	0	233	212	5	38	60	9.7	2.74	96	.246	.278	14	.175	-1	1	-3	-3	-0.8
1919	NY-N	1	1	.500	11	3	0	0	0	19	27	0	12	2	19.4	7.11	39	.386	.488	0	.000	-1	-9	-9	-0	-1.0
1920	NY-N	0	0	—	8	0	0	0	0	15	9	0	4	3	7.8	1.80	167	.167	.224	0	.000	-1	2	2	0	0.0
1921	NY-N	2	0	1.000	5	1	0	0	0	11²	17	0	5	4	14.7	3.86	95	.321	.345	0	.000	-0	-0	-1	-1	-0.1
	Det-A	1	0	1.000	4	2	0	0	0	13	18	0	7	3	18.0	4.85	88	.383	.473	2	.400	-1	-1	-1	-0	-0.1
Total	10	92	78	.541	256	178	93	23	8	1469²	1416	41	390	543	11.4	2.89	94	.259	.315	72	.151	-13	-10	-28	-11	-5.7

● **GAYLORD PERRY**   Perry, Gaylord Jackson b: 9/15/38, Williamston, N.C. BR/TR, 6'4", 215 lbs. Deb: 4/14/62 FH

YEAR	TM/L	W	L	PCT	G	GS	CG	SH	SV	IP	H	HR	BB	SO	RAT	ERA	ERA+	OAV	OOB	BH	AVG	PB	PR	/A	PD	TPI
1962	SF-N	3	1	.750	13	7	1	0	0	43	54	3	14	20	14.2	5.23	73	.310	.362	3	.231	0	-6	-7	-1	-0.6
1963	SF-N	1	6	.143	31	4	0	0	0	76	84	10	29	52	13.6	4.03	79	.279	.346	4	.222	1	-6	-7	-0	-0.6
1964	SF-N	12	11	.522	44	19	5	2	5	206¹	179	16	43	155	9.9	2.75	130	.232	.278	3	.054	-3	18	19	-2	1.6
1965	SF-N	8	12	.400	47	26	6	0	1	195²	194	21	70	170	12.4	4.19	86	.256	.324	10	.156	-0	-14	-13	3	-0.9
1966	SF-N★	21	8	.724	36	35	13	3	0	255²	242	15	40	201	10.1	2.99	123	.247	.280	16	.186	-0	17	19	1	2.1
1967	SF-N	15	17	.469	39	37	18	3	1	293	231	20	84	230	9.8	2.61	126	.214	.274	13	.143	-1	25	22	4	2.7
1968	SF-N	16	15	.516	39	38	19	1	1	291	240	10	59	173	9.4	2.44	120	.222	.265	11	.113	-3	18	16	4	2.0
1969	SF-N	19	14	.576	40	39	26	3	0	325¹	290	23	91	233	10.8	2.49	141	.237	.295	14	.120	-2	40	37	3	3.9
1970	SF-N★	23	13	.639	41	41	23	5	0	328²	292	27	84	214	10.5	3.20	124	.237	.290	14	.117	-4	31	28	5	3.0
1971	*SF-N	16	12	.571	37	37	14	2	0	280	255	20	67	158	10.5	2.76	123	.242	.290	10	.102	-3	22	20	0	1.6
1972	Cle-A★	24	16	.600	41	40	29	5	1	342²	253	17	82	234	9.1	1.92	168	.205	.261	17	.155	0	44	49	2	7.0
1973	Cle-A	19	19	.500	41	41	29	7	0	344	315	34	115	238	11.4	3.38	116	.246	.311	0	—	0	17	21	1	2.3
1974	Cle-A★	21	13	.618	37	37	28	4	0	322¹	230	25	99	216	9.4	2.51	144	.204	.272	0	—	0	40	39	1	4.4
1975	Cle-A	6	9	.400	15	15	10	1	0	121²	120	16	34	85	11.5	3.55	106	.256	.308	0	—	0	3	3	1	0.5
	Tex-A	12	8	.600	22	22	15	4	0	184	157	12	36	148	9.6	3.03	124	.227	.268	0	—	0	15	15	-1	1.5
	Yr	18	17	.514	37	37	25	5	0	305²	277	28	70	233	10.3	3.24	116	.238	.283	0	—	0	18	18	1	2.0
1976	Tex-A	15	14	.517	32	32	21	2	0	250¹	232	14	52	143	10.2	3.24	111	.247	.287	0	—	0	8	10	-3	0.6
1977	Tex-A	15	12	.556	34	34	13	4	0	238	239	21	56	177	11.3	3.37	121	.262	.308	0	—	0	18	19	-1	1.9
1978	SD-N	21	6	.778	37	37	5	2	0	260²	241	9	66	154	10.8	2.73	122	.248	.298	8	.092	-3	25	17	0	1.4
1979	SD-N★	12	11	.522	32	32	10	0	0	232²	225	12	67	140	11.4	3.06	115	.257	.313	6	.085	-2	17	12	1	1.1
1980	Tex-A	6	9	.400	24	24	6	2	0	155	159	12	46	107	12.3	3.43	114	.268	.328	0	—	0	10	8	1	1.1
	NY-N	4	4	.500	10	8	0	0	0	50²	65	2	18	28	14.9	4.44	88	.320	.378	0	—	0	-2	-3	-0	-0.3
	Yr	10	13	.435	34	32	6	2	0	205²	224	14	64	135	12.6	3.68	106	.278	.332	0	—	0	8	5	1	0.8
1981	Atl-N	8	9	.471	23	23	3	0	0	150²	182	9	24	60	12.5	3.94	91	.304	.335	12	.250	-1	-8	-6	-1	-0.5
1982	Sea-A	10	12	.455	32	32	6	0	0	216²	245	27	54	116	12.6	4.40	96	.287	.332	0	—	0	-4	-4	0	-0.4
1983	Sea-A	3	10	.231	16	16	2	0	0	102	116	8	23	42	12.5	4.94	86	.286	.329	0	—	0	-10	-8	0	-0.9
	KC-A	4	4	.500	14	14	1	1	0	84¹	98	6	26	40	13.3	4.27	95	.292	.344	0	—	0	-2	-2	0	-0.1
	Yr	7	14	.333	30	30	3	1	0	186¹	214	24	49	82	12.8	4.64	90	.286	.331	0	—	0	-12	-10	1	-1.0
Total	22	314	265	.542	777	690	303	53	11	5350¹	4938	399	1379	3534	10.8	3.11	117	.245	.297	141	.131	-16	311	305	21	34.4

● **SCOTT PERRY**   Perry, Herbert Scott b: 4/17/1891, Denison, Tex. d: 10/27/59, Kansas City, Mo. BR/TR, 6'1", 195 lbs. Deb: 5/13/15

YEAR	TM/L	W	L	PCT	G	GS	CG	SH	SV	IP	H	HR	BB	SO	RAT	ERA	ERA+	OAV	OOB	BH	AVG	PB	PR	/A	PD	TPI
1915	StL-A	0	0	—	1	1	0	0	0	2	5	0	1	0	31.5	13.50	21	.455	.538	0	—	0	-2	-2	-0	0.0
1916	Chi-N	2	1	.667	4	3	2	1	0	28¹	30	0	3	10	10.5	2.54	115	.291	.311	3	.273	1	0	1	0	0.2
1917	Cin-N	0	0	—	4	1	0	0	0	13¹	17	0	8	4	17.6	6.75	39	.321	.419	0	—	0	-6	-6	-0	-0.1
1918	Phi-A	20	19	.513	44	36	30	3	2	332¹	295	1	111	81	11.0	1.98	148	.247	.312	15	.134	-6	30	35	2	3.9
1919	Phi-A	4	17	.190	25	21	12	0	1	183²	193	4	72	38	13.1	3.58	96	.282	.352	8	.136	-3	-7	-3	6	0.1
1920	Phi-A	11	25	.306	42	34	20	1	1	263²	310	14	65	79	13.0	3.62	111	.300	.345	13	.157	-4	5	12	0	1.1
1921	Phi-A	3	6	.333	12	8	5	1	0	70	77	4	24	19	13.1	4.11	108	.288	.349	1	.038	-4	3	3	1	0.0
Total	7	40	68	.370	132	104	69	5	5	893¹	927	23	284	231	12.3	3.07	113	.277	.336	40	.135	-17	21	40	9	5.2

● **JIM PERRY**   Perry, James Evan b: 10/30/35, Williamston, N.C. BB/TR, 6'4", 200 lbs. Deb: 4/23/59 F

YEAR	TM/L	W	L	PCT	G	GS	CG	SH	SV	IP	H	HR	BB	SO	RAT	ERA	ERA+	OAV	OOB	BH	AVG	PB	PR	/A	PD	TPI
1959	Cle-A	12	10	.545	44	13	8	2	4	153	122	10	55	79	10.5	2.65	139	.225	.298	15	.300	3	21	18	-0	2.8
1960	Cle-A	18	10	.643	41	36	10	4	1	261¹	257	35	91	120	12.1	3.62	103	.260	.324	22	.242	3	7	4	0	0.6
1961	Cle-A☆	10	17	.370	35	35	6	1	0	223²	238	28	87	90	13.3	4.71	84	.273	.343	12	.164	-1	-17	-19	-0	-2.1
1962	Cle-A	12	12	.500	35	27	7	3	0	193²	213	21	59	74	12.7	4.14	94	.285	.339	11	.183	-0	-4	-6	1	-0.5
1963	Cle-A	0	0	—	5	0	0	0	0	10¹	12	0	2	7	12.2	5.23	69	.293	.326	0	.000	-0	-2	-1	0	0.0
	Min-A	9	9	.500	35	25	5	1	1	168¹	167	17	57	65	12.1	3.74	97	.256	.318	11	.216	1	-2	-2	-1	0.0
	Yr	9	9	.500	40	25	5	1	1	178²	179	17	59	72	12.1	3.83	95	.258	.318	11	.208	1	-4	-4	-1	0.0
1964	Min-A	6	3	.667	42	1	0	0	2	65¹	61	7	23	55	11.7	3.44	104	.245	.311	2	.154	-0	1	1	-0	0.1
1965	*Min-A	12	7	.632	36	19	4	2	0	167²	142	18	47	88	10.3	2.63	135	.232	.290	9	.170	1	15	17	-1	1.9
1966	Min-A	11	7	.611	33	25	8	1	0	184¹	149	17	53	120	10.3	2.54	142	.222	.284	13	.220	4	18	22	-2	2.4
1967	Min-A	8	7	.533	37	11	3	2	0	130²	123	8	50	94	12.1	3.03	114	.255	.328	8	.190	1	7	8	-0	0.7
1968	Min-A	8	6	.571	32	10	3	0	0	139	113	6	26	69	9.3	2.27	136	.219	.263	6	.143	1	11	13	1	1.7
1969	*Min-A	20	6	.769	46	36	12	3	0	261²	244	18	66	153	11.0	2.82	129	.247	.300	16	.172	1	23	24	-2	2.2
1970	*Min-A★	24	12	.667	40	40	13	4	0	278²	258	20	57	168	10.5	3.04	123	.243	.290	24	.247	5	21	21	1	3.3
1971	Min-A☆	17	17	.500	40	39	8	0	1	270	263	39	102	126	12.3	4.23	84	.259	.329	17	.185	-1	-23	-20	0	-2.3
1972	Min-A	13	16	.448	35	35	5	2	0	217²	191	14	60	86	10.3	3.35	96	.236	.295	11	.155	-2	-7	-3	-1	-0.7
1973	Det-A	14	13	.519	35	34	7	1	0	203	225	22	55	66	12.6	4.03	101	.282	.331	0	—	0	-5	1	-0	0.1
1974	Cle-A	17	12	.586	36	36	8	3	0	252	242	11	64	71	11.1	2.96	122	.254	.304	0	—	0	18	18	-1	2.0
1975	Cle-A	1	6	.143	8	6	0	0	0	37²	46	8	18	11	15.3	6.69	57	.309	.383	0	—	0	-12	-12	0	-1.8
	Oak-A	3	4	.429	15	11	2	1	0	67²	61	7	26	33	12.5	4.66	78	.237	.324	0	—	0	-7	-8	-1	-0.7
	Yr	4	10	.286	23	17	2	1	0	105¹	107	15	44	44	13.5	5.38	68	.264	.346	0	—	0	-19	-20	-1	-2.5
Total	17	215	174	.553	630	447	109	32	10	3285²	3127	308	998	1576	11.5	3.45	106	.252	.312	177	.199	23	61	75	-7	9.7

● **PAT PERRY**   Perry, William Patrick b: 2/4/59, Taylorville, Ill. BL/TL, 6'1", 170 lbs. Deb: 9/12/85

YEAR	TM/L	W	L	PCT	G	GS	CG	SH	SV	IP	H	HR	BB	SO	RAT	ERA	ERA+	OAV	OOB	BH	AVG	PB	PR	/A	PD	TPI
1985	StL-N	0	0	—	3	0	0	0	0	12¹	3	0	4	4	4.4	0.00	—	.077	.143	1	.500	0	5	5	-0	0.4
1986	StL-N	2	1	.400	46	0	0	0	2	68²	59	5	34	29	12.2	3.80	96	.239	.331	0	.000	-1	-1	-1	1	-0.1
1987	StL-N	4	2	.667	45	0	0	0	0	65²	54	7	25	33	10.6	4.39	95	.222	.289	1	.143	-0	-2	-2	0	-0.1
	Cin-N	1	0	1.000	12	0	0	0	0	15¹	6	0	4	6	6.5	0.00	—	.122	.204	0	—	0	7	7	0	0.5
	Yr	5	2	.714	57	0	0	0	0	81	60	7	25	39	9.6	3.56	117	.203	.268	1	.143	-0	5	6	1	0.4

YEAR TM/L	W	L	PCT	G	GS	CG	SH	SV	IP	H	HR	BB	SO	RAT	ERA	ERA+	OAV	OOB	BH	AVG	PB	PR	/A	PD	TPI
1988 Cin-N	2	2	.500	12	0	0	0	0	20²	21	4	9	11	13.1	5.66	63	.262	.337	0	.000	-0	-5	-5	-0	-0.9
Chi-N	2	2	.500	35	0	0	0	1	38	40	5	7	24	11.4	3.32	109	.270	.308	1	1.000	1	1	1	-0	0.3
Yr	4	4	.500	47	0	0	0	1	58²	61	9	16	35	12.0	4.14	87	.264	.315	1	.333	1	-5	-4	-0	-0.6
1989 Chi-N	0	0	.000	19	0	0	0	1	35²	23	2	16	20	9.8	1.77	213	.187	.281	1	.167	-0	7	8	-1	0.2
1990 LA-N	0	0	—	7	0	0	0	0	6²	9	0	5	2	20.3	8.10	45	.310	.429	0	.000	-0	-3	-3	-0	0.0
Total 6	12	10	.545	182	0	0	0	6	263	215	23	99	131	10.9	3.46	110	.224	.300	4	.148	0	8	10	-0	0.3

● **PARSON PERRYMAN**   Perryman, Emmett Key   b: 10/24/1888, Everett Springs, Ga.   d: 9/12/66, Starke, Fla.   BR/TR, 6'4.5", 193 lbs.   Deb: 4/14/15

YEAR TM/L	W	L	PCT	G	GS	CG	SH	SV	IP	H	HR	BB	SO	RAT	ERA	ERA+	OAV	OOB	BH	AVG	PB	PR	/A	PD	TPI
1915 StL-A	2	4	.333	24	3	0	0	0	50¹	52	2	16	19	12.3	3.93	73	.281	.342	0	.000	-1	-6	-6	1	-0.7

● **ROBERT PERSON**   Person, Robert Alan   b: 10/6/69, Lowell, Mass.   BR/TR, 5'11", 180 lbs.   Deb: 9/18/95

YEAR TM/L	W	L	PCT	G	GS	CG	SH	SV	IP	H	HR	BB	SO	RAT	ERA	ERA+	OAV	OOB	BH	AVG	PB	PR	/A	PD	TPI
1995 NY-N	1	0	1.000	3	1	0	0	0	12	5	1	2	10	5.3	0.75	539	.119	.159	2	.667	1	5	4	-0	0.4
1996 NY-N	4	5	.444	27	13	0	0	0	89²	86	16	35	76	12.3	4.52	87	.247	.319	3	.143	-0	-3	-6	-2	-0.7
Total 2	5	5	.500	30	14	0	0	0	101²	91	17	37	86	11.5	4.07	97	.233	.303	5	.208	1	-2	-2	-2	-0.3

● **BILL PERTICA**   Pertica, William Andrew   b: 3/5/1897, Santa Barbara, Cal.   d: 12/28/67, Los Angeles, Cal.   BR/TR, 5'9", 165 lbs.   Deb: 8/7/18

YEAR TM/L	W	L	PCT	G	GS	CG	SH	SV	IP	H	HR	BB	SO	RAT	ERA	ERA+	OAV	OOB	BH	AVG	PB	PR	/A	PD	TPI
1918 Bos-A	0	0	—	1	0	0	0	0	3	3	0	0	1	9.0	3.00	89	.273	.273	0	.000	-0	-0	-0	0	0.0
1921 StL-N	14	10	.583	38	31	15	2	2	208¹	212	9	70	67	12.6	3.37	109	.267	.334	10	.143	-3	10	7	-3	0.1
1922 StL-N	8	8	.500	34	15	2	0	0	117¹	153	5	65	30	17.0	5.91	65	.333	.419	6	.182	-0	-24	-27	1	-2.9
1923 StL-N	0	0	—	1	1	0	0	0	2¹	2	0	3	0	23.1	3.86	101	.250	.500	0	.000	-0	0	0	0	0.0
Total 4	22	18	.550	74	47	17	2	2	331	370	14	138	98	14.2	4.27	87	.291	.367	16	.152	-4	-14	-20	-2	-2.8

● **STAN PERZANOWSKI**   Perzanowski, Stanley   b: 8/25/50, East Chicago, Ind.   BB/TR, 6'2", 170 lbs.   Deb: 6/20/71

YEAR TM/L	W	L	PCT	G	GS	CG	SH	SV	IP	H	HR	BB	SO	RAT	ERA	ERA+	OAV	OOB	BH	AVG	PB	PR	/A	PD	TPI
1971 Chi-A	0	1	.000	5	0	0	0	1	6	14	1	3	5	25.5	12.00	30	.412	.459	0	.000	-0	-6	-6	-0	-1.0
1974 Chi-A	0	0	—	2	1	0	0	0	2¹	8	1	2	2	38.6	19.29	19	.533	.588	0	—	0	-4	-4	0	-0.1
1975 Tex-A	3	3	.500	12	8	1	0	0	66	59	1	25	26	12.1	3.00	125	.246	.330	0	—	0	6	6	1	0.7
1976 Tex-A	0	0	—	5	0	0	0	0	11²	20	3	4	6	20.1	10.03	36	.385	.448	0	—	0	-8	-8	-0	-0.1
1978 Min-A	2	7	.222	13	7	1	0	1	56²	59	1	26	31	14.1	5.24	73	.276	.365	0	—	0	-9	-9	1	-1.2
Total 5	5	11	.313	37	16	2	0	2	142²	160	7	60	70	14.6	5.11	74	.288	.369	0	.000	-0	-22	-21	2	-1.7

● **JEFF PETEREK**   Peterek, Jeffrey Allen   b: 9/22/63, Michigan City, Ind.   BR/TR, 6'2", 195 lbs.   Deb: 8/14/89

YEAR TM/L	W	L	PCT	G	GS	CG	SH	SV	IP	H	HR	BB	SO	RAT	ERA	ERA+	OAV	OOB	BH	AVG	PB	PR	/A	PD	TPI
1989 Mil-A	0	2	.000	7	4	0	0	0	31¹	31	3	14	16	12.9	4.02	95	.252	.328	0	—	0	-0	-1	0	0.0

● **CHRIS PETERS**   Peters, Christopher Michael   b: 1/28/72, Fort Thomas, Ky.   BL/TL, 6'1", 170 lbs.   Deb: 7/19/96

YEAR TM/L	W	L	PCT	G	GS	CG	SH	SV	IP	H	HR	BB	SO	RAT	ERA	ERA+	OAV	OOB	BH	AVG	PB	PR	/A	PD	TPI
1996 Pit-N	2	4	.333	16	10	0	0	0	64	72	9	25	28	13.8	5.63	78	.287	.354	4	.211	0	-10	-9	-0	-0.7

● **GARY PETERS**   Peters, Gary Charles   b: 4/21/37, Grove City, Pa.   BL/TL, 6'2", 200 lbs.   Deb: 9/10/59

YEAR TM/L	W	L	PCT	G	GS	CG	SH	SV	IP	H	HR	BB	SO	RAT	ERA	ERA+	OAV	OOB	BH	AVG	PB	PR	/A	PD	TPI
1959 Chi-A	0	0	—	2	0	0	0	0	1	2	0	2	1	36.0	0.00	—	.400	.571	0	—	0	0	0	0	0.0
1960 Chi-A	0	0	—	2	0	0	0	0	3¹	4	0	1	4	13.5	2.70	140	.286	.333	0	—	0	0	0	0	0.0
1961 Chi-A	0	0	—	3	0	0	0	1	10¹	10	0	2	6	10.5	1.74	225	.270	.308	1	.333	0	3	2	1	0.2
1962 Chi-A	0	1	.000	5	0	0	0	0	6¹	8	0	1	4	14.2	5.68	69	.308	.357	0	—	-1	-1	-1	0	-0.2
1963 Chi-A	19	8	.704	41	30	13	4	1	243	192	9	68	189	9.9	**2.33**	**150**	.216	.278	21	.259	9	**35**	32	-1	4.5
1964 Chi-A☆	**20**	8	.714	37	36	11	3	0	273²	217	20	104	205	10.8	2.50	138	.219	.297	25	.208	8	34	29	0	3.9
1965 Chi-A	10	12	.455	33	30	11	1	0	176¹	181	19	63	95	12.7	3.62	88	.265	.331	13	.181	2	-5	-8	-0	-0.8
1966 Chi-A	12	10	.545	30	27	11	4	0	204²	156	11	45	129	**9.0**	**1.98**	**160**	.212	**.261**	19	.235	6	**33**	27	1	3.9
1967 Chi-A★	16	11	.593	38	36	11	3	0	260	187	15	91	215	10.0	2.28	136	**.199**	.277	21	.212	7	27	24	3	**3.7**
1968 Chi-A	4	13	.235	31	25	6	1	1	162²	146	7	60	110	11.8	3.76	80	.242	.318	15	.208	7	-14	-13	-0	-0.7
1969 Chi-A	10	15	.400	36	32	7	3	0	218²	238	21	78	140	13.2	4.53	85	.283	.347	12	.169	1	-22	-16	-2	-1.7
1970 Bos-A	16	11	.593	34	34	10	4	0	221²	221	20	83	155	12.6	4.06	98	.257	.328	20	.244	6	-9	-2	-1	0.2
1971 Bos-A	14	11	.560	34	32	9	1	1	214	241	25	70	100	13.3	4.37	84	.288	.347	26	.271	8	-22	-16	-2	-1.2
1972 Bos-A	3	3	.500	33	4	0	0	0	85¹	91	14	38	67	13.9	4.32	74	.279	.360	6	.200	1	-12	-11	-1	-0.7
Total 14	124	103	.546	359	286	79	23	5	2081	1894	157	706	1420	11.5	3.25	106	.243	.311	179	.222	57	50	46	-1	11.1

● **JOHN PETERS**   Peters, John Paul   b: 4/8/1850, Louisiana, Mo.   d: 1/4/24, St.Louis, Mo.   BR/TR, 5'7", 180 lbs.   Deb: 5/23/1874 ◆

YEAR TM/L	W	L	PCT	G	GS	CG	SH	SV	IP	H	HR	BB	SO	RAT	ERA	ERA+	OAV	OOB	BH	AVG	PB	PR	/A	PD	TPI
1876 Chi-N	0	0	—	1	0	0	0	1	1	1	0	0	1	18.0	0.00	—	.250	.400	111	.351	0	0	0	0	0.1

● **RUBE PETERS**   Peters, Oscar Casper   b: 3/15/1885, Grantfork, Ill.   d: 2/7/65, Pequannock, N.J.   BR/TR, 6'1", 195 lbs.   Deb: 4/13/12

YEAR TM/L	W	L	PCT	G	GS	CG	SH	SV	IP	H	HR	BB	SO	RAT	ERA	ERA+	OAV	OOB	BH	AVG	PB	PR	/A	PD	TPI
1912 Chi-A	5	6	.455	28	11	4	0	0	108²	134	2	33	39	14.3	4.14	77	.309	.366	6	.194	-1	-10	-11	4	-0.6
1914 Bro-F	2	2	.500	11	3	1	0	0	37²	52	1	16	13	16.2	3.82	75	.335	.398	1	.091	-1	-4	-4	0	-0.5
Total 2	7	8	.467	39	14	5	0	0	146¹	186	3	49	52	14.8	4.06	77	.316	.374	7	.167	-1	-14	-15	4	-1.1

● **RAY PETERS**   Peters, Raymond James   b: 8/27/46, Buffalo, N.Y.   BR/TR, 6'5.5", 210 lbs.   Deb: 6/4/70

YEAR TM/L	W	L	PCT	G	GS	CG	SH	SV	IP	H	HR	BB	SO	RAT	ERA	ERA+	OAV	OOB	BH	AVG	PB	PR	/A	PD	TPI
1970 Mil-A	0	2	.000	2	2	0	0	0	2	7	0	5	1	54.0	31.50	12	.583	.706	0	—	0	-6	-6	-0	-2.8

● **STEVE PETERS**   Peters, Steven Bradley   b: 11/14/62, Oklahoma City, Okla   BL/TL, 5'10", 170 lbs.   Deb: 8/11/87

YEAR TM/L	W	L	PCT	G	GS	CG	SH	SV	IP	H	HR	BB	SO	RAT	ERA	ERA+	OAV	OOB	BH	AVG	PB	PR	/A	PD	TPI
1987 StL-N	0	0	—	12	0	0	0	1	15	17	1	6	11	13.8	1.80	231	.298	.365	0	—	-0	4	4	1	0.1
1988 StL-N	3	3	.500	44	0	0	0	0	45	57	8	22	30	15.8	6.40	54	.313	.387	0	.000	-0	-15	-15	-1	-1.9
Total 2	3	3	.500	56	0	0	0	1	60	74	9	28	41	15.3	5.25	69	.310	.382	0	.000	-1	-11	-11	0	-1.8

● **ADAM PETERSON**   Peterson, Adam Charles   b: 12/11/65, Long Beach, Cal.   BR/TR, 6'3", 190 lbs.   Deb: 9/19/87

YEAR TM/L	W	L	PCT	G	GS	CG	SH	SV	IP	H	HR	BB	SO	RAT	ERA	ERA+	OAV	OOB	BH	AVG	PB	PR	/A	PD	TPI
1987 Chi-A	0	0	—	1	1	0	0	0	4	8	1	3	1	24.8	13.50	30	.444	.524	—	—	0	-4	-4	-0	-0.1
1988 Chi-A	0	1	.000	2	2	0	0	0	6	6	0	6	3	18.0	13.50	29	.240	.387	0	—	0	-6	-6	-0	-0.8
1989 Chi-A	0	1	.000	3	2	0	0	0	5¹	13	1	2	3	25.3	15.19	25	.464	.500	0	—	0	-7	-7	-0	-1.0
1990 Chi-A	2	5	.286	20	11	2	0	0	85	90	12	26	29	12.5	4.55	84	.278	.335	0	—	0	-6	-7	-1	-0.5
1991 SD-N	3	4	.429	13	11	0	0	0	54²	50	10	28	37	12.8	4.45	85	.242	.332	0	.000	-1	-5	-4	-0	-0.6
Total 5	5	11	.313	39	27	2	0	0	155	167	24	65	75	13.6	5.46	70	.277	.350	0	.000	-1	-28	-28	-2	-3.0

● **FRITZ PETERSON**   Peterson, Fritz Fred (b: Fred Ingels Peterson)   b: 2/8/42, Chicago, Ill.   BB/TL, 6', 200 lbs.   Deb: 4/15/66

YEAR TM/L	W	L	PCT	G	GS	CG	SH	SV	IP	H	HR	BB	SO	RAT	ERA	ERA+	OAV	OOB	BH	AVG	PB	PR	/A	PD	TPI
1966 NY-A	12	11	.522	34	32	11	2	0	215	196	15	40	96	10.0	3.31	101	.241	.279	15	.224	4	3	0	-0	0.4
1967 NY-A	8	14	.364	36	30	6	1	0	181¹	179	11	43	102	11.2	3.47	90	.256	.302	7	.146	1	-5	-7	1	-0.6
1968 NY-A	12	11	.522	36	27	6	0	0	212¹	187	13	29	115	9.3	2.63	110	.241	.272	5	.079	-2	8	6	4	1.0
1969 NY-A★	17	16	.515	37	37	16	4	0	272	228	15	43	150	**9.1**	2.55	136	.229	.263	9	.112	-0	32	28	2	3.7
1970 NY-A★	20	11	.645	39	37	8	2	0	260¹	247	24	40	127	**10.0**	2.90	121	.248	**.280**	20	.222	5	23	18	2	2.9
1971 NY-A	15	13	.536	37	35	16	4	1	274	269	25	42	139	10.5	3.05	106	.258	.289	7	.082	-3	12	5	2	0.4
1972 NY-A	17	15	.531	35	35	12	3	0	250¹	270	11	44	100	11.5	3.24	91	.276	.310	19	.232	4	-5	-8	1	-0.5
1973 NY-A	8	15	.348	31	31	6	0	0	184¹	207	18	49	59	12.8	3.95	93	.286	.337	0	—	0	-3	-6	0	-0.7
1974 NY-A				3	1	0	0	0	7²	13	1	2	5	17.6	4.70	75	.361	.395	0	—	0	-1	-1	-0	0.1
Cle-A	9	14	.391	29	29	3	0	0	152²	187	16	37	52	13.4	4.36	83	.305	.349	0	—	0	-13	-13	1	-1.6
Yr	9	14	.391	32	30	3	0	0	160¹	200	17	39	57	13.6	4.38	82	.308	.351	0	—	0	-14	-14	1	-1.5
1975 Cle-A	14	8	.636	25	25	6	2	0	146¹	154	15	40	47	12.3	3.94	96	.275	.331	0	—	0	-3	-3	-1	-0.3
1976 Cle-A	0	3	.000	9	9	0	0	0	47	59	3	10	19	13.2	5.55	63	.309	.343	0	—	0	-11	-11	-0	-0.6
Tex-A	1	0	1.000	4	2	0	0	0	15	21	0	7	4	16.8	3.60	100	.344	.412	0	—	0	-0	-0	-0	-0.1
Yr	1	3	.250	13	11	0	0	0	62	80	3	17	23	14.1	5.08	69	.316	.359	0	—	0	-11	-11	-0	-0.7
Total 11	133	131	.504	355	330	90	20	1	2218¹	2217	173	426	1015	10.9	3.30	101	.261	.300	82	.159	8	40	10	15	4.1

● **JIM PETERSON**   Peterson, James Niels   b: 8/18/08, Philadelphia, Pa.   d: 4/8/75, Palm Beach, Fla.   BR/TR, 6'0.5", 200 lbs.   Deb: 7/9/31

YEAR TM/L	W	L	PCT	G	GS	CG	SH	SV	IP	H	HR	BB	SO	RAT	ERA	ERA+	OAV	OOB	BH	AVG	PB	PR	/A	PD	TPI
1931 Phi-A	0	1	.000	6	1	0	0	0	13	18	0	4	7	15.2	6.23	72	.321	.367	1	.500	1	-3	-3	-0	-0.1
1933 Phi-A	2	5	.286	32	5	0	0	0	90²	114	6	36	18	14.9	4.96	86	.305	.366	4	.148	-1	-7	-7	2	-0.3
1937 Bro-N	0	0	—	3	0	0	0	0	5²	8	3	2	4	15.9	7.94	51	.333	.385	0	—	0	-2	-2	1	0.1
Total 3	2	6	.250	41	6	0	0	0	109¹	140	9	42	29	15.0	5.27	82	.308	.367	5	.172	0	-12	-12	3	-0.3

● **KENT PETERSON**   Peterson, Kent Franklin "Pete"   b: 12/21/25, Goshen, Utah   d: 4/27/95, Highland, Utah   BR/TL, 5'10", 175 lbs.   Deb: 7/15/44

YEAR TM/L	W	L	PCT	G	GS	CG	SH	SV	IP	H	HR	BB	SO	RAT	ERA	ERA+	OAV	OOB	BH	AVG	PB	PR	/A	PD	TPI
1944 Cin-N	0	0	—	1	0	0	0	0	1	1	0	0	0	0.0	0.00	—	.000	.000	0	—	0	0	0	-0	0.0

YEAR	TM/L	W	L	PCT	G	GS	CG	SH	SV	IP	H	HR	BB	SO	RAT	ERA	ERA+	OAV	OOB	BH	AVG	PB	PR	/A	PD	TPI
1947	Cin-N	6	13	.316	37	17	3	1	2	152¹	156	8	62	78	13.1	4.25	96	.265	.338	3	.068	-3	-3	-3	-2	-0.8
1948	Cin-N	2	15	.118	43	17	2	0	1	137	146	10	59	64	13.9	4.60	85	.271	.350	5	.139	-2	-10	-10	-0	-1.3
1949	Cin-N	4	5	.444	30	7	2	0	0	66¹	66	6	46	28	15.7	6.24	67	.261	.383	1	.056	-2	-16	-15	-1	-2.0
1950	Cin-N	0	3	.000	9	2	0	0	0	20	25	4	17	6	18.9	7.20	59	.305	.424	1	.333	0	-7	-7	-1	-0.9
1951	Cin-N	1	1	.500	9	0	0	0	0	9²	13	0	8	5	20.5	6.52	63	.317	.440	0	.000	-0	-3	-3	-0	-0.5
1952	Phi-N	0	0	—	3	0	0	0	2	7	2	0	2	7	5.1	0.00	—	.091	.167	0	.000	-0	3	3	-0	0.2
1953	Phi-N	0	1	.000	15	0	0	0	0	27	26	3	21	20	16.0	6.67	63	.252	.384	0	.000	-1	-7	-7	-0	-0.3
Total	8	13	38	.255	147	43	7	1	5	420¹	434	33	215	208	14.2	4.95	82	.266	.357	10	.091	-8	-43	-42	-4	-5.6

● **SID PETERSON**   Peterson, Sidney Herbert b: 1/31/18, Havelock, N.Dak.   BR/TR, 6'3", 200 lbs.   Deb: 5/4/43

YEAR	TM/L	W	L	PCT	G	GS	CG	SH	SV	IP	H	HR	BB	SO	RAT	ERA	ERA+	OAV	OOB	BH	AVG	PB	PR	/A	PD	TPI
1943	StL-A	2	0	1.000	3	0	0	0	0	10	15	0	3	0	17.1	2.70	123	.341	.396	0	.000	-0	1	1	-0	0.1

● **MARK PETKOVSEK**   Petkovsek, Mark Joseph b: 11/18/65, Beaumont, Tex.   BR/TR, 6', 185 lbs.   Deb: 6/8/91

YEAR	TM/L	W	L	PCT	G	GS	CG	SH	SV	IP	H	HR	BB	SO	RAT	ERA	ERA+	OAV	OOB	BH	AVG	PB	PR	/A	PD	TPI
1991	Tex-A	0	1	.000	4	1	0	0	0	9¹	21	4	4	6	24.1	14.46	28	.438	.481	0	—	0	-11	-11	-0	-0.9
1993	Pit-N	3	0	1.000	26	0	0	0	0	32¹	43	7	9	14	14.5	6.96	58	.328	.371	0	—	0	-10	-10	1	-0.8
1995	StL-N	6	6	.500	26	21	1	1	0	137¹	136	11	35	71	11.6	4.00	105	.262	.316	3	.081	-1	3	3	-1	0.1
1996	*StL-N	11	2	.846	48	6	0	0	0	88²	83	9	35	45	12.5	3.55	119	.251	.332	3	.188	0	7	7	0	0.9
Total	4	20	9	.690	104	28	1	1	0	267²	283	31	83	136	12.7	4.57	91	.275	.335	6	.113	-1	-12	-12	0	-0.7

● **DAN PETRY**   Petry, Daniel Joseph b: 11/13/58, Palo Alto, Cal.   BR/TR, 6'4", 200 lbs.   Deb: 7/8/79

YEAR	TM/L	W	L	PCT	G	GS	CG	SH	SV	IP	H	HR	BB	SO	RAT	ERA	ERA+	OAV	OOB	BH	AVG	PB	PR	/A	PD	TPI
1979	Det-A	6	5	.545	15	15	2	0	0	98	90	11	33	43	11.7	3.95	110	.254	.325	0	—	0	3	4	-1	0.3
1980	Det-A	10	9	.526	27	25	4	3	0	164²	156	9	83	88	13.1	3.94	104	.253	.342	0	—	0	2	3	2	0.4
1981	Det-A	10	9	.526	23	22	7	2	0	141	115	10	57	79	11.0	3.00	126	.224	.302	0	—	0	10	12	2	1.7
1982	Det-A	15	9	.625	35	35	8	1	0	246	220	15	100	132	11.9	3.22	126	.241	.319	0	—	0	23	23	4	2.6
1983	Det-A	19	11	.633	38	38	9	2	0	266²	256	37	99	122	12.2	3.92	100	.256	.327	0	—	0	4	-0	3	0.3
1984	*Det-A	18	8	.692	35	35	7	2	0	233¹	231	21	66	144	11.6	3.24	121	.259	.312	0	—	0	19	18	3	2.2
1985	Det-A★	15	13	.536	34	34	8	0	0	238²	190	24	81	109	10.3	3.36	121	.217	.285	0	—	0	21	19	0	2.1
1986	Det-A	5	10	.333	20	20	2	0	0	116	122	15	53	56	14.0	4.66	89	.268	.350	0	—	0	-6	-7	1	-0.7
1987	*Det-A	9	7	.563	30	21	0	0	0	134²	148	22	76	93	15.6	5.61	75	.279	.379	0	—	0	-17	-21	1	-1.8
1988	Cal-A	3	9	.250	22	22	4	1	0	139²	139	18	59	64	13.1	4.38	88	.263	.344	0	—	0	-6	-8	2	-0.3
1989	Cal-A	3	2	.600	19	4	0	0	0	51	53	8	23	21	13.6	5.47	70	.275	.355	0	—	0	-9	-9	0	-0.8
1990	Det-A	10	9	.526	32	23	1	0	0	149²	148	14	77	73	13.6	4.45	89	.263	.353	0	—	0	-9	-8	2	-0.8
1991	Det-A	2	3	.400	17	6	0	0	0	54²	66	9	19	18	14.0	4.94	84	.300	.356	0	—	0	-5	-5	2	-0.3
	Atl-N	0	0	—	10	0	0	0	0	24¹	29	2	14	9	16.3	5.55	70	.296	.389	1	.200	0	-5	-4	0	0.0
	Bos-A	0	0	—	13	0	0	0	0	22¹	21	3	12	12	13.7	4.43	97	.250	.351	0	—	0	-1	-0	0	-0.1
Total	13	125	104	.546	370	300	52	11	1	2080¹	1984	218	852	1063	12.5	3.95	102	.253	.330	1	.200	0	24	16	22	4.8

● **JAY PETTIBONE**   Pettibone, Harry Jonathan b: 6/21/57, Mt.Clemens, Mich.   BR/TR, 6'4", 182 lbs.   Deb: 9/11/83

YEAR	TM/L	W	L	PCT	G	GS	CG	SH	SV	IP	H	HR	BB	SO	RAT	ERA	ERA+	OAV	OOB	BH	AVG	PB	PR	/A	PD	TPI
1983	Min-A	0	4	.000	4	4	1	0	0	27	28	4	10	12	12.7	5.33	80	.280	.345	0	—	0	-4	-3	0	-0.4

● **PAUL PETTIT**   Pettit, George William Paul "Lefty" b: 11/29/31, Los Angeles, Cal.   BL/TL, 6'2", 195 lbs.   Deb: 5/4/51

YEAR	TM/L	W	L	PCT	G	GS	CG	SH	SV	IP	H	HR	BB	SO	RAT	ERA	ERA+	OAV	OOB	BH	AVG	PB	PR	/A	PD	TPI
1951	Pit-N	0	0	—	2	0	0	0	0	2²	2	1	0	0	10.1	3.38	125	.200	.273	0	.000	-0	0	0	-0	0.0
1953	Pit-N	1	2	.333	10	5	0	0	0	28	33	1	20	14	17.0	7.71	58	.297	.405	2	.250	1	-11	-10	0	-0.8
Total	2	1	2	.333	12	5	0	0	0	30²	35	2	21	14	16.4	7.34	61	.289	.394	2	.222	1	-10	-10	0	-0.8

● **LEON PETTIT**   Pettit, Leon Arthur "Lefty" b: 6/23/02, Waynesburg, Pa. d: 11/21/74, Columbia, Tenn.   BL/TL, 5'10.5", 165 lbs.   Deb: 4/18/35

YEAR	TM/L	W	L	PCT	G	GS	CG	SH	SV	IP	H	HR	BB	SO	RAT	ERA	ERA+	OAV	OOB	BH	AVG	PB	PR	/A	PD	TPI
1935	Was-A	8	5	.615	41	7	1	0	3	109	129	6	58	45	15.8	4.45	87	.301	.390	2	.080	0	-6	-8	-0	-0.8
1937	Phi-N	0	1	.000	3	1	0	0	0	4	6	1	4	0	22.5	11.25	39	.353	.476	0	—	0	-3	-3	-0	-0.6
Total	2	8	6	.571	44	8	1	0	3	113	135	7	62	45	16.0	5.18	84	.303	.393	2	.080	0	-9	-11	-0	-1.4

● **BOB PETTIT**   Pettit, Robert Henry b: 7/19/1861, Williamstown, Mass. d: 11/1/10, Derby, Conn.   BL/TR, 5'9", 160 lbs.   Deb: 9/3/1887 ♦

YEAR	TM/L	W	L	PCT	G	GS	CG	SH	SV	IP	H	HR	BB	SO	RAT	ERA	ERA+	OAV	OOB	BH	AVG	PB	PR	/A	PD	TPI
1887	Chi-N	0	0	—	1	0	0	0	1	1	3	0	2	0	45.0	0.00	—	.375	.500	36	.261	0	0	0	0	0.1

● **ANDY PETTITTE**   Pettitte, Andrew Eugene b: 6/15/72, Baton Rouge, La.   BL/TL, 6'5", 235 lbs.   Deb: 4/29/95

YEAR	TM/L	W	L	PCT	G	GS	CG	SH	SV	IP	H	HR	BB	SO	RAT	ERA	ERA+	OAV	OOB	BH	AVG	PB	PR	/A	PD	TPI
1995	*NY-A	12	9	.571	31	26	3	0	0	175	183	15	63	114	12.7	4.17	111	.272	.336	0	—	0	11	9	0	0.9
1996	*NY-A☆	21	8	.724	35	34	2	0	0	221	229	23	72	162	12.4	3.87	131	.271	.331	0	—	0	28	29	1	3.4
Total	2	33	17	.660	66	60	5	0	0	396	412	38	135	276	12.5	4.00	121	.272	.333	0	—	0	38	38	1	4.3

● **CHARLIE PETTY**   Petty, Charles E. b: 6/28/1866, Nashville, Tenn.   TR,   Deb: 7/30/1889

YEAR	TM/L	W	L	PCT	G	GS	CG	SH	SV	IP	H	HR	BB	SO	RAT	ERA	ERA+	OAV	OOB	BH	AVG	PB	PR	/A	PD	TPI
1889	Cin-a	2	3	.400	5	5	5	0	0	44	44	3	20	10	14.3	5.52	71	.253	.350	6	.300	1	-8	-8	-0	-0.6
1893	NY-N	5	2	.714	9	5	4	0	0	54	66	0	28	12	15.8	3.33	140	.292	.373	7	.318	3	8	8	-0	1.0
1894	Was-N	3	8	.273	16	12	8	0	0	103	156	4	32	14	17.2	5.59	94	.344	.399	8	.195	-2	-3	-4	-1	-0.5
	Cle-N	0	2	.000	4	3	2	0	0	27	42	4	14	4	19.7	8.67	63	.350	.431	1	.083	-2	-10	-10	-1	-0.7
	Yr	3	10	.231	20	15	10	0	0	130	198	8	46	18	17.1	6.23	85	.340	.391	9	.170	-4	-13	-13	-1	-1.2
Total	3	10	15	.400	34	26	19	0	0	228	308	11	94	40	16.6	5.41	90	.317	.388	22	.232	-0	-13	-13	-2	-0.8

● **JESSE PETTY**   Petty, Jesse Lee "The Silver Fox" b: 11/23/1894, Orr, Okla. d: 10/23/71, St.Paul, Minn.   BR/TL, 6', 195 lbs.   Deb: 4/14/21

YEAR	TM/L	W	L	PCT	G	GS	CG	SH	SV	IP	H	HR	BB	SO	RAT	ERA	ERA+	OAV	OOB	BH	AVG	PB	PR	/A	PD	TPI
1921	Cle-A	0	0	—	4	0	0	0	0	9	10	0	0	0	10.0	2.00	213	.345	.345	0	.000	-0	2	2	1	0.0
1925	Bro-N	9	9	.500	28	21	7	0	0	153	188	15	47	39	13.9	4.88	86	.304	.355	7	.140	-3	-10	-12	-2	-1.5
1926	Bro-N	17	17	.500	38	33	23	1	1	275²	246	6	79	101	10.7	2.84	135	**.240**	.296	17	.175	-3	30	30	-4	2.7
1927	Bro-N	13	18	.419	42	33	19	2	1	271²	263	13	53	101	10.6	2.98	133	.254	.293	9	.099	-7	28	30	-3	2.1
1928	Bro-N	15	15	.500	40	31	15	2	1	234	264	18	56	74	12.5	4.04	98	.289	.334	9	.111	-5	-1	-2	-4	-1.1
1929	Pit-N	11	10	.524	36	25	12	1	0	184¹	197	12	42	58	11.7	3.71	129	.277	.317	7	.104	-5	21	22	-2	1.4
1930	Pit-N	1	6	.143	10	7	0	0	0	41¹	67	8	13	16	17.9	8.27	60	.362	.410	1	.083	-1	-15	-15	-0	-2.0
	Chi-N	1	3	.250	9	3	0	0	0	39¹	51	2	6	18	13.0	2.97	164	.317	.341	3	.231	-0	9	8	-0	0.7
	Yr	2	9	.182	19	10	0	0	0	80²	118	10	19	34	15.3	5.69	87	.339	.373	4	.160	-1	-6	-7	-0	-1.3
Total	7	67	78	.462	207	153	76	6	4	1208¹	1286	77	296	407	11.9	3.68	113	.275	.320	53	.128	-25	63	63	-14	2.3

● **PRETZEL PEZZULLO**   Pezzullo, John b: 12/10/10, Bridgeport, Conn. d: 5/16/90, Dallas, Tex.   BL/TL, 5'11.5", 180 lbs.   Deb: 4/18/35

YEAR	TM/L	W	L	PCT	G	GS	CG	SH	SV	IP	H	HR	BB	SO	RAT	ERA	ERA+	OAV	OOB	BH	AVG	PB	PR	/A	PD	TPI
1935	Phi-N	3	5	.375	41	7	2	0	1	84¹	115	5	45	24	17.8	6.40	71	.321	.407	6	.250	0	-22	-18	-2	-1.6
1936	Phi-N	0	0	—	1	0	0	0	0	2	1	0	6	0	31.5	4.50	101	.167	.583	0	—	0	0	0	-0	0.0
Total	2	3	5	.375	42	7	2	0	1	86¹	116	5	51	24	18.1	6.36	71	.319	.412	6	.250	0	-22	-18	-2	-1.6

● **BILL PFANN**   Pfann, William F. b: 6/1863, Hamilton, Ont., Can. d: 6/3/04, Hamilton, Ont., Can   6', 205 lbs.   Deb: 6/16/1894

YEAR	TM/L	W	L	PCT	G	GS	CG	SH	SV	IP	H	HR	BB	SO	RAT	ERA	ERA+	OAV	OOB	BH	AVG	PB	PR	/A	PD	TPI
1894	Cin-N	0	1	.000	1	1	0	0	0	3	10	1	4	0	42.0	27.00	21	.526	.609	0	.000	-0	-7	-7	0	-1.1

● **JEFF PFEFFER**   Pfeffer, Edward Joseph b: 3/4/1888, Seymour, Ill. d: 8/15/72, Chicago, Ill.   BR/TR, 6'3", 210 lbs.   Deb: 4/16/11 F

YEAR	TM/L	W	L	PCT	G	GS	CG	SH	SV	IP	H	HR	BB	SO	RAT	ERA	ERA+	OAV	OOB	BH	AVG	PB	PR	/A	PD	TPI
1911	StL-A	0	0	—	2	0	0	0	0	10	11	0	4	4	13.5	7.20	47	.297	.366	0	.000	-1	-4	-4	-0	-0.1
1913	Bro-N	0	1	.000	5	2	1	0	0	24¹	28	0	13	13	16.6	3.33	99	.311	.421	0	—	-0	-0	-0	-0	-0.1
1914	Bro-N	23	12	.657	43	34	27	3	4	315	264	9	91	135	10.3	1.97	145	.232	.293	23	.198	-1	29	31	-4	3.1
1915	Bro-N	19	14	.576	40	34	26	6	3	291²	243	8	76	84	10.4	2.10	132	.231	.293	27	.255	-5	21	22	-4	2.6
1916	*Bro-N	25	11	.694	41	36	30	6	1	328²	274	5	63	128	9.7	1.92	140	.230	.278	34	.279	7	26	28	-5	3.6
1917	Bro-N	11	15	.423	30	30	24	3	0	266	225	4	66	115	10.4	2.23	125	.234	.294	13	.130	-4	14	17	-2	0.9
1918	Bro-N	1	0	1.000	1	1	1	0	0	9	7	0	3	6	11.0	0.00	—	.071	.161	1	.250	0	3	3	0	0.5
1919	Bro-N	17	13	.567	30	30	26	4	0	267	270	7	49	92	11.2	2.66	112	.267	.308	20	.206	1	7	11	-1	1.2
1920	*Bro-N	16	9	.640	30	28	20	2	0	215	225	6	45	80	11.5	3.01	106	.273	.314	18	.243	1	3	5	-3	0.3
1921	Bro-N	1	5	.167	6	5	2	0	0	31²	36	0	9	8	13.1	4.55	86	.310	.365	0	.000	-2	-3	-2	-0	-0.5
	StL-N	9	3	.750	24	18	9	1	2	98²	115	3	28	22	13.5	4.29	86	.305	.361	4	.138	-1	-6	-7	-1	-0.9
	Yr	10	8	.556	24	18	9	1	2	130¹	151	3	37	30	13.3	4.35	86	.306	.360	4	.100	-2	-9	-9	-1	-1.4
1922	StL-N	19	12	.613	44	32	19	1	2	261¹	286	21	62	58	12.2	3.58	108	.279	.324	24	.245	4	15	8	1	1.3
1923	StL-N	8	9	.471	26	18	13	0	0	152¹	171	8	40	33	13.0	4.02	97	.287	.341	7	.127	-2	-0	-13	-1	-0.7
1924	StL-N	4	5	.444	16	12	3	0	0	78	102	3	30	20	15.3	5.31	71	.318	.378	2	.115	-2	-14	-13	-1	-1.6

YEAR	TM/L	W	L	PCT	G	GS	CG	SH	SV	IP	H	HR	BB	SO	RAT	ERA	ERA+	OAV	OOB	BH	AVG	PB	PR	/A	PD	TPI
	Pit-N	5	3	.625	15	4	1	0	0	58²	68	3	17	19	13.0	3.07	125	.293	.341	6	.240	-0	5	5	-1	0.5
	Yr	9	8	.529	31	16	4	0	0	136²	170	6	47	39	14.3	4.35	88	.307	.361	9	.176	-3	-7	-8	-2	-1.1
Total	13	158	112	.585	347	279	194	28	10	2407¹	2320	67	592	836	11.3	2.77	114	.258	.311	180	.206	2	97	103	-21	10.1

● **BIG JEFF PFEFFER**   Pfeffer, Francis Xavier b: 3/31/1882, Champaign, Ill. d: 12/19/54, Kankakee, Ill. BR/TR, 6'1", 185 lbs. Deb: 4/15/05 F

YEAR	TM/L	W	L	PCT	G	GS	CG	SH	SV	IP	H	HR	BB	SO	RAT	ERA	ERA+	OAV	OOB	BH	AVG	PB	PR	/A	PD	TPI
1905	Chi-N	4	4	.500	15	11	9	0	0	101	84	2	36	56	11.0	2.50	120	.240	.318	4	.200	1	6	5	-1	0.4
1906	Bos-N	13	22	.371	36	36	33	4	0	302¹	270	4	114	158	11.9	2.95	91	.246	.325	31	.196	3	-11	-9	2	-0.3
1907	Bos-N	6	8	.429	19	16	12	1	0	144	129	3	61	65	12.3	3.00	85	.253	.341	15	.250	0	-8	-7	-0	-0.4
1908	Bos-N	0	0	—	4	0	0	0	0	10	18	1	8	3	23.4	12.60	19	.383	.473	0	.000	-0	-11	-11	-0	-0.1
1910	Chi-N	1	0	1.000	13	1	0	0	0	41¹	43	1	16	11	13.1	3.27	88	.281	.353	3	.176	1	-1	-2	-1	0.0
1911	Bos-N	7	5	.583	26	6	4	1	2	97	116	3	57	24	16.1	4.73	81	.301	.391	9	.196	1	-14	-10	0	-1.0
Total	6	31	39	.443	113	70	59	6	2	695²	660	14	292	317	12.7	3.30	87	.260	.342	66	.204	8	-40	-34	-0	-1.4

● **FRED PFEFFER**   Pfeffer, Nathaniel Frederick "Fritz" or "Dandelion"
b: 3/17/1860, Louisville, Ky. d: 4/10/32, Chicago, Ill. BR/TR, 5'10.5", 184 lbs. Deb: 5/1/1882 M♦

YEAR	TM/L	W	L	PCT	G	GS	CG	SH	SV	IP	H	HR	BB	SO	RAT	ERA	ERA+	OAV	OOB	BH	AVG	PB	PR	/A	PD	TPI
1884	Chi-N	0	1	.000	1	0	0	0	0	3	3	0	1	0	36.0	9.00	33	.333	.400	135	.289	0	-1	-1	-0	0.0
1885	*Chi-N	2	1	.667	5	2	2	0	2	31²	26	1	8	13	9.7	2.56	119	.222	.272	113	.241	1	1	2	-0	0.2
1892	Lou-N	0	0	—	1	0	0	0	0	5	4	0	5	0	16.2	1.80	170	.211	.375	121	.257	1	1	1	0	0.1
1894	Lou-N	0	0	—	1	0	0	0	0	7	8	0	6	0	19.3	2.57	198	.286	.429	126	.308	0	2	2	-0	0.0
Total	4	2	1	.667	8	2	2	0	2	44²	41	1	20	13	12.5	2.62	130	.237	.320	1671	.255	2	3	4	-1	0.2

● **JACK PFIESTER**   Pfiester, John Albert "Jack The Giant Killer" (b: John Albert Hagenbush)
b: 5/24/1878, Cincinnati, Ohio d: 9/3/53, Loveland, Ohio BR/TL, 5'11", 180 lbs. Deb: 9/8/03

YEAR	TM/L	W	L	PCT	G	GS	CG	SH	SV	IP	H	HR	BB	SO	RAT	ERA	ERA+	OAV	OOB	BH	AVG	PB	PR	/A	PD	TPI
1903	Pit-N	0	3	.000	3	3	2	0	0	19	26	0	10	15	18.0	6.16	53	.321	.409	0	.000	-1	-6	-6	-0	-0.8
1904	Pit-N	1	1	.500	3	2	1	0	0	20	28	0	4	9	16.6	7.20	38	.318	.381	2	.286	1	-10	-10	-0	-0.7
1906	*Chi-N	20	8	.714	31	29	20	4	0	250²	173	3	63	153	8.9	1.51	175	.194	.258	4	.048	-7	31	32	-1	2.8
1907	*Chi-N	14	9	.609	30	22	13	3	0	195	143	1	48	90	9.0	**1.15**	**216**	.207	.263	6	.094	-3	29	29	-2	3.1
1908	*Chi-N	12	10	.545	33	29	18	3	0	252	204	1	70	117	10.2	2.00	108	.223	.287	8	.101	-4	10	10	-3	0.1
1909	Chi-N	17	6	.739	29	25	13	6	0	196²	179	1	49	73	10.7	2.43	105	.240	.291	11	.169	0	4	3	3	0.6
1910	*Chi-N	6	3	.667	14	13	5	2	0	100¹	82	0	26	34	9.8	1.79	161	.225	.279	3	.091	-2	14	12	-0	0.7
1911	Chi-N	1	4	.200	6	5	3	0	0	33²	34	0	18	15	14.4	4.01	83	.262	.360	2	.182	-0	-2	-3	1	-0.3
Total	8	71	44	.617	149	128	75	17	0	1067¹	869	6	293	503	10.1	2.02	128	.223	.284	36	.103	-15	69	67	-3	5.5

● **DAN PFISTER**   Pfister, Daniel Albin b: 12/20/36, Plainfield, N.J. BR/TR, 6', 187 lbs. Deb: 9/9/61

YEAR	TM/L	W	L	PCT	G	GS	CG	SH	SV	IP	H	HR	BB	SO	RAT	ERA	ERA+	OAV	OOB	BH	AVG	PB	PR	/A	PD	TPI
1961	KC-A	0	0	—	2	0	0	0	0	2¹	5	2	4	3	34.7	15.43	27	.417	.563	0	—	0	-3	-3	-0	0.0
1962	KC-A	4	14	.222	41	25	2	0	1	196¹	175	27	106	123	13.5	4.54	93	.238	.341	12	.185	-1	-12	-7	1	-0.6
1963	KC-A	1	0	1.000	3	1	0	0	0	9¹	8	1	3	9	11.6	1.93	202	.229	.308	0	.000	-0	2	2	0	0.2
1964	KC-A	1	5	.167	19	3	0	0	0	41¹	50	10	29	21	18.5	6.53	58	.311	.434	0	.000	-0	-13	-12	-0	-1.7
Total	4	6	19	.240	65	29	2	0	1	249	238	40	142	156	14.3	4.87	85	.252	.359	12	.162	-2	-27	-20	-1	-2.1

● **LEE PFUND**   Pfund, Le Roy Herbert b: 10/10/18, Oak Park, Ill. BR/TR, 6'1", 185 lbs. Deb: 4/21/45

YEAR	TM/L	W	L	PCT	G	GS	CG	SH	SV	IP	H	HR	BB	SO	RAT	ERA	ERA+	OAV	OOB	BH	AVG	PB	PR	/A	PD	TPI
1945	Bro-N	3	2	.600	15	10	2	0	0	62¹	69	4	35	27	15.7	5.20	72	.274	.373	4	.182	0	-10	-10	1	-0.6

● **BILL PHEBUS**   Phebus, Raymond William b: 8/2/09, Cherryvale, Kan. d: 10/11/89, Bartow, Fla. BR/TR, 5'9", 170 lbs. Deb: 9/6/36

YEAR	TM/L	W	L	PCT	G	GS	CG	SH	SV	IP	H	HR	BB	SO	RAT	ERA	ERA+	OAV	OOB	BH	AVG	PB	PR	/A	PD	TPI
1936	Was-A	0	0	—	2	1	0	0	0	7¹	4	1	4	4	11.0	2.45	195	.114	.225	0	.000	0	2	2	-0	0.0
1937	Was-A	3	2	.600	6	5	4	1	1	40²	33	2	24	13	13.1	2.21	200	.232	.351	0	.000	1	11	10	-1	1.2
1938	Was-A	0	0	—	5	0	0	0	1	6¹	9	1	7	2	22.7	11.37	40	.346	.485	0	.000	0	-5	-5	-0	-0.1
Total	3	3	2	.600	13	6	4	1	2	54¹	46	4	35	18	13.9	3.31	135	.227	.349	0	.000	1	8	7	-1	1.1

● **RAY PHELPS**   Phelps, Raymond Clifford b: 12/11/03, Dunlap, Tenn. d: 7/7/71, Fort Pierce, Fla. BR/TR, 6'2", 200 lbs. Deb: 4/23/30

YEAR	TM/L	W	L	PCT	G	GS	CG	SH	SV	IP	H	HR	BB	SO	RAT	ERA	ERA+	OAV	OOB	BH	AVG	PB	PR	/A	PD	TPI
1930	Bro-N	14	7	.667	36	24	11	2	0	179²	198	21	52	64	12.7	4.11	120	.280	.332	10	.147	-2	17	16	2	1.5
1931	Bro-N	7	9	.438	28	26	3	1	0	149¹	184	3	44	50	14.0	5.00	76	.306	.357	8	.157	-1	-19	-20	-0	-1.9
1932	Bro-N	5	4	.556	20	8	4	1	0	79¹	101	5	27	21	14.9	5.90	65	.323	.382	2	.087	-1	-18	-18	0	-1.8
1935	Chi-A	4	8	.333	27	17	4	0	1	125	126	10	55	38	13.2	4.82	96	.262	.341	5	.122	-4	-5	-3	2	-0.4
1936	Chi-A	4	6	.400	15	4	2	0	0	68²	91	9	42	17	17.7	6.03	86	.331	.423	6	.231	-1	-8	-6	1	-0.6
Total	5	33	35	.485	126	79	24	4	1	602	700	48	220	190	14.0	4.93	90	.294	.358	31	.148	-8	-32	-31	5	-3.2

● **DEACON PHILLIPPE**   Phillippe, Charles Louis b: 5/23/1872, Rural Retreat, Va. d: 3/30/52, Avalon, Pa. BR/TR, 6'0.5", 180 lbs. Deb: 4/21/1899

YEAR	TM/L	W	L	PCT	G	GS	CG	SH	SV	IP	H	HR	BB	SO	RAT	ERA	ERA+	OAV	OOB	BH	AVG	PB	PR	/A	PD	TPI
1899	Lou-N	21	17	.553	42	38	33	2	1	321	331	10	64	68	11.3	3.17	122	.266	.306	26	.203	-1	24	25	-0	2.3
1900	*Pit-N	20	13	.606	38	33	29	1	0	279	274	7	42	75	**10.4**	2.84	128	.257	**.289**	19	.181	-2	27	25	-2	2.0
1901	Pit-N	22	12	.647	37	32	30	1	2	296	274	4	28	103	9.8	2.22	147	.244	.275	26	.230	5	**36**	34	3	4.4
1902	Pit-N	20	9	.690	31	30	29	5	0	272	265	1	26	122	9.8	2.05	133	.255	.276	25	.221	3	22	21	-2	2.1
1903	*Pit-N	25	9	.735	36	33	31	4	2	289¹	269	4	29	123	**9.4**	2.43	133	.241	**.263**	26	.210	2	27	26	-2	2.7
1904	Pit-N	10	10	.500	21	19	17	3	1	166²	183	1	26	82	11.4	3.24	85	.272	.302	2	.123	-4	-9	-9	-0	-1.4
1905	Pit-N	20	13	.606	38	33	25	6	0	279	235	0	48	133	9.5	2.19	137	.233	.274	6	.093	-4	25	25	-1	2.2
1906	Pit-N	15	10	.600	33	24	19	3	0	218²	216	3	26	90	10.0	2.47	108	.252	.276	20	.244	3	4	5	0	0.8
1907	Pit-N	14	11	.560	35	26	17	1	2	214	214	2	36	61	10.7	2.61	103	.263	.300	12	.185	1	-3	-4	-2	-0.6
1908	Pit-N	0	0	—	5	0	0	0	0	12	20	0	3	1	17.3	11.25	20	.357	.390	1	.250	0	-12	-12	1	-0.1
1909	*Pit-N	8	3	.727	22	13	7	1	0	131²	121	2	14	38	9.5	2.32	117	.253	.280	3	.071	-3	4	6	-2	-0.1
1910	Pit-N	14	2	.875	31	8	5	1	4	121²	111	4	9	30	9.1	2.29	135	.239	.258	9	1.200	1	10	11	-3	1.2
1911	Pit-N	0	0	—	3	0	0	0	0	6	5	0	2	3	10.5	7.50	46	.238	.304	1	1.000	0	-3	-3	0	0.1
Total	13	189	109	.634	372	289	242	27	12	2607	2518	41	363	929	10.1	2.59	120	.253	.283	185	.189	2	153	150	-14	15.7

● **BUZ PHILLIPS**   Phillips, Albert Abernathy b: 5/25/04, Newton, N.C. d: 11/6/64, Baltimore, Md. BR/TR, 5'11.5", 185 lbs. Deb: 8/5/30

YEAR	TM/L	W	L	PCT	G	GS	CG	SH	SV	IP	H	HR	BB	SO	RAT	ERA	ERA+	OAV	OOB	BH	AVG	PB	PR	/A	PD	TPI
1930	Phi-N	0	0	—	14	1	0	0	0	43²	68	6	18	19	17.9	8.04	68	.354	.412	6	.462	2	-15	-12	-1	0.1

● **RED PHILLIPS**   Phillips, Clarence Lemuel b: 11/3/08, Pauls Valley, Okla. d: 2/1/88, Wichita, Kan. BR/TR, 6'3.5", 195 lbs. Deb: 7/24/34

YEAR	TM/L	W	L	PCT	G	GS	CG	SH	SV	IP	H	HR	BB	SO	RAT	ERA	ERA+	OAV	OOB	BH	AVG	PB	PR	/A	PD	TPI
1934	Det-A	1	0	1.000	7	1	0	0	1	23¹	31	1	6	3	14.3	6.17	71	.316	.412	3	.250	1	-4	-5	-0	-0.3
1936	Det-A	3	4	.333	22	6	3	0	0	87¹	124	12	22	15	15.0	6.49	76	.332	.370	10	.303	2	-14	-15	-0	-0.7
Total	2	4	4	.500	29	7	4	0	1	110²	155	13	28	18	15.7	6.42	75	.329	.379	13	.289	3	-18	-20	-1	-1.0

● **JACK PHILLIPS**   Phillips, Jack Dorn "Stretch" b: 9/6/21, Clarence, N.Y. BR/TR, 6'4", 193 lbs. Deb: 8/22/47 ♦

YEAR	TM/L	W	L	PCT	G	GS	CG	SH	SV	IP	H	HR	BB	SO	RAT	ERA	ERA+	OAV	OOB	BH	AVG	PB	PR	/A	PD	TPI
1950	Pit-N	0	0	—	1	0	0	0	0	5	7	0	1	2	14.4	7.20	61	.333	.364	61	.293	0	-2	-2	0	0.0

● **JACK PHILLIPS**   Phillips, John Stephen b: 5/24/19, St.Louis, Mo. d: 6/16/58, St.Louis, Mo. BR/TR, 6'1", 185 lbs. Deb: 7/13/45 ♦

YEAR	TM/L	W	L	PCT	G	GS	CG	SH	SV	IP	H	HR	BB	SO	RAT	ERA	ERA+	OAV	OOB	BH	AVG	PB	PR	/A	PD	TPI
1945	NY-N	0	0	—	1	0	0	0	0	4¹	1	0	4	2	22.8	10.38	38	.313	.500	1	.500	0	-1	-1	0	0.0

● **ED PHILLIPS**   Phillips, Norman Edwin b: 9/20/44, Ardmore, Okla. BR/TR, 6'1", 190 lbs. Deb: 4/9/70

YEAR	TM/L	W	L	PCT	G	GS	CG	SH	SV	IP	H	HR	BB	SO	RAT	ERA	ERA+	OAV	OOB	BH	AVG	PB	PR	/A	PD	TPI
1970	Bos-A	0	2	.000	18	0	0	0	0	23²	29	4	10	23	15.6	5.32	74	.312	.390	0	.000	-0	-4	-4	-0	-0.4

● **TOM PHILLIPS**   Phillips, Thomas Gerald b: 4/5/1889, Philipsburg, Pa. d: 4/12/29, Philipsburg, Pa. BR/TR, 6'2", 190 lbs. Deb: 9/13/15

YEAR	TM/L	W	L	PCT	G	GS	CG	SH	SV	IP	H	HR	BB	SO	RAT	ERA	ERA+	OAV	OOB	BH	AVG	PB	PR	/A	PD	TPI
1915	StL-A	1	3	.250	5	4	1	0	0	27¹	28	0	12	5	13.8	2.96	97	.283	.372	1	.111	-1	-0	-0	-1	-0.2
1919	Cle-A	3	2	.600	22	3	2	0	0	55	55	2	34	18	15.1	2.95	114	.272	.385	4	.364	1	**2**	**2**	-1	0.2
1921	Was-A	1	0	1.000	1	1	1	0	0	9	9	2	3	1	12.0	2.00	206	.290	.353	0	.000	0	2	2	-0	0.1
1922	Was-A	3	7	.300	17	7	2	1	0	70	72	2	22	19	12.6	4.89	79	.273	.338	3	.150	-1	-7	-8	-1	-1.1
Total	4	8	12	.400	45	15	6	1	0	161¹	164	6	71	44	13.6	3.74	95	.275	.361	8	.186	-1	-3	-3	-3	-1.0

● **BILL PHILLIPS**   Phillips, William Corcoran "Whoa Bill" or "Silver Bill"
b: 11/9/1868, Allenport, Pa. d: 10/25/41, Charleroi, Pa. BR/TR, 5'11", 180 lbs. Deb: 8/11/1890 M

YEAR	TM/L	W	L	PCT	G	GS	CG	SH	SV	IP	H	HR	BB	SO	RAT	ERA	ERA+	OAV	OOB	BH	AVG	PB	PR	/A	PD	TPI
1890	Pit-N	1	9	.100	10	10	9	0	0	82	123	4	29	26	16.8	7.57	44	.336	.386	11	.239	1	-36	-39	0	-3.2
1895	Cin-N	6	7	.462	18	9	6	0	2	109	126	6	44	15	14.6	6.03	83	.285	.359	15	.313	2	-15	-13	1	-1.0
1899	Cin-N	17	9	.654	33	27	18	1	1	227²	234	3	71	43	12.6	3.32	118	.265	.330	12	.130	-5	14	15	-0	0.9
1900	Cin-N	9	11	.450	29	24	17	3	0	208¹	229	5	67	51	13.3	4.28	86	.279	.343	13	.165	-4	-13	-14	6	-0.9

YEAR	TM/L	W	L	PCT	G	GS	CG	SH	SV	IP	H	HR	BB	SO	RAT	ERA	ERA+	OAV	OOB	BH	AVG	PB	PR	/A	PD	TPI
1901	Cin-N	14	18	.438	37	36	29	1	0	281¹	364	7	67	109	14.2	4.64	69	.311	.354	22	.202	2	-41	-45	5	-3.6
1902	Cin-N	16	16	.500	33	33	30	0	0	269	267	3	55	85	11.1	2.51	119	.259	.302	10	.342	10	8	15	3	3.1
1903	Cin-N	7	6	.538	16	13	11	1	0	118¹	134	0	30	46	13.0	3.35	106	.279	.330	10	.175	-1	-1	3	2	0.3
Total	7	70	76	.479	176	152	120	6	3	1295²	1477	32	363	374	13.2	4.09	87	.284	.338	122	.224	4	-85	-77	16	-4.4

● TAYLOR PHILLIPS
Phillips, William Taylor "Tay" b: 6/18/33, Atlanta, Ga. BL/TL, 5′11″, 185 lbs. Deb: 6/8/56

YEAR	TM/L	W	L	PCT	G	GS	CG	SH	SV	IP	H	HR	BB	SO	RAT	ERA	ERA+	OAV	OOB	BH	AVG	PB	PR	/A	PD	TPI
1956	Mil-N	5	3	.625	23	6	3	0	2	87²	69	6	33	36	11.2	2.26	153	.223	.311	0	.000	-2	15	12	2	1.1
1957	Mil-N	3	2	.600	27	6	0	0	1	73	82	3	40	36	15.2	5.55	63	.300	.392	2	.100	-1	-14	-17	0	-1.2
1958	Chi-N	7	10	.412	39	27	5	1	1	170¹	178	22	79	102	13.9	4.76	82	.266	.349	3	.056	-4	-15	-16	1	-1.7
1959	Chi-N	0	2	.000	7	2	0	0	0	16²	22	3	11	5	18.9	7.56	52	.319	.427	0	.000	-0	-7	-7	0	-0.7
	Phi-N	1	4	.200	32	3	1	0	1	63	72	4	31	35	15.3	5.00	82	.303	.392	1	.091	-1	-7	-6	0	-0.5
	Yr	1	6	.143	39	5	1	0	1	79²	94	7	42	40	15.8	5.54	74	.303	.393	1	.067	-1	-14	-13	1	-1.2
1960	Phi-N	0	1	.000	10	1	0	0	0	14	21	2	4	6	16.7	8.36	46	.356	.406	0	.000	-0	-7	-7	-0	-0.5
1963	Chi-A	0	0	—	9	0	0	0	0	14	16	2	13	13	19.3	10.29	34	.302	.448	0	.000	-0	-10	-11	0	0.0
Total	6	16	22	.421	147	45	9	1	6	438²	460	42	211	233	14.2	4.82	78	.275	.364	6	.053	-9	-46	-51	4	-3.5

● TOM PHOEBUS
Phoebus, Thomas Harold b: 4/7/42, Baltimore, Md. BR/TR, 5′8″, 185 lbs. Deb: 9/15/66

YEAR	TM/L	W	L	PCT	G	GS	CG	SH	SV	IP	H	HR	BB	SO	RAT	ERA	ERA+	OAV	OOB	BH	AVG	PB	PR	/A	PD	TPI
1966	Bal-A	2	1	.667	3	3	2	2	0	22	16	0	6	17	9.0	1.23	271	.213	.272	1	.167	0	5	5	-0	0.8
1967	Bal-A	14	9	.609	33	33	7	4	0	208	177	16	114	179	12.6	3.33	95	.227	.326	11	.145	1	-2	-4	-2	-0.6
1968	Bal-A	15	15	.500	36	36	9	3	0	240²	186	10	105	193	11.0	2.62	112	.212	.299	15	.183	3	10	8	-0	1.4
1969	Bal-A	14	7	.667	35	33	6	2	0	202	180	23	87	117	12.1	3.52	101	.241	.324	15	.200	2	2	1	-1	0.1
1970	*Bal-A	5	5	.500	27	21	3	0	0	135	106	11	62	72	11.6	3.07	119	.219	.315	7	.163	-0	10	9	0	0.6
1971	SD-N	3	11	.214	29	21	2	0	0	133¹	144	14	64	80	14.2	4.45	74	.280	.363	6	.167	1	-15	-17	-1	-1.6
1972	SD-N	0	1	.000	1	1	0	0	0	5²	3	2	6	8	14.3	7.94	41	.150	.346	0	.000	-0	-3	-3	0	-0.4
	Chi-N	3	3	.500	37	1	0	0	6	83¹	76	9	45	59	13.3	3.78	101	.247	.346	2	.133	-1	-3	0	1	0.0
	Yr	3	4	.429	38	2	0	0	6	89	79	11	51	67	13.3	4.04	93	.241	.346	2	.118	-1	-6	-3	1	-0.4
Total	7	56	52	.519	201	149	29	11	6	1030	888	85	489	725	12.2	3.33	100	.233	.324	57	.170	6	4	-1	-3	0.3

● STEVE PHOENIX
Phoenix, Steven Robert b: 1/31/68, Phoenix, Ariz. BR/TR, 6′2″, 175 lbs. Deb: 7/30/94

YEAR	TM/L	W	L	PCT	G	GS	CG	SH	SV	IP	H	HR	BB	SO	RAT	ERA	ERA+	OAV	OOB	BH	AVG	PB	PR	/A	PD	TPI
1994	Oak-A	0	0	—	2	0	0	0	0	4¹	4	0	2	3	12.5	6.23	71	.235	.316	0	—	0	-1	-1	-0	0.7
1995	Oak-A	0	0	—	1	0	0	0	0	1²	3	1	3	3	32.4	32.40	14	.429	.600	0	—	0	-5	-5	-0	0.6
Total	2	0	0	—	3	0	0	0	0	6	7	1	5	6	18.0	13.50	33	.292	.414	0	—	0	-6	-6	-0	1.3

● BILL PHYLE
Phyle, William Joseph b: 6/25/1875, Duluth, Minn. d: 8/6/53, Los Angeles, Cal. TR , Deb: 9/17/1898 ♦

YEAR	TM/L	W	L	PCT	G	GS	CG	SH	SV	IP	H	HR	BB	SO	RAT	ERA	ERA+	OAV	OOB	BH	AVG	PB	PR	/A	PD	TPI
1898	Chi-N	2	1	.667	3	3	3	2	0	23	24	3	6	4	12.5	0.78	458	.267	.327	1	.111	-0	7	7	-1	0.8
1899	Chi-N	1	8	.111	10	9	9	0	1	83²	92	2	29	10	13.4	4.20	89	.279	.344	6	.176	-2	-3	-4	1	-0.5
1901	NY-N	7	10	.412	24	19	16	0	1	168²	208	2	54	62	14.3	4.27	77	.301	.356	12	.182	-1	-18	-18	1	-1.5
Total	3	10	19	.345	37	31	28	2	2	275¹	324	4	89	76	13.9	3.96	88	.291	.350	32	.176	-4	-14	-15	2	-1.2

● DOUG PIATT
Piatt, Douglas William b: 9/26/65, Beaver, Pa. BL/TR, 6′1″, 185 lbs. Deb: 6/11/91

YEAR	TM/L	W	L	PCT	G	GS	CG	SH	SV	IP	H	HR	BB	SO	RAT	ERA	ERA+	OAV	OOB	BH	AVG	PB	PR	/A	PD	TPI
1991	Mon-N	0	0	—	21	0	0	0	0	34²	29	3	17	29	11.9	2.60	139	.230	.322	0	.000	-0	4	4	0	0.0

● WILEY PIATT
Piatt, Wiley Harold "Iron Man" b: 7/13/1874, Blue Creek, Ohio d: 9/20/46, Cincinnati, Ohio BL/TL, 5′10″, 175 lbs. Deb: 4/22/1898

YEAR	TM/L	W	L	PCT	G	GS	CG	SH	SV	IP	H	HR	BB	SO	RAT	ERA	ERA+	OAV	OOB	BH	AVG	PB	PR	/A	PD	TPI
1898	Phi-N	24	14	.632	39	37	33	6	0	306	285	2	97	121	11.8	3.18	108	.245	.314	32	.262	4	15	9	-2	1.1
1899	Phi-N	23	15	.605	39	38	31	2	0	305	323	6	86	89	12.7	3.45	107	.271	.332	33	.270	4	14	8	-5	0.8
1900	Phi-N	9	10	.474	22	20	16	1	0	160²	194	6	71	47	15.7	4.71	77	.298	.380	17	.250	2	-18	-19	-3	-1.9
1901	Phi-A	5	12	.294	18	16	15	0	1	140	176	4	60	45	15.4	4.63	82	.303	.372	13	.224	0	-15	-13	-4	-1.6
	Chi-A	4	2	.667	7	6	4	1	0	51²	42	2	14	19	10.5	2.79	125	.220	.287	2	.118	-1	5	4	-1	0.2
	Yr	9	14	.391	25	22	19	1	1	191²	218	6	74	64	13.9	4.13	89	.282	.347	15	.200	-1	-10	-9	-5	-1.4
1902	Chi-A	12	12	.500	32	30	22	2	0	246	263	3	66	96	12.4	3.51	96	.274	.327	17	.200	2	2	-3	-3	-0.4
1903	Bos-N	9	14	.391	25	23	18	0	0	181	198	5	61	100	13.1	3.18	101	.280	.340	16	.225	2	2	1	-3	0.0
Total	6	86	79	.521	182	170	139	12	1	1390¹	1481	27	455	517	13.0	3.61	97	.272	.337	130	.239	13	4	-15	-20	-1.8

● HIPOLITO PICHARDO
Pichardo, Hipolito Antonio (Balbina) b: 8/22/69, Jicome Esperanza, D.R. BR/TR, 6′1″, 160 lbs. Deb: 4/21/92

YEAR	TM/L	W	L	PCT	G	GS	CG	SH	SV	IP	H	HR	BB	SO	RAT	ERA	ERA+	OAV	OOB	BH	AVG	PB	PR	/A	PD	TPI
1992	KC-A	9	6	.600	31	24	1	1	0	143²	148	9	49	59	12.5	3.95	103	.267	.330	0	—	0	-0	2	0	0.0
1993	KC-A	7	8	.467	30	25	2	0	0	165	183	10	53	70	13.2	4.04	113	.282	.341	0	—	0	5	10	2	0.5
1994	KC-A	5	3	.625	45	0	0	0	3	67²	82	4	24	36	15.0	4.92	102	.308	.380	0	—	0	-1	1	1	-0.1
1995	KC-A	8	4	.667	44	0	0	0	1	64	66	4	30	43	14.1	4.36	110	.265	.353	0	.000	0	3	3	1	0.5
1996	KC-A	3	5	.375	57	0	0	0	3	68	74	5	26	43	13.5	5.43	90	.284	.353	0	—	0	-3	-4	1	-0.1
Total	5	32	26	.552	207	49	3	1	7	508¹	553	32	182	251	13.4	4.36	105	.279	.347	0	.000	0	3	11	5	0.8

● RON PICHE
Piche, Ronald Jacques b: 5/22/35, Verdun, Que., Canada BR/TR, 5′11″, 165 lbs. Deb: 5/30/60 C

YEAR	TM/L	W	L	PCT	G	GS	CG	SH	SV	IP	H	HR	BB	SO	RAT	ERA	ERA+	OAV	OOB	BH	AVG	PB	PR	/A	PD	TPI
1960	Mil-N	3	5	.375	37	0	0	0	9	48	48	3	23	38	13.9	3.56	96	.258	.349	0	.000	-0	1	-1	-1	-0.2
1961	Mil-N	2	2	.500	12	1	1	0	1	23¹	20	1	16	16	13.9	3.47	108	.238	.360	0	.000	-1	1	1	0	0.1
1962	Mil-N	3	2	.600	14	8	2	0	0	52	54	6	29	28	14.9	4.85	78	.273	.374	1	.056	-1	-5	-6	1	-0.6
1963	Mil-N	1	1	.500	37	1	0	0	5	53	53	6	25	40	13.2	3.40	95	.256	.336	0	.000	-1	-1	-1	0	0.0
1965	Cal-A	0	3	.000	14	1	0	0	0	19²	20	5	12	14	14.6	6.86	50	.267	.368	0	.000	-0	-7	-8	-0	-1.1
1966	StL-N	1	3	.250	20	0	0	0	2	25¹	21	4	18	21	14.2	4.26	84	.214	.342	0	.000	-0	-2	-0	0	-0.4
Total	6	10	16	.385	134	11	3	0	12	221¹	216	23	123	157	14.1	4.19	84	.255	.354	1	.024	-3	-13	-16	1	-2.2

● CHARLIE PICKETT
Pickett, Charles Albert b: 3/1/1883, Delaware, Ohio d: 5/20/69, Springfield, Ohio BR/TR, 6′1″, 175 lbs. Deb: 6/21/10

YEAR	TM/L	W	L	PCT	G	GS	CG	SH	SV	IP	H	HR	BB	SO	RAT	ERA	ERA+	OAV	OOB	BH	AVG	PB	PR	/A	PD	TPI
1910	StL-N	0	0	—	2	0	0	0	0	6	7	0	2	2	13.5	1.50	199	.280	.333	0	—	0	1	1	-0	0.0

● CLARENCE PICKREL
Pickrel, Clarence Douglas b: 3/28/11, Gretna, Va. d: 11/4/83, Rocky Mount, Va. BR/TR, 6′1″, 180 lbs. Deb: 4/22/33

YEAR	TM/L	W	L	PCT	G	GS	CG	SH	SV	IP	H	HR	BB	SO	RAT	ERA	ERA+	OAV	OOB	BH	AVG	PB	PR	/A	PD	TPI
1933	Phi-N	1	0	1.000	9	0	0	0	0	13²	22	3	6	9	15.8	3.95	97	.357	.400	0	.000	-0	-1	-2	-1	-0.1
1934	Bos-N	0	0	—	10	0	0	0	0	16	24	0	7	6	17.4	5.06	76	.333	.392	0	.000	-0	-2	-2	-1	-0.1
Total	2	1	0	1.000	19	0	0	0	0	29²	44	3	13	15	16.7	4.55	84	.344	.396	0	.000	-0	-3	-2	-2	-0.2

● JEFF PICO
Pico, Jeffrey Mark b: 2/12/66, Antioch, Cal. BR/TR, 6′1″, 190 lbs. Deb: 5/31/88

YEAR	TM/L	W	L	PCT	G	GS	CG	SH	SV	IP	H	HR	BB	SO	RAT	ERA	ERA+	OAV	OOB	BH	AVG	PB	PR	/A	PD	TPI
1988	Chi-N	6	7	.462	29	13	2	2	1	112²	108	6	37	57	11.6	4.15	87	.252	.312	5	.147	0	-9	-7	-0	-0.8
1989	Chi-N	3	1	.750	53	5	0	0	2	90²	99	8	31	38	12.9	3.77	100	.278	.336	1	.100	-1	-3	-0	1	0.1
1990	Chi-N	4	4	.500	31	8	0	0	0	92	120	7	37	37	15.5	4.79	85	.321	.383	6	.273	2	-10	-7	1	-0.3
Total	3	13	12	.520	113	26	2	2	3	295¹	327	21	105	132	13.2	4.24	90	.282	.343	12	.182	1	-22	-14	2	-1.0

● MARIO PICONE
Picone, Mario Peter "Babe" b: 7/5/26, Brooklyn, N.Y. BR/TR, 5′11″, 180 lbs. Deb: 9/27/47

YEAR	TM/L	W	L	PCT	G	GS	CG	SH	SV	IP	H	HR	BB	SO	RAT	ERA	ERA+	OAV	OOB	BH	AVG	PB	PR	/A	PD	TPI
1947	NY-N	0	0	—	2	1	0	0	0	7	10	1	2	1	15.4	7.71	53	.345	.387	1	.500	-1	-3	-3	0	0.1
1952	NY-N	0	1	.000	2	1	0	0	0	9	11	2	5	3	16.5	7.00	53	.306	.390	0	.000	-1	-3	-3	0	-0.3
1954	NY-N	0	0	—	5	0	0	0	0	13²	13	1	11	6	15.8	5.27	77	.283	.421	0	.000	-0	-2	-2	-0	0.0
	Cin-N	0	1	.000	4	1	0	0	0	10¹	9	3	7	1	13.9	6.10	69	.243	.364	0	.000	-0	-2	-2	-0	-0.1
	Yr	0	1	.000	9	1	0	0	0	24	22	4	18	7	15.0	5.63	73	.265	.396	0	.000	-0	-4	-4	-0	-0.1
Total	3	0	2	.000	13	3	0	0	0	40	43	7	25	11	15.3	6.30	64	.291	.393	1	.167	-2	-10	-10	-0	-0.3

● AL PIECHOTA
Piechota, Aloysius Edward "Pie" b: 1/19/14, Chicago, Ill. d: 6/13/96, Chicago, Ill. BR/TR, 6′, 195 lbs. Deb: 5/7/40

YEAR	TM/L	W	L	PCT	G	GS	CG	SH	SV	IP	H	HR	BB	SO	RAT	ERA	ERA+	OAV	OOB	BH	AVG	PB	PR	/A	PD	TPI
1940	Bos-N	2	5	.286	21	8	2	0	0	61	68	6	41	18	16.1	5.75	65	.278	.381	4	.200	1	-13	-14	-0	-1.3
1941	Bos-N	0	0	—	1	0	0	0	0	1	0	0	1	0	9.0	0.00	—	.000	.250	0	—	0	0	0	0	0.0
Total	2	2	5	.286	22	8	2	0	0	62	68	6	42	18	16.0	5.66	66	.274	.379	4	.200	1	-13	-13	-0	-1.3

● CY PIEH
Pieh, Edwin John b: 9/29/1886, Waunakee, Wis. d: 9/12/45, Jacksonville, Fla BR/TR, 6′2″, 190 lbs. Deb: 9/6/13

YEAR	TM/L	W	L	PCT	G	GS	CG	SH	SV	IP	H	HR	BB	SO	RAT	ERA	ERA+	OAV	OOB	BH	AVG	PB	PR	/A	PD	TPI
1913	NY-A	1	0	1.000	4	0	0	0	0	10¹	10	0	7	6	14.8	4.35	69	.250	.362	1	.250	0	-2	-1	1	0.0
1914	NY-A	4	4	.500	18	4	1	0	0	62¹	68	6	29	24	14.0	5.05	55	.289	.367	2	.133	-0	-16	-16	-1	-2.0
1915	NY-A	4	5	.444	21	8	3	2	0	94	78	2	39	46	11.7	2.87	102	.234	.324	2	.067	-3	1	1	0	-0.3
Total	3	9	9	.500	43	12	4	2	0	166²	156	8	75	76	12.7	3.78	76	.257	.343	5	.098	-3	-17	-17	-0	-2.3

YEAR	TM/L	W	L	PCT	G	GS	CG	SH	SV	IP	H	HR	BB	SO	RAT	ERA	ERA+	OAV	OOB	BH	AVG	PB	PR	/A	PD	TPI

● **ED PIERCE**   Pierce, Edward John   b: 10/6/68, Arcadia, Cal.   BL/TL, 6'1", 185 lbs.   Deb: 9/6/92

| 1992 | KC-A | 0 | 0 | — | 2 | 1 | 0 | 0 | 0 | 5¹ | 9 | 1 | 4 | 3 | 21.9 | 3.38 | 120 | .429 | .520 | 0 | — | 0 | 0 | 0 | 0 | -0.2 |

● **JEFF PIERCE**   Pierce, Jeffrey Charles   b: 6/7/69, Poughkeepsie, N.Y.   BR/TR, 6'1", 190 lbs.   Deb: 4/26/95

| 1995 | Bos-A | 0 | 3 | .000 | 15 | 0 | 0 | 0 | 0 | 15 | 16 | 1 | 14 | 12 | 18.0 | 6.60 | 74 | .286 | .429 | 0 | | 0 | -3 | -3 | -0 | -0.5 |

● **RAY PIERCE**   Pierce, Raymond Lester "Lefty"   b: 6/6/1897, Emporia, Kan.   d: 5/4/63, Denver, Colo.   BL/TL, 5'7", 156 lbs.   Deb: 5/12/24

1924	Chi-N	0	0		6	0	0	0	0	7¹	7	2	4	2	13.5	7.36	53	.269	.367	0		-0	-3	-3	-0	0.0
1925	Phi-N	5	4	.556	23	8	4	0	0	90	134	7	24	18	15.9	5.50	87	.356	.397	5	.179	-0	-12	-7	0	-0.6
1926	Phi-N	2	7	.222	37	7	1	0	0	84²	128	3	35	18	17.4	5.63	74	.348	.406	3	.125	-2	-17	-14	-1	-1.5
Total	3	7	11	.389	66	15	5	0	0	182	269	12	63	38	16.5	5.64	79	.349	.400	8	.154	-2	-32	-24	-1	-2.1

● **TONY PIERCE**   Pierce, Tony Michael   b: 1/29/46, Brunswick, Ga.   BR/TL, 6'1", 190 lbs.   Deb: 4/14/67

1967	KC-A	3	4	.429	49	6	0	0	7	97²	79	6	30	61	10.5	3.04	105	.221	.290	0	.000	-2	-2	-1	-1	-0.2
1968	Oak-A	1	2	.333	17	3	0	0	1	32²	39	3	10	16	13.8	3.86	73	.295	.350	0	.000	-1	-3	-4	1	-0.4
Total	2	4	6	.400	66	9	0	0	8	130¹	118	9	40	77	11.3	3.25	95	.241	.306	0		-3	-1	-2	-1	-0.6

● **BILLY PIERCE**   Pierce, Walter William   b: 4/2/27, Detroit, Mich.   BL/TL, 5'10", 160 lbs.   Deb: 6/1/45

1945	Det-A	0	0		5	0	0	0	0	10	6	1	10	10	15.3	1.80	195	.182	.386	0	.000	-0	2	2	0	0.0
1948	Det-A	3	0	1.000	22	5	0	0	0	55¹	47	5	51	36	16.1	6.34	69	.234	.391	5	.294	2	-13	-12	0	-0.4
1949	Chi-A	7	15	.318	32	26	8	0	0	171²	145	11	112	95	13.5	3.88	108	.228	.344	9	.176	-1	6	6	1	0.7
1950	Chi-A	12	16	.429	33	29	15	1	1	219¹	189	16	137	118	13.5	3.98	113	.228	.339	20	.260	4	15	12	2	1.6
1951	Chi-A	15	14	.517	37	28	18	1	2	240¹	237	14	73	113	11.6	3.03	133	.258	.313	16	.203	-0	29	27	-1	2.9
1952	Chi-A	15	12	.556	33	32	14	4	1	255¹	214	12	79	144	10.4	2.57	142	.227	.289	17	.187	0	31	31	0	3.2
1953	Chi-A★	18	12	.600	40	33	19	7	3	271¹	216	20	102	**186**	10.6	2.72	148	**.218**	.292	11	.126	-4	38	39	-1	3.5
1954	Chi-A	9	10	.474	36	26	12	4	3	188²	179	15	86	148	12.8	3.48	107	.249	.332	11	.193	-0	5	5	-2	0.3
1955	Chi-A★	15	10	.600	33	26	16	6	1	205²	162	16	64	157	10.0	**1.97**	**200**	.213	**.277**	12	.171	-1	**45**	**45**	-1	**5.3**
1956	Chi-A★	20	9	.690	35	33	**21**	6	0	276¹	261	24	100	192	11.9	3.32	123	.249	.316	16	.157	-4	26	24	-3	1.5
1957	Chi-A★	**20**	12	.625	37	34	**16**	4	2	257	228	18	71	171	10.5	3.26	115	.234	.287	17	.172	-2	15	14	0	1.4
1958	Chi-A☆	17	11	.607	35	32	**19**	3	2	245	204	33	66	144	10.0	2.68	136	.227	.280	17	.205	2	30	26	-3	2.8
1959	*Chi-A☆	14	15	.483	34	33	12	2	0	224	217	36	62	114	11.3	3.62	104	.253	.306	13	.191	3	6	4	-0	0.7
1960	Chi-A	14	7	.667	32	30	8	1	0	196¹	201	24	46	108	11.3	3.62	104	.266	.308	12	.179	1	5	3	-1	0.3
1961	Chi-A☆	10	9	.526	39	28	5	1	3	180	190	17	54	106	12.3	3.80	103	.275	.328	8	.143	-2	4	2	-0	0.1
1962	*SF-N	16	6	.727	30	23	7	2	1	162¹	147	19	35	76	10.3	3.49	109	.239	.284	12	.214	-2	8	5	-1	0.7
1963	SF-N	3	11	.214	38	13	3	1	8	99	106	12	20	52	11.5	4.27	75	.272	.309	4	.129	-0	-11	-12	-1	-1.8
1964	SF-N	3	0	1.000	34	1	0	0	4	49	40	6	10	29	9.2	2.20	162	.222	.263	3	.333	1	7	7	-1	0.6
Total	18	211	169	.555	585	432	193	38	32	3306²	2989	284	1178	1999	11.4	3.27	119	.240	.307	203	.184	-0	250	229	-15	23.3

● **BILL PIERCY**   Piercy, William Benton "Wild Bill"   b: 5/2/1896, ElMonte, Cal.   d: 8/28/51, Long Beach, Cal.   BR/TR, 6'1.5", 170 lbs.   Deb: 10/3/17

1917	NY-A	0	1	.000	1	1	0	0	0	9	9	0	2	4	11.0	3.00	90	.257	.297	0	.000	-0	-0	-0	-0	0.0
1921	*NY-A	5	4	.556	14	10	5	1	0	81²	82	4	28	35	12.9	2.98	142	.263	.337	6	.214	-0	12	11	-0	1.1
1922	Bos-A	3	9	.250	29	12	7	1	0	121¹	140	2	62	24	15.4	4.67	88	.304	.394	5	.147	-1	-8	-8	-2	-0.6
1923	Bos-A	8	17	.320	30	24	11	0	0	187¹	193	6	73	51	13.5	3.41	121	.277	.357	7	.132	-3	12	15	3	1.8
1924	Bos-A	5	5	.417	23	18	3	0	0	121	156	4	66	20	17.3	5.95	73	.335	.429	6	.154	-2	-23	-21	1	-1.8
1926	Chi-N	6	5	.545	19	5	2	0	0	90¹	96	1	37	31	13.8	4.48	86	.280	.360	9	.257	1	-7	-6	0	-0.6
Total	6	27	43	.386	116	70	28	2	0	610²	676	16	268	165	14.5	4.26	97	.292	.376	33	.173	-5	-15	-10	-2	-0.1

● **MARINO PIERETTI**   Pieretti, Marino Paul "Chick"   b: 9/23/20, Lucca, Italy   d: 1/30/81, San Francisco, Cal.   BR/TR, 5'7", 158 lbs.   Deb: 4/19/45

1945	Was-A	14	13	.519	44	27	14	3	2	233¹	235	3	91	66	12.6	3.32	94	.257	.325	18	.222	2	1	-6	1	-0.3
1946	Was-A	2	2	.500	30	2	1	0	0	62	70	9	40	26	16.0	5.95	56	.292	.397	3	.214	-0	-17	-18	1	-1.0
1947	Was-A	2	4	.333	23	10	2	1	0	83¹	97	3	47	32	15.8	4.21	88	.287	.377	6	.231	-0	-5	-5	-0	-0.3
1948	Was-A	0	2	.000	8	1	0	0	0	11²	18	1	7	6	19.3	10.80	40	.375	.455	0	.000	-0	-8	-8	-0	-1.2
	Chi-A	8	10	.444	21	18	4	0	1	120	117	6	52	28	12.7	4.95	86	.262	.339	7	.179	-1	-9	-9	1	-1.2
	Yr	8	12	.400	29	19	4	0	1	131²	135	7	59	34	13.3	5.47	78	.273	.351	7	.171	-1	-17	-18	1	-2.4
1949	Chi-A	4	6	.400	39	9	0	0	4	116	131	6	54	25	14.4	5.51	76	.289	.364	9	.237	1	-17	-17	1	-1.2
1950	Cle-A	0	1	.000	29	1	0	0	1	47¹	45	2	30	11	14.3	4.18	104	.253	.361	2	.286	1	2	1	1	0.1
Total	6	30	38	.441	194	68	21	4	8	673²	713	34	321	188	13.9	4.53	81	.272	.353	45	.217	2	-52	-63	5	-5.1

● **AL PIEROTTI**   Pierotti, Albert Felix   b: 10/24/1895, Boston, Mass.   d: 2/12/64, Everett, Mass.   BR/TR, 5'10.5", 195 lbs.   Deb: 8/9/20

1920	Bos-N	1	1	.500	6	2	1	0	0	25	23	3	9	12	11.5	2.88	106	.250	.317	2	.250	0	1	0	-0	0.0
1921	Bos-N	0	1	.000	2	0	0	0	0	1²	3	0	3	1	32.4	21.60	17	.375	.545	0	.000	-0	-3	-3	-0	-1.3
Total	2	1	2	.333	8	2	1	0	0	26²	26	3	12	13	12.8	4.05	76	.260	.339	2	.222	-0	-3	-3	-1	-1.3

● **BILL PIERRO**   Pierro, William Leonard "Wild Bill"   b: 4/15/26, Brooklyn, N.Y.   BR/TR, 6'1", 155 lbs.   Deb: 7/17/50

| 1950 | Pit-N | 0 | 2 | .000 | 12 | 3 | 0 | 0 | 0 | 29 | 33 | 2 | 28 | 13 | 19.6 | 10.55 | 42 | .289 | .438 | 2 | .222 | -0 | -21 | -20 | -1 | -1.2 |

● **DAVE PIERSON**   Pierson, David P.   b: 8/20/1855, Wilkes-Barre, Pa.   d: 11/11/22, Trenton, N.J.   BR/TR, 5'7", 142 lbs.   Deb: 4/25/1876   F♦

| 1876 | Cin-N | 0 | 1 | .000 | 1 | 1 | 0 | 0 | 0 | 2 | 10 | 0 | — | 0 | — | ∞ | — | 1.000 | 1.000 | 55 | .236 | -0 | -2 | -2 | 0 | -0.2 |

● **WILLIAM PIERSON**   Pierson, William Morris   b: 6/14/1899, Atlantic City, N.J.   d: 2/20/59, Atlantic City, N.J   BL/TL, 6'2", 180 lbs.   Deb: 7/4/18

1918	Phi-A	0	1	.000	8	1	0	0	0	21²	20	1	20	6	17.4	3.32	88	.286	.457	1	.250	-0	-1	-1	-1	-0.2
1919	Phi-A	0	0		2	1	0	0	0	7²	9	0	8	4	20.0	3.52	97	.333	.486	1	.333	0	-0	-0	0	0.1
1924	Phi-A	0	0		1	0	0	0	0	2²	3	0	3	0	20.3	3.38	127	.300	.462	0		0	-0	-0	-0	0.0
Total	3	0	1	.000	11	2	0	0	0	32	32	1	31	10	18.3	3.38	94	.299	.464	2	.286	0	-1	-1	-1	-0.1

● **GEORGE PIKTUZIS**   Piktuzis, George Richard   b: 1/3/32, Chicago, Ill.   BR/TL, 6'2", 200 lbs.   Deb: 4/25/56

| 1956 | Chi-N | 0 | 0 | — | 2 | 0 | 0 | 0 | 0 | 5 | 6 | 1 | 2 | 3 | 14.4 | 7.20 | 52 | .333 | .400 | 0 | | 0 | -2 | -2 | -0 | 0.0 |

● **DUANE PILLETTE**   Pillette, Duane Xavier "Dee"   b: 7/24/22, Detroit, Mich.   BR/TR, 6'3", 205 lbs.   Deb: 7/19/49   F

1949	NY-A	2	4	.333	12	3	2	0	0	37¹	43	6	19	14	14.9	4.34	93	.299	.380	0	.000	-1	-1	-1	1	-0.2
1950	NY-A	0	0		4	0	0	0	0	7	9	1	3	4	15.4	1.29	334	.321	.387	0		-0	3	2	-0	0.2
	StL-A	3	5	.375	24	7	1	0	0	73²	104	6	44	18	18.3	7.09	70	.337	.423	3	.136	-1	-21	-17	-0	-1.7
	Yr	3	5	.375	28	7	1	0	2	80²	113	6	47	22	18.1	6.58	74	.335	.420	3	.136	-1	-18	-15	-1	-1.7
1951	StL-A	6	14	.300	35	24	6	1	0	191	205	14	115	65	15.0	4.99	88	.276	.376	8	.136	-3	-19	-13	-1	-1.6
1952	StL-A	10	13	.435	30	30	3	1	0	205¹	222	14	55	62	12.4	3.59	109	.274	.325	12	.182	-1	7	3	-2	0.6
1953	StL-A	7	13	.350	31	25	5	1	0	166²	181	16	72	60	13.2	4.48	94	.277	.341	7	.132	-1	-9	-5	-1	-0.7
1954	Bal-A	10	14	.417	25	25	11	4	0	179	158	9	67	66	11.4	3.12	115	.234	.305	7	.132	-1	12	9	3	1.4
1955	Bal-A	0	3	.000	7	5	0	0	0	20²	31	6	14	13	19.6	6.53	58	.344	.433	1	.167	-1	-6	-6	0	-0.7
1956	Phi-N	0	0		20	0	0	0	2	23¹	22	2	12	10	17.0	6.56	57	.330	.404	2	.222	0	-7	-7	-0	0.0
Total	8	38	66	.365	188	119	34	4	2	904	985	67	391	305	13.9	4.40	93	.277	.352	38	.140	-7	-45	-32	-1	-2.9

● **HERMAN PILLETTE**   Pillette, Herman Polycarp "Old Folks"   b: 12/26/1895, St.Paul, Ore.   d: 4/30/60, Sacramento, Cal.   BR/TR, 6'2", 190 lbs.   Deb: 7/30/17   F

1917	Cin-N	0	0		1	0	0	0	0	1	4	0	0	0	36.0	18.00	15	.571	.571	0		0	-2	-2	-0	0.0
1922	Det-A	19	12	.613	40	37	18	4	1	274²	270	6	95	71	12.5	2.85	136	.258	.328	17	.172	-3	36	31	3	3.2
1923	Det-A	14	19	.424	47	36	14	0	1	250¹	280	7	83	64	13.3	3.85	100	.288	.347	21	.247	4	4	0	4	0.8
1924	Det-A	1	1	.500	19	3	1	0	1	37²	46	1	14	13	15.1	4.78	86	.297	.366	4	.364	1	-2	-3	-0	0.0
Total	4	34	32	.515	107	76	33	4	3	563²	600	14	192	148	13.0	3.45	113	.275	.344	42	.215	2	36	27	7	4.0

● **SQUIZ PILLION**   Pillion, Cecil Randolph   b: 4/13/1894, Hartford, Conn.   d: 9/30/62, Pittsburgh, Pa.   BL/TL, 6', 178 lbs.   Deb: 8/20/15

| 1915 | Phi-A | 0 | 0 | — | 2 | 0 | 0 | 0 | 0 | 5¹ | 10 | 0 | 2 | 0 | 21.9 | 6.75 | 43 | .400 | .464 | 0 | | -0 | -2 | -2 | 0 | 0.0 |

HORACIO PINA
Pina, Horacio (Garcia) b: 3/12/45, Coahuila, Mexico   BR/TR, 6'2", 177 lbs.   Deb: 8/14/68

YEAR	TM/L	W	L	PCT	G	GS	CG	SH	SV	IP	H	HR	BB	SO	RAT	ERA	ERA+	OAV	OOB	BH	AVG	PB	PR	/A	PD	TPI
1968	Cle-A	1	1	.500	12	3	0	0	2	31.1	24	0	15	24	11.5	1.72	172	.218	.317	0	.000	-1	4	4	-0	0.3
1969	Cle-A	4	2	.667	31	4	0	0	2	46.2	44	6	27	32	14.7	5.21	72	.256	.373	3	.500	1	-8	-7	-0	-0.8
1970	Was-A	5	3	.625	61	0	0	0	6	71	66	4	35	41	13.2	2.79	127	.250	.344	0	.000	-0	7	6	1	0.8
1971	Was-A	1	1	.500	56	0	0	0	2	57.2	47	2	31	58	12.8	3.59	92	.227	.339	0	.000	-0	-1	-2	1	0.0
1972	Tex-A	2	7	.222	60	0	0	0	15	76	61	3	43	60	13.3	3.20	94	.228	.352	1	.200	1	-1	-2	3	0.1
1973	*Oak-A	6	3	.667	47	0	0	0	8	88	58	8	34	41	10.2	2.76	128	.193	.292	0	—	0	10	8	3	1.4
1974	Chi-N	3	4	.429	34	0	0	0	4	47.1	49	4	28	32	15.0	3.99	96	.268	.371	1	.200	-0	-2	-1	1	-0.1
	Cal-A	1	2	.333	11	0	0	0	0	11.2	9	1	3	6	9.3	2.31	149	.209	.261	0	—	-0	2	1	1	0.8
1978	Phi-N	0	0	—	2	0	0	0	0	2.1	0	0	0	4	0.0	0.00	—	.000	.000	0	.000	-0	1	1	0	0.0
Total 8		23	23	.500	314	7	0	0	38	432	358	28	216	278	12.6	3.25	106	.231	.336	5	.185	-1	12	9	9	2.5

ED PINKHAM
Pinkham, Edward b: 1849, Brooklyn, N.Y.   TL, 5'7", 142 lbs.   Deb: 5/8/1871 ♦

YEAR	TM/L	W	L	PCT	G	GS	CG	SH	SV	IP	H	HR	BB	SO	RAT	ERA	ERA+	OAV	OOB	BH	AVG	PB	PR	/A	PD	TPI
1871	Chi-n	1	0	1.000	1	1	1	0	0	10.1	11	0	3	0	11.3	3.48	132	.208	.255	25	.263	1	1	1		0.1

GEORGE PINKNEY
Pinkney, George Burton b: 1/11/1862, Orange Prairie, Ill. d: 11/10/26, Peoria, Ill.   BR/TR, 5'7", 160 lbs.   Deb: 8/16/1884 ♦

YEAR	TM/L	W	L	PCT	G	GS	CG	SH	SV	IP	H	HR	BB	SO	RAT	ERA	ERA+	OAV	OOB	BH	AVG	PB	PR	/A	PD	TPI
1886	Bro-a	0	0	—	1	0	0	0	0	2	2	0	0	0	9.0	4.50	78	.400	.400	156	.261	0	-0	-0	-0	0.0

ED PINNANCE
Pinnance, Edward D. "Peanuts" b: 10/22/1879, Walpole Island, Ont., Canada d: 12/12/44, Walpole Island, Ontario, Canada   BL/TR, 6'1", 180 lbs.   Deb: 9/14/03

YEAR	TM/L	W	L	PCT	G	GS	CG	SH	SV	IP	H	HR	BB	SO	RAT	ERA	ERA+	OAV	OOB	BH	AVG	PB	PR	/A	PD	TPI
1903	Phi-A	0	0	—	2	1	0	0	1	7	5	0	2	2	9.0	2.57	119	.200	.259	0	.000	-0	0	-0		0.0

LERTON PINTO
Pinto, William Lerton b: 4/8/1899, Chillicothe, Ohio d: 5/13/83, Oxnard, Cal.   BL/TR, 6', 190 lbs.   Deb: 5/23/22

YEAR	TM/L	W	L	PCT	G	GS	CG	SH	SV	IP	H	HR	BB	SO	RAT	ERA	ERA+	OAV	OOB	BH	AVG	PB	PR	/A	PD	TPI
1922	Phi-N	0	1	.000	9	0	0	0	0	24.2	31	1	14	4	16.4	5.11	91	.320	.405	1	.111	-1	-3	-1	-1	-0.1
1924	Phi-N	0	0	—	3	0	0	0	0	4	7	1	0	1	15.8	9.00	50	.467	.467	0	.000	-0	-2	-2	0	-0.1
Total 2		0	1	.000	12	0	0	0	0	28.2	38	2	14	5	16.3	5.65	82	.339	.413	1	.100	-1	-5	-3	-1	-0.1

ED PIPGRAS
Pipgras, Edward John b: 6/15/04, Schleswig, Iowa d: 4/13/64, Currie, Minn.   BR/TR, 6'2.5", 175 lbs.   Deb: 8/25/32 F

YEAR	TM/L	W	L	PCT	G	GS	CG	SH	SV	IP	H	HR	BB	SO	RAT	ERA	ERA+	OAV	OOB	BH	AVG	PB	PR	/A	PD	TPI
1932	Bro-N	0	1	.000	5	1	0	0	0	10	16	2	6	5	19.8	5.40	71	.348	.423	0	.000	-0	-2	-2	0	-0.2

GEORGE PIPGRAS
Pipgras, George William b: 12/20/1899, Ida Grove, Iowa d: 10/19/86, Gainesville, Fla.   BR/TR, 6'1.5", 185 lbs.   Deb: 6/9/23 FU

YEAR	TM/L	W	L	PCT	G	GS	CG	SH	SV	IP	H	HR	BB	SO	RAT	ERA	ERA+	OAV	OOB	BH	AVG	PB	PR	/A	PD	TPI
1923	NY-A	1	3	.250	8	2	2	0	0	33.1	34	2	25	12	16.2	5.94	66	.276	.403	0	.000	-1	-7	-7	-0	-0.9
1924	NY-A	0	1	.000	9	1	0	0	1	15.1	20	0	18	6	24.7	9.98	42	.351	.532	1	.333	-4	-10	-10	1	-0.6
1927	*NY-A	10	3	.769	29	21	9	1	0	166.1	148	2	77	81	12.2	4.11	94	.247	.334	16	.239	2	1	-5	-1	-0.3
1928	*NY-A	24	13	.649	46	38	22	4	3	300.1	314	4	103	139	12.6	3.38	111	.272	.333	18	.157	-4	22	13	-4	0.6
1929	NY-A	18	12	.600	39	33	13	3	0	225.2	229	16	95	125	13.1	4.23	91	.264	.340	12	.143	-4	-9	-3		-1.7
1930	NY-A	15	15	.500	44	30	15	3	4	221	230	9	70	111	12.5	4.11	105	.263	.324	12	.150	-2	13	5	-2	0.0
1931	NY-A	7	6	.538	36	14	6	1	3	137.2	134	8	58	59	12.7	3.79	105	.251	.327	1	.024	-6	9	3	-2	-0.5
1932	*NY-A	16	9	.640	32	27	14	2	0	219	235	15	87	111	13.5	4.19	97	.269	.340	18	.220	1	7	-3	-2	-0.4
1933	NY-A	2	2	.500	4	4	3	0	0	33	32	1	12	14	12.0	3.27	119	.252	.317	1	.091	-1	4	2	1	0.3
	Bos-A	9	8	.529	22	17	9	2	1	128.1	140	5	45	56	13.1	4.07	108	.276	.337	9	.196	-1	3	4	-2	0.3
	Yr	11	10	.524	26	21	12	2	1	161.1	172	6	57	70	12.9	3.90	110	.271	.333	10	.175	-1	7	7	-1	0.6
1934	Bos-A	0	0	—	2	1	0	0	0	3.1	4	1	3	0	18.9	8.10	59	.308	.438	0	.000	-0	-1	-1	0	-0.1
1935	Bos-A	0	1	.000	5	1	0	0	0	5	6	0	3	2	27.0	14.40	33	.391	.517	0	—	0	-6	-5	0	-0.8
Total 11		102	73	.583	276	189	93	16	12	1488.1	1529	66	598	714	13.1	4.09	98	.266	.339	88	.163	-15	35	-14	-15	-4.0

COTTON PIPPEN
Pippen, Henry Harold b: 4/2/11, Cisco, Tex. d: 2/15/81, Williams, Cal.   BR/TR, 6'2", 180 lbs.   Deb: 8/28/36

YEAR	TM/L	W	L	PCT	G	GS	CG	SH	SV	IP	H	HR	BB	SO	RAT	ERA	ERA+	OAV	OOB	BH	AVG	PB	PR	/A	PD	TPI
1936	StL-N	0	2	.000	6	3	0	0	0	21	37	5	8	8	20.1	7.71	51	.402	.461	1	.167	0	-9	-9	1	-0.6
1939	Phi-A	4	11	.267	25	17	5	0	1	118.2	169	13	40	33	15.9	5.99	79	.329	.378	3	.086	-2	-18	-17	2	-1.8
	Det-A	0	1	.000	3	2	0	0	0	14	18	1	6	5	15.4	7.07	69	.310	.375	2	.400	-0	-4	-3	-0	-0.2
	Yr	4	12	.250	28	19	5	0	1	132.2	187	14	46	38	15.8	6.11	77	.326	.376	5	.125	-2	-22	-20	1	-2.0
1940	Det-A	1	2	.333	4	3	0	0	0	21.1	29	3	10	9	16.9	6.75	70	.326	.400	0	.000	-1	-6	-5	0	-0.6
Total 3		5	16	.238	38	25	5	0	1	175	253	22	64	55	16.5	6.38	73	.336	.391	6	.111	-3	-36	-34	2	-3.2

GERRY PIRTLE
Pirtle, Gerald Eugene b: 12/3/47, Tulsa, Okla.   BR/TR, 6'1", 185 lbs.   Deb: 7/2/78

YEAR	TM/L	W	L	PCT	G	GS	CG	SH	SV	IP	H	HR	BB	SO	RAT	ERA	ERA+	OAV	OOB	BH	AVG	PB	PR	/A	PD	TPI
1978	Mon-N	0	2	.000	19	0	0	0	0	25.2	33	5	23	14	20.3	5.96	59	.314	.446	0	—	0	-7	-7	-0	-0.5

SKIP PITLOCK
Pitlock, Lee Patrick Thomas b: 11/6/47, Hillside, Ill.   BL/TL, 6'2", 180 lbs.   Deb: 6/12/70

YEAR	TM/L	W	L	PCT	G	GS	CG	SH	SV	IP	H	HR	BB	SO	RAT	ERA	ERA+	OAV	OOB	BH	AVG	PB	PR	/A	PD	TPI
1970	SF-N	5	5	.500	18	15	1	0	0	87	92	13	48	56	14.9	4.66	85	.274	.371	2	.080	-0	-6	-7	0	-0.7
1974	Chi-A	3	3	.500	40	5	0	0	0	105.2	103	7	55	68	14.1	4.43	84	.257	.356	0	—	-0	-10	-8	-1	-0.7
1975	Chi-A	0	0	—	1	0	0	0	0	0	0	0	0	0	—	—	—	1.000	1.000	0	—	-0	0	0	-0	-0.1
Total 3		8	8	.500	59	20	1	0	1	192.2	196	20	103	124	14.5	4.53	85	.266	.364	2	.080	-1	-15	-15	-1	-1.5

TOGIE PITTINGER
Pittinger, Charles Reno b: 1/12/1872, Greencastle, Pa. d: 1/14/09, Greencastle, Pa.   BL/TR, 6'2", 175 lbs.   Deb: 4/26/00

YEAR	TM/L	W	L	PCT	G	GS	CG	SH	SV	IP	H	HR	BB	SO	RAT	ERA	ERA+	OAV	OOB	BH	AVG	PB	PR	/A	PD	TPI
1900	Bos-N	2	9	.182	18	13	8	0	0	114	135	7	54	27	15.6	5.13	80	.293	.377	6	.130	-4	-18	-13	-1	-1.4
1901	Bos-N	13	16	.448	34	33	27	1	0	281.1	288	7	76	129	11.9	3.01	120	.263	.316	11	.110	-8	10	19	3	1.2
1902	Bos-N	27	16	.628	46	40	36	7	0	389.1	360	4	128	174	11.7	2.52	112	.245	.313	20	.136	8	11	13	-2	0.2
1903	Bos-N	18	22	.450	44	39	35	3	1	351.2	396	12	143	140	14.2	3.48	92	.294	.369	14	.109	-9	-8	-11	-3	-2.1
1904	Bos-N	15	21	.417	38	37	35	5	0	335.1	298	1	144	146	12.2	2.66	104	.242	.329	13	.107	-9	3	4	5	0.0
1905	Phi-N	23	14	.622	46	37	29	4	2	337.1	311	6	104	136	11.5	3.09	94	.247	.313	19	.156	-3	-3	-6	-3	-1.3
1906	Phi-N	8	10	.444	20	16	9	2	0	129.2	128	2	50	43	13.2	3.40	77	.252	.334	4	.091	-1	-11	-11	-1	-1.8
1907	Phi-N	9	5	.643	16	12	8	1	0	102	101	3	35	37	12.4	3.00	81	.261	.330	5	.139	-1	-6	-7	-1	-1.0
Total 8		115	113	.504	262	227	187	23	3	2040.2	2017	39	734	832	12.6	3.10	98	.260	.332	92	.124	-43	-23	-13	-3	-6.2

JIM PITTSLEY
Pittsley, James Michael b: 4/3/74, DuBois, Pa.   BR/TR, 6'7", 215 lbs.   Deb: 5/23/95

YEAR	TM/L	W	L	PCT	G	GS	CG	SH	SV	IP	H	HR	BB	SO	RAT	ERA	ERA+	OAV	OOB	BH	AVG	PB	PR	/A	PD	TPI
1995	KC-A	0	0	—	1	1	0	0	0	3.1	7	3	1	0	21.6	13.50	35	.438	.471	0	—	0	-3	-3	-0	0.0

STAN PITULA
Pitula, Stanley b: 3/23/31, Hackensack, N.J. d: 8/15/65, Hackensack, N.J.   BR/TR, 5'10", 170 lbs.   Deb: 4/24/57

YEAR	TM/L	W	L	PCT	G	GS	CG	SH	SV	IP	H	HR	BB	SO	RAT	ERA	ERA+	OAV	OOB	BH	AVG	PB	PR	/A	PD	TPI
1957	Cle-A	2	2	.500	23	5	1	0	0	59.2	67	8	32	17	15.2	4.98	75	.296	.388	3	.200	0	-8	-8	-1	-0.6

JUAN PIZARRO
Pizarro, Juan Ramon (Cordova) b: 2/7/37, Santurce, P.R.   BL/TL, 5'11", 190 lbs.   Deb: 5/4/57

YEAR	TM/L	W	L	PCT	G	GS	CG	SH	SV	IP	H	HR	BB	SO	RAT	ERA	ERA+	OAV	OOB	BH	AVG	PB	PR	/A	PD	TPI
1957	*Mil-N	5	6	.455	24	10	3	0	0	99.1	99	16	51	68	13.7	4.62	76	.261	.350	9	.250	3	-8	-12	-1	-1.0
1958	*Mil-N	6	4	.600	16	10	7	1	1	96.2	75	12	47	84	11.7	2.70	130	.212	.312	8	.250	3	13	9	1	1.2
1959	Mil-N	6	2	.750	29	14	6	2	0	133.2	117	13	70	126	13.1	3.77	94	.237	.342	5	.122	-0	3	-3	0	-0.2
1960	Mil-N	6	7	.462	21	17	3	0	0	114.2	105	13	72	88	14.2	4.55	75	.244	.357	11	.275	3	-10	-14	-1	-1.2
1961	Chi-A	14	7	.667	39	25	12	1	2	194.2	164	17	89	188	11.9	3.05	128	.226	.314	5	.217		21	19	-1	2.3
1962	Chi-A	12	14	.462	36	32	9	1	2	203.1	182	16	97	173	12.4	3.81	103	.236	.322	11	.159	-0	4	2	-2	0.0
1963	Chi-A★	16	8	.667	32	28	10	3	1	214.2	177	14	63	163	10.2	2.39	147	.224	.284	13	.178	3	30	27	-3	3.0
1964	Chi-A☆	19	9	.679	33	33	11	4	0	239	193	23	56	162	9.5	2.56	135	.219	.267	19	.211	5	28	24	-1	3.1
1965	Chi-A	6	3	.667	18	18	2	1	0	97	96	9	37	65	12.4	3.43	93	.254	.322	8	.235	3	0	-3	-0	0.1
1966	Chi-A	8	6	.571	34	9	1	0	0	88.2	91	9	42	99	13.3	3.76	84	.269	.347	4	.154	0	-3	-6	-1	-0.8
1967	Pit-N	8	10	.444	50	9	1	1	0	107	107	9	52	96	12.3	3.95	85	.259	.334	7	.259	2	-7	-7	-1	-1.2
1968	Pit-N	1	1	.500	12	0	0	0	0	11	14	2	10	14	20.5	3.27	89	.311	.446	0	.000	-0	-0	-0	-0	-0.0
	Bos-A	6	8	.429	19	12	6	0	0	107.2	97	15	44	84	11.8	3.59	88	.242	.317	5	.161	1	-7	-7	-0	-0.4
1969	Bos-A	0	1	.000	3	0	0	0	0	9	14	2	4	8	20.0	6.00	63	.359	.444	1	.333		-2	-2	-0	-0.3
	Cle-A	3	3	.500	48	4	1	0	4	82.2	67	6	49	44	12.8	3.16	119	.229	.343	3	.200	-0	4	6	0	0.5
	Oak-A	1	1	.500	3	0	0	0	0	7.2	3	1	3	4	7.0	2.35	146	.125	.222	1	.500	-0	1	1	-0	0.3
	Yr	4	5	.444	57	4	1	0	4	99.1	84	9	56	52	12.9	3.35	112	.230	.335	5	.200	-1	4	6	0	0.5
1970	Chi-N	0	0	—	12	0	0	0	0	15.2	16	2	9	14	14.9	4.60	98	.256	.366	5	.000	-0	-1	-0	-0	-0.0
1971	Chi-N	7	6	.538	16	14	6	3	0	101	78	10	40	67	10.7	3.46	114	.209	.289	6	.176	1	5	1	0	0.8
1972	Chi-N	4	5	.444	16	7	1	0	0	59.1	62	7	32	24	15.0	3.94	97	.293	.384	3	.143	-0	-3	-3	1	-0.1
1973	Chi-N	0	1	.000	2	0	0	0	0	4	6	1	1	0	18.0	11.25	68	.353	.421	0	.000	-0	-3	-3	0	-0.6

YEAR	TM/L	W	L	PCT	G	GS	CG	SH	SV	IP	H	HR	BB	SO	RAT	ERA	ERA+	OAV	OOB	BH	AVG	PB	PR	/A	PD	TPI
	Hou-N	2	2	.500	15	1	0	0	0	23¹	28	1	11	10	15.4	6.56	55	.301	.381	0	.000	-0	-8	-8	1	-1.1
	Yr	2	3	.400	17	1	0	0	0	27¹	34	2	12	13	15.5	7.24	51	.304	.376	0	—	-0	-11	-11	1	-1.7
1974	*Pit-N	1	1	.500	7	2	0	0	0	24	20	2	11	7	11.6	1.88	184	.220	.304	2	.333	-1	5	4	-0	0.4
Total	18	131	105	.555	488	245	79	17	28	2034¹	1807	201	888	1522	12.1	3.43	104	.237	.320	133	.202	29	55	33	-5	4.6

● **GORDIE PLADSON**   Pladson, Gordon Cecil b: 7/31/56, New Westminster, B.C., Canada BR/TR, 6'4", 210 lbs. Deb: 9/7/79

YEAR	TM/L	W	L	PCT	G	GS	CG	SH	SV	IP	H	HR	BB	SO	RAT	ERA	ERA+	OAV	OOB	BH	AVG	PB	PR	/A	PD	TPI
1979	Hou-N	0	0	—	4	0	0	0	0	4	9	1	2	2	24.8	4.50	78	.450	.500	0	—	0	-0	-0	-0	0.0
1980	Hou-N	0	4	.000	12	6	0	0	0	41¹	38	3	16	13	11.8	4.35	75	.244	.314	0	.000	-1	-3	-5	-0	-0.5
1981	Hou-N	0	0	—	2	0	0	0	0	4	9	0	3	3	27.0	9.00	37	.429	.500	0	—	0	-2	-3	-0	0.0
1982	Hou-N	0	0	—	2	0	0	0	0	1¹	10	0	2	0	81.0	54.00	6	.769	.800	0	—	0	-7	-8	-0	0.0
Total	4	0	4	.000	20	6	0	0	0	50¹	66	4	23	18	15.8	6.04	66	.314	.382	0	.000	-1	-14	-15	-0	-0.5

● **EMIL PLANETA**   Planeta, Emil Joseph b: 1/31/09, Higganum, Conn. d: 2/2/63, Rocky Hill, Conn. BR/TR, 6', 190 lbs. Deb: 9/20/31

YEAR	TM/L	W	L	PCT	G	GS	CG	SH	SV	IP	H	HR	BB	SO	RAT	ERA	ERA+	OAV	OOB	BH	AVG	PB	PR	/A	PD	TPI
1931	NY-N	0	0	—	2	0	0	0	0	5¹	7	0	4	0	18.6	10.13	36	.292	.393	0	.000	-0	-4	-4	-0	0.0

● **ED PLANK**   Plank, Edward Arthur b: 4/9/52, Chicago, Ill. BR/TR, 6'1", 205 lbs. Deb: 9/6/78

YEAR	TM/L	W	L	PCT	G	GS	CG	SH	SV	IP	H	HR	BB	SO	RAT	ERA	ERA+	OAV	OOB	BH	AVG	PB	PR	/A	PD	TPI
1978	SF-N	0	0	—	5	0	0	0	0	6²	6	1	2	1	10.8	4.05	85	.273	.333	0	—	0	-0	-0	-0	0.0
1979	SF-N	0	0	—	4	0	0	0	0	3²	9	0	2	1	27.0	7.36	47	.450	.500	0	—	0	-1	-2	-0	0.0
Total	2	0	0	—	9	0	0	0	0	10¹	15	1	4	2	16.5	5.23	66	.357	.413	0	—	0	-2	-2	-1	0.0

● **EDDIE PLANK**   Plank, Edward Stewart "Gettysburg Eddie" b: 8/31/1875, Gettysburg, Pa. d: 2/24/26, Gettysburg, Pa. BL/TL, 5'11.5", 175 lbs. Deb: 5/13/01 H

YEAR	TM/L	W	L	PCT	G	GS	CG	SH	SV	IP	H	HR	BB	SO	RAT	ERA	ERA+	OAV	OOB	BH	AVG	PB	PR	/A	PD	TPI
1901	Phi-A	17	13	.567	33	32	28	1	0	260²	254	2	68	90	11.4	3.31	114	.252	.304	18	.182	-3	10	13	-2	0.8
1902	Phi-A	20	15	.571	36	32	31	1	0	300	319	5	61	107	11.9	3.30	111	.273	.319	35	.292	6	9	12	-2	1.6
1903	Phi-A	23	16	.590	43	40	33	3	0	336	317	5	65	176	10.8	2.38	128	.249	.297	25	.187	-1	22	25	-1	2.5
1904	Phi-A	26	17	.605	44	43	37	7	0	357¹	311	2	86	201	10.5	2.17	124	.235	.292	31	.240	3	17	20	-0	2.8
1905	*Phi-A	24	12	.667	41	41	35	4	0	346²	287	3	75	210	10.0	2.26	118	.227	.283	29	.230	3	15	15	-3	1.6
1906	Phi-A	19	6	.760	26	25	21	5	0	211²	173	1	51	108	10.2	2.25	121	.226	.288	17	.233	2	10	11	-2	1.3
1907	Phi-A	24	16	.600	43	40	33	8	0	343²	282	5	85	183	10.1	2.20	118	.226	.285	26	.211	2	13	15	-1	1.9
1908	Phi-A	14	16	.467	34	28	21	4	1	244²	202	1	46	135	9.5	2.17	118	.224	.269	16	.180	-1	6	11	-4	0.7
1909	Phi-A	19	10	.655	34	33	24	3	0	265¹	215	1	62	132	9.7	1.76	136	.224	.277	21	.219	4	21	19	1	2.7
1910	Phi-A	16	10	.615	38	32	22	1	2	250¹	218	3	55	123	10.1	2.01	118	.237	.286	11	.128	-3	14	10	-3	0.4
1911	*Phi-A	23	8	.742	40	30	24	6	4	256²	237	2	77	149	11.5	2.10	150	.255	.322	18	.191	-1	35	30	1	3.4
1912	Phi-A	26	6	.813	37	30	23	5	2	259²	234	1	83	110	11.2	2.22	139	.245	.309	24	.267	4	32	25	-2	3.2
1913	*Phi-A	18	10	.643	41	30	18	7	4	242²	211	3	57	151	10.1	2.60	106	.234	.283	8	.105	-3	9	5	-1	0.3
1914	*Phi-A	15	7	.682	34	22	12	4	3	185¹	178	2	42	110	11.0	2.87	91	.266	.315	9	.150	0	-3	-5	-3	-0.9
1915	StL-F	21	11	.656	42	31	23	6	3	268¹	212	1	54	147	9.0	2.08	138	.218	.262	24	.258	3	19	24	-3	2.9
1916	StL-A	16	15	.516	37	26	17	3	3	235²	203	2	67	88	10.5	2.33	118	.237	.297	15	.185	-1	13	11	-4	1.1
1917	StL-A	5	6	.455	20	14	8	1	1	131	105	2	38	26	10.0	1.79	145	.225	.287	4	.105	-1	13	12	-2	0.7
Total	17	326	194	.627	623	529	410	69	23	4495²	3958	41	1072	2246	10.5	2.35	122	.239	.293	331	.206	17	257	254	-32	27.0

● **ERIK PLANTENBERG**   Plantenberg, Erik John b: 10/30/68, Renton, Wash. BB/TL, 6'1", 180 lbs. Deb: 7/31/93

YEAR	TM/L	W	L	PCT	G	GS	CG	SH	SV	IP	H	HR	BB	SO	RAT	ERA	ERA+	OAV	OOB	BH	AVG	PB	PR	/A	PD	TPI
1993	Sea-A	0	0	—	20	0	0	0	1	9²	11	0	12	3	22.3	6.52	68	.282	.462	0	—	0	-2	-2	0	0.0
1994	Sea-A	0	0	—	6	0	0	0	0	7	4	0	7	1	15.4	0.00	—	.174	.387	0	—	0	4	4	0	0.0
Total	2	0	0	—	26	0	0	0	1	16²	15	0	19	4	19.4	3.78	122	.242	.434	0	—	0	1	2	0	0.0

● **BILL PLEIS**   Pleis, William b: 8/5/37, St.Louis, Mo. BL/TL, 5'10", 175 lbs. Deb: 4/16/61

YEAR	TM/L	W	L	PCT	G	GS	CG	SH	SV	IP	H	HR	BB	SO	RAT	ERA	ERA+	OAV	OOB	BH	AVG	PB	PR	/A	PD	TPI
1961	Min-A	4	2	.667	37	0	0	0	2	56¹	59	4	34	32	15.5	4.95	86	.266	.373	1	.111	-1	-6	-4	-1	-0.6
1962	Min-A	2	5	.286	21	4	0	0	3	45	46	7	14	31	12.2	4.40	93	.264	.323	4	.286	-1	-2	-2	-1	-0.2
1963	Min-A	6	2	.750	36	4	1	0	0	68	67	10	16	37	11.0	4.37	83	.258	.301	2	.125	0	-6	-5	-0	-0.6
1964	Min-A	4	1	.800	47	0	0	0	4	50²	46	3	21	42	13.3	3.91	92	.232	.346	1	.250	0	-2	-2	-0	-0.1
1965	*Min-A	4	4	.500	41	2	0	0	4	51¹	49	3	27	33	13.3	2.98	119	.250	.341	0	.000	-1	3	3	-1	0.4
1966	Min-A	1	2	.333	8	0	0	0	0	9¹	5	1	4	9	8.7	1.93	186	.152	.243	0	—	0	2	2	-0	0.5
Total	6	21	16	.568	190	10	1	0	13	280²	269	31	126	184	12.9	4.07	93	.251	.334	8	.160	0	-11	-8	-3	-0.6

● **DAN PLESAC**   Plesac, Daniel Thomas b: 2/4/62, Gary, Ind. BL/TL, 6'5", 210 lbs. Deb: 4/11/86

YEAR	TM/L	W	L	PCT	G	GS	CG	SH	SV	IP	H	HR	BB	SO	RAT	ERA	ERA+	OAV	OOB	BH	AVG	PB	PR	/A	PD	TPI
1986	Mil-A	10	7	.588	51	0	0	0	14	91	81	5	29	75	10.9	2.97	146	.240	.301	0	—	0	12	14	-1	2.7
1987	Mil-A★	5	6	.455	57	0	0	0	23	79¹	63	8	23	89	10.1	2.61	175	.213	.276	0	—	0	16	17	-0	3.2
1988	Mil-A★	1	2	.333	50	0	0	0	30	52¹	46	2	12	52	10.0	2.41	165	.234	.278	0	—	0	9	9	-0	1.4
1989	Mil-A	3	4	.429	52	0	0	0	33	61¹	47	6	17	52	9.4	2.35	163	.213	.269	0	—	0	10	10	-0	2.1
1990	Mil-A	3	7	.300	66	0	0	0	24	69	67	5	31	65	13.2	4.43	87	.257	.342	0	—	0	-4	-4	-0	-0.8
1991	Mil-A	2	7	.222	45	10	0	0	8	92¹	92	7	39	61	13.1	4.29	93	.263	.342	0	—	0	-2	-3	-2	-0.5
1992	Mil-A	4	4	.556	44	4	0	0	1	79	64	5	35	54	11.6	2.96	130	.229	.321	0	—	0	9	8	-1	0.9
1993	Chi-N	2	1	.667	57	0	0	0	0	62²	74	10	21	47	13.6	4.74	84	.298	.353	0	.000	0	-5	-5	-0	-0.3
1994	Chi-N	2	3	.400	54	0	0	0	1	54²	61	9	13	53	12.3	4.61	90	.279	.322	0	.000	0	-2	-3	-1	-0.4
1995	Pit-N	4	4	.500	58	0	0	0	3	60¹	53	3	27	57	12.1	3.58	120	.237	.321	1	.250	0	4	5	0	0.6
1996	Pit-N	6	5	.545	73	0	0	0	11	70¹	67	4	24	76	11.6	4.09	107	.247	.308	0	—	-1	1	2	-2	0.1
Total	11	43	50	.462	607	14	0	0	148	772¹	715	69	271	681	11.7	3.54	116	.246	.314	1	.071	-1	48	49	-7	9.0

● **NORMAN PLITT**   Plitt, Norman William b: 2/21/1893, York, Pa. d: 2/1/54, New York, N.Y. BR/TR, 5'11", 180 lbs. Deb: 4/26/18

YEAR	TM/L	W	L	PCT	G	GS	CG	SH	SV	IP	H	HR	BB	SO	RAT	ERA	ERA+	OAV	OOB	BH	AVG	PB	PR	/A	PD	TPI
1918	Bro-N	0	0	—	1	0	0	0	0	2	3	0	1	0	18.0	4.50	62	.429	.500	1	1.000	-0	-0	-0	-0	0.0
1927	Bro-N	2	6	.250	19	8	1	0	0	62¹	73	3	36	9	15.9	4.91	81	.303	.396	4	.222	-0	-7	-7	-0	-0.7
	NY-N	1	0	1.000	3	0	0	0	0	7¹	9	0	1	0	13.5	3.68	105	.310	.355	0	.000	-0	0	0	1	0.0
	Yr	3	6	.333	22	8	1	0	0	69²	82	3	37	9	15.5	4.78	83	.303	.388	4	.211	-0	-7	-6	1	-0.7
Total	2	3	6	.333	23	8	1	0	0	71²	85	3	38	9	15.7	4.77	82	.307	.394	5	.250	-0	-7	-7	0	-0.7

● **TIM PLODINEC**   Plodinec, Timothy Alfred b: 1/27/47, Aliquippa, Pa. BR/TR, 6'4", 190 lbs. Deb: 6/2/72

YEAR	TM/L	W	L	PCT	G	GS	CG	SH	SV	IP	H	HR	BB	SO	RAT	ERA	ERA+	OAV	OOB	BH	AVG	PB	PR	/A	PD	TPI
1972	StL-N	0	0	—	1	0	0	0	0	0¹	3	0	0	0	81.0	27.00	13	.750	.750	0	—	0	-1	-1	0	0.0

● **ERIC PLUNK**   Plunk, Eric Vaughn b: 9/3/63, Wilmington, Cal. BR/TR, 6'5", 210 lbs. Deb: 5/12/86

YEAR	TM/L	W	L	PCT	G	GS	CG	SH	SV	IP	H	HR	BB	SO	RAT	ERA	ERA+	OAV	OOB	BH	AVG	PB	PR	/A	PD	TPI
1986	Oak-A	4	7	.364	26	15	0	0	0	120¹	91	14	102	98	14.8	5.31	73	.214	.372	0	—	0	-15	-19	-2	-1.7
1987	Oak-A	4	6	.400	32	11	0	0	2	95	91	8	62	90	14.7	4.74	87	.253	.366	0	—	0	-3	-6	-1	-0.7
1988	*Oak-A	7	2	.778	49	0	0	0	5	78	62	6	39	79	11.8	3.00	126	.217	.313	0	—	0	8	7	-1	0.8
1989	Oak-A	1	1	.500	23	0	0	0	1	28²	17	1	12	24	9.4	2.20	167	.172	.268	0	—	0	5	5	-0	0.5
	NY-A	7	5	.583	27	7	0	0	0	75²	65	7	52	61	13.3	3.69	105	.237	.359	0	—	0	2	-2	-1	0.1
	Yr	8	6	.571	50	7	0	0	1	104¹	82	8	64	85	12.6	3.28	116	.219	.333	0	—	0	7	4	-1	0.6
1990	NY-A	6	3	.667	47	0	0	0	0	72²	58	6	43	67	12.8	2.72	146	.225	.340	0	—	0	10	10	2	1.3
1991	NY-A	2	5	.286	43	8	0	0	0	111²	128	18	62	103	15.4	4.76	87	.286	.374	0	—	0	-8	-8	-2	-0.6
1992	Cle-A	9	6	.600	58	0	0	0	4	71²	61	5	38	50	12.4	3.64	107	.229	.326	0	—	0	6	5	-0	0.5
1993	Cle-A	4	5	.444	70	0	0	0	15	71	61	6	30	77	11.5	2.79	155	.226	.303	0	—	0	12	12	-1	1.7
1994	Cle-A	7	2	.778	41	0	0	0	3	71	61	3	37	73	12.7	2.54	186	.231	.330	0	—	0	18	17	-1	1.9
1995	*Cle-A	6	2	.750	56	0	0	0	2	64	48	5	27	71	11.1	2.67	176	.211	.305	0	—	0	15	14	0	1.6
1996	*Cle-A	3	2	.600	56	0	0	0	2	77²	56	6	34	85	10.8	2.43	201	.203	.297	0	—	0	22	21	-0	1.2
Total	11	60	46	.566	528	41	0	0	34	937¹	799	86	538	878	13.0	3.62	115	.231	.338	0	—	0	67	57	-8	6.6

● **JEFF PLYMPTON**   Plympton, Jeffrey Hunter b: 11/24/65, Framingham, Mass. BR/TR, 6'2", 205 lbs. Deb: 6/15/91

YEAR	TM/L	W	L	PCT	G	GS	CG	SH	SV	IP	H	HR	BB	SO	RAT	ERA	ERA+	OAV	OOB	BH	AVG	PB	PR	/A	PD	TPI
1991	Bos-A	0	0	—	4	0	0	0	0	5¹	2	0	4	2	15.2	0.00	—	.263	.391	0	—	0	2	3	-0	-0.1

● **RAY POAT**   Poat, Raymond Willis b: 12/19/17, Chicago, Ill. d: 4/29/90, Oak Lawn, Ill. BR/TR, 6'2", 200 lbs. Deb: 4/15/42

YEAR	TM/L	W	L	PCT	G	GS	CG	SH	SV	IP	H	HR	BB	SO	RAT	ERA	ERA+	OAV	OOB	BH	AVG	PB	PR	/A	PD	TPI
1942	Cle-A	1	3	.250	4	4	1	0	0	18¹	24	1	9	8	16.7	5.40	64	.296	.374	0	.000	-0	-4	-4	0	-0.7
1943	Cle-A	2	5	.286	17	4	1	0	0	45	44	3	20	31	12.8	4.40	71	.259	.337	2	.154	-1	-6	-6	-0	-1.0
1944	Cle-A	4	8	.333	36	6	1	0	1	80²	82	8	37	40	13.3	5.13	64	.265	.343	0	.000	-2	-15	-16	-0	-2.5
1947	NY-N	4	3	.571	7	7	5	0	0	60	53	8	13	25	9.9	2.55	160	.238	.280	4	.190	2	10	10	-1	1.3

YEAR	TM/L	W	L	PCT	G	GS	CG	SH	SV	IP	H	HR	BB	SO	RAT	ERA	ERA+	OAV	OOB	BH	AVG	PB	PR	/A	PD	TPI
1948	NY-N	11	10	.524	39	24	7	3	0	157²	162	21	67	57	13.2	4.34	91	.262	.337	7	.125	-1	-7	-7	-2	-1.2
1949	NY-N	0	0	—	2	0	0	0	0	2¹	8	0	1	0	34.7	19.29	21	.615	.643	0	—	-0	-4	-4	-0	0.0
	Pit-N	0	1	.000	11	2	0	0	0	36	52	6	15	17	16.8	6.25	67	.335	.394	1	.100	-1	-9	-8	-0	-0.3
	Yr	0	1	.000	13	2	0	0	0	38¹	60	6	16	17	17.8	7.04	59	.357	.413	1	.100	-1	-13	-12	-0	-0.3
Total 6		22	30	.423	116	47	15	4	1	400	425	48	162	178	13.3	4.55	82	.271	.340	14	.115	-3	-34	-36	-3	-4.4

● BUD PODBIELAN Podbielan, Clarence Anthony b: 3/6/24, Curlew, Wash. d: 10/26/82, Syracuse, N.Y. BR/TR, 6'1.5", 170 lbs. Deb: 4/25/49

YEAR	TM/L	W	L	PCT	G	GS	CG	SH	SV	IP	H	HR	BB	SO	RAT	ERA	ERA+	OAV	OOB	BH	AVG	PB	PR	/A	PD	TPI
1949	Bro-N	0	1	.000	7	1	0	0	0	12¹	9	1	9	5	13.9	3.65	112	.205	.352	3	.000	-0	1	1	1	0.1
1950	Bro-N	5	4	.556	20	10	2	0	1	72²	93	10	29	28	15.4	5.33	77	.307	.371	3	.107	-1	-10	-10	1	-1.1
1951	Bro-N	2	2	.500	27	5	1	0	0	79²	67	9	36	26	11.9	3.50	112	.233	.322	7	.304	1	4	4	0	0.3
1952	Bro-N	0	0	—	3	0	0	0	0	2	4	1	3	1	31.5	18.00	20	.444	.583	0	—	-0	-3	-3	-0	0.0
	Cin-N	4	5	.444	24	7	4	1	1	86²	78	8	26	22	10.9	2.80	135	.245	.304	4	.160	0	9	9	-1	0.9
	Yr	4	5	.444	27	7	4	1	1	88²	82	9	29	23	11.4	3.15	120	.251	.314	4	.160	0	6	6	-1	0.9
1953	Cin-N	6	16	.273	36	24	8	1	1	186¹	214	21	67	74	14.0	4.73	92	.290	.356	7	.125	-3	-9	-8	-0	-1.1
1954	Cin-N	7	10	.412	27	24	4	0	0	131	157	20	58	42	14.9	5.36	78	.300	.372	6	.143	-1	-19	-17	-2	-2.1
1955	Cin-N	1	2	.333	17	2	0	0	0	42	36	4	11	26	10.3	3.21	132	.234	.289	2	.400	1	4	5	0	0.4
1957	Cin-N	0	1	.000	5	3	1	0	0	16	18	4	4	13	12.4	6.19	66	.290	.333	0	.000	-1	-4	-4	-1	-0.3
1959	Cle-A	0	1	.000	6	0	0	0	0	12¹	17	1	2	5	13.9	5.84	63	.354	.380	0	.000	-0	-3	-3	0	-0.2
Total 9		25	42	.373	172	76	20	2	3	641	693	79	245	242	13.4	4.49	92	.279	.348	29	.154	-4	-30	-26	-2	-3.1

● JOHNNY PODGAJNY Podgajny, John Sigmund "Specs" b: 6/10/20, Chester, Pa. d: 3/2/71, Chester, Pa. BR/TR, 6'2", 173 lbs. Deb: 9/15/40

YEAR	TM/L	W	L	PCT	G	GS	CG	SH	SV	IP	H	HR	BB	SO	RAT	ERA	ERA+	OAV	OOB	BH	AVG	PB	PR	/A	PD	TPI
1940	Phi-N	1	3	.250	4	4	3	0	0	35	33	0	1	12	9.0	2.83	138	.250	.261	2	.167	-0	4	4	0	0.5
1941	Phi-N	9	12	.429	34	24	8	0	0	181¹	191	8	70	53	13.2	4.62	80	.270	.339	8	.129	-3	-20	-18	1	-2.1
1942	Phi-N	6	14	.300	43	23	6	0	0	186²	191	9	63	40	12.8	3.91	85	.268	.337	11	.183	-0	-12	-12	-1	-1.4
1943	Phi-N	4	4	.500	13	5	3	0	0	64	77	4	16	13	13.1	4.22	80	.310	.352	5	.250	1	-6	-6	1	-0.5
	Pit-N	0	4	.000	15	5	0	0	0	34¹	37	1	13	7	13.1	4.72	74	.266	.329	1	.143	-0	-5	-5	2	-0.4
	Yr	4	8	.333	28	10	3	0	0	98¹	114	5	29	20	13.1	4.39	78	.295	.344	6	.222	0	-11	-11	3	-0.9
1946	Cle-A	0	0	—	6	0	0	0	0	9	13	0	4	4	15.0	5.00	66	.302	.333	0	—	-0	-1	-2	0	0.0
Total 5		20	37	.351	115	61	20	0	0	510¹	542	22	165	129	12.8	4.20	82	.273	.334	27	.168	-3	-41	-39	3	-3.9

● JOHNNY PODRES Podres, John Joseph b: 9/30/32, Witherbee, N.Y. BL/TL, 5'11", 192 lbs. Deb: 4/17/53 C

YEAR	TM/L	W	L	PCT	G	GS	CG	SH	SV	IP	H	HR	BB	SO	RAT	ERA	ERA+	OAV	OOB	BH	AVG	PB	PR	/A	PD	TPI
1953	*Bro-N	9	4	.692	33	18	3	1	0	115	126	12	64	82	14.9	4.23	101	.282	.373	11	.306	2	1	0	-0	0.2
1954	Bro-N	11	7	.611	29	21	6	2	0	151²	147	13	53	79	11.9	4.27	96	.255	.319	17	.283	5	-3	-3	-2	0.0
1955	*Bro-N	9	10	.474	27	24	5	2	0	159¹	160	15	57	114	12.5	3.95	103	.259	.326	11	.183	-0	1	2	-1	0.0
1957	Bro-N	12	9	.571	31	27	10	**6**	3	196	168	15	44	109	**9.8**	**2.66**	**156**	.230	**.274**	15	.208	1	26	33	-0	3.5
1958	LA-N☆	13	15	.464	39	31	10	2	1	210¹	208	27	78	143	12.3	3.72	110	.261	.328	9	.127	-3	5	9	-2	0.6
1959	*LA-N	14	9	.609	34	29	6	2	0	195	192	23	74	145	12.4	4.11	103	.261	.331	16	.246	3	-3	3	1	0.7
1960	LA-N★	14	12	.538	34	33	8	1	0	227²	217	25	71	159	11.4	3.08	129	.250	.308	9	.136	-1	17	22	-2	2.1
1961	LA-N	18	5	**.783**	32	29	6	1	0	182²	192	27	51	124	12.2	3.74	116	.271	.324	16	.232	1	6	12	-2	1.3
1962	LA-N★	15	13	.536	40	40	8	0	1	255	270	20	71	178	12.1	3.81	95	.272	.323	14	.159	1	4	-5	-4	-0.8
1963	*LA-N	14	12	.538	37	34	10	5	1	198¹	196	16	64	134	11.9	3.54	85	.257	.316	9	.141	1	-6	-11	-1	-1.4
1964	LA-N	0	2	.000	2	2	0	0	0	2²	5	1	3	0	27.0	16.88	19	.417	.533	0	—	-0	-4	-4	-0	-1.7
1965	LA-N	7	6	.538	27	22	2	1	1	134	126	17	39	63	11.2	3.43	95	.247	.303	8	.178	1	2	-2	-3	-0.4
1966	LA-N	0	0	—	1	0	0	0	0	1²	2	0	1	1	16.2	0.00	—	.400	.500	0	—	0	1	1	0	0.0
	Det-A	4	5	.444	36	13	2	1	4	107²	106	12	34	53	11.8	3.43	102	.259	.317	7	.233	2	0	1	-1	0.2
1967	Det-A	3	1	.750	21	8	0	1	0	63¹	58	12	11	34	9.9	3.84	85	.244	.280	2	.100	-1	-4	-4	-0	-0.4
1969	SD-N	5	6	.455	17	9	1	0	0	64²	66	7	28	17	13.2	4.31	82	.264	.341	1	.063	-1	-5	-6	-1	-1.1
Total 15		148	116	.561	440	340	77	24	11	2265	2239	242	743	1435	12.0	3.68	105	.259	.319	145	.190	12	37	45	-17	2.8

● JOE POETZ Poetz, Joseph Frank "Bull Montana" b: 6/22/1900, St.Louis, Mo. d: 2/7/42, St.Louis, Mo. BR/TR, 5'10.5", 175 lbs. Deb: 9/14/26

YEAR	TM/L	W	L	PCT	G	GS	CG	SH	SV	IP	H	HR	BB	SO	RAT	ERA	ERA+	OAV	OOB	BH	AVG	PB	PR	/A	PD	TPI
1926	NY-N	0	1	.000	2	1	0	0	0	8	9	2	8	0	15.8	3.38	111	.192	.400	0	0	0	0	0	0	0.1

● BOOTS POFFENBERGER Poffenberger, Cletus Elwood b: 7/1/15, Williamsport, Md. BR/TR, 5'10", 178 lbs. Deb: 6/11/37

YEAR	TM/L	W	L	PCT	G	GS	CG	SH	SV	IP	H	HR	BB	SO	RAT	ERA	ERA+	OAV	OOB	BH	AVG	PB	PR	/A	PD	TPI
1937	Det-A	10	5	.667	29	16	5	0	3	137¹	135	8	79	35	15.1	4.65	100	.277	.377	11	.216	-0	-1	0	1	0.1
1938	Det-A	6	7	.462	25	15	8	1	1	125	147	8	66	28	15.5	4.82	104	.297	.382	8	.182	-1	2	-2	-0	0.0
1939	Bro-N	0	0	—	3	1	0	0	0	5	19	1	4	2	19.8	5.40	75	.318	.423	0	.000	-0	-1	-1	0	0.0
Total 3		16	12	.571	57	32	13	1	4	267¹	301	17	149	65	15.4	4.75	101	.287	.379	19	.198	-2	2	0	-0	0.1

● TOM POHOLSKY Poholsky, Thomas George b: 8/26/29, Detroit, Mich. BR/TR, 6'3", 205 lbs. Deb: 4/20/50

YEAR	TM/L	W	L	PCT	G	GS	CG	SH	SV	IP	H	HR	BB	SO	RAT	ERA	ERA+	OAV	OOB	BH	AVG	PB	PR	/A	PD	TPI
1950	StL-N	0	0	—	5	1	0	0	0	14²	16	2	3	11	11.7	3.68	117	.281	.317	0	.000	-0	1	1	-0	-0.1
1951	StL-N	7	13	.350	38	26	10	1	1	195	204	15	68	70	12.6	4.43	89	.271	.331	14	.209	0	-10	-10	1	-0.8
1954	StL-N	5	7	.417	25	13	4	0	0	106	101	11	20	55	10.6	3.06	135	.254	.296	4	.148	-1	12	12	0	1.2
1955	StL-N	9	11	.450	30	24	8	2	0	151	143	26	35	66	10.7	3.81	106	.244	.289	8	.182	0	4	4	-1	0.4
1956	StL-N	9	14	.391	33	29	7	2	0	203	210	27	44	95	11.5	3.59	105	.268	.311	11	.159	-1	4	4	0	0.4
1957	Chi-N	1	7	.125	28	11	1	0	0	84	117	9	22	28	15.1	4.93	79	.330	.372	2	.105	-1	-10	-10	0	-0.9
Total 6		31	52	.373	159	104	30	5	1	753²	791	90	192	316	11.9	3.93	101	.270	.317	39	.171	-3	1	1	1	0.2

● JENNINGS POINDEXTER Poindexter, Chester Jennings "Jinx" b: 9/30/10, Pauls Valley, Okla. d: 3/3/83, Norman, Okla. BL/TL, 5'10", 165 lbs. Deb: 9/15/36

YEAR	TM/L	W	L	PCT	G	GS	CG	SH	SV	IP	H	HR	BB	SO	RAT	ERA	ERA+	OAV	OOB	BH	AVG	PB	PR	/A	PD	TPI
1936	Bos-A	0	2	.000	3	3	0	0	0	10²	13	0	16	2	24.5	6.75	79	.302	.492	0	.000	-0	-2	-2	-0	-0.3
1939	Phi-N	0	0	—	11	1	0	0	0	30¹	29	0	15	12	13.1	4.15	96	.250	.336	2	.200	-0	-1	-0	0	0.0
Total 2		0	2	.000	14	4	0	0	0	41	42	0	31	14	16.0	4.83	90	.264	.384	2	.143	-1	-3	-2	-0	-0.3

● LOU POLCHOW Polchow, Louis William b: 3/14/1881, Mankato, Minn. d: 8/15/12, Good Thunder, Minn 5'9" Deb: 9/14/02

YEAR	TM/L	W	L	PCT	G	GS	CG	SH	SV	IP	H	HR	BB	SO	RAT	ERA	ERA+	OAV	OOB	BH	AVG	PB	PR	/A	PD	TPI
1902	Cle-A	0	1	.000	1	1	1	0	0	8	9	0	4	2	14.6	5.63	61	.281	.361	0	.000	-1	-2	-2	-0	-0.2

● DICK POLE Pole, Richard Henry b: 10/13/50, Trout Creek, Mich. BR/TR, 6'3", 210 lbs. Deb: 8/3/73 C

YEAR	TM/L	W	L	PCT	G	GS	CG	SH	SV	IP	H	HR	BB	SO	RAT	ERA	ERA+	OAV	OOB	BH	AVG	PB	PR	/A	PD	TPI
1973	Bos-A	3	2	.600	12	7	0	0	0	54²	70	4	18	24	14.5	5.60	72	.318	.370	0	—	0	-11	-10	-0	-1.1
1974	Bos-A	1	1	.500	15	2	0	0	0	45	55	6	13	32	13.8	4.20	91	.304	.354	0	—	0	-3	-3	1	-0.1
1975	*Bos-A	4	6	.400	18	11	2	1	0	89²	102	11	32	42	13.7	4.42	92	.290	.352	0	—	0	-6	-3	0	-0.4
1976	Bos-A	6	5	.545	31	15	1	0	0	120²	131	8	48	49	13.5	4.33	90	.279	.348	0	—	0	-11	-6	-1	-0.6
1977	Sea-A	7	12	.368	25	24	3	0	0	122¹	127	16	57	51	14.0	5.15	80	.270	.356	0	—	0	-15	-14	-2	-2.1
1978	Sea-A	4	11	.267	21	18	2	0	0	98²	122	16	41	41	15.1	6.48	59	.306	.375	0	—	0	-30	-29	-1	-3.8
Total 6		25	37	.403	122	77	8	1	0	531	607	61	209	239	14.1	5.05	79	.290	.359	0	.000	-0	-76	-63	-5	-8.1

● KEN POLIVKA Polivka, Kenneth Lyle "Soup" b: 1/21/21, Chicago, Ill. d: 7/23/88, Aurora, Ill. BL/TL, 5'10.5", 175 lbs. Deb: 4/18/47

YEAR	TM/L	W	L	PCT	G	GS	CG	SH	SV	IP	H	HR	BB	SO	RAT	ERA	ERA+	OAV	OOB	BH	AVG	PB	PR	/A	PD	TPI
1947	Cin-N	0	0	—	2	0	0	0	0	3	3	0	3	1	18.0	3.00	137	.250	.400	0	0	0	0	0	0	0.0

● HOWIE POLLET Pollet, Howard Joseph b: 6/26/21, New Orleans, La. d: 8/8/74, Houston, Tex. BL/TL, 6'1.5", 175 lbs. Deb: 8/20/41 C

YEAR	TM/L	W	L	PCT	G	GS	CG	SH	SV	IP	H	HR	BB	SO	RAT	ERA	ERA+	OAV	OOB	BH	AVG	PB	PR	/A	PD	TPI
1941	StL-N	5	2	.714	9	8	6	2	0	70	55	1	27	37	10.7	1.93	195	.212	.289	5	.179	-0	13	14	1	1.5
1942	*StL-N	7	5	.583	27	13	5	2	0	109¹	102	7	39	42	11.8	2.88	119	.242	.309	7	.226	3	5	7	-2	0.8
1943	StL-N†	8	4	.667	16	14	12	5	0	118¹	83	3	32	41	8.9	**1.75**	192	.200	.261	7	.163	-1	21	21	-2	1.9
1946	*StL-N☆	**21**	10	.677	40	32	22	4	5	266	228	12	86	107	10.8	**2.10**	**165**	.234	.300	14	.161	-0	**39**	**40**	1	5.1
1947	StL-N	9	11	.450	37	24	9	0	2	176¹	195	11	87	73	14.5	4.34	95	.286	.369	15	.231	2	-5	-4	-0	-0.2
1948	StL-N	13	8	.619	36	26	11	0	0	186¹	216	10	67	80	13.8	4.54	90	.289	.349	8	.118	-3	-12	-9	-2	-1.1
1949	StL-N★	20	9	.690	39	28	17	5	1	230²	228	9	59	108	11.3	2.77	150	.256	.304	16	.195	1	33	**36**	-2	**4.2**
1950	StL-N	14	13	.519	37	30	14	2	2	232¹	228	19	68	117	11.5	3.29	130	.256	.310	12	.143	-2	22	26	0	2.6
1951	StL-N	0	3	.000	9	2	0	0	0	12¹	10	1	9	8	13.1	4.38	94	.208	.321	0	.000	-1	-1	-1	0	0.0
	Pit-N	6	10	.375	21	21	4	1	0	128²	149	24	51	49	14.1	5.04	84	.294	.360	5	.139	-0	-15	-12	-1	-1.3
	Yr	6	13	.316	27	23	4	1	0	141	159	25	60	57	14.0	4.98	84	.287	.357	5	.135	0	-16	-12	-1	-1.3
1952	Pit-N	7	16	.304	31	30	9	1	0	214	217	22	71	90	12.2	4.12	97	.266	.327	13	.191	2	-9	-3	1	0.0
1953	Pit-N	1	1	.500	5	2	0	0	0	12²	27	2	6	8	23.4	10.66	42	.482	.532	1	.333	0	-9	-9	-0	-1.1

YEAR TM/L	W	L	PCT	G	GS	CG	SH	SV	IP	H	HR	BB	SO	RAT	ERA	ERA+	OAV	OOB	BH	AVG	PB	PR	/A	PD	TPI
Chi-N	5	6	.455	25	17	2	0	1	111¹	120	6	44	45	13.3	4.12	108	.271	.338	4	.129	-1	2	4	-1	0.2
Yr	6	7	.462	30	19	2	0	1	124	147	8	50	53	14.4	4.79	93	.295	.360	5	.147	-1	-4	-5	-1	-0.9
1954 Chi-N	8	10	.444	20	20	4	2	0	128¹	131	4	54	58	13.0	3.58	117	.263	.335	13	.277	2	7	9	-0	1.4
1955 Chi-N	4	3	.571	24	7	1	1	5	61	62	11	27	27	13.1	5.61	73	.265	.341	6	.400	3	-11	-10	1	-0.8
1956 Chi-A	3	1	.750	11	4	0	0	0	26¹	27	2	11	14	13.0	4.10	100	.252	.322	3	.375	1	0	-0	0	0.1
Pit-N	0	4	.000	19	0	0	0	0	23¹	18	3	8	10	10.0	3.09	122	.212	.280	0	.000	0	2	2	0	0.4
Total 14	131	116	.530	403	278	116	25	20	2107¹	2096	146	745	934	12.2	3.51	113	.260	.324	129	.185	7	82	111	0	13.7

● **DALE POLLEY**   Polley, Ezra Dale   b: 8/9/65, Georgetown, Ky.   BR/TL, 6', 165 lbs.   Deb: 6/23/96

YEAR TM/L	W	L	PCT	G	GS	CG	SH	SV	IP	H	HR	BB	SO	RAT	ERA	ERA+	OAV	OOB	BH	AVG	PB	PR	/A	PD	TPI
1996 NY-A	1	3	.250	32	0	0	0	0	21²	23	5	11	14	15.4	7.89	64	.264	.366	0	—	0	-7	-7	0	-1.1

● **LOU POLLI**   Polli, Louis Americo "Crip"   b: 7/9/01, Barre, Vt.   BR/TR, 5'10.5", 165 lbs.   Deb: 4/18/32

YEAR TM/L	W	L	PCT	G	GS	CG	SH	SV	IP	H	HR	BB	SO	RAT	ERA	ERA+	OAV	OOB	BH	AVG	PB	PR	/A	PD	TPI
1932 StL-A	0	0	—	5	0	0	0	0	6²	13	0	3	5	21.6	5.40	90	.406	.457	1	.500	—	-1	-0	-0	0.0
1944 NY-N	0	2	.000	19	0	0	0	3	35²	42	3	20	6	15.6	4.54	81	.294	.380	0	.000	-1	-4	-3	-0	-0.4
Total 2	0	2	.000	24	0	0	0	3	42¹	55	3	23	11	16.6	4.68	82	.314	.394	1	.125	-1	-4	-4	-0	-0.4

● **JOHN POLONI**   Poloni, John Paul   b: 2/28/54, Dearborn, Mich.   BL/TL, 6'5", 210 lbs.   Deb: 9/16/77

YEAR TM/L	W	L	PCT	G	GS	CG	SH	SV	IP	H	HR	BB	SO	RAT	ERA	ERA+	OAV	OOB	BH	AVG	PB	PR	/A	PD	TPI
1977 Tex-A	1	0	1.000	2	1	0	0	0	7	8	1	1	5	11.6	6.43	63	.286	.310	0	—	0	-2	-2	-0	-0.3

● **JOHN POMORSKI**   Pomorski, John Leon   b: 12/30/05, Brooklyn, N.Y.   d: 12/6/77, Brampton, Ont., Can.   BR/TR, 6', 178 lbs.   Deb: 4/17/34

YEAR TM/L	W	L	PCT	G	GS	CG	SH	SV	IP	H	HR	BB	SO	RAT	ERA	ERA+	OAV	OOB	BH	AVG	PB	PR	/A	PD	TPI
1934 Chi-A	0	0	—	3	0	0	0	0	1²	1	0	2	0	16.2	5.40	88	.143	.333	0	—	0	-0	0	0	0.0

● **ARLIE POND**   Pond, Erasmus Arlington   b: 1/19/1872, Rutland, Vt.   d: 9/19/30, Cebu, Philippines   BR/TR, 5'10", 160 lbs.   Deb: 7/4/1895

YEAR TM/L	W	L	PCT	G	GS	CG	SH	SV	IP	H	HR	BB	SO	RAT	ERA	ERA+	OAV	OOB	BH	AVG	PB	PR	/A	PD	TPI
1895 Bal-N	0	1	.000	6	1	1	0	2	13²	10	0	12	13	15.1	5.93	80	.200	.365	2	.333	1	-2	-1	-0	-0.1
1896 Bal-N	16	8	.667	28	26	21	2	0	214¹	232	4	57	80	12.4	3.49	123	.274	.324	19	.235	3	21	19	-2	1.5
1897 Bal-N	18	9	.667	32	28	23	0	0	248	267	4	72	59	12.8	3.52	119	.273	.332	22	.244	2	22	18	-1	1.6
1898 Bal-N	1	1	.500	3	2	1	1	0	20	8	0	9	4	8.5	0.45	796	.123	.250	2	.286	1	7	7	-1	0.7
Total 4	35	19	.648	69	57	46	3	2	496	517	8	150	156	12.1	3.45	122	.266	.327	45	.245	7	48	42	-3	3.7

● **ELMER PONDER**   Ponder, Charles Elmer   b: 6/26/1893, Reed, Okla.   d: 4/20/74, Albuquerque, N.Mex   BR/TR, 6', 178 lbs.   Deb: 9/18/17

YEAR TM/L	W	L	PCT	G	GS	CG	SH	SV	IP	H	HR	BB	SO	RAT	ERA	ERA+	OAV	OOB	BH	AVG	PB	PR	/A	PD	TPI
1917 Pit-N	1	1	.500	3	2	1	1	0	21¹	12	0	6	11	8.0	1.69	168	.167	.241	0	.000	-1	2	3	0	0.0
1919 Pit-N	5	0	.000	9	5	0	0	0	47¹	55	0	6	12	12.2	3.99	76	.297	.330	2	.133	-1	-6	-5	-1	-0.7
1920 Pit-N	11	15	.423	33	23	13	2	0	196	182	3	40	62	10.3	2.62	123	.246	.286	7	.119	-4	11	13	1	1.3
1921 Pit-N	2	0	1.000	8	1	1	0	0	24²	29	1	3	3	11.7	2.19	175	.305	.327	0	.000	-0	4	5	0	0.2
Chi-N	3	6	.333	16	11	5	0	0	89¹	117	7	17	31	13.8	4.74	81	.321	.356	4	.121	-2	-9	-9	2	-0.9
Yr	5	6	.455	24	12	6	0	0	114	146	8	20	34	13.3	4.18	91	.317	.350	4	.093	-4	-5	-5	2	-0.7
Total 4	17	27	.386	69	42	20	3	0	378²	395	11	72	113	11.3	3.21	105	.271	.309	13	.105	-10	3	6	0	-0.1

● **ED POOLE**   Poole, Edward I.   b: 9/7/1874, Canton, Ohio   d: 3/11/19, Malvern, Ohio   BR/TR, 5'10", 175 lbs.   Deb: 10/6/00 ◆

YEAR TM/L	W	L	PCT	G	GS	CG	SH	SV	IP	H	HR	BB	SO	RAT	ERA	ERA+	OAV	OOB	BH	AVG	PB	PR	/A	PD	TPI
1900 Pit-N	1	0	1.000	1	0	0	0	0	7	4	0	0	3	5.1	1.29	283	.167	.167	2	.500	1	2	2	0	0.4
1901 Pit-N	5	4	.556	12	10	8	1	0	80	78	3	30	26	12.8	3.60	91	.254	.332	16	.205	1	-2	-3	-0	-0.2
1902 Pit-N	0	0	—	1	0	0	0	0	8	7	0	3	2	11.3	1.13	243	.233	.303	1	.250	1	1	1	0	0.1
Cin-N	12	4	.750	16	16	16	0	0	138	129	2	54	55	12.5	2.15	139	.248	.328	7	.115	-4	10	13	-0	1.0
Yr	12	4	.750	17	16	16	2	0	146	136	2	57	57	12.4	2.10	142	.247	.326	8	.123	-4	11	14	-0	1.0
1903 Cin-N	7	13	.350	25	21	18	1	0	184	188	4	77	73	13.5	3.28	109	.270	.352	17	.243	-0	0	6	2	0.7
1904 Bro-N	8	14	.364	25	23	19	1	1	178	178	6	74	67	13.1	3.39	81	.268	.349	8	.129	-3	-13	-13	3	-1.5
Total 5	33	35	.485	80	70	61	5	1	595	584	13	238	226	12.9	3.04	103	.260	.340	51	.183	-6	-2	6	6	0.4

● **JIM POOLE**   Poole, James Richard   b: 4/28/66, Rochester, N.Y.   BL/TL, 6'2", 190 lbs.   Deb: 6/15/90

YEAR TM/L	W	L	PCT	G	GS	CG	SH	SV	IP	H	HR	BB	SO	RAT	ERA	ERA+	OAV	OOB	BH	AVG	PB	PR	/A	PD	TPI
1990 LA-N	0	0	—	16	0	0	0	0	10²	7	1	3	6	12.7	4.22	87	.184	.326	0	—	0	-1	-1	-0	0.0
1991 Tex-A	0	0	—	5	0	0	0	0	6	10	3	4	4	19.5	4.50	90	.370	.433	0	—	0	-0	-0	-0	0.1
Bal-A	3	2	.600	24	0	0	0	0	36	19	3	9	34	7.0	2.00	198	.157	.215	0	—	0	8	8	0	1.4
Yr	3	2	.600	29	0	0	0	0	42	29	3	12	38	8.8	2.36	168	.195	.255	0	—	0	8	7	0	1.5
1992 Bal-A	0	0	—	6	0	0	0	0	3¹	3	0	1	3	10.8	0.00	—	.231	.286	0	—	0	1	1	-0	-0.1
1993 Bal-A	2	1	.667	55	0	0	0	2	50¹	30	2	21	29	9.1	2.15	208	.175	.266	0	—	0	12	13	0	0.5
1994 Bal-A	1	1	1.000	38	0	0	0	0	20¹	32	4	11	18	19.0	6.64	75	.372	.443	0	—	0	-4	-4	1	-0.3
1995 *Cle-A	3	3	.500	42	0	0	0	0	50¹	40	7	17	41	10.5	3.75	125	.217	.291	0	—	0	5	5	0	0.5
1996 Cle-A	4	0	1.000	32	0	0	0	0	26²	29	3	14	19	14.5	3.04	161	.274	.358	0	—	0	6	5	1	0.7
SF-N	2	1	.667	35	0	0	0	0	23²	15	2	13	19	11.0	2.66	154	.188	.309	0	.000	0	4	5	1	0.5
Total 7	15	7	.682	253	0	0	0	3	227¹	185	22	97	173	11.3	3.17	140	.224	.308	0	—	-0	32	32	2	3.3

● **TOM POORMAN**   Poorman, Thomas Iverson   b: 10/14/1857, Lock Haven, Pa.   d: 2/18/05, Lock Haven, Pa.   BL/TR, 5'7", 135 lbs.   Deb: 5/5/1880 ◆

YEAR TM/L	W	L	PCT	G	GS	CG	SH	SV	IP	H	HR	BB	SO	RAT	ERA	ERA+	OAV	OOB	BH	AVG	PB	PR	/A	PD	TPI
1880 Buf-N	1	8	.111	11	9	9	0	1	85	117	3	19	13	14.4	4.13	59	.307	.340	11	.157	-3	-17	-16	1	-1.6
Chi-N	2	0	1.000	2	1	0	0	0	15	12	0	8	0	12.0	2.40	101	.203	.299	5	.200	-0	-0	-1		-0.1
Yr	3	8	.273	13	10	9	0	1	100	129	3	27	13	14.0	3.87	63	.293	.334	16	.168	-3	-17	-16		-1.7
1884 Tol-a	0	1	.000	1	1	1	0	0	9	13	1	2	0	15.0	3.00	114	.310	.341	89	.233	0	0	0		0.0
1887 Phi-a			—	1	0	0	0	0	0²	5	1	1	2	81.0	40.50	11	.714	.750	155	.265	0	-3	-3	0	0.0
Total 3	3	9	.250	15	11	10	0	1	109²	147	5	30	14	14.5	4.02	63	.301	.341	498	.244	-2	-19	-19	1	-1.7

● **BILL POPP**   Popp, William Peter   b: 6/7/1877, St.Louis, Mo.   d: 9/5/09, St.Louis, Mo.   TR, 5'10.5", 170 lbs.   Deb: 4/19/02

YEAR TM/L	W	L	PCT	G	GS	CG	SH	SV	IP	H	HR	BB	SO	RAT	ERA	ERA+	OAV	OOB	BH	AVG	PB	PR	/A	PD	TPI
1902 StL-N	2	6	.250	9	7	5	0	0	60¹	87	2	26	20	17.6	4.92	56	.336	.407	1	.048	-3	-14	-15	1	-1.8

● **ED PORRAY**   Porray, Edmund Joseph   b: 12/5/1888, At Sea On Atlantic Ocean   d: 7/13/54, Lackawaxen, Pa.   BR/TR, 5'11", 170 lbs.   Deb: 4/17/14

YEAR TM/L	W	L	PCT	G	GS	CG	SH	SV	IP	H	HR	BB	SO	RAT	ERA	ERA+	OAV	OOB	BH	AVG	PB	PR	/A	PD	TPI
1914 Buf-F	0	1	.000	3	3	0	0	0	10¹	18	2	7	0	21.8	4.35	68	.391	.472	0	.000	-1	-2	-2	1	-0.2

● **CHUCK PORTER**   Porter, Charles William   b: 1/12/56, Baltimore, Md.   BR/TR, 6'3", 188 lbs.   Deb: 9/14/81

YEAR TM/L	W	L	PCT	G	GS	CG	SH	SV	IP	H	HR	BB	SO	RAT	ERA	ERA+	OAV	OOB	BH	AVG	PB	PR	/A	PD	TPI
1981 Mil-A	0	0	—	3	0	0	0	0	4¹	6	0	1	4	14.5	4.15	82	.316	.350	0			-0	-0	-0	0.0
1982 Mil-A	0	0	—	3	0	0	0	0	3²	3	0	1	3	9.8	4.91	77	.250	.308	0			-0	-0	-0	0.0
1983 Mil-A	7	9	.438	25	21	6	1	0	134	162	9	38	76	13.6	4.50	83	.298	.346	0			-7	-11	-0	-1.0
1984 Mil-A	6	4	.600	17	12	1	0	0	81¹	92	8	12	48	11.5	3.87	99	.284	.310	0			3	1	-0	0.0
1985 Mil-A	0	0	—	6	1	0	0	0	13²	15	1	2	8	11.2	1.98	211	.273	.298	0			3	3	-0	0.0
Total 5	13	13	.500	54	34	7	1	0	237	278	18	54	136	12.7	4.14	92	.291	.331	0			-3	-9	-0	-1.0

● **HENRY PORTER**   Porter, Henry   b: 6/1858, Vergennes, Vt.   d: 12/30/06, Brockton, Mass.   BR/TR,   Deb: 9/27/1884

YEAR TM/L	W	L	PCT	G	GS	CG	SH	SV	IP	H	HR	BB	SO	RAT	ERA	ERA+	OAV	OOB	BH	AVG	PB	PR	/A	PD	TPI
1884 Mil-U	3	3	.500	6	6	6	0	0	51	32	1	9	71	7.2	3.00	44	.168	.205	11	.275	1	-3	-9	1	-0.7
1885 Bro-a	33	21	.611	54	54	53	2	0	481²	427	11	107	197	10.3	2.78	118	.223	.270	40	.205	-2	25	27	3	2.6
1886 Bro-a	27	19	.587	48	48	48	1	0	424	439	8	120	163	12.0	3.42	102	.252	.303	33	.179	-9	2	3	-2	-0.7
1887 Bro-a	15	24	.385	40	40	38	1	0	339²	416	7	96	74	13.8	4.21	102	.297	.345	29	.199	-3	3	3	-2	-0.1
1888 KC-a	18	37	.327	55	54	53	4	0	474	507	16	120	145	12.7	4.16	83	.272	.321	28	.144	-13	-58	-38	4	-4.3
1889 KC-a	0	3	.000	4	4	3	0	0	23	52	1	14	9	26.2	12.52	33	.433	.496	1	.100	-1	-22	-21	0	-1.8
Total 6	96	107	.473	207	206	201	9	0	1793¹	1893	43	466	659	12.1	3.70	95	.259	.308	142	.184	-27	-53	-35	3	-5.0

● **NED PORTER**   Porter, Ned Swindell   b: 5/6/05, Apalachicola, Fla.   d: 6/30/68, Gainesville, Fla.   BR/TR, 6', 173 lbs.   Deb: 8/7/26

YEAR TM/L	W	L	PCT	G	GS	CG	SH	SV	IP	H	HR	BB	SO	RAT	ERA	ERA+	OAV	OOB	BH	AVG	PB	PR	/A	PD	TPI
1926 NY-N	0	0	—	2	0	0	0	0	2	2	1	0	1	9.0	4.50	83	.250	.250	0		0	-0	-0	-0	0.0
1927 NY-N	0	0	—	1	0	0	0	0	2	3	0	1	0	18.0	0.00	—	.333	.400	0		0	1	1	-0	0.0
Total 2	0	0	—	3	0	0	0	0	4	5	1	1	1	13.5	2.25	169	.294	.333	0		0	1	1	-0	0.0

● **ODIE PORTER**   Porter, Odie Oscar   b: 5/24/1877, Borden, Ind.   d: 5/2/03, Borden, Ind.   TL,   Deb: 6/16/02

YEAR TM/L	W	L	PCT	G	GS	CG	SH	SV	IP	H	HR	BB	SO	RAT	ERA	ERA+	OAV	OOB	BH	AVG	PB	PR	/A	PD	TPI
1902 Phi-A	0	1	.000	1	1	1	0	0	8	12	0	5	2	19.1	3.38	109	.343	.425	0	.000	-0	0	0	0	0.0

● **BOB PORTERFIELD**   Porterfield, Erwin Coolidge   b: 8/10/23, Newport, Va.   d: 4/28/80, Sealy, Tex.   BR/TR, 6', 190 lbs.   Deb: 8/8/48

YEAR TM/L	W	L	PCT	G	GS	CG	SH	SV	IP	H	HR	BB	SO	RAT	ERA	ERA+	OAV	OOB	BH	AVG	PB	PR	/A	PD	TPI
1948 NY-A	5	3	.625	16	12	2	1	0	78	85	5	34	30	13.7	4.50	91	.273	.345	6	.250	0	-2	-4	-1	-0.4
1949 NY-A	2	5	.286	12	8	3	0	0	57²	53	3	29	25	13.0	4.06	100	.251	.344	1	.053	-2	1	-0	-1	-0.2

YEAR	TM/L	W	L	PCT	G	GS	CG	SH	SV	IP	H	HR	BB	SO	RAT	ERA	ERA+	OAV	OOB	BH	AVG	PB	PR	/A	PD	TPI
1950	NY-A	1	1	.500	10	2	0	0	1	19²	28	2	8	9	16.5	8.69	49	.341	.400	1	.333	1	-9	-10	-0	-0.9
1951	NY-A	0	0	—	2	0	0	0	0	3	5	0	3	2	24.0	15.00	26	.385	.500	0	—	0	-4	-4	-0	0.0
	Was-A	9	8	.529	19	19	10	3	0	133¹	109	8	54	53	11.0	3.24	126	.224	.302	6	.130	-3	13	13	-0	1.1
	Yr	9	8	.529	21	19	10	3	0	136¹	114	8	57	55	11.3	3.50	117	.228	.308	6	.130	-3	9	9	-0	1.1
1952	Was-A	13	14	.481	31	29	15	3	0	231¹	222	7	85	80	12.1	2.72	131	.254	.323	15	.190	0	24	21	-3	2.2
1953	Was-A	22	10	.688	34	32	**24**	**9**	0	255	243	19	73	77	11.2	3.35	116	.257	.310	25	.255	8	18	15	2	2.9
1954	Was-A★	13	15	.464	32	31	**21**	2	0	244	249	14	77	82	12.1	3.32	107	.266	.324	9	.102	-3	11	6	3	0.7
1955	Was-A	10	17	.370	30	27	8	2	0	178	197	14	54	74	12.8	4.45	86	.282	.335	12	.190	1	-10	-12	-1	-1.6
1956	Bos-A	3	12	.200	25	18	4	1	0	126	127	21	64	53	13.7	5.14	90	.260	.347	14	.326	3	-14	-7	-2	-0.6
1957	Bos-A	4	4	.500	28	9	3	1	1	102¹	107	8	30	28	12.1	4.05	99	.272	.325	5	.172	-0	-3	-1	1	0.0
1958	Bos-A	0	0	—	2	0	0	0	0	4	3	1	4	1	6.8	4.50	89	.214	.214	0	—	-0	-0	-0	-0	0.0
	Pit-N	4	6	.400	37	6	2	1	5	87²	78	7	19	39	10.1	3.29	118	.241	.285	1	.050	-1	6	6	-0	0.6
1959	Pit-N	0	0	—	6	0	0	0	0	5¹	6	1	2	1	13.5	1.69	229	.286	.348	0	.000	-0	1	1	-0	0.0
	Chi-N	0	0	—	4	0	0	0	0	6¹	14	1	3	0	24.2	11.37	35	.424	.472	0	.000	-0	-5	-5	-0	0.0
	Pit-N	1	2	.333	30	0	0	0	1	36	45	2	17	18	15.5	4.75	81	.321	.395	0	.000	-0	-3	-4	1	-0.2
	Yr	1	2	.333	40	0	0	0	1	47²	65	4	22	19	16.4	5.29	73	.335	.403	0	.000	-0	-7	-7	1	-0.2
Total	12	87	97	.473	318	193	92	23	8	1567²	1571	113	552	572	12.3	3.79	102	.263	.327	95	.184	4	26	16	0	3.6

● **AL PORTO**   Porto, Alfred "Lefty"   b: 6/27/26, Heilwood, Pa.   BL/TL, 5'11", 176 lbs.   Deb: 4/22/48

YEAR	TM/L	W	L	PCT	G	GS	CG	SH	SV	IP	H	HR	BB	SO	RAT	ERA	ERA+	OAV	OOB	BH	AVG	PB	PR	/A	PD	TPI
1948	Phi-N	0	0	—	3	0	0	0	0	4	2	0	1	2	6.8	0.00	—	.143	.200	0	—	0	2	2	-0	0.0

● **ARNIE PORTOCARRERO**   Portocarrero, Arnold Mario   b: 7/5/31, New York, N.Y.   d: 6/21/86, Kansas City, Kan.   BR/TR, 6'3", 196 lbs.   Deb: 4/18/54

YEAR	TM/L	W	L	PCT	G	GS	CG	SH	SV	IP	H	HR	BB	SO	RAT	ERA	ERA+	OAV	OOB	BH	AVG	PB	PR	/A	PD	TPI
1954	Phi-A	9	18	.333	34	33	16	1	0	248	233	25	114	132	12.8	4.06	96	.249	.334	8	.107	-2	-9	-4	-1	-1.0
1955	KC-A	5	9	.357	24	20	4	1	0	111¹	109	12	67	34	14.6	4.77	88	.259	.366	4	.108	-1	-10	-7	-1	-1.0
1956	KC-A	0	1	.000	3	1	0	0	0	5¹	8	2	7	2	18.0	10.13	43	.300	.432	0	.000	-0	-5	-5	-0	-0.5
1957	KC-A	4	9	.308	33	17	1	0	0	114²	103	10	34	42	11.0	3.92	101	.240	.300	3	.107	-1	-0	-1	-0	-0.2
1958	Bal-A	15	11	.577	32	27	10	3	2	204²	173	17	57	90	10.2	3.25	110	.229	.286	11	.164	0	12	8	-3	0.7
1959	Bal-A	2	7	.222	27	14	1	0	0	90	107	10	32	23	14.1	6.80	56	.294	.354	0	.000	-3	-29	-30	-1	-2.8
1960	Bal-A	3	2	.600	13	5	1	0	0	40²	44	6	9	15	11.7	4.43	86	.275	.314	0	.000	-1	-2	-3	-1	-0.5
Total	7	38	57	.400	166	117	33	5	2	817¹	778	82	320	338	12.3	4.32	89	.252	.325	26	.108	-9	-47	-42	-9	-5.3

● **MARK PORTUGAL**   Portugal, Mark Steven   b: 10/30/62, Los Angeles, Cal.   BR/TR, 6', 190 lbs.   Deb: 8/14/85

YEAR	TM/L	W	L	PCT	G	GS	CG	SH	SV	IP	H	HR	BB	SO	RAT	ERA	ERA+	OAV	OOB	BH	AVG	PB	PR	/A	PD	TPI
1985	Min-A	1	3	.250	6	4	0	0	0	24¹	24	3	14	12	14.1	5.55	79	.270	.369	0	—	0	-4	-3	1	-0.4
1986	Min-A	6	10	.375	27	15	3	0	1	112²	112	10	50	67	13.0	4.31	100	.265	.345	0	—	0	-2	-0	-0	-0.1
1987	Min-A	1	3	.250	13	7	0	0	0	44	58	13	24	28	17.0	7.77	59	.326	.409	0	—	0	-16	-15	-0	-1.2
1988	Min-A	3	3	.500	26	0	0	0	3	57²	60	11	17	31	12.2	4.53	90	.274	.329	0	—	0	-4	-3	-2	-0.6
1989	Hou-N	7	1	.875	20	15	2	1	0	108	91	7	37	86	10.8	2.75	123	.232	.302	7	.206	3	9	8	0	0.9
1990	Hou-N	11	10	.524	32	32	1	0	0	196²	187	21	67	136	11.8	3.62	103	.250	.315	9	.136	-1	4	2	-0	0.1
1991	Hou-N	10	12	.455	32	27	1	0	1	168¹	163	19	59	120	12.0	4.49	78	.256	.321	9	.196	3	-15	-18	-1	-2.0
1992	Hou-N	6	3	.667	18	16	1	1	0	101¹	76	7	41	62	10.5	2.66	126	.213	.296	3	.107	-1	9	8	0	0.6
1993	Hou-N	18	4	**.818**	33	33	1	1	0	208	194	10	77	131	11.9	2.77	140	.248	.319	15	.231	4	29	25	1	3.0
1994	SF-N	10	8	.556	21	21	1	0	0	137¹	135	17	45	87	12.2	3.93	102	.260	.326	17	.354	4	4	1	-2	0.8
1995	SF-N	5	5	.500	17	17	1	0	0	104	106	10	34	63	12.3	4.15	98	.262	.323	3	.103	-0	0	-1	-1	-0.2
	*Cin-N	6	5	.545	14	14	0	0	0	77²	79	7	22	33	11.9	3.82	108	.262	.317	5	.172	1	3	3	-1	0.4
	Yr	11	10	.524	31	31	1	0	0	181²	185	17	56	96	12.0	4.01	102	.262	.318	8	.138	1	3	2	-2	0.1
1996	Cin-N	8	9	.471	27	26	1	1	0	156	146	20	42	93	11.0	3.98	104	.248	.300	8	.167	-0	4	3	-2	0.1
Total	12	92	76	.548	286	227	12	4	5	1496	1431	155	529	949	12.0	3.83	101	.254	.321	76	.193	16	23	8	-6	1.4

● **BILL POSEDEL**   Posedel, William John "Sailor Bill" or "Barnacle Bill"
b: 8/2/06, San Francisco, Cal.   d: 11/28/89, Livermore, Cal.   BR/TR, 5'11", 175 lbs.   Deb: 4/23/38   C

YEAR	TM/L	W	L	PCT	G	GS	CG	SH	SV	IP	H	HR	BB	SO	RAT	ERA	ERA+	OAV	OOB	BH	AVG	PB	PR	/A	PD	TPI
1938	Bro-N	8	9	.471	33	17	6	1	1	140	178	14	46	44	14.5	5.66	69	.311	.365	10	.227	1	-29	-27	-1	-2.9
1939	Bos-N	15	13	.536	33	29	18	5	0	220²	221	8	78	73	12.2	3.92	94	.268	.331	8	.110	-4	0	-5	-1	-1.1
1940	Bos-N	12	17	.414	35	32	18	0	1	233	263	16	81	86	13.3	4.13	90	.288	.346	14	.171	1	-7	-11	-0	-1.1
1941	Bos-N	4	4	.500	18	9	3	0	0	57¹	61	6	30	10	14.4	4.87	73	.279	.368	8	.320	2	-8	-8	-0	-0.8
1946	Bos-N	2	0	1.000	19	0	0	0	4	28¹	34	4	13	9	14.9	6.99	49	.304	.376	0	.000	-0	-11	-11	-0	-1.2
Total	5	41	43	.488	138	87	45	6	6	679¹	757	48	248	227	13.4	4.56	82	.286	.349	40	.176	0	-55	-63	-4	-7.1

● **BOB POSER**   Poser, John Falk   b: 3/16/10, Columbus, Wis.   BL/TR, 6', 173 lbs.   Deb: 4/17/32

YEAR	TM/L	W	L	PCT	G	GS	CG	SH	SV	IP	H	HR	BB	SO	RAT	ERA	ERA+	OAV	OOB	BH	AVG	PB	PR	/A	PD	TPI
1932	Chi-A	0	0	—	1	0	0	0	0	2	3	0	7	0	67.5	27.00	16	.600	.714	0	.000	-0	-2	-2	-0	0.0
1935	StL-A	1	1	.500	4	1	0	0	0	13²	26	0	4	1	19.8	9.22	52	.400	.435	1	.250	1	-7	-7	-1	-0.8
Total	2	1	1	.500	5	1	0	0	0	14¹	29	0	6	2	22.0	10.05	47	.414	.461	1	.143	1	-9	-8	-1	-0.8

● **LOU POSSEHL**   Possehl, Louis Thomas   b: 4/12/26, Chicago, Ill.   BR/TR, 6'2", 180 lbs.   Deb: 8/25/46   F

YEAR	TM/L	W	L	PCT	G	GS	CG	SH	SV	IP	H	HR	BB	SO	RAT	ERA	ERA+	OAV	OOB	BH	AVG	PB	PR	/A	PD	TPI
1946	Phi-N	1	2	.333	4	4	0	0	0	13²	19	0	10	4	19.8	5.93	58	.339	.448	0	.000	-0	-4	-4	0	-0.7
1947	Phi-N	0	0	—	2	0	0	0	0	4¹	5	0	1	2	12.5	4.15	96	.385	.429	0	—	0	-0	-0	-0	0.1
1948	Phi-N	1	1	.500	3	2	1	0	0	14²	17	3	4	7	12.9	4.91	80	.304	.350	1	.250	0	-2	-2	-0	-0.2
1951	Phi-N	0	1	.000	2	1	0	0	0	6	9	0	3	6	18.0	6.00	64	.333	.400	0	.000	-0	-1	-1	0	-0.2
1952	Phi-N	0	1	.000	4	2	0	0	0	12²	12	3	7	3	13.5	4.97	73	.235	.328	0	.000	-0	-2	-2	-0	-0.2
Total	5	2	5	.286	15	8	1	0	0	51¹	62	6	24	22	15.4	5.26	71	.305	.384	1	.100	-0	-9	-9	0	-1.2

● **NELLIE POTT**   Pott, Nelson Adolph "Lefty"   b: 7/16/1899, Cincinnati, Ohio   d: 12/3/63, Cincinnati, Ohio   BL/TL, 6', 185 lbs.   Deb: 4/19/22

YEAR	TM/L	W	L	PCT	G	GS	CG	SH	SV	IP	H	HR	BB	SO	RAT	ERA	ERA+	OAV	OOB	BH	AVG	PB	PR	/A	PD	TPI
1922	Cle-A	0	0	—	2	0	0	0	0	2	7	1	2	0	40.5	31.50	13	.583	.643	0	—	0	-6	-6	-0	0.0

● **DYKES POTTER**   Potter, Maryland Dykes   b: 9/7/10, Ashland, Ky.   BR/TR, 6', 185 lbs.   Deb: 4/26/38   F

YEAR	TM/L	W	L	PCT	G	GS	CG	SH	SV	IP	H	HR	BB	SO	RAT	ERA	ERA+	OAV	OOB	BH	AVG	PB	PR	/A	PD	TPI
1938	Bro-N	0	0	—	2	0	0	0	0	2	4	1	0	1	18.0	4.50	87	.400	.400	0	—	0	-0	-0	-0	0.0

● **NELS POTTER**   Potter, Nelson Thomas "Nellie"   b: 8/23/11, Mt. Morris, Ill.   d: 9/30/90, Mt. Morris, Ill.   BL/TR, 5'11", 180 lbs.   Deb: 4/25/36

YEAR	TM/L	W	L	PCT	G	GS	CG	SH	SV	IP	H	HR	BB	SO	RAT	ERA	ERA+	OAV	OOB	BH	AVG	PB	PR	/A	PD	TPI
1936	StL-N	0	0	—	1	0	0	0	0	1	0	0	0	0	0.0	0.00	—	.000	.000	0	—	-0	0	0	-0	0.0
1938	Phi-A	2	12	.143	35	9	4	0	5	111¹	139	15	49	43	15.4	6.47	75	.306	.376	10	.256	1	-21	-20	-1	-2.1
1939	Phi-A	8	12	.400	41	25	9	0	2	196¹	258	26	88	60	16.1	6.60	71	.321	.391	12	.179	-1	-43	-41	-1	-3.5
1940	Phi-A	9	14	.391	31	25	13	0	0	200²	213	18	71	73	12.8	4.44	100	.269	.330	18	.254	2	-1	-0	-0	0.2
1941	Phi-A	1	1	.500	10	3	1	0	2	23¹	21	3	16	7	19.7	9.26	45	.337	.425	1	.167	-0	-13	-13	-0	-1.1
	Bos-A	2	0	1.000	10	0	0	0	0	20	21	0	16	6	16.6	4.50	93	.284	.411	0	.000	-0	-1	-1	-0	-0.1
	Yr	3	1	.750	20	3	1	0	2	43¹	56	3	32	13	18.3	7.06	59	.315	.419	1	.111	-0	-14	-14	-0	-1.2
1943	StL-A	10	5	.667	33	13	8	0	1	168¹	146	11	54	80	10.9	2.78	120	.235	.299	8	.145	-1	10	10	1	0.9
1944	*StL-A	19	7	.731	32	29	16	3	0	232	211	6	70	91	10.9	2.83	127	.244	.301	13	.159	-2	15	20	2	2.1
1945	StL-A	15	11	.577	32	32	21	3	0	255¹	212	10	68	129	9.9	2.47	143	.226	.279	28	.304	4	25	30	-1	3.5
1946	StL-A	8	9	.471	23	19	10	0	0	145	152	9	47	50	12.3	3.72	100	.268	.340	12	.231	-2	-4	-0	-1	0.2
1947	StL-A	4	10	.286	32	10	3	0	2	122²	130	13	44	65	12.9	4.04	96	.277	.342	9	.257	3	-5	-2	-1	-0.2
1948	StL-A	1	1	.500	10	1	0	0	1	10¹	11	1	4	4	14.8	5.23	87	.262	.354	2	.500	1	-1	-1	1	0.0
	Phi-A	2	2	.500	10	1	0	0	0	18	17	1	5	13	11.0	4.00	107	.250	.301	1	.250	0	-0	-0	0	0.1
	Yr	3	3	.500	20	2	0	0	1	28¹	28	2	9	17	11.8	4.45	99	.255	.306	3	.375	1	-0	-0	1	0.1
	*Bos-N	5	2	.714	18	5	3	0	2	85	77	4	8	47	9.0	2.33	165	.245	.264	11	.379	3	15	14	1	1.6
1949	Bos-N	6	11	.353	41	5	0	0	9	96²	130	6	30	57	12.1	4.19	90	.265	.321	3	.130	-0	-23	-4	1	-0.7
Total	12	92	97	.487	349	177	89	6	22	1686	1721	123	582	747	12.4	3.99	99	.265	.328	128	.228	11	-23	-6	3	1.3

● **SQUIRE POTTER**   Potter, Robert   b: 3/18/02, Flatwoods, Ky.   d: 1/27/83, Ashland, Ky.   BR/TR, 6'1", 185 lbs.   Deb: 8/7/23   F

YEAR	TM/L	W	L	PCT	G	GS	CG	SH	SV	IP	H	HR	BB	SO	RAT	ERA	ERA+	OAV	OOB	BH	AVG	PB	PR	/A	PD	TPI
1923	Was-A	0	0	—	1	0	0	0	0	3	11	0	4	1	45.0	21.00	18	.688	.750	0	—	0	-6	-6	-0	0.0

● **MIKE POTTS**   Potts, Michael Larry   b: 9/5/70, Langdale, Ala.   BL/TL, 5'9", 179 lbs.   Deb: 4/6/96

YEAR	TM/L	W	L	PCT	G	GS	CG	SH	SV	IP	H	HR	BB	SO	RAT	ERA	ERA+	OAV	OOB	BH	AVG	PB	PR	/A	PD	TPI
1996	Mil-A	1	2	.333	24	0	0	0	1	45¹	58	7	30	21	17.5	7.15	74	.319	.415	0	—	0	-11	-9	-1	-0.6

YEAR	TM/L	W	L	PCT	G	GS	CG	SH	SV	IP	H	HR	BB	SO	RAT	ERA	ERA+	OAV	OOB	BH	AVG	PB	PR	/A	PD	TPI
● **BILL POUNDS**	Pounds, Jeared Wells b: 3/11/1878, Paterson, N.J. d: 7/7/36, Paterson, N.J. BR/TR, 5'10.5", 178 lbs. Deb: 5/2/03																								
1903	Cle-A	0	0	—	1	0	0	0	0	5	8	0	0	2	14.4	10.80	26	.364	.364	1	.500	1	-4	-4	-0	0.1
	Bro-N	0	0	—	1	0	0	0	0	6	8	1	2	2	15.0	6.00	53	.348	.400	2	.667	1	-2	-2	0	0.1
Total	1	0	0	—	2	0	0	0	0	11	16	1	2	4	14.7	8.18	37	.356	.383	3	.600	1	-6	-6	0	0.2
● **ABNER POWELL**	Powell, Charles Abner "Ab" b: 12/15/1860, Shenandoah, Pa. d: 8/7/53, New Orleans, La. BL/TR, 5'7", 160 lbs. Deb: 8/4/1884 ♦																								
1884	Was-U	6	12	.333	18	17	14	1	0	134	135	3	19	78	10.3	3.43	70	.245	.270	54	.283	0	-15	-15	2	-1.4
1886	Bal-a	2	5	.286	7	7	7	0	0	60	66	2	26	15	14.0	5.10	67	.264	.336	7	.179	-1	-11	-11	2	-0.9
	Cin-a	0	1	.000	4	1	1	0	0	15¹	16	0	9	4	14.7	4.70	75	.271	.368	17	.230	-0	-2	-2	-0	-0.1
	Yr	2	6	.250	11	8	8	0	0	75¹	82	2	35	19	14.0	5.02	69	.265	.339	24	.212	-1	-13	-13	1	-1.0
Total	2	8	18	.308	29	25	22	1	0	209¹	217	5	54	97	11.7	4.00	69	.252	.297	78	.257	-1	-28	-29	3	-2.4
● **DENNIS POWELL**	Powell, Dennis Clay b: 8/13/63, Moultrie, Ga. BR/TL, 6'3", 200 lbs. Deb: 7/7/85																								
1985	LA-N	1	1	.500	16	2	0	0	1	29¹	30	7	13	19	13.5	5.22	67	.263	.344	0	.000	-0	-5	-6	0	-0.4
1986	LA-N	2	7	.222	27	6	0	0	1	65¹	65	5	25	31	12.5	4.27	81	.272	.343	3	.214	1	-4	-6	-1	-0.7
1987	Sea-A	1	3	.250	16	3	0	0	0	34¹	32	3	15	17	12.3	3.15	150	.250	.329	0	—	0	5	6	0	0.5
1988	Sea-A	1	3	.250	12	2	0	0	0	18²	29	2	11	15	20.3	8.68	48	.363	.452	0	—	0	-10	-9	0	-1.8
1989	Sea-A	2	2	.500	43	1	0	0	2	45	49	6	21	27	14.4	5.00	81	.285	.369	0	—	0	-6	-5	1	-0.4
1990	Sea-A	0	0	—	2	0	0	0	0	3	5	0	2	0	24.0	9.00	44	.357	.471	0	—	0	-2	-2	-0	-0.1
	Mil-A	0	4	.000	9	7	0	0	0	39¹	59	6	19	23	18.1	6.86	56	.341	.409	0	—	0	-13	-13	1	-1.0
	Yr	0	4	.000	11	7	0	0	0	42¹	64	6	21	23	18.3	7.02	55	.340	.410	0	—	0	-15	-15	1	-1.1
1992	Sea-A	4	2	.667	49	0	0	0	3	57	49	5	29	35	12.8	4.58	87	.238	.340	0	—	0	-4	-4	-0	-0.4
1993	Sea-A	0	0	—	33	2	0	0	0	47²	42	7	24	32	12.7	4.15	106	.255	.353	0	—	0	1	1	-0	0.0
Total	8	11	22	.333	207	23	0	0	3	339²	360	35	159	199	14.1	4.95	80	.279	.363	3	.176	1	-37	-37	1	-4.4
● **GROVER POWELL**	Powell, Grover David b: 10/10/40, Sayre, Pa. d: 5/21/85, Raleigh, N.C. BL/TL, 5'10", 175 lbs. Deb: 7/13/63																								
1963	NY-N	1	1	.500	20	4	1	1	0	49²	37	3	32	39	12.7	2.72	128	.202	.324	2	.200	1	3	4	0	0.3
● **JAY POWELL**	Powell, James Willard b: 1/9/72, Meridian, Miss. BR/TR, 6'4", 220 lbs. Deb: 9/10/95																								
1995	Fla-N	0	0	—	9	0	0	0	0	8¹	7	0	6	4	16.2	1.08	390	.241	.405	0	—	0	3	3	0	0.0
1996	Fla-N	4	3	.571	67	0	0	0	2	71¹	71	5	36	52	14.0	4.54	89	.255	.349	0	.000	-1	-3	-4	-1	-0.5
Total	2	4	3	.571	76	0	0	0	2	79²	78	5	42	56	14.2	4.18	97	.254	.355	0	.000	-1	-0	-1	-0	-0.5
● **JACK POWELL**	Powell, John Joseph "Red" b: 7/9/1874, Bloomington, Ill. d: 10/17/44, Chicago, Ill. BR/TR, 5'11", 195 lbs. Deb: 6/23/1897																								
1897	Cle-N	15	10	.600	27	26	24	2	0	225	245	2	62	61	12.6	3.16	142	.275	.328	20	.206	-4	29	33	-1	2.5
1898	StL-N	23	15	.605	42	41	36	**6**	0	342	328	8	112	93	12.0	3.00	121	.251	.317	18	.132	-7	23	24	-2	1.4
1899	StL-N	23	19	.548	48	43	**40**	1	0	373	433	15	85	87	12.9	3.52	113	.290	.334	27	.201	-1	14	19	-3	1.4
1900	StL-N	17	16	.515	38	37	28	3	0	287²	325	9	77	77	12.7	4.44	82	.284	.331	31	.284	10	-24	-26	0	-1.5
1901	StL-N	19	19	.500	**45**	37	33	2	3	338¹	351	14	50	133	11.0	3.54	90	.266	.299	21	.176	1	-8	-13	-5	-1.6
1902	StL-A	22	17	.564	42	39	36	3	**2**	328¹	320	12	69	137	11.6	3.21	110	.256	.312	26	.205	4	13	12	-5	1.0
1903	StL-A	15	19	.441	38	34	33	4	**2**	306¹	294	11	58	169	10.5	2.91	100	.252	.290	25	.208	2	2	0	-1	0.2
1904	NY-A	23	19	.548	47	45	38	3	0	390¹	340	15	92	202	10.2	2.44	111	.235	.286	26	.178	-3	7	12	-6	0.3
1905	NY-A	8	13	.381	37	23	13	1	1	203	214	4	57	84	12.3	3.50	84	.272	.326	12	.185	-0	-19	-13	-6	-2.0
	StL-A	2	1	.667	3	3	3	0	0	28	22	0	5	12	9.0	1.61	158	.218	.262	1	.100	-1	3	3	-1	0.2
	Yr	10	14	.417	40	26	16	1	1	231	236	4	62	96	11.6	3.27	88	.266	.313	13	.173	-1	-16	-10	-7	-1.8
1906	StL-A	13	14	.481	28	26	25	3	1	244	196	2	55	132	9.6	1.77	146	.223	.275	21	.231	3	25	22	-4	2.5
1907	StL-A	13	16	.448	32	31	27	4	1	255²	229	4	62	96	10.4	2.68	94	.242	.292	12	.132	-3	-4	-5	-3	-1.2
1908	StL-A	16	13	.552	33	32	23	5	1	256	208	1	47	85	9.2	2.11	113	.231	.274	21	.236	3	8	8	-6	0.5
1909	StL-A	12	16	.429	34	27	18	4	3	239	221	1	42	82	10.1	2.11	115	.250	.287	14	.179	-1	10	8	-4	0.6
1910	StL-A	7	11	.389	21	18	8	3	0	129¹	121	0	28	52	10.4	2.30	108	.250	.292	7	.163	-1	3	3	-3	-0.2
1911	StL-A	8	19	.296	31	27	18	1	1	207²	224	7	44	52	11.9	3.29	102	.262	.304	12	.164	-3	1	2	-5	-0.5
1912	StL-A	9	17	.346	32	27	19	0	0	235²	248	5	52	67	11.6	3.10	107	.276	.318	15	.183	0	6	6	-4	0.3
Total	16	245	254	.491	578	516	422	46	15	4389	4319	110	1021	1621	11.2	2.97	106	.258	.305	309	.192	-1	89	94	-58	3.9
● **JACK POWELL**	Powell, Reginald Bertrand b: 8/17/1891, Holcomb, Mo. d: 3/12/30, Memphis, Tenn. TR, 6'2", Deb: 6/14/13																								
1913	StL-A	0	0	—	2	0	0	0	0	2	1	0	2	0	13.5	0.00	—	.143	.333	0	—	0	1	1	1	0.0
● **ROSS POWELL**	Powell, Ross John b: 1/24/68, Grand Rapids, Mich. BL/TL, 6', 180 lbs. Deb: 9/5/93																								
1993	Cin-N	0	3	.000	16¹	9	1	0	0	16¹	13	1	6	17	10.5	4.41	91	.224	.297	0	.000	-0	-1	-1	-0	-0.1
1994	Hou-N	0	0	—	12	0	0	0	0	7¹	7	1	5	4	14.7	1.23	322	.240	.387	0	—	0	2	2	0	0.0
1995	Hou-N	0	0	—	15	0	0	0	0	9	16	1	11	8	27.0	11.00	35	.381	.509	0	—	0	-7	-7	0	0.0
	Pit-N	0	2	.000	13	3	0	0	0	20²	20	5	10	12	13.9	5.23	82	.253	.352	0	.000	-0	-2	-2	-0	-0.2
	Yr	0	2	.000	27	3	0	0	0	29²	36	6	21	20	17.1	6.98	60	.295	.407	0	.000	-0	-9	-9	0	-0.2
Total	3	0	5	.000	48	4	0	0	0	53¹	55	7	32	42	15.2	5.40	76	.270	.377	0	.000	-0	-7	-8	0	-0.3
● **BILL POWELL**	Powell, William Burris "Big Bill" b: 5/8/1885, Richmond, Va. d: 9/28/67, E.Liverpool, Ohio BR/TR, 6'2.5", 182 lbs. Deb: 4/16/09																								
1909	Pit-N	0	1	.000	3	1	0	0	0	7¹	7	0	6	2	17.2	3.68	74	.292	.452	1	.333	0	-1	-1	0	-0.1
1910	Pit-N	4	6	.400	12	9	4	2	0	75	65	0	34	23	12.5	2.40	129	.242	.338	6	.261	1	5	6	2	1.0
1912	Chi-N	0	0	—	1	0	0	0	0	2	3	0	3	1	13.5	9.00	37	.250	.333	0	—	0	-1	-1	0	0.0
1913	Cin-N	0	1	.000	1	1	0	0	0	0¹	1	0	2	0	108.0	54.00	6	1.000	1.000	0	—	0	-2	-2	0	-2.0
Total	4	4	8	.333	17	11	4	2	0	84²	76	0	45	25	13.6	2.87	107	.251	.355	7	.269	1	1	2	2	-1.1
● **TED POWER**	Power, Ted Henry b: 1/31/55, Guthrie, Okla. BR/TR, 6'4", 225 lbs. Deb: 9/9/81																								
1981	LA-N	1	3	.250	5	2	0	0	0	14¹	14	0	7	7	15.1	3.14	106	.286	.375	0	.000	-0	1	0	-1	0.0
1982	LA-N	1	1	.500	12	4	0	0	0	33²	38	4	23	15	16.3	6.68	52	.288	.394	0	.000	-0	-12	-12	-0	-0.7
1983	Cin-N	5	6	.455	49	6	1	0	2	111	120	10	49	59	13.8	4.54	84	.284	.362	0	.000	-0	-11	-9	-2	-1.2
1984	Cin-N	9	7	.563	**78**	0	0	0	11	108²	93	4	46	81	11.5	2.82	134	.237	.317	0	.000	-0	9	12	0	1.9
1985	Cin-N	8	6	.571	64	0	0	0	27	80	65	2	45	42	12.5	2.70	140	.227	.334	0	—	0	8	10	2	2.1
1986	Cin-N	10	6	.625	56	10	0	0	1	129	115	13	52	95	11.7	3.70	105	.245	.322	3	.125	0	1	0	-0	-0.3
1987	Cin-N	10	13	.435	34	34	2	1	0	204	213	28	71	133	12.7	4.50	94	.267	.329	7	.119	0	-10	-6	-3	-0.9
1988	KC-A	5	6	.455	22	12	2	0	0	80¹	98	7	30	44	14.7	5.94	67	.305	.370	0	—	0	-18	-17	-0	-2.1
	Det-A	1	1	.500	4	2	0	0	0	18²	23	1	8	13	14.9	5.79	66	.307	.373	0	—	0	-4	-4	-0	-0.3
	Yr	6	7	.462	26	14	2	0	0	99	121	8	38	57	14.5	5.91	67	.300	.361	0	—	0	-21	-22	-0	-2.4
1989	StL-N	7	7	.500	23	15	0	0	0	97	96	7	21	43	10.9	3.71	98	.255	.296	3	.091	-2	-2	-1	-0	-0.5
1990	*Pit-N	1	3	.250	40	0	0	0	7	51²	50	5	17	42	11.7	3.66	99	.255	.315	1	.125	0	1	-0	-0	-0.1
1991	Cin-N	5	3	.625	68	0	0	0	3	87	87	6	31	51	12.4	3.62	105	.265	.332	0	—	0	1	2	0	0.1
1992	Cle-A	3	3	.500	64	0	0	0	6	99¹	88	7	35	51	11.5	2.54	154	.248	.322	0	—	0	15	15	0	1.1
1993	Cle-A	0	2	.000	20	0	0	0	0	20	30	2	8	12	17.1	7.20	60	.343	.388	0	—	0	-6	-6	-0	-0.6
	Sea-A	2	2	.500	25	0	0	0	13	25¹	21	5	19	16	12.8	3.91	113	.287	.350	0	—	0	1	1	0	0.2
	Yr	2	4	.333	45	0	0	0	13	45¹	51	7	27	28	14.7	5.36	81	.308	.366	0	—	0	-5	-5	-0	-0.4
Total	13	68	69	.496	564	85	6	3	70	1160	1159	97	452	701	12.6	4.00	97	.264	.335	14	.089	-4	-26	-14	-11	-0.7
● **JIM POWERS**	Powers, James T. b: 1868, New York, N.Y. 5'10", 150 lbs. Deb: 4/18/1890																								
1890	Bro-a	1	2	.333	4	2	2	0	0	30	38	1	16	3	16.5	5.70	68	.299	.382	2	.154	-0	-6	-6	-0	-0.5
● **IKE POWERS**	Powers, John Lloyd b: 3/13/06, Hancock, Md. d: 12/22/68, Hancock, Md. BR/TR, 6'0.5", 188 lbs. Deb: 7/26/27																								
1927	Phi-A	1	1	.500	11	1	0	0	0	26	26	1	7	3	11.4	4.50	95	.271	.320	2	.400	1	-1	-1	-0	0.0
1928	Phi-A	1	0	1.000	9	0	0	0	2	12	8	1	10	4	14.3	4.50	89	.222	.404	0	—	0	-1	-1	1	0.0
Total	2	2	1	.667	20	1	0	0	2	38	34	2	17	7	12.3	4.50	93	.258	.347	2	.400	1	-2	-1	1	0.0
● **WILLIE PRALL**	Prall, Wilfred Anthony b: 4/20/50, Hackensack, N.J. BL/TL, 6'3", 200 lbs. Deb: 9/3/75																								
1975	Chi-N	0	2	.000	3	3	0	0	0	14²	21	1	8	7	17.8	8.59	45	.339	.414	0	.000	-0	-8	-8	0	-0.9

YEAR TM/L	W	L	PCT	G	GS	CG	SH	SV	IP	H	HR	BB	SO	RAT	ERA	ERA+	OAV	OOB	BH	AVG	PB	PR	/A	PD	TPI

● **AL PRATT**   Pratt, Albert George "Uncle Al" b: 11/19/1848, Allegheny, Pa. d: 11/21/37, Pittsburgh, Pa. TR , 5'7", 140 lbs. Deb: 5/4/1871 MU

1871 Cle-n	10	17	.370	28	28	22	0	0	224²	296	9	47	**34**	13.7	3.77	110	.277	.307	34	.262	2	11	9		1.0
1872 Cle-n	2	9	.182	15	12	8	0	0	105²	150	3	14	7	14.0	5.79	61	.286	.305	18	.277	1	-25	-26		-0.5
Total 2 n	12	26	.316	43	40	30	0	0	330¹	446	12	61	41	13.8	4.41	81	.280	.306	52	.267	3	-28	-31		0.5

● **JOHN PREGENZER**   Pregenzer, John Arthur b: 8/2/35, Burlington, Wis. BR/TR, 6'5", 220 lbs. Deb: 4/20/63

1963 SF-N	0	0	—	6	0	0	0	1	9¹	8	0	8	5	16.4	4.82	66	.242	.405	0	—	0	-2	-2	-0	0.0
1964 SF-N	2	0	1.000	13	0	0	0	0	18¹	21	1	11	8	16.2	4.91	73	.296	.398	0	—	0	-3	-3	-0	-0.3
Total 2	2	0	1.000	19	0	0	0	1	27²	29	1	19	13	16.3	4.88	70	.279	.400	0	—	0	-4	-4	-0	-0.3

● **JIM PRENDERGAST**   Prendergast, James Bartholomew b: 8/23/17, Brooklyn, N.Y. d: 8/23/94, Amherst, N.Y. BL/TL, 6'1", 208 lbs. Deb: 4/25/48

| 1948 Bos-N | 1 | 1 | .500 | 10 | 2 | 0 | 0 | 1 | 16² | 30 | 1 | 5 | 3 | 18.9 | 10.26 | 37 | .380 | .417 | 0 | .000 | -1 | -12 | -12 | 0 | -1.4 |

● **MIKE PRENDERGAST**   Prendergast, Michael Thomas b: 12/15/1888, Arlington, Ill. d: 11/18/67, Omaha, Neb. BR/TR, 5'9.5", 165 lbs. Deb: 4/26/14

1914 Chi-F	5	9	.357	30	19	7	1	0	136	131	6	40	71	11.5	2.38	111	.255	.313	4	.108	-3	8	4	-2	0.0
1915 Chi-F	14	12	.538	42	30	16	3	0	253²	220	6	67	95	10.3	2.48	101	.240	.295	6	.075	-9	7	1	-3	-1.1
1916 Chi-N	6	11	.353	35	10	4	2	2	152	127	5	23	56	8.9	2.31	126	.228	.260	7	.152	-2	5	10	-1	0.9
1917 Chi-N	3	6	.333	35	8	1	0	1	99¹	112	6	21	43	12.1	3.35	86	.302	.339	7	.250	1	-7	-5	-1	-0.4
1918 Phi-N	13	14	.481	33	30	20	0	0	252¹	257	6	46	41	10.8	2.89	104	.273	.308	7	.082	-8	-4	3	-2	-0.7
1919 Phi-N	0	1	.000	5	1	0	0	0	15	20	0	10	5	18.6	8.40	38	.351	.456	1	.333	0	-9	-9	-0	-0.5
Total 6	41	53	.436	180	98	48	6	4	908¹	867	29	207	311	10.7	2.74	102	.258	.304	32	.115	-19	0	5	-8	-1.8

● **GEORGE PRENTISS**   Prentiss, George Pepper (a.k.a. George Pepper Wilson In 1901)
b: 6/10/1876, Wilmington, Del. d: 9/8/02, Wilmington, Del. BB/TR, 5'11", 175 lbs. Deb: 9/23/01

1901 Bos-A	1	0	1.000	2	1	1	0	0	10	7	0	6	0	11.7	1.80	196	.194	.310	1	.333	1	2	2	-0	0.2
1902 Bos-A	2	2	.500	7	4	3	0	0	41	55	0	10	9	14.3	5.27	68	.322	.359	5	.313	1	-8	-8	-0	-0.6
Bal-A	0	1	.000	2	2	0	0	0	6²	14	1	5	1	25.7	10.80	35	.424	.500	0	.000	-1	-5	-5	-0	-0.6
Yr	2	3	.400	9	6	3	0	0	47²	69	1	15	10	15.9	6.04	60	.338	.384	5	.263	-0	-13	-13	-0	-1.2
Total 2	3	3	.500	11	7	4	0	0	57²	76	1	21	10	15.1	5.31	68	.317	.372	6	.261	1	-11	-11	-0	-1.0

● **JOE PRESKO**   Presko, Joseph Edward "Baby Joe" b: 10/7/28, Kansas City, Mo. BR/TR, 6', 170 lbs. Deb: 5/3/51

1951 StL-N	7	4	.636	15	12	5	0	2	88²	86	9	20	38	11.0	3.45	115	.251	.296	6	.162	-1	5	5	-1	0.4
1952 StL-N	7	10	.412	28	18	5	1	0	146²	140	15	57	63	12.1	4.05	92	.247	.317	4	.093	-2	-5	-5	-1	-0.9
1953 StL-N	6	13	.316	34	25	4	0	1	161²	165	19	65	56	13.1	5.01	85	.261	.335	13	.220	1	-13	-14	-1	-1.4
1954 StL-N	4	9	.308	37	6	1	0	1	71²	97	14	41	36	18.0	6.91	60	.327	.417	4	.250	-4	-23	-22	-3	-3.4
1957 Det-A	1	1	.500	7	0	0	0	0	11	10	0	4	3	12.3	1.64	236	.278	.366	0	.000	-1	3	3	0	0.4
1958 Det-A	0	0	—	7	0	0	0	0	10²	13	0	1	6	11.8	3.38	120	.317	.333	0	—	0	1	0	0	0.1
Total 6	25	37	.403	128	61	15	2	5	490¹	511	57	188	202	13.1	4.61	87	.267	.337	27	.173	-1	-33	-33	-4	-4.8

● **TOT PRESSNELL**   Pressnell, Forest Charles b: 8/8/06, Findlay, Ohio BR/TR, 5'10", 175 lbs. Deb: 4/21/38

1938 Bro-N	11	14	.440	43	19	6	1	3	192	209	11	56	57	12.8	3.56	110	.276	.332	9	.143	-1	5	7	-1	0.7
1939 Bro-N	9	7	.563	34	18	10	2	2	156²	171	8	33	43	11.8	4.02	100	.273	.311	10	.196	-1	-2	0	-0	-0.1
1940 Bro-N	6	5	.545	24	4	1	1	2	68¹	58	4	17	21	10.1	3.69	108	.221	.274	0	—	-2	1	2	-1	0.0
1941 Chi-N	5	3	.625	29	1	0	0	1	70	69	2	23	27	12.3	3.09	114	.253	.320	3	.200	0	**4**	3	-1	0.3
1942 Chi-N	1	1	.500	27	0	0	0	4	39¹	40	5	5	9	11.4	5.49	58	.260	.305	2	.667	1	-10	-10	-0	-0.6
Total 5	32	30	.516	154	42	17	4	12	526¹	547	30	134	157	12.0	3.80	102	.264	.315	24	.161	-3	-1	3	-3	0.3

● **JOE PRICE**   Price, Joseph Walter b: 11/29/56, Inglewood, Cal. BR/TL, 6'4", 220 lbs. Deb: 6/14/80

1980 Cin-N	7	3	.700	24	13	2	0	0	111¹	95	10	37	44	10.8	3.56	101	.236	.302	5	.128	-2	1	0	-1	-0.3
1981 Cin-N	6	1	.857	41	0	0	0	4	53²	42	3	18	41	10.1	2.52	141	.222	.290	0	.000	0	6	6	1	0.9
1982 Cin-N	3	4	.429	59	1	0	0	3	72²	73	7	32	71	13.5	2.85	130	.263	.347	1	.333	0	6	7	-1	0.6
1983 Cin-N	10	6	.625	21	21	5	0	0	144	118	12	46	83	10.3	2.88	132	.225	.287	4	.098	-1	12	15	-0	1.4
1984 Cin-N	7	13	.350	30	30	3	1	0	171²	176	19	61	129	12.5	4.19	90	.261	.324	7	.146	-1	-12	-8	-3	-1.2
1985 Cin-N	2	2	.500	26	8	0	0	1	64²	59	10	23	52	11.4	3.90	97	.242	.307	0	.000	-1	-2	-1	-1	-0.3
1986 Cin-N	1	2	.333	25	2	0	0	1	41²	49	5	22	30	15.3	5.40	73	.292	.376	1	.143	-1	-8	-7	-1	-0.6
1987 *SF-N	2	2	.500	20	0	0	0	1	35	19	5	13	42	8.5	2.57	149	.154	.241	1	.167	0	6	5	-1	0.5
1988 SF-N	1	6	.143	38	3	0	0	4	61²	59	5	27	49	12.7	3.94	83	.249	.328	0	.000	0	-3	-5	-0	-0.5
1989 SF-N	1	1	.500	7	1	0	0	0	14	16	3	4	10	12.9	5.79	58	.314	.364	0	.000	0	-4	-4	-0	-0.5
Bos-A	2	5	.286	31	1	0	0	0	70¹	71	8	30	52	12.9	4.35	94	.262	.336	0	—	0	-4	-2	-1	-0.6
1990 Bal-A	3	4	.429	50	0	0	0	0	65¹	62	8	24	54	11.8	3.58	106	.253	.320	0	—	0	2	2	-0	0.3
Total 11	45	49	.479	372	84	10	1	13	906	839	95	337	657	11.8	3.65	102	.246	.316	19	.111	-5	0	8	-8	-0.4

● **BILL PRICE**   Price, William b: Philadelphia, Pa. Deb: 4/27/1890

| 1890 Phi-a | 1 | 0 | 1.000 | 1 | 1 | 1 | 0 | 0 | 9 | 6 | 0 | 7 | 1 | 14.0 | 2.00 | 192 | .182 | .341 | 1 | .250 | -0 | 2 | 2 | -0 | 0.2 |

● **BOB PRIDDY**   Priddy, Robert Simpson b: 12/10/39, Pittsburgh, Pa. BR/TR, 6'1", 200 lbs. Deb: 9/20/62

1962 Pit-N	1	0	1.000	2	0	0	0	0	3	4	0	1	1	15.0	3.00	131	.308	.357	0	—	0	0	0	-0	0.1
1964 Pit-N	1	2	.333	19	0	0	0	1	34¹	35	2	15	23	13.4	3.93	89	.282	.364	0	.000	0	-2	-2	-1	-0.2
1965 SF-N	1	0	1.000	8	0	0	0	0	10¹	6	1	2	7	7.0	1.74	207	.176	.222	0	.000	0	2	2	-0	0.2
1966 SF-N	6	3	.667	38	3	0	0	1	91	88	8	28	51	11.8	3.96	93	.259	.321	3	.176	-1	-4	-3	-1	-0.4
1967 Was-A	3	7	.300	46	8	1	0	4	110	98	12	33	57	10.7	3.44	92	.240	.297	4	.182	1	-3	3	-1	0.0
1968 Chi-A	3	11	.214	35	18	2	0	0	114	106	14	41	66	11.9	3.63	83	.244	.315	1	.042	-1	-8	-8	-2	-1.2
1969 Chi-A	0	0	—	4	0	0	0	0	8	10	2	2	6	13.5	4.50	86	.303	.343	0	—	0	-1	-1	-0	0.0
Cal-A	0	1	.000	15	0	0	0	0	26¹	24	4	7	15	10.6	4.78	73	.242	.292	0	.000	0	-3	-4	-0	-0.1
Yr	0	1	.000	19	0	0	0	0	34¹	34	6	9	20	11.3	4.72	76	.258	.305	0	.000	0	-4	-4	-0	-0.1
Atl-N	0	0	—	1	0	0	0	0	2	1	0	1	1	9.0	0.00	—	.143	.250	1	1.000	-0	1	1	-0	0.0
1970 Atl-N	5	5	.500	41	0	0	0	0	73	75	9	24	32	12.6	5.42	79	.269	.333	3	.200	-0	-11	-9	-1	-0.7
1971 Atl-N	4	9	.308	40	0	0	0	2	64	71	8	44	36	16.3	4.22	88	.289	.399	2	.182	-4	-5	-4	1	-0.7
Total 9	24	38	.387	249	29	3	0	18	536	518	60	198	294	12.2	4.00	87	.257	.327	13	.137	1	-33	-30	-2	-3.5

● **ARIEL PRIETO**   Prieto, Ariel b: 10/22/69, Havana, Cuba BR/TR, 6'3", 225 lbs. Deb: 7/2/95

1995 Oak-A	2	6	.250	14	9	1	0	0	58	57	4	32	37	14.6	4.97	90	.264	.372	0	—	0	-2	-3	-0	-0.4
1996 Oak-A	6	7	.462	21	21	2	0	0	125²	130	9	54	75	13.7	4.15	116	.273	.356	0	—	0	12	9	-0	1.0
Total 2	8	13	.381	35	30	3	0	0	183²	187	13	86	112	14.0	4.41	107	.270	.361	0	—	0	10	6	-0	0.6

● **RAY PRIM**   Prim, Raymond Lee "Pop" b: 12/30/06, Salitpa, Ala. d: 4/29/95, Monte Rio, Cal. BR/TL, 6', 178 lbs. Deb: 9/24/33

1933 Was-A	0	1	.000	2	1	0	0	0	14¹	13	0	2	6	9.4	3.14	133	.232	.259	0	.000	-1	2	2	1	0.1
1934 Was-A	0	2	.000	8	1	0	0	0	14²	19	1	8	3	16.6	6.75	64	.339	.422	0	.000	-0	-4	-4	-0	-0.4
1935 Phi-N	3	4	.429	29	6	1	0	0	73¹	110	4	15	27	15.3	5.77	79	.340	.369	2	.083	-2	-14	-10	-1	-1.1
1943 Chi-N	4	3	.571	29	5	0	0	0	60	67	2	14	27	12.2	2.55	131	.282	.321	2	.167	-0	6	5	2	0.8
1945 *Chi-N	13	8	.619	34	19	9	2	2	165¹	142	9	23	88	**9.0**	2.40	**153**	**.228**	**.256**	13	.255	3	26	23	-1	3.0
1946 Chi-N	2	3	.400	14	2	0	0	2	23¹	28	5	10	10	14.7	5.79	57	.289	.355	1	.200	0	-6	-6	1	-1.2
Total 6	22	21	.512	116	34	10	2	4	351	379	21	72	161	11.6	3.56	107	.272	.308	18	.180	-0	9	9	3	1.2

● **DON PRINCE**   Prince, Donald Mark b: 4/5/38, Clarkton, N.C. BR/TR, 6'4", 200 lbs. Deb: 9/21/62

| 1962 Chi-N | 0 | 0 | — | 1 | 0 | 0 | 0 | 0 | 1 | 0 | 0 | 1 | 0 | 18.0 | 0.00 | — | .000 | .500 | 0 | — | 0 | 0 | 0 | -0 | 0.0 |

● **JIM PROCTOR**   Proctor, James Arthur b: 9/9/35, Brandywine, Md. BR/TR, 6', 165 lbs. Deb: 9/14/59

| 1959 Det-A | 0 | 1 | .000 | 2 | 0 | 0 | 0 | 0 | 2² | 8 | 3 | 0 | 2 | 37.1 | 16.88 | 24 | .533 | .611 | 0 | — | 0 | -4 | -4 | 0 | -1.0 |

● **RED PROCTOR**   Proctor, Noah Richard b: 10/27/1900, Williamsburg, Va. d: 12/17/54, Richmond, Va. BR/TR, 6'1", 165 lbs. Deb: 8/6/23

| 1923 Chi-N | 0 | 0 | — | 2 | 0 | 0 | 0 | 0 | 4 | 11 | 0 | 2 | 0 | 29.3 | 13.50 | 29 | .550 | .591 | 0 | — | 0 | -4 | -4 | -0 | 0.0 |

YEAR	TM/L	W	L	PCT	G	GS	CG	SH	SV	IP	H	HR	BB	SO	RAT	ERA	ERA+	OAV	OOB	BH	AVG	PB	PR	/A	PD	TPI

● **GEORGE PROESER**   Proeser, George "Yatz" b: 5/30/1864, Cincinnati, Ohio d: 10/13/41, New Burlington, O. BL/TL, 5'10", 190 lbs. Deb: 9/15/1888 ♦

| | 1888 | Cle-a | 3 | 4 | .429 | 7 | 7 | 7 | 1 | 0 | 59 | 53 | 4 | 30 | 20 | 13.7 | 3.81 | 81 | .231 | .338 | 7 | .304 | 2 | -5 | -5 | -1 | -0.4 |

● **MIKE PROLY**   Proly, Michael James b: 12/15/50, Jamaica, N.Y. BR/TR, 6', 185 lbs. Deb: 4/10/76

YEAR	TM/L	W	L	PCT	G	GS	CG	SH	SV	IP	H	HR	BB	SO	RAT	ERA	ERA+	OAV	OOB	BH	AVG	PB	PR	/A	PD	TPI
1976	StL-N	1	0	1.000	14	0	0	0	0	17	21	0	6	4	14.3	3.71	95	.328	.386	0	—	0	-0	0	0	0.0
1978	Chi-A	5	2	.714	14	6	2	0	1	65²	63	4	12	19	10.3	2.74	139	.250	.284	0	—	0	7	8	-1	0.7
1979	Chi-A	3	8	.273	38	6	0	0	9	88¹	89	6	40	32	13.2	3.87	110	.260	.339	0	—	0	3	4	1	0.6
1980	Chi-A	5	10	.333	62	3	0	0	8	146²	136	7	58	56	12.1	3.07	131	.253	.329	0	—	0	16	16	2	1.8
1981	Phi-N	2	1	.667	35	2	0	0	2	63	66	6	19	19	12.3	3.86	94	.282	.339	0	.000	-1	-3	-2	0	-0.1
1982	Chi-N	5	3	.625	44	1	0	0	1	82	77	5	22	24	11.1	2.30	162	.257	.312	4	.286	1	12	13	0	1.4
1983	Chi-N	1	5	.167	60	0	0	0	1	83	79	5	38	31	12.8	3.58	106	.259	.343	1	.091	-0	2	1	0	0.1
Total	7	22	29	.431	267	18	2	0	22	545²	531	33	195	185	12.1	3.23	121	.261	.328	5	.156	-0	36	40	4	4.5

● **BILL PROUGH**   Prough, Herschel Clinton "Clint" b: 11/28/1887, Markle, Ind. d: 12/29/36, Richmond, Ind. BR/TR, 6'3", 185 lbs. Deb: 4/27/12

| 1912 | Cin-N | 0 | 0 | — | 1 | 0 | 0 | 0 | 0 | 3 | 7 | 0 | 1 | 0 | 24.0 | 6.00 | 56 | .538 | .571 | 0 | .000 | -0 | -1 | -1 | -0 | 0.0 |

● **AUGIE PRUDHOMME**   Prudhomme, John Olgus b: 11/20/02, Frierson, La. d: 10/4/92, Shreveport, La. BR/TR, 6'2", 186 lbs. Deb: 4/19/29

| 1929 | Det-A | 1 | 6 | .143 | 34 | 6 | 2 | 0 | 1 | 94 | 119 | 7 | 53 | 26 | 16.7 | 6.22 | 69 | .322 | .410 | 5 | .238 | 1 | -21 | -20 | 1 | -1.1 |

● **HUB PRUETT**   Pruett, Hubert Shelby "Shucks" b: 9/1/1900, Malden, Mo. d: 1/28/82, Ladue, Mo. BL/TL, 5'10.5", 165 lbs. Deb: 4/26/22

YEAR	TM/L	W	L	PCT	G	GS	CG	SH	SV	IP	H	HR	BB	SO	RAT	ERA	ERA+	OAV	OOB	BH	AVG	PB	PR	/A	PD	TPI
1922	StL-A	7	7	.500	39	8	4	0	7	119²	99	2	59	70	12.3	2.33	178	.235	.336	5	.147	-1	23	24	2	2.9
1923	StL-A	4	7	.364	32	8	3	0	2	104¹	109	3	64	59	15.2	4.31	97	.279	.385	3	.130	-1	-4	-2	1	-0.1
1924	StL-A	3	4	.429	33	1	0	0	0	65	64	1	42	27	15.2	4.57	99	.270	.389	1	.200	-1	-2	-0	1	0.0
1927	Phi-N	7	17	.292	31	28	12	1	0	186	238	6	89	90	16.4	6.05	68	.314	.395	13	.217	1	-44	-40	3	-3.9
1928	Phi-N	2	4	.333	13	9	4	0	0	71¹	78	2	49	35	16.4	4.54	94	.291	.406	2	.208	-0	-4	-2	0	-0.2
1930	NY-N	5	4	.556	45	8	1	0	3	135²	152	11	63	49	14.5	4.78	99	.287	.367	5	.135	-1	3	-1	1	-0.1
1932	Bos-N	1	5	.167	18	7	4	0	0	63	76	3	30	27	16.0	5.14	73	.308	.396	2	.105	-1	-9	-10	2	-0.7
Total	7	29	48	.377	211	69	28	1	13	745	816	28	396	357	15.1	4.63	92	.286	.380	36	.170	-3	-38	-29	10	-2.1

● **TEX PRUIETT**   Pruiett, Charles Le Roy b: 4/10/1883, Osgood, Ind. d: 3/6/53, Ventura, Cal. BL/TR, Deb: 4/26/07

1907	Bos-A	3	11	.214	35	17	6	2	3	173²	166	1	59	54	12.1	3.11	83	.254	.323	8	.157	-1	-11	-10	1	-0.8
1908	Bos-A	1	7	.125	13	6	1	1	2	58²	55	1	21	28	12.0	1.99	123	.275	.350	1	.063	-2	3	3	0	0.3
Total	2	4	18	.182	48	23	7	3	5	232¹	221	2	80	82	12.0	2.83	90	.259	.329	9	.134	-2	-8	-7	1	-0.5

● **TROY PUCKETT**   Puckett, Troy Levi b: 12/10/1889, Winchester, Ind. d: 4/13/71, Winchester, Ind. BL/TR, 6'2", 186 lbs. Deb: 10/4/11

| 1911 | Phi-N | 0 | 0 | — | 1 | 0 | 0 | 0 | 0 | 2 | 4 | 0 | 1 | 1 | 31.5 | 13.50 | 26 | .444 | .583 | 0 | — | 0 | -2 | -2 | -0 | 0.0 |

● **MIGUEL PUENTE**   Puente, Miguel Antonio (Aguilar) b: 5/8/48, San Luis Potosi, Mex BR/TR, 6', 160 lbs. Deb: 5/3/70

| 1970 | SF-N | 1 | 3 | .250 | 6 | 4 | 1 | 0 | 0 | 18² | 25 | 5 | 11 | 14 | 17.4 | 8.20 | 48 | .325 | .409 | 0 | .000 | -1 | -9 | -9 | 0 | -1.5 |

● **TIM PUGH**   Pugh, Timothy Dean b: 1/26/67, S.Lake Tahoe, Cal. BR/TR, 6'6", 225 lbs. Deb: 9/1/92

YEAR	TM/L	W	L	PCT	G	GS	CG	SH	SV	IP	H	HR	BB	SO	RAT	ERA	ERA+	OAV	OOB	BH	AVG	PB	PR	/A	PD	TPI
1992	Cin-N	4	2	.667	7	7	0	0	0	45¹	47	2	13	18	12.1	2.58	139	.276	.332	1	.077	-0	5	5	-0	0.6
1993	Cin-N	10	15	.400	31	27	3	1	0	164¹	200	19	59	94	14.6	5.26	77	.303	.366	12	.222	2	-22	-23	-0	-2.8
1994	Cin-N	3	3	.500	10	9	1	0	0	47²	60	5	24	24	16.8	6.04	68	.314	.405	5	.357	2	-10	-10	0	-0.2
1995	Cin-N	6	5	.545	28	12	0	0	0	98¹	100	13	32	38	12.2	3.84	107	.266	.325	4	.143	0	4	3	-1	0.2
1996	Cin-N	1	0	1.000	9	0	0	0	0	15¹	20	3	11	9	18.8	10.57	39	.317	.427	0	—	0	-11	-11	1	-0.5
	KC-A	0	1	.000	19	1	0	0	0	36¹	42	9	12	27	13.9	5.45	90	.282	.344	0	—	0	-2	-2	0	-0.2
	Cin-N	0	1	.000	1	0	0	0	0	0¹	4	0	2	0	108.0	54.00	8	.800	.800	0	—	0	-2	-2	0	-1.9
Total	5	24	27	.471	105	56	4	1	0	407²	473	51	153	210	14.2	4.97	82	.293	.360	22	.202	4	-38	-39	-1	-5.3

● **CHARLIE PULEO**   Puleo, Charles Michael b: 2/7/55, Glen Ridge, N.J. BR/TR, 6'3", 200 lbs. Deb: 9/16/81

YEAR	TM/L	W	L	PCT	G	GS	CG	SH	SV	IP	H	HR	BB	SO	RAT	ERA	ERA+	OAV	OOB	BH	AVG	PB	PR	/A	PD	TPI
1981	NY-N	0	0	—	4	1	0	0	0	13¹	8	0	8	8	10.8	0.00	—	.182	.308	0	.000	-0	5	5	0	0.0
1982	NY-N	9	9	.500	36	24	1	1	1	171	179	13	90	98	14.3	4.47	81	.275	.364	6	.125	-1	-17	-16	3	-1.4
1983	Cin-N	6	12	.333	27	24	0	0	0	143²	145	18	91	71	15.1	4.89	78	.269	.379	5	.100	-2	-20	-17	-2	-2.2
1984	Cin-N	1	2	.333	5	4	0	0	0	22	27	2	15	6	17.2	5.73	68	.297	.396	1	.200	0	-5	-5	-1	-0.6
1986	Atl-N	1	2	.333	5	3	1	0	0	24¹	13	4	12	18	9.6	2.96	134	.160	.277	2	.333	0	2	3	0	0.4
1987	Atl-N	6	8	.429	35	16	1	0	0	123¹	122	11	40	99	12.0	4.23	103	.262	.325	5	.179	1	-2	2	-2	0.1
1988	Atl-N	5	5	.500	53	3	0	0	1	106¹	101	9	47	70	12.8	3.47	106	.251	.333	3	.231	0	-0	2	0	0.2
1989	Atl-N	1	1	.500	15	1	0	0	0	29	26	2	16	17	13.0	4.66	78	.245	.344	0	.000	-0	-4	-3	-1	-0.3
Total	8	29	39	.426	180	76	3	1	2	633	621	59	319	387	13.6	4.25	90	.261	.351	22	.144	-1	-41	-30	-2	-3.8

● **ALFONSO PULIDO**   Pulido, Alfonso (Manzo) b: 1/23/57, Veracruz, Mexico BL/TL, 5'11", 170 lbs. Deb: 9/5/83

1983	Pit-N	0	0	—	1	1	0	0	0	2	4	2	1	1	22.5	9.00	41	.400	.455	0	—	0	-1	-1	-0	0.0
1984	Pit-N	0	0	—	1	0	0	0	0	2	3	0	1	2	18.0	9.00	40	.333	.400	0	—	0	-1	-1	-0	0.0
1986	NY-A	1	1	.500	10	3	0	0	1	30²	38	8	9	13	13.8	4.70	87	.306	.353	0	—	0	-2	-2	0	-0.1
Total	3	1	1	.500	12	4	0	0	1	34²	45	10	11	16	14.5	5.19	78	.315	.364	0	—	0	-4	-4	0	0.0

● **CARLOS PULIDO**   Pulido, Juan Carlos (Valera) b: 8/5/71, Caracas, Venez. BL/TL, 6', 195 lbs. Deb: 4/9/94

| 1994 | Min-A | 3 | 7 | .300 | 19 | 14 | 0 | 0 | 0 | 84¹ | 87 | 17 | 40 | 32 | 13.7 | 5.98 | 81 | .273 | .356 | | | 0 | -11 | -10 | -1 | -1.1 |

● **BILL PULSIPHER**   Pulsipher, William Thomas b: 10/9/73, Fort Benning, Ga. BL/TL, 6'3", 210 lbs. Deb: 6/17/95

| 1995 | NY-N | 5 | 7 | .417 | 17 | 17 | 2 | 0 | 0 | 126² | 122 | 11 | 45 | 81 | 12.2 | 3.98 | 102 | .255 | .324 | 4 | .105 | 0 | 3 | 1 | 0 | 0.1 |

● **SPENCER PUMPELLY**   Pumpelly, Spencer Armstrong b: 4/11/1893, Owego, N.Y. d: 12/5/73, Sayre, Pa. 5'11", 175 lbs. Deb: 7/11/25

| 1925 | Was-A | 0 | 0 | — | 1 | 0 | 0 | 0 | 0 | 1 | 1 | 1 | 0 | 0 | 18.0 | 9.00 | 47 | .333 | .500 | 0 | — | -0 | -1 | -0 | -0 | 0.0 |

● **BLONDIE PURCELL**   Purcell, William Aloysius b: Paterson, N.J. BR/TR, 5'9.5", 159 lbs. Deb: 5/1/1879 M♦

YEAR	TM/L	W	L	PCT	G	GS	CG	SH	SV	IP	H	HR	BB	SO	RAT	ERA	ERA+	OAV	OOB	BH	AVG	PB	PR	/A	PD	TPI
1879	Syr-N	4	15	.211	22	17	15	0	0	179²	245	1	19	28	13.2	3.76	63	.303	.319	72	.260	3	-25	-28	-3	-2.3
	Cin-N	0	2	.000	2	2	0	0	0	18	27	0	0	3	14.5	4.00	58	.355	.372	11	.220	-0	-3	-3	0	-0.3
	Yr	4	17	.190	24	19	17	0	0	197²	272	1	21	31	13.3	3.78	63	.308	.324	83	.254	3	-28	-31	-2	-2.6
1880	Cin-N	3	17	.150	25	21	21	0	0	196	235	1	32	47	12.3	3.21	77	.271	.297	95	.292	4	-18	-16	-0	-1.0
1881	Buf-N	4	1	.800	9	5	5	0	0	61²	62	2	9	15	10.4	2.77	100	.248	.274	33	.292	2	0	0	1	0.2
1882	Buf-N	2	1	.667	6	3	3	0	0	31	44	2	4	9	13.9	4.94	98	.338	.358	105	.276	1	-7	-7	1	-0.4
1883	Phi-N	2	6	.250	11	9	7	0	0	80	110	0	12	30	13.7	4.39	70	.306	.329	114	.268	2	-11	-12	1	-0.6
1884	Phi-N	0	0	—	1	0	0	0	0	4	3	1	0	4	6.8	2.25	133	.188	.188	108	.252	0	0	0	-0	0.0
1885	Phi-a	0	1	.000	1	0	0	0	0	6	11	0	2	3	19.5	6.00	57	.423	.464	90	.296	0	-2	-2	0	-0.2
1886	Bal-a	0	0	—	1	0	0	0	0	1	1	0	0	0	9.0	9.00	38	.200	.200	19	.224	-1	-1	-0	0	0.0
1887	Bal-a	0	0	—	1	0	0	0	0	1	8	0	4	2	29.3	15.75	26	.381	.500	142	.250	-5	-5	-0	0	0.0
Total	9	15	43	.259	79	57	52	0	0	581¹	746	7	84	138	12.9	3.73	70	.292	.314	1217	.267	12	-72	-73	-1	-4.6

● **JOHN PURDIN**   Purdin, John Nolan b: 7/16/42, Lynx, Ohio BR/TR, 6'2", 185 lbs. Deb: 9/16/64

1964	LA-N	2	0	1.000	3	2	1	1	0	16	6	1	6	8	7.3	0.56	576	.115	.207	1	.200	0	5	5	0	0.6
1965	LA-N	2	1	.667	11	2	0	0	0	22²	26	8	13	16	15.5	6.75	48	.283	.371	0	.000	-0	-8	-9	1	-1.2
1968	LA-N	2	3	.400	35	1	0	0	1	55²	42	2	21	38	10.2	3.07	90	.206	.280	3	.500	0	-1	-1	-0	-0.1
1969	LA-N	0	0	—	9	0	0	0	1	16¹	19	7	12	6	17.1	6.06	55	.292	.403	0	.000	-0	-4	-5	0	-0.1
Total	4	6	4	.600	58	5	1	1	2	110²	93	18	52	68	11.8	3.90	77	.225	.312	4	.250	1	-8	-11	1	-0.7

● **BOB PURKEY**   Purkey, Robert Thomas b: 7/14/29, Pittsburgh, Pa. BR/TR, 6'2", 195 lbs. Deb: 4/14/54

1954	Pit-N	3	8	.273	36	11	0	0	0	131¹	145	9	62	38	14.7	5.07	83	.293	.379	2	.077	-1	-15	-13	5	-0.6
1955	Pit-N	2	7	.222	34	11	2	0	0	67²	77	5	25	24	13.8	5.32	77	.287	.353	6	.316	2	-10	-9	1	-0.8
1956	Pit-N	0	0	—	2	0	0	0	0	4	2	1	1	1	4.5	2.25	168	.143	.143	0	—	1	1	1	0	0.0
1957	Pit-N	11	14	.440	48	21	6	1	2	179²	194	10	38	51	12.0	3.86	98	.278	.322	5	.111	-0	-1	-1	-2	-0.2
1958	Cin-N☆	17	11	.607	37	34	17	3	0	250	259	25	49	70	11.2	3.60	115	.268	.306	9	.111	-2	10	15	2	1.5

YEAR	TM/L	W	L	PCT	G	GS	CG	SH	SV	IP	H	HR	BB	SO	RAT	ERA	ERA+	OAV	OOB	BH	AVG	PB	PR	/A	PD	TPI
1959	Cin-N	13	18	.419	38	33	9	1	1	218	241	25	43	78	12.0	4.25	95	.279	.318	11	.167	3	-7	-5	-0	-0.4
1960	Cin-N	17	11	.607	41	33	11	1	0	252²	259	23	59	97	11.6	3.60	106	.265	.312	11	.133	-2	5	6	2	0.7
1961	*Cin-N★	16	12	.571	36	34	13	1	1	246¹	245	27	51	116	11.0	3.73	109	.255	.297	8	.100	-3	8	9	6	1.2
1962	Cin-N★	23	5	**.821**	37	37	18	2	0	288¹	260	28	64	141	10.6	2.81	143	.240	.291	11	.103	-2	36	**39**	3	3.6
1963	Cin-N	6	10	.375	21	21	4	1	0	137	143	12	33	55	11.7	3.55	94	.272	.318	4	.098	-1	-4	-3	1	-0.3
1964	Cin-N	11	9	.550	34	25	9	2	1	195²	181	16	49	78	10.9	3.04	119	.246	.299	3	.052	-4	11	13	2	1.0
1965	StL-N	10	9	.526	32	17	3	1	2	124¹	148	20	33	39	13.6	5.79	66	.294	.346	1	.029	-3	-31	-27	1	-4.0
1966	Pit-N	0	1	.000	10	0	0	0	0	19²	16	0	4	5	9.2	1.37	260	.235	.278	0	.000	-0	5	5	1	0.4
Total	13	129	115	.529	386	276	92	13	9	2114²	2170	195	510	793	11.7	3.79	103	.266	.315	71	.110	-13	9	30	21	2.1

● **OSCAR PURNER**   Purner, Oscar E. b: 1873, Washington, D.C.   Deb: 9/2/1895

YEAR	TM/L	W	L	PCT	G	GS	CG	SH	SV	IP	H	HR	BB	SO	RAT	ERA	ERA+	OAV	OOB	BH	AVG	PB	PR	/A	PD	TPI
1895	Was-N	0	0	—	1	0	0	0	0	2	4	1	3	0	31.5	9.00	53	.400	.538	0	.000	-0	-1	-1	-0	0.0

● **AMBROSE PUTTMANN**   Puttmann, Ambrose Nicholas "Putty" or "Brose"   b: 9/9/1880, Cincinnati, Ohio d: 6/21/36, Jamaica, N.Y. TL , 6'4", 185 lbs.   Deb: 9/4/03

YEAR	TM/L	W	L	PCT	G	GS	CG	SH	SV	IP	H	HR	BB	SO	RAT	ERA	ERA+	OAV	OOB	BH	AVG	PB	PR	/A	PD	TPI
1903	NY-A	2	0	1.000	3	2	1	0	0	19	16	0	4	8	9.9	0.95	330	.229	.280	1	.143	-0	4	5	1	0.6
1904	NY-A	2	0	1.000	9	3	2	1	0	49¹	40	0	17	26	10.4	2.74	99	.222	.289	5	.278	2	-1	-0	0	0.2
1905	NY-A	2	7	.222	17	9	5	1	1	86¹	79	2	37	39	12.6	4.27	69	.245	.332	10	.313	3	-16	-13	-0	-1.1
1906	StL-N	2	2	.500	4	4	0	0	0	18²	23	2	9	12	16.4	5.30	50	.303	.391	2	.333	-0	-6	-6	0	-1.0
Total	4	8	9	.471	33	18	8	2	1	173¹	158	4	67	85	12.1	3.58	80	.244	.322	18	.286	4	-18	-14	1	-1.3

● **JOHN PYECHA**   Pyecha, John Nicholas b: 11/25/31, Aliquippa, Pa. BR/TR, 6'5", 200 lbs.   Deb: 4/24/54

YEAR	TM/L	W	L	PCT	G	GS	CG	SH	SV	IP	H	HR	BB	SO	RAT	ERA	ERA+	OAV	OOB	BH	AVG	PB	PR	/A	PD	TPI
1954	Chi-N	0	1	.000	1	0	0	0	0	2²	4	1	2	2	20.3	10.13	41	.333	.429	0	.000	-0	-2	-2	-0	-0.5

● **HARLAN PYLE**   Pyle, Harlan Albert "Firpo" b: 11/29/05, Burchard, Neb. d: 1/13/93, Beatrice, Neb. BR/TR, 6'2", 180 lbs.   Deb: 9/21/28

YEAR	TM/L	W	L	PCT	G	GS	CG	SH	SV	IP	H	HR	BB	SO	RAT	ERA	ERA+	OAV	OOB	BH	AVG	PB	PR	/A	PD	TPI
1928	Cin-N	0	0	—	2	1	0	0	0	1¹	1	0	4	1	33.8	20.25	20	.143	.455	0	.000	-0	-2	-2	0	0.0

● **SHADOW PYLE**   Pyle, Harry Thomas b: 11/29/1861, Reading, Pa. d: 12/26/08, Reading, Pa. TL , 5'8", 136 lbs.   Deb: 10/15/1884

YEAR	TM/L	W	L	PCT	G	GS	CG	SH	SV	IP	H	HR	BB	SO	RAT	ERA	ERA+	OAV	OOB	BH	AVG	PB	PR	/A	PD	TPI
1884	Phi-N	0	1	.000	1	1	1	0	0	9	9	0	6	4	15.0	4.00	75	.257	.366	0	.000	-1	-1	-1	-0	-0.2
1887	Chi-N	1	3	.250	4	4	3	0	0	26²	32	1	21	5	18.6	4.73	95	.291	.414	3	.188	-0	-2	-1	1	-0.0
Total	2	1	4	.200	5	5	4	0	0	35²	41	1	27	9	17.7	4.54	90	.283	.402	3	.150	-1	-3	-2	1	-0.2

● **EWALD PYLE**   Pyle, Herbert Ewald "Lefty" b: 8/27/10, St.Louis, Mo. BL/TL, 6'0.5", 175 lbs.   Deb: 4/23/39

YEAR	TM/L	W	L	PCT	G	GS	CG	SH	SV	IP	H	HR	BB	SO	RAT	ERA	ERA+	OAV	OOB	BH	AVG	PB	PR	/A	PD	TPI
1939	StL-A	0	2	.000	6	1	0	0	0	8¹	17	3	11	5	30.2	12.96	38	.405	.528	0	.000	-0	-8	-7	1	-1.3
1942	StL-A	0	0	—	2	0	0	0	0	5¹	6	0	4	1	16.9	6.75	55	.286	.400	0	.000	-0	-2	-2	-0	-0.1
1943	Was-A	4	8	.333	18	11	2	1	1	72²	70	0	45	25	14.4	4.09	78	.254	.360	2	.100	-1	-6	-7	-1	-1.3
1944	NY-N	7	10	.412	31	21	3	0	0	164	152	7	68	79	12.4	4.34	85	.241	.321	8	.157	-0	-13	-12	0	-1.2
1945	NY-N	0	0	—	6	1	0	0	0	6¹	16	0	4	2	28.4	17.05	23	.457	.513	0	.000	-0	-9	-9	1	0.0
	Bos-N	0	1	.000	4	2	0	0	0	13²	16	1	18	10	22.4	7.24	53	.302	.479	2	.333	1	-5	-5	-0	-0.3
	Yr	0	1	.000	10	3	0	0	0	20	32	1	22	12	24.3	10.35	37	.364	.491	2	.250	0	-15	-14	-0	-0.3
Total	5	11	21	.344	67	36	5	1	1	270¹	277	16	150	122	14.4	5.03	71	.262	.357	12	.143	-2	-44	-43	-0	-4.2

● **TOM QUALTERS**   Qualters, Thomas Francis "Money Bags" b: 4/1/35, McKeesport, Pa. BR/TR, 6'0.5", 190 lbs.   Deb: 9/13/53

YEAR	TM/L	W	L	PCT	G	GS	CG	SH	SV	IP	H	HR	BB	SO	RAT	ERA	ERA+	OAV	OOB	BH	AVG	PB	PR	/A	PD	TPI
1953	Phi-N	0	0	—	1	0	0	0	0	0¹	4	1	1	0	162.0	162.00	3	.800	.857	0	—	0	-6	-6	0	0.0
1957	Phi-N	0	0	—	6	0	0	0	0	7¹	12	1	4	6	19.6	7.36	52	.400	.471	0	—	0	-3	-3	0	0.0
1958	Phi-N	0	0	—	1	0	0	0	0	2	2	0	1	0	13.5	4.50	88	.222	.300	0	—	0	-0	-0	-0	0.0
	Chi-A	0	0	—	26	0	0	0	0	43	45	1	20	14	13.6	4.19	87	.281	.361	0	.000	0	-2	-3	1	0.1
Total	3	0	0	—	34	0	0	0	0	52²	63	2	26	20	15.4	5.64	65	.309	.390	0	.000	0	-11	-11	1	0.1

● **PAUL QUANTRILL**   Quantrill, Paul John b: 11/3/68, London, Ont., Canada BL/TR, 6'1", 175 lbs.   Deb: 7/20/92

YEAR	TM/L	W	L	PCT	G	GS	CG	SH	SV	IP	H	HR	BB	SO	RAT	ERA	ERA+	OAV	OOB	BH	AVG	PB	PR	/A	PD	TPI
1992	Bos-A	2	3	.400	27	0	0	0	1	49¹	55	1	15	24	13.0	2.19	192	.288	.343	0	—	0	10	11	-0	1.1
1993	Bos-A	6	12	.333	49	14	1	1	1	138	151	13	44	66	12.8	3.91	118	.279	.335	0	—	0	6	11	-1	1.1
1994	Bos-A	1	1	.500	17	0	0	0	0	23	25	4	5	15	12.5	3.52	143	.278	.330	0	—	0	3	4	-0	0.0
	Phi-N	2	2	.500	18	1	0	0	0	30	39	3	10	13	15.6	6.00	71	.331	.397	0	.000	0	-6	-6	0	-0.7
1995	Phi-N	11	12	.478	33	29	0	0	0	179¹	212	20	44	103	13.1	4.67	91	.295	.341	6	.105	-2	-10	-9	1	-1.1
1996	Tor-A	5	14	.263	38	20	0	0	0	134¹	172	27	51	86	15.1	5.43	93	.316	.377	0	—	0	-6	-6	1	-0.6
Total	5	27	44	.380	182	64	1	1	3	554	654	68	169	307	13.6	4.47	102	.297	.351	6	.100	-3	-3	6	0	-0.2

● **BILL QUARLES**   Quarles, William H. b: 1869, Petersburg, Va. d: 3/25/1897, Petersburg, Va. 6'3"   Deb: 5/21/1891

YEAR	TM/L	W	L	PCT	G	GS	CG	SH	SV	IP	H	HR	BB	SO	RAT	ERA	ERA+	OAV	OOB	BH	AVG	PB	PR	/A	PD	TPI
1891	Was-a	1	1	.500	3	2	2	0	0	22	32	1	12	10	18.8	8.18	46	.330	.414	0	.000	-2	-11	-11	-0	-0.8
1893	Bos-N	2	1	.667	3	3	3	0	0	27	31	2	5	6	12.7	4.67	106	.279	.322	2	.222	-0	-1	1	-0	0.0
Total	2	3	2	.600	6	5	5	0	0	49	63	3	17	16	15.4	6.24	70	.303	.367	2	.100	-2	-11	-10	-1	-0.8

● **MEL QUEEN**   Queen, Melvin Douglas b: 3/26/42, Johnson City, N.Y. BL/TR, 6'1", 197 lbs.   Deb: 4/13/64 FC♦

YEAR	TM/L	W	L	PCT	G	GS	CG	SH	SV	IP	H	HR	BB	SO	RAT	ERA	ERA+	OAV	OOB	BH	AVG	PB	PR	/A	PD	TPI
1966	Cin-N	0	0	—	7	0	0	0	1	7	11	0	6	9	21.9	6.43	61	.367	.472	7	.127	0	-2	-2	0	-0.1
1967	Cin-N	14	8	.636	31	24	6	2	0	195²	155	17	52	154	9.8	2.76	136	.215	.273	17	.210	3	13	22	-2	2.6
1968	Cin-N	0	1	.000	5	4	0	0	0	18¹	25	7	6	20	15.2	5.89	54	.333	.383	1	.125	-0	-6	-6	0	-0.3
1969	Cin-N	1	0	1.000	2	1	0	0	0	12	7	2	3	7	8.3	2.25	167	.163	.234	1	.167	-0	2	2	-0	0.1
1970	Cal-A	3	6	.333	34	3	0	0	9	60	58	5	28	44	13.7	4.20	86	.261	.357	4	.250	-1	-3	-4	-1	-0.7
1971	Cal-A	2	2	.500	44	0	0	0	4	65²	49	3	29	53	11.8	1.78	182	.212	.321	0	.000	-1	12	11	-1	0.6
1972	Cal-A	0	0	—	17	0	0	0	0	31	31	2	19	19	15.4	4.35	67	.265	.381	0	.000	-0	-4	-5	-0	0.0
Total	7	20	17	.541	140	33	6	2	14	389²	336	36	143	306	11.6	3.14	113	.233	.313	49	.179	3	12	18	-4	2.2

● **MEL QUEEN**   Queen, Melvin Joseph b: 3/4/18, Maxwell, Pa. d: 4/4/82, Fort Smith, Ark. BR/TR, 6'0.5", 204 lbs.   Deb: 4/18/42 F

YEAR	TM/L	W	L	PCT	G	GS	CG	SH	SV	IP	H	HR	BB	SO	RAT	ERA	ERA+	OAV	OOB	BH	AVG	PB	PR	/A	PD	TPI
1942	NY-A	1	0	1.000	4	0	0	0	0	5²	6	0	3	0	17.5	0.00	—	.300	.440	0	.000	-0	3	3	-0	0.4
1944	NY-A	6	3	.667	10	10	4	1	0	81²	68	7	34	30	11.4	3.31	105	.227	.308	6	.194	0	1	2	-2	0.4
1946	NY-A	1	1	.500	14	3	1	0	0	30¹	40	2	21	26	18.1	6.53	53	.315	.412	1	.143	-0	-10	-10	-0	-0.7
1947	NY-A	0	0	—	5	0	0	0	0	6²	7	0	4	4	18.9	9.45	37	.321	.424	0	.000	-0	-4	-4	-0	0.0
	Pit-N	3	7	.300	14	12	2	0	0	74	70	8	51	34	14.8	4.01	105	.244	.360	2	.077	-2	0	2	-1	-0.1
1948	Pit-N	4	4	.500	25	8	0	0	1	66¹	82	8	40	34	17.0	6.65	61	.308	.405	1	.059	-2	-20	-19	-1	-2.2
1950	Pit-N	5	14	.263	33	21	4	0	0	120¹	135	18	73	76	15.7	5.98	73	.284	.381	2	.057	-3	-25	-21	-1	-3.2
1951	Pit-N	7	9	.438	39	21	4	1	0	168¹	149	21	99	123	13.3	4.44	95	.233	.337	5	.106	-3	-9	-4	-3	-0.9
1952	Pit-N	0	2	.000	2	2	0	0	0	3¹	10	0	4	3	32.4	29.70	13	.381	.480	0	—	0	-10	-10	-0	-2.6
Total	8	27	40	.403	146	77	15	3	1	556²	567	68	329	328	14.7	5.09	80	.262	.362	17	.104	-10	-74	-63	-9	-9.3

● **EDDIE QUICK**   Quick, Edward b: 12/1881, Baltimore, Md. d: 6/19/13, Rocky Ford, Colo. TR , 5'11"   Deb: 9/28/03

YEAR	TM/L	W	L	PCT	G	GS	CG	SH	SV	IP	H	HR	BB	SO	RAT	ERA	ERA+	OAV	OOB	BH	AVG	PB	PR	/A	PD	TPI
1903	NY-A	0	0	—	1	1	0	0	0	2	5	0	4	0	27.0	9.00	35	.455	.500	0	.000	-0	-1	-1	0	0.0

● **TAD QUINN**   Quinn, Clarence Carr b: 9/21/1882, Torrington, Conn. d: 8/6/46, Waterbury, Conn. TR , 6'1", 210 lbs.   Deb: 9/27/02

YEAR	TM/L	W	L	PCT	G	GS	CG	SH	SV	IP	H	HR	BB	SO	RAT	ERA	ERA+	OAV	OOB	BH	AVG	PB	PR	/A	PD	TPI
1902	Phi-A	0	1	.000	2	1	1	0	0	8	12	1	4	3	14.6	4.50	82	.343	.361	0	.000	-0	-1	-1	-0	-0.1
1903	Phi-N	0	0	—	3	0	0	0	0	9	11	0	5	1	17.0	5.00	77	.297	.395	2	.667	1	-2	-1	1	0.2
Total	2	0	1	.000	5	1	1	0	0	17	23	1	9	4	15.9	4.76	70	.319	.380	2	.333	1	-3	-3	0	0.1

● **FRANK QUINN**   Quinn, Frank William b: 11/27/27, Springfield, Mass. d: 1/11/93, Boynton Beach, Fla. BR/TR, 6'2", 180 lbs.   Deb: 5/29/49

YEAR	TM/L	W	L	PCT	G	GS	CG	SH	SV	IP	H	HR	BB	SO	RAT	ERA	ERA+	OAV	OOB	BH	AVG	PB	PR	/A	PD	TPI
1949	Bos-A	0	0	—	8	0	0	0	0	22	18	2	9	4	11.5	2.86	152	.222	.308	1	.167	-0	3	4	-0	0.3
1950	Bos-A	0	0	—	1	0	0	0	0	2	2	0	1	0	13.5	9.00	54	.250	.333	0	—	0	-1	-1	0	0.0
Total	2	0	0	—	9	0	0	0	0	24	20	2	10	4	11.6	3.38	131	.225	.310	1	.167	-0	3	3	0	0.0

● **JACK QUINN**   Quinn, John Picus (b: John Quinn Picus) b: 7/5/1883, Janesville, Pa. d: 4/17/46, Pottsville, Pa. BR/TR, 6', 196 lbs.   Deb: 4/15/09

YEAR	TM/L	W	L	PCT	G	GS	CG	SH	SV	IP	H	HR	BB	SO	RAT	ERA	ERA+	OAV	OOB	BH	AVG	PB	PR	/A	PD	TPI
1909	NY-A	9	5	.643	23	11	8	0	1	118²	110	1	24	36	10.5	1.97	128	.252	.297	7	.156	0	7	7	3	1.3
1910	NY-A	18	12	.600	35	31	20	0	0	235²	214	2	58	82	10.6	2.37	112	.247	.299	19	.232	4	4	8	7	2.2
1911	NY-A	8	10	.444	40	16	7	0	2	174²	203	8	41	71	12.8	3.76	96	.297	.341	10	.164	-1	-8	-3	3	-0.1
1912	NY-A	5	7	.417	18	11	7	0	0	102²	139	4	23	47	14.6	5.79	62	.325	.365	8	.205	-1	-28	-25	2	-2.3

YEAR	TM/L	W	L	PCT	G	GS	CG	SH	SV	IP	H	HR	BB	SO	RAT	ERA	ERA+	OAV	OOB	BH	AVG	PB	PR	/A	PD	TPI
1913	Bos-N	4	3	.571	8	7	6	1	0	56¹	55	1	7	33	10.1	2.40	137	.261	.288	4	.200	1	5	6	2	1.1
1914	Bal-F	26	14	.650	46	42	27	4	1	342¹	335	3	65	164	10.7	2.60	117	.266	.307	33	.273	6	11	16	1	0.7
1915	Bal-F	9	22	.290	44	31	21	0	1	273²	289	9	63	118	11.8	3.45	83	.278	.325	29	.264	3	-22	-18	3	-1.2
1918	Chi-A	5	1	.833	6	5	5	0	0	51	38	0	7	22	7.9	2.29	119	.216	.246	4	.222	1	3	3	0	0.5
1919	NY-A	15	14	.517	38	31	18	4	0	266	242	8	65	97	10.6	2.61	123	.244	.295	19	.209	1	18	17	1	2.0
1920	NY-A	18	10	.643	41	32	17	2	3	253¹	271	8	48	101	11.4	3.20	119	.273	.308	8	.091	-5	17	18	3	1.5
1921	*NY-A	8	7	.533	33	13	6	0	0	119	158	7	32	44	14.7	3.78	112	.327	.375	9	.220	1	7	6	1	0.8
1922	Bos-A	13	16	.448	40	32	16	4	0	256	263	9	59	67	11.4	3.48	118	.267	.311	9	.099	-5	16	18	5	1.8
1923	Bos-A	13	17	.433	42	28	16	1	7	243	302	6	53	71	13.4	3.89	106	.316	.356	18	.225	0	3	6	-1	0.6
1924	Bos-A	12	13	.480	44	25	13	2	7	228²	241	10	52	64	12.0	3.27	134	.273	.322	14	.179	-4	24	28	4	2.9
1925	Bos-A	7	8	.467	19	15	8	0	0	105	140	3	26	24	14.5	4.37	104	.315	.357	3	.094	-2	0	2	2	0.2
	Phi-A	6	3	.667	18	13	4	0	0	99²	119	3	16	19	12.5	3.88	120	.296	.328	3	.097	-3	6	8	1	0.5
	Yr	13	11	.542	37	28	12	0	0	204²	259	6	42	43	13.4	4.13	111	.305	.340	6	.095	-5	6	11	3	0.7
1926	Phi-A	10	11	.476	31	21	8	3	1	163²	191	4	36	58	12.5	3.41	122	.296	.334	8	.174	-0	11	14	1	1.7
1927	Phi-A	15	10	.600	34	25	11	3	1	201¹	211	8	37	43	11.3	3.26	131	.278	.315	6	.091	-7	20	22	-1	1.7
1928	Phi-A	18	7	.720	31	28	18	4	1	211¹	239	8	34	43	11.9	2.90	139	.286	.320	13	.165	-3	27	26	1	2.6
1929	*Phi-A	11	9	.550	35	18	7	0	2	161	182	8	39	41	12.4	3.97	107	.290	.332	8	.133	-4	5	5	0	0.7
1930	*Phi-A	9	7	.563	35	7	0	0	6	89²	109	6	22	28	13.2	4.42	106	.302	.344	9	.265	1	**2**	**3**	2	0.7
1931	Bro-N	5	4	.556	39	1	0	0	**15**	64¹	65	1	24	25	12.6	2.66	143	.266	.335	3	.200	0	9	8	1	1.6
1932	Bro-N	3	7	.300	42	0	0	0	**8**	87¹	102	1	24	28	13.1	3.30	116	.296	.343	4	.200	0	**6**	**5**	0	0.7
1933	Cin-N	0	1	.000	14	0	0	0	1	15²	20	1	5	3	14.4	4.02	84	.323	.373	0	.000	-0	-1	-1	1	0.0
Total	23	247	218	.531	756	443	243	28	57	3920¹	4238	102	860	1329	11.9	3.29	113	.280	.323	248	.184	-16	140	182	40	23.6

● **WIMPY QUINN**   Quinn, Wellington Hunt   b: 5/12/18, Birmingham, Ala.   d: 9/1/54, Santa Monica, Cal.   BR/TR, 6'2", 187 lbs.   Deb: 6/8/41

YEAR	TM/L	W	L	PCT	G	GS	CG	SH	SV	IP	H	HR	BB	SO	RAT	ERA	ERA+	OAV	OOB	BH	AVG	PB	PR	/A	PD	TPI
1941	Chi-N	0	0	—	3	0	0	0	0	5	3	0	3	2	10.8	7.20	49	.158	.273	1	.500	0	-2	-2	-0	0.0

● **LUIS QUINTANA**   Quintana, Luis Joaquin (Santos)   b: 12/25/51, Vega Baja, P.R.   BL/TL, 6'2", 175 lbs.   Deb: 7/9/74

YEAR	TM/L	W	L	PCT	G	GS	CG	SH	SV	IP	H	HR	BB	SO	RAT	ERA	ERA+	OAV	OOB	BH	AVG	PB	PR	/A	PD	TPI
1974	Cal-A	2	1	.667	18	0	0	0	0	12²	17	0	14	11	22.0	4.26	81	.337	.470	0	—	0	-1	-1	-0	0.0
1975	Cal-A	0	2	.000	4	0	0	0	0	7	13	2	6	5	24.4	6.43	55	.394	.487	0	—	0	-2	-2	-0	-0.6
Total	2	2	3	.400	22	0	0	0	0	19²	30	2	20	16	22.9	5.03	69	.353	.476	0	—	0	-3	-3	-0	-0.6

● **RAFAEL QUIRICO**   Quirico, Rafael Octavio (Dottin)   b: 9/7/69, Santo Domingo, D.R.   BL/TL, 6'3", 170 lbs.   Deb: 6/25/96

YEAR	TM/L	W	L	PCT	G	GS	CG	SH	SV	IP	H	HR	BB	SO	RAT	ERA	ERA+	OAV	OOB	BH	AVG	PB	PR	/A	PD	TPI
1996	Phi-N	0	1	.000	1	1	0	0	0	1²	4	1	5	1	48.6	37.80	12	.444	.643	0	—	0	-6	-6	0	-1.5

● **ART QUIRK**   Quirk, Arthur Lincoln   b: 4/11/38, Providence, R.I.   BR/TL, 5'11", 170 lbs.   Deb: 4/17/62

YEAR	TM/L	W	L	PCT	G	GS	CG	SH	SV	IP	H	HR	BB	SO	RAT	ERA	ERA+	OAV	OOB	BH	AVG	PB	PR	/A	PD	TPI
1962	Bal-A	2	2	.500	7	5	0	0	0	27¹	36	3	18	18	17.8	5.93	62	.308	.400	1	.143	0	-6	-7	1	-0.8
1963	Was-A	1	0	1.000	7	3	0	0	0	21	23	3	8	12	13.3	4.29	87	.280	.344	1	.250	0	-2	-1	-0	-0.1
Total	2	3	2	.600	14	8	0	0	0	48¹	59	6	26	30	15.8	5.21	71	.296	.378	2	.182	0	-7	-8	0	-0.9

● **DAN QUISENBERRY**   Quisenberry, Daniel Raymond   b: 2/7/53, Santa Monica, Cal.   BR/TR, 6'2", 180 lbs.   Deb: 7/8/79

YEAR	TM/L	W	L	PCT	G	GS	CG	SH	SV	IP	H	HR	BB	SO	RAT	ERA	ERA+	OAV	OOB	BH	AVG	PB	PR	/A	PD	TPI
1979	KC-A	3	2	.600	32	0	0	0	5	40	42	5	7	13	11.0	3.15	135	.278	.310	0	—	0	5	5	1	0.7
1980	*KC-A	12	7	.632	**75**	0	0	0	**33**	128¹	129	5	27	37	11.0	3.09	131	.265	.305	0	—	0	14	14	3	2.9
1981	*KC-A	1	4	.200	40	0	0	0	18	62¹	59	1	15	20	10.8	1.73	208	.258	.306	0	—	0	13	13	3	2.2
1982	KC-A★	9	7	.563	72	0	0	0	**35**	136²	126	12	12	46	9.1	2.57	159	.252	.270	0	—	0	23	23	6	4.5
1983	KC-A★	5	3	.625	**69**	0	0	0	**45**	139	118	6	11	48	8.4	1.94	210	.229	.245	0	—	0	**33**	**33**	2	4.2
1984	*KC-A☆	6	3	.667	72	0	0	0	**44**	129¹	121	10	12	41	9.3	2.64	152	.247	.265	0	—	0	19	20	3	2.9
1985	*KC-A	8	9	.471	**84**	0	0	0	37	129	142	8	16	54	11.1	2.37	175	.280	.303	0	—	0	25	26	1	4.6
1986	KC-A	3	7	.300	62	0	0	0	12	81¹	92	2	24	36	13.2	2.77	154	.291	.347	0	—	0	13	13	2	2.0
1987	KC-A	4	1	.800	47	0	0	0	8	49	58	3	10	17	12.7	2.76	165	.287	.324	0	—	0	9	10	2	1.3
1988	KC-A	0	1	.000	20	0	0	0	1	25¹	32	0	5	9	13.1	3.55	112	.305	.336	0	—	0	1	1	1	0.1
	StL-N	2	0	1.000	33	0	0	0	0	38	54	4	6	19	14.2	6.16	56	.344	.368	0	.000	0	-11	-11	0	-0.5
1989	StL-N	3	1	.750	63	0	0	0	6	78¹	78	2	14	37	10.6	2.64	137	.261	.294	1	.250	0	7	9	2	0.8
1990	SF-N	0	1	.000	5	0	0	0	0	6²	13	1	3	2	21.6	13.50	27	.419	.471	0	—	-0	-7	-7	-0	-0.9
Total	12	56	46	.549	674	0	0	0	244	1043¹	1064	59	162	379	10.6	2.76	146	.267	.297	1	.167	0	144	147	25	24.8

● **CHARLIE RABE**   Rabe, Charles Henry   b: 5/6/32, Boyce, Tex.   BL/TL, 6'1", 180 lbs.   Deb: 9/21/57

YEAR	TM/L	W	L	PCT	G	GS	CG	SH	SV	IP	H	HR	BB	SO	RAT	ERA	ERA+	OAV	OOB	BH	AVG	PB	PR	/A	PD	TPI
1957	Cin-N	0	1	.000	2	1	0	0	0	8¹	5	2	0	6	5.4	2.16	190	.167	.167	0	.000	-0	2	1	-0	0.1
1958	Cin-N	0	3	.000	9	1	0	0	0	18²	25	3	9	10	16.4	4.34	96	.321	.391	0	.000	-1	-1	-0	0	-0.1
Total	2	0	4	.000	11	2	0	0	0	27	30	5	9	16	13.0	3.67	113	.278	.333	0	.000	-1	1	0	0	0.0

● **STEVE RACHUNOK**   Rachunok, Stephen Stepanovich "The Mad Russian"   b: 12/5/16, Rittman, Ohio   BR/TR, 6'4.5", 205 lbs.   Deb: 9/17/40

YEAR	TM/L	W	L	PCT	G	GS	CG	SH	SV	IP	H	HR	BB	SO	RAT	ERA	ERA+	OAV	OOB	BH	AVG	PB	PR	/A	PD	TPI
1940	Bro-N	0	1	.000	4	0	0	0	0	9²	9	0	5	4	12.6	4.50	89	.243	.333	0	.000	0	-1	-1	0	0.1

● **MIKE RACZKA**   Raczka, Michael   b: 11/16/62, New Britain, Conn.   BL/TL, 6', 200 lbs.   Deb: 8/15/92

YEAR	TM/L	W	L	PCT	G	GS	CG	SH	SV	IP	H	HR	BB	SO	RAT	ERA	ERA+	OAV	OOB	BH	AVG	PB	PR	/A	PD	TPI
1992	Oak-A	0	0	—	8	0	0	0	0	6¹	8	0	5	2	18.5	8.53	44	.308	.419	0	—	0	-3	-3	-0	0.1

● **DICK RADATZ**   Radatz, Richard Raymond "The Monster"   b: 4/2/37, Detroit, Mich.   BR/TR, 6'5", 235 lbs.   Deb: 4/10/62

YEAR	TM/L	W	L	PCT	G	GS	CG	SH	SV	IP	H	HR	BB	SO	RAT	ERA	ERA+	OAV	OOB	BH	AVG	PB	PR	/A	PD	TPI
1962	Bos-A	9	6	.600	**62**	0	0	0	24	124²	95	9	40	144	10.4	2.24	184	.211	.281	3	.097	-2	**24**	**26**	-2	3.7
1963	Bos-A★	15	6	.714	66	0	0	0	25	132¹	94	9	51	162	10.2	1.97	192	.201	.286	2	.069	-2	**24**	**27**	-2	**5.0**
1964	Bos-A★	16	9	.640	79	0	0	0	**29**	157	103	13	58	181	9.6	2.29	168	.186	.271	6	.162	-0	23	27	-2	**5.1**
1965	Bos-A	9	11	.450	63	0	0	0	22	124¹	104	11	53	121	11.7	3.91	95	.227	.314	5	.185	1	-6	-5	-1	-0.4
1966	Bos-A	0	2	.000	16	0	0	0	4	19	24	3	11	19	16.6	4.74	80	.304	.389	0	.000	-0	-3	-2	-1	-0.4
	Cle-A	0	3	.000	39	0	0	0	10	56²	49	6	34	49	13.7	4.61	75	.233	.348	1	.111	-1	-7	-7	-1	-0.9
	Yr	0	5	.000	55	0	0	0	14	75²	73	9	45	68	14.4	4.64	76	.253	.359	1	.091	-1	-10	-9	-2	-1.2
1967	Cle-A	0	0	—	3	0	0	0	0	3	5	1	2	1	21.0	6.00	54	.357	.438	0	—	0	-1	-0	-0	0.0
	Chi-N	1	0	1.000	20	0	0	0	5	23¹	17	4	24	18	15.8	6.56	54	.154	.383	1	.250	0	-8	-8	-0	-0.7
1969	Det-A	2	2	.500	11	0	0	0	0	18²	14	3	5	18	9.2	3.38	111	.212	.268	0	.000	0	1	1	0	0.1
	Mon-N	0	4	.000	22	0	0	0	0	34²	32	6	18	32	13.2	5.71	64	.244	.340	1	.250	-1	-8	-8	-1	-1.0
Total	7	52	43	.547	381	0	0	0	122	693²	532	65	296	745	11.1	3.13	122	.212	.303	19	.131	-3	38	53	-9	10.6

● **CHARLEY RADBOURN**   Radbourn, Charles Gardner "Old Hoss"
b: 12/11/1854, Rochester, N.Y.   d: 2/5/1897, Bloomington, Ill.   BR/TR, 5'9", 168 lbs.   Deb: 5/5/1880   H♦

YEAR	TM/L	W	L	PCT	G	GS	CG	SH	SV	IP	H	HR	BB	SO	RAT	ERA	ERA+	OAV	OOB	BH	AVG	PB	PR	/A	PD	TPI
1881	Pro-N	25	11	**.694**	41	36	34	3	0	325¹	309	1	64	117	10.3	2.43	109	**.235**	.270	59	.219	-1	12	8	3	0.9
1882	Pro-N	33	20	.623	55	52	51	**6**	0	474	429	6	51	201	9.1	2.09	135	.226	.246	78	.239	-1	**43**	**38**	1	**3.4**
1883	Pro-N	**48**	25	.658	76	68	66	7	0	632¹	563	7	56	315	8.8	2.05	151	.227	**.244**	108	.283	14	76	73	5	8.4
1884	*Pro-N	**59**	12	**.831**	75	73	**73**	11	1	678²	528	18	98	**441**	8.3	**1.38**	**205**	.205	.234	83	.230	6	121	109	-4	**9.8**
1885	Pro-N	28	21	.571	49	49	49	2	0	445²	423	4	83	154	10.2	2.20	120	.241	.275	58	.233	12	31	22	4	3.5
1886	Bos-N	27	31	.466	58	58	57	3	0	509¹	521	18	111	218	11.2	3.00	106	.254	.292	60	.237	8	17	11	2	1.9
1887	Bos-N	24	23	.511	50	50	48	1	0	425	505	20	133	87	13.8	4.55	89	.286	.340	40	.229	1	-23	-23	-3	-2.1
1888	Bos-N	7	16	.304	24	24	24	1	0	207	187	8	45	64	10.4	2.87	99	.234	.282	17	.215	1	-0	-0	-1	-0.1
1889	Bos-N	20	11	.645	33	31	28	1	0	277	282	14	72	99	11.8	3.67	113	.256	.306	23	.189	-1	11	15	2	1.4
1890	Bos-P	27	12	.692	41	38	36	1	0	343	352	8	100	80	12.1	3.31	133	.254	.309	39	.253	0	35	42	3	3.7
1891	Cin-N	11	13	.458	26	24	23	2	0	218¹	227	13	62	35	12.8	4.25	79	.266	.323	17	.171	-1	-22	-21	-3	-2.1
Total	11	309	195	.613	528	503	489	35	2	4535¹	4335	117	875	1830	10.4	2.67	120	.241	.278	585	.235	40	302	267	7	28.7

● **GEORGE RADBOURN**   Radbourn, George B. "Dordy"   b: 4/8/1856, Bloomington, Ill.   d: 1/1/04, Bloomington, Ill.   160 lbs.   Deb: 5/30/1883

YEAR	TM/L	W	L	PCT	G	GS	CG	SH	SV	IP	H	HR	BB	SO	RAT	ERA	ERA+	OAV	OOB	BH	AVG	PB	PR	/A	PD	TPI
1883	Det-N	1	2	.333	3	3	2	0	0	22	38	1	2	2	18.4	6.55	47	.345	.385	2	.167	-1	-8	-8	-0	-0.8

● **ROY RADEBAUGH**   Radebaugh, Roy   b: 2/22/1884, Champaign, Ill.   d: 1/17/45, Cedar Rapids, Iowa   BR/TR, 5'7", 160 lbs.   Deb: 9/22/11

YEAR	TM/L	W	L	PCT	G	GS	CG	SH	SV	IP	H	HR	BB	SO	RAT	ERA	ERA+	OAV	OOB	BH	AVG	PB	PR	/A	PD	TPI
1911	StL-N	0	0	—	2	1	0	0	0	10	6	0	4	1	9.0	2.70	125	.176	.263	0	.000	-0	1	1	0	0.0

YEAR	TM/L	W	L	PCT	G	GS	CG	SH	SV	IP	H	HR	BB	SO	RAT	ERA	ERA+	OAV	OOB	BH	AVG	PB	PR	/A	PD	TPI

● DREW RADER   Rader, Drew Leon "Lefty" b: 5/14/01, Elmira, N.Y. d: 6/5/75, Catskill, N.Y. BR/TL, 6'2", 187 lbs. Deb: 7/18/21

| 1921 | Pit-N | 0 | 0 | — | 1 | 0 | 0 | 0 | 0 | 2 | 2 | 0 | 0 | 0 | 9.0 | 0.00 | — | .286 | .286 | 0 | .000 | -0 | 1 | 1 | -0 | 0.0 |

● PAUL RADFORD   Radford, Paul Revere "Shorty" b: 10/14/1861, Roxbury, Mass. d: 2/21/45, Boston, Mass. BR/TR, 5'6", 148 lbs. Deb: 5/1/1883 ◆

1884	*Pro-N	0	2	.000	2	2	1	0	0	13	27	0	3	2	20.8	7.62	37	.403	.429	70	.197	-0	-7	-7	-0	-0.7
1885	*Pro-N	0	2	.000	3	2	2	0	0	18¹	34	1	8	3	20.6	7.85	34	.378	.429	90	.243	1	-10	-11	0	-0.8
1887	NY-a	0	0	—	2	0	0	0	0	5	15	1	3	4	32.4	18.00	24	.789	.818	129	.265	1	-8	-8	-0	0.0
1890	Cle-P	0	0	—	1	0	0	0	0	5	7	1	1	3	14.4	3.60	110	.318	.348	136	.292	0	0	0	1	0.1
1891	Bos-a	0	0	—	1	0	0	0	0	1	0	0	0	0	0.0	0.00	—	.000	.000	118	.259	0	0	0	0	0.0
1893	Was-N	0	0	—	1	0	0	0	0	1	2	2	2	1	36.0	18.00	26	.400	.571	106	.228	0	-1	-1	0	0.0
Total	6	0	4	.000	10	4	3	0	0	43¹	85	5	17	13	21.2	8.52	36	.413	.457	1206	.242	2	-25	-26	0	-1.4

● SCOTT RADINSKY   Radinsky, Scott David b: 3/3/68, Glendale, Cal. BL/TL, 6'3", 190 lbs. Deb: 4/9/90

1990	Chi-A	6	1	.857	62	0	0	0	4	52¹	47	1	36	46	14.6	4.82	79	.241	.365	0	—	0	-5	-6	0	-0.7
1991	Chi-A	5	5	.500	67	0	0	0	8	71¹	53	4	23	49	9.7	2.02	197	.206	.274	0	—	0	16	15	1	2.4
1992	Chi-A	3	7	.300	68	0	0	0	15	59¹	54	3	34	48	13.7	2.73	141	.243	.349	0	—	0	8	7	0	1.6
1993	*Chi-A	8	2	.800	73	0	0	0	4	54²	61	3	19	44	13.3	4.28	98	.268	.327	0	—	0	-1	0	0	0.0
1995	Chi-A	2	1	.667	46	0	0	0	0	38	46	7	17	14	14.9	5.45	82	.309	.380	0	—	0	-3	-4	0	-0.3
1996	*LA-N	5	1	.833	58	0	0	0	2	52¹	52	1	17	48	11.9	2.41	160	.264	.322	0	.000	-0	11	8	0	0.9
Total	6	29	17	.630	374	0	0	0	33	328	313	20	146	249	12.8	3.43	117	.251	.332	0	.000	-0	27	21	1	3.9

● BRAD RADKE   Radke, Brad William b: 10/27/72, Eau Claire, Wis. BR/TR, 6'2", 180 lbs. Deb: 4/29/95

1995	Min-A	11	14	.440	29	28	2	1	0	181	195	32	47	75	12.2	5.32	90	.275	.323	0	—	0	-12	-11	-1	-1.3
1996	Min-A	11	16	.407	35	35	3	0	0	232	231	40	57	148	11.3	4.46	115	.256	.304	0	—	0	14	17	-3	1.5
Total	2	22	30	.423	64	63	5	1	0	413	426	72	104	223	11.7	4.84	103	.264	.312	0	—	0	1	6	-3	0.2

● HAL RAETHER   Raether, Harold Herman "Bud" b: 10/10/32, Lake Mills, Wis. BR/TR, 6'1", 185 lbs. Deb: 7/4/54

1954	Phi-A	0	0	—	1	0	0	0	0	2	1	0	4	0	22.5	4.50	87	.200	.556	0	—	0	-0	-0	-0	0.0
1957	KC-A	0	0	—	1	0	0	0	0	2	2	1	0	0	9.0	9.00	44	.250	.250	0	—	0	-1	-1	-0	0.0
Total	2	0	0	—	2	0	0	0	0	4	3	1	4	0	15.8	6.75	58	.231	.412	0	—	0	-1	-1	-0	0.0

● KEN RAFFENSBERGER   Raffensberger, Kenneth David b: 8/8/17, York, Pa. BR/TL, 6'2", 185 lbs. Deb: 4/25/39

1939	StL-N	0	0	—	1	0	0	0	0	1	2	0	1	0	18.0	0.00	—	.400	.400	0	—	0	0	0	0	0.0
1940	Chi-N	7	9	.438	43	10	3	0	3	114²	120	10	29	55	11.9	3.38	111	.271	.319	5	.167	-1	6	5	-1	0.5
1941	Chi-N	0	1	.000	10	1	0	0	0	18	17	0	7	5	12.0	4.50	78	.262	.333	0	.000	-1	-2	-2	1	-0.1
1943	Phi-N	0	1	.000	1	1	0	0	0	8	7	0	2	3	10.1	1.13	300	.241	.290	0	.000	-0	2	2	-0	0.2
1944	Phi-N★	13	20	.394	37	31	18	3	0	258²	257	9	45	136	10.6	3.06	118	.252	.285	11	.138	-3	16	16	-3	1.3
1945	Phi-N	0	3	.000	5	4	1	0	0	24¹	28	3	14	6	15.5	4.44	86	.283	.372	0	.000	-1	-2	-2	0	-0.3
1946	Phi-N	8	15	.348	39	23	14	2	6	196	203	10	39	73	11.2	3.63	95	.265	.302	10	.167	-1	-5	-4	-3	-0.8
1947	Phi-N	2	6	.250	10	7	3	1	0	41	50	4	8	16	13.0	5.49	73	.307	.343	4	.267	-1	-7	-7	1	-1.0
	Cin-N	6	5	.545	19	15	7	0	1	106²	132	11	29	38	13.6	4.13	99	.305	.348	6	.162	-1	-1	-0	-1	-0.2
	Yr	8	11	.421	29	22	10	1	1	147²	182	15	37	54	13.3	4.51	90	.305	.345	10	.192	-0	-7	-7	0	-1.2
1948	Cin-N	11	12	.478	40	24	7	4	0	180¹	187	15	37	57	11.2	3.84	102	.259	.296	7	.113	-3	2	1	-2	-0.3
1949	Cin-N	18	17	.514	41	38	20	5	0	284	289	23	80	103	11.8	3.39	123	.264	.315	16	.178	0	21	25	-3	2.6
1950	Cin-N	14	19	.424	38	35	18	4	0	239	271	34	40	87	11.8	4.26	100	.279	.308	11	.134	-2	-3	-1	-2	-0.4
1951	Cin-N	16	17	.485	42	33	14	5	5	248²	232	30	28	81	**10.0**	3.44	119	.246	.279	10	.122	-3	14	18	-4	1.5
1952	Cin-N	17	13	.567	38	33	18	**6**	1	247	247	18	45	93	10.7	2.81	134	.261	.295	8	.107	-2	25	27	-2	2.7
1953	Cin-N	7	14	.333	26	26	9	1	0	174	200	23	33	47	12.1	3.93	111	.289	.322	8	.140	-1	7	8	2	0.9
1954	Cin-N	0	2	.000	6	1	0	0	0	10¹	15	2	3	5	15.7	7.84	53	.333	.375	1	.500	-1	-4	-4	0	-0.7
Total	15	119	154	.436	396	282	133	31	16	2151²	2257	192	449	806	11.4	3.60	110	.267	.306	97	.141	-17	71	82	-18	5.9

● AL RAFFO   Raffo, Albert Martin b: 11/27/41, San Francisco, Cal. BR/TR, 6'5", 210 lbs. Deb: 4/29/69

| 1969 | Phi-N | 1 | 3 | .250 | 45 | 0 | 0 | 0 | 1 | 72¹ | 81 | 6 | 25 | 38 | 13.7 | 4.11 | 86 | .286 | .353 | 1 | .167 | 0 | -4 | -5 | 1 | -0.2 |

● PAT RAGAN   Ragan, Don Carlos Patrick b: 11/15/1888, Blanchard, Iowa d: 9/4/56, Los Angeles, Cal. BR/TR, 5'10.5", 185 lbs. Deb: 4/21/09 C

1909	Cin-N	0	1	.000	2	0	0	0	0	8	7	0	4	2	12.4	3.38	77	.259	.355	1	.500	-1	-1	-1	-0	-0.1
	Chi-N	0	0	—	2	0	0	0	0	3²	4	0	1	2	12.3	2.45	104	.286	.333	0	.000	-0	0	0	-0	0.0
	Yr	0	1	.000	4	0	0	0	0	11²	11	0	5	4	12.3	3.09	84	.268	.348	1	.250	0	-1	-1	-0	-0.1
1911	Bro-N	4	3	.571	22	7	5	1	1	93²	87	0	31	39	11.0	2.11	158	.252	.321	4	.138	-1	13	13	-1	0.7
1912	Bro-N	7	18	.280	36	26	12	1	1	208	211	7	65	101	12.1	3.63	92	.270	.329	4	.060	-7	-5	-7	-1	-1.5
1913	Bro-N	15	18	.455	44	32	14	0	0	264²	284	10	64	109	12.0	3.77	87	.281	.327	15	.165	-2	-17	-14	2	-1.7
1914	Bro-N	10	15	.400	38	26	14	1	3	208¹	214	5	85	106	13.0	2.98	96	.270	.343	10	.133	-3	-4	-3	0	-0.7
1915	Bro-N	1	0	1.000	5	0	0	0	0	19²	11	0	8	7	8.7	0.92	304	.164	.253	1	.167	0	4	4	0	0.3
	Bos-N	16	12	.571	33	26	13	3	0	227	208	2	59	81	10.9	2.46	105	.255	.311	12	.150	-0	7	3	-2	0.0
	Yr	17	12	.586	38	26	13	3	0	246²	219	2	67	88	10.7	2.34	112	.248	.306	13	.151	-1	11	7	-2	0.1
1916	Bos-N	9	9	.500	28	23	14	3	0	182	143	3	47	94	9.4	2.08	120	.218	.270	13	.217	3	11	8	1	1.3
1917	Bos-N	6	9	.400	30	13	5	1	1	147²	138	1	35	61	10.6	2.93	87	.250	.295	6	.125	-1	-4	-6	-0	-0.8
1918	Bos-N	8	17	.320	30	25	15	2	0	206¹	212	4	54	68	11.8	3.23	83	.270	.320	13	.183	-2	-11	-12	-0	-1.6
1919	Bos-N	0	2	.000	4	3	0	0	0	12²	16	0	3	3	13.5	7.11	40	.281	.317	1	.250	0	-6	-6	0	-0.8
	NY-N	1	0	1.000	7	1	1	0	0	22²	19	0	14	7	13.1	1.59	177	.247	.363	3	.429	1	3	3	0	0.3
	Yr	1	2	.333	11	4	1	0	0	35¹	35	0	17	10	13.2	3.57	79	.261	.344	4	.364	1	-3	-3	0	-0.5
	Chi-A	0	0	—	1	0	0	0	0	1	1	0	0	0	9.0	0.00	—	.250	.250	0	—	0	0	0	0	0.0
1923	Phi-N	0	0	—	3	0	0	0	0	3	6	1	0	0	18.0	6.00	77	.400	.400	1	.500	0	-1	-0	-0	0.0
Total	11	77	104	.425	283	182	93	12	6	1608¹	1555	38	470	680	11.5	2.99	97	.260	.317	84	.154	-13	-8	-18	-2	-4.8

● FRANK RAGLAND   Ragland, Frank Roland b: 5/26/04, Water Valley, Miss. d: 7/28/59, Paris, Miss. BR/TR, 6'1", 186 lbs. Deb: 4/17/32

1932	Was-A	1	0	1.000	12	1	0	0	0	37²	54	5	21	11	18.6	7.41	58	.346	.433	3	.273	1	-12	-13	0	-0.2
1933	Phi-N	0	4	.000	11	5	0	0	0	38¹	51	1	10	4	14.6	6.81	56	.317	.360	2	.200	-0	-15	-13	1	-1.1
Total	2	1	4	.200	23	6	0	0	0	76	105	6	31	15	16.6	7.11	58	.331	.398	5	.238	1	-27	-25	1	-1.3

● ERIC RAICH   Raich, Eric James b: 11/1/51, Detroit, Mich. BR/TR, 6'4", 225 lbs. Deb: 5/24/75

1975	Cle-A	7	8	.467	18	17	2	0	0	92²	118	12	31	34	14.6	5.54	68	.320	.374	0	—	0	-18	-18	-1	-2.6
1976	Cle-A	0	0	—	1	0	0	0	0	2²	7	1	0	1	23.6	16.88	21	.467	.467	0	—	0	-4	-4	-0	0.0
Total	2	7	8	.467	19	17	2	0	0	95¹	125	13	31	35	14.8	5.85	64	.326	.377	0	—	0	-22	-22	-1	-2.6

● CHUCK RAINEY   Rainey, Charles David b: 7/14/54, San Diego, Cal. BR/TR, 5'11", 190 lbs. Deb: 4/8/79

1979	Bos-A	8	5	.615	20	16	4	1	1	103²	97	7	41	41	12.2	3.82	116	.250	.326	0	—	0	5	7	1	0.8
1980	Bos-A	8	3	.727	16	13	2	1	0	87	92	7	41	42	14.6	4.86	87	.273	.355	0	—	0	-8	-6	-1	-0.8
1981	Bos-A	0	1	.000	11	2	0	0	0	40	39	2	13	20	11.7	2.70	143	.252	.310	0	—	0	4	5	1	0.4
1982	Bos-A	7	5	.583	27	25	3	3	0	129	146	14	58	57	14.7	5.02	86	.294	.376	0	—	0	-14	-10	1	-0.8
1983	Chi-N	14	13	.519	34	34	1	1	0	191	219	17	74	84	13.9	4.48	85	.295	.361	9	.161	-1	-18	-15	3	-1.6
1984	Chi-N	5	7	.417	17	16	0	0	0	88¹	102	4	38	45	14.5	4.28	91	.290	.362	3	.097	-1	-7	-4	1	-0.5
	Oak-A	1	1	.500	16	0	0	0	2	30²	43	2	17	10	17.6	6.75	55	.333	.411	0	—	0	-9	-10	-2	-0.7
Total	6	43	35	.551	141	106	10	6	3	669²	738	53	287	300	13.9	4.50	90	.284	.358	12	.138	-1	-47	-33	5	-3.5

● DAVE RAJSICH   Rajsich, David Christopher b: 9/28/51, Youngstown, Ohio BL/TL, 6'5", 175 lbs. Deb: 7/2/78 F

1978	NY-A	0	0	—	4	0	0	0	0	13¹	16	0	6	9	14.9	4.05	89	.320	.393	0	—	0	-0	-0	-0	0.0
1979	Tex-A	1	3	.250	27	3	0	0	0	53²	56	7	18	32	12.4	3.52	118	.267	.325	0	—	0	4	4	1	0.3
1980	Tex-A	2	1	.667	24	1	0	0	2	48¹	56	7	22	35	15.1	5.96	65	.295	.377	0	—	0	-10	-11	-0	-0.7
Total	3	3	4	.429	55	6	0	0	2	115¹	128	14	46	76	13.8	4.60	88	.284	.355	0	—	0	-7	-8	1	-0.4

YEAR	TM/L	W	L	PCT	G	GS	CG	SH	SV	IP	H	HR	BB	SO	RAT	ERA	ERA+	OAV	OOB	BH	AVG	PB	PR	/A	PD	TPI

● ED RAKOW
Rakow, Edward Charles "Rock" b: 5/30/36, Pittsburgh, Pa. BB/TR, 5'11", 178 lbs. Deb: 4/22/60

YEAR	TM/L	W	L	PCT	G	GS	CG	SH	SV	IP	H	HR	BB	SO	RAT	ERA	ERA+	OAV	OOB	BH	AVG	PB	PR	/A	PD	TPI
1960	LA-N	0	1	.000	9	2	0	0	0	22	30	5	11	9	16.8	7.36	54	.323	.394	2	.333	0	-9	-8	-0	-0.3
1961	KC-A	2	8	.200	45	11	1	0	1	124²	131	14	49	81	13.6	4.76	88	.269	.346	3	.103	-2	-10	-8	1	-0.4
1962	KC-A	14	17	.452	42	35	11	2	1	235¹	232	31	98	159	12.8	4.25	99	.260	.336	8	.098	-5	-7	-1	2	-0.4
1963	KC-A	9	10	.474	34	26	7	1	0	174¹	173	18	61	104	12.3	3.92	99	.261	.328	6	.105	-2	-6	-0	1	-0.1
1964	Det-A	8	9	.471	42	13	1	0	3	152¹	155	14	59	96	13.0	3.72	98	.266	.340	0	.000	-4	-2	-1	-2	-0.3
1965	Det-A	0	0	—	6	0	0	0	0	13¹	14	2	11	10	16.9	6.08	57	.280	.410	0	.000	-0	-4	-4	-1	-0.1
1967	Atl-N	3	2	.600	17	3	0	0	0	39¹	36	4	15	25	11.9	5.26	63	.240	.313	0	.000	-1	-8	-8	-1	-1.2
Total	7	36	47	.434	195	90	20	3	5	761¹	771	88	304	484	13.0	4.33	92	.264	.339	19	.084	-13	-46	-31	4	-3.1

● JOHN RALEIGH
Raleigh, John Austin b: 4/21/1890, Elkhorn, Wis. d: 8/24/55, Escondido, Cal. BR/TL, Deb: 8/4/09

YEAR	TM/L	W	L	PCT	G	GS	CG	SH	SV	IP	H	HR	BB	SO	RAT	ERA	ERA+	OAV	OOB	BH	AVG	PB	PR	/A	PD	TPI
1909	StL-N	1	10	.091	15	10	3	0	0	80²	85	0	21	26	12.2	3.79	67	.285	.339	2	.087	-2	-11	-11	0	-1.6
1910	StL-N	0	0	—	3	1	0	0	0	5	8	0	0	2	14.4	9.00	33	.364	.364	0	.000	-0	-3	-3	0	0.0
Total	2	1	10	.091	18	11	3	0	0	85²	93	0	21	28	12.3	4.10	62	.291	.340	2	.083	-2	-14	-15	0	-1.6

● PEP RAMBERT
Rambert, Elmer Donald b: 8/1/16, Cleveland, Ohio d: 11/16/74, W.Palm Beach, Fla. BR/TR, 6', 175 lbs. Deb: 9/23/39

YEAR	TM/L	W	L	PCT	G	GS	CG	SH	SV	IP	H	HR	BB	SO	RAT	ERA	ERA+	OAV	OOB	BH	AVG	PB	PR	/A	PD	TPI
1939	Pit-N	0	0	—	2	0	0	0	0	3²	7	0	1	4	19.6	9.82	39	.389	.421			0	-2	-2	0	0.0
1940	Pit-N	0	1	.000	3	1	0	0	0	8¹	12	0	4	0	20.5	7.56	50	.333	.442	0	.000	-0	-3	-3	0	-0.4
Total	2	0	1	.000	5	1	0	0	0	12	19	0	5	4	20.3	8.25	46	.352	.435	0	.000	0	-6	-6	0	-0.4

● PETE RAMBO
Rambo, Warren Dawson b: 11/1/06, Thorofare, N.J. d: 6/19/91, Camden, N.J. BR/TR, 5'9", 150 lbs. Deb: 9/16/26

YEAR	TM/L	W	L	PCT	G	GS	CG	SH	SV	IP	H	HR	BB	SO	RAT	ERA	ERA+	OAV	OOB	BH	AVG	PB	PR	/A	PD	TPI
1926	Phi-N	0	0	—	1	0	0	0	0	3²	6	0	4	2	24.5	14.73	28	.353	.476	1	1.000	0	-4	-4	0	0.1

● ALLAN RAMIREZ
Ramirez, Daniel Allan b: 5/1/57, Victoria, Tex. BR/TR, 5'10", 180 lbs. Deb: 6/8/83

YEAR	TM/L	W	L	PCT	G	GS	CG	SH	SV	IP	H	HR	BB	SO	RAT	ERA	ERA+	OAV	OOB	BH	AVG	PB	PR	/A	PD	TPI
1983	Bal-A	4	4	.500	11	10	1	0	0	57	46	6	30	20	12.0	3.47	114	.229	.329	0	—	0	4	3	0	0.4

● PEDRO RAMOS
Ramos, Pedro (Guerra) "Pete" b: 4/28/35, Pinar Del Rio, Cuba BB/TR, 6', 185 lbs. Deb: 4/11/55 ♦

YEAR	TM/L	W	L	PCT	G	GS	CG	SH	SV	IP	H	HR	BB	SO	RAT	ERA	ERA+	OAV	OOB	BH	AVG	PB	PR	/A	PD	TPI
1955	Was-A	5	11	.313	45	9	3	1	5	130	121	13	39	34	11.8	3.88	99	.253	.323	3	.079	-3	1	-1	-1	-0.5
1956	Was-A	12	10	.545	37	18	4	0	0	152	178	23	76	54	15.2	5.27	82	.299	.381	9	.205	0	-19	-16	-0	-2.0
1957	Was-A	12	16	.429	43	30	7	1	0	231	251	43	69	91	12.7	4.79	81	.271	.327	13	.171	-1	-26	-23	-0	-2.6
1958	Was-A	14	18	.438	43	37	10	4	3	259¹	277	38	77	132	12.5	4.23	90	.273	.327	21	.239	-1	-13	-12	-1	-1.3
1959	Was-A☆	13	19	.406	37	35	11	0	0	233²	233	29	52	95	11.3	4.16	94	.257	.304	11	.147	-0	-8	-6	-1	-0.8
1960	Was-A	11	18	.379	43	36	14	1	2	274	254	24	99	160	11.8	3.45	113	.243	.315	10	.116	-2	13	13	0	1.2
1961	Min-A	11	20	.355	42	34	9	3	2	264¹	265	39	74	174	11.8	3.95	107	.258	.313	16	.172	1	2	9	-3	0.6
1962	Cle-A	10	12	.455	37	27	7	2	1	201¹	189	28	85	96	12.5	3.71	104	.246	.326	10	.147	2	6	4	0	0.6
1963	Cle-A	9	8	.529	36	22	5	0	0	184²	156	29	41	169	9.8	3.12	116	.226	.273	6	.119	1	10	10	-2	0.6
1964	Cle-A	7	10	.412	36	19	3	1	0	133	144	18	26	98	11.8	5.14	70	.273	.312	7	.179	-2	-22	-23	-1	-2.5
	NY-A	1	0	1.000	13	0	0	0	8	21²	13	1	0	21	5.4	1.25	291	.183	.183	0	.000	-1	6	6	-1	0.6
	Yr	8	10	.444	49	19	3	1	8	154²	157	19	26	119	10.6	4.60	78	.259	.290	7	.159	1	-17	-17	-2	-1.9
1965	NY-A	5	5	.500	65	0	0	0	19	92¹	80	7	27	68	10.5	2.92	116	.237	.296	1	.083	-1	5	5	-1	0.5
1966	NY-A	3	9	.250	52	1	0	0	13	89²	98	10	18	58	11.7	3.61	92	.283	.321	2	.154	-0	-2	-3	-0	-0.5
1967	Phi-N	0	0	—	6	0	0	0	0	8	14	1	4	7	27.0	9.00	38	.412	.545	0	.000	-0	-5	-5	1	0.1
1969	Pit-N	0	1	.000	5	0	0	0	0	6	8	2	0	4	12.0	6.00	58	.320	.320	0	.000	-0	-2	-2	0	-0.3
	Cin-N	4	3	.571	38	0	0	0	2	66¹	73	8	24	40	13.8	5.16	73	.284	.357	0	.000	-1	-12	-10	-1	-1.1
	Yr	4	4	.500	43	0	0	0	2	72¹	81	10	24	44	13.7	5.23	72	.287	.354	0	.000	-1	-13	-12	-1	-1.4
1970	Was-A	0	0	—	4	0	0	0	0	8¹	10	2	4	10	15.1	7.56	47	.294	.368	0	.000	-0	-4	-4	0	0.0
Total	15	117	160	.422	582	268	73	13	55	2355²	2364	315	724	1305	12.1	4.08	95	.261	.320	109	.155	-0	-68	-58	-9	-6.9

● WILLIE RAMSDELL
Ramsdell, James Willard "The Knuck" b: 4/4/16, Williamsburg, Kan. d: 10/8/69, Wichita, Kan. BR/TR, 5'10", 180 lbs. Deb: 9/24/47

YEAR	TM/L	W	L	PCT	G	GS	CG	SH	SV	IP	H	HR	BB	SO	RAT	ERA	ERA+	OAV	OOB	BH	AVG	PB	PR	/A	PD	TPI
1947	Bro-N	1	1	.500	2	0	0	0	0	2²	4	0	3	3	27.0	6.75	61	.333	.500	1	1.000	0	-1	-1	0	-0.4
1948	Bro-N	4	4	.500	27	1	0	0	4	50¹	48	6	41	34	16.5	5.19	75	.251	.391	1	.091	-1	-7	-7	-1	-1.0
1950	Bro-N	1	2	.333	5	0	0	0	1	6¹	7	0	2	2	14.2	2.84	144	.292	.370	0	.000	-0	1	1	0	0.4
	Cin-N	7	12	.368	27	22	8	1	0	157¹	151	17	75	83	13.0	3.72	114	.255	.341	10	.200	1	7	9	-1	0.9
	Yr	8	14	.364	32	22	8	1	1	163²	158	17	77	85	13.0	3.68	115	.256	.341	10	.189	-0	8	10	-1	1.3
1951	Cin-N	9	17	.346	31	31	10	1	0	196	204	18	70	88	12.9	4.04	101	.266	.333	9	.155	-1	-2	1	-2	-0.2
1952	Chi-N	2	3	.400	19	4	0	0	0	67	41	5	24	30	9.4	2.42	159	.173	.263	1	.056	-1	10	11	-1	0.6
Total	5	24	39	.381	111	58	18	2	5	479²	455	46	215	240	12.9	3.83	107	.250	.335	22	.156	-2	9	14	-2	1.3

● TOAD RAMSEY
Ramsey, Thomas A. b: 8/8/1864, Indianapolis, Ind. d: 3/27/06, Indianapolis, Ind. BR/TL, Deb: 9/5/1885

YEAR	TM/L	W	L	PCT	G	GS	CG	SH	SV	IP	H	HR	BB	SO	RAT	ERA	ERA+	OAV	OOB	BH	AVG	PB	PR	/A	PD	TPI
1885	Lou-a	3	6	.333	9	9	9	0	0	79	44	1	28	83	8.3	1.94	167	.150	.227	4	.129	-2	12	11	-0	0.8
1886	Lou-a	38	27	.585	67	67	**66**	3	0	588²	447	3	207	499	10.2	2.45	149	**.198**	.254	58	.241	-3	66	**78**	-3	6.5
1887	Lou-a	37	27	.578	65	64	61	0	0	561	544	9	167	**355**	11.7	3.43	128	.242	.299	43	.191	-10	54	60	-9	3.1
1888	Lou-a	8	30	.211	40	40	37	1	0	342¹	362	6	86	228	12.1	3.42	90	.262	.310	17	.120	-7	-13	-13	-4	-2.1
1889	Lou-a	1	16	.059	18	18	15	0	0	140	175	7	71	60	15.9	5.59	69	.297	.374	15	.263	0	-27	-27	-2	-2.5
	StL-a	3	1	.750	5	3	3	0	0	41	44	0	10	33	12.1	3.95	107	.265	.311	5	.294	0	-1	1	-1	0.1
	Yr	4	17	.190	23	21	18	0	0	181	219	7	81	93	15.0	5.22	75	.289	.358	20	.270	1	-28	-26	-2	-2.4
1890	StL-a	24	17	.585	44	40	34	1	0	348²	325	10	102	257	11.2	3.69	117	.239	.296	33	.228	-1	7	24	-7	1.5
Total	6	114	124	.479	248	241	225	5	0	2100²	1941	40	671	1515	11.4	3.29	117	.234	.295	175	.204	-22	97	134	-25	7.8

● RIBS RANEY
Raney, Frank Robert Donald (b: Frank Robert Donald Raniszewski) b: 2/16/23, Detroit, Mich. BR/TR, 6'4", 190 lbs. Deb: 9/18/49

YEAR	TM/L	W	L	PCT	G	GS	CG	SH	SV	IP	H	HR	BB	SO	RAT	ERA	ERA+	OAV	OOB	BH	AVG	PB	PR	/A	PD	TPI
1949	StL-A	1	2	.333	3	3	1	0	0	16¹	23	2	5	5	19.3	7.71	59	.333	.432	0	.000	-1	-6	-6	-0	-0.9
1950	StL-A	0	1	.000	1	0	0	0	0	2	2	0	2	2	18.0	4.50	110	.250	.400	0	.000	0	0	0	0	0.0
Total	2	1	3	.250	4	3	1	0	0	18¹	25	2	14	7	19.1	7.36	62	.325	.429	0	.000	-1	-6	-6	-0	-0.9

● PAT RAPP
Rapp, Patrick Leland b: 7/13/67, Jennings, La. BR/TR, 6'3", 195 lbs. Deb: 7/10/92

YEAR	TM/L	W	L	PCT	G	GS	CG	SH	SV	IP	H	HR	BB	SO	RAT	ERA	ERA+	OAV	OOB	BH	AVG	PB	PR	/A	PD	TPI
1992	SF-N	0	2	.000	3	2	0	0	0	10	8	0	6	3	13.5	7.20	46	.235	.366	0	.000	-0	-4	-4	0	-0.7
1993	Fla-N	4	6	.400	16	16	1	0	0	94	101	7	39	57	13.6	4.02	107	.281	.355	6	.194	0	0	3	0	0.4
1994	Fla-N	7	8	.467	24	23	1	1	0	133¹	132	13	69	75	14.0	3.85	114	.266	.364	5	.122	-2	5	8	-1	0.5
1995	Fla-N	14	7	.667	28	28	3	2	0	167¹	158	10	76	102	13.0	3.44	122	.253	.340	6	.107	-3	14	14	-1	1.3
1996	Fla-N	8	16	.333	30	29	0	0	0	162¹	184	12	91	86	15.4	5.10	79	.301	.394	7	.121	-2	-16	-19	-0	-2.5
Total	5	33	39	.458	101	98	6	3	0	567	583	42	281	323	14.0	4.17	101	.274	.364	24	.128	-6	-1	2	-1	-1.0

● VIC RASCHI
Raschi, Victor John Angelo b: 3/28/19, W.Springfield, Mass. d: 10/14/88, Groveland, N.Y. BR/TR, 6'1", 205 lbs. Deb: 9/23/46

YEAR	TM/L	W	L	PCT	G	GS	CG	SH	SV	IP	H	HR	BB	SO	RAT	ERA	ERA+	OAV	OOB	BH	AVG	PB	PR	/A	PD	TPI
1946	NY-A	2	0	1.000	2	2	2	0	0	16	14	0	5	11	10.7	3.94	88	.230	.288	1	.250	0	-1	-1	0	-0.1
1947	*NY-A	7	2	.778	15	14	6	1	0	104²	89	11	38	51	11.0	3.87	91	.226	.296	10	.250	2	-2	-4	0	-0.2
1948	*NY-A★	19	8	.704	36	31	18	6	1	222²	208	15	74	124	11.5	3.84	106	.247	.310	19	.235	2	11	6	-1	0.7
1949	*NY-A★	21	10	.677	38	37	21	3	0	274²	247	16	138	124	12.8	3.34	121	.241	.334	13	.157	1	26	21	1	2.3
1950	*NY-A★	21	8	**.724**	33	32	17	3	1	256²	232	19	116	155	12.3	4.00	107	.243	.327	17	.198	1	17	8	-3	0.7
1951	*NY-A	21	10	.677	35	34	15	4	0	258¹	233	20	103	**164**	11.9	3.27	117	.242	.319	15	.176	1	24	16	-3	1.2
1952	*NY-A★	16	6	.727	31	31	13	4	0	223	174	23	91	127	10.9	2.78	139	.216	.300	13	.188	3	22	13	-4	1.1
1953	*NY-A	13	6	.684	28	26	7	4	1	181	150	11	55	76	**10.2**	3.33	111	.224	**.283**	9	.143	-2	13	7	-2	0.3
1954	StL-N	8	9	.471	30	29	6	0	0	179	182	24	71	73	12.7	4.73	87	.268	.337	9	.141	-2	-13	-12	-1	-1.1
1955	StL-N	0	1	1.000	3	1	0	0	0	5	12	3	3	1	32.4	21.60	19	.556	.600	0	—	0	-3	-3	-0	-1.0
	KC-A	4	6	.400	20	18	1	0	0	101¹	132	15	35	38	15.0	5.42	77	.312	.366	6	.182	-0	-16	-14	-1	-1.1
Total	10	132	66	.667	269	255	106	26	3	1819	1666	139	727	944	12.0	3.72	105	.244	.319	112	.184	3	78	38	-9	2.8

● DENNIS RASMUSSEN
Rasmussen, Dennis Lee b: 4/18/59, Los Angeles, Cal. BL/TL, 6'7", 230 lbs. Deb: 9/16/83 F

YEAR	TM/L	W	L	PCT	G	GS	CG	SH	SV	IP	H	HR	BB	SO	RAT	ERA	ERA+	OAV	OOB	BH	AVG	PB	PR	/A	PD	TPI
1983	SD-N	0	0	—	4	1	0	0	0	13²	10	1	9	13	11.9	1.98	176	.204	.310	0	.000	-0	3	2	1	0.0
1984	NY-A	9	6	.600	24	24	1	0	0	147²	127	16	60	110	11.6	4.57	83	.234	.315	0	—	0	-10	-13	-1	-1.0
1985	NY-A	3	5	.375	22	16	2	0	0	101²	97	10	42	63	12.4	3.98	100	.255	.331	0	—	0	0	0	0	0.2
1986	NY-A	18	6	.750	31	31	3	1	0	202	160	28	74	131	10.5	3.88	105	.217	.290	0	—	0	7	5	0	0.5

YEAR TM/L	W	L	PCT	G	GS	CG	SH	SV	IP	H	HR	BB	SO	RAT	ERA	ERA+	OAV	OOB	BH	AVG	PB	PR	/A	PD	TPI
1987 NY-A	9	7	.563	26	25	2	0	0	146	145	31	55	89	12.6	4.75	92	.260	.331	0	—	0	-5	-6	-0	-0.5
Cin-N	4	1	.800	7	7	0	0	0	45^1	39	5	12	39	10.3	3.97	107	.229	.284	1	.067	-1	1	1	0	0.1
1988 Cin-N	2	6	.250	11	11	1	1	0	56^1	68	8	22	27	14.7	5.75	62	.300	.367	5	.227	1	-14	-14	0	-1.6
SD-N	14	4	.778	20	20	6	0	0	148^1	131	9	36	85	10.3	2.55	133	.238	.287	9	.188	2	15	14	2	2.2
Yr	16	10	.615	31	31	7	1	0	204^2	199	17	58	112	11.4	3.43	100	.254	.308	14	.200	3	0	0	2	0.6
1989 SD-N	10	10	.500	33	33	1	0	0	183^2	190	18	72	87	13.0	4.26	82	.270	.340	11	.169	-1	-16	-16	-1	-1.6
1990 SD-N	11	15	.423	32	32	3	1	0	187^2	217	28	62	86	13.5	4.51	85	.292	.349	18	.290	5	-15	-14	0	-1.3
1991 SD-N	6	13	.316	24	24	1	1	0	146^2	155	12	49	75	12.6	3.74	101	.271	.331	6	.136	1	-1	1	2	0.4
1992 Chi-N	0	0	—	3	1	0	0	0	5	7	2	2	0	18.0	10.80	33	.350	.435	0	—	-0	-4	-4	0	0.0
KC-A	4	1	.800	5	5	1	1	0	37^2	25	0	6	12	7.4	1.43	283	.197	.233	0	—	0	10	11	1	1.5
1993 KC-A	1	2	.333	9	4	0	0	0	29	40	4	14	12	17.1	7.45	61	.328	.401	0	—	-0	-10	-9	-0	-0.8
1995 KC-A	0	1	.000	5	1	0	0	0	10	13	3	8	6	18.9	9.00	53	.302	.412	0	—	-0	-5	-5	-0	-0.4
Total 12	91	77	.542	256	235	21	5	0	1460^2	1424	175	522	835	12.2	4.15	93	.257	.324	50	.193	8	-42	-45	2	-2.3

● ERIC RASMUSSEN
Rasmussen, Eric Ralph (Born Harold Ralph Rasmussen)   b: 3/22/52, Racine, Wis.   BR/TR, 6'3", 205 lbs.   Deb: 7/21/75

YEAR TM/L	W	L	PCT	G	GS	CG	SH	SV	IP	H	HR	BB	SO	RAT	ERA	ERA+	OAV	OOB	BH	AVG	PB	PR	/A	PD	TPI
1975 StL-N	5	5	.500	14	13	2	1	0	81	86	8	20	59	11.8	3.78	99	.264	.306	4	.154	-0	-1	-0	-0	-0.1
1976 StL-N	6	12	.333	43	17	2	1	0	150^1	139	10	54	76	11.7	3.53	100	.247	.315	4	.105	-1	-1	0	3	0.2
1977 StL-N	11	17	.393	34	34	11	3	0	233	223	24	63	120	11.2	3.48	111	.254	.308	10	.139	0	11	10	-1	1.0
1978 StL-N	2	5	.286	10	10	2	1	0	60^1	61	4	20	32	12.1	4.18	84	.270	.329	2	.111	-1	-4	-4	-0	-0.6
SD-N	12	10	.545	27	24	3	2	0	146^1	154	16	43	59	12.2	4.06	82	.277	.331	7	.152	-1	-8	-12	1	-1.6
Yr	14	15	.483	37	34	5	3	0	206^2	215	20	63	91	12.1	4.09	83	.274	.329	9	.141	-2	-12	-16	1	-2.2
1979 SD-N	6	9	.400	45	20	5	3	3	156^2	142	9	42	54	10.6	3.27	108	.244	.295	2	.056	-2	8	4	-1	0.2
1980 SD-N	4	11	.267	40	14	0	0	1	111^1	130	9	33	50	13.4	4.37	79	.295	.349	2	.095	-1	-9	-12	-0	-1.6
1982 StL-N	1	2	.333	8	3	0	0	0	18^1	21	2	8	15	14.2	4.42	82	.288	.358	0	.000	-0	-2	-2	0	-0.2
1983 StL-N	0	0	—	6	0	0	0	1	7^2	16	1	4	6	23.5	11.74	31	.444	.500	0	—	-0	-7	-7	0	-0.2
KC-A	3	6	.333	11	9	2	1	0	52^2	61	4	22	18	14.2	4.78	85	.289	.356	0	—	-0	-4	-4	-0	-0.6
Total 8	50	77	.394	238	144	27	12	5	1017^2	1033	87	309	489	12.0	3.85	94	.266	.321	31	.119	-5	-17	-27	2	-3.5

● HANS RASMUSSEN
Rasmussen, Henry Florian   b: 4/18/1895, Chicago, Ill.   d: 1/1/49, Chicago, Ill.   BR/TR, 6'6", 220 lbs.   Deb: 8/11/15

YEAR TM/L	W	L	PCT	G	GS	CG	SH	SV	IP	H	HR	BB	SO	RAT	ERA	ERA+	OAV	OOB	BH	AVG	PB	PR	/A	PD	TPI
1915 Chi-F	0	0	—	2	0	0	0	0	2	3	0	2	2	22.5	13.50	19	.600	.714	0	.000	-0	-2	-2	0	0.0

● FRED RATH
Rath, Frederick Helsher   b: 9/1/43, Little Rock, Ark.   BR/TR, 6'3", 200 lbs.   Deb: 9/10/68

YEAR TM/L	W	L	PCT	G	GS	CG	SH	SV	IP	H	HR	BB	SO	RAT	ERA	ERA+	OAV	OOB	BH	AVG	PB	PR	/A	PD	TPI
1968 Chi-A	0	0	—	5	0	0	0	0	11^1	8	0	3	3	9.5	1.59	191	.182	.250	0	—	0	2	2	0	0.0
1969 Chi-A	0	2	.000	3	2	0	0	0	11^2	11	4	8	4	14.7	7.71	50	.256	.373	0	.000	-0	-5	-5	0	-0.7
Total 2	0	2	.000	8	2	0	0	0	23	19	4	11	7	12.1	4.70	73	.218	.313	0	.000	-0	-4	-3	0	-0.7

● STEVE RATZER
Ratzer, Steven Wayne   b: 9/9/53, Paterson, N.J.   BR/TR, 6'1", 192 lbs.   Deb: 10/5/80

YEAR TM/L	W	L	PCT	G	GS	CG	SH	SV	IP	H	HR	BB	SO	RAT	ERA	ERA+	OAV	OOB	BH	AVG	PB	PR	/A	PD	TPI
1980 Mon-N	0	0	—	1	1	0	0	0	4	9	0	2	0	24.8	11.25	32	.450	.500	0	.000	-0	-3	-3	0	0.0
1981 Mon-N	1	1	.500	12	0	0	0	0	17^1	23	2	7	4	15.6	6.23	56	.311	.370	0	.000	-0	-5	-5	1	-0.5
Total 2	1	1	.500	13	1	0	0	0	21^1	32	2	9	4	17.3	7.17	49	.340	.398	0	.000	-0	-9	-9	1	-0.5

● DOUG RAU
Rau, Douglas James   b: 12/15/48, Columbus, Tex.   BL/TL, 6'2", 175 lbs.   Deb: 9/2/72

YEAR TM/L	W	L	PCT	G	GS	CG	SH	SV	IP	H	HR	BB	SO	RAT	ERA	ERA+	OAV	OOB	BH	AVG	PB	PR	/A	PD	TPI
1972 LA-N	2	2	.500	7	3	2	0	0	32^2	18	1	11	19	8.3	2.20	151	.159	.240	1	.143	1	5	4	0	0.6
1973 LA-N	4	2	.667	14	6	3	0	3	63^2	64	5	28	51	13.1	3.96	87	.259	.337	1	.091	-1	-2	-4	-0	-0.5
1974 *LA-N	13	11	.542	36	35	3	1	0	198^1	191	20	70	126	13.1	3.72	91	.251	.318	9	.141	-1	-2	-7	-0	-0.9
1975 LA-N	15	9	.625	38	38	8	2	0	257^2	227	18	61	151	10.2	3.11	109	.236	.283	17	.195	2	15	8	-1	0.9
1976 LA-N	16	12	.571	34	32	8	3	0	231	221	18	69	98	11.6	2.57	132	.258	.318	9	.150	1	24	21	-0	2.6
1977 *LA-N	14	8	.636	32	32	4	2	0	212^1	232	15	49	126	12.2	3.43	111	.282	.327	10	.141	-0	11	9	-1	0.7
1978 *LA-N	15	9	.625	30	30	7	2	0	199	219	17	68	95	13.1	3.26	108	.284	.344	9	.143	-1	7	6	-2	0.3
1979 LA-N	1	5	.167	11	11	1	1	0	56	73	3	22	25	15.9	5.30	69	.320	.390	2	.143	-1	-10	-10	-0	-0.9
1981 Cal-A	1	2	.333	3	3	0	0	0	10^1	14	2	4	3	15.7	8.71	42	.341	.400	0	—	0	-6	-6	-0	-1.3
Total 9	81	60	.574	222	187	33	11	3	1261	1259	99	382	697	11.9	3.35	104	.262	.320	58	.154	2	41	21	-6	1.5

● BOB RAUCH
Rauch, Robert John   b: 6/16/49, Brookings, S.D.   BR/TR, 6'4", 200 lbs.   Deb: 6/29/72

YEAR TM/L	W	L	PCT	G	GS	CG	SH	SV	IP	H	HR	BB	SO	RAT	ERA	ERA+	OAV	OOB	BH	AVG	PB	PR	/A	PD	TPI
1972 NY-N	0	1	.000	19	0	0	0	1	27	27	3	21	23	16.0	5.00	67	.273	.400	0	.000	-0	-5	-5	0	-0.2

● LANCE RAUTZHAN
Rautzhan, Clarence George   b: 8/20/52, Pottsville, Pa.   BR/TL, 6'1", 195 lbs.   Deb: 7/23/77

YEAR TM/L	W	L	PCT	G	GS	CG	SH	SV	IP	H	HR	BB	SO	RAT	ERA	ERA+	OAV	OOB	BH	AVG	PB	PR	/A	PD	TPI
1977 *LA-N	4	1	.800	25	0	0	0	2	20^2	25	0	7	13	13.9	4.35	88	.313	.368	0	.000	-0	-1	-1	0	-0.3
1978 *LA-N	2	1	.667	43	0	0	0	4	61^1	61	1	19	25	11.9	2.93	120	.263	.321	0	.000	-0	4	4	2	0.4
1979 LA-N	0	2	.000	12	0	0	0	1	9^2	9	0	11	5	19.6	7.45	49	.273	.467	0	—	-0	-4	-4	-0	-0.8
Mil-A	0	0	—	3	0	0	0	0	3	3	0	10	2	39.0	9.00	46	.300	.650	0	—	-0	-2	-2	0	0.0
Total 3	6	4	.600	83	0	0	0	7	94^2	98	1	47	45	14.0	3.90	93	.276	.364	0	.000	-0	-2	-3	2	-0.7

● SHANE RAWLEY
Rawley, Shane William   b: 7/27/55, Racine, Wis.   BR/TL, 6', 180 lbs.   Deb: 4/6/78

YEAR TM/L	W	L	PCT	G	GS	CG	SH	SV	IP	H	HR	BB	SO	RAT	ERA	ERA+	OAV	OOB	BH	AVG	PB	PR	/A	PD	TPI
1978 Sea-A	4	9	.308	52	4	0	0	1	111^1	114	7	51	66	13.7	4.12	92	.275	.362	0	—	0	-4	-4	1	-0.3
1979 Sea-A	5	9	.357	48	3	0	0	11	84^1	88	2	40	48	13.8	3.84	113	.278	.361	0	—	0	3	5	1	0.8
1980 Sea-A	7	7	.500	59	0	0	0	13	113^2	103	3	63	68	13.4	3.33	124	.257	.363	0	—	0	9	10	2	1.6
1981 Sea-A	4	6	.400	46	0	0	0	8	68^1	64	1	38	35	13.6	3.95	97	.257	.358	0	—	0	-2	-1	0	0.1
1982 NY-A	11	10	.524	47	17	3	0	3	164	165	10	54	111	12.1	4.06	98	.267	.328	0	—	0	-1	-1	1	0.1
1983 NY-A	14	14	.500	34	33	13	2	1	238^1	246	19	79	124	12.4	3.78	103	.269	.329	0	—	0	8	3	0	0.5
1984 NY-A	2	3	.400	11	10	0	0	0	42	46	0	27	24	15.6	6.21	61	.272	.372	0	—	0	-10	-11	-0	-0.9
Phi-N	10	6	.625	18	18	3	0	0	120^1	117	13	27	58	10.8	3.81	95	.257	.300	5	.116	-2	-3	-2	-1	-0.6
1985 Phi-N	13	8	.619	36	31	6	2	0	198^2	188	16	81	106	12.3	3.31	111	.249	.323	8	.138	-1	6	8	1	1.0
1986 Phi-N☆	11	7	.611	23	23	7	1	0	157^2	166	13	50	73	12.4	3.54	109	.270	.326	9	.173	1	3	5	-0	0.6
1987 Phi-N	17	11	.607	36	36	4	1	0	229^2	250	23	86	123	13.4	4.39	97	.279	.346	12	.152	-1	-8	-4	-1	-0.6
1988 Phi-N	8	16	.333	32	32	4	1	0	198	220	27	78	87	13.7	4.18	85	.286	.355	6	.105	-1	-16	-14	-0	-1.7
1989 Min-A	5	12	.294	27	25	0	0	0	145	167	19	60	68	14.1	5.21	79	.293	.361	0	—	0	-21	-17	-1	-1.9
Total 12	111	118	.485	469	230	41	7	40	1871^1	1934	153	734	991	13.0	4.02	97	.271	.341	40	.138	-3	-36	-22	2	-1.7

● CARL RAY
Ray, Carl Grady   b: 1/31/1889, Danbury, N.C.   d: 4/3/70, Walnut Cove, N.C.   BL/TL, 5'11", 170 lbs.   Deb: 9/25/15

YEAR TM/L	W	L	PCT	G	GS	CG	SH	SV	IP	H	HR	BB	SO	RAT	ERA	ERA+	OAV	OOB	BH	AVG	PB	PR	/A	PD	TPI
1915 Phi-A	0	1	.000	2	1	0	0	0	7^1	11	0	6	6	25.8	4.91	60	.333	.488	0	.000	-0	-2	-2	-0	-0.2
1916 Phi-A	0	1	.000	3	1	0	0	0	9^1	9	0	14	5	23.1	4.82	59	.257	.480	0	.000	-0	-2	-2	-0	-0.3
Total 2	0	2	.000	5	2	0	0	0	16^2	20	0	20	11	24.3	4.86	59	.294	.484	0	.000	-0	-4	-4	-1	-0.5

● JIM RAY
Ray, James Francis "Sting"   b: 12/1/44, Rock Hill, S.C.   BR/TR, 6'1", 195 lbs.   Deb: 9/16/65

YEAR TM/L	W	L	PCT	G	GS	CG	SH	SV	IP	H	HR	BB	SO	RAT	ERA	ERA+	OAV	OOB	BH	AVG	PB	PR	/A	PD	TPI
1965 Hou-N	0	2	.000	3	2	0	0	0	7^2	11	1	6	7	20.0	10.57	32	.355	.459	0	.000	-0	-6	-6	0	-1.2
1966 Hou-N	0	0	—	1	0	0	0	0	1	0	0	1	0	—	∞	—	—	1.000	0	—	0	-1	-1	0	-0.1
1968 Hou-N	2	3	.400	41	2	1	0	1	80^2	65	5	25	71	10.2	2.68	110	.220	.283	1	.067	-1	3	2	0	0.6
1969 Hou-N	8	2	.800	40	13	0	0	0	115	105	11	48	115	12.1	3.91	90	.245	.324	3	.115	-1	-4	-5	-1	-0.6
1970 Hou-N	6	3	.667	52	2	0	0	5	105	97	13	49	67	12.5	3.26	119	.251	.336	5	.185	-0	9	7	0	0.6
1971 Hou-N	10	4	.714	47	1	0	0	8	97^2	72	3	31	46	9.7	2.12	159	.211	.281	3	.167	-1	15	14	-2	1.8
1972 Hou-N	10	9	.526	54	2	0	0	6	90^1	77	10	44	50	12.4	4.28	79	.227	.321	1	.063	-1	-8	-9	-1	-2.3
1973 Hou-N	6	4	.600	42	0	0	0	6	69	65	5	38	25	13.8	4.43	82	.254	.356	3	.231	-1	-6	-6	-1	-1.0
1974 Det-A	1	3	.250	28	0	0	0	2	52^1	49	4	29	26	13.6	4.47	85	.254	.354	0	.000	-0	-5	-4	0	-0.5
Total 9	43	30	.589	308	20	1	0	25	617^2	541	52	271	407	12.0	3.61	97	.238	.323	16	.137	-3	-4	-8	-6	-3.3

● FARMER RAY
Ray, Robert Henry   b: 9/17/1886, Ft.Lyon, Colo.   d: 3/11/63, Electra, Tex.   BL/TR, 5'11", 160 lbs.   Deb: 6/13/10

YEAR TM/L	W	L	PCT	G	GS	CG	SH	SV	IP	H	HR	BB	SO	RAT	ERA	ERA+	OAV	OOB	BH	AVG	PB	PR	/A	PD	TPI
1910 StL-A	4	10	.286	21	16	11	0	0	140^2	146	3	49	35	12.9	3.58	69	.285	.356	7	.175	0	-17	-17	-3	-1.9

● CURT RAYDON
Raydon, Curtis Lowell   b: 11/18/33, Bloomington, Ill.   BR/TR, 6'4", 190 lbs.   Deb: 4/15/58

YEAR TM/L	W	L	PCT	G	GS	CG	SH	SV	IP	H	HR	BB	SO	RAT	ERA	ERA+	OAV	OOB	BH	AVG	PB	PR	/A	PD	TPI
1958 Pit-N	8	4	.667	31	20	2	1	1	134^1	118	18	61	85	12.3	3.62	107	.236	.326	1	.026	-2	5	4	-3	-0.2

YEAR TM/L	W	L	PCT	G	GS	CG	SH	SV	IP	H	HR	BB	SO	RAT	ERA	ERA+	OAV	OOB	BH	AVG	PB	PR	/A	PD	TPI

● **BUGS RAYMOND** Raymond, Arthur Lawrence b: 2/24/1882, Chicago, Ill. d: 9/7/12, Chicago, Ill. BR/TR, 5'10", 180 lbs. Deb: 9/23/04

YEAR TM/L	W	L	PCT	G	GS	CG	SH	SV	IP	H	HR	BB	SO	RAT	ERA	ERA+	OAV	OOB	BH	AVG	PB	PR	/A	PD	TPI
1904 Det-A	0	1	.000	5	2	1	0	0	14²	14	0	6	7	13.5	3.07	83	.250	.344	0	.000	-1	-1	-1	1	0.0
1907 StL-N	2	4	.333	8	6	6	1	0	64²	56	3	21	34	10.9	1.67	150	.230	.294	5	.091	-0	6	6	0	0.6
1908 StL-N	15	25	.375	48	37	23	5	2	324¹	236	2	95	145	9.6	2.03	116	.207	.277	17	.189	1	12	13	3	2.1
1909 NY-N	18	12	.600	39	30	18	2	0	270	239	7	87	121	11.1	2.47	104	.245	.311	13	.146	0	4	3	2	0.5
1910 NY-N	4	11	.267	19	11	6	0	0	99¹	106	2	40	55	14.0	3.81	78	.280	.362	5	.156	-1	-9	-9	2	-1.1
1911 NY-N	6	4	.600	17	9	4	1	0	81²	73	1	33	39	11.9	3.31	102	.248	.328	5	.200	-0	1	1	1	0.1
Total 6	45	57	.441	136	95	58	9	2	854²	724	15	282	401	10.9	2.49	105	.235	.306	42	.160	-0	13	11	9	2.2

● **HARRY RAYMOND** Raymond, Harry H. "Jack" b: 2/20/1862, Utica, N.Y. d: 3/21/25, San Diego, Cal. 5'9", 179 lbs. Deb: 9/9/1888 ♦

YEAR TM/L	W	L	PCT	G	GS	CG	SH	SV	IP	H	HR	BB	SO	RAT	ERA	ERA+	OAV	OOB	BH	AVG	PB	PR	/A	PD	TPI
1889 Lou-a	0	1	1.000	1	1	1	0	0	9	8	0	11	1	19.0	1.00	385	.229	.413	123	.239	0	3	3	-0	0.2

● **CLAUDE RAYMOND** Raymond, Joseph Claude Marc "Frenchy" b: 5/7/37, St.Jean, Que., Canada BR/TR, 5'10", 175 lbs. Deb: 4/15/59

YEAR TM/L	W	L	PCT	G	GS	CG	SH	SV	IP	H	HR	BB	SO	RAT	ERA	ERA+	OAV	OOB	BH	AVG	PB	PR	/A	PD	TPI
1959 Chi-A	0	0	—	3	0	0	0	0	4	5	2	1	2	15.8	9.00	42	.333	.412			0	-2	-2	0	0.0
1961 Mil-N	1	0	1.000	13	0	0	0	2	20¹	22	2	9	13	14.2	3.98	94	.275	.356	0	.000	-0	0	-1	0	0.0
1962 Mil-N	5	5	.500	26	0	0	0	10	42²	37	5	15	40	11.4	2.74	138	.236	.310	0	.000	-0	6	5	-1	1.2
1963 Mil-N	4	6	.400	45	0	0	0	5	53¹	57	12	27	44	14.9	5.40	60	.268	.361	2	.500	2	-13	-13	1	-2.3
1964 Hou-N	5	5	.500	38	0	0	0	5	79²	64	3	22	56	10.1	2.82	121	.229	.292	1	.071	-0	6	5	1	0.7
1965 Hou-N	7	4	.636	33	7	2	0	5	96¹	87	6	16	79	10.1	2.90	116	.244	.286	3	.115	-1	7	5	-0	0.5
1966 Hou-N☆	7	5	.583	62	0	0	0	16	92	85	10	25	73	11.2	3.13	109	.242	.300	5	.111	0	5	3	-2	0.3
1967 Hou-N	0	4	.000	21	0	0	0	5	31	31	5	7	17	11.6	3.19	104	.256	.308	1	.200	1	1	-0	0.1
Atl-N	4	1	.800	28	0	0	0	5	34¹	33	2	11	14	11.5	2.62	127	.260	.319	0	.000	0	3	3	0	0.5
Yr	4	5	.444	49	0	0	0	10	65¹	64	7	18	31	11.3	2.89	115	.255	.305	1	.143	0	4	3	0	0.6
1968 Atl-N	3	5	.375	36	0	0	0	10	60¹	56	4	18	37	11.2	2.83	106	.256	.315	1	.143	-0	1	1	0	0.2
1969 Atl-N	2	2	.500	33	0	0	0	1	48	56	4	13	15	13.3	5.25	69	.298	.350	2	.286	-0	-9	-9	-1	-0.8
Mon-N	1	2	.333	15	0	0	0	1	22	21	2	8	11	12.7	4.09	90	.256	.337	0	.000	-0	-1	-1	-0	-0.1
Yr	3	4	.429	48	0	0	0	2	70	77	6	21	26	12.9	4.89	74	.281	.337	2	.182	-0	-10	-10	-0	-0.9
1970 Mon-N	6	7	.462	59	0	0	0	23	83¹	76	13	27	68	11.3	4.43	93	.240	.303	0	.000	-1	-4	-3	-1	-0.8
1971 Mon-N	1	7	.125	37	0	0	0	1	53²	81	5	25	29	17.8	4.70	75	.373	.438	0	.000	-0	-7	-7	1	-0.9
Total 12	46	53	.465	449	7	2	0	83	721	711	75	225	497	12.0	3.66	96	.261	.324	11	.109	-2	-7	-13	-0	-1.4

● **BARRY RAZIANO** Raziano, Barry John b: 2/5/47, New Orleans, La. BB/TR, 5'10", 175 lbs. Deb: 8/18/73

YEAR TM/L	W	L	PCT	G	GS	CG	SH	SV	IP	H	HR	BB	SO	RAT	ERA	ERA+	OAV	OOB	BH	AVG	PB	PR	/A	PD	TPI
1973 KC-A	0	0	—	2	0	0	0	0	5	6	1	1	0	14.4	5.40	76	.316	.381	0	—	0	-1	-1	0	0.0
1974 Cal-A	1	2	.333	13	0	0	0	1	16²	15	8	8	9	12.4	6.48	53	.246	.333	0	—	0	-5	-6	-0	-0.7
Total 2	1	2	.333	15	0	0	0	1	21²	21	9	9	9	12.9	6.23	58	.262	.344	0	—	0	-6	-6	-0	-0.7

● **RIP REAGAN** Reagan, Arthur (b: Arthur Edgar Ragan) b: 6/5/1878, Lincoln, Ill. d: 6/8/53, Kansas City, Mo. BR/TR, 5'11", 170 lbs. Deb: 9/19/03

YEAR TM/L	W	L	PCT	G	GS	CG	SH	SV	IP	H	HR	BB	SO	RAT	ERA	ERA+	OAV	OOB	BH	AVG	PB	PR	/A	PD	TPI
1903 Cin-N	0	2	.000	3	2	2	0	0	18	40	0	7	3	24.0	6.00	59	.455	.500	2	.250	0	-5	-5	-0	-0.4

● **JIM REARDON** Reardon, James Matthew b: 1866, Hoosick Falls, N.Y. d: 2/25/1891, Hoosick Falls, N.Y Deb: 7/17/1886

YEAR TM/L	W	L	PCT	G	GS	CG	SH	SV	IP	H	HR	BB	SO	RAT	ERA	ERA+	OAV	OOB	BH	AVG	PB	PR	/A	PD	TPI
1886 StL-N	0	1	.000	1	1	1	0	0	8	10	1	5	0	16.9	6.75	48	.323	.417	1	.250	0	-3	-3	-0	-0.3
Cin-a	0	1	.000	1	1	0	0	0	2	5	0	4	0	40.5	18.00	20	.500	.643	0	.000	-0	-3	-3	-0	-0.9
Total 1	0	2	.000	2	2	1	0	0	10	15	1	9	0	21.6	9.00	36	.366	.480	1	.143	-1	-6	-6	-0	-1.2

● **JEFF REARDON** Reardon, Jeffrey James b: 10/1/55, Dalton, Mass. BR/TR, 6'1", 195 lbs. Deb: 8/25/79

YEAR TM/L	W	L	PCT	G	GS	CG	SH	SV	IP	H	HR	BB	SO	RAT	ERA	ERA+	OAV	OOB	BH	AVG	PB	PR	/A	PD	TPI
1979 NY-N	1	2	.333	18	0	0	0	2	20²	12	2	9	10	9.1	1.74	209	.174	.269	0	—	0	5	4	-0	0.7
1980 NY-N	8	7	.533	61	0	0	0	6	110¹	96	4	47	101	11.7	2.61	136	.231	.310	0	.000	-1	12	12	-2	1.3
1981 NY-N	1	0	1.000	18	0	0	0	0	28²	27	2	12	28	12.6	3.45	101	.245	.325	0	—	0	0	0	-1	-0.1
*Mon-N	2	0	1.000	25	0	0	0	8	41²	21	3	9	21	6.7	1.30	269	.148	.204	0	.000	-0	10	10	-1	0.6
Yr	3	0	1.000	43	0	0	0	8	70¹	48	5	21	49	9.0	2.18	160	.189	.254	0	.000	-0	10	10	-2	0.5
1982 Mon-N	7	4	.636	75	0	0	0	26	109	87	6	36	86	10.3	2.06	176	.221	.289	1	.100	0	19	19	-1	2.6
1983 Mon-N	7	9	.438	66	0	0	0	21	92	87	7	44	78	12.9	3.03	118	.250	.336	1	.125	-0	6	6	-2	0.9
1984 Mon-N	7	7	.500	68	0	0	0	23	87	70	5	37	79	11.4	2.90	118	.220	.307	0	.000	-1	7	5	-2	0.8
1985 Mon-N★	2	8	.200	63	0	0	0	41	87²	68	7	26	67	9.8	3.18	107	.209	.270	2	.286	-1	4	2	-1	0.4
1986 Mon-N☆	7	9	.438	62	0	0	0	35	89	83	12	26	67	11.1	3.94	94	.251	.307	1	.125	-0	-2	-3	-0	-0.7
1987 *Min-A	8	8	.500	63	0	0	0	31	80¹	70	14	28	83	11.3	4.48	103	.232	.303	0	—	0	-1	-1	-1	0.2
1988 Min-A☆	2	4	.333	63	0	0	0	42	73	68	6	15	56	10.5	2.47	165	.245	.289	0	—	0	12	13	-2	2.0
1989 Min-A	5	4	.556	65	0	0	0	31	73	68	8	12	46	10.2	4.07	102	.246	.285	0	—	0	-2	-1	-2	-0.5
1990 *Bos-A	5	3	.625	47	0	0	0	21	51¹	39	4	9	33	8.4	3.16	129	.206	.282	0	—	0	4	5	-1	0.8
1991 Bos-A★	1	4	.200	57	0	0	0	40	59¹	54	9	16	44	10.8	3.03	142	.236	.284	0	—	0	7	8	-2	1.1
1992 Bos-A	2	2	.500	46	0	0	0	27	42¹	53	6	7	32	13.0	4.25	99	.308	.339	0	—	0	-1	-0	-0	-0.2
*Atl-N	3	0	1.000	14	0	0	0	3	15²	14	0	2	7	9.8	1.15	318	.241	.279	0	—	0	4	4	-1	1.0
1993 Cin-N	4	6	.400	58	0	0	0	8	61²	66	4	10	35	11.8	4.09	98	.270	.313	0	.000	-0	-0	-1	-2	-0.2
1994 NY-A	1	0	1.000	11	0	0	0	2	9²	17	3	4	4	18.6	8.38	55	.386	.426	0	—	0	-4	-4	-0	-0.4
Total 16	73	77	.487	880	0	0	0	367	1132¹	1000	109	358	877	11.0	3.16	121	.236	.299	5	.088	-3	80	83	-19	10.3

● **FRANK REBERGER** Reberger, Frank Beall "Crane" b: 6/7/44, Caldwell, Idaho BL/TR, 6'5", 200 lbs. Deb: 6/6/68 C

YEAR TM/L	W	L	PCT	G	GS	CG	SH	SV	IP	H	HR	BB	SO	RAT	ERA	ERA+	OAV	OOB	BH	AVG	PB	PR	/A	PD	TPI
1968 Chi-N	0	1	.000	3	1	0	0	0	6	9	1	2	3	16.5	4.50	70	.346	.393	0		0	-1	-1	-0	-0.1
1969 SD-N	1	2	.333	67	0	0	0	6	87²	83	6	41	65	12.9	3.59	98	.258	.345	1	.200	0	0	-1	2	0.2
1970 SF-N	7	8	.467	45	18	3	0	2	152	178	13	98	117	16.8	5.57	71	.293	.397	11	.234	1	-26	-27	-0	-2.3
1971 SF-N	3	0	1.000	13	7	0	0	0	43²	47	5	19	21	12.0	3.92	87	.283	.317	3	.231	0	-2	-3	-0	-0.1
1972 SF-N	3	4	.429	20	11	2	0	0	99¹	97	10	37	52	12.6	3.99	87	.257	.332	8	.229	2	-6	-6	1	-0.1
Total 5	14	15	.483	148	37	5	0	8	388²	404	35	197	258	14.3	4.52	81	.270	.361	23	.230	4	-35	-36	4	-2.3

● **JOHN RECCIUS** Reccius, John b: 10/29/1859, Louisville, Ky. d: 9/1/30, Louisville, Ky. 5'6.5", Deb: 5/2/1882 F♦

YEAR TM/L	W	L	PCT	G	GS	CG	SH	SV	IP	H	HR	BB	SO	RAT	ERA	ERA+	OAV	OOB	BH	AVG	PB	PR	/A	PD	TPI
1882 Lou-a	4	6	.400	13	10	9	1	0	95	106	3	22	31	12.1	3.03	82	.264	.303	63	.237	3	-4	-6	-1	-0.4
1883 Lou-a	0	0	—	1	0	0	0	0	4	10	0	0	0	22.5	2.25	133	.455	.455	9	.143	-0	0	0	0	0.0
Total 2	4	6	.400	14	10	9	1	0	99	116	3	22	31	12.5	3.00	83	.274	.310	72	.219	3	-3	-6	-1	-0.4

● **PHIL RECCIUS** Reccius, Phillip b: 6/7/1862, Louisville, Ky. d: 2/15/03, Louisville, Ky. 5'9", 163 lbs. Deb: 9/25/1882 F♦

YEAR TM/L	W	L	PCT	G	GS	CG	SH	SV	IP	H	HR	BB	SO	RAT	ERA	ERA+	OAV	OOB	BH	AVG	PB	PR	/A	PD	TPI
1884 Lou-a	6	7	.462	18	11	11	0	0	129¹	118	2	19	46	9.8	2.71	114	.228	.261	63	.240	2	8	5	0	0.6
1885 Lou-a	0	4	.000	7	5	4	0	1	40	46	0	11	10	13.0	3.82	84	.253	.299	97	.241	1	-3	-3	1	-0.1
1886 Lou-a	0	0	—	1	1	0	0	0	3	7	0	3	0	30.0	9.00	40	.467	.556	4	.308	0	-2	-2	-0	-0.4
1887 Cle-a	0	0	—	1	0	0	0	0	7	8	0	5	0	16.7	7.71	56	.320	.433	47	.205	4	-3	-3	-0	0.1
Total 4	6	12	.333	27	17	15	0	1	179¹	179	2	38	56	11.1	3.26	97	.242	.284	225	.231	4	1	-2	1	0.1

● **PHIL REDDING** Redding, Philip Hayden b: 1/25/1890, Crystal Springs, Miss. d: 3/30/29, Greenwood, Miss. BL/TR, 5'11.5", 190 lbs. Deb: 9/14/12

YEAR TM/L	W	L	PCT	G	GS	CG	SH	SV	IP	H	HR	BB	SO	RAT	ERA	ERA+	OAV	OOB	BH	AVG	PB	PR	/A	PD	TPI
1912 StL-N	2	1	.667	3	3	2	0	0	25¹	31	2	11	9	14.9	4.97	69	.313	.382	0	.000	-1	-4	-4	-0	-0.5
1913 StL-N	0	0	—	1	0	0	0	0	2²	2	0	1	1	10.1	6.75	48	.286	.375	0	.000	-0	-1	-1	-0	-0.0
Total 2	2	1	.667	4	3	2	0	0	28	33	2	12	10	14.5	5.14	66	.311	.381	0	.000	-1	-5	-5	-0	-0.5

● **PETE REDFERN** Redfern, Peter Irvine b: 8/25/54, Glendale, Cal. BR/TR, 6'2", 195 lbs. Deb: 5/15/76

YEAR TM/L	W	L	PCT	G	GS	CG	SH	SV	IP	H	HR	BB	SO	RAT	ERA	ERA+	OAV	OOB	BH	AVG	PB	PR	/A	PD	TPI
1976 Min-A	8	8	.500	23	23	1	1	0	118	105	6	63	74	13.0	3.51	102	.241	.341		—	0	1	1	-0	-0.1
1977 Min-A	6	9	.400	30	28	4	0	0	137¹	164	13	66	73	15.3	5.18	77	.304	.384		—	0	-17	-18	1	-1.6
1978 Min-A	0	2	.000	3	2	0	0	0	9²	10	2	6	4	14.9	6.52	59	.294	.400		—	0	-3	-3	-0	-0.6
1979 Min-A	7	3	.700	40	6	0	0	1	108¹	106	8	35	85	11.8	3.49	126	.258	.318		—	0	9	11	-1	0.5
1980 Min-A	7	7	.500	23	16	2	0	0	104²	117	11	33	73	12.9	4.56	96	.283	.336		—	0	-6	-2	-1	-0.4
1981 Min-A	9	8	.529	24	23	3	0	0	141²	140	16	52	75	12.3	4.07	97	.261	.328		—	0	-2	-1	-0	-0.6
1982 Min-A	5	11	.313	27	13	3	0	2	94¹	122	12	51	40	16.6	6.58	68	.322	.404		—	0	-26	-26	-2	-3.5
Total 7	42	48	.467	170	111	13	1	3	714	764	68	306	426	13.6	4.54	89	.278	.353	0	—	0	-50	-38	-2	-6.3

YEAR	TM/L	W	L	PCT	G	GS	CG	SH	SV	IP	H	HR	BB	SO	RAT	ERA	ERA+	OAV	OOB	BH	AVG	PB	PR	/A	PD	TPI

● **HOWIE REED**   Reed, Howard Dean "Diz"   b: 12/21/36, Dallas, Tex.   d: 12/7/84, Corpus Christi, Tex.   BR/TR, 6'1", 210 lbs.   Deb: 9/13/58

1958	KC-A	1	0	1.000	3	1	1	0	0	10¹	5	0	4	5	7.8	0.87	449	.132	.214	0	.000	-0	3	3	-0	0.3
1959	KC-A	0	3	.000	6	3	0	0	0	20²	26	3	10	11	15.7	7.40	54	.313	.387	0	.000	-0	-8	-8	-1	-1.0
1960	KC-A	0	0	—	1	0	0	0	0	1²	2	1	0	1	10.8	0.00	—	.286	.286	0	—	0	1	1	-0	0.0
1964	LA-N	3	4	.429	26	7	0	0	1	90	79	4	36	52	11.5	3.20	101	.236	.310	2	.100	-0	3	0	1	0.1
1965	*LA-N	7	5	.583	38	5	0	0	1	78	73	6	27	47	11.9	3.12	105	.243	.312	0	.000	-0	4	1	1	0.3
1966	LA-N	0	0	—	1	0	0	0	0	1²	1	0	0	0	5.4	0.00	—	.167	.167	0	—	-0	1	1	0	0.0
	Cal-A	0	1	.000	19	1	0	0	1	43	39	5	15	17	11.3	2.93	115	.247	.312	0	.000	-1	2	2	-0	-0.1
1967	Hou-N	1	1	.500	4	2	0	0	0	18¹	19	0	2	9	10.3	3.44	96	.268	.288	0	.000	-0	-0	-0	-0	-0.1
1969	Mon-N	6	7	.462	31	15	2	1	1	106	119	7	50	59	14.5	4.84	76	.290	.369	4	.125	1	-15	-14	2	-1.2
1970	Mon-N	6	5	.545	57	1	0	0	5	89	81	7	40	42	12.4	3.13	131	.252	.339	0	.000	-0	9	10	0	1.2
1971	Mon-N	2	3	.400	43	0	0	0	0	56²	66	8	24	24	14.3	4.29	82	.296	.364	0	.000	-0	-5	-5	0	-0.4
Total	10	26	29	.473	229	35	3	1	9	515¹	510	41	208	268	12.7	3.72	96	.261	.334	6	.066	-1	-5	-9	3	-0.9

● **JERRY REED**   Reed, Jerry Maxwell   b: 10/8/55, Bryson City, N.C.   BR/TR, 6'1", 190 lbs.   Deb: 9/11/81

1981	Phi-N	0	1	.000	4	0	0	0	0	4²	7	0	6	5	25.1	7.71	47	.333	.481	0	—	0	-2	-2	0	-0.4
1982	Phi-N	1	0	1.000	7	0	0	0	0	8²	11	0	3	1	15.6	5.19	71	.324	.395	0	—	0	-2	-1	-0	-0.2
	Cle-A	1	1	.500	6	1	0	0	0	15²	15	1	3	10	10.3	3.45	118	.250	.286	0	—	0	1	1	0	0.1
1983	Cle-A	0	0	—	7	0	0	0	0	21¹	26	4	9	11	14.8	7.17	59	.310	.376	0	—	0	-7	-7	1	0.1
1985	Cle-A	3	5	.375	33	5	0	0	8	72¹	67	12	19	37	11.1	4.11	101	.245	.302	0	—	0	0	1	0	0.1
1986	Sea-A	4	0	1.000	11	4	0	0	0	34²	38	3	13	16	13.2	3.12	136	.273	.336	0	—	0	4	4	-0	0.4
1987	Sea-A	1	2	.333	39	1	0	0	7	81²	79	7	24	51	11.7	3.42	138	.255	.315	0	—	0	9	12	-0	1.0
1988	Sea-A	1	1	.500	46	0	0	0	1	86¹	82	8	33	48	12.2	3.96	105	.256	.330	0	—	0	2	1	0	0.0
1989	Sea-A	7	7	.500	52	1	0	0	0	101³	89	10	43	50	11.8	3.19	126	.235	.314	0	—	0	8	9	-0	1.0
1990	Sea-A	0	1	.000	4	0	0	0	0	7¹	8	1	3	2	13.5	4.91	81	.286	.355	0	—	0	-1	-1	0	-0.1
	Bos-A	2	1	.667	29	0	0	0	2	45	55	1	16	17	14.2	4.80	85	.302	.359	0	—	0	-4	-4	-0	-0.5
	Yr	2	2	.500	33	0	0	0	2	52¹	63	2	19	19	14.1	4.82	84	.300	.358	0	—	0	-5	-4	0	-0.6
Total	9	20	19	.513	238	12	0	0	18	479¹	477	47	172	248	12.4	3.94	107	.261	.328	0	—	0	6	14	2	0.7

● **RICK REED**   Reed, Richard Allen   b: 8/16/64, Huntington, W.Va.   BR/TR, 6', 195 lbs.   Deb: 8/8/88

1988	Pit-N	1	0	1.000	2	2	0	0	0	12	10	1	2	6	9.0	3.00	113	.233	.267	0	.000	-0	1	1	0	0.0
1989	Pit-N	1	4	.200	15	7	0	0	0	54²	62	5	11	34	12.3	5.60	60	.290	.330	1	.077	-0	-13	-14	-0	-1.2
1990	Pit-N	2	3	.400	13	8	1	1	1	53²	62	6	12	27	12.6	4.36	83	.279	.319	4	.250	1	-3	-4	-1	-0.3
1991	Pit-N	0	0	—	1	1	0	0	0	4¹	11	1	0	2	18.7	10.38	34	.400	.429	1	.500	1	-3	-3	-0	0.1
1992	KC-A	3	7	.300	19	18	1	1	0	100¹	105	10	20	49	11.7	3.68	110	.271	.316	0	—	0	3	4	1	0.3
1993	KC-A	0	0	—	1	0	0	0	0	3²	6	1	1	3	19.6	9.82	47	.375	.444	0	—	0	-2	-2	0	-0.2
	Tex-A	1	0	1.000	2	0	0	0	0	4	6	1	1	2	18.0	2.25	184	.375	.444	0	—	0	1	1	0	0.3
	Yr	1	0	1.000	3	0	0	0	0	7²	12	1	2	5	17.6	5.87	74	.364	.417	0	—	0	-1	-1	0	0.1
1994	Tex-A	1	1	.500	4	4	0	0	0	16²	17	3	7	12	13.5	5.94	81	.254	.333	0	—	0	-2	-2	0	-0.2
1995	Cin-N	0	0	—	4	3	0	0	0	17	18	5	3	10	11.1	5.82	71	.273	.304	0	.000	-0	-3	-3	-0	-0.1
Total	8	9	15	.375	61	42	2	2	1	266¹	294	32	58	145	12.3	4.63	83	.280	.324	6	.158	1	-22	-23	-0	-1.3

● **BOB REED**   Reed, Robert Edward   b: 1/12/45, Boston, Mass.   BR/TR, 5'10", 175 lbs.   Deb: 9/5/69

1969	Det-A	0	0	—	8	1	0	0	0	14²	9	0	8	9	10.4	1.84	203	.184	.298	1	.500	0	3	3	0	0.1
1970	Det-A	2	4	.333	16	4	0	0	2	46¹	54	5	14	26	13.2	4.86	77	.292	.342	1	.083	-0	-6	-6	-1	-0.8
Total	2	2	4	.333	24	5	0	0	2	61	63	5	22	35	12.5	4.13	90	.269	.332	2	.143	-0	-3	-3	-0	-0.7

● **RON REED**   Reed, Ronald Lee   b: 11/2/42, LaPorte, Ind.   BR/TR, 6'6", 215 lbs.   Deb: 9/26/66

1966	Atl-N	1	1	.500	2	2	0	0	0	8¹	7	1	4	9	11.9	2.16	168	.226	.314	0	.000	-0	1	1	-0	0.3
1967	Atl-N	1	1	.500	3	3	0	0	0	21¹	21	1	3	11	11.0	2.95	112	.262	.306	0	.000	-1	1	1	1	0.1
1968	Atl-N★	11	10	.524	35	28	6	1	0	201²	189	10	49	111	10.9	3.35	89	.246	.297	10	.161	1	-8	-8	0	-0.7
1969	*Atl-N	18	10	.643	36	33	7	1	0	241¹	227	24	56	160	10.8	3.47	104	.246	.294	10	.125	-2	3	4	-1	0.1
1970	Atl-N	7	10	.412	21	18	6	0	0	134²	140	16	39	68	12.1	4.41	97	.266	.319	4	.091	-2	-5	-2	-1	-0.4
1971	Atl-N	13	14	.481	32	32	8	1	0	222¹	221	26	54	129	11.2	3.72	100	.261	.306	11	.149	-3	-6	-0	-1	-0.4
1972	Atl-N	11	15	.423	31	30	11	3	0	213	222	18	60	111	12.2	3.93	96	.270	.325	13	.178	-1	-11	-3	1	-0.4
1973	Atl-N	4	11	.267	20	19	2	0	1	116¹	133	7	31	64	12.9	4.41	89	.287	.335	9	.200	-0	-10	-6	1	-0.6
1974	Atl-N	10	11	.476	28	28	6	1	0	186	171	16	41	78	10.4	3.39	112	.243	.286	6	.105	-3	5	8	-2	0.3
1975	Atl-N	4	5	.444	10	10	1	0	0	74²	93	1	16	40	13.1	4.22	89	.304	.339	6	.231	1	-5	-4	-0	-0.3
	StL-N	9	8	.529	24	24	7	2	0	175²	181	4	37	99	11.4	3.23	116	.263	.305	9	.161	-0	8	10	-1	0.8
	Yr	13	13	.500	34	34	8	2	0	250¹	274	5	53	139	11.9	3.52	107	.275	.314	15	.183	1	3	7	-1	0.5
1976	*Phi-N	8	7	.533	59	4	1	0	14	128	88	9	32	96	8.6	2.46	144	.193	.249	4	.167	-0	15	15	1	2.1
1977	*Phi-N	7	5	.583	60	3	0	0	15	124¹	101	9	37	84	10.1	2.75	145	.223	.283	2	.111	-0	16	17	-1	1.9
1978	*Phi-N	3	4	.429	66	0	0	0	17	108²	87	6	23	85	9.5	2.24	160	.223	.275	0	.000	-0	16	16	-2	1.4
1979	Phi-N	13	8	.619	61	0	0	0	9	102	110	9	32	58	12.7	4.15	92	.278	.335	3	.300	1	-5	-4	-0	-0.6
1980	*Phi-N	7	5	.583	55	0	0	0	9	91¹	88	4	30	54	11.7	4.04	94	.253	.314	3	.300	1	-4	-3	-1	-0.2
1981	*Phi-N	5	3	.625	39	0	0	0	8	61¹	54	6	17	40	10.6	3.08	118	.237	.293	3	.500	1	3	4	-1	0.7
1982	Phi-N	5	5	.500	57	2	0	0	14	98	85	4	24	57	10.3	2.66	138	.235	.289	4	.333	2	10	11	2	1.7
1983	*Phi-N	9	1	.900	61	0	0	0	8	95²	89	5	34	73	11.7	3.48	102	.248	.315	1	.167	-0	2	1	-2	-0.1
1984	Chi-A	0	0	—	51	0	0	0	0	73	67	7	14	57	10.1	3.08	135	.248	.288	0	.000	-0	7	9	0	1.0
Total	19	146	140	.510	751	236	55	8	103	2477²	2374	182	633	1481	11.1	3.46	107	.252	.303	98	.158	-6	32	68	-3	6.7

● **STEVE REED**   Reed, Steven Vincent   b: 3/11/66, Los Angeles, Cal.   BR/TR, 6'2", 200 lbs.   Deb: 8/30/92

1992	SF-N	1	0	1.000	18	0	0	0	0	15²	13	2	3	11	9.8	2.30	144	.220	.270	0	—	0	2	2	1	0.2
1993	Col-N	9	5	.643	64	0	0	0	3	84	80	13	30	51	12.1	4.48	106	.259	.330	0	.000	-1	-4	-3	0	0.3
1994	Col-N	3	2	.600	**61**	0	0	0	3	64	79	9	26	51	15.6	3.94	126	.306	.383	0	—	0	2	7	-1	0.4
1995	*Col-N	5	2	.714	71	0	0	0	3	84	61	8	21	79	8.9	2.14	251	.203	.257	1	.333	0	19	**30**	1	2.6
1996	Col-N	4	3	.571	70	0	0	0	0	75	66	11	19	51	10.9	3.96	137	.239	.302	0	.333	1	2	12	-1	1.0
Total	5	22	12	.647	284	0	0	0	9	323	299	43	99	243	11.6	3.54	142	.249	.315	2	.118	-1	21	54	-0	4.5

● **BILL REEDER**   Reeder, William Edgar   b: 2/20/22, Dike, Texas   BR/TR, 6'5", 205 lbs.   Deb: 4/23/49

| 1949 | StL-N | 1 | 1 | .500 | 21 | 1 | 0 | 0 | 0 | 33² | 33 | 2 | 30 | 21 | 17.1 | 5.08 | 82 | .270 | .418 | 0 | — | -0 | -4 | -3 | 0 | -0.3 |

● **STAN REES**   Rees, Stanley Milton "Nellie"   b: 2/25/1899, Cynthiana, Ky.   d: 8/30/37, Lexington, Ky.   BL/TL, 6'3", 190 lbs.   Deb: 6/12/18

| 1918 | Was-A | 1 | 0 | 1.000 | 2 | 0 | 0 | 0 | 0 | 2 | 3 | 0 | 4 | 1 | 31.5 | 0.00 | — | .500 | .700 | 0 | — | 0 | 1 | 1 | 0 | 0.3 |

● **BOBBY REEVES**   Reeves, Robert Edwin "Gunner"   b: 6/24/04, Hill City, Tenn.   d: 6/4/93, Chattanooga, Tenn.   BR/TR, 5'11", 170 lbs.   Deb: 6/9/26 ◆

| 1931 | Bos-A | 0 | 0 | — | 1 | 0 | 0 | 0 | 0 | 7¹ | 6 | 0 | 1 | 0 | 8.6 | 3.68 | 117 | .214 | .241 | 14 | .167 | 1 | 1 | 1 | 0 | 0.0 |

● **MIKE REGAN**   Regan, Michael Joseph   b: 11/19/1887, Phoenix, N.Y.   d: 5/22/61, Albany, N.Y.   BR/TR, 5'11", 165 lbs.   Deb: 5/13/17

1917	Cin-N	11	10	.524	32	26	16	1	0	216	228	4	41	50	11.4	2.71	97	.273	.310	15	.200	1	0	-2	3	0.2
1918	Cin-N	5	5	.500	22	6	4	3	2	80	77	0	29	15	11.9	3.26	82	.262	.328	8	.296	2	-4	-5	-1	-0.5
1919	Cin-N	0	0	—	1	0	0	0	0	2¹	1	0	0	1	3.9	0.00	—	.143	.143	0	.000	-0	1	1	-0	0.0
Total	3	16	15	.516	55	32	20	4	2	298¹	306	4	70	66	11.5	2.84	93	.269	.314	23	.223	3	-4	-7	2	-0.3

● **PHIL REGAN**   Regan, Philip Raymond "The Vulture"   b: 4/6/37, Otsego, Mich.   BR/TR, 6'3", 200 lbs.   Deb: 7/19/60   MC

1960	Det-A	0	4	.000	17	7	0	0	1	68	70	11	25	38	12.8	4.50	88	.267	.336	1	.059	-1	-5	-4	-1	-0.4
1961	Det-A	10	7	.588	32	16	6	0	0	120	134	19	41	46	13.2	5.25	78	.281	.339	-2	.075	-2	-16	-15	-3	-2.4
1962	Det-A	11	9	.550	35	23	6	0	0	171¹	169	23	64	87	12.3	4.04	101	.254	.320	13	.206	1	-1	-0	-2	-0.1
1963	Det-A	15	9	.625	38	27	5	1	1	189	179	33	59	115	11.7	3.86	97	.245	.308	8	.143	-0	-5	-2	-3	-0.6
1964	Det-A	5	10	.333	32	21	2	0	0	146²	162	21	49	91	13.3	5.03	80	.282	.344	13	.317	5	-23	-22	-0	-1.6
1965	Det-A	1	5	.167	16	7	1	0	0	51²	57	6	20	31	13.4	5.05	69	.282	.347	1	.083	-0	-9	-7	-0	-1.1

YEAR TM/L	W	L	PCT	G	GS	CG	SH	SV	IP	H	HR	BB	SO	RAT	ERA	ERA+	OAV	OOB	BH	AVG	PB	PR	/A	PD	TPI
1966 *LA-N☆	14	1	.933	65	0	0	0	**21**	116²	85	6	24	88	8.4	1.62	203	.207	.251	3	.143	0	**26**	**22**	1	3.8
1967 LA-N	6	9	.400	55	3	0	0	6	96¹	108	2	32	53	13.3	2.99	104	.284	.343	1	.100	-0	4	1	1	0.2
1968 LA-N	2	0	1.000	5	0	0	0	0	7²	10	1	1	7	12.9	3.52	78	.313	.333	0	.000	-0	-0	-1	-0	-0.2
Chi-N	10	5	.667	68	0	0	0	25	127	109	9	24	60	9.6	2.20	144	.232	.272	3	.150	-0	11	14	0	2.4
Yr	12	5	.706	73	0	0	0	25	134²	119	10	25	67	9.8	2.27	138	.237	.276	3	.143	-0	11	13	-0	2.2
1969 Chi-N	12	6	.667	71	0	0	0	17	112	120	6	35	56	12.6	3.70	109	.282	.339	0	.000	-1	-1	4	0	0.8
1970 Chi-N	5	9	.357	54	0	0	0	12	75²	81	8	32	31	13.6	4.76	95	.287	.362	0	.000	-1	-6	-2	2	-0.3
1971 Chi-N	5	5	.500	48	1	0	0	6	73¹	84	4	33	28	14.6	3.93	100	.301	.379	0	.000	-1	-4	0	1	0.0
1972 Chi-N	0	1	.000	5	0	0	0	0	4	6	0	2	2	18.0	2.25	169	.400	.471	0	—	0	1	1	0	0.2
Chi-A	0	1	.000	10	0	0	0	1	13¹	18	1	6	4	16.9	4.05	77	.346	.424	1	1.000	-0	-1	-1	-0	0.0
Total 13	96	81	.542	551	105	20	1	92	1372²	1392	150	447	743	12.2	3.84	97	.265	.325	49	.153	1	-31	-16	-4	0.7

● EARL REID

Reid, Earl Percy b: 6/8/13, Bangor, Ala. d: 5/11/84, Cullman, Ala. BL/TR, 6'3", 190 lbs. Deb: 5/8/46

YEAR TM/L	W	L	PCT	G	GS	CG	SH	SV	IP	H	HR	BB	SO	RAT	ERA	ERA+	OAV	OOB	BH	AVG	PB	PR	/A	PD	TPI
1946 Bos-N	1	0	1.000	2	0	0	0	0	3	4	0	3	2	21.0	3.00	114	.308	.438	0	—	0	0	0	-0	0.0

● BILL REIDY

Reidy, William Joseph b: 10/9/1873, Cleveland, Ohio d: 10/14/15, Cleveland, Ohio BR/TR, 5'10", 175 lbs. Deb: 7/21/1896

YEAR TM/L	W	L	PCT	G	GS	CG	SH	SV	IP	H	HR	BB	SO	RAT	ERA	ERA+	OAV	OOB	BH	AVG	PB	PR	/A	PD	TPI
1896 NY-N	0	1	.000	2	1	1	0	0	13	24	1	1	1	20.1	7.62	55	.393	.439	0	.000	-1	-5	-5	0	-0.3
1899 Bro-N	1	0	1.000	2	1	1	0	1	7	9	0	2	1	14.1	2.57	152	.310	.355	0	.000	-1	1	1	0	0.1
1901 Mil-A	16	20	.444	37	33	28	2	0	301¹	364	14	62	50	13.0	4.21	85	.295	.333	16	.143	-6	-18	-21	-3	-2.7
1902 StL-A	5	3	.375	12	9	7	0	0	95	111	0	13	16	12.4	4.45	79	.292	.327	8	.195	-4	-9	-10	-1	-0.6
1903 StL-A	1	4	.200	5	5	5	1	0	43	53	1	7	8	13.2	3.98	73	.301	.339	1	.067	-2	-5	-5	-1	-0.8
Bro-N	6	7	.462	15	13	11	0	0	104	130	0	14	21	13.0	3.46	92	.315	.346	9	.243	1	-2	-3	-0	-0.4
1904 Bro-N	0	4	.000	6	4	2	0	0	38¹	49	0	6	11	13.4	4.46	62	.293	.326	5	.156	-0	-7	-7	-1	-0.8
Total 6	27	41	.397	79	66	55	3	2	601²	740	15	106	109	13.1	4.17	82	.301	.337	39	.159	-9	-46	-50	-5	-5.5

● ART REINHART

Reinhart, Arthur Conrad b: 5/29/1899, Ackley, Iowa d: 11/11/46, Houston, Tex. BL/TL, 6'1", 170 lbs. Deb: 4/26/19

YEAR TM/L	W	L	PCT	G	GS	CG	SH	SV	IP	H	HR	BB	SO	RAT	ERA	ERA+	OAV	OOB	BH	AVG	PB	PR	/A	PD	TPI
1919 StL-N	0	0	—	1	0	0	0	0	0	0	0	0	0	—	—	—	—	1.000	0	—	0	0	0	-0	0.0
1925 StL-N	11	5	.688	20	16	15	1	0	144²	149	7	47	26	12.4	3.05	142	.278	.341	22	.328	5	20	20	-0	2.5
1926 *StL-N	10	5	.667	27	11	9	0	0	143	159	5	47	26	13.2	4.22	93	.295	.355	20	.317	4	-6	-5	1	0.0
1927 StL-N	5	2	.714	21	9	4	2	1	81²	82	5	36	15	13.0	4.19	94	.267	.344	10	.313	2	-2	-1	-0	-0.1
1928 StL-N	4	6	.400	23	9	3	1	2	75¹	80	3	27	12	12.8	2.87	140	.272	.333	4	.167	-0	9	9	-1	1.1
Total 5	30	18	.625	92	45	31	4	3	444²	470	20	157	79	12.9	3.60	113	.280	.345	56	.301	10	20	23	-1	3.5

● JACK REIS

Reis, Harrie Crane b: 6/14/1890, Cincinnati, Ohio d: 7/20/39, Cincinnati, Ohio BR/TR, 5'10.5", 160 lbs. Deb: 9/9/11

YEAR TM/L	W	L	PCT	G	GS	CG	SH	SV	IP	H	HR	BB	SO	RAT	ERA	ERA+	OAV	OOB	BH	AVG	PB	PR	/A	PD	TPI
1911 StL-N	0	0	—	3	0	0	0	0	9¹	5	0	8	4	12.5	0.96	350	.156	.325	0	.000	-0	3	3	0	0.0

● LAURIE REIS

Reis, Lawrence P. b: 11/20/1858, Illinois d: 1/24/21, Chicago, Ill. BR/TR, 160 lbs. Deb: 10/1/1877

YEAR TM/L	W	L	PCT	G	GS	CG	SH	SV	IP	H	HR	BB	SO	RAT	ERA	ERA+	OAV	OOB	BH	AVG	PB	PR	/A	PD	TPI
1877 Chi-N	3	1	.750	4	4	4	1	0	36	29	1	6	11	8.8	0.75	396	.213	.246	2	.125	-2	8	9	-0	0.7
1878 Chi-N	1	3	.250	4	4	4	0	0	36	55	0	4	8	14.8	3.25	77	.335	.351	3	.150	-1	-4	-3	-1	-0.5
Total 2	4	4	.500	8	8	8	1	0	72	84	1	10	19	11.8	2.00	135	.280	.303	5	.139	-2	4	6	-2	0.2

● BOBBY REIS

Reis, Robert Joseph Thomas b: 1/2/09, Woodside, N.Y. d: 5/1/73, St.Paul, Minn. BR/TR, 6'1", 175 lbs. Deb: 9/19/31 ◆

YEAR TM/L	W	L	PCT	G	GS	CG	SH	SV	IP	H	HR	BB	SO	RAT	ERA	ERA+	OAV	OOB	BH	AVG	PB	PR	/A	PD	TPI
1935 Bro-N	3	2	.600	14	2	1	0	2	41¹	46	0	24	7	15.5	2.83	140	.277	.372	21	.247	1	5	5	1	0.8
1936 Bos-N	6	5	.545	35	5	3	0	0	138²	152	7	74	25	15.0	4.48	86	.283	.375	13	.217	1	-7	-10	-4	-0.2
1937 Bos-N	0	0	—	4	0	0	0	0	5	3	0	1	0	14.4	1.80	199	.158	.333	21	.244	1	1	1	-0	-0.2
1938 Bos-N	1	6	.143	16	2	1	0	0	57²	61	5	41	20	16.9	4.99	69	.271	.397	9	.184	-0	-8	-10	0	-1.0
Total 4	10	13	.435	69	9	5	0	2	242²	262	12	144	52	15.5	4.27	88	.277	.379	70	.233	3	-8	-14	5	-0.4

● TOMMY REIS

Reis, Thomas Edward b: 8/6/14, Newport, Ky. BR/TR, 6'2", 180 lbs. Deb: 4/27/38

YEAR TM/L	W	L	PCT	G	GS	CG	SH	SV	IP	H	HR	BB	SO	RAT	ERA	ERA+	OAV	OOB	BH	AVG	PB	PR	/A	PD	TPI
1938 Phi-N	0	1	.000	4	0	0	0	0	4²	8	0	8	2	30.9	19.29	20	.364	.533	0	.000	-0	-8	-8	-0	-1.3
Bos-N	0	0	—	4	0	0	0	0	6¹	8	1	1	4	12.8	7.11	48	.296	.321	0	—	0	-2	-3	-0	0.0
Yr	0	1	.000	8	0	0	0	0	11	16	1	9	6	20.5	12.27	30	.327	.431	0	—	-0	-10	-11	-0	-1.3

● BUGS REISIGL

Reisigl, Jacob b: 12/12/1887, Brooklyn, N.Y. d: 2/24/57, Amsterdam, N.Y. BR/TR, 5'10.5", 175 lbs. Deb: 9/20/11

YEAR TM/L	W	L	PCT	G	GS	CG	SH	SV	IP	H	HR	BB	SO	RAT	ERA	ERA+	OAV	OOB	BH	AVG	PB	PR	/A	PD	TPI
1911 Cle-A	0	1	.000	2	1	1	0	0	13	13	1	3	6	11.1	6.23	55	.271	.314	0	—	-1	-4	-4	-0	-0.3

● DOC REISLING

Reisling, Frank Carl b: 7/25/1874, Martins Ferry, O. d: 3/4/55, Tulsa, Okla. BR/TR, 5'10", 180 lbs. Deb: 9/10/04

YEAR TM/L	W	L	PCT	G	GS	CG	SH	SV	IP	H	HR	BB	SO	RAT	ERA	ERA+	OAV	OOB	BH	AVG	PB	PR	/A	PD	TPI
1904 Bro-N	3	4	.429	7	7	6	1	0	51	45	0	10	19	11.3	2.12	130	.238	.308	2	.154	0	4	4	0	0.5
1905 Bro-N	0	0	—	1	0	0	0	0	3	3	0	4	2	21.0	3.00	96	.273	.467	0	.000	-0	-0	0	0	0.0
1909 Was-A	2	4	.333	10	6	6	1	0	66²	70	0	17	20	11.7	2.43	100	.270	.315	4	.167	-0	0	-1	-1	-0.1
1910 Was-A	10	10	.500	30	20	13	2	1	191	185	3	44	57	11.0	2.54	98	.264	.312	12	.200	-1	-1	-0	0	0.1
Total 4	15	19	.441	49	33	25	4	1	311²	303	3	75	100	11.3	2.45	103	.261	.314	18	.184	-2	3	2	-1	0.5

● BRYAN REKAR

Rekar, Bryan Robert b: 6/3/72, Oaklawn, Ill. BR/TR, 6'3", 205 lbs. Deb: 7/19/95

YEAR TM/L	W	L	PCT	G	GS	CG	SH	SV	IP	H	HR	BB	SO	RAT	ERA	ERA+	OAV	OOB	BH	AVG	PB	PR	/A	PD	TPI
1995 Col-N	4	6	.400	15	14	1	0	0	85	95	11	24	60	12.9	4.98	108	.282	.335	1	.038	-2	-8	4	1	0.2
1996 Col-N	2	4	.333	14	11	0	0	0	58¹	87	11	26	25	18.2	8.95	62	.345	.417	4	.267	-0	-31	-23	-0	-1.9
Total 2	6	10	.375	29	25	1	0	0	143¹	182	22	50	85	15.1	6.59	82	.309	.371	5	.122	-2	-38	-19	1	-1.7

● MIKE REMLINGER

Remlinger, Michael John b: 3/23/66, Middletown, N.Y. BL/TL, 6', 195 lbs. Deb: 6/15/91

YEAR TM/L	W	L	PCT	G	GS	CG	SH	SV	IP	H	HR	BB	SO	RAT	ERA	ERA+	OAV	OOB	BH	AVG	PB	PR	/A	PD	TPI
1991 SF-N	2	1	.667	8	6	1	0	0	35	36	5	20	19	14.4	4.37	82	.271	.366	0	.000	-0	-3	-3	-0	-0.3
1994 NY-N	1	5	.167	10	9	0	0	0	54²	55	9	35	33	15.0	4.61	91	.261	.368	0	.000	-1	-2	-3	-1	-0.5
1995 NY-N	0	1	.000	5	0	0	0	0	5²	7	1	2	6	14.3	6.35	64	.292	.346	0	.000	-0	-1	-0	0	-0.2
Cin-N	0	0	—	2	0	0	0	0	1	2	0	3	1	45.0	9.00	46	.500	.714	0	—	-0	-1	-0	0	0.0
Yr	0	1	.000	7	0	0	0	0	6²	9	1	5	7	18.9	6.75	60	.321	.424	0	—	-0	-1	-0	0	-0.2
1996 Cin-N	0	0	—	19	4	0	0	0	27¹	24	4	19	19	15.1	5.60	74	.242	.380	1	.143	-0	-4	-4	0	-0.1
Total 4	3	8	.273	44	19	1	0	0	123²	124	19	79	78	15.1	4.88	82	.263	.374	1	.032	-2	-11	-12	-1	-1.1

● WIN REMMERSWAAL

Remmerswaal, Wilhelmus Abraham b: 3/8/54, The Hague, Holland BR/TR, 6'2", 160 lbs. Deb: 8/3/79

YEAR TM/L	W	L	PCT	G	GS	CG	SH	SV	IP	H	HR	BB	SO	RAT	ERA	ERA+	OAV	OOB	BH	AVG	PB	PR	/A	PD	TPI
1979 Bos-A	1	0	1.000	8	0	0	0	0	20¹	26	1	12	16	17.3	7.08	62	.317	.411		—	0	-6	-6	-0	-0.7
1980 Bos-A	2	1	.667	14	0	0	0	0	35¹	39	4	9	20	12.2	4.58	92	.295	.340		—	0	-2	-1	-1	-0.2
Total 2	3	1	.750	22	0	0	0	0	55²	65	5	21	36	14.1	5.50	78	.304	.369		—	0	-9	-7	-1	-0.9

● ALEX REMNEAS

Remneas, Alexander Norman b: 2/21/1886, Minneapolis, Minn. d: 8/27/75, Phoenix, Ariz. BR/TR, 6'1", 180 lbs. Deb: 4/15/12

YEAR TM/L	W	L	PCT	G	GS	CG	SH	SV	IP	H	HR	BB	SO	RAT	ERA	ERA+	OAV	OOB	BH	AVG	PB	PR	/A	PD	TPI
1912 Det-A	0	0	—	1	0	0	0	0	1²	3	0	4	0	27.0	27.00	12	.455	.455	0	—	-0	-4	-4	-0	0.0
1915 StL-A	0	0	—	2	0	0	0	0	6	3	0	3	10	10.5	1.50	191	.136	.269	0	.000	-0	1	1	0	0.0
Total 2	0	0	—	3	0	0	0	0	7²	6	0	7	10	14.1	7.04	42	.242	.324	0	.000	-0	-3	-3	-0	0.0

● ERWIN RENFER

Renfer, Erwin Arthur b: 12/11/1891, Elgin, Ill. d: 10/26/57, Sycamore, Ill. BR/TR, 6', 180 lbs. Deb: 9/18/13

YEAR TM/L	W	L	PCT	G	GS	CG	SH	SV	IP	H	HR	BB	SO	RAT	ERA	ERA+	OAV	OOB	BH	AVG	PB	PR	/A	PD	TPI
1913 Det-A	0	1	.000	1	1	0	0	0	6	5	0	3	1	13.5	6.00	49	.227	.346	0	—	-0	-2	-2	0	-0.3

● LADDIE RENFROE

Renfroe, Cohen Williams b: 5/9/62, Natchez, Miss. BB/TR, 5'11", 200 lbs. Deb: 7/3/91

YEAR TM/L	W	L	PCT	G	GS	CG	SH	SV	IP	H	HR	BB	SO	RAT	ERA	ERA+	OAV	OOB	BH	AVG	PB	PR	/A	PD	TPI
1991 Chi-N	0	1	.000	4	0	0	0	0	4²	11	1	2	4	25.1	13.50	29	.440	.481	0	.000	-0	-5	-5	-0	-0.9

● MARSHALL RENFROE

Renfroe, Marshall Daniel b: 5/25/36, Century, Fla. d: 12/10/70, Pensacola, Fla. BL/TL, 6', 180 lbs. Deb: 9/27/59

YEAR TM/L	W	L	PCT	G	GS	CG	SH	SV	IP	H	HR	BB	SO	RAT	ERA	ERA+	OAV	OOB	BH	AVG	PB	PR	/A	PD	TPI
1959 SF-N	0	0	—	1	1	0	0	0	2	3	1	3	3	27.0	27.00	14	.333	.500	0	—	-0	-5	-5	-0	0.0

● HAL RENIFF

Reniff, Harold Eugene "Porky" b: 7/2/38, Warren, Ohio BR/TR, 6', 215 lbs. Deb: 6/8/61

YEAR TM/L	W	L	PCT	G	GS	CG	SH	SV	IP	H	HR	BB	SO	RAT	ERA	ERA+	OAV	OOB	BH	AVG	PB	PR	/A	PD	TPI
1961 NY-A	2	0	1.000	25	0	0	0	2	45¹	31	1	31	21	12.3	2.58	144	.197	.330	0	.000	-1	7	6	-1	0.2
1962 NY-A	0	0	—	2	0	0	0	0	3²	4	0	1	1	12.3	7.36	51	.400	.571	0	—	-0	-1	-1	-0	-0.1
1963 *NY-A	4	3	.571	48	0	0	0	18	89¹	63	3	42	56	10.8	2.62	134	.202	.301	0	—	-1	10	9	3	1.2
1964 *NY-A	6	4	.600	41	0	0	0	9	69¹	47	3	30	38	10.0	3.12	116	.199	.289	1	.100	-0	4	4	0	0.6
1965 NY-A	3	4	.429	51	0	0	0	4	85¹	74	4	48	74	13.4	3.80	90	.232	.341	0	.000	-0	-3	-4	-0	-0.4
1966 NY-A	3	7	.300	56	0	0	0	9	95¹	80	2	49	79	12.7	3.21	104	.229	.333	4	.286	1	2	-1	-0	0.2

YEAR	TM/L	W	L	PCT	G	GS	CG	SH	SV	IP	H	HR	BB	SO	RAT	ERA	ERA+	OAV	OOB	BH	AVG	PB	PR	/A	PD	TPI
1967	NY-A	0	2	.000	24	0	0	0	0	40	40	0	14	24	12.8	4.27	73	.256	.329	0	.000	-0	-5	-5	-1	-0.3
	NY-N	3	3	.500	29	0	0	0	4	43	42	1	23	21	13.8	3.35	101	.266	.363	0	.000	-0	0	0	-1	-0.1
Total 7		21	23	.477	276	0	0	0	45	471¹	383	14	242	314	12.3	3.27	106	.225	.327	5	.096	-2	14	10	-0	1.4

● **JIM RENINGER**   Reninger, James David   b: 3/7/15, Aurora, Ill.   d: 8/23/93, N.Fort Myers, Fla.   BR/TR, 6'3", 210 lbs.   Deb: 9/17/38

YEAR	TM/L	W	L	PCT	G	GS	CG	SH	SV	IP	H	HR	BB	SO	RAT	ERA	ERA+	OAV	OOB	BH	AVG	PB	PR	/A	PD	TPI
1938	Phi-A	0	2	.000	4	4	1	0	0	22²	28	3	14	9	16.7	7.15	68	.295	.385	0	.000	-0	-6	-6	0	-0.4
1939	Phi-A	0	2	.000	4	2	0	0	0	16¹	24	3	12	3	19.8	7.71	61	.369	.468	1	.167	-0	-6	-5	0	-0.5
Total 2		0	4	.000	8	6	1	0	0	39	52	6	26	12	18.0	7.38	65	.325	.419	1	.077	-1	-12	-11	0	-0.9

● **STEVE RENKO**   Renko, Steven   b: 12/10/44, Kansas City, Kan.   BR/TR, 6'5", 230 lbs.   Deb: 6/27/69

YEAR	TM/L	W	L	PCT	G	GS	CG	SH	SV	IP	H	HR	BB	SO	RAT	ERA	ERA+	OAV	OOB	BH	AVG	PB	PR	/A	PD	TPI
1969	Mon-N	6	7	.462	18	15	4	0	0	103¹	94	14	50	68	12.7	4.01	92	.243	.333	6	.167	1	-5	-4	-1	-0.4
1970	Mon-N	13	11	.542	41	33	7	1	1	222²	203	27	104	142	12.7	4.32	95	.241	.329	16	.200	2	-7	-5	-0	-0.3
1971	Mon-N	15	14	.517	40	37	9	3	0	275²	256	24	135	129	12.9	3.75	94	.247	.336	21	.210	4	-9	-7	-2	-0.4
1972	Mon-N	1	10	.091	30	12	0	0	0	97	96	11	67	66	15.1	5.20	68	.262	.376	7	.292	1	-19	-18	1	-1.7
1973	Mon-N	15	11	.577	36	34	9	0	1	249²	201	26	108	164	11.2	2.81	136	.218	.300	24	.273	7	24	28	-2	3.6
1974	Mon-N	12	16	.429	37	35	8	1	0	227²	222	17	81	138	12.0	4.03	95	.257	.321	17	.210	3	-10	-5	3	0.1
1975	Mon-N	6	12	.333	31	25	3	1	1	170¹	175	20	76	99	13.3	4.07	94	.265	.341	15	.278	5	-8	-5	-0	0.0
1976	Mon-N	0	1	.000	5	1	0	0	0	13	15	2	3	4	12.5	5.54	67	.288	.327	1	.333	0	-3	-3	-1	-0.2
	Chi-N	8	11	.421	28	27	4	1	0	163¹	164	12	43	112	11.4	3.86	100	.258	.305	5	.094	-3	-6	-0	-1	-0.5
	Yr	8	12	.400	33	28	4	1	0	176¹	179	14	46	116	11.5	3.98	97	.260	.307	6	.107	-3	-9	-3	-2	-0.7
1977	Chi-N	2	2	.500	13	8	0	0	1	51¹	51	10	21	34	12.8	4.56	96	.258	.332	2	.167	0	-4	-1	-1	-0.2
	Chi-A	5	0	1.000	8	8	0	0	2	53¹	55	3	17	36	12.3	3.54	115	.274	.333	0	—	0	3	3	0	0.3
1978	Oak-A	6	12	.333	27	25	3	1	0	151	152	10	67	89	13.2	4.29	85	.265	.344	0	—	0	-9	-11	-0	-0.8
1979	Bos-A	11	9	.550	27	27	4	1	0	171	174	22	53	99	12.1	4.11	107	.260	.317	0	—	0	2	6	-1	0.3
1980	Bos-A	9	9	.500	32	23	1	0	0	165¹	180	17	56	90	12.9	4.19	101	.281	.340	0	—	0	-3	-0	-1	-0.2
1981	Cal-A	8	4	.667	22	15	0	0	1	102	93	7	42	50	12.0	3.44	106	.250	.328	0	—	0	2	2	-2	0.1
1982	Cal-A	11	6	.647	31	23	4	0	0	156	163	17	51	81	12.4	4.44	91	.269	.327	0	—	0	-6	-7	-2	-0.8
1983	KC-A	6	11	.353	25	17	1	0	1	121¹	144	9	50	53	14.3	4.30	95	.293	.341	0	—	0	-3	-3	-1	-0.5
Total 15		134	146	.479	451	365	57	9	6	2494	2438	248	1010	1455	12.5	3.99	98	.256	.329	114	.215	21	-62	-27	-9	-1.6

● **ANDY REPLOGLE**   Replogle, Andrew David   b: 10/7/53, South Bend, Ind.   BR/TR, 6'5", 205 lbs.   Deb: 4/11/78

YEAR	TM/L	W	L	PCT	G	GS	CG	SH	SV	IP	H	HR	BB	SO	RAT	ERA	ERA+	OAV	OOB	BH	AVG	PB	PR	/A	PD	TPI
1978	Mil-A	9	5	.643	32	18	3	2	0	149¹	177	14	47	61	13.6	3.92	96	.301	.353	0	—	0	-3	-3	-2	-0.5
1979	Mil-A	0	0	—	3	0	0	0	0	8	13	0	2	2	16.9	5.63	70	.382	.417	0	—	0	-1	-1	0	0.0
Total 2		9	5	.643	35	18	3	2	0	157¹	190	14	49	63	13.7	4.00	94	.305	.357	0	—	0	-4	-4	-2	-0.5

● **XAVIER RESCIGNO**   Rescigno, Xavier Frederick "Mr. X"   b: 10/13/13, New York, N.Y.   BR/TR, 5'10.5", 175 lbs.   Deb: 4/22/43

YEAR	TM/L	W	L	PCT	G	GS	CG	SH	SV	IP	H	HR	BB	SO	RAT	ERA	ERA+	OAV	OOB	BH	AVG	PB	PR	/A	PD	TPI
1943	Pit-N	6	9	.400	37	14	5	1	2	132²	125	6	45	41	11.7	2.98	117	.252	.317	5	.143	0	6	7	-2	0.6
1944	Pit-N	10	8	.556	48	6	2	0	5	124	146	9	34	45	13.1	4.35	85	.291	.337	2	.091	-1	-10	-9	-0	-1.3
1945	Pit-N	3	5	.375	44	1	0	0	9	78²	95	6	34	29	14.9	5.72	69	.303	.372	2	.133	-0	-17	-16	-0	-1.8
Total 3		19	22	.463	129	21	7	1	16	335¹	366	21	113	115	13.0	4.13	89	.279	.338	9	.125	-1	-21	-17	-3	-2.5

● **GEORGE RETTGER**   Rettger, George Edward   b: 7/29/1868, Cleveland, Ohio   d: 6/5/21, Lakewood, Ohio   BR/TR, 5'11", 175 lbs.   Deb: 8/13/1891

YEAR	TM/L	W	L	PCT	G	GS	CG	SH	SV	IP	H	HR	BB	SO	RAT	ERA	ERA+	OAV	OOB	BH	AVG	PB	PR	/A	PD	TPI
1891	StL-a	7	3	.700	14	12	10	1	1	92²	85	4	51	49	14.0	3.40	124	.235	.343	3	.071	-3	3	8	-1	0.4
1892	Cle-N	1	3	.250	6	5	3	0	0	38	32	2	31	12	15.2	4.26	80	.219	.360	2	.133	-0	-4	-4	-0	-0.4
	Cin-N	1	0	1.000	1	1	1	0	0	9	8	0	10	1	19.0	4.00	82	.229	.413	1	.125	-0	-1	-1	-0	-0.1
	Yr	2	3	.400	7	6	4	0	0	47	40	2	41	13	15.7	4.21	80	.220	.366	3	.130	-0	-5	-4	-0	-0.5
Total 2		9	6	.600	21	18	14	1	1	139²	125	6	92	62	14.6	3.67	107	.231	.352	6	.092	-3	-1	4	-1	-0.1

● **OTTO RETTIG**   Rettig, Adolph John   b: 1/29/1894, New York, N.Y.   d: 6/16/77, Stuart, Fla.   BR/TR, 5'11", 165 lbs.   Deb: 7/19/22

YEAR	TM/L	W	L	PCT	G	GS	CG	SH	SV	IP	H	HR	BB	SO	RAT	ERA	ERA+	OAV	OOB	BH	AVG	PB	PR	/A	PD	TPI
1922	Phi-A	2	1	.333	4	4	1	0	0	18¹	18	0	12	3	15.2	4.91	87	.265	.383	0	.000	-1	-2	-1	0	-0.3

● **ED REULBACH**   Reulbach, Edward Marvin "Big Ed"   b: 12/1/1882, Detroit, Mich.   d: 7/17/61, Glens Falls, N.Y.   BR/TR, 6'1", 190 lbs.   Deb: 5/16/05

YEAR	TM/L	W	L	PCT	G	GS	CG	SH	SV	IP	H	HR	BB	SO	RAT	ERA	ERA+	OAV	OOB	BH	AVG	PB	PR	/A	PD	TPI
1905	Chi-N	18	14	.563	34	29	28	5	1	291²	208	1	73	152	9.2	1.42	210	**.201**	.266	14	.127	-6	51	51	-1	4.8
1906	*Chi-N	19	4	**.826**	33	24	20	8	1	218	129	1	92	94	9.7	1.65	160	**.175**	.278	13	.157	-2	24	24	3	2.8
1907	*Chi-N	17	4	**.810**	27	22	16	4	0	192	147	1	64	96	10.3	1.69	148	.217	.294	11	.175	0	17	17	1	2.1
1908	*Chi-N	24	7	**.774**	46	35	25	7	1	297²	227	4	106	133	10.4	2.03	116	.214	.292	23	.232	7	11	11	-1	1.7
1909	*Chi-N	19	10	.655	35	32	23	6	0	262²	194	1	82	105	9.8	1.78	143	.212	.294	12	.140	-1	24	22	4	2.9
1910	*Chi-N	12	8	.600	24	23	14	1	0	173¹	161	1	49	55	11.4	3.12	92	.250	.312	6	.107	-3	-2	-5	1	-0.8
1911	Chi-N	16	9	.640	33	29	15	2	0	221²	191	3	103	79	12.1	2.96	112	.236	.325	6	.090	-1	11	9	3	1.0
1912	Chi-N	10	6	.625	39	19	8	0	4	169	161	7	60	75	12.2	3.78	88	.259	.332	6	.109	-3	-7	-8	4	-0.6
1913	Chi-N	1	3	.250	10	3	1	0	0	38²	31	2	16	14	14.7	4.42	72	.281	.375	3	.250	-1	-5	-5	0	-0.5
	Bro-N	7	6	.538	15	12	8	2	0	110	77	3	34	46	9.4	2.05	161	.202	.274	3	.143	0	14	15	-1	1.7
	Yr	8	9	.471	25	15	9	2	0	148²	118	4	55	56	10.7	2.66	123	.223	.301	6	.146	-1	9	10	-1	1.2
1914	Bro-N	11	18	.379	44	29	14	3	3	256	228	5	83	119	11.3	2.64	108	.242	.310	9	.122	-0	4	4	1	0.8
1915	New-F	21	10	.677	33	30	23	4	1	270	233	3	69	117	10.2	2.23	115	.236	.287	18	.196	-2	15	10	1	1.1
1916	Bos-N	7	6	.538	21	11	6	0	0	109¹	99	1	41	47	11.9	2.47	101	.251	.328	3	.091	-1	2	0	5	0.5
1917	Bos-N	1	0	1.000	5	2	0	0	0	22¹	21	0	15	9	14.9	2.82	90	.256	.378	0	.000	1	-0	-1	1	0.2
Total 13		182	106	.632	399	300	201	40	13	2632¹	2117	33	892	1137	10.7	2.28	124	.224	.299	127	.147	-11	159	146	22	17.7

● **PAUL REUSCHEL**   Reuschel, Paul Richard   b: 1/12/47, Quincy, Ill.   BR/TR, 6'4", 225 lbs.   Deb: 7/25/75   F

YEAR	TM/L	W	L	PCT	G	GS	CG	SH	SV	IP	H	HR	BB	SO	RAT	ERA	ERA+	OAV	OOB	BH	AVG	PB	PR	/A	PD	TPI
1975	Chi-N	1	3	.250	28	0	0	0	0	36	44	1	13	12	14.5	3.50	110	.312	.374	0	.000	-0	0	1	0	0.2
1976	Chi-N	4	2	.667	50	2	0	0	3	87	94	12	33	55	13.2	4.55	85	.278	.344	2	.154	-0	-10	-7	1	-0.4
1977	Chi-N	5	6	.455	69	0	0	0	4	107	105	9	40	62	12.2	4.37	100	.262	.329	0	.000	-1	-6	-0	2	0.1
1978	Chi-N	2	0	1.000	16	0	0	0	0	28	29	4	13	13	13.8	5.14	78	.269	.352	0	—	0	-5	-3	-0	-0.3
	Cle-A	2	4	.333	18	6	1	0	0	89²	95	4	32	24	11.9	3.11	120	.271	.318	0	—	0	6	6	1	0.5
1979	Cle-A	2	1	.667	17	1	0	0	1	45¹	73	7	11	22	16.7	7.94	54	.365	.398	0	—	0	-19	-19	1	-1.1
Total 5		16	16	.500	198	9	1	0	13	393	440	38	132	188	13.2	4.51	89	.286	.344	2	.063	-2	-32	-21	5	-1.0

● **RICK REUSCHEL**   Reuschel, Rickey Eugene   b: 5/16/49, Quincy, Ill.   BR/TR, 6'3", 235 lbs.   Deb: 6/19/72   F

YEAR	TM/L	W	L	PCT	G	GS	CG	SH	SV	IP	H	HR	BB	SO	RAT	ERA	ERA+	OAV	OOB	BH	AVG	PB	PR	/A	PD	TPI
1972	Chi-N	10	8	.556	21	18	5	4	0	129	127	3	29	87	11.0	2.93	130	.259	.303	6	.136	-1	7	13	-0	1.6
1973	Chi-N	14	15	.483	36	36	7	3	0	237	244	15	62	168	11.8	3.00	131	.263	.312	9	.123	-3	17	25	4	3.0
1974	Chi-N	13	12	.520	41	38	6	2	0	240²	262	18	83	160	13.1	4.30	89	.276	.338	19	.221	2	-18	-13	5	-0.6
1975	Chi-N	11	17	.393	38	37	6	0	1	234	244	17	67	155	12.2	3.73	103	.268	.323	16	.208	2	-3	-3	3	0.8
1976	Chi-N	14	12	.538	38	37	9	2	1	260	260	17	64	146	11.5	3.46	111	.265	.315	19	.229	4	1	11	3	1.9
1977	Chi-N★	20	10	.667	39	37	8	4	1	252	233	13	74	166	11.1	2.79	157	.247	.305	18	.207	1	31	**45**	3	5.8
1978	Chi-N	14	15	.483	35	35	9	1	0	242²	235	16	54	115	10.9	3.41	114	.254	.299	10	.137	-1	4	17	2	2.0
1979	Chi-N	18	12	.600	36	36	5	1	0	239	251	16	75	125	12.7	3.62	114	.274	.335	13	.165	1	3	13	5	2.1
1980	Chi-N	11	13	.458	38	38	6	0	0	257	281	13	76	140	12.6	3.40	115	.274	.340	13	.159	-1	6	15	5	1.8
1981	Chi-N	4	7	.364	13	13	1	0	0	85²	87	4	23	53	12.2	3.47	107	.267	.323	2	.080	-1	7	8	2	0.3
	*NY-A	4	4	.500	12	11	3	0	0	70²	75	4	10	22	11.0	2.67	134	.280	.308	0	—	0	8	7	1	0.9
1983	Chi-N	1	1	.500	4	4	1	0	0	20²	18	1	10	9	12.2	3.92	97	.234	.322	1	.143	-0	-1	-0	1	0.1
1984	Chi-N	5	5	.500	19	14	1	0	0	92¹	123	7	23	43	14.5	5.17	76	.339	.383	7	.241	-2	-16	-13	1	-1.0
1985	Pit-N	14	8	.636	31	26	9	1	1	194	153	7	52	138	9.6	2.27	157	.215	.272	10	.169	1	28	28	4	4.0
1986	Pit-N	9	16	.360	35	34	4	2	0	215²	232	20	57	125	12.4	3.96	97	.274	.326	11	.157	-0	-6	-3	3	0.0
1987	Pit-N★	8	6	.571	25	25	9	3	0	177	163	12	35	80	10.4	2.75	150	.246	.290	9	.150	-2	26	27	1	2.3
	*SF-N	5	3	.625	9	8	3	1	0	50	44	1	7	27	9.5	4.32	89	.230	.265	2	.105	-0	-1	-3	0	-0.4
	Yr	13	9	.591	34	33	**12**	**4**	0	227	207	13	42	107	**10.0**	3.09	131	.239	.276	11	.139	-2	25	24	1	1.9
1988	SF-N	19	11	.633	36	36	7	2	0	245	242	11	42	92	10.7	3.12	104	.260	.297	8	.110	-1	9	4	-2	0.0
1989	*SF-N★	17	8	.680	32	32	2	0	0	208¹	195	11	53	111	10.8	2.94	115	.247	.297	10	.164	1	13	10	-0	1.3
1990	SF-N	3	6	.333	15	15	0	0	1	87	102	8	31	49	13.9	3.93	93	.297	.357	0	.154	-0	-1	-3	0	-0.2

YEAR	TM/L	W	L	PCT	G	GS	CG	SH	SV	IP	H	HR	BB	SO	RAT	ERA	ERA+	OAV	OOB	BH	AVG	PB	PR	/A	PD	TPI
1991	SF-N	0	2	.000	4	1	0	0	0	10²	17	0	7	4	20.3	4.22	85	.370	.453	0	.000	-0	-1	-1	-0	-0.2
Total	19	214	191	.528	557	529	102	26	5	3548¹	3588	221	935	2015	11.7	3.37	114	.264	.316	187	.168	8	108	183	39	25.5

● **JERRY REUSS**   Reuss, Jerry b: 6/19/49, St.Louis, Mo.   BL/TL, 6'5", 217 lbs.   Deb: 9/27/69

YEAR	TM/L	W	L	PCT	G	GS	CG	SH	SV	IP	H	HR	BB	SO	RAT	ERA	ERA+	OAV	OOB	BH	AVG	PB	PR	/A	PD	TPI
1969	StL-N	1	0	1.000	1	1	0	0	0	7	2	0	3	3	9.0	0.00	—	.091	.259	1	.333	0	3	3	0	0.6
1970	StL-N	7	8	.467	20	20	5	2	0	127¹	132	9	49	74	12.9	4.10	100	.271	.339	2	.050	-3	-1	0	-0	-0.2
1971	StL-N	14	14	.500	36	35	7	2	0	211	228	13	109	131	14.7	4.78	75	.279	.368	8	.123	0	-31	-28	-2	-3.5
1972	Hou-N	9	13	.409	33	30	4	1	1	192	177	14	83	174	12.7	4.17	81	.246	.332	7	.106	-1	-15	-17	-1	-2.0
1973	Hou-N	16	13	.552	41	40	12	3	0	279¹	271	17	117	177	12.6	3.74	97	.256	.332	13	.137	-1	-2	-3	-1	-0.7
1974	*Pit-N	16	11	.593	35	35	14	1	0	260	259	20	101	105	12.5	3.50	99	.261	.329	13	.151	0	4	-1	-2	-0.3
1975	*Pit-N★	18	11	.621	32	32	15	6	0	237¹	224	17	78	131	11.5	2.54	139	.253	.314	14	.197	-1	28	26	2	3.7
1976	Pit-N	14	9	.609	31	29	11	3	2	209¹	209	16	51	108	11.3	3.53	99	.256	.301	16	.242	6	-1	-1	-0	0.3
1977	Pit-N	10	13	.435	33	33	8	2	0	208	225	11	77	116	13.0	4.11	97	.280	.341	12	.171	1	-5	-3	-1	-0.1
1978	Pit-N	3	2	.600	23	12	3	1	0	82²	97	5	23	42	13.4	4.90	76	.297	.348	5	.185	0	-12	-11	-0	-0.6
1979	LA-N	7	14	.333	39	21	4	1	3	160	178	4	60	83	13.6	3.54	103	.282	.347	7	.167	1	3	2	1	0.5
1980	LA-N★	18	6	.750	37	29	10	**6**	3	229¹	193	12	40	111	9.1	2.51	139	.227	.261	6	.088	-1	28	25	1	2.7
1981	*LA-N	10	4	.714	22	22	8	2	0	152²	138	6	27	51	10.0	2.30	144	.243	.282	10	.196	0	20	17	3	1.9
1982	LA-N	18	11	.621	39	37	8	4	0	254²	232	11	50	138	10.0	3.11	111	.240	.278	17	.221	3	14	10	2	1.6
1983	*LA-N	12	11	.522	32	31	7	0	0	223¹	233	11	50	143	11.5	2.94	122	.271	.313	20	.282	5	17	16	4	2.7
1984	LA-N	5	7	.417	30	15	2	0	1	99	102	4	31	44	12.1	3.82	92	.266	.321	4	.167	1	-3	-3	-0	-0.3
1985	*LA-N	14	10	.583	34	33	5	3	0	212²	210	16	58	84	11.5	2.92	119	.260	.312	10	.135	-1	16	13	-2	1.1
1986	LA-N	2	6	.250	19	13	0	0	0	74	96	13	17	29	14.0	5.84	59	.313	.353	5	.250	-1	-17	-20	1	-1.7
1987	LA-N	0	0	—	1	0	0	0	0	2	2	0	0	2	9.0	4.50	88	.333	.333	-0	—	-0	-0	-0	-0	-0
	Cin-N	0	5	.000	7	7	0	0	0	34²	52	2	12	10	16.9	7.79	54	.351	.404	1	.125	0	-14	-14	-1	-1.6
	Yr	0	5	.000	8	7	0	0	0	36²	54	2	12	12	16.4	7.61	56	.348	.399	1	.125	0	-14	-14	-1	-1.6
	Cal-A	4	5	.444	17	16	1	1	0	82¹	112	16	17	37	14.3	5.25	82	.327	.362	0	—	0	-7	-9	-2	-0.7
1988	Chi-A	13	9	.591	32	29	2	0	0	183	183	15	43	73	11.3	3.44	115	.263	.309	0	—	0	11	11	0	1.2
1989	Chi-A	8	5	.615	23	19	1	1	0	106²	135	12	21	27	13.4	5.06	75	.308	.344	0	—	0	-14	-15	-2	-1.8
	Mil-A	1	4	.200	7	7	0	0	0	33²	36	7	13	13	13.4	5.35	72	.273	.342	0	—	0	-5	-6	-0	-0.7
	Yr	9	9	.500	30	26	1	1	0	140¹	171	19	34	40	13.2	5.13	74	.295	.336	0	—	0	-19	-21	-2	-2.5
1990	Pit-N	0	0	—	4	1	0	0	0	7²	8	1	3	1	12.9	3.52	103	.267	.333	0	—	0	0	0	0	0.0
Total	22	220	191	.535	628	547	127	39	11	3669²	3734	245	1127	1907	12.1	3.64	100	.265	.322	171	.167	15	16	-7	2	2.1

● **TODD REVENIG**   Revenig, Todd Michael b: 6/28/69, Brainerd, Minn.   BR/TR, 6'1", 185 lbs.   Deb: 8/24/92

YEAR	TM/L	W	L	PCT	G	GS	CG	SH	SV	IP	H	HR	BB	SO	RAT	ERA	ERA+	OAV	OOB	BH	AVG	PB	PR	/A	PD	TPI
1992	Oak-A	0	0	—	2	0	0	0	0	2	2	0	1	1	9.0	0.00	—	.286	.286	0	—	0	1	1	-0	0.4

● **CARLOS REYES**   Reyes, Carlos Alberto b: 4/4/69, Miami, Fla.   BB/TR, 6'1", 190 lbs.   Deb: 4/7/94

YEAR	TM/L	W	L	PCT	G	GS	CG	SH	SV	IP	H	HR	BB	SO	RAT	ERA	ERA+	OAV	OOB	BH	AVG	PB	PR	/A	PD	TPI
1994	Oak-A	0	3	.000	27	9	0	0	0	78	71	10	44	57	13.5	4.15	107	.242	.345	0	—	0	6	2	-1	0.5
1995	Oak-A	4	6	.400	40	1	0	0	0	69	71	10	28	48	13.6	5.09	88	.264	.344	0	—	0	-3	-5	1	-0.4
1996	Oak-A	7	10	.412	46	10	0	0	1	122¹	134	19	61	78	14.5	4.78	101	.281	.365	0	—	0	3	0	-1	0.1
Total	3	11	19	.367	113	20	0	0	1	269¹	276	39	133	183	14.0	4.68	99	.266	.354	0	—	0	6	-2	-2	0.1

● **ALBERTO REYES**   Reyes, Rafael Alberto b: 4/10/71, San Cristobal, D.R.   BR/TR, 6'1", 195 lbs.   Deb: 4/27/95

YEAR	TM/L	W	L	PCT	G	GS	CG	SH	SV	IP	H	HR	BB	SO	RAT	ERA	ERA+	OAV	OOB	BH	AVG	PB	PR	/A	PD	TPI
1995	Mil-A	1	1	.500	27	0	0	0	0	33¹	19	3	18	29	10.8	2.43	205	.167	.296	0	—	0	8	9	0	0.4
1996	Mil-A	1	0	1.000	5	0	0	0	0	5²	8	1	2	2	15.9	7.94	66	.320	.370	0	—	0	-2	-2	-0	-0.4
Total	2	2	1	.667	32	0	0	0	0	39	27	4	20	31	11.5	3.23	155	.194	.309	0	—	0	7	8	0	0.4

● **ALLIE REYNOLDS**   Reynolds, Allie Pierce "Superchief" b: 2/10/15, Bethany, Okla.   d: 12/26/94, Oklahoma City, Okla.   BR/TR, 6', 195 lbs.   Deb: 9/17/42

YEAR	TM/L	W	L	PCT	G	GS	CG	SH	SV	IP	H	HR	BB	SO	RAT	ERA	ERA+	OAV	OOB	BH	AVG	PB	PR	/A	PD	TPI
1942	Cle-A	0	0	—	2	0	0	0	0	5	5	0	4	2	16.2	0.00	—	.250	.375	1	.000	-0	2	2	-0	0.0
1943	Cle-A	11	12	.478	34	21	11	3	3	198²	140	3	109	**151**	11.6	2.99	104	**.202**	.316	10	.149	-1	7	3	-0	0.1
1944	Cle-A	11	8	.579	28	21	5	1	1	158	141	2	91	84	13.4	3.30	100	.240	.346	7	.123	-3	2	-0	-1	-0.4
1945	Cle-A†	18	12	.600	44	30	16	2	1	247¹	227	7	130	112	13.2	3.20	101	.247	.343	8	.094	-7	5	1	-1	-0.7
1946	Cle-A	11	15	.423	31	28	9	3	0	183¹	180	10	108	107	14.2	3.88	85	.259	.359	14	.222	1	-8	-12	-1	-1.5
1947	*NY-A	19	8	**.704**	34	30	17	4	2	241²	207	23	123	129	12.4	3.20	110	.227	.322	16	.146	-2	13	9	-2	0.6
1948	NY-A	16	7	.696	39	31	11	1	3	236¹	240	17	111	101	13.5	3.77	108	.268	.351	16	.193	0	14	8	-3	0.6
1949	*NY-A☆	17	6	.739	35	31	4	2	1	213²	200	15	123	105	13.8	4.00	101	.250	.353	17	.218	6	5	1	-0	0.6
1950	*NY-A★	16	12	.571	35	29	14	2	2	240²	215	12	138	160	13.5	3.74	115	.242	.349	15	.185	1	22	15	-1	1.5
1951	*NY-A	17	8	.680	40	26	16	**7**	7	221	171	12	100	126	11.2	3.05	125	**.213**	.304	14	.184	0	26	19	-3	1.8
1952	*NY-A☆	20	8	.714	35	29	24	**6**	6	244¹	194	10	97	**160**	11.0	2.06	161	.218	.300	13	.153	-1	**44**	34	-1	3.9
1953	*NY-A★	13	7	.650	41	15	5	1	13	145	140	21	61	86	12.8	3.41	108	.253	.333	5	.122	1	9	4	-2	0.5
1954	NY-A†	13	4	.765	36	18	5	4	1	157¹	133	13	66	100	11.6	3.32	104	.233	.316	6	.160	-0	7	2	-0	0.1
Total	13	182	107	.630	434	309	137	36	49	2492¹	2193	133	1261	1423	12.7	3.30	110	.238	.333	140	.163	-5	149	87	-16	6.9

● **ARCHIE REYNOLDS**   Reynolds, Archie Edward b: 1/3/46, Glendale, Cal.   BR/TR, 6'2", 205 lbs.   Deb: 8/15/68

YEAR	TM/L	W	L	PCT	G	GS	CG	SH	SV	IP	H	HR	BB	SO	RAT	ERA	ERA+	OAV	OOB	BH	AVG	PB	PR	/A	PD	TPI
1968	Chi-N	0	1	.000	7	1	0	0	0	13¹	14	1	7	6	14.9	6.75	47	.259	.355	1	.500	1	-6	-5	-0	-0.2
1969	Chi-N	0	1	.000	2	2	0	0	0	7¹	11	1	7	4	22.1	2.45	164	.379	.500	1	.000	0	1	1	-0	0.2
1970	Chi-N	0	2	.000	7	1	0	0	0	15	17	3	9	9	16.2	6.60	68	.298	.403	0	.000	0	-4	-3	-0	-0.4
1971	Cal-A	0	3	.000	15	1	0	0	0	27¹	32	2	18	15	16.5	4.61	70	.305	.407	0	.000	-0	-3	-4	-0	-0.4
1972	Mil-A	0	1	.000	5	2	0	0	0	18²	26	1	8	13	16.4	7.23	42	.338	.400	2	.500	1	-9	-9	-0	-0.4
Total	5	0	8	.000	36	7	0	0	0	81²	100	8	49	47	16.6	5.73	61	.311	.405	3	.273	2	-21	-21	-1	-1.4

● **CHARLIE REYNOLDS**   Reynolds, Charles E. b: 7/31/1857, Allegany, N.Y.   d: 5/1/13, Buffalo, N.Y.   Deb: 5/18/1882

YEAR	TM/L	W	L	PCT	G	GS	CG	SH	SV	IP	H	HR	BB	SO	RAT	ERA	ERA+	OAV	OOB	BH	AVG	PB	PR	/A	PD	TPI
1882	Phi-a	1	1	.500	2	2	1	0	0	12	18	0	3	4	15.8	5.25	57	.327	.362	1	.125	-1	-3	-3	-1	-0.5

● **CRAIG REYNOLDS**   Reynolds, Gordon Craig b: 12/27/52, Houston, Tex.   BL/TR, 6'1", 175 lbs.   Deb: 8/1/75 ◆

YEAR	TM/L	W	L	PCT	G	GS	CG	SH	SV	IP	H	HR	BB	SO	RAT	ERA	ERA+	OAV	OOB	BH	AVG	PB	PR	/A	PD	TPI
1986	*Hou-N	0	0	—	1	0	0	0	0	1	3	0	2	1	45.0	27.00	13	.500	.625	78	.249	0	-3	-3	0	0.0
1989	Hou-N	0	0	—	1	0	0	0	0	1	3	0	1	0	45.0	27.00	13	.500	.625	38	.201	0	-3	-3	0	0.0
Total	2	0	0	—	2	0	0	0	0	2	6	0	3	1	45.0	27.00	13	.500	.625	1142	.256	0	-5	-5	0	0.0

● **KEN REYNOLDS**   Reynolds, Kenneth Lee b: 1/4/47, Trevose, Pa.   BL/TL, 6', 180 lbs.   Deb: 9/5/70

YEAR	TM/L	W	L	PCT	G	GS	CG	SH	SV	IP	H	HR	BB	SO	RAT	ERA	ERA+	OAV	OOB	BH	AVG	PB	PR	/A	PD	TPI
1970	Phi-N	0	0	—	4	0	0	0	0	2¹	3	0	4	1	27.0	0.00	—	.333	.538	0	—	0	1	1	0	0.0
1971	Phi-N	5	9	.357	35	25	2	1	0	162¹	163	11	82	81	13.9	4.49	78	.269	.361	10	.200	-2	-19	-17	-1	-1.3
1972	Phi-N	2	15	.118	33	23	2	0	0	154¹	149	17	60	87	12.2	4.26	84	.258	.329	8	.200	1	-14	-11	-0	-1.1
1973	Mil-A	0	1	.000	2	1	0	0	0	7¹	5	1	10	3	19.6	7.36	51	.200	.444	0	—	0	-3	-3	1	-0.2
1975	StL-N	0	1	.000	10	0	0	0	0	17	12	0	11	7	12.2	1.59	236	.214	.343	0	.000	-0	4	4	1	0.3
1976	SD-N	0	3	.000	19	2	0	0	0	32¹	38	0	29	18	18.6	6.40	51	.309	.441	0	.000	-1	-10	-11	-0	-1.1
Total	6	7	29	.194	103	51	4	1	1	375²	370	29	196	197	13.8	4.46	80	.265	.358	18	.186	2	-41	-38	0	-3.4

● **SHANE REYNOLDS**   Reynolds, Richard Shane b: 3/26/68, Bastrop, La.   BR/TR, 6'3", 210 lbs.   Deb: 7/20/92

YEAR	TM/L	W	L	PCT	G	GS	CG	SH	SV	IP	H	HR	BB	SO	RAT	ERA	ERA+	OAV	OOB	BH	AVG	PB	PR	/A	PD	TPI
1992	Hou-N	1	3	.250	8	5	0	0	0	25¹	42	2	6	10	17.1	7.11	47	.385	.417	2	.500	1	-10	-11	-1	-1.3
1993	Hou-N	0	0	—	5	1	0	0	0	11	11	0	6	10	13.9	0.82	473	.256	.347	1	.500	0	4	4	-0	0.6
1994	Hou-N	8	5	.615	33	14	1	0	0	124	128	10	21	110	11.3	3.05	130	.263	.302	3	.091	-2	16	12	0	1.0
1995	Hou-N	10	11	.476	30	30	3	2	0	189¹	196	15	37	175	11.2	3.47	111	.263	.300	8	.127	-2	15	8	3	1.0
1996	Hou-N	16	10	.615	35	35	4	1	0	239	227	20	44	204	10.5	3.65	105	.249	.290	14	.184	4	15	5	-1	0.8
Total	5	35	29	.547	111	85	8	3	0	588²	604	47	114	509	11.2	3.56	108	.263	.303	28	.157	3	40	19	3	1.5

● **BOB REYNOLDS**   Reynolds, Robert Allen b: 1/21/47, Seattle, Wash.   BR/TR, 6', 205 lbs.   Deb: 9/19/69

YEAR	TM/L	W	L	PCT	G	GS	CG	SH	SV	IP	H	HR	BB	SO	RAT	ERA	ERA+	OAV	OOB	BH	AVG	PB	PR	/A	PD	TPI
1969	Mon-N	0	0	—	1	1	0	0	0	1¹	3	0	3	2	40.5	20.25	18	.429	.600	0	—	0	-2	-2	-0	0.0
1971	StL-N	0	0	—	7	0	0	0	0	7	15	2	6	4	28.3	10.29	35	.441	.537	0	—	0	-5	-5	-0	0.0
	Mil-A	0	1	.000	3	0	0	0	0	6	4	0	3	4	10.5	3.00	116	.222	.333	0	—	0	0	0	0	0.0
1972	Bal-A	0	0	—	3	0	0	0	0	9²	7	2	5	5	14.0	1.86	165	.258	.395	0	.000	0	1	1	0	0.0
1973	*Bal-A	7	5	.583	42	1	0	0	9	111	88	3	31	77	9.6	1.95	192	.219	.275	0	—	0	23	22	-2	2.5

YEAR	TM/L	W	L	PCT	G	GS	CG	SH	SV	IP	H	HR	BB	SO	RAT	ERA	ERA+	OAV	OOB	BH	AVG	PB	PR	/A	PD	TPI
1974	*Bal-A	7	5	.583	54	0	0	0	7	69¹	75	4	14	43	11.7	2.73	127	.278	.316	0	—	0	7	6	-0	1.0
1975	Bal-A	0	1	.000	7	0	0	0	0	6	11	1	1	1	18.0	9.00	39	.423	.444	0	—	0	-3	-4	-0	-0.1
	Det-A	0	2	.000	21	0	0	0	3	34²	40	8	14	26	14.3	4.67	86	.288	.357	0	—	0	-3	-3	-0	-0.5
	Cle-A	0	2	.000	5	0	0	0	2	9²	11	0	3	5	13.0	4.66	81	.289	.341	0	—	0	-1	-1	-0	-0.2
	Yr	0	5	.000	33	0	0	0	5	50¹	62	9	18	32	14.3	5.19	75	.301	.357	0	—	0	-8	-7	-0	-0.8
Total 6		14	16	.467	140	2	0	0	21	254²	255	18	82	167	12.0	3.15	116	.264	.324	0	.000	-0	16	14	-3	2.7

● ROSS REYNOLDS
Reynolds, Ross Ernest "Doc"   b: 8/20/1887, Barksdale, Tex.   d: 6/23/70, Ada, Okla.   BR/TR, 6'2", 185 lbs.   Deb: 5/2/14

YEAR	TM/L	W	L	PCT	G	GS	CG	SH	SV	IP	H	HR	BB	SO	RAT	ERA	ERA+	OAV	OOB	BH	AVG	PB	PR	/A	PD	TPI
1914	Det-A	5	3	.625	26	7	3	1	0	78	62	0	39	31	12.3	2.08	135	.230	.340	1	.048	-2	6	6	-1	0.3
1915	Det-A	0	1	.000	4	2	0	0	0	11¹	17	0	5	2	18.3	6.35	48	.378	.451	0	.000	-0	-4	-4	0	-0.3
Total 2		5	4	.556	30	9	3	1	0	89¹	79	0	44	33	13.1	2.62	108	.251	.355	1	.042	-2	1	2	-1	0.0

● ARMANDO REYNOSO
Reynoso, Armando Martin (Gutierrez)   b: 5/1/66, San Luis Potosi, Mex.   BR/TR, 6', 186 lbs.   Deb: 8/11/91

YEAR	TM/L	W	L	PCT	G	GS	CG	SH	SV	IP	H	HR	BB	SO	RAT	ERA	ERA+	OAV	OOB	BH	AVG	PB	PR	/A	PD	TPI
1991	Atl-N	2	1	.667	6	5	0	0	0	23¹	26	4	10	10	15.0	6.17	63	.299	.390	0	.000	-0	-6	-6	2	-0.5
1992	Atl-N	1	0	1.000	3	1	0	0	1	7²	11	2	2	2	16.4	4.70	78	.393	.452	0	.000	-0	-1	-1	0	-0.1
1993	Col-N	12	11	.522	30	30	4	0	0	189	206	22	63	117	13.2	4.00	119	.277	.340	8	.127	-1	1	16	2	1.9
1994	Col-N	3	4	.429	9	9	1	0	0	52¹	54	5	22	25	14.1	4.82	103	.278	.369	3	.176	-0	-4	1	2	0.3
1995	*Col-N	7	7	.500	20	18	0	0	0	93	116	12	36	40	15.2	5.32	101	.316	.385	4	.133	-2	-12	1	3	0.2
1996	Col-N	8	9	.471	30	30	0	0	0	168²	195	27	49	88	13.5	4.96	109	.291	.348	9	.173	-1	-14	9	2	0.9
Total 6		33	32	.508	98	93	5	0	1	534	608	72	182	282	13.9	4.72	107	.291	.357	24	.140	-5	-36	19	11	2.7

● FLINT RHEM
Rhem, Charles Flint "Shad"   b: 1/24/01, Rhems, S.C.   d: 7/30/69, Columbia, S.C.   BR/TR, 6'2", 180 lbs.   Deb: 9/6/24

YEAR	TM/L	W	L	PCT	G	GS	CG	SH	SV	IP	H	HR	BB	SO	RAT	ERA	ERA+	OAV	OOB	BH	AVG	PB	PR	/A	PD	TPI
1924	StL-N	2	2	.500	6	3	0	1	0	32¹	31	1	17	20	13.4	4.45	85	.254	.345	2	.167	-0	-2	-2	0	-0.3
1925	StL-N	8	13	.381	30	24	8	1	1	170	204	16	58	66	14.1	4.92	88	.299	.357	14	.237	1	-12	-11	0	-1.1
1926	*StL-N	20	7	.741	34	34	20	1	0	258	241	12	75	72	11.1	3.21	122	.250	.305	18	.188	-2	18	20	1	1.8
1927	StL-N	10	12	.455	27	26	9	2	0	169¹	189	6	54	51	13.1	4.41	90	.285	.342	4	.068	-5	-9	-9	-3	-1.8
1928	*StL-N	11	8	.579	28	22	9	0	3	169²	199	13	71	47	14.5	4.14	97	.296	.365	11	.164	-1	-3	-3	2	-0.3
1930	StL-N	12	8	.600	26	19	9	0	0	139²	173	11	37	43	13.7	4.45	113	.306	.352	12	.231	-1	8	9	-3	0.7
1931	*StL-N	11	10	.524	33	26	10	2	1	207¹	214	17	60	72	12.0	3.56	111	.268	.321	9	.130	-4	7	9	-2	0.2
1932	StL-N	4	2	.667	6	6	5	1	0	50	48	3	10	18	10.4	3.06	129	.257	.294	3	.188	0	5	5	0	0.6
	Phi-N	11	7	.611	26	20	10	0	1	168²	177	13	49	35	12.1	3.74	108	.269	.319	7	.113	-3	3	13	-0	0.7
	Yr	15	9	.625	32	26	15	1	1	218²	225	16	59	53	11.7	3.58	120	.266	.314	10	.128	-5	7	18	-1	1.3
1933	Phi-N	5	14	.263	28	19	3	0	2	125	182	10	33	27	15.6	6.62	58	.340	.381	4	.087	-4	-46	-39	-0	-5.5
1934	StL-N	1	0	1.000	5	1	0	0	0	15²	26	0	7	6	19.0	4.60	92	.394	.452	0	.000	-0	-1	-1	-0	-0.1
	Bos-N	8	8	.500	25	20	5	1	0	152²	164	5	38	56	11.9	3.60	106	.273	.317	3	.058	-5	8	4	1	0.0
	Yr	9	8	.529	30	21	5	1	1	168¹	190	5	45	62	12.6	3.69	105	.285	.331	3	.056	-5	7	3	1	-0.1
1935	Bos-N	0	5	.000	10	6	0	0	0	40¹	61	4	11	10	16.1	5.36	71	.341	.379	0	.000	-1	-6	-7	-0	-0.8
1936	StL-N	2	1	.667	10	4	0	0	0	26²	49	2	9	7	19.6	6.75	58	.405	.446	1	.125	-0	-8	-8	-1	-0.7
Total 12		105	97	.520	294	230	91	8	10	1725¹	1958	113	529	534	13.1	4.20	98	.287	.340	88	.144	-28	-39	-20	-3	-6.8

● BILLY RHINES
Rhines, William Pearl "Bunker"   b: 3/14/1869, Ridgway, Pa.   d: 1/30/22, Ridgway, Pa.   BR/TR, 5'11", 168 lbs.   Deb: 4/22/1890

YEAR	TM/L	W	L	PCT	G	GS	CG	SH	SV	IP	H	HR	BB	SO	RAT	ERA	ERA+	OAV	OOB	BH	AVG	PB	PR	/A	PD	TPI
1890	Cin-N	28	17	.622	46	45	45	6	0	401¹	337	6	113	182	**10.4**	**1.95**	**182**	**.221**	**.281**	29	.188	-5	**72**	72	1	6.5
1891	Cin-N	17	24	.415	48	43	40	1	1	372²	364	4	124	138	12.3	2.87	117	.246	.314	18	.122	-9	20	21	3	1.3
1892	Cin-N	3	7	.300	11	9	6	0	0	74²	102	0	36	10	17.1	5.42	60	.313	.388	5	.185	1	-18	-18	-1	-1.8
1893	Lou-N	1	4	.200	7	5	3	0	0	31	49	3	19	0	20.6	8.71	51	.348	.436	1	.091	-2	-14	-15	0	-1.6
1895	Cin-N	19	10	.655	38	33	25	0	0	267²	322	4	76	72	14.1	4.81	103	.293	.351	25	.221	-4	-1	5	-0	0.1
1896	Cin-N	8	6	.571	19	17	11	3	0	143	128	1	48	32	**11.6**	**2.45**	**188**	**.238**	**.311**	10	.192	-3	30	34	0	2.5
1897	Cin-N	21	15	.583	41	32	26	1	0	288²	311	4	86	65	12.9	4.08	112	.273	.333	17	.159	-6	7	15	-2	0.7
1898	Pit-N	12	16	.429	31	29	27	2	0	258	289	0	61	48	12.7	3.52	101	.281	.329	15	.150	-4	2	1	5	0.2
1899	Pit-N	4	4	.500	9	9	4	0	0	54	59	3	13	6	12.7	6.00	64	.277	.330	10	.435	4	-13	-13	-1	-1.2
Total 9		113	103	.523	248	222	187	13	1	1891	1961	25	576	553	12.6	3.48	114	.262	.324	130	.177	-27	87	100	4	6.7

● BOB RHOADS
Rhoads, Robert Barton "Dusty"   b: 10/4/1879, Wooster, Ohio   d: 2/12/67, San Bernardino, Cal.   BR/TR, 6'1", 215 lbs.   Deb: 4/19/02

YEAR	TM/L	W	L	PCT	G	GS	CG	SH	SV	IP	H	HR	BB	SO	RAT	ERA	ERA+	OAV	OOB	BH	AVG	PB	PR	/A	PD	TPI
1902	Chi-N	4	8	.333	16	12	12	1	1	118	131	1	42	43	13.7	3.20	84	.281	.348	10	.222	0	-6	-7	-1	-0.7
1903	StL-N	5	8	.385	17	13	12	1	0	129	154	3	47	52	14.2	4.60	71	.303	.366	7	.140	-2	-19	-19	-1	-1.9
	Cle-A	2	3	.400	5	5	5	0	0	41	55	2	3	21	13.2	5.27	54	.320	.339	2	.118	-1	-10	-11	-0	-1.2
1904	Cle-A	10	9	.526	22	19	18	0	0	175¹	175	1	48	72	11.7	2.87	88	.261	.315	18	.196	-0	-5	-7	-1	-0.8
1905	Cle-A	16	9	.640	28	26	24	4	0	235	219	4	55	61	10.9	2.83	93	.249	.300	21	.221	4	-5	-5	-0	-0.1
1906	Cle-A	22	10	.688	38	34	31	7	0	315	259	6	92	89	10.2	1.80	145	.227	.288	19	.161	-3	31	29	-2	2.4
1907	Cle-A	15	14	.517	35	31	23	5	1	275	258	0	84	76	11.7	2.29	109	.250	.316	17	.185	-1	8	7	-1	0.4
1908	Cle-A	18	12	.600	37	30	20	1	0	270	242	3	63	62	10.3	1.77	135	.239	.298	20	.222	4	19	19	2	2.9
1909	Cle-A	5	9	.357	20	15	9	2	0	133¹	124	1	50	46	12.2	2.90	88	.281	.361	7	.163	-0	-6	-5	1	-0.5
Total 8		97	82	.542	218	185	154	21	2	1691²	1604	19	494	522	11.5	2.61	100	.256	.316	121	.188	-0	6	0	-3	0.5

● RICK RHODEN
Rhoden, Richard Alan   b: 5/16/53, Boynton Beach, Fla.   BR/TR, 6'3", 195 lbs.   Deb: 7/5/74

YEAR	TM/L	W	L	PCT	G	GS	CG	SH	SV	IP	H	HR	BB	SO	RAT	ERA	ERA+	OAV	OOB	BH	AVG	PB	PR	/A	PD	TPI
1974	LA-N	1	0	1.000	4	0	0	0	0	9	5	1	4	7	9.0	2.00	170	.161	.257	1	.500	0	2	1	-0	0.2
1975	LA-N	3	3	.500	26	11	1	0	0	99¹	94	8	32	40	11.5	3.08	110	.253	.314	2	.071	-2	6	4	0	0.2
1976	LA-N★	12	3	.800	27	26	10	3	0	181	165	17	53	77	10.9	2.98	113	.242	.298	20	.308	7	10	8	-2	1.2
1977	*LA-N	16	10	.615	31	31	4	1	0	216¹	223	20	63	122	12.0	3.74	102	.270	.323	18	.231	5	4	2	-3	0.4
1978	*LA-N	10	8	.556	30	23	6	3	0	164²	160	13	51	79	11.7	3.66	96	.255	.314	7	.135	-0	-2	-3	-1	-0.5
1979	Pit-N	0	1	.000	1	1	0	0	0	5	5	0	2	2	12.6	7.20	54	.263	.333	1	1.000	0	-2	-2	0	-0.2
1980	Pit-N	7	5	.583	20	19	2	0	0	126²	133	9	40	70	12.5	3.84	95	.273	.332	15	.375	6	-3	-3	0	0.4
1981	Pit-N	9	4	.692	21	21	4	2	0	136¹	147	6	53	76	13.3	3.89	92	.283	.352	9	.188	-1	-6	-5	1	-0.3
1982	Pit-N	11	14	.440	35	35	7	2	0	230¹	239	14	70	128	12.4	4.14	89	.267	.321	22	.265	8	-14	-11	2	0.0
1983	Pit-N	13	13	.500	36	35	7	2	1	244¹	256	13	68	153	12.0	3.09	120	.276	.327	13	.151	-2	14	17	1	1.6
1984	Pit-N	14	9	.609	33	33	6	3	0	238¹	216	13	62	136	10.5	2.72	132	.243	.293	28	.333	10	23	**23**	2	3.5
1985	Pit-N	10	15	.400	35	35	2	0	0	213¹	254	18	69	128	13.9	4.47	80	.296	.352	14	.189	2	-21	-21	-0	-2.1
1986	Pit-N☆	15	12	.556	34	34	12	1	0	253²	211	17	76	159	10.3	2.84	135	.228	.288	25	.278	9	25	28	1	4.0
1987	NY-A	16	10	.615	30	29	4	0	0	181²	184	22	61	107	12.3	3.86	113	.268	.330	0	—	0	12	10	0	1.4
1988	NY-A	12	12	.500	30	30	5	1	0	197	206	20	56	94	12.3	4.29	92	.269	.325	0	—	0	-7	-8	-1	-0.9
1989	Hou-N	2	6	.250	20	17	0	0	0	96²	108	7	41	41	14.2	4.28	79	.289	.364	6	.207	1	-8	-10	1	-0.6
Total 16		151	125	.547	413	380	69	17	1	2593²	2606	198	801	1419	12.0	3.59	103	.264	.321	181	.238	45	33	32	1	8.1

● ARTHUR LEE RHODES
Rhodes, Arthur Lee   b: 10/24/69, Waco, Tex.   BL/TL, 6'2", 190 lbs.   Deb: 8/21/91

YEAR	TM/L	W	L	PCT	G	GS	CG	SH	SV	IP	H	HR	BB	SO	RAT	ERA	ERA+	OAV	OOB	BH	AVG	PB	PR	/A	PD	TPI
1991	Bal-A	0	3	.000	8	8	0	0	0	36	47	4	23	23	17.5	8.00	49	.320	.412	0	—	0	-16	-16	-1	-0.9
1992	Bal-A	7	5	.583	15	15	2	1	0	94¹	87	6	38	77	12.0	3.63	111	.249	.325	0	—	0	3	4	0	0.4
1993	Bal-A	5	6	.455	17	17	0	0	0	85²	91	16	49	49	14.8	6.51	69	.274	.369	0	—	0	-21	-19	-2	-2.4
1994	Bal-A	3	5	.375	10	10	3	2	0	52²	51	8	30	47	14.2	5.81	86	.254	.356	0	—	0	-6	-5	-0	-0.8
1995	Bal-A	2	5	.286	19	9	1	0	0	75¹	68	13	48	77	13.9	6.21	76	.239	.349	0	—	0	-13	-12	-1	-1.0
1996	*Bal-A	9	1	.900	28	2	0	0	0	53	48	6	23	62	12.1	4.08	120	.241	.320	0	—	0	5	5	-1	0.7
Total 6		26	25	.510	97	61	5	3	1	397	392	53	211	335	13.8	5.49	82	.259	.351	0	—	0	-46	-44	-5	-4.0

● CHARLIE RHODES
Rhodes, Charles Anderson "Dusty"   b: 4/7/1885, Caney, Kan.   d: 10/26/18, Caney, Kan.   BR/TR, 5'7", 180 lbs.   Deb: 7/26/06

YEAR	TM/L	W	L	PCT	G	GS	CG	SH	SV	IP	H	HR	BB	SO	RAT	ERA	ERA+	OAV	OOB	BH	AVG	PB	PR	/A	PD	TPI
1906	StL-N	3	4	.429	9	6	3	0	0	45	37	0	20	32	12.6	3.40	77	.223	.328	3	.188	-0	-4	-4	0	-0.6
1908	Cin-N	0	0	—	1	0	0	0	0	4	1	0	2	4	9.0	0.00	—	.077	.250	0	.000	-0	1	1	0	-0.0
	StL-N	1	2	.333	4	4	3	0	0	33	23	2	12	15	9.8	3.00	79	.200	.281	3	.250	1	-2	-2	1	-0.1
	Yr	1	2	.333	5	4	3	0	0	37	24	2	14	19	9.5	2.68	88	.186	.271	3	.231	1	-1	-1	1	-0.1
1909	StL-N	3	5	.375	12	10	4	0	0	61	55	0	33	25	13.3	3.98	63	.256	.360	4	.211	1	-9	-10	2	-0.9
Total 3		7	11	.389	26	20	10	0	0	143	116	2	67	76	12.1	3.46	73	.228	.329	10	.208	2	-15	-15	4	-1.6

YEAR TM/L	W	L	PCT	G	GS	CG	SH	SV	IP	H	HR	BB	SO	RAT	ERA	ERA+	OAV	OOB	BH	AVG	PB	PR	/A	PD	TPI

● GORDON RHODES Rhodes, John Gordon "Dusty" b: 8/11/07, Winnemucca, Nev. d: 3/24/60, Long Beach, Cal. BR/TR, 6′, 187 lbs. Deb: 4/29/29

YEAR TM/L	W	L	PCT	G	GS	CG	SH	SV	IP	H	HR	BB	SO	RAT	ERA	ERA+	OAV	OOB	BH	AVG	PB	PR	/A	PD	TPI
1929 NY-A	0	4	.000	10	4	0	0	0	42²	57	3	16	13	15.8	4.85	80	.333	.397	3	.300	1	-3	-5	-1	-0.4
1930 NY-A	0	0	—	3	0	0	0	0	2	3	0	4	1	31.5	9.00	48	.500	.700	0	—	0	-1	-1	0	0.0
1931 NY-A	6	3	.667	18	11	4	0	0	87	82	3	52	36	13.9	3.41	116	.235	.334	6	.214	1	9	5	0	0.6
1932 NY-A	1	2	.333	10	2	1	0	0	24	25	0	21	15	17.3	7.88	52	.275	.411	2	.286	0	-9	-10	1	-0.8
Bos-A	1	8	.111	12	11	4	0	0	79¹	79	5	31	22	12.5	5.11	86	.261	.329	2	.074	-2	-6	-5	-0	-0.7
Yr	2	10	.167	22	13	5	0	0	103¹	104	5	52	37	13.6	5.75	76	.264	.350	4	.118	-2	-15	-16	1	-1.5
1933 Bos-A	12	15	.444	34	29	14	0	0	232	242	13	93	85	13.0	4.03	109	.265	.334	23	.267	4	6	9	-1	1.3
1934 Bos-A	12	12	.500	44	31	10	0	2	219	247	10	98	79	14.3	4.56	105	.285	.360	10	.133	-3	-2	6	1	0.3
1935 Bos-A	2	10	.167	34	19	1	0	2	146¹	195	14	60	44	15.7	5.41	88	.324	.387	7	.146	-4	-16	-11	-1	-1.1
1936 Phi-A	9	20	.310	35	28	13	1	1	216¹	266	26	102	61	15.4	5.74	89	.304	.378	16	.213	-5	-17	-15	-3	-2.0
Total 8	43	74	.368	200	135	47	1	5	1048²	1196	74	477	356	14.4	4.85	95	.286	.361	69	.194	-5	-37	-28	-3	-2.8

● BILL RHODES Rhodes, William Clarence b: Pottstown, Pa. Deb: 6/14/1893

YEAR TM/L	W	L	PCT	G	GS	CG	SH	SV	IP	H	HR	BB	SO	RAT	ERA	ERA+	OAV	OOB	BH	AVG	PB	PR	/A	PD	TPI
1893 Lou-N	5	12	.294	20	19	17	0	0	151²	244	10	66	22	19.0	7.60	58	.352	.416	9	.129	-4	-49	-54	-2	-4.4

● DENNIS RIBANT Ribant, Dennis Joseph b: 9/20/41, Detroit, Mich. BR/TR, 5′11″, 175 lbs. Deb: 8/9/64

YEAR TM/L	W	L	PCT	G	GS	CG	SH	SV	IP	H	HR	BB	SO	RAT	ERA	ERA+	OAV	OOB	BH	AVG	PB	PR	/A	PD	TPI
1964 NY-N	1	5	.167	14	7	1	1	1	57²	65	8	9	35	11.5	5.15	69	.281	.308	2	.100	-0	-10	-10	-1	-1.1
1965 NY-N	1	3	.250	19	1	0	0	3	35¹	29	5	6	13	8.9	3.82	92	.228	.263	0	.000	-1	-1	-1	-0	-0.3
1966 NY-N	11	9	.550	39	26	10	1	3	188¹	184	20	40	84	10.8	3.20	114	.254	.294	12	.197	0	8	9	0	1.1
1967 Pit-N	9	8	.529	38	22	2	0	0	172	186	16	40	75	12.0	4.08	82	.280	.324	16	.267	5	-14	-14	2	-0.6
1968 Det-A	2	2	.500	14	0	0	0	1	24¹	20	1	10	7	11.5	2.22	136	.217	.301	1	.200	0	2	2	-1	0.4
Chi-A	0	2	.000	17	0	0	0	0	31¹	42	3	17	20	17.5	6.03	50	.318	.404	-0	—	-1	-11	-10	-0	-0.4
Yr	2	4	.333	31	0	0	0	1	55²	62	4	27	27	14.7	4.37	69	.276	.358	1	.083	-0	-9	-8	-0	-0.4
1969 StL-N	0	0	—	1	0	0	0	0	1¹	4	1	0	0	33.8	13.50	26	.571	.625	-0	—	-1	-1	-0	0	0.0
Cin-N	0	0	—	7	0	0	0	0	8¹	6	1	3	7	9.7	1.08	348	.188	.257	-0	—	0	2	2	0	0.0
Yr	0	0	—	8	0	0	0	0	9²	10	2	3	7	13.0	2.79	134	.250	.318	-0	—	0	1	1	0	0.0
Total 6	24	29	.453	149	56	13	2	9	518²	536	55	126	241	11.6	3.87	90	.267	.312	31	.195	4	-24	-23	0	-1.3

● FRANK RICCELLI Riccelli, Frank Joseph b: 2/24/53, Syracuse, N.Y. BL/TL, 6′3″, 205 lbs. Deb: 9/11/76

YEAR TM/L	W	L	PCT	G	GS	CG	SH	SV	IP	H	HR	BB	SO	RAT	ERA	ERA+	OAV	OOB	BH	AVG	PB	PR	/A	PD	TPI
1976 SF-N	1	1	.500	4	3	0	0	0	16	16	1	5	11	11.8	5.63	64	.258	.313	1	.167	-0	-4	-4	-0	-0.4
1978 Hou-N	0	0	—	2	0	0	0	0	3	1	0	1	3	3.0	0.00	—	.100	.100	0	—	-0	1	1	-0	0.0
1979 Hou-N	2	2	.500	11	2	0	0	0	22	22	0	18	20	16.4	4.09	86	.262	.392	2	.333	1	-1	-1	1	-0.1
Total 3	3	3	.500	17	5	0	0	0	41	39	1	23	32	13.6	4.39	81	.250	.346	3	.250	1	-4	-3	0	-0.5

● CHUCK RICCI Ricci, Charles Mark b: 11/20/68, Abington, Pa. BR/TR, 6′2″, 180 lbs. Deb: 9/8/95

YEAR TM/L	W	L	PCT	G	GS	CG	SH	SV	IP	H	HR	BB	SO	RAT	ERA	ERA+	OAV	OOB	BH	AVG	PB	PR	/A	PD	TPI
1995 Phi-N	1	0	1.000	7	0	0	0	0	10	9	0	3	9	11.7	1.80	235	.273	.351	0	—	0	3	3	-0	0.4

● SAM RICE Rice, Edgar Charles b: 2/20/1890, Morocco, Ind. d: 10/13/74, Rossmoor, Md. BL/TR, 5′9″, 150 lbs. Deb: 8/7/15 H♦

YEAR TM/L	W	L	PCT	G	GS	CG	SH	SV	IP	H	HR	BB	SO	RAT	ERA	ERA+	OAV	OOB	BH	AVG	PB	PR	/A	PD	TPI
1915 Was-A	1	0	1.000	4	2	1	0	0	18	13	0	9	11	11.0	2.00	148	.213	.314	3	.375	1	2	2	0	0.2
1916 Was-A	0	1	.000	5	1	0	0	0	21¹	18	0	10	3	11.8	2.95	95	.237	.326	59	.299	2	-0	-0	0	0.1
Total 2	1	1	.500	9	3	1	0	0	39¹	31	0	19	12	11.4	2.52	114	.226	.321	2987	.322	2	2	2	0	0.3

● PAT RICE Rice, Patrick Edward b: 11/2/63, Rapid City, S.Dak. BR/TR, 6′2″, 200 lbs. Deb: 5/18/91

YEAR TM/L	W	L	PCT	G	GS	CG	SH	SV	IP	H	HR	BB	SO	RAT	ERA	ERA+	OAV	OOB	BH	AVG	PB	PR	/A	PD	TPI
1991 Sea-A	0	0	—	2	0	0	0	0	21	18	1	3	9	9.0	3.00	137	.234	.330	0	—	0	3	3	-0	0.2

● WOODY RICH Rich, Woodrow Earl b: 3/9/16, Morganton, N.C. d: 4/18/83, Morganton, N.C. BL/TR, 6′2″, 185 lbs. Deb: 4/22/39

YEAR TM/L	W	L	PCT	G	GS	CG	SH	SV	IP	H	HR	BB	SO	RAT	ERA	ERA+	OAV	OOB	BH	AVG	PB	PR	/A	PD	TPI
1939 Bos-A	4	3	.571	21	12	3	0	1	77	78	2	35	24	13.8	4.91	96	.264	.352	7	.259	4	-1	-0	0	0.0
1940 Bos-A	1	0	1.000	3	1	0	0	0	11²	9	2	1	8	7.7	0.77	583	.214	.233	0	.000	-1	5	5	0	0.3
1941 Bos-A	0	0	—	2	1	0	0	0	3²	8	1	2	4	24.5	17.18	24	.421	.476	0	—	-0	-5	-5	0	-0.4
1944 Bos-N	1	1	.500	7	2	1	0	0	25	32	3	12	6	16.9	5.76	66	.327	.416	1	.125	-1	-6	-7	-0	-0.4
Total 4	6	4	.600	33	16	5	0	1	117¹	127	8	50	42	14.2	5.06	89	.280	.361	8	.205	-1	-9	-7	0	-0.1

● J.R. RICHARD Richard, James Rodney b: 3/7/50, Vienna, La. BR/TR, 6′8″, 222 lbs. Deb: 9/5/71

YEAR TM/L	W	L	PCT	G	GS	CG	SH	SV	IP	H	HR	BB	SO	RAT	ERA	ERA+	OAV	OOB	BH	AVG	PB	PR	/A	PD	TPI
1971 Hou-N	2	1	.667	4	4	1	1	0	21	17	1	16	29	14.1	3.43	98	.215	.347	0	.000	-1	0	-0	0	-0.1
1972 Hou-N	1	0	1.000	4	1	0	0	0	6	10	0	8	8	30.0	13.50	25	.385	.556	0	—	0	-7	-7	-0	-0.9
1973 Hou-N	6	2	.750	16	10	2	1	0	72	54	2	38	75	11.6	4.00	91	.210	.314	5	.179	-0	-3	-3	-1	-0.4
1974 Hou-N	2	3	.400	15	9	0	0	0	64²	58	3	36	42	13.2	4.18	83	.243	.344	3	.143	0	-4	-5	-1	-0.4
1975 Hou-N	12	10	.545	33	31	7	1	0	203	178	14	138	176	14.2	4.39	77	.236	.359	15	.203	4	-17	-23	-2	-2.0
1976 Hou-N	20	15	.571	39	39	14	3	0	291	221	14	151	214	11.6	2.75	116	**.212**	.314	14	.140	0	24	14	1	1.6
1977 Hou-N	18	12	.600	36	36	13	0	0	267	212	18	104	214	10.7	2.97	107	.218	.293	20	.230	6	28	18	3	2.9
1978 Hou-N	18	11	.621	36	36	16	3	0	275¹	192	12	141	**303**	11.0	3.11	107	**.196**	.299	18	.178	1	14	6	2	1.0
1979 Hou-N	18	13	.581	38	38	19	4	0	292¹	220	13	98	**313**	9.9	**2.71**	130	**.209**	.278	12	.126	-0	**33**	**26**	-1	2.5
1980 Hou-N★	10	4	.714	17	17	4	0	0	113²	65	2	40	119	8.3	1.90	173	.166	.244	6	.154	1	21	18	-1	2.2
Total 10	107	71	.601	238	221	76	19	0	1606	1227	73	770	1493	11.3	3.15	108	.212	.306	93	.168	12	91	44	0	6.4

● DUANE RICHARDS Richards, Duane Lee b: 12/16/36, Spartanburg, Ind. BR/TR, 6′3″, 200 lbs. Deb: 9/25/60

YEAR TM/L	W	L	PCT	G	GS	CG	SH	SV	IP	H	HR	BB	SO	RAT	ERA	ERA+	OAV	OOB	BH	AVG	PB	PR	/A	PD	TPI
1960 Cin-N	0	0	—	2	0	0	0	0	3	5	0	2	2	21.0	9.00	42	.385	.467	0	—	0	-2	-2	0	0.0

● RUSTY RICHARDS Richards, Russell Earl b: 1/27/65, Houston, Tex. BL/TL, 6′4″, 200 lbs. Deb: 9/20/89

YEAR TM/L	W	L	PCT	G	GS	CG	SH	SV	IP	H	HR	BB	SO	RAT	ERA	ERA+	OAV	OOB	BH	AVG	PB	PR	/A	PD	TPI
1989 Atl-N	0	0	—	2	2	0	0	0	9¹	10	2	6	4	16.4	4.82	76	.278	.395	0	.000	-0	-1	-1	0	0.0
1990 Atl-N	0	0	—	1	0	0	0	0	1	2	1	1	0	27.0	27.00	15	.400	.500	0	—	0	-3	-3	0	0.0
Total 2	0	0	—	3	2	0	0	0	10¹	12	3	7	4	17.4	6.97	53	.293	.408	0	.000	-0	-4	-4	0	-0.3

● HARDY RICHARDSON Richardson, Abram Harding "Old True Blue" b: 4/21/1855, Clarksboro, N.J. d: 1/14/31, Utica, N.Y. BR/TR, 5′9.5″, 170 lbs. Deb: 5/1/1879 ♦

YEAR TM/L	W	L	PCT	G	GS	CG	SH	SV	IP	H	HR	BB	SO	RAT	ERA	ERA+	OAV	OOB	BH	AVG	PB	PR	/A	PD	TPI
1885 Buf-N	0	0	—	1	0	0	0	0	4	5	0	3	1	18.0	2.25	132	.294	.400	136	.319	0	0	0	0	0.0
1886 Det-N	3	0	1.000	4	1	0	0	0	12	11	1	10	5	15.8	4.50	74	.208	.333	189	.351	2	-2	-0	-0	-0.3
Total 2	3	0	1.000	5	1	0	0	0	16	16	1	13	6	16.3	3.94	82	.229	.349	1688	.299	3	-1	-0	-0	-0.3

● DANNY RICHARDSON Richardson, Daniel b: 1/25/1863, Elmira, N.Y. d: 9/12/26, New York, N.Y. BR/TR, 5′8″, 165 lbs. Deb: 5/22/1884 M♦

YEAR TM/L	W	L	PCT	G	GS	CG	SH	SV	IP	H	HR	BB	SO	RAT	ERA	ERA+	OAV	OOB	BH	AVG	PB	PR	/A	PD	TPI
1885 NY-N	7	1	.875	9	8	7	1	0	75	58	0	18	21	9.1	2.40	111	.205	.252	52	.263	2	4	2	-1	0.3
1886 NY-N	0	2	.000	5	1	1	0	0	25	33	1	11	17	15.8	5.76	56	.320	.386	55	.232	1	-7	-7	1	-0.3
1887 NY-N	0	0	—	1	0	0	0	0	0	0	0	1	0	—	—	—	—	1.000	125	.278	0	0	0	0	0.0
Total 3	7	3	.700	15	9	8	1	0	100	91	1	30	38	10.9	3.24	86	.236	.291	1129	.254	3	-3	-5	0	0.0

● GORDIE RICHARDSON Richardson, Gordon Clark b: 7/19/38, Colquitt, Ga. BR/TL, 6′, 185 lbs. Deb: 7/26/64

YEAR TM/L	W	L	PCT	G	GS	CG	SH	SV	IP	H	HR	BB	SO	RAT	ERA	ERA+	OAV	OOB	BH	AVG	PB	PR	/A	PD	TPI
1964 ★StL-N	4	2	.667	19	6	1	0	2	47	40	2	15	28	10.7	2.30	166	.231	.296	1	.077	-0	6	8	-1	0.9
1965 NY-N	2	2	.500	35	0	0	0	2	52¹	41	5	16	43	10.1	3.78	93	.224	.294	0	.000	-1	-1	-0	-1	-0.2
1966 NY-N	0	2	.000	15	1	0	0	0	18²	24	7	6	15	14.5	9.16	40	.312	.361	0	—	-0	-12	-11	-0	-1.3
Total 3	6	6	.500	69	7	1	0	4	118	105	14	37	86	11.1	4.04	90	.242	.307	1	.048	-0	-6	-5	-2	-0.6

● JEFF RICHARDSON Richardson, Jeffrey Scott b: 8/29/63, Wichita, Kan. BR/TR, 6′3″, 185 lbs. Deb: 9/19/90

YEAR TM/L	W	L	PCT	G	GS	CG	SH	SV	IP	H	HR	BB	SO	RAT	ERA	ERA+	OAV	OOB	BH	AVG	PB	PR	/A	PD	TPI
1990 Cal-A	0	0	—	1	0	0	0	0	0¹	1	0	0	0	27.0	0.00	—	.500	.500	0	—	0	0	0	0	0.2

● JACK RICHARDSON Richardson, John William b: 10/3/1891, Central City, Ill. d: 1/18/70, Marion, Ill. BB/TR, 6′3″, 197 lbs. Deb: 9/17/15

YEAR TM/L	W	L	PCT	G	GS	CG	SH	SV	IP	H	HR	BB	SO	RAT	ERA	ERA+	OAV	OOB	BH	AVG	PB	PR	/A	PD	TPI
1915 Phi-A	0	1	.000	3	3	2	0	0	24	21	0	14	11	13.5	6.23	111	.253	.367	0	.000	1	1	1	-0	-0.1
1916 Phi-A	0	0	—	1	0	0	0	0	0²	2	0	1	1	40.5	40.50	18	.667	.750	0	—	-0	-3	-3	-0	-0.1
Total 2	0	1	.000	4	3	2	0	0	24²	23	0	15	12	14.2	3.65	80	.267	.382	0	.000	1	-2	-2	-0	-0.1

● PETE RICHERT Richert, Peter Gerard b: 10/29/39, Floral Park, N.Y. BL/TL, 6′, 184 lbs. Deb: 4/12/62

YEAR TM/L	W	L	PCT	G	GS	CG	SH	SV	IP	H	HR	BB	SO	RAT	ERA	ERA+	OAV	OOB	BH	AVG	PB	PR	/A	PD	TPI
1962 LA-N	5	4	.556	19	12	1	0	0	81¹	77	6	45	75	13.6	3.87	94	.249	.346	2	.080	-1	1	-2	1	-0.3
1963 LA-N	5	3	.625	20	12	1	0	0	78	80	7	28	54	12.6	4.50	67	.262	.326	4	.182	-1	-11	-13	-1	-1.3

YEAR TM/L	W	L	PCT	G	GS	CG	SH	SV	IP	H	HR	BB	SO	RAT	ERA	ERA+	OAV	OOB	BH	AVG	PB	PR	/A	PD	TPI
1964 LA-N	2	3	.400	8	6	1	1	0	34²	38	2	18	25	15.1	4.15	78	.271	.363	1	.091	-0	-2	-4	1	-0.4
1965 Was-A★	15	12	.556	34	29	6	0	0	194	146	18	84	161	10.8	2.60	134	.210	.297	10	.156	-0	19	19	-0	2.5
1966 Was-A★	14	14	.500	36	34	7	0	0	245²	196	36	69	195	9.7	3.37	103	.215	.271	14	.163	2	2	2	-0	0.2
1967 Was-A	2	6	.250	11	10	1	1	0	54¹	49	5	15	41	10.8	4.64	68	.237	.291	1	.059	-1	-8	-9	-1	-1.5
Bal-A	7	10	.412	26	19	5	1	2	132¹	107	11	41	90	10.1	2.99	105	.220	.282	4	.108	-1	4	2	1	0.3
Yr	9	16	.360	37	29	6	2	2	186²	156	16	56	131	10.3	3.47	91	.223	.282	5	.093	-2	-5	-7	-1	-1.2
1968 Bal-A	6	3	.667	36	0	0	0	6	62¹	51	7	12	47	9.5	3.47	84	.225	.273	2	.200	0	-3	-4	1	-0.5
1969 *Bal-A	7	4	.636	44	0	0	0	12	57¹	42	7	14	54	8.8	2.20	162	.202	.252	1	.125	0	9	9	-1	2.0
1970 *Bal-A	7	2	.778	50	0	0	0	13	54²	36	5	24	66	10.0	1.98	185	.194	.289	0	.000	-0	11	10	0	2.1
1971 *Bal-A	3	5	.375	35	0	0	0	4	36¹	26	3	22	35	12.1	3.47	97	.205	.327	0	.000	-0	-0	-0	-1	-0.1
1972 LA-N	3	2	.400	37	0	0	0	6	52	42	3	18	51	10.6	2.25	148	.219	.289	3	.500	1	7	6	-0	0.8
1973 LA-N	3	3	.500	39	0	0	0	7	51	44	5	19	31	11.3	3.18	108	.234	.308	1	.200	0	3	1	1	0.3
1974 StL-N	0	0	—	13	0	0	0	1	11¹	10	1	11	4	16.7	2.38	150	.244	.404	0	—	0	2	2	-0	0.0
Phi-N	2	1	.667	21	0	0	0	0	20¹	15	0	4	9	8.4	2.21	171	.205	.247	0	—	0	3	4	-0	0.5
Yr	2	1	.667	34	0	0	0	1	31²	25	1	15	13	11.4	2.27	163	.216	.305	0	—	0	5	5	-1	0.5
Total 13	80	73	.523	429	122	22	3	51	1165²	959	116	424	925	10.8	3.19	106	.223	.295	43	.145	-1	34	24	-3	4.6

● **LEW RICHIE**   Richie, Lewis A.   b: 8/23/1883, Ambler, Pa.   d: 8/15/36, South Mountain, Pa.   BR/TR, 5'8", 165 lbs.   Deb: 5/8/06

YEAR TM/L	W	L	PCT	G	GS	CG	SH	SV	IP	H	HR	BB	SO	RAT	ERA	ERA+	OAV	OOB	BH	AVG	PB	PR	/A	PD	TPI
1906 Phi-N	9	11	.450	33	22	14	3	0	205²	170	3	79	65	11.2	2.41	109	.230	.309	3	.050	-3	5	5	-3	-0.2
1907 Phi-N	6	6	.500	25	12	9	2	0	117	88	0	38	40	10.1	1.77	137	.215	.290	7	.163	0	9	8	-1	0.8
1908 Phi-N	7	10	.412	25	15	13	2	1	157²	125	1	49	58	10.3	1.83	133	.233	.304	11	.212	2	9	10	-1	1.2
1909 Phi-N	1	1	.500	11	1	0	1	1	45	40	0	18	11	12.0	2.00	130	.263	.349	4	.250	1	3	3	-1	0.2
Bos-N	7	7	.500	22	13	9	2	2	131²	118	2	44	42	11.1	2.32	121	.247	.312	5	.114	-2	4	7	-3	0.2
Yr	8	8	.500	33	14	9	3	3	176²	158	2	62	53	11.3	2.24	123	.250	.318	9	.150	-1	7	10	-4	0.4
1910 Bos-N	0	3	.000	4	2	0	0	0	16¹	20	0	9	7	16.0	2.76	121	.317	.403	0	.000	-1	1	1	1	0.2
*Chi-N	11	4	.733	30	11	8	3	4	130	117	1	51	53	11.8	2.70	107	.257	.336	9	.225	3	5	3	1	0.6
Yr	11	7	.611	34	13	8	3	4	146¹	137	1	60	60	12.3	2.71	108	.264	.344	9	.205	2	5	4	1	0.8
1911 Chi-N	15	11	.577	36	29	18	4	1	253	213	6	103	78	11.3	2.31	143	.235	.315	14	.154	-3	31	28	0	2.4
1912 Chi-N	16	8	.667	39	27	15	4	0	238	222	5	74	69	11.4	2.95	113	.261	.324	10	.132	-3	12	10	-2	0.3
1913 Chi-N	2	4	.333	16	5	0	0	0	65	77	3	30	15	15.0	5.82	55	.304	.380	2	.118	-2	-19	-19	-1	-1.7
Total 8	74	65	.532	241	137	86	20	9	1359¹	1190	21	495	438	11.4	2.54	115	.246	.320	65	.147	-7	60	58	-11	4.0

● **BERYL RICHMOND**   Richmond, Beryl Justice   b: 8/24/07, Glen Easton, W.Va.   d: 4/24/80, Cameron, W.Va.   BB/TL, 6'1", 185 lbs.   Deb: 4/21/33

YEAR TM/L	W	L	PCT	G	GS	CG	SH	SV	IP	H	HR	BB	SO	RAT	ERA	ERA+	OAV	OOB	BH	AVG	PB	PR	/A	PD	TPI
1933 Chi-N	0	0	—	4	0	0	0	0	4²	3	0	2	2	23.1	1.93	170	.455	.500	0	.000	-0	1	1	-0	0.0
1934 Cin-N	1	2	.333	6	2	1	0	0	19¹	23	0	10	9	15.4	3.72	110	.303	.384	0	.000	-1	1	1	-0	0.0
Total 2	1	2	.333	10	2	1	0	0	24	33	0	12	11	16.9	3.38	116	.337	.409	0	.000	-1	1	1	-0	0.0

● **LEE RICHMOND**   Richmond, J Lee   b: 5/5/1857, Sheffield, Ohio   d: 10/1/29, Toledo, Ohio   TL, 5'10", 155 lbs.   Deb: 9/27/1879 ♦

YEAR TM/L	W	L	PCT	G	GS	CG	SH	SV	IP	H	HR	BB	SO	RAT	ERA	ERA+	OAV	OOB	BH	AVG	PB	PR	/A	PD	TPI
1879 Bos-N	1	0	1.000	1	1	1	0	0	9	4	0	1	11	5.0	2.00	124	.114	.139	2	.333	0	0	0	0	0.1
1880 Wor-N	32	32	.500	74	66	57	5	3	590³	541	7	74	243	9.4	2.15	121	.232	.255	70	.227	-4	15	29	-6	1.9
1881 Wor-N	25	26	.490	53	52	50	3	0	462¹	547	7	68	156	12.0	3.39	89	.284	.309	63	.250	-1	-31	-19	2	-1.5
1882 Wor-N	14	33	.298	48	46	44	0	0	411	525	11	88	123	13.4	3.74	83	.294	.327	64	.281	7	-39	-29	3	-1.7
1883 Pro-N	3	7	.300	12	12	8	0	0	92	122	2	27	13	14.6	3.33	93	.314	.358	55	.284	3	-2	-2	-0	-0.7
1886 Cin-a	0	2	.000	3	2	1	0	0	18	24	0	11	6	18.5	8.00	44	.308	.407	8	.276	4	-9	-9	-0	-0.7
Total 6	75	100	.429	191	179	161	8	3	1583	1763	27	269	552	11.6	3.06	95	.269	.298	262	.257	7	-66	-28	-1	-1.9

● **RAY RICHMOND**   Richmond, Raymond Sinclair   b: 6/15/1896, Fillmore, Ill.   d: 10/21/69, DeSoto, Mo.   BR/TR, 6', 175 lbs.   Deb: 9/25/20

YEAR TM/L	W	L	PCT	G	GS	CG	SH	SV	IP	H	HR	BB	SO	RAT	ERA	ERA+	OAV	OOB	BH	AVG	PB	PR	/A	PD	TPI
1920 StL-A	2	0	1.000	2	2	1	0	0	17	18	0	9	4	14.3	6.35	62	.273	.360	1	.167	-0	-5	-5	0	-0.4
1921 StL-A	0	1	.000	6	2	0	0	0	14¹	21	1	13	6	23.2	11.30	40	.362	.500	0	.000	-1	-11	-11	0	-0.7
Total 2	2	1	.667	8	4	1	0	0	31¹	39	1	22	10	18.4	8.62	48	.315	.430	1	.100	-1	-16	-15	0	-1.1

● **REGGIE RICHTER**   Richter, Emil Henry   b: 9/14/1888, Dusseldorf, Germany   d: 8/2/34, Winfield, Ill.   BR/TR, 6'2", 180 lbs.   Deb: 5/30/11

YEAR TM/L	W	L	PCT	G	GS	CG	SH	SV	IP	H	HR	BB	SO	RAT	ERA	ERA+	OAV	OOB	BH	AVG	PB	PR	/A	PD	TPI
1911 Chi-N	1	3	.250	22	5	0	0	2	54²	62	1	20	34	14.0	3.13	106	.307	.378	1	.100	-1	2	1	-0	0.0

● **DICK RICKETTS**   Ricketts, Richard James   b: 12/4/33, Pottstown, Pa.   d: 3/6/88, Rochester, N.Y.   BL/TR, 6'7", 215 lbs.   Deb: 6/14/59   F

YEAR TM/L	W	L	PCT	G	GS	CG	SH	SV	IP	H	HR	BB	SO	RAT	ERA	ERA+	OAV	OOB	BH	AVG	PB	PR	/A	PD	TPI
1959 StL-N	1	6	.143	12	9	0	0	0	55²	68	7	30	25	15.8	5.82	73	.301	.383	1	.056	-2	-12	-10	-2	-1.4

● **ELMER RIDDLE**   Riddle, Elmer Ray   b: 7/31/14, Columbus, Ga.   d: 5/14/84, Columbus, Ga.   BR/TR, 5'11.5", 170 lbs.   Deb: 10/1/39   F

YEAR TM/L	W	L	PCT	G	GS	CG	SH	SV	IP	H	HR	BB	SO	RAT	ERA	ERA+	OAV	OOB	BH	AVG	PB	PR	/A	PD	TPI
1939 Cin-N	0	0	—	1	0	0	0	0	2	1	0	0	4	4.5	0.00	—	.143	.143	0	—	0	1	1	-0	0.0
1940 *Cin-N	1	2	.333	15	1	1	0	2	33²	30	0	17	9	12.6	1.87	202	.250	.343	1	.143	-0	7	7	0	0.7
1941 Cin-N	19	4	**.826**	33	22	15	4	1	216²	180	8	59	80	10.1	**2.24**	**160**	.224	.282	16	.225	3	33	33	-1	3.6
1942 Cin-N	7	11	.389	29	19	7	1	0	158¹	157	7	79	78	13.6	3.69	89	.260	.349	15	.259	3	-7	-1	-0	-0.6
1943 Cin-N	21	11	.656	36	33	19	5	3	260¹	235	6	107	69	11.9	2.63	126	.245	.322	18	.194	1	22	20	-1	2.5
1944 Cin-N	2	2	.500	4	4	2	0	0	26²	25	0	12	6	12.5	4.05	86	.250	.330	1	.125	-0	-1	-2	1	-0.2
1945 Cin-N	1	4	.200	12	3	0	0	0	29²	39	4	27	5	20.0	8.19	46	.333	.458	3	.273	1	-14	-15	0	-1.9
1947 Cin-N	1	0	1.000	16	3	0	0	0	30¹	42	5	31	8	22.0	8.31	49	.333	.468	0	.000	-0	-14	-14	-1	-0.5
1948 Pit-N☆	12	10	.545	28	27	12	3	1	191	184	20	81	63	12.6	3.49	117	.250	.327	12	.188	1	10	12	0	1.5
1949 Pit-N	1	8	.111	16	12	1	0	2	74¹	81	9	45	24	15.7	5.33	79	.281	.386	3	.136	-1	-11	-9	-2	-1.2
Total 10	65	52	.556	190	124	57	13	8	1023	974	59	458	342	12.8	3.40	107	.252	.335	69	.204	7	26	25	-4	3.9

● **DENNY RIDDLEBERGER**   Riddleberger, Dennis Michael   b: 11/22/45, Clifton Forge, Va.   BR/TL, 6'3", 195 lbs.   Deb: 9/15/70

YEAR TM/L	W	L	PCT	G	GS	CG	SH	SV	IP	H	HR	BB	SO	RAT	ERA	ERA+	OAV	OOB	BH	AVG	PB	PR	/A	PD	TPI
1970 Was-A	0	0	—	8	0	0	0	0	9¹	7	1	2	5	8.7	0.96	369	.219	.265	0	—	0	3	3	-0	0.0
1971 Was-A	3	1	.750	57	0	0	0	1	69²	67	9	32	56	12.9	3.23	102	.260	.344	0	.000	-0	2	1	-0	0.0
1972 Cle-A	1	3	.250	38	0	0	0	1	54	45	5	22	34	11.5	2.50	129	.237	.322	0	.000	-0	3	4	-1	0.3
Total 3	4	4	.500	103	0	0	0	2	133	119	15	56	95	12.6	2.77	116	.248	.330	0	.000	-0	8	8	-1	0.3

● **DORSEY RIDDLEMOSER**   Riddlemoser, Dorsey Lee   b: 3/25/1875, Frederick, Md.   d: 5/11/54, Frederick, Md.   BR/TR,   Deb: 8/22/1899

YEAR TM/L	W	L	PCT	G	GS	CG	SH	SV	IP	H	HR	BB	SO	RAT	ERA	ERA+	OAV	OOB	BH	AVG	PB	PR	/A	PD	TPI
1899 Was-N	0	0	—	1	0	0	0	0	2	7	0	2	0	40.5	18.00	22	.538	.600	0	.000	-0	-3	-3	0	0.0

● **JACK RIDGWAY**   Ridgway, Jacob A.   b: 7/23/1889, Philadelphia, Pa.   d: 2/23/28, Philadelphia, Pa.   BL/TL, 5'11", 174 lbs.   Deb: 5/20/14

YEAR TM/L	W	L	PCT	G	GS	CG	SH	SV	IP	H	HR	BB	SO	RAT	ERA	ERA+	OAV	OOB	BH	AVG	PB	PR	/A	PD	TPI
1914 Bal-F	0	1	.000	4	1	0	0	0	9	20	1	3	2	24.0	11.00	28	.444	.490	0	.000	-0	-8	-8	0	-0.7

● **STEVE RIDZIK**   Ridzik, Stephen George   b: 4/29/29, Yonkers, N.Y.   BR/TR, 5'11", 170 lbs.   Deb: 9/4/50

YEAR TM/L	W	L	PCT	G	GS	CG	SH	SV	IP	H	HR	BB	SO	RAT	ERA	ERA+	OAV	OOB	BH	AVG	PB	PR	/A	PD	TPI
1950 Phi-N	0	0	—	1	0	0	0	0	3	3	1	2	1	12.0	6.00	67	.300	.364	0	—	0	-1	-1	-0	0.0
1952 Phi-N	4	2	.667	24	9	2	0	0	92²	74	10	37	43	10.9	3.01	121	.218	.297	3	.136	0	7	7	-2	0.2
1953 Phi-N	9	6	.600	42	12	1	0	0	124	119	15	48	53	12.5	3.77	112	.256	.332	7	.194	2	7	6	-1	0.8
1954 Phi-N	4	5	.444	35	6	0	0	0	80²	72	7	44	45	12.9	4.13	98	.233	.329	5	.227	1	-1	-1	-0	0.0
1955 Phi-N	0	1	.000	3	1	0	0	0	11	7	1	8	6	14.7	2.45	162	.179	.360	0	.000	-1	2	2	-0	0.1
Cin-N	0	3	.000	13	2	0	0	0	30	35	4	14	6	15.0	4.50	94	.299	.379	1	.167	-0	-2	-1	-1	-0.2
Yr	0	4	.000	16	3	0	0	0	41	42	5	22	12	15.0	3.95	105	.264	.371	1	.100	-1	0	1	-1	-0.1
1956 NY-N	6	2	.750	41	5	1	1	0	92¹	80	7	65	53	14.6	3.80	99	.240	.371	7	.250	1	-0	-0	-1	-0.1
1957 NY-N	0	2	.000	15	0	0	0	0	26²	19	3	19	13	13.5	4.73	83	.213	.364	1	.200	-0	-3	-2	0	-0.1
1958 Cle-A	0	2	.000	9	0	0	0	0	8²	9	1	4	6	14.5	2.08	176	.257	.350	0	.000	-0	2	2	-0	0.0
1963 Was-A	5	5	.455	20	10	0	0	0	89²	82	16	35	47	12.2	4.82	77	.240	.319	5	.172	0	-12	-11	-0	-1.3
1964 Was-A	5	5	.500	49	6	0	0	0	112	96	10	31	60	10.8	2.89	128	.236	.301	6	.222	1	9	10	-1	0.9
1965 Was-A	4	4	.600	63	0	0	0	0	109²	108	18	43	72	13.0	4.02	86	.265	.337	3	.167	-0	-7	-7	0	-0.6
1966 Phi-N	0	0	—	2	0	0	0	0	2¹	5	0	1	0	23.1	7.71	47	.455	.500	0	.000	-0	-1	-1	0	0.0
Total 12	39	38	.506	314	48	4	1	11	782²	709	93	351	406	12.6	3.79	101	.243	.332	38	.192	4	2	3	-4	0.2

● **ELMER RIEGER**   Rieger, Elmer Jay   b: 2/25/1889, Perris, Cal.   d: 10/21/59, Los Angeles, Cal.   BB/TR, 6', 175 lbs.   Deb: 4/20/10

YEAR TM/L	W	L	PCT	G	GS	CG	SH	SV	IP	H	HR	BB	SO	RAT	ERA	ERA+	OAV	OOB	BH	AVG	PB	PR	/A	PD	TPI
1910 StL-N	0	2	.000	13	1	0	0	0	21¹	26	1	7	9	14.3	5.48	54	.325	.386	0	.000	0	-6	-6	0	-0.5

YEAR	TM/L	W	L	PCT	G	GS	CG	SH	SV	IP	H	HR	BB	SO	RAT	ERA	ERA+	OAV	OOB	BH	AVG	PB	PR	/A	PD	TPI

● DAVE RIGHETTI   Righetti, David Allan b: 11/28/58, San Jose, Cal. BL/TL, 6'3", 198 lbs. Deb: 9/16/79

YEAR	TM/L	W	L	PCT	G	GS	CG	SH	SV	IP	H	HR	BB	SO	RAT	ERA	ERA+	OAV	OOB	BH	AVG	PB	PR	/A	PD	TPI
1979	NY-A	0	1	.000	3	3	0	0	0	17¹	10	2	10	13	10.4	3.63	112	.182	.308	0	—	0	1	1	-1	0.3
1981	*NY-A	8	4	.667	15	15	2	0	0	105¹	75	1	38	89	9.7	2.05	174	.196	.269	0	—	0	19	18	-1	2.0
1982	NY-A	11	10	.524	33	27	4	0	1	183	155	11	108	163	13.2	3.79	105	.229	.340	0	—	0	6	4	-2	0.4
1983	NY-A	14	8	.636	31	31	7	2	0	217	194	12	67	169	10.9	3.44	113	.237	.297	0	—	0	15	11	-1	0.9
1984	NY-A	5	6	.455	64	0	0	0	31	96¹	79	5	37	90	10.8	2.34	167	.223	.296	0	—	0	18	16	-0	2.7
1985	NY-A	12	7	.632	74	0	0	0	29	107	96	5	45	92	11.9	2.78	144	.241	.318	0	—	0	16	15	-1	3.3
1986	NY-A★	8	8	.500	74	0	0	0	46	106²	88	4	35	83	10.5	2.45	167	.226	.293	0	—	0	20	19	-1	4.3
1987	NY-A★	8	6	.571	60	0	0	0	31	95	95	9	44	77	13.4	3.51	125	.262	.346	0	—	0	10	9	-0	1.9
1988	NY-A	5	4	.556	60	0	0	0	25	87	86	5	37	70	12.8	3.52	112	.257	.332	0	—	0	4	4	-1	0.6
1989	NY-A	2	6	.250	55	0	0	0	25	69	73	6	26	51	13.0	3.00	129	.277	.344	0	—	0	7	7	-0	1.1
1990	NY-A	1	1	.500	53	0	0	0	36	53	48	8	26	43	12.9	3.57	111	.234	.326	0	—	0	2	2	-1	0.2
1991	SF-N	2	7	.222	61	0	0	0	24	71²	64	4	28	51	11.9	3.39	106	.240	.319	0	.000	-0	2	2	1	0.3
1992	SF-N	2	7	.222	54	0	0	0	3	78¹	79	4	36	47	13.2	5.06	65	.269	.348	1	.143	-0	-14	-15	-2	-2.0
1993	SF-N	1	1	.500	51	0	0	0	1	47¹	58	11	17	31	14.5	5.70	69	.305	.365	1	1.000	0	-9	-9	-0	-0.4
1994	Oak-A	0	0	—	7	0	0	0	0	7	13	3	9	4	29.6	16.71	26	.419	.561	0	—	0	-9	-10	-1	-0.2
	Tor-A	0	1	.000	13	0	0	0	0	13¹	9	2	10	10	12.8	6.75	71	.188	.328	0	—	0	-3	-3	0	-0.2
	Yr	0	1	.000	20	0	0	0	0	20¹	22	5	19	14	18.1	10.18	46	.272	.410	0	—	0	-12	-12	-0	-0.4
1995	Chi-A	3	2	.600	10	9	0	0	0	49¹	65	6	18	29	15.1	4.20	106	.325	.381	0	—	0	3	1	-1	0.1
Total	16	82	79	.509	718	89	13	2	252	1403²	1287	95	591	1112	12.2	3.46	113	.244	.323	2	.182	0	89	71	-10	15.7

● RON RIGHTNOWAR   Rightnowar, Ronald Gene b: 9/5/64, Toledo, Ohio BR/TR, 6'3", 190 lbs. Deb: 5/20/95

YEAR	TM/L	W	L	PCT	G	GS	CG	SH	SV	IP	H	HR	BB	SO	RAT	ERA	ERA+	OAV	OOB	BH	AVG	PB	PR	/A	PD	TPI
1995	Mil-A	2	1	.667	34	0	0	0	1	36²	35	3	18	22	14.2	5.40	92	.271	.382	0	—	0	-3	-2	1	-0.1

● JOHNNY RIGNEY   Rigney, John Dungan b: 10/28/14, Oak Park, Ill. d: 10/21/84, Lombard, Ill. BR/TR, 6'2", 190 lbs. Deb: 4/21/37

YEAR	TM/L	W	L	PCT	G	GS	CG	SH	SV	IP	H	HR	BB	SO	RAT	ERA	ERA+	OAV	OOB	BH	AVG	PB	PR	/A	PD	TPI
1937	Chi-A	2	5	.286	22	4	0	1	1	90²	107	10	46	38	15.5	4.96	93	.290	.373	5	.167	-0	-3	-4	-1	-0.3
1938	Chi-A	9	9	.500	38	12	7	1	1	167	164	16	72	84	12.8	3.56	138	.256	.333	8	.145	-3	23	25	0	2.0
1939	Chi-A	15	8	.652	35	29	11	2	0	218²	208	10	84	119	12.1	3.70	128	.247	.316	16	.200	-1	22	25	-2	2.0
1940	Chi-A	14	18	.438	39	33	19	2	3	280²	240	22	90	141	10.6	3.11	142	.230	.292	20	.215	1	40	41	-1	4.2
1941	Chi-A	13	13	.500	30	29	18	3	0	237	224	21	92	119	12.1	3.84	107	.249	.320	17	.202	8	7	-0	8	0.3
1942	Chi-A	3	3	.500	7	7	6	0	0	59	40	2	16	34	8.7	3.20	112	.185	.245	1	.053	-1	3	3	0	0.1
1946	Chi-A	5	5	.500	15	11	3	2	0	82²	76	6	35	51	12.3	4.03	85	.240	.319	4	.154	-1	-5	-6	-1	-0.8
1947	Chi-A	2	3	.400	11	2	0	0	0	50²	42	3	15	19	10.1	1.95	187	.228	.286	0	.000	-2	10	10	1	0.8
Total	8	63	64	.496	197	132	66	10	5	1186¹	1101	90	450	605	11.9	3.59	121	.244	.314	71	.177	-6	98	100	-3	8.8

● JOSE RIJO   Rijo, Jose Antonio (Abreu) b: 5/13/65, San Cristobal, D.R. BR/TR, 6'1", 200 lbs. Deb: 4/5/84

YEAR	TM/L	W	L	PCT	G	GS	CG	SH	SV	IP	H	HR	BB	SO	RAT	ERA	ERA+	OAV	OOB	BH	AVG	PB	PR	/A	PD	TPI
1984	NY-A	2	8	.200	24	5	0	0	2	62¹	74	5	33	47	15.6	4.76	80	.298	.383	0	—	0	-5	-7	1	-0.9
1985	Oak-A	6	4	.600	12	9	0	0	0	63²	57	6	28	65	12.2	3.53	109	.239	.322	0	—	0	4	2	-1	0.8
1986	Oak-A	9	11	.450	39	26	4	0	1	193²	172	24	108	176	13.2	4.65	83	.237	.339	0	—	0	-10	-17	-1	-1.0
1987	Oak-A	2	7	.222	21	14	1	0	0	82¹	106	10	41	67	16.3	5.90	70	.305	.381	0	—	0	-13	-16	0	-1.1
1988	Cin-N	13	8	.619	49	19	0	0	0	162	120	7	63	160	10.3	2.39	150	.209	.291	2	.054	-2	19	21	0	2.6
1989	Cin-N	7	6	.538	19	19	1	1	0	111	101	6	48	86	12.2	2.84	127	.249	.332	8	.211	1	8	9	-0	1.2
1990	*Cin-N	14	8	.636	29	29	7	1	0	197	151	10	78	152	10.6	2.70	146	.212	.292	10	.161	-0	24	27	1	3.1
1991	Cin-N	15	6	.714	30	30	3	1	0	204¹	165	8	55	172	9.8	2.51	151	.219	.274	14	.209	1	27	29	-0	3.0
1992	Cin-N	15	10	.600	33	33	2	0	0	211	185	15	44	171	9.9	2.56	141	.238	.282	14	.194	1	22	24	1	3.2
1993	Cin-N	14	9	.609	36	36	2	1	0	257¹	218	19	62	227	9.9	2.48	162	.230	.278	22	.268	7	45	44	3	4.8
1994	Cin-N†	9	6	.600	26	26	2	0	0	172¹	177	16	52	171	12.2	3.08	134	.265	.322	10	.204	0	22	20	2	1.9
1995	Cin-N	5	4	.556	14	14	0	0	0	69	76	6	22	62	12.8	4.17	99	.285	.339	3	.136	0	0	-0	-0	-0.1
Total	12	111	87	.561	332	260	22	4	3	1786	1602	132	634	1556	11.4	3.16	122	.240	.309	83	.193	10	142	140	5	17.5

● GEORGE RILEY   Riley, George Michael b: 10/6/56, Philadelphia, Pa. BL/TL, 6'2", 210 lbs. Deb: 9/15/79

YEAR	TM/L	W	L	PCT	G	GS	CG	SH	SV	IP	H	HR	BB	SO	RAT	ERA	ERA+	OAV	OOB	BH	AVG	PB	PR	/A	PD	TPI
1979	Chi-N	0	1	.000	4	1	0	0	0	13	16	1	6	5	16.6	5.54	74	.320	.414	0	.000	-0	-3	-2	0	-0.1
1980	Chi-N	0	4	.000	22	6	0	0	0	36	41	4	20	18	15.8	5.75	68	.293	.389	0	.000	-0	-9	-7	1	-0.7
1984	SF-N	1	0	1.000	5	4	0	0	0	29¹	39	1	7	12	14.7	3.99	88	.315	.361	1	.100	-0	-1	-2	-0	-0.1
1986	Mon-N	0	0	—	10	0	0	0	0	8²	7	0	8	5	16.6	4.15	89	.212	.381	0	—	0	-0	-0	-0	-0.0
Total	4	1	5	.167	41	5	0	0	0	87	103	4	41	40	15.6	4.97	76	.297	.382	1	.077	-1	-13	-11	1	-0.9

● ANDY RINCON   Rincon, Andrew John b: 3/5/59, Monterey Park, Cal. BR/TR, 6'3", 195 lbs. Deb: 9/15/80

YEAR	TM/L	W	L	PCT	G	GS	CG	SH	SV	IP	H	HR	BB	SO	RAT	ERA	ERA+	OAV	OOB	BH	AVG	PB	PR	/A	PD	TPI
1980	StL-N	3	1	.750	4	4	1	0	0	31	23	1	7	22	8.7	2.61	141	.215	.263	3	.250	0	3	4	0	0.6
1981	StL-N	3	1	.750	5	5	1	1	0	35²	27	0	5	13	8.6	1.77	201	.214	.256	3	.231	1	7	7	-0	0.9
1982	StL-N	2	3	.400	11	6	1	0	0	40	35	1	25	11	13.5	4.72	77	.241	.353	1	.100	-0	-5	-5	-1	-0.6
Total	3	8	5	.615	20	15	3	1	0	106²	85	2	37	46	10.5	3.12	116	.225	.297	7	.200	1	5	6	-1	0.9

● JEFF RINEER   Rineer, Jeffrey Alan b: 7/3/55, Lancaster, Pa. BL/TL, 6'4", 205 lbs. Deb: 9/30/79

YEAR	TM/L	W	L	PCT	G	GS	CG	SH	SV	IP	H	HR	BB	SO	RAT	ERA	ERA+	OAV	OOB	BH	AVG	PB	PR	/A	PD	TPI
1979	Bal-A	0	0	—	1	0	0	0	0	1	0	0	0	0	0.0	0.00	—	.000	.000	0	—	0	0	0	0	0.4

● JIMMY RING   Ring, James Joseph b: 2/15/1895, Brooklyn, N.Y. d: 7/6/65, New York, N.Y. BR/TR, 6'1", 170 lbs. Deb: 4/13/17

YEAR	TM/L	W	L	PCT	G	GS	CG	SH	SV	IP	H	HR	BB	SO	RAT	ERA	ERA+	OAV	OOB	BH	AVG	PB	PR	/A	PD	TPI
1917	Cin-N	3	7	.300	24	7	3	0	2	88	90	2	35	33	12.9	4.40	60	.273	.343	2	.077	-2	-16	-17	0	-2.2
1918	Cin-N	9	5	.643	21	18	13	4	0	142¹	130	5	48	26	11.4	2.85	94	.247	.314	6	.120	-3	-1	-3	-3	-0.9
1919	*Cin-N	10	9	.526	32	18	12	2	3	183	150	1	51	61	10.0	2.26	123	.232	.291	6	.097	-5	13	10	3	0.9
1920	Cin-N	17	16	.515	42	33	18	1	1	266²	268	4	92	73	12.3	3.54	86	.264	.329	19	.198	-0	-12	-15	1	-1.8
1921	Phi-N	10	19	.345	34	30	21	0	1	246	258	8	88	88	12.8	4.24	100	.274	.340	12	.145	-4	-13	-0	-3	-0.2
1922	Phi-N	12	18	.400	40	33	17	0	1	249¹	292	19	103	116	14.4	4.58	102	.297	.365	13	.148	-5	-13	2	4	0.2
1923	Phi-N	18	16	.529	39	36	23	0	0	304¹	336	13	115	112	13.4	3.87	113	.283	.347	12	.106	-9	4	25	3	1.8
1924	Phi-N	10	12	.455	32	31	16	1	0	215²	236	9	108	72	14.5	3.97	112	.286	.371	17	.230	-1	-2	12	2	1.3
1925	Phi-N	14	16	.467	38	37	21	1	0	270	325	14	119	93	14.8	4.37	109	.297	.367	11	.109	-7	-3	12	2	0.7
1926	NY-N	11	10	.524	39	23	5	0	2	183¹	207	12	74	76	13.8	4.57	82	.290	.357	8	.143	-3	-15	-17	-1	-2.1
1927	StL-N	0	4	.000	13	3	1	0	0	33	39	3	17	13	15.5	6.55	60	.300	.385	3	.375	1	-10	-10	1	-0.8
1928	Phi-N	4	17	.190	35	25	4	0	0	173	214	14	103	72	16.6	6.40	67	.316	.407	11	.183	-2	-46	-41	1	-4.2
Total	12	118	149	.442	389	294	154	9	11	2354¹	2545	104	953	835	13.5	4.12	95	.281	.351	120	.147	-40	-115	-50	16	-7.3

● ALLEN RIPLEY   Ripley, Allen Stevens b: 10/18/52, Norwood, Mass. BR/TR, 6'3", 190 lbs. Deb: 4/10/78 F

YEAR	TM/L	W	L	PCT	G	GS	CG	SH	SV	IP	H	HR	BB	SO	RAT	ERA	ERA+	OAV	OOB	BH	AVG	PB	PR	/A	PD	TPI
1978	Bos-A	2	5	.286	15	11	1	0	0	73	92	10	22	26	14.4	5.55	74	.311	.364	0	—	0	-14	-12	-1	-1.9
1979	Bos-A	3	1	.750	16	3	0	0	1	64²	77	9	25	34	14.6	5.15	86	.295	.363	0	—	0	-7	-5	-1	-0.9
1980	SF-N	9	10	.474	23	20	2	0	0	112²	119	10	36	65	12.7	4.15	85	.274	.335	6	.150	-0	-7	-8	0	-1.2
1981	SF-N	4	4	.500	19	14	1	0	0	90²	103	5	27	47	13.2	4.07	84	.291	.345	4	.133	-1	-6	-6	1	-0.6
1982	Chi-N	5	7	.417	28	19	0	0	0	122²	130	12	38	57	12.5	4.26	88	.285	.343	5	.132	-1	-9	-7	1	-0.7
Total	5	23	27	.460	101	67	4	0	1	463²	521	46	148	229	13.3	4.52	83	.289	.348	15	.139	-3	-43	-38	-0	-5.3

● WALT RIPLEY   Ripley, Walter Franklin b: 11/26/16, Worcester, Mass. d: 10/7/90, Attleboro, Mass. BR/TR, 6', 168 lbs. Deb: 8/17/35 F

YEAR	TM/L	W	L	PCT	G	GS	CG	SH	SV	IP	H	HR	BB	SO	RAT	ERA	ERA+	OAV	OOB	BH	AVG	PB	PR	/A	PD	TPI
1935	Bos-A	0	0	—	2	0	0	0	0	4	7	0	4	0	22.5	9.00	53	.412	.500	0	—	0	-2	-2	-0	0.0

● RAY RIPPELMEYER   Rippelmeyer, Raymond Roy b: 7/9/33, Valmeyer, Ill. BR/TR, 6'3", 200 lbs. Deb: 4/14/62 C

YEAR	TM/L	W	L	PCT	G	GS	CG	SH	SV	IP	H	HR	BB	SO	RAT	ERA	ERA+	OAV	OOB	BH	AVG	PB	PR	/A	PD	TPI
1962	Was-A	1	2	.333	18	1	0	0	0	39¹	47	7	17	17	14.6	5.49	74	.294	.362	3	.500	2	-7	-6	2	0.0

● CHARLIE RIPPLE   Ripple, Charles Dawson b: 12/1/21, Bolton, N.C. d: 5/6/79, Wilmington, N.C. BL/TL, 6'2", 210 lbs. Deb: 9/25/44

YEAR	TM/L	W	L	PCT	G	GS	CG	SH	SV	IP	H	HR	BB	SO	RAT	ERA	ERA+	OAV	OOB	BH	AVG	PB	PR	/A	PD	TPI
1944	Phi-N	0	0	—	1	0	0	0	0	2¹	6	0	3	2	38.6	15.43	23	.500	.625	1	1.000	0	-3	-3	-0	0.0
1945	Phi-N	0	1	.000	4	0	0	0	0	7²	7	0	10	5	20.0	7.04	54	.241	.436	0	.000	0	-3	-3	-0	-0.3
1946	Phi-N	1	0	1.000	6	0	0	0	0	3¹	5	0	3	2	29.7	10.80	32	.385	.579	0	—	0	-3	-3	-0	-0.7
Total	3	1	1	.500	11	0	0	0	0	13¹	18	0	16	9	25.7	9.45	34	.333	.514	1	.200	0	-9	-9	-0	-1.0

YEAR	TM/L	W	L	PCT	G	GS	CG	SH	SV	IP	H	HR	BB	SO	RAT	ERA	ERA+	OAV	OOB	BH	AVG	PB	PR	/A	PD	TPI

● BILL RISLEY Risley, William Charles b: 5/29/67, Chicago, Ill. BR/TR, 6'2", 215 lbs. Deb: 7/8/92

1992	Mon-N	1	0	1.000	1	1	0	0	0	5	4	0	1	2	9.0	1.80	193	.235	.278	0	.000	-0	1	1	0	0.2
1993	Mon-N	0	0	—	2	0	0	0	0	3	2	1	2	2	15.0	6.00	70	.200	.385	0	—	0	-1	-1	0	0.0
1994	Sea-A	9	6	.600	37	0	0	0	0	52¹	31	7	19	61	8.6	3.44	142	.170	.249	0	—	0	8	8	-0	2.0
1995	*Sea-A	2	1	.667	45	0	0	0	1	60¹	55	7	18	65	11.0	3.13	151	.244	.303	0	—	0	11	11	-1	0.4
1996	Tor-A	0	1	.000	25	0	0	0	0	41²	33	7	25	29	12.5	3.89	130	.221	.333	0	—	0	5	5	-2	0.0
Total	5		12	8	.600	110	1	0	0	1	162¹	125	22	65	159	10.6	3.44	140	.214	.295	0	.000	-0	24	25	-2	2.6

● JAY RITCHIE Ritchie, Jay Seay b: 11/20/36, Salisbury, N.C. BR/TR, 6'4", 190 lbs. Deb: 8/4/64

1964	Bos-A	1	1	.500	21	0	0	0	2	46	43	4	14	35	11.2	2.74	141	.249	.305	1	.111	-1	5	6	-0	0.2
1965	Bos-A	1	2	.333	44	0	0	0	2	71	83	3	26	55	13.9	3.17	118	.302	.364	1	.200	0	2	4	0	0.2
1966	Atl-N	0	1	.000	22	0	0	0	4	35¹	32	3	12	33	11.2	4.08	89	.241	.303	2	.500	1	-2	-2	0	0.0
1967	Atl-N	4	6	.400	52	0	0	0	2	82¹	75	6	29	57	11.8	3.17	105	.245	.319	3	.300	1	2	1	1	0.4
1968	Cin-N	2	3	.400	28	2	0	0	0	56²	68	7	13	32	13.0	4.61	69	.293	.333	0	.000	-1	-10	-9	-1	-1.0
Total	5		8	13	.381	167	2	0	0	8	291¹	301	23	94	212	12.4	3.49	101	.269	.329	7	.200	0	-3	-1	0	-0.2

● WALLY RITCHIE Ritchie, Wallace Reid b: 7/12/65, Glendale, Cal. BL/TL, 6'2", 180 lbs. Deb: 5/1/87

1987	Phi-N	3	2	.600	49	0	0	0	3	62¹	60	8	29	45	13.0	3.75	113	.254	.338	1	.250	-1	2	3	-0	0.3
1988	Phi-N	0	0	—	19	0	0	0	0	26	19	1	17	8	12.8	3.12	114	.207	.336	0	—	0	1	1	-0	0.0
1991	Phi-N	1	2	.333	39	0	0	0	0	50¹	44	4	17	26	11.3	2.50	146	.234	.304	0	.000	-0	7	7	-0	0.3
1992	Phi-N	2	1	.667	40	0	0	0	1	39	44	3	17	19	14.1	3.00	116	.288	.359	0	.000	0	2	2	-0	0.1
Total	4		6	5	.545	147	0	0	0	4	177²	167	16	80	98	12.7	3.14	121	.250	.333	1	.125	0	12	13	-1	0.7

● REGGIE RITTER Ritter, Reggie Blake b: 1/23/60, Malvern, Ark. BL/TR, 6'2", 195 lbs. Deb: 5/17/86

1986	Cle-A	0	0	—	5	0	0	0	0	10	14	1	4	6	17.1	6.30	66	.341	.413	0	—	0	-2	-2	0	0.2
1987	Cle-A	1	1	.500	14	0	0	0	0	26²	33	5	16	11	16.5	6.08	74	.300	.389	0	—	0	-5	-5	0	-0.3
Total	2		1	1	.500	19	0	0	0	0	36²	47	6	20	17	16.7	6.14	72	.311	.395	0	—	0	-7	-7	1	-0.1

● HANK RITTER Ritter, William Herbert b: 10/12/1893, McCoysville, Pa. d: 9/3/64, Akron, Ohio BR/TR, 6', 180 lbs. Deb: 8/3/12

1912	Phi-N	0	0	—	3	0	0	0	0	6	5	0	5	1	15.0	4.50	81	.192	.323	0	.000	-0	-1	-1	-0	0.0
1914	NY-N	1	0	1.000	1	0	0	0	0	8	4	0	4	4	9.0	1.13	236	.160	.276	0	.000	-0	1	1	-0	0.1
1915	NY-N	2	1	.667	22	2	0	0	2	58¹	66	4	15	35	13.3	4.63	55	.291	.348	2	.125	-1	-12	-13	-0	-0.9
1916	NY-N	1	0	1.000	3	0	0	0	0	5	3	0	0	3	7.2	0.00	—	.200	.250	0	—	0	1	1	0	0.3
Total	4		4	1	.800	29	2	0	0	2	77¹	78	4	24	43	12.6	3.96	67	.266	.334	2	.100	-1	-10	-11	-1	-0.5

● JIM RITTWAGE Rittwage, James Michael b: 10/23/44, Cleveland, Ohio BR/TR, 6'3", 190 lbs. Deb: 9/7/70

| 1970 | Cle-A | 1 | 1 | .500 | 8 | 3 | 1 | 0 | 0 | 26 | 18 | 0 | 21 | 16 | 13.5 | 4.15 | 95 | .194 | .342 | 3 | .375 | 1 | -1 | -1 | 0 | 0.1 |

● KEVIN RITZ Ritz, Kevin D b: 6/8/65, Eatontown, N.J. BR/TR, 6'4", 195 lbs. Deb: 7/15/89

1989	Det-A	4	6	.400	12	12	1	0	0	74	75	2	44	56	14.6	4.38	87	.265	.366	0	—	0	-4	-5	0	-0.5
1990	Det-A	0	4	.000	4	4	0	0	0	7¹	14	0	14	3	34.4	11.05	36	.400	.571	0	—	0	-6	-6	1	-2.1
1991	Det-A	0	3	.000	11	5	0	0	0	15¹	17	1	22	9	24.1	11.74	35	.288	.494	0	—	0	-13	-13	0	-2.1
1992	Det-A	2	5	.286	23	11	0	0	0	80¹	88	4	44	57	15.1	5.60	71	.278	.372	0	.000	-2	-15	-15	1	-1.2
1994	Col-N	5	6	.455	15	15	0	0	0	73²	88	5	35	53	15.5	5.62	88	.303	.386	0	.000	0	-12	-5	1	-0.8
1995	*Col-N	11	11	.500	31	28	0	0	2	173¹	171	16	65	120	12.6	4.21	128	.259	.332	9	.188	-1	23	23	3	2.9
1996	Col-N	17	11	.607	35	35	2	0	0	213	236	24	105	105	14.9	5.28	103	.282	.370	15	.231	1	-25	4	-1	1.0
Total	7		39	46	.459	131	110	3	0	2	637	689	52	329	403	14.8	5.19	95	.278	.369	24	.180	-2	-75	-18	9	-2.8

● BEN RIVERA Rivera, Bienvenido Santana b: 1/11/68, San Pedro De Macoris, D.R. BR/TR, 6'6", 210 lbs. Deb: 4/9/92

1992	Atl-N	0	1	.000	8	0	0	0	0	15¹	21	1	13	11	21.1	4.70	78	.339	.468	0	.000	-1	-2	-2	0	-0.1
	Phi-N	7	3	.700	20	14	4	1	0	102	78	8	32	66	9.9	2.82	124	.211	.278	3	.094	-1	8	8	-0	0.6
	Yr	7	4	.636	28	14	4	1	0	117¹	99	9	45	77	11.2	3.07	114	.228	.304	3	.091	-1	6	6	0	0.5
1993	*Phi-N	13	9	.591	30	28	1	1	0	163	175	16	85	123	14.7	5.02	79	.273	.363	5	.098	-2	-18	-19	-2	-2.6
1994	Phi-N	3	4	.429	9	7	0	0	0	38	40	7	22	19	14.4	6.87	62	.274	.373	0	.000	-1	-11	-11	0	-1.7
Total	3		23	17	.575	67	49	5	2	0	318¹	314	32	152	219	13.5	4.52	85	.258	.345	8	.086	-3	-23	-24	-2	-3.8

● MARIANO RIVERA Rivera, Mariano b: 11/29/69, Panama City, Panama BR/TR, 6'4", 170 lbs. Deb: 5/23/95

1995	*NY-A	5	3	.625	19	10	0	0	0	67	71	11	30	51	13.8	5.51	84	.266	.344	0	—	0	-6	-7	1	-0.6
1996	*NY-A	8	3	.727	61	0	0	0	5	107²	73	1	34	130	9.1	2.09	242	.189	.258	0	—	0	**35**	**35**	0	3.3
Total	2		13	6	.684	80	10	0	0	5	174²	144	12	64	181	10.9	3.40	144	.221	.294	0	—	0	29	29	1	2.7

● ROBERTO RIVERA Rivera, Roberto (Diaz) b: 1/1/69, Bayamon, P.R. BL/TL, 6', 175 lbs. Deb: 9/3/95

| 1995 | Chi-N | 0 | 0 | — | 7 | 0 | 0 | 0 | 0 | 5 | 8 | 1 | 2 | 2 | 18.0 | 5.40 | 76 | .381 | .435 | 0 | — | 0 | -1 | -1 | 0 | -0.1 |

● TINK RIVIERE Riviere, Arthur Bernard b: 8/2/1899, Liberty, Tex. d: 9/27/65, Liberty, Tex. BR/TR, 5'10", 167 lbs. Deb: 4/15/21

1921	StL-N	1	0	1.000	18	2	0	0	0	38¹	45	2	20	15	15.7	6.10	60	.280	.366	3	.375	2	-10	-10	-2	-0.2
1925	Chi-A	0	0	—	3	0	0	0	0	4²	6	0	7	1	27.0	13.50	31	.429	.636	0	.000	-0	-5	-5	1	0.0
Total	2		1	0	1.000	21	2	0	0	0	43	51	2	27	16	17.0	6.91	54	.291	.395	3	.333	2	-15	-15	-1	-0.2

● EPPA RIXEY Rixey, Eppa "Jeptha" b: 5/3/1891, Culpeper, Va. d: 2/28/63, Cincinnati, Ohio BR/TL, 6'5", 210 lbs. Deb: 6/21/12 H

1912	Phi-N	10	10	.500	23	20	10	3	0	162	147	2	54	59	11.3	2.50	145	.256	.322	9	.170	-2	16	20	-1	2.0
1913	Phi-N	9	5	.643	35	19	9	1	2	155²	148	4	56	75	12.1	3.12	107	.258	.331	9	.191	-0	1	4	-0	0.3
1914	Phi-N	2	11	.154	24	15	2	0	0	103	124	0	45	41	15.6	4.37	67	.313	.387	1	.038	-1	-18	-16	0	-2.0
1915	*Phi-N	11	12	.478	29	22	10	2	1	176³	163	6	64	88	11.7	2.39	115	.250	.319	9	.164	0	7	7	0	0.9
1916	Phi-N	22	10	.688	38	33	20	3	0	287	239	2	74	134	10.0	1.85	143	.229	.284	15	.155	-2	25	26	3	3.2
1917	Phi-N	16	21	.432	39	36	23	4	1	281²	249	1	67	121	10.3	2.27	124	.241	.290	18	.191	-1	14	17	4	2.6
1919	Phi-N	6	12	.333	23	18	11	1	0	154	160	4	50	63	12.4	3.97	81	.278	.339	7	.149	-2	-18	-13	2	-1.4
1920	Phi-N	11	22	.333	41	34	25	0	2	284¹	288	6	69	109	11.4	3.48	98	.274	.321	25	.248	1	-11	-2	3	0.3
1921	Cin-N	19	18	.514	40	36	21	2	1	301	324	1	66	76	11.8	2.78	129	.282	.324	13	.129	-5	**34**	27	3	2.8
1922	Cin-N	25	13	.658	40	38	26	2	0	**313**¹	337	13	45	80	11.1	3.53	113	.275	.303	21	.193	1	20	16	-0	1.5
1923	Cin-N	20	15	.571	42	37	23	3	1	309	334	3	65	97	11.7	2.80	138	.280	.320	17	.159	-5	41	37	2	3.4
1924	Cin-N	15	14	.517	35	29	15	4	1	238¹	219	3	47	57	10.1	2.76	137	.246	.285	18	.214	1	29	27	-1	3.1
1925	Cin-N	21	11	.656	39	36	22	2	1	287¹	302	8	47	69	11.2	2.88	143	.273	.307	22	.214	-1	44	39	-2	3.6
1926	Cin-N	14	8	.636	37	29	14	3	0	233	231	4	56	61	11.2	3.40	109	.265	.313	19	.226	-2	11	8	-2	0.5
1927	Cin-N	12	10	.545	34	29	11	1	1	219²	240	4	43	42	11.7	3.48	109	.287	.325	20	.247	4	11	7	-1	0.6
1928	Cin-N	19	18	.514	43	37	17	3	2	291¹	317	4	67	58	12.0	3.43	115	.288	.330	18	.173	-1	18	17	0	1.8
1929	Cin-N	10	13	.435	35	24	11	0	1	201	235	6	60	37	13.3	4.16	110	.296	.348	15	.231	0	12	9	-1	0.8
1930	Cin-N	9	13	.409	32	21	5	0	0	164	207	11	47	37	14.3	5.10	95	.317	.370	11	.200	-1	-2	-5	-0	-0.6
1931	Cin-N	4	7	.364	22	17	4	0	0	126²	143	4	30	22	12.3	3.91	96	.291	.332	6	.150	-1	-1	-2	4	-0.1
1932	Cin-N	5	5	.500	25	11	6	2	0	111²	109	5	20	34	10.4	2.66	145	.254	.288	9	.265	1	15	15	1	1.4
1933	Cin-N	6	3	.667	16	12	5	1	0	94¹	118	1	12	10	12.4	3.15	108	.298	.319	9	.257	2	3	1	0	0.0
Total	21		266	251	.515	692	553	290	37	14	4494²	4633	92	1082	1350	11.6	3.15	116	.272	.318	291	.191	-15	251	248	16	25.9

● JOE ROA Roa, Joseph Rodger b: 10/11/71, Southfield, Mich. BR/TR, 6'1", 194 lbs. Deb: 9/20/95

1995	Cle-A	0	1	.000	1	1	0	0	0	6	9	1	2	0	16.5	6.00	78	.360	.407	0	—	0	-1	-1	0	-0.1
1996	Cle-A	0	0	—	1	0	0	0	0	1²	4	0	3	0	37.8	10.80	45	.500	.636	0	—	0	-1	-1	0	0.0
Total	2		0	1	.000	2	1	0	0	0	7²	13	1	5	0	21.1	7.04	67	.394	.474	0	—	0	-2	-2	0	-0.1

● JOHN ROACH Roach, John F. b: Farrandsville, Pa. BR/TL, 5'9", 175 lbs. Deb: 5/14/1887

| 1887 | NY-N | 0 | 1 | .000 | 1 | 1 | 1 | 0 | 0 | 8 | 18 | 0 | 4 | 3 | 25.9 | 11.25 | 33 | .419 | .479 | 1 | .250 | -0 | -6 | -7 | -0 | -0.5 |

YEAR	TM/L	W	L	PCT	G	GS	CG	SH	SV	IP	H	HR	BB	SO	RAT	ERA	ERA+	OAV	OOB	BH	AVG	PB	PR	/A	PD	TPI

● SKEL ROACH Roach, Rudolph Charles (b: Rudolph Charles Weichbrodt) b: 10/20/1871, Danzig, Germany d: 3/9/58, Oak Park, Ill. BR/TR, 6'2", Deb: 8/9/1899

| 1899 | Chi-N | 1 | 0 | 1.000 | 1 | 1 | 1 | 0 | 0 | 9 | 13 | 0 | 1 | 0 | 14.0 | 3.00 | 125 | .333 | .350 | 0 | .000 | -1 | 1 | 1 | -0 | 0.0 |

● BRUCE ROBBINS Robbins, Bruce Duane b: 9/10/59, Portland, Ind. BL/TL, 6'1", 190 lbs. Deb: 7/28/79

1979	Det-A	3	3	.500	10	8	0	0	0	46	45	3	21	22	12.9	3.91	111	.265	.346	0	—	0	2	2	-1	0.1
1980	Det-A	4	2	.667	15	6	0	0	0	51²	60	12	28	23	15.3	6.62	62	.287	.371	0	—	0	-15	-14	-0	-1.6
Total	2	7	5	.583	25	14	0	0	0	97²	105	15	49	45	14.2	5.34	79	.277	.360	0	—	0	-13	-12	-0	-1.5

● BERT ROBERGE Roberge, Bertrand Roland b: 10/3/54, Lewiston, Maine BR/TR, 6'4", 190 lbs. Deb: 5/28/79

1979	Hou-N	3	0	1.000	26	0	0	0	4	32	20	0	17	13	10.4	1.69	208	.196	.311	0	.000	-0	7	6	-0	0.7
1980	Hou-N	2	0	1.000	14	0	0	0	0	24¹	24	2	10	13	13.3	5.92	56	.261	.346	0	.000	-0	-6	-7	0	-0.6
1982	Hou-N	1	2	.333	22	0	0	0	3	25²	29	2	6	18	12.3	4.21	79	.284	.324	0	.000	-0	-2	-3	-1	-0.3
1984	Chi-A	3	3	.500	21	0	0	0	0	40²	36	2	15	25	12.0	3.76	111	.240	.321	0	—	0	1	2	1	0.2
1985	Mon-N	3	3	.500	42	0	0	0	2	68	58	5	22	34	10.9	3.44	99	.232	.299	0	.000	-0	1	-0	0	0.0
1986	Mon-N	0	4	.000	21	0	0	0	1	28²	33	2	10	20	13.8	6.28	59	.295	.358	0	.000	-0	-8	-8	0	-1.1
Total	6	12	12	.500	146	0	0	0	10	219¹	200	11	80	119	11.8	3.98	90	.248	.321	0	.000	-1	-7	-10	1	-1.1

● SID ROBERSON Roberson, Sidney Dean b: 9/9/71, Jacksonville, Fla. BL/TL, 5'9", 170 lbs. Deb: 5/20/95

| 1995 | Mil-A | 6 | 4 | .600 | 26 | 13 | 0 | 0 | 0 | 84¹ | 102 | 16 | 37 | 40 | 15.7 | 5.76 | 86 | .307 | .390 | 0 | — | 0 | -10 | -7 | -2 | -0.9 |

● DALE ROBERTS Roberts, Dale "Mountain Man" b: 4/12/42, Owenton, Ky. BR/TL, 6'4", 180 lbs. Deb: 9/9/67

| 1967 | NY-A | 0 | 0 | — | 2 | 0 | 0 | 0 | 0 | 3 | 0 | 0 | 3 | 1 | 31.5 | 9.00 | 35 | .429 | .636 | 0 | — | 0 | -1 | -1 | 0 | 0.0 |

● DAVE ROBERTS Roberts, David Arthur b: 9/11/44, Gallipolis, Ohio BL/TL, 6'2", 197 lbs. Deb: 7/6/69

1969	SD-N	0	3	.000	22	5	0	0	1	48²	65	5	19	19	16.1	4.81	74	.322	.388	4	.267	1	-7	-7	0	-0.3
1970	SD-N	8	14	.364	43	21	3	2	1	181²	182	16	43	102	11.2	3.81	104	.261	.305	9	.153	1	5	3	-0	0.5
1971	SD-N	14	17	.452	37	34	14	2	0	269³	238	16	61	135	10.1	2.10	157	.240	.288	19	.221	2	41	36	1	4.6
1972	Hou-N	12	7	.632	35	28	7	3	2	192	227	18	57	111	13.4	4.50	75	.296	.346	16	.239	6	-22	-24	-1	-1.9
1973	Hou-N	17	11	.607	39	36	12	6	0	249¹	264	15	62	119	11.8	2.85	127	.271	.316	11	.129	-3	22	22	-1	2.0
1974	Hou-N	10	12	.455	34	30	8	2	1	204	216	6	65	72	12.5	3.40	102	.276	.333	16	.219	5	1	2	0	0.9
1975	Hou-N	8	14	.364	32	27	7	0	1	198¹	182	16	73	101	11.7	4.27	79	.244	.313	9	.143	0	-14	-20	1	-1.9
1976	Det-A	16	17	.485	36	36	18	4	0	252	254	16	63	79	11.5	4.00	93	.264	.312	0	—	0	-13	-8	2	-1.1
1977	Det-A	4	10	.286	22	22	5	0	0	129¹	143	20	41	46	12.9	5.15	83	.274	.330	0	—	0	-16	-12	-0	-1.5
	Chi-N	1	1	.500	17	6	1	0	1	53	55	1	12	23	11.5	3.23	136	.275	.319	1	.059	-2	4	7	2	0.3
1978	Chi-N	6	8	.429	35	20	2	1	1	142¹	159	17	56	54	13.8	5.25	77	.288	.357	17	.327	6	-26	-19	1	-1.1
1979	SF-N	0	2	.000	26	1	0	0	3	42	42	3	18	23	13.1	2.57	136	.262	.341	0	.000	-1	5	4	1	0.2
	*Pit-N	5	2	.714	21	3	0	0	1	38²	47	1	12	15	14.0	3.26	119	.318	.373	0	.000	-1	2	3	0	0.5
	Yr	5	4	.556	47	4	0	0	4	80²	89	4	30	38	13.4	2.90	127	.287	.352	0	.000	-1	7	7	1	0.7
1980	Pit-N	0	0	—	2	0	0	0	0	2¹	2	0	1	1	11.6	3.86	94	.250	.333	—	—	0	-0	-0	-0	0.0
	Sea-A	2	3	.400	37	4	0	0	3	80¹	86	7	27	47	12.8	4.37	95	.270	.329	0	—	0	-3	-2	-1	-0.3
1981	NY-N	0	3	.000	7	4	0	0	0	15¹	26	5	5	10	18.2	9.39	37	.366	.408	1	.250	0	-10	-10	-1	-1.6
Total	13	103	125	.452	445	277	77	20	15	2099	2188	155	615	957	12.2	3.78	97	.265	.324	103	.194	15	-27	-28	7	-0.7

● JIM ROBERTS Roberts, James Newson "Big Jim" b: 10/13/1895, Artesia, Miss. d: 6/24/84, Columbus, Miss. BR/TR, 6'3", 205 lbs. Deb: 7/27/24

1924	Bro-N	0	3	.000	11	5	0	0	0	25¹	41	1	8	10	18.1	7.46	50	.360	.411	1	.143	-0	-10	-10	-0	-1.1
1925	Bro-N	0	0	—	1	0	0	0	0	1	1	0	0	0	9.0	0.00	—	.500	.500	0	—	0	0	0	0	0.0
Total	2	0	3	.000	12	5	0	0	0	26¹	42	1	8	10	17.8	7.18	52	.362	.413	1	.143	-0	-10	-10	-1	-1.1

● LEON ROBERTS Roberts, Leon Kauffman b: 1/22/51, Vicksburg, Mich. BR/TR, 6'3", 200 lbs. Deb: 9/3/74 ♦

| 1984 | KC-A | 0 | 0 | — | 1 | 0 | 0 | 0 | 0 | 1 | 4 | 1 | 1 | 1 | 45.0 | 27.00 | 15 | .571 | .625 | 10 | .222 | 0 | -3 | -3 | -0 | -0.3 |

● RAY ROBERTS Roberts, Raymond b: 8/25/1895, Cruger, Miss. d: 1/30/62, Cruger, Miss. BL/TL, 5'11", 180 lbs. Deb: 9/12/19

| 1919 | Phi-A | 0 | 2 | .000 | 3 | 2 | 0 | 0 | 0 | 21 | 23 | 2 | 9 | 2 | 15.4 | 7.71 | 44 | .368 | .400 | 1 | .250 | 0 | -7 | -7 | -0 | -0.8 |

● ROBIN ROBERTS Roberts, Robin Evan b: 9/30/26, Springfield, Ill. BB/TR, 6', 190 lbs. Deb: 6/18/48 H

1948	Phi-N	7	9	.438	20	20	9	0	0	146²	148	10	61	84	13.1	3.19	124	.278	.356	11	.250	4	12	12	-2	1.5
1949	Phi-N	15	15	.500	43	31	11	3	4	226²	229	15	75	95	12.3	3.69	107	.273	.337	5	.075	-3	9	6	-3	0.1
1950	*Phi-N★	20	11	.645	40	39	21	**5**	1	304¹	282	29	77	146	10.7	3.02	134	.248	.297	12	.118	-4	**38**	35	-2	2.9
1951	Phi-N★	21	15	.583	44	39	22	6	2	**315**	284	20	64	127	10.0	3.03	127	.237	**.278**	15	.172	5	33	29	-3	**3.4**
1952	Phi-N☆	**28**	7	.800	39	37	**30**	3	2	**330**	292	22	45	148	9.3	2.59	141	.234	.263	14	.125	-2	**42**	**39**	-3	4.0
1953	Phi-N★	**23**	16	.590	44	41	**33**	5	2	**346²**	324	30	61	**198**	10.0	2.75	153	.242	.276	22	.179	2	59	**56**	-1	6.1
1954	Phi-N★	**23**	15	.605	45	38	**29**	4	4	**336²**	289	35	56	**185**	9.4	2.97	136	.231	**.267**	15	.123	-4	41	40	-4	3.6
1955	Phi-N★	**23**	14	.622	41	38	**26**	1	3	**305**	292	41	53	160	10.2	3.28	121	.246	**.280**	27	.252	14	26	24	-5	3.7
1956	Phi-N☆	19	18	.514	43	37	**22**	1	3	297¹	328	46	40	157	11.2	4.45	84	.282	.307	20	.200	4	-22	-24	-0	-2.4
1957	Phi-N	10	22	.313	39	32	14	2	2	249²	246	40	43	128	10.5	4.07	93	.252	.284	13	.162	-1	-5	-7	-0	-0.8
1958	Phi-N	17	14	.548	35	34	21	1	0	269²	270	30	51	130	10.8	3.24	122	.259	.294	20	.202	4	21	22	-2	2.5
1959	Phi-N	15	17	.469	35	35	19	2	0	257¹	267	34	35	137	10.7	4.27	96	.263	.291	17	.191	3	-9	-5	-0	-0.8
1960	Phi-N	12	16	.429	35	33	13	2	1	237²	256	31	34	122	11.1	4.02	97	.275	.302	12	.152	-1	-7	-4	-3	-0.8
1961	Phi-N	1	10	.091	26	18	2	0	0	117	154	19	23	54	13.8	5.85	70	.326	.360	3	.091	-2	-24	-23	-2	-2.2
1962	Bal-A	10	9	.526	27	25	6	0	0	191¹	176	17	41	102	10.4	2.78	133	.244	.289	10	.192	2	25	20	-1	2.0
1963	Bal-A	14	13	.519	35	35	9	2	0	251²	230	35	40	124	9.8	3.33	104	.240	**.272**	16	.203	2	8	4	-2	0.5
1964	Bal-A	13	7	.650	31	31	8	4	0	204	203	18	52	109	11.4	2.91	123	.261	.310	9	.132	-1	16	15	-2	1.1
1965	Bal-A	5	7	.417	20	15	5	1	0	114²	110	17	20	63	10.3	3.38	103	.252	.286	6	.171	1	1	-1	-0	0.1
	Hou-N	5	1	.714	10	10	3	2	0	76	61	1	14	34	8.4	1.89	177	.216	.243	5	.238	3	14	12	-2	1.4
1966	Hou-N	3	5	.375	13	12	1	1	1	63²	79	7	10	26	12.7	3.82	90	.307	.336	1	.063	-1	-1	-3	-0	-0.5
	Chi-N	2	3	.400	11	9	1	0	0	48¹	62	8	11	28	13.6	6.14	60	.321	.349	2	.200	1	-14	-13	-0	-1.1
	Yr	5	8	.385	24	21	2	1	1	112	141	15	21	54	13.0	4.82	73	.307	.337	3	.115	-0	-15	-16	-1	-1.6
Total	19	286	245	.539	676	609	305	45	25	4688²	4582	505	902	2357	10.6	3.41	113	.255	.293	255	.167	34	264	236	-35	24.9

● CHARLIE ROBERTSON Robertson, Charles Culbertson b: 1/31/1896, Dexter, Tex. d: 8/23/84, Fort Worth, Tex. BL/TR, 6', 175 lbs. Deb: 5/13/19

1919	Chi-A	0	1	.000	1	1	0	0	0	2	5	0	1	0	22.5	9.00	35	.556	.556	0	—	0	-1	-1	-0	-0.5
1922	Chi-A	14	15	.483	37	34	21	3	0	272	294	9	89	83	12.8	3.64	112	.286	.345	16	.184	-2	12	13	-5	0.6
1923	Chi-A	13	18	.419	38	34	18	1	0	255	262	8	104	91	13.1	3.81	104	.272	.346	21	.247	0	5	4	-2	0.2
1924	Chi-A	4	10	.286	17	14	5	0	0	97¹	108	2	54	29	15.0	4.99	83	.288	.393	6	.182	-1	-8	-9	-2	-1.4
1925	Chi-A	8	12	.400	24	23	6	2	0	137	181	8	47	27	15.1	5.26	79	.327	.381	10	.222	0	-13	-17	-2	-2.1
1926	StL-A	1	2	.333	8	7	1	0	0	28	38	4	21	13	19.6	8.36	51	.333	.445	3	.300	1	-13	-13	-0	-1.1
1927	Bos-N	7	17	.292	28	22	8	0	0	154¹	188	2	46	49	13.9	4.72	79	.308	.360	12	.240	1	-14	-17	-1	-2.4
1928	Bos-N	2	5	.286	13	7	1	0	1	59¹	73	5	16	17	13.5	5.31	74	.308	.352	0	.000	-1	-9	-9	-1	-1.1
Total	8	49	80	.380	166	142	60	6	1	1005	1149	38	377	310	13.8	4.44	90	.296	.361	68	.208	-2	-42	-49	-13	-7.6

● JERRY ROBERTSON Robertson, Jerry Lee b: 10/13/43, Winchester, Kan. d: 3/24/96, Burlington, Kan. BB/TR, 6'2", 205 lbs. Deb: 4/8/69

1969	Mon-N	5	16	.238	38	27	3	0	1	179²	186	17	81	133	13.6	3.96	93	.272	.352	5	.089	-3	-7	-6	-3	-1.1
1970	Det-A	0	0	—	11	0	0	0	0	14²	19	1	5	11	14.7	3.68	101	.304	.353	—	—	0	0	0	0	0.0
Total	2	5	16	.238	49	27	3	0	1	194¹	205	18	86	144	13.7	3.94	93	.274	.352	5	.089	-3	-7	-6	-3	-1.1

● DICK ROBERTSON Robertson, Preston b: 1891, Washington, D.C. d: 10/2/44, New Orleans, La. BR/TR, 5'9", 160 lbs. Deb: 9/16/13

1913	Cin-N	0	1	.000	2	1	0	0	0	10	13	0	9	1	19.8	7.20	45	.342	.468	0	.000	-0	-4	-4	-0	-0.4
1918	Bro-N	3	6	.333	13	9	7	1	0	87	87	0	28	18	11.9	2.59	108	.272	.330	9	.300	2	2	2	-0	0.4
1919	Was-A	0	1	.000	7	4	1	0	0	27²	25	1	9	7	11.1	2.28	141	.253	.315	0	—	0	3	3	0	0.0
Total	3	3	8	.273	22	14	8	1	0	124²	125	1	46	26	12.3	2.89	101	.274	.340	9	.225	2	0	0	-0	0.0

YEAR	TM/L	W	L	PCT	G	GS	CG	SH	SV	IP	H	HR	BB	SO	RAT	ERA	ERA+	OAV	OOB	BH	AVG	PB	PR	/A	PD	TPI

● RICH ROBERTSON   Robertson, Richard Paul b: 10/14/44, Albany, Cal. BR/TR, 6'2", 210 lbs. Deb: 9/10/66

1966	SF-N	0	0	—	1	0	0	0	0	2¹	3	0	2	2	19.3	7.71	48	.300	.417	0	—	0	-1	-1	-0	0.0
1967	SF-N	0	0	—	1	0	0	0	0	2	3	0	1	1	13.5	4.50	73	.333	.333	0	—	-0	-0	-0	0	0.0
1968	SF-N	2	0	1.000	3	1	0	0	0	9	9	0	3	8	12.0	6.00	49	.265	.324	1	.500	0	-3	-3	0	-0.6
1969	SF-N	1	3	.250	17	7	1	1	0	44¹	53	4	21	20	15.2	5.48	64	.298	.375	0	.000	-1	-9	-10	0	-0.9
1970	SF-N	8	9	.471	41	26	6	0	1	183²	199	22	96	121	14.5	4.85	82	.277	.363	6	.102	-1	-16	-18	-0	-1.6
1971	SF-N	2	2	.500	23	6	1	0	1	61	66	5	31	32	14.6	4.57	74	.267	.354	1	.067	-1	-8	-8	-1	-0.7
Total	6	13	14	.481	86	40	8	1	2	302¹	333	31	153	184	14.6	4.94	76	.278	.362	8	.093	-2	-38	-40	-1	-3.8

● RICH ROBERTSON   Robertson, Richard Wayne b: 9/15/68, Nacogdoches, Tex. BL/TL, 6'4", 175 lbs. Deb: 4/30/93

1993	Pit-N	0	1	.000	9	0	0	0	0	9	15	0	4	5	19.0	6.00	67	.385	.442	0	—	0	-2	-2	-0	-0.2
1994	Pit-N	0	0	—	8	0	0	0	0	15²	20	2	10	8	17.2	6.89	63	.313	.405	1	.250	0	-5	-4	-0	-0.2
1995	Min-A	2	0	1.000	25	4	1	0	0	51²	48	4	31	38	13.8	3.83	124	.253	.357	0	—	0	5	5	-1	0.1
1996	Min-A	7	17	.292	36	31	5	3	0	186¹	197	22	116	114	15.6	5.12	100	.273	.380	0	—	0	-3	0	2	0.2
Total	4	9	18	.333	78	35	6	3	0	262²	280	28	161	165	15.4	5.00	99	.276	.380	1	.250	0	-4	-1	1	0.1

● DEWEY ROBINSON   Robinson, Dewey Everett b: 4/28/55, Evanston, Ill. BR/TR, 6', 180 lbs. Deb: 4/6/79

1979	Chi-A	0	1	.000	11	0	0	0	0	14¹	11	1	9	5	12.6	6.28	68	.212	.328	0	—	0	-3	-3	-0	-0.2
1980	Chi-A	1	1	.500	15	0	0	0	0	35	26	2	16	28	10.8	3.09	131	.215	.307	0	—	0	4	4	0	0.2
1981	Chi-A	1	0	1.000	4	0	0	0	0	4	5	1	3	2	18.0	4.50	79	.357	.471	0	—	0	-0	-0	-0	-0.1
Total	3	2	2	.500	30	0	0	0	0	53¹	42	4	28	35	11.8	4.05	100	.225	.326	0	—	0	-0	0	-0	-0.1

● DON ROBINSON   Robinson, Don Allen b: 6/8/57, Ashland, Ky. BR/TR, 6'4", 231 lbs. Deb: 4/10/78

1978	Pit-N	14	6	.700	35	32	9	1	1	228¹	203	20	57	135	10.4	3.47	107	.236	.286	20	.235	2	3	6	-1	0.6
1979	*Pit-N	8	8	.500	29	25	4	0	0	160²	171	12	52	96	12.7	3.87	100	.277	.337	10	.204	1	-2	0	-3	-0.2
1980	Pit-N	7	10	.412	29	24	3	2	1	160¹	157	14	45	103	11.6	3.99	91	.257	.314	19	.333	6	-7	-6	0	-0.6
1981	Pit-N	0	3	.000	16	2	0	0	2	38¹	47	4	23	17	16.4	5.87	61	.313	.405	3	.250	1	-10	-10	1	-0.7
1982	Pit-N	15	13	.536	38	30	6	0	0	227	213	26	103	165	12.6	4.28	87	.250	.333	24	.282	8	-17	-15	-2	-1.0
1983	Pit-N	2	2	.500	9	6	0	0	0	36¹	43	5	21	28	15.9	4.46	83	.297	.386	2	.154	1	-3	-3	-0	-0.2
1984	Pit-N	5	6	.455	51	1	0	0	10	122	99	6	49	110	10.9	3.02	119	.226	.304	9	.290	4	8	8	1	1.3
1985	Pit-N	5	11	.313	44	6	0	0	3	95¹	95	6	42	65	13.1	3.87	92	.255	.334	5	.238	3	-3	-3	-0	-0.3
1986	Pit-N	3	4	.429	50	0	0	0	14	69¹	61	5	27	53	11.7	3.38	114	.237	.315	4	.667	3	3	4	0	0.7
1987	Pit-N	6	6	.500	42	0	0	0	12	65¹	66	6	22	53	12.1	3.86	107	.267	.327	1	.143	1	2	2	0	0.4
	*SF-N	5	1	.833	25	0	0	0	7	42²	39	1	18	26	12.0	2.74	140	.239	.315	3	.273	2	6	5	-1	1.0
	Yr	11	7	.611	67	0	0	0	19	108	105	7	40	79	12.1	3.42	117	.255	.322	4	.222	2	8	7	-1	1.4
1988	SF-N	10	5	.667	51	19	3	2	6	176²	152	11	49	122	10.4	2.45	133	.231	.287	9	.173	3	20	16	-2	1.6
1989	*SF-N	12	11	.522	34	32	5	1	0	197	184	22	37	96	10.2	3.43	98	.248	.285	15	.185	4	-2	-1	-4	-0.2
1990	SF-N	10	7	.588	26	25	4	0	0	157²	173	18	41	78	12.3	4.57	80	.280	.326	9	.143	1	-14	-16	-2	-1.6
1991	SF-N	5	9	.357	34	16	0	0	0	121¹	123	12	50	78	12.9	4.38	82	.265	.337	6	.150	0	-9	-11	-0	-1.2
1992	Cal-A	1	0	1.000	3	3	0	0	0	16¹	19	1	3	9	12.1	2.20	181	.292	.324	0	—	0	3	3	-1	0.1
	Phi-N	1	4	.200	8	8	0	0	0	43²	49	6	4	17	11.1	6.18	56	.290	.310	7	.389	3	-13	-13	-1	-1.1
Total	15	109	106	.507	524	229	34	6	57	1958¹	1894	175	643	1251	11.8	3.79	96	.255	.317	146	.231	41	-34	-34	-14	-0.8

● HUMBERTO ROBINSON   Robinson, Humberto Valentino b: 6/25/30, Colon, Panama BR/TR, 6'1", 155 lbs. Deb: 4/20/55

1955	Mil-N	3	1	.750	13	2	1	0	2	38	31	1	25	19	14.2	3.08	122	.235	.373	1	.077	-1	4	3	0	0.2
1956	Mil-N	0	0	—	1	0	0	0	0	2	1	0	2	0	13.5	0.00	—	.167	.375	0	—	0	1	1	0	0.0
1958	Mil-N	2	4	.333	19	0	0	0	1	41²	30	4	13	26	9.7	3.02	116	.203	.276	1	.167	1	4	2	1	0.5
1959	Cle-A	1	0	1.000	5	0	0	0	0	8²	9	0	4	6	13.5	4.15	89	.281	.361	0	—	0	-0	-0	-0	0.0
	Phi-N	2	4	.333	31	4	1	0	1	73	70	6	24	32	11.6	3.33	123	.251	.310	3	.231	1	5	6	0	0.7
1960	Phi-N	0	4	.000	33	1	0	0	0	49²	48	6	22	31	12.7	3.44	113	.255	.333	1	.167	-0	2	2	0	0.2
Total	5	8	13	.381	102	7	2	0	4	213	189	17	90	114	12.0	3.25	119	.241	.323	6	.158	0	16	14	2	1.6

● JEFF ROBINSON   Robinson, Jeffrey Daniel b: 12/13/60, Santa Ana, Cal. BR/TR, 6'4", 200 lbs. Deb: 4/7/84

1984	SF-N	7	15	.318	34	33	1	1	0	171²	195	12	52	102	13.3	4.56	77	.288	.345	7	.115	-2	-19	-20	-1	-2.5
1985	SF-N	0	0	—	3	0	0	0	0	12¹	16	2	10	8	19.0	5.11	67	.333	.448	0	—	0	-2	-2	-0	-0.1
1986	SF-N	6	3	.667	64	1	0	0	8	104¹	92	8	32	90	10.8	3.36	105	.234	.293	1	.067	-1	4	2	-1	0.0
1987	SF-N	6	8	.429	63	0	0	0	10	96²	69	10	48	82	11.0	2.79	138	.207	.309	2	.111	-1	14	11	1	1.7
	Pit-N	2	1	.667	18	0	0	0	4	26²	20	1	6	19	8.8	3.04	135	.215	.263	1	.250	1	3	3	0	0.6
	Yr	8	9	.471	81	0	0	0	14	123¹	89	11	54	101	10.4	2.85	137	.206	.295	3	.136	0	17	14	1	2.3
1988	Pit-N	11	5	.688	75	0	0	0	9	124²	113	6	39	87	11.2	3.03	112	.244	.307	3	.188	0	6	5	0	0.8
1989	Pit-N	7	13	.350	50	19	0	0	4	141¹	161	14	59	95	14.1	4.58	73	.283	.351	8	.229	2	-17	-19	1	-2.3
1990	NY-A	3	6	.333	54	4	1	0	0	88²	82	6	34	43	11.9	3.45	115	.248	.320	0	—	0	4	5	2	0.7
1991	Cal-A	0	3	.000	39	0	0	0	3	57	56	9	29	57	13.7	5.37	76	.259	.352	0	—	0	-8	-8	-0	-0.4
1992	Chi-N	4	3	.571	49	5	0	0	1	78	76	5	40	46	13.6	3.00	120	.263	.356	0	.000	-1	4	5	1	0.4
Total	9	46	57	.447	454	62	2	1	39	901¹	880	75	349	629	12.5	3.79	95	.258	.330	22	.137	-1	-10	-18	4	-1.0

● JEFF ROBINSON   Robinson, Jeffrey Mark b: 12/14/61, Ventura, Cal. BR/TR, 6'6", 240 lbs. Deb: 4/12/87

1987	*Det-A	9	6	.600	29	21	2	1	0	127¹	132	16	54	98	13.6	5.37	77	.262	.342	0	—	0	-13	-16	-1	-1.6
1988	Det-A	13	6	.684	24	23	6	2	0	172	121	19	72	114	10.3	2.98	128	.197	.284	0	—	0	19	16	-0	1.7
1989	Det-A	4	5	.444	16	16	1	1	0	78	76	10	46	40	14.2	4.73	81	.259	.361	0	—	0	-7	-8	-1	-0.9
1990	Det-A	10	9	.526	27	27	1	1	0	145	141	23	88	76	14.6	5.96	66	.255	.364	0	—	0	-33	-32	-1	-3.7
1991	Bal-A	4	9	.308	21	19	0	0	0	104¹	119	12	51	65	15.2	5.18	76	.289	.375	0	—	0	-13	-14	-1	-1.4
1992	Tex-A	4	4	.500	16	4	0	0	0	45²	50	6	21	18	14.0	5.72	66	.281	.357	0	—	0	-9	-10	-1	-1.4
	Pit-N	3	1	.750	8	7	0	0	0	36¹	33	2	14	12	11.4	4.46	77	.244	.325	1	.091	-1	-4	-4	-0	-0.5
Total	6	47	40	.540	141	117	10	5	0	708²	672	88	347	425	13.2	4.79	82	.250	.341	1	.091	-1	-60	-68	-4	-7.8

● JACK ROBINSON   Robinson, John Edward b: 2/20/21, Orange, N.J. BR/TR, 6', 175 lbs. Deb: 5/4/49

| 1949 | Bos-A | 0 | 0 | — | 3 | 0 | 0 | 0 | 0 | 4 | 4 | 0 | 1 | 1 | 13.5 | 2.25 | 194 | .267 | .353 | 0 | — | 0 | 1 | 1 | 0 | 0.0 |

● HANK ROBINSON   Robinson, John Henry "Rube" (b: John Henry Roberson)
b: 8/16/1889, Floyd, Ark. d: 7/3/65, N.Little Rock, Ark BR/TL, 5'11.5", 160 lbs. Deb: 9/2/11

1911	Pit-N	0	1	.000	5	0	0	0	0	13	13	0	5	8	13.2	2.77	124	.283	.365	0	.000	-0	1	1	1	0.1
1912	Pit-N	12	7	.632	33	16	11	0	2	175	146	3	30	79	9.6	2.26	144	.237	.284	15	.254	3	22	19	-1	2.1
1913	Pit-N	14	9	.609	43	23	8	1	0	196¹	184	1	41	50	10.6	2.38	126	.255	.301	11	.180	-1	18	14	-2	1.3
1914	StL-N	7	8	.467	26	16	6	1	0	126	128	1	32	30	11.7	3.00	93	.274	.325	6	.171	-0	-3	-3	2	-0.2
1915	StL-N	7	8	.467	32	15	6	1	0	143	128	1	35	57	10.7	2.45	114	.245	.301	5	.106	-2	5	5	1	0.4
1918	NY-A	2	4	.333	11	3	0	0	0	48	47	0	16	14	12.4	3.00	94	.269	.340	0	.000	-2	-1	-1	-0	-0.4
Total	6	42	37	.532	150	73	32	3	2	701¹	646	6	159	238	10.7	2.53	118	.253	.305	37	.170	-3	42	36	1	3.3

● KENNY ROBINSON   Robinson, Kenneth Neal b: 11/3/69, Barberton, Ohio BR/TR, 5'7", 175 lbs. Deb: 7/20/95

1995	Tor-A	1	2	.333	21	0	0	0	0	39	25	7	22	31	11.3	3.69	128	.179	.299	0	—	0	4	4	-1	0.2
1996	KC-A	1	0	1.000	5	0	0	0	0	6	9	0	3	5	18.0	6.00	81	.346	.414	0	—	0	-1	-1	-0	-0.1
Total	2	2	2	.500	26	0	0	0	0	45	34	7	25	36	12.2	4.00	118	.205	.316	0	—	0	4	4	-1	0.1

● RON ROBINSON   Robinson, Ronald Dean b: 3/24/62, Exeter, Cal. BR/TR, 6'4", 235 lbs. Deb: 8/14/84

1984	Cin-N	1	2	.333	12	5	1	0	0	39²	35	3	13	24	10.9	2.72	139	.232	.293	0	.000	-1	4	5	0	0.2
1985	Cin-N	7	7	.500	33	12	0	0	1	108	107	11	24	76	11.6	3.99	94	.259	.314	2	.091	-1	-5	-2	1	-0.4
1986	Cin-N	10	3	.769	70	0	0	0	14	116²	110	6	43	117	12.0	3.24	119	.253	.323	1	.071	-1	6	8	1	1.1
1987	Cin-N	7	5	.583	48	18	0	0	4	154	148	14	43	99	11.2	3.68	115	.256	.308	7	.194	-0	7	10	-2	0.5
1988	Cin-N	3	7	.300	17	16	0	0	0	78²	88	6	26	38	13.3	4.12	87	.285	.344	5	.200	1	-6	-5	-0	-0.5
1989	Cin-N	5	3	.625	15	15	0	0	0	83¹	80	8	28	36	11.9	3.35	108	.252	.317	6	.214	1	1	2	-0	0.3

YEAR	TM/L	W	L	PCT	G	GS	CG	SH	SV	IP	H	HR	BB	SO	RAT	ERA	ERA+	OAV	OOB	BH	AVG	PB	PR	/A	PD	TPI
1990	Cin-N	2	2	.500	6	5	0	0	0	31¹	36	2	14	14	14.4	4.88	81	.295	.368	1	.091	-1	-4	-3	-0	-0.4
	Mil-A	12	5	.706	22	22	7	2	0	148¹	158	5	37	57	12.2	2.91	133	.275	.326	0	—	0	16	16	-0	1.7
1991	Mil-A	0	1	.000	1	1	0	0	0	4¹	6	0	3	0	20.8	6.23	64	.353	.476	0	—	0	-1	-1	-0	-0.1
1992	Mil-A	1	4	.200	8	8	0	0	0	35¹	51	3	14	12	17.1	5.86	65	.331	.394	0	—	0	-8	-8	-0	-0.9
Total	9	48	39	.552	232	102	8	2	19	800	819	61	253	473	12.3	3.63	107	.267	.326	22	.153	-2	12	21	-1	1.5

● **BILL ROBINSON**   Robinson, William (b: William Anderson)   b: Taylorsville, Ky.   Deb: 8/12/1889

YEAR	TM/L	W	L	PCT	G	GS	CG	SH	SV	IP	H	HR	BB	SO	RAT	ERA	ERA+	OAV	OOB	BH	AVG	PB	PR	/A	PD	TPI
1889	Lou-a	0	1	.000	1	1	1	0	0	8	10	2	6	2	18.0	10.13	38	.294	.400	1	.333	0	-6	-6	0	-0.4

● **YANK ROBINSON**   Robinson, William H.   b: 9/19/1859, Philadelphia, Pa.   d: 8/25/1894, St.Louis, Mo.   BR/TR, 5'6.5", 170 lbs.   Deb: 8/24/1882   ♦

YEAR	TM/L	W	L	PCT	G	GS	CG	SH	SV	IP	H	HR	BB	SO	RAT	ERA	ERA+	OAV	OOB	BH	AVG	PB	PR	/A	PD	TPI
1882	Det-N	0	0	—	1	0	0	0	0	2	0	0	1	0	4.5	0.00	—	.000	.125	7	.179	-0	1	1	0	0.0
1884	Bal-U	3	3	.500	11	3	3	0	0	75	96	1	18	61	13.7	3.48	77	.292	.329	111	.267	-0	-9	-7	-3	-0.7
1886	*StL-a	0	1	.000	1	1	1	0	0	9	10	0	7	1	17.0	3.00	115	.286	.405	132	.274	-0	0	-0	-0	0.1
1887	*StL-a	0	0	—	1	0	0	0	1	3	3	0	3	0	21.0	3.00	151	.333	.538	131	.305	0	0	1	0	0.0
Total	4	3	4	.429	14	4	4	0	1	89	109	1	29	62	14.1	3.34	85	.287	.339	825	.241	-0	-7	-5	-3	-0.6

● **CHICK ROBITAILLE**   Robitaille, Joseph Anthony   b: 3/2/1879, Whitehall, N.Y.   d: 7/30/47, Waterford, N.Y.   BR/TR, 5'8", 150 lbs.   Deb: 9/2/04

YEAR	TM/L	W	L	PCT	G	GS	CG	SH	SV	IP	H	HR	BB	SO	RAT	ERA	ERA+	OAV	OOB	BH	AVG	PB	PR	/A	PD	TPI
1904	Pit-N	4	3	.571	9	8	8	0	0	66	52	1	13	34	9.0	1.91	144	.208	.250	2	.095	-2	6	6	-1	0.3
1905	Pit-N	8	5	.615	17	12	10	0	0	120¹	126	1	28	32	11.7	2.92	103	.276	.322	6	.133	-2	1	1	-0	-0.1
Total	2	12	8	.600	26	20	18	0	0	186¹	178	2	41	66	10.8	2.56	114	.252	.297	8	.121	-4	7	7	-1	0.2

● **ARMANDO ROCHE**   Roche, Armando (Baez)   b: 12/7/26, Havana, Cuba   BR/TR, 6', 190 lbs.   Deb: 5/10/45

YEAR	TM/L	W	L	PCT	G	GS	CG	SH	SV	IP	H	HR	BB	SO	RAT	ERA	ERA+	OAV	OOB	BH	AVG	PB	PR	/A	PD	TPI
1945	Was-A	0	0	—	2	0	0	0	0	6	10	0	2	0	18.0	6.00	52	.400	.444	0	.000	-0	-2	-2	0	0.0

● **MIKE ROCHFORD**   Rochford, Michael Joseph   b: 3/14/63, Methuen, Mass.   BL/TL, 6'4", 205 lbs.   Deb: 9/3/88

YEAR	TM/L	W	L	PCT	G	GS	CG	SH	SV	IP	H	HR	BB	SO	RAT	ERA	ERA+	OAV	OOB	BH	AVG	PB	PR	/A	PD	TPI
1988	Bos-A	0	0	—	2	0	0	0	0	2¹	4	0	1	1	19.3	—	—	.364	.417	0	—	0	1	1	0	0.0
1989	Bos-A	0	0	—	4	0	0	0	0	4	4	1	0	0	6.75	61	.267	.421	0	—	0	-1	-1	-0	0.0
1990	Bos-A	0	1	.000	2	1	0	0	0	4	10	1	4	2	31.5	18.00	23	.526	.609	0	—	0	-6	-6	-0	-1.1
Total	3	0	1	.000	8	1	0	0	0	10¹	18	2	9	2	23.5	9.58	43	.400	.500	0	—	0	-7	-6	-0	-1.1

● **RICH RODAS**   Rodas, Richard Martin   b: 11/7/59, Roseville, Cal.   BL/TL, 6'1", 180 lbs.   Deb: 9/6/83

YEAR	TM/L	W	L	PCT	G	GS	CG	SH	SV	IP	H	HR	BB	SO	RAT	ERA	ERA+	OAV	OOB	BH	AVG	PB	PR	/A	PD	TPI
1983	LA-N	0	0	—	7	0	0	0	0	4²	4	0	3	5	13.5	1.93	186	.222	.333	0	—	0	1	1	-0	0.0
1984	LA-N	0	0	—	3	0	0	0	0	5	5	2	1	1	10.8	5.40	65	.250	.286	0	.000	-0	-1	-1	0	0.0
Total	2	0	0	—	10	0	0	0	0	9²	9	2	4	6	12.1	3.72	96	.237	.310	0	.000	-0	-0	-0	-0	0.0

● **EDUARDO RODRIGUEZ**   Rodriguez, Eduardo (Reyes)   b: 3/6/52, Barceloneta, P.R.   BR/TR, 6', 185 lbs.   Deb: 6/20/73

YEAR	TM/L	W	L	PCT	G	GS	CG	SH	SV	IP	H	HR	BB	SO	RAT	ERA	ERA+	OAV	OOB	BH	AVG	PB	PR	/A	PD	TPI
1973	Mil-A	9	7	.563	30	6	2	0	6	76¹	71	6	47	49	14.1	3.30	114	.247	.357	1	1.000	1	4	4	-0	0.9
1974	Mil-A	7	4	.636	43	6	0	0	4	111²	97	7	51	58	12.3	3.63	100	.241	.333	0	—	0	3	3	-0	0.1
1975	Mil-A	7	0	1.000	43	1	0	0	7	87²	77	9	44	65	12.9	3.49	110	.235	.334	0	—	0	3	3	-0	0.1
1976	Mil-A	5	13	.278	45	12	3	0	8	136	124	10	65	77	12.7	3.64	96	.249	.339	0	—	-0	-2	-2	-1	-0.3
1977	Mil-A	5	6	.455	42	5	1	1	4	142³	126	15	56	104	11.7	4.35	93	.236	.311	0	—	0	-5	-5	-1	-0.4
1978	Mil-A	5	5	.500	32	8	0	0	2	105¹	107	9	26	51	11.5	3.93	96	.262	.310	0	—	0	-2	-2	-0	-0.2
1979	KC-A	4	1	.800	29	1	1	0	2	74¹	79	9	34	26	14.0	4.84	88	.276	.359	0	—	0	-5	-5	-1	-0.5
Total	7	42	36	.538	264	39	7	1	32	734	681	65	323	430	12.6	3.89	98	.248	.332	1	1.000	1	-7	-7	-5	-0.4

● **FELIX RODRIGUEZ**   Rodriguez, Felix Antonio   b: 12/5/72, Montecristi, D.R.   BR/TR, 6'1", 170 lbs.   Deb: 5/13/95

YEAR	TM/L	W	L	PCT	G	GS	CG	SH	SV	IP	H	HR	BB	SO	RAT	ERA	ERA+	OAV	OOB	BH	AVG	PB	PR	/A	PD	TPI
1995	LA-N	1	1	.500	11	0	0	0	0	10²	11	2	5	5	13.5	2.53	150	.275	.356	0	—	0	2	1	-0	0.2

● **FREDDY RODRIGUEZ**   Rodriguez, Fernando Pedro (Borrego)   b: 4/29/24, Havana, Cuba   BR/TR, 6', 180 lbs.   Deb: 4/18/58

YEAR	TM/L	W	L	PCT	G	GS	CG	SH	SV	IP	H	HR	BB	SO	RAT	ERA	ERA+	OAV	OOB	BH	AVG	PB	PR	/A	PD	TPI
1958	Chi-N	0	0	—	7	0	0	0	2	7¹	8	2	5	5	17.2	7.36	53	.267	.389	0	.000	-0	-3	-3	-0	-0.2
1959	Phi-N	0	0	—	1	0	0	0	0	2	4	1	0	2	22.5	13.50	30	.400	.455	0	—	0	-2	-2	-0	0.0
Total	2	0	0	—	8	0	0	0	2	9¹	12	3	5	7	18.3	8.68	46	.300	.404	0	.000	-0	-5	-5	-0	-0.2

● **FRANK RODRIGUEZ**   Rodriguez, Francisco   b: 12/11/72, Brooklyn, N.Y.   BR/TR, 6', 190 lbs.   Deb: 4/26/95

YEAR	TM/L	W	L	PCT	G	GS	CG	SH	SV	IP	H	HR	BB	SO	RAT	ERA	ERA+	OAV	OOB	BH	AVG	PB	PR	/A	PD	TPI
1995	Bos-A	0	2	.000	9	2	0	0	0	15¹	21	3	10	14	18.2	10.57	46	.323	.413	0	—	0	-10	-10	1	-1.0
	Min-A	5	6	.455	16	16	0	0	0	90¹	93	8	47	45	14.4	5.38	89	.269	.364	0	—	0	-7	-6	2	-0.4
	Yr	5	8	.385	25	18	0	0	0	105²	114	11	57	59	15.0	6.13	78	.277	.372	0	—	0	-17	-16	3	-1.4
1996	Min-A	13	14	.481	38	33	3	0	2	206²	218	27	78	110	13.1	5.05	102	.272	.340	0	—	0	-1	-2	1	0.1
Total	2	18	22	.450	63	51	3	0	2	312¹	332	38	135	169	13.7	5.42	93	.274	.351	0	—	0	-18	-14	3	-1.3

● **NERIO RODRIGUEZ**   Rodriguez, Nerio   b: 3/22/73, San Pedro De Macoris, D.R.   BR/TR, 6'1", 195 lbs.   Deb: 8/18/96

YEAR	TM/L	W	L	PCT	G	GS	CG	SH	SV	IP	H	HR	BB	SO	RAT	ERA	ERA+	OAV	OOB	BH	AVG	PB	PR	/A	PD	TPI
1996	Bal-A	0	1	.000	8	1	0	0	0	16²	18	2	7	12	14.0	4.32	113	.265	.342	0	—	0	1	1	-1	0.0

● **RICK RODRIGUEZ**   Rodriguez, Ricardo   b: 9/21/60, Oakland, Cal.   BR/TR, 6'3", 190 lbs.   Deb: 9/17/86

YEAR	TM/L	W	L	PCT	G	GS	CG	SH	SV	IP	H	HR	BB	SO	RAT	ERA	ERA+	OAV	OOB	BH	AVG	PB	PR	/A	PD	TPI
1986	Oak-A	1	2	.333	3	3	0	0	0	16¹	17	4	7	2	13.2	6.61	58	.262	.333	0	—	0	-4	-5	0	-0.5
1987	Oak-A	1	0	1.000	15	0	0	0	0	24¹	32	1	15	9	17.8	2.96	139	.337	.432	0	—	0	4	3	1	0.2
1988	Cle-A	1	2	.333	10	5	0	0	0	33	43	4	17	10	16.6	7.09	58	.323	.404	0	—	0	-11	-11	1	-0.8
1990	SF-N	0	0	—	3	0	0	0	0	3¹	5	0	2	1	18.0	8.10	45	.357	.438	0	—	0	-2	-2	0	0.0
Total	4	3	4	.429	31	8	0	0	0	77	97	9	41	22	16.4	5.73	71	.316	.400	0	—	0	-13	-14	2	-1.1

● **RICH RODRIGUEZ**   Rodriguez, Richard Anthony   b: 3/1/63, Downey, Cal.   BL/TL, 5'10", 194 lbs.   Deb: 6/30/90

YEAR	TM/L	W	L	PCT	G	GS	CG	SH	SV	IP	H	HR	BB	SO	RAT	ERA	ERA+	OAV	OOB	BH	AVG	PB	PR	/A	PD	TPI
1990	SD-N	1	1	.500	32	0	0	0	1	47²	52	2	16	22	13.0	2.83	135	.287	.348	0	.000	-0	5	5	1	0.3
1991	SD-N	3	1	.750	64	1	0	0	0	80	66	8	44	40	12.4	3.26	116	.234	.337	0	.000	-1	5	4	-0	0.2
1992	SD-N	6	3	.667	61	1	0	0	0	91	77	4	29	64	10.5	2.37	151	.229	.290	0	.000	-0	11	12	1	1.2
1993	SD-N	2	3	.400	34	0	0	0	2	30	34	2	9	22	13.2	3.30	125	.281	.336	0	.000	0	2	3	-1	0.4
	Fla-N	0	1	.000	36	0	0	0	1	46	39	8	24	21	12.5	4.11	105	.229	.328	0	.000	0	0	1	0	0.1
	Yr	2	4	.333	70	0	0	0	3	76	73	10	33	43	12.7	3.79	112	.250	.328	0	.000	0	2	4	-1	0.5
1994	StL-N	3	5	.375	56	0	0	0	0	60¹	62	6	26	43	13.3	4.03	103	.270	.346	0	.000	-0	1	1	-1	-0.1
1995	StL-N	0	0	—	1	0	0	0	0	0	0	0	0	0	—	0.00	—	.000	.000	0	—	0	0	0	0	0.0
Total	6	15	14	.517	284	2	0	0	4	356²	330	30	148	212	12.2	3.20	122	.249	.327	0	.000	-1	24	28	-0	2.1

● **ROSARIO RODRIGUEZ**   Rodriguez, Rosario Isabel (Echavarria)   b: 7/8/69, Los Mochis, Mexico   BR/TL, 6', 185 lbs.   Deb: 9/1/89

YEAR	TM/L	W	L	PCT	G	GS	CG	SH	SV	IP	H	HR	BB	SO	RAT	ERA	ERA+	OAV	OOB	BH	AVG	PB	PR	/A	PD	TPI
1989	Cin-N	1	1	.500	7	0	0	0	0	4¹	3	0	3	2	12.5	4.15	87	.188	.316	0	—	0	-0	-0	0	-0.1
1990	Cin-N	0	0	—	9	0	0	0	0	10¹	15	3	2	8	15.7	6.10	65	.357	.400	0	—	0	-3	-2	0	0.0
1991	*Pit-N	1	1	.500	18	0	0	0	6	15¹	14	1	8	10	13.5	4.11	87	.246	.348	0	—	0	-1	-1	0	-0.2
Total	3	2	2	.500	34	0	0	0	6	30	32	4	13	18	14.1	4.80	77	.278	.362	0	—	0	-4	-4	1	-0.2

● **ROBERTO RODRIQUEZ**   Rodriguez, Roberto (Munoz)   b: 11/29/41, Caracas, Venez.   BR/TR, 6'3", 185 lbs.   Deb: 5/13/67

YEAR	TM/L	W	L	PCT	G	GS	CG	SH	SV	IP	H	HR	BB	SO	RAT	ERA	ERA+	OAV	OOB	BH	AVG	PB	PR	/A	PD	TPI
1967	KC-A	1	1	.500	15	5	0	0	0	40¹	42	4	14	29	12.7	3.57	89	.268	.331	0	.000	-1	-2	-2	-0	-0.3
1970	Oak-A	0	0	—	6	0	0	0	0	12¹	10	2	3	9	9.5	2.92	121	.227	.277	0	.000	-0	0	-0	-0	0.0
	SD-N	0	0	—	10	0	0	0	3	16¹	26	1	5	8	17.1	6.61	60	.366	.408	0	.000	-0	-5	-5	-0	-0.2
	Chi-N	3	2	.600	26	0	0	0	4	43¹	50	6	15	24	13.5	5.82	77	.289	.346	1	.125	1	-9	-6	-0	-0.6
	Yr	3	2	.600	36	0	0	0	7	59²	76	7	20	34	14.5	6.03	72	.311	.364	1	.091	1	-13	-11	-0	-0.8
Total	4	4	3	.571	57	5	0	0	7	112¹	128	13	37	91	13.3	4.81	80	.288	.344	1	.048	1	-14	-12	-0	-1.1

● **PREACHER ROE**   Roe, Elwin Charles   b: 2/26/15, Ash Flat, Ark.   BR/TL, 6'2", 170 lbs.   Deb: 8/22/38

YEAR	TM/L	W	L	PCT	G	GS	CG	SH	SV	IP	H	HR	BB	SO	RAT	ERA	ERA+	OAV	OOB	BH	AVG	PB	PR	/A	PD	TPI
1938	StL-N	0	0	—	1	0	0	0	0	2²	6	0	2	1	27.0	13.50	29	.429	.500	0	.000	-0	-3	-3	-0	-0.2
1944	Pit-N	13	11	.542	39	25	7	1	1	185¹	182	7	59	88	11.8	3.11	120	.253	.311	7	.132	-2	10	13	-1	1.2
1945	Pit-N†	14	13	.519	33	31	15	3	1	235	228	8	57	**148**	10.5	2.87	137	.259	.296	8	.107	-3	24	28	1	2.8
1946	Pit-N	3	8	.273	21	10	1	0	2	70	83	5	25	44	14.1	5.14	69	.294	.356	1	.067	-1	-13	-13	-0	-1.9
1947	Pit-N	4	15	.211	38	22	4	0	2	144	156	14	67	63	13.7	5.25	80	.276	.348	5	.125	-2	-19	-16	-1	-2.2
1948	Bro-N	12	8	.600	34	22	8	2	0	177²	156	14	33	86	9.7	2.63	152	.233	.271	5	.098	-2	26	27	-1	2.6
1949	*Bro-N★	15	6	**.714**	30	27	13	3	1	212²	201	25	44	109	10.5	2.79	147	.252	.293	8	.114	-2	29	31	-2	2.4

YEAR	TM/L	W	L	PCT	G	GS	CG	SH	SV	IP	H	HR	BB	SO	RAT	ERA	ERA+	OAV	OOB	BH	AVG	PB	PR	/A	PD	TPI
1950	Bro-N☆	19	11	.633	36	32	16	2	1	250²	245	34	66	125	11.3	3.30	124	.257	.308	14	.154	-3	23	22	-2	1.9
1951	Bro-N☆	22	3	.880	34	33	19	2	0	257²	247	30	64	113	10.9	3.04	129	.258	.304	10	.112	-5	26	25	-1	1.7
1952	*Bro-N†	11	2	.846	27	25	8	2	0	158²	163	16	39	83	11.6	3.12	117	.270	.317	4	.070	-3	11	9	-1	0.2
1953	*Bro-N	11	3	.786	25	24	9	1	0	157	171	27	40	85	12.2	4.36	98	.278	.323	3	.053	-4	-1	-2	1	-0.5
1954	Bro-N	3	4	.429	15	10	1	0	0	63	69	11	23	31	13.1	5.00	82	.279	.341	3	.143	-0	-7	-6	-0	-0.7
Total	12	127	84	.602	333	261	101	17	10	1914¹	1907	199	504	956	11.4	3.43	116	.261	.310	68	.110	-27	108	115	-9	7.5

● CLAY ROE   Roe, James Clay "Shad" b: 1/7/04, Greenbriar, Tenn. d: 4/4/56, Cleveland, Miss. BL/TL, 6'1", 180 lbs. Deb: 10/3/23

YEAR	TM/L	W	L	PCT	G	GS	CG	SH	SV	IP	H	HR	BB	SO	RAT	ERA	ERA+	OAV	OOB	BH	AVG	PB	PR	/A	PD	TPI
1923	Was-A	0	1	.000	1	1	0	0	0	1²	0	0	6	2	32.4	—	—	.000	.500	0	—	0	1	1	-0	0.5

● ED ROEBUCK   Roebuck, Edward Jack b: 7/3/31, East Millsboro, Pa. BR/TR, 6'2", 185 lbs. Deb: 4/18/55

YEAR	TM/L	W	L	PCT	G	GS	CG	SH	SV	IP	H	HR	BB	SO	RAT	ERA	ERA+	OAV	OOB	BH	AVG	PB	PR	/A	PD	TPI
1955	*Bro-N	5	6	.455	47	0	0	0	12	84	96	14	24	33	13.2	4.71	86	.288	.342	2	.111	-1	-6	-6	1	-0.9
1956	*Bro-N	5	4	.556	43	0	0	0	1	89¹	83	15	29	60	11.5	3.93	101	.251	.315	6	.333	2	-2	0	1	0.3
1957	Bro-N	8	2	.800	44	1	0	0	8	96¹	70	9	46	73	11.0	2.71	154	.205	.303	5	.238	2	13	16	2	2.3
1958	LA-N	0	1	.000	32	0	0	0	5	44	45	9	15	26	12.7	3.48	118	.271	.339	2	.500	1	2	3	-0	0.2
1960	LA-N	8	3	.727	58	0	0	0	8	116²	109	13	38	77	11.3	2.78	143	.256	.317	4	.167	-0	13	15	2	1.8
1961	LA-N	2	0	1.000	5	0	0	0	0	9	12	1	2	9	14.0	5.00	87	.324	.359	0	.000	-0	-1	-1	0	-0.2
1962	LA-N	10	2	.833	64	0	0	0	9	119¹	102	11	54	72	12.2	3.09	117	.232	.325	6	.214	1	11	7	0	0.9
1963	LA-N	2	4	.333	29	0	0	0	0	40¹	54	4	21	26	17.2	4.24	71	.321	.403	1	.250	0	-4	-5	1	-0.7
	Was-A	2	1	.667	26	0	0	0	4	57¹	63	5	29	25	14.8	3.30	113	.284	.372	2	.182	-1	2	3	1	0.2
1964	Was-A	0	0	—	2	0	0	0	0	1	0	0	2	0	18.0	9.00	41	.000	.333	0	—	0	-1	-1	0	0.0
	Phi-N	5	3	.625	60	0	0	0	12	77¹	55	7	25	42	9.8	2.21	157	.196	.272	0	.000	-1	11	11	1	1.5
1965	Phi-N	5	3	.625	44	0	0	0	3	50¹	55	2	15	29	13.4	3.40	102	.288	.355	0	.000	-1	1	0	-1	-0.1
1966	Phi-N	0	2	.000	6	0	0	0	0	6	9	0	2	5	16.5	6.00	60	.333	.379	0	—	0	-2	-2	-0	-0.5
Total	11	52	31	.627	460	1	0	0	62	791	753	90	302	477	12.3	3.35	114	.254	.329	28	.204	3	38	41	7	4.8

● MIKE ROESLER   Roesler, Michael Joseph b: 9/12/63, Fort Wayne, Ind. BR/TR, 6'5", 195 lbs. Deb: 8/9/89

YEAR	TM/L	W	L	PCT	G	GS	CG	SH	SV	IP	H	HR	BB	SO	RAT	ERA	ERA+	OAV	OOB	BH	AVG	PB	PR	/A	PD	TPI
1989	Cin-N	0	1	.000	17	0	0	0	0	25	22	4	9	14	11.2	3.96	91	.239	.307	0	—	0	-1	-1	-1	-0.1
1990	Pit-N	1	0	1.000	5	0	0	0	0	6	5	1	2	4	10.5	3.00	121	.217	.280	0	—	0	1	0	0	0.0
Total	2	1	1	.500	22	0	0	0	0	31	27	5	11	18	11.0	3.77	96	.235	.302	0	.000	-0	-1	-1	-1	-0.1

● OSCAR ROETTGER   Roettger, Oscar Frederick Louis "Okkie" b: 2/19/1900, St.Louis, Mo. d: 7/4/86, St.Louis, Mo. BR/TR, 6', 170 lbs. Deb: 7/7/23 F♦

YEAR	TM/L	W	L	PCT	G	GS	CG	SH	SV	IP	H	HR	BB	SO	RAT	ERA	ERA+	OAV	OOB	BH	AVG	PB	PR	/A	PD	TPI
1923	NY-A	0	0	—	5	0	0	0	1	11²	16	3	12	7	22.4	8.49	46	.340	.483	0	.000	-0	-6	-6	0	-0.1
1924	NY-A	0	0	—	1	0	0	0	0	0	1	0	2	0	—	—	—	1.000	1.000	0	—	0	0	0	0	0.0
Total	2	0	0	—	6	0	0	0	1	11²	17	3	14	7	24.7	8.49	46	.354	.508	14	.212	-0	-6	-6	0	-0.1

● JOE ROGALSKI   Rogalski, Joseph Anthony b: 7/15/12, Ashland, Wis. d: 11/20/51, Ashland, Wis. BR/TR, 6'2", 187 lbs. Deb: 9/14/38

YEAR	TM/L	W	L	PCT	G	GS	CG	SH	SV	IP	H	HR	BB	SO	RAT	ERA	ERA+	OAV	OOB	BH	AVG	PB	PR	/A	PD	TPI
1938	Det-A	0	0	—	2	0	0	0	0	7	12	0	0	2	15.4	2.57	194	.400	.400	0	—	-0	2	2	-0	0.0

● KEVIN ROGERS   Rogers, Charles Kevin b: 8/20/68, Cleveland, Miss. BB/TL, 6'2", 190 lbs. Deb: 9/4/92

YEAR	TM/L	W	L	PCT	G	GS	CG	SH	SV	IP	H	HR	BB	SO	RAT	ERA	ERA+	OAV	OOB	BH	AVG	PB	PR	/A	PD	TPI
1992	SF-N	0	2	.000	6	6	0	0	0	34	37	4	13	26	13.5	4.24	78	.280	.349	2	.222	0	-3	-4	-1	-0.2
1993	SF-N	2	2	.500	64	0	0	0	0	80²	71	3	28	62	11.5	2.68	146	.236	.309	0	.000	-0	12	11	-1	0.4
1994	SF-N	0	0	—	9	0	0	0	0	10¹	10	1	6	7	13.9	3.48	115	.250	.348	0	—	0	1	1	-0	0.0
Total	3	2	4	.333	79	6	0	0	0	125	118	8	47	95	12.2	3.17	118	.249	.324	2	.167	-0	10	8	-2	0.2

● JIMMY ROGERS   Rogers, James Randall b: 1/3/67, Tulsa, Okla. BR/TR, 6'2", 190 lbs. Deb: 7/30/95

YEAR	TM/L	W	L	PCT	G	GS	CG	SH	SV	IP	H	HR	BB	SO	RAT	ERA	ERA+	OAV	OOB	BH	AVG	PB	PR	/A	PD	TPI
1995	Tor-A	2	4	.333	19	0	0	0	0	23²	21	4	18	13	14.8	5.70	83	.239	.368	0	—	0	-3	-3	-0	-0.6

● KENNY ROGERS   Rogers, Kenneth Scott b: 11/10/64, Savannah, Ga. BL/TL, 6'1", 200 lbs. Deb: 4/6/89

YEAR	TM/L	W	L	PCT	G	GS	CG	SH	SV	IP	H	HR	BB	SO	RAT	ERA	ERA+	OAV	OOB	BH	AVG	PB	PR	/A	PD	TPI
1989	Tex-A	3	4	.429	73	0	0	0	2	73²	60	2	42	63	13.0	2.93	135	.232	.348	0	—	0	8	8	2	1.0
1990	Tex-A	10	6	.625	69	3	0	0	15	97²	93	6	42	74	12.5	3.13	125	.249	.326	0	—	0	8	9	2	1.7
1991	Tex-A	10	10	.500	63	9	0	0	5	109²	121	14	61	73	15.4	5.42	74	.281	.378	0	—	0	-16	-17	-0	-2.8
1992	Tex-A	3	6	.333	81	0	0	0	6	78²	80	7	26	70	12.1	3.09	123	.261	.319	0	—	0	7	6	1	1.1
1993	Tex-A	16	10	.615	35	33	5	0	0	208¹	210	18	71	140	12.3	4.10	101	.263	.326	0	—	0	5	1	4	0.8
1994	Tex-A	11	8	.579	24	24	6	2	0	167¹	169	24	52	120	12.0	4.46	108	.260	.318	0	—	0	6	7	2	0.9
1995	Tex-A★	17	7	.708	31	31	3	1	0	208	192	26	76	140	11.7	3.38	143	.243	.311	0	—	0	31	34	1	3.6
1996	*NY-A	12	8	.600	30	30	2	1	0	179	179	16	83	92	13.6	4.68	108	.261	.347	0	—	0	6	7	2	0.8
Total	8	82	59	.582	406	130	16	4	28	1122¹	1104	113	453	772	12.7	4.01	111	.257	.332	0	—	0	56	54	15	7.1

● LEE ROGERS   Rogers, Lee Otis "Buck" b: 10/8/13, Tuscaloosa, Ala. d: 11/23/95, Little Rock, Ark. BR/TL, 5'11", 170 lbs. Deb: 4/27/38

YEAR	TM/L	W	L	PCT	G	GS	CG	SH	SV	IP	H	HR	BB	SO	RAT	ERA	ERA+	OAV	OOB	BH	AVG	PB	PR	/A	PD	TPI
1938	Bos-A	1	1	.500	14	2	0	0	0	27²	32	4	18	7	16.3	6.51	76	.302	.403	0	.000	-0	-5	-5	1	-0.2
	Bro-N	0	2	.000	12	2	0	0	0	23²	23	0	10	11	12.9	5.70	68	.256	.337	0	.000	0	-5	-5	1	-0.2
Total	1	1	3	.250	26	4	0	0	0	51¹	55	4	28	18	14.7	6.14	73	.281	.373	0	.000	0	-10	-10	2	-0.4

● BUCK ROGERS   Rogers, Orlin Woodrow "Lefty" b: 11/5/12, Spring Garden, Va. BR/TL, 5'8.5", 164 lbs. Deb: 9/15/35

YEAR	TM/L	W	L	PCT	G	GS	CG	SH	SV	IP	H	HR	BB	SO	RAT	ERA	ERA+	OAV	OOB	BH	AVG	PB	PR	/A	PD	TPI
1935	Was-A	0	1	.000	2	1	0	0	0	10	16	0	6	7	19.8	7.20	60	.340	.415	0	.000	-1	-3	-3	-0	-0.3

● STEVE ROGERS   Rogers, Stephen Douglas b: 10/26/49, Jefferson City, Mo. BR/TR, 6'1", 182 lbs. Deb: 7/18/73

YEAR	TM/L	W	L	PCT	G	GS	CG	SH	SV	IP	H	HR	BB	SO	RAT	ERA	ERA+	OAV	OOB	BH	AVG	PB	PR	/A	PD	TPI
1973	Mon-N	10	5	.667	17	17	7	3	0	134	93	5	49	64	9.6	1.54	247	.199	.276	4	.098	-1	31	34	1	4.1
1974	Mon-N☆	15	22	.405	38	38	11	1	0	253²	255	19	80	154	12.1	4.47	86	.265	.324	11	.139	-1	-24	-18	3	-2.2
1975	Mon-N	11	12	.478	35	35	12	3	0	251²	248	13	88	137	12.2	3.29	116	.260	.325	13	.169	1	9	15	0	1.5
1976	Mon-N	7	17	.292	33	32	8	4	1	230	212	10	69	150	11.2	3.21	116	.250	.309	11	.149	-2	7	13	5	1.7
1977	Mon-N	17	16	.515	40	40	17	4	0	301²	272	16	81	206	10.7	3.10	123	.242	.296	10	.104	-3	27	24	4	2.3
1978	Mon-N★	13	10	.565	30	29	11	1	1	219	186	12	64	126	10.4	2.47	143	.235	.294	8	.113	-2	27	26	1	2.6
1979	Mon-N★	13	12	.520	37	37	13	5	0	248²	232	14	78	143	11.4	3.00	122	.251	.312	12	.156	1	20	18	2	2.1
1980	Mon-N	16	11	.593	37	37	14	4	0	281	247	16	85	147	10.7	2.98	120	.238	.298	13	.160	1	19	18	-1	1.7
1981	*Mon-N	12	8	.600	22	22	7	4	0	160²	149	7	41	87	10.8	3.42	102	.248	.298	8	.145	-1	1	1	-1	0.0
1982	Mon-N★	19	8	.704	35	35	14	4	0	277	245	12	65	179	10.3	2.40	151	.237	.286	11	.129	0	37	38	0	3.7
1983	Mon-N☆	17	12	.586	36	36	13	5	0	273	258	14	78	146	11.2	3.23	111	.252	.308	12	.146	-1	12	11	-2	0.8
1984	Mon-N	6	15	.286	31	28	1	0	0	169¹	171	12	78	64	13.3	4.31	80	.267	.348	7	.143	1	-13	-17	-0	-1.8
1985	Mon-N	2	4	.333	7	5	1	0	0	51	51	1	8	18	16.8	5.68	60	.329	.406	2	.143	-0	-9	-10	1	-1.2
Total	13	158	152	.510	399	393	129	37	2	2837²	2619	151	876	1621	11.2	3.17	115	.248	.308	122	.138	-4	146	154	14	15.3

● TOM ROGERS   Rogers, Thomas Andrew "Shotgun" b: 2/12/1892, Sparta, Tenn. d: 3/7/36, Nashville, Tenn. BR/TR, 6'0.5", 180 lbs. Deb: 4/14/17

YEAR	TM/L	W	L	PCT	G	GS	CG	SH	SV	IP	H	HR	BB	SO	RAT	ERA	ERA+	OAV	OOB	BH	AVG	PB	PR	/A	PD	TPI
1917	StL-A	3	6	.333	24	8	3	0	2	108²	112	3	44	27	13.2	3.89	67	.277	.352	5	.172	-4	-15	-16	-0	-1.4
1918	StL-A	8	10	.444	29	16	11	3	0	154	148	3	49	29	11.7	3.27	84	.267	.330	13	.245	2	-8	-9	2	-0.7
1919	StL-A	0	1	.000	2	0	0	0	0	1	7	0	0	1	63.0	27.00	12	.700	.700	0	—	0	-3	-3	0	-1.6
	Phi-A	4	12	.250	23	18	7	1	0	140	152	9	60	37	13.8	4.31	80	.292	.369	11	.224	-0	-17	-14	4	-1.0
	Yr	4	13	.235	25	18	7	1	0	141	159	9	60	38	14.2	4.47	77	.300	.374	11	.224	-0	-19	-16	4	-2.6
1921	*NY-A	0	1	.000	5	0	0	0	1	11	12	1	9	1	18.0	7.36	58	.300	.440	1	.333	-0	-4	-4	1	-0.3
Total	4	15	30	.333	83	42	21	3	3	414²	431	6	162	94	13.1	3.95	75	.282	.354	30	.224	1	-46	-45	6	-5.0

● CLINT ROGGE   Rogge, Francis Clinton b: 7/19/1889, Memphis, Mich. d: 1/6/69, Mt.Clemens, Mich. BL/TR, 5'10", 185 lbs. Deb: 4/11/15

YEAR	TM/L	W	L	PCT	G	GS	CG	SH	SV	IP	H	HR	BB	SO	RAT	ERA	ERA+	OAV	OOB	BH	AVG	PB	PR	/A	PD	TPI
1915	Pit-F	17	11	.607	37	31	17	5	0	254¹	240	6	93	93	12.1	2.55	106	.257	.330	14	.173	-1	5	5	1	0.5
1921	Cin-N	1	2	.333	6	3	0	0	0	35¹	43	2	9	12	13.2	4.08	88	.307	.349	1	.100	0	-1	-2	0	-0.1
Total	2	18	13	.581	43	34	17	5	0	289²	283	8	102	105	12.2	2.73	103	.264	.332	15	.165	-1	3	3	1	0.4

● GARRY ROGGENBURK   Roggenburk, Garry Earl b: 4/16/40, Cleveland, Ohio. BR/TL, 6'6", 195 lbs. Deb: 4/20/63

YEAR	TM/L	W	L	PCT	G	GS	CG	SH	SV	IP	H	HR	BB	SO	RAT	ERA	ERA+	OAV	OOB	BH	AVG	PB	PR	/A	PD	TPI
1963	Min-A	2	4	.333	36	2	0	0	2	50	47	3	22	24	13.3	2.16	169	.253	.347	1	.143	0	8	8	1	1.2
1965	Min-A	1	0	1.000	21	0	0	0	2	21	21	1	12	16	14.1	3.43	104	.266	.363	0	.000	0	-0	-1	0	0.0
1966	Min-A	1	2	.333	12	0	0	0	0	12¹	14	4	10	3	17.5	5.84	62	.292	.414	0	—	0	-3	-3	-0	-0.7
	Bos-A	0	0	—	1	0	0	0	0	0¹	1	0	1	0	54.0	0.00	—	.500	.667	0	—	0	0	0	-0	0.0

YEAR	TM/L	W	L	PCT	G	GS	CG	SH	SV	IP	H	HR	BB	SO	RAT	ERA	ERA+	OAV	OOB	BH	AVG	PB	PR	/A	PD	TPI
	Yr	1	2	.333	13	0	0	0	1	12²	15	4	11	3	18.5	5.68	63	.300	.426	0	—	0	-3	-3	0	-0.7
1968	Bos-A	0	0	—	4	0	0	0	0	8¹	9	0	3	4	13.0	2.16	146	.257	.316	0	—	0	1	1	-0	0.0
1969	Bos-A	0	1	.000	7	0	0	0	0	9²	13	1	5	8	17.7	8.38	45	.342	.432	0	.000	-0	-5	-5	-0	-0.5
	Sea-A	2	2	.500	7	4	1	0	0	24¹	27	6	11	11	14.4	4.44	82	.276	.355	1	.125	-0	-2	-2	-0	-0.4
	Yr	2	3	.400	14	4	1	0	0	34	40	7	16	19	15.1	5.56	66	.292	.370	1	.100	-1	-7	-7	-0	-0.9
Total	5	6	9	.400	79	6	1	0	7	126	132	15	64	56	14.5	3.64	99	.272	.364	2	.100	-1	-1	-1	0	-0.4

● SAUL ROGOVIN
Rogovin, Saul Walter   b: 10/10/23, Brooklyn, N.Y.   d: 1/23/95, New York, N.Y.   BR/TR, 6'2", 205 lbs.   Deb: 4/28/49

YEAR	TM/L	W	L	PCT	G	GS	CG	SH	SV	IP	H	HR	BB	SO	RAT	ERA	ERA+	OAV	OOB	BH	AVG	PB	PR	/A	PD	TPI
1949	Det-A	0	1	.000	5	0	0	0	0	5²	13	1	7	2	31.8	14.29	29	.464	.571	0	—	0	-6	-6	-0	-0.9
1950	Det-A	2	1	.667	11	5	1	0	0	40	39	5	26	11	15.1	4.50	104	.258	.374	3	.188	0	1	1	-1	0.0
1951	Det-A	1	1	.500	5	4	0	0	0	24	23	4	7	5	11.3	5.25	80	.247	.300	2	.286	—	-3	-3	-0	-0.1
	Chi-A	11	7	.611	22	22	17	3	0	192²	166	11	67	77	10.9	2.48	163	.234	.301	15	.203	-0	35	33	-1	2.9
	Yr	12	8	.600	27	26	17	3	0	216²	189	15	74	82	11.0	**2.78**	**146**	.235	.301	17	.210	1	32	**31**	-0	2.8
1952	Chi-A	14	9	.609	33	30	12	3	1	231²	224	14	79	121	11.9	3.85	95	.255	.318	17	.202	3	-4	-5	-0	-0.2
1953	Chi-A	7	12	.368	22	19	4	1	1	131	151	17	48	62	13.8	5.22	77	.289	.351	5	.135	-0	-18	-17	-0	-2.2
1955	Bal-A	1	8	.111	14	12	1	0	0	71	79	5	27	35	13.7	4.56	84	.288	.356	2	.091	-1	-5	-6	-0	-0.9
	Phi-N	5	3	.625	12	11	5	2	0	73	60	3	17	27	9.5	3.08	129	.230	.277	6	.250	2	8	7	-1	0.9
1956	Phi-N	7	6	.538	22	18	3	0	0	106²	122	22	27	48	12.6	4.98	75	.282	.325	4	.111	-2	-14	-15	-1	-1.9
1957	Phi-N	0	0	—	4	0	0	0	0	8	11	1	3	0	15.8	9.00	42	.333	.389	0	—	0	-5	-5	-0	-0.4
Total	8	48	48	.500	150	121	43	9	2	883²	888	83	308	388	12.3	4.06	96	.262	.326	54	.180	-2	-12	-16	-4	-2.4

● LES ROHR
Rohr, Leslie Norvin   b: 3/5/46, Lowestoft, England   BL/TL, 6'5", 205 lbs.   Deb: 9/19/67

YEAR	TM/L	W	L	PCT	G	GS	CG	SH	SV	IP	H	HR	BB	SO	RAT	ERA	ERA+	OAV	OOB	BH	AVG	PB	PR	/A	PD	TPI
1967	NY-N	2	1	.667	3	3	0	0	0	17	13	1	9	15	11.6	2.12	160	.224	.328	0	.000	-1	2	2	-1	0.3
1968	NY-N	0	2	.000	2	1	0	0	0	6	9	0	7	5	24.0	4.50	67	.333	.471	0	—	0	-1	-1	0	-0.3
1969	NY-N	0	0	—	1	0	0	0	0	1¹	5	0	1	0	40.5	20.25	18	.625	.667	0	—	0	-2	-2	-0	-0.0
Total	3	2	3	.400	6	4	0	0	0	24¹	27	1	17	20	16.3	3.70	90	.290	.408	0	.000	-0	-1	-1	-1	0.0

● BILLY ROHR
Rohr, William Joseph   b: 7/1/45, San Diego, Cal.   BL/TL, 6'3", 170 lbs.   Deb: 4/14/67

YEAR	TM/L	W	L	PCT	G	GS	CG	SH	SV	IP	H	HR	BB	SO	RAT	ERA	ERA+	OAV	OOB	BH	AVG	PB	PR	/A	PD	TPI
1967	Bos-A	2	3	.400	10	8	2	1	0	42¹	43	4	22	16	14.2	5.10	68	.256	.349	0	.000	-1	-9	-8	-0	-0.9
1968	Cle-A	1	0	1.000	17	0	0	0	1	18¹	18	5	10	5	13.7	6.87	43	.265	.359	0	.000	-0	-8	-8	-0	-0.6
Total	2	3	3	.500	27	8	2	1	1	60²	61	9	32	21	14.1	5.64	59	.258	.352	0	.000	-1	-17	-16	-0	-1.5

● MEL ROJAS
Rojas, Melquiades (Medrano)   b: 12/10/66, Haina, D.R.   BR/TR, 5'11", 175 lbs.   Deb: 8/1/90

YEAR	TM/L	W	L	PCT	G	GS	CG	SH	SV	IP	H	HR	BB	SO	RAT	ERA	ERA+	OAV	OOB	BH	AVG	PB	PR	/A	PD	TPI
1990	Mon-N	3	1	.750	23	0	0	0	1	40	34	5	24	26	13.5	3.60	101	.234	.351	0	.000	-0	1	0	-0	-0.1
1991	Mon-N	3	3	.500	37	0	0	0	6	48	42	4	13	37	10.5	3.75	96	.228	.283	0	.000	-0	-1	-1	-0	-0.2
1992	Mon-N	7	1	.875	68	0	0	0	10	100²	71	2	34	70	9.6	1.43	242	.199	.272	1	.067	-1	**23**	**23**	-0	2.1
1993	Mon-N	5	8	.385	66	0	0	0	10	88¹	80	6	30	48	11.6	2.95	141	.242	.313	1	.083	-1	11	12	-1	1.7
1994	Mon-N	3	2	.600	58	0	0	0	16	84	71	11	21	84	10.3	3.32	127	.227	.284	2	.200	-0	8	8	0	0.8
1995	Mon-N	1	4	.200	59	0	0	0	30	67²	69	2	29	61	14.0	4.12	104	.262	.351	0	.000	-1	0	1	-0	0.1
1996	Mon-N	7	4	.636	74	0	0	0	36	81	56	5	28	92	9.6	3.22	134	.193	.269	3	.375	1	9	10	1	2.1
Total	7	29	23	.558	385	0	0	0	109	509²	423	35	179	418	11.0	3.04	131	.225	.300	7	.121	-2	52	53	-1	6.5

● MINNIE ROJAS
Rojas, Minervino Alejandro (Landin)   b: 11/26/38, Remidios, Las Villas, Cuba   BR/TR, 6'1", 170 lbs.   Deb: 5/30/66

YEAR	TM/L	W	L	PCT	G	GS	CG	SH	SV	IP	H	HR	BB	SO	RAT	ERA	ERA+	OAV	OOB	BH	AVG	PB	PR	/A	PD	TPI
1966	Cal-A	7	4	.636	47	2	0	0	10	84¹	83	9	15	37	10.6	2.88	117	.262	.297	1	.071	-0	5	4	-1	0.5
1967	Cal-A	12	9	.571	72	0	0	0	27	121²	106	7	38	83	10.9	2.52	125	.232	.296	1	.059	-1	10	8	-2	1.6
1968	Cal-A	4	3	.571	38	0	0	0	6	55	55	11	15	33	11.5	4.25	68	.252	.300	1	.100	-0	-8	-8	-1	-1.4
Total	3	23	16	.590	157	2	0	0	43	261	244	27	68	153	10.9	3.00	105	.246	.297	3	.073	-2	7	5	-4	0.7

● COOKIE ROJAS
Rojas, Octavio Victor (Rivas)   b: 3/6/39, Havana, Cuba   BR/TR, 5'10", 170 lbs.   Deb: 4/10/62   MC♦

YEAR	TM/L	W	L	PCT	G	GS	CG	SH	SV	IP	H	HR	BB	SO	RAT	ERA	ERA+	OAV	OOB	BH	AVG	PB	PR	/A	PD	TPI
1967	Phi-N	0	0	—	1	0	0	0	0	1	0	0	0	0	9.0	0.00	—	.200	.200	137	.259		0	0	0	0.0

● JIM ROLAND
Roland, James Ivan   b: 12/14/42, Franklin, N.C.   BR/TL, 6'3", 190 lbs.   Deb: 9/20/62

YEAR	TM/L	W	L	PCT	G	GS	CG	SH	SV	IP	H	HR	BB	SO	RAT	ERA	ERA+	OAV	OOB	BH	AVG	PB	PR	/A	PD	TPI
1962	Min-A	0	0	—	1	0	0	0	0	2	1	0	1	1	4.5	0.00	—	.143	.143	0	—	0	1	1	0	0.0
1963	Min-A	4	1	.800	10	7	1	0	0	49	32	4	27	34	10.8	2.57	142	.185	.295	0	.000	-2	6	6	0	0.4
1964	Min-A	2	6	.250	30	13	1	0	3	94¹	76	12	55	63	12.9	4.10	87	.218	.332	4	.148	-1	-5	-6	-1	-0.7
1966	Min-A	0	0	—	1	0	0	0	0	2	1	0	1	0	10.0	0.00	—	.000	.000	0	—	0	1	1	0	0.0
1967	Min-A	0	1	.000	25	0	0	0	0	35²	33	3	17	16	12.6	3.03	114	.244	.329	0	.000	-1	1	2	-0	0.0
1968	Min-A	4	1	.800	28	4	1	0	0	61²	55	3	24	36	11.8	3.50	88	.238	.315	0	.000	-1	-4	-3	1	-0.2
1969	Oak-A	5	1	.833	39	3	2	0	1	86¹	59	2	46	48	11.6	2.19	157	.197	.316	2	.095	-1	14	12	0	0.7
1970	Oak-A	3	3	.500	28	2	0	0	2	43¹	28	2	23	26	10.6	2.70	131	.181	.287	0	.000	-0	5	4	1	0.6
1971	Oak-A	3	3	.250	31	0	0	0	0	45¹	34	4	19	30	11.5	3.18	105	.214	.317	0	.000	-0	1	1	-0	0.0
1972	Oak-A	0	0	—	2	0	0	0	0	2¹	5	0	0	2	19.3	3.86	74	.455	.455	0	—	0	-0	-0	0	0.0
	NY-A	0	1	.000	16	0	0	0	0	25	27	3	16	13	15.8	5.04	58	.287	.396	0	—	-0	-6	-6	-0	-0.9
	Tex-A	0	0	—	5	0	0	0	0	3¹	7	1	2	4	27.0	8.10	37	.412	.500	0	—	0	-2	-2	-0	-0.3
	Yr	0	1	.000	23	0	0	0	0	30²	39	4	18	17	17.0	5.28	56	.317	.408	0	.000	-0	-8	-8	-0	-1.2
Total	10	19	17	.528	216	29	6	1	9	450¹	357	34	229	272	12.1	3.22	106	.218	.321	6	.071	-5	12	10	-1	0.5

● JOSE ROMAN
Roman, Jose Rafael (Sarita)   b: 5/21/63, Santo Domingo, D.R.   BR/TR, 6', 175 lbs.   Deb: 9/5/84

YEAR	TM/L	W	L	PCT	G	GS	CG	SH	SV	IP	H	HR	BB	SO	RAT	ERA	ERA+	OAV	OOB	BH	AVG	PB	PR	/A	PD	TPI
1984	Cle-A	0	2	.000	3	2	0	0	0	6	9	1	11	3	30.0	18.00	23	.391	.588	0	—	0	-9	-9	-0	-2.0
1985	Cle-A	0	4	.000	5	3	0	0	0	16¹	13	3	14	12	14.9	6.61	63	.200	.342	0	—	0	-4	-4	-0	-0.9
1986	Cle-A	1	2	.333	6	5	0	0	0	22	23	3	17	9	16.8	6.55	63	.280	.410	0	—	0	-6	-6	-1	-0.7
Total	3	1	8	.111	14	10	0	0	0	44¹	45	7	42	24	17.9	8.12	51	.265	.413	0	—	0	-20	-20	-1	-3.6

● RON ROMANICK
Romanick, Ronald James   b: 11/6/60, Burley, Idaho   BR/TR, 6'4", 195 lbs.   Deb: 4/5/84

YEAR	TM/L	W	L	PCT	G	GS	CG	SH	SV	IP	H	HR	BB	SO	RAT	ERA	ERA+	OAV	OOB	BH	AVG	PB	PR	/A	PD	TPI
1984	Cal-A	12	12	.500	33	33	8	2	0	229²	240	23	61	87	12.0	3.76	105	.270	.320	0	—	0	6	5	-2	0.3
1985	Cal-A	14	9	.609	31	31	6	1	0	195	210	29	62	64	12.7	4.11	100	.280	.338	0	—	0	1	0	-3	-0.3
1986	Cal-A	5	8	.385	18	18	1	1	0	106¹	124	13	44	38	14.2	5.50	75	.297	.364	0	—	0	-16	-16	-1	-1.8
Total	3	31	29	.517	82	82	15	4	0	531	574	65	167	189	12.7	4.24	96	.279	.336	0	—	0	-9	-11	-6	-1.8

● JIM ROMANO
Romano, James King   b: 4/6/27, Brooklyn, N.Y.   d: 9/12/90, New York, N.Y.   BR/TR, 6'4", 190 lbs.   Deb: 9/21/50

YEAR	TM/L	W	L	PCT	G	GS	CG	SH	SV	IP	H	HR	BB	SO	RAT	ERA	ERA+	OAV	OOB	BH	AVG	PB	PR	/A	PD	TPI
1950	Bro-N	0	0	—	3	1	0	0	0	6¹	8	0	2	8	14.2	5.68	72	.296	.345	0	.000	-0	-1	-1	0	0.0

● DUTCH ROMBERGER
Romberger, Allen Isaiah   b: 5/26/27, Klingerstown, Pa.   d: 5/26/83, Weikert, Pa.   BR/TR, 6', 185 lbs.   Deb: 5/31/54

YEAR	TM/L	W	L	PCT	G	GS	CG	SH	SV	IP	H	HR	BB	SO	RAT	ERA	ERA+	OAV	OOB	BH	AVG	PB	PR	/A	PD	TPI
1954	Phi-A	1	1	.500	10	0	0	0	0	15²	24	3	4	4	16.1	7.47	50	.358	.402	0	—	0	-14	-13	-0	-1.5

● RAMON ROMERO
Romero, Ramon (De Los Santos)   b: 1/8/59, San Pedro De Macoris, D.R.   BL/TL, 6'4", 170 lbs.   Deb: 9/18/84

YEAR	TM/L	W	L	PCT	G	GS	CG	SH	SV	IP	H	HR	BB	SO	RAT	ERA	ERA+	OAV	OOB	BH	AVG	PB	PR	/A	PD	TPI
1984	Cle-A	0	0	—	1	0	0	0	0	3	1	0	0	3	3.0	0.00	—	.000	.111	0	—	0	1	1	-0	-0.1
1985	Cle-A	2	3	.400	19	10	0	0	0	64¹	69	13	38	38	15.7	6.58	63	.276	.382	0	—	0	-17	-17	-1	-1.2
Total	2	2	3	.400	20	10	0	0	0	67¹	69	13	38	41	15.1	6.28	66	.267	.374	0	—	0	-16	-16	-1	-1.3

● EDDIE ROMMEL
Rommel, Edwin Americus   b: 9/13/1897, Baltimore, Md.   d: 8/26/70, Baltimore, Md.   BR/TR, 6'2", 197 lbs.   Deb: 4/19/20   CU

YEAR	TM/L	W	L	PCT	G	GS	CG	SH	SV	IP	H	HR	BB	SO	RAT	ERA	ERA+	OAV	OOB	BH	AVG	PB	PR	/A	PD	TPI
1920	Phi-A	7	7	.500	33	12	8	2	1	173²	165	5	43	43	11.0	2.85	141	.259	.309	11	.216	-0	18	23	5	2.2
1921	Phi-A	16	23	.410	46	32	20	0	3	285¹	312	21	87	71	12.6	3.94	113	.284	.337	18	.191	-2	11	16	3	2.0
1922	Phi-A	**27**	13	.675	**51**	33	22	3	2	294	294	21	63	54	11.1	3.28	130	.267	.309	17	.181	-3	25	32	3	4.0
1923	Phi-A	18	19	.486	**56**	31	19	3	5	297²	306	14	108	76	12.6	3.27	126	.271	.336	24	.238	1	24	28	8	**4.0**
1924	Phi-A	18	15	.545	43	34	21	3	1	278	302	8	94	72	12.9	3.95	108	.284	.344	15	.158	-6	9	10	8	1.2
1925	Phi-A	**21**	10	.677	52	28	14	1	3	261	285	10	95	67	13.3	3.69	126	.281	.346	15	.185	-1	20	28	5	3.3
1926	Phi-A	11	11	.500	37	26	12	0	0	219	225	10	54	52	11.5	3.08	139	.268	.314	6	.098	-4	23	26	2	3.2
1927	Phi-A	11	3	.786	30	17	8	2	0	146²	166	6	48	23	13.3	4.36	98	.286	.343	8	.157	-2	-4	-2	3	-0.1
1928	Phi-A	13	5	.722	43	11	6	0	7	173²	177	11	26	27	10.6	3.06	131	.266	.295	18	.243	3	19	18	3	2.3
1929	*Phi-A	12	2	.857	32	6	4	0	4	113²	135	10	34	25	13.5	2.85	148	.306	.344	8	.205	-0	18	17	1	2.0
1930	Phi-A	9	4	.692	35	5	3	0	4	130¹	142	11	27	35	11.7	4.28	109	.277	.315	10	.263	3	5	6	1	0.9

YEAR TM/L	W	L	PCT	G	GS	CG	SH	SV	IP	H	HR	BB	SO	RAT	ERA	ERA+	OAV	OOB	BH	AVG	PB	PR	/A	PD	TPI
1931 *Phi-A	7	5	.583	25	10	8	1	0	118	136	5	27	18	12.5	2.97	151	.291	.331	14	.259	2	18	20	-0	1.9
1932 Phi-A	1	2	.333	17	0	0	0	2	65¹	84	6	18	16	14.1	5.51	82	.315	.358	6	.300	2	-7	-7	2	0.0
Total 13	171	119	.590	500	249	147	18	29	2556¹	2729	138	724	599	12.3	3.54	128	.277	.329	164	.199	-7	179	217	42	26.0

● **ENRIQUE ROMO**   Romo, Enrique (Navarro) b: 7/15/47, Santa Rosalia, Mex   BR/TR, 5'11", 185 lbs.   Deb: 4/7/77   F

YEAR TM/L	W	L	PCT	G	GS	CG	SH	SV	IP	H	HR	BB	SO	RAT	ERA	ERA+	OAV	OOB	BH	AVG	PB	PR	/A	PD	TPI
1977 Sea-A	8	10	.444	58	3	0	0	16	114¹	93	8	39	105	10.8	2.83	145	.227	.302	0	—	0	16	16	1	3.0
1978 Sea-A	11	7	.611	56	0	0	0	10	107¹	88	12	39	62	11.1	3.69	103	.227	.306	0	—	0	1	1	-1	0.1
1979 *Pit-N	10	5	.667	84	0	0	0	5	129¹	122	11	43	106	11.7	2.99	130	.253	.318	2	.167	-0	11	13	2	1.7
1980 Pit-N	5	5	.500	74	0	0	0	11	123²	117	10	28	82	10.6	3.27	111	.252	.296	5	.455	3	4	5	1	0.9
1981 Pit-N	1	3	.250	33	0	0	0	9	41²	47	5	18	23	14.0	4.54	79	.288	.359	0	.000	-0	-5	-4	-0	-0.7
1982 Pit-N	9	3	.750	45	0	0	0	1	86²	81	11	36	58	12.3	4.36	85	.245	.322	3	.300	1	-7	-6	-0	-0.8
Total 6	44	33	.571	350	3	0	0	52	603	548	57	203	436	11.4	3.45	111	.245	.312	10	.270	4	19	25	2	4.2

● **VICENTE ROMO**   Romo, Vicente (Navarro) "Huevo" b: 4/12/43, Santa Rosalia, Mex.   BR/TR, 6'1", 195 lbs.   Deb: 4/11/68   F

YEAR TM/L	W	L	PCT	G	GS	CG	SH	SV	IP	H	HR	BB	SO	RAT	ERA	ERA+	OAV	OOB	BH	AVG	PB	PR	/A	PD	TPI
1968 LA-N	0	0	—	1	0	0	0	1	1	1	0	0	0	9.0	0.00	—	.250	.250	0	—	0	0	0	-0	0.0
Cle-A	5	3	.625	40	1	0	0	12	83¹	43	5	32	54	8.3	1.62	183	.154	.245	2	.143	-0	13	12	-0	1.7
1969 Cle-A	1	1	.500	3	0	0	0	0	8	7	0	3	7	11.3	2.25	167	.233	.303	1	.500	0	1	1	-0	0.4
Bos-A	7	9	.438	52	11	4	1	11	127¹	116	14	50	89	11.8	3.18	120	.247	.321	4	.129	-1	6	9	0	1.2
Yr	8	10	.444	55	11	4	1	11	135¹	123	14	53	96	11.8	3.13	122	.246	.319	5	.152	-0	7	10	0	1.6
1970 Bos-A	7	3	.700	48	10	0	0	6	108	115	14	43	71	13.2	4.08	97	.273	.340	4	.148	0	-4	-1	1	0.0
1971 Chi-A	1	7	.125	45	2	0	0	5	72	52	5	37	48	11.1	3.38	106	.202	.303	4	.364	1	1	2	1	0.5
1972 Chi-A	3	0	1.000	28	0	0	0	1	51²	47	5	18	46	11.5	3.31	94	.246	.314	0	.000	-1	-1	-1	-0	-0.1
1973 SD-N	2	3	.400	49	1	0	0	7	87²	85	11	46	51	13.4	3.70	94	.260	.351	2	.125	-0	-0	-2	0	-0.1
1974 SD-N	5	5	.500	54	1	0	0	9	71	78	6	37	26	14.8	4.56	78	.290	.380	0	.000	-1	-7	-8	2	-1.2
1982 LA-N	1	2	.333	15	6	0	0	1	35²	25	1	14	24	10.3	3.03	114	.195	.285	1	.200	0	2	2	1	0.2
Total 8	32	33	.492	335	32	4	1	52	645²	569	61	280	416	11.3	3.36	106	.239	.322	18	.149	-1	10	13	5	2.6

● **JOHN ROMONOSKY**   Romonosky, John b: 7/7/29, Harrisburg, Ill.   BR/TR, 6'2", 195 lbs.   Deb: 9/6/53

YEAR TM/L	W	L	PCT	G	GS	CG	SH	SV	IP	H	HR	BB	SO	RAT	ERA	ERA+	OAV	OOB	BH	AVG	PB	PR	/A	PD	TPI
1953 StL-N	0	0	—	2	2	0	0	0	7²	9	1	4	3	16.4	4.70	91	.281	.378	0	.000	-0	-0	-0	-0	-0.1
1958 Was-A	2	4	.333	18	5	1	0	0	55¹	52	6	28	38	13.0	6.51	59	.243	.331	4	.308	2	-17	-17	0	-1.3
1959 Was-A	1	0	1.000	12	2	0	0	0	38¹	36	4	19	22	13.6	3.29	119	.254	.354	2	.182	0	2	3	-0	0.1
Total 3	3	4	.429	32	9	1	0	0	101¹	97	11	51	63	13.5	5.15	75	.250	.343	6	.231	2	-15	-14	-0	-1.3

● **GILBERTO RONDON**   Rondon, Gilberto b: 11/18/53, Bronx, N.Y.   BR/TR, 6'2", 200 lbs.   Deb: 4/10/76   F

YEAR TM/L	W	L	PCT	G	GS	CG	SH	SV	IP	H	HR	BB	SO	RAT	ERA	ERA+	OAV	OOB	BH	AVG	PB	PR	/A	PD	TPI
1976 Hou-N	2	2	.500	19	7	0	0	0	53²	70	6	39	21	18.3	5.70	56	.315	.418	4	.286	1	-13	-15	-1	-1.0
1979 Chi-A	0	0	—	4	0	0	0	0	9²	11	2	6	3	15.8	3.72	114	.282	.378	0	—	0	1	1	-0	0.0
Total 2	2	2	.500	23	7	0	0	0	63¹	81	8	45	24	17.9	5.40	62	.310	.412	4	.286	1	-13	-14	-1	-1.0

● **JIM ROOKER**   Rooker, James Phillip b: 9/23/42, Lakeview, Ore.   BR/TL, 6', 201 lbs.   Deb: 6/30/68

YEAR TM/L	W	L	PCT	G	GS	CG	SH	SV	IP	H	HR	BB	SO	RAT	ERA	ERA+	OAV	OOB	BH	AVG	PB	PR	/A	PD	TPI
1968 Det-A	0	0	—	2	0	0	0	0	4²	4	0	1	4	9.6	3.86	78	.235	.278	0	.000	-0	-0	-0	-0	0.0
1969 KC-A	4	16	.200	28	22	8	1	0	158¹	136	13	73	108	11.9	3.75	98	.229	.315	16	.281	8	-2	-1	-1	0.6
1970 KC-A	10	15	.400	38	29	6	3	1	203²	190	11	102	117	12.9	3.54	106	.252	.341	14	.200	3	4	5	-0	0.9
1971 KC-A	2	7	.222	20	7	1	1	0	54	59	2	24	31	14.0	5.33	64	.284	.361	0	.000	-1	-11	-11	-1	-1.9
1972 KC-A	5	6	.455	18	10	4	2	0	72	78	3	24	44	12.9	4.38	69	.280	.339	2	.100	-1	-11	-11	1	-1.6
1973 Pit-N	10	6	.625	41	18	6	3	5	170¹	143	12	52	102	10.4	2.85	123	.229	.290	12	.245	-3	13	13	1	1.6
1974 *Pit-N	15	11	.577	33	33	15	1	0	262²	228	17	83	139	10.8	2.78	124	.238	.301	29	.305	11	25	20	1	3.2
1975 *Pit-N	13	11	.542	28	28	7	1	0	196²	177	16	76	102	11.7	2.97	119	.238	.311	6	.095	-3	14	12	0	1.2
1976 Pit-N	15	8	.652	30	29	10	1	1	198²	201	12	72	92	12.5	3.35	104	.263	.328	16	.216	3	3	3	-1	0.6
1977 Pit-N	14	9	.609	30	30	7	2	0	204¹	196	24	64	89	11.5	3.08	129	.253	.310	13	.186	0	19	20	-2	2.0
1978 Pit-N	9	11	.450	28	28	1	0	0	163¹	160	13	81	76	13.4	4.24	87	.259	.348	9	.161	0	-12	-10	1	-1.0
1979 Pit-N	4	7	.364	19	17	1	0	0	103²	106	11	39	44	12.6	4.60	84	.266	.331	4	.121	-1	-10	-8	-1	-1.0
1980 Pit-N	2	2	.500	4	4	0	0	0	18	16	0	12	8	14.0	3.50	104	.262	.384	1	.143	1	0	0	0	0.2
Total 13	103	109	.486	319	255	66	15	7	1810¹	1694	128	703	976	12.0	3.46	104	.249	.321	122	.201	23	34	30	-2	4.8

● **CHARLIE ROOT**   Root, Charles Henry "Chinski" b: 3/17/1899, Middletown, Ohio   d: 11/5/70, Hollister, Cal.   BR/TR, 5'10.5", 190 lbs.   Deb: 4/18/23   C

YEAR TM/L	W	L	PCT	G	GS	CG	SH	SV	IP	H	HR	BB	SO	RAT	ERA	ERA+	OAV	OOB	BH	AVG	PB	PR	/A	PD	TPI
1923 StL-A	0	4	.000	27	2	0	0	0	60	68	4	18	27	13.8	5.70	73	.302	.369	1	.077	-1	-11	-10	-1	-0.7
1926 Chi-N	18	17	.514	42	32	21	2	2	271¹	267	10	62	127	11.1	2.82	136	.264	.310	13	.143	-4	30	31	-1	3.2
1927 Chi-N	26	15	.634	48	36	21	4	2	309	296	16	117	145	12.3	3.76	103	.254	.326	27	.221	3	6	4	-4	0.3
1928 Chi-N	14	18	.438	40	30	13	1	2	237	214	15	73	122	11.2	3.57	108	.242	.305	13	.178	-0	11	7	-3	0.6
1929 *Chi-N	19	6	.760	43	31	19	4	3	272	286	12	83	124	12.3	3.47	133	.275	.330	15	.156	0	38	35	-4	2.4
1930 Chi-N	16	14	.533	37	30	15	4	3	220¹	247	16	63	124	12.9	4.33	113	.281	.334	21	.262	5	16	14	-3	1.7
1931 Chi-N	17	14	.548	39	31	19	3	2	251	240	7	71	131	11.4	3.48	111	.252	.309	20	.222	3	11	11	-3	1.2
1932 *Chi-N	15	10	.600	39	23	11	0	3	216¹	211	10	55	96	11.3	3.58	105	.253	.303	13	.171	-1	7	5	-3	0.1
1933 Chi-N	15	10	.600	35	30	20	2	0	242²	232	14	61	86	11.3	2.60	126	.252	.306	8	.094	-4	20	18	-3	1.0
1934 Chi-N	4	7	.364	34	9	2	0	0	117²	141	8	53	46	15.2	4.28	90	.298	.375	7	.175	2	-3	-5	-1	-0.4
1935 *Chi-N	15	8	.652	38	18	11	1	2	201¹	193	15	47	94	10.9	3.08	127	.252	.298	14	.203	2	21	19	-3	1.9
1936 Chi-N	3	6	.333	33	4	0	0	1	73²	81	8	20	32	12.6	4.15	96	.280	.331	5	.333	1	-1	-1	-1	-0.1
1937 Chi-N	13	5	.722	43	15	5	0	5	178²	173	18	32	74	10.5	3.38	118	.253	.290	12	.179	0	11	12	-1	1.1
1938 *Chi-N	8	7	.533	44	11	5	0	4	160²	163	10	30	70	10.9	2.86	134	.258	.294	8	.167	-0	17	17	-2	1.4
1939 Chi-N	8	8	.500	35	16	8	0	4	167¹	189	11	34	65	12.1	4.03	98	.286	.323	10	.175	2	-2	-2	-3	-0.3
1940 Chi-N	2	4	.333	36	8	1	0	1	112	118	9	33	50	12.2	3.86	97	.265	.317	4	.129	-1	-0	-1	-0	-0.2
1941 Chi-N	8	7	.533	19	15	6	0	0	106²	133	8	37	46	14.3	5.40	68	.306	.360	5	.152	2	-21	-22	-1	-2.6
Total 17	201	160	.557	632	341	177	21	40	3197¹	3252	187	889	1459	11.9	3.59	110	.264	.318	196	.180	8	148	129	-35	10.6

● **JOHN ROPER**   Roper, John Christopher b: 11/21/71, Southern Pines, N.C.   BR/TR, 6', 175 lbs.   Deb: 5/16/93

YEAR TM/L	W	L	PCT	G	GS	CG	SH	SV	IP	H	HR	BB	SO	RAT	ERA	ERA+	OAV	OOB	BH	AVG	PB	PR	/A	PD	TPI
1993 Cin-N	2	5	.286	16	15	0	0	0	80	92	10	36	54	14.8	5.62	72	.295	.375	5	.179	-0	-14	-14	-0	-1.1
1994 Cin-N	6	2	.750	16	15	0	0	0	92	90	16	30	51	12.1	4.50	92	.255	.320	6	.182	-0	-3	-4	-0	-0.3
1995 Cin-N	0	0	—	2	2	0	0	0	7	13	3	4	6	21.9	10.29	40	.406	.472	0	.000	-0	-5	-5	-0	0.0
SF-N	0	0	—	1	0	0	0	0	1	2	0	2	0	36.0	27.00	15	.500	.667	0	—	0	-3	-3	-0	0.0
Yr	0	0	—	3	2	0	0	0	8	15	3	6	6	23.6	12.38	33	.417	.500	0	.000	-0	-7	-7	-0	0.0
Total 3	8	7	.533	35	32	0	0	0	180	197	29	72	111	13.9	5.35	76	.281	.355	11	.177	-0	-24	-25	-1	-1.4

● **JOSE ROSADO**   Rosado, Jose Antonio (Rosado) b: 11/9/74, Jersey City, N.J.   BL/TL, 6', 175 lbs.   Deb: 6/12/96

YEAR TM/L	W	L	PCT	G	GS	CG	SH	SV	IP	H	HR	BB	SO	RAT	ERA	ERA+	OAV	OOB	BH	AVG	PB	PR	/A	PD	TPI
1996 KC-A	8	6	.571	16	16	2	1	0	106²	101	7	26	64	11.1	3.21	152	.249	.300	0	—	0	21	20	-0	2.3

● **CHUCK ROSE**   Rose, Charles Alfred b: 9/1/1885, Macon, Mo.   d: 8/4/61, Salina, Kan.   BL/TL, 5'8.5", 158 lbs.   Deb: 9/13/09

YEAR TM/L	W	L	PCT	G	GS	CG	SH	SV	IP	H	HR	BB	SO	RAT	ERA	ERA+	OAV	OOB	BH	AVG	PB	PR	/A	PD	TPI
1909 StL-A	1	2	.333	3	3	3	0	0	25	32	1	7	6	15.1	5.40	45	.330	.393	0	.000	-1	-8	-8	-1	-1.0

● **DON ROSE**   Rose, Donald Gary b: 3/19/47, Covina, Cal.   BR/TR, 6'3", 195 lbs.   Deb: 9/15/71

YEAR TM/L	W	L	PCT	G	GS	CG	SH	SV	IP	H	HR	BB	SO	RAT	ERA	ERA+	OAV	OOB	BH	AVG	PB	PR	/A	PD	TPI
1971 NY-N	0	0	—	1	0	0	0	0	2	2	0	0	1	9.0	0.00	—	.286	.286	0	—	0	1	1	-0	0.0
1972 Cal-A	1	4	.200	16	4	0	0	0	42²	49	9	19	39	14.3	4.22	69	.283	.354	2	.200	1	-5	-6	-0	-0.6
1974 SF-N	0	0	—	2	0	0	0	0	1	4	0	1	0	45.0	9.00	42	.667	.714	0	—	0	-1	-1	-0	0.0
Total 3	1	4	.200	19	4	0	0	0	45²	55	9	20	40	14.8	4.14	71	.296	.364	2	.200	1	-5	-6	-1	-0.6

● **ZEKE ROSEBRAUGH**   Rosebraugh, Eli Ethelbert b: 9/8/1870, Charleston, Ill.   d: 7/16/30, Fresno, Cal.   TL ,   Deb: 9/21/1898

YEAR TM/L	W	L	PCT	G	GS	CG	SH	SV	IP	H	HR	BB	SO	RAT	ERA	ERA+	OAV	OOB	BH	AVG	PB	PR	/A	PD	TPI
1898 Pit-N	0	2	.000	4	2	2	0	0	21²	23	0	9	6	14.5	3.32	107	.271	.361	3	.375	-1	1	1	-0	0.1
1899 Pit-N	0	1	.000	2	2	0	0	0	6	14	0	3	2	27.0	9.00	42	.452	.514	-0	-0	-0	-3	-3	-0	-0.5
Total 2	0	3	.000	6	4	2	0	0	27²	37	0	12	8	17.2	4.55	79	.319	.402	3	.300	-1	-3	-3	-0	-0.4

● **CHIEF ROSEMAN**   Roseman, James John b: 1856, New York, N.Y.   d: 7/4/38, Brooklyn, N.Y.   BR/TR, 5'7", 167 lbs.   Deb: 5/1/1882   M♦

YEAR TM/L	W	L	PCT	G	GS	CG	SH	SV	IP	H	HR	BB	SO	RAT	ERA	ERA+	OAV	OOB	BH	AVG	PB	PR	/A	PD	TPI
1885 NY-a	0	1	.000	1	1	0	0	0	1	3	0	2	0	45.0	27.00	11	.333	.455	114	.278		-3	-3	0	-1.2
1886 NY-a	0	0	—	1	0	0	0	0	7	6	0	0	0	7.7	5.14	66	.240	.240	127	.227	0	-1	-1	0	0.0

YEAR TM/L	W	L	PCT	G	GS	CG	SH	SV	IP	H	HR	BB	SO	RAT	ERA	ERA+	OAV	OOB	BH	AVG	PB	PR	/A	PD	TPI
1887 NY-a	0	0	—	2	0	0	0	0	8	11	0	5	1	20.3	7.88	54	.407	.529	55	.228	-0	-3	-3	-0	0.0
Total 3	0	1	.000	4	1	0	0	0	16	20	0	7	1	16.3	7.88	48	.328	.414	726	.263	0	-7	-7	-0	-1.2

● **STEVE ROSENBERG** Rosenberg, Steven Allen b: 10/31/64, Brooklyn, N.Y. BL/TL, 6', 186 lbs. Deb: 6/4/88

YEAR TM/L	W	L	PCT	G	GS	CG	SH	SV	IP	H	HR	BB	SO	RAT	ERA	ERA+	OAV	OOB	BH	AVG	PB	PR	/A	PD	TPI
1988 Chi-A	0	1	.000	33	0	0	0	1	46	53	5	19	28	14.1	4.30	92	.298	.365	0	—	0	-2	-2	-0	-0.1
1989 Chi-A	4	13	.235	38	21	2	0	0	142	148	14	58	77	13.1	4.94	77	.273	.344	0	—	0	-17	-18	0	-1.9
1990 Chi-A	1	0	1.000	6	0	0	0	0	10	10	2	5	4	13.5	5.40	71	.256	.341	0	—	-0	-2	-2	-0	-0.1
1991 SD-N	1	1	.500	10	0	0	0	0	11^2	11	3	5	6	12.3	6.94	55	.250	.327	0	.000	-0	-4	-4	-0	-0.7
Total 4	6	15	.286	87	21	2	0	1	209^2	222	24	87	115	13.3	4.94	78	.276	.348	0	.000	-0	-24	-26	-0	-2.8

● **WAYNE ROSENTHAL** Rosenthal, Wayne Scott b: 2/19/65, Brooklyn, N.Y. BR/TR, 6'5", 220 lbs. Deb: 6/26/91

YEAR TM/L	W	L	PCT	G	GS	CG	SH	SV	IP	H	HR	BB	SO	RAT	ERA	ERA+	OAV	OOB	BH	AVG	PB	PR	/A	PD	TPI
1991 Tex-A	1	4	.200	36	0	0	0	1	70^1	72	9	36	61	13.9	5.25	77	.257	.344	0	—	-0	-9	-10	-1	-0.7
1992 Tex-A	0	0	—	6	0	0	0	0	4^2	7	1	2	1	17.4	7.71	49	.333	.391	0	—	-0	-2	-2	-0	0.0
Total 2	1	4	.200	42	0	0	0	1	75	79	10	38	62	14.2	5.40	74	.262	.347	0	—	-0	-11	-12	-1	-0.7

● **STEVE ROSER** Roser, Emerson Corey b: 1/25/18, Rome, N.Y. BR/TR, 6'4", 220 lbs. Deb: 5/5/44

YEAR TM/L	W	L	PCT	G	GS	CG	SH	SV	IP	H	HR	BB	SO	RAT	ERA	ERA+	OAV	OOB	BH	AVG	PB	PR	/A	PD	TPI
1944 NY-A	4	3	.571	16	6	1	0	1	84	80	3	34	34	12.2	3.86	90	.256	.329	3	.100	-2	-4	-3	-1	-0.5
1945 NY-A	0	0	—	11	0	0	0	0	27	27	1	8	11	11.7	3.67	94	.262	.315	1	.125	-0	-1	-1	0	0.0
1946 NY-A	1	1	.500	4	1	0	0	0	3^1	7	0	4	2	29.7	16.20	21	.438	.550	0	—	-0	-5	-5	-0	-2.0
Bos-N	1	1	.500	14	1	0	0	0	35	33	1	18	18	13.1	3.60	95	.250	.340	0	.000	-1	-1	-1	-0	-0.1
Total 3	6	5	.545	45	8	1	0	2	149^1	147	5	64	64	12.7	4.04	86	.261	.336	4	.093	-3	-10	-9	-1	-2.6

● **BUSTER ROSS** Ross, Chester Franklin b: 3/11/03, Kuttawa, Ky. d: 4/24/82, Mayfield, Ky. BL/TL, 6'1", 195 lbs. Deb: 6/15/24

YEAR TM/L	W	L	PCT	G	GS	CG	SH	SV	IP	H	HR	BB	SO	RAT	ERA	ERA+	OAV	OOB	BH	AVG	PB	PR	/A	PD	TPI
1924 Bos-A	4	3	.571	30	2	1	1	1	93^1	98	3	30	16	13.4	3.47	126	.307	.361	5	.200	-0	8	9	-1	0.5
1925 Bos-A	3	8	.273	33	8	0	0	0	94^1	119	3	40	15	15.6	6.20	73	.313	.386	3	.125	-1	-19	-17	-1	-1.8
1926 Bos-A	0	1	.000	1	0	0	0	0	2^2	5	0	4	0	30.4	16.88	24	.385	.529	0	.000	-0	-4	-4	0	-0.8
Total 3	7	12	.368	64	10	1	1	1	190^1	233	6	74	31	14.8	5.01	89	.311	.377	8	.160	-2	-15	-12	-2	-2.1

● **CLIFF ROSS** Ross, Clifford Davis b: 8/3/28, Philadelphia, Pa. BL/TL, 6'4", 195 lbs. Deb: 9/11/54

YEAR TM/L	W	L	PCT	G	GS	CG	SH	SV	IP	H	HR	BB	SO	RAT	ERA	ERA+	OAV	OOB	BH	AVG	PB	PR	/A	PD	TPI
1954 Cin-N	0	0	—	4	0	0	0	1	2^2	0	0	1	0	0.0	0.00	—	.000	.000	0	—	-0	1	1	0	0.1

● **ERNIE ROSS** Ross, Ernest Bertram "Curly" b: 3/31/1880, Toronto, Ont., Can. d: 3/28/50, Toronto, Ont., Can. BL/TL, 5'8", 150 lbs. Deb: 9/17/02

YEAR TM/L	W	L	PCT	G	GS	CG	SH	SV	IP	H	HR	BB	SO	RAT	ERA	ERA+	OAV	OOB	BH	AVG	PB	PR	/A	PD	TPI
1902 Bal-A	1	1	.500	2	2	2	0	0	17	20	0	12	2	17.5	7.41	51	.294	.407	0	—	-1	-7	-7	-1	-0.7

● **BOB ROSS** Ross, Floyd Robert b: 11/2/28, Fullerton, Cal. BR/TL, 6', 165 lbs. Deb: 6/16/50

YEAR TM/L	W	L	PCT	G	GS	CG	SH	SV	IP	H	HR	BB	SO	RAT	ERA	ERA+	OAV	OOB	BH	AVG	PB	PR	/A	PD	TPI
1950 Was-A	0	1	.000	6	2	0	0	0	12^2	15	1	15	2	21.3	8.53	53	.300	.462	0	.000	-0	-6	-6	0	-0.4
1951 Was-A	0	1	.000	11	1	0	0	0	31^2	36	3	21	23	16.2	6.54	63	.295	.399	1	.111	-0	-8	-9	-1	-0.3
1956 Phi-N	0	0	—	3	0	0	0	0	3^1	4	1	2	4	16.2	8.10	46	.333	.429	0	—	-0	-2	-2	-0	0.0
Total 3	0	2	.000	20	3	0	0	0	47^2	55	5	38	29	17.6	7.17	58	.299	.419	1	.083	-1	-16	-16	-1	-0.7

● **GARY ROSS** Ross, Gary Douglas b: 9/16/47, McKeesport, Pa. BR/TR, 6'1", 190 lbs. Deb: 6/28/68

YEAR TM/L	W	L	PCT	G	GS	CG	SH	SV	IP	H	HR	BB	SO	RAT	ERA	ERA+	OAV	OOB	BH	AVG	PB	PR	/A	PD	TPI
1968 Chi-N	1	1	.500	13	5	1	0	0	41	44	3	25	31	15.1	4.17	76	.288	.388	1	.091	-1	-5	-5	0	-0.3
1969 Chi-N	0	0	—	2	1	0	0	0	2	2	0	3	2	13.5	13.50	30	.143	.333	0	—	-0	-2	-2	-0	0.0
SD-N	3	12	.200	46	7	0	0	3	109^2	104	5	56	58	13.5	4.19	84	.252	.348	0	.000	-2	-7	-8	2	-1.1
Yr	3	12	.200	48	8	0	0	3	111^2	105	5	58	60	13.5	4.35	81	.250	.348	0	.000	-2	-9	-10	2	-1.1
1970 SD-N	2	3	.400	33	2	0	0	1	62^1	72	8	36	39	16.0	5.20	76	.305	.404	4	.500	2	-8	-8	1	-0.4
1971 SD-N	1	3	.250	13	0	0	0	0	24^1	27	0	11	13	14.4	2.96	111	.300	.382	0	.000	-0	1	1	0	0.1
1972 SD-N	4	3	.571	60	0	0	0	3	91^2	87	2	49	46	13.7	2.45	134	.261	.363	2	.154	-0	10	8	1	0.8
1973 SD-N	4	4	.500	58	0	0	0	0	76^1	93	8	33	44	15.3	5.42	64	.304	.379	0	.000	-0	-15	-17	-0	-1.6
1974 SD-N	0	0	—	9	0	0	0	0	18	23	1	6	11	14.5	4.50	79	.315	.367	0	.000	-0	-2	-2	-0	-0.1
1975 Cal-A	0	1	.000	1	1	0	0	0	5	6	1	1	4	12.6	5.40	66	.273	.304	0	—	-1	-1	-1	-0	-0.1
1976 Cal-A	8	16	.333	34	31	7	2	0	225	224	12	58	100	11.5	3.00	114	.258	.308	0	—	-0	13	8	5	1.4
1977 Cal-A	2	4	.333	14	12	0	0	0	58^1	83	10	11	30	14.8	5.55	70	.337	.371	0	—	-0	-10	-11	-1	-0.9
Total 10	25	47	.347	283	59	8	2	7	713^2	764	48	288	378	13.6	3.92	89	.278	.352	7	.115	-2	-26	-36	9	-2.1

● **GEORGE ROSS** Ross, George Sidney b: 6/27/1892, San Rafael, Cal. d: 4/22/35, Amityville, N.Y. BL/TL, 5'10.5", 175 lbs. Deb: 6/27/18

YEAR TM/L	W	L	PCT	G	GS	CG	SH	SV	IP	H	HR	BB	SO	RAT	ERA	ERA+	OAV	OOB	BH	AVG	PB	PR	/A	PD	TPI
1918 NY-N	0	0	—	1	0	0	0	1	2^1	2	0	3	2	19.3	0.00	—	.222	.417	0	.000	-0	1	1	0	0.1

● **BUCK ROSS** Ross, Lee Ravon b: 2/2/15, Norwood, N.C. d: 11/23/78, Charlotte, N.C. BR/TR, 6'2", 170 lbs. Deb: 5/7/36

YEAR TM/L	W	L	PCT	G	GS	CG	SH	SV	IP	H	HR	BB	SO	RAT	ERA	ERA+	OAV	OOB	BH	AVG	PB	PR	/A	PD	TPI
1936 Phi-A	9	14	.391	30	27	12	1	0	200^2	253	17	83	47	15.1	5.83	88	.304	.367	12	.169	-1	-18	-16	-2	-1.7
1937 Phi-A	10	13	.333	28	22	7	1	0	147^1	183	12	63	37	15.0	4.89	96	.306	.373	5	.102	-3	-4	-3	0	-0.5
1938 Phi-A	9	16	.360	29	28	10	0	0	184^1	218	23	80	54	14.5	5.32	91	.289	.357	12	.190	-0	-11	-10	-0	-1.1
1939 Phi-A	6	14	.300	29	28	6	1	0	174	216	17	95	43	16.1	6.00	78	.302	.384	12	.207	-1	-27	-25	-2	-2.5
1940 Phi-A	5	10	.333	24	19	10	0	1	156^1	160	15	60	43	12.7	4.38	102	.256	.322	7	.132	-2	0	1	-1	-0.2
1941 Phi-A	0	1	.000	1	1	0	0	0	4	10	2	2	1	27.0	18.00	23	.435	.480	0	.000	-0	-6	-6	-0	-0.9
Chi-A	3	8	.273	20	11	7	0	0	108^1	99	6	43	30	11.9	3.16	139	.239	.312	7	.219	1	12	11	-2	1.0
Yr	3	9	.250	21	12	7	0	0	112^1	109	8	45	30	12.4	3.69	111	.249	.321	7	.212	1	6	5	-2	0.1
1942 Chi-A	5	7	.417	22	14	4	2	1	113^1	118	6	39	37	12.5	5.00	72	.264	.323	6	.158	-0	-17	-18	-3	-1.9
1943 Chi-A	11	7	.611	21	21	7	1	0	149^1	140	6	56	41	11.9	3.19	105	.253	.324	4	.087	-1	2	2	-1	0.5
1944 Chi-A	2	7	.222	20	9	2	0	0	90^1	97	6	35	20	13.4	5.18	66	.280	.350	2	.077	-2	-18	-18	-2	-2.0
1945 Chi-A	1	1	.500	13	2	0	0	0	37^2	51	3	17	8	16.4	5.79	57	.327	.393	2	.182	-0	-10	-10	-1	-0.6
Total 10	56	95	.371	237	182	65	6	2	1365^1	1545	114	573	360	14.0	4.94	88	.283	.351	69	.154	-11	-97	-91	-13	-10.4

● **MARK ROSS** Ross, Mark Joseph b: 8/8/57, Galveston, Tex. BR/TR, 6', 195 lbs. Deb: 9/12/82

YEAR TM/L	W	L	PCT	G	GS	CG	SH	SV	IP	H	HR	BB	SO	RAT	ERA	ERA+	OAV	OOB	BH	AVG	PB	PR	/A	PD	TPI
1982 Hou-N	0	0	—	4	0	0	0	0	6	3	0	4	4	4.5	1.50	221	.143	.143	0	—	-0	1	1	0	0.0
1984 Hou-N	1	0	1.000	2	0	0	0	0	2^1	0	0	1	2	3.9	0.00	—	.125	.125	0	—	-0	1	1	-0	0.4
1985 Hou-N	0	2	.000	8	0	0	0	0	13	12	2	4	7	9.7	4.85	71	.240	.269	0	.000	-0	-2	-2	-0	-0.3
1987 Pit-N	0	0	—	1	0	0	0	0	1	1	1	0	0	9.00	46	.250	.250	0	—	-0	-1	-1	0	0.0
1988 Tor-A	0	0	—	3	0	0	0	0	7^1	5	0	4	4	11.0	4.91	80	.185	.290	0	—	-0	-1	-1	-0	0.0
1990 Pit-N	1	0	1.000	9	0	0	0	0	12^2	11	2	4	6	10.7	3.55	102	.244	.306	0	—	-0	0	0	0	0.0
Total 6	2	2	.500	27	0	0	0	0	42^1	33	5	10	17	9.1	3.83	93	.213	.261	0	—	-0	-1	-0	0	0.0

● **JOE ROSSELLI** Rosselli, Joseph Donald b: 5/28/72, Burbank, Cal. BR/TL, 6'1", 170 lbs. Deb: 4/30/95

YEAR TM/L	W	L	PCT	G	GS	CG	SH	SV	IP	H	HR	BB	SO	RAT	ERA	ERA+	OAV	OOB	BH	AVG	PB	PR	/A	PD	TPI
1995 SF-N	2	1	.667	9	5	0	0	0	30	39	5	20	7	17.7	8.70	47	.342	.440	2	.200	0	-15	-15	-0	-1.3

● **FRANK ROSSO** Rosso, Francis James b: 3/1/21, Agawam, Mass. d: 1/26/80, Springfield, Mass. BR/TR, 5'11", 180 lbs. Deb: 9/15/44

YEAR TM/L	W	L	PCT	G	GS	CG	SH	SV	IP	H	HR	BB	SO	RAT	ERA	ERA+	OAV	OOB	BH	AVG	PB	PR	/A	PD	TPI
1944 NY-N	0	0	—	2	0	0	0	0	4	11	0	3	4	31.5	9.00	41	.550	.609	0	—	0	-2	-2	0	0.0

● **MARV ROTBLATT** Rotblatt, Marvin "Rotty" b: 10/18/27, Chicago, Ill. BB/TL, 5'7", 160 lbs. Deb: 7/4/48

YEAR TM/L	W	L	PCT	G	GS	CG	SH	SV	IP	H	HR	BB	SO	RAT	ERA	ERA+	OAV	OOB	BH	AVG	PB	PR	/A	PD	TPI
1948 Chi-A	0	1	.000	7	2	0	0	0	18^1	19	2	23	4	21.1	7.85	54	.271	.457	0	.000	-0	-7	-7	-1	-0.4
1950 Chi-A	0	0	—	2	0	0	0	0	8^2	11	2	6	6	16.6	6.23	72	.344	.432	0	.000	-0	-3	-3	0	0.0
1951 Chi-A	4	2	.667	26	2	0	0	2	47^2	44	2	23	20	12.8	3.40	119	.244	.333	0	.000	-2	4	3	1	0.3
Total 3	4	3	.571	35	4	0	0	2	74^2	74	6	51	30	15.3	4.82	86	.262	.379	0	.000	-2	-5	-6	1	-0.1

● **JACK ROTHROCK** Rothrock, John Houston b: 3/14/05, Long Beach, Cal. d: 2/2/80, San Bernardino, Cal BB/TR, 5'11.5", 165 lbs. Deb: 7/28/25 ♦

YEAR TM/L	W	L	PCT	G	GS	CG	SH	SV	IP	H	HR	BB	SO	RAT	ERA	ERA+	OAV	OOB	BH	AVG	PB	PR	/A	PD	TPI
1928 Bos-A	0	0	—	1	0	0	0	0	1	0	0	0	0	0.0	0.00	—	.000	.000	92	.267		0	0	0	0.0

● **LARRY ROTHSCHILD** Rothschild, Lawrence Lee b: 3/12/54, Chicago, Ill. BL/TR, 6'2", 180 lbs. Deb: 9/11/81 C

YEAR TM/L	W	L	PCT	G	GS	CG	SH	SV	IP	H	HR	BB	SO	RAT	ERA	ERA+	OAV	OOB	BH	AVG	PB	PR	/A	PD	TPI
1981 Det-A	0	0	—	5	0	0	0	1	5^2	4	0	6	1	15.9	1.59	237	.200	.385	0	—	0	1	1	-0	0.1
1982 Det-A	0	0	—	2	0	0	0	0	2^2	4	1	2	0	20.3	13.50	30	.333	.429	0	—	0	-3	-3	-0	0.0
Total 2	0	0	—	7	0	0	0	1	8^1	8	1	8	1	17.3	5.40	72	.250	.400	0	—	0	-1	-1	0	0.1

YEAR TM/L	W	L	PCT	G	GS	CG	SH	SV	IP	H	HR	BB	SO	RAT	ERA	ERA+	OAV	OOB	BH	AVG	PB	PR	/A	PD	TPI

● GENE ROUNSAVILLE Rounsaville, Virle Gene b: 9/27/44, Konawa, Okla. BR/TR, 6'3", 205 lbs. Deb: 4/7/70

| 1970 Chi-A | 0 | 1 | .000 | 8 | 0 | 0 | 0 | 0 | 6¹ | 10 | 1 | 2 | 3 | 17.1 | 9.95 | 39 | .357 | .400 | 0 | — | 0 | -4 | -4 | -0 | -0.6 |

● JACK ROWAN Rowan, John Albert b: 6/16/1887, New Castle, Pa. d: 9/29/66, Dayton, Ohio BR/TR, 6'1", 210 lbs. Deb: 9/6/06

1906 Det-A	0	1	.000	1	1	1	0	0	9	15	0	6	0	21.0	11.00	25	.375	.457	1	.250	0	-8	-8	-0	-0.6
1908 Cin-N	3	3	.500	8	7	4	1	0	49¹	46	0	16	24	11.3	1.82	126	.253	.313	1	.071	-1	3	3	1	0.3
1909 Cin-N	11	12	.478	38	23	14	0	0	225²	185	0	104	81	11.6	2.79	93	.233	.324	6	.092	-1	-5	-5	-5	-1.1
1910 Cin-N	14	13	.519	42	30	18	4	1	261	242	4	105	108	12.3	2.93	99	.254	.334	19	.229	3	3	-0	-4	-0.2
1911 Phi-N	2	4	.333	12	6	2	0	0	45²	59	3	20	17	15.8	4.73	73	.316	.385	1	.077	-1	-7	-7	1	-0.8
Chi-N	0	0	—	1	0	0	0	0	2	1	0	2	0	18.0	4.50	74	.143	.400	0	.000	-0	-0	-0	-0	0.0
Yr	2	4	.333	13	6	2	0	0	47²	60	3	22	17	15.7	4.72	73	.308	.381	1	.071	-1	-7	-7	1	-0.8
1913 Cin-N	0	4	.000	5	5	5	0	0	39	37	0	9	21	10.8	3.00	108	.264	.313	2	.182	1	1	-0	-0	0.2
1914 Cin-N	1	3	.250	12	2	0	0	2	39	38	1	10	16	11.1	3.46	85	.262	.310	0	.000	-1	-3	-2	-1	-0.4
Total 7	31	40	.437	119	74	44	5	3	670²	623	8	272	267	12.2	3.07	92	.255	.333	30	.151	1	-16	-19	-9	-2.6

● DAVE ROWE Rowe, David Elwood b: 10/9/1854, Harrisburg, Pa. d: 12/9/30, Glendale, Cal. BR/TR, 5'9", 180 lbs. Deb: 5/30/1877 FM♦

1877 Chi-N	0	1	.000	1	1	0	0	0	1	3	0	2	0	45.0	18.00	17	.600	.714	2	.286	0	-2	-2	0	-0.9
1882 Cle-N	0	1	.000	1	1	1	0	0	9	29	3	7	0	36.0	12.00	23	.492	.545	25	.258	0	-9	-9	-0	-0.6
1883 Bal-a	0	0	—	1	0	0	0	0	4	12	1	2	1	31.5	20.25	17	.500	.538	80	.313	0	-8	-7	-0	0.0
1884 StL-U	1	0	1.000	1	1	1	0	0	9	10	0	0	2	10.0	2.00	120	.263	.263	142	.293	0	0	0	0	0.1
Total 4	1	2	.333	4	3	2	0	0	23	54	4	11	3	25.4	9.78	28	.429	.474	383	.263	-0	-18	-18	-0	-1.4

● DON ROWE Rowe, Donald Howard b: 4/3/36, Brawley, Cal. BL/TL, 6', 180 lbs. Deb: 4/9/63 C

| 1963 NY-N | 0 | 0 | — | 26 | 1 | 0 | 0 | 0 | 54² | 59 | 6 | 21 | 27 | 13.3 | 4.28 | 81 | .280 | .348 | 3 | .231 | 0 | -6 | -5 | -1 | -0.1 |

● KEN ROWE Rowe, Kenneth Darrell b: 12/31/33, Ferndale, Mich. BR/TR, 6'2", 185 lbs. Deb: 4/14/63 C

1963 LA-N	1	1	.500	14	0	0	0	1	27²	28	2	11	12	13.0	2.93	103	.264	.339	0	.000	-1	1	0	-0	-0.1
1964 Bal-A	1	0	1.000	6	0	0	0	0	4¹	10	1	1	4	22.8	8.31	43	.455	.478	0	—	0	-2	-2	0	-0.4
1965 Bal-A	0	0	—	6	0	0	0	0	13¹	17	0	2	3	12.8	3.38	103	.321	.345	1	1.000	0	0	-1	-0	0.0
Total 3	2	1	.667	26	0	0	0	1	45¹	55	3	14	19	13.9	3.57	90	.304	.357	1	.167	-0	-1	-2	-1	-0.5

● SCHOOLBOY ROWE Rowe, Lynwood Thomas b: 1/11/10, Waco, Tex. d: 1/8/61, ElDorado, Ark. BR/TR, 6'4.5", 210 lbs. Deb: 4/15/33 C♦

1933 Det-A	7	4	.636	19	15	8	1	0	123¹	129	7	31	75	11.7	3.58	121	.269	.315	11	.220	-0	10	10	2	0.9
1934 *Det-A	24	8	.750	45	30	20	3	1	266	259	12	81	149	11.5	3.45	127	.253	.313	33	.303	12	31	28	-0	4.0
1935 *Det-A☆	19	13	.594	42	34	21	**6**	3	275²	272	11	68	140	11.2	3.69	113	.255	**.301**	34	.312	14	23	15	-2	2.6
1936 Det-A★	19	10	.655	41	35	19	4	3	245²	266	15	64	115	12.2	4.51	110	.275	.321	23	.256	7	14	12	2	2.0
1937 Det-A	1	4	.200	10	2	1	0	0	31¹	49	7	9	6	16.9	8.62	54	.350	.393	2	.200	-0	-14	-14	-0	-1.6
1938 Det-A	0	2	.000	4	3	0	0	0	21	20	1	11	4	13.3	3.00	167	.256	.348	1	.167	-0	4	5	1	0.4
1939 Det-A	10	12	.455	28	24	8	1	0	164	192	17	61	51	14.0	4.99	98	.291	.353	15	.246	2	-7	-2	0	0.0
1940 *Det-A	16	3	**.842**	27	23	11	1	0	169	170	15	43	61	11.4	3.46	137	.259	.305	18	.269	5	17	24	-0	2.9
1941 Det-A	8	6	.571	27	14	4	0	1	139	155	6	33	54	12.2	4.14	110	.278	.318	15	.273	5	0	6	1	1.1
1942 Det-A	1	0	1.000	2	1	0	0	0	10¹	9	0	2	7	9.6	0.00	—	.220	.256	0	.000	-1	4	5	0	0.4
Bro-N	0	0	1.000	9	2	0	0	0	30¹	36	2	12	6	14.5	5.34	61	.288	.355	4	.211	0	-7	-0	-0	-0.2
1943 Phi-N	14	8	.636	27	25	11	3	1	199	196	7	29	52	10.3	2.94	115	.249	.279	36	.300	16	10	10	3	3.1
1946 Phi-N	11	4	.733	17	16	9	2	0	136	112	3	21	51	9.2	2.12	162	.224	.263	11	.180	2	20	20	-2	2.3
1947 Phi-N★	14	10	.583	31	28	15	1	1	195²	232	22	45	74	12.9	4.32	93	.292	.333	22	.278	10	-6	-7	-1	0.1
1948 Phi-N	10	10	.500	30	20	8	0	0	148	167	9	31	46	12.2	4.07	97	.281	.319	10	.192	2	-2	-2	1	0.0
1949 Phi-N	3	7	.300	23	6	0	0	0	65¹	68	2	17	22	12.0	4.82	82	.300	.354	4	.235	2	-6	-6	1	-0.6
Total 15	158	101	.610	382	278	137	22	12	2219¹	2332	132	558	913	11.8	3.87	110	.269	.315	239	.263	76	93	96	2	17.4

● MIKE ROWLAND Rowland, Michael Evan b: 1/31/53, Chicago, Ill. BR/TR, 6'3", 205 lbs. Deb: 7/25/80

1980 SF-N	1	1	.500	19	0	0	0	0	27	26	2	8	8	9.7	2.33	152	.206	.274	0	—	0	4	4	-0	0.2
1981 SF-N	0	1	.000	9	1	0	0	0	15²	13	1	6	8	11.5	3.45	100	.232	.317	1	1.000	0	-0	-0	-0	0.0
Total 2	1	2	.333	28	1	0	0	0	42²	33	3	14	16	10.3	2.74	128	.216	.290	1	1.000	0	4	4	-0	0.2

● CHARLIE ROY Roy, Charles Robert b: 6/22/1884, Beaulieu, Minn. d: 2/10/50, Blackfoot, Idaho BR/TR, 5'10", 190 lbs. Deb: 6/27/06 F

| 1906 Phi-N | 0 | 1 | .000 | 7 | 1 | 0 | 0 | 0 | 18¹ | 24 | 0 | 5 | 6 | 14.7 | 4.91 | 53 | .316 | .366 | 0 | .000 | -1 | -5 | -5 | -0 | -0.3 |

● EMILE ROY Roy, Emile Arthur b: 5/26/07, Brighton, Mass. BR/TR, 5'11", 180 lbs. Deb: 9/30/33

| 1933 Phi-A | 0 | 1 | 1.000 | 1 | 0 | 0 | 0 | 0 | 2¹ | 4 | 0 | 3 | 1 | 30.9 | 27.00 | 16 | .364 | .533 | 0 | — | 0 | -6 | -6 | -0 | -1.2 |

● JEAN-PIERRE ROY Roy, Jean-Pierre b: 6/26/20, Montreal, Que., Can. BB/TR, 5'10", 160 lbs. Deb: 5/5/46

| 1946 Bro-N | 0 | 0 | — | 3 | 1 | 0 | 0 | 0 | 6¹ | 5 | 2 | 5 | 6 | 14.2 | 9.95 | 34 | .200 | .333 | 0 | — | 0 | -5 | -5 | -0 | -0.1 |

● LUTHER ROY Roy, Luther Franklin b: 7/29/02, Ooltewah, Tenn. d: 7/24/63, Grand Rapids, Mich. BR/TR, 5'10.5", 161 lbs. Deb: 6/12/24 F

1924 Cle-A	0	5	.000	16	5	2	0	0	48²	62	3	31	14	17.2	7.77	55	.318	.412	4	.267	-0	-19	-19	1	-1.5
1925 Cle-A	0	0	—	6	1	0	0	0	10	14	1	11	1	22.5	3.60	123	.368	.510	0	.000	-0	1	1	-0	-0.1
1927 Chi-N	3	1	.750	11	0	0	0	0	19²	14	0	11	5	11.9	2.29	169	.206	.329	1	.333	0	4	3	0	0.7
1929 Phi-N	3	6	.333	21	12	1	0	0	88²	137	11	37	16	18.0	8.42	62	.350	.411	9	.281	2	-37	-32	1	-2.2
Bro-N	0	0	—	2	0	0	0	0	3²	4	0	2	0	14.7	4.91	94	.286	.375	0	.000	-0	-0	-0	-0	0.0
Yr	3	6	.333	23	12	1	0	0	92¹	141	11	39	16	17.5	8.29	62	.346	.403	9	.273	2	-37	-32	1	-2.2
Total 4	6	12	.333	56	18	3	0	0	170²	231	15	92	36	17.2	7.17	66	.328	.408	14	.264	2	-51	-47	1	-3.1

● NORMIE ROY Roy, Norman Brooks "Jumbo" b: 11/15/28, Newton, Mass. BR/TR, 6', 200 lbs. Deb: 4/23/50

| 1950 Bos-N | 4 | 3 | .571 | 19 | 6 | 2 | 0 | 1 | 59² | 72 | 7 | 39 | 25 | 17.0 | 5.13 | 75 | .305 | .408 | 3 | .167 | 0 | -7 | -8 | 0 | -0.9 |

● DICK ROZEK Rozek, Richard Louis b: 3/27/27, Cedar Rapids, Iowa BL/TL, 6'0.5", 190 lbs. Deb: 4/29/50

1950 Cle-A	0	0	—	12	2	0	0	0	25¹	28	3	19	14	16.7	4.97	87	.283	.398	0	.000	-1	-1	-2	-1	-0.1
1951 Cle-A	0	0	—	7	1	0	0	0	15¹	11	1	11	5	17.6	2.93	129	.286	.400	1	.333	-0	2	1	-1	0.0
1952 Cle-A	1	0	1.000	10	1	0	0	0	12²	11	0	13	5	17.1	4.97	67	.224	.387	0	.000	-0	-2	-2	-0	-0.2
1953 Phi-A	0	0	—	2	0	0	0	0	10²	8	3	9	2	14.3	5.06	85	.222	.378	0	.000	-0	-1	-1	-0	0.0
1954 Phi-A	0	0	—	2	0	0	0	0	1¹	0	0	3	0	27.0	6.75	58	.000	.571	0	—	0	-0	-0	-0	0.0
Total 5	1	0	1.000	33	4	0	0	0	65¹	65	7	55	26	16.8	4.55	88	.260	.397	1	.083	-1	-3	-4	-2	-0.3

● DAVE ROZEMA Rozema, David Scott b: 8/5/56, Grand Rapids, Mich. BR/TR, 6'4", 200 lbs. Deb: 4/11/77

1977 Det-A	15	7	.682	28	28	16	1	0	218¹	222	25	34	92	10.8	3.09	139	.265	.299	0	—	0	23	29	3	2.8
1978 Det-A	9	12	.429	28	28	11	2	0	209¹	205	17	41	57	10.7	3.14	123	.260	.298	0	—	0	15	17	-1	1.5
1979 Det-A	4	4	.500	16	16	4	1	0	97¹	101	12	30	33	12.7	3.51	123	.270	.334	0	—	0	8	9	0	0.6
1980 Det-A	6	9	.400	42	13	2	1	4	144²	152	11	49	49	12.8	3.92	105	.277	.342	0	—	0	2	3	1	0.3
1981 Det-A	5	5	.500	28	9	2	0	0	104	99	12	25	46	11.0	3.63	104	.256	.306	0	—	0	2	-1	0	0.1
1982 Det-A	3	0	1.000	8	2	0	1	0	27²	17	2	7	16	8.1	1.63	250	.179	.243	0	—	0	8	7	1	0.9
1983 Det-A	8	3	.727	29	16	1	0	0	105	100	10	29	63	11.1	3.43	114	.248	.300	0	—	0	7	6	1	0.7
1984 Det-A	7	6	.538	29	16	0	0	0	101	110	13	18	48	11.6	3.74	105	.274	.309	0	—	0	-3	-0	1	0.3
1985 Tex-A	3	7	.300	34	4	0	0	1	88	100	10	22	42	12.7	4.19	101	.287	.333	0	—	0	1	0	-1	0.1
1986 Tex-A	0	0	—	6	0	0	0	0	10²	19	1	3	3	18.6	5.91	73	.404	.440	0	—	0	-2	-0	0	0.0
Total 10	60	53	.531	248	132	36	7	17	1106	1125	113	258	448	11.5	3.47	117	.266	.313	0	—	0	63	73	3	7.3

● JORGE RUBIO Rubio, Jorge Jesus (Chavez) b: 4/23/45, Mexicali, Mexico BR/TR, 6'3", 200 lbs. Deb: 4/21/66

1966 Cal-A	2	1	.667	7	4	1	0	0	27¹	22	2	16	27	12.8	2.96	113	.220	.333	0	.000	-1	1	1	-0	0.0
1967 Cal-A	0	2	.000	3	3	0	1	0	15	18	2	9	4	18.6	3.60	87	.316	.443	1	.333	1	-1	-1	0	0.0
Total 2	2	3	.400	10	7	1	1	0	42¹	40	4	25	31	14.9	3.19	103	.255	.374	1	.091	-0	1	-0	-0	0.0

YEAR TM/L	W	L	PCT	G	GS	CG	SH	SV	IP	H	HR	BB	SO	RAT	ERA	ERA+	OAV	OOB	BH	AVG	PB	PR	/A	PD	TPI
● **DAVE RUCKER** Rucker, David Michael b: 9/1/57, San Bernardino, Cal BL/TL, 6'1", 190 lbs. Deb: 4/12/81																									
1981 Det-A	0	0	—	2	0	0	0	0	4	3	0	1	2	11.3	6.75	56	.188	.278	0	—	0	-1	-1	-0	0.0
1982 Det-A	5	6	.455	27	4	1	0	0	64	62	4	23	31	12.2	3.38	120	.251	.320	0	—	0	5	5	0	0.8
1983 Det-A	1	2	.333	4	0	0	0	0	9	18	2	8	6	27.0	17.00	23	.419	.519	0	—	0	-13	-13	0	-2.7
StL-N	5	3	.625	34	0	0	0	0	37	36	1	18	22	13.4	2.43	149	.263	.353	0	.000	-0	5	5	0	1.0
1984 StL-N	2	4	.400	50	0	0	0	0	73	62	0	34	38	12.0	2.10	166	.237	.327	1	.143	0	12	11	-1	0.6
1985 Phi-N	3	2	.600	39	3	0	0	0	79¹	83	6	40	41	14.2	4.31	85	.279	.368	4	.333	2	-6	-6	0	-0.1
1986 Phi-N	0	2	.000	19	0	0	0	0	25	34	4	14	14	17.3	5.76	67	.340	.421	0	.000	-0	-6	-5	0	-0.4
1988 Pit-N	0	2	.000	31	0	0	0	0	28¹	39	2	9	16	15.2	4.76	71	.328	.375	0	.000	-0	-4	-4	0	-0.3
Total 7	16	20	.444	206	10	1	0	1	319²	337	19	147	170	13.9	3.94	94	.276	.357	5	.192	1	-8	-9	0	-1.1
● **NAP RUCKER** Rucker, George b: 9/30/1884, Crabapple, Ga. d: 12/19/70, Alpharetta, Ga. BR/TL, 5'11", 190 lbs. Deb: 4/15/07																									
1907 Bro-N	15	13	.536	37	30	26	4	0	275¹	242	3	80	131	10.8	2.06	114	.242	.303	15	.155	-1	13	9	-1	0.7
1908 Bro-N	17	19	.472	42	37	30	6	1	333¹	265	1	125	199	11.0	2.08	113	.231	.317	21	.179	-1	11	10	4	1.5
1909 Bro-N	13	19	.406	38	33	28	6	1	309¹	245	6	101	201	11.5	2.24	116	.228	.303	12	.119	-5	12	12	-2	0.5
1910 Bro-N	17	18	.486	41	39	**27**	**6**	0	**320¹**	293	5	84	147	10.8	2.58	117	.251	.306	23	.209	-1	16	16	-2	1.3
1911 Bro-N	22	18	.550	48	33	23	5	4	315²	255	12	110	190	10.6	2.71	123	.226	.300	21	.202	2	24	22	2	3.0
1912 Bro-N	18	21	.462	45	34	23	**6**	4	297²	272	6	72	151	10.5	2.21	152	.250	.298	25	.245	2	40	38	2	**5.2**
1913 Bro-N	14	15	.483	41	33	16	4	3	260	236	3	67	111	10.7	2.87	115	.249	.304	21	.241	2	10	12	-4	1.1
1914 Bro-N	7	6	.538	16	16	5	0	0	103²	113	2	27	35	12.3	3.39	84	.275	.323	9	.265	2	-7	-6	-0	-0.5
1915 Bro-N	9	4	.692	19	15	7	1	1	122²	134	3	28	72	12.0	2.42	115	.279	.322	6	.214	-1	4	5	1	0.8
1916 *Bro-N	2	1	.667	9	3	1	0	0	37¹	34	0	7	14	10.1	1.69	159	.241	.282	1	.091	-1	4	4	0	0.2
Total 10	134	134	.500	336	273	186	38	14	2375¹	2089	41	701	1217	10.8	2.42	119	.243	.306	157	.195	1	127	121	1	13.8
● **ERNIE RUDOLPH** Rudolph, Ernest William b: 2/13/09, Black River Falls, Wis. BL/TL, 5'8", 165 lbs. Deb: 6/16/45																									
1945 Bro-N	1	0	1.000	7	0	0	0	0	8²	12	1	7	3	19.7	5.19	72	.333	.442	0	—	1	-1	-1	0	-0.1
● **DON RUDOLPH** Rudolph, Frederick Donald b: 8/16/31, Baltimore, Md. d: 9/12/68, Granada Hills, Cal BL/TL, 5'11", 195 lbs. Deb: 9/21/57																									
1957 Chi-A	1	0	1.000	5	0	0	0	0	12	6	2	2	6	6.0	2.25	166	.146	.186	1	.500	1	2	2	-0	0.2
1958 Chi-A	1	0	1.000	7	0	0	0	1	7	4	0	5	2	11.6	2.57	141	.190	.346	0	—	0	1	1	0	0.2
1959 Chi-A	0	0	—	4	0	0	0	0	3	4	0	2	0	18.0	0.00	—	.333	.429	0	—	0	1	1	0	0.1
Cin-N	0	0	—	5	0	0	0	0	7¹	13	1	3	8	19.6	4.91	83	.394	.444	0	.000	-0	-1	-1	0	0.0
1962 Cle-A	0	0	—	1	0	0	0	0	0¹	1	0	0	0	27.0	0.00	—	1.000	1.000	0	—	0	0	0	0	0.0
Was-A	8	10	.444	37	23	6	2	0	176¹	187	13	42	68	11.8	3.62	111	.274	.319	10	.175	-1	7	8	-1	0.8
Yr	8	10	.444	38	23	6	2	0	176²	188	13	42	68	11.9	3.62	112	.275	.320	10	.175	-1	7	8	-1	0.8
1963 Was-A	7	19	.269	37	26	4	0	1	174	189	28	36	74	11.9	4.55	82	.275	.317	8	.178	-1	-18	-16	-1	-2.1
1964 Was-A	1	3	.250	28	8	0	0	0	70¹	81	10	12	32	11.9	4.09	90	.290	.320	1	.067	-1	-4	-3	-0	-0.3
Total 6	18	32	.360	124	57	10	2	3	450¹	485	54	102	182	11.9	4.00	96	.276	.319	20	.167	3	-11	-8	-1	-1.1
● **DICK RUDOLPH** Rudolph, Richard "Baldy" b: 8/25/1887, New York, N.Y. d: 10/20/49, Bronx, N.Y. BR/TR, 5'9.5", 160 lbs. Deb: 9/30/10 C																									
1910 NY-N	0	1	.000	3	1	1	0	0	12	21	0	2	9	17.3	7.50	40	.350	.371	1	.250	0	-6	-6	-0	-0.7
1911 NY-N	0	0	—	1	0	0	0	0	2	2	0	0	0	9.0	9.00	37	.250	.250	1	1.000	0	-1	-1	-0	0.0
1913 Bos-N	14	13	.519	33	22	17	2	0	249¹	258	4	59	109	11.5	2.92	112	.276	.320	21	.239	4	8	10	5	1.9
1914 *Bos-N	26	10	.722	42	36	31	6	0	336¹	288	9	61	138	**9.4**	2.35	117	.238	.276	15	.125	-1	16	15	2	1.7
1915 Bos-N	22	19	.537	44	43	30	3	1	341¹	304	4	64	147	9.9	2.37	109	.242	.282	23	.198	6	14	8	1	1.7
1916 Bos-N	19	12	.613	41	38	27	5	3	312	266	2	38	133	**8.9**	2.16	115	.235	**.261**	16	.158	1	16	11	6	1.9
1917 Bos-N	13	13	.500	31	30	22	5	0	242²	252	1	54	96	11.5	3.41	75	.272	.314	20	.230	3	-19	-23	1	-2.1
1918 Bos-N	9	10	.474	21	20	15	3	0	154	144	2	30	48	10.2	2.57	104	.255	.292	10	.185	-1	3	2	1	0.3
1919 Bos-N	13	18	.419	37	32	24	2	2	273²	282	5	54	76	11.1	2.17	132	.276	.314	17	.193	2	23	21	0	2.9
1920 Bos-N	4	8	.333	18	11	3	0	0	89	104	4	24	24	13.3	4.04	75	.294	.346	5	.185	-0	-9	-10	0	-1.2
1922 Bos-N	0	2	.000	3	3	1	0	0	16	22	2	5	3	15.2	5.06	79	.328	.375	2	.400	-1	-2	-2	-0	-0.1
1923 Bos-N	1	2	.333	4	4	1	1	0	19¹	27	0	10	3	17.7	3.72	107	.333	.413	0	.000	-1	1	1	-0	0.0
1927 Bos-N	0	0	—	1	0	0	0	0	1¹	1	0	1	0	13.5	0.00	—	.200	.333	0	—	0	1	1	-0	0.0
Total 13	121	108	.528	279	240	172	27	8	2049	1971	35	402	786	10.5	2.66	104	.258	.298	131	.188	14	44	25	15	6.3
● **MATT RUEBEL** Ruebel, Matthew Alexander b: 10/16/69, Cincinnati, Ohio BL/TL, 6'2", 180 lbs. Deb: 5/21/96																									
1996 Pit-N	1	1	.500	26	7	0	0	1	58²	64	7	25	22	14.6	4.60	95	.277	.363	3	.231	1	-3	-1	-0	0.0
● **KIRK RUETER** Rueter, Kirk Wesley b: 12/1/70, Hoyleton, Ill. BL/TL, 6'3", 190 lbs. Deb: 7/7/93																									
1993 Mon-N	8	0	1.000	14	14	1	0	0	85²	85	5	18	31	10.8	2.73	153	.264	.303	2	.077	-1	12	14	2	1.3
1994 Mon-N	7	3	.700	20	20	0	0	0	92¹	106	11	23	50	12.8	5.17	82	.294	.340	4	.118	-1	-10	-10	0	-1.0
1995 Mon-N	5	3	.625	9	9	1	1	0	47¹	38	3	9	28	9.1	3.23	133	.224	.267	0	.000	-2	5	6	1	0.8
1996 Mon-N	5	6	.455	16	16	0	0	0	78²	91	12	22	30	13.2	4.58	94	.294	.345	3	.120	-1	-6	-6	2	-0.1
SF-N	1	2	.333	4	3	0	0	0	23¹	18	0	5	16	8.9	1.93	212	.207	.250	1	.143	0	6	6	-0	0.7
Yr	6	8	.429	20	19	0	0	0	102	109	12	27	46	12.0	3.97	107	.273	.319	4	.125	-1	3	3	2	0.6
Total 4	26	14	.650	63	62	2	1	0	327¹	338	31	77	155	11.5	3.88	109	.271	.316	10	.093	-4	10	13	5	1.7
● **DUTCH RUETHER** Ruether, Walter Henry b: 9/13/1893, Alameda, Cal. d: 5/16/70, Phoenix, Ariz. BL/TL, 6'1.5", 180 lbs. Deb: 4/13/17 ◆																									
1917 Chi-N	2	0	1.000	10	4	1	0	0	36¹	37	0	12	23	12.9	2.48	117	.285	.359	12	.273	2	1	1	-0	0.4
Cin-N	1	2	.333	7	4	1	0	0	35²	43	0	14	12	14.9	3.53	74	.323	.396	5	.208	1	-3	-4	-0	-0.2
Yr	3	2	.600	17	8	2	1	0	72	80	0	26	35	13.5	3.00	92	.301	.367	17	.250	3	-2	-2	-0	0.2
1918 Cin-N	0	1	.000	2	2	1	0	0	10	10	0	3	10	12.6	2.70	99	.244	.311	0	.000	-0	0	-0	-0	-0.1
1919 *Cin-N	19	6	**.760**	33	29	20	3	0	242²	195	1	83	78	10.6	1.82	153	.223	.295	24	.261	6	30	26	-3	3.1
1920 Cin-N	16	12	.571	37	33	23	5	3	265²	235	2	96	99	11.5	2.47	123	.247	.321	20	.192	-1	20	17	0	1.7
1921 Bro-N	10	13	.435	36	27	12	1	0	211¹	247	6	67	78	13.7	4.26	91	.299	.356	34	.351	11	-11	-9	-1	0.2
1922 Bro-N	21	12	.636	35	35	26	2	0	267¹	290	11	92	89	13.1	3.53	115	.282	.345	26	.208	6	17	16	-0	2.2
1923 Bro-N	15	14	.517	34	34	20	0	0	275	308	11	86	87	13.1	4.22	92	.287	.343	32	.274	4	-7	-10	-2	-0.6
1924 Bro-N	8	13	.381	30	21	13	2	3	168	190	4	45	63	12.9	3.91	96	.282	.332	15	.242	-0	-1	-3	1	0.0
1925 *Was-A	18	7	.720	30	29	16	1	0	223¹	241	6	105	68	14.3	3.87	109	.281	.365	36	.333	6	13	9	-3	1.6
1926 Was-A	12	6	.667	23	23	9	0	0	169¹	214	5	66	48	15.1	4.84	80	.311	.375	23	.250	4	-15	-18	-2	-1.4
*NY-A	2	3	.400	5	5	1	0	0	36	32	1	18	12	12.8	3.50	110	.248	.345	2	.095	-2	2	1	-1	-0.1
Yr	14	9	.609	28	28	10	0	0	205¹	246	6	84	60	14.5	4.60	84	.300	.366	25	.221	3	-13	-17	-3	-1.5
1927 NY-A	13	6	.684	27	19	9	0	0	184	202	8	52	45	12.8	3.38	114	.287	.343	21	.262	5	10	10	0	1.4
Total 11	137	95	.591	309	272	155	18	8	2124²	2244	54	739	708	12.9	3.50	104	.277	.342	250	.258	45	60	36	-9	8.2
● **SCOTT RUFFCORN** Ruffcorn, Scott Patrick b: 12/29/69, Austin, Tex. BR/TR, 6'4", 215 lbs. Deb: 6/19/93																									
1993 Chi-A	0	2	.000	3	2	0	0	0	10	9	2	10	2	17.1	8.10	52	.265	.432	0	—	0	-4	-4	-1	-0.7
1994 Chi-A	0	2	.000	2	1	0	0	0	6¹	15	1	3	6	28.4	12.79	36	.455	.526	0	—	0	-6	-6	-0	-1.1
1995 Chi-A	0	0	—	4	0	0	0	0	8	10	0	13	5	28.1	7.88	57	.333	.556	0	—	0	-3	-3	-0	0.0
1996 Chi-A	0	1	.000	3	1	0	0	0	6¹	10	1	6	3	22.7	11.37	41	.370	.485	0	—	0	-4	-5	-0	-0.5
Total 4	0	5	.000	12	5	0	0	0	30²	44	4	34	13	23.5	9.68	46	.355	.500	0	—	0	-17	-18	-1	-2.3
● **BRUCE RUFFIN** Ruffin, Bruce Wayne b: 10/4/63, Lubbock, Tex. BB/TL, 6'2", 205 lbs. Deb: 6/28/86																									
1986 Phi-N	9	4	.692	21	21	6	0	0	146¹	138	6	44	70	11.3	2.46	157	.251	.308	4	.073	-3	20	23	-1	1.5
1987 Phi-N	11	14	.440	35	35	3	1	0	204²	236	17	73	93	13.7	4.35	97	.298	.359	4	.055	-5	-6	-3	-0	-0.8
1988 Phi-N	6	10	.375	55	15	3	0	3	144¹	151	7	80	82	14.6	4.43	80	.275	.370	4	.121	-0	-16	-14	-1	-1.5
1989 Phi-N	6	10	.375	24	23	1	0	0	125²	152	6	62	70	15.3	4.44	80	.301	.377	6	.176	-2	-13	-13	-1	-1.2
1990 Phi-N	6	13	.316	32	25	2	1	0	149	178	6	62	79	14.6	5.38	71	.297	.364	3	.068	-2	-26	-26	-0	-3.1
1991 Phi-N	4	7	.364	31	15	1	0	0	119	125	6	38	65	12.4	3.78	97	.272	.329	0	.000	-1	-1	-2	-0	-0.3
1992 Mil-A	1	6	.143	25	6	1	0	0	58	66	7	41	45	16.6	6.67	57	.293	.402	0	—	-0	-18	-18	-0	-2.0
1993 Col-N	6	5	.545	59	12	0	0	2	139¹	145	10	69	126	13.9	3.87	123	.269	.352	2	.080	-1	3	14	-0	0.9

YEAR	TM/L	W	L	PCT	G	GS	CG	SH	SV	IP	H	HR	BB	SO	RAT	ERA	ERA+	OAV	OOB	BH	AVG	PB	PR	/A	PD	TPI
1994	Col-N	4	5	.444	56	0	0	0	16	55²	55	6	30	65	13.9	4.04	123	.253	.347	1	.250	0	1	6	1	1.2
1995	*Col-N	0	1	.000	37	0	0	0	11	34	26	1	19	23	11.9	2.12	254	.222	.331	0	.000	-0	8	12	0	1.0
1996	Col-N	7	5	.583	71	0	0	0	24	69²	55	5	29	74	10.9	4.00	136	.212	.291	0	.000	0	2	11	0	2.4
Total	11	60	80	.429	446	152	17	3	56	1246	1327	89	547	812	13.6	4.17	98	.276	.351	24	.081	-10	-47	-11	1	-1.8

● **JOHNNY RUFFIN**   Ruffin, Johnny Renando b: 7/29/71, Butler, Ala.   BR/TR, 6'3", 172 lbs.   Deb: 8/8/93

YEAR	TM/L	W	L	PCT	G	GS	CG	SH	SV	IP	H	HR	BB	SO	RAT	ERA	ERA+	OAV	OOB	BH	AVG	PB	PR	/A	PD	TPI
1993	Cin-N	2	1	.667	21	0	0	0	2	37²	36	4	11	30	11.5	3.58	112	.247	.304	1	.333	0	2	2	0	0.2
1994	Cin-N	7	2	.778	51	0	0	0	1	70	57	7	27	44	10.8	3.09	134	.223	.297	0	.000	-1	9	8	-1	0.8
1995	Cin-N	0	0	—	10	0	0	0	0	13¹	4	0	11	11	10.1	1.35	305	.093	.278	0	.000	0	4	4	0	0.0
1996	Cin-N	1	3	.250	49	0	0	0	0	62¹	71	10	37	69	15.9	5.49	76	.292	.390	2	.500	1	-9	-9	-0	-0.5
Total	4	10	6	.625	131	0	0	0	3	183¹	168	21	86	154	12.6	3.88	106	.244	.331	3	.176	-0	6	5	-1	0.5

● **RED RUFFING**   Ruffing, Charles Herbert b: 5/3/04, Granville, Ill. d: 2/17/86, Mayfield Hts., O.   BR/TR, 6'1.5", 205 lbs.   Deb: 5/31/24   CH◆

YEAR	TM/L	W	L	PCT	G	GS	CG	SH	SV	IP	H	HR	BB	SO	RAT	ERA	ERA+	OAV	OOB	BH	AVG	PB	PR	/A	PD	TPI
1924	Bos-A	0	0	—	8	2	0	0	0	23	29	0	9	10	16.0	6.65	66	.333	.414	1	.143	-0	-6	-6	-1	0.0
1925	Bos-A	9	18	.333	37	27	13	3	1	217¹	253	10	75	64	13.7	5.01	91	.299	.357	17	.215	-0	-15	-11	-1	-1.2
1926	Bos-A	6	15	.286	37	22	6	0	2	166	169	4	68	58	13.1	4.39	93	.274	.351	10	.196	0	-7	-6	-1	-0.8
1927	Bos-A	5	13	.278	26	18	10	0	2	158¹	160	7	87	77	14.3	4.66	91	.277	.375	14	.255	1	-9	-8	-0	-0.6
1928	Bos-A	10	25	.286	42	34	25	1	2	289¹	303	6	96	118	12.7	3.89	106	.275	.339	38	.314	11	5	7	-3	1.7
1929	Bos-A	9	22	.290	35	30	18	1	1	244¹	280	17	118	109	14.7	4.86	88	.297	.376	35	.307	5	-17	-16	-1	-1.0
1930	Bos-A	0	3	.000	4	3	1	0	0	24	32	1	6	14	14.6	6.38	72	.323	.368	3	.273	1	-5	-5	-1	-0.5
	NY-A	15	5	.750	34	25	12	2	1	197²	200	10	62	117	12.0	4.14	104	.260	.317	37	.374	17	11	3	-2	1.6
	Yr	15	8	.652	38	28	13	2	1	221²	232	11	68	131	12.3	4.38	99	.267	.322	40	.364	18	7	-1	-3	1.1
1931	NY-A	16	14	.533	37	30	19	1	2	237	240	11	87	132	12.6	4.41	90	.256	.323	38	.330	11	-1	-3	-3	-0.3
1932	*NY-A	18	7	.720	35	29	22	3	2	259	219	16	115	**190**	11.7	3.09	132	**.226**	.311	38	.306	14	40	28	-2	3.5
1933	NY-A	9	14	.391	35	28	18	0	3	235	230	7	93	122	12.5	3.91	99	.258	.330	29	.252	8	10	-1	-0	0.7
1934	NY-A★	19	11	.633	36	31	19	5	0	256¹	232	18	104	149	11.8	3.93	103	.236	.310	28	.248	7	16	4	-3	0.7
1935	NY-A	16	11	.593	30	29	19	2	0	222	201	17	76	81	11.3	3.12	130	.239	.303	37	.339	14	33	23	-2	3.5
1936	NY-A	20	12	.625	33	33	25	3	0	271	274	22	90	102	12.2	3.85	121	.263	.323	39	.291	16	36	24	2	3.9
1937	NY-A	20	7	.741	31	31	22	4	0	256¹	242	17	68	131	10.9	2.98	149	.247	.296	26	.202	3	47	42	-4	3.1
1938	*NY-A☆	**21**	7	**.750**	31	31	22	3	0	247¹	246	16	82	127	11.9	3.31	137	.258	.317	24	.224	10	**41**	34	-2	**4.0**
1939	*NY-A★	21	7	.750	28	28	22	**5**	0	233¹	211	15	75	95	11.1	2.93	149	.240	.301	35	.307	9	44	37	-2	4.7
1940	NY-A★	15	12	.556	30	30	20	3	0	226	218	24	76	97	11.8	3.38	119	.252	.314	11	.124	-3	25	16	-3	1.1
1941	*NY-A☆	15	6	.714	23	23	13	2	0	185²	177	13	54	60	11.2	3.54	111	.252	.306	27	.303	12	13	8	-3	1.6
1942	*NY-A☆	14	7	.667	24	24	16	4	0	193²	183	10	41	82	10.5	3.21	107	.250	.292	20	.250	7	10	5	-2	1.0
1945	NY-A	7	3	.700	11	11	8	1	0	87¹	85	2	20	24	10.9	2.89	120	.251	.294	10	.217	1	5	6	-2	0.5
1946	NY-A	5	1	.833	8	8	4	2	0	61	37	2	23	19	8.9	1.77	195	.171	.251	3	.120	-1	12	11	-1	0.9
1947	Chi-A	3	5	.375	9	9	1	0	0	53	63	7	16	11	13.4	6.11	60	.290	.339	5	.208	-0	-14	-14	-0	-1.8
Total	22	273	225	.548	624	536	335	45	16	4344	4284	254	1541	1987	12.2	3.80	109	.258	.323	521	.269	143	272	174	-34	26.9

● **VERN RUHLE**   Ruhle, Vernon Gerald b: 1/25/51, Coleman, Mich.   BR/TR, 6'1", 187 lbs.   Deb: 9/9/74

YEAR	TM/L	W	L	PCT	G	GS	CG	SH	SV	IP	H	HR	BB	SO	RAT	ERA	ERA+	OAV	OOB	BH	AVG	PB	PR	/A	PD	TPI
1974	Det-A	2	0	1.000	5	3	1	0	0	33	35	1	6	10	11.5	2.73	139	.273	.311	0	—	0	3	4	-1	-0.1
1975	Det-A	11	12	.478	32	31	8	3	0	190	199	17	65	67	12.8	4.03	100	.266	.330	0	—	0	-5	-0	-2	-0.5
1976	Det-A	9	12	.429	32	32	5	1	0	199²	227	19	59	88	13.1	3.92	95	.288	.340	0	—	0	-9	-5	-0	-0.7
1977	Det-A	3	5	.375	14	10	0	0	0	66¹	83	9	15	27	13.7	5.70	75	.305	.348	0	—	0	-12	-10	-1	-1.1
1978	Hou-N	3	3	.500	13	10	2	2	0	68	57	0	20	27	10.3	2.12	156	.224	.283	1	.056	-1	11	9	-1	0.6
1979	Hou-N	2	6	.250	13	10	2	2	0	66¹	64	9	8	33	10.0	4.07	86	.249	.277	1	.053	-1	-2	-4	-1	-0.6
1980	*Hou-N	12	4	.750	28	22	6	2	0	159¹	148	7	29	55	10.2	2.37	139	.251	.289	12	.245	4	22	16	-2	1.9
1981	*Hou-N	4	6	.400	20	15	1	0	1	102	97	6	20	39	10.4	2.91	113	.250	.289	6	.250	3	7	4	-2	0.6
1982	Hou-N	9	13	.409	31	21	3	2	1	149	169	12	24	56	11.9	3.93	84	.289	.321	4	.098	-0	-5	-10	-1	-1.5
1983	Hou-N	8	5	.615	41	9	0	0	3	114²	107	13	36	43	11.5	3.69	92	.249	.312	2	.105	0	-1	-4	0	-0.3
1984	Hou-N	1	9	.100	40	6	1	0	0	90¹	112	5	29	60	14.3	4.58	72	.309	.365	1	.083	0	-10	-13	-1	-1.3
1985	Cle-A	2	10	.167	42	16	1	0	3	125	139	16	30	54	12.3	4.32	96	.283	.326	0	—	0	-2	-3	-0	-0.3
1986	*Cal-A	1	3	.250	16	3	0	0	1	47²	46	7	5	23	10.2	4.15	99	.247	.278	0	—	0	-0	-1	0	0.0
Total	13	67	88	.432	327	188	29	12	11	1411¹	1483	119	348	582	11.9	3.73	97	.270	.318	27	.148	6	-5	-16	-8	-3.3

● **ANDY RUSH**   Rush, Jesse Howard b: 12/26/1889, Longton, Kan.   d: 3/16/69, Fresno, Cal.   BR/TR, 6'3", 180 lbs.   Deb: 4/16/25

YEAR	TM/L	W	L	PCT	G	GS	CG	SH	SV	IP	H	HR	BB	SO	RAT	ERA	ERA+	OAV	OOB	BH	AVG	PB	PR	/A	PD	TPI
1925	Bro-N	0	1	.000	4	2	0	0	0	9²	16	3	5	4	19.6	9.31	45	.364	.429	0	.000	-0	-5	-6	0	-0.5

● **BOB RUSH**   Rush, Robert Ransom b: 12/21/25, Battle Creek, Mich   BR/TR, 6'4", 205 lbs.   Deb: 4/22/48

YEAR	TM/L	W	L	PCT	G	GS	CG	SH	SV	IP	H	HR	BB	SO	RAT	ERA	ERA+	OAV	OOB	BH	AVG	PB	PR	/A	PD	TPI
1948	Chi-N	5	11	.313	36	16	4	0	0	133¹	153	8	37	72	12.9	3.92	100	.287	.335	5	.128	-2	1	-0	1	-0.1
1949	Chi-N	10	18	.357	35	27	9	1	4	201	197	10	79	80	12.4	4.07	99	.255	.324	2	.032	-7	-1	-1	1	-0.7
1950	Chi-N☆	13	20	.394	39	34	19	1	1	254²	261	11	93	93	12.7	3.71	113	.265	.332	15	.167	-1	12	14	2	1.8
1951	Chi-N	11	12	.478	37	29	12	2	2	211¹	212	16	68	129	12.1	3.83	107	.254	.312	13	.191	-0	3	6	1	0.7
1952	Chi-N★	17	13	.567	34	32	17	4	0	250¹	205	14	81	157	10.5	2.70	143	.216	.282	28	.292	7	29	32	2	**5.0**
1953	Chi-N	9	14	.391	29	28	8	1	0	166²	177	17	66	84	13.4	4.54	98	.270	.341	6	.111	-2	-5	-2	1	-0.3
1954	Chi-N	13	15	.464	33	32	11	0	0	236¹	213	12	103	124	12.2	3.77	111	.243	.326	23	.277	7	8	11	3	2.3
1955	Chi-N	13	11	.542	33	33	14	3	0	234	204	19	73	130	10.7	3.50	117	.234	.295	9	.110	-3	14	15	1	1.2
1956	Chi-N	13	10	.565	32	32	13	1	0	239²	210	30	59	104	10.2	3.19	118	.233	.282	8	.098	-3	15	15	-2	0.9
1957	Chi-N	6	16	.273	31	29	5	0	0	205¹	211	16	66	103	12.2	4.38	88	.265	.323	14	.203	2	-12	-12	-2	-1.1
1958	*Mil-N	10	6	.625	28	20	5	2	0	147¹	142	18	31	84	10.6	3.42	103	.253	.293	9	.200	2	9	2	-2	0.2
1959	Mil-N	5	6	.455	31	9	1	1	0	101¹	102	5	23	64	11.2	2.40	148	.257	.299	6	.188	0	17	13	-1	1.3
1960	Mil-N	2	0	1.000	10	0	0	0	1	15	24	2	5	12	17.4	4.20	82	.369	.414	1	.333	1	-1	-1	-0	-0.1
	Chi-A	0	0	—	9	0	0	0	0	14¹	16	4	5	12	13.2	5.65	67	.302	.362	1	1.000	1	-3	-3	0	0.1
Total	13	127	152	.455	417	321	118	16	8	2410²	2327	177	789	1244	11.8	3.65	109	.251	.313	140	.173	0	88	90	7	11.2

● **AMOS RUSIE**   Rusie, Amos Wilson "The Hoosier Thunderbolt" b: 5/30/1871, Mooresville, Ind.   d: 12/6/42, Seattle, Wash.   BR/TR, 6'1", 200 lbs.   Deb: 5/9/1889   H

YEAR	TM/L	W	L	PCT	G	GS	CG	SH	SV	IP	H	HR	BB	SO	RAT	ERA	ERA+	OAV	OOB	BH	AVG	PB	PR	/A	PD	TPI
1889	Ind-N	12	10	.545	33	22	19	1	0	225	246	12	116	109	14.8	5.32	78	.270	.358	18	.175	-3	-33	-29	-2	-2.5
1890	NY-N	29	34	.460	67	62	56	1	1	548²	436	3	289	**341**	12.3	2.56	137	**.212**	.316	79	.278	10	62	58	6	**6.9**
1891	NY-N	33	20	.623	61	57	52	**6**	1	500¹	391	6	262	**337**	12.1	2.55	125	**.207**	.310	54	.245	4	44	36	2	3.7
1892	NY-N	32	31	.508	65	62	59	2	0	541	410	7	270	304	11.5	2.84	113	.202	.299	54	.211	-0	27	23	6	2.7
1893	NY-N	33	21	.611	**56**	52	**50**	4	1	**482**	451	15	218	208	12.8	3.23	144	**.240**	.324	57	.269	3	**77**	76	3	**7.2**
1894	*NY-N	**36**	13	**.735**	54	50	45	**3**	1	444	426	10	200	195	12.8	2.78	**189**	**.250**	**.330**	52	.280	3	126	122	8	**11.0**
1895	NY-N	23	23	.500	49	47	42	**4**	0	393¹	384	9	159	201	12.6	3.73	124	.252	.325	44	.246	-5	46	40	3	3.3
1897	NY-N	28	10	.737	38	37	35	2	0	322¹	314	6	87	135	11.5	2.54	164	.253	.308	40	.278	3	64	58	2	6.1
1898	NY-N	20	11	.645	37	36	33	4	1	300	288	6	103	114	12.0	3.03	115	.251	.317	29	.210	-1	19	15	-0	1.2
1901	Cin-N	0	1	.000	3	2	2	0	0	22	43	1	9	6	18.8	8.59	37	.406	.422	1	.125	-0	-13	-13	-0	-0.5
Total	10	246	174	.586	463	427	393	30	5	3778²	3389	75	1707	1950	12.6	3.07	130	.234	.319	428	.247	12	418	384	27	39.1

● **SCOTT RUSKIN**   Ruskin, Scott Drew b: 6/8/63, Jacksonville, Fla.   BR/TL, 6'2", 185 lbs.   Deb: 4/9/90

YEAR	TM/L	W	L	PCT	G	GS	CG	SH	SV	IP	H	HR	BB	SO	RAT	ERA	ERA+	OAV	OOB	BH	AVG	PB	PR	/A	PD	TPI
1990	Pit-N	2	2	.500	44	0	0	0	0	47²	50	2	28	34	15.1	3.02	120	.269	.370	2	.333	2	4	3	0	0.4
	Mon-N	1	0	1.000	23	0	0	0	0	27²	25	2	10	23	11.4	2.28	160	.243	.310	0	.000	-0	5	4	0	0.2
	Yr	3	2	.600	67	0	0	0	0	75¹	75	4	38	57	13.5	2.75	132	.256	.341	2	.250	1	9	7	0	0.6
1991	Mon-N	4	4	.500	64	0	0	0	6	63²	57	4	30	46	12.7	4.24	85	.241	.333	0	.000	-0	-4	-4	0	-0.6
1992	Cin-N	4	3	.571	57	0	0	0	0	53²	56	6	20	43	12.9	5.03	72	.275	.342	0	.000	-0	-9	-9	0	-1.1
1993	Cin-N	0	0	—	1	0	0	0	0	1	3	0	0	0	45.0	18.00	22	.500	.625	0	—	0	-2	-2	0	0.0
Total	4	11	9	.550	192	0	0	0	8	193²	191	15	90	146	13.3	3.95	92	.260	.345	2	.154	1	-6	-7	-1	-1.1

● **JOHN RUSS**   Russ, John b: 4/1/1858, Cannelton, Ind.   d: 1/18/12, Louisville, Ky.   Deb: 7/4/1882   ◆

YEAR	TM/L	W	L	PCT	G	GS	CG	SH	SV	IP	H	HR	BB	SO	RAT	ERA	ERA+	OAV	OOB	BH	AVG	PB	PR	/A	PD	TPI
1882	Bal-a	0	1	.000	1	1	0	0	0	5	10	0	1	0	19.8	7.20	38	.385	.407	1	.333	0	-3	-2	-0	-0.3

● ALLAN RUSSELL
Russell, Allan E. "Rubberarm" b: 7/31/1893, Baltimore, Md. d: 10/20/72, Baltimore, Md. BB/TR, 5'11", 165 lbs. Deb: 9/13/15 F

YEAR TM/L	W	L	PCT	G	GS	CG	SH	SV	IP	H	HR	BB	SO	RAT	ERA	ERA+	OAV	OOB	BH	AVG	PB	PR	/A	PD	TPI
1915 NY-A	1	2	.333	5	3	1	0	0	27	21	1	21	21	14.3	2.67	110	.228	.377	2	.250	0	1	1	-0	0.1
1916 NY-A	6	10	.375	34	19	8	1	6	171¹	138	1	75	104	11.6	3.20	90	.232	.324	2	.044	-3	-7	-6	0	-0.9
1917 NY-A	7	8	.467	25	10	6	0	2	104¹	89	3	39	55	11.6	2.24	120	.236	.319	10	.323	3	5	5	-1	1.1
1918 NY-A	7	11	.389	27	18	7	2	4	141	139	6	73	54	13.9	3.26	87	.267	.363	7	.167	-1	-7	-7	-1	-1.1
1919 NY-A	5	5	.500	23	9	4	1	1	90²	89	6	32	50	12.2	3.47	92	.251	.317	7	.233	0	-2	-3	0	-0.2
Bos-A	10	4	.714	21	11	9	1	4	121¹	105	0	39	63	10.8	2.52	120	.246	.310	5	.122	-1	10	7	-1	0.6
Yr	15	9	.625	44	20	13	2	5	212	194	6	71	113	11.3	2.93	106	.248	.311	12	.169	-1	7	4	-0	0.4
1920 Bos-A	5	6	.455	16	10	7	0	1	107²	100	3	38	53	11.8	3.01	121	.251	.321	5	.122	-2	9	8	1	0.6
1921 Bos-A	6	11	.353	39	14	7	0	3	173	204	10	77	60	15.1	4.11	103	.303	.382	7	.123	-5	3	2	0	-0.3
1922 Bos-A	6	7	.462	34	11	1	0	2	125²	152	6	57	34	15.5	5.01	82	.314	.392	3	.079	-3	-14	-13	2	-1.2
1923 Was-A	10	7	.588	52	5	4	0	9	181¹	177	9	77	67	12.7	3.03	124	.270	.348	10	.200	2	19	15	-3	1.2
1924 *Was-A	5	1	.833	37	0	0	0	8	82¹	83	1	45	17	14.1	4.37	92	.282	.379	5	.278	2	-1	-3	-0	-0.1
1925 Was-A	2	4	.333	32	2	0	0	0	62	85	6	37	25	16.1	5.77	73	.315	.399	2	.143	-1	-10	-12	2	-0.8
Total 11	70	76	.479	345	112	54	5	42	1394¹	1382	59	610	603	13.1	3.52	99	.269	.351	65	.157	-10	-0	-4	-0	-1.0

● LEFTY RUSSELL
Russell, Clarence Dickson b: 7/8/1890, Baltimore, Md. d: 1/22/62, Baltimore, Md. BL/TL, 6'1", 165 lbs. Deb: 10/1/10 F

YEAR TM/L	W	L	PCT	G	GS	CG	SH	SV	IP	H	HR	BB	SO	RAT	ERA	ERA+	OAV	OOB	BH	AVG	PB	PR	/A	PD	TPI
1910 Phi-A	1	0	1.000	1	1	1	0	0	9	8	0	2	5	10.0	0.00	—	.258	.303	0	.000	-0	3	2	0	0.3
1911 Phi-A	0	3	.000	7	2	0	0	0	31²	45	1	18	9	19.3	7.67	41	.357	.456	5	.385	1	-15	-16	1	-1.0
1912 Phi-A	0	2	.000	5	2	1	0	0	17¹	18	1	14	9	18.2	7.27	42	.265	.412	0	.000	-0	-8	-8	0	-0.8
Total 3	1	5	.167	13	5	2	0	0	58	71	2	34	21	17.5	6.36	47	.316	.423	5	.250	0	-20	-22	1	-1.5

● REB RUSSELL
Russell, Ewell Albert b: 4/12/1889, Jackson, Miss. d: 9/30/73, Indianapolis, Ind BL/TL, 5'11", 185 lbs. Deb: 4/18/13 ♦

YEAR TM/L	W	L	PCT	G	GS	CG	SH	SV	IP	H	HR	BB	SO	RAT	ERA	ERA+	OAV	OOB	BH	AVG	PB	PR	/A	PD	TPI
1913 Chi-A	22	16	.579	**52**	36	26	8	4	316²	250	2	79	122	9.5	1.90	154	.219	.273	20	.189	3	36	36	-5	4.2
1914 Chi-A	8	12	.400	38	23	8	1	1	167¹	168	3	33	79	11.0	2.90	92	.268	.308	17	.266	4	-3	-4	-0	-0.1
1915 Chi-A	11	10	.524	41	25	10	3	2	229¹	215	0	47	90	10.5	2.59	115	.249	.292	21	.244	4	9	10	-2	1.1
1916 Chi-A	18	11	.621	56	25	16	5	3	264¹	207	1	42	112	**8.5**	2.42	114	.220	**.254**	13	.143	-4	12	10	-2	0.5
1917 *Chi-A	15	5	**.750**	35	24	11	5	3	189¹	170	1	32	54	9.6	1.95	136	.245	.279	19	.279	5	15	15	-1	1.2
1918 Chi-A	7	5	.583	19	15	10	2	0	124²	117	0	33	38	10.8	2.60	105	.252	.302	7	.140	-1	2	2	-1	-0.2
1919 Chi-A	0	0	—	1	0	0	0	0	1	1	0	1	0	—	—	—	1.000	1.000	—	—	—	0	0	0	0.0
Total 7	81	59	.579	242	148	81	24	13	1291²	1128	7	267	495	9.8	2.33	122	.238	.281	262	.268	10	72	69	-11	7.7

● JACK RUSSELL
Russell, Jack Erwin b: 10/24/05, Paris, Tex. d: 11/3/90, Clearwater, Fla. BR/TR, 6'1.5", 178 lbs. Deb: 5/5/26

YEAR TM/L	W	L	PCT	G	GS	CG	SH	SV	IP	H	HR	BB	SO	RAT	ERA	ERA+	OAV	OOB	BH	AVG	PB	PR	/A	PD	TPI
1926 Bos-A	0	5	.000	36	5	1	0	0	98	94	2	24	17	10.9	3.58	104	.268	.316	4	.190	-0	5	5	4	0.6
1927 Bos-A	4	9	.308	34	15	4	1	0	147	172	5	40	25	13.3	4.10	103	.298	.348	6	.125	-3	1	2	1	0.0
1928 Bos-A	11	14	.440	32	26	10	2	0	201¹	233	6	41	27	12.4	3.84	107	.294	.332	13	.210	-4	8	9	4	0.8
1929 Bos-A	6	18	.250	35	32	13	0	0	227¹	263	12	40	37	12.1	3.92	109	.290	.322	9	.129	-4	8	9	4	0.8
1930 Bos-A	9	20	.310	35	30	15	0	0	229²	302	11	53	35	14.0	5.45	85	.321	.359	14	.177	-3	-20	-21	2	-2.2
1931 Bos-A	10	18	.357	36	31	13	0	0	232	298	7	65	45	14.2	5.16	83	.310	.355	16	.195	-0	-20	-22	3	-1.8
1932 Bos-A	1	7	.125	11	6	1	0	0	39²	61	2	15	7	17.2	6.81	66	.343	.394	1	.091	-1	-10	-10	0	-1.7
Cle-A	5	7	.417	18	11	6	0	1	113	146	5	27	27	13.9	4.70	101	.310	.349	12	.300	2	-3	-1	1	0.4
Yr	6	14	.300	29	17	7	0	1	152²	207	7	42	34	14.7	5.25	89	.319	.361	13	.255	1	-13	-10	2	-1.3
1933 *Was-A	12	6	.667	50	3	2	0	13	124	119	3	32	28	11.0	2.69	156	.255	.305	5	.147	-1	22	21	4	3.4
1934 Was-A☆	5	10	.333	**54**	9	3	0	7	157²	179	6	56	38	13.5	4.17	104	.287	.348	7	.159	-3	6	3	0	0.7
1935 Was-A	4	9	.308	43	7	2	0	3	126	170	10	37	30	14.9	5.71	76	.324	.371	2	.100	1	-18	-20	3	-1.4
1936 Was-A	3	2	.600	18	5	1	0	3	49²	66	3	25	6	16.5	6.34	75	.317	.391	0	.000	-2	-7	-9	1	-0.9
Bos-A	0	3	.000	23	2	0	0	0	40	57	2	16	9	16.4	5.62	94	.345	.403	2	.286	-0	-3	-1	2	0.1
Yr	3	5	.375	41	7	1	0	3	89²	123	5	41	15	16.5	6.02	83	.330	.396	2	.091	-2	-10	-10	3	-0.8
1937 Det-A	2	5	.286	25	0	0	0	4	40¹	63	4	20	10	18.7	7.59	62	.362	.431	0	.000	-2	-13	-13	1	-2.0
1938 *Chi-N	6	1	.857	42	0	0	0	3	102¹	100	1	30	29	11.5	3.34	115	.258	.313	7	.219	0	5	6	3	0.8
1939 Chi-N	4	3	.571	39	0	0	0	1	68²	78	3	24	32	13.4	3.67	107	.282	.339	0	.000	-2	2	2	1	0.1
1940 StL-N	3	4	.429	26	0	0	0	1	54	53	1	26	16	13.2	2.50	160	.252	.335	0	.000	-0	8	9	1	1.1
Total 15	85	141	.376	557	182	71	3	38	2050²	2454	83	571	418	13.4	4.46	97	.299	.346	103	.167	-11	-33	-33	36	-1.2

● JEFF RUSSELL
Russell, Jeffrey Lee b: 9/2/61, Cincinnati, Ohio BR/TR, 6'3", 210 lbs. Deb: 8/13/83

YEAR TM/L	W	L	PCT	G	GS	CG	SH	SV	IP	H	HR	BB	SO	RAT	ERA	ERA+	OAV	OOB	BH	AVG	PB	PR	/A	PD	TPI
1983 Cin-N	4	5	.444	10	10	2	0	0	68¹	58	7	22	40	10.5	3.03	126	.233	.295	3	.143	1	5	6	-0	0.8
1984 Cin-N	6	18	.250	33	30	4	2	0	181²	186	15	65	101	12.6	4.26	89	.263	.329	8	.140	-0	-14	-11	1	-1.1
1985 Tex-A	3	6	.333	13	13	0	0	0	62	85	10	27	44	16.5	7.55	56	.324	.392	0	—		-23	-23	1	-2.6
1986 Tex-A	5	2	.714	37	0	0	0	0	82	74	11	31	54	11.6	3.40	126	.244	.316	0			7	8	2	0.7
1987 Tex-A	5	4	.556	52	2	0	0	3	97¹	109	9	52	56	15.1	4.44	101	.285	.373	0			1	1	-2	0.2
1988 Tex-A★	10	9	.526	34	24	3	0	0	188²	183	15	66	88	12.2	3.82	107	.257	.326	0			3	6	2	0.7
1989 Tex-A★	6	4	.600	71	0	0	0	38	72²	45	4	24	77	8.9	1.98	200	.182	.263	0			15	16	2	3.8
1990 Tex-A	1	5	.167	27	0	0	0	10	25¹	23	1	16	16	13.9	4.26	92	.253	.364	0			-1	-1	0	-0.3
1991 Tex-A	6	4	.600	68	0	0	0	30	79¹	71	11	26	52	11.1	3.29	122	.235	.298	0			7	7	2	1.3
1992 Tex-A	2	3	.400	51	0	0	0	28	56²	51	3	22	43	11.9	1.91	199	.238	.315	0			13	12	1	2.1
*Oak-A	2	0	1.000	8	0	0	0	2	9²	4	0	3	5	6.5	0.00	—	.125	.200	0			4	4	-0	0.9
Yr	4	3	.571	59	0	0	0	30	66¹	55	3	25	48	10.9	1.63	233	.220	.291	0			17	16	0	3.0
1993 Bos-A	1	4	.200	51	0	0	0	33	46²	39	1	14	45	10.4	2.70	171	.231	.293	0			8	10	1	2.2
1994 Bos-A	0	5	.000	29	0	0	0	12	28²	36	5	13	18	14.1	5.14	98	.270	.352	0			-1	-0	-1	-0.2
Cle-A	1	1	.500	13	0	0	0	5	12²	13	2	3	10	11.4	4.97	95	.265	.308	0			-0	-0	-1	-0.1
Yr	1	6	.143	42	0	0	0	17	40²	43	5	16	28	13.1	5.09	97	.264	.330	0			-1	-1	-1	-0.3
1995 Tex-A	1	0	1.000	37	0	0	0	20	32²	36	3	9	21	12.4	3.03	159	.277	.324	0			6	7	1	0.8
1996 *Tex-A	3	3	.500	55	0	0	0	3	56	58	5	22	23	13.5	3.38	157	.269	.347	0			10	12	0	1.1
Total 14	56	73	.434	589	79	11	2	186	1099²	1065	100	415	693	12.3	3.75	112	.255	.326	11	.139	1	40	53	9	10.4

● JOHN RUSSELL
Russell, John Albert b: 10/20/1894, San Mateo, Cal. d: 11/19/30, Ely, Nev. BL/TL, 6'2", 195 lbs. Deb: 7/4/17

YEAR TM/L	W	L	PCT	G	GS	CG	SH	SV	IP	H	HR	BB	SO	RAT	ERA	ERA+	OAV	OOB	BH	AVG	PB	PR	/A	PD	TPI
1917 Bro-N	0	1	.000	5	1	1	0	0	16	12	1	6	10	11.1	4.50	62	.222	.300	1	.250	-0	-3	-3	-0	-0.2
1918 Bro-N	0	0	—	1	0	0	0	0	1	2	0	1	0	27.0	18.00	15	.500	.600	0	—	—	-2	-2	-0	-0.3
1921 Chi-A	2	5	.286	11	9	4	0	0	66¹	82	3	35	15	16.0	5.29	80	.314	.397	10	.400	3	-7	-8	-1	-0.4
1922 Chi-A	0	1	.000	4	1	0	0	1	6²	7	0	4	3	14.9	6.75	60	.280	.379	0	—	-0	-2	-2	-0	-0.3
Total 4	2	7	.222	21	11	5	0	1	90	103	4	46	19	15.0	5.40	73	.299	.384	11	.367	3	-14	-14	-1	-0.9

● JOHN RUSSELL
Russell, John William b: 1/5/61, Oklahoma City, Okla. BR/TR, 6', 200 lbs. Deb: 6/22/84 ♦

YEAR TM/L	W	L	PCT	G	GS	CG	SH	SV	IP	H	HR	BB	SO	RAT	ERA	ERA+	OAV	OOB	BH	AVG	PB	PR	/A	PD	TPI
1989 Atl-N	0	0	—	1	0	0	0	0	0¹	1	0	0	0	0.00	—	—	.000	.000	29	.182	0	0	0	0	0.0

● MARIUS RUSSO
Russo, Marius Ugo "Lefty" b: 7/19/14, Brooklyn, N.Y. BR/TL, 6'1", 190 lbs. Deb: 6/6/39

YEAR TM/L	W	L	PCT	G	GS	CG	SH	SV	IP	H	HR	BB	SO	RAT	ERA	ERA+	OAV	OOB	BH	AVG	PB	PR	/A	PD	TPI
1939 NY-A	8	3	.727	21	11	9	2	0	116	86	6	41	55	9.9	2.41	181	.210	.283	10	.244	1	29	25	2	2.5
1940 NY-A	14	8	.636	30	24	15	0	1	189¹	181	17	55	87	11.3	3.28	123	.249	.303	12	.188	2	23	16	3	2.2
1941 *NY-A☆	14	10	.583	28	27	17	3	1	209²	195	8	47	105	10.6	3.09	127	.247	.322	18	.231	3	25	20	2	2.5
1942 NY-A	4	1	.800	9	5	2	0	0	45¹	42	2	14	15	11.1	2.78	124	.244	.306	4	.235	1	4	3	0	0.5
1943 *NY-A	5	10	.333	24	14	5	1	0	101²	89	7	45	42	12.0	3.72	87	.235	.319	6	.194	1	-5	-6	-0	-0.7
1946 NY-A	0	2	.000	9	3	0	0	0	18²	26	1	11	7	17.8	4.34	80	.333	.416	0	—	-1	-2	-2	-0	-0.2
Total 6	45	34	.570	120	84	48	6	5	680²	618	41	253	311	11.6	3.13	124	.242	.312	50	.213	8	74	57	8	6.8

● DICK RUSTECK
Rusteck, Richard Frank b: 7/12/41, Chicago, Ill. BR/TL, 6'1", 175 lbs. Deb: 6/10/66

YEAR TM/L	W	L	PCT	G	GS	CG	SH	SV	IP	H	HR	BB	SO	RAT	ERA	ERA+	OAV	OOB	BH	AVG	PB	PR	/A	PD	TPI
1966 NY-N	1	2	.333	8	3	1	0	0	24	24	1	8	9	12.0	3.00	121	.276	.337	0	.000	-1	2	2	-0	0.1

● BABE RUTH
Ruth, George Herman "The Bambino" or "The Sultan Of Swat" b: 2/6/1895, Baltimore, Md. d: 8/16/48, New York, N.Y. BL/TL, 6'2", 215 lbs. Deb: 7/11/14 CH♦

YEAR TM/L	W	L	PCT	G	GS	CG	SH	SV	IP	H	HR	BB	SO	RAT	ERA	ERA+	OAV	OOB	BH	AVG	PB	PR	/A	PD	TPI
1914 Bos-A	2	1	.667	5	3	1	0	0	23	21	1	7	3	11.0	3.91	69	.236	.292	2	.200	-0	-3	-3	-0	-0.4
1915 *Bos-A	18	8	.692	32	28	16	1	0	217²	166	3	85	112	10.6	2.44	114	.212	.294	29	.315	16	12	8	1	2.8

YEAR TM/L	W	L	PCT	G	GS	CG	SH	SV	IP	H	HR	BB	SO	RAT	ERA	ERA+	OAV	OOB	BH	AVG	PB	PR	/A	PD	TPI
1916 *Bos-A	23	12	.657	44	41	23	**9**	1	323²	230	0	118	170	9.9	**1.75**	158	**.201**	.280	37	.272	14	**39**	37	0	**5.9**
1917 Bos-A	24	13	.649	41	38	**35**	6	2	326¹	244	2	108	128	10.0	2.01	128	.211	.284	40	.325	17	24	21	2	4.8
1918 *Bos-A	13	7	.650	20	19	18	1	0	166¹	125	1	49	40	9.5	2.22	121	.214	.277	95	.300	12	10	9	4	2.9
1919 Bos-A	9	5	.643	17	15	12	0	1	133¹	148	2	58	30	14.0	2.97	102	.290	.365	139	.322	14	4	1	0	1.5
1920 NY-A	1	0	1.000	1	1	0	0	0	4	3	0	2	0	11.3	4.50	85	.200	.294	172	.376	1	-0	-0	-0	0.0
1921 *NY-A	2	0	1.000	2	1	0	0	0	9	14	1	9	2	23.0	9.00	47	.350	.469	204	.378	2	-5	-5	-0	-0.7
1930 NY-A	1	0	1.000	1	1	1	0	0	9	11	0	2	3	13.0	3.00	143	.306	.342	186	.359	1	2	1	1	0.3
1933 NY-A★	1	0	1.000	1	1	1	0	0	9	12	0	3	0	15.0	5.00	78	.308	.357	138	.301	1	-1	-1	-0	0.0
Total 10	94	46	.671	163	148	107	17	4	1221¹	974	10	441	488	10.6	2.28	122	.221	.297	2873	.342	78	81	67	8	17.1

● **JOHNNY RUTHERFORD** Rutherford, John William "Doc" b: 5/5/25, Belleville, Ont., Canada BL/TR, 5′10.5″, 170 lbs. Deb: 4/30/52

YEAR TM/L	W	L	PCT	G	GS	CG	SH	SV	IP	H	HR	BB	SO	RAT	ERA	ERA+	OAV	OOB	BH	AVG	PB	PR	/A	PD	TPI
1952 *Bro-N	7	7	.500	22	11	4	0	2	97¹	97	9	29	29	11.8	4.25	86	.262	.319	9	.290	2	-6	-7	1	-0.6

● **DICK RUTHVEN** Ruthven, Richard David b: 3/27/51, Sacramento, Cal. BR/TR, 6′3″, 190 lbs. Deb: 4/17/73

YEAR TM/L	W	L	PCT	G	GS	CG	SH	SV	IP	H	HR	BB	SO	RAT	ERA	ERA+	OAV	OOB	BH	AVG	PB	PR	/A	PD	TPI
1973 Phi-N	6	9	.400	25	23	3	1	1	128¹	125	10	75	98	14.2	4.21	90	.257	.360	5	.132	-1	-8	-6	1	-0.7
1974 Phi-N	9	13	.409	35	35	6	0	0	212²	182	11	116	153	12.7	4.02	94	.231	.332	13	.191	-1	-10	-6	-1	-0.8
1975 Phi-N	2	2	.500	11	7	0	0	0	40²	37	7	22	26	13.3	4.20	89	.243	.343	2	.154	-0	-3	-2	-0	-0.3
1976 Atl-N☆	14	17	.452	36	36	8	4	0	240¹	255	14	90	142	13.2	4.19	90	.275	.345	13	.171	-0	-19	-11	2	-1.1
1977 Atl-N	7	13	.350	25	23	6	2	0	151	158	14	62	84	13.2	4.23	105	.267	.338	12	.267	3	-5	4	-2	0.6
1978 Atl-N	2	6	.250	13	13	2	1	0	81	78	8	28	45	11.8	4.11	98	.257	.319	2	.083	-3	-5	-1	-0	-0.2
*Phi-N	13	5	.722	20	20	9	2	0	150²	136	13	28	75	9.9	2.99	119	.248	.285	15	.283	4	10	10	-0	1.6
Yr	15	11	.577	33	33	11	3	0	231²	214	21	56	120	10.5	3.38	111	.250	.297	17	.221	3	5	9	-1	1.4
1979 Phi-N	7	5	.583	20	20	3	2	0	122¹	121	10	37	58	11.8	4.27	90	.256	.313	6	.146	-1	-7	-6	-2	-0.7
1980 *Phi-N	17	10	.630	33	33	6	1	0	223¹	241	9	74	86	12.8	3.55	107	.283	.342	16	.235	4	1	6	-0	1.0
1981 *Phi-N★	12	7	.632	23	22	5	0	0	146²	162	10	54	80	13.4	5.15	70	.281	.346	7	.140	-0	-27	-25	-1	-3.0
1982 Phi-N	11	11	.500	33	31	8	2	0	204¹	189	18	59	115	11.2	3.79	97	.246	.305	7	.109	-2	-4	-3	-2	-0.8
1983 Phi-N	1	3	.250	7	7	0	0	0	33²	46	5	10	26	15.0	5.61	64	.333	.378	1	.111	-1	-7	-8	-0	-0.8
Chi-N	12	9	.571	25	25	5	2	0	149¹	156	17	28	73	11.3	4.10	92	.269	.306	12	.226	2	-8	-5	2	-0.3
Yr	13	12	.520	32	32	5	2	0	183	202	22	38	99	12.0	4.38	86	.279	.318	13	.210	2	-15	-13	2	-1.1
1984 Chi-N	6	10	.375	23	22	0	0	0	126²	154	14	41	55	14.1	5.04	77	.302	.359	7	.159	0	-21	-16	-1	-1.8
1985 Chi-N	4	7	.364	20	15	0	0	0	87¹	103	6	37	26	14.4	4.53	88	.299	.367	5	.208	0	-9	-5	-1	-0.8
1986 Chi-N	0	0	—	6	0	0	0	0	10²	12	4	6	3	15.2	5.06	80	.293	.383	0	.000	-0	-2	-1	-0	-0.1
Total 14	123	127	.492	355	332	61	17	1	2109	2155	165	767	1145	12.6	4.14	92	.267	.333	123	.183	6	-123	-75	-4	-8.1

● **CYCLONE RYAN** Ryan, Daniel R. b: 1866, Cappagh White, Ireland d: 1/30/17, Medfield, Mass. TR , 6′, 200 lbs. Deb: 8/8/1887 ♦

YEAR TM/L	W	L	PCT	G	GS	CG	SH	SV	IP	H	HR	BB	SO	RAT	ERA	ERA+	OAV	OOB	BH	AVG	PB	PR	/A	PD	TPI
1887 NY-a	0	1	.000	2	1	0	0	0	2¹	5	1	6	0	42.4	23.14	18	.455	.647	7	.219	-0	-5	-5	-0	-1.2
1891 Bos-N	0	0	—	1	0	0	0	0	3	2	1	0	9.0	0.00	—	.182	.250	0	.000	-0	1	1	0	0.0
Total 2	0	1	.000	3	1	0	0	0	5¹	7	1	7	0	23.6	10.13	39	.318	.483	7	.212	-0	-4	-4	-0	-1.2

● **JACK RYAN** Ryan, Jack "Gulfport" b: 9/19/1884, Lawrenceville, Ill. d: 10/16/49, Hondsboro, Miss. BR/TR, 5′10″, 165 lbs. Deb: 7/2/08

YEAR TM/L	W	L	PCT	G	GS	CG	SH	SV	IP	H	HR	BB	SO	RAT	ERA	ERA+	OAV	OOB	BH	AVG	PB	PR	/A	PD	TPI
1908 Cle-A	1	1	.500	8	1	0	0	1	35²	27	3	2	7	7.6	2.27	105	.220	.238	1	.091	0	0	0	-0	0.1
1909 Bos-A	4	3	.571	13	8	2	0	0	61¹	65	0	20	24	13.1	3.23	77	.281	.349	4	.211	0	-5	-5	-1	-0.6
1911 Bro-N	0	1	.000	3	1	0	0	0	6	9	1	4	1	21.0	3.00	111	.375	.483	0	.000	0	0	0	-0	0.0
Total 3	5	5	.500	24	10	3	0	1	103	101	4	26	32	11.6	2.88	87	.267	.324	5	.161	1	-4	-4	-0	-0.5

● **JIMMY RYAN** Ryan, James Edward "Pony" b: 2/11/1863, Clinton, Mass. d: 10/26/23, Chicago, Ill. BR/TL, 5′9″, 162 lbs. Deb: 10/8/1885 ♦

YEAR TM/L	W	L	PCT	G	GS	CG	SH	SV	IP	H	HR	BB	SO	RAT	ERA	ERA+	OAV	OOB	BH	AVG	PB	PR	/A	PD	TPI
1886 *Chi-N	0	0	—	5	0	0	0	1	23¹	19	2	13	15	12.3	4.63	79	.257	.368	100	.306	1	-3	-3	0	0.1
1887 Chi-N	2	1	.667	8	3	2	0	0	45	53	3	17	14	15.2	4.20	107	.305	.386	145	.285	2	-1	1	2	0.3
1888 Chi-N	4	0	1.000	8	2	1	0	0	38¹	47	2	12	11	13.9	3.05	99	.297	.347	182	.332	4	-1	-0	0	0.2
1891 Chi-N	0	0	—	2	0	0	0	1	5²	11	1	2	2	20.6	1.59	210	.393	.433	140	.277	1	1	1	-0	0.1
1893 Chi-N	0	0	—	1	0	0	0	0	4²	3	1	0	1	5.8	0.00	—	.176	.176	102	.299	1	2	2	0	0.0
Total 5	6	1	.857	24	5	3	0	2	117	133	7	44	43	14.1	3.62	105	.295	.365	2502	.306	9	-1	2	2	0.6

● **JOHN RYAN** Ryan, John A. (Played 1 Game Under Real Name Of Daniel Sheehan) b: Birmingham, Mich. TR , Deb: 4/19/1884

YEAR TM/L	W	L	PCT	G	GS	CG	SH	SV	IP	H	HR	BB	SO	RAT	ERA	ERA+	OAV	OOB	BH	AVG	PB	PR	/A	PD	TPI
1884 Bal-U	3	2	.600	6	6	6	0	0	51	61	1	16	33	13.6	3.35	80	.277	.326	2	.080	-3	-5	-4	-0	-0.6

● **JOHNNY RYAN** Ryan, John Joseph b: 10/1853, Philadelphia, Pa. d: 3/22/02, Philadelphia, Pa. 5′7.5″, 150 lbs. Deb: 8/19/1873 ♦

YEAR TM/L	W	L	PCT	G	GS	CG	SH	SV	IP	H	HR	BB	SO	RAT	ERA	ERA+	OAV	OOB	BH	AVG	PB	PR	/A	PD	TPI
1874 Bal-n	0	0	—	1	0	0	0	0	3¹	13	0	0	0	35.1	16.20	14	.565	.565	35	.192	-0	-5	-5		0.0
1875 NH-n	1	5	.167	10	6	4	0	0	59¹	70	1	9	1	12.0	3.19	65	.255	.279	23	.158	-1	-6	-7		-0.7
1876 Lou-N	0	0	—	1	0	0	0	0	8	22	0	0	1	24.8	5.63	48	.449	.449	61	.253	-1	-3	-3	-0	0.0
Total 2 n	1	5	.167	11	6	4	0	0	62²	83	1	9	1	13.2	3.88	54	.279	.301	60	.179	-1	-12	-12		-0.7

● **KEN RYAN** Ryan, Kenneth Frederick b: 10/24/68, Pawtucket, R.I. BR/TR, 6′3″, 200 lbs. Deb: 8/31/92

YEAR TM/L	W	L	PCT	G	GS	CG	SH	SV	IP	H	HR	BB	SO	RAT	ERA	ERA+	OAV	OOB	BH	AVG	PB	PR	/A	PD	TPI
1992 Bos-A			—	7	0	0	0	1	7	5	1	5	5	11.6	6.43	66	.174	.344	0	—	0	-2	-2	0	0.0
1993 Bos-A	7	2	.778	47	0	0	0	1	50	43	2	29	49	13.5	3.60	128	.235	.349	0	—	0	4	6	0	0.9
1994 Bos-A	2	3	.400	42	0	0	0	13	48	46	1	17	32	12.0	2.44	206	.256	.323	0	—	0	13	14	-1	1.9
1995 Bos-A	0	4	.000	28	0	0	0	7	32²	34	4	24	34	16.3	4.96	98	.268	.388	0	—	0	-1	-0	-1	-0.1
1996 Phi-N	3	5	.375	62	0	0	0	8	89	71	4	45	70	11.8	2.43	180	.223	.321	1	.143	-0	18	19	0	1.8
Total 5	12	14	.462	186	0	0	0	30	226²	198	13	120	190	12.9	3.18	146	.238	.338	1	.143	-0	31	37	-1	4.5

● **NOLAN RYAN** Ryan, Lynn Nolan b: 1/31/47, Refugio, Tex. BR/TR, 6′2″, 195 lbs. Deb: 9/11/66

YEAR TM/L	W	L	PCT	G	GS	CG	SH	SV	IP	H	HR	BB	SO	RAT	ERA	ERA+	OAV	OOB	BH	AVG	PB	PR	/A	PD	TPI
1966 NY-N	0	1	.000	2	1	0	0	0	3	5	1	3	6	24.0	15.00	24	.357	.471	0	—	0	-4	-4	0	-0.9
1968 NY-N	6	9	.400	21	18	3	0	0	134	93	12	75	133	11.6	3.09	98	.200	.317	5	.114	-1	-2	-1	-2	-0.5
1969 *NY-N	6	3	.667	25	10	2	0	1	89¹	60	3	53	92	11.5	3.53	104	.189	.307	3	.103	-1	1	1	-2	-0.3
1970 NY-N	7	11	.389	27	19	5	2	1	131²	86	10	97	125	12.8	3.42	118	.188	.335	8	.178	-1	9	9	-1	1.0
1971 NY-N	10	14	.417	30	26	3	0	0	152	125	8	116	137	15.2	3.97	86	.219	.365	6	.128	-0	-9	-1	-1	-1.6
1972 Cal-A☆	19	16	.543	39	39	20	**9**	0	284	166	14	157	**329**	10.6	2.28	128	**.171**	.292	13	.135	-1	25	20	-2	2.4
1973 Cal-A★	21	16	.568	41	39	26	4	1	326	238	18	162	**383**	11.2	2.87	123	.203	.304	0	—	0	34	24	-2	2.9
1974 Cal-A	22	16	.579	42	41	26	3	0	332²	221	18	202	**367**	11.7	2.89	119	**.190**	.314	0	—	0	27	20	2	2.8
1975 Cal-A☆	14	12	.538	28	28	10	5	0	198	152	13	132	186	13.3	3.45	103	.213	.342	0	—	0	7	2	-0	0.5
1976 Cal-A	17	18	.486	39	39	21	**7**	0	284¹	193	13	183	**327**	12.1	3.36	99	**.195**	.323	0	—	0	5	-1	0	0.3
1977 Cal-A†	19	16	.543	37	37	22	4	0	299	198	12	204	**341**	12.4	2.77	141	**.193**	.331	0	—	0	**43**	38	0	4.2
1978 Cal-A	10	13	.435	31	31	14	3	0	234²	183	12	148	260	12.8	3.72	97	.220	.340	0	—	0	1	-3	1	0.1
1979 *Cal-A★	16	14	.533	34	34	17	**5**	0	222²	169	15	114	223	11.7	3.60	113	**.212**	.314	0	—	0	15	12	-0	1.6
1980 *Hou-N	11	10	.524	35	35	4	2	0	233²	205	10	98	200	11.8	3.35	106	.236	.316	6	.086	-1	8	8	-1	0.5
1981 *Hou-N★	11	5	.688	21	21	5	3	0	149	99	2	68	140	10.1	**1.69**	195	**.188**	.281	11	.216	3	**30**	27	-1	**3.3**
1982 Hou-N	16	12	.571	35	35	10	3	0	250¹	196	20	109	245	11.3	3.16	105	**.213**	.302	10	.120	1	12	4	0	0.3
1983 Hou-N	14	9	.609	29	29	5	2	0	196¹	134	9	101	183	11.0	2.98	114	**.195**	.302	5	.072	-4	14	9	-0	0.6
1984 Hou-N	12	11	.522	30	30	5	2	0	183²	143	12	69	197	10.6	3.04	99	.211	.288	6	.098	-2	11	6	-3	0.3
1985 Hou-N★	10	12	.455	35	35	4	0	0	232	205	14	95	209	12.0	3.80	91	.239	.322	7	.111	-1	-5	-9	-3	-1.2
1986 *Hou-N	12	8	.600	30	30	1	0	0	178	119	14	82	194	10.4	3.34	110	.188	.285	6	.102	-2	4	5	-1	0.1
1987 Hou-N	8	16	.333	34	34	0	0	0	211²	154	14	87	270	10.4	2.76	142	**.199**	.284	4	.062	-3	31	27	-1	2.5
1988 Hou-N	12	11	.522	33	33	4	1	0	220	186	18	87	228	11.5	3.52	94	.227	.307	4	.057	-3	-2	-5	-3	-1.1
1989 Tex-A★	16	10	.615	32	32	6	2	0	239¹	162	17	98	**301**	10.1	3.20	124	**.187**	.295	0	—	0	18	20	-1	1.9
1990 Tex-A	13	9	.591	30	30	5	2	0	204	137	18	74	232	9.6	3.44	114	**.188**	**.269**	0	—	0	11	11	-2	0.9
1991 Tex-A	12	6	.667	27	27	2	2	0	173	102	12	72	203	9.3	2.91	138	**.172**	**.267**	0	—	0	23	21	-1	2.0
1992 Tex-A	5	9	.357	27	27	2	0	0	157¹	138	9	69	157	12.5	3.72	102	.233	.331	0	—	0	-0	-3	-2	-0.2
1993 Tex-A	5	5	.500	13	13	0	0	0	66¹	54	5	40	46	12.9	4.88	85	.220	.331	0	—	0	-4	-5	0	-0.8
Total 27	324	292	.526	807	773	222	61	3	5386	3923	321	2795	5714	11.5	3.19	111	.204	.309	94	.110	-17	309	218	-29	20.8

● **ROSY RYAN** Ryan, Wilfred Patrick Dolan b: 3/15/1898, Worcester, Mass. d: 12/10/80, Scottsdale, Ariz. BL/TR, 6′, 185 lbs. Deb: 9/7/19

YEAR TM/L	W	L	PCT	G	GS	CG	SH	SV	IP	H	HR	BB	SO	RAT	ERA	ERA+	OAV	OOB	BH	AVG	PB	PR	/A	PD	TPI
1919 NY-N	1	2	.333	4	3	1	0	0	20¹	20	0	9	7	13.3	3.10	91	.260	.345	0	.000	-1	-0	-1	-1	-0.2

YEAR	TM/L	W	L	PCT	G	GS	CG	SH	SV	IP	H	HR	BB	SO	RAT	ERA	ERA+	OAV	OOB	BH	AVG	PB	PR	/A	PD	TPI
1920	NY-N	0	1	.000	3	1	1	0	0	15^1	14	1	4	5	10.6	1.76	170	.259	.310	0	.000	-1	2	2	0	0.1
1921	NY-N	7	10	.412	36	16	5	0	3	147^1	140	6	32	58	10.6	3.73	98	.255	.297	9	.200	1	-1	-1	-1	-0.2
1922	*NY-N	17	12	.586	46	22	12	1	3	191^2	194	5	74	75	12.7	3.01	133	.269	.338	12	.194	1	23	21	-1	2.8
1923	*NY-N	16	5	.762	**45**	15	7	0	4	172^2	169	8	46	58	11.3	3.49	109	.257	.308	11	.208	0	10	6	0	0.7
1924	*NY-N	8	6	.571	37	9	2	0	5	124^2	137	1	37	36	12.7	4.26	86	.285	.339	5	.139	-1	-5	-8	-2	-1.2
1925	Bos-N	2	8	.200	37	7	1	0	2	122^2	152	7	52	48	15.0	6.31	64	.303	.368	11	.282	3	-28	-31	-1	-2.0
1926	Bos-N	0	2	.000	7	2	0	0	0	19	29	1	7	6	17.1	7.58	47	.392	.444	1	.200	-0	-8	-9	-0	-0.8
1928	NY-A	0	0	—	3	0	0	0	0	6	17	1	1	5	27.0	16.50	23	.486	.500	0	.000	-1	-8	-8	-0	-0.1
1933	Bro-N	1	1	.500	30	0	0	0	2	61^1	69	3	16	22	12.9	4.55	71	.276	.327	2	.154	0	-8	-9	-0	-0.4
Total	10	52	47	.525	248	75	29	1	19	881	941	33	278	315	12.6	4.14	91	.277	.333	51	.190	-1	-22	-38	-5	-1.3

● MIKE RYBA
Ryba, Dominic Joseph b: 6/9/03, DeLancey, Pa. d: 12/13/71, Brookline Station, Mo. BR/TR, 5'11.5", 180 lbs. Deb: 9/22/35 C

YEAR	TM/L	W	L	PCT	G	GS	CG	SH	SV	IP	H	HR	BB	SO	RAT	ERA	ERA+	OAV	OOB	BH	AVG	PB	PR	/A	PD	TPI
1935	StL-N	1	1	.500	2	1	1	0	0	16	15	0	1	6	9.0	3.38	121	.242	.254	2	.400	1	1	1	0	0.2
1936	StL-N	5	1	.833	14	0	0	0	0	45	55	3	16	25	14.6	5.40	73	.294	.356	3	.167	-0	-7	-7	-1	-1.0
1937	StL-N	9	6	.600	38	8	5	0	0	135	152	8	40	57	12.9	4.13	96	.284	.336	15	.313	4	-3	-2	0	0.2
1938	StL-N	1	1	.500	3	0	0	0	0	5	8	0	1	0	16.2	5.40	73	.348	.375	0	—	1	-1	-1	0	-0.3
1941	Bos-A	7	3	.700	40	3	0	0	6	121	143	14	42	54	13.8	4.46	93	.297	.353	8	.216	1	-4	-4	2	0.0
1942	Bos-A	3	3	.500	18	0	0	0	3	44^1	49	5	13	16	12.8	3.86	97	.278	.332	5	.294	1	-1	-1	1	0.0
1943	Bos-A	7	5	.583	40	8	4	1	2	143^2	142	4	57	50	12.5	3.26	102	.262	.333	8	.186	0	1	1	-0	0.0
1944	Bos-A	12	7	.632	42	7	2	0	2	138	119	7	39	50	10.3	3.33	102	.233	.287	6	.146	-0	2	1	3	0.4
1945	Bos-A	7	6	.538	34	9	4	1	2	123	122	6	33	44	11.5	2.49	137	.259	.310	9	.250	1	12	13	1	1.5
1946	*Bos-A	0	1	.000	9	0	0	0	0	12^1	12	0	5	5	12.1	3.55	103	.261	.333	1	1.000	1	-0	-0	0	0.1
Total	10	52	34	.605	240	36	16	2	16	783^2	817	47	247	307	12.3	3.66	100	.269	.326	58	.235	9	-1	1	3	1.1

● GARY RYERSON
Ryerson, Gary Lawrence b: 6/7/48, Los Angeles, Cal. BR/TL, 6'1", 175 lbs. Deb: 6/28/72

YEAR	TM/L	W	L	PCT	G	GS	CG	SH	SV	IP	H	HR	BB	SO	RAT	ERA	ERA+	OAV	OOB	BH	AVG	PB	PR	/A	PD	TPI
1972	Mil-A	3	8	.273	20	14	4	1	0	102	119	9	21	45	12.4	3.62	84	.290	.324	1	.042	-1	-6	-7	-1	-1.0
1973	Mil-A	0	1	.000	9	4	0	0	0	23	32	0	7	10	15.3	7.83	48	.327	.371	0	—	0	-10	-10	0	-0.3
Total	2	3	9	.250	29	18	4	1	0	125	151	9	28	55	12.9	4.39	72	.297	.333	1	.042	-1	-17	-17	-1	-1.3

● BRET SABERHAGEN
Saberhagen, Bret William b: 4/11/64, Chicago Heights, Ill. BR/TR, 6'1", 195 lbs. Deb: 4/4/84

YEAR	TM/L	W	L	PCT	G	GS	CG	SH	SV	IP	H	HR	BB	SO	RAT	ERA	ERA+	OAV	OOB	BH	AVG	PB	PR	/A	PD	TPI
1984	*KC-A	10	11	.476	38	18	2	1	1	157^2	138	13	36	73	10.0	3.48	116	.237	.283	0	—	0	9	10	0	1.2
1985	*KC-A	20	6	.769	32	32	10	1	0	235^1	211	19	38	158	**9.6**	2.87	145	.241	**.273**	0	—	0	33	34	2	3.8
1986	KC-A	7	12	.368	30	25	4	2	0	156	165	15	29	112	11.3	4.15	102	.268	.303	0	—	0	0	2	1	0.3
1987	KC-A★	18	10	.643	33	33	15	4	0	257	246	27	53	163	10.7	3.36	135	.252	.295	0	—	0	31	34	1	3.4
1988	KC-A	14	16	.467	35	35	9	0	0	260^2	271	18	59	171	11.5	3.80	105	.269	.312	0	—	0	5	5	0	0.6
1989	*KC-A	**23**	6	**.793**	36	35	**12**	4	0	262^1	209	13	43	193	**8.7**	**2.16**	**178**	.217	**.252**	0	—	0	**50**	**49**	0	**5.5**
1990	KC-A★	5	9	.357	20	20	5	0	0	135	146	9	28	87	11.7	3.27	117	.279	.316	0	—	0	10	8	3	1.2
1991	KC-A	13	8	.619	28	28	7	2	0	196^1	165	12	45	136	10.0	3.07	134	.228	.281	0	—	0	22	23	1	2.4
1992	NY-N	3	5	.375	17	15	1	1	0	97^2	84	6	27	81	10.6	3.50	99	.233	.294	3	.107	-0	-0	3	0	0.2
1993	NY-N	7	7	.500	19	19	4	1	0	139^1	131	11	17	93	9.8	3.29	122	.250	.278	5	.111	-0	12	11	3	1.3
1994	NY-N☆	14	4	**.778**	24	24	4	0	0	177^1	169	13	13	143	9.4	2.74	152	.254	.273	10	.172	1	29	28	2	3.1
1995	NY-N	5	5	.500	16	16	3	0	0	110	105	13	20	71	10.6	3.35	121	.251	.293	4	.114	-1	10	8	2	0.8
	*Col-N	2	1	.667	9	9	0	0	0	43	60	8	13	29	16.3	6.28	86	.323	.382	1	.071	-1	-10	-4	0	-0.3
	Yr	7	6	.538	25	25	3	0	0	153	165	21	33	100	11.9	4.18	106	.269	.312	5	.102	-2	0	4	2	0.5
Total	12	141	100	.585	337	309	76	16	1	2227^2	2100	177	421	1510	10.4	3.26	126	.249	.289	23	.128	-2	201	208	19	23.5

● BRIAN SACKINSKY
Sackinsky, Brian Walter b: 6/22/71, Pittsburgh, Pa. BR/TR, 6'4", 220 lbs. Deb: 4/20/96

YEAR	TM/L	W	L	PCT	G	GS	CG	SH	SV	IP	H	HR	BB	SO	RAT	ERA	ERA+	OAV	OOB	BH	AVG	PB	PR	/A	PD	TPI
1996	Bal-A	0	0	—	3	0	0	0	0	4^2	6	1	3	2	17.4	3.86	127	.316	.409	0	—	0	1	1	-0	0.0

● RAY SADECKI
Sadecki, Raymond Michael b: 12/26/40, Kansas City, Kan. BL/TL, 5'11", 180 lbs. Deb: 5/19/60

YEAR	TM/L	W	L	PCT	G	GS	CG	SH	SV	IP	H	HR	BB	SO	RAT	ERA	ERA+	OAV	OOB	BH	AVG	PB	PR	/A	PD	TPI
1960	StL-N	9	9	.500	26	26	7	1	0	157^1	148	15	86	95	13.4	3.78	109	.249	.345	12	.211	-0	-0	6	-2	0.2
1961	StL-N	14	10	.583	31	31	13	0	0	222^2	196	28	102	114	12.3	3.72	118	.238	.324	22	.253	2	8	17	-5	1.3
1962	StL-N	6	8	.429	22	17	4	1	0	102^1	121	13	43	50	14.7	5.54	77	.296	.367	3	.081	-2	-18	-14	-2	-2.1
1963	StL-N	10	10	.500	36	28	4	1	1	193^1	198	25	78	136	13.0	4.10	87	.266	.339	9	.141	-1	-17	-12	-3	-1.6
1964	*StL-N	20	11	.645	37	32	9	2	1	220	232	16	60	119	12.0	3.68	103	.273	.322	12	.160	1	-4	3	-3	0.3
1965	StL-N	6	15	.286	36	28	4	0	1	172^2	192	26	64	122	13.3	5.21	74	.284	.346	11	.200	2	-32	-26	-2	-3.3
1966	StL-N	2	1	.667	5	3	1	0	0	24^1	16	2	9	21	9.2	2.22	162	.188	.266	3	.429	1	2	4	0	0.7
	SF-N	3	7	.300	26	19	3	1	0	105	125	20	39	62	14.4	5.40	68	.293	.358	11	.324	5	-21	-20	-2	-1.4
	Yr	5	8	.385	31	22	4	1	0	129^1	141	22	48	83	13.4	4.80	76	.276	.343	14	.341	7	-17	-17	-2	-0.7
1967	SF-N	12	6	.667	35	24	10	2	0	188	184	9	58	145	10.9	2.78	118	.238	.301	18	.247	4	13	11	1	1.4
1968	SF-N	12	18	.400	38	36	13	6	0	254	225	14	70	206	10.6	2.91	101	.237	.292	8	.094	-1	2	1	-3	-0.3
1969	SF-N	5	8	.385	38	24	4	3	0	138^1	137	18	53	104	12.5	4.23	83	.255	.329	5	.125	-2	-10	-11	-2	-0.6
1970	NY-N	8	4	.667	28	19	4	0	0	138^2	134	18	52	89	12.1	3.89	103	.255	.322	8	.205	1	2	2	-2	0.0
1971	NY-N	7	7	.500	34	20	5	2	0	163^1	139	10	44	120	10.3	2.92	117	.229	.285	10	.200	1	10	9	2	0.6
1972	NY-N	2	1	.667	34	2	0	0	1	75^2	73	3	31	62	12.6	3.09	109	.257	.334	2	.154	-0	2	1	-1	-0.1
1973	*NY-N	5	4	.556	31	11	1	0	1	116^2	109	11	41	87	11.6	3.39	107	.248	.314	7	.226	1	3	3	-3	0.1
1974	NY-N	8	8	.500	34	10	3	1	0	103	107	7	35	46	12.6	3.41	105	.274	.337	7	.259	1	2	2	0	0.3
1975	StL-N	1	0	1.000	11	0	0	0	0	11	13	0	7	8	16.4	3.27	115	.289	.385	0	—	0	1	-0	0	0.0
	Atl-N	2	3	.400	25	5	0	0	1	66^1	73	3	21	24	13.3	4.21	90	.286	.350	3	.200	0	-4	-3	-1	-0.3
	Yr	3	3	.500	33	5	0	0	1	77^1	86	3	28	32	13.7	4.07	93	.285	.353	3	.200	0	-4	-3	-0	-0.3
1976	KC-A	0	0	—	3	0	0	0	0	4^2	7	0	3	1	19.3	0.00	—	.368	.455	0	—	0	2	2	-0	0.1
	Mil-A	2	0	1.000	36	0	0	0	0	37^1	38	2	20	27	14.7	4.34	81	.262	.363	0	—	0	-3	-4	-0	-0.2
	Yr	2	0	1.000	39	0	0	0	0	42	45	2	23	28	15.2	3.86	91	.274	.374	0	—	0	-2	-2	-1	-0.3
1977	NY-N	0	1	.000	4	0	0	0	0	3	3	1	3	0	18.0	6.00	62	.300	.462	0	—	0	-1	-1	-0	-0.2
Total	18	135	131	.508	563	328	85	20	7	2500^2	2456	240	922	1614	12.3	3.78	97	.258	.326	151	.191	19	-61	-32	-30	-4.9

● JIM SADOWSKI
Sadowski, James Michael b: 8/7/51, Pittsburgh, Pa. BR/TR, 6'3", 195 lbs. Deb: 4/27/74

YEAR	TM/L	W	L	PCT	G	GS	CG	SH	SV	IP	H	HR	BB	SO	RAT	ERA	ERA+	OAV	OOB	BH	AVG	PB	PR	/A	PD	TPI
1974	Pit-N	0	1	.000	4	0	0	0	0	9	7	1	9	1	16.0	6.00	57	.233	.410	0	.000	0	-2	-3	1	-0.2

● BOB SADOWSKI
Sadowski, Robert b: 2/19/38, Pittsburgh, Pa. BR/TR, 6'2", 195 lbs. Deb: 6/19/63 F

YEAR	TM/L	W	L	PCT	G	GS	CG	SH	SV	IP	H	HR	BB	SO	RAT	ERA	ERA+	OAV	OOB	BH	AVG	PB	PR	/A	PD	TPI
1963	Mil-N	5	7	.417	19	18	5	1	0	116^2	99	8	30	72	10.3	2.62	123	.231	.289	2	.057	-2	9	8	1	0.6
1964	Mil-N	9	10	.474	51	18	5	0	5	166^2	159	18	56	96	12.0	4.10	86	.251	.319	8	.154	0	-11	-8	3	-1.0
1965	Mil-N	5	9	.357	34	13	3	0	3	123	117	11	35	78	11.3	4.32	82	.250	.306	3	.086	-2	-11	-11	-1	-1.5
1966	Bos-A	1	1	.500	11	5	0	0	0	33^1	41	4	9	11	13.8	5.40	70	.311	.359	0	—	-0	-7	-6	-0	-0.4
Total	4	20	27	.426	115	54	13	1	8	439^2	416	41	130	257	11.5	3.87	90	.250	.311	13	.101	-4	-20	-20	2	-2.3

● TED SADOWSKI
Sadowski, Theodore b: 4/1/36, Pittsburgh, Pa. d: 7/18/93, Shaler Twsp., Pa. BR/TR, 6'1.5", 190 lbs. Deb: 9/2/60 F

YEAR	TM/L	W	L	PCT	G	GS	CG	SH	SV	IP	H	HR	BB	SO	RAT	ERA	ERA+	OAV	OOB	BH	AVG	PB	PR	/A	PD	TPI
1960	Was-A	1	0	1.000	9	1	0	0	0	17^1	17	4	9	12	14.0	5.19	75	.258	.355	0	.000	—	-3	-3	0	-0.2
1961	Min-A	0	2	.000	15	1	0	0	0	33	49	6	11	16	16.6	6.82	62	.348	.399	0	.000	0	-10	-9	-1	-0.5
1962	Min-A	1	1	.500	19	0	0	0	0	34	37	6	11	15	13.0	5.03	81	.301	.363	2	.500	1	-4	-4	-0	-0.1
Total	3	2	3	.400	43	2	0	0	0	84^1	103	16	31	39	14.6	5.76	71	.312	.376	2	.154	1	-17	-16	1	-0.9

● A. J. SAGER
Sager, Anthony Joseph b: 3/3/65, Columbus, Ohio BR/TR, 6'4", 220 lbs. Deb: 4/4/94

YEAR	TM/L	W	L	PCT	G	GS	CG	SH	SV	IP	H	HR	BB	SO	RAT	ERA	ERA+	OAV	OOB	BH	AVG	PB	PR	/A	PD	TPI
1994	SD-N	1	4	.200	22	3	0	0	0	46^2	62	4	16	26	15.4	5.98	69	.325	.383	1	.100	1	-9	-10	2	-0.7
1995	Col-N	0	0	—	14	0	1	0	0	14^2	19	1	7	10	16.0	7.36	73	.311	.382	0	.000	0	-5	-3	1	-0.2
1996	Det-A	4	5	.444	22	9	0	0	0	79	91	10	29	52	13.9	5.01	101	.294	.358	0	—	0	-1	1	-1	0.2
Total	3	5	9	.357	54	12	1	0	0	140^1	172	15	52	88	14.6	5.58	86	.306	.369	1	.077	1	-15	-12	2	-0.7

● JOHNNY SAIN
Sain, John Franklin b: 9/25/17, Havana, Ark. BR/TR, 6'2", 200 lbs. Deb: 4/24/42 C

YEAR	TM/L	W	L	PCT	G	GS	CG	SH	SV	IP	H	HR	BB	SO	RAT	ERA	ERA+	OAV	OOB	BH	AVG	PB	PR	/A	PD	TPI
1942	Bos-N	4	7	.364	40	3	0	0	6	97	79	8	63	68	13.6	3.90	86	.228	.354	2	.074	-2	-6	-6	1	-0.8
1946	Bos-N	20	14	.588	37	34	**24**	3	2	265	225	8	87	129	10.7	2.21	155	.230	.294	28	.298	5	35	36	3	**5.9**

YEAR	TM/L	W	L	PCT	G	GS	CG	SH	SV	IP	H	HR	BB	SO	RAT	ERA	ERA+	OAV	OOB	BH	AVG	PB	PR	/A	PD	TPI
1947	Bos-N★	21	12	.636	38	35	22	3	1	266	265	19	79	132	11.8	3.52	111	.255	.310	37	.346	12	16	11	1	2.6
1948	*Bos-N★	24	15	.615	42	39	28	4	1	314²	297	19	83	137	11.0	2.60	147	.245	.296	25	.217	3	47	43	-2	5.3
1949	Bos-N	10	17	.370	37	36	16	1	0	243	285	15	75	73	13.5	4.81	78	.291	.344	20	.206	1	-21	-28	-2	-2.7
1950	Bos-N	20	13	.606	37	37	25	3	0	278¹	294	34	70	96	11.8	3.94	98	.269	.314	21	.206	4	6	-3	-2	-0.2
1951	Bos-N	5	13	.278	26	22	6	1	1	160¹	195	16	45	63	13.6	4.21	87	.299	.347	11	.212	1	-4	-10	0	-0.7
	*NY-A	2	1	.667	7	4	1	0	1	37	41	5	8	21	11.9	4.14	93	.281	.318	4	.286	1	-0	-1	1	0.0
1952	*NY-A	11	6	.647	35	16	8	0	7	148¹	149	15	38	57	11.5	3.46	96	.261	.310	19	.268	7	4	-2	-1	0.3
1953	*NY-A☆	14	7	.667	40	19	10	1	9	189	189	16	45	84	11.3	3.00	123	.262	.308	17	.250	5	21	15	-0	2.1
1954	NY-A	6	6	.500	45	0	0	0	22	77	66	11	15	33	9.5	3.16	109	.229	.267	6	.353	5	5	2	-0	0.7
1955	NY-A	0	0	—	3	0	0	0	0	5¹	6	4	1	5	11.8	6.75	55	.300	.333	0	.000	-0	-2	-2	0	0.0
	KC-A	2	5	.286	25	0	0	0	1	44²	54	10	10	12	12.9	5.44	77	.297	.333	0	.000	-1	-7	-6	-1	-1.1
	Yr	2	5	.286	28	0	0	0	1	50	60	14	11	17	12.8	5.58	74	.297	.333	0	.000	-1	-9	-8	-1	-1.1
Total	11	139	116	.545	412	245	140	16	51	2125²	2145	180	619	910	11.8	3.49	106	.261	.315	190	.245	40	94	50	-2	11.4

● **RANDY ST.CLAIRE**   St.Claire, Randy Anthony   b: 8/23/60, Glens Falls, N.Y.   BR/TR, 6′2″, 190 lbs.   Deb: 9/11/84   F

YEAR	TM/L	W	L	PCT	G	GS	CG	SH	SV	IP	H	HR	BB	SO	RAT	ERA	ERA+	OAV	OOB	BH	AVG	PB	PR	/A	PD	TPI
1984	Mon-N	0	0	—	4	0	0	0	0	8	11	0	4	4	15.8	4.50	76	.344	.400	0	—	0	-1	-1	-0	0.0
1985	Mon-N	5	3	.625	42	0	0	0	0	68²	69	3	26	25	12.6	3.93	86	.265	.334	1	.200	-1	-3	-4	-0	-0.3
1986	Mon-N	2	0	1.000	11	0	0	0	1	19	13	2	6	21	9.0	2.37	156	.186	.250	0	.000	-0	3	3	1	0.4
1987	Mon-N	3	3	.500	44	0	0	0	7	67	64	9	20	43	11.4	4.03	104	.249	.306	2	.333	-1	0	1	-0	0.1
1988	Mon-N	0	0	—	6	0	0	0	0	7¹	11	2	5	6	19.6	6.14	59	.344	.432	0	—	0	-2	-2	0	0.0
	Cin-N	1	0	1.000	10	0	0	0	0	13²	13	3	5	8	11.9	2.63	136	.241	.305	0	.000	-0	1	1	-0	0.1
	Yr	1	0	1.000	16	0	0	0	0	21	24	5	10	14	14.6	3.86	93	.276	.351	0	.000	-0	-1	-1	0	0.1
1989	Min-A	1	0	1.000	14	0	0	0	1	22¹	22	4	10	14	12.5	5.24	79	.226	.323	0	—	0	-3	-3	-0	-0.1
1991	*Atl-N	0	0	—	19	0	0	0	0	28²	31	4	9	30	12.6	4.08	95	.282	.336	1	.500	-1	-1	-1	0	0.1
1992	Atl-N	0	0	—	10	0	0	0	0	15¹	17	1	8	7	14.7	5.87	62	.283	.368	0	—	0	-4	-4	0	0.0
1994	Tor-A	0	0	—	2	0	0	0	0	2	4	0	2	2	27.0	9.00	54	.444	.545	0	—	0	-1	-1	-0	0.0
Total	9	12	6	.667	162	0	0	0	9	252	252	28	93	160	12.5	4.14	92	.260	.328	4	.267	1	-11	-10	2	0.3

● **JIM ST.VRAIN**   St.Vrain, James Marcellin   b: 6/6/1883, Ralls County, Mo.   d: 6/12/37, Butte, Montana   BR/TL, 5′9″, 175 lbs.   Deb: 4/20/02

| 1902 | Chi-N | 4 | 6 | .400 | 12 | 11 | 10 | 1 | 0 | 95 | 88 | 0 | 25 | 51 | 11.2 | 2.08 | 130 | .246 | .304 | 3 | .097 | -2 | 7 | 7 | 0 | 0.5 |

● **LUIS SALAZAR**   Salazar, Luis Ernesto (Garcia)   b: 5/19/56, Barcelona, Venez.   BR/TR, 5′9″, 180 lbs.   Deb: 8/15/80   ◆

| 1987 | SD-N | 0 | 0 | — | 2 | 0 | 0 | 0 | 0 | 2 | 2 | 0 | 1 | 0 | 13.5 | 4.50 | 88 | .250 | .333 | 48 | .254 | 0 | -0 | -0 | 0 | 0.0 |

● **FREDDY SALE**   Sale, Frederick Link   b: 5/2/02, Chester, S.C.   d: 5/27/56, Hermosa Beach, Cal   BR/TR, 5′9″, 160 lbs.   Deb: 6/30/24

| 1924 | Pit-N | 0 | 0 | — | 1 | 0 | 0 | 0 | 0 | 1 | 2 | 0 | 6 | 1 | 18.0 | 0.00 | — | .500 | .500 | 0 | — | 0 | 0 | 0 | -0 | 0.0 |

● **HARRY SALISBURY**   Salisbury, Henry H.   b: 5/15/1855, Providence, R.I.   d: 3/29/33, Chicago, Ill.   BL , 5′8.5″, 162 lbs.   Deb: 8/28/1879

1879	Tro-N	4	6	.400	10	10	9	0	0	89	103	0	11	31	11.5	2.22	112	.265	.285	2	.056	-4	3	3	2	0.0
1882	Pit-a	20	18	.526	38	38	38	1	0	335	315	1	37	135	9.5	2.63	99	.232	.253	22	.152	-6	2	-1	-2	-0.8
Total	2	24	24	.500	48	48	47	1	0	424	418	1	48	166	9.9	2.55	102	.239	.260	24	.133	-10	5	2	-1	-0.8

● **BILL SALISBURY**   Salisbury, William Ansel "Solly"   b: 11/12/1876, Algona, Iowa   d: 1/17/52, Rowena, Ore.   BR/TR, 6′, 180 lbs.   Deb: 4/19/02

| 1902 | Phi-N | 0 | 0 | — | 2 | 1 | 0 | 0 | 0 | 6 | 15 | 1 | 2 | 0 | 27.0 | 13.50 | 21 | .469 | .514 | 0 | .000 | -0 | -7 | -7 | -1 | -0.1 |

● **ROGER SALKELD**   Salkeld, Roger William   b: 3/6/71, Burbank, Cal.   BR/TR, 6′5″, 215 lbs.   Deb: 9/8/93   F

1993	Sea-A	0	0	—	3	0	0	0	0	14¹	13	0	4	13	11.3	2.51	175	.232	.295	0	—	0	3	3	0	0.0
1994	Sea-A	2	5	.286	13	13	0	0	0	59	76	7	45	46	18.6	7.17	68	.314	.424	0	—	0	-16	-15	-1	-1.5
1996	Cin-N	8	5	.615	29	19	1	1	0	116	114	18	54	82	13.5	5.20	80	.261	.351	1	.031	-3	-13	-13	-0	-1.6
Total	3	10	10	.500	45	34	1	1	0	189¹	203	25	103	141	14.9	5.61	78	.277	.372	1	.031	-3	-25	-26	-1	-3.1

● **SLIM SALLEE**   Sallee, Harry Franklin "Scatter"   b: 2/3/1885, Higginsport, Ohio   d: 3/23/50, Higginsport, Ohio   BL/TL, 6′3″, 180 lbs.   Deb: 4/16/08

1908	StL-N	3	8	.273	25	12	7	1	0	128²	144	1	36	39	12.8	3.15	75	.274	.324	2	.049	-11	-11	-0	-1.3
1909	StL-N	10	11	.476	32	27	12	1	0	219	223	3	59	55	11.8	2.42	104	.264	.315	8	.113	-2	4	3	-0	0.0
1910	StL-N	7	8	.467	18	13	9	1	2	115	112	4	24	46	10.7	2.97	100	.251	.290	4	.108	-2	1	0	0	-0.2
1911	StL-N	15	9	.625	36	30	18	1	3	245	234	6	64	74	11.1	2.76	123	.257	.309	15	.169	-2	18	17	-3	1.1
1912	StL-N	16	17	.485	48	32	20	3	6	294	289	6	72	108	11.2	2.60	132	.266	.315	14	.136	-4	26	27	-2	2.3
1913	StL-N	19	15	.559	50	31	18	3	5	276	257	11	60	106	10.5	2.71	119	.255	.301	20	.211	2	15	16	1	2.2
1914	StL-N	18	17	.514	46	30	18	3	6	282¹	252	5	72	105	10.4	2.10	133	.246	.302	21	.231	2	22	22	-2	2.9
1915	StL-N	13	17	.433	46	33	17	2	3	275¹	245	6	57	91	10.0	2.84	98	.238	.280	11	.120	-3	-3	-2	-1	-0.7
1916	StL-N	5	5	.500	16	7	4	2	1	70	75	2	23	28	12.9	3.47	76	.290	.352	3	.167	-0	-7	-6	-1	-1.1
	NY-N	9	4	.692	15	11	7	2	0	111²	96	2	10	35	8.5	1.37	174	.234	.252	9	.257	2	15	13	-3	1.6
	Yr	14	9	.609	31	18	11	4	1	181²	171	4	33	63	10.1	2.18	115	.255	.290	12	.226	2	9	7	-4	0.5
1917	*NY-N	18	7	.720	34	24	18	1	4	215²	199	4	34	54	9.8	2.17	118	.249	.280	17	.221	1	13	9	-4	0.8
1918	NY-N	8	8	.500	18	16	12	1	2	132	122	3	12	33	9.1	2.25	117	.241	.259	5	.122	-2	8	6	-2	0.3
1919	*Cin-N	21	7	.750	29	28	22	4	0	227²	221	4	20	24	9.6	2.06	135	.258	.276	14	.189	2	22	18	-5	2.0
1920	Cin-N	5	6	.455	21	12	6	0	2	116	129	4	16	13	11.4	3.34	91	.293	.320	6	.171	-1	-3	-3	-0	-0.8
	NY-N	1	0	1.000	5	2	1	0	0	17	16	0	0	2	8.5	1.59	189	.239	.239	1	.333	1	3	3	-0	0.2
	Yr	6	6	.500	26	14	7	0	2	133	145	4	16	15	10.9	3.11	97	.284	.306	7	.184	-0	0	-1	-4	-0.6
1921	NY-N	6	4	.600	37	0	0	0	2	96¹	115	7	14	23	12.1	3.64	101	.307	.332	8	.364	2	1	-2	-0	0.1
Total	14	174	143	.549	476	308	189	25	36	2821²	2729	68	573	836	10.7	2.56	114	.258	.299	158	.171	-8	125	109	-26	9.4

● **ROGER SALMON**   Salmon, Roger Elliott   b: 5/11/1891, Newark, N.J.   d: 6/17/74, Belfast, Me.   BL/TL, 6′2″, 170 lbs.   Deb: 5/3/12

| 1912 | Phi-A | 1 | 0 | 1.000 | 2 | 1 | 0 | 0 | 0 | 5 | 7 | 0 | 4 | 5 | 19.8 | 9.00 | 34 | .318 | .423 | 0 | .000 | -0 | -3 | -3 | -0 | -0.5 |

● **GUS SALVE**   Salve, Augustus William   b: 12/29/1885, Boston, Mass.   d: 3/29/71, Providence, R.I.   BL/TL, 6′, 190 lbs.   Deb: 9/14/08

| 1908 | Phi-A | 0 | 1 | .000 | 2 | 1 | 1 | 0 | 0 | 15¹ | 17 | 1 | 9 | 6 | 15.8 | 4.11 | 62 | .266 | .365 | 0 | .000 | -1 | -3 | -3 | -1 | -0.3 |

● **JACK SALVESON**   Salveson, John Theodore   b: 1/5/14, Fullerton, Cal.   d: 12/28/74, Norwalk, Cal.   BR/TR, 6′0.5″, 180 lbs.   Deb: 6/3/33

1933	NY-N	0	2	.000	8	2	2	0	0	30²	30	4	14	8	12.9	3.82	84	.252	.331	1	.111	-1	-2	-2	0	-0.2
1934	NY-N	3	1	.750	12	4	0	0	0	38¹	43	2	13	18	13.1	3.52	110	.281	.337	3	.300	-2	2	1	1	0.2
1935	Pit-N	0	1	.000	5	0	0	0	0	7	11	1	5	2	21.9	9.00	46	.306	.405	0	.000	-0	-4	-4	1	-0.4
	Chi-A	1	2	.333	20	2	2	0	1	66²	79	6	23	22	13.8	4.86	95	.298	.354	6	.300	2	-3	-2	-0	-0.1
1943	Cle-A	5	3	.625	23	11	4	3	3	86	87	5	26	24	11.5	3.35	93	.266	.322	6	.231	-2	-0	-0	0	0.0
1945	Cle-A	0	0	—	19	0	0	0	0	44	52	3	6	11	12.1	3.68	88	.294	.321	4	.400	3	-2	-1	0	0.4
Total	5	9	9	.500	87	19	8	3	4	272²	302	21	87	85	12.9	3.99	91	.280	.336	20	.260	7	-8	-11	2	0.1

● **MANNY SALVO**   Salvo, Manuel "Gyp"   b: 6/30/13, Sacramento, Cal.   BR/TR, 6′4″, 210 lbs.   Deb: 4/22/39

1939	NY-N	4	10	.286	32	18	4	0	1	136	150	11	75	69	15.2	4.63	85	.285	.380	4	.098	-2	-11	-11	1	-1.0
1940	Bos-N	10	9	.526	21	20	14	5	0	160²	151	9	45	70	11.0	3.08	121	.248	.306	6	.103	-3	14	11	-1	0.8
1941	Bos-N	7	16	.304	35	27	11	2	0	195	192	9	49	67	13.3	4.06	88	.255	.340	7	.113	-1	-9	-11	-0	-1.2
1942	Bos-N	7	8	.467	25	14	8	1	0	130²	129	7	41	25	12.0	3.03	110	.260	.322	5	.122	-1	4	4	-1	0.2
1943	Bos-N	0	0	1.000	1	0	0	0	0	5	5	0	1	1	9.0	7.20	47	.250	.423	2	1.000	0	-1	-1	0	-0.2
	Phi-N	0	0	—	1	0	0	0	0	0¹	2	0	1	0	81.0	27.00	12	.667	.750	0	—	0	-1	-1	0	0.0
	Bos-N	5	6	.455	20	13	5	1	0	93²	94	6	25	25	11.5	3.27	105	.261	.311	6	.214	0	1	1	1	0.2
	Yr	5	7	.417	22	14	5	1	0	99	101	6	32	26	12.2	3.55	96	.264	.322	8	.267	2	-1	-1	1	0.0
Total	5	33	50	.398	135	93	40	9	1	721¹	723	42	284	247	12.8	3.69	98	.261	.334	30	.129	-4	-4	-7	-3	-1.2

● **JOE SAMBITO**   Sambito, Joseph Charles   b: 6/28/52, Brooklyn, N.Y.   BL/TL, 6′1″, 190 lbs.   Deb: 7/20/76

1976	Hou-N	3	2	.600	20	4	1	1	1	53¹	45	4	14	26	10.0	3.54	90	.237	.289	2	.222	1	-0	-2	1	0.0
1977	Hou-N	5	5	.500	54	0	0	0	7	89	77	6	24	67	10.2	2.33	153	.235	.287	2	.154	-0	16	12	1	1.5
1978	Hou-N	4	9	.308	62	0	0	0	11	88	85	5	32	96	12.0	3.07	108	.260	.326	1	.167	-0	5	2	1	0.6

YEAR	TM/L	W	L	PCT	G	GS	CG	SH	SV	IP	H	HR	BB	SO	RAT	ERA	ERA+	OAV	OOB	BH	AVG	PB	PR	/A	PD	TPI
1979	Hou-N★	8	7	.533	63	0	0	0	22	91^1	80	8	23	83	10.5	1.77	198	.235	.292	2	.286	2	**20**	18	1	4.1
1980	*Hou-N	8	4	.667	64	0	0	0	17	90^1	65	3	22	75	8.9	2.19	150	.200	.255	0	.000	-1	14	11	0	1.8
1981	*Hou-N	5	5	.500	49	0	0	0	10	63^2	43	4	22	41	9.5	1.84	179	.192	.270	0	.000	-1	12	10	1	2.0
1982	Hou-N	0	0	—	9	0	0	0	4	12^2	7	0	2	7	6.4	0.71	467	.159	.196	0	.000	-0	4	4	0	0.3
1984	Hou-N	0	0	—	32	0	0	0	0	47^2	39	5	16	26	10.4	3.02	110	.228	.294	0	.000	-0	3	2	-1	-0.1
1985	NY-N	0	0	—	8	0	0	0	0	10^2	21	1	8	3	24.5	12.66	27	.420	.500	0	—	-0	-11	-11	-0	0.0
1986	*Bos-A	2	0	1.000	53	0	0	0	12	44^2	54	4	16	30	14.5	4.84	86	.298	.362	0	—	-0	-3	-3	-0	-0.3
1987	Bos-A	2	6	.250	47	0	0	0	0	37^2	46	8	16	35	14.8	6.93	65	.301	.367	0	—	-0	-10	-10	-0	-1.9
Total 11		37	38	.493	461	5	1	1	84	629	562	48	195	489	11.0	3.03	115	.241	.302	7	.135	2	49	32	4	8.0

● **BILL SAMPEN**   Sampen, William Albert b: 1/18/63, Lincoln, Ill. BR/TR, 6'1", 185 lbs. Deb: 4/10/90

YEAR	TM/L	W	L	PCT	G	GS	CG	SH	SV	IP	H	HR	BB	SO	RAT	ERA	ERA+	OAV	OOB	BH	AVG	PB	PR	/A	PD	TPI
1990	Mon-N	12	7	.632	59	4	0	0	2	90^1	94	7	33	69	12.9	2.99	122	.268	.334	0	.000	-1	8	7	-1	1.2
1991	Mon-N	9	5	.643	43	8	0	0	0	92^1	96	13	46	52	14.1	4.00	91	.273	.362	3	.231	0	-3	-4	-1	-0.6
1992	Mon-N	1	4	.200	44	1	0	0	0	63^1	62	4	29	23	13.1	3.13	111	.268	.352	0	.000	-1	3	2	1	0.2
	KC-A	0	2	.000	8	1	0	0	0	19^2	21	0	3	14	12.4	3.66	111	.292	.346	0	—	0	1	1	0	0.1
1993	KC-A	2	2	.500	18	0	0	0	0	18^1	25	1	9	9	18.7	5.89	78	.338	.437	0	—	0	-3	-3	0	-0.9
1994	Cal-A	1	1	.500	10	0	0	0	0	15^1	14	1	13	9	17.6	6.46	76	.241	.405	0	—	0	-3	-3	0	-0.3
Total 5		25	21	.543	182	14	0	0	2	299^1	312	26	133	176	13.9	3.73	100	.274	.358	3	.111	-1	2	0	-1	-0.3

● **JOE SAMUELS**   Samuels, Joseph Jonas "Skabotch" b: 3/21/05, Scranton, Pa. BR/TR, 6'1.5", 196 lbs. Deb: 4/23/30

YEAR	TM/L	W	L	PCT	G	GS	CG	SH	SV	IP	H	HR	BB	SO	RAT	ERA	ERA+	OAV	OOB	BH	AVG	PB	PR	/A	PD	TPI
1930	Det-A	0	0	—	2	0	0	0	0	6	10	1	6	1	24.0	16.50	29	.417	.533	0	—	0	-8	-8	-0	0.0

● **ROGER SAMUELS**   Samuels, Roger Howard b: 1/5/61, San Jose, Cal. BL/TL, 6'5", 210 lbs. Deb: 7/20/88

YEAR	TM/L	W	L	PCT	G	GS	CG	SH	SV	IP	H	HR	BB	SO	RAT	ERA	ERA+	OAV	OOB	BH	AVG	PB	PR	/A	PD	TPI
1988	SF-N	1	2	.333	15	0	0	0	0	23^1	17	4	7	22	9.6	3.47	94	.202	.272	0	.000	-0	-0	-1	0	-0.1
1989	Pit-N	0	0	—	5	0	0	0	0	3^2	9	1	4	2	31.9	9.82	34	.474	.565	0	—	0	-3	-3	-0	-0.1
Total 2		1	2	.333	20	0	0	0	0	27	26	5	11	24	12.7	4.33	76	.252	.330	0	.000	-0	-3	-3	0	-0.1

● **ALEX SANCHEZ**   Sanchez, Alex Anthony b: 4/8/66, Concord, Cal. BR/TR, 6'2", 185 lbs. Deb: 5/23/89

YEAR	TM/L	W	L	PCT	G	GS	CG	SH	SV	IP	H	HR	BB	SO	RAT	ERA	ERA+	OAV	OOB	BH	AVG	PB	PR	/A	PD	TPI
1989	Tor-A	0	1	.000	4	3	0	0	0	11^2	16	1	14	4	23.1	10.03	38	.356	.508	0	—	0	-8	-8	1	-0.5

● **ISRAEL SANCHEZ**   Sanchez, Israel (Matos) b: 8/20/63, Falcon Lasvias, Cuba BL/TL, 5'9", 170 lbs. Deb: 7/7/88

YEAR	TM/L	W	L	PCT	G	GS	CG	SH	SV	IP	H	HR	BB	SO	RAT	ERA	ERA+	OAV	OOB	BH	AVG	PB	PR	/A	PD	TPI
1988	KC-A	3	2	.600	19	1	0	0	1	35^2	36	0	18	14	13.6	4.54	88	.265	.351	0	—	0	-2	-2	-0	-0.3
1990	KC-A	0	0	—	11	0	0	0	0	9^2	16	1	3	5	18.6	8.38	46	.381	.435	0	—	0	-5	-5	-0	-0.1
Total 2		3	2	.600	30	1	0	0	1	45^1	52	1	21	19	14.7	5.36	74	.292	.370	0	—	0	-7	-7	0	-0.3

● **LUIS SANCHEZ**   Sanchez, Luis Mercedes (b: Luis Mercedes Escoba (Sanchez)) b: 8/24/53, Cariaco, Ven. BR/TR, 6'2", 210 lbs. Deb: 4/10/81

YEAR	TM/L	W	L	PCT	G	GS	CG	SH	SV	IP	H	HR	BB	SO	RAT	ERA	ERA+	OAV	OOB	BH	AVG	PB	PR	/A	PD	TPI
1981	Cal-A	0	2	.000	17	0	0	0	2	33^2	39	4	11	13	13.6	2.94	124	.287	.345	0	—	0	3	3	0	0.2
1982	*Cal-A	7	4	.636	46	0	0	0	5	92^2	89	3	34	58	12.6	3.21	126	.259	.339	0	—	0	9	9	1	1.1
1983	Cal-A	10	8	.556	56	1	0	0	7	98^1	92	6	40	49	12.4	3.66	110	.254	.333	0	—	0	4	4	2	0.9
1984	Cal-A	9	7	.563	49	0	0	0	11	83^2	84	10	33	62	12.9	3.33	119	.268	.343	0	—	0	6	6	-0	1.2
1985	Cal-A	2	0	1.000	26	0	0	0	2	61^1	67	9	27	34	13.9	5.72	72	.283	.358	0	—	0	-11	-11	-0	-0.3
Total 5		28	21	.571	194	1	0	0	27	369^2	371	32	145	216	12.9	3.75	107	.267	.342	0	—	0	11	10	2	3.1

● **RAUL SANCHEZ**   Sanchez, Raul Guadalupe (Rodriguez) b: 12/12/30, Marianao, Cuba BR/TR, 6', 150 lbs. Deb: 4/17/52

YEAR	TM/L	W	L	PCT	G	GS	CG	SH	SV	IP	H	HR	BB	SO	RAT	ERA	ERA+	OAV	OOB	BH	AVG	PB	PR	/A	PD	TPI
1952	Was-A	1	1	.500	3	2	1	1	0	12^2	13	0	7	6	14.2	3.55	100	.260	.351	0	.000	-1	0	0	0	-0.1
1957	Cin-N	3	2	.600	38	0	0	0	5	62^1	61	7	25	37	13.0	4.76	86	.262	.344	2	.286	1	-6	-5	1	-0.3
1960	Cin-N	1	0	1.000	8	0	0	0	0	14^2	12	1	11	5	16.0	4.91	78	.226	.388	1	.500	0	-2	-2	0	-0.1
Total 3		5	3	.625	49	2	1	1	5	89^2	86	8	43	48	13.7	4.62	86	.256	.352	3	.214	0	-8	-6	1	-0.5

● **BEN SANDERS**   Sanders, Alexander Bennett b: 2/16/1865, Catharpin, Va. d: 8/29/30, Memphis, Tenn. BR/TR, 6', 210 lbs. Deb: 6/6/1888 ♦

YEAR	TM/L	W	L	PCT	G	GS	CG	SH	SV	IP	H	HR	BB	SO	RAT	ERA	ERA+	OAV	OOB	BH	AVG	PB	PR	/A	PD	TPI
1888	Phi-N	19	10	.655	31	29	28	**8**	0	275^1	240	3	33	121	9.0	1.90	178	.228	.253	58	.246	5	29	33	4	4.2
1889	Phi-N	19	18	.514	44	39	34	1	1	349^1	406	9	96	123	13.0	3.55	122	.282	.328	47	.278	6	18	31	-2	3.0
1890	Phi-P	19	18	.514	43	40	37	2	1	346^2	412	13	69	107	12.7	3.76	114	.283	.320	59	.312	9	18	20	1	2.4
1891	Phi-a	11	5	.688	19	18	15	0	0	145	157	3	37	40	12.5	3.79	101	.267	.319	39	.250	2	-1	-1	-1	0.2
1892	Lou-N	12	19	.387	31	31	30	3	0	268^1	281	6	62	77	11.6	3.22	95	.259	.300	54	.273	10	2	-5	-1	0.5
Total 5		80	70	.533	168	157	144	14	2	1385	1496	34	297	468	11.8	3.24	116	.266	.306	257	.271	33	66	79	1	10.3

● **DEE SANDERS**   Sanders, Dee Wilma b: 4/8/21, Quitman, Tex. BR/TR, 6'3", 195 lbs. Deb: 8/12/45

YEAR	TM/L	W	L	PCT	G	GS	CG	SH	SV	IP	H	HR	BB	SO	RAT	ERA	ERA+	OAV	OOB	BH	AVG	PB	PR	/A	PD	TPI
1945	StL-A	0	0	—	2	0	0	0	0	1^1	7	0	1	1	54.0	40.50	9	.700	.727	0	—	0	-6	-5	0	0.0

● **KEN SANDERS**   Sanders, Kenneth George "Daffy" b: 7/8/41, St.Louis, Mo. BR/TR, 5'11", 185 lbs. Deb: 8/6/64

YEAR	TM/L	W	L	PCT	G	GS	CG	SH	SV	IP	H	HR	BB	SO	RAT	ERA	ERA+	OAV	OOB	BH	AVG	PB	PR	/A	PD	TPI
1964	KC-A	0	2	.000	21	0	0	0	1	27	23	2	17	18	13.7	3.67	104	.232	.350	0	—	0	-0	0	1	0.1
1966	Bos-A	3	6	.333	24	0	0	0	2	47^1	36	2	28	33	12.5	3.80	100	.214	.333	0	.000	-0	-2	0	0	-0.1
	KC-A	3	4	.429	38	1	0	0	0	65^1	59	7	48	41	14.9	3.72	91	.250	.379	2	.250	-2	-1	-2	1	-0.1
	Yr	6	10	.375	62	1	0	0	3	112^2	95	9	76	74	13.7	3.75	95	.233	.355	2	.143	-2	-4	-2	1	-0.1
1968	Oak-A	0	1	.000	7	0	0	0	0	10^2	8	1	8	6	13.5	3.38	84	.229	.372	0	—	0	-0	-1	0	-0.1
1970	Mil-A	5	2	.714	50	0	0	0	13	92^1	64	1	25	64	9.1	1.75	216	.201	.268	3	.231	1	20	21	1	2.4
1971	Mil-A	7	12	.368	**83**	0	0	0	**31**	136^1	111	9	34	80	9.8	1.91	181	.227	.282	0	.000	-1	**23**	**24**	2	4.7
1972	Mil-A	2	9	.182	62	0	0	0	17	92^1	88	10	31	51	11.8	3.12	97	.245	.309	1	.143	0	-1	-1	1	0.0
1973	Min-A	2	4	.333	27	0	0	0	8	44^1	53	4	21	19	15.4	6.09	65	.299	.380	0	—	0	-11	-11	-0	-1.7
	Cle-A	5	1	.833	15	0	0	0	5	27^1	18	2	9	14	8.9	1.65	238	.188	.257	0	—	0	7	7	0	1.8
	Yr	7	5	.583	42	0	0	0	13	71^2	71	6	30	33	12.7	4.40	90	.255	.328	0	—	0	-5	-4	0	0.1
1974	Cle-A	0	1	.000	9	0	0	0	1	11	21	5	5	4	21.3	9.82	37	.404	.456	0	—	0	-8	-8	-0	-0.7
	Cal-A	0	0	—	9	0	0	0	1	9^2	10	0	3	4	12.1	2.79	123	.278	.333	0	—	0	1	1	1	0.5
	Yr	0	1	.000	18	0	0	0	2	20^2	31	5	8	8	17.0	6.53	54	.352	.406	0	—	0	-7	-7	1	-0.2
1975	NY-N	1	1	.500	29	0	0	0	5	43	31	2	14	29	9.4	2.30	150	.205	.273	0	.000	-0	6	5	0	0.4
1976	NY-N	1	2	.333	31	0	0	0	0	47	39	4	12	16	10.0	2.87	115	.231	.286	0	—	0	3	2	1	0.2
	KC-A	0	0	—	3	0	0	0	0	3	3	0	3	2	18.0	0.00	—	.273	.429	0	—	0	1	1	0	-0.1
Total 10		29	45	.392	408	1	0	0	86	656^2	564	49	258	360	11.5	2.97	118	.235	.314	6	.115	-0	38	39	7	7.4

● **ROY SANDERS**   Sanders, Roy Garvin "Butch" or "Pepe" b: 8/1/1892, Stafford, Kan. d: 1/17/50, Kansas City, Mo. BR/TR, 6'0.5", 195 lbs. Deb: 4/16/17

YEAR	TM/L	W	L	PCT	G	GS	CG	SH	SV	IP	H	HR	BB	SO	RAT	ERA	ERA+	OAV	OOB	BH	AVG	PB	PR	/A	PD	TPI
1917	Cin-N	0	1	.000	2	2	1	0	0	14	12	0	16	3	18.6	4.50	58	.273	.475	0	.000	-1	-3	-3	1	-0.2
1918	Pit-N	7	9	.438	28	14	6	1	1	156	135	1	52	55	10.9	2.60	111	.239	.305	8	.151	-1	3	5	2	0.6
Total 2		7	10	.412	30	16	7	1	1	170	147	1	68	58	11.5	2.75	104	.241	.321	8	.136	-2	0	2	2	0.4

● **ROY SANDERS**   Sanders, Roy Lee "Simon" b: 6/10/1894, Missouri d: 7/8/63, Louisville, Ky. BR/TR, 6', 185 lbs. Deb: 8/6/18

YEAR	TM/L	W	L	PCT	G	GS	CG	SH	SV	IP	H	HR	BB	SO	RAT	ERA	ERA+	OAV	OOB	BH	AVG	PB	PR	/A	PD	TPI
1918	NY-A	0	2	.000	6	2	0	0	0	25^2	28	0	16	8	16.1	4.21	67	.301	.414	0	.000	-1	-4	-4	-1	-0.5
1920	StL-A	1	1	.500	8	2	0	0	0	17^1	20	1	17	2	19.7	5.19	75	.313	.463	0	.000	-1	-3	-2	-1	-0.4
Total 2		1	3	.250	14	4	0	0	0	43	48	1	33	10	17.6	4.60	71	.306	.435	0	.000	-2	-7	-6	-1	-0.9

● **SCOTT SANDERS**   Sanders, Scott Gerald b: 3/25/69, Hannibal, Mo. BR/TR, 6'4", 220 lbs. Deb: 8/6/93

YEAR	TM/L	W	L	PCT	G	GS	CG	SH	SV	IP	H	HR	BB	SO	RAT	ERA	ERA+	OAV	OOB	BH	AVG	PB	PR	/A	PD	TPI
1993	SD-N	3	3	.500	9	9	0	0	0	52^1	54	4	23	37	13.4	4.13	100	.265	.342	1	.063	-1	-1	0	-1	-0.2
1994	SD-N	4	8	.333	23	20	0	0	1	111	103	10	48	109	12.6	4.78	86	.245	.329	4	.125	-0	-7	-8	-1	-0.8
1995	SD-N	5	5	.500	17	15	1	0	0	90	79	14	31	88	11.2	4.30	94	.228	.296	8	.296	-3	-2	-3	-2	-0.2
1996	*SD-N	9	5	.643	46	16	0	0	0	144	117	16	48	157	10.4	3.38	118	.221	.288	7	.194	2	13	10	1	0.9
Total 4		21	21	.500	95	60	1	0	1	397^1	353	38	150	391	11.6	4.08	99	.235	.309	20	.180	3	5	-1	-3	-0.3

● **WAR SANDERS**   Sanders, Warren Williams b: 8/2/1877, Maynardville, Tenn. d: 8/3/62, Chattanooga, Tenn. BR/TL, 5'10", 160 lbs. Deb: 4/18/03

YEAR	TM/L	W	L	PCT	G	GS	CG	SH	SV	IP	H	HR	BB	SO	RAT	ERA	ERA+	OAV	OOB	BH	AVG	PB	PR	/A	PD	TPI
1903	StL-N	1	6	.143	8	6	3	0	0	40	48	0	21	16	16.0	6.07	54	.286	.342	1	.067	-1	-12	-12	-1	-1.9
1904	StL-N	1	2	.333	4	3	1	0	0	19	25	1	1	4	12.8	4.74	57	.298	.354	0	—	-1	-4	-4	0	-0.6
Total 2		2	8	.200	12	9	4	0	0	59	73	1	22	20	14.9	5.64	55	.290	.354	1	.048	-2	-17	-17	-0	-2.5

YEAR	TM/L	W	L	PCT	G	GS	CG	SH	SV	IP	H	HR	BB	SO	RAT	ERA	ERA+	OAV	OOB	BH	AVG	PB	PR	/A	PD	TPI

● SCOTT SANDERSON
Sanderson, Scott Douglas b: 7/22/56, Dearborn, Mich. BR/TR, 6'5", 200 lbs. Deb: 8/6/78

YEAR	TM/L	W	L	PCT	G	GS	CG	SH	SV	IP	H	HR	BB	SO	RAT	ERA	ERA+	OAV	OOB	BH	AVG	PB	PR	/A	PD	TPI
1978	Mon-N	4	2	.667	10	9	1	1	0	61	52	3	21	50	10.9	2.51	140	.232	.301	2	.105	-1	7	7	-1	0.5
1979	Mon-N	9	8	.529	34	24	5	3	1	168	148	16	54	138	11.0	3.43	107	.236	.300	8	.160	-0	6	4	-2	0.2
1980	Mon-N	16	11	.593	33	33	7	3	0	211¹	206	18	56	125	11.3	3.11	115	.257	.308	5	.078	-3	12	11	-2	0.8
1981	*Mon-N	9	7	.563	22	22	4	1	0	137¹	122	10	31	77	10.1	2.95	118	.236	.281	4	.114	2	8	8	-2	1.0
1982	Mon-N	12	12	.500	32	32	7	0	0	224	212	24	58	158	11.0	3.46	105	.251	.301	8	.140	1	4	5	-3	0.2
1983	Mon-N	6	7	.462	18	16	0	0	1	81¹	98	12	20	55	13.1	4.65	77	.303	.344	4	.143	-0	-9	-10	-1	-1.5
1984	*Chi-N	8	5	.615	24	24	3	0	0	140²	140	5	24	76	10.6	3.14	125	.264	.298	5	.119	-1	7	12	1	1.1
1985	Chi-N	5	6	.455	19	19	2	0	0	121	100	13	27	80	9.4	3.12	128	.228	.273	2	.065	-2	6	12	1	1.0
1986	Chi-N	9	11	.450	37	28	1	1	1	169²	165	21	37	124	10.8	4.19	96	.255	.297	3	.059	-3	-9	-3	-1	-0.8
1987	Chi-N	8	9	.471	32	22	0	0	0	144²	156	23	50	106	13.0	4.29	100	.274	.336	3	.075	-1	-3	-0	-1	-0.2
1988	Chi-N	1	2	.333	11	0	0	0	0	15¹	13	1	3	6	9.4	5.28	68	.232	.271	0	—	0	-0	-3	-0	-0.6
1989	*Chi-N	11	9	.550	37	23	2	0	0	146¹	155	16	31	86	11.6	3.94	95	.273	.313	2	.047	-2	-7	-3	-2	-0.8
1990	*Oak-A	17	11	.607	34	34	2	1	0	206¹	205	27	66	128	12.0	3.88	96	.255	.315	0	—	0	1	4	-2	-0.6
1991	NY-A☆	16	10	.615	34	34	2	2	0	208	200	22	29	130	10.0	3.81	109	.252	.281	0	—	0	7	8	-3	0.6
1992	NY-A	12	11	.522	33	33	2	1	0	193¹	220	28	64	104	13.4	4.93	79	.286	.344	0	—	0	-21	-22	-2	-2.5
1993	Cal-A	7	11	.389	21	21	4	1	0	135¹	153	15	27	66	12.3	4.46	101	.289	.329	0	—	0	-2	1	-1	-0.2
	SF-N	4	2	.667	11	8	0	0	0	48²	48	12	7	36	10.4	3.51	111	.255	.286	0	.000	-1	3	2	0	0.1
1994	Chi-A	8	4	.667	18	14	1	0	0	92	110	20	12	36	12.1	5.09	92	.296	.322	0	—	0	-3	-4	-1	-0.4
1995	Cal-A	1	3	.250	7	7	0	0	0	39¹	48	6	4	19	11.9	4.12	114	.298	.323	0	—	0	3	3	-0	0.2
1996	Cal-A	0	2	.000	5	4	0	0	0	18	39	5	4	7	22.5	7.50	65	.433	.469	0	—	0	-5	-5	0	-0.4
Total	19	163	143	.533	472	407	43	14	5	2561²	2590	297	625	1611	11.4	3.84	102	.263	.310	46	.097	-12	-1	19	-21	-2.3

● FRED SANFORD
Sanford, John Frederick b: 8/9/19, Garfield, Utah BB/TR, 6'1", 200 lbs. Deb: 5/5/43

YEAR	TM/L	W	L	PCT	G	GS	CG	SH	SV	IP	H	HR	BB	SO	RAT	ERA	ERA+	OAV	OOB	BH	AVG	PB	PR	/A	PD	TPI
1943	StL-A	0	0	—	3	0	0	0	0	9¹	7	0	4	2	10.6	1.93	172	.219	.306	0	—	0	1	1	0	0.0
1946	StL-A	2	1	.667	3	3	2	2	0	22	19	0	9	8	11.5	2.05	182	.235	.311	2	.286	1	4	4	-0	0.7
1947	StL-A	7	16	.304	34	23	9	0	4	186²	186	11	76	62	12.6	3.71	104	.261	.332	11	.204	-0	0	3	-1	0.2
1948	StL-A	12	21	.364	42	33	9	1	2	227	250	19	91	79	13.6	4.64	98	.279	.347	11	.151	-2	-9	-2	1	-0.4
1949	NY-A	7	3	.700	29	11	3	0	0	95¹	100	9	57	51	14.8	3.87	105	.270	.367	4	.118	-2	3	2	-0	-0.1
1950	NY-A	5	4	.556	26	12	2	0	0	112²	103	9	79	54	14.6	4.55	94	.252	.374	8	.229	1	0	-3	3	0.1
1951	NY-A	0	3	.000	11	2	0	0	0	26²	15	2	25	10	13.5	3.71	103	.169	.351	0	.000	-1	1	0	1	0.0
	Was-A	2	3	.400	7	7	0	0	0	37	51	5	27	12	19.0	6.57	62	.329	.429	1	.071	-1	-10	-10	-1	-1.3
	StL-A	2	4	.333	9	7	1	0	0	27¹	37	6	23	7	19.8	10.21	43	.308	.420	2	.286	1	-18	-18	-1	-2.9
	Yr	4	10	.286	27	16	1	0	0	91	103	13	75	29	17.6	6.82	60	.283	.405	3	.115	-1	-27	-27	-0	-4.2
Total	7	37	55	.402	164	98	26	3	6	744	768	67	391	285	14.1	4.45	94	.268	.357	39	.170	-4	-28	-21	2	-3.7

● JACK SANFORD
Sanford, John Stanley b: 5/18/29, Wellesley Hills, Mass. BR/TR, 6', 190 lbs. Deb: 9/16/56 C

YEAR	TM/L	W	L	PCT	G	GS	CG	SH	SV	IP	H	HR	BB	SO	RAT	ERA	ERA+	OAV	OOB	BH	AVG	PB	PR	/A	PD	TPI
1956	Phi-N	1	0	1.000	3	1	0	0	0	13	7	0	13	6	14.5	1.38	269	.184	.404	1	.333	0	3	3	0	0.3
1957	Phi-N★	19	8	.704	33	33	15	3	0	236²	194	22	94	**188**	11.1	3.08	124	**.221**	.298	15	.169	-1	21	19	-1	1.9
1958	Phi-N	10	13	.435	38	27	7	2	0	186¹	197	15	81	106	13.6	4.44	89	.274	.350	10	.169	-1	-10	-10	-2	-1.1
1959	SF-N	15	12	.556	36	31	10	0	1	222¹	198	22	70	132	11.1	3.16	121	.235	.300	8	.111	-1	20	16	-1	1.6
1960	SF-N	12	14	.462	37	34	11	**6**	0	219	199	11	99	125	12.3	3.82	91	.243	.326	13	.176	1	-1	-8	-1	-0.9
1961	SF-N	13	9	.591	38	33	6	0	0	217¹	203	22	87	112	12.2	4.22	90	.249	.325	16	.216	6	-5	-10	-1	-0.4
1962	*SF-N	24	7	.774	39	38	13	2	0	265¹	233	26	92	147	11.1	3.43	111	.234	.301	15	.153	0	15	11	2	1.3
1963	SF-N	16	13	.552	42	42	11	0	0	284¹	273	21	76	158	11.2	3.51	91	.251	.303	13	.138	3	-7	-10	3	-0.4
1964	SF-N	5	7	.417	18	17	3	1	1	106¹	91	7	37	64	11.2	3.30	108	.228	.300	4	.133	1	3	3	1	0.4
1965	SF-N	4	5	.444	23	16	0	0	2	91	92	11	30	42	12.8	3.96	91	.256	.325	3	.120	-0	-4	-4	-1	-0.4
	Cal-A	1	2	.333	9	5	0	0	1	29¹	35	2	10	13	13.8	4.60	74	.324	.381	1	.143	-0	-4	-4	-1	-0.4
1966	Cal-A	13	7	.650	50	6	0	0	5	108	108	11	27	54	11.6	3.83	88	.271	.323	3	.136	1	-5	-6	-1	-0.9
1967	Cal-A	3	2	.600	12	9	0	0	1	48¹	53	6	21	22	11.2	4.47	70	.288	.314	2	.200	1	-7	-7	1	-0.5
	KC-A	1	2	.333	10	1	0	0	0	22	24	1	14	13	16.4	6.55	49	.296	.412	0	.000	-0	-8	-8	1	-1.0
	Yr	4	4	.500	22	10	0	0	1	70¹	77	7	21	34	12.8	5.12	62	.288	.345	2	.167	1	-15	-15	2	-1.5
Total	12	137	101	.576	388	293	76	14	11	2049¹	1907	174	737	1182	11.8	3.69	98	.247	.316	105	.158	12	11	-14	3	-0.5

● MO SANFORD
Sanford, Meredith Leroy b: 12/24/66, Americus, Ga. BR/TR, 6'6", 220 lbs. Deb: 8/9/91

YEAR	TM/L	W	L	PCT	G	GS	CG	SH	SV	IP	H	HR	BB	SO	RAT	ERA	ERA+	OAV	OOB	BH	AVG	PB	PR	/A	PD	TPI
1991	Cin-N	1	2	.333	5	5	0	0	0	28	19	3	15	31	11.3	3.86	99	.186	.297	0	.000	-1	-1	-0	-0	-0.1
1993	Col-N	1	2	.333	11	6	0	0	0	35²	37	4	27	36	16.1	5.30	90	.278	.400	0	.000	-1	-5	-2	-1	-0.3
1995	Min-A	0	0	—	11	0	0	0	0	18²	16	7	16	17	16.4	5.30	90	.225	.382	0	—	0	-1	-1	-1	-0.1
Total	3	2	4	.333	27	11	0	0	0	82¹	72	14	58	84	14.5	4.81	92	.235	.362	0	.000	-2	-7	-3	-2	-0.5

● JOSE SANTIAGO
Santiago, Jose Guillermo (Guzman) "Pants" b: 9/4/28, Coamo, P.R. BR/TR, 5'10", 175 lbs. Deb: 4/17/54

YEAR	TM/L	W	L	PCT	G	GS	CG	SH	SV	IP	H	HR	BB	SO	RAT	ERA	ERA+	OAV	OOB	BH	AVG	PB	PR	/A	PD	TPI
1954	Cle-A	0	0	—	1	0	0	0	0	2	1	0	2	1	10.8	0.00	—	.000	.286	0	—	0	1	1	-0	0.0
1955	Cle-A	2	0	1.000	17	0	0	0	0	32²	31	1	14	19	13.8	2.48	161	.256	.357	2	.500	1	5	5	0	0.4
1956	KC-A	1	2	.333	9	5	0	0	0	21²	36	3	17	9	24.1	8.31	52	.387	.504	2	.400	0	-10	-10	-1	-1.0
Total	3	3	2	.600	27	5	0	0	0	56	67	4	33	29	17.7	4.66	88	.306	.420	4	.444	2	-4	-3	0	-0.6

● JOSE SANTIAGO
Santiago, Jose Rafael (Alfonso) b: 8/15/40, Juana Diaz, P.R. BR/TR, 6'2", 185 lbs. Deb: 9/9/63

YEAR	TM/L	W	L	PCT	G	GS	CG	SH	SV	IP	H	HR	BB	SO	RAT	ERA	ERA+	OAV	OOB	BH	AVG	PB	PR	/A	PD	TPI
1963	KC-A	1	0	1.000	4	0	0	0	0	7	8	4	2	6	12.9	9.00	43	.276	.323	0	—	0	-4	-4	0	-0.5
1964	KC-A	0	6	.000	34	8	0	0	0	83²	84	9	35	64	13.2	4.73	81	.258	.337	0	.000	-2	-10	-9	-1	-0.8
1965	KC-A	0	0	—	4	0	0	0	0	5	8	1	4	8	21.6	9.00	39	.364	.462	0	—	0	-3	-3	0	-0.4
1966	Bos-A	12	13	.480	35	28	7	1	2	172	155	17	58	119	11.3	3.66	104	.238	.302	11	.196	-1	-4	3	-1	0.3
1967	*Bos-A	12	4	.750	50	11	2	0	5	145¹	138	14	47	109	11.6	3.59	97	.251	.313	8	.190	2	4	3	-1	0.1
1968	Bos-A†	9	4	.692	18	18	7	2	0	124	96	9	42	86	10.2	2.25	140	.215	.287	7	.163	1	10	13	-0	1.4
1969	Bos-A	0	0	—	10	0	0	0	0	7²	11	2	4	4	17.6	3.52	108	.324	.395	0	—	0	-0	0	-0	0.0
1970	Bos-A	0	2	.000	8	0	0	0	1	11	18	0	8	8	20.6	10.32	38	.353	.441	2	.667	1	-8	-8	-0	-1.3
Total	8	34	29	.540	163	65	16	3	8	556	518	56	200	404	11.8	3.74	96	.246	.314	28	.173	2	-26	-10	-2	-0.8

● AL SANTORINI
Santorini, Alan Joel b: 5/19/48, Irvington, N.J. BR/TR, 6', 190 lbs. Deb: 9/10/68

YEAR	TM/L	W	L	PCT	G	GS	CG	SH	SV	IP	H	HR	BB	SO	RAT	ERA	ERA+	OAV	OOB	BH	AVG	PB	PR	/A	PD	TPI
1968	Atl-N	0	1	.000	3	1	0	0	0	3	4	1	0	0	12.0	0.00	—	.286	.286	0	—	0	1	1	-0	0.4
1969	SD-N	8	14	.364	32	30	2	1	0	184²	194	11	73	111	13.4	3.95	90	.270	.343	7	.111	-1	-7	-8	1	-1.0
1970	SD-N	1	8	.111	21	12	0	0	0	75²	91	11	43	41	16.3	6.07	66	.294	.385	0	.000	-2	-17	-18	-1	-2.1
1971	SD-N	0	2	.000	18	3	0	0	0	38¹	43	4	11	21	12.7	3.76	88	.285	.333	2	.400	1	-1	-2	-1	-0.1
	StL-N	0	2	.000	19	5	0	0	2	49²	51	2	19	51	12.9	3.81	95	.270	.340	3	.300	1	-2	-1	-0	0.0
	Yr	0	4	.000	37	8	0	0	2	88	94	6	30	72	12.8	3.78	92	.275	.335	5	.333	1	-3	-3	-1	-0.1
1972	StL-N	8	11	.421	30	19	3	0	0	133²	136	6	46	72	12.3	4.11	83	.263	.324	3	.075	-2	-10	-10	-1	-1.7
1973	StL-N	0	0	—	4	0	0	0	0	8¹	14	1	2	2	18.4	5.40	72	.400	.447	0	.000	-0	-2	-2	0	0.0
Total	6	17	38	.309	127	70	5	4	3	493¹	533	36	194	268	13.5	4.29	83	.276	.346	15	.109	-4	-38	-40	-3	-4.5

● MANNY SARMIENTO
Sarmiento, Manuel Eduardo (Aponte) b: 2/2/56, Cagua, Venez. BR/TR, 6', 170 lbs. Deb: 7/30/76

YEAR	TM/L	W	L	PCT	G	GS	CG	SH	SV	IP	H	HR	BB	SO	RAT	ERA	ERA+	OAV	OOB	BH	AVG	PB	PR	/A	PD	TPI
1976	*Cin-N	5	1	.833	22	0	0	0	0	43²	36	1	12	20	10.1	2.06	170	.222	.280	0	.000	-0	7	7	-1	0.7
1977	Cin-N	0	0	—	24	0	0	0	1	40¹	28	6	11	23	8.7	2.45	160	.196	.253	0	.000	-0	7	7	-1	-0.1
1978	Cin-N	9	7	.563	63	6	0	0	5	127¹	109	16	54	72	11.6	4.38	81	.234	.315	0	.000	-1	-11	-12	-1	-1.7
1979	Cin-N	4	0	.000	23	1	0	0	0	38²	47	2	9	19	12.8	4.66	80	.311	.346	0	.000	-1	-4	-4	-0	-0.5
1980	Sea-A	0	1	.000	9	0	0	0	1	14²	14	2	6	15	12.3	3.68	112	.255	.328	0	—	0	1	-0	0	0.0
1982	Pit-N	9	4	.692	35	17	4	0	1	164²	153	7	46	81	10.9	3.39	109	.246	.298	5	.191	1	4	6	2	0.3
1983	Pit-N	3	5	.375	52	5	0	0	4	84¹	74	8	36	49	11.7	2.99	124	.243	.324	0	.000	-1	6	7	-1	0.5
Total	7	26	22	.542	228	22	4	0	12	513²	461	42	172	283	11.1	3.49	106	.242	.306	9	.103	-3	9	11	-6	-0.8

● KEVIN SAUCIER
Saucier, Kevin Andrew b: 8/9/56, Pensacola, Fla. BR/TL, 6'1", 196 lbs. Deb: 10/1/78

YEAR	TM/L	W	L	PCT	G	GS	CG	SH	SV	IP	H	HR	BB	SO	RAT	ERA	ERA+	OAV	OOB	BH	AVG	PB	PR	/A	PD	TPI
1978	Phi-N	0	1	.000	1	0	0	0	0	2	4	0	1	2	27.0	18.00	20	.400	.500	0	—	0	-3	-3	-0	-0.9
1979	Phi-N	1	4	.200	29	2	0	0	0	62¹	68	4	35	21	15.0	4.19	91	.291	.385	1	.100	-1	-3	-3	0	-0.2

YEAR	TM/L	W	L	PCT	G	GS	CG	SH	SV	IP	H	HR	BB	SO	RAT	ERA	ERA+	OAV	OOB	BH	AVG	PB	PR	/A	PD	TPI
1980	*Phi-N	7	3	.700	40	0	0	0	13	50	50	2	20	25	13.3	3.42	111	.281	.366	0	.000	-1	1	2	0	0.3
1981	Det-A	4	2	.667	38	0	0	0	13	49	26	1	21	23	9.6	1.65	228	.160	.277	0	—	0	11	12	0	2.0
1982	Det-A	3	1	.750	31	1	0	0	5	40¹	35	0	29	23	14.7	3.12	130	.254	.391	0	—	0	4	4	0	0.5
Total	5	15	11	.577	139	3	0	0	19	203²	183	7	104	94	13.3	3.31	116	.253	.359	1	.056	-2	10	12	1	1.7

● **DENNIS SAUNDERS**   Saunders, Dennis James b: 1/4/49, Alhambra, Cal. BB/TR, 6'3", 195 lbs. Deb: 5/21/70

YEAR	TM/L	W	L	PCT	G	GS	CG	SH	SV	IP	H	HR	BB	SO	RAT	ERA	ERA+	OAV	OOB	BH	AVG	PB	PR	/A	PD	TPI
1970	Det-A	1	1	.500	8	0	0	0	0	14	16	1	5	8	14.1	3.21	116	.286	.355	0	—	-1	1	1	1	0.1

● **RICH SAUVEUR**   Sauveur, Richard Daniel b: 11/23/63, Arlington, Va. BL/TL, 6'4", 163 lbs. Deb: 7/1/86

YEAR	TM/L	W	L	PCT	G	GS	CG	SH	SV	IP	H	HR	BB	SO	RAT	ERA	ERA+	OAV	OOB	BH	AVG	PB	PR	/A	PD	TPI
1986	Pit-N	0	0	—	3	3	0	0	0	12	17	3	6	6	18.8	6.00	64	.354	.446	1	.333	0	-3	-3	1	0.1
1988	Mon-N	0	0	—	4	0	0	0	0	3	3	1	2	3	15.0	6.00	60	.250	.357	0	—	0	-1	-1	0	0.0
1991	NY-N	0	0	—	6	0	0	0	0	3¹	7	1	2	4	24.3	10.80	34	.467	.529	0	—	0	-3	-3	0	0.0
1992	KC-A	0	1	.000	8	0	0	0	0	14¹	15	1	8	7	15.7	4.40	92	.273	.385	0	—	0	-1	-1	-0	-0.1
1996	Chi-A	0	0	—	3	0	0	0	0	3	3	1	5	1	27.0	15.00	31	.333	.600	0	—	0	-3	-3	0	0.2
Total	5	0	1	.000	24	3	0	0	0	35²	45	7	23	21	18.4	6.56	60	.324	.437	1	.333	0	-11	-10	1	0.2

● **JACK SAVAGE**   Savage, John Joseph b: 4/22/64, Louisville, Ky. BR/TR, 6'3", 190 lbs. Deb: 9/14/87

YEAR	TM/L	W	L	PCT	G	GS	CG	SH	SV	IP	H	HR	BB	SO	RAT	ERA	ERA+	OAV	OOB	BH	AVG	PB	PR	/A	PD	TPI
1987	LA-N	0	0	—	3	0	0	0	0	3¹	4	0	0	0	10.8	2.70	147	.286	.286	0	—	0	1	0	-0	0.0
1990	Min-A	0	2	.000	17	0	0	0	1	26	37	3	11	12	16.6	8.31	50	.339	.400	0	—	0	-13	-12	-0	-0.9
Total	2	0	2	.000	20	0	0	0	1	29¹	41	3	11	12	16.0	7.67	54	.333	.388	0	—	0	-12	-12	-0	-0.9

● **BOB SAVAGE**   Savage, John Robert b: 12/1/21, Manchester, N.H. BR/TR, 6'2", 180 lbs. Deb: 6/24/42

YEAR	TM/L	W	L	PCT	G	GS	CG	SH	SV	IP	H	HR	BB	SO	RAT	ERA	ERA+	OAV	OOB	BH	AVG	PB	PR	/A	PD	TPI
1942	Phi-A	0	1	.000	8	3	0	0	0	30²	24	0	31	10	16.1	3.23	117	.220	.393	1	.111	0	1	2	0	0.1
1946	Phi-A	3	15	.167	40	19	7	1	2	164	164	5	93	78	14.2	4.06	87	.259	.355	5	.122	1	-10	-9	-3	-1.2
1947	Phi-A	8	10	.444	44	8	2	1	2	146	135	8	55	56	11.7	3.76	101	.245	.314	2	.050	-4	-1	1	-2	-0.5
1948	Phi-A	5	1	.833	33	1	1	0	5	75¹	98	9	33	26	15.7	6.21	69	.318	.384	1	.077	-1	-16	-16	-1	-1.4
1949	StL-A	0	0	—	4	0	0	0	0	7	12	1	3	1	19.3	6.43	70	.400	.455	0	.000	0	-2	-1	0	0.0
Total	5	16	27	.372	129	31	10	2	9	423	433	23	215	171	13.8	4.32	88	.265	.352	9	.087	-3	-27	-24	-6	-3.1

● **DON SAVIDGE**   Savidge, Donald Snyder b: 8/28/08, Berwick, Pa. d: 3/22/83, Santa Barbara, Cal BR/TR, 6'1", 180 lbs. Deb: 8/6/29 F

YEAR	TM/L	W	L	PCT	G	GS	CG	SH	SV	IP	H	HR	BB	SO	RAT	ERA	ERA+	OAV	OOB	BH	AVG	PB	PR	/A	PD	TPI
1929	Was-A	0	0	—	3	0	0	0	0	6	12	1	2	2	21.0	9.00	47	.414	.452	0	—	0	-3	-3	0	0.0

● **RALPH SAVIDGE**   Savidge, Ralph Austin "The Human Whipcord" b: 2/3/1879, Jerseytown, Pa. d: 7/22/59, Berwick, Pa. BR/TR, 6'2", 210 lbs. Deb: 9/22/08 F

YEAR	TM/L	W	L	PCT	G	GS	CG	SH	SV	IP	H	HR	BB	SO	RAT	ERA	ERA+	OAV	OOB	BH	AVG	PB	PR	/A	PD	TPI
1908	Cin-N	0	1	.000	4	1	1	0	0	21	18	0	8	7	11.1	2.57	90	.247	.321	0	.000	-1	-0	-1	-1	-0.2
1909	Cin-N	0	0	—	1	0	0	0	0	4	10	1	3	2	31.5	22.50	12	.588	.667	0	—	-0	-9	-9	0	0.0
Total	2	0	1	.000	5	1	1	0	0	25	28	1	11	9	14.4	5.76	41	.311	.392	0	.000	-1	-9	-9	-1	-0.2

● **MOE SAVRANSKY**   Savransky, Morris b: 1/13/29, Cleveland, Ohio BL/TL, 5'11", 175 lbs. Deb: 4/23/54

YEAR	TM/L	W	L	PCT	G	GS	CG	SH	SV	IP	H	HR	BB	SO	RAT	ERA	ERA+	OAV	OOB	BH	AVG	PB	PR	/A	PD	TPI
1954	Cin-N	0	2	.000	16	0	0	0	0	24	23	6	8	7	12.4	4.88	86	.247	.320	1	.500	1	-2	-2	1	0.0

● **RICK SAWYER**   Sawyer, Richard Clyde b: 4/7/48, Bakersfield, Cal. BR/TR, 6'2", 205 lbs. Deb: 4/28/74

YEAR	TM/L	W	L	PCT	G	GS	CG	SH	SV	IP	H	HR	BB	SO	RAT	ERA	ERA+	OAV	OOB	BH	AVG	PB	PR	/A	PD	TPI
1974	NY-A	0	0	—	1	0	0	0	0	1²	2	0	1	1	16.2	16.20	22	.500	.600	0	—	0	-2	-2	0	0.1
1975	NY-A	0	0	—	4	0	0	0	0	6	7	0	2	3	13.5	3.00	123	.304	.360	0	—	0	1	-0	-0	0.0
1976	SD-N	5	3	.625	13	11	4	2	0	81²	84	2	38	33	13.6	2.53	129	.272	.353	5	.208	1	9	7	-0	0.7
1977	SD-N	7	6	.538	56	9	0	0	0	111	136	15	55	45	16.1	5.84	61	.316	.402	3	.150	1	-24	-28	1	-2.7
Total	4	12	9	.571	74	20	4	2	0	200¹	229	17	96	82	15.0	4.49	76	.290	.384	8	.182	2	-17	-24	1	-1.9

● **WILL SAWYER**   Sawyer, Willard Newton b: 7/29/1864, Brimfield, Ohio d: 1/5/36, Kent, Ohio BL/TL, Deb: 7/21/1883

YEAR	TM/L	W	L	PCT	G	GS	CG	SH	SV	IP	H	HR	BB	SO	RAT	ERA	ERA+	OAV	OOB	BH	AVG	PB	PR	/A	PD	TPI
1883	Cle-N	4	10	.286	17	15	15	0	0	141	119	1	47	76	10.6	2.36	133	**.217**	.279	1	.021	-7	12	12	-3	0.1

● **BILL SAYLES**   Sayles, William Nisbeth b: 7/27/17, Portland, Ore. BR/TR, 6'2", 175 lbs. Deb: 7/17/39

YEAR	TM/L	W	L	PCT	G	GS	CG	SH	SV	IP	H	HR	BB	SO	RAT	ERA	ERA+	OAV	OOB	BH	AVG	PB	PR	/A	PD	TPI
1939	Bos-A	0	0	—	5	0	0	0	0	14	14	1	13	9	17.4	7.07	67	.264	.409	1	.143	-0	-4	-4	0	0.0
1943	NY-N	1	3	.250	18	3	1	0	0	53	60	1	23	38	14.1	4.75	72	.284	.355	4	.308	1	-8	-8	-0	-0.5
	Bro-N	0	0	—	5	0	0	0	0	11²	13	0	10	5	17.7	7.71	44	.271	.397	1	.500	0	-6	-6	-0	0.0
	Yr	1	3	.250	23	3	1	0	0	64²	73	1	33	43	14.8	5.29	65	.282	.363	5	.333	1	-14	-13	-1	-0.5
Total	2	1	3	.250	28	3	1	0	0	78²	87	2	46	52	15.2	5.61	65	.279	.372	6	.273	1	-17	-17	-0	-0.5

● **PHIL SAYLOR**   Saylor, Philip Andrew "Lefty" b: 1/2/1871, Van Wert Co., Ohio d: 7/23/37, W.Alexandria, O. TL, Deb: 7/11/1891

YEAR	TM/L	W	L	PCT	G	GS	CG	SH	SV	IP	H	HR	BB	SO	RAT	ERA	ERA+	OAV	OOB	BH	AVG	PB	PR	/A	PD	TPI
1891	Phi-N	0	0	—	1	0	0	0	0	3	2	1	0	0	6.0	6.00	57	.182	.182	0	—	-0	-1	-1	-0	0.0

● **FRANK SCANLAN**   Scanlan, Frank Aloysius b: 4/28/1890, Syracuse, N.Y. d: 4/9/69, Brooklyn, N.Y. BL/TL, 6'1.5", 175 lbs. Deb: 8/6/09 F

YEAR	TM/L	W	L	PCT	G	GS	CG	SH	SV	IP	H	HR	BB	SO	RAT	ERA	ERA+	OAV	OOB	BH	AVG	PB	PR	/A	PD	TPI
1909	Phi-N	0	0	—	6	0	0	0	1	11	8	0	5	6	10.6	1.64	159	.211	.302	0	—	-1	1	1	-0	-0.1

● **BOB SCANLAN**   Scanlan, Robert Guy b: 8/9/66, Los Angeles, Cal. BR/TR, 6'7", 215 lbs. Deb: 5/7/91

YEAR	TM/L	W	L	PCT	G	GS	CG	SH	SV	IP	H	HR	BB	SO	RAT	ERA	ERA+	OAV	OOB	BH	AVG	PB	PR	/A	PD	TPI
1991	Chi-N	7	8	.467	40	13	0	0	1	111	114	5	40	44	12.7	3.89	100	.268	.335	1	.042	-2	-3	-0	-0	-0.2
1992	Chi-N	3	6	.333	69	0	0	0	14	87¹	76	4	30	42	11.0	2.89	125	.235	.302	0	.000	-0	6	7	1	1.0
1993	Chi-N	4	5	.444	70	0	0	0	0	75¹	79	6	28	44	13.1	4.54	88	.278	.349	1	.500	0	-4	-5	-1	-0.6
1994	Mil-A	2	6	.250	30	12	0	0	2	103	117	11	28	65	13.0	4.11	122	.288	.340	—	—	0	8	11	0	0.7
1995	Mil-A	4	7	.364	17	14	0	0	0	83¹	101	9	44	29	16.4	6.59	76	.304	.397	—	—	0	-17	-15	-1	-1.6
1996	Det-A	0	0	—	8	0	0	0	0	11	16	1	9	3	21.3	10.64	48	.348	.464	0	—	0	-7	-7	-0	0.0
	KC-A	0	1	.000	9	0	0	0	0	11¹	13	1	3	3	13.5	3.18	154	.295	.354	0	—	0	2	2	0	0.2
	Yr	0	1	.000	17	0	0	0	0	22¹	29	2	12	6	16.9	6.85	73	.319	.404	0	—	0	-5	-5	-0	0.2
Total	6	20	33	.377	243	39	0	0	17	482¹	516	37	182	230	13.4	4.46	97	.277	.348	2	.067	-2	-15	-7	-0	-0.5

● **DOC SCANLAN**   Scanlan, William Dennis b: 3/7/1881, Syracuse, N.Y. d: 5/29/49, Brooklyn, N.Y. BL/TR, 5'8", 165 lbs. Deb: 9/24/03 F

YEAR	TM/L	W	L	PCT	G	GS	CG	SH	SV	IP	H	HR	BB	SO	RAT	ERA	ERA+	OAV	OOB	BH	AVG	PB	PR	/A	PD	TPI
1903	Pit-N	0	1	.000	1	1	1	0	0	9	5	0	6	4	11.0	4.00	81	.167	.306	0	.000	0	-1	-1	-0	-0.1
1904	Pit-N	1	3	.250	4	3	1	0	0	22	21	0	20	10	17.6	4.91	56	.236	.387	0	.000	-1	-5	-5	-0	-0.9
	Bro-N	6	6	.500	13	12	11	3	0	104	94	0	40	40	11.8	2.16	127	.242	.316	5	.143	-2	7	7	-2	0.4
	Yr	7	9	.438	17	15	12	3	0	126	115	0	60	50	12.6	2.64	104	.240	.327	5	.122	-2	1	1	-2	-0.5
1905	Bro-N	14	12	.538	33	28	22	2	0	249²	220	4	104	135	12.0	2.92	99	.237	.319	16	.167	-2	2	-1	-2	-0.4
1906	Bro-N	18	13	.581	38	33	28	6	2	288	230	5	127	94	11.3	3.19	79	.214	.301	18	.186	3	-18	-21	-7	-2.7
1907	Bro-N	6	8	.429	17	15	10	2	0	107	90	1	61	59	13.0	3.20	73	.239	.349	6	.265	5	-9	-10	-2	-0.9
1909	Bro-N	8	7	.533	19	17	13	1	0	141¹	125	0	65	72	12.4	2.93	88	.252	.343	12	.273	-5	-5	-1	-0	-0.1
1910	Bro-N	9	11	.450	34	25	14	0	2	217¹	175	1	116	103	12.3	2.61	116	.234	.341	14	.203	1	10	10	-2	0.7
1911	Bro-N	3	10	.231	22	15	3	1	1	113²	101	2	69	45	13.9	3.64	92	.256	.374	4	.121	-2	-2	-3	-0	-0.8
Total	8	65	71	.478	181	149	102	15	5	1252	1061	15	608	584	12.3	3.00	93	.234	.330	78	.188	8	-21	-31	-17	-4.6

● **PAT SCANTLEBURY**   Scantlebury, Patricio Athelstan b: 11/11/17, Gatun, Canal Zone d: 5/24/91, Glen Ridge, N.J. BL/TL, 6'1", 180 lbs. Deb: 4/19/56

YEAR	TM/L	W	L	PCT	G	GS	CG	SH	SV	IP	H	HR	BB	SO	RAT	ERA	ERA+	OAV	OOB	BH	AVG	PB	PR	/A	PD	TPI
1956	Cin-N	0	1	.000	6	2	0	0	0	19	24	5	10	10	13.7	6.63	60	.293	.333	0	.000	-0	-6	-6	-0	-0.3

● **RANDY SCARBERY**   Scarbery, Randy James b: 6/22/52, Fresno, Cal. BB/TR, 6'1", 185 lbs. Deb: 4/16/79

YEAR	TM/L	W	L	PCT	G	GS	CG	SH	SV	IP	H	HR	BB	SO	RAT	ERA	ERA+	OAV	OOB	BH	AVG	PB	PR	/A	PD	TPI
1979	Chi-A	2	8	.200	45	5	0	0	4	101¹	102	9	34	45	12.3	4.62	92	.262	.326	0	—	0	-5	-4	0	-0.4
1980	Chi-A	1	2	.333	15	0	0	0	2	28²	24	1	7	18	10.4	4.08	99	.238	.300	0	—	0	-0	-0	-0	0.0
Total	2	3	10	.231	60	5	0	0	6	130	126	10	41	63	11.9	4.50	93	.257	.320	0	—	0	-5	-4	-0	-0.4

● **RAY SCARBOROUGH**   Scarborough, Ray Wilson (b: Rae Wilson Scarborough) b: 7/23/17, Mt.Gilead, N.C. d: 7/1/82, Mount Olive, N.C. BR/TR, 6', 185 lbs. Deb: 6/26/42 C

YEAR	TM/L	W	L	PCT	G	GS	CG	SH	SV	IP	H	HR	BB	SO	RAT	ERA	ERA+	OAV	OOB	BH	AVG	PB	PR	/A	PD	TPI
1942	Was-A	2	1	.667	17	5	1	1	0	63¹	68	2	32	16	14.2	4.12	89	.272	.355	4	.190	0	-3	-3	1	-0.1
1943	Was-A	4	4	.500	24	6	2	0	3	86	93	2	46	43	14.5	2.83	113	.273	.359	8	.333	2	5	4	0	0.6
1946	Was-A	7	11	.389	32	20	6	1	1	155²	176	8	74	65	14.5	4.05	83	.286	.364	5	.140	-9	-12	-12	-2	-1.3
1947	Was-A	6	13	.316	38	18	8	2	0	161	165	5	67	63	13.0	3.41	109	.267	.339	6	.120	-3	6	6	-0	0.3
1948	Was-A	15	8	.652	31	26	8	0	1	185¹	166	10	72	76	11.7	2.82	154	.233	.307	14	.219	-0	30	31	3	3.8
1949	Was-A	13	11	.542	34	27	11	1	0	199²	204	10	88	81	13.5	4.60	93	.265	.346	13	.194	-0	-9	-8	1	-0.7

YEAR	TM/L	W	L	PCT	G	GS	CG	SH	SV	IP	H	HR	BB	SO	RAT	ERA	ERA+	OAV	OOB	BH	AVG	PB	PR	/A	PD	TPI
1950	Was-A	3	5	.375	8	8	4	2	0	58¹	62	1	22	24	13.3	4.01	112	.276	.345	2	.100	-1	4	3	1	0.3
	Chi-A☆	10	13	.435	27	23	8	1	1	149¹	160	10	62	70	13.6	5.30	85	.274	.347	8	.174	-1	-12	-14	-1	-1.9
	Yr	13	18	.419	35	31	12	3	1	207²	222	11	84	94	13.4	4.94	91	.273	.344	10	.152	-3	-8	-10	0	-1.6
1951	Bos-A	12	9	.571	37	22	8	0	0	184	201	21	61	71	13.5	5.09	88	.275	.342	13	.191	-2	-20	-13	1	-1.5
1952	Bos-A	1	5	.167	28	8	1	1	4	76²	79	8	35	29	13.9	4.81	82	.266	.351	4	.222	0	-10	-7	0	-0.6
	*NY-A	5	1	.833	9	4	1	0	0	34	27	4	15	11	11.4	2.91	114	.223	.314	5	.357	2	3	2	0	0.4
	Yr	6	6	.500	37	12	2	1	4	110²	106	12	50	42	12.8	4.23	89	.251	.332	9	.281	2	-7	-6	0	-0.2
1953	NY-A	2	2	.500	25	1	0	0	0	54²	52	4	26	20	13.5	3.29	112	.250	.345	1	.083	-0	4	2	0	0.2
	Det-A	0	2	.000	13	0	0	0	2	20²	34	3	11	12	20.9	8.27	49	.354	.436	0	.000	-0	-10	-10	-0	-1.1
	Yr	2	4	.333	38	1	0	0	2	75¹	86	7	37	32	15.1	4.66	81	.279	.362	1	.071	-0	-6	-7	-0	-0.9
Total 10		80	85	.485	318	168	59	9	12	1428¹	1487	88	611	564	13.5	4.13	97	.267	.344	85	.186	-6	-22	-19	4	-1.6

● MAC SCARCE
Scarce, Guerrant McCurdy b: 4/8/49, Danville, Va.   BL/TL, 6'3", 200 lbs.   Deb: 7/10/72

YEAR	TM/L	W	L	PCT	G	GS	CG	SH	SV	IP	H	HR	BB	SO	RAT	ERA	ERA+	OAV	OOB	BH	AVG	PB	PR	/A	PD	TPI
1972	Phi-N	1	2	.333	31	0	0	0	4	36²	30	6	20	40	12.8	3.44	105	.222	.331	0	.000	-1	0	1	1	0.1
1973	Phi-N	1	8	.111	52	0	0	0	12	70²	54	3	47	57	13.0	2.42	157	.220	.347	0	.000	-1	10	11	-1	1.5
1974	Phi-N	3	8	.273	58	0	0	0	5	70¹	72	6	35	50	13.9	4.99	76	.275	.365	0	.000	-1	-11	-9	-1	-1.7
1975	NY-N	0	0	—	1	0	0	0	0	0	1	0	0	0	—			1.000	1.000	0		0	0	0	0	0.0
1978	Min-A	1	1	.500	17	0	0	0	0	32	35	5	15	17	14.9	3.94	97	.292	.384	0	—	0	-1	-0	-1	-0.1
Total 5		6	19	.240	159	0	0	0	21	209²	192	20	117	164	13.6	3.69	102	.251	.357	0	.000	-2	-2	2	-2	-0.2

● AL SCHACHT
Schacht, Alexander b: 11/11/1892, New York, N.Y. d: 7/14/84, Waterbury, Conn.   BR/TR, 5'11", 142 lbs.   Deb: 9/18/19 C

YEAR	TM/L	W	L	PCT	G	GS	CG	SH	SV	IP	H	HR	BB	SO	RAT	ERA	ERA+	OAV	OOB	BH	AVG	PB	PR	/A	PD	TPI
1919	Was-A	2	0	1.000	2	2	1	0	0	15	14	0	4	4	10.8	2.40	134	.233	.281	0	.000	0	1	1	-0	0.2
1920	Was-A	6	4	.600	22	11	5	1	1	99¹	130	3	30	19	14.6	4.44	84	.319	.367	5	.192	1	-7	-8	-2	-0.4
1921	Was-A	6	6	.500	29	5	2	0	1	82²	110	2	27	15	15.1	4.90	84	.332	.386	5	.227	1	-6	-7	-3	-1.1
Total 3		14	10	.583	53	18	8	1	2	197	254	4	61	38	14.5	4.48	86	.318	.368	10	.196	2	-11	-14	-2	-1.3

● SID SCHACHT
Schacht, Sidney b: 2/3/18, Bogota, N.J. d: 3/30/91, Ft.Lauderdale, Fla.   BR/TR, 5'11", 170 lbs.   Deb: 4/23/50

YEAR	TM/L	W	L	PCT	G	GS	CG	SH	SV	IP	H	HR	BB	SO	RAT	ERA	ERA+	OAV	OOB	BH	AVG	PB	PR	/A	PD	TPI
1950	StL-A	0	0	—	8	1	0	0	0	10²	24	5	14	7	32.1	16.03	31	.429	.543	0	.000	-0	-14	-13	-0	0.0
1951	StL-A	0	0	—	6	0	0	0	0	6	14	1	5	4	28.5	21.00	21	.452	.528	0	.000	-0	-11	-11	-0	-0.4
	Bos-N	0	2	.000	5	0	0	0	0	4²	6	0	2	1	15.4	1.93	191	.300	.364	0	—	0	1	1	-0	0.3
Total 2		0	2	.000	19	1	0	0	0	21¹	44	6	21	12	27.4	14.34	31	.411	.508	0	.000	-0	-24	-23	-1	-0.1

● HAL SCHACKER
Schacker, Harold b: 4/6/25, Brooklyn, N.Y.   BR/TR, 6', 190 lbs.   Deb: 5/9/45

YEAR	TM/L	W	L	PCT	G	GS	CG	SH	SV	IP	H	HR	BB	SO	RAT	ERA	ERA+	OAV	OOB	BH	AVG	PB	PR	/A	PD	TPI
1945	Bos-N	0	1	.000	6	0	0	0	0	15¹	14	2	9	6	13.5	5.28	73	.241	.343	0	.000	-0	-3	-2	-0	-0.2

● GERMANY SCHAEFER
Schaefer, Herman A. b: 2/4/1877, Chicago, Ill. d: 5/16/19, Saranac Lake, N.Y.   BR/TR, 5'9", 175 lbs.   Deb: 10/5/01 ♦

YEAR	TM/L	W	L	PCT	G	GS	CG	SH	SV	IP	H	HR	BB	SO	RAT	ERA	ERA+	OAV	OOB	BH	AVG	PB	PR	/A	PD	TPI
1912	Was-A	0	0	—	1	0	0	0	0	1	0	0	0	0	13.5	0.00	—	.333	.333	41	.247	0	0	0	-0	0.0
1913	Was-A	0	0	—	1	0	0	0	0	0¹	2	1	0	0	54.0	54.00	5	.667	.667	32	.320	0	-2	-2	0	0.0
Total 2		0	0	—	2	0	0	0	0	1	3	1	0	0	27.0	18.00	18	.500	.500	972	.257	0	-2	-2	-0	0.0

● HARRY SCHAEFFER
Schaeffer, Harry Edward "Lefty" b: 6/23/24, Reading, Pa.   BL/TL, 6'2.5", 175 lbs.   Deb: 7/28/52

YEAR	TM/L	W	L	PCT	G	GS	CG	SH	SV	IP	H	HR	BB	SO	RAT	ERA	ERA+	OAV	OOB	BH	AVG	PB	PR	/A	PD	TPI
1952	NY-A	0	1	.000	5	2	0	0	0	17	18	2	18	15	19.1	5.29	83	.265	.419	0	.000	-0	-3	-4	0	-0.2

● MARK SCHAEFFER
Schaeffer, Mark Philip b: 6/5/48, Santa Monica, Cal.   BL/TL, 6'5", 215 lbs.   Deb: 4/18/72

YEAR	TM/L	W	L	PCT	G	GS	CG	SH	SV	IP	H	HR	BB	SO	RAT	ERA	ERA+	OAV	OOB	BH	AVG	PB	PR	/A	PD	TPI
1972	SD-N	2	0	1.000	41	0	0	0	1	41	52	3	28	25	18.0	4.61	71	.319	.425	0	.000	-0	-5	-6	1	-0.3

● JOE SCHAFFERNOTH
Schaffernoth, Joseph Arthur b: 8/6/37, Trenton, N.J.   BR/TR, 6'4.5", 195 lbs.   Deb: 4/15/59

YEAR	TM/L	W	L	PCT	G	GS	CG	SH	SV	IP	H	HR	BB	SO	RAT	ERA	ERA+	OAV	OOB	BH	AVG	PB	PR	/A	PD	TPI
1959	Chi-N	1	0	1.000	5	0	0	0	0	7²	11	1	4	3	17.6	8.22	48	.355	.429	0	.000	-0	-4	-4	-0	-0.5
1960	Chi-N	2	3	.400	33	0	0	0	3	55	46	2	17	33	10.5	2.78	136	.235	.299	2	.286	0	6	6	0	0.7
1961	Chi-N	0	4	.000	21	0	0	0	0	38¹	43	7	18	23	14.6	6.34	66	.293	.373	0	.000	-1	-10	-9	-0	-0.9
	Cle-A	0	1	.000	15	0	0	0	0	17	16	2	14	9	16.4	4.76	83	.242	.383	0	.000	-0	-1	-2	1	-0.2
Total 3		3	8	.273	74	1	0	0	0	118	116	12	53	68	13.1	4.58	86	.264	.347	2	.125	-1	-9	-8	1	-0.7

● ART SCHALLOCK
Schallock, Arthur Lawrence b: 4/25/24, Mill Valley, Cal.   BL/TL, 5'9", 160 lbs.   Deb: 7/16/51

YEAR	TM/L	W	L	PCT	G	GS	CG	SH	SV	IP	H	HR	BB	SO	RAT	ERA	ERA+	OAV	OOB	BH	AVG	PB	PR	/A	PD	TPI
1951	NY-A	3	1	.750	11	6	1	0	0	46¹	50	3	20	19	13.8	3.88	99	.272	.346	5	.294	-1	1	-0	0	0.1
1952	NY-A	0	0	—	2	0	0	0	0	2	3	0	2	1	22.5	9.00	37	.375	.500	0	—	0	-1	-1	-0	-0.1
1953	*NY-A	0	0	—	7	1	0	0	1	21¹	30	2	15	13	19.4	2.95	125	.345	.447	2	.333	0	2	2	-0	0.0
1954	NY-A	1	0	1.000	6	1	1	0	0	17¹	20	3	11	9	16.6	4.15	83	.282	.386	0	.000	-0	-1	-1	-0	-0.2
1955	NY-A	0	0	—	2	0	0	0	0	3	4	1	1	2	15.0	6.00	62	.333	.385	0	—	0	-1	-1	-0	-0.1
	Bal-A	3	5	.375	30	13	2	0	0	80¹	92	6	42	33	15.2	4.15	92	.294	.381	2	.105	-1	-2	-3	-1	-0.4
	Yr	3	5	.375	32	6	1	0	0	83¹	96	6	43	35	15.2	4.21	90	.295	.381	2	.105	-1	-2	-4	-1	-0.4
Total 5		6	7	.462	58	14	3	0	1	170¹	199	11	91	77	15.6	4.02	94	.295	.383	9	.200	1	-1	-3	-1	-0.6

● CHARLEY SCHANZ
Schanz, Charles Murrell b: 6/8/19, Anacortes, Wash. d: 5/28/92, Sacramento, Cal.   BR/TR, 6'3.5", 215 lbs.   Deb: 4/20/44

YEAR	TM/L	W	L	PCT	G	GS	CG	SH	SV	IP	H	HR	BB	SO	RAT	ERA	ERA+	OAV	OOB	BH	AVG	PB	PR	/A	PD	TPI
1944	Phi-N	13	16	.448	40	30	13	1	3	241¹	231	6	103	84	12.7	3.32	109	.254	.334	12	.148	-1	8	8	-0	0.8
1945	Phi-N	4	15	.211	35	21	5	1	5	144²	165	5	87	56	16.2	4.35	88	.285	.387	6	.154	-0	-9	-8	1	-1.0
1946	Phi-N	6	6	.500	32	15	4	0	4	116¹	130	8	71	47	15.9	5.80	59	.286	.389	1	.083	-1	-31	-31	1	-3.2
1947	Phi-N	2	4	.333	34	6	1	0	2	101²	107	7	47	42	13.9	4.16	96	.295	.380	4	.148	-1	-1	-2	-0	-0.2
1950	Bos-A	3	2	.600	14	0	0	0	0	22²	25	3	24	14	19.9	8.34	59	.281	.439	1	.091	-1	-9	-9	-0	-1.6
Total 5		28	43	.394	155	72	23	2	14	626²	658	29	332	243	14.6	4.34	86	.275	.369	26	.134	-5	-43	-42	1	-5.2

● JOHN SCHAPPERT
Schappert, John b: Brooklyn, N.Y. d: 7/29/16, Rockaway Beach, N.Y.   BR/TR, 5'10", 170 lbs.   Deb: 5/3/1882

YEAR	TM/L	W	L	PCT	G	GS	CG	SH	SV	IP	H	HR	BB	SO	RAT	ERA	ERA+	OAV	OOB	BH	AVG	PB	PR	/A	PD	TPI
1882	StL-a	8	7	.533	15	14	13	0	0	128	131	2	32	38	11.5	3.52	80	.248	.291	9	.180	0	-12	-10	-2	-1.1

● BILL SCHARDT
Schardt, Wilburt "Big Bill" b: 1/20/1886, Cleveland, Ohio d: 7/20/64, Vermilion, Ohio   BR/TR, 6'4", 210 lbs.   Deb: 4/14/11

YEAR	TM/L	W	L	PCT	G	GS	CG	SH	SV	IP	H	HR	BB	SO	RAT	ERA	ERA+	OAV	OOB	BH	AVG	PB	PR	/A	PD	TPI
1911	Bro-N	5	15	.250	39	22	10	1	4	195¹	190	4	91	77	13.3	3.59	93	.266	.355	10	.169	0	-4	-6	0	-0.5
1912	Bro-N	0	1	.000	7	0	0	0	1	20²	25	1	6	7	14.4	4.35	77	.321	.384	0	.000	-1	-2	-2	2	0.0
Total 2		5	16	.238	46	22	10	1	5	216	215	5	97	84	13.7	3.67	93	.271	.358	10	.154	0	-6	-8	2	-0.5

● JEFF SCHATTINGER
Schattinger, Jeffrey Charles b: 10/25/55, Fresno, Cal.   BL/TR, 6'5", 200 lbs.   Deb: 9/21/81

YEAR	TM/L	W	L	PCT	G	GS	CG	SH	SV	IP	H	HR	BB	SO	RAT	ERA	ERA+	OAV	OOB	BH	AVG	PB	PR	/A	PD	TPI
1981	KC-A	0	0	—	1	0	0	0	0	3	2	0	1	1	15.0	0.00	—	.182	.357	0	—	0	1	1	-0	0.0

● DAN SCHATZEDER
Schatzeder, Daniel Ernest b: 12/1/54, Elmhurst, Ill.   BL/TL, 6', 195 lbs.   Deb: 9/4/77

YEAR	TM/L	W	L	PCT	G	GS	CG	SH	SV	IP	H	HR	BB	SO	RAT	ERA	ERA+	OAV	OOB	BH	AVG	PB	PR	/A	PD	TPI
1977	Mon-N	2	1	.667	6	3	1	1	0	21²	16	0	13	14	12.0	2.49	153	.203	.315	2	.333	0	3	3	-0	0.5
1978	Mon-N	7	7	.500	29	18	2	0	0	143²	108	10	68	69	11.2	3.07	115	.213	.308	10	.222	3	8	7	-2	0.8
1979	Mon-N	10	5	.667	32	21	3	0	1	162	136	17	59	106	10.9	2.83	129	.225	.295	11	.216	4	16	15	-3	1.5
1980	Det-A	11	13	.458	32	26	9	2	0	192²	178	23	58	94	11.2	4.02	102	.246	.304	0	—	0	2	2	-0	0.0
1981	Det-A	6	8	.429	17	14	1	0	0	71¹	74	13	29	20	13.2	6.06	62	.265	.339	0	—	0	-19	-18	-0	-3.1
1982	SF-N	1	4	.200	13	3	0	0	0	33¹	47	3	12	18	15.9	7.29	49	.333	.386	1	.125	-0	-14	-14	0	-1.8
	Mon-N	0	2	.000	26	1	0	0	0	36	37	1	12	15	12.8	3.50	104	.276	.345	2	.400	3	4	4	0	0.1
	Yr	1	6	.143	39	4	0	0	0	69¹	84	4	24	33	14.3	5.32	68	.304	.364	3	.231	1	-13	-13	-1	-1.7
1983	Mon-N	5	2	.714	58	2	0	0	2	87	88	3	25	48	12.2	3.21	112	.265	.326	2	.200	0	4	4	-1	0.2
1984	Mon-N	7	7	.500	36	14	1	0	0	136	112	13	36	89	9.9	2.71	126	.224	.278	11	.314	5	13	11	-3	1.3
1985	Mon-N	3	5	.375	24	15	1	0	0	104¹	101	13	31	64	11.4	3.80	89	.259	.314	6	.194	3	-2	-5	0	0.8
1986	Mon-N	3	2	.600	30	1	0	0	0	59	53	6	19	33	11.0	3.20	115	.240	.300	9	.429	6	3	3	-0	0.8
	Phi-N	3	3	.500	25	0	0	0	0	29¹	28	3	16	14	13.5	3.38	114	.252	.346	1	.200	1	2	3	-0	0.3
	Yr	6	5	.545	55	1	0	0	0	88¹	81	9	35	47	11.8	3.26	115	.243	.314	10	.385	7	4	5	-1	1.1
1987	Phi-N	3	1	.750	26	0	0	0	0	37²	40	4	18	24	12.9	4.06	104	.278	.342	2	.167	0	1	1	-0	0.0
	*Min-A	3	1	.750	30	1	0	0	0	43²	64	8	18	30	17.1	6.39	72	.342	.403	0	.000	0	-9	-9	-0	-0.7
1988	Cle-A	0	2	.000	16	0	0	0	0	16	26	6	7	8	16.3	9.56	43	.351	.377	0	—	0	-10	-10	-0	-1.5
	Min-A	0	1	.000	10	0	0	0	0	10¹	8	1	5	17	12.2	1.74	234	.216	.326	0	—	0	3	3	0	0.1
	Yr	0	3	.000	25	0	0	0	3	26¹	34	7	7	17	14.4	6.49	63	.304	.350	0	—	0	-7	-7	-0	-1.4

YEAR	TM/L	W	L	PCT	G	GS	CG	SH	SV	IP	H	HR	BB	SO	RAT	ERA	ERA+	OAV	OOB	BH	AVG	PB	PR	/A	PD	TPI
1989	Hou-N	4	1	.800	36	0	0	0	1	56²	64	2	28	46	15.1	4.45	76	.287	.374	0	.000	-1	-6	-7	0	-0.7
1990	Hou-N	1	3	.250	45	2	0	0	0	64	61	2	23	37	11.8	2.39	155	.261	.327	1	.250	0	10	9	-0	0.5
	NY-N	0	0	—	6	0	0	0	0	5²	5	0	0	2	7.9	0.00	—	.263	.263	0	—	0	2	2	0	0.0
	Yr	1	3	.250	51	2	0	0	0	69²	66	2	23	39	11.5	2.20	169	.256	.317	1	.250	-0	12	12	-0	0.5
1991	KC-A	0	0	—	8	0	0	0	0	6²	11	0	7	4	24.3	9.45	44	.367	.486	0	—	0	-4	-4	-0	-0.2
Total 15		69	68	.504	504	121	18	4	10	1317	1257	128	475	748	12.0	3.74	99	.253	.321	58	.240	22	1	-4	-13	-1.7

● **RUBE SCHAUER**   Schauer, Alexander John (b: Dimitri Ivanovich Dimitrihoff)
b: 3/19/1891, Odessa, Russia   d: 4/15/57, Minneapolis, Minn.   BR/TR, 6'2", 192 lbs.   Deb: 8/27/13

YEAR	TM/L	W	L	PCT	G	GS	CG	SH	SV	IP	H	HR	BB	SO	RAT	ERA	ERA+	OAV	OOB	BH	AVG	PB	PR	/A	PD	TPI
1913	NY-N	0	1	.000	3	1	1	0	0	12	14	0	9	7	17.3	7.50	42	.292	.404	0	.000	-0	-6	-6	0	-0.4
1914	NY-N	0	0	—	6	0	0	0	0	22¹	16	2	8	6	9.7	3.22	82	.205	.279	1	.143	-0	-1	-1	-1	-0.1
1915	NY-N	2	8	.200	32	7	4	0	0	105¹	101	4	35	65	11.8	3.50	73	.258	.322	2	.077	-2	-9	-11	-0	-1.3
1916	NY-N	1	4	.200	19	3	1	0	0	45²	44	0	16	24	12.2	2.96	82	.257	.328	2	.222	-1	-2	-3	-0	-0.4
1917	Phi-A	7	16	.304	33	21	10	0	1	215	209	6	69	62	11.8	3.14	88	.263	.324	11	.145	-2	-11	-9	-0	-1.2
Total 5		10	29	.256	93	32	16	0	1	400¹	384	12	137	164	11.9	3.35	80	.259	.324	16	.132	-4	-29	-30	-1	-3.3

● **OWEN SCHEETZ**   Scheetz, Owen Franklin   b: 12/24/13, New Bedford, Ohio   d: 9/28/94, Kirkersville, O.   BR/TR, 6', 190 lbs.   Deb: 4/22/43

YEAR	TM/L	W	L	PCT	G	GS	CG	SH	SV	IP	H	HR	BB	SO	RAT	ERA	ERA+	OAV	OOB	BH	AVG	PB	PR	/A	PD	TPI
1943	Was-A	0	0	—	6	0	0	0	1	9	16	0	4	5	20.0	7.00	46	.381	.435	0	.000	-0	-4	-4	0	-0.1

● **LEFTY SCHEGG**   Schegg, Gilbert Eugene (b: Gilbert Eugene Price)
b: 8/28/1889, Leesville, Ohio   d: 2/27/63, Niles, Ohio   BL/TL, 5'11", 180 lbs.   Deb: 8/20/12

YEAR	TM/L	W	L	PCT	G	GS	CG	SH	SV	IP	H	HR	BB	SO	RAT	ERA	ERA+	OAV	OOB	BH	AVG	PB	PR	/A	PD	TPI
1912	Was-A	0	0	—	2	1	0	0	0	5¹	7	0	4	3	18.6	3.38	99	.333	.440	0	.000	-0	-0	-0	-1	-0.1

● **CARL SCHEIB**   Scheib, Carl Alvin   b: 1/1/27, Gratz, Pa.   BR/TR, 6'1", 192 lbs.   Deb: 9/6/43

YEAR	TM/L	W	L	PCT	G	GS	CG	SH	SV	IP	H	HR	BB	SO	RAT	ERA	ERA+	OAV	OOB	BH	AVG	PB	PR	/A	PD	TPI
1943	Phi-A	0	1	.000	6	0	0	0	0	18²	24	4	3	3	13.5	4.34	78	.308	.341	0	.000	-1	-2	-2	-1	-0.2
1944	Phi-A	0	0	—	15	0	0	0	0	36¹	36	1	11	13	12.6	4.21	83	.257	.329	3	.300	1	-3	-3	1	0.2
1945	Phi-A	0	0	—	4	0	0	0	0	8²	6	0	4	2	10.4	3.12	110	.207	.303	0	.000	-0	0	0	0	0.0
1947	Phi-A	4	6	.400	21	12	6	2	0	116	121	11	55	26	13.8	5.04	76	.274	.357	6	.133	-2	-17	-16	-2	-1.6
1948	Phi-A	14	8	.636	32	24	15	1	0	198²	219	14	76	44	13.4	3.94	109	.286	.351	31	.298	7	8	8	1	1.9
1949	Phi-A	9	12	.429	38	23	11	2	0	182²	191	16	118	43	15.3	5.12	80	.275	.382	17	.236	-3	-19	-21	-3	-2.0
1950	Phi-A	3	10	.231	43	8	1	0	3	106	138	13	70	37	17.7	7.22	63	.317	.411	13	.250	-3	-31	-31	-1	-3.2
1951	Phi-A	1	12	.077	46	11	3	0	10	143	132	7	71	49	13.3	4.47	96	.250	.347	21	.396	8	-6	-3	4	1.0
1952	Phi-A	11	7	.611	30	19	8	1	2	158	153	21	50	42	11.8	4.39	90	.253	.314	18	.220	1	-12	-8	-0	-0.7
1953	Phi-A	3	7	.300	28	8	3	0	2	96	99	9	29	25	12.7	4.88	88	.261	.325	8	.195	1	-9	-6	-0	-0.7
1954	Phi-A	0	1	.000	1	1	0	0	0	2	5	1	1	1	31.5	22.50	17	.500	.583	0	—	0	-4	-4	-0	-1.1
	StL-N	0	1	.000	3	1	0	0	0	4²	6	3	5	5	21.2	11.57	36	.300	.440	0	.000	-0	-4	-4	-0	-0.7
Total 11		45	65	.409	267	107	47	6	17	1070²	1130	99	493	290	13.9	4.88	85	.274	.355	117	.250	16	-100	-89	-0	-7.2

● **FRANK SCHEIBECK**   Scheibeck, Frank S.   b: 6/28/1865, Detroit, Mich.   d: 10/22/56, Detroit, Mich.   BR/TR, 5'7", 145 lbs.   Deb: 5/9/1887 ♦

YEAR	TM/L	W	L	PCT	G	GS	CG	SH	SV	IP	H	HR	BB	SO	RAT	ERA	ERA+	OAV	OOB	BH	AVG	PB	PR	/A	PD	TPI
1887	Cle-a	0	1	.000	1	1	1	0	0	9	17	1	4	3	22.0	12.00	36	.362	.423	2	.222	0	-8	-8	-0	-0.5

● **JACK SCHEIBLE**   Scheible, John G.   b: 2/16/1866, Youngstown, Ohio   d: 8/9/1897, Youngstown, Ohio   TL ,   Deb: 9/8/1893

YEAR	TM/L	W	L	PCT	G	GS	CG	SH	SV	IP	H	HR	BB	SO	RAT	ERA	ERA+	OAV	OOB	BH	AVG	PB	PR	/A	PD	TPI
1893	Cle-N	1	1	.500	2	2	2	1	0	18	15	0	11	1	13.0	2.00	244	.221	.329	1	.143	-0	5	6	-0	0.5
1894	Phi-N	0	1	.000	1	1	0	0	0	0¹	6	0	2	0	243.0	189.00	1	.857	.900	0	—	0	-7	-7	-0	-3.9
Total 2		1	2	.333	3	3	2	1	0	18¹	21	0	13	1	17.2	5.40	91	.280	.393	1	.143	-0	-1	-1	-0	-3.4

● **RICH SCHEID**   Scheid, Richard Paul   b: 2/3/65, Staten Island, N.Y.   BL/TL, 6'3", 185 lbs.   Deb: 9/11/92

YEAR	TM/L	W	L	PCT	G	GS	CG	SH	SV	IP	H	HR	BB	SO	RAT	ERA	ERA+	OAV	OOB	BH	AVG	PB	PR	/A	PD	TPI
1992	Hou-N	0	1	.000	7	1	0	0	0	12	14	2	6	8	15.0	6.00	56	.280	.357	0	.000	-0	-3	-4	-0	-0.3
1994	Fla-N	1	3	.250	8	5	0	0	0	32¹	35	6	8	17	12.5	3.34	131	.269	.321	0	.000	-1	3	4	-1	0.3
1995	Fla-N	0	0	—	6	0	0	0	0	10¹	14	1	7	10	18.3	6.10	69	.341	.438	0	—	0	-2	-2	1	0.1
Total 3		1	4	.200	21	6	0	0	0	54²	63	9	21	35	14.2	4.45	92	.285	.352	0	.000	-2	-2	-0	0	0.1

● **JIM SCHELLE**   Schelle, Gerard Anthony   b: 4/13/17, Baltimore, Md.   d: 5/4/90, Weymouth, Mass.   BR/TR, 6'3", 204 lbs.   Deb: 7/23/39

YEAR	TM/L	W	L	PCT	G	GS	CG	SH	SV	IP	H	HR	BB	SO	RAT	ERA	ERA+	OAV	OOB	BH	AVG	PB	PR	/A	PD	TPI
1939	Phi-A	0	0	—	1	0	0	0	0	1	3	0	3	0	—	∞	—	1.000	1.000	0	—	0	-3	-3	0	-0.2

● **FRED SCHEMANSKE**   Schemanske, Frederick George "Buck"   b: 4/28/03, Detroit, Mich.   d: 2/18/60, Detroit, Mich.   BR/TR, 6'2", 190 lbs.   Deb: 9/15/23 ♦

YEAR	TM/L	W	L	PCT	G	GS	CG	SH	SV	IP	H	HR	BB	SO	RAT	ERA	ERA+	OAV	OOB	BH	AVG	PB	PR	/A	PD	TPI
1923	Was-A	0	0	—	1	0	0	0	0	1	1	0	3	0	27.0	27.00	14	.600	.600	2	1.000	1	-3	-3	-0	0.1

● **BILL SCHENCK**   Schenck, William G.   b: Brooklyn, N.Y.   5'7", 171 lbs.   Deb: 5/29/1882 ♦

YEAR	TM/L	W	L	PCT	G	GS	CG	SH	SV	IP	H	HR	BB	SO	RAT	ERA	ERA+	OAV	OOB	BH	AVG	PB	PR	/A	PD	TPI
1882	Lou-a	1	0	1.000	2	1	1	0	0	10	6	0	1	4	6.3	0.90	275	.162	.184	60	.260	0	2	2	0	0.1

● **JOHN SCHENEBERG**   Scheneberg, John Bluford   b: 11/20/1887, Guyandotte, W.Va.   d: 9/26/50, Huntington, W.Va.   BB/TR, 6'1", 180 lbs.   Deb: 9/23/13

YEAR	TM/L	W	L	PCT	G	GS	CG	SH	SV	IP	H	HR	BB	SO	RAT	ERA	ERA+	OAV	OOB	BH	AVG	PB	PR	/A	PD	TPI
1913	Pit-N	0	1	.000	1	1	0	0	0	6	10	1	9	3	18.0	6.00	50	.400	.444	1	.500	0	-2	-2	-0	-0.2
1920	StL-A	0	0	—	1	0	0	0	0	2	7	0	1	0	36.0	27.00	15	.583	.615	0	—	0	-5	-5	-0	0.0
Total 2		0	1	.000	2	1	0	0	0	8	17	1	10	3	22.5	11.25	29	.459	.500	1	.500	0	-7	-7	-0	-0.2

● **FRED SCHERMAN**   Scherman, Frederick John   b: 7/25/44, Dayton, Ohio   BL/TL, 6'1", 195 lbs.   Deb: 4/26/69

YEAR	TM/L	W	L	PCT	G	GS	CG	SH	SV	IP	H	HR	BB	SO	RAT	ERA	ERA+	OAV	OOB	BH	AVG	PB	PR	/A	PD	TPI
1969	Det-A	1	0	1.000	4	0	0	0	0	4	6	2	0	4	13.5	6.75	55	.333	.333	0	—	0	-1	-1	0	-0.3
1970	Det-A	4	4	.500	48	0	0	0	1	69²	61	5	28	58	11.6	3.23	115	.237	.315	2	.167	-0	4	4	0	0.4
1971	Det-A	11	6	.647	69	1	1	0	20	113	91	11	49	46	11.5	2.71	133	.226	.318	5	.208	1	9	11	1	2.3
1972	*Det-A	7	3	.700	57	3	0	0	12	94	91	5	53	53	14.3	3.64	86	.269	.376	2	.091	-0	-6	-5	-1	-0.9
1973	Det-A	2	2	.500	34	0	0	0	0	61²	59	6	30	28	13.4	4.23	97	.258	.351	0	—	0	-3	-1	-0	-0.2
1974	Hou-N	2	5	.286	53	0	0	0	4	61¹	67	5	26	35	14.7	4.11	84	.284	.372	0	.000	-0	-3	-4	-0	-0.6
1975	Hou-N	0	0	—	16	0	0	0	0	16¹	21	4	13	14.3		4.96	68	.318	.366	0	.000	-0	-2	-3	-0	-0.2
	Mon-N	4	3	.571	34	7	0	0	0	76¹	84	3	41	43	15.3	3.54	108	.283	.379	1	.063	-1	2	1	0	0.2
	Yr	4	4	.500	50	7	0	0	0	92²	105	7	45	56	15.1	3.79	99	.288	.373	1	.059	-1	1	-1	0	0.1
1976	Mon-N	2	2	.500	31	0	0	0	1	40	42	5	14	18	13.3	4.95	75	.261	.331	1	.250	0	-6	-5	-1	-0.6
Total 8		33	26	.559	346	11	1	0	39	536¹	522	46	245	297	13.4	3.66	99	.260	.350	11	.134	-1	-9	-3	-1	0.1

● **BILL SCHERRER**   Scherrer, William Joseph   b: 1/20/58, Tonawanda, N.Y.   BL/TL, 6'4", 180 lbs.   Deb: 9/7/82

YEAR	TM/L	W	L	PCT	G	GS	CG	SH	SV	IP	H	HR	BB	SO	RAT	ERA	ERA+	OAV	OOB	BH	AVG	PB	PR	/A	PD	TPI
1982	Cin-N	0	1	.000	5	2	0	0	0	17¹	17	0	0	7	8.8	2.60	142	.250	.250	1	.500	1	2	2	-0	0.2
1983	Cin-N	2	3	.400	73	0	0	0	10	92	73	6	33	57	10.4	2.74	139	.225	.296	1	.091	-0	9	11	3	0.7
1984	Cin-N	1	1	.500	36	0	0	0	0	52¹	64	6	15	35	13.6	4.99	76	.300	.346	0	.000	-0	-8	-7	0	-0.3
	*Det-A	1	0	1.000	18	0	0	0	0	19	14	1	9	16	10.4	1.89	207	.206	.289	0	—	0	4	4	-0	0.2
1985	Det-A	3	2	.600	48	0	0	0	4	66	62	4	31	46	14.2	4.36	93	.248	.356	0	—	-0	-2	-2	-1	-0.1
1986	Det-A	0	0	—	13	0	0	0	0	21	19	3	22	16	18.0	7.29	57	.244	.416	0	—	0	-7	-7	-0	-0.3
1987	Cin-N	1	1	.500	23	0	0	0	0	33	43	3	16	24	16.1	4.36	97	.328	.401	0	.000	-0	-1	-1	-0	-0.1
1988	Bal-A	0	1	.000	4	0	0	0	0	4	8	2	3	1	24.8	13.50	29	.400	.478	0	—	0	-4	-4	-0	-0.7
	Phi-N	0	0	—	8	0	0	0	0	6²	7	0	2	4	12.2	5.40	66	.269	.321	0	—	0	-1	-1	-0	-0.1
Total 7		8	10	.444	228	2	0	0	11	311¹	307	31	140	207	13.0	4.08	96	.260	.340	2	.118	-0	-8	-5	1	-0.3

● **DUTCH SCHESLER**   Schesler, Charles   b: 6/1/1900, Frankfurt, Germany   d: 11/19/53, Harrisburg, Pa.   BR/TR, 6'2", 185 lbs.   Deb: 4/16/31

YEAR	TM/L	W	L	PCT	G	GS	CG	SH	SV	IP	H	HR	BB	SO	RAT	ERA	ERA+	OAV	OOB	BH	AVG	PB	PR	/A	PD	TPI
1931	Phi-N	0	0	—	17	0	0	0	0	38¹	65	4	18	14	20.4	7.28	58	.385	.455	1	.111	-0	-15	-13	-0	-0.3

● **LOU SCHETTLER**   Schettler, Louis Martin   b: 6/12/1886, Pittsburgh, Pa.   d: 5/1/60, Youngstown, Ohio   BR/TR, 5'11", 160 lbs.   Deb: 4/25/10

YEAR	TM/L	W	L	PCT	G	GS	CG	SH	SV	IP	H	HR	BB	SO	RAT	ERA	ERA+	OAV	OOB	BH	AVG	PB	PR	/A	PD	TPI
1910	Phi-N	2	6	.250	27	7	3	0	1	107	96	2	51	62	12.5	3.20	98	.247	.337	7	.171	-1	-2	-1	-0	-0.3

● **CURT SCHILLING**   Schilling, Curtis Montague   b: 11/14/66, Anchorage, Alaska   BR/TR, 6'5", 205 lbs.   Deb: 9/7/88

YEAR	TM/L	W	L	PCT	G	GS	CG	SH	SV	IP	H	HR	BB	SO	RAT	ERA	ERA+	OAV	OOB	BH	AVG	PB	PR	/A	PD	TPI
1988	Bal-A	0	3	.000	4	4	0	0	0	14²	22	3	10	4	20.3	9.82	40	.355	.452	0	—	0	-10	-10	-1	-1.4
1989	Bal-A	0	1	.000	5	1	0	0	0	8²	10	2	3	6	13.5	6.23	61	.286	.342	0	—	0	-2	-2	-0	-0.3
1990	Bal-A	1	2	.333	35	0	0	0	3	46	38	1	19	32	11.2	2.54	149	.229	.308	0	—	0	7	6	-1	0.4
1991	Hou-N	3	5	.375	56	0	0	0	8	75²	79	2	39	71	14.0	3.81	92	.271	.358	1	.333	-0	-1	-3	-0	-0.4
1992	Phi-N	14	11	.560	42	26	10	4	2	226¹	165	11	59	147	**8.9**	2.35	149	**.201**	**.256**	10	.156	-0	29	29	-3	3.0

YEAR	TM/L	W	L	PCT	G	GS	CG	SH	SV	IP	H	HR	BB	SO	RAT	ERA	ERA+	OAV	OOB	BH	AVG	PB	PR	/A	PD	TPI
1993	*Phi-N	16	7	.696	34	34	7	2	0	235¹	234	23	57	186	11.3	4.02	99	.259	.305	11	.147	-1	1	-1	0	-0.2
1994	Phi-N	2	8	.200	13	13	1	0	0	82¹	87	10	28	58	12.9	4.48	96	.270	.334	3	.107	-1	-2	-2	-1	-0.4
1995	Phi-N	7	5	.583	17	17	1	0	0	116	96	12	26	114	9.7	3.57	118	.220	.268	7	.175	0	8	8	-2	0.6
1996	Phi-N	9	10	.474	26	26	**8**	2	0	183¹	149	16	50	182	9.9	3.19	137	.223	.280	11	.175	-0	21	24	-3	1.9
Total	9	52	52	.500	232	121	27	8	13	988¹	880	80	291	800	10.8	3.49	113	.237	.296	43	.158	-2	50	49	-10	3.2

● **RED SCHILLINGS**   Schillings, Elbert Isaiah   b: 3/29/1900, Deport, Tex.   d: 1/7/54, Oklahoma City, Okla   BR/TR, 5'10", 180 lbs.   Deb: 9/11/22

YEAR	TM/L	W	L	PCT	G	GS	CG	SH	SV	IP	H	HR	BB	SO	RAT	ERA	ERA+	OAV	OOB	BH	AVG	PB	PR	/A	PD	TPI
1922	Phi-A	0	0	—	4	0	0	0	0	8	10	1	11	4	23.6	6.75	63	.313	.488	0	.000	-0	-2	-2	-0	0.0

● **CALVIN SCHIRALDI**   Schiraldi, Calvin Drew   b: 6/16/62, Houston, Tex.   BR/TR, 6'4", 200 lbs.   Deb: 9/1/84

YEAR	TM/L	W	L	PCT	G	GS	CG	SH	SV	IP	H	HR	BB	SO	RAT	ERA	ERA+	OAV	OOB	BH	AVG	PB	PR	/A	PD	TPI
1984	NY-N	0	2	.000	5	3	0	0	0	17¹	20	3	10	16	15.6	5.71	62	.286	.375	0	.000	-0	-4	-4	0	-0.4
1985	NY-N	2	1	.667	10	4	0	0	0	26¹	43	4	11	21	19.5	8.89	39	.368	.435	1	.125	-0	-15	-16	0	-1.6
1986	*Bos-A	4	2	.667	25	0	0	0	9	51	36	5	15	55	9.2	1.41	295	.201	.267	0	—	0	16	16	-1	2.2
1987	Bos-A	8	5	.615	62	1	0	0	6	83²	75	15	40	93	12.5	4.41	103	.240	.328	0	—	0	0	1	-0	0.2
1988	Chi-N	9	13	.409	29	27	2	1	1	166¹	166	13	63	140	12.5	4.38	82	.257	.325	6	.100	-2	-17	-14	-2	-2.2
1989	Chi-N	3	6	.333	54	0	0	0	4	78²	60	7	50	54	12.7	3.78	100	.209	.328	0	.000	-1	-2	-0	-1	-0.2
	SD-N	3	1	.750	5	4	0	0	0	21¹	12	1	13	17	10.5	2.53	138	.162	.287	1	.143	1	2	2	-0	0.5
	Yr	6	7	.462	59	4	0	0	4	100	72	8	63	71	12.2	3.51	105	.198	.316	1	.063	'0	-0	2	-2	0.3
1990	SD-N	3	8	.273	42	8	0	0	1	104	105	11	60	74	14.4	4.41	87	.264	.362	4	.190	2	-7	-7	-1	-0.6
1991	Tex-A	0	1	.000	3	0	0	0	0	4²	5	3	5	1	19.3	11.57	35	.263	.417	0	—	0	-4	-4	-0	-0.6
Total	8	32	39	.451	235	47	2	1	21	553¹	522	62	267	471	13.0	4.28	90	.248	.336	12	.111	-1	-32	-26	-5	-2.7

● **BIFF SCHLITZER**   Schlitzer, Victor Joseph   b: 12/4/1884, Rochester, N.Y.   d: 1/4/48, Wellesley Hills, Mass.   BR/TR, 5'11", 175 lbs.   Deb: 4/17/08

YEAR	TM/L	W	L	PCT	G	GS	CG	SH	SV	IP	H	HR	BB	SO	RAT	ERA	ERA+	OAV	OOB	BH	AVG	PB	PR	/A	PD	TPI
1908	Phi-A	6	8	.429	24	18	11	2	0	131	110	1	45	57	10.8	3.16	81	.234	.303	9	.196	-1	-11	-9	-2	-1.3
1909	Phi-A	0	3	.000	4	3	0	0	0	13¹	13	0	7	6	15.5	5.40	45	.245	.365	1	.250	0	-4	-4	1	-0.8
	Bos-A	4	4	.500	13	8	5	0	1	69²	68	0	17	23	11.1	3.49	72	.234	.279	5	.185	0	-8	-8	1	-0.8
	Yr	4	7	.364	17	11	5	0	1	83	81	0	24	29	11.5	3.80	65	.234	.286	6	.194	1	-12	-12	1	-1.6
1914	Buf-F	0	0	—	3	0	0	0	0	3¹	7	3	2	1	24.3	16.20	18	.438	.500	1	1.000	0	-5	-5	0	0.0
Total	3	10	15	.400	44	29	16	2	1	217¹	198	4	71	87	11.4	3.60	71	.239	.303	16	.205	0	-28	-26	-1	-2.9

● **GEORGE SCHMEES**   Schmees, George Edward "Rocky"   b: 9/6/24, Cincinnati, Ohio   BL/TL, 6', 190 lbs.   Deb: 4/15/52 ◆

YEAR	TM/L	W	L	PCT	G	GS	CG	SH	SV	IP	H	HR	BB	SO	RAT	ERA	ERA+	OAV	OOB	BH	AVG	PB	PR	/A	PD	TPI
1952	Bos-A	0	0	—	2	1	0	0	0	6	9	2	2	2	16.5	3.00	131	.346	.393	13	.203	0	0	1	1	0.1

● **AL SCHMELZ**   Schmelz, Alan George   b: 11/12/43, Whittier, Cal.   BR/TR, 6'4", 210 lbs.   Deb: 9/7/67

YEAR	TM/L	W	L	PCT	G	GS	CG	SH	SV	IP	H	HR	BB	SO	RAT	ERA	ERA+	OAV	OOB	BH	AVG	PB	PR	/A	PD	TPI
1967	NY-N	0	0	—	2	0	0	0	0	3	4	1	1	2	15.0	3.00	113	.364	.417	0	—	0	0	0	0	0.0

● **BUTCH SCHMIDT**   Schmidt, Charles John "Butcher Boy"   b: 7/19/1886, Baltimore, Md.   d: 9/4/52, Baltimore, Md.   BL/TL, 6'1.5", 200 lbs.   Deb: 5/11/09 ◆

YEAR	TM/L	W	L	PCT	G	GS	CG	SH	SV	IP	H	HR	BB	SO	RAT	ERA	ERA+	OAV	OOB	BH	AVG	PB	PR	/A	PD	TPI
1909	NY-A	0	0	—	1	0	0	0	0	5	10	0	1	2	19.8	7.20	35	.435	.458	0	.000	-0	-3	-3	-0	-0.1

● **CURT SCHMIDT**   Schmidt, Curtis Allen   b: 3/16/70, Miles City, Mont.   BR/TR, 6'6", 200 lbs.   Deb: 4/28/95

YEAR	TM/L	W	L	PCT	G	GS	CG	SH	SV	IP	H	HR	BB	SO	RAT	ERA	ERA+	OAV	OOB	BH	AVG	PB	PR	/A	PD	TPI
1995	Mon-N	0	0	—	11	0	0	0	0	10¹	15	1	9	2	22.6	6.97	62	.357	.491	0	—	0	-3	-3	-0	0.0

● **DAVE SCHMIDT**   Schmidt, David Joseph   b: 4/22/57, Niles, Mich.   BR/TR, 6'1", 185 lbs.   Deb: 5/1/81

YEAR	TM/L	W	L	PCT	G	GS	CG	SH	SV	IP	H	HR	BB	SO	RAT	ERA	ERA+	OAV	OOB	BH	AVG	PB	PR	/A	PD	TPI
1981	Tex-A	0	1	.000	14	1	0	0	1	31²	31	1	11	13	12.2	3.13	111	.258	.326	0	—	0	2	1	0	0.1
1982	Tex-A	4	6	.400	33	8	0	0	6	109²	118	5	25	69	12.1	3.20	121	.279	.327	0	—	0	11	8	-0	1.0
1983	Tex-A	3	3	.500	31	0	0	0	2	46¹	42	3	14	29	11.1	3.88	103	.241	.302	0	—	0	1	1	0	0.2
1984	Tex-A	6	6	.500	43	0	0	0	12	70¹	69	3	20	46	11.4	2.56	162	.262	.314	0	—	0	11	12	1	2.5
1985	Tex-A	7	6	.538	51	4	1	1	5	85²	81	6	22	46	10.8	3.15	134	.246	.293	0	—	0	9	10	1	1.6
1986	Chi-N	3	6	.333	49	1	0	0	8	92¹	94	10	27	67	12.3	3.31	130	.264	.325	0	—	0	9	10	-1	0.9
1987	Bal-A	10	5	.667	35	14	2	1	1	124	128	13	26	70	11.3	3.77	117	.263	.302	0	—	0	8	9	-1	0.8
1988	Bal-A	8	5	.615	41	9	0	0	2	129²	129	14	38	67	11.8	3.40	115	.262	.319	0	—	0	8	7	2	1.0
1989	Bal-A	10	13	.435	38	26	2	0	0	156²	196	24	36	46	13.4	5.69	67	.310	.349	0	—	0	-31	-33	1	-4.1
1990	Mon-N	3	3	.500	34	0	0	0	13	48	58	3	13	22	13.3	4.31	85	.297	.341	0	.000	-3	-4	-4	0	-0.6
1991	Mon-N	0	1	.000	4	0	0	0	0	4¹	9	2	2	3	22.8	10.38	35	.429	.478	0	—	0	-3	-3	-0	-0.6
1992	Sea-A	0	0	—	3	0	0	0	0	3¹	7	1	3	1	27.0	18.90	21	.438	.526	0	—	0	-6	-6	-0	0.0
Total	12	54	55	.495	376	63	5	3	50	902	962	85	237	479	12.1	3.88	103	.274	.323	0	.000	-3	17	13	3	2.8

● **FREDDY SCHMIDT**   Schmidt, Frederick Albert   b: 2/9/16, Hartford, Conn.   BR/TR, 6'1", 185 lbs.   Deb: 4/25/44

YEAR	TM/L	W	L	PCT	G	GS	CG	SH	SV	IP	H	HR	BB	SO	RAT	ERA	ERA+	OAV	OOB	BH	AVG	PB	PR	/A	PD	TPI
1944	*StL-N	7	3	.700	37	9	3	2	5	114¹	94	5	58	58	12.0	3.15	112	.222	.317	7	.206	0	6	5	-1	0.3
1946	StL-N	1	0	1.000	16	0	0	0	0	27¹	27	0	15	14	14.8	3.29	105	.276	.388	0	.000	0	0	0	0	0.0
1947	StL-N	0	0	—	2	0	0	0	0	4	5	1	1	2	13.5	2.25	184	.333	.375	0	—	0	1	1	-0	0.0
	Phi-N	5	8	.385	29	5	0	0	0	76²	76	4	43	24	14.4	4.70	85	.285	.392	1	.050	-2	-5	-6	-1	-1.1
	Chi-N	0	0	—	1	1	0	0	0	3	4	0	5	0	27.0	9.00	44	.333	.529	0	.000	-0	-2	-2	-0	0.0
	Yr	5	8	.385	32	6	0	0	0	83²	85	5	49	26	14.4	4.73	85	.285	.386	1	.045	-2	-6	-7	-1	-1.1
Total	3	13	11	.542	85	15	3	2	5	225¹	206	10	122	98	13.4	3.75	98	.252	.355	8	.140	-2	-0	-1	-1	-0.8

● **PETE SCHMIDT**   Schmidt, Friedrich Christoph Herman   b: 7/23/1890, Lowden, Iowa   d: 3/11/73, Pembroke, Ont., Can   BR/TR, 5'11", 175 lbs.   Deb: 7/14/13

YEAR	TM/L	W	L	PCT	G	GS	CG	SH	SV	IP	H	HR	BB	SO	RAT	ERA	ERA+	OAV	OOB	BH	AVG	PB	PR	/A	PD	TPI
1913	StL-A	0	0	—	1	0	0	0	1	2	3	0	2	0	22.5	4.50	65	.333	.455	0	—	0	-0	-0	-0	-0.1

● **HENRY SCHMIDT**   Schmidt, Henry Martin   b: 6/26/1873, Brownsville, Tex.   d: 4/23/26, Nashville, Tenn.   BR/TR, 5'11", 170 lbs.   Deb: 4/17/03

YEAR	TM/L	W	L	PCT	G	GS	CG	SH	SV	IP	H	HR	BB	SO	RAT	ERA	ERA+	OAV	OOB	BH	AVG	PB	PR	/A	PD	TPI
1903	Bro-N	22	13	.629	40	36	29	5	2	301	321	5	120	96	13.8	3.83	83	.280	.359	21	.196	3	-19	-21	6	-1.3

● **JASON SCHMIDT**   Schmidt, Jason David   b: 1/29/73, Kelso, Wash.   BR/TR, 6'5", 185 lbs.   Deb: 4/28/95

YEAR	TM/L	W	L	PCT	G	GS	CG	SH	SV	IP	H	HR	BB	SO	RAT	ERA	ERA+	OAV	OOB	BH	AVG	PB	PR	/A	PD	TPI
1995	Atl-N	2	2	.500	9	2	0	0	0	25	27	2	18	19	16.6	5.76	74	.287	.407	1	.200	0	-4	-4	0	-0.5
1996	Atl-N	3	4	.429	13	11	0	0	0	58²	69	8	32	48	15.5	6.75	65	.296	.381	0	.000	-2	-17	-15	-1	-1.7
	Pit-N	2	2	.500	6	6	1	0	0	37²	39	2	21	26	14.8	4.06	108	.271	.371	1	.083	-1	1	-0	0	-0.0
	Yr	5	6	.455	19	17	1	0	0	96¹	108	10	53	74	15.2	5.70	77	.282	.372	1	.032	-2	-16	-14	-1	-1.7
Total	2	7	8	.467	28	19	1	0	0	121¹	135	12	71	93	15.5	5.71	76	.287	.383	2	.056	-2	-20	-18	-1	-2.2

● **JEFF SCHMIDT**   Schmidt, Jeffrey Thomas   b: 2/21/71, Northfield, Minn.   BR/TR, 6'5", 205 lbs.   Deb: 5/17/96

YEAR	TM/L	W	L	PCT	G	GS	CG	SH	SV	IP	H	HR	BB	SO	RAT	ERA	ERA+	OAV	OOB	BH	AVG	PB	PR	/A	PD	TPI
1996	Cal-A	2	0	1.000	9	0	0	0	0	8	13	2	8	2	23.6	7.88	62	.394	.512	0	—	0	-3	-3	-0	-0.5

● **WILLARD SCHMIDT**   Schmidt, Willard Raymond   b: 5/29/28, Hays, Kan.   BR/TR, 6'1", 187 lbs.   Deb: 4/19/52

YEAR	TM/L	W	L	PCT	G	GS	CG	SH	SV	IP	H	HR	BB	SO	RAT	ERA	ERA+	OAV	OOB	BH	AVG	PB	PR	/A	PD	TPI
1952	StL-N	2	3	.400	18	5	0	0	0	34²	36	6	18	30	14.5	5.19	72	.267	.361	1	.125	-0	-6	-6	1	-0.7
1953	StL-N	0	2	.000	6	2	0	0	0	17²	21	1	13	11	17.8	9.17	46	.288	.402	0	.000	-1	-10	-10	-0	-0.9
1955	StL-N	7	6	.538	20	15	8	1	0	129²	89	7	57	86	10.3	2.78	146	.197	.291	5	.119	-3	18	19	1	1.5
1956	StL-N	6	8	.429	33	21	2	0	1	147²	131	18	78	52	12.8	3.84	99	.246	.344	10	.233	1	-1	-1	2	0.2
1957	StL-N	10	3	.769	40	8	1	0	0	116²	146	13	49	63	15.2	4.78	83	.312	.380	7	.212	0	-12	-11	1	-1.0
1958	Cin-N	3	5	.375	41	2	0	0	0	69¹	60	8	43	36	14.1	2.86	145	.235	.325	1	.091	-1	8	10	1	1.1
1959	Cin-N	3	2	.600	36	4	0	0	0	70²	80	4	30	40	14.1	3.95	103	.296	.369	1	.083	-0	0	1	1	0.2
Total	7	31	29	.517	194	55	11	1	2	586¹	563	57	278	323	13.1	3.93	101	.258	.344	25	.163	-2	-1	2	6	0.4

● **CRAZY SCHMIT**   Schmit, Frederick M. "Germany"   b: 2/13/1866, Chicago, Ill.   d: 10/5/40, Chicago, Ill.   BL/TL, 5'10.5", 165 lbs.   Deb: 4/21/1890

YEAR	TM/L	W	L	PCT	G	GS	CG	SH	SV	IP	H	HR	BB	SO	RAT	ERA	ERA+	OAV	OOB	BH	AVG	PB	PR	/A	PD	TPI
1890	Pit-N	1	9	.100	11	10	9	1	0	83¹	108	3	42	35	17.1	5.83	57	.304	.390	2	.061	-3	-21	-23	-0	-2.3
1892	Bal-N	1	4	.200	6	6	6	0	0	47¹	37	0	26	17	12.0	3.23	106	.207	.307	2	.105	-1	0	1	1	0.1
1893	Bal-N	3	2	.600	9	6	4	0	0	49	67	1	22	10	16.7	6.61	72	.316	.386	5	.238	-0	-11	-10	-1	-0.8
	NY-N	0	2	.000	4	4	1	0	0	20²	30	0	17	5	21.3	7.40	63	.330	.444	2	-6	-6	-0	-0.3
	Yr	3	4	.429	13	10	5	0	0	69²	97	1	39	15	17.8	6.85	69	.318	.399	9	.300	-1	-17	-16	-1	-1.1
1899	Cle-N	2	17	.105	20	19	16	0	0	138¹	197	4	59	24	17.8	5.86	63	.334	.410	11	.157	-2	-31	-33	2	-3.4
1901	Bal-A	0	2	.000	4	3	1	0	0	22²	25	0	16	2	16.3	1.99	195	.278	.387	2	.222	-0	4	5	1	0.5
Total	5	7	36	.163	54	48	37	1	0	361¹	464	7	185	93	16.8	5.45	69	.304	.391	26	.161	-4	-64	-68	2	-6.2

YEAR	TM/L	W	L	PCT	G	GS	CG	SH	SV	IP	H	HR	BB	SO	RAT	ERA	ERA+	OAV	OOB	BH	AVG	PB	PR	/A	PD	TPI
● **JOHNNY SCHMITZ**					Schmitz, John Albert "Bear Tracks"				b: 11/27/20, Wausau, Wis.		BR/TL, 6′, 170 lbs.		Deb: 9/6/41												
1941	Chi-N	2	0	1.000	5	3	1	0	0	20²	12	0	9	11	9.6	1.31	269	.182	.289	4	.571	2	5	5	1	0.8
1942	Chi-N	3	7	.300	23	10	1	0	2	86²	70	3	45	51	12.3	3.43	93	.230	.335	4	.154	-1	-1	-2	4	0.1
1946	Chi-N☆	11	11	.500	41	31	14	2	2	224¹	184	6	94	**135**	11.2	2.61	127	**.221**	.302	9	.129	-2	20	18	2	1.8
1947	Chi-N	13	18	.419	38	28	10	3	4	207	209	8	80	97	12.7	3.22	123	.262	.330	5	.132	-2	19	17	2	2.4
1948	Chi-N★	18	13	.581	34	30	18	2	1	242	186	11	97	100	10.6	2.64	148	**.215**	.295	11	.131	-2	35	34	5	4.6
1949	Chi-N	11	13	.458	36	31	9	3	3	207	227	11	92	75	14.0	4.35	93	.287	.363	10	.143	-1	-7	-7	5	-0.3
1950	Chi-N	10	16	.385	39	27	8	3	0	193	217	23	91	75	14.5	4.99	84	.284	.363	8	.119	-3	-18	-17	5	-1.7
1951	Chi-N	1	2	.333	8	3	0	0	0	18	22	1	15	6	18.5	8.00	51	.301	.420	1	.167	-0	-8	-8	1	-1.0
	Bro-N	1	4	.200	16	7	0	0	0	55²	55	4	28	20	13.7	5.34	74	.259	.351	4	.222	2	-9	-9	1	-0.4
	Yr	2	6	.250	24	10	0	0	0	73²	77	5	43	26	14.9	5.99	66	.270	.373	5	.208	1	-17	-17	2	-1.4
1952	Bro-N	1	1	.500	10	3	1	0	0	33¹	29	3	18	11	13.0	4.32	84	.238	.340	1	.125	-0	-2	-3	1	0.0
	NY-A	1	1	.500	5	2	1	0	1	15	15	0	9	3	15.0	3.60	92	.263	.373	3	.600	0	-0	-0	0	0.2
	Cin-N	1	0	1.000	3	0	0	0	0	5	3	2	3	3	10.8	0.00	—	.188	.316	0	—	0	2	2	0	0.4
1953	NY-A	0	0	—	3	0	0	0	0	4¹	2	1	3	0	10.4	2.08	178	.143	.294	0	—	0	1	1	0	0.1
	Was-A	2	7	.222	24	13	5	0	4	107²	118	9	37	39	13.3	3.68	106	.286	.351	2	.059	-4	3	1	1	-0.1
	Yr	2	7	.222	27	13	5	0	6	112	120	10	40	39	13.2	3.62	108	.282	.349	2	.059	-4	5	3	1	0.0
1954	Was-A	11	8	.579	29	23	12	2	1	185¹	176	6	64	56	11.8	2.91	122	.255	.321	7	.117	-3	17	13	2	1.2
1955	Was-A	7	10	.412	32	21	6	1	1	165	187	8	54	49	13.5	3.71	103	.291	.352	10	.185	0	5	2	2	0.5
1956	Bos-N	0	0	—	2	0	0	0	0	4¹	5	0	4	0	18.7	0.00	—	.278	.409	0	.000	-0	-1	-0	0	-0.0
	Bal-A	0	3	.000	18	3	0	0	0	38¹	49	3	14	15	15.0	3.99	98	.318	.379	0	.000	-1	1	-0	1	-0.1
	Yr	0	3	.000	20	3	0	0	0	42²	54	3	18	15	15.4	3.59	111	.314	.382	0	.000	-2	3	2	1	-0.1
Total	13	93	114	.449	366	235	86	16	21	1812²	1766	97	757	746	12.7	3.55	107	.258	.335	83	.141	-14	66	50	35	8.5
● **CHARLIE SCHMUTZ**					Schmutz, Charles Otto "King"				b: 1/1/1890, San Diego, Cal.		d: 6/27/62, Seattle, Wash.		BR/TR, 6′1.5″, 195 lbs.		Deb: 5/13/14										
1914	Bro-N	1	3	.250	18	5	1	0	0	57¹	57	1	13	21	11.1	3.30	87	.265	.310	3	.188	1	-3	-3	1	-0.1
1915	Bro-N	0	0	—	1	0	0	0	0	4	7	0	1	1	18.0	6.75	41	.438	.471	0	.000	-0	-2	-2	0	0.0
Total	2	1	3	.250	19	5	1	0	0	61¹	64	1	14	22	11.6	3.52	81	.277	.321	3	.176	0	-5	-5	1	-0.1
● **FRANK SCHNEIBERG**					Schneiberg, Frank Frederick				b: 3/12/1882, Milwaukee, Wis.		d: 5/18/48, Milwaukee, Wis.		TR		Deb: 6/8/10										
1910	Bro-N	0	0	—	1	0	0	0	0	1	5	0	4	0	81.0	63.00	5	.625	.750	0	—	0	-7	-7	-0	0.0
● **DAN SCHNEIDER**					Schneider, Daniel Louis				b: 8/29/42, Evansville, Ind.		BL/TL, 6′3″, 170 lbs.		Deb: 5/12/63											
1963	Mil-N	1	0	1.000	30	3	0	0	0	43²	36	2	20	19	11.5	3.09	104	.225	.311	0	.000	-1	1	1	1	-0.2
1964	Mil-N	1	2	.333	13	5	0	0	0	36¹	38	6	13	14	12.6	5.45	65	.270	.331	0	.000	-1	-8	-8	1	-0.6
1966	Atl-N	0	0	—	14	0	0	0	0	26¹	31	5	5	11	14.0	3.42	106	.324	.360	4	.500	1	1	1	-0	0.1
1967	Hou-N	0	2	.000	54	0	0	0	2	52²	60	5	27	39	15.2	4.96	67	.296	.384	1	.200	1	-9	-10	1	-0.3
1969	Hou-N	0	1	.000	6	0	0	0	0	7¹	16	2	5	3	25.8	13.50	26	.485	.553	0	.000	-0	-8	-8	0	-0.9
Total	5	2	5	.286	117	8	0	0	2	166¹	185	16	70	86	14.0	4.71	72	.287	.359	5	.172	-0	-24	-24	1	-1.9
● **JEFF SCHNEIDER**					Schneider, Jeffrey Theodore				b: 12/6/52, Bremerton, Wash.		BB/TL, 6′3″, 195 lbs.		Deb: 8/12/81											
1981	Bal-A	0	0	—	11	0	0	0	1	24	27	4	12	17	15.0	4.88	74	.290	.377	0	—	0	-3	-3	-0	-0.1
● **PETE SCHNEIDER**					Schneider, Peter Joseph				b: 8/20/1895, Los Angeles, Cal.		d: 6/1/57, Los Angeles, Cal.		BR/TR, 6′1″, 194 lbs.		Deb: 6/20/14										
1914	Cin-N	5	13	.278	29	20	11	1	1	144¹	143	1	56	62	12.8	2.81	104	.269	.347	8	.178	1	-0	2	-1	0.2
1915	Cin-N	14	19	.424	48	35	16	5	2	275²	254	4	104	108	11.9	2.48	115	.251	.325	23	.245	5	8	12	-1	2.0
1916	Cin-N	10	19	.345	44	31	16	2	1	274¹	259	4	82	117	11.6	2.69	96	.255	.319	21	.236	2	-2	-3	-3	-0.3
1917	Cin-N	20	19	.513	46	42	24	0	0	333²	311	4	117	138	11.6	2.10	124	.255	.326	19	.167	-0	23	19	5	1.8
1918	Cin-N	10	15	.400	33	30	17	2	0	217	213	2	117	51	14.1	3.53	76	.272	.374	24	.289	6	-18	-21	-3	-2.0
1919	NY-A	0	1	.000	7	4	0	0	0	29	19	1	22	11	13.7	3.41	94	.192	.355	1	.111	-1	-1	-1	-0	-0.2
Total	6	59	86	.407	207	162	84	10	4	1274	1199	16	498	487	12.4	2.66	102	.257	.336	96	.237	14	9	8	-13	1.5
● **KARL SCHNELL**					Schnell, Karl Otto				b: 9/20/1899, Los Angeles, Cal.		d: 5/31/92, Palo Alto, Cal.		BR/TR, 6′1″, 176 lbs.		Deb: 4/24/22										
1922	Cin-N	0	0	—	10	0	0	0	0	20	21	0	18	5	17.5	2.70	148	.300	.443	1	.250	0	3	3	0	0.0
1923	Cin-N	0	0	—	1	0	0	0	0	1	2	0	2	0	36.0	36.00	11	.667	.800	0	—	0	-4	-4	-0	0.0
Total	2	0	0	—	11	0	0	0	0	21	23	0	20	5	18.4	4.29	93	.315	.462	1	.250	0	-1	-0	0	0.0
● **GERRY SCHOEN**					Schoen, Gerald Thomas				b: 1/15/47, New Orleans, La.		BR/TR, 6′3″, 215 lbs.		Deb: 9/14/68											
1968	Was-A	0	1	.000	1	1	0	0	0	3²	6	1	1	2	17.2	7.36	40	.400	.438	0	.000	-0	-2	-2	0	-0.4
● **JUMBO SCHOENECK**					Schoeneck, Louis N.				b: 3/3/1862, Chicago, Ill.		d: 1/20/30, Chicago, Ill.		BR/TR, 6′3″, 223 lbs.		Deb: 4/20/1884 ♦										
1888	Ind-N	0	0	—	2	0	0	0	0	4¹	5	0	1	1	12.5	0.00	—	.227	.261	40	.237	0	1	1	-0	0.0
● **MIKE SCHOOLER**					Schooler, Michael Ralph				b: 8/10/62, Anaheim, Cal.		BR/TR, 6′3″, 220 lbs.		Deb: 6/10/88											
1988	Sea-A	5	8	.385	40	0	0	0	15	48¹	45	4	24	54	13.0	3.54	118	.245	.335	0		0	2	3	-0	0.7
1989	Sea-A	1	7	.125	67	0	0	0	33	77	81	3	19	69	11.9	2.81	144	.266	.314	0		0	9	10	1	1.8
1990	Sea-A	1	4	.200	49	0	0	0	30	56	47	5	16	45	10.3	2.25	176	.227	.286	0	.000	0	10	11	0	1.9
1991	Sea-A	3	3	.500	34	0	0	0	7	34¹	25	2	10	31	9.2	3.67	112	.198	.257	0		0	2	2	-0	0.3
1992	Sea-A	2	7	.222	53	0	0	0	13	51²	55	7	24	33	13.9	4.70	84	.275	.356	0		0	-4	-4	1	-0.8
1993	Tex-A	3	0	1.000	17	0	0	0	0	24¹	30	3	10	16	14.8	5.55	75	.303	.367	0		0	-3	-4	-0	-0.4
Total	6	15	29	.341	260	0	0	0	98	291²	283	23	103	248	12.1	3.49	116	.253	.318	0	.000	0	16	18	1	3.5
● **ED SCHORR**					Schorr, Edward Walter				b: 2/14/1891, Bremen, Ohio		d: 9/12/69, Atlantic City, N.J.		BR/TR, 6′2.5″, 180 lbs.		Deb: 4/26/15										
1915	Chi-N	0	0	—	2	0	0	0	0	6	9	0	5	2	21.0	7.50	37	.409	.519	1	.500	0	-3	-3	0	0.0
● **GENE SCHOTT**					Schott, Arthur Eugene				b: 7/14/13, Batavia, Ohio		d: 11/16/92, Sun City Center, Fla.		BR/TR, 6′2″, 185 lbs.		Deb: 4/16/35 ♦										
1935	Cin-N	8	11	.421	33	19	9	1	0	159	153	5	64	49	12.3	3.91	102	.253	.326	12	.200	1	2	1	3	0.5
1936	Cin-N	11	11	.500	31	22	8	0	1	180	184	7	73	65	13.1	3.80	101	.262	.335	18	.300	7	4	0	1	0.9
1937	Cin-N	4	13	.235	37	16	7	2	1	154¹	150	7	48	56	11.6	2.97	125	.253	.310	1	.143	-1	16	13	1	1.3
1938	Cin-N	5	5	.500	31	4	0	0	2	83	89	3	32	21	13.2	4.45	82	.279	.347	3	.125	-1	-6	-7	1	-0.9
1939	Phi-N	0	1	.000	4	0	0	0	0	11	14	0	5	1	17.2	4.91	82	.326	.420	2	.333	1	-1	-1	1	0.0
Total	5	28	41	.406	136	61	24	3	4	587¹	590	22	222	192	12.6	3.72	103	.261	.329	42	.211	6	15	6	6	1.8
● **PETE SCHOUREK**					Schourek, Peter Alan				b: 5/10/69, Austin, Tex.		BL/TL, 6′5″, 195 lbs.		Deb: 4/9/91											
1991	NY-N	5	4	.556	35	8	1	1	2	86¹	82	7	43	67	13.2	4.27	85	.248	.338	3	.136	0	-6	-6	1	-0.5
1992	NY-N	6	8	.429	22	21	0	0	0	136	137	9	44	60	12.1	3.64	95	.261	.321	2	.048	-3	-2	-3	-2	-0.8
1993	NY-N	5	12	.294	41	18	0	0	0	128¹	168	13	45	72	15.1	5.96	67	.319	.376	7	.219	2	-27	-28	1	-3.1
1994	Cin-N	7	2	.778	22	10	0	0	0	81¹	90	11	29	69	13.5	4.09	101	.287	.353	4	.174	1	1	0	0	0.2
1995	*Cin-N	18	7	.720	29	29	2	0	0	190¹	158	17	45	160	10.0	3.22	128	.228	.283	13	.220	2	20	19	0	2.5
1996	Cin-N	4	5	.444	12	12	0	0	0	67¹	79	7	24	54	14.2	6.01	69	.293	.357	5	.263	1	-13	-14	1	-1.4
Total	6	45	38	.542	161	98	3	1	2	689²	714	64	230	482	12.6	4.32	91	.269	.332	34	.173	3	-27	-31	-1	-3.1
● **BARNEY SCHREIBER**					Schreiber, David Henry				b: 5/8/1882, Waverly, Ohio		d: 10/6/64, Chillicothe, Ohio		BL/TL, 6′, 185 lbs.		Deb: 5/15/11										
1911	Cin-N	0	0	—	3	0	0	0	1	10	19	2	2	5	18.9	5.40	61	.413	.438	0	.000	-0	-2	-2	-0	-0.1
● **PAUL SCHREIBER**					Schreiber, Paul Frederick "Von"				b: 10/8/02, Jacksonville, Fla.		d: 1/28/82, Sarasota, Fla.		BR/TR, 6′2″, 180 lbs.		Deb: 9/2/22 C										
1922	Bro-N	0	0	—	1	0	0	0	0	1	2	0	0	0	18.0	0.00	—	.500	.500	0	—	0	1	1	0	0.1
1923	Bro-N	0	0	—	9	0	0	0	1	15	16	1	8	4	15.6	4.20	92	.276	.382	0	.000	-0	-1	-0	1	-0.1
1945	NY-A	0	0	—	2	0	0	0	0	4¹	4	0	2	1	12.5	4.15	83	.267	.353	0	.000	-0	-0	-1	0	0.1
Total	3	0	0	—	12	0	0	0	1	20¹	22	1	10	5	15.0	3.98	96	.286	.382	0	.000	0	0	0	1	0.0

YEAR TM/L	W	L	PCT	G	GS	CG	SH	SV	IP	H	HR	BB	SO	RAT	ERA	ERA+	OAV	OOB	BH	AVG	PB	PR	/A	PD	TPI
● **AL SCHROLL** Schroll, Albert Bringhurst "Bull" b: 3/22/32, New Orleans, La. BR/TR, 6'2", 210 lbs. Deb: 4/20/58																								
1958 Bos-A	0	0	—	5	0	0	0	0	10	6	1	4	7	9.0	4.50	89	.176	.263	1	1.000	0	-1	-1	0	0.1
1959 Phi-N	1	1	.500	3	0	0	0	0	9¹	12	1	6	4	17.4	8.68	47	.353	.450	1	.250	0	-5	-5	0	-0.8
Bos-A	1	4	.200	14	5	1	0	0	46	47	3	22	26	13.7	4.70	86	.269	.354	1	.111	0	-4	-3	-1	-0.3
1960 Chi-N	0	0	—	2	0	0	0	0	2²	3	1	5	2	27.0	10.13	37	.273	.500	1	1.000	0	-2	-2	-0	0.0
1961 Min-A	4	4	.500	11	8	2	0	0	50	53	5	27	24	14.8	5.22	81	.266	.360	5	.278	2	-7	-5	-0	-0.6
Total 4	6	9	.400	35	13	3	0	0	118	121	11	64	63	14.3	5.34	77	.267	.362	9	.273	4	-19	-16	-1	-1.6
● **KEN SCHROM** Schrom, Kenneth Marvin b: 11/23/54, Grangeville, Idaho BR/TR, 6'2", 195 lbs. Deb: 8/8/80																								
1980 Tor-A	1	0	1.000	17	0	0	0	1	31	32	2	19	13	14.8	5.23	82	.274	.375	0	—	0	-4	-3	0	-0.1
1982 Tor-A	1	0	1.000	6	0	0	0	0	15¹	13	3	15	8	16.4	5.87	76	.232	.394	0	—	0	-3	-2	-1	-0.6
1983 Min-A	15	8	.652	33	28	6	1	0	196¹	196	14	80	80	13.1	3.71	114	.266	.345	0	—	0	8	12	-3	0.9
1984 Min-A	5	11	.313	25	21	3	0	0	137	156	15	41	49	13.0	4.47	94	.285	.336	0	—	0	-7	-4	-2	-0.8
1985 Min-A	9	12	.429	29	26	6	0	0	160²	164	28	59	74	12.5	4.99	88	.272	.337	0	—	0	-15	-10	1	-1.2
1986 Cle-A☆	14	7	.667	34	33	3	1	0	206	217	34	49	87	12.1	4.54	91	.271	.322	0	—	0	-8	-9	-3	-1.1
1987 Cle-A	6	13	.316	32	29	4	1	0	153²	185	29	57	61	14.3	6.50	70	.298	.360	0	—	0	-35	-34	-2	-3.6
Total 7	51	51	.500	176	137	22	3	1	900	963	125	320	372	13.1	4.81	89	.276	.342	0	—	0	-65	-51	-10	-6.5
● **RON SCHUELER** Schueler, Ronald Richard b: 4/18/48, Catharine, Kan. BR/TR, 6'4", 205 lbs. Deb: 4/16/72 C																								
1972 Atl-N	5	8	.385	37	18	3	0	2	144²	122	16	60	96	11.4	3.67	103	.227	.307	8	.190	0	-3	2	-1	0.1
1973 Atl-N	8	7	.533	39	20	4	2	2	186	179	24	66	124	11.9	3.87	102	.255	.319	11	.177	-1	-4	1	-1	-0.1
1974 Phi-N	11	16	.407	44	27	5	0	1	203¹	202	17	98	109	13.5	3.72	102	.264	.351	6	.118	-2	-2	1	-2	-0.4
1975 Phi-N	4	4	.500	46	6	1	0	0	92²	88	6	40	69	12.5	5.24	71	.258	.338	2	.154	-0	-17	-16	1	-1.2
1976 Phi-N	1	0	1.000	35	0	0	0	3	49²	44	4	16	43	11.2	2.90	122	.243	.312	0	.000	0	3	4	-1	0.0
1977 Min-A	8	7	.533	52	7	0	0	3	134²	131	16	61	77	13.2	4.41	90	.260	.347	0	—	0	-5	-6	2	-0.4
1978 Chi-A	3	5	.375	30	7	0	0	0	81²	76	10	39	39	13.4	4.30	88	.251	.350	0	—	0	-5	-5	-0	-0.4
1979 Chi-A	0	1	.000	8	1	0	0	0	19²	19	3	13	6	15.6	7.32	58	.264	.391	0	—	0	-7	-7	-0	-0.3
Total 8	40	48	.455	291	86	13	2	11	912¹	861	96	393	563	12.6	4.08	94	.253	.334	27	.159	-3	-40	-25	-2	-2.7
● **DAVE SCHULER** Schuler, David Paul b: 10/4/53, Framingham, Mass. BR/TL, 6'4", 210 lbs. Deb: 9/17/79																								
1979 Cal-A	0	0	—	1	0	0	0	0	1²	2	1	0	0	10.8	10.80	38	.333	.333	0	—	0	-1	-1	-0	0.2
1980 Cal-A	0	1	.000	8	0	0	0	0	12²	13	3	2	7	10.7	3.55	111	.271	.300	0	—	0	1	1	-0	0.0
1985 Atl-N	0	0	—	9	0	0	0	0	10²	19	4	3	10	18.6	6.75	57	.404	.440	0	—	0	-4	-3	-0	0.0
Total 3	0	1	.000	18	0	0	0	0	25	34	8	5	17	14.0	5.40	72	.337	.368	0	—	0	-4	-4	-1	0.2
● **ERIK SCHULLSTROM** Schullstrom, Erik Paul b: 3/25/69, San Diego, Cal. BR/TR, 6'5", 220 lbs. Deb: 7/18/94																								
1994 Min-A	0	0	—	9	0	0	0	1	13	13	0	5	13	13.2	2.77	176	.260	.339	0	—	0	3	3	-0	0.0
1995 Min-A	0	0	—	37	0	0	0	0	47	66	8	22	21	17.0	6.89	69	.332	.401	0	—	0	-11	-11	-0	0.0
Total 2	0	0	—	46	0	0	0	1	60	79	8	27	34	16.2	6.00	80	.317	.388	0	—	0	-8	-8	-1	0.0
● **BUDDY SCHULTZ** Schultz, Charles Budd b: 9/19/50, Cleveland, Ohio BR/TL, 6', 175 lbs. Deb: 9/3/75																								
1975 Chi-N	2	0	1.000	6	0	0	0	0	5²	11	1	5	4	25.4	6.35	60	.367	.457	0	—	0	-2	-2	-0	-0.5
1976 Chi-N	1	1	.500	29	0	0	0	2	23²	37	3	9	15	17.5	6.08	63	.356	.407	0	.000	-0	-7	-6	1	-0.6
1977 StL-N	6	1	.857	40	3	0	0	1	85¹	76	5	24	66	10.5	2.32	166	.245	.299	2	.167	0	15	14	-1	1.1
1978 StL-N	2	4	.333	62	0	0	0	6	83	66	6	36	70	11.3	3.80	93	.226	.309	1	.200	1	-2	-3	-1	-0.2
1979 StL-N	4	3	.571	31	0	0	0	3	42¹	40	7	14	38	11.5	4.46	84	.256	.318	0	.000	0	-3	-3	-0	-0.6
Total 5	15	9	.625	168	3	0	0	12	240	232	21	88	193	12.0	3.68	101	.257	.324	3	.120	0	1	1	-1	-0.8
● **BARNEY SCHULTZ** Schultz, George Warren b: 8/15/26, Beverly, N.J. BR/TR, 6'2", 200 lbs. Deb: 4/12/55 C																								
1955 StL-N	1	2	.333	19	0	0	0	4	29²	28	5	15	19	14.3	7.89	52	.259	.370	0	.000	-1	-13	-13	1	-1.4
1959 Det-A	2	3	.333	13	0	0	0	0	18¹	17	1	14	17	15.7	4.42	92	.254	.390	2	1.000	1	-1	-1	-0	0.0
1961 Chi-N	7	6	.538	41	0	0	0	7	66²	57	6	25	59	11.6	2.70	155	.228	.308	1	.100	-1	10	11	0	2.1
1962 Chi-N	5	5	.500	51	0	0	0	5	77²	66	7	23	58	10.8	3.82	108	.231	.297	0	.000	-0	1	3	0	0.3
1963 Chi-N	1	0	1.000	15	0	0	0	2	27¹	25	5	9	18	11.2	3.62	97	.263	.327	0	.000	-0	-1	-0	0	0.0
StL-N	2	0	1.000	24	0	0	0	1	35¹	36	5	8	26	11.7	3.57	99	.263	.313	0	—	0	-1	-0	-0	0.0
Yr	3	0	1.000	39	0	0	0	3	62²	61	10	17	44	11.5	3.59	98	.263	.319	0	.000	-0	-2	-0	0	0.0
1964 *StL-N	1	3	.250	30	0	0	0	14	49¹	51	3	11	29	8.4	1.64	232	.201	.249	1	.167	-0	10	12	-1	1.7
1965 StL-N	2	2	.500	34	0	0	0	3	42¹	39	8	11	38	10.6	3.83	100	.242	.291	0	.000	-0	-1	-0	0	0.0
Total 7	20	20	.500	227	0	0	0	35	346²	303	38	116	264	11.3	3.63	109	.237	.308	4	.121	-1	4	12	-0	2.7
● **BOB SCHULTZ** Schultz, Robert Duffy b: 11/27/23, Louisville, Ky. d: 3/31/79, Nashville, Tenn. BL/TL, 6'3", 200 lbs. Deb: 4/20/51																								
1951 Chi-N	3	6	.333	17	10	2	0	0	77¹	75	9	51	27	14.9	5.24	78	.251	.364	4	.138	-1	-11	-10	-1	-1.2
1952 Chi-N	6	3	.667	29	5	1	0	0	74	63	3	51	31	14.1	4.01	96	.232	.357	4	.222	0	-2	-1	-2	-0.3
1953 Chi-N	2	0	.000	7	2	0	0	0	11²	13	2	11	4	19.3	5.40	82	.289	.439	0	—	0	-1	-1	-1	-0.3
Pit-N	0	2	.000	11	2	0	0	0	18²	26	3	10	5	18.3	8.20	55	.321	.409	0	.000	0	-8	-7	-0	-0.7
Yr	0	4	.000	18	4	0	0	0	30¹	39	5	21	9	18.4	7.12	63	.307	.413	0	.000	0	-10	-9	-1	-1.0
1955 Det-A	0	0	—	1	0	0	0	0	1¹	2	0	2	0	27.0	20.25	19	.333	.500	0	—	0	-2	-2	-0	0.0
Total 4	9	13	.409	65	19	3	0	0	183	179	17	125	67	15.3	5.16	79	.255	.372	8	.154	-1	-25	-23	-4	-2.5
● **WEBB SCHULTZ** Schultz, Webb Carl b: 1/31/1898, Wautoma, Wis. d: 7/26/86, Delavan, Wis. BR/TR, 5'11", 172 lbs. Deb: 8/3/24																								
1924 Chi-A	0	0	—	1	0	0	0	0	1	1	0	0	0	9.0	9.00	46	.250	.250	0	—	0	-1	-1	-0	0.0
● **MIKE SCHULTZ** Schultz, William Michael b: 12/17/20, Syracuse, N.Y. BL/TL, 6'1", 175 lbs. Deb: 4/20/47																								
1947 Cin-N	0	0	—	1	0	0	0	0	2	4	0	2	0	27.0	4.50	91	.444	.545	0	—	0	-0	-0	-0	0.0
● **JOHN SCHULTZE** Schultze, John F. b: Burlington, N.J. 6'0.5", 165 lbs. Deb: 5/6/1891																								
1891 Phi-N	0	1	.000	6	1	0	0	0	15	18	1	11	4	17.4	6.60	52	.286	.392	1	.167	-0	-5	-5	-1	-0.3
● **AL SCHULZ** Schulz, Albert Christopher b: 5/12/1889, Toledo, Ohio d: 12/13/31, Gallipolis, Ohio BR/TL, 6', 182 lbs. Deb: 9/25/12																								
1912 NY-A	1	1	.500	3	1	1	0	0	16¹	11	0	11	8	12.1	2.20	163	.183	.310	0	.000	-0	2	3	1	0.3
1913 NY-A	7	13	.350	38	22	9	0	0	193	197	4	69	77	12.6	3.73	80	.266	.333	11	.175	0	-17	-16	-1	-1.6
1914 NY-A	1	3	.250	6	4	1	0	0	28¹	27	0	10	18	12.4	4.76	58	.237	.310	0	.000	-0	-6	-6	1	-0.8
Buf-F	9	12	.429	27	23	10	1	2	171	160	3	77	87	12.6	3.37	88	.259	.343	10	.179	-1	-9	-8	2	-0.8
1915 Buf-F	21	14	.600	42	38	25	5	0	309²	264	8	149	160	12.2	3.08	91	.238	.332	18	.165	-4	-12	-10	1	-1.3
1916 Cin-N	8	19	.296	44	22	10	0	2	215	208	4	93	95	12.8	3.14	83	.268	.350	8	.125	-3	-12	-13	0	-2.0
Total 5	47	62	.431	160	110	56	5	4	933³	867	19	409	445	12.5	3.32	85	.254	.337	47	.155	-9	-55	-50	3	-6.2
● **WALT SCHULZ** Schulz, Walter Frederick b: 4/16/1900, St.Louis, Mo. d: 2/27/28, Prescott, Ark. BR/TR, 6', 170 lbs. Deb: 9/24/20																								
1920 StL-N	0	0	—	2	0	0	0	0	6	10	0	2	0	18.0	6.00	50	.370	.414	0	.000	-0	-2	-2	0	0.0
● **DON SCHULZE** Schulze, Donald Arthur b: 9/27/62, Roselle, Ill. BR/TR, 6'3", 225 lbs. Deb: 9/13/83																								
1983 Chi-N	0	1	.000	4	3	0	0	0	14	19	1	7	8	17.4	7.07	54	.322	.403	0	.000	0	-5	-5	0	-0.3
1984 Chi-N	0	0	—	1	1	0	0	0	3	8	0	1	2	27.0	12.00	33	.571	.600	0	—	0	-3	-3	0	0.0
Cle-A	3	6	.333	19	14	2	0	0	85²	105	9	27	39	13.9	4.83	85	.302	.352	0	—	0	-8	-7	-0	-0.7
1985 Cle-A	4	10	.286	19	18	1	0	0	94¹	128	10	19	37	14.4	6.01	69	.322	.360	0	—	0	-20	-20	1	-2.4
1986 Cle-A	4	4	.500	19	13	1	0	0	84²	98	9	34	33	13.5	5.00	83	.266	.343	0	—	0	-8	-8	-1	-0.7
1987 NY-N	1	2	.333	5	4	0	0	0	21²	24	4	6	5	12.9	6.23	61	.296	.352	0	.000	0	-5	-6	1	-0.6
1989 NY-A	1	1	.500	3	2	0	0	0	11	12	1	5	6	14.7	4.09	95	.300	.391	0	—	0	-0	-0	-0	-0.1
SD-N	2	1	.667	7	4	0	0	0	24¹	28	6	6	14	16.3	5.55	63	.352	.386	0	—	0	-6	-5	-0	-0.4
Total 6	15	25	.375	76	59	4	0	0	338²	422	40	105	144	14.3	5.47	74	.306	.361	0	—	0	-54	-54	1	-5.4

YEAR	TM/L	W	L	PCT	G	GS	CG	SH	SV	IP	H	HR	BB	SO	RAT	ERA	ERA+	OAV	OOB	BH	AVG	PB	PR	/A	PD	TPI

● HAL SCHUMACHER   Schumacher, Harold Henry "Prince Hal" b: 11/23/10, Hinckley, N.Y. d: 4/21/93, Cooperstown, N.Y. BR/TR, 6', 190 lbs. Deb: 4/15/31

1931	NY-N	1	1	.500	8	2	1	0	1	18¹	31	3	14	11	22.1	10.80	34	.387	.479	1	.143	-0	-14	-14	1	-1.4
1932	NY-N	5	6	.455	27	13	3	1	0	101¹	119	3	39	38	14.2	3.55	104	.288	.352	7	.226	1	4	2	0	0.5
1933	*NY-N☆	19	12	.613	35	33	21	7	1	258²	199	9	84	96	9.9	2.16	149	**.214**	.280	21	.214	1	34	30	3	4.2
1934	NY-N	23	10	.697	41	36	18	2	0	297	290	16	89	112	11.8	3.18	122	.259	.313	28	.239	10	29	23	3	3.5
1935	NY-N★	19	9	.679	33	33	19	3	0	261²	235	11	70	79	10.7	2.89	133	.238	.292	21	.196	2	33	28	7	3.7
1936	*NY-N	11	13	.458	35	30	9	3	1	215¹	234	15	69	75	12.7	3.47	112	.280	.336	16	.216	2	13	10	4	1.6
1937	*NY-N	13	12	.520	38	29	10	1	1	217²	222	11	89	100	12.9	3.60	108	.264	.335	18	.222	3	8	7	1	1.1
1938	NY-N	13	8	.619	28	28	12	3	0	185	178	12	50	54	11.2	3.50	108	.248	.299	16	.239	4	6	5	2	1.2
1939	NY-N	13	10	.565	29	27	8	0	0	181²	199	14	89	58	14.4	4.81	82	.276	.358	14	.203	1	-18	-18	-0	-1.9
1940	NY-N	13	13	.500	34	30	12	1	1	227	218	14	96	123	12.4	3.25	119	.251	.355	15	.192	2	15	16	4	2.4
1941	NY-N	12	10	.545	30	26	12	3	1	206	187	11	79	63	11.8	3.36	110	.243	.317	10	.152	-1	6	8	1	0.6
1942	NY-N	12	13	.480	29	29	12	3	0	216	208	12	82	49	12.2	3.04	111	.251	.321	13	.173	1	6	5	2	1.2
1946	NY-N	4	4	.500	24	13	2	0	1	96²	95	8	52	48	13.7	3.91	88	.255	.347	1	.038	-2	-5	-5	3	-0.4
Total	13	158	121	.566	391	329	138	27	7	2482¹	2424	139	902	906	12.1	3.36	111	.255	.321	181	.202	24	117	100	30	16.3

● HACK SCHUMANN   Schumann, Carl J. b: 8/13/1884, Buffalo, N.Y. d: 3/25/46, Mill Grove, N.Y. TR, 6'2", 230 lbs. Deb: 9/19/06

| 1906 | Phi-A | 0 | 2 | .000 | 4 | 2 | 1 | 0 | 0 | 18 | 21 | 0 | 8 | 9 | 15.5 | 4.00 | 68 | .296 | .383 | 0 | .000 | -1 | -3 | -3 | -0 | -0.4 |

● FERDIE SCHUPP   Schupp, Ferdinand Maurice b: 1/16/1891, Louisville, Ky. d: 12/16/71, Los Angeles, Cal. BR/TR, 5'10", 150 lbs. Deb: 4/19/13

1913	NY-N	0	0	—	5	1	0	0	0	12	10	1	3	2	9.8	0.75	416	.244	.295	1	.333	1	3	3	-0	0.1
1914	NY-N	0	0	—	8	0	0	1	0	17	19	0	9	5	15.9	5.82	46	.306	.411	0	.000	-0	-6	-6	-0	-0.1
1915	NY-N	1	0	1.000	23	1	0	0	0	54²	57	1	29	28	14.7	5.10	50	.281	.379	2	.200	-0	-14	-15	-0	-0.2
1916	NY-N	9	3	.750	30	11	8	4	1	140¹	79	1	37	86	7.8	0.90	271	.167	.235	4	.098	-2	27	24	-3	1.6
1917	*NY-N	21	7	**.750**	36	32	25	6	0	272	202	7	70	147	9.1	1.95	131	**.209**	.265	15	.161	1	23	18	-3	1.7
1918	NY-N	0	1	.000	10	2	1	0	0	33¹	42	1	27	22	19.4	7.56	35	.328	.456	1	.111	-0	-18	-18	-0	-0.6
1919	NY-N	1	3	.250	9	4	0	0	1	32	32	2	18	17	14.1	5.63	50	.269	.365	2	.333	-1	-10	-10	-1	-1.3
	StL-N	4	4	.500	10	10	6	0	0	69²	55	2	30	37	11.1	3.75	75	.221	.307	1	.050	-0	-6	-7	-1	-0.9
	Yr	5	7	.417	19	14	6	0	1	101²	87	4	48	54	12.0	4.34	64	.236	.326	3	.115	-1	-16	-17	-2	-2.2
1920	StL-N	16	13	.552	38	37	17	0	0	250²	246	5	127	119	13.7	3.52	85	.265	.358	22	.256	6	-11	-15	-2	-1.3
1921	StL-N	2	0	1.000	9	4	1	0	1	37¹	42	5	21	22	15.7	4.10	89	.276	.371	4	.286	-0	-1	-2	-0	-0.1
	Bro-N	3	4	.429	20	7	1	0	2	61	75	2	27	26	15.3	4.57	85	.310	.384	1	.083	-1	-5	-5	0	-0.6
	Yr	5	4	.556	29	11	2	0	3	98¹	117	7	48	48	15.3	4.39	87	.295	.374	5	.192	-0	-7	-6	-0	-0.7
1922	Chi-A	4	4	.500	18	12	3	1	0	74	79	4	56	38	17.9	6.08	67	.284	.425	5	.217	1	-17	-17	-0	-1.5
Total	10	61	39	.610	216	121	62	11	6	1054	938	30	464	553	12.3	3.32	87	.244	.331	58	.182	5	-35	-51	-10	-3.2

● WAYNE SCHURR   Schurr, Wayne Allen b: 8/6/37, Garrett, Ind. BR/TR, 6'4", 185 lbs. Deb: 4/15/64

| 1964 | Chi-N | 0 | 0 | — | 26 | 0 | 0 | 0 | 0 | 48¹ | 57 | 3 | 11 | 29 | 12.7 | 3.72 | 100 | .298 | .337 | 0 | .000 | -0 | -1 | -0 | -0 | -0.1 |

● CARL SCHUTZ   Schutz, Carl James b: 8/22/71, Hammond, La. BL/TL, 5'11", 208 lbs. Deb: 9/3/96

| 1996 | Atl-N | 0 | 0 | — | 3 | 0 | 0 | 0 | 0 | 3¹ | 3 | 0 | 2 | 5 | 13.5 | 2.70 | 163 | .273 | .385 | 0 | — | 0 | 1 | 1 | -0 | 0.0 |

● MIKE SCHWABE   Schwabe, Michael Scott b: 7/12/64, Ft.Dodge, Iowa BR/TR, 6'4", 200 lbs. Deb: 5/27/89

1989	Det-A	2	4	.333	13	4	0	0	0	44²	58	6	16	13	15.1	6.04	63	.307	.364	0	—	0	-11	-11	1	-1.2
1990	Det-A	0	0	—	1	0	0	0	0	3²	5	0	0	1	12.3	2.45	161	.357	.357	0	—	0	1	0	0	0.0
Total	2	2	4	.333	14	4	0	0	0	48¹	63	6	16	14	14.9	5.77	66	.310	.364	0	—	0	-10	-10	1	-1.2

● DON SCHWALL   Schwall, Donald Bernard b: 3/2/36, Wilkes-Barre, Pa. BR/TR, 6'6", 200 lbs. Deb: 5/21/61

1961	Bos-A★	15	7	.682	25	25	10	2	0	178²	167	8	110	91	14.3	3.22	129	.255	.368	11	.180	-0	16	19	1	2.2
1962	Bos-A	9	15	.375	33	32	5	1	0	182¹	180	18	121	89	15.4	4.94	84	.260	.378	9	.136	-2	-20	-16	-0	-2.1
1963	Pit-N	6	12	.333	33	24	3	2	0	167²	158	13	74	86	12.8	3.33	99	.255	.340	8	.160	-0	-1	-1	-2	0.1
1964	Pit-N	4	3	.571	15	9	0	0	0	49²	53	1	15	36	12.3	4.35	81	.269	.321	5	.263	-4	-5	-0	-0.4
1965	Pit-N	9	6	.600	43	1	0	0	4	77	77	5	30	55	12.7	2.92	120	.269	.343	0	.000	-2	5	5	2	1.0
1966	Pit-N	3	2	.600	11	4	0	0	0	41²	31	3	21	24	11.4	2.16	165	.209	.312	1	.100	-0	7	7	0	0.8
	Atl-N	3	3	.500	11	8	0	0	0	45¹	44	3	19	27	12.9	4.37	83	.256	.337	0	.000	-2	-4	-4	-0	-0.6
	Yr	6	5	.545	22	12	0	0	0	87	75	6	40	51	12.1	3.31	109	.234	.322	1	.043	-2	3	3	-0	0.2
1967	Atl-N	0	0	—	1	0	0	0	0	0²	0	0	1	0	13.5	0.00	—	.000	.500	0	—	0	0	0	0	0.0
Total	7	49	48	.505	172	103	18	5	4	743	710	50	391	408	13.7	3.72	102	.257	.354	34	.145	-5	-1	5	4	1.0

● BLACKIE SCHWAMB   Schwamb, Ralph Richard b: 8/6/26, Lancaster, Cal. d: 12/21/89, Los Angeles, Cal. BR/TR, 6'5.5", 198 lbs. Deb: 7/25/48

| 1948 | StL-A | 1 | 1 | .500 | 12 | 5 | 0 | 0 | 0 | 31² | 44 | 3 | 21 | 7 | 18.5 | 8.53 | 53 | .331 | .422 | 3 | .300 | 1 | -15 | -14 | 0 | -0.6 |

● JEFF SCHWARZ   Schwarz, Jeffrey William b: 5/20/64, Fort Pierce, Fla. BR/TR, 6'5", 190 lbs. Deb: 4/24/93

1993	Chi-A	2	2	.500	41	0	0	0	0	51	35	1	38	41	13.4	3.71	113	.201	.353	0	—	0	3	3	-1	0.1
1994	Chi-A	0	0	—	9	0	0	0	0	11¹	9	0	16	14	19.9	6.35	73	.205	.417	0	—	0	-2	-2	-0	-0.1
	Cal-A	0	0	—	4	0	0	0	0	6²	5	1	2	4	14.9	4.05	121	.250	.423	0	—	0	1	1	0	-0.1
	Yr	0	0	—	13	0	0	0	0	18	14	1	18	18	18.0	5.50	86	.219	.419	0	—	0	-1	-2	-0	-0.1
Total	2	2	2	.500	54	0	0	0	0	69	49	2	56	59	14.6	4.17	104	.206	.372	0	—	0	2	1	-2	0.1

● RUDY SCHWENCK   Schwenck, Rudolph Christian b: 4/6/1884, Louisville, Ky. d: 11/27/41, Anchorage, Ky. BL/TL, 6', 174 lbs. Deb: 9/23/09

| 1909 | Chi-N | 1 | 1 | .500 | 3 | 2 | 0 | 0 | 0 | 4 | 16 | 0 | 3 | 3 | 45.0 | 13.50 | 19 | .308 | .357 | 1 | .250 | -0 | -5 | -5 | 1 | -1.6 |

● HAL SCHWENK   Schwenk, Harold Edward b: 8/23/1890, Schuylkill Haven, Pa. d: 9/3/55, Kansas City, Mo. BL/TL, 6', 185 lbs. Deb: 9/4/13

| 1913 | StL-A | 1 | 0 | 1.000 | 1 | 1 | 1 | 0 | 0 | 11 | 12 | 0 | 4 | 3 | 13.1 | 3.27 | 90 | .333 | .400 | 1 | .333 | 1 | -0 | -0 | -0 | 0.0 |

● JIM SCOGGINS   Scoggins, Lynn J. "Lefty" b: 7/19/1891, Killeen, Tex. d: 8/16/23, Columbia, S.C. BL/TL, 5'11", 165 lbs. Deb: 8/26/13

| 1913 | Chi-A | 0 | 1 | .000 | 1 | 1 | 0 | 0 | 0 | 0 | 1 | 0 | 0 | 0 | — | — | — | .000 | .500 | 0 | — | 0 | 0 | 0 | 0 | 0.0 |

● HERB SCORE   Score, Herbert Jude b: 6/7/33, Rosedale, N.Y. BL/TL, 6'2", 185 lbs. Deb: 4/15/55

1955	Cle-A☆	16	10	.615	33	32	11	2	0	227¹	158	18	154	**245**	12.4	2.85	140	.194	.323	10	.119	-4	28	29	-4	2.2
1956	Cle-A★	20	9	.690	35	33	16	**5**	0	249¹	162	18	129	**263**	10.6	2.53	**166**	**.186**	.292	16	.184	1	45	46	-4	4.8
1957	Cle-A	2	1	.667	5	5	1	0	0	36	18	0	26	39	11.3	2.00	186	.149	.304	1	.091	-0	7	5	0	0.5
1958	Cle-A	2	3	.400	12	5	2	1	0	41	29	1	34	48	13.8	3.95	92	.197	.348	1	.091	-0	-1	-1	-1	-0.3
1959	Cle-A	9	11	.450	30	25	9	1	0	160²	123	24	115	147	13.4	4.71	78	**.210**	.341	5	.096	-3	-15	-18	-3	-2.6
1960	Chi-A	5	10	.333	23	22	9	0	0	113²	91	10	87	78	14.3	3.72	102	.226	.366	3	.100	-1	2	1	-0	-0.0
1961	Chi-A	1	2	.333	8	5	1	0	0	24¹	22	3	24	14	17.0	6.66	59	.259	.422	0	.000	-1	-7	-7	0	-0.8
1962	Chi-A	0	0	—	4	0	0	0	0	6	6	1	4	3	15.0	4.50	87	.261	.370	0	—	-0	-0	-0	-0	-0.0
Total	8	55	46	.545	150	127	47	11	3	858¹	609	79	573	837	12.5	3.36	117	.200	.328	36	.128	-8	59	55	-12	3.8

● DICK SCOTT   Scott, Amos Richard b: 2/5/1883, Bethel, Ohio d: 1/18/11, Chicago, Ill. BR/TR, 6', 180 lbs. Deb: 6/26/01

| 1901 | Cin-N | 0 | 2 | .000 | 3 | 2 | 2 | 0 | 0 | 21 | 26 | 2 | 11 | 6 | 16.3 | 5.14 | 62 | .302 | .388 | 0 | .000 | -1 | -4 | -5 | -1 | -0.5 |

● DARRYL SCOTT   Scott, Darryl Nelson b: 8/6/68, Fresno, Cal. BR/TR, 6'1", 185 lbs. Deb: 5/31/93

| 1993 | Cal-A | 1 | 2 | .333 | 16 | 0 | 0 | 0 | 0 | 20 | 19 | 1 | 11 | 13 | 13.9 | 5.85 | 77 | .250 | .352 | 0 | — | 0 | -3 | -3 | -1 | -0.5 |

● ED SCOTT   Scott, Edward b: 8/12/1870, Walbridge, Ohio d: 11/1/33, Toledo, Ohio BR/TR, 6'3", Deb: 4/19/00

1900	Cin-N	17	20	.459	42	35	31	0	1	315	370	10	65	87	12.8	3.86	95	.292	.334	19	.154	-5	-6	-6	9	-0.2
1901	Cle-A	6	6	.500	17	16	11	0	1	124²	149	2	38	23	14.0	4.40	81	.293	.350	10	.208	1	-10	-12	2	-0.7
Total	2	23	26	.469	59	51	42	0	2	439²	519	12	103	110	13.2	4.01	91	.292	.338	29	.170	-4	-16	-18	11	-0.9

● GEORGE SCOTT   Scott, George William b: 11/17/1896, Trenton, Mo. BR/TR, 6'1", 175 lbs. Deb: 9/13/20

| 1920 | StL-N | 0 | 0 | — | 2 | 0 | 0 | 0 | 0 | 6 | 4 | 0 | 3 | 1 | 10.5 | 4.50 | 66 | .200 | .304 | 0 | .000 | -0 | -1 | -1 | -0 | -0.1 |

● JIM SCOTT
Scott, James "Death Valley Jim"   b: 4/23/1888, Deadwood, S.Dak.   d: 4/7/57, Jacumba, Cal.   BR/TR, 6'1", 235 lbs.   Deb: 4/25/09   U

YEAR TM/L	W	L	PCT	G	GS	CG	SH	SV	IP	H	HR	BB	SO	RAT	ERA	ERA+	OAV	OOB	BH	AVG	PB	PR	/A	PD	TPI
1909 Chi-A	12	12	.500	36	29	20	4	0	250¹	194	0	93	135	10.9	2.30	102	.223	.310	9	.106	-1	5	1	-1	-0.2
1910 Chi-A	8	18	.308	41	23	14	2	1	229²	182	5	86	135	10.7	2.43	99	.226	.303	15	.203	2	2	-1	3	0.4
1911 Chi-A	14	11	.560	39	26	13	3	0	222	195	3	81	128	11.4	2.39	135	.240	.311	11	.155	-2	24	21	-4	1.5
1912 Chi-A	2	2	.500	6	4	2	1	0	37²	36	0	15	23	12.4	2.15	149	.265	.342	0	.000	-2	5	4	-0	0.2
1913 Chi-A	20	20	.500	48	38	25	4	1	312¹	252	2	86	158	10.0	1.90	154	.221	.281	7	.072	-7	36	36	-0	3.8
1914 Chi-A	14	18	.438	43	33	12	2	1	253¹	228	5	75	138	10.9	2.84	94	.246	.306	14	.163	-0	-3	-4	3	-0.4
1915 Chi-A	24	11	.686	48	35	23	7	2	296¹	256	3	78	120	10.3	2.03	146	.238	.292	12	.126	-5	30	31	2	3.4
1916 Chi-A	7	14	.333	32	21	8	1	3	165¹	155	3	53	71	11.5	2.72	101	.258	.321	6	.115	-3	2	1	-1	-0.4
1917 Chi-A	6	7	.462	24	17	6	2	1	125	126	0	42	37	12.5	1.87	142	.272	.341	5	.119	-2	11	11	0	1.0
Total 9	107	113	.486	317	226	123	26	9	1892	1624	21	609	945	10.9	2.30	120	.238	.305	79	.129	-21	111	99	3	9.3

● JACK SCOTT
Scott, John William   b: 4/18/1892, Ridgeway, N.C.   d: 11/30/59, Durham, N.C.   BL/TR, 6'2.5", 199 lbs.   Deb: 9/6/16

YEAR TM/L	W	L	PCT	G	GS	CG	SH	SV	IP	H	HR	BB	SO	RAT	ERA	ERA+	OAV	OOB	BH	AVG	PB	PR	/A	PD	TPI
1916 Pit-N	0	0	—	1	0	0	0	0	5	5	1	3	4	14.4	10.80	25	.278	.381	0	.000	-0	-5	-5	0	0.0
1917 Bos-N	1	2	.333	7	3	3	0	0	39²	36	0	5	21	10.0	1.82	141	.255	.295	2	.125	-1	4	3	-1	0.1
1919 Bos-N	6	6	.500	19	12	7	0	1	103²	109	3	39	44	12.9	3.13	91	.275	.341	7	.175	-1	-2	-3	-3	-0.7
1920 Bos-N	10	21	.323	44	33	22	3	1	291	308	6	85	94	12.6	3.53	87	.277	.336	21	.212	-0	-13	-15	-4	-2.0
1921 Bos-N	15	13	.536	47	28	16	2	3	233²	258	9	57	83	12.4	3.70	99	.283	.330	30	.341	10	2	-1	1	0.7
1922 Cin-N	0	0	—	1	0	0	0	0	2	2	0	1	0	27.0	9.00	44	.500	.600	0	.000	-0	-1	-1	-0	0.0
*NY-N	8	2	.800	17	10	5	0	2	79²	83	7	23	37	12.2	4.41	91	.265	.320	8	.267	1	-3	-4	-1	-0.4
Yr	8	2	.800	18	10	5	0	2	80²	85	7	24	37	12.4	4.46	90	.268	.324	8	.258	1	-3	-4	-1	-0.4
1923 *NY-N	16	7	.696	40	25	9	3	1	220	223	15	65	79	11.9	3.89	98	.267	.323	25	.316	7	3	-2	-2	0.3
1925 NY-N	14	15	.483	36	28	18	2	3	239²	251	10	55	87	11.6	3.15	128	.269	.313	21	.241	6	30	24	2	3.3
1926 NY-N	13	15	.464	50	22	13	0	5	226	242	13	53	82	11.9	4.34	86	.276	.319	28	.337	9	-13	-15	-1	-0.9
1927 Phi-N	9	21	.300	48	25	17	1	1	233¹	304	15	69	69	14.5	5.09	81	.330	.379	33	.289	8	-30	-25	-0	-2.0
1928 NY-N	4	1	.800	16	3	0	0	1	50¹	59	3	11	17	12.9	3.58	109	.295	.338	4	.267	1	2	2	0	0.3
1929 NY-N	7	6	.538	30	6	2	0	1	91²	89	12	27	40	11.4	3.53	130	.260	.314	8	.308	3	12	11	1	1.6
Total 12	103	109	.486	356	195	115	11	19	1814²	1969	94	493	657	12.4	3.85	96	.281	.332	187	.275	44	-13	-30	-9	0.3

● LEFTY SCOTT
Scott, Marshall   b: 7/15/15, Roswell, N.Mex.   d: 3/3/64, Houston, Tex.   BR/TL, 6'0.5", 165 lbs.   Deb: 6/15/45

YEAR TM/L	W	L	PCT	G	GS	CG	SH	SV	IP	H	HR	BB	SO	RAT	ERA	ERA+	OAV	OOB	BH	AVG	PB	PR	/A	PD	TPI
1945 Phi-N	0	2	.000	8	2	0	0	0	22¹	29	1	12	5	16.5	4.43	86	.312	.390	0	.000	-0	-2	-1	-1	-0.2

● MIKE SCOTT
Scott, Michael Warren   b: 4/26/55, Santa Monica, Cal.   BR/TR, 6'3", 215 lbs.   Deb: 4/18/79

YEAR TM/L	W	L	PCT	G	GS	CG	SH	SV	IP	H	HR	BB	SO	RAT	ERA	ERA+	OAV	OOB	BH	AVG	PB	PR	/A	PD	TPI
1979 NY-N	1	3	.250	18	9	0	0	0	52¹	59	4	20	21	13.6	5.33	68	.289	.353	0	.000	-1	-9	-10	-0	-0.8
1980 NY-N	1	1	.500	6	6	1	1	0	29¹	40	1	8	13	14.7	4.30	83	.331	.372	1	.111	-0	-2	-2	-0	-0.1
1981 NY-N	5	10	.333	23	23	1	0	0	136	130	11	34	54	10.9	3.90	89	.261	.309	3	.073	-2	-6	-6	3	-0.5
1982 NY-N	7	13	.350	37	22	1	0	3	147	185	13	60	63	15.1	5.14	71	.321	.387	7	.146	-0	-25	-25	4	-2.7
1983 Hou-N	10	6	.625	24	24	2	2	0	145	143	8	46	73	12.0	3.72	91	.258	.320	8	.167	1	-2	-5	-0	-0.4
1984 Hou-N	5	11	.313	31	29	0	0	0	154	179	7	43	83	13.1	4.68	71	.293	.343	6	.128	-0	-19	-23	-0	-2.2
1985 Hou-N	18	8	.692	36	35	4	2	0	221²	194	20	80	137	11.2	3.29	105	.235	.304	11	.153	-2	7	4	-2	0.6
1986 *Hou-N★	18	10	.643	37	37	7	5	0	275¹	182	17	72	306	8.4	2.22	162	.186	.244	12	.126	-2	46	42	2	4.3
1987 Hou-N★	16	13	.552	36	36	8	3	0	247²	199	21	79	233	9.4	3.23	121	.217	.282	10	.125	-1	23	19	0	1.9
1988 Hou-N	14	8	.636	32	32	8	5	0	218²	162	19	53	190	9.2	2.92	114	.204	.261	6	.085	-3	13	10	-1	0.6
1989 Hou-N†	20	10	.667	33	32	9	2	0	229	180	23	62	172	9.6	3.10	109	.212	.268	10	.133	-0	10	7	-2	0.6
1990 Hou-N	9	13	.409	32	32	4	2	0	205²	194	27	66	121	11.4	3.81	98	.246	.305	7	.130	-0	-2	-2	-2	-0.4
1991 Hou-N	0	2	.000	2	2	0	0	0	7	11	2	4	3	20.6	12.86	27	.367	.457	0	.000	-0	-7	-7	-0	-1.3
Total 13	124	108	.534	347	319	45	22	3	2068²	1858	173	627	1469	11.0	3.54	100	.240	.300	81	.124	-6	28	1	3	-0.4

● MILT SCOTT
Scott, Milton Parker "Mikado Milt"   b: 1/17/1866, Chicago, Ill.   d: 11/3/38, Baltimore, Md.   BR, 5'9", 160 lbs.   Deb: 9/30/1882 ♦

YEAR TM/L	W	L	PCT	G	GS	CG	SH	SV	IP	H	HR	BB	SO	RAT	ERA	ERA+	OAV	OOB	BH	AVG	PB	PR	/A	PD	TPI
1886 Bal-a	0	0	—	1	0	0	0	0	3	2	0	2	0	15.0	3.00	114	.125	.263	92	.190	-0	0	0	-0	0.0

● MICKEY SCOTT
Scott, Ralph Robert   b: 7/25/47, Weimar, Germany   BL/TL, 6'1", 165 lbs.   Deb: 5/6/72

YEAR TM/L	W	L	PCT	G	GS	CG	SH	SV	IP	H	HR	BB	SO	RAT	ERA	ERA+	OAV	OOB	BH	AVG	PB	PR	/A	PD	TPI
1972 Bal-A	0	1	.000	15	0	0	0	0	23	23	2	5	11	11.3	2.74	112	.277	.326	0	.000	1	1	1	-0	0.1
1973 Bal-A	0	0	—	1	0	0	0	0	1²	2	1	2	2	21.6	5.40	69	.286	.444	0	—	-0	-0	-0	-1	0.1
Mon-N	1	2	.333	22	0	0	0	0	24	27	3	9	11	14.3	5.25	73	.287	.362	0	.000	-0	-4	-4	-0	-0.5
1975 Cal-A	4	2	.667	50	0	0	0	1	68¹	59	8	18	31	10.3	3.29	108	.233	.287	0	—	-0	4	2	-1	0.7
1976 Cal-A	3	0	1.000	34	0	0	0	3	39	47	3	12	10	13.6	3.23	103	.307	.358	0	—	-0	1	0	-1	0.0
1977 Cal-A	0	2	.000	12	0	0	0	0	16	19	1	4	5	12.9	5.63	70	.302	.343	0	—	-0	-3	-3	-0	-0.2
Total 5	8	7	.533	133	0	0	0	4	172	177	18	50	70	12.1	3.72	94	.271	.327	0	.000	-0	-2	-4	-1	-0.2

● DICK SCOTT
Scott, Richard Lewis   b: 3/15/33, Portsmouth, N.H.   BR/TL, 6'2", 185 lbs.   Deb: 5/8/63

YEAR TM/L	W	L	PCT	G	GS	CG	SH	SV	IP	H	HR	BB	SO	RAT	ERA	ERA+	OAV	OOB	BH	AVG	PB	PR	/A	PD	TPI
1963 LA-N	0	0	—	9	0	0	0	2	12	17	6	3	6	15.0	6.75	45	.340	.377	0	—	-0	-5	-5	-0	-0.2
1964 Chi-N	0	0	—	3	0	0	0	0	4¹	10	2	1	1	22.8	12.46	30	.417	.440	0	—	-0	-4	-4	0	0.0
Total 2	0	0	—	12	0	0	0	2	16¹	27	8	4	7	17.1	8.27	39	.365	.397	0	—	-0	-9	-9	-0	-0.2

● TIM SCOTT
Scott, Timothy Dale   b: 11/16/66, Hanford, Cal.   BR/TR, 6'2", 185 lbs.   Deb: 6/25/91

YEAR TM/L	W	L	PCT	G	GS	CG	SH	SV	IP	H	HR	BB	SO	RAT	ERA	ERA+	OAV	OOB	BH	AVG	PB	PR	/A	PD	TPI
1991 SD-N	0	0	—	2	0	0	0	0	1	1	0	0	1	18.0	9.00	42	.400	.400	0	—	0	-1	-1	0	0.0
1992 SD-N	4	1	.800	34	0	0	0	0	37²	39	4	21	30	14.6	5.26	68	.267	.363	0	—	-0	-7	-7	-1	-0.9
1993 SD-N	2	0	1.000	24	0	0	0	0	37²	38	1	15	30	13.6	2.39	173	.260	.345	0	.000	-0	7	7	0	0.3
Mon-N	5	2	.714	32	0	0	0	1	34	31	3	19	35	13.2	3.71	113	.242	.340	0	.000	-0	1	2	-0	0.3
Yr	7	2	.778	56	0	0	0	1	71²	69	4	34	65	12.9	3.01	138	.246	.343	0	.000	-0	8	9	-0	0.6
1994 Mon-N	5	2	.714	40	0	0	0	1	53¹	51	6	18	37	12.0	2.70	156	.251	.318	0	.000	-0	9	9	-0	0.9
1995 Mon-N	2	0	1.000	62	0	0	0	2	63¹	52	6	23	57	11.5	3.98	108	.222	.308	1	.250	-0	1	2	-1	0.0
1996 Mon-N	3	5	.375	45	0	0	0	0	46¹	41	3	21	37	12.0	3.11	139	.238	.328	0	.000	-0	1	1	-0	0.8
SF-N	2	2	.500	20	0	0	0	0	19²	24	5	9	10	15.6	8.24	50	.316	.395	0	.000	-0	-9	-9	-1	-1.5
Yr	5	7	.417	65	0	0	0	0	66	65	8	30	47	13.1	4.64	92	.258	.339	0	.000	-1	-3	-3	-0	-0.7
Total 6	23	12	.657	259	0	0	0	5	293	278	22	126	237	12.9	3.84	108	.250	.335	1	.067	-0	8	10	-4	-0.1

● SCOTT SCUDDER
Scudder, William Scott   b: 2/14/68, Paris, Tex.   BR/TR, 6'2", 180 lbs.   Deb: 6/6/89

YEAR TM/L	W	L	PCT	G	GS	CG	SH	SV	IP	H	HR	BB	SO	RAT	ERA	ERA+	OAV	OOB	BH	AVG	PB	PR	/A	PD	TPI
1989 Cin-N	4	9	.308	23	17	0	0	0	100¹	91	14	61	66	13.7	4.49	80	.239	.346	4	.167	1	-11	-10	-1	-1.2
1990 *Cin-N	5	5	.500	21	10	0	0	0	71²	74	12	30	42	13.4	4.90	81	.265	.343	1	.056	-0	-9	-8	-1	-1.1
1991 Cin-N	6	9	.400	27	14	0	0	1	101¹	91	6	56	51	13.6	4.35	87	.246	.354	3	.103	-0	-8	-6	-1	-1.0
1992 Cle-A	6	10	.375	23	22	0	0	0	109	134	10	55	66	15.8	5.28	74	.303	.383	0	—	-0	-16	-17	0	-2.1
1993 Cle-A	0	1	.000	2	1	0	0	0	4	5	0	4	1	22.5	9.00	48	.333	.500	0	—	-0	-2	-2	-0	-0.4
Total 5	21	34	.382	96	64	0	0	1	386¹	395	42	206	226	14.3	4.80	79	.266	.360	8	.113	-0	-46	-42	-3	-5.8

● ROD SCURRY
Scurry, Rodney Grant   b: 3/17/56, Sacramento, Cal.   d: 11/5/92, Reno, Nev.   BL/TL, 6'2", 180 lbs.   Deb: 4/17/80

YEAR TM/L	W	L	PCT	G	GS	CG	SH	SV	IP	H	HR	BB	SO	RAT	ERA	ERA+	OAV	OOB	BH	AVG	PB	PR	/A	PD	TPI
1980 Pit-N	0	2	.000	20	0	0	0	0	37²	28	2	17	28	10.0	2.15	169	.176	.280	1	.250	0	6	6	-0	0.3
1981 Pit-N	4	4	.444	27	7	0	0	7	74	74	6	40	65	14.2	3.77	95	.261	.358	3	.158	0	-2	-1	-1	-0.3
1982 Pit-N	4	5	.444	76	0	0	0	14	103²	79	3	64	94	12.8	1.74	213	.212	.334	5	.238	1	21	23	-1	2.6
1983 Pit-N	4	9	.308	61	0	0	0	0	68	63	6	53	67	15.9	5.56	67	.249	.387	0	.000	-1	-15	-14	-0	-2.8
1984 Pit-N	5	6	.455	43	0	0	0	1	46¹	28	1	22	48	9.7	2.53	143	.175	.275	0	.000	0	5	6	0	1.4
1985 Pit-N	0	1	.000	30	0	0	0	0	47²	42	4	28	43	13.2	3.21	111	.236	.340	0	.000	-0	5	6	-0	1.4
NY-A	1	0	1.000	5	0	0	0	0	12²	5	2	10	17	10.7	2.84	141	.125	.300	0	—	-0	2	2	0	0.1
1986 NY-A	1	2	.333	31	0	0	0	0	39¹	38	1	22	36	14.2	3.66	112	.252	.354	0	—	-0	2	2	-0	0.0
1988 Sea-A	0	2	.000	39	0	0	0	2	31¹	32	6	18	33	15.5	4.02	103	.258	.370	0	—	-0	-0	0	-1	-0.1
Total 8	19	32	.373	332	7	0	0	39	460²	384	31	274	431	13.2	3.24	115	.227	.341	9	.164	-0	22	25	-0	1.4

● JOHNNIE SEALE
Seale, Johnny Ray "Durango Kid"   b: 11/14/38, Edgewater, Colo.   BL/TL, 5'10", 155 lbs.   Deb: 9/20/64

YEAR TM/L	W	L	PCT	G	GS	CG	SH	SV	IP	H	HR	BB	SO	RAT	ERA	ERA+	OAV	OOB	BH	AVG	PB	PR	/A	PD	TPI
1964 Det-A	1	0	1.000	4	0	0	0	0	10	6	1	4	5	9.0	3.60	102	.171	.256	0	.000	-0	0	0	1	0.0

YEAR	TM/L	W	L	PCT	G	GS	CG	SH	SV	IP	H	HR	BB	SO	RAT	ERA	ERA+	OAV	OOB	BH	AVG	PB	PR	/A	PD	TPI
1965	Det-A	0	0		4	0	0	0	0	3	7	1	2	3	27.0	12.00	29	.500	.563	0	—	0	-3	-3	-0	0.0
Total	2	1	0	1.000	8	0	0	0	0	13	13	2	6	8	13.2	5.54	65	.265	.345	0	.000	-0	-3	-3	-0	0.0

● **KIM SEAMAN** Seaman, Kim Michael b: 5/6/57, Pascagoula, Miss. BL/TL, 6'4", 205 lbs. Deb: 9/28/79

YEAR	TM/L	W	L	PCT	G	GS	CG	SH	SV	IP	H	HR	BB	SO	RAT	ERA	ERA+	OAV	OOB	BH	AVG	PB	PR	/A	PD	TPI
1979	StL-N	0	0		1	0	0	0	0	2	0	0	2	3	9.0	0.00	—	.000	.250		—	0	1	1	0	0.0
1980	StL-N	3	2	.600	26	0	0	0	4	23²	16	2	13	10	11.0	3.42	108	.188	.296	0	.000	-0	1	1	-0	0.1
Total	2	3	2	.600	27	0	0	0	4	25²	16	2	15	13	10.9	3.16	117	.176	.292	0	.000	-0	1	2	-0	0.1

● **RUDY SEANEZ** Seanez, Rudy Caballero b: 10/20/68, Brawley, Cal. BR/TR, 5'10", 185 lbs. Deb: 9/7/89

YEAR	TM/L	W	L	PCT	G	GS	CG	SH	SV	IP	H	HR	BB	SO	RAT	ERA	ERA+	OAV	OOB	BH	AVG	PB	PR	/A	PD	TPI
1989	Cle-A	0	0		5	0	0	0	0	5	1	0	4	7	9.0	3.60	110	.071	.278	0	—	0	0	0	0	0.0
1990	Cle-A	2	1	.667	24	0	0	0	0	27¹	22	2	25	24	15.8	5.60	70	.220	.381	0	—	-0	-5	-5	-1	-0.5
1991	Cle-A	0	0	—	5	0	0	0	0	5	10	2	7	3	30.6	16.20	26	.385	.515	0	—	-0	-7	-7	-0	0.0
1993	SD-N	0	0	—	3	0	0	0	0	3¹	8	1	2	1	27.0	13.50	31	.471	.526	0	—	-0	-4	-3	-0	0.0
1994	LA-N	1	1	.500	17	0	0	0	0	23²	24	2	9	18	12.9	2.66	147	.273	.347	0	.000	-0	4	4	0	0.2
1995	LA-N	1	3	.250	37	0	0	0	3	34²	39	5	18	29	15.1	6.75	56	.285	.372	0	.000	-0	-10	-11	-0	-1.4
Total	6	4	5	.444	91	0	0	0	3	99	104	12	65	86	15.6	6.00	65	.272	.382	0	.000	-0	-21	-23	-1	-1.7

● **RAY SEARAGE** Searage, Raymond Mark b: 5/1/55, Freeport, N.Y. BL/TL, 6'1", 180 lbs. Deb: 6/11/81

YEAR	TM/L	W	L	PCT	G	GS	CG	SH	SV	IP	H	HR	BB	SO	RAT	ERA	ERA+	OAV	OOB	BH	AVG	PB	PR	/A	PD	TPI
1981	NY-N	1	0	1.000	26	0	0	0	0	36²	34	2	17	16	12.5	3.68	95	.252	.336	1	1.000	0	-1	-1	-0	0.0
1984	Mil-A	2	1	.667	21	0	0	0	6	38¹	20	0	16	29	8.7	0.70	546	.155	.253	0	—	0	14	13	0	1.4
1985	Mil-A	1	4	.200	33	0	0	0	0	38	54	2	34	36	18.5	5.92	70	.338	.424	0	—	0	-7	-7	-1	-1.0
1986	Mil-A	0	1	.000	17	0	0	0	0	22	29	6	9	10	16.0	6.95	62	.315	.382	0	—	0	-7	-6	-0	-0.4
	Chi-A	1	0	1.000	29	0	0	0	1	29	15	1	19	26	10.6	0.62	694	.156	.296	0	—	0	11	12	0	0.3
	Yr	1	1	.500	46	0	0	0	1	51	44	7	28	36	12.7	3.35	129	.233	.332	0	—	0	5	5	-0	-0.1
1987	Chi-A	2	3	.400	58	0	0	0	0	55²	56	9	24	33	13.1	4.20	109	.264	.342	0	—	0	2	2	0	0.1
1989	LA-N	3	4	.429	41	0	0	0	0	35²	29	1	18	24	11.9	3.53	97	.225	.320	0	—	-0	-0	-1	1	0.1
1990	LA-N	1	0	1.000	29	0	0	0	0	32¹	30	1	10	19	11.1	2.78	131	.250	.308	0	.000	-0	4	3	1	0.1
Total	7	11	13	.458	254	0	0	0	11	287²	267	22	137	193	12.7	3.50	114	.249	.336	1	.333	0	15	15	0	0.5

● **STEVE SEARCY** Searcy, William Steven b: 6/4/64, Knoxville, Tenn. BL/TL, 6'1", 190 lbs. Deb: 8/29/88

YEAR	TM/L	W	L	PCT	G	GS	CG	SH	SV	IP	H	HR	BB	SO	RAT	ERA	ERA+	OAV	OOB	BH	AVG	PB	PR	/A	PD	TPI
1988	Det-A	0	2	.000	2	2	0	0	0	8	3	1	4	5	13.5	5.63	68	.242	.324	0	—	0	-1	-2	-0	-0.2
1989	Det-A	1	1	.500	8	2	0	0	0	22¹	27	3	12	11	15.7	6.04	63	.307	.390	0	—	0	-5	-6	-0	-0.5
1990	Det-A	2	7	.222	16	12	1	0	0	75¹	76	9	51	66	15.2	4.66	85	.270	.381	0	—	0	-6	-6	-0	-0.7
1991	Det-A	1	2	.333	16	5	0	0	0	40²	52	8	30	32	18.1	8.41	49	.313	.418	0	.000	-0	-19	-19	-1	-1.2
	Phi-N	2	1	.667	18	0	0	0	0	30¹	29	2	14	21	12.8	4.15	88	.252	.333	0	.000	-0	-2	-2	-0	-0.2
1992	Phi-N	0	0	—	10	0	0	0	0	10¹	18	2	8	5	18.3	6.10	57	.325	.438	0	—	0	-3	-3	-0	-0.1
Total	5	6	13	.316	70	21	1	0	0	187	205	25	119	140	15.6	5.68	69	.283	.384	0	.000	-0	-37	-37	-1	-2.8

● **TOM SEATON** Seaton, Thomas Gordon b: 8/30/1887, Blair, Neb. d: 4/10/40, ElPaso, Tex. BB/TR, 6', 175 lbs. Deb: 4/13/12

YEAR	TM/L	W	L	PCT	G	GS	CG	SH	SV	IP	H	HR	BB	SO	RAT	ERA	ERA+	OAV	OOB	BH	AVG	PB	PR	/A	PD	TPI
1912	Phi-N	16	12	.571	44	27	16	2	2	255	246	8	106	118	12.7	3.28	111	.261	.342	18	.217	-0	4	10	-2	0.8
1913	Phi-N	27	12	.692	52	35	21	5	1	322¹	262	6	136	168	11.4	2.60	128	.226	.313	12	.109	-5	22	26	2	2.7
1914	Bro-F	25	14	.641	44	38	26	7	2	302²	299	6	102	172	12.3	3.03	95	.259	.326	22	.206	2	-5	-5	0	-0.4
1915	Bro-F	12	11	.522	32	23	13	0	3	189¹	199	6	99	86	14.3	4.56	60	.273	.362	16	.242	3	-39	-39	1	-4.0
	New-F	2	6	.250	12	10	7	0	1	75	61	1	21	28	10.1	2.28	112	.224	.285	4	.154	0	4	3	-0	0.3
	Yr	14	17	.452	44	33	20	0	4	264¹	260	7	120	114	13.0	3.92	68	.259	.339	20	.217	3	-35	-36	2	-3.7
1916	Chi-N	6	6	.500	31	12	4	0	1	121	108	3	43	45	11.5	3.27	89	.246	.319	7	.184	-0	-9	-5	-1	-0.4
1917	Chi-N	5	4	.556	16	9	3	1	1	74²	60	0	23	27	10.1	2.53	114	.227	.292	5	.238	1	1	3	1	0.6
Total	6	93	65	.589	231	154	90	15	11	1340	1235	30	530	644	12.1	3.14	98	.249	.327	84	.186	0	-22	-8	4	-0.4

● **TOM SEATS** Seats, Thomas Edward b: 9/24/10, Farmington, N.C. d: 5/10/92, San Ramon, Cal. BR/TL, 5'11", 190 lbs. Deb: 5/4/40

YEAR	TM/L	W	L	PCT	G	GS	CG	SH	SV	IP	H	HR	BB	SO	RAT	ERA	ERA+	OAV	OOB	BH	AVG	PB	PR	/A	PD	TPI
1940	Det-A	2	2	.500	26	2	0	0	1	55²	67	4	21	25	14.2	4.69	101	.290	.349	1	.083	-1	-2	0	0	-0.1
1945	Bro-N	10	7	.588	31	18	6	2	0	121²	127	8	37	44	12.5	4.36	86	.271	.320	9	.209	0	-8	-8	0	-1.0
Total	2	12	9	.571	57	20	6	2	1	177¹	194	12	58	69	13.0	4.47	91	.271	.329	10	.182	0	-10	-8	0	-1.1

● **TOM SEAVER** Seaver, George Thomas "Tom Terrific" b: 11/17/44, Fresno, Cal. BR/TR, 6'1", 206 lbs. Deb: 4/13/67 H

YEAR	TM/L	W	L	PCT	G	GS	CG	SH	SV	IP	H	HR	BB	SO	RAT	ERA	ERA+	OAV	OOB	BH	AVG	PB	PR	/A	PD	TPI
1967	NY-N★	16	13	.552	35	34	18	2	0	251	224	19	78	170	11.0	2.76	123	.241	.303	11	.143	2	17	18	0	2.3
1968	NY-N★	16	12	.571	36	35	14	5	1	277²	224	15	48	205	9.1	2.20	137	.222	.262	15	.158	0	24	25	2	3.1
1969	*NY-N☆	25	7	.781	36	35	18	5	0	273¹	202	24	82	208	9.6	2.21	166	.207	.273	11	.121	-0	42	44	2	5.6
1970	NY-N☆	18	12	.600	37	36	19	2	0	290²	230	21	83	283	9.8	2.82	143	.214	.273	17	.179	4	40	39	2	4.5
1971	NY-N☆	20	10	.667	36	35	21	4	0	286¹	210	18	61	289	8.6	1.76	194	.206	.253	18	.196	4	54	52	1	6.5
1972	NY-N☆	21	12	.636	35	35	13	3	0	262	215	23	77	249	10.2	2.92	115	.224	.285	13	.146	4	16	13	2	2.2
1973	*NY-N★	19	10	.655	36	36	18	3	0	290	219	23	64	251	8.9	2.08	174	.206	.254	15	.161	3	51	50	-0	5.4
1974	NY-N	11	11	.500	32	32	12	5	0	236	199	19	75	201	10.6	3.20	111	.230	.293	7	.099	-2	11	9	2	0.9
1975	NY-N★	22	9	.710	36	36	15	5	0	280¹	217	11	88	243	9.9	2.38	145	.214	.280	17	.179	3	39	33	2	4.3
1976	NY-N★	14	11	.560	35	34	13	5	0	271	211	14	77	235	9.7	2.59	127	.213	.273	7	.085	0	27	21	1	1.9
1977	NY-N	7	3	.700	13	13	5	3	0	96	79	7	28	72	10.0	3.00	125	.221	.277	5	.161	-0	10	8	1	0.8
	Cin-N★	14	3	.824	20	20	14	4	0	165¹	120	12	38	124	8.6	2.34	168	.201	.249	12	.218	-1	29	29	-1	3.3
	Yr	21	6	.778	33	33	19	7	0	261¹	199	19	66	196	9.1	2.58	149	.208	.259	17	.198	-0	39	37	-0	4.1
1978	Cin-N☆	16	14	.533	36	36	8	1	0	259²	218	26	89	226	10.6	2.88	123	.227	.292	9	.122	-0	20	19	-2	1.6
1979	*Cin-N	16	6	.727	32	32	9	5	0	215	187	16	61	131	10.4	3.14	119	.236	.291	12	.158	2	14	10	1	0.8
1980	Cin-N	10	8	.556	26	26	5	1	0	168	140	24	59	101	10.7	3.64	98	.225	.293	6	.130	1	-1	-1	0	0.1
1981	Cin-N★	14	2	.875	23	23	6	1	0	166¹	120	10	66	87	10.2	2.54	140	.205	.289	11	.200	4	17	19	-1	2.1
1982	Cin-N	5	13	.278	21	21	0	0	0	111¹	136	14	44	62	14.8	5.50	67	.302	.368	6	.176	0	-23	-22	-0	-3.2
1983	NY-N	9	14	.391	34	34	5	2	0	231	201	18	86	135	11.3	3.55	102	.235	.308	10	.156	0	2	2	-1	0.3
1984	Chi-A	15	11	.577	34	33	10	4	0	236²	216	24	61	131	10.6	3.95	99	.242	.290	0	—	0	-2	-1	1	-0.2
1985	Chi-A	16	11	.593	35	33	6	1	0	238²	223	22	69	134	11.3	3.17	136	.248	.307	0	—	0	26	30	3	3.5
1986	Chi-A	2	6	.250	12	12	1	0	0	72	66	7	27	31	12.3	4.38	99	.242	.321	0	—	-0	-2	-1	-0	-0.2
	Bos-A	5	7	.417	16	16	1	0	0	104¹	114	8	29	72	12.5	3.80	110	.278	.329	0	—	0	4	4	-0	0.4
	Yr	7	13	.350	28	28	2	0	0	176¹	180	17	56	103	12.1	4.03	105	.261	.318	0	—	-0	3	3	-1	0.1
Total	20	311	205	.603	656	647	231	61	1	4782²	3971	380	1390	3640	10.2	2.86	127	.226	.285	202	.154	28	419	411	13	48.2

● **BOB SEBRA** Sebra, Robert Bush b: 12/11/61, Ridgewood, N.J. BR/TR, 6'2", 200 lbs. Deb: 6/26/85

YEAR	TM/L	W	L	PCT	G	GS	CG	SH	SV	IP	H	HR	BB	SO	RAT	ERA	ERA+	OAV	OOB	BH	AVG	PB	PR	/A	PD	TPI
1985	Tex-A	0	2	.000	7	4	0	0	0	20¹	26	4	14	13	18.1	7.52	56	.306	.410	0	—	0	-8	-7	-0	-0.6
1986	Mon-N	5	5	.500	17	13	3	1	0	91¹	82	9	25	66	10.8	3.55	104	.239	.296	6	.207	1	2	1	-1	0.2
1987	Mon-N	6	15	.286	36	27	4	1	0	177¹	184	15	67	156	12.9	4.42	95	.272	.340	8	.157	0	-7	-4	-1	-0.5
1988	Phi-N	1	2	.333	3	3	0	0	0	11¹	15	0	10	7	19.9	7.94	45	.333	.455	0	.000	-0	-4	-3	-0	-1.2
1989	Phi-N	2	3	.400	6	4	0	0	0	34¹	41	6	10	21	14.4	4.46	80	.295	.359	0	.000	-0	-4	-3	-0	-0.1
	Cin-N	0	0	—	15	0	0	0	1	21	24	2	18	14	19.3	6.43	56	.296	.441	0	.000	-0	-7	-7	-0	-0.5
	Yr	2	3	.400	21	4	0	0	1	55¹	65	8	28	35	15.6	5.20	68	.289	.375	0	.000	-0	-11	-10	-0	-0.6
1990	Mil-A	1	2	.333	10	1	0	0	0	11	20	1	5	4	21.3	8.18	47	.408	.473	0	—	-0	-5	-5	-1	-0.2
Total	6	15	29	.341	94	52	7	2	1	366²	392	37	149	281	13.6	4.71	84	.276	.351	14	.146	0	-34	-31	-2	-3.9

● **DOC SECHRIST** Sechrist, Theodore O'Hara b: 2/10/1876, Williamstown, Ky. d: 4/2/50, Louisville, Ky. BR/TR, 5'9", 160 lbs. Deb: 4/28/1899

YEAR	TM/L	W	L	PCT	G	GS	CG	SH	SV	IP	H	HR	BB	SO	RAT	ERA	ERA+	OAV	OOB	BH	AVG	PB	PR	/A	PD	TPI
1899	NY-N	0	0	—	1	0	0	0	0	2	0	0	2	0				1.000		0	—	0	0	0	0	0.0

● **DON SECRIST** Secrist, Donald Laverne b: 2/26/44, Seattle, Wash. BL/TL, 6'2", 195 lbs. Deb: 4/11/69

YEAR	TM/L	W	L	PCT	G	GS	CG	SH	SV	IP	H	HR	BB	SO	RAT	ERA	ERA+	OAV	OOB	BH	AVG	PB	PR	/A	PD	TPI
1969	Chi-A	0	1	.000	19	0	0	0	0	40	35	7	14	23	11.2	6.07	63	.227	.296	1	.143	0	-11	-10	-0	-0.2
1970	Chi-A	0	0	—	9	0	0	0	0	14²	19	1	12	9	19.0	5.52	71	.333	.449	0	—	0	-3	-3	-0	-0.0
Total	2	0	1	.000	28	0	0	0	0	54²	54	8	26	32	13.3	5.93	66	.256	.340	1	.143	0	-14	-13	-0	-0.2

● **DUKE SEDGWICK** Sedgwick, Henry Kenneth b: 6/1/1898, Martins Ferry, O. d: 12/4/82, Clearwater, Fla. BR/TR, 6', 175 lbs. Deb: 7/12/21

YEAR	TM/L	W	L	PCT	G	GS	CG	SH	SV	IP	H	HR	BB	SO	RAT	ERA	ERA+	OAV	OOB	BH	AVG	PB	PR	/A	PD	TPI
1921	Phi-N	1	3	.250	16	5	1	0	0	71¹	81	3	32	21	14.8	4.92	86	.283	.363	5	.208	-1	-9	-5	-1	-0.5

YEAR TM/L	W	L	PCT	G	GS	CG	SH	SV	IP	H	HR	BB	SO	RAT	ERA	ERA+	OAV	OOB	BH	AVG	PB	PR	/A	PD	TPI
1923 Was-A	0	1	.000	5	2	1	0	0	16	27	1	6	4	18.6	7.88	48	.415	.465	0	.000	-1	-7	-7	1	-0.4
Total 2	1	4	.200	21	7	2	0	0	87¹	108	4	38	25	15.5	5.46	76	.308	.382	5	.172	-2	-16	-13	-0	-0.9

● CHARLIE SEE See, Charles Henry "Chad" b: 10/13/1896, Pleasantville, N.Y d: 7/19/48, Bridgeport, Conn. BL/TR, 5'10.5", 175 lbs. Deb: 8/6/19 ♦

YEAR TM/L	W	L	PCT	G	GS	CG	SH	SV	IP	H	HR	BB	SO	RAT	ERA	ERA+	OAV	OOB	BH	AVG	PB	PR	/A	PD	TPI
1920 Cin-N	0	0	—	1	0	0	0	0	6	6	0	4	3	15.0	6.00	47	.286	.400	25	.305	0	-2	-2	-0	0.0

● CHUCK SEELBACH Seelbach, Charles Frederick b: 3/20/48, Lakewood, Ohio BR/TR, 6', 180 lbs. Deb: 6/29/71

YEAR TM/L	W	L	PCT	G	GS	CG	SH	SV	IP	H	HR	BB	SO	RAT	ERA	ERA+	OAV	OOB	BH	AVG	PB	PR	/A	PD	TPI
1971 Det-A	0	0	—	5	0	0	0	0	4	6	2	7	1	31.5	13.50	27	.375	.583	0	—	0	-4	-4	-0	0.0
1972 *Det-A	9	8	.529	61	3	0	0	14	112	96	6	39	76	11.1	2.89	109	.238	.310	3	.143	1	2	3	-1	0.7
1973 Det-A	1	0	1.000	5	0	0	0	0	7	7	1	2	2	11.6	3.86	106	.250	.300	0	—	0	-0	0	1	-0.4
1974 Det-A	0	0	—	4	0	0	0	0	7²	9	2	3	0	15.3	4.70	81	.300	.382	0	—	0	-1	-1	-0	-0.3
Total 4	10	8	.556	75	3	0	0	14	130²	118	11	51	79	12.0	3.38	96	.247	.326	3	.143	1	-3	-2	-0	-0.0

● EMMETT SEERY Seery, John Emmett b: 2/13/1861, Princeville, Ill. d: 8/7/30, Saranac Lake, N.Y. BL/TR, Deb: 4/17/1884 ♦

YEAR TM/L	W	L	PCT	G	GS	CG	SH	SV	IP	H	HR	BB	SO	RAT	ERA	ERA+	OAV	OOB	BH	AVG	PB	PR	/A	PD	TPI
1886 StL-N	0	0	—	2	0	0	0	0	7	8	1	3	2	14.1	7.71	42	.320	.393	108	.238	0	-3	-3	-0	0.0

● HERMAN SEGELKE Segelke, Herman Neils b: 4/24/58, San Mateo, Cal. BR/TR, 6'4", 200 lbs. Deb: 4/7/82

YEAR TM/L	W	L	PCT	G	GS	CG	SH	SV	IP	H	HR	BB	SO	RAT	ERA	ERA+	OAV	OOB	BH	AVG	PB	PR	/A	PD	TPI
1982 Chi-N	0	0	—	3	0	0	0	0	4¹	6	1	6	4	24.9	8.31	45	.316	.480	0	—	0	-2	-2	0	0.0

● DIEGO SEGUI Segui, Diego Pablo (Gonzalez) b: 8/17/37, Holguin, Cuba BR/TR, 6', 190 lbs. Deb: 4/12/62 F

YEAR TM/L	W	L	PCT	G	GS	CG	SH	SV	IP	H	HR	BB	SO	RAT	ERA	ERA+	OAV	OOB	BH	AVG	PB	PR	/A	PD	TPI
1962 KC-A	8	5	.615	37	13	2	0	6	116²	89	16	46	71	10.5	3.86	109	.211	.291	8	.235	2	1	5	0	0.7
1963 KC-A	9	6	.600	38	23	4	1	0	167	173	17	73	116	13.4	3.77	103	.267	.343	12	.218	1	-3	2	1	0.4
1964 KC-A	8	17	.320	40	35	5	2	0	217	219	30	94	155	13.0	4.56	84	.260	.335	11	.155	0	-23	-18	2	-1.7
1965 KC-A	5	15	.250	40	25	5	1	0	163	166	18	67	119	13.0	4.64	75	.261	.334	9	.191	2	-21	-21	-1	-2.2
1966 Was-A	3	7	.300	21	13	1	1	0	72	82	8	24	54	13.3	5.00	69	.291	.346	2	.111	-1	-13	-12	-1	-1.7
1967 KC-A	3	4	.429	36	3	0	0	1	70	62	4	31	52	12.2	3.09	103	.238	.324	0	.000	-1	1	1	-0	-0.1
1968 Oak-A	6	5	.545	52	0	0	0	6	83	51	7	32	72	9.0	2.39	118	.173	.255	1	.111	0	5	4	1	0.5
1969 Sea-A	12	6	.667	66	8	2	0	12	142¹	127	14	61	113	12.0	3.35	108	.238	.319	4	.148	-0	4	4	1	0.7
1970 Oak-A	10	10	.500	47	19	3	2	2	162	130	9	68	95	11.1	**2.56**	**138**	.222	.305	5	.116	-2	21	18	-1	1.8
1971 *Oak-A	10	8	.556	26	21	5	0	0	146¹	122	13	63	81	11.6	3.14	106	.229	.310	4	.085	-1	5	3	-1	0.2
1972 Oak-A	0	1	.000	7	3	0	0	0	22²	25	2	7	11	12.7	3.57	80	.287	.340	-1	.143	-0	-1	-2	-0	-0.1
StL-N	3	1	.750	33	0	0	0	9	55²	47	2	32	54	12.8	3.07	111	.229	.333	1	.143	-1	2	2	1	0.3
1973 StL-N	7	6	.538	65	0	0	0	17	100¹	78	6	53	93	11.8	2.78	131	.211	.310	0	.000	-1	10	10	1	1.3
1974 Bos-A	6	8	.429	58	0	0	0	10	108	106	9	49	76	13.0	4.00	96	.257	.337	0	—	0	-5	-2	-1	-0.8
1975 *Bos-A	2	5	.286	33	1	1	0	6	71	71	10	43	45	14.5	4.82	85	.270	.373	0	—	0	-8	-6	-1	-0.7
1977 Sea-A	0	7	.000	40	7	0	0	2	110²	108	20	43	91	12.4	5.69	72	.251	.321	0	—	-1	-20	-19	-0	-1.1
Total 15	92	111	.453	639	171	28	7	71	1807²	1656	185	786	1298	12.2	3.81	96	.243	.323	58	.151	-1	-43	-32	-3	-2.5

● JOSE SEGURA Segura, Jose Altagracia (Mota) b: 1/26/63, Fundacion, D.R. BR/TR, 5'11", 180 lbs. Deb: 4/10/88

YEAR TM/L	W	L	PCT	G	GS	CG	SH	SV	IP	H	HR	BB	SO	RAT	ERA	ERA+	OAV	OOB	BH	AVG	PB	PR	/A	PD	TPI
1988 Chi-A	0	0	—	4	0	0	0	0	8²	19	1	8	2	28.0	13.50	29	.432	.519	0	—	0	-9	-9	0	-1.0
1989 Chi-A	0	1	.000	7	0	0	0	0	6	13	2	3	4	24.0	15.00	25	.464	.516	0	—	0	-7	-7	0	-1.0
1991 SF-N	0	1	.000	11	0	0	0	0	16¹	20	1	5	10	13.8	4.41	81	.303	.352	0	—	0	-1	-2	-0	-0.1
Total 3	0	2	.000	22	0	0	0	0	31	52	4	16	16	19.7	9.00	41	.377	.442	0	—	0	-18	-18	0	-1.1

● SOCKS SEIBOLD Seibold, Harry b: 4/3/1896, Philadelphia, Pa. d: 9/21/65, Philadelphia, Pa. BR/TR, 5'8.5", 162 lbs. Deb: 9/18/15 ♦

YEAR TM/L	W	L	PCT	G	GS	CG	SH	SV	IP	H	HR	BB	SO	RAT	ERA	ERA+	OAV	OOB	BH	AVG	PB	PR	/A	PD	TPI
1916 Phi-A	1	2	.333	3	2	1	1	0	21²	22	0	9	5	12.9	4.15	69	.272	.344	2	.167	-0	-3	-3	1	-0.3
1917 Phi-A	4	16	.200	33	15	9	1	1	160	141	1	85	55	12.9	3.94	70	.243	.343	13	.220	2	-23	-21	-1	-2.5
1919 Phi-A	2	3	.400	14	4	1	0	0	45²	58	2	26	19	17.3	5.32	64	.322	.419	2	.154	-1	-11	-10	0	-1.1
1929 Bos-N	12	17	.414	33	27	16	1	1	205²	228	17	80	54	13.6	4.73	99	.285	.352	20	.286	4	-0	-1	-1	0.2
1930 Bos-N	15	16	.484	36	33	20	1	2	251	288	16	95	70	13.4	4.12	120	.298	.348	19	.211	0	24	23	-3	2.1
1931 Bos-N	10	18	.357	33	29	10	3	0	206¹	226	12	65	50	12.8	4.67	81	.279	.335	9	.129	-4	-18	-20	0	-2.7
1932 Bos-N	3	10	.231	28	20	6	1	0	136²	173	12	41	33	14.2	4.68	83	.308	.358	7	.152	-2	-12	-14	2	-1.1
1933 Bos-N	1	4	.200	11	5	1	0	1	36²	43	0	14	10	14.0	3.68	83	.295	.366	1	.111	0	-1	-3	-0	-0.3
Total 8	48	86	.358	191	135	64	8	5	1063¹	1179	60	405	296	13.5	4.43	91	.284	.350	76	.192	-0	-45	-48	-1	-5.6

● KEVIN SEITZER Seitzer, Kevin Lee b: 3/26/62, Springfield, Ill. BR/TR, 5'11", 180 lbs. Deb: 9/3/86 ♦

YEAR TM/L	W	L	PCT	G	GS	CG	SH	SV	IP	H	HR	BB	SO	RAT	ERA	ERA+	OAV	OOB	BH	AVG	PB	PR	/A	PD	TPI
1993 Oak-A	0	0	—	1	0	0	0	0	0¹	0	0	0	1	0.0	0.00	—	.000	.000	65	.255	1	0	0	0	0.0

● AARON SELE Sele, Aaron Helmer b: 6/25/70, Golden Valley, Minn. BR/TR, 6'5", 205 lbs. Deb: 6/23/93

YEAR TM/L	W	L	PCT	G	GS	CG	SH	SV	IP	H	HR	BB	SO	RAT	ERA	ERA+	OAV	OOB	BH	AVG	PB	PR	/A	PD	TPI
1993 Bos-A	7	2	.778	18	18	0	0	0	111²	100	5	48	93	12.5	2.74	168	.237	.325	0	—	0	20	23	-2	1.4
1994 Bos-A	8	7	.533	22	22	2	0	0	143¹	140	13	60	105	13.1	3.83	131	.261	.345	0	—	0	15	19	-1	1.4
1995 Bos-A	3	1	.750	6	6	0	0	0	32¹	32	3	14	21	13.6	3.06	159	.252	.340	0	—	0	6	6	-0	0.5
1996 Bos-A	7	11	.389	29	29	1	0	0	157¹	192	14	67	137	15.3	5.32	97	.303	.377	0	—	0	-6	-3	-0	-0.4
Total 4	25	21	.543	75	75	3	0	0	444²	464	35	189	356	13.8	4.03	123	.270	.351	0	—	0	35	46	-3	2.9

● EPP SELL Sell, Lester Elwood b: 4/26/1897, Llewellyn, Pa. d: 2/19/61, Reading, Pa. BR/TR, 6', 175 lbs. Deb: 9/1/22

YEAR TM/L	W	L	PCT	G	GS	CG	SH	SV	IP	H	HR	BB	SO	RAT	ERA	ERA+	OAV	OOB	BH	AVG	PB	PR	/A	PD	TPI
1922 StL-N	4	2	.667	7	5	0	0	0	33	47	2	9	5	15.0	6.82	57	.338	.374	4	.333	1	-10	-11	1	-1.3
1923 StL-N	0	1	.000	5	1	0	0	0	15	16	1	8	2	14.4	6.00	65	.291	.381	0	.000	-1	-3	-3	-0	-0.3
Total 2	4	3	.571	12	6	0	0	0	48	63	3	14	7	14.8	6.56	59	.325	.376	4	.211	0	-13	-14	0	-1.6

● JEFF SELLERS Sellers, Jeffrey Doyle b: 5/11/64, Compton, Cal. BR/TR, 6'1", 175 lbs. Deb: 9/15/85

YEAR TM/L	W	L	PCT	G	GS	CG	SH	SV	IP	H	HR	BB	SO	RAT	ERA	ERA+	OAV	OOB	BH	AVG	PB	PR	/A	PD	TPI
1985 Bos-A	2	0	1.000	4	4	1	0	0	22¹	24	1	7	6	12.5	3.63	118	.273	.326	0	—	0	1	2	-0	0.1
1986 Bos-A	3	7	.300	14	13	1	0	0	82	90	13	40	51	14.6	4.94	84	.282	.367	0	—	0	-7	-7	-0	-0.7
1987 Bos-A	7	8	.467	25	22	4	2	0	139²	161	10	61	99	14.5	5.28	86	.298	.373	0	—	0	-13	-12	1	-1.2
1988 Bos-A	1	7	.125	18	12	1	0	0	85²	89	9	56	70	15.5	4.83	85	.268	.379	0	—	0	-8	-7	-0	-0.9
Total 4	13	22	.371	61	51	7	2	0	329²	364	33	164	226	14.7	4.97	87	.285	.370	0	—	0	-27	-24	0	-2.7

● DAVE SELLS Sells, David Wayne b: 9/18/46, Vacaville, Cal. BR/TR, 5'11", 175 lbs. Deb: 8/2/72

YEAR TM/L	W	L	PCT	G	GS	CG	SH	SV	IP	H	HR	BB	SO	RAT	ERA	ERA+	OAV	OOB	BH	AVG	PB	PR	/A	PD	TPI
1972 Cal-A	2	0	1.000	10	0	0	0	0	16	11	0	5	2	9.0	2.81	103	.196	.262	0	—	0	0	0	0	0.1
1973 Cal-A	7	2	.778	51	0	0	0	10	68	72	2	35	25	14.8	3.71	96	.277	.373	0	—	0	1	-0	0	0.4
1974 Cal-A	2	3	.400	20	0	0	0	2	39	48	3	16	14	15.5	3.69	93	.312	.387	0	—	0	-0	-1	0	0.3
1975 Cal-A	0	0	—	4	0	0	0	0	8¹	9	3	4	7	18.4	8.64	41	.250	.386	0	—	0	-5	-5	-0	-0.1
LA-N	0	2	.000	5	0	0	0	0	7	6	2	7	1	11.6	3.86	88	.222	.300	1	1.000	0	-0	-0	0	0.0
Total 4	11	7	.611	90	0	0	0	12	138¹	146	10	67	49	14.4	3.90	88	.274	.363	1	1.000	0	-4	-7	1	0.8

● DICK SELMA Selma, Richard Jay b: 11/4/43, Santa Ana, Cal. BR/TR, 5'11", 175 lbs. Deb: 9/2/65

YEAR TM/L	W	L	PCT	G	GS	CG	SH	SV	IP	H	HR	BB	SO	RAT	ERA	ERA+	OAV	OOB	BH	AVG	PB	PR	/A	PD	TPI
1965 NY-N	2	1	.667	4	4	1	1	0	26²	22	1	9	26	10.8	3.71	95	.229	.302	2	.222	-1	-1	-1	1	0.0
1966 NY-N	4	6	.400	30	7	0	0	1	80²	84	11	39	58	14.1	4.24	86	.274	.361	1	.071	0	-6	-5	2	-0.4
1967 NY-N	2	4	.333	38	4	0	0	1	81¹	71	3	36	52	12.1	2.77	122	.241	.328	2	.091	-1	6	6	1	0.4
1968 NY-N	9	10	.474	33	23	4	3	0	169²	148	11	54	117	11.0	2.76	110	.233	.298	12	.207	1	4	5	2	1.0
1969 SD-N	3	0	.500	4	3	1	0	0	22	19	3	9	20	11.5	4.09	86	.229	.304	2	.286	0	-1	-1	-0	-0.2
Chi-N	10	8	.556	36	25	4	2	1	168²	137	13	72	161	11.3	3.63	111	.222	.307	8	.154	-1	7	-1	0	0.6
Yr	12	10	.545	40	28	5	2	1	190²	156	16	81	181	11.3	3.68	108	.223	.307	10	.169	-1	-2	-6	1	0.4
1970 Phi-N	8	9	.471	73	0	0	0	22	134¹	108	8	59	153	11.5	2.75	145	.226	.317	3	.150	0	**19**	**19**	2	3.0
1971 Phi-N	0	1	.000	17	0	0	0	1	24²	21	2	8	19	11.3	3.28	107	.231	.307	1	1.000	0	0	0	1	0.1
1972 Phi-N	2	9	.182	46	10	1	0	3	98²	91	13	73	58	15.4	5.56	65	.249	.381	4	.200	1	-23	-22	1	-2.3
1973 Phi-N	1	1	.500	6	0	0	0	0	8	8	1	6	4	12.4	5.63	67	.240	.367	0	—	0	-2	-1	-0	-0.3
1974 Cal-A	2	2	.500	18	0	0	0	0	23	22	5	9	16	12.9	5.09	68	.272	.404	0	—	0	-4	-4	-0	-0.2
Mil-A	0	0	—	3	0	0	0	0	2¹	5	0	8	2	23.1	19.29	19	.455	.500	0	—	0	-4	-4	-0	0.0
Yr	2	2	.500	21	0	0	0	0	25¹	27	2	17	18	16.0	6.39	54	.290	.405	0	—	0	-8	-8	-0	-0.2
Total 10	42	54	.438	307	76	16	6	31	840	734	69	381	681	12.2	3.62	100	.238	.327	35	.172	-2	-11	-/2	8	1.7

YEAR TM/L	W	L	PCT	G	GS	CG	SH	SV	IP	H	HR	BB	SO	RAT	ERA	ERA+	OAV	OOB	BH	AVG	PB	PR	/A	PD	TPI
● **FRANK SELMAN**				Selman, Frank C. (a.k.a. Frank C. Williams 1871-75)				b: Baltimore, Md.				Deb: 5/4/1871 ♦												
1873 Mar-n	0	1	.000	1	1	1	0	0	9	21	0	0	0	21.0	8.00	40	.350	.350	1	.333	0	-5	-5		-0.3
● **CARROLL SEMBERA**				Sembera, Carroll William				b: 7/26/41, Shiner, Tex.		BR/TR, 6', 155 lbs.		Deb: 9/28/65												
1965 Hou-N	0	1	.000	2	1	0	0	0	7¹	5	0	3	4	9.8	3.68	91	.185	.267	0	.000	-0	-0	-0	0	0.0
1966 Hou-N	1	2	.333	24	0	0	0	1	33	36	3	16	21	14.2	3.00	114	.288	.369	0	.000	-0	2	2	0	0.1
1967 Hou-N	2	6	.250	45	0	0	0	3	59²	66	7	19	48	13.0	4.83	69	.269	.325	1	.143	-0	-10	-10	1	-1.3
1969 Mon-N	2	2	.000	23	0	0	0	0	33	28	1	24	15	14.7	3.55	104	.246	.386	1	.250	0	0	-0	0	0.0
1970 Mon-N	0	0	—	5	0	0	0	0	6²	14	2	11	6	35.1	18.90	22	.424	.578	0	—	0	-11	-11	-0	0.0
Total 5	3	11	.214	99	1	0	0	4	139²	149	13	73	94	14.6	4.47	74	.274	.364	2	.133	-0	-19	-19	1	-1.2
● **FRANK SEMINARA**				Seminara, Frank Peter				b: 5/16/67, Brooklyn, N.Y.		BR/TR, 6'2", 205 lbs.		Deb: 6/2/92												
1992 SD-N	9	4	.692	19	18	0	0	0	100¹	98	5	46	61	13.2	3.68	97	.257	.342	4	.118	-1	-2	-1	2	-0.1
1993 SD-N	3	3	.500	18	7	0	0	0	46¹	53	5	21	22	15.0	4.47	93	.294	.377	2	.200	0	-2	-2	0	-0.2
1994 NY-N	0	2	.000	10	1	0	0	0	17	20	2	8	7	14.8	5.82	72	.303	.378	0	.000	-0	-3	-3	-1	-0.4
Total 3	12	9	.571	47	26	0	0	0	163²	171	12	75	90	13.9	4.12	92	.273	.356	6	.128	-1	-7	-6	1	-0.7
● **RAY SEMPROCH**				Semproch, Roman Anthony "Baby"				b: 1/7/31, Cleveland, Ohio		BR/TR, 5'11", 180 lbs.		Deb: 4/15/58												
1958 Phi-N	13	11	.542	36	30	12	6	0	204¹	211	25	58	92	12.4	3.92	101	.264	.319	7	.095	-5	1	1	-1	-0.4
1959 Phi-N	3	10	.231	30	18	2	0	3	111²	119	12	59	54	14.6	5.40	76	.277	.368	6	.176	-0	-18	-16	1	-1.7
1960 Det-A	3	0	1.000	17	0	0	0	0	27	29	2	16	9	15.0	4.00	99	.269	.363	0	.000	-0	-0	-0	1	0.1
1961 LA-A	0	0	—	2	0	0	0	0	1	1	0	3	1	36.0	9.00	50	.333	.667	0	—	0	-1	-0	0	0.0
Total 4	19	21	.475	85	48	14	2	3	344	360	39	136	156	13.2	4.42	91	.269	.340	13	.116	-5	-18	-16	1	-2.0
● **STEVE SENTENEY**				Senteney, Stephen Leonard				b: 8/7/55, Indianapolis, Ind.		d: 6/19/89, Colusa, Cal.		BR/TR, 6'2", 205 lbs.		Deb: 6/6/82										
1982 Tor-A	0	0	—	11	0	0	0	0	22	23	5	6	20	11.9	4.91	91	.247	.293	0	—	0	-2	-1	-0	-0.1
● **MANNY SEOANE**				Seoane, Manuel Modesto				b: 6/26/55, Tampa, Fla.		BR/TR, 6'3", 187 lbs.		Deb: 9/18/77												
1977 Phi-N	0	0	—	2	1	0	0	0	6	11	0	3	4	21.0	6.00	67	.407	.467	1	.500	-0	-1	-1	-0	-0.2
1978 Chi-N	1	0	1.000	7	1	0	0	0	8¹	11	0	6	5	18.4	5.40	75	.297	.395	0	—	0	-2	-1	-0	-0.2
Total 2	1	0	1.000	9	2	0	0	0	14¹	22	0	9	9	19.5	5.65	71	.344	.425	1	.500	-0	-3	-3	-1	-0.2
● **BILLY SERAD**				Serad, William I.				b: 1863, Philadelphia, Pa.		d: 11/1/25, Chester, Pa.		BR/TR, 5'7", 156 lbs.		Deb: 5/5/1884										
1884 Buf-N	16	20	.444	37	37	34	2	0	308	373	21	111	150	14.1	4.27	74	.281	.336	24	.175	-7	-44	-38	-3	-4.2
1885 Buf-N	9	21	.250	30	29	27	0	0	241¹	299	5	80	90	14.1	4.10	73	.293	.344	16	.154	-6	-34	-30	-3	-3.5
1887 Cin-a	10	11	.476	22	21	20	1	0	187¹	201	7	80	34	13.9	4.08	106	.266	.343	14	.177	-4	4	5	-1	0.1
1888 Cin-a	2	3	.400	6	5	5	0	0	50²	62	1	19	4	15.5	3.55	89	.291	.366	3	.130	-1	-3	-2	-1	-0.4
Total 4	35	55	.389	95	92	86	4	1	787¹	935	34	290	278	14.2	4.13	82	.282	.342	57	.166	-17	-77	-64	-7	-8.0
● **DAN SERAFINI**				Serafini, Daniel Joseph				b: 1/25/74, San Francisco, Cal.		BB/TL, 6'1", 185 lbs.		Deb: 6/25/96												
1996 Min-A	0	1	.000	3	1	0	0	0	4¹	7	1	2	1	20.8	10.38	49	.368	.455			0	-3	-3	-0	-0.4
● **GARY SERUM**				Serum, Gary Wayne				b: 10/24/56, Fargo, N.D.		BR/TR, 6'1", 180 lbs.		Deb: 7/22/77												
1977 Min-A	0	0	—	8	0	0	0	0	22²	22	4	10	14	13.5	4.37	91	.268	.362	0		0	-1	-1	-0	0.0
1978 Min-A	9	9	.500	34	23	6	1	1	184¹	188	14	44	80	11.5	4.10	93	.266	.311	0		0	-7	-6	-0	-0.9
1979 Min-A	1	3	.250	20	5	0	0	0	64	93	10	20	31	15.9	6.61	66	.354	.399	0		0	-17	-16	-0	-0.6
Total 3	10	12	.455	62	28	6	1	1	271	303	28	74	125	12.7	4.72	84	.288	.337	0		0	-25	-23	-0	-1.5
● **SCOTT SERVICE**				Service, Scott David				b: 2/26/67, Cincinnati, Ohio		BR/TR, 6'6", 230 lbs.		Deb: 9/5/88												
1988 Phi-N	0	0	—	5	0	0	0	0	5¹	7	0	1	6	15.2	1.69	211	.333	.391	0		0	1	1	-0	0.0
1992 Mon-N	0	0	—	5	0	0	0	0	7	15	1	5	11	25.7	14.14	25	.417	.488	0	.000	-0	-8	-8	-0	-0.9
1993 Col-N	0	0	—	3	0	0	0	0	4²	7	1	1	3	19.3	9.64	49	.400	.455	0		0	-3	-3	-0	0.0
Cin-N	2	2	.500	26	0	0	0	2	41¹	36	5	15	40	11.3	3.70	109	.235	.308	1	.143	-0	2	1	-0	0.1
Yr	2	2	.500	29	0	0	0	2	46	44	6	16	43	11.9	4.30	95	.250	.316	1	.143	-0	-1	-1	-0	0.1
1994 Cin-N	0	1	.333	6	0	0	0	0	7¹	8	2	3	5	13.5	7.36	56	.267	.333	0		0	-3	-3	-0	-0.9
1995 SF-N	3	1	.750	28	0	0	0	0	31	18	4	20	30	11.6	3.19	128	.176	.323	0	.000	-0	3	3	-0	0.1
1996 Cin-N	1	0	1.000	34	1	0	0	0	48	51	7	18	46	14.1	3.94	105	.277	.361	0	.000	-0	1	1	-0	0.0
Total 6	7	5	.583	107	1	0	0	4	144²	143	20	63	141	13.5	4.48	91	.262	.350	1	.067	-1	-6	-7	0	-0.5
● **MERLE SETTLEMIRE**				Settlemire, Edgar Merle "Lefty"				b: 1/19/03, Santa Fe, Ohio		d: 6/12/88, Russells Point, Ohio		BL/TL, 5'9", 156 lbs.		Deb: 4/13/28										
1928 Bos-A	0	6	.000	30	9	0	0	0	82¹	116	2	34	12	17.1	5.47	75	.345	.415	3	.176	-1	-13	-12	2	-0.6
● **AL SEVERINSEN**				Severinsen, Albert Henry				b: 11/9/44, Brooklyn, N.Y.		BR/TR, 6'3", 220 lbs.		Deb: 7/1/69												
1969 Bal-A	1	1	.500	12	0	0	0	0	19²	14	2	10	13	11.0	2.29	156	.206	.308	1	.333	0	3	3	0	0.3
1971 SD-N	2	5	.286	59	0	0	0	8	70	77	4	30	31	14.0	3.47	95	.292	.368	0	.000	-0	-1	1	1	0.0
1972 SD-N	0	1	.000	17	0	0	0	1	21¹	13	1	7	9	9.3	2.53	130	.173	.262	0	.000	-0	2	1	0	0.1
Total 3	3	7	.300	88	0	0	0	9	111	104	7	47	53	12.6	3.08	108	.256	.338	1	.200	0	5	3	2	0.4
● **ED SEWARD**				Seward, Edward William (b: Edward William Sourhardt)																					
				b: 6/29/1867, Cleveland, Ohio				d: 7/30/47, Cleveland, Ohio		TR, 5'7", 175 lbs.		Deb: 9/30/1885 U ♦												
1885 Pro-N	0	0	—	1	0	0	0	0	6	2	0	1	0	3.0	.00		.100	.100	0	.000	-0	2	2	1	0.0
1887 Phi-a	25	25	.500	55	52	52	3	0	470²	445	7	140	155	11.6	4.13	104	.244	.306	50	.188	-4	9	8	-2	0.0
1888 Phi-a	35	19	.648	57	57	57	**6**	0	518²	388	4	127	**272**	9.3	2.01	149	.200	.258	32	.142	-4	61	56	3	4.9
1889 Phi-a	21	15	.583	39	38	35	3	0	320	353	9	101	102	13.1	3.97	95	.271	.330	11	.217	6	-4	-6	-2	-0.2
1890 Phi-a	6	12	.333	21	19	15	1	0	154	165	4	72	55	14.3	4.73	81	.266	.349	10	.139	-1	-15	-15	-0	-1.5
1891 Cle-N	2	1	.667	3	3	0	0	0	16¹	16	0	1	4	9.4	3.86	90	.246	.258	4	.211	0	-1	-1	-1	-0.1
Total 6	89	72	.553	176	169	159	13	0	1485²	1369	23	441	589	11.4	3.40	108	.237	.299	127	.174	-3	51	43	-2	3.1
● **FRANK SEWARD**				Seward, Frank Martin				b: 4/7/21, Pennsauken, N.J.		BR/TR, 6'3", 200 lbs.		Deb: 9/28/43												
1943 NY-N	0	1	.000	1	1	0	0	0	9	12	0	5	2	17.0	3.00	115	.324	.405	0	.000	-1	-0	-0	-0	-0.1
1944 NY-N	3	2	.600	25	7	2	0	0	78¹	98	8	32	16	15.2	5.40	68	.306	.373	2	.083	-2	-16	-15	-1	-1.2
Total 2	3	3	.500	26	8	2	0	0	87¹	110	8	37	18	15.4	5.15	71	.308	.376	2	.071	-2	-15	-15	-2	-1.3
● **RIP SEWELL**				Sewell, Truett Banks				b: 5/11/07, Decatur, Ala.		d: 9/3/89, Plant City, Fla.		BL/TR, 6'1", 180 lbs.		Deb: 6/14/32 C										
1932 Det-A	0	0	—	5	0	0	0	0	10²	19	2	8	2	22.8	12.66	37	.388	.474	1	.500	0	-10	-9	0	0.0
1938 Pit-N	0	1	.000	17	0	0	0	0	38¹	41	3	21	18	15.0	4.23	90	.275	.372	1	.083	-1	-2	-2	1	0.0
1939 Pit-N	10	9	.526	52	12	5	1	2	176¹	177	10	73	69	12.8	4.08	94	.265	.339	11	.200	1	-3	-5	3	-0.1
1940 Pit-N	16	5	.762	33	23	14	2	1	189²	169	6	67	60	11.3	2.80	136	.238	.307	14	.192	2	22	21	2	2.7
1941 Pit-N	14	17	.452	39	32	18	2	2	249	225	18	84	76	11.3	3.72	97	.235	.299	16	.174	0	-2	-3	2	-0.1
1942 Pit-N	17	15	.531	40	33	18	5	2	248	259	8	75	62	12.4	3.41	99	.265	.317	13	.149	-3	-0	-3	2	-0.4
1943 Pit-N★	**21**	9	.700	35	31	**25**	3	2	265¹	267	6	75	85	11.7	2.54	137	.260	.312	30	.286	6	25	28	1	**4.0**
1944 Pit-N★	21	12	.636	38	33	24	3	0	286	263	15	99	87	11.5	3.18	117	.240	.304	25	.223	3	14	17	-1	2.1
1945 Pit-N†	11	9	.550	33	24	9	1	1	188	212	9	91	60	14.6	4.07	97	.279	.357	20	.313	6	-6	-3	-0	0.3
1946 Pit-N★	8	12	.400	25	20	11	2	0	149¹	140	6	53	30	13.1	3.68	96	.245	.310	9	.180	0	-4	-3	-1	-0.4
1947 Pit-N	6	4	.600	24	12	4	1	0	121	121	7	36	26	11.9	3.57	118	.263	.321	5	.125	-1	7	9	1	0.7
1948 Pit-N	13	3	.813	21	17	7	0	0	121²	126	9	37	36	12.1	3.48	117	.262	.317	6	.143	1	6	6	1	1.1
1949 Pit-N	6	1	.857	14	2	1	0	0	76	80	8	32	26	13.5	3.91	108	.280	.351	1	.063	-0	1	2	-1	0.1
Total 13	143	97	.596	390	243	137	20	15	2119¹	2101	116	748	636	12.2	3.48	107	.256	.320	152	.203	16	45	60	7	10.1
● **ELMER SEXAUER**				Sexauer, Elmer George				b: 5/21/26, St.Louis Co., Mo.		BR/TR, 6'4", 220 lbs.		Deb: 9/6/48												
1948 Bro-N	0	0	—	2	0	0	0	0	0²	1	0	2	0	27.0	13.50	30	.000	.500	0	—	0	-1	-1	-0	0.0

YEAR TM/L	W	L	PCT	G	GS	CG	SH	SV	IP	H	HR	BB	SO	RAT	ERA	ERA+	OAV	OOB	BH	AVG	PB	PR	/A	PD	TPI
● FRANK SEXTON	Sexton, Frank Joseph b: 7/8/1872, Brockton, Mass. d: 1/4/38, Brighton, Mass. 160 lbs. Deb: 6/21/1895																								
1895 Bos-N	1	5	.167	7	5	4	0	0	49	59	4	22	14	15.2	5.69	90	.294	.369	5	.227	-1	-5	-3	-1	-0.4
● GORDON SEYFRIED	Seyfried, Gordon Clay b: 7/4/37, Long Beach, Cal. BR/TR, 6', 185 lbs. Deb: 9/13/63																								
1963 Cle-A	0	1	.000	3	1	0	0	0	7¹	9	0	3	1	14.7	1.23	295	.300	.364	0	.000	-0	2	2	0	0.3
1964 Cle-A	0	0	—	2	0	0	0	0	2¹	4	0	0	0	15.4	0.00	—	.444	.444	0	—	0	1	1	0	0.0
Total 2	0	1	.000	5	1	0	0	0	9²	13	0	3	1	14.9	0.93	388	.333	.381	0	.000	-0	3	3	0	0.3
● JAKE SEYMOUR	Seymour, Jacob (b: Jacob Semer) b: 1854, Pittsburgh, Pa. d: 8/1/1897, Allegheny, Pa. Deb: 9/23/1882																								
1882 Pit-a	0	1	.000	1	1	1	0	0	8	16	0	2	2	20.3	7.88	33	.390	.419	0	.000	-1	-5	-5	-0	-0.4
● CY SEYMOUR	Seymour, James Bentley b: 12/9/1872, Albany, N.Y. d: 9/20/19, New York, N.Y. BL/TL, 6', 200 lbs. Deb: 4/22/1896 ◆																								
1896 NY-N	2	4	.333	11	8	4	0	0	70¹	75	8	51	33	16.5	6.40	66	.271	.390	7	.219	-1	-16	-17	1	-1.1
1897 NY-N	18	14	.563	38	33	28	2	1	277²	254	4	164	149	14.2	3.37	123	.242	.355	33	.241	1	29	24	8	3.0
1898 NY-N	25	19	.568	45	43	39	4	0	356²	313	4	213	239	14.1	3.18	109	.234	.353	82	.276	7	17	12	8	2.7
1899 NY-N	14	18	.438	32	32	31	0	0	268¹	247	5	170	142	14.7	3.56	106	.245	.364	12	.300	1	9	6	5	1.9
1900 NY-N	2	1	.667	13	7	2	0	0	53	58	4	54	19	20.7	6.96	52	.278	.447	12	.300	1	-19	-20	-1	-0.7
1902 Cin-N	0	0	—	1	0	0	0	0	3	4	0	3	2	21.0	9.00	33	.308	.438	83	.340	0	-2	-2	-0	0.1
Total 6	61	56	.521	140	123	104	6	1	1029	951	25	655	584	14.8	3.76	101	.244	.365	1723	.303	16	18	3	23	5.8
● JOHN SHAFFER	Shaffer, John W. "Cannon Ball" b: 2/18/1864, Lock Haven, Pa. d: 11/21/26, Endicott, N.Y. Deb: 9/13/1886																								
1886 NY-a	5	3	.625	8	8	8	1	0	69	40	0	29	36	9.1	1.96	174	.164	.255	6	.240	1	11	11	-1	1.1
1887 NY-a	2	11	.154	13	13	13	0	0	112	148	3	53	22	17.0	6.19	69	.310	.391	8	.167	-3	-24	-24	2	-2.0
Total 2	7	14	.333	21	21	21	1	0	181	188	3	82	58	14.0	4.57	86	.260	.346	14	.192	-2	-12	-13	1	-0.9
● GUS SHALLIX	Shallix, August (b: August Schallick) b: 3/29/1858, Paderborn, Westphalia, Germany d: 10/28/37, Cincinnati, Ohio BR/TR, 5'11", 165 lbs. Deb: 6/22/1884																								
1884 Cin-a	11	10	.524	23	23	23	0	0	199²	163	6	53	78	10.9	3.70	90	.212	.286	3	.036	-10	-10	-8	1	-1.5
1885 Cin-a	6	4	.600	13	12	7	0	0	91¹	95	1	33	15	13.9	3.25	100	.265	.349	5	.128	-2	-0	0	1	-0.1
Total 2	17	14	.548	36	35	30	0	0	291	258	7	86	93	11.8	3.56	93	.229	.306	8	.065	-12	-10	-8	2	-1.6
● GREG SHANAHAN	Shanahan, Paul Gregory b: 12/11/47, Eureka, Cal. BR/TR, 6'2", 190 lbs. Deb: 9/4/73																								
1973 LA-N	0	0	—	7	0	0	0	0	15²	14	2	4	11	10.3	3.45	100	.230	.277	0	.000	0	-0	-0	-0	0.0
1974 LA-N	0	0	—	4	0	0	0	0	7	7	1	5	2	15.4	3.86	88	.259	.375	0	—	0	-0	-0	-0	0.0
Total 2	0	0	—	11	0	0	0	0	22²	21	3	9	13	11.9	3.57	96	.239	.309	0	.000	0	-0	-0	-0	0.0
● HARVEY SHANK	Shank, Harvey Tillman b: 7/29/46, Toronto, Ont., Can. BR/TR, 6'4", 220 lbs. Deb: 5/16/70																								
1970 Cal-A	0	0	—	1	0	0	0	0	3	2	0	1	2	12.8			.182	.308	0		0	1	1	-0	0.0
● BILL SHANNER	Shanner, Wilfred William b: 11/4/1894, Oakland City, Ind. d: 12/18/86, Evansville, Ind. BL/TR, Deb: 10/1/20																								
1920 Phi-A	0	0	—	1	0	0	0	0	4	6	2	1	1	15.8	6.75	60	.353	.389	0	.000	-0	-1	-1	-0	0.0
● BOBBY SHANTZ	Shantz, Robert Clayton b: 9/26/25, Pottstown, Pa. BR/TL, 5'6", 142 lbs. Deb: 5/1/49 F																								
1949 Phi-A	6	8	.429	33	7	4	1	2	127	100	9	74	58	12.5	3.40	121	.221	.334	7	.189	1	11	10	4	1.5
1950 Phi-A	8	14	.364	36	23	6	1	0	214²	251	18	85	93	14.4	4.61	99	.294	.362	11	.167	-0	-1	-1	4	0.2
1951 Phi-A☆	18	10	.643	32	25	13	3	0	205¹	213	15	70	77	12.6	3.94	108	.270	.333	18	.250	2	4	8	3	1.5
1952 Phi-A★	24	7	.774	33	33	27	5	0	279²	230	21	63	152	9.6	2.48	160	.225	.272	19	.198	2	37	46	2	5.5
1953 Phi-A	5	9	.357	16	16	6	0	0	105²	107	10	26	58	11.3	4.09	105	.263	.307	9	.237	1	-1	2	2	0.6
1954 Phi-A	1	0	1.000	2	1	0	0	0	8	12	2	3	0	18.0	7.88	50	.364	.432	1	.333	0	-4	-4	-0	-0.3
1955 KC-A	5	10	.333	23	17	4	1	0	125	124	8	66	58	13.8	4.54	92	.264	.356	6	.146	-2	-8	-5	1	-0.6
1956 KC-A	2	7	.222	45	2	1	0	9	101¹	95	12	37	67	12.0	4.35	99	.248	.319	2	.091	-1	-2	-0	1	0.0
1957 *NY-A☆	11	5	.688	30	21	9	1	5	173	157	15	40	72	10.6	2.45	147	.248	.299	10	.179	2	26	22	6	3.1
1958 NY-A	7	6	.538	33	13	3	0	0	126	127	16	35	80	11.7	3.36	105	.262	.315	8	.229	2	6	2	3	0.8
1959 NY-A	7	3	.700	33	4	2	2	3	94²	64	8	33	66	9.2	2.38	153	.189	.261	5	.217	2	16	13	1	1.7
1960 *NY-A	5	4	.556	42	0	0	0	11	67²	57	5	24	54	11.0	2.79	128	.235	.309	1	.100	-0	8	6	1	1.0
1961 Pit-N	6	3	.667	43	6	2	1	2	89¹	91	6	26	61	12.2	3.32	120	.271	.331	7	.438	3	7	7	2	1.1
1962 Hou-N	1	1	.500	3	3	1	0	0	20²	15	1	5	14	8.7	1.31	286	.208	.260	0	.000	-1	6	6	2	0.7
StL-N	5	3	.625	28	0	0	0	4	57²	45	7	20	47	10.3	2.18	195	.211	.282	2	.154	-0	11	13	1	2.0
Yr	6	4	.600	31	3	1	0	4	78¹	60	8	25	61	9.9	1.95	211	.210	.276	2	.095	-1	17	19	3	2.7
1963 StL-N	6	4	.600	55	0	0	0	11	79¹	60	7	17	70	8.4	2.61	136	.192	.243	1	.143	0	6	8	3	1.6
1964 StL-N	1	3	.250	16	0	0	0	0	17¹	14	2	7	18	11.9	3.12	122	.226	.304	0	—	0	1	1	1	0.4
Chi-N	0	1	.000	20	0	0	0	1	11¹	15	2	6	12	16.7	5.56	67	.319	.396	0	—	0	-3	-2	0	-0.2
Phi-N	1	1	.500	14	0	0	0	0	32	23	1	6	18	8.2	2.25	154	.204	.244	0	.000	0	5	4	2	0.5
Yr	2	5	.286	50	0	0	0	1	60²	52	5	19	48	10.5	3.12	116	.233	.293	0	.000	-0	3	3	4	0.7
Total 16	119	99	.546	537	171	78	15	48	1935²	1795	151	643	1072	11.5	3.38	119	.248	.313	107	.195	11	125	137	39	21.1
● GEORGE SHARROTT	Sharrott, George Oscar b: 11/2/1869, Staten Island, N.Y. d: 1/6/32, Jamaica, N.Y. BL/TL, 5'8", 164 lbs. Deb: 7/27/1893																								
1893 Bro-N	4	6	.400	13	10	10	0	1	95	114	4	58	24	17.1	5.87	75	.289	.390	9	.231	0	-13	-15	-1	-1.2
1894 Bro-N	0	1	.000	2	2	1	0	0	9	7	0	5	2	15.0	7.00	71	.212	.366	1	.333	0	-2	-2	-0	-0.2
Total 2	4	7	.364	15	12	11	0	1	104	121	4	63	26	16.9	5.97	75	.283	.388	10	.238	0	-14	-17	-1	-1.4
● JACK SHARROTT	Sharrott, John Henry b: 8/13/1869, Bangor, Me. d: 12/31/27, Los Angeles, Cal. BR/TR, 5'9", 165 lbs. Deb: 4/22/1890 ◆																								
1890 NY-N	11	10	.524	25	19	18	0	0	184	162	3	88	84	12.7	2.89	121	.229	.322	22	.202	-2	14	13	3	1.2
1891 NY-N	5	5	.500	10	9	6	0	1	69¹	47	2	35	41	11.2	2.60	123	.185	.294	10	.333	4	6	5	1	1.0
1892 NY-N	0	0	—	1	0	0	0	0	2	2	0	1	1	13.5	4.50	72	.250	.333	1	.125	-0	-0	-0	-0	0.0
1893 Phi-N	4	2	.667	12	4	2	0	0	56	53	1	33	11	14.5	4.50	102	.242	.352	38	.250	0	1	0	0	0.1
Total 4	20	17	.541	48	32	26	0	1	311¹	264	6	157	137	12.7	3.12	116	.222	.322	71	.237	2	21	17	3	2.3
● JOE SHAUTE	Shaute, Joseph Benjamin "Lefty" b: 8/1/1899, Peckville, Pa. d: 2/21/70, Scranton, Pa. BL/TL, 6', 190 lbs. Deb: 7/6/22																								
1922 Cle-A	0	0	—	2	0	0	0	0	3²	7	2	3	2	24.5	19.64	20	.389	.476	0	.000	-0	-6	-6	-0	-0.1
1923 Cle-A	10	8	.556	33	16	7	0	0	172	176	4	53	61	12.0	3.51	113	.275	.332	11	.162	-4	9	9	-2	0.3
1924 Cle-A	20	17	.541	46	34	21	2	2	283	317	6	83	68	12.9	3.75	114	.287	.340	34	.318	9	15	16	-2	2.6
1925 Cle-A	4	12	.250	26	17	10	1	0	131	160	6	44	34	14.1	5.43	81	.304	.358	16	.302	3	-15	-15	-2	-1.4
1926 Cle-A	14	10	.583	34	25	15	1	1	206²	215	9	65	47	12.3	3.53	115	.278	.337	20	.274	4	11	12	-5	1.2
1927 Cle-A	9	16	.360	45	28	14	0	2	230¹	255	9	75	63	13.0	4.22	100	.286	.343	27	.325	6	-2	-0	-2	0.3
1928 Cle-A	13	17	.433	36	31	21	1	2	253²	295	6	68	81	13.1	4.40	102	.299	.348	21	.228	3	-0	3	1	0.7
1929 Cle-A	8	8	.500	26	24	8	0	0	162	211	6	52	43	14.7	4.28	104	.320	.370	17	.293	3	-1	-3	-3	0.0
1930 Cle-A	0	0	—	4	0	0	0	0	4²	8	0	4	2	23.1	15.43	31	.333	.429	0	—	0	-6	-5	-0	0.0
1931 Bro-N	8	8	.579	25	19	6	0	0	128²	162	9	32	50	13.6	4.83	79	.305	.346	8	.178	-0	-14	-14	0	-1.9
1932 Bro-N	7	7	.500	34	9	1	0	0	117	147	8	21	38	13.1	4.54	84	.301	.333	9	.200	1	-9	-9	-2	-1.1
1933 Bro-N	3	4	.429	41	6	1	0	2	108¹	125	4	31	26	13.0	3.49	92	.287	.336	6	.222	1	-2	-3	1	-1.0
1934 Cin-N	2	2	.000	8	0	0	0	0	18	19	1	2	2	11.4	4.15	98	.268	.297	1	.250	0	-0	-0	-0	-0.1
Total 13	99	109	.476	360	208	103	5	18	1818¹	2097	75	534	512	13.1	4.15	99	.293	.345	170	.258	25	-18	-12	-14	0.8
● JEFF SHAVER	Shaver, Jeffrey Thomas b: 7/30/63, Beaver, Pa. BR/TR, 6'3", 195 lbs. Deb: 7/6/88																								
1988 Oak-A	0	0	—	1	0	0	0	0	2	1	0	0	0	9.0	0.00	—	.000	.333	0		0	0	0	0	0.3
● DON SHAW	Shaw, Donald Wellington b: 2/23/44, Pittsburgh, Pa. BL/TL, 6', 185 lbs. Deb: 4/11/67																								
1967 NY-N	4	5	.444	40	0	0	0	3	51¹	40	5	23	44	11.0	2.98	114	.219	.306	0	.000	0	2	2	-1	0.4
1968 NY-N	0	0	—	7	0	0	0	0	12¹	11	1	5	8	5.8	0.73	414	.086	.200	0	—	0	3	3	0	0.0
1969 Mon-N	2	5	.286	35	1	0	0	1	65²	61	9	37	45	13.7	5.21	71	.254	.358	0	.000	-0	-12	-11	1	-1.1
1971 StL-N	7	2	.778	45	0	0	0	2	51	45	1	31	19	13.6	2.65	136	.237	.347	0	.000	-0	5	5	-0	0.9

YEAR TM/L	W	L	PCT	G	GS	CG	SH	SV	IP	H	HR	BB	SO	RAT	ERA	ERA+	OAV	OOB	BH	AVG	PB	PR	/A	PD	TPI
1972 StL-N	0	1	.000	8	0	0	0	0	3	5	1	3	0	24.0	9.00	38	.417	.533	0	.000	-0	-2	-2	-0	-0.6
Oak-A	0	1	.000	3	0	0	0	0	5¹	12	2	2	4	23.6	16.88	17	.500	.538	0	—	-0	-8	-8	-0	-1.2
Total 5	13	14	.481	138	1	0	0	6	188²	166	19	101	123	12.9	4.01	87	.243	.343	0	.000	-0	-12	-11	-0	-1.6

● DUPEE SHAW   Shaw, Frederick Lander   b: 5/31/1859, Charlestown, Mass.   d: 6/11/38, Wakefield, Mass.   BL/TL, 5'8", 165 lbs.   Deb: 6/18/1883

YEAR TM/L	W	L	PCT	G	GS	CG	SH	SV	IP	H	HR	BB	SO	RAT	ERA	ERA+	OAV	OOB	BH	AVG	PB	PR	/A	PD	TPI
1883 Det-N	10	15	.400	26	25	23	1	0	227	238	3	44	73	11.2	2.50	124	.256	.290	39	.206	-3	16	15	0	1.2
1884 Det-N	9	18	.333	28	28	25	0	0	227²	219	8	72	142	11.5	3.04	95	.237	.292	26	.191	-1	-2	-4	2	-0.3
Bos-U	21	15	.583	39	38	35	5	0	315²	227	1	37	309	7.5	1.77	135	.188	.212	37	.242	-5	**24**	22	-0	1.5
1885 Pro-N	23	26	.469	49	49	47	6	0	399²	343	7	99	194	10.0	2.57	103	.209	.254	22	.133	-10	11	4	-2	-0.7
1886 Was-N	13	31	.295	45	44	43	1	0	385²	384	12	91	177	11.1	3.34	98	.250	.291	13	.088	-10	-1	-2	-1	-1.3
1887 Was-N	7	13	.350	21	20	20	0	0	181¹	263	8	46	47	15.5	6.45	63	.328	.366	13	.186	-2	-48	-48	-2	-4.0
1888 Was-N	0	3	.000	3	3	3	0	0	25	36	2	7	8	15.5	6.48	43	.333	.374	0	.000	-1	-10	-10	-1	-1.1
Total 6	83	121	.407	211	207	196	13	0	1762	1710	41	396	950	11.0	3.10	96	.239	.279	140	.170	-32	-10	-25	-5	-4.7

● JIM SHAW   Shaw, James Aloysius "Grunting Jim"   b: 8/19/1893, Pittsburgh, Pa.   d: 1/27/62, Washington, D.C.   BR/TR, 6', 180 lbs.   Deb: 9/15/13

YEAR TM/L	W	L	PCT	G	GS	CG	SH	SV	IP	H	HR	BB	SO	RAT	ERA	ERA+	OAV	OOB	BH	AVG	PB	PR	/A	PD	TPI
1913 Was-A	0	1	.000	2	1	1	0	0	13	8	0	7	14	11.1	2.08	142	.205	.340	0	.000	-0	1	1	1	0.2
1914 Was-A	15	17	.469	48	31	15	5	**4**	257	198	3	137	164	12.0	2.70	104	.216	.324	10	.118	-3	1	3	1	0.2
1915 Was-A	6	11	.353	25	18	7	1	1	133	102	2	76	78	12.2	2.50	119	.220	.333	10	.233	1	6	7	-1	0.9
1916 Was-A	3	8	.273	26	9	5	2	1	106¹	86	1	50	44	11.7	2.62	106	.227	.320	5	.156	-0	2	2	-3	-0.1
1917 Was-A	15	14	.517	47	31	15	2	1	266¹	233	1	123	118	12.1	3.21	82	.242	.328	14	.154	-2	-16	-17	-3	-2.4
1918 Was-A	16	12	.571	41	30	14	4	1	241¹	201	2	90	129	10.9	2.42	113	.228	.300	11	.133	-5	9	8	-5	-0.1
1919 Was-A	17	17	.500	**45**	37	23	3	**5**	306²	274	5	101	128	11.2	2.73	118	.244	.309	17	.160	-1	17	16	-6	1.1
1920 Was-A	11	18	.379	38	32	17	0	1	236¹	285	12	87	88	14.3	4.27	87	.314	.376	14	.189	0	-12	-14	-4	-1.8
1921 Was-A	1	0	1.000	15	5	0	0	3	41	59	2	17	4	16.7	7.36	56	.345	.404	2	.417	2	-14	-15	0	-0.3
Total 9	84	98	.462	287	194	96	17	17	1600¹	1446	28	688	767	12.1	3.07	99	.247	.329	86	.163	-8	-4	-7	-19	-2.3

● JEFF SHAW   Shaw, Jeffrey Lee   b: 7/7/66, Washington Court House, Ohio   BR/TR, 6'2", 185 lbs.   Deb: 4/30/90

YEAR TM/L	W	L	PCT	G	GS	CG	SH	SV	IP	H	HR	BB	SO	RAT	ERA	ERA+	OAV	OOB	BH	AVG	PB	PR	/A	PD	TPI
1990 Cle-A	3	4	.429	12	9	0	0	0	48²	73	11	20	25	17.2	6.66	59	.356	.413	0	—	0	-15	-15	0	-1.7
1991 Cle-A	0	5	.000	29	1	0	0	1	72¹	72	6	27	31	12.8	3.36	124	.262	.337	0	—	0	6	6	0	0.4
1992 Cle-A	0	1	.000	2	1	0	0	0	7²	7	2	4	3	12.9	8.22	48	.259	.355	0	—	0	-4	-4	0	-0.3
1993 Mon-N	2	7	.222	55	8	0	0	0	95²	91	12	32	50	12.2	4.14	101	.254	.327	1	.067	-1	-1	0	1	0.0
1994 Mon-N	5	2	.714	46	0	0	0	1	67¹	67	8	15	47	11.2	3.88	109	.254	.299	2	.286	1	3	3	1	0.4
1995 Mon-N	1	6	.143	50	0	0	0	3	62¹	58	4	26	45	12.6	4.62	93	.250	.333	0	.000	-0	-3	-2	1	-0.2
Chi-A	0	0	—	9	0	0	0	0	9²	12	1	2	6	13.0	6.52	68	.316	.350	0	—	0	-2	-2	0	0.4
1996 Cin-N	8	6	.571	78	0	0	0	4	104²	99	8	29	69	11.2	2.49	166	.252	.307	0	—	0	20	19	1	2.5
Total 7	19	31	.380	281	19	0	0	9	468¹	479	53	154	276	12.5	4.05	103	.267	.332	3	.091	-1	4	6	3	1.5

● BOB SHAW   Shaw, Robert John   b: 6/29/33, Bronx, N.Y.   BR/TR, 6'2", 195 lbs.   Deb: 8/11/57   C

YEAR TM/L	W	L	PCT	G	GS	CG	SH	SV	IP	H	HR	BB	SO	RAT	ERA	ERA+	OAV	OOB	BH	AVG	PB	PR	/A	PD	TPI
1957 Det-A	0	1	.000	7	0	0	0	0	9²	7	1	2	7	16.8	7.45	52	.289	.400	0	.000	-0	-4	-4	-0	-0.4
1958 Det-A	1	2	.333	11	2	0	0	0	26²	32	2	13	17	15.2	5.06	80	.302	.378	3	.375	1	-4	-3	1	-0.2
Chi-A	4	2	.667	29	3	0	0	1	64	67	8	28	18	13.6	4.64	78	.271	.350	0	.000	-1	-6	-7	-2	-0.6
Yr	5	4	.556	40	5	0	0	1	90²	99	10	41	35	14.1	4.76	79	.280	.358	3	.136	-0	-10	-10	-1	-0.8
1959 *Chi-A	18	6	**.750**	47	26	8	3	3	230²	217	15	54	89	10.8	2.69	140	.249	.297	9	.123	-2	30	27	1	2.6
1960 Chi-A	13	13	.500	36	32	7	1	0	192²	221	16	62	64	13.4	4.06	93	.292	.348	8	.138	-0	-4	-4	-0	-0.9
1961 Chi-A	3	4	.429	14	10	3	0	0	71¹	85	11	20	31	13.4	3.79	103	.302	.351	0	.000	-1	2	1	-0	-0.1
KC-A	9	10	.474	26	24	6	0	0	150¹	165	13	58	60	13.8	4.31	97	.281	.352	11	.200	-1	-5	-2	-0	-0.3
Yr	12	14	.462	40	34	9	0	0	221²	250	24	78	91	13.6	4.14	99	.286	.349	11	.151	-2	-3	-1	-0	-0.4
1962 Mil-N★	15	9	.625	38	29	12	3	2	225	223	20	44	124	11.2	2.80	136	.260	.305	10	.137	1	29	25	2	2.6
1963 Mil-N	7	11	.389	48	16	3	3	13	159	144	10	55	105	11.5	2.66	121	.243	.312	5	.122	0	11	10	-2	1.2
1964 SF-N	7	6	.538	61	1	0	0	11	93¹	105	5	31	57	13.6	3.76	95	.286	.350	0	.000	-1	-2	-2	-0	-0.6
1965 SF-N	16	9	.640	42	33	6	1	2	235	213	14	53	148	10.3	2.64	136	.236	.280	8	.101	-3	23	25	1	2.4
1966 SF-N	1	4	.200	13	6	0	0	0	31²	45	9	7	14	14.8	6.25	59	.324	.356	0	.000	-0	-9	-9	-1	-1.4
NY-N	11	10	.524	26	25	7	2	0	167²	171	12	42	104	11.3	3.92	93	.261	.313	13	.260	3	-6	-5	-1	-0.2
Yr	12	14	.462	39	31	7	2	0	199¹	216	21	49	125	12.3	4.29	85	.272	.320	13	.232	2	-15	-14	-2	-1.6
1967 NY-N	3	9	.250	23	13	3	1	0	98²	105	9	28	49	12.3	4.29	79	.273	.326	1	.040	-2	-10	-10	-1	-1.4
Chi-N	0	2	.000	9	3	0	0	0	22¹	33	0	9	7	18.5	6.04	59	.351	.430	1	.250	-1	-7	-6	-1	-0.6
Yr	3	11	.214	32	16	3	1	0	121	138	9	37	56	13.3	4.61	74	.286	.342	2	.069	-1	-17	-16	-2	-2.0
Total 11	108	98	.524	430	223	55	14	32	1778	1837	149	511	880	12.2	3.52	105	.267	.323	69	.133	-7	38	34	-2	2.1

● SAM SHAW   Shaw, Samuel E.   b: 5/1864, Baltimore, Md.   BR/TR, 5'5", 140 lbs.   Deb: 5/3/1888

YEAR TM/L	W	L	PCT	G	GS	CG	SH	SV	IP	H	HR	BB	SO	RAT	ERA	ERA+	OAV	OOB	BH	AVG	PB	PR	/A	PD	TPI
1888 Bal-a	2	4	.333	6	6	6	0	0	53	65	2	15	22	14.3	3.40	88	.291	.347	3	.150	-1	-2	-2	-1	-0.4
1893 Chi-N	1	0	1.000	2	1	1	0	0	16	12	2	13	1	19.1	5.63	82	.203	.420	2	.286	-0	-2	-2	-0	-0.1
Total 2	3	4	.429	8	8	7	0	0	69	77	4	28	23	15.4	3.91	86	.273	.365	5	.185	-1	-4	-4	-1	-0.5

● BOB SHAWKEY   Shawkey, James Robert   b: 12/4/1890, Sigel, Pa.   d: 12/31/80, Syracuse, N.Y.   BR/TR, 5'11", 168 lbs.   Deb: 7/16/13   MC

YEAR TM/L	W	L	PCT	G	GS	CG	SH	SV	IP	H	HR	BB	SO	RAT	ERA	ERA+	OAV	OOB	BH	AVG	PB	PR	/A	PD	TPI
1913 Phi-A	6	5	.545	18	15	8	1	0	111¹	92	2	50	52	11.7	2.34	118	.207	.291	6	.136	-2	7	5	1	0.4
1914 *Phi-A	16	8	.667	38	31	18	5	2	237	223	4	75	89	11.4	2.73	96	.262	.323	17	.205	2	0	-3	-2	-0.3
1915 Phi-A	6	6	.500	17	13	7	1	0	100	103	8	38	56	12.8	4.05	72	.278	.346	4	.129	-1	-12	-12	0	-1.4
NY-A	4	7	.364	16	9	5	1	0	85²	78	7	35	31	12.1	3.26	90	.265	.347	7	.241	-1	-3	-3	-1	-0.3
Yr	10	13	.435	33	22	12	2	0	185²	181	15	73	87	12.4	3.68	80	.272	.345	11	.183	-1	-15	-16	-1	-1.7
1916 NY-A	24	14	.632	53	27	21	6	**8**	276²	204	4	81	122	9.5	2.21	131	.209	.273	17	.183	-1	19	21	0	2.9
1917 NY-A	13	15	.464	32	26	16	2	0	236¹	207	2	72	97	10.9	2.44	110	.243	.306	16	.190	-0	6	7	3	1.1
1918 NY-A	1	1	.500	3	2	1	1	0	16	7	1	3	9	9.6	1.13	251	.143	.288	3	.750	2	8	8	0	0.7
1919 NY-A	20	11	.645	41	27	22	3	**5**	261¹	218	7	92	122	10.8	2.72	117	.231	.303	22	.234	-0	15	14	-1	1.5
1920 NY-A	20	13	.606	38	31	20	5	2	267²	246	10	85	126	11.2	**2.45**	**156**	.248	.308	23	.230	-0	40	41	-3	4.3
1921 *NY-A	18	12	.600	38	31	22	3	1	245	245	15	86	126	12.4	4.08	104	.263	.329	27	.300	4	4	4	0	0.4
1922 *NY-A	20	12	.625	39	34	22	3	1	299²	286	16	98	130	11.5	2.91	138	.256	.316	21	.183	-3	38	36	-0	3.2
1923 *NY-A	16	11	.593	36	31	17	1	1	258²	232	17	102	125	11.8	3.51	112	**.246**	.322	20	.202	-3	14	12	-1	0.8
1924 NY-A	16	11	.593	38	25	19	0	3	207²	226	11	74	114	13.1	4.12	101	.286	.349	11	.186	-0	1	1	1	0.7
1925 NY-A	6	14	.300	33	19	9	1	0	186	209	12	67	81	13.6	4.11	104	.294	.359	10	.147	-4	3	3	-1	-0.2
1926 *NY-A	8	7	.533	29	10	3	1	3	104¹	102	8	37	63	12.2	3.62	106	.263	.330	9	.257	2	5	5	0	0.5
1927 *NY-A	2	3	.400	19	2	0	0	1	43²	44	1	16	23	12.4	2.89	134	.262	.330	1	.091	-1	6	6	0	0.5
Total 15	196	150	.566	488	333	197	33	28	2937	2722	114	1018	1360	11.6	3.09	114	.251	.319	225	.214	4	151	136	-10	14.8

● SPEC SHEA   Shea, Francis Joseph "The Naugatuck Nugget" (b: Francis Joseph O'shea)   b: 10/2/20, Naugatuck, Conn.   BR/TR, 6', 195 lbs.   Deb: 4/19/47

YEAR TM/L	W	L	PCT	G	GS	CG	SH	SV	IP	H	HR	BB	SO	RAT	ERA	ERA+	OAV	OOB	BH	AVG	PB	PR	/A	PD	TPI
1947 *NY-A★	14	5	.737	27	23	13	3	1	178²	127	10	89	89	11.1	3.07	115	**.200**	.303	11	.196	2	13	9	-3	0.8
1948 NY-A	9	10	.474	28	22	8	3	1	155²	117	10	87	71	11.9	3.41	120	**.208**	.316	7	.149	1	15	12	-2	1.1
1949 NY-A	1	1	.500	20	3	0	0	1	52¹	48	5	43	22	15.6	5.33	76	.250	.387	3	.250	-1	-7	-7	-0	-0.2
1951 NY-A	5	5	.500	25	11	2	0	0	95²	112	11	50	38	15.6	4.33	88	.300	.389	6	.214	-1	-5	-5	-0	-0.4
1952 Was-A	11	7	.611	22	21	12	2	0	169	144	8	49	65	12.7	2.93	121	.231	.331	15	.238	2	14	12	-1	1.3
1953 Was-A	12	7	.632	23	23	11	1	0	164²	151	11	75	38	12.6	3.94	99	.244	.329	11	.177	-1	1	-1	-1	-0.3
1954 Was-A	2	9	.182	23	11	0	0	0	71¹	97	9	34	21	16.8	6.18	58	.340	.414	1	.050	-2	-19	-21	1	-2.9
1955 Was-A	2	2	.500	27	4	1	0	2	56¹	53	4	27	16	12.9	3.99	96	.251	.339	4	.400	1	-4	-3	-0	-0.6
Total 8	56	46	.549	195	118	48	12	5	943²	849	66	497	361	13.0	3.80	99	.243	.340	58	.195	6	7	-3	-8	-0.6

● JOHN SHEA   Shea, John Michael Joseph "Lefty"   b: 12/27/04, Everett, Mass.   d: 11/30/56, Malden, Mass.   BL/TL, 5'10.5", 171 lbs.   Deb: 6/30/28

YEAR TM/L	W	L	PCT	G	GS	CG	SH	SV	IP	H	HR	BB	SO	RAT	ERA	ERA+	OAV	OOB	BH	AVG	PB	PR	/A	PD	TPI
1928 Bos-A	0	0	—	1	0	0	0	0	1	1	0	1	1	18.0	18.00	23	.250	.400	0	—	0	-2	-2	0	0.0

● MIKE SHEA   Shea, Michael Joseph   b: 3/10/1867, New Orleans, La.   d: 8/22/27, New Orleans, La.   TR, 5'10", 170 lbs.   Deb: 4/20/1887

YEAR TM/L	W	L	PCT	G	GS	CG	SH	SV	IP	H	HR	BB	SO	RAT	ERA	ERA+	OAV	OOB	BH	AVG	PB	PR	/A	PD	TPI
1887 Cin-a	1	1	.500	2	2	2	0	0	16²	26	0	10	0	19.4	7.02	62	.333	.409	2	.250	0	-5	-5	1	-0.3

YEAR	TM/L	W	L	PCT	G	GS	CG	SH	SV	IP	H	HR	BB	SO	RAT	ERA	ERA+	OAV	OOB	BH	AVG	PB	PR	/A	PD	TPI

● RED SHEA
Shea, Patrick Henry b: 11/29/1898, Ware, Mass. d: 11/17/81, Stafford Springs, Conn. BR/TR, 6', 165 lbs. Deb: 5/6/18

1918	Phi-A	0	0	—	3	0	0	0	0	9	14	0	2	2	16.0	4.00	73	.378	.410	0	.000	-0	-1	-1	-0	-0.1
1921	NY-N	5	2	.714	9	2	1	0	0	32	28	2	2	10	9.3	3.09	119	.239	.270	1	.111	-1	2	2	-1	0.3
1922	NY-N	0	3	.000	11	2	0	0	0	23	22	2	11	5	12.9	4.70	85	.256	.340	0	.000	-1	-2	-2	1	-0.2
Total	3	5	5	.500	23	4	1	0	0	64	64	4	15	17	11.5	3.80	97	.267	.318	1	.053	-2	-0	-1	-0	0.0

● STEVE SHEA
Shea, Steven Francis b: 12/5/42, Worcester, Mass. BR/TR, 6'3", 215 lbs. Deb: 7/14/68

1968	Hou-N	4	4	.500	30	0	0	0	6	34²	27	0	11	15	10.6	3.38	88	.229	.311	0	.000	-1	-2	-2	1	-0.4
1969	Mon-N	0	0	—	10	0	0	0	0	15²	18	2	8	11	14.9	2.87	128	.300	.382	0	—	0	1	1	0	0.0
Total	2	4	4	.500	40	0	0	0	6	50¹	45	2	19	26	12.0	3.22	99	.253	.335	0	.000	-1	-0	-0	1	-0.4

● AL SHEALY
Shealy, Albert Berley b: 3/20/1900, Chapin, S.C. d: 3/7/67, Hagerstown, Md. BR/TR, 5'11", 175 lbs. Deb: 4/13/28

1928	NY-A	8	6	.571	23	12	3	0	2	96	124	4	42	39	15.7	5.06	74	.308	.375	9	.237	2	-11	-14	0	-1.6
1930	Chi-N	0	0	—	24	0	0	0	0	27	37	2	14	14	17.0	8.00	61	.327	.402	3	.600	1	-9	-9	-0	0.1
Total	2	8	6	.571	47	12	3	0	2	123	161	6	56	53	16.0	5.71	70	.313	.381	12	.279	4	-20	-23	-0	-1.5

● JOHN SHEARON
Shearon, John M. b: 1870, Pittsburgh, Pa. d: 2/1/23, Bradford, Pa. Deb: 7/28/1891 ♦

1891	Cle-N	1	3	.250	6	5	4	0	0	46	57	2	24	19	16.0	3.52	98	.292	.373	30	.242	-0	-1	-0	-0	0.0

● GEORGE SHEARS
Shears, George Penfield b: 4/13/1890, Marshall, Mo. d: 11/12/78, Loveland, Colo. BR/TL, 6'3", 180 lbs. Deb: 4/24/12

1912	NY-A	0	0	—	4	0	0	0	0	15	24	1	11	9	21.0	5.40	67	.364	.455	1	.167	0	-3	-3	0	0.0

● TOM SHEEHAN
Sheehan, Thomas Clancy b: 3/31/1894, Grand Ridge, Ill. d: 10/29/82, Chillicothe, Ohio BR/TR, 6'2.5", 190 lbs. Deb: 7/14/15 MC

1915	Phi-A	4	9	.308	15	13	8	1	0	102	131	1	38	22	15.0	4.15	71	.335	.395	4	.118	-3	-14	-14	-1	-1.9
1916	Phi-A	1	16	.059	38	17	8	0	0	188	197	2	94	54	14.0	3.69	78	.287	.374	7	.125	-2	-18	-17	3	-1.4
1921	NY-A	1	0	1.000	12	1	0	0	1	33	43	1	19	7	17.2	5.45	78	.326	.414	5	.625	2	-4	-4	2	0.2
1924	Cin-N	9	11	.450	39	14	8	2	1	166²	170	5	54	52	12.1	3.24	116	.269	.328	18	.310	4	12	10	-2	1.2
1925	Cin-N	1	0	1.000	10	3	1	0	1	29	37	3	12	5	15.2	8.07	51	.298	.360	1	.200	1	-12	-13	-1	-0.4
	Pit-N	1	1	.500	23	0	0	0	2	57¹	63	2	13	13	11.9	2.67	167	.286	.326	3	.150	-1	10	11	0	0.3
	Yr	2	1	.667	33	3	1	0	3	86¹	100	5	25	18	13.0	4.48	97	.291	.339	4	.160	-0	-2	-1	-1	-0.1
1926	Pit-N	0	2	.000	9	4	1	0	0	31	36	0	12	16	14.5	6.68	59	.298	.370	1	.111	-1	-10	-9	-0	-0.6
Total	6	17	39	.304	146	52	26	3	5	607	677	14	242	169	13.7	4.00	86	.294	.362	39	.205	0	-36	-36	1	-2.6

● ROLLIE SHELDON
Sheldon, Roland Frank b: 12/17/36, Putnam, Conn. BR/TR, 6'4", 190 lbs. Deb: 4/23/61

1961	NY-A	11	5	.688	35	21	6	2	0	162²	149	17	55	84	11.4	3.60	103	.246	.311	7	.125	-2	8	2	1	0.1
1962	NY-A	7	8	.467	34	16	2	0	1	118	136	12	36	54	12.6	5.49	68	.289	.331	2	.077	-0	-20	-23	-2	-2.7
1964	*NY-A	5	2	.714	19	12	3	0	1	102¹	92	18	18	57	9.8	3.61	100	.243	.279	3	.088	-2	0	0	-1	-0.1
1965	NY-A	0	0	—	3	0	0	0	0	6¹	5	0	1	7	8.5	1.42	240	.238	.273	0	.000	-0	1	1	0	0.0
	KC-A	10	8	.556	32	29	4	1	0	186²	180	22	56	105	11.7	3.95	88	.251	.312	4	.078	-3	-10	-10	-0	-1.2
	Yr	10	8	.556	35	29	4	1	0	193	185	22	57	112	11.6	3.87	90	.251	.310	4	.077	-3	-9	-8	0	-1.2
1966	KC-A	4	7	.364	14	13	1	1	0	69	73	3	26	26	13.0	3.13	109	.275	.342	2	.087	-1	2	2	0	0.2
	Bos-A	1	6	.143	23	10	1	0	0	79²	106	15	23	38	14.8	4.97	77	.320	.368	2	.111	-1	-14	-10	0	-0.9
	Yr	5	13	.278	37	23	2	1	0	148²	179	18	49	64	13.9	4.12	88	.297	.352	4	.098	-2	-11	-8	1	-0.7
Total	5	38	36	.514	160	101	17	4	2	724²	741	87	207	371	11.9	4.09	89	.266	.320	20	.096	-9	-32	-36	0	-4.6

● FRANK SHELLENBACK
Shellenback, Frank Victor b: 12/16/1898, Joplin, Mo. d: 8/17/69, Newton, Mass. BR/TR, 6'2", 192 lbs. Deb: 5/8/18 C

1918	Chi-A	9	12	.429	28	21	10	2	2	182²	180	1	74	47	12.7	2.66	103	.262	.338	7	.130	-1	2	2	-5	-0.5
1919	Chi-A	1	3	.250	8	4	2	0	0	35	40	1	16	10	14.4	5.14	62	.303	.378	1	.091	-0	-7	-8	-0	-0.8
Total	2	10	15	.400	36	25	12	2	2	217²	220	2	90	57	13.0	3.06	92	.269	.344	8	.123	-1	-5	-6	-5	-1.3

● JIM SHELLENBACK
Shellenback, James Philip b: 11/18/43, Riverside, Cal. BL/TL, 6'2", 200 lbs. Deb: 9/15/66 C

1966	Pit-N	0	0	—	2	0	0	0	0	3	3	3	1	3	0	18.0	9.00	40	.300	.462	0	—	0	-2	-2	0	0.0
1967	Pit-N	1	1	.500	6	2	1	0	0	23¹	23	1	12	11	13.9	2.70	125	.250	.343	1	.167	-0	2	2	-0	0.1
1969	Pit-N	0	0	—	8	0	0	0	0	16²	14	1	4	7	9.7	3.24	108	.233	.281	0	.000	-0	1	0	1	0.1
	Was-A	4	7	.364	30	11	2	0	1	84²	87	8	48	50	14.5	4.04	86	.268	.364	5	.185	-0	-4	-5	2	-0.5
1970	Was-A	6	7	.462	39	14	2	1	0	117¹	107	6	51	57	12.1	3.68	97	.246	.325	2	.067	-2	0	-2	-1	-0.4
1971	Was-A	3	11	.214	40	15	3	1	0	120	123	10	49	47	13.1	3.53	94	.267	.342	1	.100	-1	-3	-3	1	-0.2
1972	Tex-A	2	4	.333	22	6	0	0	1	57	46	6	16	30	10.1	3.47	87	.221	.283	1	.100	-0	-3	-3	-1	-0.4
1973	Tex-A	0	0	—	2	0	0	0	0	1²	3	0	0	2	21.6	0.00	—	.000	.000	0	—	1	1	1	0	0.1
1974	Tex-A	0	0	—	11	0	0	0	0	24²	30	4	12	14	15.7	5.84	61	.306	.387	0	—	-1	-6	-6	0	0.0
1977	Min-A	0	0	—	5	0	0	0	0	5²	10	1	5	3	23.8	7.94	50	.385	.484	0	—	0	-2	-2	0	0.0
Total	9	16	30	.348	165	48	8	2	2	454	443	40	200	222	12.9	3.81	88	.258	.338	14	.135	-2	-14	-21	3	-1.2

● BERT SHEPARD
Shepard, Bert Robert b: 6/28/20, Dana, Ind. BL/TL, 5'11", 185 lbs. Deb: 8/4/45

1945	Was-A	0	0	—	1	0	0	0	0	5¹	3	0	1	2	8.4	1.69	184	.167	.250	0	.000	-0	1	1	0	0.0

● KEITH SHEPHERD
Shepherd, Keith Wayne b: 1/21/68, Wabash, Ind. BR/TR, 6'2", 205 lbs. Deb: 9/6/92

1992	Phi-N	1	1	.500	12	0	0	0	2	22	19	0	6	10	10.2	3.27	107	.244	.298	0	—	0	1	1	0	0.1
1993	Col-N	1	3	.250	14	1	0	0	1	19¹	26	4	4	7	14.4	6.98	68	.333	.373	0	.000	-0	-6	-5	-0	-0.9
1995	Bos-A	0	0	—	2	0	0	0	0	1	4	0	2	0	54.0	36.00	14	.571	.667	0	—	0	-3	-3	-0	-0.2
1996	Bal-A	0	1	.000	13	0	0	0	0	20²	31	6	18	17	21.3	8.71	56	.341	.450	0	—	0	-9	-9	-0	-0.3
Total	4	2	5	.286	41	1	0	0	3	63	80	10	30	34	15.9	6.71	65	.315	.389	0	.000	0	-18	-16	0	-1.3

● BILL SHERDEL
Sherdel, William Henry "Wee Willie" b: 8/15/1896, McSherrystown, Pa d: 11/14/68, McSherrystown, Pa BL/TL, 5'10", 160 lbs. Deb: 4/22/18

1918	StL-N	6	12	.333	35	16	9	1	0	182¹	174	3	49	40	11.2	2.71	100	.259	.313	15	.242	3	1	-0	-2	0.2
1919	StL-N	5	9	.357	36	11	7	0	1	137¹	137	3	42	52	11.9	3.47	80	.270	.328	13	.271	2	-9	-10	1	-0.7
1920	StL-N	11	10	.524	43	7	4	0	6	170	183	1	40	74	12.4	3.28	91	.297	.350	14	.222	2	-3	-6	1	-0.4
1921	StL-N	9	8	.529	38	8	5	1	1	144¹	137	7	38	57	11.1	3.18	115	.247	.299	5	.114	-2	10	8	1	0.6
1922	StL-N	17	13	.567	47	31	15	2	2	242	298	12	62	79	13.6	3.87	100	.303	.348	17	.193	1	6	-0	-3	-0.3
1923	StL-N	15	13	.536	39	26	14	0	2	225	270	15	59	78	13.4	4.32	90	.296	.343	28	.337	9	-8	-10	-3	-0.6
1924	StL-N	8	9	.471	35	10	6	0	1	168²	188	9	38	57	12.3	3.42	111	.291	.335	15	.200	2	8	7	-2	0.7
1925	StL-N	15	6	.714	32	21	17	2	1	200	216	6	42	53	11.7	3.11	139	.277	.316	15	.205	2	26	27	-1	2.6
1926	*StL-N	16	12	.571	34	29	17	3	0	234²	255	15	49	59	11.9	3.49	112	.278	.318	22	.244	2	9	11	-3	1.1
1927	StL-N	17	12	.586	39	28	18	0	6	232¹	241	17	48	59	11.3	3.53	112	.269	.308	14	.194	1	10	11	-4	1.0
1928	*StL-N	21	10	.677	38	27	20	0	5	248²	251	17	56	72	11.2	2.86	140	.261	.303	19	.226	4	31	32	-5	3.7
1929	StL-N	10	15	.400	33	22	11	0	0	195²	278	14	58	69	15.5	5.93	79	.337	.382	16	.229	2	-26	-28	-2	-2.8
1930	StL-N	3	2	.600	13	7	1	0	0	64	86	5	13	29	14.1	4.64	108	.325	.358	2	.105	-2	2	3	-1	0.0
	Bos-N	6	5	.545	21	14	7	0	1	119	131	10	30	26	12.3	4.75	104	.283	.329	4	.095	-4	3	2	-1	-0.2
	Yr	9	7	.563	34	21	8	0	1	183¹	217	15	43	55	12.9	4.71	105	.298	.339	6	.098	-5	5	5	-1	-0.2
1931	Bos-N	6	10	.375	27	16	8	0	0	137²	163	13	30	45	13.0	4.25	89	.294	.337	14	.304	4	-6	-7	-2	-0.6
1932	Bos-N	0	0	—	1	0	0	0	0	1²	3	0	1	0	21.6	0.00	—	.375	.444	0	—	-0	1	1	-0	0.0
	StL-N	0	0	—	3	0	0	0	0	5²	7	0	1	1	12.7	4.76	83	.304	.333	1	1.000	1	-1	-0	0	0.1
	Yr	0	0	—	4	0	0	0	0	7¹	10	0	2	1	14.7	3.68	106	.323	.364	1	1.000	1	0	0	0	0.1
Total	15	165	146	.531	514	273	159	11	26	2709¹	3018	149	661	839	12.4	3.72	103	.285	.330	214	.223	27	55	38	-25	4.4

● ROY SHERID
Sherid, Royden Richard b: 1/25/07, Norristown, Pa. d: 2/28/82, Parker Ford, Pa. BR/TR, 6'2", 185 lbs. Deb: 5/11/29

1929	NY-A	6	6	.500	33	15	9	0	1	154²	165	6	55	51	13.1	3.61	107	.277	.343	9	.180	-1	11	4	-1	0.2
1930	NY-A	12	13	.480	37	21	8	0	4	184	214	13	87	59	15.0	5.23	82	.289	.368	7	.101	-6	-12	-19	-1	-2.7
1931	NY-A	5	5	.500	17	8	3	0	2	74¹	94	4	24	39	14.7	5.69	70	.306	.362	10	.333	2	-11	-14	-0	-1.4
Total	3	23	24	.489	87	44	20	0	7	413	473	23	166	149	14.2	4.71	88	.288	.358	26	.174	-4	-12	-29	-2	-3.9

YEAR	TM/L	W	L	PCT	G	GS	CG	SH	SV	IP	H	HR	BB	SO	RAT	ERA	ERA+	OAV	OOB	BH	AVG	PB	PR	/A	PD	TPI

● JOE SHERMAN Sherman, Joel Powers b: 11/4/1890, Yarmouth, Mass. d: 12/21/87, Cape Coral, Fla. BR/TR, 6′, 165 lbs. Deb: 9/24/15

| | 1915 Phi-A | 1 | 0 | 1.000 | 2 | 1 | 1 | 0 | 0 | 15 | 15 | 0 | 1 | 5 | 10.8 | 2.40 | 122 | .259 | .295 | 2 | .333 | 1 | 1 | 1 | -0 | 0.0 |

● DAN SHERMAN Sherman, Lester Daniel "Babe" b: 5/9/1890, Hubbardsville, N.Y. d: 9/16/55, Highland Park, Mich. BR/TR, 5′6″, 145 lbs. Deb: 6/4/14

| | 1914 Chi-F | 0 | 1 | .000 | 1 | 0 | 0 | 0 | 0 | 0¹ | 0 | 0 | 2 | 0 | 54.0 | 0.00 | — | .000 | .667 | 0 | | 0 | 0 | 0 | 0 | 0.3 |

● TIM SHERRILL Sherrill, Timothy Shawn b: 9/10/65, Harrison, Ark. BL/TL, 5′11″, 170 lbs. Deb: 8/14/90

	1990 StL-N	0	0	—	8	0	0	0	0	4¹	10	1	0	3	27.0	6.23	61	.476	.542	0	—	0	-1	-1	0	0.0
	1991 StL-N	0	0	—	10	0	0	0	0	14¹	20	2	3	4	15.7	8.16	46	.339	.391	0	—	0	-7	-7	0	0.0
	Total 2	0	0	—	18	0	0	0	0	18²	30	2	6	7	18.3	7.71	48	.375	.432	0	—	0	-8	-8	0	0.0

● FRED SHERRY Sherry, Fred Peter (b: Fred Peter Schuerholz) b: 1/13/1889, Honesdale, Pa. d: 7/27/75, Honesdale, Pa. BR/TR, 6′, 170 lbs. Deb: 4/25/11

| | 1911 Was-A | 0 | 4 | .000 | 10 | 3 | 2 | 0 | 0 | 52¹ | 63 | 1 | 19 | 20 | 14.1 | 4.30 | 76 | .310 | .369 | 3 | .158 | -0 | -6 | -6 | 0 | -0.4 |

● LARRY SHERRY Sherry, Lawrence b: 7/25/35, Los Angeles, Cal. BR/TR, 6′2″, 204 lbs. Deb: 4/17/58 FC

	1958 LA-N	0	0	—	5	0	0	0	0	4¹	10	0	7	2	37.4	12.46	33	.476	.621	0	—	0	-4	-4	0	0.0
	1959 *LA-N	7	2	.778	23	9	1	1	3	94¹	75	9	43	72	11.4	2.19	193	.218	.308	7	.219	2	18	21	-1	2.2
	1960 LA-N	14	10	.583	57	3	1	0	7	142¹	125	14	82	114	13.5	3.79	105	.238	.347	6	.162	1	-1	3	1	0.6
	1961 LA-N	4	4	.500	53	1	0	0	15	94²	90	10	39	79	12.6	3.90	111	.252	.333	2	.154	-0	1	5	-2	0.0
	1962 LA-N	7	3	.700	58	0	0	0	11	90	81	8	44	71	13.1	3.20	113	.241	.339	2	.118	-0	7	4	-0	0.5
	1963 LA-N	2	6	.250	36	3	0	0	3	79²	82	8	24	47	12.4	3.73	81	.265	.325	1	.111	-1	-4	-6	-0	-0.6
	1964 Det-A	7	5	.583	38	0	0	0	11	66¹	52	7	37	58	12.5	3.66	100	.216	.327	0	.000	-2	-0	-0	-0	-0.2
	1965 Det-A	3	6	.333	39	0	0	0	5	78¹	71	5	40	46	12.9	3.10	112	.254	.349	3	.300	2	3	3	0	0.5
	1966 Det-A	8	5	.615	55	0	0	0	20	77²	66	8	36	63	12.2	3.82	91	.232	.325	4	.400	2	-3	-3	-1	-0.5
	1967 Det-A	0	1	.000	20	0	0	0	1	28	35	3	7	20	13.8	6.43	51	.289	.333	0	.000	-0	-10	-10	-0	-0.4
	Hou-N	1	2	.333	29	0	0	0	6	40²	53	4	13	32	14.8	4.87	68	.327	.381	0	.000	-1	-7	-7	1	-0.7
	1968 Cal-A	0	0	—	3	0	0	0	0	3	7	2	2	2	27.0	6.00	49	.467	.529	0	—	-1	-1	-0	0	0.0
	Total 11	53	44	.546	416	16	2	1	82	799¹	747	78	374	606	13.0	3.67	101	.249	.339	25	.169	4	0	5	-2	1.8

● BEN SHIELDS Shields, Benjamin Cowan "Big Ben" or "Lefty" b: 6/17/03, Huntersville, N.C. d: 1/24/82, Woodruff, S.C. BR/TL, 6′1.5″, 195 lbs. Deb: 4/17/24

	1924 NY-A	0	0	—	2	0	0	0	0	2	6	0	2	3	36.0	27.00	15	.545	.615	0	—	0	-5	-5	-0	0.0
	1925 NY-A	3	0	1.000	4	2	2	0	0	24	24	2	12	5	14.3	4.88	87	.267	.365	1	.125	-1	-1	-2	-1	-0.3
	1930 Bos-A	0	0	—	3	0	0	0	0	10	16	0	6	1	19.8	9.00	51	.400	.478	0	.000	-1	-5	-5	-0	0.0
	1931 Phi-N	1	0	1.000	4	0	0	0	0	5¹	9	1	7	0	27.0	15.19	28	.391	.533	0	.000	-0	-7	-6	-0	-1.0
	Total 4	4	0	1.000	13	2	2	0	0	41¹	55	3	27	9	18.3	8.27	53	.335	.435	1	.077	-2	-18	-18	-1	-1.3

● CHARLIE SHIELDS Shields, Charles Jessamine b: 12/10/1879, Jackson, Tenn. d: 8/27/53, Memphis, Tenn. BL/TL. Deb: 4/23/02

	1902 Bal-A	4	11	.267	23	15	10	1	1	142¹	201	4	32	28	14.9	4.24	89	.333	.368	8	.167	-1	-10	-7	-4	-1.1
	StL-A	3	0	1.000	4	4	3	0	0	30	37	1	7	6	13.2	3.30	107	.303	.341	6	.462	2	1	1	-1	0.3
	Yr	7	11	.389	27	19	13	1	1	172¹	238	8	39	34	14.5	4.07	92	.327	.361	14	.230	1	-10	-7	-5	-0.8
	1907 StL-N	0	2	.000	3	2	0	0	0	6²	12	0	7	1	28.4	9.45	26	.444	.583	0	.000	-0	-5	-5	0	-1.2
	Total 2	7	13	.350	30	21	13	1	1	179	250	8	46	35	15.1	4.27	86	.332	.374	14	.222	1	-15	-12	-4	-2.0

● STEVE SHIELDS Shields, Stephen Mack b: 11/30/58, Gadsden, Ala. BR/TR, 6′5″, 230 lbs. Deb: 6/1/85

	1985 Atl-N	1	2	.333	23	6	0	0	0	68	86	9	32	29	15.8	5.16	75	.320	.394	2	.111	-1	-12	-10	-1	-0.6
	1986 Atl-N	0	0	—	6	0	0	0	0	12²	13	4	7	6	14.2	7.11	56	.271	.364	0	.000	-0	-5	-4	-0	0.0
	KC-A	0	0	—	3	0	0	0	0	8²	3	1	4	2	7.3	2.08	205	.111	.226	0	—	0	2	2	-0	-0.1
	1987 Sea-A	2	0	1.000	20	0	0	0	3	30	43	7	12	22	16.5	6.60	71	.333	.390	0	—	0	-7	-6	0	-0.8
	1988 NY-A	5	5	.500	39	0	0	0	0	82¹	96	8	30	55	14.0	4.37	90	.298	.362	0	—	0	-4	-4	-0	-0.4
	1989 Min-A	0	1	.000	11	0	0	0	0	17¹	28	3	6	12	17.7	7.79	53	.354	.400	0	—	0	-8	-7	-0	-0.5
	Total 5	8	8	.500	102	6	0	0	3	219	269	32	91	126	14.9	5.26	77	.308	.375	2	.105	-1	-33	-29	-1	-2.4

● VINCE SHIELDS Shields, Vincent William b: 11/18/1900, Fredericton, N.B., Canada d: 10/17/52, Plaster Rock, N.B., Canada BL/TR, 5′11″, 185 lbs. Deb: 9/20/24

| | 1924 StL-N | 1 | 1 | .500 | 2 | 1 | 0 | 0 | 0 | 7 | 10 | 1 | 3 | 0 | 18.0 | 3.00 | 126 | .227 | .320 | 2 | .400 | 0 | 1 | 1 | -1 | 0.2 |

● GARLAND SHIFFLETT Shifflett, Garland Jessie "Duck" b: 3/28/35, Elkton, Va. BR/TR, 5′10.5″, 165 lbs. Deb: 4/22/57

	1957 Was-A	0	0	—	6	1	0	0	0	8	6	0	10	2	18.0	10.13	38	.222	.432	0	—	0	-6	-6	-0	0.0
	1964 Min-A	0	2	.000	10	1	0	0	1	17²	22	1	7	8	15.3	4.58	78	.297	.366	0	.000	-0	-2	-2	-0	-0.2
	Total 2	0	2	.000	16	1	0	0	1	25²	28	1	17	10	16.1	6.31	58	.277	.387	0	.000	-0	-8	-8	-0	-0.2

● STEVE SHIFFLETT Shifflett, Stephen Earl b: 1/5/66, Kansas City, Mo. BR/TR, 6′1″, 205 lbs. Deb: 7/3/92

| | 1992 KC-A | 1 | 4 | .200 | 34 | 0 | 0 | 0 | 1 | 52 | 55 | 2 | 15 | 25 | 12.8 | 2.60 | 156 | .279 | .343 | 0 | — | 0 | 8 | 8 | 0 | 0.8 |

● ZAK SHINALL Shinall, Zakary Sebastien b: 10/14/68, St.Louis, Mo. BR/TR, 6′3″, 215 lbs. Deb: 5/12/93

| | 1993 Sea-A | 0 | 0 | — | 1 | 0 | 0 | 0 | 0 | 2² | 4 | 1 | 2 | 0 | 20.3 | 3.38 | 130 | .333 | .429 | 0 | — | 0 | 0 | -0 | 0 | 0.0 |

● RAZOR SHINES Shines, Anthony Raymond "Ray" b: 7/18/56, Durham, N.C. BB/TR, 6′1″, 210 lbs. Deb: 9/9/83 ◆

| | 1985 Mon-N | 0 | 0 | — | 1 | 0 | 0 | 0 | 0 | 1 | 0 | 0 | 2 | 0 | 9.0 | 0.00 | — | .250 | .250 | 6 | .120 | -0 | 0 | -0 | -0 | 0.0 |

● DAVE SHIPANOFF Shipanoff, David Noel b: 11/13/59, Edmonton, Alberta, Can. BR/TR, 6′2″, 185 lbs. Deb: 8/9/85

| | 1985 Phi-N | 1 | 2 | .333 | 26 | 0 | 0 | 0 | 3 | 36¹ | 33 | 3 | 16 | 26 | 12.4 | 3.22 | 114 | .231 | .313 | 0 | .000 | -0 | 1 | 2 | -0 | 0.1 |

● JOE SHIPLEY Shipley, Joseph Clark "Moses" b: 5/9/35, Morristown, Tenn. BR/TR, 6′4″, 210 lbs. Deb: 7/14/58

	1958 SF-N	0	0	—	1	0	0	0	0	1¹	0	0	3	0	54.0	33.75	11	.429	.667	0	—	0	-4	-4	0	0.0
	1959 SF-N	0	0	—	10	1	0	0	0	18	16	2	17	11	17.0	4.50	85	.239	.400	0	.000	-0	-4	-4	-0	-0.1
	1960 SF-N	0	0	—	15	0	0	0	0	20	20	2	9	9	14.4	5.40	64	.274	.376	0	—	0	-4	-4	1	0.1
	1963 Chi-A	0	1	.000	4	0	0	0	0	4²	9	0	3	3	28.9	5.79	61	.409	.536	0	—	0	-1	-1	-0	-0.3
	Total 4	0	1	.000	29	1	0	0	0	44	48	4	35	23	18.2	5.93	61	.284	.424	0	—	-1	-10	-11	-0	-0.3

● DUKE SHIREY Shirey, Clair Lee b: 6/20/1898, Jersey Shore, Pa. d: 9/1/62, Hagerstown, Md. BR/TR, 6′1″, 175 lbs. Deb: 9/28/20

| | 1920 Was-A | 0 | 1 | .000 | 4 | 0 | 0 | 0 | 0 | 4 | 5 | 0 | 2 | 0 | 18.0 | 6.75 | 55 | .313 | .421 | 0 | .000 | -0 | -1 | -1 | -0 | -0.3 |

● TEX SHIRLEY Shirley, Alvis Newman b: 4/25/18, Birthright, Tex. d: 11/7/93, DeSoto, Tex. BB/TR, 6′1″, 175 lbs. Deb: 9/6/41

	1941 Phi-A	0	1	.000	5	0	0	0	1	7¹	8	1	4	3	17.2	2.45	171	.286	.412	0	.000	-0	1	1	0	0.2
	1942 Phi-A	0	1	.000	15	1	0	0	1	35²	37	0	22	10	15.4	5.30	71	.272	.381	0	.000	-1	-7	-6	-1	-0.4
	1944 *StL-A	5	4	.556	23	11	2	1	0	80¹	59	4	64	35	13.9	4.15	87	.203	.348	4	.143	-2	-6	-5	-1	-0.8
	1945 StL-A	8	12	.400	32	24	10	2	0	183²	191	8	93	77	14.0	3.63	97	.274	.360	20	.286	-2	-5	-2	-1	-0.1
	1946 StL-A	6	12	.333	27	18	7	0	0	139²	148	7	105	45	16.4	4.96	75	.273	.391	10	.196	-0	-23	-19	-1	-2.3
	Total 5	19	30	.388	102	54	19	3	2	446²	443	20	290	168	14.9	4.25	85	.261	.371	34	.214	-5	-39	-31	-3	-3.4

● BOB SHIRLEY Shirley, Robert Charles b: 6/25/54, Cushing, Okla. BR/TL, 5′11″, 185 lbs. Deb: 4/10/77

	1977 SD-N	12	18	.400	39	35	1	0	0	214	215	22	100	146	13.4	3.70	96	.259	.341	9	.122	-2	5	-4	1	-0.6
	1978 SD-N	8	11	.421	50	20	2	0	5	166	164	10	61	102	12.4	3.69	90	.262	.330	5	.125	-0	-2	-7	2	-0.6
	1979 SD-N	8	16	.333	49	25	3	1	0	205	196	15	59	117	11.5	3.38	104	.257	.316	5	.091	-2	8	3	0	0.2
	1980 SD-N	11	12	.478	59	12	3	0	7	137	137	4	54	67	12.9	3.55	97	.276	.344	1	.033	-1	1	-2	2	-0.3
	1981 StL-N	6	4	.600	28	11	1	0	0	79¹	78	6	34	36	12.8	4.08	87	.260	.337	3	.136	-1	-5	-5	-1	-0.8
	1982 Cin-N	8	13	.381	41	20	1	0	0	152²	138	17	73	89	12.6	3.60	103	.248	.338	6	.143	-0	-12	-14	1	-1.3
	1983 NY-A	5	8	.385	25	11	1	0	0	108	122	10	36	53	13.2	5.08	77	.293	.350	0	—	0	-12	-14	-2	-1.3
	1984 NY-A	3	3	.500	41	7	1	0	0	114¹	119	6	38	70	12.4	3.38	112	.274	.333	0	—	0	8	5	0	0.5
	1985 NY-A	5	5	.500	48	8	2	0	0	109	103	5	26	55	10.7	2.64	151	.251	.295	0	—	0	18	16	-1	1.4
	1986 NY-A	0	4	.000	39	6	0	0	3	105¹	108	13	40	64	12.9	5.04	81	.271	.342	0	—	0	-10	-11	-1	-0.3
	1987 NY-A	1	0	1.000	12	1	0	0	0	34	36	4	16	12	13.8	4.50	97	.277	.356	0	—	0	-0	-1	-0	0.0

YEAR	TM/L	W	L	PCT	G	GS	CG	SH	SV	IP	H	HR	BB	SO	RAT	ERA	ERA+	OAV	OOB	BH	AVG	PB	PR	/A	PD	TPI
	KC-A	0	0	—	3	0	0	0	0	7¹	10	5	6	1	19.6	14.73	31	.323	.432	0	—	0	-8	-8	-0	-0.2
	Yr	1	0	1.000	15	1	0	0	0	41¹	46	9	22	13	14.8	6.31	70	.275	.360	0	—	-1	-9	-9	-1	-0.2
Total	11	67	94	.416	434	162	16	2	18	1432	1432	127	543	790	12.5	3.82	96	.264	.334	29	.110	-8	2	-24	5	-1.8

● STEVE SHIRLEY
Shirley, Steven Brian b: 10/12/56, San Francisco, Cal. BL/TL, 6', 185 lbs. Deb: 6/21/82

YEAR	TM/L	W	L	PCT	G	GS	CG	SH	SV	IP	H	HR	BB	SO	RAT	ERA	ERA+	OAV	OOB	BH	AVG	PB	PR	/A	PD	TPI
1982	LA-N	1	1	.500	11	0	0	0	0	12²	15	0	7	8	15.6	4.26	81	.300	.386	1	1.000	0	-1	-1	0	-0.1

● GEORGE SHOCH
Shoch, George Quintus b: 1/6/1859, Philadelphia, Pa. d: 9/30/37, Philadelphia, Pa. BR/TR, 5'6", 158 lbs. Deb: 9/10/1886 ♦

YEAR	TM/L	W	L	PCT	G	GS	CG	SH	SV	IP	H	HR	BB	SO	RAT	ERA	ERA+	OAV	OOB	BH	AVG	PB	PR	/A	PD	TPI
1888	Was-N	0	0	—	1	0	0	0	0	3	2	0	1	0	9.0	0.00	—	.167	.231	58	.183	♦	1	1	-0	0.0

● URBAN SHOCKER
Shocker, Urban James (b: Urbain Jacques Shockcor)
b: 8/22/1890, Cleveland, Ohio d: 9/9/28, Denver, Colo. BR/TR, 5'10", 170 lbs. Deb: 4/24/16

YEAR	TM/L	W	L	PCT	G	GS	CG	SH	SV	IP	H	HR	BB	SO	RAT	ERA	ERA+	OAV	OOB	BH	AVG	PB	PR	/A	PD	TPI
1916	NY-A	4	3	.571	12	9	4	1	0	82¹	67	2	32	43	11.5	2.62	110	.230	.319	4	.190	1	2	2	-0	0.3
1917	NY-A	8	5	.615	26	13	7	0	1	145	124	2	46	68	10.6	2.61	103	.241	.303	8	.178	-1	1	1	2	0.2
1918	StL-A	6	5	.545	14	9	7	0	2	94²	69	0	40	33	10.5	1.81	152	.209	.296	11	.324	4	10	10	1	1.8
1919	StL-A	13	11	.542	30	25	14	5	0	211	193	6	55	86	10.7	2.69	123	.244	.296	8	.138	-0	13	15	-1	1.4
1920	StL-A	20	10	.667	38	28	22	5	5	245²	224	10	70	107	10.9	2.71	145	.248	.305	18	.225	2	30	33	-0	4.0
1921	StL-A	27	12	.692	47	38	30	4	4	326²	345	21	86	132	12.0	3.55	126	.270	.319	27	.260	5	26	34	3	4.3
1922	StL-A	24	17	.585	48	38	29	2	3	348	365	22	57	149	11.0	2.97	139	.272	.304	22	.191	2	41	45	-3	4.8
1923	StL-A	20	12	.625	43	35	24	3	5	277¹	292	12	49	109	11.2	3.41	122	.272	.306	16	.200	2	18	24	-3	2.4
1924	StL-A	16	13	.552	40	33	17	4	1	246¹	270	11	52	88	11.9	4.20	107	.277	.315	16	.239	5	1	9	-2	1.2
1925	NY-A	12	12	.500	41	30	15	2	2	244¹	278	17	58	74	12.5	3.65	117	.294	.336	11	.172	5	20	17	-2	1.7
1926	*NY-A	19	11	.633	41	32	18	0	2	258¹	272	13	71	59	12.0	3.38	114	.269	.318	13	.171	1	18	14	-2	1.3
1927	NY-A	18	6	.750	31	27	13	2	0	200	207	8	41	35	11.2	2.84	136	.268	.306	13	.241	3	29	23	-2	2.5
1928	NY-A	0	0	—	1	0	0	0	0	2	3	0	0	0	13.5	0.00	—	.429	.429	0	—	0	1	1	-0	0.0
Total	13	187	117	.615	412	317	200	28	25	2681²	2709	126	657	983	11.4	3.17	124	.265	.311	167	.209	28	210	226	-9	25.9

● MILT SHOFFNER
Shoffner, Milburn James b: 11/13/05, Sherman, Tex. d: 1/19/78, Madison, Ohio BL/TL, 6'1.5", 184 lbs. Deb: 7/20/29

YEAR	TM/L	W	L	PCT	G	GS	CG	SH	SV	IP	H	HR	BB	SO	RAT	ERA	ERA+	OAV	OOB	BH	AVG	PB	PR	/A	PD	TPI
1929	Cle-A	2	3	.400	11	3	1	0	0	44²	46	4	22	15	14.3	5.04	88	.284	.380	0	.000	-2	-4	-3	0	-0.5
1930	Cle-A	3	4	.429	24	10	1	0	0	84²	129	8	50	17	19.1	7.97	61	.362	.442	7	.212	1	-31	-30	-0	-1.8
1931	Cle-A	2	3	.400	12	4	1	0	0	41	55	4	26	12	18.2	7.24	64	.320	.415	1	.077	-1	-13	-12	-0	-1.3
1937	Bos-N	3	1	.750	6	5	3	1	1	42²	38	1	9	13	10.1	2.53	142	.239	.284	2	.125	1	7	5	1	0.6
1938	Bos-N	8	7	.533	26	15	9	1	1	139²	147	7	36	49	11.9	3.54	97	.270	.317	12	.211	3	4	-2	-0	-0.1
1939	Bos-N	4	6	.400	25	11	7	0	1	132¹	133	4	42	51	12.0	3.13	118	.265	.324	7	.159	-0	12	8	0	0.6
	Cin-N	2	2	.500	10	3	0	0	0	37²	43	3	11	6	13.4	3.35	115	.289	.346	1	.091	-1	2	2	-0	0.1
	Yr	6	8	.429	35	14	7	0	1	170	176	7	53	57	12.2	3.18	117	.270	.327	8	.145	-1	14	10	0	0.7
1940	Cin-N	1	0	1.000	20	0	0	0	0	54¹	56	3	18	17	12.3	5.63	67	.268	.326	2	.125	-1	-11	-11	-1	-0.3
Total	7	25	26	.490	134	51	22	2	3	577	647	34	214	180	13.6	4.59	85	.287	.352	32	.156	-0	-35	-43	-2	-2.7

● ERNIE SHORE
Shore, Ernest Grady b: 3/24/1891, East Bend, N.C. d: 9/24/80, Winston-Salem, N.C. BR/TR, 6'4", 220 lbs. Deb: 6/20/12

YEAR	TM/L	W	L	PCT	G	GS	CG	SH	SV	IP	H	HR	BB	SO	RAT	ERA	ERA+	OAV	OOB	BH	AVG	PB	PR	/A	PD	TPI
1912	NY-N	0	0	—	1	0	0	0	0	1	1	0	1	0	81.0	27.00	13	.667	.692	0	—	0	-3	-3	-0	-0.5
1914	Bos-A	10	5	.667	20	16	10	1	0	139²	103	1	34	51	9.2	2.00	135	.204	.261	5	.102	-3	12	11	2	1.1
1915	*Bos-A	19	8	.704	38	32	17	4	0	247	207	3	66	102	10.1	1.64	169	.228	.283	8	.101	-3	36	31	4	3.5
1916	*Bos-A	16	10	.615	38	28	10	3	1	225²	221	1	49	62	10.9	2.63	105	.259	.302	7	.091	-5	5	3	5	0.4
1917	Bos-A	13	10	.565	29	27	14	1	1	226²	201	1	55	57	10.6	2.22	116	.240	.297	13	.167	-1	11	9	3	1.1
1919	NY-A	5	8	.385	20	13	3	0	0	95	105	4	44	24	14.2	4.17	77	.288	.366	4	.143	-2	-10	-10	-0	-1.4
1920	NY-A	2	2	.500	14	5	2	0	1	44¹	68	1	21	12	16.8	4.87	78	.333	.405	2	.182	0	-5	-5	1	-0.4
Total	7	65	43	.602	160	121	56	9	5	979¹	906	12	270	309	11.1	2.47	113	.247	.304	39	.121	-14	45	36	14	3.8

● RAY SHORE
Shore, Raymond Everett b: 6/9/21, Cincinnati, Ohio d: 8/13/96, St.Louis, Mo. BR/TR, 6'3", 210 lbs. Deb: 9/21/46 C

YEAR	TM/L	W	L	PCT	G	GS	CG	SH	SV	IP	H	HR	BB	SO	RAT	ERA	ERA+	OAV	OOB	BH	AVG	PB	PR	/A	PD	TPI
1946	StL-A	0	0	—	1	0	0	0	0	1	3	0	1	1	36.0	18.00	21	.500	.571			0	-2	-2	0	-0.1
1948	StL-A	1	2	.333	17	4	0	0	0	38	40	2	35	12	18.7	6.39	71	.270	.422	0	.000	-1	-9	-8	0	-0.6
1949	StL-A	0	1	.000	13	0	0	0	0	23¹	27	3	31	13	23.1	10.80	42	.297	.484	0	.000	-1	-17	-16	1	-0.6
Total	3	1	3	.250	31	4	0	0	0	62¹	70	5	67	26	20.6	8.23	55	.286	.450	0	.000	-2	-28	-26	1	-1.2

● BILL SHORES
Shores, William David b: 5/26/04, Abilene, Tex. d: 2/19/84, Purcell, Okla. BR/TR, 6', 185 lbs. Deb: 4/11/28

YEAR	TM/L	W	L	PCT	G	GS	CG	SH	SV	IP	H	HR	BB	SO	RAT	ERA	ERA+	OAV	OOB	BH	AVG	PB	PR	/A	PD	TPI
1928	Phi-A	1	1	.500	3	2	1	0	0	14	13	1	6	5	12.9	3.21	125	.250	.339	0	.000	-1	1	1	-0	0.0
1929	Phi-A	11	6	.647	39	13	5	1	7	152²	150	9	59	49	12.5	3.60	118	.262	.334	5	.125	-2	11	11	-1	0.9
1930	*Phi-A	12	4	.750	31	19	7	1	0	159	169	11	70	48	13.7	4.19	112	.276	.353	11	.193	-2	8	9	0	0.5
1931	Phi-A	0	3	.000	6	2	0	0	0	16	26	3	10	2	20.3	5.06	89	.361	.439	1	.333	0	-1	-1	-0	-0.1
1933	NY-N	2	1	.667	8	3	1	0	0	36²	41	4	14	20	13.5	3.93	82	.291	.355	3	.273	1	-2	-3	1	0.0
1936	Chi-A	0	0	—	9	0	0	0	0	17	26	1	8	5	18.0	9.53	55	.356	.420	1	.000	-0	-8	-8	0	0.0
Total	6	26	15	.634	96	39	14	2	7	395¹	425	28	168	129	13.6	4.17	105	.279	.353	21	.174	-4	8	8	1	1.3

● CHRIS SHORT
Short, Christopher Joseph b: 9/19/37, Milford, Del. d: 8/1/91, Wilmington, Del. BR/TL, 6'4", 205 lbs. Deb: 4/19/59

YEAR	TM/L	W	L	PCT	G	GS	CG	SH	SV	IP	H	HR	BB	SO	RAT	ERA	ERA+	OAV	OOB	BH	AVG	PB	PR	/A	PD	TPI
1959	Phi-N	0	0	—	3	2	0	0	0	14¹	19	3	10	8	18.8	8.16	50	.317	.423	0	.000	-1	-7	-6	-0	-0.1
1960	Phi-N	6	9	.400	42	10	2	0	3	107¹	101	8	52	54	13.1	3.94	99	.249	.339	0	.000	-3	-2	-1	0	-0.4
1961	Phi-N	6	12	.333	39	16	1	0	1	127¹	157	12	71	80	16.3	5.94	69	.304	.391	6	.162	-1	-27	-26	-1	-3.3
1962	Phi-N	11	9	.550	47	12	4	0	3	142	149	13	56	91	13.5	3.42	113	.272	.348	8	.222	1	8	7	0	1.1
1963	Phi-N	9	12	.429	38	27	6	3	0	198	185	12	69	160	11.7	2.95	109	.248	.315	7	.106	-2	7	6	4	0.8
1964	Phi-N★	17	9	.654	42	31	12	4	2	220²	174	10	51	181	9.3	2.20	158	.217	.268	7	.108	-1	33	31	-1	3.5
1965	Phi-N	18	11	.621	47	40	15	5	2	297¹	260	18	89	237	10.7	2.82	123	.235	.295	13	.131	-2	24	21	-3	1.5
1966	Phi-N	20	10	.667	42	39	19	4	0	272	257	28	68	177	11.1	3.54	102	.250	.302	22	.208	1	7	6	-3	0.3
1967	Phi-N★	9	11	.450	29	26	8	2	1	199²	163	9	74	142	10.9	2.39	142	.225	.300	6	.091	-2	22	22	0	2.1
1968	Phi-N	19	13	.594	42	36	9	2	1	269²	236	25	81	202	10.9	2.94	102	.236	.299	12	.152	0	1	-1	0	0.0
1969	Phi-N	0	0	—	2	0	0	0	0	10	11	2	4	5	14.4	7.20	49	.282	.364	0	.000	-4	-4	-0	0	0.0
1970	Phi-N	9	16	.360	36	34	7	2	1	199	211	13	66	133	12.8	4.30	93	.272	.334	3	.049	-5	-6	-7	-2	-1.5
1971	Phi-N	7	14	.333	31	26	5	2	1	173	182	22	63	95	12.9	3.85	92	.274	.339	4	.083	-1	-7	-6	-1	-0.9
1972	Phi-N	1	1	.500	19	0	0	0	1	23	24	3	8	20	12.5	3.91	92	.267	.327		—	-1	-1	-0	-0.1	
1973	Mil-A	3	5	.375	42	7	0	0	0	72	86	5	44	44	16.5	5.13	73	.299	.395	0	—	0	-10	-11	-0	-1.2
Total	15	135	132	.506	501	308	88	24	18	2325	2215	183	806	1629	11.9	3.43	103	.252	.319	88	.126	-17	33	30	-4	2.0

● BILL SHORT
Short, William Ross b: 11/27/37, Kingston, N.Y. BL/TL, 5'9", 170 lbs. Deb: 4/23/60

YEAR	TM/L	W	L	PCT	G	GS	CG	SH	SV	IP	H	HR	BB	SO	RAT	ERA	ERA+	OAV	OOB	BH	AVG	PB	PR	/A	PD	TPI
1960	NY-A	3	5	.375	10	10	2	0	0	47	49	5	30	14	15.3	4.79	75	.282	.390	3	.200	1	-5	-6	-1	-0.9
1962	Bal-A	0	0	—	5	0	0	0	0	4	8	0	6	3	33.8	15.75	23	.381	.536	0	.000	-0	-5	-5	0	0.0
1966	Bal-A	2	3	.400	6	6	1	1	0	37²	34	2	10	27	10.5	2.87	116	.239	.289	1	.091	-1	2	2	1	0.2
	Bos-A	0	0	—	8	0	0	0	0	8¹	10	2	2	2	13.0	4.32	88	.294	.333	0	.000	-1	-1	-1	-0	0.0
	Yr	2	3	.400	14	6	1	1	0	46	44	4	12	29	11.0	3.13	109	.247	.295	1	.083	-2	1	1	1	0.2
1967	Pit-N	0	0	—	6	0	0	0	0	2¹	1	0	1	1	7.7	3.86	87	.143	.250	0	—	-0	-0	-0	-0	0.0
1968	NY-N	0	3	.000	34	0	0	0	0	30¹	24	1	14	24	11.6	4.75	64	.220	.315	0	.000	-0	-6	-6	1	-0.6
1969	Cin-N	0	0	—	4	0	0	0	0	2¹	4	0	1	0	19.3	15.43	24	.400	.455	0	.000	-0	-2	-2	0	0.0
Total	6	5	11	.313	73	16	3	1	0	132	130	8	64	71	13.4	4.70	73	.262	.349	4	.125	-1	-18	-19	2	-1.3

● CLYDE SHOUN
Shoun, Clyde Mitchell "Hardrock" b: 3/20/12, Mountain City, Tenn. d: 3/20/68, Mountain Home, Tenn. BL/TL, 6'1", 188 lbs. Deb: 8/7/35

YEAR	TM/L	W	L	PCT	G	GS	CG	SH	SV	IP	H	HR	BB	SO	RAT	ERA	ERA+	OAV	OOB	BH	AVG	PB	PR	/A	PD	TPI
1935	Chi-N	1	0	1.000	5	0	0	0	0	12²	14	2	5	5	13.5	2.84	138	.298	.365	0	.000	-1	2	2	-0	0.0
1936	Chi-N	0	0	—	4	0	0	0	0	4¹	9	2	4	1	18.7	12.46	32	.429	.429	0	—	0	-4	-4	-0	0.0
1937	Chi-N	7	7	.500	37	9	2	0	0	93	118	9	45	43	15.8	5.61	71	.309	.382	4	.138	-1	-18	-17	-1	-2.4
1938	StL-N	6	6	.500	40	12	3	0	1	117¹	130	8	43	37	13.3	4.14	96	.283	.345	8	.258	-0	-5	-2	-1	-0.3
1939	StL-N	3	1	.750	53	2	0	0	9	103	98	4	42	52	12.5	3.76	109	.248	.323	3	.115	-1	2	4	-0	0.1
1940	StL-N	13	11	.542	54	19	13	1	5	197¹	193	13	46	82	11.0	3.92	102	.255	.299	12	.190	-1	-2	1	-0	0.0
1941	StL-N	3	5	.375	26	6	1	0	0	70	98	7	20	34	15.2	5.66	67	.337	.379	4	.182	0	-16	-15	-1	-1.4
1942	StL-N	0	0	—	2	0	0	0	0	1²	1	0	1	0	5.4	0.00	—	.167	.167	0	—	1	1	1	-0	0.0

YEAR	TM/L	W	L	PCT	G	GS	CG	SH	SV	IP	H	HR	BB	SO	RAT	ERA	ERA+	OAV	OOB	BH	AVG	PB	PR	/A	PD	TPI
	Cin-N	1	3	.250	34	0	0	0	0	72²	55	2	24	32	9.8	2.23	147	.216	.283	4	.308	1	9	9	1	0.6
	Yr	1	3	.250	36	0	0	0	0	74¹	56	2	24	32	9.7	2.18	151	.215	.281	4	.308	1	9	9	1	0.6
1943	Cin-N	14	5	.737	45	5	2	0	7	147	131	6	46	61	10.8	3.06	108	.241	.300	13	.310	4	5	4	1	1.0
1944	Cin-N	13	10	.565	38	21	12	1	2	202²	193	10	42	55	10.6	3.02	116	.248	.290	15	.224	1	13	11	-3	0.9
1946	Cin-N	1	6	.143	27	5	0	0	0	79	87	3	26	20	13.0	4.10	82	.292	.351	2	.095	-1	-6	-7	-2	-0.9
1947	Cin-N	0	0	—	10	0	0	0	0	14¹	16	2	5	7	13.8	5.02	82	.320	.393	0	—	0	-2	-1	0	0.0
	Bos-N	5	3	.625	26	3	1	1	1	73²	73	6	21	23	11.5	4.40	89	.254	.305	3	.158	-1	-3	-4	-1	-0.6
	Yr	5	3	.625	36	3	1	1	1	88	89	8	26	30	11.8	4.50	87	.263	.316	3	.158	-1	-4	-6	-1	-0.6
1948	Bos-N	5	1	.833	36	2	1	0	4	74	77	7	20	25	11.8	4.01	96	.267	.315	4	.190	-1	-0	-1	-2	-0.3
1949	Bos-N	0	0	—	1	0	0	0	0	1	1	0	0	0	9.0	0.00	—	.250	.250	0	—	0	0	0	-0	0.0
	Chi-A	1	1	.500	16	0	0	0	0	23¹	37	1	13	13	19.3	5.79	72	.370	.442	1	.200	0	-4	-4	0	-0.3
Total	14	73	59	.553	454	85	34	3	29	1287	1325	81	404	483	12.2	3.91	96	.267	.324	73	.202	1	-27	-25	-9	-3.6

● **BRIAN SHOUSE**   Shouse, Brian Douglas b: 9/26/68, Effingham, Ill. BL/TL, 5'11", 180 lbs. Deb: 7/31/93 ◆

1993	Pit-N	0	0	—	6	0	0	0	0	4	7	1	2	3	20.3	9.00	45	.368	.429	0	—	0	-2	-2	0	0.0

● **ERIC SHOW**   Show, Eric Vaughn b: 5/19/56, Riverside, Cal. d: 3/16/94, Dulzura, Cal. BR/TR, 6'1", 185 lbs. Deb: 9/2/81

1981	SD-N	1	3	.250	15	0	0	0	3	23	17	2	9	22	10.6	3.13	104	.213	.300	0	—	0	1	0	0	0.1
1982	SD-N	10	6	.625	47	14	2	2	3	150	117	10	48	88	10.2	2.64	130	.217	.287	6	.146	-1	16	13	2	1.5
1983	SD-N	15	12	.556	35	33	4	2	0	200²	201	25	74	120	12.6	4.17	84	.263	.333	11	.172	1	-12	-15	-2	-2.0
1984	*SD-N	15	9	.625	32	32	3	1	0	206²	175	18	88	104	11.6	3.40	105	.234	.317	17	.246	6	4	4	-1	1.0
1985	SD-N	12	11	.522	35	35	5	2	0	233	212	16	87	141	11.7	3.09	114	.243	.316	10	.127	-1	13	11	-3	0.7
1986	SD-N	9	5	.643	24	22	2	0	0	136¹	109	11	69	94	12.0	2.97	123	.225	.326	7	.163	1	11	10	-2	0.9
1987	SD-N	8	16	.333	34	34	5	3	0	206¹	188	26	85	117	12.3	3.84	103	.241	.323	5	.071	-1	6	3	-1	-0.2
1988	SD-N	16	11	.593	32	32	13	1	0	234²	201	22	53	144	10.0	3.26	104	.231	.280	12	.148	-0	5	4	-4	-0.1
1989	SD-N	8	6	.571	16	16	1	0	0	106¹	113	9	39	66	13.0	4.23	83	.274	.340	8	.235	2	-9	-9	-1	-1.0
1990	SD-N	6	8	.429	39	12	0	0	1	106¹	131	16	41	55	14.9	5.76	66	.306	.372	5	.200	1	-23	-23	-1	-2.7
1991	Oak-A	1	2	.333	23	5	0	0	0	51²	62	5	17	20	13.8	5.92	65	.298	.351	0	—	0	-10	-12	-1	-0.6
Total	11	101	89	.532	332	235	35	11	7	1655	1526	171	610	971	11.9	3.66	98	.247	.319	81	.160	3	1	-13	-13	-2.4

● **LEV SHREVE**   Shreve, Leven Lawrence b: 1/14/1869, Louisville, Ky. d: 10/18/42, Detroit, Mich. BR/TR, 5'11", 150 lbs. Deb: 5/2/1887

1887	Bal-a	3	1	.750	5	5	4	1	0	38	33	0	19	13	12.6	3.79	108	.228	.321	4	.167	-1	2	1	0	0.0
	Ind-N	5	9	.357	14	14	14	1	0	122	141	5	65	22	15.5	4.72	88	.278	.365	13	.265	0	-9	-8	-2	-0.8
1888	Ind-N	11	24	.314	35	35	34	1	0	297²	352	23	93	101	13.7	4.63	64	.288	.342	21	.183	-1	-59	-55	0	-5.4
1889	Ind-N	0	3	.000	3	3	1	0	0	15²	25	3	12	5	21.8	13.79	30	.352	.452	0	—	-0	-17	-17	0	-1.9
Total	3	19	37	.339	57	57	53	3	0	473¹	551	31	189	141	14.3	4.89	70	.283	.351	38	.195	-3	-82	-78	-1	-8.1

● **HARRY SHRIVER**   Shriver, Harry Graydon "Pop" b: 9/2/1896, Wadestown, W.Va. d: 1/21/70, Morgantown, W.Va. BR/TR, 6'2", 180 lbs. Deb: 4/14/22

1922	Bro-N	4	6	.400	25	13	4	2	0	108¹	114	5	48	38	13.6	2.99	136	.287	.367	1	.037	-3	13	13	-2	0.5
1923	Bro-N	0	0	—	1	1	0	0	0	4	8	0	0	1	18.0	6.75	58	.444	.444	0	.000	-0	-1	-1	-0	0.0
Total	2	4	6	.400	26	14	4	2	0	112¹	122	5	48	39	13.8	3.12	130	.294	.370	1	.036	-3	12	12	-3	0.5

● **PAUL SHUEY**   Shuey, Paul Kenneth b: 9/16/70, Lima, Ohio BR/TR, 6'3", 215 lbs. Deb: 5/8/94

1994	Cle-A	0	1	.000	14	0	0	0	5	11²	14	1	12	16	20.1	8.49	56	.280	.419	0	—	0	-5	-5	-0	-0.7
1995	Cle-A	2	0	1.000	7	0	0	0	0	6¹	5	0	5	5	14.2	4.26	110	.238	.385	0	—	0	0	0	-0	0.0
1996	*Cle-A	5	2	.714	42	0	0	0	4	53²	45	6	26	44	11.9	2.85	172	.231	.321	0	—	0	13	12	-0	1.5
Total	3	5	5	.500	63	0	0	0	9	71²	64	7	43	65	13.4	3.89	124	.241	.346	0	—	0	8	6	-0	0.8

● **TOOTS SHULTZ**   Shultz, Wallace Luther b: 10/10/1888, Homestead, Pa. d: 1/30/59, McKeesport, Pa. BR/TR, 5'10", 175 lbs. Deb: 5/5/11

1911	Phi-N	0	3	.000	5	3	2	0	0	25	30	5	15	19	17.6	9.36	37	.300	.412	2	.250	0	-17	-16	0	-1.5
1912	Phi-N	1	4	.200	22	4	1	0	1	59	75	2	35	20	17.2	4.58	79	.333	.430	5	.238	0	-8	-6	0	-0.4
Total	2	1	7	.125	27	7	3	0	1	84	105	7	50	29	17.4	6.00	60	.323	.424	7	.241	0	-24	-23	1	-1.9

● **HARRY SHUMAN**   Shuman, Harry b: 3/5/15, Philadelphia, Pa. d: 10/25/96, Philadelphia, Pa. BR/TR, 6'2", 195 lbs. Deb: 9/14/42

1942	Pit-N	0	0	—	1	0	0	0	0	2	0	0	1	1	4.5	0.00	—	.000	.167	0	—	0	1	1	-0	0.0
1943	Pit-N	0	0	—	11	0	0	0	0	22	30	0	8	5	16.4	5.32	65	.337	.404	0	.000	-0	-5	-4	0	0.0
1944	Phi-N	0	0	—	18	0	0	0	0	26²	26	1	11	4	12.5	4.05	89	.245	.316	0	.000	-0	-1	-1	0	0.0
Total	3	0	0	—	30	0	0	0	0	50²	56	1	20	10	13.9	4.44	80	.280	.351	0	—	0	-5	-5	0	0.0

● **PAUL SIEBERT**   Siebert, Paul Edward b: 6/5/53, Minneapolis, Minn. BL/TL, 6'2", 205 lbs. Deb: 9/7/74 F

1974	Hou-N	1	1	.500	5	5	1	0	2	25¹	21	3	11	10	11.4	3.55	97	.236	.320			-1	0	-0	1	0.1
1975	Hou-N	0	2	.000	7	5	0	0	0	18¹	20	1	6	13	13.3	2.95	114	.294	.360	0	.000	-0	1	1	-0	0.1
1976	Hou-N	0	2	.000	19	0	0	0	0	25²	29	0	18	10	16.8	3.16	101	.296	.410	0	—	0	0	-1	-0	-0.1
1977	SD-N	0	0	—	4	0	0	0	0	3²	3	1	4	1	17.2	2.45	144	.214	.389	0	—	-0	1	1	-0	0.1
	NY-N	2	1	.667	25	0	0	0	0	28	27	0	13	20	13.2	3.86	97	.257	.345	0	.000	-0	0	-0	-0	-0.1
	Yr	2	1	.667	29	0	0	0	0	31²	30	1	17	21	13.2	3.69	101	.250	.348	0	.000	-0	1	0	-0	-0.1
1978	NY-N	0	2	.000	27	0	0	0	0	28	30	2	21	12	16.7	5.14	68	.283	.406	0	.000	-0	-5	-5	0	-0.4
Total	5	3	8	.273	87	7	1	1	3	129	130	6	73	59	14.4	3.77	92	.271	.372	0	.000	-2	-2	-4	0	-0.5

● **SONNY SIEBERT**   Siebert, Wilfred Charles b: 1/14/37, St.Marys, Mo. BR/TR, 6'3", 198 lbs. Deb: 4/26/64 C

1964	Cle-A	7	9	.438	41	14	3	1	3	156	142	15	57	144	11.6	3.23	111	.243	.313	13	.265	5	7	6	-2	1.1
1965	Cle-A	16	8	.667	39	27	4	1	1	188²	139	14	46	191	9.1	2.43	143	.206	**.262**	7	.106	-2	22	22	1	2.7
1966	Cle-A★	16	8	**.667**	34	32	11	1	1	241	193	26	62	163	9.7	2.80	123	.221	.278	11	.129	-2	17	17	2	1.7
1967	Cle-A	10	12	.455	34	26	7	1	4	185	136	17	54	136	9.5	2.38	137	.202	.268	7	.135	1	18	18	-2	2.3
1968	Cle-A	12	10	.545	31	30	8	4	0	206	145	12	88	146	10.5	2.97	100	.198	.290	11	.157	1	0	1	0	0.2
1969	Cle-A	0	1	.000	2	2	0	0	0	14	10	1	4	8	11.6	3.21	117	.196	.305	1	.250	1	-1	-0	0	0.1
	Bos-A	14	10	.583	43	22	4	2	0	163¹	151	21	68	127	12.3	3.80	100	.245	.324	8	.151	1	-3	0	0	0.3
	Yr	14	11	.560	45	24	2	0	5	177¹	161	22	76	133	12.2	3.76	101	.241	.322	9	.158	1	-3	1	2	0.4
1970	Bos-A	15	8	.652	33	33	7	2	0	222²	207	29	60	142	11.0	3.44	115	.248	.303	10	.130	-2	7	13	0	1.1
1971	Bos-A☆	16	10	.615	32	32	12	4	0	235¹	220	20	60	131	10.8	2.91	127	.245	.294	21	.266	10	15	21	1	3.5
1972	Bos-A	12	12	.500	32	30	7	3	0	196¹	204	17	59	123	12.4	3.80	84	.264	.322	17	.236	6	-16	-13	1	-0.8
1973	Bos-A	0	1	.000	2	1	0	0	0	2¹	5	1	1	5	23.1	7.71	52	.417	.462	0	—	0	-1	-1	0	-0.3
	Tex-A	7	11	.389	25	20	1	1	2	119²	120	11	37	76	12.0	3.99	93	.288	.317	0	—	-2	-2	-4	2	-0.3
	Yr	7	12	.368	27	21	1	1	2	122	125	12	38	81	12.2	4.06	92	.262	.320	0	—	-2	-3	-4	2	-0.6
1974	StL-N	8	8	.500	28	20	5	0	0	133²	150	4	51	68	13.7	3.84	93	.288	.355	5	.114	-2	-3	-4	-1	-0.7
1975	SD-N	3	2	.600	6	6	0	0	0	26²	37	3	10	10	16.2	4.39	79	.330	.390	3	.375	2	-2	-3	0	-0.3
	Oak-A	4	4	.500	17	13	0	0	0	61	66	4	31	44	13.4	3.69	98	.252	.338	0	—	-0	-1	-2	0	-0.3
Total	12	140	114	.551	399	307	67	21	16	2152	1919	197	692	1512	11.1	3.21	110	.238	.303	114	.173	18	57	73	5	10.4

● **DWIGHT SIEBLER**   Siebler, Dwight Leroy b: 8/5/37, Columbus, Neb. BR/TR, 6'2", 184 lbs. Deb: 8/26/63

1963	Min-A	2	1	.667	7	5	2	0	0	38²	25	6	12	12	8.8	2.79	130	.182	.253	2	.133	-0	4	4	-1	0.1
1964	Min-A	0	0	—	9	0	0	0	0	11	11	1	6	10	13.1	4.91	78	.256	.356	0	—	-0	-2	-2	-0	0.0
1965	Min-A	0	0	—	7	1	0	0	0	15	11	2	11	13	13.2	4.20	85	.193	.324	0	.000	-0	-1	-1	-0	-0.1
1966	Min-A	2	2	.500	23	2	0	0	0	49²	47	6	14	24	11.2	3.44	104	.253	.308	0	.000	-1	-1	-1	-0	-0.1
1967	Min-A	0	0	—	2	0	0	0	0	3	4	0	1	12	15.0	3.00	115	.364	.417	0	—	-0	-1	-1	-0	0.0
Total	5	4	3	.571	48	8	2	0	0	117¹	97	15	44	71	11.0	3.45	104	.226	.300	2	.074	-1	-1	-2	-2	0.0

● **CANDY SIERRA**   Sierra, Ulises (Pizarro) b: 3/27/67, Rio Piedras, P.R. BR/TR, 6'2", 190 lbs. Deb: 4/6/88

1988	SD-N	0	1	.000	15	0	0	0	0	23²	36	2	11	20	17.9	5.70	60	.379	.443	0	.000	-0	-6	-6	0	-0.3
	Cin-N	0	0	—	1	0	0	0	0	4	5	0	1	4	13.5	4.50	80	.294	.333	0	.000	-0	-0	-0	-0	0.0
	Yr	0	1	.000	16	0	0	0	0	27²	41	2	12	24	17.2	5.53	62	.363	.424	0	—	-0	-6	-6	0	-0.3

YEAR	TM/L	W	L	PCT	G	GS	CG	SH	SV	IP	H	HR	BB	SO	RAT	ERA	ERA+	OAV	OOB	BH	AVG	PB	PR	/A	PD	TPI
● ED SIEVER	Siever, Edward Tilden b: 4/2/1877, Goddard, Kan. d: 2/4/20, Detroit, Mich. BL/TL, 5'11.5", 190 lbs. Deb: 4/26/01																								
1901	Det-A	18	15	.545	38	33	30	2	0	288²	334	9	65	85	12.7	3.24	119	.286	.328	18	.168	-5	14	19	-1	1.3
1902	Det-A	8	11	.421	25	23	17	4	1	188¹	166	0	32	36	9.6	1.91	191	.237	.272	10	.152	-4	35	36	-4	2.6
1903	StL-A	13	14	.481	31	27	24	1	0	254	245	6	39	90	10.2	2.48	117	.253	.285	13	.140	-4	14	12	2	1.0
1904	StL-A	10	15	.400	29	24	19	2	0	217	235	3	65	77	12.6	2.65	93	.277	.330	11	.155	-1	-1	-4	1	-0.6
1906	Det-A	14	11	.560	30	25	20	1	0	222²	240	5	45	71	11.9	2.71	102	.278	.321	12	.156	-3	-0	1	-2	-0.4
1907	*Det-A	18	11	.621	39	33	22	3	1	274²	256	1	52	88	10.5	2.16	120	.249	.293	15	.160	-3	12	14	-3	0.7
1908	Det-A	2	6	.250	11	9	4	1	0	61²	74	0	13	23	12.7	3.50	69	.302	.337	3	.167	-1	-8	-7	-1	-1.1
Total	7	83	83	.500	203	174	136	14	2	1507	1550	24	311	470	11.3	2.60	116	.266	.308	82	.156	-21	64	70	-8	3.5
● WALTER SIGNER	Signer, Walter Donald Aloysius b: 10/12/10, New York, N.Y. d: 7/23/74, Greenwich, Conn. BR/TR, 6', 185 lbs. Deb: 9/18/43																								
1943	Chi-N	2	1	.667	4	2	1	0	0	25	24	3	4	5	10.1	2.88	116	.245	.275	2	.250	-1	1	1	-0	0.2
1945	Chi-N	0	0	—	6	0	0	0	1	8	11	1	5	0	18.0	3.38	108	.256	.333	0	.000	-0	0	0	-0	0.0
Total	2	2	1	.667	10	2	1	0	1	33	35	4	9	5	12.0	3.00	114	.248	.293	2	.222	0	2	2	-0	0.2
● SETH SIGSBY	Sigsby, Seth De Witt (b: Seth De Witt) b: 4/30/1874, Cobleskill, N.Y. d: 9/15/53, Schenectady, N.Y 6', 175 lbs. Deb: 6/27/1893																								
1893	NY-N	0	0	—	1	0	0	0	0	3	4	0	2	1	18.0	9.00	52	.100	.400	0	.000	-0	-1	-1	-0	0.0
● JOSE SILVA	Silva, Jose Leonel b: 12/19/73, Tijuana, Mex. BR/TR, 6'5", 210 lbs. Deb: 9/10/96																								
1996	Tor-A	0	0	—	2	0	0	0	0	2	5	1	0	0	22.5	13.50	37	.455	.455	0	—	0	-2	-2	0	0.0
● AL SIMA	Sima, Albert b: 10/7/21, Mahwah, N.J. d: 8/17/93, Suffern, N.Y. BR/TL, 6', 187 lbs. Deb: 6/28/50																								
1950	Was-A	4	5	.444	17	9	1	0	0	77	89	4	26	23	13.6	4.79	94	.291	.348	3	.115	-2	-2	-3	-1	-0.6
1951	Was-A	3	7	.300	18	8	1	0	0	77	79	5	41	26	14.0	4.79	85	.261	.349	3	.176	1	-6	-6	-1	-0.6
1953	Was-A	3	4	.400	31	5	1	0	1	68¹	63	7	31	25	12.8	3.42	114	.249	.338	2	.118	-1	4	4	1	0.2
1954	Chi-A	0	1	.000	5	1	0	0	1	7	11	1	2	1	16.7	5.14	73	.393	.433	0	.000	-0	-1	-1	-0	-0.2
	Phi-N	2	5	.286	29	7	1	0	2	79¹	101	9	32	36	15.1	5.22	75	.309	.370	1	.050	-2	-13	-12	-1	-1.3
	Yr	2	6	.250	34	8	1	0	3	86¹	112	10	34	37	15.2	5.21	75	.314	.373	1	.045	-2	-14	-13	-1	-1.5
Total	4	11	21	.344	100	30	4	0	4	308²	343	31	132	111	14.0	4.61	89	.282	.354	9	.110	-5	-18	-17	-2	-2.5
● BILL SIMAS	Simas, William Anthony b: 11/28/71, Hanford, Cal. BL/TR, 6'3", 220 lbs. Deb: 8/15/95																								
1995	Chi-A	1	1	.500	14	0	0	0	0	14	15	1	10	16	16.7	2.57	173	.273	.394	0	—	0	3	3	-0	0.3
1996	Chi-A	2	8	.200	64	0	0	0	2	72²	75	5	39	65	14.5	4.58	103	.265	.360	0	—	0	3	1	-0	0.2
Total	2	3	9	.250	78	0	0	0	2	86²	90	6	49	81	14.8	4.26	109	.266	.366	0	—	0	7	4	-1	0.5
● CURT SIMMONS	Simmons, Curtis Thomas b: 5/19/29, Egypt, Pa. BL/TL, 6', 187 lbs. Deb: 9/28/47																								
1947	Phi-N	1	0	1.000	1	1	1	0	0	9	5	0	6	9	11.0	1.00	401	.161	.297	1	.500	0	3	3	-0	0.4
1948	Phi-N	7	13	.350	31	22	7	0	0	170	169	8	108	86	14.8	4.87	81	.266	.374	7	.137	-1	-17	-17	1	-1.8
1949	Phi-N	4	10	.286	38	14	2	0	1	131¹	133	7	55	83	13.0	4.59	86	.275	.350	7	.171	-1	-8	-9	-0	-1.0
1950	Phi-N	17	8	.680	31	27	11	2	1	214²	178	19	88	146	11.2	3.40	119	.223	.302	12	.156	-1	18	16	0	1.5
1952	Phi-N★	14	8	.636	28	28	15	6	0	201¹	170	11	70	141	10.8	2.82	130	.227	.294	11	.164	2	20	19	-3	1.9
1953	Phi-N★	16	13	.552	32	30	19	4	0	238	211	17	82	138	11.2	3.21	131	.236	.302	13	.140	-3	28	26	-3	2.4
1954	Phi-N	14	15	.483	34	33	21	3	1	253	226	14	98	125	11.7	2.81	144	.239	.314	16	.176	-3	35	35	-3	3.3
1955	Phi-N	8	8	.500	25	22	3	0	0	130	148	15	50	58	13.9	4.92	81	.290	.356	8	.174	-1	-13	-14	-1	-1.6
1956	Phi-N	15	10	.600	33	27	14	0	0	198	186	17	65	88	11.5	3.36	111	.248	.311	17	.236	3	9	8	-1	1.3
1957	Phi-N★	12	11	.522	32	29	9	2	0	212	214	14	50	92	11.3	3.44	111	.264	.309	17	.239	4	10	9	-3	1.0
1958	Phi-N	7	14	.333	29	27	7	1	1	168¹	196	11	40	78	12.8	4.38	90	.293	.336	12	.203	0	-8	-8	-1	-1.0
1959	Phi-N	0	0	—	7	0	0	0	0	10	16	2	4	9	15.3	4.50	91	.400	.415	0	—	0	-1	-0	0	0.0
1960	Phi-N	0	0	—	4	2	0	0	0	4	13	3	6	4	42.8	18.00	22	.542	.633	0	—	0	-6	-6	1	0.0
	StL-N	7	4	.636	23	17	3	1	0	152	149	11	31	63	10.7	2.66	154	.257	.295	10	.213	1	19	24	0	1.8
	Yr	7	4	.636	27	19	3	1	0	156	162	14	37	67	11.5	3.06	134	.269	.311	10	.213	1	12	18	1	1.8
1961	StL-N	9	10	.474	30	29	6	2	0	195²	203	14	64	99	12.5	3.13	141	.269	.329	20	.303	5	20	28	-0	3.0
1962	StL-N	10	10	.500	31	22	9	4	0	154	167	18	32	74	11.8	3.51	122	.280	.320	8	.160	0	7	13	-1	1.5
1963	StL-N	15	9	.625	32	32	11	6	0	232²	209	13	48	127	10.2	2.48	143	.239	.283	13	.160	0	21	28	-4	2.5
1964	*StL-N	18	9	.667	34	34	12	3	0	244	233	24	49	104	10.6	3.43	111	.249	.290	10	.106	-3	3	10	-1	0.6
1965	StL-N	9	15	.375	34	32	5	0	0	203	229	19	54	96	12.7	4.08	94	.283	.331	3	.047	-5	-12	-5	-2	-1.3
1966	StL-N	1	1	.500	10	5	1	0	0	33¹	35	3	14	14	13.2	4.59	78	.269	.340	1	.125	-0	-4	-4	-1	-0.2
	Chi-N	4	7	.364	19	10	3	1	0	77¹	79	7	21	24	11.8	4.07	90	.268	.319	2	.111	-0	-4	-3	-2	-0.4
	Yr	5	8	.385	29	15	4	1	0	110²	114	10	35	38	12.2	4.23	86	.268	.325	3	.115	-0	-8	-7	1	-0.6
1967	Chi-N	3	7	.300	17	14	3	0	0	82	100	10	23	36	13.7	4.94	72	.300	.349	4	.143	-1	-14	-13	-0	-1.5
	Cal-A	2	1	.667	14	4	1	1	1	34²	44	4	9	13	14.3	2.60	121	.321	.372	2	.222	1	2	2	-1	0.2
Total	20	193	183	.513	569	461	163	36	5	3348¹	3313	255	1063	1697	11.9	3.54	111	.259	.319	194	.171	1	109	142	-21	12.6
● PAT SIMMONS	Simmons, Patrick Clement (b: Patrick Clement Simoni) b: 11/29/08, Watervliet, N.Y. d: 7/3/68, Albany, N.Y. BR/TR, 5'11", 172 lbs. Deb: 4/18/28																								
1928	Bos-A	0	2	.000	31	3	0	0	0	69	69	4	38	16	14.1	4.04	102	.271	.367	2	.133	-1	0	1	-0	-0.1
1929	Bos-A	0	0	—	2	0	0	0	1	7	6	0	3	2	11.6	0.00	—	.231	.310	0	.000	-0	3	3	0	0.1
Total	2	0	2	.000	33	3	0	0	1	76	75	4	41	18	13.9	3.67	112	.267	.362	2	.125	-1	3	4	-0	0.0
● DOUG SIMONS	Simons, Douglas Eugene b: 9/15/66, Bakersfield, Cal. BL/TL, 6', 170 lbs. Deb: 4/9/91																								
1991	NY-N	2	3	.400	42	1	0	0	0	60²	55	9	19	38	11.3	5.19	70	.246	.310	0	.000	0	-10	-10	2	-0.7
1992	Mon-N	0	0	—	7	0	0	0	0	5¹	15	3	2	6	30.4	23.63	15	.500	.545	0	—	0	-12	-12	-0	0.0
Total	2	2	3	.400	49	1	0	0	0	66	70	8	21	44	12.8	6.68	54	.276	.338	0	.000	0	-22	-22	2	-0.7
● JOE SIMPSON	Simpson, Joe Allen b: 12/31/51, Purcell, Okla. BL/TL, 6'3", 175 lbs. Deb: 9/2/75 ♦																								
1983	KC-A	0	0	—	2	0	0	0	0	3	4	0	2	1	18.0	3.00	136	.308	.400	20	.168	-0	1	1	0	0.0
● STEVE SIMPSON	Simpson, Steven Edward b: 8/30/48, St.Joseph, Mo. d: 11/2/89, Omaha, Neb. BR/TR, 6'3", 200 lbs. Deb: 9/10/72																								
1972	SD-N	0	2	.000	9	0	0	0	2	11¹	10	0	8	9	14.3	4.76	69	.238	.360	0	—	0	-2	-2	-0	-0.4
● DUKE SIMPSON	Simpson, Thomas Leo b: 9/15/27, Columbus, Ohio BR/TR, 6'1.5", 190 lbs. Deb: 5/6/53																								
1953	Chi-N	1	2	.333	30	1	0	0	0	45	60	8	25	21	17.2	8.00	56	.314	.396	2	.250	0	-19	-18	-1	-1.0
● WAYNE SIMPSON	Simpson, Wayne Kirby b: 12/2/48, Los Angeles, Cal. BR/TR, 6'3", 220 lbs. Deb: 4/9/70																								
1970	Cin-N☆	14	3	.824	26	26	10	2	0	176	125	15	81	119	11.0	3.02	134	.198	.298	6	.094	-4	20	20	2	1.6
1971	Cin-N	4	7	.364	22	21	1	0	0	117¹	106	9	77	61	14.3	4.76	71	.244	.361	1	.031	-2	-17	-18	2	-1.6
1972	Cin-N	8	5	.615	24	22	1	0	0	130¹	124	17	49	70	12.1	4.14	78	.247	.316	3	.063	-3	-10	-13	-3	-1.8
1973	KC-A	3	4	.429	16	10	1	0	0	59²	66	7	35	29	15.4	5.73	72	.284	.381	0	—	0	-13	-11	-2	-1.1
1975	Phi-N	0	1	.000	7	2	0	0	0	30²	31	1	11	19	12.6	3.23	116	.263	.331	2	.222	0	1	2	0	0.1
1977	Cal-A	6	12	.333	27	23	0	0	0	122	154	14	62	55	16.5	5.83	67	.308	.392	0	—	0	-24	-26	-1	-3.3
Total	6	36	31	.537	122	107	13	2	0	636	606	57	315	353	13.4	4.37	85	.251	.343	12	.078	-8	-42	-47	2	-6.1
● PETE SIMS	Sims, Clarence b: 5/24/1891, Crown City, Ohio d: 12/2/68, Dallas, Tex. BR/TR, 5'11.5", 165 lbs. Deb: 9/16/15																								
1915	StL-A	1	0	1.000	3	2	0	0	0	8¹	6	0	6	4	13.0	4.32	66	.214	.353	1	1.000	1	-1	-1	-0	-0.1
● BERT SINCOCK	Sincock, Herbert Sylvester b: 9/8/1887, Barkerville, B.C., Canada d: 8/1/46, Houghton, Mich. BL/TL, 5'10.5", 165 lbs. Deb: 6/25/08																								
1908	Cin-N	0	0	—	1	0	0	0	0	4²	3	0	4	1	5.8	3.86	60	.176	.176	0	.000	-0	-1	-1	-0	0.0
● BILL SINGER	Singer, William Robert "The Singer Throwing Machine" b: 4/24/44, Los Angeles, Cal. BR/TR, 6'4", 200 lbs. Deb: 9/24/64																								
1964	LA-N	0	1	.000	2	2	0	0	0	14	11	0	12	3	14.8	3.21	101	.216	.365	1	.167	0	1	0	-0	0.0
1965	LA-N	0	0	—	2	0	0	0	0	1	2	0	4	1	36.0	0.00	—	.400	.571	0	—	0	0	0	-0	0.0
1966	LA-N	0	0	—	3	0	0	0	0	4	4	0	2	4	13.5	0.00	—	.286	.375	0	—	0	2	1	0	0.0

YEAR	TM/L	W	L	PCT	G	GS	CG	SH	SV	IP	H	HR	BB	SO	RAT	ERA	ERA+	OAV	OOB	BH	AVG	PB	PR	/A	PD	TPI
1967	LA-N	12	8	.600	32	29	7	3	0	204^1	185	5	61	169	11.2	2.64	117	.239	.301	6	.090	-3	17	10	1	0.7
1968	LA-N	13	17	.433	37	36	12	6	0	256^1	227	14	78	227	10.9	2.88	96	.237	.298	12	.148	3	3	-3	0	0.4
1969	LA-N★	20	12	.625	41	40	16	2	1	315^2	244	22	74	247	9.4	2.34	142	.210	.263	11	.102	-4	44	35	-2	2.8
1970	LA-N	8	5	.615	16	16	5	3	0	106^1	79	10	32	93	9.6	3.13	122	.203	.267	5	.132	-0	11	8	1	0.8
1971	LA-N	10	17	.370	31	31	8	1	0	203^1	195	19	71	144	12.0	4.16	78	.252	.318	6	.103	-0	-16	-21	-1	-2.7
1972	LA-N	6	16	.273	26	25	4	3	0	169^1	148	8	60	101	11.3	3.67	91	.237	.309	4	.073	-3	-4	-6	1	-1.0
1973	Cal-A★	20	14	.588	40	40	19	2	0	315^2	280	15	130	241	11.9	3.22	110	.235	.314	0	—	0	21	11	-2	1.0
1974	Cal-A	7	4	.636	14	14	8	0	0	108^2	102	3	43	77	12.1	2.98	115	.250	.323	0	—	0	8	5	0	0.6
1975	Cal-A	7	15	.318	29	27	8	0	1	179	171	18	81	78	13.0	4.98	71	.257	.343	0	—	0	-24	-28	-1	-3.1
1976	Tex-A	4	1	.800	10	10	2	1	0	64^2	56	4	27	34	12.2	3.48	103	.239	.331	0	—	0	1	-1	0	-1.0
	Min-A	9	9	.500	26	26	5	3	0	172	177	9	69	63	13.2	3.77	95	.274	.349	0	—	0	-5	-4	-2	-0.5
	Yr	13	10	.565	36	36	7	4	0	236^2	233	13	96	97	12.7	3.69	97	.262	.338	0	—	0	-4	-3	-2	-0.5
1977	Tor-A	2	8	.200	13	12	0	0	0	59^2	71	5	39	33	16.9	6.79	62	.296	.399	0	—	0	-18	-17	-0	-2.3
Total 14		118	127	.482	322	308	94	24	2	2174	1952	132	781	1515	11.6	3.39	99	.240	.311	45	.109	-7	39	-8	-7	-3.7

● **ELMER SINGLETON** Singleton, Bert Elmer "Smoky" b: 6/26/18, Ogden, Utah d: 1/5/96, Ogden, Utah BR/TR, 6'2", 174 lbs. Deb: 8/20/45

YEAR	TM/L	W	L	PCT	G	GS	CG	SH	SV	IP	H	HR	BB	SO	RAT	ERA	ERA+	OAV	OOB	BH	AVG	PB	PR	/A	PD	TPI
1945	Bos-N	1	4	.200	7	5	1	0	0	37^1	35	1	14	14	12.1	4.82	79	.248	.321	0	.000	-1	-4	-4	-0	-0.6
1946	Bos-N	0	1	.000	15	2	0	0	1	33^2	27	3	21	17	13.1	3.74	92	.221	.340	0	.000	-1	-1	-1	-0	-0.1
1947	Pit-N	2	2	.500	36	3	0	0	1	67	70	9	39	24	14.9	6.31	67	.267	.366	4	.308	1	-17	-16	0	-0.7
1948	Pit-N	4	6	.400	38	5	1	0	0	92^1	90	11	40	53	12.8	4.97	82	.253	.330	2	.087	-2	-10	-9	1	-1.0
1950	Was-A	1	2	.333	21	1	0	0	0	36^1	39	4	17	19	13.9	5.20	86	.291	.371	3	.429	1	-3	-3	1	0.0
1957	Chi-N	0	1	.000	5	2	0	0	0	13^1	20	3	1	6	14.9	6.75	57	.333	.355	0	.000	-0	-4	-4	-0	-0.3
1958	Chi-N	1	0	1.000	2	0	0	0	0	4^2	1	0	2	2	3.9	0.00	—	.071	.133	0	.000	-0	2	2	0	0.4
1959	Chi-N	2	1	.667	21	1	0	0	0	43	40	2	12	25	10.9	2.72	145	.252	.304	0	.000	-1	6	6	1	0.4
Total 8		11	17	.393	145	19	2	0	4	327^2	322	33	146	160	13.0	4.83	83	.258	.338	9	.132	-3	-32	-29	3	-1.9

● **JOHN SINGLETON** Singleton, John Edward "Sheriff" b: 11/27/1896, Gallipolis, Ohio d: 10/23/37, Dayton, Ohio BR/TR, 5'11", 171 lbs. Deb: 6/8/22

YEAR	TM/L	W	L	PCT	G	GS	CG	SH	SV	IP	H	HR	BB	SO	RAT	ERA	ERA+	OAV	OOB	BH	AVG	PB	PR	/A	PD	TPI
1922	Phi-N	1	10	.091	22	9	3	1	0	93	127	6	38	27	16.5	5.90	79	.346	.415	5	.139	-2	-19	-13	-1	-1.5

● **MIKE SIROTKA** Sirotka, Michael Robert b: 5/13/71, Houston, Tex. BL/TL, 6'1", 190 lbs. Deb: 7/19/95

YEAR	TM/L	W	L	PCT	G	GS	CG	SH	SV	IP	H	HR	BB	SO	RAT	ERA	ERA+	OAV	OOB	BH	AVG	PB	PR	/A	PD	TPI
1995	Chi-A	1	2	.333	6	6	0	0	0	34^1	39	2	17	19	14.7	4.19	106	.298	.378	0	—	0	2	1	-0	0.1
1996	Chi-A	1	2	.333	15	4	0	0	0	26^1	34	3	12	11	15.7	7.18	65	.315	.383	0	—	0	-6	-7	-1	-0.7
Total 2		2	4	.333	21	10	0	0	0	60^2	73	5	29	30	15.1	5.49	83	.305	.381	0	—	0	-4	-6	-1	-0.6

● **DOUG SISK** Sisk, Douglas Randall b: 9/26/57, Renton, Wash. BR/TR, 6'2", 210 lbs. Deb: 9/6/82

YEAR	TM/L	W	L	PCT	G	GS	CG	SH	SV	IP	H	HR	BB	SO	RAT	ERA	ERA+	OAV	OOB	BH	AVG	PB	PR	/A	PD	TPI
1982	NY-N	0	1	.000	8	0	0	0	1	8^2	5	1	4	4	10.4	1.04	349	.172	.294	0	—	0	2	2	0	0.3
1983	NY-N	5	4	.556	67	0	0	0	11	104^1	88	1	59	33	13.0	2.24	162	.235	.346	3	.500	1	16	16	-1	1.7
1984	NY-N	1	3	.250	50	0	0	0	15	77^2	57	1	54	32	13.2	2.09	169	.215	.354	1	.091	-0	13	12	0	1.1
1985	NY-N	4	5	.444	42	0	0	0	2	73	86	3	40	26	15.8	5.30	86	.291	.379	0	.000	-1	-14	-15	1	-1.9
1986	*NY-N	4	2	.667	41	0	0	0	1	70^2	77	0	31	31	14.4	3.06	116	.282	.366	0	.000	-0	5	4	-1	0.2
1987	NY-N	3	1	.750	55	0	0	0	3	78	83	5	22	37	12.5	3.46	109	.270	.325	0	.000	-1	5	3	1	0.2
1988	Bal-A	3	3	.500	52	0	0	0	0	94^1	109	3	45	26	14.9	3.72	105	.306	.387	0	—	0	3	2	1	0.2
1990	Atl-N	0	0	—	3	0	0	0	0	2^1	1	0	4	1	19.3	3.86	105	.143	.455	0	—	0	0	0	0	0.0
1991	Atl-N	2	1	.667	14	0	0	0	0	14^1	21	1	8	5	18.2	5.02	77	.333	.408	0	—	0	-2	-2	-0	-0.3
Total 9		22	20	.524	332	0	0	0	33	523^1	527	15	267	195	14.0	3.27	112	.268	.361	4	.105	-1	29	23	2	1.5

● **TOMMIE SISK** Sisk, Tommie Wayne b: 4/12/42, Ardmore, Okla. BR/TR, 6'3", 195 lbs. Deb: 7/19/62

YEAR	TM/L	W	L	PCT	G	GS	CG	SH	SV	IP	H	HR	BB	SO	RAT	ERA	ERA+	OAV	OOB	BH	AVG	PB	PR	/A	PD	TPI
1962	Pit-N	0	2	.000	5	3	1	0	0	17^2	18	1	8	6	13.8	4.08	97	.257	.342	1	.200	0	-0	-0	-0	-0.1
1963	Pit-N	1	3	.250	57	4	1	0	1	108	85	6	45	73	10.9	2.92	113	.222	.305	1	.063	-0	4	5	1	0.2
1964	Pit-N	1	4	.200	42	1	0	0	0	61^1	91	4	29	35	18.0	6.16	57	.364	.436	0	.000	-1	-18	-18	2	-1.3
1965	Pit-N	7	3	.700	38	12	1	1	0	111^1	103	6	50	66	12.4	3.40	103	.248	.330	2	.061	-2	2	1	-1	-0.2
1966	Pit-N	10	5	.667	34	23	4	1	1	150	146	14	52	60	12.1	4.14	86	.256	.323	5	.098	-1	-9	-9	0	-1.0
1967	Pit-N	13	13	.500	37	31	11	2	1	207^2	196	6	78	85	12.0	3.34	101	.253	.324	7	.101	-2	2	1	-1	-0.1
1968	Pit-N	5	5	.500	33	11	0	0	1	96	101	3	35	41	13.0	3.28	89	.282	.351	6	.083	-1	4	3	-1	-0.5
1969	SD-N	2	13	.133	53	13	1	0	6	143	160	11	48	59	13.2	4.78	74	.285	.342	3	.120	-1	-19	-20	0	-2.0
1970	Chi-A	1	1	.500	17	1	0	0	0	33^1	37	6	13	16	13.5	5.40	72	.276	.340	1	.250	0	-6	-6	1	-0.2
Total 9		40	49	.449	316	99	19	4	10	928^1	937	57	358	441	12.7	3.92	88	.266	.337	22	.094	-7	-48	-50	3	-5.2

● **DAVE SISLER** Sisler, David Michael b: 10/16/31, St.Louis, Mo. BR/TR, 6'4", 200 lbs. Deb: 4/21/56 F

YEAR	TM/L	W	L	PCT	G	GS	CG	SH	SV	IP	H	HR	BB	SO	RAT	ERA	ERA+	OAV	OOB	BH	AVG	PB	PR	/A	PD	TPI
1956	Bos-A	9	8	.529	39	14	3	0	3	142^1	120	13	72	93	14.6	4.62	100	.227	.328	5	.119	-2	-7	-7	0	-0.2
1957	Bos-A	7	8	.467	22	19	5	0	1	122^1	135	15	61	55	14.6	4.71	85	.280	.363	7	.167	-0	-12	-10	-1	-1.1
1958	Bos-A	8	9	.471	30	25	4	1	0	149^1	157	22	79	71	14.3	4.94	81	.276	.366	9	.196	-0	-19	-16	-1	-1.6
1959	Bos-A	0	0	—	3	0	0	0	0	6^2	9	3	1	3	13.5	6.75	60	.310	.333	1	.500	-0	-2	-2	-0	0.0
	Det-A	1	3	.250	32	0	0	0	7	51^2	46	4	36	29	14.5	4.01	101	.242	.366	1	.200	-0	-1	-0	-1	0.0
	Yr	1	3	.250	35	0	0	0	7	58^1	55	7	37	32	14.3	4.32	94	.251	.362	2	.286	-1	-3	-2	-1	0.0
1960	Det-A	7	5	.583	41	0	0	0	6	80	56	9	45	47	11.6	2.47	160	.199	.314	2	.125	-0	12	13	1	2.2
1961	Was-A	2	8	.200	45	1	0	0	11	60^1	55	6	48	30	15.8	4.18	96	.251	.393	0	.000	-0	-1	-1	-0	-0.2
1962	Cin-N	4	3	.571	35	0	0	0	1	43^2	44	7	26	27	14.4	3.92	103	.270	.370	0	—	0	-1	-1	-0	-0.0
Total 7		38	44	.463	247	59	12	1	29	656^1	622	70	368	355	13.8	4.33	95	.253	.354	25	.157	-2	-31	-15	1	-0.9

● **GEORGE SISLER** Sisler, George Harold "Georgeous George" b: 3/24/1893, Manchester, Ohio d: 3/26/73, Richmond Heights, Mo. BL/TL, 5'11", 170 lbs. Deb: 6/28/15 FMCH♦

YEAR	TM/L	W	L	PCT	G	GS	CG	SH	SV	IP	H	HR	BB	SO	RAT	ERA	ERA+	OAV	OOB	BH	AVG	PB	PR	/A	PD	TPI
1915	StL-A	4	4	.500	15	8	6	0	0	70	62	0	38	41	13.4	2.83	101	.247	.355	78	.285	3	1	0	0	0.2
1916	StL-A	1	2	.333	3	3	3	0	0	27	18	0*	6	12	8.3	1.00	275	.198	.255	177	.305	1	5	5	1	0.9
1918	StL-A	0	0	—	2	1	0	0	0	8	10	0	4	4	16.9	4.50	61	.286	.375	154	.341	1	-2	-2	0	0.0
1920	StL-A	0	0	—	1	0	0	0	0	1	2	0	1	0	9.0	0.00	—	.000	.000	257	.407	4	0	0	0	0.1
1925	StL-A	0	0	—	1	0	0	0	0	2	1	0	1	1	9.0	0.00	—	.167	.286	224	.345	4	0	0	0	0.1
1926	StL-A	0	0	—	1	0	0	0	0	1	2	0	1	1	9.0	0.00	—	.286	.286	178	.290	0	0	0	0	0.1
1928	Bos-N	0	0	—	1	0	0	0	0	1	1	0	1	0	9.0	0.00	—	.000	.333	167	.340	0	0	0	0	0.0
Total 7		5	6	.455	24	12	9	1	3	111	91	0	52	63	12.1	2.35	123	.231	.330	2812	.340	7	8	7	1	1.3

● **CARL SITTON** Sitton, Carl Vetter b: 9/22/1882, Pendleton, S.C. d: 9/11/31, Valdosta, Ga. BR/TR, 5'10.5", 170 lbs. Deb: 4/24/09

YEAR	TM/L	W	L	PCT	G	GS	CG	SH	SV	IP	H	HR	BB	SO	RAT	ERA	ERA+	OAV	OOB	BH	AVG	PB	PR	/A	PD	TPI
1909	Cle-A	3	2	.600	14	5	3	0	0	50	50	1	16	16	12.2	2.88	89	.263	.327	2	.154	0	-2	-2	-1	-0.2

● **PETE SIVESS** Sivess, Peter b: 9/23/13, South River, N.J. BR/TR, 6'3.5", 195 lbs. Deb: 6/13/36

YEAR	TM/L	W	L	PCT	G	GS	CG	SH	SV	IP	H	HR	BB	SO	RAT	ERA	ERA+	OAV	OOB	BH	AVG	PB	PR	/A	PD	TPI
1936	Phi-N	3	4	.429	17	6	2	0	0	65	84	6	36	22	16.8	4.57	99	.310	.393	3	.120	-2	-4	-4	-2	-0.4
1937	Phi-N	1	1	.500	6	2	1	0	0	23	30	5	11	4	16.6	7.04	62	.330	.402	0	.000	-1	-8	-7	-1	-0.6
1938	Phi-N	3	6	.333	39	8	2	0	0	116	143	12	69	32	16.5	5.51	71	.306	.397	6	.188	-1	-22	-21	-1	-1.7
Total 3		7	11	.389	62	16	5	0	0	204	257	23	116	58	16.5	5.38	77	.310	.396	9	.143	-4	-34	-28	-3	-2.7

● **JIM SIWY** Siwy, James Gerard b: 9/20/58, Central Falls, R.I BR/TR, 6'4", 200 lbs. Deb: 8/20/82

YEAR	TM/L	W	L	PCT	G	GS	CG	SH	SV	IP	H	HR	BB	SO	RAT	ERA	ERA+	OAV	OOB	BH	AVG	PB	PR	/A	PD	TPI
1982	Chi-A	0	0	—	2	1	0	0	0	7	10	1	5	3	19.3	10.29	39	.385	.484	0	—	0	-5	-5	-0	0.0
1984	Chi-A	0	0	—	1	0	0	0	0	4^1	3	1	2	4	10.4	2.08	200	.231	.333	0	—	0	1	1	0	-0.2
Total 2		0	0	—	3	1	0	0	0	11^1	13	2	7	7	15.9	7.15	57	.333	.435	0	—	0	-4	-4	-0	-0.2

● **JOE SKALSKI** Skalski, Joseph Douglas b: 9/26/64, Burnham, Ill. BR/TR, 6'3", 190 lbs. Deb: 4/10/89

YEAR	TM/L	W	L	PCT	G	GS	CG	SH	SV	IP	H	HR	BB	SO	RAT	ERA	ERA+	OAV	OOB	BH	AVG	PB	PR	/A	PD	TPI
1989	Cle-A	0	2	.000	2	1	0	0	0	6^2	7	0	4	3	17.6	6.75	59	.259	.394	0	—	0	-2	-2	-0	-0.5

● **DAVE SKAUGSTAD** Skaugstad, David Wendell b: 1/10/40, Algona, Iowa BL/TL, 6'1", 179 lbs. Deb: 9/25/57

YEAR	TM/L	W	L	PCT	G	GS	CG	SH	SV	IP	H	HR	BB	SO	RAT	ERA	ERA+	OAV	OOB	BH	AVG	PB	PR	/A	PD	TPI
1957	Cin-N	0	0	—	2	0	0	0	0	5^2	4	0	6	4	15.9	1.59	259	.190	.370	0	.000	0	1	2	0	0.0

YEAR TM/L	W	L	PCT	G	GS	CG	SH	SV	IP	H	HR	BB	SO	RAT	ERA	ERA+	OAV	OOB	BH	AVG	PB	PR	/A	PD	TPI
● **DAVE SKEELS**			Skeels, David b: 12/29/1892, Addy, Wash. d: 12/2/26, Spokane, Wash. BL/TR, 6'1", 187 lbs. Deb: 9/14/10																						
1910 Det-A	0	0	—	1	1	0	0	0	6	9	0	4	2	21.0	12.00	22	.333	.438	0	.000	-0	-6	-6	0	0.0
● **CRAIG SKOK**			Skok, Craig Richard b: 9/1/47, Dobbs Ferry, N.Y. BR/TL, 6', 190 lbs. Deb: 5/4/73																						
1973 Bos-A	0	1	.000	11	0	0	0	1	28²	35	2	11	22	14.4	6.28	64	.304	.365	0	—	0	-8	-7	-0	-0.3
1976 Tex-A	0	1	.000	9	0	0	0	0	5	13	2	3	5	28.8	12.60	28	.481	.533	0	—	0	-5	-5	-0	-1.0
1978 Atl-N	3	2	.600	43	0	0	0	2	62	64	8	27	28	13.2	4.35	93	.266	.340	2	.250	0	-5	-2	-0	-0.2
1979 Atl-N	1	3	.250	44	0	0	0	2	54¹	58	7	17	30	12.9	3.98	102	.282	.345	0	.000	-0	-1	0	0	0.1
Total 4	4	7	.364	107	0	0	0	5	150	170	19	58	85	13.9	4.86	83	.289	.355	2	.182	-0	-20	-14	-0	-1.4
● **JOHN SKOPEC**			Skopec, John S. "Buckshot" b: 5/8/1880, Chicago, Ill. d: 10/20/12, Chicago, Ill. BR/TL, 5'10", 190 lbs. Deb: 4/25/01																						
1901 Chi-A	6	3	.667	9	9	6	0	0	68¹	62	1	45	24	15.1	3.16	110	.239	.369	10	.333	3	4	2	3	0.8
1903 Det-A	2	2	.500	6	5	3	0	0	39¹	46	0	13	14	14.0	3.43	85	.291	.353	2	.154	-0	-2	-2	0	-0.2
Total 2	8	5	.615	15	14	9	0	0	107²	108	1	58	38	14.7	3.26	101	.259	.363	12	.279	3	2	0	3	0.6
● **JOHN SLAGLE**			Slagle, John A. b: Lawrence, Ind. BL/TR, Deb: 4/30/1891																						
1891 Cin-a	0	0	—	1	0	0	0	1	1¹	3	0	1	1	27.0	0.00	—	.429	.500	0	.000	-0	1	1	0	0.1
● **ROGER SLAGLE**			Slagle, Roger Lee b: 11/4/53, Wichita, Kan. BR/TR, 6'3", 190 lbs. Deb: 9/7/79																						
1979 NY-A	0	0	—	1	0	0	0	0	2	0	0	2	0	9.0	0.00	—	.000	.000	0	—	0	1	1	0	0.0
● **WALT SLAGLE**			Slagle, Walter Jennings b: 12/15/1878, Kenton, Ohio d: 6/17/74, San Gabriel, Cal. BB/TR, 6', 165 lbs. Deb: 5/4/10																						
1910 Cin-N	0	0	—	1	0	0	0	0	1	0	0	3	0	36.0	9.00	32	.000	.571	0	—	0	-1	-1	-0	0.0
● **CY SLAPNICKA**			Slapnicka, Cyril Charles b: 3/23/1886, Cedar Rapids, Iowa d: 10/20/79, Cedar Rapids, Iowa BB/TR, 5'10", 165 lbs. Deb: 9/26/11																						
1911 Chi-N	0	2	.000	3	2	1	0	0	24	21	0	7	10	11.6	3.38	98	.236	.313	2	.222	-0	0	-0	1	0.1
1918 Pit-N	1	4	.200	7	6	4	0	1	49¹	50	2	22	3	14.0	4.74	61	.269	.362	1	.071	-1	-11	-10	-0	-1.1
Total 2	1	6	.143	10	8	5	0	1	73¹	71	2	29	13	13.3	4.30	70	.258	.346	3	.130	-1	-11	-10	-0	-1.0
● **JOHN SLAPPEY**			Slappey, John Henry b: 8/8/1898, Albany, Ga. d: 6/10/57, Marietta, Ga. BL/TL, 6'4", 170 lbs. Deb: 8/23/20																						
1920 Phi-A	0	1	.000	3	1	0	0	0	6¹	15	0	4	1	27.0	7.11	57	.441	.500	1	.500	1	-2	-2	-0	-0.2
● **JIM SLATON**			Slaton, James Michael b: 6/19/50, Long Beach, Cal. BR/TR, 6', 185 lbs. Deb: 4/14/71																						
1971 Mil-A	10	8	.556	26	23	5	4	0	147²	140	16	71	63	12.9	3.78	92	.253	.339	5	.109	-1	-5	-5	-2	-0.9
1972 Mil-A	1	6	.143	9	8	0	0	0	44	50	3	21	17	14.7	5.52	55	.287	.367	1	.091	-1	-12	-12	1	-1.8
1973 Mil-A	13	15	.464	38	38	13	3	0	276¹	266	30	99	134	11.9	3.71	101	.251	.316	0	—	0	3	1	-3	-0.2
1974 Mil-A	13	16	.448	40	35	10	3	0	250	255	22	102	126	13.0	3.92	92	.268	.341	0	—	0	-9	-9	0	-0.9
1975 Mil-A	11	18	.379	37	33	10	3	0	217	238	28	90	119	13.7	4.52	85	.276	.346	0	—	0	-18	-17	1	-2.0
1976 Mil-A	14	15	.483	38	38	12	2	0	292²	287	14	94	138	11.9	3.44	101	.259	.320	0	—	0	2	1	1	0.3
1977 Mil-A☆	10	14	.417	32	31	7	1	0	221	223	25	77	104	12.7	3.58	113	.266	.336	0	—	0	12	12	1	1.2
1978 Det-A	17	11	.607	35	34	11	2	0	233²	235	27	85	92	12.6	4.12	94	.263	.332	0	—	0	-9	-7	-1	-0.9
1979 Mil-A	15	9	.625	32	31	12	3	0	213	229	15	54	80	12.0	3.63	115	.278	.323	0	—	0	14	13	1	1.3
1980 Mil-A	1	1	.500	3	3	0	0	0	16¹	17	3	5	4	12.1	4.41	88	.270	.324	0	—	0	-1	-1	0	-0.1
1981 *Mil-A	5	7	.417	24	21	0	0	0	117¹	120	10	50	47	13.2	4.37	78	.273	.350	0	—	0	-9	-12	-0	-0.9
1982 *Mil-A	10	6	.625	39	7	0	0	6	117²	117	14	41	59	12.2	3.29	115	.264	.327	0	—	0	10	6	0	0.8
1983 Mil-A	14	6	.700	46	0	0	0	0	112¹	112	12	36	64	13.8	4.33	86	.272	.363	0	—	0	-3	-1	-1	-1.2
1984 Cal-A	7	10	.412	32	22	5	1	0	163	192	22	56	67	13.8	4.97	80	.295	.353	0	—	0	-18	-18	-0	-1.6
1985 Cal-A	6	10	.375	29	24	1	0	1	148¹	162	22	63	60	13.8	4.37	94	.284	.357	0	—	0	-4	-5	-0	-0.4
1986 Cal-A	6	4	.400	14	12	0	0	0	73¹	84	9	29	31	14.1	5.65	73	.295	.364	0	—	0	-12	-13	1	-1.4
Det-A	0	0	—	22	0	0	0	2	40	46	5	11	12	13.0	4.05	102	.287	.337	0	—	0	1	0	0	0.0
Yr	4	6	.400	36	12	0	0	2	113¹	130	14	40	43	13.6	5.08	81	.287	.346	0	—	0	-11	-12	1	-1.4
Total 16	151	158	.489	496	360	86	22	14	2683²	2773	277	1004	1191	12.8	4.03	94	.270	.337	6	.105	-2	-58	-70	-4	-8.7
● **PHIL SLATTERY**			Slattery, Philip Ryan b: 2/25/1893, Harper, Iowa d: 3/2/68, Long Beach, Cal. BR/TL, 5'11", 160 lbs. Deb: 9/16/15																						
1915 Pit-N	0	0	—	3	0	0	0	0	8	5	0	1	1	9.0	0.00	—	.185	.267	0	.000	-0	2	1	-1	-0.1
● **BARNEY SLAUGHTER**			Slaughter, Byron Atkins b: 10/6/1884, Smyrna, Del. d: 5/17/61, Philadelphia, Pa. BR/TR, 5'11.5", 165 lbs. Deb: 8/9/10																						
1910 Phi-N	0	1	.000	8	1	0	0	1	18	21	0	11	7	16.0	5.50	57	.318	.416	1	.200	0	-5	-5	-0	-0.3
● **STERLING SLAUGHTER**			Slaughter, Sterling Feore b: 11/18/41, Danville, Ill. BR/TR, 5'11", 165 lbs. Deb: 4/19/64																						
1964 Chi-N	2	4	.333	20	6	1	0	0	51²	64	8	32	32	16.7	5.75	65	.305	.397	1	.083	0	-13	-12	-1	-1.4
● **BILL SLAYBACK**			Slayback, William Grover b: 2/21/48, Hollywood, Cal. BR/TR, 6'4", 200 lbs. Deb: 6/26/72																						
1972 Det-A	5	6	.455	23	13	3	1	0	81²	74	4	25	65	11.0	3.20	98	.239	.298	4	.174	0	-1	-0	1	0.0
1973 Det-A	0	0	—	3	0	0	0	0	2	5	1	0	1	27.0	4.50	91	.417	.462	0	—	0	-0	-0	-0	0.0
1974 Det-A	1	3	.250	16	4	0	0	0	54²	57	1	26	23	14.2	4.77	80	.273	.361	0	—	0	-7	-6	-0	-0.5
Total 3	6	9	.400	42	17	3	1	0	138¹	136	5	51	89	12.5	3.84	89	.256	.327	4	.174	0	-8	-7	0	-0.5
● **STEVE SLAYTON**			Slayton, Foster Herbert b: 4/26/02, Barre, Vt. d: 12/20/84, Manchester, N.H. BR/TR, 6', 163 lbs. Deb: 7/21/28																						
1928 Bos-A	0	0	—	3	0	0	0	0	7	6	0	3	2	11.6	3.86	107	.240	.321	0	.000	-0	0	0	-0	0.0
● **LOU SLEATER**			Sleater, Louis Mortimer b: 9/8/26, St.Louis, Mo. BL/TL, 5'10", 185 lbs. Deb: 4/25/50																						
1950 StL-A	0	0	—	1	0	0	0	0	1	0	0	0	1	0.0	0.00	—	.000	.000	0	—	0	1	1	0	0.0
1951 StL-A	1	9	.100	20	8	4	0	1	81	88	7	53	33	16.2	5.11	86	.271	.381	7	.226	0	-9	-6	-1	-0.8
1952 StL-A	0	1	.000	4	2	0	0	0	8²	9	1	5	1	14.5	7.27	54	.265	.359	0	.000	0	-3	-3	-0	-0.4
Was-A	4	2	.667	14	9	3	1	0	57	56	4	30	22	13.9	3.63	98	.260	.356	1	.050	-2	-0	-1	-0	-0.4
Yr	4	3	.571	18	11	3	1	0	65²	65	5	35	23	14.0	4.11	88	.261	.357	1	.045	-2	-3	-4	-0	-0.8
1955 KC-A	1	1	.500	16	1	0	0	0	25²	33	5	21	11	18.9	7.71	54	.324	.439	2	.154	-1	-11	-10	-0	-1.4
1956 Mil-N	2	2	.500	25	1	0	0	0	45²	42	6	27	32	13.6	3.15	110	.240	.342	5	.500	3	3	2	1	0.5
1957 Det-A	3	3	.500	41	0	0	0	0	69¹	67	9	28	43	11.7	3.76	102	.237	.315	5	.250	3	0	1	-0	0.4
1958 Det-A	0	0	—	4	0	0	0	0	5¹	3	0	6	2	15.2	6.75	60	.158	.360	1	1.000	1	-2	-2	-0	0.2
Bal-A	1	0	1.000	6	0	0	0	0	7	14	0	2	5	20.6	12.86	28	.438	.471	0	.000	-1	-7	-7	-0	-0.9
Yr	1	0	1.000	10	0	0	0	0	12¹	17	0	8	7	18.2	10.22	37	.333	.424	1	.143	0	-9	-9	-0	-0.7
Total 7	12	18	.400	131	21	7	1	5	300²	306	32	172	152	14.5	4.70	83	.263	.362	21	.204	3	-28	-26	-2	-2.2
● **LEFTY SLOAT**			Sloat, Dwain Clifford b: 12/1/18, Nokomis, Ill. BR/TL, 6', 168 lbs. Deb: 4/24/48																						
1948 Bro-N	0	1	.000	4	1	0	0	0	7¹	7	0	8	1	18.4	6.14	65	.280	.455	0	.000	-0	-2	-5	1	-0.2
1949 Chi-N	0	0	—	5	1	0	0	0	9	14	0	3	3	17.0	7.00	58	.400	.447	0	—	0	-3	-3	0	0.0
Total 2	0	1	.000	9	2	0	0	0	16¹	21	0	11	4	17.6	6.61	61	.350	.451	0	.000	-0	-5	-8	1	-0.2
● **HEATHCLIFF SLOCUMB**			Slocumb, Heath b: 6/7/66, Jamaica, N.Y. BR/TR, 6'3", 210 lbs. Deb: 4/11/91																						
1991 Chi-N	2	1	.667	52	0	0	0	1	62²	53	3	30	34	12.4	3.45	113	.231	.328	0	.000	-0	2	3	0	0.1
1992 Chi-N	0	3	.000	30	0	0	0	1	36	52	3	21	27	18.5	6.50	55	.351	.435	0	.000	-0	-12	-12	-0	-1.1
1993 Chi-N	1	0	1.000	10	0	0	0	0	10²	7	0	4	4	9.3	3.38	118	.189	.268	0	.000	-0	1	1	0	0.1
Cle-A	3	1	.750	20	0	0	0	0	27¹	28	3	16	18	14.5	4.28	101	.272	.370	0	—	0	0	-0	-0	0.0
1994 Phi-N	5	1	.833	52	0	0	0	0	72¹	75	2	28	58	13.1	2.86	150	.262	.332	1	.250	-0	11	11	0	0.9
1995 Phi-N★	5	6	.455	61	0	0	0	32	65¹	64	2	35	63	13.8	2.89	146	.257	.351	0	.000	-0	10	12	2	2.5
1996 Bos-A	5	5	.500	75	0	0	0	31	83¹	68	2	55	88	13.6	3.02	170	.222	.346	0	—	0	18	20	1	3.4
Total 6	21	17	.553	300	0	0	0	65	357²	347	13	189	292	13.7	3.50	124	.256	.351	1	.091	-1	29	33	3	5.9
● **JOE SLUSARSKI**			Slusarski, Joseph Andrew b: 12/19/66, Indianapolis, Ind. BR/TR, 6'4", 195 lbs. Deb: 4/11/91																						
1991 Oak-A	5	7	.417	20	19	1	0	0	109¹	121	14	52	60	14.6	5.27	73	.283	.366	0	—	0	-14	-17	-1	-1.6
1992 Oak-A	5	5	.500	15	14	0	0	0	76	85	15	27	38	14.0	5.45	69	.284	.355	0	—	0	-13	-14	-1	-1.7

YEAR	TM/L	W	L	PCT	G	GS	CG	SH	SV	IP	H	HR	BB	SO	RAT	ERA	ERA+	OAV	OOB	BH	AVG	PB	PR	/A	PD	TPI
1993	Oak-A	0	0	—	2	1	0	0	0	8²	9	1	11	1	20.8	5.19	78	.300	.488	0	—	0	-1	-1	0	0.0
1995	Mil-A	1	1	.500	12	0	0	0	0	15	21	3	6	6	17.4	5.40	92	.333	.408	0	—	0	-1	-1	-0	-0.1
Total	4	11	13	.458	49	34	1	0	0	209	236	33	96	105	14.8	5.34	73	.288	.371	0	—	0	-29	-34	-2	-3.4

● **AARON SMALL**   Small, Aaron James   b: 11/23/71, Oxnard, Cal.   BR/TR, 6'5", 200 lbs.   Deb: 6/11/94

YEAR	TM/L	W	L	PCT	G	GS	CG	SH	SV	IP	H	HR	BB	SO	RAT	ERA	ERA+	OAV	OOB	BH	AVG	PB	PR	/A	PD	TPI
1994	Tor-A	0	0	—	1	0	0	0	0	2	5	1	2	0	31.5	9.00	54	.500	.583	0	—	0	-1	-1	0	0.0
1995	Fla-N	0	1	1.000	7	0	0	0	0	6¹	7	1	6	5	18.5	1.42	296	.269	.406	0	—	0	2	2	0	0.3
1996	Oak-A	1	3	.250	12	3	0	0	0	28²	37	3	22	17	18.8	8.16	59	.308	.420	0	—	0	-10	-11	0	-1.1
Total	3	2	3	.400	20	3	0	0	0	37	49	5	30	22	19.5	7.05	67	.314	.428	0	—	0	-9	-10	0	-0.8

● **MARK SMALL**   Small, Mark Allen   b: 11/12/67, Portland, Ore.   BR/TR, 6'3", 205 lbs.   Deb: 4/5/96

YEAR	TM/L	W	L	PCT	G	GS	CG	SH	SV	IP	H	HR	BB	SO	RAT	ERA	ERA+	OAV	OOB	BH	AVG	PB	PR	/A	PD	TPI
1996	Hou-N	0	1	.000	16	0	0	0	0	24¹	33	1	13	16	17.4	5.92	65	.308	.388	0	.000	-0	-5	-6	-1	-0.3

● **WALT SMALLWOOD**   Smallwood, Walter Clayton   b: 4/24/1893, Dayton, Md.   d: 4/29/67, Baltimore, Md.   BR/TR, 6'2", 190 lbs.   Deb: 9/19/17

YEAR	TM/L	W	L	PCT	G	GS	CG	SH	SV	IP	H	HR	BB	SO	RAT	ERA	ERA+	OAV	OOB	BH	AVG	PB	PR	/A	PD	TPI
1917	NY-A	0	0	—	2	0	0	0	0	2	1	0	1	1	9.0	0.00	—	.167	.286	0	—	1	1	1	0	0.0
1919	NY-A	0	0	—	6	0	0	0	0	21²	20	1	9	6	12.9	4.98	64	.263	.356	0	.000	-1	-4	-4	-0	-0.1
Total	2	0	0	—	8	0	0	0	0	23²	21	1	10	7	12.5	4.56	69	.256	.351	0	.000	-1	-4	-4	-0	-0.1

● **JOHN SMILEY**   Smiley, John Patrick   b: 3/17/65, Phoenixville, Pa.   BL/TL, 6'4", 195 lbs.   Deb: 9/1/86

YEAR	TM/L	W	L	PCT	G	GS	CG	SH	SV	IP	H	HR	BB	SO	RAT	ERA	ERA+	OAV	OOB	BH	AVG	PB	PR	/A	PD	TPI
1986	Pit-N	1	0	1.000	12	0	0	0	0	11²	4	2	4	9	6.2	3.86	99	.105	.190	0	—	-0	-0	-0	0	0.0
1987	Pit-N	5	5	.500	63	0	0	0	4	75	69	7	50	58	14.3	5.76	71	.244	.357	1	.143	0	-14	-14	0	-1.7
1988	Pit-N	13	11	.542	34	32	5	1	0	205	185	15	46	129	10.3	3.25	105	.241	.287	5	.079	-2	5	3	-1	0.1
1989	Pit-N	12	8	.600	28	28	8	1	0	205¹	174	22	49	123	9.9	2.81	120	.226	.276	9	.138	1	16	13	-2	1.0
1990	*Pit-N	9	10	.474	26	25	2	0	0	149¹	161	15	36	86	12.0	4.64	78	.275	.319	6	.122	0	-14	-17	0	-1.9
1991	*Pit-N★	**20**	8	.714	33	32	2	1	0	207²	194	17	44	129	10.4	3.08	116	.251	.294	7	.100	-2	14	11	-0	1.2
1992	Min-A	16	9	.640	34	34	5	2	0	241	205	17	65	163	10.3	3.21	126	.231	.288	0	—	0	19	23	0	2.2
1993	Cin-N	3	9	.250	18	18	2	0	0	105²	117	15	31	60	12.8	5.62	72	.286	.339	8	.250	-2	-19	-19	0	-1.6
1994	Cin-N	11	10	.524	24	24	1	1	0	158²	169	18	37	112	11.9	3.86	107	.275	.320	11	.200	3	6	5	-1	0.7
1995	*Cin-N★	12	5	.706	28	27	1	0	0	176²	173	11	39	124	11.0	3.46	119	.263	.308	9	.164	2	14	13	-0	1.3
1996	Cin-N	13	14	.481	35	34	2	2	0	217¹	207	20	54	171	11.0	3.64	114	.256	.306	13	.191	1	14	12	-1	1.5
Total	11	115	89	.564	335	254	28	8	4	1753¹	1658	159	455	1164	11.0	3.67	104	.251	.303	69	.149	5	41	30	-4	2.8

● **SMITH**   Smith   Deb: 6/5/1884

YEAR	TM/L	W	L	PCT	G	GS	CG	SH	SV	IP	H	HR	BB	SO	RAT	ERA	ERA+	OAV	OOB	BH	AVG	PB	PR	/A	PD	TPI
1884	Bal-U	0	0	—	1	1	0	0	0	6	12	0	2	2	21.0	9.00	30	.387	.424	1	.200	-1	-4	-4	-0	-0.1

● **SMITH**   Smith   Deb: 5/31/1886

YEAR	TM/L	W	L	PCT	G	GS	CG	SH	SV	IP	H	HR	BB	SO	RAT	ERA	ERA+	OAV	OOB	BH	AVG	PB	PR	/A	PD	TPI
1886	Cin-a	0	1	.000	1	1	1	0	0	9	8	0	10	1	18.0	4.00	88	.229	.400	1	.250	-0	-1	-0	-0	-0.1

● **AL SMITH**   Smith, Alfred John   b: 10/12/07, Belleville, Ill.   d: 4/28/77, Brownsville, Tex.   BL/TL, 5'11", 180 lbs.   Deb: 5/5/34   C

YEAR	TM/L	W	L	PCT	G	GS	CG	SH	SV	IP	H	HR	BB	SO	RAT	ERA	ERA+	OAV	OOB	BH	AVG	PB	PR	/A	PD	TPI
1934	NY-N	3	5	.375	30	5	0	0	5	66²	70	2	21	27	12.3	4.32	90	.266	.320	4	.286	1	-2	-3	-0	-0.4
1935	NY-N	10	8	.556	40	10	4	1	5	124	125	6	32	44	11.9	3.41	113	.263	.319	4	.118	-0	8	6	-1	0.7
1936	*NY-N	14	13	.519	43	30	9	4	2	209¹	217	16	69	89	12.5	3.78	103	.274	.335	10	.137	-1	6	3	-1	0.1
1937	*NY-N	5	4	.556	39	2	0	0	0	85²	91	8	30	41	12.9	4.20	93	.275	.339	3	.120	-2	-3	-3	-1	-0.5
1938	Phi-N	1	4	.200	37	1	0	0	0	86	115	7	40	46	16.2	6.28	62	.320	.388	0	.000	—	-24	-23	0	-1.4
1939	Phi-N	0	0	—	5	0	0	0	0	9	11	1	5	2	18.0	4.00	100	.314	.429	0	.000	-0	-0	-0	-0	0.0
1940	Cle-A	15	7	.682	31	24	11	1	2	183	187	12	55	46	12.2	3.44	123	.270	.329	19	.306	7	19	16	2	2.6
1941	Cle-A	12	13	.480	29	27	13	2	0	206²	204	12	75	76	12.2	3.83	103	.256	.321	11	.155	2	7	2	0	0.6
1942	Cle-A	10	15	.400	30	24	7	1	1	168¹	163	9	71	66	12.8	3.96	87	.251	.329	15	.250	3	-6	-9	-1	-1.0
1943	Cle-A☆	17	7	.708	29	27	14	3	1	208¹	186	7	72	72	11.1	2.55	122	.239	.303	14	.206	3	17	13	-0	1.9
1944	Cle-A	7	13	.350	28	26	7	1	0	181²	197	6	69	44	13.3	3.42	96	.280	.347	10	.156	-1	0	-2	1	-0.2
1945	Cle-A	5	12	.294	21	19	8	1	1	133²	141	6	48	34	12.9	3.84	85	.275	.340	12	.293	4	-7	-9	2	-0.4
Total	12	99	101	.495	356	202	75	16	17	1662¹	1707	94	587	587	12.6	3.72	99	.267	.332	102	.191	14	17	-10	4	2.0

● **AL SMITH**   Smith, Alfred Kendricks   b: 12/13/03, Norristown, Pa.   d: 8/11/95, San Diego, Cal.   BR/TR, 6', 170 lbs.   Deb: 6/18/26

YEAR	TM/L	W	L	PCT	G	GS	CG	SH	SV	IP	H	HR	BB	SO	RAT	ERA	ERA+	OAV	OOB	BH	AVG	PB	PR	/A	PD	TPI
1926	NY-N	0	0	—	1	0	0	0	0	2	4	0	2	0	27.0	9.00	42	.444	.545	0	—	0	-1	-1	-0	-0.1

● **ART SMITH**   Smith, Arthur Laird   b: 6/21/06, Boston, Mass.   d: 11/22/95, Norwalk, Conn.   BR/TR, 6', 175 lbs.   Deb: 6/9/32

YEAR	TM/L	W	L	PCT	G	GS	CG	SH	SV	IP	H	HR	BB	SO	RAT	ERA	ERA+	OAV	OOB	BH	AVG	PB	PR	/A	PD	TPI
1932	Chi-A	0	1	.000	3	2	0	0	0	7	17	1	4	1	27.0	11.57	37	.500	.553	0	.000	-0	-6	-6	1	-0.6

● **BILLY SMITH**   Smith, Billy Lavern   b: 9/13/54, LaMarque, Tex.   BR/TR, 6'7", 200 lbs.   Deb: 6/9/81

YEAR	TM/L	W	L	PCT	G	GS	CG	SH	SV	IP	H	HR	BB	SO	RAT	ERA	ERA+	OAV	OOB	BH	AVG	PB	PR	/A	PD	TPI
1981	*Hou-N	1	1	.500	10	1	0	0	0	20²	20	3	3	3	10.0	3.05	108	.263	.291	0	.000	-0	1	1	0	0.0

● **BRYN SMITH**   Smith, Bryn Nelson   b: 8/11/55, Marietta, Ga.   BR/TR, 6'2", 205 lbs.   Deb: 9/8/81

YEAR	TM/L	W	L	PCT	G	GS	CG	SH	SV	IP	H	HR	BB	SO	RAT	ERA	ERA+	OAV	OOB	BH	AVG	PB	PR	/A	PD	TPI
1981	Mon-N	1	0	1.000	7	0	0	0	0	13	14	1	3	9	11.8	2.77	126	.280	.321	0	.000	-0	1	1	-0	0.0
1982	Mon-N	2	4	.333	47	1	0	0	3	79¹	81	5	23	50	11.8	4.20	87	.264	.315	0	.000	-0	-5	-5	-0	-0.4
1983	Mon-N	6	11	.353	49	12	5	3	3	155¹	142	13	43	101	11.0	2.49	144	.248	.306	5	.167	-0	20	19	0	2.1
1984	Mon-N	12	13	.480	28	28	4	2	0	179	178	15	51	101	11.7	3.32	103	.259	.313	7	.132	-1	5	2	2	0.6
1985	Mon-N	18	5	.783	32	32	4	2	0	222¹	193	17	41	127	9.5	2.91	145	.232	.269	14	.194	3	17	12	-1	1.4
1986	Mon-N	10	8	.556	30	30	1	0	0	187¹	182	15	63	105	12.1	3.94	94	.251	.316	8	.138	1	-5	-5	3	0.0
1987	Mon-N	10	9	.526	26	26	2	1	0	150¹	164	16	31	94	11.8	4.37	96	.274	.312	6	.136	-0	-5	-3	-0	-0.3
1988	Mon-N	12	10	.545	32	32	1	0	0	198	179	15	32	122	10.0	3.00	120	.243	.284	6	.109	-1	10	13	-2	1.1
1989	Mon-N	10	11	.476	33	32	3	1	0	215²	177	16	54	129	9.8	2.84	124	.223	.276	4	.065	-2	16	17	2	1.6
1990	StL-N	9	8	.529	26	25	0	0	0	141¹	160	11	30	78	12.4	4.27	89	.286	.327	10	.256	3	-7	-7	-1	-0.5
1991	StL-N	12	9	.571	31	31	3	0	0	198²	188	16	45	94	10.9	3.85	97	.251	.300	16	.246	3	-4	-3	-1	-0.1
1992	StL-N	4	2	.667	13	1	0	0	0	21¹	20	3	5	9	11.8	4.64	73	.247	.315	0	.000	-0	-3	-3	0	-0.8
1993	Col-N	2	4	.333	11	5	0	0	0	29²	47	2	11	19	18.5	8.49	56	.362	.424	0	.000	-0	-15	-12	1	-2.0
Total	13	108	94	.535	365	255	23	8	6	1791¹	1725	140	432	1028	11.1	3.53	104	.253	.305	76	.153	7	25	25	4	2.7

● **CHARLIE SMITH**   Smith, Charles Edwin   b: 4/20/1880, Cleveland, Ohio   d: 1/3/29, Wickliffe, Ohio   BR/TR, 6'1", 185 lbs.   Deb: 8/6/02   F

YEAR	TM/L	W	L	PCT	G	GS	CG	SH	SV	IP	H	HR	BB	SO	RAT	ERA	ERA+	OAV	OOB	BH	AVG	PB	PR	/A	PD	TPI
1902	Cle-A	2	1	.667	3	3	2	1	0	20	23	0	5	12	12.6	4.05	85	.287	.329	1	.125	-0	-1	-1	0	-0.2
1906	Was-A	9	16	.360	33	22	17	2	0	235¹	250	0	75	105	12.7	2.91	91	.275	.336	16	.184	-1	-6	-7	-3	-1.1
1907	Was-A	10	20	.333	36	31	21	3	0	258²	254	0	51	119	10.6	2.61	93	.259	.297	12	.143	-3	-2	-6	3	-0.6
1908	Was-A	9	13	.409	26	23	14	1	1	183	166	2	60	83	11.3	2.41	95	.247	.311	8	.123	-2	-0	-3	-1	-0.6
1909	Was-A	3	12	.200	23	15	7	1	0	145²	140	4	37	72	11.1	3.27	74	.250	.303	7	.156	-1	-13	-14	-1	-1.4
	Bos-A	3	0	1.000	3	3	2	1	0	25	23	2	2	11	9.4	2.16	116	.247	.260	3	.300	1	1	1	0	0.2
	Yr	6	12	.333	26	18	9	2	0	170²	163	6	39	83	10.7	3.11	78	.247	.290	10	.182	-0	-12	-13	-1	-1.2
1910	Bos-A	11	6	.647	24	18	11	0	1	156¹	141	4	35	53	10.2	2.30	111	.248	.294	5	.114	-2	4	4	-2	-0.1
1911	Bos-A	0	0	—	1	1	0	0	0	2	2	1	1	0	13.5	9.00	36	.250	.333	0	—	-0	-1	-1	0	0.0
	Chi-N	3	2	.600	7	5	1	1	0	38	31	0	7	11	9.2	1.42	233	.228	.271	1	.077	-1	8	8	1	0.8
1912	Chi-N	7	4	.636	20	7	3	1	0	94	92	3	41	47	12.1	4.21	79	.269	.335	9	.257	1	-8	-9	-1	-0.7
1913	Chi-N	7	9	.438	20	17	8	1	0	137²	138	2	34	47	11.5	2.55	125	.274	.325	4	.089	-3	10	10	0	0.9
1914	Chi-N	0	3	.000	16	5	1	0	0	53²	49	3	15	17	10.9	3.86	72	.251	.308	1	.091	-0	-6	-6	-1	-0.9
Total	10	66	87	.431	212	148	87	10	3	1349¹	1309	22	353	570	11.3	2.81	94	.259	.311	67	.150	-13	-15	-24	-3	-3.9

● **POP SMITH**   Smith, Charles Marvin   b: 10/12/1856, Digby, N.S., Canada   d: 4/18/27, Boston, Mass.   BR/TR, 5'11", 170 lbs.   Deb: 5/1/1880   U♦

YEAR	TM/L	W	L	PCT	G	GS	CG	SH	SV	IP	H	HR	BB	SO	RAT	ERA	ERA+	OAV	OOB	BH	AVG	PB	PR	/A	PD	TPI
1883	Col-a	0	0	—	3	0	0	0	0	5²	10	0	0	0	15.9	6.35	48	.357	.357	106	.262	1	-2	-2	-0	0.0

● **POP-BOY SMITH**   Smith, Clarence Ossie   b: 5/23/1892, Newport, Tenn.   d: 2/16/24, Sweetwater, Tex.   BR/TR, 6'1", 176 lbs.   Deb: 4/19/13

YEAR	TM/L	W	L	PCT	G	GS	CG	SH	SV	IP	H	HR	BB	SO	RAT	ERA	ERA+	OAV	OOB	BH	AVG	PB	PR	/A	PD	TPI
1913	Chi-A	0	1	.000	15	2	0	0	1	32	26	1	13	13	12.7	3.38	87	.261	.338	0	.000	-1	-2	-1	0	0.0
1916	Cle-A	1	2	.333	5	3	0	0	0	25²	21	5	11	4	13.0	3.86	78	.253	.333	2	.286	-0	-3	-3	-0	-0.3
1917	Cle-A	0	1	.000	6	0	0	0	0	8²	14	0	4	3	19.7	8.31	34	.368	.442	0	.000	-0	-5	-5	1	-0.5
Total	3	1	4	.200	26	5	0	0	1	66¹	70	6	26	20	13.7	4.21	70	.273	.352	2	.154	-1	-10	-9	2	-0.8

YEAR TM/L	W	L	PCT	G	GS	CG	SH	SV	IP	H	HR	BB	SO	RAT	ERA	ERA+	OAV	OOB	BH	AVG	PB	PR	/A	PD	TPI

● CLAY SMITH Smith, Clay Jamieson b: 9/11/14, Cambridge, Kan. BR/TR, 6'2", 190 lbs. Deb: 9/13/38

1938 Cle-A	0	0	—	4	0	0	0	0	11	18	1	2	3	16.4	6.55	71	.367	.392	0	.000	-0	-2	-2	0	0.0
1940 *Det-A	1	1	.500	14	1	0	0	0	28¹	32	3	13	14	14.6	5.08	94	.283	.362	0	—	-1	-2	-1	1	-0.1
Total 2	1	1	.500	18	1	0	0	0	39¹	50	4	15	17	15.1	5.49	86	.309	.371	0	.000	-1	-4	-3	1	-0.1

● DAN SMITH Smith, Daniel Scott b: 4/20/69, St.Paul, Minn. BL/TL, 6'5", 190 lbs. Deb: 9/12/92

1992 Tex-A	0	3	.000	4	2	0	0	0	14¹	18	1	8	5	16.3	5.02	76	.321	.406	0	—	0	-2	-2	-0	-0.4
1994 Tex-A	1	2	.333	13	0	0	0	0	14²	18	2	12	9	18.4	4.30	112	.281	.395	0	—	0	1	1	-0	0.1
Total 2	1	5	.167	17	2	0	0	0	29	36	3	20	14	17.4	4.66	92	.300	.400	0	—	0	-1	-1	-1	-0.3

● DARYL SMITH Smith, Daryl Clinton b: 7/29/60, Baltimore, Md. BR/TR, 6'4", 185 lbs. Deb: 9/18/90

| 1990 KC-A | 0 | 1 | .000 | 6² | 5 | 0 | 4 | 6 | 12.2 | 4.05 | 95 | .238 | .360 | 0 | — | 0 | -0 | -0 | -0 | 0.0 |

● DAVE SMITH Smith, David Merwin b: 12/17/14, Sellers, S.C. BR/TR, 5'10", 170 lbs. Deb: 6/16/38

1938 Phi-A	2	1	.667	21	0	0	0	0	44¹	50	0	28	13	16.0	5.08	95	.284	.385	0	.000	-1	-1	-1	-0	-0.2
1939 Phi-A	0	0	—	1	0	0	0	0	0	1	0	2	0	—	—	—	1.000	1.000	0	—	0	0	0	0	0.0
Total 2	2	1	.667	22	0	0	0	0	44¹	51	0	30	13	16.6	5.08	95	.288	.394	0	.000	-1	-1	-1	-0	-0.2

● DAVE SMITH Smith, David Stanley b: 1/21/55, Richmond, Cal. BR/TR, 6'1", 195 lbs. Deb: 4/11/80

1980 *Hou-N	7	5	.583	57	0	0	0	10	102²	90	1	32	85	11.0	1.93	170	.237	.304	0	.000	-1	19	15	-1	1.8
1981 *Hou-N	5	3	.625	42	0	0	0	8	75	54	2	23	52	9.5	2.76	119	.198	.265	2	.250	0	6	4	-0	0.6
1982 Hou-N	5	4	.556	49	1	0	0	11	63¹	69	4	31	28	14.2	3.84	86	.285	.366	0	.000	-0	-2	-4	-1	-0.7
1983 Hou-N	3	1	.750	42	0	0	0	6	72²	72	4	36	41	13.4	3.10	110	.258	.343	0	.000	-1	4	2	-2	-0.1
1984 Hou-N	5	4	.556	53	0	0	0	5	77¹	60	5	20	45	9.4	2.21	150	.214	.269	0	.000	-0	12	10	-1	1.1
1985 Hou-N	9	5	.643	64	0	0	0	27	79¹	69	3	17	40	9.9	2.27	153	.235	.280	0	.000	-0	12	11	-1	2.4
1986 *Hou-N☆	4	7	.364	54	0	0	0	33	56	39	5	22	46	10.0	2.73	132	.200	.284	0	.000	-0	6	5	0	1.6
1987 Hou-N	2	3	.400	50	0	0	0	24	60	39	0	21	73	9.2	1.65	237	.182	.258	1	.500	1	16	15	-0	2.3
1988 Hou-N	4	5	.444	51	0	0	0	27	57¹	60	1	19	38	12.6	2.67	124	.268	.328	0	.000	-0	5	4	-0	1.0
1989 Hou-N	3	4	.429	52	0	0	0	25	58	49	1	19	31	10.7	2.64	128	.233	.300	0	.000	-0	6	5	1	1.0
1990 Hou-N★	6	6	.500	49	0	0	0	23	60¹	45	4	20	50	9.7	2.39	156	.210	.278	0	.000	-0	9	9	-1	2.2
1991 Chi-N	0	6	.000	35	0	0	0	17	33	39	6	19	16	16.1	6.00	65	.302	.396	0	.000	-0	-8	-8	-0	-2.0
1992 Chi-N	0	0	—	11	0	0	0	0	14¹	15	0	4	3	11.9	2.51	143	.273	.322	0	.000	-0	2	2	-0	0.0
Total 13	53	53	.500	609	1	0	0	216	809¹	700	34	283	548	11.1	2.67	130	.234	.303	3	.068	-2	87	71	-7	11.2

● DAVE SMITH Smith, David Wayne b: 8/30/57, Tomball, Tex. BR/TR, 6'1", 190 lbs. Deb: 9/18/84

1984 Cal-A	0	0	—	1	0	0	0	0	1	4	1	0	0	36.0	18.00	22	.571	.571	0	—	0	-2	-2	0	0.0
1985 Cal-A	0	0	—	4	0	0	0	0	5	5	1	1	3	10.8	7.20	57	.278	.316	0	—	0	-1	-1	0	0.0
Total 2	0	0	—	5	0	0	0	0	6	9	2	1	3	15.0	9.00	45	.360	.385	0	—	0	-3	-3	0	0.0

● DOUG SMITH Smith, Douglass Weldon b: 5/25/1892, Millers Falls, Mass. d: 9/18/73, Greenfield, Mass. BL/TL, 5'10", 168 lbs. Deb: 7/10/12

| 1912 Bos-A | 0 | 0 | — | 1 | 0 | 0 | 0 | 0 | 3 | 4 | 0 | 1 | 0 | 12.0 | 3.00 | 113 | .364 | .364 | 0 | — | 0 | 0 | 0 | -0 | 0.0 |

● EDDIE SMITH Smith, Edgar b: 12/14/13, Mansfield, N.J. d: 1/2/94, Willingboro, N.J. BB/TL, 5'10", 174 lbs. Deb: 9/20/36

1936 Phi-A	1	1	.500	2	2	2	0	0	19	22	3	8	7	14.2	1.89	269	.341	.341	1	.125	-1	7	7	0	0.6
1937 Phi-A	4	17	.190	38	23	14	1	5	196²	178	18	90	79	12.4	3.94	120	.242	.327	17	.233	1	15	17	-2	1.7
1938 Phi-A	3	10	.231	43	7	0	0	4	130²	151	13	76	78	15.9	5.92	82	.287	.381	12	.286	3	-16	-16	0	-1.1
1939 Phi-A	1	0	1.000	3	0	0	0	0	3²	7	0	2	3	22.1	9.82	48	.412	.474	0	—	-0	-2	-0	-0	-0.4
Chi-A	9	11	.450	29	22	7	1	0	176²	161	11	90	67	13.0	3.67	129	.247	.342	6	.115	-1	19	21	-2	1.7
Yr	10	11	.476	32	22	7	1	0	180¹	168	11	92	70	13.2	3.79	125	.251	.346	6	.115	-1	17	19	-2	1.3
1940 Chi-A	14	9	.609	32	28	12	0	0	207¹	179	16	95	119	12.0	3.21	138	.228	.313	15	.217	2	27	28	-1	2.9
1941 Chi-A★	13	17	.433	34	33	21	1	1	263¹	243	13	114	111	12.4	3.18	129	.246	.328	19	.216	4	28	27	0	3.2
1942 Chi-A☆	7	20	.259	29	28	18	2	1	215	223	17	81	78	13.1	3.98	90	.269	.341	9	.123	-2	-8	-9	2	-1.0
1943 Chi-A	11	11	.500	25	25	14	2	0	187²	197	2	76	66	13.3	3.69	90	.277	.351	11	.159	-1	-8	-7	0	-0.9
1946 Chi-A	8	11	.421	24	21	3	1	1	145¹	135	9	60	59	12.3	2.85	120	.246	.325	8	.178	-1	11	9	-0	1.2
1947 Chi-A	1	3	.250	15	5	0	0	0	33¹	40	1	24	12	17.3	7.29	50	.299	.405	1	.167	-0	-13	-13	-1	-1.5
Bos-A	1	3	.250	8	3	0	0	0	17	18	3	18	15	19.1	7.41	52	.269	.424	1	.167	-0	-7	-7	-0	-1.3
Yr	2	6	.250	23	8	0	0	0	50¹	58	4	42	27	17.9	7.33	51	.289	.412	2	.167	-0	-20	-20	-1	-2.8
Total 10	73	113	.392	282	197	91	8	12	1595²	1554	106	739	694	13.1	3.82	108	.256	.340	100	.188	5	51	53	-3	5.1

● EDGAR SMITH Smith, Edgar Eugene b: 6/12/1862, Providence, R.I. d: 11/3/1892, Providence, R.I. BR/TR, 5'10", 160 lbs. Deb: 5/25/1883 ◆

1883 Phi-N	0	1	.000	1	1	1	0	0	7	18	1	3	2	27.0	15.43	20	.409	.447	3	.750	1	-10	-10	-0	-0.7
1884 Was-a	2	0	.000	3	2	2	0	0	22	27	0	5	4	13.5	4.91	62	.276	.317	5	.088	-1	-4	-5	-0	-0.4
1885 Pro-N	1	0	1.000	1	1	1	0	0	9	9	0	0	1	9.0	1.00	265	.273	.273	1	.250	0	1	0	0	0.0
1890 Cle-N	1	4	.200	6	6	5	0	0	44	42	1	10	11	10.8	4.30	83	.244	.290	7	.292	-1	-4	-3	2	0.0
Total 4	2	7	.222	11	10	8	0	0	82	96	1	18	18	12.7	5.05	65	.277	.316	18	.184	-1	-15	-16	1	-0.9

● ELMER SMITH Smith, Elmer Ellsworth b: 3/23/1868, Pittsburgh, Pa. d: 11/3/45, Pittsburgh, Pa. BL/TL, 5'11", 178 lbs. Deb: 9/10/1886 ◆

1886 Cin-a	4	4	.500	8	8	8	0	0	72²	57	1	44	40	12.9	3.72	95	.211	.328	8	.286	4	-2	-2	-2	0.0
1887 Cin-a	34	17	.667	52	52	49	3	0	447¹	400	5	126	176	**10.8**	**2.94**	**148**	**.230**	**.286**	47	.253	5	68	**70**	-5	6.0
1888 Cin-a	22	17	.564	40	40	37	5	0	348¹	309	1	89	154	10.8	2.74	116	.229	.286	29	.225	4	13	17	-5	1.4
1889 Cin-a	9	12	.429	29	22	16	0	0	203	253	11	101	104	16.0	4.88	80	.296	.375	23	.277	4	-23	-22	-4	-1.6
1892 Pit-N	6	7	.462	17	13	12	1	0	134	140	2	58	51	13.4	3.63	91	.258	.331	140	.274	6	-5	-5	-1	-0.1
1894 Pit-N	0	0	—	1	0	0	0	0	4	6	0	1	0	18.0	4.50	116	.333	.400	174	.356	0	0	0	0	0.0
1898 Cin-N	0	0	—	1	0	0	0	0	1	2	1	3	0	45.0	18.00	21	.400	.625	166	.342	0	-2	-2	0	0.0
Total 7	75	57	.568	149	136	122	9	0	1210¹	1167	21	422	525	12.1	3.35	113	.244	.311	1454	.310	25	48	58	-19	5.7

● BILL SMITH Smith, F. William b: 1863, New Orleans, La. TR, 5'8", 152 lbs. Deb: 7/6/1886

| 1886 Det-N | 5 | 4 | .556 | 9 | 9 | 9 | 0 | 0 | 77 | 81 | 0 | 30 | 36 | 13.0 | 4.09 | 81 | .259 | .324 | 7 | .184 | -1 | -7 | -7 | -1 | -0.8 |

● FRANK SMITH Smith, Frank Elmer "Nig" or "Piano Mover" (b: Frank Elmer Schmidt) b: 10/28/1879, Pittsburgh, Pa. d: 11/3/52, Pittsburgh, Pa. BR/TR, 5'10.5", 194 lbs. Deb: 4/22/04

1904 Chi-A	16	9	.640	26	23	22	4	0	202¹	157	0	58	107	10.1	2.09	117	.215	.284	18	.250	4	11	8	-2	1.3
1905 Chi-A	19	13	.594	39	31	27	4	0	291²	215	0	107	171	10.2	2.13	116	.208	.287	24	.226	7	17	11	0	2.0
1906 Chi-A	5	5	.500	20	13	8	1	1	122	124	3	57	53	12.2	3.39	75	.267	.327	12	.293	5	-10	-12	1	-0.3
1907 Chi-A	23	10	.697	41	37	29	3	0	310	280	3	111	139	11.4	2.47	97	.243	.311	18	.196	5	-3	-3	0	0.6
1908 Chi-A	16	17	.485	41	35	24	3	1	297²	213	2	73	129	8.7	2.03	114	.203	.256	20	.189	1	12	10	3	1.7
1909 Chi-A	25	17	.595	**51**	40	**37**	7	1	365	278	1	70	**177**	8.7	1.80	130	.216	.257	22	.173	6	27	22	10	**4.6**
1910 Chi-A	4	9	.308	19	15	9	7	1	128²	91	4	40	50	9.3	2.03	118	.204	.272	8	.186	2	-7	-7	-0	-0.7
Bos-A	1	2	.333	4	3	2	0	0	28	22	0	11	8	10.9	4.82	53	.234	.321	1	.111	-0	-7	-7	-0	-0.7
Yr	5	11	.313	23	18	11	3	0	156²	113	1	51	58	9.3	2.53	96	.208	.277	9	.173	2	-4	-4	-0	0.5
1911 Bos-A	0	0	—	1	1	0	0	0	2¹	6	0	3	1	34.7	15.43	21	.500	.600	—	—	-0	-3	-3	0	0.1
Cin-N	10	14	.417	34	18	10	0	1	176¹	198	1	55	67	13.1	3.98	83	.289	.345	12	.214	3	-11	-13	4	-0.9
1912 Cin-N	1	1	.500	7	3	1	0	0	22²	34	1	15	5	19.5	6.35	53	.370	.458	2	.250	-0	-8	-8	-1	-0.6
1914 Bal-F	10	8	.556	39	22	9	1	2	174²	180	8	47	83	11.7	2.99	101	.259	.306	12	.203	-0	-2	-3	0	0.3
1915 Bal-F	4	4	.500	17	9	2	0	0	88²	108	6	31	37	14.1	4.67	61	.312	.369	5	.172	-0	-19	-18	1	-1.4
Bro-F	5	2	.714	15	5	4	1	0	63	69	1	18	24	13.4	3.14	87	.290	.344	4	.200	-0	-3	-3	1	-0.2
Yr	9	6	.600	32	14	6	1	0	151²	177	7	49	61	13.4	4.04	70	.303	.357	9	.184	1	-22	-21	1	-1.6
Total 11	139	111	.556	354	255	184	27	6	2273	1975	27	676	1051	10.7	2.59	99	.237	.297	156	.204	35	15	-10	26	7.7

● FRANK SMITH Smith, Frank Thomas b: 4/4/28, Pierrepont Manor, N.Y. BR/TR, 6'3", 200 lbs. Deb: 4/18/50

| 1950 Cin-N | 2 | 7 | .222 | 38 | 4 | 0 | 0 | 3 | 90² | 73 | 12 | 39 | 55 | 11.9 | 3.87 | 109 | .216 | .312 | 2 | .095 | -2 | 3 | 4 | -1 | 0.1 |
| 1951 Cin-N | 5 | 5 | .500 | 50 | 0 | 0 | 0 | 11 | 76 | 65 | 7 | 22 | 34 | 10.8 | 3.20 | 128 | .230 | .295 | 0 | .000 | -1 | 6 | 7 | 0 | 1.1 |

YEAR TM/L	W	L	PCT	G	GS	CG	SH	SV	IP	H	HR	BB	SO	RAT	ERA	ERA+	OAV	OOB	BH	AVG	PB	PR	/A	PD	TPI
1952 Cin-N	12	11	.522	53	2	1	0	7	122^1	109	13	41	77	11.6	3.75	101	.242	.315	5	.172	0	-0	-0	-2	-0.1
1953 Cin-N	8	1	.889	50	1	0	0	2	83^2	89	15	25	42	12.6	5.49	79	.272	.330	2	.154	-1	-11	-11	1	-1.0
1954 Cin-N	5	8	.385	50	0	0	0	20	81	60	15	29	51	10.2	2.67	157	.211	.291	1	.100	-1	13	14	0	2.9
1955 StL-N	3	1	.750	28	0	0	0	1	39	27	3	23	17	12.7	3.23	126	.205	.344	0	.000	-1	3	4	-0	0.3
1956 Cin-N	0	0	—	2	0	0	0	0	3	3	2	2	1	15.0	12.00	33	.300	.417	0	—	0	-3	-3	0	0.0
Total 7	35	33	.515	271	7	1	0	44	495^2	426	67	181	277	11.6	3.81	107	.234	.313	10	.115	-3	11	16	-2	3.3

● **FRED SMITH** Smith, Frederick b: 11/24/1878, New Diggings, Wis. d: 2/4/64, Los Angeles, Cal. BL/TR, 6', 186 lbs. Deb: 6/14/07

YEAR TM/L	W	L	PCT	G	GS	CG	SH	SV	IP	H	HR	BB	SO	RAT	ERA	ERA+	OAV	OOB	BH	AVG	PB	PR	/A	PD	TPI
1907 Cin-N	2	7	.222	18	9	5	0	1	85^1	90	3	24	19	12.4	2.85	91	.274	.331	3	.107	-2	-4	-2	0	-0.4

● **FRED SMITH** Smith, Frederick C. b: 3/25/1863, Greene, N.Y. d: 1/9/41, Syracuse, N.Y. BL/TR, 5'11", 156 lbs. Deb: 4/18/1890

YEAR TM/L	W	L	PCT	G	GS	CG	SH	SV	IP	H	HR	BB	SO	RAT	ERA	ERA+	OAV	OOB	BH	AVG	PB	PR	/A	PD	TPI
1890 Tol-a	19	13	.594	35	34	31	2	0	286	273	13	90	116	11.8	3.27	121	.244	.307	21	.167	-2	19	22	3	2.0

● **GEORGE SMITH** Smith, George Allen "Columbia George" b: 5/31/1892, Byram, Conn. d: 1/7/65, Greenwich, Conn. BR/TR, 6'2", 163 lbs. Deb: 8/9/16

YEAR TM/L	W	L	PCT	G	GS	CG	SH	SV	IP	H	HR	BB	SO	RAT	ERA	ERA+	OAV	OOB	BH	AVG	PB	PR	/A	PD	TPI
1916 NY-N	3	0	1.000	9	1	0	0	0	20^2	14	0	6	9	9.1	2.61	93	.197	.269	0	.000		-0	-0	0	0.0
1917 NY-N	0	3	.000	14	1	1	0	0	38	38	1	11	16	11.8	2.84	90	.270	.327	0	.000	-1	-1	-1	-0	-0.2
1918 Cin-N	2	3	.400	10	6	4	1	0	55^1	71	3	11	19	13.3	4.07	66	.329	.361	0	.000	-2	-8	-9	1	-0.9
NY-N	2	3	.400	5	2	1	0	0	26^2	26	0	6	4	11.1	4.05	65	.255	.303	2	.250	-0	-4	-4	-1	-0.8
Bro-N	4	1	.800	8	5	4	0	0	50	43	0	5	18	9.0	2.34	119	.249	.278	3	.200	0	2	2	1	0.4
Yr	8	7	.533	23	13	9	1	0	132	140	3	22	41	11.2	3.41	79	.285	.318	5	.125	-2	-9	-10	-1	-1.3
1919 NY-N	0	2	.000	3	2	0	0	0	11	18	1	4	0	18.0	5.73	49	.383	.431	0	.000	-0	-3	-4	-0	-0.7
Phi-N	5	11	.313	31	19	11	1	0	184^2	194	7	46	42	11.8	3.22	100	.278	.326	8	.133	-3	-6	0	-1	-0.4
Yr	5	13	.278	34	21	11	1	0	195^2	212	8	50	42	12.2	3.36	95	.285	.332	8	.127	-4	-10	-3	-1	-1.1
1920 Phi-N	13	18	.419	43	28	10	1	2	250^2	265	10	51	51	11.6	3.45	99	.283	.324	7	.097	-6	-9	-1	-2	-0.9
1921 Phi-N	4	20	.167	39	28	12	1	1	221^1	303	12	52	45	14.6	4.76	89	.335	.373	4	.056	-8	-24	-13	-2	-2.1
1922 Phi-N	5	14	.263	42	16	6	1	0	194	250	16	35	44	13.5	4.78	98	.316	.350	5	.076	-7	-15	-2	-2	-1.0
1923 Bro-N	3	6	.333	25	7	3	0	1	91	99	4	28	15	12.9	3.66	106	.278	.336	5	.192	-1	3	2	-1	-0.1
Total 8	41	81	.336	229	115	52	5	4	1143^1	1321	54	255	263	12.6	3.89	94	.298	.340	34	.097	-29	-63	-31	-8	-6.7

● **HEINIE SMITH** Smith, George Henry b: 10/24/1871, Pittsburgh, Pa. d: 6/25/39, Buffalo, N.Y. BR/TR, 5'9.5", 160 lbs. Deb: 9/8/1897 M♦

YEAR TM/L	W	L	PCT	G	GS	CG	SH	SV	IP	H	HR	BB	SO	RAT	ERA	ERA+	OAV	OOB	BH	AVG	PB	PR	/A	PD	TPI
1901 NY-N	0	1	.000	2	1	1	0	0	13^1	24	0	5	5	21.6	8.10	41	.387	.457	6	.207	0	-7	-7	-0	-0.4

● **GERMANY SMITH** Smith, George J. b: 4/21/1863, Pittsburgh, Pa. d: 12/1/27, Altoona, Pa. BR/TR, 6', 175 lbs. Deb: 4/17/1884 ♦

YEAR TM/L	W	L	PCT	G	GS	CG	SH	SV	IP	H	HR	BB	SO	RAT	ERA	ERA+	OAV	OOB	BH	AVG	PB	PR	/A	PD	TPI
1884 Alt-U	0	0	—	1	0	0	0	0	1	3	0	0	1	27.0	9.00	30	.500	.500	34	.315	0	-1	-1	0	0.0

● **GEORGE SMITH** Smith, George Shelby b: 10/27/01, Louisville, Ky. d: 5/26/81, Richmond, Va. BR/TR, 6'1", 175 lbs. Deb: 4/21/26

YEAR TM/L	W	L	PCT	G	GS	CG	SH	SV	IP	H	HR	BB	SO	RAT	ERA	ERA+	OAV	OOB	BH	AVG	PB	PR	/A	PD	TPI
1926 Det-A	1	2	.333	23	1	0	0	0	44	55	3	33	15	18.4	6.95	68	.318	.433	0	.000	-0	-14	-14	-1	-0.9
1927 Det-A	4	1	.800	29	0	0	0	0	71^1	62	3	50	32	14.4	3.91	108	.240	.368	7	.368	3	2	2	-1	0.4
1928 Det-A	1	1	.500	39	2	0	0	3	106	103	3	50	54	13.0	4.42	93	.263	.346	3	.111	-2	-4	-4	-2	-0.5
1929 Det-A	3	2	.600	14	2	1	0	0	35^2	42	1	36	13	19.7	5.80	74	.307	.451	5	.417	2	-6	-6	-1	-0.4
1930 Bos-A	1	2	.333	27	2	0	0	0	73^2	92	4	49	21	17.3	6.60	70	.317	.418	8	.333	2	-16	-16	-0	-0.3
Total 5	10	8	.556	132	7	1	0	3	330^2	354	17	218	135	15.7	5.28	81	.283	.392	23	.264	4	-39	-38	-2	-1.7

● **HAL SMITH** Smith, Harold Laverne b: 6/30/02, Creston, Iowa d: 9/27/92, Ft.Lauderdale, Fla. BR/TR, 6'3", 195 lbs. Deb: 9/14/32

YEAR TM/L	W	L	PCT	G	GS	CG	SH	SV	IP	H	HR	BB	SO	RAT	ERA	ERA+	OAV	OOB	BH	AVG	PB	PR	/A	PD	TPI
1932 Pit-N	1	0	1.000	2	1	1	1	0	12	9	4	6	8	8.3	0.75	508	.209	.244	0	.000	-0	4	4	0	0.3
1933 Pit-N	8	7	.533	28	19	8	2	1	145	149	5	31	40	11.5	2.86	116	.261	.305	6	.128	-2	8	7	-2	0.4
1934 Pit-N	3	4	.429	20	5	1	0	0	50	72	3	18	15	16.9	7.20	57	.343	.405	1	.059	-2	-17	-17	-0	-2.2
1935 Pit-N	0	0	—	1	0	0	0	0	3	2	0	1	0	9.0	3.00	137	.200	.273	0	.000	-0	0	0	0	0.0
Total 4	12	11	.522	51	25	10	3	1	210	232	8	52	59	12.6	3.77	94	.279	.328	7	.104	-4	-5	-5	-2	-1.5

● **HARRY SMITH** Smith, Harrison Morton b: 8/15/1889, Union, Neb. d: 7/26/64, Dunbar, Neb. BR/TR, 5'9", 160 lbs. Deb: 10/6/12

YEAR TM/L	W	L	PCT	G	GS	CG	SH	SV	IP	H	HR	BB	SO	RAT	ERA	ERA+	OAV	OOB	BH	AVG	PB	PR	/A	PD	TPI
1912 Chi-A	1	0	1.000	1	1	0	0	0	5	6	0	0	1	10.8	1.80	178	.333	.333	0	.000	-0	1	1	-0	0.1

● **JACK SMITH** Smith, Jack Hatfield b: 11/15/35, Pikeville, Ky. BR/TR, 6', 185 lbs. Deb: 9/10/62

YEAR TM/L	W	L	PCT	G	GS	CG	SH	SV	IP	H	HR	BB	SO	RAT	ERA	ERA+	OAV	OOB	BH	AVG	PB	PR	/A	PD	TPI
1962 LA-N	0	0	—	8	0	0	0	1	10	10	0	4	7	12.6	4.50	81	.263	.333	0	.000	-0	-1	-1	-0	-0.1
1963 LA-N	0	0	—	4	0	0	0	0	8^1	10	2	3	4	15.1	7.56	40	.303	.378	0	.000	-0	-4	-4	0	0.0
1964 Mil-N	2	2	.500	22	0	0	0	1	31	28	3	11	19	11.3	3.77	93	.237	.302	1	.333	-1	-1	-1	0	0.0
Total 3	2	2	.500	34	0	0	0	1	49^1	48	5	17	31	12.2	4.56	76	.254	.322	1	.167	-0	-5	-6	1	-0.1

● **JAKE SMITH** Smith, Jacob (b: Jacob Schmidt) b: 6/10/1887, Dravosburg, Pa d: 11/7/48, E.McKeesport, Pa. BB/TL, 6'5", 200 lbs. Deb: 10/3/11

YEAR TM/L	W	L	PCT	G	GS	CG	SH	SV	IP	H	HR	BB	SO	RAT	ERA	ERA+	OAV	OOB	BH	AVG	PB	PR	/A	PD	TPI
1911 Phi-N	0	0	—	2	0	0	0	0	5	3	0	2	1	9.0	0.00	—	.176	.263	0	.000	-0	2	2	0	0.0

● **PHENOMENAL SMITH** Smith, John Francis (b: John Francis Gammon)
b: 12/12/1864, Philadelphia, Pa. d: 4/3/52, Manchester, N.H. BL/TL, 5'6.5", 161 lbs. Deb: 4/18/1884

YEAR TM/L	W	L	PCT	G	GS	CG	SH	SV	IP	H	HR	BB	SO	RAT	ERA	ERA+	OAV	OOB	BH	AVG	PB	PR	/A	PD	TPI
1884 Bal-U	3	4	.429	9	8	5	0	0	62	86	2	17	13	15.0	3.48	77	.308	.348	5	.147	-4	-7	-6	-1	-0.9
Phi-a	0	1	.000	1	1	1	0	0	9	14	0	1	3	15.0	4.00	85	.368	.385	1	.250	-0	-1	-1	0	0.0
Pit-a	0	1	.000	1	1	0	0	0	8	11	0	2	4	15.8	9.00	37	.306	.359	0	.000	-0	-5	-5	0	-0.5
Yr	0	2	.000	2	2	1	0	0	17	25	0	3	7	15.4	6.35	53	.338	.372	1	.125	-1	-6	-6	0	-0.5
1885 Bro-a	0	1	.000	1	1	1	0	0	8	12	0	6	2	21.4	12.38	27	.300	.404	1	.333	0	-8	-8	-0	-0.6
Phi-a	0	1	.000	1	1	0	0	0	4	7	0	4	8	27.0	9.00	38	.368	.500	0	.000	-0	-3	-2	-0	-0.4
Yr	0	2	.000	2	2	1	0	0	12	19	0	10	9	22.5	11.25	30	.317	.423	1	.200	-0	-11	-11	-0	-1.0
1886 Det-N	1	1	.500	3	3	3	0	0	25	16	0	8	15	8.6	2.16	153	.174	.240	1	.111	-1	3	3	-1	0.1
1887 Bal-a	25	30	.455	58	55	54	1	0	491^1	526	7	176	206	13.1	3.79	108	.261	.325	48	.234	-8	28	17	-1	2.0
1888 Bal-a	14	19	.424	35	32	31	0	0	292	249	5	137	152	12.6	3.61	83	.222	.320	27	.248	-8	-18	-20	-4	-1.5
Phi-a	2	1	.667	3	3	3	0	0	22	21	0	10	19	12.7	2.86	104	.241	.320	3	.333	-1	0	0	-0	0.1
Yr	16	20	.444	38	35	34	0	0	314	270	5	147	171	12.0	3.55	84	.219	.303	30	.254	-9	-18	-20	-1	-1.4
1889 Phi-a	3	4	.429	5	5	5	0	0	43	53	2	25	12	17.0	4.40	86	.294	.389	1	.188	-0	-3	-3	-1	-0.3
1890 Phi-N	8	12	.400	24	20	19	1	0	204	209	6	89	81	13.5	4.28	85	.257	.336	24	.279	4	-16	-14	-2	-0.9
Pit-N	1	3	.250	5	5	5	0	0	44	39	0	13	15	10.8	3.07	107	.231	.290	7	.412	2	2	1	-0	0.3
Yr	9	15	.375	29	25	24	1	0	248	248	6	102	96	12.7	4.06	88	.251	.321	31	.301	6	-14	-13	-3	-0.6
1891 Phi-N	1	1	.500	3	2	0	0	0	19	20	1	8	3	13.3	4.26	80	.260	.329	3	.375	1	-2	-2	-1	-0.1
Total 8	57	78	.422	149	137	128	3	0	1231^1	1263	22	496	532	13.2	3.87	93	.254	.329	123	.243	19	-28	-38	-10	-2.7

● **CHICK SMITH** Smith, John William (b: Jan Smadt) b: 12/2/1892, Dayton, Ky. d: 10/11/35, Dayton, Ky. BL/TL, 5'8", 165 lbs. Deb: 4/12/13

YEAR TM/L	W	L	PCT	G	GS	CG	SH	SV	IP	H	HR	BB	SO	RAT	ERA	ERA+	OAV	OOB	BH	AVG	PB	PR	/A	PD	TPI
1913 Cin-N	0	1	.000						17^2	15	1	11	11	13.2	3.57	91	.238	.351	0	.000	-0	-1	-1	0	-0.1

● **LEE SMITH** Smith, Lee Arthur b: 12/4/57, Shreveport, La. BR/TR, 6'6", 225 lbs. Deb: 9/1/80

YEAR TM/L	W	L	PCT	G	GS	CG	SH	SV	IP	H	HR	BB	SO	RAT	ERA	ERA+	OAV	OOB	BH	AVG	PB	PR	/A	PD	TPI
1980 Chi-N	2	0	1.000	18	0	0	0	0	21^2	21	0	14	17	14.5	2.91	135	.259	.368	0	—	0	2	2	-0	0.2
1981 Chi-N	3	6	.333	40	1	0	0	0	66^2	57	2	31	50	12.0	3.51	105	.239	.330	0	.000	-1	-0	1	-0	0.0
1982 Chi-N	2	5	.286	72	5	0	0	0	117	105	5	37	99	11.2	2.69	139	.245	.309	1	.063	-0	12	14	-1	1.1
1983 Chi-N★	4	10	.286	66	0	0	0	29	103^1	70	5	41	91	9.8	1.65	229	.194	.279	1	.111	-1	23	25	-1	4.6
1984 *Chi-N	9	7	.563	69	0	0	0	33	101	98	6	35	86	11.9	3.65	107	.255	.317	1	.077	-1	-1	3	0	0.5
1985 Chi-N	7	4	.636	65	0	0	0	33	97^2	87	5	32	112	11.1	3.04	131	.242	.305	0	.000	-0	6	10	-1	1.7
1986 Chi-N	9	9	.500	66	0	0	0	31	90^1	69	7	42	93	11.1	3.09	131	.215	.306	1	.000	-0	6	10	0	2.4
1987 Chi-N★	4	10	.286	62	0	0	0	36	83^2	84	7	32	96	12.5	3.12	137	.259	.326	9	.265	-1	9	11	-1	2.4
1988 *Bos-A	4	5	.444	64	0	0	0	29	83^2	72	7	37	96	11.0	2.80	147	.225	.307	0	—	0	11	12	-1	1.9
1989 Bos-A	6	1	.857	64	0	0	0	25	70^2	53	6	33	96	11.0	3.57	115	.209	.301	0	.000	-0	2	4	-0	0.2
1990 Bos-A	2	1	.667	11	0	0	0	4	14^1	13	0	9	17	13.8	1.88	216	.236	.344	0	.000	-0	3	3	0	0.8
StL-N	3	4	.429	53	0	0	0	27	68^2	58	9	20	70	10.2	2.10	182	.227	.284	0	—	0	13	13	-2	2.1
1991 StL-N☆	6	3	.667	67	0	0	0	47	73	70	5	13	67	10.2	2.34	159	.249	.284	0	.000	0	11	11	-1	2.5
1992 StL-N☆	4	9	.308	70	0	0	0	43	75	62	9	26	60	10.6	3.12	109	.221	.287	1	.333	-0	2	2	-1	0.5
1993 StL-N☆	2	4	.333	55	0	0	0	43	50	49	11	9	49	10.4	4.50	88	.251	.284	0	—	0	-3	-1	-0	-0.9

YEAR	TM/L	W	L	PCT	G	GS	CG	SH	SV	IP	H	HR	BB	SO	RAT	ERA	ERA+	OAV	OOB	BH	AVG	PB	PR	/A	PD	TPI
	NY-A	0	0	—	8	0	0	0	3	8	4	0	5	11	10.1	0.00	—	.148	.281	0	—	0	4	4	0	0.2
1994	Bal-A★	1	4	.200	41	0	0	0	**33**	38¹	34	6	11	42	10.6	3.29	152	.239	.294	0	—	0	6	7	-1	1.9
1995	Cal-A☆	0	5	.000	52	0	0	0	37	49¹	42	3	25	43	12.4	3.47	135	.237	.335	0	—	0	7	7	-1	1.4
1996	Cal-A	0	0	—	11	0	0	0	0	11	8	0	3	6	9.0	2.45	199	.205	.262	0	—	0	3	3	-0	0.0
	Cin-N	3	4	.429	43	0	0	0	0	44¹	49	4	23	35	14.8	4.06	102	.277	.363	0	—	0	1	0	0	0.0
Total 17		71	91	.438	997	6	0	0	473	1267²	1105	87	478	1236	11.3	2.98	133	.235	.307	3	.047	-4	118	141	-11	23.5

● **ROY SMITH**   Smith, Le Roy Purdy   b: 9/6/61, Mt.Vernon, N.Y.   BR/TR, 6'3", 200 lbs.   Deb: 6/23/84

YEAR	TM/L	W	L	PCT	G	GS	CG	SH	SV	IP	H	HR	BB	SO	RAT	ERA	ERA+	OAV	OOB	BH	AVG	PB	PR	/A	PD	TPI
1984	Cle-A	5	5	.500	22	14	0	0	0	86¹	91	14	40	55	13.8	4.59	89	.270	.349	0	—	0	-6	-5	-2	-0.7
1985	Cle-A	1	4	.200	12	11	1	0	0	62¹	84	8	17	28	14.7	5.34	77	.321	.364	0	—	0	-8	-8	-1	-0.6
1986	Min-A	0	2	.000	5	0	0	0	0	10¹	13	1	5	8	16.5	6.97	62	.295	.380	0	—	0	-3	-3	-0	-0.6
1987	Min-A	1	0	1.000	5	0	0	0	0	16¹	20	3	1	8	15.4	4.96	93	.290	.364	0	—	0	-1	-1	-0	-0.1
1988	Min-A	3	0	1.000	9	4	0	0	0	37	29	3	12	17	10.2	2.68	152	.210	.278	0	—	0	5	6	-1	0.4
1989	Min-A	10	6	.625	32	26	2	0	1	172¹	180	22	51	92	12.3	3.92	106	.269	.326	0	—	0	-1	4	-3	-0.2
1990	Min-A	5	10	.333	32	23	1	1	0	153¹	191	24	47	87	14.0	4.81	86	.313	.362	0	—	0	-15	-11	-2	-1.3
1991	Bal-A	5	4	.556	17	14	0	0	0	80¹	99	9	24	25	13.9	5.60	71	.311	.362	0	—	0	-13	-15	-1	-1.3
Total 8		30	31	.492	136	93	4	1	1	618¹	707	80	202	320	13.4	4.60	90	.289	.346	0	—	0	-42	-33	-9	-4.4

● **MARK SMITH**   Smith, Mark Christopher   b: 11/23/55, Arlington, Va.   BR/TR, 6'2", 215 lbs.   Deb: 8/12/83

YEAR	TM/L	W	L	PCT	G	GS	CG	SH	SV	IP	H	HR	BB	SO	RAT	ERA	ERA+	OAV	OOB	BH	AVG	PB	PR	/A	PD	TPI
1983	Oak-A	1	0	1.000	8	1	0	0	0	14²	24	0	6	10	19.0	6.75	57	.387	.449	0	—	0	-4	-5	-0	0.0

● **MIKE SMITH**   Smith, Michael Anthony   b: 2/23/61, Jackson, Miss.   BR/TR, 6'1", 195 lbs.   Deb: 4/6/84

YEAR	TM/L	W	L	PCT	G	GS	CG	SH	SV	IP	H	HR	BB	SO	RAT	ERA	ERA+	OAV	OOB	BH	AVG	PB	PR	/A	PD	TPI
1984	Cin-N	1	0	1.000	8	0	0	0	0	10¹	12	1	5	7	14.8	5.23	72	.286	.362	0	—	0	-2	-2	-0	-0.2
1985	Cin-N	0	0	—	2	0	0	0	0	3¹	2	1	2	8	8.1	5.40	70	.167	.231	0	—	0	-1	-1	-0	0.0
1986	Cin-N	0	0	—	2	1	0	0	0	3¹	7	0	1	1	21.6	13.50	29	.412	.444	0	—	0	-4	-4	-0	-0.4
1988	Mon-N	0	0	—	5	0	0	0	0	8²	6	0	5	4	11.4	3.12	115	.207	.324	0	—	0	0	0	0	0.0
1989	Pit-N	0	1	.000	16	0	0	0	1	24	28	1	10	12	14.3	3.75	89	.301	.369	0	.000	-0	-1	-1	1	0.0
Total 5		1	1	.500	33	1	0	0	1	49²	55	4	22	26	14.0	4.71	75	.285	.358	0	.000	-1	-7	-6	0	-0.2

● **MIKE SMITH**   Smith, Michael Anthony   b: 10/31/63, San Antonio, Tex.   BR/TR, 6'3", 180 lbs.   Deb: 6/30/89

YEAR	TM/L	W	L	PCT	G	GS	CG	SH	SV	IP	H	HR	BB	SO	RAT	ERA	ERA+	OAV	OOB	BH	AVG	PB	PR	/A	PD	TPI
1989	Bal-A	2	0	1.000	13	1	0	0	0	20	25	3	14	12	17.5	7.65	50	.313	.415	0	—	0	-8	-9	-0	-0.6
1990	Bal-A	0	0	—	2	0	0	0	0	3	4	2	1	2	15.0	12.00	32	.308	.357	0	—	0	-3	-3	-0	0.0
Total 2		2	0	1.000	15	1	0	0	0	23	29	5	15	14	17.2	8.22	46	.312	.407	0	—	0	-11	-11	-0	-0.6

● **PETE SMITH**   Smith, Peter John   b: 2/27/66, Abington, Mass.   BR/TR, 6'3", 200 lbs.   Deb: 9/8/87

YEAR	TM/L	W	L	PCT	G	GS	CG	SH	SV	IP	H	HR	BB	SO	RAT	ERA	ERA+	OAV	OOB	BH	AVG	PB	PR	/A	PD	TPI
1987	Atl-N	1	2	.333	6	6	0	0	0	31²	39	3	14	11	15.1	4.83	90	.307	.376	1	.091	-1	-3	-2	-1	-0.3
1988	Atl-N	7	15	.318	32	32	5	3	0	195¹	183	15	88	124	12.5	3.69	100	.250	.331	6	.113	-1	-5	-0	-3	-0.4
1989	Atl-N	5	14	.263	28	27	1	0	0	142	144	13	57	115	12.7	4.75	77	.263	.333	4	.098	-0	-20	-17	-1	-2.3
1990	Atl-N	5	6	.455	13	13	3	0	0	77	77	11	24	56	11.8	4.79	84	.260	.316	2	.087	-1	-9	-6	-1	-1.0
1991	Atl-N	1	3	.250	14	10	0	0	0	48	48	5	22	29	13.1	5.06	77	.262	.341	2	.167	-1	-7	-6	1	-0.4
1992	*Atl-N	7	0	1.000	12	11	2	1	0	79	63	3	28	43	10.4	2.05	178	.217	.286	1	.038	-1	13	14	-0	1.1
1993	Atl-N	4	8	.333	20	14	0	0	0	90²	92	15	36	53	12.9	4.37	92	.270	.343	6	.222	-1	-3	-4	-0	-0.3
1994	NY-N	4	10	.286	21	21	1	0	0	131¹	145	25	42	62	13.0	5.55	75	.285	.342	5	.135	0	-20	-20	1	-1.7
1995	Cin-N	1	2	.333	11	2	0	0	0	24¹	30	8	7	14	14.1	6.66	62	.319	.373	0	.000	0	-7	-7	0	-0.7
Total 9		35	60	.368	157	136	12	4	0	819¹	821	98	318	507	12.6	4.40	88	.263	.333	27	.116	-3	-60	-48	-4	-6.0

● **PETE SMITH**   Smith, Peter Luke   b: 3/19/40, Natick, Mass.   BR/TR, 6'2", 190 lbs.   Deb: 9/13/62

YEAR	TM/L	W	L	PCT	G	GS	CG	SH	SV	IP	H	HR	BB	SO	RAT	ERA	ERA+	OAV	OOB	BH	AVG	PB	PR	/A	PD	TPI
1962	Bos-A	0	1	.000	1	1	0	0	0	3²	7	3	2	1	22.1	19.64	21	.438	.500	0	.000	-0	-6	-6	0	-0.9
1963	Bos-A	0	0	—	6	1	0	0	0	15	11	2	6	6	10.2	3.60	105	.212	.293	0	.000	0	0	0	0	0.0
Total 2		0	1	.000	7	2	0	0	0	18²	18	5	8	7	12.5	6.75	57	.265	.342	0	.000	-0	-6	-6	0	-0.9

● **REX SMITH**   Smith, Rex (b: Henry W. Schmidt)   b: 1864, Louisville, Ky.   d: 6/21/1895, Louisville, Ky.   Deb: 7/11/1886

YEAR	TM/L	W	L	PCT	G	GS	CG	SH	SV	IP	H	HR	BB	SO	RAT	ERA	ERA+	OAV	OOB	BH	AVG	PB	PR	/A	PD	TPI
1886	Phi-a	0	1	.000	1	1	1	0	0	9	15	0	5	4	20.0	7.00	50	.385	.455	0	.000	-1	-4	-3	-0	-0.3

● **ED SMITH**   Smith, Rhesa Edward   b: 2/21/1879, Mentone, Ind.   d: 3/20/55, Tarpon Springs, Fla.   BR/TR, 5'11", 170 lbs.   Deb: 4/27/06

YEAR	TM/L	W	L	PCT	G	GS	CG	SH	SV	IP	H	HR	BB	SO	RAT	ERA	ERA+	OAV	OOB	BH	AVG	PB	PR	/A	PD	TPI
1906	StL-A	8	11	.421	19	18	13	0	0	154²	153	3	53	45	12.5	3.72	69	.261	.331	11	.204	2	-18	-20	1	-1.9

● **BOB SMITH**   Smith, Robert Ashley (a.k.a. Robert M. Brown in 1914)   b: 7/20/1890, Woodbury, Vt.   d: 12/27/65, West Los Angeles, Cal.   BR/TR, 5'11", 160 lbs.   Deb: 4/19/13

YEAR	TM/L	W	L	PCT	G	GS	CG	SH	SV	IP	H	HR	BB	SO	RAT	ERA	ERA+	OAV	OOB	BH	AVG	PB	PR	/A	PD	TPI
1913	Chi-A	0	0	—	1	0	0	0	0	2	3	0	1	3	27.0	13.50	22	.273	.429	0	—	0	-2	-2	-0	0.0
1914	Buf-F	0	0	—	15	1	0	0	3	36²	39	3	16	13	14.0	3.44	86	.281	.363	2	.222	0	-2	-2	1	0.1
1915	Buf-F	0	0	—	1	0	0	0	0	1	1	0	2	0	36.0	18.00	16	.333	.667	0	—	0	-2	-2	-0	0.0
Total 3		0	0	—	17	1	0	0	3	39²	43	3	21	14	15.2	4.31	69	.281	.379	2	.222	0	-6	-6	1	0.1

● **BOB SMITH**   Smith, Robert Eldridge   b: 4/22/1895, Rogersville, Tenn.   d: 7/19/87, Waycross, Ga.   BR/TR, 5'10", 175 lbs.   Deb: 4/19/23 ♦

YEAR	TM/L	W	L	PCT	G	GS	CG	SH	SV	IP	H	HR	BB	SO	RAT	ERA	ERA+	OAV	OOB	BH	AVG	PB	PR	/A	PD	TPI
1925	Bos-N	5	3	.625	13	10	6	0	0	92²	110	6	36	19	14.2	4.47	90	.304	.367	49	.282	3	-2	-5	-0	-0.1
1926	Bos-N	10	13	.435	33	23	14	4	1	201¹	199	10	75	44	12.2	3.75	94	.269	.336	25	.298	7	2	-5	2	0.5
1927	Bos-N	10	18	.357	41	32	16	1	3	260²	297	9	75	81	12.9	3.76	99	.301	.351	27	.248	4	4	-1	2	0.6
1928	Bos-N	13	17	.433	38	25	14	0	2	244¹	274	6	74	59	12.9	3.87	101	.289	.342	23	.250	3	3	-0	1	0.7
1929	Bos-N	11	17	.393	34	29	19	1	3	231	256	20	71	65	12.8	4.68	100	.285	.338	17	.172	-1	1	0	1	0.1
1930	Bos-N	10	14	.417	38	24	14	2	5	219²	247	25	85	84	13.7	4.26	116	.290	.357	19	.235	-1	17	16	2	1.6
1931	Chi-N	15	12	.556	36	29	18	2	2	240¹	239	10	62	63	11.3	3.22	120	.256	.303	19	.218	2	17	17	1	2.0
1932	*Chi-N	4	3	.571	34	11	4	1	2	119	148	4	36	35	14.1	4.61	82	.303	.355	10	.238	2	-10	-11	1	-0.4
1933	Cin-N	4	4	.500	16	6	4	0	0	73²	75	3	11	18	10.5	2.20	154	.260	.287	5	.200	0	10	10	0	1.0
	Bos-N	4	3	.571	14	4	3	1	1	58²	68	3	7	17	11.5	3.22	95	.296	.316	4	.200	1	-1	-1	0	0.0
	Yr	8	7	.533	30	10	7	1	1	132¹	143	6	18	35	10.9	2.65	123	.276	.300	9	.200	1	10	9	1	1.0
1934	Bos-N	6	9	.400	39	5	3	0	5	121²	133	9	36	26	12.5	4.66	82	.277	.328	5	.250	1	-8	-11	1	-1.1
1935	Bos-N	8	18	.308	46	20	8	1	0	203¹	232	13	61	38	13.1	3.94	96	.285	.337	17	.270	2	-2	-3	-1	-0.2
1936	Bos-N	6	7	.462	35	11	5	2	8	136	142	3	35	36	11.8	3.77	102	.264	.311	10	.222	0	4	1	0	0.2
1937	Bos-N	0	1	.000	18	0	0	0	1	35	42	1	14	12	12.3	4.09	88	.295	.326	2	.200	0	-1	-2	-1	-0.1
Total 13		106	139	.433	435	229	128	16	40	2246¹	2472	132	670	618	12.7	3.94	100	.283	.335	409	.242	23	40	4	12	4.8

● **BOB SMITH**   Smith, Robert Gilchrist   b: 2/1/31, Woodsville, N.H.   BR/TL, 6'1.5", 190 lbs.   Deb: 4/29/55

YEAR	TM/L	W	L	PCT	G	GS	CG	SH	SV	IP	H	HR	BB	SO	RAT	ERA	ERA+	OAV	OOB	BH	AVG	PB	PR	/A	PD	TPI
1955	Bos-A	0	0	—	1	0	0	0	0	1²	1	0	1	1	10.8	0.00	—	.200	.333	0	—	0	1	1	-0	0.0
1957	StL-N	0	0	—	6	0	0	0	1	9	12	0	6	13	17.7	4.66	85	.267	.365	0	.000	-0	-1	-1	0	0.0
	Pit-N	2	4	.333	20	4	2	0	0	55	48	2	25	33	12.1	3.11	122	.229	.314	1	.077	-1	5	4	-1	0.2
	Yr	2	4	.333	26	4	2	0	1	64²	60	2	31	46	12.8	3.34	114	.234	.319	1	.067	-1	4	3	-1	0.2
1958	Pit-N	2	2	.500	35	4	0	0	1	61	61	6	31	24	13.9	4.43	87	.262	.353	1	.091	-1	-3	-4	-1	-0.2
1959	Pit-N	0	0	—	18	0	0	0	0	28¹	32	1	17	22	15.6	3.49	111	.291	.386	0	.000	-0	1	1	-0	-0.1
	Det-A	0	0	.000	11	0	0	0	0	11	20	3	4	4	18.8	8.18	50	.417	.451	0	—	-0	-5	-5	0	-1.2
Total 4		4	9	.308	91	6	2	0	2	166²	174	14	83	93	14.1	4.05	95	.267	.354	2	.069	-2	-3	-3	-0	-1.3

● **BOB SMITH**   Smith, Robert Walkay "Riverboat"   b: 5/13/28, Clarence, Mo.   BL/TL, 6', 185 lbs.   Deb: 4/22/58

YEAR	TM/L	W	L	PCT	G	GS	CG	SH	SV	IP	H	HR	BB	SO	RAT	ERA	ERA+	OAV	OOB	BH	AVG	PB	PR	/A	PD	TPI
1958	Bos-A	4	3	.571	17	7	1	0	0	66²	61	4	45	43	14.3	3.78	106	.248	.364	2	.105	-1	-0	2	1	0.1
1959	Chi-N	0	0	—	1	0	0	0	0	0²	3	1	2	0	94.5	81.00	5	.833	.875	0	—	-0	-6	-6	0	0.0
	Cle-A	0	1	.000	12	3	0	0	0	29¹	31	2	12	17	13.2	5.22	71	.282	.352	0	.000	-1	-4	-5	-0	-0.2
Total 2		4	4	.500	30	10	1	0	0	96²	97	6	59	60	14.5	4.75	82	.268	.371	2	.080	-2	-10	-9	-1	-0.1

● **RUFUS SMITH**   Smith, Rufus Frazier "Shirt"   b: 1/24/05, Guilford College, N.C.   d: 8/21/84, Aiken, S.C.   BR/TL, 5'8", 165 lbs.   Deb: 10/2/27

YEAR	TM/L	W	L	PCT	G	GS	CG	SH	SV	IP	H	HR	BB	SO	RAT	ERA	ERA+	OAV	OOB	BH	AVG	PB	PR	/A	PD	TPI
1927	Det-A	0	0	—	1	1	0	0	0	8	9	0	3	2	13.5	3.38	125	.242	.324	0	.000	1	1	-0	-1	-0.1

● **SHERRY SMITH**   Smith, Sherrod Malone   b: 2/18/1891, Monticello, Ga.   d: 9/12/49, Reidsville, Ga.   BR/TL, 6'1", 170 lbs.   Deb: 5/11/11

YEAR	TM/L	W	L	PCT	G	GS	CG	SH	SV	IP	H	HR	BB	SO	RAT	ERA	ERA+	OAV	OOB	BH	AVG	PB	PR	/A	PD	TPI
1911	Pit-N	0	0	—	1	0	0	0	0	0²	4	0	1	0	67.5	54.00	6	.667	.714	0	—	0	-4	-4	-0	0.0

YEAR TM/L	W	L	PCT	G	GS	CG	SH	SV	IP	H	HR	BB	SO	RAT	ERA	ERA+	OAV	OOB	BH	AVG	PB	PR	/A	PD	TPI
1912 Pit-N	0	0	—	3	0	0	0	1	4	6	0	1	3	15.8	6.75	48	.600	.636	0	—		-1	-2	-0	-0.1
1915 Bro-N	14	8	.636	29	20	11	2	2	173⅔	169	3	42	52	11.2	2.59	107	.264	.315	14	.246	3	3	4	-0	0.7
1916 *Bro-N	14	10	.583	36	25	15	4	1	219	193	5	45	67	9.9	2.34	114	.239	.282	21	.273	5	7	8	0	1.6
1917 Bro-N	12	12	.500	38	23	15	0	3	211⅓	210	5	51	58	11.2	3.32	84	.265	.311	15	.195	2	-14	-12	3	-0.8
1919 Bro-N	7	12	.368	30	19	13	2	1	173	181	3	29	40	11.1	2.24	133	.278	.313	8	.148	-2	13	14	3	1.7
1920 *Bro-N	11	9	.550	33	13	6	2	3	136⅓	134	1	27	33	10.8	1.85	173	.264	.304	10	.233	2	19	21	5	4.0
1921 Bro-N	7	11	.389	35	17	9	0	4	175⅓	232	4	34	36	13.7	3.90	100	.319	.350	13	.228	1	-2	-0	5	0.5
1922 Bro-N	8	8	.333	28	8	3	1	2	108⅔	128	6	35	15	14.1	4.56	89	.309	.373	9	.257	2	-5	-6	1	-0.3
Cle-A	1	0	1.000	2	2	1	0	0	15⅔	18	0	3	4	12.1	3.45	116	.295	.328	2	.333	1	1	1	0	0.1
1923 Cle-A	9	6	.600	30	16	10	1	1	124	129	4	37	23	12.2	3.27	121	.269	.324	11	.244	1	10	10	2	1.3
1924 Cle-A	12	14	.462	39	27	20	2	1	247⅔	267	5	42	34	11.5	3.02	142	.277	.312	18	.202	-1	33	35	3	3.4
1925 Cle-A	11	14	.440	31	30	**22**	1	1	237	296	11	48	30	13.3	4.86	91	.306	.342	28	.304	7	-12	-12	-0	-0.4
1926 Cle-A	11	10	.524	27	24	16	1	0	188⅓	214	8	31	25	11.9	3.73	109	.292	.324	14	.215	2	6	7	3	1.2
1927 Cle-A	1	4	.200	11	2	1	0	1	38	53	1	14	8	15.9	5.45	77	.342	.396	2	.167	-0	-6	-5	-0	-0.6
Total 14	114	118	.491	373	226	142	16	21	2052⅔	2234	57	440	428	11.9	3.32	108	.282	.324	165	.233	22	48	59	26	12.3

● **TOM SMITH**   Smith, Thomas Edward   b: 12/5/1871, Boston, Mass.   d: 3/2/29, Dorchester, Mass.   BR/TR, 5'7.5", 165 lbs.   Deb: 6/6/1894

YEAR TM/L	W	L	PCT	G	GS	CG	SH	SV	IP	H	HR	BB	SO	RAT	ERA	ERA+	OAV	OOB	BH	AVG	PB	PR	/A	PD	TPI
1894 Bos-N	0	0	—	2	0	0	0	1	4	6	2	6	2	27.0	15.00	38	.320	.514	0	.000	-0	-6	-6	-0	-0.2
1895 Phi-N	2	3	.400	11	7	4	0	0	68	76	1	53	21	18.0	6.88	70	.278	.408	8	.242	-0	-16	-16	-1	-0.9
1896 Lou-N	2	3	.400	11	5	4	0	0	55	73	2	25	14	16.7	5.40	80	.316	.392	8	.205	-0	-6	-7	1	-0.4
1898 StL-N	0	1	.000	1	1	1	0	0	9	9	0	5	1	16.0	2.00	189	.257	.381	1	.500	1	2	2	0	0.3
Total 4	4	7	.364	25	13	9	0	1	138	166	5	89	38	17.7	6.33	72	.294	.406	17	.224	-0	-27	-27	-0	-1.2

● **BILL SMITH**   Smith, William Garland   b: 6/8/34, Washington, D.C.   BL/TL, 6', 190 lbs.   Deb: 9/13/58

YEAR TM/L	W	L	PCT	G	GS	CG	SH	SV	IP	H	HR	BB	SO	RAT	ERA	ERA+	OAV	OOB	BH	AVG	PB	PR	/A	PD	TPI
1958 StL-N	0	1	.000	2	1	0	0	0	9⅔	12	0	4	4	14.9	6.52	63	.324	.390	0	.000	-0	-3	-3	0	-0.2
1959 StL-N	0	0	—	6	0	0	0	1	8⅓	11	0	3	4	15.1	1.08	393	.333	.389	0	.000	-0	3	3	0	0.1
1962 Phi-N	1	5	.167	24	5	0	0	0	50⅓	59	8	10	26	12.5	4.29	90	.295	.332	2	.182	-1	-2	-2	-0	-0.2
Total 3	1	6	.143	32	6	0	0	1	68⅓	82	8	17	34	13.2	4.21	94	.304	.347	2	.143	-0	-2	-2	-0	-0.3

● **WILLIE SMITH**   Smith, Willie   b: 2/11/39, Anniston, Ala.   BL/TL, 6', 190 lbs.   Deb: 6/18/63   ♦

YEAR TM/L	W	L	PCT	G	GS	CG	SH	SV	IP	H	HR	BB	SO	RAT	ERA	ERA+	OAV	OOB	BH	AVG	PB	PR	/A	PD	TPI
1963 Det-A	1	0	1.000	11	2	0	0	0	21⅔	24	2	13	16	15.4	4.57	82	.300	.398	1	.125	-0	-2	-2	-0	-0.2
1964 LA-A	1	4	.200	15	1	0	0	0	31⅔	34	5	10	20	12.8	2.84	116	.293	.354	108	.301	6	3	2	0	0.5
1968 Cle-A	0	0	—	2	0	0	0	0	5	2	0	1	1	5.4	0.00	—	.125	.176	6	.143	0	2	2	0	0.0
Chi-N	0	0	—	1	0	0	0	0	2⅔	0	0	0	2	0.0	0.00	—	.000	.000	39	.275	0	1	1	0	0.1
Total 3	2	4	.333	29	3	0	0	0	61	60	7	24	39	12.5	3.10	110	.273	.347	410	.248	6	3	2	1	0.4

● **WILLIE SMITH**   Smith, Willie Everett   b: 8/27/67, Savannah, Ga.   BR/TR, 6'6", 250 lbs.   Deb: 4/25/94

YEAR TM/L	W	L	PCT	G	GS	CG	SH	SV	IP	H	HR	BB	SO	RAT	ERA	ERA+	OAV	OOB	BH	AVG	PB	PR	/A	PD	TPI
1994 StL-N	1	1	.500	8	0	0	0	0	7	9	4	3	7	15.4	9.00	46	.300	.364	0	—	0	-4	-4		-0.9

● **ZANE SMITH**   Smith, Zane William   b: 12/28/60, Madison, Wis.   BL/TL, 6'2", 195 lbs.   Deb: 9/10/84

YEAR TM/L	W	L	PCT	G	GS	CG	SH	SV	IP	H	HR	BB	SO	RAT	ERA	ERA+	OAV	OOB	BH	AVG	PB	PR	/A	PD	TPI
1984 Atl-N	1	0	1.000	3	3	0	0	0	20	16	1	13	16	13.0	2.25	171	.219	.337	5	.556	2	3	4	0	0.4
1985 Atl-N	9	10	.474	42	18	2	2	0	147	135	4	80	85	13.3	3.80	101	.254	.355	6	.162	-0	-3	1	2	0.3
1986 Atl-N	8	16	.333	38	32	3	1	1	204⅔	209	8	105	139	14.0	4.05	98	.275	.367	5	.085	-3	-7	-3	3	-0.2
1987 Atl-N	15	10	.600	36	36	9	3	0	242	245	19	91	130	12.7	4.09	106	.266	.335	10	.132	-1	-0	7	3	0.8
1988 Atl-N	5	10	.333	23	22	3	0	0	140⅓	159	8	44	59	13.2	4.30	86	.292	.348	7	.167	-0	-13	-10	3	-0.6
1989 Atl-N	1	12	.077	17	17	0	0	0	99	102	5	33	58	12.5	4.45	82	.267	.329	5	.179	-0	-11	-9	2	-0.9
Mon-N	0	1	.000	31	0	0	0	2	48	39	2	19	35	11.1	1.50	235	.220	.299	1	.250	0	11	11	1	0.5
Yr	1	13	.071	48	17	0	0	2	147	141	7	52	93	11.9	3.49	103	.249	.313	6	.188	0	0	2	3	-0.4
1990 Mon-N	6	7	.462	22	21	1	0	0	139⅓	141	11	41	80	11.9	3.23	113	.266	.322	7	.175	1	9	6	1	0.8
*Pit-N	6	2	.750	11	10	3	2	0	76	55	4	9	50	7.6	1.30	278	.203	.229	4	.143	1	21	20	-0	2.2
Yr	12	9	.571	33	31	4	2	0	215⅓	196	15	50	130	10.5	2.55	143	.243	.287	11	.162	2	30	26	1	3.0
1991 *Pit-N	16	10	.615	35	35	5	3	0	228	234	15	29	120	10.5	3.20	112	.268	.293	13	.183	3	12	9	1	1.4
1992 Pit-N	8	8	.500	23	22	1	0	0	141	138	8	19	56	10.1	3.06	112	.261	.289	6	.122	-0	7	6	0	0.7
1993 Pit-N	3	7	.300	14	14	3	0	0	83	97	9	22	32	12.9	4.55	89	.298	.343	2	.080	-2	-5	-5	-1	-0.7
1994 Pit-N	10	8	.556	25	24	7	1	0	157	162	18	34	57	11.2	3.27	132	.270	.309	12	.211	1	16	18	3	2.3
1995 *Bos-A	8	8	.500	24	21	0	0	0	110⅔	144	7	23	47	13.7	5.61	87	.316	.351	0	—	0	-11	-9	-0	-1.1
1996 Pit-N	4	6	.400	16	16	1	0	0	83⅓	104	7	21	47	13.9	5.08	86	.309	.356	4	.154	-1	-8	-6	-0	-0.8
Total 13	100	115	.465	360	291	35	16	3	1919⅓	1980	122	583	1011	12.2	3.74	105	.271	.327	87	.158	0	20	41	17	5.1

● **ROGER SMITHBERG**   Smithberg, Roger Craig   b: 3/21/66, Elgin, Ill.   BR/TR, 6'3", 205 lbs.   Deb: 9/1/93

YEAR TM/L	W	L	PCT	G	GS	CG	SH	SV	IP	H	HR	BB	SO	RAT	ERA	ERA+	OAV	OOB	BH	AVG	PB	PR	/A	PD	TPI
1993 Oak-A	1	2	.333	13	0	0	0	3	19⅔	13	2	7	4	9.6	2.75	148	.197	.284	—		0	3	3	1	0.6
1994 Oak-A	0	0	—	2	0	0	0	0	2⅓	6	1	1	3	27.0	15.43	29	.500	.538	—		0	-3	-3	-0	0.0
Total 2	1	2	.333	15	0	0	0	3	22	19	3	8	7	11.5	4.09	101	.244	.322	—		0	1	0	1	0.6

● **MIKE SMITHSON**   Smithson, Billy Mike   b: 1/21/55, Centerville, Tenn.   BL/TR, 6'8", 215 lbs.   Deb: 8/27/82

YEAR TM/L	W	L	PCT	G	GS	CG	SH	SV	IP	H	HR	BB	SO	RAT	ERA	ERA+	OAV	OOB	BH	AVG	PB	PR	/A	PD	TPI
1982 Tex-A	3	4	.429	8	8	3	0	0	46⅔	51	5	13	24	12.9	5.01	77	.282	.340	—		0	-5	-6	-1	-0.8
1983 Tex-A	10	14	.417	33	33	10	0	0	223⅓	233	14	71	135	12.6	3.91	102	.269	.330	—		0	4	2	1	0.4
1984 Min-A	15	13	.536	36	36	10	0	1	252	246	35	54	144	11.0	3.68	114	.252	.296	—		0	9	15	-1	1.4
1985 Min-A	15	14	.517	37	37	8	3	0	257	264	25	78	127	12.5	4.34	101	.266	.333	—		0	-6	2	-2	0.0
1986 Min-A	13	14	.481	34	33	8	1	0	198	234	26	57	114	13.9	4.77	90	.294	.352	—		0	-13	-10	-1	-1.3
1987 Min-A	4	7	.364	21	20	0	0	0	109	126	17	38	53	14.3	5.94	78	.286	.355	—		0	-18	-16	-1	-1.5
1988 *Bos-A	9	6	.600	31	18	1	0	0	126⅔	149	25	37	73	13.6	5.97	69	.292	.347	—		0	-28	-26	-1	-2.8
1989 Bos-A	7	14	.333	40	19	1	1	2	143⅔	170	21	35	61	13.5	4.95	83	.297	.348	—		0	-17	-14	-1	-2.1
Total 8	76	86	.469	240	204	41	6	2	1356⅓	1473	168	383	731	12.8	4.58	92	.277	.334	—		0	-74	-53	-4	-6.7

● **LEFTY SMOLL**   Smoll, Clyde Hetrick   b: 4/17/14, Quakertown, Pa.   d: 8/31/85, Quakertown, Pa.   BB/TL, 5'10", 175 lbs.   Deb: 4/26/40

YEAR TM/L	W	L	PCT	G	GS	CG	SH	SV	IP	H	HR	BB	SO	RAT	ERA	ERA+	OAV	OOB	BH	AVG	PB	PR	/A	PD	TPI
1940 Phi-N	2	8	.200	33	9	0	0	0	109	145	6	36	31	15.3	5.37	73	.322	.378	5	.161	-1	-18	-18	-2	-1.7

● **JOHN SMOLTZ**   Smoltz, John Andrew   b: 5/15/67, Detroit, Mich.   BR/TR, 6'3", 210 lbs.   Deb: 7/23/88

YEAR TM/L	W	L	PCT	G	GS	CG	SH	SV	IP	H	HR	BB	SO	RAT	ERA	ERA+	OAV	OOB	BH	AVG	PB	PR	/A	PD	TPI
1988 Atl-N	2	7	.222	12	12	0	0	0	64	74	10	33	37	15.3	5.48	67	.285	.369	2	.118	-0	-14	-13	-1	-1.7
1989 Atl-N★	12	11	.522	29	29	5	0	0	208	160	15	72	168	10.1	2.94	124	.212	.282	7	.113	-1	13	16	2	2.1
1990 Atl-N	14	11	.560	34	34	6	2	0	231⅓	206	20	90	170	11.6	3.85	105	.240	.313	12	.162	1	-2	5	1	0.7
1991 *Atl-N	14	13	.519	36	36	5	0	0	229⅔	206	16	77	148	11.2	3.80	102	.243	.308	7	.108	-1	-3	2	0	0.2
1992 *Atl-N★	15	12	.556	35	35	9	3	0	246⅔	206	17	80	**215**	10.6	2.85	129	.224	.289	12	.160	2	18	22	-1	2.6
1993 *Atl-N★	15	11	.577	35	35	3	1	0	243⅔	208	23	100	208	11.6	3.62	111	.230	.311	13	.183	3	11	11	-0	1.3
1994 Atl-N	6	10	.375	21	21	1	0	0	134⅔	120	15	48	113	11.5	4.14	102	.239	.310	6	.162	1	1	4	1	0.3
1995 *Atl-N	12	7	.632	29	29	2	1	0	192⅔	166	15	72	193	11.3	3.18	134	.232	.306	6	.107	-1	21	23	-1	1.9
1996 *Atl-N★	**24**	8	**.750**	35	35	6	2	0	253⅔	199	19	55	**276**	**9.1**	2.94	149	.216	**.261**	17	.218	4	36	41	1	5.4
Total 9	114	90	.559	266	266	37	9	0	1804⅓	1545	150	627	1528	11.0	3.45	116	.231	.300	82	.153	10	81	110	2	12.8

● **HARRY SMYTHE**   Smythe, William Henry   b: 10/24/04, Augusta, Ga.   d: 8/28/80, Augusta, Ga.   BL/TL, 5'10.5", 179 lbs.   Deb: 7/21/29

YEAR TM/L	W	L	PCT	G	GS	CG	SH	SV	IP	H	HR	BB	SO	RAT	ERA	ERA+	OAV	OOB	BH	AVG	PB	PR	/A	PD	TPI
1929 Phi-N	4	6	.400	19	7	2	0	1	68⅔	94	3	15	12	14.4	5.24	99	.330	.365	5	.192	-1	-4	-0	2	0.0
1930 Phi-N	0	3	.000	25	3	0	0	2	49⅔	84	3	31	9	21.4	7.79	70	.368	.450	4	.286	-0	-16	-13	-1	-0.8
1934 NY-A	0	2	.000	8	0	0	0	0	15	24	1	8	7	19.2	7.80	52	.381	.451	1	.200	-0	-6	-6	-1	-0.7
Bro-N	1	1	.500	8	0	0	0	1	21⅓	30	3	8	5	16.5	5.91	66	.337	.398	3	.333	1	-2	-2	-0	-0.2
Total 3	5	12	.294	60	10	2	0	4	154⅔	232	10	62	33	17.4	6.40	66	.349	.408	13	.241	-0	-29	-24	2	-1.7

● **NATE SNELL**   Snell, Nathaniel   b: 9/2/52, Orangeburg, S.C.   BR/TR, 6'4", 190 lbs.   Deb: 9/20/84

YEAR TM/L	W	L	PCT	G	GS	CG	SH	SV	IP	H	HR	BB	SO	RAT	ERA	ERA+	OAV	OOB	BH	AVG	PB	PR	/A	PD	TPI
1984 Bal-A	1	1	.500	5	0	0	0	0	7⅔	8	1	1	7	10.6	2.35	165	.258	.281	—		0	1	1	-0	0.3
1985 Bal-A	3	2	.600	43	0	0	0	5	100⅓	100	4	30	41	11.8	2.69	150	.260	.315	—		0	16	15	1	0.9
1986 Bal-A	2	1	.667	34	0	0	0	1	72⅓	69	9	22	29	11.4	3.86	107	.257	.316	—		0	3	2	1	0.3

YEAR TM/L	W	L	PCT	G	GS	CG	SH	SV	IP	H	HR	BB	SO	RAT	ERA	ERA+	OAV	OOB	BH	AVG	PB	PR	/A	PD	TPI
1987 Det-A	1	2	.333	22	2	0	0	0	38²	39	5	19	19	13.5	3.96	107	.267	.352	0	—	0	2	1	-1	0.1
Total 4	7	6	.538	104	2	0	0	5	219	216	19	72	96	11.9	3.29	125	.260	.321	0	—	0	22	20	1	1.6

● **FRANK SNOOK** Snook, Frank Walter b: 3/28/49, Somerville, N.J. BR/TR, 6'2", 180 lbs. Deb: 7/13/73

YEAR TM/L	W	L	PCT	G	GS	CG	SH	SV	IP	H	HR	BB	SO	RAT	ERA	ERA+	OAV	OOB	BH	AVG	PB	PR	/A	PD	TPI
1973 SD-N	0	2	.000	18	0	0	0	1	27¹	19	4	18	13	12.2	3.62	96	.200	.327	0	.000	-0	0	-0	1	0.0

● **COLONEL SNOVER** Snover, Colonel Lester "Bosco" b: 5/16/1895, Hallstead, Pa. d: 4/30/69, Rochester, N.Y. BL/TL, 6'0.5", 200 lbs. Deb: 9/18/19

YEAR TM/L	W	L	PCT	G	GS	CG	SH	SV	IP	H	HR	BB	SO	RAT	ERA	ERA+	OAV	OOB	BH	AVG	PB	PR	/A	PD	TPI
1919 NY-N	0	1	.000	2	1	0	0	0	9	7	0	3	4	11.0	1.00	281	.212	.297	0	.000	0	2	2	-0	0.2

● **BRIAN SNYDER** Snyder, Brian Robert b: 2/20/58, Flemington, N.J. BL/TL, 6'3", 185 lbs. Deb: 5/25/85

YEAR TM/L	W	L	PCT	G	GS	CG	SH	SV	IP	H	HR	BB	SO	RAT	ERA	ERA+	OAV	OOB	BH	AVG	PB	PR	/A	PD	TPI
1985 Sea-A	1	2	.333	15	6	0	0	0	35¹	44	4	19	23	16.3	6.37	66	.306	.390	0	—	0	-9	-8	1	-0.6
1989 Oak-A	0	0	—	2	0	0	0	0	0²	2	1	2	1	54.0	27.00	14	.500	.667	0	—	0	-2	-2	0	0.2
Total 2	1	2	.333	17	6	0	0	0	36	46	3	21	24	17.0	6.75	62	.311	.400	0	—	0	-10	-10	1	-0.4

● **GENE SNYDER** Snyder, Gene Walter b: 3/31/31, York, Pa. d: 6/2/96, York, Pa. BR/TL, 5'11", 175 lbs. Deb: 4/26/59

YEAR TM/L	W	L	PCT	G	GS	CG	SH	SV	IP	H	HR	BB	SO	RAT	ERA	ERA+	OAV	OOB	BH	AVG	PB	PR	/A	PD	TPI
1959 LA-N	1	1	.500	11	2	0	0	0	26¹	32	1	20	20	17.8	5.47	77	.299	.409	0	.000	-0	-4	-4	-0	-0.3

● **GEORGE SNYDER** Snyder, George T. b: 8/1848, Philadelphia, Pa. d: 8/2/05, Philadelphia, Pa. Deb: 9/30/1882

YEAR TM/L	W	L	PCT	G	GS	CG	SH	SV	IP	H	HR	BB	SO	RAT	ERA	ERA+	OAV	OOB	BH	AVG	PB	PR	/A	PD	TPI
1882 Phi-a	1	0	1.000	1	1	1	0	0	9	4	0	2	0	6.0	0.00	—	.125	.176	1	.333	0	3	3	0	0.3

● **BILL SNYDER** Snyder, William Nicholas b: 1/28/1898, Mansfield, Ohio d: 10/8/34, Vicksburg, Mich. BR/TR, Deb: 9/4/19

YEAR TM/L	W	L	PCT	G	GS	CG	SH	SV	IP	H	HR	BB	SO	RAT	ERA	ERA+	OAV	OOB	BH	AVG	PB	PR	/A	PD	TPI
1919 Was-A	0	1	.000	2	1	0	0	0	8	6	0	3	5	10.1	1.13	285	.200	.273	0	.000	-0	2	2	-0	0.2
1920 Was-A	2	1	.667	16	4	1	0	1	54	59	1	28	17	15.5	4.17	90	.280	.380	6	.316	1	-2	-3	-1	-0.1
Total 2	2	2	.500	18	5	1	0	1	62	65	1	31	22	14.8	3.77	97	.270	.367	6	.286	1	-1	-1	-1	0.1

● **STEVE SODERSTROM** Soderstrom, Stephen Andrew b: 4/3/72, Turlock, Cal. BR/TR, 6'3", 215 lbs. Deb: 9/17/96

YEAR TM/L	W	L	PCT	G	GS	CG	SH	SV	IP	H	HR	BB	SO	RAT	ERA	ERA+	OAV	OOB	BH	AVG	PB	PR	/A	PD	TPI
1996 SF-N	2	0	1.000	3	3	0	0	0	13²	16	1	6	9	15.8	5.27	78	.302	.393	0	.000	-1	-2	-2	-0	-0.3

● **CLINT SODOWSKY** Sodowsky, Clint Rea b: 7/13/72, Ponca City, Okla. BL/TR, 6'3", 180 lbs. Deb: 9/4/95

YEAR TM/L	W	L	PCT	G	GS	CG	SH	SV	IP	H	HR	BB	SO	RAT	ERA	ERA+	OAV	OOB	BH	AVG	PB	PR	/A	PD	TPI
1995 Det-A	2	2	.500	6	6	0	0	0	23¹	24	4	18	14	16.2	5.01	95	.258	.378	0	—	0	-1	-1	-0	-0.1
1996 Det-A	1	3	.250	7	7	0	0	0	24¹	40	5	20	9	23.3	11.84	43	.370	.481	0	—	0	-19	-18	-0	-2.1
Total 2	3	5	.375	13	13	0	0	0	47²	64	9	38	23	19.8	8.50	58	.318	.434	0	—	0	-19	-19	-1	-2.2

● **RAY SOFF** Soff, Raymond John b: 10/31/58, Adrian, Mich. BR/TR, 6', 185 lbs. Deb: 7/17/86

YEAR TM/L	W	L	PCT	G	GS	CG	SH	SV	IP	H	HR	BB	SO	RAT	ERA	ERA+	OAV	OOB	BH	AVG	PB	PR	/A	PD	TPI
1986 StL-N	4	2	.667	30	0	0	0	0	38¹	37	4	13	22	11.7	3.29	111	.255	.316	0	.000	-0	2	1	0	0.2
1987 StL-N	1	0	1.000	12	0	0	0	0	15¹	18	3	5	9	14.1	6.46	64	.295	.358	0	.000	-0	-4	-4	-0	-0.2
Total 2	5	2	.714	42	0	0	0	0	53²	55	7	18	31	12.4	4.19	90	.267	.329	0	.000	-0	-2	-2	0	0.0

● **JULIO SOLANO** Solano, Julio Cesar b: 1/8/60, Aqua Blanca, D.R. BR/TR, 6'1", 160 lbs. Deb: 4/5/83

YEAR TM/L	W	L	PCT	G	GS	CG	SH	SV	IP	H	HR	BB	SO	RAT	ERA	ERA+	OAV	OOB	BH	AVG	PB	PR	/A	PD	TPI
1983 Hou-N	0	2	.000	4	0	0	0	0	6¹	4	1	3	3	13.5	6.00	57	.217	.333	0	—	0	-2	-2	-0	-0.5
1984 Hou-N	1	3	.250	31	0	0	0	0	50²	31	3	18	33	8.7	1.95	170	.179	.257	1	.333	0	9	8	-1	0.5
1985 Hou-N	2	2	.500	20	0	0	0	0	33²	34	5	13	17	12.6	3.48	100	.262	.329	0	.000	0	0	-0	-1	-0.1
1986 Hou-N	3	1	.750	16	1	0	0	0	32	39	5	22	21	18.0	7.59	47	.310	.424	0	—	-1	-14	-14	-0	-1.7
1987 Hou-N	0	0	—	11	0	0	0	0	20	25	5	9	12	15.3	7.65	51	.298	.366	0	.000	-0	-8	-8	-0	-0.8
1988 Sea-A	0	0	—	17	0	0	0	3	22	22	3	12	10	13.9	4.09	102	.268	.362	0	—	0	-0	-0	-0	-0.2
1989 Sea-A	0	0	—	7	0	0	0	0	9²	6	1	4	6	10.2	5.59	72	.176	.282	0	—	0	-2	-2	-0	-0.2
Total 7	6	8	.429	106	1	0	0	3	174	162	23	82	102	12.8	4.55	79	.248	.336	1	.077	-1	-16	-18	-2	-2.2

● **MARCELINO SOLIS** Solis, Marcelino b: 7/19/30, San Luis Potosi, Mexico BL/TL, 6'1", 185 lbs. Deb: 7/16/58

YEAR TM/L	W	L	PCT	G	GS	CG	SH	SV	IP	H	HR	BB	SO	RAT	ERA	ERA+	OAV	OOB	BH	AVG	PB	PR	/A	PD	TPI
1958 Chi-N	3	3	.500	15	4	0	0	0	52	74	5	20	15	17.0	6.06	65	.339	.405	5	.250	1	-12	-12	-0	-1.1

● **EDDIE SOLOMON** Solomon, Eddie "Buddy" b: 2/9/51, Perry, Ga. d: 1/12/86, Macon, Ga. BR/TR, 6'3", 190 lbs. Deb: 9/2/73

YEAR TM/L	W	L	PCT	G	GS	CG	SH	SV	IP	H	HR	BB	SO	RAT	ERA	ERA+	OAV	OOB	BH	AVG	PB	PR	/A	PD	TPI
1973 LA-N	0	0	—	4	0	0	0	0	6¹	10	3	4	6	21.3	7.11	48	.357	.455	0	.000	—	-2	-3	-0	0.0
1974 *LA-N	0	0	—	4	0	0	0	1	6	5	1	2	2	10.5	1.50	227	.217	.280	0	—	0	1	1	0	0.1
1975 Chi-N	0	0	—	6	0	0	0	0	6²	7	1	6	3	17.6	1.35	285	.269	.406	0	—	0	2	2	0	0.0
1976 StL-N	1	1	.500	26	2	0	0	0	37	45	2	16	19	15.1	4.86	73	.306	.378	2	.400	1	-6	-5	1	-0.1
1977 Atl-N	6	6	.500	18	16	0	0	0	88²	110	10	34	54	14.8	4.57	97	.305	.368	4	.129	-1	-6	-1	-0	-0.3
1978 Atl-N	4	6	.400	37	8	0	0	2	106	98	12	50	64	12.7	4.08	99	.247	.335	4	.138	-1	-6	-0	-0	-0.1
1979 Atl-N	7	14	.333	31	30	4	0	0	186	184	19	51	96	11.7	4.21	96	.254	.308	13	.203	1	-10	-3	-1	-0.4
1980 Pit-N	7	3	.700	26	12	2	0	0	100¹	96	8	37	35	12.3	2.69	135	.253	.325	7	.219	1	10	11	-0	1.1
1981 Pit-N	8	6	.571	22	17	2	0	1	127	133	10	27	38	11.6	3.12	115	.278	.321	7	.163	-1	5	7	-1	0.5
1982 Pit-N	2	6	.250	11	10	0	0	0	46²	59	7	18	18	17.0	6.75	55	.347	.404	2	.133	-1	-16	-16	-2	-2.4
Chi-A	1	0	1.000	6	0	0	0	0	7¹	7	1	2	2	11.0	3.68	110	.241	.290	0	—	0	0	0	0	0.0
Total 10	36	42	.462	191	95	8	0	4	718	764	76	247	337	12.9	4.00	97	.274	.337	39	.177	-1	-28	-8	-3	-1.6

● **JOE SOMMER** Sommer, Joseph John b: 11/20/1858, Covington, Ky. d: 1/16/38, Cincinnati, Ohio BR/TR, Deb: 7/8/1880 ♦

YEAR TM/L	W	L	PCT	G	GS	CG	SH	SV	IP	H	HR	BB	SO	RAT	ERA	ERA+	OAV	OOB	BH	AVG	PB	PR	/A	PD	TPI
1883 Cin-a	0	0	—	1	0	0	0	0	5	9	0	1	2	18.0	5.40	60	.360	.385	115	.278	0	-1	-1	-0	0.0
1885 Bal-a	0	0	—	2	0	0	0	1	2	3	0	1	0	18.0	9.00	36	.429	.429	118	.251	0	-2	-2	-0	-0.1
1886 Bal-a	0	0	—	4	0	0	0	0	3	7	0	3	1	38.3	18.00	19	.519	.567	117	.209	-0	-6	-6	-0	-0.1
1887 Bal-a	0	0	—	1	0	0	0	0	1	2	1	0	0	27.0	9.00	46	.333	.429	123	.266	0	-1	-1	-0	0.0
1890 Cle-N	0	0	—	1	0	0	0	0	1	2	0	2	0	36.0	0.00	—	.400	.571	8	.229	1	0	-0	-0	0.0
Total 5	0	0	—	6	0	0	0	1	14	33	1	7	3	25.7	9.64	35	.429	.476	911	.248	1	-10	-10	-1	-0.1

● **RUDY SOMMERS** Sommers, Rudolph b: 10/30/1888, Cincinnati, Ohio d: 3/18/49, Louisville, Ky. BB/TL, 5'11", 165 lbs. Deb: 9/8/12

YEAR TM/L	W	L	PCT	G	GS	CG	SH	SV	IP	H	HR	BB	SO	RAT	ERA	ERA+	OAV	OOB	BH	AVG	PB	PR	/A	PD	TPI
1912 Chi-N	0	1	.000	1	0	0	0	0	3	4	0	2	2	18.0	3.00	111	.333	.429	0	.000	0	0	-0	-0	0.0
1914 Bro-F	2	7	.222	23	8	2	0	2	82	88	2	34	40	13.7	4.06	71	.282	.358	6	.250	2	-11	-11	-1	-1.0
1926 Bos-A	0	0	—	2	0	0	0	0	2	3	0	3	0	27.0	13.50	30	.333	.500	0	—	-0	-2	-2	0	-0.1
1927 Bos-A	0	0	—	7	0	0	0	0	14	18	2	14	2	20.6	8.36	51	.353	.492	1	.500	0	-7	-6	1	0.1
Total 4	2	8	.200	33	8	2	0	2	101	113	4	53	44	15.1	4.81	64	.294	.384	7	.259	2	-19	-19	-0	-0.9

● **ANDY SOMMERVILLE** Sommerville, Andrew Henry (b: Henry Travers Summersgill) b: 2/6/1876, Brooklyn, N.Y. d: 6/16/31, Richmond Hill, N.Y. Deb: 8/8/1894

YEAR TM/L	W	L	PCT	G	GS	CG	SH	SV	IP	H	HR	BB	SO	RAT	ERA	ERA+	OAV	OOB	BH	AVG	PB	PR	/A	PD	TPI
1894 Bro-N	0	1	.000	1	1	0	0	0	0¹	4	0	5	0	162.0	162.00	3	.500	.857	0	—	0	-6	-6	0	-3.6

● **DON SONGER** Songer, Donald C. b: 1/31/1900, Walnut, Kan. d: 10/3/62, Kansas City, Mo. BL/TL, 6', 165 lbs. Deb: 9/21/24

YEAR TM/L	W	L	PCT	G	GS	CG	SH	SV	IP	H	HR	BB	SO	RAT	ERA	ERA+	OAV	OOB	BH	AVG	PB	PR	/A	PD	TPI
1924 Pit-N	0	0	—	4	1	0	0	1	9¹	14	1	3	3	16.4	6.75	57	.333	.378	0	.000	-0	-3	-3	0	-0.1
1925 Pit-N	1	0	1.000	11²	14	0	8	4	17.0	2.31	193	.298	.400	0	3	3	-0	0.2
1926 Pit-N	7	8	.467	35	14	5	1	2	126¹	118	4	52	27	12.9	3.13	126	.252	.340	4	.105	-2	10	11	1	1.1
1927 Pit-N	0	0	—	2	0	0	0	0	4²	10	4	0	1	28.9	11.57	36	.526	.625	0	.000	-0	-4	-4	-0	-0.1
NY-N	3	5	.375	22	1	0	0	1	50¹	48	4	31	9	14.3	2.86	135	.261	.370	3	.300	1	6	6	1	1.0
Yr	3	5	.375	24	1	0	0	1	55	58	8	35	10	15.4	3.60	108	.284	.392	3	.273	1	2	2	1	1.0
Total 4	10	14	.417	71	16	5	1	4	202¹	204	9	98	44	14.0	3.38	117	.268	.361	7	.132	-2	11	13	2	2.2

● **LARY SORENSEN** Sorensen, Lary Alan b: 10/4/55, Detroit, Mich. BR/TR, 6'2", 210 lbs. Deb: 6/7/77

YEAR TM/L	W	L	PCT	G	GS	CG	SH	SV	IP	H	HR	BB	SO	RAT	ERA	ERA+	OAV	OOB	BH	AVG	PB	PR	/A	PD	TPI
1977 Mil-A	7	10	.412	23	20	9	1	0	142¹	147	10	36	57	11.6	4.36	93	.270	.316	0	—	0	-5	-5	1	-0.4
1978 Mil-A★	18	12	.600	37	36	17	3	1	280²	277	16	50	78	10.6	3.21	117	.259	.295	0	—	0	17	17	1	1.8
1979 Mil-A	15	14	.517	34	34	16	2	0	235¹	250	30	42	63	11.3	3.98	105	.275	.310	0	—	0	4	4	1	0.6
1980 Mil-A	12	10	.545	35	29	8	2	0	195²	242	13	45	54	13.3	3.68	105	.311	.351	0	—	0	8	4	1	0.7
1981 StL-N	7	7	.500	23	23	3	1	0	140¹	149	8	26	52	11.3	3.27	109	.271	.305	3	.065	-3	2	4	1	0.1
1982 Cle-A	10	15	.400	32	30	6	1	0	189¹	251	19	55	62	14.7	5.61	73	.322	.369	0	—	0	-32	-32	1	-3.7
1983 Cle-A	12	11	.522	36	34	8	1	0	222²	238	21	65	76	12.3	4.24	100	.276	.328	0	—	0	-5	-0	2	0.1
1984 Oak-A	6	13	.316	46	21	8	0	0	183¹	240	11	44	60	14.2	4.91	91	.317	.359	0	—	0	-19	-24	-1	-2.3
1985 Chi-N	3	7	.300	45	3	0	0	0	82¹	86	8	24	34	12.5	4.26	94	.274	.333	0	.000	-0	-6	-3	-0	-0.3

YEAR	TM/L	W	L	PCT	G	GS	CG	SH	SV	IP	H	HR	BB	SO	RAT	ERA	ERA+	OAV	OOB	BH	AVG	PB	PR	/A	PD	TPI
1987	Mon-N	3	4	.429	23	5	0	0	0	47²	56	7	12	21	13.4	4.72	89	.286	.336	0	.000	-5	-3	-3	-1	-0.5
1988	SF-N	0	0	—	12	0	0	0	2	16²	24	1	3	9	14.6	4.86	67	.329	.355	0	.000	-0	-3	-3	-0	-0.1
Total	11	93	103	.474	346	235	69	10	6	1736¹	1960	147	402	569	12.4	4.15	95	.287	.329	3	.049	-4	-38	-38	1	-4.0

● VIC SORRELL
Sorrell, Victor Garland b: 4/9/01, Morrisville, N.C. d: 5/4/72, Raleigh, N.C. BR/TR, 5'10", 180 lbs. Deb: 4/22/28

YEAR	TM/L	W	L	PCT	G	GS	CG	SH	SV	IP	H	HR	BB	SO	RAT	ERA	ERA+	OAV	OOB	BH	AVG	PB	PR	/A	PD	TPI
1928	Det-A	8	11	.421	29	23	8	0	0	171	182	9	83	67	14.2	4.79	86	.277	.363	6	.109	-5	-14	-13	-3	-1.9
1929	Det-A	14	15	.483	36	31	13	1	1	226	270	15	106	81	15.1	5.18	83	.302	.377	12	.145	-6	-23	-22	-1	-3.0
1930	Det-A	16	11	.593	35	30	14	2	1	233¹	245	13	106	97	13.5	3.86	124	.274	.351	15	.188	-3	21	24	-3	1.8
1931	Det-A	13	14	.481	35	32	19	1	1	245	267	8	114	99	14.0	4.15	110	.278	.355	14	.159	-4	6	12	1	0.8
1932	Det-A	14	14	.500	32	31	13	1	0	234¹	234	11	77	84	12.1	4.03	117	.259	.319	9	.118	-4	12	17	-2	1.3
1933	Det-A	11	15	.423	36	28	13	1	0	232²	233	18	78	75	12.1	3.79	114	.260	.321	11	.149	-2	13	13	-0	1.0
1934	Det-A	6	9	.400	28	19	6	1	2	129²	146	13	45	46	13.5	4.79	92	.283	.345	4	.108	-1	-4	-6	-2	-0.5
1935	Det-A	3	3	.571	12	6	4	0	0	51¹	65	2	25	22	16.1	4.03	103	.319	.398	0	.000	-0	3	2	1	-0.2
1936	Det-A	6	7	.462	30	14	5	1	3	131¹	153	9	64	37	15.0	5.28	94	.294	.373	6	.154	1	-3	-5	2	-0.2
1937	Det-A	0	2	.000	7	2	0	0	1	17	25	3	8	11	17.5	9.00	52	.338	.402	0	.000	-0	-8	-8	-0	-0.9
Total	10	92	101	.477	280	216	95	8	10	1671²	1820	101	706	619	13.7	4.43	102	.279	.351	77	.139	-27	0	14	-4	-1.8

● ELIAS SOSA
Sosa, Elias (Martinez) b: 6/10/50, LaVega, D.R. BR/TR, 6'2", 190 lbs. Deb: 9/8/72

YEAR	TM/L	W	L	PCT	G	GS	CG	SH	SV	IP	H	HR	BB	SO	RAT	ERA	ERA+	OAV	OOB	BH	AVG	PB	PR	/A	PD	TPI
1972	SF-N	0	1	.000	8	0	0	0	3	15²	10	0	12	10	12.6	2.30	152	.189	.338	0	.000	-0	2	2	-0	0.2
1973	SF-N	10	4	.714	71	1	0	0	18	107	95	7	41	70	11.8	3.28	116	.241	.318	1	.071	-0	5	6	-1	0.9
1974	SF-N	9	7	.563	68	0	0	0	6	101	94	8	45	48	12.5	3.48	109	.252	.334	1	.067	-1	2	4	-1	0.4
1975	StL-N	0	3	.000	14	1	0	0	0	27¹	22	3	14	15	12.2	3.95	95	.227	.330	1	.125	-0	-1	-1	-0	-0.1
	Atl-N	2	5	.500	43	0	0	0	2	62¹	70	3	29	31	14.7	4.48	84	.294	.378	1	.143	-0	-6	-5	-1	-0.4
	Yr	2	5	.286	57	1	0	0	2	89²	92	6	43	46	13.9	4.32	87	.271	.358	2	.133	-1	-7	-5	-0	-0.5
1976	Atl-N	4	4	.500	21	0	0	0	1	35¹	41	3	13	32	14.0	5.35	71	.287	.350	1	.143	-0	-7	-6	-0	-1.5
	LA-N	2	4	.333	24	0	0	0	1	33²	30	0	12	20	11.2	3.48	97	.242	.309	0	—	-0	-0	-0	-1	-0.1
	Yr	6	8	.429	45	0	0	0	2	69	71	3	25	52	12.5	4.43	81	.263	.325	1	.143	-0	-7	-6	-0	-1.6
1977	*LA-N	2	2	.500	44	0	0	0	1	63²	42	7	12	47	7.8	1.98	193	.189	.234	1	.250	-0	14	13	0	0.8
1978	Oak-A	8	2	.800	68	0	0	0	14	109	106	5	44	61	12.5	2.64	138	.264	.338	0	—	-0	14	12	0	1.5
1979	Mon-N	8	7	.533	62	0	0	0	18	96²	77	2	37	59	10.8	1.96	187	.219	.297	2	.154	-0	19	18	-1	3.3
1980	Mon-N	9	6	.600	67	0	0	0	9	93²	104	5	19	58	11.9	3.07	116	.286	.323	1	.091	-1	5	5	-0	0.8
1981	*Mon-N	1	2	.333	32	0	0	0	3	39¹	46	3	8	18	12.6	3.66	95	.297	.335	2	1.000	-1	-1	-1	-0	0.1
1982	Det-A	3	3	.500	38	0	0	0	4	61	64	11	18	24	12.4	4.43	92	.270	.327	0	—	-0	-2	-2	1	-0.2
1983	SD-N	1	4	.200	41	1	0	0	1	72¹	72	7	30	45	13.1	4.35	80	.268	.348	1	.143	-0	-6	-7	-1	-0.6
Total	12	59	51	.536	601	3	0	0	83	918	873	64	334	538	12.0	3.32	111	.255	.325	12	.130	-3	37	39	-3	5.1

● JOSE SOSA
Sosa, Jose Ynocencio (b: Jose Ynocencio (Sosa)) b: 12/28/52, Santo Domingo, D.R. BR/TR, 5'11", 158 lbs. Deb: 7/22/75

YEAR	TM/L	W	L	PCT	G	GS	CG	SH	SV	IP	H	HR	BB	SO	RAT	ERA	ERA+	OAV	OOB	BH	AVG	PB	PR	/A	PD	TPI
1975	Hou-N	1	3	.250	25	2	0	0	1	47	51	5	23	31	14.4	4.02	84	.291	.377	3	.333	2	-2	-3	-1	-0.2
1976	Hou-N	0	0	—	9	0	0	0	0	11²	16	0	6	5	19.3	6.94	46	.340	.446	0	—	-0	-4	-5	1	0.1
Total	2	1	3	.250	34	2	0	0	1	58²	67	5	29	36	15.3	4.60	72	.302	.392	3	.333	2	-7	-8	-0	-0.1

● ALLEN SOTHORON
Sothoron, Allen Sutton b: 4/27/1893, Bradford, Ohio d: 6/17/39, St.Louis, Mo. BB/TR, 5'11", 182 lbs. Deb: 9/17/14 MC

YEAR	TM/L	W	L	PCT	G	GS	CG	SH	SV	IP	H	HR	BB	SO	RAT	ERA	ERA+	OAV	OOB	BH	AVG	PB	PR	/A	PD	TPI
1914	StL-A	0	0	—	1	0	0	0	0	6	4	0	4	3	15.0	6.00	45	.261	.370	0	.000	-0	-2	-2	-0	0.0
1915	StL-A	0	1	.000	3	1	0	0	0	3²	8	0	5	2	31.9	7.36	39	.400	.520	0	.000	-0	-2	-2	-0	-0.4
1917	StL-A	14	19	.424	48	32	17	3	4	276²	259	2	96	85	11.8	2.83	92	.251	.320	20	.217	3	-5	-7	-1	-0.6
1918	StL-A	12	12	.500	29	24	14	2	0	209	152	3	67	71	9.6	1.94	141	**.205**	.274	10	.159	-2	20	19	-3	1.6
1919	StL-A	20	13	.606	40	30	21	3	3	270	256	4	87	106	11.8	2.20	151	.246	.311	17	.175	-2	31	34	-7	3.1
1920	StL-A	8	15	.348	36	26	17	1	2	218¹	263	6	89	81	14.8	4.70	83	.307	.376	16	.222	-1	-22	-19	-2	-2.1
1921	StL-A	1	2	.333	5	4	1	0	0	27²	33	0	8	12	13.7	5.20	86	.314	.368	1	.111	-0	-3	-2	-0	-0.3
	Bos-A	0	2	.000	2	2	0	0	0	6	15	0	3	2	30.0	13.50	31	.455	.526	1	.500	-1	-6	-6	-0	-1.2
	Cle-A	12	4	.750	22	16	10	2	0	144²	146	0	58	61	13.1	3.24	132	.279	.358	16	.276	4	17	17	-2	1.5
	Yr	13	8	.619	29	22	11	2	0	178¹	194	0	71	72	13.7	3.89	111	.293	.367	18	.261	2	8	8	-2	0.0
1922	Cle-A	1	3	.250	6	4	2	0	0	25¹	26	1	14	8	14.9	6.39	63	.274	.378	4	.444	1	-7	-7	-0	-0.8
1924	StL-N	10	16	.385	29	28	16	**4**	0	196²	209	9	84	62	13.0	3.57	106	.275	.354	14	.194	-2	7	5	-3	0.0
1925	StL-N	10	10	.500	28	22	8	2	0	155²	173	7	63	67	14.0	4.05	107	.280	.353	11	.196	-1	4	5	-4	0.0
1926	StL-N	3	3	.500	15	4	1	0	0	42²	37	2	16	19	11.2	4.22	93	.247	.319	3	.231	-2	-1	-1	-0	-0.5
Total	11	91	100	.476	264	193	102	17	9	1582¹	1583	34	596	576	12.7	3.31	105	.264	.336	113	.207	-2	29	30	-24	0.5

● MARIO SOTO
Soto, Mario Melvin b: 7/12/56, Bani, D.R. BR/TR, 6', 185 lbs. Deb: 7/21/77

YEAR	TM/L	W	L	PCT	G	GS	CG	SH	SV	IP	H	HR	BB	SO	RAT	ERA	ERA+	OAV	OOB	BH	AVG	PB	PR	/A	PD	TPI
1977	Cin-N	2	6	.250	12	10	2	0	0	60²	60	12	26	44	13.2	5.34	74	.258	.340	1	.077	-0	-10	-10	0	-1.1
1978	Cin-N	1	0	1.000	5	1	0	0	0	18	13	1	13	13	13.0	2.50	142	.197	.329	0	.000	-0	2	2	0	0.0
1979	*Cin-N	3	2	.600	25	0	0	0	0	37¹	33	2	30	32	15.4	5.30	70	.243	.383	4	.571	-2	-7	-7	-0	-0.7
1980	Cin-N	10	8	.556	53	12	3	0	2	190¹	126	11	84	182	10.0	3.07	116	**.187**	.279	2	.043	-4	11	11	0	0.6
1981	Cin-N	12	9	.571	25	25	10	3	0	175	142	13	61	151	10.6	3.29	108	.220	.290	4	.068	-4	4	5	-1	0.0
1982	Cin-N★	14	13	.519	35	34	13	2	0	257²	202	19	71	274	**9.7**	2.79	132	.215	**.273**	14	.167	-1	23	26	1	2.7
1983	Cin-N★	17	13	.567	34	34	**18**	3	0	273²	207	28	95	242	10.1	2.70	141	.208	.280	11	.125	-2	28	34	-1	3.3
1984	Cin-N★	18	7	.720	33	33	**13**	0	0	237¹	181	26	87	185	10.4	3.53	107	.209	.286	18	.207	3	2	7	-3	0.7
1985	Cin-N	12	15	.444	36	36	9	1	0	256²	190	30	104	214	10.6	3.58	106	.211	.292	11	.133	-2	2	6	-1	0.3
1986	Cin-N	5	10	.333	19	19	1	0	0	105	113	16	46	67	13.7	4.71	82	.280	.355	3	.111	-1	-12	-10	-1	-1.4
1987	Cin-N	3	2	.600	6	6	0	0	0	31²	34	7	12	11	13.1	5.12	83	.279	.343	1	.083	-1	-3	-3	-0	-0.5
1988	Cin-N	3	7	.300	14	14	3	1	0	87	88	8	28	34	12.2	4.66	77	.267	.328	1	.045	-1	-12	-10	-1	-1.3
Total	12	100	92	.521	297	224	72	13	4	1730¹	1395	172	657	1449	10.8	3.47	108	.220	.296	70	.132	-10	27	51	-8	2.6

● MARK SOUZA
Souza, Kenneth Mark b: 2/1/55, Redwood City, Cal. BL/TL, 6', 180 lbs. Deb: 4/22/80

YEAR	TM/L	W	L	PCT	G	GS	CG	SH	SV	IP	H	HR	BB	SO	RAT	ERA	ERA+	OAV	OOB	BH	AVG	PB	PR	/A	PD	TPI
1980	Oak-A	0	0	—	5	0	0	0	0	7	9	1	5	2	18.0	7.71	49	.310	.412	0	—	0	-3	-3	-0	0.4

● JOHN SOWDERS
Sowders, John b: 12/10/1866, Louisville, Ky. d: 7/29/39, Indianapolis, Ind BR/TL, 6', Deb: 6/28/1887 F♦

YEAR	TM/L	W	L	PCT	G	GS	CG	SH	SV	IP	H	HR	BB	SO	RAT	ERA	ERA+	OAV	OOB	BH	AVG	PB	PR	/A	PD	TPI
1887	Ind-N	0	0	—	1	0	0	0	0	3	11	0	5	0	48.0	21.00	20	.500	.593	0	.000	-0	-6	-6	-0	-0.1
1889	KC-a	6	16	.273	25	23	20	0	1	185	204	9	105	104	15.4	4.82	87	.271	.366	19	.218	-4	-20	-13	-2	-1.4
1890	Bro-P	19	16	.543	39	37	28	1	0	309	358	6	161	91	15.4	3.82	117	.278	.363	25	.189	-5	14	22	-2	1.3
Total	3	25	32	.439	65	60	48	1	1	497	573	12	271	195	15.6	4.29	102	.278	.366	44	.199	-7	-11	4	-4	-0.1

● BILL SOWDERS
Sowders, William Jefferson "Little Bill"
b: 11/29/1864, Louisville, Ky. d: 2/2/51, Indianapolis, Ind. BR/TR, 6', 155 lbs. Deb: 4/24/1888 F

YEAR	TM/L	W	L	PCT	G	GS	CG	SH	SV	IP	H	HR	BB	SO	RAT	ERA	ERA+	OAV	OOB	BH	AVG	PB	PR	/A	PD	TPI
1888	Bos-N	19	15	.559	36	35	34	2	0	317	278	8	73	132	10.2	2.07	138	.226	.275	18	.148	-4	27	27	1	2.3
1889	Bos-N	1	2	.333	7	4	3	0	0	42	53	3	23	10	16.7	5.14	81	.299	.386	4	.235	-0	-5	-5	1	-0.3
	Pit-N	6	5	.545	13	11	9	0	3	52²	94	4	29	33	21.7	7.35	51	.376	.449	13	.271	2	-19	-21	2	-2.7
	Yr	7	7	.500	20	15	12	0	**3**	94²	147	4	52	43	19.3	6.37	62	.343	.419	17	.262	2	-25	-26	3	-3.0
1890	Pit-N	3	8	.273	15	11	9	0	0	106	117	1	24	50	12.1	4.42	75	.271	.313	9	.180	-4	-10	-13	-0	-1.4
Total	3	29	30	.492	71	61	55	2	3	517²	542	14	149	205	12.3	3.34	95	.264	.340	44	.186	-4	-7	-11	2	-2.1

● BOB SPADE
Spade, Robert b: 1/4/1877, Akron, Ohio d: 9/7/24, Cincinnati, Ohio BR/TR, 5'10", 190 lbs. Deb: 9/22/07

YEAR	TM/L	W	L	PCT	G	GS	CG	SH	SV	IP	H	HR	BB	SO	RAT	ERA	ERA+	OAV	OOB	BH	AVG	PB	PR	/A	PD	TPI
1907	Cin-N	1	2	.333	3	3	1	0	0	27	21	0	9	7	10.0	1.00	260	.219	.292	2	.286	1	4	5	-1	0.7
1908	Cin-N	17	12	.586	35	28	22	2	1	249¹	230	2	85	74	11.6	2.74	84	.250	.317	17	.195	-1	-11	-12	-4	-1.8
1909	Cin-N	5	5	.500	14	13	8	0	0	98	91	0	39	31	12.3	2.85	91	.236	.313	10	.294	4	-3	-3	-0	-0.3
1910	Cin-N	1	2	.333	7	5	1	0	0	17¹	35	1	9	7	23.4	6.75	43	.479	.542	0	.000	-1	-7	-7	-0	-1.1
	StL-A	1	3	.250	7	5	2	0	1	34²	34	1	17	8	13.5	4.41	56	.270	.361	3	.273	-2	-7	-7	-1	-0.7
Total	4	25	24	.510	62	52	36	4	1	426¹	411	4	159	127	12.3	2.96	82	.257	.329	32	.222	-7	-23	-25	-9	-3.2

● WARREN SPAHN
Spahn, Warren Edward b: 4/23/21, Buffalo, N.Y. BL/TL, 6', 175 lbs. Deb: 4/19/42 CH

YEAR	TM/L	W	L	PCT	G	GS	CG	SH	SV	IP	H	HR	BB	SO	RAT	ERA	ERA+	OAV	OOB	BH	AVG	PB	PR	/A	PD	TPI
1942	Bos-N	0	0	—	4	2	1	0	0	15²	25	0	11	7	20.7	5.74	58	.368	.456	1	.167	-0	-4	-4	-0	0.0
1946	Bos-N	8	5	.615	24	16	8	0	1	125²	107	6	36	67	10.3	2.94	117	.228	.285	7	.163	-1	7	7	-2	0.4

YEAR TM/L	W	L	PCT	G	GS	CG	SH	SV	IP	H	HR	BB	SO	RAT	ERA	ERA+	OAV	OOB	BH	AVG	PB	PR	/A	PD	TPI
1947 Bos-N★	21	10	.677	40	35	22	7	3	289²	245	15	84	123	10.3	2.33	167	.226	.283	16	.163	1	56	50	-2	5.1
1948 *Bos-N	15	12	.556	36	35	16	3	1	257	237	19	77	114	11.0	3.71	103	.242	.298	15	.167	2	7	3	0	0.5
1949 Bos-N★	21	14	.600	38	38	25	4	0	302¹	283	27	86	151	11.1	3.07	123	.245	.299	18	.162	-0	33	24	-2	2.3
1950 Bos-N☆	21	17	.553	41	39	25	1	1	293	248	22	111	191	11.1	3.16	123	.227	.299	23	.217	4	32	22	0	3.1
1951 Bos-N☆	22	14	.611	39	36	26	7	0	310²	278	20	109	164	11.2	2.98	123	.238	.304	22	.190	5	34	24	2	2.9
1952 Bos-N☆	14	19	.424	40	35	19	5	3	290	263	19	73	183	10.6	2.98	121	.240	.291	18	.161	2	24	20	1	2.7
1953 Mil-N★	23	7	.767	35	32	24	5	3	265²	211	14	70	148	9.6	2.10	187	.217	.270	23	.219	5	65	54	2	6.6
1954 Mil-N★	21	12	.636	39	34	23	1	3	283¹	262	24	86	136	11.1	3.14	118	.245	.302	21	.208	6	29	18	1	2.7
1955 Mil-N	17	14	.548	39	32	16	1	1	245²	249	25	65	110	11.6	3.26	115	.265	.314	17	.210	5	21	14	0	2.1
1956 Mil-N	20	11	.645	39	35	20	3	3	281¹	249	25	52	128	9.7	2.78	124	.238	.276	22	.210	6	31	21	-1	2.9
1957 *Mil-N☆	21	11	.656	39	35	18	4	3	271	241	23	78	111	10.7	2.69	130	.237	.293	13	.138	5	36	24	0	3.0
1958 *Mil-N★	22	11	.667	38	36	23	2	1	290	257	29	76	150	10.4	3.07	115	.237	.288	36	.333	18	28	14	4	3.9
1959 Mil-N☆	21	15	.583	40	36	21	4	0	292	282	21	70	143	10.9	2.96	120	.253	.298	24	.231	7	32	19	-1	2.8
1960 Mil-N	21	10	.677	40	33	18	4	2	267²	254	24	74	154	11.2	3.50	98	.250	.303	14	.147	3	8	-2	3	0.3
1961 Mil-N★	21	13	.618	38	34	21	4	0	262²	236	24	64	115	10.4	3.02	124	.243	.293	21	.223	10	30	21	3	3.9
1962 Mil-N	18	14	.563	34	34	22	0	0	269¹	248	25	55	118	10.2	3.04	125	.246	.287	18	.184	4	27	23	1	3.1
1963 Mil-N☆	23	7	.767	33	33	22	7	0	259²	241	23	49	102	10.1	2.60	124	.248	.284	16	.178	5	20	18	4	3.2
1964 Mil-N	6	13	.316	38	25	4	1	4	173²	204	23	52	78	13.4	5.29	67	.297	.348	11	.186	2	-34	-34	-1	-3.5
1965 NY-N	4	12	.250	20	19	5	0	0	126	140	18	35	56	12.6	4.36	81	.281	.331	4	.114	1	-11	-12	0	-1.2
SF-N	3	4	.429	16	11	3	0	0	71²	70	8	21	34	11.6	3.39	106	.256	.312	3	.143	1	1	2	1	0.2
Yr	7	16	.304	36	30	8	0	0	197²	210	26	56	90	12.2	4.01	89	.271	.321	7	.125	2	-10	-10	1	-1.0
Total 21	363	245	.597	750	665	382	63	29	5243²	4830	434	1434	2583	10.8	3.09	118	.244	.297	363	.194	88	470	330	9	47.0

● **AL SPALDING** Spalding, Albert Goodwill b: 9/2/1850, Byron, Ill. d: 9/9/15, San Diego, Cal. BR/TR, 6'1", 170 lbs. Deb: 5/5/1871 MH♦

YEAR TM/L	W	L	PCT	G	GS	CG	SH	SV	IP	H	HR	BB	SO	RAT	ERA	ERA+	OAV	OOB	BH	AVG	PB	PR	/A	PD	TPI
1871 Bos-n	19	10	.655	31	31	22	1	0	257¹	333	2	38	23	13.0	3.36	124	.268	.290	39	.271	2	25	23		1.6
1872 Bos-n	38	8	.826	48	48	41	3	0	404²	417	0	27	27	9.9	1.87	195	.244	.255	84	.354	18	80	80		7.1
1873 Bos-n	41	14	.745	60	55	47	1	2	497²	643	5	28	31	12.1	2.46	135	.283	.292	106	.329	21	44	47		5.4
1874 Bos-n	52	16	.765	71	69	65	4	0	617¹	755	1	19	30	11.3	1.92	112	.273	.278	119	.329	21	18	16		2.9
1875 Bos-n	54	5	.915	72	62	52	7	9	570²	573	1	18	75	9.3	1.59	135	.245	.251	107	.312	22	40	35		4.7
1876 Chi-N	47	12	.797	61	60	53	8	0	528²	542	6	26	39	9.7	1.75	139	.247	.256	91	.312	9	33	41	4	4.6
1877 Chi-N	1	0	1.000	4	1	0	0	1	11	11	0	0	2	13.9	3.27	91	.321	.321	6	.256	-0	1	-1	1	0.0
Total 5 n	204	53	.794	282	265	227	16	11	2347²	2721	9	130	186	10.9	2.10	136	.264	.273	455	.323	85	206	199		21.7
Total 2	48	12	.800	65	61	53	8	1	539²	559	6	26	41	9.8	1.78	138	.249	.257	158	.287	9	32	40	5	4.6

● **BILL SPANSWICK** Spanswick, William Henry b: 7/8/38, Springfield, Mass. BL/TL, 6'3", 195 lbs. Deb: 4/18/64

YEAR TM/L	W	L	PCT	G	GS	CG	SH	SV	IP	H	HR	BB	SO	RAT	ERA	ERA+	OAV	OOB	BH	AVG	PB	PR	/A	PD	TPI
1964 Bos-A	2	3	.400	29	7	0	0	0	65¹	75	9	44	55	16.8	6.89	56	.306	.418	4	.286	1	-24	-22	1	-1.3

● **STEVE SPARKS** Sparks, Steven William b: 7/2/65, Tulsa, Okla. BR/TR, 6', 180 lbs. Deb: 4/28/95

YEAR TM/L	W	L	PCT	G	GS	CG	SH	SV	IP	H	HR	BB	SO	RAT	ERA	ERA+	OAV	OOB	BH	AVG	PB	PR	/A	PD	TPI
1995 Mil-A	9	11	.450	33	27	3	0	0	202	210	17	86	96	13.4	4.63	108	.274	.351	0	—	0	2	8	4	0.8
1996 Mil-A	4	7	.364	20	13	1	0	0	88²	103	19	52	21	16.0	6.60	80	.297	.393	0	—	0	-16	-13	2	-1.5
Total 2	13	18	.419	53	40	4	0	0	290²	313	36	138	117	14.2	5.23	97	.281	.364	0	—	0	-14	-5	6	-0.7

● **TULLY SPARKS** Sparks, Thomas Frank b: 12/12/1874, Etna, Ga. d: 7/15/37, Anniston, Ala. BR/TR, Deb: 9/15/1897

YEAR TM/L	W	L	PCT	G	GS	CG	SH	SV	IP	H	HR	BB	SO	RAT	ERA	ERA+	OAV	OOB	BH	AVG	PB	PR	/A	PD	TPI
1897 Phi-N	0	1	.000	1	1	1	0	0	8	12	0	4	4	18.0	10.13	41	.343	.410	0	.000	-1	-5	-5	0	-0.4
1899 Pit-N	8	6	.571	28	17	8	0	0	170	180	1	82	53	14.4	3.86	99	.271	.360	8	.129	-2	-0	-1	-1	-0.3
1901 Mil-A	7	16	.304	29	26	18	0	0	210	228	5	93	62	14.4	3.51	102	.273	.356	12	.169	-1	4	2	-0	0.1
1902 NY-N	4	10	.286	15	13	11	0	1	115	123	2	40	40	13.1	3.76	75	.273	.338	5	.135	-1	-12	-12	3	-1.2
Bos-N	7	9	.438	17	15	15	1	0	142²	151	4	40	37	12.5	3.47	103	.272	.329	8	.154	-1	2	2	0	0.0
1903 Phi-N	11	15	.423	28	28	27	0	0	248	248	3	56	88	11.3	2.72	120	.263	.310	10	.109	-5	15	15	-2	0.7
1904 Phi-N	7	16	.304	26	25	19	3	0	200²	208	1	43	67	11.5	2.65	101	.260	.302	8	.105	-5	2	1	-4	-0.8
1905 Phi-N	14	11	.560	34	26	20	3	1	259²	217	2	73	90	10.4	2.18	134	.236	.298	12	.128	-2	24	21	-6	1.1
1906 Phi-N	19	16	.543	42	37	29	6	3	316²	244	6	62	114	9.0	2.16	121	.211	.257	16	.154	-0	17	16	-4	1.4
1907 Phi-N	22	8	.733	33	31	24	5	0	265	221	2	51	90	9.5	2.00	121	.228	.271	3	.034	-8	14	12	-5	-0.1
1908 Phi-N	16	15	.516	33	31	24	2	0	263¹	251	3	51	85	10.6	2.60	93	.257	.300	4	.052	-5	-7	-5	-2	-1.5
1909 Phi-N	6	11	.353	24	16	6	1	0	121²	126	4	32	40	11.9	2.96	88	.280	.332	5	.139	-1	-5	-5	-1	-0.9
1910 Phi-N	0	2	.000	3	3	0	0	0	15	22	2	4	8	15.6	6.00	52	.324	.361	0	.000	-1	-5	-5	-0	-0.6
Total 12	121	136	.471	313	269	202	19	8	2335²	2231	33	629	778	11.4	2.79	105	.253	.309	91	.114	-33	42	37	-20	-2.5

● **JOE SPARMA** Sparma, Joseph Blase b: 2/4/42, Massillon, Ohio d: 5/14/86, Columbus, Ohio BR/TR, 6', 195 lbs. Deb: 5/20/64

YEAR TM/L	W	L	PCT	G	GS	CG	SH	SV	IP	H	HR	BB	SO	RAT	ERA	ERA+	OAV	OOB	BH	AVG	PB	PR	/A	PD	TPI
1964 Det-A	5	6	.455	21	11	3	2	0	84	62	4	45	71	11.8	3.00	122	.207	.316	4	.160	-1	5	5	1	1.0
1965 Det-A	13	8	.619	30	28	6	0	0	167	142	13	75	127	11.9	3.18	109	.228	.314	7	.135	-0	5	6	-1	0.6
1966 Det-A	2	7	.222	29	13	0	0	0	91²	103	14	52	61	15.5	5.30	66	.288	.383	5	.217	-1	-19	-19	-2	-1.8
1967 Det-A	16	9	.640	37	37	11	5	0	217²	186	20	85	153	11.5	3.76	87	.227	.306	4	.054	-5	-13	-12	-2	-2.1
1968 *Det-A	10	10	.500	34	31	7	1	0	182¹	169	14	77	110	12.5	3.70	81	.246	.328	8	.133	-1	-15	-14	-1	-1.9
1969 Det-A	6	8	.429	23	16	3	2	0	92²	78	5	77	41	15.2	4.76	78	.231	.375	4	.138	-1	-12	-11	-1	-1.6
1970 Mon-N	0	4	.000	9	6	1	0	0	29¹	34	7	25	23	18.7	7.06	58	.296	.430	0	.000	-0	-10	-10	-0	-1.2
Total 7	52	52	.500	183	142	31	10	0	864²	774	77	436	586	12.9	3.94	86	.239	.334	32	.119	-6	-57	-53	-7	-7.0

● **TRIS SPEAKER** Speaker, Tristram E "The Grey Eagle" b: 4/4/1888, Hubbard, Tex. d: 12/8/58, Lake Whitney, Tex. BL/TL, 5'11.5", 193 lbs. Deb: 9/14/07 MH♦

YEAR TM/L	W	L	PCT	G	GS	CG	SH	SV	IP	H	HR	BB	SO	RAT	ERA	ERA+	OAV	OOB	BH	AVG	PB	PR	/A	PD	TPI
1914 Bos-A	0	0	—	1	0	0	0	0	1	2	0	0	0	18.0	9.00	30	.500	.500	193	.338	1	-1	-1	0	0.0

● **CLIFF SPECK** Speck, Robert Clifford b: 8/8/56, Portland, Ore. BR/TR, 6'4", 195 lbs. Deb: 7/30/86

YEAR TM/L	W	L	PCT	G	GS	CG	SH	SV	IP	H	HR	BB	SO	RAT	ERA	ERA+	OAV	OOB	BH	AVG	PB	PR	/A	PD	TPI
1986 Atl-N	2	1	.667	28¹	25	2	15	21	13.0	4.13	96	.238	.339	0	.000	—	-1	-0	-1		0.0

● **BY SPEECE** Speece, Byron Franklin b: 1/6/1897, West Baden, Ind. d: 9/29/74, Elgin, Ore. BR/TR, 5'11", 170 lbs. Deb: 4/21/24

YEAR TM/L	W	L	PCT	G	GS	CG	SH	SV	IP	H	HR	BB	SO	RAT	ERA	ERA+	OAV	OOB	BH	AVG	PB	PR	/A	PD	TPI
1924 *Was-A	2	1	.667	21	1	0	0	0	54¹	60	0	27	15	14.7	2.65	152	.303	.392	3	.150	-1	10	8	1	0.4
1925 Cle-A	3	5	.375	28	3	3	0	1	90¹	106	0	28	26	13.6	4.28	103	.297	.353	5	.161	-1	8	16	0	0.2
1926 Cle-A	0	0	—	2	0	0	0	0	3	1	0	2	1	9.0	0.00	—	.125	.300	0	—	0	1	1	0	0.0
1930 Phi-N	0	0	—	11	0	0	0	0	19²	41	1	4	9	20.6	13.27	41	.432	.455	1	.333	-0	-18	-17	-0	-0.2
Total 4	5	6	.455	62	4	3	0	1	167¹	208	1	61	51	14.7	4.73	93	.316	.378	9	.167	-2	-6	-6	2	0.4

● **FLOYD SPEER** Speer, Floyd Vernie b: 1/27/13, Booneville, Ark. d: 3/22/69, Little Rock, Ark. BR/TR, 6', 180 lbs. Deb: 4/25/43

YEAR TM/L	W	L	PCT	G	GS	CG	SH	SV	IP	H	HR	BB	SO	RAT	ERA	ERA+	OAV	OOB	BH	AVG	PB	PR	/A	PD	TPI
1943 Chi-A	0	0	—	1	0	0	0	0	1	1	0	1	1	27.0	9.00	37	.250	.500	0	—	0	-1	-1	0	0.0
1944 Chi-A	0	0	—	2	0	0	0	0	2	4	0	1	1	18.0	9.00	38	.500	.500	0	—	0	-1	-1	-0	0.0
Total 2	0	0	—	3	0	0	0	0	3	5	0	2	2	21.0	9.00	38	.417	.500	0	—	0	-1	-1	0	0.0

● **KID SPEER** Speer, George Nathan b: 6/16/1886, Corning, Mo. d: 1/13/46, Edmonton, Alberta, Canada BL/TL, 5'9", 152 lbs. Deb: 4/24/09

YEAR TM/L	W	L	PCT	G	GS	CG	SH	SV	IP	H	HR	BB	SO	RAT	ERA	ERA+	OAV	OOB	BH	AVG	PB	PR	/A	PD	TPI
1909 Det-A	4	4	.500	12	8	4	0	1	76¹	88	2	13	12	12.4	2.83	89	.293	.331	3	.120	-0	-3	-3	1	-0.3

● **HACK SPENCER** Spencer, Fred Calvin b: 4/25/1885, St.Cloud, Minn. d: 2/5/69, St.Anthony, Minn. BR/TR, 5'10.5", 172 lbs. Deb: 4/18/12

YEAR TM/L	W	L	PCT	G	GS	CG	SH	SV	IP	H	HR	BB	SO	RAT	ERA	ERA+	OAV	OOB	BH	AVG	PB	PR	/A	PD	TPI
1912 StL-A	0	0	—	1	0	0	0	0	1²	2	0	0	0	10.8	0.00	—	.286	.286	0	—	0	1	1	0	0.0

● **GEORGE SPENCER** Spencer, George Elwell b: 7/7/26, Columbus, Ohio BR/TR, 6'1", 215 lbs. Deb: 8/17/50

YEAR TM/L	W	L	PCT	G	GS	CG	SH	SV	IP	H	HR	BB	SO	RAT	ERA	ERA+	OAV	OOB	BH	AVG	PB	PR	/A	PD	TPI
1950 NY-N	1	0	1.000	10	1	1	0	0	25¹	12	3	7	5	6.8	2.49	165	.141	.207	0	.000	-1	5	5	0	0.1
1951 *NY-N	10	4	.714	57	4	2	0	6	132	125	21	56	36	12.4	3.75	104	.254	.282	4	.125	-1	3	2	1	0.3
1952 NY-N	3	5	.375	35	4	0	0	6	60	57	13	21	27	12.2	5.55	67	.251	.323	2	.200	-2	-12	-12	-0	-1.6
1953 NY-N	0	0	—	1	0	0	0	0	2¹	3	0	2	1	19.3	7.71	56	.300	.417				-1	-1	0	0.0
1954 NY-N	1	0	1.000	6	0	0	0	0	14¹	10	3	6	9	13.2	3.65	111	.209	.313	0	.000	-1	1	1	0	0.1
1955 NY-N	0	0	—	1	0	0	0	0	1²	1	1	2	0	21.6	5.40	75	.167	.444				-0	-0	0	0.0
1958 Det-A	1	0	1.000	7	0	0	0	0	10	11	0	4	5	13.5	2.70	149	.289	.357				1	1	0	0.2
1960 Det-A	0	1	.000	5	0	0	0	1	7²	9	0	8	4	17.6	3.52	112	.323	.417				0	0	0	0.0
Total 8	16	10	.615	122	9	3	0	9	251¹	228	40	106	82	12.1	4.05	96	.245	.324	6	.120	-2	-3	-4	2	-0.9

YEAR TM/L	W	L	PCT	G	GS	CG	SH	SV	IP	H	HR	BB	SO	RAT	ERA	ERA+	OAV	OOB	BH	AVG	PB	PR	/A	PD	TPI

● GLENN SPENCER   Spencer, Glenn Edward   b: 9/11/05, Corning, N.Y.   d: 12/30/58, Binghamton, N.Y.   BR/TR, 5'11″, 155 lbs.   Deb: 4/11/28

1928 Pit-N	0	0	—	4	0	0	0	0	5²	4	0	3	2	11.1	1.59	256	.200	.304	0	—	-0	2	2	-0	-0.1
1930 Pit-N	8	9	.471	41	10	5	0	4	156²	185	16	63	60	14.4	5.40	92	.305	.372	6	.113	-4	-7	-7	-2	-1.2
1931 Pit-N	11	12	.478	38	18	11	1	3	186²	180	8	65	51	12.1	3.42	112	.260	.328	5	.096	-0	9	9	-0	0.7
1932 Pit-N	4	8	.333	39	13	5	1	1	137²	167	10	44	35	14.0	4.97	77	.288	.341	6	.162	-1	-17	-18	-1	-1.6
1933 NY-N	0	2	.000	17	3	1	0	0	47¹	52	3	26	14	15.0	5.13	63	.284	.376	2	.167	-0	-9	-10	-0	-0.4
Total 5	23	31	.426	139	44	22	2	8	534	588	37	201	162	13.5	4.53	91	.282	.349	19	.123	-9	-23	-25	-3	-2.6

● BOB SPICER   Spicer, Robert Oberton   b: 4/11/25, Richmond, Va.   BL/TR, 5'10″, 173 lbs.   Deb: 4/17/55

1955 KC-A	0	0	—	2	0	0	0	0	2²	9	2	4	2	47.3	33.75	12	.529	.636	0	.000	-0	-9	-9	-0	0.0
1956 KC-A	0	0	—	2	0	0	0	0	2¹	6	1	1	0	30.9	19.29	22	.545	.615	0	—	0	-4	-4	-0	0.0
Total 2	0	0	—	4	0	0	0	0	5	15	3	5	2	39.6	27.00	16	.536	.629	0	.000	-0	-13	-13	-0	0.0

● DAN SPILLNER   Spillner, Daniel Ray   b: 11/27/51, Casper, Wyo.   BR/TR, 6'1″, 190 lbs.   Deb: 5/21/74

1974 SD-N	9	11	.450	30	25	5	2	0	148	153	15	70	95	13.6	4.01	89	.267	.346	1	.023	-4	-7	-8	-1	-1.5
1975 SD-N	5	13	.278	37	25	3	0	1	166²	194	14	63	104	14.0	4.27	81	.293	.356	6	.133	1	-12	-15	0	-1.4
1976 SD-N	2	11	.154	32	14	0	0	1	106²	120	11	55	57	14.8	5.06	65	.291	.374	1	.040	-1	-19	-21	1	-2.4
1977 SD-N	7	6	.538	76	0	0	0	6	123	130	12	60	74	14.0	3.73	95	.280	.363	2	.118	1	2	-3	-2	-0.4
1978 SD-N	1	0	1.000	17	0	0	0	0	25²	32	2	7	16	13.7	4.56	73	.317	.361	0	—	0	-3	-4	-0	-0.1
Cle-A	3	1	.750	36	0	0	0	3	56¹	54	7	21	48	12.1	3.67	102	.254	.323	0	—	0	1	0	-1	-0.1
1979 Cle-A	9	5	.643	49	13	3	0	1	157²	153	16	64	97	12.6	4.62	92	.256	.331	0	—	0	-7	-6	-1	-0.6
1980 Cle-A	16	11	.593	34	30	7	1	0	194¹	225	23	74	100	14.0	5.28	77	.288	.352	0	—	0	-27	-26	-2	-3.3
1981 Cle-A	4	4	.500	32	5	1	0	7	97¹	86	3	39	59	11.6	3.14	115	.240	.314	0	—	0	6	5	0	0.5
1982 Cle-A	12	10	.545	65	0	0	0	21	133²	117	9	45	90	10.9	2.49	164	.235	.299	0	—	0	**24**	**24**	-3	4.2
1983 Cle-A	2	9	.182	60	0	0	0	8	92¹	117	7	38	48	15.3	5.07	84	.315	.382	0	—	0	-10	-9	-1	-1.2
1984 Cle-A	0	5	.000	14	8	0	0	0	51	70	3	22	23	16.2	5.65	72	.332	.395	0	—	0	-9	-9	-1	-0.7
Chi-A	1	0	1.000	22	0	0	0	0	48¹	51	4	14	26	12.3	4.10	101	.276	.330	0	—	0	-1	-0	-0	0.0
Yr	1	5	.167	36	8	0	0	0	99¹	121	10	36	49	14.3	4.89	84	.301	.360	0	—	0	-10	-9	-1	-0.7
1985 Chi-A	4	3	.571	52	3	0	0	1	91²	83	10	33	41	11.4	3.44	126	.245	.312	0	—	0	7	9	-3	0.4
Total 12	75	89	.457	556	123	19	3	50	1492²	1585	134	605	878	13.3	4.21	91	.275	.345	10	.077	-3	-55	-62	-12	-6.6

● SCIPIO SPINKS   Spinks, Scipio Ronald   b: 7/12/47, Chicago, Ill.   BR/TR, 6'1″, 185 lbs.   Deb: 9/16/69

1969 Hou-N	0	0	—	1	0	0	0	0	2	1	0	1	4	9.0	0.00	—	.143	.250	0	—	0	1	1	0	0.0
1970 Hou-N	0	1	.000	5	2	0	0	0	13²	17	5	9	6	17.1	9.88	39	.293	.388	0	.000	-0	-9	-9	-1	-0.6
1971 Hou-N	1	0	1.000	5	3	1	0	0	29¹	22	2	13	26	11.0	3.68	91	.210	.303	2	.222	1	-1	-1	0	0.0
1972 StL-N	5	5	.500	16	16	6	0	0	118	96	5	59	93	12.0	2.67	127	.221	.317	7	.167	-1	10	11	1	0.8
1973 StL-N	1	5	.167	8	8	0	0	0	38²	39	4	25	25	14.9	4.89	75	.269	.376	2	.182	1	-5	-5	1	-0.6
Total 5	7	11	.389	35	29	7	0	0	201²	175	16	107	154	12.7	3.70	94	.234	.332	11	.169	0	-4	-5	1	-0.4

● PAUL SPLITTORFF   Splittorff, Paul William   b: 10/8/46, Evansville, Ind.   BL/TL, 6'3″, 210 lbs.   Deb: 9/23/70

1970 KC-A	0	1	.000	2	1	0	0	0	8²	16	1	5	10	21.8	7.27	51	.390	.457	1	.500	1	-3	-3	0	-0.3
1971 KC-A	8	9	.471	22	22	6	3	0	144¹	129	4	35	80	10.5	2.68	128	.243	.295	5	.104	-1	13	12	2	1.5
1972 KC-A	12	12	.500	35	33	12	2	0	216	189	11	67	140	10.8	3.13	97	.241	.304	16	.225	4	-2	-2	4	0.6
1973 KC-A	20	11	.645	38	38	12	3	0	262	279	19	78	110	12.4	3.98	103	.272	.327	0	—	0	-5	-4	1	0.0
1974 KC-A	13	19	.406	36	36	8	1	0	226	252	20	75	90	13.1	4.10	93	.285	.342	0	—	0	-12	-7	0	-1.3
1975 KC-A	9	10	.474	35	23	6	3	1	159	156	10	56	76	12.1	3.17	121	.255	.319	0	—	0	11	12	2	1.5
1976 *KC-A	11	8	.579	26	23	5	1	0	158²	169	11	59	59	13.1	3.97	88	.277	.343	0	—	0	-8	-8	1	-0.8
1977 *KC-A	16	6	**.727**	37	37	6	2	0	229	243	11	83	99	12.9	3.69	109	.278	.342	0	—	0	9	9	-0	0.7
1978 *KC-A	19	13	.594	39	38	13	2	0	262	244	22	60	76	10.5	3.40	112	.247	.293	0	—	0	11	12	1	1.5
1979 KC-A	15	17	.469	36	35	11	0	0	240	248	25	77	77	12.4	4.24	101	.268	.328	0	—	0	-1	-1	-2	-0.2
1980 *KC-A	14	11	.560	34	33	4	0	0	204	236	17	43	53	12.4	4.15	98	.296	.333	0	—	0	-3	-2	-0	-0.3
1981 KC-A	5	5	.500	21	15	1	0	0	99	111	12	23	48	12.3	4.36	83	.294	.337	0	—	0	-8	-8	1	-0.7
1982 KC-A	10	10	.500	29	28	0	0	0	162	166	14	57	74	12.6	4.28	95	.266	.330	0	—	0	-4	-4	0	-0.4
1983 KC-A	13	8	.619	24	27	4	0	0	156	159	9	52	61	12.2	3.63	112	.262	.322	0	—	0	7	8	0	0.9
1984 KC-A	1	3	.250	12	3	0	0	0	28	47	3	10	4	18.3	7.71	52	.376	.422	0	—	0	-12	-11	1	-1.3
Total 15	166	143	.537	429	392	88	17	1	2554²	2644	192	780	1057	12.2	3.81	101	.270	.326	22	.182	3	-6	10	10	1.4

● PAUL SPOLJARIC   Spoljaric, Paul Nikola   b: 9/24/70, Kelowna, B.C., Canada   BR/TL, 6'3″, 205 lbs.   Deb: 4/6/94

1994 Tor-A	0	1	.000	2	1	0	0	0	2¹	5	1	4	3	54.0	38.57	12	.417	.667	0	—	0	-9	-9	-0	-1.9
1996 Tor-A	2	2	.500	28	0	0	0	1	38	30	8	24	37	12.1	3.08	164	.214	.317	0	—	0	8	8	0	0.8
Total 2	2	3	.400	30	1	0	0	1	40¹	35	9	28	40	14.5	5.13	98	.230	.357	0	—	0	-1	-0	-0	-1.1

● CARL SPONGBERG   Spongberg, Carl Gustav   b: 5/21/1884, Idaho Falls, Idaho   d: 7/21/38, Los Angeles, Cal.   BR/TR, 6'2″, 208 lbs.   Deb: 8/1/08

| 1908 Chi-N | 0 | 0 | — | 1 | 0 | 0 | 0 | 0 | 7 | 9 | 1 | 6 | 4 | 21.9 | 9.00 | 26 | .321 | .472 | 2 | .667 | 1 | -5 | -5 | 0 | 0.1 |

● KARL SPOONER   Spooner, Karl Benjamin   b: 6/23/31, Oriskany Falls, N.Y.   d: 4/10/84, Vero Beach, Fla.   BR/TL, 6', 185 lbs.   Deb: 9/22/54

1954 Bro-N	2	0	1.000	2	2	2	2	0	18	7	0	6	27	6.5	0.00	—	.113	.191	1	.167	0	8	9	-0	1.1
1955 *Bro-N	8	6	.571	29	14	2	1	2	98²	79	8	41	78	11.4	3.65	111	.215	.302	8	.286	3	4	5	-0	0.8
Total 2	10	6	.625	31	16	4	3	2	116²	86	8	47	105	10.6	3.09	132	.200	.286	9	.265	3	12	13	-1	1.9

● JERRY SPRADLIN   Spradlin, Jerry Carl   b: 6/14/67, Fullerton, Cal.   BB/TR, 6'7″, 230 lbs.   Deb: 7/2/93

1993 Cin-N	2	1	.667	37	0	0	0	2	49	44	4	9	24	9.7	3.49	115	.249	.285	0	.000	-0	3	3	-1	0.0
1994 Cin-N	0	0	—	6	0	0	0	0	8	12	2	2	4	15.8	10.13	41	.353	.389	0	—	0	-5	-5	0	-0.4
1996 Cin-N	0	0	—	1	0	0	0	0	0¹	0	0	0	0	0.0	0.00	—	.000	.000	0	—	0	0	0	-0	0.0
Total 3	2	1	.667	44	0	0	0	2	57¹	56	6	11	28	10.5	4.40	92	.264	.300	0	.000	-0	-2	-2	-1	-0.4

● HOMER SPRAGINS   Spragins, Homer Franklin   b: 11/9/20, Grenada, Miss.   BR/TR, 6'1″, 190 lbs.   Deb: 9/13/47

| 1947 Phi-N | 0 | 0 | — | 4 | 0 | 0 | 0 | 0 | 5¹ | 3 | 0 | 3 | 3 | 10.1 | 6.75 | 59 | .158 | .273 | 0 | — | 0 | -2 | -2 | 0 | 0.0 |

● CHARLIE SPRAGUE   Sprague, Charles Wellington   b: 10/10/1864, Cleveland, Ohio   d: 12/31/12, Des Moines, Iowa   BL/TL, 5'11″, 150 lbs.   Deb: 9/17/1887   ♦

1887 Chi-N	1	0	1.000	3	3	2	0	0	22	24	1	13	9	16.8	4.91	77	.276	.394	2	.154	-1	-2	-1	-1	-0.2
1889 Cle-N	0	2	.000	2	2	2	0	0	17	27	1	10	8	20.6	8.47	48	.351	.438	1	.143	-0	-8	-8	1	-0.6
1890 Tol-a	9	5	.643	19	12	9	0	0	122²	111	0	78	59	15.2	3.89	102	.234	.363	47	.236	3	-0	1	-2	0.1
Total 3	10	7	.588	24	17	13	0	0	161²	162	1	101	76	16.0	4.51	89	.254	.376	50	.228	2	-11	-9	-2	-0.7

● ED SPRAGUE   Sprague, Edward Nelson Sr.   b: 9/16/45, Boston, Mass.   BR/TR, 6'4″, 195 lbs.   Deb: 4/10/68   F

1968 Oak-A	3	4	.429	47	1	0	0	4	68²	51	5	34	34	11.4	3.28	86	.209	.311	0	.000	-1	-2	-3	1	-0.4
1969 Oak-A	1	1	.500	27	0	0	0	0	46¹	47	4	31	20	15.5	4.47	77	.267	.383	1	.200	0	-4	-5	2	0.4
1971 Cin-N	1	0	1.000	7	0	0	0	0	11	8	0	7	6	7.4	0.00	—	.195	.214	0	—	0	4	4	-1	0.3
1972 Cin-N	1	3	.500	33	1	0	0	0	56²	55	6	26	25	13.3	4.13	78	.261	.350	0	.000	-1	-4	-6	-1	-0.7
1973 Cin-N	1	3	.250	28	0	0	0	0	38²	35	3	22	19	13.7	5.12	66	.246	.355	0	.000	-0	-6	-7	-0	-0.7
StL-N	0	0	—	8	0	0	0	0	8	8	1	4	2	13.5	2.25	162	.276	.364	0	—	0	1	1	0	0.0
Yr	1	3	.250	36	0	0	0	0	46²	43	4	26	21	13.3	4.63	74	.247	.345	0	.000	-0	-5	-6	-1	-0.7
Mil-A	0	1	.000	7	0	0	0	0	9²	13	0	14	3	27.0	9.31	40	.317	.509	0	—	0	-6	-6	-0	-0.6
1974 Mil-A	7	2	.778	20	10	3	0	0	94	94	3	31	57	12.4	2.39	151	.266	.332	0	—	0	13	13	-1	1.2
1975 Mil-A	4	7	.125	18	11	0	0	1	67¹	81	6	40	21	16.4	4.68	82	.297	.390	0	—	0	-7	-6	-1	-0.8
1976 Mil-A	0	2	.000	3	0	0	0	0	7²	14	0	7	1	20.0	7.04	50	.438	.486	0	—	0	-3	-3	-0	-0.6
Total 8	17	23	.425	198	23	3	0	9	408	406	27	206	188	13.9	3.84	89	.263	.356	1	.045	-2	-15	-19	-2	-2.3

● JACK SPRING   Spring, Jack Russell   b: 3/11/33, Spokane, Wash.   BR/TR, 6'1″, 180 lbs.   Deb: 4/16/55

| 1955 Phi-N | 0 | 1 | .000 | 2 | 0 | 0 | 0 | 0 | 2² | 2 | 1 | 1 | 2 | 10.1 | 6.75 | 59 | .200 | .273 | 0 | .000 | -0 | -1 | -1 | -0 | -0.3 |
| 1957 Bos-A | 0 | 0 | — | 1 | 0 | 0 | 0 | 0 | 1 | 0 | 0 | 0 | 0 | 0.0 | 0.00 | — | .000 | .000 | 0 | — | 0 | 0 | 0 | -0 | 0.0 |

YEAR	TM/L	W	L	PCT	G	GS	CG	SH	SV	IP	H	HR	BB	SO	RAT	ERA	ERA+	OAV	OOB	BH	AVG	PB	PR	/A	PD	TPI
1958	Was-A	0	0	—	3	1	0	0	0	7	16	1	7	1	29.6	14.14	27	.457	.548	0	.000	-0	-8	-8	0	0.0
1961	LA-A	3	0	1.000	18	4	0	0	0	38	35	4	15	27	12.6	4.26	106	.243	.327	0	.000	-1	-1	1	-0	0.0
1962	LA-A	4	2	.667	57	0	0	0	6	65	66	7	30	31	13.6	4.02	96	.270	.355	1	.091	-1	-0	-1	1	-0.1
1963	LA-A	3	0	1.000	45	0	0	0	2	38¹	40	3	9	13	11.5	3.05	112	.268	.310	1	.333	0	2	2	1	0.2
1964	LA-A	1	0	1.000	6	0	0	0	0	3¹	3	1	3	0	16.2	2.70	122	.273	.429	0	—	0	0	0	-0	0.0
	Chi-N	0	0	—	7	0	0	0	0	6	4	0	2	1	9.0	6.00	62	.200	.273	0	—	0	-2	-2	0	0.0
	StL-N	0	0	—	2	0	0	0	0	3	8	1	1	0	27.0	3.00	127	.471	.500	0	—	0	0	0	0	0.0
	Yr	0	0	—	9	0	0	0	0	9	12	1	3	1	15.0	5.00	75	.316	.366	0	—	0	-1	-1	0	0.0
1965	Cle-A	1	2	.333	14	0	0	0	0	21²	21	2	10	12	12.9	3.74	93	.259	.341	1	.333	-1	-1	-1	-1	-0.1
Total	8	12	5	.706	155	5	0	0	8	186	195	21	78	86	13.5	4.26	90	.273	.349	3	.107	-1	-9	-9	1	-0.3

● **BRAD SPRINGER** Springer, Bradford Louis b: 5/9/04, Detroit, Mich. d: 1/4/70, Birmingham, Mich. BL/TL, 6', 155 lbs. Deb: 5/1/25

YEAR	TM/L	W	L	PCT	G	GS	CG	SH	SV	IP	H	HR	BB	SO	RAT	ERA	ERA+	OAV	OOB	BH	AVG	PB	PR	/A	PD	TPI
1925	StL-A	0	0	—	2	0	0	0	0	3	1	0	7	0	24.0	3.00	156	.200	.667	0	—	0	1	1	0	0.0
1926	Cin-N	0	0	—	1	0	0	0	0	1¹	2	0	2	1	33.8	6.75	55	.286	.500	0	.000	-0	0	0	0	0.0
Total	2	0	0	—	3	0	0	0	0	4¹	3	0	9	1	27.0	4.15	105	.250	.591	0	.000	-0	0	0	0	0.0

● **DENNIS SPRINGER** Springer, Dennis Leroy b: 2/12/65, Fresno, Cal. BR/TR, 5'10", 185 lbs. Deb: 9/14/95

YEAR	TM/L	W	L	PCT	G	GS	CG	SH	SV	IP	H	HR	BB	SO	RAT	ERA	ERA+	OAV	OOB	BH	AVG	PB	PR	/A	PD	TPI
1995	Phi-N	0	3	.000	4	4	0	0	0	22¹	21	3	9	15	12.5	4.84	87	.256	.337	1	.125	-0	-2	-2	-1	-0.3
1996	Cal-A	5	6	.455	20	15	2	1	0	94²	91	24	43	64	13.3	5.51	89	.251	.340	0	—	0	-5	-7	-1	-0.6
Total	2	5	9	.357	24	19	2	1	0	117	112	27	52	79	13.2	5.38	89	.252	.339	1	.125	-0	-7	-8	-2	-0.7

● **ED SPRINGER** Springer, Edward H. b: 2/9/1861, California d: 4/24/26, Los Angeles Co., Cal. 6'2", 187 lbs. Deb: 7/12/1889

YEAR	TM/L	W	L	PCT	G	GS	CG	SH	SV	IP	H	HR	BB	SO	RAT	ERA	ERA+	OAV	OOB	BH	AVG	PB	PR	/A	PD	TPI
1889	Lou-a	0	1	.000	1	1	1	0	0	5	8	0	2	1	21.6	9.00	43	.348	.444	0	.000	-0	-3	-3	-0	-0.4

● **RUSS SPRINGER** Springer, Russell Paul b: 11/7/68, Alexandria, La. BR/TR, 6'4", 195 lbs. Deb: 4/17/92

YEAR	TM/L	W	L	PCT	G	GS	CG	SH	SV	IP	H	HR	BB	SO	RAT	ERA	ERA+	OAV	OOB	BH	AVG	PB	PR	/A	PD	TPI
1992	NY-A	0	0	—	14	0	0	0	0	16	18	0	10	12	16.3	6.19	63	.281	.387	0	—	0	-4	-4	-0	0.0
1993	Cal-A	1	6	.143	14	9	1	0	0	60	73	11	32	31	16.2	7.20	63	.303	.391	0	—	0	-19	-18	-1	-2.0
1994	Cal-A	2	2	.500	18	5	0	0	2	45²	53	9	14	28	13.2	5.52	89	.291	.342	0	—	0	-4	-3	-0	-0.4
1995	Cal-A	1	2	.333	19	6	0	0	1	51²	60	11	25	38	15.7	6.10	77	.290	.380	0	—	0	-8	-8	-0	-0.4
	Phi-N	0	0	—	14	0	0	0	0	26²	22	5	10	32	11.5	3.71	114	.227	.312	0	.000	-0	1	2	1	0.0
1996	Phi-N	3	10	.231	51	7	0	0	0	96²	106	12	38	94	13.5	4.66	94	.272	.338	1	.059	-1	-5	-3	-0	-0.6
Total	5	7	20	.259	130	27	1	0	3	296²	332	48	129	235	14.3	5.55	81	.281	.358	1	.056	-1	-38	-35	-3	-3.4

● **CHARLIE SPROULL** Sproull, Charles William b: 1/9/19, Taylorsville, Ga. d: 1/13/80, Rockford, Ill. BR/TR, 6'3", 185 lbs. Deb: 4/19/45

YEAR	TM/L	W	L	PCT	G	GS	CG	SH	SV	IP	H	HR	BB	SO	RAT	ERA	ERA+	OAV	OOB	BH	AVG	PB	PR	/A	PD	TPI
1945	Phi-N	4	10	.286	34	19	2	0	1	130¹	158	10	80	47	16.4	5.94	65	.298	.390	5	.143	-1	-31	-31	-1	-3.1

● **BOB SPROUT** Sprout, Robert Samuel b: 12/5/41, Florin, Pa. BL/TL, 6', 165 lbs. Deb: 9/27/61

YEAR	TM/L	W	L	PCT	G	GS	CG	SH	SV	IP	H	HR	BB	SO	RAT	ERA	ERA+	OAV	OOB	BH	AVG	PB	PR	/A	PD	TPI
1961	LA-A	0	0	—	1	1	0	0	0	4	4	0	3	2	15.8	4.50	100	.267	.389	0	—	0	-0	-0	-0	0.0

● **BOBBY SPROWL** Sprowl, Robert John b: 4/14/56, Sandusky, Ohio BL/TL, 6'2", 190 lbs. Deb: 9/5/78

YEAR	TM/L	W	L	PCT	G	GS	CG	SH	SV	IP	H	HR	BB	SO	RAT	ERA	ERA+	OAV	OOB	BH	AVG	PB	PR	/A	PD	TPI
1978	Bos-A	0	2	.000	3	3	0	0	0	12²	12	3	10	10	15.6	6.39	64	.245	.373	0	—	0	-4	-3	-0	-0.5
1979	Hou-N	0	0	—	3	0	0	0	0	4	1	0	2	3	6.8	0.00	—	.083	.214	0	—	0	2	2	-0	0.2
1980	Hou-N	0	0	—	1	0	0	0	0	1	1	0	1	3	18.0	0.00	—	.250	.400	0	—	0	0	0	0	0.0
1981	Hou-N	0	1	.000	15	1	0	0	0	28²	40	1	14	18	17.0	5.97	55	.333	.403	1	.167	-0	-8	-9	-0	-0.3
Total	4	0	3	.000	22	4	0	0	0	46¹	54	4	27	34	15.7	5.44	65	.292	.382	1	.167	-0	-10	-10	-0	-0.8

● **MIKE SQUIRES** Squires, Michael Lynn b: 3/5/52, Kalamazoo, Mich. BL/TL, 5'11", 185 lbs. Deb: 9/1/75 C♦

YEAR	TM/L	W	L	PCT	G	GS	CG	SH	SV	IP	H	HR	BB	SO	RAT	ERA	ERA+	OAV	OOB	BH	AVG	PB	PR	/A	PD	TPI
1984	Chi-A	0	0	—	1	0	0	0	0	0¹	0	0	0	0	0.0	0.0	—	.000	.000	15	.183	0	0	0	0	0.0

● **GEORGE STABLEIN** Stablein, George Charles b: 10/29/57, Inglewood, Cal. BR/TR, 6'4", 185 lbs. Deb: 9/20/80

YEAR	TM/L	W	L	PCT	G	GS	CG	SH	SV	IP	H	HR	BB	SO	RAT	ERA	ERA+	OAV	OOB	BH	AVG	PB	PR	/A	PD	TPI
1980	SD-N	0	1	.000	4	2	0	0	0	11²	16	0	3	4	14.7	3.09	111	.340	.380	0	.000	-0	1	0	-0	0.0

● **EDDIE STACK** Stack, William Edward b: 10/24/1887, Chicago, Ill. d: 8/28/58, Chicago, Ill. BR/TR, 6', 175 lbs. Deb: 6/7/10

YEAR	TM/L	W	L	PCT	G	GS	CG	SH	SV	IP	H	HR	BB	SO	RAT	ERA	ERA+	OAV	OOB	BH	AVG	PB	PR	/A	PD	TPI
1910	Phi-N	6	7	.462	20	16	8	1	0	117	115	7	34	48	11.8	4.00	78	.266	.326	3	.083	-3	-13	-11	-1	-1.6
1911	Phi-N	5	5	.500	13	10	5	0	0	77²	67	3	41	36	13.2	3.59	96	.234	.342	2	.083	-2	-2	-1	0	-0.3
1912	Bro-N	7	5	.583	28	17	4	0	1	142	139	3	55	45	12.9	3.36	100	.264	.343	7	.135	-3	1	0	-1	-0.4
1913	Bro-N	4	4	.500	23	9	4	1	0	87	79	0	32	34	11.6	2.38	138	.250	.321	4	.160	-1	8	9	-2	0.4
	Chi-N	4	2	.667	11	7	3	1	1	51	56	1	15	28	12.9	4.24	75	.280	.336	1	.063	-1	-6	-6	-1	-0.9
	Yr	8	6	.571	34	16	7	2	1	138	135	1	47	62	12.0	3.07	106	.261	.325	5	.122	-2	2	3	-3	-0.5
1914	Chi-N	0	1	.000	7	1	0	0	0	16¹	13	0	11	9	13.2	4.96	56	.220	.343	0	.000	-0	-4	-4	-0	-0.2
Total	5	26	24	.520	102	60	24	3	2	491	469	14	188	200	12.4	3.52	93	.258	.334	17	.108	-10	-15	-14	-4	-3.0

● **GENERAL STAFFORD** Stafford, James Joseph "Jamsey" b: 7/9/1868, Webster, Mass. d: 9/18/23, Worcester, Mass. BR/TR, 5'8", 165 lbs. Deb: 8/27/1890 F♦

YEAR	TM/L	W	L	PCT	G	GS	CG	SH	SV	IP	H	HR	BB	SO	RAT	ERA	ERA+	OAV	OOB	BH	AVG	PB	PR	/A	PD	TPI
1890	Buf-P	3	9	.250	12	12	11	0	0	98	123	8	43	21	15.6	5.14	80	.294	.366	7	.143	-2	-10	-11	-1	-1.1

● **JOHN STAFFORD** Stafford, John Henry "Doc" b: 4/8/1870, Dudley, Mass. d: 7/3/40, Worcester, Mass. BR/TR, 5'10", 170 lbs. Deb: 6/15/1893 F

YEAR	TM/L	W	L	PCT	G	GS	CG	SH	SV	IP	H	HR	BB	SO	RAT	ERA	ERA+	OAV	OOB	BH	AVG	PB	PR	/A	PD	TPI
1893	Cle-N	0	1	.000	2	0	0	0	0	7	12	1	7	4	24.4	14.14	35	.364	.475	0	.000	-1	-7	-7	-0	-0.7

● **BILL STAFFORD** Stafford, William Charles b: 8/13/39, Catskill, N.Y. BR/TR, 6'2", 193 lbs. Deb: 4/17/60

YEAR	TM/L	W	L	PCT	G	GS	CG	SH	SV	IP	H	HR	BB	SO	RAT	ERA	ERA+	OAV	OOB	BH	AVG	PB	PR	/A	PD	TPI
1960	*NY-A	3	1	.750	11	8	2	1	0	60	50	3	18	36	10.4	2.25	159	.226	.287	1	.045	-2	11	9	1	0.4
1961	*NY-A	14	9	.609	36	25	8	3	2	195	168	13	59	101	10.7	2.68	139	.232	.294	12	.179	2	29	23	-1	2.6
1962	*NY-A	14	9	.609	35	33	7	2	0	213¹	188	20	77	109	11.3	3.67	102	.233	.303	17	.218	3	7	2	-1	0.3
1963	NY-A	4	8	.333	28	14	0	0	3	89²	104	16	42	52	15.0	6.02	58	.287	.366	7	.292	3	-24	-25	-0	-3.0
1964	NY-A	5	0	1.000	31	1	0	0	4	60²	54	4	22	39	11.0	2.67	136	.231	.308	1	.077	-1	6	6	0	0.5
1965	NY-A	3	8	.273	22	15	1	0	0	111¹	93	16	31	71	10.2	3.56	96	.229	.286	0	—	-3	-1	-2	-0	-0.5
1966	KC-A	0	4	.000	9	8	0	0	0	39²	42	2	12	31	12.7	4.99	68	.273	.333	0	.000	-1	-7	-7	-1	-0.8
1967	KC-A	0	1	.000	14	0	0	0	0	16	12	0	9	10	11.8	1.69	189	.214	.323	0	.000	-0	3	3	0	0.2
Total	8	43	40	.518	186	104	18	6	9	785²	707	77	270	449	11.4	3.52	103	.240	.308	38	.155	0	24	9	-2	-0.3

● **CHICK STAHL** Stahl, Charles Sylvester b: 1/10/1873, Avilla, Ind. d: 3/28/07, W.Baden, Ind. BL/TL, 5'10", 160 lbs. Deb: 4/19/1897 M♦

YEAR	TM/L	W	L	PCT	G	GS	CG	SH	SV	IP	H	HR	BB	SO	RAT	ERA	ERA+	OAV	OOB	BH	AVG	PB	PR	/A	PD	TPI
1899	Bos-N	0	0	—	1	0	0	0	0	2	2	0	3	0	22.5	9.00	46	.250	.455	202	.351	0	-1	-1	0	0.0

● **GERRY STALEY** Staley, Gerald Lee b: 8/21/20, Brush Prairie, Wash. BR/TR, 6', 195 lbs. Deb: 4/20/47

YEAR	TM/L	W	L	PCT	G	GS	CG	SH	SV	IP	H	HR	BB	SO	RAT	ERA	ERA+	OAV	OOB	BH	AVG	PB	PR	/A	PD	TPI
1947	StL-N	1	0	1.000	18	1	1	0	0	29¹	33	2	8	14	12.9	2.76	150	.287	.339	0	.000	-1	4	4	1	0.1
1948	StL-N	4	4	.500	31	3	0	0	0	52	61	5	21	23	14.2	6.92	59	.288	.352	2	.222	-1	-17	-16	1	-2.0
1949	StL-N	10	10	.500	45	17	5	2	6	171¹	154	7	41	55	10.4	2.73	152	**.238**	.286	5	.122	-0	25	27	3	3.5
1950	StL-N	13	13	.500	42	22	7	1	3	169²	201	14	61	62	14.3	4.99	86	.300	.365	8	.145	-1	-16	-13	3	-1.6
1951	StL-N	19	13	.594	42	30	16	4	3	227	244	14	74	67	12.9	3.81	104	.275	.337	13	.160	-1	4	4	2	0.6
1952	StL-N☆	17	14	.548	35	33	15	0	0	239²	238	21	52	93	11.2	3.27	114	.256	.301	13	.153	-2	12	12	4	1.6
1953	StL-N☆	18	9	.667	40	32	10	1	4	230	243	31	54	88	12.3	3.99	107	.269	.322	8	.103	-5	8	7	2	0.5
1954	StL-N	7	13	.350	48	24	3	1	2	155²	198	21	47	50	14.5	5.26	78	.308	.361	6	.139	-0	-21	-20	2	-2.1
1955	Cin-N	5	8	.385	30	18	2	0	0	119²	146	22	28	40	13.3	4.66	91	.309	.351	2	.056	-4	-8	-6	1	-0.8
	NY-A	0	0	—	2	0	0	0	0	2	5	1	1	0	27.0	13.50	28	.417	.462	0	—	0	-2	-2	-0	0.0
1956	NY-A	0	0	—	1	0	0	0	0	0¹	4	0	1	0	108.0	108.00	4	.800	.800	0	—	0	-4	-4	-0	0.0
	Chi-A	8	3	.727	26	10	5	0	0	101²	98	11	20	25	11.0	2.92	140	.251	.298	3	.094	-2	14	13	1	1.1
	Yr	8	3	.727	27	10	5	0	0	102	102	11	20	26	11.3	3.26	126	.258	.304	3	.091	-3	10	9	1	1.1
1957	Chi-A	5	1	.833	47	0	0	0	7	105	95	7	27	44	10.5	2.06	182	.244	.293	1	.045	-1	**20**	**20**	2	1.4
1958	Chi-A	4	4	.444	50	0	0	0	8	85¹	81	10	24	27	11.1	3.16	115	.259	.312	0	.000	-1	6	4	0	0.7
1959	*Chi-A★	8	5	.615	**67**	0	0	0	14	116¹	111	9	25	54	10.5	2.24	167	.259	.300	2	.154	0	**21**	**20**	-0	2.6
1960	Chi-A★	13	8	.619	64	0	0	0	10	115¹	94	8	25	43	9.5	2.42	156	.227	.276	4	.235	1	**19**	**17**	3	**3.7**
1961	Chi-A	0	3	.000	16	0	0	0	0	18	17	3	5	8	11.0	5.00	78	.246	.297	0	.000	-0	-3	-3	-0	-0.3
	KC-A	1	1	.500	23	0	0	0	2	30	32	4	10	16	13.2	3.60	116	.278	.346	0	.000	-0	1	2	1	0.2
	Det-A	1	1	.500	13	0	0	0	0	13¹	15	1	6	8	14.2	3.38	121	.288	.362	0	.000	-0	1	1	0	0.2

YEAR TM/L	W	L	PCT	G	GS	CG	SH	SV	IP	H	HR	BB	SO	RAT	ERA	ERA+	OAV	OOB	BH	AVG	PB	PR	/A	PD	TPI
Yr	2	5	.286	52	0	0	0	4	61¹	64	8	21	32	12.5	3.96	103	.267	.326	0	.000	0	0	1	1	0.1
Total 15	134	111	.547	640	186	58	9	61	1981²	2070	187	529	727	12.1	3.70	108	.270	.322	66	.126	-16	65	68	29	9.4

● **HARRY STALEY** Staley, Henry Eli b: 11/3/1866, Jacksonville, Ill. d: 1/12/10, Battle Creek, Mich BR/TR, 5'10", 175 lbs. Deb: 6/23/1888

YEAR TM/L	W	L	PCT	G	GS	CG	SH	SV	IP	H	HR	BB	SO	RAT	ERA	ERA+	OAV	OOB	BH	AVG	PB	PR	/A	PD	TPI
1888 Pit-N	12	12	.500	25	24	24	2	0	207¹	185	6	53	89	10.6	2.69	99	.235	.289	11	.129	-4	4	-1	-1	-0.5
1889 Pit-N	21	26	.447	49	47	46	1	1	420	433	11	116	159	11.9	3.51	107	.258	.309	30	.161	-7	23	11	2	0.6
1890 Pit-P	21	25	.457	46	46	44	3	0	387²	392	5	74	145	**11.1**	3.23	121	.251	**.290**	34	.207	1	43	29	-2	2.5
1891 Pit-N	4	5	.444	9	7	6	0	0	71²	77	4	11	25	11.3	2.89	114	.265	.296	4	.226	1	4	3	-0	0.4
Bos-N	20	8	.714	31	30	26	1	0	252¹	236	11	69	114	**11.0**	2.50	146	.238	.290	17	.167	-2	24	33	-1	2.7
Yr	24	13	.649	40	37	32	1	0	324	313	15	80	139	**11.0**	2.58	138	.244	**.290**	28	.180	-1	28	36	-1	3.1
1892 *Bos-N	22	10	.688	37	35	31	3	0	299²	273	10	97	93	11.2	3.03	116	.233	.293	16	.131	-6	8	16	-2	0.7
1893 Bos-N	18	10	.643	36	31	23	0	0	263	344	22	81	61	14.7	5.13	86	.307	.356	30	.265	3	-14	-6	-1	-0.4
1894 Bos-N	12	10	.545	27	21	18	0	1	208²	305	15	61	32	16.0	6.81	83	.337	.382	20	.235	0	-35	-26	-3	-2.1
1895 StL-N	6	13	.316	23	16	13	0	0	158²	223	8	39	28	15.0	5.22	93	.327	.365	9	.134	-6	-8	-7	-2	-1.2
Total 8	136	119	.533	283	257	231	10	2	2269	2468	92	601	746	12.4	3.80	105	.269	.317	174	.182	-19	51	51	-9	2.7

● **TRACY STALLARD** Stallard, Evan Tracy b: 8/31/37, Coeburn, Va. BR/TR, 6'5", 205 lbs. Deb: 9/24/60

YEAR TM/L	W	L	PCT	G	GS	CG	SH	SV	IP	H	HR	BB	SO	RAT	ERA	ERA+	OAV	OOB	BH	AVG	PB	PR	/A	PD	TPI
1960 Bos-A	0	0	—	4	0	0	0	0	4	0	0	2	6	4.5	0.00	—	.000	.133	0	—	0	2	2	0	0.0
1961 Bos-A	2	7	.222	43	14	1	0	2	132²	110	15	96	109	14.0	4.88	85	.229	.359	3	.083	-2	-13	-11	-2	-1.1
1962 Bos-A	0	0	—	1	0	0	0	0	1	0	0	0	0	0.0	0.00	—	.000	.000	0	—	0	0	0	-0	0.0
1963 NY-N	6	17	.261	39	23	5	0	1	154²	156	23	77	110	13.6	4.71	74	.262	.347	3	.063	-3	-24	-21	-1	-3.3
1964 NY-N	10	20	.333	36	34	11	2	0	225²	213	26	73	118	11.6	3.79	94	.252	.316	15	.190	-4	-6	-5	-2	-0.7
1965 StL-N	11	8	.579	40	26	4	1	0	194¹	172	25	70	99	11.5	3.38	114	.235	.307	6	.088	-4	3	10	-2	0.3
1966 StL-N	1	5	.167	20	7	0	0	1	52¹	65	9	25	35	15.8	5.68	63	.305	.383	0	.000	-0	-12	-12	-0	-1.5
Total 7	30	57	.345	183	104	21	3	4	764²	716	92	343	477	12.7	4.17	90	.248	.332	27	.110	-9	-50	-37	-7	-6.3

● **CHARLEY STANCEU** Stanceu, Charles b: 1/9/16, Canton, Ohio d: 4/3/69, Canton, Ohio BR/TR, 6'2", 190 lbs. Deb: 4/16/41

YEAR TM/L	W	L	PCT	G	GS	CG	SH	SV	IP	H	HR	BB	SO	RAT	ERA	ERA+	OAV	OOB	BH	AVG	PB	PR	/A	PD	TPI
1941 NY-A	3	3	.500	22	8	0	0	0	48	58	3	35	21	17.6	5.63	70	.296	.405	0	.000	-4	-9	-1	-1	-1.2
1946 NY-A	0	0	—	3	0	0	0	0	4	6	0	5	2	24.8	9.00	38	.316	.458	0	—	0	-2	-2	-0	0.0
Phi-N	2	4	.333	14	11	1	0	0	70¹	71	4	39	23	14.1	4.22	81	.270	.364	0	.000	-2	-6	-6	-1	-0.8
Total 2	5	7	.417	39	19	1	0	0	122¹	135	7	79	47	15.8	4.93	74	.282	.385	0	.000	-4	-17	-18	-2	-2.0

● **PETE STANDRIDGE** Standridge, Alfred Peter b: 4/25/1891, Black Diamond, Wash. d: 8/2/63, San Francisco, Cal. BR/TR, 5'10.5", 165 lbs. Deb: 9/19/11

YEAR TM/L	W	L	PCT	G	GS	CG	SH	SV	IP	H	HR	BB	SO	RAT	ERA	ERA+	OAV	OOB	BH	AVG	PB	PR	/A	PD	TPI
1911 StL-N	0	0	—	2	0	0	0	0	4²	10	0	4	3	28.9	9.64	35	.435	.536	0	.000	-0	-3	-3	0	0.0
1915 Chi-N	4	1	.800	29	3	2	0	0	112¹	120	6	36	42	13.7	3.61	77	.274	.332	9	.225	3	-11	-10	-0	-0.2
Total 2	4	1	.800	31	3	2	0	0	117	130	6	40	45	15.3	3.85	73	.282	.343	9	.220	3	-14	-14	-0	-0.2

● **AL STANEK** Stanek, Albert Wilfred "Lefty" b: 12/24/43, Springfield, Mass. BL/TL, 5'11.5", 190 lbs. Deb: 4/26/63

YEAR TM/L	W	L	PCT	G	GS	CG	SH	SV	IP	H	HR	BB	SO	RAT	ERA	ERA+	OAV	OOB	BH	AVG	PB	PR	/A	PD	TPI
1963 SF-N	0	0	—	11	0	0	0	0	13¹	10	1	12	5	14.9	4.73	68	.217	.379	0	.000	-0	-2	-2	1	0.1

● **KEVIN STANFIELD** Stanfield, Kevin Bruce b: 12/19/55, Huron, S.Dak. BL/TL, 6', 190 lbs. Deb: 9/14/79

YEAR TM/L	W	L	PCT	G	GS	CG	SH	SV	IP	H	HR	BB	SO	RAT	ERA	ERA+	OAV	OOB	BH	AVG	PB	PR	/A	PD	TPI
1979 Min-A	0	0	—	3	0	0	0	0	3	2	0	0	0	6.0	6.00	73	.200	.200	0	—	0	-1	-1	0	0.0

● **LEE STANGE** Stange, Albert Lee b: 10/27/36, Chicago, Ill. BR/TR, 5'10", 170 lbs. Deb: 4/15/61 C

YEAR TM/L	W	L	PCT	G	GS	CG	SH	SV	IP	H	HR	BB	SO	RAT	ERA	ERA+	OAV	OOB	BH	AVG	PB	PR	/A	PD	TPI
1961 Min-A	1	0	1.000	7	0	0	0	0	12¹	15	1	10	10	18.2	2.92	145	.294	.410	0	.000	-1	2	2	0	0.1
1962 Min-A	4	3	.571	44	6	1	0	3	95	98	14	39	70	13.1	4.45	92	.271	.343	1	.059	-1	-5	-4	-0	-0.4
1963 Min-A	12	5	.706	32	20	7	2	0	164²	145	21	43	100	13.0	2.62	139	.233	.283	5	.096	-1	18	19	-0	1.7
1964 Min-A	3	6	.333	14	11	2	0	0	79²	78	13	19	54	11.0	4.74	75	.255	.298	1	.040	-1	-10	-10	1	-1.1
Cle-A	4	8	.333	23	14	0	0	0	91²	98	14	31	78	12.8	4.12	87	.270	.329	2	.080	-1	-5	-5	-0	-0.8
Yr	7	14	.333	37	25	2	0	0	171¹	176	27	50	132	11.9	4.41	81	.262	.314	3	.060	-2	-15	-16	0	-1.9
1965 Cle-A	8	4	.667	41	12	4	2	0	132	122	19	26	80	10.2	3.34	104	.247	.286	3	.107	-1	2	2	-2	0.1
1966 Cle-A	1	0	1.000	8	2	1	0	0	16	17	1	3	6	11.8	2.81	122	.279	.323	1	.250	0	1	1	-0	0.1
Bos-A	7	9	.438	28	19	8	2	0	153¹	140	17	43	77	10.8	3.35	114	.246	.300	3	.063	-3	2	8	-1	0.3
Yr	8	9	.471	36	21	9	2	0	169¹	157	18	46	85	10.8	3.30	114	.248	.300	4	.077	-3	3	9	-2	0.4
1967 *Bos-A	8	10	.444	35	24	6	2	1	181²	171	14	32	101	10.2	2.77	126	.246	.282	3	.061	-3	9	14	-3	0.9
1968 Bos-A	5	5	.500	50	2	0	0	12	103	89	10	25	53	10.0	3.93	80	.237	.286	2	.133	-0	-11	-9	-1	-1.3
1969 Bos-A	6	9	.400	41	15	2	0	3	137	137	14	56	59	13.1	3.68	103	.256	.333	3	.086	-2	1	6	-2	-0.1
1970 Bos-A	2	2	.500	20	0	0	0	2	27¹	34	5	12	14	16.4	5.60	71	.301	.378	0	.000	-0	-4	-5	-0	-0.8
Chi-A	1	0	1.000	16	0	0	0	0	22¹	28	5	5	14	13.3	5.24	74	.295	.330	0	.000	-0	-4	-3	-0	-0.2
Yr	3	2	.600	36	0	0	0	2	49²	62	10	17	28	14.3	5.44	72	.291	.343	0	.000	-0	-8	-8	-0	-1.0
Total 10	62	61	.504	359	125	32	8	21	1216	1172	142	344	710	11.5	3.56	102	.252	.306	24	.079	-11	-2	4	-11	-1.5

● **DON STANHOUSE** Stanhouse, Donald Joseph b: 2/12/51, DuQuoin, Ill. BR/TR, 6'2", 195 lbs. Deb: 4/19/72

YEAR TM/L	W	L	PCT	G	GS	CG	SH	SV	IP	H	HR	BB	SO	RAT	ERA	ERA+	OAV	OOB	BH	AVG	PB	PR	/A	PD	TPI
1972 Tex-A	2	9	.182	24	16	1	0	0	104²	83	8	73	78	13.5	3.78	80	.223	.351	4	.129	-0	-8	-9	2	-0.8
1973 Tex-A	1	7	.125	21	5	1	0	0	70	70	5	44	42	14.9	4.76	78	.262	.371	0	—	0	-7	-8	2	-0.6
1974 Tex-A	1	1	.500	18	0	0	0	0	31¹	38	4	17	26	16.4	4.88	73	.302	.393	0	—	0	-4	-5	1	0.0
1975 Mon-N	0	0	—	4	3	0	0	0	13	19	1	11	20	20.8	8.31	46	.345	.455	1	.333	-0	-7	-6	-0	0.0
1976 Mon-N	9	12	.429	34	26	8	1	1	184	182	7	92	79	13.6	3.77	99	.263	.352	11	.212	2	-5	-1	3	0.4
1977 Mon-N	10	10	.500	47	16	1	1	10	158¹	147	12	84	89	13.4	3.41	112	.251	.349	9	.191	-1	9	7	-1	0.9
1978 Bal-A	6	9	.400	56	0	0	0	24	74²	60	0	52	42	13.5	2.89	121	.230	.358	0	—	0	7	5	0	1.4
1979 *Bal-A☆	7	3	.700	52	0	0	0	21	72²	49	4	51	34	12.5	2.85	141	.202	.342	0	.000	-0	11	9	1	1.9
1980 LA-N	2	2	.500	21	0	0	0	7	25	30	4	16	6	15.6	5.04	69	.306	.404	0	.000	-0	-4	-4	1	-0.8
1982 Bal-A	0	1	.000	17	0	0	0	0	26²	29	3	15	8	15.5	5.40	75	.276	.377	0	—	0	-4	-4	-0	-0.1
Total 10	38	54	.413	294	66	11	2	64	760¹	707	48	455	408	13.9	3.84	95	.252	.359	25	.185	-0	-13	-16	8	2.3

● **JOE STANKA** Stanka, Joe Donald b: 7/23/31, Hammon, Okla. BR/TR, 6'5", 201 lbs. Deb: 9/2/59

YEAR TM/L	W	L	PCT	G	GS	CG	SH	SV	IP	H	HR	BB	SO	RAT	ERA	ERA+	OAV	OOB	BH	AVG	PB	PR	/A	PD	TPI
1959 Chi-A	1	0	1.000	2	0	0	0	0	5¹	2	1	4	3	10.1	3.38	111	.111	.273	1	.333	0	0	-0	-0	0.0

● **BUCK STANLEY** Stanley, John Leonard b: 11/13/1889, Washington, D.C. d: 8/13/40, Norfolk, Va. BL/TL, 5'10", 160 lbs. Deb: 9/12/11 F

YEAR TM/L	W	L	PCT	G	GS	CG	SH	SV	IP	H	HR	BB	SO	RAT	ERA	ERA+	OAV	OOB	BH	AVG	PB	PR	/A	PD	TPI
1911 Phi-N	0	0	—	4	0	0	0	0	11¹	14	0	9	5	18.3	6.35	54	.326	.442	0	.000	-1	-4	-4	1	-0.1

● **JOE STANLEY** Stanley, Joseph Bernard b: 4/2/1881, Washington, D.C. d: 9/13/67, Detroit, Mich. BB/TR, 5'9.5", 150 lbs. Deb: 9/11/1897 F♦

YEAR TM/L	W	L	PCT	G	GS	CG	SH	SV	IP	H	HR	BB	SO	RAT	ERA	ERA+	OAV	OOB	BH	AVG	PB	PR	/A	PD	TPI
1897 Was-N	0	0	—	1	0	0	0	0	0²	2	0	0	0	—			.000	.000	0	—	-0	0	-0	-0	0.0
1903 Bos-N	0	0	—	1	0	0	0	0	4	4	0	1	2	20.3	9.00	36	.286	.474	77	.250	-	-3	-3	-0	0.0
1906 Was-A	0	0	—	1	0	0	0	0	3	3	1	0	2	15.0	12.00	22	.273	.385	36	.163	-0	-3	-3	-0	0.0
Total 3	0	0	—	3	0	0	0	0	7	9	1	1	6	16.4	9.39	33	.259	.412	148	.213	0	-5	-5	-1	0.0

● **BOB STANLEY** Stanley, Robert William b: 11/10/54, Portland, Maine BR/TR, 6'4", 215 lbs. Deb: 4/16/77

YEAR TM/L	W	L	PCT	G	GS	CG	SH	SV	IP	H	HR	BB	SO	RAT	ERA	ERA+	OAV	OOB	BH	AVG	PB	PR	/A	PD	TPI
1977 Bos-A	8	7	.533	41	13	3	1	3	151	176	10	43	44	13.2	3.99	112	.294	.344	0	—	0	1	8	4	0.8
1978 Bos-A	15	2	.882	52	3	0	0	10	141²	142	6	34	38	11.2	2.60	158	.266	.312	0	—	0	18	24	2	3.2
1979 Bos-A★	16	12	.571	40	30	9	4	1	216²	250	14	44	56	12.4	3.99	111	.294	.332	0	—	0	5	10	2	1.3
1980 Bos-A	10	8	.556	52	17	5	1	14	175	186	11	52	71	12.6	3.39	124	.278	.337	0	—	0	12	16	3	2.1
1981 Bos-A	10	8	.556	35	1	0	0	0	98²	110	3	38	28	14.0	3.83	101	.294	.368	0	—	0	-2	0	3	0.3
1982 Bos-A	12	7	.632	48	0	0	0	14	168¹	161	11	50	83	11.5	3.10	**139**	.263	.313	0	—	0	18	23	4	3.1
1983 Bos-A★	8	10	.444	64	0	0	0	33	145¹	145	7	38	65	11.9	2.85	153	.266	.317	0	—	0	20	24	-1	3.7
1984 Bos-A	9	10	.474	57	0	0	0	22	106²	113	9	23	52	11.6	3.54	117	.267	.308	0	—	0	5	7	3	1.7
1985 Bos-A	6	6	.500	48	0	0	0	10	87²	76	7	30	42	11.3	2.87	149	.237	.306	0	—	0	12	14	0	2.0
1986 *Bos-A	6	6	.500	66	1	0	0	16	82¹	109	9	22	54	14.3	4.37	95	.322	.364	0	—	0	-2	-1	1	-0.3
1987 Bos-A	4	15	.211	34	20	4	1	0	152¹	198	17	42	67	14.2	5.01	91	.321	.366	0	—	0	-9	-8	1	-0.9
1988 *Bos-A	6	4	.600	57	0	0	0	5	101²	90	6	29	57	13.2	3.19	129	.242	.309	0	—	0	9	10	-0	0.9
1989 Bos-A	5	2	.714	43	0	0	0	4	79¹	102	8	26	32	14.6	4.88	91	.321	.374	0	—	0	-9	-7	0	-0.6
Total 13	115	97	.542	637	85	21	7	132	1707	1858	113	471	693	12.5	3.64	117	.282	.334	0	—	0	80	121	22	17.3

YEAR	TM/L	W	L	PCT	G	GS	CG	SH	SV	IP	H	HR	BB	SO	RAT	ERA	ERA+	OAV	OOB	BH	AVG	PB	PR	/A	PD	TPI

● MIKE STANTON
Stanton, Michael Thomas b: 9/25/52, Phenix City, Ala. BB/TR, 6'2", 205 lbs. Deb: 7/9/75

YEAR	TM/L	W	L	PCT	G	GS	CG	SH	SV	IP	H	HR	BB	SO	RAT	ERA	ERA+	OAV	OOB	BH	AVG	PB	PR	/A	PD	TPI
1975	Hou-N	0	2	.000	7	2	0	0	1	17¹	20	1	20	16	20.8	7.27	46	.290	.449	1	.250	0	-7	-8	0	-0.8
1980	Cle-A	1	3	.250	51	0	0	0	5	85²	98	5	44	74	15.2	5.46	75	.297	.385	0	—	0	-14	-13	1	-0.6
1981	Cle-A	3	3	.500	24	0	0	0	2	43¹	43	4	18	34	12.7	4.36	83	.262	.335	0	—	0	-3	-4	-1	-0.5
1982	Sea-A	2	4	.333	56	1	0	0	7	71¹	70	5	21	49	11.5	4.16	102	.260	.314	0	—	0	-1	-1	1	0.1
1983	Sea-A	2	3	.400	50	0	0	0	7	65	65	3	28	47	13.0	3.32	128	.273	.352	0	—	0	5	7	-0	0.5
1984	Sea-A	4	4	.500	54	0	0	0	8	61	55	3	22	55	11.7	3.54	113	.241	.313	0	—	0	3	3	-1	0.4
1985	Sea-A	1	2	.333	24	0	0	0	1	29	32	4	21	17	17.4	5.28	80	.278	.403	0	—	0	-4	-3	1	-0.3
	Chi-A	0	1	.000	11	0	0	0	0	11²	15	2	8	12	17.7	9.26	47	.294	.390	0	—	0	-7	-6	-0	-0.5
	Yr	1	3	.250	35	0	0	0	1	40²	47	6	29	29	16.8	6.42	66	.278	.384	0	—	0	-10	-10	1	-0.8
Total	7	13	22	.371	277	3	0	0	31	384¹	398	27	182	304	13.8	4.61	88	.272	.356	1	.250	0	-27	-24	1	-1.7

● MIKE STANTON
Stanton, William Michael b: 6/2/67, Houston, Tex. BL/TL, 6'1", 190 lbs. Deb: 8/24/89

YEAR	TM/L	W	L	PCT	G	GS	CG	SH	SV	IP	H	HR	BB	SO	RAT	ERA	ERA+	OAV	OOB	BH	AVG	PB	PR	/A	PD	TPI
1989	Atl-N	0	1	.000	20	0	0	0	7	24	17	0	8	27	9.4	1.50	243	.207	.278	0	—	0	5	6	-0	0.5
1990	Atl-N	0	3	.000	7	0	0	0	2	7	16	1	4	7	27.0	18.00	22	.444	.512	0	—	0	-11	-11	0	-3.6
1991	*Atl-N	5	5	.500	74	0	0	0	7	78	62	6	21	54	9.7	2.88	135	.217	.273	3	.500	2	7	9	1	1.5
1992	*Atl-N	5	4	.556	65	0	0	0	8	63²	59	6	20	44	11.5	4.10	89	.247	.310	1	.500	0	-4	-3	-0	-0.4
1993	*Atl-N	4	6	.400	63	0	0	0	27	52	51	4	29	43	13.8	4.67	86	.255	.349	0	—	0	-4	-4	-0	-1.0
1994	Atl-N	3	1	.750	49	0	0	0	3	45²	41	2	26	35	13.8	3.55	120	.248	.361	2	.667	1	3	4	1	0.5
1995	Atl-N	1	1	.500	26	0	0	0	1	19¹	31	3	6	13	17.7	5.59	76	.369	.418	0	—	0	-3	-3	-0	-0.3
	*Bos-A	1	0	1.000	22	0	0	0	0	21	17	3	8	10	10.7	3.00	162	.224	.298	0	—	0	4	4	-0	0.0
1996	Bos-A	4	3	.571	59	0	0	0	1	56¹	58	5	24	46	12.9	3.83	134	.275	.346	0	—	0	7	8	0	0.6
	*Tex-A	0	1	.000	22	0	0	0	0	22¹	20	2	4	14	9.7	3.22	165	.241	.276	0	—	0	4	5	-1	-0.3
	Yr	4	4	.500	81	0	0	0	1	78²	78	11	27	60	12.2	3.66	142	.264	.325	0	—	0	12	13	-1	0.3
Total	8	23	25	.479	407	0	0	0	56	389¹	372	36	149	293	12.2	3.88	109	.254	.327	6	.545	3	9	15	1	-2.5

● DAVE STAPLETON
Stapleton, David Earl b: 10/16/61, Miami, Ariz. BL/TL, 6'1", 185 lbs. Deb: 9/14/87

YEAR	TM/L	W	L	PCT	G	GS	CG	SH	SV	IP	H	HR	BB	SO	RAT	ERA	ERA+	OAV	OOB	BH	AVG	PB	PR	/A	PD	TPI
1987	Mil-A	2	0	1.000	4	0	0	0	0	14²	13	0	3	14	9.8	1.84	248	.241	.281	0	—	0	4	4	-0	0.5
1988	Mil-A	0	0	—	6	0	0	0	0	13²	20	1	9	6	19.8	5.93	67	.339	.435	0	—	0	-3	-3	-0	0.0
Total	2	2	0	1.000	10	0	0	0	0	28¹	33	1	12	20	14.6	3.81	112	.292	.365	0	—	0	1	1	-0	0.5

● CON STARKEL
Starkel, Conrad b: 11/16/1880, Germany d: 1/19/33, Tacoma, Wash. BR/TR, 6', 200 lbs. Deb: 4/19/06

YEAR	TM/L	W	L	PCT	G	GS	CG	SH	SV	IP	H	HR	BB	SO	RAT	ERA	ERA+	OAV	OOB	BH	AVG	PB	PR	/A	PD	TPI
1906	Was-A	0	0	—	1	0	0	0	0	3	7	1	2	1	27.0	18.00	15	.467	.529	0	—	0	-5	-5	0	0.0

● RAY STARR
Starr, Raymond Francis "Iron Man" b: 4/23/06, Nowata, Okla. d: 2/9/63, Baylis, Ill. BR/TR, 6'1", 178 lbs. Deb: 9/11/32

YEAR	TM/L	W	L	PCT	G	GS	CG	SH	SV	IP	H	HR	BB	SO	RAT	ERA	ERA+	OAV	OOB	BH	AVG	PB	PR	/A	PD	TPI
1932	StL-N	1	1	.500	3	2	1	1	0	20	19	2	10	6	13.5	2.70	146	.284	.385	1	.250	0	3	3	1	0.3
1933	NY-N	0	1	.000	6	2	0	0	0	13¹	19	0	10	2	20.3	5.40	59	.339	.448	0	.000	-0	-3	-3	-0	-0.3
	Bos-N	0	1	.000	9	1	0	0	0	28	32	4	9	15	13.5	3.86	79	.296	.356	1	.143	0	-2	-2	0	0.0
	Yr	0	2	.000	15	3	0	0	0	41¹	51	4	19	17	15.5	4.35	71	.309	.384	1	.100	0	-5	-6	0	-0.3
1941	Cin-N	3	2	.600	7	4	3	2	0	34	28	1	6	11	9.3	2.65	136	.219	.259	2	.182	-0	4	4	0	0.5
1942	Cin-N☆	15	13	.536	37	33	17	4	0	276²	228	10	106	83	11.0	2.67	123	.226	.301	8	.091	-5	20	19	-2	1.2
1943	Cin-N	11	10	.524	36	33	9	2	1	217¹	201	9	91	42	12.3	3.64	91	.248	.328	9	.122	-4	-6	-8	-0	-1.2
1944	Pit-N	6	5	.545	27	12	5	0	3	89²	116	6	36	25	15.4	5.02	74	.314	.377	3	.136	-1	-14	-13	-1	-1.5
1945	Pit-N	0	2	.000	4	0	0	0	0	6²	10	0	4	0	18.9	9.45	42	.370	.452	1	1.000	1	-4	-4	0	-0.9
	Chi-N	1	0	1.000	9	1	0	0	0	13¹	17	1	7	5	16.2	7.43	49	.298	.375	1	.500	1	-5	-6	-0	-0.3
	Yr	1	2	.333	13	1	0	0	0	20	27	1	11	5	17.1	8.10	46	.321	.400	2	.667	1	-10	-10	0	-1.2
Total	7	37	35	.514	138	88	35	9	4	699	670	33	279	189	12.4	3.53	96	.255	.329	26	.123	-7	-8	-11	-1	-2.2

● DICK STARR
Starr, Richard Eugene b: 3/2/21, Kittanning, Pa. BR/TR, 6'3", 190 lbs. Deb: 9/5/47

YEAR	TM/L	W	L	PCT	G	GS	CG	SH	SV	IP	H	HR	BB	SO	RAT	ERA	ERA+	OAV	OOB	BH	AVG	PB	PR	/A	PD	TPI
1947	NY-A	1	0	1.000	4	1	1	0	0	12¹	12	1	8	1	14.6	1.46	242	.250	.357	1	.333	1	3	3	0	0.3
1948	NY-A	0	0	—	1	0	0	0	0	2	0	0	2	2	9.0	4.50	91	.000	.250	0	—	0	-0	-0	-0	0.0
1949	StL-A	1	7	.125	30	8	1	1	0	83¹	96	6	48	44	15.7	4.32	105	.292	.384	2	.087	-1	-1	-2	-1	-0.4
1950	StL-A	7	5	.583	32	16	4	1	2	123²	140	11	74	30	16.1	5.02	99	.287	.389	5	.139	-3	-6	-1	-1	-0.4
1951	StL-A	2	5	.286	15	9	0	0	0	62	66	10	42	26	16.0	7.40	59	.273	.385	4	.222	0	-23	-21	-1	-2.0
	Was-A	1	7	.125	11	11	0	0	0	61¹	76	12	24	17	14.7	5.58	73	.304	.365	3	.176	1	-10	-10	-2	-1.2
	Yr	3	12	.200	26	20	0	0	0	123¹	142	22	66	43	15.2	6.49	65	.287	.371	7	.200	1	-33	-31	-2	-3.2
Total	5	12	24	.333	93	45	7	2	2	344²	390	40	198	120	15.6	5.25	86	.286	.381	15	.155	-2	-37	-27	-4	-3.3

● HERMAN STARRETTE
Starrette, Herman Paul b: 11/20/38, Statesville, N.C. BR/TR, 6', 175 lbs. Deb: 7/1/63 C

YEAR	TM/L	W	L	PCT	G	GS	CG	SH	SV	IP	H	HR	BB	SO	RAT	ERA	ERA+	OAV	OOB	BH	AVG	PB	PR	/A	PD	TPI
1963	Bal-A	0	1	.000	18	0	0	0	0	26	26	1	7	13	12.1	3.46	100	.271	.333	0	.000	0	0	0	1	0.1
1964	Bal-A	1	0	1.000	5	0	0	0	0	11	9	0	6	5	12.3	1.64	218	.250	.357	0	.000	-0	2	2	-0	0.1
1965	Bal-A	0	0	—	4	0	0	0	0	9	8	0	3	3	11.0	1.00	347	.258	.324	0	.000	-0	3	3	0	0.2
Total	3	1	1	.500	27	0	0	0	0	46	43	1	16	21	11.9	2.54	137	.264	.337	0	.000	-0	5	5	1	0.2

● ED STAUFFER
Stauffer, Charles Edward b: 1/10/1898, Emsworth, Pa. d: 7/2/79, St.Petersburg, Fla BR/TR, 5'11", 185 lbs. Deb: 4/26/23

YEAR	TM/L	W	L	PCT	G	GS	CG	SH	SV	IP	H	HR	BB	SO	RAT	ERA	ERA+	OAV	OOB	BH	AVG	PB	PR	/A	PD	TPI
1923	Chi-N	0	0	—	1	0	0	0	0	2	5	0	1	0	27.0	13.50	30	.556	.600	0	—	0	-2	-2	0	0.0
1925	StL-A	0	1	.000	20	1	0	0	0	30¹	34	1	21	13	16.3	5.34	87	.283	.390	1	.250	-0	-3	-2	-1	-0.2
Total	2	0	1	.000	21	1	0	0	0	32¹	39	1	22	13	17.0	5.85	79	.302	.404	1	.250	-0	-5	-4	-1	-0.2

● BILL STEARNS
Stearns, William E. b: 3/20/1853, Washington, D.C. d: 12/30/1898, Washington, D.C. TR, Deb: 6/26/1871

YEAR	TM/L	W	L	PCT	G	GS	CG	SH	SV	IP	H	HR	BB	SO	RAT	ERA	ERA+	OAV	OOB	BH	AVG	PB	PR	/A	PD	TPI
1871	Oly-n	2	0	1.000	2	2	2	0	0	18	10	0	8	0	9.0	2.50	167	.149	.240	0	.000	-1	3	3		0.1
1872	Nat-n	0	11	.000	11	11	11	0	0	99	193	2	3	2	17.8	6.18	75	.339	.343	12	.267	-3	-28	-17		-1.8
1873	Was-n	7	25	.219	32	32	32	0	0	283	481	3	15	4	15.8	4.55	74	.330	.337	24	.180	-6	-41	-38		-3.2
1874	Har-n	3	14	.176	22	18	14	0	0	158²	238	0	14	14	14.3	3.01	76	.298	.310	21	.159	-5	-15	-13		-1.4
1875	Was-n	1	14	.067	17	16	14	0	0	141	246	3	4	3	16.0	4.02	59	.332	.336	20	.256	-0	-28	-26		-2.2
Total	5 n	13	64	.169	84	79	73	0	0	699²	1168	12	44	23	15.6	4.27	56	.321	.330	77	.194	-16	-159	-148		-8.5

● CHARLIE STECHER
Stecher, Charles b: Bordentown, N.J. Deb: 9/6/1890

YEAR	TM/L	W	L	PCT	G	GS	CG	SH	SV	IP	H	HR	BB	SO	RAT	ERA	ERA+	OAV	OOB	BH	AVG	PB	PR	/A	PD	TPI
1890	Phi-a	0	10	.000	10	10	9	0	0	68	111	1	60	18	24.5	10.32	37	.356	.479	7	.241	1	-49	-49	2	-4.4

● ELMER STEELE
Steele, Elmer Rae b: 5/17/1886, Poughkeepsie, N.Y. d: 3/9/66, Rhinebeck, N.Y. BB/TR, 5'11", 200 lbs. Deb: 9/12/07

YEAR	TM/L	W	L	PCT	G	GS	CG	SH	SV	IP	H	HR	BB	SO	RAT	ERA	ERA+	OAV	OOB	BH	AVG	PB	PR	/A	PD	TPI
1907	Bos-A	0	1	.000	4	1	0	0	0	11¹	11	0	1	9	9.5	1.59	162	.256	.273	0	.000	-1	1	1	-0	0.1
1908	Bos-A	5	7	.417	16	13	9	1	0	118	85	1	13	37	7.7	1.83	134	.209	.239	2	.051	-4	7	8	-1	0.3
1909	Bos-A	4	4	.500	16	8	2	0	0	75²	75	1	15	32	10.8	2.85	88	.255	.294	5	.227	1	-3	-3	1	-0.1
1910	Pit-N	0	0	—	3	2	0	0	0	24	19	0	3	7	8.3	2.25	138	.221	.247	0	.000	-0	2	2	1	0.1
1911	Pit-N	9	9	.500	31	16	7	2	2	166	153	5	31	52	10.2	2.60	132	.256	.297	11	.180	-0	15	15	2	1.7
	Bro-N	0	0	—	2	0	0	0	0	23	24	0	5	9	11.3	3.13	107	.258	.296	0	.000	0	1	1	0	-0.1
	Yr	9	9	.500	33	16	7	2	2	189	177	5	36	61	10.1	2.67	128	.255	.292	11	.157	-1	15	16	2	1.6
Total	5	18	24	.429	75	43	20	3	3	418	367	7	68	147	9.5	2.41	122	.241	.278	18	.127	-6	23	25	3	2.2

● BOB STEELE
Steele, Robert Wesley b: 1/5/1894, Cassburn, Ont., Can. d: 1/27/62, Ocala, Fla. BB/TL, 5'10.5", 175 lbs. Deb: 4/17/16

YEAR	TM/L	W	L	PCT	G	GS	CG	SH	SV	IP	H	HR	BB	SO	RAT	ERA	ERA+	OAV	OOB	BH	AVG	PB	PR	/A	PD	TPI
1916	StL-N	5	15	.250	29	21	7	1	0	148	156	6	42	67	12.2	3.41	78	.285	.340	10	.196	-1	-13	-13	-3	-2.0
1917	StL-N	1	3	.250	12	6	1	0	0	42	33	1	19	23	11.1	3.21	84	.223	.315	5	.385	2	-2	-2	-1	-0.1
	Pit-N	5	11	.313	27	19	13	1	1	179²	158	0	53	82	10.8	2.76	103	.237	.298	17	.224	1	-1	2	-2	0.1
	Yr	6	14	.300	39	25	14	1	1	221²	191	1	72	105	10.9	2.84	99	.235	.301	22	.247	3	-3	-1	-2	-0.1
1918	Pit-N	2	3	.400	10	4	2	1	1	49	44	2	17	21	11.6	3.31	87	.240	.312	2	.125	-0	-1	-0	-1	-0.3
	NY-N	3	5	.375	12	7	5	1	1	66	56	1	11	24	9.5	2.59	101	.226	.267	6	.286	2	1	2	-1	-0.0
	Yr	5	8	.385	22	11	7	2	2	115	100	3	28	45	10.3	2.90	94	.231	.282	8	.216	2	-2	-3	-3	-0.3
1919	NY-N	0	1	.000	1	0	0	0	0	3	3	0	2	0	15.0	6.00	47	.250	.357	0	—	0	-1	-1	-0	-0.3
Total	4	16	38	.296	91	57	28	4	3	487²	450	10	144	217	11.2	3.05	90	.249	.310	40	.225	3	-19	-16	-8	-2.7

YEAR	TM/L	W	L	PCT	G	GS	CG	SH	SV	IP	H	HR	BB	SO	RAT	ERA	ERA+	OAV	OOB	BH	AVG	PB	PR	/A	PD	TPI
● **BILL STEELE**					Steele, William Mitchell "Big Bill"			b: 10/5/1885, Milford, Pa.		d: 10/19/49, Overland, Mo.			BR/TR, 5'11", 200 lbs.				Deb: 9/10/10								
1910	StL-N	4	4	.500	9	8	8	0	1	71²	71	1	24	25	12.7	3.27	91	.264	.338	8	.258	1	-2	-2	1	0.0
1911	StL-N	18	19	.486	43	34	23	1	3	287¹	287	8	113	115	12.8	3.73	91	.269	.345	21	.208	4	-10	-11	3	-0.6
1912	StL-N	9	13	.409	40	25	7	0	2	194	245	5	66	67	14.8	4.69	73	.322	.381	11	.180	1	-27	-27	-4	-2.2
1913	StL-N	4	4	.500	12	9	2	0	0	54	58	3	18	10	13.2	5.00	65	.286	.353	4	.056	-1	-11	-11	-1	-1.6
1914	StL-N	1	2	.333	17	2	0	0	0	53¹	55	3	7	16	11.0	2.70	104	.274	.308	5	.294	2	1	1	1	0.3
	Bro-N	1	1	.500	8	1	0	0	1	16¹	17	1	7	3	13.2	5.51	52	.258	.329	1	.333	1	-5	-5	-0	-0.6
	Yr	2	3	.400	25	3	0	0	1	69²	72	4	14	19	11.1	3.36	84	.267	.303	6	.300	2	-4	-4	1	-0.3
Total	5	37	43	.463	129	79	40	1	7	676²	733	21	235	236	13.3	4.02	82	.286	.352	47	.203	8	-55	-55	8	-4.7
● **BILL STEEN**					Steen, William John			b: 11/11/1887, Pittsburgh, Pa.		d: 3/13/79, Signal Hill, Cal.			BR/TR, 6'0.5", 180 lbs.				Deb: 4/15/12								
1912	Cle-A	9	8	.529	26	16	6	1	0	143¹	163	3	45	61	13.1	3.77	90	.298	.352	13	.271	2	-7	-6	-1	-0.5
1913	Cle-A	4	5	.444	22	13	7	2	2	128¹	113	3	49	57	11.6	2.45	124	.237	.313	7	.171	-0	7	8	-0	0.5
1914	Cle-A	9	14	.391	30	22	13	1	0	200²	201	6	68	97	12.2	2.60	111	.272	.337	14	.200	1	3	6	0	0.8
1915	Cle-A	1	4	.200	10	7	2	0	0	45¹	51	1	15	22	13.5	4.96	61	.290	.352	3	.188	-0	-10	-10	2	-0.8
	Det-A	5	1	.833	20	7	3	0	4	79¹	83	0	22	28	12.0	2.72	111	.269	.319	5	.179	-1	2	3	2	0.3
	Yr	6	5	.545	30	14	5	0	4	124²	134	1	37	50	12.4	3.54	86	.275	.328	8	.182	-1	-8	-7	4	-0.5
Total	4	28	32	.467	108	65	31	4	6	597	611	7	199	265	12.4	3.05	101	.272	.334	42	.207	1	-6	2	2	0.3
● **MILT STEENGRAFE**					Steengrafe, Milton Henry			b: 5/26/1900, San Francisco, Cal		d: 6/2/77, Oklahoma City, Okla.			BR/TR, 6', 170 lbs.			Deb: 5/5/24									
1924	Chi-A	0	0	—	3	0	0	0	0	5²	15	0	4	3	30.2	12.71	32	.484	.543	0	.000	-0	-5	-5	0	0.0
1926	Chi-A	1	1	.500	13	1	0	0	0	38¹	43	1	19	10	15.0	3.99	97	.295	.383	0	.000	-2	0	-1	-1	-0.3
Total	2	1	1	.500	16	1	0	0	0	44	58	1	23	13	17.0	5.11	76	.328	.411	0	.000	-2	-5	-6	-1	-0.3
● **MORRIE STEEVENS**					Steevens, Morris Dale			b: 10/7/40, Salem, Ill.		BL/TL, 6'2", 175 lbs.			Deb: 4/13/62											
1962	Chi-N	0	1	.000	12	1	0	0	0	15	10	0	11	5	13.2	2.40	173	.196	.349	0	.000	-0	3	3	0	0.2
1964	Phi-N	0	0	—	4	0	0	0	0	2²	5	0	1	3	20.3	3.38	103	.385	.429	0	—	0	0	0	0	0.0
1965	Phi-N	0	1	.000	6	0	0	0	0	2²	5	1	4	3	30.4	16.88	20	.417	.563	0	—	-0	-4	-4	-0	-1.3
Total	3	0	2	.000	22	1	0	0	0	20¹	20	1	16	11	16.4	4.43	90	.263	.398	0	.000	-0	-1	-1	0	-1.1
● **ED STEIN**					Stein, Edward F.			b: 9/5/1869, Detroit, Mich.		d: 5/10/28, Detroit, Mich.			BR/TR, 5'11", 170 lbs.			Deb: 7/24/1890								
1890	Chi-N	12	6	.667	20	18	14	1	0	160²	147	9	83	65	13.5	3.81	96	.236	.336	9	.153	-2	-4	-3	-1	-0.5
1891	Chi-N	7	6	.538	14	10	9	1	0	101	99	7	57	38	14.1	3.74	89	.247	.343	7	.163	-1	-4	-5	2	-0.4
1892	Bro-N	27	16	.628	48	42	38	6	1	377¹	310	6	150	190	11.3	2.84	111	.215	.296	31	.215	4	19	14	2	1.8
1893	Bro-N	19	15	.559	37	34	28	1	0	298¹	294	4	193	84	14.7	3.77	117	.250	.323	25	.212	-3	30	22	2	1.7
1894	Bro-N	26	14	.650	44	40	37	2	1	350	388	10	170	84	14.7	4.63	107	.278	.362	38	.259	5	27	12	-0	1.3
1895	Bro-N	15	13	.536	32	27	24	1	0	255¹	282	9	93	55	13.4	4.72	93	.276	.340	26	.250	2	2	-9	1	-0.5
1896	Bro-N	3	6	.333	17	10	6	0	0	90¹	130	6	51	16	18.2	4.88	84	.334	.414	10	.256	0	-5	-8	-0	-0.5
1898	Bro-N	0	2	.000	3	2	2	0	0	23	39	0	9	6	18.8	5.48	65	.371	.421	4	.400	1	-5	-5	-0	-0.3
Total	8	109	78	.583	215	183	158	12	3	1656	1689	51	732	535	13.5	3.97	103	.258	.338	150	.226	5	59	22	5	2.6
● **IRV STEIN**					Stein, Irvin Michael			b: 5/21/11, Madisonville, La.		d: 1/7/81, Covington, La.			BR/TR, 6'2", 170 lbs.			Deb: 7/7/32								
1932	Phi-A	0	0	—	1	0	0	0	0	3	7	2	1	0	24.0	12.00	38	.500	.533	0	.000	-0	-3	-2	0	0.0
● **RANDY STEIN**					Stein, William Randolph			b: 3/7/53, Pomona, Cal.		BR/TR, 6'4", 210 lbs.			Deb: 4/17/78											
1978	Mil-A	3	2	.600	31	1	0	0	1	72²	78	5	39	42	15.0	5.33	71	.280	.376	0	—	0	-13	-13	-0	-0.8
1979	Sea-A	2	3	.400	23	1	0	0	0	41¹	48	7	27	39	16.5	5.88	74	.291	.394	0	—	0	-8	-7	-1	-0.8
1981	Sea-A	0	1	.000	5	0	0	0	0	9¹	18	1	8	6	25.1	10.61	36	.429	.520	0	—	0	-7	-7	-0	-0.7
1982	Chi-N	0	0	—	6	0	0	0	0	10¹	7	2	7	6	12.2	3.48	107	.200	.333	0	—	0	0	-0	-0	0.0
Total	4	5	6	.455	65	2	0	0	1	133²	151	15	81	93	16.0	5.72	69	.290	.390	0	—	0	-27	-26	-1	-2.3
● **RAY STEINEDER**					Steineder, Raymond J.			b: 11/13/1895, Salem, N.J.		d: 8/25/82, Vineland, N.J.			BR/TR, 6'0.5", 160 lbs.			Deb: 7/16/23								
1923	Pit-N	2	0	1.000	15	2	1	0	0	55	58	3	18	23	12.8	4.75	85	.278	.341	7	.467	3	-5	-4	-1	-0.2
1924	Pit-N	0	1	.000	5	0	0	0	0	2²	6	0	5	0	37.1	13.50	28	.400	.550	0	—	0	-3	-3	-0	-0.9
	Phi-N	1	1	.500	9	0	0	0	0	28²	29	1	16	11	14.1	4.40	101	.266	.360	3	.300	0	-2	-0	-0	0.1
	Yr	1	2	.333	14	0	0	0	0	31¹	35	1	21	11	16.1	5.17	86	.282	.386	3	.300	0	-5	-3	-0	-0.8
Total	2	3	2	.600	29	2	1	0	0	86¹	93	4	39	34	14.0	4.90	85	.279	.358	10	.400	3	-9	-7	-1	-0.8
● **RICK STEIRER**					Steirer, Ricky Francis			b: 8/27/56, Baltimore, Md.		BR/TR, 6'4", 200 lbs.			Deb: 8/5/82											
1982	Cal-A	1	0	1.000	10	1	0	0	0	26¹	25	2	11	14	12.6	3.76	108	.243	.322	0	—	1	1	1	0	0.1
1983	Cal-A	3	2	.600	19	5	0	0	0	61²	77	3	18	25	14.3	4.82	83	.302	.355	0	—	-5	-6	-1	-3	-0.3
1984	Cal-A	0	1	.000	1	1	0	0	0	2²	6	0	2	2	27.0	16.88	24	.500	.571	0	—	0	-4	-4	-0	-0.8
Total	3	4	3	.571	30	7	0	0	0	90²	108	5	31	41	14.2	4.86	83	.292	.353	0	—	-4	-8	-8	-1	-1.0
● **BILL STELLBERGER**					Stellberger, William F.			b: 4/22/1865, Detroit, Mich.		d: 11/9/36, Detroit, Mich.			BL/TL,		Deb: 10/1/1885									
1885	Pro-N	0	1	.000	1	1	1	0	0	8	14	0	4	0	20.3	7.88	34	.389	.450	0	.000	-1	-4	-5	0	-0.4
● **JEFF STEMBER**					Stember, Jeffrey Alan			b: 3/2/58, Elizabeth, N.J.		BR/TR, 6'5", 220 lbs.			Deb: 8/5/80											
1980	SF-N	0	0	—	1	1	0	0	0	3	2	1	2	0	12.4	3.00	118	.167	.286	0	.000	-0	0	0	0	0.0
● **BILL STEMMEYER**					Stemmeyer, William "Cannon Ball"			b: 5/6/1865, Cleveland, Ohio		d: 5/3/45, Cleveland, Ohio			BR/TR, 6'2", 190 lbs.			Deb: 10/3/1885								
1885	Bos-N	1	1	.500	2	2	2	1	0	11	7	0	11	8	14.7	0.00	—	.194	.383	3	.429	1	3	3	0	0.8
1886	Bos-N	22	18	.550	41	41	41	0	0	348²	300	11	144	239	11.5	3.02	106	.218	.292	41	.277	9	11	7	-3	1.2
1887	Bos-N	6	8	.429	15	14	14	0	1	119¹	138	4	41	41	13.7	5.20	78	.274	.331	12	.255	2	-15	-15	-2	-1.3
1888	Cle-a	0	2	.000	2	2	2	0	0	16	37	0	9	7	26.4	9.00	34	.435	.495	4	.400	1	-11	-11	-0	-0.8
Total	4	29	29	.500	60	59	59	1	1	495	482	15	205	295	12.5	3.67	92	.241	.312	60	.283	14	-11	-16	-4	-0.1
● **DAVE STENHOUSE**					Stenhouse, David Rotchford			b: 9/12/33, Westerly, R.I.		BR/TR, 6', 195 lbs.			Deb: 4/18/62 F											
1962	Was-A★	11	12	.478	34	26	9	2	0	197	169	24	90	123	11.9	3.65	110	.234	.320	3	.052	-5	7	8	2	0.6
1963	Was-A	3	9	.250	16	16	2	1	0	87	90	12	45	47	14.1	4.55	82	.260	.347	2	.080	-1	-9	-8	-0	-1.1
1964	Was-A	2	7	.222	26	14	1	0	1	88	80	12	39	44	12.3	4.81	77	.239	.320	6	.300	2	-12	-11	-0	-0.9
Total	3	16	28	.364	76	56	12	3	1	372	339	48	174	214	12.5	4.14	94	.241	.327	11	.107	-4	-14	-11	1	-1.4
● **BUZZ STEPHEN**					Stephen, Louis Roberts			b: 7/13/44, Porterville, Cal.		BR/TR, 6'4", 205 lbs.			Deb: 9/20/68											
1968	Min-A	1	1	.500	2	2	0	0	0	11¹	11	0	4	9	15.1	4.76	65	.268	.396	0	.000	-0	-2	-2	0	-0.4
● **BRYAN STEPHENS**					Stephens, Bryan Maris			b: 7/14/20, Fayetteville, Ark		d: 11/21/91, Santa Ana, Cal.			BR/TR, 6'4", 175 lbs.			Deb: 5/15/47								
1947	Cle-A	5	10	.333	31	5	1	0	1	92	79	6	39	34	11.7	4.01	97	.230	.312	3	.111	-2	-3	-5	-1	-1.1
1948	StL-A	3	6	.333	43	12	2	0	3	122²	141	14	67	35	15.6	6.02	76	.289	.379	4	.125	-1	-24	-20	-1	-1.5
Total	2	8	16	.333	74	17	3	0	4	214²	220	20	106	69	13.9	5.16	79	.264	.352	7	.119	-3	-27	-26	-2	-2.6
● **CLARENCE STEPHENS**					Stephens, Clarence Wright			b: 8/19/1863, Cincinnati, Ohio		d: 2/28/45, Cincinnati, Ohio		TR,		Deb: 10/8/1886									
1886	Cin-a	1	0	1.000	1	1	1	0	0	8	9	0	5	6	16.9	5.63	63	.273	.385	3	.600	1	-2	-2	-0	-0.1
1891	Cin-N	0	1	.000	1	1	1	0	0	8	9	1	3	2	13.5	7.88	43	.273	.333	0	.000	-0	-4	-4	-0	-0.4
1892	Cin-N	0	1	.000	1	1	1	0	0	7	12	0	4	1	20.6	1.29	254	.364	.432	0	.000	-0	2	2	0	0.2
Total	3	1	2	.333	3	3	3	0	0	23	30	1	12	10	16.8	5.09	67	.303	.384	3	.300	1	-4	-4	-0	-0.3
● **BEN STEPHENS**					Stephens, George Benjamin			b: 9/28/1867, Romeo, Mich.		d: 8/5/1896, Armada, Mich.			5'10.5", 170 lbs.			Deb: 8/5/1892								
1892	Bal-N	1	1	.500	5	2	2	0	1	29	39	1	23	7	16.3	2.79	123	.298	.353	0	.000	-2	2	2	-0	0.0
1893	Was-N	0	6	.000	9	6	6	0	0	63²	81	3	31	14	16.7	5.80	80	.306	.386	3	.103	-4	-8	-8	1	-0.8
1894	Was-N	0	0	—	3	2	1	0	0	11	19	1	8	1	22.9	4.91	107	.373	.467	1	.250	-0	0	0	-0	0.0
Total	3	1	7	.125	17	10	9	0	1	103²	139	4	48	22	16.8	4.86	90	.312	.386	4	.087	-5	-6	-6	1	-0.8

YEAR TM/L	W	L	PCT	G	GS	CG	SH	SV	IP	H	HR	BB	SO	RAT	ERA	ERA+	OAV	OOB	BH	AVG	PB	PR	/A	PD	TPI
● EARL STEPHENSON									Stephenson, Chester Earl b: 7/31/47, Benson, N.C. BL/TL, 6'3", 175 lbs. Deb: 4/7/71																
1971 Chi-N	1	0	1.000	16	0	0	0	1	20¹	24	1	11	11	15.5	4.43	89	.316	.402	0	.000	-0	-2	-1	-0	-0.1
1972 Mil-A	3	5	.375	35	8	0	0	0	80¹	79	5	33	33	12.9	3.25	93	.262	.340	0	.000	-2	-2	-0	-0	-0.4
1977 Bal-A	0	0	—	1	0	0	0	0	3	5	1	0	2	15.0	9.00	42	.357	.357	0	—	-0	-2	-2	-0	0.6
1978 Bal-A	0	0	—	2	0	0	0	0	9²	10	0	5	4	14.0	2.79	125	.294	.385	0	—	-0	1	1	-0	0.3
Total 4	4	5	.444	54	8	1	0	1	113¹	118	7	49	50	13.5	3.57	91	.277	.356	0	.000	-2	-4	-4	-0	0.4
● GARRETT STEPHENSON									Stephenson, Garrett Charles b: 1/2/72, Takoma Park, Md. BR/TR, 6'4", 185 lbs. Deb: 7/25/96																
1996 Bal-A	0	1	.000	3	0	0	0	0	6¹	13	1	3	3	24.2	12.79	38	.433	.500	0	—	0	-5	-6	0	-0.6
● JERRY STEPHENSON									Stephenson, Jerry Joseph b: 10/6/43, Detroit, Mich. BL/TR, 6'2", 185 lbs. Deb: 4/14/63 F																
1963 Bos-A	0	0	—	1	1	0	0	0	2¹	5	0	2	3	27.0	7.71	49	.556	.636	0	.000	-0	-1	-1	-0	0.0
1965 Bos-A	1	5	.167	15	8	0	0	0	52	62	7	33	49	16.6	6.23	60	.287	.384	3	.231	-0	-16	-14	-0	-1.4
1966 Bos-A	2	5	.286	15	11	0	0	0	66¹	68	6	44	50	15.3	5.83	65	.264	.373	2	.118	-1	-18	-15	-0	-1.5
1967 *Bos-A	3	1	.750	8	6	0	0	0	39²	32	4	16	24	11.1	3.86	90	.227	.310	4	.250	0	-3	-2	0	-0.1
1968 Bos-A	2	8	.200	23	7	2	0	0	68²	81	4	42	51	16.4	5.64	56	.295	.392	6	.353	2	-20	-19	1	-2.4
1969 Sea-A	0	0	—	2	0	0	0	0	2²	6	0	3	1	33.8	10.13	36	.429	.556	0	.000	-0	-2	-2	-0	0.0
1970 LA-N	0	0	—	3	0	0	0	0	6²	11	0	5	6	21.6	9.45	41	.379	.471	0	.000	-0	-4	-4	-0	0.0
Total 7	8	19	.296	67	33	3	0	1	238¹	265	21	145	184	15.7	5.70	62	.281	.381	15	.231	2	-64	-57	1	-5.4
● JOHN STERLING									Sterling, John A. b: Philadelphia, Pa. Deb: 10/12/1890																
1890 Phi-a	0	1	.000	1	1	1	0	0	5	16	1	4	1	37.8	21.60	18	.516	.583	0	.000	-0	-10	-10	-0	-1.0
● RANDY STERLING									Sterling, Randall Wayne b: 4/21/51, Key West, Fla. BB/TR, 6'2", 195 lbs. Deb: 9/16/74																
1974 NY-N	1	1	.500	3	2	0	0	0	9¹	13	0	3	2	16.4	4.82	74	.351	.415	0	.000	0	-1	-1	0	-0.2
● DAVE STEVENS									Stevens, David James b: 3/4/70, Fullerton, Cal. BR/TR, 6'3", 210 lbs. Deb: 5/20/94																
1994 Min-A	5	2	.714	24	0	0	0	0	45	55	6	23	24	15.8	6.80	72	.302	.383	0	—	0	-10	-10	-0	-1.2
1995 Min-A	5	4	.556	56	0	0	0	10	65²	74	14	32	47	14.7	5.07	94	.285	.365	0	—	0	-3	-2	-0	-0.3
1996 Min-A	3	3	.500	49	0	0	0	11	58	58	12	25	29	12.9	4.66	110	.264	.339	0	—	0	2	3	-0	0.2
Total 3	13	9	.591	129	0	0	0	21	168²	187	32	80	100	14.4	5.39	91	.282	.362	0	—	0	-10	-9	-0	-1.3
● JIM STEVENS									Stevens, James Arthur "Steve" b: 8/25/1889, Williamsburg, Md. d: 9/25/66, Baltimore, Md. BR/TR, 5'11", 180 lbs. Deb: 8/24/14																
1914 Was-A	0	0	—	2	0	0	0	0	3	4	0	2	0	21.0	9.00	31	.364	.500	0	.000	-0	-2	-2	-0	0.0
● DAVE STEWART									Stewart, David Keith b: 2/19/57, Oakland, Cal. BR/TR, 6'2", 200 lbs. Deb: 9/22/78																
1978 LA-N	0	0	—	1	0	0	0	0	2	1	0	0	1	4.5	0.00	—	.167	.167	0	—	0	1	1	-0	0.0
1981 *LA-N	4	3	.571	32	0	0	0	6	43¹	40	3	14	29	11.2	2.49	133	.250	.310	2	.400	2	5	4	-0	1.0
1982 LA-N	9	8	.529	45	14	0	0	1	146¹	137	14	49	80	11.6	3.81	91	.249	.313	7	.179	1	-3	-6	-1	-0.6
1983 LA-N	5	2	.714	46	1	0	0	0	76	67	4	33	54	12.1	2.96	121	.237	.321	1	.143	-0	6	5	-1	0.5
Tex-A	5	2	.714	8	8	2	0	0	59	50	2	17	24	10.5	2.14	188	.233	.295	0	—	0	13	12	0	1.5
1984 Tex-A	7	14	.333	32	27	3	0	0	192¹	193	26	87	119	13.3	4.73	88	.258	.339	0	—	0	-16	-12	-1	-1.4
1985 Tex-A	0	6	.000	42	5	0	0	4	81¹	86	13	37	64	13.8	5.42	78	.273	.353	0	—	0	-12	-11	0	-0.8
Phi-N	0	0	—	4	0	0	0	0	4¹	4	2	4	2	18.7	6.23	59	.278	.409	0	—	0	-1	-1	-0	0.0
1986 Phi-N	0	0	—	8	0	0	0	0	12¹	15	1	4	9	13.9	6.57	59	.306	.358	0	—	0	-3	-4	-0	0.0
Oak-A	9	5	.643	29	17	4	1	0	149¹	137	15	65	102	12.4	3.74	103	.241	.322	0	—	0	7	2	-0	0.2
1987 Oak-A	20	13	.606	37	37	8	1	0	261¹	224	24	105	205	11.5	3.68	112	.229	.307	0	—	0	22	13	-3	1.5
1988 *Oak-A	21	12	.636	37	37	14	2	0	275²	240	14	110	192	11.5	3.23	117	.234	.310	0	—	0	22	17	-3	1.7
1989 *Oak-A★	21	9	.700	36	36	8	0	0	257²	260	23	69	155	11.7	3.32	111	.263	.315	0	—	0	16	10	-1	1.2
1990 *Oak-A	22	11	.667	36	36	11	4	0	267	226	16	83	166	10.6	2.56	145	.231	.294	0	—	0	40	34	-2	4.1
1991 Oak-A	11	11	.500	35	35	2	1	0	226	245	24	105	144	14.3	5.18	74	.278	.361	0	—	0	-27	-34	-2	-3.0
1992 *Oak-A	12	10	.545	31	31	2	0	0	199¹	175	25	79	130	11.8	3.66	102	.237	.318	0	—	0	6	2	-3	0.1
1993 *Tor-A	12	8	.600	26	26	0	0	0	162	146	23	72	96	12.3	4.44	97	.242	.326	0	—	0	-2	-2	-2	-0.5
1994 Tor-A	7	8	.467	22	22	1	0	0	133¹	151	26	62	111	14.6	5.87	82	.285	.364	0	—	0	-16	-16	-2	-1.6
1995 Oak-A	3	7	.300	16	16	0	0	0	81	101	11	39	58	15.8	6.89	65	.305	.382	0	—	0	-20	-22	0	-2.1
Total 16	168	129	.566	523	348	55	9	19	2629²	2499	264	1034	1741	12.3	3.95	99	.251	.325	10	.196	2	37	-7	-21	1.8
● FRANK STEWART									Stewart, Frank "Stewy" b: 9/8/06, Minneapolis, Minn. BR/TR, 6'1.5", 180 lbs. Deb: 10/2/27																
1927 Chi-A	0	1	.000	1	1	0	0	0	4	5	0	4	0	20.3	9.00	45	.357	.500	0	.000	-0	-2	-2	-1	-0.4
● JOE STEWART									Stewart, Joseph Lawrence "Ace" b: 3/11/1879, Monroe, N.C. d: 2/9/13, Youngstown, Ohio TR, 5'11", 175 lbs. Deb: 9/13/04																
1904 Bos-N	0	0	—	2	0	0	0	0	9¹	12	0	4	1	16.4	9.64	29	.286	.362	1	.200	-0	-7	-7	-0	0.0
● SAMMY STEWART									Stewart, Samuel Lee b: 10/28/54, Asheville, N.C. BR/TR, 6'3", 208 lbs. Deb: 9/1/78																
1978 Bal-A	1	1	.500	2	2	0	0	0	11¹	10	0	3	11	10.3	3.18	110	.238	.289	0	—	0	1	0	0	0.4
1979 *Bal-A	8	5	.615	31	3	1	0	1	117²	96	11	71	71	13.2	3.52	114	.232	.351	0	—	0	9	6	3	1.0
1980 Bal-A	7	7	.500	33	3	2	0	3	118²	103	9	60	78	12.5	3.56	111	.235	.330	0	—	0	6	5	-0	0.6
1981 Bal-A	4	8	.333	29	3	0	0	4	112¹	89	8	57	57	11.9	2.32	156	.225	.327	0	—	0	17	16	-0	1.8
1982 Bal-A	10	9	.526	38	12	1	1	5	139	140	9	61	77	13.2	4.14	97	.263	.342	0	—	0	-1	-2	1	-0.2
1983 *Bal-A	9	4	.692	58	1	0	0	7	144¹	138	6	67	95	12.8	3.62	109	.253	.336	0	—	0	7	5	-1	0.4
1984 Bal-A	7	4	.636	60	0	0	0	13	93	81	7	47	56	12.5	3.29	118	.241	.336	0	—	0	7	6	0	0.8
1985 Bal-A	5	7	.417	56	1	0	0	9	129²	117	15	66	77	12.8	3.61	112	.246	.339	0	—	0	8	6	1	0.6
1986 Bos-A	4	1	.800	27	0	0	0	0	63²	64	7	48	47	15.8	4.38	95	.266	.388	0	—	0	-1	-2	-0	-0.2
1987 Cle-A	4	2	.667	25	0	0	0	3	27	25	4	21	25	15.7	5.67	80	.234	.364	0	—	0	-4	-3	0	-0.7
Total 10	59	48	.551	359	25	4	1	45	956²	863	77	502	586	13.0	3.59	110	.245	.341	0	—	0	49	39	1	4.5
● BUNKY STEWART									Stewart, Veston Goff b: 1/7/31, Jasper, N.C. BL/TL, 6', 155 lbs. Deb: 5/4/52																
1952 Was-A	0	0	—	1	0	0	0	0	1	2	0	1	2	27.0	18.00	20	.500	.600	0	—	0	-2	-2	-0	0.0
1953 Was-A	0	2	.000	2	2	1	0	0	15¹	17	1	11	3	17.0	4.70	83	.283	.403	1	.200	-0	-1	-1	-0	-0.2
1954 Was-A	0	2	.000	29	2	0	0	1	50²	67	3	27	27	17.4	7.64	47	.324	.412	0	.000	0	-22	-23	1	-0.8
1955 Was-A	0	0	—	7	1	0	0	0	15¹	18	0	6	10	14.1	4.11	93	.295	.358	0	.000	-0	-0	-0	-0	0.0
1956 Was-A	5	7	.417	33	9	1	0	2	105	111	15	82	36	17.0	5.57	78	.276	.405	7	.250	-0	-16	-15	1	-1.4
Total 5	5	11	.313	72	14	2	0	3	187¹	215	19	127	77	16.9	6.01	67	.293	.404	8	.211	-0	-42	-41	2	-2.4
● LEFTY STEWART									Stewart, Walter Cleveland b: 9/23/1900, Sparta, Tenn. d: 9/26/74, Knoxville, Tenn. BR/TL, 5'10", 160 lbs. Deb: 4/20/21																
1921 Det-A	0	0	—	5	0	0	0	1	9	20	0	5	4	25.0	12.00	36	.455	.510	0	.000	-0	-8	-8	0	-0.2
1927 StL-A	8	11	.421	27	19	11	0	1	155²	187	7	43	43	13.4	4.28	102	.310	.357	15	.306	3	-2	1	2	0.5
1928 StL-A	7	9	.438	29	17	7	1	3	142²	173	5	32	25	13.1	4.67	90	.310	.350	14	.275	2	-10	-7	-0	-0.5
1929 StL-A	9	6	.600	23	18	8	1	0	149²	137	11	49	47	11.4	3.25	136	.246	.312	6	.118	-4	17	20	-0	1.3
1930 StL-A	20	12	.625	35	33	23	1	0	271	281	21	70	79	11.7	3.45	141	.268	.315	22	.244	2	36	43	0	4.7
1931 StL-A	14	17	.452	36	33	20	1	0	258	287	17	68	89	13.1	4.40	105	.277	.334	22	.250	6	-0	7	1	1.4
1932 StL-A	15	19	.441	41	32	18	2	1	259²	269	22	99	86	12.9	4.61	105	.270	.338	12	.146	-2	-4	7	1	0.6
1933 *Was-A	15	6	.714	34	31	11	1	0	230²	227	19	60	69	11.2	3.82	109	.256	.304	11	.143	1	12	9	1	0.8
1934 Was-A	7	11	.389	24	22	7	1	0	152	184	8	36	36	13.1	4.03	107	.303	.343	7	.156	-1	5	5	-0	0.5
1935 Was-A	0	1	.000	1	1	0	0	0	2²	8	1	0	2	33.8	13.50	32	.533	.588	0	.000	-0	-3	-3	-0	-0.6
Cle-A	6	6	.500	24	10	2	0	2	91	122	6	17	24	13.5	5.44	83	.312	.342	6	.250	-1	-10	-9	-1	-1.3
Yr	6	7	.462	25	11	2	0	2	93²	130	7	19	25	14.4	5.67	79	.320	.352	6	.194	-1	-13	-12	-1	-1.9
Total 10	101	98	.508	279	216	107	8	8	1722	1895	117	498	503	12.6	4.19	108	.281	.332	115	.204	6	35	64	0	7.0
● MACK STEWART									Stewart, William Macklin b: 9/23/14, Stevenson, Ala. d: 3/21/60, Macon, Ga. BR/TR, 6', 167 lbs. Deb: 7/7/44																
1944 Chi-N	0	0	—	8	0	0	0	0	12¹	11	1	4	3	10.9	1.46	242	.239	.300	0	.000	-0	3	3	-0	0.0

YEAR TM/L	W	L	PCT	G	GS	CG	SH	SV	IP	H	HR	BB	SO	RAT	ERA	ERA+	OAV	OOB	BH	AVG	PB	PR	/A	PD	TPI
1945 Chi-N	0	1	.000	16	1	0	0	0	28¹	37	0	14	9	16.2	4.76	77	.322	.395	1	.333	0	-3	-4	0	-0.1
Total 2	0	1	.000	24	1	0	0	0	40²	48	1	18	12	14.6	3.76	96	.298	.369	1	.250	0	-0	-1	0	-0.1

● **PHIL STIDHAM** Stidham, Phillip Wayne b: 11/18/68, Tulsa, Okla. BR/TR, 6′, 180 lbs. Deb: 6/4/94

YEAR TM/L	W	L	PCT	G	GS	CG	SH	SV	IP	H	HR	BB	SO	RAT	ERA	ERA+	OAV	OOB	BH	AVG	PB	PR	/A	PD	TPI
1994 Det-A	0	0	—	5	0	0	0	0	4¹	12	3	4	4	33.2	24.92	19	.571	.640	0	—	0	-10	-10	-0	0.0

● **DAVE STIEB** Stieb, David Andrew b: 7/22/57, Santa Ana, Cal. BR/TR, 6′1″, 195 lbs. Deb: 6/29/79

YEAR TM/L	W	L	PCT	G	GS	CG	SH	SV	IP	H	HR	BB	SO	RAT	ERA	ERA+	OAV	OOB	BH	AVG	PB	PR	/A	PD	TPI
1979 Tor-A	8	8	.500	18	18	7	1	0	129¹	139	11	48	52	13.3	4.31	101	.276	.344	0	—	0	-1	0	3	0.3
1980 Tor-A★	12	15	.444	34	32	14	4	0	242²	232	12	83	108	11.9	3.71	116	.260	.327	0	.000	0	9	16	5	2.2
1981 Tor-A★	11	10	.524	25	25	11	2	0	183²	148	10	61	89	10.8	3.19	124	.223	.299	0	—	0	10	15	2	1.9
1982 Tor-A	17	14	.548	38	38	**19**	**5**	0	**288¹**	271	27	75	141	11.0	3.25	138	.248	.299	0	—	0	27	**39**	4	4.2
1983 Tor-A	17	12	.586	36	36	14	4	0	278	223	21	93	187	10.7	3.04	141	.219	.293	0	—	0	31	**39**	1	3.9
1984 Tor-A	16	8	.667	35	35	11	2	0	267	215	19	88	198	10.6	2.83	**145**	**.221**	.293	0	—	0	34	37	1	3.3
1985 *Tor-A★	14	13	.519	36	36	8	2	0	265	206	22	96	167	10.6	**2.48**	**170**	**.213**	.290	0	—	0	49	51	5	**5.5**
1986 Tor-A	7	12	.368	37	34	1	1	1	205	239	29	87	127	15.0	4.74	89	.297	.376	0	—	0	-13	-12	1	-0.8
1987 Tor-A	13	9	.591	33	31	3	1	0	185	164	16	87	115	12.6	4.09	110	.239	.331	0	—	0	8	8	1	1.0
1988 Tor-A★	16	8	.667	32	31	8	4	0	207¹	157	15	79	147	10.8	3.04	129	.210	.296	0	—	0	21	21	1	2.3
1989 *Tor-A	17	8	.680	33	33	3	2	0	206²	164	12	76	101	11.0	3.35	112	.219	.302	0	—	0	12	10	0	1.2
1990 Tor-A★	18	6	.750	33	33	2	2	0	208²	179	11	64	125	10.9	2.93	134	.230	.297	0	—	0	23	23	3	2.9
1991 Tor-A	4	3	.571	9	9	1	0	0	59²	52	4	23	29	11.6	3.17	133	.243	.322	0	—	0	6	7	1	0.8
1992 Tor-A	4	6	.400	21	14	1	0	0	96¹	98	9	43	45	13.5	5.04	81	.275	.359	0	—	0	-12	-10	2	-0.9
1993 Chi-A	1	3	.250	4	4	0	0	0	22¹	27	1	14	11	16.5	6.04	69	.300	.394	0	—	0	-4	-5	-0	-0.6
Total 15	175	135	.565	424	409	103	30	1	2845	2514	219	1017	1642	11.6	3.41	122	.239	.313	0	.000	0	199	240	29	27.2

● **FRED STIELY** Stiely, Fred Warren "Lefty" b: 6/1/01, Pillow, Pa. d: 1/6/81, Valley View, Pa. BL/TL, 5′8″, 170 lbs. Deb: 10/6/29

YEAR TM/L	W	L	PCT	G	GS	CG	SH	SV	IP	H	HR	BB	SO	RAT	ERA	ERA+	OAV	OOB	BH	AVG	PB	PR	/A	PD	TPI
1929 StL-A	1	0	1.000	1	1	1	0	0	9	11	0	3	2	15.0	0.00	—	.297	.366	2	.667	1	4	4	0	0.7
1930 StL-A	0	1	.000	4	2	1	0	0	19	27	4	9	5	17.1	8.53	57	.346	.414	3	.429	1	-8	-8	-0	-0.2
1931 StL-A	0	0	—	4	0	0	0	0	6²	7	0	3	2	14.9	6.75	69	.269	.367	0	—	0	-2	-2	-0	0.0
Total 3	1	1	.500	9	3	2	0	0	34²	45	4	14	9	16.1	5.97	79	.319	.392	5	.500	2	-6	-5	-1	0.5

● **DICK STIGMAN** Stigman, Richard Lewis b: 1/24/36, Nimrod, Minn. BR/TL, 6′3″, 200 lbs. Deb: 4/22/60

YEAR TM/L	W	L	PCT	G	GS	CG	SH	SV	IP	H	HR	BB	SO	RAT	ERA	ERA+	OAV	OOB	BH	AVG	PB	PR	/A	PD	TPI
1960 Cle-A☆	5	11	.313	41	18	3	0	9	133²	118	13	87	104	13.8	4.51	83	.238	.352	8	.222	1	-9	-11	-2	-1.4
1961 Cle-A	2	5	.286	22	6	0	0	0	64¹	65	7	25	48	12.6	4.62	85	.264	.332	2	.125	-1	-4	-5	0	-0.5
1962 Min-A	12	5	.706	40	15	6	0	3	142²	122	19	64	116	11.9	3.66	112	.233	.319	2	.044	-4	5	7	-2	0.2
1963 Min-A	15	15	.500	33	33	15	3	0	241	210	32	81	193	10.9	3.25	112	.231	.294	9	.107	-2	10	11	-4	0.6
1964 Min-A	6	15	.286	32	29	5	1	0	190	160	31	70	159	11.1	4.03	89	.225	.299	7	.101	-3	-8	-9	-3	-1.5
1965 Min-A	4	2	.667	33	8	0	0	4	70	59	14	33	70	11.8	4.37	81	.227	.314	2	.133	-0	-7	-6	-1	-0.7
1966 Bos-A	2	1	.667	34	10	1	1	0	81	85	15	46	65	14.7	5.44	70	.268	.363	2	.118	-1	-18	-15	-1	-0.7
Total 7	46	54	.460	235	119	30	5	16	922²	819	133	406	755	12.0	4.03	93	.237	.318	32	.113	-8	-32	-29	-13	-4.0

● **ROLLIE STILES** Stiles, Rolland Mays "Lena" b: 11/17/06, Ratcliff, Ark. BR/TR, 6′1.5″, 180 lbs. Deb: 6/19/30

YEAR TM/L	W	L	PCT	G	GS	CG	SH	SV	IP	H	HR	BB	SO	RAT	ERA	ERA+	OAV	OOB	BH	AVG	PB	PR	/A	PD	TPI
1930 StL-A	3	6	.333	20	7	3	0	0	102	136	10	41	25	15.7	5.91	82	.337	.399	10	.270	0	-14	-12	-1	-0.9
1931 StL-A	3	1	.750	34	2	0	0	0	81	112	2	60	32	19.3	7.22	64	.352	.458	1	.045	-2	-26	-23	-0	-1.2
1933 StL-A	3	7	.300	31	9	6	1	1	115	154	4	47	29	16.5	5.01	93	.327	.390	2	.061	-3	-9	-5	-1	-0.7
Total 3	9	14	.391	85	18	9	1	1	298	402	16	148	86	16.8	5.92	80	.337	.412	13	.141	-5	-49	-40	-2	-2.8

● **ARCHIE STIMMEL** Stimmel, Archibald May "Lumbago" b: 5/30/1873, Woodsboro, Md. d: 8/18/58, Frederick, Md. BR/TR, 6′, 175 lbs. Deb: 7/3/00

YEAR TM/L	W	L	PCT	G	GS	CG	SH	SV	IP	H	HR	BB	SO	RAT	ERA	ERA+	OAV	OOB	BH	AVG	PB	PR	/A	PD	TPI
1900 Cin-N	1	1	.500	2	1	1	0	0	13	18	1	4	2	15.2	6.92	53	.327	.373	1	.200	-0	-5	-5	-0	-0.6
1901 Cin-N	4	14	.222	20	18	14	1	0	153¹	170	10	44	55	13.3	4.11	78	.279	.339	5	.081	-5	-13	-15	-3	-2.2
1902 Cin-N	0	4	.000	4	3	3	0	0	26	37	1	12	7	17.7	3.46	87	.333	.408	2	.200	-0	-2	-1	-0	-0.2
Total 3	5	19	.208	26	22	18	1	0	192¹	225	12	60	64	14.0	4.21	76	.290	.352	8	.104	-5	-20	-21	-3	-3.0

● **CARL STIMSON** Stimson, Carl Remus b: 7/18/1894, Hamburg, Iowa d: 11/9/36, Omaha, Neb. BB/TR, 6′5″, 190 lbs. Deb: 6/6/23

YEAR TM/L	W	L	PCT	G	GS	CG	SH	SV	IP	H	HR	BB	SO	RAT	ERA	ERA+	OAV	OOB	BH	AVG	PB	PR	/A	PD	TPI
1923 Bos-A	0	0	—	2	0	0	0	0	4	12	0	5	1	40.5	22.50	18	.750	.818	0	.000	0	-8	-8	0	0.0

● **HARRY STINE** Stine, Harry C. b: 2/20/1864, Shenandoah, Pa. d: 6/5/24, Niagara Falls, N.Y TL, 5′6″, 150 lbs. Deb: 7/22/1890

YEAR TM/L	W	L	PCT	G	GS	CG	SH	SV	IP	H	HR	BB	SO	RAT	ERA	ERA+	OAV	OOB	BH	AVG	PB	PR	/A	PD	TPI
1890 Phi-a	0	1	.000	1	1	1	0	0	8	17	0	4	1	23.6	9.00	43	.415	.467	1	.250	0	-5	-5	-0	-0.4

● **LEE STINE** Stine, Lee Elbert b: 11/17/13, Stillwater, Okla. BR/TR, 5′11″, 185 lbs. Deb: 4/17/34

YEAR TM/L	W	L	PCT	G	GS	CG	SH	SV	IP	H	HR	BB	SO	RAT	ERA	ERA+	OAV	OOB	BH	AVG	PB	PR	/A	PD	TPI
1934 Chi-A	0	0	—	4	0	0	0	0	11	12	2	10	8	18.0	8.18	58	.268	.423	0	.000	0	-5	-4	-0	0.0
1935 Chi-A	0	0	—	1	0	0	0	0	2	3	1	2	1	22.5	9.00	51	.286	.500	0	—	0	-1	-1	1	0.1
1936 Cin-N	3	8	.273	40	13	5	1	2	121²	157	6	41	26	15.2	5.03	76	.318	.379	8	.296	3	-14	-16	2	-0.9
1938 NY-A	0	0	—	4	0	0	0	0	8²	7	0	2	4	10.4	1.04	437	.333	.357	1	.500	0	4	3	-0	0.1
Total 4	3	8	.273	49	13	5	1	2	143¹	179	9	55	39	15.3	5.09	78	.315	.384	9	.300	4	-16	-18	2	-0.8

● **JACK STIVETTS** Stivetts, John Elmer "Happy Jack" b: 3/31/1868, Ashland, Pa. d: 4/18/30, Ashland, Pa. BR/TR, 6′2″, 185 lbs. Deb: 6/26/1889 ♦

YEAR TM/L	W	L	PCT	G	GS	CG	SH	SV	IP	H	HR	BB	SO	RAT	ERA	ERA+	OAV	OOB	BH	AVG	PB	PR	/A	PD	TPI
1889 StL-a	12	7	.632	26	20	18	2	1	191²	153	4	68	143	**10.6**	**2.25**	**188**	**.212**	**.285**	18	.228	-1	34	42	0	3.3
1890 StL-a	27	21	.563	54	46	41	3	0	419¹	399	14	179	289	12.8	3.52	123	.243	.324	65	.288	14	16	37	3	4.9
1891 StL-a	33	22	.600	**64**	56	40	3	1	440	357	15	232	**259**	12.4	2.86	147	.214	.317	92	.305	9	42	**66**	3	**7.7**
1892 *Bos-N	35	16	.686	54	48	45	3	1	415²	346	12	171	180	11.4	3.03	116	.217	.297	71	.296	15	12	22	1	3.7
1893 Bos-N	20	12	.625	38	34	29	1	1	283²	315	17	115	61	14.0	4.41	112	.273	.344	51	.297	5	8	17	-2	1.7
1894 Bos-N	26	14	.650	45	39	30	0	0	338	429	24	127	76	15.2	4.90	116	.306	.369	80	.328	10	16	29	-3	3.0
1895 Bos-N	17	17	.500	38	34	30	0	0	291	341	15	89	111	13.7	4.64	110	.288	.344	30	.190	-7	5	15	-1	0.5
1896 Bos-N	22	14	.611	42	36	31	2	0	329	353	20	99	71	12.6	4.10	111	.272	.327	76	.344	11	9	16	-3	2.1
1897 *Bos-N	11	4	.733	18	15	10	0	0	129¹	147	5	43	27	13.6	3.41	131	.284	.345	73	.367	7	13	15	1	2.1
1898 Bos-N	0	1	.000	2	1	1	0	0	12	17	2	7	1	18.0	8.25	45	.333	.414	28	.252	0	-6	-6	0	-0.3
1899 Cle-N	0	4	.000	7	4	3	0	0	38	48	2	25	5	17.8	5.68	65	.308	.410	8	.205	1	-8	-8	2	-0.3
Total 11	203	132	.606	388	333	278	14	4	2887²	2905	131	1155	1223	13.0	3.74	121	.255	.329	592	.297	65	141	247	0	28.2

● **CHUCK STOBBS** Stobbs, Charles Klein b: 7/2/29, Wheeling, W.Va. BL/TL, 6′1″, 185 lbs. Deb: 9/15/47

YEAR TM/L	W	L	PCT	G	GS	CG	SH	SV	IP	H	HR	BB	SO	RAT	ERA	ERA+	OAV	OOB	BH	AVG	PB	PR	/A	PD	TPI
1947 Bos-A	0	1	.000	4	1	0	0	0	9	10	1	10	5	20.0	6.00	65	.294	.455	0	.000	-0	-2	-2	-0	-0.2
1948 Bos-A	0	0	—	6	0	0	0	0	7	9	0	7	4	20.6	6.43	68	.321	.457	0	.000	-0	-2	-2	0	0.0
1949 Bos-A	11	6	.647	26	19	10	0	0	152	145	10	75	70	13.1	4.03	108	.254	.343	11	.208	0	3	6	-1	0.5
1950 Bos-A	12	7	.632	32	21	6	0	0	169¹	158	17	88	78	13.3	5.10	96	.250	.346	14	.246	3	-10	-4	1	0.0
1951 Bos-A	10	9	.526	34	25	6	0	0	170	180	15	74	75	13.7	4.76	94	.271	.349	11	.180	-2	-12	-6	-1	-1.0
1952 Chi-A	7	12	.368	38	17	2	0	0	135	118	9	72	73	13.0	3.13	116	.237	.339	4	.079	-1	8	7	1	1.0
1953 Was-A	11	8	.579	27	20	8	0	0	153	146	11	44	67	11.2	3.29	118	.246	.299	10	.227	1	12	10	1	1.3
1954 Was-A	11	11	.500	31	24	10	3	0	182	189	6	67	67	12.7	4.10	87	.270	.335	7	.137	-0	-8	-11	-1	-1.1
1955 Was-A	4	14	.222	41	16	2	0	3	140¹	169	18	57	60	14.6	5.00	77	.302	.368	6	.171	2	-16	-18	1	-1.8
1956 Was-A	15	15	.500	37	33	15	2	0	240	264	26	54	67	12.0	3.60	120	.279	.318	15	.179	-2	15	19	1	2.1
1957 Was-A	8	20	.286	42	31	5	2	0	211²	235	28	80	114	13.6	5.36	73	.279	.345	16	.211	-1	-37	-34	-3	-4.2
1958 Was-A	6	2	.250	19	8	0	0	0	56²	87	7	16	23	16.7	6.04	63	.369	.413	0	.000	-2	-14	-14	0	-1.9
StL-N	1	3	.250	17	0	0	0	0	39²	40	4	14	25	12.3	3.63	114	.261	.323	1	.250	-1	3	3	0	0.3
1959 Was-A	1	8	.111	41	7	0	0	7	90²	82	13	24	50	10.7	2.98	131	.238	.291	2	.105	-1	9	9	0	0.9
1960 Was-A	12	7	.632	40	13	1	1	2	119¹	115	9	38	72	11.8	3.32	117	.252	.313	3	.088	-2	7	8	-2	0.8
1961 Min-A	2	3	.400	24	2	0	0	2	44²	56	7	15	17	14.7	7.46	57	.311	.371	3	.375	1	-17	-16	-1	-1.7
Total 15	107	130	.451	459	238	65	7	19	1920²	2003	183	735	897	13.0	4.29	95	.269	.338	102	.176	-4	-63	-46	-5	-5.0

● **WES STOCK** Stock, Wesley Gay b: 4/10/34, Longview, Wash. BR/TR, 6′2″, 188 lbs. Deb: 4/19/59 C

YEAR TM/L	W	L	PCT	G	GS	CG	SH	SV	IP	H	HR	BB	SO	RAT	ERA	ERA+	OAV	OOB	BH	AVG	PB	PR	/A	PD	TPI
1959 Bal-A	0	0	—	7	0	0	0	0	12²	16	1	2	8	12.8	3.55	107	.302	.327	0	—	-0	0	-0	-0	0.0
1960 Bal-A	2	2	.500	17	0	0	0	2	34¹	26	2	14	25	10.7	2.88	132	.218	.306	0	.000	-1	4	4	1	0.4
1961 Bal-A	5	0	1.000	35	1	0	0	3	71²	58	3	27	47	10.9	3.01	128	.225	.303	0	.000	-1	8	7	2	0.6

YEAR	TM/L	W	L	PCT	G	GS	CG	SH	SV	IP	H	HR	BB	SO	RAT	ERA	ERA+	OAV	OOB	BH	AVG	PB	PR	/A	PD	TPI
1962	Bal-A	3	2	.600	53	0	0	0	3	65	50	7	36	34	12.0	4.43	83	.217	.326	0	.000	-0	-3	-5	3	-0.1
1963	Bal-A	7	0	1.000	47	0	0	0	0	75¹	69	11	31	55	11.9	3.94	88	.246	.321	0	.000	-1	-3	-4	1	-0.4
1964	Bal-A	2	0	1.000	14	0	0	0	0	20²	17	5	8	14	10.9	3.92	91	.233	.309	0	.000	-0	-1	-1	0	-0.1
	KC-A	6	3	.667	50	0	0	0	5	93	69	10	34	101	10.4	1.94	197	.213	.296	3	.200	0	17	19	-1	2.0
	Yr	8	3	.727	64	0	0	0	5	113²	86	15	42	115	10.5	2.30	164	.216	.297	3	.158	-0	17	19	-0	1.9
1965	KC-A	0	4	.000	62	2	0	0	4	99²	96	18	40	52	12.6	5.24	67	.251	.328	0	.000	-1	-20	-19	2	-0.8
1966	KC-A	2	2	.500	35	0	0	0	3	44	30	3	21	31	11.0	2.66	128	.199	.309	0	.000	-0	4	4	0	0.3
1967	KC-A	0	0	—	1	0	0	0	0	1	3	0	2	0	45.0	18.00	18	.500	.625	0	—	0	-2	-2	0	-0.1
Total	9	27	13	.675	321	3	0	0	22	517¹	434	60	215	365	11.6	3.60	101	.231	.315	3	.051	-4	6	3	7	1.9

● OTIS STOCKSDALE
Stocksdale, Otis Hinkley "Old Gray Fox" b: 8/7/1871, Arcadia, Md. d: 3/15/33, Pennsville, N.J. BL/TR, 5'10.5", 180 lbs. Deb: 7/24/1893

YEAR	TM/L	W	L	PCT	G	GS	CG	SH	SV	IP	H	HR	BB	SO	RAT	ERA	ERA+	OAV	OOB	BH	AVG	PB	PR	/A	PD	TPI
1893	Was-N	2	8	.200	11	11	7	0	0	69	111	4	32	12	19.3	8.22	56	.352	.420	12	.300	2	-27	-28	1	-2.5
1894	Was-N	5	9	.357	18	14	11	0	0	117¹	176	10	42	10	17.8	5.06	104	.342	.407	23	.324	1	3	3	1	0.3
1895	Was-N	6	11	.353	20	17	11	0	1	136	199	7	52	23	17.1	6.09	79	.336	.397	23	.311	2	-20	-19	-0	-1.5
	Bos-N	2	2	.500	4	4	1	0	0	23	31	2	8	2	15.3	5.87	81	.316	.368	4	.267	-0	-3	-2	-0	-0.3
	Yr	8	13	.381	24	21	12	0	1	159	230	9	60	25	16.4	6.06	80	.329	.382	27	.303	2	-23	-21	-1	-1.8
1896	Bal-N	0	1	.000	1	0	0	0	0	1²	4	0	2	1	37.8	16.20	26	.444	.583	1	.333	1	-2	-2	0	-0.7
Total	4	15	31	.326	54	46	30	0	1	347	521	23	136	48	17.8	6.20	80	.341	.405	63	.310	5	-49	-48	1	-4.7

● BOB STODDARD
Stoddard, Robert Lyle b: 3/8/57, San Jose, Cal. BR/TR, 6'1", 200 lbs. Deb: 9/4/81

YEAR	TM/L	W	L	PCT	G	GS	CG	SH	SV	IP	H	HR	BB	SO	RAT	ERA	ERA+	OAV	OOB	BH	AVG	PB	PR	/A	PD	TPI
1981	Sea-A	2	1	.667	5	5	1	0	0	34²	35	3	9	22	11.7	2.60	148	.269	.321	0	—	0	4	5	-0	0.4
1982	Sea-A	3	3	.500	9	9	2	1	0	67¹	48	7	18	24	9.2	2.41	176	.205	.271	0	—	0	12	14	0	1.2
1983	Sea-A	9	17	.346	35	23	2	1	0	175²	182	29	58	87	12.5	4.41	97	.274	.336	0	—	0	-7	-3	3	-0.1
1984	Sea-A	2	3	.400	27	6	0	0	0	79	86	10	37	39	14.2	5.13	78	.278	.359	0	—	0	-10	-10	1	-0.5
1985	Det-A	0	0	—	8	0	0	0	1	13¹	15	3	5	11	13.5	6.75	60	.268	.328	0	—	0	-4	-4	1	-0.2
1986	SD-N	1	0	1.000	18	0	0	0	1	23¹	20	1	11	17	12.3	2.31	158	.227	.320	0	.000	0	4	3	-0	0.1
1987	KC-A	1	3	.250	17	2	0	0	1	40	51	3	22	23	17.1	4.27	107	.313	.404	0	—	0	1	1	1	0.2
Total	7	18	27	.400	119	45	5	2	3	433¹	437	56	160	223	12.7	4.03	103	.266	.336	0	.000	-0	0	6	5	1.3

● TIM STODDARD
Stoddard, Timothy Paul b: 1/24/53, E.Chicago, Ind. BR/TR, 6'7", 250 lbs. Deb: 9/7/75

YEAR	TM/L	W	L	PCT	G	GS	CG	SH	SV	IP	H	HR	BB	SO	RAT	ERA	ERA+	OAV	OOB	BH	AVG	PB	PR	/A	PD	TPI
1975	Chi-A	0	0	—	1	0	0	0	0	1	2	1	0	0	18.0	9.00	43	.400	.400	0	—	0	-1	-1	0	0.0
1978	Bal-A	0	1	.000	8	0	0	0	0	18	22	3	8	14	16.0	6.00	58	.301	.386	0	—	0	-4	-5	0	0.0
1979	*Bal-A	3	1	.750	29	0	0	0	3	58	44	3	19	47	9.8	1.71	235	.212	.278	0	—	0	16	15	-0	1.2
1980	Bal-A	5	3	.625	64	0	0	0	26	86	72	6	38	64	11.6	2.51	157	.233	.319	0	—	0	15	14	-1	2.1
1981	Bal-A	4	2	.667	31	0	0	0	7	37¹	34	6	22	29	13.5	3.86	94	.268	.358	0	—	0	-1	-1	-0	-0.2
1982	Bal-A	3	4	.429	50	0	0	0	12	56	53	4	29	42	13.3	4.02	100	.249	.342	0	—	0	0	0	-0	0.0
1983	Bal-A	4	3	.571	47	0	0	0	9	57²	65	10	29	50	14.8	6.09	65	.293	.377	0	—	0	-13	-14	0	-1.9
1984	*Chi-A	10	6	.625	58	0	0	0	7	92	77	9	57	87	13.2	3.82	102	.236	.352	1	.091	-1	-2	1	-1	0.0
1985	SD-N	1	6	.143	44	0	0	0	1	60	63	3	37	42	15.0	4.65	76	.269	.369	0	—	0	-7	-7	-1	-1.0
1986	SD-N	1	3	.250	30	0	0	0	0	45¹	33	6	34	37	13.3	3.77	97	.200	.337	1	.250	1	-0	-1	0	0.1
	NY-A	4	1	.800	24	0	0	0	0	49¹	41	6	23	34	11.7	3.83	107	.232	.320	0	—	0	2	1	0	0.1
1987	NY-A	4	3	.571	57	0	0	0	8	92²	83	13	30	78	11.0	3.50	125	.235	.295	0	—	0	10	9	1	0.7
1988	NY-A	2	2	.500	28	0	0	0	3	55	62	5	27	33	14.9	6.38	62	.286	.370	0	—	0	-15	-15	0	-1.0
1989	Cle-A	0	0	—	14	0	0	0	0	21¹	25	1	7	12	13.5	2.95	134	.313	.368	0	—	0	2	2	0	-0.1
Total	13	41	35	.539	485	0	0	0	76	729²	680	72	356	582	12.9	3.95	100	.250	.339	2	.100	-0	2	-0	-3	-0.2

● ART STOKES
Stokes, Arthur Milton b: 9/13/1896, Emmitsburg, Md. d: 6/3/62, Titusville, Pa. BR/TR, 5'10.5", 155 lbs. Deb: 5/5/25

YEAR	TM/L	W	L	PCT	G	GS	CG	SH	SV	IP	H	HR	BB	SO	RAT	ERA	ERA+	OAV	OOB	BH	AVG	PB	PR	/A	PD	TPI
1925	Phi-A	1	1	.500	12	0	0	0	0	24¹	24	0	10	7	13.3	4.07	114	.270	.356	0	.000	-0	1	2	-0	0.0

● DICK STONE
Stone, Charles Richard b: 12/5/11, Oklahoma City, Okla d: 2/18/80, Oklahoma City, Okla. BL/TL, 5'9", 153 lbs. Deb: 8/26/45

YEAR	TM/L	W	L	PCT	G	GS	CG	SH	SV	IP	H	HR	BB	SO	RAT	ERA	ERA+	OAV	OOB	BH	AVG	PB	PR	/A	PD	TPI
1945	Was-A	0	0	—	3	0	0	0	0	5	6	0	2	1	14.4	0.00	—	.316	.381	0	—	0	2	2	0	0.0

● DEAN STONE
Stone, Darrah Dean b: 9/1/30, Moline, Ill. BL/TL, 6'4", 205 lbs. Deb: 9/13/53

YEAR	TM/L	W	L	PCT	G	GS	CG	SH	SV	IP	H	HR	BB	SO	RAT	ERA	ERA+	OAV	OOB	BH	AVG	PB	PR	/A	PD	TPI
1953	Was-A	0	1	.000	3	1	0	0	0	8²	13	0	5	5	18.7	8.31	47	.361	.439	0	.000	-0	-4	-4	-0	-0.4
1954	Was-A★	12	10	.545	31	23	10	2	0	178²	161	9	69	87	11.6	3.22	110	.240	.312	5	.096	-0	10	7	-3	0.5
1955	Was-A	6	13	.316	43	24	5	1	1	180	180	14	114	84	14.9	4.15	92	.267	.375	2	.043	-4	-4	-6	-2	-1.1
1956	Was-A	5	7	.417	41	21	2	0	3	132	148	10	93	86	16.9	6.27	69	.282	.397	3	.088	-1	-31	-29	-1	-2.5
1957	Was-A	0	0	—	3	0	0	0	0	3¹	5	0	2	3	18.9	8.10	48	.357	.438	0	—	-0	-2	-2	-0	0.0
	Bos-A	1	3	.250	17	8	0	0	0	51¹	56	5	35	32	16.0	5.08	78	.284	.392	0	.000	-1	-7	-6	1	-0.5
	Yr	1	3	.250	20	8	0	0	0	54²	61	5	37	35	16.1	5.27	76	.288	.394	0	.000	-1	-9	-8	1	-0.5
1959	StL-N	0	1	.000	18	1	0	0	1	30	30	4	16	17	13.8	4.20	101	.273	.365	0	.000	-0	-1	-0	-0	-0.1
1962	Hou-N	3	2	.600	15	7	2	2	0	52¹	61	4	20	31	14.1	4.47	84	.295	.360	4	.250	1	-3	-4	0	-0.2
	Chi-A	1	0	1.000	27	0	0	0	5	30¹	28	3	9	23	11.3	3.26	120	.255	.317	1	.500	1	2	2	0	0.3
1963	Bal-A	1	2	.333	17	0	0	0	1	19¹	23	0	10	12	15.4	5.12	68	.307	.388	0	—	0	-3	-4	0	-0.5
Total	8	29	39	.426	215	85	19	5	12	686	705	47	373	380	14.3	4.47	86	.269	.363	15	.088	-6	-43	-46	-5	-4.6

● DWIGHT STONE
Stone, Dwight Ely b: 8/2/1886, Holt Co., Neb. d: 6/3/76, Glendale, Cal. BR/TR, 6'1.5", 170 lbs. Deb: 4/13/13

YEAR	TM/L	W	L	PCT	G	GS	CG	SH	SV	IP	H	HR	BB	SO	RAT	ERA	ERA+	OAV	OOB	BH	AVG	PB	PR	/A	PD	TPI
1913	StL-A	2	6	.250	18	7	4	1	0	91	94	4	46	37	14.5	3.56	82	.267	.363	9	.273	2	-6	-6	1	-0.2
1914	KC-F	8	14	.364	39	22	6	0	0	186²	205	8	77	88	14.0	4.34	64	.281	.356	7	.121	-4	-30	-32	1	-3.7
Total	2	10	20	.333	57	29	10	1	0	277²	299	8	123	125	14.2	4.08	69	.276	.358	16	.176	-2	-36	-39	2	-3.9

● ARNIE STONE
Stone, Edwin Arnold b: 10/9/1892, North Creek, N.Y. d: 7/29/48, Hudson Falls, N.Y BR/TL, 6', 180 lbs. Deb: 8/7/23

YEAR	TM/L	W	L	PCT	G	GS	CG	SH	SV	IP	H	HR	BB	SO	RAT	ERA	ERA+	OAV	OOB	BH	AVG	PB	PR	/A	PD	TPI
1923	Pit-N	0	1	.000	9	0	0	0	0	12¹	19	1	9	4	16.8	8.03	50	.352	.397	0	.000	-0	-6	-6	1	-0.4
1924	Pit-N	4	2	.667	26	2	1	0	0	64	57	0	15	7	10.1	2.95	130	.259	.306	2	.133	-1	6	6	0	0.4
Total	2	4	3	.571	35	2	1	0	0	76¹	76	0	19	11	11.2	3.77	102	.277	.324	2	.125	-1	1	1	-0	0.0

● GEORGE STONE
Stone, George Heard b: 7/9/46, Ruston, La. BL/TL, 6'3", 205 lbs. Deb: 9/15/67

YEAR	TM/L	W	L	PCT	G	GS	CG	SH	SV	IP	H	HR	BB	SO	RAT	ERA	ERA+	OAV	OOB	BH	AVG	PB	PR	/A	PD	TPI
1967	Atl-N	0	0	—	2	1	0	0	0	7¹	8	1	0	5	11.0	4.91	68	.267	.290	0	.000	-0	-1	-1	0	0.0
1968	Atl-N	7	4	.636	17	10	2	0	0	75	63	9	19	52	9.8	2.76	108	.222	.271	9	.333	3	2	2	-1	0.5
1969	*Atl-N	13	10	.565	36	20	3	0	3	165¹	166	20	48	102	11.9	3.65	99	.260	.317	11	.186	1	-1	-1	-1	0.0
1970	Atl-N	11	11	.500	35	30	9	2	0	207¹	218	27	50	131	11.9	3.86	111	.267	.314	11	.236	4	4	10	3	1.6
1971	Atl-N	6	8	.429	27	24	4	2	0	172²	186	19	35	110	11.8	3.60	103	.274	.315	11	.177	-0	-3	2	-0	0.1
1972	Atl-N	6	11	.353	31	16	2	1	1	111	143	18	14	40	12.9	5.51	69	.315	.380	5	.200	1	-25	-21	1	-2.8
1973	*NY-N	12	3	.800	27	20	2	0	0	148	157	16	31	77	11.4	2.80	129	.274	.311	13	.271	2	14	13	1	1.7
1974	NY-N	2	7	.222	15	13	1	0	0	77	103	4	21	29	14.5	5.03	71	.322	.364	3	.115	-1	-12	-13	0	-1.4
1975	NY-N	3	3	.500	13	11	1	0	1	57	75	3	21	21	15.2	5.05	68	.323	.379	3	.143	0	-9	-10	1	-0.9
Total	9	60	57	.513	203	145	24	5	5	1020²	1119	122	270	590	12.4	3.89	96	.278	.326	72	.212	10	-31	-19	4	-1.2

● ROCKY STONE
Stone, John Vernon b: 8/23/18, Redding, Cal. d: 11/12/86, Fountain Valley, Cal. BR/TR, 6', 200 lbs. Deb: 5/2/43

YEAR	TM/L	W	L	PCT	G	GS	CG	SH	SV	IP	H	HR	BB	SO	RAT	ERA	ERA+	OAV	OOB	BH	AVG	PB	PR	/A	PD	TPI
1943	Cin-N	0	1	.000	13	0	0	0	0	24²	23	0	8	11	11.3	4.38	76	.237	.295	1	.250	0	-3	-3	-1	-0.2

● STEVE STONE
Stone, Steven Michael b: 7/14/47, Euclid, Ohio BR/TR, 5'10", 175 lbs. Deb: 4/8/71

YEAR	TM/L	W	L	PCT	G	GS	CG	SH	SV	IP	H	HR	BB	SO	RAT	ERA	ERA+	OAV	OOB	BH	AVG	PB	PR	/A	PD	TPI
1971	SF-N	5	9	.357	24	19	2	2	0	110²	110	9	55	63	13.7	4.15	82	.259	.349	0	.000	-2	-8	-9	2	-1.2
1972	SF-N	6	8	.429	27	16	4	1	0	123²	97	11	49	85	10.8	2.98	117	.218	.298	4	.118	-1	6	7	0	0.7
1973	Chi-N	6	11	.353	36	22	3	0	1	176¹	163	11	82	138	12.9	4.24	93	.245	.335	0	—	0	-8	-5	0	-0.5
1974	Chi-N	8	6	.571	38	23	4	0	0	169²	185	19	64	90	13.4	4.14	92	.278	.345	7	.121	-3	-10	-6	1	-0.7
1975	Chi-N	12	8	.600	33	32	6	1	0	214¹	198	20	80	139	11.9	3.95	97	.245	.316	8	.111	-2	-4	-3	0	-0.4
1976	Chi-N	3	6	.333	17	15	1	0	0	75	70	6	21	33	11.3	4.08	95	.250	.309	3	.143	-1	-5	-2	-0	-0.4
1977	Chi-A	15	12	.556	31	31	8	0	0	207¹	228	25	80	124	13.6	4.51	90	.281	.350	0	PB	0	-10	-10	-0	-1.1
1978	Chi-A	12	12	.500	30	30	6	1	0	212	196	19	84	118	12.0	4.37	87	.247	.321	0	PB	0	-14	-13	0	-1.5
1979	*Bal-A	11	7	.611	32	32	3	0	0	186	173	31	73	96	12.0	3.77	106	.248	.320	0	—	0	9	5	1	0.6

YEAR TM/L	W	L	PCT	G	GS	CG	SH	SV	IP	H	HR	BB	SO	RAT	ERA	ERA+	OAV	OOB	BH	AVG	PB	PR	/A	PD	TPI
1980 Bal-A★	25	7	.781	37	37	9	1	0	250²	224	22	101	149	11.9	3.23	122	.240	.319	0	—	0	22	20	-2	2.2
1981 Bal-A	4	7	.364	15	12	0	0	0	62²	63	7	27	30	13.1	4.60	79	.266	.343	0	—	-0	-7	-7	-0	-1.1
Total 11	107	93	.535	320	269	43	7	1	1788¹	1707	184	716	1065	12.4	3.97	97	.253	.328	22	.100	-9	-32	-22	-0	-3.4

● **TIGE STONE**   Stone, William Arthur   b: 9/18/01, Macon, Ga.   d: 1/1/60, Jacksonville, Fla.   BR/TR, 5'8", 145 lbs.   Deb: 8/23/23 ♦

YEAR TM/L	W	L	PCT	G	GS	CG	SH	SV	IP	H	HR	BB	SO	RAT	ERA	ERA+	OAV	OOB	BH	AVG	PB	PR	/A	PD	TPI
1923 StL-N	0	0	—	1	0	0	0	0	3	5	1	3	1	24.0	12.00	33	.455	.571	1	1.000	0	-3	-3	0	0.1

● **BILL STONEMAN**   Stoneman, William Hambly   b: 4/7/44, Oak Park, Ill.   BR/TR, 5'10", 170 lbs.   Deb: 7/16/67

YEAR TM/L	W	L	PCT	G	GS	CG	SH	SV	IP	H	HR	BB	SO	RAT	ERA	ERA+	OAV	OOB	BH	AVG	PB	PR	/A	PD	TPI
1967 Chi-N	2	4	.333	28	2	0	0	4	63	51	7	22	52	10.4	3.29	108	.223	.291	0	.000	-1	1	2	-1	0.0
1968 Chi-N	0	1	.000	18	0	0	0	0	29¹	35	6	14	18	15.3	5.52	57	.310	.391	0	—	-0	-8	-8	-0	-0.3
1969 Mon-N	11	19	.367	42	36	8	5	0	235²	233	26	123	185	14.1	4.39	84	.261	.358	4	.055	-3	-21	-19	-1	-2.6
1970 Mon-N	7	15	.318	40	30	5	3	0	207²	209	26	109	176	14.4	4.59	90	.263	.361	6	.100	-1	-13	-11	-1	-1.4
1971 Mon-N	17	16	.515	39	39	20	3	0	294²	243	20	146	251	12.0	3.15	112	.225	.321	12	.129	-1	10	12	0	1.4
1972 Mon-N★	12	14	.462	36	35	13	4	0	250	213	15	102	171	11.4	2.98	119	.229	.308	6	.080	-4	13	16	0	1.1
1973 Mon-N	4	8	.333	29	17	0	0	1	96²	120	12	55	48	16.9	6.80	56	.310	.404	1	.050	-1	-34	-32	0	-3.6
1974 Cal-A	1	8	.111	13	11	0	0	0	58²	78	8	31	33	17.0	6.14	56	.322	.404	0	—	-0	-16	-18	-0	-2.3
Total 8	54	85	.388	245	170	46	15	5	1236¹	1182	120	602	934	13.3	4.08	90	.253	.344	29	.086	-13	-68	-57	-3	-7.7

● **LIL STONER**   Stoner, Ulysses Simpson Grant   b: 2/28/1899, Bowie, Tex.   d: 6/26/66, Enid, Okla.   BR/TR, 5'9.5", 180 lbs.   Deb: 4/15/22

YEAR TM/L	W	L	PCT	G	GS	CG	SH	SV	IP	H	HR	BB	SO	RAT	ERA	ERA+	OAV	OOB	BH	AVG	PB	PR	/A	PD	TPI
1922 Det-A	4	4	.500	17	7	2	0	0	62²	76	3	35	18	16.4	7.04	55	.315	.409	2	.100	-1	-21	-22	1	-2.3
1924 Det-A	11	11	.500	36	25	10	1	0	215²	271	13	65	66	14.2	4.72	87	.316	.367	15	.195	1	-12	-14	-1	-1.2
1925 Det-A	10	9	.526	34	18	8	0	1	152	166	6	53	51	13.5	4.26	101	.283	.352	16	.291	4	2	1	-3	0.1
1926 Det-A	7	10	.412	32	22	7	0	0	159²	179	11	63	57	13.8	5.47	74	.291	.359	9	.170	-2	-26	-25	-0	-2.4
1927 Det-A	10	13	.435	38	24	13	0	5	215	251	9	77	63	13.9	3.98	106	.301	.362	8	.108	-6	4	6	-2	-0.2
1928 Det-A	5	8	.385	36	11	4	0	4	126¹	151	16	42	29	14.0	4.35	95	.296	.353	7	.179	-1	-4	-3	-2	-0.6
1929 Det-A	3	3	.500	24	3	1	0	4	53	57	7	31	12	15.3	5.26	82	.288	.390	1	.067	-1	-6	-6	2	-0.7
1930 Pit-N	0	0	—	5	0	0	0	0	5²	7	2	3	1	15.9	4.76	105	.318	.400	0	—	0	0	0	0	0.0
1931 Phi-N	0	0	—	7	1	0	0	0	13²	22	0	5	2	17.8	6.59	64	.373	.422	0	.000	-1	-4	-4	0	-0.1
Total 9	50	58	.463	229	111	45	1	14	1003²	1180	62	374	299	14.2	4.76	87	.301	.366	58	.172	-7	-66	-67	-5	-7.4

● **MEL STOTTLEMYRE**   Stottlemyre, Melvin Leon Jr.   b: 12/28/63, Prosser, Wash.   BR/TR, 6', 190 lbs.   Deb: 7/17/90 F

YEAR TM/L	W	L	PCT	G	GS	CG	SH	SV	IP	H	HR	BB	SO	RAT	ERA	ERA+	OAV	OOB	BH	AVG	PB	PR	/A	PD	TPI
1990 KC-A	0	1	.000	13	2	0	0	0	31¹	35	3	12	14	13.5	4.88	78	.280	.343	0	—	0	-3	-4	0	-0.1

● **MEL STOTTLEMYRE**   Stottlemyre, Melvin Leon Sr.   b: 11/13/41, Hazleton, Mo.   BR/TR, 6'2", 190 lbs.   Deb: 8/12/64 FC

YEAR TM/L	W	L	PCT	G	GS	CG	SH	SV	IP	H	HR	BB	SO	RAT	ERA	ERA+	OAV	OOB	BH	AVG	PB	PR	/A	PD	TPI
1964 *NY-A	9	3	.750	13	12	5	2	0	96	77	3	35	49	10.7	2.06	176	.219	.294	9	.243	2	17	17	1	2.5
1965 NY-A☆	20	9	.690	37	37	18	4	0	291	250	18	88	155	10.7	2.63	129	.233	.295	13	.131	1	27	25	6	3.2
1966 NY-A★	12	20	.375	37	35	9	3	1	251	239	18	82	146	11.5	3.80	87	.253	.313	11	.138	1	-10	-13	4	-1.1
1967 NY-A	15	15	.500	36	36	10	4	0	255	235	20	88	151	11.5	2.96	105	.248	.313	8	.098	-3	8	5	6	0.8
1968 NY-A★	21	12	.636	36	36	19	6	0	278²	243	21	65	140	10.0	2.45	118	.234	.281	13	.143	2	16	14	2	2.2
1969 NY-A★	20	14	.588	39	39	24	3	0	303	267	19	97	113	11.0	2.82	123	.239	.303	18	.178	5	27	22	8	3.8
1970 NY-A★	15	13	.536	37	37	14	4	0	271	262	23	84	126	11.7	3.09	114	.255	.315	16	.188	9	19	13	2	2.5
1971 NY-A	16	12	.571	35	35	19	7	0	269²	234	16	69	132	10.2	2.87	113	.233	.285	16	.170	2	18	11	3	1.7
1972 NY-A	14	18	.438	36	36	9	7	0	260	250	13	85	110	11.7	3.22	92	.254	.316	16	.200	3	-5	-8	3	-0.3
1973 NY-A	16	16	.500	38	38	19	4	0	273	259	13	79	95	11.3	3.07	119	.253	.310	0	—	0	23	18	2	2.2
1974 NY-A	6	7	.462	16	15	6	0	0	113	119	7	37	40	12.7	3.58	98	.272	.335	0	—	0	-1	-1	-1	-0.2
Total 11	164	139	.541	360	356	152	40	1	2661¹	2435	171	809	1257	11.1	2.97	112	.245	.304	120	.160	21	139	102	36	17.3

● **TODD STOTTLEMYRE**   Stottlemyre, Todd Vernon   b: 5/20/65, Sunnyside, Wash.   BL/TR, 6'3", 195 lbs.   Deb: 4/6/88 F

YEAR TM/L	W	L	PCT	G	GS	CG	SH	SV	IP	H	HR	BB	SO	RAT	ERA	ERA+	OAV	OOB	BH	AVG	PB	PR	/A	PD	TPI
1988 Tor-A	4	8	.333	28	16	0	0	0	98	109	15	46	67	14.6	5.69	69	.283	.366	0	—	0	-19	-19	-0	-2.1
1989 *Tor-A	7	7	.500	27	18	0	0	0	127²	137	11	44	63	13.1	3.88	97	.282	.348	0	—	0	-2	-1	-0	-0.3
1990 Tor-A	13	17	.433	33	33	4	0	0	203	214	16	69	115	12.9	4.34	91	.274	.339	0	—	0	-10	-9	-1	-1.1
1991 Tor-A	15	8	.652	34	34	1	0	0	219	194	21	75	116	11.5	3.78	111	.235	.308	0	—	0	8	10	-0	0.8
1992 *Tor-A	12	11	.522	28	27	6	2	0	174	175	24	63	98	12.8	4.50	91	.262	.334	0	—	0	-11	-8	-1	-1.2
1993 *Tor-A	11	12	.478	30	28	1	1	0	176²	204	11	69	98	14.1	4.84	89	.292	.358	0	—	0	-10	-10	-1	-1.2
1994 Tor-A	7	7	.500	26	19	1	1	1	140²	149	19	48	105	13.1	4.22	114	.275	.342	0	—	0	9	9	-1	0.7
1995 Oak-A	14	7	.667	31	31	2	0	0	209²	228	26	80	205	13.5	4.55	98	.276	.344	0	.000	0	4	-2	-1	-0.3
1996 *StL-N	14	11	.560	34	33	5	2	0	223¹	191	30	93	194	11.6	3.87	109	.231	.312	15	.227	3	9	9	1	1.3
Total 9	97	88	.524	271	239	22	6	1	1572	1601	171	587	1061	12.9	4.33	97	.265	.336	15	.224	3	-21	-21	-3	-3.4

● **ALLYN STOUT**   Stout, Allyn McClelland "Fish Hook"   b: 10/31/04, Peoria, Ill.   d: 12/22/74, Sikeston, Mo.   BR/TR, 5'10", 167 lbs.   Deb: 5/16/31

YEAR TM/L	W	L	PCT	G	GS	CG	SH	SV	IP	H	HR	BB	SO	RAT	ERA	ERA+	OAV	OOB	BH	AVG	PB	PR	/A	PD	TPI
1931 StL-N	6	0	1.000	30	3	1	0	3	72²	77	2	34	40	15.1	4.21	93	.305	.381	2	.105	-1	-3	-3	1	-0.2
1932 StL-N	4	5	.444	36	3	1	0	1	73²	87	5	28	32	14.5	4.40	89	.305	.375	2	.100	-1	-4	-4	1	-0.5
1933 StL-N	0	0	—	1	0	0	0	0	2	1	0	1	1	9.0	0.00	—	.167	.286	0	—	0	1	1	0	0.0
Cin-N	2	3	.400	23	5	2	0	0	71¹	85	3	26	29	14.0	3.79	90	.295	.354	4	.182	-0	-4	-3	-1	-0.3
Yr	2	3	.400	24	5	2	0	0	73¹	86	3	27	30	13.9	3.68	92	.293	.352	4	.182	-0	-3	-2	-1	-0.3
1934 Cin-N	6	8	.429	41	16	4	0	1	140²	170	10	47	51	14.1	4.86	84	.297	.354	8	.186	0	-13	-12	-0	-1.1
1935 NY-N	1	4	.200	40	2	0	0	5	88	99	7	37	29	14.3	4.91	79	.289	.365	2	.133	0	-9	-10	-1	-0.7
1943 Bos-N	1	0	1.000	9	0	0	0	1	9¹	17	1	4	3	20.3	6.75	51	.378	.429	0	.000	0	-4	-4	-0	-0.5
Total 6	20	20	.500	180	29	8	0	11	457²	546	28	177	185	14.5	4.54	85	.299	.365	18	.149	-1	-35	-34	-1	-3.3

● **JESSE STOVALL**   Stovall, Jesse Cramer "Scout"   b: 7/24/1875, Leeds, Mo.   d: 7/12/55, San Diego, Cal.   BL/TR, 6', 175 lbs.   Deb: 8/31/03 F

YEAR TM/L	W	L	PCT	G	GS	CG	SH	SV	IP	H	HR	BB	SO	RAT	ERA	ERA+	OAV	OOB	BH	AVG	PB	PR	/A	PD	TPI
1903 Cle-A	5	1	.833	6	6	6	2	0	57	44	0	21	12	10.7	2.05	139	.213	.294	1	.045	-2	6	5	-1	0.2
1904 Det-A	3	13	.188	22	17	13	1	0	146²	170	3	45	41	14.2	4.42	58	.291	.358	11	.196	0	-30	-30	0	-3.0
Total 2	8	14	.364	28	23	19	3	0	203²	214	3	66	53	13.2	3.76	70	.270	.341	12	.154	-2	-24	-25	-0	-2.8

● **HARRY STOVEY**   Stovey, Harry Duffield (b: Harry Duffield Stowe)   b: 12/20/1856, Philadelphia, Pa.   d: 9/20/37, New Bedford, Mass   BR/TR, 5'11.5", 175 lbs.   Deb: 5/1/1880 M♦

YEAR TM/L	W	L	PCT	G	GS	CG	SH	SV	IP	H	HR	BB	SO	RAT	ERA	ERA+	OAV	OOB	BH	AVG	PB	PR	/A	PD	TPI
1880 Wor-N	0	0	—	2	0	0	0	0	6	8	0	3	2	16.5	4.50	58	.308	.379	94	.265	0	-1	-1	-0	0.0
1883 Phi-a	0	0	—	1	0	0	0	0	3	5	0	0	4	15.0	9.00	39	.357	.357	128	.304	0	-2	-2	-0	-0.1
1886 Phi-a	0	0	—	1	0	0	0	0	0¹	2	0	0	0	54.0	27.00	13	.667	.667	144	.294	0	-1	-1	-0	0.0
Total 3	0	0	—	4	0	0	0	0	9¹	15	0	3	7	17.4	6.75	43	.349	.391	1771	.289	0	-4	-4	-0	0.0

● **HAL STOWE**   Stowe, Harold Rudolph   b: 8/29/37, Gastonia, N.C.   BL/TL, 6', 170 lbs.   Deb: 9/30/60

YEAR TM/L	W	L	PCT	G	GS	CG	SH	SV	IP	H	HR	BB	SO	RAT	ERA	ERA+	OAV	OOB	BH	AVG	PB	PR	/A	PD	TPI
1960 NY-A	0	0	—	1	0	0	0	0	1	1	0	1	0	9.0	9.00	40	.000	.500	0	—	0	-1	-1	-0	0.0

● **MIKE STRAHLER**   Strahler, Michael Wayne   b: 3/14/47, Chicago, Ill.   BR/TR, 6'4", 180 lbs.   Deb: 9/12/70

YEAR TM/L	W	L	PCT	G	GS	CG	SH	SV	IP	H	HR	BB	SO	RAT	ERA	ERA+	OAV	OOB	BH	AVG	PB	PR	/A	PD	TPI
1970 LA-N	1	1	.500	6	0	0	0	1	18²	13	1	10	11	11.1	1.45	265	.194	.299	2	.250	0	5	5	0	0.6
1971 LA-N	0	0	—	6	0	0	0	0	12²	10	1	8	7	12.8	2.84	114	.217	.333	0	.000	0	1	1	0	0.0
1972 LA-N	1	2	.333	19	2	1	0	0	47	42	5	22	25	13.2	3.26	102	.237	.325	2	.182	1	1	1	0	0.1
1973 Det-A	4	5	.444	22	11	1	0	0	80¹	84	7	39	37	13.9	4.37	94	.273	.356	0	—	-0	-5	-3	-1	-0.3
Total 4	6	8	.429	53	13	2	0	1	158²	149	14	79	80	13.0	3.57	105	.249	.339	4	.200	1	2	3	-1	0.4

● **DICK STRAHS**   Strahs, Richard Bernard   b: 12/4/23, Evanston, Ill.   d: 5/26/88, Las Vegas, Nev.   BL/TR, 6', 192 lbs.   Deb: 7/24/54

YEAR TM/L	W	L	PCT	G	GS	CG	SH	SV	IP	H	HR	BB	SO	RAT	ERA	ERA+	OAV	OOB	BH	AVG	PB	PR	/A	PD	TPI
1954 Chi-A	0	0	—	9	0	0	0	1	14¹	16	0	8	8	15.1	5.65	66	.271	.358	0	.000	0	-3	-3	-0	0.0

● **LES STRAKER**   Straker, Lester Paul (Bolnalda)   b: 10/10/59, Ciudad Bolivar, Venezuela   BR/TR, 6'1", 193 lbs.   Deb: 4/11/87

YEAR TM/L	W	L	PCT	G	GS	CG	SH	SV	IP	H	HR	BB	SO	RAT	ERA	ERA+	OAV	OOB	BH	AVG	PB	PR	/A	PD	TPI
1987 *Min-A	8	10	.444	31	26	1	0	0	154	150	24	59	76	12.3	4.37	106	.257	.328	0	—	0	4	-2	0	0.3
1988 Min-A	2	5	.286	16	14	1	1	0	82²	86	8	25	23	12.1	3.92	104	.276	.329	0	—	0	1	0	0	0.1
Total 2	10	15	.400	47	40	2	1	0	237	236	32	84	99	12.2	4.22	105	.264	.328	0	—	0	2	5	-1	0.4

● **BOB STRAMPE**   Strampe, Robert Edwin   b: 6/13/50, Janesville, Wis.   BB/TR, 6'1", 185 lbs.   Deb: 5/10/72

YEAR TM/L	W	L	PCT	G	GS	CG	SH	SV	IP	H	HR	BB	SO	RAT	ERA	ERA+	OAV	OOB	BH	AVG	PB	PR	/A	PD	TPI
1972 Det-A	0	0	—	7	0	0	0	0	4²	6	0	7	4	25.1	11.57	27	.300	.481	0	—	0	-4	-4	-0	0.0

YEAR	TM/L	W	L	PCT	G	GS	CG	SH	SV	IP	H	HR	BB	SO	RAT	ERA	ERA+	OAV	OOB	BH	AVG	PB	PR	/A	PD	TPI

● PAUL STRAND Strand, Paul Edward b: 12/19/1893, Carbonado, Wash. d: 7/2/74, Salt Lake City, Utah BL/TL, 6'0.5", 190 lbs. Deb: 5/15/13 ♦

1913	Bos-N	0	0	—	7	0	0	0	0	17	22	1	12	6	18.0	2.12	155	.393	.500	1	.167	-0	2	2	0	0.0
1914	Bos-N	6	2	.750	16	3	1	0	0	55¹	47	1	23	33	11.5	2.44	113	.235	.317	8	.333	2	2	2	-0	0.5
1915	Bos-N	1	1	.500	6	2	2	0	1	22²	26	0	3	13	11.5	2.38	109	.295	.319	2	.091	-0	1	1	-1	-0.1
Total	3	7	3	.700	29	5	3	0	1	95	95	2	38	52	12.7	2.37	119	.276	.350	49	.224	2	5	5	-1	0.4

● SCOTT STRATTON Stratton, C. Scott b: 10/2/1869, Campbellsburg, Ky. d: 3/8/39, Louisville, Ky. BL/TR, 6', 180 lbs. Deb: 4/21/1888 ♦

1888	Lou-a	10	17	.370	33	28	28	2	0	269²	287	7	53	97	11.8	3.64	85	.263	.306	64	.257	5	-17	-17	-1	-1.0
1889	Lou-a	3	13	.188	19	17	13	0	1	133²	157	6	42	42	13.9	3.23	119	.284	.342	66	.288	4	9	9	2	1.4
1890	*Lou-a	34	14	.708	50	49	44	4	0	431	398	3	61	207	9.9	2.36	163	.238	.270	61	.323	16	72	71	6	8.9
1891	Pit-N	0	2	.000	2	2	2	0	0	18¹	16	0	5	5	10.3	2.45	134	.225	.276	1	.125	-1	2	2	1	0.2
	Lou-a	6	13	.316	20	20	20	1	0	172	204	4	30	52	12.8	4.08	90	.285	.324	27	.235	1	-7	-8	3	-0.4
1892	Lou-N	21	19	.525	42	40	39	2	0	351²	342	1	70	93	10.8	2.92	105	.245	.285	56	.256	10	14	6	2	1.8
1893	Lou-N	12	23	.343	37	35	34	1	0	314²	445	8	100	43	15.8	5.43	81	.323	.373	49	.226	3	-27	-36	6	-2.1
1894	Lou-N	1	5	.167	7	5	4	0	0	43	72	3	13	13	18.4	8.37	61	.367	.415	12	.324	2	-15	-16	0	-1.2
	Chi-N	8	5	.615	15	12	11	0	0	119¹	198	5	40	23	18.2	6.03	93	.365	.412	36	.375	7	-9	-6	0	0.1
	Yr	9	10	.474	22	17	15	0	0	162¹	270	8	53	26	18.1	6.65	82	.364	.409	48	.361	8	-24	-21	1	-1.1
1895	Chi-N	2	3	.400	5	5	3	0	0	30	51	1	14	4	20.7	9.60	53	.370	.442	7	.292	1	-16	-15	1	-1.5
Total	8	97	114	.460	230	213	198	10	1	1883¹	2170	44	432	569	12.8	3.87	99	.280	.323	379	.274	48	7	-10	20	6.2

● MONTY STRATTON Stratton, Monty Franklin Pierce "Gander" b: 5/21/12, Celeste, Tex. d: 9/29/82, Greenville, Tex. BR/TR, 6'5", 180 lbs. Deb: 6/2/34 C

1934	Chi-A	0	0	—	1	0	0	0	0	3¹	4	0	1	0	13.5	5.40	88	.333	.385	0	.000	-0	-0	-0	-0	0.0
1935	Chi-A	1	2	.333	5	5	2	0	0	38	40	0	9	8	12.1	4.03	115	.274	.325	2	.143	-1	2	3	0	0.1
1936	Chi-A	5	7	.417	16	14	3	0	0	95	117	8	46	37	15.5	5.21	100	.305	.381	8	.216	1	-2	-0	2	0.2
1937	Chi-A†	15	5	.750	22	21	14	5	0	164²	142	6	37	69	9.9	2.40	191	.234	.280	12	.200	-0	41	40	1	4.5
1938	Chi-A	15	9	.625	26	22	17	0	2	186¹	186	18	56	82	12.0	4.01	122	.255	.315	21	.266	5	16	18	0	2.6
Total	5	36	23	.610	70	62	36	5	2	487¹	489	32	149	196	12.0	3.71	130	.261	.319	43	.224	5	56	61	3	7.4

● ED STRATTON Stratton, William Edward b: Baltimore, Md. Deb: 5/14/1873

| 1873 | Mar-n | 0 | 3 | .000 | 3 | 3 | 3 | 0 | 0 | 27 | 75 | 1 | 1 | 0 | 25.3 | 8.33 | 39 | .412 | .415 | 2 | .125 | -1 | -15 | -15 | | -1.0 |

● JOE STRAUSS Strauss, Joseph "Dutch" or "The Socker" (b: Joseph Strasser)
b: 11/16/1858, Cincinnati, Ohio d: 6/24/06, Cincinnati, Ohio BR/TR, Deb: 7/27/1884 ♦

| 1886 | Lou-a | 0 | 0 | — | 2 | 0 | 0 | 1 | 0 | 4 | 6 | 0 | 3 | 0 | 20.3 | 4.50 | 81 | .231 | .310 | 64 | .215 | -0 | -0 | -0 | -0 | 0.0 |

● OSCAR STREIT Streit, Oscar William b: 7/7/1873, Florence, Ala. d: 10/10/35, Birmingham, Ala. BL/TL, 6'5", 190 lbs. Deb: 4/21/1899

1899	Bos-N	1	0	1.000	2	1	1	0	0	14²	15	1	15	10	19.6	6.75	62	.263	.432	0	.000	-1	-5	-4	0	-0.3
1902	Cle-A	0	7	.000	8	7	4	0	0	51²	72	3	25	10	17.4	5.23	66	.330	.407	4	.211	1	-9	-10	-1	-1.1
Total	2	1	7	.125	10	8	5	0	0	66¹	87	4	40	10	17.6	5.56	65	.316	.412	4	.154	-0	-14	-14	-1	-1.4

● ED STRELECKI Strelecki, Edward Harold b: 4/10/05, Newark, N.J. d: 1/9/68, Newark, N.J. BR/TR, 5'11.5", 180 lbs. Deb: 4/16/28

1928	StL-A	0	2	.000	22	2	1	0	1	50¹	49	4	17	8	12.0	4.29	98	.269	.335	2	.200	-1	-1	-1	0	-0.1
1929	StL-A	1	1	.500	7	0	0	0	0	11	12	1	6	2	15.5	4.91	90	.279	.380	0	.000	-0	-1	-1	0	-0.1
1931	Cin-N	0	0	—	13	0	0	0	0	24¹	37	2	9	3	18.1	9.25	40	.394	.462	1	.200	0	-15	-15	0	0.1
Total	3	1	3	.250	42	2	1	0	1	85²	98	7	32	13	14.2	5.78	71	.307	.379	3	.176	-1	-17	-16	1	0.0

● PHIL STREMMEL Stremmel, Philip b: 4/16/1880, Zanesville, Ohio d: 12/26/47, Chicago, Ill. BR/TR, 6', 175 lbs. Deb: 9/16/09

1909	StL-A	0	2	.000	2	2	2	0	0	18	20	0	4	6	12.5	4.50	54	.308	.357	0	.000	-1	-4	-4	0	-0.4
1910	StL-A	0	2	.000	5	2	2	0	0	29	31	0	16	7	14.6	3.72	66	.287	.379	1	.125	-0	-4	-4	2	-0.1
Total	2	0	4	.000	7	4	4	0	0	47	51	0	20	13	13.8	4.02	61	.295	.371	1	.071	-1	-8	-8	2	-0.5

● CUB STRICKER Stricker, John A. (b: John A. Streaker)
b: 2/15/1860, Philadelphia, Pa. d: 11/19/37, Philadelphia, Pa. BR/TR, 5'3", 138 lbs. Deb: 5/2/1882 M♦

1882	Phi-a	1	0	1.000	7	3	0	1	2	7	3	0	1	2	5.1	1.29	232	.120	.154	59	.217	-0	1	1	-0	0.1
1884	Phi-a	0	0	—	1	0	0	0	0	3	6	1	0	1	21.0	6.00	56	.333	.368	92	.231	-1	-1	-0	0	0.1
1887	Cle-a	0	0	—	3	0	0	0	1	5²	5	0	7	2	19.1	3.18	137	.238	.429	141	.264	0	1	1	0	0.1
1888	Cle-a	1	0	1.000	2	0	0	0	0	12	16	0	2	5	14.3	4.50	69	.308	.345	115	.233	0	-2	-2	0	-0.1
Total	4	2	0	1.000	8	0	0	1	3	27²	30	1	10	11	13.7	3.58	94	.259	.328	1106	.239	1	-1	-1	-0	0.1

● JIM STRICKLAND Strickland, James Michael b: 6/12/46, Los Angeles, Cal. BL/TL, 6', 175 lbs. Deb: 5/19/71

1971	Min-A	1	0	1.000	24	0	0	0	1	31¹	20	2	18	21	11.5	1.44	247	.183	.310	0	.000	0	7	7	0	0.3
1972	Min-A	3	1	.750	25	0	0	0	1	36	28	7	19	30	11.8	2.50	128	.214	.313	1	.333	1	2	3	0	0.5
1973	Min-A	0	1	.000	7	0	0	0	0	5¹	11	0	5	6	27.0	11.81	34	.440	.533	0	—	-0	-5	-5	0	-0.7
1975	Cle-A	0	0	—	4	0	0	0	1	4²	4	0	2	3	13.5	1.93	196	.222	.333	0	—	1	1	1	0	0.0
Total	4	4	2	.667	60	0	0	0	5	77¹	63	9	44	60	12.8	2.68	128	.223	.333	1	.250	1	6	7	0	0.1

● BILL STRICKLAND Strickland, William Goss b: 3/29/08, Nashville, Ga. BR/TR, 6'2", 170 lbs. Deb: 9/16/37

| 1937 | StL-A | 0 | 0 | — | 9 | 0 | 0 | 0 | 0 | 21¹ | 28 | 2 | 15 | 6 | 19.0 | 5.91 | 82 | .341 | .455 | 1 | .167 | -0 | -3 | -3 | -0 | 0.0 |

● ELMER STRICKLETT Stricklett, Elmer Griffin "Spitball" b: 8/29/1876, Glasco, Kan. d: 6/7/64, Santa Cruz, Cal. BR/TR, 5'6", 140 lbs. Deb: 4/22/04

1904	Chi-A	0	1	.000	1	1	0	0	0	7	12	0	2	3	18.0	10.29	24	.375	.412	0	.000	-0	-6	-6	0	-0.6
1905	Bro-N	9	18	.333	33	28	25	1	1	237¹	259	0	71	77	13.0	3.34	87	.282	.343	13	.148	-1	-9	-12	9	-0.4
1906	Bro-N	14	18	.438	41	35	28	5	5	291²	273	2	77	88	11.0	2.72	93	.253	.306	20	.206	-5	-3	-9	9	0.9
1907	Bro-N	12	14	.462	29	26	25	4	0	229²	211	1	65	69	11.1	2.27	103	.255	.315	12	.148	1	5	2	7	1.1
Total	4	35	51	.407	104	90	78	10	6	765²	755	3	215	237	11.7	2.84	91	.264	.322	45	.167	-4	-12	-22	25	1.0

● JOHN STRIKE Strike, John b: 1865, Pennsylvania Deb: 9/24/1886

| 1886 | Phi-N | 1 | 1 | .500 | 2 | 2 | 1 | 0 | 0 | 15 | 19 | 1 | 7 | 11 | 15.6 | 4.80 | 69 | .311 | .382 | 0 | .000 | -1 | -2 | -2 | -1 | -0.4 |

● JAKE STRIKER Striker, Wilbur Scott b: 10/23/33, New Washington, O. BL/TL, 6'2", 200 lbs. Deb: 9/25/59

1959	Cle-A	1	0	1.000	2	1	1	0	0	6²	8	0	4	5	16.2	2.70	136	.296	.387	0	.000	1	1	1	0	0.2
1960	Chi-A	0	0	—	2	0	0	0	0	3²	5	1	1	1	17.2	4.91	77	.357	.438	0	—	0	-0	-0	0	0.0
Total	2	1	0	1.000	3	1	1	0	0	10¹	13	1	5	6	16.8	3.48	107	.317	.404	0	—	1	0	0	0	0.2

● NICK STRINCEVICH Strincevich, Nicholas "Jumbo" b: 3/1/15, Gary, Ind. BR/TR, 6'1", 180 lbs. Deb: 4/23/40

1940	Bos-N	4	8	.333	32	14	5	0	1	128²	142	17	63	54	14.9	5.53	67	.278	.367	5	.116	-2	-24	-26	-2	-2.5
1941	Bos-N	0	0	—	3	0	0	0	0	3¹	7	0	6	1	37.8	10.80	33	.412	.583	0	—	-2	-3	-3	0	-0.4
	Pit-N	1	2	.333	12	3	0	0	0	31	35	4	13	12	14.2	5.23	69	.280	.353	3	.429	1	-5	-6	0	-0.4
	Yr	1	2	.333	15	3	0	0	0	34¹	42	4	19	13	16.3	5.77	63	.294	.380	3	.429	1	-8	-8	0	-0.4
1942	Pit-N	0	0	—	7	0	0	0	0	22¹	19	2	9	9	11.7	2.82	120	.229	.312	0	.000	-1	1	1	-0	-0.1
1944	Pit-N	14	7	.667	40	26	11	0	2	190	190	5	37	47	10.9	3.08	121	.257	.296	9	.158	-1	11	13	5	1.9
1945	Pit-N	16	10	.615	36	29	18	0	1	228¹	235	7	49	74	11.3	3.31	119	.260	.301	17	.202	0	12	16	-2	1.6
1946	Pit-N	10	15	.400	32	22	11	3	1	176	185	7	44	49	11.9	3.58	98	.268	.316	8	.154	1	-3	-1	-2	-0.3
1947	Pit-N	1	6	.143	32	7	1	0	0	89	111	9	37	22	15.2	5.26	80	.316	.385	1	.048	-2	-12	-10	-0	-0.9
1948	Pit-N	0	0	—	3	0	0	0	0	4¹	8	2	1	0	20.8	8.31	49	.444	.500	0	—	-1	-2	-2	-0	-0.3
	Phi-N	0	1	.000	6	1	0	0	0	16²	26	1	10	4	19.4	9.18	43	.347	.424	0	—	-1	-10	-10	-1	-0.6
	Yr	0	1	.000	9	1	0	0	0	21	34	3	11	4	19.7	9.00	44	.366	.438	0	—	-2	-12	-12	-0	-0.6
Total	8	46	49	.484	203	103	46	4	6	889²	958	52	270	274	12.7	4.05	93	.273	.329	43	.158	-4	-34	-26	-1	-1.3

● JOHN STROHMAYER Strohmayer, John Emery b: 10/13/46, Belle Fourche, S.D. BR/TR, 6'1", 181 lbs. Deb: 4/29/70

1970	Mon-N	3	1	.750	42	0	0	0	0	76	85	7	39	74	14.9	4.86	85	.279	.364	1	.167	-0	-7	-6	-0	-0.3
1971	Mon-N	7	5	.583	27	14	2	0	1	114	124	16	31	56	12.6	4.34	81	.281	.333	8	.229	1	-11	-10	-1	-1.1
1972	Mon-N	2	3	.333	48	0	0	0	0	76²	73	6	31	50	12.3	3.52	101	.256	.331	0	.000	-0	-1	0	1	0.1

YEAR	TM/L	W	L	PCT	G	GS	CG	SH	SV	IP	H	HR	BB	SO	RAT	ERA	ERA+	OAV	OOB	BH	AVG	PB	PR	/A	PD	TPI
1973	Mon-N	0	1	.000	17	3	0	0	0	34²	34	4	22	15	14.8	5.19	73	.260	.370	1	.200	0	-6	-5	-0	-0.1
	NY-N	0	0	—	7	0	0	0	0	10	13	2	4	5	15.3	8.10	45	.310	.370	0	—	0	-5	-5	-0	0.0
	Yr	0	1	.000	24	3	0	0	0	44²	47	6	26	20	14.7	5.84	65	.270	.365	1	.200	0	-11	-10	-0	-0.1
1974	NY-N	0	0	—	1	0	0	0	0	1	0	0	1	0	9.0	0.00	—	.000	.250	0	—	0	0	0	0	0.0
Total	5	11	9	.550	142	17	2	0	4	312¹	329	35	128	200	13.4	4.47	83	.272	.346	10	.200	1	-29	-26	-0	-1.4

● BRENT STROM Strom, Brent Terry b: 10/14/48, San Diego, Cal. BR/TL, 6'3", 190 lbs. Deb: 7/31/72 C

YEAR	TM/L	W	L	PCT	G	GS	CG	SH	SV	IP	H	HR	BB	SO	RAT	ERA	ERA+	OAV	OOB	BH	AVG	PB	PR	/A	PD	TPI
1972	NY-N	0	3	.000	11	5	0	0	0	30¹	34	7	15	20	14.5	6.82	49	.296	.377	0	.000	-1	-11	-12	-1	-1.2
1973	Cle-A	2	10	.167	27	18	2	0	0	123	134	18	47	91	13.5	4.61	85	.278	.346	0	—	-1	-11	-9	1	-0.8
1975	SD-N	8	8	.500	18	16	6	2	0	120¹	111	6	33	56	10.3	2.54	137	.233	.289	3	.100	-1	14	12	0	1.6
1976	SD-N	12	16	.429	36	33	8	1	0	210²	188	15	73	103	11.2	3.29	99	.239	.305	4	.063	-2	5	-0	0	-0.3
1977	SD-N	0	2	.000	8	3	0	0	0	16²	24	5	12	8	18.9	12.42	28	.329	.427	1	.333	0	-16	-16	-0	-1.6
Total	5	22	39	.361	100	75	16	3	0	501	482	51	180	278	12.0	3.95	88	.254	.321	8	.078	-3	-19	-26	-0	-2.3

● FLOYD STROMME Stromme, Floyd Marvin "Rock" b: 8/1/16, Cooperstown, N.Dak. d: 2/7/93, Wenatchee, Wash. BR/TR, 5'11", 170 lbs. Deb: 7/5/39

YEAR	TM/L	W	L	PCT	G	GS	CG	SH	SV	IP	H	HR	BB	SO	RAT	ERA	ERA+	OAV	OOB	BH	AVG	PB	PR	/A	PD	TPI
1939	Cle-A	0	1	.000	5	0	0	0	0	13	13	1	13	4	18.0	4.85	91	.265	.419	1	.333	0	-0	-1	0	0.0

● SAILOR STROUD Stroud, Ralph Vivian b: 5/15/1885, Ironia, N.J. d: 4/11/70, Stockton, Cal. BR/TR, 6', 160 lbs. Deb: 4/29/10

YEAR	TM/L	W	L	PCT	G	GS	CG	SH	SV	IP	H	HR	BB	SO	RAT	ERA	ERA+	OAV	OOB	BH	AVG	PB	PR	/A	PD	TPI
1910	Det-A	5	9	.357	28	15	7	3	1	130¹	123	9	41	63	11.8	3.25	81	.257	.325	1	.026	-4	-11	-9	-4	-1.8
1915	NY-N	12	9	.571	32	22	8	0	1	184	194	3	35	62	11.5	2.79	92	.281	.321	9	.161	-1	-1	-5	-0	-0.6
1916	NY-N	3	2	.600	10	4	0	0	1	46²	47	1	9	16	11.0	2.70	90	.266	.305	1	.071	-1	-0	-1	-0	-0.3
Total	3	20	20	.500	70	41	15	3	3	361	364	13	85	141	11.5	2.94	88	.271	.321	11	.101	-6	-12	-15	-4	-2.7

● STEAMBOAT STRUSS Struss, Clarence Herbert b: 2/24/09, Riverdale, Ill. d: 9/12/85, Grand Rapids, Mich. BR/TR, 5'11", 163 lbs. Deb: 9/30/34

YEAR	TM/L	W	L	PCT	G	GS	CG	SH	SV	IP	H	HR	BB	SO	RAT	ERA	ERA+	OAV	OOB	BH	AVG	PB	PR	/A	PD	TPI
1934	Pit-N	0	1	.000	1	1	0	0	0	7	7	0	6	3	16.7	6.43	64	.250	.382	1	.333	0	-2	-2	0	-0.2

● DUTCH STRYKER Stryker, Sterling Alpa b: 7/29/1895, Atlantic Highlands, N.J. d: 11/5/64, Red Bank, N.J. BR/TR, 5'11.5", 180 lbs. Deb: 4/16/24

YEAR	TM/L	W	L	PCT	G	GS	CG	SH	SV	IP	H	HR	BB	SO	RAT	ERA	ERA+	OAV	OOB	BH	AVG	PB	PR	/A	PD	TPI
1924	Bos-N	3	8	.273	20	10	2	0	0	73¹	90	4	22	22	13.9	6.01	64	.314	.365	5	.217	-0	-17	-18	2	-2.1
1926	Bro-N	0	0	—	2	0	0	0	0	2	8	0	1	0	40.5	27.00	14	.571	.600	0	—	-0	-5	-5	-0	0.0
Total	2	3	8	.273	22	10	2	0	0	75¹	98	4	23	22	14.6	6.57	58	.326	.375	5	.217	-0	-23	-23	2	-2.1

● JOHNNY STUART Stuart, John Davis "Stud" b: 4/27/01, Clinton, Tenn. d: 5/13/70, Charleston, W.Va. BR/TR, 5'11", 170 lbs. Deb: 7/27/22

YEAR	TM/L	W	L	PCT	G	GS	CG	SH	SV	IP	H	HR	BB	SO	RAT	ERA	ERA+	OAV	OOB	BH	AVG	PB	PR	/A	PD	TPI
1922	StL-N	0	0	—	2	1	0	0	0	2	2	0	2	1	22.5	9.00	43	.222	.417			0	-1	-1	-0	0.0
1923	StL-N	9	5	.643	37	10	7	1	3	149²	139	11	70	55	13.1	4.27	91	.252	.345	14	.246	-1	-4	-6	-1	-0.6
1924	StL-N	9	11	.450	28	22	13	0	0	159	167	12	60	54	13.1	4.75	80	.273	.343	11	.204	-1	-16	-17	-3	-2.2
1925	StL-N	2	2	.500	15	1	1	0	0	47	52	6	24	14	14.9	6.13	71	.278	.366	4	.250	1	-10	-9	-0	-0.6
Total	4	20	18	.526	82	34	21	1	3	357²	360	29	156	124	13.4	4.76	82	.265	.348	29	.228	-1	-31	-34	-5	-3.4

● MARLIN STUART Stuart, Marlin Henry b: 8/8/18, Paragould, Ark. d: 6/16/94, Paragould, Ark. BL/TR, 6'2", 185 lbs. Deb: 4/26/49

YEAR	TM/L	W	L	PCT	G	GS	CG	SH	SV	IP	H	HR	BB	SO	RAT	ERA	ERA+	OAV	OOB	BH	AVG	PB	PR	/A	PD	TPI
1949	Det-A	0	2	.000	14	2	0	0	0	29²	39	3	35	14	22.4	9.10	46	.348	.503	2	.333	1	-16	-16	0	-0.9
1950	Det-A	3	1	.750	19	1	0	0	0	43²	59	6	22	19	16.9	5.56	84	.330	.406	1	.083	-1	-5	-4	0	-0.5
1951	Det-A	4	6	.400	29	15	5	0	1	124	119	9	71	46	14.3	3.77	111	.258	.365	10	.233	-1	5	6	0	0.6
1952	Det-A	3	2	.600	30	9	2	0	1	91¹	91	8	48	32	14.0	4.93	77	.265	.360	2	.087	-1	-13	-11	-0	-0.7
	StL-A	1	2	.333	12	2	0	0	1	26	26	3	9	13	12.1	4.15	94	.260	.321	0	.000	-1	-1	-1	-1	-0.2
	Yr	4	4	.500	42	11	2	0	2	117¹	117	11	57	45	13.3	4.76	81	.262	.346	2	.069	-2	-14	-12	-1	-0.9
1953	StL-A	8	2	.800	60	2	0	0	7	114¹	136	6	44	46	14.2	3.94	107	.300	.363	5	.192	-1	1	3	-0	0.2
1954	Bal-A	1	2	.333	22	0	0	0	0	38¹	46	2	15	13	14.8	4.46	80	.303	.373	2	.333	-0	-3	-4	0	-0.3
	NY-A	3	0	1.000	10	0	0	0	1	18¹	28	0	12	12	19.6	5.40	64	.350	.435	2	.333	0	-3	-4	0	-0.6
	Yr	4	2	.667	32	0	0	0	3	56²	74	2	27	25	16.0	4.76	74	.315	.385	4	.222	1	-7	-8	1	-0.9
Total	6	23	17	.575	196	31	7	0	15	485²	544	37	256	185	15.1	4.65	87	.289	.378	22	.176	-1	-36	-31	-0	-2.4

● GEORGE STUELAND Stueland, George Anton b: 3/2/1899, Algona, Iowa d: 9/9/64, Onawa, Iowa BB/TR, 6'1.5", 174 lbs. Deb: 9/15/21

YEAR	TM/L	W	L	PCT	G	GS	CG	SH	SV	IP	H	HR	BB	SO	RAT	ERA	ERA+	OAV	OOB	BH	AVG	PB	PR	/A	PD	TPI
1921	Chi-N	0	1	.000	2	1	0	0	0	11	11	0	7	4	14.7	5.73	67	.282	.391	1	.333	0	-2	-2	0	-0.2
1922	Chi-N	9	4	.692	35	11	4	0	0	113	129	9	49	44	14.6	5.81	72	.297	.374	4	.129	-2	-22	-20	-1	-2.2
1923	Chi-N	0	1	.000	6	0	0	0	0	8	11	0	5	2	18.0	5.63	71	.478	.571	0	—	-1	-1	-1	0	-0.1
1925	Chi-N	0	0	—	2	0	0	0	0	3	2	0	3	2	15.0	3.00	144	.182	.357	1	1.000	0	0	0	0	0.1
Total	4	9	6	.600	45	12	4	0	0	135	153	9	64	52	14.8	5.73	73	.301	.385	6	.171	-1	-25	-24	-1	-2.4

● PAUL STUFFEL Stuffel, Paul Harrington "Stu" b: 3/22/27, Canton, Ohio BR/TR, 6'2", 185 lbs. Deb: 9/16/50

YEAR	TM/L	W	L	PCT	G	GS	CG	SH	SV	IP	H	HR	BB	SO	RAT	ERA	ERA+	OAV	OOB	BH	AVG	PB	PR	/A	PD	TPI
1950	Phi-N	0	0	—	3	0	0	0	0	5	4	0	1	3	10.8	1.80	225	.211	.286			0	1	1	0	0.0
1952	Phi-N	1	0	1.000	2	1	0	0	0	6	5	0	7	3	18.0	3.00	122	.217	.400	0	.000	-0	0	0	0	0.1
1953	Phi-N	0	0	—	2	0	0	0	0	0	4	0	4	0	∞	∞	—	1.000		0	—	0	-4	-4	0	-0.4
Total	3	1	0	1.000	7	1	0	0	0	11	9	0	12	6	18.0	3.55	67	.214	.400	0	.000	-0	-2	-2	0	-0.3

● GEORGE STULTZ Stultz, George Irvin b: 6/30/1873, Louisville, Ky. d: 3/19/55, Louisville, Ky. 5'10", 150 lbs. Deb: 9/22/1894

YEAR	TM/L	W	L	PCT	G	GS	CG	SH	SV	IP	H	HR	BB	SO	RAT	ERA	ERA+	OAV	OOB	BH	AVG	PB	PR	/A	PD	TPI
1894	Bos-N	1	0	1.000	1	1	1	0	0	9	4	1	5	1	9.0	0.00	—	.133	.257	1	.333	-0	5	6	1	0.6

● JIM STUMP Stump, James Gilbert b: 2/10/32, Lansing, Mich. BR/TR, 6', 188 lbs. Deb: 8/29/57

YEAR	TM/L	W	L	PCT	G	GS	CG	SH	SV	IP	H	HR	BB	SO	RAT	ERA	ERA+	OAV	OOB	BH	AVG	PB	PR	/A	PD	TPI
1957	Det-A	1	0	1.000	6	0	0	0	0	13¹	11	0	8	2	12.8	2.03	190	.220	.328	1	.500	0	3	3	0	0.2
1959	Det-A	0	0	—	5	0	0	0	0	11¹	12	1	4	6	12.7	2.38	170	.279	.340	1	1.000	1	2	2	0	0.1
Total	2	1	0	1.000	11	0	0	0	0	24²	23	1	12	8	12.8	2.19	180	.247	.333	2	.667	1	4	5	0	0.3

● JOHN STUPER Stuper, John Anton b: 5/9/57, Butler, Pa. BR/TR, 6'2", 200 lbs. Deb: 6/1/82

YEAR	TM/L	W	L	PCT	G	GS	CG	SH	SV	IP	H	HR	BB	SO	RAT	ERA	ERA+	OAV	OOB	BH	AVG	PB	PR	/A	PD	TPI
1982	*StL-N	9	7	.563	23	21	2	0	0	136²	137	8	55	53	12.6	3.36	108	.266	.337	5	.119	-1	4	4	-3	0.0
1983	StL-N	12	11	.522	40	30	6	1	1	198	202	15	71	81	12.5	3.68	98	.265	.329	8	.136	-1	-1	-1	-1	-0.4
1984	StL-N	3	5	.375	15	12	0	0	0	61²	73	4	20	19	13.9	5.28	66	.297	.364	1	.063	-0	-12	-12	0	-1.5
1985	Cin-N	8	5	.615	33	13	1	0	0	99	116	8	37	38	13.9	4.55	83	.303	.364	1	.059	-0	-10	-8	0	-1.1
Total	4	32	28	.533	111	76	9	1	1	495	528	35	183	191	13.0	3.96	92	.277	.341	15	.112	-3	-20	-18	-4	-3.0

● TOM STURDIVANT Sturdivant, Thomas Virgil "Snake" b: 4/28/30, Gordon, Kan. BL/TR, 6'1", 186 lbs. Deb: 4/14/55

YEAR	TM/L	W	L	PCT	G	GS	CG	SH	SV	IP	H	HR	BB	SO	RAT	ERA	ERA+	OAV	OOB	BH	AVG	PB	PR	/A	PD	TPI
1955	*NY-A	1	3	.250	33	1	0	0	0	68¹	48	6	42	48	12.1	3.16	118	.203	.329	1	.083	-1	6	4	-0	0.1
1956	*NY-A	16	8	.667	32	17	6	2	5	158¹	134	15	52	110	10.8	3.30	117	.224	**.291**	20	.313	4	15	10	-2	1.7
1957	*NY-A	16	6	**.727**	28	28	7	2	0	201²	170	14	80	118	11.3	2.54	141	.232	.311	13	.183	1	28	23	-2	2.3
1958	NY-A	3	6	.333	15	10	0	0	0	70²	77	6	38	41	15.0	4.20	84	.276	.366	4	.190	0	-3	-5	-2	-0.7
1959	NY-A	0	2	.000	7	3	0	0	0	25¹	20	4	9	16	11.0	4.97	73	.222	.293	0	.000	-1	-6	-5	0	-0.3
	KC-A	2	6	.250	36	3	0	0	1	71²	70	9	34	57	13.8	4.65	86	.258	.354	1	.059	-2	-6	-5	1	-0.6
	Yr	2	8	.200	43	6	0	0	1	97	90	13	43	73	12.9	4.73	83	.249	.338	1	.043	-3	-9	-9	-2	-0.9
1960	Bos-A	3	3	.500	40	3	0	0	1	101¹	106	16	45	67	13.6	4.97	81	.279	.358	4	.182	-1	-12	-10	-0	-0.7
1961	Was-A	2	6	.250	15	10	1	1	0	80	67	6	40	39	12.4	4.61	87	.233	.332	2	.077	-1	-5	-5	1	-0.5
	Pit-N	5	2	.714	13	11	6	1	0	85²	81	6	17	45	10.4	2.84	141	.249	.289	8	.250	1	11	11	-1	0.8
1962	Pit-N	9	5	.643	49	12	2	1	2	125¹	120	12	39	76	11.6	3.73	105	.260	.321	6	.182	0	3	3	0	0.3
1963	Pit-N	0	0	—	3	0	0	0	0	8¹	8	1	4	6	13.0	6.48	51	.267	.353	0	.000	0	-3	-3	0	-0.1
	Det-A	1	2	.333	28	0	0	0	0	55	43	7	24	36	11.1	3.76	99	.221	.309	0	.000	0	-1	-1	0	-0.1
	KC-A	1	2	.333	14	3	0	0	0	53	47	3	13	26	11.0	3.74	104	.237	.301	0	.000	0	-1	-1	0	-0.1
	Yr	2	4	.333	45	3	0	0	0	108	90	10	41	62	11.0	3.75	102	.226	.300	0	.000	-2	-1	1	0	-0.2
1964	KC-A	0	0	—	3	0	0	0	0	3²	4	0	1	4	17.2	9.82	39	.308	.438	1	1.000	0	-3	-2	-0	-0.1
	NY-N	0	0	—	3	0	0	0	0	6	9	0	3	4	18.0	5.97	60	.306	.358	0	.000	0	-1	-1	0	-0.1
Total	10	59	51	.536	335	101	22	7	17	1137	1029	107	449	704	12.0	3.74	102	.244	.322	60	.183	-1	18	10	-4	2.1

● TANYON STURTZE Sturtze, Tanyon James b: 10/12/70, Worcester, Mass. BR/TR, 6'5", 190 lbs. Deb: 5/3/95

YEAR	TM/L	W	L	PCT	G	GS	CG	SH	SV	IP	H	HR	BB	SO	RAT	ERA	ERA+	OAV	OOB	BH	AVG	PB	PR	/A	PD	TPI
1995	Chi-N	0	0	—	2	0	0	0	0	2	2	1	1	0	13.5	9.00	46	.250	.333	0	—	0	-1	-1	-0	0.0

YEAR	TM/L	W	L	PCT	G	GS	CG	SH	SV	IP	H	HR	BB	SO	RAT	ERA	ERA+	OAV	OOB	BH	AVG	PB	PR	/A	PD	TPI
1996	Chi-N	1	0	1.000	6	0	0	0	0	11	16	3	5	7	17.2	9.00	47	.348	.412	0	.000	-0	-6	-6	0	-0.4
Total	2	1	0	1.000	8	0	0	0	0	13	18	4	6	7	16.6	9.00	47	.333	.400	0	.000	-0	-7	-7	0	-0.4

● DICK SUCH   Such, Richard Stanley b: 10/15/44, Sanford, N.C. BL/TR, 6'4", 190 lbs. Deb: 4/6/70 C

| 1970 | Was-A | 1 | 5 | .167 | 21 | 5 | 0 | 0 | 0 | 50 | 48 | 8 | 45 | 41 | 17.3 | 7.56 | 47 | .258 | .410 | 3 | .231 | 1 | -21 | -22 | 0 | -2.2 |

● CHARLEY SUCHE   Suche, Charles Morris b: 8/5/15, Cranes Mill, Tex. d: 2/11/84, San Antonio, Tex. BR/TL, 6'2", 190 lbs. Deb: 9/18/38

| 1938 | Cle-A | 0 | 0 | — | 1 | 0 | 0 | 0 | 0 | 1¹ | 4 | 0 | 3 | 1 | 47.3 | 27.00 | 17 | .571 | .700 | 1 | 1.000 | | -3 | -3 | 0 | 0.1 |

● JIM SUCHECKI   Suchecki, James Joseph b: 8/25/27, Chicago, Ill. BR/TR, 6', 185 lbs. Deb: 5/20/50

1950	Bos-A	0	0		4	0	0	0	0	4	3	0	4	3	15.8	4.50	109	.231	.412	0	—	0	0	0	-0	0.0
1951	StL-A	0	6	.000	29	6	0	0	0	89²	113	8	42	47	15.7	5.42	81	.299	.371	2	.100	-2	-13	-10	-1	-0.8
1952	Pit-N	0	0		5	0	0	0	0	10	14	1	4	6	17.1	5.40	74	.326	.396	0	.000	-0	-2	-2	-0	0.0
Total	3	0	6	.000	38	6	0	0	0	103²	130	9	50	56	15.8	5.38	81	.300	.374	2	.091	-2	-15	-12	-1	-0.8

● WILLIE SUDHOFF   Sudhoff, John William "Wee Willie" b: 9/17/1874, St.Louis, Mo. d: 5/25/17, St.Louis, Mo. BR/TR, 5'7", 165 lbs. Deb: 8/20/1897

1897	StL-N	2	7	.222	11	9	9	0	0	92²	126	8	21	19	14.3	4.47	99	.321	.356	10	.238	-1	-2	-1	2	0.0
1898	StL-N	11	27	.289	41	38	35	0	1	315	355	11	102	65	13.8	4.34	87	.282	.349	19	.158	-6	-26	-19	8	-1.8
1899	Cle-A	3	8	.273	11	10	8	0	0	86¹	131	3	25	10	17.0	6.98	53	.347	.399	2	.065	-4	-30	-32	2	-2.9
	StL-N	12	10	.545	25	23	16	0	0	178¹	193	5	62	29	13.6	4.04	99	.276	.347	13	.203	-0	-4	-1	4	0.3
	Yr	15	18	.455	36	33	24	0	0	264²	324	8	87	39	14.5	5.00	78	.299	.359	15	.158	-3	-34	-33	7	-2.6
1900	StL-N	6	8	.429	16	14	13	2	0	127	128	3	37	29	12.3	2.76	132	.261	.323	20	.189	-0	13	12	1	1.2
1901	StL-N	17	11	.607	38	26	25	1	2	276¹	281	6	92	78	12.7	3.52	90	.262	.331	19	.176	3	-6	-10	2	-0.4
1902	StL-A	12	12	.500	30	25	20	0	0	220	213	6	67	44	11.9	2.86	123	.254	.319	13	.169	-2	17	16	3	1.7
1903	StL-A	21	15	.583	38	35	30	5	0	293²	262	4	56	104	11.0	2.27	128	.238	.281	20	.182	-1	23	21	3	2.7
1904	StL-A	8	15	.348	27	24	20	1	0	222¹	232	8	54	63	12.0	3.76	66	.269	.320	14	.165	0	-29	-32	5	-2.5
1905	StL-A	10	20	.333	32	30	23	1	0	244	222	8	78	70	11.5	2.99	85	.244	.313	16	.186	2	-9	-12	4	-0.8
1906	Was-A	0	2	.000	9	5	0	0	0	19²	30	1	9	7	18.8	9.15	29	.353	.427	1	.429	1	-14	-14	1	-1.1
Total	10	102	135	.430	278	239	199	10	3	2075¹	2173	61	603	516	12.6	3.60	91	.269	.329	149	.178	-7	-65	-74	35	-3.6

● JOE SUGDEN   Sugden, Joseph b: 7/31/1870, Philadelphia, Pa. d: 6/28/59, Philadelphia, Pa. BB/TR, 5'10", 180 lbs. Deb: 7/20/1893 C◆

| 1902 | StL-A | 0 | 0 | — | 1 | 0 | 0 | 0 | 0 | 1 | 1 | 0 | 0 | 0 | 9.0 | 0.00 | — | .250 | .250 | 50 | .250 | | 0 | 0 | 0 | 0.0 |

● GEORGE SUGGS   Suggs, George Franklin b: 7/7/1882, Kinston, N.C. d: 4/4/49, Kinston, N.C. BR/TR, 5'7.5", 168 lbs. Deb: 4/21/08

1908	Det-A	1	1	.500	6	1	1	0	1	27	32	2	8	11.3	1.67	145	.299	.312	2	.200	-1	2	2	-1	0.1
1909	Det-A	1	3	.250	9	4	2	0	1	44¹	34	1	10	19	9.5	2.03	124	.228	.290	1	.067	-1	2	2	-0	0.1
1910	Cin-N	20	12	.625	35	30	23	2	3	266	248	6	48	109	10.5	2.40	121	.253	.297	14	.165	2	19	15	1	2.1
1911	Cin-N	15	13	.536	36	29	17	1	0	260²	258	3	79	91	12.0	3.00	110	.268	.330	23	.256	6	12	9	3	1.9
1912	Cin-N	19	16	.543	42	36	25	5	3	303	320	6	56	104	11.5	2.94	114	.278	.318	17	.160	-1	16	14	1	1.5
1913	Cin-N	8	15	.348	36	22	9	2	2	199	220	6	35	73	11.8	4.03	81	.292	.329	17	.254	2	-18	-17	3	-1.3
1914	Bal-F	24	14	.632	46	38	26	6	4	319¹	322	6	57	132	11.0	2.90	104	.266	.304	21	.212	2	-1	-5	6	1.3
1915	Bal-F	11	17	.393	35	25	12	0	3	232²	288	12	68	71	14.0	4.14	69	.318	.370	17	.221	0	-36	-33	2	-3.5
Total	8	99	91	.521	245	185	115	16	17	1652	1722	40	355	588	11.7	3.11	100	.277	.322	112	.204	11	-5	-1	14	2.2

● ED SUKLA   Sukla, Edward Anthony (b: Edward Anthony Suckla) b: 3/3/43, Long Beach, Cal. BR/TR, 5'11", 170 lbs. Deb: 9/17/64

1964	LA-A	0	1	.000	2	0	0	0	0	2²	2	1	3	1	10.1	6.75	49	.200	.273	0		0	-1	-1	0	-0.3
1965	Cal-A	2	3	.400	25	0	0	0	3	32	32	3	10	15	12.1	4.50	76	.264	.326	0	—	0	-4	-4	1	-0.6
1966	Cal-A	1	1	.500	12	0	0	0	1	16²	18	4	6	8	13.0	6.48	52	.281	.343	0	.000	-0	-6	-6	-1	-0.8
Total	3	3	5	.375	39	0	0	0	4	51¹	52	8	17	26	12.3	5.26	64	.267	.329	0	.000	-0	-10	-11	0	-1.7

● CHARLIE SULLIVAN   Sullivan, Charles Edward b: 5/23/03, Yadkin Valley, N.C d: 5/28/35, Maiden, N.C. BL/TR, 6'1", 185 lbs. Deb: 4/21/28

1928	Det-A	0	2	.000	3	2	0	0	0	12¹	18	1	6	2	17.5	6.57	63	.360	.429	0	.000	-1	-3	-3	-0	-0.5
1930	Det-A	1	5	.167	40	3	2	0	0	93²	112	9	53	38	16.0	6.53	73	.311	.401	7	.292	2	-20	-18	1	-0.9
1931	Det-A	3	2	.600	31	4	2	0	0	95	109	6	46	28	14.8	4.93	93	.288	.366	4	.167	-1	-6	-4	-0	-0.3
Total	3	4	9	.308	74	9	4	0	0	201	239	16	105	68	15.5	5.78	81	.303	.386	11	.212	-0	-29	-25	1	-1.7

● FLEURY SULLIVAN   Sullivan, Florence P. b: 1862, E.St.Louis, Ill. d: 2/15/1897, E.St.Louis, Ill. Deb: 5/3/1884

| 1884 | Pit-a | 16 | 35 | .314 | 51 | 51 | 51 | 2 | 0 | 441 | 496 | 15 | 96 | 189 | 12.5 | 4.20 | 80 | .268 | .311 | 29 | .153 | -9 | -47 | -41 | 1 | -4.5 |

● FRANK SULLIVAN   Sullivan, Franklin Leal b: 1/23/30, Hollywood, Cal. BR/TR, 6'6.5", 215 lbs. Deb: 7/31/53

1953	Bos-A	1	1	.500	14	0	0	0	0	25²	24	3	11	17	12.6	5.61	75	.264	.350	1	.250	0	-5	-4	-0	-0.3
1954	Bos-A	15	12	.556	36	26	11	3	1	206¹	185	18	66	124	11.2	3.14	131	.240	.305	7	.103	-3	13	22	1	2.7
1955	Bos-A★	18	13	.581	35	35	16	3	0	260	235	23	100	129	11.8	2.91	147	.241	.316	10	.112	-4	30	40	1	4.2
1956	Bos-A☆	14	7	.667	34	33	12	1	0	242	253	22	82	116	12.8	3.42	135	.268	.332	12	.141	-5	20	32	0	2.0
1957	Bos-A	14	11	.560	31	30	14	3	0	240²	206	16	48	127	9.8	2.73	146	.230	.275	13	.165	-2	28	34	2	3.5
1958	Bos-A	13	9	.591	32	29	10	2	3	199¹	216	12	49	103	12.1	3.57	112	.278	.324	11	.164	-1	4	10	-1	0.9
1959	Bos-A	9	11	.450	30	26	5	2	1	177²	172	17	67	107	12.5	3.95	103	.258	.332	2	.200	-1	-2	1	-0	-0.0
1960	Bos-A	6	16	.273	40	22	4	0	1	153²	164	12	52	98	13.0	5.10	79	.269	.332	5	.125	-1	-21	-18	-1	-2.5
1961	Phi-N	3	16	.158	49	18	1	1	6	159¹	161	19	55	114	12.5	4.29	95	.262	.327	5	.152	-1	-5	-4	1	-0.3
1962	Phi-N	0	2	.000	19	0	0	0	0	23	38	2	12	12	20.3	6.26	62	.396	.473	0	—	0	-6	-6	-0	-0.4
	Min-A	4	1	.800	21	0	0	0	5	33¹	33	7	13	10	12.4	3.24	126	.258	.326	0	.000	-0	3	3	0	0.5
1963	Min-A	0	1	.000	10	0	0	0	0	11	15	1	4	2	15.5	5.73	64	.349	.404	0	—	0	-3	-3	-0	-0.2
Total	11	97	100	.492	351	219	73	15	18	1732	1702	148	559	959	12.0	3.60	116	.257	.320	76	.144	-17	59	108	3	10.1

● HARRY SULLIVAN   Sullivan, Harry Andrew b: 4/12/1888, Rockford, Ill. d: 9/22/19, Rockford, Ill. BL/TL, Deb: 8/11/09

| 1909 | StL-N | 0 | 0 | — | 2 | 1 | 0 | 0 | 0 | 1 | 4 | 1 | 1 | 0 | 54.0 | 36.00 | 7 | .500 | .600 | 0 | .000 | -0 | -4 | -4 | 0 | 0.0 |

● JIM SULLIVAN   Sullivan, James E. b: 4/25/1869, Charlestown, Mass. d: 11/30/01, Roxbury, Mass. BR/TR, 5'10", 155 lbs. Deb: 4/22/1891

1891	Bos-N	0	0	—	1	0	0	0	0	0¹	2	0	5	0	189.0	81.00	5	.667	.875		—	0	-3	-3	-0	0.0
	Col-a	0	1	.000	1	1	0	0	0	9	10	1	5	1	16.0	4.00	87	.270	.372	0	.000	-1	-0	-1	1	-0.1
1895	Bos-N	11	9	.550	21	19	16	0	0	179¹	236	10	58	46	15.6	4.82	106	.312	.373	15	.176	-6	-1	6	-2	-0.2
1896	Bos-N	11	12	.478	31	26	21	1	1	225¹	268	12	68	33	13.7	4.03	113	.293	.346	19	.216	-2	8	13	-3	0.5
1897	*Bos-N	4	5	.444	13	9	8	2	1	89	91	1	26	17	12.0	3.94	113	.263	.318	6	.182	-3	4	5	-1	0.1
Total	4	26	27	.491	67	55	46	2	3	503	607	24	162	97	14.2	4.35	108	.295	.354	40	.190	-11	8	20	-6	0.3

● JIM SULLIVAN   Sullivan, James Richard b: 4/5/1894, Mine Run, Va. d: 2/12/72, Burtonsville, Md. BR/TR, 5'11", 165 lbs. Deb: 9/27/21

1921	Phi-A	0	2	.000	2	2	2	0	0	17	20	1	4	6	14.3	3.18	140	.294	.360	0	.000	-1	2	2	0	0.1
1922	Phi-A	0	2	.000	20	2	1	0	0	51¹	76	3	25	15	17.9	5.44	78	.373	.443	1	.091	-1	-8	-7	-0	-0.3
1923	Cle-A	0	1	.000	3	0	0	0	0	5	10	2	8	6	14.40	14.40	28	.476	.593	0	.000	-0	-6	-6	-0	-0.9
Total	3	0	5	.000	25	4	3	0	0	73¹	106	3	37	27	17.8	5.52	78	.362	.437	1	.056	-2	-12	-10	-1	-1.1

● JOE SULLIVAN   Sullivan, Joe b: 9/26/10, Mason City, Ill. d: 4/8/85, Sequim, Wash. BL/TL, 5'11", 175 lbs. Deb: 4/20/35

1935	Det-A	6	6	.500	25	12	5	0	0	125²	119	4	71	53	13.8	3.51	119	.244	.344	7	.163	-1	13	9	-1	0.6
1936	Det-A	2	5	.286	26	4	1	0	1	79²	111	4	40	32	17.3	6.78	73	.331	.406	5	.179	-1	-15	-16	-1	-1.3
1939	Bos-N	6	9	.400	31	11	7	0	2	113²	114	8	50	46	13.1	3.64	101	.266	.346	12	.300	3	0	1	0	0.4
1940	Bos-N	10	14	.417	36	22	8	0	0	177¹	157	6	89	64	12.9	3.55	105	.240	.339	14	.197	-0	6	6	0	0.4
1941	Bos-N	2	2	.500	16	2	0	0	0	52¹	60	3	26	11	15.1	4.13	86	.290	.374	1	.067	-1	-3	-1	-0	-0.3
	Pit-N	4	1	.800	16	4	0	0	1	39¹	40	7	22	10	14.2	2.97	121	.258	.350	4	.364	1	3	4	0	0.5
	Yr	6	3	.667	32	6	0	0	1	91²	100	10	48	21	14.5	3.63	99	.275	.359	5	.192	-0	-0	1	0	0.2
Total	5	30	37	.448	150	55	20	0	5	588	601	25	298	216	14.0	4.01	99	.265	.355	43	.207	1	7	-3	0	0.3

● JOHN SULLIVAN   Sullivan, John Jeremiah "Lefty" b: 5/31/1894, Chicago, Ill. d: 7/7/58, Chicago, Ill. BL/TL, 5'11", 165 lbs. Deb: 7/18/19

| 1919 | Chi-A | 0 | 1 | .000 | 4 | 2 | 1 | 0 | 0 | 15 | 24 | 0 | 8 | 9 | 19.8 | 4.20 | 76 | .364 | .440 | 0 | .000 | -0 | -2 | -2 | -1 | -0.2 |

YEAR TM/L	W	L	PCT	G	GS	CG	SH	SV	IP	H	HR	BB	SO	RAT	ERA	ERA+	OAV	OOB	BH	AVG	PB	PR	/A	PD	TPI
● **MARTY SULLIVAN** Sullivan, Martin C. b: 10/20/1862, Lowell, Mass. d: 1/6/1894, Lowell, Mass. BR/TR, Deb: 4/30/1887 ♦																									
1887 Chi-N	0	0	—	1	0	0	0	0	2¹	6	0	1	1	27.0	7.71	58	.500	.538	134	.284	0	-1	-1	-0	0.0
● **MIKE SULLIVAN** Sullivan, Michael Joseph "Big Mike" b: 10/23/1866, Boston, Mass. d: 6/14/06, Boston, Mass. BL, 6'1", 210 lbs. Deb: 6/17/1889																									
1889 Was-N	0	3	.000	9	3	3	0	0	41	47	2	32	15	18.0	7.24	54	.280	.404	1	.053	-3	-15	-15	-0	-1.0
1890 Chi-N	5	6	.455	12	12	10	0	0	96	108	3	58	33	15.9	4.59	80	.276	.374	3	.125	-3	-11	-10	-0	-1.2
1891 Phi-a	0	2	.000	2	2	2	0	0	18	17	2	10	7	15.0	3.50	109	.239	.357	0	.000	-1	0	1	-0	-0.1
NY-N	1	2	.333	3	3	3	0	0	24	24	0	8	11	12.4	3.38	95	.250	.314	2	.200	-0	-0	-0	-0	-0.1
1892 Cin-N	12	4	.750	21	16	15	0	0	166¹	179	8	74	56	14.2	3.08	106	.264	.344	13	.176	-2	4	3	-2	-0.1
1893 Cin-N	8	11	.421	27	18	14	0	1	183²	200	5	103	40	15.7	5.05	95	.269	.370	16	.203	-3	-8	-5	-0	-0.7
1894 Was-N	2	10	.167	20	12	11	0	1	117²	166	10	74	21	19.0	6.58	80	.329	.422	9	.158	-4	-16	-17	-0	-1.5
Cle-N	6	5	.545	13	11	9	0	0	90²	128	4	47	19	17.7	6.35	86	.329	.405	13	.295	-0	-10	-9	-1	-0.8
Yr	8	15	.348	33	23	20	0	1	208¹	294	14	121	40	18.1	6.48	83	.326	.407	22	.218	-4	-27	-26	-1	-2.3
1895 Cle-N	1	2	.333	4	3	2	0	0	31	42	1	16	5	17.1	8.42	59	.318	.396	2	.133	-2	-13	-12	-1	-0.9
1896 NY-N	10	13	.435	25	22	18	0	0	185¹	188	3	71	42	13.2	4.66	90	.261	.338	16	.208	-3	-6	-9	-0	-1.2
1897 NY-N	8	7	.533	23	16	11	1	2	148²	183	6	71	35	16.2	5.09	82	.300	.386	18	.273	-0	-13	-15	1	-1.1
1898 Bos-N	0	1	.000	3	2	0	0	0	12	19	1	9	1	21.8	12.00	31	.358	.460	1	.333	0	-11	-11	-0	-0.7
1899 Bos-N	1	0	1.000	1	1	1	0	0	9	10	1	4	1	15.0	5.00	83	.278	.366	1	.333	0	-1	-1	-0	-0.1
Total 11	54	66	.450	163	121	99	1	4	1123¹	1311	46	577	286	15.8	5.11	84	.285	.375	97	.196	-21	-100	-102	-5	-9.5
● **PAT SULLIVAN** Sullivan, Patrick J. b: 12/22/1862, Milwaukee, Wis. TR, 5'11", 165 lbs. Deb: 8/30/1884 ♦																									
1884 KC-U	0	1	.000	1	1	0	0	0	7	15	1	5	1	25.7	11.57	19	.405	.476	22	.193	0	-7	-7	-0	-0.6
● **LEFTY SULLIVAN** Sullivan, Paul Thomas b: 9/7/16, Nashville, Tenn. d: 11/1/88, Scottsdale, Ariz. BL/TL, 6'3", 204 lbs. Deb: 5/6/39																									
1939 Cle-A	0	1	.000	7	1	0	0	0	12²	9	0	9	4	13.5	4.26	103	.214	.365	0	.000	-0	1	0	-1	-0.1
● **SUTER SULLIVAN** Sullivan, Suter G. b: 10/14/1872, Baltimore, Md. d: 4/19/25, Baltimore, Md. 6', 170 lbs. Deb: 7/24/1898 ♦																									
1898 StL-N	0	0	—	1	0	0	0	0	6	10	4	3	0	21.0	1.50	253	.370	.452	32	.222	0	1	2	-0	0.0
● **TOM SULLIVAN** Sullivan, Thomas b: 3/1/1860, New York, N.Y. d: 4/12/47, Cincinnati, Ohio Deb: 9/27/1884																									
1884 Col-a	2	2	.500	4	4	4	0	0	31	42	3	12	12	13.1	4.06	75	.318	.333	1	.091	-1	-3	-4	-1	-0.5
1886 Lou-a	2	7	.222	9	9	8	0	0	75	94	6	33	27	15.5	3.96	92	.305	.376	3	.111	-2	-4	-3	0	-0.4
1888 KC-a	8	16	.333	24	24	24	0	0	214²	227	2	68	84	13.4	3.40	101	.262	.332	10	.109	-6	-8	1	5	0.0
1889 KC-a	2	8	.200	10	10	10	0	0	87¹	111	4	38	24	17.1	5.67	74	.300	.391	5	.152	-1	-18	-14	-1	-1.3
Total 4	14	33	.298	47	47	46	0	0	408	474	12	152	147	14.5	4.04	89	.282	.354	19	.117	-9	-33	-20	4	-2.2
● **TOM SULLIVAN** Sullivan, Thomas Augustin b: 10/18/1895, Boston, Mass. d: 9/23/62, Boston, Mass. BL/TL, 5'11", 178 lbs. Deb: 5/15/22																									
1922 Phi-N	0	0	—	3	0	0	0	0	8	16	0	5	2	24.8	11.25	41	.410	.489	1	.250	1	-6	-6	-0	0.1
● **SLEEPER SULLIVAN** Sullivan, Thomas Jefferson "Old Iron Hands" b: St.Louis, Mo. d: 9/25/1899, Camden, N.J. BR/TR, 175 lbs. Deb: 5/3/1881 ♦																									
1884 StL-U	1	0	1.000	1	1	0	0	0	6	10	0	3	3	15.0	4.50	53	.345	.345	1	.111	-1	-1	-1	-0	-0.2
● **BILL SULLIVAN** Sullivan, William F. b: 12/1868, Providence, R.I. d: 10/8/05, Providence, R.I. BR/TR, Deb: 4/19/1890																									
1890 Syr-a	1	4	.200	6	6	6	0	0	42	51	2	27	8	16.5	7.93	58	.291	.404	2	.091	-2	-19	-21	-0	-1.8
● **SCOTT SULLIVAN** Sullivan, William Scott b: 3/13/71, Tuscaloosa, Ala. BR/TR, 6'3", 210 lbs. Deb: 5/6/95																									
1995 Cin-N	0	0	—	3	0	0	0	0	3²	3	0	2	4	14.7	4.91	84	.286	.375	0	.000	-0	-0	-0	-0	0.0
1996 Cin-N	0	0	—	7	0	0	0	0	8	7	0	5	3	14.6	2.25	185	.250	.382	0	.000	-0	2	2	-0	0.0
Total 2	0	0	—	10	0	0	0	0	11²	11	0	7	7	14.7	3.09	134	.262	.380	0	.000	-0	2	2	-0	0.0
● **ED SUMMERS** Summers, Oron Edgar "Kickapoo Ed" or "Chief" b: 12/5/1884, Ladoga, Ind. d: 5/12/53, Indianapolis, Ind. BB/TR, 6'2", 180 lbs. Deb: 4/16/08																									
1908 *Det-A	24	12	.667	40	32	23	5	1	301	271	3	55	103	10.3	1.64	147	.242	.290	14	.124	-6	25	26	-1	2.4
1909 *Det-A	19	9	.679	35	32	24	3	1	281²	243	4	52	107	9.7	2.24	113	.227	.269	4	.106	-4	8	9	1	0.5
1910 Det-A	13	12	.520	30	25	18	1	0	220¹	211	8	60	82	11.3	2.53	104	.254	.308	14	.184	-0	-2	1	0	0.3
1911 Det-A	11	11	.500	30	20	13	0	0	179¹	189	3	51	65	12.6	3.66	95	.274	.334	16	.254	1	-6	-4	-1	-0.5
1912 Det-A	1	1	.500	3	3	1	0	0	16²	16	1	3	5	10.3	4.86	67	.250	.284	3	.500	1	-3	-3	-0	-0.2
Total 5	68	45	.602	138	112	79	9	3	999	930	19	221	362	10.8	2.42	111	.246	.296	57	.162	-9	23	30	-0	2.5
● **BILLY SUNDAY** Sunday, William Ashley "Parson" or "The Evangelist" b: 11/19/1862, Ames, Iowa d: 11/6/35, Chicago, Ill. BL/TR, 5'10", 160 lbs. Deb: 5/22/1883 ♦																									
1890 Pit-N	0	0	—	1	0	0	0	0	2	6	0	3	0	—	∞		1.000	1.000	92	.257	0	-2	-2	-0	-0.2
● **GORDIE SUNDIN** Sundin, Gordon Vincent b: 10/10/37, Minneapolis, Minn. BR/TR, 6'4", 215 lbs. Deb: 9/19/56																									
1956 Bal-A	0	0	—	1	0	0	0	0	0	0	0	2	0	—	∞	—	—	1.000	0		0	-1	-1	0	-0.1
● **STEVE SUNDRA** Sundra, Stephen Richard "Smokey" b: 3/27/10, Luxor, Pa. d: 3/23/52, Cleveland, Ohio BR/TR, 6'2", 190 lbs. Deb: 4/17/36																									
1936 NY-A	0	0	—	1	0	0	0	0	2	2	0	2	1	18.0	0.00		.286	.444	0	.000	-0	1	1	-0	0.0
1938 NY-A	6	4	.600	25	8	3	0	0	93²	107	7	43	33	14.4	4.80	94	.291	.365	6	.182	1	-0	-3	-1	-0.1
1939 *NY-A	11	1	.917	24	11	8	1	0	120¹	110	7	56	27	12.4	2.76	158	.240	.323	13	.265	4	25	21	1	2.2
1940 NY-A	4	6	.400	27	8	2	0	2	99¹	121	11	42	26	14.9	5.53	73	.299	.366	4	.138	-1	-13	-16	0	-1.5
1941 Was-A	9	13	.409	28	23	11	0	0	168¹	203	11	61	50	14.2	5.29	76	.294	.352	13	.217	2	-21	-23	-1	-2.4
1942 Was-A	1	3	.250	6	4	2	0	0	33²	43	1	15	5	15.8	5.61	65	.305	.376	2	.167	-0	-7	-7	-0	-0.8
StL-A	8	3	.727	20	13	6	1	0	110²	122	8	29	26	12.3	3.82	97	.275	.319	9	.225	3	-2	-1	-0	0.1
Yr	9	6	.600	26	17	8	1	0	144¹	165	9	44	31	13.0	4.24	87	.282	.332	11	.212	2	-9	-9	-0	-0.7
1943 StL-A	15	11	.577	32	29	13	3	0	208	212	10	66	44	12.0	3.25	103	.266	.322	16	.219	1	1	2	-0	0.4
1944 StL-A	2	0	1.000	3	3	2	0	0	19	15	1	4	1	9.0	1.42	253	.211	.253	0	.000	0	4	5	-0	0.5
1946 StL-A	0	0	—	2	0	0	0	0	4	9	3	0	3	27.0	11.25	34	.409	.480	0		-0	-3	-3	0	0.0
Total 9	56	41	.577	168	99	47	4	2	859¹	944	50	321	214	13.3	4.17	94	.277	.340	63	.209	10	-16	-24	1	-1.6
● **TOM SUNKEL** Sunkel, Thomas Jacob "Lefty" b: 8/9/12, Paris, Ill. BL/TL, 6'1", 190 lbs. Deb: 8/26/37																									
1937 StL-N	0	0	—	9	1	0	0	0	29¹	24	0	11	9	10.7	2.76	144	.214	.285	1	.111	-1	4	4	-0	-0.1
1939 StL-N	4	4	.500	20	11	2	1	0	85¹	79	4	56	54	14.3	4.22	98	.242	.354	9	.321	2	-3	-1	-1	0.0
1941 NY-N	1	1	.500	2	2	1	0	0	15¹	7	0	12	14	11.7	2.93	126	.140	.317	2	.333	1	1	1	-0	0.2
1942 NY-N	3	6	.333	19	11	3	0	0	63²	65	5	41	29	15.0	4.81	70	.269	.375	2	.105	-1	-11	-10	-2	-1.6
1943 NY-N	0	1	.000	1	1	0	0	0	2²	4	1	3	2	23.6	10.13	34	.308	.438	0	—	-0	-2	-2	-0	-0.5
1944 Bro-N	1	3	.250	12	3	0	0	2	24	39	1	10	6	18.4	7.50	47	.368	.422	0	.000	-1	-10	-11	-1	-1.7
Total 6	9	15	.375	63	29	6	2	2	220¹	218	11	133	112	14.4	4.53	83	.256	.358	14	.212	0	-21	-19	-4	-3.7
● **JEFF SUPPAN** Suppan, Jeffrey Scot b: 1/2/75, Oklahoma City, Okla. BR/TR, 6'1", 200 lbs. Deb: 7/17/95																									
1995 Bos-A	1	2	.333	8	3	0	0	0	22²	29	4	5	19	13.5	5.96	82	.312	.347	0		-0	-3	-3	-0	-0.3
1996 Bos-A	1	1	.500	8	4	0	0	0	22²	29	3	13	13	17.1	7.54	68	.330	.422	0		-0	-6	-6	-0	-0.5
Total 2	2	3	.400	16	7	0	0	0	45¹	58	7	18	32	15.3	6.75	74	.320	.385	0		-1	-10	-9	-1	-0.8
● **RICK SURHOFF** Surhoff, Richard Clifford b: 10/3/62, Bronx, N.Y. BR/TR, 6'3", 210 lbs. Deb: 9/8/85 F																									
1985 Phi-N	1	0	1.000	2	0	0	0	0	1	0	0	1	0	18.0	0.00	—	.500	.500	0		0	0	0	-0	0.4
Tex-A	0	1	.000	7	0	0	0	2	8¹	12	2	3	6	16.4	7.56	56	.343	.395	0		-0	-3	-4	-0	-0.5
Total 1	1	1	.500	9	0	0	0	2	9¹	12	2	4	6	16.4	6.75	62	.359	.405	0		-0	-3	-3	-0	-0.1
● **MAX SURKONT** Surkont, Matthew Constantine b: 6/16/22, Central Falls, R.I. d: 10/8/86, Largo, Fla. BR/TR, 6', 205 lbs. Deb: 4/19/49																									
1949 Chi-A	3	5	.375	44	6	0	0	4	96	92	9	60	38	14.5	4.78	87	.255	.366	1	.045	-1	-6	-7	-1	-0.8
1950 Bos-N	5	2	.714	9	6	2	0	0	55²	63	5	20	21	13.7	3.23	119	.285	.350	10	.435	5	6	4	-1	0.9
1951 Bos-N	12	16	.429	37	33	11	2	1	237	230	21	89	110	12.4	3.99	92	.252	.323	11	.151	0	-1	-8	-3	-1.1
1952 Bos-N	12	13	.480	37	31	12	1	0	215	201	19	76	84	11.7	3.77	96	.245	.311	7	.111	-1	-1	-4	-1	-0.6

YEAR	TM/L	W	L	PCT	G	GS	CG	SH	SV	IP	H	HR	BB	SO	RAT	ERA	ERA+	OAV	OOB	BH	AVG	PB	PR	/A	PD	TPI
1953	Mil-N	11	5	.688	28	24	11	2	0	170	168	22	64	83	12.3	4.18	94	.255	.321	16	.286	7	2	-5	1	0.3
1954	Pit-N	9	18	.333	33	29	11	0	0	208¹	216	25	78	78	12.9	4.41	95	.268	.335	10	.167	0	-8	-5	0	-0.5
1955	Pit-N	7	14	.333	35	22	5	0	2	166¹	194	23	78	84	14.9	5.57	74	.298	.376	7	.140	-0	-28	-27	-2	-3.2
1956	Pit-N	0	0	—	1	0	0	0	0	2	2	0	3	1	22.5	4.50	84	.333	.556	0	—	-0	-0	-0	-0	0.0
	StL-N	0	0	—	5	0	0	0	0	5²	10	3	2	5	19.1	9.53	40	.417	.462	0	.000	-0	-4	-4	0	0.0
	NY-N	2	2	.500	8	4	1	0	1	32	24	5	9	18	9.3	4.78	79	.202	.258	1	.111	-0	-4	-4	-0	-0.5
	Yr	2	2	.500	14	4	1	0	1	39²	36	8	14	24	11.3	5.45	69	.240	.305	1	.100	-0	-7	-7	-1	-0.5
1957	NY-N	0	1	.000	5	0	0	0	0	6¹	9	2	2	8	15.6	9.95	40	.321	.367	0	.	-0	-4	-4	-0	0.0
Total 9		61	76	.445	236	149	53	7	8	1194¹	1209	134	481	571	12.9	4.38	89	.262	.335	63	.176	8	-48	-63	-5	-6.1

● **GEORGE SUSCE**   Susce, George Daniel   b: 9/13/31, Pittsburgh, Pa.   BR/TR, 6'1", 180 lbs.   Deb: 4/15/55   F

YEAR	TM/L	W	L	PCT	G	GS	CG	SH	SV	IP	H	HR	BB	SO	RAT	ERA	ERA+	OAV	OOB	BH	AVG	PB	PR	/A	PD	TPI
1955	Bos-A	9	7	.563	29	15	6	1	4	144¹	123	12	49	60	11.2	3.06	140	.232	.306	7	.143	-2	15	20	-0	1.8
1956	Bos-A	2	4	.333	21	6	0	0	0	69²	71	14	44	26	15.4	6.20	74	.262	.373	4	.222	1	-16	-12	-0	-0.8
1957	Bos-A	7	3	.700	29	5	0	0	1	88¹	93	6	41	40	14.0	4.28	93	.274	.358	3	.120	-1	-5	-3	-1	-0.5
1958	Bos-A	0	0	—	2	0	0	0	0	2	6	1	1	0	31.5	18.00	22	.600	.636	0	—	-0	-3	-3	-0	0.0
	Det-A	4	3	.571	27	10	2	0	1	90²	90	7	26	42	11.8	3.67	110	.259	.316	3	.125	-1	1	4	-2	0.0
	Yr	4	3	.571	29	10	2	0	1	92²	96	8	27	42	12.2	3.98	101	.268	.325	3	.125	-1	-2	1	-2	0.0
1959	Det-A	0	0	—	9	0	0	0	0	14²	24	4	9	21	21.5	12.89	32	.358	.449	0	.000	-0	-15	-14	-0	0.0
Total 5		22	17	.564	117	36	8	1	3	409²	407	44	170	177	13.1	4.42	95	.260	.340	17	.145	-2	-23	-9	-4	0.5

● **RICK SUTCLIFFE**   Sutcliffe, Richard Lee   b: 6/21/56, Independence, Mo.   BL/TR, 6'7", 215 lbs.   Deb: 9/29/76

YEAR	TM/L	W	L	PCT	G	GS	CG	SH	SV	IP	H	HR	BB	SO	RAT	ERA	ERA+	OAV	OOB	BH	AVG	PB	PR	/A	PD	TPI
1976	LA-N	0	0	—	1	1	0	0	0	5	2	0	1	3	5.4	0.00	—	.125	.176	0	.000	-0	2	2	-0	0.0
1978	LA-N	0	0	—	2	0	0	0	0	1²	2	0	1	2	21.6	0.00	—	.286	.444	0	.000	-0	1	1	-0	0.0
1979	LA-N	17	10	.630	39	30	5	1	0	242	217	16	97	117	11.8	3.46	105	.243	.319	21	.247	5	7	5	-2	0.8
1980	LA-N	3	9	.250	42	10	1	1	5	110	122	10	55	59	14.6	5.56	63	.285	.368	4	.148	-0	-24	-25	-1	-2.9
1981	LA-N	2	2	.500	14	6	0	0	0	47	41	5	20	16	12.1	4.02	83	.238	.325	2	.182	1	-3	-4	0	-0.2
1982	Cle-A	14	8	.636	34	27	6	1	1	216	174	16	98	142	11.5	**2.96**	138	**.226**	.317	0	—	0	**27**	27	1	2.7
1983	Cle-A☆	17	11	.607	36	35	10	2	0	243¹	251	23	102	160	13.3	4.29	99	.268	.344	0	—	0	-6	-1	2	-0.2
1984	Cle-A	4	5	.444	15	15	2	0	0	94¹	111	7	46	58	15.2	5.15	79	.298	.378	0	—	0	-12	-11	-0	-1.0
	*Chi-N	16	1	**.941**	20	20	7	3	0	150¹	123	9	39	155	9.8	2.69	145	.220	.272	14	.250	3	15	20	2	2.8
1985	Chi-N	8	8	.500	20	20	6	3	0	130	119	12	44	102	11.5	3.18	125	.240	.306	10	.233	2	6	12	1	1.8
1986	Chi-N	5	14	.263	28	27	4	1	0	176²	166	19	96	122	13.4	4.64	87	.252	.348	11	.208	2	-18	-12	1	-0.8
1987	Chi-N★	**18**	10	.643	34	34	6	1	0	237¹	223	24	106	174	12.6	3.68	116	.252	.335	12	.148	2	11	16	4	2.4
1988	Chi-N	13	14	.481	32	32	12	2	0	226	232	16	70	144	12.1	3.86	93	.269	.325	12	.160	1	-10	-6	1	-0.3
1989	*Chi-N★	16	11	.593	35	34	5	1	0	229	202	18	69	153	10.7	3.66	103	.240	.299	10	.143	1	-4	3	1	0.6
1990	Chi-N	0	2	.000	5	5	0	0	0	21¹	25	1	12	7	15.6	5.91	69	.305	.394	0	.000	0	-5	-4	-0	-0.3
1991	Chi-N	6	5	.545	19	18	0	0	0	96²	96	4	45	52	13.2	4.10	95	.264	.345	3	.094	-1	-4	-2	0	-0.3
1992	Bal-A	16	15	.516	36	36	5	2	0	237¹	251	20	74	109	12.6	4.47	90	.273	.332	0	—	0	-14	-12	-2	-1.8
1993	Bal-A	10	10	.500	29	28	3	0	0	166	212	23	74	80	15.8	5.75	78	.314	.386	0	—	0	-26	-24	1	-2.5
1994	StL-N	6	4	.600	16	14	0	0	0	67²	93	11	32	26	16.9	6.52	64	.331	.403	3	.130	-1	-17	-18	1	-2.1
Total 18		171	139	.552	457	392	72	18	6	2697²	2662	236	1081	1679	12.6	4.08	97	.260	.334	102	.181	17	-77	-34	10	-1.4

● **HARRY SUTER**   Suter, Harry Richard "Handsome Harry" or "Rube"   b: 9/15/1887, Independence, Mo.   d: 7/24/71, Topeka, Kan.   BL/TL, 5'10", 190 lbs.   Deb: 4/16/09

YEAR	TM/L	W	L	PCT	G	GS	CG	SH	SV	IP	H	HR	BB	SO	RAT	ERA	ERA+	OAV	OOB	BH	AVG	PB	PR	/A	PD	TPI
1909	Chi-A	2	3	.400	18	7	3	1	1	87¹	72	2	28	53	10.7	2.47	95	.199	.264	3	.094	-1	0	-1	-1	-0.3

● **DARRELL SUTHERLAND**   Sutherland, Darrell Wayne   b: 11/14/41, Glendale, Cal.   BR/TR, 6'4", 169 lbs.   Deb: 6/28/64   F

YEAR	TM/L	W	L	PCT	G	GS	CG	SH	SV	IP	H	HR	BB	SO	RAT	ERA	ERA+	OAV	OOB	BH	AVG	PB	PR	/A	PD	TPI
1964	NY-N	0	3	.000	10	4	0	0	0	26²	32	1	12	9	15.5	7.76	46	.302	.383	1	.200	0	-13	-12	1	-1.1
1965	NY-N	3	1	.750	18	2	0	0	0	48	33	1	17	16	10.1	2.81	125	.199	.289	2	.154	0	4	4	2	0.5
1966	NY-N	2	0	1.000	31	0	0	0	1	44¹	60	6	25	23	17.7	4.87	75	.339	.426	2	.667	1	-6	-6	1	-0.1
1968	Cle-A	0	0	—	3	0	0	0	0	3¹	6	0	4	2	27.0	8.10	37	.375	.500	0	—	-0	-2	-2	-0	0.0
Total 4		5	4	.556	62	6	0	0	1	122¹	131	8	58	50	14.5	4.78	75	.282	.371	5	.238	1	-17	-17	3	-0.7

● **SUDS SUTHERLAND**   Sutherland, Harvey Scott   b: 2/20/1894, Beaverton, Ore.   d: 5/11/72, Portland, Ore.   BR/TR, 6', 180 lbs.   Deb: 4/14/21

YEAR	TM/L	W	L	PCT	G	GS	CG	SH	SV	IP	H	HR	BB	SO	RAT	ERA	ERA+	OAV	OOB	BH	AVG	PB	PR	/A	PD	TPI
1921	Det-A	6	2	.750	13	8	3	0	0	58	80	1	18	18	15.2	4.97	86	.328	.374	11	.407	2	-4	-4	2	-0.1

● **DIZZY SUTHERLAND**   Sutherland, Howard Alvin   b: 4/9/22, Washington, D.C.   d: 8/26/79, Washington, D.C.   BL/TL, 6', 200 lbs.   Deb: 9/20/49

YEAR	TM/L	W	L	PCT	G	GS	CG	SH	SV	IP	H	HR	BB	SO	RAT	ERA	ERA+	OAV	OOB	BH	AVG	PB	PR	/A	PD	TPI
1949	Was-A	0	1	.000	1	1	0	0	0	1	2	0	6	0	72.0	45.00	9	.400	.727	0	—	-0	-5	-5	0	-1.7

● **BRUCE SUTTER**   Sutter, Howard Bruce   b: 1/8/53, Lancaster, Pa.   BR/TR, 6'2", 190 lbs.   Deb: 5/9/76

YEAR	TM/L	W	L	PCT	G	GS	CG	SH	SV	IP	H	HR	BB	SO	RAT	ERA	ERA+	OAV	OOB	BH	AVG	PB	PR	/A	PD	TPI
1976	Chi-N	6	3	.667	52	0	0	0	10	83¹	63	4	26	73	9.6	2.70	143	.209	.272	0	.000	-1	7	11	-0	1.3
1977	Chi-N†	7	3	.700	62	0	0	0	31	107¹	69	5	23	129	7.8	1.34	327	.183	.232	3	.150	-0	31	**36**	1	5.6
1978	Chi-N★	8	10	.444	64	0	0	0	27	99	82	10	34	106	10.6	3.18	127	.220	.287	1	.077	-0	1	-0	1	2.2
1979	Chi-N★	6	6	.500	62	0	0	0	37	101¹	67	3	32	110	8.8	2.22	185	.186	.252	3	.250	0	17	21	1	**4.3**
1980	Chi-N★	5	8	.385	60	0	0	0	28	102¹	90	5	34	76	11.0	2.64	148	.242	.307	1	.111	-1	11	14	-0	2.6
1981	StL-N★	3	5	.375	48	0	0	0	25	82¹	64	5	24	57	9.7	2.62	136	.218	.279	0	.000	-1	8	9	-1	1.2
1982	*StL-N	9	8	.529	70	0	0	0	36	102¹	88	8	34	61	11.0	2.90	125	.235	.303	1	.125	0	8	8	0	1.9
1983	StL-N	9	10	.474	60	0	0	0	21	89¹	90	8	30	64	12.2	4.23	86	.262	.324	0	.000	-1	-6	-6	2	-1.4
1984	StL-N☆	5	7	.417	71	0	0	0	**45**	122²	109	9	23	77	9.8	1.54	225	.245	.284	0	.000	-1	**28**	26	1	**4.4**
1985	Atl-N	7	7	.500	58	0	0	0	23	88¹	91	13	29	52	12.5	4.48	86	.267	.330	0	.000	-1	-9	-6	-0	-1.3
1986	Atl-N	2	0	1.000	16	0	0	0	3	18²	17	3	9	16	12.5	4.34	92	.243	.329	0	.000	-1	-1	-0	1	-0.1
1988	Atl-N	1	4	.200	38	0	0	0	14	45¹	49	4	11	40	12.1	4.76	77	.275	.321	0	.000	-1	-7	-5	-0	-0.9
Total 12		68	71	.489	661	0	0	0	300	1042¹	879	77	309	861	10.4	2.83	135	.230	.289	9	.088	-5	91	116	4	19.8

● **JACK SUTTHOFF**   Sutthoff, John Gerhard "Sunny Jack"   b: 6/29/1873, Cincinnati, Ohio   d: 8/3/42, Cincinnati, Ohio   BL/TR, 5'9", 175 lbs.   Deb: 9/15/1898

YEAR	TM/L	W	L	PCT	G	GS	CG	SH	SV	IP	H	HR	BB	SO	RAT	ERA	ERA+	OAV	OOB	BH	AVG	PB	PR	/A	PD	TPI
1898	Was-N	0	0	—	2	1	0	0	0	8¹	16	1	8	3	25.9	12.96	38	.400	.500	1	.333	-1	-9	-9	-0	0.0
1899	StL-N	1	2	.333	3	3	1	0	0	24	29	1	15	8	16.5	4.13	97	.299	.393	1	.100	-1	-1	-0	0	-0.1
1901	Cin-N	1	6	.143	10	4	0	0	0	70¹	82	2	39	12	15.7	5.50	58	.289	.378	3	.107	-2	-17	-18	-1	-1.7
1903	Cin-N	16	9	.640	30	27	21	3	0	224²	207	2	79	76	12.1	2.80	127	.246	.323	12	.143	-3	12	19	-1	1.4
1904	Cin-N	5	6	.455	12	10	8	0	0	90	83	1	43	27	12.9	2.30	127	.255	.348	6	.182	-0	4	6	-2	0.5
	Phi-N	6	13	.316	19	18	17	0	0	163²	172	2	71	46	13.9	3.68	73	.272	.354	10	.164	-0	-17	-18	-1	-2.1
	Yr	11	19	.367	31	28	25	0	0	253²	255	3	114	73	13.4	3.19	87	.266	.349	16	.170	-1	-13	-12	-3	-1.6
1905	Phi-N	3	4	.429	13	6	4	1	0	77²	82	2	36	26	14.1	3.82	76	.290	.378	2	.080	-1	-7	-8	0	-0.7
Total 6		32	40	.444	89	69	57	4	0	658²	671	11	291	198	13.6	3.54	89	.268	.352	35	.143	-7	-35	-28	-5	-2.7

● **DON SUTTON**   Sutton, Donald Howard   b: 4/2/45, Clio, Ala.   BR/TR, 6'1", 185 lbs.   Deb: 4/14/66

YEAR	TM/L	W	L	PCT	G	GS	CG	SH	SV	IP	H	HR	BB	SO	RAT	ERA	ERA+	OAV	OOB	BH	AVG	PB	PR	/A	PD	TPI
1966	LA-N	12	12	.500	37	35	6	2	0	225²	192	19	52	209	9.9	2.99	110	.228	.276	15	.183	1	15	8	-0	0.9
1967	LA-N	11	15	.423	37	34	11	3	1	232²	223	18	57	169	11.1	3.95	79	.250	.300	10	.133	-0	-15	-22	-2	-2.5
1968	LA-N	11	15	.423	35	27	7	2	1	207²	179	6	59	162	10.4	2.60	106	.232	.288	11	.177	1	9	4	-1	0.5
1969	LA-N	17	18	.486	41	41	11	4	0	293¹	269	25	91	217	11.1	3.47	96	.242	.301	15	.153	-1	4	-5	0	-0.6
1970	LA-N	15	13	.536	38	38	11	4	0	260¹	251	38	78	201	11.7	4.08	94	.249	.310	13	.155	3	-1	-7	-1	-0.5
1971	LA-N	17	12	.586	38	37	12	4	1	265¹	231	10	55	194	9.9	2.54	127	.238	.282	19	.216	3	27	20	-1	2.5
1972	LA-N★	19	9	.679	33	33	18	**9**	0	272²	186	13	63	207	**8.4**	2.08	160	**.189**	**.240**	13	.143	-1	42	38	-0	3.9
1973	LA-N	18	10	.643	33	33	14	3	0	256¹	196	18	56	200	9.0	2.42	142	.209	.258	10	.119	-2	35	29	-1	2.9
1974	*LA-N	19	9	.679	40	40	10	5	0	276	241	23	80	179	10.7	3.23	105	.229	.288	18	.184	5	12	5	-1	0.4
1975	LA-N	16	13	.552	35	35	11	4	1	254¹	202	17	62	175	9.4	2.87	119	.213	**.264**	11	.138	-1	21	15	-1	1.4
1976	LA-N	21	10	.677	35	34	15	3	0	267²	231	22	82	161	10.6	3.06	111	.234	.295	7	.083	-3	13	10	-3	0.5
1977	*LA-N★	14	8	.636	33	33	9	3	0	240¹	207	23	69	150	10.4	3.18	120	.233	.291	11	.151	-1	19	17	-1	1.4
1978	*LA-N	15	11	.577	34	34	12	2	0	238¹	228	29	69	154	10.9	3.55	99	.236	.295	6	.083	-3	1	-1	-2	-0.7
1979	LA-N	12	15	.444	33	32	6	1	0	226	201	24	61	146	10.5	3.82	95	.239	.291	11	.143	-0	1	-1	-2	-0.8
1980	LA-N	13	5	.722	32	31	4	2	1	212¹	163	20	47	128	9.0	**2.20**	159	.211	**.258**	5	.078	-4	33	30	-0	2.1

YEAR	TM/L	W	L	PCT	G	GS	CG	SH	SV	IP	H	HR	BB	SO	RAT	ERA	ERA+	OAV	OOB	BH	AVG	PB	PR	/A	PD	TPI
1981	Hou-N	11	9	.550	23	23	6	3	0	158²	132	6	29	104	**9.2**	2.61	126	.230	**.268**	7	.137	0	16	12	0	1.6
1982	Hou-N	13	8	.619	27	27	4	0	0	195	169	10	46	139	10.0	3.00	111	.232	.279	11	.162	-0	13	7	-1	0.6
	*Mil-A	4	1	.800	7	7	1	0	0	54²	55	8	18	36	12.0	3.29	115	.263	.322	0	—	0	5	3	1	0.7
1983	Mil-A	8	13	.381	31	31	4	0	0	220¹	209	21	54	134	10.9	4.08	97	.246	.295	0	—	0	-1	-9	-1	-0.5
1984	Mil-A	14	12	.538	33	33	1	0	0	212²	224	24	51	143	11.8	3.77	102	.266	.310	0	—	0	5	2	-2	0.2
1985	Oak-A	13	8	.619	29	29	1	1	0	194¹	194	19	51	91	11.3	3.89	99	.256	.302	0	—	0	6	-1	0	0.3
	Cal-A	2	2	.500	5	5	0	0	0	31²	27	6	8	16	9.9	3.69	111	.233	.282	0	—	0	2	1	-1	0.1
	Yr	15	10	.600	34	34	1	1	0	226	221	25	59	107	11.2	3.86	101	.251	.298	0	—	0	7	1	-1	0.4
1986	*Cal-A	15	11	.577	34	34	3	1	0	207	192	31	49	116	10.6	3.74	110	.242	.288	0	—	0	10	9	-3	0.8
1987	Cal-A	11	11	.500	35	34	1	0	0	191²	199	38	41	99	11.6	4.70	92	.269	.313	0	—	0	-8	-3	-0.9	
1988	LA-N	3	6	.333	16	16	0	0	0	87¹	91	7	30	44	12.6	3.92	85	.270	.332	2	.087	-1	-5	-6	-1	0.0
Total	23	324	256	.559	774	756	178	58	5	5282¹	4692	472	1343	3574	10.4	3.26	108	.236	.287	195	.144	-7	259	146	-26	13.6

● **EZRA SUTTON** Sutton, Ezra Ballou b: 9/17/1850, Palmyra, N.Y. d: 6/20/07, Braintree, Mass. BR/TR, 5'8.5", 153 lbs. Deb: 5/4/1871 ♦

YEAR	TM/L	W	L	PCT	G	GS	CG	SH	SV	IP	H	HR	BB	SO	RAT	ERA	ERA+	OAV	OOB	BH	AVG	PB	PR	/A	PD	TPI
1875	Ath-n	0	0	—	2	0	0	0	0	6	14	0	0	0	21.0	10.50	23	.412	.412	116	.324	1	-6	-5		0.0

● **JOHN SUTTON** Sutton, Johnny Ike b: 11/13/52, Dallas, Tex. BR/TR, 5'11", 185 lbs. Deb: 4/7/77

YEAR	TM/L	W	L	PCT	G	GS	CG	SH	SV	IP	H	HR	BB	SO	RAT	ERA	ERA+	OAV	OOB	BH	AVG	PB	PR	/A	PD	TPI
1977	StL-N	2	1	.667	14	0	0	0	0	24¹	28	1	9	9	13.7	2.59	149	.315	.378	0	.000	-0	4	3	0	0.4
1978	Min-A	0	0	—	17	0	0	0	0	44¹	46	3	15	18	12.6	3.45	111	.264	.326	0	—	0	2	2	-0	-0.2
Total	2	2	1	.667	31	0	0	0	0	68²	74	4	24	27	13.0	3.15	122	.281	.344	0	.000	-0	5	5	0	0.2

● **MAC SUZUKI** Suzuki, Makoto b: 5/31/75, Kobe, Japan BR/TR, 6'3", 195 lbs. Deb: 7/7/96

YEAR	TM/L	W	L	PCT	G	GS	CG	SH	SV	IP	H	HR	BB	SO	RAT	ERA	ERA+	OAV	OOB	BH	AVG	PB	PR	/A	PD	TPI
1996	Sea-A	0	0	—	1	0	0	0	0	1¹	2	0	2	1	27.0	20.25	24	.333	.500	0	—	0	-2	-2	0	0.0

● **BILL SWABACH** Swabach, William Deb: 7/9/1887

YEAR	TM/L	W	L	PCT	G	GS	CG	SH	SV	IP	H	HR	BB	SO	RAT	ERA	ERA+	OAV	OOB	BH	AVG	PB	PR	/A	PD	TPI
1887	NY-N	0	2	.000	2	2	2	0	0	16	27	1	6	6	19.1	5.06	74	.346	.400	0	.000	-1	-2	-2	0	-0.3

● **BILL SWAGGERTY** Swaggerty, William David b: 12/5/56, Sanford, Fla. BR/TR, 6'2", 186 lbs. Deb: 8/13/83

YEAR	TM/L	W	L	PCT	G	GS	CG	SH	SV	IP	H	HR	BB	SO	RAT	ERA	ERA+	OAV	OOB	BH	AVG	PB	PR	/A	PD	TPI
1983	Bal-A	1	1	.500	7	2	0	0	0	21²	23	1	6	7	12.0	2.91	136	.267	.315	0	—	0	3	3	1	0.4
1984	Bal-A	3	2	.600	23	6	0	0	0	57	68	7	21	18	14.1	5.21	74	.302	.362	0	—	0	-8	-8	-1	-0.7
1985	Bal-A	0	0	—	1	0	0	0	0	1²	3	0	2	2	27.0	5.40	75	.375	.500	0	—	0	-0	-0	0	0.1
1986	Bal-A	0	0	—	1	0	0	0	0	1	6	0	1	1	63.0	18.00	23	.750	.778	0	—	0	-2	-2	0	0.1
Total	4	4	3	.571	32	8	0	0	0	81¹	100	8	30	28	14.4	4.76	82	.306	.364	0	—	0	-7	-8	0	-0.1

● **CY SWAIM** Swaim, John Hillary b: 3/11/1874, Cadwallader, Ohio d: 12/27/45, Eustis, Fla. 6'6", 180 lbs. Deb: 5/3/1897

YEAR	TM/L	W	L	PCT	G	GS	CG	SH	SV	IP	H	HR	BB	SO	RAT	ERA	ERA+	OAV	OOB	BH	AVG	PB	PR	/A	PD	TPI
1897	Was-N	9	11	.450	26	19	14	0	0	184	219	6	59	52	14.1	4.60	94	.293	.353	16	.225	-3	-6	-5	-4	-1.0
1898	Was-N	3	11	.214	16	13	9	0	1	101¹	119	4	28	30	13.4	4.26	86	.290	.342	5	.143	-3	-7	-7	-1	-1.1
Total	2	12	22	.353	42	32	23	0	1	285¹	338	9	87	82	13.8	4.48	92	.292	.349	21	.198	-6	-13	-12	-5	-2.1

● **CRAIG SWAN** Swan, Craig Steven b: 11/30/50, Van Nuys, Cal. BR/TR, 6'3", 215 lbs. Deb: 9/3/73

YEAR	TM/L	W	L	PCT	G	GS	CG	SH	SV	IP	H	HR	BB	SO	RAT	ERA	ERA+	OAV	OOB	BH	AVG	PB	PR	/A	PD	TPI
1973	NY-N	0	1	.000	3	1	0	0	0	8¹	16	2	2	4	19.4	8.64	42	.432	.462	0	.000	—	-5	-5	0	-0.5
1974	NY-N	1	3	.250	7	5	0	0	0	30¹	28	1	21	10	14.5	4.45	80	.255	.374	4	.364	1	-3	-3	0	-0.2
1975	NY-N	1	3	.250	6	6	0	0	0	31	38	4	13	19	15.1	6.39	54	.302	.371	0	.000	-1	-10	-10	-1	-1.2
1976	NY-N	6	9	.400	23	22	2	1	0	132¹	129	11	44	89	12.1	3.54	93	.254	.320	4	.103	-1	-1	-4	-1	-0.5
1977	NY-N	9	10	.474	26	24	2	1	0	146²	153	10	56	71	12.9	4.23	88	.268	.334	9	.188	-0	-5	-8	-2	-1.2
1978	NY-N	9	6	.600	29	28	5	1	0	207¹	164	12	58	125	**9.7**	2.43	143	.219	.277	10	.154	-0	26	24	1	1.8
1979	NY-N	14	13	.519	35	35	10	3	0	251¹	241	20	57	145	10.2	3.29	110	.255	.299	10	.123	-1	12	10	-1	0.8
1980	NY-N	5	9	.357	21	21	4	1	0	128¹	117	20	30	79	10.3	3.58	99	.247	.292	7	.219	2	-0	-2	0	-0.1
1981	NY-N	1	1	.500	5	3	0	0	0	13²	10	0	1	9	7.2	3.29	106	.204	.220	0	.000	-0	1	1	0	0.0
1982	NY-N	11	7	.611	37	21	2	0	1	166¹	165	13	37	67	10.9	3.35	108	.256	.297	8	.182	3	5	5	-1	0.7
1983	NY-N	2	8	.200	27	18	0	0	1	96¹	112	14	42	43	14.4	5.51	66	.299	.369	1	.077	-2	-20	-20	-1	-2.2
1984	NY-N	1	0	1.000	10	0	0	0	0	18²	18	5	7	10	12.1	8.20	43	.247	.313	0	—	-0	-10	-10	-0	-0.5
	Cal-A	0	1	.000	2	1	0	0	0	5	8	3	2	4	14.4	10.80	37	.348	.348	0	—	0	-4	-4	0	-0.6
Total	12	59	72	.450	231	185	25	7	2	1235²	1199	115	368	673	11.5	3.74	95	.256	.312	54	.151	1	-13	-24	-10	-3.7

● **DUCKY SWAN** Swan, Harry Gordon b: 8/11/1887, Lancaster, Pa. d: 5/8/46, Pittsburgh, Pa. BR/TR, 5'10", 165 lbs. Deb: 4/28/14

YEAR	TM/L	W	L	PCT	G	GS	CG	SH	SV	IP	H	HR	BB	SO	RAT	ERA	ERA+	OAV	OOB	BH	AVG	PB	PR	/A	PD	TPI
1914	KC-F	0	0	—	1	0	0	0	0	1	0	0	1	1	9.0	0.00	—	.000	.250	0	—	0	0	0	0	0.0

● **RUSS SWAN** Swan, Russell Howard b: 1/3/64, Fremont, Cal. BL/TL, 6'4", 210 lbs. Deb: 8/3/89

YEAR	TM/L	W	L	PCT	G	GS	CG	SH	SV	IP	H	HR	BB	SO	RAT	ERA	ERA+	OAV	OOB	BH	AVG	PB	PR	/A	PD	TPI
1989	SF-N	0	2	.000	2	2	0	0	0	6²	11	4	2	4	20.3	10.80	31	.393	.469	0	.000	-0	-5	-6	0	-1.2
1990	SF-N	0	2	1.000	2	1	0	0	0	2¹	5	0	2	1	38.6	3.86	94	.429	.556	0	.000	-0	1	2	0	0.1
	Sea-A	2	3	.400	11	8	0	0	0	47	42	3	18	15	11.5	3.64	109	.244	.316	0	—	0	1	2	0	0.1
1991	Sea-A	6	2	.750	63	0	0	0	0	78²	81	8	28	33	12.5	3.43	120	.269	.331	0	—	0	6	6	1	0.6
1992	Sea-A	3	10	.231	55	9	1	0	9	104¹	104	8	45	45	13.1	4.74	84	.262	.342	0	—	0	-9	-9	2	-1.0
1993	Sea-A	3	3	.500	23	0	0	0	0	19²	25	2	18	10	20.6	9.15	48	.316	.455	0	—	0	-11	-10	1	-2.6
1994	Cle-A	0	0	—	12	0	0	0	0	8	13	1	7	2	22.5	11.25	42	.382	.488	0	—	0	-6	-6	0	-0.6
Total	6	14	22	.389	168	20	1	0	11	266²	282	26	124	108	13.9	4.83	84	.275	.356	0	.000	-0	-24	-23	3	-4.7

● **RED SWANSON** Swanson, Arthur Leonard b: 10/15/36, Baton Rouge, La. BR/TR, 6'1.5", 175 lbs. Deb: 9/10/55

YEAR	TM/L	W	L	PCT	G	GS	CG	SH	SV	IP	H	HR	BB	SO	RAT	ERA	ERA+	OAV	OOB	BH	AVG	PB	PR	/A	PD	TPI
1955	Pit-N	0	0	—	1	0	0	0	0	2	3	0	2	1	22.5	18.00	30	.286	.500	0	—	0	-3	-3	-0	0.0
1956	Pit-N	0	0	—	9	0	0	0	0	11²	21	1	8	5	22.4	10.03	38	.438	.518	0	—	0	-8	-8	1	0.1
1957	Pit-N	3	3	.500	32	8	1	0	0	72²	68	9	31	29	12.4	3.72	102	.248	.327	0	.000	-1	1	1	-1	-0.2
Total	3	3	3	.500	42	8	1	0	0	86¹	91	11	42	34	14.0	4.90	77	.277	.360	0	.000	-1	-10	-11	-0	-0.1

● **ED SWARTWOOD** Swartwood, Cyrus Edward b: 1/12/1859, Rockford, Ill. d: 5/15/24, Pittsburgh, Pa. BL/TR, 5'11", 198 lbs. Deb: 8/11/1881 U♦

YEAR	TM/L	W	L	PCT	G	GS	CG	SH	SV	IP	H	HR	BB	SO	RAT	ERA	ERA+	OAV	OOB	BH	AVG	PB	PR	/A	PD	TPI
1884	Pit-a	0	0	—	1	0	0	0	0	2¹	6	0	1	0	27.0	11.57	29	.400	.438	115	.288	0	-2	-2	0	0.0
1890	Tol-a	0	0	—	1	0	0	0	0	3	2	0	1	1	15.0	3.00	132	.182	.182	151	.327	0	0	0	0	0.0
Total	2	0	0	—	2	0	0	0	0	5¹	8	0	1	1	15.2	6.75	54	.308	.333	861	.299	1	-2	-2	0	0.0

● **BUD SWARTZ** Swartz, Sherwin Merle b: 6/13/29, Tulsa, Okla. d: 6/24/91, Los Angeles, Cal. BL/TL, 6'2.5", 180 lbs. Deb: 7/12/47

YEAR	TM/L	W	L	PCT	G	GS	CG	SH	SV	IP	H	HR	BB	SO	RAT	ERA	ERA+	OAV	OOB	BH	AVG	PB	PR	/A	PD	TPI
1947	StL-A	0	0	—	5	0	0	0	0	5¹	9	1	7	1	27.0	6.75	57	.360	.500	1	1.000	0	-2	-2	0	0.0

● **MONTY SWARTZ** Swartz, Vernon Monroe "Dazzy" b: 1/1/1897, Farmersville, Ohio d: 1/13/80, Germantown, Ohio BR/TR, 5'11", 182 lbs. Deb: 10/3/20

YEAR	TM/L	W	L	PCT	G	GS	CG	SH	SV	IP	H	HR	BB	SO	RAT	ERA	ERA+	OAV	OOB	BH	AVG	PB	PR	/A	PD	TPI
1920	Cin-N	0	1	.000	1	1	1	0	0	12	17	0	2	2	14.3	4.50	68	.333	.358	2	.500	-2	-2	-2	0	-0.1

● **DAVE SWARTZBAUGH** Swartzbaugh, David Theodore b: 2/11/68, Middletown, Ohio BR/TR, 6'2", 195 lbs. Deb: 9/3/95

YEAR	TM/L	W	L	PCT	G	GS	CG	SH	SV	IP	H	HR	BB	SO	RAT	ERA	ERA+	OAV	OOB	BH	AVG	PB	PR	/A	PD	TPI
1995	Chi-N	0	0	—	7	0	0	0	0	7¹	5	1	3	5	9.8	—	.208	.296	0	—	0	3	3	0	0.0	
1996	Chi-N	0	2	.000	6	5	0	0	0	24	26	3	14	13	15.0	6.38	87	.277	.370	0	.000	-0	-6	-6	0	-0.4
Total	2	0	2	.000	13	5	0	0	0	31¹	31	3	17	18	13.8	4.88	87	.263	.356	0	.000	-0	-3	-3	0	-0.4

● **PARK SWARTZEL** Swartzel, Park B. b: 11/21/1865, Knightstown, Ind. d: 1/3/40, Los Angeles, Cal. BR/TR, 5'10", Deb: 4/17/1889

YEAR	TM/L	W	L	PCT	G	GS	CG	SH	SV	IP	H	HR	BB	SO	RAT	ERA	ERA+	OAV	OOB	BH	AVG	PB	PR	/A	PD	TPI
1889	KC-a	19	27	.413	48	47	45	0	1	410¹	481	21	117	147	13.6	4.32	97	.283	.338	25	.144	-9	-22	-6	9	-0.5

● **CHARLIE SWEENEY** Sweeney, Charles J. b: 4/13/1863, San Francisco, Cal d: 4/4/02, San Francisco, Cal. BR/TR, 5'10.5", 181 lbs. Deb: 5/11/1882 ♦

YEAR	TM/L	W	L	PCT	G	GS	CG	SH	SV	IP	H	HR	BB	SO	RAT	ERA	ERA+	OAV	OOB	BH	AVG	PB	PR	/A	PD	TPI
1883	Pro-N	7	7	.500	20	18	14	0	0	146²	142	3	28	48	10.4	3.13	99	.237	.272	19	.218	-1	0	-1	1	-0.1
1884	Pro-N	17	8	.680	27	24	22	4	1	221	153	4	29	145	**7.4**	1.55	182	**.187**	**.215**	50	.298	8	35	31	1	3.9
	StL-U	24	7	.774	33	32	31	2	0	271	207	4	19	192	7.3	1.83	131	.197	.207	54	.316	6	19	17	5	2.4
1885	StL-N	11	21	.344	35	35	32	2	0	275	276	6	50	84	10.7	3.93	70	.250	.282	55	.206	-0	-34	-36	1	-3.3
1886	StL-N	5	6	.455	11	11	11	0	0	93	108	3	12	29	11.7	4.16	78	.285	.350	5	.250	-9	-10	-10	0	-0.8
1887	Cle-a	0	3	.000	3	3	3	0	0	24	42	0	13	8	20.6	8.25	53	.372	.437	30	.226	-4	-11	-10	0	-0.8
Total	5	64	52	.552	129	123	113	8	1	1030²	928	24	172	505	9.6	2.87	97	.228	.260	224	.251	14	1	-8	8	1.3

● BILL SWEENEY   Sweeney, William J.   b: Philadelphia, Pa.   d: 8/2/03, Philadelphia, Pa.   TR,   Deb: 6/27/1882

YEAR TM/L	W	L	PCT	G	GS	CG	SH	SV	IP	H	HR	BB	SO	RAT	ERA	ERA+	OAV	OOB	BH	AVG	PB	PR	/A	PD	TPI
1882 Phi-a	9	10	.474	20	20	18	0	0	170	178	4	42	48	11.6	2.91	102	.252	.294	14	.159	-3	-4	1	-1	-0.2
1884 Bal-U	**40**	21	.656	**62**	60	**58**	4	0	**538**	522	13	74	374	10.0	2.59	103	.238	.263	71	.240	-16	-9	5	1	-0.7
Total 2	49	31	.613	82	80	76	4	0	708	700	17	116	422	10.4	2.67	103	.241	.270	85	.221	-19	-13	7	1	-0.9

● LES SWEETLAND   Sweetland, Lester Leo (Born Leo Sweetland)   b: 8/15/01, St.Ignace, Mich.   d: 3/4/74, Melbourne, Fla.   BR/TL, 5'11.5", 155 lbs.   Deb: 7/4/27

YEAR TM/L	W	L	PCT	G	GS	CG	SH	SV	IP	H	HR	BB	SO	RAT	ERA	ERA+	OAV	OOB	BH	AVG	PB	PR	/A	PD	TPI
1927 Phi-N	2	10	.167	21	13	6	0	0	103²	147	3	53	21	17.6	6.16	67	.348	.425	12	.316	3	-26	-23	5	-1.5
1928 Phi-N	3	15	.167	37	18	5	0	0	135¹	163	15	97	23	18.3	6.58	65	.306	.426	9	.191	1	-39	-35	2	-3.7
1929 Phi-N	13	11	.542	43	25	10	2	2	204¹	255	23	87	47	15.5	5.11	102	.316	.389	26	.292	3	-9	2	4	0.8
1930 Phi-N	7	15	.318	34	25	8	1	0	167	271	24	60	36	18.1	7.71	71	.373	.425	16	.281	4	-51	-42	1	-3.7
1931 Chi-N	8	7	.533	26	14	9	0	0	130¹	156	3	61	32	15.3	5.04	77	.297	.375	15	.268	5	-17	-17	0	-1.3
Total 5	33	58	.363	161	95	38	3	4	740²	992	68	358	159	16.9	6.10	77	.329	.407	78	.272	16	-142	-116	12	-9.4

● STEVE SWETONIC   Swetonic, Stephen Albert   b: 8/13/03, Mt.Pleasant, Pa.   d: 4/22/74, Canonsburg, Pa.   BR/TR, 5'11", 185 lbs.   Deb: 4/17/29   ◆

YEAR TM/L	W	L	PCT	G	GS	CG	SH	SV	IP	H	HR	BB	SO	RAT	ERA	ERA+	OAV	OOB	BH	AVG	PB	PR	/A	PD	TPI
1929 Pit-N	8	10	.444	41	12	3	0	5	143²	172	6	50	35	14.2	4.82	99	.299	.360	13	.271	3	-2	-1	2	0.3
1930 Pit-N	6	6	.500	23	6	3	1	0	96²	107	7	20	35	12.5	4.47	111	.276	.323	4	.111	-3	5	5	-1	0.3
1931 Pit-N	0	2	.000	14	0	0	0	1	27²	28	0	16	8	14.3	3.90	99	.264	.361	1	.143	-0	-0	-0	-0	0.0
1932 Pit-N	11	6	.647	24	19	11	**4**	0	162²	134	11	55	39	10.5	2.82	135	**.221**	.286	19	.093	-4	19	18	-1	1.2
1933 Pit-N	12	12	.500	31	21	8	3	0	164²	166	10	64	37	12.7	3.50	95	.260	.330	11	.200	1	-3	-3	-1	-0.5
Total 5	37	36	.507	133	58	25	8	11	595¹	607	34	212	154	12.5	3.81	107	.262	.326	34	.170	-3	20	19	-2	1.3

● BILL SWIFT   Swift, William Charles   b: 10/27/61, Portland, Maine   BR/TR, 6', 180 lbs.   Deb: 6/7/85

YEAR TM/L	W	L	PCT	G	GS	CG	SH	SV	IP	H	HR	BB	SO	RAT	ERA	ERA+	OAV	OOB	BH	AVG	PB	PR	/A	PD	TPI
1985 Sea-A	6	10	.375	23	21	0	0	0	120²	131	8	48	55	13.7	4.77	88	.279	.352	0	—	0	-8	-8	0	-0.9
1986 Sea-A	2	9	.182	29	17	1	0	0	115¹	148	5	55	55	16.4	5.46	78	.319	.399	0	—	0	-16	-16	1	-1.2
1988 Sea-A	8	12	.400	38	24	6	1	0	174²	199	10	65	47	14.0	4.59	91	.294	.363	0	—	0	-12	-8	2	-0.9
1989 Sea-A	7	3	.700	37	16	0	0	1	130	140	7	38	45	12.5	4.43	91	.278	.331	0	—	0	-8	-6	5	-0.1
1990 Sea-A	6	4	.600	55	8	0	0	6	128	135	4	21	42	11.5	2.39	166	.272	.311	0	—	0	22	22	0	1.8
1991 Sea-A	1	2	.333	71	0	0	0	17	90¹	74	3	26	48	10.1	1.99	207	.224	.283	0	—	0	21	21	3	1.6
1992 SF-N	10	4	.714	30	22	3	2	1	164²	144	6	43	77	10.4	**2.08**	159	.239	.293	8	.157	1	26	22	2	2.3
1993 SF-N	21	8	.724	34	34	1	1	0	232²	195	18	55	157	9.9	2.82	138	.226	.278	21	.262	6	31	28	2	4.2
1994 SF-N	8	7	.533	17	17	0	0	0	109¹	109	10	31	62	11.6	3.38	119	.262	.315	2	.188	-1	2	8	-1	1.1
1995 *Col-N	9	3	.750	19	19	0	0	0	105²	122	12	43	68	14.1	4.94	109	.296	.364	7	.194	0	-9	5	3	0.8
1996 Col-N	1	1	.500	7	3	0	0	0	18¹	23	1	5	5	13.7	5.40	101	.307	.350	2	.333	0	-2	0	0	0.1
Total 11	79	63	.556	360	181	11	4	27	1389²	1420	84	430	661	12.2	3.64	112	.268	.327	44	.215	9	54	69	18	8.8

● BILL SWIFT   Swift, William Vincent   b: 1/10/08, Elmira, N.Y.   d: 2/23/69, Bartow, Fla.   BR/TR, 6'1.5", 192 lbs.   Deb: 4/12/32

YEAR TM/L	W	L	PCT	G	GS	CG	SH	SV	IP	H	HR	BB	SO	RAT	ERA	ERA+	OAV	OOB	BH	AVG	PB	PR	/A	PD	TPI
1932 Pit-N	14	10	.583	39	23	11	0	4	214¹	205	15	26	64	9.8	3.61	106	.248	.272	15	.192	-1	6	5	-4	0.0
1933 Pit-N	14	10	.583	37	29	13	2	0	218¹	214	11	36	64	10.5	3.13	106	.251	.285	20	.244	3	5	5	-2	0.6
1934 Pit-N	11	13	.458	37	24	13	1	0	212²	244	15	46	81	12.6	3.98	103	.284	.326	18	.214	2	2	3	-1	0.3
1935 Pit-N	15	8	.652	39	21	11	3	1	203²	193	6	37	74	10.2	2.70	152	.247	.282	19	.244	3	30	32	-4	3.2
1936 Pit-N	16	16	.500	45	31	17	0	2	262²	275	18	63	92	11.6	4.01	101	.265	.310	31	.295	9	0	1	-5	0.5
1937 Pit-N	9	10	.474	36	17	9	0	3	164	160	14	34	84	10.8	3.95	98	.256	.297	9	.167	-1	-1	-2	-3	-0.5
1938 Pit-N	7	5	.583	36	9	2	0	0	150	155	9	40	77	11.9	3.24	117	.271	.323	10	.200	2	9	9	-1	0.8
1939 Pit-N	5	7	.417	36	8	2	1	4	129²	150	6	28	56	12.6	3.89	99	.293	.333	10	.238	2	0	-1	-3	-0.2
1940 Bos-N	1	1	.500	4	0	0	0	0	9¹	12	0	7	7	18.3	2.89	129	.308	.413	0	.000	-0	1	1	0	0.2
1941 Bro-N	3	0	1.000	9	0	0	0	0	22	26	4	7	9	13.5	3.27	112	.289	.340	1	.200	-0	1	1	-0	0.1
1943 Chi-A	0	2	.000	18	1	0	0	0	51¹	48	5	27	22	13.5	4.21	79	.246	.355	1	.100	-0	-5	-5	-2	-0.4
Total 11	95	82	.537	336	163	78	7	20	1637²	1682	103	351	636	11.4	3.58	108	.263	.305	134	.227	18	49	49	-25	4.6

● OAD SWIGART   Swigart, Oadis Vaughn   b: 2/13/15, Archie, Mo.   BL/TR, 6', 175 lbs.   Deb: 9/14/39

YEAR TM/L	W	L	PCT	G	GS	CG	SH	SV	IP	H	HR	BB	SO	RAT	ERA	ERA+	OAV	OOB	BH	AVG	PB	PR	/A	PD	TPI
1939 Pit-N	1	1	.500	3	3	1	0	0	24¹	27	1	6	8	12.2	4.44	87	.293	.337	2	.250	0	-1	-2	-0	-0.1
1940 Pit-N	0	2	.000	7	2	0	0	0	22¹	27	1	10	9	14.9	4.43	86	.297	.366	1	.200	-0	-1	-2	-0	-0.1
Total 2	1	3	.250	10	5	1	0	0	46²	54	2	16	17	13.5	4.44	86	.295	.352	3	.231	0	-3	-3	-0	-0.2

● AD SWIGLER   Swigler, Adam William "Doc"   b: 9/21/1895, Philadelphia, Pa.   d: 2/5/75, Philadelphia, Pa.   BR/TR, 5'10", 180 lbs.   Deb: 9/25/17

YEAR TM/L	W	L	PCT	G	GS	CG	SH	SV	IP	H	HR	BB	SO	RAT	ERA	ERA+	OAV	OOB	BH	AVG	PB	PR	/A	PD	TPI
1917 NY-N	0	1	.000	1	1	0	0	0	6	7	0	8	4	22.5	6.00	43	.333	.517	0	.000	-0	-2	-2	-0	-0.3

● GREG SWINDELL   Swindell, Forest Gregory   b: 1/2/65, Fort Worth, Tex.   BR/TL, 6'2", 225 lbs.   Deb: 8/21/86

YEAR TM/L	W	L	PCT	G	GS	CG	SH	SV	IP	H	HR	BB	SO	RAT	ERA	ERA+	OAV	OOB	BH	AVG	PB	PR	/A	PD	TPI
1986 Cle-A	5	2	.714	9	9	1	0	0	61²	57	9	15	46	10.7	4.23	98	.243	.291	0	—	0	-0	-1	1	0.1
1987 Cle-A	3	8	.273	16	15	4	1	0	102¹	112	18	37	97	13.2	5.10	89	.283	.346	0	—	0	-7	-7	-0	-0.7
1988 Cle-A	18	14	.563	33	33	12	4	0	242	234	18	45	180	10.4	3.20	129	.252	.287	0	—	0	21	25	-1	2.9
1989 Cle-A★	13	6	.684	28	28	5	2	0	184¹	170	16	51	129	10.8	3.37	118	.246	.298	0	—	0	11	12	-0	1.0
1990 Cle-A	12	9	.571	34	34	3	0	0	214²	245	27	47	135	12.3	4.40	89	.288	.326	0	—	0	-12	-12	-2	-1.2
1991 Cle-A	9	16	.360	33	33	7	0	0	238	241	21	31	169	10.4	3.48	119	.263	.289	0	—	0	16	18	-1	1.6
1992 Cin-N	12	8	.600	31	30	5	1	0	213²	210	14	41	138	10.7	2.70	133	.260	.297	10	.125	-2	19	21	-1	1.8
1993 Hou-N	12	13	.480	31	31	1	1	0	190¹	215	24	40	124	12.1	4.16	93	.283	.319	11	.183	-0	-3	-6	-0	-0.7
1994 Hou-N	8	9	.471	24	24	1	0	0	148¹	175	20	26	74	12.3	4.37	90	.302	.333	1	.250	-3	-3	-7	-2	-0.6
1995 Hou-N	10	9	.526	33	26	1	0	0	153	180	21	39	96	13.0	4.47	86	.297	.342	12	.240	4	-5	-10	2	-0.6
1996 Hou-N	0	3	.000	8	4	0	0	0	23	35	5	11	15	18.4	7.83	49	.340	.409	2	.333	1	-9	-10	-0	-1.0
Cle-A	1	1	.500	13	2	0	0	0	28¹	37	4	8	21	12.2	6.59	74	.279	.328	0	—	0	-5	-5	0	-0.3
Total 11	103	98	.512	293	268	40	12	0	1800	1905	201	391	1224	11.6	3.90	102	.273	.313	46	.192	7	23	19	-5	2.3

● JOSH SWINDELL   Swindell, Joshua Ernest   b: 7/5/1883, Rose Hill, Kan.   d: 3/19/69, Fruita, Colo.   BR/TR, 6', 180 lbs.   Deb: 9/16/11   ◆

YEAR TM/L	W	L	PCT	G	GS	CG	SH	SV	IP	H	HR	BB	SO	RAT	ERA	ERA+	OAV	OOB	BH	AVG	PB	PR	/A	PD	TPI
1911 Cle-A	0	1	.000	4	1	1	0	0	17¹	19	0	4	6	12.5	2.08	164	.257	.304	1	.250	-0	2	3	-0	0.1

● PAUL SWINGLE   Swingle, Paul Christopher   b: 12/21/66, Inglewood, Cal.   BR/TR, 6', 185 lbs.   Deb: 9/7/93

YEAR TM/L	W	L	PCT	G	GS	CG	SH	SV	IP	H	HR	BB	SO	RAT	ERA	ERA+	OAV	OOB	BH	AVG	PB	PR	/A	PD	TPI
1993 Cal-A	0	1	.000	9	0	0	0	0	9²	15	2	6	6	19.6	8.38	54	.357	.438	0	—	0	-4	-4	-0	-0.4

● LEN SWORMSTEDT   Swormstedt, Leonard Jordan   b: 10/6/1878, Cincinnati, Ohio   d: 7/19/64, Salem, Mass.   BR/TR, 5'11.5", 165 lbs.   Deb: 9/29/01

YEAR TM/L	W	L	PCT	G	GS	CG	SH	SV	IP	H	HR	BB	SO	RAT	ERA	ERA+	OAV	OOB	BH	AVG	PB	PR	/A	PD	TPI
1901 Cin-N	2	1	.667	3	3	3	0	0	26	19	2	5	13	9.0	1.73	185	.202	.257	0	.000	-1	5	4	0	0.3
1902 Cin-N	0	2	.000	2	2	1	0	0	18	22	1	5	6	13.5	4.00	75	.301	.346				-2	-2	-0	-0.3
1906 Bos-A	1	1	.500	3	2	1	0	0	21	17	0		6	7.7	1.29	214	.224	.234	1	.125	-1	3	3	-1	0.2
Total 3	3	4	.429	8	7	7	0	0	65	58	3	10	22	9.8	2.22	136	.239	.277	1	.043	-3	5	6	-1	0.2

● BOB SYKES   Sykes, Robert Joseph   b: 12/11/54, Neptune, N.J.   BB/TL, 6'2", 200 lbs.   Deb: 4/9/77

YEAR TM/L	W	L	PCT	G	GS	CG	SH	SV	IP	H	HR	BB	SO	RAT	ERA	ERA+	OAV	OOB	BH	AVG	PB	PR	/A	PD	TPI
1977 Det-A	5	7	.417	32	20	3	0	0	132²	141	15	50	58	13.1	4.41	97	.271	.337	0	—	0	-5	-2	-0	-0.5
1978 Det-A	6	6	.500	22	10	3	2	2	93²	94	14	34	58	12.9	3.94	98	.275	.339	0	—	0	-2	-1	-2	-0.5
1979 StL-N	4	3	.571	13	11	0	0	0	67	86	11	34	35	16.3	6.18	61	.315	.393	2	.095	-0	-18	-18	-1	-1.7
1980 StL-N	6	10	.375	27	19	4	3	0	126	140	5	54	50	13.4	4.64	79	.277	.350	4	.103	-2	-15	-13	-1	-1.9
1981 StL-N	2	0	1.000	22	1	0	0	0	37¹	37	2	18	14	13.5	4.58	78	.266	.354	0	.000	-0	-5	-4	1	-0.1
Total 5	23	26	.469	116	61	10	5	2	456²	497	54	190	215	13.6	4.65	84	.280	.351	6	.097	-2	-44	-38	-4	-4.7

● LOU SYLVESTER   Sylvester, Louis J.   b: 2/14/1855, Springfield, Ill.   BR/TR, 5'3", 165 lbs.   Deb: 4/18/1884   ◆

YEAR TM/L	W	L	PCT	G	GS	CG	SH	SV	IP	H	HR	BB	SO	RAT	ERA	ERA+	OAV	OOB	BH	AVG	PB	PR	/A	PD	TPI
1884 Cin-U	0	1	.000	6	1	1	0	1	32²	32	0	6	7	10.5	3.58	72	.239	.271	89	.267	-0	-4	-4	-1	-0.2

● JEFF TABAKA   Tabaka, Jeffrey Jon   b: 1/17/64, Barberton, Ohio   BR/TL, 6'2", 195 lbs.   Deb: 4/19/94

YEAR TM/L	W	L	PCT	G	GS	CG	SH	SV	IP	H	HR	BB	SO	RAT	ERA	ERA+	OAV	OOB	BH	AVG	PB	PR	/A	PD	TPI
1994 Pit-N	0	0	—	5	0	0	0	0	4	4	1	2	8	27.0	18.00	24	.250	.500	0	—	0	-6	-6	-0	0.0
SD-N	3	1	.750	34	0	0	0	0	37	28	0	19	30	11.4	3.89	106	.209	.307	1	1.000	1	1	1	-0	0.2
Yr	3	1	.750	39	0	0	0	0	41	32	1	21	32	13.0	5.27	78	.213	.333	1	1.000	1	-5	-5	0	0.2
1995 SD-N	0	0	—	10	0	0	0	0	6¹	10	1	5	6	21.3	7.11	57	.370	.469	0	—	0	-2	-2	-0	0.0
Hou-N	1	0	1.000	24	0	0	0	0	24¹	17	1	12	19	10.7	2.22	174	.202	.302	0	.000	-0	5	4	-0	0.1

YEAR TM/L	W	L	PCT	G	GS	CG	SH	SV	IP	H	HR	BB	SO	RAT	ERA	ERA+	OAV	OOB	BH	AVG	PB	PR	/A	PD	TPI
Yr	1	0	1.000	34	0	0	0	0	30²	27	2	17	25	12.9	3.23	121	.243	.344	0	.000	-0	3	2	-0	0.1
1996 Hou-N	0	2	.000	18	0	0	0	1	20¹	28	5	14	18	19.9	6.64	82	.322	.433	0	.000	-0	-5	-6	-1	-0.7
Total 3	4	3	.571	91	0	0	0	2	92	87	8	58	75	14.5	4.89	81	.250	.362	1	.333	1	-7	-9	-1	-0.4

● **LEFTY TABER**   Taber, Edward Timothy b: 1/11/1900, Rock Island, Ill. d: 11/5/83, Lincoln, Neb. BL/TL, 6', 180 lbs. Deb: 9/4/26

YEAR TM/L	W	L	PCT	G	GS	CG	SH	SV	IP	H	HR	BB	SO	RAT	ERA	ERA+	OAV	OOB	BH	AVG	PB	PR	/A	PD	TPI
1926 Phi-N	0	0	—	6	0	0	0	0	8¹	8	0	5	0	16.2	7.56	55	.242	.375	0	.000	-0	-3	-3	-0	0.0
1927 Phi-N	0	1	.000	3	1	0	0	0	3¹	8	0	5	0	37.8	18.90	22	.533	.667	0	.000	-0	-6	-5	-0	-1.2
Total 2	0	1	.000	9	1	0	0	0	11²	16	0	10	0	22.4	10.80	38	.333	.475	0	.000	-0	-9	-9	-0	-1.2

● **JOHN TABER**   Taber, John Pardon b: 6/28/1868, Acushnet, Mass. d: 2/21/40, Boston, Mass. BR/TR, 5'8", Deb: 4/30/1890

YEAR TM/L	W	L	PCT	G	GS	CG	SH	SV	IP	H	HR	BB	SO	RAT	ERA	ERA+	OAV	OOB	BH	AVG	PB	PR	/A	PD	TPI
1890 Bos-N	0	1	.000	2	1	1	0	0	13	11	0	8	3	13.2	4.15	90	.220	.328	0	.000	-1	-1	-1	0	-0.1

● **JEFF TACKETT**   Tackett, Jeffrey Wilson b: 12/1/65, Fresno, Cal. BR/TR, 6'2", 200 lbs. Deb: 9/11/91 ♦

YEAR TM/L	W	L	PCT	G	GS	CG	SH	SV	IP	H	HR	BB	SO	RAT	ERA	ERA+	OAV	OOB	BH	AVG	PB	PR	/A	PD	TPI
1993 Bal-A	0	0	—	1	0	0	0	0	1	1	0	1	0	18.0	0.00	—	.250	.400	15	.172	1	0	0	0	0.0

● **JOHN TAFF**   Taff, John Gallatin b: 6/3/1890, Austin, Tex. d: 5/15/61, Houston, Tex. BR/TR, 6', 170 lbs. Deb: 5/11/13

YEAR TM/L	W	L	PCT	G	GS	CG	SH	SV	IP	H	HR	BB	SO	RAT	ERA	ERA+	OAV	OOB	BH	AVG	PB	PR	/A	PD	TPI
1913 Phi-A	0	1	.000	7	1	0	0	1	17²	22	0	5	9	13.8	6.62	42	.293	.338	1	.200	-0	-7	-8	0	-0.5

● **DOUG TAITT**   Taitt, Douglas John "Poco" b: 8/3/02, Bay City, Mich. d: 12/12/70, Portland, Ore. BL/TR, 6', 176 lbs. Deb: 4/10/28 ♦

YEAR TM/L	W	L	PCT	G	GS	CG	SH	SV	IP	H	HR	BB	SO	RAT	ERA	ERA+	OAV	OOB	BH	AVG	PB	PR	/A	PD	TPI
1928 Bos-A	0	0	—	1	0	0	0	0	1	2	0	1	1	36.0	27.00	15	.400	.571	144	.299	0	-3	-3	-0	0.0

● **FRED TALBOT**   Talbot, Frederick Lealand "Bubby" b: 6/28/41, Washington, D.C. BR/TR, 6'2", 195 lbs. Deb: 9/28/63

YEAR TM/L	W	L	PCT	G	GS	CG	SH	SV	IP	H	HR	BB	SO	RAT	ERA	ERA+	OAV	OOB	BH	AVG	PB	PR	/A	PD	TPI
1963 Chi-A	0	0	—	1	0	0	0	0	3	2	0	4	2	18.0	3.00	117	.222	.462	0	.000	-0	0	0	0	0.0
1964 Chi-A	4	5	.444	17	12	3	2	0	75¹	83	7	20	34	12.8	3.70	93	.288	.343	5	.263	3	-1	-2	-1	0.0
1965 KC-A	10	12	.455	39	33	2	1	0	198	188	25	86	117	12.7	4.14	84	.251	.333	14	.200	3	-15	-14	-1	-1.2
1966 KC-A	4	4	.500	11	11	0	0	0	67²	65	6	28	37	12.6	4.79	71	.248	.325	3	.150	-0	-10	-10	-0	-1.1
NY-A	7	7	.500	23	19	3	0	0	124¹	123	16	45	48	12.4	4.13	81	.262	.331	5	.143	1	-10	-11	-0	-1.1
Yr	11	11	.500	34	30	3	0	0	192	188	22	73	85	12.4	4.36	77	.256	.326	8	.145	1	-20	-22	-0	-2.2
1967 NY-A	6	8	.429	29	22	2	0	0	138²	132	20	54	61	12.5	4.22	74	.252	.329	6	.158	3	-15	-17	-2	-1.0
1968 NY-A	1	9	.100	29	11	1	0	0	99	89	6	42	67	12.1	3.36	86	.241	.322	2	.118	-1	-4	-5	-1	-0.4
1969 NY-A	0	0	—	8	0	0	0	0	12¹	13	1	6	7	13.9	5.11	68	.283	.365	0	.000	-0	-2	-2	0	-0.5
Sea-A	5	8	.385	25	16	1	1	0	114²	125	12	41	67	13.3	4.16	87	.278	.343	6	.162	2	-7	-7	-0	-0.5
Oak-A	1	2	.333	12	2	0	0	0	19	22	2	7	9	13.7	5.21	66	.297	.358	1	.333	-0	-3	-4	0	-0.6
Yr	6	10	.375	45	18	1	1	0	146	160	15	54	83	13.2	4.38	82	.277	.339	7	.171	2	-12	-13	-0	-1.1
1970 Oak-A	0	1	.000	1	0	0	0	0	1²	2	1	1	0	16.2	10.80	38	.286	.375	0	—	-0	-1	-1	0	-0.5
Total 8	38	56	.404	195	126	12	4	1	853²	844	96	334	449	12.7	4.12	81	.260	.334	42	.174	13	-68	-74	2	-6.4

● **ROY TALCOTT**   Talcott, Le Roy Everett b: 1/16/20, Brookline, Mass. BR/TR, 6'1.5", 180 lbs. Deb: 6/24/43

YEAR TM/L	W	L	PCT	G	GS	CG	SH	SV	IP	H	HR	BB	SO	RAT	ERA	ERA+	OAV	OOB	BH	AVG	PB	PR	/A	PD	TPI
1943 Bos-N	0	0	—	1	0	0	0	0	0²	1	0	2	0	40.5	27.00	13	.333	.600	0	—	0	-2	-2	0	0.0

● **VITO TAMULIS**   Tamulis, Vitautis Casimirus b: 7/11/11, Cambridge, Mass. d: 5/5/74, Nashville, Tenn. BL/TL, 5'9", 170 lbs. Deb: 9/25/34

YEAR TM/L	W	L	PCT	G	GS	CG	SH	SV	IP	H	HR	BB	SO	RAT	ERA	ERA+	OAV	OOB	BH	AVG	PB	PR	/A	PD	TPI
1934 NY-A	1	0	1.000	1	1	1	0	0	9	7	0	1	5	8.0	0.00	—	.219	.242	1	.250	0	4	4	0	0.5
1935 NY-A	10	5	.667	30	19	9	3	1	160²	178	7	55	57	13.2	4.09	90	.280	.339	14	.246	4	7	-1	-1	0.2
1938 StL-A	0	3	.000	3	2	0	0	0	15¹	26	2	10	11	21.1	7.63	65	.366	.444	2	.400	-1	-5	-5	-0	-0.6
Bro-N	12	6	.667	38	18	9	0	2	159²	181	11	40	70	12.6	3.83	102	.288	.333	7	.127	-3	-1	1	-2	-0.3
1939 Bro-N	9	8	.529	39	17	8	1	4	158²	177	10	45	83	13.0	4.37	92	.287	.343	10	.182	-1	-8	-6	-0	-0.7
1940 Bro-N	8	5	.615	41	12	4	0	2	154¹	147	6	34	55	12.0	3.09	129	.244	.288	6	.130	-1	13	16	-1	1.0
1941 Phi-N	0	1	.000	6	1	0	0	0	12	21	1	7	5	21.8	9.00	41	.382	.460	0	.000	-0	-7	-7	0	-0.5
Bro-N	0	0	—	12	0	0	0	1	22	21	1	10	8	12.7	3.68	100	.244	.323	0	.000	-1	-0	-0	-0	-0.1
Yr	0	1	.000	18	1	0	0	1	34	42	2	17	13	15.6	5.56	66	.296	.371	0	.000	-1	-7	-7	-0	-0.6
Total 6	40	28	.588	170	70	31	6	10	691²	758	37	202	294	12.7	3.97	101	.278	.331	40	.175	-1	3	4	-2	-0.5

● **FRANK TANANA**   Tanana, Frank Daryl b: 7/3/53, Detroit, Mich. BL/TL, 6'3", 195 lbs. Deb: 9/9/73

YEAR TM/L	W	L	PCT	G	GS	CG	SH	SV	IP	H	HR	BB	SO	RAT	ERA	ERA+	OAV	OOB	BH	AVG	PB	PR	/A	PD	TPI
1973 Cal-A	2	2	.500	4	4	2	1	0	26¹	20	2	8	22	9.6	3.08	115	.200	.259	0	—	0	2	1	0	0.3
1974 Cal-A	14	19	.424	39	35	12	4	0	268²	262	27	77	180	11.6	3.12	110	.255	.312	0	—	0	15	10	0	1.6
1975 Cal-A	16	9	.640	34	33	16	5	0	257¹	211	21	73	**269**	10.2	2.62	135	.226	.288	0	—	0	33	26	3	3.3
1976 Cal-A★	19	10	.655	34	34	23	2	0	288¹	212	24	73	261	**9.2**	2.43	137	.203	**.261**	0	—	0	35	29	1	3.2
1977 Cal-A†	15	9	.625	31	31	20	**7**	0	241¹	201	19	61	205	10.2	**2.54**	**154**	.227	.286	0	—	0	41	37	1	3.7
1978 Cal-A☆	18	12	.600	33	33	10	4	0	239	239	26	60	137	11.6	3.65	99	.258	.309	0	—	0	3	-1	-2	-0.4
1979 *Cal-A	7	5	.583	18	17	2	1	0	90¹	93	9	25	46	12.0	3.89	105	.264	.317	0	—	0	3	-2	-1	0.4
1980 Cal-A	11	12	.478	32	31	7	0	0	204	223	18	45	113	12.2	4.15	95	.277	.322	0	—	0	-3	-5	-1	-0.6
1981 Bos-A	4	10	.286	24	23	5	3	0	141¹	142	11	43	78	12.0	4.01	96	.265	.324	0	—	0	-6	-2	1	-0.2
1982 Tex-A	7	18	.280	30	30	7	0	0	194¹	199	16	55	87	12.1	4.21	92	.264	.320	0	—	0	-3	-7	-0	-0.7
1983 Tex-A	7	9	.438	29	22	3	0	0	159¹	144	14	49	108	11.3	3.16	127	.240	.304	0	—	0	16	15	3	1.8
1984 Tex-A	15	15	.500	35	35	3	1	0	246¹	234	30	81	141	11.7	3.25	127	.245	.308	0	—	0	20	24	1	2.7
1985 Tex-A	2	7	.222	13	13	0	0	0	77²	98	15	23	52	13.1	5.91	72	.287	.338	0	—	0	-15	-15	-0	-1.5
Det-A	10	7	.588	20	20	4	0	0	137¹	131	13	34	107	10.9	3.34	122	.250	.298	0	—	0	12	11	1	1.4
Yr	12	14	.462	33	33	4	0	0	215	220	28	57	159	11.7	4.27	97	.262	.311	0	—	0	-3	-3	-1	-0.1
1986 Det-A	12	9	.571	32	31	3	1	0	188¹	196	23	65	119	12.6	4.16	99	.268	.330	0	—	0	1	0	0	0.1
1987 *Det-A	15	10	.600	34	34	3	0	0	218²	216	27	56	146	11.4	3.91	108	.256	.306	0	—	0	13	8	0	0.9
1988 Det-A	14	11	.560	32	32	2	0	0	203	213	26	64	127	12.5	4.21	91	.267	.324	0	—	0	-6	-9	-0	-0.7
1989 Det-A	10	14	.417	33	33	6	1	0	223²	227	21	74	147	12.4	3.58	107	.265	.329	0	—	0	7	6	2	1.0
1990 Det-A	9	8	.529	34	29	3	0	0	176¹	190	25	66	114	13.5	5.31	75	.280	.352	0	—	0	-27	-26	-0	-2.2
1991 Det-A	13	12	.520	33	33	3	0	0	217¹	217	26	78	124	12.3	3.77	110	.265	.330	0	.000	0	8	9	-1	1.1
1992 Det-A	13	11	.542	32	31	3	0	0	186²	188	22	90	91	13.7	4.39	90	.267	.356	0	—	0	-9	-11	-0	-1.0
1993 NY-N	7	15	.318	29	29	0	0	0	183	198	26	48	104	12.5	4.48	90	.278	.332	9	.155	-0	-9	-9	-1	-1.1
NY-A	0	2	.000	3	3	0	0	0	19²	18	2	7	12	11.4	3.20	130	.222	.284	0	—	0	2	2	-1	0.2
Total 21	240	236	.504	638	616	143	34	0	4188¹	4063	448	1255	2773	11.7	3.66	106	.254	.314	9	.153	-1	134	95	14	13.3

● **JESSE TANNEHILL**   Tannehill, Jesse Niles "Powder" b: 7/14/1874, Dayton, Ky. d: 9/22/56, Dayton, Ky. BB/TL, 5'8", 150 lbs. Deb: 6/17/1894 FC♦

YEAR TM/L	W	L	PCT	G	GS	CG	SH	SV	IP	H	HR	BB	SO	RAT	ERA	ERA+	OAV	OOB	BH	AVG	PB	PR	/A	PD	TPI
1894 Cin-N	1	1	.500	5	2	1	0	1	29	37	1	16	7	16.8	7.14	78	.306	.391	0	.000	-2	-6	-5	-1	-0.5
1897 Pit-N	9	9	.500	21	16	11	1	1	142	172	1	24	40	12.9	4.25	98	.297	.333	49	.266	3	1	-1	3	0.3
1898 Pit-N	25	13	.658	43	38	34	5	2	326²	338	2	63	93	11.4	2.95	121	.265	.306	44	.289	7	24	22	3	3.5
1899 Pit-N	24	14	.632	40	35	32	3	1	313	354	4	51	61	12.0	2.73	140	.285	.320	34	.258	5	39	38	4	4.8
1900 Pit-N	20	6	.769	29	27	23	2	0	234	247	3	43	50	11.8	2.88	126	.271	.316	37	.336	8	21	19	1	2.7
1901 Pit-N	18	10	.643	32	30	25	4	1	252¹	240	1	36	118	10.2	**2.18**	150	.249	.283	33	.244	5	32	31	-3	3.2
1902 Pit-N	20	6	.769	26	24	23	2	0	231	203	0	25	100	9.3	1.95	140	.236	.266	43	.291	7	21	20	-0	3.1
1903 NY-A	15	15	.500	32	31	22	2	0	239²	258	3	34	106	11.3	3.27	96	.274	.307	26	.234	5	-8	-4	-2	0.3
1904 Bos-A	21	11	.656	33	31	30	6	0	281²	256	5	33	116	9.6	2.04	131	.243	.275	24	.197	5	17	20	3	3.0
1905 Bos-A	22	9	.710	37	32	27	6	0	271²	238	7	59	113	10.3	2.48	109	.237	.288	21	.226	6	4	3	1	1.6
1906 Bos-A	13	11	.542	27	26	18	2	0	196¹	207	9	39	82	11.7	3.16	87	.274	.318	22	.278	4	-10	-9	-0	-0.4
1907 Bos-A	6	7	.462	18	16	10	2	0	131	131	3	20	29	10.7	2.47	104	.263	.298	10	.196	1	1	1	0	0.3
1908 Bos-A	0	0	—	5	4	0	1	0	20	18	0	3	4	9.5	3.60	68	.200	.304	1	.500	-0	-1	0	0	0.1
Was-A	2	4	.333	10	9	5	0	0	71²	77	0	23	14	13.3	3.77	61	.278	.346	11	.256	1	-11	-12	-1	-0.6
Yr	2	4	.333	11	10	5	1	0	76²	81	0	26	14	13.3	3.76	61	.273	.343	12	.267	1	-12	-12	-1	-0.5
1909 Was-A	1	1	.500	7	6	1	0	0	21	19	1	5	8	12.0	3.43	71	.268	.325	6	.167	0	-1	-1	-0	-0.0
1911 Cin-N	0	0	—	1	0	0	0	0	4¹	7	0	3	1	18.7	6.23	53	.316	.409	0	.000	-0	-1	-1	0	0.0
Total 15	197	117	.627	358	320	263	34	7	2750¹	2787	40	477	940	11.1	2.79	115	.263	.303	361	.256	55	123	124	16	21.3

● **BRUCE TANNER**   Tanner, Bruce Matthew b: 12/9/61, New Castle, Pa. BL/TR, 6'3", 220 lbs. Deb: 6/12/85 F

YEAR TM/L	W	L	PCT	G	GS	CG	SH	SV	IP	H	HR	BB	SO	RAT	ERA	ERA+	OAV	OOB	BH	AVG	PB	PR	/A	PD	TPI
1985 Chi-A	1	2	.333	10	4	0	0	0	27	34	1	13	9	16.3	5.33	81	.309	.392	0	—	0	-4	-3	1	-0.4

YEAR	TM/L	W	L	PCT	G	GS	CG	SH	SV	IP	H	HR	BB	SO	RAT	ERA	ERA+	OAV	OOB	BH	AVG	PB	PR	/A	PD	TPI
● **KEVIN TAPANI**	Tapani, Kevin Ray b: 2/18/64, Des Moines, Iowa BR/TR, 6', 180 lbs. Deb: 7/4/89																									
1989	NY-N	0	0	—	3	0	0	0	0	7¹	5	1	4	2	11.0	3.68	89	.192	.300	0	.000	-0	-0	-0	0	0.0
	Min-A	2	2	.500	5	5	0	0	0	32²	34	2	8	21	11.6	3.86	107	.266	.309	0	—	0	0	1	-0	-0.2
1990	Min-A	12	8	.600	28	28	1	1	0	159¹	164	12	29	101	11.0	4.07	102	.264	.299	0	—	0	-3	2	0	-0.1
1991	*Min-A	16	9	.640	34	34	4	1	0	244	225	23	40	135	9.8	2.99	143	.245	.278	0	—	0	30	35	-0	3.3
1992	Min-A	16	11	.593	34	34	4	1	0	220	226	17	48	138	11.4	3.97	102	.269	.313	0	—	0	-3	2	-0	0.1
1993	Min-A	12	15	.444	36	35	3	1	0	225²	243	21	57	150	12.2	4.43	98	.272	.320	0	—	0	-3	-2	1	-0.1
1994	Min-A	11	7	.611	24	24	4	1	0	156	181	13	39	91	12.9	4.62	105	.291	.337	0	—	0	3	4	1	0.6
1995	Min-A	6	11	.353	20	20	1	0	0	133²	155	21	34	88	13.0	4.92	97	.290	.337	0	—	0	-3	-2	-1	-0.3
	*LA-N	4	2	.667	13	11	0	0	0	57	72	8	14	43	13.7	5.05	75	.306	.348	3	.176	0	-6	-8	0	-0.7
1996	Chi-A	13	10	.565	34	34	1	0	0	225¹	236	34	76	150	12.6	4.59	102	.268	.328	0	—	0	10	3	-1	0.3
Total	8	92	75	.551	231	225	20	6	0	1461	1541	152	349	919	11.8	4.18	105	.271	.316	3	.158	0	28	36	1	3.0
● **RANDY TATE**	Tate, Randall Lee b: 10/23/52, Florence, Ala. BR/TR, 6'3", 190 lbs. Deb: 4/14/75																									
1975	NY-N	5	13	.278	26	23	2	0	0	137²	121	8	86	99	13.9	4.45	78	.240	.356	0	.000	-4	-13	-15	0	-2.3
● **STU TATE**	Tate, Stuart Douglas b: 6/17/62, Huntsville, Ala. BR/TR, 6'3", 205 lbs. Deb: 9/20/89																									
1989	SF-N	0	0	—	2	0	0	0	0	2²	3	0	0	4	10.1	3.38	100	.250	.250	0	—	0	-0	-0	-0	0.0
● **AL TATE**	Tate, Walter Alvin b: 7/1/18, Coleman, Okla. d: 5/8/93, Bountiful, Utah BR/TR, 6', 180 lbs. Deb: 9/27/46																									
1946	Pit-N	0	1	.000	2	1	1	0	0	9	8	0	7	2	15.0	5.00	70	.267	.405	1	.333	0	-2	-1	0	-0.1
● **KEN TATUM**	Tatum, Kenneth Ray b: 4/25/44, Alexandria, La. BR/TR, 6'2", 205 lbs. Deb: 5/28/69																									
1969	Cal-A	7	2	.778	45	0	0	0	22	86¹	51	1	39	65	9.8	1.36	257	.172	.277	6	.286	4	**22**	20	-0	3.8
1970	Cal-A	7	4	.636	62	0	0	0	17	88²	68	12	26	50	10.0	2.94	123	.208	.277	2	.182	1	8	7	0	1.1
1971	Bos-A	2	4	.333	36	1	0	0	9	53²	50	3	25	21	13.9	4.19	88	.255	.362	3	.300	2	-4	-3	0	-0.2
1972	Bos-A	0	2	.000	22	0	0	0	4	29¹	32	3	15	15	15.0	3.07	105	.283	.377	0	.000	0	-0	-0	-0	0.0
1973	Bos-A	0	0	—	1	0	0	0	0	4	6	2	3	0	20.3	9.00	45	.462	.563	0	—	0	-2	-2	-0	0.0
1974	Chi-A	0	0	—	10	1	0	0	0	20²	23	3	9	5	13.9	4.79	78	.274	.344	0	.000	0	-3	-2	1	0.0
Total	6	16	12	.571	176	2	0	0	52	282²	230	24	117	156	11.7	2.93	122	.224	.314	11	.244	7	20	20	0	4.7
● **WALT TAUSCHER**	Tauscher, Walter Edward b: 11/22/01, LaSalle, Ill. d: 11/27/92, Winter Park, Fla. BR/TR, 6'1", 186 lbs. Deb: 4/19/28																									
1928	Pit-N	0	0	—	17	0	0	0	1	29¹	28	0	12	7	13.2	4.91	83	.280	.374	1	.167	-0	-3	-3	0	-0.1
1931	Was-A	1	0	1.000	6	0	0	0	0	12	24	2	4	5	21.0	7.50	57	.429	.467	0	—	-0	-4	-4	2	-0.2
Total	2	1	0	1.000	23	0	0	0	1	41¹	52	2	16	12	15.5	5.66	73	.333	.406	1	.167	-0	-7	-7	1	-0.3
● **JULIAN TAVAREZ**	Tavarez, Julian (Carmen) b: 5/22/73, Santiago, D.R. BR/TR, 6'2", 165 lbs. Deb: 8/7/93																									
1993	Cle-A	2	2	.500	8	7	0	0	0	37	53	7	13	19	16.5	6.57	66	.340	.398	0	—	0	-9	-9	-0	-0.8
1994	Cle-A	0	1	.000	1	1	0	0	0	1²	6	1	1	0	37.8	21.60	22	.500	.538	0	—	0	-3	-3	-0	-1.0
1995	*Cle-A	10	2	.833	57	0	0	0	0	85	76	7	21	68	10.6	2.44	193	.235	.287	0	—	0	22	21	0	2.6
1996	*Cle-A	4	7	.364	51	4	0	0	0	80²	101	9	22	46	13.8	5.36	91	.315	.360	0	—	0	-3	-4	-1	-0.5
Total	4	16	12	.571	117	12	0	0	0	204¹	236	24	57	133	13.2	4.49	105	.290	.341	0	—	0	6	5	-1	0.3
● **ARLAS TAYLOR**	Taylor, Arlas Walter "Lefty" or "Foxy" b: 3/16/1896, Warrick County, Ind. d: 9/10/58, Dade City, Fla. BR/TL, 5'11", Deb: 9/15/21																									
1921	Phi-A	0	1	.000	1	1	0	0	0	2	7	1	2	1	40.5	22.50	20	.636	.692	0	—	0	-4	-4	0	-1.0
● **BEN TAYLOR**	Taylor, Benjamin Harrison b: 4/2/1889, Paoli, Ind. d: 11/3/46, Martin County, Ind. BR/TR, 5'11", 163 lbs. Deb: 6/28/12																									
1912	Cin-N	0	0	—	2	0	0	0	0	5²	9	0	3	2	20.6	3.18	106	.360	.448	0	.000	0	0	0	-0	0.0
● **BRUCE TAYLOR**	Taylor, Bruce Bell b: 4/16/53, Holden, Mass. BR/TR, 6', 178 lbs. Deb: 8/5/77																									
1977	Det-A	1	0	1.000	19	0	0	0	0	29¹	23	2	10	19	10.4	3.38	127	.219	.293	0	—	0	2	3	0	0.0
1978	Det-A	0	0	—	1	0	0	0	0	1	0	0	0	0	0.0	0.00	—	.000	.000	0	—	0	0	0	0	0.0
1979	Det-A	1	2	.333	10	0	0	0	0	18²	16	1	7	8	12.1	4.82	90	.242	.333	0	—	0	-1	-1	-0	-0.3
Total	3	2	2	.500	30	0	0	0	2	49	39	3	17	27	10.8	3.86	111	.224	.304	0	—	0	1	2	0	-0.3
● **CHUCK TAYLOR**	Taylor, Charles Gilbert b: 4/18/42, Murfreesboro, Tenn. BR/TR, 6'2", 195 lbs. Deb: 5/27/69																									
1969	StL-N	7	5	.583	27	13	5	1	0	126²	108	8	30	62	10.0	2.56	140	.235	.287	7	.179	1	15	14	-2	1.2
1970	StL-N	6	7	.462	56	7	1	1	8	124¹	116	5	31	64	10.8	3.11	132	.256	.306	3	.115	-1	13	14	1	1.5
1971	StL-N	3	1	.750	43	1	0	0	3	71¹	72	7	25	46	12.4	3.53	102	.267	.331	2	.167	0	-1	1	0	0.1
1972	NY-N	0	0	—	20	0	0	0	2	31	44	2	9	9	15.7	5.52	61	.341	.388	0	.000	-0	-7	-7	1	0.0
	Mil-A	0	0	—	5	0	0	0	1	11²	8	0	3	5	9.3	1.54	196	.200	.273	1	.500	0	2	2	0	0.1
1973	Mon-N	2	0	1.000	8	0	0	0	0	20¹	17	3	2	10	8.4	1.77	215	.230	.250	0	—	-0	4	5	1	0.5
1974	Mon-N	6	2	.750	61	0	0	0	11	107²	101	8	25	43	10.8	2.17	177	.256	.305	3	.300	-0	17	20	-0	2.0
1975	Mon-N	2	2	.500	54	0	0	0	6	74	72	6	24	29	11.8	3.53	108	.264	.326	0	.000	-0	1	2	0	0.1
1976	Mon-N	2	3	.400	31	0	0	0	0	40	38	4	13	14	11.5	4.50	83	.273	.336	0	.000	-0	-4	-3	-0	-0.5
Total	8	28	20	.583	305	21	6	2	31	607	576	43	162	282	11.1	3.07	123	.258	.312	16	.158	0	40	47	1	5.0
● **DORN TAYLOR**	Taylor, Donald Clyde b: 8/11/58, Abington, Pa. BR/TR, 6'2", 180 lbs. Deb: 4/30/87																									
1987	Pit-N	2	3	.400	14	8	0	0	0	53¹	48	10	28	37	13.0	5.74	72	.247	.345	3	.167	-0	-10	-10	-1	-0.8
1989	Pit-N	1	1	.500	9	0	0	0	1	10²	14	0	5	3	16.0	5.06	66	.333	.404	0	.000	-0	-2	-2	-0	-0.4
1990	Bal-A	0	1	.000	4	0	0	0	0	3²	4	0	2	4	14.7	2.45	155	.250	.333	0	—	0	1	1	-0	0.3
Total	3	3	5	.375	27	8	0	0	1	67²	66	10	35	44	13.6	5.45	73	.262	.354	3	.158	-0	-11	-11	-1	-0.9
● **ED TAYLOR**	Taylor, Edgar Ruben "Rube" b: 3/23/1877, Palestine, Tex. d: 1/31/12, Dallas, Tex. TL, Deb: 8/8/03																									
1903	StL-N	0	0	—	1	0	0	0	0	1	0	0	0	0	0.0	0.00	—	.000	.000	0	—	0	1	1	0	0.0
● **GARY TAYLOR**	Taylor, Gary William b: 10/19/45, Detroit, Mich. BR/TR, 6'2", 190 lbs. Deb: 9/2/69																									
1969	Det-A	0	1	.000	7	0	0	0	0	10¹	10	2	6	3	13.9	5.23	71	.244	.340	0	—	-0	-2	-2	0	-0.2
● **HARRY TAYLOR**	Taylor, Harry Evans b: 12/2/35, San Angelo, Tex. BR/TR, 6', 185 lbs. Deb: 9/17/57																									
1957	KC-A	0	0	—	2	0	0	0	0	8²	11	0	4	4	16.6	3.12	127	.314	.400	1	.250	0	1	1	-0	0.0
● **HARRY TAYLOR**	Taylor, James Harry b: 5/20/19, E.Glenn, Ind. BR/TR, 6'1", 175 lbs. Deb: 9/22/46																									
1946	Bro-N	0	0	—	4	0	0	0	1	4²	5	0	1	6	11.6	3.86	88	.313	.353	0	—	0	-0	-0	0	0.0
1947	*Bro-N	10	5	.667	33	20	10	2	1	162	130	10	83	58	12.1	3.11	133	**.225**	.327	8	.129	-2	17	18	1	1.5
1948	Bro-N	2	7	.222	17	13	2	0	0	80²	90	8	61	32	17.2	5.36	75	.288	.408	6	.273	1	-13	-12	2	-0.9
1950	Bos-A	2	0	1.000	3	2	1	0	0	19	13	0	8	8	9.9	1.42	345	.197	.284	2	.286	0	7	7	0	0.8
1951	Bos-A	4	9	.308	31	8	1	0	2	81¹	100	6	42	22	15.8	5.75	78	.307	.388	3	.103	-3	-15	-12	1	-1.8
1952	Bos-A	1	0	1.000	2	1	0	0	0	10	6	1	6	1	11.7	1.80	219	.176	.317	1	.250	0	2	2	0	0.2
Total	6	19	21	.475	90	44	16	3	4	357²	344	25	201	127	14.0	4.10	102	.258	.359	20	.161	-3	-2	4	4	-0.2
● **JACK TAYLOR**	Taylor, John Budd "Brewery Jack" b: 5/23/1873, Staten Island, N.Y. d: 2/7/1900, Staten Island, N.Y. BR/TR, 6'1", 190 lbs. Deb: 9/16/1891																									
1891	NY-N	0	1	.000	1	1	0	0	0	8	4	1	3	3	7.9	1.13	285	.143	.226	0	.000	0	2	2	-0	0.2
1892	Phi-N	1	0	1.000	3	3	2	0	0	26	28	2	10	7	13.2	1.38	234	.264	.328	2	.167	-0	5	5	-1	0.0
1893	Phi-N	10	9	.526	25	16	14	0	0	170	187	8	77	41	14.5	4.24	108	.271	.353	20	.215	-2	8	6	2	0.5
1894	Phi-N	23	13	.639	41	34	31	0	0	298	347	13	96	76	13.9	4.08	125	.288	.349	48	.333	9	41	34	2	3.7
1895	Phi-N	26	14	.650	41	37	33	1	1	335	403	7	83	93	13.5	4.49	107	.293	.340	45	.290	7	11	11	4	1.9
1896	Phi-N	20	21	.488	45	41	35	1	0	359	459	17	112	97	14.8	4.79	90	.308	.365	29	.185	-6	-17	-19	4	-1.9
1897	Phi-N	16	20	.444	40	37	35	2	2	317¹	376	5	76	88	13.6	4.23	99	.292	.345	35	.252	2	3	-1	3	0.3
1898	StL-N	15	29	.341	50	47	42	0	1	397	465	14	83	99	13.0	3.90	97	.290	.335	38	.242	13	-13	-5	8	0.7
1899	Cin-N	9	10	.474	24	18	15	2	1	168¹	197	7	41	34	13.3	4.12	95	.291	.341	17	.250	-0	-5	-4	-1	-0.5
Total	9	120	117	.506	270	234	208	7	9	2079	2466	74	581	528	13.7	4.23	103	.291	.346	234	.252	11	36	34	21	4.9

YEAR TM/L	W	L	PCT	G	GS	CG	SH	SV	IP	H	HR	BB	SO	RAT	ERA	ERA+	OAV	OOB	BH	AVG	PB	PR	/A	PD	TPI

● JACK TAYLOR
Taylor, John W. b: 1/14/1874, New Straitsville, Ohio d: 3/4/38, Columbus, Ohio BR/TR, 5'10", 170 lbs. Deb: 9/25/1898

YEAR TM/L	W	L	PCT	G	GS	CG	SH	SV	IP	H	HR	BB	SO	RAT	ERA	ERA+	OAV	OOB	BH	AVG	PB	PR	/A	PD	TPI
1898 Chi-N	5	0	1.000	5	5	5	0	0	41	32	0	10	11	9.4	2.20	163	.213	.267	3	.200		6	6	-0	0.8
1899 Chi-N	18	21	.462	41	39	39	1	0	354²	380	6	84	67	12.3	3.76	100	.274	.325	37	.266	10	4	-0	1	1.0
1900 Chi-N	10	17	.370	28	26	26	2	1	222¹	226	4	58	57	11.8	2.55	141	.263	.316	19	.235	2	28	26	-3	2.7
1901 Chi-N	13	19	.406	33	31	30	0	1	275²	341	5	44	68	12.8	3.36	96	.302	.332	23	.217	2	-1	-4	2	0.0
1902 Chi-N	23	11	.676	36	33	33	7	1	324²	271	2	43	83	9.0	1.33	203	.227	.260	44	.237	3	52	49	4	6.3
1903 Chi-N	21	14	.600	37	33	33	1	1	312¹	277	2	57	83	9.8	2.45	128	.235	.273	28	.222	4	28	24	1	2.9
1904 StL-N	20	19	.513	41	39	39	2	1	352	297	6	82	103	10.0	2.22	121	.220	.271	28	.211	4	20	19	1	2.6
1905 StL-N	15	21	.417	37	34	34	3	1	309	302	10	85	102	11.6	3.44	87	.259	.315	23	.190	4	-15	-16	-2	-1.5
1906 StL-N	8	9	.471	17	17	17	1	0	155	133	3	47	27	10.9	2.15	122	.227	.292	11	.208	3	8	8	1	1.4
Chi-N	12	3	.800	17	16	15	2	0	147¹	116	1	39	34	9.8	1.83	144	.223	.285	11	.208	2	13	13	-0	1.5
Yr	20	12	.625	34	33	32	3	0	302¹	249	4	86	61	10.2	1.99	132	.224	.283	22	.208	5	21	21	0	2.9
1907 Chi-N	7	5	.583	18	13	8	0	0	123	127	3	33	22	11.8	3.29	76	.268	.318	9	.191	0	-11	-11	1	-1.0
Total 10	152	139	.522	310	286	278	19	5	2617	2502	41	582	657	10.9	2.66	115	.250	.298	236	.223	35	134	116	5	16.7

● KERRY TAYLOR
Taylor, Kerry Thomas b: 1/25/71, Bemidji, Minn. BR/TR, 6'3", 200 lbs. Deb: 4/13/93

YEAR TM/L	W	L	PCT	G	GS	CG	SH	SV	IP	H	HR	BB	SO	RAT	ERA	ERA+	OAV	OOB	BH	AVG	PB	PR	/A	PD	TPI
1993 SD-N	0	5	.000	36	7	0	0	0	68¹	72	5	49	45	16.5	6.45	64	.277	.399	0	.000	-1	-18	-18	-1	-1.3
1994 SD-N	0	0	—	1	1	0	0	0	4¹	9	1	1	3	22.8	8.31	49	.409	.458	0	.000	-0	-2	-2	-0	0.0
Total 2	0	5	.000	37	8	0	0	0	72²	81	6	50	48	16.6	6.56	63	.287	.404	0	.000	-2	-20	-20	-1	-1.3

● DUMMY TAYLOR
Taylor, Luther Haden b: 2/21/1875, Oskaloosa, Kan. d: 8/22/58, Jacksonville, Ill. BR/TR, 6'1", 160 lbs. Deb: 8/27/00

YEAR TM/L	W	L	PCT	G	GS	CG	SH	SV	IP	H	HR	BB	SO	RAT	ERA	ERA+	OAV	OOB	BH	AVG	PB	PR	/A	PD	TPI
1900 NY-N	4	3	.571	11	7	6	0	0	62¹	74	0	24	16	14.9	2.45	147	.294	.367	3	.136	-1	9	8	-2	0.5
1901 NY-N	18	27	.400	45	43	37	4	0	353¹	377	8	112	136	12.9	3.18	104	.271	.333	18	.132	-8	5	5	1	-0.2
1902 Cle-A	1	3	.250	4	4	4	1	0	34	37	0	8	12	12.4	1.59	217	.278	.329	1	.100	-0	8	7	1	0.9
NY-N	7	15	.318	26	25	18	0	0	200²	194	4	55	87	11.8	2.29	123	.254	.317	6	.092	-5	11	12	-1	0.6
1903 NY-N	13	13	.500	33	31	18	1	0	244²	306	6	89	94	14.7	4.23	79	.314	.374	12	.146	-2	-26	-24	-1	-2.4
1904 NY-N	21	15	.583	37	36	29	5	0	296¹	231	6	75	138	9.6	2.34	117	.214	.270	16	.157	-1	13	13	3	1.6
1905 NY-N	16	9	.640	32	28	18	4	0	213¹	200	5	51	91	10.0	2.66	110	.247	.298	9	.130	-1	8	6	1	0.6
1906 NY-N	17	9	.654	31	27	13	2	0	213	186	4	57	91	10.5	2.20	119	.233	.289	14	.184	0	10	10	-1	1.1
1907 NY-N	11	7	.611	28	21	11	3	1	171	145	1	46	56	10.2	2.42	102	.232	.288	6	.125	-1	1	1	-0	-0.1
1908 NY-N	8	5	.615	27	15	6	1	2	127²	127	5	34	50	11.6	2.33	104	.253	.306	8	.229	2	1	1	-0	0.3
Total 9	116	106	.523	274	237	160	21	3	1916¹	1877	39	551	767	11.7	2.75	107	.256	.314	93	.144	-17	40	39	0	2.9

● WILEY TAYLOR
Taylor, Philip Wiley b: 3/18/1888, Wamego, Kan. d: 7/8/54, Westmoreland, Kan. BR/TR, 6'1", 175 lbs. Deb: 9/6/11

YEAR TM/L	W	L	PCT	G	GS	CG	SH	SV	IP	H	HR	BB	SO	RAT	ERA	ERA+	OAV	OOB	BH	AVG	PB	PR	/A	PD	TPI
1911 Det-A	0	2	.000	3	2	1	0	0	19	18	0	10	9	13.7	3.79	91	.247	.345	0	.000	-1	-1	-1	-1	-0.2
1912 Chi-A	0	1	.000	3	3	0	0	0	20	21	0	14	4	15.7	4.95	65	.309	.427	0	.000	-1	-4	-4	-0	-0.2
1913 StL-A	0	2	.000	5	4	1	0	0	31²	33	0	16	12	13.9	4.83	61	.280	.366	0	.000	-1	-7	-7	-0	-0.5
1914 StL-A	2	5	.286	16	8	2	1	0	50	41	0	25	20	12.2	3.42	79	.209	.305	2	.167	-0	-4	-4	-0	-0.6
Total 4	2	10	.167	27	17	4	1	0	120²	113	0	65	45	13.5	4.10	72	.248	.346	2	.061	-3	-15	-15	-0	-1.5

● SCOTT TAYLOR
Taylor, Rodney Scott b: 8/2/67, Defiance, Ohio BL/TL, 6'1", 185 lbs. Deb: 9/17/92

YEAR TM/L	W	L	PCT	G	GS	CG	SH	SV	IP	H	HR	BB	SO	RAT	ERA	ERA+	OAV	OOB	BH	AVG	PB	PR	/A	PD	TPI
1992 Bos-A	1	1	.500	4	1	0	0	0	14²	13	4	4	7	10.4	4.91	86	.245	.298	0	—	0	-2	-1	-0	-0.1
1993 Bos-A	0	1	.000	16	0	0	0	0	11	14	1	12	8	22.1	8.18	56	.311	.466	0	—	0	-5	-4	-0	-0.8
Total 2	1	2	.333	20	1	0	0	0	25²	27	5	16	15	15.4	6.31	69	.276	.383	0	—	0	-6	-5	-0	-0.9

● RON TAYLOR
Taylor, Ronald Wesley b: 12/13/37, Toronto, Ont., Can. BR/TR, 6'1", 195 lbs. Deb: 4/11/62

YEAR TM/L	W	L	PCT	G	GS	CG	SH	SV	IP	H	HR	BB	SO	RAT	ERA	ERA+	OAV	OOB	BH	AVG	PB	PR	/A	PD	TPI
1962 Cle-A	2	2	.500	8	4	1	0	0	33¹	36	6	13	15	13.5	5.94	65	.281	.352	3	.273	-0	-7	-8	-0	-0.8
1963 StL-N	9	7	.563	54	9	2	0	11	133¹	119	10	30	91	10.3	2.84	125	.243	.293	1	.031	-3	7	11	-3	0.9
1964 *StL-N	8	4	.667	63	2	0	0	7	101¹	109	15	33	69	12.7	4.62	82	.274	.331	2	.133	-0	-12	-9	2	-1.0
1965 StL-N	2	1	.667	25	0	0	0	4	43²	43	6	15	26	12.2	4.53	85	.261	.326	2	.400	1	-5	-3	-0	-0.2
Hou-N	1	5	.167	32	1	0	0	4	57²	68	5	16	37	13.9	6.40	52	.305	.365	0	.000	-1	-18	-19	-1	-2.4
Yr	3	6	.333	57	1	0	0	5	101¹	111	11	31	63	13.1	5.60	64	.283	.343	2	.111	-1	-23	-23	-1	-2.6
1966 Hou-N	2	3	.400	36	1	0	0	4	64²	89	5	10	29	14.5	5.71	60	.333	.369	2	.167	-0	-15	-16	-1	-1.3
1967 NY-N	4	6	.400	50	0	0	0	8	73	60	5	23	46	10.4	2.34	145	.230	.295	0	.000	-1	8	8	0	1.3
1968 NY-N	1	5	.167	58	0	0	0	13	76²	64	4	18	49	9.7	2.70	112	.228	.277	0	.000	-1	3	3	1	0.3
1969 *NY-N	9	4	.692	59	0	0	0	13	76	61	7	24	42	10.2	2.72	134	.228	.294	1	.250	-1	7	8	0	1.7
1970 NY-N	5	4	.556	57	0	0	0	13	66¹	65	5	16	28	11.0	3.93	102	.265	.310	0	.000	-0	1	1	0	0.1
1971 NY-N	2	2	.500	45	0	0	0	6	69	71	7	11	32	10.8	3.65	93	.269	.301	1	.250	-1	-1	-2	-0	-0.1
1972 SD-N	0	0	—	4	0	0	0	0	5	9	5	0	1	16.2	12.60	26	.375	.375	0	—	0	-5	-5	0	0.0
Total 11	45	43	.511	491	17	3	0	72	800	794	76	209	464	11.5	3.93	91	.264	.316	12	.103	-5	-39	-32	-2	-1.5

● SCOTT TAYLOR
Taylor, Scott Michael b: 10/3/66, Topeka, Kan. BR/TR, 6'3", 200 lbs. Deb: 7/28/95

YEAR TM/L	W	L	PCT	G	GS	CG	SH	SV	IP	H	HR	BB	SO	RAT	ERA	ERA+	OAV	OOB	BH	AVG	PB	PR	/A	PD	TPI
1995 Tex-A	1	2	.333	3	3	0	0	0	15¹	25	6	5	10	17.6	9.39	51	.379	.423	0	—	0	-8	-8	0	-1.1

● TERRY TAYLOR
Taylor, Terry Derrell b: 7/28/64, Crestview, Fla. BR/TR, 6'1", 180 lbs. Deb: 8/19/88

YEAR TM/L	W	L	PCT	G	GS	CG	SH	SV	IP	H	HR	BB	SO	RAT	ERA	ERA+	OAV	OOB	BH	AVG	PB	PR	/A	PD	TPI
1988 Sea-A	0	1	.000	5	5	0	0	0	23	26	2	11	9	14.5	6.26	66	.295	.374	0	—	0	-6	-5	-1	-0.6

● PETE TAYLOR
Taylor, Vernon Charles b: 11/26/27, Severn, Md. BR/TR, 6'1", 170 lbs. Deb: 5/2/52

YEAR TM/L	W	L	PCT	G	GS	CG	SH	SV	IP	H	HR	BB	SO	RAT	ERA	ERA+	OAV	OOB	BH	AVG	PB	PR	/A	PD	TPI
1952 StL-A	0	0	—	1	0	0	0	0	2	4	0	3	0	31.5	13.50	29	.500	.636	0	—	0	-2	-2	0	0.0

● WADE TAYLOR
Taylor, Wade Eric b: 10/19/65, Mobile, Ala. BR/TR, 6'1", 185 lbs. Deb: 6/2/91

YEAR TM/L	W	L	PCT	G	GS	CG	SH	SV	IP	H	HR	BB	SO	RAT	ERA	ERA+	OAV	OOB	BH	AVG	PB	PR	/A	PD	TPI
1991 NY-A	7	12	.368	23	22	0	0	0	116¹	144	13	53	72	15.8	6.27	66	.314	.393	0	—	0	-28	-27	1	-3.6

● BILLY TAYLOR
Taylor, William Henry "Bollicky Bill" b: 1855, Washington, D.C. d: 5/14/1900, Jacksonville, Fla. BR/TR, 5'11.5", 204 lbs. Deb: 5/21/1881 ♦

YEAR TM/L	W	L	PCT	G	GS	CG	SH	SV	IP	H	HR	BB	SO	RAT	ERA	ERA+	OAV	OOB	BH	AVG	PB	PR	/A	PD	TPI
1881 Wor-N	0	1	.000	1	1	1	0	0	8	15	0	6	0	23.6	7.88	38	.366	.447	3	.107	-0	-5	-4	-0	-0.4
Cle-N	0	0	—	1	0	0	0	0	3	0	0	1	2	3.0	0.00	—	.000	.100	25	.243	-0	1	1	-0	0.0
Yr	0	1	.000	2	1	1	0	0	11	15	0	7	2	18.0	5.73	51	.300	.386	28	.214	-0	-4	-3	-0	-0.4
1882 Pit-a	0	1	.000	1	1	0	0	0	5	11	0	4	1	27.0	16.20	16	.407	.484	84	.281	0	-8	-8	-0	-0.8
1883 Pit-a	4	7	.364	19	19	8	0	0	127	166	4	34	41	14.2	5.39	60	.296	.337	96	.260	3	-29	-31	-2	-1.9
1884 StL-U	25	4	.862	33	29	29	2	4	263	222	6	40	154	9.0	1.68	143	.213	.243	68	.366	13	22	21	-1	2.8
Phi-a	18	12	.600	30	30	30	1	0	260	232	3	44	130	10.0	2.53	134	.219	.258	28	.252	3	21	25	2	2.9
1885 Phi-a	1	5	.167	6	6	6	0	0	52¹	68	0	9	11	13.4	3.27	105	.343	.375	4	.190	-1	-0	1	-1	-0.1
1886 Bal-a	1	6	.143	8	8	8	0	0	72¹	87	1	20	37	13.6	5.72	60	.284	.332	12	.308	1	-18	-18	-0	-1.2
1887 Phi-a	1	0	1.000	1	1	1	0	0	9	10	1	7	0	17.0	3.00	143	.286	.405	1	.250	-0	1	1	-0	0.1
Total 7	50	36	.581	100	84	83	3	4	799²	811	11	165	376	11.2	3.17	96	.248	.287	323	.277	20	-14	-13	-4	1.4

● BILLY TAYLOR
Taylor, William Howell b: 10/16/61, Monticello, Fla. BR/TR, 6'8", 200 lbs. Deb: 4/5/94

YEAR TM/L	W	L	PCT	G	GS	CG	SH	SV	IP	H	HR	BB	SO	RAT	ERA	ERA+	OAV	OOB	BH	AVG	PB	PR	/A	PD	TPI
1994 Oak-A	1	3	.250	41	0	0	0	1	46¹	38	4	18	48	11.3	3.50	127	.220	.301	0	—	0	7	5	-0	0.8
1996 Oak-A	6	3	.667	55	0	0	0	17	60¹	52	5	25	67	12.1	4.33	111	.231	.319	0	—	0	4	3	1	0.6
Total 2	7	6	.538	96	0	0	0	18	106²	90	9	43	115	11.7	3.97	117	.226	.311	0	—	0	11	8	0	1.4

● BUD TEACHOUT
Teachout, Arthur John b: 2/27/04, Los Angeles, Cal. d: 5/11/85, Laguna Beach, Cal BR/TL, 6'2", 183 lbs. Deb: 5/12/30

YEAR TM/L	W	L	PCT	G	GS	CG	SH	SV	IP	H	HR	BB	SO	RAT	ERA	ERA+	OAV	OOB	BH	AVG	PB	PR	/A	PD	TPI
1930 Chi-N	11	4	.733	40	16	6	0	0	153	178	16	48	59	13.3	4.06	120	.296	.348	17	.270	3	16	14	1	1.3
1931 Chi-N	1	2	.333	27	3	1	0	0	61¹	79	6	28	14	15.8	5.72	67	.305	.375	5	.238	-0	-13	-13	1	-0.4
1932 StL-N	0	0	—	1	0	0	0	0	1	2	0	0	0	18.0	0.00	—	.400	.400	0	—	0	0	0	-0	0.0
Total 3	12	6	.667	68	19	7	0	0	215¹	259	22	76	73	14.0	4.51	102	.299	.356	22	.262	3	2	0	0.9

● GEORGE TEBEAU
Tebeau, George E. "White Wings" b: 12/26/1861, St.Louis, Mo. d: 2/4/23, Denver, Colo. BR/TR, 5'9", 175 lbs. Deb: 4/16/1887 F♦

YEAR TM/L	W	L	PCT	G	GS	CG	SH	SV	IP	H	HR	BB	SO	RAT	ERA	ERA+	OAV	OOB	BH	AVG	PB	PR	/A	PD	TPI
1887 Cin-a	0	0	—	1	1	1	0	1	8	21	0	3	1	28.1	13.50	32	.447	.532	94	.296	-0	-8	-8	-0	-0.5
1890 Tol-a	0	1	.000	1	0	0	0	0	5	9	0	5	0	25.2	9.00	44	.375	.483	102	.268	1	-3	-3	-0	0.0
Total 2	0	1	.000	2	1	1	0	0	13	30	0	8	1	27.0	11.77	36	.448	.513	622	.269	1	-11	-11	0	-0.5

YEAR	TM/L	W	L	PCT	G	GS	CG	SH	SV	IP	H	HR	BB	SO	RAT	ERA	ERA+	OAV	OOB	BH	AVG	PB	PR	/A	PD	TPI

● PATSY TEBEAU   Tebeau, Oliver Wendell   b: 12/5/1864, St.Louis, Mo.   d: 5/15/18, St.Louis, Mo.   BR/TR, 5'8", 163 lbs.   Deb: 9/20/1887   FM♦

| 1896 | *Cle-N | 0 | 0 | — | 1 | 0 | 0 | 0 | 0 | 0 | 1 | 0 | 0 | 0 | — | 1.000 | 1.000 | 146 | .269 | 0 | | 0 | 0 | 0 | 0 | 0.0 |

● AL TEDROW   Tedrow, Allen Seymour   b: 12/14/1891, Westerville, Ohio   d: 1/23/58, Westerville, Ohio   BR/TL, 6', 180 lbs.   Deb: 9/15/14

| 1914 | Cle-A | 1 | 2 | .333 | 4 | 3 | 1 | 0 | 0 | 22¹ | 19 | 0 | 14 | 4 | 14.5 | 1.21 | 239 | .235 | .367 | 1 | .167 | 0 | 4 | 4 | -0 | 0.6 |

● KENT TEKULVE   Tekulve, Kenton Charles   b: 3/5/47, Cincinnati, Ohio   BR/TR, 6'4", 180 lbs.   Deb: 5/20/74

1974	Pit-N	1	1	.500	8	0	0	0	0	9	12	1	5	6	18.0	6.00	57	.343	.439	0	—	0	-2	-3	1	-0.5
1975	*Pit-N	1	2	.333	34	0	0	0	5	56	43	2	23	28	10.8	2.25	157	.215	.299	1	.091	-0	9	8	2	0.7
1976	Pit-N	5	3	.625	64	0	0	0	9	102²	91	3	25	68	10.2	2.45	142	.241	.288	0	.000	-1	12	12	2	1.2
1977	Pit-N	10	1	.909	72	0	0	0	7	103	89	5	33	59	10.7	3.06	130	.236	.299	3	.250	0	10	11	3	1.6
1978	Pit-N	8	7	.533	91	0	0	0	31	135	115	6	55	77	11.5	2.33	159	.228	.306	2	.095	-1	19	21	3	3.5
1979	*Pit-N	10	8	.556	94	0	0	0	31	134¹	109	5	49	75	10.7	2.75	141	.222	.296	2	.133	-0	15	17	2	3.1
1980	Pit-N☆	8	12	.400	78	0	0	0	21	93	96	6	40	47	13.3	3.39	107	.267	.342	0	.000	-1	2	3	1	0.6
1981	Pit-N	5	5	.500	45	0	0	0	3	65	61	1	17	34	10.9	2.49	144	.250	.302	0	.000	-0	7	8	1	1.4
1982	Pit-N	12	8	.600	85	0	0	0	20	128²	113	7	46	66	11.3	2.87	129	.237	.309	1	.071	-1	10	12	2	2.2
1983	Pit-N	7	5	.583	76	0	0	0	18	99	78	1	36	52	10.4	1.64	226	.223	.296	0	.000	-1	22	23	1	3.5
1984	Pit-N	3	9	.250	72	0	0	0	13	88	86	4	33	36	12.3	2.66	135	.262	.331	0	.000	-1	9	9	3	1.6
1985	Pit-N	0	0	—	3	0	0	0	0	7¹	7	1	5	4	32.4	16.20	22	.467	.600	0	—	0	-5	-5	0	0.0
	Phi-N	4	10	.286	58	0	0	0	14	72¹	67	4	25	36	11.7	2.99	123	.246	.314	0	.000	-0	5	6	0	1.3
	Yr	4	10	.286	61	0	0	0	14	75²	74	5	30	40	12.6	3.57	103	.258	.332	0	.000	-0	0	1	0	1.3
1986	Phi-N	11	5	.688	73	0	0	0	4	110	99	2	25	57	10.1	2.54	152	.240	.283	0	.000	-0	14	16	0	2.4
1987	Phi-N	6	4	.600	90	0	0	0	3	105	96	8	29	60	10.7	3.09	137	.243	.295	0	.000	-0	12	13	1	1.4
1988	Phi-N	3	7	.300	70	0	0	0	4	80	87	3	22	43	12.5	3.60	99	.276	.327	0	.000	-0	-1	-0	1	0.0
1989	Cin-N	0	3	.000	37	0	0	0	1	52	56	5	23	31	13.7	5.02	72	.272	.345	1	.500	0	-9	-8	0	-0.8
Total	16	94	90	.511	1050	0	0	0	184	1436¹	1305	63	491	779	11.4	2.85	131	.244	.309	10	.083	-6	128	141	22	23.6

● AMAURY TELEMACO   Telemaco, Amaury (Regalado)   b: 1/19/74, Higuey, D.R.   BR/TR, 6'4", 220 lbs.   Deb: 5/16/96

| 1996 | Chi-N | 5 | 7 | .417 | 25 | 17 | 0 | 0 | 0 | 97¹ | 108 | 20 | 31 | 64 | 13.1 | 5.46 | 78 | .281 | .339 | 3 | .103 | -1 | -13 | -13 | -1 | -1.6 |

● ANTHONY TELFORD   Telford, Anthony Charles   b: 3/6/66, San Jose, Cal.   BR/TR, 6', 175 lbs.   Deb: 8/19/90

1990	Bal-A	3	3	.500	8	8	0	0	0	36¹	43	4	19	20	15.6	4.95	77	.295	.380	0	—	0	-4	-5	0	-0.5
1991	Bal-A	0	0	—	9	1	0	0	0	26²	27	3	6	24	11.1	4.05	98	.265	.306	0	—	0	-0	-0	-0	-0.1
1993	Bal-A	0	0	—	3	0	0	0	0	7¹	11	3	1	6	16.0	9.82	46	.344	.382	0	—	0	-4	-4	0	-0.3
Total	3	3	3	.500	20	9	0	0	0	70¹	81	10	26	50	13.9	5.12	77	.289	.354	0	—	0	-9	-9	0	-0.8

● DAVE TELGHEDER   Telgheder, David William   b: 11/11/66, Middletown, N.Y.   BR/TR, 6'3", 212 lbs.   Deb: 6/12/93

1993	NY-N	6	2	.750	24	7	0	0	0	75²	82	10	21	35	12.7	4.76	84	.276	.332	1	.067	-0	-6	-6	-1	-0.7
1994	NY-N	0	1	.000	6	0	0	0	0	10	11	2	4	8	17.1	7.20	58	.282	.404	0	—	0	-3	-3	-1	-0.3
1995	NY-N	1	2	.333	7	4	0	0	0	25²	34	4	7	16	14.4	5.61	72	.318	.360	2	.333	1	-4	-4	1	-0.4
1996	Oak-A	4	7	.364	16	14	1	1	0	79¹	92	12	26	43	13.5	4.65	103	.292	.348	0	—	0	3	1	0	0.2
Total	4	11	12	.478	53	25	1	1	0	190²	219	28	62	98	13.5	4.96	88	.289	.347	3	.143	0	-10	-13	-0	-1.2

● TOM TELLMANN   Tellmann, Thomas John   b: 3/29/54, Warren, Pa.   BR/TR, 6'3", 195 lbs.   Deb: 6/9/79

1979	SD-N	0	0	—	1	0	0	0	0	2²	7	1	0	1	23.6	16.88	21	.467	.467	0	.000	-0	-4	-4	0	0.0
1980	SD-N	3	0	1.000	6	2	2	0	1	22¹	23	0	8	9	12.5	1.61	213	.264	.326	1	.125	-0	5	5	0	0.6
1983	Mil-A	9	4	.692	44	0	0	0	8	99²	95	7	35	48	11.9	2.80	133	.259	.327	0	—	0	14	10	3	2.1
1984	Mil-A	6	3	.667	50	0	0	0	4	81	82	6	31	28	12.7	2.78	138	.272	.342	0	—	0	11	10	1	1.1
1985	Oak-A	0	0	—	11	0	0	0	0	21¹	33	3	9	8	18.1	5.06	76	.347	.410	0	—	0	-2	-3	0	0.1
Total	5	18	7	.720	112	2	2	0	13	227	240	17	83	94	13.0	3.05	123	.277	.343	1	.111	0	24	18	4	3.9

● CHUCK TEMPLETON   Templeton, Charles Sherman   b: 6/1/32, Detroit, Mich.   BR/TL, 6'3", 210 lbs.   Deb: 9/9/55

1955	Bro-N	0	1	.000	4	0	0	0	0	4²	5	2	5	3	21.2	11.57	35	.294	.478	0	—	0	-4	-4	0	-0.7
1956	Bro-N	0	1	.000	6	2	0	0	0	16¹	20	2	10	8	16.5	6.61	60	.294	.385	0	.000	-0	-5	-5	-0	-0.3
Total	2	0	2	.000	10	2	0	0	0	21	25	4	15	11	17.6	7.71	52	.294	.406	0	.000	-0	-9	-9	-0	-1.0

● JOHN TENER   Tener, John Kinley   b: 7/25/1863, County Tyrone, Ireland   d: 5/19/46, Pittsburgh, Pa.   BR/TR, 6'4", 180 lbs.   Deb: 6/8/1885   ♦

1888	Chi-N	7	5	.583	12	12	11	1	0	102	90	6	25	39	10.9	2.74	117	.228	.288	9	.196	-0	1	3	1	0.4
1889	Chi-N	15	15	.500	35	30	28	1	0	287	302	16	105	105	13.0	3.64	114	.262	.328	41	.273	5	12	17	3	2.1
1890	Pit-P	3	11	.214	14	14	13	0	0	117	160	6	70	30	18.1	7.31	53	.312	.400	12	.190	2	-40	-44	4	-3.1
Total	3	25	31	.446	61	56	52	2	0	506	552	28	200	174	13.7	4.30	90	.268	.339	62	.236	6	-27	-23	8	-0.6

● JIM TENNANT   Tennant, James McDonnell   b: 3/3/07, Shepherdstown, W.Va   d: 4/16/67, Trumbull, Conn.   BR/TR, 6'1", 190 lbs.   Deb: 9/28/29

| 1929 | NY-N | 0 | 0 | — | 1 | 0 | 0 | 0 | 0 | 1 | 1 | 0 | 1 | 0 | 9.0 | 0.00 | — | .333 | .333 | 0 | — | 0 | 1 | 1 | 0 | 0.0 |

● FRED TENNEY   Tenney, Fred Clay   b: 7/9/1859, Marlborough, N.H.   d: 6/15/19, Fall River, Mass.   Deb: 4/28/1884   ♦

1884	Bos-U	3	1	.750	4	4	4	0	0	35	31	0	5	18	9.3	2.31	103	.221	.248	2	.118	-3	0	0	-1	-0.3
	Wil-U	0	1	.000	1	1	1	0	0	8	6	0	4	10	11.3	1.13	237	.194	.286	0	.000	-1	2	2	0	0.1
	Yr	3	2	.600	5	5	5	0	0	43	37	0	9	28	9.6	2.09	116	.216	.256	2	.100	-3	2	2	-1	-0.2

● FRED TENNEY   Tenney, Frederick   b: 11/26/1871, Georgetown, Mass.   d: 7/3/52, Boston, Mass.   BL/TL, 5'9", 155 lbs.   Deb: 6/16/1894   M♦

| 1905 | Bos-N | 0 | 0 | — | 1 | 0 | 0 | 0 | 0 | 2 | 2 | 0 | 1 | 0 | 27.0 | 4.50 | 69 | .417 | .462 | 158 | .288 | | 0 | -0 | -0 | 0.0 |

● BOB TERLECKI   Terlecki, Robert Joseph   b: 2/14/45, Trenton, N.J.   BR/TR, 5'8", 185 lbs.   Deb: 8/16/72

| 1972 | Phi-N | 0 | 0 | — | 9 | 0 | 0 | 0 | 0 | 13¹ | 16 | 2 | 10 | 5 | 17.6 | 4.73 | 76 | .308 | .419 | 0 | — | 0 | -2 | -1 | 0 | 0.0 |

● GREG TERLECKY   Terlecky, Gregory John   b: 3/20/52, Culver City, Cal.   BR/TR, 6'3", 200 lbs.   Deb: 6/12/75

| 1975 | StL-N | 0 | 1 | .000 | 20 | 0 | 0 | 0 | 0 | 30¹ | 38 | 4 | 12 | 13 | 14.8 | 4.45 | 84 | .306 | .368 | 1 | .333 | 0 | -3 | -2 | 0 | 0.0 |

● JEFF TERPKO   Terpko, Jeffrey Michael   b: 10/16/50, Sayre, Pa.   BR/TR, 6', 180 lbs.   Deb: 9/21/74

1974	Tex-A	0	0	—	3	0	0	0	0	7	6	0	4	3	12.9	1.29	277	.231	.333	0	—	0	2	2	-0	0.2
1976	Tex-A	3	3	.500	32	0	0	0	0	52²	42	3	29	24	12.1	2.39	150	.223	.327	0	—	0	7	7	-0	0.6
1977	Mon-N	0	1	.000	13	0	0	0	0	20²	28	2	15	14	18.7	5.66	67	.346	.448	0	.000	-0	-4	-4	-0	-0.2
Total	3	3	4	.429	48	0	0	0	0	80¹	76	5	48	41	13.9	3.14	116	.258	.362	0	.000	-0	4	5	-1	0.6

● WALT TERRELL   Terrell, Charles Walter   b: 5/11/58, Jeffersonville, Ind   BL/TR, 6'2", 205 lbs.   Deb: 9/8/82

1982	NY-N	0	3	.000	3	3	0	0	0	21	22	2	14	8	15.4	3.43	106	.268	.375	2	.400	1	0	0	-0	0.1
1983	NY-N	8	8	.500	21	20	4	2	0	133²	123	7	55	59	12.1	3.57	102	.251	.329	8	.182	3	1	1	-0	0.4
1984	NY-N	11	12	.478	33	33	3	1	0	215	232	16	80	114	13.2	3.52	101	.282	.348	6	.080	-4	2	0	-0	0.3
1985	Det-A	15	10	.600	34	34	5	3	0	229	221	19	95	130	12.6	3.85	106	.255	.332	0	—	0	7	6	3	0.9
1986	Det-A	15	12	.556	34	33	9	0	0	217¹	199	30	98	93	12.4	4.56	90	.245	.329	0	—	0	-9	-10	2	-1.0
1987	*Det-A	17	10	.630	35	35	10	1	0	244²	254	30	94	143	12.9	4.05	104	.268	.336	0	—	0	11	5	1	0.7
1988	Det-A	7	16	.304	29	29	11	1	0	206¹	199	20	78	84	12.2	3.97	96	.258	.328	0	—	0	-0	-4	0	0.0
1989	SD-N	5	13	.278	19	19	4	1	0	123¹	134	14	26	63	11.7	4.01	87	.277	.314	4	.100	0	-7	-7	3	-0.7
	NY-A	6	5	.545	13	13	1	0	0	83	102	9	24	30	13.9	5.20	74	.307	.358	0	—	0	-12	-12	0	-1.4
1990	Pit-N	2	7	.222	16	16	0	0	0	82²	98	13	33	34	14.7	5.88	62	.295	.366	3	.107	-1	-19	-21	1	-2.0
	Det-A	6	4	.600	13	13	2	0	0	75¹	86	7	24	30	14.1	4.54	87	.290	.359	0	—	0	-5	-5	-1	-0.7
1991	Det-A	12	14	.462	35	33	8	2	0	218²	257	16	79	80	13.9	4.24	98	.301	.361	0	—	0	-4	-2	-1	-0.5
1992	Det-A	7	10	.412	36	14	1	0	0	136²	163	14	48	61	14.1	5.20	76	.298	.358	0	—	0	-19	-19	1	-2.0
Total	11	111	124	.472	321	294	56	12	0	1986²	2090	187	748	929	13.4	4.22	93	.274	.341	23	.120	-1	-54	-68	8	-6.3

● JERRY TERRELL   Terrell, Jerry Wayne   b: 7/13/46, Waseca, Minn.   BR/TR, 6', 170 lbs.   Deb: 4/14/73   ♦

| 1979 | KC-A | 0 | 0 | — | 1 | 0 | 0 | 0 | 0 | 1 | 0 | 0 | 0 | 0 | 0.0 | 0.00 | — | .000 | .000 | 12 | .300 | 0 | 0 | 0 | 0 | 0.0 |

YEAR TM/L	W	L	PCT	G	GS	CG	SH	SV	IP	H	HR	BB	SO	RAT	ERA	ERA+	OAV	OOB	BH	AVG	PB	PR	/A	PD	TPI
1980 KC-A	0	0	—	1	0	0	0	0	1	1	0	1	0	18.0	0.00	—	.250	.400	1	.063	0	0	0	0	0.0
Total 2	0	0	—	2	0	0	0	0	2	1	0	1	0	9.0	0.00	—	.143	.250	412	.253	0	1	1	0	0.0

● **JOHN TERRY**   Terry, John Burchard b: 11/1/1879, Waterbury, Conn. d: 4/27/33, Kansas City, Mo.   Deb: 9/17/02

YEAR TM/L	W	L	PCT	G	GS	CG	SH	SV	IP	H	HR	BB	SO	RAT	ERA	ERA+	OAV	OOB	BH	AVG	PB	PR	/A	PD	TPI
1902 Det-A	0	1	.000	1	1	1	0	0	5	8	0	1	0	16.2	3.60	101	.364	.391	0	.000	-0	-0	-0	-0	-0.1
1903 StL-A	1	1	.500	3	1	1	0	0	17²	21	0	4	2	14.3	2.55	114	.296	.359	0	.000	-1	1	1	-0	-0.1
Total 2	1	2	.333	4	2	2	0	0	22²	29	0	5	2	14.7	2.78	111	.312	.366	0	.000	-2	1	1	-1	-0.2

● **YANK TERRY**   Terry, Lancelot Yank b: 2/11/11, Bedford, Ind. d: 11/4/79, Bloomington, Ind. BR/TR, 6'1", 180 lbs. Deb: 8/3/40

YEAR TM/L	W	L	PCT	G	GS	CG	SH	SV	IP	H	HR	BB	SO	RAT	ERA	ERA+	OAV	OOB	BH	AVG	PB	PR	/A	PD	TPI
1940 Bos-A	1	0	1.000	4	1	0	0	0	19¹	24	2	11	9	16.3	8.84	51	.304	.389	2	.250	0	-10	-9	-0	-0.4
1942 Bos-A	6	5	.545	20	11	3	0	1	85	82	5	43	37	13.4	3.92	95	.248	.339	3	.111	-1	-2	-2	-0	-0.4
1943 Bos-A	7	9	.438	30	22	7	0	1	163²	147	8	63	63	13.0	3.52	94	.242	.314	3	.067	-3	-4	-4	-0	-0.6
1944 Bos-A	6	10	.375	27	17	3	0	0	132²	142	10	65	30	14.2	4.21	81	.276	.361	11	.234	1	-11	-12	-1	-1.2
1945 Bos-A	0	4	.000	12	4	1	0	0	56²	68	8	14	28	13.0	4.13	82	.296	.336	2	.111	-2	-5	-5	-1	-0.5
Total 5	20	28	.417	93	55	14	0	2	457¹	463	33	196	167	13.1	4.09	85	.263	.339	21	.145	-4	-32	-31	-1	-3.1

● **RALPH TERRY**   Terry, Ralph Willard b: 1/9/36, Big Cabin, Okla. BR/TR, 6'3", 195 lbs. Deb: 8/6/56

YEAR TM/L	W	L	PCT	G	GS	CG	SH	SV	IP	H	HR	BB	SO	RAT	ERA	ERA+	OAV	OOB	BH	AVG	PB	PR	/A	PD	TPI
1956 NY-A	1	2	.333	3	3	0	0	0	13¹	17	2	11	8	18.9	9.45	41	.347	.467	1	.167	-0	-8	-8	-0	-1.3
1957 NY-A	1	1	.500	7	2	1	0	0	20²	18	1	7	11	11.3	3.05	118	.240	.313	1	.250	0	2	1	0	0.2
KC-A	4	11	.267	21	19	3	1	0	130²	119	15	47	80	11.7	3.38	117	.239	.310	6	.143	-2	6	8	0	0.7
Yr	5	12	.294	28	21	4	2	0	151	137	16	55	87	11.7	3.33	117	.239	.310	7	.152	-2	8	10	0	0.9
1958 KC-A	11	13	.458	40	33	8	3	2	216²	217	29	61	134	11.6	4.24	92	.262	.314	14	.197	-0	-11	-8	-2	-1.1
1959 KC-A	2	4	.333	9	7	2	0	0	46¹	56	9	19	35	14.8	5.24	76	.308	.376	3	.176	-1	-7	-6	-1	-0.7
NY-A	3	7	.300	24	16	5	1	0	127¹	130	7	30	55	11.5	3.39	107	.270	.316	4	.098	-3	7	4	-0	-0.1
Yr	5	11	.313	33	23	7	1	0	173²	186	16	49	90	12.3	3.89	96	.280	.331	7	.121	-3	-0	-3	0	-0.8
1960 *NY-A	10	8	.556	35	23	7	3	1	166²	149	15	52	92	11.1	3.40	105	.237	.300	6	.122	-2	9	3	0	0.1
1961 *NY-A	16	3	.842	31	27	9	2	0	188¹	162	19	42	86	9.8	3.15	118	.232	.277	15	.227	2	18	12	1	1.4
1962 *NY-A☆	**23**	12	.657	43	39	14	3	2	298²	257	40	57	176	**9.6**	3.19	117	.231	.270	20	.189	1	26	18	-4	1.7
1963 *NY-A	17	15	.531	40	37	**18**	3	1	268	246	29	39	114	**9.7**	3.22	109	.242	.273	7	.080	-6	12	9	-1	0.2
1964 *NY-A	7	11	.389	27	14	2	1	4	115	130	20	31	77	12.7	4.54	80	.283	.329	7	.200	1	-12	-12	-0	-1.7
1965 Cle-A	11	6	.647	30	26	6	2	0	165²	154	22	23	84	9.7	3.69	94	.242	.269	7	.143	2	-4	-4	-4	-0.6
1966 KC-A	1	5	.167	15	10	0	0	1	64	65	7	15	33	11.4	3.80	89	.263	.308	3	.214	1	-3	-3	-1	-0.2
NY-N	0	0	1.000	11	1	0	0	1	24²	27	1	11	14	13.9	4.74	77	.293	.369	1	.167	0	-3	-3	-0	-0.2
1967 NY-N	0	0	—	2	0	0	0	0	3¹	1	0	1	2	5.7	0.00	—	.091	.091	0	—	-0	1	1	0	0.0
Total 12	107	99	.519	338	257	75	20	11	1849¹	1748	216	446	1000	10.8	3.62	102	.249	.296	95	.160	-6	32	13	-11	-1.6

● **SCOTT TERRY**   Terry, Scott Ray b: 11/21/59, Hobbs, N.Mex. BR/TR, 5'11", 195 lbs. Deb: 4/9/86

YEAR TM/L	W	L	PCT	G	GS	CG	SH	SV	IP	H	HR	BB	SO	RAT	ERA	ERA+	OAV	OOB	BH	AVG	PB	PR	/A	PD	TPI
1986 Cin-N	1	2	.333	28	3	0	0	0	55²	66	8	32	32	15.8	6.14	63	.300	.389	1	.250	0	-15	-14	0	-0.7
1987 StL-N	0	0	—	11	0	0	0	0	13¹	13	0	9	14	14.2	3.38	123	.260	.362	0	.000	-0	1	1	0	0.0
1988 StL-N	9	6	.600	51	11	1	0	3	129¹	119	5	34	65	10.6	2.92	119	.247	.297	7	.250	2	8	8	0	1.2
1989 StL-N	8	10	.444	31	24	1	0	2	148²	142	14	43	69	11.4	3.57	102	.253	.310	5	.156	-1	-1	1	2	0.5
1990 StL-N	2	6	.250	50	2	0	0	2	72	75	7	27	35	13.3	4.75	80	.264	.337	5	.455	2	-8	-7	0	-0.6
1991 StL-N	4	4	.500	65	0	0	0	1	80¹	76	1	32	52	12.1	2.80	133	.249	.320	1	.143	-0	8	8	1	0.9
Total 6	24	28	.462	236	40	2	0	8	499¹	491	35	176	262	12.1	3.73	98	.258	.323	21	.216	6	-7	-3	4	1.3

● **ADONIS TERRY**   Terry, William H b: 8/7/1864, Westfield, Mass. d: 2/24/15, Milwaukee, Wis. BR/TR, 5'11.5", 168 lbs. Deb: 5/1/1884 U♦

YEAR TM/L	W	L	PCT	G	GS	CG	SH	SV	IP	H	HR	BB	SO	RAT	ERA	ERA+	OAV	OOB	BH	AVG	PB	PR	/A	PD	TPI
1884 Bro-a	19	35	.352	56	55	54	2	0	476	486	10	72	230	10.7	3.55	93	.248	.277	3	.233	-3	-16	-12	-3	-1.2
1885 Bro-a	6	17	.261	25	23	23	0	1	209	213	6	42	96	11.2	4.26	77	.262	.301	45	.170	-3	-24	-22	1	-2.1
1886 Bro-a	18	16	.529	34	34	32	5	0	288¹	263	1	115	162	12.3	3.09	113	.231	.310	71	.237	2	12	13	4	1.8
1887 Bro-a	16	16	.500	40	35	35	1	**3**	318	331	10	99	138	12.4	4.02	107	.262	.320	103	.293	7	10	10	5	1.6
1888 Bro-a	13	8	.619	23	23	20	2	0	195	145	2	67	138	10.2	2.03	147	**.199**	.275	29	.252	3	22	21	1	2.2
1889 *Bro-a	22	15	.595	41	39	35	4	0	326	285	6	126	186	11.8	3.29	113	.228	.307	48	.300	12	20	16	6	2.9
1890 *Bro-N	26	16	.619	46	44	38	1	0	370	362	3	133	185	12.4	2.94	117	.248	.318	101	.278	15	26	20	1	3.1
1891 Bro-N	6	16	.273	25	22	18	1	1	194	207	3	80	65	13.6	4.22	78	.263	.336	19	.209	3	-19	-20	-1	-1.5
1892 Bal-N	0	1	.000	1	1	1	0	0	9	7	0	7	3	14.0	4.00	86	.206	.341	0	.000	-1	-1	-1	0	-0.1
Pit-N	18	7	.720	30	26	24	2	1	240	185	3	106	95	11.2	2.51	131	.204	.293	16	.160	1	21	21	1	2.1
Yr	18	8	.692	31	27	25	2	1	249	192	3	113	98	11.3	2.57	129	.204	.295	16	.154	1	20	20	1	2.0
1893 Pit-N	12	8	.600	26	19	14	0	0	170	177	5	99	52	15.2	4.45	102	.260	.363	18	.254	2	-5	-5	0	-2.1
1894 Pit-N	0	1	.000	1	1	0	0	0	0²	2	0	1	0	81.0	67.50	8	.500	.750	0	.500	-0	-5	-5	0	-2.1
Chi-N	5	11	.313	23	21	16	0	0	163¹	232	12	123	88	20.4	5.84	96	.330	.441	33	.347	4	-9	-4	-1	-2.1
Yr	5	12	.294	24	22	16	0	0	164	234	12	127	88	20.7	6.09	92	.331	.444	33	.347	4	-14	-9	-1	-2.1
1895 Chi-N	21	14	.600	38	34	31	0	0	311¹	386	4	131	88	14.3	4.80	106	.277	.354	30	.219	-6	-1	10	2	0.5
1896 Chi-N	15	14	.517	30	28	25	1	0	235¹	268	6	88	74	14.0	4.28	106	.284	.351	26	.263	2	2	2	3	0.7
1897 Chi-N	0	1	.000	1	1	0	0	0	8	11	0	6	1	21.4	10.13	44	.324	.452	0	.000	-0	-5	-5	-0	-0.4
Total 14	197	196	.501	440	406	367	17	6	3514	3520	76	1298	1552	12.7	3.73	103	.252	.322	594	.249	45	38	47	15	7.9

● **DICK TERWILLIGER**   Terwilliger, Richard Martin b: 6/27/06, Sand Lake, Mich. d: 1/21/69, Greenville, Mich. BR/TR, 5'11", 178 lbs. Deb: 8/18/32

YEAR TM/L	W	L	PCT	G	GS	CG	SH	SV	IP	H	HR	BB	SO	RAT	ERA	ERA+	OAV	OOB	BH	AVG	PB	PR	/A	PD	TPI
1932 StL-N	0	0	—	1	0	0	0	0	3	1	0	2	2	12.0	12.00	—	.143	.400	0	.000	-0	1	1	0	0.0

● **JEFF TESREAU**   Tesreau, Charles Monroe b: 3/5/1889, Silver Mine, Mo. d: 9/24/46, Hanover, N.H. BR/TR, 6'2", 218 lbs. Deb: 4/12/12

YEAR TM/L	W	L	PCT	G	GS	CG	SH	SV	IP	H	HR	BB	SO	RAT	ERA	ERA+	OAV	OOB	BH	AVG	PB	PR	/A	PD	TPI
1912 *NY-N	17	7	.708	36	28	19	3	1	243	177	2	106	119	10.9	**1.96**	172	**.204**	.298	12	.146	-2	39	38	1	3.3
1913 *NY-N	22	13	.629	41	38	17	1	0	282	222	7	119	167	11.1	2.17	144	**.220**	.306	21	.221	2	32	30	1	3.9
1914 NY-N	26	10	.722	42	40	26	**8**	1	322²	238	8	128	189	10.4	2.37	112	**.209**	.293	15	.210	-2	15	10	-2	1.5
1915 NY-N	19	16	.543	43	38	24	8	0	306	235	4	75	176	9.3	2.29	112	.215	.269	24	.233	6	16	9	1	1.8
1916 NY-N	14	14	.500	40	32	23	5	2	268¹	249	6	95	113	10.7	2.92	83	.250	.300	18	.191	-4	-8	-14	-0	-1.4
1917 NY-N	13	8	.619	33	20	11	1	2	183²	168	6	58	85	11.3	3.09	83	.249	.312	14	.230	-2	-8	-11	2	-1.0
1918 NY-N	4	4	.500	12	9	3	0	0	73²	61	1	*21	31	10.0	2.32	113	.227	.283	7	.318	2	4	3	1	0.6
Total 7	115	72	.615	247	205	123	27	9	1679	1350	37	572	880	10.5	2.43	114	.223	.295	124	.216	17	89	63	3	8.7

● **BOB TEWKSBURY**   Tewksbury, Robert Alan b: 11/30/60, Concord, N.H. BR/TR, 6'4", 200 lbs. Deb: 4/11/86

YEAR TM/L	W	L	PCT	G	GS	CG	SH	SV	IP	H	HR	BB	SO	RAT	ERA	ERA+	OAV	OOB	BH	AVG	PB	PR	/A	PD	TPI
1986 NY-A	9	5	.643	23	20	2	0	0	130¹	144	8	31	49	12.4	3.31	123	.282	.329	0	—	0	12	11	2	1.3
1987 NY-A	1	4	.200	8	6	0	0	0	33¹	47	5	7	12	14.9	6.75	65	.338	.374	0	.000	0	-9	-9	-0	-1.0
Chi-N	0	4	.000	7	3	0	0	0	18	32	1	13	10	22.5	6.50	66	.421	.506	0	.000	-1	-5	-4	-1	-0.9
1988 Chi-N	0	0	—	1	1	0	0	0	3¹	1	0	2	1	21.6	8.10	45	.400	.471	0	.000	-0	-2	-2	-0	-0.2
1989 StL-N	0	0	1.000	7	4	1	0	0	30	25	2	10	17	11.1	3.30	110	.225	.301	1	.111	-0	1	1	-0	0.1
1990 StL-N	10	9	.526	28	20	1	1	0	145¹	151	7	15	50	10.5	3.47	110	.267	.290	7	.171	1	5	6	-1	0.8
1991 StL-N	11	12	.478	30	30	3	0	0	191	206	13	38	75	11.7	3.25	114	.281	.321	9	.155	1	9	10	1	1.3
1992 StL-N★	16	5	**.762**	33	32	5	0	0	233	217	15	20	91	9.3	2.16	157	.248	.267	6	.086	-2	35	32	2	2.7
1993 StL-N	17	10	.630	32	32	2	0	0	213²	258	15	20	97	12.0	3.83	103	.301	.322	14	.203	5	5	3	3	0.9
1994 StL-N	12	10	.545	24	24	1	0	0	155²	190	19	22	79	12.4	5.32	78	.304	.330	10	.185	1	-19	-20	-2	-2.1
1995 Tex-A	8	7	.533	21	21	4	1	0	129²	169	8	20	53	13.3	4.58	105	.319	.348	0	.000	0	2	2	0	0.5
1996 SD-N	10	10	.500	36	33	1	0	0	206²	224	17	43	126	11.8	4.31	92	.275	.314	2	.031	-5	-2	-7	4	-0.7
Total 11	95	76	.556	250	226	25	5	1	1490	1669	111	241	660	11.7	3.80	104	.285	.317	49	.131	-2	33	24	12	2.8

● **GRANT THATCHER**   Thatcher, Ulysses Grant b: 2/23/1877, Maytown, Pa. d: 3/17/36, Lancaster, Pa. TR, 5'10.5", 180 lbs. Deb: 9/9/03

YEAR TM/L	W	L	PCT	G	GS	CG	SH	SV	IP	H	HR	BB	SO	RAT	ERA	ERA+	OAV	OOB	BH	AVG	PB	PR	/A	PD	TPI
1903 Bro-N	3	1	.750	4	4	4	0	0	28	33	1	7	9	12.9	2.89	110	.292	.333	2	.182	0	1	1	-0	0.1
1904 Bro-N	1	0	1.000	1	0	0	0	0	9	9	0	2	0	11.0	4.00	69	.281	.324	1	.250	-0	-1	-0	-0	-0.1
Total 2	4	1	.800	5	4	4	0	0	37	42	1	9	9	12.4	3.16	98	.290	.331	3	.200	-0	-0	-0	-0	0.0

● **GREG THAYER**   Thayer, Gregory Allen b: 10/23/49, Cedar Rapids, Iowa BR/TR, 5'11", 182 lbs. Deb: 4/7/78

YEAR TM/L	W	L	PCT	G	GS	CG	SH	SV	IP	H	HR	BB	SO	RAT	ERA	ERA+	OAV	OOB	BH	AVG	PB	PR	/A	PD	TPI
1978 Min-A	1	1	.500	20	0	0	0	0	45	40	5	30	30	14.6	3.80	100	.258	.388	0	—	0	-0	-0	-0	0.0

YEAR TM/L	W	L	PCT	G	GS	CG	SH	SV	IP	H	HR	BB	SO	RAT	ERA	ERA+	OAV	OOB	BH	AVG	PB	PR	/A	PD	TPI

● **JACK THEIS**   Theis, John Louis b: 7/23/1891, Georgetown, Ohio d: 7/6/41, Georgetown, Ohio BR/TR, 6′, 190 lbs. Deb: 7/5/20

| 1920 Cin-N | 0 | 0 | — | 1 | 0 | 0 | 0 | 0 | 2 | 1 | 0 | 3 | 0 | 18.0 | 0.00 | — | .143 | .400 | 0 | — | 0 | 1 | 1 | -0 | 0.0 |

● **DUANE THEISS**   Theiss, Duane Charles b: 11/20/53, Zanesville, Ohio BR/TR, 6′3″, 185 lbs. Deb: 8/5/77

1977 Atl-N	1	1	.500	17	0	0	0	0	20²	26	1	16	7	18.7	6.53	68	.338	.457	0	.000	-0	-6	-5	0	-0.4
1978 Atl-N	0	0	—	3	0	0	0	0	6¹	3	0	3	3	9.9	1.42	285	.158	.304	0	.000	-0	2	2	0	0.0
Total 2	1	1	.500	20	0	0	0	0	27	29	1	19	10	16.7	5.33	82	.302	.427	0	.000	-0	-5	-3	0	-0.4

● **JUG THESENGA**   Thesenga, Arnold Joseph b: 4/27/14, Jefferson, S.Dak. BR/TR, 6′, 200 lbs. Deb: 9/1/44

| 1944 Was-A | 0 | 0 | — | 5 | 1 | 0 | 0 | 0 | 12¹ | 18 | 0 | 12 | 2 | 21.9 | 5.11 | 64 | .340 | .462 | 0 | .000 | -0 | -2 | -3 | 0 | 0.0 |

● **BERT THIEL**   Thiel, Maynard Bert b: 5/4/26, Marion, Wis. BR/TR, 5′10″, 185 lbs. Deb: 4/17/52

| 1952 Bos-N | 1 | 1 | .500 | 4 | 0 | 0 | 0 | 0 | 7 | 11 | 1 | 6 | 2 | 21.9 | 7.71 | 47 | .344 | .447 | 0 | — | 0 | -3 | -3 | -0 | -0.8 |

● **HENRY THIELMAN**   Thielman, Henry Joseph b: 10/3/1880, St.Cloud, Minn. d: 9/2/42, New York, N.Y. BR/TR, 5′11″, 175 lbs. Deb: 4/17/02 F♦

1902 NY-N	0	1	.000	2	2	0	0	0	6	8	0	6	5	21.0	1.50	187	.320	.452	1	.111	-4	1	1	0	0.2
Cin-N	9	15	.375	25	23	22	0	1	211	201	2	78	49	12.7	3.24	92	.251	.332	12	.132	-4	-11	-6	-1	-1.1
Yr	9	16	.360	27	25	22	0	1	217	209	2	84	54	12.9	3.19	94	.253	.336	13	.130	-4	-10	-5	-0	-0.9
1903 Bro-N	0	3	.000	4	3	3	0	0	29	31	3	14	10	14.6	4.66	69	.330	.427	5	.217	1	-4	-5	1	-0.2
Total 2	9	19	.321	31	28	25	0	1	246	240	5	98	64	13.1	3.37	90	.261	.346	18	.146	-3	-14	-9	-1	-1.1

● **JAKE THIELMAN**   Thielman, John Peter b: 5/20/1879, St.Cloud, Minn. d: 1/28/28, Minneapolis, Minn. BR/TR, 5′11″, 175 lbs. Deb: 4/23/05 F

1905 StL-N	15	16	.484	32	29	26	0	0	242	265	4	62	87	12.6	3.50	85	.281	.333	21	.231	8	-13	-14	3	-0.5
1906 StL-N	0	1	.000	1	1	0	0	0	5	5	0	2	0	12.6	3.60	73	.263	.333	1	.500	-1	-1	-0	-0	-0.1
1907 Cle-A	11	8	.579	20	18	18	3	0	166	151	2	34	56	10.4	2.33	107	.245	.292	12	.203	1	4	3	-3	0.2
1908 Cle-A	4	3	.571	11	8	5	0	0	61²	59	2	9	15	10.5	3.65	65	.260	.300	8	.348	4	-9	-9	2	-0.4
Bos-A	0	0	—	1	0	0	0	0	0²	3	1	0	0	40.5	40.50	6	.600	.600	0	—	0	-3	-3	-0	0.0
Yr	4	3	.571	12	8	5	0	0	62¹	62	3	9	15	10.3	4.04	59	.263	.290	8	.348	4	-11	-11	1	-0.4
Total 4	30	28	.517	65	56	49	3	0	475¹	483	9	107	158	11.6	3.16	86	.267	.316	42	.240	13	-21	-23	2	-0.8

● **DAVE THIES**   Thies, David Robert b: 3/21/37, Minneapolis, Minn. BR/TR, 6′4″, 205 lbs. Deb: 4/20/63

| 1963 KC-A | 0 | 1 | .000 | 9 | 2 | 0 | 0 | 0 | 25¹ | 26 | 2 | 12 | 9 | 14.2 | 4.62 | 84 | .274 | .367 | 2 | .333 | 1 | -3 | -2 | 0 | 0.0 |

● **JAKE THIES**   Thies, Vernon Arthur b: 4/1/26, St.Louis, Mo. BR/TR, 5′11″, 170 lbs. Deb: 4/24/54

1954 Pit-N	3	9	.250	33	18	3	1	0	130¹	120	13	49	57	11.9	3.87	108	.244	.317	1	.030	-2	3	5	0	0.2
1955 Pit-N	0	1	.000	1	1	0	0	0	3²	5	0	3	0	22.1	4.91	84	.357	.500	0	—	0	-0	-0	-0	-0.1
Total 2	3	10	.231	34	19	3	1	0	134	125	13	52	57	12.2	3.90	107	.248	.323	1	.030	-2	3	4	0	0.1

● **BOBBY THIGPEN**   Thigpen, Robert Thomas b: 7/17/63, Tallahassee, Fla. BR/TR, 6′3″, 195 lbs. Deb: 8/6/86

1986 Chi-A	2	0	1.000	20	0	0	0	7	35²	26	1	12	20	9.8	1.77	244	.205	.279	0	—	0	10	10	-0	0.8
1987 Chi-A	7	5	.583	51	0	0	0	16	89	86	10	24	52	11.4	2.73	168	.256	.311	0	—	0	17	18	0	2.8
1988 Chi-A	5	8	.385	68	0	0	0	34	90	96	6	33	62	13.3	3.30	120	.273	.342	0	—	0	7	7	0	1.4
1989 Chi-A	2	6	.250	61	0	0	0	34	79	62	10	40	47	11.7	3.76	101	.218	.316	0	—	0	1	0	-1	0.1
1990 Chi-A★	4	6	.400	77	0	0	0	57	88²	60	5	32	70	9.4	1.83	209	.195	.274	0	—	0	20	20	0	4.4
1991 Chi-A	7	5	.583	67	0	0	0	30	69²	63	10	38	47	13.6	3.49	114	.245	.351	0	—	0	5	4	1	1.1
1992 Chi-A	1	3	.250	55	0	0	0	22	55	58	4	33	45	15.4	4.75	81	.275	.381	0	—	0	-5	-5	1	-0.6
1993 Chi-A	0	0	—	25	0	0	0	1	34²	51	5	12	19	17.7	5.71	73	.349	.417	0	—	0	-5	-6	-1	0.1
*Phi-N	3	1	.750	17	0	0	0	0	19¹	23	4	9	10	15.4	6.05	66	.307	.388	0	.000	0	-4	-4	0	-0.8
1994 Sea-A	0	2	.000	9	0	0	0	0	7²	12	3	5	4	17.7	9.39	52	.353	.436	0	—	0	-4	-4	-0	-0.9
Total 9	31	36	.463	448	0	0	0	201	568²	537	56	238	376	12.6	3.43	118	.252	.334	0	.000	0	41	39	0	8.4

● **J. J. THOBE**   Thobe, John Joseph b: 11/19/70, Covington, Ky. BR/TR, 6′6″, 200 lbs. Deb: 9/18/95 F

| 1995 Mon-N | 0 | 0 | — | 4 | 0 | 0 | 0 | 0 | 4 | 6 | 0 | 3 | 0 | 20.3 | 9.00 | 48 | .333 | .429 | 0 | — | 0 | -2 | -2 | 0 | 0.0 |

● **TOM THOBE**   Thobe, Thomas Neal b: 9/3/69, Covington, Ky. BL/TL, 6′6″, 195 lbs. Deb: 9/12/95 F

1995 Atl-N	0	0	—	3	0	0	0	0	3¹	7	0	0	2	18.9	10.80	39	.412	.412	0	—	0	-2	-2	-0	0.0
1996 Atl-N	0	1	.000	4	0	0	0	0	6	5	1	0	1	7.5	1.50	293	.217	.217	0	.000	-0	2	2	-1	0.2
Total 2	0	1	.000	7	0	0	0	0	9¹	12	1	0	3	11.6	4.82	90	.300	.300	0	.000	-0	-1	-0	-1	0.2

● **DICK THOENEN**   Thoenen, Richard Crispin b: 1/9/44, Mexico, Mo. BR/TR, 6′6″, 215 lbs. Deb: 9/16/67

| 1967 Phi-N | 0 | 0 | — | 1 | 0 | 0 | 0 | 0 | 1 | 2 | 0 | 0 | 1 | 18.0 | 9.00 | 38 | .500 | .500 | 0 | — | 0 | -1 | -1 | 0 | 0.0 |

● **TOMMY THOMAS**   Thomas, Alphonse b: 12/23/1899, Baltimore, Md. d: 4/27/88, Dallastown, Pa. BR/TR, 5′10″, 175 lbs. Deb: 4/17/26

1926 Chi-A	15	12	.556	44	32	13	2	2	249	225	7	110	127	12.1	3.80	102	**.244**	.325	16	.186	-1	6	2	-3	-0.2
1927 Chi-A	19	16	.543	40	36	24	3	1	307²	271	16	94	107	10.7	2.98	136	.244	.303	14	.147	-3	40	36	-4	2.9
1928 Chi-A	17	16	.515	36	32	24	3	2	283	277	14	76	129	11.4	3.08	131	.259	.310	21	.219	3	30	30	-3	3.3
1929 Chi-A	14	18	.438	36	31	**24**	2	1	259²	270	17	60	62	11.4	3.19	134	.269	.310	25	.255	2	30	32	-3	3.4
1930 Chi-A	5	13	.278	34	27	7	0	0	169	229	13	44	58	14.6	5.22	89	.323	.364	7	.125	-4	-11	-11	0	-1.3
1931 Chi-A	10	14	.417	43	36	11	2	2	245¹	298	17	69	72	13.6	4.73	90	.292	.340	21	.241	1	-10	-13	-1	-1.0
1932 Chi-A	3	3	.500	12	3	1	0	0	43²	55	4	15	11	14.6	6.18	70	.307	.364	1	.077	-1	-8	-9	-0	-1.1
Was-A	8	7	.533	18	14	7	1	0	117	114	5	46	36	12.3	3.54	122	.255	.325	10	.238	1	12	10	-2	1.0
Yr	11	10	.524	30	17	8	1	0	160²	169	11	61	47	12.9	4.26	101	.270	.334	11	.200	0	4	1	-2	-0.1
1933 *Was-A	7	7	.500	35	14	8	0	3	135	149	9	49	35	13.3	4.80	87	.273	.336	10	.238	1	-8	-9	-2	-0.9
1934 Was-A	8	9	.471	33	18	7	1	1	133¹	154	10	54	42	14.5	5.47	79	.294	.368	7	.184	-0	-14	-17	-2	-2.0
1935 Was-A	0	0	—	1	0	0	0	0	0¹	3	0	1	0	81.0	54.00	8	.750	.750	0	—	0	-1	-1	-0	-0.1
Phi-N	0	1	.000	4	1	0	0	0	12	15	2	5	3	15.0	5.25	86	.313	.377	0	.000	-0	-2	-1	-0	-0.1
1936 StL-A	11	9	.550	36	21	8	1	0	179²	245	9	52	40	14.8	5.26	102	.297	.362	8	.138	-3	-4	-2	-0	-0.3
1937 StL-A	0	1	.000	17	2	0	0	0	30²	46	2	10	10	16.7	7.04	69	.348	.399	0	.000	-0	-4	-5	-0	-0.3
Bos-A	0	2	.000	9	0	0	0	0	11	16	2	4	4	17.2	4.09	116	.340	.404	1	.250	-0	1	1	0	0.1
Yr	0	3	.000	26	2	0	0	0	41²	62	4	14	14	16.6	6.26	77	.344	.395	1	.125	-1	-4	-7	-0	-0.2
Total 12	117	128	.478	398	267	128	15	12	2176¹	2341	144	712	736	12.7	4.11	104	.275	.333	141	.195	-5	52	43	-22	3.5

● **BLAINE THOMAS**   Thomas, Blaine M. "Baldy" b: 8/1888, Glendora, Cal. d: 8/21/15, Glendora, Cal. BR/TR, 5′10″, 165 lbs. Deb: 8/25/11

| 1911 Bos-A | 0 | 0 | — | 2 | 0 | 0 | 0 | 0 | 4² | 3 | 0 | 7 | 2 | 21.2 | 0.00 | — | .273 | .579 | 1 | .500 | 0 | 2 | 2 | 0 | 0.0 |

● **CARL THOMAS**   Thomas, Carl Leslie b: 5/28/32, Minneapolis, Minn. BR/TR, 6′5″, 245 lbs. Deb: 4/19/60

| 1960 Cle-A | 1 | 0 | 1.000 | 4 | 0 | 0 | 0 | 0 | 9² | 8 | 1 | 10 | 5 | 17.7 | 7.45 | 50 | .229 | .413 | 1 | .333 | 1 | -4 | -4 | 0 | -0.3 |

● **LEFTY THOMAS**   Thomas, Clarence Fletcher b: 10/4/03, Glade Spring, Va. d: 3/21/52, Charlottesville, Va. BL/TL, 6′, 183 lbs. Deb: 9/26/25

1925 Was-A	0	2	.000	2	1	0	0	0	13	14	0	7	10	14.5	2.08	204	.264	.350	0	.000	-1	3	3	0	0.3
1926 Was-A	0	0	—	6	0	0	0	0	8²	8	0	10	3	18.7	5.19	74	.267	.450	0	.000	-0	-1	-1	0	0.0
Total 2	0	2	.000	8	1	0	0	0	21²	22	0	17	13	16.2	3.32	123	.265	.390	0	.000	-1	2	2	0	0.3

● **CLAUDE THOMAS**   Thomas, Claude Alfred "Lefty" b: 5/15/1890, Stanberry, Mo. d: 3/6/46, Sulphur, Okla. BL/TL, 6′1″, 180 lbs. Deb: 9/14/16

| 1916 Was-A | 1 | 2 | .333 | 7 | 4 | 1 | 0 | 0 | 28¹ | 27 | 1 | 12 | 7 | 13.0 | 4.13 | 68 | .265 | .353 | 1 | .100 | -1 | -4 | -4 | -0 | -0.5 |

● **FAY THOMAS**   Thomas, Fay Wesley "Scow" b: 10/10/04, Holyrood, Kan. d: 8/16/90, Chatsworth, Cal. BR/TR, 6′2″, 195 lbs. Deb: 6/27/27

1927 NY-N	0	0	—	9	0	0	0	0	16¹	19	3	4	11	13.2	3.31	117	.302	.353	0	.000	-0	1	1	-0	-0.1
1931 Cle-A	4	4	.333	12	4	2	0	0	48²	62	2	32	25	17.8	5.18	89	.323	.421	2	.154	-1	-5	-3	-0	-0.4
1932 Bro-N	0	1	.000	7	2	0	0	0	17	23	0	8	9	15.9	7.41	51	.306	.375	-0	—	-0	-7	-7	0	-0.4
1935 StL-A	7	15	.318	49	19	4	0	1	147	165	11	89	67	15.7	4.78	100	.289	.388	4	.105	-3	2	2	1	0.0
Total 4	9	20	.310	81	23	6	0	1	229	269	16	133	112	16.0	4.95	93	.299	.392	6	.107	-4	-15	-9	1	-0.9

YEAR TM/L	W	L	PCT	G	GS	CG	SH	SV	IP	H	HR	BB	SO	RAT	ERA	ERA+	OAV	OOB	BH	AVG	PB	PR	/A	PD	TPI
● **FROSTY THOMAS** Thomas, Forrest b: 5/23/1881, Faucett, Mo. d: 3/18/70, St.Joseph, Mo. BR/TR, 6′, 185 lbs. Deb: 5/1/05																									
1905 Det-A	0	1	.000	2	1	0	0	0	6	10	0	3	5	21.0	7.50	36	.370	.452	0	.000	0	-3	-3	0	-0.4
● **LARRY THOMAS** Thomas, Larry Wayne b: 10/25/69, Miami, Fla. BR/TL, 6′1″, 190 lbs. Deb: 8/11/95																									
1995 Chi-A	0	0	—	17	0	0	0	0	13²	8	1	6	12	9.2	1.32	338	.167	.259	0	—	0	5	5	-0	0.3
1996 Chi-A	2	3	.400	57	0	0	0	0	30²	32	1	14	20	14.4	3.23	146	.281	.374	0	—	0	6	5	-0	1.1
Total 2	2	3	.400	74	0	0	0	0	44¹	40	2	20	32	12.8	2.64	175	.247	.341	0	—	0	11	10	-0	1.4
● **BUD THOMAS** Thomas, Luther Baxter b: 9/9/10, Faber, Va. BR/TR, 6′, 180 lbs. Deb: 9/13/32																									
1932 Was-A	0	0	—	2	0	0	0	0	3	1	0	2	1	9.0	0.00	—	.100	.250	0	—	0	1	1	-0	0.0
1933 Was-A	0	0	—	2	0	0	0	0	4	11	1	2	1	31.5	15.75	27	.550	.609	0	.000	-0	-5	-5	0	-0.3
1937 Phi-A	8	15	.348	35	26	6	1	0	169²	208	15	52	54	13.8	4.99	95	.295	.344	6	.128	-1	-7	-5	-3	-0.9
1938 Phi-A	9	14	.391	42	29	7	1	0	212¹	259	23	62	48	13.7	4.92	98	.299	.347	9	.130	-3	-3	-2	-1	-0.5
1939 Phi-A	0	1	.000	2	2	0	0	0	4	8	2	1	0	20.3	15.75	30	.421	.450	0	.000	-0	-5	-5	0	-0.9
Was-A	0	0	—	4	0	0	0	0	9	11	0	2	0	13.0	6.00	72	.306	.342	0	.000	-0	-1	-2	0	0.0
Det-A	7	0	1.000	27	0	0	0	1	47¹	45	7	20	14	12.4	4.18	117	.254	.330	1	.111	-1	2	4	-0	0.4
Yr	7	1	.875	33	2	0	0	1	60¹	64	9	23	14	13.0	5.22	92	.276	.341	1	.071	-2	-4	-3	-0	-0.5
1940 Det-A	0	1	.000	3	0	0	0	0	4	8	1	3	0	24.8	9.00	53	.421	.500	0	—	0	-2	-2	1	-0.3
1941 Det-A	1	3	.250	26	1	0	0	2	72²	74	4	22	17	11.9	4.21	108	.260	.313	2	.105	-0	-1	-3	2	0.2
Total 7	25	34	.424	143	58	13	2	3	526	625	53	166	135	13.6	4.96	96	.292	.345	18	.120	-7	-20	-13	-1	-2.0
● **MIKE THOMAS** Thomas, Michael Steven b: 9/2/69, Sacramento, Cal. BL/TL, 6′2″, 205 lbs. Deb: 7/12/95																									
1995 Mil-A	0	0	—	1	0	0	0	0	1¹	2	0	1	0	20.3	0.00	—	.333	.429	0	—	0	1	1	0	-0.4
● **MYLES THOMAS** Thomas, Myles Lewis b: 10/22/1897, State College, Pa. d: 12/12/63, Toledo, Ohio BR/TR, 5′9.5″, 170 lbs. Deb: 4/18/26																									
1926 *NY-A	6	6	.500	33	13	3	0	0	140¹	140	6	65	38	13.3	4.23	91	.271	.356	5	.116	-3	-3	-6	1	-0.7
1927 NY-A	7	4	.636	21	9	1	0	0	88²	111	4	43	25	15.7	4.87	79	.322	.398	9	.333	2	-7	-10	0	-0.9
1928 NY-A	1	0	1.000	12	1	0	0	0	31²	33	3	9	10	11.9	3.41	110	.277	.328	4	.400	1	2	1	-0	0.1
1929 NY-A	0	2	.000	5	1	0	0	0	15	27	1	9	3	21.6	10.80	36	.409	.480	1	.143	-1	-11	-12	1	-1.2
Was-A	7	8	.467	22	14	7	0	2	125¹	139	3	48	33	13.4	3.52	121	.288	.352	14	.292	2	10	10	1	1.3
Yr	7	10	.412	27	15	7	0	2	140¹	166	4	57	36	14.3	4.30	98	.302	.368	15	.273	1	-1	-2	1	0.1
1930 Was-A	2	2	.500	12	2	0	0	0	33²	49	3	15	12	17.1	8.29	55	.358	.421	2	.182	-1	-14	-14	-1	-1.4
Total 5	23	22	.511	105	40	11	0	2	434²	499	20	189	121	14.3	4.64	87	.299	.372	35	.240	0	-23	-30	1	-2.8
● **ROY THOMAS** Thomas, Roy Allen b: 3/24/1874, Norristown, Pa. d: 11/20/59, Norristown, Pa. BL/TL, 5′11″, 150 lbs. Deb: 4/14/1899 FC♦																									
1900 Phi-N	0	0	—	1	0	0	0	0	2²	4	0	0	0	13.5	3.38	107	.333	.333	168	.316	0	0	0	-0	0.0
● **ROY THOMAS** Thomas, Roy Justin b: 6/22/53, Quantico, Va. BR/TR, 6′6″, 200 lbs. Deb: 9/21/77																									
1977 Hou-N	0	0	—	4	0	0	0	0	6¹	5	0	3	4	11.4	2.84	125	.208	.296	0	—	0	1	1	0	0.0
1978 StL-N	1	1	.500	16	1	0	0	3	28¹	21	0	16	16	11.8	3.81	92	.216	.327	1	.250	0	-1	-1	1	0.0
1979 StL-N	3	4	.429	26	6	0	0	1	77	66	3	24	44	10.5	2.92	129	.237	.298	1	.059	-1	7	7	1	0.6
1980 StL-N	3	2	.400	24	5	0	0	1	55	59	3	25	22	14.2	4.75	78	.274	.358	2	.154	-0	-7	-6	1	-0.5
1983 Sea-A	3	1	.750	43	0	0	0	1	88²	95	4	32	77	13.1	3.45	123	.275	.340	0	—	0	6	8	-0	0.1
1984 Sea-A	3	2	.600	21	1	0	0	1	49²	52	8	37	42	16.9	5.26	76	.280	.410	0	—	0	-7	-7	-0	-0.6
1985 Sea-A	7	0	1.000	40	0	0	0	1	93²	66	8	48	70	11.1	3.36	125	.202	.309	0	—	0	8	9	-1	0.5
1987 Sea-A	1	0	1.000	8	0	0	0	0	20²	23	7	11	14	15.2	5.23	90	.299	.393	0	—	0	-2	-1	-1	-0.2
Total 8	20	11	.645	182	13	0	0	7	419¹	387	33	196	289	12.8	3.82	105	.250	.339	4	.118	-1	5	9	1	-0.1
● **STAN THOMAS** Thomas, Stanley Brown b: 7/11/49, Rumford, Me. BR/TR, 6′2″, 185 lbs. Deb: 7/5/74																									
1974 Tex-A	0	0	—	12	0	0	0	0	13²	22	1	6	8	18.4	6.59	54	.379	.438	0	—	0	-5	-5	0	-0.5
1975 Tex-A	4	4	.500	46	1	0	0	0	81¹	72	2	34	46	12.1	3.10	121	.239	.322	0	—	0	6	6	0	0.7
1976 Cle-A	4	4	.500	37	7	2	0	6	105²	88	5	41	54	11.3	2.30	152	.229	.310	0	—	0	14	14	3	1.6
1977 Sea-A	2	6	.250	13	9	1	0	0	58¹	74	8	25	14	15.7	6.02	68	.310	.382	0	—	0	-13	-12	-0	-1.4
NY-A	1	0	1.000	3	0	0	0	0	6¹	7	0	4	1	15.6	7.11	55	.280	.379	0	—	0	-2	-2	-0	-0.3
Yr	3	6	.333	16	9	1	0	0	64²	81	8	29	15	15.3	6.12	67	.300	.368	0	—	0	-15	-15	-1	-1.7
Total 4	11	14	.440	111	17	3	0	6	265¹	263	16	110	123	13.0	3.70	101	.261	.340	0	—	0	1	1	3	0.6
● **TOM THOMAS** Thomas, Thomas R. "Savage Tom" b: 12/27/1873, Shawnee, Ohio d: 9/23/42, Shawnee, Ohio BR/TR, 6′4″, 195 lbs. Deb: 9/20/1894																									
1894 Cle-N	0	0	—	1	0	0	0	0	0¹	3	0	0	0	54.0	27.00	20	.000	.667	0	—	0	-1	-1	0	0.0
1899 StL-N	1	1	.500	4	2	2	0	0	25	22	1	4	8	9.4	2.52	158	.237	.268	3	.250	0	4	4	0	0.3
1900 StL-N	2	2	.500	5	1	1	0	0	26¹	38	2	4	7	14.7	3.76	97	.336	.364	1	.091	-1	-0	-0	-1	-0.2
Total 3	3	3	.500	10	3	3	0	0	51²	60	3	8	15	12.4	3.31	115	.290	.326	4	.174	-1	3	3	-1	0.1
● **ERSKINE THOMASON** Thomason, Melvin Erskine b: 8/13/48, Laurens, S.C. BR/TR, 6′1″, 190 lbs. Deb: 9/18/74																									
1974 Phi-N	0	0	—	1	0	0	0	0	1	0	0	1	0	9.0	0.00	—	.000	.000	0	—	0	0	0	0	0.0
● **ART THOMPSON** Thompson, Arthur J. Deb: 6/17/1884																									
1884 Was-U	0	1	.000	1	1	1	0	0	8	10	1	3	8	14.6	6.75	36	.286	.342	0	.000	-1	-4	-4	0	-0.4
● **FORREST THOMPSON** Thompson, David Forrest b: 3/3/18, Mooresville, N.C. d: 2/26/79, Charlotte, N.C. BL/TL, 5′11″, 195 lbs. Deb: 4/26/48																									
1948 Was-A	6	10	.375	46	7	0	0	4	131¹	134	9	54	40	13.0	3.84	113	.262	.334	10	.286	2	7	7	-0	1.1
1949 Was-A	1	3	.250	9	1	0	0	0	16¹	22	1	9	8	17.6	4.41	97	.328	.416	3	.600	2	-0	-0	-0	0.1
Total 2	7	13	.350	55	8	0	0	4	147²	156	10	63	48	13.5	3.90	111	.270	.344	13	.325	4	6	7	-0	1.2
● **JUNIOR THOMPSON** Thompson, Eugene Earl b: 6/7/17, Latham, Ill. BR/TR, 6′1″, 185 lbs. Deb: 4/26/39																									
1939 *Cin-N	13	5	.722	42	11	5	3	2	152¹	130	6	55	87	11.1	2.54	151	.236	.309	11	.229	0	23	22	-1	2.3
1940 *Cin-N	16	9	.640	33	31	17	3	0	225¹	197	10	96	103	11.8	3.32	114	.233	.313	18	.228	3	13	12	-1	1.4
1941 Cin-N	6	6	.500	27	15	4	1	0	109	117	6	57	46	14.6	4.87	74	.272	.361	7	.233	1	-15	-15	2	-1.3
1942 Cin-N	4	7	.364	29	10	1	0	0	101²	86	5	53	35	12.5	3.36	98	.226	.324	8	.267	2	-1	-1	4	0.5
1946 NY-N	4	6	.400	39	1	0	0	4	62²	36	6	40	31	10.9	1.29	266	.190	.332	1	.143	-0	15	15	2	2.8
1947 NY-N	4	2	.667	15	0	0	0	0	35²	36	3	27	13	16.1	4.29	95	.279	.408	0	.000	-1	-1	-1	-0	-0.1
Total 6	47	35	.573	185	68	27	6	7	686²	602	35	328	315	12.3	3.26	113	.239	.329	45	.225	6	35	32	6	5.6
● **FULLER THOMPSON** Thompson, Fuller Weidner b: 5/1/1889, Los Angeles, Cal. d: 2/19/72, Los Angeles, Cal. BR/TR, 5′11.5″, 164 lbs. Deb: 8/19/11																									
1911 Bos-N	0	0	—	3	0	0	0	0	4²	5	0	2	0	13.5	3.86	99	.294	.368	0	—	0	-0	-0	0	0.0
● **HARRY THOMPSON** Thompson, Harold b: 9/9/1889, Nanticoke, Pa. d: 2/14/51, Reno, Nev. BL/TL, 5′8″, 150 lbs. Deb: 4/24/19																									
1919 Was-A	0	3	.000	12	2	0	0	1	43¹	48	0	8	10	12.0	3.53	91	.293	.333	8	.250	1	-1	-2	0	0.0
Phi-A	0	1	.000	3	0	0	0	0	12	16	4	3	1	14.3	6.75	51	.327	.365	0	.000	-1	-5	-4	0	-0.4
Yr	0	4	.000	15	2	0	0	1	55¹	64	4	11	11	12.2	4.23	77	.298	.332	8	.211	-0	-6	-6	1	-0.4
● **LEE THOMPSON** Thompson, John Dudley "Lefty" b: 2/26/1898, Smithfield, Utah d: 2/17/63, Santa Barbara, Cal BL/TL, 6′1″, 185 lbs. Deb: 9/4/21																									
1921 Chi-A	0	3	.000	4	4	0	0	0	20²	32	1	6	4	16.5	8.27	51	.333	.373	2	.286	0	-9	-9	-1	-1.0
● **GUS THOMPSON** Thompson, John Gustav b: 6/22/1877, Humboldt, Iowa d: 3/28/58, Kalispell, Mont. 6′2″, 185 lbs. Deb: 8/31/03																									
1903 *Pit-N	2	2	.500	5	4	3	0	0	43	52	1	16	22	14.4	3.56	91	.295	.358	4	.250	0	-1	-1	1	-0.2
1906 StL-N	2	11	.154	17	12	8	0	0	103	111	2	25	36	12.3	4.31	57	.285	.336	6	.176	-0	-19	-19	1	-2.2
Total 2	4	13	.235	22	16	11	0	0	146	163	3	41	58	12.9	4.07	69	.288	.343	10	.200	-0	-20	-20	1	-2.4
● **JOCKO THOMPSON** Thompson, John Samuel b: 1/17/17, Beverly, Mass. d: 2/3/88, Olney, Md. BL/TL, 6′, 185 lbs. Deb: 9/21/48																									
1948 Phi-N	1	0	1.000	2	2	1	0	0	13	10	1	9	7	13.2	2.77	142	.233	.365	0	.000	0	2	2	-0	0.1
1949 Phi-N	1	3	.250	8	5	1	0	0	31¹	38	6	11	12	14.1	6.89	57	.314	.371	2	.182	-0	-10	-10	-0	-1.1
1950 Phi-N	0	0	—	2	0	0	0	0	4	1	0	4	2	11.3	0.00	—	.077	.294	0	—	0	2	2	0	0.0

YEAR	TM/L	W	L	PCT	G	GS	CG	SH	SV	IP	H	HR	BB	SO	RAT	ERA	ERA+	OAV	OOB	BH	AVG	PB	PR	/A	PD	TPI
1951	Phi-N	4	8	.333	29	14	3	2	1	119¹	102	12	59	60	12.3	3.85	100	.231	.325	4	.103	-1	2	0	-1	-0.2
Total	4	6	11	.353	41	21	5	2	1	167²	151	18	83	81	12.7	4.24	91	.244	.336	6	.113	-1	-5	-7	-1	-1.2

● JUSTIN THOMPSON
Thompson, Justin Willard b: 3/8/73, San Antonio, Tex. BL/TL, 6'4", 215 lbs. Deb: 5/27/96

YEAR	TM/L	W	L	PCT	G	GS	CG	SH	SV	IP	H	HR	BB	SO	RAT	ERA	ERA+	OAV	OOB	BH	AVG	PB	PR	/A	PD	TPI
1996	Det-A	1	6	.143	11	11	0	0	0	59	62	7	31	44	14.5	4.58	111	.267	.358	0	—	0	3	3	1	0.5

● MARK THOMPSON
Thompson, Mark Radford b: 4/7/71, Russellville, Ky. BR/TR, 6'2", 205 lbs. Deb: 7/26/94

YEAR	TM/L	W	L	PCT	G	GS	CG	SH	SV	IP	H	HR	BB	SO	RAT	ERA	ERA+	OAV	OOB	BH	AVG	PB	PR	/A	PD	TPI
1994	Col-N	1	1	.500	2	2	0	0	0	9	16	2	8	5	25.0	9.00	55	.400	.510	0	.000	-0	-5	-4	-0	-0.7
1995	*Col-N	2	3	.400	21	5	0	0	0	51	73	7	22	30	16.9	6.53	82	.349	.414	5	.385	1	-13	-6	-1	-0.4
1996	Col-N	9	11	.450	34	28	3	1	0	169²	189	25	74	99	14.6	5.30	102	.285	.368	8	.138	-3	-21	-2	-1	-0.1
Total	3	12	15	.444	57	35	3	1	0	229²	278	34	104	134	15.6	5.72	94	.305	.385	13	.173	-2	-39	-8	-1	-1.2

● MIKE THOMPSON
Thompson, Michael Wayne b: 9/6/49, Denver, Colo. BR/TR, 6'3", 190 lbs. Deb: 5/19/71

YEAR	TM/L	W	L	PCT	G	GS	CG	SH	SV	IP	H	HR	BB	SO	RAT	ERA	ERA+	OAV	OOB	BH	AVG	PB	PR	/A	PD	TPI
1971	Was-A	1	6	.143	16	12	0	0	0	66²	53	3	54	41	14.9	4.86	68	.222	.372	2	.118	0	-10	-12	0	-1.1
1973	StL-N	0	0	—	2	2	0	0	0	4	1	0	5	3	13.5	—	—	.077	.333	0	.000	-0	2	2	-0	0.0
1974	StL-N	0	3	.000	19	4	0	0	0	38¹	37	1	35	25	17.4	5.63	63	.274	.430	0	.000	-2	-9	-9	-0	-0.7
	Atl-N	0	0	—	1	1	0	0	0	4	7	0	2	2	20.3	4.50	84	.412	.474	1	1.000	0	-0	-0	-0	0.1
	Yr	0	3	.000	20	5	0	0	0	42¹	44	1	37	27	17.2	5.53	65	.286	.424	1	.111	-1	-9	-9	-0	-0.6
1975	Atl-N	0	6	.000	16	10	0	0	0	51²	60	2	32	42	16.0	4.70	80	.305	.402	1	.071	-1	-6	-5	-1	-0.6
Total	4	1	15	.063	54	29	0	0	0	164²	158	6	128	113	15.9	4.86	73	.263	.396	4	.098	-1	-24	-24	1	-2.3

● RICH THOMPSON
Thompson, Richard Neil b: 11/1/58, New York, N.Y. BR/TR, 6'3", 225 lbs. Deb: 4/28/85

YEAR	TM/L	W	L	PCT	G	GS	CG	SH	SV	IP	H	HR	BB	SO	RAT	ERA	ERA+	OAV	OOB	BH	AVG	PB	PR	/A	PD	TPI
1985	Cle-A	3	8	.273	57	0	0	0	5	80	95	8	48	30	16.8	6.30	66	.303	.405	0	—	0	-19	-19	-2	-2.6
1989	Mon-N	0	2	.000	19	1	0	0	0	33	27	2	11	15	10.9	2.18	162	.241	.320	0	.000	0	5	5	0	0.3
1990	Mon-N	0	0	—	1	0	0	0	0	1	1	0	0	0	9.0	0.00	—	.250	.250	0	—	0	0	0	0	0.0
Total	3	3	10	.231	77	1	0	0	5	114	123	10	59	45	15.0	5.05	78	.286	.382	0	.000	0	-14	-14	-2	-2.3

● TOMMY THOMPSON
Thompson, Thomas Carl b: 11/7/1889, Spring City, Tenn. d: 1/16/63, LaJolla, Cal. BR/TR, 5'9.5", 170 lbs. Deb: 6/5/12 F

YEAR	TM/L	W	L	PCT	G	GS	CG	SH	SV	IP	H	HR	BB	SO	RAT	ERA	ERA+	OAV	OOB	BH	AVG	PB	PR	/A	PD	TPI
1912	NY-N	0	2	.000	7	2	1	0	0	32²	43	0	13	16	16.3	6.06	59	.341	.415	3	.300	1	-10	-9	-1	-0.5

● WILL THOMPSON
Thompson, Will McLain b: 8/30/1870, Pittsburgh, Pa. d: 6/9/62, Pittsburgh, Pa. BR/TR, 5'11.5", 190 lbs. Deb: 7/9/1892

YEAR	TM/L	W	L	PCT	G	GS	CG	SH	SV	IP	H	HR	BB	SO	RAT	ERA	ERA+	OAV	OOB	BH	AVG	PB	PR	/A	PD	TPI
1892	Pit-N	0	1	.000	1	1	0	0	0	3	3	0	3	2	15.0	3.00	110	.250	.500	0	—	0	0	0	0	0.1

● HANK THORMAHLEN
Thormahlen, Herbert Ehler "Lefty" b: 7/5/1896, Jersey City, N.J. d: 2/6/55, Los Angeles, Cal. BL/TL, 6', 180 lbs. Deb: 9/29/17

YEAR	TM/L	W	L	PCT	G	GS	CG	SH	SV	IP	H	HR	BB	SO	RAT	ERA	ERA+	OAV	OOB	BH	AVG	PB	PR	/A	PD	TPI
1917	NY-A	0	1	.000	1	1	0	0	0	8	9	0	4	5	15.8	2.25	119	.281	.378	0	.000	-0	1	1	-0	0.0
1918	NY-A	7	3	.700	16	12	5	2	0	112²	85	1	52	22	11.4	2.48	114	.217	.318	3	.077	-3	4	4	0	0.0
1919	NY-A	12	10	.545	30	25	13	2	1	188²	155	10	61	62	10.5	2.62	122	.228	.295	11	.186	-0	13	12	-1	1.2
1920	NY-A	9	6	.600	29	15	6	0	0	143¹	178	5	43	35	14.0	4.14	92	.312	.362	10	.222	1	-6	-5	-1	-0.3
1921	Bos-A	1	7	.125	23	9	3	0	0	96¹	101	3	34	17	13.2	4.48	94	.277	.349	4	.174	-1	-2	-3	-0	-0.2
1925	Bro-N	0	3	.000	5	2	0	0	0	16	22	0	9	7	18.6	3.94	106	.333	.429	1	.200	1	0	0	0	0.2
Total	6	29	30	.492	104	64	27	4	2	565	550	19	203	148	12.3	3.33	105	.261	.332	29	.168	-3	10	9	0	0.9

● PAUL THORMODSGARD
Thormodsgard, Paul Gayton b: 11/10/53, San Francisco, Cal. BR/TR, 6'2", 190 lbs. Deb: 4/10/77

YEAR	TM/L	W	L	PCT	G	GS	CG	SH	SV	IP	H	HR	BB	SO	RAT	ERA	ERA+	OAV	OOB	BH	AVG	PB	PR	/A	PD	TPI
1977	Min-A	11	15	.423	37	37	8	1	0	218	236	25	65	94	12.6	4.62	86	.280	.333	0	—	0	-14	-16	-1	-1.6
1978	Min-A	1	6	.143	12	12	1	0	0	66	81	7	17	23	13.5	5.05	76	.308	.352	0	—	0	-9	-9	-1	-1.0
1979	Min-A	0	0	—	1	0	0	0	0	1	3	1	0	1	27.0	9.00	49	.500	.500	0	—	0	-1	-1	0	0.0
Total	3	12	21	.364	50	49	9	1	0	285	320	33	82	118	12.8	4.74	83	.288	.339	0	—	0	-24	-25	-2	-2.6

● JOHN THORNTON
Thornton, John b: 1870, Washington, D.C. 5'10.5", 175 lbs. Deb: 8/14/1889 ♦

YEAR	TM/L	W	L	PCT	G	GS	CG	SH	SV	IP	H	HR	BB	SO	RAT	ERA	ERA+	OAV	OOB	BH	AVG	PB	PR	/A	PD	TPI
1889	Was-N	0	1	.000	1	1	1	0	0	9	7	0	7	3	15.0	5.00	79	.229	.357	0	.000	-1	-1	-1	-0	-0.2
1891	Phi-N	15	16	.484	37	32	23	1	2	269	268	3	115	52	13.1	3.68	93	.250	.328	17	.138	-7	-10	-8	2	-1.3
1892	Phi-N	0	2	.000	3	2	1	0	0	12	16	1	17	2	24.8	12.75	25	.308	.478	5	.385	1	-13	-13	-0	-1.3
Total	3	15	19	.441	41	35	25	1	2	290	292	4	139	57	13.7	4.10	83	.252	.337	22	.154	-7	-24	-22	2	-2.8

● WALTER THORNTON
Thornton, Walter Miller b: 2/18/1875, Lewiston, Maine d: 7/14/60, Los Angeles, Cal. BL/TL, 6'1", 180 lbs. Deb: 7/1/1895 ♦

YEAR	TM/L	W	L	PCT	G	GS	CG	SH	SV	IP	H	HR	BB	SO	RAT	ERA	ERA+	OAV	OOB	BH	AVG	PB	PR	/A	PD	TPI
1895	Chi-N	2	0	1.000	7	2	2	0	1	40	58	3	31	13	21.1	6.07	84	.333	.448	7	.318	2	-6	-4	-1	-0.1
1896	Chi-N	2	1	.667	5	5	2	0	0	23²	30	1	13	10	16.4	5.70	80	.306	.387	2	.364	2	-4	-3	-1	-0.2
1897	Chi-N	6	7	.462	16	16	15	0	0	130	164	4	51	55	15.3	4.70	95	.305	.371	85	.321	4	-6	-3	-0	0.1
1898	Chi-N	13	10	.565	28	25	21	2	0	215¹	226	4	56	56	12.5	3.34	107	.268	.327	62	.295	6	-8	-6	-1	0.9
Total	4	23	18	.561	56	48	40	2	1	409¹	478	12	151	134	14.5	4.18	97	.289	.357	162	.312	13	-8	-6	-2	0.7

● BOB THORPE
Thorpe, Robert Joseph b: 1/12/35, San Diego, Cal. d: 3/17/60, San Diego, Cal. BR/TR, 6'1", 170 lbs. Deb: 4/17/55

YEAR	TM/L	W	L	PCT	G	GS	CG	SH	SV	IP	H	HR	BB	SO	RAT	ERA	ERA+	OAV	OOB	BH	AVG	PB	PR	/A	PD	TPI
1955	Chi-N	0	0	—	2	0	0	0	0	3	4	0	0	4	12.0	3.00	136	.333	.333	0	—	0	0	0	0	0.0

● GEORGE THROOP
Throop, George Lynford b: 11/24/50, Pasadena, Cal. BR/TR, 6'7", 205 lbs. Deb: 9/7/75

YEAR	TM/L	W	L	PCT	G	GS	CG	SH	SV	IP	H	HR	BB	SO	RAT	ERA	ERA+	OAV	OOB	BH	AVG	PB	PR	/A	PD	TPI
1975	KC-A	0	0	—	7	0	0	0	0	9	8	1	2	8	10.0	4.00	96	.250	.294	0	—	0	-0	-0	0	-0.1
1977	KC-A	0	0	—	4	0	0	0	1	5¹	1	1	4	1	8.4	3.38	120	.059	.238	0	—	0	1	1	0	0.0
1978	KC-A	1	0	1.000	1	0	0	0	0	3	2	0	3	2	15.0	0.00	—	.222	.417	0	—	0	1	1	0	0.3
1979	KC-A	0	0	—	4	0	0	0	0	2²	7	0	5	1	40.5	13.50	32	.467	.600	0	—	0	-3	-3	-0	-0.1
	Hou-N	1	0	1.000	14	0	0	0	2	22¹	23	4	11	15	14.1	3.22	109	.271	.361	0	—	0	1	1	0	0.0
Total	4	2	0	1.000	30	0	0	0	3	42¹	41	6	25	27	14.2	3.83	97	.259	.364	0	.000	-0	-1	-0	0	0.1

● LOU THUMAN
Thuman, Louis Charles Frank b: 12/13/16, Baltimore, Md. BR/TR, 6'2", 185 lbs. Deb: 9/8/39

YEAR	TM/L	W	L	PCT	G	GS	CG	SH	SV	IP	H	HR	BB	SO	RAT	ERA	ERA+	OAV	OOB	BH	AVG	PB	PR	/A	PD	TPI
1939	Was-A	0	0	—	3	0	0	0	0	4	5	0	2	1	15.8	9.00	48	.278	.350	0	—	0	-2	-2	0	0.0
1940	Was-A	0	1	.000	2	0	0	0	0	5	10	0	7	0	30.6	14.40	29	.400	.531	0	—	0	-6	-6	-0	-0.8
Total	2	0	1	.000	5	0	0	0	0	9	15	0	9	1	24.0	12.00	35	.349	.462	0	.000	0	-8	-8	0	-0.8

● MARK THURMOND
Thurmond, Mark Anthony b: 9/12/56, Houston, Tex. BL/TL, 6', 193 lbs. Deb: 5/14/83

YEAR	TM/L	W	L	PCT	G	GS	CG	SH	SV	IP	H	HR	BB	SO	RAT	ERA	ERA+	OAV	OOB	BH	AVG	PB	PR	/A	PD	TPI
1983	SD-N	7	3	.700	21	18	2	0	0	115	104	7	33	49	10.8	2.65	131	.248	.306	2	.054	-2	12	11	1	0.8
1984	*SD-N	14	8	.636	32	29	1	1	0	178²	174	12	55	57	11.5	2.97	120	.256	.311	11	.190	1	12	12	2	1.8
1985	SD-N	7	11	.389	36	23	1	1	2	138¹	154	9	44	57	13.1	3.97	89	.291	.349	3	.088	-2	-6	-7	1	-0.9
1986	SD-N	3	7	.300	17	15	2	1	0	70²	96	7	27	32	15.7	6.50	56	.325	.382	6	.250	1	-22	-22	0	-2.6
	Det-A	4	1	.800	25	4	0	0	0	51²	44	7	17	17	10.6	1.92	215	.234	.298	0	—	0	13	13	1	1.2
1987	*Det-A	0	1	.000	48	0	0	0	0	61²	83	5	24	21	15.6	4.23	100	.331	.389	0	—	0	2	-0	-0	0.0
1988	Bal-A	1	8	.111	43	6	0	0	0	74²	70	7	29	13	11.4	4.58	85	.277	.343	0	—	0	-5	-6	-1	-0.7
1989	Bal-A	2	4	.333	49	2	0	0	4	90	102	6	17	34	12.0	3.90	97	.288	.323	0	—	0	-0	-1	-1	-0.1
1990	SF-N	2	3	.400	43	0	0	0	0	56²	53	6	18	24	11.3	3.34	109	.257	.317	0	.000	-1	3	1	1	0.3
Total	8	40	46	.465	314	97	6	3	21	837²	890	69	262	322	12.5	3.69	100	.277	.333	22	.139	-1	1	2	2	-0.2

● SLOPPY THURSTON
Thurston, Hollis John b: 6/2/1899, Fremont, Neb. d: 9/14/73, Los Angeles, Cal. BR/TR, 5'11", 165 lbs. Deb: 4/19/23

YEAR	TM/L	W	L	PCT	G	GS	CG	SH	SV	IP	H	HR	BB	SO	RAT	ERA	ERA+	OAV	OOB	BH	AVG	PB	PR	/A	PD	TPI
1923	StL-A	0	0	—	2	1	0	0	0	4	8	0	2	0	22.5	6.75	62	.421	.476	0	—	0	-1	-1	-0	0.0
	Chi-A	7	8	.467	44	12	8	0	4	191²	223	11	36	55	12.2	3.05	130	.308	.341	25	.316	6	20	19	-0	2.0
	Yr	7	8	.467	46	13	8	0	4	195²	231	11	38	55	12.4	3.13	127	.310	.345	25	.316	6	19	18	-1	2.0
1924	Chi-A	20	14	.588	38	36	28	1	1	291	330	17	60	37	12.2	3.80	108	.290	.329	31	.254	4	14	10	1	1.6
1925	Chi-A	10	14	.417	36	25	9	0	1	183	250	14	47	35	14.9	5.95	70	.335	.378	24	.286	7	-32	-37	2	-3.1
1926	Chi-A	6	8	.429	31	13	6	1	3	134¹	164	10	36	35	13.5	5.02	77	.311	.356	19	.311	6	-15	-17	-1	-1.3
1927	Was-A	13	13	.500	29	28	13	2	0	205¹	254	16	60	38	13.9	4.47	91	.308	.356	29	.315	9	-8	-9	-1	-0.2
1930	Bro-N	6	4	.600	24	11	5	0	0	106	110	4	17	26	10.8	3.40	145	.266	.295	10	.200	-0	19	18	2	1.5
1931	Bro-N	4	6	.400	30	9	2	0	0	143	175	5	38	34	13.8	3.97	96	.301	.346	13	.271	-1	-0	-1	-0	-0.1
1932	Bro-N	12	8	.600	28	20	12	0	0	153	173	7	38	35	12.5	4.06	94	.287	.330	17	.304	5	-3	-4	1	0.3
1933	Bro-N	6	8	.429	32	15	6	0	3	131¹	171	4	34	22	14.5	4.52	71	.319	.366	7	.159	-1	-17	-19	-2	-1.9
Total	9	89	86	.509	288	178	95	8	13	1542²	1859	93	369	306	13.1	4.24	94	.304	.346	175	.270	38	-25	-42	3	-1.4

YEAR	TM/L	W	L	PCT	G	GS	CG	SH	SV	IP	H	HR	BB	SO	RAT	ERA	ERA+	OAV	OOB	BH	AVG	PB	PR	/A	PD	TPI

● **LUIS TIANT**   Tiant, Luis Clemente (Vega)   b: 11/23/40, Marianao, Cuba   BR/TR, 5'11", 190 lbs.   Deb: 7/19/64

1964	Cle-A	10	4	.714	19	16	9	3	1	127	94	13	47	105	10.1	2.83	127	.207	.284	5	.111	-1	11	11	-0	1.1
1965	Cle-A	11	11	.500	41	30	10	2	1	196¹	166	20	66	152	10.8	3.53	99	.228	.295	6	.088	-2	-2	-1	-0	-0.3
1966	Cle-A	12	11	.522	46	16	7	**5**	8	155	121	16	50	145	10.0	2.79	123	.213	.279	4	.111	-1	11	11	-1	1.5
1967	Cle-A	12	9	.571	33	29	9	1	2	213²	177	24	67	219	10.3	2.74	119	.221	.282	18	.254	5	12	13	-2	1.5
1968	Cle-A★	21	9	.700	34	32	19	**9**	0	258¹	152	16	73	264	8.0	**1.60**	185	**.168**	**.233**	7	.080	-5	**40**	39	-3	4.2
1969	Cle-A	9	20	.310	38	37	9	1	0	249²	229	37	129	156	13.2	3.71	101	.246	.343	19	.235	6	-3	-1	-0	0.7
1970	*Min-A	7	3	.700	18	17	2	1	0	92²	84	12	41	50	12.3	3.40	109	.246	.330	13	.406	9	5	3	-0	0.9
1971	Bos-A	1	7	.125	21	10	1	0	0	72¹	73	8	32	59	13.2	4.85	76	.259	.337	6	.158	-0	-11	-9	-0	-1.0
1972	Bos-A	15	6	.714	43	19	12	6	3	179	128	7	65	123	9.7	**1.91**	168	.202	.277	6	.107	-2	23	26	-1	3.0
1973	Bos-A	20	13	.606	35	35	23	0	0	272	217	32	78	206	**10.0**	3.34	120	.219	**.281**	0	—	0	14	20	-1	2.0
1974	Bos-A★	22	13	.629	38	38	25	**7**	0	311¹	281	21	82	176	10.6	2.92	132	.241	.293	0	.000	0	24	32	-3	3.0
1975	*Bos-A	18	14	.563	35	35	18	2	0	260	262	25	72	142	11.7	4.02	101	.264	.316	0	.000	0	-7	-2	-3	-0.2
1976	Bos-A★	21	12	.636	38	38	19	3	0	279	274	25	64	131	11.0	3.06	128	.260	.304	0	.000	0	14	26	-2	2.8
1977	Bos-A	12	8	.600	32	32	3	0	0	188²	210	26	51	124	12.5	4.53	99	.279	.327	0	—	0	-10	-1	-2	-1.0
1978	Bos-A	13	8	.619	32	31	12	5	0	212¹	185	26	57	114	10.5	3.31	124	.234	.290	0	—	0	11	19	-2	0.8
1979	NY-A	13	8	.619	30	30	5	1	0	195²	190	22	53	104	11.2	3.91	104	.251	.300	0	—	0	7	4	-0	0.5
1980	NY-A	8	9	.471	25	25	3	0	0	136¹	139	10	50	84	12.5	4.89	80	.265	.330	0	—	0	-13	-15	1	-1.4
1981	Pit-N	2	5	.286	9	9	1	0	0	57¹	54	3	19	32	11.5	3.92	92	.243	.303	3	.188	1	-3	-2	-1	-0.3
1982	Cal-A	2	2	.500	6	5	0	0	0	29²	39	3	8	30	14.3	5.76	70	.310	.351	0	—	0	-6	-6	-1	-0.7
Total	19	229	172	.571	573	484	187	49	15	3486¹	3075	346	1104	2416	10.9	3.30	113	.236	.298	84	.164	6	116	173	-21	17.1

● **JAY TIBBS**   Tibbs, Jay Lindsey   b: 1/4/62, Birmingham, Ala.   BR/TR, 6'3", 185 lbs.   Deb: 7/15/84

1984	Cin-N	6	2	.750	14	14	3	1	0	100²	87	4	33	40	10.7	2.86	132	.238	.302	5	.139	-1	8	10	-1	0.6
1985	Cin-N	10	16	.385	35	34	5	2	0	218	216	14	83	98	12.3	3.92	97	.262	.329	6	.092	-3	-8	-3	1	-0.6
1986	Mon-N	7	9	.438	35	31	3	2	0	190¹	181	16	70	117	12.0	3.97	93	.256	.326	7	.130	-0	-5	-6	-1	-0.5
1987	Mon-N	4	5	.444	19	12	0	0	0	83	95	10	34	54	14.0	4.99	84	.289	.355	3	.120	-1	-8	-7	-1	-0.7
1988	Bal-A	4	15	.211	30	24	1	0	0	158²	184	18	63	82	14.2	5.39	72	.293	.360	0	—	0	-25	-26	0	-2.7
1989	Bal-A	1	0	1.000	10	8	1	0	0	54¹	62	2	20	30	13.6	2.82	135	.287	.347	0	—	0	6	6	-0	0.5
1990	Bal-A	2	7	.222	10	10	0	0	0	50²	55	8	14	23	12.3	5.68	67	.279	.327	0	—	0	-10	-11	0	-1.5
	Pit-N	1	0	1.000	5	0	0	0	0	7	7	0	2	4	11.6	2.57	141	.259	.310	0	—	0	1	1	0	0.1
Total	7	39	54	.419	158	133	13	5	0	862²	887	68	319	448	12.6	4.20	91	.269	.335	21	.117	-4	-41	-36	-1	-4.8

● **DICK TIDROW**   Tidrow, Richard William   b: 5/14/47, San Francisco, Cal.   BR/TR, 6'4", 213 lbs.   Deb: 4/18/72

1972	Cle-A	14	15	.483	39	34	10	3	0	237¹	200	21	70	123	10.5	2.77	116	.230	.291	7	.100	-3	8	12	-4	0.7
1973	Cle-A	14	16	.467	42	40	13	2	0	274²	289	31	95	138	12.8	4.42	89	.270	.334	0	—	0	-19	-15	-2	-1.7
1974	Cle-A	1	3	.250	4	4	0	0	0	19	21	4	13	6	17.1	7.11	51	.276	.396	0	—	0	-7	-7	-0	-1.2
	NY-A	11	9	.550	33	25	5	0	1	190²	205	14	53	100	12.4	3.87	91	.279	.331	0	—	0	-5	-7	-2	-0.8
	Yr	12	12	.500	37	29	5	0	1	209²	226	18	66	108	12.7	4.16	85	.278	.335	0	—	0	-13	-15	-1	-2.0
1975	NY-A	6	3	.667	37	0	0	0	5	69¹	65	5	31	38	12.9	3.12	118	.256	.344	0	—	0	5	4	-0	0.5
1976	*NY-A	4	5	.444	47	2	0	0	10	92¹	80	5	24	65	10.2	2.63	130	.233	.285	0	—	0	9	8	-1	0.8
1977	*NY-A	11	4	.733	49	7	0	0	5	151	143	20	41	83	11.1	3.16	125	.250	.303	0	—	0	15	13	-1	1.3
1978	*NY-A	7	11	.389	31	25	4	0	0	185¹	191	13	53	73	12.1	3.84	94	.267	.322	0	—	0	-2	-4	-2	-0.4
1979	NY-A	1	0	1.000	14	0	0	0	2	22³	38	4	7	16	16.7	7.94	51	.409	.433	0	—	0	-9	-10	1	-1.0
	Chi-N	11	5	.688	63	0	0	0	4	102²	86	5	42	68	11.4	2.72	151	.231	.313	2	.200	1	12	16	1	2.7
1980	Chi-N	6	5	.545	**84**	0	0	0	6	116	97	10	53	97	12.0	2.79	140	.229	.322	0	.000	-0	10	14	-1	1.4
1981	Chi-N	3	10	.231	51	0	0	0	0	74²	73	6	30	39	12.5	5.06	73	.256	.329	0	.000	-1	-13	-11	-1	-2.3
1982	Chi-N	8	3	.727	65	0	0	0	7	103²	106	6	29	62	12.0	3.39	110	.265	.319	0	.000	-1	2	4	-2	0.2
1983	*Chi-A	2	4	.333	50	1	0	0	7	91²	86	13	34	66	11.9	4.22	99	.242	.310	0	—	0	-2	-0	-1	-0.2
1984	NY-N	0	0	—	11	0	0	0	0	15²	25	7	5	8	18.4	9.19	38	.357	.416	0	—	0	-10	-10	0	-0.7
Total	13	100	94	.515	620	138	32	5	55	1746²	1705	163	579	975	12.0	3.68	101	.257	.321	9	.095	-5	-5	7	-11	0.0

● **BOBBY TIEFENAUER**   Tiefenauer, Bobby Gene   b: 10/10/29, Desloge, Mo.   BR/TR, 6'2", 185 lbs.   Deb: 7/14/52   C

1952	StL-N	0	0	—	6	0	0	0	0	8	12	1	7	3	21.4	7.88	47	.343	.452	0	.000	-0	-4	-4	0	-0.4
1955	StL-N	1	4	.200	18	0	0	0	0	32²	31	6	10	16	12.4	4.41	92	.261	.338	0	.000	-0	-1	-1	-0	-0.2
1960	Cle-A	0	1	.000	6	0	0	0	0	9	8	0	3	2	11.0	2.00	187	.242	.306	0	.000	0	2	2	-0	0.2
1961	StL-N	0	0	—	3	0	0	0	0	4¹	9	0	4	3	27.0	6.23	71	.450	.542	0	—	0	-1	-1	-0	-0.0
1962	Hou-N	2	4	.333	43	0	0	0	2	85	91	6	21	60	12.1	4.34	86	.277	.324	1	.111	-0	-4	-6	-2	-0.5
1963	Mil-N	1	1	.500	12	0	0	0	1	29²	20	1	4	22	7.3	1.21	265	.194	.224	0	—	0	7	7	1	0.6
1964	Mil-N	4	6	.400	46	0	0	0	13	73	61	6	15	48	9.7	3.21	110	.225	.273	0	—	-1	3	3	-1	0.2
1965	Mil-N	0	1	.000	7	0	0	0	0	7	8	3	7	7	15.4	7.71	46	.286	.375	0	—	0	-3	-3	0	-0.4
	NY-A	1	1	.500	10	0	0	0	2	20¹	19	3	5	15	11.1	3.54	96	.253	.309	0	—	-0	-0	-0	-0	-0.0
	Cle-A	0	5	.000	15	0	0	0	4	22¹	24	3	10	13	14.1	4.84	72	.273	.354	0	.000	-0	-3	-3	-0	-0.9
	Yr	1	6	.143	25	0	0	0	6	42²	43	6	15	28	12.4	4.22	82	.259	.324	0	.000	-0	-4	-4	-0	-0.9
1967	Cle-A	0	1	.000	5	0	0	0	0	11¹	9	0	3	6	9.5	0.79	411	.225	.279	0	—	0	3	3	-1	0.2
1968	Chi-N	0	1	.000	5	0	0	0	0	13¹	20	2	5	9	17.6	6.08	52	.351	.373	0	—	0	-5	-4	-0	-0.4
Total	10	9	25	.265	179	0	0	0	23	316	312	29	87	204	11.7	3.84	94	.260	.317	1	.026	-1	-9	-7	-2	-1.2

● **VERLE TIEFENTHALER**   Tiefenthaler, Verle Matthew   b: 7/11/37, Breda, Iowa   BL/TR, 6'1", 190 lbs.   Deb: 4/19/62

| 1962 | Chi-A | 0 | 0 | — | 3 | 0 | 0 | 0 | 0 | 3² | 6 | 1 | 7 | 1 | 31.9 | 9.82 | 40 | .353 | .542 | 0 | — | 0 | -2 | -2 | -0 | 0.0 |

● **EDDIE TIEMEYER**   Tiemeyer, Edward Carl   b: 5/9/1885, Cincinnati, Ohio   d: 9/27/46, Cincinnati, Ohio   BR/TR, 5'11.5", 185 lbs.   Deb: 8/19/06 ◆

| 1906 | Cin-N | 0 | 0 | — | 1 | 0 | 0 | 0 | 0 | 1 | 1 | 0 | 1 | 0 | 18.0 | 0.00 | — | .500 | .667 | 2 | .182 | 0 | 0 | 0 | -0 | 0.0 |

● **MIKE TIERNAN**   Tiernan, Michael Joseph "Silent Mike"   b: 1/21/1867, Trenton, N.J.   d: 11/9/18, New York, N.Y.   BL/TL, 5'11", 165 lbs.   Deb: 4/30/1887 ◆

| 1887 | NY-N | 1 | 2 | .333 | 5 | 0 | 0 | 0 | **1** | 19² | 33 | 2 | 7 | 3 | 18.8 | 8.69 | 43 | .398 | .451 | 117 | .287 | 2 | -10 | -11 | -0 | -1.2 |

● **LES TIETJE**   Tietje, Leslie William "Toots"   b: 9/11/11, Sumner, Iowa   d: 10/2/96, Rochester, Minn.   BR/TR, 6'0.5", 178 lbs.   Deb: 9/18/33

1933	Chi-A	2	0	1.000	3	3	1	0	0	22¹	16	1	9	12	12.5	2.42	175	.203	.330	1	.125	0	5	5	0	0.4
1934	Chi-A	5	14	.263	34	22	8	1	0	176	174	20	96	81	13.9	4.81	98	.257	.351	1	.017	-7	-6	-1	2	-0.7
1935	Chi-A	9	15	.375	30	21	9	1	0	169²	184	14	81	64	14.2	4.30	108	.277	.357	12	.197	-1	3	6	-2	0.5
1936	Chi-A	0	0	—	2	0	0	0	0	2¹	9	0	5	3	42.4	27.00	19	.462	.611	0	—	0	-6	-6	-0	0.0
	StL-A	3	5	.375	14	7	2	0	0	50¹	65	2	30	16	17.3	6.62	81	.310	.401	1	.067	-1	-9	-7	1	-0.9
	Yr	3	5	.375	16	7	2	0	0	52²	71	2	35	19	18.5	7.52	71	.318	.415	1	.067	-1	-15	-13	1	-0.9
1937	StL-A	1	2	.333	5	4	1	0	0	30	32	0	17	5	14.7	4.20	115	.283	.377	0	.000	-1	2	2	-1	0.0
1938	StL-A	2	5	.286	17	8	1	0	0	62	83	8	38	15	17.6	7.55	66	.327	.414	2	.111	-1	-19	-18	-0	-1.7
Total	6	22	41	.349	105	65	22	3	0	512²	560	45	282	193	14.9	5.11	93	.279	.369	17	.099	-12	-31	-19	0	-2.4

● **RAY TIFT**   Tift, Raymond Frank   b: 6/21/1884, Fitchburg, Mass.   d: 3/29/45, Verona, N.J.   TL ,   Deb: 8/7/07

| 1907 | NY-A | 0 | 0 | — | 4 | 1 | 0 | 0 | 0 | 19 | 33 | 1 | 6 | 4 | 17.5 | 4.74 | 59 | .384 | .411 | 0 | .000 | -0 | -5 | -4 | -1 | -0.1 |

● **JOHNNY TILLMAN**   Tillman, John Lawrence "Ducky"   b: 10/6/1893, Bridgeport, Conn.   d: 4/7/64, Harrisburg, Pa.   BB/TR, 5'11", 170 lbs.   Deb: 9/20/15

| 1915 | StL-A | 1 | 0 | 1.000 | 2 | 1 | 0 | 0 | 0 | 10 | 6 | 0 | 4 | 6 | 9.0 | 0.90 | 318 | .176 | .263 | 0 | .000 | -0 | 2 | 2 | 0 | 0.2 |

● **THAD TILLOTSON**   Tillotson, Thaddeus Asa   b: 12/20/40, Merced, Cal.   BR/TR, 6'2.5", 195 lbs.   Deb: 4/14/67

1967	NY-A	3	9	.250	43	5	1	0	2	98¹	99	9	39	62	12.8	4.03	78	.261	.333	1	.063	-0	-9	-10	0	-1.2
1968	NY-A	1	0	1.000	7	0	0	0	0	10¹	11	0	7	1	15.7	4.35	67	.282	.391	0	.000	-0	-2	-2	0	-0.1
Total	2	4	9	.308	50	5	1	0	2	108²	110	9	46	63	13.1	4.06	77	.263	.339	1	.059	-1	-10	-11	1	-1.3

● **GARY TIMBERLAKE**   Timberlake, Gary Dale   b: 8/8/48, Laconia, Ind.   BR/TL, 6'2", 205 lbs.   Deb: 6/18/69

| 1969 | Sea-A | 0 | 0 | — | 2 | 2 | 0 | 0 | 0 | 6 | 7 | 0 | 9 | 4 | 24.0 | 7.50 | 48 | .269 | .457 | 0 | .000 | -0 | -3 | -3 | -0 | 0.0 |

YEAR	TM/L	W	L	PCT	G	GS	CG	SH	SV	IP	H	HR	BB	SO	RAT	ERA	ERA+	OAV	OOB	BH	AVG	PB	PR	/A	PD	TPI
● MIKE TIMLIN	Timlin, Michael August b: 3/10/66, Midland, Tex. BR/TR, 6'4", 205 lbs. Deb: 4/8/91																								
1991	*Tor-A	11	6	.647	63	3	0	0	3	108¹	94	6	50	85	12.0	3.16	133	.233	.319	0	—	0	11	13	1	1.9
1992	Tor-A	0	2	.000	26	0	0	0	1	43²	45	0	20	35	13.6	4.12	99	.271	.353	0	—	0	-1	-0	0	-0.1
1993	*Tor-A	4	2	.667	54	0	0	0	1	55²	63	7	27	49	14.7	4.69	92	.284	.364	0	—	0	-2	-2	1	-0.1
1994	Tor-A	0	1	.000	34	0	0	0	2	40	41	5	20	38	14.2	5.17	93	.261	.352	0	—	0	-2	-2	0	0.0
1995	Tor-A	4	3	.571	31	0	0	0	5	42	38	1	17	36	12.2	2.14	220	.242	.324	0	—	0	12	12	1	2.1
1996	Tor-A	1	6	.143	59	0	0	0	31	56²	47	4	18	52	10.6	3.65	138	.229	.298	0	—	0	8	9	-0	1.7
Total	6	20	20	.500	267	3	0	0	43	346¹	328	23	152	295	12.7	3.72	121	.250	.332	0	—	0	27	29	3	5.5
● TOM TIMMERMANN	Timmermann, Thomas Henry b: 5/12/40, Breese, Ill. BR/TR, 6'4", 215 lbs. Deb: 6/18/69																								
1969	Det-A	4	3	.571	31	1	1	0	1	55²	50	1	26	42	12.6	2.75	136	.238	.328	1	.111	-0	5	6	-1	0.6
1970	Det-A	6	7	.462	61	0	0	0	27	85¹	90	3	34	49	13.3	4.11	91	.273	.344	0	.000	-2	-4	-4	-0	-1.0
1971	Det-A	7	6	.538	52	2	0	0	4	84	82	6	37	51	13.1	3.86	93	.262	.346	1	.053	-1	-4	-2	-0	-0.5
1972	Det-A	8	10	.444	34	25	3	2	0	149²	121	12	41	88	10.0	2.89	109	.216	.276	6	.136	-0	3	4	-2	0.3
1973	Det-A	1	1	.500	17	1	0	0	1	39	39	4	11	21	11.5	3.69	111	.258	.309	0	—	0	1	2	-1	-0.2
	Cle-A	8	7	.533	29	15	4	0	2	124¹	117	15	54	62	12.6	4.92	80	.251	.332	0	—	0	-15	-14	-0	-1.6
	Yr	9	8	.529	46	16	4	0	3	163¹	156	19	65	83	12.3	4.63	86	.252	.327	0	—	0	-15	-12	-1	-1.8
1974	Cle-A	1	1	.500	4	0	0	0	0	10	9	1	5	2	12.6	5.40	67	.250	.341	0	—	0	-2	-2	1	-0.3
Total	6	35	35	.500	228	44	8	2	35	548	508	42	208	315	12.0	3.78	96	.246	.319	8	.091	-4	-16	-10	-3	-2.7
● BEN TINCUP	Tincup, Austin Ben b: 12/14/1890, Adair, Okla. d: 7/5/80, Claremore, Okla. BL/TR, 6'1", 180 lbs. Deb: 5/22/14 C◆																								
1914	Phi-N	8	10	.444	28	17	9	3	2	155	165	0	62	108	13.4	2.61	113	.286	.359	9	.170	-1	3	6	1	0.7
1915	Phi-N	0	0	—	10	0	0	0	0	31	26	1	9	10	10.2	2.03	135	.263	.324	0	.000	-1	2	2	0	-0.1
1918	Phi-N	0	1	.000	8	1	0	0	0	16²	24	1	6	6	16.2	7.56	40	.329	.380	1	.125	-0	-9	-8	1	-0.4
1928	Chi-N	0	0	—	2	0	0	0	0	9	14	0	1	3	15.0	7.00	55	.378	.395	0	.000	-0	-3	-3	0	0.0
Total	4	8	11	.421	48	18	9	3	2	211²	229	2	78	127	13.2	3.40	95	.291	.358	10	.135	-3	-6	-3	2	0.2
● BUD TINNING	Tinning, Lyle Forrest b: 3/12/06, Pilger, Neb. d: 1/17/61, Evansville, Ind. BB/TR, 5'11", 198 lbs. Deb: 4/20/32																								
1932	*Chi-N	5	3	.625	24	7	2	0	0	93¹	93	3	24	30	11.5	2.80	135	.263	.313	2	.087	-1	11	10	0	0.7
1933	Chi-N	13	6	.684	32	21	10	3	1	175¹	169	3	60	59	12.0	3.18	103	.255	.320	14	.209	1	3	2	-2	0.0
1934	Chi-N	4	6	.400	39	7	1	1	3	129¹	134	9	46	44	12.6	3.34	116	.269	.332	7	.179	-1	10	8	-1	0.4
1935	StL-N	0	0	—	4	0	0	0	0	7²	9	1	5	2	17.6	5.87	70	.300	.417	0	.000	-0	-2	-2	0	0.0
Total	4	22	15	.595	99	35	13	4	4	405²	405	16	135	135	12.2	3.19	113	.262	.325	23	.177	-1	23	18	-4	1.1
● DAN TIPPLE	Tipple, Daniel E. "Big Dan" or "Rusty" b: 2/13/1890, Rockford, Ill. d: 3/26/60, Omaha, Neb. BR/TR, 6', 176 lbs. Deb: 9/18/15																								
1915	NY-A	1	1	.500	3	2	2	0	0	19	14	1	11	14	11.8	0.95	310	.203	.313	0	.000	-1	4	4	-1	0.2
● JACK TISING	Tising, Johnnie Joseph b: 10/9/03, High Point, Mo. d: 9/5/67, Leadville, Colo. BL/TR, 6'2", 180 lbs. Deb: 4/24/36																								
1936	Pit-N	1	3	.250	10	6	1	0	0	47	52	5	24	27	14.6	4.21	96	.272	.353	3	.273	0	-1	-1	-0	-0.1
● CANNONBALL TITCOMB	Titcomb, Ledell b: 8/21/1866, W.Baldwin, Me. d: 6/8/50, Kingston, N.H. BL/TL, 5'6", 157 lbs. Deb: 5/5/1886																								
1886	Phi-N	0	5	.000	5	5	5	0	0	41	43	1	24	24	14.7	3.73	88	.244	.335	1	.063	-2	-2	-2	-1	-0.3
1887	Phi-a	1	2	.333	3	3	3	0	0	24	31	1	19	16	18.8	6.75	64	.298	.407	0	.000	-1	-7	-7	-1	-0.7
	NY-N	4	3	.571	9	9	9	0	0	72	68	3	37	34	13.3	3.88	97	.233	.321	2	.069	-4	2	-1	-1	-0.5
1888	*NY-N	14	8	.636	23	23	22	4	0	197	149	4	46	129	9.1	2.24	122	.201	.253	10	.122	-4	13	11	-4	0.2
1889	NY-N	1	2	.333	3	3	3	0	0	26	27	1	16	7	15.6	6.58	60	.260	.369	1	.083	-1	-7	-8	-0	-0.7
1890	Roc-a	10	9	.526	20	19	19	1	0	168²	168	6	97	73	14.9	3.74	95	.251	.358	8	.107	-5	3	-3	-3	-1.0
Total	5	30	29	.508	63	62	61	5	0	528²	486	16	239	283	12.7	3.47	96	.233	.318	22	.098	-18	2	-9	-8	-3.0
● DAVE TOBIK	Tobik, David Vance b: 3/2/53, Euclid, Ohio BR/TR, 6'1", 195 lbs. Deb: 8/26/78																								
1978	Det-A	0	0	—	5	0	0	0	0	12	12	1	3	11	11.3	3.75	103	.261	.306	0	—	0	0	0	-0	-0.2
1979	Det-A	3	5	.375	37	0	0	0	3	68²	59	12	25	48	11.0	4.33	100	.231	.300	0	—	0	-1	-0	-1	-0.3
1980	Det-A	1	0	1.000	17	1	0	0	0	61	61	7	21	34	12.1	3.98	103	.266	.328	0	—	0	0	1	-0	-0.1
1981	Det-A	2	2	.500	27	0	0	0	1	60¹	47	7	33	32	11.9	2.69	140	.215	.317	0	—	0	7	7	-1	0.2
1982	Det-A	4	9	.308	51	1	0	0	9	98²	86	8	38	63	11.4	3.56	114	.241	.316	0	—	0	6	6	-1	0.7
1983	Tex-A	2	1	.667	27	0	0	0	9	44	36	2	13	30	10.0	3.68	109	.222	.280	0	—	0	2	2	0	0.3
1984	Tex-A	1	6	.143	24	0	0	0	5	42¹	44	5	17	30	13.2	3.61	115	.265	.337	0	—	0	2	2	1	0.2
1985	Sea-A	1	0	1.000	8	0	0	0	1	9	10	2	3	8	13.0	6.00	70	.286	.342	0	—	0	-2	-2	-0	-0.2
Total	8	14	23	.378	196	2	0	0	28	396	355	44	153	256	11.6	3.70	110	.242	.314	0	—	0	13	16	-3	0.6
● JIM TOBIN	Tobin, James Anthony "Abba Dabba" b: 12/27/12, Oakland, Cal. d: 5/19/69, Oakland, Cal. BR/TR, 6', 185 lbs. Deb: 4/30/37 F◆																								
1937	Pit-N	6	3	.667	20	8	7	0	1	87	74	1	20	37	10.7	3.00	129	.226	.289	15	.441	7	9	8	-2	1.4
1938	Pit-N	14	12	.538	40	33	14	2	0	241¹	254	17	66	70	12.2	3.47	109	.270	.321	25	.243	7	9	9	-2	1.3
1939	Pit-N	9	9	.500	25	19	8	0	0	145¹	194	7	33	43	14.2	4.52	85	.319	.356	18	.243	5	-10	-11	-1	-0.8
1940	Bos-N	7	3	.700	15	11	9	0	0	96¹	102	8	24	29	11.8	3.83	97	.264	.307	12	.279	3	0	-1	-1	0.2
1941	Bos-N	12	12	.500	33	26	20	3	0	238	229	12	60	61	10.9	3.10	115	.253	.300	19	.184	3	14	12	4	2.0
1942	Bos-N	12	21	.364	37	33	**28**	1	0	**287²**	283	20	96	71	12.0	3.97	84	.257	.320	28	.246	14	-21	-20	6	-0.1
1943	Bos-N	14	14	.500	33	30	24	1	0	250	241	12	69	52	11.2	2.66	128	.251	.303	30	.280	6	20	21	2	3.5
1944	Bos-N★	18	19	.486	43	36	**28**	5	3	299¹	271	18	97	81	11.2	3.01	127	.240	.302	22	.190	5	20	27	7	4.7
1945	Bos-N	9	14	.391	27	25	16	0	0	196²	220	10	56	38	12.9	3.84	100	.282	.334	11	.143	5	-1	-0	2	0.7
	*Det-A	4	5	.444	14	12	2	0	1	58¹	61	2	28	14	14.3	3.55	99	.274	.365	3	.120	1	0	-0	1	0.1
Total	9	105	112	.484	287	227	156	12	5	1900	1929	107	557	498	11.9	3.44	106	.262	.316	183	.230	54	39	45	16	13.0
● PAT TOBIN	Tobin, Marion Brooks b: 1/28/16, Hermitage, Ark. d: 1/21/75, Shreveport, La. BR/TR, 6'1", 198 lbs. Deb: 8/21/41																								
1941	Phi-A	0	0	—	1	0	0	0	0	1	4	0	2	0	54.0	36.00	12	.571	.667	0	—	0	-4	-4	0	0.0
● FRANK TODD	Todd, George Franklin b: 10/18/1869, Aberdeen, Md. d: 8/11/19, Havre De Grace, Md. TL , Deb: 7/14/1898																								
1898	Lou-N	0	2	.000	4	2	0	0	0	11	23	0	8	5	27.0	13.91	26	.418	.508	1	.200	0	-13	-13	-1	-1.6
● JACKSON TODD	Todd, Jackson A b: 11/20/51, Tulsa, Okla. BR/TR, 6'2", 180 lbs. Deb: 5/5/77																								
1977	NY-N	3	6	.333	19	10	0	0	0	71²	78	8	20	39	12.6	4.77	78	.273	.325	1	.059	-1	-7	-8	0	-1.0
1979	Tor-A	1	0	1.000	12	1	0	0	0	32¹	40	7	7	14	13.4	5.85	74	.299	.338	0	—	0	-6	-5	0	-0.2
1980	Tor-A	5	2	.714	12	12	4	0	0	85	90	14	30	44	12.9	4.02	107	.276	.341	0	—	0	0	3	1	0.1
1981	Tor-A	1	7	.222	21	13	3	0	0	97²	94	10	31	41	11.9	3.96	99	.251	.315	0	—	0	-3	-0	1	-0.1
Total	4	10	16	.385	64	36	7	0	0	286²	302	39	88	138	12.6	4.40	89	.270	.328	1	.059	-1	-16	-11	2	-1.2
● JIM TODD	Todd, James Richard b: 9/21/47, Lancaster, Pa. BL/TR, 6'2", 190 lbs. Deb: 4/29/74																								
1974	Chi-N	4	2	.667	43	6	0	0	0	88	82	7	41	42	12.9	3.89	98	.252	.341	1	.063	-1	-3	-1	-1	-0.1
1975	*Oak-A	8	3	.727	58	0	0	0	12	122	104	4	33	50	10.3	2.29	159	.234	.292	0	—	0	20	18	4	2.3
1976	Oak-A	7	8	.467	49	0	0	0	4	82²	84	2	32	22	12.8	3.81	88	.276	.358	0	—	0	-3	-4	-2	-0.6
1977	Chi-N	1	1	.500	20	0	0	0	0	30²	47	1	19	17	20.0	9.10	48	.336	.422	0	—	-0	-18	-16	0	-0.9
1978	Sea-A	3	4	.429	49	0	0	0	0	106²	113	4	61	37	14.7	3.88	98	.280	.375	0	—	0	-1	-1	0	0.0
1979	Oak-A	2	5	.286	51	0	0	0	8	81	108	12	51	26	17.9	6.56	62	.329	.423	0	—	0	-21	-23	7	-1.4
Total	6	25	23	.521	270	8	0	0	24	511	541	34	239	194	14.0	4.23	89	.280	.360	1	.059	-2	-25	-26	7	-0.7
● HAL TOENES	Toenes, William Harrel b: 10/8/17, Mobile, Ala. BR/TR, 5'11.5", 175 lbs. Deb: 9/17/47																								
1947	Was-A	0	1	.000	3	1	0	0	0	6²	11	0	5	2	17.6	6.75	55	.379	.419	0	.000	0	-2	-2	-0	-0.3
● FREDDIE TOLIVER	Toliver, Freddie Lee b: 2/3/61, Natchez, Miss. BR/TR, 6'1", 170 lbs. Deb: 9/15/84																								
1984	Cin-N	0	0	—	3	1	0	0	0	10	7	0	7	4	12.6	0.90	420	.206	.341	0	.000	-0	3	3	-0	0.0
1985	Phi-N	0	4	.000	11	3	0	0	1	25	27	2	17	23	15.8	4.68	79	.273	.379	2	.500	1	-3	-3	-0	-0.4
1986	Phi-N	0	0	—	5	5	0	0	0	25²	28	0	11	20	13.7	3.51	110	.286	.358	0	.000	-0	1	1	0	0.1

YEAR	TM/L	W	L	PCT	G	GS	CG	SH	SV	IP	H	HR	BB	SO	RAT	ERA	ERA+	OAV	OOB	BH	AVG	PB	PR	/A	PD	TPI
1987	Phi-N	1	1	.500	10	4	0	0	0	30¹	34	2	17	25	15.4	5.64	75	.291	.385	0	.000	-1	-5	-5	0	-0.2
1988	Min-A	7	6	.538	21	19	0	0	0	114²	116	8	52	69	13.3	4.24	96	.270	.350	0	—	0	-3	-2	0	-0.2
1989	Min-A	1	3	.250	7	5	0	0	0	29	39	2	15	11	17.1	7.76	53	.317	.396	0	—	0	-12	-12	1	-1.2
	SD-N	0	0	—	9	0	0	0	0	14	17	5	9	14	17.4	7.07	49	.321	.429	0	—	0	-6	-6	0	0.0
1993	Pit-N	1	0	1.000	12	0	0	0	0	21²	20	2	8	14	12.5	3.74	108	.267	.353	0	.000	-0	1	1	-1	0.0
Total	7	10	16	.385	78	37	0	0	1	270¹	288	21	136	180	14.3	4.73	85	.280	.367	2	.111	-0	-25	-22	1	-2.0

● **DICK TOMANEK**   Tomanek, Richard Carl "Bones" b: 1/6/31, Avon Lake, Ohio BL/TL, 6'1", 175 lbs. Deb: 9/25/53

YEAR	TM/L	W	L	PCT	G	GS	CG	SH	SV	IP	H	HR	BB	SO	RAT	ERA	ERA+	OAV	OOB	BH	AVG	PB	PR	/A	PD	TPI
1953	Cle-A	1	0	1.000	1	1	1	0	0	9	6	1	6	6	13.0	2.00	188	.176	.317	0	.000	-1	2	2	-0	0.1
1954	Cle-A	1	0	—	1	0	0	0	0	1²	1	1	1	0	10.8	5.40	68	.167	.286	0	—	-0	-0	-0	-0	0.0
1957	Cle-A	2	1	.667	34	2	0	0	0	69²	67	13	37	55	13.6	5.68	65	.248	.341	3	.231	0	-15	-15	-0	-0.5
1958	Cle-A	2	3	.400	18	6	2	0	0	57²	61	8	28	42	14.2	5.62	65	.276	.363	2	.118	-0	-12	-13	-0	-0.9
	KC-A	5	5	.500	36	2	1	0	5	72¹	69	5	28	50	12.1	3.61	108	.252	.321	3	.231	1	1	2	-0	0.4
	Yr	7	8	.467	54	8	3	0	5	130	130	13	56	92	12.9	4.50	84	.261	.336	5	.167	1	-11	-10	-0	-0.5
1959	KC-A	0	1	.000	16	0	0	0	2	20²	27	6	12	13	17.9	6.53	61	.310	.406	1	.500	-0	-6	-6	-0	-0.3
Total	5	10	10	.500	106	11	4	0	7	231	231	34	112	166	13.6	4.95	77	.259	.346	9	.180	1	-30	-30	1	-1.2

● **ANDY TOMASIC**   Tomasic, Andrew John b: 12/10/19, Hokendauqua, Pa. BR/TR, 6', 175 lbs. Deb: 4/28/49

YEAR	TM/L	W	L	PCT	G	GS	CG	SH	SV	IP	H	HR	BB	SO	RAT	ERA	ERA+	OAV	OOB	BH	AVG	PB	PR	/A	PD	TPI
1949	NY-N	0	1	.000	2	0	0	0	0	5	9	2	5	2	25.2	18.00	22	.375	.483	0	.000	-0	-8	-8	-0	-1.1

● **ANDY TOMBERLIN**   Tomberlin, Andy Lee b: 11/7/66, Monroe, N.C. BL/TL, 5'11", 160 lbs. Deb: 8/12/93 ♦

YEAR	TM/L	W	L	PCT	G	GS	CG	SH	SV	IP	H	HR	BB	SO	RAT	ERA	ERA+	OAV	OOB	BH	AVG	PB	PR	/A	PD	TPI
1994	Bos-A	0	0	—	1	0	0	0	0	2	1	0	1	1	9.0	0.00	—	.143	.250	7	.194	1	1	1	-0	0.0

● **DAVE TOMLIN**   Tomlin, David Allen b: 6/22/49, Maysville, Ky. BL/TL, 6'3", 185 lbs. Deb: 9/2/72

YEAR	TM/L	W	L	PCT	G	GS	CG	SH	SV	IP	H	HR	BB	SO	RAT	ERA	ERA+	OAV	OOB	BH	AVG	PB	PR	/A	PD	TPI
1972	Cin-N	0	0	—	3	0	0	0	0	4	7	2	1	2	18.0	9.00	36	.412	.444	0	—	0	-2	-3	0	0.0
1973	*Cin-N	1	2	.333	16	0	0	0	1	27²	24	5	15	20	12.7	4.88	70	.238	.336	0	.000	-0	-4	-5	0	-0.5
1974	SD-N	2	0	1.000	47	0	0	0	2	58	59	4	30	29	14.1	4.34	82	.271	.364	0	.000	-0	-5	-5	1	-0.2
1975	SD-N	2	1	.667	67	0	0	0	1	83	87	5	31	48	13.0	3.25	107	.275	.344	1	.200	1	3	2	3	0.6
1976	SD-N	0	1	.000	49	1	0	0	0	73	62	4	20	43	10.2	2.84	115	.235	.291	0	.000	-1	5	4	2	0.2
1977	SD-N	4	4	.500	76	0	0	0	3	101²	98	3	32	55	11.7	3.01	118	.259	.320	2	.286	0	10	6	1	0.6
1978	Cin-N	9	1	.900	57	0	0	0	4	62¹	88	3	30	32	17.5	5.78	61	.326	.399	1	.200	-0	-15	-15	-1	-2.5
1979	*Cin-N	2	2	.500	53	0	0	0	1	58¹	59	3	18	30	12.2	2.62	142	.269	.328	1	.500	1	7	7	0	0.5
1980	Cin-N	3	0	1.000	27	0	0	0	0	26	38	2	11	6	17.0	5.54	65	.355	.415	0	—	-0	-6	-6	-0	-0.5
1982	Mon-N	0	0	—	1	0	0	0	0	2	1	0	1	2	9.0	4.50	81	.167	.286	0	—	-0	-0	-0	-0	0.0
1983	Pit-N	0	0	—	5	0	0	0	0	4	6	0	1	5	15.8	6.75	55	.316	.350	0	—	-1	-1	-0	-0	0.0
1985	Pit-N	0	0	—	1	0	0	0	0	1	0	0	1	0	18.0	0.00	—	.333	.500	0	—	-0	0	-0	0	0.0
1986	Mon-N	0	0	—	7	0	0	0	0	10¹	13	1	7	6	18.3	5.23	71	.317	.429	0	—	0	-2	-0	0	0.0
Total	13	25	12	.676	409	1	0	0	12	511¹	543	32	198	278	13.3	3.82	92	.277	.347	5	.147	1	-17	-9	-1.8

● **RANDY TOMLIN**   Tomlin, Randy Leon b: 6/14/66, Bainbridge, Md. BL/TL, 5'11", 179 lbs. Deb: 8/6/90

YEAR	TM/L	W	L	PCT	G	GS	CG	SH	SV	IP	H	HR	BB	SO	RAT	ERA	ERA+	OAV	OOB	BH	AVG	PB	PR	/A	PD	TPI
1990	Pit-N	4	4	.500	12	12	2	0	0	77²	62	5	12	42	8.7	2.55	142	.221	.256	1	.040	-1	11	9	1	0.9
1991	*Pit-N	8	7	.533	31	27	4	2	0	175	170	9	54	104	11.8	2.98	120	.254	.316	10	.192	1	14	11	2	1.3
1992	*Pit-N	14	9	.609	35	33	1	1	0	208²	226	11	42	90	11.8	3.41	101	.282	.322	9	.138	0	2	3	3	0.4
1993	Pit-N	4	8	.333	18	18	1	0	0	98¹	109	11	15	44	11.8	4.85	83	.291	.327	6	.182	-0	-9	-9	1	-0.8
1994	Pit-N	0	3	.000	10	4	0	0	0	20²	23	1	10	17	14.4	3.92	110	.291	.371	3	.500	1	1	1	0	0.2
Total	5	30	31	.492	106	94	8	3	0	580¹	590	37	133	297	11.5	3.43	106	.268	.314	29	.160	1	18	13	7	2.0

● **CHUCK TOMPKINS**   Tompkins, Charles Herbert b: 9/1/1889, Prescott, Ark. d: 9/20/75, Prescott, Ark. BR/TR, 6', 185 lbs. Deb: 6/25/12

YEAR	TM/L	W	L	PCT	G	GS	CG	SH	SV	IP	H	HR	BB	SO	RAT	ERA	ERA+	OAV	OOB	BH	AVG	PB	PR	/A	PD	TPI
1912	Cin-N	0	0	—	1	0	0	0	0	3	5	0	1	1	15.0	0.00	—	.357	.357	1	1.000	-0	1	1	-0	0.0

● **RON TOMPKINS**   Tompkins, Ronald Everett "Stretch" b: 11/27/44, San Diego, Cal. BR/TR, 6'4", 198 lbs. Deb: 9/9/65

YEAR	TM/L	W	L	PCT	G	GS	CG	SH	SV	IP	H	HR	BB	SO	RAT	ERA	ERA+	OAV	OOB	BH	AVG	PB	PR	/A	PD	TPI
1965	KC-A	0	0	—	5	1	0	0	0	10¹	9	3	4	11.3	3.48	100	.237	.310	0	.000	-0	-0	-0	0	0.0
1971	Chi-N	0	2	.000	35	0	0	0	3	39²	31	3	21	20	12.5	4.08	96	.214	.325	0	—	0	-3	-1	1	0.1
Total	2	0	2	.000	40	1	0	0	3	50	40	3	24	24	12.2	3.96	97	.219	.322	0	.000	-0	-3	-1	1	0.1

● **TOMMY TOMS**   Toms, Thomas Howard b: 10/15/51, Charlottesville, Va BR/TR, 6'4", 195 lbs. Deb: 5/4/75

YEAR	TM/L	W	L	PCT	G	GS	CG	SH	SV	IP	H	HR	BB	SO	RAT	ERA	ERA+	OAV	OOB	BH	AVG	PB	PR	/A	PD	TPI
1975	SF-N	0	1	.000	7	0	0	0	0	10¹	13	1	6	6	16.5	6.10	62	.317	.404	0	—	0	-3	-3	-0	-0.2
1976	SF-N	0	1	.000	7	0	0	0	0	8²	11	4	1	4	14.5	6.23	58	.351	.368	0	—	-0	-3	-3	-0	-0.2
1977	SF-N	0	1	.000	4	0	0	0	0	4¹	7	0	2	4	18.7	2.08	188	.333	.391	0	—	0	1	1	-0	0.2
Total	3	0	3	.000	18	0	0	0	0	23¹	33	2	9	16	16.2	5.40	70	.333	.389	0	—	0	-5	-4	-0	-0.2

● **FRED TONEY**   Toney, Fred Alexandra b: 12/11/1888, Nashville, Tenn. d: 3/11/53, Nashville, Tenn. BR/TR, 6'1", 195 lbs. Deb: 4/15/11

YEAR	TM/L	W	L	PCT	G	GS	CG	SH	SV	IP	H	HR	BB	SO	RAT	ERA	ERA+	OAV	OOB	BH	AVG	PB	PR	/A	PD	TPI
1911	Chi-N	1	1	.500	18	4	1	0	0	67	55	2	35	27	12.8	2.42	137	.229	.339	2	.111	-1	7	7	1	0.1
1912	Chi-N	1	2	.333	9	2	0	0	0	24	21	0	11	9	12.4	5.25	63	.247	.340	0	.000	-0	-5	-5	-1	-0.6
1913	Chi-N	2	2	.500	7	5	2	0	0	39	52	1	22	12	17.3	6.00	53	.327	.412	3	.250	1	-12	-12	0	-1.0
1915	Cin-N	17	6	.739	36	23	18	6	2	222²	160	1	73	108	9.5	1.58	181	.207	.278	7	.095	-3	29	32	1	3.1
1916	Cin-N	14	17	.452	41	38	21	3	1	300	247	6	78	146	10.0	2.28	114	.231	.288	12	.121	-4	11	11	-4	0.7
1917	Cin-N	24	16	.600	43	42	31	7	1	339²	300	4	77	123	10.1	2.20	119	.238	.286	13	.112	-6	19	16	-5	0.7
1918	Cin-N	6	10	.375	21	19	9	1	2	136²	148	2	31	32	11.8	2.90	92	.282	.322	9	.214	-2	2	-3	-1	-0.3
	NY-N	6	2	.750	11	9	7	1	1	85¹	55	1	7	19	6.8	1.69	156	.192	.216	6	.188	-1	10	9	-1	0.7
	Yr	12	12	.500	32	28	16	2	**3**	222	203	3	38	51	9.9	2.43	109	.250	.285	15	.203	-0	8	5	0	0.4
1919	NY-N	13	6	.684	24	20	14	4	1	181	157	6	35	40	9.6	1.84	152	.235	.276	15	.227	1	22	19	-3	1.9
1920	NY-N	21	11	.656	42	37	17	4	1	278¹	266	8	57	81	10.6	2.65	113	.259	.302	23	.240	3	15	11	-2	1.2
1921	*NY-N	18	11	.621	42	32	16	1	3	249¹	274	14	65	62	12.4	3.61	102	.289	.328	18	.209	2	5	-2	-1	0.3
1922	NY-N	5	6	.455	13	12	6	0	0	86¹	91	5	31	17	12.9	4.17	96	.277	.343	2	.067	-2	-1	-2	0	-0.6
1923	StL-N	11	12	.478	29	28	16	1	0	196²	211	8	61	28	12.7	3.84	102	.282	.341	8	.116	-5	3	1	3	0.0
Total	12	139	102	.577	336	271	158	28	12	2206	2037	59	583	718	10.9	2.69	113	.251	.305	118	.159	-18	102	85	-12	5.7

● **DOC TONKIN**   Tonkin, Harry Glenville b: 8/11/1881, Concord, N.H. d: 5/30/59, Miami, Fla. BL/TL, 5'9", 165 lbs. Deb: 8/19/07

YEAR	TM/L	W	L	PCT	G	GS	CG	SH	SV	IP	H	HR	BB	SO	RAT	ERA	ERA+	OAV	OOB	BH	AVG	PB	PR	/A	PD	TPI
1907	Was-A	0	0	—	1	0	0	0	0	2²	6	0	5	0	37.1	6.75	36	.462	.611	2	1.000	1	-1	-1	0	0.1

● **STEVE TOOLE**   Toole, Stephen John b: 4/9/1859, New Orleans, La. d: 3/28/19, Pittsburgh, Pa. BR/TL, 6', 170 lbs. Deb: 4/20/1886 U

YEAR	TM/L	W	L	PCT	G	GS	CG	SH	SV	IP	H	HR	BB	SO	RAT	ERA	ERA+	OAV	OOB	BH	AVG	PB	PR	/A	PD	TPI
1886	Bro-a	6	6	.500	13	12	11	0	0	104	100	0	64	48	14.9	4.41	79	.246	.359	20	.351	4	-11	-11	2	-0.5
1887	Bro-a	14	10	.583	24	24	22	1	0	194	186	4	106	48	14.1	4.31	100	.254	.358	24	.233	-1	-0	-1	-1	-0.2
1888	KC-a	5	6	.455	12	10	10	0	0	91²	124	4	50	35	17.6	6.68	51	.312	.395	10	.208	-0	-37	-33	0	-2.9
1890	Bro-a	2	4	.333	6	6	6	0	0	53¹	47	0	39	10	15.2	4.05	96	.229	.363	6	.300	-2	-1	-1	0	0.1
Total	4	27	26	.509	55	52	49	1	0	443	457	8	259	141	15.1	4.79	81	.262	.367	60	.263	0	-49	-44	2	-3.5

● **RUPE TOPPIN**   Toppin, Ruperto b: 12/7/41, Panama City, Panama BR/TR, 6', 185 lbs. Deb: 7/28/62

YEAR	TM/L	W	L	PCT	G	GS	CG	SH	SV	IP	H	HR	BB	SO	RAT	ERA	ERA+	OAV	OOB	BH	AVG	PB	PR	/A	PD	TPI
1962	KC-A	0	0	—	2	0	0	0	0	2	1	0	5	1	27.0	13.50	31	.167	.545	1	1.000	0	-2	-2	-0	0.0

● **RED TORKELSON**   Torkelson, Chester Leroy b: 3/19/1894, Chicago, Ill. d: 9/22/64, Chicago, Ill. BR/TR, 6', 175 lbs. Deb: 8/29/17

YEAR	TM/L	W	L	PCT	G	GS	CG	SH	SV	IP	H	HR	BB	SO	RAT	ERA	ERA+	OAV	OOB	BH	AVG	PB	PR	/A	PD	TPI
1917	Cle-A	2	1	.667	4	3	0	0	0	22¹	33	1	13	10	19.3	7.66	37	.333	.421	2	.222	-0	-12	-12	0	-1.3

● **PABLO TORREALBA**   Torrealba, Pablo Arnoldo (Torrealba) b: 4/28/48, Barquisimeto, Ven. BL/TL, 5'9", 175 lbs. Deb: 4/9/75

YEAR	TM/L	W	L	PCT	G	GS	CG	SH	SV	IP	H	HR	BB	SO	RAT	ERA	ERA+	OAV	OOB	BH	AVG	PB	PR	/A	PD	TPI
1975	Atl-N	0	1	.000	6	0	0	0	0	6²	7	0	3	5	13.5	1.35	274	.250	.323	1	1.000	0	2	1	1	0.4
1976	Atl-N	0	2	.000	36	0	0	0	2	53	67	0	22	33	15.6	3.57	106	.315	.387	0	.000	-0	-0	1	1	0.1
1977	Oak-A	4	6	.400	41	10	3	0	2	116²	127	6	38	51	12.9	2.62	153	.279	.337	0	—	0	19	18	2	1.7
1978	Chi-A	2	4	.333	25	3	1	0	1	57¹	69	6	39	22	17.4	4.71	81	.301	.410	0	—	-0	-6	-1	-0	-0.8
1979	Chi-A	0	0	—	3	0	0	0	0	5²	5	1	2	2	11.1	1.59	268	.250	.318	0	—	0	1	-0	1	0.2
Total	5	6	13	.316	111	13	4	0	5	239¹	275	12	104	113	14.6	3.27	120	.291	.366	1	.200	-0	16	17	2	1.4

YEAR	TM/L	W	L	PCT	G	GS	CG	SH	SV	IP	H	HR	BB	SO	RAT	ERA	ERA+	OAV	OOB	BH	AVG	PB	PR	/A	PD	TPI

● **ANGEL TORRES** Torres, Angel Rafael (Ruiz) b: 10/24/52, Las Ciengas, Azua, D.R. BL/TL, 5'11", 168 lbs. Deb: 9/12/77

| 1977 | Cin-N | 0 | 0 | — | 5 | 0 | 0 | 0 | 0 | 8¹ | 7 | 2 | 8 | 8 | 16.2 | 2.16 | 182 | .233 | .395 | 0 | — | 0 | 2 | 2 | 0 | 0.0 |

● **DILSON TORRES** Torres, Dilson Dario b: 5/31/70, Sur Edo Aragua, Venez. BR/TR, 6'3", 200 lbs. Deb: 4/29/95

| 1995 | KC-A | 1 | 2 | .333 | 24 | 2 | 0 | 0 | 0 | 44¹ | 56 | 6 | 17 | 28 | 15.0 | 6.09 | 79 | .311 | .374 | 0 | — | 0 | -7 | -6 | 2 | -0.2 |

● **GIL TORRES** Torres, Don Gilberto (Nunez) b: 8/23/15, Regla, Cuba d: 1/10/83, Regla, Cuba BR/TR, 6', 155 lbs. Deb: 4/25/40 F♦

1940	Was-A	0	0	—	2	0	0	0	0	2²	3	0	0	1	10.1	0.00	—	.273	.273	0	—	0	1	1	0	0.0
1946	Was-A	0	0	—	3	0	0	0	1	7	9	0	3	2	15.4	7.71	43	.310	.375	47	.254	1	-3	-3	-0	-0.1
Total	2	0	0	—	5	0	0	0	1	9²	12	0	3	3	14.0	5.59	64	.300	.349	320	.252	1	-2	-2	-0	-0.1

● **HECTOR TORRES** Torres, Hector Epitacio (Marroquin) b: 9/16/45, Monterrey, Mexico BR/TR, 6', 175 lbs. Deb: 4/10/68 C♦

| 1972 | Mon-N | 0 | 0 | — | 1 | 0 | 0 | 0 | 0 | 0² | 5 | 0 | 0 | 0 | 67.5 | 27.00 | 13 | .714 | .714 | 28 | .155 | 0 | -2 | -2 | 0 | 0.0 |

● **SALOMON TORRES** Torres, Salomon (Ramirez) b: 3/11/72, San Pedro De Macoris, D.R. BR/TR, 5'11", 150 lbs. Deb: 8/29/93

1993	SF-N	3	5	.375	8	8	0	0	0	44²	43	5	27	23	13.1	4.03	97	.231	.346	3	.231	0	0	-1	1	0.0
1994	SF-N	2	8	.200	16	14	1	0	0	84¹	95	10	34	42	14.5	5.44	74	.292	.372	4	.154	-0	-12	-13	-2	-1.5
1995	SF-N	0	1	.000	4	1	0	0	0	8	13	4	7	2	22.5	9.00	45	.394	.500	0	.000	-0	-4	-4	0	-0.5
	Sea-A	3	8	.273	16	13	1	0	0	72	87	12	42	45	16.4	6.00	79	.291	.382	0	—	0	-10	-10	1	-1.1
1996	Sea-A	3	3	.500	10	7	1	1	0	49	44	5	23	36	12.9	4.59	107	.242	.337	0	—	-0	2	2	-1	0.1
Total	4	11	25	.306	54	43	3	1	0	258	276	36	133	148	14.7	5.30	82	.276	.369	7	.175	-0	-24	-27	-0	-3.0

● **MIKE TORREZ** Torrez, Michael Augustine b: 8/28/46, Topeka, Kan. BR/TR, 6'5", 220 lbs. Deb: 9/10/67

1967	StL-N	.0	1	.000	3	1	0	0	0	5²	5	0	1	5	11.1	3.18	103	.238	.304	0	.000	-0	0	-0	-0	0.0
1968	StL-N	2	1	.667	5	2	0	0	0	19¹	20	1	12	6	15.4	2.79	104	.286	.398	2	.286	0	0	-0	0	0.1
1969	StL-N	10	4	.714	24	15	3	0	0	107²	96	7	62	61	13.5	3.59	99	.240	.346	3	.073	-2	-0	-0	0	-0.2
1970	StL-N	8	10	.444	30	28	5	1	0	179¹	168	13	103	100	13.8	4.22	98	.248	.350	17	.270	4	-3	-2	-0	0.2
1971	StL-N	1	2	.333	9	6	0	0	0	36	41	2	30	8	18.0	6.00	60	.304	.434	1	.143	1	-10	-10	0	-0.6
	Mon-N	0	0	—	1	0	0	0	0	3	4	0	1	2	15.0	0.00	—	.308	.357	0	—	0	1	1	0	0.1
	Yr	1	2	.333	10	6	0	0	0	39	45	2	31	10	17.5	5.54	65	.300	.420	1	.143	1	-9	-8	1	-0.6
1972	Mon-N	16	12	.571	34	33	13	0	0	243¹	215	15	103	112	12.0	3.33	107	.242	.325	15	.176	0	3	6	2	1.0
1973	Mon-N	9	12	.429	35	34	3	1	0	208	207	17	115	90	14.1	4.46	86	.262	.359	12	.174	-1	-18	-15	2	-1.3
1974	Mon-N	15	8	.652	32	30	6	1	0	186¹	184	10	84	92	13.1	3.57	107	.257	.337	8	.125	-3	1	5	5	0.8
1975	Bal-A	20	9	**.690**	36	36	16	2	0	270²	238	15	133	119	12.5	3.06	115	.239	.332	0	—	0	22	14	1	1.4
1976	Oak-A	16	12	.571	39	39	13	4	0	266¹	231	15	87	115	10.9	2.50	134	.235	.301	0	—	0	30	25	-1	2.7
1977	Oak-A	3	1	.750	4	4	2	0	0	26¹	24	1	11	12	12.0	4.44	91	.242	.327	0	—	0	-1	-0	-0	-0.2
	*NY-A	14	12	.538	31	31	15	2	0	217	212	20	75	90	12.2	3.82	103	.259	.326	0	—	0	6	3	-2	0.1
	Yr	17	13	.567	35	35	17	2	0	243¹	235	23	86	102	12.1	3.88	102	.256	.324	0	—	0	5	2	-2	-0.1
1978	Bos-A	16	13	.552	36	36	15	2	0	250	272	19	99	120	13.5	3.96	104	.281	.349	0	—	0	-6	-4	-2	0.2
1979	Bos-A	16	13	.552	36	36	12	1	0	252¹	254	20	121	125	13.6	4.49	98	.264	.349	0	—	0	-8	-2	-0	-0.4
1980	Bos-A	9	16	.360	36	32	6	1	0	207¹	256	18	75	97	14.4	5.08	83	.313	.371	0	—	0	-24	-20	2	-2.0
1981	Bos-A	10	3	.769	22	22	2	0	0	127¹	130	10	51	54	12.8	3.68	105	.267	.337	0	—	0	3	-1	-1	0.1
1982	Bos-A	9	9	.500	31	31	1	0	0	175²	196	20	74	84	14.1	5.23	82	.282	.356	0	—	0	-22	-18	-2	-1.9
1983	NY-N	10	17	.370	39	34	5	0	0	222¹	227	16	113	94	13.8	4.37	83	.271	.358	3	.046	-5	-18	-18	0	-2.5
1984	NY-N	1	5	.167	9	8	0	0	0	37²	55	3	18	16	17.9	5.02	70	.369	.444	3	.300	1	-6	-6	0	-0.8
	Oak-A	0	0	—	2	0	0	0	0	2¹	9	0	3	2	46.3	27.00	14	.563	.632	0	—	0	-6	-6	-0	0.3
Total	18	185	160	.536	494	458	117	15	0	3044	3043	223	1371	1404	13.2	3.96	97	.264	.345	64	.155	-4	-60	-38	3	-3.0

● **LOU TOST** Tost, Louis Eugene b: 6/1/11, Cumberland, Wash. d: 2/22/67, Santa Clara, Cal. BL/TL, 6', 175 lbs. Deb: 4/20/42

1942	Bos-N	10	10	.500	35	22	5	1	0	147²	146	12	52	43	12.3	3.53	94	.256	.322	9	.176	0	-4	-3	-1	-0.5
1943	Bos-N	0	1	.000	3	1	0	0	0	6²	10	2	4	3	18.9	5.40	63	.357	.438	0	.000	-0	-1	-1	0	-0.2
1947	Pit-N	0	0	—	1	0	0	0	0	1	3	0	0	0	27.0	9.00	47	.600	.600	0	—	-1	-1	-0	0	0.0
Total	3	10	11	.476	39	23	5	1	0	155¹	159	14	56	46	12.7	3.65	92	.263	.330	9	.173	-1	-6	-5	-1	-0.7

● **PAUL TOTH** Toth, Paul Louis b: 6/30/35, McRoberts, Ky. BR/TR, 6'1", 175 lbs. Deb: 4/22/62

1962	StL-N	1	0	1.000	6	1	0	0	0	16²	18	1	4	5	11.9	5.40	79	.295	.338	2	.400	-2	-3	-2	-0	-0.1
	Chi-N	3	1	.750	6	4	1	0	0	34	29	2	10	11	10.9	4.24	98	.240	.308	2	.182	0	-1	-0	-0	-0.1
	Yr	4	1	.800	12	5	1	0	0	50²	47	3	14	16	11.2	4.62	91	.257	.317	4	.250	1	-4	-2	-1	-0.2
1963	Chi-N	5	9	.357	27	14	3	2	0	130²	115	9	35	66	10.5	3.10	113	.240	.294	1	.026	-3	3	6	-1	0.2
1964	Chi-N	0	2	.000	4	2	0	0	0	10²	15	2	5	0	16.9	8.44	44	.341	.408	1	.333	0	-6	-6	1	-0.4
Total	3	9	12	.429	43	21	5	2	0	192	177	14	54	82	11.0	3.80	97	.251	.308	6	.103	-2	-7	-2	-1	-0.8

● **CLAY TOUCHSTONE** Touchstone, Clayland Maffitt b: 1/24/03, Moore Twsp., Pa. d: 4/28/49, Beaumont, Tex. BR/TR, 5'9", 175 lbs. Deb: 9/4/28

1928	Bos-N	0	0	—	5	0	0	0	0	8	15	1	2	1	20.3	4.50	87	.417	.462	0	.000	-0	-0	-1	0	0.0
1929	Bos-N	0	0	—	1	0	0	0	0	2²	6	1	2	1	20.3	16.88	28	.429	.429	1	1.000	0	-4	-4	-0	0.0
1945	Chi-A	0	0	—	6	0	0	0	0	10	14	1	6	4	18.9	5.40	61	.311	.404	0	.000	-0	-2	-2	0	0.0
Total	3	0	0	—	12	0	0	0	0	20²	35	3	8	6	19.6	6.53	57	.368	.429	1	.250	-0	-6	-6	0	0.0

● **CESAR TOVAR** Tovar, Cesar Leonardo "Pepito" (b: Cesar Leonard Perez (Tovar)) b: 7/3/40, Caracas, Venez. d: 7/14/94, Caracas, Venez. BR/TR, 5'9", 155 lbs. Deb: 4/12/65 ♦

| 1968 | Min-A | 0 | 0 | — | 1 | 1 | 0 | 0 | 0 | 1 | 0 | 0 | 1 | 0 | 9.0 | 0.00 | — | .000 | .250 | 167 | .272 | 0 | 0 | 0 | 0 | 0.0 |

● **IRA TOWNSEND** Townsend, Ira Dance "Pat" b: 1/9/1894, Weimar, Tex. d: 7/21/65, Schulenburg, Tex. BR/TR, 6'1", 180 lbs. Deb: 8/25/20

1920	Bos-N	0	0	—	4	1	0	0	0	6²	10	1	2	1	17.6	1.35	226	.370	.433	0	.000	-0	1	1	-0	0.0
1921	Bos-N	0	0	—	4	0	0	0	0	7¹	11	1	4	0	20.9	6.14	59	.344	.447	0	.000	-0	-2	-2	0	0.0
Total	2	0	0	—	8	1	0	0	0	14	21	1	6	1	19.3	3.86	87	.356	.441	0	.000	-0	-1	-1	-0	0.0

● **HAPPY TOWNSEND** Townsend, John b: 4/9/1879, Townsend, Del. d: 12/21/63, Wilmington, Del. BR/TR, 6', 190 lbs. Deb: 4/19/01

1901	Phi-N	9	6	.600	19	16	14	2	0	143²	118	3	64	72	11.7	3.45	99	**.223**	.312	7	.109	-4	-2	-1	-2	-0.7
1902	Was-A	9	16	.360	27	26	22	0	0	220¹	233	12	89	71	13.7	4.45	83	.272	.349	23	.264	3	-21	-18	-1	-1.5
1903	Was-A	2	11	.154	20	13	10	0	0	126²	145	3	48	54	14.4	4.76	66	.287	.359	2	.045	-4	-25	-23	-0	-2.4
1904	Was-A	5	26	.161	36	34	31	0	0	291¹	319	4	100	143	13.2	3.58	74	.279	.342	20	.168	-2	-32	-30	-1	-3.3
1905	Was-A	7	16	.304	34	24	22	0	0	263	247	2	102	102	11.8	2.63	100	.250	.318	15	.181	1	1	0	-3	-0.1
1906	Cle-A	3	7	.300	17	12	8	1	0	93²	92	1	31	31	12.5	2.91	90	.262	.332	4	.133	-1	-4	-2	-0	-0.5
Total	6	35	82	.299	153	125	107	5	0	1137²	1154	24	416	473	12.9	3.59	83	.264	.336	71	.166	-8	-82	-75	-7	-8.5

● **LEO TOWNSEND** Townsend, Leo Alphonse "Lefty" b: 1/15/1891, Mobile, Ala. d: 12/3/76, Mobile, Ala. BL/TL, 5'10", 160 lbs. Deb: 9/8/20

1920	Bos-N	2	2	.500	7	1	1	0	0	24¹	18	1	2	0	7.4	1.48	206	.220	.238	1	.167	0	4	4	0	0.7
1921	Bos-N	0	1	.000	1	1	0	0	0	1	2	0	3	0	33.8	27.00	14	.400	.625	0	—	0	-3	-3	0	-1.2
Total	2	2	3	.400	8	2	1	0	0	25²	20	1	5	0	8.8	2.81	110	.230	.272	1	.167	0	1	1	0	-0.5

● **BILL TOZER** Tozer, William Louis b: 7/3/1882, St.Louis, Mo. d: 2/23/55, Belmont, Cal. BR/TR, 6', 200 lbs. Deb: 4/16/08

| 1908 | Cin-N | 0 | 0 | — | 4 | 0 | 0 | 0 | 0 | 10² | 11 | 0 | 4 | 5 | 13.5 | 1.69 | 137 | .268 | .348 | 0 | .000 | -0 | 1 | 1 | 0 | 0.0 |

● **STEVE TRACHSEL** Trachsel, Stephen Christopher b: 10/31/70, Oxnard, Cal. BR/TR, 6'3", 185 lbs. Deb: 9/19/93

1993	Chi-N	0	2	.000	3	3	0	0	0	19²	16	4	3	14	8.7	4.58	87	.219	.250	1	.167	0	-1	-1	0	-0.1
1994	Chi-N	9	7	.563	22	22	1	0	0	146	133	19	54	108	11.7	3.21	130	.242	.314	8	.186	1	16	15	2	1.8
1995	Chi-N	7	13	.350	30	29	2	0	0	160²	174	25	76	117	14.0	5.15	80	.277	.355	13	.265	3	-17	-19	-2	-1.9
1996	Chi-N★	13	9	.591	31	31	3	2	0	205	181	30	62	132	11.0	3.03	141	.235	.299	7	.106	-2	27	28	0	2.6
Total	4	29	31	.483	86	85	6	2	0	531¹	504	78	195	371	12.0	3.78	110	.250	.319	29	.177	3	25	23	1	2.5

YEAR TM/L	W	L	PCT	G	GS	CG	SH	SV	IP	H	HR	BB	SO	RAT	ERA	ERA+	OAV	OOB	BH	AVG	PB	PR	/A	PD	TPI
● FRED TRAUTMAN Trautman, Frederick Orlando b: 3/24/1892, Bucyrus, Ohio d: 2/15/64, Bucyrus, Ohio BR/TR, 6'1", 175 lbs. Deb: 4/27/15																								
1915 New-F	0	0	—	1	0	0	0	0	3	4	0	1	2	18.0	6.00	43	.364	.462	0	.000	-0	-1	-1	-0	0.0
● JOHN TRAUTWEIN Trautwein, John Howard b: 8/7/62, Lafayette Hill, Pa. BR/TR, 6'3", 205 lbs. Deb: 4/7/88																								
1988 Bos-A	0	1	.000	9	0	0	0	0	16	26	2	9	8	20.3	9.00	46	.382	.462	0	—	0	-9	-9	-0	-0.7
● ALLAN TRAVERS Travers, Aloysius Joseph "Joe" b: 5/7/1892, Philadelphia, Pa. d: 4/19/68, Philadelphia, Pa. BR/TR, 6'1", 180 lbs. Deb: 5/18/12																								
1912 Det-A	0	1	.000	1	1	1	0	0	8	26	0	7	1	37.1	15.75	21	.605	.660	0	.000	-0	-11	-11	1	-0.8
● BILL TRAVERS Travers, William Edward b: 10/27/52, Norwood, Mass. BL/TL, 6'6", 200 lbs. Deb: 5/19/74																								
1974 Mil-A	2	3	.400	23	1	0	0	0	53	59	6	30	31	15.3	4.92	73	.296	.391	0	—	0	-8	-8	0	-0.6
1975 Mil-A	6	11	.353	28	23	5	0	1	136¹	130	15	60	57	13.3	4.29	89	.251	.342	1	.150	-0	-7	-1	-0	-0.9
1976 Mil-A☆	15	16	.484	34	34	15	3	0	240	211	21	95	120	11.8	2.81	124	.237	.316	0	—	0	19	18	-1	2.3
1977 Mil-A	4	12	.250	19	19	2	1	0	121²	140	13	57	49	15.1	5.25	77	.291	.374	0	—	0	-16	-16	-0	-1.8
1978 Mil-A	12	11	.522	28	28	8	3	0	175²	184	20	58	66	12.7	4.41	85	.268	.331	0	—	0	-13	-13	-1	-1.4
1979 Mil-A	14	8	.636	30	27	9	2	0	187¹	196	33	45	74	11.7	3.89	107	.270	.315	0	—	0	7	6	-2	0.4
1980 Mil-A	12	6	.667	29	25	7	1	0	154¹	147	20	47	62	11.7	3.91	99	.249	.311	0	—	0	2	-1	-1	0.1
1981 Cal-A	0	1	.000	4	4	0	0	0	9²	14	2	4	5	16.8	8.38	44	.333	.391	0	—	0	-5	-5	-0	-0.5
1983 Cal-A	0	3	.000	10	7	0	0	0	42²	58	4	19	24	16.7	5.91	68	.331	.403	0	—	0	-9	-9	-0	-0.5
Total 9	65	71	.478	205	168	46	10	1	1120²	1139	134	415	488	12.8	4.10	93	.264	.335	0	—	0	-30	-34	-3	-2.9
● HARRY TREKELL Trekell, Harry Roy b: 11/18/1892, Breda, Ill. d: 11/4/65, Spokane, Wash. BR/TR, 6'1.5", 170 lbs. Deb: 8/16/13																								
1913 StL-N	0	1	.000	7	1	0	0	0	30	25	2	8	15	10.5	4.50	72	.221	.285	1	.111	-0	-4	-4	-0	-0.2
● BILL TREMEL Tremel, William Leonard "Mumbles" b: 7/4/29, Lilly, Pa. BR/TR, 5'11", 180 lbs. Deb: 6/12/54																								
1954 Chi-N	1	2	.333	33	0	0	0	4	51¹	45	3	28	21	12.8	4.21	100	.243	.343	2	.250	0	-1	-0	-1	-0.1
1955 Chi-N	3	0	1.000	23	0	0	0	2	38²	33	2	18	13	11.9	3.72	110	.239	.327	2	.286	0	1	2	-1	0.1
1956 Chi-N	0	0	—	1	0	0	0	0	1	3	0	0	0	27.0	9.00	42	.600	.600	0	—	0	-1	-1	-0	0.0
Total 3	4	2	.667	57	0	0	0	6	91	81	5	46	34	12.6	4.05	102	.247	.340	4	.267	1	-0	1	-2	0.1
● BOB TRICE Trice, Robert Lee b: 8/28/26, Newton, Ga. d: 9/16/88, Weirton, W.Va. BR/TR, 6'3", 190 lbs. Deb: 9/13/53																								
1953 Phi-A	2	1	.667	3	3	1	0	0	23	25	4	6	4	12.1	5.48	78	.275	.320	1	.143	-0	-4	-3	-1	-0.2
1954 Phi-A	7	8	.467	19	18	8	1	0	119	146	14	48	22	14.7	5.60	70	.305	.369	12	.286	4	-25	-22	0	-2.0
1955 KC-A	0	0	—	4	0	0	0	0	10	14	4	6	2	18.0	9.00	46	.326	.408	2	.667	1	-6	-5	1	0.1
Total 3	9	9	.500	26	21	9	1	0	152	185	22	60	28	14.5	5.80	69	.302	.365	15	.288	5	-34	-31	2	-2.1
● JOE TRIMBLE Trimble, Joseph Gerard b: 10/12/30, Providence, R.I. BR/TR, 6'1", 190 lbs. Deb: 4/29/55																								
1955 Bos-A	0	0	—	2	0	0	0	0	2	0	0	3	1	13.5	0.00	—	.000	.375	0	—	0	1	1	0	0.0
1957 Pit-N	0	2	.000	5	4	0	0	0	19²	23	7	13	9	16.9	8.24	46	.291	.398	1	.143	-0	-10	-10	-0	-0.8
Total 2	0	2	.000	7	4	0	0	0	21²	23	7	16	10	16.6	7.48	51	.274	.396	1	.143	-0	-9	-9	-0	-0.8
● KEN TRINKLE Trinkle, Kenneth Wayne b: 12/15/19, Paoli, Ind. d: 5/10/76, Paoli, Ind. BR/TR, 6'1.5", 175 lbs. Deb: 4/25/43																								
1943 NY-N	1	5	.167	11	6	1	0	0	45²	51	3	15	10	13.2	3.74	92	.276	.333	3	.250	1	-2	-2	1	-0.1
1946 NY-N	7	14	.333	48	13	2	0	2	151	146	8	74	49	13.2	3.87	89	.253	.340	3	.079	-2	-8	-7	-0	-1.2
1947 NY-N	8	4	.667	62	0	0	0	10	93²	100	3	48	37	14.3	3.75	109	.278	.364	3	.188	-0	3	3	2	0.6
1948 NY-N	4	5	.444	53	0	0	0	7	70²	66	6	41	20	14.0	3.18	124	.244	.350	2	.250	0	6	6	1	1.0
1949 Phi-N	1	1	.500	42	0	0	0	2	74¹	79	3	30	14	13.6	4.00	99	.299	.377	0	.000	0	1	1	1	0.1
Total 5	21	29	.420	216	19	3	0	21	435¹	442	23	208	130	13.6	3.74	100	.267	.352	11	.138	-2	0	0	6	0.5
● RICKY TRLICEK Trlicek, Richard Alan b: 4/26/69, Houston, Tex. BR/TR, 6'3", 200 lbs. Deb: 4/8/92																								
1992 Tor-A	0	0	—	2	0	0	0	0	1²	2	0	2	1	21.6	10.80	38	.286	.444	0	—	0	-1	-1	0	-0.1
1993 LA-N	1	2	.333	41	0	0	0	0	64	59	3	21	41	11.5	4.08	94	.244	.309	1	.250	0	-0	-2	1	0.0
1994 Bos-A	1	1	.500	12	1	0	0	0	22¹	32	5	16	7	19.3	8.06	62	.330	.425	0	—	0	-8	-8	-0	-0.7
1996 NY-N	0	1	.000	5	0	0	0	0	5¹	3	0	3	3	11.8	3.38	116	.214	.389	0	—	0	0	0	0	0.1
Total 4	2	4	.333	60	1	0	0	1	93¹	96	8	42	52	13.6	5.11	80	.267	.348	1	.250	0	-9	-10	1	-0.7
● RICH TROEDSON Troedson, Richard La Monte b: 5/1/50, Palo Alto, Cal. BL/TL, 6'1", 170 lbs. Deb: 4/9/73																								
1973 SD-N	7	9	.438	50	18	2	0	1	152¹	167	12	59	81	13.4	4.25	82	.284	.351	7	.175	0	-10	-13	2	-1.1
1974 SD-N	1	1	.500	15	1	0	0	1	18²	24	6	8	11	15.9	8.68	41	.300	.371	0	.000	-0	-10	-11	0	-1.1
Total 2	8	10	.444	65	19	2	0	2	171	191	18	67	92	13.7	4.74	73	.286	.353	7	.171	-0	-21	-24	2	-2.2
● MIKE TROMBLEY Trombley, Michael Scott b: 4/14/67, Springfield, Mass. BR/TR, 6'2", 200 lbs. Deb: 8/19/92																								
1992 Min-A	3	2	.600	10	7	0	0	0	46¹	43	5	17	38	11.8	3.30	123	.247	.318	0	—	0	3	4	0	0.3
1993 Min-A	6	6	.500	44	10	0	0	0	114¹	131	15	41	85	13.8	4.88	89	.290	.353	0	—	0	-7	-7	1	-0.5
1994 Min-A	2	0	1.000	24	0	0	0	0	48¹	56	10	18	32	14.3	6.33	77	.287	.356	0	—	0	-8	-8	-1	-0.3
1995 Min-A	4	8	.333	20	18	0	0	0	97²	107	18	42	68	14.0	5.62	85	.273	.348	0	—	0	-10	-9	-1	-1.1
1996 Min-A	5	1	.833	43	0	0	0	6	68²	61	9	25	57	11.9	3.01	170	.236	.315	0	—	0	15	16	-0	1.3
Total 5	20	17	.541	141	35	0	0	6	375¹	398	50	143	280	13.3	4.72	98	.270	.341	0	—	0	-7	-4	-1	-0.3
● HAL TROSKY Trosky, Harold Arthur Jr. "Hoot" (b: Harold Arthur Troyavesky Jr.) b: 9/29/36, Cleveland, Ohio BR/TR, 6'3", 205 lbs. Deb: 9/25/58 F																								
1958 Chi-A	1	0	1.000	2	0	0	0	0	3	5	0	2	1	21.0	6.00	61	.385	.467	0	—	0	-1	-1	0	-0.2
● BILL TROTTER Trotter, William Felix b: 8/10/08, Cisne, Ill. d: 8/26/84, Arlington, Mass. BR/TR, 6'2", 195 lbs. Deb: 4/23/37																								
1937 StL-A	2	9	.182	34	12	3	0	1	122¹	150	14	50	37	15.2	5.81	83	.304	.376	1	.030	-3	-16	-13	-2	-1.4
1938 StL-A	0	1	.000	1	1	1	0	0	8	8	0	1	9	9.0	5.63	88	.242	.242	0	.000	0	-1	-1	0	0.0
1939 StL-A	6	13	.316	41	13	4	0	0	156²	205	16	54	61	15.2	5.34	91	.318	.376	4	.108	-1	-13	-8	1	-0.8
1940 StL-A	7	6	.538	36	4	1	0	2	98	107	5	31	29	13.7	3.77	122	.300	.353	1	.045	-2	7	9	1	0.9
1941 StL-A	4	2	.667	29	2	0	0	0	49²	68	2	19	17	16.1	5.98	72	.332	.394	0	.000	-1	-10	-9	1	-1.0
1942 StL-A	0	1	.000	3	0	0	0	0	2	5	0	2	0	31.5	18.00	21	.385	.467	0	—	0	-3	-3	0	-1.2
Was-A	3	1	.750	17	4	0	0	0	40²	52	4	14	13	14.6	5.75	63	.304	.357	0	.000	-0	-10	-10	1	-0.8
Yr	3	2	.600	20	4	0	0	0	42²	57	4	16	13	15.4	6.33	58	.310	.365	0	.000	-0	-13	-13	1	-2.0
1944 StL-N	0	1	.000	2	1	0	0	0	6	14	5	4	0	27.0	13.50	26	.467	.529	0	—	0	-7	-7	0	-0.8
Total 7	22	34	.393	163	31	9	0	3	483¹	619	46	174	158	15.0	5.40	85	.313	.373	6	.055	-7	-52	-42	2	-5.1
● DIZZY TROUT Trout, Paul Howard b: 6/29/15, Sandcut, Ind. d: 2/28/72, Harvey, Ill. BR/TR, 6'2.5", 195 lbs. Deb: 4/25/39 F																								
1939 Det-A	9	10	.474	33	22	6	0	2	162	168	5	74	72	13.7	3.61	135	.270	.351	12	.211	-0	18	23	-1	2.2
1940 *Det-A	3	7	.300	33	10	1	0	2	100²	125	4	54	64	16.3	4.47	106	.307	.392	4	.129	-2	-1	3	2	0.3
1941 Det-A	9	9	.500	37	18	6	1	2	151²	144	7	84	88	13.6	3.74	122	.252	.350	9	.180	0	7	14	1	1.6
1942 Det-A	12	18	.400	35	29	13	1	0	223	214	15	89	91	12.4	3.43	115	.249	.322	16	.213	2	6	13	4	2.3
1943 Det-A	20	12	.625	44	30	18	5	6	246²	204	9	101	111	11.1	2.48	142	.227	.305	20	.220	4	22	29	4	4.7
1944 Det-A☆	27	14	.659	49	40	33	7	0	352¹	314	9	83	144	10.2	2.12	168	.237	.284	36	.271	12	51	57	7	9.1
1945 *Det-A	18	15	.545	41	31	18	4	0	246¹	252	8	79	97	12.1	3.14	112	.267	.324	25	.245	4	6	10	3	2.1
1946 Det-A	17	13	.567	38	32	23	5	3	276¹	244	11	97	151	11.2	2.34	156	.238	.306	20	.194	3	36	40	4	5.3
1947 Det-A☆	10	11	.476	32	26	9	2	0	186¹	186	6	65	74	12.3	3.48	108	.261	.325	11	.162	3	5	11	3	1.4
1948 Det-A	10	14	.417	32	23	11	2	2	183²	193	7	73	91	13.1	3.43	127	.269	.338	15	.217	2	18	19	2	2.6
1949 Det-A	3	6	.333	33	4	0	0	4	59¹	68	7	21	19	13.5	4.40	95	.292	.350	2	.143	0	-1	-2	0	-0.1
1950 Det-A	13	5	.722	34	20	11	1	4	184²	190	13	64	88	12.6	3.75	125	.267	.332	12	.190	-1	17	19	3	2.1
1951 Det-A	9	14	.391	42	22	7	0	6	191²	172	13	75	89	11.6	4.04	103	.240	.312	14	.269	4	2	3	4	1.2
1952 Det-A	1	5	.167	10	2	0	0	0	27	30	4	19	20	16.3	5.33	71	.286	.388	1	.333	-0	-5	-5	1	-0.8
Bos-A	9	8	.529	26	17	2	1	0	133²	133	3	68	57	13.7	3.64	108	.263	.354	8	.136	-1	1	1	0	0.5
Yr	10	13	.435	36	19	2	1	0	160²	163	7	87	77	14.2	3.92	100	.267	.361	9	.170	-1	-4	-/A	-2	-0.3

YEAR	TM/L	W	L	PCT	G	GS	CG	SH	SV	IP	H	HR	BB	SO	RAT	ERA	ERA+	OAV	OOB	BH	AVG	PB	PR	/A	PD	TPI
1957	Bal-A	0	0	—	2	0	0	0	0	4	4	0	0	0	108.0	81.00	4	.800	.800	0	—	0	-3	-3	0	0.0
Total	15	170	161	.514	521	322	158	28	35	2725²	2641	112	1046	1256	12.3	3.23	124	.255	.325	205	.213	31	177	232	38	34.5

● STEVE TROUT
Trout, Steven Russell b: 7/30/57, Detroit, Mich. BL/TL, 6'4", 195 lbs. Deb: 7/1/78 F

YEAR	TM/L	W	L	PCT	G	GS	CG	SH	SV	IP	H	HR	BB	SO	RAT	ERA	ERA+	OAV	OOB	BH	AVG	PB	PR	/A	PD	TPI
1978	Chi-A	3	0	1.000	4	3	1	0	0	22¹	19	0	11	11	12.1	4.03	94	.229	.319	0	—	0	-1	-1	-0	-0.1
1979	Chi-A	11	8	.579	34	18	6	2	4	155	165	10	59	76	13.3	3.89	109	.273	.343	0	—	0	6	6	2	0.9
1980	Chi-A	9	16	.360	32	30	7	2	0	199²	229	14	49	89	12.9	3.70	109	.290	.338	0	—	0	8	7	3	1.1
1981	Chi-A	8	7	.533	20	18	3	0	0	124²	122	7	38	54	11.8	3.47	103	.261	.322	0	—	0	3	2	0	0.3
1982	Chi-A	6	9	.400	25	19	2	0	0	120¹	130	9	50	62	13.6	4.26	95	.273	.344	0	—	0	-3	-3	0	-0.3
1983	Chi-N	10	14	.417	34	32	1	0	0	180	217	13	59	80	13.9	4.65	82	.305	.360	12	.194	1	-20	-17	-2	-1.8
1984	*Chi-N	13	7	.650	32	31	6	2	0	190	205	7	59	81	12.6	3.41	115	.285	.341	8	.131	-1	4	10	4	1.3
1985	Chi-N	9	7	.563	24	24	3	1	0	140²	142	8	63	68	13.2	3.39	118	.270	.350	5	.109	-2	3	9	2	1.1
1986	Chi-N	5	7	.417	37	25	0	0	0	161	184	6	78	69	14.7	4.75	85	.298	.378	9	.209	1	-19	-13	1	-0.7
1987	Chi-N	6	3	.667	11	11	3	2	0	75	72	6	27	32	12.0	3.00	143	.260	.328	4	.154	-1	9	11	0	1.2
	NY-A	0	4	.000	14	9	0	0	0	46¹	51	4	37	27	17.3	6.60	66	.274	.397	0	—	0	-11	-11	0	-0.7
1988	Sea-A	4	7	.364	15	13	0	0	0	56¹	86	6	31	14	19.5	7.83	53	.361	.445	0	—	0	-24	-23	0	-3.8
1989	Sea-A	4	3	.571	19	3	0	0	0	30	43	3	17	17	18.0	6.60	61	.333	.411	0	—	0	-9	-9	0	-1.9
Total	12	88	92	.489	301	236	32	9	4	1501¹	1665	90	578	656	13.6	4.18	96	.286	.354	38	.160	-2	-55	-30	14	-3.4

● BOB TROWBRIDGE
Trowbridge, Robert b: 6/27/30, Hudson, N.Y. d: 4/3/80, Hudson, N.Y. BR/TR, 6'1", 190 lbs. Deb: 4/22/56

YEAR	TM/L	W	L	PCT	G	GS	CG	SH	SV	IP	H	HR	BB	SO	RAT	ERA	ERA+	OAV	OOB	BH	AVG	PB	PR	/A	PD	TPI
1956	Mil-N	3	2	.600	19	4	1	0	0	50²	38	4	34	40	13.1	2.66	130	.210	.341	0	.000	-1	6	4	0	0.4
1957	*Mil-N	7	5	.583	32	16	3	1	1	126	118	9	52	75	12.2	3.64	96	.248	.323	4	.103	-2	3	-2	-1	-0.4
1958	Mil-N	1	3	.250	27	4	0	0	1	55	53	4	26	31	13.1	3.93	90	.252	.338	1	.111	-1	0	-2	-1	-0.3
1959	Mil-N	1	0	1.000	16	0	0	0	1	30¹	45	2	10	22	16.3	5.93	60	.344	.390	0	.000	-0	-7	-8	-0	-0.4
1960	KC-A	1	3	.250	22	1	0	0	2	68¹	70	6	34	33	13.8	4.61	86	.281	.370	1	.056	-1	-6	-5	0	-0.4
Total	5	13	13	.500	116	25	4	1	5	330¹	324	25	156	201	13.2	3.95	91	.260	.344	6	.078	-5	-3	-13	-1	-1.1

● BUN TROY
Troy, Robert b: 8/27/1888, Bad Wurzach, Ger. d: 10/7/18, Petit Maujouym, France BR/TR, 6'4", 195 lbs. Deb: 9/15/12

YEAR	TM/L	W	L	PCT	G	GS	CG	SH	SV	IP	H	HR	BB	SO	RAT	ERA	ERA+	OAV	OOB	BH	AVG	PB	PR	/A	PD	TPI
1912	Det-A	0	1	.000	1	1	0	0	0	6²	9	0	3	1	17.6	5.40	60	.346	.433	0	.000	-0	-2	-2	-0	-0.2

● VIRGIL TRUCKS
Trucks, Virgil Oliver "Fire" b: 4/26/17, Birmingham, Ala. BR/TR, 5'11", 198 lbs. Deb: 9/27/41 C

YEAR	TM/L	W	L	PCT	G	GS	CG	SH	SV	IP	H	HR	BB	SO	RAT	ERA	ERA+	OAV	OOB	BH	AVG	PB	PR	/A	PD	TPI
1941	Det-A	0	0	—	1	0	0	0	0	2	4	0	0	3	18.0	9.00	50	.500	.500	0	—	0	-1	-1	0	0.0
1942	Det-A	14	8	.636	28	20	8	2	0	167²	147	3	74	91	12.0	2.74	144	.231	.314	8	.123	-4	17	23	-2	2.3
1943	Det-A	16	10	.615	33	25	10	2	2	202²	170	11	52	118	9.9	2.84	124	.225	.276	13	.181	-2	10	15	-2	1.6
1945	*Det-A	0	0	—	1	1	0	0	0	5¹	3	0	2	3	8.4	1.69	208	.176	.263	0	.000	-0	1	1	0	0.0
1946	Det-A	14	9	.609	32	29	15	6	0	236²	217	9	75	161	11.2	3.23	113	.241	.302	17	.179	-1	7	11	-1	0.8
1947	Det-A	10	12	.455	36	26	8	2	2	180²	186	14	79	108	13.3	4.53	83	.263	.339	19	.271	2	-17	-15	-1	-1.6
1948	Det-A	14	13	.519	43	26	7	0	2	211²	190	14	85	123	11.8	3.78	116	.240	.315	13	.165	-3	12	14	-1	1.1
1949	Det-A★	19	11	.633	41	32	17	6	4	275	209	16	124	153	11.0	2.81	148	.211	.301	12	.120	-6	42	41	-3	3.3
1950	Det-A	3	1	.750	7	7	2	1	0	48¹	45	6	21	25	12.5	3.54	133	.243	.324	3	.150	-1	6	6	1	0.4
1951	Det-A	13	8	.619	37	18	6	1	1	153²	153	9	75	89	13.6	4.33	96	.262	.350	13	.236	-0	-4	-3	2	-0.3
1952	Det-A	5	19	.208	35	29	8	3	1	197	190	12	82	129	12.7	3.97	96	.251	.330	12	.188	-0	-7	-4	-2	-0.2
1953	StL-A	5	4	.556	16	12	4	2	2	88	83	4	32	47	12.2	3.07	137	.249	.322	4	.160	-1	9	11	-1	0.9
	Chi-A	15	6	.714	24	21	13	3	1	176¹	151	14	67	102	11.3	2.86	141	.232	.306	15	.238	2	22	23	1	2.9
	Yr	20	10	.667	40	33	17	5	3	264¹	234	18	99	149	11.4	2.93	139	.237	.308	19	.216	1	31	34	0	3.8
1954	Chi-A★	19	12	.613	40	33	16	5	3	264²	224	13	95	152	10.9	2.79	134	.228	.297	17	.183	-1	27	28	1	3.2
1955	Chi-A	13	8	.619	32	26	7	3	0	175	176	19	61	91	12.3	3.96	100	.260	.323	8	.125	-3	-0	-0	-0	-0.3
1956	Det-A	6	5	.545	22	16	3	1	1	120	104	15	63	43	13.0	3.83	108	.239	.343	11	.244	-1	4	4	-1	0.2
1957	KC-A	9	7	.563	48	7	0	0	7	116	106	12	62	55	13.2	3.03	131	.248	.346	4	.143	-1	10	12	0	1.6
1958	KC-A	0	1	.000	16	0	0	0	3	22	18	1	15	15	13.5	2.05	191	.222	.344	0	.000	-0	4	5	0	0.3
	NY-A	2	1	.667	25	0	0	0	1	39²	40	1	24	26	15.0	4.54	78	.265	.373	2	.250	-0	-3	-4	-0	-0.4
	Yr	2	2	.500	41	0	0	0	4	61²	58	3	39	41	14.4	3.65	100	.249	.361	2	.222	0	1	0	-0	-0.1
Total	17	177	135	.567	517	328	124	33	30	2682¹	2416	188	1088	1534	11.9	3.39	117	.240	.317	171	.180	-19	141	167	-5	15.9

● MIKE TRUJILLO
Trujillo, Michael Andrew b: 1/12/60, Denver, Colo. BR/TR, 6'1", 180 lbs. Deb: 4/14/85

YEAR	TM/L	W	L	PCT	G	GS	CG	SH	SV	IP	H	HR	BB	SO	RAT	ERA	ERA+	OAV	OOB	BH	AVG	PB	PR	/A	PD	TPI
1985	Bos-A	4	4	.500	27	7	1	0	1	84	112	7	23	19	14.8	4.82	89	.320	.367	0	—	0	-6	-5	2	-0.6
1986	Bos-A	0	0	—	3	0	0	0	0	5²	7	1	6	4	20.6	9.53	44	.304	.448	0	—	0	-3	-3	1	-0.3
	Sea-A	3	2	.600	11	4	1	1	0	41¹	32	5	15	19	10.2	2.40	177	.215	.287	0	—	0	8	8	-0	0.9
	Yr	3	2	.600	14	4	1	1	0	47	39	5	21	23	11.3	3.26	130	.227	.311	0	—	0	5	5	0	0.9
1987	Sea-A	4	4	.500	28	7	0	0	1	65²	70	7	26	36	13.4	6.17	76	.277	.349	0	—	0	-12	-11	-1	-1.6
1988	Det-A	0	0	—	6	0	0	0	0	12¹	11	2	5	5	11.7	5.11	75	.234	.308	0	—	0	-2	-2	0	0.3
1989	Det-A	1	2	.333	8	4	1	0	0	25²	35	3	13	13	16.8	5.96	64	.333	.407	0	—	0	-6	-6	0	-0.5
Total	5	12	12	.500	83	22	3	1	3	234²	267	29	88	96	13.8	5.02	86	.288	.353	0	—	0	-21	-19	2	-1.5

● ED TRUMBULL
Trumbull, Edward J. (b: Edward J. Trembly) b: 11/3/1860, Chicopee, Mass. d: 1/14/37, Kingston, Pa. Deb: 5/10/1884 ♦

YEAR	TM/L	W	L	PCT	G	GS	CG	SH	SV	IP	H	HR	BB	SO	RAT	ERA	ERA+	OAV	OOB	BH	AVG	PB	PR	/A	PD	TPI
1884	Was-a	1	9	.100	10	10	10	0	0	84	108	4	31	43	15.0	4.71	64	.295	.352	10	.116	-2	-14	-16	-1	-1.7

● GEORGE TSAMIS
Tsamis, George Alex b: 6/14/67, Campbell, Cal. BR/TL, 6'2", 190 lbs. Deb: 4/26/93

YEAR	TM/L	W	L	PCT	G	GS	CG	SH	SV	IP	H	HR	BB	SO	RAT	ERA	ERA+	OAV	OOB	BH	AVG	PB	PR	/A	PD	TPI
1993	Min-A	1	2	.333	41	0	0	0	1	68¹	86	9	27	30	15.3	6.19	70	.317	.385	0	—	0	-14	-14	1	-0.5

● JOHN TSITOURIS
Tsitouris, John Philip b: 5/4/36, Monroe, N.C. BR/TR, 6', 175 lbs. Deb: 6/13/57

YEAR	TM/L	W	L	PCT	G	GS	CG	SH	SV	IP	H	HR	BB	SO	RAT	ERA	ERA+	OAV	OOB	BH	AVG	PB	PR	/A	PD	TPI
1957	Det-A	1	0	1.000	2	0	0	0	0	3¹	8	0	2	2	27.0	8.10	48	.500	.556	0	.000	-0	-2	-2	0	-0.4
1958	KC-A	0	0	—	1	1	0	0	0	3	2	0	2	1	12.0	3.00	130	.182	.308	0	.000	0	0	0	0	0.0
1959	KC-A	4	3	.571	24	10	0	0	0	83¹	90	3	35	50	13.8	4.97	81	.271	.346	3	.150	-1	-10	-9	-1	-0.8
1960	KC-A	2	6	.250	33	8	1	0	0	33	38	3	21	12	18.3	6.55	61	.297	.427	0	.000	-1	-10	-10	0	-0.6
1962	Cin-N	1	0	1.000	4	2	1	0	0	21¹	13	0	7	7	9.7	0.84	477	.181	.280	0	.000	-1	7	8	-0	0.2
1963	Cin-N	12	8	.600	30	21	8	3	0	191	167	20	38	113	10.2	3.16	106	.232	.281	5	.081	-3	3	4	-3	-0.3
1964	Cin-N	9	13	.409	37	24	6	1	2	175¹	178	20	75	146	13.2	3.80	95	.263	.340	11	.190	2	-5	-4	-1	-0.3
1965	Cin-N	6	9	.400	31	20	3	1	0	131	134	18	65	91	14.3	4.95	76	.265	.359	3	.070	-2	-20	-17	-1	-2.2
1966	Cin-N	0	0	—	1	0	0	0	0	1	3	0	1	0	36.0	18.00	22	.750	.800	0	—	0	-2	-2	0	0.0
1967	Cin-N	1	0	1.000	2	0	0	0	1	8¹	5	1	6	4	11.3	3.38	111	.154	.313	0	—	0	0	0	0	0.1
1968	Cin-N	0	3	.000	3	0	0	0	0	12²	16	6	8	6	17.8	7.11	44	.302	.403	0	.000	-0	-6	-6	0	-1.1
Total	11	34	38	.472	149	84	18	3	3	663	653	71	260	432	12.9	4.13	88	.257	.335	22	.111	-6	-44	-36	-5	-5.4

● TOMMY TUCKER
Tucker, Thomas Joseph "Foghorn" b: 10/28/1863, Holyoke, Mass. d: 10/22/35, Montague, Mass. BB/TR, 5'11", 165 lbs. Deb: 4/16/1887 ♦

YEAR	TM/L	W	L	PCT	G	GS	CG	SH	SV	IP	H	HR	BB	SO	RAT	ERA	ERA+	OAV	OOB	BH	AVG	PB	PR	/A	PD	TPI
1888	Bal-a	0	0	—	1	0	0	0	0	2¹	4	0	0	2	15.4	3.86	77	.364	.364	149	.287	0	-0	-0	-0	0.0
1891	Bos-N	0	0	—	1	0	0	0	0	1	3	0	0	0	27.0	9.00	41	.500	.500	148	.270	-1	-1	-1	-0	0.0
Total	2	0	0	—	2	0	0	0	0	3¹	7	0	0	2	18.9	5.40	59	.412	.412	1882	.290	0	-1	-1	-0	0.0

● TOM TUCKEY
Tuckey, Thomas H. "Tabasco Tom" b: 10/7/1883, Birmingham, England d: 10/17/50, New York, N.Y. TL, 6'3", Deb: 8/11/08

YEAR	TM/L	W	L	PCT	G	GS	CG	SH	SV	IP	H	HR	BB	SO	RAT	ERA	ERA+	OAV	OOB	BH	AVG	PB	PR	/A	PD	TPI
1908	Bos-N	3	3	.500	8	8	3	0	0	72	60	2	20	26	10.5	2.50	96	.265	.336	1	.050	-2	-1	-1	0	-0.2
1909	Bos-N	0	9	.000	17	10	4	0	0	90²	104	3	22	16	12.8	4.27	66	.295	.342	4	.138	-1	-17	-15	1	-1.4
Total	2	3	12	.200	25	18	7	0	0	162²	164	5	42	42	11.8	3.49	76	.284	.340	5	.102	-3	-18	-15	1	-1.6

● JOHN TUDOR
Tudor, John Thomas b: 2/2/54, Schenectady, N.Y. BL/TL, 6', 185 lbs. Deb: 8/16/79

YEAR	TM/L	W	L	PCT	G	GS	CG	SH	SV	IP	H	HR	BB	SO	RAT	ERA	ERA+	OAV	OOB	BH	AVG	PB	PR	/A	PD	TPI
1979	Bos-A	1	2	.333	6	6	1	0	0	28	39	2	9	11	15.4	6.43	69	.345	.393	0	—	0	-7	-6	1	-0.5
1980	Bos-A	8	5	.615	16	13	5	0	0	92¹	81	4	31	45	11.2	3.02	140	.238	.307	0	—	0	10	12	2	1.4
1981	Bos-A	4	3	.571	18	11	2	0	0	78²	74	11	28	44	12.0	4.58	85	.252	.323	0	—	0	-8	-6	1	-0.8
1982	Bos-A	13	10	.565	32	30	6	1	0	195²	215	24	59	146	13.0	3.63	119	.280	.338	0	—	0	10	15	2	1.4
1983	Bos-A	13	12	.520	34	34	7	2	0	242	236	31	81	136	11.9	4.09	106	.255	.317	0	—	1	-1	7	-1	0.2
1984	Pit-N	12	11	.522	32	32	6	1	0	212	200	19	56	117	10.9	3.27	110	.248	.297	16	.211	2	8	8	-1	1.0
1985	*StL-N	21	8	.724	36	36	14	10	0	275	209	14	49	169	8.6	1.93	183	.209	.249	13	.138	1	51	49	1	5.5

YEAR	TM/L	W	L	PCT	G	GS	CG	SH	SV	IP	H	HR	BB	SO	RAT	ERA	ERA+	OAV	OOB	BH	AVG	PB	PR	/A	PD	TPI
1986	StL-N	13	7	.650	30	30	3	0	0	219	197	22	53	107	10.3	2.92	125	.244	.291	11	.153	-0	19	18	1	1.6
1987	*StL-N	10	2	.833	16	16	0	0	0	96	100	11	32	54	12.5	3.84	108	.272	.333	7	.200	1	3	3	1	0.6
1988	StL-N	6	5	.545	21	21	4	1	0	145¹	131	5	31	55	10.1	2.29	152	.247	.290	5	.109	-1	19	19	1	1.5
	*LA-N	4	3	.571	9	9	1	0	0	52¹	58	5	10	32	11.7	2.41	138	.284	.318	0	.000	-0	6	5	0	0.6
	Yr	10	8	.556	30	30	5	1	0	197²	189	10	41	87	10.5	2.32	148	.255	.294	5	.085	-2	25	24	1	2.1
1989	LA-N	0	0	—	6	3	0	0	0	14¹	17	1	6	9	14.4	3.14	109	.309	.377	0	.000	-0	1	0	0	0.0
1990	StL-N	12	4	.750	25	22	1	1	0	146¹	120	10	30	63	9.3	2.40	159	.225	.269	7	.152	-0	23	23	2	2.7
Total	12	117	72	.619	281	263	50	16	1	1797	1677	156	475	988	10.9	3.12	123	.248	.301	59	.154	3	132	146	9	15.2

● **OSCAR TUERO**   Tuero, Oscar (Monzon) (b: Oscar Tuero Monzon) b: 12/17/1898, Canada d: 10/21/60, Houston, Tex.   BR/TR, 5'8.5", 158 lbs. Deb: 5/30/18

YEAR	TM/L	W	L	PCT	G	GS	CG	SH	SV	IP	H	HR	BB	SO	RAT	ERA	ERA+	OAV	OOB	BH	AVG	PB	PR	/A	PD	TPI
1918	StL-N	1	2	.333	11	3	2	0	0	44¹	32	0	10	13	9.1	1.02	267	.208	.269	3	.250	0	9	8	-1	0.5
1919	StL-N	5	7	.417	**45**	16	4	0	**4**	154²	137	4	42	45	11.0	3.20	87	.242	.306	8	.205	1	-5	-7	-0	-0.5
1920	StL-N	0	0	—	2	0	0	0	0	0²	5	0	1	0	81.0	54.00	6	.833	.857	0	—	-0	-4	-4	-0	0.0
Total	3	6	9	.400	58	19	6	0	4	199²	174	4	53	58	10.8	2.88	96	.240	.303	11	.216	1	-0	-2	-1	0.0

● **BOB TUFTS**   Tufts, Robert Malcolm b: 11/2/55, Medford, Mass.   BL/TL, 6'5", 215 lbs. Deb: 8/10/81

YEAR	TM/L	W	L	PCT	G	GS	CG	SH	SV	IP	H	HR	BB	SO	RAT	ERA	ERA+	OAV	OOB	BH	AVG	PB	PR	/A	PD	TPI
1981	SF-N	0	0	—	11	0	0	0	0	15¹	20	1	6	12	15.8	3.52	97	.308	.375	0	.000	-0	-0	-0	1	0.1
1982	KC-A	2	0	1.000	10	0	0	0	2	20	24	3	3	13	12.1	4.50	91	.293	.318	0	—	-1	-1	-1	-1	-0.2
1983	KC-A	0	0	—	6	0	0	0	0	6²	16	1	5	3	29.7	8.10	50	.444	.524	0	—	-0	-3	-3	0	-0.1
Total	3	2	0	1.000	27	0	0	0	2	42	60	5	14	28	16.3	4.71	81	.328	.382	0	.000	-0	-4	-4	0	-0.1

● **LEE TUNNELL**   Tunnell, Byron Lee b: 10/30/60, Tyler, Tex.   BR/TR, 6'1", 180 lbs. Deb: 9/4/82

YEAR	TM/L	W	L	PCT	G	GS	CG	SH	SV	IP	H	HR	BB	SO	RAT	ERA	ERA+	OAV	OOB	BH	AVG	PB	PR	/A	PD	TPI
1982	Pit-N	1	1	.500	5	3	0	0	0	18¹	17	1	5	4	11.8	3.93	94	.254	.324	0	.000	-1	-1	-1	0	-0.1
1983	Pit-N	11	6	.647	35	25	5	3	0	177²	167	15	58	95	11.5	3.65	102	.252	.314	7	.121	-1	-1	1	2	0.2
1984	Pit-N	1	7	.125	26	6	0	0	0	68¹	81	6	40	51	15.9	5.27	68	.298	.388	1	.083	-1	-13	-13	1	-1.3
1985	Pit-N	4	10	.286	24	23	0	0	0	132¹	126	11	57	74	12.5	4.01	89	.251	.329	4	.085	-2	-6	-6	1	-0.8
1987	*StL-N	4	4	.500	32	9	0	0	0	74¹	90	5	34	49	15.1	4.84	86	.307	.381	4	.235	-1	-6	-6	-0	-0.5
1989	Min-A	1	0	1.000	10	0	0	0	0	12	18	1	6	7	18.0	6.00	69	.340	.407	0	—	0	-3	-2	-0	-0.6
Total	6	22	28	.440	132	66	5	3	1	483	499	39	200	280	13.1	4.23	88	.270	.343	16	.116	-4	-29	-27	4	-3.1

● **GEORGE TURBEVILLE**   Turbeville, George Elkins b: 8/24/14, Turbeville, S.C.   d: 10/5/83, Salisbury, N.C.   BR/TL, 6'1", 175 lbs. Deb: 7/20/35

YEAR	TM/L	W	L	PCT	G	GS	CG	SH	SV	IP	H	HR	BB	SO	RAT	ERA	ERA+	OAV	OOB	BH	AVG	PB	PR	/A	PD	TPI
1935	Phi-A	0	3	.000	19	6	2	0	0	63²	74	2	69	20	20.2	7.63	60	.312	.467	2	.105	-2	-22	-22	-1	-1.1
1936	Phi-A	2	5	.286	12	6	2	0	0	43²	42	6	32	10	16.5	6.39	68	.258	.398	2	.143	-1	-7	-6	-0	-0.8
1937	Phi-A	0	4	.000	31	3	0	0	0	77¹	80	2	56	17	15.8	4.77	99	.266	.381	6	.231	0	-1	-1	-1	-0.1
Total	3	2	12	.143	62	15	4	0	0	184²	196	10	157	47	17.5	6.14	77	.280	.416	10	.169	-3	-30	-29	-2	-2.0

● **LUCAS TURK**   Turk, Lucas Newton "Harlem" or "Chief" b: 5/2/1898, Homer, Ga.   d: 1/11/94, Homer, Ga.   BR/TR, 6', 165 lbs. Deb: 6/7/22

YEAR	TM/L	W	L	PCT	G	GS	CG	SH	SV	IP	H	HR	BB	SO	RAT	ERA	ERA+	OAV	OOB	BH	AVG	PB	PR	/A	PD	TPI
1922	Was-A	0	0	—	5	0	0	0	0	11²	14	0	5	1	16.2	6.94	56	.340	.404	1	.250	-0	-4	-4	-1	-0.1

● **BOB TURLEY**   Turley, Robert Lee "Bullet Bob" b: 9/19/30, Troy, Ill.   BR/TR, 6'2", 215 lbs. Deb: 9/29/51   C

YEAR	TM/L	W	L	PCT	G	GS	CG	SH	SV	IP	H	HR	BB	SO	RAT	ERA	ERA+	OAV	OOB	BH	AVG	PB	PR	/A	PD	TPI
1951	StL-A	0	1	.000	1	1	0	0	0	7¹	11	0	3	5	17.2	7.36	66	.355	.412	0	.000	-0	-3	-2	0	-0.3
1953	StL-A	2	6	.250	10	7	3	1	0	60¹	39	4	44	61	12.7	3.28	128	.184	.329	5	.278	1	5	6	-1	0.9
1954	Bal-A☆	14	15	.483	35	35	14	0	0	247¹	178	7	181	**185**	13.3	3.46	104	**.203**	.343	11	.136	-3	7	3	-1	0.1
1955	*NY-A☆	17	13	.567	36	34	13	6	1	246²	168	16	177	210	12.8	3.06	122	**.193**	.333	11	.134	-0	25	19	-2	1.9
1956	*NY-A	8	4	.667	27	21	5	1	1	132	138	13	103	91	16.7	5.05	77	.273	.400	8	.174	-0	-13	-17	-1	-1.5
1957	*NY-A	13	6	.684	32	23	9	4	3	176¹	120	17	85	152	10.9	2.71	133	**.194**	.300	5	.088	-2	21	17	-0	1.6
1958	*NY-A★	**21**	7	**.750**	33	31	**19**	6	1	245¹	178	24	128	168	11.5	2.97	119	**.206**	.313	12	.136	-1	22	15	-2	1.4
1959	NY-A	8	11	.421	33	22	7	3	0	154¹	141	15	83	111	13.2	4.32	84	.245	.343	4	.087	-2	-8	-11	-1	-1.5
1960	*NY-A	9	3	.750	34	24	4	1	5	173¹	138	14	87	87	11.9	3.27	110	.222	.322	4	.073	-4	12	6	-1	-0.1
1961	NY-A	3	5	.375	15	12	1	0	0	72	74	11	51	48	16.1	5.75	65	.269	.391	2	.095	-1	-14	-16	-1	-1.7
1962	NY-A	3	3	.500	24	8	0	0	1	69	68	8	47	42	15.5	4.57	82	.263	.384	0	.000	-1	-5	-6	1	-0.6
1963	LA-A	2	7	.222	19	12	3	2	0	87¹	71	5	51	70	12.8	3.30	104	.222	.332	4	.160	1	3	1	-0	0.2
	Bos-A	1	4	.200	11	7	0	0	0	41¹	42	6	28	35	15.5	6.10	64	.256	.368	3	.214	0	-11	-11	-0	-1.2
	Yr	3	11	.214	30	19	3	2	0	128²	113	11	79	105	13.5	4.20	84	.232	.340	7	.179	1	-8	-9	-1	-1.0
Total	12	101	85	.543	310	237	78	24	12	1712²	1366	140	1068	1265	13.1	3.64	101	.220	.340	69	.126	-12	41	4	-9	-0.8

● **TUCK TURNER**   Turner, George A. b: 2/13/1873, W.New Brighton, N.Y.   d: 7/16/45, Staten Island, N.Y.   BB/TL, 5'6.5", 155 lbs. Deb: 8/18/1893 ♦

YEAR	TM/L	W	L	PCT	G	GS	CG	SH	SV	IP	H	HR	BB	SO	RAT	ERA	ERA+	OAV	OOB	BH	AVG	PB	PR	/A	PD	TPI
1894	Phi-N	0	0	—	1	1	1	0	0	8	18	0	6	1	27.0	7.50	68	.346	.414	141	.416	1	-1	-2	-0	0.6

● **JIM TURNER**   Turner, James Riley "Milkman Jim" b: 8/6/03, Antioch, Tenn.   BL/TR, 6', 185 lbs. Deb: 4/30/37   C

YEAR	TM/L	W	L	PCT	G	GS	CG	SH	SV	IP	H	HR	BB	SO	RAT	ERA	ERA+	OAV	OOB	BH	AVG	PB	PR	/A	PD	TPI
1937	Bos-N	20	11	.645	33	30	**24**	**5**	1	256²	228	13	52	69	**9.8**	**2.38**	150	.235	**.274**	24	.250	4	**44**	34	-0	**4.5**
1938	Bos-N☆	14	18	.438	35	34	22	3	0	268	267	21	54	71	10.9	3.46	99	.259	.299	22	.229	4	10	-1	4	0.7
1939	Bos-N	4	11	.267	25	22	9	0	0	157²	181	10	51	50	13.5	4.28	86	.293	.351	13	.236	2	-6	-10	1	-0.5
1940	*Cin-N	14	7	.667	24	23	11	0	0	187	187	9	32	53	10.5	2.89	131	.264	.296	18	.240	3	20	19	-2	2.2
1941	Cin-N	6	4	.600	23	10	3	0	0	113	120	5	24	34	11.5	3.11	116	.277	.317	6	.146	-1	7	6	2	0.6
1942	Cin-N	0	0	—	3	0	0	0	0	3¹	5	1	3	2	21.6	10.80	30	.333	.444	0	.000	-0	-3	-3	-0	-0.2
	*NY-A	1	1	.500	5	0	0	0	0	7	7	4	2	2	11.6	1.29	268	.167	.200	0	.000	-0	2	2	0	0.6
1943	NY-A	3	0	1.000	18	0	0	0	1	43¹	44	1	13	15	11.8	3.53	91	.260	.313	1	.077	-1	-1	-2	-0	-0.3
1944	NY-A	4	4	.500	35	0	0	0	0	41²	42	3	13	13	13.4	3.46	101	.264	.354	2	.200	-1	-0	-1	1	-0.2
1945	NY-A	3	4	.429	30	0	0	0	10	54¹	45	4	31	22	12.6	3.64	95	.225	.329	1	.091	-1	-2	-1	1	-0.2
Total	9	69	60	.535	231	119	69	8	20	1132	1123	67	283	329	11.3	3.22	111	.260	.307	87	.218	12	70	45	6	7.6

● **KEN TURNER**   Turner, Kenneth Charles b: 8/17/43, Framingham, Mass.   BR/TL, 6'2", 190 lbs. Deb: 6/11/67

YEAR	TM/L	W	L	PCT	G	GS	CG	SH	SV	IP	H	HR	BB	SO	RAT	ERA	ERA+	OAV	OOB	BH	AVG	PB	PR	/A	PD	TPI
1967	Cal-A	1	2	.333	13	1	0	0	0	17¹	16	4	4	6	10.9	4.15	76	.239	.292	0	.000	-0	-2	-2	0	-0.3

● **TED TURNER**   Turner, Theodore Holhot b: 5/4/1892, Lawrenceburg, Ky.   d: 2/4/58, Lexington, Ky.   BR/TR, 6', 180 lbs. Deb: 4/20/20

YEAR	TM/L	W	L	PCT	G	GS	CG	SH	SV	IP	H	HR	BB	SO	RAT	ERA	ERA+	OAV	OOB	BH	AVG	PB	PR	/A	PD	TPI
1920	Chi-N	0	0	—	1	0	0	0	0	1¹	2	0	1	0	20.3	13.50	24	.400	.500	0	.000	-0	-2	-2	-0	0.0

● **TINK TURNER**   Turner, Thomas Lovatt b: 2/20/1890, Swarthmore, Pa.   d: 2/25/62, Philadelphia, Pa.   BR/TR, 6'1", 190 lbs. Deb: 9/24/15

YEAR	TM/L	W	L	PCT	G	GS	CG	SH	SV	IP	H	HR	BB	SO	RAT	ERA	ERA+	OAV	OOB	BH	AVG	PB	PR	/A	PD	TPI
1915	Phi-A	0	1	.000	1	1	0	0	0	2	5	1	3	0	36.0	22.50	13	.500	.615	0	—	0	-4	-4	-0	-1.1

● **MATT TURNER**   Turner, William Matthew b: 2/18/67, Lexington, Ky.   BR/TR, 6'5", 215 lbs. Deb: 4/23/93

YEAR	TM/L	W	L	PCT	G	GS	CG	SH	SV	IP	H	HR	BB	SO	RAT	ERA	ERA+	OAV	OOB	BH	AVG	PB	PR	/A	PD	TPI
1993	Fla-N	4	5	.444	55	0	0	0	0	68	52	7	26	59	10.9	2.91	148	.227	.305	0	.000	-0	9	11	0	1.3
1994	Cle-A	1	0	1.000	9	0	0	0	0	12²	16	0	7	5	16.3	2.13	221	.241	.359	0	—	-0	4	4	-1	0.2
Total	2	5	5	.500	64	0	0	0	0	80²	68	7	33	64	11.7	2.79	157	.230	.315	0	.000	-0	12	14	-0	1.5

● **ELMER TUTWILER**   Tutwiler, Elmer Strange b: 11/19/05, Carbon Hill, Ala.   d: 5/3/76, Pensacola, Fla.   BR/TR, 5'11", 158 lbs. Deb: 8/20/28

YEAR	TM/L	W	L	PCT	G	GS	CG	SH	SV	IP	H	HR	BB	SO	RAT	ERA	ERA+	OAV	OOB	BH	AVG	PB	PR	/A	PD	TPI
1928	Pit-N	0	0	—	2	0	0	0	0	3²	4	0	1	0	9.8	4.91	83	.267	.267	0	—	-0	-0	-0	0	0.0

● **TWINK TWINING**   Twining, Howard Earle "Doc" b: 5/30/1894, Horsham, Pa.   d: 6/14/73, Lansdale, Pa.   BR/TR, 6', 168 lbs. Deb: 7/9/16

YEAR	TM/L	W	L	PCT	G	GS	CG	SH	SV	IP	H	HR	BB	SO	RAT	ERA	ERA+	OAV	OOB	BH	AVG	PB	PR	/A	PD	TPI
1916	Cin-N	0	0	—	1	0	0	0	0	1	2	0	0	0	18.0	13.50	19	.444	.545	0	—	0	-2	-2	-0	0.0

● **LARRY TWITCHELL**   Twitchell, Lawrence Grant b: 2/18/1864, Cleveland, Ohio   d: 8/23/30, Cleveland, Ohio   BR/TR, 6', 185 lbs. Deb: 4/30/1886 ♦

YEAR	TM/L	W	L	PCT	G	GS	CG	SH	SV	IP	H	HR	BB	SO	RAT	ERA	ERA+	OAV	OOB	BH	AVG	PB	PR	/A	PD	TPI
1886	Det-N	0	2	.000	4	4	2	0	0	25	35	1	12	6	16.9	6.48	51	.347	.416	1	.063	-2	-9	-9	1	-0.6
1887	*Det-N	11	1	.917	15	12	11	0	1	112¹	120	3	36	24	13.3	4.33	94	.268	.336	88	.333	4	-3	-3	-1	-0.2
1888	Det-N	0	0	—	2	0	0	0	0	4	6	1	0	3	6.75	41	.375	.375	128	.244	-0	-2	-2	0	-0.1
1889	Cle-N	0	0	—	1	0	0	0	0	1	0	0	0	0	9.0	0.00	—	.000	.250	151	.275	0	0	-0	0	0.0
1890	Buf-P	5	7	.417	13	12	12	0	0	104¹	112	3	72	29	17.2	4.57	90	.262	.387	38	.221	-4	-5	2	-0.2
1891	Col-a	1	1	.500	6	1	1	0	1	31	29	1	15	8	13.3	4.06	85	.240	.328	62	.277	0	-0	-0	0	0.0
1894	Lou-N	0	0	—	1	0	0	0	0	3	5	1	0	0	18.0	6.00	85	.357	.400	56	.267	-0	-0	-0	0	0.0
Total	7	17	11	.607	42	29	26	0	2	280²	307	10	135	70	15.1	4.62	85	.272	.363	676	.263	7	-19	-21	1	-1.1

YEAR	TM/L	W	L	PCT	G	GS	CG	SH	SV	IP	H	HR	BB	SO	RAT	ERA	ERA+	OAV	OOB	BH	AVG	PB	PR	/A	PD	TPI

● WAYNE TWITCHELL
Twitchell, Wayne Lee b: 3/10/48, Portland, Ore. BR/TR, 6'6", 220 lbs. Deb: 9/7/70

YEAR	TM/L	W	L	PCT	G	GS	CG	SH	SV	IP	H	HR	BB	SO	RAT	ERA	ERA+	OAV	OOB	BH	AVG	PB	PR	/A	PD	TPI
1970	Mil-A	0	0	—	2	0	0	0	0	1²	3	0	1	5	21.6	10.80	35	.333	.400	0	—	0	-1	-1	0	0.0
1971	Phi-N	1	0	1.000	6	1	0	0	0	16	8	1	10	15	10.7	0.00	—	.145	.288	0	.000	-0	6	6	-0	0.3
1972	Phi-N	5	9	.357	49	15	1	1	1	139²	138	6	56	112	12.6	4.06	88	.259	.332	2	.071	-2	-9	-7	-1	-1.0
1973	Phi-N★	13	9	.591	34	28	10	5	0	223¹	172	16	99	169	11.3	2.50	152	.219	.314	7	.097	-4	29	32	-3	2.3
1974	Phi-N	6	9	.400	25	18	2	0	0	112¹	122	11	65	72	15.5	5.21	73	.276	.377	6	.171	-1	-20	-18	-2	-2.3
1975	Phi-N	5	10	.333	36	20	0	0	0	134¹	132	10	78	101	14.1	4.42	84	.261	.361	3	.088	-2	-12	-10	-3	-1.5
1976	Phi-N	3	1	.750	26	2	0	0	1	61²	55	3	18	67	11.1	1.75	203	.241	.305	1	.167	0	12	12	0	0.9
1977	Phi-N	0	5	.000	12	8	0	0	0	45²	50	3	25	37	14.8	4.53	88	.287	.377	1	.091	-0	-3	-3	1	-0.3
	Mon-N	6	5	.545	22	22	2	0	0	139	116	18	49	93	11.0	4.21	90	.230	.304	8	.205	2	-5	-6	-1	-0.3
	Yr	6	10	.375	34	30	2	0	0	184²	166	21	74	130	11.9	4.29	90	.244	.323	9	.180	2	-8	-9	-0	-0.6
1978	Mon-N	4	12	.250	33	15	0	0	0	112	121	6	71	69	15.8	5.38	65	.286	.395	2	.083	-1	-22	-23	-1	-3.2
1979	NY-N	5	3	.625	33	2	0	0	0	63²	55	6	55	44	16.1	5.23	70	.243	.400	3	.375	1	-11	-11	-0	-1.2
	Sea-A	0	2	.000	4	2	0	0	0	7	12	1	5	5	15.1	5.27	83	.375	.220	.371	0	—	-0	-2	-1	-0	-0.2
Total	10	48	65	.425	282	133	15	6	2	1063	983	92	537	789	13.2	3.98	94	.250	.346	33	.127	-6	-38	-31	-10	-6.5

● JEFF TWITTY
Twitty, Jeffrey Dean b: 11/10/57, Lancaster, S.C. BL/TL, 6'2", 185 lbs. Deb: 7/5/80

YEAR	TM/L	W	L	PCT	G	GS	CG	SH	SV	IP	H	HR	BB	SO	RAT	ERA	ERA+	OAV	OOB	BH	AVG	PB	PR	/A	PD	TPI
1980	KC-A	2	1	.667	13	0	0	0	0	22¹	33	4	7	9	16.1	6.04	67	.351	.396	0	—	0	-5	-5	0	-0.6

● CY TWOMBLY
Twombly, Edwin Parker b: 6/15/1897, Groveland, Mass. d: 12/3/74, Savannah, Ga. BL/TL, 5'10.5", 170 lbs. Deb: 6/25/21

YEAR	TM/L	W	L	PCT	G	GS	CG	SH	SV	IP	H	HR	BB	SO	RAT	ERA	ERA+	OAV	OOB	BH	AVG	PB	PR	/A	PD	TPI
1921	Chi-A	1	2	.333	7	4	0	0	0	27²	26	1	25	2	17.2	5.86	72	.283	.445	0	.000	-2	-5	-5	1	-0.5

● LEFTY TYLER
Tyler, George Albert b: 12/14/1889, Derry, N.H. d: 9/29/53, Lowell, Mass. BL/TL, 6', 175 lbs. Deb: 9/20/10 F

YEAR	TM/L	W	L	PCT	G	GS	CG	SH	SV	IP	H	HR	BB	SO	RAT	ERA	ERA+	OAV	OOB	BH	AVG	PB	PR	/A	PD	TPI
1910	Bos-N	0	0	—	2	0	0	0	0	11¹	11	1	6	6	13.5	2.38	140	.275	.370	2	.500	1	1	1	-0	0.1
1911	Bos-N	7	10	.412	28	20	10	1	0	165¹	150	11	109	90	14.6	5.06	76	.243	.365	10	.164	-1	-31	-23	4	-1.8
1912	Bos-N	12	22	.353	42	31	15	1	0	256¹	262	8	126	144	14.0	4.18	86	.276	.367	19	.198	-1	-22	-17	4	-1.8
1913	Bos-N	16	17	.485	39	34	**28**	4	2	290¹	245	6	108	143	11.3	2.79	118	.235	.313	21	.206	4	13	16	7	2.9
1914	*Bos-N	16	13	.552	38	34	21	5	2	271¹	247	7	101	140	12.0	2.69	103	.243	.327	19	.202	1	3	2	-2	0.1
1915	Bos-N	10	9	.526	32	24	15	1	0	204²	182	6	84	89	11.9	2.86	91	.243	.324	23	.261	8	-2	-6	-1	0.2
1916	Bos-N	17	9	.654	34	28	21	6	1	249	200	6	58	117	9.4	2.02	123	.226	.276	19	.204	7	17	13	2	2.5
1917	Bos-N	14	12	.538	32	28	22	4	1	239	203	1	86	98	11.1	2.52	101	.240	.314	31	.231	4	5	1	3	1.1
1918	*Chi-N	19	8	.704	33	30	22	6	1	269¹	218	1	67	102	9.7	2.00	139	.226	.279	21	.210	1	23	23	3	3.0
1919	Chi-N	2	2	.500	6	5	3	0	0	30	20	0	13	9	9.9	2.10	137	.196	.287	1	.143	1	3	3	1	0.6
1920	Chi-N	11	12	.478	27	27	18	2	0	193	193	6	57	57	11.8	3.31	97	.268	.324	17	.262	4	-4	-2	3	0.5
1921	Chi-N	3	2	.600	10	6	4	0	0	50	59	2	14	8	13.1	3.24	118	.294	.340	6	.231	1	3	3	-1	0.3
Total	12	127	116	.523	323	267	179	30	7	2230	1990	51	829	1003	11.6	2.95	101	.245	.320	189	.217	30	9	11	21	7.7

● JIM TYNG
Tyng, James Alexander b: 3/27/1856, Philadelphia, Pa. d: 10/30/31, New York, N.Y. 5'9", 155 lbs. Deb: 9/23/1879

YEAR	TM/L	W	L	PCT	G	GS	CG	SH	SV	IP	H	HR	BB	SO	RAT	ERA	ERA+	OAV	OOB	BH	AVG	PB	PR	/A	PD	TPI
1879	Bos-N	1	2	.333	3	3	3	0	0	27	35	0	6	7	13.7	5.00	54	.292	.325	5	.357	1	-8	-8	0	-0.5
1888	Phi-N	0	0	—	1	0	0	0	1	4	8	0	2	2	24.8	4.50	66	.381	.458	0	.000	-0	-1	-1	0	0.0
Total	2	1	2	.333	4	3	3	0	1	31	43	0	8	9	15.1	4.94	51	.305	.347	5	.333	1	-8	-8	0	-0.5

● DAVE TYRIVER
Tyriver, David Burton b: 10/31/37, Oshkosh, Wis. d: 10/28/88, Oshkosh, Wis. BR/TR, 6' ", 175 lbs. Deb: 8/21/62

YEAR	TM/L	W	L	PCT	G	GS	CG	SH	SV	IP	H	HR	BB	SO	RAT	ERA	ERA+	OAV	OOB	BH	AVG	PB	PR	/A	PD	TPI
1962	Cle-A	0	0	—	4	0	0	0	0	10²	10	2	7	7	15.2	4.22	92	.250	.375	0	.000	-0	-0	-0	0	0.0

● JIMMY UCHRINSCKO
Uchrinscko, James Emerson b: 10/20/1900, W.Newton, Pa. d: 3/17/95, Mt.Pleasant, Pa. BL/TR, 6', 180 lbs. Deb: 7/20/26

YEAR	TM/L	W	L	PCT	G	GS	CG	SH	SV	IP	H	HR	BB	SO	RAT	ERA	ERA+	OAV	OOB	BH	AVG	PB	PR	/A	PD	TPI
1926	Was-A	0	0	—	3	0	0	0	0	8	13	0	8	0	23.6	10.13	38	.433	.553	0	.000	-0	-5	-6	0	0.0

● BOB UHL
Uhl, Robert Ellwood "Lefty" b: 9/17/13, San Francisco, Cal. d: 8/21/90, Santa Rosa, Cal. BB/TL, 5'11", 175 lbs. Deb: 5/8/38

YEAR	TM/L	W	L	PCT	G	GS	CG	SH	SV	IP	H	HR	BB	SO	RAT	ERA	ERA+	OAV	OOB	BH	AVG	PB	PR	/A	PD	TPI
1938	Chi-A	0	0	—	1	0	0	0	0	2	1	0	0	4	4.5	0.00	—	.167	.167	0	—	0	1	1	-0	0.0
1940	Det-A	0	0	—	1	0	0	0	0	0	4	0	2	0	—	∞	—	1.000	1.000	0	—	0	-4	-4	0	-0.3
Total	2	0	0	—	2	0	0	0	0	2	5	0	2	4	31.5	18.00	27	.500	.583	0	—	0	-3	-3	-0	-0.3

● GEORGE UHLE
Uhle, George Ernest "The Bull" b: 9/18/1898, Cleveland, Ohio d: 2/26/85, Lakewood, Ohio BR/TR, 6', 190 lbs. Deb: 4/30/19 C♦

YEAR	TM/L	W	L	PCT	G	GS	CG	SH	SV	IP	H	HR	BB	SO	RAT	ERA	ERA+	OAV	OOB	BH	AVG	PB	PR	/A	PD	TPI
1919	Cle-A	10	5	.667	26	12	7	1	0	127	129	1	43	50	12.7	2.91	115	.261	.329	13	.302	3	5	6	0	1.0
1920	*Cle-A	4	5	.444	27	6	2	0	1	84²	98	3	29	27	14.4	5.21	73	.296	.367	11	.344	2	-13	-13	0	-1.0
1921	Cle-A	16	13	.552	41	28	13	2	2	238	288	9	63	63	13.4	4.01	106	.306	.352	23	.245	3	7	7	-3	0.7
1922	Cle-A	22	16	.579	50	40	23	**5**	3	287¹	328	6	89	82	13.5	4.07	98	.290	.348	29	.266	9	-1	-2	-3	0.1
1923	Cle-A	26	16	.619	54	44	**29**	1	5	357²	378	8	102	109	12.4	3.77	105	.271	.326	52	.361	16	8	8	0	2.4
1924	Cle-A	9	15	.375	28	25	15	0	1	196¹	238	6	75	57	14.9	4.77	90	.306	.376	33	.308	7	-12	-11	1	-0.4
1925	Cle-A	13	11	.542	29	26	17	1	0	210²	218	5	78	68	13.0	4.10	108	.268	.339	29	.287	6	7	7	-3	1.0
1926	Cle-A	27	11	**.711**	39	36	**32**	3	1	318¹	300	7	118	159	12.2	2.83	143	.253	.328	30	.227	4	42	43	-0	**5.2**
1927	Cle-A	8	9	.471	25	22	10	1	1	153¹	187	3	59	69	15.0	4.34	97	.310	.379	21	.266	4	-3	-2	-1	-0.9
1928	Cle-A	12	17	.414	31	28	18	2	1	214¹	252	8	74	72	13.0	4.07	102	.300	.344	28	.286	7	-1	-2	3	1.1
1929	Det-A	15	11	.577	32	30	23	1	0	249	283	9	58	100	12.4	4.08	105	.287	.328	37	.343	8	4	6	-3	1.1
1930	Det-A	12	12	.500	33	29	18	1	3	239	239	18	75	117	12.0	3.65	131	.264	.323	36	.308	8	26	30	-3	3.2
1931	Det-A	11	12	.478	29	18	15	2	1	193	190	4	49	63	11.3	3.50	131	.255	.304	22	.244	5	19	23	-1	2.9
1932	Det-A	6	6	.500	33	15	4	1	5	146²	152	15	42	51	12.1	4.48	105	.266	.320	10	.182	1	-0	4	-1	0.3
1933	Det-A	0	0	—	1	0	0	0	0	0²	2	1	0	1	27.0	27.00	16	.500	.500	0	—	-0	-2	-2	-0	-0.9
	NY-N	1	1	.500	6	1	0	0	0	13²	14	5	6	4	14.5	7.90	41	.302	.373	0	.000	-0	-7	-7	-0	-0.9
	NY-A	6	1	.857	12	6	4	0	0	61	63	4	20	26	12.7	5.16	75	.257	.321	8	.400	4	-6	-9	-1	-0.5
1934	NY-A	2	4	.333	10	2	0	0	0	16¹	30	3	7	10	20.4	9.92	41	.400	.451	3	.600	2	-10	-11	-0	-2.7
1936	Cle-A	0	1	.000	2	0	0	0	0	6²	8	1	5	3	22.0	8.53	59	.419	.463	8	.381	4	-5	-5	-1	0.0
Total	17	200	166	.546	513	368	232	21	25	3119²	3417	119	966	1135	13.0	3.99	104	.281	.340	393	.289	92	60	74	-15	13.5

● JERRY UJDUR
Ujdur, Gerald Raymond b: 3/5/57, Duluth, Minn. BR/TR, 6'1", 195 lbs. Deb: 8/17/80

YEAR	TM/L	W	L	PCT	G	GS	CG	SH	SV	IP	H	HR	BB	SO	RAT	ERA	ERA+	OAV	OOB	BH	AVG	PB	PR	/A	PD	TPI
1980	Det-A	1	0	1.000	9	2	0	0	0	21¹	36	5	10	8	19.8	7.59	54	.383	.448	0	—	0	-8	-8	-1	-0.6
1981	Det-A	0	0	—	4	4	0	0	0	14	19	2	5	5	15.4	6.43	59	.322	.375	0	—	0	-4	-4	0	0.0
1982	Det-A	10	10	.500	25	25	7	0	0	178	150	29	69	86	11.2	3.69	110	.230	.306	0	—	0	8	7	-1	0.6
1983	Det-A	0	4	.000	11	6	0	0	0	34	41	6	20	13	16.4	7.15	55	.293	.385	0	—	0	-12	-12	-1	-1.2
1984	Cle-A	1	2	.333	4	3	0	0	0	14¹	22	1	6	6	18.8	6.91	59	.355	.429	0	—	0	-5	-4	-1	-0.9
Total	5	12	16	.429	53	40	7	0	0	261²	268	43	110	118	13.2	4.78	84	.266	.342	0	—	0	-21	-22	-3	-2.1

● SANDY ULLRICH
Ullrich, Carlos Santiago (Castello) b: 7/25/21, Havana, Cuba BR/TR, 6'1", 180 lbs. Deb: 5/3/44

YEAR	TM/L	W	L	PCT	G	GS	CG	SH	SV	IP	H	HR	BB	SO	RAT	ERA	ERA+	OAV	OOB	BH	AVG	PB	PR	/A	PD	TPI
1944	Was-A	0	0	—	3	0	0	0	0	9²	17	2	4	2	20.5	9.31	45	.386	.449	1	.333	—	-6	-7	0	0.0
1945	Was-A	3	3	.500	28	6	0	0	1	81¹	91	3	34	26	13.8	4.54	68	.276	.343	6	.273	1	-11	-13	1	-0.7
Total	2	3	3	.500	31	6	0	0	1	91	108	5	38	28	14.5	5.04	62	.289	.356	7	.280	1	-17	-19	2	-0.7

● DUTCH ULRICH
Ulrich, Frank W. b: 11/18/1899, Baltimore, Md. d: 2/11/29, Baltimore, Md. BR/TR, 6'2", 195 lbs. Deb: 4/18/25

YEAR	TM/L	W	L	PCT	G	GS	CG	SH	SV	IP	H	HR	BB	SO	RAT	ERA	ERA+	OAV	OOB	BH	AVG	PB	PR	/A	PD	TPI
1925	Phi-N	3	3	.500	21	4	2	0	0	65	73	8	12	29	11.9	3.05	157	.285	.320	2	.125	-1	9	12	1	1.0
1926	Phi-N	8	13	.381	45	17	8	1	1	147²	178	9	37	52	13.2	4.08	101	.304	.347	12	.245	-1	-4	1	-0	0.3
1927	Phi-N	8	11	.421	32	18	14	1	1	193¹	201	6	40	42	11.2	3.17	131	.271	.308	9	.123	-6	16	21	-2	1.1
Total	3	19	27	.413	98	39	24	2	2	406	452	23	89	123	12.0	3.48	122	.286	.324	23	.167	-5	21	34	-2	2.4

● ARNOLD UMBACH
Umbach, Arnold William b: 12/6/42, Williamsburg, Va. BR/TR, 6'1", 180 lbs. Deb: 10/3/64

YEAR	TM/L	W	L	PCT	G	GS	CG	SH	SV	IP	H	HR	BB	SO	RAT	ERA	ERA+	OAV	OOB	BH	AVG	PB	PR	/A	PD	TPI
1964	Mil-N	1	0	1.000	1	1	0	0	0	9	4	0	4	7	16.2	3.24	109	.333	.405	0	.000	-0	0	0	-0	0.1
1966	Atl-N	0	2	.000	22	3	0	0	1	40²	40	1	18	23	13.3	3.10	117	.256	.341	1	.200	3	2	2	-0	0.1
Total	2	1	2	.333	23	4	0	0	1	49	51	1	22	30	13.8	3.12	116	.270	.352	1	.125	3	3	3	-0	0.1

● JIM UMBARGER
Umbarger, James Harold b: 2/17/53, Burbank, Cal. BL/TL, 6'6", 200 lbs. Deb: 4/8/75

YEAR	TM/L	W	L	PCT	G	GS	CG	SH	SV	IP	H	HR	BB	SO	RAT	ERA	ERA+	OAV	OOB	BH	AVG	PB	PR	/A	PD	TPI
1975	Tex-A	8	7	.533	56	12	3	2	2	131	134	11	59	50	13.4	4.12	91	.276	.357	0	—	0	-5	-5	1	-0.5
1976	Tex-A	10	12	.455	30	30	10	3	0	197¹	208	12	54	105	12.0	3.15	114	.274	.324	0	—	0	8	10	-0	1.0

YEAR TM/L	W	L	PCT	G	GS	CG	SH	SV	IP	H	HR	BB	SO	RAT	ERA	ERA+	OAV	OOB	BH	AVG	PB	PR	/A	PD	TPI
1977 Oak-A	1	5	.167	12	8	1	0	0	44	62	3	28	24	19.2	6.55	61	.354	.454	0	—	0	-12	-12	0	-1.3
Tex-A	1	1	.500	3	2	0	0	0	13	14	2	4	5	12.5	5.54	74	.275	.327	0	—	-0	-2	-2	-0	-0.3
Yr	2	6	.250	15	10	1	0	0	57	76	5	32	29	17.1	6.32	64	.326	.408	0	—	-0	-14	-14	0	-1.6
1978 Tex-A	5	8	.385	32	9	1	0	1	97¹	116	9	36	60	14.2	4.88	77	.299	.362	0	—	0	-12	-12	1	-1.5
Total 4	25	33	.431	133	61	15	5	3	483	534	37	181	244	13.5	4.14	90	.287	.354	0	—	0	-23	-22	2	-2.6

● JIM UMBRICHT Umbricht, James b: 9/17/30, Chicago, Ill. d: 4/8/64, Houston, Tex. BR/TR, 6'4", 215 lbs. Deb: 9/26/59

YEAR TM/L	W	L	PCT	G	GS	CG	SH	SV	IP	H	HR	BB	SO	RAT	ERA	ERA+	OAV	OOB	BH	AVG	PB	PR	/A	PD	TPI
1959 Pit-N	0	0	—	1	1	0	0	0	7	7	3	4	3	14.1	6.43	60	.259	.355	0	.000	-0	-2	-2	0	0.0
1960 Pit-N	1	2	.333	17	3	0	0	1	40²	40	5	27	26	14.8	5.09	74	.270	.383	2	.333	0	-6	-6	-1	-0.5
1961 Pit-N	0	0	—	1	0	0	0	0	3¹	5	0	2	1	18.9	2.70	148	.333	.412	1	1.000	0	0	0	-0	0.0
1962 Hou-N	4	0	1.000	34	0	0	0	2	67	51	3	17	55	9.4	2.01	185	.213	.270	1	.111	-0	14	13	1	0.8
1963 Hou-N	4	3	.571	35	3	0	0	0	76	52	6	21	48	8.8	2.61	121	.195	.256	1	.111	-0	6	5	1	0.5
Total 5	9	5	.643	88	7	0	0	3	194	155	17	71	133	11.6	3.06	115	.222	.297	5	.179	-0	13	10	0	0.8

● WILLIE UNDERHILL Underhill, Willie Vern b: 9/6/04, Yowell, Tex. d: 10/26/70, Bay City, Tex. BR/TR, 6'2", 185 lbs. Deb: 9/8/27

YEAR TM/L	W	L	PCT	G	GS	CG	SH	SV	IP	H	HR	BB	SO	RAT	ERA	ERA+	OAV	OOB	BH	AVG	PB	PR	/A	PD	TPI
1927 Cle-A	0	2	.000	4	1	0	0	0	8¹	12	0	11	4	24.8	9.72	43	.375	.535	0	.000	-0	-5	-5	0	-0.9
1928 Cle-A	1	2	.333	11	3	1	0	0	28	33	0	20	16	17.4	4.50	92	.306	.419	4	.364	2	-1	-1	0	0.1
Total 2	1	4	.200	15	4	1	0	0	36¹	45	0	31	20	19.1	5.70	73	.321	.448	4	.333	1	-7	-6	0	-0.8

● FRED UNDERWOOD Underwood, Frederick Theodore b: 10/14/1868, St.Louis Co., Mo. d: 1/26/06, Kansas City, Mo. 170 lbs. Deb: 7/18/1894

YEAR TM/L	W	L	PCT	G	GS	CG	SH	SV	IP	H	HR	BB	SO	RAT	ERA	ERA+	OAV	OOB	BH	AVG	PB	PR	/A	PD	TPI
1894 Bro-N	2	4	.333	7	6	5	0	0	47	80	1	30	10	21.4	7.85	63	.372	.453	7	.389	2	-13	-15	-0	-1.1

● PAT UNDERWOOD Underwood, Patrick John b: 2/9/57, Kokomo, Ind. BL/TL, 6', 175 lbs. Deb: 5/31/79 F

YEAR TM/L	W	L	PCT	G	GS	CG	SH	SV	IP	H	HR	BB	SO	RAT	ERA	ERA+	OAV	OOB	BH	AVG	PB	PR	/A	PD	TPI
1979 Det-A	6	4	.600	27	15	1	0	0	121²	126	17	29	83	11.6	4.59	94	.269	.314	0	—	0	-5	-4	-1	-0.4
1980 Det-A	3	6	.333	49	7	0	0	5	112²	121	19	35	60	12.6	3.59	114	.277	.333	0	—	0	6	6	0	0.3
1982 Det-A	4	8	.333	33	12	2	0	3	99	108	17	22	43	11.8	4.73	86	.269	.307	0	—	0	-7	-7	1	-0.8
1983 Det-A	0	0	—	4	0	0	0	0	10¹	11	1	6	2	14.8	8.71	45	.289	.386	0	—	0	-5	-6	0	0.0
Total 4	13	18	.419	113	34	3	0	8	343²	366	47	92	188	12.1	4.43	94	.272	.320	0	—	0	-12	-10	-1	-0.9

● TOM UNDERWOOD Underwood, Thomas Gerald b: 12/22/53, Kokomo, Ind. BR/TL, 5'11", 170 lbs. Deb: 8/19/74 F

YEAR TM/L	W	L	PCT	G	GS	CG	SH	SV	IP	H	HR	BB	SO	RAT	ERA	ERA+	OAV	OOB	BH	AVG	PB	PR	/A	PD	TPI
1974 Phi-N	1	0	1.000	7	0	0	0	0	13	15	1	5	8	13.8	4.85	78	.313	.377	0	.000	-0	-2	-2	-0	-0.2
1975 Phi-N	14	13	.519	35	35	7	2	0	219¹	221	12	84	123	12.8	4.14	90	.262	.333	9	.122	-2	-13	-10	-4	-1.7
1976 *Phi-N	10	5	.667	33	25	3	0	2	155²	154	9	63	94	12.6	3.53	101	.260	.332	5	.109	-1	-3	-0	-3	-0.3
1977 Phi-N	3	2	.600	14	0	0	0	1	33¹	44	2	18	20	16.7	5.13	78	.328	.408	0	.000	-0	-5	-4	0	-0.6
StL-N	6	9	.400	19	17	1	0	0	100	104	7	57	66	14.6	4.95	78	.278	.375	4	.133	-1	-12	-12	-1	-1.7
Yr	9	11	.450	33	17	1	0	1	133¹	148	9	75	86	15.1	4.99	78	.290	.382	4	.121	-1	-16	-16	-2	-2.3
1978 Tor-A	6	14	.300	31	30	7	1	0	197²	201	14	87	139	13.2	4.10	96	.263	.340	0	—	0	-7	-4	-3	-0.7
1979 Tor-A	9	16	.360	33	32	12	1	0	227	213	23	95	127	12.6	3.69	118	.253	.335	0	—	0	13	17	-0	1.6
1980 *NY-A	13	9	.591	38	27	2	2	2	187	163	15	66	116	11.2	3.66	107	.237	.307	0	—	0	8	5	0	0.7
1981 NY-A	1	4	.200	9	6	0	0	0	32²	32	2	13	29	12.4	4.41	81	.262	.333	0	—	0	-3	-3	-0	-0.4
*Oak-A	3	2	.600	16	5	1	0	1	51	37	4	25	46	11.3	3.18	120	.202	.305	0	—	0	3	2	0	0.2
Yr	4	6	.400	25	11	1	0	1	83²	69	6	38	75	11.7	3.66	96	.226	.316	0	—	0	-0	-1	-0	-0.2
1982 Oak-A	10	6	.625	56	10	2	0	7	153	136	11	68	79	12.1	3.29	119	.241	.324	0	—	0	13	10	-2	1.0
1983 Oak-A	9	7	.563	51	15	0	0	4	144²	156	13	50	62	12.9	4.04	95	.277	.338	0	—	0	-3	-3	-0	-0.5
1984 Bal-A	1	0	1.000	37	1	0	0	0	71²	78	8	31	39	13.7	3.52	110	.282	.354	0	—	0	4	3	1	0.3
Total 11	86	87	.497	379	203	35	6	18	1586	1554	130	662	948	12.7	3.89	100	.259	.336	18	.117	-4	-0	-0	-15	-2.3

● WOODY UPCHURCH Upchurch, Jefferson Woodrow b: 4/13/11, Buies Creek, N.C. d: 10/23/71, Buies Creek, N.C. BR/TL, 6', 180 lbs. Deb: 9/14/35

YEAR TM/L	W	L	PCT	G	GS	CG	SH	SV	IP	H	HR	BB	SO	RAT	ERA	ERA+	OAV	OOB	BH	AVG	PB	PR	/A	PD	TPI
1935 Phi-A	0	2	.000	3	3	1	0	0	21¹	23	3	12	2	14.8	5.06	90	.271	.361	2	.286	-1	-1	-1	-0	-0.1
1936 Phi-A	0	2	.000	7	2	1	0	0	22¹	36	7	14	6	20.1	9.67	53	.353	.431	1	.143	-0	-12	-11	-1	-0.9
Total 2	0	4	.000	10	5	2	0	0	43²	59	10	26	8	17.5	7.42	65	.316	.399	3	.214	-0	-13	-13	-1	-1.0

● JOHN UPHAM Upham, John Leslie b: 12/29/41, Windsor, Ont., Can. BL/TL, 6', 180 lbs. Deb: 4/16/67 ◆

YEAR TM/L	W	L	PCT	G	GS	CG	SH	SV	IP	H	HR	BB	SO	RAT	ERA	ERA+	OAV	OOB	BH	AVG	PB	PR	/A	PD	TPI
1967 Chi-N	0	1	.000	5	0	0	0	0	1¹	4	1	2	2	40.5	33.75	11	.571	.667	2	.667	1	-5	-4	0	-2.4
1968 Chi-N	0	0	—	2	0	0	0	0	7	2	0	3	2	7.7	0.00	—	.087	.222	2	.200	0	2	2	0	0.0
Total 2	0	1	.000	7	0	0	0	0	8¹	6	1	5	4	13.0	5.40	60	.200	.333	4	.308	1	-2	-2	0	-2.4

● BILL UPHAM Upham, William Lawrence b: 4/4/1888, Akron, Ohio d: 9/14/59, Newark, N.J. BB/TR, 6', 178 lbs. Deb: 4/10/15

YEAR TM/L	W	L	PCT	G	GS	CG	SH	SV	IP	H	HR	BB	SO	RAT	ERA	ERA+	OAV	OOB	BH	AVG	PB	PR	/A	PD	TPI
1915 Bro-F	6	8	.429	33	11	4	2	5	121	129	0	40	46	12.6	3.05	89	.274	.331	4	.111	-2	-4	-4	2	-0.6
1918 Bos-N	1	1	.500	3	2	1	0	0	20²	28	2	1	8	12.6	5.23	51	.326	.333	2	.222	0	-6	-6	-0	-0.5
Total 2	7	9	.438	36	13	6	2	5	141²	157	2	41	54	12.6	3.37	81	.282	.332	6	.133	-2	-10	-10	2	-1.1

● JERRY UPP Upp, George Henry b: 12/10/1883, Sandusky, Ohio d: 6/30/37, Sandusky, Ohio TL, Deb: 9/2/09

YEAR TM/L	W	L	PCT	G	GS	CG	SH	SV	IP	H	HR	BB	SO	RAT	ERA	ERA+	OAV	OOB	BH	AVG	PB	PR	/A	PD	TPI
1909 Cle-A	2	1	.667	7	4	2	0	0	26²	26	0	12	13	12.8	1.69	152	.260	.339	2	.222	0	2	3	1	0.4

● CECIL UPSHAW Upshaw, Cecil Lee b: 10/22/42, Spearsville, La. d: 2/7/95, Lawrenceville, Ga. BR/TR, 6'6", 205 lbs. Deb: 10/1/66

YEAR TM/L	W	L	PCT	G	GS	CG	SH	SV	IP	H	HR	BB	SO	RAT	ERA	ERA+	OAV	OOB	BH	AVG	PB	PR	/A	PD	TPI
1966 Atl-N	0	0	—	1	0	0	0	0	3	0	0	3	2	9.0	0.00	—	.000	.273	1	1.000	0	1	1	-0	0.0
1967 Atl-N	2	3	.400	30	0	0	0	8	45¹	42	4	8	31	10.7	2.58	129	.247	.297	1	.167	1	4	4	0	0.6
1968 Atl-N	8	7	.533	52	0	0	0	13	116²	98	6	24	74	9.7	2.47	121	.229	.276	4	.174	0	7	7	-1	1.1
1969 *Atl-N	6	4	.600	62	0	0	0	27	105¹	102	7	29	57	11.3	2.91	124	.259	.311	5	.238	2	8	8	1	1.5
1971 Atl-N	11	6	.647	49	0	0	0	17	82	95	5	28	56	13.7	3.51	106	.292	.352	0	.000	-2	-0	2	-1	0.2
1972 Atl-N	3	5	.375	42	0	0	0	13	53²	50	5	19	23	11.7	3.69	103	.249	.317	1	.143	-0	-1	-1	1	0.2
1973 Atl-N	0	1	.000	5	0	0	0	0	3²	9	0	2	3	24.5	9.82	40	.444	.500	0	—	0	-3	-2	-0	-0.6
Hou-N	2	3	.400	35	0	0	0	1	38¹	38	3	15	24	12.7	4.46	81	.259	.331	0	.000	0	-3	-4	1	-0.4
Yr	2	4	.333	40	0	0	0	1	42	47	3	17	27	13.7	4.93	74	.277	.348	0	.000	0	-6	-6	-1	-1.0
1974 Cle-A	0	1	.000	7	0	0	0	0	8	10	1	4	7	15.8	3.38	107	.345	.424	0	—	0	0	0	0	0.0
NY-A	1	5	.167	36	0	0	0	6	59²	53	1	24	27	12.1	3.02	117	.254	.339	0	—	0	4	3	1	0.5
Yr	1	6	.143	43	0	0	0	6	67²	63	2	28	34	12.5	3.06	116	.262	.347	0	—	0	4	4	1	0.5
1975 Chi-A	1	1	.500	29	0	0	0	1	47¹	49	5	21	22	14.1	3.23	120	.271	.359	0	—	0	3	3	0	0.1
Total 9	34	36	.486	348	0	0	0	86	563	545	37	177	323	11.9	3.13	112	.258	.322	12	.160	1	19	23	2	3.2

● BILL UPTON Upton, William Ray b: 6/18/29, Esther, Mo. d: 1/2/87, San Diego, Cal. BR/TR, 6', 167 lbs. Deb: 4/13/54 F

YEAR TM/L	W	L	PCT	G	GS	CG	SH	SV	IP	H	HR	BB	SO	RAT	ERA	ERA+	OAV	OOB	BH	AVG	PB	PR	/A	PD	TPI
1954 Phi-A	0	0	—	2	0	0	0	1	5	6	1	4	2	12.6	1.80	217	.300	.333	0	—	0	1	1	0	0.1

● JACK URBAN Urban, Jack Elmer b: 12/5/28, Omaha, Neb. BR/TR, 5'8", 155 lbs. Deb: 6/13/57

YEAR TM/L	W	L	PCT	G	GS	CG	SH	SV	IP	H	HR	BB	SO	RAT	ERA	ERA+	OAV	OOB	BH	AVG	PB	PR	/A	PD	TPI
1957 KC-A	7	4	.636	31	13	3	0	0	129¹	111	7	45	55	10.9	3.34	118	.237	.305	11	.282	2	6	9	2	1.1
1958 KC-A	8	11	.421	30	24	5	1	1	132	150	17	51	54	13.8	5.93	66	.286	.351	7	.152	-2	-32	-30	-1	-4.0
1959 StL-N	0	0	—	8	0	0	0	0	10²	18	1	7	4	21.1	9.28	46	.409	.490	0	.000	-0	-6	-6	-0	0.0
Total 3	15	15	.500	69	37	8	1	1	272	279	25	103	113	12.7	4.83	82	.269	.337	18	.209	-0	-32	-27	-2	-2.9

● TOM URBANI Urbani, Thomas James b: 1/21/68, Santa Cruz, Cal. BL/TL, 6'1", 190 lbs. Deb: 4/21/93

YEAR TM/L	W	L	PCT	G	GS	CG	SH	SV	IP	H	HR	BB	SO	RAT	ERA	ERA+	OAV	OOB	BH	AVG	PB	PR	/A	PD	TPI
1993 StL-N	1	3	.250	18	9	0	0	0	62	73	4	26	33	14.4	4.65	85	.296	.363	3	.188	1	-4	-5	0	-0.2
1994 StL-N	3	7	.300	20	10	0	0	0	80¹	98	12	21	43	13.7	5.15	81	.302	.350	6	.250	1	-8	-9	0	-0.8
1995 StL-N	3	5	.375	24	13	0	0	0	82²	99	11	21	62	13.3	3.70	113	.305	.351	6	.316	3	4	4	1	0.9
1996 StL-N	1	0	1.000	3	0	0	0	0	11²	19	7	4	11	14.7	7.71	55	.319	.373	1	.167	0	-5	-5	-1	-0.4
Det-A	2	2	.500	16	4	0	0	0	23²	31	4	14	20	17.9	8.37	61	.310	.405	0	—	0	-9	-9	0	-1.2
Total 4	10	17	.370	81	36	0	0	0	260¹	316	38	86	149	14.1	4.98	84	.303	.360	16	.246	1	-22	-22	1	-1.7

● UGUETH URBINA Urbina, Ugueth Urtain (Villarreal) b: 2/15/74, Caracas, Venez. BR/TR, 6'2", 185 lbs. Deb: 5/9/95

YEAR TM/L	W	L	PCT	G	GS	CG	SH	SV	IP	H	HR	BB	SO	RAT	ERA	ERA+	OAV	OOB	BH	AVG	PB	PR	/A	PD	TPI
1995 Mon-N	2	2	.500	7	4	0	0	0	23¹	26	6	14	15	15.4	6.17	70	.280	.374	2	.333	-0	-5	-5	-1	-0.6
1996 Mon-N	10	5	.667	33	17	0	0	0	114	102	18	44	108	11.6	3.71	116	.234	.306	3	.103	-1	6	8	-1	0.7
Total 2	12	7	.632	40	21	0	0	0	137¹	128	24	58	123	12.3	4.13	104	.242	.319	5	.143	-1	1	3	-0	0.1

YEAR	TM/L	W	L	PCT	G	GS	CG	SH	SV	IP	H	HR	BB	SO	RAT	ERA	ERA+	OAV	OOB	BH	AVG	PB	PR	/A	PD	TPI

● JOHN URREA   Urrea, John Godoy b: 2/9/55, Los Angeles, Cal.   BR/TR, 6'3", 205 lbs.   Deb: 4/10/77

YEAR	TM/L	W	L	PCT	G	GS	CG	SH	SV	IP	H	HR	BB	SO	RAT	ERA	ERA+	OAV	OOB	BH	AVG	PB	PR	/A	PD	TPI
1977	StL-N	7	6	.538	41	12	2	1	4	139²	126	13	35	61	10.4	3.16	122	.244	.292	4	.138	2	12	11	1	1.2
1978	StL-N	4	9	.308	27	12	1	0	0	98²	108	4	47	61	14.8	5.38	65	.284	.373	3	.125	-1	-20	-20	0	-2.5
1979	StL-N	0	0	—	3	2	0	0	0	11¹	13	0	9	5	17.5	3.97	95	.310	.431	1	.250	0	-0	-0	0	0.0
1980	StL-N	4	1	.800	30	1	0	0	3	64²	57	2	41	36	13.9	3.48	106	.239	.356	3	.231	0	1	2	-1	0.0
1981	SD-N	2	2	.500	38	0	0	0	2	49	43	1	28	19	13.6	2.39	136	.239	.351	1	.250	0	6	5	-1	0.3
Total	5	17	18	.486	139	27	3	1	9	363¹	347	20	160	202	12.9	3.74	97	.256	.339	12	.162	2	-2	-4	-1	-1.0

● BOB VAIL   Vail, Robert Garfield "Doc" b: 9/24/1881, Linneus, Maine   d: 3/22/42, Philadelphia, Pa.   BR/TR, 5'10", 165 lbs.   Deb: 8/27/08

YEAR	TM/L	W	L	PCT	G	GS	CG	SH	SV	IP	H	HR	BB	SO	RAT	ERA	ERA+	OAV	OOB	BH	AVG	PB	PR	/A	PD	TPI
1908	Pit-N	1	2	.333	4	1	0	0	0	15	15	0	7	9	13.8	6.00	38	.268	.359	1	.333	1	-6	-6	-1	-1.1

● ISMAEL VALDES   Valdes, Ismael (Alvarez) b: 8/21/73, Victoria, Mex.   BR/TR, 6'3", 185 lbs.   Deb: 6/15/94

YEAR	TM/L	W	L	PCT	G	GS	CG	SH	SV	IP	H	HR	BB	SO	RAT	ERA	ERA+	OAV	OOB	BH	AVG	PB	PR	/A	PD	TPI
1994	LA-N	3	1	.750	21	1	0	0	0	28¹	21	2	10	28	9.8	3.18	123	.206	.277	0	.000	-0	3	2	1	0.4
1995	*LA-N	13	11	.542	33	27	6	2	1	197²	168	17	51	150	10.5	3.05	124	.228	.279	6	.097	-3	25	16	1	1.6
1996	*LA-N	15	7	.682	33	33	0	0	0	225	219	20	54	173	11.0	3.32	116	.251	.296	10	.143	-1	22	13	-0	1.1
Total	3	31	19	.620	87	61	6	2	1	451	408	39	115	351	10.5	3.19	120	.238	.288	16	.119	-4	50	32	2	3.1

● MARC VALDES   Valdes, Marc Christopher b: 12/20/71, Dayton, Ohio   BR/TR, 6', 170 lbs.   Deb: 8/28/95

YEAR	TM/L	W	L	PCT	G	GS	CG	SH	SV	IP	H	HR	BB	SO	RAT	ERA	ERA+	OAV	OOB	BH	AVG	PB	PR	/A	PD	TPI
1995	Fla-N	0	0	—	3	3	0	0	0	7	17	1	9	2	34.7	14.14	30	.459	.574	0	.000	-0	-8	-8	-0	-0.1
1996	Fla-N	1	3	.250	11	8	0	0	0	48²	63	5	23	13	16.1	4.81	84	.315	.388	0	.000	-1	-3	-4	-1	-0.5
Total	2	1	3	.250	14	11	0	0	0	55²	80	6	32	15	18.4	5.98	68	.338	.421	0	.000	-1	-11	-12	-1	-0.6

● CARLOS VALDEZ   Valdez, Carlos Luis (Lorenzo) b: 12/26/71, Bani, D.R.   BR/TR, 5'11", 165 lbs.   Deb: 7/18/95

YEAR	TM/L	W	L	PCT	G	GS	CG	SH	SV	IP	H	HR	BB	SO	RAT	ERA	ERA+	OAV	OOB	BH	AVG	PB	PR	/A	PD	TPI
1995	SF-N	0	1	.000	11	0	0	0	0	14²	19	1	8	7	17.2	6.14	67	.322	.412	0	.000	-0	-3	-3	-0	-0.2

● EFRAIN VALDEZ   Valdez, Efrain Antonio b: 7/11/66, Nizao Bani, D.R.   BL/TL, 5'11", 180 lbs.   Deb: 8/13/90

YEAR	TM/L	W	L	PCT	G	GS	CG	SH	SV	IP	H	HR	BB	SO	RAT	ERA	ERA+	OAV	OOB	BH	AVG	PB	PR	/A	PD	TPI
1990	Cle-A	1	1	.500	13	0	0	0	0	23²	20	2	14	13	12.9	3.04	129	.233	.340	0	—	0	2	2	-0	0.2
1991	Cle-A	0	0	—	7	0	0	0	0	6	5	0	3	1	13.5	1.50	277	.238	.360	0	—	0	2	2	0	0.0
Total	2	1	1	.500	20	0	0	0	0	29²	25	2	17	14	13.0	2.73	145	.234	.344	0	—	0	4	4	-0	0.2

● RAFAEL VALDEZ   Valdez, Rafael Emilio (Diaz) b: 12/17/67, Nizao Bani, D.R.   BR/TR, 5'11", 165 lbs.   Deb: 4/18/90

YEAR	TM/L	W	L	PCT	G	GS	CG	SH	SV	IP	H	HR	BB	SO	RAT	ERA	ERA+	OAV	OOB	BH	AVG	PB	PR	/A	PD	TPI
1990	SD-N	0	1	.000	3	0	0	0	0	5²	11	4	2	3	20.6	11.12	34	.393	.433	0	.000	-0	-5	-5	-0	-0.7

● RENE VALDEZ   Valdez, Rene Gutierrez (b: Rene Gutierrez (Valdez)) b: 6/2/29, Guanabacoa, Cuba   BR/TR, 6'3", 175 lbs.   Deb: 4/21/57

YEAR	TM/L	W	L	PCT	G	GS	CG	SH	SV	IP	H	HR	BB	SO	RAT	ERA	ERA+	OAV	OOB	BH	AVG	PB	PR	/A	PD	TPI
1957	Bro-N	1	1	.500	5	1	0	0	0	13	18	1	6	9	13.8	5.54	75	.265	.357	0	—	0	-2	-2	-0	-0.3

● SERGIO VALDEZ   Valdez, Sergio Sanchez (b: Sergio Sanchez (Valdez)) b: 9/7/64, Elias Pina, D.R.   BR/TR, 6', 165 lbs.   Deb: 9/10/86

YEAR	TM/L	W	L	PCT	G	GS	CG	SH	SV	IP	H	HR	BB	SO	RAT	ERA	ERA+	OAV	OOB	BH	AVG	PB	PR	/A	PD	TPI
1986	Mon-N	0	4	.000	5	5	0	0	0	25	39	2	11	20	18.4	6.84	54	.361	.425	1	.125	-0	-9	-9	-1	-1.2
1989	Atl-N	1	2	.333	19	1	0	0	0	32²	31	5	17	26	13.2	6.06	60	.246	.336	1	1.000	0	-9	-9	-1	-0.8
1990	Atl-N	0	0	—	6	0	0	0	0	5¹	6	2	3	6	15.2	6.75	60	.273	.360	0	—	0	-2	-2	-0	0.0
	Cle-A	6	6	.500	24	13	0	0	0	102¹	109	17	35	63	12.8	4.75	82	.276	.336	0	—	0	-10	-9	-0	-1.0
1991	Cle-A	1	0	1.000	6	0	0	0	0	16¹	15	4	5	11	11.0	5.51	75	.238	.294	0	—	0	-3	-2	-1	-0.2
1992	Mon-N	0	2	.000	27	0	0	0	0	37¹	25	2	12	32	8.9	2.41	144	.185	.252	1	.000	0	5	4	0	0.2
1993	Mon-N	0	0	—	4	0	0	0	0	3	4	1	1	2	15.0	9.00	46	.308	.357	0	—	0	-2	-2	-0	0.0
1994	Bos-A	0	1	.000	12	1	0	0	0	14¹	25	4	8	4	20.7	8.16	62	.391	.458	0	—	0	-5	-5	-0	-0.3
1995	SF-N	4	5	.444	13	11	1	0	0	66¹	78	12	17	29	13.3	4.75	86	.298	.348	2	.095	-1	-4	-5	-0	-0.6
Total	8	12	20	.375	116	31	1	0	0	302²	332	46	109	190	13.3	5.06	78	.279	.343	4	.121	-1	-39	-38	-1	-3.9

● CORKY VALENTINE   Valentine, Harold Lewis b: 1/4/29, Troy, Ohio   BR/TR, 6'1", 203 lbs.   Deb: 4/17/54

YEAR	TM/L	W	L	PCT	G	GS	CG	SH	SV	IP	H	HR	BB	SO	RAT	ERA	ERA+	OAV	OOB	BH	AVG	PB	PR	/A	PD	TPI
1954	Cin-N	12	11	.522	36	28	7	3	1	194¹	211	24	60	73	12.7	4.45	94	.282	.339	9	.138	-2	-8	-5	-2	-0.9
1955	Cin-N	2	1	.667	10	5	0	0	0	26²	29	5	16	14	15.5	7.43	57	.276	.377	0	.000	-1	-10	-9	1	-0.9
Total	2	14	12	.538	46	33	7	3	1	221	240	29	76	87	13.1	4.81	87	.282	.344	9	.125	-3	-18	-15	-1	-1.8

● JOHN VALENTINE   Valentine, John Gill b: 11/21/1855, Brooklyn, N.Y.   d: 10/10/03, Central Islip, N.Y   Deb: 5/3/1883

YEAR	TM/L	W	L	PCT	G	GS	CG	SH	SV	IP	H	HR	BB	SO	RAT	ERA	ERA+	OAV	OOB	BH	AVG	PB	PR	/A	PD	TPI
1883	Col-a	2	10	.167	13	12	11	0	0	102	130	0	17	13	13.0	3.53	87	.317	.291	17	.283	3	-3	-1	-0	-0.1

● VITO VALENTINETTI   Valentinetti, Vito John b: 9/16/28, W.New York, N.J.   BR/TR, 6', 195 lbs.   Deb: 6/20/54

YEAR	TM/L	W	L	PCT	G	GS	CG	SH	SV	IP	H	HR	BB	SO	RAT	ERA	ERA+	OAV	OOB	BH	AVG	PB	PR	/A	PD	TPI
1954	Chi-A	0	0	—	1	0	0	0	0	1	4	1	2	1	54.0	54.00	7	.571	.667	0	—	0	-6	-6	0	0.0
1956	Chi-N	6	4	.600	42	2	0	0	1	95¹	84	10	36	26	11.4	3.78	100	.243	.317	2	.100	-1	-0	-0	-1	-0.3
1957	Chi-N	0	0	—	9	0	0	0	0	12	12	1	7	4	14.3	2.25	172	.255	.352	0	.000	0	2	2	-0	0.0
	Cle-A	2	2	.500	11	2	1	0	0	23²	26	3	13	9	15.2	4.94	75	.289	.385	1	.200	-0	-3	-3	-0	-0.5
1958	Det-A	1	0	1.000	15	0	0	0	2	18²	18	4	5	10	11.6	3.38	120	.257	.316	0	—	0	1	1	-0	0.1
	Was-A	4	6	.400	23	10	2	0	0	95²	106	16	49	33	14.8	5.08	75	.286	.373	9	.321	2	-14	-13	2	-0.9
	Yr	5	6	.455	38	10	2	0	2	114¹	124	20	54	43	14.2	4.80	80	.281	.362	9	.321	2	-13	-12	1	-0.8
1959	Was-A	0	2	.000	7	1	0	0	0	10²	16	0	10	7	22.8	10.13	39	.356	.482	0	—	0	-7	-7	0	-1.1
Total	5	13	14	.481	112	15	3	0	3	257	266	35	122	94	13.8	4.54	81	.273	.358	12	.218	1	-27	-26	0	-2.7

● FERNANDO VALENZUELA   Valenzuela, Fernando (Anguamea) b: 11/1/60, Navojoa, Mexico   BL/TL, 5'11", 195 lbs.   Deb: 9/15/80

YEAR	TM/L	W	L	PCT	G	GS	CG	SH	SV	IP	H	HR	BB	SO	RAT	ERA	ERA+	OAV	OOB	BH	AVG	PB	PR	/A	PD	TPI
1980	LA-N	2	0	1.000	10	0	0	0	0	17²	8	0	5	16	6.6	0.00	—	.136	.203	0	.000	-0	7	7	0	0.9
1981	*LA-N★	13	7	.650	25	25	**11**	**8**	0	**192**¹	140	11	61	**180**	9.5	2.48	134	.205	.271	16	.250	3	22	18	2	2.5
1982	LA-N★	19	13	.594	37	37	18	4	0	285	247	13	83	199	10.5	2.87	121	.236	.294	16	.168	1	23	19	5	2.7
1983	*LA-N☆	15	10	.600	35	35	9	4	0	257	245	16	99	189	12.2	3.75	96	.255	.327	17	.187	2	-3	-4	4	0.2
1984	LA-N★	12	17	.414	34	34	12	2	0	261	218	14	106	240	11.2	3.03	116	.229	.308	15	.190	4	16	14	2	2.5
1985	*LA-N★	17	10	.630	35	35	14	5	0	272¹	211	14	101	208	10.3	2.45	142	.214	.288	21	.216	4	35	31	2	3.6
1986	LA-N★	**21**	11	.656	34	34	**20**	3	0	269¹	226	18	85	242	10.4	3.14	110	.226	.288	5	.220	5	17	9	4	1.9
1987	LA-N	14	14	.500	34	34	**12**	1	0	251	254	25	124	190	13.7	3.98	100	.262	.349	13	.141	-1	3	-5	3	0.2
1988	LA-N	5	8	.385	23	22	3	0	1	142¹	142	11	76	64	13.8	4.24	80	.268	.360	8	.182	1	-12	-14	3	-0.8
1989	LA-N	10	13	.435	31	31	3	0	0	196²	185	11	98	116	13.0	3.43	99	.251	.340	12	.182	1	-1	-0	2	-0.1
1990	LA-N	13	13	.500	33	33	5	2	0	204	223	19	77	115	13.2	4.59	80	.276	.339	21	.304	8	-18	-21	-0	-1.6
1991	Cal-A	0	2	.000	2	2	0	0	0	6²	14	3	3	5	23.0	12.15	34	.452	.500	0	—	0	-6	-6	0	-1.2
1993	Bal-A	8	10	.444	32	31	5	2	0	178²	179	18	79	78	13.2	4.94	91	.266	.346	0	—	0	-12	-9	-2	-0.7
1994	Phi-N	1	2	.333	8	7	0	0	0	45	42	8	7	19	9.8	3.00	143	.247	.277	3	.250	1	6	6	0	0.5
1995	SD-N	8	3	.727	29	15	0	0	0	90¹	101	16	34	57	13.5	4.98	81	.289	.352	8	.250	3	-8	-10	3	-0.4
1996	*SD-N	13	8	.619	33	31	0	0	0	171²	177	17	67	95	12.8	3.62	110	.269	.336	9	.143	-1	11	7	2	0.9
Total	16	171	141	.548	435	406	112	31	2	2841	2612	214	1105	2013	11.8	3.50	104	.246	.318	183	.200	32	81	46	34	11.4

● JULIO VALERA   Valera, Julio Enrique (Torres) b: 10/13/68, Aguadilla, P.R.   BR/TR, 6'2", 185 lbs.   Deb: 9/1/90

YEAR	TM/L	W	L	PCT	G	GS	CG	SH	SV	IP	H	HR	BB	SO	RAT	ERA	ERA+	OAV	OOB	BH	AVG	PB	PR	/A	PD	TPI
1990	NY-N	1	1	.500	3	3	0	0	0	13	20	1	7	4	18.7	6.92	54	.351	.422	1	.200	0	-5	-5	-1	-0.6
1991	NY-N	0	0	—	2	0	0	0	0	2	1	1	0	3	22.5	0.00	—	.143	.455	0	—	0	1	1	0	0.0
1992	Cal-A	8	11	.421	30	28	4	2	0	188	188	16	64	113	12.2	3.73	107	.262	.324	0	—	0	4	5	-2	0.2
1993	Cal-A	3	6	.333	19	5	0	0	4	53	77	8	15	28	16.0	6.62	68	.344	.390	0	—	0	-14	-12	-0	-2.0
1996	KC-A	3	2	.600	31	2	0	0	1	61¹	75	7	21	31	15.3	6.46	76	.307	.381	0	—	0	-10	-11	-0	-0.6
Total	5	15	20	.429	85	38	4	2	5	317¹	361	31	117	179	13.7	4.85	87	.289	.353	1	.200	0	-23	-22	-4	-3.0

● CLAY Van ALSTYNE   Van Alstyne, Clayton Emory "Spike" b: 5/24/1900, Stuyvesant, N.Y.   d: 1/5/60, Hudson, N.Y.   BR/TR, 5'11", 180 lbs.   Deb: 8/20/27

YEAR	TM/L	W	L	PCT	G	GS	CG	SH	SV	IP	H	HR	BB	SO	RAT	ERA	ERA+	OAV	OOB	BH	AVG	PB	PR	/A	PD	TPI
1927	Was-A	0	0	—	2	0	0	0	0	3	3	0	1	0	9.0	3.00	136	.250	.250	0	—	0	-0	-0	-0	0.0
1928	Was-A	0	0	—	4	0	0	0	0	21¹	26	0	13	5	16.9	5.48	73	.329	.430	2	.250	1	-3	-3	1	0.2
Total	2	0	0	—	6	0	0	0	0	24¹	29	0	13	5	15.9	5.18	78	.319	.410	2	.250	1	-3	-3	1	0.2

● RUSS Van ATTA   Van Atta, Russell "Sheriff" b: 6/21/06, Augusta, N.J.   d: 10/10/86, Andover, N.J.   BL/TL, 6', 184 lbs.   Deb: 4/25/33

YEAR	TM/L	W	L	PCT	G	GS	CG	SH	SV	IP	H	HR	BB	SO	RAT	ERA	ERA+	OAV	OOB	BH	AVG	PB	PR	/A	PD	TPI
1933	NY-A	12	4	.750	26	22	10	2	1	157	160	3	63	76	12.8	4.18	93	.262	.332	17	.283	4	2	-5	0	-0.1
1934	NY-A	3	5	.375	28	9	0	0	0	88	107	3	46	39	15.9	6.34	64	.307	.390	6	.207	1	-18	-22	-1	-1.6

YEAR TM/L	W	L	PCT	G	GS	CG	SH	SV	IP	H	HR	BB	SO	RAT	ERA	ERA+	OAV	OOB	BH	AVG	PB	PR	/A	PD	TPI
1935 NY-A	0	0	—	5	0	0	0	0	4²	5	0	4	3	17.4	3.86	105	.263	.391	0	.000	-0	0	-0	-0	0.0
StL-A	9	16	.360	53	17	1	0	3	170¹	201	10	87	87	15.4	5.34	90	.292	.374	9	.214	-1	-17	-10	-1	-1.5
Yr	9	16	.360	**58**	17	1	0	3	175	206	10	91	90	15.4	5.30	90	.291	.375	9	.209	-1	-16	-10	-2	-1.5
1936 StL-A	4	7	.364	**52**	9	2	0	2	122²	164	9	68	59	17.2	6.60	81	.320	.401	5	.172	-1	-21	-17	1	-1.2
1937 StL-A	1	2	.333	16	6	1	0	0	58²	74	2	32	34	16.3	5.52	87	.307	.388	6	.462	3	-6	-5	1	0.2
1938 StL-A	4	7	.364	25	12	3	1	0	104	118	7	61	35	15.6	6.06	82	.289	.382	4	.133	-1	-15	-13	-0	-1.1
1939 StL-A	0	0	—	2	1	0	0	0	7	9	0	7	2	21.9	11.57	42	.310	.459	0	.000	-0	-5	-5	-0	0.0
Total 7	33	41	.446	207	76	17	3	6	712¹	838	39	368	339	15.4	5.60	82	.293	.376	47	.228	5	-80	-78	-1	-5.3

● **OZZIE Van BRABANT**   Van Brabant, Camille Oscar   b: 9/28/26, Kingsville, Ont., Canada   BR/TR, 6'1", 165 lbs.   Deb: 4/13/54

YEAR TM/L	W	L	PCT	G	GS	CG	SH	SV	IP	H	HR	BB	SO	RAT	ERA	ERA+	OAV	OOB	BH	AVG	PB	PR	/A	PD	TPI
1954 Phi-A	0	2	.000	9	2	0	0	0	26²	35	3	18	10	18.2	7.09	55	.347	.450	1	.200	0	-10	-9	1	-0.5
1955 KC-A	0	0	—	2	0	0	0	0	2	4	1	2	1	27.0	18.00	23	.400	.500	0	—	-0	-3	-3	-0	0.0
Total 2	0	2	.000	11	2	0	0	0	28²	39	4	20	11	18.8	7.85	50	.351	.455	1	.200	-0	-13	-13	1	-0.5

● **DAZZY VANCE**   Vance, Clarence Arthur   b: 3/4/1891, Orient, Iowa   d: 2/16/61, Homosassa Springs, Fla.   BR/TR, 6'2", 200 lbs.   Deb: 4/16/15   H

YEAR TM/L	W	L	PCT	G	GS	CG	SH	SV	IP	H	HR	BB	SO	RAT	ERA	ERA+	OAV	OOB	BH	AVG	PB	PR	/A	PD	TPI
1915 Pit-N	0	1	.000	1	1	0	0	0	2²	3	0	5	0	30.4	10.13	27	.375	.643	0	.000	-0	-2	-2	0	-0.6
NY-A	0	3	.000	8	3	1	0	0	28	23	1	16	18	13.2	3.54	83	.232	.350	2	.667	-2	-2	-2	-0	0.0
1918 NY-A	0	0	—	2	0	0	0	0	2¹	9	0	2	0	42.4	15.43	18	.692	.733	0	—	-0	-3	-3	-0	0.0
1922 Bro-N	18	12	.600	36	31	16	**5**	0	245²	259	9	94	**134**	13.2	3.70	110	.276	.347	20	.225	1	11	10	0	1.3
1923 Bro-N	18	15	.545	37	35	21	3	0	280¹	263	10	100	**197**	12.0	3.50	111	.250	.322	7	.084	-3	16	12	0	0.9
1924 Bro-N	**28**	6	.824	35	34	**30**	3	0	308¹	238	11	77	**262**	9.5	**2.16**	**173**	**.213**	**.269**	16	.151	-2	**58**	**54**	1	**5.7**
1925 Bro-N	**22**	9	.710	31	31	26	**4**	0	265¹	247	8	66	**221**	11.0	3.53	118	.250	.304	14	.143	-0	22	19	1	2.1
1926 Bro-N	9	10	.474	24	22	12	0	1	169	172	9	58	**140**	12.3	3.89	98	.271	.333	10	.182	-1	-1	-2	0	-0.1
1927 Bro-N	16	15	.516	34	32	**25**	2	1	273¹	242	12	69	**184**	10.4	2.70	147	**.239**	.291	15	.167	-2	37	38	-2	3.8
1928 Bro-N	22	10	.688	38	32	24	**4**	2	280¹	226	11	72	**200**	9.8	**2.09**	**191**	**.221**	**.277**	17	.177	2	**59**	**59**	1	**7.0**
1929 Bro-N	14	13	.519	31	26	17	1	0	231¹	244	15	47	126	11.7	3.89	119	.274	.316	10	.135	-1	21	19	1	1.7
1930 Bro-N	17	15	.531	35	31	20	**4**	0	258²	241	15	55	173	10.5	**2.61**	**188**	.246	**.289**	12	.135	-5	68	66	-1	6.6
1931 Bro-N	11	13	.458	30	29	12	2	0	218²	221	12	53	150	11.3	3.38	113	.261	.304	9	.134	-2	12	11	1	0.9
1932 Bro-N	12	11	.522	27	24	9	1	1	175²	171	10	57	103	11.7	4.20	91	.256	.315	5	.089	-4	-6	-7	-0	-1.2
1933 StL-N	6	2	.750	28	11	2	0	3	99	105	3	28	67	12.2	3.55	98	.267	.318	5	.179	-1	-2	-1	-0	-0.2
1934 Cin-N	0	2	.000	6	2	0	0	0	18	28	1	11	9	20.0	7.50	54	.350	.435	1	.250	-0	-7	-7	-0	-0.6
*StL-N	1	1	.500	19	4	1	0	1	59	62	4	14	33	11.9	3.66	115	.271	.318	2	.133	-0	3	4	0	0.1
Yr	1	3	.250	25	6	1	0	1	77	90	5	25	42	13.7	4.56	92	.290	.347	3	.158	0	-4	-3	-0	-0.5
1935 Bro-N	3	2	.600	20	0	0	0	2	51	55	3	16	28	13.1	4.41	90	.268	.330	1	.059	-2	-2	-2	-0	-0.4
Total 16	197	140	.585	442	348	216	29	11	2966²	2809	132	840	2045	11.3	3.24	125	.251	.308	146	.150	-18	281	266	3	27.0

● **SANDY VANCE**   Vance, Gene Covington   b: 1/5/47, Lamar, Colo.   BR/TR, 6'2", 180 lbs.   Deb: 4/26/70

YEAR TM/L	W	L	PCT	G	GS	CG	SH	SV	IP	H	HR	BB	SO	RAT	ERA	ERA+	OAV	OOB	BH	AVG	PB	PR	/A	PD	TPI
1970 LA-N	7	7	.500	20	18	2	0	0	115	109	9	37	45	11.5	3.13	122	.248	.308	7	.189	1	12	9	-3	0.8
1971 LA-N	2	1	.667	10	3	0	0	0	26	38	1	9	11	16.3	6.92	47	.355	.405	0	.000	-0	-10	-11	-0	-1.2
Total 2	9	8	.529	30	21	2	0	0	141	147	10	46	56	12.4	3.83	97	.269	.327	7	.167	0	2	-2	-3	-0.4

● **JOE VANCE**   Vance, Joseph Albert "Sandy"   b: 9/16/05, Devine, Tex.   d: 7/4/78, Devine, Tex.   BR/TR, 6'1.5", 190 lbs.   Deb: 4/18/35

YEAR TM/L	W	L	PCT	G	GS	CG	SH	SV	IP	H	HR	BB	SO	RAT	ERA	ERA+	OAV	OOB	BH	AVG	PB	PR	/A	PD	TPI
1935 Chi-A	2	2	.500	10	0	0	0	0	31	36	1	21	12	16.5	6.68	69	.295	.399	2	.182	-1	-8	-7	1	-0.8
1937 NY-A	1	0	1.000	2	2	0	0	0	15	11	2	9	3	12.0	3.00	148	.204	.317	0	.000	-1	3	2	1	0.1
1938 NY-A	0	0	—	3	1	0	0	0	11¹	20	2	4	2	19.1	7.15	63	.408	.453	3	.750	-2	-3	-3	0	0.2
Total 3	3	2	.600	15	3	0	0	0	57¹	67	5	34	17	15.9	5.81	79	.298	.390	5	.250	-4	-8	-8	1	-0.5

● **CHRIS Van CUYK**   Van Cuyk, Christian Gerald   b: 1/3/27, Kimberly, Wis.   d: 11/3/92, Hudson, Fla.   BL/TL, 6'6", 215 lbs.   Deb: 7/16/50   F

YEAR TM/L	W	L	PCT	G	GS	CG	SH	SV	IP	H	HR	BB	SO	RAT	ERA	ERA+	OAV	OOB	BH	AVG	PB	PR	/A	PD	TPI
1950 Bro-N	1	3	.250	12	4	1	0	0	33¹	33	3	12	21	12.4	4.86	84	.266	.336	1	.100	-1	-3	-3	-1	-0.4
1951 Bro-N	1	2	.333	9	6	0	0	0	29¹	33	4	11	16	14.7	5.52	71	.295	.378	2	.250	-0	-5	-5	-0	-0.4
1952 Bro-N	5	6	.455	23	16	4	0	1	97²	104	12	40	66	13.7	5.16	71	.271	.347	8	.242	2	-16	-17	-1	-1.7
Total 3	7	11	.389	44	26	5	0	1	160¹	170	19	63	103	13.6	5.16	73	.274	.351	11	.216	1	-23	-25	-2	-2.5

● **JOHNNY Van CUYK**   Van Cuyk, John Henry   b: 7/7/21, Little Chute, Wis.   BL/TL, 6'1", 190 lbs.   Deb: 9/18/47   F

YEAR TM/L	W	L	PCT	G	GS	CG	SH	SV	IP	H	HR	BB	SO	RAT	ERA	ERA+	OAV	OOB	BH	AVG	PB	PR	/A	PD	TPI
1947 Bro-N	0	0	—	2	0	0	0	0	3¹	5	0	1	2	16.2	5.40	77	.357	.400	0	—	0	-0	-0	0	0.0
1948 Bro-N	0	0	—	3	0	0	0	0	5	4	1	1	0	9.0	3.60	111	.200	.238	0	—	-0	0	0	0	0.0
1949 Bro-N	0	0	—	2	0	0	0	0	2	3	0	1	1	18.0	9.00	46	.429	.500	0	—	-0	-1	-1	-0	0.0
Total 3	0	0	—	7	0	0	0	0	10¹	12	1	3	3	13.1	5.23	78	.293	.341	0	—	0	-1	-1	-0	0.0

● **ED VANDE BERG**   Vande Berg, Edward John   b: 10/26/58, Redlands, Cal.   BR/TL, 6'2", 180 lbs.   Deb: 4/7/82

YEAR TM/L	W	L	PCT	G	GS	CG	SH	SV	IP	H	HR	BB	SO	RAT	ERA	ERA+	OAV	OOB	BH	AVG	PB	PR	/A	PD	TPI
1982 Sea-A	9	4	.692	**78**	0	0	0	5	76	54	5	32	60	10.4	2.37	176	.207	.298	0	—	0	14	16	2	2.9
1983 Sea-A	2	4	.333	68	0	0	0	1	64¹	59	6	22	49	11.5	3.36	127	.246	.312	0	—	0	5	6	0	0.5
1984 Sea-A	8	12	.400	50	17	2	0	7	130¹	165	18	50	71	14.8	4.76	84	.313	.373	0	—	-0	-11	-11	-0	-1.7
1985 Sea-A	2	1	.667	76	0	0	0	3	67²	71	4	31	34	13.7	3.72	113	.274	.354	0	—	0	3	4	1	0.2
1986 LA-N	1	5	.167	60	0	0	0	0	71¹	83	8	33	45	14.8	3.41	101	.290	.366	0	.000	-0	2	0	1	0.1
1987 Cle-A	1	0	1.000	55	0	0	0	4	72¹	96	9	21	40	14.6	5.10	89	.325	.370	0	—	0	-5	-5	0	-0.0
1988 Tex-A	2	2	.500	26	0	0	0	2	37	44	2	11	18	13.4	4.14	99	.308	.357	0	—	-0	-1	-0	-1	-0.2
Total 7	25	28	.472	413	17	2	0	22	519	572	52	200	314	13.5	3.92	104	.284	.351	0	.000	-0	8	10	3	1.8

● **HY VANDENBERG**   Vandenberg, Harold Harris   b: 3/17/06, Abilene, Kan.   d: 7/31/94, Bloomington, Minn.   BR/TR, 6'4", 220 lbs.   Deb: 6/8/35

YEAR TM/L	W	L	PCT	G	GS	CG	SH	SV	IP	H	HR	BB	SO	RAT	ERA	ERA+	OAV	OOB	BH	AVG	PB	PR	/A	PD	TPI
1935 Bos-A	0	0	—	3	0	0	0	0	5¹	15	1	4	2	32.1	20.25	23	.500	.559	1	1.000	0	-9	-9	0	0.0
1937 NY-N	0	1	.000	1	1	0	0	0	8	10	1	6	2	18.0	7.88	49	.313	.421	0	.000	-1	-4	-4	1	-0.3
1938 NY-N	0	1	.000	6	1	0	0	0	18	28	2	12	7	20.0	7.50	50	.368	.455	0	.000	-1	-7	-7	1	-0.3
1939 NY-N	0	0	—	2	1	0	0	0	6¹	10	0	6	3	22.7	5.68	69	.345	.457	1	.125	-0	-1	-0	0	0.0
1940 NY-N	1	1	.500	13	3	1	0	1	32¹	27	2	16	17	12.2	3.90	100	.227	.324	1	.125	-0	-0	-0	-1	-0.1
1944 Chi-N	7	4	.636	35	9	2	0	2	126¹	123	8	51	54	12.5	3.63	97	.255	.327	9	.237	-1	2	2	0	-0.1
1945 *Chi-N	7	3	.700	30	7	3	1	2	95¹	91	4	33	35	12.1	3.49	105	.259	.330	4	.125	-1	3	2	0	0.1
Total 7	15	10	.600	90	22	7	1	5	291²	304	17	128	120	13.5	4.32	85	.271	.349	15	.169	-1	-19	-21	2	-0.7

● **JOHNNY VANDER MEER**   Vander Meer, John Samuel "Double No-Hit" or "The Dutch Master"   b: 11/2/14, Prospect Park, N.J.   BB/TL, 6'1", 190 lbs.   Deb: 4/22/37

YEAR TM/L	W	L	PCT	G	GS	CG	SH	SV	IP	H	HR	BB	SO	RAT	ERA	ERA+	OAV	OOB	BH	AVG	PB	PR	/A	PD	TPI
1937 Cin-N	3	5	.375	19	10	4	0	0	84¹	63	0	69	52	14.3	3.84	97	.209	.359	5	.217	1	1	-1	2	0.2
1938 Cin-N★	15	10	.600	32	29	16	3	0	225¹	177	12	103	125	11.3	3.12	117	**.213**	.302	15	.181	-2	17	13	-1	1.0
1939 Cin-N☆	5	9	.357	30	21	8	0	0	129	128	7	95	102	15.7	4.67	82	.264	.387	4	.111	-1	-11	-12	-1	-1.4
1940 *Cin-N	3	1	.750	10	7	2	0	1	48	38	3	41	41	15.0	3.75	101	.211	.360	4	.300	-1	1	0	0	0.2
1941 Cin-N	16	13	.552	33	32	18	6	0	226¹	172	8	126	**202**	11.9	2.82	127	.214	.321	10	.132	-3	20	19	2	2.3
1942 Cin-N★	18	12	.600	33	33	21	4	0	244	188	6	102	**186**	10.7	2.43	135	.208	.290	11	.147	-1	24	23	1	2.9
1943 Cin-N★	15	16	.484	36	36	21	3	0	289	228	5	162	**174**	12.2	2.87	116	.224	.332	13	.137	-2	17	14	3	1.6
1946 Cin-N	10	12	.455	29	25	11	4	0	204¹	175	11	78	94	11.1	3.17	105	.233	.325	18	.247	-4	5	4	-2	0.5
1947 Cin-N	9	14	.391	30	29	9	3	0	186	186	11	87	79	13.4	4.40	93	.261	.343	5	.088	-3	-6	-7	-1	-1.0
1948 Cin-N	17	14	.548	33	33	14	3	0	232	204	15	124	120	12.8	3.41	115	.239	.336	11	.141	-1	14	13	-1	1.6
1949 Cin-N	5	10	.333	28	24	7	0	0	159²	172	6	85	70	14.6	4.90	85	.281	.370	4	.077	-3	-15	-13	1	-1.2
1950 Chi-N	3	4	.429	32	7	1	0	0	73²	60	10	59	41	14.9	3.79	111	.221	.363	2	.125	-0	3	3	0	0.3
1951 Cle-A	0	1	.000	1	1	0	0	0	1	2	0	1	2	27.0	18.00	21	.500	.529	0	.000	-0	-5	-5	-0	-0.9
Total 13	119	121	.496	346	286	131	29	2	2104²	1799	100	1132	1294	12.6	3.44	107	.232	.332	104	.152	-9	63	53	3	6.1

● **BEN Van DYKE**   Van Dyke, Benjamin Harrison   b: 8/15/1888, Clintonville, Pa.   d: 10/22/73, Sarasota, Fla.   BR/TL, 6'1", 150 lbs.   Deb: 5/11/09

YEAR TM/L	W	L	PCT	G	GS	CG	SH	SV	IP	H	HR	BB	SO	RAT	ERA	ERA+	OAV	OOB	BH	AVG	PB	PR	/A	PD	TPI
1909 Phi-N	0	0	—	2	0	0	0	0	7¹	7	0	4	5	13.5	3.68	71	.269	.367	0	—	-0	-1	-0	-1	-0.1
1912 Bos-A	0	0	—	3	1	0	0	0	14¹	13	0	7	8	13.2	3.14	108	.245	.344	1	.250	0	0	-0	-0	-0.1
Total 2	0	0	—	5	1	0	0	0	21²	20	0	11	13	13.3	3.32	94	.253	.352	1	.143	-0	-1	-0	-1	-0.2

YEAR	TM/L	W	L	PCT	G	GS	CG	SH	SV	IP	H	HR	BB	SO	RAT	ERA	ERA+	OAV	OOB	BH	AVG	PB	PR	/A	PD	TPI

● TIM Van EGMOND   Van Egmond, Timothy Layne b: 5/31/69, Shreveport, La. BR/TR, 6'2", 185 lbs. Deb: 6/26/94

1994	Bos-A	2	3	.400	7	7	1	0	0	38¹	38	7	21	22	13.9	6.34	79	.255	.347	0	—	0	-7	-6	-1	-0.7
1995	Bos-A	0	1	.000	4	1	0	0	0	6²	9	2	6	5	20.3	9.45	52	.310	.429	0	—	0	-4	-3	-0	-0.4
1996	Mil-A	3	5	.375	12	9	0	0	0	54²	58	6	23	33	13.5	5.27	100	.274	.347	0	—	0	-2	-0	-0	-0.1
Total	3	5	9	.357	23	17	1	0	0	99²	105	15	50	60	14.1	5.96	86	.269	.354	0	—	0	-12	-9	-1	-1.2

● ELAM VANGILDER   Vangilder, Elam Russell b: 4/23/1896, Cape Girardeau, Mo d: 4/30/77, Cape Girardeau, Mo BR/TR, 6'1", 192 lbs. Deb: 9/18/19

1919	StL-A	1	0	1.000	3	1	0	0	0	13	16	0	3	6	12.5	2.08	160	.306	.346	2	.667	1	2	2	1	0.3
1920	StL-A	3	8	.273	24	13	4	0	0	104²	131	7	40	25	15.0	5.50	71	.310	.373	4	.133	-2	-20	-18	-0	-1.8
1921	StL-A	11	12	.478	31	21	10	1	0	180¹	196	10	67	48	13.2	3.94	114	.278	.342	13	.200	-2	7	11	-0	1.0
1922	StL-A	19	13	.594	43	30	19	3	4	245	248	13	48	63	11.1	3.42	121	.270	.310	32	.344	13	17	20	-3	3.4
1923	StL-A	16	17	.485	41	35	20	4	1	282²	276	11	120	74	12.8	3.06	136	.266	.345	24	.218	-0	29	35	-3	3.4
1924	StL-A	5	10	.333	43	18	5	0	1	145	183	10	55	49	15.3	5.64	80	.317	.385	13	.295	3	-23	-18	2	-1.2
1925	StL-A	14	8	.636	52	16	4	1	6	193	225	11	92	61	15.0	4.70	99	.303	.385	13	.183	-5	-7	-1	-0	-0.3
1926	StL-A	9	11	.450	42	19	8	1	1	181	196	12	98	49	14.7	5.17	83	.285	.376	11	.190	1	-23	-18	-2	-1.8
1927	StL-A	10	12	.455	44	23	12	3	1	203	245	13	102	62	15.6	4.79	91	.310	.392	19	.279	2	-15	-10	-4	-1.0
1928	Det-A	11	10	.524	38	11	7	0	5	156¹	163	4	67	43	13.4	3.91	105	.272	.348	15	.259	2	2	3	0	0.6
1929	Det-A	0	1	.000	6	0	0	0	0	11¹	16	1	7	3	18.3	6.35	68	.348	.434	0	.000	-0	-3	-3	1	-0.1
Total	11	99	102	.493	367	187	90	13	19	1715²	1894	92	699	474	13.8	4.28	100	.288	.360	146	.243	15	-33	3	-9	2.5

● GEORGE Van HALTREN   Van Haltren, George Edward Martin "Rip" b: 3/30/1866, St.Louis, Mo. d: 9/29/45, Oakland, Cal. BL/TL, 5'11", 170 lbs. Deb: 6/27/1887 M ◆

1887	Chi-N	11	7	.611	20	18	18	0	1	161	177	7	66	76	14.5	3.86	116	.277	.359	35	.203	-2	4	11	-0	0.8
1888	Chi-N	13	13	.500	30	24	24	4	1	245²	263	15	60	139	12.3	3.52	86	.267	.318	90	.283	11	-18	-13	2	-0.1
1890	Bro-P	15	10	.600	28	25	23	0	2	223	272	8	89	48	15.4	4.28	104	.288	.362	126	.335	10	-1	4	3	1.3
1891	Bal-a	0	1	.000	6	1	0	1	0	23	38	1	10	7	20.3	5.09	73	.358	.433	180	.318	3	-3	-3	-0	0.1
1892	Bal-N	0	0	—	4	0	0	0	0	14²	28	1	7	5	21.5	9.20	37	.389	.443	168	.302	2	-10	-9	0	0.1
1895	NY-N	1	0	0	1	0	0	0	0	5	13	0	2	1	30.6	12.60	37	.481	.548	177	.340	0	-4	-4	-0	0.0
1896	NY-N	1	0	1.000	2	0	0	0	0	8	5	1	1	3	6.8	2.25	187	.179	.207	197	.351	1	2	2	-0	0.2
1900	NY-N	0	0	—	3	0	0	0	0	3	1	0	3	0	12.0	0.00	—	.100	.308	180	.315	0	1	1	-0	0.0
1901	NY-N	0	0	—	1	0	0	0	0	6	12	0	6	2	28.5	3.00	110	.414	.528	182	.335	0	0	1	1	0.1
Total	9	40	31	.563	93	68	65	5	4	689¹	809	33	244	281	14.5	4.05	96	.285	.353	2532	.316	25	-30	-12	6	2.4

● WILLIAM Van LANDINGHAM   Van Landingham, William Joseph b: 7/16/70, Columbia, Tenn. BR/TR, 6'2", 210 lbs. Deb: 5/21/94

1994	SF-N	8	2	.800	16	14	0	0	0	84	70	4	43	56	12.3	3.54	113	.223	.320	2	.065	-2	6	4	-0	0.2
1995	SF-N	6	3	.667	18	18	1	0	0	122²	124	14	40	95	12.2	3.67	111	.264	.324	7	.152	0	7	6	0	0.5
1996	SF-N	9	14	.391	32	32	0	0	0	181²	196	17	78	97	14.0	5.40	76	.276	.355	8	.131	-1	-24	-26	-3	-3.1
Total	3	23	19	.548	66	64	1	0	0	388¹	390	35	161	248	13.1	4.45	91	.261	.338	17	.123	-3	-11	-16	-3	-2.4

● TODD Van POPPEL   Van Poppel, Todd Matthew b: 12/9/71, Hinsdale, Ill. BR/TR, 6'5", 210 lbs. Deb: 9/11/91

1991	Oak-A	0	0	—	1	1	0	0	0	4²	7	1	2	6	17.4	9.64	40	.368	.429	0	—	0	-3	-3	0	0.3
1993	Oak-A	6	6	.500	16	16	0	0	0	84	76	10	62	47	15.0	5.04	81	.243	.371	0	—	0	-7	-9	-1	-1.2
1994	Oak-A	7	10	.412	23	23	0	0	0	116²	108	20	89	83	15.4	6.09	73	.250	.382	0	—	0	-17	-22	-1	-2.5
1995	Oak-A	4	8	.333	36	14	0	0	0	138²	125	16	56	122	12.0	4.88	92	.244	.323	0	—	0	-3	-6	-2	-0.6
1996	Oak-A	1	5	.167	28	6	0	0	1	63	86	13	33	37	17.3	7.71	62	.333	.413	0	—	0	-19	-20	-1	-1.7
	Det-A	2	4	.333	9	9	1	1	0	36¹	53	11	29	16	20.6	11.39	44	.338	.444	0	—	0	-26	-26	-0	-2.9
	Yr	3	9	.250	37	15	1	1	1	99¹	139	24	62	53	18.3	9.06	54	.329	.416	0	—	0	-45	-46	-1	-4.6
Total	5	20	33	.377	113	69	2	1	1	443	455	71	271	311	15.0	6.22	72	.269	.374	0	—	0	-74	-86	-5	-8.6

● BEN Van RYN   Van Ryn, Benjamin Ashley b: 8/9/71, Fort Wayne, Ind. BL/TL, 6'5", 185 lbs. Deb: 5/9/96

| 1996 | Cal-A | 0 | 0 | — | 2 | 0 | 0 | 0 | 0 | 1 | 1 | 0 | 1 | 0 | 18.0 | 0.00 | — | .250 | .400 | 0 | — | 0 | 1 | 1 | 0 | 0.0 |

● IKE Van ZANDT   Van Zandt, Charles Isaac b: 1877, Brooklyn, N.Y. d: 9/14/08, Nashua, N.H. BL, Deb: 8/5/01 ◆

1901	NY-N	0	0	—	2	0	0	0	0	12²	16	0	8	2	17.8	7.11	47	.308	.410	1	.167	-0	-5	-5	-1	-0.1
1905	StL-A	0	0	—	1	0	0	0	0	6²	2	0	2	3	6.8	0.00	—	.095	.208	75	.233	0	2	2	0	0.0
Total	2	0	0	—	3	0	0	0	0	19¹	18	0	10	5	14.0	4.66	65	.247	.353	76	.224	-0	-3	-3	-1	-0.1

● ANDY VARGA   Varga, Andrew William b: 12/11/30, Chicago, Ill. d: 11/4/92, Orlando, Fla. BR/TL, 6'4", 187 lbs. Deb: 9/9/50

1950	Chi-N	0	0	—	1	0	0	0	0	1	0	0	2	1	9.0	0.00	—	.000	.333	0	—	0	-0	-0	-0	0.0
1951	Chi-N	0	0	—	2	0	0	0	0	3	2	0	6	1	24.0	3.00	136	.200	.500	0	—	0	-0	-0	-0	0.0
Total	2	0	0	—	3	0	0	0	0	4	2	0	7	2	20.3	2.25	183	.167	.474	0	—	0	1	1	0	0.0

● ROBERTO VARGAS   Vargas, Roberto Enrique (Velez) b: 5/29/29, Santurce, P.R. BL/TL, 5'11", 170 lbs. Deb: 4/17/55

| 1955 | Mil-N | 0 | 0 | — | 25 | 0 | 0 | 0 | 2 | 24² | 39 | 4 | 14 | 13 | 19.7 | 8.76 | 43 | .355 | .432 | 1 | .500 | 0 | -13 | -14 | 1 | -0.1 |

● BILL VARGUS   Vargus, William Fay b: 11/11/1899, N.Scituate, Mass. d: 2/12/79, Hyannis, Mass. BL/TL, 6', 165 lbs. Deb: 6/23/25

1925	Bos-N	1	1	.500	11	2	1	0	0	36¹	45	1	13	5	14.9	3.96	101	.302	.366	3	.250	0	1	1	0	0.0
1926	Bos-N	0	0	—	4	0	0	0	0	3	4	0	1	0	15.0	3.00	118	.333	.385	0	—	0	0	0	0	0.0
Total	2	1	1	.500	15	2	1	0	0	39¹	49	1	14	5	14.9	3.89	102	.304	.367	3	.250	0	1	1	0	0.0

● DIKE VARNEY   Varney, Lawrence Delano (b: Lawrence Delano De Varney) b: 8/9/1880, Dover, N.H. d: 4/23/50, Long Island City, N.Y. BL/TL, 6', 165 lbs. Deb: 7/3/02

| 1902 | Cle-A | 1 | 1 | .500 | 3 | 0 | 0 | 0 | 0 | 14 | 10 | 0 | 12 | 7 | 19.0 | 6.14 | 56 | .250 | .425 | 1 | .167 | -0 | -4 | -4 | 0 | -0.5 |

● CAL VASBINDER   Vasbinder, Moses Calhoun b: 7/19/1880, Scio, Ohio d: 12/22/50, Cadiz, Ohio BR/TR, 6'2", Deb: 4/27/02

| 1902 | Cle-A | 0 | 0 | — | 2 | 0 | 0 | 0 | 0 | 5 | 5 | 1 | 8 | 2 | 23.4 | 9.00 | 38 | .263 | .481 | 1 | .500 | 0 | -3 | -3 | 0 | 0.0 |

● RAFAEL VASQUEZ   Vasquez, Rafael b: 6/28/58, LaRomana, D.R. BR/TR, 6', 160 lbs. Deb: 4/6/79

| 1979 | Sea-A | 1 | 0 | 1.000 | 9 | 0 | 0 | 0 | 0 | 16 | 23 | 4 | 6 | 9 | 16.9 | 5.06 | 86 | .354 | .417 | 0 | — | 0 | -2 | -1 | -0 | -0.1 |

● PORTER VAUGHAN   Vaughan, Cecil Porter "Lefty" b: 5/11/19, Stevensville, Va. BR/TL, 6'1", 178 lbs. Deb: 6/16/40

1940	Phi-A	2	9	.182	18	15	5	0	2	99¹	104	9	61	46	15.2	5.35	83	.264	.367	8	.235	0	-11	-10	-1	-1.0
1941	Phi-A	0	2	.000	5	3	1	0	0	22²	32	3	12	6	17.5	7.94	53	.327	.400	1	.143	-0	-10	-9	-0	-0.7
1946	Phi-A	0	0	—	1	0	0	0	0	0	1	0	1	0	—	—	—	1.000	1.000	0	—	0	-0	-0	0	0.0
Total	3	2	11	.154	24	18	6	0	2	122	137	12	74	52	15.8	5.83	75	.278	.375	9	.220	-0	-20	-19	-1	-1.7

● CHARLIE VAUGHAN   Vaughan, Charles Wayne b: 10/6/47, Mercedes, Tex. BR/TL, 6'1.5", 185 lbs. Deb: 9/3/66

1966	Atl-N	1	0	1.000	1	1	0	0	0	7	8	0	3	6	14.1	2.57	141	.296	.367	1	.250	0	1	1	0	0.1
1969	Atl-N	0	0	—	1	0	0	0	0	1	1	0	3	0	36.0	18.00	20	.250	.571	0	—	0	-2	-2	0	0.0
Total	2	1	0	1.000	2	1	0	0	0	8	9	0	6	6	16.9	4.50	81	.290	.405	1	.250	0	-1	-1	0	0.1

● ROY VAUGHN   Vaughn, Clarence Leroy b: 9/4/11, Sedalia, Mo. d: 3/1/37, Martinsville, Va. BB/TR, 6'0.5", 178 lbs. Deb: 7/1/34

| 1934 | Phi-A | 0 | 0 | — | 2 | 0 | 0 | 0 | 0 | 4¹ | 3 | 1 | 3 | 1 | 12.5 | 2.08 | 211 | .176 | .300 | 0 | .000 | -0 | 1 | 1 | -0 | 0.0 |

● DE WAYNE VAUGHN   Vaughn, De Wayne Mathew b: 7/22/59, Oklahoma City, Okla BR/TR, 5'11", 180 lbs. Deb: 4/17/88

| 1988 | Tex-A | 0 | 0 | — | 8 | 0 | 0 | 0 | 0 | 15¹ | 24 | 4 | 4 | 8 | 16.4 | 7.63 | 53 | .348 | .384 | 0 | — | 0 | -6 | -6 | -1 | -0.1 |

● FARMER VAUGHN   Vaughn, Harry Francis b: 3/1/1864, Ruraldale, Ohio d: 2/21/14, Cincinnati, Ohio BR/TR, 6'3", 177 lbs. Deb: 10/7/1886 ◆

| 1891 | Cin-a | 0 | 0 | — | 1 | 0 | 0 | 0 | 0 | 7 | 12 | 0 | 7 | 0 | 24.4 | 3.86 | 107 | .364 | .400 | 45 | .257 | — | -0 | -0 | — | 0.0 |

● HIPPO VAUGHN   Vaughn, James Leslie b: 4/9/1888, Weatherford, Tex. d: 5/29/66, Chicago, Ill. BB/TL, 6'4", 215 lbs. Deb: 6/19/08

| 1908 | NY-A | 2 | 1 | .667 | 6 | 4 | 2 | 1 | 0 | 39¹ | 25 | 0 | 19 | 21 | 9.3 | 3.86 | 64 | .167 | .500 | 0 | .000 | -0 | -0 | -0 | -0 | 0.0 |
| 1910 | NY-A | 13 | 11 | .542 | 30 | 25 | 18 | 5 | 1 | 221² | 190 | 1 | 58 | 107 | 10.5 | 1.83 | 146 | .237 | .297 | 10 | .133 | -2 | 17 | 20 | -0 | 2.0 |

YEAR TM/L	W	L	PCT	G	GS	CG	SH	SV	IP	H	HR	BB	SO	RAT	ERA	ERA+	OAV	OOB	BH	AVG	PB	PR	/A	PD	TPI
1911 NY-A	8	10	.444	26	19	10	0	0	145²	158	2	54	74	13.5	4.39	82	.284	.354	7	.143	-1	-17	-13	1	-1.4
1912 NY-A	2	8	.200	15	10	5	1	0	63	66	1	37	46	14.9	5.14	70	.264	.361	2	.095	-1	-13	-11	1	-1.5
Was-A	4	3	.571	12	8	4	0	0	81	75	0	43	49	13.6	2.89	115	.253	.356	6	.200	-1	4	4	2	0.4
Yr	6	11	.353	27	18	9	1	0	144	141	1	80	95	14.1	3.88	89	.258	.357	8	.157	-2	-9	-7	3	-1.1
1913 Chi-N	5	1	.833	7	6	5	2	0	56	37	0	27	36	10.6	1.45	207	.182	.284	4	.190	-1	11	11	0	1.1
1914 Chi-N	21	13	.618	42	35	23	4	1	293²	236	1	109	165	10.8	2.05	135	.222	.299	14	.144	-0	24	24	-0	2.7
1915 Chi-N	20	12	.625	41	34	18	4	1	269²	240	4	77	148	10.9	2.87	97	.238	.299	14	.163	1	-4	-3	-1	-0.3
1916 Chi-N	17	15	.531	44	35	21	4	1	294	269	4	67	144	10.5	2.20	132	.250	.298	14	.135	-4	14	23	1	2.2
1917 Chi-N	23	13	.639	41	38	27	5	0	295²	255	3	91	195	10.8	2.01	144	.235	.300	16	.160	1	23	29	3	4.1
1918 *Chi-N	**22**	10	.688	35	33	27	**8**	0	**290¹**	216	4	76	**148**	9.3	**1.74**	**160**	**.208**	.266	23	.240	4	**33**	**34**	-1	**4.4**
1919 Chi-N	21	14	.600	38	37	25	4	1	**306²**	264	3	62	**141**	9.7	1.79	161	.234	.278	17	.173	-0	**38**	**37**	-3	4.2
1920 Chi-N	19	16	.543	40	38	30	0	1	301	301	6	81	131	11.7	2.54	126	.264	.318	22	.216	4	20	22	-0	2.7
1921 Chi-N	3	11	.214	17	14	7	0	0	109¹	153	6	31	30	15.6	6.01	64	.341	.390	10	.244	2	-27	-27	-1	-2.7
Total 13	178	137	.565	390	332	214	41	5	2730	2461	39	817	1416	11.1	2.49	120	.244	.306	159	.173	-1	123	152	-1	17.9

● **AL VEACH** Veach, Alvis Lindel b: 8/6/09, Maylene, Ala. d: 9/6/90, Charlotte, N.C. BR/TR, 5'11", 178 lbs. Deb: 9/22/35

YEAR TM/L	W	L	PCT	G	GS	CG	SH	SV	IP	H	HR	BB	SO	RAT	ERA	ERA+	OAV	OOB	BH	AVG	PB	PR	/A	PD	TPI
1935 Phi-A	0	2	.000	2	1	0	0	0	10	20	1	9	3	26.1	11.70	39	.417	.509	0	.000	-1	-8	-8	0	-1.1

● **BOBBY VEACH** Veach, Robert Hayes b: 6/29/1888, Island, Ky. d: 8/7/45, Detroit, Mich. BL/TR, 5'11", 160 lbs. Deb: 8/6/12 ♦

YEAR TM/L	W	L	PCT	G	GS	CG	SH	SV	IP	H	HR	BB	SO	RAT	ERA	ERA+	OAV	OOB	BH	AVG	PB	PR	/A	PD	TPI
1918 Det-A	0	0	—	1	0	0	0	1	2	2	0	2	0		4.50	59	.286	.444	139	.279	0	-0	-0	-0	-0.1

● **PEEK-A-BOO VEACH** Veach, William Walter b: 6/15/1862, Indianapolis, Ind d: 11/12/37, Indianapolis, Ind. Deb: 8/24/1884 ♦

YEAR TM/L	W	L	PCT	G	GS	CG	SH	SV	IP	H	HR	BB	SO	RAT	ERA	ERA+	OAV	OOB	BH	AVG	PB	PR	/A	PD	TPI
1884 KC-U	3	9	.250	12	12	12	0	0	104	95	1	10	62	9.1	2.42	92	.227	.245	11	.134	-3	0	-2	1	-0.4
1887 Lou-a	0	1	.000	1	1	1	0	0	9	5	1	8	2	13.0	4.00	110	.172	.351	0	.000	-5	0	0	-0	0.0
Total 2	3	10	.231	13	13	13	0	0	113	100	2	18	64	9.4	2.55	94	.223	.253	76	.215	-4	0	-2	1	-0.4

● **BOB VEALE** Veale, Robert Andrew b: 10/28/35, Birmingham, Ala. BB/TL, 6'6", 212 lbs. Deb: 4/16/62

YEAR TM/L	W	L	PCT	G	GS	CG	SH	SV	IP	H	HR	BB	SO	RAT	ERA	ERA+	OAV	OOB	BH	AVG	PB	PR	/A	PD	TPI
1962 Pit-N	2	2	.500	11	6	2	0	1	45²	39	2	25	42	12.6	3.74	105	.235	.335	4	.250	1	1	1	-0	0.1
1963 Pit-N	5	2	.714	34	7	3	2	3	77²	59	1	40	68	11.6	1.04	316	.215	.317	2	.087	-0	19	**19**	0	1.9
1964 Pit-N	18	12	.600	40	38	14	1	0	279²	222	8	124	**250**	11.2	2.74	128	.217	.303	15	.156	-0	25	24	-1	2.4
1965 Pit-N☆	17	12	.586	39	37	14	7	0	266	221	5	119	276	11.7	2.84	124	.225	.313	8	.086	-1	21	20	-2	1.5
1966 Pit-N☆	16	12	.571	38	37	12	3	0	268¹	228	18	102	229	11.2	3.02	118	.232	.307	13	.138	-2	18	17	-2	1.2
1967 Pit-N	16	8	.667	33	31	6	1	0	203	184	12	119	179	13.7	3.64	93	.245	.352	3	.043	-5	-6	-6	1	-1.1
1968 Pit-N	13	14	.481	36	33	13	4	0	245²	187	13	94	171	10.4	2.05	142	.211	.288	9	.110	-2	25	24	-0	2.3
1969 Pit-N	13	14	.481	34	34	9	1	0	225²	232	8	91	213	13.0	3.23	108	.267	.338	4	.051	-5	9	6	-0	0.1
1970 Pit-N	10	15	.400	34	32	5	1	0	202	189	15	94	178	12.7	3.92	100	.246	.331	1	.164	-1	-2	-2	-0	-0.1
1971 *Pit-N	6	0	1.000	37	0	0	0	0	46¹	59	5	24	40	16.1	6.99	48	.314	.392	3	.333	-1	-18	-19	-2	-2.5
1972 Pit-N	0	0	—	5	0	0	0	0	9	10	0	7	6	17.0	6.00	55	.313	.436	0	.000	-0	-3	-3	-0	-0.1
Bos-A	2	0	1.000	6	0	0	0	0	8	3	0	10	5	16.0	0.00	—	.083	.185	0	.000	-0	3	3	1	1.0
1973 Bos-A	3	3	.400	32	0	0	0	11	36¹	37	2	12	25	12.1	3.47	116	.268	.327	0	—	0	0	0	0	0.5
1974 Bos-A	0	1	.000	18	0	0	0	2	13	15	2	4	16	13.2	5.54	69	.283	.333	0	—	0	-3	-2	-0	-0.3
Total 13	120	95	.558	397	255	78	20	21	1926	1684	91	858	1703	12.0	3.07	113	.236	.320	72	.114	-17	96	86	-9	6.9

● **LOU VEDDER** Vedder, Louis Edward b: 4/20/1897, Oakville, Mich. d: 3/9/90, Lake Placid, Fla. BR/TR, 5'10.5", 175 lbs. Deb: 9/18/20

YEAR TM/L	W	L	PCT	G	GS	CG	SH	SV	IP	H	HR	BB	SO	RAT	ERA	ERA+	OAV	OOB	BH	AVG	PB	PR	/A	PD	TPI
1920 Det-A	0	0	—	1	0	0	0	0	2	0	0	1	0	1.0	0.00	—	.000	.000	0	—	0	1	1	0	0.0

● **AL VEIGEL** Veigel, Allen Francis b: 1/30/17, Dover, Ohio BR/TR, 6'1", 180 lbs. Deb: 9/21/39

YEAR TM/L	W	L	PCT	G	GS	CG	SH	SV	IP	H	HR	BB	SO	RAT	ERA	ERA+	OAV	OOB	BH	AVG	PB	PR	/A	PD	TPI
1939 Bos-N	0	1	.000	2	0	0	0	0	2²	3	0	5	2	27.0	6.75	55	.250	.471	0	.000	-1	-0	-0	-0	-0.3

● **BUCKY VEIL** Veil, Frederick William b: 8/2/1881, Tyrone, Pa. d: 4/16/31, Altoona, Pa. BR/TR, 5'10", 165 lbs. Deb: 4/19/03

YEAR TM/L	W	L	PCT	G	GS	CG	SH	SV	IP	H	HR	BB	SO	RAT	ERA	ERA+	OAV	OOB	BH	AVG	PB	PR	/A	PD	TPI
1903 *Pit-N	5	3	.625	12	6	4	0	0	70²	70	1	36	20	13.8	3.82	85	.269	.362	6	.207	-0	-4	-5	0	-0.5
1904 Pit-N	0	0	—	1	1	0	0	0	4²	4	0	4	1	17.4	5.79	47	.250	.429	1	1.000	0	-2	-2	0	0.1
Total 2	5	3	.625	13	7	4	0	0	75¹	74	1	40	21	14.0	3.94	81	.268	.367	7	.233	0	-6	-6	0	-0.4

● **CARLOS VELAZQUEZ** Velazquez, Carlos (Quinones) b: 3/22/48, Loiza, P.R. BR/TR, 5'11", 180 lbs. Deb: 7/20/73

YEAR TM/L	W	L	PCT	G	GS	CG	SH	SV	IP	H	HR	BB	SO	RAT	ERA	ERA+	OAV	OOB	BH	AVG	PB	PR	/A	PD	TPI
1973 Mil-A	2	2	.500	12	0	0	0	2	38¹	24	3	10	12	13.1	2.58	146	.297	.339	0	—	0	5	5	0	0.6

● **DARIO VERAS** Veras, Dario Antonio b: 3/13/73, Santiago, D.R. BR/TR, 6'2", 165 lbs. Deb: 7/31/96

YEAR TM/L	W	L	PCT	G	GS	CG	SH	SV	IP	H	HR	BB	SO	RAT	ERA	ERA+	OAV	OOB	BH	AVG	PB	PR	/A	PD	TPI
1996 *SD-N	3	1	.750	23	0	0	0	0	29	24	3	10	23	10.9	2.79	143	.231	.304	0	—	0	5	4	0	0.5

● **JOE VERBANIC** Verbanic, Joseph Michael b: 4/24/43, Washington, Pa. BR/TR, 6', 155 lbs. Deb: 7/22/66

YEAR TM/L	W	L	PCT	G	GS	CG	SH	SV	IP	H	HR	BB	SO	RAT	ERA	ERA+	OAV	OOB	BH	AVG	PB	PR	/A	PD	TPI
1966 Phi-N	1	1	.500	17	0	0	0	0	14	12	1	2	10	14.1	5.14	70	.226	.349	0	—	0	-2	-2	-0	-0.3
1967 NY-A	4	3	.571	28	6	1	1	2	80¹	74	6	21	39	10.9	2.80	112	.249	.303	2	.111	-0	4	3	2	0.4
1968 NY-A	6	7	.462	40	11	2	1	4	97	104	6	41	40	14.0	3.15	92	.284	.366	2	.080	-1	-2	-3	1	-0.4
1970 NY-A	1	0	1.000	7	0	0	0	0	15²	20	1	12	8	19.0	4.60	76	.323	.440	1	.333	0	-2	-2	1	0.0
Total 4	12	11	.522	92	17	3	2	6	207	210	15	84	94	13.2	3.26	95	.270	.348	5	.109	-1	-2	-4	4	-0.3

● **AL VERDEL** Verdel, Albert Alfred "Stumpy" b: 6/10/21, Punxsutawney, Pa. d: 4/16/91, Sarasota, Fla. BR/TR, 5'9.5", 186 lbs. Deb: 4/20/44

YEAR TM/L	W	L	PCT	G	GS	CG	SH	SV	IP	H	HR	BB	SO	RAT	ERA	ERA+	OAV	OOB	BH	AVG	PB	PR	/A	PD	TPI
1944 Phi-N	0	0	—	1	0	0	0	0	1	0	0	1	0		0.00	—	.000	.000	0	—	0	0	0	-0	0.0

● **TOMMY VEREKER** Vereker, John James b: 12/2/1893, Baltimore, Md. d: 4/2/74, Baltimore, Md. 5'10", 185 lbs. Deb: 6/17/15

YEAR TM/L	W	L	PCT	G	GS	CG	SH	SV	IP	H	HR	BB	SO	RAT	ERA	ERA+	OAV	OOB	BH	AVG	PB	PR	/A	PD	TPI
1915 Bal-F	0	0	—	2	0	0	0	0	3	3	1	2	1	18.0	15.00	19	.273	.429	0	—	0	-4	-4	-0	0.0

● **DAVE VERES** Veres, David Scott b: 10/19/66, Montgomery, Ala. BR/TR, 6'2", 195 lbs. Deb: 5/10/94

YEAR TM/L	W	L	PCT	G	GS	CG	SH	SV	IP	H	HR	BB	SO	RAT	ERA	ERA+	OAV	OOB	BH	AVG	PB	PR	/A	PD	TPI
1994 Hou-N	3	3	.500	32	0	0	0	1	41	39	4	7	28	10.3	2.41	164	.247	.283	1	.500	1	8	7	-1	1.0
1995 Hou-N	5	1	.833	72	0	0	0	1	103¹	89	5	30	94	10.7	2.26	171	.241	.304	0	.000	-1	**22**	18	-1	0.9
1996 Mon-N	6	3	.667	68	0	0	0	4	77²	85	10	32	81	14.3	4.17	103	.277	.366	3	.375	-0	1	0	-0	0.2
Total 3	14	7	.667	172	0	0	0	6	222	213	19	69	203	11.9	2.96	136	.255	.320	4	.267	1	31	27	-2	2.1

● **RANDY VERES** Veres, Randolph Ruhland b: 11/25/65, Sacramento, Cal. BR/TR, 6'3", 190 lbs. Deb: 7/1/89

YEAR TM/L	W	L	PCT	G	GS	CG	SH	SV	IP	H	HR	BB	SO	RAT	ERA	ERA+	OAV	OOB	BH	AVG	PB	PR	/A	PD	TPI
1989 Mil-A	0	1	.000	3	1	0	0	0	8¹	9	0	4	4	14.0	4.32	89	.290	.371	0	—	0	-0	-0	0	0.0
1990 Mil-A	0	3	.000	26	0	0	0	1	41²	38	5	16	16	11.9	3.67	105	.247	.322	0	—	0	1	1	1	0.2
1994 Chi-N	1	1	.500	10	0	0	0	0	9²	12	3	2	5	14.0	5.59	74	.308	.357	0	—	0	-1	-1	-0	-0.3
1995 Fla-N	4	4	.500	47	0	0	0	1	48²	46	6	22	31	12.8	3.88	108	.251	.335	0	.000	-0	2	2	-1	0.1
1996 Det-A	0	4	.000	25	0	0	0	0	30¹	38	6	23	28	18.7	8.31	61	.306	.423	0	—	0	-11	-11	-1	-1.2
Total 5	5	13	.278	111	1	0	0	2	138²	143	20	67	84	13.8	4.93	86	.269	.357	0	—	0	-10	-10	-1	-0.9

● **JOHN VERHOEVEN** Verhoeven, John C b: 7/3/53, Long Beach, Cal. BR/TR, 6'5", 200 lbs. Deb: 7/6/76

YEAR TM/L	W	L	PCT	G	GS	CG	SH	SV	IP	H	HR	BB	SO	RAT	ERA	ERA+	OAV	OOB	BH	AVG	PB	PR	/A	PD	TPI
1976 Cal-A	0	2	.000	21	0	0	0	4	37¹	35	2	14	23	11.8	3.38	99	.252	.320	0	—	0	1	-0	1	0.2
1977 Cal-A	0	2	.000	3	0	0	0	0	4²	4	0	4	3	17.4	3.86	101	.222	.391	0	—	0	0	0	0	0.2
Chi-N	0	0	—	6	0	0	0	0	10¹	9	1	6	3	9.6	2.61	156	.231	.268	0	—	0	2	2	0	0.1
Yr	0	2	.000	9	0	0	0	0	15	13	1	10	6	11.4	3.00	134	.224	.297	0	—	0	2	2	0	0.3
1980 Min-A	3	4	.429	44	0	0	0	5	99²	109	10	29	42	12.7	3.97	110	.289	.345	1		0	4	4	0	-0.1
1981 Min-A	0	0	—	25	0	0	0	2	52	57	4	14	16	12.6	3.98	98	.288	.341	0	—	0	1	2	0	-0.2
Total 4	3	8	.273	99	0	0	0	11	204	214	16	63	90	12.5	3.79	106	.278	.337	1		0	5	2	0	0.2

● **JOE VERNON** Vernon, Joseph Henry b: 11/25/1889, Mansfield, Mass. d: 3/13/55, Philadelphia, Pa. BR/TR, 5'11", 160 lbs. Deb: 7/20/12

YEAR TM/L	W	L	PCT	G	GS	CG	SH	SV	IP	H	HR	BB	SO	RAT	ERA	ERA+	OAV	OOB	BH	AVG	PB	PR	/A	PD	TPI
1912 Chi-N	0	0	—	4	0	0	0	0	4	4	0	6	4	24.8	11.25	30	.286	.524	0	.000	-0	-3	-4	-0	-0.1
1914 Bro-F	0	0	—	1	1	0	0	0	3¹	4	0	5	0	24.3	10.80	27	.308	.500	0	—	0	-3	-3	0	-0.1
Total 2	0	0	—	5	1	0	0	0	7¹	8	0	11	4	24.5	11.05	28	.296	.513	0	.000	-0	-6	-6	-0	-0.3

● **BOB VESELIC** Veselic, Robert Michael b: 9/27/55, Pittsburgh, Pa. d: 12/26/95, Los Angeles, Cal. BR/TR, 6', 175 lbs. Deb: 9/18/80

YEAR TM/L	W	L	PCT	G	GS	CG	SH	SV	IP	H	HR	BB	SO	RAT	ERA	ERA+	OAV	OOB	BH	AVG	PB	PR	/A	PD	TPI
1980 Min-A	0	0	—	1	0	0	0	0	4	3	1	1	2	9.0	4.50	97	.214	.267	0		0	-0	-0	-0	-0.3

YEAR	TM/L	W	L	PCT	G	GS	CG	SH	SV	IP	H	HR	BB	SO	RAT	ERA	ERA+	OAV	OOB	BH	AVG	PB	PR	/A	PD	TPI
1981	Min-A	1	1	.500	5	0	0	0	0	22²	22	1	12	13	13.5	3.18	124	.250	.340	0	—	0	1	2	-1	-0.1
Total	2	1	1	.500	6	0	0	0	0	26²	25	2	13	15	12.8	3.38	119	.245	.330	0	—	0	1	2	-1	-0.4

● **LEE VIAU**   Viau, Leon A. b: 7/5/1866, Corinth, Vt. d: 12/17/47, Hopewell, N.J. BR/TR, 5'4", 160 lbs. Deb: 4/22/1888

YEAR	TM/L	W	L	PCT	G	GS	CG	SH	SV	IP	H	HR	BB	SO	RAT	ERA	ERA+	OAV	OOB	BH	AVG	PB	PR	/A	PD	TPI
1888	Cin-a	27	14	.659	42	42	42	1	0	387²	331	7	110	164	10.7	2.65	120	.222	.285	13	.087	-11	18	23	-2	0.7
1889	Cin-a	22	20	.524	47	42	38	1	1	373	379	8	136	152	12.7	3.79	103	.255	.322	21	.143	-9	3	5	-3	-0.6
1890	Cin-N	7	5	.583	13	10	7	1	0	90	97	8	39	41	13.7	4.50	79	.266	.339	5	.139	-2	-9	-9	1	-1.1
	Cle-N	4	9	.308	13	13	13	1	0	107	101	4	42	30	12.4	3.36	106	.242	.318	7	.163	-2	2	3	-1	0.0
	Yr	11	14	.440	26	23	20	2	0	197	198	12	81	71	13.0	3.88	92	.253	.327	12	.152	-4	-7	-7	0	-1.1
1891	Cle-N	18	17	.514	45	38	31	0	0	343²	367	3	138	130	13.6	3.01	115	.263	.336	23	.160	-3	13	17	1	1.2
1892	Cle-N	0	1	.000	1	1	0	0	0	1	5	0	1	0	54.0	36.00	9	.625	.667	0	—	-0	-4	-4	0	-1.5
	Lou-N	4	11	.267	16	15	14	1	0	130²	156	7	56	36	14.6	3.99	77	.285	.351	13	.197	1	-10	-13	2	-0.9
	Bos-N	1	0	1.000	1	1	1	0	0	9	5	0	4	1	9.0	0.00	—	.156	.250	0	.000	-0	3	4	-0	0.3
	Yr	5	12	.294	18	17	15	1	0	140²	166	7	61	37	14.5	3.97	78	.282	.350	13	.188	1	-11	-14	2	-2.1
Total	5	83	77	.519	178	162	146	5	1	1442	1441	37	526	554	12.6	3.33	105	.251	.320	82	.139	-27	16	25	-1	-1.9

● **RUBE VICKERS**   Vickers, Harry Porter b: 5/17/1878, St.Marys, Ont., Can d: 12/9/58, Belleville, Mich. BL/TR, 6'2", 225 lbs. Deb: 9/21/02

YEAR	TM/L	W	L	PCT	G	GS	CG	SH	SV	IP	H	HR	BB	SO	RAT	ERA	ERA+	OAV	OOB	BH	AVG	PB	PR	/A	PD	TPI
1902	Cin-N	0	3	.000	3	3	3	0	0	21	31	0	8	6	17.1	6.00	50	.341	.400	1	.364	1	-8	-7	-1	-0.8
1903	Bro-N	0	1	.000	4	1	1	0	0	14	27	0	9	5	23.8	10.93	29	.415	.493	1	.100	-1	-12	-12	1	-0.6
1907	Phi-A	2	2	.500	10	4	3	1	0	50¹	44	1	12	21	10.2	3.40	77	.238	.288	3	.150	-1	-5	-4	0	-0.4
1908	Phi-A	18	19	.486	53	34	21	6	1	317	264	0	71	156	9.8	2.21	116	.231	.282	17	.160	-1	6	12	-3	1.0
1909	Phi-A	2	2	.500	18	3	1	0	1	55²	60	0	19	25	13.1	3.40	71	.274	.338	1	.063	-1	-6	-6	-1	-0.8
Total	5	22	27	.449	88	45	29	7	2	458	426	1	119	213	11.0	2.93	88	.250	.305	26	.160	-3	-24	-17	-4	-1.6

● **TOM VICKERY**   Vickery, Thomas Gill "Vinegar Tom" b: 5/5/1867, Milford, N.J. d: 3/21/21, Burlington, N.J. TR, 6', 170 lbs. Deb: 4/21/1890

YEAR	TM/L	W	L	PCT	G	GS	CG	SH	SV	IP	H	HR	BB	SO	RAT	ERA	ERA+	OAV	OOB	BH	AVG	PB	PR	/A	PD	TPI
1890	Phi-N	24	22	.522	46	46	41	2	0	382	405	8	184	162	14.6	3.44	106	.264	.353	33	.208	-4	6	9	-2	0.3
1891	Chi-N	6	5	.545	14	12	7	0	0	79²	72	4	44	39	13.7	4.07	82	.232	.337	7	.179	-2	-6	-7	1	-0.8
1892	Bal-N	8	10	.444	24	21	17	0	0	176	189	3	87	49	14.6	3.53	97	.264	.351	18	.243	-2	-5	-2	-2	-0.1
1893	Phi-N	4	5	.444	13	11	7	0	0	80	100	1	37	15	16.1	5.40	85	.297	.376	11	.314	1	-7	-7	2	-0.3
Total	4	42	42	.500	97	90	72	2	0	717²	766	16	352	265	14.6	3.75	98	.264	.354	69	.225	-3	-12	-6	-1	-0.9

● **RON VILLONE**   Villone, Ronald Thomas b: 1/16/70, Englewood, N.J. BL/TL, 6'3", 230 lbs. Deb: 4/28/95

YEAR	TM/L	W	L	PCT	G	GS	CG	SH	SV	IP	H	HR	BB	SO	RAT	ERA	ERA+	OAV	OOB	BH	AVG	PB	PR	/A	PD	TPI
1995	Sea-A	0	2	.000	19	0	0	0	0	19¹	20	6	23	26	20.5	7.91	60	.270	.449	0	—	0	-7	-7	-0	-0.7
	SD-N	2	1	.667	19	0	0	0	1	25²	24	5	11	37	12.3	4.21	96	.242	.318	0	.000	-0	-0	-1	-0	-0.1
1996	SD-N	1	1	.500	21	0	0	0	0	18¹	17	2	7	19	12.3	2.95	135	.243	.321	0	—	0	3	2	0	0.2
	Mil-A	0	0	—	23	0	0	0	2	24²	14	4	18	19	13.1	3.28	160	.175	.353	0	—	-0	5	5	-1	-0.4
Total	3	4	4	.429	82	0	0	0	0	88	75	17	59	101	14.3	4.50	100	.232	.361	0	.000	-0	1	-1	-1	-1.0

● **BOB VINES**   Vines, Robert Earl b: 2/25/1897, Waxahachie, Tex. d: 10/18/82, Orlando, Fla. BR/TR, 6'4", 184 lbs. Deb: 9/3/24

YEAR	TM/L	W	L	PCT	G	GS	CG	SH	SV	IP	H	HR	BB	SO	RAT	ERA	ERA+	OAV	OOB	BH	AVG	PB	PR	/A	PD	TPI
1924	StL-N	0	0	—	2	0	0	0	0	10²	23	1	4	0	19.4	9.28	41	.426	.426	0	—	-1	-6	-7	-0	-0.1
1925	Phi-N	0	0	—	3	0	0	0	0	4	9	0	3	0	27.0	11.25	42	.450	.522	0	—	0	-3	-3	0	-0.0
Total	2	0	0	—	5	0	0	0	0	14²	32	1	3	0	21.5	9.82	41	.432	.455	0	.000	-1	-10	-9	-0	-0.1

● **DAVE VINEYARD**   Vineyard, David Kent b: 2/25/41, Clay, W.Va. BR/TR, 6'3", 195 lbs. Deb: 7/18/64

YEAR	TM/L	W	L	PCT	G	GS	CG	SH	SV	IP	H	HR	BB	SO	RAT	ERA	ERA+	OAV	OOB	BH	AVG	PB	PR	/A	PD	TPI
1964	Bal-A	2	5	.286	19	6	1	0	0	54	57	5	33	49	15.0	4.17	86	.274	.357	2	.167	0	-3	-4	-1	-0.5

● **BILL VINTON**   Vinton, William Miller b: 4/27/1865, Winthrop, Mass. d: 9/3/1893, Pawtucket, R.I. BR/TR, 6'1", 160 lbs. Deb: 7/3/1884

YEAR	TM/L	W	L	PCT	G	GS	CG	SH	SV	IP	H	HR	BB	SO	RAT	ERA	ERA+	OAV	OOB	BH	AVG	PB	PR	/A	PD	TPI
1884	Phi-N	10	10	.500	21	21	20	0	0	182	166	6	35	105	9.9	2.23	134	.220	.255	9	.115	-6	15	15	3	1.1
1885	Phi-N	3	6	.333	9	9	8	0	0	77	90	0	23	21	13.2	3.04	92	.269	.317	2	.067	-3	-2	-2	0	-0.5
	Phi-a	4	3	.571	7	7	6	2	0	55	46	1	15	34	10.6	2.45	140	.200	.261	4	.154	-1	5	6	-0	0.6
Total	2	17	19	.472	37	37	34	2	0	314	302	7	73	160	10.9	2.46	122	.229	.272	15	.112	-10	18	19	3	1.2

● **FRANK VIOLA**   Viola, Frank John b: 4/19/60, Hempstead, N.Y. BL/TL, 6'4", 209 lbs. Deb: 6/6/82

YEAR	TM/L	W	L	PCT	G	GS	CG	SH	SV	IP	H	HR	BB	SO	RAT	ERA	ERA+	OAV	OOB	BH	AVG	PB	PR	/A	PD	TPI
1982	Min-A	4	10	.286	22	22	3	1	0	126	152	22	38	84	13.6	5.21	81	.302	.351	0	—	0	-16	-14	-1	-1.4
1983	Min-A	7	15	.318	35	34	4	0	0	210	242	34	92	127	14.7	5.49	77	.287	.363	0	—	0	-33	-29	-1	-2.7
1984	Min-A	18	12	.600	35	35	10	4	0	257²	225	28	73	149	10.5	3.21	131	.233	.290	0	—	0	22	28	-3	2.8
1985	Min-A	18	14	.563	36	36	9	0	0	250²	262	26	68	135	11.9	4.09	108	.268	.316	0	—	0	1	9	-2	0.8
1986	Min-A	16	13	.552	37	37	7	1	0	245²	257	37	83	191	12.6	4.51	96	.268	.329	0	—	0	-9	-5	-3	-0.9
1987	*Min-A	17	10	.630	36	36	7	1	0	251²	230	29	66	197	10.8	2.90	159	.241	.294	0	—	0	44	48	-1	4.6
1988	Min-A★	24	7	**.774**	35	35	7	2	0	255¹	236	20	54	193	10.3	2.64	154	.245	.288	0	—	0	38	**40**	-1	4.6
1989	Min-A	8	12	.400	24	24	7	1	0	175²	171	14	47	138	11.3	3.79	109	.256	.308	0	—	0	2	7	0	0.7
	NY-N	5	5	.500	12	12	2	1	0	85¹	75	5	27	73	10.9	3.38	97	.236	.298	3	.130	-0	1	-1	-1	-0.2
1990	NY-N★	20	12	.625	35	35	7	3	0	249²	227	15	60	182	10.4	2.67	140	.242	.289	13	.153	-1	**31**	30	-0	**3.6**
1991	NY-N★	13	15	.464	35	35	3	0	0	231¹	259	25	54	132	12.2	3.97	92	.286	.327	9	.127	-1	-7	-8	-1	-1.2
1992	Bos-A	13	12	.520	35	35	6	1	0	238	214	13	89	121	11.7	3.44	122	.242	.316	0	—	0	13	20	3	1.8
1993	Bos-A	11	8	.579	29	29	2	1	0	183²	180	12	72	91	12.6	3.14	147	.259	.334	0	—	0	24	30	0	2.9
1994	Bos-A	1	1	.500	6	6	0	0	0	31	34	2	17	9	14.8	4.65	108	.296	.386	0	—	0	1	1	-0	-0.2
1995	Cin-N	0	1	.000	3	3	0	0	0	14¹	20	3	3	4	14.4	6.28	66	.333	.365	1	.167	-0	-3	-3	-0	-0.2
1996	Tor-A	1	3	.250	6	6	0	0	0	30¹	43	6	21	18	19.6	7.71	65	.350	.452	0	—	0	-9	-9	-0	-1.0
Total	15	176	150	.540	421	420	74	16	0	2836¹	2827	294	864	1844	11.9	3.73	112	.260	.317	26	.141	-2	99	143	-12	14.0

● **JAKE VIRTUE**   Virtue, Jacob Kitchline "Guesses" b: 3/2/1865, Philadelphia, Pa. d: 2/3/43, Camden, N.J. BB/TL, 5'9.5", 165 lbs. Deb: 7/21/1890 ♦

YEAR	TM/L	W	L	PCT	G	GS	CG	SH	SV	IP	H	HR	BB	SO	RAT	ERA	ERA+	OAV	OOB	BH	AVG	PB	PR	/A	PD	TPI
1893	Cle-N	0	0	—	1	0	0	0	0	5	3	0	3	2	10.8	1.80	271	.167	.286	100	.265	0	2	2	-0	0.0
1894	Cle-N	0	0	—	1	0	0	0	0	0	0	0	1	0	—	—	—	—	1.000	23	.258	0	0	0	0	0.0
Total	2	0	0	—	2	0	0	0	0	5	3	0	4	2	12.6	1.80	271	.167	.318	483	.274	0	2	2	-0	0.0

● **JOE VITELLI**   Vitelli, Antonio Joseph b: 4/12/08, McKees Rocks, Pa. d: 2/7/67, Pittsburgh, Pa. BR/TR, 6'1", 195 lbs. Deb: 5/30/44 ♦

YEAR	TM/L	W	L	PCT	G	GS	CG	SH	SV	IP	H	HR	BB	SO	RAT	ERA	ERA+	OAV	OOB	BH	AVG	PB	PR	/A	PD	TPI
1944	Pit-N	0	0	—	4	0	0	0	0	7	5	1	7	2	16.7	2.57	145	.185	.371	0	.000	-0	1	1	0	0.0

● **JOE VITKO**   Vitko, Joseph John b: 2/1/70, Somerville, N.J. BR/TR, 6'8", 210 lbs. Deb: 9/18/92

YEAR	TM/L	W	L	PCT	G	GS	CG	SH	SV	IP	H	HR	BB	SO	RAT	ERA	ERA+	OAV	OOB	BH	AVG	PB	PR	/A	PD	TPI
1992	NY-N	0	1	.000	3	1	0	0	0	4²	12	1	1	6	25.1	13.50	26	.444	.464	0	—	0	-5	-5	-0	-0.9

● **OLLIE VOIGT**   Voigt, Olen Edward "Ode" b: 1/29/1900, Wheaton, Ill. d: 4/7/70, Scottsdale, Ariz. BL/TR, 6'1", 170 lbs. Deb: 4/19/24

YEAR	TM/L	W	L	PCT	G	GS	CG	SH	SV	IP	H	HR	BB	SO	RAT	ERA	ERA+	OAV	OOB	BH	AVG	PB	PR	/A	PD	TPI
1924	StL-A	1	0	1.000	8	1	0	0	0	16¹	21	1	13	4	18.7	5.51	82	.356	.472	1	.250	0	-2	-2	1	0.1

● **BILL VOISELLE**   Voiselle, William Symmes "Big Bill" or "Ninety-Six" b: 1/29/19, Greenwood, S.C. BR/TR, 6'4", 200 lbs. Deb: 9/1/42

YEAR	TM/L	W	L	PCT	G	GS	CG	SH	SV	IP	H	HR	BB	SO	RAT	ERA	ERA+	OAV	OOB	BH	AVG	PB	PR	/A	PD	TPI
1942	NY-N	0	0	—	2	1	0	0	0	9	6	1	4	5	10.0	2.00	168	.176	.263	0	.000	0	1	1	0	0.2
1943	NY-N	1	2	.333	4	4	3	0	0	31	18	1	14	19	9.3	2.03	170	.154	.244	1	.111	-1	5	5	-1	0.3
1944	NY-N☆	21	16	.568	43	41	25	1	0	312²	276	31	118	**161**	11.5	3.02	121	.232	.303	22	.210	3	20	22	-3	2.5
1945	NY-N	14	14	.500	41	35	14	4	0	232²	249	16	97	115	13.6	4.49	87	.273	.345	10	.127	-3	-18	-15	-0	-1.9
1946	NY-N	9	15	.375	36	25	10	2	0	178	171	14	85	89	12.9	3.74	92	.248	.330	9	.164	-1	-7	-6	-0	-0.9
1947	NY-N	4	4	.200	11	5	1	0	0	42²	44	7	22	20	14.1	4.64	88	.284	.376	2	.133	-1	-3	-3	-0	-0.4
	Bos-N	8	7	.533	22	20	7	0	0	131¹	146	10	51	59	13.6	4.32	90	.280	.345	9	.170	-1	-4	-6	1	-1.0
	Yr	9	11	.450	33	25	8	0	0	174	190	14	73	79	13.7	4.40	90	.280	.351	11	.162	-1	-7	-9	1	-1.0
1948	*Bos-N	13	13	.500	37	30	9	2	2	215²	226	18	90	89	13.3	3.63	106	.272	.345	7	.097	-4	8	5	-3	-0.1
1949	Bos-N	8	7	.467	30	22	5	4	0	169¹	170	14	78	63	13.2	4.04	94	.263	.343	7	.115	-2	-0	-5	1	-0.5
1950	Chi-N	0	4	.000	19	7	0	0	0	51¹	64	9	29	25	16.5	5.79	73	.303	.390	1	.077	-1	-9	-9	-1	-0.8
Total	9	74	84	.468	245	190	74	13	3	1373¹	1370	115	588	645	12.9	3.83	98	.258	.334	68	.147	-10	-6	-10	-6	-2.2

● **JAKE VOLZ**   Volz, Jacob Phillip "Silent Jake" b: 4/4/1878, San Antonio, Tex. d: 8/11/62, San Antonio, Tex. BR/TR, 5'10", 175 lbs. Deb: 9/28/01

YEAR	TM/L	W	L	PCT	G	GS	CG	SH	SV	IP	H	HR	BB	SO	RAT	ERA	ERA+	OAV	OOB	BH	AVG	PB	PR	/A	PD	TPI
1901	Bos-A	1	0	1.000	1	1	1	0	0	7	6	2	9	5	19.3	9.00	39	.231	.429	0	.000	-0	-4	-4	-1	-0.5
1905	Bos-N	0	2	.000	3	2	0	0	0	8²	12	0	8	11	21.8	10.38	30	.364	.500	0	.000	-0	-7	-7	-1	-1.3

YEAR TM/L	W	L	PCT	G	GS	CG	SH	SV	IP	H	HR	BB	SO	RAT	ERA	ERA+	OAV	OOB	BH	AVG	PB	PR	/A	PD	TPI
1908 Cin-N	1	2	.333	7	4	1	0	0	22²	16	1	12	6	11.9	3.57	65	.195	.313	1	.250	0	-3	-3	-1	-0.5
Total 3	2	4	.333	11	7	2	0	0	38¹	34	1	29	12	15.5	6.10	44	.241	.382	1	.100	-1	-14	-14	-2	-2.3

● **TONY Von FRICKEN** — Von Fricken, Anthony b: 5/30/1870, Brooklyn, N.Y. d: 3/22/47, Troy, N.Y. BB/TR, 5'11.5", 160 lbs. Deb: 5/9/1890

YEAR TM/L	W	L	PCT	G	GS	CG	SH	SV	IP	H	HR	BB	SO	RAT	ERA	ERA+	OAV	OOB	BH	AVG	PB	PR	/A	PD	TPI
1890 Bos-N	0	1	.000	1	1	0	0	0	8	23	0	8	2	34.9	10.13	37	.489	.564	0	.000	-1	-6	-6	-0	-0.5

● **BRUCE Von HOFF** — Von Hoff, Bruce Frederick b: 11/17/43, Oakland, Cal. BR/TR, 6', 187 lbs. Deb: 9/28/65

YEAR TM/L	W	L	PCT	G	GS	CG	SH	SV	IP	H	HR	BB	SO	RAT	ERA	ERA+	OAV	OOB	BH	AVG	PB	PR	/A	PD	TPI
1965 Hou-N	0	0	—	3	0	0	0	0	3	3	0	2	1	15.0	9.00	37	.250	.357	0	—	0	-2	-2	-0	0.0
1967 Hou-N	0	3	.000	10	10	0	0	0	50¹	52	3	28	22	14.3	4.83	69	.268	.360	1	.067	-1	-8	-8	-1	-0.6
Total 2	0	3	.000	13	10	0	0	0	53¹	55	3	30	23	14.3	5.06	65	.267	.360	1	.067	-1	-10	-10	-1	-0.6

● **DAVE Von OHLEN** — Von Ohlen, David b: 10/25/58, Flushing, N.Y. BL/TL, 6'2", 200 lbs. Deb: 5/13/83

YEAR TM/L	W	L	PCT	G	GS	CG	SH	SV	IP	H	HR	BB	SO	RAT	ERA	ERA+	OAV	OOB	BH	AVG	PB	PR	/A	PD	TPI
1983 StL-N	3	2	.600	46	0	0	0	2	68¹	71	3	25	21	13.0	3.29	110	.280	.351	1	.143	0	2	3	-0	0.2
1984 StL-N	1	0	1.000	27	0	0	0	0	34²	39	0	8	19	12.2	3.12	111	.300	.341	1	1.000	0	2	1	1	0.2
1985 Cle-A	3	2	.600	26	0	0	0	0	43¹	47	3	20	12	13.9	2.91	142	.288	.366	0	—	0	6	6	1	0.7
1986 Oak-A	0	3	.000	24	0	0	0	1	15¹	18	0	7	4	14.7	3.52	110	.300	.373	0	—	0	1	1	0	0.2
1987 Oak-A	0	0	—	4	0	0	0	0	6	10	1	1	3	16.5	7.50	55	.400	.423	0	—	0	-2	-2	-0	-0.1
Total 5	7	7	.500	127	0	0	0	4	167²	185	7	61	59	13.4	3.33	113	.293	.358	2	.250	1	9	8	1	1.3

● **CY VORHEES** — Vorhees, Henry Bert b: 9/30/1874, Lodi, Ohio d: 2/8/10, Perry, Ohio 6'3", 200 lbs. Deb: 4/17/02

YEAR TM/L	W	L	PCT	G	GS	CG	SH	SV	IP	H	HR	BB	SO	RAT	ERA	ERA+	OAV	OOB	BH	AVG	PB	PR	/A	PD	TPI
1902 Phi-N	3	3	.500	10	5	3	1	0	53²	63	1	20	24	14.1	3.86	73	.292	.354	7	.350	2	-6	-6	-1	-0.5
Was-A	0	1	.000	1	1	1	0	0	8	10	0	2	1	13.5	4.50	82	.303	.343	2	.667	1	-1	-1	-0	-0.1
Total 1	3	4	.429	11	6	4	1	0	61²	73	1	22	25	14.0	3.94	74	.293	.353	9	.391	3	-7	-7	-1	-0.5

● **ED VOSBERG** — Vosberg, Edward John b: 9/28/61, Tucson, Ariz. BL/TL, 6'1", 190 lbs. Deb: 9/17/86

YEAR TM/L	W	L	PCT	G	GS	CG	SH	SV	IP	H	HR	BB	SO	RAT	ERA	ERA+	OAV	OOB	BH	AVG	PB	PR	/A	PD	TPI
1986 SD-N	0	1	.000	5	3	0	0	0	13²	17	1	9	8	17.1	6.59	55	.304	.400	0	.000	-0	-4	-4	-0	-0.4
1990 SF-N	1	1	.500	18	0	0	0	0	24¹	21	3	12	12	12.2	5.55	66	.233	.324	0	—	-0	-5	-5	-0	-0.4
1994 Oak-A	0	2	.000	16	0	0	0	0	13²	16	2	5	12	13.8	3.95	112	.320	.382	0	—	0	1	1	1	0.3
1995 Tex-A	5	5	.500	44	0	0	0	4	36	32	3	16	36	12.0	3.00	161	.241	.322	0	—	0	7	7	-1	1.8
1996 *Tex-A	1	1	.500	52	0	0	0	8	44	51	4	21	32	14.7	3.27	162	.298	.375	0	—	0	8	10	1	0.8
Total 5	7	10	.412	135	3	0	0	12	131²	137	13	63	100	13.7	4.03	114	.274	.355	0	.000	0	7	8	1	2.1

● **ALEX VOSS** — Voss, Alexander b: 5/16/1858, Roswell, Ga. d: 8/31/06, Cincinnati, Ohio BR/TR, 6'1", 180 lbs. Deb: 4/17/1884 ◆

YEAR TM/L	W	L	PCT	G	GS	CG	SH	SV	IP	H	HR	BB	SO	RAT	ERA	ERA+	OAV	OOB	BH	AVG	PB	PR	/A	PD	TPI
1884 Was-U	5	14	.263	27	20	18	0	0	186¹	206	2	32	112	11.5	3.57	67	.262	.291	47	.192	-9	-23	-24	3	-2.2
KC-U	0	6	.000	7	6	6	0	0	53	74	2	7	17	13.8	4.25	53	.310	.329	4	.089	-4	-11	-12	1	-1.3
Yr	5	20	.200	34	26	24	0	0	239¹	280	4	39	129	12.0	3.72	63	.273	.300	51	.176	-13	-34	-36	3	-3.5

● **RIP VOWINKEL** — Vowinkel, John Henry b: 11/18/1884, Oswego, N.Y. d: 7/13/66, Oswego, N.Y. BR/TR, 5'10", 195 lbs. Deb: 9/5/05

YEAR TM/L	W	L	PCT	G	GS	CG	SH	SV	IP	H	HR	BB	SO	RAT	ERA	ERA+	OAV	OOB	BH	AVG	PB	PR	/A	PD	TPI
1905 Cin-N	3	3	.500	6	6	4	0	0	45¹	52	2	10	7	12.5	4.17	79	.302	.344	1	.071	-0	-6	-6	-1	-0.7

● **PETE VUCKOVICH** — Vuckovich, Peter Dennis b: 10/27/52, Johnstown, Pa. BR/TR, 6'4", 220 lbs. Deb: 8/3/75

YEAR TM/L	W	L	PCT	G	GS	CG	SH	SV	IP	H	HR	BB	SO	RAT	ERA	ERA+	OAV	OOB	BH	AVG	PB	PR	/A	PD	TPI
1975 Chi-A	0	1	.000	4	0	0	0	0	10¹	17	0	7	7	20.9	13.06	30	.386	.471	0	—	0	-11	-11	0	-0.9
1976 Chi-A	7	4	.636	33	7	1	0	0	110¹	122	3	60	62	15.2	4.65	77	.287	.380	0	—	0	-14	-13	0	-1.3
1977 Tor-A	7	7	.500	53	8	3	1	8	148	143	13	59	123	12.6	3.47	121	.257	.333	0	—	0	10	12	1	1.2
1978 StL-N	12	12	.500	45	23	6	2	1	198¹	187	9	59	149	11.3	2.54	138	.253	.310	8	.138	-1	23	21	2	2.6
1979 StL-N	15	10	.600	34	32	9	0	0	233	229	22	64	145	11.4	3.59	105	.260	.312	12	.152	-2	4	4	-1	0.1
1980 StL-N	12	9	.571	32	30	7	3	1	222¹	203	18	68	132	11.1	3.40	109	.247	.306	13	.183	1	5	7	-1	0.8
1981 *Mil-A	**14**	4	**.778**	24	23	2	1	0	149²	137	9	57	84	11.9	3.55	96	.249	.324	0	—	0	2	-2	1	-0.2
1982 *Mil-A	18	6	**.750**	30	30	9	1	0	223²	234	14	102	105	13.7	3.34	113	.275	.356	0	—	0	18	11	1	1.2
1983 Mil-A	0	2	.000	3	3	0	0	0	14²	15	0	10	10	16.0	4.91	76	.259	.377	0	—	0	-1	-2	-0	-0.2
1985 Mil-A	6	10	.375	22	22	1	0	0	112²	134	16	48	55	15.1	5.51	76	.298	.374	0	—	0	-17	-17	-1	-2.1
1986 Mil-A	2	4	.333	6	6	0	0	0	35¹	35	3	11	12	12.8	3.06	141	.273	.343	0	—	0	4	5	0	0.2
Total 11	93	69	.574	286	186	38	8	10	1455¹	1454	107	545	882	12.6	3.66	103	.264	.334	33	.159	-2	22	16	2	2.2

● **PAUL WACHTEL** — Wachtel, Paul Horine b: 4/30/1888, Myersville, Md. d: 12/15/64, San Antonio, Tex. BR/TR, 5'11", 175 lbs. Deb: 9/18/17

YEAR TM/L	W	L	PCT	G	GS	CG	SH	SV	IP	H	HR	BB	SO	RAT	ERA	ERA+	OAV	OOB	BH	AVG	PB	PR	/A	PD	TPI
1917 Bro-N	0	0	—	2	0	0	0	0	6	9	0	4	3	19.5	10.50	27	.375	.464	1	.333	—	-5	-5	-0	0.0

● **CHARLIE WACKER** — Wacker, Charles James b: 12/8/1883, Jeffersonville, Ind d: 8/7/48, Evansville, Ind. BL/TL, 5'9", Deb: 4/28/09

YEAR TM/L	W	L	PCT	G	GS	CG	SH	SV	IP	H	HR	BB	SO	RAT	ERA	ERA+	OAV	OOB	BH	AVG	PB	PR	/A	PD	TPI
1909 Pit-N	0	0	—	1	0	0	0	0	2	2	0	1	0	13.5	0.00	—	.400	.500	0	—	0	1	1	0	0.0

● **RUBE WADDELL** — Waddell, George Edward b: 10/13/1876, Bradford, Pa. d: 4/1/14, San Antonio, Tex. BR/TL, 6'1.5", 196 lbs. Deb: 9/8/1897 H

YEAR TM/L	W	L	PCT	G	GS	CG	SH	SV	IP	H	HR	BB	SO	RAT	ERA	ERA+	OAV	OOB	BH	AVG	PB	PR	/A	PD	TPI
1897 Lou-N	0	1	.000	2	1	1	0	0	14	17	1	6	5	15.4	3.21	133	.298	.375	0	.000	-1	2	2	0	0.0
1899 Lou-N	7	2	.778	10	9	9	1	1	79	69	4	14	44	10.4	3.08	125	.235	.288	8	.235	-0	7	7	-1	0.6
1900 *Pit-N	8	13	.381	29	22	16	2	0	208²	176	3	55	130	10.5	**2.37**	**153**	**.229**	.291	14	.173	-2	31	29	1	2.4
1901 Pit-N	0	2	.000	2	2	0	0	0	7²	10	0	2	4	23.5	9.39	35	.313	.476	0	.000	-0	-5	-5	0	-0.9
Chi-N	14	14	.500	29	28	26	0	0	243²	239	5	66	168	11.6	2.81	115	.255	.310	25	.255	6	14	12	3	2.2
Yr	14	16	.467	31	30	26	0	0	251²	249	5	75	172	11.9	3.01	108	.256	.316	25	.248	6	9	6	4	1.3
1902 Phi-A	24	7	.774	33	27	26	3	0	276¹	224	7	64	**210**	9.7	2.05	179	.222	.276	32	.286	7	47	50	-0	**5.9**
1903 Phi-A	21	16	.568	39	38	**34**	4	0	324	274	3	85	**302**	10.2	2.44	125	.229	.284	14	.122	-6	19	22	-0	1.7
1904 Phi-A	25	19	.568	46	46	39	8	0	383	307	5	91	**349**	9.7	1.62	**165**	.221	.275	17	.122	-7	**42**	45	2	4.9
1905 Phi-A	**27**	10	**.730**	**46**	34	27	7	0	328²	231	5	90	**287**	9.1	**1.48**	**180**	**.200**	.263	20	.172	-1	**43**	43	-0	4.9
1906 Phi-A	15	17	.469	43	34	22	8	0	272²	221	1	92	**196**	10.7	2.21	123	.225	.297	14	.163	-0	15	16	-2	0.8
1907 Phi-A	19	13	.594	44	33	20	7	0	284²	234	2	73	**232**	10.2	2.15	121	.227	.287	12	.119	-5	12	14	-2	0.8
1908 StL-A	19	14	.576	43	36	25	5	3	285²	223	4	90	232	10.1	1.89	127	.213	.281	10	.110	-1	16	16	-1	1.7
1909 StL-A	11	14	.440	31	28	16	5	0	220¹	204	1	57	141	10.2	2.37	102	.247	.323	5	.067	-5	3	1	-1	-0.6
1910 StL-A	3	1	.750	10	2	1	0	1	33	31	1	16	16	11.7	3.55	70	.242	.307	1	.111	-0	-4	-4	-1	-0.6
Total 13	193	143	.574	407	340	261	50	5	2961¹	2460	37	803	2316	10.3	2.16	135	.228	.288	172	.161	-17	240	247	-1	24.6

● **TOM WADDELL** — Waddell, Thomas David b: 9/17/58, Dundee, Scotland BR/TR, 6'1", 185 lbs. Deb: 4/15/84

YEAR TM/L	W	L	PCT	G	GS	CG	SH	SV	IP	H	HR	BB	SO	RAT	ERA	ERA+	OAV	OOB	BH	AVG	PB	PR	/A	PD	TPI
1984 Cle-A	7	4	.636	58	0	0	0	6	97	68	12	37	59	9.8	3.06	133	.202	.283	0	—	0	10	11	-1	1.1
1985 Cle-A	8	6	.571	49	9	1	0	9	112²	104	20	39	53	11.5	4.87	85	.246	.312	0	—	0	-9	-9	0	-1.1
1987 Cle-A	0	1	.000	6	0	0	0	0	5²	7	1	7	6	23.8	14.29	32	.292	.469	0	—	0	-6	-6	-0	-0.9
Total 3	15	11	.577	113	9	1	0	15	215¹	179	33	83	118	11.1	4.30	96	.229	.305	0	—	0	-5	-4	-1	-0.9

● **BEN WADE** — Wade, Benjamin Styron b: 11/26/22, Morehead City, N.C BR/TR, 6'3", 205 lbs. Deb: 4/30/48 F

YEAR TM/L	W	L	PCT	G	GS	CG	SH	SV	IP	H	HR	BB	SO	RAT	ERA	ERA+	OAV	OOB	BH	AVG	PB	PR	/A	PD	TPI
1948 Chi-N	0	1	.000	2	0	0	0	0	5	4	0	4	1	14.4	7.20	54	.211	.348	0	—	-0	-2	-0	-0	-0.3
1952 Bro-N	11	9	.550	37	24	5	1	3	180	166	19	94	118	13.1	3.60	101	.246	.340	7	.117	1	3	1	-2	0.4
1953 *Bro-N	7	5	.583	32	9	2	0	3	90¹	79	15	33	65	11.6	3.79	113	.232	.308	4	.167	0	5	5	-2	0.4
1954 Bro-N	1	1	.500	23	0	0	0	0	45	62	9	21	25	16.6	8.20	50	.339	.407	0	.000	-1	-21	-21	-1	-1.2
StL-N	0	0	—	13	0	0	0	0	23	27	5	15	19	17.2	5.48	75	.303	.415	0	.000	-0	-4	-3	-0	
Yr	1	1	.500	36	0	0	0	0	68	89	14	36	44	16.8	7.28	56	.319	.401	0	.000	-1	-24	-24	-1	-1.2
1955 Pit-N	0	0	—	11	1	0	0	0	28	23	2	14	7	13.2	3.21	128	.232	.318	0	.000	-0	3	3	0	0.1
Total 5	19	17	.528	118	25	5	1	10	371¹	364	49	181	235	13.4	4.34	90	.259	.347	11	.112	0	-16	-18	-5	-1.0

● **TERRELL WADE** — Wade, Hawatha Terrell b: 1/25/73, Rembert, S.C. BL/TL, 6'3", 205 lbs. Deb: 9/12/95

YEAR TM/L	W	L	PCT	G	GS	CG	SH	SV	IP	H	HR	BB	SO	RAT	ERA	ERA+	OAV	OOB	BH	AVG	PB	PR	/A	PD	TPI
1995 Atl-N	0	1	.000	3	0	0	0	0	4	3	1	4	3	15.8	4.50	95	.214	.389	0	—	-0	-0	-0	-0	0.0
1996 *Atl-N	5	0	1.000	44	8	0	0	1	69²	57	9	47	79	13.6	2.97	148	.228	.351	2	.154	0	10	11	0	0.7
Total 2	5	1	.833	47	8	0	0	1	73²	60	10	51	82	13.7	3.05	144	.226	.353	2	.154	0	10	11	0	0.7

● **JAKE WADE** — Wade, Jacob Fields "Whistling Jake" b: 4/1/12, Morehead City, N.C. BL/TL, 6'2", 175 lbs. Deb: 4/22/36 F

YEAR TM/L	W	L	PCT	G	GS	CG	SH	SV	IP	H	HR	BB	SO	RAT	ERA	ERA+	OAV	OOB	BH	AVG	PB	PR	/A	PD	TPI
1936 Det-A	4	5	.444	13	11	4	1	0	78¹	93	7	52	30	16.8	5.29	94	.296	.398	5	.172	-2	-2	-3	1	-0.4
1937 Det-A	7	10	.412	33	25	7	1	0	165¹	160	13	107	69	14.7	5.39	87	.257	.368	11	.186	-1	-14	-13	1	-1.2
1938 Det-A	3	2	.600	27	4	0	0	0	70	73	9	48	23	15.6	6.56	76	.268	.378	1	.048	-2	-14	-12	-0	-0.9

YEAR	TM/L	W	L	PCT	G	GS	CG	SH	SV	IP	H	HR	BB	SO	RAT	ERA	ERA+	OAV	OOB	BH	AVG	PB	PR	/A	PD	TPI
1939	Bos-A	1	4	.200	20	6	1	0	0	47²	68	1	37	21	19.8	6.23	76	.358	.463	0	.000	-2	-9	-8	-0	-0.9
	StL-A	0	2	.000	4	2	1	0	0	16¹	26	1	19	9	24.8	11.02	44	.356	.489	0	.000	-1	-12	-11	0	-1.0
	Yr	1	6	.143	24	8	2	0	0	64	94	2	56	30	21.1	7.45	64	.357	.470	0	.000	-3	-20	-19	0	-1.9
1942	Chi-A	5	5	.500	15	10	3	0	0	85²	84	2	56	32	14.7	4.10	88	.255	.363	7	.241	1	-4	-5	1	-0.3
1943	Chi-A	3	7	.300	21	9	3	1	0	83²	84	3	54	41	13.3	3.01	111	.222	.349	4	.148	0	3	3	-1	0.2
1944	Chi-A	2	4	.333	19	5	1	0	2	74²	75	3	41	35	14.0	4.82	71	.261	.354	7	.292	1	-12	-12	-2	-1.0
1946	NY-A	2	1	.667	13	1	0	0	1	35¹	33	2	14	22	12.2	2.29	151	.250	.327	1	.111	-0	5	5	0	0.4
	Was-A	0	0	—	6	0	0	0	0	11¹	12	1	12	9	19.1	4.76	70	.279	.436	0	—	-0	-2	-2	0	0.0
	Yr	2	1	.667	19	1	0	0	1	46²	45	3	26	31	13.7	2.89	118	.256	.351	1	.100	-0	3	3	0	0.4
Total 8		27	40	.403	171	71	20	3	3	668¹	690	42	440	291	15.3	5.00	84	.269	.378	36	.167	-5	-60	-58	-1	-5.1

● **JACK WADSWORTH**   Wadsworth, John L. b: 12/17/1867, Wellington, Ohio d: 7/8/41, Elyria, Ohio BL/TR, 180 lbs. Deb: 5/1/1890

YEAR	TM/L	W	L	PCT	G	GS	CG	SH	SV	IP	H	HR	BB	SO	RAT	ERA	ERA+	OAV	OOB	BH	AVG	PB	PR	/A	PD	TPI
1890	Cle-N	2	16	.111	20	19	19	0	0	169²	202	6	81	26	15.3	5.20	69	.287	.365	12	.176	-3	-31	-30	-1	-2.7
1893	Bal-N	0	3	.000	3	3	0	0	0	16	37	0	8	2	25.3	11.25	42	.440	.489	3	.429	1	-12	-12	-1	-1.3
1894	Lou-N	4	18	.182	22	22	20	0	0	173	261	10	103	57	19.1	7.60	67	.344	.425	19	.257	-0	-44	-48	-0	-3.9
1895	Lou-N	0	1	.000	2	0	0	0	0	9	24	0	7	2	31.0	16.00	29	.480	.544	1	.250	-0	-11	-11	0	-0.8
Total 4		6	38	.136	47	44	39	0	0	367²	524	16	199	87	17.9	6.85	64	.328	.406	35	.229	-2	-97	-101	-1	-8.7

● **CHARLIE WAGNER**   Wagner, Charles Thomas "Broadway" b: 12/3/12, Reading, Pa. BR/TR, 5'11", 170 lbs. Deb: 4/19/38 C

YEAR	TM/L	W	L	PCT	G	GS	CG	SH	SV	IP	H	HR	BB	SO	RAT	ERA	ERA+	OAV	OOB	BH	AVG	PB	PR	/A	PD	TPI
1938	Bos-A	1	3	.250	13	6	1	0	0	36²	47	5	24	14	17.7	8.35	59	.309	.407	2	.167	-1	-14	-14	-1	-1.3
1939	Bos-A	3	1	.750	9	5	0	0	0	38¹	49	3	14	13	14.8	4.23	112	.320	.377	1	.071	-2	2	2	-0	0.0
1940	Bos-A	1	0	1.000	12	1	0	0	0	29¹	45	5	8	13	16.3	5.52	81	.344	.381	1	.200	-0	-4	-3	-0	-0.1
1941	Bos-A	12	8	.600	29	25	12	3	0	187¹	175	14	85	51	12.5	3.07	136	.245	.326	10	.159	-1	22	23	-0	2.1
1942	Bos-A	14	11	.560	29	26	17	2	0	205¹	184	5	95	52	12.4	3.29	113	.247	.336	5	.077	-5	8	10	1	0.7
1946	Bos-A	1	0	1.000	8	4	0	0	0	30²	52	6	19	14	15.0	5.87	62	.276	.378	1	.091	-0	-8	-8	-0	-0.3
Total 6		32	23	.582	100	67	30	5	0	527²	532	38	245	157	13.4	3.91	104	.264	.346	20	.118	-9	6	10	-1	1.1

● **GARY WAGNER**   Wagner, Gary Edward b: 6/28/40, Bridgeport, Ill. BR/TR, 6'4", 191 lbs. Deb: 4/18/65

YEAR	TM/L	W	L	PCT	G	GS	CG	SH	SV	IP	H	HR	BB	SO	RAT	ERA	ERA+	OAV	OOB	BH	AVG	PB	PR	/A	PD	TPI
1965	Phi-N	7	7	.500	59	0	0	0	7	105	87	6	49	91	11.8	3.00	115	.233	.325	1	.077	-0	6	5	1	0.8
1966	Phi-N	0	1	.000	5	1	0	0	0	6¹	8	1	5	2	18.5	8.53	42	.333	.448	0	—	-0	-3	-3	-0	-0.5
1967	Phi-N	0	0	—	1	0	0	0	0	2	1	0	1	1	4.5	0.00	—	.167	.167	0	—	0	1	1	0	0.0
1968	Phi-N	4	4	.500	44	0	0	0	8	78	69	4	31	43	12.1	3.00	100	.243	.328	1	.083	-1	-0	0	1	0.0
1969	Phi-N	0	3	.000	9	2	0	0	0	19¹	31	3	7	8	17.7	7.91	45	.365	.413	0	.000	-0	-9	-9	-1	-1.4
	Bos-A	1	3	.250	6	1	0	0	0	16¹	19	1	9	13	18.2	6.06	63	.300	.440	0	.000	-0	-4	-4	-0	-0.9
1970	Bos-A	3	1	.750	38	0	0	0	7	40¹	36	5	19	20	12.7	3.35	118	.232	.324	1	.167	-0	2	3	-1	0.3
Total 6		15	19	.441	162	4	0	0	22	267¹	250	14	126	174	13.0	3.70	93	.253	.343	3	.081	-2	-9	-8	1	-1.7

● **HECTOR WAGNER**   Wagner, Hector Raul Guerrero (b: Hector Raul Guerrero (Wagner)) b: 11/26/68, San Juan, D.R. BR/TR, 6'3", 185 lbs. Deb: 9/10/90

YEAR	TM/L	W	L	PCT	G	GS	CG	SH	SV	IP	H	HR	BB	SO	RAT	ERA	ERA+	OAV	OOB	BH	AVG	PB	PR	/A	PD	TPI
1990	KC-A	0	2	.000	5	5	0	0	0	23¹	32	4	11	14	16.6	8.10	47	.323	.391	0	—	0	-11	-11	-0	-0.7
1991	KC-A	1	1	.500	2	2	0	0	0	10	16	2	3	5	17.1	7.20	57	.348	.388	0	—	0	-3	-3	-0	-0.6
Total 2		1	3	.250	7	7	0	0	0	33¹	48	6	14	19	16.7	7.83	50	.331	.390	0	—	0	-14	-14	0	-1.3

● **HONUS WAGNER**   Wagner, John Peter "The Flying Dutchman" b: 2/24/1874, Chartiers, Pa. d: 12/6/55, Carnegie, Pa. BR/TR, 5'11", 200 lbs. Deb: 7/19/1897 FMCH♦

YEAR	TM/L	W	L	PCT	G	GS	CG	SH	SV	IP	H	HR	BB	SO	RAT	ERA	ERA+	OAV	OOB	BH	AVG	PB	PR	/A	PD	TPI
1900	*Pit-N	0	0	—	1	0	0	0	0	3	3	0	4	1	21.0	0.00	—	.250	.438	201	.381	1	1	1	-0	0.0
1902	Pit-N	0	0	—	1	0	0	0	0	5¹	4	0	2	5	10.1	0.00	—	.211	.286	176	.330	1	2	2	-0	0.0
Total 2		0	0	—	2	0	0	0	0	8¹	7	0	6	6	14.0	0.00	—	.226	.351	3415	.327	1	3	3	-0	0.0

● **MARK WAGNER**   Wagner, Mark Duane b: 3/4/54, Conneaut, Ohio BR/TR, 6'1", 175 lbs. Deb: 8/20/76 ♦

YEAR	TM/L	W	L	PCT	G	GS	CG	SH	SV	IP	H	HR	BB	SO	RAT	ERA	ERA+	OAV	OOB	BH	AVG	PB	PR	/A	PD	TPI
1984	Oak-A	0	0	—	1	0	0	0	0	1²	2	0	1	1	16.2	0.00	—	.400	.500	20	.230	-0	1	1	-0	0.0

● **MATT WAGNER**   Wagner, Matthew William b: 4/4/72, Cedar Falls, Ia. BR/TR, 6'5", 215 lbs. Deb: 6/5/96

YEAR	TM/L	W	L	PCT	G	GS	CG	SH	SV	IP	H	HR	BB	SO	RAT	ERA	ERA+	OAV	OOB	BH	AVG	PB	PR	/A	PD	TPI
1996	Sea-A	3	5	.375	15	14	1	0	0	80	91	13	41	58	14.8	6.79	71	.285	.367	0	—	0	-18	-18	-1	-1.5

● **PAUL WAGNER**   Wagner, Paul Alan b: 11/14/67, Milwaukee, Wis. BR/TR, 6'3", 205 lbs. Deb: 7/26/92

YEAR	TM/L	W	L	PCT	G	GS	CG	SH	SV	IP	H	HR	BB	SO	RAT	ERA	ERA+	OAV	OOB	BH	AVG	PB	PR	/A	PD	TPI
1992	Pit-N	2	0	1.000	6	1	0	0	0	13	9	0	5	5	9.7	0.69	497	.191	.269	1	.333	0	4	4	0	0.7
1993	Pit-N	8	8	.500	44	17	1	1	2	141¹	143	15	42	114	11.8	4.27	95	.263	.317	8	.190	0	-4	-3	-1	-0.4
1994	Pit-N	7	8	.467	29	17	1	0	0	119²	136	7	50	86	14.6	4.59	94	.293	.372	6	.162	-0	-5	-4	2	-0.2
1995	Pit-N	5	16	.238	33	25	3	1	1	165	174	18	72	120	13.8	4.80	90	.273	.353	9	.214	2	-11	-9	1	-0.8
1996	Pit-N	4	8	.333	16	15	1	0	0	81²	86	10	39	81	14.1	5.40	81	.275	.361	1	.040	-2	-11	-9	1	-1.2
Total 5		26	40	.394	128	75	6	2	3	520²	548	50	208	406	13.4	4.60	92	.273	.347	25	.168	0	-27	-22	3	-1.9

● **BILLY WAGNER**   Wagner, William Edward b: 7/25/71, Tannersville, Va. BL/TL, 5'10", 180 lbs. Deb: 9/13/95

YEAR	TM/L	W	L	PCT	G	GS	CG	SH	SV	IP	H	HR	BB	SO	RAT	ERA	ERA+	OAV	OOB	BH	AVG	PB	PR	/A	PD	TPI
1995	Hou-N	0	0	—	1	0	0	0	0	0¹	0	0	0	0	0.0	0.00	—	.000	—	0	—	0	0	0	0	0.0
1996	Hou-N	2	2	.500	37	0	0	0	9	51²	28	6	30	67	10.6	2.44	157	.165	.300	0	.000	-1	10	8	-1	0.7
Total 2		2	2	.500	38	0	0	0	9	52	28	6	30	67	10.6	2.42	158	.164	.299	0	.000	-1	10	8	-1	0.7

● **BULL WAGNER**   Wagner, William George b: 12/25/1887, Lilley, Mich. d: 10/2/67, Muskegon, Mich. BR/TR, 6'0.5", 225 lbs. Deb: 6/2/13

YEAR	TM/L	W	L	PCT	G	GS	CG	SH	SV	IP	H	HR	BB	SO	RAT	ERA	ERA+	OAV	OOB	BH	AVG	PB	PR	/A	PD	TPI
1913	Bro-N	4	2	.667	18	1	0	0	0	70²	75	5	30	11	14.0	5.48	60	.285	.363	6	.231	-1	-18	-17	-2	-1.4
1914	Bro-N	0	1	.000	6	0	0	0	0	12¹	14	0	12	4	19.7	6.57	44	.311	.466	0	.000	-0	-5	-5	-0	-0.4
Total 2		4	3	.571	24	1	0	0	0	83	91	5	42	15	14.9	5.64	57	.289	.380	6	.222	0	-23	-22	-2	-1.8

● **DAVE WAINHOUSE**   Wainhouse, David Paul b: 11/7/67, Toronto, Ont., Can. BL/TR, 6'2", 190 lbs. Deb: 8/3/91

YEAR	TM/L	W	L	PCT	G	GS	CG	SH	SV	IP	H	HR	BB	SO	RAT	ERA	ERA+	OAV	OOB	BH	AVG	PB	PR	/A	PD	TPI
1991	Mon-N	0	1	.000	2	0	0	0	0	2²	2	0	4	1	20.3	6.75	54	.222	.462	0	—	0	-1	-1	-0	-0.3
1993	Sea-A	0	0	—	3	0	0	0	0	2¹	7	1	5	2	50.1	27.00	16	.500	.650	0	—	0	-6	-6	-0	0.0
1996	Pit-N	1	0	1.000	17	0	0	0	0	23²	22	3	10	16	12.2	5.70	77	.250	.327	0	.000	-0	-4	-3	-1	-0.1
Total 3		1	1	.500	22	0	0	0	0	28²	31	4	19	19	16.0	7.53	57	.279	.389	0	.000	-0	-11	-10	-1	-0.4

● **RICK WAITS**   Waits, Michael Richard b: 5/15/52, Atlanta, Ga. BL/TL, 6'3", 195 lbs. Deb: 9/17/73

YEAR	TM/L	W	L	PCT	G	GS	CG	SH	SV	IP	H	HR	BB	SO	RAT	ERA	ERA+	OAV	OOB	BH	AVG	PB	PR	/A	PD	TPI
1973	Tex-A	0	0	—	1	0	0	0	1	1	1	0	1	0	18.0	9.00	41	.333	.500	0	—	0	-1	-1	0	-0.1
1975	Cle-A	6	2	.750	16	7	3	0	1	70¹	57	3	25	34	10.6	2.94	128	.221	.292	0	—	0	7	7	0	0.8
1976	Cle-A	7	9	.438	26	22	4	2	0	123²	143	7	54	65	14.3	4.00	87	.297	.368	0	—	0	-7	-7	1	-0.9
1977	Cle-A	9	7	.563	37	16	1	0	2	135¹	132	8	64	62	13.1	3.99	99	.262	.347	0	—	0	-1	-0	-0	-0.1
1978	Cle-A	13	15	.464	34	33	15	2	0	230¹	206	16	86	97	11.5	3.20	117	.240	.310	0	—	0	14	14	3	2.0
1979	Cle-A	16	13	.552	34	34	8	3	0	231	230	26	91	91	12.7	4.44	96	.264	.336	0	—	0	-6	-5	2	-0.4
1980	Cle-A	13	14	.481	33	33	9	2	0	224¹	231	18	82	109	12.6	4.45	91	.270	.335	0	—	0	-10	-10	-1	-1.1
1981	Cle-A	8	10	.444	22	21	5	1	0	126¹	173	7	44	51	15.5	4.92	74	.330	.383	0	—	0	-18	-18	2	-2.1
1982	Cle-A	2	13	.133	25	21	2	0	0	115	128	13	57	44	14.6	5.40	76	.290	.372	0	—	0	-17	-17	1	-1.8
1983	Cle-A	0	1	.000	8	0	0	0	0	19²	23	1	9	13	14.6	4.58	93	.307	.381	0	—	0	-1	-0	0	0.0
	Mil-A	0	2	.000	10	2	0	0	0	30	39	1	11	20	15.0	5.10	73	.320	.376	0	—	0	-3	-5	-0	-0.3
	Yr	0	3	.000	18	2	0	0	0	49²	62	2	20	33	14.9	4.89	80	.308	.371	0	—	0	-5	-5	-0	-0.3
1984	Mil-A	2	4	.333	47	1	0	0	0	73	84	7	24	49	13.3	3.58	108	.297	.352	0	—	0	3	2	0	0.3
1985	Mil-A	3	2	.600	24	0	0	0	0	47	67	3	20	24	16.7	6.51	64	.340	.401	0	.000	0	-12	-12	0	-1.2
Total 12		79	92	.462	317	190	47	10	8	1427	1514	110	568	659	13.2	4.25	92	.277	.346	0	.000	0	-50	-53	8	-4.9

● **TIM WAKEFIELD**   Wakefield, Timothy Stephen b: 8/2/66, Melbourne, Fla. BR/TR, 6'2", 195 lbs. Deb: 7/31/92

YEAR	TM/L	W	L	PCT	G	GS	CG	SH	SV	IP	H	HR	BB	SO	RAT	ERA	ERA+	OAV	OOB	BH	AVG	PB	PR	/A	PD	TPI
1992	*Pit-N	8	1	.889	13	13	4	1	0	92	76	3	35	51	11.0	2.15	160	.232	.309	2	.071	-1	14	13	1	1.3
1993	Pit-N	6	11	.353	24	20	3	2	0	128¹	145	14	75	59	16.1	5.61	72	.291	.393	7	.163	1	-22	-22	-1	-2.5
1995	*Bos-A	16	8	.667	27	27	6	1	0	195¹	163	22	68	119	11.1	2.95	165	.227	.302	0	—	0	38	42	-1	4.5
1996	Bos-A	14	13	.519	32	32	6	0	0	211²	238	38	90	140	14.5	5.14	100	.280	.357	0	—	0	-4	-0	-2	-0.2
Total 4		44	33	.571	96	92	19	4	0	627¹	622	77	268	369	13.2	4.12	111	.260	.342	9	.127	-0	26	32	-4	3.1

YEAR TM/L	W	L	PCT	G	GS	CG	SH	SV	IP	H	HR	BB	SO	RAT	ERA	ERA+	OAV	OOB	BH	AVG	PB	PR	/A	PD	TPI
● **BILL WAKEFIELD** Wakefield, William Sumner b: 5/24/41, Kansas City, Mo. BR/TR, 6', 175 lbs. Deb: 4/18/64																									
1964 NY-N	3	5	.375	62	4	0	0	2	119²	103	10	61	61	13.0	3.61	99	.235	.341	4	.167	-0	-1	-0	0	0.0
● **RUBE WALBERG** Walberg, George Elvin b: 7/27/1896, Pine City, Minn. d: 10/27/78, Tempe, Ariz. BL/TR, 6'1.5", 190 lbs. Deb: 4/29/23																									
1923 NY-N	0	0	—	2	0	0	0	0	5	4	0	1	1	9.0	1.80	212	.211	.250	0	.000	-0	1	1	-0	0.0
Phi-A	4	8	.333	26	10	4	0	0	115	122	10	60	38	14.4	5.32	77	.280	.369	13	.317	3	-17	-16	1	-1.1
1924 Phi-A	0	0	—	6	2	0	0	0	7	10	0	10	3	25.7	12.86	33	.345	.513	1	.500	0	-7	-7	0	0.0
1925 Phi-A	8	14	.364	53	20	7	0	7	191²	197	11	77	82	13.0	3.99	117	.269	.340	10	.156	-4	9	14	1	1.2
1926 Phi-A	12	10	.545	40	19	5	2	2	151	168	4	60	72	13.9	2.80	149	.292	.365	7	.152	-2	20	23	-1	2.8
1927 Phi-A	16	12	.571	46	34	15	0	4	249¹	257	18	91	136	12.7	3.93	108	.271	.337	18	.207	3	6	9	-0	1.2
1928 Phi-A	17	12	.586	38	30	15	3	1	235²	236	19	64	112	11.6	3.55	113	.265	.317	18	.209	1	13	12	1	1.5
1929 *Phi-A	18	11	.621	40	33	20	3	4	267²	256	22	99	94	11.9	3.60	118	.254	.320	23	.223	-0	19	19	-2	1.6
1930 *Phi-A	13	12	.520	38	30	12	2	1	205¹	207	6	85	100	12.9	4.69	100	.262	.335	12	.164	-3	-1	-0	-1	-0.4
1931 *Phi-A	20	12	.625	44	35	19	1	3	**291**	298	16	109	106	12.6	3.74	120	.266	.331	13	.124	-6	21	24	-1	1.6
1932 Phi-A	17	10	.630	41	34	19	3	1	272	305	16	103	96	13.5	4.73	96	.282	.344	16	.170	-3	-8	-0	-1	-0.7
1933 Phi-A	9	13	.409	40	20	10	1	4	201	224	12	95	68	14.3	4.88	88	.278	.354	9	.132	-1	-13	-13	1	-1.4
1934 Bos-A	6	7	.462	30	10	2	0	1	104³	118	5	41	38	13.8	4.04	119	.284	.350	6	.188	-1	5	9	1	1.0
1935 Bos-A	5	9	.357	44	10	4	0	3	142³	152	10	54	44	13.1	3.91	121	.273	.340	6	.162	-2	9	13	-1	0.9
1936 Bos-A	5	4	.556	24	9	5	0	0	100¹	98	7	36	49	12.1	4.40	121	.257	.323	5	.156	-1	7	10	1	0.7
1937 Bos-A	5	7	.417	32	11	3	0	1	104²	117	4	47	46	16.5	5.59	85	.332	.400	5	.147	-1	-11	-10	-0	-1.1
Total 15	155	141	.524	544	307	140	15	32	2644	2795	163	1031	1085	13.1	4.16	107	.273	.341	162	.179	-18	53	82	-2	7.7
● **DOC WALDBAUER** Waldbauer, Albert Charles b: 2/22/1892, Richmond, Va. d: 7/16/69, Yakima, Wash. BR/TR, 6', 172 lbs. Deb: 9/24/17																									
1917 Was-A	0	0	—	2	0	0	0	1	5	10	0	2	2	21.6	7.20	36	.476	.522	0	.000	-0	-3	-3	0	-0.1
● **BOB WALK** Walk, Robert Vernon b: 11/26/56, Van Nuys, Cal. BR/TR, 6'4", 208 lbs. Deb: 5/26/80																									
1980 *Phi-N	11	7	.611	27	27	2	0	0	151²	163	8	71	94	14.0	4.57	83	.276	.356	7	.140	-0	-16	-13	-1	-1.5
1981 Atl-N	1	4	.200	12	8	0	0	0	43¹	41	6	23	16	13.3	4.57	78	.250	.342	1	.143	-0	-5	-5	-1	-0.6
1982 *Atl-N	11	9	.550	32	27	3	1	0	164³	179	19	59	84	13.4	4.87	75	.280	.347	10	.196	-2	-23	-21	-2	-2.4
1983 Atl-N	0	0	—	1	1	0	0	0	3²	7	0	2	4	22.1	7.36	53	.412	.474	0	.000	-0	-2	-1	0	0.0
1984 Pit-N	1	1	.500	2	2	0	0	0	10¹	8	1	4	10	10.5	2.61	138	.200	.273	0	.000	-0	1	1	-0	0.1
1985 Pit-N	2	3	.400	9	9	1	1	0	58²	60	3	18	40	12.0	3.68	97	.265	.320	0	.000	-1	-1	-1	-1	-0.3
1986 Pit-N	7	8	.467	44	15	1	1	2	141²	129	14	64	78	12.5	3.75	102	.251	.337	6	.154	0	-0	1	2	0.3
1987 Pit-N	8	2	.800	39	12	1	1	0	117	107	11	51	78	12.4	3.31	124	.245	.329	6	.231	1	10	10	1	1.0
1988 Pit-N★	12	10	.545	32	32	1	1	0	212²	183	6	65	81	10.6	2.71	126	.230	.290	-2	.087	-2	17	16	0	1.5
1989 Pit-N	13	10	.565	33	31	2	0	0	196	208	13	65	83	12.7	4.41	76	.271	.331	13	.186	-3	-20	-23	-1	-2.2
1990 *Pit-N	7	5	.583	26	24	1	1	1	129²	136	17	36	73	12.2	3.75	97	.270	.324	6	.162	1	-2	-1	-0	-0.2
1991 *Pit-N	9	2	.818	25	20	0	0	0	115	104	10	35	67	11.3	3.60	99	.240	.304	8	.205	2	1	-0	-0	0.2
1992 *Pit-N	10	6	.625	36	19	1	0	0	135	132	16	43	60	12.1	3.20	108	.258	.323	4	.093	-2	5	4	1	0.4
1993 Pit-N	13	14	.481	32	32	3	0	0	187	214	23	70	80	13.9	5.68	71	.294	.360	7	.121	-2	-34	-34	-1	-4.3
Total 14	105	81	.565	350	259	16	6	5	1666	1671	143	606	848	12.5	4.03	91	.263	.330	74	.145	-66	-67	-1	-8.0	
● **ED WALKER** Walker, Edward Harrison b: 8/11/1874, Cambois, England d: 9/29/47, Akron, Ohio BL/TL, 6'5", 242 lbs. Deb: 9/26/02																									
1902 Cle-A	0	1	.000	1	1	1	0	0	8	11	0	3	1	15.8	3.38	102	.324	.378	1	.333	-0	0	0	0	0.0
1903 Cle-A	0	0	—	3	3	0	0	0	12	13	0	10	4	17.3	5.25	54	.277	.404	0	.000	-0	-3	-3	-1	-0.1
Total 2	0	1	.000	4	4	1	0	0	20	24	0	13	5	16.6	4.50	67	.296	.394	1	.167	-0	-3	-3	-1	-0.1
● **DIXIE WALKER** Walker, Ewart Gladstone b: 6/1/1887, Brownsville, Pa. d: 11/14/65, Leeds, Ala. BL/TR, 6', 192 lbs. Deb: 9/17/09 F																									
1909 Was-A	3	1	.750	4	4	3	0	0	36	31	0	6	25	9.3	2.50	97	.217	.248	2	.154	-0	-0	-0	-1	-0.1
1910 Was-A	11	11	.500	29	26	16	3	0	199¹	177	2	68	84	11.4	3.30	76	.245	.317	9	.130	-3	-17	-18	-1	-2.3
1911 Was-A	8	13	.381	32	24	15	2	0	185²	205	2	50	65	12.7	3.39	97	.286	.339	20	.303	4	-1	-2	-1	-1.0
1912 Was-A	3	6	.333	9	8	5	0	0	60	72	2	18	29	14.1	5.25	64	.300	.359	2	.125	-1	-13	-13	-0	-1.5
Total 4	25	31	.446	74	62	40	5	0	481	485	6	142	203	12.1	3.52	82	.266	.326	33	.201	2	-31	-33	-3	-3.9
● **MYSTERIOUS WALKER** Walker, Frederick Mitchell b: 3/21/1884, Utica, Neb. d: 2/1/58, Oak Park, Ill. BR/TR, 5'10.5", 185 lbs. Deb: 6/28/10																									
1910 Cin-N	0	0	—	1	0	0	0	0	3	4	0	4	1	24.0	3.00	97	.333	.500	0	.000	-0	-0	-0	-0	0.0
1912 Cle-A	0	0	—	1	0	0	0	0	1	0	0	1	0	9.0	0.00	—	.000	.200	0	—	-0	0	0	-0	0.0
1913 Bro-N	1	3	.250	11	8	3	0	0	58¹	44	3	35	35	13.0	3.55	93	.233	.367	3	.167	-0	-2	-2	2	0.0
1914 Pit-F	4	16	.200	35	21	12	0	0	169¹	197	3	74	79	14.6	4.31	67	.294	.367	6	.113	-3	-27	-27	3	-2.8
1915 Bro-F	2	4	.333	13	7	2	0	1	65²	61	3	22	28	11.4	3.70	73	.242	.303	6	.222	1	-7	-7	1	-0.5
Total 5	7	23	.233	61	36	17	0	1	297¹	306	9	136	143	13.6	4.00	73	.272	.354	15	.152	-4	-36	-36	6	-3.3
● **GEORGE WALKER** Walker, George A. b: 1863, Hamilton, Ontario, Canada TR, 5'9", 184 lbs. Deb: 8/1/1888																									
1888 Bal-a	1	3	.250	4	4	4	1	0	35	36	2	14	18	12.9	5.91	50	.257	.325	1	.077	-1	-11	-11	-0	-1.1
● **LUKE WALKER** Walker, James Luke b: 9/2/43, DeKalb, Tex. BL/TL, 6'1.5", 192 lbs. Deb: 9/7/65																									
1965 Pit-N	0	0	—	2	0	0	0	0	5	2	0	1	5	5.4	0.00	—	.118	.167	0	—	0	2	2	0	0.2
1966 Pit-N	0	1	.000	10	1	0	0	0	10	8	0	15	7	21.6	4.50	79	.205	.436	0	.000	-0	-1	-1	-0	-0.1
1968 Pit-N	0	3	.000	39	1	0	0	3	61²	42	1	39	66	12.0	2.04	143	.190	.314	0	.000	-1	6	6	1	0.4
1969 Pit-N	4	6	.400	31	15	3	1	0	118²	98	5	57	96	11.9	3.64	96	.226	.319	0	.000	-3	-1	-2	1	-0.4
1970 *Pit-N	15	6	.714	42	19	5	3	3	163	129	6	89	124	12.1	3.04	128	.219	.323	6	.130	-1	18	16	-0	1.8
1971 *Pit-N	10	8	.556	28	24	4	2	0	159²	157	9	53	86	11.9	3.55	95	.262	.324	1	.022	-3	-2	-3	-2	-0.8
1972 *Pit-N	4	6	.400	26	12	2	0	2	92²	98	4	34	48	12.8	3.40	98	.274	.342	2	.083	-1	-1	-1	-0	-0.3
1973 Pit-N	7	12	.368	37	18	2	1	1	122	129	6	66	74	14.5	4.65	76	.270	.360	2	.067	-2	-13	-15	-1	-2.5
1974 Det-A	5	5	.500	28	9	0	0	0	92	100	9	54	52	15.3	4.99	76	.278	.375	0	—	0	-14	-12	0	-1.3
Total 9	45	47	.489	243	100	16	7	9	824²	763	43	408	558	12.9	3.65	94	.247	.337	11	.059	-11	-3	-11	-2	-3.2
● **ROY WALKER** Walker, James Roy "Dixie" b: 4/13/1893, Lawrenceburg, Tenn. d: 2/10/62, New Orleans, La. BR/TR, 6'1.5", 180 lbs. Deb: 9/16/12																									
1912 Cle-A	0	0	—	1	0	0	0	0	2	0	0	2	1	9.0	0.00	—	.000	.250	0	—	0	1	1	-0	0.0
1915 Cle-A	4	9	.308	25	15	4	0	1	131	122	1	65	57	13.3	3.98	77	.261	.360	5	.132	-2	-15	-14	-2	-1.8
1917 Chi-N	0	1	.000	2	1	0	0	0	7	8	0	5	4	16.7	3.86	75	.286	.394	0	.000	-0	-1	-1	-0	-0.1
1918 Chi-N	1	3	.250	13	7	2	0	1	43¹	50	1	15	20	13.7	2.70	103	.298	.359	0	.000	-1	0	0	0	-0.1
1921 StL-N	11	12	.478	38	23	11	0	3	170²	194	10	53	52	13.1	4.22	87	.293	.347	11	.204	-0	-8	-10	-1	-1.4
1922 StL-N	1	2	.333	12	2	0	0	0	32	34	1	15	14	13.8	4.78	81	.293	.374	1	.143	-2	-2	-3	-1	-0.4
Total 6	17	27	.386	91	48	17	0	5	386	408	13	155	148	13.3	3.99	85	.282	.355	17	.153	-4	-26	-26	-5	-3.8
● **JERRY WALKER** Walker, Jerry Allen b: 2/12/39, Ada, Okla. BB/TR, 6'1", 195 lbs. Deb: 7/6/57 C																									
1957 Bal-A	1	0	1.000	13	3	1	1	1	27²	24	1	14	13	12.4	2.93	123	.245	.339	0	.000	-0	3	3	0	0.0
1958 Bal-A	0	0	—	6	0	0	0	0	10¹	16	2	5	6	18.3	6.97	52	.340	.404	0	.000	-0	-4	-4	0	-0.3
1959 Bal-A★	11	10	.524	30	22	7	2	4	182	160	13	52	100	10.6	2.92	130	.240	.297	11	.169	-1	19	18	-0	1.9
1960 Bal-A	3	4	.429	29	18	1	0	5	118	107	15	56	48	12.7	3.74	102	.247	.337	14	.368	5	-2	-1	-2	0.6
1961 KC-A	8	14	.364	36	24	4	0	1	168	161	23	96	56	14.3	4.82	87	.253	.359	16	.250	3	-15	-12	-1	-1.1
1962 KC-A	9	8	.471	31	21	3	1	0	143¹	165	27	78	57	15.7	5.90	72	.288	.381	15	.263	5	-31	-27	-2	-2.2
1963 Cle-A	6	6	.500	39	2	0	0	2	88	92	15	36	41	13.3	4.91	74	.265	.338	2	.105	-0	-13	-13	-0	-1.7
1964 Cle-A	0	1	.000	6	0	0	0	0	9²	9	1	4	5	12.1	4.66	77	.257	.333	0	—	-0	-1	-1	-0	-0.1
Total 8	37	44	.457	190	90	16	4	13	747	734	97	341	326	13.3	4.36	90	.259	.343	58	.230	10	-39	-36	1	-2.7
● **MARTY WALKER** Walker, Martin Van Buren "Buddy" b: 3/27/1899, Philadelphia, Pa. d: 4/24/78, Philadelphia, Pa. BL/TL, 6', 170 lbs. Deb: 9/30/28																									
1928 Phi-N	0	1	.000	1	1	0	0	0	2	0	3	0	—	∞	—	1.000	1.000	0	—	0	-2	-2	0	-0.2	
● **MIKE WALKER** Walker, Michael Aaron b: 6/23/65, Houston, Tex. BR/TR, 6'3", 205 lbs. Deb: 6/16/92																									
1992 Sea-A	0	3	.000	5	3	0	0	0	14²	21	4	9	5	18.4	7.36	54	.333	.417	0	—	0	-6	-6	0	-0.9

YEAR	TM/L	W	L	PCT	G	GS	CG	SH	SV	IP	H	HR	BB	SO	RAT	ERA	ERA+	OAV	OOB	BH	AVG	PB	PR	/A	PD	TPI
● **MIKE WALKER**					Walker, Michael Charles b: 10/4/66, Chicago, Ill. BR/TR, 6'2", 195 lbs. Deb: 9/9/88																					
1988	Cle-A	0	1	.000	3	1	0	0	0	8²	8	0	10	7	18.7	7.27	57	.258	.439	0	—	0	-3	-3	0	-0.4
1990	Cle-A	2	6	.250	18	11	0	0	0	75²	82	6	42	34	15.5	4.88	80	.277	.378	0	—	0	-8	-8	-0	-0.8
1991	Cle-A	0	1	.000	5	0	0	0	0	4¹	6	0	2	2	18.7	2.08	200	.316	.409	0	—	0	1	1	0	0.2
1995	Chi-N	1	3	.250	42	0	0	0	1	44²	45	2	24	20	13.9	3.22	127	.259	.348	0	.000	-0	5	4	-0	0.3
1996	Det-A			—	20	0	0	0	1	27²	40	10	17	13	18.9	8.46	60	.351	.439	0	—	-0	-11	-10	-1	-0.1
Total	5	3	11	.214	88	12	0	0	2	161	181	18	95	76	15.9	5.09	82	.285	.385	0	.000	-0	-16	-16	-0	-0.8
● **PETE WALKER**					Walker, Peter Brian b: 4/8/69, Beverly, Mass. BR/TR, 6'2", 195 lbs. Deb: 6/7/95																					
1995	NY-N	1	0	1.000	13	0	0	0	0	17²	24	3	5	5	14.8	4.58	88	.329	.372	0	—	0	-1	-1	-0	-0.1
1996	SD-N	0	0	—	1	0	0	0	0	0²	0	0	3	1	40.5	0.00	—	.000	.600	0	—	0	0	0	0	0.0
Total	2	1	0	1.000	14	0	0	0	0	18¹	24	3	8	6	15.7	4.42	92	.300	.386	0	—	0	-0	-1	-0	-0.1
● **TOM WALKER**					Walker, Robert Thomas b: 11/7/48, Tampa, Fla. BR/TR, 6'1", 188 lbs. Deb: 4/23/72																					
1972	Mon-N	2	2	.500	46	0	0	0	0	74²	71	4	22	42	11.3	2.89	123	.248	.304	0	.000	-0	5	5	-0	0.3
1973	Mon-N	7	5	.583	54	0	0	0	4	91²	95	7	42	68	13.7	3.63	105	.274	.357	0	.000	-1	0	2	-0	0.2
1974	Mon-N	4	5	.444	33	8	1	0	2	91²	96	7	28	70	12.4	3.83	100	.266	.322	3	.188	-0	-2	0	-1	0.0
1975	Det-A	3	8	.273	36	9	1	0	0	115¹	116	16	40	60	12.6	4.45	90	.261	.329	0	—	0	-9	-6	-2	-0.9
1976	StL-N	1	2	.333	10	0	0	0	3	19²	22	2	3	11	11.4	4.12	86	.265	.291	2	.400	1	-1	-1	-1	-0.2
1977	Mon-N	1	1	.500	11	0	0	0	0	19	15	2	7	10	10.4	4.74	80	.221	.293	0	.000	-0	-2	-2	-0	-0.2
	Cal-A	0	0	—	1	0	0	0	0	2	3	2	0	1	13.5	9.00	43	.375	.375	0	—	-0	-1	-1	-0	-0.1
Total	6	18	23	.439	191	17	2	0	11	414	418	40	142	262	12.4	3.87	99	.262	.326	5	.152	-0	-10	-3	-3	-0.8
● **TOM WALKER**					Walker, Thomas William b: 8/1/1881, Philadelphia, Pa. d: 7/10/44, Woodbury Heights, N.J. BR/TR, 5'11", 170 lbs. Deb: 9/27/02																					
1902	Phi-A	0	1	.000	1	1	1	0	0	8	10	0	2	2	12.4	5.63	65	.303	.324	1	.250	-0	-2	-2	-1	-0.1
1904	Cin-N	15	8	.652	24	24	22	2	0	217	196	2	53	64	11.1	2.24	131	.238	.299	9	.117	-4	12	17	-2	1.0
1905	Cin-N	9	7	.563	23	19	12	1	0	144²	171	3	44	28	13.7	3.24	102	.305	.362	7	.137	-1	-4	1	-0	-0.1
Total	3	24	16	.600	48	44	35	3	0	369²	377	5	97	94	12.1	2.70	114	.266	.325	17	.129	-6	6	16	-1	0.8
● **BILL WALKER**					Walker, William Henry b: 10/7/03, E.St.Louis, Ill. d: 6/14/66, E.St.Louis, Ill. BR/TL, 6', 175 lbs. Deb: 9/13/27																					
1927	NY-N	0	0	—	3	0	0	0	0	4	6	0	5	4	24.8	9.00	43	.429	.579	0	—	0	-2	-2	-0	0.0
1928	NY-N	3	6	.333	22	8	1	0	0	76¹	79	9	31	39	13.1	4.72	83	.275	.348	2	.091	-2	-6	-7	-0	-0.9
1929	NY-N	14	7	.667	29	23	13	1	0	177²	188	11	57	65	12.6	**3.09**	148	.274	.334	7	.115	-3	32	29	-3	2.3
1930	NY-N	17	15	.531	39	34	13	2	1	245¹	258	19	88	105	12.9	3.93	121	.268	.334	16	.186	-1	29	22	-1	2.1
1931	NY-N	16	9	.640	37	28	19	**6**	3	239¹	212	6	64	121	10.5	**2.26**	164	.231	.283	5	.065	-6	**43**	38	-4	2.8
1932	NY-N	8	12	.400	31	22	9	0	2	163	177	23	55	74	13.0	4.14	90	.274	.334	7	.135	-2	-5	-8	2	-0.9
1933	StL-N	9	10	.474	29	20	6	2	0	158	168	8	67	41	13.4	3.42	102	.273	.346	7	.132	-2	-1	-1	1	0.0
1934	*StL-N	12	4	.750	24	19	10	1	0	153	160	11	66	76	13.4	3.12	136	.270	.345	6	.093	-4	16	19	-1	1.2
1935	StL-N★	13	8	.619	37	25	8	2	1	193¹	222	7	78	79	14.2	3.82	107	.288	.357	6	.102	-4	4	6	-1	0.2
1936	StL-N	5	6	.455	21	13	4	1	1	79²	106	5	27	22	15.3	5.87	67	.318	.373	7	.280	1	-16	-17	-1	-1.8
Total	10	97	77	.557	272	192	83	15	8	1489²	1576	99	538	626	12.9	3.59	114	.271	.335	62	.127	-23	93	83	-7	5.0
● **JIM WALKUP**					Walkup, James Elton b: 12/14/09, Havana, Ark. BR/TR, 6'1", 170 lbs. Deb: 9/22/34																					
1934	StL-A	0	0	—	3	0	0	0	0	8¹	6	0	5	6	11.9	2.16	231	.200	.314	1	.333	0	2	3	-0	0.0
1935	StL-A	6	9	.400	55	20	4	1	0	181¹	226	17	104	44	16.5	6.25	77	.305	.392	6	.128	-3	-36	-29	-1	-2.4
1936	StL-A	0	3	.000	5	2	0	0	0	15²	20	0	6	5	14.9	8.04	67	.308	.366	0	.000	-1	-5	-5	1	-0.7
1937	StL-A	9	12	.429	27	18	6	0	0	150¹	218	16	83	46	18.0	7.36	66	.347	.423	14	.241	-1	-46	-42	2	-4.4
1938	StL-A	1	12	.077	18	13	1	0	0	94	127	13	53	28	17.5	6.80	73	.329	.414	4	.138	-2	-21	-19	0	-2.1
1939	StL-A	0	1	.000	1	0	0	0	0	0²	2	0	1	0	40.5	0.00	—	.500	.600	0	—	0	0	0	0	0.6
	Det-A	0	1	.000	7	0	0	0	0	12	15	3	8	5	17.3	7.50	65	.319	.418	1	.500	-0	-4	-3	-0	-0.2
	Yr	0	2	.000	8	0	0	0	0	12²	17	3	9	5	18.5	7.11	69	.333	.433	1	.500	-0	-3	-3	-0	0.4
Total	6	16	38	.296	116	53	11	1	0	462¹	614	49	260	134	17.1	6.74	72	.323	.406	26	.182	-6	-110	-96	1	-9.2
● **JIM WALKUP**					Walkup, James Huey b: 11/3/1895, Havana, Ark. d: 6/12/90, Duncan, Okla. BR/TL, 5'8", 150 lbs. Deb: 4/30/27																					
1927	Det-A	0	0	—	2	0	0	0	0	1²	3	0	0	0	16.2	5.40	74	.429	.429	0	.000	-0	-0	-0	0	-0.1
● **DONNE WALL**					Wall, Donnell Lee b: 7/11/67, Potosi, Mo. BR/TR, 6'1", 180 lbs. Deb: 9/2/95																					
1995	Hou-N	3	1	.750	6	5	0	0	0	24¹	33	5	5	16	14.1	5.55	70	.320	.352	0	.000	-1	-4	-5	-0	-0.7
1996	Hou-N	9	8	.529	26	23	2	1	0	150	170	17	34	99	12.6	4.56	86	.286	.331	9	.205	2	-6	-12	-0	-1.0
Total	2	12	9	.571	32	28	2	1	0	174¹	203	22	39	115	12.9	4.70	82	.291	.334	9	.184	1	-9	-17	-0	-1.7
● **MURRAY WALL**					Wall, Murray Wesley b: 9/19/26, Dallas, Tex. d: 10/8/71, Lone Oak, Tex. BR/TR, 6'3", 185 lbs. Deb: 7/4/50																					
1950	Bos-N	0	0	—	1	0	0	0	0	4	6	0	2	2	18.0	9.00	43	.333	.400	0	—	-0	-2	-2	-0	0.0
1957	Bos-A	3	0	1.000	11	0	0	0	1	24¹	21	3	2	13	8.5	3.33	120	.233	.250	2	.333	0	1	2	1	0.4
1958	Bos-A	8	9	.471	52	1	0	0	10	114¹	109	14	33	53	11.6	3.62	111	.255	.316	3	.107	0	2	5	3	0.9
1959	Bos-A	1	4	.200	15	0	0	0	0	31²	31	5	15	8	13.1	5.40	75	.267	.351	0	.000	-1	-5	-5	1	-0.8
	Was-A	0	0	—	1	0	0	0	0	4¹	3	1	0	6	20.3	6.75	58	.600	.600	0	.000	-0	-0	-0	-0	-0.0
	Bos-A	1	1	.500	11	0	0	0	0	17¹	26	2	11	6	19.7	5.71	71	.371	.463	0	.000	-0	-4	-3	-0	-0.4
	Yr	2	5	.286	27	0	0	0	0	50¹	60	8	26	14	15.6	5.54	73	.313	.397	0	.000	-1	-9	-8	1	-1.2
Total	4	13	14	.481	91	1	0	0	14	193	196	25	63	82	12.4	4.20	96	.270	.333	5	.109	-3	-8	-4	5	0.1
● **STAN WALL**					Wall, Stanley Arthur b: 6/16/51, Butler, Mo. BL/TL, 6'1", 175 lbs. Deb: 7/19/75																					
1975	LA-N	0	1	.000	10	0	0	0	0	16	12	0	7	6	11.3	1.69	201	.222	.323	0	—	0	3	3	0	0.2
1976	LA-N	2	2	.500	31	0	0	0	1	50	50	5	15	27	12.1	3.60	94	.269	.330	0	.000	-0	-1	-1	-1	-0.2
1977	LA-N	2	3	.400	25	0	0	0	0	32	36	3	13	22	14.1	5.34	72	.279	.350	0	.000	-0	-5	-5	-0	-0.8
Total	3	4	6	.400	66	0	0	0	1	98	98	8	35	55	12.6	3.86	91	.266	.336	0	.000	-0	-2	-4	-1	-0.8
● **DAVE WALLACE**					Wallace, David William b: 9/7/47, Waterbury, Conn. BR/TR, 5'10", 185 lbs. Deb: 7/18/73																					
1973	Phi-N	0	0	—	4	0	0	0	0	3²	7	1	2	2	36.8	22.09	17	.591	.625	0	—	-0	-8	-7	0	0.0
1974	Phi-N	0	1	.000	3	0	0	0	0	3	4	2	3	3	21.0	9.00	42	.308	.438	0	—	-0	-2	-2	0	-0.5
1978	Tor-A	0	0	—	6	0	0	0	0	14	12	1	11	7	14.8	3.86	102	.245	.383	0	—	-0	-0	-0	0	0.0
Total	3	0	1	.000	13	0	0	0	0	20²	23	4	16	12	19.6	7.84	49	.345	.450	0	—	-0	-9	-9	0	-0.5
● **DEREK WALLACE**					Wallace, Derek Robert b: 9/1/71, Van Nuys, Cal. BR/TR, 6'3", 200 lbs. Deb: 8/13/96																					
1996	NY-N	2	3	.400	19	0	0	0	3	24²	29	2	14	15	15.7	4.01	98	.290	.377	0	—	0	1	-0	-0	-0.1
● **HUCK WALLACE**					Wallace, Harry Clinton "Lefty" b: 7/27/1882, Richmond, Ind. d: 7/6/51, Cleveland, Ohio BL/TL, 5'6", 160 lbs. Deb: 6/5/12																					
1912	Phi-N	0	0	—	4	0	0	0	0	4²	7	0	4	2	21.2	0.00	—	.350	.458	0	—	0	2	2	-0	0.1
● **LEFTY WALLACE**					Wallace, James Harold b: 8/12/21, Evansville, Ind. d: 7/28/82, Evansville, Ind. BL/TL, 5'11", 160 lbs. Deb: 5/5/42																					
1942	Bos-N	1	3	.250	19	3	1	0	0	49¹	39	3	24	20	11.9	3.83	87	.217	.316	2	.143	-0	-3	-3	-1	-0.3
1945	Bos-N	1	0	1.000	5	3	1	0	0	20	18	1	9	4	12.6	4.50	85	.240	.329	0	.000	-1	-2	-1	0	-0.1
1946	Bos-N	3	3	.500	27	8	2	0	0	75¹	76	5	31	27	12.9	4.18	82	.253	.325	1	.056	-1	-6	-6	2	-0.4
Total	3	5	6	.455	51	14	4	0	0	144²	133	9	64	51	12.5	4.11	84	.240	.323	3	.079	-2	-11	-10	1	-0.8
● **MIKE WALLACE**					Wallace, Michael Sherman b: 2/3/51, Gastonia, N.C. BL/TL, 6'2", 204 lbs. Deb: 6/27/73																					
1973	Phi-N	1	1	.500	20	3	1	0	1	33¹	38	1	15	20	14.3	3.78	100	.304	.379	0	.000	-0	-0	-0	-0	-0.1
1974	Phi-N	0	1	1.000	8	0	0	0	0	8¹	12	2	11	2	15.1	5.40	70	.324	.359	0	—	-0	-2	-2	-0	-0.2
	NY-A	6	0	1.000	23	1	0	0	0	52¹	42	3	35	24	13.2	2.41	146	.222	.344	0	—	0	7	6	-1	0.6
1975	NY-A	0	0	—	9	0	0	0	0	4¹	11	1	6	2	24.9	14.54	25	.458	.480	0	—	-0	-5	-5	-0	0.1
	StL-N	0	0	—	9	0	0	0	0	8²	9	0	5	6	14.5	2.08	181	.281	.378	0	—	0	1	2	0	0.0
1976	StL-N	3	2	.600	49	0	0	0	3	66¹	66	3	39	40	14.2	4.07	87	.264	.363	1	.333	0	-4	-4	0	-0.3

YEAR	TM/L	W	L	PCT	G	GS	CG	SH	SV	IP	H	HR	BB	SO	RAT	ERA	ERA+	OAV	OOB	BH	AVG	PB	PR	/A	PD	TPI
1977	Tex-A	0	0	—		5	0	0	0	0	8¹	10	1	10	2	21.6	7.56	54	.323	.488	0	—	0	-3	-3	0	0.0
Total	5	11	3	.786		117	4	1	0	3	181²	188	9	107	105	14.6	3.91	93	.273	.371	1	.143	0	-6	-6	-1	0.1

● **BOBBY WALLACE**   Wallace, Rhoderick John b: 11/4/1873, Pittsburgh, Pa. d: 11/3/60, Torrance, Cal. BR/TR, 5'8", 170 lbs. Deb: 9/15/1894 MUCH♦

1894	Cle-N	2	1	.667		4	3	2	0	0	26	28	1	20	10	17.0	5.19	105	.272	.395	2	.154	-1	0	1	1	0.0
1895	Cle-N	12	14	.462		30	28	22	1	1	228²	271	3	87	63	14.4	4.09	122	.290	.356	21	.214	-3	17	23	3	2.0
1896	*Cle-N	10	7	.588		22	16	13	2	0	145¹	167	2	49	46	13.6	3.34	136	.286	.345	35	.235	0	16	19	-0	1.8
1902	StL-A					1	1	0	0	0	2	3	0	0	1	13.5		—	.333	.333	141	.285	0	1	1	0	0.0
Total	4	24	22	.522		57	48	37	3	1	402	469	6	156	120	14.3	3.87	125	.288	.355	2309	.268	-3	35	44	4	3.8

● **TIM WALLACH**   Wallach, Timothy Charles b: 9/14/57, Huntington Park, Cal. BR/TR, 6'3", 200 lbs. Deb: 9/6/80 ♦

1987	Mon-N★	0	0	—		1	0	0	0	0	1	1	0	0	0	9.0	0.00	—	.333	.333	177	.298	1	-0	-0	-0	0.0
1989	Mon-N★	0	0	—		1	0	0	0	0	1	2	0	0	0	18.0	9.00	39	.500	.500	159	.277	0	-1	-1	0	0.0
Total	2	0	0	—		2	0	0	0	0	2	3	0	0	0	13.5	4.50	86	.429	.429	2085	.257	1	-0	-0	-0	0.0

● **RED WALLER**   Waller, John Francis b: 6/16/1883, Washington, D.C. d: 2/9/15, Secaucus, N.J. Deb: 4/27/09

| 1909 | NY-N | 0 | 0 | — | | 1 | 0 | 0 | 0 | 0 | 1 | 3 | 0 | 1 | 0 | 36.0 | 0.00 | — | .429 | .500 | 0 | — | 0 | 0 | 0 | 0 | 0.0 |

● **AUGIE WALSH**   Walsh, August Sothley b: 8/17/04, Wilmington, Del. d: 11/12/85, San Rafael, Cal. BR/TR, 6', 175 lbs. Deb: 10/2/27

1927	Phi-N	0	1	.000		1	1	1	0	0	10	12	3	5	0	15.3	4.50	92	.333	.415	1	.250	-0	-1	-1	0	-0.1
1928	Phi-N	4	9	.308		38	11	2	0	2	122¹	160	14	40	38	15.1	6.18	69	.321	.378	10	.256	2	-30	-26	-2	-2.4
Total	2	4	10	.286		39	12	3	0	2	132¹	172	16	45	38	15.1	6.05	70	.322	.380	11	.256	2	-30	-26	-2	-2.5

● **CONNIE WALSH**   Walsh, Cornelius R. b: 4/23/1882, St.Louis, Mo. d: 4/5/53, St.Louis, Mo. Deb: 9/16/07

| 1907 | Pit-N | 0 | 0 | — | | 1 | 0 | 0 | 0 | 0 | 1 | 1 | 0 | 1 | 0 | 18.0 | 9.00 | 27 | .250 | .400 | 0 | — | 0 | -1 | -1 | -0 | 0.0 |

● **DAVE WALSH**   Walsh, David Peter b: 9/25/60, Arlington, Mass. BL/TL, 6'1", 185 lbs. Deb: 8/13/90

| 1990 | LA-N | 1 | 0 | 1.000 | | 20 | 0 | 0 | 0 | 1 | 16¹ | 15 | 1 | 6 | 15 | 11.6 | 3.86 | 95 | .242 | .309 | 0 | — | 0 | -0 | -0 | 0 | 0.0 |

● **ED WALSH**   Walsh, Edward Arthur b: 2/11/05, Meriden, Conn. d: 10/31/37, Meriden, Conn. BR/TR, 6'1", 180 lbs. Deb: 7/4/28 F

1928	Chi-A	4	7	.364		14	10	3	0	0	78	86	2	42	32	15.3	4.96	82	.290	.387	3	.111	-2	-8	-8	-1	-1.2
1929	Chi-A	6	11	.353		24	20	7	0	0	129	156	9	64	31	15.6	5.65	76	.312	.394	10	.233	2	-20	-20	1	-1.9
1930	Chi-A	1	4	.200		37	4	0	0	0	103²	131	4	30	37	14.3	5.38	86	.316	.367	9	.265	1	-8	-9	1	-0.2
1932	Chi-A	0	2	.000		4	4	1	0	0	20¹	26	3	13	7	17.3	8.41	51	.299	.390	2	.286	0	-9	-9	-0	-0.7
Total	4	11	24	.314		79	38	11	0	0	331	399	22	149	107	15.3	5.57	78	.307	.384	24	.216	1	-45	-45	1	-4.0

● **ED WALSH**   Walsh, Edward Augustine "Big Ed" b: 5/14/1881, Plains, Pa. d: 5/26/59, Pompano Beach, Fla BR/TR, 6'1", 193 lbs. Deb: 5/7/04 FMUCH

1904	Chi-A	6	3	.667		18	8	6	1	0	110²	90	1	32	57	10.2	2.60	94	.223	.285	9	.220	3	-0	-2	0	0.2
1905	Chi-A	8	3	.727		22	13	9	1	0	136²	121	0	29	71	10.1	2.17	131	.239	.284	9	.155	-0	7	4	0	0.4
1906	*Chi-A	17	13	.567		41	31	24	**10**	1	278¹	215	1	58	171	9.1	1.88	135	.217	.265	14	.141	-2	25	21	8	3.0
1907	Chi-A	24	18	.571		**56**	46	**37**	5	4	422¹	341	3	87	206	9.3	**1.60**	150	.223	.269	25	.162	-1	**44**	37	22	6.4
1908	Chi-A	**40**	15	**.727**		**66**	49	**42**	**11**	**6**	**464**	343	2	56	**269**	7.9	1.42	163	.203	.232	27	.172	2	**50**	46	14	8.1
1909	Chi-A	15	11	.577		31	28	20	8	2	230¹	166	0	50	127	**8.6**	1.41	166	.203	**.253**	18	.214	4	**27**	24	7	4.4
1910	Chi-A	18	20	.474		**45**	36	33	7	5	369²	242	5	61	258	**7.5**	**1.27**	**189**	**.187**	**.226**	30	.217	4	**52**	46	10	7.1
1911	Chi-A	27	18	.600		**56**	37	33	5	4	368²	327	4	72	255	9.9	2.22	145	.239	**.280**	34	.215	-1	46	41	15	6.2
1912	Chi-A	27	17	.614		**62**	41	32	6	**10**	**393**	332	6	94	254	9.8	2.15	149	.231	.279	33	.243	6	51	46	7	6.6
1913	Chi-A	8	3	.727		16	14	7	1	0	97²	91	1	39	34	12.3	2.58	113	.243	.321	5	.156	-1	4	4	1	0.4
1914	Chi-A	2	3	.400		8	5	3	1	0	44²	33	0	20	15	10.9	2.82	95	.212	.305	1	.063	-1	-0	-1	1	-0.1
1915	Chi-A	3	0	1.000		3	3	3	1	0	27	19	0	7	12	8.7	1.33	223	.202	.257	4	.364	1	5	5	1	0.6
1916	Chi-A	0	1	.000		2	1	0	0	0	3¹	4	0	3	3	18.9	2.70	102	.286	.412	0	—	0	0	0	0	0.0
1917	Bos-N	0	1	.000		4	2	0	0	0	18	22	0	9	4	16.0	3.50	73	.314	.400	1	.250	-1	-2	-2	0	0.0
Total	14	195	126	.607		430	315	250	57	34	2964¹	2346	23	617	1736	9.2	1.82	145	.218	.264	210	.193	14	310	270	83	43.3

● **JUNIOR WALSH**   Walsh, James Gerald b: 3/7/19, Newark, N.J. d: 11/12/90, Olyphant, Pa. BR/TR, 5'11", 185 lbs. Deb: 9/14/46

1946	Pit-N	0	1	.000		4	2	0	0	0	10¹	9	0	10	2	17.4	5.23	67	.237	.408	0	.000	-1	-2	-2	-0	-0.2
1948	Pit-N	1	0	1.000		2	0	0	0	0	4¹	4	1	5	0	18.7	10.38	39	.235	.409	0	.000	-0	-3	-3	0	-0.5
1949	Pit-N	1	4	.200		9	7	1	1	0	42²	40	5	16	24	11.8	5.06	83	.244	.311	0	.000	-1	-5	-4	-1	-0.6
1950	Pit-N	1	1	.500		38	2	0	0	0	62¹	56	6	34	33	13.1	5.05	87	.246	.346	1	.167	1	-6	-5	0	-0.1
1951	Pit-N	1	4	.200		36	1	0	0	2	73¹	92	9	46	32	17.1	6.87	61	.304	.397	1	.143	0	-24	-22	0	-1.3
Total	5	4	10	.286		89	12	1	1	2	193	201	21	111	91	14.7	5.92	72	.268	.365	2	.065	-0	-40	-35	-2	-2.7

● **JIM WALSH**   Walsh, James Thomas b: 7/10/1894, Roxbury, Mass. d: 5/13/67, Boston, Mass. BL/TL, 5'11", 175 lbs. Deb: 8/25/21

| 1921 | Det-A | 0 | 0 | — | | 3 | 0 | 0 | 0 | 0 | 4 | 2 | 0 | 1 | 3 | 6.8 | 2.25 | 190 | .125 | .176 | 0 | — | 0 | 1 | 1 | 0 | 0.1 |

● **DEE WALSH**   Walsh, Leo Thomas b: 3/28/1890, St.Louis, Mo. d: 7/14/71, St.Louis, Mo. BB/TR, 5'9.5", 165 lbs. Deb: 4/10/13 ♦

| 1915 | StL-A | 0 | 0 | — | | 1 | 0 | 0 | 0 | 0 | 2 | 2 | 0 | 2 | 0 | 18.0 | 13.50 | 21 | .222 | .364 | 33 | .220 | 0 | -2 | -2 | 0 | 0.0 |

● **JIMMY WALSH**   Walsh, Michael Timothy "Runt" b: 3/25/1886, Lima, Ohio d: 1/21/47, Baltimore, Md. BR/TR, 5'9", 174 lbs. Deb: 4/25/10 ♦

| 1911 | Phi-N | 0 | 1 | .000 | | 1 | 0 | 0 | 0 | 0 | 2² | 7 | 1 | 1 | 0 | 27.0 | 13.50 | 26 | .500 | .533 | 78 | .270 | 0 | -3 | -3 | -0 | -0.7 |

● **GENE WALTER**   Walter, Gene Winston b: 11/22/60, Chicago, Ill. BL/TL, 6'4", 200 lbs. Deb: 8/9/85

1985	SD-N	0	2	.000		15	0	0	0	3	22	12	0	8	18	8.2	2.05	173	.158	.238	0	.000	0	4	4	0	0.5
1986	SD-N	2	2	.500		57	0	0	0	1	98	89	7	49	84	13.0	3.86	95	.247	.343	2	.200	1	-2	-2	1	0.1
1987	NY-N	1	2	.333		21	0	0	0	0	19²	18	1	13	11	14.6	3.20	118	.243	.364	0	.000	0	2	2	0	0.2
1988	NY-N	0	1	.000		19	0	0	0	0	16²	21	0	11	14	17.3	3.78	85	.309	.405	0	—	0	-1	-1	-0	-0.1
	Sea-A	1	0	1.000		16	0	0	0	0	26¹	21	0	15	13	13.0	5.13	81	.216	.333	0	—	0	-3	-0	-0	-0.3
Total	4	4	7	.364		128	0	0	0	4	182²	161	8	96	140	13.0	3.74	98	.238	.339	2	.167	1	-0	2	1	-0.2

● **BERNIE WALTER**   Walter, James Bernard b: 8/15/08, Dover, Tenn. d: 10/30/88, Nashville, Tenn. BR/TR, 6'1", 175 lbs. Deb: 8/16/30

| 1930 | Pit-N | 0 | 0 | — | | 1 | 0 | 0 | 0 | 0 | 1 | 0 | 0 | 0 | 0 | 0.0 | 0.00 | — | .000 | .000 | 0 | — | 0 | 1 | 1 | 0 | 0.1 |

● **CHARLIE WALTERS**   Walters, Charles Leonard b: 2/21/47, Minneapolis, Minn. BR/TR, 6'4", 190 lbs. Deb: 4/11/69

| 1969 | Min-A | 0 | 0 | — | | 6 | 0 | 0 | 0 | 0 | 6² | 6 | 1 | 3 | 2 | 13.5 | 5.40 | 68 | .240 | .345 | 0 | — | 0 | -1 | -1 | -0 | 0.0 |

● **MIKE WALTERS**   Walters, Michael Charles b: 10/18/57, St.Louis, Mo. BR/TR, 6'5", 203 lbs. Deb: 7/8/83

1983	Min-A	1	1	.500		23	0	0	0	2	59	52	4	20	21	11.3	4.12	103	.243	.314	0	—	0	-0	1	0	-0.1
1984	Min-A	0	3	.000		23	0	0	0	2	29	31	1	14	10	14.3	3.72	113	.287	.374	0	—	0	0	2	-0	-0.1
Total	2	1	4	.200		46	0	0	0	4	88	83	5	34	31	12.3	3.99	106	.258	.334	0	—	0	0	2	0	-0.2

● **BUCKY WALTERS**   Walters, William Henry b: 4/19/09, Philadelphia, Pa. d: 4/20/91, Abington, Pa. BR/TR, 6'1", 180 lbs. Deb: 9/18/31 MC♦

1934	Phi-N	0	0	—		2	1	0	0	0	7	8	2	4	2	14.1	1.29	367	.296	.367	78	.260	0	2	3	1	0.1
1935	Phi-N	9	9	.500		24	22	8	2	0	151	168	9	60	40	14.5	4.17	109	.289	.370	24	.250	1	-3	6	2	1.1
1936	Phi-N	11	21	.344		40	33	15	**4**	0	258	284	11	115	66	14.1	4.26	107	.277	.353	29	.240	3	-7	8	9	2.2
1937	Phi-N★	14	15	.483		37	34	15	3	0	246¹	292	14	86	87	13.9	4.75	91	.295	.353	38	.277	4	-23	-11	5	-0.2
1938	Phi-N	4	8	.333		12	12	9	1	0	82²	91	8	42	28	14.8	5.23	74	.276	.363	10	.286	3	-13	-12	0	-1.2
	Cin-N	11	6	.647		27	22	11	2	1	168¹	168	5	66	65	12.6	3.69	99	.255	.324	9	.141	0	2	-1	2	0.1
	Yr	15	14	.517		39	34	20	3	1	251	259	13	108	93	13.2	4.20	89	.261	.335	19	.192	3	-11	-13	2	-1.1
1939	*Cin-N☆	**27**	11	.711		39	36	**31**	2	0	**319**	250	15	109	**137**	10.3	**2.29**	**168**	.220	.291	39	.325	13	**58**	55	4	8.5
1940	*Cin-N★	**22**	10	.688		36	36	**29**	3	0	**305**	241	19	92	115	10.0	**2.48**	**153**	.220	.283	24	.205	4	**46**	44	-1	4.7
1941	Cin-N★	19	15	.559		37	35	**27**	5	1	**302**	292	10	88	129	11.4	2.83	127	.255	.320	20	.179	3	27	26	2	3.3
1942	Cin-N★	15	14	.517		34	32	21	2	0	253²	253	8	73	109	10.7	2.66	112	.263	.289	24	.231	6	18	18	1	3.0
1943	Cin-N	15	15	.500		36	36	24	2	0	246¹	244	8	109	80	12.9	3.54	94	.264	.342	35	.267	4	-4	-6	0	0.7
1944	Cin-N★	**23**	8	.742		34	32	27	6	1	285	233	10	87	77	10.2	2.40	145	**.219**	.281	30	.280	8	**38**	34	1	4.7

YEAR	TM/L	W	L	PCT	G	GS	CG	SH	SV	IP	H	HR	BB	SO	RAT	ERA	ERA+	OAV	OOB	BH	AVG	PB	PR	/A	PD	TPI
1945	Cin-N	10	10	.500	22	22	12	3	0	168	166	6	51	45	11.7	2.68	140	.259	.316	14	.230	5	21	20	-0	2.9
1946	Cin-N	10	7	.588	22	22	10	2	0	151⅓	146	9	64	60	12.6	2.56	131	.258	.336	7	.127	-1	14	13	2	1.6
1947	Cin-N	8	8	.500	20	20	5	2	0	122	137	15	49	43	13.9	5.75	71	.278	.347	12	.267	3	-23	-22	-1	-2.3
1948	Cin-N	0	3	.000	7	5	1	0	0	35	42	6	18	19	15.4	4.63	84	.316	.397	4	.267	-0	-3	-3	1	-0.1
1950	Bos-N	0	0	—	1	0	0	0	0	4	5	0	2	0	15.8	4.50	86	.313	.389	0	.000	-0	-0	-0	-0	0.0
Total	16	198	160	.553	428	398	242	42	4	3104⅔	2990	154	1121	1107	12.1	3.30	115	.253	.321	477	.243	57	152	168	27	28.6

● BRUCE WALTON — Walton, Bruce Kenneth b: 12/25/62, Bakersfield, Cal. BR/TR, 6'2", 195 lbs. Deb: 5/11/91

YEAR	TM/L	W	L	PCT	G	GS	CG	SH	SV	IP	H	HR	BB	SO	RAT	ERA	ERA+	OAV	OOB	BH	AVG	PB	PR	/A	PD	TPI
1991	Oak-A	1	0	1.000	12	0	0	0	0	13	11	3	6	10	12.5	6.23	62	.229	.327	0	—	0	-3	-3	-0	-0.2
1992	Oak-A	0	0	—	7	0	0	0	0	10	17	1	3	7	18.0	9.90	38	.378	.417	0	—	0	-7	-7	-0	0.0
1993	Mon-N	0	0	—	4	0	0	0	0	5⅔	11	1	3	0	22.2	9.53	44	.407	.467	0	.000	-0	-3	-3	-0	0.0
1994	Col-N	1	0	1.000	4	0	0	0	0	5⅓	6	1	3	1	15.2	8.44	59	.273	.360	0	—	0	-3	-2	-0	-0.3
Total	4	2	0	1.000	27	0	0	0	0	34	45	6	15	18	16.1	8.21	49	.317	.386	0	.000	-0	-16	-16	-1	-0.5

● DICK WANTZ — Wantz, Richard Carter b: 4/11/40, South Gate, Cal. d: 5/13/65, Inglewood, Cal. BR/TR, 6'5", 175 lbs. Deb: 4/13/65

YEAR	TM/L	W	L	PCT	G	GS	CG	SH	SV	IP	H	HR	BB	SO	RAT	ERA	ERA+	OAV	OOB	BH	AVG	PB	PR	/A	PD	TPI
1965	Cal-A				1	0	0	0	—	1	3	0	0	0	27.0	18.00	11	.500	.500	0	—	0	-2	-2	0	0.0

● STEVE WAPNICK — Wapnick, Steven Lee b: 9/25/65, Panorama City, Cal. BR/TR, 6'2", 200 lbs. Deb: 4/14/90

YEAR	TM/L	W	L	PCT	G	GS	CG	SH	SV	IP	H	HR	BB	SO	RAT	ERA	ERA+	OAV	OOB	BH	AVG	PB	PR	/A	PD	TPI
1990	Det-A	0	0	—	4	0	0	0	0	7	8	0	10	6	23.1	6.43	62	.296	.486	0	—	0	-2	-2	-0	0.0
1991	Chi-A	0	1	.000	6	0	0	0	0	5	2	0	4	1	10.8	1.80	221	.111	.273	0	—	0	1	1	-0	0.2
Total	2	0	1	.000	10	0	0	0	0	12	10	0	14	7	18.0	4.50	88	.222	.407	0	—	0	-1	-1	-0	0.2

● COLIN WARD — Ward, Colin Norval b: 11/22/60, Los Angeles, Cal. BL/TL, 6'3", 190 lbs. Deb: 9/21/85

YEAR	TM/L	W	L	PCT	G	GS	CG	SH	SV	IP	H	HR	BB	SO	RAT	ERA	ERA+	OAV	OOB	BH	AVG	PB	PR	/A	PD	TPI
1985	SF-N	0	0	—	6	2	0	0	0	12⅓	10	0	7	8	12.4	4.38	78	.233	.340	0	.000	-0	-1	-1	-0	0.0

● JOHNNY WARD — Ward, John b: East St.Louis, Ill. Deb: 9/19/1885

YEAR	TM/L	W	L	PCT	G	GS	CG	SH	SV	IP	H	HR	BB	SO	RAT	ERA	ERA+	OAV	OOB	BH	AVG	PB	PR	/A	PD	TPI
1885	Pro-N	0	1	.000	1	1	1	0	0	8	10	0	1	3	12.4	4.50	59	.286	.306	0	.000	-0	-1	-2	-0	-0.2

● JOHN WARD — Ward, John Montgomery b: 3/3/1860, Bellefonte, Pa. d: 3/4/25, Augusta, Ga. BL/TR, 5'9", 165 lbs. Deb: 7/15/1878 MH♦

YEAR	TM/L	W	L	PCT	G	GS	CG	SH	SV	IP	H	HR	BB	SO	RAT	ERA	ERA+	OAV	OOB	BH	AVG	PB	PR	/A	PD	TPI
1878	Pro-N	22	13	.629	37	37	37	6	0	334	308	3	34	116	9.2	**1.51**	146	.231	.251	27	.196	2	**30**	26	2	2.6
1879	Pro-N	**47**	19	**.712**	70	60	58	2	1	587	571	5	36	**239**	9.3	2.15	110	.239	.250	104	.286	17	23	13	4	2.9
1880	Pro-N	39	24	.619	70	67	59	**8**	1	595	501	5	45	230	8.3	1.74	127	.217	.232	81	.228	1	**42**	31	5	3.4
1881	Pro-N	18	18	.500	39	35	32	3	0	330	326	6	53	119	10.3	2.13	125	.242	.271	87	.244	3	24	19	5	2.5
1882	Pro-N	19	12	.613	33	32	29	4	1	278	261	6	36	72	9.6	2.59	109	.232	.256	87	.245	1	10	7	4	1.0
1883	NY-N	16	13	.552	34	25	24	1	0	277	278	3	31	121	10.0	2.70	115	.246	.267	97	.255	6	14	12	4	1.8
1884	NY-N	3	3	.500	9	5	5	0	0	60⅔	72	4	18	23	13.4	3.41	87	.280	.327	122	.253	1	-3	-3	1	-0.1
Total	7	164	102	.617	292	261	244	24	3	2461⅔	2317	26	253	920	9.4	2.10	118	.235	.254	2104	.275	31	138	105	24	14.1

● DICK WARD — Ward, Richard Ole b: 5/21/09, Herrick, S.Dak. d: 5/30/66, Freeland, Wash. BR/TR, 6'1", 198 lbs. Deb: 5/3/34

YEAR	TM/L	W	L	PCT	G	GS	CG	SH	SV	IP	H	HR	BB	SO	RAT	ERA	ERA+	OAV	OOB	BH	AVG	PB	PR	/A	PD	TPI
1934	Chi-N	0	0	—	3	0	0	0	0	6	9	0	2	1	16.5	3.00	129	.375	.423	0	.000	-0	1	1	-0	0.0
1935	StL-N	0	0	—	1	0	0	0	0	0	0	0	1	0	—	—	—	—	1.000	0	—	-0	0	0	-0	0.0
Total	2	0	0	—	4	0	0	0	0	6	9	0	3	1	18.0	3.00	129	.375	.444	0	.000	-0	1	1	-0	0.0

● COLBY WARD — Ward, Robert Colby b: 1/2/64, Lansing, Mich. BR/TR, 6'2", 185 lbs. Deb: 7/27/90

YEAR	TM/L	W	L	PCT	G	GS	CG	SH	SV	IP	H	HR	BB	SO	RAT	ERA	ERA+	OAV	OOB	BH	AVG	PB	PR	/A	PD	TPI
1990	Cle-A	1	3	.250	22	0	0	0	1	36	31	3	21	23	13.3	4.25	92	.238	.349	0	—	0	-1	-1	-0	-0.1

● DUANE WARD — Ward, Roy Duane b: 5/28/64, Park View, N.Mex. BR/TR, 6'4", 215 lbs. Deb: 4/12/86

YEAR	TM/L	W	L	PCT	G	GS	CG	SH	SV	IP	H	HR	BB	SO	RAT	ERA	ERA+	OAV	OOB	BH	AVG	PB	PR	/A	PD	TPI
1986	Atl-N	0	1	.000	10	0	0	0	0	16	22	2	8		16.9	7.31	54	.349	.423	0	.000	-0	-6	-6	1	-0.3
	Tor-A	0	1	.000	2	1	0	0	0	2	3	0	4	1	36.0	13.50	31	.300	.533	0	—	0	-2	-2	-0	-0.8
1987	Tor-A	1	0	1.000	12	1	0	0	0	11⅔	14	0	12	10	20.1	6.94	65	.326	.473	0	—	0	-3	-3	-0	-0.3
1988	Tor-A	9	3	.750	64	0	0	0	15	111⅔	101	5	60	91	13.4	3.30	119	.245	.347	0	—	0	8	8	-0	0.9
1989	*Tor-A	4	10	.286	66	0	0	0	15	114⅔	94	4	58	122	12.3	3.77	100	.230	.333	0	—	0	1	0	2	0.2
1990	*Tor-A	2	8	.200	73	0	0	0	11	127⅔	101	9	42	112	10.2	3.45	114	.221	.288	0	—	0	6	7	1	0.6
1991	*Tor-A	7	6	.538	81	0	0	0	23	107⅓	80	3	33	132	9.6	2.77	152	.207	.273	0	—	0	16	17	0	2.5
1992	*Tor-A	7	4	.636	79	0	0	0	12	101⅓	76	5	39	103	10.3	1.95	209	.207	.285	0	—	0	22	24	2	2.9
1993	*Tor-A★	2	3	.400	71	0	0	0	**45**	71⅔	49	4	25	97	9.4	2.13	202	.193	.268	0	—	0	17	17	-1	2.9
1995	Tor-A	0	1	.000	4	0	0	0	0	2⅔	11	0	5	3	57.4	27.00	17	.579	.680	0	—	0	-7	-7	-0	-1.7
Total	9	32	37	.464	462	2	0	0	121	666⅔	551	32	286	679	11.5	3.28	123	.228	.314	0	.000	-0	53	55	2	6.9

● JON WARDEN — Warden, Jonathan Edgar "Warbler" b: 10/1/46, Columbus, Ohio BB/TL, 6', 205 lbs. Deb: 4/11/68

YEAR	TM/L	W	L	PCT	G	GS	CG	SH	SV	IP	H	HR	BB	SO	RAT	ERA	ERA+	OAV	OOB	BH	AVG	PB	PR	/A	PD	TPI
1968	Det-A	4	1	.800	28	0	0	0	5	37⅓	30	5	15	25	10.8	3.62	83	.217	.294	0	.000	-0	-3	-3	-1	-0.5

● CURT WARDLE — Wardle, Curtis Ray b: 11/16/60, Downey, Cal. BL/TL, 6'5", 220 lbs. Deb: 8/30/84

YEAR	TM/L	W	L	PCT	G	GS	CG	SH	SV	IP	H	HR	BB	SO	RAT	ERA	ERA+	OAV	OOB	BH	AVG	PB	PR	/A	PD	TPI
1984	Min-A	0	0	—	2	0	0	0	0	4	3	2	0	5	6.8	4.50	93	.200	.200	0	—	0	-0	-0	0	-0.3
1985	Min-A	1	3	.250	35	0	0	0	1	49	49	9	28	47	14.3	5.51	80	.266	.366	0	—	0	-7	-6	-1	-0.8
	Cle-A	7	6	.538	15	12	0	0	0	66	78	11	34	37	15.4	6.68	62	.297	.379	0	—	0	-19	-19	-1	-3.0
	Yr	8	9	.471	50	12	0	0	1	115	127	20	62	84	14.9	6.18	69	.283	.371	0	—	0	-26	-25	-0	-3.8
Total	2	8	9	.471	52	12	0	0	1	119	130	22	62	89	14.7	6.13	69	.281	.369	0	—	0	-26	-25	0	-4.1

● JEFF WARE — Ware, Jeffrey Allan b: 11/11/70, Norfolk, Va. BR/TR, 6'3", 190 lbs. Deb: 9/2/95

YEAR	TM/L	W	L	PCT	G	GS	CG	SH	SV	IP	H	HR	BB	SO	RAT	ERA	ERA+	OAV	OOB	BH	AVG	PB	PR	/A	PD	TPI
1995	Tor-A	2	1	.667	5	5	0	0	0	26⅓	28	2	21	18	17.1	5.47	86	.277	.407	0	—	0	-2	-2	-0	-0.2
1996	Tor-A	1	5	.167	13	4	0	0	0	32⅔	35	6	31	11	18.7	9.09	56	.271	.420	0	—	0	-15	-15	-0	-2.0
Total	2	3	6	.333	18	9	0	0	0	59	63	8	52	29	18.0	7.47	66	.274	.414	0	—	0	-17	-17	0	-2.2

● JACK WARHOP — Warhop, John Milton "Chief" or "Crab" (b: John Milton Wauhop) b: 7/4/1884, Hinton, W.Va. d: 10/4/60, Freeport, Ill. BR/TR, 5'9.5", 168 lbs. Deb: 9/19/08

YEAR	TM/L	W	L	PCT	G	GS	CG	SH	SV	IP	H	HR	BB	SO	RAT	ERA	ERA+	OAV	OOB	BH	AVG	PB	PR	/A	PD	TPI
1908	NY-A	1	2	.333	5	4	4	0	0	36⅓	40	4	8	11	12.9	4.46	56	.292	.349	1	.063	-1	-8	-8	0	-0.7
1909	NY-A	13	15	.464	36	23	21	3	2	243⅓	197	2	81	95	11.2	2.40	105	.233	.319	11	.128	-2	2	3	1	0.3
1910	NY-A	14	14	.500	37	27	20	0	2	243	219	1	79	75	11.7	3.00	89	.246	.320	14	.177	-1	-13	-9	-4	-1.6
1911	NY-A	12	13	.480	31	25	17	1	0	209⅔	239	6	44	71	12.8	4.16	86	.286	.333	12	.156	-4	-19	-13	-2	-1.9
1912	NY-A	10	19	.345	39	22	16	0	3	258	256	3	59	110	11.5	2.86	126	.266	.319	19	.207	-1	13	21	-3	1.9
1913	NY-A	4	6	.400	15	7	1	0	0	62⅓	69	1	33	11	16.5	3.75	80	.292	.406	3	.130	-1	-6	-5	-2	-1.0
1914	NY-A	8	15	.348	37	23	15	0	0	216⅔	182	8	44	56	9.8	2.37	117	.235	.286	10	.141	-1	9	9	-2	0.7
1915	NY-A	7	9	.438	21	19	12	0	0	143⅓	164	7	52	34	14.3	3.96	74	.309	.384	7	.137	-2	-16	-16	-3	-2.0
Total	8	69	93	.426	221	150	105	4	7	1412⅔	1366	28	400	463	12.0	3.12	96	.262	.328	77	.156	-12	-38	-19	-13	-4.3

● CY WARMOTH — Warmoth, Wallace Walter b: 2/2/1893, Bone Gap, Ill. d: 6/20/57, Mt.Carmel, Ill. BL/TL, 5'11", 158 lbs. Deb: 8/31/16

YEAR	TM/L	W	L	PCT	G	GS	CG	SH	SV	IP	H	HR	BB	SO	RAT	ERA	ERA+	OAV	OOB	BH	AVG	PB	PR	/A	PD	TPI
1916	StL-N	0	0	—	3	0	0	0	0	5	12	0	4	1	30.6	14.40	18	.500	.586	0	.000	-0	-7	-7	-0	-0.1
1922	Was-A	1	0	1.000	5	1	0	0	0	19	15	0	9	8	11.4	1.42	272	.205	.293	1	.143	-0	6	5	-0	0.2
1923	Was-A	7	5	.583	21	13	4	0	0	105	103	8	76	45	15.4	4.29	88	.261	.381	8	.222	2	-4	-6	-0	-0.4
Total	3	8	5	.615	29	14	4	0	0	129	130	8	89	54	15.4	4.26	88	.264	.379	9	.200	1	-5	-7	-0	-0.3

● LON WARNEKE — Warneke, Lonnie "The Arkansas Hummingbird" b: 3/28/09, Mt.Ida, Ark. d: 6/23/76, Hot Springs, Ark. BR/TR, 6'2", 185 lbs. Deb: 4/18/30 U

YEAR	TM/L	W	L	PCT	G	GS	CG	SH	SV	IP	H	HR	BB	SO	RAT	ERA	ERA+	OAV	OOB	BH	AVG	PB	PR	/A	PD	TPI
1930	Chi-N	0	0	—	1	0	0	0	0	1⅓	2	0	5	0	47.3	33.75	14	.400	.700	0	—	0	-4	-4	0	0.0
1931	Chi-N	2	4	.333	20	7	3	0	0	64⅓	67	1	37	27	15.0	3.22	120	.269	.370	5	.263	1	5	5	-1	0.4
1932	*Chi-N	22	6	.786	35	32	25	**4**	0	277	247	12	64	106	10.2	2.37	159	.237	.283	19	.192	-0	**46**	43	-0	4.1
1933	Chi-N★	18	13	.581	36	34	**26**	4	0	287⅓	262	6	75	133	10.6	2.00	163	.244	.295	30	.300	10	43	43	2	6.2
1934	Chi-N★	22	10	.688	43	35	23	6	0	291⅓	273	16	66	143	10.5	3.21	121	.244	.287	22	.195	-1	27	21	0	2.1
1935	Chi-N★	20	13	.606	42	30	18	4	0	261⅔	257	10	64	120	10.4	3.06	128	.257	.294	21	.220	1	20	13	0	3.0
1936	Chi-N★	16	13	.552	40	29	13	**4**	1	240⅓	246	16	76	100	12.2	3.45	116	.264	.322	17	.202	0	15	14	-1	1.5
1937	StL-N	18	11	.621	36	33	18	2	0	238⅔	280	32	69	87	13.2	4.53	88	.287	.335	21	.262	4	-16	-14	-3	-1.4
1938	StL-N	13	8	.619	31	26	12	4	0	197	199	14	64	89	12.1	3.97	100	.256	.314	23	.324	5	-4	-0	-2	0.3
1939	StL-N☆	13	7	.650	34	21	6	2	0	162	160	14	49	59	11.7	3.78	109	.259	.316	10	.192	1	3	6	-0	0.7

YEAR	TM/L	W	L	PCT	G	GS	CG	SH	SV	IP	H	HR	BB	SO	RAT	ERA	ERA+	OAV	OOB	BH	AVG	PB	PR	/A	PD	TPI
1940	StL-N	16	10	.615	33	31	17	1	0	232	235	17	47	85	11.1	3.14	127	.257	.296	18	.209	2	18	22	1	2.6
1941	StL-N☆	17	9	.654	37	30	12	4	0	246	227	19	82	83	11.4	3.15	120	.249	.313	9	.117	-2	13	17	-2	1.3
1942	StL-N	6	4	.600	12	12	5	0	0	82	76	8	15	31	10.0	3.29	104	.238	.272	10	.333	3	0	1	-1	0.3
	Chi-N	5	7	.417	15	12	8	1	2	99	97	2	21	28	10.7	2.27	141	.259	.298	6	.188	-0	11	10	-0	1.2
	Yr	11	11	.500	27	24	13	1	2	181	173	10	36	59	10.4	2.73	121	.249	.286	16	.258	2	12	11	-1	1.5
1943	Chi-N	4	5	.444	21	10	4	0	0	88¹	82	3	18	30	10.2	3.16	106	.246	.285	5	.192	1	2	2	1	0.4
1945	Chi-N	0	1	.000	9	1	0	0	0	14	16	0	1	6	10.9	3.86	95	.267	.279	0	.000	0	-0	-0	0	0.0
Total	15	192	121	.613	445	343	192	30	13	2782¹	2726	175	739	1140	11.1	3.18	119	.255	.304	215	.223	27	188	188	-5	22.7

● **ED WARNER**   Warner, Edward Emory b: 6/20/1889, Fitchburg, Mass. d: 2/5/54, New York, N.Y. BR/TL, 5'10.5", 165 lbs. Deb: 7/2/12

YEAR	TM/L	W	L	PCT	G	GS	CG	SH	SV	IP	H	HR	BB	SO	RAT	ERA	ERA+	OAV	OOB	BH	AVG	PB	PR	/A	PD	TPI
1912	Pit-N	1	1	.500	11	3	1	1	0	45	40	0	18	13	12.2	3.60	91	.242	.328	1	.133	-1	-1	-2	1	-0.1

● **JACK WARNER**   Warner, Jack Dyer b: 7/12/40, Brandywine, W.Va. BR/TR, 5'11", 190 lbs. Deb: 4/10/62

YEAR	TM/L	W	L	PCT	G	GS	CG	SH	SV	IP	H	HR	BB	SO	RAT	ERA	ERA+	OAV	OOB	BH	AVG	PB	PR	/A	PD	TPI
1962	Chi-N	0	0	—	7	0	0	0	0	7	9	3	0	3	11.6	7.71	54	.321	.321	0	—	0	-3	-3	0	0.0
1963	Chi-N	0	1	.000	8	0	0	0	0	22²	21	1	8	7	11.5	2.78	126	.256	.322	1	.250	0	1	2	-0	0.1
1964	Chi-N	0	0	—	7	0	0	0	0	9¹	12	0	4	6	15.4	2.89	128	.333	.400	0	—	0	1	1	0	0.0
1965	Chi-N	0	1	.000	11	0	0	0	0	15²	22	1	9	7	17.8	8.62	43	.355	.437	0	.000	-0	-9	-9	0	-0.5
Total	4	0	2	.000	33	0	0	0	0	54²	64	5	21	23	14.0	5.10	72	.308	.371	1	.200	0	-10	-9	0	-0.4

● **MIKE WARREN**   Warren, Michael Bruce b: 3/26/61, Inglewood, Cal. BR/TR, 6'1", 175 lbs. Deb: 6/12/83

YEAR	TM/L	W	L	PCT	G	GS	CG	SH	SV	IP	H	HR	BB	SO	RAT	ERA	ERA+	OAV	OOB	BH	AVG	PB	PR	/A	PD	TPI
1983	Oak-A	5	3	.625	12	9	3	1	0	65³	51	4	24	39	9.6	4.11	94	—	.215	.273	0	—	-0	-2	-1	0.2
1984	Oak-A	3	6	.333	24	12	0	0	0	90	104	11	44	61	15.1	4.90	76	.291	.373	0	—	0	-9	-12	-2	-0.7
1985	Oak-A	1	4	.200	16	6	0	0	0	49	52	13	38	48	17.3	6.61	58	.261	.390	0	—	0	-13	-15	-1	-0.9
Total	3	9	13	.409	52	27	3	1	0	204²	207	28	100	139	13.9	5.06	75	.261	.349	0	—	0	-23	-28	-4	-1.4

● **TOMMY WARREN**   Warren, Thomas Gentry b: 7/5/17, Tulsa, Okla. d: 1/2/68, Tulsa, Okla. BB/TL, 6'1", 190 lbs. Deb: 4/18/44

YEAR	TM/L	W	L	PCT	G	GS	CG	SH	SV	IP	H	HR	BB	SO	RAT	ERA	ERA+	OAV	OOB	BH	AVG	PB	PR	/A	PD	TPI
1944	Bro-N	1	4	.200	22	4	2	0	0	68²	74	4	40	18	14.9	4.98	71	.270	.363	11	.256	2	-10	-11	0	-0.6

● **DAN WARTHEN**   Warthen, Daniel Dean b: 12/1/52, Omaha, Neb. BB/TL, 6', 200 lbs. Deb: 5/18/75 C

YEAR	TM/L	W	L	PCT	G	GS	CG	SH	SV	IP	H	HR	BB	SO	RAT	ERA	ERA+	OAV	OOB	BH	AVG	PB	PR	/A	PD	TPI
1975	Mon-N	8	6	.571	40	18	2	0	3	167²	130	8	87	128	11.7	3.11	123	.217	.317	6	.118	-2	9	13	1	0.9
1976	Mon-N	2	10	.167	23	16	2	1	0	90	90	8	66	67	14.4	5.30	70	.232	.364	0	.000	-3	-18	-16	0	-2.2
1977	Mon-N	2	3	.400	12	6	1	0	0	35	33	7	38	26	18.3	7.97	48	.262	.433	1	.111	-0	-16	-16	1	-1.9
	Phi-N	0	1	.000	3	0	0	0	0	3²	4	0	5	1	22.1	0.00	—	.267	.450	0	—	0	2	0	-0	0.4
	Yr	2	4	.333	15	6	1	0	0	38²	37	7	43	27	18.6	7.22	53	.261	.432	1	.111	-0	-14	-15	1	-1.5
1978	Hou-N	0	1	.000	5	1	0	0	0	10²	10	3	2	2	10.1	4.22	78	.250	.286	0	.000	-0	-1	-1	0	-0.1
Total	4	12	21	.364	83	41	5	1	3	307	253	26	198	224	13.3	4.31	88	.228	.347	7	.079	-6	-23	-18	1	-2.9

● **JOHN WASDIN**   Wasdin, John Truman b: 8/5/72, Fort Belvoir, Va. BR/TR, 6'2", 190 lbs. Deb: 8/24/95

YEAR	TM/L	W	L	PCT	G	GS	CG	SH	SV	IP	H	HR	BB	SO	RAT	ERA	ERA+	OAV	OOB	BH	AVG	PB	PR	/A	PD	TPI
1995	Oak-A	1	1	.500	5	2	0	0	0	17¹	14	4	3	6	9.3	4.67	96	.215	.261	0	—	0	0	-0	-1	0.0
1996	Oak-A	8	7	.533	25	21	1	0	0	131¹	145	24	50	75	13.6	5.96	81	.283	.352	0	—	0	-14	-17	-1	-1.6
Total	2	9	8	.529	30	23	1	0	0	148²	159	28	53	81	13.1	5.81	82	.276	.342	0	—	0	-14	-17	-2	-1.6

● **GEORGE WASHBURN**   Washburn, George Edward b: 10/6/14, Solon, Me. d: 1/5/79, Baton Rouge, La. BL/TR, 6'1", 175 lbs. Deb: 5/4/41

YEAR	TM/L	W	L	PCT	G	GS	CG	SH	SV	IP	H	HR	BB	SO	RAT	ERA	ERA+	OAV	OOB	BH	AVG	PB	PR	/A	PD	TPI
1941	NY-A	0	0	—	1	1	0	0	0	2	2	0	5	1	31.5	13.50	29	.286	.583	0	.000	-0	-2	-2	0	-0.7

● **GREG WASHBURN**   Washburn, Gregory James b: 12/3/46, Coal City, Ill. BR/TR, 6', 190 lbs. Deb: 6/7/69

YEAR	TM/L	W	L	PCT	G	GS	CG	SH	SV	IP	H	HR	BB	SO	RAT	ERA	ERA+	OAV	OOB	BH	AVG	PB	PR	/A	PD	TPI
1969	Cal-A	0	2	.000	8	2	0	0	0	11¹	21	0	5	4	21.4	7.94	44	.404	.466	0	—	0	-5	-6	0	-0.9

● **LIBE WASHBURN**   Washburn, Libeus b: 6/16/1874, Lyme, N.H. d: 3/22/40, Malone, N.Y. BB/TL, 5'10", 180 lbs. Deb: 5/30/02 ♦

YEAR	TM/L	W	L	PCT	G	GS	CG	SH	SV	IP	H	HR	BB	SO	RAT	ERA	ERA+	OAV	OOB	BH	AVG	PB	PR	/A	PD	TPI
1903	Phi-N	0	4	.000	4	4	4	0	0	35	44	0	11	9	14.1	4.37	75	.326	.377	3	.167	-0	-4	-4	-1	-0.5

● **RAY WASHBURN**   Washburn, Ray Clark b: 5/31/38, Pasco, Wash. BR/TR, 6'1", 205 lbs. Deb: 9/20/61

YEAR	TM/L	W	L	PCT	G	GS	CG	SH	SV	IP	H	HR	BB	SO	RAT	ERA	ERA+	OAV	OOB	BH	AVG	PB	PR	/A	PD	TPI
1961	StL-N	1	1	.500	3	2	1	0	0	20¹	10	1	7	12	8.0	1.77	248	.152	.243	1	.125	-1	5	6	0	0.5
1962	StL-N	12	9	.571	34	25	2	1	0	175²	187	25	58	109	12.7	4.10	104	.273	.332	10	.179	1	-3	3	1	0.5
1963	StL-N	5	3	.625	11	11	4	2	0	64¹	50	5	14	47	9.1	3.08	115	.212	.259	1	.053	-1	2	3	1	0.4
1964	StL-N	3	4	.429	15	10	0	0	2	60	60	7	17	28	12.3	4.05	94	.264	.329	2	.133	-0	-3	-2	1	-0.1
1965	StL-N	9	11	.450	28	16	1	1	2	119¹	114	15	28	67	10.8	3.62	106	.254	.300	5	.152	0	-1	3	-1	-0.4
1966	StL-N	11	9	.550	27	26	4	1	0	170	183	15	44	98	12.1	3.76	95	.280	.326	5	.093	-1	-3	-3	1	-0.4
1967	*StL-N	10	7	.588	27	27	3	1	0	186¹	190	14	42	98	11.4	3.53	93	.265	.309	6	.091	-2	-3	-5	2	-0.4
1968	*StL-N	14	8	.636	31	30	8	4	0	215	191	9	47	124	10.0	2.26	128	.239	.283	5	.083	0	17	15	-2	1.4
1969	StL-N	3	8	.273	28	16	2	0	0	132¹	133	9	49	80	12.4	3.06	117	.261	.327	4	.081	-0	8	8	1	0.5
1970	*Cin-N	4	4	.500	35	3	0	0	0	66¹	90	7	48	37	18.7	6.92	58	.324	.423	0	.000	-1	-21	-21	1	-2.2
Total	10	72	64	.529	239	166	25	10	5	1209²	1208	107	354	700	11.8	3.53	101	.261	.316	38	.105	-7	-3	6	4	0.6

● **BUCK WASHER**   Washer, William b: 10/11/1882, Akron, Ohio d: 12/8/55, Akron, Ohio BR/TR, 5'10", 175 lbs. Deb: 4/25/05

YEAR	TM/L	W	L	PCT	G	GS	CG	SH	SV	IP	H	HR	BB	SO	RAT	ERA	ERA+	OAV	OOB	BH	AVG	PB	PR	/A	PD	TPI
1905	Phi-N	0	0	—	1	0	0	0	0	3	4	0	2	0	27.0	6.00	49	.333	.529	0	.000	-0	-1	-1	0	0.0

● **GARY WASLEWSKI**   Waslewski, Gary Lee b: 7/21/41, Meriden, Conn. BR/TR, 6'4", 195 lbs. Deb: 6/11/67

YEAR	TM/L	W	L	PCT	G	GS	CG	SH	SV	IP	H	HR	BB	SO	RAT	ERA	ERA+	OAV	OOB	BH	AVG	PB	PR	/A	PD	TPI
1967	*Bos-A	2	2	.500	12	8	0	0	0	42	34	3	20	20	11.8	3.21	108	.225	.320	1	.091	-1	0	1	0	0.1
1968	Bos-A	4	7	.364	34	11	0	0	2	105¹	108	9	40	59	13.2	3.67	86	.269	.344	1	.038	-2	-8	-6	2	-0.7
1969	StL-N	0	2	.000	12	0	0	0	1	20²	19	3	8	16	12.2	3.92	91	.244	.322	0	.000	-0	-1	-1	1	0.0
	Mon-N	3	7	.300	30	14	3	1	0	109¹	102	5	63	63	13.4	3.29	112	.252	.364	1	.033	-2	4	5	1	0.2
	Yr	3	9	.250	42	14	3	1	1	130	121	8	71	79	13.8	3.39	108	.250	.355	1	.032	-2	3	4	1	0.2
1970	Mon-N	0	2	.000	6	4	0	0	0	24²	23	3	15	19	13.9	5.11	80	.247	.352	0	.000	-0	-3	-3	1	-0.2
	NY-A	2	2	.500	26	5	0	0	4	55	42	4	27	27	11.9	3.11	113	.219	.327	1	.100	-1	4	2	1	0.2
1971	NY-A	0	1	.000	24	0	0	0	0	35²	28	2	16	17	11.4	3.28	98	.214	.304	1	—	-0	-0	-0	0	0.0
1972	Oak-A	0	0	—	2	0	0	0	0	17²	12	3	8	8	10.2	2.04	140	.190	.282	0	—	-0	2	0	0	0.3
Total	6	11	26	.297	152	42	5	1	5	410¹	368	32	197	229	12.9	3.44	100	.243	.338	4	.045	-6	-2	1	4	-0.1

● **STEVE WATERBURY**   Waterbury, Steven Craig b: 4/6/52, Carbondale, Ill. BR/TR, 6'5", 190 lbs. Deb: 9/14/76

YEAR	TM/L	W	L	PCT	G	GS	CG	SH	SV	IP	H	HR	BB	SO	RAT	ERA	ERA+	OAV	OOB	BH	AVG	PB	PR	/A	PD	TPI
1976	StL-N	0	0	—	5	0	0	0	0	6	7	0	3	4	15.0	6.00	59	.304	.385	0	—	0	-2	-2	-0	0.0

● **FRED WATERS**   Waters, Fred Warren b: 2/2/27, Benton, Miss. d: 8/28/89, Pensacola, Fla. BL/TL, 5'11", 185 lbs. Deb: 9/20/55

YEAR	TM/L	W	L	PCT	G	GS	CG	SH	SV	IP	H	HR	BB	SO	RAT	ERA	ERA+	OAV	OOB	BH	AVG	PB	PR	/A	PD	TPI
1955	Pit-N	0	0	—	2	0	0	0	0	5	7	1	2	0	16.2	3.60	114	.318	.375	0	.000	-0	0	0	0	0.0
1956	Pit-N	2	2	.500	23	5	1	0	0	51	48	3	30	14	13.9	2.82	134	.258	.364	1	.050	-1	5	5	-1	0.1
Total	2	2	2	.500	25	5	1	0	0	56	55	4	32	14	14.1	2.89	131	.264	.365	1	.048	-1	6	6	-1	0.1

● **BOB WATKINS**   Watkins, Robert Cecil b: 3/12/48, San Francisco, Cal. BR/TR, 6'1", 170 lbs. Deb: 9/6/69

YEAR	TM/L	W	L	PCT	G	GS	CG	SH	SV	IP	H	HR	BB	SO	RAT	ERA	ERA+	OAV	OOB	BH	AVG	PB	PR	/A	PD	TPI
1969	Hou-N	0	0	—	5	0	0	0	0	15²	13	1	13	11	14.9	5.17	68	.241	.388	0	.000	-0	-3	-3	0	-0.1

● **SCOTT WATKINS**   Watkins, Scott Allen b: 5/15/70, Tulsa, Okla. BL/TL, 6'3", 180 lbs. Deb: 8/1/95

YEAR	TM/L	W	L	PCT	G	GS	CG	SH	SV	IP	H	HR	BB	SO	RAT	ERA	ERA+	OAV	OOB	BH	AVG	PB	PR	/A	PD	TPI
1995	Min-A	0	0	—	27	0	0	0	0	21²	22	1	6	11	13.7	5.40	88	.278	.367	0	—	0	-2	-2	0	0.0

● **ALLEN WATSON**   Watson, Allen Kenneth b: 11/18/70, Jamaica, N.Y. BL/TL, 6'3", 195 lbs. Deb: 7/8/93

YEAR	TM/L	W	L	PCT	G	GS	CG	SH	SV	IP	H	HR	BB	SO	RAT	ERA	ERA+	OAV	OOB	BH	AVG	PB	PR	/A	PD	TPI
1993	StL-N	6	7	.462	16	15	0	0	0	86	90	11	28	49	12.7	4.60	86	.271	.333	6	.231	2	-5	-6	-1	-0.7
1994	StL-N	6	5	.545	22	22	0	0	0	115²	130	15	53	74	14.3	5.52	75	.286	.370	6	.158	1	-17	-18	-1	-1.4
1995	StL-N	7	9	.438	21	19	0	0	0	114¹	126	17	41	49	13.5	4.96	84	.285	.352	15	.417	6	-10	-10	-1	-0.5
1996	SF-N	8	12	.400	29	29	2	0	0	185²	189	28	69	128	12.7	4.61	89	.273	.343	15	.231	4	-8	-11	-2	-0.7
Total	4	27	33	.450	88	85	2	0	0	501²	535	71	191	300	13.4	4.88	84	.279	.350	42	.255	14	-40	-44	-3	-3.3

● **DOC WATSON**   Watson, Charles John b: 1/30/1886, Kensington, Ohio d: 12/30/49, San Diego, Cal. BR/TL, 6', 170 lbs. Deb: 9/3/13

YEAR	TM/L	W	L	PCT	G	GS	CG	SH	SV	IP	H	HR	BB	SO	RAT	ERA	ERA+	OAV	OOB	BH	AVG	PB	PR	/A	PD	TPI
1913	Chi-N	1	0	1.000	1	1	1	0	0	9	8	0	6	1	14.4	1.00	318	.242	.375	0	.000	0	2	2	1	0.2
1914	Chi-F	9	8	.529	26	18	10	3	1	172	145	2	49	69	10.3	2.04	130	.236	.295	5	.093	-5	16	12	-1	0.5

YEAR	TM/L	W	L	PCT	G	GS	CG	SH	SV	IP	H	HR	BB	SO	RAT	ERA	ERA+	OAV	OOB	BH	AVG	PB	PR	/A	PD	TPI
	StL-F	3	4	.429	9	7	4	2	0	56	41	1	24	18	11.1	1.93	158	.211	.311	2	.125	-1	6	7	-1	0.6
	Yr	12	12	.500	35	25	14	5	1	228	186	3	73	87	10.4	2.01	137	.229	.296	7	.100	-6	22	19	-2	1.1
1915	StL-F	9	9	.500	33	20	6	0	0	135²	132	1	58	45	12.9	3.98	72	.273	.355	5	.125	-3	-19	-17	-4	-2.8
Total 3		22	21	.512	69	46	21	5	1	372²	326	4	137	133	11.5	2.70	104	.246	.322	12	.107	-9	5	4	-7	-1.5

● MULE WATSON
Watson, John Reeves　b: 10/15/1896, Homer, La.　d: 8/25/49, Shreveport, La.　BR/TR, 6'1.5", 185 lbs.　Deb: 7/4/18

YEAR	TM/L	W	L	PCT	G	GS	CG	SH	SV	IP	H	HR	BB	SO	RAT	ERA	ERA+	OAV	OOB	BH	AVG	PB	PR	/A	PD	TPI
1918	Phi-A	7	10	.412	21	19	11	3	0	141²	139	0	44	30	11.8	3.37	87	.288	.350	6	.128	-3	-9	-7	-2	-1.3
1919	Phi-A	0	1	.000	4	2	0	0	0	14¹	17	2	7	6	15.1	6.91	50	.309	.387	0	.000	-1	-6	-6	1	-0.3
1920	Bos-N	0	0	—	1	0	0	0	0	3	0	0	0	0	0.0	0.00	—	.000	.000	0	.000	-0	1	1	0	0.0
	Pit-N	0	0	—	5	0	0	0	0	11¹	15	2	7	1	17.5	8.74	37	.326	.415	0	.000	-0	-7	-7	0	-0.1
	Bos-N	5	4	.556	12	10	4	2	0	71²	79	0	17	16	12.2	3.77	81	.298	.343	3	.130	-1	-5	-6	-0	-0.8
	Yr	5	4	.556	18	10	4	2	0	86	94	2	24	17	12.5	4.29	72	.294	.345	3	.111	-2	-11	-12	-0	-0.9
1921	Bos-N	14	13	.519	44	31	15	1	2	259¹	269	11	57	48	11.6	3.85	95	.270	.314	12	.138	-4	-2	-6	-1	-1.0
1922	Bos-N	8	14	.364	41	27	8	1	1	201	262	9	59	53	14.6	4.70	85	.317	.366	13	.197	-4	-13	-16	-0	-1.5
1923	Bos-N	1	2	.333	11	4	1	0	0	31¹	42	2	20	10	17.8	5.17	77	.339	.431	2	.250	-0	-4	-4	-0	-0.4
	*NY-N	8	5	.615	17	15	8	0	0	108¹	117	11	21	26	11.5	3.41	112	.280	.316	8	.174	-1	7	5	-1	0.3
	Yr	9	7	.563	28	19	9	0	1	139²	159	13	41	36	13.0	3.80	101	.293	.344	10	.185	-1	3	1	-1	-0.1
1924	*NY-N	7	4	.636	22	16	6	1	0	99²	122	7	24	18	13.3	3.79	97	.303	.343	9	.257	4	1	-1	-1	0.2
Total 7		50	53	.485	178	124	53	8	4	941²	1062	44	256	208	12.8	4.03	89	.293	.342	53	.165	-8	-38	-45	-3	-4.9

● MILT WATSON
Watson, Milton Wilson "Mule"　b: 1/10/1890, Flovilla, Ga.　d: 4/10/62, Pine Bluff, Ark.　BR/TR, 6'1", 180 lbs.　Deb: 7/26/16

YEAR	TM/L	W	L	PCT	G	GS	CG	SH	SV	IP	H	HR	BB	SO	RAT	ERA	ERA+	OAV	OOB	BH	AVG	PB	PR	/A	PD	TPI
1916	StL-N	4	6	.400	18	13	5	2	0	103	109	3	33	27	12.8	3.06	86	.283	.346	7	.219	0	-5	-5	-1	-0.5
1917	StL-N	10	13	.435	41	20	5	3	0	161¹	149	3	51	45	11.7	3.51	77	.252	.321	5	.098	-4	-14	-15	-1	-2.3
1918	Phi-N	5	7	.417	23	11	6	0	0	112²	126	1	36	29	13.1	3.43	87	.293	.350	3	.075	-4	-8	-5	-1	-1.1
1919	Phi-N	2	4	.333	8	4	3	0	0	47	51	3	19	12	13.8	5.17	62	.282	.356	1	.063	-2	-12	-10	-1	-1.3
Total 4		21	30	.412	90	48	19	5	0	424	435	10	139	113	12.5	3.57	79	.274	.339	16	.115	-9	-40	-35	-0	-5.2

● MOTHER WATSON
Watson, Walter L.　b: 1/27/1865, Middleport, Ohio　d: 11/23/1898, Middleport, Ohio　5'9", 145 lbs.　Deb: 5/19/1887

YEAR	TM/L	W	L	PCT	G	GS	CG	SH	SV	IP	H	HR	BB	SO	RAT	ERA	ERA+	OAV	OOB	BH	AVG	PB	PR	/A	PD	TPI
1887	Cin-a	0	1	.000	2	2	1	0	0	14	22	0	6	1	18.0	5.79	75	.328	.384	1	.125	-0	-2	-2	-1	-0.2

● EDDIE WATT
Watt, Edward Dean　b: 4/4/41, Lamoni, Iowa　BR/TR, 5'10", 197 lbs.　Deb: 4/12/66

YEAR	TM/L	W	L	PCT	G	GS	CG	SH	SV	IP	H	HR	BB	SO	RAT	ERA	ERA+	OAV	OOB	BH	AVG	PB	PR	/A	PD	TPI
1966	Bal-A	9	7	.563	43	13	1	0	4	145²	123	11	44	102	10.6	3.83	87	.230	.295	14	.304	6	-6	-8	-2	-0.5
1967	Bal-A	3	5	.375	49	0	0	0	8	103²	67	5	37	93	9.3	2.26	140	.183	.263	4	.182	2	11	10	0	1.2
1968	Bal-A	5	5	.500	59	0	0	0	11	83¹	63	1	35	72	10.8	2.27	129	.209	.295	0	.000	-0	7	6	0	0.9
1969	*Bal-A	5	2	.714	56	0	0	0	16	71	49	3	26	46	9.8	1.65	216	.194	.274	0	.000	-0	16	15	-0	2.2
1970	*Bal-A	7	7	.500	53	0	0	0	12	55¹	44	3	29	33	12.7	3.25	112	.239	.358	1	.125	-0	3	2	-0	0.7
1971	*Bal-A	3	1	.750	35	0	0	0	11	39²	39	1	8	26	10.7	1.82	185	.260	.297	0	—	-0	7	7	-1	1.1
1972	Bal-A	2	3	.400	38	0	0	0	7	45²	30	2	20	23	10.2	2.17	142	.191	.291	0	.000	-0	5	5	-0	0.7
1973	*Bal-A	3	4	.429	30	0	0	0	5	71	62	8	21	38	10.8	3.30	113	.235	.296	0	—	-0	4	3	-1	0.3
1974	Phi-N	1	1	.500	42	0	0	0	6	38¹	39	3	26	21	15.7	3.99	95	.275	.394	0	—	-0	-2	-1	-0	-0.1
1975	Chi-N	0	1	.000	6	0	0	0	0	6	14	0	8	6	34.5	13.50	28	.452	.575	0	—	-0	-7	-6	-0	-0.9
Total 10		38	36	.514	411	13	1	0	80	659²	530	37	254	462	11.0	2.91	116	.222	.304	19	.190	6	38	33	-3	5.6

● FRANK WATT
Watt, Frank Marion "Kilo"　b: 12/15/02, Washington, D.C.　d: 8/31/56, Washington, D.C.　BR/TR, 6'1", 205 lbs.　Deb: 4/14/31　F

YEAR	TM/L	W	L	PCT	G	GS	CG	SH	SV	IP	H	HR	BB	SO	RAT	ERA	ERA+	OAV	OOB	BH	AVG	PB	PR	/A	PD	TPI
1931	Phi-N	5	5	.500	38	12	5	0	2	122²	147	5	49	25	14.6	4.84	88	.296	.362	8	.205		-13	-8	-2	-0.8

● JIM WAUGH
Waugh, James Elden　b: 11/25/33, Lancaster, Ohio　BR/TR, 6'3", 185 lbs.　Deb: 4/19/52

YEAR	TM/L	W	L	PCT	G	GS	CG	SH	SV	IP	H	HR	BB	SO	RAT	ERA	ERA+	OAV	OOB	BH	AVG	PB	PR	/A	PD	TPI
1952	Pit-N	1	6	.143	17	7	1	0	0	52¹	61	4	32	18	16.3	6.36	63	.285	.383	1	.100	-0	-15	-14	-0	-1.6
1953	Pit-N	4	5	.444	29	11	1	0	0	90¹	108	21	56	23	16.3	6.48	69	.295	.389	5	.227	0	-22	-20	-1	-1.7
Total 2		5	11	.313	46	18	2	0	0	142²	169	25	88	41	16.3	6.43	67	.291	.387	6	.188	-0	-37	-34	-1	-3.3

● FRANK WAYENBERG
Wayenberg, Frank　b: 8/27/1898, Franklin, Kan.　d: 4/16/75, Zanesville, Ohio　BR/TR, 6'0.5", 172 lbs.　Deb: 8/25/24

YEAR	TM/L	W	L	PCT	G	GS	CG	SH	SV	IP	H	HR	BB	SO	RAT	ERA	ERA+	OAV	OOB	BH	AVG	PB	PR	/A	PD	TPI
1924	Cle-A	0	0	—	2	1	0	0	0	6²	7	0	5	3	17.6	5.40	79	.259	.394	1	.500		-1	-1	-0	0.0

● GARY WAYNE
Wayne, Gary Anthony　b: 11/30/62, Dearborn, Mich.　BL/TL, 6'3", 185 lbs.　Deb: 4/7/89

YEAR	TM/L	W	L	PCT	G	GS	CG	SH	SV	IP	H	HR	BB	SO	RAT	ERA	ERA+	OAV	OOB	BH	AVG	PB	PR	/A	PD	TPI
1989	Min-A	3	4	.429	60	0	0	0	1	71	55	4	36	41	11.7	3.30	126	.212	.311	0	—	0	5	7	-0	0.3
1990	Min-A	1	1	.500	38	0	0	0	1	38²	38	5	13	28	12.1	4.19	99	.255	.319	0	—	0	-1	-0	-0	-0.1
1991	Min-A	0	1	.000	8	0	0	0	0	12¹	11	1	4	7	11.7	5.11	84	.244	.320	0	—	0	-1	-0	-0	-0.1
1992	Min-A	3	3	.500	41	0	0	0	0	48	46	2	19	29	12.8	2.63	154	.260	.342	0	—	0	7	8	1	1.0
1993	Col-N	5	3	.625	65	0	0	0	0	62¹	68	3	26	49	13.7	5.05	94	.276	.348	1	1.000	0	-7	-2	-0	-0.2
1994	LA-N	1	3	.250	19	0	0	0	0	17¹	19	2	6	10	14.5	4.67	84	.279	.364	0	.000	-0	-1	-1	-0	-0.3
Total 6		14	14	.500	231	0	0	0	4	249²	237	22	104	164	12.7	3.93	109	.251	.332	1	.500	0	1	10	1	0.6

● KEN WEAFER
Weafer, Kenneth Albert "Al"　b: 2/6/14, Woburn, Mass.　BR/TR, 6'0.5", 183 lbs.　Deb: 5/29/36

YEAR	TM/L	W	L	PCT	G	GS	CG	SH	SV	IP	H	HR	BB	SO	RAT	ERA	ERA+	OAV	OOB	BH	AVG	PB	PR	/A	PD	TPI
1936	Bos-N	0	0	—	1	0	0	0	0	3	6	1	3	0	27.0	12.00	32	.375	.474	0	.000	-0	-3	-3	-0	0.0

● DAVE WEATHERS
Weathers, John David　b: 9/25/69, Lawrenceburg, Tenn.　BR/TR, 6'3", 205 lbs.　Deb: 8/2/91

YEAR	TM/L	W	L	PCT	G	GS	CG	SH	SV	IP	H	HR	BB	SO	RAT	ERA	ERA+	OAV	OOB	BH	AVG	PB	PR	/A	PD	TPI
1991	Tor-A	1	0	1.000	15	0	0	0	0	14²	15	1	17	13	20.9	4.91	86	.263	.447	0	—	0	-1	-1	-0	-0.1
1992	Tor-A	0	0	—	2	0	0	0	0	3¹	5	1	2	3	18.9	8.10	50	.385	.467	0	—	0	-2	-1	-0	0.0
1993	Fla-N	2	3	.400	14	6	0	0	0	45²	57	3	13	34	14.0	5.12	84	.306	.355	1	.100	-1	-5	-4	-0	-0.5
1994	Fla-N	8	12	.400	24	24	0	0	0	135	166	13	59	72	15.3	5.27	83	.306	.379	3	.068	-2	-16	-13	-1	-2.0
1995	Fla-N	4	5	.444	28	15	0	0	0	90¹	104	8	52	60	16.0	5.98	70	.295	.394	4	.154	-1	-18	-18	-1	-1.6
1996	Fla-N	2	2	.500	31	8	0	0	0	71¹	85	7	28	40	14.8	4.54	89	.302	.374	3	.158	1	-3	-4	-0	-0.1
	*NY-A	0	2	.000	11	4	0	0	0	17¹	23	1	14	13	20.3	9.35	54	.315	.438	0	—	0	-8	-8	-0	-0.8
Total 6		17	24	.415	125	57	0	0	0	377²	455	34	185	235	15.7	5.48	78	.303	.385	11	.111	-3	-53	-50	-2	-5.1

● FLOYD WEAVER
Weaver, David Floyd　b: 5/12/41, Ben Franklin, Tex.　BR/TR, 6'4", 195 lbs.　Deb: 9/30/62

YEAR	TM/L	W	L	PCT	G	GS	CG	SH	SV	IP	H	HR	BB	SO	RAT	ERA	ERA+	OAV	OOB	BH	AVG	PB	PR	/A	PD	TPI
1962	Cle-A	1	0	1.000	1	1	0	0	0	5	3	1	0	8	5.4	1.80	215	.167	.167	1	.500	0	1	1	-0	0.3
1965	Cle-A	2	2	.500	32	1	0	0	1	61¹	61	10	24	37	13.2	5.43	64	.265	.347	1	.091	0	-13	-13	-0	-0.9
1970	Chi-A	1	2	.333	31	3	0	0	0	61²	52	7	31	51	12.4	4.38	89	.233	.332	0	.000	-1	-5	-3	-1	-0.3
1971	Mil-A	0	1	.000	21	0	0	0	0	27¹	33	3	18	12	17.1	7.24	48	.320	.426	0	—	-0	-11	-11	-0	-0.4
Total 4		4	5	.444	85	5	0	0	1	155¹	149	21	73	108	13.3	5.21	70	.260	.351	2	.100	-0	-28	-27	-1	-1.3

● HARRY WEAVER
Weaver, Harry Abraham　b: 2/26/1892, Clarendon, Pa.　d: 5/30/83, Rochester, N.Y.　BR/TR, 5'11", 160 lbs.　Deb: 9/18/15

YEAR	TM/L	W	L	PCT	G	GS	CG	SH	SV	IP	H	HR	BB	SO	RAT	ERA	ERA+	OAV	OOB	BH	AVG	PB	PR	/A	PD	TPI
1915	Phi-A	0	2	.000	2	2	2	0	0	18	18	1	10	1	14.5	3.00	98	.290	.397	1	.167	0	-0	-0	1	0.1
1916	Phi-A	0	0	—	3	0	0	0	0	8	14	0	5	2	21.4	10.13	28	.424	.500	1	.500	0	-6	-6	0	0.0
1917	Chi-N	1	1	.500	4	2	1	1	0	19²	17	0	7	8	11.0	2.75	105	.230	.296	1	.200	0	-0	0	1	0.1
1918	Chi-N	2	2	.500	8	3	1	0	1	32²	27	1	7	9	9.4	2.20	126	.227	.270	2	.250	-1	2	2	0	0.4
1919	Chi-N	0	0	—	2	1	0	0	0	3¹	6	0	2	1	24.3	10.80	27	.375	.474	0	.000	-0	-3	-3	-0	-0.7
Total 5		3	5	.333	19	8	4	2	1	81²	82	2	31	21	12.7	3.64	78	.270	.341	5	.227	-1	-8	-7	2	-0.1

● JIM WEAVER
Weaver, James Brian "Fluff"　b: 2/19/39, Lancaster, Pa.　BL/TL, 6', 178 lbs.　Deb: 8/13/67

YEAR	TM/L	W	L	PCT	G	GS	CG	SH	SV	IP	H	HR	BB	SO	RAT	ERA	ERA+	OAV	OOB	BH	AVG	PB	PR	/A	PD	TPI
1967	Cal-A	3	0	1.000	13	2	0	0	0	30¹	26	2	9	20	10.7	2.67	118	.232	.295	0	.000	-1	2	2	2	0.3
1968	Cal-A	0	1	.000	14	0	0	0	0	22²	22	4	10	8	12.7	2.38	122	.259	.337	0	.000	-0	2	1	-1	0.0
Total 2		3	1	.750	27	2	0	0	0	53	48	6	19	28	11.5	2.55	119	.244	.313	0	.000	-1	3	3	1	0.3

● JIM WEAVER
Weaver, James Dement "Big Jim"　b: 11/25/03, Obion County, Tenn.　d: 12/12/83, Lakeland, Fla.　BR/TR, 6'6", 230 lbs.　Deb: 8/27/28

YEAR	TM/L	W	L	PCT	G	GS	CG	SH	SV	IP	H	HR	BB	SO	RAT	ERA	ERA+	OAV	OOB	BH	AVG	PB	PR	/A	PD	TPI
1928	Was-A	0	0	—	3	0	0	0	0	6	2	0	6	2	13.5	1.50	267	.143	.429	0	.000	-0	2	2	0	0.4
1931	NY-A	2	1	.667	17	5	2	0	0	57²	66	3	29	28	15.0	5.31	75	.280	.361	1	.050	-3	-6	-9	0	-0.6
1934	StL-A	0	1	.000	5	2	0	0	0	19²	17	3	20	11	16.9	6.41	78	.236	.402	1	.143	-0	-4	-3	1	-0.2
	Chi-N	11	9	.550	27	20	8	1	0	159	160	8	54	98	12.5	3.91	99	.263	.326	3	.058	-5	2	-1	-1	-0.6
1935	Pit-N	14	8	.636	33	22	11	**4**	0	176¹	177	9	58	87	12.1	3.42	110	.254	.313	4	.071	-4	12	13	1	1.2

YEAR	TM/L	W	L	PCT	G	GS	CG	SH	SV	IP	H	HR	BB	SO	RAT	ERA	ERA+	OAV	OOB	BH	AVG	PB	PR	/A	PD	TPI
1936	Pit-N	14	8	.636	38	31	11	1	0	225²	239	12	74	108	12.5	4.31	94	.272	.329	8	.101	-5	-7	-6	-2	-1.2
1937	Pit-N	8	5	.615	32	9	2	1	0	109²	106	2	31	44	11.2	3.20	121	.255	.307	4	.148	-0	9	8	-2	0.7
1938	StL-A	0	1	.000	1	1	0	0	0	7	9	0	4	4	23.1	9.00	55	.321	.486	0	.000	-0	-3	-3	-0	-0.3
	Cin-N	6	4	.600	30	15	2	0	3	129¹	109	6	54	64	11.4	3.13	117	.227	.306	9	.205	-0	9	7	-1	0.5
1939	Cin-N				3	0	0	0	0	3	3	0	1	3	12.0	3.00	128	.250	.308	0	.000	-0	0	0	-0	0.0
Total 8		57	36	.613	189	108	38	7	3	893¹	891	38	336	449	12.5	3.88	102	.258	.326	30	.104	-17	14	9	-4	-0.5

● MONTE WEAVER
Weaver, Montie Morton "Prof" b: 6/15/06, Helton, N.C. d: 6/14/94, Orlando, Fla. BL/TR, 6', 170 lbs. Deb: 9/20/31

YEAR	TM/L	W	L	PCT	G	GS	CG	SH	SV	IP	H	HR	BB	SO	RAT	ERA	ERA+	OAV	OOB	BH	AVG	PB	PR	/A	PD	TPI
1931	Was-A	1	0	1.000	3	1	1	0	0	10	11	0	6	6	15.3	4.50	95	.268	.362	0	.000	-0	-0	-0	0	0.0
1932	Was-A	22	10	.688	43	30	13	1	2	234	236	9	112	83	13.4	4.08	106	.261	.342	27	.287	6	10	6	-2	1.0
1933	*Was-A	10	5	.667	23	21	12	1	0	152¹	147	3	53	45	11.9	3.25	129	.257	.322	7	.125	-3	17	16	-1	1.0
1934	Was-A	11	15	.423	31	31	11	0	0	204²	255	16	63	51	14.0	4.79	90	.306	.355	13	.162	-2	-7	-11	-2	-1.5
1935	Was-A	1	1	.500	5	2	0	0	0	12	16	1	6	4	16.5	5.25	82	.320	.393	1	.333	-0	-1	-1	-0	-0.2
1936	Was-A	6	4	.600	26	5	3	0	1	91	92	3	38	15	12.9	4.35	110	.262	.334	5	.200	1	7	4	-0	0.4
1937	Was-A	12	9	.571	30	26	9	0	0	188²	197	21	70	44	12.7	4.20	105	.266	.330	14	.206	1	9	5	1	0.6
1938	Was-A	7	6	.538	31	18	7	0	1	139	157	9	74	43	15.2	5.24	86	.282	.370	12	.267	4	-7	-11	-1	-0.6
1939	Bos-A	1	0	1.000	9	1	1	0	1	20¹	26	0	13	6	17.7	6.64	71	.321	.421	0	.000	-1	-5	-4	-1	-0.3
Total 9		71	50	.587	201	135	57	2	4	1052	1137	62	435	297	13.5	4.36	101	.276	.345	79	.209	5	24	3	-6	0.4

● ORLIE WEAVER
Weaver, Orville Forest b: 6/4/1886, Newport, Ky. d: 11/28/70, New Orleans, La. BR/TR, 6', 180 lbs. Deb: 9/14/10

YEAR	TM/L	W	L	PCT	G	GS	CG	SH	SV	IP	H	HR	BB	SO	RAT	ERA	ERA+	OAV	OOB	BH	AVG	PB	PR	/A	PD	TPI
1910	Chi-N	1	1	.500	7	2	2	0	0	32	34	3	15	22	14.1	3.66	79	.270	.352	2	.154	-1	-2	-3	-1	-0.3
1911	Chi-N	2	2	.500	6	3	1	1	0	43²	29	0	17	20	10.3	2.06	161	.196	.296	1	.059	-1	7	6	-0	0.3
	Bos-N	3	12	.200	27	17	4	0	1	121	140	9	84	50	17.2	6.47	59	.303	.418	5	.122	-4	-41	-36	-2	-4.1
	Yr	5	14	.263	33	20	5	1	1	164²	169	9	101	70	15.1	5.30	70	.275	.384	6	.103	-4	-35	-29	-3	-3.8
Total 2		6	15	.286	40	22	7	1	0	196²	203	11	116	92	15.1	5.03	71	.276	.383	8	.113	-4	-37	-32	-4	-4.1

● ROGER WEAVER
Weaver, Roger Edward b: 10/6/54, Amsterdam, N.Y. BR/TR, 6'3", 190 lbs. Deb: 6/6/80

YEAR	TM/L	W	L	PCT	G	GS	CG	SH	SV	IP	H	HR	BB	SO	RAT	ERA	ERA+	OAV	OOB	BH	AVG	PB	PR	/A	PD	TPI
1980	Det-A	3	4	.429	19	8	1	0	0	63²	56	5	34	42	12.9	4.10	100	.247	.347	0	—	0	-0	0	1	-0.1

● SAM WEAVER
Weaver, Samuel H. b: 7/10/1855, Philadelphia, Pa. d: 2/1/14, Philadelphia, Pa. BR/TR, 5'10", 175 lbs. Deb: 10/25/1875

YEAR	TM/L	W	L	PCT	G	GS	CG	SH	SV	IP	H	HR	BB	SO	RAT	ERA	ERA+	OAV	OOB	BH	AVG	PB	PR	/A	PD	TPI
1875	Phi-n	1	0	1.000	1	1	1	0	0	6	6	0	2	2	12.0	1.50	152	.240	.296	1	.250	0	0	1		0.1
1878	Mil-N	12	31	.279	45	43	39	1	0	383	371	2	21	95	**9.2**	1.95	135	.237	**.247**	34	.200	-3	15	**29**	0	**2.7**
1882	Phi-a	26	15	.634	42	41	41	2	0	371	374	6	35	104	9.9	2.74	109	.245	.262	36	.232	1	-2	10	1	1.1
1883	Lou-a	24	22	.522	46	46	45	4	0	400²	451	3	35	105	10.9	3.71	81	.266	.281	37	.192	0	-18	-32	-1	-3.0
1884	Phi-U	5	10	.333	17	17	14	0	0	136	206	3	11	40	14.4	5.76	40	.328	.339	18	.214	-5	-50	-52	-1	-4.4
1886	Phi-a	2	2	.000	2	2	1	0	0	11	30	0	2	2	27.0	14.73	26	.423	.446	1	.143	-1	-14	-14	-0	-1.4
Total 5		67	80	.456	152	149	140	7	0	1301²	1432	14	104	346	10.6	3.22	88	.261	.275	126	.207	-7	-69	-54	-1	-5.0

● LEFTY WEBB
Webb, Cleon Earl b: 3/1/1885, Mt.Gilead, Ohio d: 1/12/58, Circleville, Ohio BB/TL, 5'11", 165 lbs. Deb: 5/23/10

YEAR	TM/L	W	L	PCT	G	GS	CG	SH	SV	IP	H	HR	BB	SO	RAT	ERA	ERA+	OAV	OOB	BH	AVG	PB	PR	/A	PD	TPI
1910	Pit-N	2	1	.667	7	3	2	0	0	27	29	0	6	13	13.3	5.67	55	.266	.333	2	.200	-0	-8	-8	-0	-0.8

● HANK WEBB
Webb, Henry Gaylord Matthew b: 5/21/50, Copiague, N.Y. BR/TR, 6'3", 175 lbs. Deb: 9/5/72

YEAR	TM/L	W	L	PCT	G	GS	CG	SH	SV	IP	H	HR	BB	SO	RAT	ERA	ERA+	OAV	OOB	BH	AVG	PB	PR	/A	PD	TPI
1972	NY-N	0	0	—	6	2	0	0	0	18¹	9	1	9	15	13.3	4.42	76	.261	.346	0	.000	-1	-2	-2	1	0.0
1973	NY-N	0	0	—	2	0	0	0	0	1²	2	1	2	1	21.6	10.80	33	.286	.444	0	—	0	-1	-1	-0	0.0
1974	NY-N	0	2	.000	3	2	0	0	0	10	15	1	10	8	23.4	7.20	49	.341	.473	0	.000	-0	-4	-4	-0	-0.7
1975	NY-N	7	6	.538	29	15	3	1	0	115	102	6	62	38	12.9	4.07	85	.236	.333	8	.258	2	-6	-8	-1	-0.7
1976	NY-N	0	1	.000	8	0	0	0	0	16	17	2	7	7	14.6	4.50	73	.274	.366	0	.000	-0	-2	-2	-0	-0.1
1977	LA-N	0	0	—	5	0	0	0	0	8	5	1	1	2	7.9	2.25	170	.192	.250	0	—	-0	1	1	-0	0.0
Total 6		7	9	.438	53	19	3	1	0	169	159	18	91	71	13.6	4.31	80	.248	.346	8	.200	1	-13	-16	-1	-1.5

● RED WEBB
Webb, Samuel Henry b: 9/25/24, Washington, D.C. d: 2/7/96, Hyattsville, Md. BL/TR, 6', 175 lbs. Deb: 9/15/48

YEAR	TM/L	W	L	PCT	G	GS	CG	SH	SV	IP	H	HR	BB	SO	RAT	ERA	ERA+	OAV	OOB	BH	AVG	PB	PR	/A	PD	TPI
1948	NY-N	2	1	.667	5	3	2	0	0	28	27	2	10	9	12.2	3.21	122	.248	.317	2	.222	-0	2	2	0	0.2
1949	NY-N	1	1	.500	20	0	0	0	0	44²	41	3	21	9	12.5	4.03	99	.248	.333	4	.400	2	-0	-0	2	0.4
Total 2		3	2	.600	25	3	2	0	0	72²	68	5	31	18	12.4	3.72	107	.248	.327	6	.316	2	2	2	2	0.6

● BILL WEBB
Webb, William Frederick b: 12/12/13, Atlanta, Ga. d: 6/1/94, Austell, Ga. BR/TR, 6'2", 180 lbs. Deb: 5/15/43

YEAR	TM/L	W	L	PCT	G	GS	CG	SH	SV	IP	H	HR	BB	SO	RAT	ERA	ERA+	OAV	OOB	BH	AVG	PB	PR	/A	PD	TPI
1943	Phi-N	0	0	—	1	0	0	0	0	1	1	1	1	0	18.0	9.00	37	.333	.500	0	—	0	-1	-1	-0	0.0

● LES WEBBER
Webber, Lester Elmer b: 5/6/15, Kelseyville, Cal. d: 11/13/86, Santa Maria, Cal. BR/TR, 6'0.5", 185 lbs. Deb: 5/17/42

YEAR	TM/L	W	L	PCT	G	GS	CG	SH	SV	IP	H	HR	BB	SO	RAT	ERA	ERA+	OAV	OOB	BH	AVG	PB	PR	/A	PD	TPI
1942	Bro-N	3	2	.600	19	3	1	0	1	51²	46	2	22	23	11.8	2.96	110	.230	.306	1	.071	-1	2	1	-1	0.1
1943	Bro-N	2	2	.500	54	0	0	0	10	115²	112	6	69	24	14.5	3.81	88	.264	.373	3	.120	-1	-6	-6	2	-0.2
1944	Bro-N	7	8	.467	48	9	1	0	0	140¹	157	9	64	42	14.4	4.94	72	.282	.357	8	.205	1	-21	-22	4	-1.7
1945	Bro-N	7	3	.700	17	5	5	0	0	75¹	69	3	25	30	11.3	3.58	105	.237	.300	2	.091	-1	2	1	-1	0.0
1946	Bro-N	3	3	.500	11	4	0	0	0	43	34	5	15	16	10.3	2.30	147	.225	.295	1	.100	-1	5	5	-1	0.6
	Cle-A	1	1	.500	4	2	0	0	0	5¹	13	0	5	0	30.4	23.63	14	.464	.545	0	.000	-0	-12	-12	0	-2.8
1948	Cle-A	0	0	—	1	0	0	0	0	0²	1	0	0	1	54.0	40.50	10	.750	.800	0	—	-0	-3	-3	0	0.0
Total 6		23	19	.548	154	25	7	0	14	432	434	25	201	141	13.4	4.33	88	.262	.344	15	.135	-2	-32	-34	5	-4.0

● CHARLIE WEBER
Weber, Charles P. "Count" b: 10/22/1868, Cincinnati, Ohio d: 6/13/14, Beaumont, Tex. Deb: 7/30/1898

YEAR	TM/L	W	L	PCT	G	GS	CG	SH	SV	IP	H	HR	BB	SO	RAT	ERA	ERA+	OAV	OOB	BH	AVG	PB	PR	/A	PD	TPI
1898	Was-N	0	1	.000	1	1	0	0	0	4	9	0	1	0	27.0	15.75	23	.450	.522	0	.000	-0	-5	-5	-0	-0.8

● MIKE WEGENER
Wegener, Michael Denis b: 10/8/46, Denver, Colo. BR/TR, 6'4", 215 lbs. Deb: 4/9/69

YEAR	TM/L	W	L	PCT	G	GS	CG	SH	SV	IP	H	HR	BB	SO	RAT	ERA	ERA+	OAV	OOB	BH	AVG	PB	PR	/A	PD	TPI
1969	Mon-N	5	14	.263	32	26	4	1	0	165²	150	10	96	124	13.6	4.40	84	.243	.349	13	.241	2	-15	-13	1	-1.0
1970	Mon-N	3	6	.333	25	16	1	0	0	104¹	100	16	56	35	13.8	5.26	78	.252	.350	4	.118	-2	-14	-13	-1	-1.2
Total 2		8	20	.286	57	42	5	1	0	270	250	26	152	159	13.7	4.73	81	.247	.349	17	.193	-0	-29	-27	1	-2.2

● BILL WEGMAN
Wegman, William Edward b: 12/19/62, Cincinnati, Ohio BR/TR, 6'5", 200 lbs. Deb: 9/14/85

YEAR	TM/L	W	L	PCT	G	GS	CG	SH	SV	IP	H	HR	BB	SO	RAT	ERA	ERA+	OAV	OOB	BH	AVG	PB	PR	/A	PD	TPI
1985	Mil-A	2	0	1.000	3	3	0	0	0	17²	17	3	6	6	10.2	3.57	117	.246	.278	0	—	0	1	1	-0	0.1
1986	Mil-A	5	12	.294	35	32	2	0	0	198¹	217	32	43	82	12.1	5.13	84	.279	.323	0	—	0	-21	-18	-1	-1.4
1987	Mil-A	12	11	.522	34	33	7	0	0	225	229	31	53	102	11.5	4.24	108	.265	.312	0	—	0	5	8	-0	0.7
1988	Mil-A	13	13	.500	32	31	4	1	0	199	207	24	50	84	11.8	4.12	97	.265	.313	0	—	0	-3	-3	-1	-0.5
1989	Mil-A	2	6	.250	11	8	1	0	0	51	69	6	21	27	15.9	6.71	57	.321	.381	0	—	0	-16	-16	1	-2.0
1990	Mil-A	2	2	.500	8	5	1	0	0	29²	37	6	6	20	13.0	4.85	80	.298	.331	0	—	0	-3	-3	-1	-0.4
1991	Mil-A	15	7	.682	28	28	7	2	0	193¹	176	16	40	89	10.4	2.84	140	.242	.288	0	—	0	27	24	2	2.9
1992	Mil-A	13	14	.481	35	35	7	0	0	261²	251	29	55	127	10.8	3.20	120	.250	.295	0	—	0	22	19	2	2.2
1993	Mil-A	4	14	.222	20	18	5	0	0	120²	135	13	34	50	12.8	4.48	95	.291	.342	0	—	0	-1	-3	-0	-0.3
1994	Mil-A	8	4	.667	19	19	0	0	0	115²	140	14	26	59	13.1	4.51	111	.303	.343	0	—	0	4	7	2	0.7
1995	Mil-A	5	7	.417	37	4	0	0	2	70²	89	14	21	50	14.4	5.35	93	.312	.366	0	—	0	-5	-3	-1	-0.5
Total 11		81	90	.474	262	216	33	4	2	1482²	1567	187	352	696	11.9	4.16	102	.271	.318	0	—	0	8	12	6	1.5

● BIGGS WEHDE
Wehde, Wilbur b: 11/23/06, Holstein, Iowa d: 9/21/70, Sioux Falls, S.Dak. BR/TR, 5'10.5", 180 lbs. Deb: 9/15/30

YEAR	TM/L	W	L	PCT	G	GS	CG	SH	SV	IP	H	HR	BB	SO	RAT	ERA	ERA+	OAV	OOB	BH	AVG	PB	PR	/A	PD	TPI
1930	Chi-A	0	0	—	4	0	0	0	0	6¹	7	1	7	3	21.3	9.95	46	.304	.484	0	.000	-0	-4	-4	1	0.1
1931	Chi-A	1	0	1.000	8	0	0	0	0	16	19	0	10	3	17.4	6.75	63	.333	.449	0	.000	-0	-4	-4	1	-0.2
Total 2		1	0	1.000	12	0	0	0	0	22¹	26	1	17	6	18.5	7.66	57	.325	.460	0	.000	-1	-8	-8	1	-0.1

● HERM WEHMEIER
Wehmeier, Herman Ralph b: 2/18/27, Cincinnati, Ohio d: 5/21/73, Dallas, Tex. BR/TR, 6'2", 200 lbs. Deb: 9/7/45

YEAR	TM/L	W	L	PCT	G	GS	CG	SH	SV	IP	H	HR	BB	SO	RAT	ERA	ERA+	OAV	OOB	BH	AVG	PB	PR	/A	PD	TPI
1945	Cin-N	0	1	.000	2	2	0	0	0	5	10	0	4	0	25.2	12.60	30	.435	.519	0	.000	-0	-5	-5	-0	-0.7
1947	Cin-N	0	0	—	1	0	0	0	0	1	0	0	0	0	.000		.000	.000	-0	0	0	-0	0.0			
1948	Cin-N	11	8	.579	33	24	6	0	0	147¹	179	21	75	56	15.6	5.86	67	.299	.379	3	.091	-3	-31	-32	-0	-3.8
1949	Cin-N	11	12	.478	33	29	11	1	0	213¹	202	20	117	89	13.8	4.68	89	.253	.353	20	.256	2	-15	-12	-2	-1.1
1950	Cin-N	10	18	.357	41	32	12	0	0	230	255	27	135	121	15.4	5.67	75	.281	.376	14	.152	-3	-39	-37	-3	-4.4
1951	Cin-N	7	10	.412	39	22	10	2	2	184²	167	15	89	93	12.7	3.70	110	.241	.330	17	.288	3	5	8	-2	0.8

YEAR	TM/L	W	L	PCT	G	GS	CG	SH	SV	IP	H	HR	BB	SO	RAT	ERA	ERA+	OAV	OOB	BH	AVG	PB	PR	/A	PD	TPI
1952	Cin-N	9	11	.450	33	26	6	1	0	190¹	197	23	103	83	14.5	5.15	73	.269	.365	12	.188	2	-30	-29	-4	-2.9
1953	Cin-N	1	6	.143	28	10	2	0	0	81²	100	20	47	32	16.2	7.16	61	.299	.385	4	.200	-0	-26	-25	-1	-1.9
1954	Cin-N	0	3	.000	12	3	0	0	2	33²	36	6	21	13	15.5	6.68	63	.271	.374	0	.000	-1	-10	-9	1	-0.8
	Phi-N	10	8	.556	25	17	10	2	0	138	117	10	51	49	11.0	3.85	105	.231	.302	6	.120	-2	3	3	-0	0.1
	Yr	10	11	.476	37	20	10	2	2	171²	153	16	72	62	11.8	4.40	92	.238	.316	6	.102	-3	-6	-6	1	-0.7
1955	Phi-N	10	12	.455	31	29	10	1	0	193²	176	21	67	85	11.4	4.41	90	.241	.307	20	.278	4	-8	-10	-1	-0.7
1956	Phi-N	0	2	.000	3	3	0	0	0	20	18	2	11	8	13.0	4.05	92	.240	.337	0	.000	-1	-1	-1	-1	-0.2
	StL-N	12	9	.571	34	19	7	2	1	170²	150	16	71	68	11.7	3.69	102	.240	.319	13	.224	4	2	2	-1	0.5
	Yr	12	11	.522	37	22	7	2	1	190²	168	18	82	76	11.8	3.73	101	.240	.320	13	.197	3	1	1	-2	0.3
1957	StL-N	10	7	.588	36	18	5	0	0	165	165	25	54	91	12.1	4.31	92	.253	.312	12	.203	0	-8	-6	-0	-0.6
1958	StL-N	1	0	1.000	3	3	0	0	0	6	13	2	2	4	22.5	13.50	31	.448	.484	1	.500	1	-6	-6	-0	-0.8
	Det-A	1	0	1.000	7	3	0	0	0	22²	21	2	5	11	10.3	2.38	169	.241	.283	0	.000	-1	3	4	-0	0.1
Total	13	92	108	.460	361	240	79	9	9	1803	1806	210	852	794	13.4	4.80	84	.260	.344	124	.196	5	-165	-156	-14	-16.4

● DAVE WEHRMEISTER
Wehrmeister, David Thomas   b: 11/9/52, Berwyn, Ill.   BR/TR, 6'4", 195 lbs.   Deb: 4/16/76

YEAR	TM/L	W	L	PCT	G	GS	CG	SH	SV	IP	H	HR	BB	SO	RAT	ERA	ERA+	OAV	OOB	BH	AVG	PB	PR	/A	PD	TPI
1976	SD-N	0	4	.000	7	4	0	0	0	19¹	27	0	11	10	17.7	7.45	44	.333	.413	0	.000	-1	-8	-9	0	-1.6
1977	SD-N	1	3	.250	30	6	0	0	0	69²	81	8	44	32	16.5	6.07	58	.293	.396	2	.167	0	-17	-20	-0	-1.0
1978	SD-N	1	0	1.000	4	0	0	0	0	7¹	8	1	5	2	16.0	6.14	54	.276	.382	0	—	0	-2	-2	-0	-0.3
1981	NY-A	0	0	—	5	0	0	0	0	7	6	0	7	7	16.7	5.14	69	.240	.406	0	—	0	-1	-1	0	0.1
1984	Phi-N	0	0	—	7	0	0	0	0	15	18	1	7	13	15.6	7.20	50	.300	.382	0	.000	-0	-6	-6	0	0.0
1985	Chi-A	2	2	.500	23	0	0	0	2	39¹	35	4	10	32	11.0	3.43	126	.241	.304	0	—	-1	3	4	-0	0.4
Total	6	4	9	.308	76	10	0	0	2	157²	175	14	84	96	15.2	5.65	65	.284	.376	2	.100	-1	-31	-34	0	-2.4

● DICK WEIK
Weik, Richard Henry "Legs"   b: 11/17/27, Waterloo, Iowa   d: 4/21/91, Harvey, Ill.   BR/TR, 6'3.5", 184 lbs.   Deb: 9/8/48   ♦

YEAR	TM/L	W	L	PCT	G	GS	CG	SH	SV	IP	H	HR	BB	SO	RAT	ERA	ERA+	OAV	OOB	BH	AVG	PB	PR	/A	PD	TPI
1948	Was-A	1	2	.333	3	3	0	0	0	12²	14	1	22	8	25.6	5.68	76	.311	.537	3	.750	-2	-2	-2	-0	-0.2
1949	Was-A	3	12	.200	27	14	2	1	0	95¹	78	5	103	58	17.1	5.38	79	.230	.410	5	.179	-1	-13	-12	1	-1.6
1950	Was-A	1	3	.250	14	5	1	0	0	44	38	2	47	26	17.4	4.30	105	.236	.409	2	.154	-1	1	1	-1	-0.1
	Cle-A	1	3	.250	11	2	0	0	0	26	18	1	26	16	15.6	3.81	114	.205	.391	1	.200	0	2	2	0	0.2
	Yr	2	6	.250	25	7	1	0	0	70	56	3	73	42	16.7	4.11	108	.225	.402	3	.167	-1	4	2	-1	0.1
1953	Det-A	0	1	.000	12	1	0	0	0	19¹	32	3	23	6	25.6	13.97	29	.386	.519	1	.500	1	-21	-21	0	-0.9
1954	Det-A	0	1	.000	9	1	0	0	0	16¹	23	3	16	9	22.0	7.16	52	.354	.488	0	.000	-0	-6	-6	-1	-0.4
Total	5	6	22	.214	76	26	3	2	1	213²	203	15	237	123	18.6	5.90	72	.260	.433	12	.226	1	-39	-39	-0	-3.0

● ED WEILAND
Weiland, Edwin Nicholas   b: 11/26/14, Evanston, Ill.   d: 7/12/71, Chicago, Ill.   BL/TR, 5'11", 180 lbs.   Deb: 5/1/40   F

YEAR	TM/L	W	L	PCT	G	GS	CG	SH	SV	IP	H	HR	BB	SO	RAT	ERA	ERA+	OAV	OOB	BH	AVG	PB	PR	/A	PD	TPI
1940	Chi-A	0	0	—	5	0	0	0	0	14¹	15	5	7	3	13.8	8.79	50	.263	.344	1	.200	-0	-7	-7	-0	-0.1
1942	Chi-A	0	0	—	5	0	0	0	0	9²	18	0	3	4	19.6	7.45	48	.383	.420	0	.000	-0	-4	-4	-0	-0.1
Total	2	0	0	—	10	0	0	0	0	24	33	5	10	7	16.1	8.25	50	.317	.377	1	.143	-0	-11	-11	-1	-0.2

● BOB WEILAND
Weiland, Robert George "Lefty"   b: 12/14/05, Chicago, Ill.   d: 11/9/88, Chicago, Ill.   BL/TL, 6'4", 215 lbs.   Deb: 9/30/28   F

YEAR	TM/L	W	L	PCT	G	GS	CG	SH	SV	IP	H	HR	BB	SO	RAT	ERA	ERA+	OAV	OOB	BH	AVG	PB	PR	/A	PD	TPI
1928	Chi-A	1	0	1.000	1	1	1	0	0	9	7	0	5	3	13.0	0.00	—	.212	.333	1	.333	0	4	4	0	0.5
1929	Chi-A	2	4	.333	15	9	1	0	1	62	62	3	43	25	15.7	5.81	74	.268	.390	2	.111	-1	-11	-10	-1	-1.1
1930	Chi-A	0	4	.000	14	3	0	0	0	32²	38	1	21	15	16.8	6.61	70	.297	.404	0	.000	-1	-7	-7	-0	-0.8
1931	Chi-A	2	7	.222	15	8	3	0	0	75	75	3	46	38	15.0	5.16	83	.259	.368	4	.182	1	-7	-8	1	-0.6
1932	Bos-A	6	16	.273	43	27	7	0	1	195²	231	11	97	63	15.4	4.51	100	.295	.377	9	.148	-1	-1	-0	3	0.2
1933	Bos-A	8	14	.364	39	27	12	0	3	216¹	197	19	100	97	12.6	3.87	113	.244	.331	7	.108	-4	10	12	-2	0.6
1934	Bos-A	1	5	.167	11	7	2	0	0	55²	63	4	27	29	14.6	5.50	87	.293	.372	2	.105	-1	-6	-4	0	-0.4
	Cle-A	1	5	.167	16	7	2	0	0	70	71	5	30	42	13.0	4.11	111	.262	.336	3	.125	-0	3	3	-1	0.2
	Yr	2	10	.167	27	14	4	0	0	125²	134	9	57	71	13.7	4.73	99	.276	.352	5	.116	-1	-3	-1	-0	-0.2
1935	StL-N	0	2	.000	14	4	0	0	0	32	39	6	31	11	20.0	9.56	50	.298	.436	0	.000	-1	-18	-17	-1	-1.0
1937	StL-N	15	14	.517	41	34	21	2	0	264¹	283	14	94	105	13.0	3.54	112	.276	.339	15	.169	0	11	13	-2	1.1
1938	StL-N	16	11	.593	35	29	11	1	1	228¹	248	14	67	117	12.6	3.59	110	.272	.324	11	.138	-3	5	9	-1	0.6
1939	StL-N	10	12	.455	32	23	6	3	1	146¹	146	4	50	63	12.4	3.57	115	.264	.331	3	.065	-3	6	9	-1	0.7
1940	StL-N	0	0	—	1	0	0	0	0	1	3	1	0	0	27.0	27.00	15	.600	.600	0	—	0	-3	-3	-0	-0.1
Total	12	62	94	.397	277	179	66	7	7	1388¹	1463	85	611	614	13.7	4.24	100	.272	.350	57	.129	-16	-13	-2	-4	0.0

● CARL WEILMAN
Weilman, Carl Woolworth "Zeke" (b: Carl Woolworth Weilenmann)
b: 11/29/1889, Hamilton, Ohio   d: 5/25/24, Hamilton, Ohio   BL/TL, 6'5.5", 187 lbs.   Deb: 8/24/12

YEAR	TM/L	W	L	PCT	G	GS	CG	SH	SV	IP	H	HR	BB	SO	RAT	ERA	ERA+	OAV	OOB	BH	AVG	PB	PR	/A	PD	TPI
1912	StL-A	2	4	.333	8	6	5	2	0	48¹	42	0	3	24	8.4	2.79	119	.227	.239	2	.118	-1	3	3	0	0.3
1913	StL-A	10	20	.333	39	28	17	2	0	251²	262	2	60	79	11.7	3.40	86	.281	.328	12	.146	-3	-13	-13	1	-1.6
1914	StL-A	18	13	.581	44	36	20	3	1	299	260	1	84	119	10.7	2.08	130	.237	.298	15	.149	-1	22	21	1	2.2
1915	StL-A	18	19	.486	47	31	19	3	4	295²	240	6	83	125	9.9	2.34	122	.229	.287	23	.230	2	19	17	-1	2.3
1916	StL-A	17	18	.486	46	31	19	1	2	276	237	3	76	91	10.5	2.15	128	.242	.301	14	.154	-1	21	18	-3	1.9
1917	StL-A	1	2	.333	5	3	0	0	0	19	19	1	6	9	11.8	1.89	137	.268	.325	0	.000	-1	2	1	0	0.3
1919	StL-A	10	6	.625	20	20	12	3	0	148	133	3	45	44	11.0	2.07	160	.244	.305	9	.191	0	19	21	-0	2.2
1920	StL-A	9	13	.409	30	24	13	1	2	183¹	201	6	61	45	13.0	4.47	88	.291	.351	11	.175	-2	-14	-11	1	-1.3
Total	8	85	95	.472	239	179	105	15	10	1521	1394	22	418	536	10.9	2.67	112	.251	.307	86	.170	-7	59	56	1	6.3

● JAKE WEIMER
Weimer, Jacob "Tornado Jake"   b: 11/29/1873, Ottumwa, Iowa   d: 6/19/28, Chicago, Ill.   BR/TL, 5'11", 175 lbs.   Deb: 4/17/03

YEAR	TM/L	W	L	PCT	G	GS	CG	SH	SV	IP	H	HR	BB	SO	RAT	ERA	ERA+	OAV	OOB	BH	AVG	PB	PR	/A	PD	TPI
1903	Chi-N	20	8	.714	35	33	27	3	0	282	241	4	104	128	11.4	2.30	136	**.225**	.301	21	.196	2	30	26	-1	2.4
1904	Chi-N	20	14	.588	37	37	31	5	0	307	229	4	97	177	9.8	1.91	140	.204	.272	21	.183	-1	28	26	3	2.9
1905	Chi-N	18	12	.600	33	30	26	2	1	250¹	212	1	80	107	10.9	2.26	132	.229	.299	19	.207	2	21	20	-1	2.4
1906	Cin-N	20	14	.588	41	39	31	6	1	304²	263	9	99	141	11.1	2.22	124	.236	.306	29	.269	6	14	18	1	2.9
1907	Cin-N	11	14	.440	29	26	19	3	0	209	165	6	63	67	10.8	2.41	108	.226	.308	14	.194	2	1	4	2	1.0
1908	Cin-N	8	7	.533	15	15	9	2	0	116²	110	2	50	36	12.8	2.39	96	.255	.341	11	.244	2	-0	-1	1	0.2
1909	NY-A	0	0	—	1	0	0	0	0	3	7	0	0	1	24.0	9.00	28	.467	.500	0	.000	-0	-2	-2	-0	0.0
Total	7	97	69	.584	191	180	143	21	2	1472²	1227	14	493	657	11.0	2.23	125	.227	.300	115	.213	11	92	93	5	11.8

● LEFTY WEINERT
Weinert, Phillip Walter   b: 4/21/02, Philadelphia, Pa.   d: 4/17/73, Rockledge, Fla.   BL/TL, 6'1", 195 lbs.   Deb: 9/24/19

YEAR	TM/L	W	L	PCT	G	GS	CG	SH	SV	IP	H	HR	BB	SO	RAT	ERA	ERA+	OAV	OOB	BH	AVG	PB	PR	/A	PD	TPI
1919	Phi-N	0	0	—	1	0	0	0	0	4	11	0	2	0	29.3	18.00	18	.478	.520	2	1.000	1	-7	-7	-0	0.2
1920	Phi-N	1	1	.500	10	2	0	0	0	22	27	1	19	10	19.2	6.14	56	.333	.465	0	.000	-1	-7	-7	-0	-0.7
1921	Phi-N	1	0	1.000	8	0	0	0	0	12¹	8	1	5	2	10.2	1.46	290	.216	.326	1	1.000	0	3	4	-1	0.3
1922	Phi-N	8	11	.421	34	22	10	0	1	166²	189	10	70	58	14.3	3.40	137	.289	.362	14	.241	-0	13	23	-2	2.3
1923	Phi-N	4	17	.190	38	20	8	0	1	156	207	10	81	46	17.1	5.42	85	.327	.410	19	.322	2	-25	-14	-3	-1.7
1924	Phi-N	0	1	.000	14²	10	1	0	0	14²	10	1	11	7	12.9	2.45	182	.204	.350	0	.000	-1	2	3	-0	0.2
1927	Phi-N	1	1	.500	5	3	1	0	0	19²	21	2	6	5	12.4	4.58	84	.259	.310	1	.200	-0	-1	-2	-0	-0.2
1928	Chi-N	1	0	1.000	10	1	0	0	0	17	24	0	9	8	18.0	5.29	73	.393	.479	0	.000	-0	-2	-3	-1	-0.2
1931	NY-A	2	2	.500	17	6	0	0	2	24²	31	2	19	24	20.1	6.20	64	.316	.451	0	.000	-0	-5	-6	-0	-0.8
Total	9	18	33	.353	131	49	19	0	2	437	528	26	222	160	15.9	4.59	97	.308	.393	37	.261	2	-29	-7	-6	-0.6

● ROY WEIR
Weir, William Franklin "Bill"   b: 2/25/11, Portland, Maine   d: 9/30/89, Anaheim, Cal.   BL/TL, 5'8.5", 170 lbs.   Deb: 6/25/36

YEAR	TM/L	W	L	PCT	G	GS	CG	SH	SV	IP	H	HR	BB	SO	RAT	ERA	ERA+	OAV	OOB	BH	AVG	PB	PR	/A	PD	TPI
1936	Bos-N	4	3	.571	12	7	3	2	0	57¹	53	0	24	29	12.1	2.83	136	.241	.316	5	.278	2	8	6	1	1.0
1937	Bos-N	1	1	.500	10	4	1	0	0	33	27	0	19	8	12.5	3.82	94	.227	.333	0	.000	-1	0	-1	-1	-0.1
1938	Bos-N	1	0	1.000	5	0	0	0	0	13¹	14	4	6	3	13.5	6.75	54	.269	.345	1	.333	0	-4	-5	0	-0.3
1939	Bos-N	0	0	—	2	0	0	0	0	2²	1	0	1	2	6.8	0.00	—	.125	.222	0	—	0	1	1	0	0.0
Total	4	6	4	.600	29	11	4	2	0	106¹	95	4	50	42	12.3	3.55	104	.238	.323	6	.188	1	5	2	2	0.6

● CURT WELCH
Welch, Curtis Benton   b: 2/11/1862, E.Liverpool, Ohio   d: 8/29/1896, E.Liverpool, Ohio   BR/TR, 5'10", 175 lbs.   Deb: 5/1/1884   ♦

YEAR	TM/L	W	L	PCT	G	GS	CG	SH	SV	IP	H	HR	BB	SO	RAT	ERA	ERA+	OAV	OOB	BH	AVG	PB	PR	/A	PD	TPI
1890	Phi-a	0	0	—	1	1	0	0	0	1	6	0	1	0	54.0	54.00	7	.667	.667	106	.268	0	-6	-6	0	0.0

● TED WELCH
Welch, Floyd John   b: 10/17/1892, Coyville, Kan.   d: 1/6/43, Great Bend, Kan.   BL/TR, 5'9.5", 160 lbs.   Deb: 5/15/14

YEAR	TM/L	W	L	PCT	G	GS	CG	SH	SV	IP	H	HR	BB	SO	RAT	ERA	ERA+	OAV	OOB	BH	AVG	PB	PR	/A	PD	TPI
1914	StL-F	0	0	—	3	0	0	0	0	6	6	0	3	2	18.0	6.00	51	.273	.429	0	.000	-0	-2	-2	-0	0.0

YEAR	TM/L	W	L	PCT	G	GS	CG	SH	SV	IP	H	HR	BB	SO	RAT	ERA	ERA+	OAV	OOB	BH	AVG	PB	PR	/A	PD	TPI

● JOHNNY WELCH   Welch, John Vernon b: 12/2/06, Washington, D.C. d: 9/2/40, St.Louis, Mo. BL/TR, 6'3", 184 lbs. Deb: 5/22/26

YEAR	TM/L	W	L	PCT	G	GS	CG	SH	SV	IP	H	HR	BB	SO	RAT	ERA	ERA+	OAV	OOB	BH	AVG	PB	PR	/A	PD	TPI
1926	Chi-N	0	0	—	3	0	0	0	0	4¹	5	0	1	0	12.5	2.08	185	.357	.400	1	1.000	0	1	1	-0	0.0
1927	Chi-N	0	0	—	1	0	0	0	0	1	0	0	3	1	27.0	9.00	43	.000	.500	0	—	0	-1	-1	0	0.0
1928	Chi-N	0	0	—	3	0	0	0	0	4	13	0	0	2	29.3	15.75	24	.591	.591	0	—	0	-5	-5	0	0.0
1931	Chi-N	2	1	.667	8	3	1	0	0	33²	39	3	10	7	13.4	3.74	103	.291	.345	5	.417	2	0	0	0	0.2
1932	Bos-A	4	6	.400	20	8	3	1	0	72¹	93	3	38	26	16.7	5.23	86	.312	.395	9	.250	2	-6	-6	0	-0.5
1933	Bos-A	4	9	.308	47	7	1	0	3	129	142	6	67	68	14.7	4.60	95	.283	.370	6	.162	-1	-5	-3	1	-0.3
1934	Bos-A	13	15	.464	41	22	8	1	0	206¹	223	14	76	91	13.4	4.49	107	.274	.342	15	.203	-1	0	7	1	0.7
1935	Bos-A	10	9	.526	31	19	10	1	2	143	155	4	53	48	13.3	4.47	106	.273	.339	9	.180	-0	-0	4	0	0.5
1936	Bos-A	2	1	.667	9	3	1	0	0	32²	43	4	8	9	14.1	5.51	96	.305	.342	3	.273	1	-2	-1	0	0.0
	Pit-N	0	0	—	9	0	0	0	1	22	22	3	6	5	11.5	4.50	90	.265	.315	2	.286	1	-18	-1	-1	0.0
Total 9		35	41	.461	172	63	24	3	6	648¹	735	36	262	257	14.1	4.66	97	.280	.350	50	.219	3	-18	-4	1	0.6

● MICKEY WELCH   Welch, Michael Francis "Smiling Mickey" b: 7/4/1859, Brooklyn, N.Y. d: 7/30/41, Concord, N.H. BR/TR, 5'8", 160 lbs. Deb: 5/1/1880   H

YEAR	TM/L	W	L	PCT	G	GS	CG	SH	SV	IP	H	HR	BB	SO	RAT	ERA	ERA+	OAV	OOB	BH	AVG	PB	PR	/A	PD	TPI
1880	Tro-N	34	30	.531	65	64	64	4	0	574	575	7	80	123	10.3	2.54	99	.249	.274	72	.287	10	-11	-1	-7	0.3
1881	Tro-N	21	18	.538	40	40	40	4	0	368	371	7	78	104	11.0	2.67	111	.255	.293	30	.203	-4	4	12	-6	0.1
1882	Tro-N	14	16	.467	33	33	30	5	0	281	334	7	62	53	12.7	3.46	82	.280	.315	37	.245	1	-17	-20	-3	-1.9
1883	NY-N	25	23	.521	54	52	46	4	0	426	431	11	66	144	10.5	2.73	114	.244	.272	75	.234	3	20	18	-6	1.3
1884	NY-N	39	21	.650	65	65	62	4	0	557¹	528	12	146	345	10.9	2.50	119	.237	.284	60	.241	9	30	29	-5	2.9
1885	NY-N	44	11	**.800**	56	55	55	7	1	492	372	4	131	258	9.2	1.66	160	.203	.256	41	.206	5	63	55	-8	5.0
1886	NY-N	33	22	.600	59	59	56	1	0	500	514	13	163	272	12.2	2.99	108	.259	.315	46	.216	1	18	12	-2	0.8
1887	NY-N	22	15	.595	40	40	39	2	0	346	339	7	91	115	11.3	3.36	112	.253	.303	36	.243	4	28	16	2	1.3
1888	*NY-N	26	19	.578	47	47	47	5	0	425¹	328	12	108	167	9.5	1.93	147	.207	.263	32	.189	1	44	38	-4	3.3
1889	*NY-N	27	12	.692	45	41	39	3	2	375	340	16	149	125	12.0	3.02	130	.234	.310	30	.192	-2	41	38	-3	2.8
1890	NY-N	17	14	.548	37	37	33	2	0	292¹	268	5	122	97	12.4	2.99	117	.236	.317	22	.179	-3	19	17	-3	0.8
1891	NY-N	5	9	.357	22	15	14	0	1	160	177	7	97	46	16.0	4.27	75	.270	.373	10	.141	-4	-16	-19	-3	-1.9
1892	NY-N	0	0	—	1	1	0	0	0	5	11	0	4	1	27.0	14.40	22	.423	.500	1	.333	0	-6	-6	-0	0.0
Total 13		307	210	.594	564	549	525	41	4	4802	4588	106	1297	1850	11.1	2.71	114	.242	.292	492	.224	21	216	196	-52	14.8

● BOB WELCH   Welch, Robert Lynn b: 11/3/56, Detroit, Mich. BR/TR, 6'3", 190 lbs. Deb: 6/20/78

YEAR	TM/L	W	L	PCT	G	GS	CG	SH	SV	IP	H	HR	BB	SO	RAT	ERA	ERA+	OAV	OOB	BH	AVG	PB	PR	/A	PD	TPI
1978	*LA-N	7	4	.636	23	13	4	3	3	111¹	92	6	26	66	9.6	2.02	174	.229	.277	5	.172	0	19	18	-1	1.8
1979	LA-N	5	6	.455	25	12	1	0	5	81¹	82	7	32	64	12.9	3.98	91	.265	.340	3	.158	-0	-2	-3	-1	-0.5
1980	LA-N★	14	9	.609	32	32	3	2	0	213²	190	15	79	141	11.5	3.29	106	.242	.314	17	.243	3	7	5	-1	0.8
1981	*LA-N	9	5	.643	23	23	2	1	0	141¹	141	11	41	88	11.8	3.44	96	.259	.315	10	.222	2	1	-2	-1	-0.1
1982	LA-N	16	11	.593	36	36	9	3	0	235²	199	19	81	176	10.9	3.36	103	.229	.299	12	.141	-1	6	3	-1	0.0
1983	*LA-N	15	12	.556	31	31	4	3	0	204	164	13	72	156	10.5	2.65	136	.222	.294	7	.096	-2	22	21	0	2.5
1984	LA-N	13	13	.500	31	29	4	1	0	178²	191	11	58	120	12.6	3.78	93	.273	.331	4	.078	-3	-4	-5	-2	-0.8
1985	*LA-N	14	4	.778	23	23	8	3	0	167¹	141	16	35	96	9.8	2.31	150	.225	.273	9	.180	1	24	22	1	2.6
1986	LA-N	7	13	.350	33	33	7	3	0	235²	227	14	55	183	11.0	3.28	105	.251	.299	8	.105	-0	11	4	-1	0.2
1987	LA-N	15	9	.625	35	35	6	**4**	0	251²	204	21	86	196	10.5	3.22	123	.221	.291	13	.157	1	24	21	2	2.2
1988	*Oak-A	17	9	.654	36	36	4	2	0	244²	237	22	81	158	12.1	3.64	104	.257	.323	0	—	0	9	4	0	0.6
1989	*Oak-A	17	8	.680	33	33	1	0	0	209²	191	13	78	137	11.8	3.00	122	.241	.314	0	—	0	20	16	-1	1.8
1990	*Oak-A★	**27**	6	**.818**	35	35	2	2	0	238	214	26	77	127	11.2	2.95	126	.242	.306	0	—	0	25	20	0	3.0
1991	Oak-A	12	13	.480	35	35	7	1	0	220	220	25	91	101	13.2	4.58	84	.263	.343	0	—	0	-12	-18	-1	-1.9
1992	*Oak-A	11	7	.611	20	20	0	0	0	123²	114	13	43	47	11.6	3.27	114	.247	.314	0	—	0	9	6	-1	1.0
1993	Oak-A	9	11	.450	30	28	0	0	0	166²	208	25	56	63	14.6	5.29	77	.310	.370	0	—	0	-18	-23	1	-2.1
1994	Oak-A	4	6	.333	25	8	0	0	0	68²	79	10	43	46	14.6	7.08	63	.290	.389	0	.000	0	-17	-20	-1	-2.2
Total 17		211	146	.591	506	462	61	28	8	3092	2894	267	1034	1969	11.7	3.47	106	.249	.314	88	.151	2	126	70	-4	8.9

● DON WELCHEL   Welchel, Donald Ray b: 2/3/57, Atlanta, Tex. BR/TR, 6'4", 205 lbs. Deb: 9/15/82

YEAR	TM/L	W	L	PCT	G	GS	CG	SH	SV	IP	H	HR	BB	SO	RAT	ERA	ERA+	OAV	OOB	BH	AVG	PB	PR	/A	PD	TPI
1982	Bal-A	1	0	1.000	2	0	0	0	0	4¹	6	0	2	3	16.6	8.31	49	.300	.364	0	—	0	-2	-2	-0	-0.4
1983	Bal-A	0	2	.000	11	0	0	0	0	26²	33	1	10	16	14.5	5.40	73	.297	.355	0	—	0	-4	-4	-0	-0.3
Total 2		1	2	.333	13	0	0	0	0	31	39	1	12	19	14.8	5.81	68	.298	.357	0	—	0	-6	-6	-0	-0.7

● DAVID WELLS   Wells, David Lee b: 5/20/63, Torrance, Cal. BL/TL, 6'3", 225 lbs. Deb: 6/30/87

YEAR	TM/L	W	L	PCT	G	GS	CG	SH	SV	IP	H	HR	BB	SO	RAT	ERA	ERA+	OAV	OOB	BH	AVG	PB	PR	/A	PD	TPI
1987	Tor-A	4	3	.571	18	2	0	0	0	29¹	37	0	12	32	15.0	3.99	113	.311	.374	0	—	0	2	2	-0	0.4
1988	Tor-A	3	5	.375	41	0	0	0	4	64¹	65	12	31	56	13.7	4.62	85	.269	.356	0	—	0	-5	-5	-0	-0.6
1989	*Tor-A	7	4	.636	54	0	0	0	2	86¹	66	5	28	78	9.8	2.40	157	.207	.271	0	—	0	14	13	0	1.7
1990	Tor-A	11	6	.647	43	25	0	0	3	189	165	14	45	115	10.1	3.14	125	.235	.283	0	—	0	16	17	1	1.4
1991	*Tor-A	15	10	.600	40	28	2	0	1	198¹	188	24	49	106	10.8	3.72	113	.251	.299	0	—	0	8	11	1	1.3
1992	Tor-A	7	9	.438	41	14	0	0	2	120	138	16	36	62	13.7	5.40	76	.289	.349	0	—	0	-19	-18	-0	-2.3
1993	Det-A	11	9	.550	32	30	0	0	0	187	183	26	42	139	11.2	4.19	102	.254	.301	0	—	0	3	-2	-1	0.1
1994	Det-A	5	7	.417	16	16	0	0	0	111¹	113	13	24	71	11.2	3.96	122	.260	.302	0	—	0	10	11	-1	0.9
1995	Det-A★	10	3	.769	18	18	3	0	0	130¹	120	17	37	83	11.0	3.04	157	.242	.298	0	—	0	24	25	-0	2.2
	*Cin-N	6	5	.545	11	11	3	0	0	72²	74	6	16	50	11.1	3.59	115	.265	.305	4	.143	-1	5	4	-1	0.4
1996	*Bal-A	11	14	.440	34	34	3	0	0	224¹	247	32	51	130	12.2	5.14	95	.285	.330	0	—	0	-4	-6	2	-0.4
Total 10		90	75	.545	348	178	16	1	13	1413	1396	165	371	922	11.5	4.10	103	.258	.316	4	.143	-1	54	56	1	5.1

● ED WELLS   Wells, Edwin Lee "Satchelfoot" b: 6/7/1900, Ashland, Ohio d: 5/1/86, Montgomery, Ala. BL/TL, 6'1.5", 183 lbs. Deb: 6/16/23

YEAR	TM/L	W	L	PCT	G	GS	CG	SH	SV	IP	H	HR	BB	SO	RAT	ERA	ERA+	OAV	OOB	BH	AVG	PB	PR	/A	PD	TPI
1923	Det-A	0	0	—	7	0	0	0	0	10	11	0	6	6	15.3	5.40	72	.306	.405	0	.000	-0	-2	-2	-0	-0.1
1924	Det-A	6	8	.429	29	15	5	0	4	102	117	0	42	33	14.1	4.06	101	.291	.360	7	.212	-1	2	1	1	0.1
1925	Det-A	6	9	.400	35	14	5	0	2	134¹	190	8	62	45	17.0	6.23	69	.345	.413	12	.279	3	-27	-29	1	-2.5
1926	Det-A	12	10	.545	36	26	9	**4**	0	178	201	7	76	58	14.1	4.15	98	.297	.370	15	.205	-0	-2	-2	-3	-0.4
1927	Det-A	0	1	.000	8	1	0	0	0	20	28	3	5	12	14.8	6.75	62	.333	.371	0	.286	-0	-6	-6	-1	-0.2
1929	NY-A	13	9	.591	31	23	10	3	0	193¹	179	19	81	78	12.1	4.33	89	.248	.324	17	.233	2	-2	-10	-4	-1.2
1930	NY-A	12	3	.800	27	21	7	0	0	150²	185	11	49	46	14.2	5.20	83	.302	.358	15	.259	-0	-9	-15	-2	-1.4
1931	NY-A	9	5	.643	27	10	6	0	2	116²	130	7	37	34	13.0	4.32	92	.286	.341	10	.222	1	1	-5	-1	-0.5
1932	NY-A	3	3	.500	22	0	0	0	2	31²	38	1	12	13	14.2	4.26	96	.302	.362	0	.000	-1	1	-1	-0	-0.2
1933	StL-A	6	14	.300	36	22	10	0	1	203²	230	13	63	58	13.0	4.20	111	.278	.330	14	.197	-1	2	10	-3	0.5
1934	StL-A	1	7	.125	33	8	2	0	1	92	108	7	35	27	14.0	4.79	104	.292	.353	4	.045	-2	-3	2	1	0.1
Total 11		68	69	.496	291	140	54	7	13	1232¹	1417	78	468	403	13.9	4.65	91	.291	.355	93	.215	1	-46	-55	-10	-5.7

● JOHN WELLS   Wells, John Frederick b: 11/25/22, Junction City, Kan. d: 10/23/93, Olean, N.Y. BR/TR, 5'11.5", 180 lbs. Deb: 9/14/44

YEAR	TM/L	W	L	PCT	G	GS	CG	SH	SV	IP	H	HR	BB	SO	RAT	ERA	ERA+	OAV	OOB	BH	AVG	PB	PR	/A	PD	TPI
1944	Bro-N	0	2	.000	4	2	0	0	0	15	18	1	11	7	17.4	5.40	66	.316	.426	1	.250	0	-3	-3	-0	-0.4

● BOB WELLS   Wells, Robert Lee b: 11/1/66, Yakima, Wash. BR/TR, 6', 180 lbs. Deb: 5/16/94

YEAR	TM/L	W	L	PCT	G	GS	CG	SH	SV	IP	H	HR	BB	SO	RAT	ERA	ERA+	OAV	OOB	BH	AVG	PB	PR	/A	PD	TPI
1994	Phi-N	1	0	1.000	6	0	0	0	0	5	4	0	3	3	14.4	1.80	238	.235	.381	0	—	0	1	1	-0	0.2
	Sea-A	1	0	1.000	1	0	0	0	0	4	4	1	1	3	11.3	2.25	217	.250	.294	0	—	0	1	1	-0	0.3
1995	*Sea-A	4	3	.571	30	4	0	0	0	76²	88	14	39	38	15.3	5.75	82	.284	.369	0	—	0	-9	-9	-0	-0.7
1996	Sea-A	12	7	.632	36	16	1	1	0	130²	141	25	46	94	13.3	5.30	93	.274	.340	0	—	0	-5	-5	-1	-0.7
Total 3		18	10	.643	73	20	1	1	0	216¹	237	36	89	138	14.0	5.33	91	.276	.351	0	—	0	-11	-12	-2	-0.9

● TERRY WELLS   Wells, Terry b: 9/10/63, Kankakee, Ill. BL/TL, 6'3", 205 lbs. Deb: 7/3/90

YEAR	TM/L	W	L	PCT	G	GS	CG	SH	SV	IP	H	HR	BB	SO	RAT	ERA	ERA+	OAV	OOB	BH	AVG	PB	PR	/A	PD	TPI
1990	LA-N	1	2	.333	5	5	0	0	0	20²	25	4	14	18	17.0	7.84	47	.287	.386	0	.000	-1	-9	-10	-1	-1.3

● CHRIS WELSH   Welsh, Christopher Charles b: 4/14/55, Wilmington, Del. BL/TL, 6'2", 185 lbs. Deb: 4/12/81

YEAR	TM/L	W	L	PCT	G	GS	CG	SH	SV	IP	H	HR	BB	SO	RAT	ERA	ERA+	OAV	OOB	BH	AVG	PB	PR	/A	PD	TPI
1981	SD-N	6	7	.462	22	19	4	2	0	123²	122	9	41	51	11.9	3.78	86	.264	.325	6	.146	-0	-4	-7	1	-0.6
1982	SD-N	8	8	.500	28	20	1	0	0	139¹	141	16	63	48	13.7	4.91	70	.268	.347	11	.262	4	-20	-23	1	-2.0
1983	SD-N	0	1	.000	7	1	0	0	0	14¹	13	2	2	5	9.4	2.51	139	.236	.263	0	.000	-0	2	2	-0	0.1
	Mon-N	0	1	.000	16	5	0	0	0	44²	46	5	18	17	13.7	5.04	71	.267	.351	4	.286	1	-7	-7	1	0.1
	Yr	0	2	.000	23	6	0	0	0	59	59	7	20	22	12.7	4.42	81	.260	.331	4	.222	1	-5	-6	1	0.1

YEAR	TM/L	W	L	PCT	G	GS	CG	SH	SV	IP	H	HR	BB	SO	RAT	ERA	ERA+	OAV	OOB	BH	AVG	PB	PR	/A	PD	TPI
1985	Tex-A	2	5	.286	25	6	0	0	0	76¹	101	11	25	31	15.3	4.13	102	.316	.372	0	—	0	0	1	-1	0.0
1986	Cin-N	6	9	.400	24	24	1	0	0	139¹	163	9	40	40	13.3	4.78	81	.301	.353	5	.119	0	-16	-14	-1	-1.4
Total 5		22	31	.415	122	75	8	3	0	537²	591	52	189	192	13.3	4.45	81	.282	.346	26	.182	5	-46	-49	2	-3.9

● **DICK WELTEROTH** Welteroth, Richard John b: 8/3/27, Williamsport, Pa. BR/TR, 5'11", 165 lbs. Deb: 5/16/48

YEAR	TM/L	W	L	PCT	G	GS	CG	SH	SV	IP	H	HR	BB	SO	RAT	ERA	ERA+	OAV	OOB	BH	AVG	PB	PR	/A	PD	TPI
1948	Was-A	2	1	.667	33	2	0	0	0	65¹	73	6	50	16	17.1	5.51	79	.286	.405	1	.100	-1	-9	-8	-0	-0.5
1949	Was-A	2	5	.286	52	2	0	0	2	95¹	107	6	89	37	18.6	7.36	58	.296	.437	1	.059	-1	-34	-33	0	-2.3
1950	Was-A	0	0	—	5	0	0	0	0	5	6	0	6	2	16.5	3.00	150	.217	.379	0	—	0	1	1	0	0.0
Total 3		4	6	.400	90	4	0	0	3	166²	185	12	145	55	17.9	6.48	66	.290	.422	2	.074	-2	-41	-40	-0	-2.8

● **TONY WELZER** Welzer, Anton Frank b: 4/5/1899, Germany d: 3/18/71, Milwaukee, Wis. BR/TR, 5'11", 160 lbs. Deb: 4/13/26

YEAR	TM/L	W	L	PCT	G	GS	CG	SH	SV	IP	H	HR	BB	SO	RAT	ERA	ERA+	OAV	OOB	BH	AVG	PB	PR	/A	PD	TPI
1926	Bos-A	4	3	.571	39	6	1	0	1	139	167	5	53	29	14.4	4.86	84	.308	.373	8	.211	2	-13	-12	4	0.0
1927	Bos-A	6	11	.353	37	19	8	0	1	171²	214	10	71	56	15.2	4.72	89	.318	.386	4	.095	-2	-11	-9	1	-0.9
Total 2		10	14	.417	76	25	9	1	1	310²	381	15	124	85	14.8	4.78	87	.313	.380	12	.150	-0	-24	-22	4	-0.9

● **TURK WENDELL** Wendell, Steven John b: 5/19/67, Pittsfield, Mass. BB/TR, 6'2", 180 lbs. Deb: 6/17/93

YEAR	TM/L	W	L	PCT	G	GS	CG	SH	SV	IP	H	HR	BB	SO	RAT	ERA	ERA+	OAV	OOB	BH	AVG	PB	PR	/A	PD	TPI
1993	Chi-N	1	2	.333	7	4	0	0	0	22²	24	3	8	15	12.7	4.37	91	.273	.333	1	.143	-0	-1	-1	0	-0.1
1994	Chi-N	0	1	.000	6	2	0	0	0	14¹	22	3	10	9	20.1	11.93	35	.349	.438	0	.000	0	-12	-12	0	-0.7
1995	Chi-N	3	1	.750	43	0	0	0	0	60¹	71	11	24	50	14.5	4.92	83	.298	.367	0	.000	-0	-5	-5	1	-0.2
1996	Chi-N	4	5	.444	70	0	0	0	18	79¹	58	8	44	75	11.9	2.84	150	.201	.313	1	.500	1	12	13	0	1.9
Total 4		8	9	.471	126	6	0	0	18	176²	175	22	86	149	13.6	4.48	93	.258	.346	2	.111	0	-6	-6	2	0.9

● **DON WENGERT** Wengert, Donald Paul b: 11/6/69, Sioux City, Iowa BR/TR, 6'2", 205 lbs. Deb: 4/30/95

YEAR	TM/L	W	L	PCT	G	GS	CG	SH	SV	IP	H	HR	BB	SO	RAT	ERA	ERA+	OAV	OOB	BH	AVG	PB	PR	/A	PD	TPI
1995	Oak-A	1	1	.500	19	0	0	0	0	29²	30	3	12	16	13.0	3.34	134	.263	.339	0	—	0	5	4	-1	0.2
1996	Oak-A	7	11	.389	36	25	1	1	0	161¹	200	29	60	75	14.8	5.58	86	.307	.371	0	—	0	-11	-14	-2	-1.4
Total 2		8	12	.400	55	25	1	1	0	191	230	32	72	91	14.6	5.23	91	.301	.366	0	—	0	-6	-10	-3	-1.2

● **BUTCH WENSLOFF** Wensloff, Charles William b: 12/3/15, Sausalito, Cal. BR/TR, 5'11", 185 lbs. Deb: 5/2/43

YEAR	TM/L	W	L	PCT	G	GS	CG	SH	SV	IP	H	HR	BB	SO	RAT	ERA	ERA+	OAV	OOB	BH	AVG	PB	PR	/A	PD	TPI
1943	NY-A	13	11	.542	29	27	18	1	1	223¹	179	7	70	105	10.1	2.54	127	.219	.282	14	.177	-0	19	17	-1	1.7
1947	*NY-A	3	1	.750	11	5	1	0	0	51²	41	3	22	18	11.0	2.61	135	.217	.299	5	.263	1	6	5	-1	0.4
1948	Cle-A	0	1	.000	1	0	0	0	0	1²	2	1	3	2	27.0	10.80	38	.286	.500	0	—	0	-1	-1	-0	-0.5
Total 3		16	13	.552	41	32	19	1	1	276²	222	11	95	125	10.3	2.60	126	.219	.287	19	.194	0	24	21	-2	1.6

● **FRED WENZ** Wenz, Frederick Charles "Fireball" b: 8/26/41, Bound Brook, N.J. BR/TR, 6'3", 214 lbs. Deb: 6/4/68

YEAR	TM/L	W	L	PCT	G	GS	CG	SH	SV	IP	H	HR	BB	SO	RAT	ERA	ERA+	OAV	OOB	BH	AVG	PB	PR	/A	PD	TPI
1968	Bos-A	0	0	—	1	0	0	0	0	1	0	0	2	3	18.0	0.00	—	.000	.400	0	—	0	0	0	0	0.0
1969	Bos-A	1	0	1.000	8	0	0	0	0	11	9	7	10	11	15.5	5.73	66	.225	.380	0	—	0	-3	-2	0	-0.2
1970	Phi-N	2	0	1.000	22	0	0	0	1	30¹	27	2	13	24	12.2	4.45	90	.237	.320	0	.000	-1	-1	-2	-1	-0.2
Total 3		3	0	1.000	31	0	0	0	1	42¹	36	9	25	38	13.2	4.68	84	.229	.339	0	.000	-0	-4	-4	-1	-0.4

● **PERRY WERDEN** Werden, Percival Wheritt b: 7/21/1865, St.Louis, Mo. d: 1/9/34, Minneapolis, Minn. BR/TR, 6'2", 220 lbs. Deb: 4/24/1884 ♦

YEAR	TM/L	W	L	PCT	G	GS	CG	SH	SV	IP	H	HR	BB	SO	RAT	ERA	ERA+	OAV	OOB	BH	AVG	PB	PR	/A	PD	TPI
1884	StL-U	12	1	.923	16	16	12	1	0	141¹	113	1	22	51	8.6	1.97	121	.204	.235	18	.237	-4	7	7	1	0.2

● **BILL WERLE** Werle, William George "Bugs" b: 12/21/20, Oakland, Cal. BL/TL, 6'2.5", 182 lbs. Deb: 4/22/49 C

YEAR	TM/L	W	L	PCT	G	GS	CG	SH	SV	IP	H	HR	BB	SO	RAT	ERA	ERA+	OAV	OOB	BH	AVG	PB	PR	/A	PD	TPI
1949	Pit-N	12	13	.480	35	29	10	2	0	221	243	22	51	106	12.3	4.24	99	.278	.324	9	.117	-3	-5	-1	1	-0.3
1950	Pit-N	8	16	.333	48	22	6	0	8	215¹	249	25	65	78	13.4	4.60	95	.290	.344	13	.194	1	-11	-5	4	-0.1
1951	Pit-N	8	6	.571	59	9	2	0	6	149²	181	20	51	57	14.3	5.65	75	.304	.364	12	.300	3	-28	-24	3	-1.5
1952	Pit-N	0	0	—	5	0	0	0	0	4	9	1	1	1	22.5	9.00	44	.429	.455	0	—	0	-2	-2	0	0.0
	StL-N	1	2	.333	19	0	0	0	1	39	40	6	15	23	12.9	4.85	77	.268	.339	1	.111	-0	-5	-5	1	-0.3
	Yr	1	2	.333	24	0	0	0	1	43	49	7	16	24	13.8	5.23	71	.288	.353	1	.111	-0	-7	-7	2	-0.3
1953	Bos-A	0	1	.000	5	0	0	0	0	11²	7	1	1	4	6.2	1.54	273	.179	.200	0	.000	-0	3	3	1	0.4
1954	Bos-A	0	1	.000	14	0	0	0	0	24¹	41	5	10	14	19.3	4.38	94	.376	.438	0	—	-0	-2	-1	-0	-0.1
Total 6		29	39	.426	185	60	18	2	15	665¹	770	80	194	283	13.4	4.69	90	.291	.345	35	.176	1	-50	-34	10	-1.9

● **GEORGE WERLEY** Werley, George William b: 9/8/38, St.Louis, Mo. BR/TR, 6'2", 196 lbs. Deb: 9/29/56

YEAR	TM/L	W	L	PCT	G	GS	CG	SH	SV	IP	H	HR	BB	SO	RAT	ERA	ERA+	OAV	OOB	BH	AVG	PB	PR	/A	PD	TPI
1956	Bal-A	0	0	—	1	0	0	0	0	1	1	0	2	0	27.0	9.00	44	.250	.500	0	—	0	-1	-1	0	0.0

● **JOHNNY WERTS** Werts, Henry Levi b: 4/20/1898, Pomaria, S.C. d: 9/24/90, Newberry, S.C. BR/TR, 5'10", 180 lbs. Deb: 4/14/26

YEAR	TM/L	W	L	PCT	G	GS	CG	SH	SV	IP	H	HR	BB	SO	RAT	ERA	ERA+	OAV	OOB	BH	AVG	PB	PR	/A	PD	TPI
1926	Bos-N	11	9	.550	32	23	7	1	0	189¹	212	6	47	65	12.8	3.28	108	.287	.338	17	.266	4	11	6	2	1.2
1927	Bos-N	4	10	.286	42	15	4	1	0	164¹	204	5	52	39	14.2	4.55	82	.315	.369	7	.163	-0	-11	-15	-1	-1.3
1928	Bos-N	0	2	.000	10	2	0	0	0	18¹	31	4	8	5	19.1	10.31	38	.369	.424	1	.333	0	-13	-13	0	-1.1
1929	Bos-N	0	0	—	4	0	0	0	1	6	13	1	4	2	25.5	10.50	45	.433	.500	1	1.000	-1	-4	-4	-0	-0.1
Total 4		15	21	.417	88	40	11	1	2	378	460	14	111	111	13.9	4.29	85	.307	.360	26	.234	4	-17	-27	1	-1.3

● **BILL WERTZ** Wertz, William Charles b: 1/15/67, Cleveland, Ohio BR/TR, 6'6", 220 lbs. Deb: 5/22/93

YEAR	TM/L	W	L	PCT	G	GS	CG	SH	SV	IP	H	HR	BB	SO	RAT	ERA	ERA+	OAV	OOB	BH	AVG	PB	PR	/A	PD	TPI
1993	Cle-A	2	3	.400	34	0	0	0	0	59²	54	5	32	53	13.1	3.62	119	.238	.335	0	—	0	5	5	-2	0.2
1994	Cle-A	0	0	—	1	0	0	0	0	4¹	9	0	1	1	20.8	10.38	45	.409	.435	0	—	0	-3	-3	-0	0.0
Total 2		2	3	.400	35	0	0	0	0	64	63	5	33	54	13.6	4.08	107	.253	.343	0	—	0	2	2	-2	0.2

● **DAVID WEST** West, David Lee b: 9/1/64, Memphis, Tenn. BL/TL, 6'6", 230 lbs. Deb: 9/24/88

YEAR	TM/L	W	L	PCT	G	GS	CG	SH	SV	IP	H	HR	BB	SO	RAT	ERA	ERA+	OAV	OOB	BH	AVG	PB	PR	/A	PD	TPI
1988	NY-N	1	0	1.000	2	1	0	0	0	6	6	0	3	3	13.5	3.00	107	.273	.360	2	1.000	1	0	0	-0	0.2
1989	NY-N	0	2	.000	11	2	0	0	0	24¹	25	4	14	19	14.8	7.40	44	.260	.360	1	.200	0	-11	-11	-1	-0.9
	Min-A	3	2	.600	10	5	0	0	0	39¹	48	5	19	31	15.8	6.41	65	.306	.388	0	—	0	-11	-10	-1	-1.3
1990	Min-A	7	9	.438	29	27	2	0	0	146¹	142	21	78	92	13.8	5.10	81	.256	.352	0	—	0	-19	-15	-1	-2.0
1991	*Min-A	4	4	.500	15	12	0	0	0	71¹	66	13	28	52	12.0	4.54	94	.244	.317	0	—	0	-4	-2	-0	-0.2
1992	Min-A	1	3	.250	9	3	0	0	0	28¹	32	3	20	19	16.8	6.99	58	.276	.387	0	—	0	-10	-9	-1	-1.2
1993	*Phi-N	6	4	.600	76	0	0	0	3	86¹	60	6	51	87	12.1	2.92	136	.194	.318	2	.400	1	11	10	-2	1.0
1994	Phi-N	4	10	.286	31	14	0	0	0	99	74	7	61	83	12.4	3.55	121	.205	.322	2	.071	-2	7	8	-2	0.7
1995	Phi-N	3	2	.600	8	8	0	0	0	38	34	5	19	25	12.8	3.79	111	.241	.335	1	.125	1	2	2	-1	0.2
1996	Phi-N	2	2	.500	7	6	0	0	0	28¹	31	0	11	22	13.3	4.76	92	.272	.336	1	.286	1	-2	-1	-0	-0.1
Total 9		31	38	.449	198	78	2	0	3	567¹	518	64	304	433	13.3	4.58	90	.242	.341	10	.182	2	-36	-29	-7	-3.6

● **FRANK WEST** West, J. Franklin b: 1/1874, Johnstown, Pa. d: 9/6/32, Wilmerding, Pa. 180 lbs. Deb: 7/11/1894

YEAR	TM/L	W	L	PCT	G	GS	CG	SH	SV	IP	H	HR	BB	SO	RAT	ERA	ERA+	OAV	OOB	BH	AVG	PB	PR	/A	PD	TPI
1894	Bos-N	0	0	—	1	0	0	0	0	3	5	0	2	1	21.0	9.00	63	.357	.438	0	.000	-0	-1	-1	-0	0.0

● **HI WEST** West, James Hiram b: 8/8/1884, Roseville, Ill. d: 5/25/63, Los Angeles, Cal. BR/TR, 6', 185 lbs. Deb: 9/8/05

YEAR	TM/L	W	L	PCT	G	GS	CG	SH	SV	IP	H	HR	BB	SO	RAT	ERA	ERA+	OAV	OOB	BH	AVG	PB	PR	/A	PD	TPI
1905	Cle-A	2	2	.500	6	4	4	1	0	33	43	0	10	15	15.3	4.09	64	.316	.376	1	.077	-1	-5	-5	-2	-0.9
1911	Cle-A	3	4	.429	13	8	3	0	0	64²	84	1	18	17	14.6	3.76	91	.343	.395	3	.130	-2	-3	-2	-1	-0.5
Total 2		5	6	.455	19	12	7	1	0	97²	127	1	28	32	14.8	3.87	81	.333	.388	4	.111	-3	-8	-8	-3	-1.4

● **LEFTY WEST** West, Weldon Edison b: 9/3/15, Gibsonville, N.C. d: 7/23/79, Hendersonville, N.C. BR/TL, 6', 165 lbs. Deb: 4/30/44

YEAR	TM/L	W	L	PCT	G	GS	CG	SH	SV	IP	H	HR	BB	SO	RAT	ERA	ERA+	OAV	OOB	BH	AVG	PB	PR	/A	PD	TPI
1944	StL-A	0	0	—	11	0	0	0	0	24¹	34	1	19	11	20.0	6.29	57	.366	.478	1	.143	-3	-8	-7	-0	-0.1
1945	StL-A	3	4	.429	24	8	1	0	0	74¹	71	2	31	38	12.3	3.63	97	.245	.318	2	.074	-3	-2	-1	-2	-0.5
Total 2		3	4	.429	35	8	1	0	0	98²	105	3	50	49	14.2	4.29	83	.274	.359	3	.088	-3	-10	-8	-2	-0.6

● **HUYLER WESTERVELT** Westervelt, Huyler b: 10/1/1870, Piermont, N.Y. 5'9", 170 lbs. Deb: 4/21/1894

YEAR	TM/L	W	L	PCT	G	GS	CG	SH	SV	IP	H	HR	BB	SO	RAT	ERA	ERA+	OAV	OOB	BH	AVG	PB	PR	/A	PD	TPI
1894	NY-N	7	10	.412	23	18	11	1	0	141	170	4	76	35	16.0	5.04	104	.295	.382	8	.143	-5	4	3	0	-0.1

● **MICKEY WESTON** Weston, Michael Lee b: 3/26/61, Flint, Mich. BR/TR, 6'1", 180 lbs. Deb: 6/18/89

YEAR	TM/L	W	L	PCT	G	GS	CG	SH	SV	IP	H	HR	BB	SO	RAT	ERA	ERA+	OAV	OOB	BH	AVG	PB	PR	/A	PD	TPI
1989	Bal-A	1	0	1.000	7	0	0	0	1	13	18	1	2	7	14.5	5.54	68	.346	.382	0	—	0	-2	-3	-0	-0.2
1990	Bal-A	1	0	1.000	9	1	0	0	0	21	28	6	6	9	14.6	7.71	49	.322	.366	0	—	0	-9	-9	-0	-0.3
1991	Tor-A	0	0	—	2	0	0	0	0	2	1	0	1	1	9.0	0.00	—	.143	.250	0	—	0	1	1	-0	0.0
1992	Phi-N	0	1	.000	3	2	0	0	0	3²	7	1	5	0	22.1	12.27	28	.412	.474	0	.000	-0	-4	-4	-0	-0.7

YEAR	TM/L	W	L	PCT	G	GS	CG	SH	SV	IP	H	HR	BB	SO	RAT	ERA	ERA+	OAV	OOB	BH	AVG	PB	PR	/A	PD	TPI
1993	NY-N	0	0	—	4	0	0	0	0	5²	11	0	1	2	20.6	7.94	51	.393	.433	0	—	0	-2	-2	0	0.0
Total	5	1	2	.333	23	3	0	0	1	45¹	65	8	11	19	15.7	7.15	53	.340	.385	0	.000	-0	-16	-17	-1	-1.2

● JOHN WETTELAND
Wetteland, John Karl b: 8/21/66, San Mateo, Cal. BR/TR, 6'2", 195 lbs. Deb: 5/31/89

YEAR	TM/L	W	L	PCT	G	GS	CG	SH	SV	IP	H	HR	BB	SO	RAT	ERA	ERA+	OAV	OOB	BH	AVG	PB	PR	/A	PD	TPI
1989	LA-N	5	8	.385	31	12	0	0	1	102²	81	8	34	96	10.1	3.77	91	.218	.284	3	.143	-0	-3	-4	-1	-0.6
1990	LA-N	2	4	.333	22	5	0	0	0	43	44	6	17	36	13.6	4.81	76	.263	.346	1	.143	1	-5	-6	-1	-0.7
1991	LA-N	1	0	1.000	6	0	0	0	0	9	5	0	3	9	9.0	0.00	—	.161	.257	0	—	0	4	4	0	0.4
1992	Mon-N	4	4	.500	67	0	0	0	37	83¹	64	6	36	99	11.2	2.92	119	.213	.305	1	.200	0	5	5	-1	0.9
1993	Mon-N	9	3	.750	70	0	0	0	43	85¹	58	3	28	113	9.3	1.37	304	.188	.260	0	.000	0	25	27	-1	5.7
1994	Mon-N	4	6	.400	52	0	0	0	25	63²	46	5	21	68	9.9	2.83	149	.202	.278	1	.250	0	10	10	-1	2.0
1995	*NY-A	1	5	.167	60	0	0	0	31	61¹	40	6	14	66	7.9	2.93	157	.185	.235	0	—	0	12	11	-1	1.9
1996	*NY-A☆	2	3	.400	62	0	0	0	**43**	63²	54	9	21	69	10.6	2.83	179	.224	.286	0	—	0	15	16	-0	2.9
Total	8	28	33	.459	370	17	0	0	180	512	392	43	174	556	10.2	2.92	138	.210	.283	6	.146	0	64	62	-6	12.5

● BUZZ WETZEL
Wetzel, Charles Edward b: 8/25/1894, Jay, Okla. d: 3/7/41, Globe, Ariz. BR/TR, 6'1", 162 lbs. Deb: 7/25/27

YEAR	TM/L	W	L	PCT	G	GS	CG	SH	SV	IP	H	HR	BB	SO	RAT	ERA	ERA+	OAV	OOB	BH	AVG	PB	PR	/A	PD	TPI
1927	Phi-A	0	0	—	2	1	0	0	0	4²	8	0	5	0	25.1	7.71	55	.400	.520	1	1.000	0	-2	-2	0	0.1

● SHORTY WETZEL
Wetzel, George William b: 1868, Philadelphia, Pa. d: 2/25/1899, Dayton, Ohio Deb: 8/26/1885

YEAR	TM/L	W	L	PCT	G	GS	CG	SH	SV	IP	H	HR	BB	SO	RAT	ERA	ERA+	OAV	OOB	BH	AVG	PB	PR	/A	PD	TPI
1885	Bal-a	0	2	.000	2	1	1	0	0	17	27	0	9	6	20.6	8.47	38	.333	.419	0	.000	-1	-10	-10	1	-0.8

● STEFAN WEVER
Wever, Stefan Matthew b: 4/22/58, Marburg, W.Ger. BR/TR, 6'8", 245 lbs. Deb: 9/17/82

YEAR	TM/L	W	L	PCT	G	GS	CG	SH	SV	IP	H	HR	BB	SO	RAT	ERA	ERA+	OAV	OOB	BH	AVG	PB	PR	/A	PD	TPI
1982	NY-A	0	1	.000	1	1	0	0	0	2²	6	1	3	2	30.4	27.00	15	.429	.529	0	—	0	-7	-7	-0	-1.2

● GUS WEYHING
Weyhing, August "Cannonball" b: 9/29/1866, Louisville, Ky. d: 9/4/55, Louisville, Ky. BR/TR, 5'10", 145 lbs. Deb: 5/2/1887 F

YEAR	TM/L	W	L	PCT	G	GS	CG	SH	SV	IP	H	HR	BB	SO	RAT	ERA	ERA+	OAV	OOB	BH	AVG	PB	PR	/A	PD	TPI
1887	Phi-a	26	28	.481	55	55	53	2	0	466¹	465	12	167	193	12.9	4.27	101	.253	.328	42	.201	-9	2	1	-2	-0.8
1888	Phi-a	28	18	.609	47	47	45	3	0	404	314	4	111	204	10.4	2.25	133	.207	.279	40	.217	4	36	33	1	3.7
1889	Phi-a	30	21	.588	54	53	50	4	0	449	382	15	212	213	12.6	2.95	128	.223	.321	25	.131	-15	45	42	-3	2.1
1890	Bro-P	30	16	.652	49	46	38	3	0	390	419	10	179	177	14.2	3.60	124	.263	.343	27	.164	-6	27	37	-9	1.9
1891	Phi-a	31	20	.608	52	51	51	3	0	450	428	12	161	219	12.4	3.18	120	.242	.316	22	.111	-16	27	32	-5	1.0
1892	Phi-N	32	21	.604	59	49	46	6	**3**	469²	411	9	168	202	11.4	2.66	122	.226	.298	29	.136	-10	33	30	-9	1.1
1893	Phi-N	23	16	.590	42	40	33	2	0	345¹	399	10	145	101	14.7	4.74	96	.281	.356	22	.150	-9	-3	-6	-2	-1.5
1894	Phi-N	16	14	.533	38	34	28	2	1	266¹	365	12	116	81	16.8	5.81	88	.322	.393	20	.174	-9	-14	-21	-3	-2.5
1895	Phi-N	0	2	.000	4	2	0	0	0	9	23	1	13	5	36.0	20.00	24	.469	.581	0	.000	-1	-15	-15	0	-1.7
	Pit-N	1	0	1.000	1	1	1	0	0	9	10	1	5	3	15.0	1.00	452	.278	.366	1	.250	0	4	4	1	0.4
	Lou-N	7	19	.269	28	25	22	1	0	213	285	14	66	53	15.2	5.41	86	.316	.367	20	.225	0	-15	-18	0	-1.6
	Yr	8	21	.276	31	28	23	1	0	231	318	9	84	61	16.0	5.81	80	.322	.380	21	.223	-1	-26	-30	-1	-2.9
1896	Lou-N	2	3	.400	5	5	4	0	0	42	62	6	15	9	16.9	6.64	65	.339	.395	2	.133	-2	-11	-11	1	-0.9
1898	Was-N	15	26	.366	45	42	39	0	0	361	428	10	84	92	13.2	4.51	82	.292	.338	25	.177	-5	-36	-34	-2	-3.8
1899	Was-N	17	21	.447	43	38	34	2	0	334²	414	8	76	96	13.9	4.54	86	.301	.352	26	.206	-1	-26	-24	-6	-2.9
1900	StL-N	3	2	.600	7	5	3	0	0	46²	60	2	21	6	15.8	4.63	79	.311	.381	2	.095	-2	-5	-5	-1	-0.7
	Bro-N	3	4	.429	8	3	3	0	0	48	66	1	20	8	16.5	4.31	89	.325	.391	4	.222	-0	-3	-3	-1	-0.4
	Yr	6	6	.500	15	13	6	0	0	94²	126	3	41	14	16.1	4.47	84	.318	.384	6	.154	-3	-8	-8	-1	-1.1
1901	Cle-A	0	0	—	2	1	0	0	0	11¹	20	0	6	2	23.0	7.94	45	.377	.468	0	.000	-1	-5	-6	-0	-0.1
	Cin-N	0	1	.000	1	1	1	0	0	3	3	0	2	3	15.0	3.00	107	.297	.366	0	.000	-0	0	0	-0	-0.1
Total	14	264	232	.532	538	503	448	28	4	4324¹	4562	120	1566	1665	13.3	3.89	102	.264	.335	307	.166	-83	41	38	-39	-6.7

● JOHN WEYHING
Weyhing, John b: 6/24/1869, Louisville, Ky. d: 6/20/1890, Louisville, Ky. BL/TL, 6'2", 185 lbs. Deb: 7/13/1888 F

YEAR	TM/L	W	L	PCT	G	GS	CG	SH	SV	IP	H	HR	BB	SO	RAT	ERA	ERA+	OAV	OOB	BH	AVG	PB	PR	/A	PD	TPI
1888	Cin-a	3	4	.429	8	8	7	0	0	65²	52	0	17	30	9.6	1.23	257	.210	.263	3	.130	-2	13	14	-1	1.1
1889	Col-a	0	0	—	1	1	0	0	0	1	1	0	4	0	45.0	27.00	13	.250	.625	0	—	0	-3	-3	-0	0.0
Total	2	3	4	.429	9	9	7	0	0	66²	53	0	21	30	10.1	1.62	196	.210	.274	3	.130	-2	11	12	-1	1.1

● LEE WHEAT
Wheat, Leroy William b: 9/15/29, Edwardsville, Ill BR/TR, 6'4", 200 lbs. Deb: 4/21/54

YEAR	TM/L	W	L	PCT	G	GS	CG	SH	SV	IP	H	HR	BB	SO	RAT	ERA	ERA+	OAV	OOB	BH	AVG	PB	PR	/A	PD	TPI
1954	Phi-A	0	2	.000	8	1	0	0	0	28¹	38	1	9	7	15.2	5.72	68	.304	.356	1	.125	-0	-6	-6	-0	-0.4
1955	KC-A	0	0	—	3	0	0	0	0	2	8	1	3	1	49.5	22.50	19	.533	.611	0	—	0	-4	-4	0	0.0
Total	2	0	2	.000	11	1	0	0	0	30¹	46	2	12	8	17.5	6.82	57	.329	.386	1	.125	-0	-10	-10	-0	-0.4

● CHARLIE WHEATLEY
Wheatley, Charles b: 6/27/1893, Rosedale, Kan. d: 12/10/82, Tulsa, Okla. BR/TR, 5'11", 174 lbs. Deb: 9/6/12

YEAR	TM/L	W	L	PCT	G	GS	CG	SH	SV	IP	H	HR	BB	SO	RAT	ERA	ERA+	OAV	OOB	BH	AVG	PB	PR	/A	PD	TPI
1912	Det-A	1	4	.200	5	5	2	0	0	35	45	1	17	14	16.5	6.17	53	.331	.413	0	.000	-2	-11	-11	-0	-1.4

● WOODY WHEATON
Wheaton, Elwood Pierce b: 10/3/14, Philadelphia, Pa. d: 12/11/95, Lancaster, Pa. BL/TL, 5'8.5", 160 lbs. Deb: 9/28/43 ♦

YEAR	TM/L	W	L	PCT	G	GS	CG	SH	SV	IP	H	HR	BB	SO	RAT	ERA	ERA+	OAV	OOB	BH	AVG	PB	PR	/A	PD	TPI
1944	Phi-a	0	1	.000	11	1	1	0	0	38	36	1	20	15	13.5	3.55	98	.255	.352	11	.186	-1	-0	-0	-1	-0.1

● RIP WHEELER
Wheeler, Floyd Clark b: 3/2/1898, Marion, Ky. d: 9/18/68, Marion, Ky. BR/TR, 6', 180 lbs. Deb: 9/30/21

YEAR	TM/L	W	L	PCT	G	GS	CG	SH	SV	IP	H	HR	BB	SO	RAT	ERA	ERA+	OAV	OOB	BH	AVG	PB	PR	/A	PD	TPI
1921	Pit-N	0	0	—	1	0	0	0	0	3	6	0	1	0	24.0	9.00	43	.500	.571	0	.000	-0	-2	-2	0	0.0
1922	Pit-N	0	0	—	1	0	0	0	0	1	1	0	2	0	27.0	0.00	—	.333	.600	0	—	0	0	0	0	0.0
1923	Chi-N	1	2	.333	3	3	1	0	0	24	28	2	5	5	13.5	4.88	82	.298	.353	1	.111	-1	-2	-1	0	-0.2
1924	Chi-N	3	6	.333	29	4	0	0	0	101¹	103	8	21	16	11.0	3.91	100	.265	.303	7	.219	-1	-0	-0	-0	-0.1
Total	4	4	8	.333	34	7	1	0	0	129¹	138	10	29	21	11.9	4.18	94	.278	.323	8	.190	-2	-4	-4	2	-0.3

● GEORGE WHEELER
Wheeler, George L. (b: George L. Heroux) b: 8/3/1869, Methuen, Mass. d: 3/23/46, Santa Ana, Cal. BB/TR Deb: 9/18/1896

YEAR	TM/L	W	L	PCT	G	GS	CG	SH	SV	IP	H	HR	BB	SO	RAT	ERA	ERA+	OAV	OOB	BH	AVG	PB	PR	/A	PD	TPI
1896	Phi-N	1	1	.500	3	2	2	0	0	16¹	18	0	5	2	13.8	3.86	112	.277	.347	1	.111	-1	1	1	0	0.0
1897	Phi-N	11	10	.524	26	19	17	0	0	191	229	3	62	35	13.9	3.96	106	.295	.349	16	.203	-1	8	5	1	0.4
1898	Phi-N	6	8	.429	15	13	10	0	0	112³	155	1	36	20	15.8	4.17	82	.325	.380	8	.186	-1	-7	-9	3	-0.8
1899	Phi-N	3	1	.750	6	5	3	0	0	39	44	1	13	3	13.8	6.00	61	.284	.351	4	.235	1	-9	-10	-0	-0.7
Total	4	21	20	.512	50	39	32	0	0	358²	446	5	116	60	14.5	4.24	92	.303	.359	29	.196	-2	-8	-13	4	-1.1

● HARRY WHEELER
Wheeler, Harry Eugene b: 3/3/1858, Versailles, Ind. d: 10/9/1900, Cincinnati, Ohio BR/TR, 5'11", 165 lbs. Deb: 6/19/1878 M♦

YEAR	TM/L	W	L	PCT	G	GS	CG	SH	SV	IP	H	HR	BB	SO	RAT	ERA	ERA+	OAV	OOB	BH	AVG	PB	PR	/A	PD	TPI
1878	Pro-N	6	1	.857	7	6	6	0	0	62	70	1	25	25	13.8	3.48	63	.275	.339	4	.148	-1	-8	-9	-2	-1.0
1879	Cin-N	0	1	.000	1	0	0	0	0	1	6	0	4	0	90.0	81.00	3	.667	.769	0	—	0	-9	-9	-0	-2.5
1882	Cin-a	1	2	.333	4	1	1	0	0	21²	21	0	12	10	13.7	5.40	49	.239	.330	86	.250	1	-7	-7	-0	-0.7
1883	Col-a	0	1	.000	1	1	1	0	0	5	13	0	2	0	27.0	7.20	47	.448	.484	84	.226	0	-2	-2	-0	-0.3
1884	KC-U	0	1	.000	1	1	0	0	0	8	7	0	0	6	7.9	1.13	199	.219	.219	16	.258	-1	1	0	1	0.1
Total	5	7	6	.538	14	10	8	0	0	97²	117	1	43	41	14.7	4.70	50	.283	.351	256	.228	-1	-24	-26	-2	-4.4

● GARY WHEELOCK
Wheelock, Gary Richard b: 11/29/51, Bakersfield, Cal. BR/TR, 6'3", 205 lbs. Deb: 9/17/76

YEAR	TM/L	W	L	PCT	G	GS	CG	SH	SV	IP	H	HR	BB	SO	RAT	ERA	ERA+	OAV	OOB	BH	AVG	PB	PR	/A	PD	TPI
1976	Cal-A	0	0	—	2	0	0	0	0	2	6	1	2	0	36.0	27.00	12	.500	.571	0	—	0	-5	-5	-0	0.0
1977	Sea-A	6	9	.400	17	17	2	0	0	88¹	94	16	26	47	12.4	4.89	84	.268	.322	0	—	0	-8	-8	-1	-1.2
1980	Sea-A	0	0	—	1	1	0	0	0	3	4	0	1	1	15.0	6.00	69	.333	.385	0	—	0	-1	-1	0	0.0
Total	3	6	9	.400	20	18	2	0	0	93¹	104	16	28	50	13.0	5.40	76	.277	.333	0	—	0	-14	-14	-1	-1.2

● JACK WHILLOCK
Whillock, Jack Franklin b: 11/4/42, Clinton, Ark. BR/TR, 6'3", 195 lbs. Deb: 8/29/71

YEAR	TM/L	W	L	PCT	G	GS	CG	SH	SV	IP	H	HR	BB	SO	RAT	ERA	ERA+	OAV	OOB	BH	AVG	PB	PR	/A	PD	TPI
1971	Det-A	0	0	—	6	0	0	0	0	8	6	2	6	6	13.5	5.63	64	.323	.364	0	.000	0	-1	-1	-0	-0.5

● PAT WHITAKER
Whitaker, William H. b: 11/1864, St.Louis, Mo. d: 7/15/02, St.Louis, Mo. TR Deb: 10/11/1888

YEAR	TM/L	W	L	PCT	G	GS	CG	SH	SV	IP	H	HR	BB	SO	RAT	ERA	ERA+	OAV	OOB	BH	AVG	PB	PR	/A	PD	TPI
1888	Bal-a	1	1	.500	2	2	2	0	0	14	10	0	6	5	13.5	5.14	49	.236	.333	0	.000	-1	-3	-3	2	-0.3
1889	Bal-a	1	0	1.000	1	1	1	0	0	9	10	0	4	1	14.0	2.00	197	.270	.341	1	.250	0	2	2	0	0.2
Total	2	2	1	.667	3	3	3	0	0	23	20	0	10	6	13.7	3.91	86	.250	.337	1	.100	-1	-1	-1	2	-0.1

● BILL WHITBY
Whitby, William Edward b: 7/29/43, Crewe, Va. BR/TR, 6'1", 190 lbs. Deb: 6/17/64

YEAR	TM/L	W	L	PCT	G	GS	CG	SH	SV	IP	H	HR	BB	SO	RAT	ERA	ERA+	OAV	OOB	BH	AVG	PB	PR	/A	PD	TPI
1964	Min-a	0	0	—	4	0	0	0	0	6¹	7	1	4	2	12.8	8.53	42	.308	.333	0	.000	-0	-3	-3	-0	0.0

● BOB WHITCHER
Whitcher, Robert Arthur b: 4/29/17, Berlin, N.H. BL/TL, 5'8", 165 lbs. Deb: 8/20/45

YEAR	TM/L	W	L	PCT	G	GS	CG	SH	SV	IP	H	HR	BB	SO	RAT	ERA	ERA+	OAV	OOB	BH	AVG	PB	PR	/A	PD	TPI
1945	Bos-N	0	2	.000	6	3	0	0	0	15²	12	1	12	6	13.8	2.87	133	.235	.381	1	.333	0	2	2	-0	0.2

YEAR TM/L	W	L	PCT	G	GS	CG	SH	SV	IP	H	HR	BB	SO	RAT	ERA	ERA+	OAV	OOB	BH	AVG	PB	PR	/A	PD	TPI

● ABE WHITE
White, Adel b: 5/16/04, Winder, Ga. d: 10/1/78, Atlanta, Ga. BR/TL, 6', 185 lbs. Deb: 7/10/37

YEAR TM/L	W	L	PCT	G	GS	CG	SH	SV	IP	H	HR	BB	SO	RAT	ERA	ERA+	OAV	OOB	BH	AVG	PB	PR	/A	PD	TPI
1937 StL-N	0	1	.000	5	0	0	0	0	9¹	14	1	3	2	16.4	6.75	59	.341	.386	1	1.000	0	-3	-3	-0	-0.2

● ERNIE WHITE
White, Ernest Daniel b: 9/5/16, Pacolet Mills, S.C d: 5/22/74, Augusta, Ga. BR/TL, 5'11.5", 175 lbs. Deb: 5/9/40 C

YEAR TM/L	W	L	PCT	G	GS	CG	SH	SV	IP	H	HR	BB	SO	RAT	ERA	ERA+	OAV	OOB	BH	AVG	PB	PR	/A	PD	TPI
1940 StL-N	1	1	.500	8	1	0	0	0	21²	29	0	14	15	18.3	4.15	96	.315	.411	3	.429	1	-1	-0	1	0.1
1941 StL-N	17	7	.708	32	25	12	3	2	210	169	12	70	117	10.5	2.40	157	.217	.287	15	.190	0	29	32	-4	3.3
1942 *StL-N	7	5	.583	26	19	7	1	2	128¹	113	11	41	67	10.9	2.52	136	.232	.294	8	.195	0	11	13	-2	1.0
1943 *StL-N	5	5	.500	14	10	5	1	0	78²	78	4	33	28	12.8	3.78	89	.257	.332	6	.214	0	-3	-4	-1	-0.5
1946 Bos-N	0	1	.000	12	1	0	0	0	23²	22	1	12	8	12.9	4.18	82	.256	.347	1	.250	0	-2	-2	-1	-0.1
1947 Bos-N	0	0	—	1	1	0	0	0	4	1	0	1	1	4.5	0.00	—	.083	.154	1	1.000	0	2	2	-0	0.0
1948 Bos-N	0	2	.000	15	0	0	0	0	23	13	0	17	8	11.7	1.96	196	.167	.316	0	.000	-0	5	5	-1	0.4
Total 7	30	21	.588	108	57	24	5	6	489¹	425	28	188	244	11.5	2.78	130	.231	.306	34	.209	2	41	45	-8	4.2

● GABE WHITE
White, Gabriel Allen b: 11/20/71, Sebring, Fla. BL/TL, 6'2", 200 lbs. Deb: 5/27/94

YEAR TM/L	W	L	PCT	G	GS	CG	SH	SV	IP	H	HR	BB	SO	RAT	ERA	ERA+	OAV	OOB	BH	AVG	PB	PR	/A	PD	TPI
1994 Mon-N	1	1	.500	7	5	0	0	0	23²	24	4	11	17	13.7	6.08	69	.261	.346	0	.000	-0	-5	-5	-0	-0.4
1995 Mon-N	1	2	.333	19	1	0	0	0	25²	26	7	9	25	12.6	7.01	61	.260	.327	0	.000	-0	-8	-8	-0	-0.9
Total 2	2	3	.400	26	6	0	0	0	49¹	50	11	20	42	13.1	6.57	65	.260	.336	0	.000	-0	-13	-13	-1	-1.3

● DEKE WHITE
White, George Frederick b: 9/8/1872, Albany, N.Y. d: 11/5/57, Ilion, N.Y. BB/TL, Deb: 9/14/1895

YEAR TM/L	W	L	PCT	G	GS	CG	SH	SV	IP	H	HR	BB	SO	RAT	ERA	ERA+	OAV	OOB	BH	AVG	PB	PR	/A	PD	TPI
1895 Phi-N	1	0	1.000	3	1	1	0	0	17¹	17	1	13	6	16.6	9.87	49	.254	.390	1	.125	-1	-10	-10	-0	-0.6

● DOC WHITE
White, Guy Harris b: 4/9/1879, Washington, D.C. d: 2/19/69, Silver Spring, Md. BL/TL, 6'1", 150 lbs. Deb: 4/22/01 ♦

YEAR TM/L	W	L	PCT	G	GS	CG	SH	SV	IP	H	HR	BB	SO	RAT	ERA	ERA+	OAV	OOB	BH	AVG	PB	PR	/A	PD	TPI
1901 Phi-N	14	13	.519	31	27	22	0	0	236²	241	0	56	132	11.8	3.19	106	.262	.314	27	.276	5	3	5	3	1.3
1902 Phi-N	16	20	.444	36	35	34	3	1	306	277	3	72	185	10.6	2.53	111	.241	.294	47	.263	4	9	10	2	2.0
1903 Chi-A	17	16	.515	37	36	29	3	0	300	258	4	69	114	10.2	2.13	132	.232	.285	22	.202	6	28	23	3	3.3
1904 Chi-A	16	12	.571	30	30	23	7	0	228	201	6	68	115	11.0	1.78	138	.238	.301	12	.158	0	21	17	1	2.4
1905 Chi-A	17	13	.567	36	33	25	4	0	260¹	204	2	58	120	9.4	1.76	140	.218	.270	15	.167	0	26	20	0	2.4
1906 *Chi-A	18	6	.750	28	24	20	7	1	219¹	160	2	38	95	8.3	1.52	167	.207	.249	12	.185	4	29	25	2	3.6
1907 Chi-A	27	13	.675	46	35	24	6	1	291	270	4	38	141	9.7	2.26	106	.248	.278	20	.222	4	9	4	5	1.6
1908 Chi-A	18	13	.581	41	37	24	5	0	296	262	6	69	126	10.3	2.55	91	.240	.291	25	.229	4	-5	-8	7	0.4
1909 Chi-A	11	9	.550	24	21	14	3	0	177²	149	1	31	77	9.5	1.72	136	.226	.269	25	.234	6	15	12	-1	2.1
1910 Chi-A	15	13	.536	33	29	20	2	1	236²	219	2	50	111	10.7	2.66	90	.243	.291	25	.198	2	-4	-7	2	-0.3
1911 Chi-A	10	14	.417	34	29	16	4	2	214¹	219	2	35	72	11.0	2.98	108	.271	.309	20	.256	3	9	6	-1	0.8
1912 Chi-A	8	10	.444	32	19	9	1	0	172	172	1	47	57	11.9	3.24	99	.267	.325	7	.125	-1	1	-1	-1	-0.3
1913 Chi-A	2	4	.333	19	8	2	0	0	103	106	2	39	39	13.1	3.50	84	.278	.353	3	.120	-1	-6	-7	2	-0.2
Total 13	189	156	.548	427	363	262	45	5	3041	2738	33	670	1384	10.4	2.39	112	.242	.292	278	.217	37	134	99	25	19.1

● HAL WHITE
White, Harold George b: 3/18/19, Utica, N.Y. BR/TR, 5'10", 170 lbs. Deb: 4/22/41

YEAR TM/L	W	L	PCT	G	GS	CG	SH	SV	IP	H	HR	BB	SO	RAT	ERA	ERA+	OAV	OOB	BH	AVG	PB	PR	/A	PD	TPI
1941 Det-A	0	0	—	4	0	0	0	0	9	11	0	6	2	17.0	6.00	76	.306	.405	0	.000	-0	-2	-1	0	0.0
1942 Det-A	12	12	.500	34	25	12	4	1	216²	212	6	82	93	12.4	2.91	136	.252	.323	13	.169	-1	18	25	0	2.6
1943 Det-A	7	12	.368	32	24	7	2	2	177²	150	6	71	58	11.2	3.39	104	.228	.304	8	.140	-1	-2	3	0	0.2
1946 Det-A	1	1	.500	11	1	1	0	0	27¹	34	5	15	12	16.1	5.60	65	.312	.395	0	.000	-1	-6	-6	1	-0.4
1947 Det-A	4	5	.444	35	5	0	0	2	84²	91	4	47	33	14.9	3.61	104	.279	.373	3	.167	0	1	1	1	0.3
1948 Det-A	2	1	.667	27	0	0	0	1	42²	46	2	26	17	15.4	6.12	71	.272	.372	2	.154	0	-9	-8	-1	-0.6
1949 Det-A	1	0	1.000	9	0	0	0	2	12	5	0	4	6	6.8	0.00	—	.125	.205	1	.333	0	6	6	1	0.7
1950 Det-A	9	6	.600	42	8	3	1	1	111	96	7	65	53	13.1	4.54	103	.239	.347	4	.121	-2	2	0	0	0.0
1951 Det-A	3	4	.429	38	4	0	0	4	76	74	7	49	23	14.8	4.74	88	.264	.378	4	.250	0	-5	-5	2	-0.3
1952 Det-A	1	8	.111	41	0	0	0	5	63¹	53	1	39	18	13.1	3.69	103	.237	.350	2	.182	-0	-1	1	1	0.2
1953 StL-A	0	0	—	10	0	0	0	0	10¹	7	1	3	2	10.5	2.61	161	.205	.279	0	.000	0	2	2	0	0.1
StL-N	6	5	.545	49	0	0	0	7	84²	84	5	39	32	13.1	2.98	143	.272	.353	0	.000	-2	12	12	1	1.5
1954 StL-N	0	0	—	5	0	0	0	1	11	14	2	4	2	28.8	19.80	21	.440	.533	0	.000	-0	-9	-9	-0	0.0
Total 12	46	54	.460	336	67	23	7	25	920¹	875	47	450	349	13.1	3.78	106	.253	.342	37	.145	-7	6	23	6	4.3

● DEACON WHITE
White, James Laurie b: 12/7/1847, Caton, N.Y. d: 7/7/39, Aurora, Ill. BL/TR, 5'11", 175 lbs. Deb: 5/4/1871 FM♦

YEAR TM/L	W	L	PCT	G	GS	CG	SH	SV	IP	H	HR	BB	SO	RAT	ERA	ERA+	OAV	OOB	BH	AVG	PB	PR	/A	PD	TPI
1876 Chi-N	0	0	—	1	0	0	0	0	2	1	0	0	3	4.5	0.00	—	.143	.143	104	.343	0	1	1	0	0.1
1890 Buf-P	0	0	—	1	0	0	0	0	8	18	0	2	0	22.5	9.00	46	.429	.455	114	.260	0	-4	-4	-1	0.0
Total 2	0	0	—	2	0	0	0	0	10	19	0	2	3	18.9	7.20	53	.388	.412	1619	.303	1	-4	-4	-0	0.1

● LARRY WHITE
White, Larry David b: 9/25/58, San Fernando, Cal. BR/TR, 6'5", 190 lbs. Deb: 9/20/83

YEAR TM/L	W	L	PCT	G	GS	CG	SH	SV	IP	H	HR	BB	SO	RAT	ERA	ERA+	OAV	OOB	BH	AVG	PB	PR	/A	PD	TPI
1983 LA-N	0	0	—	4	0	0	0	0	7	4	0	3	5	9.0	1.29	279	.174	.269	0	—	0	2	2	0	0.0
1984 LA-N	0	1	.000	7	1	0	0	0	12	9	2	6	10	11.3	3.00	118	.209	.306	0	.000	-0	1	1	-0	0.1
Total 2	0	1	.000	11	1	0	0	0	19	13	2	9	15	10.4	2.37	150	.197	.293	0	.000	-0	3	3	-0	0.1

● KIRBY WHITE
White, Oliver Kirby "Red" or "Buck" b: 1/3/1884, Hillsboro, Ohio d: 4/22/43, Hillsboro, Ohio BL/TR, 6', 190 lbs. Deb: 5/4/09

YEAR TM/L	W	L	PCT	G	GS	CG	SH	SV	IP	H	HR	BB	SO	RAT	ERA	ERA+	OAV	OOB	BH	AVG	PB	PR	/A	PD	TPI
1909 Bos-N	6	13	.316	23	19	11	1	0	148¹	134	5	80	53	13.0	3.22	88	.245	.343	8	.160	-1	-10	-7	4	-1.0
1910 Bos-N	1	2	.333	3	3	1	0	0	26	15	2	12	6	10.4	1.38	240	.188	.316	2	.333	1	5	6	0	0.8
Pit-N	10	9	.526	30	21	7	3	2	153¹	142	2	75	42	13.0	3.46	90	.258	.352	12	.261	3	-7	-6	-3	-0.7
Yr	11	11	.500	33	24	10	3	2	179¹	157	4	87	48	12.5	3.16	99	.248	.343	14	.269	4	-3	-1	-3	0.1
1911 Pit-N	0	1	.000	2	1	0	0	0	3	3	1	1	1	12.0	9.00	38	.250	.308	0	.000	-0	-2	-2	0	-0.5
Total 3	17	25	.405	58	44	21	4	2	330²	294	10	168	102	12.8	3.24	93	.247	.345	22	.214	3	-15	-9	-4	-1.4

● RICK WHITE
White, Richard Allen b: 12/23/68, Springfield, Ohio BR/TR, 6'4", 215 lbs. Deb: 4/6/94

YEAR TM/L	W	L	PCT	G	GS	CG	SH	SV	IP	H	HR	BB	SO	RAT	ERA	ERA+	OAV	OOB	BH	AVG	PB	PR	/A	PD	TPI
1994 Pit-N	4	5	.444	43	5	0	0	6	75¹	79	9	17	38	12.2	3.82	113	.280	.334	1	.077	-1	3	4	-1	0.4
1995 Pit-N	2	3	.400	15	9	0	0	0	55	66	3	18	29	14.1	4.75	91	.299	.357	1	.067	-1	-3	-3	0	-0.3
Total 2	6	8	.429	58	14	0	0	6	130¹	145	12	35	67	13.4	4.21	102	.288	.344	2	.071	-1	-0	-1	-1	0.1

● STEVE WHITE
White, Stephen Vincent b: 12/21/1884, Dorchester, Mass. d: 1/29/75, Braintree, Mass. BR/TR, 5'10", 160 lbs. Deb: 5/29/12

YEAR TM/L	W	L	PCT	G	GS	CG	SH	SV	IP	H	HR	BB	SO	RAT	ERA	ERA+	OAV	OOB	BH	AVG	PB	PR	/A	PD	TPI
1912 Was-A	0	0	—	1	0	0	0	0	0²	2	1	0	1	27.0	0.00	—	.667	.667	0	—	0	0	0	-0	0.0
Bos-N	0	0	—	3	0	0	0	0	6	9	0	5	2	22.5	6.00	60	.429	.556	0	.000	-0	-2	-2	0	0.0
Total 1	0	0	—	4	0	0	0	0	6²	11	1	5	3	23.0	5.40	66	.458	.567	0	.000	-0	-1	-1	-0	0.0

● BILL WHITE
White, William Dighton b: 5/1/1860, Bridgeport, Ohio d: 12/29/24, Bellaire, Ohio TR, Deb: 5/3/1884 ♦

YEAR TM/L	W	L	PCT	G	GS	CG	SH	SV	IP	H	HR	BB	SO	RAT	ERA	ERA+	OAV	OOB	BH	AVG	PB	PR	/A	PD	TPI
1886 Lou-a	0	0	—	1	0	0	0	0	1	2	0	2	1	36.0	9.00	40	.400	.571	143	.257	0	-1	-1	0	0.0

● WILL WHITE
White, William Henry "Whoop-La" b: 10/11/1854, Caton, N.Y. d: 8/31/11, Port Carling, Ont., Canada BB/TR, 5'9.5", 175 lbs. Deb: 7/20/1877 FM

YEAR TM/L	W	L	PCT	G	GS	CG	SH	SV	IP	H	HR	BB	SO	RAT	ERA	ERA+	OAV	OOB	BH	AVG	PB	PR	/A	PD	TPI
1877 Bos-N	2	1	.667	3	3	3	0	0	27	27	0	6	9	9.7	3.00	94	.243	.257	3	.200	-1	-1	-1	-1	-0.2
1878 Cin-N	30	21	.588	52	52	52	3	0	468	477	1	45	169	10.0	1.79	119	.252	.252	28	.142	-8	27	18	-2	0.7
1879 Cin-N	43	31	.581	76	75	75	4	0	680	676	10	68	232	9.8	1.99	117	.238	.256	40	.136	-17	38	26	-7	0.2
1880 Cin-N	18	42	.300	62	62	58	3	0	517¹	550	9	56	161	10.5	2.14	116	.255	.273	35	.169	-9	13	20	-7	0.5
1881 Det-N	0	2	.000	2	2	2	0	0	18	24	0	5	2	13.0	5.00	58	.296	.313	0	.000	-1	-4	-4	-1	-0.5
1882 Cin-a	40	12	.769	54	54	52	8	0	480	411	3	71	122	9.0	1.54	172	.216	.244	55	.266	6	61	59	13	7.3
1883 Cin-a	43	22	.662	65	64	64	6	0	577	473	16	104	141	9.0	2.09	155	.209	.244	54	.225	3	78	74	-3	6.6
1884 Cin-a	34	18	.654	52	52	52	7	0	456	479	16	74	118	11.6	3.32	101	.255	.290	35	.190	-2	-3	1	-6	-0.8
1885 Cin-a	18	15	.545	34	34	33	2	0	293¹	295	9	64	80	11.8	3.53	92	.255	.309	20	.169	-3	-9	-9	-3	-1.4
1886 Cin-a	1	2	.333	3	3	3	0	0	26	28	1	4	6	15.2	4.15	85	.280	.379	1	.111	-1	-2	-2	-0	-0.2
Total 10	229	166	.580	403	401	394	36	0	3542²	3440	65	496	1041	10.2	2.28	126	.239	.268	271	.183	-33	198	179	-18	12.2

● JOHN WHITEHEAD
Whitehead, John Henderson "Silent John" b: 4/27/09, Coleman, Tex. d: 10/20/64, Bonham, Tex. BR/TR, 6'2", 195 lbs. Deb: 4/19/35

YEAR TM/L	W	L	PCT	G	GS	CG	SH	SV	IP	H	HR	BB	SO	RAT	ERA	ERA+	OAV	OOB	BH	AVG	PB	PR	/A	PD	TPI
1935 Chi-A	13	13	.500	28	27	18	1	0	222¹	249	17	101	72	12.6	3.72	124	.250	.332	12	.146	-5	18	22	3	2.0
1936 Chi-A	13	13	.500	34	32	15	1	1	230²	254	9	98	70	13.9	4.64	112	.276	.349	21	.142	-8	17	14	3	1.7
1937 Chi-A	11	8	.579	26	24	8	4	0	165²	191	14	56	45	13.7	4.07	113	.294	.354	13	.224	1	10	10	-1	0.9
1938 Chi-A	10	11	.476	32	24	10	2	1	183¹	218	12	80	38	14.8	4.76	103	.299	.370	6	.100	-4	1	3	-1	-0.1

YEAR	TM/L	W	L	PCT	G	GS	CG	SH	SV	IP	H	HR	BB	SO	RAT	ERA	ERA+	OAV	OOB	BH	AVG	PB	PR	/A	PD	TPI
1939	Chi-A	0	3	.000	7	4	0	0	0	32	60	4	5	9	18.3	8.16	58	.408	.428	0	.000	-1	-13	-12	0	-1.0
	StL-A	1	3	.250	26	4	0	0	1	66	88	10	17	9	14.6	5.86	83	.321	.365	1	.059	-1	-9	-7	1	-0.4
	Yr	1	6	.143	33	8	0	0	1	98	148	14	22	18	15.8	6.61	73	.352	.387	1	.038	-3	-22	-20	1	-1.4
1940	StL-A	1	3	.250	15	4	1	1	0	40	46	3	14	11	13.5	5.40	85	.286	.343	2	.167	-1	-5	-4	-1	-0.4
1942	StL-A	0	0	—	4	0	0	0	0	8	8	0	1	0	22.5	6.75	55	.421	.476	0	—	0	-1	-1	0	0.0
Total	7	49	54	.476	172	119	52	9	4	944	1074	69	372	254	14.0	4.60	105	.287	.355	55	.169	-11	11	24	5	2.7

● MILT WHITEHEAD
Whitehead, Milton P. b: 1862, Canada d: 8/15/01, Highland, Cal. BB, Deb: 4/20/1884 ♦

YEAR	TM/L	W	L	PCT	G	GS	CG	SH	SV	IP	H	HR	BB	SO	RAT	ERA	ERA+	OAV	OOB	BH	AVG	PB	PR	/A	PD	TPI
1884	StL-U	0	1	.000	1	1	1	0	0	8	14	0	2	2	18.0	9.00	27	.359	.390	83	.211	-0	-6	-6	0	-0.5

● EARL WHITEHILL
Whitehill, Earl Oliver b: 2/7/1900, Cedar Rapids, Iowa d: 10/22/54, Omaha, Neb. BL/TL, 5'9.5", 174 lbs. Deb: 9/15/23 C

YEAR	TM/L	W	L	PCT	G	GS	CG	SH	SV	IP	H	HR	BB	SO	RAT	ERA	ERA+	OAV	OOB	BH	AVG	PB	PR	/A	PD	TPI
1923	Det-A	2	0	1.000	8	3	1	0	0	33	22	2	15	19	10.9	2.73	142	.188	.296	4	.364	1	5	4	-0	0.3
1924	Det-A	17	9	.654	35	32	16	2	0	233	260	8	79	65	13.6	3.86	106	.288	.353	19	.213	1	10	6	-0	0.7
1925	Det-A	11	11	.500	35	33	15	1	2	239¹	267	13	88	83	13.7	4.66	92	.293	.361	19	.218	-0	-7	-9	-1	-0.8
1926	Det-A	16	13	.552	36	34	13	0	0	252¹	271	7	79	109	12.8	3.99	102	.277	.336	23	.253	4	1	2	-1	0.5
1927	Det-A	16	14	.533	41	31	17	3	3	236	238	4	105	95	13.4	3.36	125	.267	.350	16	.205	-0	21	22	-3	2.3
1928	Det-A	11	16	.407	31	30	12	1	0	196¹	214	8	78	93	13.4	4.31	95	.277	.344	13	.194	-1	-6	-4	-1	-0.6
1929	Det-A	14	15	.483	38	28	18	1	1	245¹	267	16	96	103	13.4	4.62	93	.280	.348	23	.256	5	-10	-9	-0	-0.5
1930	Det-A	17	13	.567	34	31	16	0	1	220²	248	8	80	109	13.7	4.24	113	.280	.351	16	.193	-4	10	14	-2	1.0
1931	Det-A	13	16	.448	34	34	22	0	0	271¹	287	22	118	81	13.6	4.08	112	.274	.351	15	.155	-5	9	15	2	1.1
1932	Det-A	16	12	.571	33	31	17	3	0	244	255	17	93	81	13.0	4.54	104	.269	.337	22	.244	1	-2	5	-2	0.4
1933	*Was-A	22	8	.733	39	37	19	2	1	270	271	9	100	96	12.5	3.33	125	.262	.329	24	.222	2	28	25	-2	2.5
1934	Was-A	14	11	.560	32	31	15	0	0	235	269	10	94	96	14.0	4.52	96	.290	.357	17	.200	4	-1	-5	-0	-0.2
1935	Was-A	14	13	.519	34	34	19	1	0	279¹	318	16	104	102	13.8	4.29	101	.289	.354	19	.183	-1	5	1	1	0.1
1936	Was-A	14	11	.560	28	28	14	0	0	212¹	252	17	89	63	14.5	4.87	98	.294	.362	13	.169	-0	4	-2	-1	-0.3
1937	Cle-A	8	8	.500	33	22	6	1	2	147	189	9	80	53	16.8	6.49	71	.322	.409	11	.224	1	-31	-31	1	-2.5
1938	Cle-A	9	8	.529	26	23	4	0	0	160¹	187	18	83	60	15.7	5.56	83	.289	.378	7	.125	-2	-14	-16	-2	-1.6
1939	Chi-N	4	7	.364	24	11	2	1	1	89¹	102	8	50	42	15.8	5.14	77	.292	.389	3	.103	-2	-12	-12	-1	-1.6
Total	17	218	185	.541	541	473	226	16	11	3564²	3917	192	1431	1350	13.8	4.36	100	.282	.353	264	.204	4	10	6	-9	0.7

● CHARLIE WHITEHOUSE
Whitehouse, Charles Evis "Lefty" b: 1/25/1894, Charleston, Ill. d: 7/19/60, Indianapolis, Ind BB/TL, 6', 152 lbs. Deb: 8/29/14

YEAR	TM/L	W	L	PCT	G	GS	CG	SH	SV	IP	H	HR	BB	SO	RAT	ERA	ERA+	OAV	OOB	BH	AVG	PB	PR	/A	PD	TPI
1914	Ind-F	2	0	1.000	8	2	2	0	0	26	34	0	5	10	13.8	4.85	64	.324	.360	0	.000	-1	-6	-5	-0	-0.5
1915	New-F	2	2	.500	11	3	1	0	0	39²	46	0	17	18	15.4	4.31	59	.299	.386	0	.000	-1	-7	-8	-1	-0.9
1919	Was-A	0	1	.000	6	1	0	0	0	12	13	1	6	5	14.3	4.50	71	.283	.365	0	.000	0	-2	-2	-0	-0.2
Total	3	4	3	.571	25	6	3	0	0	77²	93	1	28	33	14.7	4.52	63	.305	.375	0	.000	-2	-14	-14	-1	-1.6

● GIL WHITEHOUSE
Whitehouse, Gilbert Arthur b: 10/15/1893, Somerville, Mass. d: 2/14/26, Brewer, Me. BB/TR, 5'10", 170 lbs. Deb: 6/20/12 ♦

YEAR	TM/L	W	L	PCT	G	GS	CG	SH	SV	IP	H	HR	BB	SO	RAT	ERA	ERA+	OAV	OOB	BH	AVG	PB	PR	/A	PD	TPI
1915	New-F	0	0	—	1	0	0	0	0	1	0	0	1	0	9.0	0.00	—	.000	.250	27	.225	0	0	0	-0	0.0

● LEN WHITEHOUSE
Whitehouse, Leonard Joseph b: 9/10/57, Burlington, Vt. BL/TL, 5'11", 175 lbs. Deb: 9/1/81

YEAR	TM/L	W	L	PCT	G	GS	CG	SH	SV	IP	H	HR	BB	SO	RAT	ERA	ERA+	OAV	OOB	BH	AVG	PB	PR	/A	PD	TPI
1981	Tex-A	0	1	.000	2	1	0	0	0	3¹	8	1	2	2	27.0	16.20	21	.500	.556	0	—	0	-5	-5	-0	-0.9
1983	Min-A	7	1	.875	60	0	0	0	2	73²	70	6	44	44	14.2	4.15	102	.261	.369	0	—	0	-1	1	-1	-0.3
1984	Min-A	2	2	.500	30	0	0	0	1	31¹	29	3	17	18	13.8	3.16	133	.254	.361	0	—	0	3	4	-0	0.1
1985	Min-A	0	0	—	5	0	0	0	1	7¹	12	4	2	4	17.2	11.05	40	.353	.389	0	—	0	-6	-5	-0	-0.5
Total	4	9	4	.692	97	1	0	0	4	115²	119	14	65	68	14.6	4.67	90	.275	.375	0	—	0	-8	-6	-1	-1.6

● WALLY WHITEHURST
Whitehurst, Walter Richard b: 4/11/64, Shreveport, La. BR/TR, 6'3", 180 lbs. Deb: 7/17/89

YEAR	TM/L	W	L	PCT	G	GS	CG	SH	SV	IP	H	HR	BB	SO	RAT	ERA	ERA+	OAV	OOB	BH	AVG	PB	PR	/A	PD	TPI
1989	NY-N	0	1	.000	9	1	0	0	0	14	17	2	5	9	14.1	4.50	73	.293	.349	2	.000	0	-2	-2	-0	-0.1
1990	NY-N	1	0	1.000	38	0	0	0	2	65²	63	5	9	46	9.9	3.29	114	.251	.277	2	.250	4	3	0	0	0.1
1991	NY-N	7	12	.368	36	20	0	0	1	133¹	142	12	25	87	11.5	4.18	87	.274	.313	6	.182	1	-7	-8	1	-0.8
1992	NY-N	3	9	.250	44	11	0	0	0	97	99	4	33	70	12.6	3.62	96	.264	.330	4	.182	1	-1	-2	1	-0.1
1993	SD-N	4	7	.364	21	19	0	0	0	105²	109	11	30	57	12.1	3.83	108	.276	.332	2	.083	-2	2	4	0	0.3
1994	SD-N	4	7	.364	13	13	0	0	0	64	84	8	26	43	15.6	4.92	83	.319	.383	2	.105	0	-5	-6	0	-0.8
1996	NY-A	1	1	.500	2	2	0	0	0	8	11	1	2	1	14.6	6.75	75	.324	.361	0	—	0	-2	-2	-0	-0.3
Total	7	20	37	.351	163	66	0	0	3	487²	525	43	130	313	12.3	4.02	94	.277	.328	16	.150	1	-11	-12	2	-1.8

● SEAN WHITESIDE
Whiteside, David Sean b: 4/19/71, Lakeland, Fla. BL/TL, 6'4", 190 lbs. Deb: 4/29/95

YEAR	TM/L	W	L	PCT	G	GS	CG	SH	SV	IP	H	HR	BB	SO	RAT	ERA	ERA+	OAV	OOB	BH	AVG	PB	PR	/A	PD	TPI
1995	Det-A	0	0	—	2	0	0	0	0	3²	7	1	4	2	27.0	14.73	32	.438	.550	0	—	0	-4	-4	-0	0.0

● MATT WHITESIDE
Whiteside, Matthew Christopher b: 8/8/67, Charleston, Mo. BR/TR, 6', 185 lbs. Deb: 8/5/92

YEAR	TM/L	W	L	PCT	G	GS	CG	SH	SV	IP	H	HR	BB	SO	RAT	ERA	ERA+	OAV	OOB	BH	AVG	PB	PR	/A	PD	TPI
1992	Tex-A	1	1	.500	20	0	0	0	4	28	26	1	11	13	11.9	1.93	197	.245	.316	0	—	0	6	6	-0	0.7
1993	Tex-A	2	1	.667	60	0	0	0	1	73	78	7	23	39	12.6	4.32	96	.281	.338	0	—	0	0	-1	-1	0.2
1994	Tex-A	2	2	.500	47	0	0	0	1	61	68	6	28	37	14.5	5.02	96	.286	.363	0	—	0	-1	-1	-1	-0.1
1995	Tex-A	5	4	.556	40	0	0	0	3	53	48	5	19	46	11.5	4.08	118	.242	.312	0	—	0	4	4	-1	0.6
1996	Tex-A	0	1	.000	14	0	0	0	0	32¹	43	8	11	15	15.0	6.68	80	.321	.372	0	—	0	-6	-5	-0	-0.3
Total	5	10	9	.526	181	0	0	0	9	247¹	263	27	92	150	13.0	4.48	102	.276	.341	0	—	0	3	2	-2	1.1

● JESSE WHITING
Whiting, Jesse W. b: 5/30/1879, Philadelphia, Pa. d: 10/28/37, Philadelphia, Pa. Deb: 9/27/02

YEAR	TM/L	W	L	PCT	G	GS	CG	SH	SV	IP	H	HR	BB	SO	RAT	ERA	ERA+	OAV	OOB	BH	AVG	PB	PR	/A	PD	TPI
1902	Phi-N	0	1	.000	1	1	1	0	0	9	13	1	6	0	19.0	5.00	56	.333	.422	1	.333	0	-2	-2	0	-0.2
1906	Bro-N	1	1	.500	3	2	2	1	0	24²	26	2	6	7	12.0	2.92	86	.286	.337	3	.300	1	-1	-1	1	0.1
1907	Bro-N	0	0	—	1	0	0	0	0	3	3	0	3	2	18.0	12.00	20	.273	.429	0	—	-0	-3	-3	0	-0.1
Total	3	1	2	.333	5	3	3	1	0	36²	42	3	15	9	14.2	4.17	62	.298	.369	4	.267	0	-6	-6	1	-0.1

● ART WHITNEY
Whitney, Arthur Wilson b: 1/16/1858, Brockton, Mass. d: 8/15/43, Lowell, Mass. BR/TR, 5'8", 155 lbs. Deb: 5/1/1880 F♦

YEAR	TM/L	W	L	PCT	G	GS	CG	SH	SV	IP	H	HR	BB	SO	RAT	ERA	ERA+	OAV	OOB	BH	AVG	PB	PR	/A	PD	TPI
1882	Det-N	0	1	.000	3	2	1	0	0	18	31	1	8	11	19.5	6.00	49	.373	.429	21	.183	-1	-6	-6	-1	-0.3
1886	Pit-a	0	0	—	1	0	0	0	0	6	7	0	3	2	15.0	3.00	113	.304	.385	122	.239	0	0	-0	-0	0.0
1889	*NY-N	0	1	.000	1	0	0	0	0	6	7	0	3	3	15.0	3.00	131	.280	.357	103	.218	0	1	1	-0	0.1
Total	3	0	2	.000	5	2	1	0	0	30	45	1	14	16	17.7	4.80	67	.344	.407	820	.223	-1	-5	-5	-1	-0.2

● JIM WHITNEY
Whitney, James Evans "Grasshopper Jim" b: 11/10/1857, Conklin, N.Y. d: 5/21/1891, Binghamton, N.Y. BL/TR, 6'2", 172 lbs. Deb: 5/2/1881 ♦

YEAR	TM/L	W	L	PCT	G	GS	CG	SH	SV	IP	H	HR	BB	SO	RAT	ERA	ERA+	OAV	OOB	BH	AVG	PB	PR	/A	PD	TPI
1881	Bos-N	31	33	.484	66	63	57	6	0	552¹	548	6	90	162	10.4	2.48	107	.248	.277	72	.255	11	18	11	-4	1.9
1882	Bos-N	24	21	.533	49	48	46	3	0	420	404	3	41	180	9.5	2.64	109	.251	.255	81	.323	23	12	11	1	3.1
1883	Bos-N	37	21	.638	62	56	54	1	2	514	492	7	35	345	9.2	2.24	138	.238	.251	115	.281	20	51	49	0	6.0
1884	Bos-N	23	14	.622	38	37	35	6	0	336	272	14	27	270	8.0	2.09	138	.207	.223	70	.259	10	33	30	4	4.0
1885	Bos-N	18	32	.360	51	50	50	2	0	441¹	503	14	37	200	11.0	2.98	90	.277	.286	68	.234	7	-8	-14	6	-0.2
1886	KC-N	12	32	.273	46	44	42	3	0	393	465	9	55	167	11.9	4.49	84	.284	.308	59	.239	6	-51	-31	6	-1.7
1887	Was-N	24	21	.533	47	47	46	2	0	404²	430	16	42	146	10.9	3.22	126	.259	.284	53	.264	9	38	38	4	4.7
1888	Was-N	18	21	.462	39	39	37	3	0	325	317	7	54	99	10.5	3.05	92	.245	.280	24	.170	-1	-7	-9	-1	-1.1
1889	Ind-N	2	7	.222	9	8	7	0	0	70	106	4	19	16	16.3	6.81	61	.339	.380	12	.375	-5	-22	-21	-1	-1.5
1890	Phi-a	2	2	.500	6	4	3	0	0	40	61	1	11	6	16.4	5.17	74	.341	.382	5	.238	-0	-6	-6	0	-0.5
Total	10	191	204	.484	413	396	377	26	2	3496¹	3598	79	411	1571	10.4	2.97	105	.253	.275	559	.261	89	60	55	15	14.7

● BILL WHITROCK
Whitrock, William Franklin b: 3/4/1870, Cincinnati, Ohio d: 7/26/35, Derby, Conn. TR, 5'7.5", 170 lbs. Deb: 5/3/1890

YEAR	TM/L	W	L	PCT	G	GS	CG	SH	SV	IP	H	HR	BB	SO	RAT	ERA	ERA+	OAV	OOB	BH	AVG	PB	PR	/A	PD	TPI
1890	StL-a	5	6	.455	16	11	10	0	1	105	104	2	40	39	12.9	3.51	123	.251	.327	7	.146	-3	4	9	0	0.6
1893	Lou-N	2	5	.286	9	8	5	0	0	46²	64	5	19	8	16.8	8.10	53	.317	.387	7	.280	-1	-18	-19	0	-1.8
1894	Lou-N	0	1	.000	1	1	0	0	0	4	8	0	2	0	22.5	9.00	57	.400	.455	0	.000	-0	-2	-2	-0	-0.3
	Cin-N	2	6	.250	10	8	8	0	0	70¹	110	7	39	9	20.2	6.65	84	.351	.438	13	.217	-2	-10	-8	0	-0.8
	Yr	2	7	.222	11	9	8	0	0	74¹	118	7	41	9	20.3	6.78	82	.354	.439	13	.210	-3	-12	-10	0	-1.1
1896	Phi-N	0	1	.000	2	1	1	0	0	9	10	0	3	1	13.0	3.00	144	.278	.333	0	.000	-0	1	1	-0	0.1
Total	4	9	19	.321	37	29	24	0	1	235	296	12	103	57	16.0	5.44	87	.300	.378	27	.196	-5	-24	-18	1	-2.2

YEAR	TM/L	W	L	PCT	G	GS	CG	SH	SV	IP	H	HR	BB	SO	RAT	ERA	ERA+	OAV	OOB	BH	AVG	PB	PR	/A	PD	TPI

● ED WHITSON
Whitson, Eddie Lee b: 5/19/55, Johnson City, Tenn. BR/TR, 6'3", 195 lbs. Deb: 9/4/77

YEAR	TM/L	W	L	PCT	G	GS	CG	SH	SV	IP	H	HR	BB	SO	RAT	ERA	ERA+	OAV	OOB	BH	AVG	PB	PR	/A	PD	TPI
1977	Pit-N	1	0	1.000	5	2	0	0	0	15²	11	0	9	10	11.5	3.45	116	.204	.317	0	.000	-0	1	1	-0	0.0
1978	Pit-N	5	6	.455	43	0	0	0	4	74¹	66	5	37	64	12.7	3.27	113	.243	.338	2	.182	-0	3	4	-1	0.5
1979	Pit-N	2	3	.400	19	7	0	0	1	57²	53	6	36	31	14.0	4.37	89	.238	.346	0	.000	-1	-4	-3	-1	-0.4
	SF-N	5	8	.385	18	17	2	0	0	100¹	98	5	39	62	12.6	3.95	89	.254	.329	5	.156	-1	-2	-5	-0	-0.7
	Yr	7	11	.389	37	24	2	0	1	158	151	11	75	93	13.1	4.10	89	.248	.338	5	.111	-2	-6	-8	-1	-1.1
1980	SF-N☆	11	13	.458	34	34	6	2	0	211²	222	7	56	90	12.0	3.10	114	.271	.321	6	.091	-4	12	10	-2	0.5
1981	SF-N	6	9	.400	22	22	2	1	0	123	130	10	47	65	13.1	4.02	85	.273	.340	3	.091	-1	-7	-8	-2	-1.2
1982	Cle-A	4	2	.667	40	9	1	1	2	107²	91	6	58	61	12.5	3.26	125	.231	.330	0	—	0	10	10	-2	0.4
1983	SD-N	5	7	.417	31	21	2	0	1	144¹	143	23	50	81	12.1	4.30	81	.256	.318	8	.182	1	-13	-13	-4	-1.3
1984	*SD-N	14	8	.636	31	31	1	0	0	189	181	16	42	103	10.8	3.24	110	.255	.299	3	.049	-5	7	7	1	0.4
1985	NY-A	10	8	.556	30	30	2	2	0	158²	201	19	43	89	14.0	4.88	82	.309	.354	0	—	0	-13	-15	-2	-1.5
1986	NY-A	5	2	.714	14	4	0	0	0	37	54	5	23	27	18.7	7.54	54	.335	.418	0	—	0	-14	-14	0	-2.1
	SD-N	1	7	.125	17	12	0	0	0	75²	85	8	37	46	14.5	5.59	65	.287	.366	3	.167	-0	-16	-16	0	-1.5
1987	SD-N	10	13	.435	36	34	3	1	0	205²	197	36	64	135	11.6	4.73	84	.251	.310	8	.123	-1	-15	-18	-2	-2.1
1988	SD-N	13	11	.542	34	33	3	1	0	205¹	202	17	45	118	10.9	3.77	90	.259	.301	11	.167	1	-7	-9	-1	-0.9
1989	SD-N	16	11	.593	33	33	5	1	0	227	198	22	48	117	10.0	2.66	132	.235	.281	10	.139	1	21	21	-2	2.4
1990	SD-N	14	9	.609	32	32	6	3	0	228²	215	13	47	127	10.4	2.60	147	.251	.291	10	.149	1	30	**31**	3	3.4
1991	SD-N	4	6	.400	13	12	2	0	0	78²	93	13	17	40	12.6	5.03	75	.299	.335	3	.125	-1	-12	-11	-1	-1.3
Total	15	126	123	.506	452	333	35	12	8	2240¹	2240	211	698	1266	11.9	3.79	97	.261	.319	72	.125	-11	-17	-28	-14	-5.4

● WALT WHITTAKER
Whittaker, Walter Elton "Doc" b: 6/11/1894, Chelsea, Mass. d: 8/9/65, Pembroke, Mass. BL/TR, 5'9.5", 165 lbs. Deb: 7/6/16

YEAR	TM/L	W	L	PCT	G	GS	CG	SH	SV	IP	H	HR	BB	SO	RAT	ERA	ERA+	OAV	OOB	BH	AVG	PB	PR	/A	PD	TPI
1916	Phi-A	0	0	—	1	0	0	0	0	2	3	0	2	0	22.5	4.50	63	.375	.500	0	—	0	-0	-0	0	0.0

● KEVIN WICKANDER
Wickander, Kevin Dean b: 1/4/65, Fort Dodge, Iowa BL/TL, 6'2", 202 lbs. Deb: 8/10/89

YEAR	TM/L	W	L	PCT	G	GS	CG	SH	SV	IP	H	HR	BB	SO	RAT	ERA	ERA+	OAV	OOB	BH	AVG	PB	PR	/A	PD	TPI
1989	Cle-A	0	0	—	2	0	0	0	0	2²	6	0	2	0	27.0	3.38	117	.462	.533	0	—	0	0	0	-0	-0.1
1990	Cle-A	0	1	.000	10	0	0	0	0	12¹	14	0	4	10	13.9	3.65	107	.304	.373	0	—	0	0	0	-0	0.0
1992	Cle-A	2	0	1.000	44	0	0	0	1	41	39	1	28	38	15.6	3.07	127	.258	.388	0	—	0	4	4	0	0.3
1993	Cle-A	0	0	—	11	0	0	0	0	8²	15	3	3	3	18.7	4.15	104	.366	.409	0	—	0	0	0	-0	0.0
	Cin-N	1	0	1.000	33	0	0	0	0	25¹	32	5	19	20	18.8	6.75	60	.308	.424	0	.000	-0	-8	-8	-0	-0.3
1995	Det-A	0	0	—	21	0	0	0	1	17¹	18	1	9	9	14.5	2.60	183	.273	.368	0	—	0	4	4	0	0.1
	Mil-A	0	0	—	8	0	0	0	0	6	1	0	3	2	6.0	0.00	—	.059	.200	0	—	0	3	3	-0	-0.1
	Yr	0	0	—	29	0	0	0	1	23¹	19	1	12	11	12.0	1.93	250	.224	.320	0	—	0	7	7	0	0.0
1996	Mil-A	2	0	1.000	21	0	0	0	0	25¹	26	2	17	19	15.3	4.97	106	.265	.374	0	—	0	0	1	-0	0.0
Total	6	5	1	.833	138²	12				138²	151	12	85	101	15.8	4.02	108	.282	.388	0	.000	-0	4	5	-1	-0.1

● KEMP WICKER
Wicker, Kemp Caswell (b: Kemp Caswell Whicker)
b: 8/13/06, Kernersville, N.C. d: 6/11/73, Kernersville, N.C BR/TL, 5'11", 182 lbs. Deb: 8/14/36

YEAR	TM/L	W	L	PCT	G	GS	CG	SH	SV	IP	H	HR	BB	SO	RAT	ERA	ERA+	OAV	OOB	BH	AVG	PB	PR	/A	PD	TPI
1936	NY-A	1	2	.333	7	0	0	0	0	20	31	2	11	5	18.9	7.65	61	.356	.429	1	.143	-0	-6	-7	0	-0.8
1937	*NY-A	7	3	.700	16	10	6	1	0	88	107	8	26	14	13.6	4.40	101	.296	.343	4	.114	-3	2	0	-2	-0.4
1938	NY-A	1	0	1.000	1	0	0	0	0	1	0	0	1	0	9.0	0.00	—	.000	.250	0	—	0	1	1	0	0.5
1941	Bro-N	1	2	.333	16	2	0	0	1	32	30	3	14	8	12.4	3.66	100	.252	.331	1	.250	0	-0	-0	-0	0.0
Total	4	10	7	.588	40	12	6	1	1	141	168	13	52	27	14.0	4.66	92	.294	.353	6	.130	-2	-3	-5	-2	-0.7

● BOB WICKER
Wicker, Robert Kitridge b: 5/24/1878, Bedford, Ind. d: 1/22/55, Evanston, Ill. BR/TR, 6'2", 180 lbs. Deb: 8/11/01

YEAR	TM/L	W	L	PCT	G	GS	CG	SH	SV	IP	H	HR	BB	SO	RAT	ERA	ERA+	OAV	OOB	BH	AVG	PB	PR	/A	PD	TPI
1901	StL-N	0	0	—	1	0	0	0	0	6	3	0	1	2	15.0	0.00	—	.308	.357	1	.333	0	1	1	-0	0.1
1902	StL-N	5	12	.294	22	16	14	1	0	152¹	159	1	45	78	12.2	3.19	86	.269	.322	18	.234	1	-7	-8	3	-0.4
1903	StL-N	0	0	—	1	0	0	0	0	5	4	0	3	3	12.6	0.00	—	.174	.269	0	.000	-0	2	2	1	0.0
	Chi-N	20	9	.690	32	27	24	1	0	247	236	3	74	110	11.4	3.02	104	.253	.311	24	.245	6	7	3	-5	0.4
	Yr	20	9	.690	33	27	24	1	1	252	240	3	77	113	11.4	2.96	106	.252	.309	24	.240	6	9	5	-4	0.4
1904	Chi-N	17	9	.654	30	27	23	4	0	229	201	6	58	99	10.3	2.67	100	.232	.282	34	.219	1	2	-0	-5	-0.5
1905	Chi-N	13	6	.684	22	22	17	4	0	178	139	3	47	86	9.5	2.02	147	.221	.276	10	.139	-2	19	19	-3	1.4
1906	Chi-N	3	5	.375	10	8	5	0	0	72¹	70	0	19	25	11.1	2.99	88	.257	.306	2	.100	-1	-3	-3	-1	-0.5
	Cin-N	6	11	.353	20	17	14	0	0	150	150	3	46	69	11.8	2.70	102	.263	.319	9	.180	2	-1	-1	-4	-0.1
	Yr	9	16	.360	30	25	19	0	0	222¹	220	3	65	94	11.6	2.79	97	.261	.315	11	.157	1	-4	-2	-5	-0.6
Total	6	64	52	.552	138	117	97	10	1	1036²	963	16	293	472	11.0	2.73	105	.247	.301	98	.205	6	20	16	-15	0.3

● DAVE WICKERSHAM
Wickersham, David Clifford b: 9/27/35, Erie, Pa. BR/TR, 6'3", 190 lbs. Deb: 9/18/60

YEAR	TM/L	W	L	PCT	G	GS	CG	SH	SV	IP	H	HR	BB	SO	RAT	ERA	ERA+	OAV	OOB	BH	AVG	PB	PR	/A	PD	TPI
1960	KC-A	0	0	—	5	0	0	0	2	8¹	4	0	1	3	5.4	1.08	369	.148	.179	0	.000	-0	3	3	0	0.1
1961	KC-A	2	1	.667	17	0	0	0	2	21	25	0	5	13	13.7	5.14	81	.309	.364	2	.667	-1	-3	-2	0	-0.2
1962	KC-A	11	4	.733	30	9	3	0	1	110	105	13	43	61	12.8	4.17	101	.257	.340	2	.057	-3	-2	1	1	-0.1
1963	KC-A	12	15	.444	38	34	4	1	1	237²	244	21	79	118	12.6	4.09	95	.268	.333	11	.138	-3	-12	-5	1	-0.8
1964	Det-A	19	12	.613	40	36	11	1	1	254	224	28	81	164	11.2	3.44	106	.232	.299	6	.073	-5	5	6	-0	0.1
1965	Det-A	9	14	.391	34	27	8	3	0	195¹	179	12	61	109	11.6	3.78	92	.241	.308	4	.069	-4	-7	-7	-1	-1.0
1966	Det-A	8	3	.727	38	14	3	0	1	140²	139	14	54	93	12.9	3.20	109	.261	.338	2	.044	-3	4	4	1	0.1
1967	Det-A	4	5	.444	36	4	0	0	4	85¹	72	6	33	44	11.5	2.74	119	.235	.318	0	.000	-2	5	5	1	0.5
1968	Pit-N	1	0	1.000	11	0	0	0	0	20²	21	0	13	9	14.8	3.48	84	.276	.382	1	.333	-0	-1	-0	-0	-0.1
1969	KC-A	2	3	.400	34	0	0	0	5	50	58	6	14	27	13.3	3.96	93	.294	.347	0	.000	0	-2	-2	0	-0.1
Total	10	68	57	.544	283	124	29	5	18	1123	1071	100	384	601	12.4	3.66	100	.252	.323	28	.086	-18	-11	2	4	-1.5

● BOB WICKMAN
Wickman, Robert Joe b: 2/6/69, Green Bay, Wis. BR/TR, 6'1", 207 lbs. Deb: 8/24/92

YEAR	TM/L	W	L	PCT	G	GS	CG	SH	SV	IP	H	HR	BB	SO	RAT	ERA	ERA+	OAV	OOB	BH	AVG	PB	PR	/A	PD	TPI
1992	NY-A	6	1	.857	8	8	0	0	0	50¹	51	2	20	21	13.1	4.11	95	.273	.349	0	—	0	-1	-1	-0	-0.1
1993	NY-A	14	4	.778	41	19	1	1	4	140	156	13	69	70	14.8	4.63	90	.284	.369	0	—	0	-5	-7	-1	-0.6
1994	NY-A	5	4	.556	**53**	0	0	0	6	70	54	3	27	56	10.5	3.09	148	.213	.292	0	—	0	13	12	-0	1.6
1995	*NY-A	2	4	.333	63	1	0	0	1	80	77	6	33	51	12.9	4.05	114	.253	.336	0	—	0	6	5	0	0.4
1996	NY-A	4	1	.800	58	0	0	0	0	79	94	7	34	61	15.2	4.67	108	.299	.377	0	—	0	3	3	3	0.4
	Mil-A	3	0	1.000	12	0	0	0	0	16²	12	3	10	14	11.9	3.24	162	.200	.314	0	—	0	3	4	0	0.4
	Yr	7	1	.875	70	0	0	0	0	95²	106	10	44	75	14.1	4.42	115	.277	.351	0	—	0	6	7	3	0.8
Total	5	34	14	.708	235	28	1	1	11	436	444	34	193	273	13.5	4.17	107	.266	.349	0	—	0	20	15	2	2.1

● AL WIDMAR
Widmar, Albert Joseph b: 3/20/25, Cleveland, Ohio BR/TR, 6'3", 185 lbs. Deb: 4/25/47 C

YEAR	TM/L	W	L	PCT	G	GS	CG	SH	SV	IP	H	HR	BB	SO	RAT	ERA	ERA+	OAV	OOB	BH	AVG	PB	PR	/A	PD	TPI
1947	Bos-A	0	0	—	2	0	0	0	0	1¹	1	1	2	1	20.3	13.50	29	.200	.429	0	—	0	-1	-1	0	0.0
1948	StL-A	2	6	.250	49	6	0	0	2	82²	84	8	48	34	14.8	4.46	102	.275	.370	3	.300	1	-2	1	2	0.3
1950	StL-A	7	15	.318	36	26	8	1	4	194²	211	16	74	78	13.3	4.76	104	.271	.337	10	.149	-3	-4	4	1	0.2
1951	StL-A	4	9	.308	26	16	4	0	0	107²	157	19	52	28	17.6	6.52	67	.344	.414	5	.167	-1	-29	-25	1	-2.6
1952	Chi-A	0	0	—	1	0	0	0	0	2	4	1	0	2	18.0	4.50	81	.444	.444	0	—	0	-0	-0	-0	0.0
Total	5	13	30	.302	114	42	12	1	5	388¹	461	41	176	143	14.9	5.21	90	.294	.367	18	.168	-4	-36	-22	3	-2.1

● WILD BILL WIDNER
Widner, William Waterfield b: 6/3/1867, Cincinnati, Ohio d: 12/10/08, Cincinnati, Ohio BR/TR, 6', 180 lbs. Deb: 6/8/1887

YEAR	TM/L	W	L	PCT	G	GS	CG	SH	SV	IP	H	HR	BB	SO	RAT	ERA	ERA+	OAV	OOB	BH	AVG	PB	PR	/A	PD	TPI
1887	Cin-a	1	0	1.000	1	1	1	0	0	9	11	2	2	4	14.0	5.00	87	.275	.326	1	.250	-0	-1	-1	0	0.0
1888	Was-N	5	7	.417	13	13	13	0	0	115	111	7	22	33	10.9	2.82	100	.247	.291	12	.200	-1	0	-0	-0	-0.1
1889	Col-a	12	20	.375	41	34	25	2	1	294	368	11	85	63	14.4	5.20	70	.297	.351	28	.211	-2	-44	-52	0	-4.2
1890	Col-a	4	8	.333	13	10	8	1	0	96	103	3	24	14	12.2	3.28	109	.266	.314	8	.195	-1	6	3	2	0.4
1891	Cin-a	1	0	1.000	1	1	1	0	0	8	13	0	4	2	21.4	7.88	52	.351	.442	1	.250	-0	-4	-3	-0	-0.3
Total	5	22	36	.379	69	59	48	3	1	522	606	23	137	110	13.3	4.36	79	.283	.333	50	.207	-3	-42	-52	2	-4.2

● TED WIEAND
Wieand, Franklin Delano Roosevelt b: 4/4/33, Walnutport, Pa. BR/TR, 6'2", 195 lbs. Deb: 9/27/58

YEAR	TM/L	W	L	PCT	G	GS	CG	SH	SV	IP	H	HR	BB	SO	RAT	ERA	ERA+	OAV	OOB	BH	AVG	PB	PR	/A	PD	TPI
1958	Cin-N	0	0	—	2	0	0	0	0	2	4	1	2	2	18.0	9.00	46	.400	.400	0	—	0	-1	-1	-0	0.0
1960	Cin-N	0	1	.000	4	0	0	0	0	4¹	4	2	3	3	18.7	10.38	37	.250	.429	0	—	0	-3	-3	-0	-0.6
Total	2	0	1	.000	6	0	0	0	0	6¹	8	3	5	5	18.5	9.95	39	.308	.419	0	—	0	-4	-4	-0	-0.6

YEAR	TM/L	W	L	PCT	G	GS	CG	SH	SV	IP	H	HR	BB	SO	RAT	ERA	ERA+	OAV	OOB	BH	AVG	PB	PR	/A	PD	TPI
● CHARLIE WIEDEMEYER	Wiedemeyer, Charles John "Chick" b: 1/31/14, Chicago, Ill. d: 10/27/79, Lake Geneva, Fla. BL/TL, 6'3", 180 lbs. Deb: 9/9/34																								
1934	Chi-N	0	0	—	4	1	0	0	0	8¹	16	1	4	2	22.7	9.72	40	.432	.500	0	.000	-0	-5	-5	0	0.0
● STUMP WIEDMAN	Wiedman, George E. b: 2/17/1861, Rochester, N.Y. d: 3/2/05, New York, N.Y. BR/TR, 5'7.5", 165 lbs. Deb: 8/26/1880 U♦																								
1880	Buf-N	0	9	.000	17	13	9	0	0	113²	141	1	9	25	11.9	3.40	72	.291	.304	8	.103	-5	-13	-12	-1	-1.3
1881	Det-N	8	5	.615	13	13	13	1	0	115	108	1	12	26	**9.4**	**1.80**	162	.238	**.258**	12	.255	-5	12	14	-2	1.3
1882	Det-N	25	20	.556	46	45	43	4	0	411	391	10	39	161	9.4	2.63	112	.236	.253	42	.218	-5	12	14	-0	0.7
1883	Det-N	20	24	.455	52	47	41	3	2	402¹	435	8	72	183	11.3	3.53	88	.257	.288	58	.185	-8	-18	-19	-0	-2.2
1884	Det-N	4	21	.160	26	26	24	0	0	212²	257	9	57	96	13.3	3.72	78	.273	.314	49	.163	-4	-18	-20	-1	-2.1
1885	Det-N	14	24	.368	38	38	37	3	0	330	343	7	63	149	11.1	3.14	91	.252	.286	24	.157	-4	-12	-11	-3	-1.7
1886	KC-N	12	36	.250	51	51	48	1	0	427²	549	11	112	168	13.9	4.50	84	.303	.344	30	.168	-10	-57	-35	-4	-3.5
1887	Det-N	13	7	.650	21	21	20	0	0	183	221	6	60	56	14.3	5.36	76	.296	.356	17	.207	-3	-26	-27	-2	-2.4
	NY-a	4	8	.333	12	12	11	1	0	97	122	3	25	37	13.7	4.64	92	.292	.333	7	.152	-2	-4	-4	1	-0.4
	NY-N	0	1	.000	1	1	1	0	0	8	10	0	2	4	13.5	1.13	335	.286	.324	1	.333	-0	3	2	-0	0.2
1888	NY-N	1	1	.500	2	2	2	0	0	18	17	2	8	5	13.5	3.50	78	.230	.321	0	.000	-0	-1	-2	0	-0.2
Total	9	101	156	.393	279	269	249	13	2	2318¹	2594	61	459	910	11.9	3.60	89	.268	.302	248	.177	-42	-120	-98	-2	-11.6
● JACK WIENEKE	Wieneke, John b: 3/10/1894, Saltsburg, Pa. d: 3/16/33, Pleasant Ridge, Mich. BR/TL, 6', 182 lbs. Deb: 7/4/21																								
1921	Chi-A	0	1	.000	10	3	0	0	0	25¹	39	4	17	10	20.3	8.17	52	.351	.442	1	.111	-1	-11	-11	0	-0.4
● BOB WIESLER	Wiesler, Robert George b: 8/13/30, St.Louis, Mo. BB/TL, 6'2", 195 lbs. Deb: 8/3/51																								
1951	NY-A	0	2	.000	4	3	0	0	0	9¹	13	0	11	3	23.1	13.50	28	.361	.511	0	.000	-1	-10	-10	-1	-1.6
1954	NY-A	3	2	.600	6	5	0	0	0	30¹	28	0	30	25	17.2	4.15	83	.259	.420	3	.273	1	-1	-2	-1	-0.3
1955	NY-A	0	2	.000	16	7	0	0	0	53	39	1	49	22	15.1	3.91	96	.212	.380	2	.143	-1	0	-1	1	0.0
1956	Was-A	3	12	.200	37	21	3	0	0	123	141	11	112	49	18.7	6.44	67	.300	.438	3	.091	-3	-31	-29	1	-3.1
1957	Was-A	1	1	.500	3	2	1	0	0	16¹	15	2	11	9	14.9	4.41	88	.250	.375	1	.167	-0	-1	-1	-0	-0.1
1958	Was-A	0	0	—	4	0	0	0	0	9¹	14	2	5	5	19.3	6.75	56	.359	.444	0	.000	-0	-3	-3	1	0.0
Total	6	7	19	.269	70	38	4	0	0	241¹	250	16	218	113	17.7	5.74	70	.279	.423	9	.130	-3	-46	-46	3	-5.1
● WHITEY WIETELMANN	Wietelmann, William Frederick b: 3/15/19, Zanesville, Ohio BB/TR, 6', 170 lbs. Deb: 9/6/39 C♦																								
1945	Bos-N	0	0	—	1	0	0	0	0	1	6	0	2	0	72.0	54.00	7	.667	.727	116	.271	0	-6	-6	0	0.0
1946	Bos-N	0	0	—	3	0	0	0	0	6²	9	1	4	2	18.9	8.10	42	.310	.412	16	.205	0	-3	-3	-0	0.0
Total	2	0	0	—	4	0	0	0	0	7²	15	1	6	2	25.8	14.09	25	.395	.489	409	.232	1	-9	-9	-0	0.0
● JIMMY WIGGS	Wiggs, James Alvin "Big Jim" b: 9/1/1876, Trondheim, Norway d: 1/20/63, Xenia, Ohio BB/TR, 6'4", 200 lbs. Deb: 4/23/03																								
1903	Cin-N	0	0	—	2	1	0	0	0	5	12	0	2	2	27.0	5.40	66	.500	.556	0	.000	-0	-1	-1	-0	-0.2
1905	Det-A	3	3	.500	7	7	4	0	0	41¹	30	0	29	37	13.1	3.27	84	.205	.341	2	.133	-0	-3	-2	-0	-0.4
1906	Det-A	0	0	—	4	1	0	0	0	10¹	11	1	7	7	17.4	5.23	53	.275	.408	1	.333	-0	-3	-3	-0	0.1
Total	3	3	4	.429	13	9	4	0	0	56²	53	1	38	46	15.1	3.81	74	.252	.377	3	.158	-0	-7	-6	-0	-0.5
● BILL WIGHT	Wight, William Robert "Lefty" b: 4/12/22, Rio Vista, Cal. BL/TL, 6'1", 180 lbs. Deb: 4/17/46																								
1946	NY-A	2	2	.500	14	4	1	0	0	40¹	44	1	30	11	16.7	4.46	77	.289	.410	0	.000	-1	-4	-5	0	-0.5
1947	NY-A	1	0	1.000	1	1	1	0	0	9	8	0	2	3	10.0	1.00	353	.242	.286	0	.000	-0	3	3	0	0.4
1948	Chi-A	9	20	.310	34	32	7	1	1	223¹	238	9	135	66	15.1	4.80	89	.278	.377	6	.082	-7	-13	-13	1	-2.0
1949	Chi-A	15	13	.536	35	33	14	3	1	245	254	9	96	78	12.9	3.31	126	.275	.343	14	.165	-1	24	24	0	2.3
1950	Chi-A	10	16	.385	30	28	13	3	0	206	213	10	79	62	12.8	3.58	125	.270	.336	0	.000	-9	23	21	2	1.6
1951	Bos-A	7	7	.500	34	17	4	2	0	118¹	128	5	63	38	14.5	5.10	88	.282	.369	3	.073	-4	-13	-8	1	-1.2
1952	Bos-A	2	1	.667	10	2	0	0	0	24¹	14	3	14	5	10.7	2.96	133	.169	.296	1	.143	-0	2	3	0	0.3
	Det-A	5	9	.357	23	19	8	3	0	143²	167	7	55	65	13.9	3.88	98	.291	.354	11	.220	1	-3	-1	2	0.2
	Yr	7	10	.412	33	21	8	3	0	168	181	10	69	70	13.4	3.75	102	.281	.344	12	.211	1	-1	1	2	0.5
1953	Det-A	0	3	.000	13	4	0	0	0	25¹	35	4	14	10	17.4	8.88	46	.333	.412	3	.429	1	-14	-14	-1	-1.3
	Cle-A	2	1	.667	20	0	0	0	1	26²	29	1	16	14	15.2	3.71	101	.282	.378	0	.000	-1	1	0	0	0.0
	Yr	2	4	.333	33	4	0	0	1	52	64	5	30	24	16.3	6.23	60	.308	.395	3	.250	-0	-13	-13	-0	-1.3
1955	Cle-A	0	0	—	17	0	0	0	1	24	24	0	9	9	12.4	2.63	152	.261	.327	0	—	0	4	4	2	0.2
	Bal-A	6	8	.429	19	14	8	2	2	117¹	111	6	39	54	11.6	2.45	155	.252	.315	3	.083	-2	20	18	2	2.1
	Yr	6	8	.429	36	14	8	2	3	141¹	135	6	48	63	11.7	2.48	155	.254	.317	3	.083	-2	23	21	4	2.3
1956	Bal-A	9	12	.429	35	26	7	1	0	174²	198	7	72	84	14.2	4.02	98	.289	.362	12	.200	-1	3	-2	-1	-0.3
1957	Bal-A	6	6	.500	27	17	2	0	0	121	122	4	54	50	13.4	3.64	99	.271	.354	1	.029	-3	2	-1	-0	-0.5
1958	Cin-N	0	1	.000	7	0	0	0	0	6²	7	1	4	5	14.9	4.05	102	.292	.393	0	—	0	-0	-0	0	0.0
	StL-N	3	0	1.000	28	1	0	0	2	57¹	64	7	32	18	15.1	5.02	82	.290	.379	1	.100	-0	-7	-6	1	-0.3
	Yr	3	1	.750	35	1	0	0	2	64	71	8	36	23	15.0	4.92	84	.290	.381	1	.100	-0	-7	-6	1	-0.3
Total	12	77	99	.438	347	198	66	15	8	1563	1656	74	714	574	13.7	3.95	103	.277	.355	55	.115	-28	27	22	9	1.0
● FRED WIGINGTON	Wigington, Fred Thomas b: 12/16/1897, Rogers, Neb. d: 5/8/80, Mesa, Ariz. BR/TR, 5'10", 168 lbs. Deb: 4/20/23																								
1923	StL-N	0	0	—	4	0	0	0	0	9²	17	2	4	2	17.3	3.24	121	.367	.457	0	.000	-0	1	1	0	0.0
● SANDY WIHTOL	Wihtol, Alexander Ames b: 6/1/55, Palo Alto, Cal. BR/TR, 6'1", 195 lbs. Deb: 9/7/79																								
1979	Cle-A	0	0	—	5	0	0	0	0	10²	10	0	3	6	11.0	3.38	126	.238	.289	0	—	0	1	1	0	0.0
1980	Cle-A	1	0	1.000	17	0	0	0	1	35¹	35	2	14	20	13.0	3.57	114	.257	.336	0	—	0	2	2	-1	0.0
1982	Cle-A	0	0	—	6	0	0	0	0	11²	9	1	7	8	13.1	4.63	88	.220	.347	0	—	0	-1	-0	0	0.0
Total	3	1	0	1.000	28	0	0	0	1	57²	54	3	24	34	12.6	3.75	110	.247	.329	0	—	0	2	2	-1	0.0
● MILT WILCOX	Wilcox, Milton Edward b: 4/20/50, Honolulu, Hawaii BR/TR, 6'2", 185 lbs. Deb: 9/5/70																								
1970	*Cin-N	3	1	.750	5	2	1	1	0	22¹	19	2	7	13	10.9	2.42	167	.229	.297	1	.200	0	4	4	0	0.8
1971	Cin-N	2	2	.500	18	3	0	0	1	43¹	43	2	17	21	12.9	3.32	101	.269	.346	0	.000	0	1	0	-0	-0.1
1972	Cle-A	7	14	.333	32	27	4	2	0	156	145	18	72	90	12.8	3.40	94	.251	.339	9	.200	1	-6	-3	-3	-0.4
1973	Cle-A	8	10	.444	26	19	4	0	0	134¹	143	14	68	82	14.7	5.83	67	.275	.367	0	—	0	-30	-29	1	-3.2
1974	Cle-A	2	2	.500	41	2	1	0	0	71¹	74	10	24	33	13.0	4.67	77	.271	.341	0	—	0	-8	-8	1	-0.5
1975	Chi-N	0	1	.000	25	0	0	0	0	38¹	50	4	17	21	16.0	5.63	68	.323	.393	1	.333	0	-9	-8	-0	-0.1
1977	Det-A	6	2	.750	20	13	1	0	0	106¹	96	13	37	82	11.3	3.64	118	.241	.307	0	—	0	5	8	-0	0.5
1978	Det-A	13	12	.520	29	27	16	2	0	215¹	208	22	68	132	11.9	3.76	103	.255	.318	0	—	0	2	1	0	0.4
1979	Det-A	12	10	.545	33	29	7	0	0	196¹	201	18	73	109	13.1	4.35	99	.267	.341	0	—	0	-0	-1	3	0.0
1980	Det-A	13	11	.542	32	31	13	4	0	198²	201	24	68	97	12.5	4.48	92	.262	.327	0	—	0	-10	-8	1	-0.8
1981	Det-A	12	9	.571	24	24	8	1	0	166¹	152	10	52	79	11.4	3.03	124	.247	.312	0	—	0	12	14	1	1.7
1982	Det-A	12	10	.545	29	29	9	1	0	193²	187	18	85	112	13.0	3.62	112	.257	.340	0	—	0	10	9	3	1.2
1983	Det-A	11	10	.524	26	26	9	0	0	186	164	19	74	101	11.7	3.97	98	.237	.314	0	—	0	2	-1	3	0.3
1984	*Det-A	17	8	.680	33	33	0	0	0	193²	183	16	66	119	11.9	4.00	98	.252	.321	0	—	0	-0	-2	1	0.0
1985	Det-A	1	3	.250	9	8	0	0	0	39	51	6	14	20	15.0	4.85	84	.315	.369	0	—	0	-3	-3	-1	-0.1
1986	Sea-A	0	8	.000	13	10	0	0	0	55²	74	11	28	26	16.7	5.50	77	.327	.404	0	—	0	-8	-6	-0	-0.9
Total	16	119	113	.513	394	283	73	10	6	2016²	1991	204	770	1137	12.7	4.07	96	.260	.334	11	.177	0	-44	-33	14	-1.2
● RANDY WILES	Wiles, Randall E b: 9/10/51, Fort Belvoir, Va. BL/TL, 6'1", 185 lbs. Deb: 8/7/77																								
1977	Chi-A	1	1	.500	5	0	0	0	0	2²	5	1	3	0	27.0	10.13	40	.417	.533	0	—	0	-2	-2	0	-1.1
● MARK WILEY	Wiley, Mark Eugene b: 2/28/48, National City, Cal. BR/TR, 6'1", 200 lbs. Deb: 6/17/75 C																								
1975	Min-A	1	3	.250	15	3	1	0	2	38²	50	4	13	15	14.9	6.05	63	.325	.381	0	—	0	-10	-10	-1	-1.1
1978	SD-N	1	0	1.000	4	1	0	0	0	7²	11	1	1	4	14.1	5.87	57	.324	.343	0	.000	-0	-2	-2	-0	-0.3
	Tor-A	0	0	—	2	0	0	0	0	2²	4	2	1	2	13.5	6.75	58	.273	.333	0	—	0	-1	-1	-0	0.0
Total	2	2	3	.400	21	4	1	0	2	49	64	5	15	18	14.7	6.06	62	.322	.372	0	.000	-0	-13	-13	-1	-1.4
● HARRY WILHELM	Wilhelm, Harry Lester b: 4/7/1874, Uniontown, Pa. d: 2/20/44, Republic, Pa. BR/TR, 5'7", 155 lbs. Deb: 8/12/1899																								
1899	Lou-N	1	1	.500	5	3	2	0	0	25	30	1	3	6	14.4	6.12	63	.336	.360	3	.250	2	-6	-6	0	-0.2

KAISER WILHELM
Wilhelm, Irvin Key b: 1/26/1874, Wooster, Ohio d: 5/21/36, Rochester, N.Y. BR/TR, 6', 162 lbs. Deb: 4/18/03 MUC

YEAR TM/L	W	L	PCT	G	GS	CG	SH	SV	IP	H	HR	BB	SO	RAT	ERA	ERA+	OAV	OOB	BH	AVG	PB	PR	/A	PD	TPI
1903 Pit-N	5	3	.625	12	9	7	1	0	86	88	0	25	20	12.1	3.24	100	.264	.321	3	.088	-2	0	-0	2	-0.1
1904 Bos-N	14	20	.412	39	36	30	3	0	288	316	8	74	73	12.4	3.69	75	.285	.333	7	.070	-8	-30	-30	1	-3.9
1905 Bos-N	3	23	.115	34	28	23	0	0	242¹	287	7	75	76	13.6	4.53	68	.295	.349	16	.160	-2	-41	-39	2	-3.7
1908 Bro-N	16	22	.421	42	36	33	6	0	332	266	3	83	99	9.6	1.87	125	.217	.271	12	.108	-4	18	18	3	1.9
1909 Bro-N	3	13	.188	22	17	14	1	0	163	176	3	59	45	13.1	3.26	80	.289	.353	13	.228	2	-12	-12	1	-0.8
1910 Bro-N	3	7	.300	15	5	0	0	0	68¹	88	3	18	17	14.1	4.74	64	.314	.358	6	.316	2	-13	-13	1	-1.4
1914 Bal-F	12	17	.414	47	27	11	1	5	243²	263	10	81	113	12.7	4.03	75	.291	.349	21	.250	1	-31	-27	3	-2.6
1915 Bal-F	0	0	—	1	0	0	0	0	1	0	0	0	0	0.0	0.00	—	.000	.000	0	—	0	0	0	-0	0.0
1921 Phi-N	0	0	—	4	0	0	0	0	8	11	0	3	1	15.8	3.38	125	.393	.452	0	.000	-0	0	1	-0	0.0
Total 9	56	105	.348	216	158	118	12	5	1432¹	1495	34	418	444	12.2	3.44	81	.274	.328	78	.154	-12	-108	-102	11	-10.6

HOYT WILHELM
Wilhelm, James Hoyt b: 7/26/23, Huntersville, N.C. BR/TR, 6', 195 lbs. Deb: 4/19/52 H

YEAR TM/L	W	L	PCT	G	GS	CG	SH	SV	IP	H	HR	BB	SO	RAT	ERA	ERA+	OAV	OOB	BH	AVG	PB	PR	/A	PD	TPI
1952 NY-N	15	3	.833	71	0	0	0	11	159¹	127	12	57	108	10.7	2.43	152	.220	.296	6	.158	0	23	23	1	2.9
1953 NY-N☆	7	8	.467	68	0	0	0	15	145	127	13	77	71	12.9	3.04	141	.238	.339	5	.152	1	20	20	-1	2.3
1954 *NY-N	12	4	.750	57	0	0	0	7	111¹	77	5	52	64	10.8	2.10	192	.198	.300	1	.048	-2	24	24	1	3.4
1955 NY-N	4	1	.800	59	0	0	0	0	103	104	10	40	71	12.8	3.93	102	.266	.337	1	.158	-1	1	1	3	0.2
1956 NY-N	4	9	.308	64	0	0	0	8	89¹	97	7	43	71	14.3	3.83	99	.280	.362	2	.222	-0	-1	-0	2	0.1
1957 StL-N	1	4	.200	40	0	0	0	11	55	52	7	21	29	12.4	4.25	93	.254	.332	0	.000	-1	-2	-2	-0	-0.3
Cle-A	1	0	1.000	2	0	0	0	0	3²	2	1	1	0	9.8	2.45	151	.154	.267	0	—	-0	1	1	-0	0.1
1958 Cle-A	2	7	.222	30	6	1	0	5	90¹	70	4	35	57	10.6	2.49	146	.215	.294	2	.095	-1	13	12	1	1.2
Bal-A	1	3	.250	9	4	3	1	0	40²	25	2	10	35	8.0	1.99	180	.179	.238	1	.091	-1	8	7	-0	0.6
Yr	3	10	.231	39	10	4	1	5	131	95	6	45	92	9.7	2.34	155	.203	.274	3	.094	-2	21	19	1	1.8
1959 Bal-A★	15	11	.577	32	27	13	3	0	226	178	13	77	139	10.6	2.19	173	.224	.301	4	.053	-6	42	40	-1	3.7
1960 Bal-A	11	8	.579	41	11	3	1	7	147	125	13	39	107	10.1	3.31	115	.228	.280	3	.071	-3	9	8	1	0.9
1961 Bal-A★	9	7	.563	51	1	0	0	18	109²	89	5	41	87	11.0	2.30	167	.219	.296	1	.050	-1	21	19	1	3.2
1962 Bal-A†	7	10	.412	52	0	0	0	15	93	64	5	34	90	9.8	1.94	191	.197	.279	2	.125	-0	21	18	0	3.8
1963 Chi-A	5	8	.385	55	3	0	0	21	136¹	106	8	30	111	9.2	2.64	133	.215	.265	2	.069	-1	15	13	1	1.6
1964 Chi-A	12	9	.571	73	0	0	0	27	131¹	94	7	30	95	8.6	1.99	174	.202	.254	3	.143	-0	24	21	-1	4.2
1965 Chi-A	7	7	.500	66	0	0	0	20	144	88	11	32	106	7.6	1.81	176	.177	.229	0	.000	-2	26	22	1	2.5
1966 Chi-A	5	2	.714	46	0	0	0	6	81¹	50	4	17	61	7.5	1.66	191	.178	.227	1	.125	0	16	14	-1	1.3
1967 Chi-A	8	3	.727	49	0	0	0	12	89	58	2	34	76	9.7	1.31	236	.183	.270	1	.077	-1	19	18	-1	2.6
1968 Chi-A	4	4	.500	72	0	0	0	12	93²	69	4	24	72	9.1	1.73	175	.205	.262	0	.000	-0	13	13	-1	1.5
1969 Cal-A	5	7	.417	44	0	0	0	10	65²	45	4	18	53	9.0	2.47	141	.194	.261	0	.000	-1	8	7	-0	1.4
Atl-N	2	0	1.000	8	0	0	0	4	12¹	5	1	4	14	7.3	0.73	494	.119	.213	0	.000	-0	4	4	0	1.0
1970 Atl-N☆	6	4	.600	50	0	0	0	13	78¹	69	7	39	67	12.5	3.10	138	.234	.325	1	.091	-0	8	10	0	1.6
Chi-N	0	1	.000	3	0	0	0	0	3²	4	1	3	1	17.2	9.82	46	.286	.412	0	—	0	-2	-2	0	-0.4
Yr	6	5	.545	53	0	0	0	13	82	73	8	42	68	12.6	3.40	126	.234	.325	1	.091	-0	6	8	1	1.2
1971 Atl-N	0	0	—	3	0	0	0	0	2¹	6	2	1	1	27.0	15.43	24	.500	.538	0	—	0	-3	-3	0	0.0
LA-N	0	1	.000	9	0	0	0	3	17²	6	1	4	15	5.1	1.02	317	.111	.172	0	.000	-0	5	4	-0	0.4
Yr	0	1	.000	12	0	0	0	3	20	12	3	5	16	7.6	2.70	122	.182	.239	0	.000	-0	2	1	0	0.4
1972 LA-N	0	1	.000	16	0	0	0	1	25¹	20	0	15	9	12.4	4.62	72	.217	.327	0	.000	-0	-3	-4	0	-0.1
Total 21	143	122	.540	1070	52	20	5	227	2254¹	1757	150	778	1610	10.4	2.52	146	.216	.290	38	.088	-21	310	288	5	39.7

LEFTY WILKIE
Wilkie, Aldon Jay b: 10/30/14, Zealandia, Sask., Canada d: 8/5/92, Tualatin, Ore. BL/TL, 5'11.5", 175 lbs. Deb: 4/22/41

YEAR TM/L	W	L	PCT	G	GS	CG	SH	SV	IP	H	HR	BB	SO	RAT	ERA	ERA+	OAV	OOB	BH	AVG	PB	PR	/A	PD	TPI
1941 Pit-N	2	4	.333	26	6	2	1	2	79	94	1	40	16	14.9	4.56	79	.289	.372	7	.292	1	-8	-8	1	-0.4
1942 Pit-N	6	7	.462	35	6	3	0	1	107¹	112	4	37	18	12.6	4.19	81	.269	.330	10	.263	2	-10	-10	2	-0.7
1946 Pit-N	0	0	—	7	0	0	0	0	7²	13	0	3	3	18.8	10.57	33	.382	.432	0	—	-0	-6	-6	-0	0.0
Total 3	8	11	.421	68	12	5	1	3	194	215	5	80	37	13.8	4.59	76	.283	.352	17	.274	3	-25	-24	3	-1.1

DEAN WILKINS
Wilkins, Dean Allan b: 8/24/66, Blue Island, Ill. BR/TR, 6'1", 170 lbs. Deb: 8/21/89

YEAR TM/L	W	L	PCT	G	GS	CG	SH	SV	IP	H	HR	BB	SO	RAT	ERA	ERA+	OAV	OOB	BH	AVG	PB	PR	/A	PD	TPI
1989 Chi-N	1	0	1.000	11	0	0	0	0	15²	13	2	9	14	12.6	4.60	82	.228	.333	0	.000	-0	-2	-1	-0	-0.1
1990 Chi-N	0	0	—	7	0	0	0	0	7¹	11	1	7	3	23.3	9.82	42	.333	.463	0	—	-0	-5	-5	-0	-0.1
1991 Hou-N	2	1	.667	7	0	0	0	0	8	16	0	10	4	29.3	11.25	31	.410	.531	0	.000	-0	-7	-7	-0	-2.2
Total 3	3	1	.750	25	0	0	0	0	31	40	3	26	21	19.5	7.55	50	.310	.429	0	.000	-0	-14	-13	-0	-2.4

ERIC WILKINS
Wilkins, Eric Lamoine b: 12/9/56, St.Louis, Mo. BR/TR, 6'1", 190 lbs. Deb: 4/11/79

YEAR TM/L	W	L	PCT	G	GS	CG	SH	SV	IP	H	HR	BB	SO	RAT	ERA	ERA+	OAV	OOB	BH	AVG	PB	PR	/A	PD	TPI
1979 Cle-A	2	4	.333	16	14	0	0	0	69²	84	8	38	52	15.4	4.39	97	.289	.386	0	—	-0	-1	-1	0	-0.3

MARC WILKINS
Wilkins, Marc Allen b: 10/21/70, Mansfield, Ohio BR/TR, 5'11", 200 lbs. Deb: 5/11/96

YEAR TM/L	W	L	PCT	G	GS	CG	SH	SV	IP	H	HR	BB	SO	RAT	ERA	ERA+	OAV	OOB	BH	AVG	PB	PR	/A	PD	TPI
1996 Pit-N	4	3	.571	47	0	0	0	1	75	75	6	36	62	14.0	3.84	114	.266	.361	2	.222	0	3	4	-0	0.4

ROY WILKINSON
Wilkinson, Roy Hamilton b: 5/8/1893, Canandaigua, N.Y. d: 7/2/56, Louisville, Ky. BR/TR, 6'1", 170 lbs. Deb: 4/29/18

YEAR TM/L	W	L	PCT	G	GS	CG	SH	SV	IP	H	HR	BB	SO	RAT	ERA	ERA+	OAV	OOB	BH	AVG	PB	PR	/A	PD	TPI
1918 Cle-A	0	0	—	1	0	0	0	0	1	0	0	0	0	0.0	0.00	—	.000	.000	0	—	-0	0	0	-0	0.0
1919 *Chi-A	1	1	.500	4	1	1	1	0	22	21	0	10	5	12.7	2.05	156	.266	.348	3	.375	2	3	3	1	0.5
1920 Chi-A	7	9	.438	34	12	8	0	2	145	162	6	48	30	13.2	4.03	93	.297	.356	7	.146	-3	-4	-4	-3	-0.9
1921 Chi-A	4	20	.167	36	23	11	0	3	198¹	259	4	78	50	15.5	5.13	83	.334	.397	8	.123	-4	-19	-20	5	-1.8
1922 Chi-A	0	1	.000	4	1	0	0	0	14¹	24	1	6	3	19.5	8.79	46	.393	.456	0	.000	-0	-8	-8	-0	-0.6
Total 5	12	31	.279	79	37	20	1	6	380²	466	11	142	88	14.5	4.66	86	.318	.381	18	.145	-5	-27	-28	4	-2.8

BILL WILKINSON
Wilkinson, William Carl b: 8/10/64, Greybull, Wyoming BR/TL, 5'10", 160 lbs. Deb: 6/13/85 F

YEAR TM/L	W	L	PCT	G	GS	CG	SH	SV	IP	H	HR	BB	SO	RAT	ERA	ERA+	OAV	OOB	BH	AVG	PB	PR	/A	PD	TPI
1985 Sea-A	0	2	.000	2	0	0	0	0	6	8	2	5	5	21.0	13.50	31	.333	.467	0	—	0	-6	-6	0	-1.3
1987 Sea-A	3	4	.429	56	0	0	0	10	76¹	61	8	21	73	9.7	3.66	129	.223	.278	0	—	0	7	9	-1	0.8
1988 Sea-A	2	2	.500	30	0	0	0	2	31	28	3	15	25	12.5	3.48	119	.233	.319	0	—	0	2	2	-1	0.1
Total 3	5	8	.385	88	2	0	0	12	113¹	97	13	42	103	11.0	4.13	110	.232	.302	0	—	0	2	1	-1	-0.4

TED WILKS
Wilks, Theodore "Cork" b: 11/13/15, Fulton, N.Y. d: 8/21/89, Houston, Tex. BR/TR, 5'9.5", 178 lbs. Deb: 4/25/44 C

YEAR TM/L	W	L	PCT	G	GS	CG	SH	SV	IP	H	HR	BB	SO	RAT	ERA	ERA+	OAV	OOB	BH	AVG	PB	PR	/A	PD	TPI
1944 *StL-N	17	4	.810	36	21	16	4	0	207²	173	12	49	70	9.7	2.64	133	.227	.275	9	.141	-1	22	20	-4	1.4
1945 StL-N	4	7	.364	18	16	4	1	0	98¹	103	9	29	28	12.2	2.93	128	.270	.324	4	.133	-0	10	9	-2	0.7
1946 *StL-N	8	0	1.000	40	4	0	0	5	95	88	13	38	40	12.1	3.41	101	.248	.324	5	.208	0	0	-0	-1	0.0
1947 StL-N	4	1	.800	37	0	0	0	5	50¹	57	10	11	28	12.5	5.01	83	.279	.323	1	.167	-0	-5	-5	-0	-0.4
1948 StL-N	6	6	.500	57	2	0	0	13	130²	113	5	39	71	10.5	2.62	156	.235	.293	5	.167	-0	19	21	-1	2.2
1949 StL-N	10	3	.769	59	0	0	0	9	118¹	105	7	38	71	10.9	3.73	112	.240	.301	1	.037	-3	4	6	-2	0.1
1950 StL-N	2	0	1.000	18	0	0	0	0	24¹	27	4	9	15	13.7	6.66	65	.287	.356	0	.000	-1	-7	-6	0	-0.5
1951 StL-N	0	0	—	17	0	0	0	0	18	19	1	5	5	12.0	3.00	132	.279	.329	0	.000	-1	2	2	-1	0.0
Pit-N	3	5	.375	48	1	1	0	12	82²	69	6	24	43	10.3	2.83	149	.231	.292	1	.083	-1	10	13	1	1.6
Yr	3	5	.375	65	1	1	0	13	100²	88	7	29	48	10.6	2.86	146	.240	.299	1	.077	-1	12	15	0	1.6
1952 Pit-N	5	5	.500	44	0	0	0	4	72¹	65	9	31	24	12.2	3.61	111	.245	.329	1	.125	-0	1	3	-1	0.3
Cle-A	0	0	—	7	0	0	0	0	11²	12	0	6	2	11.6	3.86	87	.186	.300	0	—	0	-1	-1	-0	-0.1
1953 Cle-A	0	0	—	4	0	0	0	0	3²	5	0	3	2	19.6	7.36	51	.278	.381	0	—	-0	-1	-1	-0	0.0
Total 10	59	30	.663	385	44	22	5	46	913	832	76	283	403	11.1	3.26	118	.244	.304	27	.131	-5	55	61	-11	5.4

ED WILLETT
Willett, Robert Edgar b: 3/7/1884, Norfolk, Va. d: 5/10/34, Wellington, Kan. BR/TR, 6', 183 lbs. Deb: 9/5/06

YEAR TM/L	W	L	PCT	G	GS	CG	SH	SV	IP	H	HR	BB	SO	RAT	ERA	ERA+	OAV	OOB	BH	AVG	PB	PR	/A	PD	TPI
1906 Det-A	0	3	.000	3	3	3	0	0	25	24	0	8	16	12.2	3.96	70	.255	.327	1	.000	-0	-4	-3	1	-0.4
1907 Det-A	1	5	.167	10	6	1	0	0	48²	47	0	20	27	12.8	3.70	70	.255	.335	1	.077	-1	-6	-6	1	-0.7
1908 Det-A	15	8	.652	30	23	18	2	1	197¹	186	2	60	77	11.9	2.28	106	.261	.331	11	.164	-2	2	3	5	0.6
1909 *Det-A	21	10	.677	41	34	25	3	1	292²	239	5	76	89	10.1	2.34	108	.221	.281	22	.196	3	5	6	-1	0.8
1910 Det-A	16	11	.593	37	25	18	4	0	224¹	175	2	74	65	10.7	2.37	111	.217	.296	11	.133	-2	4	7	7	1.3
1911 Det-A	13	14	.481	38	27	15	2	1	231¹	261	3	80	86	13.8	3.66	95	.295	.363	22	.268	7	-8	-5	3	0.4
1912 Det-A	17	15	.531	37	31	28	1	0	284¹	281	8	84	89	12.1	3.29	99	.262	.326	19	.165	-2	1	-1	5	0.3
1913 Det-A	13	14	.481	34	31	20	0	0	242	237	6	89	59	12.5	3.09	95	.260	.333	26	.283	7	-4	-5	3	0.7

YEAR	TM/L	W	L	PCT	G	GS	CG	SH	SV	IP	H	HR	BB	SO	RAT	ERA	ERA+	OAV	OOB	BH	AVG	PB	PR	/A	PD	TPI
1914	StL-F	4	16	.200	27	21	14	0	0	175	208	5	56	73	14.1	4.22	72	.295	.355	15	.234	2	-26	-23	5	-1.7
1915	StL-F	2	3	.400	17	2	1	0	2	52²	61	2	18	19	14.0	4.61	62	.295	.360	3	.200	0	-11	-10	0	-1.0
Total 10		102	99	.507	274	202	142	12	5	1773¹	1719	24	565	600	12.1	3.08	94	.258	.326	130	.199	11	-47	-37	28	0.3

● CARL WILLEY
Willey, Carlton Francis b: 6/6/31, Cherryfield, Me. BR/TR, 6', 175 lbs. Deb: 4/30/58

YEAR	TM/L	W	L	PCT	G	GS	CG	SH	SV	IP	H	HR	BB	SO	RAT	ERA	ERA+	OAV	OOB	BH	AVG	PB	PR	/A	PD	TPI
1958	*Mil-N	9	7	.563	23	19	9	**4**	0	140	110	14	53	74	10.6	2.70	130	.215	.291	5	.104	-2	19	13	-2	0.9
1959	Mil-N	5	9	.357	26	15	5	2	0	117	126	12	31	51	12.2	4.15	85	.273	.322	4	.103	-1	-3	-8	-1	-1.1
1960	Mil-N	6	7	.462	28	21	2	1	0	144²	136	19	65	109	12.9	4.35	79	.248	.335	7	.146	1	-10	-15	-1	-1.2
1961	Mil-N	6	12	.333	35	22	4	0	0	159²	147	20	65	91	12.1	3.83	98	.247	.323	1	.019	-6	4	-2	3	-0.5
1962	Mil-N	2	5	.286	30	6	0	0	1	73¹	95	9	20	40	14.2	5.40	70	.319	.364	3	.273	1	-12	-13	-0	-1.1
1963	NY-N	9	14	.391	30	28	7	4	0	183	149	24	69	101	10.9	3.10	113	.220	.296	6	.111	-1	4	8	0	0.9
1964	NY-N	0	2	.000	14	3	0	0	0	30	37	5	8	14	13.8	3.60	94	.301	.348	0	.000	-0	-0	-1	-0	-0.2
1965	NY-N	1	2	.333	13	3	1	0	0	28	30	2	15	13	15.1	4.18	84	.270	.367	0	.000	-0	-2	-2	-0	-0.3
Total 8		38	58	.396	199	117	28	11	1	875²	830	105	326	493	12.1	3.76	95	.250	.320	26	.099	-9	1	-17	-3	-2.6

● NICK WILLHITE
Willhite, Jon Nicholas b: 1/27/41, Tulsa, Okla. BL/TL, 6'2", 195 lbs. Deb: 6/16/63

YEAR	TM/L	W	L	PCT	G	GS	CG	SH	SV	IP	H	HR	BB	SO	RAT	ERA	ERA+	OAV	OOB	BH	AVG	PB	PR	/A	PD	TPI
1963	LA-N	2	3	.400	8	5	1	1	0	38	44	5	10	28	12.8	3.79	80	.286	.329	3	.300	1	-2	-3	-1	-0.4
1964	LA-N	2	4	.333	10	7	2	0	0	43²	43	4	13	24	11.5	3.71	87	.264	.318	0	.000	-0	-1	-2	1	-0.2
1965	Was-A			—	5	0	0	0	0	6¹	10	2	4	3	19.9	7.11	49	.345	.424	0	—	0	-3	-3	-0	-0.6
	LA-N	2	2	.500	15	6	0	0	1	42	47	7	22	28	15.2	5.36	61	.288	.380	4	.400	3	-8	-10	-1	-0.6
1966	LA-N	0	0	—	6	0	0	0	0	4¹	3	0	5	4	16.6	2.08	159	.214	.421	0	—	-0	1	1	0	0.0
1967	Cal-A	0	2	.000	10	7	0	0	0	39¹	39	8	16	22	12.6	4.35	72	.258	.329	0	.000	-1	-5	-5	-0	-0.5
	NY-N	0	1	.000	4	1	0	0	0	8¹	9	1	5	9	15.1	8.64	39	.257	.350	0	.000	-0	-5	-5	-0	-0.5
Total 5		6	12	.333	58	29	3	1	1	182	195	27	75	118	13.5	4.55	70	.275	.346	7	.163	2	-23	-27	-0	-2.1

● ALBERT WILLIAMS
Williams, Albert Hamilton (De Souza) b: 5/6/54, Lagunas De Perlas, Nic. BR/TR, 6'4", 190 lbs. Deb: 5/7/80

YEAR	TM/L	W	L	PCT	G	GS	CG	SH	SV	IP	H	HR	BB	SO	RAT	ERA	ERA+	OAV	OOB	BH	AVG	PB	PR	/A	PD	TPI
1980	Min-A	6	2	.750	18	9	3	0	1	77	73	9	30	35	12.0	3.51	124	.255	.323	0	—	0	5	7	-1	0.2
1981	Min-A	6	10	.375	23	22	4	0	0	150	160	11	52	76	12.8	4.08	97	.276	.337	0	—	0	-7	-2	-2	-0.7
1982	Min-A	9	7	.563	26	26	3	0	0	153²	166	18	55	61	12.9	4.22	101	.276	.337	0	—	0	-2	0	0	0.0
1983	Min-A	11	14	.440	36	29	4	1	1	193¹	196	21	68	68	12.5	4.14	103	.262	.327	0	—	0	-2	2	-2	0.1
1984	Min-A	3	5	.375	17	11	1	0	0	68²	75	9	22	22	13.6	5.77	73	.284	.355	0	—	0	-14	-12	-0	-1.3
Total 5		35	38	.479	120	97	15	1	2	642²	670	68	227	262	12.7	4.24	99	.270	.334	0	—	0	-20	-4	-4	-1.7

● AL WILLIAMS
Williams, Almon Edward b: 5/11/14, Valhermoso Springs, Ala. d: 7/19/69, Groves, Tex. BR/TR, 6'3", 200 lbs. Deb: 4/19/37

YEAR	TM/L	W	L	PCT	G	GS	CG	SH	SV	IP	H	HR	BB	SO	RAT	ERA	ERA+	OAV	OOB	BH	AVG	PB	PR	/A	PD	TPI
1937	Phi-A	4	1	.800	16	8	2	0	1	75¹	88	0	49	27	16.5	5.38	88	.300	.402	2	.083	-2	-6	-6	0	-0.5
1938	Phi-A	0	7	.000	30	8	1	0	0	93¹	128	6	54	25	17.6	6.94	70	.324	.407	1	.040	-3	-22	-22	-0	-1.5
Total 2		4	8	.333	46	16	3	0	1	168²	216	6	103	52	17.1	6.24	77	.314	.405	3	.061	-5	-29	-27	-0	-2.0

● GUS WILLIAMS
Williams, Augustine H. b: 1870, New York, N.Y. d: 10/14/1890, New York, N.Y. 5'11", 170 lbs. Deb: 4/18/1890

YEAR	TM/L	W	L	PCT	G	GS	CG	SH	SV	IP	H	HR	BB	SO	RAT	ERA	ERA+	OAV	OOB	BH	AVG	PB	PR	/A	PD	TPI
1890	Bro-a	0	1	.000	2	2	1	0	0	12	13	0	12	2	18.8	7.50	52	.265	.410	2	.500	1	-5	-5	-1	-0.3

● BRIAN WILLIAMS
Williams, Brian O'Neal b: 2/15/69, Lancaster, S.C. BR/TR, 6'3", 205 lbs. Deb: 9/16/91

YEAR	TM/L	W	L	PCT	G	GS	CG	SH	SV	IP	H	HR	BB	SO	RAT	ERA	ERA+	OAV	OOB	BH	AVG	PB	PR	/A	PD	TPI
1991	Hou-N	0	1	.000	2	2	0	0	0	12	11	4	4	4	12.0	3.75	94	.250	.327	0	.000	-0	-0	-0	-1	-0.1
1992	Hou-N	7	6	.538	16	16	0	0	0	96¹	92	10	42	54	12.5	3.92	86	.255	.333	4	.133	-0	-4	-6	-0	-0.8
1993	Hou-N	4	4	.500	42	5	0	0	3	82	76	7	38	56	13.0	4.83	80	.248	.338	2	.200	-0	-7	-9	2	-0.6
1994	Hou-N	6	5	.545	20	13	0	0	0	78¹	112	9	41	49	18.0	5.74	69	.343	.422	6	.261	-4	-13	-16	-1	-1.8
1995	SD-N	3	10	.231	44	6	0	0	0	72	79	3	38	75	15.6	6.00	67	.279	.380	1	.071	-0	-15	-16	-0	-2.5
1996	Det-A	3	10	.231	40	17	2	1	2	121	145	21	64	72	17.6	6.77	75	.304	.415	0	—	0	-24	-23	-0	-2.0
Total 6		23	36	.390	164	59	2	1	5	461²	515	52	248	310	15.3	5.46	75	.286	.380	13	.162	0	-64	-70	1	-7.8

● CHARLIE WILLIAMS
Williams, Charles Prosek b: 10/11/47, Flushing, N.Y. BR/TR, 6'2", 200 lbs. Deb: 4/23/71

YEAR	TM/L	W	L	PCT	G	GS	CG	SH	SV	IP	H	HR	BB	SO	RAT	ERA	ERA+	OAV	OOB	BH	AVG	PB	PR	/A	PD	TPI
1971	NY-N	5	6	.455	31	9	1	0	0	90¹	92	7	41	53	13.5	4.78	71	.267	.348	2	.087	-1	-13	-14	-1	-1.8
1972	SF-N	0	2	.000	3	2	0	0	0	9¹	14	3	3	3	16.4	8.68	40	.333	.378	0	.000	-0	-5	-5	-0	-1.0
1973	SF-N	3	0	1.000	12	0	0	0	0	23	32	2	7	11	15.3	6.65	57	.330	.375	1	.333	0	-8	-7	0	-0.8
1974	SF-N	1	3	.250	39	7	0	0	0	100¹	93	4	31	48	11.3	2.78	137	.250	.311	3	.136	-1	9	11	3	0.6
1975	SF-N	5	3	.625	55	2	0	0	3	98	94	2	66	45	15.1	3.49	109	.261	.381	2	.125	0	1	3	2	0.5
1976	SF-N	2	0	1.000	48	2	0	0	1	85	80	4	39	34	12.8	2.96	122	.256	.343	1	.125	-0	5	6	1	0.4
1977	SF-N	6	5	.545	55	1	0	0	0	119¹	116	9	60	41	13.5	4.00	98	.262	.354	4	.222	0	-1	-1	-0	-0.1
1978	SF-N	1	3	.250	25	1	0	0	0	48	60	5	28	22	16.7	5.44	63	.314	.405	0	.000	-1	-10	-11	-0	-0.9
Total 8		23	22	.511	268	33	2	0	4	573¹	581	38	275	257	13.7	3.97	93	.269	.355	13	.134	-2	-22	-17	-3	-3.3

● LEFTY WILLIAMS
Williams, Claude Preston b: 3/9/1893, Aurora, Mo. d: 11/4/59, Laguna Beach, Cal. BR/TL, 5'9", 160 lbs. Deb: 9/17/13

YEAR	TM/L	W	L	PCT	G	GS	CG	SH	SV	IP	H	HR	BB	SO	RAT	ERA	ERA+	OAV	OOB	BH	AVG	PB	PR	/A	PD	TPI
1913	Det-A	1	3	.250	5	4	3	0	0	29	34	1	4	9	12.1	4.97	59	.286	.315	1	.100	-0	-7	-7	-1	-1.0
1914	Det-A	0	1	.000	1	1	0	0	0	3	3	0	2	0	45.0	0.00	—	.429	.556	0	—	0	0	-0	0	0.4
1916	Chi-A	13	7	.650	43	26	10	2	1	224¹	220	5	65	138	11.8	2.89	96	.267	.327	10	.135	-0	-1	-3	-4	-0.8
1917	*Chi-A	17	8	.680	45	29	8	1	1	230	221	3	81	85	12.2	2.97	89	.252	.321	6	.090	-3	-8	-8	-5	-1.7
1918	Chi-A	6	4	.600	15	14	7	2	1	105²	76	0	47	30	10.9	2.73	100	.209	.308	5	.132	-2	1	-0	-2	-0.5
1919	*Chi-A	23	11	.676	41	40	27	5	1	297	265	7	58	125	10.1	2.64	121	.244	.289	17	.181	1	20	18	-5	1.5
1920	Chi-A	22	14	.611	39	38	25	0	0	299	302	15	90	128	12.2	3.91	96	.271	.332	22	.218	0	-4	-5	-3	-0.8
Total 7		82	48	.631	189	152	80	10	5	1186	1121	30	347	515	11.5	3.13	99	.255	.316	61	.159	-4	1	-4	-21	-2.9

● MUTT WILLIAMS
Williams, David Carter b: 7/31/1891, Ozark, Ark. d: 3/30/62, Fayetteville, Ark. BR/TR, 6'3.5", 195 lbs. Deb: 10/4/13

YEAR	TM/L	W	L	PCT	G	GS	CG	SH	SV	IP	H	HR	BB	SO	RAT	ERA	ERA+	OAV	OOB	BH	AVG	PB	PR	/A	PD	TPI
1913	Was-A	1	0	1.000	1	1	0	0	0	4	4	1	2	1	13.5	4.50	66	.286	.375	1	.500	0	-1	-1	0	-0.1
1914	Was-A	0	0	—	5	0	0	0	1	7	5	0	4	3	11.6	5.14	58	.227	.346	0	—	0	-2	-1	-0	-0.1
Total 2		1	0	1.000	6	1	0	0	1	11	9	1	6	4	12.3	4.91	58	.250	.357	1	.500	0	-3	-2	-0	-0.2

● DAVE WILLIAMS
Williams, David Owen b: 2/7/1881, Scranton, Pa. d: 4/25/18, Hot Springs, Ark. BR/TL, 5'11.5", 167 lbs. Deb: 7/2/02

YEAR	TM/L	W	L	PCT	G	GS	CG	SH	SV	IP	H	HR	BB	SO	RAT	ERA	ERA+	OAV	OOB	BH	AVG	PB	PR	/A	PD	TPI
1902	Bos-A	0	0	—	3	0	0	0	0	18²	22	0	11	7	16.4	5.30	67	.293	.391	3	.333	1	-4	-4	-1	0.0

● DON WILLIAMS
Williams, Donald Fred b: 9/14/31, Floyd, Va. BR/TR, 6'2", 180 lbs. Deb: 9/12/58

YEAR	TM/L	W	L	PCT	G	GS	CG	SH	SV	IP	H	HR	BB	SO	RAT	ERA	ERA+	OAV	OOB	BH	AVG	PB	PR	/A	PD	TPI
1958	Pit-N	0	0	—	2	0	0	0	0	4	6	1	1	3	15.8	6.75	57	.375	.412	0	—	0	-1	-1	-0	0.0
1959	Pit-N	0	0	—	6	0	0	0	0	12	17	1	3	5	15.0	6.75	57	.362	.400	1	.333	1	-4	-4	-1	0.0
1962	KC-A	0	0	—	3	0	0	0	0	4	6	0	1	5	15.8	9.00	47	.353	.389	0	.000	-0	-2	-2	-0	0.0
Total 3		0	0	—	11	0	0	0	0	20	29	2	4	7	15.3	7.20	53	.363	.400	1	.250	1	-7	-7	-1	0.0

● DON WILLIAMS
Williams, Donald Reid "Dino" b: 9/2/35, Los Angeles, Cal. d: 12/20/91, LaJolla, Cal. BR/TR, 6'5", 218 lbs. Deb: 8/4/63

YEAR	TM/L	W	L	PCT	G	GS	CG	SH	SV	IP	H	HR	BB	SO	RAT	ERA	ERA+	OAV	OOB	BH	AVG	PB	PR	/A	PD	TPI
1963	Min-A	0	0	—	3	0	0	0	0	4¹	9	2	5	3	29.1	10.38	35	.381	.519	0	—	0	-3	-3	-0	0.0

● DALE WILLIAMS
Williams, Elisha Alphonso b: 10/6/1855, Ludlow, Ky. d: 10/22/39, Covington, Ky. BR/TR, 5'9", 175 lbs. Deb: 8/12/1876

YEAR	TM/L	W	L	PCT	G	GS	CG	SH	SV	IP	H	HR	BB	SO	RAT	ERA	ERA+	OAV	OOB	BH	AVG	PB	PR	/A	PD	TPI
1876	Cin-N	1	8	.111	9	9	9	0	0	83	123	1	4	9	13.8	4.23	52	.339	.346	7	.200	-2	-18	-19	-0	-1.6

● FRANK WILLIAMS
Williams, Frank Lee b: 2/13/58, Seattle, Wash. BR/TR, 6'1", 190 lbs. Deb: 4/5/84

YEAR	TM/L	W	L	PCT	G	GS	CG	SH	SV	IP	H	HR	BB	SO	RAT	ERA	ERA+	OAV	OOB	BH	AVG	PB	PR	/A	PD	TPI
1984	SF-N	9	4	.692	61	1	1	1	3	106¹	88	2	51	91	12.0	3.55	99	.226	.321	4	.222	1	0	-1	4	0.5
1985	SF-N	2	4	.333	49	0	0	0	0	73	65	5	35	52	13.1	4.19	82	.242	.342	0	.000	-0	-5	-6	-0	-0.5
1986	SF-N	3	1	.750	36	0	0	0	0	52¹	35	0	21	33	10.3	1.20	292	.212	.316	1	.500	0	15	13	1	1.1
1987	Cin-N	4	0	1.000	85	0	0	0	2	105²	101	5	39	60	12.1	2.30	185	.254	.324	0	.000	-1	21	23	1	0.9
1988	Cin-N	3	2	.600	60	0	0	0	3	62²	59	6	35	43	13.8	2.59	139	.252	.354	0	.000	0	6	7	0	0.6
1989	Det-A	3	3	.500	42	0	0	0	0	71²	70	5	46	33	14.9	3.64	105	.254	.366	0	—	0	2	1	-0	0.1
Total 6		24	14	.632	333	1	1	1	8	471²	418	23	227	314	12.7	3.00	124	.242	.336	5	.172	0	39	38	5	2.7

● WOODY WILLIAMS
Williams, Gregory Scott b: 8/19/66, Houston, Tex. BR/TR, 6', 180 lbs. Deb: 5/14/93

YEAR	TM/L	W	L	PCT	G	GS	CG	SH	SV	IP	H	HR	BB	SO	RAT	ERA	ERA+	OAV	OOB	BH	AVG	PB	PR	/A	PD	TPI
1993	Tor-A	3	1	.750	30	0	0	0	0	37	40	2	22	24	15.3	4.38	99	.274	.373	0	—	0	-0	-0	1	0.0
1994	Tor-A	1	3	.250	38	0	0	0	0	59¹	44	5	33	56	12.0	3.64	132	.205	.316	0	—	0	8	8	-0	0.4

YEAR TM/L	W	L	PCT	G	GS	CG	SH	SV	IP	H	HR	BB	SO	RAT	ERA	ERA+	OAV	OOB	BH	AVG	PB	PR	/A	PD	TPI
1995 Tor-A	1	2	.333	23	3	0	0	0	53²	44	6	28	41	12.4	3.69	128	.220	.322	0	—	0	6	6	0	0.3
1996 Tor-A	4	5	.444	12	10	1	0	0	59	64	8	21	43	13.1	4.73	107	.278	.341	0	—	0	2	2	-0	0.3
Total 4	9	11	.450	103	13	1	0	0	209	192	21	104	164	13.0	4.09	117	.243	.335	0	—	0	15	16	0	1.0

● **JOHNNIE WILLIAMS**   Williams, John Brodie "Honolulu Johnnie"
b: 7/16/1889, Honolulu, Hawaii d: 9/8/63, Long Beach, Cal.   BR/TR, 6', 180 lbs.   Deb: 4/21/14

| 1914 Det-A | 0 | 2 | .000 | 4 | 3 | 1 | 0 | 0 | 11¹ | 17 | 0 | 5 | 4 | 17.5 | 6.35 | 44 | .378 | .440 | 0 | .000 | -0 | -5 | -4 | -0 | -0.8 |

● **LEON WILLIAMS**   Williams, Leon Theo "Lefty"   b: 12/2/05, Macon, Ga.   d: 11/20/84, Atlanta, Ga.   BL/TR, 5'10.5", 154 lbs.   Deb: 6/2/26

| 1926 Bro-N | 0 | 0 | — | 8 | 0 | 0 | 0 | 0 | 8¹ | 16 | 0 | 2 | 3 | 19.4 | 5.40 | 71 | .421 | .450 | 1 | .200 | 0 | -1 | -1 | 1 | 0.1 |

● **MARSH WILLIAMS**   Williams, Marshall McDiarmid "Cap"   b: 2/21/1893, Faison, N.C.   d: 2/22/35, Tucson, Ariz.   BR/TR, 6', 180 lbs.   Deb: 7/7/16

| 1916 Phi-A | 0 | 6 | .000 | 10 | 4 | 3 | 0 | 0 | 51¹ | 71 | 4 | 31 | 17 | 17.9 | 7.89 | 36 | .350 | .436 | 2 | .105 | -1 | -29 | -29 | -1 | -3.0 |

● **MATT WILLIAMS**   Williams, Matthew Evan   b: 7/25/59, Houston, Tex.   BR/TR, 6'1", 200 lbs.   Deb: 8/2/83

1983 Tor-A	1	1	.500	4	3	0	0	0	8	13	5	7	3	23.6	14.63	29	.361	.477	0	—	0	-9	-9	-0	-1.6
1985 Tex-A	2	1	.667	6	3	0	0	0	26	20	3	10	22	10.4	2.42	175	.211	.286	0	—	0	5	5	-1	0.4
Total 2	3	2	.600	10	6	0	0	0	34	33	8	17	27	13.5	5.29	80	.252	.342	0	—	0	-4	-4	-0	-1.2

● **MIKE WILLIAMS**   Williams, Michael Darren   b: 7/29/69, Radford, Va.   BR/TR, 6'2", 190 lbs.   Deb: 6/30/92

1992 Phi-N	1	1	.500	5	5	1	0	0	28²	29	3	7	5	11.3	5.34	65	.259	.303	4	.400	1	-6	-6	-0	-0.3
1993 Phi-N	1	3	.250	17	4	0	0	0	51	50	5	22	33	12.7	5.29	75	.253	.327	1	.083	-1	-7	-8	-0	-0.6
1994 Phi-N	2	4	.333	12	6	0	0	0	50¹	61	7	20	29	14.5	5.01	86	.310	.373	2	.167	0	-4	-4	-0	-0.4
1995 Phi-N	3	3	.500	33	8	0	0	0	87²	78	10	29	57	11.3	3.29	129	.239	.306	2	.125	-0	9	9	1	0.6
1996 Phi-N	6	14	.300	32	29	0	0	0	167	188	25	67	103	14.1	5.44	80	.290	.362	8	.157	-1	-23	-20	3	-1.8
Total 5	13	25	.342	99	54	1	0	0	384²	406	50	145	227	13.1	4.87	86	.274	.342	17	.168	-0	-31	-28	3	-2.5

● **MITCH WILLIAMS**   Williams, Mitchell Steven "Wild Thing"   b: 11/17/64, Santa Ana, Cal.   BL/TL, 6'4", 205 lbs.   Deb: 4/9/86

1986 Tex-A	8	6	.571	**80**	0	0	0	8	98	69	8	79	90	14.6	3.58	120	.202	.369	0	—	0	6	8	-1	1.0
1987 Tex-A	8	6	.571	85	1	0	0	6	108²	63	9	94	129	13.6	3.23	138	.175	.355	0	—	0	15	15	1	1.9
1988 Tex-A	2	7	.222	67	0	0	0	18	68	48	4	47	61	13.4	4.63	88	.203	.349	0	—	0	-5	-4	0	-0.7
1989 *Chi-N★	4	4	.500	76	0	0	0	36	81²	71	6	52	67	14.4	2.76	136	.238	.366	1	.200	1	7	9	-1	1.7
1990 Chi-N	1	8	.111	59	2	0	0	16	66¹	60	4	50	55	15.1	3.93	104	.239	.368	0	.000	-1	-1	-1	-0	-0.0
1991 Phi-N	12	5	.706	69	0	0	0	30	88¹	56	4	62	84	12.8	2.34	156	.182	.333	0	.000	-1	13	13	-1	3.1
1992 Phi-N	5	8	.385	66	0	0	0	29	81	69	4	64	74	15.4	3.78	92	.240	.389	1	.250	-1	-2	-3	-1	-0.6
1993 *Phi-N	3	7	.300	65	0	0	0	43	62	56	3	44	60	14.8	3.34	119	.245	.371	1	1.000	0	5	4	-1	1.1
1994 Hou-N	1	4	.200	25	0	0	0	6	20	21	4	21	24	20.7	7.65	52	.269	.447	0	—	0	-8	-8	-0	-2.2
1995 Cal-A	1	2	.333	20	0	0	0	1	10²	11	3	21	9	30.4	6.75	70	.317	.563	0	—	0	-2	-2	-0	-0.5
Total 10	45	57	.441	612	3	0	0	192	684²	526	47	537	650	14.7	3.58	112	.216	.369	3	.188	1	27	33	-5	4.8

● **STEAMBOAT WILLIAMS**   Williams, Rees Gephardt   b: 1/31/1892, Cascade, Mont.   d: 6/29/79, Deer River, Minn.   BL/TR, 5'11", 170 lbs.   Deb: 7/12/14

1914 StL-N	0	1	.000	5	1	0	0	0	11	13	1	6	2	15.5	6.55	43	.295	.380	0	.000	-0	-5	-5	-0	-0.4
1916 StL-N	6	7	.462	36	8	5	0	1	105	121	6	27	25	12.8	4.20	63	.291	.336	5	.208	1	-18	-18	-0	-2.2
Total 2	6	8	.429	41	9	5	0	1	116	134	7	33	27	13.0	4.42	60	.291	.340	5	.200	1	-23	-23	-0	-2.6

● **RICK WILLIAMS**   Williams, Richard Allen   b: 11/9/52, Merced, Cal.   BR/TR, 6'1", 180 lbs.   Deb: 6/12/78

1978 Hou-N	1	2	.333	17	1	0	0	0	34²	43	2	10	17	13.8	4.67	71	.301	.346	0	.000	-1	-4	-5	0	-0.5
1979 Hou-N	4	7	.364	31	16	2	2	0	121¹	122	6	30	37	11.4	3.26	108	.261	.308	8	.258	3	6	3	0	0.6
Total 2	5	9	.357	48	17	2	2	0	156	165	8	40	54	11.9	3.58	97	.270	.317	8	.222	2	2	-2	1	0.1

● **ACE WILLIAMS**   Williams, Robert Fulton   b: 3/18/17, Montclair, N.J.   BR/TL, 6'2", 174 lbs.   Deb: 7/15/40

1940 Bos-N	0	0	—	5	0	0	0	0	9	21	0	12	5	34.0	16.00	23	.375	.493	0	.000	-0	-12	-12	0	0.0
1946 Bos-N	0	0	—	1	0	0	0	0	0	1	0	1	0	—	—	—	1.000	1.000	0	—	0	-0	-0	0	0.0
Total 2	0	0	—	6	0	0	0	0	9	22	0	13	5	36.0	16.00	23	.386	.507	0	.000	-0	-12	-12	0	0.0

● **SHAD WILLIAMS**   Williams, Shad Clayton   b: 3/10/71, Fresno, Cal.   BR/TR, 6', 198 lbs.   Deb: 5/18/96

| 1996 Cal-A | 0 | 2 | .000 | 13 | 2 | 0 | 0 | 0 | 28¹ | 42 | 7 | 21 | 26 | 20.6 | 8.89 | 55 | .341 | .445 | 0 | — | 0 | -12 | -13 | -1 | -0.7 |

● **STAN WILLIAMS**   Williams, Stanley Wilson   b: 9/14/36, Enfield, N.H.   BR/TR, 6'5", 230 lbs.   Deb: 5/17/58   C

1958 LA-N	9	7	.563	27	21	3	2	0	119	99	11	65	80	12.9	4.01	102	.228	.338	2	.050	-3	-1	1	0	-0.1
1959 *LA-N	5	5	.500	35	15	2	0	0	124²	102	12	86	89	14.2	3.97	106	.228	.363	7	.194	1	-0	4	0	0.3
1960 LA-N★	14	10	.583	38	30	9	2	1	207¹	162	26	72	175	10.4	3.00	133	.210	.282	9	.141	0	18	22	1	2.6
1961 LA-N	15	12	.556	41	35	6	2	0	235¹	213	17	108	205	12.5	3.90	111	.242	.329	13	.167	-1	3	12	-1	1.1
1962 LA-N	14	12	.538	40	28	4	1	1	185²	184	16	98	108	13.7	4.46	81	.253	.341	5	.076	-2	-11	-17	-1	-2.4
1963 *NY-A	9	8	.529	29	21	6	1	0	146	137	7	57	98	12.3	3.21	110	.249	.326	5	.102	-1	7	5	1	0.5
1964 NY-A	1	5	.167	21	10	1	0	0	82	76	7	38	54	12.5	3.84	94	.248	.330	3	.143	-0	-2	-2	1	-0.1
1965 Cle-A	0	0	—	3	0	0	0	0	4¹	6	1	3	1	18.7	6.23	56	.353	.450	0	—	0	-1	-1	0	0.0
1967 Cle-A	6	4	.600	16	8	2	1	1	79	64	6	24	75	10.1	2.62	125	.218	.279	2	.091	-1	5	6	-2	0.4
1968 Cle-A	13	11	.542	44	24	6	2	0	194¹	163	14	51	147	10.4	2.50	118	.225	.285	4	.069	-1	10	10	-1	1.5
1969 Cle-A	6	14	.300	61	15	3	0	12	178¹	155	25	67	139	11.8	3.94	96	.235	.317	4	.100	-1	-6	-3	-1	-0.5
1970 *Min-A	10	1	.909	68	0	0	0	15	113¹	85	8	32	76	9.7	1.99	187	.208	.274	0	.000	-2	22	22	-2	2.2
1971 Min-A	4	5	.444	46	1	0	0	4	78	64	7	44	47	13.3	4.15	86	.220	.340	0	.000	-0	-6	-5	-1	-0.8
StL-N	3	0	1.000	10	0	0	0	0	12²	13	0	2	8	12.1	1.42	253	.265	.321	0	.000	-0	3	3	0	0.3
1972 Bos-A	0	0	—	4	0	0	0	0	4¹	5	0	1	3	12.5	6.23	52	.294	.333	0	—	0	-2	-1	0	0.0
Total 14	109	94	.537	482	208	42	11	43	1764¹	1527	160	748	1305	12.0	3.48	108	.232	.317	59	.118	-10	39	53	-4	5.5

● **TED WILLIAMS**   Williams, Theodore Samuel "The Kid', "The Thumper" or "The Splendid Splinter"
b: 8/30/18, San Diego, Cal.   BL/TR, 6'3", 205 lbs.   Deb: 4/20/39   MH♦

| 1940 Bos-A★ | 0 | 0 | — | 1 | 0 | 0 | 0 | 0 | 2 | 3 | 0 | 1 | 1 | 13.5 | 4.50 | 100 | .333 | .333 | 193 | .344 | 1 | -0 | -0 | 0 | 0.0 |

● **TOM WILLIAMS**   Williams, Thomas C.   b: 8/19/1870, Minersville, Ohio   d: 7/27/40, Columbus, Ohio   Deb: 5/1/1892

1892 Cle-N	1	0	1.000	2	1	1	0	0	9	9	1	6	3	10.0	3.00	113	.250	.270	1	.100	-1	0	0	-0	0.0
1893 Cle-N	1	1	.500	5	2	2	0	0	24	33	1	10	6	16.5	4.88	100	.317	.383	5	.278	0	-1	0	0	0.0
Total 2	2	1	.667	7	3	3	0	0	33	42	2	11	9	14.7	4.36	102	.300	.355	6	.214	-0	-1	0	-0	0.0

● **TODD WILLIAMS**   Williams, Todd Michael   b: 2/13/71, Syracuse, N.Y.   BR/TR, 6'3", 185 lbs.   Deb: 4/29/95

| 1995 LA-N | 2 | 2 | .500 | 16 | 0 | 0 | 0 | 0 | 19¹ | 19 | 3 | 7 | 8 | 12.1 | 5.12 | 74 | .264 | .329 | 1 | .500 | 0 | -2 | -3 | 1 | -0.4 |

● **POP WILLIAMS**   Williams, Walter Merrill   b: 5/19/1874, Bowdoinham, Me.   d: 8/4/59, Topsham, Maine   BL/TR, 5'11", 190 lbs.   Deb: 9/14/1898

1898 Was-N	0	2	.000	2	2	2	0	0	17	32	0	7	3	20.6	8.47	43	.395	.443	3	.375	1	-9	-9	-1	-0.7
1902 Chi-N	11	16	.407	31	31	26	1	0	254¹	259	6	63	94	11.7	2.51	107	.264	.313	23	.198	2	8	5	3	1.1
1903 Chi-N	0	1	.000	1	1	1	0	0	6	9	2	0	0	16.2	5.40	58	.409	.409	0	—	-1	-1	-0	-2	-0.2
Phi-N	1	1	.500	2	2	1	0	0	18	21	0	6	6	14.0	3.00	109	.304	.368	2	.286	1	1	1	1	0.2
Bos-N	4	5	.444	10	10	9	1	0	83	97	3	37	20	15.5	4.12	78	.295	.381	10	.238	-0	-8	-8	-1	-0.8
Yr	5	7	.417	13	13	11	1	0	106	127	5	43	30	15.2	3.99	81	.302	.378	12	.235	0	-8	-9	-0	-0.8
Total 3	16	25	.390	46	46	40	2	0	377¹	418	11	113	127	13.1	3.20	90	.282	.340	38	.217	4	-10	-13	2	-0.4

● **WASH WILLIAMS**   Williams, Washington J.   b: Philadelphia, Pa.   d: 1/1890, Philadelphia, Pa.   5'11", 180 lbs.   Deb: 8/5/1884   ♦

| 1885 Chi-N | 0 | 0 | — | 1 | 1 | 0 | 0 | 0 | 2 | 2 | 0 | 2 | 5 | 31.5 | 13.50 | 22 | .400 | .700 | 1 | .250 | -0 | -2 | -2 | 0 | 0.0 |

● **NED WILLIAMSON**   Williamson, Edward Nagle   b: 10/24/1857, Philadelphia, Pa.   d: 3/3/1894, Willow Springs, Ark   BR/TR, 5'11", 210 lbs.   Deb: 5/1/1878   ♦

| 1881 Chi-N | 1 | 1 | .500 | 3 | 1 | 1 | 0 | 0 | 18 | 14 | 0 | 2 | 2 | 7.0 | 2.00 | 137 | .209 | .209 | 92 | .268 | 1 | 2 | 1 | -0 | 0.1 |
| 1882 Chi-N | 0 | 1 | .000 | 1 | 1 | 0 | 0 | 0 | 3 | 9 | 1 | 1 | 0 | 30.0 | 6.00 | 48 | .500 | .526 | 98 | .282 | -0 | -1 | -1 | 0 | 0.0 |

YEAR	TM/L	W	L	PCT	G	GS	CG	SH	SV	IP	H	HR	BB	SO	RAT	ERA	ERA+	OAV	OOB	BH	AVG	PB	PR	/A	PD	TPI
1883	Chi-N	0	0	—	1	0	0	0	0	1	1	0	1	1	18.0	9.00	35	.167	.286	111	.276	0	-1	-1	0	0.0
1884	Chi-N	0	0	—	2	0	0	0	0	2	8	0	2	0	45.0	18.00	17	.500	.556	116	.278	1	-3	-3	0	0.0
1885	*Chi-N	0	0	—	2	0	0	0	2	6	2	0	0	3	3.0	0.00	—	.080	.080	97	.238	0	2	2	0	0.2
1886	*Chi-N	0	0	—	2	0	0	0	1	3	2	0	0	1	6.0	0.00	—	.143	.143	93	.216	0	1	1	-0	0.1
1887	Chi-N	0	0	—	1	0	0	0	0	2	2	1	0	1	13.5	9.00	50	.222	.300	117	.267	0	-1	-1	0	0.0
Total	7	1	1	.500	12	1	1	0	3	35	38	1	5	7	11.1	3.34	90	.245	.269	1159	.255	3	-2	-1	0	0.4

● **MARK WILLIAMSON**   Williamson, Mark Alan b: 7/21/59, Corpus Christi, Tex.   BR/TR, 6', 171 lbs.   Deb: 4/8/87

YEAR	TM/L	W	L	PCT	G	GS	CG	SH	SV	IP	H	HR	BB	SO	RAT	ERA	ERA+	OAV	OOB	BH	AVG	PB	PR	/A	PD	TPI
1987	Bal-A	8	9	.471	61	2	0	0	3	125	122	12	41	73	12.0	4.03	109	.261	.324	0	—	0	6	5	1	0.8
1988	Bal-A	5	8	.385	37	10	2	0	2	117²	125	14	40	69	12.8	4.90	80	.272	.333	0	—	0	-12	-13	-0	-1.3
1989	Bal-A	10	5	.667	65	0	0	0	9	107¹	105	4	30	55	11.5	2.93	129	.261	.315	0	—	0	11	10	-1	1.5
1990	Bal-A	8	2	.800	49	0	0	0	1	85¹	65	8	28	60	9.8	2.21	171	.215	.282	0	—	0	16	15	1	1.8
1991	Bal-A	5	5	.500	65	0	0	0	4	80¹	87	9	35	53	13.7	4.48	88	.275	.348	0	—	0	-3	-5	-0	-0.6
1992	Bal-A	0	0	—	12	0	0	0	1	18²	16	1	10	14	12.5	0.96	417	.239	.338	0	—	0	6	6	-1	0.0
1993	Bal-A	7	5	.583	48	1	0	0	1	88	106	5	25	45	13.4	4.91	91	.304	.350	0	—	0	-6	-4	-0	-0.6
1994	Bal-A	3	1	.750	28	2	0	0	1	67¹	75	9	17	28	12.6	4.01	125	.278	.325	0	—	0	6	7	-1	0.2
Total	8	46	35	.568	365	15	2	0	21	689²	701	62	226	397	12.2	3.86	107	.266	.326	0	—	0	24	22	-1	1.8

● **AL WILLIAMSON**   Williamson, Silas Albert b: 2/20/1900, Buckville, Ark.   d: 11/29/78, Hot Springs, Ark.   BR/TR, 5'11", 160 lbs.   Deb: 4/27/28

YEAR	TM/L	W	L	PCT	G	GS	CG	SH	SV	IP	H	HR	BB	SO	RAT	ERA	ERA+	OAV	OOB	BH	AVG	PB	PR	/A	PD	TPI
1928	Chi-A	0	0	—	1	0	0	0	0	2	1	0	0	4	4.5	0.00	—	.167	.167	0	—	0	1	1	0	0.0

● **CARL WILLIS**   Willis, Carl Blake b: 12/28/60, Danville, Va.   BL/TR, 6'4", 210 lbs.   Deb: 6/9/84

YEAR	TM/L	W	L	PCT	G	GS	CG	SH	SV	IP	H	HR	BB	SO	RAT	ERA	ERA+	OAV	OOB	BH	AVG	PB	PR	/A	PD	TPI
1984	Det-A	0	2	.000	10	2	0	0	0	16	25	1	5	4	16.9	7.31	54	.362	.405	0	—	0	-6	-6	0	-0.6
	Cin-N	0	1	.000	7	0	0	0	1	9²	8	1	2	3	9.3	3.72	101	.222	.263	0	—	0	-0	-0	0	0.0
1985	Cin-N	1	0	1.000	11	0	0	0	1	13²	21	3	5	6	17.1	9.22	41	.344	.394	0	.000	0	-9	-8	-0	-0.7
1986	Cin-N	1	3	.250	29	0	0	0	1	52¹	54	4	32	24	15.0	4.47	87	.278	.383	1	.333	0	-4	-4	1	-0.2
1988	Chi-A	0	0	—	6	0	0	0	0	12	17	3	7	6	18.0	8.25	48	.362	.444	0	—	0	-6	-6	0	0.0
1991	*Min-A	8	3	.727	40	0	0	0	2	89	76	4	19	53	9.7	2.63	162	.232	.276	0	—	0	14	16	-1	1.8
1992	Min-A	7	3	.700	59	0	0	0	1	79¹	73	4	11	45	9.5	2.72	149	.246	.273	0	—	0	11	12	-1	1.3
1993	Min-A	3	0	1.000	53	0	0	0	5	58	56	2	17	44	11.3	3.10	140	.259	.313	0	—	0	8	8	0	0.4
1994	Min-A	2	4	.333	49	0	0	0	3	59¹	89	6	12	37	15.3	5.92	82	.335	.363	0	—	0	-7	-7	-1	-0.7
1995	Min-A	0	0	—	3	0	0	0	0	0²	5	0	5	0	135.0	94.50	5	.833	.909	0	—	0	-7	-7	0	0.0
Total	9	22	16	.579	267	2	0	0	13	390	424	28	115	222	12.5	4.25	100	.279	.330	1	.250	0	-6	-1	-3	1.3

● **LEFTY WILLIS**   Willis, Charles William b: 11/4/05, Leetown, W.Va.   d: 5/10/62, Bethesda, Md.   BL/TL, 6'1", 175 lbs.   Deb: 10/3/25

YEAR	TM/L	W	L	PCT	G	GS	CG	SH	SV	IP	H	HR	BB	SO	RAT	ERA	ERA+	OAV	OOB	BH	AVG	PB	PR	/A	PD	TPI
1925	Phi-A	0	0	—	1	1	0	0	0	5	9	2	1	2	19.8	10.80	43	.409	.458	0	.000	-1	-4	-3	0	0.0
1926	Phi-A	0	0	—	13	1	0	0	1	32¹	31	0	12	13	12.2	1.39	300	.270	.344	2	.222	-1	9	10	0	0.0
1927	Phi-A	3	1	.750	15	2	1	0	0	27	32	2	11	7	14.3	5.67	75	.308	.374	0	.000	-1	-5	-4	1	-0.5
Total	3	3	1	.750	29	4	1	0	1	64¹	72	4	25	23	13.7	3.92	108	.299	.367	2	.111	-1	1	2	1	-0.5

● **DALE WILLIS**   Willis, Dale Jerome b: 5/29/38, Calhoun, Ga.   BR/TR, 5'11", 165 lbs.   Deb: 4/14/63

YEAR	TM/L	W	L	PCT	G	GS	CG	SH	SV	IP	H	HR	BB	SO	RAT	ERA	ERA+	OAV	OOB	BH	AVG	PB	PR	/A	PD	TPI
1963	KC-A	0	2	.000	25	0	0	0	1	44²	46	3	25	47	15.1	5.04	77	.266	.371	1	.167	-1	-7	-6	1	-0.2

● **JIM WILLIS**   Willis, James Gladden b: 3/20/27, Doyline, La.   BL/TR, 6'3", 175 lbs.   Deb: 4/22/53

YEAR	TM/L	W	L	PCT	G	GS	CG	SH	SV	IP	H	HR	BB	SO	RAT	ERA	ERA+	OAV	OOB	BH	AVG	PB	PR	/A	PD	TPI
1953	Chi-N	2	1	.667	13	3	2	0	0	43¹	37	1	17	15	11.8	3.12	143	.228	.313	0	.000	-1	6	6	1	0.4
1954	Chi-N	0	1	.000	14	1	0	0	0	23	22	1	18	5	16.8	3.91	107	.256	.402	0	.000	-1	0	1	1	0.0
Total	2	2	2	.500	27	4	2	0	0	66¹	59	2	35	20	13.6	3.39	129	.238	.346	0	.000	-2	6	7	2	0.4

● **JOE WILLIS**   Willis, Joseph Denk b: 4/9/1890, Coal Grove, Ohio   d: 12/4/66, Ironton, Ohio   BR/TL, 6'1", 185 lbs.   Deb: 5/3/11

YEAR	TM/L	W	L	PCT	G	GS	CG	SH	SV	IP	H	HR	BB	SO	RAT	ERA	ERA+	OAV	OOB	BH	AVG	PB	PR	/A	PD	TPI
1911	StL-A	0	1	.000	1	1	0	0	0	7	8	0	3	0	14.1	5.14	66	.308	.379	0	—	0	-1	-1	-1	-0.2
	StL-N	0	1	.000	2	2	1	0	0	15	13	0	4	5	10.2	4.20	80	.232	.283	0	.000	-1	-1	-1	0	-0.1
1912	StL-N	4	9	.308	31	17	4	0	2	129²	143	3	62	55	14.6	4.44	77	.288	.372	6	.158	-2	-15	-15	-1	-1.5
1913	StL-N	0	0	—	7	0	0	0	1	9²	9	0	11	6	18.6	7.45	43	.257	.435	0	.000	-0	-5	-5	-0	-0.2
Total	3	4	11	.267	41	20	5	0	3	161¹	173	3	80	66	14.4	4.63	74	.282	.369	6	.125	-2	-22	-22	-1	-2.0

● **LES WILLIS**   Willis, Lester Evans "Wimpy" or "Lefty" b: 1/17/08, Nacogdoches, Tex.   d: 1/22/82, Jasper, Tex.   BL/TL, 5'9.5", 195 lbs.   Deb: 4/28/47

YEAR	TM/L	W	L	PCT	G	GS	CG	SH	SV	IP	H	HR	BB	SO	RAT	ERA	ERA+	OAV	OOB	BH	AVG	PB	PR	/A	PD	TPI
1947	Cle-A	0	2	.000	22	0	0	0	0	44	58	3	24	10	16.8	3.48	100	.324	.404	1	.091	-1	1	0	-1	-0.2

● **MIKE WILLIS**   Willis, Michael Henry b: 12/26/50, Oklahoma City, Okla.   BL/TL, 6'2", 210 lbs.   Deb: 4/13/77

YEAR	TM/L	W	L	PCT	G	GS	CG	SH	SV	IP	H	HR	BB	SO	RAT	ERA	ERA+	OAV	OOB	BH	AVG	PB	PR	/A	PD	TPI
1977	Tor-A	2	6	.250	43	3	0	0	5	107¹	105	15	38	59	12.0	3.94	106	.260	.324	0	—	0	1	3	1	0.3
1978	Tor-A	3	7	.300	44	2	1	0	7	100²	104	11	39	52	12.8	4.56	86	.271	.338	0	—	0	-9	-7	-0	-0.8
1979	Tor-A	0	3	.000	17	1	0	0	0	26²	35	1	16	18	17.6	8.44	51	.333	.426	0	—	0	-13	-12	-1	-1.2
1980	Tor-A	2	1	.667	20	0	0	0	3	26¹	25	3	11	14	12.6	1.71	252	.248	.327	0	—	0	7	8	0	0.7
1981	Tor-A	0	4	.000	20	0	0	0	0	35	43	6	20	16	16.5	5.91	67	.301	.390	0	—	0	-9	-8	0	-0.8
Total	5	7	21	.250	144	6	1	0	15	296	312	36	124	149	13.3	4.59	89	.274	.347	0	—	0	-22	-16	1	-1.8

● **RON WILLIS**   Willis, Ronald Earl b: 7/12/43, Willisville, Tenn.   d: 11/21/77, Memphis, Tenn.   BR/TR, 6'2", 195 lbs.   Deb: 9/20/66

YEAR	TM/L	W	L	PCT	G	GS	CG	SH	SV	IP	H	HR	BB	SO	RAT	ERA	ERA+	OAV	OOB	BH	AVG	PB	PR	/A	PD	TPI
1966	StL-N	0	0	—	4	0	0	0	1	3	1	0	1	2	6.0	0.00	—	.100	.182	0	—	0	1	1	-0	0.1
1967	*StL-N	6	5	.545	65	0	0	0	10	81	76	3	43	43	13.6	2.67	123	.257	.357	3	.375	1	6	6	2	1.3
1968	*StL-N	2	3	.400	48	0	0	0	4	63²	50	4	28	39	11.2	3.39	85	.213	.299	0	.000	-1	-3	-4	1	-0.4
1969	StL-N	1	2	.333	26	0	0	0	1	32¹	26	4	19	23	12.8	4.18	86	.224	.338	1	1.000	0	-2	-2	1	0.0
	Hou-N	0	0	—	3	0	0	0	0	2¹	3	0	2	2	11.6	0.00	—	.300	.300	0	—	0	1	1	-0	0.0
	Yr	1	2	.333	29	0	0	0	1	34²	29	4	19	25	12.5	3.89	92	.223	.322	1	1.000	0	-1	-1	1	0.0
1970	SD-N	2	2	.500	42	0	0	0	4	56	53	4	28	20	13.7	4.02	99	.247	.344	0	.000	1	0	-0	1	0.1
Total	5	11	12	.478	188	0	0	0	19	238¹	209	15	119	124	12.7	3.32	102	.237	.334	4	.160	1	4	2	5	1.1

● **VIC WILLIS**   Willis, Victor Gazaway b: 4/12/1876, Cecil Co., Md.   d: 8/3/47, Elkton, Md.   BR/TR, 6'2", 185 lbs.   Deb: 4/20/1898   H

YEAR	TM/L	W	L	PCT	G	GS	CG	SH	SV	IP	H	HR	BB	SO	RAT	ERA	ERA+	OAV	OOB	BH	AVG	PB	PR	/A	PD	TPI
1898	Bos-N	25	13	.658	41	38	29	1	0	311	264	5	148	160	12.8	2.84	130	.228	.331	17	.145	-6	27	30	-0	2.5
1899	Bos-N	27	8	.771	41	38	35	5	2	342²	277	6	117	120	11.1	2.50	167	.221	.303	29	.216	-4	52	63	0	5.3
1900	Bos-N	10	17	.370	32	29	22	2	0	236	258	11	106	53	14.3	4.19	98	.277	.359	12	.136	-6	-13	-2	-2	-0.9
1901	Bos-N	20	17	.541	38	35	33	6	0	305¹	262	6	78	133	10.3	2.36	153	.238	.286	20	.187	-1	33	43	-1	4.6
1902	Bos-N	27	20	.574	51	46	45	4	3	410	372	6	101	225	10.7	2.20	129	.242	.295	23	.153	-6	27	29	4	3.1
1903	Bos-N	12	18	.400	33	32	29	2	0	278	256	1	88	125	11.5	2.98	108	.251	.317	24	.188	-1	9	7	3	0.8
1904	Bos-N	18	25	.419	43	43	39	2	0	350	357	7	109	196	12.3	2.85	97	.266	.327	27	.182	1	-4	-7	4	0.0
1905	Bos-N	12	29	.293	41	41	36	4	0	342	340	7	107	149	12.1	3.21	90	.265	.328	20	.153	-3	-8	-4	6	-0.1
1906	Pit-N	23	13	.639	41	36	32	6	1	322	295	0	76	124	10.5	1.73	154	.250	.298	20	.174	-1	32	34	5	4.5
1907	Pit-N	21	11	.656	39	37	27	6	1	292²	234	4	69	107	9.5	2.34	104	.219	.271	14	.136	-2	4	3	2	0.3
1908	Pit-N	23	11	.676	41	38	25	7	0	304²	239	2	69	97	9.3	2.07	111	.213	.262	17	.165	-1	10	8	-1	0.7
1909	*Pit-N	22	11	.667	39	35	24	4	1	289²	243	3	83	95	10.3	2.24	122	.231	.289	14	.136	-2	12	16	1	1.6
1910	StL-N	9	12	.429	33	33	19	1	1	212	224	6	61	67	12.1	3.35	89	.275	.326	11	.167	-2	-8	-9	2	-0.8
Total	13	249	205	.548	513	471	388	50	11	3996	3621	66	1212	1651	11.2	2.63	118	.243	.307	248	.166	-33	172	208	27	22.0

● **CLAUDE WILLOUGHBY**   Willoughby, Claude William "Flunky" or "Weeping Willie"
b: 11/14/1898, Buffalo, Kan.   d: 8/14/73, McPherson, Kan.   BR/TR, 5'9.5", 165 lbs.   Deb: 9/18/25

YEAR	TM/L	W	L	PCT	G	GS	CG	SH	SV	IP	H	HR	BB	SO	RAT	ERA	ERA+	OAV	OOB	BH	AVG	PB	PR	/A	PD	TPI
1925	Phi-N	2	1	.667	3	3	1	0	0	23	26	0	11	6	14.9	1.96	244	.295	.380	0	.000	-1	6	7	1	0.7
1926	Phi-N	8	12	.400	47	18	6	0	1	168	218	7	71	37	15.8	5.95	70	.327	.396	11	.212	-1	-40	-34	3	-3.3
1927	Phi-N	3	7	.300	35	6	1	1	2	97²	126	7	53	14	16.7	6.54	63	.321	.404	2	.077	-2	-28	-26	-1	-2.6
1928	Phi-N	6	5	.545	35	13	5	1	1	130²	180	6	43	26	18.3	5.30	81	.340	.432	6	.150	-1	-19	-15	-1	-1.2
1929	Phi-N	15	14	.517	49	34	14	1	4	243¹	288	15	108	50	14.8	4.99	104	.296	.370	13	.143	-5	-7	-5	1	0.5
1930	Phi-N	4	17	.190	41	24	5	1	1	153	241	17	68	38	18.3	7.59	72	.369	.430	5	.104	-4	-44	-36	2	-3.9
1931	Pit-N	0	2	.000	9	2	1	0	0	25²	32	4	12	4	15.4	6.31	61	.305	.376	2	.286	0	-7	-7	0	-0.4
Total	7	38	58	.396	219	100	33	4	9	841¹	1111	56	406	175	16.4	5.84	81	.326	.401	39	.143	-14	-140	-106	8	-10.2

YEAR TM/L	W	L	PCT	G	GS	CG	SH	SV	IP	H	HR	BB	SO	RAT	ERA	ERA+	OAV	OOB	BH	AVG	PB	PR	/A	PD	TPI

● JIM WILLOUGHBY — Willoughby, James Arthur b: 1/31/49, Salinas, Cal. BR/TR, 6'2", 185 lbs. Deb: 9/5/71

YEAR TM/L	W	L	PCT	G	GS	CG	SH	SV	IP	H	HR	BB	SO	RAT	ERA	ERA+	OAV	OOB	BH	AVG	PB	PR	/A	PD	TPI
1971 SF-N	0	1	.000	2	1	0	0	0	4	8	0	1	3	20.3	9.00	38	.400	.429	0	.000	-0	-2	-2	0	-0.5
1972 SF-N	6	4	.600	11	11	7	0	0	87²	72	8	14	40	9.0	2.36	148	.222	.259	5	.185	0	11	11	0	1.4
1973 SF-N	4	5	.444	39	12	1	1	1	123	138	21	37	60	13.0	4.68	82	.295	.350	4	.143	1	-14	-12	-1	-0.8
1974 SF-N	1	4	.200	18	4	0	0	0	40²	51	7	9	12	13.3	4.65	82	.304	.339	1	.100	-0	-5	-4	1	-0.4
1975 *Bos-A	5	2	.714	24	0	0	0	8	48¹	46	6	16	29	11.9	3.54	115	.247	.314	0	—	0	1	1	0	0.3
1976 Bos-A	3	12	.200	54	0	0	0	10	99	94	4	31	37	12.1	2.82	139	.256	.328	0	.000	0	8	12	1	2.2
1977 Bos-A	6	2	.750	31	0	0	0	2	54²	54	5	18	33	12.2	4.94	91	.258	.323	0	—	0	-5	-3	1	-0.3
1978 Chi-A	1	6	.143	59	0	0	0	13	93¹	95	6	19	36	11.4	3.86	99	.275	.320	0	—	0	-1	-1	2	0.1
Total 8	26	36	.419	238	28	8	1	34	550²	558	57	145	250	11.8	3.79	102	.267	.321	10	.149	1	-8	4	5	2.0

● FRANK WILLS — Wills, Frank Lee b: 10/26/58, New Orleans, La. BR/TR, 6'2", 202 lbs. Deb: 7/31/83

YEAR TM/L	W	L	PCT	G	GS	CG	SH	SV	IP	H	HR	BB	SO	RAT	ERA	ERA+	OAV	OOB	BH	AVG	PB	PR	/A	PD	TPI
1983 KC-A	2	1	.667	6	4	0	0	0	34²	35	2	15	23	13.0	4.15	98	.259	.333	0	—	0	-0	-0	-0	-0.1
1984 KC-A	2	3	.400	10	5	0	0	0	37	39	3	13	21	12.6	5.11	79	.271	.331	0	—	0	-5	-4	-1	-0.6
1985 Sea-A	5	11	.313	24	18	1	0	1	123	122	18	68	67	14.1	6.00	70	.266	.365	0	—	0	-25	-24	0	-2.7
1986 Cle-A	4	4	.500	26	0	0	0	4	40¹	43	6	16	32	13.2	4.91	84	.272	.339	0	—	0	-3	-3	0	-0.6
1987 Cle-A	0	1	.000	6	0	0	0	1	5¹	3	0	7	4	16.9	5.06	89	.176	.417	0	—	0	-0	-0	0	-0.1
1988 Tor-A	0	0	—	10	0	0	0	0	20²	22	2	6	19	12.2	5.23	75	.272	.322	0	—	0	-3	-3	1	0.0
1989 Tor-A	3	1	.750	24	4	0	0	0	71¹	65	4	30	41	12.1	3.66	103	.242	.320	0	—	0	2	1	-0	0.1
1990 Tor-A	6	4	.600	44	4	0	0	0	99	101	13	38	72	12.7	4.73	83	.266	.334	0	—	0	-9	-9	0	-0.8
1991 Tor-A	0	1	.000	4	0	0	0	0	4¹	9	2	3	2	29.1	16.62	25	.421	.560	0	—	0	-6	-6	0	-1.1
Total 9	22	26	.458	154	35	1	0	6	435²	438	50	198	281	13.3	5.06	80	.264	.344	0	—	0	-50	-50	0	-5.9

● TED WILLS — Wills, Theodore Carl b: 2/9/34, Fresno, Cal. BL/TL, 6'2", 200 lbs. Deb: 5/24/59

YEAR TM/L	W	L	PCT	G	GS	CG	SH	SV	IP	H	HR	BB	SO	RAT	ERA	ERA+	OAV	OOB	BH	AVG	PB	PR	/A	PD	TPI
1959 Bos-A	2	6	.250	9	8	2	0	0	56¹	68	9	24	24	14.9	5.27	77	.302	.372	4	.250	1	-9	-8	-0	-0.9
1960 Bos-A	1	1	.500	15	0	0	0	1	30¹	38	4	16	28	16.9	7.42	55	.317	.410	2	.250	1	-12	-11	1	-0.6
1961 Bos-A	3	2	.600	17	0	0	0	0	19²	24	2	19	11	19.7	5.95	70	.304	.439	0	.000	-0	-4	-4	0	-0.9
1962 Bos-A	0	0	—	1	0	0	0	0	0²	2	0	1	0	—	∞	—	1.000	1.000	0	—	-0	-1	-1	0	-0.1
Cin-N	0	2	.000	26	5	0	0	3	61	61	12	23	58	13.1	5.31	76	.266	.346	5	.313	1	-9	-9	-0	-0.3
1965 Chi-A	2	0	1.000	15	0	0	0	1	19	17	2	14	12	15.2	2.84	112	.258	.395	0	.000	0	1	1	0	0.1
Total 5	8	11	.421	83	13	2	0	5	186¹	210	29	97	133	15.3	5.51	72	.291	.383	11	.250	3	-34	-32	1	-2.7

● PAUL WILMET — Wilmet, Paul Richard b: 11/8/58, Green Bay, Wis. BR/TR, 5'11", 170 lbs. Deb: 7/25/89

YEAR TM/L	W	L	PCT	G	GS	CG	SH	SV	IP	H	HR	BB	SO	RAT	ERA	ERA+	OAV	OOB	BH	AVG	PB	PR	/A	PD	TPI
1989 Tex-A	0	0	—	3	0	0	0	0	2¹	5	0	2	1	27.0	15.43	26	.417	.500	0	—	0	-3	-3	0	0.0

● WHITEY WILSHERE — Wilshere, Vernon Sprague b: 8/3/12, Poplar Ridge, N.Y. d: 5/23/85, Cooperstown, N.Y. BL/TL, 6', 180 lbs. Deb: 6/24/34

YEAR TM/L	W	L	PCT	G	GS	CG	SH	SV	IP	H	HR	BB	SO	RAT	ERA	ERA+	OAV	OOB	BH	AVG	PB	PR	/A	PD	TPI
1934 Phi-A	0	1	.000	9	2	0	0	0	21²	39	0	15	19	22.8	12.05	36	.394	.478	0	.000	-0	-18	-18	-1	-0.8
1935 Phi-A	9	9	.500	27	18	7	3	1	142¹	136	8	78	80	14.2	4.05	112	.253	.358	4	.093	-4	6	8	-0	0.5
1936 Phi-A	1	2	.333	5	3	0	0	0	18¹	21	1	19	4	19.6	6.87	74	.288	.435	0	.000	-0	-4	-4	-0	-0.5
Total 3	10	12	.455	41	23	7	3	1	182¹	196	9	112	103	15.7	5.28	87	.276	.383	4	.080	-4	-15	-14	-1	-0.8

● TERRY WILSHUSEN — Wilshusen, Terry Wayne b: 3/22/49, Atascadero, Cal. BR/TR, 6'2", 210 lbs. Deb: 4/7/73

YEAR TM/L	W	L	PCT	G	GS	CG	SH	SV	IP	H	HR	BB	SO	RAT	ERA	ERA+	OAV	OOB	BH	AVG	PB	PR	/A	PD	TPI
1973 Cal-A	0	0	—	1	0	0	0	0	0¹	1	0	0	0	81.0	81.00	4	.000	.750	0	—	0	-3	-3	0	0.4

● DON WILSON — Wilson, Donald Edward b: 2/12/45, Monroe, La. d: 1/5/75, Houston, Tex. BR/TR, 6'3", 205 lbs. Deb: 9/29/66

YEAR TM/L	W	L	PCT	G	GS	CG	SH	SV	IP	H	HR	BB	SO	RAT	ERA	ERA+	OAV	OOB	BH	AVG	PB	PR	/A	PD	TPI
1966 Hou-N	1	0	1.000	1	0	0	0	0	6	5	1	1	7	9.0	3.00	114	.238	.273	1	.500	1	0	0	0	0.1
1967 Hou-N	10	9	.526	31	28	7	3	0	184	141	10	69	159	10.6	2.79	119	.209	.289	6	.091	-2	12	11	-2	0.7
1968 Hou-N	13	16	.448	33	30	9	3	0	208²	187	9	70	175	11.3	3.28	90	.236	.302	15	.214	4	-7	-7	-2	-0.8
1969 Hou-N	16	12	.571	34	34	13	1	0	225	210	16	97	235	12.6	4.00	89	.245	.328	8	.099	-1	-10	-11	-0	-1.5
1970 Hou-N	11	6	.647	29	27	3	0	0	184¹	188	15	66	94	12.7	3.91	99	.259	.327	8	.116	-2	-3	-1	-3	-0.6
1971 Hou-N★	16	10	.615	35	34	18	3	0	268	195	15	79	180	9.4	2.45	137	**.202**	.268	14	.154	-1	30	27	-3	2.2
1972 Hou-N	15	10	.600	33	33	13	3	0	228¹	196	16	66	172	10.4	2.68	125	.233	.290	8	.105	-2	20	17	1	1.7
1973 Hou-N	11	16	.407	37	32	10	3	2	239¹	187	21	92	149	10.8	3.20	114	.213	.293	14	.177	1	12	12	-2	1.1
1974 Hou-N	11	13	.458	33	27	5	1	0	204²	170	16	100	112	12.0	3.08	112	.227	.321	13	.206	2	12	9	-3	1.0
Total 9	104	92	.531	266	245	78	20	2	1748¹	1479	119	640	1283	11.2	3.15	109	.228	.301	87	.146	-1	73	57	-14	3.9

● DUANE WILSON — Wilson, Duane Lewis b: 6/29/34, Wichita, Kan. BL/TL, 6'1", 185 lbs. Deb: 7/3/58

YEAR TM/L	W	L	PCT	G	GS	CG	SH	SV	IP	H	HR	BB	SO	RAT	ERA	ERA+	OAV	OOB	BH	AVG	PB	PR	/A	PD	TPI
1958 Bos-A	0	0	—	2	2	0	0	0	6¹	10	0	7	3	24.2	5.68	70	.400	.531	0	.000	-0	-1	-1	0	0.0

● FIN WILSON — Wilson, Finis Elbert b: 12/9/1889, East Fork, Ky. d: 3/9/59, Coral Gables, Fla. BL/TL, 6'1", 194 lbs. Deb: 9/26/14

YEAR TM/L	W	L	PCT	G	GS	CG	SH	SV	IP	H	HR	BB	SO	RAT	ERA	ERA+	OAV	OOB	BH	AVG	PB	PR	/A	PD	TPI
1914 Bro-F	0	1	.000	2	1	0	0	0	7	9	0	11	4	23.1	7.71	37	.269	.486	1	.500	1	-4	-4	-0	-0.4
1915 Bro-F	1	8	.111	18	11	5	0	0	102¹	85	2	53	47	12.5	3.78	72	.249	.356	11	.314	2	-12	-12	-0	-0.7
Total 2	1	9	.100	20	12	6	0	0	109¹	92	2	64	51	13.2	4.03	68	.250	.367	12	.324	3	-16	-16	-0	-1.1

● ZEKE WILSON — Wilson, Frank Ealton b: 12/24/1869, Benton, Ala. d: 4/26/28, Montgomery, Ala. BR/TR, 5'10", 165 lbs. Deb: 4/23/1895

YEAR TM/L	W	L	PCT	G	GS	CG	SH	SV	IP	H	HR	BB	SO	RAT	ERA	ERA+	OAV	OOB	BH	AVG	PB	PR	/A	PD	TPI
1895 Bos-N	2	4	.333	6	6	4	0	0	45	54	1	27	5	16.2	5.20	98	.293	.384	6	.316	1	-2	-0	1	0.1
Cle-N	3	1	.750	8	7	3	0	0	44²	63	3	20	16	17.1	4.23	118	.328	.397	2	.111	-2	3	4	-0	0.0
Yr	5	5	.500	14	13	7	0	0	89²	117	4	47	21	16.7	4.72	107	.311	.391	8	.216	-2	1	3	1	0.1
1896 Cle-N	17	9	.654	33	29	20	1	1	240	265	9	81	56	13.3	4.01	113	.278	.339	27	.270	2	9	14	6	1.8
1897 Cle-N	16	11	.593	34	30	26	1	0	263²	323	9	83	69	14.2	4.16	108	.299	.354	26	.224	-3	4	10	1	0.6
1898 Cle-N	13	18	.419	33	31	28	1	0	254²	307	4	51	45	12.9	3.60	100	.296	.354	21	.178	-3	0	4	0	0.1
1899 StL-N	1	1	.500	5	2	2	0	0	26	30	0	4	3	12.5	4.50	88	.288	.327	0	.000	-1	-2	-1	0	-0.1
Total 5	52	44	.542	119	105	83	3	1	874	1042	26	266	194	13.8	4.03	106	.293	.347	82	.215	-8	13	25	14	2.5

● GARY WILSON — Wilson, Gary Morris b: 1/1/70, Arcata, Cal. BR/TR, 6'3", 190 lbs. Deb: 4/28/95

YEAR TM/L	W	L	PCT	G	GS	CG	SH	SV	IP	H	HR	BB	SO	RAT	ERA	ERA+	OAV	OOB	BH	AVG	PB	PR	/A	PD	TPI
1995 Pit-N	0	1	.000	10	0	0	0	0	14¹	13	2	6	8	12.6	5.02	86	.241	.328	0	—	0	-1	-1	-0	-0.1

● GARY WILSON — Wilson, Gary Steven b: 11/21/54, Camden, Ark. BR/TR, 6'2", 185 lbs. Deb: 4/13/79

YEAR TM/L	W	L	PCT	G	GS	CG	SH	SV	IP	H	HR	BB	SO	RAT	ERA	ERA+	OAV	OOB	BH	AVG	PB	PR	/A	PD	TPI
1979 Hou-N	0	0	—	6	0	0	0	0	7¹	15	2	6	6	25.8	12.27	29	.441	.525	0	—	0	-7	-7	-0	-0.7

● GLENN WILSON — Wilson, Glenn Dwight b: 12/22/58, Baytown, Tex. BR/TR, 6'1", 190 lbs. Deb: 4/15/82 ♦

YEAR TM/L	W	L	PCT	G	GS	CG	SH	SV	IP	H	HR	BB	SO	RAT	ERA	ERA+	OAV	OOB	BH	AVG	PB	PR	/A	PD	TPI
1987 Phi-N	0	0	—	1	0	0	0	0	1								.000	.000	150	.264	0	0	0	0	0.0

● TEX WILSON — Wilson, Gomer Russell b: 7/8/01, Trenton, Tex. d: 9/15/46, Sulphur Springs, Tex. BR/TL, 5'10", 170 lbs. Deb: 9/2/24

YEAR TM/L	W	L	PCT	G	GS	CG	SH	SV	IP	H	HR	BB	SO	RAT	ERA	ERA+	OAV	OOB	BH	AVG	PB	PR	/A	PD	TPI
1924 Bro-N	0	0	—	2	0	0	0	0	3²	7	0	1	2	19.6	14.73	25	.412	.444	0	.000	-0	-4	-4	0	0.0

● HIGHBALL WILSON — Wilson, Howard Paul b: 8/9/1878, Philadelphia, Pa. d: 10/16/34, Havre De Grace, Md TR, Deb: 9/13/1899

YEAR TM/L	W	L	PCT	G	GS	CG	SH	SV	IP	H	HR	BB	SO	RAT	ERA	ERA+	OAV	OOB	BH	AVG	PB	PR	/A	PD	TPI
1899 Cle-N	0	1	.000	1	1	1	0	0	8	12	0	6	1	19.1	9.00	41	.343	.425	1	.333	0	-5	-5	-0	-0.4
1902 Phi-A	7	5	.583	13	10	8	0	0	96¹	103	1	19	18	12.2	2.43	151	.274	.324	6	.171	-1	12	13	-1	1.2
1903 Was-A	7	18	.280	30	28	25	1	0	242¹	269	7	43	56	12.0	3.31	95	.280	.318	17	.200	2	-9	-5	-4	-0.6
1904 Was-A	0	3	.000	3	3	3	0	0	25	33	0	4	11	14.0	4.68	57	.317	.355	2	.222	1	-6	-6	0	-0.5
Total 4	14	27	.341	47	42	37	1	0	371²	417	8	71	86	12.3	3.29	99	.283	.325	26	.197	2	-7	-2	-5	-0.3

● JIM WILSON — Wilson, James Alger b: 2/20/22, San Diego, Cal. d: 9/2/86, Newport Beach, Cal BR/TR, 6'1.5", 200 lbs. Deb: 4/18/45

YEAR TM/L	W	L	PCT	G	GS	CG	SH	SV	IP	H	HR	BB	SO	RAT	ERA	ERA+	OAV	OOB	BH	AVG	PB	PR	/A	PD	TPI
1945 Bos-A	6	8	.429	23	21	8	2	0	144¹	121	7	88	50	13.1	3.30	103	.228	.339	13	.245	2	1	2	-2	0.1
1946 Bos-A	0	0	—	1	0	0	0	0	0²	2	0	1	0	27.0	27.00	14	.500	.500	0	—	-0	-2	-2	-0	0.0
1948 StL-A	0	0	—	4	0	0	0	0	2²	5	0	5	1	33.8	13.50	34	.417	.588	0	—	0	-3	-3	0	-0.1
1949 Phi-A	0	0	—	2	0	0	0	0	2	5	0	6	2	21.6	14.40	29	.350	.480	0	—	-0	-6	-6	-0	-0.1
1951 Bos-N	7	7	.500	20	15	5	0	1	110	131	14	40	33	14.3	5.40	68	.294	.357	7	.179	-1	-18	-21	-1	-2.4
1952 Bos-N	12	14	.462	33	33	14	0	0	234	234	16	50	104	12.6	4.23	85	.262	.333	14	.163	-0	-13	-16	-1	-1.8
1953 Mil-N	4	9	.308	20	18	5	0	0	114	107	16	43	71	12.1	4.34	90	.243	.315	6	.167	0	-1	-5	1	-0.3
1954 Mil-N☆	8	2	.800	27	19	6	4	0	127²	129	12	36	52	12.0	3.52	106	.266	.323	7	.159	0	8	3	1	0.3

YEAR	TM/L	W	L	PCT	G	GS	CG	SH	SV	IP	H	HR	BB	SO	RAT	ERA	ERA+	OAV	OOB	BH	AVG	PB	PR	/A	PD	TPI
1955	Bal-A☆	12	18	.400	34	31	14	4	0	235¹	200	17	87	96	11.1	3.44	111	.228	.300	15	.169	-2	14	10	-0	1.0
1956	Bal-A	4	2	.667	7	7	1	0	0	48¹	49	5	16	31	12.5	5.03	78	.268	.333	4	.267	2	-5	-6	-0	-0.4
	Chi-A★	9	12	.429	28	21	6	3	0	159²	149	15	70	82	12.5	4.06	101	.248	.329	19	.306	4	2	1	-0	0.5
	Yr	13	14	.481	35	28	7	3	0	208	198	20	86	113	12.4	4.28	95	.252	.327	23	.299	6	-3	-5	-0	0.1
1957	Chi-A	15	8	.652	30	29	12	**5**	0	201²	189	22	65	100	11.5	3.48	107	.249	.310	10	.147	-0	7	6	-2	0.4
1958	Chi-A	9	9	.500	28	23	8	1	1	155²	156	21	63	70	12.7	4.10	89	.268	.341	4	.078	-6	-8	-1	-1.3
Total	12	86	89	.491	257	217	75	19	2	1539	1479	151	608	692	12.4	4.01	93	.254	.327	99	.181	4	-21	-45	-5	-4.0

● **JACK WILSON** Wilson, John Francis "Black Jack" b: 4/12/12, Portland, Ore. d: 4/19/95, Edmonds, Wash. BR/TR, 5'11", 210 lbs. Deb: 9/9/34

YEAR	TM/L	W	L	PCT	G	GS	CG	SH	SV	IP	H	HR	BB	SO	RAT	ERA	ERA+	OAV	OOB	BH	AVG	PB	PR	/A	PD	TPI
1934	Phi-A	0	1	.000	2	2	1	0	0	9	15	1	9	2	24.0	12.00	37	.405	.522		.000	-0	-8	-8	-0	-0.6
1935	Bos-A	3	4	.429	23	6	2	0	1	64	72	0	36	19	15.5	4.22	112	.290	.385	5	.313	2	2	4	1	0.7
1936	Bos-A	6	8	.429	43	9	2	0	3	136¹	152	4	86	74	15.8	4.42	120	.284	.384	11	.220	-0	9	13	0	1.1
1937	Bos-A	16	10	.615	42	21	14	1	7	221¹	209	13	119	137	13.5	3.70	128	.248	.343	14	.165	-3	23	26	1	1.5
1938	Bos-A	15	15	.500	37	27	11	3	1	194²	200	16	91	96	13.5	4.30	115	.262	.342	15	.221	0	11	14	-1	1.7
1939	Bos-A	11	11	.500	36	22	6	0	2	177¹	198	10	75	80	13.9	4.67	101	.281	.351	10	.159	-4	-1	1	-0	-0.2
1940	Bos-A	12	6	.667	41	16	9	0	5	157²	170	17	87	102	14.8	5.08	89	.270	.362	18	.273	4	-12	-10	-2	-0.8
1941	Bos-A	4	13	.235	27	12	4	1	1	116¹	140	7	70	55	16.6	5.03	83	.300	.397	7	.159	-1	-11	-11	-2	-1.3
1942	Was-A	1	4	.200	12	6	1	0	0	42	57	2	23	18	17.4	6.64	55	.322	.403	2	.118	-1	-14	-14	-1	-1.6
	Det-A	0	0	—	9	0	0	0	0	13	20	3	5	7	17.3	4.85	81	.351	.403	0	.000	-0	-2	-1	0	0.0
	Yr	1	4	.200	21	6	1	0	0	55	77	5	28	25	17.2	6.22	60	.328	.399	2	.111	-1	-16	-15	-0	-1.6
Total	9	68	72	.486	281	121	50	5	20	1131²	1233	73	601	590	14.7	4.59	102	.276	.364	82	.199	-3	-4	13	1	1.5

● **JOHN WILSON** Wilson, John Nicodemus b: 6/15/1890, Boonsboro, Md. d: 9/23/54, Annapolis, Md. BR/TL, 6'1", 185 lbs. Deb: 6/11/13

YEAR	TM/L	W	L	PCT	G	GS	CG	SH	SV	IP	H	HR	BB	SO	RAT	ERA	ERA+	OAV	OOB	BH	AVG	PB	PR	/A	PD	TPI
1913	Was-A	0	0	—	3	0	0	0	0	4	4	0	3	1	15.8	4.50	66	.267	.389	0	—	0	-1	-1	0	0.0

● **JOHN WILSON** Wilson, John Samuel b: 4/25/03, Coal City, Ala. d: 8/27/80, Chattanooga, Tenn. BR/TR, 6'2", 164 lbs. Deb: 5/9/27

YEAR	TM/L	W	L	PCT	G	GS	CG	SH	SV	IP	H	HR	BB	SO	RAT	ERA	ERA+	OAV	OOB	BH	AVG	PB	PR	/A	PD	TPI
1927	Bos-A	0	2	.000	5	2	2	0	0	25¹	31	1	13	8	15.6	3.55	119	.326	.407	1	.111	-1	2	2	-0	0.0
1928	Bos-A	0	0	—	2	0	0	0	0	5	6	0	6	1	21.6	9.00	46	.333	.500	0	.000	-0	-3	-3	0	0.0
Total	2	0	2	.000	7	2	2	0	0	30¹	37	1	19	9	16.6	4.45	94	.327	.424	1	.100	-1	-1	-1	0	0.0

● **MAX WILSON** Wilson, Max b: 6/3/16, Haw River, N.C. d: 1/2/77, Greensboro, N.C. BL/TL, 5'7", 160 lbs. Deb: 9/10/40

YEAR	TM/L	W	L	PCT	G	GS	CG	SH	SV	IP	H	HR	BB	SO	RAT	ERA	ERA+	OAV	OOB	BH	AVG	PB	PR	/A	PD	TPI
1940	Phi-N	0	0	—	3	0	0	0	0	7	16	1	2	3	23.1	12.86	30	.444	.474	0	.000	-0	-7	-7	0	0.0
1946	Was-A	0	1	.000	9	0	0	0	0	12²	16	1	9	8	17.8	7.11	47	.320	.424	0	.000	-0	-5	-5	-0	-0.4
Total	2	0	1	.000	12	0	0	0	0	19²	32	2	11	11	19.7	9.15	39	.372	.443	0	.000	-0	-12	-12	-0	-0.4

● **PAUL WILSON** Wilson, Paul Anthony b: 3/28/73, Orlando, Fla. BR/TR, 6'5", 235 lbs. Deb: 4/4/96

YEAR	TM/L	W	L	PCT	G	GS	CG	SH	SV	IP	H	HR	BB	SO	RAT	ERA	ERA+	OAV	OOB	BH	AVG	PB	PR	/A	PD	TPI
1996	NY-N	5	12	.294	26	26	1	0	0	149	157	15	71	109	14.4	5.38	73	.268	.357	4	.080	-1	-19	-24	-2	-2.6

● **PETE WILSON** Wilson, Peter Alex b: 10/9/1885, Springfield, Mass. d: 6/5/57, St.Petersburg, Fla TL, Deb: 9/15/08

YEAR	TM/L	W	L	PCT	G	GS	CG	SH	SV	IP	H	HR	BB	SO	RAT	ERA	ERA+	OAV	OOB	BH	AVG	PB	PR	/A	PD	TPI
1908	NY-A	3	3	.500	6	6	4	1	0	39	27	0	33	28	14.1	3.46	72	.191	.349	1	.071	-1	-5	-4	-0	-0.7
1909	NY-A	6	5	.545	14	13	7	1	0	93²	82	2	43	44	12.4	3.17	80	.230	.320	4	.118	-1	-7	-7	-1	-1.0
Total	2	9	8	.529	20	19	11	2	0	132²	109	2	76	72	12.9	3.26	77	.219	.329	5	.104	-2	-12	-11	-1	-1.7

● **EARL WILSON** Wilson, Robert Earl (Name Changed From Wilson, Earl Lawrence) b: 10/2/34, Ponchatoula, La. BR/TR, 6'3", 216 lbs. Deb: 7/28/59

YEAR	TM/L	W	L	PCT	G	GS	CG	SH	SV	IP	H	HR	BB	SO	RAT	ERA	ERA+	OAV	OOB	BH	AVG	PB	PR	/A	PD	TPI
1959	Bos-A	1	1	.500	9	4	0	0	0	23²	21	2	31	17	19.8	6.08	67	.241	.441	4	.500	2	-6	-5	0	-0.2
1960	Bos-A	3	2	.600	13	9	2	0	0	65	61	4	48	40	15.1	4.71	86	.247	.369	4	.174	-0	-6	-5	0	-0.3
1962	Bos-A	12	8	.600	31	28	4	1	0	191¹	163	21	111	137	13.2	3.90	106	.231	.340	12	.174	3	1	5	-1	0.7
1963	Bos-A	11	16	.407	37	34	6	3	0	210²	184	18	105	123	12.4	3.76	101	.234	.325	15	.208	5	-3	1	1	0.7
1964	Bos-A	11	12	.478	33	31	5	0	0	202¹	213	37	73	166	12.8	4.49	86	.269	.332	15	.205	8	-20	-14	-0	-0.7
1965	Bos-A	13	14	.481	36	36	8	1	0	230²	221	27	77	164	11.6	3.98	94	.250	.313	14	.177	8	-13	-7	-1	0.0
1966	Bos-A	5	5	.500	15	14	5	1	0	100²	88	14	36	67	11.3	3.84	99	.235	.306	8	.250	-2	-5	-0	-0	0.3
	Det-A	13	6	.684	23	23	8	2	0	163¹	126	16	38	133	9.3	2.59	134	.213	.265	15	.234	9	15	16	2	3.2
	Yr	18	11	.621	38	37	13	3	0	264	214	30	74	200	10.0	3.07	117	.220	.278	23	.240	12	11	16	2	3.5
1967	Det-A	**22**	11	.667	39	38	12	0	0	264	216	34	92	184	10.6	3.27	100	.224	.294	20	.185	7	-1	-0	2	0.9
1968	*Det-A	13	12	.520	34	33	10	3	0	224¹	192	20	65	168	10.3	2.85	106	.231	.287	20	.227	10	3	4	1	1.7
1969	Det-A	12	10	.545	35	35	5	1	0	214²	209	23	69	150	11.8	3.31	113	.256	.317	10	.132	-0	7	10	1	1.1
1970	Det-A	4	6	.400	18	16	4	1	0	96	87	15	32	74	11.3	4.41	85	.238	.303	6	.194	2	-7	-7	-0	-0.5
	SD-N	1	6	.143	18	17	1	0	0	65	82	5	19	24	14.3	4.85	82	.300	.360	1	.059	-6	-6	-1		-0.7
Total	11	121	109	.526	338	310	69	13	0	2051²	1863	236	796	1452	11.8	3.69	99	.242	.315	144	.195	57	-39	-10	2	6.2

● **ROY WILSON** Wilson, Roy Edward "Lefty" b: 9/13/1896, Foster, Iowa d: 12/3/69, Clarion, Iowa BL/TL, 6', 175 lbs. Deb: 4/18/28

YEAR	TM/L	W	L	PCT	G	GS	CG	SH	SV	IP	H	HR	BB	SO	RAT	ERA	ERA+	OAV	OOB	BH	AVG	PB	PR	/A	PD	TPI
1928	Chi-A	0	0	—	1	0	0	0	0	3¹	2	0	3	2	13.5	0.00	—	.167	.333	0	.000	-0	1	2	0	0.0

● **STEVE WILSON** Wilson, Stephen Douglas b: 12/13/64, Victoria, B.C., Can. BL/TL, 6'4", 205 lbs. Deb: 9/16/88

YEAR	TM/L	W	L	PCT	G	GS	CG	SH	SV	IP	H	HR	BB	SO	RAT	ERA	ERA+	OAV	OOB	BH	AVG	PB	PR	/A	PD	TPI
1988	Tex-A	0	0	—	3	0	0	0	0	7²	7	1	4	11	12.9	5.87	70	.259	.355	0	—	0	-2	-2	-0	-0.1
1989	*Chi-N	6	4	.600	53	8	0	0	2	85²	83	6	31	65	12.1	4.20	89	.257	.324	1	.063	-1	-7	-4	-0	-0.6
1990	Chi-N	4	9	.308	45	15	1	0	0	139	140	17	43	95	12.0	4.79	85	.259	.316	6	.162	-0	-15	-11	-1	-1.0
1991	Chi-N	0	0	—	8	0	0	0	0	12¹	13	1	5	9	13.1	4.38	89	.277	.346	0	.000	-0	-1	-1	-0	-0.1
	LA-N	0	0	—	11	0	0	0	2	8¹	1	0	4	5	5.4	0.00	—	.042	.179	0	.000	-0	3	3	-0	0.1
	Yr	0	0	—	19	0	0	0	2	20²	14	1	9	14	10.0	2.61	144	.194	.284	0	.000	-0	2	3	-0	0.0
1992	LA-N	2	5	.286	60	0	0	0	0	66²	74	6	29	54	14.0	4.18	82	.282	.356	1	.333	-0	-5	-5	-0	-0.6
1993	LA-N	1	0	1.000	25	0	0	0	0	25²	30	2	14	23	15.8	4.56	84	.288	.378	0	.000	-0	-1	-2	-0	-0.1
Total	6	13	18	.419	205	23	1	0	6	345¹	348	33	130	252	12.6	4.40	87	.262	.330	8	.133	-1	-28	-22	-2	-2.4

● **TREVOR WILSON** Wilson, Trevor Kirk b: 6/7/66, Torrance, Cal. BL/TL, 6', 190 lbs. Deb: 9/5/88

YEAR	TM/L	W	L	PCT	G	GS	CG	SH	SV	IP	H	HR	BB	SO	RAT	ERA	ERA+	OAV	OOB	BH	AVG	PB	PR	/A	PD	TPI
1988	SF-N	0	2	.000	4	4	0	0	0	22	25	1	8	15	13.5	4.09	80	.298	.359	2	.286	1	-2	-1	-0	-0.2
1989	SF-N	2	3	.400	14	4	0	0	0	39¹	28	2	24	22	12.8	4.35	78	.207	.344	1	.250	-0	-4	-4	-0	-0.4
1990	SF-N	8	7	.533	27	17	3	2	0	110¹	87	11	49	66	11.2	4.00	91	.218	.305	4	.138	-0	-3	-4	2	-0.4
1991	SF-N	13	11	.542	44	29	2	1	0	202	173	13	77	139	11.4	3.56	100	.234	.310	12	.235	5	3	0	3	0.8
1992	SF-N	8	14	.364	26	26	1	1	0	154	152	18	64	88	13.0	4.21	79	.265	.345	3	.077	-1	-12	-15	-1	-2.0
1993	SF-N	7	5	.583	22	18	1	1	0	110	110	8	40	57	12.8	3.60	100	.275	.350	4	.138	1	5	4	-1	0.3
1995	SF-N	3	4	.429	17	17	0	0	0	82²	82	8	38	38	13.5	3.92	104	.269	.357	7	.233	1	2	1	0	0.3
Total	7	41	46	.471	154	115	7	4	0	720¹	657	61	300	425	12.3	3.87	93	.249	.332	34	.176	7	-9	-21	5	-1.5

● **WALTER WILSON** Wilson, Walter Wood b: 11/24/13, Glenn, Ga. d: 4/17/94, Bremen, Ga. BL/TR, 6'4", 190 lbs. Deb: 4/17/45

YEAR	TM/L	W	L	PCT	G	GS	CG	SH	SV	IP	H	HR	BB	SO	RAT	ERA	ERA+	OAV	OOB	BH	AVG	PB	PR	/A	PD	TPI
1945	Det-A	1	3	.250	25	4	1	0	0	70¹	76	4	35	28	14.6	4.61	76	.284	.373	1	.053	-2	-10	-9	1	-0.6

● **WILLY WILSON** Wilson, William b: 1/7/1884, Columbus, Ohio d: 10/28/25, Seattle, Wash. BR/TR, Deb: 10/3/06

YEAR	TM/L	W	L	PCT	G	GS	CG	SH	SV	IP	H	HR	BB	SO	RAT	ERA	ERA+	OAV	OOB	BH	AVG	PB	PR	/A	PD	TPI
1906	Was-A	0	1	.000	1	1	1	0	0	7	3	0	2	1	7.7	2.57	102	.130	.231	0	.000	-0	0	0	0	0.0

● **MUTT WILSON** Wilson, William Clarence "Lank" b: 7/20/1896, Kiser, N.C. d: 8/31/62, Wildwood, Fla. BR/TR, 6'3", 167 lbs. Deb: 9/11/20

YEAR	TM/L	W	L	PCT	G	GS	CG	SH	SV	IP	H	HR	BB	SO	RAT	ERA	ERA+	OAV	OOB	BH	AVG	PB	PR	/A	PD	TPI
1920	Det-A	1	1	.500	3	2	1	0	0	12¹	16	0	8	4	17.5	4.38	108	.240	.309	1	.250	-0	-0	-0	-0	0.0

● **BILL WILSON** Wilson, William Donald b: 11/6/28, Central City, Neb. BR/TR, 6'2", 200 lbs. Deb: 9/24/50 ♦

YEAR	TM/L	W	L	PCT	G	GS	CG	SH	SV	IP	H	HR	BB	SO	RAT	ERA	ERA+	OAV	OOB	BH	AVG	PB	PR	/A	PD	TPI
1955	KC-A	0	0	—	1	0	0	0	0	1	1	0	1	1	18.0	—		.250	.400	61	.223	0	0	0	0	0.0

● **BILL WILSON** Wilson, William Harlan b: 9/21/42, Pomeroy, Ohio d: 93, BR/TR, 6'2", 200 lbs. Deb: 4/8/69

YEAR	TM/L	W	L	PCT	G	GS	CG	SH	SV	IP	H	HR	BB	SO	RAT	ERA	ERA+	OAV	OOB	BH	AVG	PB	PR	/A	PD	TPI
1969	Phi-N	2	5	.286	37	0	0	0	6	62¹	53	6	36	48	13.0	3.32	107	.231	.338	0	.000	-0	2	2	-1	0.0
1970	Phi-N	1	0	1.000	37	0	0	0	0	58¹	57	5	33	41	13.9	4.78	88	.263	.360	1	.250	-0	-5	-5	-0	-0.1
1971	Phi-N	4	6	.400	40	0	0	0	2	58²	39	4	22	40	9.5	3.07	115	.188	.268	1	.100	-1	8	8	3	0.7
1972	Phi-N	1	1	.500	23	0	0	0	0	30	26	1	11	18	11.1	3.30	109	.234	.303		—	-0	1	1	0	0.1
1973	Phi-N	1	3	.250	44	0	0	0	9	48²	54	7	29	24	15.3	6.66	44	.293	.390	0	.000	-0	-16	-15	-0	-1.5
Total	5	9	15	.375	179	0	0	0	17	258	229	23	131	171	12.6	4.22	88	.241	.335	2	.083	-1	-16	-15	0	-0.8

YEAR TM/L	W	L	PCT	G	GS	CG	SH	SV	IP	H	HR	BB	SO	RAT	ERA	ERA+	OAV	OOB	BH	AVG	PB	PR	/A	PD	TPI

● **HOOKS WILTSE**   Wiltse, George Leroy   b: 9/7/1880, Hamilton, N.Y.   d: 1/21/59, Long Beach, N.Y.   BR/TL, 6′, 185 lbs.   Deb: 4/21/04   FC

YEAR TM/L	W	L	PCT	G	GS	CG	SH	SV	IP	H	HR	BB	SO	RAT	ERA	ERA+	OAV	OOB	BH	AVG	PB	PR	/A	PD	TPI
1904 NY-N	13	3	.813	24	16	14	2	3	164²	150	8	61	105	11.8	2.84	96	.240	.313	15	.224	3	-2	-2	3	0.4
1905 NY-N	15	6	.714	32	19	18	1	4	197	158	5	61	120	10.2	2.47	119	.219	.284	20	.278	7	12	10	5	2.4
1906 NY-N	16	11	.593	38	26	21	4	6	249¹	227	3	58	125	10.4	2.27	115	.241	.288	18	.191	2	10	9	-1	1.2
1907 NY-N	13	12	.520	33	21	14	3	2	190¹	171	4	48	79	10.6	2.18	114	.241	.294	9	.134	0	6	6	2	1.1
1908 NY-N	23	14	.622	44	38	30	7	2	330	266	4	73	118	9.5	2.24	108	.224	.274	26	.236	6	5	7	-0	1.4
1909 NY-N	20	11	.645	37	30	22	4	3	269¹	228	9	51	119	9.5	2.00	128	.233	.275	19	.200	2	18	17	-2	1.9
1910 NY-N	14	12	.538	36	30	18	2	2	235¹	232	4	52	88	10.9	2.72	109	.261	.303	13	.176	0	8	7	-3	0.4
1911 *NY-N	12	9	.571	30	24	11	4	0	187¹	177	7	39	92	10.5	3.27	103	.251	.292	13	.188	-1	3	2	0	0.1
1912 NY-N	9	6	.600	28	17	5	0	3	134	140	7	28	58	11.4	3.16	107	.273	.312	15	.326	4	4	3	2	0.8
1913 *NY-N	0	0	—	17	2	0	0	3	57²	53	1	8	25	9.7	1.56	200	.237	.266	5	.208	0	11	10	0	0.2
1914 NY-N	1	1	.500	20	0	0	0	1	38	41	2	12	19	12.6	2.84	93	.289	.344	2	.667	-2	-0	-1	0	0.1
1915 Bro-F	3	5	.375	18	3	1	0	5	59¹	49	1	7	17	8.8	2.28	120	.226	.257	1	.045	-3	3	3	-1	0.1
Total 12	139	90	.607	357	226	154	27	34	2112¹	1892	54	498	965	10.4	2.47	112	.241	.290	156	.210	22	77	72	5	10.1

● **HAL WILTSE**   Wiltse, Harold James "Whitey"   b: 8/6/03, Clay City, Ill.   d: 11/2/83, Bunkie, La.   BL/TL, 5′9″, 168 lbs.   Deb: 4/13/26

YEAR TM/L	W	L	PCT	G	GS	CG	SH	SV	IP	H	HR	BB	SO	RAT	ERA	ERA+	OAV	OOB	BH	AVG	PB	PR	/A	PD	TPI
1926 Bos-A	8	15	.348	37	29	9	1	0	196¹	201	6	99	59	14.0	4.22	97	.273	.363	5	.085	-5	-4	-3	0	-0.7
1927 Bos-A	10	18	.357	36	29	13	1	1	219	276	5	76	47	14.6	5.10	83	.321	.379	16	.208	-2	-23	-21	1	-2.3
1928 Bos-A	0	2	.000	2	2	1	0	0	12	16	1	1	5	15.0	9.00	46	.314	.364	0	.000	-1	-7	-7	-0	-0.8
StL-A	2	5	.286	26	5	0	0	0	72	93	4	35	23	16.4	5.25	80	.316	.395	5	.227	0	-10	-8	-0	-0.7
Yr	2	7	.222	28	7	1	0	0	84	109	5	36	28	15.9	5.79	72	.313	.382	5	.192	-1	-16	-15	-0	-1.5
1931 Phi-N	0	0	—	1	0	0	0	0	1	3	0	0	0	27.0	9.00	47	.600	.600	0	—	0	-1	-1	0	0.0
Total 4	20	40	.333	102	65	23	2	1	500¹	589	16	211	134	14.7	4.87	85	.303	.375	26	.160	-7	-44	-40	2	-4.5

● **SNAKE WILTSE**   Wiltse, Lewis De Witt   b: 12/5/1871, Bouckville, N.Y.   d: 8/25/28, Harrisburg, Pa.   BR/TL,   Deb: 5/5/01   F

YEAR TM/L	W	L	PCT	G	GS	CG	SH	SV	IP	H	HR	BB	SO	RAT	ERA	ERA+	OAV	OOB	BH	AVG	PB	PR	/A	PD	TPI
1901 Pit-N	1	4	.200	7	5	3	0	0	44¹	57	2	13	10	15.2	4.26	77	.310	.371	3	.158	-1	-5	-5	1	-0.5
Phi-A	13	5	.722	19	19	18	0	1	166	185	3	35	40	12.3	3.58	105	.279	.322	25	.373	8	2	4	1	1.2
1902 Phi-A	8	8	.500	19	17	13	0	1	138	182	7	41	28	14.9	5.15	71	.318	.368	10	.175	-0	-24	-23	-1	-2.3
Bal-A	7	11	.389	19	18	18	0	0	164	215	4	51	37	15.0	5.10	74	.316	.371	39	.295	6	-28	-24	-0	-1.7
Yr	15	19	.441	38	35	31	0	1	302	397	11	92	65	14.8	5.13	73	.316	.366	49	.259	5	-52	-47	-1	-4.0
1903 NY-A	0	3	.000	4	3	2	0	1	25	35	1	6	6	15.1	5.40	58	.330	.372	2	.222	0	-7	-6	-0	-0.7
Total 3	29	31	.483	68	62	54	2	2	537¹	674	15	146	121	14.2	4.59	80	.305	.356	79	.278	13	-62	-55	-1	-4.0

● **FRED WINCHELL**   Winchell, Frederick Russell (b: Frederick Cook)
b: 1/23/1882, Arlington, Mass.   d: 8/8/58, Toronto, Ont., Can.   TR , 5′8″,   Deb: 9/16/09

YEAR TM/L	W	L	PCT	G	GS	CG	SH	SV	IP	H	HR	BB	SO	RAT	ERA	ERA+	OAV	OOB	BH	AVG	PB	PR	/A	PD	TPI
1909 Cle-A	0	3	.000	4	3	0	0	1	14¹	16	1	0	2	7	11.3	6.28	41	.296	.321	1	.200	0	-6	-6	-0	-1.2

● **ED WINEAPPLE**   Wineapple, Edward "Lefty"   b: 8/10/05, Boston, Mass.   d: 7/23/96, Delray Beach, Fla.   BL/TL, 6′, 210 lbs.   Deb: 9/15/29

YEAR TM/L	W	L	PCT	G	GS	CG	SH	SV	IP	H	HR	BB	SO	RAT	ERA	ERA+	OAV	OOB	BH	AVG	PB	PR	/A	PD	TPI
1929 Was-A	0	0	—	1	0	0	0	0	4	7	0	3	1	22.5	4.50	94	.467	.556	0	.000	-0	-0	-0	-0	0.0

● **RALPH WINEGARNER**   Winegarner, Ralph Lee   b: 10/29/09, Benton, Kan.   d: 4/14/88, Wichita, Kan.   BR/TR, 6′, 182 lbs.   Deb: 9/20/30   C♦

YEAR TM/L	W	L	PCT	G	GS	CG	SH	SV	IP	H	HR	BB	SO	RAT	ERA	ERA+	OAV	OOB	BH	AVG	PB	PR	/A	PD	TPI
1932 Cle-A	1	0	1.000	5	1	1	0	0	17¹	7	0	13	5	10.4	1.04	457	.123	.286	1	.143	—	7	7	-0	0.3
1934 Cle-A	5	4	.556	22	6	4	0	0	78¹	91	4	39	32	15.2	5.51	82	.289	.371	10	.196	1	-9	-8	-0	-0.7
1935 Cle-A	2	2	.500	25	4	2	0	0	67¹	89	10	29	41	15.9	5.75	78	.313	.379	26	.310	4	-10	-9	0	-0.7
1936 Cle-A	0	0	—	9	0	0	0	0	14²	18	0	6	3	14.7	4.91	103	.295	.358	2	.125	-1	0	-0	-0	-0.1
1949 StL-A	0	0	—	9	0	0	0	0	16²	24	2	2	8	14.0	7.56	60	.329	.347	2	.400	2	-6	-6	-0	0.1
Total 5	8	6	.571	70	11	7	0	0	194¹	229	13	89	89	14.9	5.33	86	.290	.364	51	.276	5	-18	-16	-1	-0.4

● **JIM WINFORD**   Winford, James Head "Cowboy"   b: 10/9/09, Shelbyville, Tenn.   d: 12/16/70, Miami, Okla.   BR/TR, 6′1″, 180 lbs.   Deb: 9/10/32

YEAR TM/L	W	L	PCT	G	GS	CG	SH	SV	IP	H	HR	BB	SO	RAT	ERA	ERA+	OAV	OOB	BH	AVG	PB	PR	/A	PD	TPI
1932 StL-N	1	1	.500	4	1	0	0	0	8¹	9	0	5	4	15.1	6.48	61	.273	.368	2	.667	1	-2	-2	0	-0.4
1934 StL-N	0	2	.000	5	1	0	0	0	12²	17	0	6	3	17.8	7.82	54	.327	.417	0	.000	-0	-5	-5	-0	-0.6
1935 StL-N	0	0	—	2	1	0	0	0	11¹	13	1	5	7	14.3	3.97	103	.283	.353	0	.000	-0	0	0	-1	-0.1
1936 StL-N	11	10	.524	39	23	10	1	3	192	203	10	68	72	12.9	3.80	104	.269	.333	5	.085	-4	5	3	-4	-0.5
1937 StL-N	2	4	.333	16	4	0	0	0	46¹	56	2	27	17	16.1	5.83	68	.311	.401	1	.125	-1	-10	-10	-0	-1.1
1938 Bro-N	0	1	.000	2	1	0	0	0	5²	9	1	4	4	20.6	11.12	35	.346	.433	0	.000	-0	-5	-5	-0	-0.6
Total 6	14	18	.438	68	31	10	1	3	276¹	307	14	115	107	14.0	4.56	87	.281	.353	8	.108	-3	-17	-18	-5	-3.3

● **ERNIE WINGARD**   Wingard, Ernest James "Jim"   b: 10/17/1900, Prattville, Ala.   d: 1/17/77, Prattville, Ala.   BL/TL, 6′2″, 176 lbs.   Deb: 5/1/24

YEAR TM/L	W	L	PCT	G	GS	CG	SH	SV	IP	H	HR	BB	SO	RAT	ERA	ERA+	OAV	OOB	BH	AVG	PB	PR	/A	PD	TPI
1924 StL-A	13	12	.520	36	26	14	0	1	218	215	6	85	23	12.5	3.51	129	.262	.334	18	.234	-3	17	24	-3	2.4
1925 StL-A	9	10	.474	32	18	8	0	0	145	183	10	77	20	16.3	5.52	85	.319	.403	15	.288	3	-18	-14	2	-1.0
1926 StL-A	5	8	.385	39	16	7	0	0	169	188	9	76	30	14.3	3.57	120	.290	.369	14	.230	1	8	14	3	1.4
1927 StL-A	2	13	.133	38	17	7	0	0	156¹	213	7	79	28	16.9	6.56	66	.340	.415	10	.179	1	-42	-38	2	-2.7
Total 4	29	43	.403	145	77	36	0	4	688¹	799	32	317	101	14.8	4.64	96	.299	.377	57	.232	2	-34	-14	4	0.1

● **TED WINGFIELD**   Wingfield, Frederick Davis   b: 8/7/1899, Bedford, Va.   d: 7/18/75, Johnson City, Tenn.   BR/TR, 5′11″, 168 lbs.   Deb: 9/23/23

YEAR TM/L	W	L	PCT	G	GS	CG	SH	SV	IP	H	HR	BB	SO	RAT	ERA	ERA+	OAV	OOB	BH	AVG	PB	PR	/A	PD	TPI
1923 Was-A	0	0	—	1	0	0	0	0	1	0	0	0	0	0.00	—	.000	.000	0	—	0	0	0	0	0.0
1924 Was-A	0	0	—	4	0	0	0	0	7	9	0	4	2	16.7	2.57	157	.300	.382	0	.000	-0	1	1	-0	0.0
Bos-A	0	2	.000	4	3	2	0	0	25²	23	0	8	4	10.9	2.45	178	.240	.298	3	.333	1	5	5	-0	0.5
Yr	0	2	.000	8	3	2	0	0	32²	32	0	12	6	12.1	2.48	173	.254	.319	3	.273	0	6	7	-0	0.5
1925 Bos-A	12	19	.387	41	27	18	2	2	254¹	267	11	92	30	13.0	3.96	115	.278	.346	23	.245	1	12	16	7	2.5
1926 Bos-A	11	16	.407	43	20	9	1	3	190²	220	11	50	30	12.8	4.44	92	.298	.344	15	.217	-0	-9	-8	2	-0.8
1927 Bos-A	1	7	.125	20	8	2	0	0	74²	105	4	27	11	16.3	5.06	83	.357	.417	4	.222	0	-8	-7	2	-0.4
Total 5	24	44	.353	113	58	31	3	5	553¹	624	24	181	68	13.3	4.18	103	.294	.353	45	.234	1	3	9	11	1.8

● **LAVE WINHAM**   Winham, Lafayette Sharkey "Lefty"   b: 10/23/1881, Brooklyn, N.Y.   d: 9/12/51, Brooklyn, N.Y.   BL/TL, 5′11″, 200 lbs.   Deb: 4/21/02

YEAR TM/L	W	L	PCT	G	GS	CG	SH	SV	IP	H	HR	BB	SO	RAT	ERA	ERA+	OAV	OOB	BH	AVG	PB	PR	/A	PD	TPI
1902 Bro-N	0	0	—	1	0	0	0	0	3	4	0	2	1	18.0	0.00	—	.308	.400	1	—	0	1	1	0	0.0
1903 Pit-N	3	1	.750	5	4	3	1	0	36	33	0	21	22	13.5	2.25	144	.231	.329	1	.071	-1	4	4	-1	0.1
Total 2	3	1	.750	6	4	3	1	0	39	37	0	23	23	13.8	2.08	154	.237	.335	1	.063	-2	5	5	-1	0.1

● **GEORGE WINKELMAN**   Winkelman, George Edward   b: 2/18/1865, Washington, D.C.   d: 5/19/60, Washington, D.C.   BL/TL,   Deb: 8/4/1883   ♦

YEAR TM/L	W	L	PCT	G	GS	CG	SH	SV	IP	H	HR	BB	SO	RAT	ERA	ERA+	OAV	OOB	BH	AVG	PB	PR	/A	PD	TPI
1886 Was-N	0	1	.000	1	1	0	0	0	6	12	0	5	4	25.5	10.50	31	.400	.486	1	.200	-0	-5	-5	-0	-0.5

● **GEORGE WINN**   Winn, George Benjamin "Breezy" or "Lefty"   b: 10/26/1897, Perry, Ga.   d: 11/1/69, Roberta, Ga.   BL/TL, 5′11″, 170 lbs.   Deb: 4/29/19

YEAR TM/L	W	L	PCT	G	GS	CG	SH	SV	IP	H	HR	BB	SO	RAT	ERA	ERA+	OAV	OOB	BH	AVG	PB	PR	/A	PD	TPI
1919 Bos-A	0	0	—	3	0	0	0	0	4²	9	0	3	0	13.5	7.71	39	.353	.389	0	.000	-0	-2	-2	-0	0.0
1922 Cle-A	1	2	.333	8	3	1	0	0	33²	44	5	7	5	13.1	4.54	88	.317	.340	3	.333	-1	-2	-2	-0	-0.1
1923 Cle-A	0	0	—	1	0	0	0	0	2	0	0	1	0	4.5	0.00	—	.000	.143	0	—	0	1	1	-0	0.0
Total 3	1	2	.333	12	3	1	0	0	40¹	50	2	7	7	12.7	4.69	83	.309	.337	3	.300	1	-3	-4	-0	-0.1

● **JIM WINN**   Winn, James Francis   b: 9/23/59, Stockton, Cal.   BR/TR, 6′3″, 210 lbs.   Deb: 4/10/83

YEAR TM/L	W	L	PCT	G	GS	CG	SH	SV	IP	H	HR	BB	SO	RAT	ERA	ERA+	OAV	OOB	BH	AVG	PB	PR	/A	PD	TPI
1983 Pit-N	1	0	—	4	0	0	0	0	11	12	2	4	3	14.7	7.36	50	.267	.353	—	0	-5	-4	0	0.0
1984 Pit-N	1	0	1.000	9	0	0	0	0	18²	19	2	9	11	13.5	3.86	93	.264	.346	0	.000	-0	-1	-1	-0	0.0
1985 Pit-N	3	6	.333	30	7	0	0	0	75²	77	4	31	22	13.1	5.23	68	.266	.341	2	.111	-0	-14	-14	2	-1.4
1986 Pit-N	3	5	.375	50	3	0	0	0	88	85	9	38	70	12.8	3.58	107	.258	.338	1	.063	-1	1	2	1	0.3
1987 Chi-A	4	6	.400	56	0	0	0	10	94	95	10	62	44	15.6	4.79	96	.271	.390	—	0	-3	-2	3	-0.1
1988 Min-A	0	0	1.000	12	0	0	0	0	21	33	4	10	9	18.4	6.00	68	.355	.417	—	0	-5	-5	0	-0.4
Total 6	12	17	.414	161	10	0	0	10	308¹	321	31	156	159	14.2	4.67	85	.272	.362	3	.088	-2	-26	-23	6	-1.6

● **TOM WINSETT**   Winsett, John Thomas "Long Tom"   b: 11/24/09, McKenzie, Tenn.   d: 7/20/87, Memphis, Tenn.   BL/TR, 6′2″, 190 lbs.   Deb: 4/20/30   ♦

YEAR TM/L	W	L	PCT	G	GS	CG	SH	SV	IP	H	HR	BB	SO	RAT	ERA	ERA+	OAV	OOB	BH	AVG	PB	PR	/A	PD	TPI
1937 Bro-N	0	0	—	1	0	0	0	0	1	3	0	2	0	45.0	18.00	22	.600	.714	83	.237	0	-2	-2	-0	0.0

● **HANK WINSTON**   Winston, Henry Rudolph   b: 6/15/04, Youngsville, N.C.   d: 2/4/74, Jacksonville, Fla.   BL/TR, 6′3.5″, 226 lbs.   Deb: 9/30/33

YEAR TM/L	W	L	PCT	G	GS	CG	SH	SV	IP	H	HR	BB	SO	RAT	ERA	ERA+	OAV	OOB	BH	AVG	PB	PR	/A	PD	TPI
1933 Phi-A	0	0	—	1	0	0	0	0	6²	7	0	6	2	17.6	6.75	63	.280	.419	0	—	-0	-2	-2	0	0.0

YEAR	TM/L	W	L	PCT	G	GS	CG	SH	SV	IP	H	HR	BB	SO	RAT	ERA	ERA+	OAV	OOB	BH	AVG	PB	PR	/A	PD	TPI
1936	Bro-N	1	3	.250	14	0	0	0	0	32¹	40	2	16	8	15.9	6.12	67	.301	.380	1	.091	-1	-8	-7	-0	-0.8
Total	2	1	3	.250	15	0	0	0	0	39	47	2	22	10	16.2	6.23	67	.297	.387	1	.071	-1	-9	-9	0	-0.8

● **GEORGE WINTER**   Winter, George Lovington "Sassafras"
b: 4/27/1878, New Providence, Pa   d: 5/26/51, Franklin Lakes, N.J.   TR, 5'8", 155 lbs.   Deb: 6/15/01

YEAR	TM/L	W	L	PCT	G	GS	CG	SH	SV	IP	H	HR	BB	SO	RAT	ERA	ERA+	OAV	OOB	BH	AVG	PB	PR	/A	PD	TPI
1901	Bos-A	16	12	.571	28	28	26	1	0	241	234	4	66	63	11.4	2.80	126	.252	.304	19	.190	-4	23	20	-1	1.5
1902	Bos-A	11	9	.550	20	20	18	0	0	168¹	149	2	53	51	11.2	2.99	119	.238	.305	10	.164	-2	11	11	-0	0.8
1903	Bos-A	9	8	.529	24	19	14	0	0	178¹	182	4	37	64	11.4	3.08	99	.263	.307	7	.106	-4	-2	-1	-1	-0.6
1904	Bos-A	8	4	.667	20	16	12	1	0	135²	126	4	27	31	10.5	2.32	115	.247	.293	5	.116	-2	4	5	-2	0.1
1905	Bos-A	16	17	.485	35	27	24	2	0	264¹	249	5	54	119	10.5	2.96	91	.251	.293	24	.261	3	-9	-8	1	-0.5
1906	Bos-A	6	18	.250	29	22	18	1	2	207²	215	8	38	72	11.2	4.12	67	.270	.308	17	.246	2	-33	-32	-0	-3.3
1907	Bos-A	12	15	.444	35	27	21	4	1	256²	198	2	61	88	9.2	2.07	124	.215	.267	21	.223	1	14	14	-0	1.5
1908	Bos-A	4	14	.222	22	17	8	0	0	147²	150	3	34	55	11.5	3.05	81	.274	.321	9	.184	-1	-11	-10	-0	-1.3
	*Det-A	1	5	.167	7	6	5	0	1	56¹	49	0	7	25	9.4	1.60	151	.240	.276	2	.111	-1	5	5	1	0.6
	Yr	5	19	.208	29	23	13	0	1	204	199	3	41	80	10.7	2.65	93	.263	.304	11	.164	-2	-6	-4	1	-0.7
Total	8	83	102	.449	220	182	146	9	4	1656	1552	32	377	568	10.7	2.87	101	.250	.297	114	.193	-8	2	7	-4	-1.2

● **CLARENCE WINTERS**   Winters, Clarence John   b: 9/7/1898, Detroit, Mich.   d: 6/29/45, Detroit, Mich.   Deb: 8/28/24

YEAR	TM/L	W	L	PCT	G	GS	CG	SH	SV	IP	H	HR	BB	SO	RAT	ERA	ERA+	OAV	OOB	BH	AVG	PB	PR	/A	PD	TPI
1924	Bos-A	0	1	.000	4	2	0	0	0	7	22	0	4	3	33.4	20.57	21	.512	.553	1	.333	0	-13	-13	-0	-1.3

● **JESSE WINTERS**   Winters, Jesse Franklin "Buck" or "T-Bone"
b: 12/22/1893, Stephenville, Tex.   d: 6/5/86, Abilene, Texas   BR/TR, 6'1", 165 lbs.   Deb: 5/3/19

YEAR	TM/L	W	L	PCT	G	GS	CG	SH	SV	IP	H	HR	BB	SO	RAT	ERA	ERA+	OAV	OOB	BH	AVG	PB	PR	/A	PD	TPI
1919	NY-N	1	2	.333	16	2	0	0	3	28	39	1	13	6	17.7	5.46	51	.339	.420	0	.000	-0	-8	-8	-0	-1.1
1920	NY-N	0	0	—	21	0	0	0	0	46¹	37	1	28	14	13.4	3.50	86	.233	.361	0	.000	-1	-2	-3	1	0.0
1921	Phi-N	5	10	.333	18	14	10	0	0	114	142	4	28	22	13.7	3.63	116	.310	.355	5	.128	-3	2	8	2	0.8
1922	Phi-N	6	6	.500	34	9	4	0	2	138¹	176	8	56	29	15.4	5.33	87	.319	.386	11	.256	-1	-19	-10	1	-0.7
1923	Phi-N	1	6	.143	21	6	1	0	1	78¹	116	7	39	23	18.3	7.35	63	.348	.423	4	.160	-1	-29	-24	-1	-1.9
Total	5	13	24	.351	110	31	15	0	6	405	510	21	164	94	15.4	5.04	83	.316	.385	20	.171	-5	-56	-39	2	-2.9

● **ALAN WIRTH**   Wirth, Alan Lee   b: 12/8/56, Mesa, Ariz.   BR/TR, 6'4", 190 lbs.   Deb: 4/9/78

YEAR	TM/L	W	L	PCT	G	GS	CG	SH	SV	IP	H	HR	BB	SO	RAT	ERA	ERA+	OAV	OOB	BH	AVG	PB	PR	/A	PD	TPI
1978	Oak-A	5	6	.455	16	14	2	1	0	81¹	72	6	34	31	12.1	3.43	106	.252	.337	0	—	0	3	2	-1	0.3
1979	Oak-A	1	0	1.000	5	1	0	0	0	12	14	2	8	7	17.3	6.00	67	.298	.411	0	—	0	-2	-3	-0	0.2
1980	Oak-A	0	0	—	2	0	0	0	0	2	3	0	0	1	13.5	4.50	84	.333	.333	0	—	0	-0	-0	-0	0.7
Total	3	6	6	.500	23	15	2	1	0	95¹	89	8	42	39	12.7	3.78	98	.260	.348	0	—	0	1	-1	-1	1.2

● **ARCHIE WISE**   Wise, Archibald Edwin   b: 7/31/12, Waxahachie, Tex.   d: 2/2/78, Dallas, Tex.   BR/TR, 6', 165 lbs.   Deb: 7/24/32

YEAR	TM/L	W	L	PCT	G	GS	CG	SH	SV	IP	H	HR	BB	SO	RAT	ERA	ERA+	OAV	OOB	BH	AVG	PB	PR	/A	PD	TPI
1932	Chi-A	0	0	—	2	0	0	0	0	7¹	8	1	5	2	17.2	4.91	88	.258	.378	1	.000	-1	-0	-0	0	-0.1

● **RICK WISE**   Wise, Richard Charles   b: 9/13/45, Jackson, Mich.   BR/TR, 6'2", 195 lbs.   Deb: 4/18/64

YEAR	TM/L	W	L	PCT	G	GS	CG	SH	SV	IP	H	HR	BB	SO	RAT	ERA	ERA+	OAV	OOB	BH	AVG	PB	PR	/A	PD	TPI
1964	Phi-N	5	3	.625	25	8	0	0	0	69	78	7	25	39	13.8	4.04	86	.277	.342	5	.294	2	-4	-4	-2	-0.4
1966	Phi-N	5	6	.455	22	13	3	0	0	99¹	100	5	24	58	11.5	3.71	97	.262	.311	0	—	-4	-1	-1	-1	-0.6
1967	Phi-N	11	11	.500	36	25	6	3	0	181¹	177	8	45	111	11.2	3.28	104	.259	.308	11	.208	3	2	3	1	0.7
1968	Phi-N	9	15	.375	30	30	7	1	0	182	210	12	37	97	12.5	4.55	66	.292	.332	14	.241	7	-32	-31	-1	-3.2
1969	Phi-N	15	13	.536	33	31	14	4	0	220	215	17	61	144	11.4	3.23	110	.257	.309	20	.270	7	9	8	1	1.9
1970	Phi-N	13	14	.481	35	34	5	1	0	220¹	253	15	65	113	13.1	4.17	96	.287	.338	15	.200	5	-3	-4	1	0.1
1971	Phi-N☆	17	14	.548	38	37	17	4	0	272¹	261	20	70	155	11.1	2.88	123	.254	.304	23	.237	10	18	20	0	3.4
1972	StL-N	16	16	.500	35	35	20	2	0	269	250	16	71	142	10.8	3.11	109	.251	.301	16	.172	1	10	9	2	1.4
1973	StL-N★	16	12	.571	35	34	14	5	0	259	259	18	59	144	11.2	3.37	108	.257	.300	17	.193	6	8	8	-1	1.4
1974	Bos-A	3	4	.429	9	9	1	0	0	49	47	2	16	25	11.8	3.86	100	.251	.314	0	—	-1	-0	-0	-0	-0.1
1975	*Bos-A	19	12	.613	35	35	17	1	0	255¹	262	34	72	141	11.9	3.95	103	.263	.315	0	—	0	-5	-4	-1	0.1
1976	Bos-A	14	11	.560	34	34	11	4	0	224¹	218	18	48	93	10.8	3.53	111	.255	.296	0	—	0	-0	9	2	1.2
1977	Bos-A	11	5	.688	26	20	4	2	0	128¹	151	19	28	85	12.8	4.77	94	.291	.332	0	—	0	-10	-4	-1	-0.4
1978	Cle-A	9	19	.321	33	31	9	1	0	211²	226	22	59	106	12.2	4.34	86	.275	.325	0	—	0	-14	-14	-0	-1.7
1979	Cle-A	15	10	.600	34	34	9	2	0	231²	229	24	68	108	11.6	3.73	114	.256	.309	0	—	0	12	13	4	1.7
1980	SD-N	6	8	.429	27	27	1	0	0	154¹	172	14	37	59	12.2	3.67	93	.285	.326	8	.138	-1	-1	-4	-1	-0.5
1981	SD-N	4	8	.333	18	18	0	0	0	98	116	10	19	27	12.4	3.77	86	.296	.328	1	.040	-2	-3	-6	-0	-0.8
1982	SD-N	0	0	—	1	0	0	0	0	2	3	0	0	0	13.5	9.00	38	.333	.333	0	—	0	-1	-1	-0	0.0
Total	18	188	181	.509	506	455	138	30	0	3127	3227	261	804	1647	11.7	3.69	100	.267	.315	130	.195	34	-15	2	9	4.2

● **ROY WISE**   Wise, Roy Ogden   b: 11/18/24, Springfield, Ill.   BB/TR, 6'2", 170 lbs.   Deb: 5/13/44

YEAR	TM/L	W	L	PCT	G	GS	CG	SH	SV	IP	H	HR	BB	SO	RAT	ERA	ERA+	OAV	OOB	BH	AVG	PB	PR	/A	PD	TPI
1944	Pit-N	0	0	—	2	0	0	0	0	3	4	0	3	1	21.0	9.00	41	.333	.467	0	—	0	-2	-2	-0	0.0

● **BILL WISE**   Wise, William E.   b: 3/15/1861, Washington, D.C.   d: 5/5/40, Washington, D.C.   Deb: 5/2/1882

YEAR	TM/L	W	L	PCT	G	GS	CG	SH	SV	IP	H	HR	BB	SO	RAT	ERA	ERA+	OAV	OOB	BH	AVG	PB	PR	/A	PD	TPI
1882	Bal-a	1	2	.333	3	3	3	0	0	26	30	1	4	9	11.8	2.77	99	.270	.296	2	.100	-1	-0	-0	-0	-0.1
1884	Was-U	23	18	.561	50	41	34	4	0	364¹	383	5	60	268	10.9	3.04	79	.252	.281	79	.233	-8	-24	-26	5	-2.4
1886	Was-N	0	1	.000	1	1	0	0	0	3	6	0	2	0	24.0	9.00	37	.400	.471	0	—	-0	-2	-2	-0	-0.4
Total	3	24	21	.533	54	45	37	4	0	393¹	419	6	66	277	11.1	3.07	79	.255	.284	81	.224	-9	-26	-28	4	-2.9

● **JACK WISNER**   Wisner, John Henry   b: 11/5/1899, Grand Rapids, Mich.   d: 12/15/81, Jackson, Mich.   BR/TR, 6'3", 195 lbs.   Deb: 9/12/19

YEAR	TM/L	W	L	PCT	G	GS	CG	SH	SV	IP	H	HR	BB	SO	RAT	ERA	ERA+	OAV	OOB	BH	AVG	PB	PR	/A	PD	TPI
1919	Pit-N	1	0	1.000	4	1	1	0	0	18²	12	0	7	4	9.6	0.96	313	.185	.274	0	.000	-1	4	4	-0	0.1
1920	Pit-N	1	3	.250	17	2	1	0	0	44²	46	1	10	13	11.5	3.43	94	.274	.318	0	.000	-1	-1	-1	-1	-0.1
1925	NY-N	0	0	—	25	0	0	0	0	40¹	33	4	14	13	10.9	3.79	106	.228	.304	0	.000	-1	1	1	-0	-0.1
1926	NY-N	2	2	.500	5	3	1	0	0	28	21	4	10	5	10.0	3.54	106	.208	.279	2	.200	-0	1	1	-0	-0.1
Total	4	4	5	.444	51	6	4	0	0	131²	112	9	41	35	10.7	3.21	111	.234	.300	2	.065	-3	6	5	1	-0.1

● **WHITEY WISTERT**   Wistert, Francis Michael   b: 2/20/12, Chicago, Ill.   d: 4/23/85, Painesville, Ohio   BR/TR, 6'4", 210 lbs.   Deb: 9/11/34

YEAR	TM/L	W	L	PCT	G	GS	CG	SH	SV	IP	H	HR	BB	SO	RAT	ERA	ERA+	OAV	OOB	BH	AVG	PB	PR	/A	PD	TPI
1934	Cin-N	0	1	.000	2	1	0	0	0	8	5	1	5	1	11.3	1.13	363	.185	.313	0	.000	-0	3	3	-0	0.2

● **JAY WITASICK**   Witasick, Gerald Alfonse   b: 8/28/72, Baltimore, Md.   BR/TR, 6'4", 205 lbs.   Deb: 7/7/96

YEAR	TM/L	W	L	PCT	G	GS	CG	SH	SV	IP	H	HR	BB	SO	RAT	ERA	ERA+	OAV	OOB	BH	AVG	PB	PR	/A	PD	TPI
1996	Oak-A	1	1	.500	12	0	0	0	0	13	12	5	5	12	11.8	6.23	77	.245	.315	0	—	0	-2	-2	-0	-0.3

● **CHARLES WITHEROW**   Witherow, Charles Samuel   Deb: 7/1/1875

YEAR	TM/L	W	L	PCT	G	GS	CG	SH	SV	IP	H	HR	BB	SO	RAT	ERA	ERA+	OAV	OOB	BH	AVG	PB	PR	/A	PD	TPI
1875	Was-n	0	1	.000	1	1	1	0	0	4	4	0	0	0	36.0	18.00	13	.444	.444	0	.000	-0	-2	-2	-0	-0.9

● **ROY WITHERUP**   Witherup, Foster Leroy   b: 7/26/1886, N.Washington, Pa.   d: 12/23/41, New Bethlehem, Pa.   BR/TR, 6', 185 lbs.   Deb: 5/14/06

YEAR	TM/L	W	L	PCT	G	GS	CG	SH	SV	IP	H	HR	BB	SO	RAT	ERA	ERA+	OAV	OOB	BH	AVG	PB	PR	/A	PD	TPI
1906	Bos-N	0	3	.000	14	7	3	0	0	46	59	2	19	14	15.5	6.26	43	.322	.389	2	.133	-1	-19	-18	-1	-1.2
1908	Was-A	2	4	.333	6	6	4	0	0	48¹	51	0	8	31	11.2	2.98	77	.264	.297	3	.167	-1	-3	-4	-0	-0.5
1909	Was-A	1	5	.167	6	4	5	0	0	68	79	1	20	26	13.1	4.24	57	.306	.356	1	.053	-2	-13	-14	-2	-1.5
Total	3	3	12	.200	26	17	12	0	0	162¹	189	3	47	71	13.2	4.44	55	.298	.348	6	.115	-3	-35	-36	-2	-3.2

● **GEORGE WITT**   Witt, George Adrian "Red"   b: 11/9/33, Long Beach, Cal.   BR/TR, 6'3", 200 lbs.   Deb: 9/21/57

YEAR	TM/L	W	L	PCT	G	GS	CG	SH	SV	IP	H	HR	BB	SO	RAT	ERA	ERA+	OAV	OOB	BH	AVG	PB	PR	/A	PD	TPI
1957	Pit-N	0	1	.000	1	1	0	0	0	1¹	4	1	5	1	60.8	40.50	9	.500	.692	0	—	0	-5	-5	0	-1.6
1958	Pit-N	9	2	.818	18	15	5	3	0	106	78	2	59	81	11.8	1.61	240	.207	.320	6	.154	-1	28	27	-0	2.5
1959	Pit-N	0	7	.000	15	11	0	0	0	50²	58	7	32	30	16.2	6.93	56	.293	.394	0	.000	-1	-17	-17	-0	-2.1
1960	*Pit-N	1	2	.333	10	6	0	0	0	30	29	3	12	15	13.5	4.20	89	.300	.369	0	.000	-1	-1	-1	-0	-0.3
1961	Pit-N	0	1	.000	9	1	0	0	0	15²	17	5	9	11	12.6	6.32	63	.274	.328	1	.500	1	-4	-4	-1	-0.2
1962	LA-A	1	2	.333	10	1	0	0	0	10	15	4	6	9	18.9	8.10	48	.349	.417	1	.333	0	-5	-5	-0	-0.8
	Hou-N	0	2	.000	4	3	0	0	0	15²	20	2	9	10	17.6	7.04	53	.339	.435	1	.250	0	-5	-6	-0	-0.6
Total	6	11	16	.407	66	38	5	3	0	229	225	24	127	156	14.0	4.32	89	.263	.361	9	.130	-2	-10	-12	-1	-3.1

● **MIKE WITT**   Witt, Michael Atwater   b: 7/20/60, Fullerton, Cal.   BR/TR, 6'7", 192 lbs.   Deb: 4/11/81

YEAR	TM/L	W	L	PCT	G	GS	CG	SH	SV	IP	H	HR	BB	SO	RAT	ERA	ERA+	OAV	OOB	BH	AVG	PB	PR	/A	PD	TPI
1981	Cal-A	8	9	.471	22	21	7	1	0	129	123	9	47	75	12.6	3.28	111	.251	.330	0	—	0	5	5	-1	0.5
1982	*Cal-A	8	6	.571	33	26	5	1	0	179²	177	8	47	85	11.6	3.51	116	.260	.314	0	—	0	11	11	-0	0.7

YEAR	TM/L	W	L	PCT	G	GS	CG	SH	SV	IP	H	HR	BB	SO	RAT	ERA	ERA+	OAV	OOB	BH	AVG	PB	PR	/A	PD	TPI
1983	Cal-A	7	14	.333	43	19	2	0	5	154	173	14	75	77	14.8	4.91	82	.293	.379	0	—	0	-14	-15	0	-1.9
1984	Cal-A	15	11	.577	34	34	9	2	0	246²	227	17	84	196	11.5	3.47	114	.244	.310	0	—	0	14	14	-1	1.3
1985	Cal-A	15	9	.625	35	35	6	1	0	250	228	17	98	180	11.9	3.56	115	.243	.317	0	—	0	16	15	0	1.4
1986	*Cal-A☆	18	10	.643	34	34	14	3	0	269	218	22	73	208	9.8	2.84	144	.221	.277	0	—	0	40	38	2	4.0
1987	Cal-A☆	16	14	.533	36	36	10	0	0	247	252	34	84	192	12.4	4.01	107	.261	.323	0	—	0	12	8	-1	1.1
1988	Cal-A	13	16	.448	34	34	12	2	0	249²	263	14	87	133	12.8	4.15	93	.272	.335	0	—	0	-5	-8	-0	-0.7
1989	Cal-A	9	15	.375	33	33	5	0	0	220	252	26	48	123	12.4	4.54	84	.292	.330	0	—	0	-16	-18	4	-1.3
1990	Cal-A	0	3	.000	10	0	0	0	1	20¹	19	1	13	14	14.6	1.77	216	.250	.367	0	—	0	5	5	1	0.9
	NY-A	5	6	.455	16	16	2	1	0	96²	87	8	34	60	11.6	4.47	89	.240	.312	0	—	0	-6	-5	0	-0.5
	Yr	5	9	.357	26	16	2	1	1	117	106	9	47	74	12.1	4.00	99	.240	.319	0	—	0	-1	-1	1	0.4
1991	NY-A	0	1	.000	2	2	0	0	0	5¹	8	1	1	0	15.2	10.13	41	.320	.346	0	—	0	-4	-4	0	-0.5
1993	NY-A	3	2	.600	9	9	0	0	0	41	39	7	22	30	14.0	5.27	79	.248	.352	0	—	0	-4	-5	0	-0.3
Total	12	117	116	.502	341	299	72	11	6	2108¹	2066	183	713	1373	12.1	3.83	105	.257	.322	0	—	0	55	41	4	4.7

● BOBBY WITT
Witt, Robert Andrew   b: 5/11/64, Arlington, Mass.   BR/TR, 6'2", 205 lbs.   Deb: 4/10/86

YEAR	TM/L	W	L	PCT	G	GS	CG	SH	SV	IP	H	HR	BB	SO	RAT	ERA	ERA+	OAV	OOB	BH	AVG	PB	PR	/A	PD	TPI
1986	Tex-A	11	9	.550	31	31	0	0	0	157²	130	18	143	174	15.8	5.48	78	.223	.379	0	—	0	-23	-21	0	-2.4
1987	Tex-A	8	10	.444	26	25	1	0	0	143	114	10	140	160	16.2	4.91	91	.219	.388	0	.000	0	-7	-7	0	-0.7
1988	Tex-A	8	10	.444	22	22	13	2	0	174¹	134	13	101	148	12.2	3.92	104	.216	.326	0	—	0	1	3	-1	0.0
1989	Tex-A	12	13	.480	31	31	5	1	0	194¹	182	14	114	166	13.8	5.14	77	.248	.351	0	—	0	-27	-25	-0	-2.9
1990	Tex-A	17	10	.630	33	32	7	1	0	222	197	12	110	221	12.6	3.36	116	.238	.330	0	—	0	13	14	-1	1.5
1991	Tex-A	3	7	.300	17	16	1	1	0	88²	84	4	74	82	16.1	6.09	66	.254	.392	0	—	0	-20	-20	-1	-2.0
1992	Tex-A	9	13	.409	25	25	0	0	0	161¹	152	14	95	100	13.9	4.46	85	.254	.358	0	—	0	-9	-12	-0	-1.4
	*Oak-A	1	1	.500	6	6	0	0	0	31²	31	2	19	25	14.2	3.41	110	.265	.368	0	—	0	2	1	0	0.2
	Yr	10	14	.417	31	31	0	0	0	193	183	16	114	125	13.8	4.29	88	.252	.354	0	—	0	-8	-11	0	-1.2
1993	Oak-A	14	13	.519	35	33	5	1	0	220	226	16	91	131	13.1	4.21	97	.269	.343	0	—	0	3	-3	2	0.2
1994	Oak-A	8	10	.444	24	24	5	3	0	135²	151	22	70	111	15.0	5.04	88	.283	.371	0	—	0	-4	-9	-1	-0.8
1995	Fla-N	2	7	.222	19	19	1	0	0	110²	104	8	47	95	12.4	3.90	108	.251	.330	2	.063	-2	3	4	0	0.1
	Tex-A	3	4	.429	10	10	1	0	0	61¹	81	4	21	46	15.1	4.55	106	.324	.379	0	—	0	1	2	-1	0.1
1996	*Tex-A	16	12	.571	33	32	2	0	0	199²	235	28	96	157	15.0	5.41	98	.295	.372	0	—	0	-9	-2	1	-0.2
Total	11	112	119	.485	312	306	41	9	0	1900¹	1821	165	1121	1616	14.1	4.61	92	.254	.357	2	.061	-2	-76	-77	-2	-8.3

● JOHNNIE WITTIG
Wittig, John Carl "Hans"   b: 6/16/14, Baltimore, Md.   BR/TR, 6', 180 lbs.   Deb: 8/4/38

YEAR	TM/L	W	L	PCT	G	GS	CG	SH	SV	IP	H	HR	BB	SO	RAT	ERA	ERA+	OAV	OOB	BH	AVG	PB	PR	/A	PD	TPI
1938	NY-N	2	3	.400	13	6	2	0	0	39¹	41	4	26	14	15.3	4.81	78	.263	.368	0	.000	-1	-4	-5	-1	-0.8
1939	NY-N	0	2	.000	5	2	1	0	0	16²	18	0	14	4	17.8	7.56	52	.281	.418	0	—	-1	-7	-7	-0	-0.7
1941	NY-N	3	5	.375	25	9	0	0	0	85¹	111	4	45	47	16.6	5.59	66	.319	.398	5	.200	-1	-19	-18	-2	-1.7
1943	NY-N	5	15	.250	40	22	4	1	4	164	172	14	76	56	13.6	4.23	82	.273	.352	5	.098	-3	-15	-14	-3	-2.3
1949	Bos-A	0	0	—	1	0	0	0	0	2	2	1	2	0	18.0	9.00	48	.286	.444	0	—	-1	-1	0	0	0.0
Total	5	10	25	.286	84	39	7	1	4	307¹	344	23	163	121	14.9	4.89	73	.286	.372	10	.110	-6	-46	-44	-6	-5.5

● MARK WOHLERS
Wohlers, Mark Edward   b: 1/23/70, Holyoke, Mass.   BR/TR, 6'4", 207 lbs.   Deb: 8/17/91

YEAR	TM/L	W	L	PCT	G	GS	CG	SH	SV	IP	H	HR	BB	SO	RAT	ERA	ERA+	OAV	OOB	BH	AVG	PB	PR	/A	PD	TPI
1991	*Atl-N	3	1	.750	17	0	0	0	2	19²	17	1	13	13	14.6	3.20	121	.239	.372	0	.000	-0	1	1	0	0.3
1992	*Atl-N	1	2	.333	32	0	0	0	4	35¹	28	0	14	17	11.0	2.55	144	.235	.321	0	.000	-0	4	4	0	0.5
1993	*Atl-N	6	2	.750	46	0	0	0	0	48	37	2	22	45	11.3	4.50	89	.218	.311	0	—	0	-2	-3	0	-0.3
1994	Atl-N	7	2	.778	51	0	0	0	1	51	51	1	33	58	14.8	4.59	92	.264	.372	1	1.000	0	-2	-2	0	-0.2
1995	*Atl-N	7	3	.700	65	0	0	0	25	64²	51	2	24	90	10.6	2.09	204	.211	.285	0	.000	-0	15	16	-1	3.2
1996	*Atl-N★	2	4	.333	77	0	0	0	39	77¹	71	8	21	100	10.9	3.03	145	.240	.295	0	.000	0	10	12	-1	1.7
Total	6	26	14	.650	288	0	0	0	71	296	255	14	127	323	11.8	3.28	127	.234	.318	1	.100	-1	25	29	-1	5.2

● STEVE WOJCIECHOWSKI
Wojciechowski, Steven Joseph   b: 7/29/70, Blue Island, Ill.   BL/TL, 6'2", 185 lbs.   Deb: 7/18/95

YEAR	TM/L	W	L	PCT	G	GS	CG	SH	SV	IP	H	HR	BB	SO	RAT	ERA	ERA+	OAV	OOB	BH	AVG	PB	PR	/A	PD	TPI
1995	Oak-A	2	3	.400	14	7	0	0	0	48²	51	7	28	13	14.8	5.18	86	.273	.370	0	—	0	-3	-4	-0	-0.3
1996	Oak-A	5	5	.500	16	15	0	0	0	79²	97	10	28	30	14.3	5.65	85	.300	.360	0	—	0	-6	-7	-1	-0.8
Total	2	7	8	.467	30	22	0	0	0	128¹	148	17	56	43	14.5	5.47	86	.290	.364	0	—	0	-8	-11	-1	-1.1

● PETE WOJEY
Wojey, Peter Paul   b: 12/1/19, Stowe, Pa.   BR/TR, 5'11", 185 lbs.   Deb: 7/2/54

YEAR	TM/L	W	L	PCT	G	GS	CG	SH	SV	IP	H	HR	BB	SO	RAT	ERA	ERA+	OAV	OOB	BH	AVG	PB	PR	/A	PD	TPI
1954	Bro-N	1	1	.500	14	1	0	0	1	27²	24	3	14	21	13.0	3.25	126	.242	.348	0	.000	-0	3	3	1	0.2
1956	Det-A	0	0	—	2	0	0	0	0	4	2	0	1	1	6.8	2.25	183	.167	.231	0	—	0	1	1	0	0.0
1957	Det-A	0	0	—	2	0	0	0	0	1¹	1	0	0	0	6.8	0.00	—	.200	.200	0	—	0	0	0	0	0.0
Total	3	1	1	.500	18	1	0	0	1	33	27	3	15	22	12.0	3.00	136	.233	.331	0	.000	-0	4	4	1	0.2

● ED WOJNA
Wojna, Edward David   b: 8/20/60, Bridgeport, Conn.   BR/TR, 6'1", 185 lbs.   Deb: 6/16/85

YEAR	TM/L	W	L	PCT	G	GS	CG	SH	SV	IP	H	HR	BB	SO	RAT	ERA	ERA+	OAV	OOB	BH	AVG	PB	PR	/A	PD	TPI
1985	SD-N	2	4	.333	15	7	0	0	0	42	53	6	19	18	16.1	5.79	61	.312	.391	2	.167	-0	-10	-11	0	-1.3
1986	SD-N	2	2	.500	7	7	1	0	0	39	42	2	16	19	13.6	3.23	113	.268	.339	2	.143	-0	2	2	-1	0.1
1987	SD-N	0	3	.000	5	3	0	0	0	18¹	25	2	6	13	15.7	5.89	67	.333	.390	0	.000	-1	-4	-4	1	-0.5
1989	Cle-A	0	1	.000	9	3	0	0	0	33	31	0	14	10	12.3	4.09	97	.254	.331	0	—	0	-1	-0	1	0.0
Total	4	4	10	.286	36	20	1	0	0	132¹	151	10	55	60	14.4	4.62	81	.288	.361	4	.129	-1	-13	-13	1	-1.7

● BOB WOLCOTT
Wolcott, Robert William   b: 9/8/73, Huntington Beach, Cal.   BR/TR, 6', 190 lbs.   Deb: 8/18/95

YEAR	TM/L	W	L	PCT	G	GS	CG	SH	SV	IP	H	HR	BB	SO	RAT	ERA	ERA+	OAV	OOB	BH	AVG	PB	PR	/A	PD	TPI
1995	*Sea-A	3	2	.600	7	6	0	0	0	36²	43	6	14	19	14.5	4.42	107	.297	.366	0	—	0	1	1	-1	0.1
1996	Sea-A	7	10	.412	30	28	1	0	0	149¹	179	26	54	78	14.5	5.73	86	.297	.361	0	—	0	-12	-13	-0	-1.2
Total	2	10	12	.455	37	34	1	0	0	186	222	32	68	97	14.5	5.47	89	.297	.362	0	—	0	-11	-12	-1	-1.1

● ERNIE WOLF
Wolf, Ernest Adolph   b: 2/2/1889, Newark, N.J.   d: 5/23/64, Atlantic Highlands, N.J.   BR/TR, 5'11", 174 lbs.   Deb: 9/10/12

YEAR	TM/L	W	L	PCT	G	GS	CG	SH	SV	IP	H	HR	BB	SO	RAT	ERA	ERA+	OAV	OOB	BH	AVG	PB	PR	/A	PD	TPI
1912	Cle-A	0	0	—	1	0	0	0	0	5²	7	0	4	4	19.1	6.35	54	.348	.444	0	.000	—	-2	-2	-0	-0.1

● WALLY WOLF
Wolf, Walter Beck   b: 1/5/42, Los Angeles, Cal.   BR/TR, 6'0.5", 191 lbs.   Deb: 9/27/69

YEAR	TM/L	W	L	PCT	G	GS	CG	SH	SV	IP	H	HR	BB	SO	RAT	ERA	ERA+	OAV	OOB	BH	AVG	PB	PR	/A	PD	TPI
1969	Cal-A	0	0	—	2	0	0	0	0	2¹	3	1	3	2	23.1	11.57	30	.333	.500	0	—	-0	-2	-2	-0	-0.1
1970	Cal-A	0	0	—	4	0	0	0	0	5¹	3	1	4	5	11.8	5.06	71	.176	.333	0	—	0	-1	-1	-0	-0.1
Total	2	0	0	—	6	0	0	0	0	7²	6	2	7	7	15.3	7.04	51	.231	.394	0	—	0	-3	-3	-0	-0.1

● LEFTY WOLF
Wolf, Walter Francis   b: 6/10/1900, Hartford, Conn.   d: 9/25/71, New Orleans, La.   BR/TL, 5'10", 163 lbs.   Deb: 7/4/21

YEAR	TM/L	W	L	PCT	G	GS	CG	SH	SV	IP	H	HR	BB	SO	RAT	ERA	ERA+	OAV	OOB	BH	AVG	PB	PR	/A	PD	TPI
1921	Phi-A	0	0	—	8	0	0	0	0	15	15	0	16	11	19.8	7.20	62	.273	.452	1	.250	-0	-5	-5	-0	0.0

● JIMMY WOLF
Wolf, William Van Winkle "Chicken"   b: 5/12/1862, Louisville, Ky.   d: 5/16/03, Louisville, Ky.   BR/TR, 5'9", 190 lbs.   Deb: 5/2/1882   M◆

YEAR	TM/L	W	L	PCT	G	GS	CG	SH	SV	IP	H	HR	BB	SO	RAT	ERA	ERA+	OAV	OOB	BH	AVG	PB	PR	/A	PD	TPI
1882	Lou-a	0	0	—	1	0	0	0	0	6	11	0	3	1	21.0	9.00	28	.367	.299	95	.299	0	-4	-4	-0	0.0
1885	Lou-a	0	0	—	1	0	0	0	0	1	1	0	0	1	9.0	9.00	36	.200	.200	141	.292	0	-1	-1	-0	0.0
1886	Lou-a	0	0	—	1	0	0	0	0	3	7	0	1	0	21.0	15.00	24	.350	.350	148	.272	0	-4	-4	-0	0.0
Total	3	0	0	—	3	0	0	0	0	10	19	0	3	2	19.8	10.80	27	.345	.379	1440	.290	1	-9	-9	-0	0.0

● CHUCK WOLFE
Wolfe, Charles Hunt   b: 2/15/1897, Wolfsburg, Pa.   d: 11/27/57, Schellsburg, Pa.   BL/TR, 5'7", 175 lbs.   Deb: 8/2/23

YEAR	TM/L	W	L	PCT	G	GS	CG	SH	SV	IP	H	HR	BB	SO	RAT	ERA	ERA+	OAV	OOB	BH	AVG	PB	PR	/A	PD	TPI
1923	Phi-A	0	0	—	3	0	0	0	0	9²	6	1	8	1	13.0	3.72	110	.194	.359	1	.333	0	0	0	-0	0.0

● ED WOLFE
Wolfe, Edward Anthony   b: 1/2/29, Los Angeles, Cal.   BR/TR, 6'3", 185 lbs.   Deb: 4/19/52

YEAR	TM/L	W	L	PCT	G	GS	CG	SH	SV	IP	H	HR	BB	SO	RAT	ERA	ERA+	OAV	OOB	BH	AVG	PB	PR	/A	PD	TPI
1952	Pit-N	0	0	—	3	0	0	0	0	3²	7	1	5	1	31.9	7.36	54	.467	.619	0	—	0	-1	-1	0	0.0

● BARNEY WOLFE
Wolfe, Wilbert Otto   b: 1/9/1876, Independence, Pa.   d: 2/27/53, N.Charleroi, Pa.   BR/TR, 6'1"   Deb: 4/24/03

YEAR	TM/L	W	L	PCT	G	GS	CG	SH	SV	IP	H	HR	BB	SO	RAT	ERA	ERA+	OAV	OOB	BH	AVG	PB	PR	/A	PD	TPI
1903	NY-A	6	9	.400	20	16	12	1	0	148¹	143	1	26	48	10.6	2.97	105	.253	.293	4	.075	-4	-0	2	-0	-0.2
1904	NY-A	0	3	.000	7	3	2	0	0	33²	31	1	4	8	9.9	3.21	85	.246	.280	0	.000	0	-2	-0	-0	-0.3
	Was-A	6	9	.400	17	16	13	2	0	126²	131	0	22	44	11.7	3.27	81	.268	.314	5	.119	-2	-9	-9	-2	-1.3
	Yr	6	12	.333	24	19	15	2	0	160¹	162	1	26	52	11.2	3.26	82	.263	.304	5	.096	-3	-12	-10	-2	-1.6
1905	Was-A	9	13	.409	28	23	17	1	1	182	162	1	37	52	10.2	2.57	103	.240	.287	8	.127	-1	2	2	-2	-0.2
1906	Was-A	0	3	.000	4	3	2	0	0	20	17	0	10	8	13.0	4.05	65	.233	.341	2	.286	0	-3	-3	-0	-0.4
Total	4	21	37	.362	76	61	46	4	1	510²	484	3	99	160	10.8	2.96	94	.251	.298	19	.109	-8	-13	-10	-4	-2.4

● BILL WOLFE   Wolfe, William   b: Jersey City, N.J.   Deb: 9/10/02

YEAR TM/L	W	L	PCT	G	GS	CG	SH	SV	IP	H	HR	BB	SO	RAT	ERA	ERA+	OAV	OOB	BH	AVG	PB	PR	/A	PD	TPI
1902 Phi-N	0	1	.000	1	1	1	0	0	9	11	0	4	3	16.0	4.00	70	.297	.381	1	.333	0	-1	-1	0	-0.1

● ROGER WOLFF   Wolff, Roger Francis   b: 4/10/11, Evansville, Ill.   d: 3/23/94, Chester, Ill.   BR/TR, 6'0.5", 208 lbs.   Deb: 9/20/41

YEAR TM/L	W	L	PCT	G	GS	CG	SH	SV	IP	H	HR	BB	SO	RAT	ERA	ERA+	OAV	OOB	BH	AVG	PB	PR	/A	PD	TPI
1941 Phi-A	0	2	.000	2	2	2	0	0	17	15	0	4	3	10.1	3.18	132	.231	.275	1	.200	-0	2	2	-0	0.2
1942 Phi-A	12	15	.444	32	25	15	2	3	214¹	206	16	69	94	11.7	3.32	114	.249	.309	6	.088	-3	8	11	0	1.0
1943 Phi-A	10	15	.400	41	26	13	2	6	221	232	11	72	91	12.5	3.54	96	.274	.334	9	.122	-4	-6	-4	-3	-1.1
1944 Was-A	4	15	.211	33	21	5	0	0	155	186	9	60	73	14.6	4.99	65	.295	.362	12	.218	1	-27	-30	2	-3.1
1945 Was-A	20	10	.667	33	29	21	4	2	250	200	7	53	108	9.1	2.12	146	.215	.258	9	.107	-5	35	27	-1	2.7
1946 Was-A	5	8	.385	21	17	6	0	0	122	115	8	30	50	11.1	2.58	130	.249	.302	4	.103	-1	12	10	-1	0.9
1947 Cle-A	0	0	—	7	2	0	0	0	16	15	1	10	5	15.2	3.94	88	.259	.386	0	.000	-0	-0	-1	1	0.0
Pit-N	1	4	.200	13	6	1	0	0	30	29	4	18	7	20.4	8.70	49	.368	.447	0	.000	-1	-15	-15	-1	-2.1
Total 7	52	69	.430	182	128	63	8	13	1025¹	1018	56	316	430	11.9	3.41	100	.258	.316	41	.122	-13	8	1	-3	-1.5

● MELLIE WOLFGANG   Wolfgang, Meldon John "Red"   b: 3/20/1890, Albany, N.Y.   d: 6/30/47, Albany, N.Y.   BR/TR, 5'9", 160 lbs.   Deb: 4/18/14

YEAR TM/L	W	L	PCT	G	GS	CG	SH	SV	IP	H	HR	BB	SO	RAT	ERA	ERA+	OAV	OOB	BH	AVG	PB	PR	/A	PD	TPI
1914 Chi-A	9	5	.643	24	11	9	2	0	119¹	96	0	32	50	9.7	1.89	142	.219	.272	7	.175	-0	11	11	4	1.7
1915 Chi-A	2	2	.500	17	2	0	0	0	53²	39	0	12	21	8.7	1.84	161	.211	.263	2	.118	-1	7	7	-1	0.2
1916 Chi-A	4	6	.400	27	14	6	1	0	127	103	2	42	36	10.4	1.98	139	.228	.296	9	.225	0	12	11	1	1.0
1917 Chi-A	0	0	—	5	0	0	0	0	17²	18	1	6	3	12.7	5.09	52	.305	.379	0	.000	-1	-5	-5	-0	-0.1
1918 Chi-A	0	1	.000	4	0	0	0	0	8¹	12	0	3	1	16.2	5.40	51	.333	.385	1	.500	0	-2	-2	0	-0.2
Total 5	15	14	.517	77	27	15	3	0	326	268	3	95	111	10.1	2.18	127	.229	.289	19	.184	-1	23	21	4	2.6

● HARRY WOLTER   Wolter, Harry Meigs   b: 7/11/1884, Monterey, Cal.   d: 7/7/70, Palo Alto, Cal.   BL/TL, 5'10", 175 lbs.   Deb: 5/14/07 ♦

YEAR TM/L	W	L	PCT	G	GS	CG	SH	SV	IP	H	HR	BB	SO	RAT	ERA	ERA+	OAV	OOB	BH	AVG	PB	PR	/A	PD	TPI
1907 Pit-N	0	0	—	1	0	0	0	0	2	3	0	2	0	22.5	4.50	54	.333	.455	0	.000	-0	-0	-0	-0	0.0
StL-N	0	2	.000	3	3	1	0	0	23	27	1	18	8	18.1	4.30	58	.318	.448	16	.340	1	-5	-5	-1	-0.4
Yr	0	2	.000	4	3	1	0	0	25	30	1	20	8	18.7	4.32	58	.319	.448	16	.333	1	-5	-5	-1	-0.4
1909 Bos-A	4	4	.500	11	6	0	0	0	59	66	0	31	21	15.3	3.51	71	.303	.397	29	.240	-1	-7	-7	-1	-0.8
Total 2	4	6	.400	15	9	1	0	0	84	96	1	50	29	16.3	3.75	67	.308	.413	514	.270	3	-12	-12	-2	-1.2

● RYNIE WOLTERS   Wolters, Reinder Albertus   b: 12/18/1842, U.S.A.   d: 1/3/17, Newark, N.J.   TR, 6', 165 lbs.   Deb: 5/18/1871

YEAR TM/L	W	L	PCT	G	GS	CG	SH	SV	IP	H	HR	BB	SO	RAT	ERA	ERA+	OAV	OOB	BH	AVG	PB	PR	/A	PD	TPI
1871 Mut-n	16	16	.500	32	32	31	1	0	283	345	7	39	22	12.2	3.43	110	.263	.285	51	.370	20	25	11		1.9
1872 Cle-n	3	6	.333	12	8	5	0	0	75¹	115	3	7	4	14.6	6.09	58	.304	.317	16	.232	-0	-21	-21		-0.9
1873 Res-n	0	1	.000	1	1	1	0	0	9²	13	0	1	1	14.0	0.00	—	.220	.233	0		-1	3	3		0.2
Total 3 n	19	23	.452	45	41	37	1	0	367¹	473	10	47	27	12.7	3.90	86	.271	.290	67	.318	19	-26	-22		1.2

● DOOLEY WOMACK   Womack, Horace Guy   b: 8/25/39, Columbia, S.C.   BL/TR, 6', 170 lbs.   Deb: 4/14/66

YEAR TM/L	W	L	PCT	G	GS	CG	SH	SV	IP	H	HR	BB	SO	RAT	ERA	ERA+	OAV	OOB	BH	AVG	PB	PR	/A	PD	TPI
1966 NY-A	7	3	.700	42	1	0	0	6	75	52	6	23	50	9.4	2.64	126	.198	.270	1	.200	-0	7	6	2	1.1
1967 NY-A	5	6	.455	65	0	0	0	18	97	80	6	35	50	10.9	2.41	130	.230	.306	4	.286	1	9	8	4	1.8
1968 NY-A	3	7	.300	45	0	0	0	4	61²	53	6	29	27	12.1	3.21	90	.244	.336	1	.200	-0	-2	-2	-2	-0.1
1969 Hou-N	2	1	.667	30	0	0	0	2	51²	49	1	20	32	12.6	3.51	101	.259	.340	1	.167	-0	0	0	2	0.2
Sea-A	2	1	.667	9	0	0	0	0	14¹	15	0	3	8	11.3	2.51	145	.273	.310	0	.000	-0	2	2	0	0.4
1970 Oak-A	0	0	—	2	0	0	0	0	3	4	2	1	3	15.0	15.00	24	.308	.357	0		-0	-4	-4	-0	0.0
Total 5	19	18	.514	193	1	0	0	24	302¹	253	21	111	177	11.1	2.95	110	.233	.310	7	.226	1	12	9	11	3.4

● SPADES WOOD   Wood, Charles Asher   b: 1/13/09, Spartanburg, S.C.   d: 5/18/86, Wichita, Kan.   BL/TL, 5'10.5", 150 lbs.   Deb: 8/16/30

YEAR TM/L	W	L	PCT	G	GS	CG	SH	SV	IP	H	HR	BB	SO	RAT	ERA	ERA+	OAV	OOB	BH	AVG	PB	PR	/A	PD	TPI
1930 Pit-N	4	3	.571	9	7	4	2	0	58	61	4	32	23	14.4	5.12	97	.270	.360	5	.250	1	-1	-1	-2	-0.2
1931 Pit-N	2	6	.250	15	10	2	0	0	64	69	2	46	33	16.3	6.05	64	.273	.387	5	.227	1	-16	-16	-0	-1.6
Total 2	6	9	.400	24	17	6	2	0	122	130	6	78	56	15.4	5.61	78	.271	.375	10	.238	1	-16	-17	-2	-1.8

● GEORGE WOOD   Wood, George A. "Dandy"   b: 11/9/1858, Boston, Mass.   d: 4/4/24, Harrisburg, Pa.   BL/TR, 5'10.5", 175 lbs.   Deb: 5/1/1880   MU♦

YEAR TM/L	W	L	PCT	G	GS	CG	SH	SV	IP	H	HR	BB	SO	RAT	ERA	ERA+	OAV	OOB	BH	AVG	PB	PR	/A	PD	TPI
1883 Det-N	0	0	—	1	0	0	0	0	5	8	0	3	0	19.8	7.20	43	.348	.423	133	.302	-0	-2	-2	0	0.1
1885 Det-N	0	0	—	1	0	0	0	0	4	5	0	1	0	13.5	0.00	—	.333	.375	105	.290	0	1	1	-0	0.0
1888 Phi-N	0	0	—	2	0	0	0	2	2	2	0	0	0		4.50	66	.300	.364	99	.229	1	-0	-0	-0	-0.1
1889 Phi-N	0	0	—	1	0	0	0	0	1	3	0	2	0	18.0	18.00	24	.400	.400	106	.251	0	-2	-2	0	0.0
Total 4	0	0	—	5	0	0	0	2	12	18	0	5	3	17.3	5.25	59	.340	.397	1467	.273	1	-3	-3	0	0.0

● JOE WOOD   Wood, Joe "Smokey Joe" (b: Howard Ellsworth Wood)   b: 10/25/1889, Kansas City, Mo.   d: 7/27/85, West Haven, Conn   BR/TR, 5'11", 180 lbs.   Deb: 8/24/08   F♦

YEAR TM/L	W	L	PCT	G	GS	CG	SH	SV	IP	H	HR	BB	SO	RAT	ERA	ERA+	OAV	OOB	BH	AVG	PB	PR	/A	PD	TPI
1908 Bos-A	1	1	.500	6	2	1	0	0	22²	14	0	16	11	12.3	2.38	103	.161	.298	0	.000	-1	0	-0	-0	-0.1
1909 Bos-A	11	7	.611	24	19	13	4	0	160²	121	1	43	88	9.5	2.18	114	.209	.270	9	.164	-5	6	-4	0	0.2
1910 Bos-A	12	13	.480	35	17	14	3	0	196²	155	3	56	145	10.1	1.69	151	.220	.287	18	.261	5	18	19	2	3.3
1911 Bos-A	23	17	.575	44	33	25	5	3	275²	226	2	76	231	10.2	2.02	162	.223	.284	23	.261	9	40	38	2	6.5
1912 *Bos-A	**34**	5	**.872**	43	38	**35**	**10**	1	344	267	2	82	258	9.4	1.91	178	.216	.272	36	.290	11	54	57	8	8.6
1913 Bos-A	11	5	.688	23	18	12	1	2	145²	120	0	61	123	11.7	2.29	129	.229	.319	15	.268	4	10	11	4	2.1
1914 Bos-A	9	3	.750	18	14	11	1	0	113¹	94	1	34	67	10.2	2.62	103	.229	.288	6	.140	0	2	1	0	0.3
1915 Bos-A	15	5	**.750**	25	16	10	3	2	157¹	120	1	44	63	9.4	**1.49**	187	.216	.275	14	.259	4	25	23	1	3.6
1917 Cle-A	0	1	.000	5	1	0	0	0	15²	17	0	7	2	13.8	3.45	82	.309	.387	0	.000	-1	-1	-0	-0	-0.2
1919 Cle-A	0	0	—	1	0	0	0	0	0²	0	0	0	0			—	.000	.000	49	.255	-1	0	0	0	0.1
1920 *Cle-A	0	0	—	1	0	0	0	0	2	4	0	2	1	27.0	22.50	17	.444	.545	37	.270	0	-4	-4	-0	0.0
Total 11	116	57	.671	225	158	121	28	11	1434¹	1138	10	421	989	10.1	2.03	146	.220	.285	553	.283	31	150	149	14	24.2

● JOHN WOOD   Wood, John B.   b: 1871, 5'7", 142 lbs.   Deb: 5/9/1896

YEAR TM/L	W	L	PCT	G	GS	CG	SH	SV	IP	H	HR	BB	SO	RAT	ERA	ERA+	OAV	OOB	BH	AVG	PB	PR	/A	PD	TPI
1896 StL-N	0	0	—	1	0	0	0	0	0	1	0	2	0	—	∞	—	1.000	1.000	0		-1	-1	-1	0	-0.1

● JOE WOOD   Wood, Joseph Frank   b: 5/20/16, Shohola, Pa.   BR/TR, 6', 190 lbs.   Deb: 5/1/44   F

YEAR TM/L	W	L	PCT	G	GS	CG	SH	SV	IP	H	HR	BB	SO	RAT	ERA	ERA+	OAV	OOB	BH	AVG	PB	PR	/A	PD	TPI
1944 Bos-A	0	1	.000	3	1	0	0	0	9²	13	0	3	5	14.9	6.52	52	.317	.364	0	.000		-3	-3	0	-0.3

● PETE WOOD   Wood, Peter Burke   b: 2/1/1857, Hamilton, Ont., Can.   d: 3/15/23, Chicago, Ill.   TR, 5'7", 185 lbs.   Deb: 7/15/1885   F

YEAR TM/L	W	L	PCT	G	GS	CG	SH	SV	IP	H	HR	BB	SO	RAT	ERA	ERA+	OAV	OOB	BH	AVG	PB	PR	/A	PD	TPI
1885 Buf-N	8	15	.348	24	22	21	0	0	198²	235	8	66	38	13.6	4.44	67	.280	.332	23	.221	-1	-36	-32	-1	-3.1
1889 Phi-N	1	1	.500	3	2	2	0	0	19	28	0	3	8	14.7	5.21	83	.333	.356	0	.000	-1	-3	-2	-0	-0.3
Total 2	9	16	.360	27	24	23	0	0	217²	263	8	69	46	13.7	4.51	69	.285	.334	23	.205	-1	-38	-34	-1	-3.4

● WILBUR WOOD   Wood, Wilbur Forrester   b: 10/22/41, Cambridge, Mass.   BR/TL, 6', 180 lbs.   Deb: 6/30/61

YEAR TM/L	W	L	PCT	G	GS	CG	SH	SV	IP	H	HR	BB	SO	RAT	ERA	ERA+	OAV	OOB	BH	AVG	PB	PR	/A	PD	TPI
1961 Bos-A	0	0	—	6	1	0	0	0	13	14	2	7	4	14.5	5.54	75	.269	.356	0	.000	-0	-2	-2	-0	-0.1
1962 Bos-A	0	0	—	1	1	0	0	0	7²	7	0	3	3	10.6	3.52	117	.214	.290	0	.000	0	0	0	0	0.0
1963 Bos-A	0	5	.000	25	6	0	0	0	64²	67	10	13	28	11.6	3.76	101	.270	.314	0	.000	-0	-0	-0	1	-0.2
1964 Bos-A	0	0	—	4	0	0	0	0	5²	13	1	3	3	25.4	17.47	22	.433	.485	0	.000	-0	-9	-9	-0	-0.1
Pit-N	0	2	.000	3	1	0	0	0	17¹	16	0	11	7	15.1	3.63	97	.246	.372	0	.000	-0	-0	-0	-1	-0.1
1965 Pit-N	1	1	.500	34	1	0	0	0	51¹	49	6	19	26	10.7	3.16	111	.237	.300	0	.000	-0	0	0	0	0.0
1967 Chi-A	4	2	.667	51	8	0	0	4	95¹	95	2	28	47	11.7	2.45	126	.260	.315	1	.063	0	8	7	1	0.4
1968 Chi-A	13	12	.520	**88**	2	0	0	16	159	127	8	33	74	9.2	1.87	162	.222	.268	2	.091	-1	**20**	**20**	-0	3.9
1969 Chi-A	10	11	.476	76	0	0	0	15	119²	113	13	40	73	11.7	3.01	128	.248	.313	0	.000	-1	8	11	1	2.1
1970 Chi-A	9	13	.409	**77**	0	0	0	21	121²	118	7	36	85	11.5	2.81	139	.258	.315	2	.111	-1	12	15	2	3.2
1971 Chi-A☆	22	13	.629	44	42	22	7	1	334	272	21	62	210	9.2	1.91	**188**	.222	.264	5	.052	-5	**57**	62	6	**6.6**
1972 Chi-A★	**24**	17	.585	49	49	20	8	0	376²	325	28	74	193	9.7	2.51	125	.277	.277	17	.136	-2	23	26	4	3.1
1973 Chi-A	**24**	20	.545	49	48	21	4	0	359¹	381	25	91	199	12.0	3.46	114	.270	.318	0		0	14	20	1	2.3
1974 Chi-A☆	20	19	.513	42	42	21	1	0	320¹	305	27	80	169	11.1	3.60	104	.254	.305	0		-1	5	3	0	0.7
1975 Chi-A	16	20	.444	43	43	9	2	1	291¹	309	26	91	140	12.8	4.11	94	.272	.329	0		0	1	1	8	1.1
1976 Chi-A	4	3	.571	7	7	1	1	0	56¹	56	1	11	31	9.9	2.24	159	.242	.279	0		-0	8	9	0	1.1
1977 Chi-A	7	8	.467	24	18	0	0	0	122²	139	10	50	42	14.6	4.99	85	.293	.373	0		-0	-13	-12	2	-1.1
1978 Chi-A	10	10	.500	28	20	0	0	0	168	187	23	74	69	14.1	5.20	73	.285	.361	0		-0	-27	-26	2	-2.5
Total 17	164	156	.512	651	297	114	24	57	2684	2582	209	724	1411	11.3	3.24	112	.254	.308	27	.084	-14	92	120	15	18.5

YEAR TM/L	W	L	PCT	G	GS	CG	SH	SV	IP	H	HR	BB	SO	RAT	ERA	ERA+	OAV	OOB	BH	AVG	PB	PR	/A	PD	TPI
● **BRAD WOODALL**   Woodall, David Bradley b: 6/25/69, Atlanta, Ga. BB/TL, 6′, 175 lbs. Deb: 7/22/94
1994 Atl-N	0	1	.000	1	1	0	0	0	6	5	2	2	2	10.5	4.50	94	.227	.292	1	.500	0	-0	-0	1	0.1
1995 Atl-N	1	1	.500	9	0	0	0	0	10¹	13	1	8	5	18.3	6.10	70	.310	.420	1	1.000	0	-2	-2	0	-0.3
1996 Atl-N	2	2	.500	8	3	0	0	0	19²	28	4	4	20	14.6	7.32	60	.368	.400	1	.200	-0	-7	-6	-0	-1.1
Total 3	3	4	.429	18	4	0	0	0	36	46	7	14	27	15.0	6.50	67	.329	.390	3	.375	1	-9	-9	0	-1.3
● **GENE WOODBURN**   Woodburn, Eugene Stewart b: 8/20/1886, Bellaire, Ohio d: 1/18/61, Sandusky, Ohio BR/TR, 6′, 175 lbs. Deb: 7/27/11
1911 StL-N	1	5	.167	11	6	1	0	0	38¹	22	0	40	23	16.0	5.40	63	.167	.382	1	.167	1	-9	-9	1	-1.0
1912 StL-N	1	4	.200	20	5	1	0	0	48¹	60	0	42	25	19.7	5.59	61	.306	.438	-2	.000	-2	-12	-12	-1	-1.3
Total 2	2	9	.182	31	11	2	0	0	86²	82	0	82	48	18.1	5.50	62	.250	.414	1	.053	-0	-20	-20	0	-2.3
● **FRED WOODCOCK**   Woodcock, Fred Wayland b: 5/17/1868, Winchendon, Mass. d: 8/11/43, Ashburnham, Mass. BL/TL, 6′2″, 190 lbs. Deb: 5/17/1892
1892 Pit-N	1	2	.333	5	4	3	0	0	33	42	1	17	8	16.6	3.55	93	.298	.381	3	.200	0	-1	-1	0	0.0
● **GEORGE WOODEND**   Woodend, George Anthony b: 12/9/17, Hartford, Conn. d: 2/6/80, Hartford, Conn. BR/TR, 6′, 200 lbs. Deb: 4/22/44
1944 Bos-N	0	0	—	3	0	0	0	0	5	9	0	45.0	13.50	28	.556	.714	0	—	0	-2	-2	0	0.0
● **HAL WOODESHICK**   Woodeshick, Harold Joseph b: 8/24/32, Wilkes-Barre, Pa. BR/TL, 6′3″, 200 lbs. Deb: 9/14/56
1956 Det-A	0	2	.000	2	2	0	0	0	5¹	12	1	3	1	25.3	13.50	30	.444	.500	0	—	0	-6	-6	0	-1.3
1958 Cle-A	6	6	.500	14	9	3	0	0	71²	71	4	25	27	12.8	3.64	100	.265	.341	4	.167	-1	1	0	3	0.2
1959 Was-A	2	4	.333	31	3	0	0	0	61	58	2	36	30	14.0	3.69	106	.253	.357	0	.000	-1	1	2	1	0.1
1960 Was-A	4	5	.444	41	14	1	0	4	115	131	7	60	46	15.2	4.70	83	.289	.375	-2	.069	-2	-11	-10	2	-0.8
1961 Was-A	3	2	.600	7	6	1	0	0	40¹	38	3	24	24	14.5	4.02	100	.257	.371	2	.125	-1	0	-0	1	0.0
Det-A	1	1	.500	12	2	0	0	0	18¹	25	3	17	13	20.6	7.85	52	.316	.438	0	.000	-0	-8	-8	1	-0.7
Yr	4	3	.571	19	8	1	0	0	58²	63	6	41	37	16.0	5.22	77	.273	.382	2	.100	-1	-8	-8	2	-0.7
1962 Hou-N★	5	16	.238	31	26	2	1	0	139¹	161	3	54	82	14.1	4.39	85	.290	.356	3	.081	-1	-7	-10	0	-1.5
1963 Hou-N★	11	9	.550	55	0	0	0	10	114	75	3	42	94	9.7	1.97	160	.186	.273	1	.130	-0	17	15	3	3.3
1964 Hou-N	2	9	.182	61	0	0	0	**23**	78¹	73	5	32	58	12.9	2.76	124	.249	.337	0	.000	-1	7	6	2	1.3
1965 Hou-N	3	4	.429	27	0	0	0	3	32¹	27	3	18	22	12.5	3.06	110	.227	.328	1	.167	-0	2	1	1	0.3
StL-N	3	2	.600	51	0	0	0	15	59²	47	1	27	37	11.5	1.81	212	.221	.314	0	.000	-1	11	13	2	2.0
Yr	6	6	.500	78	0	0	0	18	92	74	4	45	59	11.8	2.25	163	.223	.319	1	.071	-1	13	15	2	2.3
1966 StL-N	2	1	.667	59	0	0	0	4	70¹	57	5	23	30	10.4	1.92	187	.224	.290	1	.200	0	13	13	3	1.1
1967 *StL-N	2	1	.667	36	0	0	0	2	41²	41	2	28	20	15.6	5.18	63	.252	.371	0	.000	-0	-9	-1	-0	-0.7
Total 11	44	62	.415	427	62	7	1	61	847¹	816	40	389	484	13.2	3.56	102	.254	.342	16	.092	-7	13	7	18	3.3
● **DAN WOODMAN**   Woodman, Daniel Courtenay "Cocoa" b: 7/8/1893, Danvers, Mass. d: 12/14/62, Danvers, Mass. BR/TR, 5′8″, 160 lbs. Deb: 7/10/14
1914 Buf-F	0	0	—	13	6	0	0	0	33²	30	0	11	13	11.2	2.41	123	.246	.313	1	.143	2	2	-1	-0.1
1915 Buf-F	0	0	—	5	1	0	0	0	15¹	14	0	9	1	13.5	4.11	68	.246	.348	0	.250	-2	-2	2	1	0.1
Total 2	0	0	—	18	1	0	0	0	49	44	0	20	14	11.9	2.94	99	.246	.325	2	.182	-1	-0	-0	0
● **CLARENCE WOODS**   Woods, Clarence Cofield b: 6/11/1892, Woods Ridge, Ohio County, Ind. d: 7/2/69, Rising Sun, Ind. BR/TR, 6′5″, 230 lbs. Deb: 8/8/14
1914 Ind-F	0	0	—	2	0	0	1	0	2	1	0	2	1	13.5	4.50	69	.167	.375	0	-0	-0	-0	-0	0	0.0
● **PINKY WOODS**   Woods, George Rowland b: 5/22/15, Waterbury, Conn. d: 10/30/82, Los Angeles, Cal. BR/TR, 6′5″, 225 lbs. Deb: 6/20/43
1943 Bos-A	5	6	.455	23	12	2	0	1	100²	109	6	55	32	14.8	4.92	67	.284	.375	8	.222	-0	-18	-18	-0	-1.9
1944 Bos-A	4	8	.333	38	20	5	1	0	170²	171	4	88	56	14.0	3.27	104	.266	.360	7	.146	-1	3	2	2	0.2
1945 Bos-A	4	7	.364	24	12	3	0	2	107¹	108	3	63	36	14.4	4.19	81	.268	.368	9	.214	-1	-9	-9	-1	-0.7
Total 3	13	21	.382	85	44	10	1	3	378²	388	13	206	124	14.3	3.97	85	.272	.366	24	.190	-1	-25	-25	3	-2.4
● **JOHN WOODS**   Woods, John Fulton "Abe" b: 1/18/1898, Princeton, W.Va. d: 10/4/46, Norfolk, Va. BR/TR, 6′, 175 lbs. Deb: 9/16/24
1924 Bos-A	0	0	—	1	0	0	0	0	1	0	0	3	0	27.0	0.00	—	.000	.500	0	—	0	-0	-0	0	0.0
● **WALT WOODS**   Woods, Walter Sydney b: 4/28/1875, Rye, N.H. d: 10/30/51, Portsmouth, N.H. BR/TR, 5′9.5″, 165 lbs. Deb: 4/20/1898
1898 Chi-N	9	13	.409	27	22	18	3	0	215	224	7	59	26	12.3	3.14	114	.266	.322	27	.175	-4	11	11	1	0.6
1899 Lou-N	9	13	.409	26	21	17	0	0	186¹	216	9	37	21	12.6	3.28	117	.290	.329	19	.151	-3	12	12	5	1.3
1900 Pit-N	0	0	—	1	0	0	0	0	3	9	0	1	1	30.0	21.00	17	.500	.526	0	.000	-0	-6	-6	-0	-0.0
Total 3	18	26	.409	54	43	35	3	0	404¹	449	16	97	48	12.5	3.34	111	.280	.328	46	.164	-7	17	17	5	1.9
● **DICK WOODSON**   Woodson, Richard Lee b: 3/30/45, Oelwein, Iowa BR/TR, 6′5″, 207 lbs. Deb: 4/8/69
1969 *Min-A	7	5	.583	44	10	2	0	1	110¹	99	11	49	66	12.3	3.67	99	.237	.322	2	.074	-1	-1	-0	1	-0.1
1970 *Min-A	1	2	.333	21	0	0	0	0	30²	29	2	19	12	14.1	3.82	98	.244	.348	0	.000	-0	-0	-0	-1	-0.3
1972 Min-A	14	14	.500	36	36	9	3	0	251²	193	19	101	150	10.6	2.72	118	.211	.291	7	.080	-5	10	14	1	1.1
1973 Min-A	10	8	.556	23	23	4	2	0	141¹	137	12	68	53	13.2	3.95	100	.254	.339	0	—	-0	-2	-0	-2	-0.2
1974 Min-A	1	1	.500	5	4	0	0	0	27	30	5	4	12	11.7	4.33	86	.273	.304	0	—	-2	-2	-2	-1	-0.3
NY-A	1	2	.333	8	3	0	0	0	28	34	6	12	12	15.1	5.79	61	.301	.373	0	—	-0	-7	-7	-1	-0.6
Yr	2	3	.400	13	7	0	0	0	55	64	11	16	24	13.3	5.07	71	.286	.336	0	—	-0	-9	-9	-0	-0.9
Total 5	34	32	.515	137	76	15	5	2	589	522	55	253	315	12.0	3.47	102	.236	.317	9	.077	-7	-2	-0	0	-0.1
● **KERRY WOODSON**   Woodson, Walter Browne b: 5/18/69, Jacksonville, Fla. BR/TR, 6′2″, 190 lbs. Deb: 7/19/92
1992 Sea-A	0	1	.000	8	1	0	0	0	13²	12	0	11	6	16.5	3.29	121	.245	.403	0	—	0	1	1	0	0.1
● **FRANK WOODWARD**   Woodward, Frank Russell b: 5/17/1894, New Haven, Conn. d: 6/11/61, New Haven, Conn. BR/TR, 5′10″, 175 lbs. Deb: 4/17/18
1918 Phi-N	0	0	—	2	0	0	0	0	6	6	0	4	4	15.0	6.00	50	.250	.357	1	.333	-2	-2	-0	0.0
1919 Phi-N	6	9	.400	17	12	6	0	0	100²	109	5	35	27	13.3	4.74	68	.291	.359	6	.207	-1	-20	-17	-2	-2.4
StL-N	3	5	.375	17	7	2	0	1	72	65	1	28	18	11.8	2.63	106	.248	.323	1	.048	-2	1	-0	-0	-0.1
Yr	9	14	.391	34	19	8	0	1	172²	174	6	63	45	12.4	3.86	79	.271	.337	7	.140	-1	-18	-16	-2	-2.5
1921 Was-A	0	0	—	3	1	0	0	0	10²	14	3	3	4	11.8	5.91	70	.282	.333	1	.333	-0	-2	-2	0	0.0
1922 Was-A	0	0	—	1	0	0	0	0	2¹	3	0	3	2	23.1	11.57	33	.375	.545	0	.000	-0	-2	-2	0	-0.7
1923 Chi-A	0	1	.000	2	1	0	0	0	2	5	0	1	2	27.0	13.50	29	.500	.545	0	—	-2	-2	0
Total 5	9	15	.375	42	21	8	0	1	193²	199	6	74	55	13.0	4.23	74	.277	.350	9	.158	-1	-26	-24	-2	-3.2
● **BOB WOODWARD**   Woodward, Robert John b: 9/28/62, Hanover, N.H. BR/TR, 6′3″, 185 lbs. Deb: 9/5/85
1985 Bos-A	1	0	1.000	5	2	0	0	0	26²	17	0	9	16	9.5	1.69	254	.168	.250	0	—	0	7	8	-1	-0.1
1986 Bos-A	2	3	.400	9	6	0	0	0	35²	46	4	11	14	14.6	5.30	79	.313	.365	0	—	0	-4	-5	0	-0.5
1987 Bos-A	1	1	.500	9	6	0	0	0	37	53	6	15	15	16.8	7.05	64	.338	.399	0	—	0	-11	-10	-1	-0.6
1988 Bos-A	0	0	—	1	0	0	0	0	0²	2	0	1	0	40.5	13.50	30	.500	.600	0	—	0	-1	-1	0	0.0
Total 4	4	4	.500	24	14	0	0	0	100	118	10	36	45	14.2	5.04	86	.289	.352	0	—	0	-9	-9	-1	-1.2
● **FLOYD WOOLDRIDGE**   Wooldridge, Floyd Lewis b: 8/25/28, Jerico Springs, Mo BR/TR, 6′1″, 185 lbs. Deb: 5/1/55
1955 StL-N	2	4	.333	18	8	2	0	0	57²	64	6	27	14	14.4	4.84	84	.281	.359	4	.222	0	-5	-5	-1	-0.6
● **JUNIOR WOOTEN**   Wooten, Earl Hazwell b: 1/16/24, Pelzer, S.C. BR/TL, 5′11″, 160 lbs. Deb: 9/16/47 ◆
1948 Was-A	0	0	—	1	0	0	0	0	2	2	0	2	1	18.0	9.00	48	.250	.400	66	.256	0	-1	-1	0	0.0
● **FRED WORDEN**   Worden, Frederick Bamford b: 9/4/1894, St.Louis, Mo. d: 11/9/41, St.Louis, Mo. BR/TR, Deb: 9/28/14
1914 Phi-A	0	0	—	1	0	0	0	0	2	8	0	0	1	36.0	18.00	15	.615	.615	0	.000	-0	-3	-3	0	0.0
● **HOGE WORKMAN**   Workman, Harry Hall b: 9/25/1899, Huntington, W.Va. d: 5/20/72, Ft.Myers, Fla. BR/TR, 5′11″, 170 lbs. Deb: 6/27/24
1924 Bos-A	0	0	—	1	1	0	0	0	18	25	2	11	7	19.0	8.50	58	.325	.422	0	—	0	-6	-6	0	0.0
● **RALPH WORKS**   Works, Ralph Talmadge "Judge" b: 3/16/1888, Payson, Ill. d: 8/4/41, Pasadena, Cal. BL/TR, 6′2.5″, 185 lbs. Deb: 5/1/09
1909 *Det-A	4	1	.800	16	4	0	0	2	64	60	0	17	31	11.3	1.97	128	.261	.313	-2	.059	-2	4	4	-1	0.1
1910 Det-A	3	6	.333	18	10	5	0	1	85²	73	1	39	36	12.2	3.57	74	.235	.328	8	.267	1	-10	-9	-1	-0.9

YEAR	TM/L	W	L	PCT	G	GS	CG	SH	SV	IP	H	HR	BB	SO	RAT	ERA	ERA+	OAV	OOB	BH	AVG	PB	PR	/A	PD	TPI
1911	Det-A	11	5	.688	30	15	9	3	0	167¹	173	3	67	68	13.2	3.87	89	.268	.342	9	.148	-3	-10	-8	-4	-1.4
1912	Det-A	5	10	.333	27	16	9	1	1	157	185	1	66	64	14.8	4.24	77	.308	.383	8	.143	-3	-16	-17	-0	-1.7
	Cin-N	1	1	.500	3	1	1	0	0	9²	4	0	5	5	9.3	2.79	120	.133	.278	1	.200	-0	1	1	-0	0.1
1913	Cin-N	0	1	.000	5	2	0	0	0	15	15	0	8	4	15.6	7.80	42	.242	.356	1	.167	-0	-8	-8	-0	-0.4
Total	5	24	24	.500	99	48	28	4	4	498²	512	5	202	208	13.3	3.79	83	.271	.348	28	.160	-8	-39	-37	-6	-4.2

● TIM WORRELL
Worrell, Timothy Howard b: 7/5/67, Pasadena, Cal. BR/TR, 6'4", 215 lbs. Deb: 6/25/93 F

YEAR	TM/L	W	L	PCT	G	GS	CG	SH	SV	IP	H	HR	BB	SO	RAT	ERA	ERA+	OAV	OOB	BH	AVG	PB	PR	/A	PD	TPI
1993	SD-N	2	7	.222	21	16	0	0	0	100²	104	11	43	52	13.1	4.92	84	.269	.342	1	.032	-3	-10	-9	-1	-1.0
1994	SD-N	0	1	.000	3	3	0	0	0	14²	9	0	5	14	8.6	3.68	112	.170	.241	1	.500	1	1	1	0	0.1
1995	SD-N	1	0	1.000	9	0	0	0	0	13¹	16	2	6	13	15.5	4.73	85	.291	.371	0	.000	-0	-1	-1	-0	-0.1
1996	*SD-N	9	7	.563	50	11	0	0	1	121	109	9	39	99	11.5	3.05	131	.236	.304	3	.150	-0	16	13	-2	1.3
Total	4	12	15	.444	83	30	0	0	1	249²	238	22	93	178	12.2	3.93	103	.249	.320	5	.093	-2	6	4	-2	0.3

● TODD WORRELL
Worrell, Todd Roland b: 9/28/59, Arcadia, Cal. BR/TR, 6'5", 215 lbs. Deb: 8/28/85 F

YEAR	TM/L	W	L	PCT	G	GS	CG	SH	SV	IP	H	HR	BB	SO	RAT	ERA	ERA+	OAV	OOB	BH	AVG	PB	PR	/A	PD	TPI
1985	*StL-N	3	0	1.000	17	0	0	0	5	21²	17	2	7	17	10.0	2.91	122	.215	.279	0	.000	-0	2	2	-0	0.2
1986	StL-N	9	10	.474	74	0	0	0	36	103²	86	9	41	73	11.1	2.08	175	.229	.307	1	.143	0	19	18	-2	4.2
1987	*StL-N	8	6	.571	75	0	0	0	33	94²	86	8	34	92	11.4	2.66	156	.242	.308	1	.100	-0	15	16	0	3.1
1988	StL-N★	5	9	.357	68	0	0	0	32	90	69	7	34	78	10.4	3.00	116	.214	.291	0	.000	-0	4	5	0	1.0
1989	StL-N	3	5	.375	47	0	0	0	20	51²	42	4	26	41	11.8	2.96	123	.222	.316	0	.000	-0	3	4	1	0.9
1992	StL-N	5	3	.625	67	0	0	0	3	64	45	4	25	64	10.0	2.11	161	.198	.281	0	—	0	10	9	-1	1.0
1993	LA-N	1	1	.500	35	0	0	0	5	38²	46	6	11	31	13.3	6.05	63	.313	.361	0	—	-0	-9	-10	-0	-0.7
1994	LA-N	6	5	.545	38	0	0	0	11	42	37	4	12	44	10.7	4.29	91	.236	.294	0	—	-0	-0	-2	-0	-0.5
1995	LA-N†	4	1	.800	59	0	0	0	32	62¹	50	4	19	61	10.1	2.02	188	.221	.285	0	.000	-0	15	12	-1	2.1
1996	*LA-N★	4	6	.400	72	0	0	0	44	65¹	70	5	15	66	12.0	3.03	127	.265	.310	0	—	-0	9	6	-1	1.4
Total	10	48	46	.511	552	0	0	0	221	634	548	53	224	567	11.1	2.88	130	.234	.303	2	.074	-1	67	60	-3	12.7

● RICH WORTHAM
Wortham, Richard Cooper b: 10/22/53, Odessa, Tex. BR/TL, 6', 185 lbs. Deb: 5/3/78

YEAR	TM/L	W	L	PCT	G	GS	CG	SH	SV	IP	H	HR	BB	SO	RAT	ERA	ERA+	OAV	OOB	BH	AVG	PB	PR	/A	PD	TPI
1978	Chi-A	3	2	.600	8	8	2	0	0	59	59	1	23	25	12.5	3.05	125	.267	.336	0	—	0	5	5	-0	0.4
1979	Chi-A	14	14	.500	34	33	5	0	0	204	195	21	100	119	13.1	4.90	87	.255	.343	0	—	0	-15	-15	-2	-1.9
1980	Chi-A	4	7	.364	41	10	0	0	1	92	102	4	58	45	15.9	5.97	67	.285	.389	0	—	0	-20	-20	1	-2.0
1983	Oak-A	0	0	—	1	0	0	0	0	3	3	0	1	0	—	∞	—	1.000	1.000	0	—	0	-1	-1	0	0.1
Total	4	21	23	.477	84	51	7	0	1	355	359	26	182	189	13.9	4.89	84	.266	.356	0	—	0	-32	-31	-1	-3.4

● AL WORTHINGTON
Worthington, Allan Fulton "Red" b: 2/5/29, Birmingham, Ala. BR/TR, 6'2", 205 lbs. Deb: 7/6/53 C

YEAR	TM/L	W	L	PCT	G	GS	CG	SH	SV	IP	H	HR	BB	SO	RAT	ERA	ERA+	OAV	OOB	BH	AVG	PB	PR	/A	PD	TPI
1953	NY-N	4	8	.333	20	17	5	2	0	102	103	6	54	52	14.0	3.44	125	.258	.349	2	.065	-2	10	10	0	0.8
1954	NY-N	0	2	.000	10	1	0	0	0	18	21	0	15	8	18.0	3.50	115	.333	.462	0	.000	-1	1	1	0	0.1
1956	NY-N	7	14	.333	28	24	4	0	0	165²	158	20	74	95	12.8	3.97	95	.254	.338	12	.235	2	-4	-3	2	0.0
1957	NY-N	8	11	.421	55	12	1	1	4	157²	140	19	56	90	11.5	4.22	93	.237	.309	4	.100	-2	-6	-5	0	-0.8
1958	SF-N	11	7	.611	54	12	1	0	6	151¹	152	17	57	76	12.5	3.63	105	.255	.322	8	.182	0	5	3	0	0.1
1959	SF-N	2	3	.400	42	3	0	0	2	73¹	68	8	37	45	13.5	3.68	103	.253	.354	1	.077	-1	2	1	1	0.1
1960	Bos-A	0	1	.000	6	0	0	0	0	11²	17	1	11	7	21.6	7.71	52	.340	.459	0	.000	-0	-5	-5	0	-0.4
	Chi-A	1	1	.500	4	0	0	0	0	5¹	3	0	4	1	11.8	3.38	112	.176	.333	2	1.000	0	0	0	0	0.2
	Yr	1	2	.333	10	0	0	0	0	17	20	1	15	8	18.5	6.35	62	.299	.427	2	.667	1	-5	-5	0	-0.2
1963	Cin-N	4	4	.500	50	0	0	0	10	81¹	75	6	31	55	12.1	2.99	112	.248	.324	1	.083	-0	3	3	2	0.6
1964	Cin-N	1	0	1.000	7	0	0	0	0	7	14	0	2	6	21.9	10.29	35	.400	.447	0	—	-0	-5	-5	-0	-0.7
	Min-A	5	6	.455	41	0	0	0	14	72¹	47	4	28	59	9.3	1.37	261	.183	.263	1	.063	-1	18	18	1	3.4
1965	*Min-A	10	7	.588	62	0	0	0	21	80¹	57	4	41	59	11.3	2.13	167	.207	.316	1	.100	0	12	13	2	3.6
1966	Min-A	6	3	.667	65	0	0	0	16	91¹	66	6	27	93	9.3	2.46	146	.199	.261	3	.273	1	10	11	1	1.8
1967	Min-A	8	9	.471	59	0	0	0	16	92	77	6	38	80	11.3	2.84	122	.229	.309	0	.000	-1	4	6	0	1.4
1968	Min-A	4	5	.444	54	0	0	0	18	76¹	67	1	32	57	11.7	2.71	114	.238	.315	0	.000	-0	2	3	0	0.5
1969	*Min-A	4	1	.800	46	0	0	0	0	61	65	7	20	51	12.5	4.57	80	.278	.335	0	.000	-0	-6	-6	-1	-0.7
Total	14	75	82	.478	602	69	11	3	110	1246²	1130	105	527	834	12.2	3.39	110	.243	.323	35	.137	-5	41	46	7	10.3

● GENE WRIGHT
Wright, Clarence Eugene "Big Gene" b: 12/11/1878, Cleveland, Ohio d: 10/29/30, Barberton, Ohio BR/TR, 6'2", 185 lbs. Deb: 10/5/01

YEAR	TM/L	W	L	PCT	G	GS	CG	SH	SV	IP	H	HR	BB	SO	RAT	ERA	ERA+	OAV	OOB	BH	AVG	PB	PR	/A	PD	TPI
1901	Bro-N	1	0	1.000	1	1	1	0	0	9	6	0	1	6	7.0	1.00	335	.188	.212	1	.333	0	2	2	-0	0.3
1902	Cle-A	7	11	.389	21	18	15	1	1	148	150	6	75	52	14.2	3.95	87	.263	.357	10	.143	-2	-6	-8	-2	-1.2
1903	Cle-A	3	9	.250	15	12	8	0	0	101²	122	1	58	42	16.3	5.75	50	.296	.388	2	.209	2	-32	-33	2	-2.9
	StL-A	3	5	.375	8	8	7	1	0	61	73	2	16	37	13.7	3.69	79	.296	.348	3	.143	-1	-5	-5	1	-0.6
	Yr	6	14	.300	23	20	15	1	0	162²	195	3	74	79	15.1	4.98	58	.296	.368	12	.188	1	-36	-38	3	-3.4
1904	StL-A	0	1	.000	1	1	0	0	0	4	10	0	2	3	27.0	13.50	18	.476	.522	0	.000	-0	-5	-5	1	-0.8
Total	4	14	26	.350	46	40	31	2	1	323²	361	9	152	140	14.7	4.50	70	.282	.365	23	.167	-1	-45	-49	1	-5.2

● CLYDE WRIGHT
Wright, Clyde b: 2/20/41, Jefferson City, Tenn. BR/TL, 6'1", 185 lbs. Deb: 6/15/66

YEAR	TM/L	W	L	PCT	G	GS	CG	SH	SV	IP	H	HR	BB	SO	RAT	ERA	ERA+	OAV	OOB	BH	AVG	PB	PR	/A	PD	TPI
1966	Cal-A	4	7	.364	20	13	3	1	0	91¹	92	11	25	37	11.6	3.74	90	.265	.316	3	.103	-1	-3	-4	0	-0.6
1967	Cal-A	5	5	.500	20	11	1	0	0	77¹	76	5	24	35	11.4	3.26	96	.260	.319	6	.273	2	-0	-0	1	0.1
1968	Cal-A	10	6	.625	41	13	2	1	3	125²	123	13	44	71	12.1	3.94	74	.256	.321	8	.216	2	-13	-14	-1	-1.8
1969	Cal-A	1	8	.111	37	5	0	0	0	63²	66	4	30	31	13.7	4.10	85	.278	.362	2	—	-0	-3	-4	-0	-0.5
1970	Cal-A★	22	12	.647	39	39	7	2	0	260²	226	24	88	110	11.1	2.83	128	.232	.300	18	.171	3	26	23	-2	3.0
1971	Cal-A	16	17	.485	37	37	10	2	0	276²	225	17	82	135	10.1	2.99	108	.226	.287	14	.154	2	14	8	4	1.5
1972	Cal-A	18	11	.621	35	35	15	2	0	251	229	14	80	87	11.2	2.98	98	.246	.308	18	.217	7	2	-2	3	0.9
1973	Cal-A	11	19	.367	37	36	13	1	0	257	273	26	76	65	12.3	3.68	96	.273	.326	0	—	0	4	4	4	0.2
1974	Mil-A	9	20	.310	38	32	15	0	0	232	264	22	54	64	12.3	4.42	82	.284	.323	0	—	0	-21	-21	2	-2.2
1975	Tex-A	4	6	.400	25	14	1	0	0	93¹	105	7	47	32	14.8	4.44	85	.294	.378	0	—	0	-7	-7	2	-0.5
Total	10	100	111	.474	329	235	67	9	3	1728²	1679	143	550	667	11.7	3.50	96	.256	.316	69	.183	14	-1	-27	13	0.1

● DAVE WRIGHT
Wright, David William b: 8/27/1875, Dennison, Ohio d: 1/18/46, Dennison, Ohio BR/TR, 6', 185 lbs. Deb: 7/22/1895

YEAR	TM/L	W	L	PCT	G	GS	CG	SH	SV	IP	H	HR	BB	SO	RAT	ERA	ERA+	OAV	OOB	BH	AVG	PB	PR	/A	PD	TPI
1895	Pit-N	0	0	—	1	0	0	0	0	2	6	0	1	0	31.5	27.00	17	.500	.538	0	.000	-0	-5	-5	0	0.0
1897	Chi-N	1	0	1.000	1	1	1	0	0	7	17	1	2	4	27.0	15.43	29	.459	.512	1	.333	0	-9	-9	0	-0.7
Total	2	1	0	1.000	2	1	1	0	0	9	23	1	3	4	28.0	18.00	25	.469	.519	1	.250	0	-14	-14	0	-0.7

● GEORGE WRIGHT
Wright, George b: 1/28/1847, Yonkers, N.Y. d: 8/21/37, Boston, Mass. BR/TR, 5'9.5", 150 lbs. Deb: 5/5/1871 FMH♦

YEAR	TM/L	W	L	PCT	G	GS	CG	SH	SV	IP	H	HR	BB	SO	RAT	ERA	ERA+	OAV	OOB	BH	AVG	PB	PR	/A	PD	TPI
1875	Bos-n	0	1	.000	2	0	0	0	0	4	5	0	0	1	11.3	6.75	32	.294	.294	136	.333	1	-2	-2		-0.3
1876	Bos-N	0	0	—	1	0	0	0	0	1	1	0	0	1	9.0	0.00	—	.250	.250	100	.299	0	0	0	0	0.0

● ED WRIGHT
Wright, Henderson Edward b: 5/15/19, Dyersburg, Tenn. d: 11/19/95, Dyersburg, Tenn. BR/TR, 6'1", 180 lbs. Deb: 7/29/45

YEAR	TM/L	W	L	PCT	G	GS	CG	SH	SV	IP	H	HR	BB	SO	RAT	ERA	ERA+	OAV	OOB	BH	AVG	PB	PR	/A	PD	TPI
1945	Bos-N	8	3	.727	15	12	7	1	0	111¹	104	7	33	24	11.1	2.51	153	.254	.310	5	.128	-2	16	16	-1	1.2
1946	Bos-N	12	9	.571	36	21	8	2	0	176¹	164	8	71	44	12.1	3.52	97	.250	.325	18	.305	6	-2	-2	0	-0.4
1947	Bos-N	3	3	.500	23	6	1	0	0	64²	80	9	35	14	16.3	6.40	61	.305	.391	3	.130	-0	-17	-18	-1	-1.5
1948	Bos-N	0	0	—	3	0	0	0	0	4²	9	0	2	2	21.2	1.93	199	.474	.524	0	—	0	1	0	0	0.1
1952	Phi-A	2	1	.667	24	0	0	0	1	41¹	55	6	20	9	17.0	6.53	61	.320	.400	1	.143	-0	-13	-12	-0	-0.9
Total	5	25	16	.610	101	39	16	3	1	398¹	412	30	161	93	13.1	4.00	92	.271	.344	27	.211	3	-15	-14	-2	-0.8

● JIM WRIGHT
Wright, James "Jiggs" b: 9/19/1900, Hyde, England d: 4/10/63, Oakland, Cal. BR/TR, 6'2.5", 195 lbs. Deb: 9/14/27

YEAR	TM/L	W	L	PCT	G	GS	CG	SH	SV	IP	H	HR	BB	SO	RAT	ERA	ERA+	OAV	OOB	BH	AVG	PB	PR	/A	PD	TPI
1927	StL-A	1	0	1.000	3	1	1	0	0	12	9	0	4	4	9.0	4.50	97	.182	.250	0	.000	-0	-2	-0	-0	-0.1
1928	StL-A	0	0	—	1	0	0	0	0	2	3	0	2	2	22.5	13.50	31	.375	.500	0	—	0	-1	-0	-0	-0.1
Total	2	1	0	1.000	4	1	1	0	0	14	11	0	6	6	10.9	5.79	75	.212	.293	0	.000	-0	-3	-0	-0	-0.1

● JIM WRIGHT
Wright, James Clifton b: 12/21/50, Reed City, Mich. BR/TR, 6'1", 165 lbs. Deb: 4/15/78

YEAR	TM/L	W	L	PCT	G	GS	CG	SH	SV	IP	H	HR	BB	SO	RAT	ERA	ERA+	OAV	OOB	BH	AVG	PB	PR	/A	PD	TPI
1978	Bos-A	8	4	.667	24	16	5	3	0	116	122	8	24	56	11.9	3.57	115	.276	.323	0	—	0	2	7	-2	0.5
1979	Bos-A	1	0	1.000	11	1	0	0	0	23	19	5	7	15	11.3	5.09	87	.226	.309	0	—	0	-2	-2	-0	-0.4
Total	2	9	4	.692	35	17	5	3	0	139	141	13	31	71	11.8	3.82	109	.268	.321	0	—	0	0	5	-2	0.1

YEAR	TM/L	W	L	PCT	G	GS	CG	SH	SV	IP	H	HR	BB	SO	RAT	ERA	ERA+	OAV	OOB	BH	AVG	PB	PR	/A	PD	TPI
● **JIM WRIGHT**					Wright, James Leon b: 3/3/55, St.Joseph, Mo. BR/TR, 6'5", 205 lbs. Deb: 4/22/81 C																					
1981	KC-A	2	3	.400	17	4	0	0	0	52	57	5	21	27	13.8	3.46	104	.277	.349	0	—	0	1	1	-1	0.0
1982	KC-A	0	0	—	7	0	0	0	0	23²	32	3	6	9	14.5	5.32	77	.320	.358	0	—	0	-3	-3	-1	-0.1
Total	2	2	3	.400	24	4	0	0	0	75²	89	8	27	36	14.0	4.04	93	.291	.352	0	—	0	-2	-2	-1	-0.1
● **RICKY WRIGHT**					Wright, James Richard b: 11/22/58, Paris, Tex. BL/TL, 6'3", 175 lbs. Deb: 7/28/82																					
1982	LA-N	2	1	.667	14	5	0	0	0	32²	28	1	20	24	13.2	3.03	114	.233	.343	1	.125	0	2	2	0	0.2
1983	LA-N	0	0	—	6	0	0	0	0	6¹	5	0	2	5	9.9	2.84	126	.227	.292	0	—	0	1	1	0	0.0
	Tex-A	0	0	—	1	0	0	0	0	2	0	0	1	2	4.5	0.00	—	.000	.167	0	—	0	1	1	0	0.2
1984	Tex-A	0	2	.000	8	1	0	0	0	14²	20	3	11	6	19.0	6.14	68	.357	.463	0	—	0	-3	-3	0	-0.5
1985	Tex-A	0	0	—	5	0	0	0	0	7²	5	1	7	3	11.7	4.70	90	.185	.313	0	—	0	-0	-0	0	-0.1
1986	Tex-A	1	0	1.000	21	1	0	0	0	39¹	44	1	21	27	14.9	5.03	85	.284	.369	0	—	0	-4	-3	1	-0.1
Total	5	3	3	.500	55	7	0	0	0	102²	102	5	60	67	14.2	4.30	92	.265	.364	1	.125	0	-4	-4	1	-0.2
● **JAMEY WRIGHT**					Wright, Jamey Alan b: 12/24/74, Oklahoma City, Okla. BR/TR, 6'6", 205 lbs. Deb: 7/3/96																					
1996	Col-N	4	4	.500	16	15	0	0	0	91¹	105	8	41	45	15.1	4.93	110	.298	.382	2	.077	-1	-7	5	1	0.4
● **KEN WRIGHT**					Wright, Kenneth Warren b: 9/4/46, Pensacola, Fla. BR/TR, 6'2", 210 lbs. Deb: 4/10/70																					
1970	KC-A	1	2	.333	47	0	0	0	3	53¹	49	2	29	30	14.3	5.23	71	.261	.379	0	.000	-0	-9	-9	-0	-0.6
1971	KC-A	3	6	.333	21	12	1	1	1	78	66	6	47	56	13.4	3.69	93	.230	.344	2	.091	-1	-2	-2	1	-0.3
1972	KC-A	1	2	.333	17	0	0	0	4	18¹	15	0	15	18	15.2	4.91	62	.231	.383	0	—	-0	-4	-4	0	-0.9
1973	KC-A	6	5	.545	25	12	1	0	0	80²	64	6	42	75	15.8	4.91	84	.210	.386	0	—	0	-10	-7	-1	-1.1
1974	NY-A	0	0	—	3	0	0	0	0	5²	5	0	7	2	19.1	3.18	111	.227	.414	0	—	0	0	0	0	0.1
Total	5	11	15	.423	113	24	2	1	8	236	195	14	180	181	14.7	4.54	81	.230	.372	2	.071	-2	-24	-22	-1	-2.8
● **MEL WRIGHT**					Wright, Melvin James b: 5/11/28, Manila, Ark. d: 5/16/83, Houston, Tex. BR/TR, 6'3", 210 lbs. Deb: 4/17/54 C																					
1954	StL-N	0	0	—	9	0	0	0	0	10¹	16	2	11	4	25.3	10.45	39	.348	.492	0	.000	-0	-7	-7	0	0.0
1955	StL-N	2	2	.500	29	0	0	0	1	36¹	44	4	9	18	13.4	6.19	66	.308	.353	0	.000	-1	-9	-9	0	-0.9
1960	Chi-N	0	0	—	9	0	0	0	2	16¹	17	1	3	8	11.0	4.96	76	.279	.313	0	.000	-0	-2	-2	-1	-0.3
1961	Chi-N	0	1	.000	11	0	0	0	0	21	42	3	4	6	19.7	10.71	39	.416	.438	0	.000	-0	-16	-15	1	-0.6
Total	4	2	4	.333	58	0	0	0	3	84	119	10	27	36	16.0	7.61	53	.339	.391	0	.000	-2	-34	-33	1	-1.8
● **BOB WRIGHT**					Wright, Robert Cassius b: 12/13/1891, Decatur Co., Ind. d: 7/30/93, Carmichael, Cal. BR/TR, 6'1.5", 175 lbs. Deb: 9/21/15																					
1915	Chi-N	0	0	—	2	0	0	0	0	4	6	0	3	2	13.5	2.25	123	.353	.353	0	—	0	0	0	0	0.0
● **ROY WRIGHT**					Wright, Roy Earl b: 9/26/33, Buchtel, Ohio BR/TR, 6'2", 170 lbs. Deb: 9/30/56																					
1956	NY-N	0	1	.000	1	1	0	0	0	2²	8	1	2	0	33.8	16.88	22	.533	.588	0	.000	-0	-4	-4	0	-0.9
● **RASTY WRIGHT**					Wright, Wayne Bromley b: 11/5/1895, Ceredo, W.Va. d: 6/12/48, Columbus, Ohio BR/TR, 5'11", 160 lbs. Deb: 6/22/17																					
1917	StL-A	0	1	.000	16	1	0	0	0	39²	48	0	10	5	13.4	5.45	48	.300	.345	2	.200	0	-12	-13	0	-0.2
1918	StL-A	8	2	.800	18	13	6	1	0	111¹	99	1	18	25	9.9	2.51	109	.244	.285	10	.294	3	3	3	-1	0.5
1919	StL-A	0	5	.000	24	5	2	0	0	63¹	79	1	20	14	14.2	5.54	60	.315	.368	1	.083	-1	-16	-16	0	-1.2
1922	StL-A	9	7	.563	31	16	5	0	5	154	148	7	50	44	12.0	2.92	142	.262	.331	7	.140	-2	19	21	1	2.0
1923	StL-A	7	4	.636	20	8	4	0	0	82²	107	6	34	26	15.9	6.42	65	.317	.387	6	.222	0	-22	-21	0	-2.2
Total	5	24	19	.558	109	43	17	1	5	451	481	15	132	114	12.6	4.05	87	.280	.338	26	.195	1	-28	-26	0	-1.1
● **HARRY WRIGHT**					Wright, William Henry b: 1/10/1835, Sheffield, England d: 10/3/1895, Atlantic City, N.J. BR/TR, 5'9.5", 157 lbs. Deb: 5/5/1871 FMH♦																					
1871	Bos-n	1	0	1.000	9	0	0	0	**3**	18²	34	0	4	0	18.3	6.27	66	.337	.362	44	.299		-4	-4		-0.2
1872	Bos-n	1	0	1.000	7	0	0	0	**4**	25²	26	0	0	1	9.1	2.10	173	.239	.239	52	.250	-0	**4**	**4**		0.1
1873	Bos-n	2	2	.500	13	5	0	0	**4**	38¹	65	0	7	6	16.9	4.23	78	.330	.353	67	.252	2	-4	-4		-0.3
1874	Bos-n	0	2	.000	6	2	0	0	**3**	16²	24	0	4	0	15.1	2.16	100	.324	.359	58	.315	1	0	-0		0.1
Total	4 n	4	4	.500	35	7	0	0	14	99¹	149	0	15	1	14.9	3.71	58	.310	.331	222	.274	5	-17	-17		-0.3
● **LUCKY WRIGHT**					Wright, William Simmons "William The Red" or "Deacon" b: 2/21/1880, Tontogany, Ohio d: 7/6/41, Tontogany, Ohio BR/TR, 6', 178 lbs. Deb: 4/18/09																					
1909	Cle-A	0	4	.000	5	4	3	0	0	28	21	0	7	5	9.0	3.21	80	.223	.277	0	.000	-1	-2	-2	-0	-0.4
● **FRANK WURM**					Wurm, Frank James b: 4/27/24, Cambridge, N.Y. d: 9/19/93, Glens Falls, N.Y. BB/TL, 6'1", 175 lbs. Deb: 9/4/44																					
1944	Bro-N	0	0	—	1	1	0	0	0	0¹	1	0	5	1	162.0	108.00	3	.500	.857	0	—	0	-4	-4	0	0.0
● **JOHN WYATT**					Wyatt, John Thomas b: 4/19/35, Chicago, Ill. BR/TR, 5'11.5", 200 lbs. Deb: 9/8/61																					
1961	KC-A	0	0	—	5	0	0	0	1	7¹	8	0	4	6	16.0	2.45	170	.296	.406	0	—	0	1	1	0	0.1
1962	KC-A	10	7	.588	59	9	0	0	11	125	121	12	80	106	14.8	4.46	95	.253	.366	3	.103	-2	-7	-3	-1	-0.7
1963	KC-A	6	4	.600	63	0	0	0	21	92	83	12	43	81	12.3	3.13	125	.239	.323	0	.000	-1	5	8	-1	1.1
1964	KC-A★	9	8	.529	**81**	0	0	0	20	128	111	23	52	74	11.5	3.59	106	.236	.314	0	.000	-1	1	3	-1	0.3
1965	KC-A	2	6	.250	65	0	0	0	18	88²	78	8	53	70	13.7	3.25	107	.241	.354	0	.000	-0	2	2	0	0.3
1966	KC-A	3	3	.500	19	0	0	0	0	23²	19	3	16	25	14.1	5.32	64	.213	.346	0	—	-1	-5	-5	1	-0.6
	Bos-A	3	4	.429	42	0	0	0	8	71²	59	3	27	63	11.3	3.14	121	.229	.311	0	.000	-1	2	5	-1	0.4
	Yr	3	7	.300	61	0	0	0	10	95¹	78	6	43	88	11.8	3.68	101	.223	.316	0	.000	-1	-3	-0	-1	-0.2
1967	*Bos-A	10	7	.588	60	0	0	0	20	93¹	71	6	39	68	10.8	2.60	134	.217	.304	1	.083	-0	7	9	1	2.2
1968	Bos-A	1	2	.333	8	0	0	0	0	10²	9	2	6	11	13.5	4.22	75	.231	.348	0	—	0	-1	-1	0	-0.3
	NY-A	2	0	1.000	7	0	0	0	0	8¹	7	1	9	6	17.3	2.16	134	.219	.390	0	—	0	1	1	0	0.2
	Det-A	1	0	1.000	22	0	0	0	2	30¹	26	2	11	25	11.3	2.37	127	.236	.311	0	—	0	2	2	0	0.1
	Yr	2	4	.333	37	0	0	0	2	49¹	42	5	26	42	12.6	2.74	110	.230	.329	0	—	0	1	2	0	-0.0
1969	Oak-A	1	0	1.000	20	0	0	0	1	8¹	14	2	6	5	17.3	5.40	64	.250	.400	0	—	0	-2	-2	-0	-0.2
Total	9	42	44	.488	435	9	0	0	103	687¹	600	72	346	540	12.7	3.47	108	.237	.334	4	.048	-6	6	21	-2	2.9
● **WHIT WYATT**					Wyatt, John Whitlow b: 9/27/07, Kensington, Ga. BR/TR, 6'1", 185 lbs. Deb: 9/16/29 C																					
1929	Det-A	0	1	.000	4	4	1	0	0	25¹	30	1	18	14	17.4	6.75	64	.309	.422	1	.100	-1	-7	-7	1	-0.3
1930	Det-A	4	5	.444	21	7	2	0	2	85²	76	6	35	68	12.0	3.57	134	.239	.320	12	.353	3	10	12	0	1.4
1931	Det-A	2	0	.000	4	1	1	0	0	20¹	30	2	12	8	19.0	8.85	52	.361	.448	2	.286	-0	-10	-10	-1	-0.8
1932	Det-A	9	13	.409	43	22	10	0	2	205²	228	12	102	82	14.6	5.03	93	.286	.369	15	.192	-0	-13	-8	-1	-0.8
1933	Det-A	0	1	.000	10	0	0	0	0	17	20	1	9	9	16.4	4.24	102	.299	.397	0	.000	-0	0	-0	-0	-0.0
	Chi-A	3	4	.429	26	7	2	0	1	87²	91	7	45	31	14.2	4.62	92	.266	.355	6	.214	-0	-3	-4	-0	-0.2
	Yr	3	5	.375	36	7	2	0	1	104²	111	8	54	40	14.4	4.56	93	.270	.358	6	.200	-0	-3	-4	-0	-0.2
1934	Chi-A	4	11	.267	23	6	2	0	2	67²	83	10	37	36	16.1	7.18	66	.303	.388	6	.231	0	-20	-18	-1	-3.2
1935	Chi-A	4	3	.571	30	1	0	0	6	52	65	6	25	22	15.9	6.75	68	.308	.387	3	.231	1	-13	-12	1	-1.4
1936	Chi-A	0	0	—	3	0	0	0	0	3	3	0	0	0	9.0	0.00	—	.273	.273	0	—	-0	2	2	0	0.1
1937	Cle-A	2	3	.400	29	4	2	0	0	73	73	8	37	44	13.2	4.44	104	.244	.340	7	.389	1	1	1	0	0.3
1939	Bro-N☆	8	3	.727	16	14	8	2	0	109	88	3	39	52	10.7	2.31	174	.224	.297	6	.167	-0	19	21	1	2.1
1940	Bro-N★	15	14	.517	37	34	16	**5**	2	239¹	233	16	62	124	11.3	3.46	116	.254	.304	14	.175	-0	10	14	-2	1.3
1941	*Bro-N★	**22**	10	.688	38	35	23	**7**	1	288¹	223	10	82	176	**9.6**	2.34	157	**.212**	**.270**	26	.239	7	**41**	**42**	-1	**5.3**
1942	Bro-N☆	19	7	.731	31	30	16	0	0	217¹	185	9	63	104	10.6	2.73	119	.225	.286	14	.182	1	14	13	-1	1.4
1943	Bro-N	14	5	.737	26	26	13	0	0	180²	139	5	43	80	**9.1**	2.49	135	**.207**	**.255**	17	.283	4	18	17	-2	2.1
1944	Bro-N	2	6	.250	10	5	1	0	0	37²	51	1	16	4	16.5	7.17	50	.311	.379	2	.154	-0	-15	-15	-0	-2.6
1945	Phi-N	0	7	.000	10	10	1	0	0	51¹	72	3	14	10	15.1	5.26	73	.330	.371	2	.125	0	-8	-8	1	-0.9
Total	16	106	95	.527	360	210	97	17	13	1761	1684	98	642	872	12.1	3.79	105	.251	.319	133	.219	18	27	39	-6	3.8
● **WELDON WYCKOFF**					Wyckoff, John Weldon b: 2/19/1892, Williamsport, Pa. d: 5/8/61, Sheboygan Falls, Wis. BR/TR, 6'1", 175 lbs. Deb: 4/19/13																					
1913	Phi-A	2	4	.333	17	7	4	0	0	61²	56	1	46	31	15.3	4.38	63	.233	.363	4	.190	-0	-10	-11	0	-1.0
1914	*Phi-A	11	7	.611	32	20	11	0	2	185	153	2	103	86	12.6	3.02	87	.228	.334	11	.147	-0	-6	-8	-5	-1.3
1915	Phi-A	10	22	.313	43	34	20	1	0	276	238	1	165	157	13.3	3.52	83	.246	.359	12	.125	-4	-18	-18	2	-2.2

YEAR	TM/L	W	L	PCT	G	GS	CG	SH	SV	IP	H	HR	BB	SO	RAT	ERA	ERA+	OAV	OOB	BH	AVG	PB	PR	/A	PD	TPI
1916	Phi-A	0	1	.000	7	2	1	0	0	21¹	20	1	20	4	17.3	5.48	52	.247	.402	3	.375	1	-6	-6	0	-0.2
	Bos-A	0	0	—	8	0	0	0	1	22²	19	0	18	18	14.7	4.76	58	.232	.370	1	.167	-0	-5	-5	-1	-0.2
	Yr	0	1	.000	15	2	1	0	1	44	39	1	38	22	15.8	5.11	55	.238	.381	4	.286	1	-11	-11	-1	-0.4
1917	Bos-A	0	0	—	1	0	0	0	0	5	4	0	4	1	16.2	1.80	143	.222	.391	0	.000	-0	0	0	0	0.0
1918	Bos-A	0	0	—	1	0	0	0	0	2	4	0	1	2	22.5	0.00	∞	.400	.455	0	.000	-0	1	1	0	0.0
Total	6	23	34	.404	109	63	36	1	3	573²	494	5	357	299	13.6	3.55	79	.239	.355	31	.149	-4	-44	-48	-3	-4.9

● **FRANK WYMAN** Wyman, Frank H. b: 5/10/1862, Haverhill, Mass. d: 2/4/16, Everett, Mass. Deb: 6/10/1884 ♦

YEAR	TM/L	W	L	PCT	G	GS	CG	SH	SV	IP	H	HR	BB	SO	RAT	ERA	ERA+	OAV	OOB	BH	AVG	PB	PR	/A	PD	TPI
1884	KC-U	0	1	.000	3	1	1	0	0	21	37	0	3	9	17.1	6.86	33	.363	.381	27	.218	-1	-10	-11	-1	-0.5

● **EARLY WYNN** Wynn, Early "Gus" b: 1/6/20, Hartford, Ala. BB/TR, 6', 200 lbs. Deb: 9/13/39 CH♦

YEAR	TM/L	W	L	PCT	G	GS	CG	SH	SV	IP	H	HR	BB	SO	RAT	ERA	ERA+	OAV	OOB	BH	AVG	PB	PR	/A	PD	TPI
1939	Was-A	0	2	.000	3	3	1	0	0	20¹	26	0	10	1	15.9	5.75	76	.313	.387	1	.167	-0	-3	-3	-1	-0.3
1941	Was-A	3	1	.750	5	5	4	0	0	40	35	1	10	15	10.1	1.57	257	.226	.273	2	.133	-0	11	11	0	1.1
1942	Was-A	10	16	.385	30	28	10	1	0	190	246	6	73	58	15.3	5.12	71	.314	.374	15	.217	2	-31	-31	-1	-3.6
1943	Was-A	18	12	.600	37	33	12	3	0	256²	232	15	83	89	11.1	2.91	96	.240	.301	29	.296	7	11	8	-2	1.6
1944	Was-A	8	17	.320	33	25	19	2	2	207²	221	3	67	65	12.6	3.38	96	.277	.334	19	.207	7	2	1	-3	-0.4
1946	Was-A	8	5	.615	17	12	9	0	0	107	112	8	33	36	12.4	3.11	108	.267	.325	15	.319	7	5	3	-0	1.1
1947	Was-A☆	17	15	.531	33	31	22	2	0	247	251	13	90	73	12.6	3.64	102	.262	.329	33	.275	7	2	2	-1	0.9
1948	Was-A	8	19	.296	33	31	15	1	0	198	236	19	94	49	15.0	5.82	75	.295	.370	23	.217	8	-34	-32	-1	-3.4
1949	Cle-A	11	7	.611	26	23	6	0	0	164²	186	8	57	62	13.3	4.15	96	.282	.340	10	.143	-2	1	-3	1	-0.3
1950	Cle-A	18	8	.692	32	28	14	2	0	213²	166	20	101	143	**11.4**	**3.20**	135	**.212**	**.305**	18	.234	7	33	27	0	3.6
1951	Cle-A	20	13	.606	37	34	21	3	1	**274¹**	227	18	107	133	11.1	3.02	126	.225	.301	20	.185	2	**34**	23	-1	2.6
1952	Cle-A	23	12	.657	42	33	19	4	3	285²	239	23	132	153	11.7	2.90	115	.231	.318	22	.222	5	25	14	-1	2.1
1953	Cle-A	17	12	.586	36	34	16	1	0	251²	234	17	107	138	12.3	3.93	95	.245	.324	25	.275	9	2	-5	-1	-0.2
1954	*Cle-A	**23**	11	.676	40	36	20	3	2	**270²**	225	21	83	155	10.2	2.73	135	.225	.284	17	.183	1	30	29	-3	3.3
1955	Cle-A★	17	11	.607	32	31	16	6	0	230	207	19	80	122	11.3	2.82	142	.240	.307	15	.179	1	29	30	-3	3.3
1956	Cle-A★	20	9	.690	38	35	18	4	2	277²	233	19	91	158	10.7	2.72	154	.228	.294	23	.228	3	44	46	1	5.1
1957	Cle-A★	14	17	.452	40	37	13	1	1	263	270	32	104	**184**	13.0	4.31	86	.265	.336	10	.116	-9	-15	-17	-1	-2.1
1958	Chi-A★	14	16	.467	40	34	11	4	2	239²	214	27	104	**179**	12.2	4.13	88	.242	.325	15	.200	3	-10	-13	-2	-1.5
1959	*Chi-A★	**22**	10	.688	37	37	14	5	0	**255²**	202	20	119	179	11.6	3.17	119	.216	.310	22	.244	9	20	17	-1	2.8
1960	Chi-A★	13	12	.520	36	35	13	**4**	1	237¹	220	20	112	158	12.7	3.49	108	.247	.334	15	.200	1	7	8	-2	1.2
1961	Chi-A	8	2	.800	17	16	5	0	0	110¹	88	11	47	64	11.1	3.51	112	.220	.304	6	.162	-0	6	5	-2	0.2
1962	Chi-A	7	15	.318	27	26	11	3	0	167²	171	15	56	91	12.3	4.46	88	.264	.326	7	.130	-0	-9	-10	-2	-1.4
1963	Cle-A	1	2	.333	20	5	1	0	0	55¹	50	2	15	29	10.6	2.28	159	.250	.302	3	.273	1	8	8	-0	0.5
Total	23	300	244	.551	691	612	290	49	15	4564	4291	338	1775	2334	12.1	3.54	106	.248	.321	365	.214	72	170	112	-25	16.6

● **BILLY WYNNE** Wynne, Billy Vernon b: 7/31/43, Williamston, N.C. BL/TR, 6'5", 206 lbs. Deb: 8/6/67

YEAR	TM/L	W	L	PCT	G	GS	CG	SH	SV	IP	H	HR	BB	SO	RAT	ERA	ERA+	OAV	OOB	BH	AVG	PB	PR	/A	PD	TPI
1967	NY-N	0	0	—	6	1	0	0	0	8²	12	0	2	4	14.5	3.12	109	.324	.359	0	.000	-0	0	0	0	0.0
1968	Chi-A	0	0	—	1	0	0	0	0	2	2	0	2	1	18.0	4.50	67	.250	.400	0	—	-0	-0	-0	0	0.0
1969	Chi-A	7	7	.500	20	20	6	1	0	128²	143	14	50	67	13.7	4.06	95	.283	.351	5	.122	-1	-6	-3	0	-0.3
1970	Chi-A	1	4	.200	12	9	0	0	0	44	54	8	22	19	15.8	5.32	73	.298	.377	1	.077	-1	-8	-7	1	-0.7
1971	Cal-A	0	0	—	3	0	0	0	0	3²	6	0	2	6	19.6	4.91	66	.375	.444	0	—	-1	-1	-0	0	0.0
Total	5	8	11	.421	42	30	6	1	0	187	217	22	78	97	14.4	4.33	88	.290	.361	6	.109	-2	-15	-11	1	-1.0

● **BILL WYNNE** Wynne, William Andrew b: 3/27/1869, Neuse, N.C. d: 8/7/51, Raleigh, N.C. BR/TR, 5'11.5", 161 lbs. Deb: 8/31/1894

YEAR	TM/L	W	L	PCT	G	GS	CG	SH	SV	IP	H	HR	BB	SO	RAT	ERA	ERA+	OAV	OOB	BH	AVG	PB	PR	/A	PD	TPI
1894	Was-N	0	1	.000	1	1	1	0	0	8	10	1	3	2	22.5	6.75	78	.303	.465	0	.000	-0	-1	-1	-0	-0.1

● **HANK WYSE** Wyse, Henry Washington "Hooks" b: 3/1/18, Lunsford, Ark. BR/TR, 5'11.5", 185 lbs. Deb: 9/7/42

YEAR	TM/L	W	L	PCT	G	GS	CG	SH	SV	IP	H	HR	BB	SO	RAT	ERA	ERA+	OAV	OOB	BH	AVG	PB	PR	/A	PD	TPI
1942	Chi-N	2	1	.667	4	4	1	0	0	28	33	1	6	8	12.5	1.93	166	.287	.322	1	.125	-0	4	4	-0	0.4
1943	Chi-N	9	7	.563	38	15	8	2	5	156	159	4	34	45	11.3	2.94	113	.264	.306	4	.080	-4	8	7	3	0.7
1944	Chi-N	16	15	.516	41	34	14	3	1	257¹	277	9	57	86	11.8	3.15	112	.278	.318	16	.178	-1	13	11	0	1.1
1945	*Chi-N†	22	10	.688	38	34	23	2	0	278¹	272	17	55	77	10.7	2.68	136	.256	.296	17	.168	-2	**35**	30	2	3.2
1946	Chi-N	14	12	.538	40	27	12	2	1	201¹	206	7	52	52	11.7	2.68	124	.265	.313	18	.243	1	16	14	2	2.2
1947	Chi-N	6	9	.400	37	19	5	1	1	142	158	12	64	53	14.3	4.31	92	.286	.363	5	.111	-0	-4	-6	1	-0.5
1950	Phi-A	9	14	.391	41	23	4	0	0	170²	192	16	87	33	15.1	5.85	78	.287	.376	9	.153	-3	-24	-25	-0	-3.0
1951	Phi-A	1	2	.333	9	1	0	0	0	14²	24	0	8	5	19.6	7.98	54	.381	.451	1	.250	-0	-6	-6	-0	-1.0
	Was-A	0	0	—	3	2	0	0	0	9¹	17	0	10	3	27.0	9.64	42	.378	.500	0	.000	-0	-6	-6	-0	-0.1
	Yr	1	2	.333	12	3	0	0	0	24	41	0	18	8	22.5	8.63	49	.380	.472	1	.125	-1	-12	-12	-0	-1.1
Total	8	79	70	.530	251	159	67	11	8	1257²	1338	66	373	362	12.4	3.52	105	.274	.329	71	.163	-11	36	24	9	3.0

● **BIFF WYSONG** Wysong, Harlan b: 4/13/05, Clarksville, Ohio d: 8/8/51, Xenia, Ohio BL/TL, 6'3", 195 lbs. Deb: 8/10/30

YEAR	TM/L	W	L	PCT	G	GS	CG	SH	SV	IP	H	HR	BB	SO	RAT	ERA	ERA+	OAV	OOB	BH	AVG	PB	PR	/A	PD	TPI
1930	Cin-N	0	1	.000	1	1	0	0	0	2¹	6	0	3	1	34.7	19.29	25	.545	.643	0	—	0	-4	-4	-0	-0.9
1931	Cin-N	0	2	.000	12	2	0	0	0	21²	25	2	23	5	19.9	7.89	47	.298	.449	1	.250	-0	-10	-10	-1	-0.8
1932	Cin-N	1	0	1.000	7	0	0	0	0	12¹	13	0	8	5	15.3	3.65	106	.277	.382	0	.000	-0	1	1	-0	0.0
Total	3	1	3	.250	20	3	0	0	0	36¹	44	2	34	11	19.3	7.18	54	.310	.443	1	.167	-0	-13	-13	-1	-1.7

● **ESTEBAN YAN** Yan, Esteban Luis b: 6/22/74, Campina Del Seibo, D.R. BR/TR, 6'4", 230 lbs. Deb: 5/20/96

YEAR	TM/L	W	L	PCT	G	GS	CG	SH	SV	IP	H	HR	BB	SO	RAT	ERA	ERA+	OAV	OOB	BH	AVG	PB	PR	/A	PD	TPI
1996	Bal-A	0	0	—	4	0	0	0	0	9¹	13	3	3	7	15.4	5.79	85	.333	.381		0	—	-1	-1	-0	0.0

● **RUSTY YARNALL** Yarnall, Waldo William b: 10/22/02, Chicago, Ill. d: 10/9/85, Lowell, Mass. BR/TR, 6', 175 lbs. Deb: 6/30/26

YEAR	TM/L	W	L	PCT	G	GS	CG	SH	SV	IP	H	HR	BB	SO	RAT	ERA	ERA+	OAV	OOB	BH	AVG	PB	PR	/A	PD	TPI
1926	Phi-N	0	1	.000	1	0	0	0	0	3	3	0	1	0	36.0	18.00	23	.500	.571	0	.000	-0	-2	-2	0	-0.9

● **RUBE YARRISON** Yarrison, Byron Wardsworth b: 3/9/1896, Montgomery, Pa. d: 4/22/77, Williamsport, Pa. BR/TR, 5'11", 165 lbs. Deb: 4/13/22

YEAR	TM/L	W	L	PCT	G	GS	CG	SH	SV	IP	H	HR	BB	SO	RAT	ERA	ERA+	OAV	OOB	BH	AVG	PB	PR	/A	PD	TPI
1922	Phi-A	1	2	.333	18	3	0	0	0	33²	50	4	12	10	17.1	8.29	51	.362	.421	1	.167	-0	-16	-15	-0	-1.2
1924	Bro-N	0	2	.000	3	0	0	0	0	11	12	0	3	2	12.3	6.55	57	.267	.327	0	—	-0	-3	-3	0	-0.5
Total	2	1	4	.200	21	3	0	0	0	44²	62	4	15	12	16.1	7.86	53	.339	.398	1	.125	-0	-19	-19	0	-1.7

● **EMIL YDE** Yde, Emil Ogden b: 1/28/1900, Great Lakes, Ill. d: 12/4/68, Leesburg, Fla. BB/TL, 5'11", 165 lbs. Deb: 4/21/24

YEAR	TM/L	W	L	PCT	G	GS	CG	SH	SV	IP	H	HR	BB	SO	RAT	ERA	ERA+	OAV	OOB	BH	AVG	PB	PR	/A	PD	TPI
1924	Pit-N	16	3	**.842**	33	22	14	**4**	0	194	171	3	62	53	11.1	2.83	136	.244	.311	21	.239	2	22	22	1	2.3
1925	*Pit-N	17	9	.654	33	28	13	0	0	207	254	11	75	41	14.4	4.13	108	.309	.369	17	.191	-2	3	8	-0	0.6
1926	Pit-N	8	7	.533	37	22	12	1	0	187¹	181	3	81	34	12.7	3.65	108	.260	.339	17	.230	3	4	6	0	0.7
1927	*Pit-N	1	3	.250	9	2	0	0	0	29²	45	1	15	9	18.8	9.71	42	.375	.453	3	.167	-0	-19	-18	1	-1.9
1929	Det-A	7	3	.700	29	6	4	1	0	86²	100	8	63	23	16.9	5.30	81	.296	.406	16	.333	2	-10	-10	-1	-0.7
Total	5	49	25	.662	141	80	43	6	0	704²	751	26	296	160	13.6	4.02	102	.281	.355	74	.233	5	-0	7	1	1.0

● **JOE YEAGER** Yeager, Joseph F. "Little Joe" b: 8/28/1875, Philadelphia, Pa. d: 7/2/37, Detroit, Mich. BR/TR, 5'10", 160 lbs. Deb: 4/22/1898 ♦

YEAR	TM/L	W	L	PCT	G	GS	CG	SH	SV	IP	H	HR	BB	SO	RAT	ERA	ERA+	OAV	OOB	BH	AVG	PB	PR	/A	PD	TPI
1898	Bro-N	12	22	.353	36	33	32	0	0	291¹	333	4	80	70	12.9	3.65	98	.285	.334	23	.172	-3	-1	-2	5	0.0
1899	Bro-N	2	2	.500	10	4	2	1	1	47²	56	1	16	6	14.0	4.72	83	.292	.352	9	.191	1	-5	-4	1	-0.2
1900	Bro-N	1	1	.500	2	1	1	0	0	17	21	1	5	2	14.3	6.88	50	.304	.351	3	.333	-0	-6	-6	-0	-0.5
1901	Det-A	12	11	.522	26	25	22	2	1	199²	209	4	46	38	11.9	2.61	147	.266	.313	25	.296	5	23	27	3	3.5
1902	Det-A	6	12	.333	19	15	14	0	0	140	171	4	41	28	13.9	4.82	76	.301	.353	39	.242	-3	-19	-18	1	-1.4
1903	Det-A	0	1	.000	1	1	1	0	0	9	15	1	0	1	15.0	4.00	73	.366	.366	103	.162	5	-0	-1	-0	-0.1
Total	6	33	49	.402	94	80	73	3	2	704²	805	15	188	145	13.0	3.74	99	.285	.334	467	.252	5	-9	-4	11	1.3

● **AL YEARGIN** Yeargin, James Almond b: 10/16/01, Mauldin, S.C. d: 5/8/37, Greenville, S.C. BR/TR, 5'11", 170 lbs. Deb: 10/1/22

YEAR	TM/L	W	L	PCT	G	GS	CG	SH	SV	IP	H	HR	BB	SO	RAT	ERA	ERA+	OAV	OOB	BH	AVG	PB	PR	/A	PD	TPI
1922	Bos-N	0	1	.000	1	1	1	0	0	7	3	1	2	1	9.0	1.29	311	.192	.250	0	.000	-0	2	2	0	0.2
1924	Bos-N	1	11	.083	32	12	6	0	0	141¹	162	7	42	34	13.2	5.09	75	.293	.346	6	.143	-2	-19	-20	4	-1.3
Total	2	1	12	.077	33	13	7	0	0	148¹	167	8	44	35	13.0	4.91	78	.288	.342	6	.133	-2	-17	-18	4	-1.1

● **LARRY YELLEN** Yellen, Lawrence Alan b: 1/4/43, Brooklyn, N.Y. BR/TR, 5'11", 190 lbs. Deb: 9/26/63

YEAR	TM/L	W	L	PCT	G	GS	CG	SH	SV	IP	H	HR	BB	SO	RAT	ERA	ERA+	OAV	OOB	BH	AVG	PB	PR	/A	PD	TPI
1963	Hou-N	0	0	—	1	1	0	0	0	5	7	0	1	3	14.4	3.60	88	.280	.308	0	.000	-0	-0	-0	0	0.0

YEAR	TM/L	W	L	PCT	G	GS	CG	SH	SV	IP	H	HR	BB	SO	RAT	ERA	ERA+	OAV	OOB	BH	AVG	PB	PR	/A	PD	TPI
1964	Hou-N	0	0	—	13	1	0	0	0	21	27	4	10	9	15.9	6.86	50	.297	.366	0	.000	-0	-8	-8	-0	0.0
Total	2	0	0	—	14	2	0	0	0	26	34	4	11	12	15.6	6.23	54	.293	.354	0	.000	-0	-8	-8	0	0.0

● **CHIEF YELLOWHORSE**   Yellowhorse, Moses J.   b: 1/28/1898, Pawnee, Okla. d: 4/10/64, Pawnee, Okla.   BR/TR, 5'10", 180 lbs. Deb: 4/15/21

YEAR	TM/L	W	L	PCT	G	GS	CG	SH	SV	IP	H	HR	BB	SO	RAT	ERA	ERA+	OAV	OOB	BH	AVG	PB	PR	/A	PD	TPI
1921	Pit-N	5	3	.625	10	4	1	0	1	48¹	45	1	13	19	10.8	2.98	129	.254	.305	0	.000	-2	4	5	-2	0.3
1922	Pit-N	3	1	.750	28	4	2	0	0	77²	92	0	20	24	13.2	4.52	90	.305	.352	6	.316	1	-4	-4	-1	-0.1
Total	2	8	4	.667	38	8	3	0	1	126	137	1	33	43	12.3	3.93	101	.286	.335	6	.167	-2	1	1	-3	0.2

● **CARROLL YERKES**   Yerkes, Charles Carroll "Lefty"   b: 6/13/03, McSherrystown, Pa.   d: 12/20/50, Oakland, Cal.   BR/TL, 5'11", 180 lbs.   Deb: 5/31/27

YEAR	TM/L	W	L	PCT	G	GS	CG	SH	SV	IP	H	HR	BB	SO	RAT	ERA	ERA+	OAV	OOB	BH	AVG	PB	PR	/A	PD	TPI
1927	Phi-A	0	0	—	1	0	0	0	0	1	0	0	1	0	9.0	0.00	—	.000	.333	0	—	0	0	0	-0	0.0
1928	Phi-A	0	1	.000	2	1	1	0	0	8³	7	0	2	1	9.3	2.08	193	.233	.281	0	.000	-0	2	2	1	0.2
1929	Phi-A	1	0	1.000	19	2	0	0	1	37¹	47	0	13	11	14.7	4.58	92	.329	.389	0	.000	-2	-1	-1	2	0.1
1932	Chi-N	0	0	—	2	0	0	0	0	9	5	2	3	4	8.0	3.00	126	.167	.242	1	.333	0	1	1	-0	0.0
1933	Chi-N	0	0	—	1	0	0	0	0	2	2	0	1	0	13.5	4.50	73	.286	.375	0	—	-0	-0	-0	0	0.0
Total	5	1	1	.500	25	3	1	0	1	58	61	2	20	16	12.7	3.88	106	.288	.352	1	.063	-2	2	1	3	0.2

● **STAN YERKES**   Yerkes, Stanley Lewis "Yank"   b: 11/28/1874, Cheltenham, Pa.   d: 7/28/40, Boston, Mass.   BR/TR, 5'10", 165 lbs.   Deb: 5/3/01

YEAR	TM/L	W	L	PCT	G	GS	CG	SH	SV	IP	H	HR	BB	SO	RAT	ERA	ERA+	OAV	OOB	BH	AVG	PB	PR	/A	PD	TPI
1901	Bal-A	0	1	.000	1	1	1	0	0	8	12	0	2	4	15.8	6.75	57	.343	.378	1	.333	0	-3	-3	0	-0.2
	StL-N	3	1	.750	4	4	4	0	0	34	35	2	6	15	11.1	3.18	100	.265	.302	1	.083	-1	0	-0	-0	-0.1
1902	StL-N	12	21	.364	39	37	27	1	0	272²	341	4	79	81	13.9	3.66	75	.306	.353	12	.132	-3	-27	-28	-2	-3.6
1903	StL-N	0	1	.000	1	1	0	0	0	5	8	0	0	3	14.4	1.80	181	.333	.333	0	.000	-0	1	1	-0	0.1
Total	3	15	24	.385	45	43	32	1	0	396	392	5	87	103	13.7	3.66	77	.303	.348	14	.130	-4	-28	-30	-3	-3.8

● **RICH YETT**   Yett, Richard Martin   b: 10/6/62, Pomona, Cal.   BR/TR, 6'2", 187 lbs.   Deb: 4/13/85

YEAR	TM/L	W	L	PCT	G	GS	CG	SH	SV	IP	H	HR	BB	SO	RAT	ERA	ERA+	OAV	OOB	BH	AVG	PB	PR	/A	PD	TPI
1985	Min-A	0	0	—	1	1	0	0	0	0¹	1	0	2	0	81.0	27.00	16	.333	.600	0	—	0	-1	-1	-0	-0.2
1986	Cle-A	5	3	.625	39	3	1	1	1	78²	84	10	37	50	14.0	5.15	80	.275	.355	0	—	0	-8	-9	-1	-0.9
1987	Cle-A	3	9	.250	37	11	2	0	1	97²	96	21	49	59	13.6	5.25	86	.257	.347	0	—	0	-9	-8	-1	-0.9
1988	Cle-A	9	6	.600	23	22	0	0	0	134¹	146	11	55	71	13.5	4.62	89	.275	.344	0	—	0	-10	-8	-2	-1.0
1989	Cle-A	5	6	.455	32	12	1	0	0	99	111	10	47	47	14.5	5.00	79	.283	.363	0	—	0	-12	-11	-1	-1.4
1990	Min-A	0	0	—	4	0	0	0	0	4¹	6	1	1	2	14.5	2.08	200	.353	.389	0	—	0	1	1	0	-0.3
Total	6	22	24	.478	136	49	4	1	2	414¹	444	53	191	229	13.9	4.95	84	.274	.353	0	—	0	-39	-36	-5	-4.7

● **EARL YINGLING**   Yingling, Earl Hershey "Chink"   b: 10/29/1888, Chillicothe, Ohio   d: 10/2/62, Columbus, Ohio   BL/TL, 5'11.5", 180 lbs.   Deb: 4/12/11

YEAR	TM/L	W	L	PCT	G	GS	CG	SH	SV	IP	H	HR	BB	SO	RAT	ERA	ERA+	OAV	OOB	BH	AVG	PB	PR	/A	PD	TPI
1911	Cle-A	1	0	1.000	4	3	1	0	0	22¹	30	1	9	6	16.1	4.43	77	.326	.392	3	.273	1	-3	-3	0	-0.1
1912	Bro-N	6	11	.353	25	16	12	0	0	163	186	10	56	51	13.4	3.59	93	.293	.351	16	.250	3	-3	-4	-1	-0.2
1913	Bro-N	8	8	.500	26	13	8	2	0	146²	158	2	10	40	10.4	2.58	128	.280	.295	23	.383	8	10	12	-1	2.0
1914	Cin-N	9	13	.409	34	27	8	3	0	198	207	6	54	80	12.1	3.45	85	.274	.328	23	.192	1	-15	-12	-2	-1.2
1918	Was-A	1	2	.333	5	2	0	0	0	38	30	0	12	15	9.9	2.13	128	.238	.304	7	.467	3	3	3	1	0.7
Total	5	25	34	.424	94	61	31	5	0	568	611	19	141	192	12.1	3.22	98	.281	.328	72	.267	16	-8	-4	-3	1.2

● **JOE YINGLING**   Yingling, Joseph Granville   b: 7/23/1866, Westminster, Md.   d: 10/24/46, Manchester, Md.   BR/TL, 5'7.5", 145 lbs.   Deb: 5/28/1886 ♦

YEAR	TM/L	W	L	PCT	G	GS	CG	SH	SV	IP	H	HR	BB	SO	RAT	ERA	ERA+	OAV	OOB	BH	AVG	PB	PR	/A	PD	TPI
1886	Was-N	0	0	—	1	0	0	0	0	3	4	1	5	0	24.0	12.00	27	.412	.444	0	.000	-0	-3	-3	0	-0.6

● **LEN YOCHIM**   Yochim, Leonard Joseph   b: 10/16/28, New Orleans, La.   BL/TL, 6'2", 200 lbs.   Deb: 9/18/51   F

YEAR	TM/L	W	L	PCT	G	GS	CG	SH	SV	IP	H	HR	BB	SO	RAT	ERA	ERA+	OAV	OOB	BH	AVG	PB	PR	/A	PD	TPI
1951	Pit-N	1	1	.500	2	2	0	0	0	8²	10	1	11	5	22.8	8.31	51	.278	.458	0	.000	-0	-4	-4	0	-0.7
1954	Pit-N	0	1	.000	10	1	0	0	0	19²	30	1	8	7	17.4	7.32	57	.361	.418	1	.500	0	-7	-7	1	-0.2
Total	2	1	2	.333	12	3	0	0	0	28¹	40	2	19	12	19.1	7.62	55	.336	.432	1	.200	-0	-11	-11	1	-0.9

● **RAY YOCHIM**   Yochim, Raymond Austin Aloysius   b: 7/19/22, New Orleans, La.   BR/TR, 6'1", 170 lbs.   Deb: 5/2/48   F

YEAR	TM/L	W	L	PCT	G	GS	CG	SH	SV	IP	H	HR	BB	SO	RAT	ERA	ERA+	OAV	OOB	BH	AVG	PB	PR	/A	PD	TPI
1948	StL-N	0	0	—	1	0	0	0	0	1	0	0	3	1	27.0	0.00	—	.000	.500	0	—	0	0	0	-0	0.0
1949	StL-N	0	0	—	3	0	0	0	0	2¹	3	1	4	3	27.0	15.43	27	.273	.467	0	—	0	-3	-3	-0	0.0
Total	2	0	0	—	4	0	0	0	0	3¹	3	1	7	4	27.0	10.80	38	.214	.476	0	—	0	-3	-2	-0	0.0

● **LEFTY YORK**   York, James Edward   b: 11/1/1892, West Fork, Ark.   d: 4/9/61, York, Pa.   BL/TL, 5'10", 185 lbs.   Deb: 9/12/19

YEAR	TM/L	W	L	PCT	G	GS	CG	SH	SV	IP	H	HR	BB	SO	RAT	ERA	ERA+	OAV	OOB	BH	AVG	PB	PR	/A	PD	TPI
1919	Phi-A	0	2	.000	2	2	0	0	0	4¹	11	0	5	2	37.4	24.92	14	.500	.581	0	.000	-0	-10	-10	0	-2.4
1921	Chi-N	5	9	.357	40	11	4	1	1	139	170	5	63	57	15.4	4.73	81	.308	.384	5	.128	-2	-15	-14	-3	-1.8
Total	2	5	11	.313	42	13	4	1	1	143¹	183	5	68	59	16.1	5.34	71	.317	.393	5	.125	-2	-25	-24	-3	-4.2

● **JIM YORK**   York, James Harlan   b: 8/27/47, Maywood, Cal.   BR/TR, 6'3", 200 lbs.   Deb: 9/21/70

YEAR	TM/L	W	L	PCT	G	GS	CG	SH	SV	IP	H	HR	BB	SO	RAT	ERA	ERA+	OAV	OOB	BH	AVG	PB	PR	/A	PD	TPI
1970	KC-A	1	1	.500	4	0	0	0	0	8	5	2	6	7	7.9	3.38	111	.179	.233	0	.000	-0	0	0	-0	0.0
1971	KC-A	5	5	.500	53	0	0	0	3	93¹	70	7	44	103	11.3	2.89	119	.203	.299	2	.118	1	6	6	-0	0.7
1972	Hou-N	0	1	.000	26	0	0	0	0	36	45	3	18	25	16.0	5.25	64	.321	.403	0	.000	-0	-7	-8	-0	-0.2
1973	Hou-N	3	4	.429	41	0	0	0	6	53	65	4	20	22	14.6	4.42	82	.305	.368	0	.000	-0	-4	-4	-0	-0.7
1974	Hou-N	2	2	.500	28	0	0	0	1	38¹	48	1	19	15	16.0	3.29	105	.298	.376	0	.000	-1	1	1	-0	0.2
1975	Hou-N	4	4	.500	19	4	0	0	0	46²	43	1	25	17	14.1	3.86	87	.251	.363	1	.091	-0	-1	-3	-1	-0.6
1976	NY-A	1	0	1.000	3	0	0	0	0	9²	14	1	6	4	17.7	5.59	61	.333	.404	0	—	0	-2	-2	-0	-0.2
Total	7	16	17	.485	174	4	0	0	10	285	290	19	132	194	13.7	3.79	91	.264	.349	3	.075	-0	-7	-10	-1	-1.0

● **MIKE YORK**   York, Michael David   b: 9/6/64, Oak Park, Ill.   BR/TR, 6'1", 187 lbs.   Deb: 8/17/90

YEAR	TM/L	W	L	PCT	G	GS	CG	SH	SV	IP	H	HR	BB	SO	RAT	ERA	ERA+	OAV	OOB	BH	AVG	PB	PR	/A	PD	TPI
1990	Pit-N	1	1	.500	4	1	0	0	0	12²	13	0	5	4	13.5	2.84	127	.277	.358	1	.333	0	1	1	-0	0.2
1991	Cle-A	1	4	.200	14	4	0	0	0	34²	45	2	19	19	17.1	6.75	62	.333	.423	0	—	0	-10	-10	-0	-1.3
Total	2	2	5	.286	18	5	0	0	0	47¹	58	2	24	23	16.2	5.70	70	.319	.407	1	.333	0	-9	-9	-0	-1.1

● **GUS YOST**   Yost, August   6'5".   Deb: 6/12/1893

YEAR	TM/L	W	L	PCT	G	GS	CG	SH	SV	IP	H	HR	BB	SO	RAT	ERA	ERA+	OAV	OOB	BH	AVG	PB	PR	/A	PD	TPI
1893	Chi-N	0	1	.000	1	1	0	0	0	2²	3	0	8	1	37.1	13.50	34	.273	.579	0	—	0	-3	-3	-0	-0.6

● **FLOYD YOUMANS**   Youmans, Floyd Everett   b: 5/11/64, Tampa, Fla.   BR/TR, 6'1", 190 lbs.   Deb: 7/1/85

YEAR	TM/L	W	L	PCT	G	GS	CG	SH	SV	IP	H	HR	BB	SO	RAT	ERA	ERA+	OAV	OOB	BH	AVG	PB	PR	/A	PD	TPI
1985	Mon-N	4	3	.571	14	12	1	0	0	77	57	3	49	54	12.5	2.45	138	.206	.327	1	.053	-0	10	8	-2	0.5
1986	Mon-N	13	12	.520	33	32	6	2	0	219	145	14	118	202	11.0	3.53	104	.188	.299	12	.160	2	4	4	-3	0.2
1987	Mon-N	9	8	.529	23	23	3	3	0	116¹	112	13	47	94	12.4	4.64	91	.251	.324	6	.150	1	-7	-6	-0	-0.7
1988	Mon-N	3	6	.333	14	13	1	0	0	84	64	8	41	54	11.5	3.21	112	.213	.311	4	.154	-0	2	4	-1	0.3
1989	Phi-N	1	5	.167	10	10	0	0	0	42²	50	7	25	20	16.2	5.70	62	.299	.397	1	.077	-1	-10	-10	-0	-1.3
Total	5	30	34	.469	94	90	11	6	0	539	428	45	280	424	12.0	3.74	100	.218	.319	24	.139	1	-1	-1	-6	-1.0

● **ANTHONY YOUNG**   Young, Anthony Wayne   b: 1/19/66, Houston, Tex.   BR/TR, 6'2", 200 lbs.   Deb: 8/5/91

YEAR	TM/L	W	L	PCT	G	GS	CG	SH	SV	IP	H	HR	BB	SO	RAT	ERA	ERA+	OAV	OOB	BH	AVG	PB	PR	/A	PD	TPI
1991	NY-N	2	5	.286	10	8	0	0	0	49¹	48	4	12	20	11.1	3.10	117	.257	.305	2	.143	-0	3	3	-1	0.3
1992	NY-N	2	14	.125	52	13	0	0	15	121	134	8	31	64	12.3	4.17	83	.285	.331	3	.111	-1	-9	-9	-0	-1.5
1993	NY-N	1	16	.059	39	10	1	0	3	100¹	103	8	42	62	13.1	3.77	107	.265	.339	2	.143	-0	4	3	0	0.4
1994	Chi-N	4	6	.400	20	19	0	0	0	114²	103	12	46	65	11.7	3.92	106	.246	.320	6	.176	0	4	3	1	0.3
1995	Chi-N	3	4	.429	32	1	0	0	2	41¹	47	5	14	15	13.9	3.70	111	.288	.356	2	.667	1	2	2	1	0.3
1996	Hou-N	3	3	.500	28	0	0	0	0	33¹	36	4	22	19	16.7	4.59	83	.279	.400	0	.000	-0	-3	-3	-0	-0.5
Total	6	15	48	.238	181	51	2	0	20	460	471	41	167	245	12.7	3.89	99	.268	.335	15	.160	-0	-0	-1	-0	-0.7

● **PETE YOUNG**   Young, Bryan Owen   b: 3/19/68, Meadville, Miss.   BR/TR, 6', 225 lbs.   Deb: 6/5/92

YEAR	TM/L	W	L	PCT	G	GS	CG	SH	SV	IP	H	HR	BB	SO	RAT	ERA	ERA+	OAV	OOB	BH	AVG	PB	PR	/A	PD	TPI
1992	Mon-N	0	0	—	13	0	0	0	0	20¹	18	0	9	11	12.4	3.98	87	.247	.337	0	—	0	-1	-1	-0	0.0
1993	Mon-N	1	0	1.000	5	0	0	0	0	5¹	4	1	0	3	6.8	3.38	124	.211	.211	0	.000	-0	0	0	0	0.1
Total	1	0	1.000	17	0	0	0	0	25²	22	1	9	14	11.2	3.86	94	.239	.314	0	—	0	-0	-1	-0	0.1

● **CHARLIE YOUNG**   Young, Charles "Cy"   b: 1/12/1893, Philadelphia, Pa.   d: 5/12/52, Riverside, N.J.   BB/TR, 5'10.5", 155 lbs.   Deb: 9/5/15

YEAR	TM/L	W	L	PCT	G	GS	CG	SH	SV	IP	H	HR	BB	SO	RAT	ERA	ERA+	OAV	OOB	BH	AVG	PB	PR	/A	PD	TPI
1915	Bal-F	2	3	.400	9	5	1	0	0	35	39	0	21	13	16.5	5.91	49	.289	.400	2	.222	1	-12	-12	2	-1.3

● **CLIFF YOUNG**   Young, Clifford Raphael   b: 8/2/64, Willis, Tex.   d: 11/4/93, Montgomery Co., Tex.   BL/TL, 6'4", 200 lbs.   Deb: 7/14/90

YEAR	TM/L	W	L	PCT	G	GS	CG	SH	SV	IP	H	HR	BB	SO	RAT	ERA	ERA+	OAV	OOB	BH	AVG	PB	PR	/A	PD	TPI
1990	Cal-A	1	1	.500	17	0	0	0	0	30²	40	2	7	19	14.1	3.52	108	.325	.366	0	—	0	1	1	-0	0.2

YEAR	TM/L	W	L	PCT	G	GS	CG	SH	SV	IP	H	HR	BB	SO	RAT	ERA	ERA+	OAV	OOB	BH	AVG	PB	PR	/A	PD	TPI
1991	Cal-A	1	0	1.000	11	0	0	0	0	12²	12	3	3	6	10.7	4.26	96	.261	.306	0	—	0	-0	-0	-0	0.0
1993	Cle-A	3	3	.500	21	7	0	0	1	60¹	74	9	18	31	14.2	4.62	94	.298	.353	0	—	0	-2	-2	-1	-0.2
Total 3		5	4	.556	49	7	0	0	1	103²	126	14	28	56	13.7	4.25	97	.302	.352	0	—	0	-1	-1	-1	0.0

● CURT YOUNG   Young, Curtis Allen b: 4/16/60, Saginaw, Mich. BR/TL, 6'1", 180 lbs. Deb: 6/24/83

YEAR	TM/L	W	L	PCT	G	GS	CG	SH	SV	IP	H	HR	BB	SO	RAT	ERA	ERA+	OAV	OOB	BH	AVG	PB	PR	/A	PD	TPI
1983	Oak-A	0	1	.000	8	2	0	0	0	9	17	1	5	5	23.0	16.00	24	.386	.460	0	—	0	-12	-12	-0	-1.0
1984	Oak-A	9	4	.692	20	17	2	1	0	108²	118	9	31	41	13.0	4.06	92	.274	.334	0	—	0	-1	-4	-1	-0.3
1985	Oak-A	0	4	.000	19	7	0	0	0	46	57	15	22	19	15.7	7.24	53	.300	.376	0	—	0	-16	-17	-1	-1.0
1986	Oak-A	13	9	.591	29	27	5	2	0	198	176	19	57	116	10.9	3.45	112	.236	.297	0	—	0	16	9	0	1.1
1987	Oak-A	13	7	.650	31	31	6	0	0	203	194	38	44	124	10.7	4.08	101	.252	.295	0	.000	0	8	1	0	0.1
1988	*Oak-A	11	8	.579	26	26	1	0	0	156¹	162	23	50	69	12.4	4.14	91	.275	.336	0	—	0	-3	-6	-1	-0.8
1989	Oak-A	5	9	.357	25	20	1	0	0	111	117	10	47	55	13.5	3.73	99	.264	.338	0	—	0	2	-1	-1	0.1
1990	*Oak-A	9	6	.600	26	21	0	0	0	124¹	124	17	53	56	13.0	4.85	77	.266	.344	0	—	0	-13	-16	-1	-1.5
1991	Oak-A	4	2	.667	41	1	0	0	0	68¹	74	8	34	27	14.5	5.00	77	.278	.364	0	—	0	-7	-9	-1	-0.6
1992	KC-A	1	2	.333	10	2	0	0	0	24¹	29	1	7	7	13.3	5.18	78	.293	.340	0	—	0	-3	-3	-0	-0.4
	NY-A	3	0	1.000	13	5	0	0	0	43¹	51	1	10	13	13.1	3.32	118	.298	.344	0	—	0	3	3	0	0.2
	Yr	4	2	.667	23	7	0	0	0	67²	80	2	17	20	13.2	3.99	99	.295	.341	0	—	0	-0	-0	-0	-0.2
1993	Oak-A	1	1	.500	3	3	0	0	0	14²	14	5	6	4	12.3	4.30	95	.241	.313	0	—	0	-0	-0	-0	0.0
Total 11		69	53	.566	251	162	15	3	0	1107	1133	147	366	536	12.5	4.25	97	.261	.330	0	—	0	-26	-55	-1	-4.1

● CY YOUNG   Young, Denton True b: 3/29/1867, Gilmore, Ohio d: 11/4/55, Newcomerstown, Ohio BR/TR, 6'2", 210 lbs. Deb: 8/6/1890 MH

YEAR	TM/L	W	L	PCT	G	GS	CG	SH	SV	IP	H	HR	BB	SO	RAT	ERA	ERA+	OAV	OOB	BH	AVG	PB	PR	/A	PD	TPI
1890	Cle-N	9	7	.563	17	16	16	0	0	147²	145	6	30	39	11.2	3.47	103	.249	.295	8	.123	-6	2	2	1	-0.3
1891	Cle-N	27	22	.551	55	46	43	0	2	423²	431	4	140	147	12.3	2.85	122	.254	.314	29	.167	-3	24	29	-1	2.4
1892	*Cle-N	36	12	.750	53	49	48	9	0	453	363	8	118	168	9.8	1.93	176	.211	.266	31	.158	-8	68	74	5	6.6
1893	Cle-N	34	16	.680	53	46	42	1	1	422²	442	10	103	102	11.8	3.36	145	.261	.307	44	.235	-6	61	71	4	6.4
1894	Cle-N	26	21	.553	52	47	44	2	1	408²	488	19	106	108	13.1	3.94	139	.293	.337	40	.215	-8	63	69	7	5.6
1895	*Cle-N	35	10	.778	47	40	36	4	0	369²	363	10	75	121	10.9	3.26	153	.253	.294	30	.214	-4	62	71	8	7.0
1896	*Cle-N	28	15	.651	51	46	42	5	3	414¹	477	7	62	140	11.9	3.24	140	.286	.316	52	.289	7	52	60	8	6.4
1897	Cle-N	21	19	.525	46	38	35	2	0	335²	391	4	49	88	12.0	3.78	119	.289	.318	34	.222	-4	20	27	3	2.3
1898	Cle-N	25	13	.658	46	41	40	1	0	377²	387	6	41	101	10.4	2.53	143	.263	.287	39	.253	5	45	46	7	5.3
1899	StL-N	26	16	.619	44	42	40	4	1	369¹	368	10	44	111	10.2	2.58	154	.260	.285	32	.216	-1	52	57	6	6.2
1900	StL-N	19	19	.500	41	35	32	4	0	321¹	337	7	36	115	10.5	3.00	121	.269	.291	22	.177	-2	25	23	0	2.1
1901	Bos-A	33	10	.767	43	41	38	5	0	371¹	324	6	37	158	8.9	1.62	217	.232	.256	32	.209	0	84	79	1	8.3
1902	Bos-A	32	11	.744	45	43	41	3	0	384²	350	6	53	160	9.7	2.15	166	.243	.276	34	.230	-8	61	61	-6	5.8
1903	*Bos-A	28	9	.757	40	35	34	7	2	341²	294	6	37	176	9.0	2.08	146	.232	.259	44	.321	12	34	36	-3	4.9
1904	Bos-A	26	16	.619	43	41	40	10	1	380	327	6	29	200	8.5	1.97	136	.233	.251	33	.223	2	27	30	-5	3.1
1905	Bos-A	18	19	.486	38	33	31	4	0	320²	248	3	30	210	8.0	1.82	148	.215	.241	18	.150	-2	30	31	-2	3.3
1906	Bos-A	13	21	.382	39	34	28	0	0	287²	288	3	25	140	10.0	3.19	86	.263	.285	16	.154	-2	-16	-14	-1	-2.0
1907	Bos-A	21	15	.583	43	37	33	6	2	343¹	286	3	51	147	9.0	1.99	129	.229	.263	27	.216	0	21	22	-6	1.8
1908	Bos-A	21	11	.656	36	33	30	3	0	299	230	1	37	150	8.1	1.26	195	.213	.240	26	.226	1	38	40	-6	4.1
1909	Cle-A	19	15	.559	35	34	30	3	0	294¹	267	4	59	109	10.2	2.26	113	.250	.294	21	.196	-0	7	10	-1	0.9
1910	Cle-A	7	10	.412	21	20	14	1	0	163¹	149	0	27	58	9.9	2.53	102	.252	.289	8	.145	-0	1	1	0	0.2
1911	Cle-A	3	4	.429	7	7	4	0	0	46¹	54	2	13	20	13.2	3.88	98	.298	.349	1	.063	-2	-3	-2	-0	-0.5
	Bos-N	4	5	.444	11	11	8	2	0	80	83	4	15	35	11.4	3.71	103	.268	.308	2	.080	-2	-3	1	-1	-0.1
Total 22		511	316	.618	906	815	749	76	17	7356	7092	138	1217	2803	10.4	2.63	138	.252	.287	623	.210	-22	753	819	19	79.8

● HARLEY YOUNG   Young, Harlan Edward "Cy The Third" b: 9/28/1883, Portland, Ind. d: 3/26/75, Jacksonville, Fla. BR/TR, 6'2", Deb: 4/21/08

YEAR	TM/L	W	L	PCT	G	GS	CG	SH	SV	IP	H	HR	BB	SO	RAT	ERA	ERA+	OAV	OOB	BH	AVG	PB	PR	/A	PD	TPI
1908	Pit-N	0	2	.000	8	3	0	0	0	48¹	40	0	10	17	10.2	2.23	103	.234	.296	1	.083	-1	1	1	0	0.0
	Bos-N	0	1	.000	6	2	1	0	0	27¹	29	0	4	12	11.9	3.29	73	.269	.313	2	.200	-0	-3	-3	-0	-0.1
	Yr	0	3	.000	14	5	1	0	0	75²	69	0	14	29	10.2	2.62	89	.243	.286	3	.136	-0	-2	-2	1	-0.1

● IRV YOUNG   Young, Irving Melrose "Young Cy" or "Cy The Second"
b: 7/21/1877, Columbia Falls, Maine d: 1/14/35, Brewer, Maine BL/TL, 5'10", 170 lbs. Deb: 4/14/05

YEAR	TM/L	W	L	PCT	G	GS	CG	SH	SV	IP	H	HR	BB	SO	RAT	ERA	ERA+	OAV	OOB	BH	AVG	PB	PR	/A	PD	TPI
1905	Bos-N	20	21	.488	43	42	41	7	0	378	337	6	71	156	9.9	2.90	107	.241	.282	14	.103	-8	4	8	4	0.4
1906	Bos-N	16	25	.390	43	41	37	4	0	358¹	349	7	83	151	11.0	2.91	92	.263	.309	12	.096	-7	-11	-9	3	-1.5
1907	Bos-N	10	23	.303	40	32	22	3	1	245¹	287	5	58	86	13.1	3.96	64	.289	.354	13	.162	-1	-41	-38	-1	-4.9
1908	Bos-N	4	9	.308	16	11	7	1	0	85	94	2	19	32	12.2	2.86	84	.289	.332	5	.156	-1	-5	-4	-1	-0.9
	Pit-N	4	3	.571	16	7	3	1	1	89²	73	1	21	31	9.9	2.01	115	.225	.283	6	.200	1	4	3	-1	0.3
	Yr	8	12	.400	32	18	10	2	1	174²	167	3	40	63	10.9	2.42	97	.257	.305	11	.177	-0	-1	-1	-2	-0.6
1910	Chi-A	4	8	.333	27	17	7	2	0	135²	120	0	39	64	10.9	2.72	88	.247	.306	5	.114	-2	-3	-5	-0	-0.7
1911	Chi-A	5	6	.455	24	11	3	1	2	92²	99	2	25	40	12.0	4.37	74	.229	.271	5	.179	-0	-11	-12	1	-1.2
Total 6		63	95	.399	209	161	120	21	4	1384²	1361	23	316	560	11.1	3.11	88	.260	.307	60	.126	-18	-62	-57	0	-8.5

● J. B. YOUNG   Young, J. B. b: Mt.Carmel, Pa. Deb: 6/10/1892

YEAR	TM/L	W	L	PCT	G	GS	CG	SH	SV	IP	H	HR	BB	SO	RAT	ERA	ERA+	OAV	OOB	BH	AVG	PB	PR	/A	PD	TPI
1892	StL-N	0	0	—	1	0	0	0	0	2	9	0	2	1	49.5	22.50	14	.600	.647	0	.000	—	-4	-4	-0	0.0

● KIP YOUNG   Young, Kip Lane b: 10/29/54, Georgetown, Ohio BR/TR, 5'11", 175 lbs. Deb: 7/21/78

YEAR	TM/L	W	L	PCT	G	GS	CG	SH	SV	IP	H	HR	BB	SO	RAT	ERA	ERA+	OAV	OOB	BH	AVG	PB	PR	/A	PD	TPI
1978	Det-A	6	7	.462	14	13	7	0	0	105²	94	9	30	49	10.7	2.81	137	.246	.304	0	—	0	11	12	-2	1.1
1979	Det-A	2	2	.500	13	7	0	0	0	43²	60	11	11	22	14.8	6.39	68	.323	.364	0	—	0	-11	-10	1	-0.9
Total 2		8	9	.471	27	20	7	0	0	149¹	154	20	41	71	11.9	3.86	104	.271	.324	0	—	0	1	2	-1	0.2

● MATT YOUNG   Young, Matthew John b: 8/9/58, Pasadena, Cal. BL/TL, 6'3", 205 lbs. Deb: 4/6/83

YEAR	TM/L	W	L	PCT	G	GS	CG	SH	SV	IP	H	HR	BB	SO	RAT	ERA	ERA+	OAV	OOB	BH	AVG	PB	PR	/A	PD	TPI
1983	Sea-A★	11	15	.423	33	32	5	2	0	203²	178	17	79	130	11.7	3.27	130	.236	.315	0	—	0	18	22	2	2.8
1984	Sea-A	6	8	.429	22	22	1	0	0	113¹	141	11	57	73	15.4	5.72	70	.307	.384	0	—	0	-22	-22	1	-2.2
1985	Sea-A	12	19	.387	37	35	5	2	1	218¹	242	23	76	136	13.4	4.91	86	.284	.345	0	—	0	-18	-17	-2	-2.3
1986	Sea-A	8	6	.571	65	5	1	0	13	103²	108	9	46	82	14.1	3.82	111	.272	.359	0	—	0	4	5	-1	0.9
1987	LA-N	5	8	.385	47	0	0	0	11	54¹	62	5	17	42	13.1	4.47	89	.288	.341	0	.000	0	-2	-3	-2	-0.9
1989	*Oak-A	1	4	.200	26	4	0	0	0	37¹	42	3	31	27	17.6	6.75	55	.284	.410	0	—	0	-12	-13	-0	-1.3
1990	Sea-A	8	18	.308	34	33	7	1	0	225¹	198	15	107	176	12.4	3.51	113	.237	.328	0	—	0	10	11	-0	1.2
1991	Bos-A	3	7	.300	19	16	0	0	0	88²	92	4	53	69	14.9	5.18	83	.266	.367	0	—	0	-11	-9	-0	-1.0
1992	Bos-A	0	4	.000	28	8	1	0	0	70²	69	7	42	57	14.5	4.58	92	.266	.363	0	—	0	-5	-3	-1	-0.3
1993	Cle-A	1	6	.143	28	12	0	0	0	74¹	75	8	57	65	16.3	5.21	83	.266	.395	0	—	0	-7	-7	0	-0.6
Total 10		55	95	.367	333	163	20	5	25	1189²	1207	99	565	857	13.7	4.40	94	.265	.350	0	.000	0	-46	-35	-3	-4.1

● CHIEF YOUNGBLOOD   Youngblood, Albert Clyde b: 6/13/1900, Hillsboro, Tex. d: 7/6/68, Amarillo, Tex. BL/TR, 6'3", 202 lbs. Deb: 7/16/22

YEAR	TM/L	W	L	PCT	G	GS	CG	SH	SV	IP	H	HR	BB	SO	RAT	ERA	ERA+	OAV	OOB	BH	AVG	PB	PR	/A	PD	TPI
1922	Was-A	0	0	—	2	0	0	0	0	4¹	9	0	7	0	37.4	14.54	27	.429	.600	0	.000	-0	-5	-5	0	0.0

● DUCKY YOUNT   Yount, Herbert Macon "Hub" b: 12/7/1885, Iredell Co., N.C. d: 5/9/70, Winston-Salem, N.C. BR/TR, 6'2", 178 lbs. Deb: 5/20/14

YEAR	TM/L	W	L	PCT	G	GS	CG	SH	SV	IP	H	HR	BB	SO	RAT	ERA	ERA+	OAV	OOB	BH	AVG	PB	PR	/A	PD	TPI
1914	Bal-F	1	1	.500	13	1	1	0	0	41¹	44	2	19	19	14.2	4.14	73	.280	.365	1	.083	-1	-6	-5	1	-0.3

● LARRY YOUNT   Yount, Lawrence King b: 2/15/50, Houston, Tex. BR/TR, 6'2", 185 lbs. Deb: 9/15/71 F

YEAR	TM/L	W	L	PCT	G	GS	CG	SH	SV	IP	H	HR	BB	SO	RAT	ERA	ERA+	OAV	OOB	BH	AVG	PB	PR	/A	PD	TPI
1971	Hou-N	0	0	—	1	0	0	0	0	0	0	0	0	0	—	—	—	—	—	0	—	-0	0	0	0	0.0

● CARL YOWELL   Yowell, Carl Columbus "Sundown" b: 12/20/02, Madison, Va. d: 7/27/85, Jacksonville, Tex. BL/TL, 6'4", 180 lbs. Deb: 9/5/24

YEAR	TM/L	W	L	PCT	G	GS	CG	SH	SV	IP	H	HR	BB	SO	RAT	ERA	ERA+	OAV	OOB	BH	AVG	PB	PR	/A	PD	TPI
1924	Cle-A	1	1	.500	4	2	2	0	0	27	37	1	13	8	16.7	6.67	64	.343	.413	2	.182	-1	-7	-7	-0	-0.5
1925	Cle-A	2	3	.400	12	4	1	0	0	36¹	40	1	17	12	14.4	4.46	99	.310	.395	1	.125	-0	-0	-0	-0	-0.1
Total 2		3	4	.429	16	6	3	0	0	63¹	77	2	30	20	15.3	5.40	81	.325	.403	3	.158	-1	-8	-7	0	-0.6

● EDDIE YUHAS   Yuhas, John Edward b: 8/5/24, Youngstown, Ohio d: 7/6/86, Winston-Salem, N.C BR/TR, 6'1", 180 lbs. Deb: 4/17/52

YEAR	TM/L	W	L	PCT	G	GS	CG	SH	SV	IP	H	HR	BB	SO	RAT	ERA	ERA+	OAV	OOB	BH	AVG	PB	PR	/A	PD	TPI
1952	StL-N	12	2	.857	54	2	0	0	6	99¹	90	5	35	39	11.5	2.72	137	.243	.312	4	.190	1	11	11	-1	1.6
1953	StL-N	0	0	—	2	0	0	0	0	1	3	0	0	0	27.0	18.00	24	.500	.500	0	—	0	-2	-2	-0	0.0
Total 2		12	2	.857	56	2	0	0	6	100¹	93	5	35	39	11.7	2.87	130	.247	.315	4	.190	1	10	9	-1	1.6

YEAR TM/L	W	L	PCT	G	GS	CG	SH	SV	IP	H	HR	BB	SO	RAT	ERA	ERA+	OAV	OOB	BH	AVG	PB	PR	/A	PD	TPI

● ADRIAN ZABALA   Zabala, Adrian (Rodriguez)   b: 8/26/16, San Antonio De Los Banos, Cuba   BL/TL, 5'11", 165 lbs.   Deb: 8/11/45

YEAR TM/L	W	L	PCT	G	GS	CG	SH	SV	IP	H	HR	BB	SO	RAT	ERA	ERA+	OAV	OOB	BH	AVG	PB	PR	/A	PD	TPI
1945 NY-N	2	4	.333	11	5	1	0	0	43¹	46	2	20	14	13.7	4.78	82	.284	.363	3	.231	1	-5	-4	0	-0.4
1949 NY-N	2	3	.400	15	4	2	1	1	41	44	5	10	13	12.1	5.27	76	.278	.325	1	.077	-1	-6	-6	-1	-0.9
Total 2	4	7	.364	26	9	3	1	1	84¹	90	7	30	27	12.9	5.02	79	.281	.345	4	.154	-0	-10	-10	-1	-1.3

● ZIP ZABEL   Zabel, George Washington   b: 2/18/1891, Wetmore, Kan.   d: 5/31/70, Beloit, Wis.   BR/TR, 6'1.5", 185 lbs.   Deb: 10/5/13

YEAR TM/L	W	L	PCT	G	GS	CG	SH	SV	IP	H	HR	BB	SO	RAT	ERA	ERA+	OAV	OOB	BH	AVG	PB	PR	/A	PD	TPI
1913 Chi-N	1	0	1.000	1	1	0	0	0	5	3	0	1	0	7.2	0.00	—	.167	.211	0	.000	0	2	2	0	0.4
1914 Chi-N	4	4	.500	29	7	2	0	3	128	104	5	45	50	10.6	2.18	128	.235	.309	7	.184	-1	9	9	-1	0.4
1915 Chi-N	7	10	.412	36	17	8	3	0	163	124	3	84	60	11.7	3.20	87	.218	.323	4	.074	-1	-8	-8	3	-0.8
Total 3	12	14	.462	66	25	10	3	3	296	231	8	130	110	11.2	2.71	103	.224	.315	11	.117	-4	2	3	2	0.4

● CHINK ZACHARY   Zachary, Albert Myron (b: Albert Myron Zarski)   b: 10/19/17, Brooklyn, N.Y.   BR/TR, 5'11", 182 lbs.   Deb: 4/23/44

YEAR TM/L	W	L	PCT	G	GS	CG	SH	SV	IP	H	HR	BB	SO	RAT	ERA	ERA+	OAV	OOB	BH	AVG	PB	PR	/A	PD	TPI
1944 Bro-N	0	2	.000	4	2	0	0	0	10¹	10	7	3	7	15.7	9.58	37	.238	.360	0	.000	-0	-7	-7	-0	-1.1

● TOM ZACHARY   Zachary, Jonathan Thompson Walton (a.k.a. Zach Walton in 1918)   b: 5/7/1896, Graham, N.C.   d: 1/24/69, Burlington, N.C.   BL/TL, 6'1", 187 lbs.   Deb: 7/11/18

YEAR TM/L	W	L	PCT	G	GS	CG	SH	SV	IP	H	HR	BB	SO	RAT	ERA	ERA+	OAV	OOB	BH	AVG	PB	PR	/A	PD	TPI
1918 Phi-A	2	0	1.000	2	2	0	0	0	8	9	0	7	1	18.0	5.63	52	.321	.457	2	.500	1	-3	-2	-0	-0.5
1919 Was-A	1	5	.167	17	7	0	0	0	61²	68	9	20	9	13.0	2.92	110	.292	.350	5	.333	2	2	2	-1	0.3
1920 Was-A	15	16	.484	44	31	19	3	2	262²	289	7	78	53	12.7	3.77	99	.285	.339	29	.261	6	1	-1	0	0.4
1921 Was-A	18	16	.529	39	30	17	2	1	250	314	10	59	53	13.6	3.96	104	.319	.361	23	.256	3	9	4	-0	0.8
1922 Was-A	15	10	.600	32	25	13	1	1	184²	190	6	43	37	11.5	3.12	124	.275	.321	21	.296	5	19	15	0	2.4
1923 Was-A	10	16	.385	35	29	10	0	0	204¹	270	9	63	40	14.8	4.49	84	.321	.372	15	.192	-0	-12	-17	-1	-1.9
1924 *Was-A	15	9	.625	33	27	13	1	2	202²	198	6	53	45	11.3	2.75	147	.264	.315	22	.306	4	33	29	2	3.7
1925 *Was-A	12	15	.444	38	33	11	1	2	217²	247	10	74	58	13.4	3.85	110	.296	.355	12	.174	-2	13	9	-0	0.8
1926 StL-A	14	15	.483	34	31	18	3	0	247¹	264	14	97	53	13.4	3.60	119	.288	.359	23	.267	4	11	19	3	2.7
1927 StL-A	4	6	.400	13	12	6	0	0	78¹	110	4	27	13	15.7	4.37	100	.345	.396	1	.107	-2	-2	-0	-1	-0.3
Was-A	4	7	.364	15	14	5	1	0	102²	116	2	30	13	13.0	3.94	103	.290	.343	5	.139	-2	2	1	-3	-0.3
Yr	8	13	.381	28	26	11	1	0	181	226	6	57	26	14.2	4.13	102	.314	.366	8	.125	-4	0	1	-3	-0.6
1928 Was-A	6	9	.400	20	14	5	1	0	102²	130	5	40	19	15.0	5.44	74	.322	.384	10	.303	1	-16	-16	1	-1.7
*NY-A	3	3	.500	7	6	3	0	1	45²	54	1	15	7	13.6	3.94	95	.320	.375	2	.133	-0	1	-1	1	-0.1
Yr	9	12	.429	27	20	8	1	1	148¹	184	6	55	26	14.5	4.98	79	.321	.380	12	.250	1	-15	-17	2	-1.8
1929 NY-A	12	0	1.000	26	11	7	2	2	119²	131	6	30	35	12.3	2.48	155	.277	.323	10	.238	1	23	18	-3	1.5
1930 NY-A	1	1	.500	3	3	0	0	0	16²	18	0	9	1	14.6	6.48	66	.269	.355	2	.250	-1	-3	-4	-1	-0.3
Bos-N	11	5	.688	24	22	10	1	0	151¹	192	9	50	57	14.4	4.58	108	.317	.369	13	.241	2	7	6	-1	0.6
1931 Bos-N	11	15	.423	33	28	16	3	0	229	243	6	53	64	11.7	3.10	122	.272	.314	14	.167	-1	19	17	2	2.0
1932 Bos-N	12	11	.522	32	24	12	1	0	212	231	6	55	67	12.2	3.10	121	.280	.326	21	.273	5	18	16	-2	1.9
1933 Bos-N	7	9	.438	26	20	6	2	2	125	134	1	35	22	12.2	3.53	87	.276	.325	5	.119	-2	-3	-6	-0	-1.0
1934 Bos-N	1	2	.333	5	4	2	1	0	24	27	1	8	4	13.1	3.38	113	.278	.333	0	.000	-1	2	1	-0	0.0
Bro-N	5	6	.455	22	12	4	0	2	101²	122	5	21	28	12.8	4.43	88	.301	.339	7	.184	1	-4	-6	-1	-0.5
Yr	6	8	.429	27	16	6	1	2	125²	149	6	29	32	12.9	4.23	92	.297	.338	7	.152	-0	-2	-5	-1	-0.5
1935 Bro-N	7	12	.368	25	21	9	1	4	158	193	10	35	33	13.1	3.59	111	.297	.335	7	.135	-1	8	7	0	0.7
1936 Bro-N	0	0	—	1	0	0	0	0	0¹	2	0	1	0	81.0	54.00	8	1.000	1.000	0	—	0	-2	-2	0	-0.0
Phi-N	0	3	.000	7	2	0	0	1	20¹	30	2	11	8	17.3	7.97	57	.329	.406	3	.333	1	-9	-8	0	-0.9
Yr	0	3	.000	8	2	0	0	1	20²	32	2	12	8	18.3	8.71	52	.345	.424	3	.333	1	-11	-10	0	-0.9
Total 19	186	191	.493	533	408	186	24	22	3126¹	3580	119	914	720	13.1	3.73	106	.294	.345	254	.226	25	116	82	-2	10.3

● CHRIS ZACHARY   Zachary, William Christopher   b: 2/19/44, Knoxville, Tenn.   BL/TR, 6'2", 200 lbs.   Deb: 4/11/63

YEAR TM/L	W	L	PCT	G	GS	CG	SH	SV	IP	H	HR	BB	SO	RAT	ERA	ERA+	OAV	OOB	BH	AVG	PB	PR	/A	PD	TPI
1963 Hou-N	2	2	.500	22	7	0	0	0	57	62	5	22	42	13.7	4.89	64	.272	.344	0	.000	-0	-10	-11	1	-0.7
1964 Hou-N	0	1	.000	1	1	0	0	0	4	6	1	1	2	15.8	9.00	38	.333	.368	0	.000	-0	-2	-2	-0	-0.4
1965 Hou-N	0	2	.000	4	2	0	0	0	10²	12	0	6	4	15.2	4.22	80	.273	.360	0	.000	-0	-1	-1	-0	-0.2
1966 Hou-N	3	5	.375	10	8	0	0	0	55	44	3	24	37	12.6	3.44	100	.221	.332	4	.222	1	1	-0	-1	0.0
1967 Hou-N	1	6	.143	9	7	0	0	0	36¹	42	5	12	18	13.9	5.70	58	.290	.352	1	.100	-0	-9	-10	-0	-1.7
1969 KC-A	0	1	.000	8	2	0	0	0	18¹	27	4	7	6	16.7	7.85	47	.346	.400	1	.500	0	-9	-8	-0	-0.4
1971 StL-N	3	10	.231	23	12	1	1	0	89²	114	3	26	48	14.5	5.32	68	.316	.368	8	.242	1	-18	-17	0	-2.2
1972 *Det-A	1	1	.500	25	1	0	0	1	38¹	27	2	15	21	10.1	1.41	223	.201	.287	1	.500	1	7	7	-0	0.5
1973 Pit-N	0	1	.000	6	0	0	0	1	12	10	1	1	6	8.3	3.00	117	.222	.239	0	.000	-0	1	1	-0	0.0
Total 9	10	29	.256	108	40	1	1	2	321¹	344	22	122	184	13.4	4.57	74	.275	.344	15	.181	1	-41	-42	-1	-5.1

● PAT ZACHRY   Zachry, Patrick Paul   b: 4/24/52, Richmond, Tex.   BR/TR, 6'5", 180 lbs.   Deb: 4/11/76

YEAR TM/L	W	L	PCT	G	GS	CG	SH	SV	IP	H	HR	BB	SO	RAT	ERA	ERA+	OAV	OOB	BH	AVG	PB	PR	/A	PD	TPI
1976 *Cin-N	14	7	.667	38	28	6	1	0	204	170	8	83	143	11.3	2.74	128	.228	.307	7	.113	-2	17	17	-2	1.4
1977 Cin-N	3	7	.300	12	12	3	0	0	75	78	7	29	36	13.0	5.04	78	.273	.342	3	.136	-1	-9	-9	1	-1.0
NY-N	7	6	.538	19	19	2	1	0	119²	129	14	48	63	13.5	3.76	99	.278	.350	6	.143	-1	2	-0	-2	-0.3
Yr	10	13	.435	31	31	5	1	0	194²	207	21	77	99	13.3	4.25	90	.274	.344	9	.141	-2	-7	-10	-0	-1.3
1978 NY-N☆	10	6	.625	21	21	5	2	0	138	120	9	60	78	11.8	3.33	105	.236	.318	3	.070	-2	4	2	1	0.2
1979 NY-N	5	1	.833	7	7	1	0	0	42²	44	3	21	17	14.1	3.59	101	.267	.356	2	.125	-1	1	0	0	0.2
1980 NY-N	6	10	.375	28	26	7	3	0	164²	145	16	58	88	11.4	3.01	118	.240	.312	2	.043	-4	11	10	-2	0.4
1981 NY-N	7	14	.333	24	24	3	0	0	139	151	13	56	76	13.7	4.14	84	.282	.354	6	.158	-0	-10	-10	-1	-1.4
1982 NY-N	6	9	.400	36	16	2	0	1	137²	149	10	57	69	13.5	4.05	90	.279	.349	3	.079	-2	-7	-6	-0	-0.9
1983 *LA-N	6	1	.857	40	1	0	0	0	61¹	63	4	21	36	12.5	2.49	144	.278	.341	2	.500	1	8	7	0	0.9
1984 LA-N	5	6	.455	58	0	0	0	2	82²	84	3	51	55	14.9	3.81	93	.267	.372	2	.333	1	-2	-3	1	-0.2
1985 Phi-N	0	0	—	10	0	0	0	0	12²	14	1	11	8	17.8	4.26	86	.280	.410	0	.000	-0	-1	-1	1	-0.2
Total 10	69	67	.507	293	154	29	7	3	1177¹	1147	88	495	669	12.7	3.52	102	.259	.336	36	.113	-11	13	8	-1	-0.9

● GEORGE ZACKERT   Zackert, George Carl "Zeke"   b: 12/24/1884, Buchanan Co., Mo.   d: 2/18/77, Burlington, Iowa   BL/TL, 6', 177 lbs.   Deb: 9/22/11

YEAR TM/L	W	L	PCT	G	GS	CG	SH	SV	IP	H	HR	BB	SO	RAT	ERA	ERA+	OAV	OOB	BH	AVG	PB	PR	/A	PD	TPI
1911 StL-N	0	2	.000	4	1	0	0	0	7¹	17	0	6	6	28.2	11.05	31	.486	.561	0	.000	-0	-6	-6	1	-1.3
1912 StL-N	0	0	—	1	0	0	0	0	1	2	0	1	0	36.0	18.00	19	.667	.800	0	—	-0	-2	-2	0	-0.0
Total 2	0	2	.000	5	1	0	0	0	8¹	19	0	7	6	29.2	11.88	28	.500	.587	0	.000	-0	-8	-8	1	-1.3

● GEOFF ZAHN   Zahn, Geoffrey Clayton   b: 12/19/45, Baltimore, Md.   BL/TL, 6'1", 180 lbs.   Deb: 9/2/73

YEAR TM/L	W	L	PCT	G	GS	CG	SH	SV	IP	H	HR	BB	SO	RAT	ERA	ERA+	OAV	OOB	BH	AVG	PB	PR	/A	PD	TPI
1973 LA-N	1	0	1.000	6	1	0	0	0	13¹	5	2	2	9	4.7	1.35	255	.116	.156	0	.000	-0	3	3	0	0.2
1974 LA-N	3	5	.375	21	10	1	0	0	79²	78	3	16	33	10.8	2.03	167	.254	.295	4	.174	-0	14	12	0	1.1
1975 LA-N	0	1	.000	2	0	0	0	0	3	2	0	5	1	21.0	9.00	38	.222	.500	0	—	0	-2	-2	-0	-0.5
Chi-N	2	7	.222	16	10	0	0	0	62²	67	2	26	21	13.4	4.45	86	.282	.352	2	.133	-1	-6	-4	1	-0.5
Yr	2	8	.200	18	10	0	0	0	65²	69	2	31	22	13.7	4.66	82	.279	.360	2	.133	-1	-8	-6	1	-1.0
1976 Chi-N	0	1	.000	10	1	0	0	0	8¹	16	0	4	4	20.5	10.80	36	.410	.452	0	.000	-0	-7	-6	0	-0.7
1977 Min-A	12	14	.462	34	32	7	1	0	198	234	20	66	88	13.9	4.68	85	.299	.358	0	—	0	-14	-15	2	-1.4
1978 Min-A	14	14	.500	35	35	12	1	0	252²	260	18	81	106	12.3	3.03	126	.274	.334	0	—	0	20	22	-0	2.3
1979 Min-A	13	7	.650	26	24	4	0	0	169	181	13	41	58	11.8	3.57	123	.279	.322	0	—	0	12	15	2	1.5
1980 Min-A	14	18	.438	38	35	13	5	0	232²	273	17	66	69	11.8	4.41	99	.302	.351	0	—	0	-10	-10	-0	-0.7
1981 Cal-A	10	11	.476	25	25	9	0	0	161¹	181	18	43	62	12.5	4.41	83	.285	.330	0	—	0	-13	-14	-0	-1.6
1982 *Cal-A	18	8	.692	34	34	12	4	0	229¹	225	18	65	81	11.5	3.73	109	.259	.314	0	—	0	9	8	-1	0.7
1983 Cal-A	9	11	.450	29	28	11	1	0	203	212	22	51	81	11.7	3.33	121	.269	.314	0	—	0	17	16	-2	1.3
1984 Cal-A	13	10	.565	28	27	9	**5**	0	199²	200	11	48	61	11.2	3.12	127	.263	.308	0	—	0	19	19	1	2.2
1985 Cal-A	2	2	.500	7	7	1	0	0	37	44	5	14	14	14.1	4.38	94	.299	.360	0	—	0	-1	-1	0	0.0
Total 13	111	109	.505	304	270	79	20	1	1849	1978	149	526	705	12.3	3.74	107	.278	.329	6	.140	-2	43	51	4	3.9

● PAUL ZAHNISER   Zahniser, Paul Vernon   b: 9/6/1896, Sac City, Iowa   d: 9/26/64, Klamath Falls, Ore.   BR/TR, 5'10.5", 170 lbs.   Deb: 5/18/23

YEAR TM/L	W	L	PCT	G	GS	CG	SH	SV	IP	H	HR	BB	SO	RAT	ERA	ERA+	OAV	OOB	BH	AVG	PB	PR	/A	PD	TPI
1923 Was-A	9	10	.474	33	21	11	0	0	177	201	7	76	52	14.2	3.86	97	.291	.364	5	.096	-1	2	-2	-0	-0.5
1924 Was-A	5	7	.417	24	14	5	1	0	92	98	2	49	28	14.8	4.40	92	.283	.378	4	.129	-2	-2	-4	-2	-0.7
1925 Bos-A	5	12	.294	37	21	7	1	1	176²	232	6	89	30	16.4	5.15	82	.327	.403	8	.138	-4	-15	-12	-2	-1.5
1926 Bos-A	6	18	.250	30	24	7	1	0	172	213	6	69	34	14.9	4.97	82	.321	.387	8	.163	-1	-18	-17	3	-1.8

YEAR TM/L	W	L	PCT	G	GS	CG	SH	SV	IP	H	HR	BB	SO	RAT	ERA	ERA+	OAV	OOB	BH	AVG	PB	PR	/A	PD	TPI
1929 Cin-N	0	0	—	1	0	0	0	0	1	2	1	1	0	27.0	27.00	17	.400	.500	0	.000	0	-2	-2	-0	0.0
Total 5	25	47	.347	125	80	29	4	1	618²	746	21	284	145	15.1	4.66	88	.309	.384	25	.132	-8	-35	-37	-3	-4.5

● CARL ZAMLOCH
Zamloch, Carl Eugene b: 10/6/1889, Oakland, Cal. d: 8/19/63, Santa Barbara, Cal BR/TR, 6'1", 176 lbs. Deb: 5/7/13

YEAR TM/L	W	L	PCT	G	GS	CG	SH	SV	IP	H	HR	BB	SO	RAT	ERA	ERA+	OAV	OOB	BH	AVG	PB	PR	/A	PD	TPI
1913 Det-A	1	6	.143	17	5	3	0	1	69²	66	1	23	28	11.9	2.45	119	.257	.325	4	.182	-1	4	4	-1	0.2

● OSCAR ZAMORA
Zamora, Oscar Jose (Sosa) b: 9/23/44, Camaguey, Cuba BR/TR, 5'10", 178 lbs. Deb: 6/18/74

YEAR TM/L	W	L	PCT	G	GS	CG	SH	SV	IP	H	HR	BB	SO	RAT	ERA	ERA+	OAV	OOB	BH	AVG	PB	PR	/A	PD	TPI
1974 Chi-N	3	9	.250	56	0	0	0	10	83²	82	6	19	38	10.9	3.12	122	.264	.306	2	.182	-0	5	6	-0	1.0
1975 Chi-N	5	2	.714	52	0	0	0	10	71	84	17	15	28	12.5	5.07	76	.298	.333	1	.167	-0	-11	-10	-0	-1.3
1976 Chi-N	5	3	.625	40	0	0	0	3	55	70	8	17	27	14.4	5.24	74	.317	.368	0	.000	-1	-11	-8	-1	-1.4
1978 Hou-N	0	0	—	10	0	0	0	0	15	20	2	7	6	16.2	7.20	46	.328	.397	0	.000	-0	-6	-6	0	0.0
Total 4	13	14	.481	158	2	0	0	23	224²	256	33	58	99	12.6	4.53	84	.293	.337	3	.107	-2	-23	-18	-1	-1.7

● DOM ZANNI
Zanni, Dominick Thomas b: 3/1/32, Bronx, N.Y. BR/TR, 5'11", 180 lbs. Deb: 9/28/58

YEAR TM/L	W	L	PCT	G	GS	CG	SH	SV	IP	H	HR	BB	SO	RAT	ERA	ERA+	OAV	OOB	BH	AVG	PB	PR	/A	PD	TPI
1958 SF-N	1	0	1.000	1	0	0	0	0	4	7	1	1	3	18.0	2.25	169	.412	.444	0	.000	-0	1	1	-0	0.1
1959 SF-N	0	0	—	9	0	0	0	0	11	12	2	1	8	17.2	6.55	58	.273	.396	0	—	0	-3	-3	1	0.1
1961 SF-N	1	0	1.000	8	0	0	0	0	13²	13	1	12	11	16.5	3.95	96	.277	.424	0	—	0	-0	-0	0	0.0
1962 Chi-A	6	5	.545	44	2	0	0	5	86¹	67	12	31	66	10.3	3.75	104	.214	.287	5	.278	2	2	1	2	0.6
1963 Chi-A	0	0	—	5	0	0	0	0	4¹	5	1	4	2	18.7	8.31	42	.294	.429	0	—	0	-2	-2	0	-0.2
Cin-N	1	1	.500	31	1	0	0	5	43	39	2	21	40	13.4	4.19	80	.247	.350	1	.333	1	-4	-4	1	-0.2
1965 Cin-N	0	0	—	8	0	0	0	0	13¹	7	1	5	10	8.1	1.35	278	.159	.245	0	—	0	3	3	0	0.0
1966 Cin-N	0	0	—	5	0	0	0	0	7¹	5	0	5	3	11.0	0.00	—	.192	.300	1	1.000	1	3	3	0	0.0
Total 7	9	6	.600	111	3	0	0	10	183	155	20	85	148	12.1	3.79	99	.233	.326	7	.280	2	-1	-1	4	0.6

● JEFF ZASKE
Zaske, Lloyd Jeffrey b: 10/6/60, Seattle, Wash. BR/TR, 6'5", 180 lbs. Deb: 7/21/84

YEAR TM/L	W	L	PCT	G	GS	CG	SH	SV	IP	H	HR	BB	SO	RAT	ERA	ERA+	OAV	OOB	BH	AVG	PB	PR	/A	PD	TPI
1984 Pit-N	0	0	—	3	0	0	0	0	5	4	0	1	2	9.0	0.00	—	.211	.250	0	—	0	2	2	0	0.0

● CLINT ZAVARAS
Zavaras, Clinton Wayne b: 1/4/67, Denver, Colo. BR/TR, 6'1", 175 lbs. Deb: 6/3/89

YEAR TM/L	W	L	PCT	G	GS	CG	SH	SV	IP	H	HR	BB	SO	RAT	ERA	ERA+	OAV	OOB	BH	AVG	PB	PR	/A	PD	TPI
1989 Sea-A	1	6	.143	10	10	0	0	0	52	49	4	30	31	14.0	5.19	78	.253	.358	0	—	0	-8	-7	-0	-1.1

● ZAY
Zay Deb: 10/7/1886 ♦

YEAR TM/L	W	L	PCT	G	GS	CG	SH	SV	IP	H	HR	BB	SO	RAT	ERA	ERA+	OAV	OOB	BH	AVG	PB	PR	/A	PD	TPI
1886 Bal-a	1	0	1.000	1	1	0	0	0	2	4	0	4	2	36.0	9.00	38	.333	.500	0	.000	-0	-1	-1	-0	-0.4

● MATT ZEISER
Zeiser, Matthew J. b: 9/25/1888, Chicago, Ill. d: 6/10/42, Chicago, Ill BR/TR, 5'10", 170 lbs. Deb: 4/27/14

YEAR TM/L	W	L	PCT	G	GS	CG	SH	SV	IP	H	HR	BB	SO	RAT	ERA	ERA+	OAV	OOB	BH	AVG	PB	PR	/A	PD	TPI
1914 Bos-A	0	0	—	2	0	0	0	0	10	9	0	8	6	16.2	1.80	150	.281	.439	0	.000	-0	1	1	-1	-0.1

● BILL ZEPP
Zepp, William Clinton b: 7/22/46, Detroit, Mich. BR/TR, 6'2", 185 lbs. Deb: 8/12/69

YEAR TM/L	W	L	PCT	G	GS	CG	SH	SV	IP	H	HR	BB	SO	RAT	ERA	ERA+	OAV	OOB	BH	AVG	PB	PR	/A	PD	TPI
1969 Min-A	0	0	—	4	0	0	0	0	5¹	6	1	4	2	16.9	6.75	54	.286	.400	0	.000	-0	-2	-2	-0	0.0
1970 *Min-A	9	4	.692	43	20	1	1	2	151	154	9	51	64	12.8	3.22	116	.266	.335	6	.136	-1	8	8	-2	0.4
1971 Det-A	1	1	.500	16	4	0	0	2	31²	41	2	17	15	17.3	5.12	70	.328	.421	0	.000	-0	-6	-5	-0	-0.4
Total 3	10	5	.667	63	24	1	1	4	188	201	12	72	81	13.6	3.64	102	.278	.353	6	.122	-2	1	1	-2	0.0

● GEORGE ZETTLEIN
Zettlein, George "Charmer" b: 7/18/1844, Brooklyn, N.Y. d: 5/23/05, Patchogue, N.Y. BR/TR, 5'9", 162 lbs. Deb: 5/8/1871

YEAR TM/L	W	L	PCT	G	GS	CG	SH	SV	IP	H	HR	BB	SO	RAT	ERA	ERA+	OAV	OOB	BH	AVG	PB	PR	/A	PD	TPI
1871 Chi-n	18	9	.667	28	28	25	0	0	240²	298	6	25	22	12.1	2.73	168	.267	.283	32	.250	-7	40	50		2.9
1872 Tro-n	14	8	.636	25	22	17	2	1	187²	207	2	8	17	10.3	2.16	168	.250	.257	29	.257	1	31	31		1.8
Eck-n	1	8	.111	9	9	8	0	0	75¹	106	1	6	8	13.4	2.75	123	.300	.312	3	.088	-4	7	5		0.0
Yr	15	16	.484	34	31	25	2	1	263	313	3	14	25	11.2	2.33	153	.265	.274	32	.218	-4	38	36		1.8
1873 Phi-n	36	15	.706	51	51	49	0	0	460	593	3	41	28	12.4	2.70	122	.283	.297	50	.207	-8	28	31		1.9
1874 Chi-n	27	30	.474	57	57	57	3	0	515²	640	3	43	26	11.9	2.43	92	.273	.286	47	.193	-9	-14	-12		-1.6
1875 Chi-n	17	14	.548	31	31	29	6	0	282	266	0	6	18	8.7	1.28	178	.230	.234	29	.218	-3	30	31		2.5
Phi-n	12	8	.600	21	21	20	1	0	181¹	209	0	10	13	10.9	2.08	109	.264	.273	15	.181	-4	3	4		-0.1
Yr	29	22	.569	52	52	49	7	0	463¹	475	0	16	31	9.5	1.59	143	.244	.250	44	.204	-7	33	35		2.4
1876 Phi-N	4	20	.167	28	25	23	1	2	234	358	2	6	10	14.0	3.88	62	.331	.334	27	.211	-5	-41	-38	-1	-3.4
Total 5 n	125	92	.576	222	219	205	12	1	1942²	2319	15	139	132	11.4	2.32	128	.267	.278	205	.210	-35	125	138		7.4

● BOB ZICK
Zick, Robert George b: 4/26/27, Chicago, Ill. BL/TR, 6', 168 lbs. Deb: 5/2/54

YEAR TM/L	W	L	PCT	G	GS	CG	SH	SV	IP	H	HR	BB	SO	RAT	ERA	ERA+	OAV	OOB	BH	AVG	PB	PR	/A	PD	TPI
1954 Chi-N	0	0	—	8	0	0	0	0	16¹	23	1	7	9	16.5	8.27	51	.343	.405	1	.250	0	-8	-7	-0	-0.8

● GEORGE ZIEGLER
Ziegler, George J. b: 1872, Chicago, Ill. d: 7/22/16, Kankakee, Ill. Deb: 6/19/1890

YEAR TM/L	W	L	PCT	G	GS	CG	SH	SV	IP	H	HR	BB	SO	RAT	ERA	ERA+	OAV	OOB	BH	AVG	PB	PR	/A	PD	TPI
1890 Pit-N	0	1	.000	1	1	0	0	0	6	12	0	1	0	18.0	10.50	31	.400	.400	0	.000	-0	-5	-5	-0	-0.5

● STEVE ZIEM
Ziem, Stephen Graeling b: 10/24/61, Milwaukee, Wis. BR/TR, 6'2", 210 lbs. Deb: 4/30/87

YEAR TM/L	W	L	PCT	G	GS	CG	SH	SV	IP	H	HR	BB	SO	RAT	ERA	ERA+	OAV	OOB	BH	AVG	PB	PR	/A	PD	TPI
1987 Atl-N	0	1	.000	2	0	0	0	0	2¹	4	0	1	0	19.3	7.71	56	.364	.417	0	—	0	-1	-1	-0	-0.3

● WALTER ZINK
Zink, Walter Noble b: 11/21/1899, Pittsfield, Mass. d: 6/12/64, Quincy, Mass. BR/TR, 6', 165 lbs. Deb: 7/6/21

YEAR TM/L	W	L	PCT	G	GS	CG	SH	SV	IP	H	HR	BB	SO	RAT	ERA	ERA+	OAV	OOB	BH	AVG	PB	PR	/A	PD	TPI
1921 NY-N	0	0	—	2	0	0	0	0	4	4	0	3	1	15.8	2.25	163	.235	.350	0	.000	-0	1	1	-0	0.0

● JIMMY ZINN
Zinn, James Edward b: 1/21/1895, Benton, Ark. d: 2/26/91, Memphis, Tenn. BL/TR, 6'0.5", 195 lbs. Deb: 9/4/19

YEAR TM/L	W	L	PCT	G	GS	CG	SH	SV	IP	H	HR	BB	SO	RAT	ERA	ERA+	OAV	OOB	BH	AVG	PB	PR	/A	PD	TPI
1919 Phi-A	1	3	.250	5	3	2	0	0	25²	38	1	10	9	17.2	6.31	54	.365	.426	4	.308	2	-9	-8	-0	-0.9
1920 Pit-N	1	1	.500	6	3	2	0	0	31	32	2	5	18	11.0	3.48	92	.260	.295	3	.200	-1	-1	-0	-0	0.0
1921 Pit-N	7	6	.538	32	9	5	1	4	127¹	159	3	30	49	13.5	3.68	104	.318	.359	11	.224	1	2	2	-0	0.0
1922 Pit-N	0	0	—	5	0	0	0	1	9²	11	1	2	3	12.1	1.86	219	.297	.333	0	.000	-0	2	2	-0	0.0
1929 Cle-A	4	6	.400	18	11	6	1	2	105¹	150	8	33	29	15.9	5.04	88	.340	.390	16	.381	7	-9	-7	-0	-0.0
Total 5	13	16	.448	66	26	15	2	7	299	390	15	80	108	14.4	4.30	92	.324	.369	34	.283	9	-15	-12	-2	-0.9

● BILL ZINSER
Zinser, William Francis b: 1/6/18, Astoria, N.Y. BR/TR, 6'1", 185 lbs. Deb: 8/19/44

YEAR TM/L	W	L	PCT	G	GS	CG	SH	SV	IP	H	HR	BB	SO	RAT	ERA	ERA+	OAV	OOB	BH	AVG	PB	PR	/A	PD	TPI
1944 Was-A	0	0	—	2	0	0	0	0	0²	1	0	5	1	81.0	27.00	12	.333	.750	0	—	0	-2	-2	0	-0.4

● ED ZMICH
Zmich, Edward Albert b: 10/1/1884, Cleveland, Ohio d: 8/20/50, Cleveland, Ohio BL/TL, 6', 180 lbs. Deb: 7/23/10

YEAR TM/L	W	L	PCT	G	GS	CG	SH	SV	IP	H	HR	BB	SO	RAT	ERA	ERA+	OAV	OOB	BH	AVG	PB	PR	/A	PD	TPI
1910 StL-N	0	5	.000	9	6	2	0	0	36	38	0	29	19	17.5	6.25	48	.304	.446	1	.077	-1	-13	-13	1	-1.6
1911 StL-N	1	0	1.000	4	0	0	0	0	12²	8	0	8	4	12.1	2.13	158	.182	.321	0	.000	-1	2	2	-1	0.0
Total 2	1	5	.167	13	6	2	0	0	48²	46	0	37	23	16.1	5.18	60	.272	.414	1	.059	-2	-11	-11	0	-1.6

● SAM ZOLDAK
Zoldak, Samuel Walter "Sad Sam" b: 12/8/18, Brooklyn, N.Y. d: 8/25/66, New Hyde Park, N.Y BL/TL, 5'11.5", 185 lbs. Deb: 5/13/44

YEAR TM/L	W	L	PCT	G	GS	CG	SH	SV	IP	H	HR	BB	SO	RAT	ERA	ERA+	OAV	OOB	BH	AVG	PB	PR	/A	PD	TPI
1944 StL-A	0	0	—	18	0	0	0	0	38²	49	1	19	16	15.8	3.72	97	.310	.384	2	.333	0	-1	-1	0	0.0
1945 StL-A	3	2	.600	26	1	1	0	0	69²	74	3	18	19	11.9	3.36	105	.267	.312	1	.050	-2	0	1	-1	-0.3
1946 StL-A	9	11	.450	35	21	9	2	2	170¹	166	11	57	51	11.8	3.43	109	.256	.317	9	.173	-0	1	6	1	0.7
1947 StL-A	9	10	.474	35	19	6	1	1	171	162	7	76	36	12.5	3.47	112	.254	.334	10	.172	-1	4	8	3	1.0
1948 StL-A	2	4	.333	11	9	0	0	0	54	64	4	19	13	14.0	4.67	98	.296	.356	6	.273	0	-2	-1	-0	0.0
Cle-A	9	6	.600	23	12	4	1	0	105²	104	6	24	17	10.9	2.81	144	.261	.303	5	.139	-2	17	15	2	1.9
Yr	11	10	.524	34	21	4	1	0	159²	168	10	43	30	11.9	3.44	123	.273	.321	11	.190	-2	15	14	2	1.9
1949 Cle-A	1	2	.333	27	0	0	0	0	53	60	4	18	11	13.2	4.25	94	.291	.348	3	.375	1	-0	1	-0	0.2
1950 Cle-A	4	2	.667	33	3	0	0	4	63²	64	6	21	15	12.2	3.96	109	.259	.320	3	.188	0	4	3	-0	0.2
1951 Phi-A	6	10	.375	26	18	7	0	0	128	127	9	24	18	10.6	3.16	135	.257	.292	7	.156	-3	14	16	-2	1.3
1952 Phi-A	0	0	—	16	10	2	1	0	75¹	86	3	25	12	13.3	4.06	97	.290	.345	4	.174	-1	1	1	0	0.1
Total 9	43	53	.448	250	93	30	5	8	929¹	956	54	301	207	12.2	3.54	112	.267	.325	50	.175	-7	34	45	3	5.2

● BILL ZUBER
Zuber, William Henry "Goober" b: 3/26/13, Middle Amana, Iowa d: 11/2/82, Cedar Rapids, Iowa BR/TR, 6'2", 195 lbs. Deb: 9/16/36

YEAR TM/L	W	L	PCT	G	GS	CG	SH	SV	IP	H	HR	BB	SO	RAT	ERA	ERA+	OAV	OOB	BH	AVG	PB	PR	/A	PD	TPI
1936 Cle-A	1	1	.500	2	1	0	0	0	13²	14	0	15	9	19.1	6.59	76	.269	.433	1	.200	-0	-2	-2	-0	-0.3
1938 Cle-A	0	3	.000	15	0	0	0	1	28²	33	0	20	14	16.6	5.02	92	.295	.402	0	.000	-1	-2	-2	-0	-0.2
1939 Cle-A	2	0	1.000	31²	0	0	0	0	31²	41	2	15	19	15.9	5.97	74	.323	.415	1	.200	-1	-5	-6	1	-0.4
1940 Cle-A	1	1	.500	17	0	0	0	0	24	25	3	14	12	14.6	5.63	75	.260	.355	1	.333	-0	-3	-4	1	-0.3
1941 Was-A	6	4	.600	36	7	1	0	2	96¹	110	5	61	51	16.2	5.42	75	.291	.392	0	.000	-3	-14	-15	-1	-1.8

YEAR	TM/L	W	L	PCT	G	GS	CG	SH	SV	IP	H	HR	BB	SO	RAT	ERA	ERA+	OAV	OOB	BH	AVG	PB	PR	/A	PD	TPI
1942	Was-A	9	9	.500	37	7	3	1	1	126²	115	5	82	64	14.0	3.84	95	.243	.355	6	.154	0	-3	-3	-3	-0.5
1943	NY-A	8	4	.667	20	13	7	0	1	118	100	3	74	57	13.3	3.89	83	.234	.347	7	.184	2	-8	-9	-2	-0.8
1944	NY-A	5	7	.417	22	13	2	1	0	107	101	5	54	59	13.1	4.21	83	.255	.346	4	.129	-2	-9	-9	-1	-1.1
1945	NY-A	5	11	.313	21	14	7	0	1	127	121	2	56	50	12.5	3.19	109	.259	.338	7	.167	-1	2	4	-1	0.2
1946	NY-A	0	1	.000	3	0	0	0	0	5²	10	2	3	3	20.6	12.71	27	.385	.448	0	.000	-0	-6	-6	-0	-0.9
	*Bos-A	5	1	.833	15	7	2	1	0	56²	37	4	39	29	12.1	2.54	144	.187	.321	2	.111	-1	6	7	0	0.6
	Yr	5	2	.714	18	7	2	1	0	62¹	47	6	42	32	12.9	3.47	105	.210	.335	2	.100	-1	0	1	-0	-0.3
1947	Bos-A	1	0	1.000	20	1	0	0	0	50²	60	4	31	23	16.2	5.33	73	.311	.406	2	.154	-0	-9	-8	-0	-0.2
Total 11		43	42	.506	224	65	23	3	6	786	767	35	468	383	14.2	4.28	87	.260	.362	31	.135	-6	-51	-50	-8	-5.5

● **GEORGE ZUVERINK** Zuverink, George b: 8/20/24, Holland, Mich. BR/TR, 6'4", 200 lbs. Deb: 4/21/51

YEAR	TM/L	W	L	PCT	G	GS	CG	SH	SV	IP	H	HR	BB	SO	RAT	ERA	ERA+	OAV	OOB	BH	AVG	PB	PR	/A	PD	TPI
1951	Cle-A	0	0	—	16	0	0	0	0	25¹	24	2	13	14	13.5	5.33	71	.253	.349	0	—	0	-3	-4	0	0.0
1952	Cle-A	0	0	—	1	0	0	0	0	1¹	1	0	0	1	6.8	0.00	—	.200	.200	0	—	0	1	0	0	0.0
1954	Cin-N	0	0	—	2	0	0	0	0	6	10	1	1	2	16.5	9.00	47	.385	.407	1	.500	0	-3	-3	-0	0.0
	Det-A	9	13	.409	35	25	9	2	4	203	201	22	62	70	12.0	3.59	103	.257	.318	8	.125	-3	3	2	3	0.2
1955	Det-A	0	5	.000	14	1	0	0	0	28¹	38	6	14	13	16.8	6.99	50	.309	.384	0	.000	-1	-10	-10	0	-1.5
	Bal-A	4	3	.571	28	5	0	0	4	86¹	80	5	17	31	10.5	2.19	174	.264	.312	5	.217	1	17	16	1	1.5
	Yr	4	8	.333	42	6	0	0	4	114²	118	11	31	44	12.0	3.38	113	.276	.331	5	.185	0	7	6	1	0.0
1956	Bal-A	7	6	.538	**62**	0	0	0	**16**	97¹	112	6	34	33	13.8	4.16	94	.294	.356	2	.118	-1	-0	-3	1	-0.4
1957	Bal-A	10	6	.625	**56**	0	0	0	9	112²	105	9	39	36	11.8	2.48	145	.257	.327	2	.130	-0	16	14	1	2.2
1958	Bal-A	2	2	.500	45	0	0	0	7	69	74	4	17	22	12.7	3.39	106	.286	.344	2	.222	1	3	2	1	0.4
1959	Bal-A	0	1	.000	6	0	0	0	0	13	15	1	6	1	14.5	4.15	91	.306	.382	0	—	1	-0	-1	0	0.0
Total 8		32	36	.471	265	31	9	2	40	642¹	660	56	203	223	12.5	3.54	105	.271	.334	21	.148	-2	23	13	7	2.4

The Annual Record: Introduction

his section contains the season-by-season standings and records for all teams since 1871, plus 28 statistical categories for each team's batting and baserunning, and 26 categories for its pitching and fielding. In those years in which major league play consisted of more than one league, the statistics are presented in the order of the leagues' founding: that is, the National Association comes first; the National League record precedes those of all its rivals; the American Association precedes the Union Association and Players League; and the American League follows the National League but precedes the Federal League.

New to this edition in an additional page for each league season, thus doubling the size of the Annual Record. The new page will present daily highlights and team rosters. An asterisk following a date signifies a non-major league event. The rosters are complete for all years of major league play until the expansion of 1961, with the exception of the 1884 Union Association, which featured massive player movement, and the twelve-team National League of 1892-99. For those league years the criteria for listing a player here are 60 at bats or 15 innings pitched. For the AL since 1961 and the NL since 1962, the criteria are 200 at bats or 50 innings pitched. Substitute players are listed at their main positions, up to two if they played in 10 or more games at the position; if a man played fewer than 10 games at his main position, he is shown with a slash preceding his position.

On the statistical page, the figure for the leading team in a given category is displayed in boldface. Where data are unavailable, the statistical column is blank. Also presented here are the top three to five players/pitchers in up to 48 categories per season. When fewer than 48 categories are shown, it means that official records are lacking; that data is not reconstructible at present; or that available data is not meaningful, such as for Relief Runs or Relief Ranking in the early years of this century. When fewer than five individuals appear in a given category, credible standouts are lacking, as in the case of Stolen Base Wins in most years. The criterion used for identifying pitching leaders is a minimum of one inning pitched per scheduled game; for batters the criterion employed is the one officially in place at the time or, in the absence of any known practice, 3.1 plate appearances per scheduled game.

Ties in counting stats are common, and occasionally they are so numerous that space does not permit listing all the players by name; ties for fifth place are not shown. Highly uncommon are ties in stats based on a large array of data, as with batting averages, on base percentages, earned run averages, and sabermetric stats such as Runs

Created, Total Average, or the various Linear Weights measures. Where rounding off has created the appearance of a tie, the true leader—as extra decimal places for a complete calculation would have revealed—is listed first. An example is the AL batting race of 1949, in which George Kell and Ted Williams are both shown as hitting .343; Kell in fact hit .3429 and Williams .3428. Both men are credited with batting averages of .343, but Kell, the actual leader, is listed first. (This procedure does not hold for calculated stats based on pitchers' won-lost percentages, where the narrow array of data frequently produces actual ties.)

For additional useful information about a team in a given year, we refer the reader to the various registers and the rosters. Team abbreviations used in the Annual Record are to be found on the last page of this book.

Following are the abbreviations employed in the team statistical reviews of the Annual Record, aside from those that are defined adequately in the introductions to the Player or Pitcher Registers, plus brief descriptions of what the less common statistics measure. For information about formulas and computation, see the Glossary.

Batting and Baserunning

PCT	Percentage of games won
GB	Games Behind the league or division leader
OR	Opponents' Runs scored
PRO	Production (On Base Percentage plus Slugging Average)
PRO+	Normalized and park-adjusted Production. A figure of 100 is a league-average performance.
BR	Batting Runs (Linear Weights measure of runs contributed beyond what a league-average batter or team might have contributed, defined as zero.)
/A	Adjusted (Signifies that the stat to the immediate left, in this instance Batting Runs, is here normalized to league average and adjusted for home-park factor. A mark of 100 is a league-average performance. Pitcher batting is removed from all league batting statistics before normalization for a variety of reasons expanded upon in the Glossary.)

PF   Park Factor (Calculated separately for batters and pitchers: above 100 signifies a park favorable to hitters, below 100 signifies a park favorable to pitchers; see Glossary for further data and technical information.)

CHI   Clutch Hitting Index (Calculated for individuals, actual RBI over expected RBI, adjusted for league average and position in batting order; calculated for teams, actual runs scored divided by Batting Runs. Marks above the median of 100 are superior. See Glossary for precise formula.)

RC   Runs Created (Bill James's formulation for run contribution from a variety of batting and baserunning events; many different formulas are applied, depending on data available; see Glossary.)

SBA   Stolen Base Average (Stolen bases divided by attempts; availability dependent upon CS, as shown above.)

SBR   Stolen Base Runs (Linear Weights measure of runs contributed *beyond* what a league-average base stealer or team might have gained, defined as zero; individual SBRs are calculated on the basis of a 66.7 percent success rate, the rate necessary to produce benefit, while team SBRs are normalized to the success rate for the league in that season; availability dependent upon CS.)

Pitching and Fielding

SH   Shutouts (Individual and combined when calculated for teams; individual only for top five leaders.)

H/G   Hits allowed per Game (Game defined as nine innings.)

CPI   Clutch Pitching Index (Expected runs over actual runs, with 100 being a league-average performance and marks above 100 indicating better than expected results. See Glossary.)

E   Errors

DP   Double Plays

FW   Fielding Wins (Fielding Runs divided by the number of runs required to create an additional win beyond average; average is defined as a team record of .500 because a league won-lost average must be .500. For more technical data about Runs Per Win and Fielding Run formulas, see Glossary.)

PW   Pitching Wins (Adjusted Pitching Runs divided by the number of runs required to create an additional win beyond average; average is defined as a team record of .500 because a league won-lost average must be .500. For more technical data about Runs Per Win and Pitching Run formulas, see Glossary.)

BW   Batting Wins (Adjusted Batting Runs divided by the number of runs required to create an additional win beyond average; average is defined as a team record of .500 because a league won-lost average must be .500. For more technical data about Runs Per Win and Batting Run formulas, see Glossary.)

SBW   Stolen Base Wins (Stolen Base Runs divided by the number of runs required to create an additional win beyond average; average is defined as a team record of .500 because a league won-lost average must be .500. For more technical data about Runs Per Win and Stolen Base Run formulas, see Glossary.)

DIF   Differential (Difference between the team's actual won-lost record and that predicted by the total of its Pitching Wins, Batting Wins, Fielding Wins, and Stolen Base Wins; indicates the extent to which a team outperformed or underperformed its talent.)

Other stats carried only on an individual basis in the Annual Record portion of *Total Baseball* are as follows (definitions supplied only when not available from Player or Pitcher Register introductions):

Total Average   Tom Boswell's formulation for offensive contribution from a variety of batting and baserunning events; calculated to make use of the maximum available data.

Fielding Runs

Total Player Rating

Bases on Balls Per Game   Game defined as nine innings; league leaders calculated on the basis of fewest walks per nine innings.

Strikeouts Per Game   Game defined as nine innings; league leaders calculated on the basis of most strikeouts per nine innings.

Starter Runs   Identical to Pitching Runs but confined to starting pitchers, defined as pitchers who average more than three innings per appearance.

Relief Runs   Identical to Pitching Runs but confined to relief pitchers.

Relief Ranking   Adjusted Relief Runs, weighted for the greater value of a bullpen "closer" who limits his opponents' scoring in the late innings; see Glossary for formula. Relief Runs will tend to benefit long and middle relievers, who are effective over many innings, while Relief Ranking will tend to benefit relievers with perhaps fewer innings but more saves and decisions.

Total Pitcher Index

Total Baseball Ranking   The "MVP" of statistics, this ranks pitchers and position players by the total runs contributed in all their endeavors, revealing the most valuable performers in a given year. For rare individuals like Babe Ruth in his Red Sox years, or Bob Caruthers, both of whom played a position in the field when they were not pitching, the TPR will sum up their records in both endeavors.

How to Read a Team Line

TEAM	G	W	L	PCT	GB	R	OR	AB	H	2B	3B	HR	BB	SO	AVG	OBP	SLG	PRO	PRO+	BR	/A	PF	CHI	RC	SB	CS	SBA	SBR
EAST																												
NY	160	100	60	.625		**703**	532	5408	1387	251	24	**152**	544	842	.256	**.328**	**.396**	**.724**	120	95	131	95	97	**717**	140	51	73	11
PIT	160	85	75	.531	15	651	616	5379	1327	240	45	110	**553**	947	.247	.321	.369	.690	105	33	42	99	99	648	119	60	66	0
MON	163	81	81	.500	20	628	592	5573	1400	260	48	107	454	1053	.251	.311	.373	.684	98	12	-18	105	97	636	189	89	68	3
CHI	163	77	85	.475	24	660	694	5675	**1481**	262	46	113	403	910	**.261**	.312	.383	.695	100	31	1	105	99	673	120	46	72	8
STL	162	76	86	.469	25	578	633	5518	1373	207	33	71	484	**827**	.249	.312	.337	.649	92	-47	-53	101	98	601	**234**	64	**79**	**32**
PHI	162	65	96	.404	35.5	597	734	5403	1294	246	31	106	489	981	.239	.308	.355	.663	94	-22	-35	102	100	599	112	49	70	4
WEST																												
LA	162	94	67	.584		628	544	5431	1346	217	25	99	437	947	.248	.308	.352	.660	99	-32	-14	97	**107**	590	131	46	74	12
CIN	161	87	74	.540	7	641	596	5426	1334	246	25	122	479	922	.246	.311	.368	.679	97	6	-19	104	102	639	207	56	**79**	29
SD	161	83	78	.516	11	594	583	5366	1325	205	35	94	494	892	.247	.313	.351	.664	99	-19	-8	98	99	594	123	50	71	7
SF	162	83	79	.512	11.5	670	626	5450	1353	227	44	113	550	1023	.248	.321	.368	.689	109	32	61	96	101	650	121	78	61	-11
HOU	162	82	80	.506	12.5	617	631	5494	1338	239	31	96	474	840	.244	.308	.351	.659	99	-32	-9	96	103	604	198	71	74	17
ATL	160	54	106	.338	39.5	555	741	5319	1319	228	28	96	432	848	.242	.301	.348	.649	88	-56	-84	105	99	549	95	69	58	-13
TOT	969					7522		65563	16277	2828	415	1279	5793	11032	.248	.313	.363	.675							1789	729	71	99

TEAM	CG	SH	SV	IP	H	H/G	HR	BB	SO	RAT	ERA	ERA+	OAV	OOB	PR	/A	PF	CPI	FA	E	DP	FW	PW	BW	SBW	DIF
EAST																										
NY	31	22	46	1439	**1253**	7.8	78	404	1100	10.6	**2.91**	111	**.235**	**.293**	86	50	93	97	**.981**	115	127	**.9**	5.4	-1.5	.3	-.7
PIT	12	11	46	1440²	1349	8.4	108	469	790	11.6	3.47	98	.250	.314	-3	-10	99	101	.980	125	128	.3	-1.1	4.5	-.9	2.1
MON	18	12	43	1482²	1310	8.0	122	476	923	11.1	3.08	**117**	.238	.303	60	**84**	104	**105**	.978	142	145	-.5	**9.1**	-1.9	-.6	-6.0
CHI	30	10	29	1464¹	1494	9.2	115	490	897	12.4	3.84	94	.265	.327	-64	-38	105	102	.980	125	128	.5	-4.1	.1	-.0	-.4
STL	17	14	42	1470²	1387	8.5	91	486	881	11.6	3.47	100	.265	.314	-4	1	101	99	**.981**	121	131	.6	.1	-5.7	**2.6**	-2.6
PHI	16	6	36	1433	1447	9.1	118	628	859	13.3	4.14	86	.265	.344	-110	-92	103	102	.976	145	134	-.7	-9.9	-3.8	-.5	-.6
WEST																										
LA	**32**	**24**	**49**	1463¹	1291	7.9	84	473	1029	11.0	2.96	112	.237	.301	78	59	97	102	.977	142	126	-.5	6.4	-1.5	.4	8.8
CIN	24	13	43	1455	1271	7.9	121	504	934	11.1	3.35	107	.237	.306	16	38	104	98	.980	125	131	.4	4.1	-2.0	2.2	1.9
SD	30	9	39	1449	1332	8.3	112	439	885	11.1	3.28	104	.247	.306	27	19	99	102	**.981**	120	**147**	.6	2.0	-.9	-.1	.8
SF	25	13	42	1462¹	1323	8.1	99	422	875	10.9	3.39	104	.242	.300	10	-20	95	93	.980	129	145	.2	-2.2	6.6	-2.1	-.5
HOU	21	15	40	1474²	1339	8.2	123	478	1049	11.3	3.41	97	.242	.307	7	-14	96	99	.978	138	124	-.3	-1.5	-1.0	.9	2.9
ATL	14	4	25	1446	1481	9.2	108	524	810	12.7	4.09	90	.268	.336	-103	-67	107	100	.976	151	138	-1.1	-7.2	-9.1	-2.3	-6.3
TOT	270	153	480	17480²		8.4				11.6	3.45		.248	.313					.979	1578	1609					

The Los Angeles Dodgers had a miracle season in 1988, winning the National League pennant and the World Series against seemingly far superior opponents, the New York Mets and the Oakland Athletics, respectively. But their first miracle was to win the National League's Western Division title after finishing 73-89 in each of the previous two seasons. How did they win the West so easily? With mirrors, mostly, for they had below-average fielding and hitting that should have partially negated their outstanding pitching.

Let's just track the Dodgers' performance in some of the key categories to show how illuminating a close examination of team data in the Annual Record can be. The Dodgers' on base percentage (OBP) and slugging average (SLG) reveal them to have been a weak hitting club, though their Adjusted Production (PRO+) is a bit better, for they scored more runs in their park than might have been expected from the total run-scoring picture at Chavez Ravine (Park Factor 97). However, their Clutch Hitting Index (CHI) was the best in their division, testifying to their character, their good fortune, or both. Their Stolen Base Average was above average, but still only accounted for 12 extra runs over the course of the season, so this wasn't the secret of their success.

The pitching numbers are superlative—fewest runs allowed in the West and lowest ERA—despite the fact that Cincinnati held opponents to the same batting average (OAV) and San Francisco to the same on base percentage (OOB). Their Clutch Pitching Index (CPI) suggests that Dodger hurlers pulled their belts a notch tighter when men were on base, and their Home Runs allowed (HR) gives another tip that they knew how to stay away from the big inning. And maybe all those Shutouts (SH) are indicative of the many games they won while scoring few runs themselves.

Look at their batting (which cost them 1.5 wins in the BW, or Batting Wins, column) and baserunning and fielding (which are a virtual wash at +0.4 and −0.5, respectively, in the SBW and FW columns), and notice that their pitching, good as it was, only supplied 6.4 wins beyond average (.500). On balance, then, their offense and defense combined to produce only five wins beyond average. They should have finished with a record of 86–76, or five games beyond the 81–81 league average. Instead they finished 94–67, eight wins beyond their expectations, as indicated in the Differential (DIF) column. Maybe it was manager Tommy Lasorda's doing after all.

March 17 The National Association of Professional Base Ball Players is formed in New York. Each club will play best-of-five series with the other clubs. The championship will be awarded to the team winning the most series against the other teams and not on a total wins or percentage basis. Teams represented are: Athletics of Philadelphia, Boston Red Stockings (who hired Harry Wright to represent them after the Cincinnati Reds disbanded); Chicago White Stockings, Eckford of Brooklyn, Forest Citys of Cleveland; Forest Citys of Rockford, Illinois, Atlantics of Brooklyn, Mutuals of New York; Nationals of Washington, D.C., Olympics of Washington, D.C., Kekiongas of Fort Wayne, Indiana, and the Union Club of Troy, New York, also known as the Haymakers.

April 29 The new ball grounds in Chicago, located at Randolph and Michigan on the lakefront, are opened as the White Stockings and a picked nine play before 1,500 people. The New York *Clipper* says: "They will have accommodations on their grounds to seat 6,500 people. With the single exception of being somewhat narrow, they will have one of the finest ballparks in the country."

May 4 The first National Association game is played at Fort Wayne, Indiana, between the Kekiongas and the Forest Citys of Cleveland. Bobby Mathews shuts out the Cleveland team 2-0, one of only four shutouts in 1871.

May 8 The visiting Boston Reds demolish the Brooklyn Atlantics 25–0 at Union Grounds, the single worst defeat the Brooklyn club will suffer in its brief history.

May 16 The first professional game ever played in Boston is played between the Red Stockings and the visiting Haymakers before 5,000. Boston has Harry Wright playing shortstop in place of his injured brother George. George will miss half the games played by the Reds, severely hampering their pennant chances. Troy wins 29-14.

May 25 The heavily favored Mutuals are soundly defeated by the Haymakers of Troy, at a game played on Brooklyn's Union Grounds, 25–10. Troy's player-manager Lipman Pike collects six hits.

June 5 The eagerly awaited series opens between the White Stockings and the Mutuals before 10,000 at the Union Grounds in Brooklyn. Five of the old Eckfords play for Chicago while five of last year's Atlantics play for the Mutuals. Fielding decides the game, as Chicago makes 19 errors to "only" 7 for the Mutuals. New York wins 8–5.

July 6* An early baseball game between a black team and a white team takes place in Chicago, when the black Uniques beat the white Alerts 17-16.

August 28 At the Union Grounds in Brooklyn, the Chicago White Stockings clinch the season's series with a 6–4 victory. The Whites could have insured a fifth and deciding game of the series played on their own grounds by losing today's game.

October 7 The Chicago Fire breaks out at 10 p.m. As the Rockford club travels toward Chicago the next day, they see the glow of the fire, turn around, and return home. Chicago loses its ballpark and equipment in the Fire. The Whites are leading in the pennant race and must defeat the Haymakers in their remaining three games to clinch.

October 30 The final championship match takes place on the Union Grounds in Brooklyn between the Athletics and the Chicago White Stockings. The Championship Committee decrees that today's game will decide the winner of the pennant. The 4-1 victory by the Athletics gives them the championship for 1871.

ATHLETICS		BOSTON		CHICAGO		CLEVELAND		KEKIONGAS	
M	D.McBride	M	H.Wright	M	J.Wood	M	C.Pabor	M	B.Lennon
1B	W.Fisler	1B	C.Gould	1B	B.McAtee	1B	J.Carleton	M	H.Deane
2B	A.Reach	2B	R.Barnes	2B	J.Wood	2B	G.Kimball	1B	J.Foran
SS	J.Radcliff	SS	G.Wright	SS	E.Duffy	SS	J.Bass	2B	T.Carey
3B	L.Meyerle	3B	H.Schafer	3B	E.Pinkham	3B	E.Sutton	SS	W.Goldsmith
LF	N.Cuthbert	LF	F.Cone	LF	F.Treacey	CF	C.Pabor	3B	F.Selman
CF	C.Sensenderfer	CF	H.Wright	CF	T.Foley	CF	A.Allison	LF	E.Mincher
RF	G.Heubel	RF	D.Birdsall	RF	J.Simmons	RF	E.White	CF	S.Armstrong
C	F.Malone	C	C.McVey	C	C.Hodes	C	D.White	RF	B.Kelly
								C	B.Lennon
O	G.Bechtel	O	F.Barrows	O	M.King	2	C.Johnson		
/1	T.Pratt	2	S.Jackson	/3	M.Brannock	/2	J.Quest	/O	P.Donnelly
/O	N.Berkenstock	P	A.Spalding	P	G.Zettlein	/O	J.Battin	/S	J.Hallinan
/O	T.Berry					/O	G.Ewell	/O	H.Deane
								/C	J.Quinn
P	D.McBride					P	A.Pratt	/C	H.Kohler
								/O	J.McDermott
								/C	B.Barrett
								/1	N.Phelps
								/1	C.Bierman
								P	B.Mathews

MUTUALS		OLYMPICS		ROCKFORD		TROY	
M	B.Ferguson	M	N.Young	M	S.Hastings	M	L.Pike
1B	J.Start	1B	E.Mills	1B	D.Mack	M	B.Craver
2B	D.Higham	2B	A.Leonard	2B	B.Addy	1B	C.Flynn
SS	D.Pearce	SS	D.Force	SS	C.Fulmer	2B	B.Craver
3B	B.Ferguson	3B	F.Waterman	3B	C.Anson	SS	D.Flowers
LF	J.Hatfield	LF	H.Berthrong	LF	R.Ham	3B	S.Bellan
CF	D.Eggler	CF	G.Hall	CF	G.Bird	LF	S.King
RF	D.Patterson	RF	J.Glenn	RF	G.Stires	CF	T.York
C	C.Mills	C	D.Allison	C	S.Hastings	RF	L.Pike
						C	M.McGeary
3	C.Smith	/O	H.Burroughs	/S	P.Sager		
		/O	T.Beals	/O	A.Barker	/1	N.Connor
P	R.Wolters	/2	C.Sweasy			/2	E.Beavens
		/2	W.White	P	C.Fisher	/S	D.Abercrombie
/P	F.Fleet	/3	F.Norton				
						P	J.McMullin
		P	A.Brainard				
		P	B.Stearns				

TEAM	G	W	L	PCT	GB	R	OR	AB	H	2B	3B	HR	BB	SO	AVG	OBP	SLG	PRO	PRO+	BR	/A	PF	CHI	RC	SB	CS	SBA	SBR
ATH	28	21	7	.750		376	266	1281	410	66	27	9	46	23	.320	.344	.435	.779	125	38	42	99	107	206	56	12	82	10
BOS	31	20	10	.667	2	401	303	1372	426	70	37	3	60	19	.310	.339	.422	.761	115	33	21	103	108	216	73	16	82	12
CHI	28	19	9	.679	2	302	241	1196	323	52	21	10	60	22	.270	.305	.374	.679	86	-7	-38	111	104	150	69	21	77	8
MUT	33	16	17	.485	7.5	302	313	1404	403	43	21	1	33	15	.287	.303	.350	.653	97	-20	8	91	94	159	46	15	75	5
OLY	32	15	15	.500	7	310	303	1353	375	54	26	6	48	13	.277	.302	.369	.671	98	-12	4	95	97	160	48	13	79	7
TRO	29	13	15	.464	8	351	362	1248	384	51	34	6	49	19	.308	.334	.417	.751	114	25	20	101	106	184	62	24	72	4
CLE	29	10	19	.345	11.5	249	341	1186	328	35	40	7	26	25	.277	.292	.391	.683	102	-7	8	95	89	136	18	8	69	1
KEK	19	7	12	.368	9.5	137	243	746	178	19	8	2	33	9	.239	.271	.294	.565	63	-34	-37	102	91	63	16	4	80	2
ROK	25	4	21	.160	15.5	231	287	1036	274	44	25	3	38	30	.264	.291	.364	.655	92	-16	-5	96	97	121	53	10	84	10
TOT	127					2659		10822	3101	434	239	47	393	175	.287	.312	.384	.695							441	123	78	59

TEAM	CG	SH	SV	IP	H	H/G	HR	BB	SO	RAT	ERA	ERA+	OAV	OOB	PR	/A	PF	CPI	FA	E	DP	FW	PW	BW	SBW	DIF
ATH	27	0	0	249	329	11.9	3	53	16	13.8	4.95	81	.284	.315	-20	-26	95	85	.845	194	13	1.1	-1.7	2.7	.2	4.6
BOS	22	1	3	276	367	12.0	2	42	23	13.3	3.55	117	.273	.296	20	18	99	101	.834	243	24	-.3	1.2	1.4	.4	2.4
CHI	25	0	1	251	308	11.0	6	28	22	12.0	2.76	166	.264	.281	41	51	109	121	.829	229	16	-.8	3.3	-2.5	.0	4.8
MUT	32	1	0	293	373	11.5	7	42	12	12.7	3.72	102	.271	.292	16	2	90	98	.840	235	14	1.0	.1	.5	-.0	-2.0
OLY	32	0	0	282	371	11.8	4	45	13	13.3	4.37	95	.281	.305	-5	-6	99	90	.850	218	20	1.5	-.4	.3	.0	-1.4
TRO	28	0	0	250	431	15.5	4	75	12	18.2	5.51	76	.342	.378	-36	-36	100	118	.845	198	22	1.3	-2.3	1.3	-.2	-1.1
CLE	23	0	0	254	346	12.3	13	53	34	14.1	4.11	100	.283	.312	3	0	98	107	.818	234	15	-.6	.0	.5	-.4	-4.0
KEK	19	1	0	169	261	13.9	5	21	17	15.0	5.17	88	.305	.322	-18	-11	108	93	.803	163	8	-.9	-.7	-2.4	-.3	1.8
ROK	23	1	0	226	315	12.5	3	34	16	13.9	4.30	95	.282	.303	-2	-5	97	91	.821	220	14	-1.5	-.3	-.3	.2	-6.6
TOT	231	4	4	2250		12.4				14.0	4.22		.287	.312					.833	1934	146					

Runs
Barnes-Bos 66
Birdsall-Bos 51
Radcliff-Ath 47
Cuthbert-Ath 47
Waterman-Oly 46

Hits
McVey-Bos 66
Meyerle-Ath 64
Barnes-Bos 63
Start-Mut 58
King-Tro 57

Doubles
Anson-Rok 11

Triples
Bass-Cle 10
Wolters-Mut 9
Barnes-Bos 9
Pratt-Cle 8

Home Runs
Treacey-Chi 4
Pike-Tro 4
Meyerle-Ath 4

Total Bases
Meyerle-Ath 91
Barnes-Bos 91
Pike-Tro 85
McVey-Bos 85
King-Tro 79

Runs Batted In
Wolters-Mut 44
McVey-Bos 43
Meyerle-Ath 40
Pike-Tro 39

Runs Produced
Barnes-Bos 100
McVey-Bos 86
Meyerle-Ath 81
King-Tro 79
Pike-Tro 78

Bases On Balls
Pinkham-Chi 18
H.Wright-Bos 13
Barnes-Bos 13
Wood-Chi 11

Batting Average
Meyerle-Ath .... .492
McVey-Bos .... .431
Barnes-Bos .... .401
King-Tro .... .396
Wood-Chi .... .378

On Base Percentage
Meyerle-Ath .... .500
G.Wright-Bos .... .453
Barnes-Bos .... .447
McVey-Bos .... .435
Wood-Chi .... .425

Slugging Average
Meyerle-Ath .... .700
Pike-Tro .... .654
Bass-Cle .... .640
Barnes-Bos .... .580
Treacey-Chi .... .573

Production
Meyerle-Ath 1.200
G.Wright-Bos 1.078
Pike-Tro 1.054
Barnes-Bos 1.027
McVey-Bos .... .991

Adjusted Production
Meyerle-Ath 243
G.Wright-Bos 200
Pike-Tro 194
Wolters-Mut 189
Barnes-Bos 186

Batter Runs
Meyerle-Ath 22.6
Barnes-Bos 18.9
Pike-Tro 15.5
McVey-Bos 15.5
Wood-Chi 14.2

Adjusted Batter Runs
Meyerle-Ath 23.2
Wolters-Mut 17.2
Barnes-Bos 17.0
Pike-Tro 14.9
McVey-Bos 13.9

Clutch Hitting Index
Goldsmith-Kek 169
Barrows-Bos 150
McMullin-Tro 149
Brainard-Oly 143
Fisher-Rok 137

Runs Created
Meyerle-Ath 49
Barnes-Bos 42
McVey-Bos 41
Wood-Chi 40
Pike-Tro 33

Total Average
Meyerle-Ath 1.470
G.Wright-Bos 1.306
Wood-Chi 1.198
Barnes-Bos 1.079
Pike-Tro 1.071

Stolen Bases
McGeary-Tro 20
Wood-Chi 18
Cuthbert-Ath 16
Leonard-Oly 14
Eggler-Mut 14

Stolen Base Average
Wood-Chi 90.0
Cuthbert-Ath 88.9
McGeary-Tro 83.3

Stolen Base Runs
Wood-Chi 4.2
McGeary-Tro 3.6
Mack-Rok 3.6
Cuthbert-Ath 3.6
Cone-Bos 3.0

Fielding Runs
Force-Oly 17.6
Barnes-Bos 13.4
Pinkham-Chi 9.4
Malone-Ath 9.1
Wood-Chi 8.6

Total Player Rating
Barnes-Bos 1.8
Force-Oly 1.3
Wood-Chi 1.3
G.Wright-Bos 1.1
McVey-Bos 1.0

Wins
Spalding-Bos 19
Zettlein-Chi 18
McBride-Ath 18
Wolters-Mut 16

Win Percentage
McBride-Ath .... .783
Zettlein-Chi .... .667
Spalding-Bos .... .655
Wolters-Mut .... .500

Games
Wolters-Mut 32
Spalding-Bos 31
Brainard-Oly 30
McMullin-Tro 29

Complete Games
Wolters-Mut 31
Brainard-Oly 30
McMullin-Tro 28
Zettlein-Chi 25
McBride-Ath 25

Shutouts
Wolters-Mut 1
Spalding-Bos 1
Mathews-Kek 1
Fisher-Rok 1

Saves
H.Wright-Bos 3
Pinkham-Chi 1

Innings Pitched
Wolters-Mut 283.0
Brainard-Oly 264.0
Spalding-Bos 257.1
McMullin-Tro 249.0
Zettlein-Chi 240.2

Fewest Hits/Game
Wolters-Mut 10.97
Zettlein-Chi 11.14
McBride-Ath 11.55
Spalding-Bos 11.65
Pratt-Cle 11.86

Fewest BB/Game
Zettlein-Chi .... .93
Mathews-Kek 1.12
Wolters-Mut 1.24
Brainard-Oly 1.26
Fisher-Rok 1.31

Strikeouts
Pratt-Cle 34
Spalding-Bos 23
Zettlein-Chi 22
Wolters-Mut 22
Mathews-Kek 17

Strikeouts/Game
Pratt-Cle 1.36
Mathews-Kek .... .91
Zettlein-Chi .... .82
Spalding-Bos .... .80
Wolters-Mut .... .70

Ratio
Zettlein-Chi 12.08
Wolters-Mut 12.21
Spalding-Bos 12.98
McBride-Ath 13.18
Brainard-Oly 13.57

Earned Run Average
Zettlein-Chi 2.73
Spalding-Bos 3.36
Wolters-Mut 3.43
Pratt-Cle 3.77
Fisher-Rok 4.35

Adjusted ERA
Zettlein-Chi 168
Spalding-Bos 124
Wolters-Mut 110
Pratt-Cle 110
Fisher-Rok 94

Opponents' Batting Avg.
Wolters-Mut .... .263
Zettlein-Chi .... .267
Spalding-Bos .... .268
Pratt-Cle .... .277
McBride-Ath .... .280

Opponents' On Base Pct.
Zettlein-Chi .... .283
Wolters-Mut .... .285
Spalding-Bos .... .290
Fisher-Rok .... .302
McBride-Ath .... .307

Starter Runs
Zettlein-Chi 39.8
Wolters-Mut 24.7
Spalding-Bos 24.7
Pratt-Cle 11.3
Stearns-Oly 3.4

Adjusted Starter Runs
Zettlein-Chi 49.7
Spalding-Bos 22.9
Wolters-Mut 11.2
Pratt-Cle 9.0
Stearns-Oly 3.3

Clutch Pitching Index
Zettlein-Chi 124
McMullin-Tro 118
Pratt-Cle 110
Spalding-Bos 101
Wolters-Mut 99

Relief Runs
Pinkham-Chi 8

Adjusted Relief Runs
Pinkham-Chi 1.3

Relief Ranking
Pinkham-Chi 1.4

Total Pitcher Index
Zettlein-Chi 2.9
Wolters-Mut 1.9
Spalding-Bos 1.6
Pratt-Cle 1.0
Stearns-Oly 1

Total Baseball Ranking
Zettlein-Chi 2.8
Wolters-Mut 1.9
Barnes-Bos 1.8
Spalding-Bos 1.4
Force-Oly 1.3

March 4 The National Association of Professional Base Ball Players holds its annual convention in Cleveland. Eight clubs send delegates. Bob Ferguson, Atlantics infielder/manager, is elected president. Each team is required to play a series of five games with each club. Whoever wins the most games will be declared champion. The rules will now permit the snap of the wrist in pitching.

April 13 A gathering of Cincinnatians takes place on the old Union Grounds to witness the auction of the trophies of the famous Cincinnati Red Stockings Base Ball Club. Balls from the Reds' victories of 1869 and 1870 sell for an average of $2–$4 each.

May 29 The first game to be played in Chicago since the Great Fire is played on the new grounds of the Chicago Base Ball Association before an enthusiastic crowd of 4,000. Baltimore defeats Cleveland 5-3.

June 15 During the Athletics-Atlantics game, Tom Barlow bunts the ball and reaches first safely. The New York *Clipper* describes the play: "After the first two strikers had been retired, Barlow, amid much laughter and applause, 'blocked' a ball in front of the home plate and reached first base before the ball did." That is one of only three hits off Dick McBride, as the Athletics win 11–1.

July 26 The National Association holds a special meeting, resolving that, because some teams have dropped out of the race (Troy, Nationals, and Olympics), nine games will be played between contending teams this season instead of five.

August 19 After the defeat of the Forest Citys of Cleveland by Boston 18-7 at Cleveland, the club disbands. There are now only six clubs left playing for the pennant.

September 1 Albert Thake, 22-year-old left fielder of the Brooklyn Atlantics, drowns off Fort Hamilton, in New York Harbor, while fishing. A benefit game is arranged by Bob Ferguson between the old Brooklyn Atlantics and members of the 1869 Cincinnati Red Stockings.

September 14 An unusual play highlights the Athletics-Boston match in Philadelphia. With the Athletics leading 4–1 in the seventh inning, and runners on first and second, Fergy Malone pops up to shortstop George Wright. Wright catches the ball in his hat and then throws the ball to third base after which it is thrown to second base. Wright claims a double play has been completed, as a batter cannot be retired with a "hat catch," and thus runners Cap Anson and Bob Reach are forced out. The umpire finally gives Malone another at-bat, declaring nobody out. The Athletics win 6–4.

October 8 The "Grand Base Ball Tournament" begins, a series of games played on the Union Grounds in Brooklyn among the three major professional clubs: Mutuals, Athletics, and the Reds of Boston. First prize will be $1,800. Today's game ends in a tie: Mutuals 7, Boston 7. The tournament will end October 17 with Philadelphia and Boston splitting the prize money.

October 22 The Boston Red Stockings win the championship of the season, winning their 39th game by defeating the Eckfords 4-3.

	ATHLETICS		ATLANTICS		BALTIMORE		BOSTON		CLEVELAND		ECKFORDS
M	D.McBride	M	B.Ferguson	M	B.Craver	M	H.Wright	M	S.Hastings	M	A.Allison
1B	D.Mack	1B	H.Dehlman	M	E.Mills	1B	C.Gould	M	D.White	M	J.Wood
2B	W.Fisler	2B	J.Hall	1B	E.Mills	2B	R.Barnes	1B	J.Simmons	M	P.Martin
SS	M.McGeary	SS	J.Burdock	2B	T.Carey	SS	G.Wright	2B	C.Sweasy	1B	A.Allison
3B	C.Anson	3B	B.Ferguson	SS	J.Radcliff	3B	H.Schafer	SS	J.Holdsworth	2B	C.Nelson
LF	N.Cuthbert	LF	A.Thake	3B	D.Force	LF	A.Leonard	3B	E.Sutton	SS	Ja.Snyder
CF	F.Treacey	CF	J.Remsen	LF	T.York	CF	H.Wright	LF	C.Pabor	3B	J.Clinton
RF	L.Meyerle	RF	J.McDonald	CF	G.Hall	RF	F.Rogers	CF	A.Allison	LF	C.Gedney
C	F.Malone	C	T.Barlow	RF	L.Pike	C	C.McVey	RF	R.Wolters	CF	D.Patterson
				C	B.Craver			C	D.White	RF	D.Hunt
O	A.Reach	O	E.Booth			C	D.Birdsall			C	D.Allison
/S	D.Flowers	2	E.Beavens	CO	D.Higham			C	S.Hastings		
/O	C.Sensenderfer	/O	Barrett	C	S.Hastings	P	A.Spalding	/1	J.Carleton	3	F.Fleet
		/2	C.Lowe					/O	Mullen	/3	M.Swandell
P	D.McBride	/O	H.Doscher	P	B.Mathews					/O	Ji.Snyder
		/2	J.Kenney	P	C.Fisher			P	A.Pratt	/2	J.Wood
		/O	O.Brown					P	R.Wolters	/1	Kavanaugh
		/O	S.Jackson							/1	B.Allison
		/O	J.Bass							/2	A.Martin
		/2	D.Clare							/C	Bestick
		/O	H.Worth							/C	Leutz
		/2	J.Galvin							/O	G.Fletcher
		/O	Higby							/C	N.Jewett
										/S	J.Holdsworth
		P	J.Britt							/S	McDonald
										P	P.Martin
										P	G.Zettlein
										P	J.McDermott
										P	M.Malone
										/P	O'Rourke

	MANSFIELDS		MUTUALS		NATIONALS		OLYMPICS		TROY
M	J.Clapp	M	D.Pearce	M	W.White	M	F.Waterman	M	J.Wood
1B	T.Murnane	M	J.Hatfield	1B	P.Hines	1B	C.Flynn	1B	B.McAtee
2B	E.Booth	1B	J.Start	2B	H.Hollingshead	2B	T.Beals	2B	J.Wood
SS	J.O'Rourke	2B	J.Hatfield	SS	J.Doyle	SS	W.Goldsmith	SS	S.Bellan
3B	G.Fields	SS	D.Pearce	3B	W.White	3B	F.Waterman	3B	D.Force
LF	J.Tipper	3B	B.Boyd	LF	E.Mincher	LF	J.Glenn	LF	S.King
CF	F.McCarton	LF	J.McMullin	CF	S.Studley	CF	G.Heubel	CF	C.Gedney
RF	C.Bentley	CF	D.Eggler	RF	O.Bielaski	RF	V.Robinson	RF	P.Martin
C	J.Clapp	RF	G.Bechtel	C	B.Lennon	C	F.Selman	C	D.Allison
		C	N.Hicks						
OP	F.Buttery			O1	D.Coughlin	/S	B.Reach	/S	C.Hodes
OS	H.Allen	3S	C.Fulmer	/O	J.Glenn	/O	H.Burroughs	/O	C.Nelson
/2	A.Brainard	/O	C.Mills	/1	J.Miller	/O	D.Hurley	/O	M.King
/O	B.Arnold			/S	Spencer	/C	B.Barrett		
		P	C.Cummings	/O	B.Yeatman			P	G.Zettlein
P	C.Bentley					P	A.Brainard		
				P	B.Stearns				

TEAM	G	W	L	PCT	GB	R	OR	AB	H	2B	3B	HR	BB	SO	AVG	OBP	SLG	PRO	PRO+	BR	/A	PF	CHI	RC	SB	CS	SBA	SBR
BOS	48	39	8	.830		521	236	2122	672	106	30	7	29	26	.317	.326	.405	.731	120	61	34	105	100	293	47	14	77	6
BAL	58	35	19	.648	7.5	617	434	2576	752	105	30	14	27	28	.292	.299	.372	.671	103	22	-4	105	107	294	36	18	67	0
MUT	56	34	20	.630	8.5	523	362	2431	674	85	12	4	55	52	.277	.293	.327	.620	99	-18	15	94	102	241	58	21	73	5
ATH	47	30	14	.682	7.5	539	349	2141	679	79	25	4	69	47	.317	.338	.383	.721	124	60	58	100	102	287	58	31	65	-1
TRO	25	15	10	.600	13	273	191	1098	330	58	8	5	7	14	.301	.305	.382	.687	111	15	11	101	109	127	9	7	56	-2
ATL	37	9	28	.243	25	237	473	1460	374	37	10	0	19	24	.256	.266	.295	.561	64	-41	-89	117	87	117	19	14	58	-3
CLE	22	6	16	.273	20.5	174	254	943	272	28	5	0	17	13	.288	.301	.329	.630	102	-4	7	95	87	96	12	3	80	2
MAN	24	5	19	.208	22.5	220	348	1022	294	29	9	1	5	12	.288	.291	.337	.628	101	-6	6	94	103	100	5	3	63	0
ECK	29	3	26	.103	27	152	413	1070	241	24	6	0	14	29	.225	.235	.259	.494	64	-55	-30	85	86	66	8	4	67	0
OLY	9	2	7	.222	18	54	140	365	91	10	3	0	4	4	.249	.257	.293	.550	75	-12	-9	95	81	26	0	3	0	-2
NAT	11	0	11	.0	21	80	190	451	108	6	1	0	1	3	.239	.241	.257	.498	47	-22	-35	117	108	29				
TOT	183					3390		15679	4487	567	139	35	247	252	.286	.297	.347	.644							252	118	68	5

TEAM	CG	SH	SV	IP	H	H/G	HR	BB	SO	RAT	ERA	ERA+	OAV	OOB	PR	/A	PF	CPI	FA	E	DP	FW	PW	BW	SBW	DIF
BOS	41	4	4	430¹	443	9.3	0	27	28	9.8	1.88	194	.243	.254	84	85	100	124	.876	278	43	4.5	5.9	2.4	.4	2.3
BAL	48	1	1	516	573	10.0	3	63	75	11.1	2.90	127	.245	.264	43	44	101	85	.829	432	22	.4	3.1	-.3	-.0	4.8
MUT	54	3	1	512	623	11.0	2	32	44	11.5	2.99	113	.272	.282	37	22	93	105	.867	326	33	5.2	1.5	1.0	.3	-1.0
ATH	47	1	0	419¹	508	10.9	3	26	44	11.5	2.85	124	.265	.275	37	32	98	103	.858	298	20	3.1	2.2	4.0	-.0	-1.2
TRO	17	2	1	225	277	11.1	2	10	18	11.5	2.60	140	.269	.276	26	26	100	117	.859	154	9	1.9	1.8	.8	-.2	-1.8
ATL	37	0	0	336	570	15.3	6	19	13	15.8	4.34	104	.328	.335	-26	6	124	117	.810	358	14	-4.0	.4	-6.2	-.2	.5
CLE	15	0	0	199	285	12.9	6	24	11	14.0	5.74	62	.290	.307	-47	-48	98	70	.816	184	17	-.9	-3.3	.5	.1	-1.4
MAN	21	0	0	211	373	15.9	5	14	5	16.5	5.67	63	.332	.340	-48	-49	99	94	.806	224	8	-2.2	-3.4	.4	-.0	-1.8
ECK	28	0	0	259¹	494	17.1	6	24	11	18.0	5.52	61	.348	.358	-54	-61	93	109	.797	284	5	-3.3	-4.2	-2.1	-.0	-1.8
OLY	9	0	0	79	148	16.9	0	5	1	17.4	6.38	56	.333	.341	-24	-24	99	82	.786	96	7	-1.4	-1.7	-.6	-.2	1.4
NAT	11	0	0	99	193	17.5	2	3	2	17.8	6.18	75	.339	.343	-28	-17	127	90	.774	120	2	-1.9	-1.2	-2.4	-.0	.0
TOT	328	11	7	3286		12.3				13.0	3.64		.286	.297					.836	2754	180					

Runs
Eggler-Mut 94
G.Wright-Bos 87
Cuthbert-Ath 83
Barnes-Bos 81
Hatfield-Mut 76

Hits
Barnes-Bos 99
Eggler-Mut 98
Force-Tro-Bal 94
Hatfield-Mut 92
Anson-Ath 90

Doubles
Barnes-Bos 28
Eggler-Mut 20
Hall-Bal 17
G.Wright-Bos 16

Triples
Gould-Bos 8
Anson-Ath 7
G.Wright-Bos 6
Hall-Bal 6

Home Runs
Pike-Bal 6
Gedney-Tro-Eck 3

Total Bases
Barnes-Bos 134
Pike-Bal 127
G.Wright-Bos 120
Eggler-Mut 118
Hall-Bal 116

Runs Batted In
Pike-Bal 60
Start-Mut 50
Anson-Ath 50
Fisler-Ath 48

Runs Produced
Cuthbert-Ath 129
Barnes-Bos 124
Pike-Bal 121
Hatfield-Mut 120
G.Wright-Bos 117

Bases On Balls
Mack-Ath 23
Anson-Ath 16
McMullin-Mut 11

Batting Average
Barnes-Bos .... .432
Force-Tro-Bal .... .418
Anson-Ath .... .415
Hastings-Cle-Bal ..362
McGeary-Ath ...... .360

On Base Percentage
Anson-Ath .... .455
Barnes-Bos .... .454
Force-Tro-Bal .... .423
Hastings-Cle-Bal ..376
McGeary-Ath ...... .366

Slugging Average
Barnes-Bos .... .585
Anson-Ath .... .525
Wood-Tro-Eck ..... .503
Force-Tro-Bal .... .493
Meyerle-Ath ...... .486

Production
Barnes-Bos 1.039
Anson-Ath .... .980
Force-Tro-Bal .... .916
Wood-Tro-Eck ..... .839
G.Wright-Bos ..... .816

Adjusted Production
Barnes-Bos 206
Anson-Ath 200
Force-Tro-Bal 176
Wood-Tro-Eck 158
Meyerle-Ath 147

Batter Runs
Barnes-Bos 30.8
Anson-Ath 26.0
Force-Tro-Bal ... 20.5
G.Wright-Bos 13.7
Hall-Bal 12.8

Adjusted Batter Runs
Barnes-Bos 26.6
Anson-Ath 25.7
Force-Tro-Bal ... 18.6
Eggler-Mut 16.2
Hatfield-Mut 12.6

Clutch Hitting Index
Start-Mut 168
White-Cle 150
Zettlein-Tro-Eck . 144
Cuthbert-Ath 135
Boyd-Mut 135

Runs Created
Barnes-Bos 65
Anson-Ath 52
Force-Tro-Bal 49
Eggler-Mut 47
G.Wright-Bos 45

Total Average
Barnes-Bos 1.133
Anson-Ath .... .963
Force-Tro-Bal .... .866
Wood-Tro-Eck ..... .828
G.Wright-Bos ..... .769

Stolen Bases
Eggler-Mut 18
G.Wright-Bos 14
Cuthbert-Ath 14
McGeary-Ath 13

Stolen Base Average
Eggler-Mut 78.3

Stolen Base Runs
Eggler-Mut 2.4
Barnes-Bos 2.4
Bechtel-Mut 2.1

Fielding Runs
Ferguson-Atl 36.3
Barnes-Bos 25.4
G.Wright-Bos 21.8
Eggler-Mut 15.4
York-Bal 10.5

Total Player Rating
Barnes-Bos 3.4
Eggler-Mut 2.5
G.Wright-Bos 2.3
Ferguson-Atl 1.7
Force-Tro-Bal 1.7

Wins
Spalding-Bos 38
Cummings-Mut ... 33
McBride-Ath 30
Mathews-Bal 25
Zettlein-Tro-Eck .. 15

Win Percentage
Spalding-Bos .... .826
McBride-Ath ..... .682
Cummings-Mut ... .623
Mathews-Bal ..... .581
Zettlein-Tro-Eck . .500

Games
Cummings-Mut 55
Mathews-Bal 49
Spalding-Bos 48
McBride-Ath 47
Britt-Atl 37

Complete Games
Cummings-Mut ... 53
McBride-Ath 47
Spalding-Bos 41
Mathews-Bal 39
Britt-Atl 37

Shutouts
Spalding-Bos 3
Cummings-Mut 3
Zettlein-Tro-Eck .. 2
McBride-Ath 1
Fisher-Bal 1

Saves
H.Wright-Bos 4
Zettlein-Tro-Eck .. 1
McMullin-Mut 1
Fisher-Bal 1

Innings Pitched
Cummings-Mut .. 497.0
McBride-Ath 419.1
Mathews-Bal 406.0
Spalding-Bos ... 404.2
Britt-Atl 336.0

Fewest Hits/Game
Fisher-Bal 7.61
Spalding-Bos 9.27
Mathews-Bal ... 10.64
Zettlein-Tro-Eck 10.71
McBride-Ath ... 10.90

Fewest BB/Game
Stearns-Nat ...... .27
Buttery-Man ...... .33
P.Martin-Tro-Eck . .44
Zettlein-Tro-Eck . .48
Britt-Atl .... .51

Strikeouts
Mathews-Bal 55
McBride-Ath 44
Cummings-Mut 43
Spalding-Bos 27
Zettlein-Tro-Eck .. 25

Strikeouts/Game
Fisher-Bal 1.64
Mathews-Bal 1.22
McBride-Ath ...... .94
Zettlein-Tro-Eck . .86
Cummings-Mut .... .78

Ratio
Fisher-Bal 8.51
Spalding-Bos 9.87
Zettlein-Tro-Eck 11.19
McBride-Ath 11.46
Cummings-Mut .. 11.50

Earned Run Average
Fisher-Bal 1.80
Spalding-Bos 1.87
Zettlein-Tro-Eck 2.33
McBride-Ath 2.85
Cummings-Mut ... 2.97

Adjusted ERA
Fisher-Bal 204
Spalding-Bos 195
Zettlein-Tro-Eck . 153
McBride-Ath 124
Mathews-Bal 115

Opponents' Batting Avg.
Fisher-Bal ...... .197
Spalding-Bos .... .244
Mathews-Bal ..... .257
McBride-Ath ..... .265
Zettlein-Tro-Eck .265

Opponents' On Base Pct.
Fisher-Bal ...... .216
Spalding-Bos .... .255
Zettlein-Tro-Eck .274
McBride-Ath ..... .275
Mathews-Bal ..... .277

Starter Runs
Spalding-Bos 79.7
Zettlein-Tro-Eck 38.4
Cummings-Mut ... 37.0
McBride-Ath 36.6
Fisher-Bal 22.5

Adjusted Starter Runs
Spalding-Bos 80.2
Zettlein-Tro-Eck 36.2
McBride-Ath 32.4
Fisher-Bal 22.8
Cummings-Mut ... 22.1

Clutch Pitching Index
Zettlein-Tro-Eck . 127
Spalding-Bos 126
Britt-Atl 117
P.Martin-Tro-Eck 115
Buttery-Man 109

Relief Runs
H.Wright-Bos 4.4

Adjusted Relief Runs
H.Wright-Bos 4.4

Relief Ranking
H.Wright-Bos 3.1

Total Pitcher Index
Spalding-Bos 7.8
McBride-Ath 2.7
Zettlein-Tro-Eck .. 2.5
Fisher-Bal 1.5
Cummings-Mut 9

Total Baseball Ranking
Spalding-Bos 7.6
Barnes-Bos 3.4
McBride-Ath 2.7
Eggler-Mut 2.5
Zettlein-Tro-Eck .. 2.5

March 3 Delegates from the existing professional clubs of the country assemble in Baltimore to establish a permanent Professional Association. A constitution is adopted along with Henry Chadwick's code of rules. For the first time a uniform ball must be used in all games.

May 5 Two thousand spectators pay 50¢ at the Union Grounds in Brooklyn and watch Baltimore play the Mutuals. Baltimore scores three in the first inning without a base hit and wins 6–1.

June 11 The largest crowd of the year, 10,000, jams the Jefferson Street Grounds at 25th Street and Jefferson to see the Athletics play the Philadelphias. The Philadelphias score five runs in the seventh to win 7–5.

June 14 In Boston, 2,000 spectators watch the Reds suffer a shutout for the first time in their history. Dick McBride of the Athletics holds the champions to only two hits.

July 4 The Resolutes of Elizabeth, New Jersey, upset the Red Stockings 11–2 in a morning game. The afternoon game is close for six innings but Boston scores five runs in the seventh, two in the eighth, and 21 in the ninth to roll to a 32–3 win.

July 10 In Philadelphia, 3,000 people see the Philadelphias, favorites for this year's pennant, and Boston, last year's champions, play a wild game with the home team winning 18–17. The teams have decided to cut short the number of games they will play in August due to poor attendance during that month.

July 21 One thousand people witness an extraordinary game in Philadelphia between the Athletics and the Lord Baltimores. Lipman Pike's three-base hit and Tom York's groundout tie the game at the end of nine innings. The Athletics' three runs in the top of the tenth and two in the top of the eleventh are matched by Baltimore, and it is not until the 13th that Everett Mills scores the winning run for the Baltimores on John Radcliffe's hit, winning 12–11.

July 24 Brooklyn's Bob Ferguson umpires a close game between the Mutuals and the Baltimores that ends in a three-run rally by the Mutes in the last of the ninth to win 11–10. A police escort is needed to get the umpire to the clubhouse. Nat Hicks of the Mutuals and Ferguson get into an altercation, the end result of which is the striking of Hicks's left arm with a bat wielded by the umpire. The men are reconciled after the game, but Hicks's arm is broken in two places, and he will not play for the next two months.

July 30 The Philadelphia Athletics play their first game in three weeks after spending a holiday at Cape May, New Jersey, to rest from the rigors of the season. They are roughly handled at Boston, with the Reds defeating them 24–10.

August 16 At Baltimore's Newington Park, Baltimore outfielder Lipman Pike races against a horse named "Clarence." Pike has a short lead after 75 yards when the trotter breaks into a run. Pike holds on to win in 10 seconds flat.

October 22 The Boston Red Stockings clinch the pennant for 1873 by defeating the Washington Nationals 11–8 in Washington. George Wright leads the attack with a triple and two singles.

November 6 The first game under the proposed new rule of 10 men and 10 innings is played between the Athletics and the Phillies as a benefit for Ned Cuthbert. The majority present thought the 10th man (a so-called "right shortstop") was an unnecessary innovation.

ATHLETICS		ATLANTICS		BALTIMORE		BOSTON		MARYLANDS	
M	D.McBride	M	B.Ferguson	M	C.McVey	M	H.Wright	M	B.Smith
1B	C.Anson	1B	H.Dehlman	M	T.Carey	1B	J.O'Rourke	1B	B.Lennon
2B	W.Fisler	2B	J.Burdock	1B	E.Mills	2B	R.Barnes	2B	M.Simpson
SS	M.McGeary	SS	D.Pearce	2B	T.Carey	SS	G.Wright	SS	L.Say
3B	E.Sutton	3B	B.Ferguson	SS	J.Radcliff	3B	H.Schafer	3B	H.Kohler
LF	J.McMullin	LF	C.Pabor	3B	D.Force	LF	A.Leonard	LF	M.Hooper
CF	T.Murnane	CF	J.Remsen	LF	T.York	CF	H.Wright	CF	J.Smith
RF	C.Fisher	RF	B.Boyd	CF	G.Hall	RF	B.Addy	RF	B.French
C	J.Clapp	C	T.Barlow	RF	L.Pike	C	D.White	C	B.Smith
				C	C.McVey				
O	C.Sensenderfer	O	E.Booth			1	J.Manning	/O	J.Sheppard
/2	A.Reach	/O	H.Doscher	CS	B.Craver	/O	D.Birdsall	/2	J.Kernan
/O	J.Battin	/1	H.Kessler	CO	S.Hastings	/1	F.Rogers	/2	R.Woodhead
				/S	B.Barrett	/2	C.Sweasy	/2	W.Goldsmith
P	D.McBride	P	J.Britt					/O	T.Johns
				P	C.Cummings	P	A.Spalding	/O	Jones
				P	A.Brainard			/S	G.Popplein
								/O	Eland
								P	E.Stratton
								P	F.Selman
								P	Mc Doolan

MUTUALS		PHILADELPHIA		RESOLUTES		WASHINGTON	
M	J.Hatfield	M	F.Malone	M	D.Allison	M	N.Young
M	J.Start	1B	D.Mack	1B	M.Campbell	1B	J.Glenn
1B	J.Start	2B	J.Wood	2B	B.Laughlin	2B	T.Beals
2B	C.Nelson	SS	C.Fulmer	SS	F.Wordsworth	SS	J.Gerhardt
SS	J.Holdsworth	3B	L.Meyerle	3B	A.Nevin	3B	W.White
3B	J.Hatfield	LF	N.Cuthbert	LF	E.Booth	LF	P.Hines
LF	C.Gedney	CF	F.Treacey	CF	A.Allison	CF	H.Hollingshead
CF	D.Eggler	RF	G.Bechtel	RF	H.Austin	RF	O.Bielaski
RF	P.Martin	C	F.Malone	C	D.Allison	C	P.Snyder
C	N.Hicks						
		1	J.Devlin	2S	F.Fleet	S2	J.Donnelly
O2	D.Higham	2	B.Addy	/C	J.Farrow	/S	F.Waterman
C	D.Allison	/1	J.Ryan	/3	J.Clinton	/O	E.Atkinson
/3	S.Bellan			/1	M.Swandell	/S	B.Reach
/1	N.Phelps	P	G.Zettlein	/2	F.Crane	/S	H.Wall
P	B.Mathews			P	H.Campbell	P	B.Stearns
						P	Greyson
				/P	L.Lovett		
				/P	R.Wolters		

TEAM	G	W	L	PCT	GB	R	OR	AB	H	2B	3B	HR	BB	SO	AVG	OBP	SLG	PRO	PRO+	BR	/A	PF	CHI	RC	SB	CS	SBA	SBR
BOS	60	43	16	.729		739	460	2755	930	146	44	12	62	24	.338	.352	.436	.788	128	122	64	108	105	428	39	27	59	-5
PHI	53	36	17	.679	4	526	396	2325	645	83	20	8	62	39	.277	.296	.341	.637	91	-17	-35	104	110	243	44	14	76	5
BAL	57	34	22	.607	7.5	644	451	2562	810	106	38	9	41	25	.316	.327	.398	.725	121	57	60	100	108	340	22	11	67	0
MUT	53	29	24	.547	11	424	385	2214	622	51	36	5	42	22	.281	.294	.343	.637	94	-16	-13	99	94	227	15	6	71	1
ATH	52	28	23	.549	11	474	403	2266	683	71	20	4	35	32	.301	.312	.356	.668	96	8	-28	108	98	251	29	24	55	-6
ATL	55	17	37	.315	23.5	366	549	2210	588	42	23	6	53	43	.266	.283	.314	.597	92	-46	-2	89	87	198	19	11	63	-1
WAS	39	8	31	.205	25	283	485	1563	408	38	19	2	19	33	.261	.270	.313	.583	80	-41	-32	97	99	132	5	5	50	-2
RES	23	2	21	.87	23	98	299	868	204	18	8	0	8	22	.235	.242	.274	.516	62	-43	-33	92	71	58	2	1	67	0
MAR	6	0	6	.0	16.5	26	152	211	33	1	0	0	0	3	.156	.156	.161	.317	-4	-25	-22	77	139	5				
TOT	199					3580		16974	4923	556	208	46	322	243	.290	.303	.355	.659							175	99	64	-7

TEAM	CG	SH	SV	IP	H	H/G	HR	BB	SO	RAT	ERA	ERA+	OAV	OOB	PR	/A	PF	CPI	FA	E	DP	FW	PW	BW	SBW	DIF
BOS	47	1	6	536	708	11.9	5	35	31	12.5	2.59	128	.287	.297	40	44	102	118	.838	465	46	.8	3.1	4.5	-.3	5.4
PHI	50	0	0	481	627	11.7	3	44	28	12.6	2.77	119	.284	.298	26	28	101	110	.848	379	43	2.3	2.0	-2.5	.4	7.3
BAL	55	1	0	508[2]	680	12.0	4	42	37	12.8	3.01	108	.285	.297	14	14	100	101	.855	366	33	4.6	1.0	4.2	.0	-3.9
MUT	48	2	0	477	539	10.2	5	69	76	11.5	2.62	121	.254	.278	33	29	97	88	.821	419	28	.3	2.1	-.9	.1	1.0
ATH	44	3	2	475	553	10.5	4	58	41	11.6	3.03	113	.257	.276	12	20	105	75	.842	383	30	1.7	1.4	-2.0	-.4	1.7
ATL	52	1	0	500	737	13.3	8	42	15	14.0	3.98	76	.303	.315	-40	-52	93	93	.820	505	30	-3.3	-3.7	-.1	-.0	-2.9
WAS	39	0	0	346	593	15.4	10	22	7	16.0	4.71	71	.335	.343	-56	-52	103	103	.818	334	27	-1.1	-3.7	-2.3	-.0	-4.4
RES	22	0	0	207	342	14.9	6	9	8	15.3	3.22	104	.310	.316	1	3	103	123	.787	247	9	-3.2	.2	-2.3	.0	-4.2
MAR	6	0	0	54	144	24.0	1	1	0	24.2	8.00	40	.393	.395	-28	-29	100	97	.761	74	0	-1.3	-2.1	-1.6	.0	1.9
TOT	363	8	8	3584[2]		12.4				13.2	3.25		.290	.303					.831	3172	246					

Runs	Hits	Doubles	Triples	Home Runs	Total Bases
Barnes-Bos 125	Barnes-Bos 137	Barnes-Bos 29	Mills-Bal 9	Pike-Bal 4	Barnes-Bos 188
G.Wright-Bos 99	G.Wright-Bos 126	G.Wright-Bos 19	G.Wright-Bos 8	G.Wright-Bos 3	G.Wright-Bos 170
Spalding-Bos 83	White-Bos 121	O'Rourke-Bos 19	Pike-Bal 8	Meyerle-Phi 3	White-Bos 148
Eggler-Mut 82	Spalding-Bos 106	Mills-Bal 19	Holdsworth-Mut ... 8		Pike-Bal 132
Leonard-Bos 81	Anson-Ath 101	Carey-Bal 19	Barnes-Bos 8		Spalding-Bos 131

Runs Batted In	Runs Produced	Bases On Balls	Batting Average	On Base Percentage	Slugging Average
White-Bos 66	Barnes-Bos 185	Barnes-Bos 18	Barnes-Bos 425	Barnes-Bos .... .456	Barnes-Bos .... .584
Barnes-Bos 62	G.Wright-Bos 146	Mack-Phi 15	Anson-Ath .... .398	Anson-Ath .... .409	G.Wright-Bos ..... .523
Leonard-Bos 61	White-Bos 145	O'Rourke-Bos 14	White-Bos .... .390	G.Wright-Bos ..... .402	McVey-Bal .... .484
Spalding-Bos 60	Spalding-Bos 142	Malone-Phi 14	G.Wright-Bos ..... .388	Force-Bal .... .391	Meyerle-Phi .... .479
Meyerle-Phi 58	Leonard-Bos 142		McVey-Bal .... .380	White-Bos .... .390	White-Bos .... .477

Production	Adjusted Production	Batter Runs	Adjusted Batter Runs	Clutch Hitting Index	Runs Created
Barnes-Bos 1.040	Barnes-Bos 191	Barnes-Bos 41.9	Barnes-Bos 32.8	Cummings-Bal 168	Barnes-Bos 91
G.Wright-Bos ..... .925	G.Wright-Bos 160	G.Wright-Bos 28.1	G.Wright-Bos 20.3	McBride-Ath 156	G.Wright-Bos 69
McVey-Bal .... .874	McVey-Bal 159	White-Bos 20.4	Pabor-Atl 16.4	Donnelly-Was 136	White-Bos 61
White-Bos .... .868	Pabor-Atl 153	Anson-Ath 16.8	White-Bos 13.5	Hollingshead-Was .. 131	O'Rourke-Bos 49
Anson-Ath .... .858	White-Bos 144	O'Rourke-Bos 15.9	McVey-Bal 13.5	Addy-Phi-Bos 131	Pike-Bal 47

Total Average	Stolen Bases	Stolen Base Average	Stolen Base Runs	Fielding Runs	Total Player Rating
Barnes-Bos 1.132	Cuthbert-Phi 13		Cuthbert-Phi 2.7	Ferguson-Atl 31.5	Barnes-Bos 3.4
G.Wright-Bos ..... .863	Barnes-Bos 13		McMullin-Ath 2.1	Barnes-Bos 19.9	G.Wright-Bos 2.2
McVey-Bal .... .808	McMullin-Ath 9		Pike-Bal 1.8	Fulmer-Phi 18.5	Ferguson-Atl 1.8
White-Bos .... .796	Wood-Phi 8			Gedney-Mut 14.6	York-Bal 1.2
Meyerle-Phi ...... .771	Pike-Bal 8			G.Wright-Bos 14.5	Mills-Bal 1.1

Wins	Win Percentage	Games	Complete Games	Shutouts	Saves
Spalding-Bos 41	Spalding-Bos ...... .745	Spalding-Bos 60	Britt-Atl 51	McBride-Ath 3	H.Wright-Bos 4
Zettlein-Phi 36	Zettlein-Phi ...... .706	Britt-Atl 54	Zettlein-Phi 49	Mathews-Mut 2	Spalding-Bos 2
Mathews-Mut 29	Cummings-Bal ... .667	Mathews-Mut 52	Spalding-Bos 47	Spalding-Bos 1	Fisher-Ath 2
Cummings-Bal 28	McBride-Ath ...... .558	Zettlein-Phi 51	Mathews-Mut 47	Cummings-Bal 1	
McBride-Ath 24	Mathews-Mut ...... .558	McBride-Ath 46	Cummings-Bal 42	Britt-Atl 1	

Innings Pitched	Fewest Hits/Game	Fewest BB/Game	Strikeouts	Strikeouts/Game	Ratio
Spalding-Bos 497.2	Fisher-Ath 9.60	H.Campbell-Res 38	Mathews-Mut 75	Mathews-Mut 1.52	Fisher-Ath 10.67
Britt-Atl 480.2	Mathews-Mut 9.93	Stearns-Was ...... .48	Cummings-Bal 34	Fisher-Ath 1.49	Mathews-Mut 11.19
Zettlein-Phi 460.0	McBride-Ath 10.65	Spalding-Bos ...... .51	Spalding-Bos 31	Cummings-Bal .... .80	McBride-Ath 11.76
Mathews-Mut 443.0	Cummings-Bal ... 11.19	Brainard-Bal .... .75	Zettlein-Phi 28	McBride-Ath .... .59	Cummings-Bal ... 11.97
McBride-Ath 382.2	Zettlein-Phi 11.60	Britt-Atl .... .75	McBride-Ath 25	Spalding-Bos .... .56	Spalding-Bos 12.13

Earned Run Average	Adjusted ERA	Opponents' Batting Avg.	Opponents' On Base Pct.	Starter Runs	Adjusted Starter Runs
Fisher-Ath 1.81	Fisher-Ath 188	Fisher-Ath .... .227	Fisher-Ath .... .246	Spalding-Bos 43.8	Spalding-Bos 47.4
Spalding-Bos 2.46	Spalding-Bos 135	Mathews-Mut ..... .251	Mathews-Mut ..... .274	Mathews-Mut 34.0	Zettlein-Phi 30.5
Mathews-Mut 2.56	Mathews-Mut 124	McBride-Ath ..... .263	McBride-Ath ..... .282	Zettlein-Phi 28.2	Mathews-Mut 29.7
Cummings-Bal ... 2.66	Cummings-Bal ... 122	Cummings-Bal .... .274	Cummings-Bal ..... .287	Cummings-Bal ... 25.0	Cummings-Bal ... 25.0
Zettlein-Phi 2.70	Zettlein-Phi 122	Zettlein-Phi ...... .283	Spalding-Bos ..... .292	Fisher-Ath 13.5	Fisher-Ath 15.0

Clutch Pitching Index	Relief Runs	Adjusted Relief Runs	Relief Ranking	Total Pitcher Index	Total Baseball Ranking
H.Campbell-Res ... 123				Spalding-Bos 5.4	Spalding-Bos 5.1
Spalding-Bos 119				Zettlein-Phi 1.9	Barnes-Bos 3.4
Zettlein-Phi 111				Mathews-Mut 1.8	G.Wright-Bos 2.2
Greyson -Was 108				Cummings-Bal ... 1.7	Zettlein-Phi 1.9
Brainard-Bal 103				Fisher-Ath 8	Mathews-Mut 1.7

January 29 A. G. Spalding arrives in England where he will call on sporting editors and athletes pursuing his plan to bring two baseball clubs to England this summer to exhibit American baseball and to play some cricket matches.

February 27 The first match of American baseball ever played in England takes place at the Kennington Oval Cricket Field in London.

March 2 The fourth meeting of the Professional Association takes place at the United States Hotel in Boston. New rules include the adoption of the batter's box and the prohibition of any player betting on his own team (expulsion) or any other team (forfeiture of pay).

March 14 A. G. Spalding comes home from his visit to England after arranging the tour of the Athletic and Boston teams this summer. Plans call for the teams to depart from the U.S. on July 16, play baseball and cricket matches in England during August, and leave Liverpool for home on August 26th. The full number of championship matches during the regular baseball season will be played.

May 5 Tommy Bond pitches for the Atlantics in their 1874 opener. It is his first appearance in the National Association. Bond will later win 40 or more games in three consecutive seasons in the NL. Today he limits Baltimore to four hits as the Atlantics win the game, played at the Union Grounds, 24–3.

May 13 The first professional championship match in Chicago, by a Chicago team, since the Great Fire is played before 4,000 spectators. George Zettlein and the White Stockings defeat the Athletics of Philadelphia 4-0. The Athletics have 10 hits and 21 base runners and yet fail to score.

June 15 Candy Cummings strikes out six consecutive Chicago White Stocking batters during an 8–6 victory at Philadelphia.

June 18 One of the poorest games of baseball ever played between two professional clubs occurs in New York as the Mutuals defeat the Chicago White Stockings 38–1. Of the 33 hits collected by the Mutes, Tom Carey makes six and scores six runs. Chicago had just two hits and commits 36 errors.

July 10 Joe Start, the Mutual first baseman, misses the train to Hartford, and the Mutes are forced to play with only eight players. Hartford wins 13–4.

August 3 The American visitors play their first game of baseball in London at the Lord's Cricket Grounds as Boston defeats the Athletics 24-7. In the morning, a cricket match between the Americans and the Marylebone Club is started. At the completion of the match on the 4th, the Americans are victorious 107–105. The American ballplayers will play in seven cricket matches during the

tour and will win all seven. However, the Americans field 18 players while their opponents use 11.

September 9 The stockholders of the Philadelphias baseball club vote 26–15 to expel player John J. Radcliffe. Umpire William McLean has testified that Radcliffe approached him before the game at Chicago on July 15 and offered him $175 if he would help Chicago win the game. Four other players were in on the plot: Candy Cummings, Nat Hicks, Bill Craver, and Denny Mack.

September 14 To the surprise of 1,000 Boston spectators, Chicago bats Spalding all over the lot with 10 runs on 22 hits while George Zettlein limits the Reds to no runs on four hits. Boston's George Wright makes three errors.

September 16* The Globes, Louisville's first black baseball team, play a charity game for yellow fever sufferers, shaming a pair of local white clubs into following suit to avoid, in the words of the Louisville *Courier-Journal,* being "outdone by the darkly-complected portion of the human race."

November 1 The season ends today with the Boston Red Stockings being declared the champions with a record of 43-17. Boston actually had a record of 52-18 but the Committee throws out the Baltimore games because the team did not complete its schedule.

ATHLETICS		ATLANTICS		BALTIMORE		BOSTON		CHICAGO		HARTFORD		MUTUALS		PHILADELPHIA	
M	D.McBride	M	B.Ferguson	M	W.White	M	H.Wright	M	F.Malone	M	L.Pike	M	T.Carey	M	N.Hicks
1B	W.Fisler	1B	H.Dehlman	1B	C.Gould	1B	J.O'Rourke	M	J.Wood	1B	E.Mills	M	D.Higham	1B	D.Mack
2B	J.Battin	2B	J.Farrow	2B	J.Manning	2B	R.Barnes	1B	J.Glenn	2B	B.Addy	1B	J.Start	2B	B.Craver
SS	E.Sutton	SS	D.Pearce	SS	L.Say	SS	G.Wright	2B	L.Meyerle	SS	T.Barlow	2B	C.Nelson	SS	C.Fulmer
3B	C.Anson	3B	B.Ferguson	3B	W.White	3B	H.Schafer	SS	J.Peters	3B	B.Boyd	SS	T.Carey	3B	J.Holdsworth
LF	C.Gedney	LF	E.Booth	LF	J.Ryan	LF	A.Leonard	3B	D.Force	LF	J.Tipper	3B	J.Burdock	LF	T.York
CF	J.McMullin	CF	B.Clack	CF	H.Deane	CF	G.Hall	LF	N.Cuthbert	CF	L.Pike	LF	J.Hatfield	CF	D.Eggler
RF	J.Clapp	RF	J.Chapman	RF	O.Bielaski	RF	C.McVey	CF	P.Hines	RF	B.Barnie	CF	J.Remsen	RF	G.Bechtel
C	M.McGeary	C	J.Knowdell	C	P.Snyder	C	D.White	RF	F.Treacey	C	S.Hastings	RF	D.Allison	C	N.Hicks
								C	F.Malone			C	D.Higham		
O	T.Murnane	C2	F.Fleet	S	J.Gerhardt	O	H.Wright			3O	S.Brady			O	J.Radcliff
O	A.Reach	O	C.Hodes	/C	F.Selman	2	T.Beals	1O	J.Devlin	/O	O.Shaffer	/O	N.Phelps	O	C.Pabor
/C	T.Miller	O	P.McGee	1	Z.Taylor			/C	Gilroy	/O	J.Farrell	/O	B.Geer	/O	J.Donnelly
/O	C.Sensenderfer	/C	H.Kessler	/2	C.Sweasy	P	A.Spalding	/C	T.Connell	/3	J.Manning	/1	D.Patterson	/1	E.McKenna
		2	C.Sweasy	/S	J.Smith					/O	O'Neal	/O	O.Shaffer	/S	Quinlan
P	D.McBride	/2	B.West	/S	Brown			P	G.Zettlein						
		/2	A.Martin	/C	Jones					P	C.Fisher	P	B.Mathews	P	C.Cummings
		/2	J.Clinton	/3	B.Smiley			/P	D.Collins	P	B.Stearns				
		/2	J.Hall	/2	Wood										
		/2	Gavern	/O	F.Boardman										
		/C	M.Ledwith	/1	H.Kohler										
		/C	C.Snow	/O	H.Reed										
				/O	H.Reville										
		P	T.Bond	/C	L.Carl										
				P	A.Brainard										
				P	J.Manning										

TEAM	G	W	L	PCT	GB	R	OR	AB	H	2B	3B	HR	BB	SO	AVG	OBP	SLG	PRO	PRO+	BR	/A	PF	CHI	RC	SB	CS	SBA	SBR
BOS	71	52	18	.743		735	415	3130	979	121	61	17	33	27	.313	.320	.407	.727	128	115	77	106	108	418	45	18	71	3
MUT	65	42	23	.646	7.5	501	377	2729	714	89	28	7	36	39	.262	.271	.322	.593	90	-20	-35	103	105	253	36	3	92	9
ATH	55	33	22	.600	11.5	441	344	2258	647	83	18	6	24	49	.287	.294	.347	.641	99	19	-18	109	103	237	36	14	72	2
PHI	58	29	29	.500	17	476	428	2435	677	78	50	2	28	33	.278	.286	.354	.640	103	19	3	104	103	248	27	18	60	-3
CHI	59	28	31	.475	18.5	418	480	2462	685	87	4	4	32	54	.278	.287	.322	.609	97	-4	-8	101	94	232	32	12	73	2
ATL	56	22	33	.400	22.5	301	450	2169	498	45	8	1	31	51	.230	.240	.259	.499	71	-84	-49	88	97	136	11	4	73	1
HAR	53	16	37	.302	27.5	371	471	2143	591	85	18	2	30	56	.276	.286	.335	.621	97	4	-16	105	94	207	27	17	61	-2
BAL	47	9	38	.191	31.5	227	505	1778	435	45	7	1	22	36	.245	.254	.280	.534	75	-49	-47	99	83	127	12	5	71	1
TOT	232					3470		19104	5226	633	194	40	236	345	.274	.282	.333	.616							226	91	71	13

TEAM	CG	SH	SV	IP	H	H/G	HR	BB	SO	RAT	ERA	ERA+	OAV	OOB	PR	/A	PF	CPI	FA	E	DP	FW	PW	BW	SBW	DIF
BOS	65	4	3	634	779	11.1	1	23	30	11.4	1.93	112	.274	.280	18	16	99	108	.850	490	53	4.7	1.2	6.0	.1	5.0
MUT	62	4	0	586	663	10.2	3	41	100	10.8	1.89	119	.261	.273	19	23	103	98	.846	443	22	4.5	1.8	-2.7	.6	5.3
ATH	55	0	0	487	514	9.5	6	32	36	10.1	1.64	140	.240	.251	29	36	106	77	.839	396	34	2.8	2.8	-1.4	.0	1.6
PHI	56	3	0	522	673	11.6	4	19	61	11.9	1.93	114	.278	.284	15	16	101	116	.809	518	38	-2.1	1.2	.2	-.4	1.0
CHI	58	3	0	533²	684	11.5	7	45	26	12.3	2.65	84	.279	.292	-28	-25	102	93	.829	477	27	.4	-1.9	-.6	.0	.7
ATL	56	1	0	506	618	11.0	15	11	39	11.2	2.06	99	.266	.269	7	-1	94	97	.820	504	14	-2.2	-.0	-3.8	-.0	.6
HAR	45	0	0	481	655	12.3	1	27	34	12.8	2.51	92	.285	.293	-17	-11	105	99	.793	532	17	-4.8	-.9	-1.2	-.3	-3.3
BAL	42	0	0	420	640	13.7	3	38	19	14.5	3.09	72	.305	.318	-42	-41	102	107	.807	450	15	-3.2	-3.2	-3.6	-.0	-4.4
TOT	439	15	3	4169²		11.3				11.8	2.18		.274	.282					.825	3810	220					

Runs
McVey-Bos 91
O'Rourke-Bos 82
Spalding-Bos 80
G.Wright-Bos 76
White-Bos 75

Hits
McVey-Bos 123
Spalding-Bos 119
Leonard-Bos 108
White-Bos 106
O'Rourke-Bos 104

Doubles
Pike-Har 22
McVey-Bos 21
Meyerle-Chi 19
Craver-Phi 19
Leonard-Bos 18

Triples
G.Wright-Bos 15
Craver-Phi 11
Holdsworth-Phi ... 9

Home Runs
O'Rourke-Bos 5
White-Bos 3
McVey-Bos 3
Clapp-Ath 3

Total Bases
McVey-Bos 165
O'Rourke-Bos 150
G.Wright-Bos 149

Runs Batted In
McVey-Bos 71
O'Rourke-Bos 61
Craver-Phi 56
Spalding-Bos 54
White-Bos 52

Runs Produced
McVey-Bos 159
O'Rourke-Bos 138
Spalding-Bos 134
White-Bos 124
Craver-Phi 124

Bases On Balls
Nelson-Mut 9
McMullin-Ath 8
Barnes-Bos 8

Batting Average
Meyerle-Chi ...... .394
McVey-Bos .... .359
Pike-Har .... .355
Manning-Bal-Har .. .346
McMullin-Ath ..... .346

On Base Percentage
Meyerle-Chi ...... .401
Pike-Har .... .368
McMullin-Ath ..... .366
McVey-Bos .... .360
Barnes-Bos .... .360

Slugging Average
Pike-Har .... .504
Craver-Phi .... .498
Meyerle-Chi ...... .488
McVey-Bos .... .481
G.Wright-Bos ..... .476

Production
Meyerle-Chi ...... .889
Pike-Har .... .872
Craver-Phi .... .851
McVey-Bos .... .842
G.Wright-Bos ..... .816

Adjusted Production
Meyerle-Chi 182
Pike-Har 168
Craver-Phi 164
McVey-Bos 158
G.Wright-Bos 150

Batter Runs
McVey-Bos 24.3
Meyerle-Chi 22.6
Craver-Phi 19.7
G.Wright-Bos 19.5
Pike-Har 19.3

Adjusted Batter Runs
Meyerle-Chi 22.0
McVey-Bos 19.6
Craver-Phi 17.3
Pike-Har 16.2
G.Wright-Bos 15.3

Clutch Hitting Index
McBride-Ath 152
Malone-Chi 140
York-Phi 139
Fisher-Har 135
Fulmer-Phi 130

Runs Created
McVey-Bos 62
G.Wright-Bos 52
O'Rourke-Bos 52
Meyerle-Chi 51
Craver-Phi 49

Total Average
Meyerle-Chi ...... .822
Pike-Har .... .817
Craver-Phi .... .804
McVey-Bos .... .774
G.Wright-Bos ..... .739

Stolen Bases
O'Rourke-Bos 11
Leonard-Bos 11
Craver-Phi 11
McGeary-Ath 10
Barlow-Har 9

Stolen Base Average

Stolen Base Runs
O'Rourke-Bos 2.7
Cuthbert-Chi 2.4

Fielding Runs
White-Bal 24.6
Barnes-Bos 19.1
Pike-Har 13.6
Ryan-Bal 12.7
Force-Chi 11.1

Total Player Rating
Pike-Har 2.3
Barnes-Bos 1.9
Craver-Phi 1.7
McVey-Bos 1.6
White-Bal 1.5

Wins
Spalding-Bos 52
Mathews-Mut 42
McBride-Ath 33
Cummings-Phi 28
Zettlein-Chi 27

Win Percentage
Spalding-Bos ..... .765
Mathews-Mut ...... .656
McBride-Ath ...... .600
Cummings-Phi ..... .519
Zettlein-Chi ..... .474

Games
Spalding-Bos 71
Mathews-Mut 65
Zettlein-Chi 57
McBride-Ath 55
Bond-Atl 55

Complete Games
Spalding-Bos 65
Mathews-Mut 62
Zettlein-Chi 57
McBride-Ath 55
Bond-Atl 55

Shutouts
Spalding-Bos 4
Mathews-Mut 4
Zettlein-Chi 3
Cummings-Phi 3
Bond-Atl 1

Saves
H.Wright-Bos 3

Innings Pitched
Spalding-Bos 617.1
Mathews-Mut 578.0
Zettlein-Chi 515.2
Bond-Atl 497.0
McBride-Ath 487.0

Fewest Hits/Game
McBride-Ath 9.50
Mathews-Mut 10.15
Bond-Atl 10.97
Spalding-Bos 11.01
Zettlein-Chi 11.17

Fewest BB/Game
Bond-Atl .... .14
Spalding-Bos ..... .28
Cummings-Phi ..... .34
Fisher-Har .... .36
McBride-Ath ...... .59

Strikeouts
Mathews-Mut 100
Cummings-Phi 61
Bond-Atl 39
McBride-Ath 36
Spalding-Bos 30

Strikeouts/Game
Mathews-Mut 1.56
Cummings-Phi 1.14
Stearns-Har ...... .79
Bond-Atl .... .71
McBride-Ath ...... .67

Ratio
McBride-Ath 10.09
Mathews-Mut 10.79
Bond-Atl 11.12
Spalding-Bos 11.28
Cummings-Phi 11.81

Earned Run Average
McBride-Ath 1.64
Mathews-Mut 1.88
Spalding-Bos 1.92
Cummings-Phi 1.96
Bond-Atl 2.03

Adjusted ERA
McBride-Ath 140
Mathews-Mut 119
Cummings-Phi 113
Spalding-Bos 112
Fisher-Har 102

Opponents' Batting Avg.
McBride-Ath ...... .240
Mathews-Mut ...... .261
Bond-Atl .... .266
Spalding-Bos ..... .273
Zettlein-Chi ..... .273

Opponents' On Base Pct.
McBride-Ath ...... .251
Bond-Atl .... .268
Mathews-Mut ...... .273
Spalding-Bos ..... .278
Cummings-Phi ..... .282

Starter Runs
McBride-Ath 29.1
Mathews-Mut 19.1
Spalding-Bos 17.7
Cummings-Phi 12.1
Bond-Atl 8.5

Adjusted Starter Runs
McBride-Ath 35.7
Mathews-Mut 22.8
Spalding-Bos 16.0
Cummings-Phi 13.6
Bechtel-Phi 2.6

Clutch Pitching Index
Cummings-Phi 113
Brainard-Bal 111
Spalding-Bos 106
Stearns-Har 99
Bond-Atl 98

Relief Runs

Adjusted Relief Runs

Relief Ranking

Total Pitcher Index
Spalding-Bos 2.9
McBride-Ath 1.8
Mathews-Mut 1.5
Bond-Atl 9
Cummings-Phi 4

Total Baseball Ranking
Spalding-Bos 2.8
Pike-Har 2.3
Barnes-Bos 1.9
McBride-Ath 1.8
Craver-Phi 1.7

January 9* The first game of baseball played on ice this winter in the New York area takes place at Prospect Park in Brooklyn. Only two outs per team constitute an inning.

May 26 The Centennial club of Philadelphia becomes the first professional club of 1875 to disband. The Centennials have the honor of becoming the first team to sell a ballplayer. The rival Athletics wanted Bill Craver and George Bechtel, so the Athletics paid an official of the Centennials to have the two players released and transferred to the Athletic club.

June 5 In St. Louis, the Boston Reds suffer their first defeat of the season after 21 victories and one draw. The Browns' George Bradley holds the Reds to eight hits. After Bradley makes the last putout, the crowd rushes on the field and lifts him to their shoulders.

June 19 Henry Chadwick has this to say about today's game: "the finest display of baseball playing and the most exciting contest yet recorded in the annals of the national game." The Chicago Whites and the Dark Blues of Hartford battle 10 scoreless innings before Jim Devlin scores on a fly out by Paul Hines in the eleventh to win for Chicago 1–0.

July 28 Philadelphia's Joseph E. Borden, also known by the name Josephs, pitches the first no-hitter in major league history, beating the Chicago White Stockings 4-0. The game takes one hour and 35 minutes to play.

September 11* The first baseball game played with women professionals takes place in Springfield, Illinois. The diamond is half-sized and a 9-foot high canvas surrounds the entire field. The uniforms are similar to the male version except the pants are shorter. Final score: "Blondes" 42, "Brunettes" 38.

October 24 The Chicago *Tribune* calls for the formation of an organization of major professional teams: Chicago, Cincinnati, Louisville, Philadelphia, New York, Boston, and Hartford.

ATHLETICS		ATLANTICS		BOSTON		CENTENNIALS		CHICAGO		HARTFORD		MUTUALS	
M	D.McBride	M	C.Pabor	M	H.Wright	M	B.Craver	M	J.Wood	M	B.Ferguson	M	N.Hicks
M	C.Anson	M	B.Boyd	1B	J.Abadie	1B	J.Devlin	1B	J.Devlin	1B	E.Mills	1B	J.Start
1B	W.Fisler	1B	F.Crane	2B	R.Barnes	2B	E.Somerville	2B	J.Miller	2B	J.Burdock	2B	C.Nelson
2B	B.Craver	2B	F.Fleet	SS	G.Wright	SS	B.Craver	SS	J.Peters	SS	T.Carey	SS	J.Hallinan
SS	D.Force	SS	H.Kessler	3B	H.Schafer	3B	G.Trenwith	3B	W.White	3B	B.Ferguson	3B	J.Gerhardt
3B	E.Sutton	3B	A.Nichols	LF	A.Leonard	LF	F.Treacey	LF	J.Glenn	LF	T.York	LF	C.Gedney
LF	G.Hall	LF	C.Pabor	CF	J.O'Rourke	CF	F.Warner	CF	P.Hines	CF	J.Remsen	CF	J.Holdsworth
CF	D.Eggler	CF	B.Clack	RF	J.Manning	RF	C.Mason	RF	O.Bielaski	RF	A.Allison	RF	E.Booth
RF	G.Bechtel	RF	B.Boyd	C	D.White	C	T.McGinley	C	S.Hastings	C	D.Allison	C	N.Hicks
C	J.Clapp	C	J.Knowdell										
				O	T.Beals	/S	J.Radcliff	CO	D.Higham	CO	B.Harbidge	O	P.McGee
1O	C.Anson	S	M.Moore	1	J.Latham	/O	L.Lovett	OP	M.Golden	/C	P.Quinn	/C	D.Higham
2O	J.Richmond	O	P.McGee	/1	F.Heifer	/C	S.Field	CO	P.Quinn	/O	S.Brady	/C	B.Barnie
O	A.Rocap	/2	D.Patterson	/O	H.Wright			/2	G.Keerl	/O	C.Jones	/3	A.Metcalf
/O	A.Reach	/O	A.Martin			P	G.Bechtel	/3	F.Waterman			/O	N.Phelps
/C	W.Coon	/2	T.Smith	P	A.Spalding			/3	W.Foley	P	C.Cummings	/O	J.Hatfield
/C	Gilroy	/1	O.Brown					/3	M.Brannock	P	T.Bond		
		/O	Stoddard					/O	Brady			P	B.Mathews
P	D.McBride	/O	J.Dailey										
P	L.Knight	/C	B.Gilligan					P	G.Zettlein				
		/O	P.Quinn										
		/C	D.Bushong										
		/O	F.Thompson										
		/1	J.Abadie										
		/2	T.Barlow										
		/3	Boland										
		/O	W.Fulmer										
		/2	Hellings										
		/2	H.Munn										
		/O	W.Rexter										
		/O	Shaffer										
		/O	Sheridan										
		/1	O.Walker										
		P	J.Cassidy										
		P	J.Clinton										
		P	J.O'Neill										
		/P	H.Arundel										
		/P	Edwards										

NEW HAVEN		PHILADELPHIA		RED STOCKINGS		ST.LOUIS		WASHINGTON		WESTERNS	
M	C.Gould	M	M.McGeary	M	C.Sweasy	M	D.Pearce	M	H.Hollingshead	M	J.Simmons
M	J.Latham	M	B.Addy	1B	C.Hautz	1B	H.Dehlman	M	B.Parks	1B	J.Carbine
M	C.Pabor	1B	T.Murnane	2B	C.Sweasy	2B	J.Battin	1B	A.Allison	2B	J.Miller
1B	C.Gould	2B	L.Meyerle	SS	B.Redmon	SS	D.Pearce	2B	S.Brady	SS	J.Hallinan
2B	E.Somerville	SS	C.Fulmer	3B	T.McSorley	3B	B.Hague	SS	J.Dailey	3B	W.Goldsmith
SS	S.Wright	3B	M.McGeary	LF	A.Croft	LF	N.Cuthbert	3B	H.Doscher	LF	C.Jones
3B	H.Luff	LF	F.Treacey	CF	B.Morgan	CF	L.Pike	LF	B.Parks	CF	J.Simmons
LF	J.Ryan	CF	J.McMullin	RF	T.Oran	RF	J.Chapman	CF	H.Hollingshead	RF	B.Riley
CF	J.Tipper	RF	B.Addy	C	S.Flint	C	T.Miller	RF	L.Ressler	C	P.Quinn
RF	J.McKelvey	C	P.Snyder					C	A.Thompson		
C	T.McGinley			/3	J.Ellick	O	C.Waitt			OC	B.Barnie
		1	F.Malone	/C	P.Dillon	C	G.Seward	C	McCloskey	/O	J.Hall
O2	B.Geer	O	O.Shaffer	/S	J.Dillon			/S	L.Say		
1	J.Latham	/3	B.Crowley			P	G.Bradley	/O	C.Mason	P	M.Golden
C	S.Bancker			P	J.Blong	P	P.Galvin	/O	J.Lowry		
/3	G.Trenwith	P	C.Fisher					/1	Terry		
/O	C.Pabor	P	G.Zettlein			/P	F.Fleet	/C	S.Field		
/1	J.Cassidy	P	J.Borden					/C	J.Gilmore		
/C	J.Keenan							/O	R.Stevens		
/O	Sullivan	/P	S.Weaver					/1	F.Selman		
/S	T.Barlow	/P	B.Parks								
/O	L.Dole							P	B.Stearns		
/O	Evans										
/2	F.Goldsmith							/P	Witherow		
/C	R.Harrison										
/S	J.Smith										
/S	Booth										
P	T.Nichols										
/P	G.Knight										

TEAM	G	W	L	PCT	GB	R	OR	AB	H	2B	3B	HR	BB	SO	AVG	OBP	SLG	PRO	PRO+	BR	/A	PF	CHI	RC	SB	CS	SBA	SBR
BOS	82	71	8	.899		831	343	3515	1128	167	51	15	33	52	.321	.327	.410	.737	153	191	164	104	111	494	93	37	72	6
HAR	86	54	28	.659	18.5	557	343	3356	871	92	35	2	34	64	.260	.267	.310	.577	97	7	-20	105	104	284	65	33	66	0
ATH	77	53	20	.726	15	699	402	3250	941	124	57	7	38	55	.290	.298	.369	.667	120	102	35	111	113	365	75	46	62	-5
STL	70	39	29	.574	26.5	386	369	2674	643	85	29	0	32	102	.240	.249	.294	.543	99	-23	13	91	96	220	108	56	75	11
PHI	70	37	31	.544	28.5	470	376	2721	683	67	27	5	21	58	.251	.257	.301	.558	92	-12	-28	104	113	220	105	51	67	1
MUT	71	30	38	.441	35.5	328	425	2685	633	82	21	7	19	47	.236	.241	.290	.531	82	-36	-57	105	85	185	20	24	45	-8
CHI	69	30	37	.448	35	379	416	2685	699	83	16	0	21	65	.260	.266	.303	.569	99	-1	-5	101	90	220	69	50	58	-9
NH	47	7	40	.149	48	170	397	1714	373	41	13	2	14	62	.218	.224	.260	.484	80	-49	-22	87	77	103	35	16	69	1
WAS	28	5	23	.179	40.5	107	338	1004	194	14	8	0	6	42	.193	.198	.223	.421	50	-49	-45	96	98	47	23	7	77	3
RS	19	4	15	.211	37	60	161	688	137	20	1	0	12	45	.199	.213	.231	.444	62	-28	-20	90	74	37	27	9	75	3
CEN	14	2	12	.143	36.5	70	138	530	125	22	3	0	10	25	.236	.250	.289	.539	97	-5	1	92	88	40	4			
ATL	44	2	42	.45	51.5	132	438	1562	304	33	6	2	8	36	.195	.199	.227	.426	57	-74	-53	87	77	69	1	5	17	-3
WES	13	1	12	.77		45	88	449	81	9	6	0	1	22	.180	.182	.227	.409	41	-24	-27	105	97	17	4	6	40	-2
TOT	345					4234		26833	6812	839	273	40	249	675	.254	.261	.310	.571							629	320	66	-3

TEAM	CG	SH	SV	IP	H	H/G	HR	BB	SO	RAT	ERA	ERA+	OAV	OOB	PR	/A	PF	CPI	FA	E	DP	FW	PW	BW	SBW	DIF
BOS	60	10	17	732	751	9.2	2	33	110	9.6	1.87	115	.248	.256	29	22	96	110	.870	483	56	4.3	1.9	14.0	.5	10.8
HAR	83	13	0	770	708	8.3	4	11	152	8.4	1.57	150	.228	.231	56	67	105	94	.881	438	47	7.8	5.7	-1.7	.0	1.2
ATH	75	6	0	687	776	10.2	4	39	45	10.7	2.40	100	.268	.278	-13	-1	107	111	.876	419	51	5.7	-.0	3.0	-.4	8.3
STL	67	5	1	630	636	9.1	3	21	71	9.4	2.10	96	.241	.247	9	-6	90	87	.869	425	36	3.0	-.5	1.1	1.0	.4
PHI	64	5	0	628	652	9.3	6	30	42	9.8	2.12	107	.243	.251	7	11	102	93	.848	477	32	.5	.9	-2.4	.1	3.8
MUT	70	3	0	636²	718	10.1	4	21	77	10.4	2.46	95	.258	.264	-17	-9	105	95	.838	526	30	-1.5	-.8	-4.9	-.7	3.8
CHI	65	7	0	625	649	9.3	0	26	55	9.7	1.63	139	.243	.250	42	45	102	115	.853	478	30	.1	3.8	-.4	-.7	-6.3
NH	40	0	0	425	501	10.6	5	21	54	11.1	2.65	78	.254	.262	-20	-27	93	87	.814	447	24	-5.7	-2.3	-1.9	.1	-6.7
WAS	23	0	0	250²	397	14.3	6	10	6	14.6	3.77	63	.311	.317	-43	-39	107	112	.791	285	8	-4.3	-3.3	-3.8	.3	-2.5
RS	16	2	0	171	209	11.0	0	3	21	11.2	2.63	83	.267	.269	-8	-8	98	94	.833	150	6	-.8	-.7	-1.7	.0	-1.2
CEN	14	0	0	126	169	12.1	0	5	6	12.4	2.71	80	.274	.280	-7	-8	98	103	.769	164	5	-3.2	-.7	.0	.0	-1.2
ATL	31	0	0	396	535	12.2	6	17	16	12.5	3.16	66	.285	.291	-41	-47	94	103	.801	432	20	-6.0	-4.0	-4.5	-.2	-5.2
WES	13	0	0	113	111	8.8	0	12	20	10.3	1.83	133	.225	.243	5	8	110	84	.860	78	5	.6	.7	-2.3	-.1	-4.3
TOT	621	51	18	6190¹		9.9				10.3	2.23		.254	.261					.849	4802	350					

Runs
Barnes-Bos 115
G.Wright-Bos . . . 106
O'Rourke-Bos . . . 97
McVey-Bos 89
Leonard-Bos . . . 87

Hits
Barnes-Bos 143
McVey-Bos 138
G.Wright-Bos . . . 136
White-Bos 136
Leonard-Bos . . . 127

Doubles
McVey-Bos 36
White-Bos 23
Pike-StL 22
Force-Ath 22

Triples
Craver-Cen-Ath . . 13
Pike-StL 12
Hall-Ath 12
McVey-Bos 9
Meyerle-Phi . . . 8

Home Runs
O'Rourke-Bos . . . 6
Start-Mut 4
Hall-Ath 4
Hallinan-Wes-Mut . 3
McVey-Bos 3

Total Bases
McVey-Bos 201
G.Wright-Bos . . . 176
Barnes-Bos 174
White-Bos 168
Leonard-Bos . . . 156

Runs Batted In
McVey-Bos 87
Leonard-Bos . . . 74
O'Rourke-Bos . . . 72
Hall-Ath 62
G.Wright-Bos . . . 61

Runs Produced
McVey-Bos 173
Barnes-Bos 172
G.Wright-Bos . . . 165
O'Rourke-Bos . . . 163
Leonard-Bos . . . 160

Bases On Balls
Dehlman-StL . . . 11
O'Rourke-Bos . . . 9
Nelson-Mut . . . 9
Hastings-Chi . . . 9
Harbidge-Har . . . 9

Batting Average
White-Bos 367
Barnes-Bos 364
McVey-Bos 355
Pike-StL 346
G.Wright-Bos 333

On Base Percentage
Barnes-Bos 375
White-Bos 372
McVey-Bos 356
Pike-StL 352
G.Wright-Bos 337

Slugging Average
McVey-Bos 517
Pike-StL 494
Craver-Cen-Ath . . .455
White-Bos 453
Barnes-Bos 443

Production
McVey-Bos 873
Pike-StL 846
White-Bos 824
Barnes-Bos 818
Craver-Cen-Ath . . .779

Adjusted Production
Pike-StL 210
McVey-Bos 193
White-Bos 178
Barnes-Bos 177
G.Wright-Bos . . . 159

Batter Runs
McVey-Bos 36.9
Barnes-Bos 31.4
White-Bos 30.0
Pike-StL 27.1
G.Wright-Bos . . . 25.1

Adjusted Batter Runs
Pike-StL 34.3
McVey-Bos 33.4
Barnes-Bos 28.0
White-Bos 26.9
G.Wright-Bos . . . 22.0

Clutch Hitting Index
Chapman-StL . . . 189
McBride-Ath . . . 164
Leonard-Bos . . . 148
Addy-Phi 142
Clapp-Ath 136

Runs Created
McVey-Bos 76
Barnes-Bos 75
White-Bos 62
G.Wright-Bos . . . 62
Pike-StL 58

Total Average
McVey-Bos 833
Pike-StL 800
Barnes-Bos 797
White-Bos 708
Craver-Cen-Ath . . .694

Stolen Bases
Murnane-Phi . . . 30
Barnes-Bos 29
Pike-StL 25
Dehlman-StL . . . 23
Burdock-Har . . . 20

Stolen Base Average
Cuthbert-StL . . . 94.7
Barnes-Bos 82.9
McGeary-Phi . . . 82.6
O'Rourke-Bos . . . 77.3
Murnane-Phi . . . 76.9

Stolen Base Runs
Barnes-Bos 5.1
Cuthbert-StL . . . 4.8
Murnane-Phi . . . 3.6
McGeary-Phi . . . 3.3
Battin-StL 2.7

Fielding Runs
Barnes-Bos 19.2
Clapp-Ath 18.1
D.Allison-Har . . 17.3
White-Bos 14.5
Sutton-Ath . . . 13.9

Total Player Rating
Barnes-Bos 4.3
White-Bos 3.6
McVey-Bos 3.4
Pike-StL 2.9
G.Wright-Bos . . . 2.0

Wins
Spalding-Bos . . . 54
McBride-Ath . . . 44
Cummings-Har . . . 35
Bradley-StL . . . 33

Win Percentage
Spalding-Bos 915
Manning-Bos 889
McBride-Ath 759
Cummings-Har 745
Zettlein-Chi-Phi . .569

Games
Spalding-Bos . . . 72
Mathews-Mut . . . 70
McBride-Ath . . . 60
Bradley-StL . . . 60
Zettlein-Chi-Phi . 52

Complete Games
Mathews-Mut . . . 69
McBride-Ath . . . 59
Bradley-StL . . . 57
Spalding-Bos . . . 52
Zettlein-Chi-Phi . 49

Shutouts
Zettlein-Chi-Phi . 7
Spalding-Bos . . . 7
Cummings-Har . . . 7
McBride-Ath . . . 6
Bond-Har 6

Saves
Spalding-Bos . . . 9
Manning-Bos . . . 6
McVey-Bos 1
Heifer-Bos 1
Galvin-StL 1

Innings Pitched
Mathews-Mut . . . 625.2
Spalding-Bos . . . 570.2
McBride-Ath . . . 538.0
Bradley-StL . . . 535.2
Zettlein-Chi-Phi . 463.1

Fewest Hits/Game
Borden-Phi 6.41
Galvin-StL 7.69
Bond-Har 7.72
Cummings-Har . . . 8.59
Fisher-Phi 8.67

Fewest BB/Game
Cummings-Har 09
Blong-RS 14
Galvin-StL 15
Bond-Har 18
Fisher-Phi 23

Strikeouts
Cummings-Har . . . 82
Spalding-Bos . . . 75
Mathews-Mut . . . 75
Bond-Har 70
Bradley-StL . . . 60

Strikeouts/Game
Manning-Bos . . . 2.13
Bond-Har 1.79
Cummings-Har . . . 1.77
Nichols-NH 1.50
Golden-Wes-Chi . . 1.32

Ratio
Borden-Phi 7.36
Galvin-StL 7.84
Bond-Har 7.90
Cummings-Har . . . 8.68
Fisher-Phi 8.90

Earned Run Average
Galvin-StL 1.16
Bond-Har 1.41
Borden-Phi 1.50
Zettlein-Chi-Phi . 1.59
Spalding-Bos . . . 1.59

Adjusted ERA
Galvin-StL 173
Bond-Har 167
Borden-Phi 152
Cummings-Har . . . 146
Zettlein-Chi-Phi . 143

Opponents' Batting Avg.
Borden-Phi 181
Galvin-StL 209
Bond-Har 216
Fisher-Phi 229
Cummings-Har 235

Opponents' On Base Pct.
Borden-Phi 203
Galvin-StL 212
Bond-Har 219
Fisher-Phi 233
Cummings-Har 236

Starter Runs
Spalding-Bos . . . 40.1
Zettlein-Chi-Phi . 32.6
Bond-Har 32.1
Cummings-Har . . . 28.9
Fisher-Phi 9.5

Adjusted Starter Runs
Bond-Har 36.7
Spalding-Bos . . . 34.9
Zettlein-Chi-Phi . 34.9
Cummings-Har . . . 34.3
Golden-Wes-Chi . . 12.6

Clutch Pitching Index
Stearns-Was . . . 123
Spalding-Bos . . . 122
Zettlein-Chi-Phi . 118
Devlin-Chi 117
McBride-Ath . . . 113

Relief Runs

Adjusted Relief Runs

Relief Ranking

Total Pitcher Index
Spalding-Bos . . . 4.7
Bond-Har 3.7
Cummings-Har . . . 2.8
Zettlein-Chi-Phi . 2.4
Devlin-Chi 1.3

Total Baseball Ranking
Spalding-Bos . . . 4.3
Barnes-Bos 4.3
Bond-Har 4.0
White-Bos 3.6
McVey-Bos 3.2

January 12 Al Spalding, pitching star of the National Association, moves from his home in Rockford, IL, with his brother J. Walter Spalding, to Chicago to "open a large emporium where they will sell all kinds of baseball goods." This will be the start of the Spalding sporting goods enterprise.

February 2 Chicago president William Hulbert organizes a meeting in New York to establish a new league. To win the support of four eastern clubs, Hulbert proposes that Morgan Bulkeley of the Hartford club be president and Nick Young of Washington be secretary. The National League is officially organized.

April 22 In the first National League game, Boston is a 6-5 winner over Philadelphia at Athletic Park. Jim O'Rourke makes the first hit and Joseph Borden, pitching under the name Josephs, is the winning pitcher.

April 24 Chicago manager Al Spalding pitches the NL's first shutout, 4–0 at Louisville.

May 2 Chicago's Ross Barnes, the great batting star of the National Association, hits the first NL homer, an inside-the-park drive off William "Cherokee" Fisher against the Cincinnati Red Stockings in Cincinnati. Barnes also hits a triple, single, steals two bases, and scores four runs.

May 10 Chicago plays its first National League home game as Albert Spalding shuts out the Cincinnati Reds 6-0.

May 13 Dick Higham of the Hartford Dark Blues hits into the first NL triple play against New York. It is the only bright spot for the Mutuals, who lose 28–3.

June 14 George Hall of the Athletics hits three triples and a home run in a 20-5 shellacking of Cincinnati. Teammate Ezra Sutton also hits three triples, the only time two players have done this in the same game.

June 27 Little Davey Force of the Athletics goes 6-for-6 against Spalding of Chicago, and Philadelphia scores four runs in the ninth to pull out a 14–13 victory. He is the first major leaguer to collect six hits in a nine-inning game.

July 8 The Boston *Herald* carries the midseason averages showing hits and errors per game (not per at bat nor per chance). Chicago's Ross Barnes is the top batter with 2.1 hits per game, and Dave Eggler of the Athletics is the leading fielder with .19 errors per game.

July 15 George Bradley of St. Louis pitches the National League's first no-hitter, defeating Hartford and Tommy Bond 2-0. It is his third shutout over Hartford in the three-game series.

July 25 For the second consecutive game, Cal McVey of Chicago collects six hits in seven trips.

August 4 Louisville, trailing Chicago by a wide margin with rain threatening in the fifth, decides to stall. They make error after error until the umpire forfeits the game to Chicago. The contest would later be ruled "no game."

September 9 Curveballer Candy Cummings of Hartford wins two games over Cincinnati, 14-4 in the morning and 8-1 in the afternoon. This marks the first time two games are played in the same day.

September 16 After only 200 watch the New York Mutuals lose to Cincinnati, the club announces that they, like the Athletics, will not make their western trip.

October 6 Louisville closes out its season with an 11–2 loss to Hartford. Jim Devlin, injured severely during yesterday's game, does not pitch for the first time this season. He will still lead the league in games (68), complete games (66), and innings pitched (622).

October 23 The Chicago *Tribune* publishes season-ending batting percentages based on the new method of dividing number of at bats into number of hits. Ross Barnes leads with a .429 average.

December 10 After a five-day league meeting in Cleveland, these results are announced: the Philadelphia Athletics and New York Mutuals are expelled by unanimous vote; a uniform and lively baseball is agreed upon.

	BOSTON		CHICAGO		CINCINNATI		HARTFORD		LOUISVILLE		NEW YORK		PHILADELPHIA		ST.LOUIS
M	H.Wright	M	A.Spalding	M	C.Gould	M	B.Ferguson	M	J.Chapman	M	B.Craver	M	A.Wright	M	M.Graffen
1B	T.Murnane	1B	C.McVey	1B	C.Gould	1B	E.Mills	1B	J.Gerhardt	1B	J.Start	1B	E.Sutton	M	G.McManus
2B	J.Morrill	2B	R.Barnes	2B	C.Sweasy	2B	J.Burdock	2B	E.Somerville	2B	B.Craver	2B	W.Fisler	1B	H.Dehlman
SS	G.Wright	SS	J.Peters	SS	H.Kessler	SS	T.Carey	SS	C.Fulmer	SS	J.Hallinan	SS	D.Force	2B	M.McGeary
3B	H.Schafer	3B	C.Anson	3B	W.Foley	3B	B.Ferguson	3B	B.Hague	3B	A.Nichols	3B	L.Meyerle	SS	D.Mack
LF	A.Leonard	LF	J.Glenn	LF	R.Snyder	LF	T.York	LF	J.Ryan	LF	F.Treacey	LF	G.Hall	3B	J.Battin
CF	J.O'Rourke	CF	P.Hines	CF	C.Jones	CF	J.Remsen	CF	S.Hastings	CF	J.Holdsworth	CF	D.Eggler	LF	N.Cuthbert
RF	J.Manning	RF	O.Bielaski	RF	D.Pierson	RF	D.Higham	RF	A.Allison	RF	E.Booth	RF	W.Coon	CF	L.Pike
C	L.Brown	C	D.White	C	A.Booth	C	D.Allison	C	P.Snyder	C	N.Hicks	C	F.Malone	RF	J.Blong
														C	J.Clapp
O	F.Whitney	O	B.Addy	O	B.Clack	C	B.Harbidge	O	J.Chapman	/O	M.Hayes	2	B.Fouser	S	D.Pearce
/O	T.McGinley	/O	F.Andrus	/C	S.Field	/O	J.Cassidy	O	J.Clinton	/O	G.Bechtel	C	W.Ritterson		
/S	S.Wright							O	G.Bechtel	/O	J.Shandley	/C	D.Bushong		
/O	B.Parks	P	A.Spalding	P	D.Dean	P	T.Bond	C	B.Holbert	/O	J.Maloney	/C	P.Curren	P	G.Bradley
/O	H.Wright			P	C.Fisher	P	C.Cummings	/O	D.Collins	/S	P.Treacey	/C	L.Paul		
				P	D.Williams			/1	J.Carbine	/2	G.Fair	/O	J.Bergh		
P	J.Borden									/2	J.Hatfield	/C	N.Phelps		
P	F.Bradley							P	J.Devlin	/1	G.Heubel	/C	J.Ward		
										/2	J.McGuinness	/C	J.Mullen		
/P	D.McBride							/P	F.Pearce	/2	B.West	/O	F.Warner		
/P	T.Nichols									/S	D.Force				
										/O	N.Phelps	P	L.Knight		
										/2	G.Seward	P	G.Zettlein		
										/C	B.Valentine				
												/P	F.Lafferty		
										P	B.Mathews				
										/P	T.Larkin				

TEAM	G	W	L	PCT	GB	R	OR	AB	H	2B	3B	HR	BB	SO	AVG	OBP	SLG	PRO	PRO+	BR	/A	PF	CHI	RC	SB	CS	SBA	SBR
CHI	66	52	14	.788		624	257	2748	926	131	32	8	70	45	.337	.353	.417	.770	140	160	93	112	107	415				
STL	64	45	19	.703	6	386	229	2478	642	73	27	2	59	63	.259	.276	.313	.589	102	-6	14	95	103	219				
HAR	69	47	21	.691	6	429	261	2664	711	96	22	2	39	78	.267	.277	.322	.599	92	1	-33	108	106	244				
BOS	70	39	31	.557	15	471	450	2722	723	96	24	9	58	98	.266	.281	.328	.609	102	11	4	102	110	257				
LOU	69	30	36	.455	22	280	344	2570	641	68	14	6	24	98	.249	.256	.294	.550	71	-42	-105	118	81	198				
NY	57	21	35	.375	26	260	412	2180	494	39	15	2	18	35	.227	.233	.261	.494	75	-76	-45	87	103	136				
PHI	60	14	45	.237	34.5	378	534	2387	646	79	35	7	27	36	.271	.279	.342	.621	108	16	19	99	100	233				
CIN	65	9	56	.138	42.5	238	579	2372	555	51	12	4	41	136	.234	.247	.271	.518	86	-63	-22	86	80	163				
TOT	260					3066		20121	5338	633	181	40	336	589	.265	.277	.321	.598										

TEAM	CG	SH	SV	IP	H	H/G	HR	BB	SO	RAT	ERA	ERA+	OAV	OOB	PR	/A	PF	CPI	FA	E	DP	FW	PW	BW	SBW	DIF
CHI	58	9	4	592¹	608	9.2	6	29	51	9.7	1.76	139	.247	.256	36	45	106	100	.899	282	33	6.0	4.0	8.2		.9
STL	63	16	0	577	472	7.4	3	39	103	8.0	1.22	175	.210	.224	70	59	93	74	.902	268	33	6.1	5.2	1.2		.5
HAR	69	11	0	624	570	8.2	2	27	114	8.6	1.67	142	.227	.235	44	49	103	72	.888	337	27	4.0	4.3	-2.9		7.6
BOS	49	3	7	632	732	10.4	7	104	77	11.9	2.51	90	.268	.295	-14	-18	98	106	.860	442	42	-1.1	-1.6	.4		6.3
LOU	67	5	0	643	605	8.5	3	38	125	9.0	1.69	160	.229	.240	44	73	118	75	.875	397	44	.9	6.4	-9.2		-1.1
NY	56	2	0	530	718	12.2	8	24	37	12.6	2.94	73	.302	.309	-37	-47	93	114	.825	473	18	-6.8	-4.1	-4.0		7.9
PHI	53	1	2	550	783	12.8	9	41	22	13.5	3.22	75	.310	.321	-56	-49	105	112	.839	456	32	-5.0	-4.3	1.7		-7.9
CIN	57	0	0	591	850	12.9	9	34	60	13.5	3.62	61	.313	.322	-86	-94	95	103	.841	469	45	-4.1	-8.3	-1.9		-9.2
TOT	472	47	13	4739¹		10.1				10.8	2.31		.265	.277					.866	3124	274					

Runs
Barnes-Chi	126
G.Wright-Bos	72
Peters-Chi	70
White-Chi	66
Burdock-Har	66

Hits
Barnes-Chi	138
Peters-Chi	111
Anson-Chi	110
McVey-Chi	107
White-Chi	104

Doubles
Hines-Chi	21
Higham-Har	21
Barnes-Chi	21
Pike-StL	19

Triples
Barnes-Chi	14
Hall-Phi	13
Pike-StL	10
Meyerle-Phi	8

Home Runs
Hall-Phi	5
Jones-Cin	4

Total Bases
Barnes-Chi	190
Hall-Phi	146
Anson-Chi	139
Hines-Chi	134

Runs Batted In
White-Chi	60
Hines-Chi	59
Barnes-Chi	59
Anson-Chi	59
McVey-Chi	53

Runs Produced
Barnes-Chi	184
White-Chi	125
Anson-Chi	120
Hines-Chi	119
Peters-Chi	116

Bases On Balls
Barnes-Chi	20
O'Rourke-Bos	15
Burdock-Har	13
Glenn-Chi	12
Anson-Chi	12

Batting Average
Barnes-Chi	.429
Hall-Phi	.366
Anson-Chi	.356
Peters-Chi	.351
McVey-Chi	.347

On Base Percentage
Barnes-Chi	.462
Hall-Phi	.384
Anson-Chi	.380
White-Chi	.358
O'Rourke-Bos	.358

Slugging Average
Barnes-Chi	.590
Hall-Phi	.545
Pike-StL	.472
Anson-Chi	.450
Meyerle-Phi	.449

Production
Barnes-Chi	1.052
Hall-Phi	.929
Anson-Chi	.830
Pike-StL	.813
Meyerle-Phi	.797

Adjusted Production
Barnes-Chi	222
Hall-Phi	208
Pike-StL	178
Meyerle-Phi	165
Jones-Cin	162

Batter Runs
Barnes-Chi	50.0
Hall-Phi	29.1
Anson-Chi	24.2
Pike-StL	19.7
O'Rourke-Bos	19.1

Adjusted Batter Runs
Barnes-Chi	38.7
Hall-Phi	29.7
Pike-StL	23.1
Jones-Cin	18.9
O'Rourke-Bos	18.1

Clutch Hitting Index
Battin-StL	150
White-Chi	142
McVey-Chi	140
Anson-Chi	138
McGeary-StL	135

Runs Created
Barnes-Chi	90
Hall-Phi	57
Anson-Chi	54
Peters-Chi	48
O'Rourke-Bos	48

Total Average
Barnes-Chi	1.141
Hall-Phi	.906
Anson-Chi	.759
Pike-StL	.738
Meyerle-Phi	.698

Stolen Bases

Stolen Base Average

Stolen Base Runs

Fielding Runs
Somerville-Lou	29.7
Force-Phi-NY	21.3
Battin-StL	13.6
G.Wright-Bos	13.1
Anson-Chi	12.8

Total Player Rating
Barnes-Chi	3.7
Anson-Chi	2.6
Hall-Phi	2.4
Battin-StL	2.2
G.Wright-Bos	2.1

Wins
Spalding-Chi	47
Bradley-StL	45
Bond-Har	31
Devlin-Lou	30
Mathews-NY	21

Win Percentage
Spalding-Chi	.797
Manning-Bos	.783
Bond-Har	.705
Bradley-StL	.703
Cummings-Har	.667

Games
Devlin-Lou	68
Bradley-StL	64
Spalding-Chi	61
Mathews-NY	56
Bond-Har	45

Complete Games
Devlin-Lou	66
Bradley-StL	63
Mathews-NY	55
Spalding-Chi	53
Bond-Har	45

Shutouts
Bradley-StL	16
Spalding-Chi	8
Bond-Har	6
Devlin-Lou	5
Cummings-Har	5

Saves
Manning-Bos	5
Zettlein-Phi	2
McVey-Chi	2

Innings Pitched
Devlin-Lou	622.0
Bradley-StL	573.0
Spalding-Chi	528.2
Mathews-NY	516.0
Bond-Har	408.0

Fewest Hits/Game
Bradley-StL	7.38
Bond-Har	7.83
Devlin-Lou	8.19
Cummings-Har	8.96
Spalding-Chi	9.23

Fewest BB/Game
Zettlein-Phi	.23
Fisher-Cin	.24
Bond-Har	.29
Mathews-NY	.42
Williams-Cin	.43

Strikeouts
Devlin-Lou	122
Bradley-StL	103
Bond-Har	88
Spalding-Chi	39
Mathews-NY	37

Strikeouts/Game
Bond-Har	1.94
Devlin-Lou	1.77
Bradley-StL	1.62
Borden-Bos	1.40
Fisher-Cin	1.14

Ratio
Bradley-StL	7.98
Bond-Har	8.12
Devlin-Lou	8.73
Cummings-Har	9.54
Spalding-Chi	9.67

Earned Run Average
Bradley-StL	1.23
Devlin-Lou	1.56
Cummings-Har	1.67
Bond-Har	1.68
Spalding-Chi	1.75

Adjusted ERA
Bradley-StL	174
Devlin-Lou	174
Cummings-Har	142
Bond-Har	141
Spalding-Chi	139

Opponents' Batting Avg.
Bradley-StL	.211
Bond-Har	.220
Devlin-Lou	.224
Cummings-Har	.239
Spalding-Chi	.247

Opponents' On Base Pct.
Bradley-StL	.224
Bond-Har	.227
Devlin-Lou	.235
Cummings-Har	.251
Spalding-Chi	.256

Starter Runs
Bradley-StL	68.9
Devlin-Lou	51.5
Spalding-Chi	32.5
Bond-Har	28.6
Cummings-Har	15.4

Adjusted Starter Runs
Devlin-Lou	79.8
Bradley-StL	57.9
Spalding-Chi	40.5
Bond-Har	31.5
Cummings-Har	16.9

Clutch Pitching Index
Knight-Phi	126
Mathews-NY	116
Borden-Bos	108
Dean-Cin	108
Zettlein-Phi	107

Relief Runs

Adjusted Relief Runs

Relief Ranking

Total Pitcher Index
Devlin-Lou	7.3
Bradley-StL	5.8
Spalding-Chi	4.6
Bond-Har	3.2
McVey-Chi	.8

Total Baseball Ranking
Devlin-Lou	7.3
Bradley-StL	5.8
Spalding-Chi	4.4
Barnes-Chi	3.7
Bond-Har	3.2

January 6 Joe Battin reportedly will not sign with the St. Louis Brown Stockings because of the new NL policy of charging players $30 for uniforms and, during road trips, deducting 50¢ a day from salaries to help offset the cost of meals.

February 3 Cherokee Fisher admits he was paid $100 to lose a game last September while pitching for the West Ends in Milwaukee.

February 20* The International Association is organized at a meeting of representatives of 17 clubs held in Pittsburgh. Although set up as an alternative to the NL, the IA will go down in history as the first minor league. A day later, the IA adopts a $10 admission fee, with an additional $10 required to enter the pennant race. Candy Cummings, pitcher-manager of the Live Oaks of Lynn, Massachusetts, is elected president.

March 5 The Hartford club completes arrangements to play its NL home games in Brooklyn. The club will still be called "Hartford."

March 22 The NL publishes its game schedule, the first league-wide schedule ever issued. The failure of the Athletics and the Mutuals to finish the 1876 season has convinced the league of the necessity of agreeing on a schedule.

April 26* The IA's opening game is played in Lynn, MA. The Manchester, NH, team beats the Live Oaks 14–3.

May 2* The Allegheny (IA) club of Pittsburgh upsets the Boston Red Stockings behind the brilliant work of Jim Galvin. Not only does he pitch a one-hit shutout, he hits a homer said to be the first ball to clear the fence at Pittsburgh's Union Park (also known as Recreation Park and the Coliseum).

May 17 At a special meeting, the league adopts a livelier version of the Spalding ball for all games.

June 5 Making his last start as a pitcher, Chicago's Al Spalding fails to retire any of the five Cincinnati batters he faces. Spalding's old Rockford teammate, Bob Addy, literally knocks Spalding out of the box with a line drive to the chest.

June 10 The St. Louis Browns and Cincinnati Reds stage a Sunday exhibition game, the only Sunday game between NL teams that would be played until 1892.

June 18 Lacking the funds to start their scheduled eastern trip, the Cincinnati club disbands. Cincinnati stockholders move to reorganize the club three days later.

June 25 Hard luck continues to dog the Cincinnati club, as a heavy windstorm nearly destroys the pavilion at the Cincinnati Baseball Park.

July 3 The reorganized Cincinnati Red Stockings reappear in action versus the Louisville Grays, losing 6-3. Whether their games will count or not in the NL standings will not be resolved until the NL meeting in December.

July 13 After pitching in 88 consecutive games since the start of the NL, an all-time record, George Bradley steps aside for Cal McVey, and Chicago beats Hartford 6-3. The revamped lineup shows Bradley at third base, Spalding at first base, and Cap Anson catching.

August 6 The NL rule calls for the home team to submit three names of approved local men as a possible umpire for each game, with the visiting team choosing one of them at random. Today in Louisville, Chicago's Cal McVey reaches into the hat and picks out a slip bearing the name of Dan Devinney, who accused St. Louis of trying to bribe him five days earlier. Disgusted, McVey then grabs the hat and finds that all 3 slips have Devinney's name on them. The incensed White Stockings demand a new umpire and then snap the Grays' six-game winning streak 7-2.

August 8 After St. Louis catcher John Clapp has his cheek smashed by a foul tip, replacement Mike Dorgan goes behind the plate wearing a mask. This is perhaps the first use of a catcher's mask in an official NL game.

September 6* Sam "Buck" Weaver of Milwaukee no-hits the Mutuals of Janesville, to win the Wisconsin state championship. The Janesville battery consists of future stars John Montgomery Ward and Albert Bushong.

October 26 Louisville club vice president Charles Chase confronts George Hall and Jim Devlin with charges that they threw road games in August and September. Both admit to throwing non-league games and implicate teammates Al Nichols and Bill Craver. The Louisville club formally expels Devlin, Hall, and Nichols for selling games and tampering with other players and expels Craver for "disobedience to positive orders." Craver will deny any wrongdoing.

December 4 At the formal meeting in Cleveland, the NL directors meet and confirm the expulsions of the four Louisville players. The directors also vote to throw out all Cincinnati games from the standings on the grounds that Cincinnati never paid its $100 dues.

	BOSTON		CHICAGO		CINCINNATI		HARTFORD		LOUISVILLE		ST.LOUIS
M	H.Wright	M	A.Spalding	M	L.Pike	M	B.Ferguson	M	J.Chapman	M	G.McManus
1B	D.White	1B	A.Spalding	M	B.Addy	1B	J.Start	1B	J.Latham	1B	H.Dehlman
2B	G.Wright	2B	R.Barnes	M	J.Manning	2B	J.Burdock	2B	J.Gerhardt	2B	M.McGeary
SS	E.Sutton	SS	J.Peters	1B	C.Gould	SS	T.Carey	SS	B.Craver	SS	D.Force
3B	J.Morrill	3B	C.Anson	2B	J.Hallinan	3B	B.Ferguson	3B	B.Hague	3B	J.Battin
LF	A.Leonard	LF	J.Glenn	SS	J.Manning	LF	T.York	LF	G.Hall	LF	J.Blong
CF	J.O'Rourke	CF	D.Eggler	3B	W.Foley	CF	J.Holdsworth	CF	B.Crowley	CF	J.Remsen
RF	H.Schafer	RF	P.Hines	LF	C.Jones	RF	J.Cassidy	RF	O.Shaffer	RF	M.Dorgan
C	L.Brown	C	C.McVey	CF	L.Pike	C	B.Harbidge	C	P.Snyder	C	J.Clapp
				RF	B.Addy						
O	T.Murnane	2O	H.Smith	C	S.Hastings	C	D.Allison	/2	A.Nichols	1O	A.Croft
/O	H.Wright	O	J.Hallinan			/O	L.Taylor	/O	F.Lafferty	/S	D.Pearce
		O	C.Eden	SC	A.Booth	/O	J.Bass	/2	J.Haldeman	/O	L.Lee
P	T.Bond	O	C.Waitt	S2	L.Meyerle	/O	J.Bunce	/2	H.Little	/O	H.Little
		/O	J.Quinn	O	N.Cuthbert	/O	J.Maloney			/O	T.Loftus
/P	W.White	/O	C.Jones	C	G.Miller	/O	J.Pike	P	J.Devlin	/O	E.McKenna
		/O	D.Rowe	/C	H.Smith					/O	J.Gleason
		/3	C.Fisher	/C	N.Hicks	P	T.Larkin			/S	T.Newell
				/1	C.Sullivan						
		P	G.Bradley	/O	J.Ryan					P	T.Nichols
		P	L.Reis	/C	H.Kessler						
				/S	B.Redmon						
				P	C.Cummings						
				P	B.Mathews						
				P	B.Mitchell						

TEAM	G	W	L	PCT	GB	R	OR	AB	H	2B	3B	HR	BB	SO	AVG	OBP	SLG	PRO	PRO+	BR	/A	PF	CHI	RC	SB	CS	SBA	SBR
BOS	61	42	18	.700		419	263	2368	700	91	37	4	65	121	.296	.314	.370	.684	114	47	33	104	104	283				
LOU	61	35	25	.583	7	339	288	2355	659	75	36	9	58	140	.280	.297	.354	.651	92	19	-47	118	92	254				
HAR	60	31	27	.534	10	341	311	2358	637	63	31	4	30	97	.270	.279	.328	.607	105	-17	18	89	103	222				
STL	60	28	32	.467	14	284	318	2178	531	51	36	1	57	147	.244	.263	.302	.565	84	-46	-31	95	102	177				
CHI	60	26	33	.441	15.5	366	375	2273	633	79	30	0	57	111	.278	.296	.340	.636	92	8	-33	112	105	234				
CIN	58	15	42	.263	25.5	291	485	2135	545	72	34	6	78	110	.255	.282	.329	.611	107	-11	24	89	94	203				
TOT	180					2040		13667	3705	431	204	24	345	726	.271	.289	.338	.627										

TEAM	CG	SH	SV	IP	H	H/G	HR	BB	SO	RAT	ERA	ERA+	OAV	OOB	PR	/A	PF	CPI	FA	E	DP	FW	PW	BW	SBW	DIF
BOS	61	7	0	548	557	9.1	5	38	177	9.8	2.15	130	.249	.261	40	40	100	98	.889	290	36	1.2	3.6	2.9		4.3
LOU	61	4	0	559	617	9.9	4	41	141	10.6	2.25	147	.270	.283	34	65	118	119	.904	267	37	2.4	5.8	-4.2		1.0
HAR	59	4	0	544	572	9.5	2	56	99	10.4	2.32	105	.253	.271	30	7	87	97	.885	313	32	-.2	.6	1.6		-.0
STL	52	1	0	541	582	9.7	2	92	132	11.2	2.66	98	.262	.291	9	-4	93	102	.892	281	29	1.4	-.4	-2.8		-.3
CHI	45	3	3	534	630	10.6	7	58	92	11.6	3.37	88	.274	.292	-33	-24	106	87	.883	313	43	-.2	-2.1	-2.9		1.7
CIN	48	1	1	515	747	13.1	4	61	85	14.1	4.19	63	.318	.335	-79	-89	94	102	.851	394	33	-4.7	-7.9	2.1		-3.0
TOT	326	20	4	3241		10.3				11.2	2.81		.271	.289					.884	1858	210					

Runs
O'Rourke-Bos 68
G.Wright-Bos 58
McVey-Chi 58
Start-Har 55

Hits
D.White-Bos 103
McVey-Chi 98
O'Rourke-Bos 96
Cassidy-Har 95
Start-Har 90

Doubles
Anson-Chi 19
York-Har 16
Manning-Cin 16
G.Wright-Bos 15
Hall-Lou 15

Triples
D.White-Bos 11
Jones-Cin-Chi-Cin . 10
Hall-Lou 8
Brown-Bos 8

Home Runs
Pike-Cin 4
Shaffer-Lou 3
Jones-Cin-Chi-Cin . 2
D.White-Bos 2
Snyder-Lou 2

Total Bases
D.White-Bos 145
McVey-Chi 121
O'Rourke-Bos 118
Hall-Lou 118
Cassidy-Har 115

Runs Batted In
D.White-Bos 49
Peters-Chi 41
Sutton-Bos 39
Jones-Cin-Chi-Cin . 38
York-Har 37

Runs Produced
D.White-Bos 98
McVey-Chi 94
G.Wright-Bos 93
O'Rourke-Bos 91
Jones-Cin-Chi-Cin . 89

Bases On Balls
O'Rourke-Bos 20
Jones-Cin-Chi-Cin . 15
Hall-Lou 12
Booth-Cin 12
Force-StL 11

Batting Average
D.White-Bos ...... .387
Cassidy-Har ...... .378
McVey-Chi .... .368
O'Rourke-Bos ..... .362
Anson-Chi .... .337

On Base Percentage
O'Rourke-Bos ..... .407
D.White-Bos ...... .405
McVey-Chi .... .387
Cassidy-Har ...... .386
Anson-Chi .... .360

Slugging Average
D.White-Bos ...... .545
Jones-Cin-Chi-Cin . .471
Cassidy-Har ...... .458
McVey-Chi .... .455
O'Rourke-Bos ..... .445

Production
D.White-Bos ...... .950
O'Rourke-Bos ..... .852
Cassidy-Har ...... .844
McVey-Chi .... .842
Jones-Cin-Chi-Cin . .824

Adjusted Production
D.White-Bos 190
Cassidy-Har 184
Jones-Cin-Chi-Cin . 175
O'Rourke-Bos 162
Manning-Cin 157

Batter Runs
D.White-Bos 28.2
O'Rourke-Bos 21.2
McVey-Chi 18.9
Cassidy-Har 17.6
Jones-Cin-Chi-Cin . 15.6

Adjusted Batter Runs
D.White-Bos 25.8
Cassidy-Har 23.7
Jones-Cin-Chi-Cin . 21.2
O'Rourke-Bos 18.9
Manning-Cin 16.4

Clutch Hitting Index
Ferguson-Har 142
Peters-Chi 139
Bond-Bos 139
Croft-StL 139
Addy-Cin 138

Runs Created
D.White-Bos 60
O'Rourke-Bos 49
McVey-Chi 48
Cassidy-Har 45
Hall-Lou 43

Total Average
D.White-Bos ...... .939
O'Rourke-Bos ..... .817
Jones-Cin-Chi-Cin . .776
McVey-Chi .... .768
Cassidy-Har ...... .756

Stolen Bases

Stolen Base Average

Stolen Base Runs

Fielding Runs
Gerhardt-Lou 19.8
Peters-Chi 19.1
Ferguson-Har 17.2
Brown-Bos 15.4
Snyder-Lou 15.2

Total Player Rating
Jones-Cin-Chi-Cin .. 2.7
D.White-Bos 2.3
Peters-Chi 1.8
Gerhardt-Lou 1.7
Brown-Bos 1.6

Wins
Bond-Bos 40
Devlin-Lou 35
Larkin-Har 29
Nichols-StL 18
Bradley-Chi 18

Win Percentage
Bond-Bos .... .702
Devlin-Lou .... .583
Larkin-Har .... .537
Nichols-StL ...... .439
Bradley-Chi ...... .439

Games
Devlin-Lou 61
Bond-Bos 58
Larkin-Har 56
Bradley-Chi 50
Nichols-StL 42

Complete Games
Devlin-Lou 61
Bond-Bos 58
Larkin-Har 55
Nichols-StL 35
Bradley-Chi 35

Shutouts
Bond-Bos 6
Larkin-Har 4
Devlin-Lou 4
Bradley-Chi 2

Saves
McVey-Chi 2
Spalding-Chi 1
Manning-Cin 1

Innings Pitched
Devlin-Lou 559.0
Bond-Bos 521.0
Larkin-Har 501.0
Bradley-Chi 394.0
Nichols-StL 350.0

Fewest Hits/Game
Bond-Bos 9.16
Larkin-Har 9.16
Nichols-StL 9.67
Blong-StL 9.75
Devlin-Lou 9.93

Fewest BB/Game
Bond-Bos .... .62
Devlin-Lou .... .66
Cummings-Cin ..... .75
Bradley-Chi ...... .89
Larkin-Har .... .95

Strikeouts
Bond-Bos 170
Devlin-Lou 141
Larkin-Har 96
Nichols-StL 80
Bradley-Chi 59

Strikeouts/Game
Mitchell-Cin 3.69
Bond-Bos 2.94
Blong-StL 2.45
Devlin-Lou 2.27
Nichols-StL 2.06

Ratio
Bond-Bos 9.78
Larkin-Har 10.11
Devlin-Lou 10.59
Nichols-StL 11.03
Bradley-Chi 11.22

Earned Run Average
Bond-Bos 2.11
Larkin-Har 2.14
Devlin-Lou 2.25
Nichols-StL 2.60
Blong-StL 2.74

Adjusted ERA
Devlin-Lou 147
Bond-Bos 133
Larkin-Har 114
Nichols-StL 100
Blong-StL 95

Opponents' Batting Avg.
Larkin-Har .... .245
Bond-Bos .... .249
Blong-StL .... .262
Nichols-StL ...... .263
Bradley-Chi ...... .269

Opponents' On Base Pct.
Bond-Bos .... .261
Larkin-Har .... .264
Devlin-Lou .... .283
Bradley-Chi ...... .286
Nichols-StL ...... .289

Starter Runs
Bond-Bos 40.5
Larkin-Har 37.3
Devlin-Lou 34.4
Reis-Chi 8.2
Nichols-StL 8.2

Adjusted Starter Runs
Devlin-Lou 65.4
Bond-Bos 40.5
Larkin-Har 16.3
Reis-Chi 8.9

Clutch Pitching Index
Mathews-Cin 123
Devlin-Lou 119
Booth-Cin 104
Nichols-StL 104
Blong-StL 101

Relief Runs

Adjusted Relief Runs

Relief Ranking

Total Pitcher Index
Devlin-Lou 5.9
Bond-Bos 3.5
Larkin-Har 1.8
Reis-Chi 7
Spalding-Chi 0

Total Baseball Ranking
Devlin-Lou 5.9
Bond-Bos 3.4
Jones-Cin-Chi-Cin . 2.7
D.White-Bos 2.3
Peters-Chi 1.8

January 16 The Grays, a new club that Benjamin Douglas put together in Providence, is finally organized with Henry Root as president, Douglas is hired as manager, and veteran Tom Carey is signed as captain.

February 9* Official averages compiled by the IA list Rochester's Steve Brady as the first-ever minor league batting champion with a .373 average.

March 27* The National Association of Amateur Base Ball Players disbands. This organization had traced its roots back to the first National Association founded in 1858.

April 1* The NL sign an agreement with six of the stronger IA clubs agreeing to drop their demand of a $100 guarantee for exhibition games and agree to split the gate receipts 50/50.

April 20 Chicago's new Lake Front Park is opened with a practice game. This field with its very short right field fence (180 feet from the plate) will house the White Stockings (NL) for eight years.

April 24 John "Bud" Fowler, a young black hurler with the Chelsea team, wins a 2–1 exhibition game from the Boston Nationals, the 1877 NL champs. Fowler will sign with the Lynn Live Oaks of the International Association. There are claims that Fowler played professionally in New Castle, Pennsylvania, as early as 1872.

May 8 Providence center fielder Paul Hines pulls off a spectacular and, perhaps, unassisted triple play. With men on second base and third base and none out in the eighth inning, Boston's Jack Burdock lines one over shortstop as both runners go. Hines, racing in, catches the ball and keeps going until he touches third base. This retires the runner who started on third base, but did it retire the runner who started on second base but had already rounded third base? To make sure, Hines throws back to Charley Sweasy to touch second base. This touches off a lively debate over whether the triple play was unassisted or not, a debate that still continues over a century later.

May 9 Sam Weaver pitches a no-hitter to lead the Milwaukee Cream Citys to their first NL win, beating Indianapolis 2–1, one run scoring after a walk. One scorer gave a hit to John Clapp of the Blues, but Weaver is generally credited with a no-hitter.

May 14 A crowd of 1,500 attends the first NL game in Milwaukee and sees the Grays end the Cincinnati Reds' six-game winning streak with an 8-5 decision.

July 15 John Montgomery Ward makes his NL debut pitching for Providence in Cincinnati. The first game is a fiasco, the Grays losing 13-9 thanks to 17 battery errors by Monte Ward and Brown. But the 18-year-old rookie will pitch every inning of every league game for the Grays for the rest of the season.

August 26* The Manchester IA club plays an exhibition at the state reform school. During the game, their dressing room is robbed of jewelry and $48 in cash.

September 14 The Red Stockings and Blues play an exhibition game in which they experiment with calling every pitch a ball or a strike and allowing only six balls for a walk. (The rules up to this time provide for the umpire to call a "warning pitch" on the first wide delivery). The reaction is favorable.

September 30 The NL season ends with a Providence win over Boston. For the first time ever, a league completes its entire schedule.

November 9 The official NL averages give Milwaukee's Abner Dalrymple the batting championship with a .356 average. These figures do not include tie games, however, and counting ties, Providence's Paul Hines would have the lead .358 to .354. The calculations giving Hines the batting crown, as well as research showing he led in RBIs, were not made until long after his death in 1935, so Hines did not know he was the ML's first triple crown winner.

December 4 The full NL meets and admits the Stars of Syracuse, Buffalo, and Cleveland. Indianapolis resigns, and the Milwaukee club is given 20 days to pay its creditors and resign honorably or be expelled. New rules include the following: The pitcher's box is narrowed from 6 feet wide to 4 feet wide. Every pitch is called either a ball, a strike, or a foul and 9 balls are required for a walk, as opposed to the old rule in which every third bad pitch was a called ball and 3 called balls gave the batter his base. A system of fines is established against pitchers who hit batsmen with pitches. Pitchers are barred from turning their backs completely to the batters during delivery. Batting-order rules are altered to make the first batter in a new inning follow the last batter in the previous inning, rather than the last man to be retired, who might have been put out on the basepaths.

BOSTON		CHICAGO		CINCINNATI		INDIANAPOLIS		MILWAUKEE		PROVIDENCE	
M	H.Wright	M	B.Ferguson	M	C.McVey	M	J.Clapp	M	J.Chapman	M	T.York
1B	J.Morrill	1B	J.Start	1B	C.Sullivan	1B	A.Croft	1B	J.Goodman	1B	T.Murnane
2B	J.Burdock	2B	B.McClellan	2B	J.Gerhardt	2B	J.Quest	2B	J.Peters	2B	C.Sweasy
SS	G.Wright	SS	B.Ferguson	SS	B.Geer	SS	F.Warner	SS	B.Redmon	SS	T.Carey
3B	E.Sutton	3B	F.Hankinson	3B	C.McVey	3B	N.Williamson	3B	W.Foley	3B	B.Hague
LF	A.Leonard	LF	C.Anson	LF	C.Jones	LF	J.Clapp	LF	A.Dalrymple	LF	T.York
CF	J.O'Rourke	CF	J.Remsen	CF	L.Pike	CF	R.McKelvy	CF	M.Golden	CF	P.Hines
RF	J.Manning	RF	J.Cassidy	RF	K.Kelly	RF	O.Shaffer	RF	B.Holbert	RF	D.Higham
C	P.Snyder	C	B.Harbidge	C	D.White	C	S.Flint	C	C.Bennett	C	L.Brown
/O	H.Schafer	O	J.Hallinan	O	B.Dickerson	S	C.Nelson	2O	G.Creamer	C	D.Allison
		/C	P.Powers			/O	J.Hallinan	O	B.Morgan	/2	L.Pike
P	T.Bond	/C	B.Traffley	P	W.White			/C	J.Knowdell		
		/O	B.Sullivan	P	B.Mitchell	P	T.Nolan	/C	J.Ellick	P	J.Ward
		/2	A.Spalding			P	J.McCormick	/3	F.Bliss	P	T.Nichols
						P	T.Healey	/C	A.Jennings	P	H.Wheeler
		P	T.Larkin								
		P	L.Reis					P	S.Weaver	/P	T.Healey
										/P	F.Corey
										/P	C.Fisher

TEAM	G	W	L	PCT	GB		R	OR	AB	H	2B	3B	HR	BB	SO		AVG	OBP	SLG	PRO	PRO+		BR	/A	PF	CHI	RC		SB	CS	SBA	SBR
BOS	60	41	19	.683			298	**241**	2220	535	75	25	2	35	154		.241	.253	.300	.553	79		-35	-56	108	**110**	173					
CIN	61	37	23	.617	4		333	281	2281	629	67	22	5	58	**141**		.276	.294	.331	.625	120		21	**53**	91	98	227					
PRO	62	33	27	.550	8		353	337	2298	604	**107**	**30**	**8**	50	218		.263	.279	.346	.625	109		19	20	100	104	227					
CHI	61	30	30	.500	11		**371**	331	2333	**677**	91	20	3	**88**	157		**.290**	**.316**	**.350**	**.666**	115		**56**	31	107	96	**265**					
IND	63	24	36	.400	17		293	328	2300	542	76	15	3	64	197		.236	.256	.286	.542	95		-43	-6	87	105	173					
MIL	61	15	45	.250	26		256	386	2212	552	65	20	4	69	214		.250	.272	.300	.572	86		-18	-38	107	88	185					
TOT	184						1904		13644	3539	481	132	23	364	1081		.259	.279	.319	.598												

TEAM	CG	SH	SV	IP		H	H/G	HR	BB	SO	RAT		ERA	ERA+	OAV	OOB		PR	/A	PF	CPI		FA	E	DP		FW	PW	BW	SBW	DIF
BOS	58	**9**	0	544		595	9.8	6	38	184	10.5		2.32	102	.272	.284		-1	2	102	**111**		**.914**	228	48		**3.5**	.2	-5.2		12.5
CIN	61	6	0	548		546	9.0	2	63	220	10.0		**1.84**	116	.248	.269		28	17	92	108		.900	269	37		1.5	**1.6**	**5.0**		-1.1
PRO	59	6	0	556		609	9.9	5	86	173	11.3		2.38	93	.265	.291		-5	-11	96	108		.892	311	42		-.5	-1.0	1.9		2.7
CHI	**61**	1	0	551		577	9.4	4	**35**	175	10.0		2.37	102	.253	**.265**		-4	3	105	85		.891	304	37		-.4	.3	2.9		-2.8
IND	59	2	**1**	578		621	9.7	3	87	182	11.0		2.32	87	.262	.288		-1	-19	88	106		.898	290	37		.9	-1.8	-.6		-4.6
MIL	54	1	0	547		589	9.7	3	55	147	10.6		2.60	101	.255	.272		-18	1	114	82		.866	376	32		-4.4	.0	-3.6		-7.1
TOT	352	25	1	3324			9.6				10.6		2.30		.259	.279							.893	1778	233						

Runs
Higham-Pro 60
Start-Chi 58
York-Pro 56
Anson-Chi 55
Dalrymple-Mil 52

Hits
Start-Chi 100
Dalrymple-Mil 96
Hines-Pro 92
Ferguson-Chi 91

Doubles
Higham-Pro 22
Brown-Pro 21
York-Pro 19
Shaffer-Ind 19
O'Rourke-Bos 17

Triples
York-Pro 10
O'Rourke-Bos 7
Jones-Cin 7

Home Runs
Hines-Pro 4
Jones-Cin 3
McVey-Cin 2
McKelvy-Ind 2

Total Bases
York-Pro 125
Start-Chi 125
Hines-Pro 125
Shaffer-Ind 121
Higham-Pro 117

Runs Batted In
Hines-Pro 50
Brown-Pro 43
Anson-Chi 40
Jones-Cin 39
Ferguson-Chi 39

Runs Produced
Anson-Chi 95
Hines-Pro 88
Higham-Pro 88
Jones-Cin 86
Brown-Pro 86

Bases On Balls
Remsen-Chi 17
Larkin-Chi 17
Shaffer-Ind 13
Clapp-Ind 13
Anson-Chi 13

Batting Average
Dalrymple-Mil 354
Hines-Pro 358
Ferguson-Chi 351
Start-Chi 351
Anson-Chi 341

On Base Percentage
Ferguson-Chi......375
Anson-Chi 372
Shaffer-Ind 369
Dalrymple-Mil 368
Hines-Pro 363

Slugging Average
Hines-Pro 486
York-Pro 465
Shaffer-Ind 455
Brown-Pro 453
Jones-Cin 441

Production
Hines-Pro 849
Shaffer-Ind 824
Start-Chi 794
York-Pro 793
Dalrymple-Mil 789

Adjusted Production
Shaffer-Ind 196
Hines-Pro 177
Jones-Cin 163
York-Pro 159
Brown-Pro 153

Batter Runs
Hines-Pro 20.0
Shaffer-Ind 19.6
Start-Chi 17.2
Dalrymple-Mil .. 16.4
York-Pro 16.1

Adjusted Batter Runs
Shaffer-Ind 27.8
Hines-Pro 20.2
Jones-Cin 17.4
York-Pro 16.3
Clapp-Ind 14.5

Clutch Hitting Index
McClellan-Chi ... 165
Harbidge-Pro ... 151
Hague-Pro 142
McKelvy-Ind 140
Bond-Bos 131

Runs Created
Hines-Pro 47
Shaffer-Ind 46
Start-Chi 46
Dalrymple-Mil ... 43
York-Pro 42

Total Average
Hines-Pro 770
Shaffer-Ind 761
York-Pro 715
Brown-Pro 692
Start-Chi 686

Stolen Bases

Stolen Base Average

Stolen Base Runs

Fielding Runs
Burdock-Bos 21.3
Hague-Pro 18.7
Ferguson-Chi ... 15.9
Kelly-Cin 11.1
Wright-Bos 10.5

Total Player Rating
Shaffer-Ind 2.9
Ferguson-Chi 2.8
Burdock-Bos 2.2
Jones-Cin 1.9
Hines-Pro 1.8

Wins
Bond-Bos 40
W.White-Cin 30
Larkin-Chi 29
Ward-Pro 22
Nolan-Ind 13

Win Percentage
Bond-Bos .... .678
Ward-Pro .... .629
W.White-Cin ..... .588
Larkin-Chi ...... .527

Games
Bond-Bos 59
Larkin-Chi 56
W.White-Cin 52
Weaver-Mil 45
Nolan-Ind 38

Complete Games
Bond-Bos 57
Larkin-Chi 56
W.White-Cin 52
Weaver-Mil 39

Shutouts
Bond-Bos 9
Ward-Pro 6
W.White-Cin 5

Saves
Healey-Pro-Ind 1

Innings Pitched
Bond-Bos 532.2
Larkin-Chi 506.0
W.White-Cin 468.0
Weaver-Mil 383.0
Nolan-Ind 347.0

Fewest Hits/Game
Mitchell-Cin 7.76
Ward-Pro 8.30
Weaver-Mil 8.72
Larkin-Chi 9.09
W.White-Cin 9.17

Fewest BB/Game
Weaver-Mil 49
Larkin-Chi 55
Bond-Bos 56
Nichols-Pro 73
W.White-Cin 87

Strikeouts
Bond-Bos 182
W.White-Cin 169
Larkin-Chi 163
Nolan-Ind 125
Ward-Pro 116

Strikeouts/Game
Mitchell-Cin 5.74
Wheeler-Pro 3.63
W.White-Cin 3.25
Nolan-Ind 3.24
Ward-Pro 3.13

Ratio
Weaver-Mil 9.21
Ward-Pro 9.22
Larkin-Chi 9.64
Mitchell-Cin 9.79
W.White-Cin 10.04

Earned Run Average
Ward-Pro 1.51
McCormick-Ind ...1.69
W.White-Cin 1.79
Weaver-Mil 1.95
Bond-Bos 2.06

Adjusted ERA
Ward-Pro 146
Weaver-Mil 134
McCormick-Ind ... 120
W.White-Cin 119
Bond-Bos 114

Opponents' Batting Avg.
Mitchell-Cin 223
Ward-Pro 231
Weaver-Mil 237
Larkin-Chi 246
W.White-Cin 252

Opponents' On Base Pct.
Weaver-Mil 247
Ward-Pro 251
Larkin-Chi 257
Mitchell-Cin 265
W.White-Cin 269

Starter Runs
Ward-Pro 29.5
W.White-Cin 26.8
Weaver-Mil 15.1
Bond-Bos 14.4
McCormick-Ind ... 8.0

Adjusted Starter Runs
Weaver-Mil 28.6
Ward-Pro 25.7
Bond-Bos 17.6
W.White-Cin 17.6
Larkin-Chi 10.2

Clutch Pitching Index
McCormick-Ind ... 152
Healey-Pro-Ind 122
Bond-Bos 119
W.White-Cin 114
Nichols-Pro 112

Relief Runs

Adjusted Relief Runs

Relief Ranking

Total Pitcher Index
Weaver-Mil........ 2.7
Ward-Pro 2.6
Larkin-Chi 1.8
Bond-Bos 1.3
W.White-Cin 7

Total Baseball Ranking
Shaffer-Ind 2.9
Ferguson-Chi 2.8
Ward-Pro 2.6
Weaver-Mil 2.4
Burdock-Bos 2.2

January 26 Troy receives notification of its admission into the NL. The Trojans are already committed to salaries totaling $10,240 for 11 players and a manager.

February 14 The Milwaukee NL club's property (Cream Citys) is sold to satisfy a bankruptcy judgment of $125.61.

February 18* At the International Association meeting, the 1878 pennant is awarded to Buffalo with a 24-8 record; Syracuse was 23-9. With no Canadian clubs in attendance, the league changes its name to the National Association.

March 25 Despite some vocal opposition from some members, the NL votes to retain its 50 cent minimum admission price. It also reinstitutes the rule making outs of fouls on third strikes caught on the first bounce.

April 1* The Northwest League is formed with Davenport, Omaha, Dubuque, and Rockford. This league refuses to affiliate with the NA or NL, setting its sights at limited attendance and salary standards. In this sense, it is the first minor league.

April 4 The Providence Grays vote to establish a "bull pen" in CF for which 15¢ admissions can be purchased starting in the fifth inning. This will become a very popular ticket, with a daily rush in the fifth.

May 30 John Ward of Providence beats Buffalo 4-0 and saves his own shutout with the innovative tactic of backing up home plate on a throw coming in from the outfield.

June 2* J. Lee Richmond, Brown University baseball star, makes his pro debut with the Worcester Brown Stockings by no-hitting Chicago in a 7-inning game 11–0. A week later, Richmond pitches Brown to the College Championship by beating Yale 3–2. Worcester will join the NL in 1880.

July 4* A holiday crowd of more than 5,000 turns out in Philadelphia to see a widely advertised game between two women's teams, the New York Blue Stockings and the Philadelphia Red Stockings. The teams, connected with variety theaters, are playing for "the championship of the U.S." The Blue Stockings win 36–24 in a loosely played game cut short when the unruly crowd gets out of control.

July 26 Syracuse's Harry McCormick hits a home run in the first and then makes it stand up by beating Boston's Tommy Bond 1-0. This will be the only time in major league history that a pitcher wins his own 1-0 game with a first-inning home run.

August 5 After Providence pitcher Bobby Mathews gives up six runs in the first two innings, he switches positions with third base Monte Ward, who pitches shutout ball the rest of the way to rally the Grays to a 7–6 win. Captain George Wright would successfully employ this pitching scheme several more times in the season.

August 7 An unusual base-path occurrence is the feature in Syracuse. Mike Dorgan, the Star runner from second base, passes Hick Carpenter, the man from third base, and crosses the plate before Carpenter is tagged out. There is as yet no specific rule about passing preceding runners, but the umpire calls both men out. The Stars beat Boston 6–5.

September 29 Will White pitches his 74th complete game of the season for Cincinnati, beating Cleveland 13-1. He will finish with 75 complete games and 680 innings pitched, establishing ML season records that will never be broken.

September 30 From the second day of the NL meeting, word leaks out of a secret agreement among the owners allowing each club to "reserve" 5 players with whom the other clubs agree not to negotiate to keep their salaries at or below current levels.

December 4 NL owners again vote to retain the 50 cent minimum admission charge despite opposition from Troy and Buffalo. The following rule changes are made: the number of balls for a walk is reduced from nine to eight. the catcher must catch the third strike on the fly to put the batter out (the first bounce no longer counting), the final outs of the last half inning need no longer be completed if the team batting last is already ahead.

BOSTON	BUFFALO	CHICAGO	CINCINNATI	CLEVELAND	PROVIDENCE	SYRACUSE	TROY
M H.Wright	M J.Clapp	M C.Anson	M D.White	M J.McCormick	M G.Wright	M M.Dorgan	M H.Phillips
1B E.Cogswell	1B O.Walker	M S.Flint	M C.McVey	1B B.Phillips	1B J.Start	M B.Holbert	M B.Ferguson
2B J.Burdock	2B C.Fulmer	1B C.Anson	1B C.McVey	2B J.Glasscock	2B M.McGeary	M J.Macullar	1B D.Brothers
SS E.Sutton	SS D.Force	2B J.Quest	2B J.Gerhardt	SS T.Carey	SS G.Wright	1B H.Carpenter	2B T.Hawkes
3B J.Morrill	3B H.Richardson	SS J.Peters	SS R.Barnes	3B F.Warner	3B B.Hague	2B J.Farrell	SS E.Caskin
LF C.Jones	LF J.Hornung	3B N.Williamson	3B W.Foley	LF B.Riley	LF T.York	SS J.Macullar	3B H.Doscher
CF J.O'Rourke	CF D.Eggler	LF A.Dalrymple	LF B.Dickerson	CF G.Strief	CF P.Hines	3B R.Woodhead	LF T.Mansell
RF S.Houck	RF B.Crowley	CF G.Gore	CF P.Hotaling	RF C.Eden	RF J.O'Rourke	LF M.Mansell	CF A.Hall
C P.Snyder	C J.Clapp	RF O.Shaffer	RF K.Kelly	C D.Kennedy	C L.Brown	CF J.Richmond	RF J.Evans
O B.Hawes	OP B.McGunnigle	C S.Flint	C D.White	CO B.Gilligan	C E.Gross	RF B.Purcell	C C.Reilley
P T.Bond	/C J.Rowe	S M.Burke	O B.Purcell	3 J.Allen	2 J.Farrell	C B.Holbert	1O A.Clapp
P C.Foley	/1 S.Libby	O1 J.Remsen	/O J.Neagle	/C H.Hoffman	/3 D.Sullivan	1O M.Dorgan	3 B.Ferguson
/P J.Tyng	P P.Galvin	/1 L.Brown	/O J.Magner	/O L.Stockwell	/C R.Kemmler	2 G.Creamer	S C.Nelson
/P L.Richmond		/O B.Harbidge	/O H.Wheeler	/O F.Gunkle	1 D.O'Leary	1 J.McGuinness	O S.Taylor
		/3 J.Stedronsky	P W.White	P J.McCormick	/C D.Allison	/3 J.Allen	S J.Shoupe
		/3 H.Doscher		P B.Mitchell	/1 B.White	/C K.Kelly	/O J.Cassidy
		/C T.Dolan			P J.Ward	/O G.Adams	/C K.Kelly
		P T.Larkin			P B.Mathews	/C F.Decker	/C B.Holbert
		P F.Hankinson				/O C.Osterhout	P G.Bradley
						/O T.Mansell	P H.Salisbury
						P H.McCormick	P F.Goldsmith
							/P P.McManus
							/P G.Gardner

TEAM	G	W	L	PCT	GB	R	OR	AB	H	2B	3B	HR	BB	SO	AVG	OBP	SLG	PRO	PRO+	BR	/A	PF	CHI	RC	SB	CS	SBA	SBR
PRO	85	59	25	.702		612	355	3392	1003	142	55	12	91	172	.296	.314	.381	.695	134	110	119	98	103	416				
BOS	84	54	30	.643	5	562	348	3217	883	138	51	20	90	222	.274	.294	.368	.662	118	68	56	102	107	357				
BUF	79	46	32	.590	10	394	365	2906	733	105	54	2	78	314	.252	.272	.328	.600	98	1	-9	102	95	265				
CHI	83	46	33	.582	10.5	437	411	3116	808	167	32	3	73	294	.259	.276	.336	.612	98	14	-13	106	96	297				
CIN	81	43	37	.538	14	485	464	3085	813	127	53	8	66	207	.264	.279	.347	.626	115	27	50	95	105	306				
CLE	82	27	55	.329	31	322	461	2987	666	116	29	4	37	214	.223	.232	.285	.517	73	-83	-80	99	96	203				
SYR	71	22	48	.314	30	276	462	2611	592	61	19	5	28	238	.227	.235	.270	.505	78	-82	-51	89	98	170				
TRO	77	19	56	.253	35.5	321	543	2841	673	102	24	4	45	182	.237	.249	.294	.543	87	-54	-31	93	93	213				
TOT	321					3409		24155	6171	958	317	58	508	1843	.255	.271	.329	.599										

TEAM	CG	SH	SV	IP	H	H/G	HR	BB	SO	RAT	ERA	ERA+	OAV	OOB	PR	/A	PF	CPI	FA	E	DP	FW	PW	BW	SBW	DIF
PRO	73	3	2	776	765	8.9	9	62	329	9.6	2.18	108	.243	.258	27	15	94	99	.902	382	41	1.8	1.4	11.0		2.8
BOS	80	13	0	753	757	9.0	9	46	230	9.6	2.19	114	.251	.262	26	25	100	107	.913	319	58	4.9	2.3	5.2		-.3
BUF	78	8	0	713	698	8.8	3	47	198	9.4	2.34	112	.242	.254	13	22	100	87	.906	331	62	2.9	2.0	-.8		2.9
CHI	82	6	0	744	762	9.2	5	57	211	9.9	2.46	105	.244	.258	3	9	103	86	.900	381	52	1.3	.8	-1.2		5.5
CIN	79	4	0	726	756	9.4	11	81	246	10.4	2.29	102	.248	.267	16	4	93	104	.877	454	48	-3.1	.4	4.6		1.1
CLE	79	3	0	741	818	9.9	4	116	287	11.3	2.65	95	.265	.292	-12	-12	100	111	.889	406	42	-.3	-1.1	-7.4		-5.3
SYR	64	5	0	649	775	10.7	4	52	132	11.5	3.19	74	.277	.290	-50	-59	95	96	.873	398	37	-2.7	-5.4	-4.7		-.2
TRO	75	3	0	695	840	10.9	13	47	210	11.5	2.80	89	.275	.286	-23	-22	100	110	.875	460	44	-4.4	-2.0	-2.9		-9.2
TOT	610	45	2	5797		9.6				10.4	2.50		.255	.271					.892	3131	384					

Runs		Hits		Doubles		Triples		Home Runs		Total Bases	
Jones-Bos	85	Hines-Pro	146	Eden-Cle	31	Dickerson-Cin	14	Jones-Bos	9	Hines-Pro	197
Hines-Pro	81	O'Rourke-Pro	126	York-Pro	25	Williamson-Chi	13	O'Rourke-Pro	6	Jones-Bos	181
Wright-Pro	79	Kelly-Cin	120	Hines-Pro	25	Kelly-Cin	12	Brouthers-Tro	4	Kelly-Cin	170
Kelly-Cin	78	Jones-Bos	112	Dalrymple-Chi	25	O'Rourke-Bos	11	Eden-Cle	3	O'Rourke-Pro	166
Dickerson-Cin	73	D.White-Cin	110	Houck-Bos	24					O'Rourke-Bos	165

Runs Batted In		Runs Produced		Bases On Balls		Batting Average		On Base Percentage		Slugging Average	
O'Rourke-Bos	62	Jones-Bos	138	Jones-Bos	29	Anson-Chi	.317	O'Rourke-Pro	.371	O'Rourke-Bos	.521
Jones-Bos	62	Hines-Pro	131	Williamson-Chi	24	Hines-Pro	.357	Hines-Pro	.369	Jones-Bos	.510
Dickerson-Cin	57	Dickerson-Cin	128	York-Pro	19	O'Rourke-Pro	.348	Jones-Bos	.367	Kelly-Cin	.493
McVey-Cin	55	O'Rourke-Bos	125	Richardson-Buf	16	Kelly-Cin	.348	Kelly-Cin	.363	Hines-Pro	.482
		Kelly-Cin	123	Barnes-Cin	16	O'Rourke-Bos	.341	O'Rourke-Bos	.357	O'Rourke-Pro	.459

Production		Adjusted Production		Batter Runs		Adjusted Batter Runs		Clutch Hitting Index		Runs Created	
O'Rourke-Bos	.877	Kelly-Cin	188	Jones-Bos	33.1	Hines-Pro	34.3	Gerhardt-Cin	150	Hines-Pro	75
Jones-Bos	.877	Jones-Bos	182	Hines-Pro	32.9	Kelly-Cin	32.1	McVey-Cin	143	Jones-Bos	68
Kelly-Cin	.855	O'Rourke-Bos	181	Kelly-Cin	28.1	Jones-Bos	31.2	Brown-Pro-Chi	137	Kelly-Cin	63
Hines-Pro	.851	Hines-Pro	181	O'Rourke-Bos	28.0	O'Rourke-Pro	28.4	Morrill-Bos	124	O'Rourke-Pro	63
O'Rourke-Pro	.829	O'Rourke-Pro	174	O'Rourke-Pro	27.2	O'Rourke-Bos	26.4	W.White-Cin	122	O'Rourke-Bos	60

Total Average		Stolen Bases		Stolen Base Average		Stolen Base Runs		Fielding Runs		Total Player Rating	
Jones-Bos	.864							Snyder-Bos	23.9	Kelly-Cin	3.9
O'Rourke-Bos	.828							Wright-Pro	20.5	Jones-Bos	3.5
Kelly-Cin	.791							Shaffer-Chi	20.3	Hines-Pro	3.3
Hines-Pro	.779							Evans-Tro	17.7	Williamson-Chi	3.2
O'Rourke-Pro	.758							Fulmer-Buf	17.4	Wright-Pro	3.2

Wins		Win Percentage		Games		Complete Games		Shutouts		Saves	
Ward-Pro	47	Ward-Pro	.712	W.White-Cin	76	W.White-Cin	75	Bond-Bos	11	Ward-Pro	1
W.White-Cin	43	Bond-Bos	.694	Ward-Pro	70	Galvin-Buf	65	Galvin-Buf	6	Mathews-Pro	1
Bond-Bos	43	Hankinson-Chi	.600	Galvin-Buf	66	McCormick-Cle	59	McCormick-Syr	5		
Galvin-Buf	37	W.White-Cin	.581	Bond-Bos	64	Bond-Bos	59	W.White-Cin	4		
Larkin-Chi	31	Galvin-Buf	.578	McCormick-Cle	62	Ward-Pro	58	Larkin-Chi	4		

Innings Pitched		Fewest Hits/Game		Fewest BB/Game		Strikeouts		Strikeouts/Game		Ratio	
W.White-Cin	680.0	McGunnigle-Buf	8.48	Bond-Bos	.39	Ward-Pro	239	McGunnigle-Buf	4.65	Bond-Bos	9.19
Galvin-Buf	593.0	Ward-Pro	8.75	Galvin-Buf	.47	W.White-Cin	232	Mathews-Pro	4.29	Ward-Pro	9.31
Ward-Pro	587.0	Bond-Bos	8.80	Bradley-Tro	.48	McCormick-Cle	197	Mitchell-Cle	4.16	Galvin-Buf	9.35
Bond-Bos	555.1	Galvin-Buf	8.88	Larkin-Chi	.53	Bond-Bos	155	Ward-Pro	3.66	Larkin-Chi	9.54
McCormick-Cle	546.1	W.White-Cin	8.95	Ward-Pro	.55	Larkin-Chi	142	McCormick-Cle	3.25	McGunnigle-Buf	9.68

Earned Run Average		Adjusted ERA		Opponents' Batting Avg.		Opponents' On Base Pct.		Starter Runs		Adjusted Starter Runs	
Bond-Bos	1.96	Bond-Bos	127	McGunnigle-Buf	.235	Larkin-Chi	.250	W.White-Cin	38.6	Bond-Bos	32.3
W.White-Cin	1.99	W.White-Cin	117	W.White-Cin	.238	Ward-Pro	.250	Bond-Bos	33.0	W.White-Cin	26.2
Ward-Pro	2.15	Galvin-Buf	115	Galvin-Buf	.239	Galvin-Buf	.253	Ward-Pro	22.8	Galvin-Buf	22.2
Salisbury-Tro	2.22	Salisbury-Tro	112	Larkin-Chi	.240	W.White-Cin	.256	Galvin-Buf	14.5	Ward-Pro	13.7
Galvin-Buf	2.28	Ward-Pro	110	Galvin-Buf	.243	Bond-Bos	.259	Goldsmith-Tro	6.5	Larkin-Chi	7.4

Clutch Pitching Index		Relief Runs		Adjusted Relief Runs		Relief Ranking		Total Pitcher Index		Total Baseball Ranking	
Salisbury-Tro	125							Bond-Bos	3.8	Kelly-Cin	3.9
Mathews-Pro	122							Ward-Pro	2.9	Bond-Bos	3.6
Bond-Bos	117							Galvin-Buf	2.8	Jones-Bos	3.5
McCormick-Cle	111							McCormick-Cle	.7	Hines-Pro	3.3
Mitchell-Cle	109							Goldsmith-Tro	.6	Williamson-Chi	3.2

February 12 The Boston club cuts the price of season tickets from $14 to $12 after the Red Stockings failed to win their third straight pennant last season.

February 25* Yale chooses not to join the American Collegiate Baseball Association because of professional players on other teams.

April 14 The new Cincinnati ballpark on Bank Street and Western Avenue (three blocks north of where Crosley Field will be located) is opened with an exhibition game between the Reds and the Washington Nationals. The park seats 3,490 and will serve professional teams in three leagues: NL in 1880, AA in 1882–83, and UA in 1884.

May 1 Opening Day in the NL. In Cincinnati, the Chicagos spoil the official opening of the Reds' new park by beating them 4-3 with two runs in the bottom of the ninth. This is the first pro game ended in "sudden death," as the old rules required that the full inning be played out even if the team batting last was already ahead.

May 20 Chicago captain Cap Anson begins using hurlers Larry Corcoran and Fred Goldsmith in alternating games, thereby establishing the first "pitching rotation" ever.

June 2 Buffalo fines first baseman Oscar Walker $50 for breaking his temperance pledge.

June 10 Boston's Charley Jones, last year's home run king with nine, hits two home runs in one inning, becoming the first big leaguer to accomplish this feat. Both come off Buffalo's Tom Poorman in the eighth inning of a 19-3 rout.

June 12 John Lee Richmond pitches the first perfect game in professional history, leading Worcester to a 1–0 victory over Cleveland. Right fielder Lon Knight saves the no-hitter by throwing out a batter at first base. Six days later, John Montgomery Ward pitches a perfect game in Providence against Buffalo, winning 5–0, the second perfect game in NL history. The third will not be pitched until 1964, when Jim Bunning turns the trick.

July 8 Chicago wins its 21st consecutive decision, beating Providence 5-4. This streak will be surpassed only once in major league history, by the New York Giants in 1916. The victory raises Chicago's won-lost record to 35-3, far ahead of second-place Providence's 21-16 mark.

August 28 Cincinnati commits 9 errors in the fourth inning and 16 in the game as the Reds are trounced by Troy 13-2. Second baseman Charlie Smith makes four errors on his way to an NL record 89 errors by a second baseman in one season.

September 2 The first night baseball is played in Nantasket Beach, Massachusetts, between teams from two Boston department stores, Jordan Marsh and R. H. White. The Boston *Post* reports the next day that "A clear, pure, bright light was produced, very strong and yet very pleasant to the sight" by the 12 carbon-arc electric lamps. The game ends in a 16-16 tie.

September 8* The Polo Grounds in New York at 110th Street between Fifth and Sixth Avenues is leased by the new Metropolitan club. The grounds, which have been used for polo matches, will be converted into the first commercial baseball park to be built on Manhattan Island. It opens three weeks later with a 4-2 Mets victory over the NA champion Nationals.

September 29* The Polo Grounds is opened with a 4–2 victory by the non-league Mets over the NA champion Nationals. The crowd of around 2,500 is the largest for a ball game in the New York area in several years.

September 30 Chicago wins its final game to finish the season with a 67-17 record, establishing an NL record for winning percentage (.798), although winning percentage will not be used officially in the league until 1884. Providence is second, 15 games behind.

December 9 The NL adopts several new rules, including: moving the pitcher's box back 5 feet so that its front line is 50 feet from the back point of home plate; reducing the number of called balls for a walk, from 8 to 7; eliminating substitutions (except in the case of illness or injury), the old rule having allowed subs in the first inning but not thereafter; prohibiting all pinch runners (this rule will be ignored many times).

	BOSTON		BUFFALO		CHICAGO		CINCINNATI		CLEVELAND		PROVIDENCE		TROY		WORCESTER
M	H.Wright	M	S.Crane	M	C.Anson	M	J.Clapp	M	J.McCormick	M	M.McGeary	M	B.Ferguson	M	F.Bancroft
1B	C.Foley	1B	D.Esterbrook	1B	C.Anson	1B	J.Reilly	1B	B.Phillips	M	M.Ward	1B	E.Cogswell	1B	C.Sullivan
2B	J.Burdock	2B	D.Force	2B	J.Quest	2B	P.Smith	2B	F.Dunlap	M	M.Dorgan	2B	B.Ferguson	2B	G.Creamer
SS	E.Sutton	SS	M.Moynahan	SS	T.Burns	SS	L.Say	SS	J.Glasscock	1B	J.Start	SS	E.Caskin	SS	A.Irwin
3B	J.Morrill	3B	H.Richardson	3B	N.Williamson	3B	H.Carpenter	3B	F.Hankinson	2B	J.Farrell	3B	R.Connor	3B	A.Whitney
LF	C.Jones	LF	J.Hornung	LF	A.Dalrymple	LF	M.Mansell	LF	N.Hanlon	SS	J.Peters	LF	P.Gillespie	LF	G.Wood
CF	Jo.O'Rourke	CF	B.Crowley	CF	G.Gore	CF	B.Purcell	CF	P.Hotaling	3B	G.Bradley	CF	J.Cassidy	CF	H.Stovey
RF	Ja.O'Rourke	RF	E.Stearns	RF	K.Kelly	RF	J.Manning	RF	O.Shaffer	LF	T.York	RF	J.Evans	RF	L.Knight
C	P.Powers	C	J.Rowe	C	S.Flint	C	J.Clapp	C	D.Kennedy	CF	P.Hines	C	B.Holbert	C	C.Bennett
										RF	M.Dorgan				
S	J.Richmond	1O	O.Walker	O	T.Beals	3	D.White	3	M.McGeary	C	E.Gross	1	B.Tobin	C	D.Bushong
C	S.Trott	SO	A.Latham	/O	T.Poorman	S3	A.Leonard	C	B.Gilligan			O	B.Dickerson	OP	F.Corey
O	S.Houck	O	D.Driscoll	OC	C.Reilley	/O	A.Hall	O	S.Houck	C	B.Ewing	O	B.Dickerson
C	J.Bergh	S	D.Mack	P	L.Corcoran	O	J.Sommer	/O	H.Wheeler	3	M.McGeary	/C	B.Harbidge	/O	J.Dorgan
/O	S.Dignan	2	C.Fulmer	P	F.Goldsmith	O	H.Wheeler					/1	D.Brouthers	/3	J.Ellick
/O	D.O'Leary	2	S.Crane			/S	S.Wright	P	J.McCormick	P	J.Ward	/C	J.Straub	/1	B.Tobin
/C	D.Sullivan	/O	C.Radbourn	/P	C.Guth	/3	A.Booth	P	G.Gardner			/C	M.Lawlor	/O	S.Dignan
/S	G.Wright	/C	T.Kearns									/C	F.Haley	/O	B.Geer
/O	J.Leary	/C	J.Keenan			P	W.White					/O	D.Higham	/O	B.McGunnigle
												/C	C.Ahearn		
P	T.Bond	P	P.Galvin									/C	F.Briody	P	L.Richmond
P	C.Foley	P	S.Wiedman												
		P	T.Poorman									P	M.Welch	/P	T.Nichols
												P	T.Keefe		
		/P	B.McGunnigle												
												/P	T.Larkin		
												/P	F.Mountain		

TEAM	G	W	L	PCT	GB	R	OR	AB	H	2B	3B	HR	BB	SO	AVG	OBP	SLG	PRO	PRO+	BR	/A	PF	CHI	RC	SB	CS	SBA	SBR
CHI	86	67	17	.798		538	317	3135	876	164	39	4	104	217	.279	.303	.360	.663	119	81	52	106	109	350				
PRO	87	52	32	.619	15	419	299	3196	793	114	34	8	89	186	.248	.268	.313	.581	101	-6	7	97	102	275				
CLE	85	47	37	.560	20	387	337	3002	726	130	52	7	76	237	.242	.261	.327	.588	102	-1	7	98	99	262				
TRO	83	41	42	.494	25.5	392	438	3007	755	114	37	5	120	260	.251	.280	.319	.599	100	15	-6	105	95	275				
WOR	85	40	43	.482	26.5	412	370	3024	699	129	52	8	81	278	.231	.251	.316	.567	86	-21	-54	109	110	246				
BOS	86	40	44	.476	27	416	456	3080	779	134	41	20	105	221	.253	.278	.343	.621	115	34	48	97	95	300				
BUF	85	24	58	.293	42	331	502	2962	669	104	37	3	90	327	.226	.249	.289	.538	82	-48	-54	102	97	218				
CIN	83	21	59	.263	44	296	472	2895	649	91	36	7	75	267	.224	.244	.288	.532	82	-54	-50	99	91	208				
TOT	340					3191		24301	5946	980	328	62	740	1993	.245	.267	.320	.587										

TEAM	CG	SH	SV	IP	H	H/G	HR	BB	SO	RAT	ERA	ERA+	OAV	OOB	PR	/A	PF	CPI	FA	E	DP	FW	PW	BW	SBW	DIF
CHI	80	8	3	775	622	7.2	8	129	367	8.7	1.93	126	.209	.242	38	43	102	83	.913	329	41	2.3	4.2	5.1		13.4
PRO	75	13	2	799	663	7.5	7	51	286	8.0	1.64	134	.215	.228	65	49	93	87	.910	357	53	1.1	4.8	.7		3.5
CLE	83	7	1	759²	685	8.1	4	98	289	9.3	1.90	124	.228	.253	40	39	99	101	.910	330	52	2.0	3.8	.7		-1.5
TRO	81	4	0	738	760	9.3	8	112	169	10.6	2.74	92	.255	.282	-30	-18	106	100	.900	366	58	-.3	-1.7	-.6		2.2
WOR	68	7	5	762²	709	8.4	13	97	297	9.5	2.27	115	.233	.257	9	28	109	94	.906	355	49	.7	2.7	-5.2		.3
BOS	70	4	0	744²	840	10.2	2	86	187	11.2	3.08	96	.276	.276	-59	-67	96	102	.901	367	54	.3	-6.5	4.7		-.5
BUF	72	6	1	739	879	10.7	10	78	186	11.7	3.09	79	.279	.297	-59	-52	104	108	.891	408	55	-2.1	-5.1	-5.2		-4.6
CIN	79	3	0	713¹	785	9.9	10	88	208	11.0	2.44	102	.259	.280	-5	5	105	116	.877	437	49	-4.1	.5	-4.9		-10.6
TOT	608	52	12	6031¹		8.9				10.0	2.37		.245	.267					.901	2949	411					

Runs	Hits	Doubles	Triples	Home Runs	Total Bases
Dalrymple-Chi 91	Dalrymple-Chi 126	Dunlap-Cle 27	Stovey-Wor 14	Stovey-Wor 6	Dalrymple-Chi 175
Stovey-Wor 76	Anson-Chi 120	Dalrymple-Chi 25	Dalrymple-Chi 12	J.O'Rourke-Bos 6	Stovey-Wor 161
Kelly-Chi 72	Gore-Chi 116	Anson-Chi 24	J.O'Rourke-Bos 11	Jones-Bos 5	J.O'Rourke-Bos ... 160
J.O'Rourke-Bos 71	Hines-Pro 115	Gore-Chi 23	Hornung-Buf 11	Dunlap-Cle 4	Dunlap-Cle 160
Gore-Chi 70	Connor-Tro 113	J.O'Rourke-Bos 22	Phillips-Cle 10		Connor-Tro 156

Runs Batted In	Runs Produced	Bases On Balls	Batting Average	On Base Percentage	Slugging Average
Anson-Chi 74	Kelly-Chi 131	Ferguson-Tro 24	Gore-Chi ..... .360	Gore-Chi ..... .399	Gore-Chi ..... .463
Kelly-Chi 60	Dalrymple-Chi 127	J.O'Rourke-Bos 21	Anson-Chi ..... .337	Anson-Chi ..... .362	Connor-Tro ..... .459
Gore-Chi 47	Anson-Chi 127	Gore-Chi 21	Connor-Tro ..... .332	Connor-Tro ..... .357	Dalrymple-Chi ..... .458
Connor-Tro 47	Gore-Chi 115	Clapp-Cin 21	Dalrymple-Chi ..... .330	Dalrymple-Chi ..... .335	Stovey-Wor ..... .454
J.O'Rourke-Bos 45	J.O'Rourke-Bos ... 110	Crowley-Buf 19	Burns-Chi ..... .309	Burns-Chi ..... .333	J.O'Rourke-Bos ..... .441

Production	Adjusted Production	Batter Runs	Adjusted Batter Runs	Clutch Hitting Index	Runs Created
Gore-Chi ..... .862	Gore-Chi 180	Gore-Chi 30.4	Gore-Chi 26.0	Anson-Chi 178	Gore-Chi 61
Connor-Tro ..... .816	Connor-Tro 166	Connor-Tro 25.4	J.O'Rourke-Bos ... 22.2	Hotaling-Cle 147	Dalrymple-Chi 60
Dalrymple-Chi ..... .793	Jones-Bos 159	Dalrymple-Chi 24.5	Connor-Tro 21.8	Kelly-Chi 141	Connor-Tro 57
Anson-Chi ..... .781	J.O'Rourke-Bos ... 158	Anson-Chi 22.9	Dalrymple-Chi 20.2	Richmond-Wor 131	Anson-Chi 55
J.O'Rourke-Bos ..... .756	Dalrymple-Chi ... 156	J.O'Rourke-Bos ... 19.9	Hines-Pro 19.1	Creamer-Wor 127	J.O'Rourke-Bos 52

Total Average	Stolen Bases	Stolen Base Average	Stolen Base Runs	Fielding Runs	Total Player Rating
Gore-Chi ..... .825				Irwin-Wor 31.2	Irwin-Wor 3.4
Connor-Tro ..... .744				Force-Buf 30.9	Clapp-Cin 2.9
Dalrymple-Chi ..... .695				Bradley-Pro 19.2	Gore-Chi 2.8
Anson-Chi ..... .691				Shaffer-Cle 17.2	Dunlap-Cle 2.7
J.O'Rourke-Bos ..... .688				Clapp-Cin 17.2	Hines-Pro 2.4

Wins	Win Percentage	Games	Complete Games	Shutouts	Saves
McCormick-Cle 45	Goldsmith-Chi ..... .875	Richmond-Wor 74	McCormick-Cle 72	Ward-Pro 8	Richmond-Wor 3
Corcoran-Chi 43	Corcoran-Chi ..... .754	McCormick-Cle 74	Welch-Tro 64	McCormick-Cle 7	Corey-Wor 2
Ward-Pro 39	Ward-Pro ..... .619	Ward-Pro 70	Ward-Pro 59	Richmond-Wor 5	Corcoran-Chi 2
Welch-Tro 34	McCormick-Cle ..... .616	Welch-Tro 65	W.White-Cin 58	Galvin-Buf 5	
Richmond-Wor 32	Welch-Tro ..... .531				

Innings Pitched	Fewest Hits/Game	Fewest BB/Game	Strikeouts	Strikeouts/Game	Ratio
McCormick-Cle .. 657.2	Keefe-Tro 5.83	Bradley-Pro ..... .28	Corcoran-Chi 268	Corcoran-Chi 4.50	Keefe-Tro 7.20
Ward-Pro 595.0	Corcoran-Chi 6.78	Galvin-Buf ..... .63	McCormick-Cle 260	Goldsmith-Chi 3.85	Bradley-Pro 7.53
Richmond-Wor 590.2	Bradley-Pro 7.26	Ward-Pro ..... .68	Richmond-Wor 243	Richmond-Wor 3.70	Ward-Pro 8.26
Welch-Tro 574.0	Ward-Pro 7.58	Wiedman-Buf ..... .71	Ward-Pro 230	McCormick-Cle 3.56	Corcoran-Chi 8.44
Corcoran-Chi 536.1	Corey-Wor 7.95	Goldsmith-Chi ..... .77	W.White-Cin 161	Ward-Pro 3.48	Goldsmith-Chi 8.86

Earned Run Average	Adjusted ERA	Opponents' Batting Avg.	Opponents' On Base Pct.	Starter Runs	Adjusted Starter Runs
Keefe-Tro ..... .86	Keefe-Tro 294	Keefe-Tro ..... .178	Keefe-Tro ..... .212	Ward-Pro 42.0	McCormick-Cle 36.8
Bradley-Pro 1.38	Bradley-Pro 160	Corcoran-Chi ..... .199	Bradley-Pro ..... .217	McCormick-Cle 38.5	Ward-Pro 30.8
Ward-Pro 1.74	Goldsmith-Chi 138	Bradley-Pro ..... .210	Ward-Pro ..... .232	Corcoran-Chi 25.5	Richmond-Wor 29.5
Goldsmith-Chi 1.75	McCormick-Cle 127	Ward-Pro ..... .217	Corcoran-Chi ..... .236	Bradley-Pro 21.7	Corcoran-Chi 28.3
McCormick-Cle 1.85	Ward-Pro 127	Corey-Wor ..... .219	Corey-Wor ..... .239	Keefe-Tro 17.7	W.White-Cin 19.6

Clutch Pitching Index	Relief Runs	Adjusted Relief Runs	Relief Ranking	Total Pitcher Index	Total Baseball Ranking
W.White-Cin 124				McCormick-Cle 4.0	Ward-Pro 4.1
Bond-Bos 114				Ward-Pro 3.4	McCormick-Cle 3.7
Poorman-Buf-Chi 112				Corcoran-Chi 3.1	Irwin-Wor 3.4
Galvin-Buf 111				Keefe-Tro 2.2	Bradley-Pro 3.4
Goldsmith-Chi 109				Goldsmith-Chi 1.9	Clapp-Cin 2.9

March 8 The NL meets and adopts an 84-game schedule. An enterprising newsman gets the various magnates to predict the winner in the coming pennant race, Chicago the consensus choice with five votes.

April 11* The Eastern Association is organized to link independent clubs in a loose pennant race. The clubs include the Nationals, Mets, Atlantics, Athletics, New Yorks, Quicksteps (of NY), and New Bostons.

May 4 Boston pitcher Jim Whitney shuts out Providence 4-0. The hardworking righthander will wind up leading the NL in both wins and losses (with a 31-33 record), a feat not repeated in the major leagues until Phil Niekro does it in 1979.

May 20 Chicago resorts to trickery to beat Boston 5–4. Mike Kelly scores the go-ahead run from second base on a groundout by cutting third base by some 30 feet.

June 20 A new Red Stocking team in Cincinnati takes the field for the first time. This club would be among the founders of the new league, the American Association, next year and would eventually become the NL Reds.

June 25 Chicago's George Gore steals seven bases as the Whites beat Providence, second five times and third twice. This record will be tied only once, by Billy Hamilton on August 31, 1894.

August 14 Statistics published in the Chicago *Tribune* put Dan Brouthers at the top of the batting list with a .390 average. Cap Anson is second with .377. Official figures at the end of the season will declare Anson batting champ with a .399 average, Brouthers finishing seventh at .318.

August 21* The Eclipse club refuses to allow a black man, catcher M. Fleetwood Walker, to play for the visiting Cleveland Whites in a game in Louisville, much to the disgust of many fans and sportswriters.

August 23 Boston left fielder Joe Hornung makes 10 putouts and one assist as the Reds beat Buffalo 4–3. This one-game record of 11 chances accepted by a left fielder still stands.

September 10 In a game in Albany, Troy's Roger Connor hits the first grand slam in NL history. The blow comes off Worcester's Lee Richmond with two out in the bottom of the ninth inning and wins the game 8-7.

September 25 Although the league has offered membership to the Mets and the Athletics and been turned down, it is announced that all eight teams from this year will be back in the NL next season, a first for the league.

September 30 The NL meeting adopts an "ironclad" contract that gives the club the right to fine a player for any conduct the club deems detrimental to its interest. Furthermore, the player assumes the responsibility for all risks of injury or illness and must pay for his own medical treatment.

October 8 Chris Von der Ahe, president of the corporation that runs Sportsman's Park in St. Louis, signs the members of the previously independent St. Louis Browns semiprofessional club, giving Von der Ahe control over the players for the first time, a key step toward the establishment of the club that will eventually become the four-time champion of the American Association.

October 10 Cincinnati baseball backers meet in Pittsburgh with H. Denny McKnight and issue a call to other independent club operators to meet November 2 to form a major league independent of the NL. A few weeks later, he organizes a new Allegheny Baseball Club of Pittsburgh in anticipation of the proposed new league.

BOSTON	BUFFALO	CHICAGO	CLEVELAND	DETROIT	PROVIDENCE	TROY	WORCESTER
M H.Wright	M J.O'Rourke	M C.Anson	M M.McGeary	M F.Bancroft	M J.Farrell	M B.Ferguson	M M.Dorgan
1B J.Morrill	1B D.Brouthers	1B C.Anson	M J.Clapp	1B M.Powell	M T.York	1B R.Connor	M H.Stovey
2B J.Burdock	2B D.Force	2B J.Quest	1B B.Phillips	2B J.Gerhardt	1B J.Start	2B B.Ferguson	1B H.Stovey
SS R.Barnes	SS J.Peters	SS T.Burns	2B F.Dunlap	SS S.Houck	2B J.Farrell	SS E.Caskin	2B G.Creamer
3B E.Sutton	3B J.O'Rourke	3B N.Williamson	SS J.Glasscock	3B A.Whitney	SS B.McClellan	3B F.Hankinson	SS A.Irwin
LF J.Hornung	LF B.Purcell	LF A.Dalrymple	3B G.Bradley	LF G.Wood	3B J.Denny	LF P.Gillespie	3B H.Carpenter
CF B.Crowley	CF H.Richardson	CF G.Gore	LF M.Moynahan	CF N.Hanlon	LF T.York	CF J.Cassidy	LF B.Dickerson
RF F.Lewis	RF C.Foley	RF K.Kelly	CF J.Remsen	RF L.Knight	CF P.Hines	RF J.Evans	CF P.Hotaling
C P.Snyder	C J.Rowe	C S.Flint	RF O.Shaffer	C C.Bennett	RF J.Ward	C B.Ewing	RF F.Corey
			C J.Clapp		C E.Gross		C D.Bushong
C P.Deasley	12 D.White	O H.Nicol	1 L.Brown	1 L.Brown		C B.Holbert	
O J.Richmond	C S.Sullivan	/3 A.Piercy	C D.Kennedy	C D.Reilley	CS B.Gilligan		1O M.Dorgan
O B.Mathews	3 J.Morrissey		O B.Taylor	/3 D.Troy	O L.Brown		S C.Nelson
/S G.Wright	/2 P.Smith	P L.Corcoran	O B.Purcell	/O M.Dorgan	/S H.Myers		/O P.Smith
/1 P.Quinn	/O E.Swartwood	P F.Goldsmith	3 M.McGeary	/C S.Trott			/O B.Taylor
/S S.Wright	/O J.Manning		3 P.Smith	/3 W.Foley	P C.Radbourn		/O L.Pike
			/3 H.Doscher	/O J.Leary	P B.Mathews		/C C.Reilley
P J.Whitney	P P.Galvin		/C P.Powers	/S E.Stearns			/C P.Quinn
P J.Fox	P J.Lynch		/C R.Kemmler	/O D.O'Leary			/S A.Stratton
				/S G.Bradley			/O M.Flaherty
/P T.Bond			P J.McCormick	/3 M.Moynahan			
			P T.Nolan	/3 B.Taylor			P L.Richmond
				/3 S.Wise			P H.McCormick
				P G.Derby			
				P S.Wiedman			
				P F.Mountain			
				/P T.Mullane			
				/P W.White			

TEAM	G	W	L	PCT	GB	R	OR	AB	H	2B	3B	HR	BB	SO	AVG	OBP	SLG	PRO	PRO+	BR	/A	PF	CHI	RC	SB	CS	SBA	SBR
CHI	84	56	28	.667		550	379	3114	918	157	36	12	140	224	.295	.325	.380	.705	119	85	60	105	105	394				
PRO	85	47	37	.560	9	447	426	3077	780	144	37	11	146	214	.253	.287	.335	.622	100	-4	3	98	104	304				
BUF	83	45	38	.542	10.5	440	447	3019	797	157	50	12	108	270	.264	.289	.361	.650	109	22	28	99	99	323				
DET	84	41	43	.488	15	439	429	2995	780	131	53	17	136	250	.260	.293	.357	.650	103	22	4	104	99	320				
TRO	85	39	45	.464	17	399	429	3046	754	124	31	5	140	240	.248	.281	.314	.595	86	-32	-53	105	100	275				
BOS	83	38	45	.458	17.5	349	410	2916	733	121	27	5	110	193	.251	.279	.317	.596	94	-31	-14	91	93	264				
CLE	85	36	48	.429	20	392	414	3117	796	120	39	7	132	224	.255	.286	.326	.612	100	-16	6	95	93	297				
WOR	83	32	50	.390	23	410	492	3093	781	114	31	7	121	169	.253	.281	.316	.597	86	-31	-54	106	102	281				
TOT	336					3426		24377	6339	1068	304	76	1033	1784	.260	.289	.338	.627										

TEAM	CG	SH	SV	IP	H	H/G	HR	BB	SO	RAT	ERA	ERA+	OAV	OOB	PR	/A	PF	CPI	FA	E	DP	FW	PW	BW	SBW	DIF
CHI	81	9	0	744²	722	8.7	14	122	228	10.2	2.43	113	.243	.273	29	26	99	97	.916	309	54	2.1	2.4	5.6		3.9
PRO	76	7	0	757²	756	9.0	5	138	264	10.6	2.40	111	.243	.275	32	22	96	94	.896	390	66	-2.0	2.1	.3		4.7
BUF	72	5	0	742¹	881	10.7	9	89	185	11.8	2.84	98	.281	.301	-5	-5	100	114	.892	408	48	-3.4	2.6	.4		4.8
DET	83	10	0	744²	785	9.5	8	137	265	11.1	2.65	110	.257	.289	11	22	105	102	.906	338	80	.5	2.1	.4		-3.9
TRO	85	8	0	770	813	9.5	11	159	207	11.4	2.97	99	.265	.301	-17	-2	106	102	.917	311	70	2.2	-.2	-5.0		-.0
BOS	72	6	3	730²	763	9.4	9	143	199	11.2	2.71	98	.258	.292	5	-4	96	103	.909	325	54	1.0	-.4	-1.3		-2.8
CLE	82	2	0	760	737	8.7	9	126	240	10.2	2.68	98	.258	.274	8	-5	94	87	.904	348	68	.2	-.5	-6.3		.6
WOR	80	5	0	737¹	882	10.8	11	120	196	12.2	3.54	85	.288	.315	-63	-43	109	101	.903	353	50	-.5	-4.0	-5.0		.6
TOT	631	52	3	5987¹		9.5				11.1	2.77		.260	.289					.905	2782	490					

Runs		Hits		Doubles		Triples		Home Runs		Total Bases	
Gore-Chi	86	Anson-Chi	137	Kelly-Chi	27	Rowe-Buf	11	Brouthers-Buf	8	Anson-Chi	175
Kelly-Chi	84	Dalrymple-Chi	117	Hines-Pro	27	Phillips-Cle	10	Bennett-Det	7	Dunlap-Cle	156
Dalrymple-Chi	72	Dickerson-Wor	116	Stovey-Wor	25			Farrell-Pro	5	Kelly-Chi	153
O'Rourke-Buf	71			Dunlap-Cle	25			Burns-Chi	4	Dalrymple-Chi	150
Farrell-Pro	69			White-Buf	24					Dickerson-Wor	149

Runs Batted In		Runs Produced		Bases On Balls		Batting Average		On Base Percentage		Slugging Average	
Anson-Chi	82	Anson-Chi	148	Clapp-Cle	35	Anson-Chi	.399	Anson-Chi	.442	Brouthers-Buf	.541
Bennett-Det	64	Kelly-Chi	137	York-Pro	29	Powell-Det	.338	York-Pro	.362	Anson-Chi	.510
Kelly-Chi	55	Gore-Chi	129	Ferguson-Tro	29	Rowe-Buf	.333	Brouthers-Buf	.361	Rowe-Buf	.480
		Knight-Det	118	Farrell-Pro	29	Start-Pro	.328	Dunlap-Cle	.358	Bennett-Det	.478
		Richardson-Buf	113			Dunlap-Cle	.325	Gore-Chi	.354	Dunlap-Cle	.444

Production		Adjusted Production		Batter Runs		Adjusted Batter Runs		Clutch Hitting Index		Runs Created	
Anson-Chi	.952	Anson-Chi	189	Anson-Chi	38.9	Anson-Chi	34.7	Knight-Det	164	Anson-Chi	79
Brouthers-Buf	.902	Brouthers-Buf	182	Brouthers-Buf	24.1	Brouthers-Buf	25.0	Anson-Chi	145	Dunlap-Cle	57
Bennett-Det	.819	Dunlap-Cle	159	Dunlap-Cle	20.0	Dunlap-Cle	23.8	Ward-Pro	143	Kelly-Chi	55
Dunlap-Cle	.802	York-Pro	150	Bennett-Det	18.3	York-Pro	18.9	Radbourn-Pro	135	Brouthers-Buf	54
York-Pro	.790	Bennett-Det	149	Kelly-Chi	18.0	O'Rourke-Buf	16.0	White-Buf	128	Dalrymple-Chi	54

Total Average		Stolen Bases		Stolen Base Average		Stolen Base Runs		Fielding Runs		Total Player Rating	
Anson-Chi	.976							Ewing-Tro	25.3	Bennett-Det	3.3
Brouthers-Buf	.891							Richardson-Buf	24.6	Anson-Chi	3.1
Bennett-Det	.770							Force-Buf	24.3	Richardson-Buf	3.1
York-Pro	.745							Williamson-Chi	22.2	Dunlap-Cle	3.0
Dunlap-Cle	.734							Bennett-Det	18.3	Ewing-Tro	2.2

Wins		Win Percentage		Games		Complete Games		Shutouts		Saves	
Whitney-Bos	31	Radbourn-Pro	.694	Whitney-Bos	66	Whitney-Bos	57	Derby-Det	9	Mathews-Pro-Bos	2
Corcoran-Chi	31	Corcoran-Chi	.689	McCormick-Cle	59	McCormick-Cle	57	Whitney-Bos	6	Morrill-Bos	1
Derby-Det	29	Goldsmith-Chi	.649	Galvin-Buf	56	Derby-Det	55	Goldsmith-Chi	5		
Galvin-Buf	28	Welch-Tro	.538	Derby-Det	56	Richmond-Wor	50	Galvin-Buf	5		
McCormick-Cle	26	Galvin-Buf	.538	Richmond-Wor	53	Galvin-Buf	48				

Innings Pitched		Fewest Hits/Game		Fewest BB/Game		Strikeouts		Strikeouts/Game		Ratio	
Whitney-Bos	552.1	McCormick-Cle	8.28	Galvin-Buf	.87	Derby-Det	212	Derby-Det	3.86	Wiedman-Det	9.39
McCormick-Cle	526.0	Wiedman-Det	8.45	Wiedman-Det	.94	McCormick-Cle	178	Corcoran-Chi	3.40	McCormick-Cle	9.72
Derby-Det	494.2	Radbourn-Pro	8.55	Goldsmith-Chi	1.20	Whitney-Bos	162	Ward-Pro	3.25	Goldsmith-Chi	10.15
Galvin-Buf	474.0	Corcoran-Chi	8.62	Richmond-Wor	1.32	Richmond-Wor	156	Radbourn-Pro	3.24	Radbourn-Pro	10.32
Richmond-Wor	462.1	Ward-Pro	8.89	McCormick-Cle	1.44	Corcoran-Chi	150	McCormick-Cle	3.05	Ward-Pro	10.34

Earned Run Average		Adjusted ERA		Opponents' Batting Avg.		Opponents' On Base Pct.		Starter Runs		Adjusted Starter Runs	
Wiedman-Det	1.80	Wiedman-Det	162	Radbourn-Pro	.235	Wiedman-Det	.258	Derby-Det	31.5	Derby-Det	39.3
Ward-Pro	2.13	Derby-Det	132	McCormick-Cle	.235	McCormick-Cle	.265	Ward-Pro	23.7	Galvin-Buf	21.3
Derby-Det	2.20	Ward-Pro	125	Wiedman-Det	.238	Radbourn-Pro	.270	Galvin-Buf	21.1	Ward-Pro	19.4
Corcoran-Chi	2.31	Corcoran-Chi	118	Corcoran-Chi	.242	Goldsmith-Chi	.271	Corcoran-Chi	20.3	Corcoran-Chi	18.7
Galvin-Buf	2.37	Galvin-Buf	117	Ward-Pro	.242	Ward-Pro	.271	McCormick-Cle	19.2	Wiedman-Det	14.3

Clutch Pitching Index		Relief Runs		Adjusted Relief Runs		Relief Ranking		Total Pitcher Index		Total Baseball Ranking	
Galvin-Buf	123							Derby-Det	3.0	Bennett-Det	3.3
Derby-Det	112							Galvin-Buf	2.6	Anson-Chi	3.1
Wiedman-Det	109							Ward-Pro	2.5	Richardson-Buf	3.1
Fox-Bos	108							Whitney-Bos	1.9	Dunlap-Cle	3.0
Lynch-Buf	106							Corcoran-Chi	1.4	Derby-Det	2.8

January 7 The NL will continue the practice of using different color patterns on uniforms for the different positions. Third basemen will wear gray and white uniforms, as the blue and white uniforms originally sought were "impossible to obtain."

January 20* The Kentucky Legislature modifies a recently passed law which inadvertently prohibited the playing of baseball games in the commonwealth.

February 4 NL players are now responsible for carrying their own bats and uniforms on road trips. They are also required to purchase and keep clean two complete uniforms, including the white linen ties to be worn on the field at all times.

February 25 Providence players and their opponents will be expected to parade down the streets of Providence in full uniform, accompanied by a brass band, on game days in order to encourage attendance.

May 5 Adrian "Cap" Anson is called out for walking back to his base after a foul ball, instead of running, as the rule specifies. This rule will be amended at the end of the season.

May 13 NL players are told that next season they will not be required to wear the uniforms known as "clown costumes," with different color combinations for each fielding position.

June 5 Boston defeats Detroit 10–2. According to the Chicago *Tribune*, this is the first time a team scoring in double figures does so entirely with earned runs.

June 6 William "Blondie" Purcell of Buffalo is fined $10 for slicing open a soggy baseball. He did this to compel the umpire to put a fresh ball in play so his pitcher Pud Galvin might be able to throw a curve.

July 24 Chicago sets a NL record for runs by beating Cleveland 35–4. Seven Chicago players get 4 or more hits and six score 4 or more runs. The record will last until June 29, 1897, when Chicago will run up 36 runs against Louisville.

August 17 In what is considered one of the greatest games in the century, Providence beats Detroit 1-0 on an 18th-inning home run by right fielder Charles Radbourn. This game will serve as the longest shutout in major league history until September 1, 1967, when San Francisco blanks Cincinnati 1-0 in 20 innings.

September 20 Chicago's Larry Corcoran pitches the second no-hitter of his career by shutting out Worcester 5–0.

September 22 In a special NL meeting Troy and Worcester are kicked out of the league, to be replaced by teams from Philadelphia and New York. When the expelled clubs threaten to boycott the rest of the season, Chicago and Providence agree to play a best-of-nine series after the season to determine the league championship.

September 25 The NL Worcester Brown Stockings come up with a baseball innovation—the doubleheader. It is the first instance of two games for the price of one admission: all previous doubleheaders called for two separate admissions. The last place Brown Stockings will end their third and final season in Worcester by drawing a scant 25 and 18 fans for games against Troy on September 28 and 29.

October 6 In the first postseason matchup between AA and NL champions, Cincinnati (AA) shuts out Chicago (NL) 4–0. The next day Chicago returns the favor by blanking Cincinnati 2–0. At this point Cincinnati, under pressure from the AA, reluctantly cancels the series to avoid expulsion from the league.

December 6 At the NL meeting, Troy and Worcester are officially replaced by New York and Philadelphia. Starting in 1883, pitchers will be charged with an error after a walk, balk, wild pitch, or hit by pitch. Catchers will be charged with an error after a passed ball.

BOSTON	BUFFALO	CHICAGO	CLEVELAND	DETROIT	PROVIDENCE	TROY	WORCESTER
M J.Morrill	M J.O'Rourke	M C.Anson	M J.McCormick	M F.Bancroft	M H.Wright	M B.Ferguson	M F.Brown
1B J.Morrill	1B D.Brouthers	1B C.Anson	M F.Dunlap	1B M.Powell	1B J.Start	1B J.Smith	M T.Bond
2B J.Burdock	2B H.Richardson	2B T.Burns	1B B.Phillips	2B D.Troy	2B J.Farrell	2B B.Ferguson	M J.Chapman
SS S.Wise	SS D.Force	SS K.Kelly	2B F.Dunlap	SS M.McGeary	SS G.Wright	SS F.Pfeffer	1B H.Stovey
3B E.Sutton	3B D.White	3B N.Williamson	SS J.Glasscock	3B J.Farrell	3B J.Denny	3B B.Ewing	2B G.Creamer
LF J.Hornung	LF B.Purcell	LF A.Dalrymple	3B M.Muldoon	LF G.Wood	LF T.York	LF P.Gillespie	SS A.Irwin
CF P.Hotaling	CF J.O'Rourke	CF G.Gore	LF D.Esterbrook	CF N.Hanlon	CF P.Hines	CF R.Connor	3B F.Mann
RF E.Rowen	RF C.Foley	RF H.Nicol	CF J.Richmond	RF L.Knight	RF J.Ward	RF C.Roseman	LF J.Clinton
C P.Deasley	C J.Rowe	C S.Flint	RF O.Shaffer	C C.Bennett	C B.Gilligan	C B.Holbert	CF J.Hayes
			C F.Briody				RF J.Evans
/O C.Buffinton	C T.Dolan	2 J.Quest	3 H.Doscher	C S.Trott	C S.Nava	O B.Harbidge	C D.Bushong
/O H.McClure		/1 M.Scott	C J.Kelly	3 A.Whitney	S T.Manning	O3 J.Cassidy	
	P P.Galvin		O D.Rowe	2 T.Forster	S C.Carroll	OP J.Egan	SP F.Corey
P J.Whitney	P H.Daily	P F.Goldsmith	O J.Tilley	S W.Kinzie	S A.Whitney	/O J.Holdsworth	O T.O'Brien
P B.Mathews		P L.Corcoran	O J.Willigrod	S B.Casey	/S D.Troy		1 J.Smith
	/P J.Burke		/O B.McGunnigle	S Y.Robinson	/C C.Reilley	P T.Keefe	S F.McLaughlin
			/O J.Dwyer	/2 T.Kearns	/O C.Sweeney	P M.Welch	1 E.Cogswell
			/C D.Kennedy	/2 H.Luff	P C.Radbourn		/O T.Bond
				/3 J.Morrissey			/O D.O'Leary
				/S J.Willigrod			/3 J.Halpin
			P J.McCormick				/3 E.Merrill
			P G.Bradley	P S.Wiedman			/1 J.Irwin
				P G.Derby			
							P L.Richmond
							P F.Mountain
							/P J.Clarkson

TEAM	G	W	L	PCT	GB	R	OR	AB	H	2B	3B	HR	BB	SO	AVG	OBP	SLG	PRO	PRO+	BR	/A	PF	CHI	RC	SB	CS	SBA	SBR
CHI	84	55	29	.655		604	353	3225	892	209	54	15	142	262	.277	.307	.389	.696	119	82	56	105	108	395				
PRO	84	52	32	.619	3	463	356	3104	776	121	53	11	102	255	.250	.274	.334	.608	96	-16	-15	100	105	291				
BUF	84	45	39	.536	10	500	461	3128	858	146	47	18	116	228	.274	.300	.368	.668	113	50	41	102	98	355				
BOS	85	45	39	.536	10	472	414	3118	823	114	50	15	134	244	.264	.294	.347	.641	107	23	22	100	97	326				
CLE	84	42	40	.512	12	402	411	3009	716	139	40	20	122	261	.238	.268	.331	.599	96	-24	-10	97	95	273				
DET	86	42	41	.506	12.5	407	488	3144	724	117	44	19	122	308	.230	.259	.314	.573	84	-53	-52	100	99	262				
TRO	85	35	48	.422	19.5	430	522	3057	747	116	59	12	109	298	.244	.270	.333	.603	99	-20	1	95	100	282				
WOR	84	18	66	.214	37	379	652	2984	689	109	57	16	113	303	.231	.259	.322	.581	85	-43	-53	102	95	255				
TOT	338					3657		24769	6225	1071	404	126	960	2159	.251	.279	.342	.622										

TEAM	CG	SH	SV	IP	H	H/G	HR	BB	SO	RAT	ERA	ERA+	OAV	OOB	PR	/A	PF	CPI	FA	E	DP	FW	PW	BW	SBW	DIF
CHI	83	7	0	763²	667	7.9	13	102	279	9.1	2.22	129	.221	.246	57	51	99	87	.898	376	54	.1	4.6	5.1		3.1
PRO	80	10	1	752	690	8.3	12	87	273	9.3	2.27	123	.228	.250	51	47	97	94	.901	371	67	.4	4.3	-1.4		6.7
BUF	79	3	0	737	778	9.5	16	114	287	10.9	3.25	90	.254	.280	-30	-30	101	89	.910	315	42	3.3	-2.7	3.7		-1.3
BOS	81	4	0	749	738	8.9	10	77	352	9.8	2.80	102	.239	.258	7	4	99	83	.910	314	37	3.6	.4	2.0		-2.9
CLE	81	4	0	751²	743	8.9	22	132	232	10.5	2.75	101	.249	.280	11	1	97	106	.905	358	71	1.1	.0	-.9		.7
DET	82	7	0	793	808	9.2	19	129	354	10.6	2.98	98	.248	.277	-9	-8	101	94	.893	396	44	-.4	-.7	-4.7		6.4
TRO	81	6	0	757	837	10.0	13	168	189	11.9	3.08	91	.268	.305	-16	-24	98	113	.887	432	70	-2.5	-2.2	.0		-1.9
WOR	75	0	0	738¹	964	11.8	21	151	195	13.6	3.75	83	.294	.325	-71	-54	107	115	.878	468	66	-4.6	-4.9	-4.8		-9.7
TOT	642	41	1	6041²		9.3				10.7	2.89		.251	.279					.897	3030	451					

Runs
Gore-Chi	99
Dalrymple-Chi	96
Stovey-Wor	90
Kelly-Chi	81
Purcell-Buf	79

Hits
Brouthers-Buf	129
Anson-Chi	126

Doubles
Kelly-Chi	37
Anson-Chi	29
Hines-Pro	28
Williamson-Chi	27
Glasscock-Cle	27

Triples
Connor-Tro	18
Wood-Det	12
Corey-Wor	12

Home Runs
Wood-Det	7
Muldoon-Cle	6
Brouthers-Buf	6

Total Bases
Brouthers-Buf	192
Connor-Tro	185
Hines-Pro	177
Anson-Chi	174
Dalrymple-Chi	167

Runs Batted In
Anson-Chi	83
Brouthers-Buf	63
Williamson-Chi	60
Richardson-Buf	57
Kelly-Chi	55

Runs Produced
Anson-Chi	151
Gore-Chi	147
Kelly-Chi	135
Dalrymple-Chi	131
Brouthers-Buf	128

Bases On Balls
Gore-Chi	29
Williamson-Chi	27
Shaffer-Cle	27
Hanlon-Det	26

Batting Average
Brouthers-Buf	.368
Anson-Chi	.362
Connor-Tro	.330
Start-Pro	.329
Whitney-Bos	.323

On Base Percentage
Brouthers-Buf	.403
Anson-Chi	.397
Whitney-Bos	.382
Gore-Chi	.369
Connor-Tro	.354

Slugging Average
Brouthers-Buf	.547
Connor-Tro	.530
Whitney-Bos	.510
Anson-Chi	.500
Hines-Pro	.467

Production
Brouthers-Buf	.950
Anson-Chi	.897
Whitney-Bos	.892
Connor-Tro	.884
Hines-Pro	.793

Adjusted Production
Brouthers-Buf	198
Connor-Tro	188
Whitney-Bos	183
Anson-Chi	177
Hines-Pro	151

Batter Runs
Brouthers-Buf	39.1
Anson-Chi	32.7
Connor-Tro	29.7
Whitney-Bos	23.7
Gore-Chi	22.2

Adjusted Batter Runs
Brouthers-Buf	37.5
Connor-Tro	33.6
Anson-Chi	28.9
Whitney-Bos	23.5
Hines-Pro	20.7

Clutch Hitting Index
Pfeffer-Chi	147
Holbert-Tro	146
Anson-Chi	143
Rowen-Bos	129
Hayes-Wor	128

Runs Created
Brouthers-Buf	79
Anson-Chi	71
Connor-Tro	67
Hines-Pro	59
Gore-Chi	59

Total Average
Brouthers-Buf	.959
Whitney-Bos	.894
Anson-Chi	.874
Connor-Tro	.846
Gore-Chi	.736

Fielding Runs
Glasscock-Cle	24.0
A.Irwin-Wor	20.5
Evans-Wor	19.8
Dunlap-Cle	17.6
Williamson-Chi	16.2

Total Player Rating
Glasscock-Cle	4.1
Connor-Tro	2.9
Williamson-Chi	2.6
Brouthers-Buf	2.6
Dunlap-Cle	2.6

Wins
McCormick-Cle	36
Radbourn-Pro	33
Goldsmith-Chi	28
Galvin-Buf	28
Corcoran-Chi	27

Win Percentage
Corcoran-Chi	.692
Radbourn-Pro	.623
Goldsmith-Chi	.622
Ward-Pro	.613
Mathews-Bos	.559

Games
McCormick-Cle	68
Radbourn-Pro	55
Galvin-Buf	52
Whitney-Bos	49
Richmond-Wor	48

Complete Games
McCormick-Cle	65
Radbourn-Pro	51
Galvin-Buf	48
Whitney-Bos	46
Goldsmith-Chi	45

Shutouts
Radbourn-Pro	6
Welch-Tro	5

Saves
Ward-Pro	1

Innings Pitched
McCormick-Cle	595.2
Radbourn-Pro	474.0
Galvin-Buf	445.1
Whitney-Bos	420.0

Fewest Hits/Game
Corcoran-Chi	7.11
Radbourn-Pro	8.15
McCormick-Cle	8.31
Goldsmith-Chi	8.38
Ward-Pro	8.45

Fewest BB/Game
Mathews-Bos	.69
Galvin-Buf	.81
Goldsmith-Chi	.84
Wiedman-Det	.85
Whitney-Bos	.88

Strikeouts
Radbourn-Pro	201
McCormick-Cle	200
Derby-Det	182
Whitney-Bos	180
Corcoran-Chi	170

Strikeouts/Game
Mathews-Bos	4.83
Derby-Det	4.52
Corcoran-Chi	4.30
Daily-Buf	4.08
Whitney-Bos	3.86

Ratio
Corcoran-Chi	8.70
Radbourn-Pro	9.11
Goldsmith-Chi	9.22
Wiedman-Det	9.42
Mathews-Bos	9.47

Earned Run Average
Corcoran-Chi	1.95
Radbourn-Pro	2.09
McCormick-Cle	2.37
Goldsmith-Chi	2.42
Keefe-Tro	2.50

Adjusted ERA
Corcoran-Chi	147
Radbourn-Pro	134
Goldsmith-Chi	118
McCormick-Cle	118
Keefe-Tro	113

Opponents' Batting Avg.
Corcoran-Chi	.200
Radbourn-Pro	.226
Mathews-Bos	.232
Ward-Pro	.232
Daily-Buf	.234

Opponents' On Base Pct.
Corcoran-Chi	.234
Mathews-Bos	.246
Radbourn-Pro	.246
Wiedman-Det	.253
Goldsmith-Chi	.254

Starter Runs
Radbourn-Pro	42.0
Corcoran-Chi	37.0
McCormick-Cle	34.0
Goldsmith-Chi	20.8
Keefe-Tro	16.2

Adjusted Starter Runs
Radbourn-Pro	37.6
Corcoran-Chi	35.9
McCormick-Cle	27.5
Goldsmith-Chi	19.5
Wiedman-Det	13.5

Clutch Pitching Index
Egan-Tro	120
Richmond-Wor	116
F.Mountain-Wor-Wor	115
Welch-Tro	113
Corey-Wor	112

Relief Runs

Adjusted Relief Runs

Relief Ranking

Total Pitcher Index
Radbourn-Pro	3.4
Corcoran-Chi	3.1
Whitney-Bos	3.1
Keefe-Tro	2.2
McCormick-Cle	2.0

Total Baseball Ranking
Glasscock-Cle	4.1
Radbourn-Pro	3.3
Corcoran-Chi	3.1
Whitney-Bos	3.1
Connor-Tro	2.9

March 11 In retaliation for the "theft" of Sam Wise and Dasher Troy by the NL, the American Association creates a loophole that allows all players either expelled or blacklisted by the NL to join AA clubs after appealing to a special commission.

May 2 The American Association plays its first game, as visiting Pittsburgh beats Cincinnati, 10-9. The other teams are Baltimore, Louisville, Philadelphia, and St. Louis. Pittsburgh will play its games at Exposition Park, which was later used for games in the Union Association, National League, and Federal League.

July 18 Louisville hurler Tony Mullane pitches both righthanded and lefthanded in a game against Baltimore, the first time the feat is performed in the major leagues. Starting in the fourth inning he pitches lefthanded whenever Baltimore's lefty hitters are at bat. In addition to continuing to pitch righthanded to righthanded hitters. It works until the ninth when, with 2 outs, Charlie Householder hits his only homer of the year to beat Mullane 9–8. A "dandy" whose impeccable grooming and well-waxed mustache earned for him the nickname of "The Count," Tony Mullane won 285 major league games, and the handsome pitcher was equally adept at pitching woo: his drawing power among females is credited with initiating the practice of Ladies Day.

September 5 Baltimore plays the first four innings of its game against Pittsburgh without its uniforms, which have been delayed at the Baltimore train station. Allegheny wins the game 3–1.

September 11 Tony Mullane pitches a no-hitter over Cincinnati 2–0. The next day Mullane does not allow a hit until the seventh inning, and wins 10–4.

October 14 Columbus, which will join the AA in 1883, is officially incorporated with $5,000 in capital stock.

October 28 The Athletics reveal that in their first AA season they reaped a $22,000 profit, more than any NL team earned. This helps convince the NL that the AA is a viable league.

November 18 The case of the Allegheny Club versus Charles Bennett is won by Bennett. Prior to the 1882 season Allegheny (Pittsburgh) signed Bennett to a $100 agreement which stated that he would sign an 1883 contract with Allegheny after the season. Instead, Bennett re-signed with Detroit. This case will later have bearing on the fight over the reserve rule during the Players' League War of 1889-90.

December 9* James H. Dudley, manager of a top black club in Richmond, Virginia, initiates discussion concerning the formation of a black league with teams from New York, Philadelphia, Pittsburgh, Cincinnati, Baltimore, Washington, DC, and Richmond, but nothing comes of it.

December 14 At its first annual convention, the AA establishes the first permanent staff of umpires in major league history. Previously, the NL and AA umpires were local men hired on game day by the home club.

BALTIMORE		CINCINNATI		LOUISVILLE		PHILADELPHIA		PITTSBURGH		ST.LOUIS	
M	H.Myers	M	P.Snyder	M	D.Mack	M	J.Latham	M	A.Pratt	M	N.Cuthbert
1B	C.Householder	1B	E.Stearns	1B	G.Hecker	1B	J.Latham	1B	C.Lane	1B	C.Comiskey
2B	G.Pierce	2B	B.McPhee	2B	P.Browning	2B	C.Stricker	2B	G.Strief	2B	B.Smiley
SS	H.Myers	SS	C.Fulmer	SS	D.Mack	SS	L.Say	SS	J.Peters	SS	B.Gleason
3B	J.Shetzline	3B	H.Carpenter	3B	B.Schenck	3B	F.Mann	3B	J.Battin	3B	J.Gleason
LF	C.Waitt	LF	J.Sommer	LF	L.Maskrey	LF	J.Birchall	LF	M.Mansell	LF	N.Cuthbert
CF	M.Cline	CF	J.Macullar	CF	J.Reccius	CF	J.Mansell	CF	E.Swartwood	CF	O.Walker
RF	T.Brown	RF	H.Wheeler	RF	J.Wolf	RF	B.Blakiston	RF	J.Leary	RF	G.Seward
C	E.Whiting	C	P.Snyder	C	D.Sullivan	C	J.O'Brien	O	B.Taylor	C	S.Sullivan
3O	H.Jacoby	1	H.Luff	C	J.Strick	CO	J.Dorgan	O	C.Morton	O	H.McCaffery
2	B.Smiley	C	P.Powers	/2	G.Pierce	S	J.Say	C	R.Kemmler	CO	E.Fusselback
/O	N.Scharf	/C	R.Kemmler	/C	J.Crotty	O	J.Richmond	C	J.Keenan	O	E.Brown
O	F.Burt	/O	T.Thompson	/O	P.Reccius	3	P.Smith	O	B.Morgan	/2	C.Morton
/O	B.Jones	/1	B.Tierney	/O	C.Bohn	/O	B.Kienzle	1	J.Goodman	/C	J.Crotty
/3	H.East			/S	P.Smith	/C	J.Straub	/O	R.McKelvy	/2	F.Decker
/2	T.Evers	P	W.White	/2	A.Booth	/O	B.Greenwood	/O	R.Wylie	/2	J.Shoupe
/3	A.Booth	P	H.McCormick	/O	J.Dyler	/O	B.Farrell			/O	B.Mitchell
/O	J.Russ			/O	H.Maskrey	/C	T.Arundel	P	H.Salisbury		
/O	L.Smith			/2	H.McCaffery			P	D.Driscoll	P	J.McGinnis
				/3	J.Say	P	S.Weaver	P	H.Arundel	P	J.Schappert
P	D.Landis			/O	E.Merrill	P	B.Sweeney			P	B.Dorr
P	T.Nichols					P	F.Mountain	/P	M.Critchley		
P	E.Geis			P	T.Mullane			/P	J.Seymour	/P	M.Critchley
						/P	D.Landis			/P	J.Doyle
/P	J.Leary					/P	C.Reynolds			/P	E.Hogan
/P	B.Wise					/P	G.Snyder				
						/P	E.Halbriter				

TEAM	G	W	L	PCT	GB	R	OR	AB	H	2B	3B	HR	BB	SO	AVG	OBP	SLG	PRO	PRO+	BR	/A	PF	CHI	RC	SB	CS	SBA	SBR
CIN	80	55	25	.688		489	268	3007	795	95	47	5	102	204	.264	.289	.332	.621	107	38	12	106	104	295				
PHI	75	41	34	.547	11.5	406	389	2707	660	89	21	5	125	164	.244	.277	.298	.575	88	-4	-50	112	104	229				
LOU	80	42	38	.525	13	443	352	2806	728	110	28	9	128	193	.259	.292	.328	.620	120	37	62	95	99	275				
PIT	79	39	39	.500	15	428	418	2904	730	110	59	18	90	183	.251	.274	.348	.622	118	35	56	95	95	284				
STL	80	37	43	.463	18	399	496	2865	663	87	41	11	112	226	.231	.260	.302	.562	90	-19	-34	104	101	231				
BAL	74	19	54	.260	32.5	273	515	2583	535	60	24	4	72	215	.207	.229	.254	.483	72	-87	-66	92	97	153				
TOT	234					2438		16872	4111	551	220	52	629	1185	.244	.271	.312	.582										

TEAM	CG	SH	SV	IP	H	H/G	HR	BB	SO	RAT	ERA	ERA+	OAV	OOB	PR	/A	PF	CPI	FA	E	DP	FW	PW	BW	SBW	DIF
CIN	77	11	0	721[1]	609	7.6	7	125	165	9.2	1.65	160	.214	.247	83	79	98	119	.907	332	41	3.7	7.3	1.1		2.9
PHI	72	2	0	663	682	9.3	13	99	190	10.6	2.97	100	.249	.275	-21	0	111	97	.895	361	36	1.2	.0	-4.6		6.9
LOU	73	6	0	693[1]	637	8.3	6	112	240	9.7	2.03	122	.229	.259	51	34	92	113	.893	385	57	1.3	3.1	5.7		-8.1
PIT	77	2	0	696[2]	694	9.0	4	82	252	10.0	2.79	93	.243	.264	-8	-14	97	90	.889	397	40	.5	-1.3	5.1		-4.3
STL	75	3	1	688[1]	729	9.5	7	103	225	10.9	2.92	96	.254	.280	-18	-9	105	101	.875	446	41	-1.6	-.8	-3.1		2.5
BAL	64	1	0	646[1]	760	10.6	15	108	113	12.1	3.88	71	.275	.302	-86	-82	102	94	.859	490	41	-5.0	-7.5	-6.1		1.1
TOT	438	25	1	4109		9.0				10.4	2.68		.244	.271					.886	2411	256					

Runs		Hits		Doubles		Triples		Home Runs		Total Bases	
Swartwood-Pit	86	Carpenter-Cin	120	Swartwood-Pit	18	Mansell-Pit	16	Walker-StL	7	Swartwood-Pit	159
Sommer-Cin	82	Browning-Lou	109	Mansell-Pit	18	Taylor-Pit	13	Browning-Lou	5	Mansell-Pit	152
Carpenter-Cin	78	Swartwood-Pit	107	Browning-Lou	17	Wheeler-Pit	11	Swartwood-Pit	4	Carpenter-Cin	148
Browning-Lou	67	Sommer-Cin	102	Taylor-Pit	16	Swartwood-Pit	11			Browning-Lou	147
Birchall-Phi	65	B.Gleason-StL	100	Cuthbert-StL	16	Wolf-Lou	8			Taylor-Pit	135

Runs Batted In		Runs Produced		Bases On Balls		Batting Average		On Base Percentage		Slugging Average	
		Carpenter-Cin	144	J.Gleason-StL	27	Browning-Lou	.378	Browning-Lou	.430	Browning-Lou	.510
		Sommer-Cin	110	Browning-Lou	26	Carpenter-Cin	.342	Swartwood-Pit	.370	Swartwood-Pit	.489
		Comiskey-StL	102	Sommer-Cin	24	Swartwood-Pit	.329	Carpenter-Cin	.360	Taylor-Pit	.452
		Snyder-Cin	98	J.Reccius-Lou	23	O'Brien-Phi	.303	O'Brien-Phi	.339	Mansell-Pit	.438
		Birchall-Phi	92	Swartwood-Pit	21	Wolf-Lou	.299	Sommer-Cin	.333	Carpenter-Cin	.422

Production		Adjusted Production		Batter Runs		Adjusted Batter Runs		Clutch Hitting Index		Runs Created	
Browning-Lou	.940	Browning-Lou	228	Browning-Lou	35.3	Browning-Lou	39.7			Browning-Lou	65
Swartwood-Pit	.859	Swartwood-Pit	197	Swartwood-Pit	29.3	Swartwood-Pit	33.0			Swartwood-Pit	60
Carpenter-Cin	.782	Taylor-Pit	157	Carpenter-Cin	22.0	Carpenter-Cin	18.1			Carpenter-Cin	55
O'Brien-Phi	.758	Carpenter-Cin	154	Taylor-Pit	14.5	Mansell-Pit	17.4			Mansell-Pit	45
Taylor-Pit	.749	Mansell-Pit	150	Mansell-Pit	14.5	Taylor-Pit	17.1			Sommer-Cin	44

Total Average		Stolen Bases		Stolen Base Average		Stolen Base Runs		Fielding Runs		Total Player Rating	
Browning-Lou	.966							Stricker-Phi	22.5	Browning-Lou	4.7
Swartwood-Pit	.826							Snyder-Cin	19.4	Snyder-Cin	2.3
Carpenter-Cin	.684							White-Cin	12.0	Swartwood-Pit	2.2
O'Brien-Phi	.679							Browning-Lou	11.8	O'Brien-Phi	1.9
Taylor-Pit	.660							O'Brien-Phi	11.4	Mansell-Pit	1.8

Wins		Win Percentage		Games		Complete Games		Shutouts		Saves	
White-Cin	40	White-Cin	.769	Mullane-Lou	55	White-Cin	52	White-Cin	8	Fusselback-StL	1
Mullane-Lou	30	Weaver-Phi	.634	White-Cin	54	Mullane-Lou	51	Mullane-Lou	5		
Weaver-Phi	26	McGinnis-StL	.581	McGinnis-StL	45	McGinnis-StL	43	McGinnis-StL	3		
McGinnis-StL	25	Mullane-Lou	.556	Landis-Phi-Bal	44	Weaver-Phi	41	McCormick-Cin	3		
Salisbury-Pit	20	Salisbury-Pit	.526	Weaver-Phi	42	Salisbury-Pit	38	Weaver-Phi	2		

Innings Pitched		Fewest Hits/Game		Fewest BB/Game		Strikeouts		Strikeouts/Game		Ratio	
White-Cin	480.0	Hecker-Lou	6.49	Hecker-Lou	.43	Mullane-Lou	170	Salisbury-Pit	3.63	Hecker-Lou	6.92
Mullane-Lou	460.1	McCormick-Cin	7.25	Driscoll-Pit	.54	Salisbury-Pit	135	Arundel-Pit	3.53	Driscoll-Pit	7.79
McGinnis-StL	388.1	Driscoll-Pit	7.25	Weaver-Phi	.85	McGinnis-StL	134	Mullane-Lou	3.32	McCormick-Cin	8.97
Weaver-Phi	371.0	White-Cin	7.71	Salisbury-Pit	.99	White-Cin	122	McGinnis-StL	3.11	White-Cin	9.04
Landis-Phi-Bal	358.0	Geis-Bal	7.90	Landis-Phi-Bal	1.18	Weaver-Phi	104	J.Reccius-Lou	2.94	Salisbury-Pit	9.46

Earned Run Average		Adjusted ERA		Opponents' Batting Avg.		Opponents' On Base Pct.		Starter Runs		Adjusted Starter Runs	
Driscoll-Pit	1.21	Driscoll-Pit	216	Hecker-Lou	.188	Hecker-Lou	.199	White-Cin	61.1	White-Cin	58.7
Hecker-Lou	1.30	Hecker-Lou	191	McCormick-Cin	.206	Driscoll-Pit	.218	Mullane-Lou	41.2	Driscoll-Pit	31.2
McCormick-Cin	1.52	McCormick-Cin	174	Driscoll-Pit	.206	McCormick-Cin	.243	Driscoll-Pit	32.9	Mullane-Lou	30.7
White-Cin	1.54	White-Cin	172	White-Cin	.216	White-Cin	.244	McCormick-Cin	28.5	McCormick-Cin	27.4
Mullane-Lou	1.88	Mullane-Lou	132	Geis-Bal	.220	Salisbury-Pit	.253	Hecker-Lou	16.0	Hecker-Lou	13.6

Clutch Pitching Index		Relief Runs		Adjusted Relief Runs		Relief Ranking		Total Pitcher Index		Total Baseball Ranking	
White-Cin	124							White-Cin	7.3	White-Cin	7.2
McCormick-Cin	124							Mullane-Lou	5.1	Mullane-Lou	5.0
Mullane-Lou	120							Driscoll-Pit	2.4	Browning-Lou	4.7
J.Reccius-Lou	119							McCormick-Cin	2.1	Driscoll-Pit	2.4
Driscoll-Pit	113							Hecker-Lou	2.1	Snyder-Cin	2.3

February 17 At a meeting between the AA and the NL, the Tripartite Agreement (or the National Agreement) is drafted. In it the leagues, along with the Northwestern League, agree to respect each other's contracts, ending a brief period of player raids. Also, the reserve rule is amended to allow each team to reserve 11 players, an increase of 6. The National Agreement will usher in a period of peaceful coexistence, lasting until the Players' League war of 1890.

March 31* The Olympic Town-Ball Club of Philadelphia, the nation's oldest ball club, celebrates its 50th anniversary.

April 3 The Cleveland club visits the White House, where President Chester A. Arthur greets them by telling them that "Good ball-players make good citizens."

April 15 The first weekly issue of *Sporting Life,* edited by Francis Richter, is published in Philadelphia. This outstanding magazine will last until 1917.

May 3 John Montgomery Ward becomes the first pitcher in history to hit two home runs in a game, giving him a 10-9 victory over Boston.

May 5 In the first game in Chicago's spectacular new ballpark, featuring 41 uniformed attendants, Detroit scores with two out in the bottom of the ninth to win 3-2.

May 22 Future evangelist Billy Sunday, playing for the Chicago White Stockings has a miserable major league debut, going 0-for-4 with 4 strikeouts.

May 28* The first of two games between Fort Wayne and Indianapolis is played under electric lights.

June 9 Philadelphia (NL) receives permission to charge 25 cents for admission, instead of 50 cents, to allow them to compete with their popular cross-town rivals, the AA-leading Athletics. Philadelphia's attendance quadruples for the rest of the season.

June 16 The New York Gothams introduce the concept of "Ladies Day," which will become a baseball staple for nearly a hundred years. Ladies, escorted or not, are admitted free. New York whips the Cleveland Spiders 5-2.

July 28* In the first recorded game in Hawaii, the Honolulu Club wins over the Oceanic Club 14-13.

August 21 In the most decisive shutout in major league history, Philadelphia routs Providence 28-0.

September 6 Chicago concludes an extraordinarily successful series against Detroit with a 26–6 win. Chicago tallies six doubles in one inning, a record that won't be topped until Boston hits 7 on August 25, 1936. Chicago sets a major league record by scoring 18 runs in the seventh inning.

September 12 At a meeting in Pittsburgh, the Union Association is formed. The UA states its intention to ignore the reserve rule.

September 25* The Union League, later known as the Eastern League (and distinct from the Union Association) is officially formed in New York.

September 27 Boston beats Cleveland 4-1 to officially clinch the NL title.

October 10 Jim Devlin, a former star pitcher for the Louisville Grays (who was expelled from baseball in 1877 for his role in throwing a series of games at the request of gamblers), dies in Philadelphia. Before his death he served as a policeman.

BOSTON		BUFFALO		CHICAGO		CLEVELAND		DETROIT		NEW YORK		PHILADELPHIA		PROVIDENCE	
M	J.Burdock	M	J.O'Rourke	M	C.Anson	M	F.Bancroft	M	J.Chapman	M	J.Clapp	M	B.Ferguson	M	H.Wright
M	J.Morrill	1B	D.Brouthers	1B	C.Anson	1B	B.Phillips	1B	M.Powell	1B	R.Connor	M	B.Purcell	1B	J.Start
1B	J.Morrill	2B	H.Richardson	2B	F.Pfeffer	2B	F.Dunlap	2B	S.Trott	2B	D.Troy	1B	S.Farrar	2B	J.Farrell
2B	J.Burdock	SS	D.Force	SS	T.Burns	SS	J.Glasscock	SS	S.Houck	SS	E.Caskin	2B	B.Ferguson	SS	A.Irwin
SS	S.Wise	3B	D.White	3B	N.Williamson	3B	M.Muldoon	3B	J.Farrell	3B	F.Hankinson	SS	B.McClellan	3B	J.Denny
3B	E.Sutton	LF	J.O'Rourke	LF	A.Dalrymple	LF	T.York	LF	G.Wood	LF	P.Gillespie	3B	F.Warner	LF	C.Carroll
LF	J.Hornung	CF	J.Lillie	CF	G.Gore	CF	P.Hotaling	CF	N.Hanlon	CF	J.Ward	LF	B.Purcell	CF	P.Hines
CF	E.Smith	RF	O.Shaffer	RF	K.Kelly	RF	J.Evans	RF	S.Wiedman	RF	M.Dorgan	CF	B.Harbidge	RF	J.Cassidy
RF	P.Radford	C	J.Rowe	C	S.Flint	C	D.Bushong	C	C.Bennett	C	B.Ewing	RF	J.Manning	C	B.Gilligan
C	M.Hines											C	E.Gross		
		O	D.Eggler	O	B.Sunday	C	F.Briody	OP	D.Burns	CO	J.Humphries			OP	L.Richmond
OP	C.Buffinton	O	C.Foley			O	B.Crowley	2	J.Quest	C	J.Clapp	CO	F.Ringo	C	S.Nava
C	M.Hackett	/O	D.Kennedy	P	L.Corcoran	/S	G.Bradley	O	T.Mansell		G.Pierce	O	F.Lewis	/S	J.Mulvey
1	L.Brown	/C	D.Darling	P	F.Goldsmith	/O	C.Cady	/O	B.Guiney	/O	D.Cramer	O	J.Neagle	/1	E.Smith
		/O	T.Suck			/C	C.Broughton			/O	D.Orr	O	C.Doyle		
P	J.Whitney					/O	L.Hunter	P	S.Wiedman			/S	J.Pirie	P	C.Radbourn
		P	P.Galvin					P	D.Shaw	P	M.Welch	/2	A.Benedict	P	C.Sweeney
		P	G.Derby	P	H.Daily	P	J.Jones	P	T.O'Neill	/3	J.Mulvey		
				P	J.McCormick				/C	A.Wolstenholme		
		/P	E.Cushman	P	W.Sawyer	/P	G.Radbourn	/P	M.Allen	/O	B.Gallagher		
		/P	A.Hagan			/P	F.McIntyre			/3	C.Kelly		
		/P	J.Burke							/3	P.Ward		
										/3	B.Gladman		
										/O	J.Kelly		
										/O	C.Waitt		
										/S	C.White		
										P	J.Coleman		
										P	A.Hagan		
										/P	C.Hilsey		
										/P	H.Henderson		
										/P	E.Smith		
										/P	A.Breitenstein		

TEAM	G	W	L	PCT	GB	R	OR	AB	H	2B	3B	HR	BB	SO	AVG	OBP	SLG	PRO	PRO+	BR	/A	PF	CHI	RC	SB	CS	SBA	SBR
BOS	98	63	35	.643		669	456	3657	1010	209	86	34	123	423	.276	.300	.408	.708	114	68	53	102	104	459				
CHI	98	59	39	.602	4	679	540	3658	1000	277	61	13	129	399	.273	.298	.393	.691	106	49	13	106	109	439				
PRO	98	58	40	.592	5	636	436	3685	1001	189	59	21	149	309	.272	.300	.372	.672	104	29	13	103	104	422				
CLE	100	55	42	.567	7.5	476	443	3457	852	184	38	8	139	374	.246	.276	.329	.605	88	-53	-47	99	97	321				
BUF	98	52	45	.536	10.5	614	576	3729	1058	184	59	8	147	342	.284	.311	.371	.682	108	44	30	102	97	441				
NY	98	46	50	.479	16	530	577	3524	900	139	69	24	127	297	.255	.281	.354	.635	96	-18	-12	99	99	360				
DET	101	40	58	.408	23	524	650	3726	931	164	48	13	166	378	.250	.282	.330	.612	93	-46	-21	95	96	355				
PHI	99	17	81	.173	46	437	887	3576	859	181	48	3	141	355	.240	.269	.320	.589	90	-74	-32	91	89	316				
TOT	395					4565		29012	7611	1527	468	124	1121	2877	.262	.290	.360	.650										

TEAM	CG	SH	SV	IP	H	H/G	HR	BB	SO	RAT	ERA	ERA+	OAV	OOB	PR	/A	PF	CPI	FA	E	DP	FW	PW	BW	SBW	DIF
BOS	89	6	3	860	853	8.9	11	90	538	9.9	2.55	121	.245	.264	56	52	99	96	.901	409	58	3.1	4.5	4.6		1.7
CHI	91	5	1	862	942	9.8	21	123	299	11.1	2.78	115	.260	.284	34	37	102	109	.879	543	76	-3.5	3.2	1.1		9.1
PRO	88	4	1	871	827	8.5	12	111	376	9.7	2.37	130	.238	.262	75	68	98	99	.903	419	75	2.7	5.9	1.1		-.7
CLE	92	5	2	879	818	8.4	7	217	402	10.6	2.22	142	.237	.282	89	92	100	118	.909	389	69	4.6	8.0	-4.1		-2.0
BUF	90	5	2	859¹	971	10.2	12	101	362	11.2	3.32	96	.268	.288	-17	-8	101	97	.896	445	52	1.4	-.7	2.6		.2
NY	87	5	0	866	907	9.4	19	170	323	11.2	2.94	105	.253	.287	19	11	99	101	.889	468	52	.2	1.0	-1.0		-2.1
DET	89	5	2	894¹	1026	10.3	22	184	324	12.2	3.58	87	.270	.303	-44	-49	99	98	.893	470	77	.9	-4.3	-1.8		-3.7
PHI	91	3	0	864²	1267	13.2	20	125	253	14.5	5.34	58	.318	.338	-212	-216	98	92	.858	639	62	-8.0	-18.9	-2.8		-2.4
TOT	717	38	11	6956¹		9.8				11.3	3.14		.262	.290					.891	3782	521					

Runs		Hits		Doubles		Triples		Home Runs		Total Bases	
Hornung-Bos	107	Brouthers-Buf	159	Williamson-Chi	49	Brouthers-Buf	17	Ewing-NY	10	Brouthers-Buf	243
Gore-Chi	105	Connor-NY	146	Brouthers-Buf	41	Morrill-Bos	16	Hornung-Bos	8	Morrill-Bos	212
O'Rourke-Buf	102	O'Rourke-Buf	143	Burns-Chi	37	Sutton-Bos	15	Denny-Pro	8	Connor-NY	207
Sutton-Bos	101	Sutton-Bos	134	Anson-Chi	36	Connor-NY	15	Ward-NY	7	Sutton-Bos	201
Hines-Pro	94	Wood-Det	133					Morrill-Bos	6	Hornung-Bos	199

Runs Batted In		Runs Produced		Bases On Balls		Batting Average		On Base Percentage		Slugging Average	
Brouthers-Buf	97	Brouthers-Buf	179	York-Cle	37	Brouthers-Buf	.374	Brouthers-Buf	.397	Brouthers-Buf	.572
Burdock-Bos	88	Sutton-Bos	171	Hanlon-Det	34	Connor-NY	.357	Connor-NY	.394	Morrill-Bos	.525
Sutton-Bos	73	Hornung-Bos	165	Powell-Det	28	Gore-Chi	.334	Gore-Chi	.377	Connor-NY	.506
Morrill-Bos	68	Burdock-Bos	163	Shaffer-Buf	27	Burdock-Bos	.330	Dunlap-Cle	.361	Sutton-Bos	.486
Anson-Chi	68	Gore-Chi	155	Gore-Chi	27	O'Rourke-Buf	.328	Burdock-Bos	.353	Ewing-NY	.481

Production		Adjusted Production		Batter Runs		Adjusted Batter Runs		Clutch Hitting Index		Runs Created	
Brouthers-Buf	.969	Brouthers-Buf	186	Brouthers-Buf	44.4	Brouthers-Buf	41.9	Start-Pro	140	Brouthers-Buf	99
Connor-NY	.900	Connor-NY	173	Connor-NY	34.6	Connor-NY	35.7	Burdock-Bos	135	Connor-NY	84
Morrill-Bos	.868	Morrill-Bos	155	Morrill-Bos	27.6	Morrill-Bos	25.4	Kelly-Chi	131	Morrill-Bos	75
Gore-Chi	.849	Bennett-Det	155	Gore-Chi	26.5	Bennett-Det	25.0	Sutton-Bos	131	Sutton-Bos	72
Sutton-Bos	.836	Gore-Chi	148	Sutton-Bos	24.4	Wood-Det	22.9	Anson-Chi	124	Gore-Chi	72

Total Average		Stolen Bases	Stolen Base Average	Stolen Base Runs	Fielding Runs		Total Player Rating	
Brouthers-Buf	.974				Farrell-Pro	24.9	Farrell-Pro	3.3
Connor-NY	.882				Shaffer-Buf	20.0	Richardson-Buf	3.1
Morrill-Bos	.825				Ward-NY	19.3	Brouthers-Buf	2.9
Gore-Chi	.812				Richardson-Buf	18.7	Gore-Chi	2.7
Bennett-Det	.783				Williamson-Chi	17.8	Dunlap-Cle	2.7

Wins		Win Percentage		Games		Complete Games		Shutouts		Saves	
Radbourn-Pro	48	McCormick-Cle	.700	Radbourn-Pro	76	Galvin-Buf	72	Galvin-Buf	5	Wiedman-Det	2
Galvin-Buf	46	Radbourn-Pro	.658	Galvin-Buf	76	Radbourn-Pro	66	Welch-NY	4	Whitney-Bos	2
Whitney-Bos	37	Buffinton-Bos	.641	Coleman-Phi	65	Coleman-Phi	59	Radbourn-Pro	4		
Corcoran-Chi	34	Whitney-Bos	.638	Whitney-Bos	62	Whitney-Bos	54	Daily-Cle	4		
McCormick-Cle	28	Corcoran-Chi	.630	Corcoran-Chi	56	Corcoran-Chi	51	Buffinton-Bos	4		

Innings Pitched		Fewest Hits/Game		Fewest BB/Game		Strikeouts		Strikeouts/Game		Ratio	
Galvin-Buf	656.1	Sawyer-Cle	7.60	Whitney-Bos	.61	Whitney-Bos	345	Whitney-Bos	6.04	Radbourn-Pro	8.81
Radbourn-Pro	632.1	Radbourn-Pro	8.01	Galvin-Buf	.69	Radbourn-Pro	315	Buffinton-Bos	5.08	Whitney-Bos	9.23
Coleman-Phi	538.1	McCormick-Cle	8.32	Radbourn-Pro	.80	Galvin-Buf	279	Sawyer-Cle	4.85	Galvin-Buf	9.96
Whitney-Bos	514.0	Daily-Cle	8.56	Coleman-Phi	.80	Corcoran-Chi	216	Radbourn-Pro	4.48	McCormick-Cle	10.03
Corcoran-Chi	473.2	Whitney-Bos	8.61	Goldsmith-Chi	.92	Buffinton-Bos	188	Corcoran-Chi	4.10	Ward-NY	10.04

Earned Run Average		Adjusted ERA		Opponents' Batting Avg.		Opponents' On Base Pct.		Starter Runs		Adjusted Starter Runs	
McCormick-Cle	1.84	McCormick-Cle	171	Sawyer-Cle	.217	Radbourn-Pro	.244	Radbourn-Pro	76.4	Radbourn-Pro	72.7
Radbourn-Pro	2.05	Radbourn-Pro	150	Radbourn-Pro	.227	Whitney-Bos	.251	Whitney-Bos	51.2	McCormick-Cle	49.7
Whitney-Bos	2.24	Whitney-Bos	138	McCormick-Cle	.233	Galvin-Buf	.265	McCormick-Cle	49.2	Whitney-Bos	49.0
Sawyer-Cle	2.36	Sawyer-Cle	133	Sweeney-Pro	.237	Ward-NY	.267	Corcoran-Chi	34.1	Corcoran-Chi	36.8
Daily-Cle	2.42	Daily-Cle	130	Whitney-Bos	.238	McCormick-Cle	.268	Galvin-Buf	30.8	Galvin-Buf	33.5

Clutch Pitching Index		Relief Runs	Adjusted Relief Runs	Relief Ranking	Total Pitcher Index		Total Baseball Ranking	
McCormick-Cle	125				Radbourn-Pro	8.4	Radbourn-Pro	8.1
Shaw-Det	121				Whitney-Bos	6.0	Whitney-Bos	6.1
Daily-Cle	119				McCormick-Cle	5.4	McCormick-Cle	5.3
O'Neill-NY	118				Corcoran-Chi	3.3	Farrell-Pro	3.3
Goldsmith-Chi	113				Galvin-Buf	2.6	Ward-NY	3.1

January 13 Both of the New York major league clubs will play games simultaneously at the Polo Grounds. Their fields will be separated by an eight-foot fence.

January 31* A Baltimore fan loses a suit against Baltimore player Andrew Burns, who, while batting, accidentally let his bat slip from his hands, hitting the spectator. The judge rules fans had been warned to keep a safe distance from the field.

March 14* In a Northwestern League meeting, Peoria moves to ban blacks in order to prevent Toledo from playing star catcher Moses Fleetwood Walker. After an "exciting discussion" the motion is withdrawn and Walker is allowed to play.

May 28 Heavyweight boxing champion John L. Sullivan pitches the Mets to a 20–15 victory in an exhibition game. For his efforts Sullivan pockets half of the proceeds—$1,595. On November 4 Sullivan will pitch another game.

June 13 The Allegheny field is partially underwater following a series of floods in Pittsburgh. Columbus scores in every inning to overcome the water-logged home club by a count of 25-10.

July 4 Tim Keefe of New York wins both ends of a doubleheader against Columbus 9–3 and 1–0, allowing a total of three hits.

July 6 Cincinnati thrashes Baltimore 23–0, setting a major league record for the most decisive shutout. The record lasts for 46 days.

August 20 After the Eclipse-Allegheny game, Allegheny players Billy Taylor, Mike Mansell, and George Creamer are each fined $100 and suspended indefinitely for drunkenness.

September 4 Columbus crushes Baltimore 21-4 behind Tom Brown, who goes 6-for-7 with 5 runs and 4 extra-base hits.

September 6 The Athletics cling to their lead in the AA by defeating second-place St. Louis for the third consecutive game. Over 45,000 fans attend the series.

September 12 Cincinnati mauls Allegheny 27-5. Hick Carpenter and Long John Reilly each get 6 hits, while Reilly also scores 6 runs and hits for the cycle.

September 19 Cincinnati first baseman Long John Reilly again hits for the cycle against Philadelphia.

September 28 After losing two straight games to the Eclipse, the Athletics rally in the 10th inning for a 7-6 win to clinch the AA championship.

November 22 New York owner John B. Day proposes a resolution to prohibit a team from signing a player who has broken the reserve clause in his contract. This resolution, eventually adopted by both the AA and the NL, effectively changes the reserve rule from a device designed to protect owners from their own greediness to a vindictive weapon to be used against uncooperative players.

November 24 The AA agrees to expand to 12 teams by admitting Brooklyn, Washington, Indianapolis and Toledo.

December 15* In Louisville a "first-class colored team" is formed. The team, later known as the Falls Cities, becomes one of the nation's best black teams. It joins the National Colored Base Ball League (NCBBL) in 1887, but apparently disbands shortly after the collapse of the NCBBL in the first week of its season.

	BALTIMORE		CINCINNATI		COLUMBUS		LOUISVILLE		NEW YORK		PHILADELPHIA		PITTSBURGH		ST.LOUIS
M	B.Barnie	M	P.Snyder	M	H.Phillips	M	J.Gerhardt	M	J.Mutrie	M	L.Knight	M	A.Pratt	M	T.Sullivan
1B	E.Stearns	1B	J.Reilly	1B	J.Field	1B	J.Latham	1B	S.Brady	1B	H.Stovey	M	O.Butler	M	C.Comiskey
2B	T.Manning	2B	B.McPhee	2B	P.Smith	2B	J.Gerhardt	2B	S.Crane	2B	C.Stricker	M	J.Battin	1B	C.Comiskey
SS	L.Say	SS	C.Fulmer	SS	J.Richmond	SS	J.Leary	SS	C.Nelson	SS	M.Moynahan	1B	E.Swartwood	2B	G.Strief
3B	J.McCormick	3B	H.Carpenter	3B	B.Kuehne	3B	J.Gleason	3B	D.Esterbrook	3B	G.Bradley	2B	G.Creamer	SS	B.Gleason
LF	J.Clinton	LF	J.Sommer	LF	H.Wheeler	LF	P.Browning	LF	E.Kennedy	LF	J.Birchall	SS	D.Mack	3B	A.Latham
CF	D.Eggler	CF	C.Jones	CF	F.Mann	CF	L.Maskrey	CF	J.O'Rourke	CF	B.Blakiston	3B	J.Battin	LF	T.Dolan
RF	D.Rowe	RF	P.Corkhill	RF	T.Brown	RF	J.Wolf	RF	C.Roseman	RF	L.Knight	LF	M.Mansell	CF	F.Lewis
C	J.Kelly	C	P.Snyder	C	R.Kemmler	C	E.Whiting	C	B.Holbert	C	J.O'Brien	CF	B.Dickerson	RF	H.Nicol
												RF	B.Taylor	C	P.Deasley
O	G.Gardner	CO	P.Powers	C1	J.Straub	C	D.Sullivan	C	C.Reipschlager	3P	F.Corey	C	J.Hayes		
2	T.O'Brien	C	B.Traffley	/2	G.Pierce	SO	T.McLaughlin	/1	D.Orr	C	E.Rowen			O	T.Mansell
CO	P.Baker	O	J.Macullar	/1	B.Schwartz	O	J.Reccius			O	B.Crowley	S	F.McLaughlin	2	J.Quest
C	R.Sweeney	/O	P.Weihe			1	L.Brown	P	T.Keefe	/S	A.Hubbard	S	B.Morgan	O	N.Cuthbert
2	B.Reid			P	F.Mountain	/1	H.Luff	P	J.Lynch	/O	C.Mason	/C	W.Blogg	/O	J.Gleason
/O	B.Gallagher	P	W.White	P	E.Dundon	/O	G.Winkelman					/S	J.Peters	/C	S.Sullivan
C	B.Barnie	P	R.Deagle	P	J.Valentine	/O	W.Prince			P	B.Mathews	/1	H.Oberbeck	/O	T.Loftus
/C	C.Broughton	P	H.McCormick			/O	J.Jones			P	J.Jones			/O	H.McCaffery
/S	G.Baker			/P	P.Fries	/O	P.Reccius			P	J.Bakely	P	D.Driscoll	/O	H.Oberbeck
/S	N.Scharf	/P	B.Mountjoy	/P	F.McIntyre							P	B.Barr	/O	J.Ewing
/2	J.Leary					P	G.Hecker					P	J.Neagle	/O	J.Gorman
/S	B.Farrell					P	S.Weaver								
/O	B.Loughlin											/P	T.Nolan	P	T.Mullane
/C	C.Ingraham											/P	N.Baker	P	J.McGinnis
/C	D.Oldfield														
/O	D.Allison													/P	C.Hodnett
P	H.Henderson														
P	B.Emslie														
P	J.Fox														
/P	J.Neagle														
/P	J.Devine														

TEAM	G	W	L	PCT	GB	R	OR	AB	H	2B	3B	HR	BB	SO	AVG	OBP	SLG	PRO	PRO+	BR	/A	PF	CHI	RC	SB	CS	SBA	SBR
PHI	98	66	32	.673		**720**	547	3712	**974**	**149**	50	20	**200**	268	**.262**	**.300**	.346	.646	103	45	-5	108	**114**	**395**				
STL	98	65	33	.663	1	549	409	3495	891	118	46	7	124	**240**	.255	.280	.321	.601	91	-14	-44	106	104	323				
CIN	98	61	37	.622	5	662	413	3669	961	122	74	**34**	139	261	.262	.289	**.363**	**.652**	106	**46**	12	106	108	**395**				
NY	97	54	42	.563	11	498	**405**	3534	883	111	58	6	142	259	.250	.279	.319	.598	91	-17	-40	104	93	322				
LOU	98	52	45	.536	13.5	564	562	3553	892	114	64	14	141	304	.251	.280	.331	.611	**107**	-3	**38**	93	103	337				
COL	97	32	65	.330	33.5	476	659	3553	854	101	79	15	134	409	.240	.268	.326	.594	102	-25	17	92	90	318				
PIT	98	31	67	.316	35	525	728	3607	892	120	58	13	164	345	.247	.280	.324	.604	102	-10	15	95	95	335				
BAL	96	28	68	.292	37	471	742	3532	870	125	49	5	164	331	.246	.280	.314	.594	91	-21	-37	103	89	318				
TOT	390					4465		28655	7217	960	478	114	1208	2417	.252	.282	.331	.613										

TEAM	CG	SH	SV	IP	H	H/G	HR	BB	SO	RAT	ERA	ERA+	OAV	OOB	PR	/A	PF	CPI	FA	E	DP	FW	PW	BW	SBW	DIF
PHI	92	1	0	873	921	9.5	22	**95**	347	10.5	2.88	121	.254	.273	41	57	105	113	.865	584	40	-4.1	5.0	-.4		16.5
STL	93	**9**	1	879¹	729	**7.5**	7	150	325	**9.0**	**2.23**	**156**	**.211**	.244	104	**122**	106	97	**.909**	388	62	4.5	**10.7**	-3.9		4.6
CIN	96	8	0	866²	766	8.0	17	168	215	9.7	2.26	143	.222	.258	100	94	98	**114**	.905	**383**	57	**4.7**	8.3	1.1		-2.0
NY	**97**	6	0	874	751	7.7	12	123	**490**	**9.0**	2.90	115	.218	.244	38	41	101	78	.905	391	45	4.1	3.6	-3.5		1.8
LOU	96	7	0	873²	987	10.2	**7**	110	269	11.3	3.50	85	.267	.288	-20	-50	91	101	.886	478	67	.6	-4.4	**3.3**		4.0
COL	90	4	0	840¹	980	10.5	16	211	222	12.8	3.96	78	.274	.314	-62	-83	93	105	.874	535	**69**	-2.1	-7.3	1.5		-8.5
PIT	82	1	**1**	867²	1140	11.8	21	151	271	13.4	4.62	69	.298	.325	-127	-137	97	102	.884	504	55	-.6	-12.1	1.3		-6.7
BAL	86	1	0	844²	943	10.0	12	190	290	12.1	4.08	85	.265	.303	-74	-58	105	93	.855	624	44	-6.3	-5.1	-3.3		-5.4
TOT	732	37	2	6919¹		9.4				10.9	3.30		.252	.282					.885	3887	439					

Runs
Stovey-Phi 110
Reilly-Cin 103
Carpenter-Cin 99
Knight-Phi 98

Hits
Swartwood-Pit 147
Reilly-Cin 136
Carpenter-Cin 130
Stovey-Phi 128
Nelson-NY 127

Doubles
Stovey-Phi 31
Swartwood-Pit 24
Knight-Phi 23
Hayes-Pit 23

Triples
Smith-Col 17
Reilly-Cin 14
Kuehne-Col 14
Mansell-Pit 13
Mann-Col 13

Home Runs
Stovey-Phi 14
Jones-Cin 10
Reilly-Cin 9
Fulmer-Cin 5
Brown-Col 5

Total Bases
Stovey-Phi 213
Reilly-Cin 212
Swartwood-Pit 196
Jones-Cin 184
B.Gleason-StL 167

Runs Batted In

Runs Produced
Reilly-Cin 173
Stovey-Phi 162
Moynahan-Phi 156
Jones-Cin 154
Knight-Phi 150

Bases On Balls
Stearns-Bal 34
Nelson-NY 31
Moynahan-Phi 31
J.Gleason-StL-Lou . . 29

Batting Average
Swartwood-Pit 357
Browning-Lou 338
Clinton-Bal 313
Rowe-Bal 313
Reilly-Cin 311

On Base Percentage
Swartwood-Pit 394
Browning-Lou 378
Moynahan-Phi 360
Clinton-Bal 357
Nelson-NY 353

Slugging Average
Stovey-Phi 506
Reilly-Cin 485
Swartwood-Pit 476
Jones-Cin 471
Browning-Lou 464

Production
Swartwood-Pit 869
Stovey-Phi 852
Browning-Lou 842
Reilly-Cin 810
Jones-Cin 799

Adjusted Production
Swartwood-Pit 187
Browning-Lou 183
Stovey-Phi 158
Reilly-Cin 149
Jones-Cin 146

Batter Runs
Swartwood-Pit 35.5
Stovey-Phi 32.4
Browning-Lou 27.4
Reilly-Cin 26.1
Jones-Cin 22.8

Adjusted Batter Runs
Swartwood-Pit 40.2
Browning-Lou 33.8
Stovey-Phi 24.7
Reilly-Cin 21.0
Jones-Cin 18.2

Clutch Hitting Index

Runs Created
Swartwood-Pit 79
Stovey-Phi 76
Reilly-Cin 71
Browning-Lou 64
Jones-Cin 62

Total Average
Swartwood-Pit 834
Stovey-Phi 819
Browning-Lou 797
Jones-Cin 739
Reilly-Cin 734

Stolen Bases

Stolen Base Average

Stolen Base Runs

Fielding Runs
Holbert-NY 34.4
Battin-Pit 28.9
Richmond-Col 25.5
Latham-StL 21.8
Gerhardt-Lou 20.3

Total Player Rating
Richmond-Col 3.5
Smith-Col 3.1
Swartwood-Pit 3.1
Gerhardt-Lou 2.4
Browning-Lou 2.3

Wins
White-Cin 43
Keefe-NY 41
Mullane-StL 35
Mathews-Phi 30

Win Percentage
Mullane-StL 700
Mathews-Phi 698
Bradley-Phi 696
White-Cin 662
McGinnis-StL 636

Games
Keefe-NY 68
White-Cin 65
Mountain-Col 59
Mullane-StL 53
Hecker-Lou 53

Complete Games
Keefe-NY 68
White-Cin 64
Mountain-Col 57
Hecker-Lou 51
Mullane-StL 49

Shutouts
White-Cin 6
McGinnis-StL 6
Keefe-NY 5
Weaver-Lou 4
Mountain-Col 4

Saves
Mullane-StL 1
Barr-Pit 1

Innings Pitched
Keefe-NY 619.0
White-Cin 577.0
Mountain-Col 503.0
Hecker-Lou 469.0
Mullane-StL 460.2

Fewest Hits/Game
Keefe-NY 7.10
Mullane-StL 7.27
White-Cin 7.38
McGinnis-StL 7.64
Deagle-Cin 8.27

Fewest BB/Game
Mathews-Phi 73
Weaver-Lou 79
Lynch-NY 88
Bradley-Phi 92
Driscoll-Pit 1.04

Strikeouts
Keefe-NY 359
Mathews-Phi 203
Lynch-NY 191
Hecker-Lou 164
Mountain-Col 159

Strikeouts/Game
Keefe-NY 5.22
Mathews-Phi 4.80
Lynch-NY 4.20
Mullane-StL 3.73
Henderson-Bal 3.64

Ratio
Keefe-NY 8.67
Mullane-StL 8.71
White-Cin 9.00
McGinnis-StL 9.27
Bradley-Phi 9.95

Earned Run Average
White-Cin 2.09
Mullane-StL 2.19
Deagle-Cin 2.31
McGinnis-StL 2.33
Keefe-NY 2.41

Adjusted ERA
Mullane-StL 159
White-Cin 155
McGinnis-StL 149
Mathews-Phi 141
Deagle-Cin 140

Opponents' Batting Avg.
Keefe-NY 203
Mullane-StL 207
White-Cin 209
McGinnis-StL 215
Deagle-Cin 229

Opponents' On Base Pct.
Keefe-NY 237
Mullane-StL 238
White-Cin 244
McGinnis-StL 249
Bradley-Phi 263

Starter Runs
White-Cin 77.4
Keefe-NY 60.8
Mullane-StL 56.8
McGinnis-StL 41.2
Mathews-Phi 35.6

Adjusted Starter Runs
White-Cin 73.8
Mullane-StL 66.1
Keefe-NY 63.5
McGinnis-StL 48.9
Mathews-Phi 42.8

Clutch Pitching Index
Mathews-Phi 127
Corey-Phi 124
McCormick-Cin . . . 123
Valentine-Col 122
Deagle-Cin 117

Relief Runs

Adjusted Relief Runs

Relief Ranking

Total Pitcher Index
White-Cin 6.6
Keefe-NY 6.6
Mullane-StL 6.2
McGinnis-StL 4.2
Mathews-Phi 3.2

Total Baseball Ranking
White-Cin 6.6
Keefe-NY 6.6
Mullane-StL 5.9
McGinnis-StL 4.0
Richmond-Col 3.5

January 4* The newly organized Union League changes its name to Eastern League to avoid confusion with the new Union Association. The EL continues today as the AAA International League.

January 4 Larry Corcoran, who had signed with Chicago of the outlaw UA, breaks his contract to re-sign with his old club, Chicago's NL White Stockings.

March 4 The NL, meeting in Buffalo, reduces the number of balls required for a walk from seven to six. Club owners also agree to provide separate team benches to minimize fraternizing among opposing players during games.

March 6 High winds in New York destroy much of the fence and blow off part of the Polo Grounds grandstand roof, depositing it a block away.

May 14 P Charles Radbourn gets 5 hits—the same number he allows Detroit—to spur a 25–3 rout, the most decisive victory in the NL this year. Detroit contributes to its own demise by committing 18 errors, including 5 by right fielder Fred Wood, whose major league career will total only 13 games.

May 16 When a foul tip from a Detroit batter sticks in the mask of Boston C Mike Hines, umpire Van Court calls the batter out on a foul catch. NL Secretary Nick Young will later instruct league umpires not to rule an out in such cases.

May 29 Taking advantage of a ground rule change which scores balls hit over the close right field Chicago fence as HRs (instead of doubles), five players hit homers in the White Stockings' home opener against Detroit. Chicago will hit 142 during the 112-game season (more than 90 percent of them at home) to set a record that will be broken by the 1927 New York Yankees.

May 30 In the afternoon game of Chicago's doubleheader with Detroit, White Stocking Ned Williamson doubles and hits a major league record 3 home runs as Chicago overwhelms the Wolverines 12–2. Williamson's homers are his first of 27 (25 at home), which will set a major league season record not broken until Babe Ruth hits 29 in 1919.

June 7 Charlie Sweeney of Providence strikes out 19 Boston Red Stockings to establish a major league record for a nine-inning game. It will be tied one month later but not broken until Roger Clemens fans 20 on April 29, 1986. Providence's 2–1 win moves it into first place, but Boston will take the next 4 from the Grays to regain the lead.

June 27 Chicago ace Larry Corcoran ends the Providence Grays' 10-game winning streak with the NL's first no-hitter of the season. The 6–0 win is Corcoran's third major league no-hitter.

July 22 Providence star Charles Sweeney is suspended without pay after he refuses to move from the mound to right field in the ninth inning with a safe lead over Philadelphia. Sweeney quits the Grays and jumps to St. Louis (UA), for which he wins 24 games for a season's total of 41. As a result, Charles Radbourn is forced to pitch almost every game for the rest of the year. Sweeney's stubbornness has an immediate effect as substitute pitcher Joseph "Cyclone" Miller surrenders 8 runs and gives the Athletics a 10–6 win.

August 28 Mickey Welch, who will win 39 games in 1884 and 307 in just 13 years, sets the all-time major league record by fanning the first nine Philadelphia batters he faces.

October 22 The weekly *Sporting Life* announces—just one day before the start of the event—that the two pennant winners have agreed to meet in a 3-game series October 23–25 at New York's Polo Grounds to decide "the championship of America."

October 25 Hoss Radbourn of Providence wins his third straight over the AA Mets to sweep the three-games series to capture the first World Series.

November 20 The NL agrees to allow overhand pitching, but rules that pitchers must keep both feet on the ground throughout their pitching motion in order to reduce the velocity of their pitches. They still must throw the ball at the height requested by the batter.

	BOSTON		BUFFALO		CHICAGO		CLEVELAND		DETROIT		NEW YORK		PHILADELPHIA		PROVIDENCE
M	J.Morrill	M	J.O'Rourke	M	C.Anson	M	C.Hackett	M	J.Chapman	M	J.Price	M	H.Wright	M	F.Bancroft
1B	J.Morrill	1B	D.Brouthers	1B	C.Anson	1B	B.Phillips	1B	M.Scott	M	M.Ward	1B	S.Farrar	1B	J.Start
2B	J.Burdock	2B	H.Richardson	2B	F.Pfeffer	2B	G.Smith	2B	B.Geis	1B	A.McKinnon	2B	E.Andrews	2B	J.Farrell
SS	S.Wise	SS	D.Force	SS	T.Burns	SS	J.Glasscock	SS	F.Meinke	2B	R.Connor	SS	B.McClellan	SS	A.Irwin
3B	E.Sutton	3B	D.White	3B	N.Williamson	3B	M.Muldoon	3B	J.Farrell	SS	E.Caskin	3B	J.Mulvey	3B	J.Denny
LF	J.Hornung	LF	J.O'Rourke	LF	A.Dalrymple	LF	W.Murphy	LF	G.Wood	3B	F.Hankinson	LF	B.Purcell	LF	C.Carroll
CF	J.Manning	CF	D.Eggler	CF	G.Gore	CF	P.Hotaling	CF	N.Hanlon	LF	P.Gillespie	CF	J.Fogarty	CF	P.Hines
RF	B.Crowley	RF	J.Lillie	RF	K.Kelly	RF	J.Evans	RF	S.Wiedman	CF	J.Ward	RF	J.Manning	RF	P.Radford
C	M.Hackett	C	J.Rowe	C	S.Flint	C	D.Bushong	C	C.Bennett	RF	M.Dorgan	C	J.Crowley	C	B.Gilligan
										C	B.Ewing				
C	M.Hines	CO	G.Myers	O	B.Sunday	OP	S.Moffett	2O	H.Jones			OP	J.Coleman	C	S.Nava
O	B.Annis	2	C.Collins	S	W.Kinzie	C	F.Briody	SO	H.Buker	OS	D.Richardson	C	F.Ringo	3	C.Bassett
T.Gunning		/O	E.Coughlin	/O	J.Brown	2S	G.Pinkney	S	F.Cox	C	J.Humphries	/C	T.Lynch	/C	M.Murray
/O	G.Moriarity	/O	B.Ely	/C	S.Sutcliffe	O	E.Burch	C	E.Gastfield	O	S.Griffin	O	J.Remsen		
/C	M.Barrett					2	J.Ardner	2	T.Kearns	/C	Loughran	O	B.Hoover	P	C.Radbourn
		P	P.Galvin	P	L.Corcoran	/2	M.Moynahan	/C	F.Wood	/C	C.Manlove	/C	J.Clements	P	C.Sweeney
P	C.Buffinton	P	B.Serad	P	F.Goldsmith	/O	G.Whiteley	/C	C.Zimmer	/C	H.Oxley	/C	T.Cusick	P	E.Conley
P	J.Whitney			P	J.Clarkson	/C	J.Moore	/S	E.Santry			/C	J.Kappel		
		/P	A.Hagan			/O	G.Strief	/O	W.Prince	P	M.Welch	/C	G.Vadeboncoeur	/P	C.Miller
/P	J.Connor			/P	T.Lee	/2	G.Fisher	/S	F.Jones	P	E.Begley	/C	P.Cook	/P	H.Arundel
/P	D.Davis			/P	G.Crosby	/O	P.Gilman	/O	J.Weber			/C	M.DePangher	/P	J.Cattanach
				/P	J.Hibbard	/O	B.Smith	/C	B.Guiney	/P	J.Brown	/C	L.Hardie		
				/P	F.Andrus			C	W.Walker			/C	B.Conway		
				/P	M.Corcoran	P	J.Harkins	/C	D.Lowe			/C	H.Allen		
				/P	T.Lynch	P	J.McCormick	P	D.Shaw			/C	E.Sixsmith		
				/P	J.Henry			P	C.Getzien			P	C.Ferguson		
								P	F.Brill			P	B.Vinton		
												P	J.McElroy		
												/P	J.Knight		
												/P	C.Murphy		
												/P	S.Morton		
												/P	C.Miller		
												/P	S.Pyle		

TEAM	G	W	L	PCT	GB	R	OR	AB	H	2B	3B	HR	BB	SO	AVG	OBP	SLG	PRO	PRO+	BR	/A	PF	CHI	RC	SB	CS	SBA	SBR
PRO	114	84	28	.750		665	388	4093	987	153	43	21	300	469	.241	.293	.315	.608	97	-18	-2	98	107	387				
BOS	116	73	38	.658	10.5	684	468	4189	1063	179	60	36	207	660	.254	.289	.351	.640	105	17	20	100	104	435				
BUF	115	64	47	.577	19.5	700	626	4197	1099	163	69	39	215	458	.262	.298	.361	.659	106	46	23	103	102	463				
NY	116	62	50	.554	22	693	623	4124	1053	149	67	23	249	492	.255	.298	.341	.639	102	20	4	102	105	429				
CHI	113	62	50	.554	22	834	647	4182	1176	162	50	142	264	469	.281	.324	.446	.770	133	201	133	108	98	619				
PHI	113	39	73	.348	45	549	824	3998	934	149	39	14	209	512	.234	.272	.301	.573	88	-72	-47	95	101	335				
CLE	113	35	77	.313	49	458	716	3934	934	147	49	16	170	576	.237	.269	.312	.581	83	-63	-81	103	86	338				
DET	114	28	84	.250	56	445	736	3970	825	114	47	31	207	699	.208	.247	.284	.531	74	-132	-104	94	93	285				
TOT	457					5028		32687	8071	1216	424	322	1821	4335	.247	.287	.340	.626										

TEAM	CG	SH	SV	IP	H	H/G	HR	BB	SO	RAT	ERA	ERA+	OAV	OOB	PR	/A	PF	CPI	FA	E	DP	FW	PW	BW	SBW	DIF
PRO	107	16	2	1036¹	825	7.2	26	172	639	8.7	1.61	176	.209	.242	158	141	95	110	.918	398	50	5.1	12.6	-.2		10.4
BOS	109	14	2	1037	932	8.1	30	135	742	9.3	2.47	117	.226	.250	58	49	97	84	.922	384	46	6.3	4.4	1.8		5.0
BUF	108	14	1	1001	1041	9.4	46	189	534	11.1	2.95	107	.254	.286	3	21	106	105	.905	462	71	1.9	1.9	2.1		2.6
NY	111	4	0	1014	1011	9.0	28	326	567	11.9	3.12	95	.245	.300	-16	-19	100	98	.895	514	69	-.6	-1.7	.4		8.0
CHI	106	9	0	997¹	1028	9.3	83	231	472	11.4	3.03	103	.250	.290	-6	11	105	112	.886	595	107	-5.6	1.0	11.9		-1.2
PHI	106	3	1	981	1090	10.0	38	254	411	12.3	3.93	76	.261	.304	-103	-106	100	87	.888	536	67	-2.5	-9.5	-4.2		-.8
CLE	107	7	0	994²	1046	9.5	35	269	482	11.9	3.43	92	.256	.302	-50	-32	106	97	.897	512	75	-1.2	-2.9	-7.2		-9.7
DET	109	3	0	984²	1097	10.0	36	245	488	12.3	3.38	86	.262	.302	-44	-54	97	100	.886	550	62	-3.0	-4.8	-9.3		-10.9
TOT	863	70	6	8046		9.0				11.1	2.98		.247	.287					.899	3951	547					

Runs	Hits	Doubles	Triples	Home Runs	Total Bases
Kelly-Chi 120	Sutton-Bos 162	Hines-Pro 36	Ewing-NY 20	Williamson-Chi 27	Dalrymple-Chi 263
O'Rourke-Buf 119	O'Rourke-Buf 162	O'Rourke-Buf 33	Brouthers-Buf 15	Pfeffer-Chi 25	Anson-Chi 258
Hornung-Bos 119	Dalrymple-Chi 161	Anson-Chi 30	Rowe-Buf 14	Dalrymple-Chi 22	Pfeffer-Chi 240
Dalrymple-Chi 111	Kelly-Chi 160	Manning-Phi 29	Phillips-Cle 12	Anson-Chi 21	Kelly-Chi 237
Anson-Chi 108	Anson-Chi 159		McKinnon-NY 12	Brouthers-Buf 14	Williamson-Chi 231

Runs Batted In	Runs Produced	Bases On Balls	Batting Average	On Base Percentage	Slugging Average
Anson-Chi 102	Kelly-Chi 202	Gore-Chi 61	O'Rourke-Buf .347	Kelly-Chi .414	Brouthers-Buf .563
Pfeffer-Chi 101	Anson-Chi 189	Kelly-Chi 46	Kelly-Chi .354	Gore-Chi .404	Williamson-Chi .554
Kelly-Chi 95	Pfeffer-Chi 181	Hines-Pro 44	Sutton-Bos .346	O'Rourke-Buf .392	Anson-Chi .543
Williamson-Chi 84	O'Rourke-Buf 177	Williamson-Chi 42	Anson-Chi .335	Sutton-Bos .384	Kelly-Chi .524
Connor-NY 82	Connor-NY 176		Brouthers-Buf .327	Brouthers-Buf .378	Pfeffer-Chi .514

Production	Adjusted Production	Batter Runs	Adjusted Batter Runs	Clutch Hitting Index	Runs Created
Brouthers-Buf .941	Brouthers-Buf 186	Kelly-Chi 48.8	Kelly-Chi 39.2	Connor-NY 148	Kelly-Chi 100
Kelly-Chi .938	Kelly-Chi 178	Anson-Chi 44.6	Brouthers-Buf 37.8	Radbourn-Pro 132	Anson-Chi 99
Anson-Chi .916	Anson-Chi 170	Brouthers-Buf 41.2	Anson-Chi 35.2	Caskin-NY 132	O'Rourke-Buf 90
Williamson-Chi .898	O'Rourke-Buf 167	O'Rourke-Buf 38.8	O'Rourke-Buf 35.0	Kelly-Chi 131	Dalrymple-Chi 88
O'Rourke-Buf .872	Williamson-Chi 164	Williamson-Chi 36.7	Sutton-Bos 33.8	Dorgan-NY 124	Brouthers-Buf 87

Total Average	Stolen Bases	Stolen Base Average	Stolen Base Runs	Fielding Runs	Total Player Rating
Kelly-Chi .969				Pfeffer-Chi 45.5	Pfeffer-Chi 6.1
Brouthers-Buf .959				Williamson-Chi 23.8	Williamson-Chi 4.7
Anson-Chi .908				Gilligan-Pro 17.2	Kelly-Chi 3.1
Williamson-Chi .907				Lillie-Buf 16.0	Sutton-Bos 2.7
O'Rourke-Buf .849				Hanlon-Det 13.3	Hines-Pro 2.6

Wins	Win Percentage	Games	Complete Games	Shutouts	Saves
Radbourn-Pro 59	Radbourn-Pro .831	Radbourn-Pro 75	Radbourn-Pro 73	Galvin-Buf 12	Morrill-Bos 2
Buffinton-Bos 48	Buffinton-Bos .750	Galvin-Buf 72	Galvin-Buf 71	Radbourn-Pro 11	Sweeney-Pro 1
Galvin-Buf 46	Sweeney-Pro .680	Buffinton-Bos 67	Buffinton-Bos 63	Buffinton-Bos 8	Radbourn-Pro 1
Welch-NY 39	Galvin-Buf .676	Welch-NY 65	Welch-NY 62	L.Corcoran-Chi 7	O'Rourke-Buf 1
L.Corcoran-Chi 35	Welch-NY .650	L.Corcoran-Chi 60	L.Corcoran-Chi 57	Whitney-Bos 6	Ferguson-Phi 1

Innings Pitched	Fewest Hits/Game	Fewest BB/Game	Strikeouts	Strikeouts/Game	Ratio
Radbourn-Pro 678.2	Sweeney-Pro 6.23	Whitney-Bos .72	Radbourn-Pro 441	Clarkson-Chi 7.78	Sweeney-Pro 7.41
Galvin-Buf 636.1	Radbourn-Pro 7.00	Galvin-Buf .89	Buffinton-Bos 417	Whitney-Bos 7.23	Whitney-Bos 8.01
Buffinton-Bos 587.0	Clarkson-Chi 7.17	Buffinton-Bos 1.17	Galvin-Buf 369	Getzien-Det 6.54	Radbourn-Pro 8.30
Welch-NY 557.1	Getzien-Det 7.21	Sweeney-Pro 1.18	Welch-NY 345	Buffinton-Bos 6.39	Getzien-Det 8.74
L.Corcoran-Chi 516.2	Whitney-Bos 7.29	Coleman-Phi 1.28	L.Corcoran-Chi 272	Sweeney-Pro 5.90	Galvin-Buf 8.90

Earned Run Average	Adjusted ERA	Opponents' Batting Avg.	Opponents' On Base Pct.	Starter Runs	Adjusted Starter Runs
Radbourn-Pro 1.38	Radbourn-Pro 204	Sweeney-Pro .187	Sweeney-Pro .215	Radbourn-Pro 120.5	Radbourn-Pro 108.6
Sweeney-Pro 1.55	Sweeney-Pro 182	Getzien-Det .204	Whitney-Bos .223	Galvin-Buf 69.5	Galvin-Buf 81.5
Getzien-Det 1.95	Galvin-Buf 158	Radbourn-Pro .205	Radbourn-Pro .234	Buffinton-Bos 54.2	Buffinton-Bos 48.2
Galvin-Buf 1.99	Getzien-Det 148	Whitney-Bos .207	Getzien-Det .237	Sweeney-Pro 35.1	L.Corcoran-Chi 41.7
Whitney-Bos 2.09	Clarkson-Chi 147	Clarkson-Chi .208	Buffinton-Bos .244	Whitney-Bos 33.2	Sweeney-Pro 31.2

Clutch Pitching Index	Relief Runs	Adjusted Relief Runs	Relief Ranking	Total Pitcher Index	Total Baseball Ranking
Radbourn-Pro 117				Radbourn-Pro 9.8	Radbourn-Pro 9.5
Meinke-Det 116				Galvin-Buf 6.8	Galvin-Buf 6.8
L.Corcoran-Chi 113				Buffinton-Bos 5.7	Pfeffer-Chi 6.1
Moffett-Cle 110				L.Corcoran-Chi 4.6	Buffinton-Bos 5.2
Welch-NY 107				Whitney-Bos 4.0	Williamson-Chi 4.7

May 1 Moses Fleetwood Walker becomes the first black in the major leagues when he plays for the Toledo club in the American Association. He goes 0-for-3 in his major league debut, allowing two passed balls and committing four errors, as his team bows to Louisville 5-1. He will do better in 41 subsequent games before injuries force Toledo to release him in late September. Only one other black player—Fleet's brother Weldy—appears in a major league uniform until Jackie Robinson in 1947.

May 1 One person is killed and several others injured when a section of bleachers collapses following Cincinnati's Opening Day loss to Columbus.

May 10 Washington catcher Alex Gardner's first major league game is also his last, as he allows 12 passed balls, a major league record that still stands. Washington loses the game to New York's Mets 11–3.

May 24 Against Pittsburgh, Philadelphia Athletics pitcher Al Atkinson hits the leadoff batter, Ed Swartwood, who steals second base, takes third base on a putout, and scores on a passed ball. But Atkinson sets down the next 27 Alleghenies for a near-perfect, no-hit 10–1 win.

June 13 Baltimore management surrounds the playing field with a barbed wire fence to restrain the crowd. Baltimore fans had surged onto the field and manhandled the umpire following a 13-inning tie with Louisville the day before.

July 4 Louisville ace Guy Hecker defeats Brooklyn in a morning game (5–4) and again in the afternoon (8–2) en route to a season total of 52 wins, an AA record.

October 30 Financially troubled despite finishing second to New York in the AA, the Columbus club decides to sell its players to Allegheny of Pittsburgh (AA)—for $6,000—and go out of business.

December 11 The AA votes to keep its ban on overhand pitching and to continue to allow fouls caught on one bounce to count as outs. It does abolish the tradition of team captains flipping for the honor of batting first. Now the home team will automatically bat first.

	BALTIMORE		BROOKLYN		CINCINNATI		COLUMBUS		INDIANAPOLIS		LOUISVILLE		NEW YORK
M	B.Barnie	M	G.Taylor	M	W.White	M	G.Schmelz	M	J.Gifford	M	M.Walsh	M	J.Mutrie
1B	E.Stearns	1B	C.Householder	M	P.Snyder	1B	J.Field	M	B.Watkins	1B	J.Latham	1B	D.Orr
2B	T.Manning	2B	B.Greenwood	1B	J.Reilly	2B	P.Smith	1B	J.Kerins	2B	J.Gerhardt	2B	D.Troy
SS	J.Macullar	SS	B.Geer	2B	B.McPhee	SS	J.Richmond	2B	E.Merrill	SS	T.McLaughlin	SS	C.Nelson
3B	J.Sommer	3B	F.Warner	SS	J.Peoples	3B	B.Kuehne	SS	M.Phillips	3B	P.Browning	3B	D.Esterbrook
LF	T.York	LF	I.Benners	3B	H.Carpenter	LF	J.Cahill	3B	P.Callahan	LF	L.Maskrey	LF	E.Kennedy
CF	J.Clinton	CF	J.Remsen	LF	T.Mansell	CF	F.Mann	LF	J.Peltz	CF	M.Cline	CF	C.Roseman
RF	G.Gardner	RF	J.Cassidy	CF	C.Jones	RF	T.Brown	CF	J.Morrison	RF	J.Wolf	RF	S.Brady
C	S.Trott	C	J.Corcoran	RF	P.Corkhill	C	R.Kemmler	RF	P.Weihe	C	D.Sullivan	C	B.Holbert
				C	P.Snyder			C	J.Keenan				
C	B.Traffley	O1	O.Walker			CO	F.Carroll			3P	P.Reccius	C	C.Reipschlager
O	D.Casey	13	J.Knowles	O	B.West	OP	E.Dundon	O	J.Dorgan	C	E.Whiting	/O	G.Pierce
O2	O.Burns	23	C.Jones	C	P.Powers	O	T.Mansell	2	C.Collins	/1	W.Andrews	/C	T.Murphy
O	B.Dickerson	OC	T.Wilson	S	F.Fennelly			3	J.Donnelly	/O	B.Dickerson	/C	H.Oxley
/3	J.Ake	C	J.Farrow	S	C.Fulmer	P	E.Morris	3	B.Watkins	/O	L.Stockwell		
/1	P.Burns	C	J.Hayes	/O	J.Woulfe	P	F.Mountain	O	J.Sneed	/C	B.Hunter	P	J.Lynch
/C	J.Roxburgh	/C	J.Dorgan	/O	F.Berkelbach			OC	T.Thompson			P	T.Keefe
				/C	G.Miller	/P	T.Sullivan	C	C.Robinson	P	G.Hecker		
P	B.Emslie	P	A.Terry	/O	I.Reeder	/P	A.Bauers	/O	G.Moriarity	P	D.Driscoll	/P	B.Becannon
P	H.Henderson	P	S.Kimber	/O	J.Parsons			/O	B.Butler	P	R.Deagle		
		P	J.Conway					/O	M.Locke				
/P	F.Goldsmith			P	W.White			/O	J.Tray				
/P	J.McLaughlin			P	B.Mountjoy			/1	B.Blakiston				
				P	G.Shallix			/O	J.Holdsworth				
								/C	H.Decker				
				/P	R.Deagle			/C	M.Barrett				
								/1	C.Levis				

	PHILADELPHIA		PITTSBURGH		RICHMOND		ST.LOUIS	/O	F.Monroe		TOLEDO		WASHINGTON
M	L.Knight	M	D.McKnight	M	F.Moses	M	J.Williams	/C	G.Mundinger	M	C.Morton	M	H.Hollingshead
1B	H.Stovey	M	B.Ferguson	1B	J.Powell	M	C.Comiskey	/O	C.Reising	1B	C.Lane	M	Bickerson
2B	C.Stricker	M	J.Battin	2B	T.Larkin	1B	C.Comiskey	/C	H.Weber	2B	S.Barkley	1B	W.Prince
SS	S.Houck	M	G.Creamer	SS	B.Schenck	2B	J.Quest	/O	P.Fries	SS	J.Miller	2B	T.Hawkes
3B	F.Corey	M	H.Phillips	3B	B.Nash	SS	B.Gleason			3B	E.Brown	SS	F.Fennelly
LF	J.Birchall	1B	J.Knowles	LF	E.Glenn	3B	A.Latham	P	L.McKeon	LF	F.Olin	3B	B.Gladman
CF	H.Larkin	2B	G.Creamer	CF	D.Johnston	LF	T.O'Neill	P	B.Barr	CF	C.Welch	LF	B.Morgan
RF	L.Knight	SS	B.White	RF	M.Mansell	CF	F.Lewis	P	J.Aydelott	RF	T.Poorman	CF	H.Mullin
C	J.Milligan	3B	J.Battin	C	J.Hanna	RF	H.Nicol	P	A.McCauley	C	F.Walker	RF	E.Trumbull
		LF	D.Miller			C	P.Deasley					C	J.Humphries
C	J.O'Brien	CF	L.Taylor	CO	M.Quinton			/P	M.MacArthur	13	J.Moffett		
O	B.Blakiston	RF	E.Swartwood	O	W.Goldsby	O	G.Strief	/P	T.Bond	C	D.McGuire	2	E.Yewell
O	J.Coleman	C	E.Colgan	/C	B.Dugan	C	T.Dolan			3	G.Meister	2O	F.Olin
O	M.Mansell			/C	B.Morgan	OP	B.Caruthers			3O	C.Morton	C	J.Hanna
/O	C.Hilsey	3O	J.McDonald	/1	A.Swan	O	C.Krehmeyer			1	T.McSorley	O	E.Smith
/C	F.Siffell	S	T.Forster	/O	W.Williams	O	J.Lavin			O	J.Tilley	O	J.Kiley
/C	E.Rowen	C	J.Hayes	/S	E.Ford	/O	W.Goldsby			C	T.Arundel	O	T.Farley
/C	E.Foster	O	C.Eden			/O	H.Wheeler			C	S.Bullas	1	S.King
/C	F.Ringo	1	J.Faatz	P	P.Meegan	/2	W.Kinzie			/O	E.Miller	/O	J.Beach
/O	M.Moynahan	O	M.Mansell	P	E.Dugan	/O	A.Struve			/O	W.Walker	/O	W.Goldsby
		3	A.Whitney			/2	C.Fulmer					/O	W.Murphy
P	B.Mathews	O	B.Reid	/P	W.Curry	/C	N.Alexander			P	T.Mullane	/1	A.Swan
P	B.Taylor	O	C.Doyle	/P	T.Firth	/C	J.McCauley			P	H.O'Day	/O	Jones
P	A.Atkinson	O	J.Woulfe									/O	Wills
		O	C.Lauer			P	J.McGinnis			/P	E.Kent	/O	L.Drake
/P	P.Smith	/2	J.Quest			P	D.Foutz					/C	A.Gardner
		/O	B.Ferguson			P	D.Davis						
		S	J.Dee									P	B.Barr
		/C	F.Smith									P	J.Hamill
		/1	C.Hautz										
		/S	G.Alberts										
		/S	J.Peters										
		/3	J.Gray										
		P	F.Sullivan										
		P	J.Neagle										
		/P	J.Fox										
		/P	B.Nelson										
		/P	F.Beck										
		/P	J.Gorman										
		/P	P.Smith										

TEAM	G	W	L	PCT	GB	R	OR	AB	H	2B	3B	HR	BB	SO	AVG	OBP	SLG	PRO	PRO+	BR	/A	PF	CHI	RC	SB	CS	SBA	SBR
NY	112	75	32	.701		734	**423**	4012	1052	155	64	22	203	315	.262	**.304**	.349	.653	120	70	87	98	109	436				
COL	110	69	39	.639	6.5	585	459	3759	901	107	96	40	196	629	.240	.288	.351	.639	108	47	97	92	95	390				
LOU	110	68	40	.630	7.5	573	425	3957	1004	152	69	17	146	408	.254	.286	.340	.626	112	29	57	96	93	395				
STL	110	67	40	.626	8	658	539	3952	987	151	60	11	172	339	.250	.288	.327	.615	100	16	-5	104	109	381				
CIN	110	68	41	.624	8	**754**	512	4090	1037	109	96	36	154	409	.254	.289	.354	.643	108	53	21	105	**114**	429				
BAL	108	63	43	.594	11.5	636	515	3845	896	133	84	32	**211**	545	.233	.284	.336	.620	101	25	1	104	105	377				
PHI	108	61	46	.570	14	700	546	3959	**1057**	**167**	**100**	26	153	434	**.267**	.301	**.379**	**.680**	117	**100**	56	106	102	**463**				
TOL	110	46	58	.442	27.5	463	571	3712	859	153	48	8	157	545	.231	.268	.305	.573	87	-39	-57	104	90	310				
BRO	109	40	64	.385	33.5	476	644	3763	845	112	47	16	179	417	.225	.263	.292	.555	83	-61	-64	101	95	296				
RIC	46	12	30	.286	30.5	194	294	1469	326	40	33	7	53	282	.222	.261	.308	.569	89	-18	-16	99	97	121				
PIT	110	30	78	.278	45.5	406	725	3689	777	105	50	2	143	411	.211	.248	.268	.516	71	-109	-116	102	92	251				
IND	110	29	78	.271	46	462	755	3813	890	129	62	20	125	561	.233	.262	.315	.577	93	-38	-24	97	88	323				
WAS	63	12	51	.190	41	248	481	2166	434	61	24	6	100	377	.200	.241	.259	.500	75	-75	-47	88	100	139				
TOT	659					6889		46186	11065	1574	833	243	1992	5672	.240	.278	.326	.604										

TEAM	CG	SH	SV	IP	H	H/G	HR	BB	SO	RAT	ERA	ERA+	OAV	OOB	PR	/A	PF	CPI	FA	E	DP	FW	PW	BW	SBW	DIF
NY	110	9	0	985	**802**	7.3	15	115	628	8.6	2.46	127	**.209**	.237	86	72	96	89	.907	441	42	2.3	6.6	7.9		4.6
COL	102	8	1	962[1]	815	7.6	22	172	526	9.5	2.68	113	.217	.256	60	36	93	98	.908	433	74	2.3	3.3	**8.9**		.5
LOU	101	6	0	989[2]	836	7.6	**9**	**97**	470	8.8	**2.17**	**142**	.216	.241	**118**	**100**	95	106	**.912**	**426**	84	2.6	**9.1**	5.2		-2.9
STL	99	8	0	987	881	8.0	16	172	477	10.0	2.67	122	.226	.266	63	63	100	106	.900	490	65	-.2	5.8	-.5		8.4
CIN	**111**	**11**	0	983[2]	956	8.7	27	181	308	11.1	3.33	100	.243	.290	-10	-1	103	106	.909	430	82	**2.8**	-.0	1.9		8.9
BAL	105	4	1	955[2]	869	8.2	16	219	**635**	10.5	2.71	128	.224	.271	56	79	107	**107**	.899	461	61	.7	7.2	.0		2.0
PHI	105	5	0	948[2]	920	8.7	16	127	530	10.3	3.42	99	.237	.269	-18	-4	104	99	.901	457	63	.9	-.4	5.1		1.9
TOL	103	9	1	946	885	8.4	12	169	501	10.5	3.06	111	.233	.275	19	35	105	99	.900	469	67	.7	3.2	-5.2		-4.7
BRO	105	6	0	948[2]	996	9.4	20	163	378	11.2	3.79	87	.254	.288	-58	-51	102	94	.889	520	68	-1.6	-4.7	-5.8		.2
RIC	45	1	0	370[1]	402	9.8	14	52	167	11.4	4.52	73	.257	.288	-53	-50	102	83	.874	239	27	-1.5	-4.6	-1.5		-1.4
PIT	108	4	0	943[1]	1059	10.1	25	216	338	12.7	4.35	77	.265	.312	-116	-104	104	96	.889	523	71	-1.6	-9.5	-10.6		-2.3
IND	107	2	0	937[2]	1001	9.6	30	199	479	11.8	4.20	78	.255	.295	-100	-97	101	90	.889	515	45	-1.2	-8.9	-2.2		-12.2
WAS	62	3	0	543[2]	643	10.6	21	110	235	12.8	4.01	76	.273	.311	-46	-59	93	109	.858	400	40	-5.3	-5.4	-4.3		-4.6
TOT	1263	80	3	11501[2]		8.7				10.6	3.24		.240	.278					.897	5804	789					

Runs		Hits		Doubles		Triples		Home Runs		Total Bases	
Stovey-Phi	124	Orr-NY	162	Barkley-Tol	39	Stovey-Phi	23	Reilly-Cin	11	Reilly-Cin	247
Jones-Cin	117	Reilly-Cin	152	Browning-Lou	33	Reilly-Cin	19	Stovey-Phi	10	Orr-NY	247
Latham-StL	115	Esterbrook-NY	150	Mann-Col	32	Orr-NY	18	Orr-NY	9	Stovey-Phi	244
Reilly-Cin	114	Browning-Lou	150	Esterbrook-NY	29	Peltz-Ind	17	Mann-Col	7	Jones-Cin	222
Nelson-NY	114	Jones-Cin	148	Lewis-StL	25	Jones-Cin	17	Jones-Cin	7	Browning-Lou	211

Runs Batted In		Runs Produced		Bases On Balls		Batting Average		On Base Percentage		Slugging Average	
Stovey-Phi	197	Nelson-NY	74	Orr-NY	.354	Jones-Cin	.376	Reilly-Cin	.551		
Reilly-Cin	194	Geer-Bro	38	Reilly-Cin	.339	Nelson-NY	.375	Stovey-Phi	.545		
Orr-NY	185	Jones-Cin	37	Browning-Lou	.336	Stovey-Phi	.368	Orr-NY	.539		
Jones-Cin	181	Macullar-Bal	36	Stovey-Phi	.326	Fennelly-Was-Cin	.367	Fennelly-Was-Cin	.480		
McPhee-Cin	166	Richmond-Col	35	Lewis-StL	.323	Reilly-Cin	.366	Browning-Lou	.472		

Production		Adjusted Production		Batter Runs		Adjusted Batter Runs		Clutch Hitting Index		Runs Created	
Reilly-Cin	.918	Orr-NY	195	Stovey-Phi	44.8	Orr-NY	44.9			Reilly-Cin	93
Stovey-Phi	.913	Reilly-Cin	186	Reilly-Cin	44.6	Reilly-Cin	39.4			Stovey-Phi	92
Orr-NY	.901	Fennelly-Was-Cin	186	Orr-NY	42.1	Stovey-Phi	37.8			Orr-NY	92
Fennelly-Was-Cin	.847	Stovey-Phi	182	Jones-Cin	39.0	Fennelly-Was-Cin	36.6			Jones-Cin	85
Jones-Cin	.846	Browning-Lou	176	Browning-Lou	31.6	Browning-Lou	36.1			Browning-Lou	77

Total Average		Stolen Bases		Stolen Base Average		Stolen Base Runs		Fielding Runs		Total Player Rating	
Stovey-Phi	.907							Latham-StL	39.5	Barkley-Tol	4.4
Reilly-Cin	.899							Smith-Col	29.1	Latham-StL	4.2
Orr-NY	.855							Snyder-Col	27.4	Fennelly-Was-Cin	4.0
Jones-Cin	.830							Gerhardt-Lou	27.3	Smith-Col	3.9
Fennelly-Was-Cin	.824							Barkley-Tol	24.6	Esterbrook-NY	3.4

Wins		Win Percentage		Games		Complete Games		Shutouts		Saves	
Hecker-Lou	52	Morris-Col	.723	Hecker-Lou	75	Hecker-Lou	72	White-Cin	7	O'Day-Tol	1
Lynch-NY	37	Hecker-Lou	.722	Mullane-Tol	67	Mullane-Tol	64	Mullane-Tol	7	Mountain-Col	1
Keefe-NY	37	Foutz-StL	.714	McKeon-Ind	61	McKeon-Ind	59	Hecker-Lou	6	O.Burns-Bal	1
Mullane-Tol	36	Lynch-NY	.712	Keefe-NY	58	Keefe-NY	56				
		Keefe-NY	.685	Terry-Bro	56	Terry-Bro	54				

Innings Pitched		Fewest Hits/Game		Fewest BB/Game		Strikeouts		Strikeouts/Game		Ratio	
Hecker-Lou	670.2	Morris-Col	7.02	Driscoll-Lou	.62	Hecker-Lou	385	Henderson-Bal	7.09	Hecker-Lou	8.02
Mullane-Tol	567.0	Hecker-Lou	7.06	Hecker-Lou	.75	Henderson-Bal	346	Davis-StL	6.49	Morris-Col	8.36
McKeon-Ind	512.0	Keefe-NY	7.08	Lynch-NY	.76	Keefe-NY	334	Morris-Col	6.33	Lynch-NY	8.56
Lynch-NY	496.0	Mountain-Col	7.21	E.Dugan-Ric	.81	Mullane-Tol	325	Keefe-NY	6.22	Keefe-NY	8.68
Keefe-NY	483.0	Foutz-StL	7.27	McGinnis-StL	.89	McKeon-Ind	308	Mathews-Phi	5.98	Foutz-StL	9.23

Earned Run Average		Adjusted ERA		Opponents' Batting Avg.		Opponents' On Base Pct.		Starter Runs		Adjusted Starter Runs	
Hecker-Lou	1.80	Hecker-Lou	171	Keefe-NY	.204	Hecker-Lou	.226	Hecker-Lou	107.6	Hecker-Lou	95.6
Foutz-StL	2.18	Foutz-StL	149	Hecker-Lou	.204	Morris-Col	.234	Keefe-NY	53.0	Mullane-Tol	55.7
Morris-Col	2.18	Morris-Col	139	Morris-Col	.204	Lynch-NY	.236	Morris-Col	50.8	Keefe-NY	46.2
Keefe-NY	2.25	Keefe-NY	138	Mountain-Col	.209	Keefe-NY	.239	Mullane-Tol	45.3	Henderson-Bal	40.9
Mountain-Col	2.45	Mullane-Tol	135	Foutz-StL	.212	Foutz-StL	.255	Mountain-Col	31.9	Morris-Col	40.3

Clutch Pitching Index		Relief Runs		Adjusted Relief Runs		Relief Ranking		Total Pitcher Index		Total Baseball Ranking	
Comiskey-StL	127							Hecker-Lou	12.6	Hecker-Lou	12.5
Foutz-StL	122							Mullane-Tol	7.7	Mullane-Tol	7.7
Davis-StL	120							Keefe-NY	5.5	Keefe-NY	5.6
O'Neill-StL	118							Henderson-Bal	4.4	Barkley-Tol	4.4
White-Cin	116							Morris-Col	4.2	Henderson-Bal	4.3

February 9 The grounds of Cincinnati's UA club are flooded under 20 feet of water from the Ohio River. It will cost $3,000 to rebuild the fallen pavilions and fences and restore the field.

March 17 The UA is very busy. The league admits a Boston club organized by George Wright to bring the number of teams to eight, expands its schedule to 112 games, decides to stick with the seven-ball walk rule and adopts the percentage system to determine the champion. The season also gets started, as Bill Sweeney pitches Baltimore to a 7-3 win over Washington.

May 10 Altoona wins its first major league game after 11 straight losses, 9–4 over Boston. They will win only 5 more times before disbanding at the end of May.

May 24 After 20 consecutive wins St. Louis finally falls 8–1 to Boston. The Maroons will finish the season with an .832 percentage, the highest in major league history.

May 31 The Altoona club disbands, the first casualty of the UA, and is replaced by a new club formed in Kansas City.

July 5 After a 17–2 loss at Cincinnati, Philadelphia Athletics (AA) pitcher Al Atkinson deserts his club for Chicago (UA)—the first player to break his contract and join the UA.

July 19 Boston's Fred "Dupee" Shaw holds pennant-bound St. Louis to one hit while fanning 18 batters, but loses the game 1–0 when batter Bill Gleason gets all the way to second base on a dropped third strike and scores on a wild pitch. In his outings of July 16, 19, and 21, Shaw will amass 48 strikeouts, a major league record for three consecutive games.

September 15 In their final home game, against the Kansas City Unions, the last place Wilmington Quick Steps have exactly zero fans in the stands at game time. Manager Joe Simmons decides to forfeit the game rather than play. Wilmington then disbands, and, four days later, Pittsburg disbands as well.

September 16 Jim McCormick picks off 4 Boston Unions in an 8–4 Cincinnati victory, one of McCormick's 21 UA wins. Earlier in the season he won 19 games for Cleveland (NL). He will lead the UA in winning percentage and in ERA.

September 19 The UA decides to drop Pittsburgh and Wilmington and replace them with Milwaukee and Omaha. The latter club will last only eight days before St. Paul picks up the banner anew.

October 5 St. Louis pitchers Charlie Sweeney and Henry Boyle stop St. Paul without a hit or walk, striking out 9 men, before rain halts play after 5 innings. But the Maroons lose the game when 2 St. Louis errors allow the game's only run. The Sweeney-Boyle performance caps what is still the premier major league season for no-hitters: 12 in all, including one of 10 innings and 7 nine-inning games.

October 9 Fred Dunlap's 13th homer helps his St. Louis Maroons bury the Washington Nationals 11–1. The second baseman will add the homer championship to his UA titles in batting, slugging, on base percentage, hits, doubles, and total bases, the most dominant season by any nonpitcher of the century. He also leads all UA second basemen in fielding average, putouts, assists, double plays, and total chances per game.

December 18 Only five clubs attend the "annual" meeting, one by proxy. The UA will die early in 1885.

ALTOONA		BALTIMORE		BOSTON		CINCINNATI		CHI-PITT		KANSAS CITY	
M	E.Curtis	M	B.Henderson	M	T.Murnane	M	D.O'Leary	M	E.Hengle	M	H.Wheeler
1B	F.Harris	1B	C.Levis	1B	T.Murnane	M	S.Crane	1B	J.Schoeneck	M	M.Porter
2B	C.Dougherty	2B	D.Phelan	2B	T.O'Brien	1B	M.Powell	2B	M.Hengle	M	T.Sullivan
SS	G.Smith	SS	L.Say	SS	W.Hackett	2B	S.Crane	SS	S.Matthias	1B	J.Sweeney
3B	H.Koons	3B	Y.Robinson	3B	J.Irwin	SS	J.Jones	3B	W.Foley	2B	C.Berry
LF	J.Murphy	LF	E.Seery	LF	K.Butler	3B	C.Barber	LF	C.Householder	SS	C.Cross
CF	F.Shaffer	CF	N.Cuthbert	CF	M.Slattery	LF	L.Sylvester	CF	H.Wheeler	3B	P.Sullivan
RF	J.Brown	RF	B.Graham	RF	E.Crane	CF	B.Harbidge	RF	J.Ellick	LF	F.Wyman
C	J.Moore	C	E.Fusselback	C	L.Brown	RF	B.Hawes	C	B.Krieg	CF	B.McLaughlin
						C	J.Kelly			RF	F.Shaffer
P	J.Murphy	CO	R.Sweeney	O	T.McCarthy			O2	C.Briggs	C	K.Baldwin
		O	H.Oberbeck	C	J.McKeever	OP	D.Burns	CS	T.Suck		
		O	J.O'Brien			S	J.Glasscock	O	G.Gardner	OP	B.Black
		O	H.Wheeler	P	J.Burke	1	M.McQuery	C	E.Gross	1	J.Gorman
		1	J.Schoeneck	P	D.Shaw	O	D.O'Leary	2	C.McGarr	2O	F.McLaughlin
				P	T.Bond	3	E.Cleveland	3	J.Battin	1O	J.Cudworth
		P	B.Sweeney			C	B.Schwartz	2	F.McLaughlin	3	H.Oberbeck
		P	T.Lee	/P	F.Tenney	C	F.Briody			OP	P.Veach
		P	A.Atkinson	/P	C.Daniels	C	J.Crotty	P	H.Daily	OC	H.Decker
						S	F.McLaughlin	P	A.Atkinson	S	L.Say
		/P	P.Smith					P	J.Horan	C	N.Alexander
		/P	J.Ryan			P	G.Bradley			O	H.Wheeler
						P	J.McCormick	/P	C.Cady	O	J.Strauss
								/P	F.Foreman		
										P	E.Hickman
										/P	J.Bakely
										/P	D.Blaisdell
										/P	D.Crothers
										/P	B.Hutchison

MILWAUKEE		PHILADELPHIA		ST.LOUIS		ST.PAUL		WASHINGTON		WILMINGTON	
M	T.Loftus	M	F.Malone	M	T.Sullivan	M	A.Thompson	M	M.Scanlon	M	J.Simmons
1B	T.Griffin	1B	J.McGuinness	M	F.Dunlap	1B	S.Dunn	1B	P.Joy	1B	R.Snyder
2B	A.Myers	2B	E.Peak	1B	J.Quinn	2B	M.Hengle	2B	T.Evers	2B	C.Bastian
SS	T.Sexton	SS	H.Easterday	2B	F.Dunlap	SS	J.Werrick	SS	J.Halpin	SS	H.Myers
3B	T.Morrissey	3B	J.McCormick	SS	M.Whitehead	3B	B.O'Brien	3B	J.McCormick	3B	J.Say
LF	S.Behel	LF	B.Hoover	3B	J.Gleason	LF	J.Tilley	LF	H.Moore	LF	T.Lynch
CF	L.Baldwin	CF	B.Kienzle	LF	H.Boyle	CF	B.Barnes	CF	P.Baker	CF	G.Fisher
RF	E.Hogan	RF	J.Flynn	CF	D.Rowe	RF	S.Carroll	RF	B.Wise	RF	J.Munce
C	C.Broughton	C	T.Gillen	RF	O.Shaffer	C	C.Ganzel	C	C.Fulmer	C	T.Cusick
				C	G.Baker						
P	H.Porter	OC	J.Clements			P	J.Brown	OP	A.Powell	P	J.Murphy
P	E.Cushman	O	H.Luff	CO	J.Brennan	P	L.Galvin	CO	J.Gunson	P	T.Nolan
				O	B.Dickerson			S	J.Deasley	P	D.Casey
		P	J.Bakely	C	T.Dolan			O	F.Tenney	P	J.Bakely
		P	S.Weaver					CO	E.McKenna		
		P	Fisher	P	C.Sweeney			3	T.Larkin		
				P	B.Taylor			OP	M.Lockwood		
		/P	B.Gallagher	P	P.Werden						
				P	C.Hodnett			P	B.Wise		
								P	A.Voss		
				/P	J.Cattanach			P	C.Gagus		
								/P	H.Daily		

TEAM	G	W	L	PCT	GB	R	OR	AB	H	2B	3B	HR	BB	SO	AVG	OBP	SLG	PRO	PRO+	BR	/A	PF	CHI	RC	SB	CS	SBA	SBR
STL	114	94	19	.832		887	429	4285	1251	259	41	32	181	542	.292	.321	.394	.715	113	-33	-56	104	103	555				
MIL	12	8	4	.667	35.5	53	34	395	88	25	0	0	20	70	.223	.260	.286	.546	124	-27	-21	54	91	30				
CIN	105	69	36	.657	21	703	466	3786	1027	118	63	26	147	482	.271	.298	.356	.654	92	-111	-150	108	102	413				
BAL	106	58	47	.552	32	662	627	3883	952	150	26	17	144	652	.245	.272	.310	.582	71	-215	-259	110	109	336				
BOS	111	58	51	.532	34	636	558	3940	928	168	32	19	118	787	.236	.260	.309	.569	74	-242	-258	98	107	324				
CP	93	41	50	.451	42	438	482	3212	742	127	26	10	119	505	.231	.258	.296	.554	69	-211	-209	99	93	252				
WAS	114	47	65	.420	46.5	572	679	3926	931	120	26	4	118	558	.237	.259	.284	.543	68	-271	-260	97	102	296				
PHI	67	21	46	.313	50	414	545	2518	618	108	35	7	103	405	.245	.275	.324	.599	89	-125	-105	93	101	230				
STP	9	2	6	.250	39.5	24	57	272	49	13	1	0	7	47	.180	.201	.235	.436	61	-30	-36	54	84	13				
ALT	25	6	19	.240	44	90	216	899	223	30	6	2	22	130	.248	.266	.301	.567	72	-55	-56	101	67	74				
KC	82	16	63	.203	61	311	618	2802	557	104	15	6	123	529	.199	.232	.253	.485	55	-255	-235	87	88	169				
WIL	18	2	16	.111	44.5	35	114	521	91	8	8	2	22	123	.175	.208	.232	.440	33	-56	-57	103	61	26				
TOT	428					4825		30439	7457	1230	279	125	1134	4830	.245	.272	.316	.588										

TEAM	CG	SH	SV	IP	H	H/G	HR	BB	SO	RAT	ERA	ERA+	OAV	OOB	PR	/A	PF	CPI	FA	E	DP	FW	PW	BW	SBW	DIF
STL	104	8	6	993	838	7.6	9	110	550	8.6	1.96	122	.214	.235	53	47	98	106	.888	554	79	3.7	4.1	-4.9		34.6
MIL	12	3	0	104	49	4.2	1	13	139	5.4	2.25	59	.132	.161	2	-11	54	12	.892	53	4	.6	-1.0	-1.8		4.2
CIN	95	11	1	914¹	831	8.2	17	90	503	9.1	2.38	107	.226	.245	6	18	105	102	.882	532	45	2.5	1.6	-13.1		25.5
BAL	92	4	0	946²	1002	9.5	24	177	628	11.2	3.01	89	.254	.286	-61	-36	110	115	.872	616	53	-.8	-3.2	-22.7		32.1
BOS	100	5	1	953¹	885	8.4	17	110	753	9.4	2.70	88	.231	.252	-28	-35	98	95	.868	633	39	-.3	-3.1	-20.7		27.6
CP	86	6	0	803²	743	8.3	12	137	679	9.9	2.72	90	.230	.261	-25	-24	100	98	.882	459	38	2.7	-2.3	-18.3		13.3
WAS	94	5	0	953¹	992	9.4	16	168	684	10.9	3.44	70	.251	.282	-106	-110	98	95	.869	625	55	.7	-9.6	-22.8		22.7
PHI	64	1	0	593¹	726	11.0	7	105	310	12.6	4.63	57	.248	.283	-144	-152	95	89	.841	501	36	-5.2	-13.3	-9.2		15.2
STP	7	1	0	71	72	9.1	1	27	44	12.5	3.17	42	.248	.312	-6	-15	54	117	.872	47	6	.2	-1.3	-3.2		2.3
ALT	20	0	0	219²	292	12.0	3	52	91	11.4	4.67	57	.300	.335	-55	-49	109	104	.862	156	4	-.6	-4.3	-4.9		3.3
KC	70	0	0	702²	862	11.0	14	127	334	12.7	4.07	55	.283	.312	-128	-144	92	104	.861	520	51	-2.5	-12.6	-20.6		12.1
WIL	15	0	0	142	165	10.5	4	18	113	11.6	3.04	87	.273	.294	-10	-6	109	126	.860	104	10	-.1	-.5	-5.0		-1.4
TOT	759	44	8	7397¹		9.1				10.5	3.05		.245	.272					.872	4800	420					

Runs	Hits	Doubles	Triples	Home Runs	Total Bases
Dunlap-StL 160	Dunlap-StL 185	Shaffer-StL 40	Burns-Cin 12	Dunlap-StL 13	Dunlap-StL 279
Shaffer-StL 130	Shaffer-StL 168	Dunlap-StL 39	Rowe-StL 11	Crane-Bos 12	Shaffer-StL 234
Seery-Bal-KC 115	Moore-Was 155	Rowe-StL 32	Shaffer-StL 10	Levis-Bal-Was 6	Rowe-StL 208
Robinson-Bal 101	Seery-Bal-KC 146	O'Brien-Bos 31			Crane-Bos 193
Rowe-StL 95	Rowe-StL 142	Gleason-StL 30			Seery-Bal-KC 192

Runs Batted In	Runs Produced	Bases On Balls	Batting Average	On Base Percentage	Slugging Average
	Dunlap-StL 147	Robinson-Bal 37	Dunlap-StL .412	Dunlap-StL .448	Dunlap-StL .621
	Shaffer-StL 128	Shaffer-StL 30	Taylor-StL .366	Shaffer-StL .398	Taylor-StL .548
	Seery-Bal-KC 113	Dunlap-StL 29	Dickerson-StL .365	Hoover-Phi .390	Shaffer-StL .501
	Robinson-Bal 99	Harbidge-Cin 25	Hoover-Phi .364	Moore-Was .363	Hoover-Phi .495
	Rowe-StL 91	Gleason-StL 23	Shaffer-StL .360	Gleason-StL .361	Burns-Cin .457

Production	Adjusted Production	Batter Runs	Adjusted Batter Runs	Clutch Hitting Index	Runs Created
Dunlap-StL 1.069	Dunlap-StL 213	Dunlap-StL 53.4	Dunlap-StL 49.1		Dunlap-StL 128
Shaffer-StL .899	Hoover-Phi 180	Shaffer-StL 27.6	Shaffer-StL 24.0		Shaffer-StL 96
Hoover-Phi .885	Shaffer-StL 165	Glasscock-Cin 16.9	Hoover-Phi 18.8		Moore-Was 71
Gleason-StL .802	Moore-Was 139	Hoover-Phi 14.4	Glasscock-Cin 13.5		Seery-Bal-KC 67
Moore-Was .777	Gleason-StL 137	Taylor-StL 12.6	Taylor-StL 11.2		Rowe-StL 65

Total Average	Stolen Bases	Stolen Base Average	Stolen Base Runs	Fielding Runs	Total Player Rating
Dunlap-StL 1.167				Dunlap-StL 30.5	Dunlap-StL 6.9
Shaffer-StL .883				Fusselback-Bal 19.3	Shaffer-StL 1.7
Hoover-Phi .846				Baker-StL 16.3	Briody-Cin 1.5
Gleason-StL .738				Robinson-Bal 16.1	Hoover-Phi 1.5
Moore-Was .686				Krieg-CP 14.9	Glasscock-Cin 1.3

Wins	Win Percentage	Games	Complete Games	Shutouts	Saves
B.Sweeney-Bal 40	McCormick-Cin .875	B.Sweeney-Bal 62	B.Sweeney-Bal 58	McCormick-Cin 7	Taylor-StL 4
Daily-CP-Was 28	Taylor-StL .862	Daily-CP-Was 58	Daily-CP-Was 56	Daily-CP-Was 5	Sylvester-Cin 1
Taylor-StL 25	Boyle-StL .833	Wise-Was 50	Bakely-Phi-Wil-KC 43	Shaw-Bos 5	Dunlap-StL 1
Bradley-Cin 25	Sweeney-StL .774	Bakely-Phi-Wil-KC 46	Bradley-Cin 36	Wise-Was 4	Brown-Bos 1
Sweeney-StL 24	B.Sweeney-Bal .656	Bradley-Cin 41	Shaw-Bos 35	B.Sweeney-Bal 4	Boyle-StL 1

Innings Pitched	Fewest Hits/Game	Fewest BB/Game	Strikeouts	Strikeouts/Game	Ratio
B.Sweeney-Bal 538.0	McCormick-Cin 6.47	Sweeney-StL .43	Daily-CP-Was 483	Shaw-Bos 8.81	McCormick-Cin 7.07
Daily-CP-Was 500.2	Shaw-Bos 6.47	McCormick-Cin .60	B.Sweeney-Bal 374	Daily-CP-Was 8.68	Sweeney-StL 7.31
Bakely-Phi-Wil-KC 394.2	Sweeney-StL 6.87	Boyle-StL .60	Shaw-Bos 309	Gagus-Was 7.92	Shaw-Bos 7.53
Wise-Was 364.1	Boyle-StL 7.08	Bradley-Cin .61	Wise-Was 268	Robinson-Bal 7.32	Boyle-StL 7.68
Bradley-Cin 342.0	Werden-StL 7.20	Murphy-Wil-Alt .62	Burke-Bos 255	Burke-Bos 7.13	Werden-StL 8.60

Earned Run Average	Adjusted ERA	Opponents' Batting Avg.	Opponents' On Base Pct.	Starter Runs	Adjusted Starter Runs
McCormick-Cin 1.54	McCormick-Cin 166	McCormick-Cin .188	McCormick-Cin .202	Shaw-Bos 23.5	McCormick-Cin 23.7
Taylor-StL 1.68	Taylor-StL 143	Shaw-Bos .188	Sweeney-StL .207	Taylor-StL 22.2	Shaw-Bos 21.3
Boyle-StL 1.74	Boyle-StL 137	Sweeney-StL .197	Shaw-Bos .212	McCormick-Cin 20.9	Taylor-StL 20.9
Shaw-Bos 1.77	Shaw-Bos 134	Boyle-StL .202	Boyle-StL .215	Sweeney-StL 18.4	Sweeney-StL 17.0
Sweeney-StL 1.83	Sweeney-StL 131	Werden-StL .205	Werden-StL .235	Boyle-StL 11.6	Boyle-StL 10.8

Clutch Pitching Index	Relief Runs	Adjusted Relief Runs	Relief Ranking	Total Pitcher Index	Total Baseball Ranking
Hodnett-StL 140				Taylor-StL 2.8	Dunlap-StL 6.7
Robinson-Bal 132				Sweeney-StL 2.4	Taylor-StL 3.2
Taylor-StL 129				McCormick-Cin 1.8	Sweeney-StL 2.4
B.Sweeney-Bal 111				Shaw-Bos 1.5	McCormick-Cin 1.8
Murphy-Wil-Alt 110				Boyle-StL .8	Shaffer-StL 1.7

January 6 Millionaire Henry V. Lucas, creator of the failed Union Association, purchases the Cleveland club and eventually fills the vacancy in the NL with his own St. Louis Maroons.

January 10 At an NL meeting, St. Louis is admitted to the League, Cleveland's registration is formally accepted, and Detroit has its request to remain in the NL granted, leaving only one opening for the season.

February 22 Boston pitcher Charlie Buffinton invents a baseball "roller skate" that gives pitchers greater impetus and swing in their delivery while still allowing them to keep both feet on the ground.

March 15 A lower court in New York decides that playing baseball on Sunday is a crime. This decision will be overturned, but it will be appealed.

May 2 In the NY Giants' opener, Mickey Welch throws a one-hitter against Boston for his first of 44 wins. He and Tim Keefe will combine for 76 victories this year, second in history only to the Grays' Hoss Radbourn and Charlie Sweeney, who won 77 in 1884.

June 6 The first game played at Chicago's new West Side Park proves victorious for the White Stockings, as they beat St. Louis 9–2. Hugh "One-Arm" Daily makes his debut as a Maroon before more than 10,000 spectators.

July 11 Chicago releases injured pitcher Larry Corcoran. After averaging 34 wins the last 5 seasons, Corcoran wins only 7 games in 1885.

August 1 The largest paying crowd to date gathers at the Polo Grounds; 13,427 fans watch the Giants defeat the Chicago White Stockings 7–6.

August 27 Providence lays off former batting champ Paul Hines and accuses him of intentionally playing poorly to receive his release. His .358 in 1878 led the NL.

September 9 The Grays end their 13-game losing streak with a 3-1 win over the Phillies. This will be the last major league game ever played in Providence.

October 7 The last NL game ever played in Buffalo's Olympic Park attracts 12 fans as Providence takes two from the Bisons 4–0 and 6–1. Grays pitcher Dupee Shaw goes the distance in both victories (each five innings), throwing a no-hitter in the first game.

October 14 The White Stockings (NL) and Browns (AA) engage in a "World's Championship" series. The winner of the 7-game series is to receive a $1,000 prize. Darkness ends Game 1 after eight innings, at a 5–5 stalemate.

October 22 John Ward and several teammates secretly form the Brotherhood of Professional Base Ball Players. The Brotherhood is strengthened by fights against salary restrictions and abuses of the reserve clause. It will become a force to reckoned with by the end of the decade.

October 24 The St. Louis Browns defeat Chicago 13-4 in the seventh and last game in their series. The AA Browns and NL White Stockings agree to throw out Game 2 of the series before the start of the seventh game. Each club wins three, loses and has a tie; each club receives $500.

November 28 President Soden buys the Providence franchise and players for $6,000.

December 18 The Washington Nationals are admitted to the NL, in place of Providence.

BOSTON		BUFFALO		CHICAGO		DETROIT		NEW YORK		PHILADELPHIA		PROVIDENCE		ST.LOUIS	
M	J.Morrill	M	J.Galvin	M	C.Anson	M	C.Morton	M	J.Mutrie	M	H.Wright	M	F.Bancroft	M	F.Dunlap
1B	J.Morrill	M	J.Chapman	1B	C.Anson	M	B.Watkins	1B	R.Connor	1B	S.Farrar	1B	J.Start	M	A.McKinnon
2B	J.Burdock	1B	D.Brouthers	2B	F.Pfeffer	1B	M.McQuery	2B	J.Gerhardt	2B	A.Myers	2B	J.Farrell	M	F.Dunlap
SS	S.Wise	2B	D.Force	SS	T.Burns	2B	S.Crane	SS	J.Ward	SS	C.Bastian	SS	A.Irwin	1B	A.McKinnon
3B	E.Sutton	SS	J.Rowe	3B	N.Williamson	SS	M.Phillips	3B	D.Esterbrook	3B	J.Mulvey	3B	J.Denny	2B	F.Dunlap
LF	T.McCarthy	3B	D.White	LF	A.Dalrymple	3B	D.Esterbrook	LF	P.Gillespie	LF	E.Andrews	LF	C.Carroll	SS	J.Glasscock
CF	J.Manning	LF	B.Crowley	CF	G.Gore	LF	J.Donnelly	CF	J.O'Rourke	CF	J.Fogarty	CF	P.Hines	3B	E.Caskin
RF	T.Poorman	CF	H.Richardson	RF	K.Kelly	CF	G.Wood	RF	M.Dorgan	RF	J.Manning	RF	P.Radford	LF	E.Seery
C	T.Gunning	RF	J.Lillie	C	S.Flint	RF	N.Hanlon	C	B.Ewing	C	J.Clements	C	B.Gilligan	CF	F.Lewis
O	G.Whiteley	C	G.Myers	O	B.Sunday	RF	S.Thompson	C	P.Deasley	C	T.Cusick	2S	C.Bassett	RF	O.Shaffer
C	P.Dealy	S1	E.Stearns	C	S.Sutcliffe	C	C.Bennett	O3	D.Richardson	C	C.Ganzel	C	C.Daily	C	F.Briody
2S	W.Hackett	C	J.McCauley	/S	J.Ryan	C	P.Deasly	P	M.Welch	O	T.Lynch	O	L.Knight	O	C.Sweeney
C	M.Hackett	O	E.Crane	/C	J.McCauley	2S	J.Quest	P	T.Keefe	/2	J.Hiland	S	T.Manning	O3	J.Quinn
O	D.Johnston	O	S.Carroll	C	W.Williams	O	J.Dorgan	/P	L.Corcoran	P	E.Daily	/3	D.Lyons	C	G.Baker
O	J.Hornung	O	W.Williams	/O	E.Gastfield	1	M.Scott			P	C.Ferguson	/3	W.Andrus	O	D.Rowe
3	B.Nash	/3	G.Hatfield	/O	B.Krieg	C	D.McGuire			P	B.Vinton	/C	M.Hines	O	D.Burns
O	B.Purcell	/2	M.Hengle	P	J.Clarkson	3	C.Morton			/P	T.Nolan	/O	E.Crane	C	S.Sutcliffe
O	M.Hines	/O	D.Eggler	P	J.McCormick	S	J.Manning					P	C.Radbourn	/O	R.Sweeney
/C	P.Tate	/O	J.Staples	P	T.Kennedy	/C	F.Ringo					P	D.Shaw	/O	J.Brennan
/O	B.Collver	/O	B.Dickerson	/P	L.Corcoran	S	C.Collins					/P	J.McCormick	/C	T.Dolan
P	J.Whitney	/2	D.Driscoll			S	J.Halpin					/P	C.Hallstrom	O	J.Fogarty
P	C.Buffinton	/2	D.Phelan			/O	G.Moriarity					/P	E.Smith	/3	J.Gleason
P	D.Davis	/S	J.McDonald			/C	J.Moore					/P	J.Foley	/3	T.McSorley
/P	B.Stemmeyer	/2	C.Ritter			/S	N.Kellogg					/P	S.Kimber	/3	B.Alvord
		/C	F.Wood			/2	G.Bryant					/P	B.Stellberger	/3	D.Phelan
		P	P.Galvin			/3	F.Olin					/P	J.Ward	/C	C.Krehmeyer
		P	B.Serad			/C	E.Gastfield					/P	E.Seward	P	H.Boyle
		P	P.Conway			/O	F.Meinke							P	J.Kirby
		P	P.Wood			P	S.Wiedman							P	H.Daily
		/P	J.Connor			P	C.Getzien							P	J.Healy
		/P	Fisher			P	L.Baldwin							/P	Palmer
						P	D.Casey								

TEAM	G	W	L	PCT	GB	R	OR	AB	H	2B	3B	HR	BB	SO	AVG	OBP	SLG	PRO	PRO+	BR	/A	PF	CHI	RC	SB	CS	SBA	SBR
CHI	113	87	25	.777		834	470	4093	1079	184	75	54	340	429	.264	.320	.385	.705	115	143	36	115	113	517				
NY	112	85	27	.759	2	691	370	4029	1085	150	82	16	221	312	.269	.307	.359	.666	122	82	91	99	106	456				
PHI	111	56	54	.509	30	513	511	3893	891	156	35	20	220	401	.229	.270	.302	.572	91	-45	-35	98	102	326				
PRO	110	53	57	.482	33	442	531	3727	820	114	30	6	265	430	.220	.272	.272	.544	83	-74	-56	96	96	282				
BOS	113	46	66	.411	41	528	589	3950	915	144	53	22	190	522	.232	.267	.312	.579	94	-41	-23	96	103	337				
DET	108	41	67	.380	44	514	582	3773	917	149	66	25	216	451	.243	.284	.337	.621	105	17	16	100	93	371				
BUF	112	38	74	.339	49	495	761	3900	980	149	50	23	179	380	.251	.284	.333	.617	100	11	-8	103	89	378				
STL	111	36	72	.333	49	390	593	3758	829	121	21	8	214	412	.221	.263	.270	.533	81	-92	-64	94	89	273				
TOT	445					4407		31123	7516	1167	412	174	1845	3337	.241	.284	.322	.606										

TEAM	CG	SH	SV	IP	H	H/G	HR	BB	SO	RAT	ERA	ERA+	OAV	OOB	PR	/A	PF	CPI	FA	E	DP	FW	PW	BW	SBW	DIF
CHI	108	14	4	1015²	868	7.7	37	202	458	9.5	2.23	136	.221	.259	66	89	108	102	.903	496	80	-2.4	8.4	3.4		21.6
NY	109	16	1	994	758	6.9	11	265	516	9.3	1.72	155	.205	.258	121	106	95	114	.929	331	85	6.0	10.0	8.6		4.5
PHI	108	10	0	976	860	7.9	18	218	378	9.9	2.39	117	.224	.266	46	41	99	96	.905	447	66	-.3	3.9	-3.3		.7
PRO	108	8	0	960²	912	8.5	18	235	371	10.7	2.71	98	.235	.278	12	-7	94	96	.903	459	70	-1.1	-.7	-5.3		5.0
BOS	111	10	0	981	1045	9.6	26	188	480	11.3	3.03	89	.261	.294	-23	-38	95	107	.901	478	79	-1.5	-3.6	-2.2		-2.8
DET	105	6	1	954¹	966	9.1	18	224	475	11.2	2.88	99	.249	.290	-6	-2	101	104	.901	463	61	-1.7	-.2	1.5		-12.6
BUF	107	4	1	956	1175	11.1	31	234	320	13.3	4.29	69	.289	.328	-157	-140	106	99	.901	464	65	-.9	-13.2	-.8		-3.1
STL	107	4	0	965¹	935	8.7	15	278	337	11.3	3.37	82	.245	.296	-59	-68	97	89	.916	398	67	2.3	-6.4	-6.0		-7.9
TOT	863	72	7	7803		8.7				10.8	2.82		.241	.284					.908	3536	573					

Runs		Hits		Doubles		Triples		Home Runs		Total Bases	
Kelly-Chi	124	Connor-NY	169	Anson-Chi	35	O'Rourke-NY	16	Dalrymple-Chi	11	Connor-NY	225
O'Rourke-NY	119	Brouthers-Buf	146	Brouthers-Buf	32	Connor-NY	15	Kelly-Chi	9	Brouthers-Buf	221
Gore-Chi	115	Anson-Chi	144	Rowe-Buf	28	Gore-Chi	13			Dalrymple-Chi	219
Dalrymple-Chi	109	Sutton-Bos	143	Dalrymple-Chi	27	Bennett-Det	13			Anson-Chi	214
Connor-NY	102	O'Rourke-NY	143	Mulvey-Phi	25					O'Rourke-NY	211

Runs Batted In		Runs Produced		Bases On Balls		Batting Average		On Base Percentage		Slugging Average	
Anson-Chi	108	Anson-Chi	201	Williamson-Chi	75	Connor-NY	.371	Connor-NY	.435	Brouthers-Buf	.543
Kelly-Chi	75	Kelly-Chi	190	Gore-Chi	68	Brouthers-Buf	.359	Brouthers-Buf	.408	Connor-NY	.495
Pfeffer-Chi	73	Gore-Chi	167	Morrill-Bos	64	Dorgan-NY	.326	Gore-Chi	.405	Ewing-NY	.471
Burns-Chi	71	Connor-NY	166	Connor-NY	51	Richardson-Buf	.319	Hanlon-Det	.372	Anson-Chi	.461
		Dalrymple-Chi	159			Gore-Chi	.313	Anson-Chi	.357	Richardson-Buf	.458

Production		Adjusted Production		Batter Runs		Adjusted Batter Runs		Clutch Hitting Index		Runs Created	
Brouthers-Buf	.951	Connor-NY	203	Connor-NY	51.7	Connor-NY	53.3	White-Buf	146	Connor-NY	100
Connor-NY	.929	Brouthers-Buf	199	Brouthers-Buf	46.8	Brouthers-Buf	43.2	Williamson-Chi	146	Brouthers-Buf	92
Gore-Chi	.858	Bennett-Det	161	Gore-Chi	40.6	O'Rourke-NY	30.9	Anson-Chi	145	Gore-Chi	83
Anson-Chi	.819	Ewing-NY	159	Anson-Chi	31.7	Gore-Chi	25.2	Gerhardt-NY	139	Anson-Chi	78
Bennett-Det	.812	O'Rourke-NY	158	O'Rourke-NY	29.5	Sutton-Bos	24.5	Pfeffer-Chi	136	O'Rourke-NY	77

Total Average		Stolen Bases		Stolen Base Average		Stolen Base Runs		Fielding Runs		Total Player Rating	
Brouthers-Buf	.977							Dunlap-StL	25.8	Connor-NY	4.0
Connor-NY	.965							Pfeffer-Chi	25.4	Dunlap-StL	4.0
Gore-Chi	.884							Fogarty-Phi	24.8	Richardson-Buf	3.4
Bennett-Det	.808							Glasscock-StL	19.4	Ewing-NY	3.2
Anson-Chi	.775							Richardson-Buf	13.1	Glasscock-StL	3.1

Wins		Win Percentage		Games		Complete Games		Shutouts		Saves	
Clarkson-Chi	53	Welch-NY	.800	Clarkson-Chi	70	Clarkson-Chi	68	Clarkson-Chi	10	Williamson-Chi	2
Welch-NY	44	Clarkson-Chi	.768	Welch-NY	56	Welch-NY	55	Welch-NY	7	Pfeffer-Chi	2
Keefe-NY	32	McCormick-Pro-Chi	.750	Whitney-Bos	51	Whitney-Bos	50	Keefe-NY	7	Welch-NY	1
Radbourn-Pro	28	Keefe-NY	.711	Buffinton-Bos	51			Shaw-Pro	6	Galvin-Buf	1
		Radbourn-Pro	.571	Daily-Phi	50			Buffinton-Bos	6	Baldwin-Det	1

Innings Pitched		Fewest Hits/Game		Fewest BB/Game		Strikeouts		Strikeouts/Game		Ratio	
Clarkson-Chi	623.0	Keefe-NY	6.75	Whitney-Bos	.75	Clarkson-Chi	308	Baldwin-Det	6.78	Baldwin-Det	8.28
Welch-NY	492.0	Welch-NY	6.80	Galvin-Buf	1.17	Welch-NY	258	Keefe-NY	5.11	Clarkson-Chi	8.58
Radbourn-Pro	445.2	Baldwin-Det	6.88	Clarkson-Chi	1.40	Buffinton-Bos	242	Buffinton-Bos	5.01	Keefe-NY	9.05
Whitney-Bos	441.1	Clarkson-Chi	7.18	Baldwin-Det	1.41	Keefe-NY	227	Welch-NY	4.72	Welch-NY	9.20
Daily-Phi	440.0	Daily-Phi	7.57	C.Sweeney-StL	1.64	Whitney-Bos	200	Clarkson-Chi	4.45	Daily-Phi	9.41

Earned Run Average		Adjusted ERA		Opponents' Batting Avg.		Opponents' On Base Pct.		Starter Runs		Adjusted Starter Runs	
Keefe-NY	1.58	Keefe-NY	169	Baldwin-Det	.197	Baldwin-Det	.228	Clarkson-Chi	67.0	Clarkson-Chi	82.0
Welch-NY	1.66	Clarkson-Chi	164	Welch-NY	.203	Clarkson-Chi	.239	Welch-NY	63.0	Welch-NY	54.7
Clarkson-Chi	1.85	Welch-NY	160	Keefe-NY	.203	Shaw-Pro	.254	Keefe-NY	55.2	Keefe-NY	48.4
Baldwin-Det	1.86	Baldwin-Det	153	Clarkson-Chi	.208	Keefe-NY	.255	Radbourn-Pro	30.5	Daily-Phi	28.2
Radbourn-Pro	2.20	Daily-Phi	126	Shaw-Pro	.209	Daily-Phi	.256	Daily-Phi	29.7	Ferguson-Phi	25.4

Clutch Pitching Index		Relief Runs		Adjusted Relief Runs		Relief Ranking		Total Pitcher Index		Total Baseball Ranking	
Keefe-NY	121							Clarkson-Chi	8.9	Clarkson-Chi	8.8
Getzien-Det	118							Welch-NY	5.0	Welch-NY	5.0
Radbourn-Pro	116							Keefe-NY	4.7	Keefe-NY	4.7
Welch-NY	112							Ferguson-Phi	4.3	Ferguson-Phi	4.5
Whitney-Bos	111							Radbourn-Pro	3.5	Connor-NY	4.0

January 20 The AA is reorganized, with clubs from St. Louis, Cincinnati, Pittsburgh, Brooklyn, Louisville, New York, and Baltimore.

February 12* The Western League is officially formed, with Indianapolis, Kansas City, Cleveland, Milwaukee, Toledo, and Omaha as the original clubs. It will last until June 23.

April 3 The Metropolitans release Tim Keefe and Dude Esterbrook; both players later sign with the NY Giants.

June 7 The AA wipes out all restrictions on pitchers using an overhand delivery.

June 17 Brooklyn's "Phenomenal" Smith loses his AA debut to St. Louis by a score of 18-5. Every run against the brash lefthander is unearned due to 14 Brooklyn errors. Smith, who gave himself his nickname, brings it on himself. When he arrived in Brooklyn, he said he didn't need his teammates to win. The intentional misplays lead to a $500 fine for each player, but Smith will be re-

leased to ensure team harmony.

July 4* An exhibition between two "old-time" teams is played at the Polo Grounds. The Old Mutual Nine (with pitcher Rynie Wolters) beats the Old Eckford club (with outfielder Dave Eggler and first baseman Andy Allison) by a score of 25-17.

July 18 The Browns lose to the Athletics in St. Louis, snapping their 27-game consecutive-win streak at home, still a major league record.

August 2 Allegheny pitcher Ed "Cannonball" Morris strikes out 15 Colonels, but still loses 4–1. Morris will lead the league in complete games (63), innings pitched (581), and strikeouts (298) this year.

August 8 All games are canceled in New York City today because of General Ulysses S. Grant's funeral.

September 28 Harry Stovey hits his AA-leading 13th homer off Pittsburgh's John Hofford. This is also Stovey's 51st career homer, which is the current major

league record.

October 1* The first black professional team is organized by Frank P. Thompson. The team is called the Athletics but will shortly become known as the Cuban Giants.

October 15 Game 2 of the championship series is forfeited to Chicago. In the top of the sixth inning, Browns manager Charlie Comiskey calls his men off the field to protest a ruling made by umpire Sullivan. The series played in four (4) cities. (also played in NY and St. Louis). Chicago takes a 3–2 series lead by beating the Browns 9–2.

October 17 At a joint meeting in New York between both leagues, a salary maximum of $2,000 and a minimum of $1,000 is set for the upcoming season.

December 8 At a meeting in Philadelphia, the AA decides to remove the Metropolitan club and admit the National club of Washington. The Mets will be readmitted by court order.

	BALTIMORE		BROOKLYN		CINCINNATI		LOUISVILLE		NEW YORK		PHILADELPHIA		PITTSBURGH		ST.LOUIS
M	B.Barnie	M	C.Hackett	M	O.Caylor	M	J.Hart	M	J.Gifford	M	H.Stovey	M	H.Phillips	M	C.Comiskey
1B	E.Stearns	M	C.Byrne	1B	J.Reilly	1B	J.Kerins	1B	D.Orr	1B	H.Stovey	1B	J.Field	1B	C.Comiskey
2B	T.Manning	1B	B.Phillips	2B	B.McPhee	2B	T.McLaughlin	2B	T.Forster	2B	C.Stricker	2B	P.Smith	2B	S.Barkley
SS	J.Macullar	2B	G.Pinkney	SS	F.Fennelly	SS	J.Miller	SS	C.Nelson	SS	S.Houck	SS	A.Whitney	SS	B.Gleason
3B	M.Muldoon	SS	G.Smith	3B	H.Carpenter	3B	P.Reccius	3B	F.Hankinson	3B	F.Corey	3B	B.Kuehne	3B	A.Latham
LF	J.Sommer	3B	B.McClellan	LF	C.Jones	LF	L.Maskrey	LF	E.Kennedy	LF	B.Purcell	LF	C.Eden	LF	Y.Robinson
CF	D.Casey	LF	E.Swartwood	CF	J.Clinton	CF	P.Browning	CF	C.Roseman	CF	H.Larkin	CF	F.Mann	CF	C.Welch
RF	O.Burns	CF	P.Hotaling	RF	P.Corkhill	RF	J.Wolf	RF	S.Brady	RF	J.Coleman	RF	T.Brown	RF	H.Nicol
C	B.Traffley	RF	J.Cassidy	C	P.Snyder	C	J.Crotty	C	C.Reipschlager	C	J.Milligan	C	F.Carroll	C	D.Bushong
		C	J.Hayes												
OC	E.Greer			C	J.Keenan	C	A.Cross	CO	B.Holbert	C	J.O'Brien	1	M.Scott	O	T.O'Neill
2	G.Gardner	OP	A.Terry	C	K.Baldwin	S	B.Geer	2	D.Troy	3S	G.Strief	C	D.Miller	D	D.Sullivan
1	J.Field	C	J.Peoples	C	P.Powers	C	D.Sullivan	C	C.Broughton	O	L.Knight	SO	J.Richmond	/C	M.Drissel
C	S.Trott	O	J.McTamany	/C	J.Peoples	C	M.Murray	/2	J.Reilly	1	M.Powell	C	R.Kemmler	/C	C.Broughton
O	T.York	C	B.Krieg			2	R.Mack	/2	D.Pierson	C	M.Quinton	/S	M.Phillips		
O	J.Evans	C	C.Robinson	P	W.White	/C	C.Krehmeyer	/3	Jones	/C	E.Fusselback	/C	F.Ringo	P	B.Caruthers
2	H.Jacoby	/C	F.Bell	P	L.McKeon	/O	M.Cline			/O	B.Hughes			P	D.Foutz
/C	P.Powers	/C	D.Oldfield	P	B.Mountjoy	/O	J.Strauss	P	J.Lynch	/O	F.Siffell	P	E.Morris	P	J.McGinnis
/1	T.O'Brien	/1	G.McVey	P	G.Pechiney			P	E.Cushman	O	O.Shaffer	P	P.Meegan		
/C	G.Derby	/C	M.Hines	P	G.Shallix			P	D.Crothers			P	H.O'Day		
/C	S.Nava	/3	B.Schenck			P	G.Hecker	P	N.Baker	P	B.Mathews	P	P.Galvin		
/2	G.Mappes			/P	H.McCaffery	P	A.Mays	P	B.Becannon	P	T.Lovett				
/O	J.Visner	P	H.Porter			P	T.Ramsey			P	E.Knouff	/P	F.Mountain		
/O	O.Walker	P	J.Harkins							P	E.Cushman	/P	J.Hofford		
/1	C.Levis					/P	J.Connor								
/O	J.Tener	/P	P.Smith							/P	B.Vinton				
/2	S.McDermott									/P	B.Taylor				
										/P	B.Emslie				
P	H.Henderson									/P	J.Conway				
P	B.Emslie									/P	P.Smith				
P	J.Henry														
/P	B.Mountjoy														
/P	J.Brown														
/P	F.Foreman														
/P	S.Wetzel														

TEAM	G	W	L	PCT	GB	R	OR	AB	H	2B	3B	HR	BB	SO	AVG	OBP	SLG	PRO	PRO+	BR	/A	PF	CHI	RC	SB	CS	SBA	SBR
STL	112	79	33	.705		677	**461**	3972	979	132	57	17	234	**282**	.246	.297	.321	.618	96	1	-27	105	**109**	388				
CIN	112	63	49	.563	16	642	575	4050	1046	108	77	26	153	420	.258	.294	.342	.636	103	18	6	102	101	417				
PIT	111	56	55	.505	22.5	547	539	3975	955	123	79	5	189	537	.240	.282	.315	.597	94	-32	-24	99	94	362				
PHI	113	55	57	.491	24	764	691	4142	1099	169	76	30	223	410	.265	.310	.365	.675	111	77	34	106	106	480				
LOU	112	53	59	.473	26	564	598	3969	986	126	83	19	152	448	.248	.281	.321	.617	99	-11	-10	100	95	384				
BRO	112	53	59	.473	26	624	650	3943	966	121	65	14	238	324	.245	.295	.319	.614	97	-4	-8	101	102	381				
NY	108	44	64	.407	33	526	688	3731	921	123	57	21	217	428	.247	.295	.327	.622	110	4	**50**	92	90	369				
BAL	110	41	68	.376	36.5	541	683	3820	837	124	59	17	**279**	529	.219	.280	.296	.576	87	-53	-45	99	99	324				
TOT	445					4885		31602	7789	1026	553	149	1685	3378	.246	.292	.328	.620										

TEAM	CG	SH	SV	IP	H	H/G	HR	BB	SO	RAT	ERA	ERA+	OAV	OOB	PR	/A	PF	CPI	FA	E	DP	FW	PW	BW	SBW	DIF
STL	111	11	0	1002	**879**	7.9	12	**168**	378	9.8	**2.44**	134	**.228**	.268	89	91	101	106	**.920**	381	64	3.0	8.2	-2.4		14.2
CIN	102	7	1	999¹	998	9.0	24	250	330	11.9	3.26	100	.253	.309	-2	-1	100	**112**	.911	423	**86**	.8	-.0	.5		5.8
PIT	104	8	0	1011	918	8.2	14	201	454	10.3	2.92	110	.232	.275	36	32	99	95	.912	422	77	.6	2.9	-2.2		-.9
PHI	105	5	0	1003¹	1038	9.3	11	212	**506**	11.6	3.23	106	.254	.298	2	23	106	104	.901	483	79	-2.2	2.1	3.1		-4.0
LOU	109	3	1	1002	927	8.3	13	217	462	10.6	2.68	120	.232	.278	63	60	99	104	.905	460	75	-1.2	5.4	-.9		-6.3
BRO	110	3	1	991²	955	8.7	27	211	436	10.8	3.46	95	.240	.283	-24	-19	102	89	.910	434	56	.2	-1.7	-.7		-.8
NY	103	2	0	937	1015	9.7	36	204	408	11.9	4.15	71	.262	.303	-94	-125	91	91	.901	452	62	-1.6	-11.3	4.5		-1.7
BAL	103	2	**4**	971	1059	9.8	12	222	395	12.3	3.90	83	.269	.316	-71	-71	100	100	.910	418	71	.6	-6.4	-4.1		-3.7
TOT	847	41	7	7917¹		8.9				11.1	3.24		.246	.292					.909	3473	570					

Runs		Hits		Doubles		Triples		Home Runs		Total Bases	
Stovey-Phi	130	Browning-Lou	174	Larkin-Phi	37	Orr-NY	21	Stovey-Phi	13	Browning-Lou	255
Larkin-Phi	114	Jones-Cin	157	Browning-Lou	34	Kuehne-Pit	19	Fennelly-Cin	10	Orr-NY	241
Jones-Cin	108	Stovey-Phi	153	Orr-NY	27	Wolf-Lou	17	Browning-Lou	9	Larkin-Phi	238
Nelson-NY	98	Orr-NY	152	Stovey-Phi	27	Jones-Cin	17	Larkin-Phi	8	Stovey-Phi	237
Browning-Lou	98	Larkin-Phi	149			Fennelly-Cin	17	Orr-NY	6	Jones-Cin	225

Runs Batted In		Runs Produced		Bases On Balls		Batting Average		On Base Percentage		Slugging Average	
Fennelly-Cin	89	Larkin-Phi	194	Nelson-NY	61	Browning-Lou	.362	Browning-Lou	.393	Orr-NY	.543
Larkin-Phi	88	Stovey-Phi	192	Macullar-Bal	49	Orr-NY	.342	Larkin-Phi	.372	Browning-Lou	.530
Orr-NY	77	Browning-Lou	162	Hotaling-Bro	49	Larkin-Phi	.329	Stovey-Phi	.371	Larkin-Phi	.525
Stovey-Phi	75	Fennelly-Cin	161	Stovey-Phi	39	Jones-Cin	.322	Brown-Pit	.366	Stovey-Phi	.488
Browning-Lou	73	Welch-StL	150			Stovey-Phi	.315	Phillips-Bro	.364	Jones-Cin	.462

Production		Adjusted Production		Batter Runs		Adjusted Batter Runs		Clutch Hitting Index		Runs Created	
Browning-Lou	.923	Orr-NY	197	Browning-Lou	47.0	Browning-Lou	47.3	Nicol-StL	131	Browning-Lou	103
Orr-NY	.901	Browning-Lou	190	Larkin-Phi	40.3	Orr-NY	46.6	Swartwood-Bro	131	Larkin-Phi	91
Larkin-Phi	.897	Larkin-Phi	171	Orr-NY	38.1	Larkin-Phi	33.8	Houck-Pit	125	Stovey-Phi	90
Stovey-Phi	.858	Stovey-Phi	160	Stovey-Phi	37.9	Stovey-Phi	31.2	Fennelly-Cin	125	Orr-NY	88
Jones-Cin	.824	Jones-Cin	156	Jones-Cin	31.5	Jones-Cin	29.5	Gleason-StL	123	Jones-Cin	83

Total Average		Stolen Bases		Stolen Base Average		Stolen Base Runs		Fielding Runs		Total Player Rating	
Browning-Lou	.912							G.Smith-Bro	39.9	Browning-Lou	4.3
Larkin-Phi	.885							Smith-Pit	33.2	Larkin-Phi	3.8
Orr-NY	.863							Houck-Pit	21.8	G.Smith-Bro	3.7
Stovey-Phi	.841							Hankinson-NY	18.0	Jones-Cin	3.4
Jones-Cin	.773							Corkhill-Cin	17.1	Smith-Pit	3.2

Wins		Win Percentage		Games		Complete Games		Shutouts		Saves	
Caruthers-StL	40	Caruthers-StL	.755	Morris-Pit	63	Morris-Pit	63	Morris-Pit	7	Burns-Bal	3
Morris-Pit	39	Foutz-StL	.702	Henderson-Bal	61	Henderson-Bal	59	Caruthers-StL	6	Terry-Bro	1
Porter-Bro	33	Mathews-Phi	.638	Porter-Bro	54	Porter-Bro	53	McGinnis-StL	3	Sommer-Bal	1
Foutz-StL	33	Morris-Pit	.619	Hecker-Lou	53	Caruthers-StL	53			Reccius-Lou	1
		Porter-Bro	.611	Caruthers-StL	53	Hecker-Lou	51			Corkhill-Cin	1

Innings Pitched		Fewest Hits/Game		Fewest BB/Game		Strikeouts		Strikeouts/Game		Ratio	
Morris-Pit	581.0	Morris-Pit	7.11	Lynch-NY	1.00	Morris-Pit	298	Mathews-Phi	6.09	Morris-Pit	8.89
Henderson-Bal	539.1	Mays-Lou	7.74	Hecker-Lou	1.01	Mathews-Phi	286	Cushman-Phi-NY	5.50	Caruthers-StL	9.44
Caruthers-StL	482.1	Foutz-StL	7.75	Caruthers-StL	1.06	Henderson-Bal	263	Morris-Pit	4.62	Hecker-Lou	9.86
Porter-Bro	481.2	McGinnis-StL	7.87	Mathews-Phi	1.21	Hecker-Lou	209	Henderson-Bal	4.39	McGinnis-StL	9.88
Hecker-Lou	480.0	Porter-Bro	7.98	McGinnis-StL	1.53	Porter-Bro	197	Harkins-Bro	4.33	Mathews-Phi	10.04

Earned Run Average		Adjusted ERA		Opponents' Batting Avg.		Opponents' On Base Pct.		Starter Runs		Adjusted Starter Runs	
Caruthers-StL	2.07	Caruthers-StL	158	Morris-Pit	.208	Morris-Pit	.247	Caruthers-StL	62.9	Caruthers-StL	64.1
Hecker-Lou	2.17	Hecker-Lou	148	Mays-Lou	.219	Caruthers-StL	.260	Morris-Pit	57.4	Hecker-Lou	55.8
Morris-Pit	2.35	Mathews-Phi	141	Porter-Bro	.223	Hecker-Lou	.265	Hecker-Lou	57.0	Morris-Pit	55.6
Mathews-Phi	2.43	Morris-Pit	137	McGinnis-StL	.225	Cushman-Phi-NY	.266	Mathews-Phi	38.2	Mathews-Phi	47.2
Foutz-StL	2.63	Foutz-StL	124	Foutz-StL	.227	Mathews-Phi	.267	Foutz-StL	28.0	Foutz-StL	29.0

Clutch Pitching Index		Relief Runs		Adjusted Relief Runs		Relief Ranking		Total Pitcher Index		Total Baseball Ranking	
Knight-Phi	283							Hecker-Lou	6.6	Caruthers-StL	6.5
Hecker-Lou	121							Caruthers-StL	6.6	Hecker-Lou	6.3
Caruthers-StL	118							Morris-Pit	4.5	Morris-Pit	4.5
Mountjoy-Cin-Bal	111							Foutz-StL	3.8	Browning-Lou	4.3
Foutz-StL	107							Mathews-Phi	3.8	Larkin-Phi	3.8

January 16 Washington is admitted to the NL, bringing the membership up to seven teams.

February 9 Kansas City is admitted to the NL on a one-year trial basis.

March 4 The NL adopts the stolen base and the 4-foot by 7-foot pitcher's box.

March 18* The New York State League admits Buffalo, Toronto, and Hamilton. The inclusion of the Canadian teams causes the league to change its name to the International League.

April 29 Opening Day for the NL. The New York *World* carries woodcuts of live action photographs taken by a "detective" camera, perhaps the first "live" pictures of baseball ever taken.

May 31 The first major league crowd of over 20,000 pays to see the afternoon game in New York versus Detroit. The Giants had snapped the Wolverines' 15-game winning streak in the morning game, but Detroit wins the nightcap before 20,632.

June 12 Detroit hits seven homers in one game. This record is broken by the Yankees on June 28, 1939.

June 26* Black lefthander George Stovey makes his pitching debut with Jersey City of the Eastern League after being purchased from the Cuban Giants, the pioneer all-black touring team.

July 3* Behind the pitching of Amos Alonzo Stagg, who will make his mark as a football coach, Yale beats Harvard in the deciding game of the college championship.

August 18 St. Louis Maroon owner Henry Lucas quits baseball, announcing that the club has cost him $27,000 in 3 years.

September 11 Connie Mack makes his major league debut with Washington, catching flawlessly and contributing a single as the Senators beat the Phillies 4-3.

September 30 Spalding accepts Von der Ahe's challenge for a "World Series" and proposes a best-of-9 series with the winning club getting the total gross gate receipts. St. Louis will accept the winner-take-all provision, but the series will be best-of-7.

October 8 Detroit's Lady Baldwin beats Philadelphia 11-0 in eight innings for his 42nd win of the season—the all-time record for a southpaw and one more than rival lefthander Ed Morris of Pittsburgh. The game marks the eighth time in 1886 that Baldwin has beaten the Phillies, including five shutouts. No one else shut out Philadelphia all season.

October 18 The World Championship Series opens in Chicago, with the White Stockings beating the Browns 6–0 behind John Clarkson's 5-hitter.

November 16 The AA and NL Joint Rules Committee announces the new rules code, which includes four strikes for an out, five balls for a walk, and establishes a 55½-foot pitching distance.

November 18 The NL meets and admits Pittsburgh, which had been looking to leave the AA since last spring.

BOSTON		CHICAGO		DETROIT		KANSAS CITY		NEW YORK		PHILADELPHIA		ST.LOUIS		WASHINGTON	
M	J.Morrill	M	C.Anson	M	B.Watkins	M	D.Rowe	M	J.Mutrie	M	H.Wright	M	G.Schmelz	M	M.Scanlon
1B	S.Wise	1B	C.Anson	1B	D.Brouthers	1B	M.McQuery	1B	R.Connor	1B	S.Farrar	1B	A.McKinnon	M	J.Gaffney
2B	J.Burdock	2B	F.Pfeffer	2B	F.Dunlap	2B	A.Myers	2B	J.Gerhardt	2B	C.Bastian	2B	F.Dunlap	1B	P.Baker
SS	J.Morrill	SS	N.Williamson	SS	J.Rowe	SS	C.Bassett	SS	J.Ward	SS	A.Irwin	SS	J.Glasscock	2B	J.Farrell
3B	B.Nash	3B	T.Burns	3B	D.White	3B	J.Donnelly	3B	D.Esterbrook	3B	J.Mulvey	3B	J.Denny	SS	D.Force
LF	J.Hornung	LF	A.Dalrymple	LF	H.Richardson	LF	J.Lillie	LF	P.Gillespie	LF	G.Wood	LF	E.Seery	3B	J.Knowles
CF	D.Johnston	CF	G.Gore	CF	N.Hanlon	CF	D.Rowe	CF	D.Richardson	CF	E.Andrews	CF	J.McGeachy	LF	C.Carroll
RF	T.Poorman	RF	K.Kelly	RF	S.Thompson	RF	P.Radford	RF	M.Dorgan	RF	J.Fogarty	RF	J.Cahill	CF	P.Hines
C	C.Daily	C	S.Flint	C	C.Bennett	C	F.Briody	C	B.Ewing	C	D.McGuire	C	G.Myers	RF	E.Crane
														C	B.Gilligan
OS	E.Sutton	O	J.Ryan	C	C.Ganzel	CO	M.Hackett	OC	J.O'Rourke	OP	E.Daily	O2	J.Quinn		
1P	C.Buffinton	O	B.Sunday	2	S.Crane	OP	P.Conway	CO	P.Deasley	C	J.Clements	C	F.Graves	S	S.Houck
C	P.Tate	C	G.Moolic	O	J.Manning	C	F.Ringo	/O	B.Finley	C	T.Cusick	2	S.Crane	3	B.Gladman
C	T.Gunning	C	L.Hardie	C	H.Decker	/C	D.Dugdale	/C	G.Begley	2	J.Farrell	1	T.Dolan	1	J.Start
C	P.Dealy			/O	J.McGeachy	/C	G.Baker	/S	E.Caskin	/O	T.McCarthy	/C	G.Mappes	1	B.Krieg
/2	M.Allen	P	J.Clarkson	/S	B.Shindle			/O	L.Corcoran	/C	C.Ganzel	/O	R.Connolly	O	G.Shoch
		P	J.McCormick	/C	T.Gillen	P	S.Wiedman	/O	J.Devine			/O	L.Pelouze	CO	J.Hayes
P	C.Radbourn	P	J.Flynn			P	J.Whitney			P	C.Ferguson			O	L.Corcoran
P	B.Stemmeyer			P	L.Baldwin			P	T.Keefe	P	D.Casey	P	J.Healy	C	D.Oldfield
				P	C.Getzien	/P	S.King	P	M.Welch			P	J.Kirby	C	C.Mack
/P	C.Parsons			P	P.Conway	/P	L.McKeon			/P	C.Titcomb	P	H.Boyle	/C	H.Decker
				P	B.Smith			/P	J.Devlin	/P	J.Strike	P	C.Sweeney	/C	E.Whiting
														/O	W.Goldsby
				/P	P.Smith							/P	J.Murphy	/3	J.McGlone
				/P	L.Twitchell							/P	A.Bauers	/C	T.Kinslow
												/P	J.Reardon	/S	J.Gallagher
														/O	G.Winkelman
														/O	Joyce
														P	D.Shaw
														P	B.Barr
														P	T.Madigan
														P	F.Gilmore
														/P	H.Daily
														/P	H.O'Day
														/P	G.Keefe
														/P	J.Henry
														/P	E.Fuller
														/P	J.Fox
														/P	B.Wise
														/P	J.Yingling

TEAM	G	W	L	PCT	GB	R	OR	AB	H	2B	3B	HR	BB	SO	AVG	OBP	SLG	PRO	PRO+	BR	/A	PF	CHI	RC	SB	CS	SBA	SBR
CHI	126	90	34	.726		900	555	4378	1223	198	87	53	460	513	.279	.348	.401	.749	115	176	48	115	104	701	213			
DET	126	87	36	.707	2.5	829	538	4501	1260	176	81	53	374	426	.280	.335	.390	.725	122	137	113	103	100	670	194			
NY	124	75	44	.630	12.5	692	558	4298	1156	175	68	21	237	410	.269	.307	.356	.663	106	29	22	101	102	531	155			
PHI	119	71	43	.623	14	621	498	4072	976	145	66	26	282	516	.240	.289	.327	.616	91	-37	-42	101	106	461	226			
BOS	118	56	61	.479	30.5	657	661	4180	1085	151	59	24	250	537	.260	.301	.341	.642	104	0	23	96	104	489	156			
STL	126	43	79	.352	46	547	712	4250	1001	183	46	30	235	656	.236	.276	.321	.597	92	-71	-35	94	96	430	156			
KC	126	30	91	.248	58.5	494	872	4236	967	177	48	19	269	608	.228	.274	.306	.580	76	-92	-128	106	90	392	96			
WAS	125	28	92	.233	60	445	791	4082	856	135	51	23	265	582	.210	.258	.285	.543	73	-143	-116	94	93	345	143			
TOT	495					5185		33997	8524	1340	506	249	2372	4248	.251	.300	.342	.641							1339			

TEAM	CG	SH	SV	IP	H	H/G	HR	BB	SO	RAT	ERA	ERA+	OAV	OOB	PR	/A	PF	CPI	FA	E	DP	FW	PW	BW	SBW	DIF
CHI	116	8	3	1097²	988	8.1	49	262	647	10.2	2.54	142	.232	.277	91	131	110	111	.912	475	82	-1.8	11.9	4.4		13.5
DET	122	8	0	1103²	995	8.1	20	270	592	10.3	2.85	115	.231	.276	53	52	100	90	.928	373	82	3.8	4.7	10.2		6.8
NY	119	3	1	1062	1029	8.7	23	280	588	11.1	2.86	111	.247	.294	50	26	97	104	.927	359	70	4.2	2.4	2.0		7.0
PHI	110	10	2	1045²	923	7.9	29	264	540	10.2	2.45	134	.224	.271	97	94	100	101	.921	393	46	1.4	8.5	-3.8		7.9
BOS	116	3	0	1029	1049	9.2	33	298	511	11.8	3.24	98	.252	.302	5	-7	97	104	.905	465	63	-2.7	-.6	2.1		-1.2
STL	118	6	0	1077¹	1050	8.8	34	392	501	12.0	3.24	99	.246	.309	5	-7	97	105	.914	452	92	-.5	-.6	-3.2		-13.7
KC	117	4	0	1066²	1345	11.3	27	246	442	13.4	4.84	77	.295	.331	-184	-132	114	90	.910	482	79	-2.1	-12.0	-11.6		-4.8
WAS	115	4	0	1041	1147	9.9	34	379	500	13.2	4.30	76	.271	.331	-117	-124	99	95	.910	458	69	-1.0	-11.2	-10.5		-9.2
TOT	933	46	6	8523		9.0				11.5	3.29		.251	.300					.916	3457	583					

Runs		Hits		Doubles		Triples		Home Runs		Total Bases	
Kelly-Chi	155	Richardson-Det	189	Brouthers-Det	40	Connor-NY	20	Richardson-Det	11	Brouthers-Det	284
Gore-Chi	150	Anson-Chi	187	Anson-Chi	35	Wood-Phi	15	Brouthers-Det	11	Anson-Chi	274
Brouthers-Det	139	Brouthers-Det	181	Kelly-Chi	32	Brouthers-Det	15	Anson-Chi	10	Richardson-Det	271
Richardson-Det	125	Kelly-Chi	175	Hines-Was	30	Thompson-Det	13	Hines-Was	9	Connor-NY	262
Anson-Chi	117	Connor-NY	172					Denny-StL	9	Kelly-Chi	241

Runs Batted In		Runs Produced		Bases On Balls		Batting Average		On Base Percentage		Slugging Average	
Anson-Chi	147	Anson-Chi	254	Gore-Chi	102	Kelly-Chi	.388	Kelly-Chi	.483	Brouthers-Det	.581
Pfeffer-Chi	95	Kelly-Chi	230	Kelly-Chi	83	Anson-Chi	.371	Brouthers-Det	.445	Anson-Chi	.544
Thompson-Det	89	Gore-Chi	207	Williamson-Chi	80	Brouthers-Det	.370	Gore-Chi	.434	Connor-NY	.540
Rowe-Det	87	Brouthers-Det	200	Brouthers-Det	66	Connor-NY	.355	Anson-Chi	.433	Kelly-Chi	.534
Ward-NY	81	Thompson-Det	182	Radford-KC	58	Richardson-Det	.351	Connor-NY	.405	Richardson-Det	.504

Production		Adjusted Production		Batter Runs		Adjusted Batter Runs		Clutch Hitting Index		Runs Created	
Brouthers-Det	1.026	Brouthers-Det	204	Brouthers-Det	65.9	Brouthers-Det	61.7	Anson-Chi	158	Kelly-Chi	146
Kelly-Chi	1.018	Connor-NY	183	Kelly-Chi	64.3	Connor-NY	47.5	Ward-NY	153	Brouthers-Det	139
Anson-Chi	.977	Kelly-Chi	182	Anson-Chi	58.3	Kelly-Chi	44.3	Pfeffer-Chi	141	Anson-Chi	134
Connor-NY	.945	Anson-Chi	170	Connor-NY	48.7	Richardson-Det	43.7	Dorgan-NY	139	Richardson-Det	129
Richardson-Det	.906	Richardson-Det	169	Richardson-Det	47.4	Anson-Chi	38.5	Gillespie-NY	138	Connor-NY	116

Total Average		Stolen Bases		Stolen Base Average	Stolen Base Runs	Fielding Runs		Total Player Rating	
Kelly-Chi	1.366	Andrews-Phi	56			Knowles-Was	27.7	Richardson-Det	4.8
Brouthers-Det	1.205	Kelly-Chi	53			Denny-StL	22.7	Kelly-Chi	4.5
Anson-Chi	1.129	Hanlon-Det	50			Dunlap-StL-Det	19.3	Glasscock-StL	4.2
Gore-Chi	1.042	Richardson-Det	42			Johnston-Bos	16.6	Connor-NY	3.9
Richardson-Det	1.029	Radford-KC	39			Glasscock-StL	13.8	Brouthers-Det	3.5

Wins		Win Percentage		Games		Complete Games		Shutouts		Saves	
Keefe-NY	42	Flynn-Chi	.793	Keefe-NY	64	Keefe-NY	62	Baldwin-Det	7	Ferguson-Phi	2
Baldwin-Det	42	Ferguson-Phi	.769	Welch-NY	59	Radbourn-Bos	57	Ferguson-Phi	4	Williamson-Chi	1
Clarkson-Chi	36	Baldwin-Det	.764	Radbourn-Bos	58	Welch-NY	56	Casey-Phi	4	Ryan-Chi	1
Welch-NY	33	McCormick-Chi	.738	Baldwin-Det	56	Baldwin-Det	55			Flynn-Chi	1
McCormick-Chi	31	Getzien-Det	.732	Clarkson-Chi	55	Clarkson-Chi	50			Devlin-NY	1

Innings Pitched		Fewest Hits/Game		Fewest BB/Game		Strikeouts		Strikeouts/Game		Ratio	
Keefe-NY	535.0	Baldwin-Det	6.86	Whitney-KC	1.26	Baldwin-Det	323	Stemmeyer-Bos	6.17	Baldwin-Det	8.70
Radbourn-Bos	509.1	Ferguson-Phi	7.21	Ferguson-Phi	1.57	Clarkson-Chi	313	Clarkson-Chi	6.04	Ferguson-Phi	8.78
Welch-NY	500.0	Flynn-Chi	7.25	Clarkson-Chi	1.66	Keefe-NY	297	Baldwin-Det	5.97	Flynn-Chi	9.46
Baldwin-Det	487.0	Stemmeyer-Bos	7.74	Keefe-NY	1.72	Welch-NY	272	Healy-StL	5.42	Clarkson-Chi	9.74
Clarkson-Chi	466.2	Boyle-StL	7.84	Baldwin-Det	1.85	Stemmeyer-Bos	239	Flynn-Chi	5.11	Keefe-NY	9.77

Earned Run Average		Adjusted ERA		Opponents' Batting Avg.		Opponents' On Base Pct.		Starter Runs		Adjusted Starter Runs	
Boyle-StL	1.76	Boyle-StL	182	Baldwin-Det	.202	Baldwin-Det	.243	Ferguson-Phi	57.5	Clarkson-Chi	62.7
Ferguson-Phi	1.98	Ferguson-Phi	166	Ferguson-Phi	.210	Ferguson-Phi	.244	Baldwin-Det	56.9	Ferguson-Phi	57.1
Baldwin-Det	2.24	Flynn-Chi	161	Flynn-Chi	.210	Flynn-Chi	.257	Clarkson-Chi	45.4	Baldwin-Det	57.1
Flynn-Chi	2.24	Clarkson-Chi	150	Stemmeyer-Bos	.218	Boyle-StL	.261	Keefe-NY	43.4	Flynn-Chi	39.3
Clarkson-Chi	2.41	Baldwin-Det	147	Boyle-StL	.220	Clarkson-Chi	.264	Casey-Phi	35.8	Keefe-NY	37.5

Clutch Pitching Index		Relief Runs	Adjusted Relief Runs	Relief Ranking	Total Pitcher Index		Total Baseball Ranking	
Boyle-StL	127				Ferguson-Phi	6.5	Ferguson-Phi	6.4
McCormick-Chi	126				Clarkson-Chi	6.5	Clarkson-Chi	6.3
Welch-NY	121				Baldwin-Det	6.1	Baldwin-Det	6.0
Kirby-StL	112				Flynn-Chi	4.1	Kelly-Chi	4.5
Radbourn-Bos	108				Boyle-StL	3.9	Richardson-Det	4.5

February 5* The patent dispute between Thayer & Wright and A. G. Spalding & Brothers goes to court in Chicago. Thayer is the Harvard player who claimed to have invented the catcher's mask, while George Wright and Spalding are former teammates on the champion Boston Red Stockings. In the eventual settlement, Thayer's claims will be upheld, and he will receive a royalty on masks sold by Spalding's company.

March 17 *The Sporting News,* the weekly that will become "The Baseball Paper of the World," publishes its first issue.

April 22 The Mets' lavish new park on Staten Island is opened with a loss to the Athletics 7–6. Later this summer, cranks (fans) will be able to look at N.Y. harbor from the St. George grandstand and see the Statue of Liberty being assembled.

May 14 Charles Comiskey of the Browns prevents a double play by running full tilt into Reds second baseman Bid McPhee, enabling the Browns to win 2-1. The Cincinnati fans are irate, but the umpire allows the play. The Browns are gradually making "breaking up the double play" an accepted part of the game.

June 16* On Opening Day in the Southern League of Colored Base Ballists, the Eclipse of Memphis beats the home Unions of New Orleans 3-1. The SLCBB, the first black professional sports league, will collapse in August.

July 7 Five of the top seven spots in the AA batting race belong to pitchers, according to *Sporting Life.*

August 15 Louisville's Guy Hecker scores 7 runs in a game, establishing a major league record. In addition, he hits 3 home runs, all inside the park, to tie the existing record.

August 22 Just as he reaches the ball on a long hit by Chicken Wolf, Reds center fielder Abner Powell's pants are grabbed by a stray dog. Wolf circles the bases with the homer that wins the game for Louisville 5–3 in 11 innings.

August 24 Baltimore's Matt Kilroy fans 16 Athletics, his high in a season in which he will set the all-time major league record with 513 strikeouts.

October 23 The St. Louis Browns win the World Championship by beating Chicago 4–3 in 10 innings. Pitching his fourth game in 6 days, Clarkson holds St. Louis hitless for 6 innings as Chicago builds a 3–0 lead. The Browns tie the game in the eighth, and Curt Welch scores the "$15,000" run on a wild pitch in the tenth. St. Louis wins the entire gate receipts from the series ($13,920), with each of 12 players getting about $580.

November 11 The Executive Council of the Brotherhood of Professional Base Ball Players, formed the previous year, meets and chooses officers. John M. Ward is re-elected president, Dan Brouthers vice president, and Tim Keefe secretary-treasurer.

November 22 The AA admits Cleveland four days after Pittsburgh fled the league to join the NL.

December 15 The AA approves the new clause that allows a club to reserve a player for as long as it wants, not just for next year's contract.

BALTIMORE		BROOKLYN		CINCINNATI		LOUISVILLE		NEW YORK		PHILADELPHIA		PITTSBURGH		ST.LOUIS	
M	B.Barnie	M	C.Byrne	M	O.Caylor	M	J.Hart	M	J.Gifford	M	L.Simmons	M	H.Phillips	M	C.Comiskey
1B	M.Scott	1B	B.Phillips	1B	J.Reilly	1B	J.Kerins	M	B.Ferguson	M	B.Sharsig	1B	O.Schomberg	1B	C.Comiskey
2B	M.Muldoon	2B	B.McClellan	2B	B.McPhee	2B	R.Mack	1B	D.Orr	1B	H.Stovey	2B	S.Barkley	2B	Y.Robinson
SS	J.Macullar	SS	G.Smith	SS	F.Fennelly	SS	B.White	2B	T.Forster	2B	L.Bierbauer	SS	P.Smith	SS	B.Gleason
3B	J.Davis	3B	G.Pinkney	3B	H.Carpenter	3B	J.Werrick	SS	C.Nelson	SS	C.McGarr	3B	A.Whitney	3B	A.Latham
LF	J.Sommer	LF	E.Burch	LF	C.Jones	LF	J.Strauss	3B	F.Hankinson	3B	J.Gleason	LF	E.Glenn	LF	T.O'Neill
CF	P.O'Connell	CF	J.McTamany	CF	F.Lewis	CF	P.Browning	LF	C.Roseman	LF	H.Larkin	CF	F.Mann	CF	C.Welch
RF	J.Manning	RF	E.Swartwood	RF	P.Corkhill	RF	J.Wolf	CF	S.Behel	CF	E.Greer	RF	T.Brown	RF	H.Nicol
C	C.Fulmer	C	J.Peoples	C	K.Baldwin	C	A.Cross	RF	S.Brady	RF	J.Coleman	C	F.Carroll	C	D.Bushong
								C	C.Reipschlager	C	W.Robinson				
23	J.Farrell	CO	B.Clark	C1	P.Snyder	1C	P.Cook	S2	T.McLaughlin	C3	J.O'Brien	O3	B.Kuehne	C	R.Kemmler
S	S.Houck	C	D.Oldfield	C	J.Keenan	O	L.Sylvester	OC	J.Donahue	C1	J.Milligan	CO	D.Miller	/S	T.McSorley
O	B.Hoover	/O	J.Strauss	O	L.Maskrey	O	H.Collins	2	J.Meister	S	J.Quest	/1	F.Ringo	/C	L.Harding
C	T.Dolan	C	J.McCauley	O	A.Powell	/O	L.Maskrey	O	B.Holbert	3	D.Lyons	1	F.Mountain		
O	B.Purcell	/O	E.Kennedy	O	L.Sylvester	/O	P.Reccius	2O	E.Foster	O	O.Shaffer	O	J.Coleman	P	D.Foutz
C	B.Traffley	/O	P.Schriver	/O	L.Marr	/1	J.Heinzman	C	J.Crotty	S	G.Bradley	/C	T.Quinn	P	B.Caruthers
O	J.Clinton			/O	L.Richmond	/O	J.Neale	/C	C.Zimmer	/O	J.Irwin	/C	D.Sullivan	P	N.Hudson
O	L.Sowders	P	H.Porter	/C	J.Boyle	/O	T.Terrell	/3	P.Connell	/O	J.Hyndman	P	E.Morris	P	J.McGinnis
/O	E.Greer	P	J.Harkins	/C	F.Vaughn	/O	C.Murphy	/O	H.Brooks	/S	C.Kelly	P	P.Galvin	/P	J.Murphy
/C	B.Conway		A.Terry									P	J.Handiboe		
/C	N.Bligh	P	H.Henderson	P	T.Mullane	P	T.Ramsey	P	J.Lynch	P	A.Atkinson				
/O	B.Barnie	P	S.Toole	P	G.Pechiney	P	G.Hecker	P	A.Mays	P	B.Mathews	/P	J.Hofford		
/S	S.Nava			P	L.McKeon			P	E.Cushman	P	B.Hart	/P	B.Bishop		
/C	T.Hellman					/P	T.Sullivan			P	T.Kennedy				
/O	Zay			P	E.Smith	/P	B.Ely			P	C.Miller				
				/P	J.Murphy	/P	T.Kennedy	/P	J.Shaffer						
P	M.Kilroy			/P	W.White	/P	E.Chamberlain			/P	J.Aydelott				
P	J.McGinnis			/P	B.Irwin					/P	S.Weaver				
P	H.Henderson			/P	D.Bickham					/P	R.Smith				
				/P	Smith					/P	J.Brown				
/P	D.Conway			/P	C.Stephens					/P	E.Clark				
/P	B.Taylor			/P	J.Reardon					/P	C.Gessner				
/P	A.Powell														
/P	E.Knouff														
/P	F.Houseman														

TEAM	G	W	L	PCT	GB	R	OR	AB	H	2B	3B	HR	BB	SO	AVG	OBP	SLG	PRO	PRO+	BR	/A	PF	CHI	RC	SB	CS	SBA	SBR
STL	139	93	46	.669		944	592	5009	1365	206	85	20	400	425	.273	.333	.360	.693	116	114	71	105	102	729	336			
PIT	140	80	57	.584	12	810	647	4854	1171	186	96	16	478	713	.241	.314	.329	.643	106	31	35	100	97	598	260			
BRO	141	76	61	.555	16	832	832	5053	1261	196	80	16	433	523	.250	.311	.330	.641	103	22	14	101	99	610	248			
LOU	138	66	70	.485	25.5	833	805	4921	1294	182	88	20	410	558	.263	.323	.348	.671	108	74	24	106	95	634	202			
CIN	141	65	73	.471	27.5	883	865	4915	1225	145	95	45	394	633	.249	.311	.345	.656	106	45	18	103	105	599	185			
PHI	139	63	72	.467	28	772	942	4856	1142	192	82	21	378	697	.235	.296	.321	.617	95	-22	-30	101	101	560	284			
NY	137	53	82	.393	38	628	766	4683	1047	108	72	18	330	578	.224	.279	.289	.568	85	-101	-73	96	96	422	120			
BAL	139	48	83	.366	41	625	878	4639	945	124	51	8	379	603	.204	.269	.258	.527	70	-163	-148	98	106	404	269			
TOT	557					6327		38930	9450	1339	649	164	3182	4730	.243	.305	.323	.628							1904			

TEAM	CG	SH	SV	IP	H	H/G	HR	BB	SO	RAT	ERA	ERA+	OAV	OOB	PR	/A	PF	CPI	FA	E	DP	FW	PW	BW	SBW	DIF
STL	134	14	2	1229¹	1087	8.0	13	329	583	10.6	2.49	138	.227	.281	130	128	100	113	.915	494	96	3.3	11.2	6.2		2.7
PIT	137	15	1	1226	1130	8.3	10	299	515	10.7	2.83	120	.235	.285	84	74	98	104	.917	487	90	3.9	6.5	3.1		-1.9
BRO	138	6	0	1234²	1202	8.8	17	464	540	12.4	3.42	102	.243	.312	3	9	101	104	.900	610	87	-2.2	.8	1.2		7.7
LOU	131	5	2	1209²	1109	8.3	4	432	720	11.7	3.07	118	.230	.297	51	75	106	101	.901	593	89	-2.0	6.6	2.1		-8.7
CIN	129	3	0	1247²	1267	9.1	25	481	495	13.0	4.18	84	.255	.327	-103	-94	102	95	.905	582	122	-.8	-8.3	1.6		3.4
PHI	134	4	0	1218²	1308	9.7	35	388	513	13.0	3.97	88	.259	.319	-72	-66	102	100	.894	637	99	-4.0	-5.8	-2.6		7.9
NY	134	5	0	1186	1148	8.7	23	386	559	11.8	3.50	97	.243	.304	-8	-14	99	98	.907	544	81	.3	-1.2	-6.4		-7.2
BAL	134	5	0	1206²	1197	8.9	25	403	805	12.3	4.08	84	.244	.308	-85	-90	99	87	.910	523	59	1.8	-7.9	-13.0		1.6
TOT	1071	57	5	9759		8.7				11.9	3.44		.243	.305					.906	4470	723					

Runs		Hits		Doubles		Triples		Home Runs		Total Bases	
Latham-StL	152	Orr-NY	193	Larkin-Phi	36	Orr-NY	31	McPhee-Cin	8	Orr-NY	301
McPhee-Cin	139	O'Neill-StL	190	McClellan-Bro	33	Coleman-Phi-Pit	17	Stovey-Phi	7	O'Neill-StL	255
Larkin-Phi	133	Larkin-Phi	180	Welch-StL	31	Kuehne-Pit	17	Orr-NY	7	Larkin-Phi	254
McClellan-Bro	131	Latham-StL	174	Barkley-Pit	31	Fennelly-Cin	17			Welch-StL	221
Pinkney-Bro	119	Phillips-Bro	160	Browning-Lou	29	Larkin-Phi	16			McPhee-Cin	221

Runs Batted In		Runs Produced		Bases On Balls		Batting Average		On Base Percentage		Slugging Average	
O'Neill-StL	107	O'Neill-StL	210	Swartwood-Bro	70	Hecker-Lou	.341	Larkin-Phi	.390	Orr-NY	.527
Corkhill-Cin	97	Welch-StL	207	Pinkney-Bro	70	Browning-Lou	.340	Browning-Lou	.389	Caruthers-StL	.527
Welch-StL	95	Larkin-Phi	205	Mack-Lou	68	Orr-NY	.338	O'Neill-StL	.385	Larkin-Phi	.450
Orr-NY	91	McPhee-Cin	201	Kerins-Lou	66	Caruthers-StL	.334	Stovey-Phi	.377	Hecker-Lou	.446
Reilly-Cin	79					O'Neill-StL	.328	Swartwood-Bro	.377	Browning-Lou	.441

Production		Adjusted Production		Batter Runs		Adjusted Batter Runs		Clutch Hitting Index		Runs Created	
Orr-NY	.890	Orr-NY	186	Orr-NY	45.9	Orr-NY	51.9	Corkhill-Cin	151	Orr-NY	118
Larkin-Phi	.839	Larkin-Phi	161	Caruthers-StL	41.4	Larkin-Phi	39.9	Carpenter-Cin	142	Larkin-Phi	114
Browning-Lou	.830	Stovey-Phi	154	Larkin-Phi	41.3	Caruthers-StL	36.8	Coleman-Phi-Pit	129	Stovey-Phi	109
O'Neill-StL	.826	O'Neill-StL	151	O'Neill-StL	38.6	O'Neill-StL	32.4	O'Brien-Phi	128	O'Neill-StL	104
Stovey-Phi	.817	Browning-Lou	151	Stovey-Phi	32.1	Stovey-Phi	31.0	O'Neill-StL	124	Latham-StL	104

Total Average		Stolen Bases		Stolen Base Average		Stolen Base Runs		Fielding Runs		Total Player Rating	
Stovey-Phi	1.009	Stovey-Phi	68					Kerins-Lou	39.0	Kerins-Lou	4.6
Larkin-Phi	.914	Latham-StL	60					McPhee-Cin	30.5	McPhee-Cin	4.6
Robinson-StL	.903	Welch-StL	59					Hankinson-NY	25.4	Larkin-Phi	3.6
Orr-NY	.897	Robinson-StL	51					Smith-Pit	21.0	Carroll-Pit	3.6
Browning-Lou	.873	McClellan-Bro	43					Peoples-Bro	18.5	O'Neill-StL	3.2

Wins		Win Percentage		Games		Complete Games		Shutouts		Saves	
Morris-Pit	41	Foutz-StL	.719	Kilroy-Bal	68	Ramsey-Lou	66	Morris-Pit	12	Morris-Pit	1
Foutz-StL	41	Caruthers-StL	.682	Ramsey-Lou	67	Kilroy-Bal	66	Foutz-StL	11	Hudson-StL	1
Ramsey-Lou	38	Morris-Pit	.672	Morris-Pit	64	Morris-Pit	63	Terry-Bro	5	Foutz-StL	1
Mullane-Cin	33	Hudson-StL	.615	Mullane-Cin	63	Mullane-Cin	55	Kilroy-Bal	5	Ely-Lou	1
Caruthers-StL	30	Atkinson-Phi	.595	Foutz-StL	59	Foutz-StL	55	Ramsey-Lou	3		

Innings Pitched		Fewest Hits/Game		Fewest BB/Game		Strikeouts		Strikeouts/Game		Ratio	
Ramsey-Lou	588.2	Ramsey-Lou	6.83	Galvin-Pit	1.55	Kilroy-Bal	513	Kilroy-Bal	7.92	Morris-Pit	9.40
Kilroy-Bal	583.0	Kilroy-Bal	7.35	Morris-Pit	1.91	Ramsey-Lou	499	Ramsey-Lou	7.63	Caruthers-StL	9.67
Morris-Pit	555.1	Morris-Pit	7.37	Caruthers-StL	2.00	Morris-Pit	326	Morris-Pit	5.28	Ramsey-Lou	10.18
Mullane-Cin	529.2	Foutz-StL	7.46	McGinnis-StL-Bal	2.27	Foutz-StL	283	Miller-Phi	5.25	Foutz-StL	10.21
Foutz-StL	504.0	Caruthers-StL	7.51	Atkinson-Phi	2.29	Mullane-Cin	250	Terry-Bro	5.06	Cushman-NY	10.45

Earned Run Average		Adjusted ERA		Opponents' Batting Avg.		Opponents' On Base Pct.		Starter Runs		Adjusted Starter Runs	
Foutz-StL	2.11	Foutz-StL	163	Ramsey-Lou	.198	Morris-Pit	.258	Foutz-StL	74.8	Ramsey-Lou	77.6
Caruthers-StL	2.32	Ramsey-Lou	148	Kilroy-Bal	.210	Caruthers-StL	.263	Ramsey-Lou	65.2	Foutz-StL	74.2
Ramsey-Lou	2.45	Caruthers-StL	148	Morris-Pit	.214	Ramsey-Lou	.269	Morris-Pit	61.4	Morris-Pit	57.6
Morris-Pit	2.45	Morris-Pit	138	Foutz-StL	.216	Foutz-StL	.274	Caruthers-StL	48.2	Caruthers-StL	47.7
Galvin-Pit	2.67	Hecker-Lou	127	Caruthers-StL	.217	Kilroy-Bal	.274	Galvin-Pit	37.3	Hecker-Lou	35.8

Clutch Pitching Index		Relief Runs	Adjusted Relief Runs	Relief Ranking		Total Pitcher Index		Total Baseball Ranking	
Galvin-Pit	130					Foutz-StL	8.1	Foutz-StL	8.1
McGinnis-StL-Bal	127					Caruthers-StL	6.8	Caruthers-StL	7.9
Foutz-StL	122					Ramsey-Lou	6.5	Ramsey-Lou	6.5
Miller-Phi	119					Hecker-Lou	5.2	Hecker-Lou	5.2
Mays-NY	107					Morris-Pit	4.4	Kerins-Lou	4.6

February 16 Chicago announces the sale of Mike "King" Kelly to Boston for $10,000, more than twice the amount ever paid for a player before. With the contract and bonus, Kelly is dubbed a "$15,000 Beauty."

March 8 The NL franchise in St. Louis is sold to a group from Indianapolis for $12,000, including players. The Maroons will now become the Hoosiers.

March 9 The Kansas City Cowboys go out of business with the sale of their players to the league for $6,000. The club's spot in the league has already been taken by Pittsburgh.

March 13 After a week of conditioning in Macon, Georgia, the Detroit team begins a six-week spring exhibition tour through the South and Midwest.

April 30 The Phillies open their new $80,000 wooden ballpark on Huntingdon Avenue and Broad Street, later known as the Baker Bowl, with a 19-10 win over NY. After a fire in 1894, the park is the first to be rebuilt using steel and concrete. The Phils will remain on this site until 1938.

May 6* The National Colored League, patterned after the NL, opens with a game in Pittsburgh, the Gorhams beating the Keystones 11–8 before a crowd of 1,200. Because of rainouts and small crowds the league, which has been recognized by the National Agreement as a legitimate minor league, will fold on May 16 after only 13 games.

May 7 Sam Thompson of Detroit becomes the first major leaguer to hit two bases-loaded triples in one game.

May 20* Nearly two weeks after defeating the Falls Citys in their NCBBL opener in Louisville, the Boston Resolutes finally leave for home after earning enough money for train fare by working as waiters. Their departure, and the circumstances surrounding it, sounds the death knell for the second professional baseball league organized by African Americans.

May 30 Chicago walks to a 12–11 victory in a morning holiday game in New York. Giants pitcher Bill George walks 16 batters to establish a major league mark. He walked 13 against Indianapolis on May 15 and would hand out another 13 passes against them on June 15.

June 5 Today's Chicago *Tribune* publishes NL batting figures through May 31 that show Fred Carroll (.476), Sam Thompson (.454), and Paul Hines (.438) leading the league. Walks are being counted as hits this year.

June 19 Cap Anson refuses to allow his NL champion White Sox to play against Newark's George Stovey, an outstanding black pitcher in the International League.

June 20* The International League passes a ban on black players. Although not strictly enforced this season, this action spells the end of the IL as a haven for black ballplayers.

October 10 The World Series opens in St. Louis with the Browns beating the Detroits 6–1. Bob Caruthers holds the Wolverines to five hits and has three hits himself.

October 13 The best-of-15 WS begins its tour of the other cities with a game in Pittsburgh, Detroit winning 8–0 behind the 2-hit pitching of Lady Baldwin.

October 27 The Brotherhood of Professional Base Ball Players holds a meeting and club representatives pledge not to sign standard contracts until negotiations are held concerning the wording of those documents.

November 16 The Joint Rules Committee does away with the 4-strike rule and with the scoring of walks as hits. Five balls for a walk remains the rule.

November 17 The NL officially recognizes the Brotherhood of Professional Base Ball Players at a meeting with a committee of three players: Dan Brouthers, Ned Hanlon and John Ward.

November 18 The NL adopts a new contract that spells out reserve provisions for the first time. The NL refuses to accept the players' demand that the salary be written out on all contracts, however.

December 2* The International League disbands. Syracuse, Toronto, Hamilton, and Buffalo split off to form the International Association, while Newark, Jersey City, Wilkes-Barre, and Scranton become the nucleus of the Central League.

BOSTON		CHICAGO		DETROIT		INDIANAPOLIS		NEW YORK		PHILADELPHIA		PITTSBURGH		WASHINGTON	
M	K.Kelly	M	C.Anson	M	B.Watkins	M	W.Burnham	M	J.Mutrie	M	H.Wright	M	H.Phillips	M	J.Gaffney
M	J.Morrill	1B	C.Anson	1B	D.Brouthers	M	F.Thomas	1B	R.Connor	1B	S.Farrar	1B	S.Barkley	1B	B.O'Brien
1B	J.Morrill	2B	F.Pfeffer	2B	F.Dunlap	M	H.Fogel	2B	D.Richardson	2B	B.McLaughlin	2B	P.Smith	2B	A.Myers
2B	J.Burdock	SS	N.Williamson	SS	J.Rowe	1B	O.Schomberg	SS	J.Ward	SS	A.Irwin	SS	B.Kuehne	SS	J.Farrell
SS	S.Wise	3B	T.Burns	3B	D.White	2B	C.Bassett	3B	B.Ewing	3B	J.Mulvey	3B	A.Whitney	3B	J.Donnelly
3B	B.Nash	LF	M.Sullivan	LF	H.Richardson	SS	J.Glasscock	LF	P.Gillespie	LF	G.Wood	LF	A.Dalrymple	LF	C.Carroll
LF	J.Hornung	CF	J.Ryan	CF	N.Hanlon	3B	J.Denny	CF	G.Gore	CF	E.Andrews	CF	T.Brown	CF	P.Hines
CF	D.Johnston	RF	B.Sunday	RF	S.Thompson	LF	E.Seery	RF	M.Tiernan	RF	J.Fogarty	RF	J.Coleman	RF	E.Daily
RF	K.Kelly	C	T.Daly	C	C.Ganzel	CF	J.McGeachy	C	W.Brown	C	J.Clements	C	D.Miller	C	C.Mack
C	P.Tate					RF	J.Cahill								
		C	S.Flint	OP	L.Twitchell	C	G.Myers	C3	J.O'Rourke	2S	C.Bastian	OC	F.Carroll	O	G.Shoch
SO	E.Sutton	OP	G.Van Haltren	C	C.Bennett			O	M.Dorgan	C	D.McGuire	1	A.McKinnon	CS	P.Dealy
OS	B.Wheelock	OC	D.Darling	C	F.Briody	C	T.Arundel	C	P.Deasley	C	E.Daily	O	E.Beecher	1	B.Krieg
C	C.Daily	O	B.Pettit	3	B.Shindle	C	M.Hackett	3	J.Rainey	C	T.Gunning	OC	J.Fields	C	B.Gilligan
C	T.O'Rourke	3	P.Tebeau	O	J.Manning	O	T.Brown	O	P.Murphy	/O	T.McCarthy			/S	J.Irwin
		/2	E.Geiss			O	M.Polhemus	/3	G.Hatfield	/3	A.Maul			/S	S.Crane
P	C.Radbourn	/O	J.Flynn	P	C.Getzien	O	G.Gardner	O	B.Becannon	/C	T.Cusick	P	P.Galvin	/2	J.O'Brien
P	K.Madden	P	J.Clarkson	P	L.Baldwin	O	B.Johnson	O	R.Carey	/O	H.Lyons	P	J.McCormick	/C	B.Wright
P	D.Conway	P	M.Baldwin	P	S.Wiedman	1	H.Jackson	/3	J.Gerhardt	P	D.Casey	P	E.Morris	P	J.Whitney
P	B.Stemmeyer			P	P.Conway	/O	L.Corcoran	/3	C.Nelson	P	C.Buffinton	/P	B.Bishop	P	H.O'Day
		/P	S.Pyle	/P	H.Gruber	/O	J.Sowders			P	C.Ferguson			P	F.Gilmore
		/P	C.Sprague	/P	E.Beatin			P	T.Keefe	/P	J.Devlin			P	D.Shaw
				/P	B.Burke	P	J.Healy	P	M.Welch						
						P	H.Boyle	P	B.George					/P	G.Keefe
						P	L.Shreve								
								/P	C.Titcomb						
						/P	D.Leitner	/P	M.Mattimore						
						/P	J.Kirby	/P	B.Swabach						
						/P	H.Morrison	/P	J.Roach						
						/P	S.Moffett	/P	S.Wiedman						
						/P	Fast								

TEAM	G	W	L	PCT	GB	R	OR	AB	H	2B	3B	HR	BB	SO	AVG	OBP	SLG	PRO	PRO+	BR	/A	PF	CHI	RC	SB	CS	SBA	SBR
DET	127	79	45	.637		969	714	4689	1404	213	126	55	352	258	.299	.353	.434	.787	118	134	104	103	103	833	267			
PHI	128	75	48	.610	3.5	901	702	4630	1269	213	89	47	385	346	.274	.337	.389	.726	99	35	-13	106	107	744	355			
CHI	127	71	50	.587	6.5	813	716	4350	1177	178	98	80	407	400	.271	.336	.412	.748	98	62	-44	113	99	748	382			
NY	129	68	55	.553	10.5	816	723	4516	1259	167	93	48	361	326	.279	.339	.389	.728	111	37	76	95	100	753	415			
BOS	127	61	60	.504	16.5	831	792	4531	1255	185	94	53	340	392	.277	.333	.394	.727	106	32	31	100	102	736	373			
PIT	125	55	69	.444	24	621	750	4414	1141	183	78	20	319	381	.258	.314	.349	.663	94	-69	-27	94	90	567	221			
WAS	126	46	76	.377	32	601	818	4314	1039	149	63	47	269	339	.241	.292	.337	.629	82	-126	-95	95	99	535	334			
IND	127	37	89	.294	43	628	965	4368	1080	162	70	33	300	379	.247	.302	.339	.641	85	-105	-82	96	97	562	334			
TOT	508					6180		35812	9624	1450	711	383	2733	2821	.269	.326	.381	.707							2681			

TEAM	CG	SH	SV	IP	H	H/G	HR	BB	SO	RAT	ERA	ERA+	OAV	OOB	PR	/A	PF	CPI	FA	E	DP	FW	PW	BW	SBW	DIF
DET	122	3	1	1116¹	1172	9.4	52	344	337	12.5	3.95	102	.264	.322	12	-3	99	97	.925	394	92	3.3	-.3	8.8		5.1
PHI	119	7	1	1132²	1173	9.3	48	305	435	12.0	3.47	121	.259	.311	72	89	104	104	.912	471	76	-.4	7.5	-1.1		7.5
CHI	117	4	3	1126	1156	9.2	55	338	510	12.4	3.46	129	.257	.317	73	120	110	108	.914	472	99	-.6	10.2	-3.7		4.7
NY	123	5	1	1113²	1096	8.9	27	373	415	12.2	3.57	105	.250	.314	59	18	93	96	.920	431	83	1.8	1.5	6.4		-3.3
BOS	123	4	1	1100²	1226	10.0	55	396	254	13.6	4.41	91	.273	.338	-44	-46	100	99	.905	522	94	-3.1	-3.9	2.6		4.9
PIT	123	4	0	1108²	1287	10.4	39	246	248	12.7	4.12	94	.281	.322	-9	-32	95	99	.921	425	70	1.4	-2.7	-2.3		-3.4
WAS	124	3	0	1090¹	1216	10.0	47	299	396	12.9	4.19	96	.272	.323	-18	-21	100	96	.909	483	77	-1.4	-1.8	-8.1		-3.8
IND	118	4	1	1088	1289	10.7	60	431	245	14.6	5.24	79	.284	.352	-145	-139	102	92	.912	479	105	-1.0	-11.8	-6.9		-6.3
TOT	969	34	8	8876¹		9.7				12.8	4.05		.269	.326					.915	3677	696					

Runs		Hits		Doubles		Triples		Home Runs		Total Bases	
Brouthers-Det	153	Thompson-Det	203	Brouthers-Det	36	Thompson-Det	23	B.O'Brien-Was	19	Thompson-Det	311
Rowe-Det	135	Ward-NY	184	Kelly-Bos	34	Connor-NY	22	Connor-NY	17	Brouthers-Det	281
Richardson-Det	131	Richardson-Det	178	Denny-Ind	34	Johnston-Bos	20	Pfeffer-Chi	16	Richardson-Det	263
Kelly-Bos	120	Rowe-Det	171	Anson-Chi	33	Brouthers-Det	20	Wood-Phi	14	Denny-Ind	256
		Brouthers-Det	169			Wood-Phi	19			Connor-NY	255

Runs Batted In		Runs Produced		Bases On Balls		Batting Average		On Base Percentage		Slugging Average	
Thompson-Det	166	Thompson-Det	273	Fogarty-Phi	82	Anson-Chi	.347	Brouthers-Det	.426	Thompson-Det	.571
Connor-NY	104	Brouthers-Det	242	Connor-NY	75	Thompson-Det	.372	Anson-Chi	.422	Brouthers-Det	.562
Anson-Chi	102	Rowe-Det	225	Williamson-Chi	73	Brouthers-Det	.338	Thompson-Det	.416	Connor-NY	.541
Brouthers-Det	101	Richardson-Det	217	Seery-Ind	71	Ward-NY	.338	Schomberg-Ind	.397	Wise-Bos	.522
Denny-Ind	97	Anson-Chi	202	Brouthers-Det	71	Wise-Bos	.334	Kelly-Bos	.393	Anson-Chi	.517

Production		Adjusted Production		Batter Runs		Adjusted Batter Runs		Clutch Hitting Index		Runs Created	
Brouthers-Det	.988	Brouthers-Det	167	Thompson-Det	51.2	Thompson-Det	46.6	Thompson-Det	149	Thompson-Det	142
Thompson-Det	.987	Thompson-Det	166	Brouthers-Det	50.5	Brouthers-Det	46.0	O'Rourke-NY	143	Brouthers-Det	138
Anson-Chi	.939	Connor-NY	164	Anson-Chi	39.3	Connor-NY	43.1	Nash-Bos	129	Kelly-Bos	129
Connor-NY	.933	Carroll-Pit	152	Connor-NY	37.1	Wise-Bos	31.6	Rowe-Det	125	Ward-NY	125
Wise-Bos	.913	Wise-Bos	151	Wise-Bos	31.7	Carroll-Pit	30.1	Schomberg-Ind	122	Connor-NY	120

Total Average		Stolen Bases		Stolen Base Average	Stolen Base Runs	Fielding Runs		Total Player Rating	
Brouthers-Det	1.184	Ward-NY	111			Glasscock-Ind	35.0	Thompson-Det	4.3
Kelly-Bos	1.146	Fogarty-Phi	102			Fogarty-Phi	31.7	Denny-Ind	4.0
Connor-NY	1.131	Kelly-Bos	84			Ward-NY	29.8	Ward-NY	3.9
Thompson-Det	1.094	Hanlon-Det	69			Johnston-Bos	25.3	Glasscock-Ind	3.5
Fogarty-Phi	1.085	Glasscock-Ind	62			Pfeffer-Chi	24.6	Fogarty-Phi	3.3

Wins		Win Percentage		Games		Complete Games		Shutouts		Saves	
Clarkson-Chi	38	Getzien-Det	.690	Clarkson-Chi	60	Clarkson-Chi	56	Casey-Phi	4	VanHaltren-Chi	1
Keefe-NY	35	Ferguson-Phi	.688	Keefe-NY	56	Keefe-NY	54	Madden-Bos	3	Twitchell-Det	1
Getzien-Det	29	Casey-Phi	.683	Radbourn-Bos	50	Radbourn-Bos	48	Healy-Ind	3	Tiernan-NY	1
Galvin-Pit	28	Keefe-NY	.648	Galvin-Pit	49	Galvin-Pit	47	Galvin-Pit	3	Stemmeyer-Bos	1
Casey-Phi	28	Clarkson-Chi	.644	Whitney-Was	47	Whitney-Was	46			Pettit-Chi	1
										Ferguson-Phi	1
										Fast-Ind	1
										Baldwin-Chi	1

Innings Pitched		Fewest Hits/Game		Fewest BB/Game		Strikeouts		Strikeouts/Game		Ratio	
Clarkson-Chi	523.0	Keefe-NY	8.08	Whitney-Was	.93	Clarkson-Chi	237	Baldwin-Chi	4.42	Keefe-NY	10.33
Keefe-NY	476.2	Conway-Det	8.14	Galvin-Pit	1.37	Keefe-NY	189	Gilmore-Was	4.37	Clarkson-Chi	10.55
Galvin-Pit	440.2	Casey-Phi	8.69	Ferguson-Phi	1.42	Baldwin-Chi	164	Buffinton-Phi	4.33	Ferguson-Phi	10.75
Radbourn-Bos	425.0	Welch-NY	8.82	Clarkson-Chi	1.58	Buffinton-Phi	160	VanHaltren-Chi	4.25	Whitney-Was	10.85
Whitney-Was	404.2	Clarkson-Chi	8.83	Boyle-Ind	1.89	Whitney-Was	146	Clarkson-Chi	4.08	Welch-NY	11.32

Earned Run Average		Adjusted ERA		Opponents' Batting Avg.		Opponents' On Base Pct.		Starter Runs		Adjusted Starter Runs	
Casey-Phi	2.86	Casey-Phi	147	Keefe-NY	.230	Keefe-NY	.276	Clarkson-Chi	56.1	Clarkson-Chi	80.1
Conway-Det	2.90	Clarkson-Chi	145	Conway-Det	.235	Clarkson-Chi	.281	Casey-Phi	51.5	Casey-Phi	58.3
Ferguson-Phi	3.00	Ferguson-Phi	140	Casey-Phi	.246	Whitney-Was	.284	Keefe-NY	49.3	Ferguson-Phi	39.9
Clarkson-Chi	3.08	Conway-Det	139	Clarkson-Chi	.246	Ferguson-Phi	.289	Galvin-Pit	37.1	Baldwin-Chi	39.5
Keefe-NY	3.12	Baldwin-Chi	131	Baldwin-Chi	.248	Galvin-Pit	.299	Whitney-Was	36.9	Whitney-Was	36.4

Clutch Pitching Index		Relief Runs	Adjusted Relief Runs	Relief Ranking	Total Pitcher Index		Total Baseball Ranking	
VanHaltren-Chi	123				Clarkson-Chi	8.3	Clarkson-Chi	8.1
Casey-Phi	117				Ferguson-Phi	4.7	Ferguson-Phi	4.7
Baldwin-Chi	114				Whitney-Was	4.7	Whitney-Was	4.5
Ferguson-Phi	108				Keefe-NY	3.8	Thompson-Det	4.3
Madden-Bos	105				Casey-Phi	3.7	Denny-Ind	4.0

April 16 Two rookies, Mike Griffin of the Baltimore Orioles and George "White Wings" Tebeau of Cincinnati, hit home runs in their first major league at bats on Opening Day. They are the first of many to accomplish this.

April 21 Pop Snyder, the only catcher from the National Association still behind the plate, allows Louisville to steal 10 bases in just 3 innings before being replaced by Jim Toy. The Colonels beat the Cleveland "Babies" 14–7.

April 22 Tony Mullane pitches a regular-season game in Missouri for the first time since 1883. The Missouri injunction obtained against him by the St. Louis Unions in 1884 having finally been resolved, Tony leads the Reds to a 5–2 victory over the Browns.

May 1 Charlie Comiskey triples and homers to lead the Browns to a 14–13 victory over Cleveland. St. Louis scores 74 runs in a 4-game sweep and is on its way to becoming the first team to score over 1,000 runs in a season.

June 9 Mets right fielder Candy Nelson sets a major league record by starting three double plays, two on throws to home and one to start an infield rundown. Only two other major league outfielders have tied this record: Jack McCarthy (4/26/05) and Ira Flagstead (4/19/26).

June 13 Sportswriter O. P. Caylor takes over as manager of the Mets. Caylor had managed Cincinnati in 1885 and 1886 while writing for the Cincinnati *Enquirer,* now he is with the New York *Tribune* and managing again.

June 16 Before a riotous Baltimore club, Curt Welch of the Browns topples Orioles second baseman Bill Greenwood to prevent a double play and is promptly arrested for assault by a policeman on duty at the park. He will be fined $4.50 by a local judge.

July 4 Dave Foutz of the Browns has a banner day at the plate, driving in nine runs with two homers and five hits in the afternoon game of a doubleheader against the Mets after having hit a homer in the morning game. St. Louis wins both 15–2 and 20–3.

July 22 Master Fred Chapman, age 14, pitches for Philadelphia against Cleveland in a 9-0 forfeited game. This is his only major league appearance.

August 12 At the Mets' grounds on Staten Island, Athletic batter Gus Weyhing hits an apparent triple that Mets' right fielder Eddie Hogan kicks onto the stage of the play "The Fall of Babylon." Since the ground rules at the park call for a double on hits into the theatrical set, the umpire orders Weyhing back to second. After a futile argument, the Athletics

leave and forfeit the game.

August 17 Managing from the press table costs Ollie Caylor and the Mets a game. With a Baltimore runner on third base in the bottom of the tenth inning, manager Caylor yells last-second instructions to catcher Bill Holbert. Just as Holbert turns around to look at the press stand, Al Mays begins his delivery. When Mays sees Holbert turned away, however, he stops, committing a balk that sends the winning run across the plate for the Orioles.

August 29 Denny Lyons of Philadelphia (AA) is held hitless for the first time since May 23 to end a 52-game hitting streak. In two of those games, however, Lyons's only hits were actually bases on balls, scored as hits this year.

October 1 Matt Kilroy pitches and wins both games of a doubleheader to close the home season at Oriole Park. The fastballer would finish the season with a 46-20 record, the major league season record for a lefthander.

October 8 The Metropolitan franchise and player contracts are sold to AA rival Brooklyn for $15,000.

December 12* A baseball reporters association is organized. It pledges to work to standardize scoring practices, especially in the gray area of stolen bases.

	BALTIMORE		BROOKLYN		CINCINNATI		CLEVELAND		LOUISVILLE		NEW YORK		PHILADELPHIA		ST.LOUIS
M	B.Barnie	M	C.Byrne	M	G.Schmelz	M	J.Williams	M	J.Kelly	M	B.Ferguson	M	F.Bancroft	M	C.Comiskey
1B	T.Tucker	1B	B.Phillips	1B	J.Reilly	1B	J.Toy	1B	J.Kerins	M	D.Orr	M	C.Mason	1B	C.Comiskey
2B	B.Greenwood	2B	B.McClellan	2B	B.McPhee	2B	C.Stricker	2B	R.Mack	M	O.Caylor	1B	J.Milligan	2B	Y.Robinson
SS	O.Burns	SS	G.Smith	SS	F.Fennelly	SS	E.McKean	SS	B.White	1B	D.Orr	2B	L.Bierbauer	SS	B.Gleason
3B	J.Davis	3B	G.Pinkney	3B	H.Carpenter	3B	P.Reccius	3B	J.Werrick	2B	J.Gerhardt	SS	C.McGarr	3B	A.Latham
LF	J.Sommer	LF	E.Greer	LF	G.Tebeau	LF	F.Mann	LF	H.Collins	SS	P.Radford	3B	D.Lyons	LF	T.O'Neill
CF	M.Griffin	CF	J.McTamany	CF	P.Corkhill	CF	P.Hotaling	CF	P.Browning	3B	F.Hankinson	LF	H.Larkin	CF	C.Welch
RF	B.Purcell	RF	E.Swartwood	RF	H.Nicol	RF	M.Allen	RF	J.Wolf	LF	D.O'Brien	CF	H.Stovey	RF	B.Caruthers
C	S.Trott	C	J.Peoples	C	K.Baldwin	C	P.Snyder	C	P.Cook	CF	C.Jones	RF	T.Poorman	C	J.Boyle
										RF	C.Roseman	C	W.Robinson		
C	C.Fulmer	OP	A.Terry	C1	J.Keenan	C1	C.Reipschlager	1P	G.Hecker	C	B.Holbert			OP	D.Foutz
CO	L.Daniels	O	E.Burch	O	C.Jones	CO	S.Carroll	CO	L.Cross			O	F.Mann	O	D.Bushong
/O	J.Hayes	C	B.Clark	/3	H.Kappel	1O	C.Sweeney	O	P.Reccius	OS	C.Nelson	C	G.Townsend	O	L.Sylvester
		C	J.O'Brien	/O	J.O'Connor	3	J.McGlone	/C	A.Cross	C	J.Donahue	1	E.Flanagan	/O	E.Knouff
P	M.Kilroy	S	B.Otterson			3	J.Say	/O	D.Hemp	O2	J.Meister	O	C.Roseman	/2	H.Lyons
P	P.Smith	/O	C.Roseman	P	E.Smith	C	J.Munyan			1	T.O'Brien	/O	E.Greer	/C	M.Goodfellow
				P	T.Mullane	C	C.Zimmer	P	T.Ramsey	O	E.Hogan	/C	J.Roxburgh		
/P	E.Knouff	P	H.Porter	P	B.Serad	3	E.Herr	P	E.Chamberlain	/1	D.Esterbrook	P	E.Seward	P	S.King
/P	L.Shreve	P	J.Harkins			/3	E.Flynn			2	J.Knowles	P	G.Weyhing	/P	N.Hudson
/P	B.Gardner	P	S.Toole	/P	J.McGinnis	/O	H.Simon	/P	J.Neale	S	C.Cross	P	A.Atkinson	/P	J.Murphy
/P	B.Keating	P	H.Henderson	P	M.Shea	/S	F.Scheibeck	/P	P.Veach	/O	J.Morrison				
				/P	M.Watson					S	S.Houck	/P	B.Mathews		
		/P	B.Cunningham	/P	W.Widner	P	B.Crowell			/1	C.Ryan	/P	B.Hart		
						P	M.Morrison			/O	F.O'Neill	/P	C.Titcomb		
						P	H.Daily			/O	C.Hall	/P	B.Taylor		
						P	B.Gilks			/C	T.Kinslow	/P	F.Chapman		
						P	G.Pechiney			/C	H.Collins	/P	B.Casey		
										/O	L.Pike				
						/P	J.Kirby			P	A.Mays				
										P	E.Cushman				
										P	J.Lynch				
										P	J.Shaffer				
										P	S.Wiedman				
										/P	B.Fagan				
										/P	C.Parsons				
										/P	G.McMullen				

TEAM	G	W	L	PCT	GB	R	OR	AB	H	2B	3B	HR	BB	SO	AVG	OBP	SLG	PRO	PRO+	BR	/A	PF	CHI	RC	SB	CS	SBA	SBR
STL	138	95	40	.704		1131	761	5048	1550	261	78	39	442	340	.307	.371	.413	.784	111	151	37	111	103	1012	581			
CIN	136	81	54	.600	14	892	745	4797	1285	179	102	37	382	366	.268	.329	.371	.700	97	-11	-31	102	102	778	527			
BAL	141	77	58	.570	18	975	861	4825	1337	202	100	31	469	334	.277	.349	.380	.729	114	50	106	94	102	852	545			
LOU	139	76	60	.559	19.5	956	854	4916	1420	194	98	27	436	356	.289	.352	.385	.737	107	61	42	102	98	850	466			
PHI	137	64	69	.481	30	893	890	4954	1370	231	84	29	321	388	.277	.327	.375	.702	99	-13	-14	100	100	782	476			
BRO	138	60	74	.448	34.5	904	918	4913	1281	200	82	25	456	365	.261	.330	.350	.680	92	-40	-51	101	103	720	409			
NY	138	44	89	.331	50	754	1093	4820	1197	193	66	21	439	463	.248	.318	.329	.647	88	-98	-63	96	94	615	305			
CLE	133	39	92	.298	54	729	1112	4649	1170	178	77	14	375	463	.252	.314	.332	.646	87	-99	-77	97	96	611	355			
TOT	550					7234		38922	10610	1638	687	223	3320	3075	.273	.337	.367	.704							3664			

TEAM	CG	SH	SV	IP	H	H/G	HR	BB	SO	RAT	ERA	ERA+	OAV	OOB	PR	/A	PF	CPI	FA	E	DP	FW	PW	BW	SBW	DIF
STL	132	6	2	1199¹	1254	9.4	19	323	334	12.2	3.77	120	.258	.311	69	100	106	94	.916	481	86	3.6	8.1	3.0		12.8
CIN	129	11	1	1182²	1202	9.1	28	396	330	12.6	3.58	121	.257	.322	93	99	101	107	.916	484	106	3.0	8.0	-2.5		5.0
BAL	132	8	0	1220	1288	9.5	16	418	470	13.0	3.87	106	.262	.326	58	30	95	100	.907	549	66	.8	2.4	8.6		-2.3
LOU	133	3	1	1205²	1274	9.5	31	357	544	12.5	3.82	115	.260	.316	63	75	102	98	.903	574	83	-.9	6.1	3.4		-.6
PHI	131	5	1	1186¹	1227	9.3	29	433	417	13.1	4.59	93	.259	.331	-39	-41	100	100	.907	528	95	1.0	-3.3	-1.1		.9
BRO	132	3	3	1185¹	1348	10.2	27	454	332	14.0	4.47	96	.281	.348	-24	-24	100	103	.905	562	88	-.5	-1.9	-4.1		-.4
NY	132	1	0	1180¹	1545	11.8	39	406	316	15.3	5.28	80	.308	.365	-130	-138	99	102	.894	632	102	-4.0	-11.2	-5.1		-2.2
CLE	127	2	1	1136	1472	11.7	34	533	332	16.4	4.99	87	.308	.384	-88	-84	101	115	.898	576	97	-2.2	-6.8	-6.2		-11.3
TOT	1048	39	9	9495²		10.1				13.6	4.29		.273	.337					.906	4386	723					

Runs		Hits		Doubles		Triples		Home Runs		Total Bases	
O'Neill-StL	167	O'Neill-StL	225	O'Neill-StL	52	Poorman-Phi	19	O'Neill-StL	14	O'Neill-StL	357
Latham-StL	163	Browning-Lou	220	Lyons-Phi	43	O'Neill-StL	19	Reilly-Cin	10	Browning-Lou	299
Griffin-Bal	142	Lyons-Phi	209	Reilly-Cin	35	McPhee-Cin	19	Burns-Bal	9	Lyons-Phi	298
Poorman-Phi	140	Latham-StL	198	Latham-StL	35	Kerins-Lou	19			Burns-Bal	286
Comiskey-StL	139	Burns-Bal	188	Browning-Lou	35	Davis-Bal	19			Reilly-Cin	263
						Burns-Bal	19				

Runs Batted In		Runs Produced		Bases On Balls		Batting Average		On Base Percentage		Slugging Average	
O'Neill-StL	123	O'Neill-StL	276	Radford-NY	106	O'Neill-StL	.435	O'Neill-StL	.490	O'Neill-StL	.691
Browning-Lou	118	Browning-Lou	251	Robinson-StL	92	Browning-Lou	.402	Browning-Lou	.464	Caruthers-StL	.547
Davis-Bal	109	Latham-StL	244	Nicol-Cin	86	Orr-NY	.368	Caruthers-StL	.463	Browning-Lou	.547
Welch-StL	108	Comiskey-StL	238	Mack-Lou	83	Lyons-Phi	.367	Robinson-StL	.445	Lyons-Phi	.523
Foutz-StL	108	Griffin-Bal	233	Fennelly-Cin	82	Caruthers-StL	.357	Lyons-Phi	.421	Burns-Bal	.519

Production		Adjusted Production		Batter Runs		Adjusted Batter Runs		Clutch Hitting Index		Runs Created	
O'Neill-StL	1.180	O'Neill-StL	205	O'Neill-StL	86.4	O'Neill-StL	67.9	Purcell-Phi	140	O'Neill-StL	194
Browning-Lou	1.011	Browning-Lou	178	Browning-Lou	60.9	Browning-Lou	57.6	Hotaling-Cle	128	Browning-Lou	191
Caruthers-StL	1.010	Burns-Bal	169	Lyons-Phi	46.7	Burns-Bal	52.5	Greenwood-Bal	127	Lyons-Phi	160
Lyons-Phi	.943	Caruthers-StL	164	Burns-Bal	43.7	Lyons-Phi	46.5	Welch-StL	127	Burns-Bal	146
Burns-Bal	.933	Lyons-Phi	162	Caruthers-StL	42.9	Caruthers-StL	30.9	Wolf-Lou	126	Latham-StL	146

Total Average		Stolen Bases		Stolen Base Average	Stolen Base Runs	Fielding Runs		Total Player Rating	
O'Neill-StL	1.514	Nicol-Cin	138			Smith-Bro	32.0	O'Neill-StL	4.7
Browning-Lou	1.422	Latham-StL	129			McPhee-Cin	26.2	Browning-Lou	4.2
Caruthers-StL	1.368	Comiskey-StL	117			Kerins-Lou	24.8	Lyons-Phi	3.5
Robinson-StL	1.197	Browning-Lou	103			White-Lou	21.5	McPhee-Cin	3.0
Lyons-Phi	1.175	McPhee-Cin	95			Welch-StL	19.4	Burns-Bal	2.8

Wins		Win Percentage		Games		Complete Games		Shutouts		Saves	
Kilroy-Bal	46	Caruthers-StL	.763	Kilroy-Bal	69	Kilroy-Bal	66	Mullane-Cin	6	Terry-Bro	3
Ramsey-Lou	37	King-StL	.727	Ramsey-Lou	65	Ramsey-Lou	61	Kilroy-Bal	6		
Smith-Cin	34	Kilroy-Bal	.708	Smith-Bal	58	Smith-Bal	54	Smith-Cin	3		
King-StL	32	Foutz-StL	.676	Weyhing-Phi	55	Weyhing-Phi	53	Seward-Phi	3		
Mullane-Cin	31	Smith-Cin	.667	Seward-Phi	55	Seward-Phi	52				

Innings Pitched		Fewest Hits/Game		Fewest BB/Game		Strikeouts		Strikeouts/Game		Ratio	
Kilroy-Bal	589.1	Smith-Cin	8.05	Hecker-Lou	1.58	Ramsey-Lou	355	Ramsey-Lou	5.70	Smith-Cin	10.76
Ramsey-Lou	561.0	Seward-Phi	8.51	Caruthers-StL	1.61	Kilroy-Bal	217	Morrison-Cle	4.49	Caruthers-StL	10.93
Smith-Bal	491.1	Toole-Bro	8.63	Lynch-NY	1.73	Smith-Bal	206	Terry-Bro	3.91	Kilroy-Bal	11.64
Seward-Phi	470.2	Ramsey-Lou	8.73	Foutz-StL	2.39	Weyhing-Phi	193	Smith-Bal	3.77	Seward-Phi	11.65
Weyhing-Phi	466.1	Caruthers-StL	8.89	Kilroy-Bal	2.40	Smith-Cin	176	Weyhing-Phi	3.72	Ramsey-Lou	11.66

Earned Run Average		Adjusted ERA		Opponents' Batting Avg.		Opponents' On Base Pct.		Starter Runs		Adjusted Starter Runs	
Smith-Cin	2.94	Smith-Cin	148	Smith-Cin	.230	Smith-Cin	.286	Kilroy-Bal	80.0	Smith-Cin	69.6
Kilroy-Bal	3.07	Caruthers-StL	137	Ramsey-Lou	.242	Caruthers-StL	.287	Smith-Cin	67.3	Kilroy-Bal	67.0
Mullane-Cin	3.24	Mullane-Cin	134	Seward-Phi	.244	Ramsey-Lou	.299	Ramsey-Lou	53.5	Ramsey-Lou	59.3
Caruthers-StL	3.30	Kilroy-Bal	133	Caruthers-StL	.247	Kilroy-Bal	.306	Mullane-Cin	48.5	Mullane-Cin	50.7
Ramsey-Lou	3.43	Ramsey-Lou	128	Kilroy-Bal	.253	Foutz-StL	.306	Caruthers-StL	37.6	Caruthers-StL	46.7

Clutch Pitching Index		Relief Runs	Adjusted Relief Runs	Relief Ranking	Total Pitcher Index		Total Baseball Ranking	
Daily-Cle	140				Kilroy-Bal	7.3	Caruthers-StL	7.7
Crowell-Cle	122				Caruthers-StL	6.2	Kilroy-Bal	7.1
Morrison-Cle	121				Smith-Cin	6.0	Smith-Cin	5.9
Mullane-Cin	119				Mullane-Cin	4.5	O'Neill-StL	4.7
Chamberlain-Lou	117				Ramsey-Lou	3.5	Mullane-Cin	4.3

February 2 Indianapolis announces that the roof of its new grandstand will hold 42 private boxes, to be sold to season subscribers only, the first sky boxes.

March 2 The NL meets in New York and abolishes all discounts from the 50-cent minimum admission price.

April 1* The Texas League plays its first game, Houston winning at home 3–1 over Galveston before 3,000 fans.

April 3 Chicago pitching star John Clarkson is sold to Boston for $10,000. With last year's deal for King Kelly, the Beaneaters have acquired a "$20,000 Battery" from the White Stockings.

May 1 After holding out for a $4,000 salary, Tim Keefe wins his 1888 debut for the Giants, beating Boston 6–1.

May 3 In New York, George Gore goes to left field to start the game, but box-seat holders scream for Mike Slattery, and captain Buck Ewing makes the change.

May 22 Future Hall of Fame slugger Ed Delahanty makes his major league debut with the Phillies, going hitless and making two errors at second base. His contract had been purchased from Wheeling in the Tri-State League for $2,000.

May 25 Boston opens its new Grand Pavilion, an elaborate double-decked structure, better known as South End Grounds. Though the Pavilion seats 2,800, 12,000 see the Beaneaters lose their home opener to the Phillies 4–1.

June 20 Future Hall of Famer first base

Jake Beckley makes his major league debut with Pittsburgh, with a double, triple, and stolen base.

June 30 With permission from the NL, the Phillies reduce admission to 25 cents. Twelve thousand fans turn out to see a one-hit 7–0 victory over Boston by Charlie Buffinton. After an average of 1,123 admissions at the 50-cent rate, attendance at Huntingdon Street Baseball Grounds will now jump to an average of 4,010.

July 28 Jimmy Ryan hits two triples, two singles, and a homer and pitches seven innings in relief to lead Chicago to a 21–17 decision over Detroit, dropping Detroit into a first-place tie with the Giants. The Colts (Cubs) trail by 2½ games.

August 14 Tim Keefe's winning streak is stopped at 19 games when Gus Krock and the Colts beat the Giants 4–2 before a crowd of 10,240 at New York.

September 6 Indianapolis tries its second experimental night game (the first was August 22) but the natural-gas illumination is inadequate, and the idea is dropped.

September 12 New York forfeits a game in Chicago when Buck Ewing is injured and cannot continue. With no uniformed substitutes available, the Giants simply leave the field in the fifth.

September 15 Ed Morris of Pittsburgh

pitches his fourth consecutive shutout, a record that will be unsurpassed in the NL until 1968. Morris's gems include 1-0 and 2-0 victories over the Phillies, a 7-inning 2-0 win over the Senators, and today's 1-0 win over the Giants.

October 1 When Indianapolis scores three runs in the top of the eighth inning to take a 4–2 lead at Washington, Senator catcher Connie Mack suddenly complains of a sore finger. The ensuing delay lasts until darkness and forces the game's end, the score reverting to a 7-inning 2–1 Senator victory.

October 16 The 10-game World Series opens in New York with the Giants and Tim Keefe edging the Browns and Silver King, 2–1. Each hurler allows only three hits.

October 25 The Giants clinch New York's first World Championship six games to two by trouncing the Browns 11-3. Tim Keefe gets his fourth win of the series.

November 20 The Joint Rules Committee reduces the number of balls for a walk from five to four, establishing the four balls/three strikes count that remains in effect more than a century later.

November 22 The NL adopts a salary classification plan that puts all players into five categories with a standard salary for each ranging from $1,500 to $2,500.

	BOSTON		CHICAGO		DETROIT		INDIANAPOLIS		NEW YORK		PHILADELPHIA		PITTSBURGH		WASHINGTON
M	J.Morrill	M	C.Anson	M	B.Watkins	M	H.Spence	M	J.Mutrie	M	H.Wright	M	H.Phillips	M	W.Hewett
1B	J.Morrill	1B	C.Anson	M	B.Leadley	1B	D.Esterbrook	1B	R.Connor	1B	S.Farrar	1B	J.Beckley	M	T.Sullivan
2B	J.Quinn	2B	F.Pfeffer	1B	D.Brouthers	2B	C.Bassett	2B	D.Richardson	2B	C.Bastian	2B	F.Dunlap	1B	B.O'Brien
SS	S.Wise	SS	N.Williamson	2B	H.Richardson	SS	J.Glasscock	SS	J.Ward	SS	A.Irwin	SS	P.Smith	2B	A.Myers
3B	B.Nash	3B	T.Burns	SS	J.Rowe	3B	J.Denny	3B	A.Whitney	3B	J.Mulvey	3B	B.Kuehne	SS	G.Shoch
LF	J.Hornung	LF	M.Sullivan	3B	D.White	LF	E.Seery	LF	J.O'Rourke	LF	G.Wood	LF	A.Dalrymple	3B	J.Donnelly
CF	D.Johnston	CF	J.Ryan	LF	L.Twitchell	CF	P.Hines	CF	M.Slattery	CF	E.Andrews	CF	B.Sunday	LF	W.Wilmot
RF	T.Brown	RF	H.Duffy	CF	N.Hanlon	RF	J.McGeachy	RF	M.Tiernan	RF	J.Fogarty	RF	J.Coleman	CF	D.Hoy
C	K.Kelly	C	T.Daly	RF	C.Campau	C	D.Buckley	C	B.Ewing	C	J.Clements	C	D.Miller	RF	E.Daily
				C	C.Bennett									C	C.Mack
S	I.Ray	OP	G.Van Haltren			C3	G.Myers	O	G.Gore	2O	E.Delahanty	CO	F.Carroll		
C	P.Tate	CO	D.Farrell	2C	C.Ganzel	C	C.Daily	O	E.Foster	C	P.Schriver	1O	A.Maul	S	S.Fuller
3	E.Sutton	O	B.Pettit	O	S.Thompson	1	J.Schoeneck	C	P.Murphy	C	B.Hallman	OC	J.Fields	C	P.Deasley
2	B.Klusman	C	S.Flint	SC	S.Sutcliffe	O1	O.Schomberg	3S	G.Hatfield	C	D.McGuire	3	E.Cleveland	S3	J.Irwin
2	J.Burdock	C	D.Darling	O	T.Scheffler			C	W.Brown	/3	W.Wagenhorst	C	P.McShannic	3	T.Arundel
C	T.O'Rourke			2	P.Nicholson	P	H.Boyle	/O	B.George	/O	J.Grim	/O	S.Nichol	/3	P.Sweeney
O	E.Glenn	P	G.Krock	C	J.Wells	P	J.Healy	/3	E.Cleveland	/2	C.Childs	/O	C.Carroll	C	M.Murray
2	B.Higgins	P	M.Baldwin	/C	D.McGuire	P	L.Shreve			/2	G.Gardner	/O	H.Yaik	/O	P.Werden
/O	M.Hines	P	J.Tener	/2	S.LaRoque	P	B.Burdick	P	T.Keefe			/C	B.Farmer	/S	G.Gardner
/C	P.Sommers			/C	B.Gilligan			P	M.Welch	P	C.Buffinton			/C	J.Banning
/O	N.Wise	P	G.Borchers	/C	C.Broughton	/P	S.Moffett	P	C.Titcomb	P	D.Casey	P	E.Morris		
		/P	A.Gumbert	/S	F.Scheibeck			P	E.Crane	P	B.Sanders	P	P.Galvin	P	H.O'Day
P	J.Clarkson	/P	F.Dwyer					P	S.Wiedman	P	K.Gleason	P	H.Staley	P	J.Whitney
P	B.Sowders	/P	T.Brynan	P	C.Getzien									P	W.Widner
P	C.Radbourn	/P	D.Clarke	P	P.Conway					/P	J.Tyng	/P	H.Henderson	P	G.Keefe
P	K.Madden	/P	W.Mains	P	H.Gruber							/P	P.Knell	P	F.Gilmore
				P	E.Beatin										
/P	D.Conway													/P	D.Shaw
				/P	L.Baldwin									/P	G.Haddock
														/P	J.Greening

TEAM	G	W	L	PCT	GB	R	OR	AB	H	2B	3B	HR	BB	SO	AVG	OBP	SLG	PRO	PRO+	BR	/A	PF	CHI	RC	SB	CS	SBA	SBR
NY	138	84	47	.641		659	479	4747	1149	130	76	55	270	456	.242	.287	.336	.623	105	21	29	99	102	562	314			
CHI	136	77	58	.570	9	734	659	4616	1201	147	95	77	290	563	.260	.308	.383	.691	118	127	74	107	99	649	287			
PHI	132	69	61	.531	14.5	535	509	4528	1021	151	46	16	268	485	.225	.276	.290	.566	82	-63	-91	105	100	441	246			
BOS	137	70	64	.522	15.5	669	619	4834	1183	167	89	56	282	524	.245	.291	.351	.642	108	51	39	102	97	593	293			
DET	134	68	63	.519	16	721	629	4849	1275	177	72	51	307	396	.263	.313	.361	.674	121	110	111	100	96	623	193			
PIT	139	66	68	.493	19.5	534	580	4713	1070	150	49	14	194	583	.227	.264	.289	.553	89	-93	-54	92	103	446	287			
IND	136	50	85	.370	36	603	731	4623	1100	180	33	34	236	492	.238	.281	.313	.594	93	-24	-35	102	103	518	350			
WAS	136	48	86	.358	37.5	482	731	4546	944	98	49	30	246	499	.208	.255	.271	.526	77	-129	-103	94	103	408	331			
TOT	544					4937		37456	8943	1200	509	333	2093	3998	.239	.285	.325	.609							2301			

TEAM	CG	SH	SV	IP	H	H/G	HR	BB	SO	RAT	ERA	ERA+	OAV	OOB	PR	/A	PF	CPI	FA	E	DP	FW	PW	BW	SBW	DIF
NY	133	20	1	1208	907	6.8	27	307	726	9.3	1.96	139	.199	.255	117	103	96	95	.924	432	76	1.2	10.1	2.9		4.3
CHI	123	13	1	1186¹	1139	8.6	63	308	588	11.4	2.96	102	.246	.301	-17	6	106	112	.927	417	112	1.7	.6	7.3		-.0
PHI	125	16	3	1167	1072	8.3	26	196	519	10.0	2.38	124	.236	.271	58	69	104	103	.923	424	70	.6	6.8	-9.0		5.6
BOS	134	7	0	1225¹	1104	8.1	36	269	484	10.4	2.61	109	.232	.280	30	27	100	100	.917	494	91	-2.2	2.7	3.8		-1.3
DET	130	10	1	1199	1115	8.4	44	183	522	10.0	2.74	100	.234	.266	12	-2	97	90	.919	463	83	-1.1	-.2	10.9		-7.1
PIT	135	13	0	1203¹	1190	8.9	23	223	367	10.8	2.67	99	.249	.287	22	-4	94	107	.927	416	88	2.3	-.4	-5.3		2.5
IND	132	6	0	1187²	1260	9.5	64	308	388	12.2	3.81	77	.263	.313	-129	-117	104	98	.921	449	84	-.0	-11.5	-3.4		-2.5
WAS	133	6	0	1179¹	1157	8.8	50	298	406	11.5	3.54	79	.248	.300	-93	-104	98	91	.912	494	69	-2.4	-10.2	-10.1		3.8
TOT	1045	91	6	9556		8.4				10.7	2.83		.239	.285					.921	3589	673					

Runs		Hits		Doubles		Triples		Home Runs		Total Bases	
Brouthers-Det	118	Ryan-Chi	182	Ryan-Chi	33	Johnston-Bos	18	Ryan-Chi	16	Ryan-Chi	283
Ryan-Chi	115	Anson-Chi	177	Brouthers-Det	33	Connor-NY	17	Connor-NY	14	Johnston-Bos	276
Johnston-Bos	102	Johnston-Bos	173	Johnston-Bos	31	Nash-Bos	15	Johnston-Bos	12	Anson-Chi	257
Anson-Chi	101	Brouthers-Det	160	Denny-Ind	27	Ewing-NY	15	Denny-Ind	12	Brouthers-Det	242
Connor-NY	98	White-Det	157	Hines-Ind	26			Anson-Chi	12	Connor-NY	231

Runs Batted In		Runs Produced		Bases On Balls		Batting Average		On Base Percentage		Slugging Average	
Anson-Chi	84	Brouthers-Det	175	Connor-NY	73	Anson-Chi	.344	Anson-Chi	.400	Ryan-Chi	.515
Nash-Bos	75	Anson-Chi	173	Hoy-Was	69	Ryan-Chi	.332	Brouthers-Det	.399	Anson-Chi	.499
Rowe-Det	74	Ryan-Chi	163	Brouthers-Det	68	Kelly-Bos	.318	Connor-NY	.389	Connor-NY	.480
Williamson-Chi	73	Johnston-Bos	158	Williamson-Chi	65	Brouthers-Det	.307	Ryan-Chi	.377	Kelly-Bos	.480
		Connor-NY	155	Seery-Ind	64	Ewing-NY	.306	Hoy-Was	.374	Johnston-Bos	.472

Production		Adjusted Production		Batter Runs		Adjusted Batter Runs		Clutch Hitting Index		Runs Created	
Anson-Chi	.899	Connor-NY	178	Ryan-Chi	49.4	Brouthers-Det	46.8	Rowe-Det	153	Ryan-Chi	133
Ryan-Chi	.892	Brouthers-Det	174	Anson-Chi	49.3	Connor-NY	45.0	Burns-Chi	150	Anson-Chi	117
Connor-NY	.869	Anson-Chi	173	Brouthers-Det	46.6	Anson-Chi	41.0	Bassett-Ind	126	Brouthers-Det	113
Brouthers-Det	.862	Ryan-Chi	170	Connor-NY	43.7	Ryan-Chi	40.8	Wood-Phi	122	Connor-NY	103
Kelly-Bos	.848	Kelly-Bos	166	Kelly-Bos	33.4	Kelly-Bos	31.8	Nash-Bos	121	Kelly-Bos	101

Total Average		Stolen Bases		Stolen Base Average	Stolen Base Runs	Fielding Runs		Total Player Rating	
Ryan-Chi	1.044	Hoy-Was	82			Pfeffer-Chi	38.3	Nash-Bos	4.9
Kelly-Bos	1.007	Seery-Ind	80			Nash-Bos	25.6	Pfeffer-Chi	4.4
Anson-Chi	.985	Sunday-Pit	71			Denny-Ind	24.5	Ewing-NY	3.9
Brouthers-Det	.983	Pfeffer-Chi	64			Burns-Chi	17.1	Ryan-Chi	3.8
Connor-NY	.982	Ryan-Chi	60			Sunday-Pit	16.6	Anson-Chi	3.6

Wins		Win Percentage		Games		Complete Games		Shutouts		Saves	
Keefe-NY	35	Keefe-NY	.745	Morris-Pit	55	Morris-Pit	54	Sanders-Phi	8	Wood-Phi	2
Clarkson-Bos	33	Conway-Det	.682	Clarkson-Bos	54	Clarkson-Bos	53	Keefe-NY	8	VanHaltren-Chi	1
Conway-Det	30	Sanders-Phi	.655	Keefe-NY	51	Galvin-Pit	49	Galvin-Pit	6	Tyng-Phi	1
Morris-Pit	29	Krock-Chi	.641	Galvin-Pit	50	Keefe-NY	48	Buffinton-Phi	6	Twitchell-Det	1
Buffinton-Phi	28	Clarkson-Bos	.623	Welch-NY	47	Welch-NY	47			Crane-NY	1

Innings Pitched		Fewest Hits/Game		Fewest BB/Game		Strikeouts		Strikeouts/Game		Ratio	
Clarkson-Bos	483.1	Keefe-NY	6.57	Sanders-Phi	1.08	Keefe-NY	335	Keefe-NY	6.94	Keefe-NY	8.68
Morris-Pit	480.0	Titcomb-NY	6.81	Galvin-Pit	1.09	Clarkson-Bos	223	Titcomb-NY	5.89	Buffinton-Phi	8.70
Galvin-Pit	437.1	Welch-NY	6.94	Krock-Chi	1.19	Getzien-Det	202	Baldwin-NY	5.63	Conway-Det	8.86
Keefe-NY	434.1	Conway-Det	7.25	Getzien-Det	1.20	Buffinton-Phi	199	VanHaltren-Chi	5.09	Sanders-Phi	9.02
Welch-NY	425.1	Buffinton-Phi	7.28	Madden-Bos	1.31	O'Day-Was	186	Getzien-Det	4.50	Gruber-Det	9.04

Earned Run Average		Adjusted ERA		Opponents' Batting Avg.		Opponents' On Base Pct.		Starter Runs		Adjusted Starter Runs	
Keefe-NY	1.74	Keefe-NY	156	Keefe-NY	.196	Conway-Det	.243	Keefe-NY	52.6	Keefe-NY	47.3
Sanders-Phi	1.90	Sanders-Phi	156	Titcomb-NY	.201	Keefe-NY	.243	Welch-NY	42.8	Buffinton-Phi	46.2
Buffinton-Phi	1.91	Buffinton-Phi	154	Welch-NY	.207	Buffinton-Phi	.244	Buffinton-Phi	40.9	Welch-NY	37.6
Welch-NY	1.93	Welch-NY	141	Conway-Det	.208	Gruber-Det	.249	Sanders-Phi	28.6	Sanders-Phi	32.2
Sowders-Bos	2.07	Sowders-Bos	137	Buffinton-Phi	.213	Titcomb-NY	.253	Morris-Pit	28.0	Sowders-Bos	26.7

Clutch Pitching Index		Relief Runs	Adjusted Relief Runs	Relief Ranking	Total Pitcher Index		Total Baseball Ranking	
Baldwin-Chi	137				Buffinton-Phi	5.8	Buffinton-Phi	5.7
Gleason-Phi	125				Sanders-Phi	4.2	Nash-Bos	4.9
Burdick-Ind	116				Keefe-NY	4.2	Pfeffer-Chi	4.4
Sowders-Bos	113				Conway-Det	3.9	Keefe-NY	4.1
Morris-Pit	112				Welch-NY	3.3	Ryan-Chi	4.0

April 18 On Opening Day in the AA, umpire John Gaffney makes news by standing behind the pitcher with men on base.

May 6 Long John Reilly hits two homers, giving him four in Cincinnati's four-game series versus Kansas City. Reilly will finish the season with an AA-leading 13 homers.

May 10 The Athletics play their first official Sunday home game at Gloucester, New Jersey, or so they think. The league secretary will later rule the game illegally rescheduled and throw it out of official records.

May 30 The Brooklyn Bridegrooms, so called because many players married over the winter, move into first place by winning two games from previous leader Cincinnati.

June 3 *Casey at the Bat* by Ernest Lawrence Thayer is published in the San Francisco *Examiner*. The poem will not become popular until later in the year, when actor DeWolf Hopper recites it.

June 18 Two AA umpires work the Cleveland-Athletic game. The two-umpire system had worked well in last fall's postseason series, but this is believed to be a regular-season first.

June 22 Lou Bierbauer of the Athletics establishes the record for second basemen by making 12 putouts in a 9-inning game. This record will not be tied until August 30, 1966.

July 5 The AA meets in St. Louis and refuses to allow its clubs to reduce admission prices from 50 cents to 25 cents. It also adopts a system of double substitute umpires in case the assigned umpire fails to show up for a game, one substitute player from each club sharing the duties.

July 20 St. Louis regains the lead by beating Kansas City 18–5. The Browns will stay in first place the rest of the season.

August 2 Claiming illness, Brooklyn captain Dave Orr misses the practice session. But later in the day he is spotted at Coney Island, and owner Charles Byrne removes him as captain.

August 3 Kansas City rookie Billy Hamilton, recently purchased from Worcester, steals his first base in the major leagues. Before returning to the mi-

nors in 1902, "Sliding Billy" will amass 912 stolen bases, a record broken by Lou Brock in 1979.

August 7 At a stormy session in Philadelphia, owners finally vote to allow 25-cent admission again but drop the percentage system of paying visitors and replace it with a $130-per-game guarantee.

August 20 St. Louis nudges past Brooklyn 1–0 on brilliant baserunning by Arlie Latham. He opens the game with a single, steals second base, and scores from second on an infield out. Silver King wins the pitchers' duel against Mickey Hughes.

October 9 The St. Louis Browns end the season with a 95-40 record. The mark is two better than the Browns' 1886 mark and it will not be topped until the adoption of the 154-game schedule.

December 5 Columbus is admitted to replace Cleveland.

December 6 The AA votes against adopting the NL's salary classification system, to the surprise of the press and the delight of the Brotherhood.

BALTIMORE		BROOKLYN		CINCINNATI		CLEVELAND		KANSAS CITY		LOUISVILLE		PHILADELPHIA		ST.LOUIS	
M	B.Barnie	M	B.McGunnigle	M	G.Schmelz	M	J.Williams	M	D.Rowe	M	J.Kelly	M	B.Sharsig	M	C.Comiskey
1B	T.Tucker	1B	D.Orr	1B	J.Reilly	M	T.Loftus	M	S.Barkley	M	M.Davidson	1B	H.Larkin	1B	C.Comiskey
2B	B.Greenwood	2B	J.Burdock	2B	B.McPhee	1B	J.Faatz	M	B.Watkins	M	J.Kerins	2B	L.Bierbauer	2B	Y.Robinson
SS	J.Farrell	SS	G.Smith	SS	F.Fennelly	2B	C.Stricker	1B	B.Phillips	M	M.Davidson	SS	B.Gleason	SS	B.White
3B	B.Shindle	3B	G.Pinkney	3B	H.Carpenter	SS	E.McKean	2B	S.Barkley	1B	S.Smith	3B	D.Lyons	3B	A.Latham
LF	O.Burns	LF	D.O'Brien	LF	G.Tebeau	3B	G.Alberts	SS	H.Easterday	2B	R.Mack	LF	H.Stovey	LF	T.O'Neill
CF	M.Griffin	CF	P.Radford	CF	P.Corkhill	LF	B.Gilks	3B	J.Davis	SS	B.White	CF	C.Welch	CF	H.Lyons
RF	B.Purcell	RF	D.Foutz	RF	H.Nicol	CF	P.Hotaling	LF	M.Cline	3B	J.Werrick	RF	T.Poorman	RF	T.McCarthy
C	C.Fulmer	C	D.Bushong	C	J.Keenan	RF	E.Hogan	CF	J.McTamany	LF	H.Collins	C	W.Robinson	C	J.Boyle
						C	C.Zimmer	RF	B.Hamilton	CF	P.Browning				
OS	J.Sommer	OP	B.Caruthers	C	K.Baldwin			C	J.Donahue	RF	J.Wolf	C	G.Townsend	C	J.Milligan
CO	J.O'Brien	2O	B.McClellan	S2	H.Kappel	O	M.Goodfellow			C	P.Cook	O3	M.Sullivan	SO	E.Herr
O	W.Goldsby	SO	O.Burns	O	J.O'Connor	OC	L.Daniels	2	F.Hankinson			O	T.Gunning	2	C.McGarr
C	B.Cantz	C	B.Clark	/C	N.Bligh	3	J.McGlone	2		OC	J.Kerins	C	B.Purcell	C	T.Dolan
C	S.Trott	C	J.Peoples			C	D.McGuire	O	M.Allen	OP	S.Stratton	S	F.Fennelly		
/O	J.Peltz	C	P.Corkhill	P	L.Viau	O	B.McClellan	O	D.Rowe	1P	G.Hecker	/C	B.Farmer	P	S.King
/S	G.Bradley	C	B.Holbert	P	T.Mullane	3	D.Van Zant	OC	J.Brennan	OC	F.Vaughn	/C	F.Zinn	P	N.Hudson
		O	E.Silch	P	E.Smith			O	J.Burns	CO	L.Cross	/C	W.Gibson	P	E.Chamberlain
P	B.Cunningham	2	H.Collins			P	J.Bakely	O	R.Ehret	3	H.Raymond			P	J.Devlin
P	Ma.Kilroy					P	D.O'Brien	C	F.Briody	S	P.Tomney	P	E.Seward	P	E.Knouff
P	P.Smith	P	M.Hughes	/P	J.Weyhing	/O	C.Jones	O	F.Weaver	P	G.Weyhing		
		P	A.Terry	/P	B.Serad	P	B.Crowell	/C	C.Hoover	1	W.Andrews	P	M.Mattimore	/P	J.Freeman
/P	S.Shaw	P	A.Mays			/O	E.Glenn	1	D.Esterbrook				
/P	G.Walker					/P	G.Proeser			/3	P.Reccius	/P	B.Blair		
/P	P.Whitaker					/P	E.Keas	P	H.Porter	/O	H.Burnett	P	P.Smith		
/P	Mi.Kilroy					/P	M.Morrison	P	T.Sullivan	/O	E.Fusselback	/P	B.Gamble		
/P	J.Harkins					/P	D.Oberlander	P	B.Fagan	/O	Long				
						/P	B.Stemmeyer	P	F.Hoffman						
						/P	E.Knouff	P	S.Toole	P	T.Ramsey				
										P	E.Chamberlain				
								/P	J.Kirby	P	J.Ewing				
								/P	F.Hafner						
										/P	B.Crowell				

TEAM	G	W	L	PCT	GB	R	OR	AB	H	2B	3B	HR	BB	SO	AVG	OBP	SLG	PRO	PRO+	BR	/A	PF	CHI	RC	SB	CS	SBA	SBR
STL	137	92	43	.681		789	501	4755	1189	149	47	36	410	521	.250	.316	.324	.640	98	54	-30	111	102	651	468			
BRO	143	88	52	.629	6.5	758	584	4871	1177	172	70	25	353	439	.242	.300	.321	.621	103	17	19	100	101	584	334			
PHI	136	81	52	.609	10	827	594	4828	1209	183	89	31	303	473	.250	.305	.344	.649	113	60	65	99	106	656	434			
CIN	137	80	54	.597	11.5	745	628	4801	1161	132	82	32	345	555	.242	.301	.323	.624	99	21	-18	105	100	623	469			
BAL	137	57	80	.416	36	653	779	4656	1068	162	70	19	298	479	.229	.284	.306	.590	96	-37	-19	97	99	511	326			
CLE	135	50	82	.379	40.5	651	839	4603	1076	128	59	12	315	559	.234	.294	.295	.589	96	-32	-13	97	99	516	353			
LOU	139	48	87	.356	44	689	870	4881	1177	183	67	14	322	604	.241	.297	.315	.612	102	1	16	98	94	565	318			
KC	132	43	89	.326	47.5	579	896	4588	1000	142	61	19	288	604	.218	.273	.288	.561	78	-84	-122	106	97	441	257			
TOT	548					5691		37983	9057	1251	545	188	2634	4234	.238	.297	.315	.612							2959			

TEAM	CG	SH	SV	IP	H	H/G	HR	BB	SO	RAT	ERA	ERA+	OAV	OOB	PR	/A	PF	CPI	FA	E	DP	FW	PW	BW	SBW	DIF
STL	132	12	0	1212²	939	7.0	19	225	517	9.1	2.09	156	.206	.254	130	156	107	96	.924	430	73	3.4	14.4	-2.8		9.4
BRO	138	9	0	1286¹	1059	7.4	15	285	577	9.7	2.33	128	.217	.266	104	92	97	97	.918	502	88	.6	8.5	1.8		7.2
PHI	133	13	0	1208²	988	7.4	14	324	596	10.4	2.41	124	.216	.279	87	76	98	102	.919	475	73	.7	7.0	6.0		.8
CIN	132	10	2	1237²	1103	8.0	19	310	539	10.8	2.73	116	.230	.288	46	60	104	102	.923	456	100	2.0	5.5	-1.7		7.2
BAL	130	3	0	1200¹	1162	8.7	23	419	525	12.5	3.78	79	.245	.318	-96	-108	97	93	.920	461	88	1.7	-10.0	-1.8		-1.5
CLE	131	6	1	1171	1235	9.5	38	389	500	12.9	3.72	83	.261	.324	-86	-82	101	105	.915	488	87	-.2	-7.6	-1.2		-7.0
LOU	133	6	0	1231¹	1264	9.2	28	281	599	11.7	3.25	95	.256	.304	-26	-24	100	105	.900	609	75	-6.2	-2.2	1.5		-12.5
KC	128	4	0	1157²	1306	10.2	32	401	381	13.8	4.29	80	.275	.340	-159	-112	112	101	.914	507	95	-1.9	-10.3	-11.3		.5
TOT	1057	63	3	9705²		8.4				11.3	3.06		.238	.297					.917	3928	679					

Runs
Pinkney-Bro	134
Collins-Lou-Bro	133
Stovey-Phi	127
Welch-Phi	125
Latham-StL	119

Hits
O'Neill-StL	177
Reilly-Cin	169
McKean-Cle	164
Collins-Lou-Bro	162
Corkhill-Cin-Bro	160

Doubles
Collins-Lou-Bro	31
Wolf-Lou	28
Reilly-Cin	28
Larkin-Phi	28

Triples
Stovey-Phi	20
Burns-Bal-Bro	15
McKean-Cle	15
Reilly-Cin	14
Foutz-Bro	13

Home Runs
Reilly-Cin	13
Stovey-Phi	9
Larkin-Phi	7

Total Bases
Reilly-Cin	264
Stovey-Phi	244
O'Neill-StL	236
McKean-Cle	233
Burns-Bal-Bro	230

Runs Batted In
Reilly-Cin	103
Larkin-Phi	101
Foutz-Bro	99
O'Neill-StL	98
Corkhill-Cin-Bro	93

Runs Produced
Reilly-Cin	202
O'Neill-StL	189
Foutz-Bro	187
Larkin-Phi	186
Welch-Phi	185

Bases On Balls
Robinson-StL	116
Fennelly-Cin-Phi	72
Nicol-Cin	67
McTamany-KC	67
Pinkney-Bro	66

Batting Average
O'Neill-StL	.335
Reilly-Cin	.321
Browning-Lou	.313
Collins-Lou-Bro	.307
Orr-Bro	.305

On Base Percentage
Robinson-StL	.400
O'Neill-StL	.390
Browning-Lou	.380
Collins-Lou-Bro	.373
Stovey-Phi	.365

Slugging Average
Reilly-Cin	.501
Stovey-Phi	.460
O'Neill-StL	.446
Browning-Lou	.436
Burns-Bal-Bro	.435

Production
Reilly-Cin	.864
O'Neill-StL	.836
Stovey-Phi	.825
Browning-Lou	.816
Collins-Lou-Bro	.796

Adjusted Production
Reilly-Cin	167
Stovey-Phi	165
Browning-Lou	164
Collins-Lou-Bro	158
Burns-Bal-Bro	152

Batter Runs
Reilly-Cin	41.7
O'Neill-StL	39.7
Stovey-Phi	37.8
Collins-Lou-Bro	32.6
Burns-Bal-Bro	27.7

Adjusted Batter Runs
Stovey-Phi	38.6
Reilly-Cin	35.5
Collins-Lou-Bro	34.8
Burns-Bal-Bro	29.5
McKean-Cle	28.5

Clutch Hitting Index
Hotaling-Cle	153
Foutz-Bro	135
Lyons-Phi	133
Gleason-Phi	132
Smith-Bro	130

Runs Created
Reilly-Cin	129
Stovey-Phi	124
Collins-Lou-Bro	112
Welch-Phi	106
O'Neill-StL	105

Total Average
Reilly-Cin	1.064
Stovey-Phi	1.048
Collins-Lou-Bro	.956
Robinson-StL	.934
Browning-Lou	.928

Stolen Bases
Latham-StL	109
Nicol-Cin	103
Welch-Phi	95
McCarthy-StL	93
Stovey-Phi	87

Stolen Base Average

Stolen Base Runs

Fielding Runs
Shindle-Bal	36.8
McPhee-Cin	31.3
Davis-KC	29.8
McCarthy-StL	29.8
Easterday-KC	26.4

Total Player Rating
Collins-Lou-Bro	4.0
Stovey-Phi	3.5
McPhee-Cin	3.3
Davis-KC	3.0
McKean-Cle	3.0

Wins
King-StL	45
Seward-Phi	35
Caruthers-Bro	29
Weyhing-Phi	28
Viau-Cin	27

Win Percentage
Hudson-StL	.714
Chamberlain-Lou-SL	.694
King-StL	.682
Caruthers-Bro	.659
Viau-Cin	.659

Games
King-StL	66
Bakely-Cle	61
Seward-Phi	57
Porter-KC	55
Cunningham-Bal	51

Complete Games
King-StL	64
Bakely-Cle	60
Seward-Phi	57
Porter-KC	53
Cunningham-Bal	50

Shutouts
Seward-Phi	6
King-StL	6
Smith-Cin	5
Hudson-StL	5

Saves
Mullane-Cin	1
Gilks-Cle	1

Innings Pitched
King-StL	585.2
Bakely-Cle	532.2
Seward-Phi	518.2
Porter-KC	474.0
Cunningham-Bal	453.1

Fewest Hits/Game
Terry-Bro	6.69
King-StL	6.72
Seward-Phi	6.73
Chamberlain-Lou-SL	6.95
Hughes-Bro	6.97

Fewest BB/Game
King-StL	1.17
Caruthers-Bro	1.22
Hudson-StL	1.59
Ewing-Lou	1.60
Hecker-Lou	1.73

Strikeouts
Seward-Phi	272
King-StL	258
Ramsey-Lou	228
Bakely-Cle	212
Weyhing-Phi	204

Strikeouts/Game
Terry-Bro	6.37
Ramsey-Lou	5.99
Chamberlain-Lou-SL	5.14
Smith-Bal-Phi	4.90
Seward-Phi	4.72

Ratio
King-StL	8.34
Caruthers-Bro	9.19
Seward-Phi	9.32
Foutz-Bro	9.51
Hughes-Bro	9.55

Earned Run Average
King-StL	1.64
Seward-Phi	2.01
Terry-Bro	2.03
Hughes-Bro	2.13
Chamberlain-Lou-SL	2.19

Adjusted ERA
King-StL	198
Seward-Phi	148
Terry-Bro	147
Chamberlain-Lou-SL	143
Hughes-Bro	140

Opponents' Batting Avg.
Terry-Bro	.200
King-StL	.200
Seward-Phi	.201
Chamberlain-Lou-SL	.206
Hughes-Bro	.206

Opponents' On Base Pct.
King-StL	.237
Caruthers-Bro	.255
Seward-Phi	.258
Foutz-Bro	.262
Hughes-Bro	.262

Starter Runs
King-StL	92.0
Seward-Phi	60.2
Hughes-Bro	37.3
Weyhing-Phi	36.3
Chamberlain-Lou-SL	29.7

Adjusted Starter Runs
King-StL	104.9
Seward-Phi	56.0
Hughes-Bro	34.1
Weyhing-Phi	33.0
Chamberlain-Lou-SL	32.4

Clutch Pitching Index
Sullivan-KC	115
Hecker-Lou	112
Terry-Bro	110
Ramsey-Lou	106
Bakely-Cle	106

Relief Runs

Adjusted Relief Runs

Relief Ranking

Total Pitcher Index
King-StL	11.4
Seward-Phi	4.9
Weyhing-Phi	3.7
Caruthers-Bro	3.5
Chamberlain-Lou-SL	3.1

Total Baseball Ranking
King-StL	11.3
Seward-Phi	4.8
Collins-Lou-Bro	4.0
Weyhing-Phi	3.6
Caruthers-Bro	3.6

January 22 Facing over $30,000 in debts, the Indianapolis team goes bankrupt and surrenders its franchise to the NL. A new Indianapolis group, headed by John T. Brush is later granted an NL franchise.

February 8 In New York City, workers are dismantling fences at the Polo Grounds to cut a street through the property, leaving the Giants without a home for the coming season.

March 22* The All America team beats Chicago 7–6 in England's Old Trafford Cricket Stadium. The Manchester *Guardian* said the "general verdict of the more than 1,000 spectators was that the American game was 'slow' and 'wanting in variety.' "

April 15* Invited to the White House after their world tour, the Chicago and All-America squads meet with new President Benjamin Harrison. Harrison proves to be quite a baseball fan and would attend many Washington games during his term in office.

April 24 Opening Day. The New York Giants open their season in Jersey City's Oakland Park, losing to Boston 8–7 before a crowd of 3,042. After just one more game in Jersey City, the Giants are forced to relocate at the Mets' old grounds in Staten Island. A rule currently in effect mandates that teams must play in the state in which their franchise is located.

April 29 The New York Giants play and win their first game 4-2 at St. George

Grounds on Staten Island. This picturesque park, home of the AA Mets in 1886 and 1887, houses the Giants and a production of the play *Nero*. The right fielder is obliged to play out on top of the stage platform, necessitating the use of rubber-soled shoes in wet weather.

May 19 Washington center fielder William "Dummy" Hoy throws out three Indianapolis runners at home plate, setting a major league record. Hoy also has a single, two doubles, and a stolen base, but the Senators still lose 8–3.

July 8 The New York Giants finally open the new Polo Grounds at 155th Street and 8th Avenue with a 7–5 victory over Pittsburgh. In 25 games in exile on Staten Island and in Jersey City, the Giants drew 57,000 fans. In 38 games in their new Manhattan home, they will draw 144,000.

July 14 A. G. Spalding's plan for classifying minor leagues is printed across the nation. It calls for strict salary and draft-price limits according to the class of the leagues, features that will serve as the basis for a century to come.

July 26 Cleveland loses 8–4 despite a fluke homer by Jay Faatz, who hits a ball that ricochets off the foot of Pittsburgh third baseman Jim White and goes into the stands, giving Faatz time to circle the bases.

August 15 Cleveland's Larry Twitchell has a 6-for-6 day at the plate with a single, double, three triples, and a homer.

The five extra- base hits tie a record set in 1885. Twitchell also pitches to two batters in the third inning before returning to the outfield. Cleveland wins 19–8 over Boston, and becomes the first team in NL history to score in all nine innings in a single game.

September 10 New York Giants pitcher Mickey Welch strikes out as the first pinch hitter in major league history.

October 4 Both contenders win again, setting up the final day with New York in front of Boston by percentage points .656 to .654. Each team has the option of playing one or two games tomorrow, so New York manager Jim Mutrie travels to Pittsburgh to watch the Boston game. If the Beaneaters play an extra game, he is ready to wire to Cleveland, where the Giants are playing, so that the Giants can also play an additional one.

October 5 New York wins the pennant on the final day by beating Cleveland 5–3 while Boston loses in Pittsburgh 6–1, making doubleheaders unnecessary.

October 18 The best-of-11 World Series between Brooklyn and New York opens at the Polo Grounds with the Bridegrooms winning, 12–10, in eight innings.

October 29 The Giants win their second consecutive World Series by earning their sixth victory in nine games. After spotting Brooklyn two runs in the first, the Giants rally to win 3-2 behind O'Day's pitching.

	BOSTON		CHICAGO		CLEVELAND		INDIANAPOLIS		NEW YORK		PHILADELPHIA		PITTSBURGH		WASHINGTON
M	J.Hart	M	C.Anson	M	T.Loftus	M	F.Bancroft	M	J.Mutrie	M	H.Wright	M	H.Phillips	M	J.Morrill
1B	D.Brouthers	1B	C.Anson	1B	J.Faatz	M	J.Glasscock	1B	R.Connor	1B	S.Farrar	M	F.Dunlap	M	A.Irwin
2B	H.Richardson	2B	F.Pfeffer	2B	C.Stricker	1B	P.Hines	2B	D.Richardson	2B	A.Myers	M	N.Hanlon	1B	J.Carney
SS	J.Quinn	SS	N.Williamson	SS	E.McKean	2B	C.Bassett	SS	J.Ward	SS	B.Hallman	1B	J.Beckley	2B	S.Wise
3B	B.Nash	3B	T.Burns	3B	P.Tebeau	SS	J.Glasscock	3B	A.Whitney	3B	J.Mulvey	2B	F.Dunlap	SS	A.Irwin
LF	T.Brown	LF	G.Van Haltren	LF	L.Twitchell	3B	J.Denny	LF	J.O'Rourke	LF	G.Wood	SS	J.Rowe	3B	J.Irwin
CF	D.Johnston	CF	J.Ryan	CF	J.McAleer	LF	E.Seery	CF	G.Gore	CF	J.Fogarty	3B	B.Kuehne	LF	W.Wilmot
RF	K.Kelly	RF	H.Duffy	RF	P.Radford	CF	M.Sullivan	RF	M.Tiernan	RF	S.Thompson	LF	A.Maul	CF	D.Hoy
C	C.Bennett	C	D.Farrell	C	C.Zimmer	RF	J.McGeachy	C	B.Ewing	C	J.Clements	CF	N.Hanlon	RF	E.Beecher
						C	D.Buckley					RF	B.Sunday	C	T.Daly
CO	C.Ganzel	S	C.Bastian	OS	B.Gilks			C	W.Brown	O2	E.Delahanty	C	D.Miller		
S	P.Smith	C	D.Darling	C	S.Sutcliffe	C	C.Daily	S	G.Hatfield	C	P.Schriver			CO	C.Mack
/S	I.Ray	C	S.Flint	C	P.Snyder	O	E.Andrews	O	M.Slattery	S	A.Irwin	CO	F.Carroll	3	P.Sweeney
/O	J.Hurley	C	P.Sommers			OC	G.Myers	/C	P.Murphy	/O	E.Andrews	OC	J.Fields	2	A.Myers
				P	D.O'Brien	C	P.Sommers	/2	H.Lyons	/2	H.Decker	S	P.Smith	1	J.Morrill
P	J.Clarkson	P	B.Hutchison	P	E.Beatin	1	J.Schoeneck	/O	B.George	/2	P.Ward	3	D.White	CS	S.Clark
P	C.Radbourn	P	J.Tener	P	J.Bakely	/C	P.Weckbecker	/O	E.Foster			/C	C.Lauer	O	G.Shoch
P	K.Madden	P	F.Dwyer	P	H.Gruber					P	C.Buffinton			/C	H.Ebright
		P	A.Gumbert			P	H.Boyle	P	M.Welch	P	B.Sanders	P	H.Staley	/C	J.Riddle
/P	B.Daley			/P	C.Sprague	P	C.Getzien	P	T.Keefe	P	K.Gleason	P	P.Galvin	/3	J.Donnelly
/P	B.Sowders	/P	G.Krock			P	A.Rusie	P	E.Crane	P	D.Casey	P	E.Morris	/1	B.O'Brien
		/P	J.Healy					P	H.O'Day					/2	A.McCoy
		/P	B.Bishop			/P	J.Whitney			/P	D.Anderson	P	B.Sowders	/O	H.Clarke
						P	B.Burdick	/P	C.Titcomb	/P	B.Day	/P	B.Garfield	/C	J.Banning
						/P	J.Fee			/P	P.Wood	/P	P.Conway		
						/P	G.Krock					/P	A.Beam	P	A.Ferson
						P	L.Shreve					/P	A.Dunning	P	G.Haddock
						/P	V.Anderson					/P	A.Jones	P	G.Keefe
						/P	J.Fanning					/P	A.Krumm	P	H.O'Day
														P	J.Healy
														/P	G.Krock
														/P	M.Sullivan
														/P	J.Thornton

TEAM	G	W	L	PCT	GB	R	OR	AB	H	2B	3B	HR	BB	SO	AVG	OBP	SLG	PRO	PRO+	BR	/A	PF	CHI	RC	SB	CS	SBA	SBR
BRO	150	101	47	.682		892	658	4937	1436	178	97	27	477	263	.291	.368	.383	.751	110	87	68	102	103	824	271			
BOS	153	95	57	.625	8	858	645	5290	1517	178	90	39	431	269	.287	.345	.377	.722	94	21	-59	110	103	787	185			
PHI	154	94	58	.618	9	916	743	5353	1613	241	83	31	441	341	.301	.363	.395	.758	118	96	128	97	99	879	212			
BAL	152	86	62	.581	15	827	691	5073	1509	204	71	17	418	383	.297	.365	.376	.741	104	68	24	105	97	861	364			
STL	155	84	67	.556	18.5	819	739	5304	1514	172	88	47	468	262	.285	.347	.378	.725	102	28	9	102	97	801	210			
CIN	156	83	67	.553	19	856	770	5225	1439	194	105	13	485	295	.275	.345	.360	.705	97	-5	-20	102	106	762	228			
PIT	154	76	73	.510	25.5	834	765	5450	1574	196	121	27	384	345	.289	.343	.384	.727	105	26	29	100	97	815	179			
CHI	152	75	73	.507	26	812	763	5148	1428	173	82	27	406	342	.277	.338	.359	.697	99	-26	-5	97	105	743	247			
LOU	155	75	77	.493	28	827	775	5307	1484	192	68	40	436	375	.280	.343	.364	.707	99	-3	-2	100	101	781	233			
NY	152	60	90	.400	42	734	863	5092	1431	161	65	23	387	360	.281	.337	.352	.689	97	-39	-13	97	100	708	234			
WAS	155	54	98	.355	49	743	983	5256	1429	162	87	47	350	341	.272	.328	.363	.691	96	-45	-37	99	99	710	176			
CLE	154	20	134	.130	84	529	1252	5279	1333	142	50	12	289	280	.253	.299	.305	.604	76	-209	-168	93	92	541	127			
TOT	921					9647		62714	17707	2193	1007	350	4972	3856	.282	.343	.366	.710							2666			

TEAM	CG	SH	SV	IP	H	H/G	HR	BB	SO	RAT	ERA	ERA+	OAV	OOB	PR	/A	PF	CPI	FA	E	DP	FW	PW	BW	SBW	DIF
BRO	121	9	9	1269¹	1320	9.4	32	463	331	13.0	3.25	120	.268	.337	85	92	102	111	.948	314	125	2.9	8.3	6.2		9.6
BOS	138	13	4	1348	1273	8.5	44	432	385	11.8	3.26	127	.250	.317	88	133	108	95	.952	303	124	4.0	12.1	-5.3		8.3
PHI	129	15	2	1333¹	1398	9.4	17	370	281	12.5	3.47	106	.270	.328	56	30	96	97	.940	379	110	-.4	2.7	11.6		4.0
BAL	132	9	4	1304¹	1403	9.7	13	349	294	12.6	3.31	119	.275	.330	78	93	103	103	.949	308	96	3.5	8.4	2.2		-2.1
STL	134	7	1	1340²	1476	9.9	41	321	331	12.4	3.36	118	.280	.327	73	91	103	107	.939	397	117	-1.3	8.2	.8		.7
CIN	130	8	5	1361	1484	9.8	26	370	360	12.8	3.70	106	.278	.333	23	32	102	97	.947	339	111	2.3	2.9	-1.8		4.6
PIT	117	9	4	1364	1464	9.7	27	437	334	13.0	3.60	106	.274	.337	38	32	99	101	.945	361	98	.7	2.9	2.6		-4.7
CHI	147	8	1	1331¹	1433	9.7	20	330	313	12.5	3.37	111	.275	.328	71	55	97	102	.935	428	145	-3.5	5.0	-.5		-.0
LOU	134	5	2	1351²	1509	10.0	33	323	287	12.6	3.45	112	.282	.331	60	60	100	106	.939	394	101	-1.1	5.4	-.2		-5.2
NY	138	4	0	1278¹	1454	10.2	19	628	397	15.3	4.29	87	.286	.375	-63	-78	97	103	.932	433	140	-3.8	-7.1	-1.2		-3.0
WAS	131	3	0	1300¹	1649	11.4	35	422	328	14.9	4.93	79	.309	.368	-157	-149	102	95	.935	403	99	-1.6	-13.5	-3.4		-3.5
CLE	138	0	0	1264	1844	13.1	43	527	215	17.7	6.37	58	.340	.409	-353	-378	94	94	.937	388	121	-.9	-34.3	-15.2		-6.6
TOT	1589	90	32	15846¹		10.1				13.4	3.85		.282	.343					.942	4447	1387					

Runs		Hits		Doubles		Triples		Home Runs		Total Bases	
McGraw-Bal	140	Delahanty-Phi	238	Delahanty-Phi	55	Williams-Pit	27	Freeman-Was	25	Delahanty-Phi	338
Keeler-Bro	140	Burkett-StL	221	Wagner-Lou	43	Freeman-Was	25	Wallace-StL	12	Freeman-Was	331
Thomas-Phi	137	Williams-Pit	219	Holmes-Bal	31	Stahl-Bos	19	Williams-Pit	9	Williams-Pit	328
Delahanty-Phi	135	Keeler-Bro	216	Long-Bos	30	Tenney-Bos	17	Mertes-Chi	9	Stahl-Bos	284
Williams-Pit	126	Tenney-Bos	209	Duffy-Bos	29	McCarthy-Pit	17	Delahanty-Phi	9	Wagner-Lou	282

Runs Batted In		Runs Produced		Bases On Balls		Batting Average		On Base Percentage		Slugging Average	
Delahanty-Phi	137	Delahanty-Phi	263	McGraw-Bal	124	Delahanty-Phi	.410	McGraw-Bal	.547	Delahanty-Phi	.582
Freeman-Was	122	Williams-Pit	233	Thomas-Phi	115	Burkett-StL	.396	Delahanty-Phi	.464	Freeman-Was	.563
Williams-Pit	116	Wagner-Lou	204	VanHaltren-NY	74	McGraw-Bal	.391	Burkett-StL	.463	Williams-Pit	.532
Wagner-Lou	113	Freeman-Was	204	Childs-StL	74	Keeler-Bro	.379	Thomas-Phi	.457	Burkett-StL	.500
Wallace-StL	108					Williams-Pit	.355	Stahl-Bos	.426	Wagner-Lou	.494

Production		Adjusted Production		Batter Runs		Adjusted Batter Runs		Clutch Hitting Index		Runs Created	
Delahanty-Phi	1.046	Delahanty-Phi	193	Delahanty-Phi	67.9	Delahanty-Phi	73.5	Brodie-Bal	139	Delahanty-Phi	175
McGraw-Bal	.994	McGraw-Bal	165	McGraw-Bal	56.8	McGraw-Bal	50.2	Long-Bos	131	Williams-Pit	152
Burkett-StL	.963	Burkett-StL	160	Burkett-StL	51.6	Williams-Pit	49.5	Magoon-Bal-Chi	129	Burkett-StL	145
Williams-Pit	.949	Williams-Pit	160	Williams-Pit	49.0	Burkett-StL	48.4	Lauder-Phi	128	McGraw-Bal	141
Freeman-Was	.925	Freeman-Was	154	Stahl-Bos	42.2	Freeman-Was	37.6	Corcoran-Cin	128	Stahl-Bos	139

Total Average		Stolen Bases		Stolen Base Average		Stolen Base Runs		Fielding Runs		Total Player Rating	
McGraw-Bal	1.601	Sheckard-Bal	77					G.Davis-NY	46.3	G.Davis-NY	6.2
Delahanty-Phi	1.245	McGraw-Bal	73					Wallace-StL	38.8	Delahanty-Phi	5.6
Burkett-StL	1.107	Heidrick-StL	55					Cross-Cle-StL	32.7	Wallace-StL	5.3
Williams-Pit	1.055	Holmes-Bal	50					Gleason-NY	25.7	Williams-Pit	5.2
Stahl-Bos	1.051	Clarke-Lou	49					Collins-Bos	20.9	Lajoie-Phi	4.9

Wins		Win Percentage		Games		Complete Games		Shutouts		Saves	
McGinnity-Bal	28	Hughes-Bro	.824	Leever-Pit	51	Young-StL	40	Willis-Bos	5	Leever-Pit	3
Hughes-Bro	28	Willis-Bos	.771	Powell-StL	48	Powell-StL	40				
Willis-Bos	27	Hahn-Cin	.742	McGinnity-Bal	48	Carrick-NY	40				
Young-StL	26	Donahue-Phi	.724	Young-StL	44	Taylor-Chi	39				
Tannehill-Pit	24	Kennedy-Bro	.710	Carrick-NY	44	McGinnity-Bal	38				

Innings Pitched		Fewest Hits/Game		Fewest BB/Game		Strikeouts		Strikeouts/Game		Ratio	
Leever-Pit	379.0	Willis-Bos	7.28	Young-StL	1.07	Hahn-Cin	145	Seymour-NY	4.76	Young-StL	10.19
Powell-StL	373.0	Hughes-Bro	7.71	Cuppy-StL	1.36	Seymour-NY	142	Hahn-Cin	4.22	Hahn-Cin	10.43
Young-StL	369.1	Hahn-Cin	8.16	Tannehill-Pit	1.47	Leever-Pit	121	Doheny-NY	3.90	Nichols-Bos	10.85
McGinnity-Bal	366.1	Seymour-NY	8.28	Kitson-Bal	1.79	Willis-Bos	120	McJames-Bro	3.43	Willis-Bos	11.14
Carrick-NY	361.2	Leever-Pit	8.38	Woods-Lou	1.79	Doheny-NY	115	Willis-Bos	3.15	Kitson-Bal	11.15

Earned Run Average		Adjusted ERA		Opponents' Batting Avg.		Opponents' On Base Pct.		Starter Runs		Adjusted Starter Runs	
Orth-Phi	2.49	Willis-Bos	166	Willis-Bos	.222	Young-StL	.285	Young-StL	52.0	Willis-Bos	63.1
Willis-Bos	2.50	Young-StL	154	Hughes-Bro	.232	Hahn-Cin	.290	Willis-Bos	51.6	Young-StL	57.2
Young-StL	2.58	McGinnity-Bal	148	Hahn-Cin	.242	Nichols-Bos	.298	McGinnity-Bal	47.7	McGinnity-Bal	52.1
Bernhard-Phi	2.65	Hahn-Cin	146	Seymour-NY	.245	Willis-Bos	.303	Hahn-Cin	40.2	Nichols-Bos	44.5
McGinnity-Bal	2.68	Hughes-Bro	146	Leever-Pit	.247	Kitson-Bal	.304	Kitson-Bal	39.2	Kitson-Bal	43.1

Clutch Pitching Index		Relief Runs	Adjusted Relief Runs	Relief Ranking	Total Pitcher Index		Total Baseball Ranking	
Kennedy-Bro	130				Young-StL	6.2	G.Davis-NY	6.2
Tannehill-Pit	124				Willis-Bos	5.3	Young-StL	6.2
Dowling-Lou	121				McGinnity-Bal	5.0	Delahanty-Phi	5.6
Callahan-Chi	121				Tannehill-Pit	4.8	Willis-Bos	5.3
Woods-Lou	118				Hughes-Bro	4.7	Wallace-StL	5.3

April 9 Pete Browning signs with Louisville for $1,600. Browning also delivers a signed pledge of abstinence sworn out before a local judge.

May 19 Fire destroys most of the stand at Brooklyn's Washington Park while the Bridegrooms are on a road trip.

May 20 The Kansas City Cowboys, after choosing to bat first, score at least one run in every inning against Brooklyn, winning 18–12. The Cowboys become the second team in AA history to score in all nine innings, Columbus having done so on June 14, 1883.

May 30 Brooklyn draws the largest crowd in AA history, 22,122, for the Bridegrooms' afternoon game against the Browns. An additional 8,462 saw the opener as the two teams split the pair.

June 13 After the Colonels lose for the 19th straight time, Louisville owner-manager Mordecai Davidson tells the players he will fine them $25 if they lose the next game.

June 15 Only six Louisville players show up for the game in Baltimore, the others sit out in protest against owner Davidson, who owes back pay and is now threatening them with fines.

June 22 Louisville's losing streak reaches 26 in a row, the all-time major league record, when the Colonels lose two heartbreakers to St. Louis, 7–6, and 3–2 in 10 innings.

June 23 The Colonels finally win, defeating St. Louis, 7–3.

September 7 The most controversial game in AA history is held in Brooklyn. The Browns hold a 4-2 lead in the ninth and claim it is too dark to continue, but the lighted candles in front of their bench make umpire Fred Goldsmith determined to finish the game no matter what. Several St. Louis players are hit with bottles as they leave the grounds. The Browns will forfeit their game the next day because they fear for their safety.

September 23 An emergency meeting of the American Association Board of Directors reverses the St. Louis forfeit of September 7, the game being ruled as a 4–2 Browns victory, although the forfeit of September 8 still stands.

October 6 Brooklyn wins its last home game 9–0 over the Athletics in six innings before a crowd of 2,488, bringing the Bridegrooms' home attendance for the season to 353,690, a major league record.

October 9 Charlie Reilly hits two home runs in his major league debut with Columbus to lead the Babies to a 10–6 victory over the Athletics. Only Bob Nieman (9/14/51) and Bert Campaneris (7/23/64) will match this feat.

November 14 Disgusted by the conduct of the Association and especially the perceived dominance of St. Louis president Von der Ahe, Brooklyn president Charles Byrne and Cincinnati owner Aaron Stern withdraw from the AA and join the NL. The next day, Kansas City also drops out of the AA.

December 16 The Players League is officially formed with Colonel E.A. McAlpin of New York as president. The league will not allow player transfers without the player's consent, excess profits will be split between the capitalists and the players, while prize money will be awarded to teams in order of finish.

December 18 The Brotherhood, a players' group, begins preliminary work on the organization of the Players' League and expels members who have signed NL contracts, including Jack Glasscock, John Clarkson, Kid Gleason, and George Miller. Among those expelled, Jake Beckley, Joe Mulvey, and Ed Delahanty would eventually jump back to the Players League and would be reinstated.

BALTIMORE	BROOKLYN	CINCINNATI	COLUMBUS	KANSAS CITY	LOUISVILLE	PHILADELPHIA	ST.LOUIS
M B.Barnie	M B.McGunnigle	M G.Schmelz	M A.Buckenberger	M B.Watkins	M D.Esterbrook	M B.Sharsig	M C.Comiskey
1B T.Tucker	1B D.Foutz	1B J.Reilly	1B D.Orr	1B E.Stearns	C.Wolf	1B H.Larkin	1B C.Comiskey
2B R.Mack	2B H.Collins	2B B.McPhee	2B B.Greenwood	2B S.Barkley	D.Shannon	2B L.Bierbauer	2B Y.Robinson
SS J.Farrell	SS G.Smith	SS O.Beard	SS H.Easterday	SS H.Long	J.Chapman	SS F.Fennelly	SS S.Fuller
3B B.Shindle	3B G.Pinkney	3B H.Carpenter	3B L.Marr	3B J.Davis	1B G.Hecker	3B D.Lyons	3B A.Latham
LF J.Hornung	LF D.O'Brien	LF G.Tebeau	LF E.Daily	LF J.Manning	2B D.Shannon	LF H.Stovey	LF T.O'Neill
CF M.Griffin	CF P.Corkhill	CF B.Holliday	CF J.McTamany	CF J.Burns	SS P.Tomney	CF C.Welch	CF C.Duffee
RF J.Sommer	RF O.Burns	RF H.Nicol	RF S.Johnson	RF B.Hamilton	3B H.Raymond	RF B.Purcell	RF T.McCarthy
C P.Tate	C J.Visner	C J.Keenan	C J.O'Connor	C C.Hoover	LF P.Browning	C W.Robinson	C J.Boyle
					CF F.Weaver		
C T.Quinn	C B.Clark	C K.Baldwin	S3 H.Kappel	CO J.Donahue	RF J.Wolf	C L.Cross	C J.Milligan
S W.Holland	C D.Bushong	OC B.Earle	C J.Peoples	O3 J.Pickett	C P.Cook	C J.Brennan	/3 P.Sweeney
S I.Ray	C C.Reynolds	C.Reynolds	C N.Bligh	3 B.Alvord	CO F.Vaughn	O M.Mattimore	/O T.Gettinger
O J.Dowie		P J.Duryea	2 J.Crooks	C J.Gunson	OP S.Stratton	C T.Gunning	/O J.Gill
C B.Cantz	P B.Caruthers	P L.Viau	/C J.Doyle	3 C.McGarr	O J.Galligan	/3 B.Graham	/S J.Davis
O C.Fulmer	P A.Terry	P T.Mullane	/C R.Kemmler	O M.Mattimore	O F.Carl	/C B.Collins	/C J.Bellman
/1 J.Kerins	P T.Lovett	P E.Smith	/3 C.Reilly	/2 R.Bittman	1 E.Flanagan	P G.Weyhing	/C D.Meek
/S D.Miller	P M.Hughes		/O B.George	/O C.Bell	/O J.Ryan	P E.Seward	
/O G.Wood		/P C.Petty	/C S.McCaffrey	C S.Ladew	C B.Gleason	P S.McMahon	P S.King
/S C.McGarr		/P T.Conovar		/C C.Reynolds	/1 D.Esterbrook		P E.Chamberlain
			P M.Baldwin		/O J.Kerins		P J.Stivetts
P M.Kilroy			P W.Widner	P P.Swartzel	/O H.Scherer	/P G.Bausewine	
P F.Foreman			P H.Gastright	P J.Conway	/O C.Fisher	/P P.Smith	/P J.Devlin
P B.Cunningham			P A.Mays	P J.Sowders	/O M.Gaule	/P J.Coleman	/P N.Hudson
				P J.McCarty	/O H.Smith	/P E.Knouff	/P T.Ramsey
/P G.Goetz			/P J.Easton	P T.Sullivan	/O J.Traffley		
/P P.Whitaker			/P J.Weyhing				
				/P H.Porter	P R.Ehret		
				/P F.Pears	P J.Ewing		
				/P J.Bates	P T.Ramsey		
					P M.McDermott		
					/P B.Robinson		
					/P E.Springer		

TEAM	G	W	L	PCT	GB	R	OR	AB	H	2B	3B	HR	BB	SO	AVG	OBP	SLG	PRO	PRO+	BR	/A	PF	CHI	RC	SB	CS	SBA	SBR
BRO	140	93	44	.679		**995**	706	4815	1265	188	79	47	**550**	401	.263	.344	.364	.708	106	43	40	100	**111**	756	389			
STL	141	90	45	.667	2	957	**680**	4939	1312	211	64	**58**	493	477	.266	.339	.370	.709	94	38	-79	113	106	751	336			
PHI	138	75	58	.564	16	880	787	4868	**1339**	239	65	43	534	496	**.275**	**.354**	.377	**.731**	114	85	97	99	93	758	252			
CIN	141	76	63	.547	18	897	769	4844	1307	197	**96**	52	452	511	.270	.340	**.382**	.722	107	57	30	103	100	**806**	462			
BAL	139	70	65	.519	22	791	795	4756	1209	155	68	20	418	536	.254	.325	.328	.653	88	-56	-69	102	103	624	311			
COL	140	60	78	.435	33.5	779	924	4816	1247	171	95	36	507	609	.259	.335	.356	.691	104	8	51	95	91	693	304			
KC	139	55	82	.401	38	852	1031	4947	1256	162	76	18	430	626	.254	.322	.328	.650	84	-66	-112	106	108	692	**472**			
LOU	140	27	111	.196	66.5	632	1091	4955	1249	170	75	22	320	521	.252	.303	.330	.633	86	-109	-95	98	87	571	203			
TOT	559					6783		38940	10184	1493	618	296	3704	4177	.262	.333	.354	.687							2729			

TEAM	CG	SH	SV	IP	H	H/G	HR	BB	SO	RAT	ERA	ERA+	OAV	OOB	PR	/A	PF	CPI	FA	E	DP	FW	PW	BW	SBW	DIF
BRO	120	10	1	1212²	1205	8.9	33	**400**	471	12.2	3.61	103	.251	.315	31	14	97	93	**.928**	**421**	92	**4.6**	1.2	3.4		15.4
STL	121	7	3	1237²	1166	**8.5**	39	413	**617**	**11.9**	**3.00**	141	**.242**	.309	116	**167**	110	106	.925	438	100	3.8	**14.1**	-6.7		11.2
PHI	**130**	9	1	1199¹	1200	9.0	35	509	479	13.4	3.53	107	.253	.335	42	33	98	**107**	.920	465	120	1.7	2.8	**8.2**		-4.2
CIN	114	3	**8**	1243	1270	9.2	35	475	562	13.0	3.50	111	.257	.328	47	54	102	105	.926	440	118	3.7	4.6	2.5		-4.3
BAL	128	**10**	1	1192	1168	8.8	**27**	424	540	12.6	3.56	111	.249	.322	38	49	103	104	.907	536	104	-2.1	4.1	-5.8		6.3
COL	114	9	4	1199	1274	9.6	33	551	610	14.1	4.39	82	.264	.346	-73	-103	94	93	.915	497	92	.3	-8.7	4.3		-4.9
KC	128	0	2	1204¹	1373	10.3	51	457	447	14.1	4.36	96	.278	.347	-69	-25	109	101	.899	611	109	-6.3	-2.1	-9.5		4.3
LOU	127	2	1	1226¹	1529	11.2	43	475	451	15.1	4.81	80	.297	.362	-132	-133	100	101	.906	584	117	-4.5	-11.3	-8.0		-18.2
TOT	982	50	21	9714¹		9.4				13.3	3.84		.262	.333					.916	3992	855					

Runs
Stovey-Phi 152
Griffin-Bal 152
O'Brien-Bro 146
Hamilton-KC 144
Collins-Bro 139

Hits
Tucker-Bal 196
Orr-Col 183
Holliday-Cin 181
O'Neill-StL 179
Shindle-Bal 178

Doubles
Welch-Phi 39
Stovey-Phi 38
Lyons-Phi 36
O'Neill-StL 33
Long-KC 32

Triples
Marr-Col 15
Griffin-Bal 14
Beard-Cin 14

Home Runs
Stovey-Phi 19
Holliday-Cin 19
Duffee-StL 16
Milligan-StL 12

Total Bases
Stovey-Phi 292
Holliday-Cin 280
Tucker-Bal 255
O'Neill-StL 255
Orr-Col 250

Runs Batted In
Stovey-Phi 119
Foutz-Bro 113
O'Neill-StL 110
Bierbauer-Phi 105
Holliday-Cin 104

Runs Produced
Stovey-Phi 252
Foutz-Bro 225
O'Neill-StL 224
O'Brien-Bro 221
Hamilton-KC 218

Bases On Balls
Robinson-StL 118
McTamany-Col . . . 116
Griffin-Bal 91
Marr-Col 87
Hamilton-KC 87

Batting Average
Tucker-Bal 372
O'Neill-StL 335
Lyons-Phi 329
Orr-Col 327
Holliday-Cin 321

On Base Percentage
Tucker-Bal 450
Larkin-Phi 428
Lyons-Phi 426
O'Neill-StL 419
Hamilton-KC 413

Slugging Average
Stovey-Phi 525
Holliday-Cin 497
Tucker-Bal 484
O'Neill-StL 478
Lyons-Phi 469

Production
Tucker-Bal 934
Stovey-Phi 918
O'Neill-StL 897
Lyons-Phi 895
Holliday-Cin 869

Adjusted Production
Tucker-Bal 163
Stovey-Phi 162
Lyons-Phi 157
Larkin-Phi 145
Holliday-Cin 142

Batter Runs
Tucker-Bal 48.2
Stovey-Phi 42.6
O'Neill-StL 39.9
Lyons-Phi 39.3
Larkin-Phi 34.2

Adjusted Batter Runs
Tucker-Bal 45.8
Stovey-Phi 44.5
Lyons-Phi 41.0
Larkin-Phi 35.9
Marr-Col 34.2

Clutch Hitting Index
Mack-Bal 147
Foutz-Bro 145
Johnson-Col 128
Hornung-Bal 127
Collins-Bro 126

Runs Created
Tucker-Bal 147
Stovey-Phi 143
Hamilton-KC 136
O'Brien-Bro 129
Holliday-Cin 124

Total Average
Tucker-Bal 1.187
Hamilton-KC 1.134
Stovey-Phi 1.125
O'Brien-Bro 1.020
O'Neill-StL 1.014

Stolen Bases
Hamilton-KC 111
O'Brien-Bro 91
Long-KC 89
Nicol-Cin 80
Latham-StL 69

Stolen Base Average

Stolen Base Runs

Fielding Runs
McPhee-Cin 41.1
Bierbauer-Phi 36.6
Long-KC 32.2
Tomney-Lou 26.7
Shindle-Bal 20.3

Total Player Rating
Stovey-Phi 4.9
Bierbauer-Phi 4.5
Lyons-Phi 4.5
Marr-Col 4.1
McPhee-Cin 4.0

Wins
Caruthers-Bro 40
King-StL 35
Duryea-Cin 32
Chamberlain-StL . . 32
Weyhing-Phi 30

Win Percentage
Caruthers-Bro 784
King-StL 686
Chamberlain-StL . . .681
Lovett-Bro 630
Duryea-Cin 627

Games
Baldwin-Col 63
Kilroy-Bal 59
King-StL 56
Caruthers-Bro 56
Weyhing-Phi 54

Complete Games
Kilroy-Bal 55
Baldwin-Col 54
Weyhing-Phi 50
King-StL 47
Caruthers-Bro 46

Shutouts
Caruthers-Bro 7
Baldwin-Col 6
Kilroy-Bal 5
Foreman-Bal 5
Weyhing-Phi 4

Saves
Mullane-Cin 5

Innings Pitched
Baldwin-Col 513.2
Kilroy-Bal 480.2
King-StL 458.0
Weyhing-Phi 449.0
Caruthers-Bro . . . 445.0

Fewest Hits/Game
Stivetts-StL 7.18
Weyhing-Phi 7.66
Terry-Bro 7.87
Foreman-Bal 7.91
Baldwin-Col 8.02

Fewest BB/Game
Caruthers-Bro 2.10
Conway-KC 2.42
King-StL 2.46
Lovett-Bro 2.55
Swartzel-KC 2.57

Strikeouts
Baldwin-Col 368
Kilroy-Bal 217
Weyhing-Phi 213
Chamberlain-StL . . 202
King-StL 188

Strikeouts/Game
Stivetts-StL 6.71
Baldwin-Col 6.45
Terry-Bro 5.13
Sowders-KC 5.06
Gastright-Col 4.65

Ratio
Stivetts-StL 10.61
Caruthers-Bro . . . 11.35
Duryea-Cin 11.56
Foreman-Bal 11.76
Conway-KC 11.77

Earned Run Average
Stivetts-StL 2.25
Duryea-Cin 2.56
Kilroy-Bal 2.85
Weyhing-Phi 2.95
Chamberlain-StL . . 2.97

Adjusted ERA
Stivetts-StL 187
Duryea-Cin 152
Chamberlain-StL . . 142
Kilroy-Bal 138
King-StL 134

Opponents' Batting Avg.
Stivetts-StL 212
Weyhing-Phi 223
Terry-Bro 228
Foreman-Bal 229
Baldwin-Col 231

Opponents' On Base Pct.
Stivetts-StL 285
Caruthers-Bro 299
Duryea-Cin 303
Foreman-Bal 306
Conway-KC 306

Starter Runs
Duryea-Cin 57.3
Kilroy-Bal 53.3
Weyhing-Phi 44.8
Chamberlain-StL . . 41.1
King-StL 35.6

Adjusted Starter Runs
Duryea-Cin 59.8
Chamberlain-StL . . 58.7
Kilroy-Bal 58.4
King-StL 54.8
Stivetts-StL 41.9

Clutch Pitching Index
Mullane-Cin 119
Duryea-Cin 116
Kilroy-Bal 114
Hughes-Bro 110
Weyhing-Phi 109

Relief Runs

Adjusted Relief Runs

Relief Ranking

Total Pitcher Index
Kilroy-Bal 6.9
Duryea-Cin 6.7
Chamberlain-StL . . 4.7
King-StL 4.5
Caruthers-Bro 4.2

Total Baseball Ranking
Kilroy-Bal 6.9
Duryea-Cin 6.6
Stovey-Phi 4.9
Chamberlain-StL . . 4.7
Bierbauer-Phi 4.5

February 1 The NL Schedule Committee meets in Pittsburgh and decides on a schedule, but for security reasons does not release it. Pittsburgh NL president Nimick comments that "if I had my way, I would duplicate all the home games of the Brotherhood clubs." Hence the reason for security.

February 17 New York NL officials fail in an effort to woo star player and Brotherhood officer Buck Ewing to rejoin the Giants. Although he has rejected an offer reported at $33,000 for three years, Ewing is later accused by some players of spying for the NL.

March 6 The NL releases a schedule with 10 teams, including the Brooklyn and Cincinnati franchises formerly in the AA. Since the NL is expected to trim back down to eight teams, the release of this schedule is seen as a ruse to throw off the PL.

April 19 The NL's biggest Opening Day crowd, 6,311 at Chicago, watches 30-year-old righthander Wild Bill Hutchison beat Cincinnati 5–4, the first of his 42 wins and 65 complete games out of 66 starts. He'll work 603 innings and relieve five times.

May 1 The 577 consecutive-game streak of third baseman George Pinckney of Brooklyn (NL) comes to an end after he is spiked in a game in Boston, which is later rained out. He has played every inning of the 577 games, a record that would last until surpassed by Cal Ripken, Jr. of Baltimore in 1985.

May 12 A scoreless pitching duel between future Hall of Famers Amos Rusie and Charles "Kid" Nichols is broken up by a tape-measure homer by New York outfielder Mike Tiernan in the 13th inning.

May 23 New York and Pittsburgh combine for an NL-record 17 stolen bases in a single game.

June 6 Harry Wright, manager of Philadelphia, is now said to be able to see while wearing colored glasses. A serious illness five days earlier had blinded him temporarily, making him the only blind manager in major league history.

July 15 New York Giants owner John B. Day tells other NL owners he must have $80,000 or sell out to the PL. Spalding, Anson, Brush, and others come to the rescue to prevent New York's withdrawal from the league.

August 16 It's a bad day for Pittsburgh's Bill Phillips as he becomes the only pitcher in major league history to give up two grand slams in one inning. Tommy Burns and Malachi Kittredge each hit one in the fifth inning en route to an 18-5 victory at Chicago's West Side Park.

October 9 Cincinnati owner Aaron Stern sells to PL owners for $40,000. Committees from the three leagues meet to begin negotiations toward a settlement of the war. PL owners from Cleveland, Brooklyn, and New York seek consolidation with the NL. A truce, during which all contracts will be respected, is agreed upon. It is left to owners in each city to arrange their own deals.

December 29 After the New York and Pittsburgh PL clubs combine with their NL rivals, Spalding buys out Chicago's PL backer Addison for $18,000, some of which goes to pay off unpaid salaries and reimburse players half of their investments. Spalding gets the club's grandstand, equipment, and player contracts.

BOSTON	BROOKLYN	CHICAGO	CINCINNATI	CLEVELAND	NEW YORK	PHILADELPHIA	PITTSBURGH
M F.Selee	M B.McGunnigle	M C.Anson	M T.Loftus	M G.Schmelz	M J.Mutrie	M H.Wright	M G.Hecker
1B T.Tucker	1B D.Foutz	1B C.Anson	1B J.Reilly	M B.Leadley	1B L.Whistler	M J.Clements	1B G.Hecker
2B P.Smith	2B H.Collins	2B B.Glenalvin	2B B.McPhee	1B P.Veach	2B C.Bassett	M A.Reach	2B S.LaRoque
SS H.Long	SS G.Smith	SS J.Cooney	SS O.Beard	2B J.Ardner	SS J.Glasscock	M B.Allen	SS E.Sales
3B C.McGarr	3B G.Pinkney	3B T.Burns	3B L.Marr	SS E.McKean	3B J.Denny	M H.Wright	3B D.Miller
LF M.Sullivan	LF A.Terry	LF C.Carroll	LF J.Knight	3B W.Smalley	LF J.Hornung	1B A.McCauley	LF J.Kelty
CF P.Hines	CF D.O'Brien	CF W.Wilmot	CF B.Holliday	LF B.Gilks	CF M.Tiernan	2B A.Myers	CF B.Sunday
RF S.Brodie	RF O.Burns	RF J.Andrews	RF H.Nicol	CF G.Davis	RF J.Burkett	SS B.Allen	RF T.Berger
C C.Bennett	C T.Daly	C M.Kittridge	C J.Harrington	RF V.Dailey	C D.Buckley	3B E.Mayer	C H.Decker
SO B.Lowe	OP B.Caruthers	O2 H.Earl	OP T.Mullane	C C.Zimmer	CO A.Clarke	LF B.Hamilton	CO B.Wilson
CO L.Hardie	O P.Corkhill	C T.Nagle	C J.Keenan	1 J.Virtue	RF D.Esterbrook	CF E.Burke	3 F.Roat
CO C.Ganzel	C B.Clark	2 P.O'Brien	3 A.Latham	O1 T.Dowse	O J.Henry	RF S.Thompson	O F.Osborne
O P.Donovan	O P.Donovan	O E.Foster	C K.Baldwin	2 B.West	C P.Murphy	C J.Clements	O M.Jordan
/O A.Schellhase	C D.Bushong	/O J.Stenzel	/S B.Clingman	O R.Wright	2 S.Howe	C1 P.Schriver	O E.Burke
P K.Nichols	/C G.Stallings	/2 E.Hutchinson	P B.Rhines	2 P.Lyons	O P.Sommers	O B.Grey	10 P.Hines
P J.Clarkson	P T.Lovett	/C C.Lauer	P J.Duryea	/O J.Sommer	C G.McMillan	O B.Sunday	2 S.Crane
P C.Getzien	/P M.Hughes	/O D.Lytle	P F.Foreman	/C P.Sommers	/O E.Daily	/1 H.Decker	O D.Hemp
/P J.Taber	/P L.Baldwin	/C M.Honan	P L.Viau	/1 L.Stockwell	/1 S.Crane	/1 F.Motz	2 F.Dunlap
/P A.Lawson		/2 P.Wright	/P J.Dolan	P E.Beatin	/1 M.Scanlan	P K.Gleason	/2 D.Lytle
/P T.Von Fricken		P B.Hutchison		P J.Wadsworth	/C T.O'Rourke	P T.Vickery	/3 H.Youngman
		P P.Luby		P C.Young	P A.Rusie	P P.Smith	/O C.Heard
		P E.Stein		P E.Lincoln	P M.Welch	/P D.Esper	/1 P.Veach
		P M.Sullivan		P L.Viau	P J.Sharrott	/P B.Day	/O J.Coleman
		P R.Coughlin		/P B.Garfield	/P B.Murphy	/P D.Anderson	/2 H.Gilbert
		/P R.Gibson		/P E.Smith		/P J.McFetridge	/S J.Gilbert
		/P F.Demarais		/P C.Parsons		/P S.Bowman	/O F.McGinn
		/P E.Eiteljorge				/P J.Coleman	/O P.Routcliffe
		/P O.France					/O R.Gray
							/O F.Truax
							/S E.Clements
							P K.Baker
							P D.Anderson
							P B.Sowders
							P C.Schmit
							P B.Phillips
							P B.Gumbert
							/P S.Bowman
							/P B.Day
							/P P.Smith
							/P C.Gray
							/P H.Jones
							/P P.Daniels
							/P D.Esper
							/P R.Gibson
							/P A.Lawson
							/P G.Ziegler
							/P J.Heyner

TEAM	G	W	L	PCT	GB	R	OR	AB	H	2B	3B	HR	BB	SO	AVG	OBP	SLG	PRO	PRO+	BR	/A	PF	CHI	RC	SB	CS	SBA	SBR
BRO	129	86	43	.667		**884**	620	4419	1166	184	75	43	517	361	.264	.346	**.369**	**.715**	113	74	**71**	100	**112**	702	**349**			
CHI	139	84	53	.613	6	847	692	4891	**1271**	147		**67**	516	514	.260	.336	.356	.692	102	37	4	104	103	713	329			
PHI	133	78	54	.591	9.5	823	707	4707	1267	**220**	78	23	522	403	**.269**	**.350**	.364	.714	110	**79**	58	103	98	**735**	335			
CIN	134	77	55	.583	10.5	753	633	4644	1203	150	**120**	27	433	377	.259	.329	.360	.689	106	25	29	100	99	670	312			
BOS	134	76	57	.571	12	763	633	4722	1220	175	62	31	**530**	515	.258	.342	.341	.683	96	30	-33	108	96	665	285			
NY	135	63	68	.481	24	713	698	4832	1250	208	89	25	350	479	.259	.315	.354	.669	99	-16	-17	100	97	647	289			
CLE	136	44	88	.333	43.5	630	832	4633	1073	132	59	21	497	474	.232	.312	.299	.611	84	-96	-84	98	97	491	152			
PIT	138	23	113	.169	66.5	597	1235	4739	1088	160	43	20	408	458	.230	.300	.294	.594	87	-134	-65	88	97	492	208			
TOT	539					6010		37587	9538	1376	586	257	3773	3581	.254	.329	.342	.671							2259			

TEAM	CG	SH	SV	IP	H	H/G	HR	BB	SO	RAT	ERA	ERA+	OAV	OOB	PR	/A	PF	CPI	FA	E	DP	FW	PW	BW	SBW	DIF
BRO	115	6	2	1145	1102	8.7	27	401	403	12.2	3.06	112	.246	.315	64	47	96	104	**.940**	**320**	92	4.5	4.2	**6.3**		6.5
CHI	126	6	**3**	1237¹	1103	8.0	41	481	504	11.9	3.24	113	.234	.311	44	50	103	93	**.940**	344	89	**4.9**	4.4	.4		5.8
PHI	122	9	2	1194²	1210	9.1	22	486	507	13.2	3.32	110	.255	.331	32	43	102	107	.929	398	**122**	.4	3.8	5.2		2.6
CIN	124	9	1	1190²	1097	8.3	41	407	488	11.8	**2.79**	127	.238	.307	**102**	100	100	**109**	.932	382	106	1.6	8.9	2.6		-2.1
BOS	**132**	**13**	1	1187	1132	8.6	27	354	506	11.5	2.93	**128**	.245	**.303**	83	**104**	105	101	.935	359	77	3.0	**9.2**	-2.9		.2
NY	115	6	1	1177	**1029**	7.9	**14**	607	**612**	13.0	3.06	114	**.230**	.331	66	52	98	104	.921	449	104	-2.3	4.6	-1.5		-3.3
CLE	129	2	0	1184¹	1322	10.0	33	462	306	14.0	4.13	86	.273	.342	-75	-70	100	99	.930	405	108	.6	-6.2	-7.5		-8.9
PIT	119	3	0	1176¹	1520	11.6	52	573	381	16.6	5.97	55	.304	.384	-315	-350	92	91	.897	607	94	-11.5	-31.1	-5.8		3.3
TOT	982	54	10	9492¹		9.0				13.0	3.56		.254	.329					.928	3264	792					

Runs
Collins-Bro 148
Carroll-Chi 134
Hamilton-Phi 133
Tiernan-NY 132
McPhee-Cin 125

Hits
Thompson-Phi 172
Glasscock-NY 172
Tiernan-NY 168
Reilly-Cin 166
Carroll-Chi 166

Doubles
Thompson-Phi 41
Glasscock-NY 32
Collins-Bro 32
Myers-Phi 29
O'Brien-Bro 28

Triples
Reilly-Cin 26
McPhee-Cin 22
Tiernan-NY 21
Beard-Cin 15

Home Runs
Wilmot-Chi 13
Tiernan-NY 13
Burns-Bro 13
Long-Bos 8

Total Bases
Tiernan-NY 274
Reilly-Cin 261
Thompson-Phi 243
Wilmot-Chi 239
Glasscock-NY 225

Runs Batted In
Burns-Bro 128
Anson-Chi 107
Thompson-Phi 102
Wilmot-Chi 99
Foutz-Bro 98

Runs Produced
Burns-Bro 217
Thompson-Phi 214
Collins-Bro 214
Wilmot-Chi 200
Foutz-Bro 199

Bases On Balls
Anson-Chi 113
McKean-Cle 87
Allen-Phi 87
Collins-Bro 85
Hamilton-Phi 83

Batting Average
Glasscock-NY ..... .336
Hamilton-Phi ...... .325
Clements-Phi ..... .315
O'Brien-Bro ...... .314
Thompson-Phi .... .313

On Base Percentage
Anson-Chi .... .443
Hamilton-Phi ...... .430
Pinkney-Bro ...... .411
McKean-Cle .... .401
Glasscock-NY ..... .395

Slugging Average
Tiernan-NY .... .495
Clements-Phi ..... .472
Reilly-Cin .... .472
Burns-Bro .... .464
Burkett-NY .... .461

Production
Tiernan-NY .... .880
Clements-Phi ..... .864
Anson-Chi .... .844
Pinkney-Bro ...... .842
Glasscock-NY ..... .834

Adjusted Production
Tiernan-NY 156
Clements-Phi 148
Pinkney-Bro 145
Glasscock-NY 143
McKean-Cle 141

Batter Runs
Tiernan-NY 37.9
Anson-Chi 37.6
Hamilton-Phi 31.7
Pinkney-Bro 30.8
McKean-Cle 28.9

Adjusted Batter Runs
Tiernan-NY 37.7
Anson-Chi 32.6
McKean-Cle 31.2
Pinkney-Bro 30.4
Hamilton-Phi 28.8

Clutch Hitting Index
Burns-Bro 150
Anson-Chi 145
Myers-Phi 140
Hines-Pit-Bos 138
Bassett-NY 129

Runs Created
Hamilton-Phi 132
Tiernan-NY 130
Wilmot-Chi 114
Glasscock-NY 113
Collins-Bro 111

Total Average
Hamilton-Phi 1.170
Tiernan-NY 1.047
Pinkney-Bro 1.015
Anson-Chi 1.009
Collins-Bro 1.005

Stolen Bases
Hamilton-Phi 102
Collins-Bro 85
Sunday-Pit-Phi 84
Wilmot-Chi 76
Tiernan-NY 56

Stolen Base Average

Stolen Base Runs

Fielding Runs
Allen-Phi 38.6
McPhee-Cin 30.0
Glasscock-NY 22.0
Smalley-Cle 16.6
Carroll-Chi 14.5

Total Player Rating
Glasscock-NY 4.9
McPhee-Cin 4.5
Allen-Phi 4.0
Clements-Phi 2.9
Collins-Bro 2.7

Wins
Hutchison-Chi 42
Gleason-Phi 38
Lovett-Bro 30
Rusie-NY 29
Rhines-Cin 28

Win Percentage
Lovett-Bro .... .732
Gleason-Phi ...... .691
Luby-Chi .... .690
Caruthers-Bro .... .676
Hutchison-Chi .... .627

Games
Hutchison-Chi 71
Rusie-NY 67
Gleason-Phi 60
Beatin-Cle 54
Nichols-Bos 48

Complete Games
Hutchison-Chi 65
Rusie-NY 56
Gleason-Phi 54
Beatin-Cle 53
Nichols-Bos 47

Shutouts
Nichols-Bos 7
Rhines-Cin 6
Gleason-Phi 6
Hutchison-Chi 5

Saves
Hutchison-Chi 2
Gleason-Phi 2
Foutz-Bro 2

Innings Pitched
Hutchison-Chi ... 603.0
Rusie-NY 548.2
Gleason-Phi 506.0
Beatin-Cle 474.1
Nichols-Bos 424.0

Fewest Hits/Game
Rusie-NY 7.15
Mullane-Cin 7.54
Hutchison-Chi 7.54
Rhines-Cin 7.56
Luby-Chi 7.60

Fewest BB/Game
Young-Cle 1.83
Duryea-Cin 1.97
Getzien-Bos 2.11
Nichols-Bos 2.38
Rhines-Cin 2.53

Strikeouts
Rusie-NY 341
Hutchison-Chi 289
Nichols-Bos 222
Gleason-Phi 222
Terry-Bro 185

Strikeouts/Game
Rusie-NY 5.59
Nichols-Bos 4.71
Terry-Bro 4.50
Hutchison-Chi 4.31
Sharrott-NY 4.11

Ratio
Rhines-Cin 10.43
Nichols-Bos 10.55
Hutchison-Chi ... 10.70
Getzien-Bos 10.98
Duryea-Cin 11.10

Earned Run Average
Rhines-Cin 1.95
Nichols-Bos 2.23
Mullane-Cin 2.24
Rusie-NY 2.56
Gleason-Phi 2.63

Adjusted ERA
Rhines-Cin 182
Nichols-Bos 168
Mullane-Cin 159
Gleason-Phi 139
Rusie-NY 137

Opponents' Batting Avg.
Rusie-NY .... .212
Mullane-Cin ...... .221
Hutchison-Chi .... .221
Rhines-Cin .... .221
Luby-Chi .... .222

Opponents' On Base Pct.
Rhines-Cin .... .282
Nichols-Bos ...... .284
Hutchison-Chi .... .287
Getzien-Bos ...... .292
Duryea-Cin .... .295

Starter Runs
Rhines-Cin 71.8
Nichols-Bos 62.8
Rusie-NY 61.1
Hutchison-Chi ... 57.6
Gleason-Phi 52.2

Adjusted Starter Runs
Nichols-Bos 71.3
Rhines-Cin 71.3
Hutchison-Chi ... 63.6
Gleason-Phi 57.0
Rusie-NY 57.0

Clutch Pitching Index
Mullane-Cin 131
Vickery-Phi 120
Rhines-Cin 118
Gleason-Phi 112
Nichols-Bos 110

Relief Runs

Adjusted Relief Runs

Relief Ranking

Total Pitcher Index
Rusie-NY 6.9
Nichols-Bos 6.7
Rhines-Cin 6.5
Hutchison-Chi 5.9
Gleason-Phi 4.6

Total Baseball Ranking
Rusie-NY 6.7
Nichols-Bos 6.6
Rhines-Cin 6.5
Hutchison-Chi 5.9
Glasscock-NY 4.9

April 22 Philadelphia and Syracuse combine for an AA record 19 stolen bases in one game.

April 27 St. Louis pitcher Jack Stivetts strikes out the first seven Columbus batters he faces. He finishes the game with 12 K's.

May 25 After a Louisville-Syracuse game played in Three Rivers, New York, part of the grandstand collapses, throwing 50 or more people to the ground. No deaths are reported, but many are injured.

June 10 St. Louis pitcher Jack Stivetts hits two homers in a game. He later dup-licates this effort on August 6, 1891, and on June 12, 1896, making him the first pitcher to achieve this feat three times. The only two pitchers to match this achievement are Wes Ferrell (who had five such games) and Don Newcombe.

July 20 After Rochester beats Columbus in a Sunday game 8–3 at Windsor Beach, both teams are arrested.

July 27 Brooklyn's AA club holds a 13-8 lead over Columbus in the eighth inning at Long Island Grounds in a Sunday game when they run out of baseballs and are forced to forfeit. Brooklyn will only win 26 of 100 games and will disband on August 25.

September 17 Philadelphia (AA) is out of money and disbands. The team releases several players and sells the others, including Wilbert Robinson, Curt Welch and Sadie McMahon. The team will reorganize, but lose the remaining 22 games on the schedule.

November 22 At the AA annual meeting in Lousiville, Philadelphia is expelled for violating the league's constitution. A new team in Philadelphia is admitted, plus entries from Boston, Washington and Chicago to replace Syracuse, Toledo and Rochester.

BALTIMORE		BROOKLYN		COLUMBUS		LOUISVILLE		PHILADELPHIA			
M	B.Barnie	M	J.Kennedy	M	A.Buckenberger	M	J.Chapman	M	B.Sharsig	/O	J.McBride
1B	T.Power	1B	B.O'Brien	M	G.Schmelz	1B	H.Taylor	1B	J.O'Brien	/O	B.Stafford
2B	R.Mack	2B	J.Gerhardt	M	J.Sullivan	2B	T.Shinnick	2B	T.Shaffer	/S	B.Collins
SS	I.Ray	SS	C.Nelson	1B	M.Lehane	SS	P.Tomney	SS	B.Conroy	/C	Macey
3B	P.Gilbert	3B	J.Davis	2B	J.Crooks	3B	H.Raymond	3B	D.Lyons	/O	H.Sweigert
LF	J.Sommer	LF	H.Simon	SS	H.Easterday	LF	C.Hamburg	LF	B.Purcell		
CF	D.Long	CF	J.Peltz	3B	C.Reilly	CF	F.Weaver	CF	C.Welch	P	S.McMahon
RF	B.Johnson	RF	E.Daily	LF	S.Johnson	RF	J.Wolf	RF	O.Shaffer	P	E.Green
C	G.Townsend	C	J.Toy	CF	J.McTamany	C	J.Ryan	C	W.Robinson	P	E.Seward
				RF	J.Sneed					P	D.Esper
C	P.Tate	CO	F.Bowes	C	J.O'Connor	C	P.Weckbecker	OS	J.Kappel		
O	C.Welch	C3	H.Pitz			C	N.Bligh	SO	G.Carman	P	C.Stecher
C	W.Robinson	S	F.Fennelly	CS	J.Doyle	/1	D.Phelan	C	K.Baldwin	/P	E.O'Neil
O	J.McGuckin	3	F.Siefke	S	B.Wheelock	/1	D.O'Connor	CO	J.Riddle	/P	M.Hughes
/3	B.Hill	3	P.O'Connell	O	S.Nichol	/S	H.Easterday	O	J.Daly	/P	J.Whitney
		/O	H.Church	/C	N.Bligh	/1	C.Roseman	1	A.Knox	/P	B.Price
P	L.German			/O	J.Munyan	/S	P.Sweeney	S	H.Easterday	/P	H.Stine
P	S.McMahon	P	C.McCullough					/2	P.Sweeney	/P	H.Helmbold
P	M.O'Rourke	P	M.Mattimore	P	H.Gastright	P	S.Stratton	3	A.Sauters	/P	J.Sterling
P	M.Morrison	P	B.Murphy	P	F.Knauss	P	R.Ehret	/O	C.Snyder	/P	Lackey
				P	J.Easton	P	G.Meakim	/O	E.Pabst		
/P	N.Baker	/P	S.Toole	P	E.Chamberlain	P	H.Goodall	/C	B.Cantz		
		/P	T.Ford	P	W.Widner	P	E.Daily	/3	H.Meyers		
		/P	J.Powers					/O	G.Crawford		
		/P	G.Williams	/P	A.Mays	/P	M.Jones	/S	D.Fitzgerald		
		/P	J.Lynch	/P	T.Ford			/O	P.Hasney		
								/2	S.Campbell		

ROCHESTER		ST.LOUIS		SYRACUSE		TOLEDO	
M	P.Powers	M	T.McCarthy	M	G.Frazer	M	C.Morton
1B	T.O'Brien	M	J.Kerins	M	W.Fessenden	1B	P.Werden
2B	B.Greenwood	M	C.Roseman	M	G.Frazer	2B	P.Nicholson
SS	M.Phillips	M	C.Campau	1B	M.McQuery	SS	F.Scheibeck
3B	J.Knowles	M	T.McCarthy	2B	C.Childs	3B	B.Alvord
LF	H.Lyons	M	J.Gerhardt	SS	B.McLaughlin	LF	B.Van Dyke
CF	S.Griffin	1B	E.Cartwright	3B	Ti.O'Rourke	CF	G.Tebeau
RF	T.Scheffler	2B	B.Higgins	LF	B.Ely	RF	E.Swartwood
C	D.McGuire	SS	S.Fuller	CF	R.Wright	C	H.Sage
		3B	C.Duffee	RF	P.Friel		
CS	D.McKeough	LF	C.Campau	C	G.Briggs	OP	C.Sprague
SC	J.Grim	CF	C.Roseman			C	E.Rogers
1	J.Field	RF	T.McCarthy	C	To.O'Rourke	C1	T.Welch
S	L.Smith	C	J.Munyan	O	H.Simon	O	J.Peltz
O	D.Burke			O	M.Dorgan	/O	J.Sneed
/O	P.Reccius	O	T.Gettinger	3	J.Battin	/C	F.Ritter
		23	P.Sweeney	C	H.Pitz		
P	B.Barr	23	J.Gerhardt	C	P.Dealy	P	J.Healy
P	W.Calihan	C	J.Wells	O	G.Proeser	P	E.Cushman
P	C.Titcomb	O	D.Miller	/O	D.Hemp	P	F.Smith
P	B.Miller	C	B.Earle	/O	J.Leighton		
		3	J.Davis	/C	D.Burke	/P	E.O'Neil
P	J.Fitzgerald	2	B.Klusman	/O	J.Peltz	/P	D.Abbott
/P	H.Blauvelt	1	J.Kerins	/C	L.Graff	/P	B.Doty
		1	P.Hartnett	/2	B.Higgins		
		C	M.Trost				
		3	J.Donnelly	P	D.Casey		
		/2	E.Herr	P	J.Keefe		
		/1	J.Kane	P	M.Morrison		
		/C	D.Meek	P	E.Mars		
		/S	G.Creely				
		/O	E.Pabst	/P	B.Sullivan		
		/3	J.Burke	/P	C.McCullough		
		/C	J.Adams	/P	T.Lyons		
		/2	F.Millard	/P	E.Lincoln		
				/P	F.Keffer		
		P	J.Stivetts				
		P	T.Ramsey				
		P	B.Hart				
		P	B.Whitrock				
		P	J.Neale				
		/P	E.Chamberlain				
		/P	G.Nicol				

TEAM	G	W	L	PCT	GB	R	OR	AB	H	2B	3B	HR	BB	SO	AVG	OBP	SLG	PRO	PRO+	BR	/A	PF	CHI	RC	SB	CS	SBA	SBR
LOU	136	88	44	.667		819	588	4687	1310	156	65	15	410	460	.279	.344	.350	.694	113	53	72	98	101	699	341			
COL	140	79	55	.590	10	831	617	4741	1225	159	77	16	545	557	.258	.341	.335	.676	112	29	85	93	103	677	353			
STL	139	78	58	.574	12	870	736	4800	1308	178	73	48	474	490	.273	.350	.370	.720	103	100	-23	114	98	746	307			
TOL	134	68	64	.515	20	739	689	4575	1152	152	108	24	486	558	.252	.333	.348	.681	103	31	9	103	94	687	421			
ROC	133	63	63	.500	22	709	711	4553	1088	131	64	31	446	538	.239	.315	.316	.631	98	-53	-2	93	103	564	310			
BAL	38	15	19	.441	24	182	192	1213	278	34	16	2	125	152	.229	.316	.289	.605	79	-23	-31	105	103	146	101			
SYR	128	55	72	.433	30.5	698	831	4469	1158	151	59	14	457	482	.259	.333	.329	.662	112	1	77	90	96	600	292			
PHI	132	54	78	.409	34	702	945	4490	1057	181	51	24	475	540	.235	.320	.314	.634	94	-41	-25	98	100	564	305			
BRO	100	26	73	.263	45.5	492	733	3475	769	116	47	13	328	456	.221	.294	.293	.587	80	-98	-82	97	106	362	182			
TOT	540					6042		37003	9345	1258	560	187	3746	4233	.253	.330	.332	.662						2612				

TEAM	CG	SH	SV	IP	H	H/G	HR	BB	SO	RAT	ERA	ERA+	OAV	OOB	PR	/A	PF	CPI	FA	E	DP	FW	PW	BW	SBW	DIF
LOU	114	13	7	1206	1120	8.4	18	293	587	10.9	2.57	149	.239	.291	173	169	100	117	.934	380	79	2.8	14.9	6.3		-2.0
COL	120	14	3	1214²	976	7.2	20	471	624	11.2	2.99	120	.214	.297	118	80	93	95	.932	396	101	2.6	7.0	7.5		-5.1
STL	118	4	1	1195¹	1127	8.5	38	447	733	12.3	3.67	117	.242	.316	25	82	112	98	.916	478	93	-1.8	7.2	-2.0		6.6
TOL	122	4	2	1159¹	1122	8.7	23	429	533	12.6	3.56	111	.247	.321	39	49	102	102	.925	419	75	.4	4.3	.8		-3.5
ROC	122	5	2	1161²	1115	8.6	19	530	477	13.2	3.56	100	.246	.331	39	-2	92	106	.926	416	95	.4	-.2	-.2		-.0
BAL	36	1	0	315¹	307	8.8	3	123	134	13.0	4.00	101	.244	.328	-5	2	105	92	.928	109	21	.6	.2	-2.7		-.0
SYR	115	5	0	1089²	1158	9.6	28	518	454	14.4	4.98	71	.265	.351	-135	-176	91	89	.925	391	90	.9	-15.5	6.8		-.7
PHI	119	3	2	1132	1405	11.2	17	514	461	15.8	5.22	73	.296	.373	-171	-176	99	99	.918	452	93	-1.6	-15.5	-2.2		7.3
BRO	96	0	0	879	1011	10.4	21	421	230	15.2	4.71	83	.281	.365	-83	-81	101	104	.909	404	92	-4.4	-7.1	-7.2		-4.8
TOT	962	49	17	9353		9.0				13.1	3.86		.253	.330					.923	3445	739					

Runs	Hits	Doubles	Triples	Home Runs	Total Bases
McTamany-Col 140	Wolf-Lou 197	Childs-Syr 33	Werden-Tol 20	Campau-StL 9	Wolf-Lou 260
McCarthy-StL 137	McCarthy-StL 192	Wolf-Lou 29	Johnson-Col 18	Cartwright-StL 8	McCarthy-StL ... 256
Fuller-StL 118	Johnson-Col 186	Lyons-Phi 29	Alvord-Tol 16	Stivetts-StL 7	Johnson-Col ... 248
Sneed-Tol-Col ... 117	Childs-Syr 170		Sneed-Tol-Col 15	Lyons-Phi 7	Childs-Syr 237
Welch-Phi-Bal 116	Taylor-Lou 169				Werden-Tol 227

Runs Batted In	Runs Produced	Bases On Balls	Batting Average	On Base Percentage	Slugging Average
Johnson-Col 113	Johnson-Col 218	McTamany-Col 112	Wolf-Lou .... .363	Lyons-Phi .... .461	Lyons-Phi .... .531
Wolf-Lou 98	McCarthy-StL 200	Crooks-Col 96	Lyons-Phi .... .354	Swartwood-Tol .... .444	Campau-StL .... .513
Childs-Syr 89	Childs-Syr 196	Swartwood-Tol 80	McCarthy-StL .... .350	Childs-Syr .... .434	Childs-Syr .... .481
Knowles-Roc 84	Wolf-Lou 194	Werden-Tol 78	Johnson-Col ...... .346	McCarthy-StL ..... .430	Wolf-Lou .... .479
Shinnick-Lou 82	McTamany-Col 187	Scheffler-Roc 78	Childs-Syr .... .345	Wright-Syr .... .428	McCarthy-StL .... .467

Production	Adjusted Production	Batter Runs	Adjusted Batter Runs	Clutch Hitting Index	Runs Created
Lyons-Phi 992	Lyons-Phi 197	McCarthy-StL 45.6	Childs-Syr 58.5	Crooks-Col 148	McCarthy-StL 150
Childs-Syr 915	Childs-Syr 189	Childs-Syr 44.7	Wolf-Lou 46.3	Knowles-Roc 141	Wolf-Lou 132
Wolf-Lou 900	Wolf-Lou 169	Wolf-Lou......... 43.3	Johnson-Col 46.0	O'Brien-Phi 139	Childs-Syr 130
McCarthy-StL 898	Johnson-Col 168	Lyons-Phi 41.4	Lyons-Phi 43.7	Johnson-Col 136	Johnson-Col 122
Swartwood-Tol 887	Swartwood-Tol 157	Swartwood-Tol 40.6	Swartwood-Tol 37.2	Shinnick-Lou 132	Werden-Tol 118

Total Average	Stolen Bases	Stolen Base Average	Stolen Base Runs	Fielding Runs	Total Player Rating
Lyons-Phi 1.224	McCarthy-StL 83			Gerhardt-Bro-StL .. 41.5	Childs-Syr 6.7
McCarthy-StL ... 1.169	Scheffler-Roc 77			Reilly-Col 28.2	Lyons-Phi 4.8
Childs-Syr 1.149	VanDyke-Tol 73			Ely-Syr 19.3	O'Connor-Col 3.7
Swartwood-Tol ... 1.141	Welch-Phi-Bal 72			Tomney-Lou 17.6	Wolf-Lou 3.6
Werden-Tol 1.074				Welch-Phi-Bal 15.7	Swartwood-Tol 3.5

Wins	Win Percentage	Games	Complete Games	Shutouts	Saves
McMahon-Phi-Bal 36	Stratton-Lou 708	McMahon-Phi-Bal 60	McMahon-Phi-Bal 55	Chamberlain-SL-Col ... 6	Goodall-Lou 4
Stratton-Lou 34	Chamberlain-SL-Col ... .682	Barr-Roc 57	Barr-Roc 52	Stratton-Lou 4	Knauss-Col 2
Gastright-Col 30	Gastright-Col ...... .682	Stivetts-StL 54	Stratton-Lou 44	Gastright-Col 4	Ehret-Lou 2
Barr-Roc 28	Ehret-Lou .... .641	Stratton-Lou 50	Healy-Tol 44	Ehret-Lou 4	
Stivetts-StL 27	McMahon-Phi-Bal ... .632	Gastright-Col 48			

Innings Pitched	Fewest Hits/Game	Fewest BB/Game	Strikeouts	Strikeouts/Game	Ratio
McMahon-Phi-Bal ...509.0	Knauss-Col 6.73	Stratton-Lou...... 1.27	McMahon-Phi-Bal ... 291	Ramsey-StL 6.63	Stratton-Lou 9.86
Barr-Roc 493.1	Gastright-Col 7.00	Ehret-Lou........ 1.98	Stivetts-StL 289	Stivetts-StL 6.20	Gastright-Col 10.43
Stratton-Lou 431.0	Easton-Col 7.50	Ramsey-StL 2.63	Ramsey-StL 257	Meakim-Lou 5.77	Knauss-Col 10.87
Stivetts-StL....... 419.1	Chamberlain-SL-Col .. 7.50	Smith-Tol 2.83	Healy-Tol 225	Chamberlain-SL-Col .. 5.49	Healy-Tol 11.04
Gastright-Col 401.1	Healy-Tol 7.54	McMahon-Phi-Bal ... 2.94	Barr-Roc 209	Healy-Tol 5.21	Ehret-Lou 11.21

Earned Run Average	Adjusted ERA	Opponents' Batting Avg.	Opponents' On Base Pct.	Starter Runs	Adjusted Starter Runs
Stratton-Lou 2.36	Stratton-Lou 163	Knauss-Col ...... .202	Stratton-Lou ...... .270	Stratton-Lou 72.0	Stratton-Lou 71.1
Ehret-Lou 2.53	Ehret-Lou......... 152	Gastright-Col ..... .208	Gastright-Col ..... .282	Ehret-Lou 53.1	Ehret-Lou 52.3
Knauss-Col 2.81	Healy-Tol 136	Easton-Col ...... .220	Knauss-Col ...... .290	Healy-Tol 42.0	Healy-Tol 45.5
Chamberlain-SL-Col ... 2.83	Meakim-Lou 132	Chamberlain-SL-Col ... .220	Healy-Tol .... .293	Gastright-Col 41.3	Stivetts-StL 36.7
Healy-Tol 2.89	Chamberlain-SL-Col 131	Healy-Tol .... .221	Ehret-Lou .... .296	Barr-Roc 33.8	McMahon-Phi-Bal ... 33.8

Clutch Pitching Index	Relief Runs	Adjusted Relief Runs	Relief Ranking	Total Pitcher Index	Total Baseball Ranking
Ehret-Lou 126				Stratton-Lou 8.9	Stratton-Lou 8.9
Titcomb-Roc 121				Stivetts-StL 4.9	Childs-Syr 6.7
Daily-Bro-Lou 113				Healy-Tol 4.7	Stivetts-StL 5.0
Stratton-Lou 110				Ehret-Lou 4.3	Lyons-Phi 4.8
Chamberlain-SL-Col 110				McMahon-Phi-Bal ... 4.0	Healy-Tol 4.6

January 16 Samuel Gompers, president of the American Federation of Labor, and three other labor leaders pledge support for the PL at a league meeting in Philadelphia.

January 28 In the first of many lawsuits filed against PL players by their former teams, the judge refuses to grant an injunction against John Ward, president of the Brotherhood. His decision, echoed frequently by other judges, states that the "want of fairness and mutuality" in the standard NL contract, specifically the clauses relating to the reserve rule, "[is] apparent."

March 27* The application of an all-black club made up of ex–Cuban Giants is rejected by the Inter-State League.

May 8 Cleveland's Willie McGill hurls a complete-game 14-5 victory over Buffalo in a Players League game at age 16, the youngest ever to perform this feat.

May 31 New York players George Gore, Buck Ewing, and Roger Connor hit consecutive homers in the eighth inning against Cincinnati. This feat will not be matched until May 10, 1894.

June 1* Professional baseball is born in England as four teams—Derby, Preston, Stoke, and Birmingham—form a league. Four Americans are imported to provide instruction.

June 2 Ed Delahanty of Cleveland goes 6-for-6 with five runs as his club crashes Chicago 20–7.

June 21 Charles "Silver" King of Chicago pitches an eight-inning no-hitter, but loses to Brooklyn 1–0. Chicago bats first, and King does not pitch the last of the ninth.

July 23 Harry Stovey of Boston's PL club becomes the first major league player to reach 100 career home runs.

September 14 When Buffalo (PL) captain Jay Faatz disagrees with management, Connie Mack becomes captain of the team. This unofficially marks the start of Connie Mack's managing career that spans more than half a century.

October 9 Cincinnati (NL) owner Aaron Stern sells his team to PL owners for $40,000 (Giants owner John B. Day had threatened the same action in July, but received help from other owners to prevent it). Committees from the three leagues begin negotiations towards a settlement of the war. PL owners from New York, Cleveland and Brooklyn seek consolidation with the NL. A truce, during which all contracts will be respected, is agreed upon. It is up to owners in each city to arrange their own deals.

October 17* The AA and NL refuse to permit the Players League champion to take part in a World Series. Interest in the postseason meeting of league champions is lukewarm as Brooklyn wins a 9-0 opener over Louisville behind Adonis Terry (26-16). After breaking even in seven games, with one tie, the teams abandon the series.

October 20 Upset over PL backers seeking deals without consulting them, the Brotherhood meets and votes to add a players' committee to the three league committees for the next meeting. John M. Ward, Ned Hanlon, and Arthur Irwin are elected. Ward makes a long, spirited plea for the players' participation. Al Spalding, eager to split the backers and players, argues against him. The original three league committees vote 2–1 against the players' involvement. Each PL backer is now out to make his own deal and the league is dead.

BOSTON		BROOKLYN		BUFFALO		CHICAGO		CLEVELAND		NEW YORK		PHILADELPHIA		PITTSBURGH	
M	K.Kelly	M	M.Ward	M	J.Rowe	M	C.Comiskey	M	T.Larkin	M	B.Ewing	M	J.Fogarty	M	N.Hanlon
1B	D.Brouthers	1B	D.Orr	M	J.Faatz	1B	C.Comiskey	M	P.Tebeau	1B	R.Connor	M	C.Buffinton	1B	J.Beckley
2B	J.Quinn	2B	L.Bierbauer	M	J.Rowe	2B	F.Pfeffer	1B	H.Larkin	2B	D.Shannon	1B	S.Farrar	2B	Y.Robinson
SS	A.Irwin	SS	J.Ward	1B	D.White	SS	C.Bastian	2B	C.Stricker	SS	D.Richardson	2B	J.Pickett	SS	T.Corcoran
3B	B.Nash	3B	B.Joyce	2B	S.Wise	3B	N.Williamson	SS	E.Delahanty	3B	A.Whitney	SS	B.Shindle	3B	B.Kuehne
LF	H.Richardson	LF	E.Seery	SS	J.Rowe	LF	T.O'Neill	3B	P.Tebeau	LF	G.Gore	3B	J.Mulvey	LF	J.Fields
CF	T.Brown	CF	E.Andrews	3B	J.Irwin	CF	J.Ryan	LF	P.Browning	CF	M.Slattery	LF	G.Wood	CF	N.Hanlon
RF	H.Stovey	RF	J.McGeachy	CF	D.Hoy	RF	H.Duffy	CF	J.McAleer	RF	J.O'Rourke	CF	M.Griffin	RF	J.Visner
C	M.Murphy	C	T.Kinslow	RF	J.Halligan	C	D.Farrell	RF	P.Radford	C	B.Ewing	RF	J.Fogarty	C	F.Carroll
				C	C.Mack			C	S.Sutcliffe			C	J.Milligan		
CS	K.Kelly	OP	G.Van Haltren			C3	J.Boyle			O	D.Johnston			C	T.Quinn
C	P.Swett	C1	P.Cook			1S	D.Darling	C3	J.Brennan	3S	G.Hatfield	OC	B.Hallman	/C	J.Hurley
/O	D.Johnston	C	D.Daily	OC	S.Clark	3	A.Latham	O	L.Twitchell	CO	W.Brown	CO	L.Cross	/2	R.Gray
/S	J.Morrill	O	A.Sunday	OP	L.Twitchell	S	F.Shugart	O	J.Carney	CO	F.Vaughn	2	D.Shannon		
		/O	J.Hayes	O	J.Rainey			C	P.Snyder	/2	F.Dunlap				
P	C.Radbourn			1	J.Faatz	P	M.Baldwin	/C	N.Stynes			P	B.Sanders	P	H.Staley
P	A.Gumbert	P	G.Weyhing	1	J.Carney	P	S.King	/O	Budd	P	E.Crane	P	P.Knell	P	A.Maul
P	B.Daley	P	J.Sowders	/O	Lewis	P	C.Bartson			P	H.O'Day	P	C.Buffinton	P	P.Galvin
P	M.Kilroy	P	C.Murphy	/O	J.Gillespie			P	H.Gruber	P	J.Ewing	P	B.Husted	P	E.Morris
		P	G.Hemming			P	F.Dwyer	P	J.Bakely	P	T.Keefe	P	B.Cunningham	P	J.Tener
P	K.Madden			P	G.Haddock			P	D.O'Brien						
				P	B.Cunningham			P	W.McGill					/P	F.Doe
				P	G.Keefe			/P	G.Hemming						
				P	G.Stafford			/P	C.Dewald						
								/P	B.Gleason						
				P	A.Ferson										
				/P	L.Baldwin										
				/P	J.Buckley										
				/P	G.Krock										
				/P	B.Duzen										
				/P	D.Cotter										
				/P	F.Doe										

TEAM	G	W	L	PCT	GB	R	OR	AB	H	2B	3B	HR	BB	SO	AVG	OBP	SLG	PRO	PRO+	BR	/A	PF	CHI	RC	SB	CS	SBA	SBR
BOS	130	81	48	.628		992	767	4626	1306	**223**	76	54	**652**	435	.282	**.376**	.398	**.774**	105	**90**	24	107	100	**869**	**412**			
BRO	133	76	56	.576	6.5	964	893	4887	1352	186	93	34	502	369	.277	.349	.374	.723	92	-13	-68	106	**106**	751	272			
NY	132	74	57	.565	8	**1018**	875	4913	**1393**	204	97	**66**	486	364	.284	.352	**.405**	.757	98	40	-44	109	**106**	800	231			
CHI	138	75	62	.547	10	886	770	4968	1311	200	95	31	492	410	.264	.335	.361	.696	87	-65	-101	104	102	712	276			
PHI	132	68	63	.519	14	941	855	4855	1350	187	**113**	49	431	**321**	.278	.343	.393	.736	100	2	-19	102	104	743	203			
PIT	128	60	68	.469	20.5	835	892	4577	1192	168	**113**	35	569	375	.260	.349	.369	.718	106	-15	56	92	97	694	249			
CLE	131	55	75	.423	26.5	849	1027	4804	1370	213	94	27	509	345	**.285**	.360	.386	.746	114	30	**107**	92	91	749	180			
BUF	134	36	96	.273	46.5	793	1199	4795	1249	180	64	20	541	367	.260	.347	.337	.684	96	-68	2	92	93	632	160			
TOT	529					7278		38425	10523	1561	745	316	4182	2986	.274	.351	.378	.729							1983			

TEAM	CG	SH	SV	IP	H	H/G	HR	BB	SO	RAT	ERA	ERA+	OAV	OOB	PR	/A	PF	CPI	FA	E	DP	FW	PW	BW	SBW	DIF
BOS	105	6	4	1137¹	1291	10.2	49	467	345	14.3	3.79	116	.274	.346	55	76	104	111	.918	460	109	1.7	6.1	1.9		6.8
BRO	111	4	**7**	1184	1334	10.1	**26**	570	377	14.9	3.95	113	.273	.356	37	65	105	106	.909	531	114	-1.8	5.2	-5.4		12.0
NY	111	3	6	1172¹	**1216**	9.3	37	569	449	14.1	4.17	109	.257	.343	8	47	107	92	**.921**	450	94	**2.8**	3.8	-3.5		5.5
CHI	124	5	2	1219¹	1238	**9.1**	27	503	**460**	13.2	**3.39**	**128**	**.252**	**.327**	114	**128**	103	100	.918	492	107	1.6	**10.2**	-8.1		2.7
PHI	118	4	2	1154¹	1292	10.1	33	495	361	14.4	4.05	105	.271	.347	22	27	101	100	.910	510	118	-.7	2.2	-1.5		2.6
PIT	121	**7**	0	1116²	1267	10.2	32	**334**	318	13.2	4.22	93	.274	.328	2	-39	92	89	.907	512	80	-1.7	-3.1	4.5		-3.6
CLE	115	1	0	1143²	1386	10.9	45	571	325	15.8	4.23	94	.287	.369	0	-33	94	114	.907	533	103	-2.3	-2.6	**8.5**		-13.6
BUF	**125**	2	0	1141	1499	11.8	67	673	351	17.5	6.11	67	.304	.393	-239	-257	97	93	.914	491	116	.8	-20.5	.2		-10.5
TOT	930	32	21	9268²		10.2				14.7	4.23		.274	.351					.913	3979	841					

Runs
Duffy-Chi 161
Brown-Bos 146
Stovey-Bos 142
Ward-Bro 134
Connor-NY 133

Hits
Duffy-Chi 191
Shindle-Phi 189
Ward-Bro 188
Browning-Cle 184
Richardson-Bos ... 181

Doubles
Browning-Cle 40
Beckley-Pit 38
O'Rourke-NY 37
Duffy-Chi 36
Brouthers-Bos 36

Triples
Visner-Pit 22
Beckley-Pit 22
Shindle-Phi 21
Fields-Pit 20
Joyce-Bro 18

Home Runs
Connor-NY 14
Richardson-Bos ... 13
Stovey-Bos 12
Shindle-Phi 10
Gore-NY 10

Total Bases
Shindle-Phi 282
Duffy-Chi 280
Beckley-Pit 276
Richardson-Bos ... 274
Connor-NY 265

Runs Batted In
Richardson-Bos ... 146
Orr-Bro 124
Beckley-Pit 120
O'Rourke-NY 115
Larkin-Cle 112

Runs Produced
Richardson-Bos ... 259
Duffy-Chi 236
Connor-NY 222
Bierbauer-Bro 220
Beckley-Pit 220

Bases On Balls
Joyce-Bro 123
Robinson-Pit 101
Brouthers-Bos 99
Hoy-Buf 94

Batting Average
Browning-Cle ..... .373
Orr-Bro .... .371
O'Rourke-NY ...... .360
Connor-NY .... .349
Ryan-Chi .... .340

On Base Percentage
Brouthers-Bos .... .466
Browning-Cle ..... .459
Connor-NY .... .450
Robinson-Pit ..... .434
Gore-NY .... .432

Slugging Average
Connor-NY .... .548
B.Ewing-NY .... .545
Beckley-Pit ...... .535
Orr-Bro .... .534
Browning-Cle ..... .517

Production
Connor-NY .... .998
Browning-Cle ..... .976
Orr-Bro .... .948
Gore-NY .... .931
O'Rourke-NY ...... .925

Adjusted Production
Browning-Cle 175
Beckley-Pit 156
Larkin-Cle 153
Connor-NY 152
Orr-Bro 144

Batter Runs
Connor-NY 47.6
Browning-Cle 45.2
Brouthers-Bos 38.2
Orr-Bro 32.3
Larkin-Cle 30.2

Adjusted Batter Runs
Browning-Cle 57.1
Larkin-Cle 41.0
Beckley-Pit 38.7
Connor-NY 35.2
Brouthers-Bos 29.2

Clutch Hitting Index
Richardson-Bos ... 128
Orr-Bro 128
Brouthers-Bos 125
Wise-Buf 119
Larkin-Cle 118

Runs Created
Duffy-Chi 141
Browning-Cle 136
Stovey-Bos 135
Connor-NY 132
Shindle-Phi 127

Total Average
Stovey-Bos 1.217
Connor-NY 1.194
Browning-Cle 1.191
Brouthers-Bos 1.149
Gore-NY 1.129

Stolen Bases
Stovey-Bos 97
Brown-Bos 79
Duffy-Chi 78
Hanlon-Pit 65
Ward-Bro 63

Stolen Base Average

Stolen Base Runs

Fielding Runs
Farrell-Chi 26.5
Richardson-Bos ... 25.3
Bierbauer-Bro 24.8
Pfeffer-Chi 24.1
Ward-Bro 21.3

Total Player Rating
Browning-Cle 4.5
Connor-NY 3.1
B.Ewing-NY 3.0
Ward-Bro 2.9
Shindle-Phi 2.6

Wins
Baldwin-Chi 33
Weyhing-Bro 30
King-Chi 30
Radbourn-Bos 27
Gumbert-Bos 23

Win Percentage
Daley-Bos .... .720
Radbourn-Bos ..... .692
Knell-Phi .... .667
Gumbert-Bos ...... .657
Weyhing-Bro ...... .652

Games
Baldwin-Chi 58
King-Chi 56
Weyhing-Bro 49
Gruber-Cle 48
Staley-Pit 46

Complete Games
Baldwin-Chi 53
King-Chi 48
Staley-Pit 44
Gruber-Cle 39
Weyhing-Bro 38

Shutouts
King-Chi 4
Weyhing-Bro 3
Staley-Pit 3

Saves
Hemming-Cle-Bro .. 3
O'Day-NY 3

Innings Pitched
Baldwin-Chi 492.0
King-Chi 461.0
Weyhing-Bro 390.0
Staley-Pit 387.2
Gruber-Cle 383.1

Fewest Hits/Game
King-Chi 8.20
Crane-NY 8.80
Keefe-NY 8.84
Hemming-Cle-Bro .. 8.88
Knell-Phi 9.01

Fewest BB/Game
Staley-Pit 1.72
Sanders-Phi 1.79
Galvin-Pit 2.03
Morris-Pit 2.18
Radbourn-Bos 2.62

Strikeouts
Baldwin-Chi 206
King-Chi 185
Weyhing-Bro 177
Staley-Pit 145
J.Ewing-NY 145

Strikeouts/Game
J.Ewing-NY 4.88
Daley-Bos 4.21
Weyhing-Bro 4.08
McGill-Cle 4.02
Haddock-Buf 3.81

Ratio
Staley-Pit 11.07
King-Chi 11.67
Radbourn-Bos 12.15
Keefe-NY 12.66
Sanders-Phi 12.75

Earned Run Average
King-Chi 2.69
Staley-Pit 3.23
Radbourn-Bos 3.31
Baldwin-Chi 3.35
Keefe-NY 3.38

Adjusted ERA
King-Chi 161
Keefe-NY 134
Radbourn-Bos 133
Baldwin-Chi 130
Weyhing-Bro 124

Opponents' Batting Avg.
King-Chi .... .232
Crane-NY .... .245
Keefe-NY .... .246
Hemming-Cle-Bro .. .247
Knell-Phi .... .250

Opponents' On Base Pct.
Staley-Pit .... .290
King-Chi .... .301
Radbourn-Bos ..... .310
Keefe-NY .... .318
Sanders-Phi ...... .320

Starter Runs
King-Chi 78.6
Baldwin-Chi 48.2
Staley-Pit 43.2
Radbourn-Bos 35.2
Weyhing-Bro 27.2

Adjusted Starter Runs
King-Chi 84.2
Baldwin-Chi 54.2
Radbourn-Bos 41.4
Weyhing-Bro 37.0
Keefe-NY 29.5

Clutch Pitching Index
O'Brien-Cle 127
Daley-Bos 124
McGill-Cle 117
Kilroy-Bos 114
Gruber-Cle 114

Relief Runs

Adjusted Relief Runs

Relief Ranking

Total Pitcher Index
King-Chi 7.1
Baldwin-Chi 4.8
Radbourn-Bos 3.7
Staley-Pit 2.5
Sanders-Phi 2.4

Total Baseball Ranking
King-Chi 7.1
Baldwin-Chi 4.8
Browning-Cle 4.5
Radbourn-Bos 3.5
Connor-NY 3.1

January 14 The NL votes to allow the AA to place a team in Boston, despite the vehement opposition of the owners of the Boston NL club.

January 16 The NL, AA, and Western Association sign a new National Agreement calling for the creation of a three-man Board of Control to settle disputes between clubs and leagues.

February 6 The New York Giants' salary list is leaked to the press. It shows a total player payroll of $54,600 with Buck Ewing's $5,500 salary topping the scale.

February 14 The National Board of Control "reluctantly" awards three disputed players (Lou Bierbauer, Harry Stovey, and Connie Mack) to the NL clubs that signed them despite the prior claims of the AA.

April 3 The Cleveland Spiders beat Pittsburgh 6-3 in St. Augustine in the first spring training game ever played in Florida between two major league teams.

April 27 The Bridegrooms play their home opener at Eastern Park in the East New York section of Brooklyn. The park was used by the PL club in 1890, and the NL club will occupy it for seven years. It is located near a complex of streetcar and suburban railroad lines, forcing fans to "dodge trolleys" to get to the gates. This spawns the name "Trolley Dodgers" or "Dodgers" for the ball club.

May 1 Cleveland opens new League Park at 66th and Lexington with Cy Young pitching the Spiders to a 12-3 victory over the Reds before a crowd of about 9,500.

June 13 A new major league attendance record is set as 22,289 jam the Polo Grounds to see the Giants nip the Colts 8-7.

July 25 An over-the-fence drive by Cliff Carroll caps a four-run rally in the bottom of the ninth to give the Chicago Colts a 15–14 victory in Cleveland. Although the ground rules at this park call for a homer on balls hit over all outfielder fences, the winning run scores from second base, so Carroll gets credit for only a double.

August 25 The Boston NL club shocks the baseball world by announcing the signing of King Kelly away from the rival Boston AA club, thereby wrecking peace talks between the leagues. Kelly signs through the 1892 season for a total of $25,000, a figure that will not be topped by any player until the Federal League war of 1914 and 1915.

September 4 "Old Man" Cap Anson shows up for today's game wearing a wig and a long white beard, much to the delight of the Chicago crowd. Anson wears this costume throughout the game, which his Colts win over the Beaneaters 5-3, stretching Chicago's lead to seven games over Boston.

September 18 Billy Hamilton steals four bases to pace the Phillies to an 11-6 decision over the Cincinnati Reds. Hamilton will finish the season with a league-leading 115 steals, breaking the 100 mark for the third year in a row.

October 1 Boston clinches the NL pennant with its 17th consecutive victory, 6–1, in Philadelphia, while Chicago is losing to Cincinnati by the same score.

November 11 The NL meets and dismisses the charges of collusion and game throwing against the eastern clubs brought by Chicago, thereby formally giving Boston the pennant. The league also plans its strategy for conquering the Association by consolidating the four strongest AA clubs into a 12-team league for next year.

December 17 The NL gains four new teams from the folding AA (St. Louis, Louisville, Washington, and Baltimore) and conducts other business as well. The NL allows Sunday games for the first time but will retain its 50-cent minimum admission price.

BOSTON	BROOKLYN	CHICAGO	CINCINNATI	CLEVELAND	NEW YORK	PHILADELPHIA	PITTSBURGH
M F.Selee	M M.Ward	M C.Anson	M T.Loftus	M B.Leadley	M J.Mutrie	M H.Wright	M N.Hanlon
1B T.Tucker	1B D.Foutz	1B C.Anson	1B J.Reilly	M P.Tebeau	1B R.Connor	1B W.Brown	M B.McGunnigle
2B J.Quinn	2B H.Collins	2B F.Pfeffer	2B B.McPhee	1B J.Virtue	2B D.Richardson	2B A.Myers	1B J.Beckley
SS H.Long	SS J.Ward	SS J.Cooney	SS G.Smith	2B C.Childs	SS J.Glasscock	SS B.Allen	2B L.Bierbauer
3B B.Nash	3B G.Pinkney	3B B.Dahlen	3B A.Latham	SS E.McKean	3B C.Bassett	3B B.Shindle	SS F.Shugart
LF B.Lowe	LF D.O'Brien	LF W.Wilmot	LF P.Browning	3B P.Tebeau	LF J.O'Rourke	LF B.Hamilton	3B C.Reilly
CF S.Brodie	CF M.Griffin	CF J.Ryan	CF B.Holliday	LF J.McAleer	CF G.Gore	CF E.Delahanty	LF P.Browning
RF H.Stovey	RF O.Burns	RF C.Carroll	RF L.Marr	CF G.Davis	RF M.Tiernan	RF S.Thompson	CF N.Hanlon
C C.Bennett	C T.Kinslow	C M.Kittridge	C J.Harrington	RF S.Johnson	C D.Buckley	C J.Clements	RF F.Carroll
				C C.Zimmer			C C.Mack
CO C.Ganzel	C C.Daily	3 T.Burns	1C J.Keenan	CO J.Doyle	SO L.Whistler	3O E.Mayer	CS D.Miller
O M.Sullivan	C1 T.Daly	C P.Schriver	O J.Halligan	O J.Burkett	C A.Clarke	CO B.Grey	O A.Maul
C K.Kelly	2 J.O'Brien	C B.Bowman	O M.Slattery	3 J.Denny	C B.Burrell	1 J.Denny	O P.Corkhill
O J.Kelley	S B.Ely	C B.Merritt	O E.Curtis	O J.Clark	/2 B.Ewing	/C J.Fields	O D.Lally
/O G.Rooks	/2 J.Burdock	C B.Clark	C P.Corkhill	3 B.Alvord	/3 J.Denny	/O L.Graulich	C2 T.Berger
/C F.Lake	/O D.Esterbrook	/O E.Foster	/O F.Foreman	/O E.Seward		/O J.Donohue	C J.Fields
		/C M.Honan		/O M.Sullivan		/S H.Morelock	/3 J.Newell
				/O B.Collins		/O W.Plock	/O P.Ward
				/O J.Daly		/S C.Bastian	/S E.Spurney
							/3 S.LaRoque
P J.Clarkson	P T.Lovett	P B.Hutchison	P T.Mullane	P C.Young	P A.Rusie	P K.Gleason	P M.Baldwin
P K.Nichols	P B.Caruthers	P A.Gumbert	P B.Rhines	P H.Gruber	P J.Ewing	P D.Esper	P S.King
P H.Staley	P G.Hemming	P P.Luby	P C.Radbourn	P L.Viau	P M.Welch	P J.Thornton	P P.Galvin
P C.Getzien	P A.Terry	P E.Stein	P E.Crane				
	P B.Inks				P J.Sharrott	P T.Keefe	
/P J.Kiley		P T.Vickery	P J.Duryea	/P E.Beatin	/P R.Coughlin	P B.Kling	/P H.Staley
/P C.Ryan		/P G.Nicol	/P C.Stephens	/P F.Knauss	/P T.Keefe	/P E.Cassian	/P S.Stratton
/P T.Brynan				/P C.Getzien	/P D.Clarkson	/P P.Smith	
/P J.Sullivan				/P H.Killeen	/P B.Barr	/P J.Schultze	
					/P M.Sullivan	/P M.Kilroy	
					/P J.Taylor	/P J.Gormley	
					/P A.Dunning	/P P.Saylor	

TEAM	G	W	L	PCT	GB	R	OR	AB	H	2B	3B	HR	BB	SO	AVG	OBP	SLG	PRO	PRO+	BR	/A	PF	CHI	RC	SB	CS	SBA	SBR
BOS	140	87	51	.630		847	658	4956	1264	181	81	53	533	537	.255	.337	.356	.693	97	52	-47	112	101	710	289			
CHI	137	82	53	.607	3.5	832	730	4873	1231	159	88	60	526	457	.253	.332	.358	.690	107	41	42	100	102	674	238			
NY	136	71	61	.538	13	754	711	4833	1271	189	72	46	438	394	.263	.329	.360	.689	111	34	66	96	96	663	224			
PHI	138	68	69	.496	18.5	756	773	4929	1244	180	51	21	482	412	.252	.326	.322	.648	92	-27	-46	103	101	609	232			
CLE	141	65	74	.468	22.5	835	888	5074	1295	183	88	22	519	464	.255	.330	.339	.669	97	7	-26	104	104	663	242			
BRO	137	61	76	.445	25.5	765	820	4748	1233	200	69	23	465	435	.260	.330	.345	.675	103	16	21	99	101	669	337			
CIN	138	56	81	.409	30.5	646	790	4791	1158	148	90	40	414	439	.242	.308	.335	.643	92	-49	-54	101	93	584	244			
PIT	137	55	80	.407	30.5	679	744	4794	1148	148	71	29	427	503	.239	.308	.318	.626	90	-73	-56	98	101	547	205			
TOT	552					6114		38998	9844	1388	610	294	3804	3641	.252	.325	.342	.667						2011				

TEAM	CG	SH	SV	IP	H	H/G	HR	BB	SO	RAT	ERA	ERA+	OAV	OOB	PR	/A	PF	CPI	FA	E	DP	FW	PW	BW	SBW	DIF
BOS	126	9	6	1241²	1223	8.9	51	364	525	11.8	2.76	132	.248	.305	80	122	109	109	.938	358	96	4.7	10.9	-4.2		6.6
CHI	114	6	3	1220²	1207	8.9	53	475	477	12.7	3.47	96	.249	.322	-17	-21	100	96	.932	397	119	1.5	-1.9	3.8		11.1
NY	117	11	3	1204	1098	8.2	26	593	651	13.1	2.99	107	.234	.327	47	28	96	104	.933	384	104	2.2	2.5	5.9		-5.5
PHI	105	3	5	1229¹	1279	9.4	29	507	342	13.4	3.73	91	.259	.333	-53	-46	102	94	.925	443	108	-1.3	-4.1	-4.1		9.0
CLE	118	1	3	1244	1371	9.9	24	466	400	13.6	3.50	99	.270	.336	-22	-7	103	105	.920	485	86	-3.5	-.6	-2.3		1.9
BRO	121	8	3	1204²	1272	9.5	40	459	407	13.4	3.86	86	.261	.332	-68	-75	99	93	.924	432	73	-.8	-6.7	1.9		-1.9
CIN	125	6	1	1218²	1234	9.1	40	465	393	13.0	3.55	95	.253	.326	-28	-25	101	96	.931	409	101	.9	-2.2	-4.8		-6.4
PIT	122	7	2	1197²	1160	8.7	31	465	446	12.7	2.89	114	.245	.320	61	51	98	109	.917	475	76	-3.6	4.6	-5.0		-8.4
TOT	948	51	26	9760²		9.1				12.9	3.34		.252	.325					.928	3383	763					

Runs		Hits		Doubles		Triples		Home Runs		Total Bases	
Hamilton-Phi	141	Hamilton-Phi	179	Griffin-Bro	36	Stovey-Bos	20	Tiernan-NY	16	Stovey-Bos	271
Long-Bos	129	McKean-Cle	170	Davis-Cle	35	Beckley-Pit	19	Stovey-Bos	16	Tiernan-NY	268
Childs-Cle	120	Tiernan-NY	166	Stovey-Bos	31	McPhee-Cin	16	Wilmot-Chi	11	Long-Bos	235
Latham-Cin	119	Davis-Cle	165	Tiernan-NY	30	Ryan-Chi	15			Davis-Cle	233
Stovey-Bos	118	O'Rourke-NY	164			Virtue-Cle	14			Beckley-Pit	232

Runs Batted In		Runs Produced		Bases On Balls		Batting Average		On Base Percentage		Slugging Average	
Anson-Chi	120	Davis-Cle	201	Hamilton-Phi	102	Hamilton-Phi	.340	Hamilton-Phi	.453	Stovey-Bos	.498
Stovey-Bos	95	Childs-Cle	201	Childs-Cle	97	Holliday-Cin	.319	Connor-NY	.399	Tiernan-NY	.494
O'Rourke-NY	95	Hamilton-Phi	199	Connor-NY	83	Browning-Pit-Cin	.317	Childs-Cle	.395	Holliday-Cin	.473
Nash-Bos	95	Connor-NY	199	Long-Bos	80	Clements-Phi	.310	Browning-Pit-Cin	.395	Connor-NY	.449
Connor-NY	94	Stovey-Bos	197			Tiernan-NY	.306	Tiernan-NY	.388	Ryan-Chi	.434

Production		Adjusted Production		Batter Runs		Adjusted Batter Runs		Clutch Hitting Index		Runs Created	
Tiernan-NY	.882	Tiernan-NY	163	Hamilton-Phi	44.1	Tiernan-NY	43.0	Anson-Chi	130	Hamilton-Phi	155
Hamilton-Phi	.874	Connor-NY	153	Tiernan-NY	37.8	Hamilton-Phi	40.8	Delahanty-Phi	126	Tiernan-NY	128
Stovey-Bos	.871	Hamilton-Phi	151	Stovey-Bos	35.2	Connor-NY	35.3	Brodie-Bos	119	Stovey-Bos	125
Holliday-Cin	.848	Holliday-Cin	145	Connor-NY	30.7	Holliday-Cin	23.7	Zimmer-Cle	119	Long-Bos	114
Connor-NY	.848	Browning-Pit-Cin	139	Holliday-Cin	24.4	Browning-Pit-Cin	22.0	Allen-Phi	119	Latham-Cin	112

Total Average		Stolen Bases		Stolen Base Average	Stolen Base Runs	Fielding Runs		Total Player Rating	
Hamilton-Phi	1.270	Hamilton-Phi	111			Richardson-NY	49.1	Richardson-NY	4.5
Tiernan-NY	1.045	Latham-Cin	87			Griffin-Bro	25.7	Latham-Cin	3.7
Stovey-Bos	1.043	Griffin-Bro	65			Pfeffer-Chi	25.0	Hamilton-Phi	3.7
Latham-Cin	.974	Long-Bos	60			McPhee-Cin	23.3	Pfeffer-Chi	3.2
Connor-NY	.968					Latham-Cin	20.4	McPhee-Cin	3.1

Wins		Win Percentage		Games		Complete Games		Shutouts		Saves	
Hutchison-Chi	44	J.Ewing-NY	.724	Hutchison-Chi	66	Hutchison-Chi	56	Rusie-NY	6	Nichols-Bos	3
Rusie-NY	33	Hutchison-Chi	.698	Rusie-NY	61	Rusie-NY	52	Nichols-Bos	5	Clarkson-Bos	3
Clarkson-Bos	33	Staley-Pit-Bos	.649	Young-Cle	55	Baldwin-Pit	48	J.Ewing-NY	4	Young-Cle	2
Nichols-Bos	30	Nichols-Bos	.638	Clarkson-Bos	55	Clarkson-Bos	47	Hutchison-Chi	4	Thornton-Phi	2
Young-Cle	27	Clarkson-Bos	.635			Nichols-Bos	45				

Innings Pitched		Fewest Hits/Game		Fewest BB/Game		Strikeouts		Strikeouts/Game		Ratio	
Hutchison-Chi	561.0	Rusie-NY	7.03	Nichols-Bos	2.18	Rusie-NY	337	Rusie-NY	6.06	Staley-Pit-Bos	11.08
Rusie-NY	500.1	Baldwin-Pit	7.92	Staley-Pit-Bos	2.22	Hutchison-Chi	261	Nichols-Bos	5.08	Hutchison-Chi	11.12
Clarkson-Bos	460.2	J.Ewing-NY	7.92	Galvin-Pit	2.26	Nichols-Bos	240	J.Ewing-NY	4.61	Nichols-Bos	11.28
Baldwin-Pit	437.2	Hutchison-Chi	8.15	Radbourn-Cin	2.56	Baldwin-Pit	197	Hutchison-Chi	4.19	J.Ewing-NY	11.80
Mullane-Cin	426.1	Mullane-Cin	8.23	Hutchison-Chi	2.86	King-Pit	160	Baldwin-Pit	4.05	Clarkson-Bos	11.80

Earned Run Average		Adjusted ERA		Opponents' Batting Avg.		Opponents' On Base Pct.		Starter Runs		Adjusted Starter Runs	
J.Ewing-NY	2.27	Nichols-Bos	153	Rusie-NY	.207	Staley-Pit-Bos	.292	Nichols-Bos	45.1	Nichols-Bos	59.6
Nichols-Bos	2.39	J.Ewing-NY	141	Baldwin-Pit	.228	Hutchison-Chi	.293	Rusie-NY	43.9	Clarkson-Bos	43.9
Rusie-NY	2.55	Staley-Pit-Bos	138	J.Ewing-NY	.228	Nichols-Bos	.296	Hutchison-Chi	33.5	Rusie-NY	35.7
Staley-Pit-Bos	2.58	Clarkson-Bos	131	Hutchison-Chi	.233	J.Ewing-NY	.305	J.Ewing-NY	32.1	Staley-Pit-Bos	35.5
Baldwin-Pit	2.76	Rusie-NY	125	Mullane-Cin	.234	Clarkson-Bos	.305	Baldwin-Pit	28.6	Hutchison-Chi	32.4

Clutch Pitching Index		Relief Runs	Adjusted Relief Runs	Relief Ranking	Total Pitcher Index		Total Baseball Ranking	
Viau-Cle	117				Nichols-Bos	5.8	Nichols-Bos	5.8
Nichols-Bos	116				Clarkson-Bos	4.8	Clarkson-Bos	4.7
Caruthers-Bro	116				Rusie-NY	3.7	Richardson-NY	4.5
Galvin-Pit	112				Staley-Pit-Bos	3.1	Latham-Cin	3.7
J.Ewing-NY	111				Hutchison-Chi	2.7	Hamilton-Phi	3.7

February 17 The AA meets and indignantly unseats President Thurman, then withdraws from the National Agreement. This means "war," and the AA's first move is to switch its franchise from Chicago to Cincinnati to compete with the NL in the Queen City.

August 17 The AA franchise in Cincinnati folds. Milwaukee of the Western Association is elected to take its place, a move that dooms that minor league. The Brewers sign four of the Kellys and several players from other WA clubs. "The King of Ballplayers," Mike Kelly, joins the Boston Reds and is appointed captain.

October 2 In the first-ever major league game in Minnesota, the Milwaukee Brewers beat the Columbus Buckeyes 5–0 in Minneapolis's Athletic Park.

October 4 Browns rookie Ted Breitenstein gets his first start on the final day of the season and hurls a no-hitter versus Louisville. He wins 8–0 while walking one and facing the minimum 27 batters.

December 17 Four AA clubs (St. Louis, Louisville, Washington, and Baltimore) join with the NL eight in a 12-club league formally styled "The National League and American Association of Professional Base Ball Clubs." The other four AA clubs are bought out for about $130,000.

	BALTIMORE		BOSTON		CINCINNATI		COLUMBUS		LOUISVILLE
M	B.Barnie	M	A.Irwin	M	K.Kelly	M	G.Schmelz	M	J.Chapman
1B	P.Werden	1B	D.Brouthers	1B	J.Carney	1B	M.Lehane	1B	H.Taylor
2B	S.Wise	2B	C.Stricker	2B	Y.Robinson	2B	J.Crooks	2B	T.Shinnick
SS	G.Van Haltren	SS	P.Radford	SS	J.Canavan	SS	B.Wheelock	SS	H.Jennings
3B	P.Gilbert	3B	D.Farrell	3B	A.Whitney	3B	B.Kuehne	3B	O.Beard
LF	B.Johnson	LF	H.Richardson	LF	E.Andrews	LF	C.Duffee	LF	P.Donovan
CF	C.Welch	CF	T.Brown	CF	D.Johnston	CF	J.McTamany	CF	F.Weaver
RF	I.Ray	RF	H.Duffy	RF	E.Seery	RF	J.Sneed	RF	J.Wolf
C	W.Robinson	C	M.Murphy	C	K.Kelly	C	J.Donahue	C	J.Ryan
C	G.Townsend	3	B.Joyce	C	F.Vaughn	OC	J.O'Connor	CS	T.Cahill
S	J.McGraw	O	J.McGeachy	O	J.Hurley	O	L.Twitchell	3	B.Kuehne
S2	J.Walsh	O	J.Irwin	O	L.Marr	C	T.Dowse	C1	P.Cook
O	L.Hardie	/S	H.Irwin	/2	B.Clingman	3	T.O'Rourke	O	M.Cline
/S	J.O'Connell	/C	K.Kelly	/2	C.Bastian	3	J.Donnelly	S	H.Raymond
		/C	T.Cotter	/2	J.Burke	3	E.Cleveland	3	J.Irwin
P	S.McMahon	/O	T.Dowd					2	S.LaRoque
P	B.Cunningham	/C	T.Donahue	P	F.Dwyer	P	P.Knell	/O	J.Long
P	K.Madden	/C	F.Quinlan	P	E.Crane	P	H.Gastright	/C	A.Schellhase
P	J.Healy	/C	M.Flynn	P	W.Mains	P	J.Dolan	/3	P.Fox
				P	W.McGill	P	J.Easton	/2	J.Gerhardt
/P	J.Bakely	P	G.Haddock					/2	P.Pettee
		P	C.Buffinton	/P	M.Kilroy	/P	J.Leiper	/C	G.Briggs
		P	D.O'Brien	/P	C.Bell	/P	D.Clarke	/2	J.Wentz
		P	B.Daley	/P	K.Keenan	/P	J.Sullivan	/1	J.Darragh
				/P	W.Widner	/P	B.Lyston	/3	N.Reeder
		/P	C.Griffith	/P	J.Slagle	/P	E.Clark		
		/P	J.Fitzgerald					P	J.Fitzgerald
		/P	K.Madden					P	J.Meekin
								P	R.Ehret
								P	S.Stratton
								P	J.Doran
								P	E.Daily
								P	C.Bell
								/P	G.Boone

	MILWAUKEE		PHILADELPHIA		ST.LOUIS		WASHINGTON
M	C.Cushman	M	B.Sharsig	M	C.Comiskey	M	S.Trott
1B	J.Carney	M	G.Wood	1B	C.Comiskey	M	P.Snyder
2B	J.Canavan	1B	H.Larkin	2B	B.Eagan	M	D.Shannon
SS	G.Shoch	2B	B.Hallman	SS	S.Fuller	M	S.Griffin
3B	G.Alberts	SS	T.Corcoran	3B	D.Lyons	1B	M.McQuery
LF	A.Dalrymple	3B	J.Mulvey	LF	T.O'Neill	2B	T.Dowd
CF	E.Burke	LF	G.Wood	CF	D.Hoy	SS	G.Hatfield
RF	H.Earl	CF	P.Corkhill	RF	T.McCarthy	3B	B.Alvord
C	F.Vaughn	RF	L.Cross	C	J.Boyle	LF	E.Beecher
		C	J.Milligan			CF	P.Hines
C3	J.Grim			CO	J.Munyan	RF	L.Murphy
/2	B.Pettit	O	J.McTamany	C	D.Darling	C	D.McGuire
/O	T.Letcher	O	J.McGeachy	/O	J.Visner		
		OP	B.Sanders	/C	P.Cook	1	A.McCauley
P	G.Davies	O	E.Beecher	/3	J.Ricks	OC	S.Sutcliffe
P	F.Killen	C	D.McKeough	/2	P.McSweeney	C	P.Lohman
P	F.Dwyer	/S	B.Clymer	/2	M.McQuaid	O	E.Curtis
		/O	P.Friel	/3	A.Whitney	2	P.Smith
/P	J.Hughey	/O	B.Matthews	/2	Y.Robinson	O	J.Burns
/P	W.Mains			/C	B.Zies	O	E.Daily
		P	G.Weyhing	/3	H.Fuller	O	P.Donovan
		P	E.Chamberlain	/C	J.Schultz	O	S.Griffin
		P	W.Calihan			O	J.Visner
				P	J.Stivetts	S	D.Shannon
		/P	S.Bowman	P	W.McGill	O	M.Slattery
		/P	G.Meakim	P	C.Griffith	3	J.Davis
		/P	M.Sullivan	P	J.Neale	S	T.McLaughlin
				P	G.Rettger	/3	W.Smalley
						/1	P.Snyder
				/P	J.Easton	/2	F.Dunlap
				/P	H.Burrell	/C	T.Hart
				/P	T.Breitenstein	/C	M.Murray
				/P	J.Duryea		
						P	K.Carsey
						P	F.Foreman
						P	J.Bakely
						/P	E.Eiteljorge
						/P	E.Cassian
						/P	B.Freeman
						/P	B.Miller
						/P	G.Keefe
						/P	M.Duke
						/P	B.Quarles
						/P	J.Mace

TEAM	G	W	L	PCT	GB	R	OR	AB	H	2B	3B	HR	BB	SO	AVG	OBP	SLG	PRO	PRO+	BR	/A	PF	CHI	RC	SB	CS	SBA	SBR
BOS	139	93	42	.689		1028	675	4889	1341	163	100	52	651	499	.274	.367	.380	.747	121	127	142	99	106	868	447			
STL	141	86	52	.623	8.5	976	753	5005	1330	169	51	58	625	440	.266	.357	.355	.712	95	65	-72	115	106	753	283			
MIL	36	21	15	.583	22.5	227	156	1271	332	58	15	13	107	114	.261	.333	.345	.694	86	3	-40	120	106	173	47			
BAL	139	71	64	.526	22	850	798	4771	1217	142	99	30	551	553	.255	.346	.345	.691	102	22	13	101	101	705	342			
PHI	143	73	66	.525	22	817	794	5039	1301	182	123	55	447	548	.258	.328	.376	.704	103	23	-3	103	95	686	149			
COL	138	61	76	.445	33	702	777	4697	1113	154	61	20	529	530	.237	.319	.308	.627	89	-93	-54	94	101	565	280			
CIN	102	43	57	.430	32.5	549	643	3574	838	105	58	28	428	385	.234	.322	.320	.642	81	-52	-101	109	99	432	164			
LOU	141	55	84	.396	40	713	890	4833	1247	130	69	17	443	473	.258	.329	.324	.653	93	-52	-42	99	95	606	230			
WAS	139	44	91	.326	49	691	1067	4715	1183	147	84	19	468	485	.251	.328	.330	.658	97	-43	-9	96	93	597	219			
TOT	559					6553		38794	9902	1250	660	292	4249	4027	.255	.338	.344	.682							2161			

TEAM	CG	SH	SV	IP	H	H/G	HR	BB	SO	RAT	ERA	ERA+	OAV	OOB	PR	/A	PF	CPI	FA	E	DP	FW	PW	BW	SBW	DIF
BOS	108	9	7	1219²	1158	8.5	42	497	524	12.6	3.03	115	.242	.321	94	62	94	109	.934	392	115	4.0	5.3	12.2		4.0
STL	103	8	5	1222²	1106	8.1	50	576	621	12.9	3.27	129	.234	.325	61	126	113	102	.920	468	91	-.2	10.9	-6.2		12.5
MIL	35	3	0	309²	291	8.5	6	120	137	12.2	2.50	176	.241	.314	42	65	118	122	.922	116	20	.2	5.6	-3.4		.7
BAL	118	6	2	1217	1238	9.2	33	472	408	13.1	3.43	109	.255	.329	39	40	100	103	.915	503	103	-2.6	3.4	1.1		1.6
PHI	135	3	0	1233²	1274	9.3	35	520	533	13.6	4.01	95	.258	.338	-40	-27	103	93	.933	389	109	4.9	-2.3	-.3		1.2
COL	118	6	0	1213¹	1141	8.5	29	588	502	13.5	3.75	92	.241	.336	-4	-39	93	93	.935	379	126	4.5	-3.4	-4.7		-4.0
CIN	86	2	1	902	921	9.2	20	446	331	14.2	3.43	120	.256	.347	29	68	111	112	.913	389	68	-3.1	5.9	-8.7		-1.1
LOU	128	9	1	1226	1353	9.9	33	464	485	13.8	4.27	83	.271	.341	-75	-85	98	92	.922	458	113	.4	-7.3	-3.6		-4.0
WAS	123	2	2	1181	1420	10.8	44	566	486	15.9	4.83	77	.288	.374	-146	-144	101	101	.900	589	95	-7.7	-12.4	-.8		-2.6
TOT	954	48	18	9725		9.2				13.6	3.72		.255	.338					.922	3683	840					

Runs		Hits		Doubles		Triples		Home Runs		Total Bases	
Brown-Bos	177	Brown-Bos	189	Milligan-Phi	35	Brouthers-Bos	21	Farrell-Bos	12	Brown-Bos	276
VanHaltren-Bal	136	VanHaltren-Bal	180	Brown-Bos	30	Brouthers-Bos	19	Milligan-Phi	11	VanHaltren-Bal	251
Hoy-StL	136	Duffy-Bos	180	O'Neill-StL	28	Canavan-Cin-Mil	18	Lyons-StL	11	Brouthers-Bos	249
Duffy-Bos	134	McCarthy-StL	179	Duffee-Col	28	Werden-Bal	18			Duffy-Bos	243
McCarthy-StL	127	Brouthers-Bos	170	Larkin-Phi	27					McCarthy-StL	236

Runs Batted In		Runs Produced		Bases On Balls		Batting Average		On Base Percentage		Slugging Average	
Farrell-Bos	110	Brown-Bos	244	Hoy-StL	119	Brouthers-Bos	.350	Brouthers-Bos	.471	Brouthers-Bos	.512
Duffy-Bos	110	Duffy-Bos	235	Crooks-Col	103	Duffy-Bos	.336	Lyons-StL	.445	Milligan-Phi	.505
Brouthers-Bos	109	Brouthers-Bos	221	McTamany-Col-Phi	101	Brown-Bos	.321	Hoy-StL	.424	Farrell-Bos	.474
Milligan-Phi	106	McCarthy-StL	214	Radford-Bos	96	O'Neill-StL	.321	Seery-Cin	.423	Brown-Bos	.469
Werden-Bal	104	VanHaltren-Bal	210	Johnson-Bal	89	VanHaltren-Bal	.318	Duffy-Bos	.408	Cross-Phi	.458

Production		Adjusted Production		Batter Runs		Adjusted Batter Runs		Clutch Hitting Index		Runs Created	
Brouthers-Bos	.983	Brouthers-Bos	184	Brouthers-Bos	57.0	Brouthers-Bos	59.2	Sneed-Col	132	Brown-Bos	155
Milligan-Phi	.903	Milligan-Phi	153	Lyons-StL	39.2	Brown-Bos	37.2	Comiskey-StL	128	Duffy-Bos	137
Lyons-StL	.900	Brown-Bos	150	Brown-Bos	35.2	Duffy-Bos	34.0	Duffy-Bos	128	Brouthers-Bos	135
Brown-Bos	.865	Duffy-Bos	149	Milligan-Phi	33.3	Milligan-Phi	30.0	Ray-Bal	128	VanHaltren-Bal	133
Duffy-Bos	.861	Farrell-Bos	147	Duffy-Bos	32.1	Joyce-Bos	28.9	Radford-Bos	127	Hoy-StL	114

Total Average		Stolen Bases		Stolen Base Average		Stolen Base Runs		Fielding Runs		Total Player Rating	
Brouthers-Bos	1.237	Brown-Bos	106					Stricker-Bos	24.2	Farrell-Bos	4.4
Brown-Bos	1.140	Duffy-Bos	85					Radford-Bos	19.9	Brouthers-Bos	3.8
Duffy-Bos	1.104	VanHaltren-Bal	75					Crooks-Col	19.6	Crooks-Col	3.3
VanHaltren-Bal	1.039	Hoy-StL	59					Eagan-StL	19.5	Milligan-Phi	3.1
Lyons-StL	1.036	Radford-Bos	55					Farrell-Bos	19.0	Radford-Bos	2.9

Wins		Win Percentage		Games		Complete Games		Shutouts		Saves	
McMahon-Bal	35	Buffinton-Bos	.763	Stivetts-StL	64	McMahon-Bal	53	McMahon-Bal	5	O'Brien-Bos	2
Haddock-Bos	34	Haddock-Bos	.756	McMahon-Bal	61	Weyhing-Phi	51	Knell-Col	5	Daley-Bos	2
Stivetts-StL	33	Weyhing-Phi	.608	Knell-Col	58	Knell-Col	47	Haddock-Bos	5		
Weyhing-Phi	31	Stivetts-StL	.600	Carsey-Was	54	Carsey-Was	46				
Buffinton-Bos	29	McMahon-Bal	.593	Weyhing-Phi	52	Chamberlain-Phi	44				

Innings Pitched		Fewest Hits/Game		Fewest BB/Game		Strikeouts		Strikeouts/Game		Ratio	
McMahon-Bal	503.0	Knell-Col	7.07	Stratton-Lou	1.78	Stivetts-StL	259	Meekin-Lou	5.68	Buffinton-Bos	10.64
Knell-Col	462.0	Stivetts-StL	7.30	Sanders-Phi	2.30	Knell-Col	228	Stivetts-StL	5.30	Haddock-Bos	11.40
Weyhing-Phi	450.0	Buffinton-Bos	7.50	McMahon-Bal	2.67	Weyhing-Phi	219	McGill-Cin-StL	4.96	McMahon-Bal	11.79
Stivetts-StL	440.0	Crane-Cin	7.78	Ehret-Lou	2.85	McMahon-Bal	219	Daley-Bos	4.83	Weyhing-Phi	12.40
Carsey-Was	415.0	Haddock-Bos	7.82	Griffith-StL-Bos	2.90	Chamberlain-Phi	204	Chamberlain-Phi	4.53	Stivetts-StL	12.42

Earned Run Average		Adjusted ERA		Opponents' Batting Avg.		Opponents' On Base Pct.		Starter Runs		Adjusted Starter Runs	
Crane-Cin	2.45	Crane-Cin	168	Knell-Col	.209	Buffinton-Bos	.285	Haddock-Bos	51.9	Stivetts-StL	65.5
Haddock-Bos	2.49	Stivetts-StL	147	Stivetts-StL	.215	Haddock-Bos	.299	McMahon-Bal	50.9	McMahon-Bal	51.7
Buffinton-Bos	2.55	Haddock-Bos	140	Buffinton-Bos	.219	McMahon-Bal	.306	Buffinton-Bos	47.3	Crane-Cin	46.3
McMahon-Bal	2.81	Buffinton-Bos	137	Crane-Cin	.225	Weyhing-Phi	.317	Stivetts-StL	41.8	Haddock-Bos	42.0
Stivetts-StL	2.86	Mains-Cin-Mil	134	Haddock-Bos	.226	Stivetts-StL	.317	Knell-Col	40.9	Buffinton-Bos	37.8

Clutch Pitching Index		Relief Runs		Adjusted Relief Runs		Relief Ranking		Total Pitcher Index		Total Baseball Ranking	
Daley-Bos	134							Stivetts-StL	7.7	Stivetts-StL	7.5
Crane-Cin	128							Haddock-Bos	5.3	Haddock-Bos	5.0
O'Brien-Bos	123							McMahon-Bal	5.0	McMahon-Bal	4.9
Mains-Cin-Mil	122							Buffinton-Bos	3.6	Farrell-Bos	4.4
Foreman-Was	113							Crane-Cin	3.5	Brouthers-Bos	3.8

January 9 "Slide, Kelly, Slide," by George Gaskin, makes the pop music charts, the first baseball song to do so.

March 1 The first meeting of the united NL and AA takes place in New York. Only four teams from the collapsed American Association are invited to join the NL, which will expand to 12 teams with a 154-game schedule split into two championship series.

April 17 The first Sunday game in NL history features the hometown Cincinnati Reds defeating the St. Louis Browns 5-1. Bid McPhee contributes a home run.

April 30 Dr. S. B. Talcott, superintendent of the State Lunatic Asylum in New York, declares in the New York *Clipper* that "I believe that baseball is a homeopathic cure for lunacy. It is a kind of craze in itself, and gives the lunatics a new kind of crazing to relieve them of the malady which afflicts their minds."

June 6 President Benjamin Harrison watches Washington go down to a 7-4 defeat to Cincinnati in 11 innings. It marks the first visit to a major league game by a U.S. president.

June 10 Wilbert Robinson, Orioles catcher, goes 7-for-7 and bats in 11 runs, as Baltimore defeats the St. Louis Browns 25-7.

June 30 Tony Mullane of Cincinnati and Ad Gumbert of Chicago pitch 20 innings in a 7–7 standoff. It is the longest major league game played in the nineteenth century.

July 11 Boston, having clinched the first-half championship, plays an unusual game at Chicago with team members, led by King Kelly, dressed in outlandish costumes and wearing beards.

August 18 In the course of a 13-4 win over Baltimore, Browns left fielder Cliff Carroll attempts to field a ground ball, but he misjudges it, and the ball becomes lodged in his shirt pocket. Before he can extricate it the Oriole batter makes it to third base. St. Louis owner Chris Von der Ahe is so outraged that he fines Carroll $50 and suspends him without pay for the rest of the season. Carroll appeals the fine and the suspension at the end of the season but is turned down.

October 15 Charles "Bumpus" Jones of Cincinnati, making his major league debut, pitches a no-hit game over Pittsburgh, winning 7–1. Jones, who won 16 games in a row in the minors, will have a tough time the following season when the pitching distance is increased. He will go 1-4 with a 10.93 ERA and never pitch in the majors again.

October 17 To settle the championship of baseball's first split season, Boston, the first-half winner, starts a five-game series with Cleveland, the second-half champ. Jack Stivetts and Cy Young battle to an 11-inning scoreless tie.

November 17 NL magnates conclude a four-day meeting in Chicago where they agree to shorten the 1893 schedule to 132 games and drop the double championship concept.

BALTIMORE		BOSTON		BROOKLYN		CHICAGO		CINCINNATI		CLEVELAND	
M	G.Van Haltren	M	F.Selee	M	M.Ward	M	C.Anson	M	C.Comiskey	M	P.Tebeau
M	J.Waltz	1B	T.Tucker	1B	D.Brouthers	1B	C.Anson	1B	C.Comiskey	1B	J.Virtue
M	N.Hanlon	2B	J.Quinn	2B	J.Ward	2B	J.Canavan	2B	B.McPhee	2B	C.Childs
1B	S.Sutcliffe	SS	H.Long	SS	T.Corcoran	SS	B.Dahlen	SS	G.Smith	SS	E.McKean
2B	C.Stricker	3B	B.Nash	3B	B.Joyce	3B	J.Parrott	3B	A.Latham	3B	G.Davis
SS	T.O'Rourke	LF	B.Lowe	LF	D.O'Brien	LF	W.Wilmot	LF	T.O'Neill	LF	J.Burkett
3B	B.Shindle	CF	H.Duffy	CF	M.Griffin	CF	J.Ryan	CF	P.Browning	CF	J.McAleer
LF	H.Stovey	RF	T.McCarthy	RF	O.Burns	RF	S.Dungan	RF	B.Holliday	RF	J.O'Connor
CF	C.Welch	C	K.Kelly	C	C.Daily	C	P.Schriver	C	M.Murphy	C	C.Zimmer
RF	G.Van Haltren										
C	W.Robinson	C	C.Ganzel	3O	T.Daly	O2	G.Decker	C1	F.Vaughn	3	P.Tebeau
		O	H.Stovey	C	T.Kinslow	S	J.Cooney	SO	F.Genins	O	J.Doyle
CO	J.Gunson	C	C.Bennett	OP	D.Foutz	C	M.Kittridge	O	G.Wood		
SO	G.Shoch			O	H.Collins	O	C.Newman	O	J.Halligan	P	C.Young
O2	J.McGraw	P	K.Nichols					O	C.Welch	P	N.Cuppy
1	L.Whistler	P	J.Stivetts	P	G.Haddock	P	B.Hutchison	C	J.Harrington	P	J.Clarkson
O	P.Ward	P	H.Staley	P	E.Stein	P	A.Gumbert			P	G.Davies
O1	J.Halligan	P	J.Clarkson	P	B.Hart	P	P.Luby	P	E.Chamberlain		
2	J.Pickett			P	B.Kennedy			P	T.Mullane	/P	G.Rettger
O	G.Wood					/P	H.DeMiller	P	F.Dwyer		
				/P	B.Inks			P	M.Sullivan		
P	S.McMahon										
P	G.Cobb							P	B.Rhines		
P	T.Vickery							/P	J.Duryea		
P	C.Buffinton							/P	D.Daub		
								/P	W.McGill		
/P	J.Healy										
/P	C.Schmit										
/P	B.Stephens										

LOUISVILLE		NEW YORK		PHILADELPHIA		PITTSBURGH		ST.LOUIS		WASHINGTON	
M	J.Chapman	M	P.Powers	M	H.Wright	M	A.Buckenberger	M	J.Glasscock	M	B.Barnie
M	F.Pfeffer	1B	B.Ewing	1B	R.Connor	M	T.Burns	M	C.Stricker	M	A.Irwin
1B	L.Whistler	2B	E.Burke	2B	B.Hallman	M	A.Buckenberger	M	J.Crooks	M	D.Richardson
2B	F.Pfeffer	SS	S.Fuller	SS	B.Allen	1B	J.Beckley	M	G.Gore	1B	H.Larkin
SS	H.Jennings	3B	D.Lyons	3B	C.Reilly	2B	L.Bierbauer	B	B.Caruthers	2B	T.Dowd
3B	B.Kuehne	LF	J.O'Rourke	LF	B.Hamilton	SS	F.Shugart	1B	P.Werden	SS	D.Richardson
LF	F.Weaver	CF	H.Lyons	CF	E.Delahanty	3B	D.Farrell	2B	J.Crooks	3B	Y.Robinson
CF	T.Brown	RF	M.Tiernan	RF	S.Thompson	LF	E.Smith	SS	J.Glasscock	LF	C.Duffee
RF	H.Taylor	C	J.Boyle	C	J.Clements	CF	D.Miller	3B	G.Pinkney	CF	D.Hoy
C	J.Grim					RF	P.Donovan	LF	C.Carroll	RF	P.Radford
		2C	J.Doyle	3C	L.Cross	C	C.Mack	CF	S.Brodie	C	D.McGuire
3	C.Bassett	2O	H.Richardson	3	J.Mulvey			RF	B.Caruthers		
C	B.Merritt	O	G.Gore			O	P.Corkhill	C	D.Buckley	C1	J.Milligan
O	E.Seery	1	J.McMahon	P	G.Weyhing	O	J.Kelley			O	L.Twitchell
C1	T.Dowse	2	C.Bassett	P	K.Carsey			O	G.Moriarity	O	P.Donovan
O	P.Browning	OC	J.Fields	P	T.Keefe	P	M.Baldwin	3	L.Camp	S	T.Berger
				P	D.Esper	P	R.Ehret	2	C.Stricker		
P	S.Stratton	P	A.Rusie			P	A.Terry	C	B.Moran	P	F.Killen
P	B.Sanders	P	S.King	P	P.Knell	P	P.Galvin	O	G.Gore	P	B.Abbey
P	F.Clausen	P	E.Crane	/P	J.Taylor					P	P.Knell
P	J.Meekin					/P	B.Gumbert	P	K.Gleason	P	J.Duryea
P	A.Jones					/P	F.Woodcock	P	T.Breitenstein	P	J.Meekin
						/P	K.Camp	P	P.Hawley		
P	L.Viau					/P	D.Esper	P	C.Getzien	P	H.Gastright
/P	G.Hemming							P	B.Hawke	P	F.Foreman
/P	J.Fitzgerald									/P	J.Dolan
/P	J.Healy							P	P.Galvin	/P	A.Jones
								P	F.Dwyer	/P	M.Kilroy
								/P	J.Easton	/P	B.Inks

TEAM	G	W	L	PCT	GB	R	OR	AB	H	2B	3B	HR	BB	SO	AVG	OBP	SLG	PRO	PRO+	BR	/A	PF	CHI	RC	SB	CS	SBA	SBR
BOS	152	102	48	.680	—	862	649	5301	1324	203	51	34	526	492	.250	.325	.327	.652	93	18	-55	109	108	689	338			
CLE	153	93	56	.624	8.5	855	613	5412	1375	196	96	26	552	536	.254	.328	.340	.668	103	48	14	104	101	694	225			
BRO	158	95	59	.617	9	935	733	5485	1439	183	105	30	629	506	.262	.344	.350	.694	120	109	144	96	101	822	409			
PHI	155	87	66	.569	16.5	860	690	5413	1420	225	95	50	528	515	.262	.334	.367	.701	118	107	110	100	95	753	216			
CIN	155	82	68	.547	20	766	731	5349	1288	155	75	44	503	474	.241	.311	.322	.633	98	-23	-12	99	101	635	270			
PIT	155	80	73	.523	23.5	802	796	5469	1288	143	108	38	435	453	.236	.297	.322	.619	92	-59	-62	100	110	604	222			
CHI	147	70	76	.479	30	635	735	5063	1188	149	92	26	427	482	.235	.299	.316	.615	90	-60	-67	101	94	561	233			
NY	153	71	80	.470	31.5	811	826	5291	1326	173	85	39	510	494	.251	.320	.338	.658	106	25	38	98	101	686	301			
LOU	154	63	89	.414	40	649	804	5334	1208	133	61	18	433	508	.226	.290	.284	.574	85	-135	-85	92	102	533	275			
WAS	153	58	93	.384	44.5	731	869	5204	1245	149	78	37	529	553	.239	.314	.319	.633	100	-18	4	97	98	624	276			
STL	155	56	94	.373	46	703	922	5259	1187	138	53	45	607	491	.226	.312	.298	.610	95	-55	-19	95	96	568	209			
BAL	152	46	101	.313	54.5	779	1020	5296	1342	160	111	30	499	480	.253	.325	.343	.668	104	44	22	103	95	680	227			
TOT	921					9388		63876	15630	2007	1010	417	6178	5964	.245	.317	.327	.644						3201				

TEAM	CG	SH	SV	IP	H	H/G	HR	BB	SO	RAT	ERA	ERA+	OAV	OOB	PR	/A	PF	CPI	FA	E	DP	FW	PW	BW	SBW	DIF
BOS	142	15	1	1336	1156	7.8	41	460	514	11.1	2.86	123	.224	.292	64	96	107	93	.929	454	127	.5	8.9	-5.1		22.7
CLE	140	11	2	1336	1178	7.9	28	413	472	10.9	2.41	140	.228	.289	130	143	103	107	.935	407	95	3.4	13.2	1.3		.6
BRO	132	12	5	1405²	1285	8.2	26	600	597	12.4	3.25	97	.234	.315	6	-14	96	95	.940	398	98	4.8	-1.3	13.3		1.2
PHI	131	10	5	1379	1297	8.5	24	492	502	12.0	2.93	111	.239	.309	54	47	99	103	.939	393	128	4.5	4.4	10.2		-8.6
CIN	130	8	2	1377¹	1327	8.7	39	535	437	12.5	3.17	103	.243	.317	18	15	99	104	.939	402	140	4.0	1.4	-1.1		2.7
PIT	130	3	1	1347¹	1300	8.7	28	537	455	12.7	3.10	106	.244	.320	28	27	100	106	.927	483	113	-.7	2.5	-5.7		7.4
CHI	133	6	1	1298	1269	8.8	35	424	518	12.0	3.16	105	.246	.308	18	22	101	100	.932	424	117	1.3	2.0	-6.2		-.2
NY	139	5	1	1322²	1165	7.9	32	635	650	12.6	3.29	98	.227	.318	-1	-11	98	94	.912	565	97	-5.8	-1.0	3.5		-1.2
LOU	147	9	0	1346	1358	9.1	26	447	430	12.3	3.34	92	.252	.313	-8	-41	93	97	.928	471	133	-.2	-3.8	-7.9		-1.2
WAS	129	5	3	1315¹	1293	8.8	40	556	479	13.1	3.46	94	.247	.327	-26	-32	99	102	.916	547	122	-4.8	-3.0	.4		-10.1
STL	139	4	1	1344²	1466	9.8	47	543	478	13.8	4.20	76	.267	.339	-137	-151	97	96	.929	452	100	1.1	-14.0	-1.8		-4.4
BAL	131	2	2	1298²	1537	10.7	51	536	437	14.7	4.28	80	.284	.353	-144	-124	104	106	.910	584	100	-7.1	-11.5	2.0		-10.9
TOT	1623	90	24	16106²		8.7				12.5	3.28		.245	.317					.928	5580	1338					

Split Season: First-half Winner BOS (52-22); Second-half Winner CLE (53-23).

Runs
Childs-Cle	136
Hamilton-Phi	132
Duffy-Bos	125
Connor-Phi	123
Brouthers-Bro	121

Hits
Brouthers-Bro	197
Thompson-Phi	186
Duffy-Bos	184
Hamilton-Phi	183
Long-Bos	181

Doubles
Connor-Phi	37
Long-Bos	33
Delahanty-Phi	30
Brouthers-Bro	30
Zimmer-Cle	29

Triples
Delahanty-Phi	21
Virtue-Cle	20
Brouthers-Bro	20
Dahlen-Chi	19
Beckley-Pit	19

Home Runs
Holliday-Cin	13
Connor-Phi	12
Ryan-Chi	10
Beckley-Pit	10
Thompson-Phi	9

Total Bases
Brouthers-Bro	282
Holliday-Cin	270
Thompson-Phi	263
Connor-Phi	261
Duffy-Bos	251

Runs Batted In
Brouthers-Bro	124
Thompson-Phi	104
Larkin-Was	96
Burns-Bro	96
Beckley-Pit	96

Runs Produced
Brouthers-Bro	240
Thompson-Phi	204
Duffy-Bos	201
Holliday-Cin	192

Bases On Balls
Crooks-StL	136
Childs-Cle	117
Connor-Phi	116
McCarthy-Bos	93

Batting Average
Brouthers-Bro	.335
Hamilton-Phi	.330
Childs-Cle	.317
Burns-Bro	.315
Ewing-NY	.310

On Base Percentage
Childs-Cle	.443
Brouthers-Bro	.432
Hamilton-Phi	.423
Connor-Phi	.420
Crooks-StL	.400

Slugging Average
Delahanty-Phi	.495
Brouthers-Bro	.480
Ewing-NY	.473
Connor-Phi	.463
Burns-Bro	.454

Production
Brouthers-Bro	.911
Connor-Phi	.883
Delahanty-Phi	.855
Burns-Bro	.849
Childs-Cle	.841

Adjusted Production
Brouthers-Bro	182
Connor-Phi	167
Burns-Bro	163
Delahanty-Phi	158
Hamilton-Phi	153

Batter Runs
Brouthers-Bro	56.9
Connor-Phi	50.6
Childs-Cle	45.5
Hamilton-Phi	39.0
Burns-Bro	37.3

Adjusted Batter Runs
Brouthers-Bro	62.5
Connor-Phi	51.0
Burns-Bro	41.8
Childs-Cle	40.1
Hamilton-Phi	39.3

Clutch Hitting Index
McKean-Cle	165
Pfeffer-Lou	142
Nash-Bos	135
Larkin-Was	131
Brouthers-Bro	128

Runs Created
Brouthers-Bro	138
Hamilton-Phi	123
Connor-Phi	122
VanHaltren-Bal-Pit	117
Holliday-Cin	114

Total Average
Brouthers-Bro	1.056
Connor-Phi	1.018
Hamilton-Phi	1.005
Childs-Cle	.982
Burns-Bro	.943

Stolen Bases
Ward-Bro	88
Brown-Lou	78
Latham-Cin	66
Hoy-Was	60
Dahlen-Chi	60

Stolen Base Average

Stolen Base Runs

Fielding Runs
D.Richardson-Was	57.6
Shindle-Bal	35.5
Bierbauer-Pit	31.7
McPhee-Cin	25.3
Dahlen-Chi	25.2

Total Player Rating
Brouthers-Bro	6.1
Dahlen-Chi	4.6
McPhee-Cin	4.5
Hamilton-Phi	4.3
D.Richardson-Was	4.0

Wins
Young-Cle	36
Hutchison-Chi	36
Stivetts-Bos	35
Nichols-Bos	35

Win Percentage
Young-Cle	.750
Terry-Bal-Pit	.692
Haddock-Bro	.690
Staley-Bos	.688

Games
Hutchison-Chi	75
Rusie-NY	65
Killen-Was	60
Weyhing-Phi	59
Baldwin-Pit	56

Complete Games
Hutchison-Chi	67
Rusie-NY	59
Nichols-Bos	49
Young-Cle	48

Shutouts
Young-Cle	9
Weyhing-Phi	6
Stein-Bro	6

Saves
Weyhing-Phi	3
Duryea-Cin-Was	2

Innings Pitched
Hutchison-Chi	622.0
Rusie-NY	541.0
Weyhing-Phi	469.2
Killen-Was	459.2

Fewest Hits/Game
Mullane-Cin	6.77
Rusie-NY	6.82
Terry-Bal-Pit	6.94
Young-Cle	7.21
Duryea-Cin-Was	7.25

Fewest BB/Game
Stratton-Lou	1.79
Dwyer-StL-Cin	1.98
Sanders-Lou	2.08
Young-Cle	2.34
Ehret-Pit	2.36

Strikeouts
Hutchison-Chi	312
Rusie-NY	304
Weyhing-Phi	202
Nichols-Bos	192
Stein-Bro	190

Strikeouts/Game
Kennedy-Bro	5.09
Rusie-NY	5.06
Stein-Bro	4.53
Hutchison-Chi	4.51
Crane-NY	4.30

Ratio
Young-Cle	9.77
Nichols-Bos	10.63
Stratton-Lou	10.77
Keefe-Phi	10.83
Mullane-Cin	11.01

Earned Run Average
Young-Cle	1.93
Keefe-Phi	2.36
J.Clarkson-Bos-Cle	2.48
Cuppy-Cle	2.51
Terry-Bal-Pit	2.57

Adjusted ERA
Young-Cle	176
J.Clarkson-Bos-Cle	139
Keefe-Phi	138
Cuppy-Cle	135
Davies-Cle	131

Opponents' Batting Avg.
Mullane-Cin	.201
Rusie-NY	.202
Terry-Bal-Pit	.205
Young-Cle	.211
Duryea-Cin-Was	.212

Opponents' On Base Pct.
Young-Cle	.266
Nichols-Bos	.283
Stratton-Lou	.286
Keefe-Phi	.287
Mullane-Cin	.290

Starter Runs
Young-Cle	68.3
Hutchison-Chi	36.0
J.Clarkson-Bos-Cle	35.0
Weyhing-Phi	32.4
Keefe-Phi	32.3

Adjusted Starter Runs
Young-Cle	73.4
J.Clarkson-Bos-Cle	41.3
Hutchison-Chi	38.5
Cuppy-Cle	36.5
Nichols-Bos	33.6

Clutch Pitching Index
Sullivan-Cin	136
Galvin-Pit-StL	122
Vickery-Bal	116
McMahon-Bal	115
Luby-Chi	115

Relief Runs

Adjusted Relief Runs

Relief Ranking

Total Pitcher Index
Young-Cle	6.6
Hutchison-Chi	4.6
Cuppy-Cle	3.8
Stivetts-Bos	3.7
J.Clarkson-Bos-Cle	3.3

Total Baseball Ranking
Young-Cle	6.6
Brouthers-Bro	6.1
Dahlen-Chi	4.6
McPhee-Cin	4.5
Hutchison-Chi	4.5

January 14* The Cuban Giants, perhaps the nation's best black baseball team, announce their desire to join the proposed Middle States League. Their application is rejected.

February 4* The first recorded version of "Casey at the Bat," as recited by Russell Hunting, hits the charts. DeWolf Hopper's more famous version will not be released until October 1906.

March 7 In arguably the most significant rule change in major league history, the NL eliminates the pitching box and adds a pitcher's rubber five feet behind the previous back line of the box, establishing the modern pitching distance of 60 feet six inches. In addition, bats flattened on one side to facilitate bunting are banned.

May 19 Held scoreless for the first eight innings, both Brooklyn and the Boston Beaneaters score three runs in the ninth to send the game into extra innings. Boston's Billy Nash hits the ball over the left field fence in the bottom of the ninth, but he stays on third base "to bother the pitcher." The tactic works, as Nash does

score. Both teams score one run in the tenth—Boston scoring on another Nash blow over the left field fence, which he runs out this time. Boston finally claims the game after a 12-inning struggle 5–4.

June 14 George Davis becomes the first player in major league history to hit a home run and a triple in the same inning as his Giants overcome the Chicago Colts 11-10. Davis's feat will not be matched until 1926, when the Detroit Tigers' Bob Fothergill turns the trick.

July 7 Louisville officials, frustrated by their inability to sell alcohol or play Sunday baseball in their new ballpark—located in the suburb of Parkland, whose laws proscribe such activities—get permission from the Kentucky Legislature to annex the land on which the ballpark is located without the consent of Parkland residents. Alcohol sales and Sunday baseball commence almost immediately.

August 7 Facing a left-handed Brooklyn pitcher, New York first baseman Roger Connor bats righthanded for the first time in his career and slugs two homers and a single in a 10–3 win.

September 28 After moving into the lead with three runs in the top of the ninth, Philadelphia players allow themselves to be retired quickly in order to finish the game before it is called on account of darkness. However, Cleveland foils their plans by scoring four runs in the bottom of the ninth to win 11–10.

September 30 It's a good day for Joe Quinn. In pregame ceremonies, the Cardinals second baseman is honored by *The Sporting News* as the most popular baseball player in America, and receives a gold watch. He then collects eight hits in the doubleheader against Boston, the first player to accomplish that feat.

October 14 Baseball legend Harry Wright suggests that umpires keep the ball-strike count a secret until the at bat is concluded. He feels this rule change will increase offense.

November 21* Ban Johnson is named president, secretary, and treasurer of the recently reorganized Western League. Under Johnson's leadership the Western League will prosper.

	BALTIMORE		BOSTON		BROOKLYN		CHICAGO		CINCINNATI		CLEVELAND
M	N.Hanlon	M	F.Selee	M	D.Foutz	M	C.Anson	M	C.Comiskey	M	P.Tebeau
1B	H.Taylor	1B	T.Tucker	1B	D.Brouthers	1B	C.Anson	1B	C.Comiskey	1B	J.Virtue
2B	H.Reitz	2B	B.Lowe	2B	D.Richardson	2B	B.Lange	2B	B.McPhee	2B	C.Childs
SS	J.McGraw	SS	H.Long	SS	T.Corcoran	SS	B.Dahlen	SS	G.Smith	SS	E.McKean
3B	B.Shindle	3B	B.Nash	3B	T.Daly	3B	J.Parrott	3B	A.Latham	3B	C.McGarr
LF	J.Long	LF	T.McCarthy	LF	D.Foutz	LF	W.Wilmot	LF	J.Canavan	LF	J.Burkett
CF	J.Kelley	CF	H.Duffy	CF	M.Griffin	CF	J.Ryan	CF	B.Holliday	CF	J.McAleer
RF	G.Treadway	RF	C.Carroll	RF	O.Burns	RF	S.Dungan	RF	J.McCarthy	RF	B.Ewing
C	W.Robinson	C	C.Bennett	C	T.Kinslow	C	M.Kittridge	C	F.Vaughn	C	C.Zimmer
C1	B.Clarke	CO	C.Ganzel	O3	G.Shoch	O1	G.Decker	C	M.Murphy	CO	J.O'Connor
O	T.O'Rourke	C	B.Merritt	C	C.Daily	C	P.Schriver	1	F.Motz	13	P.Tebeau
1	J.Milligan			O	H.Stovey	3O	L.Camp	O	P.Ward	C	J.Gunson
O	S.Brodie	P	K.Nichols	3	G.Hatfield	S	C.Irwin	O	G.Henry		
O	B.Gilks	P	J.Stivetts	3	W.Keeler	2	B.Glenalvin			P	C.Young
		P	H.Staley							P	J.Clarkson
P	S.McMahon	P	H.Gastright	P	B.Kennedy	P	B.Hutchison	P	E.Chamberlain	P	N.Cuppy
P	T.Mullane			P	E.Stein	P	W.McGill	P	M.Sullivan	P	C.Hastings
P	B.Hawke	/P	B.Quarles	P	G.Haddock	P	H.Mauck	P	T.Parrott		
P	E.McNabb			P	D.Daub			P	T.Mullane	/P	T.Williams
P	K.Baker			P	T.Lovett	P	F.Clausen			/P	C.Fisher
						P	G.McGinnis	P	S.King	/P	J.Scheible
/P	C.Schmit			P	G.Sharrott	/P	B.Abbey	/P	G.Darby	/P	G.Davies
/P	J.Wadsworth					/P	F.Donnelly	/P	B.Jones		
						/P	T.Parrott	/P	L.Cross		
						/P	C.Griffith				
						/P	S.Shaw				

	LOUISVILLE		NEW YORK		PHILADELPHIA		PITTSBURGH		ST.LOUIS		WASHINGTON
M	B.Barnie	M	M.Ward	M	H.Wright	M	A.Buckenberger	M	B.Watkins	M	J.O'Rourke
1B	W.Brown	1B	R.Connor	1B	J.Boyle	1B	J.Beckley	1B	P.Werden	1B	H.Larkin
2B	F.Pfeffer	2B	J.Ward	2B	B.Hallman	2B	L.Bierbauer	2B	J.Quinn	2B	S.Wise
SS	T.O'Rourke	SS	S.Fuller	SS	B.Allen	SS	J.Glasscock	SS	J.Glasscock	SS	J.Sullivan
3B	G.Pinkney	3B	G.Davis	3B	C.Reilly	3B	D.Lyons	3B	J.Crooks	3B	J.Mulvey
LF	P.Browning	LF	E.Burke	LF	E.Delahanty	LF	E.Smith	LF	C.Frank	LF	J.O'Rourke
CF	T.Brown	CF	G.Stafford	CF	B.Hamilton	CF	G.Van Haltren	CF	S.Brodie	CF	D.Hoy
RF	F.Weaver	RF	M.Tiernan	RF	S.Thompson	RF	P.Donovan	RF	T.Dowd	RF	P.Radford
C	J.Grim	C	J.Doyle	C	J.Clements	C	D.Miller	C	H.Peitz	C	D.Farrell
O	L.Twitchell	O	H.Lyons	C3	L.Cross	OC	J.Stenzel	OS	F.Shugart	C1	D.McGuire
S	J.Denny	C	J.Milligan	O	T.Turner	S	F.Shugart	S	B.Ely	2O	C.Stricker
S	H.Jennings	C	P.Wilson	OP	J.Sharrott	C	C.Mack	C	J.Gunson	O	C.Abbey
		C	K.Kelly			C	B.Earle	O	J.Bannon		
P	G.Hemming			P	G.Weyhing	C	J.Sugden	OC	D.Cooley	P	D.Esper
P	S.Stratton	P	A.Rusie	P	K.Carsey			O	S.Griffin	P	A.Maul
P	B.Rhodes	P	M.Baldwin	P	T.Keefe	P	F.Killen			P	J.Meekin
P	J.Menefee	P	L.German	P	J.Taylor	P	R.Ehret	P	T.Breitenstein	P	J.Duryea
						P	A.Terry	P	K.Gleason		
/P	B.Whitrock	P	E.Crane	P	T.Vickery	P	A.Gumbert	P	P.Hawley	P	O.Stocksdale
/P	M.Kilroy	/P	C.Petty	/P	G.McGinnis			P	D.Clarkson	/P	B.Stephens
/P	F.Clausen	/P	S.King			/P	H.Gastright				
/P	B.Rhines	/P	G.Davies			/P	T.Colcolough	/P	J.Dolan		
		/P	C.Schmit								

TEAM	G	W	L	PCT	GB	R	OR	AB	H	2B	3B	HR	BB	SO	AVG	OBP	SLG	PRO	PRO+	BR	/A	PF	CHI	RC	SB	CS	SBA	SBR
BOS	131	86	43	.667		1008	795	4678	1358	178	50	65	561	292	.290	.372	.391	.763	99	54	-18	108	111	790	243			
PIT	131	81	48	.628	5	970	766	4834	1447	176	127	32	537	274	.299	.377	.411	.788	116	96	115	98	99	848	210			
CLE	129	73	55	.570	12.5	976	839	4747	1425	222	98	32	532	229	.300	.374	.408	.782	106	84	28	106	103	841	252			
PHI	133	72	57	.558	14	1011	841	5151	1553	246	90	80	468	335	.301	.368	.431	.799	117	108	111	100	98	912	202			
NY	136	68	64	.515	19.5	941	845	4858	1424	182	101	61	504	281	.293	.346	.410	.776	111	69	66	100	99	860	299			
CIN	131	65	63	.508	20.5	759	814	4617	1195	161	65	29	532	256	.259	.342	.341	.683	84	-88	-106	102	101	634	238			
BRO	130	65	63	.508	20.5	775	845	4511	1200	173	83	45	473	296	.266	.341	.371	.712	97	-46	-11	95	101	659	213			
BAL	130	60	70	.462	26.5	820	893	4651	1281	164	86	27	539	323	.275	.359	.365	.724	95	-12	-25	102	98	711	233			
CHI	128	56	71	.441	29	829	874	4664	1299	186	93	32	465	262	.279	.348	.379	.727	99	-20	-8	99	102	722	255			
STL	135	57	75	.432	30.5	745	829	4879	1288	152	98	10	524	251	.264	.343	.341	.684	86	-89	-91	100	94	674	250			
LOU	126	50	75	.400	34	759	942	4566	1185	177	73	19	485	306	.260	.338	.343	.681	92	-94	-37	92	104	612	203			
WAS	130	40	89	.310	46	722	1032	4742	1258	180	83	23	523	237	.265	.346	.353	.699	92	-62	-40	97	90	648	154			
TOT	785					10315		56898	15913	2197	1047	460	6143	3342	.280	.356	.379	.736							2752			

TEAM	CG	SH	SV	IP	H	H/G	HR	BB	SO	RAT	ERA	ERA+	OAV	OOB	PR	/A	PF	CPI	FA	E	DP	FW	PW	BW	SBW	DIF
BOS	114	2	2	1163²	1314	10.2	66	402	253	13.6	4.43	111	.277	.339	30	64	106	100	.936	353	118	1.8	5.2	-1.5		16.0
PIT	104	8	2	1167	1232	9.5	29	504	280	13.8	4.08	112	.263	.342	75	60	98	101	.938	347	112	2.1	4.9	9.4		.0
CLE	110	2	2	1140¹	1361	10.7	35	356	242	13.8	4.20	116	.288	.342	59	86	105	106	.929	395	92	-.9	7.1	2.3		.6
PHI	107	4	2	1189	1357	10.3	30	521	283	14.8	4.68	98	.279	.357	-2	-14	98	98	.944	318	121	4.1	-1.1	9.1		-4.5
NY	111	6	4	1211¹	1271	9.4	36	581	395	14.2	4.29	108	.262	.347	49	48	100	99	.927	432	95	-1.8	3.9	5.4		-5.5
CIN	97	4	5	1172	1305	10.0	38	549	258	14.8	4.55	105	.274	.357	15	30	103	101	.943	321	138	3.6	2.5	-8.7		3.7
BRO	109	3	3	1154	1262	9.8	41	547	297	14.4	4.55	97	.270	.352	15	-16	95	98	.930	385	88	-.2	-1.3	-.9		3.4
BAL	104	1	2	1123²	1325	10.6	29	534	275	15.2	4.97	95	.285	.364	-39	-30	102	97	.929	384	95	-.1	-2.5	-2.0		-.4
CHI	101	4	5	1117¹	1278	10.3	26	553	273	15.3	4.81	96	.279	.365	-18	-24	99	99	.922	421	92	-2.5	-2.0	-.7		-2.3
STL	114	3	4	1207	1292	9.6	38	542	301	14.1	4.06	116	.266	.346	80	88	101	105	.930	398	110	-.0	7.2	-7.5		-8.7
LOU	113	4	1	1080	1431	11.9	38	479	190	16.1	5.90	74	.310	.380	-149	-181	94	94	.937	330	111	-2.2	-14.8	-3.0		3.1
WAS	110	2	0	1139	1485	11.7	54	574	292	16.7	5.56	83	.306	.387	-114	-120	99	103	.912	497	96	-6.5	-9.8	-3.3		-4.9
TOT	1294	43	32	13864¹		10.3				14.7	4.66		.280	.356					.931	4581	1268					

Runs		Hits		Doubles		Triples		Home Runs		Total Bases	
Long-Bos	149	Thompson-Phi	222	Thompson-Phi	37	Werden-StL	29	Delahanty-Phi	19	Delahanty-Phi	347
Duffy-Bos	147	Delahanty-Phi	219	Delahanty-Phi	35	Davis-NY	27	Clements-Phi	17	Thompson-Phi	318
Delahanty-Phi	145	Duffy-Bos	203	Tebeau-Cle	32	McKean-Cle	24	Tiernan-NY	14	Davis-NY	304
Childs-Cle	145	Davis-NY	195	Beckley-Pit	32	Smith-Pit	23	Lowe-Bos	14	Smith-Pit	272
Burkett-Cle	145	Ward-NY	193			Beckley-Pit	19				

Runs Batted In		Runs Produced		Bases On Balls		Batting Average		On Base Percentage		Slugging Average	
Delahanty-Phi	146	Delahanty-Phi	272	Crooks-StL	121	Duffy-Bos	.363	Hamilton-Phi	.490	Delahanty-Phi	.583
McKean-Cle	133	Duffy-Bos	259	Childs-Cle	120	Hamilton-Phi	.380	Childs-Cle	.463	Davis-NY	.554
Thompson-Phi	126	Thompson-Phi	245	Radford-Was	104	Thompson-Phi	.370	Burkett-Cle	.459	Thompson-Phi	.530
Nash-Bos	123	Ewing-Cle	233	McGraw-Bal	101	Delahanty-Phi	.368	McGraw-Bal	.454	Smith-Pit	.525
Ewing-Cle	122	McKean-Cle	232	Burkett-Cle	98	Davis-NY	.355	Smith-Pit	.435	Hamilton-Phi	.524

Production		Adjusted Production		Batter Runs		Adjusted Batter Runs		Clutch Hitting Index		Runs Created	
Hamilton-Phi	1.014	Hamilton-Phi	170	Delahanty-Phi	52.7	Delahanty-Phi	53.2	Anson-Chi	148	Delahanty-Phi	167
Delahanty-Phi	1.007	Delahanty-Phi	167	Burkett-Cle	43.6	Smith-Pit	44.0	Vaughn-Cin	147	Thompson-Phi	146
Davis-NY	.964	Smith-Pit	158	Thompson-Phi	43.3	Thompson-Phi	43.8	McKean-Cle	135	Davis-NY	143
Smith-Pit	.960	Davis-NY	155	Smith-Pit	41.4	Hamilton-Phi	40.2	Glasscock-StL-Pit	132	Burkett-Cle	137
Thompson-Phi	.954	Thompson-Phi	153	Davis-NY	40.0	Davis-NY	39.6	O'Rourke-Was	129	Smith-Pit	133

Total Average		Stolen Bases		Stolen Base Average		Stolen Base Runs		Fielding Runs		Total Player Rating	
Hamilton-Phi	1.386	T.Brown-Lou	66					McPhee-Cin	34.0	Delahanty-Phi	6.3
Burkett-Cle	1.186	Dowd-StL	59					Delahanty-Phi	30.8	McPhee-Cin	3.5
Delahanty-Phi	1.173	Latham-Cin	57					T.Brown-Lou	27.1	Davis-NY	3.4
Smith-Pit	1.121	Burke-NY	54					G.Smith-Cin	19.5	Smith-Pit	3.3
Davis-NY	1.107	Brodie-StL-Bal	49					Allen-Phi	18.4	Hamilton-Phi	3.3

Wins		Win Percentage		Games		Complete Games		Shutouts		Saves	
Killen-Pit	36	Gastright-Pit-Bos	.750	Rusie-NY	56	Rusie-NY	50	Rusie-NY	4	Mullane-Cin-Bal	2
Young-Cle	34	Killen-Pit	.720	Killen-Pit	55	Nichols-Bos	43	Ehret-Pit	4	Baldwin-Pit-NY	2
Nichols-Bos	34	Nichols-Bos	.708	Young-Cle	53	Young-Cle	42			Dwyer-Cin	2
Rusie-NY	33	Young-Cle	.680	Nichols-Bos	52	Kennedy-Bro	40			Donnelly-Chi	2
Kennedy-Bro	25	Staley-Bos	.643	Mullane-Cin-Bal	49					Colcolough-Pit	2

Innings Pitched		Fewest Hits/Game		Fewest BB/Game		Strikeouts		Strikeouts/Game		Ratio	
Rusie-NY	482.0	Rusie-NY	8.42	Young-Cle	2.19	Rusie-NY	208	Rusie-NY	3.88	Young-Cle	11.82
Nichols-Bos	425.0	Breitenstein-StL	8.44	Nichols-Bos	2.50	Kennedy-Bro	107	Meekin-Was	3.34	Nichols-Bos	11.84
Young-Cle	422.2	Killen-Pit	8.70	Cuppy-Cle	2.77	Young-Cle	102	Hawley-StL	2.89	Killen-Pit	12.06
Killen-Pit	415.0	Kennedy-Bro	8.84	Staley-Bos	2.77	Breitenstein-StL	102	Keefe-Phi	2.83	Breitenstein-StL	12.30
		Stein-Bro	8.87	Stratton-Lou	2.86	Weyhing-Phi	101	Terry-Pit	2.75	Stein-Bro	12.70

Earned Run Average		Adjusted ERA		Opponents' Batting Avg.		Opponents' On Base Pct.		Starter Runs		Adjusted Starter Runs	
Breitenstein-StL	3.18	Breitenstein-StL	149	Rusie-NY	.240	Young-Cle	.308	Rusie-NY	76.6	Rusie-NY	76.1
Rusie-NY	3.23	Young-Cle	145	Breitenstein-StL	.241	Nichols-Bos	.308	Breitenstein-StL	63.2	Young-Cle	71.2
Young-Cle	3.36	Rusie-NY	144	Killen-Pit	.246	Killen-Pit	.312	Young-Cle	60.9	Nichols-Bos	66.9
Ehret-Pit	3.44	Nichols-Bos	140	Kennedy-Bro	.249	Breitenstein-StL	.316	Nichols-Bos	54.1	Breitenstein-StL	65.9
Clarkson-StL	3.48	Clarkson-StL	136	Stein-Bro	.250	Stein-Bro	.323	Killen-Pit	46.9	Killen-Pit	41.8

Clutch Pitching Index		Relief Runs		Adjusted Relief Runs		Relief Ranking		Total Pitcher Index		Total Baseball Ranking	
Esper-Was	120							Rusie-NY	7.2	Rusie-NY	7.2
Clarkson-StL	117							Young-Cle	6.4	Young-Cle	6.4
McNabb-Bal	113							Breitenstein-StL	5.5	Delahanty-Phi	6.3
Cuppy-Cle	111							Nichols-Bos	5.5	Breitenstein-StL	5.5
Rusie-NY	111							Killen-Pit	5.2	Nichols-Bos	5.4

January 9 Boston's veteran catcher Charlie Bennett loses both legs in a horrible train accident. In 1900, Detroit, his prior team, will rename its ballpark Bennett Park, the site of Tiger Stadium.

February 26 In a series of rule changes designed to help pitchers, foul bunts will now be called strikes, and the infield fly rule is instituted.

March 14* U.S. Immigration Inspector De Barry will ask the Treasury Department if baseball is a "recognized profession" in order to determine if Buffalo has violated the alien contract labor law by signing two Canadians. Before De Barry gets a reply, Buffalo decides to play only Americans.

May 15 In the aftermath of a fierce fight between Baltimore's John McGraw and Boston's Tommy Tucker in the third inning, a devastating fire starts in the right field stands at Boston's South End Grounds. The fire destroys $70,000 worth of equipment as well as the park, the only truly double-decked grandstand Boston would ever have.

May 30 Boston second baseman Bobby Lowe hits homers in four consecutive at bats, including two in the third inning, to lead his team to a 20–11 conquest of Cincinnati and a sweep of the double-header. Lowe also adds a single to total 17 bases for the game, a record tied but not beaten until Joe Adcock in 1954. In the two games Lowe's teammate Herman Long sets a major league record by scoring nine runs, which has since been tied only once.

June 30 Future Hall of Famer Fred Clarke sets a record by going 5-for-5 in his first major league game.

July 20 Cincinnati benefits from bottom-of-the-tenth-inning home runs by Harry "Farmer" Vaughn and George "Germany" Smith, the latter with two outs, to squeak past Pittsburgh 7-6. Pirate outfielder Elmer Smith, who is allowed to retrieve the game-winning hit in the left field bleachers according to Cincinnati ground rules, is prevented from doing so by overzealous Reds fans, one of whom even draws a revolver on him.

August 6 Fire again strikes the major leagues as sparks from a plumber's torch starts a blaze that destroys the grandstand at Philadelphia's Huntingdon Grounds, better known as Baker Bowl. It will be rebuilt with concrete and steel.

August 7 Boston's Jimmy "Foxy Grandpa" Bannon becomes the first player to hit grand slams in consecutive games. Bannon's feat will not be matched until September 24, 1901.

August 14 Taking advantage of the unusually small University of Pennsylvania field, visiting Louisville tags six homers, including two by Tom Brown, to beat Philadelphia 13–7.

August 24 Chicago catcher William "Pop" Schriver becomes the first ballplayer to catch a ball dropped from the top of the Washington Monument. Later in the day the Colts top Washington 10-5, and Schriver is 2-for-2.

September 30 Losing to Cincinnati 16–1 in the bottom of the sixth, Cleveland stages a furious comeback, including an 11-run outburst in the seventh, to conclude the season with a 16–16 tie.

October 8 New York whips NL regular season champion Baltimore 16–3 to sweep the best-of-seven Temple Cup postseason series.

November 8 Mike "King" Kelly dies of pneumonia in Boston.

December 15 Veteran manager John Chapman expresses his support of a proposed rule change forbidding all but catchers and first base from wearing gloves. Chapman remarks that "as it is now, inferior players with big gloves can get into the game and force good men out."

	BALTIMORE		BOSTON		BROOKLYN		CHICAGO		CINCINNATI		CLEVELAND
M	N.Hanlon	M	F.Selee	M	D.Foutz	M	C.Anson	M	C.Comiskey	M	P.Tebeau
1B	D.Brouthers	1B	T.Tucker	1B	D.Foutz	1B	C.Anson	1B	C.Comiskey	1B	P.Tebeau
2B	H.Reitz	2B	B.Lowe	2B	T.Daly	2B	J.Parrott	2B	B.McPhee	2B	C.Childs
SS	H.Jennings	SS	H.Long	SS	T.Corcoran	SS	B.Dahlen	SS	G.Smith	SS	E.McKean
3B	J.McGraw	3B	B.Nash	3B	B.Shindle	3B	C.Irwin	3B	A.Latham	3B	C.McGarr
LF	J.Kelley	LF	T.McCarthy	LF	G.Treadway	LF	W.Wilmot	LF	B.Holliday	LF	J.Burkett
CF	S.Brodie	CF	H.Duffy	CF	M.Griffin	CF	B.Lange	CF	D.Hoy	CF	J.McAleer
RF	W.Keeler	RF	J.Bannon	RF	O.Burns	RF	J.Ryan	RF	J.Canavan	RF	H.Blake
C	W.Robinson	C	C.Ganzel	C	T.Kinslow	C	P.Schriver	C	M.Murphy	C	C.Zimmer
2	F.Bonner	C	J.Ryan	1C	C.LaChance	1O	G.Decker	C1	F.Vaughn	CO	J.O'Connor
C	B.Clarke	S	F.Connaughton	O3	G.Shoch	C	M.Kittridge	O1	J.McCarthy	O	B.Ewing
		C	F.Tenney	C	C.Daily			C	B.Merritt	O1	G.Tebeau
P	S.McMahon			O	J.Anderson	P	B.Hutchison	1	F.Motz	O	J.Virtue
P	B.Hawke	P	K.Nichols			P	C.Griffith				
P	K.Gleason	P	J.Stivetts	P	B.Kennedy	P	W.McGill	P	F.Dwyer	P	C.Young
P	B.Inks	P	H.Staley	P	E.Stein	P	A.Terry	P	T.Parrott	P	N.Cuppy
P	T.Mullane	P	T.Lovett	P	D.Daub	P	S.Stratton	P	E.Chamberlain	P	J.Clarkson
				P	H.Gastright			P	C.Fisher	P	M.Sullivan
P	D.Esper	P	G.Hodson			P	B.Abbey				
/P	S.Brown			P	C.Lucid	/P	K.Camp	P	B.Whitrock	/P	F.Griffith
/P	G.Hemming			/P	F.Underwood			/P	L.Cross	/P	T.Mullane
								/P	H.Fournier	/P	C.Petty
								/P	J.Tannehill	/P	B.Wallace

	LOUISVILLE		NEW YORK		PHILADELPHIA		PITTSBURGH		ST.LOUIS		WASHINGTON
M	B.Barnie	M	M.Ward	M	A.Irwin	M	A.Buckenberger	M	G.Miller	M	G.Schmelz
1B	L.Lutenberg	1B	J.Doyle	1B	J.Boyle	M	C.Mack	1B	R.Connor	1B	E.Cartwright
2B	F.Pfeffer	2B	J.Ward	2B	B.Hallman	1B	J.Beckley	2B	J.Quinn	2B	P.Ward
SS	D.Richardson	SS	S.Fuller	SS	J.Sullivan	2B	L.Bierbauer	SS	B.Ely	SS	F.Scheibeck
3B	J.Denny	3B	G.Davis	3B	L.Cross	SS	J.Glasscock	3B	H.Peitz	3B	B.Joyce
LF	F.Clarke	LF	E.Burke	LF	E.Delahanty	3B	D.Lyons	LF	C.Frank	LF	K.Selbach
CF	T.Brown	CF	G.Van Haltren	CF	B.Hamilton	LF	E.Smith	CF	F.Shugart	CF	C.Abbey
RF	O.Smith	RF	M.Tiernan	RF	S.Thompson	CF	J.Stenzel	RF	T.Dowd	RF	B.Hassamaer
C	J.Grim	C	D.Farrell	C	J.Clements	RF	P.Donovan	C	D.Miller	C	D.McGuire
						C	C.Mack				
OC	F.Weaver	SO	Y.Murphy	O	T.Turner	O3	D.Cooley	O3	D.Cooley	S2	P.Radford
1O	T.O'Rourke	C1	P.Wilson	C1	M.Grady	3	F.Hartman	C	A.Twineham	O	G.Tebeau
O	L.Twitchell	1	R.Connor	C	D.Buckley	C	J.Sugden	O	M.Hogan	C	D.Dugdale
3	P.Flaherty			S	B.Allen	CS	F.Weaver	C	D.Buckley	/2	J.Sullivan
3	P.Gilbert			3	C.Reilly	C	B.Merritt	3	T.O'Rourke		
O	G.Nicol	P	A.Rusie			S	F.Scheibeck			P	W.Mercer
C	B.Earle	P	J.Meekin	P	J.Taylor			P	T.Breitenstein	P	A.Maul
		P	H.Westervelt	P	K.Carsey	P	R.Ehret	P	P.Hawley	P	M.Sullivan
		P	L.German	P	G.Weyhing	P	A.Gumbert	P	D.Clarkson	P	O.Stocksdale
P	G.Hemming	P	D.Clarke	P	G.Harper	P	F.Killen			P	D.Esper
P	P.Knell			P	T.Colcolough						
P	J.Menefee			P	J.Menefee	/P	K.Gleason				
P	J.Wadsworth			P	G.Haddock			/P	E.Mason	P	C.Petty
				/P	N.Callahan					/P	G.Haddock
/P	B.Inks	P	G.Haddock	/P	J.Johnson	/P	G.Nicol			/P	J.Malarkey
/P	S.Stratton	/P	J.Fanning	/P	J.Easton						
/P	M.Kilroy	/P	A.Lukens								

TEAM	G	W	L	PCT	GB	R	OR	AB	H	2B	3B	HR	BB	SO	AVG	OBP	SLG	PRO	PRO+	BR	/A	PF	CHI	RC	SB	CS	SBA	SBR
BAL	129	89	39	.695		1171	819	4799	1647	271	150	33	516	200	.343	.418	.483	.901	116	173	122	104	99	1146	324			
NY	137	88	44	.667	3	940	789	4806	1446	197	96	43	476	217	.301	.368	.409	.777	92	-68	-61	99	104	869	319			
BOS	133	83	49	.629	8	1220	1002	5011	1658	272	94	103	535	261	.331	.401	.484	.885	108	135	44	108	106	1102	241			
PHI	129	71	57	.555	18	1143	966	4967	1732	252	131	40	496	245	.349	.414	.476	.890	122	156	187	97	97	1132	273			
BRO	134	70	61	.534	20.5	1021	1007	4816	1507	228	130	42	466	294	.313	.378	.440	.818	109	5	75	93	104	941	282			
CLE	130	68	61	.527	21.5	932	964	4764	1442	241	90	37	471	301	.303	.368	.414	.782	89	-57	-92	104	103	837	220			
PIT	132	65	65	.500	25	955	972	4676	1458	222	124	48	434	208	.312	.379	.443	.822	103	11	21	99	98	921	256			
CHI	135	57	75	.432	34	1041	1066	4960	1555	265	86	65	496	298	.314	.380	.441	.821	97	12	-43	105	102	987	327			
STL	133	56	76	.424	35	771	953	4610	1320	171	113	54	442	289	.286	.354	.408	.762	87	-100	-100	100	92	763	190			
CIN	132	55	75	.423	35	910	1085	4671	1374	224	67	61	508	252	.294	.368	.410	.778	88	-62	-96	104	102	812	215			
WAS	132	45	87	.341	46	882	1122	4581	1317	218	118	59	617	375	.287	.381	.425	.806	101	-7	24	97	92	864	249			
LOU	130	36	94	.277	54	692	1001	4482	1206	173	88	42	350	364	.269	.330	.375	.705	78	-199	-152	93	99	652	217			
TOT	793					11678		57143	17662	2734	1287	627	5807	3304	.309	.379	.435	.814							3113			

TEAM	CG	SH	SV	IP	H	H/G	HR	BB	SO	RAT	ERA	ERA+	OAV	OOB	PR	/A	PF	CPI	FA	E	DP	FW	PW	BW	SBW	DIF
BAL	97	1	11	1116¹	1371	11.1	31	472	275	15.2	5.00	109	.299	.371	39	55	103	98	.944	293	105	5.6	4.2	9.4		5.8
NY	111	5	5	1212	1292	9.6	37	539	395	13.8	3.83	137	.271	.349	200	187	99	107	.924	443	101	-1.6	14.3	-4.7		13.9
BOS	108	3	2	1166	1529	11.8	89	411	262	15.3	5.41	105	.314	.372	-12	33	107	101	.925	415	120	-.7	2.5	3.4		11.8
PHI	102	3	4	1125²	1482	11.8	62	469	262	16.1	5.63	90	.314	.384	-39	-68	96	99	.935	338	111	3.0	-5.2	14.3		-5.2
BRO	105	3	5	1162¹	1447	11.2	41	555	285	16.0	5.51	90	.302	.382	-25	-75	93	95	.928	390	85	.9	-5.8	5.8		3.6
CLE	106	6	1	1124¹	1390	11.1	54	435	254	14.9	4.97	110	.301	.366	43	59	103	100	.935	344	107	2.9	4.5	-7.1		3.2
PIT	106	2	0	1164²	1552	12.0	39	457	304	15.8	5.60	93	.317	.380	-37	-50	98	96	.936	354	106	2.6	-3.8	1.6		-.4
CHI	117	0	0	1148	1561	12.2	48	557	281	17.1	5.68	99	.322	.398	-47	-11	106	103	.918	452	113	-2.4	-.8	-3.3		-2.4
STL	114	2	0	1161	1418	11.0	48	500	319	15.2	5.29	102	.299	.371	4	14	102	94	.923	426	109	-1.3	1.1	-7.7		-2.1
CIN	110	4	3	1147¹	1585	12.4	85	491	219	16.7	5.99	93	.325	.393	-85	-56	104	101	.925	423	119	-1.3	-4.3	-7.4		2.9
WAS	101	0	4	1107	1573	12.8	59	446	190	16.3	5.51	95	.331	.396	-24	-32	99	110	.908	499	81	-5.6	-2.5	1.8		-14.8
LOU	113	2	1	1096²	1462	12.0	39	475	258	16.3	5.45	93	.317	.386	-16	-44	96	101	.920	428	130	-1.9	-3.4	-11.7		-12.1
TOT	1290	31	36	13731¹		11.6				15.8	5.32		.309	.379					.927	4805	1287					

Runs		Hits		Doubles		Triples		Home Runs		Total Bases	
Hamilton-Phi	192	Duffy-Bos	237	Duffy-Bos	51	Reitz-Bal	31	Duffy-Bos	18	Duffy-Bos	374
Kelley-Bal	165	Hamilton-Phi	220	Kelley-Bal	48	Thompson-Phi	27	Lowe-Bos	17	Lowe-Bos	319
Keeler-Bal	165	Keeler-Bal	219	Wilmot-Chi	45	Treadway-Bro	26	Joyce-Was	17	Kelley-Bal	305
Duffy-Bos	160	Lowe-Bos	212			Connor-NY-StL	25	Dahlen-Chi	15	Keeler-Bal	305
Lowe-Bos	158	Brodie-Bal	210			Brouthers-Bal	23			Stenzel-Pit	303

Runs Batted In		Runs Produced		Bases On Balls		Batting Average		On Base Percentage		Slugging Average	
Duffy-Bos	145	Duffy-Bos	287	Hamilton-Phi	126	Duffy-Bos	.440	Hamilton-Phi	.523	Duffy-Bos	.694
Thompson-Phi	141	Hamilton-Phi	275	Kelley-Bal	107	Turner-Phi	.416	Kelley-Bal	.502	Thompson-Phi	.686
E.Delahanty-Phi	131	E.Delahanty-Phi	274	Childs-Cle	107	Thompson-Phi	.407	Duffy-Bos	.502	Joyce-Was	.648
Wilmot-Chi	130	Kelley-Bal	270	Nash-Bos	91	E.Delahanty-Phi	.407	Joyce-Was	.496	Kelley-Bal	.602
		Wilmot-Chi	259	McGraw-Bal	91	Hamilton-Phi	.404	E.Delahanty-Phi	.478	E.Delahanty-Phi	.585

Production		Adjusted Production		Batter Runs		Adjusted Batter Runs		Clutch Hitting Index		Runs Created	
Duffy-Bos	1.196	Joyce-Was	180	Duffy-Bos	75.7	Hamilton-Phi	64.7	Robinson-Bal	141	Duffy-Bos	217
Thompson-Phi	1.145	Thompson-Phi	177	Kelley-Bal	60.2	Duffy-Bos	61.4	Wilmot-Chi	132	Hamilton-Phi	207
Joyce-Was	1.143	Duffy-Bos	172	Hamilton-Phi	59.9	Thompson-Phi	52.9	McGraw-Bal	122	Kelley-Bal	182
Kelley-Bal	1.104	E.Delahanty-Phi	159	Thompson-Phi	49.3	Kelley-Bal	52.6	Bierbauer-Pit	121	Stenzel-Pit	165
E.Delahanty-Phi	1.063	Kelley-Bal	158	Joyce-Was	47.1	Joyce-Was	51.3	Reitz-Bal	118	Thompson-Phi	152

Total Average		Stolen Bases		Stolen Base Average		Stolen Base Runs		Fielding Runs		Total Player Rating	
Duffy-Bos	1.619	Hamilton-Phi	98					Jennings-Bal	33.1	Dahlen-Chi	4.8
Hamilton-Phi	1.605	McGraw-Bal	78					Dahlen-Chi	31.6	E.Delahanty-Phi	4.7
Joyce-Was	1.528	Wilmot-Chi	74					McPhee-Cin	31.2	Hamilton-Phi	4.6
Kelley-Bal	1.503	T.Brown-Lou	66					Farrell-NY	29.4	Duffy-Bos	4.3
Thompson-Phi	1.409	Lange-Chi	65					Reitz-Bal	26.9	Joyce-Was	3.7

Wins		Win Percentage		Games		Complete Games		Shutouts		Saves	
Rusie-NY	36	Meekin-NY	.786	Breitenstein-StL	56	Breitenstein-StL	46	Rusie-NY	3	Mullane-Bal-Cle	4
Meekin-NY	33	McMahon-Bal	.758	Rusie-NY	54	Rusie-NY	45	Nichols-Bos	3	Mercer-Was	3
Nichols-Bos	32	Rusie-NY	.735	Hawley-StL	53	Young-Cle	44	Cuppy-Cle	3	Hawke-Bal	3
Breitenstein-StL	27	Nichols-Bos	.711	Young-Cle	52	Nichols-Bos	40				
				Meekin-NY	52	Meekin-NY	40				

Innings Pitched		Fewest Hits/Game		Fewest BB/Game		Strikeouts		Strikeouts/Game		Ratio	
Breitenstein-StL	447.1	Rusie-NY	8.64	Young-Cle	2.33	Rusie-NY	195	Rusie-NY	3.95	Rusie-NY	12.79
Rusie-NY	444.0	Meekin-NY	8.89	Menefee-Lou-Pit	2.48	Breitenstein-StL	140	Hawke-Bal	2.97	Meekin-NY	12.89
Meekin-NY	409.0	Stein-Bro	9.98	Gleason-StL-Bal	2.54	Meekin-NY	133	Wadsworth-Lou	2.97	Clarkson-Cle	13.08
Young-Cle	408.2	Breitenstein-StL	10.00	Staley-Bos	2.63	Hawley-StL	120	Meekin-NY	2.93	Young-Cle	13.19
Nichols-Bos	407.0	Clarkson-Cle	10.33	Nichols-Bos	2.68	Nichols-Bos	113	Chamberlain-Cin	2.89	Nichols-Bos	13.67

Earned Run Average		Adjusted ERA		Opponents' Batting Avg.		Opponents' On Base Pct.		Starter Runs		Adjusted Starter Runs	
Rusie-NY	2.78	Rusie-NY	189	Rusie-NY	.250	Rusie-NY	.331	Rusie-NY	125.3	Rusie-NY	121.3
Meekin-NY	3.70	Meekin-NY	142	Meekin-NY	.256	Meekin-NY	.333	Meekin-NY	73.6	Meekin-NY	70.0
Mercer-Was	3.85	Young-Cle	138	Stein-Bro	.278	Clarkson-Cle	.336	Young-Cle	62.4	Young-Cle	68.7
Young-Cle	3.94	Mercer-Was	137	Breitenstein-StL	.279	Young-Cle	.338	Mercer-Was	55.4	Mercer-Was	53.2
Taylor-Phi	4.08	McMahon-Bal	129	Clarkson-Cle	.285	Nichols-Bos	.346	Taylor-Phi	41.0	Nichols-Bos	41.5

Clutch Pitching Index		Relief Runs		Adjusted Relief Runs		Relief Ranking		Total Pitcher Index		Total Baseball Ranking	
Mercer-Was	134							Rusie-NY	11.0	Rusie-NY	11.0
Rusie-NY	125							Young-Cle	5.6	Young-Cle	5.6
Terry-Pit-Chi	121							Meekin-NY	5.5	Meekin-NY	5.5
Hemming-Lou-Bal	112							Mercer-Was	5.0	Mercer-Was	5.0
Killen-Pit	111							Taylor-Phi	3.7	Dahlen-Chi	4.8

February 2 The New York *Clipper* and the Cincinnati *Times-Star* both express disapproval of the proposal of putting numbers on uniforms as a means of identifying individual players. The *Times-Star* advocates a return to the use of "distinctive colors in club uniforms," or the practice of assigning to each position a specific color pattern, first enacted in 1882.

February 9 New York owner Andrew Freedman institutes reserved grandstand seats to attract businessmen.

March 16 John Brush, owner of the Cincinnati Reds and the Indianapolis team of the Western League, transfers six Reds to his minor league team. This sort of exchange becomes increasingly common in the 1890s as owners of more than one team shuttle their players between their teams throughout each season in an attempt to stock their most profitable team of the moment.

April 12 In a rare matchup between a major league team and a black team, Cincinnati beats the Page Fence Giants for the second consecutive day.

April 19* Holy Cross defeats Brown University 13–4 in a game between two of the top college teams. The Crusaders have five future major league players in their lineup, while the losers have two. Louis Sockalexis plays left field for the victors and has six stolen bases.

May 23 The Louisville Colonels drop a game to Brooklyn because they run out of baseballs. The home team is responsible for supplying balls, but the game begins with just three on hand, two of them practice balls borrowed from Brooklyn. By the third inning, the balls are worn out and a messenger sent for new ones does not come back in time. Louisville is forced to forfeit.

May 29 Jake Beckley hits a three-run homer to give Pittsburgh an 8–6 win over Washington. Under the rules of the era, which do not allow a team batting in the bottom of the last inning to win by more than one run, Beckley should be credited only with a triple. Apparently the rule is not strictly enforced.

June 3 Roger Connor becomes the major leagues' all-time home run leader, passing Harry Stovey with his fourth round-tripper of the season, and the 122nd of his career. This historic home run drives in St. Louis's only two runs in a 5-2 loss to Brooklyn.

June 15 Future novelist Zane Grey makes his minor league debut playing left field for Findlay, Ohio, against Wheeling (Tri-State League). The Pennsylvania University athlete, playing under the name Zane, fails to get a hit, but walks and scores on a grand slam by brother Romer "Reddy" Grey.

August 3* The Capital Colored All-Americans set sail for England with a team of players from Western League clubs.

August 12* Heavyweight boxing champion Jim Corbett, a good ballplayer and a great gate attraction, plays first base for the Scranton team in an Eastern League victory over Buffalo. Corbett collects two singles and knocks in two runs. His brother Joe, who will become a major league pitcher, plays shortstop.

October 8 Cleveland takes the Temple Cup by beating the Baltimore Orioles for the fourth time in five games. The lack of respect accorded the Cup is reflected in the "very cold reception" Cleveland receives after returning from Baltimore on October 9.

November 15 Cap Anson makes his stage debut in *A Runaway Colt*. Aside from forgetting a few lines Anson does quite well.

BALTIMORE		BOSTON		BROOKLYN		CHICAGO		CINCINNATI		CLEVELAND	
M	N.Hanlon	M	F.Selee	M	D.Foutz	M	C.Anson	M	B.Ewing	M	P.Tebeau
1B	S.Carey	1B	T.Tucker	1B	C.LaChance	1B	C.Anson	1B	B.Ewing	1B	P.Tebeau
2B	K.Gleason	2B	B.Lowe	2B	T.Daly	2B	A.Stewart	2B	B.McPhee	2B	C.Childs
SS	H.Jennings	SS	H.Long	SS	T.Corcoran	SS	B.Dahlen	SS	G.Smith	SS	E.McKean
3B	J.McGraw	3B	B.Nash	3B	B.Shindle	3B	B.Everitt	3B	A.Latham	3B	C.McGarr
LF	J.Kelley	LF	T.McCarthy	LF	J.Anderson	LF	W.Wilmot	LF	D.Hoy	LF	J.Burkett
CF	S.Brodie	CF	H.Duffy	CF	M.Griffin	CF	B.Lange	CF	G.Hogriever	CF	J.McAleer
RF	W.Keeler	RF	J.Bannon	RF	G.Treadway	RF	J.Ryan	RF	D.Miller	RF	H.Blake
C	W.Robinson	C	C.Ganzel	C	J.Grim	C	T.Donahue	C	F.Vaughn	C	C.Zimmer
23	H.Reitz	C	J.Ryan	O2	G.Shoch	O1	G.Decker	O	E.Burke	C1	J.O'Connor
C	B.Clarke	OC	F.Tenney	C	C.Daily	C	M.Kittridge	32	B.Grey	O1	G.Tebeau
		2	J.Harrington	O	D.Foutz	2	H.Truby	O	B.Holliday	3	E.Gremminger
P	B.Hoffer			O	O.Burns			C	M.Murphy		
P	G.Hemming	P	K.Nichols			P	C.Griffith	C	B.Merritt	P	C.Young
P	D.Esper	P	J.Stivetts	P	B.Kennedy	P	A.Terry			P	N.Cuppy
P	D.Clarkson	P	C.Dolan	P	E.Stein	P	B.Hutchison	P	F.Dwyer	P	B.Wallace
P	S.McMahon	P	J.Sullivan	P	A.Gumbert			P	B.Rhines	P	P.Knell
				P	D.Daub	/P	D.Parker	P	T.Parrott		
		/P	F.Sexton	P	C.Lucid	/P	D.Friend	P	F.Foreman	/P	Z.Wilson
		/P	Z.Wilson			/P	W.Thornton	P	B.Phillips	/P	M.Sullivan
		/P	O.Stocksdale	/P	B.Abbey	/P	S.Stratton				

LOUISVILLE		NEW YORK		PHILADELPHIA		PITTSBURGH		ST.LOUIS		WASHINGTON	
M	J.McCloskey	M	G.Davis	M	A.Irwin	M	C.Mack	M	A.Buckenberger	M	G.Schmelz
1B	H.Spies	M	J.Doyle	1B	J.Boyle	1B	J.Beckley	M	C.Von Der Ahe	1B	E.Cartwright
2B	J.O'Brien	M	H.Watkins	2B	B.Hallman	2B	L.Bierbauer	M	J.Quinn	2B	J.Crooks
SS	F.Shugart	1B	J.Doyle	SS	J.Sullivan	SS	M.Cross	M	L.Phelan	SS	F.Scheibeck
3B	J.Collins	2B	G.Stafford	3B	L.Cross	3B	B.Clingman	1B	R.Connor	3B	B.Joyce
LF	F.Clarke	SS	S.Fuller	LF	E.Delahanty	LF	E.Smith	2B	J.Quinn	LF	K.Selbach
CF	J.Wright	3B	G.Davis	CF	B.Hamilton	CF	J.Stenzel	SS	B.Ely	CF	C.Abbey
RF	T.Gettinger	LF	E.Burke	RF	S.Thompson	RF	P.Donovan	3B	D.Miller	RF	B.Hassamaer
C	J.Warner	CF	G.Van Haltren	C	J.Clements	C	B.Merritt	LF	D.Cooley	C	D.McGuire
		RF	M.Tiernan					CF	T.Brown		
O3	W.Preston	C	D.Farrell	O	T.Turner	O3	F.Genins	RF	T.Dowd	OP	J.Boyd
O	D.Holmes			S3	C.Reilly	C	J.Sugden	C	H.Peitz	O	T.Brown
C1	T.Welch	C1	P.Wilson	C	M.Grady	S	B.S_tuart_			S	J.Glasscock
O	T.McCreery	O	Y.Murphy	C	D.Buckley	C	T.Kinslow	O1	B.Sheehan	S	D.Coogan
1	D.Brouthers	O1	T.Bannon					3	D.Lyons		
1	B.Hassamaer	O	O.Burns	P	K.Carsey	P	P.Hawley	C	J.Otten	P	W.Mercer
O	D.Sweeney	C	P.Schriver	P	J.Taylor	P	B.Hart	3	I.Samuls	P	V.Anderson
S	J.Glasscock	1	W.Clark	P	W.McGill	P	B.Foreman			P	O.Stocksdale
/S	A.McGann			P	A.Orth	P	F.Killen	P	T.Breitenstein	P	A.Maul
		P	A.Rusie			P	J.Gardner	P	R.Ehret	P	J.Malarkey
P	B.Cunningham	P	D.Clarke	P	C.Lucid			P	H.Staley		
P	G.Weyhing	P	J.Meekin	P	T.Smith	P	S.Moran	P	B.Kissinger	/P	J.Gilroy
P	M.McDermott	P	L.German	P	H.Lampe	/P	T.Colcolough	P	D.McDougal	/P	A.Boswell
P	B.Inks			/P	E.Beam	/P	H.Jordan			/P	J.Corbett
		/P	A.Boswell	/P	G.Hodson					/P	D.McJames
		/P	E.Doheny	/P	D.White			/P	D.Clarkson	/P	C.Molesworth
P	P.Luby										
P	P.Knell										
/P	D.McFarlan										

TEAM	G	W	L	PCT	GB	R	OR	AB	H	2B	3B	HR	BB	SO	AVG	OBP	SLG	PRO	PRO+	BR	/A	PF	CHI	RC	SB	CS	SBA	SBR
BAL	132	87	43	.669		1009	646	4725	1530	235	89	25	355	243	.324	.384	.427	.811	110	92	65	103	104	930	310			
CLE	131	84	46	.646	3	917	720	4658	1423	194	67	29	472	361	.305	.375	.395	.770	97	26	-26	106	102	790	187			
PHI	133	78	53	.595	9.5	1068	957	5037	1664	272	73	61	463	262	.330	.394	.450	.844	122	161	157	100	97	1040	276			
CHI	133	72	58	.554	15	866	854	4708	1401	171	85	55	422	344	.298	.361	.405	.766	95	6	-49	106	99	810	260			
BRO	133	71	60	.542	16.5	867	834	4717	1330	189	77	39	397	318	.282	.346	.379	.725	99	-66	-2	92	108	707	183			
BOS	132	71	60	.542	16.5	907	826	4715	1369	197	57	54	500	236	.290	.365	.391	.756	92	-4	-73	108	102	778	199			
PIT	134	71	61	.538	17	811	787	4645	1349	190	89	26	376	299	.290	.352	.386	.738	99	-41	3	95	99	753	257			
CIN	132	66	64	.508	21	903	854	4684	1395	235	105	36	414	249	.298	.359	.416	.775	99	18	-18	104	103	844	326			
NY	132	66	65	.504	21.5	852	834	4605	1324	191	90	32	454	292	.288	.355	.389	.744	98	-29	-9	98	104	763	292			
WAS	132	43	85	.336	43	837	1048	4577	1314	207	101	55	518	396	.287	.366	.412	.778	105	31	43	99	94	805	237			
STL	135	39	92	.298	48.5	747	1032	4781	1344	155	88	38	384	279	.281	.338	.374	.712	88	-94	-84	99	96	699	205			
LOU	133	35	96	.267	52.5	698	1090	4724	1320	171	73	34	346	323	.279	.339	.368	.707	92	-100	-52	94	92	665	156			
TOT	796					10482		56576	16763	2407	994	484	5101	3602	.296	.361	.400	.761							2888			

TEAM	CG	SH	SV	IP	H	H/G	HR	BB	SO	RAT	ERA	ERA+	OAV	OOB	PR	/A	PF	CPI	FA	E	DP	FW	PW	BW	SBW	DIF
BAL	104	10	4	1134¹	1216	9.6	31	430	244	13.4	3.80	125	.271	.340	123	118	100	105	.946	288	108	5.4	9.6	5.3		1.8
CLE	108	6	3	1143²	1272	10.0	33	346	326	13.0	3.91	127	.278	.333	110	135	104	101	.936	348	77	1.8	10.9	-2.1		8.3
PHI	106	2	7	1161	1467	11.4	36	485	330	15.6	5.47	88	.304	.375	-89	-88	100	94	.933	369	93	1.0	-7.1	12.7		5.9
CHI	119	3	1	1150²	1422	11.1	38	432	297	15.0	4.67	109	.300	.366	14	52	106	105	.928	401	113	-.8	4.2	-4.0		7.6
BRO	103	5	6	1150²	1360	10.6	41	395	216	14.1	4.94	89	.290	.351	-21	-71	92	91	.941	325	96	3.5	-5.8	-.2		8.0
BOS	116	4	4	1175¹	1364	10.4	56	363	370	13.6	4.27	119	.286	.343	66	107	107	103	.934	364	104	1.1	8.7	-5.9		1.6
PIT	106	4	6	1171²	1263	9.7	17	500	382	14.2	4.05	112	.272	.353	95	60	95	102	.930	392	95	-.1	4.9	.2		.0
CIN	97	2	6	1147¹	1451	11.4	39	362	245	14.7	4.81	103	.304	.361	4	19	104	101	.931	377	112	.4	1.5	-1.5		.5
NY	115	6	1	1147¹	1359	10.7	34	415	409	14.3	4.51	103	.291	.354	34	16	97	100	.922	438	106	-3.0	1.3	-.7		3.0
WAS	99	0	5	1101²	1507	12.3	55	465	258	16.7	5.28	91	.321	.391	-61	-60	100	110	.917	447	96	-3.5	-4.9	3.5		-16.1
STL	105	1	1	1152¹	1562	12.2	64	439	280	16.0	5.76	84	.319	.381	-126	-120	101	98	.930	380	94	.7	-9.7	-6.8		-10.7
LOU	104	3	1	1117¹	1520	12.2	40	470	245	16.5	5.90	78	.320	.389	-139	-158	97	96	.913	477	104	-5.1	-12.8	-4.2		-8.4
TOT	1282	46	45	13753¹		11.0				14.7	4.78		.296	.361					.930	4606	1198					

Runs		Hits		Doubles		Triples		Home Runs		Total Bases	
Hamilton-Phi	166	Burkett-Cle	225	Delahanty-Phi	49	Selbach-Was	22	Thompson-Phi	18	Thompson-Phi	352
Keeler-Bal	162	Keeler-Bal	213	Thompson-Phi	45	Tiernan-NY	21	Joyce-Was	17	Delahanty-Phi	296
Jennings-Bal	159	Thompson-Phi	211	Jennings-Bal	41	Thompson-Phi	21	Clements-Phi	13	Burkett-Cle	288
Burkett-Cle	153	Jennings-Bal	204	Stenzel-Pit	38	Cooley-StL	20	Delahanty-Phi	11	McKean-Cle	283
Delahanty-Phi	149	Hamilton-Phi	201	Griffin-Bro	38					Kelley-Bal	283

Runs Batted In		Runs Produced		Bases On Balls		Batting Average		On Base Percentage		Slugging Average	
Thompson-Phi	165	Jennings-Bal	280	Joyce-Was	96	Burkett-Cle	.409	Delahanty-Phi	.500	Thompson-Phi	.654
Kelley-Bal	134	Thompson-Phi	278	Hamilton-Phi	96	Delahanty-Phi	.404	Hamilton-Phi	.490	Delahanty-Phi	.617
Brodie-Bal	134	Kelley-Bal	272	Griffin-Bro	93	Clements-Phi	.394	Burkett-Cle	.486	Clements-Phi	.612
Jennings-Bal	125	Delahanty-Phi	244	Delahanty-Phi	86	Thompson-Phi	.392	McGraw-Bal	.459	Lange-Chi	.575
McKean-Cle	119	McKean-Cle	242	Kelley-Bal	77	Lange-Chi	.389	Lange-Chi	.456	Kelley-Bal	.546

Production		Adjusted Production		Batter Runs		Adjusted Batter Runs		Clutch Hitting Index		Runs Created	
Delahanty-Phi	1.117	Delahanty-Phi	186	Delahanty-Phi	66.4	Delahanty-Phi	65.8	Childs-Cle	141	Hamilton-Phi	178
Thompson-Phi	1.085	Thompson-Phi	177	Thompson-Phi	56.9	Thompson-Phi	56.3	Brodie-Bal	140	Delahanty-Phi	176
Lange-Chi	1.032	Stenzel-Pit	162	Burkett-Cle	54.2	Stenzel-Pit	49.7	Kelley-Bal	130	Thompson-Phi	167
Burkett-Cle	1.009	Lange-Chi	155	Hamilton-Phi	49.6	Hamilton-Phi	49.0	Cross-Phi	128	Burkett-Cle	165
Kelley-Bal	1.003	Hamilton-Phi	154	Kelley-Bal	47.3	Burkett-Cle	45.1	Jennings-Bal	124	Lange-Chi	160

Total Average		Stolen Bases		Stolen Base Average		Stolen Base Runs		Fielding Runs		Total Player Rating	
Delahanty-Phi	1.517	Hamilton-Phi	97					Jennings-Bal	35.7	Jennings-Bal	6.0
Hamilton-Phi	1.443	Lange-Chi	67					Dahlen-Chi	35.6	Thompson-Phi	4.7
Lange-Chi	1.373	McGraw-Bal	61					Fuller-NY	34.0	Delahanty-Phi	4.7
Kelley-Bal	1.289	Kelley-Bal	54					Cross-Phi	33.5	Griffin-Bro	3.6
Thompson-Phi	1.269							Collins-Bos-Lou	18.9	Kelley-Bal	3.5

Wins		Win Percentage		Games		Complete Games		Shutouts		Saves	
Young-Cle	35	Hoffer-Bal	.838	Hawley-Pit	56	Breitenstein-StL	46	Young-Cle	4	Parrott-Cin	3
Hoffer-Bal	31	Young-Cle	.778	Breitenstein-StL	54	Hawley-Pit	44	Rusie-NY	4	Nichols-Bos	3
Hawley-Pit	31	Rhines-Cin	.655	Rusie-NY	49	Rusie-NY	42	McMahon-Bal	4	Beam-Phi	3
						Nichols-Bos	42	Hoffer-Bal	4		
						Griffith-Chi	39	Hawley-Pit	4		

Innings Pitched		Fewest Hits/Game		Fewest BB/Game		Strikeouts		Strikeouts/Game		Ratio	
Hawley-Pit	444.1	Foreman-Pit	8.44	Young-Cle	1.83	Rusie-NY	201	Rusie-NY	4.60	Young-Cle	10.86
Breitenstein-StL	429.2	Hoffer-Bal	8.48	Clarke-NY	1.92	Hawley-Pit	142	McGill-Pit	4.32	Maul-Was	11.68
Rusie-NY	393.1	Rusie-NY	8.79	Nichols-Bos	2.04	Nichols-Bos	140	Foreman-Pit	3.48	Nichols-Bos	12.04
Nichols-Bos	379.2	Young-Cle	8.84	Staley-StL	2.21	Breitenstein-StL	127	Stivetts-Bos	3.43	Hawley-Pit	12.23
Young-Cle	369.2	Maul-Was	9.02	Taylor-Phi	2.23	Young-Cle	121	Nichols-Bos	3.32	Cuppy-Cle	12.42

Earned Run Average		Adjusted ERA		Opponents' Batting Avg.		Opponents' On Base Pct.		Starter Runs		Adjusted Starter Runs	
Maul-Was	2.45	Maul-Was	195	Foreman-Pit	.245	Young-Cle	.294	Hawley-Pit	78.8	Nichols-Bos	71.0
McMahon-Bal	2.94	Young-Cle	153	Hoffer-Bal	.246	Maul-Was	.309	Young-Cle	62.2	Young-Cle	70.6
Hawley-Pit	3.18	Nichols-Bos	149	Rusie-NY	.252	Nichols-Bos	.316	Nichols-Bos	57.5	Hawley-Pit	65.8
Hoffer-Bal	3.21	Hoffer-Bal	148	Young-Cle	.253	Hawley-Pit	.320	Hoffer-Bal	54.6	Cuppy-Cle	56.4
Foreman-Pit	3.22	Hawley-Pit	142	Maul-Was	.257	Cuppy-Cle	.323	Cuppy-Cle	48.3	Hoffer-Bal	53.8

Clutch Pitching Index		Relief Runs		Adjusted Relief Runs		Relief Ranking		Total Pitcher Index		Total Baseball Ranking	
Maul-Was	137							Hawley-Pit	7.4	Hawley-Pit	7.4
Mercer-Was	126							Young-Cle	7.0	Young-Cle	7.0
Clarke-NY	119							Cuppy-Cle	5.8	Jennings-Bal	6.0
Foreman-Cin	116							Nichols-Bos	5.7	Cuppy-Cle	5.8
Griffith-Chi	115							Griffith-Chi	4.5	Nichols-Bos	5.7

January 18 John Ward, who hasn't played or managed for the last two seasons, objects to being reserved by New York. At the NL meeting in February his appeal is upheld, and Ward becomes a free agent.

February 1 NL umpires oppose the proposed rule giving them the authority to eject "obstreperous players." They claim that the imposition of fines is a more effective form of discipline.

March 15 The Louisville infield is being rebuilt with base lines of blue clay. In addition, blue semicircles will radiate out from first base and third base, joining at second base to form, along with the bottom half of the diamond—a heart.

March 24 The NL adopts changes in the National Agreement. The minor leagues are divided into six classifications based on population, and new draft fees are instituted. The NL forbids players from deliberately soiling baseballs, declares that "a ball cutting the corners of the home plate, and being requisite height, must be called a strike," and empowers umpires to eject players.

April 7 Louisville's Pete Cassidy becomes the first baseball player in history to be X-rayed, as a splinter of bone is removed from his wrist.

April 16 The 12-team NL season opens, with no franchise changes from last year. The largest Opening Day crowd in the century, 24,500, sees the opener in Philadelphia. Veteran Cincinnati Reds second baseman Bid McPhee opens the season sporting a glove for the first time and survives several weeks of good-natured ribbing by opponents. He is the last player to convert to wearing a mitt.

May 8 In the top of the ninth inning, Philadelphia's Billy Nash starts to argue with the umpire over a called strike but stays in the batter's box. Quick-witted pitcher Clark Griffith throws a pitch in the midst of the argument which nicks Nash's bat, resulting in a double play. His quick thinking helps the Chicago Colts take a 5-3 victory.

September 7 On Labor Day, Baltimore wins a rare tripleheader from Louisville 4-3, 9-1, and 12-1, the last game in eight innings.

September 19 Kid Nichols wins his 30th game for the sixth straight year in Boston's 3-1 victory over Brooklyn.

September 26 Jesse Burkett gets three hits for Cleveland in the final game of the season to finish at .410, becoming the first major leaguer to hit .400 in consecutive seasons, a feat later duplicated by Ty Cobb and Rogers Hornsby.

October 4* The Cuban Giants defeat the Chicago Unions 11-9 and claim the title of black champions of America.

October 8 Following another rainout, the Orioles defeat Cleveland 5-0 to win the Temple Cup in a 4-game sweep. The Cup games are poorly attended, while the rowdy behavior of both teams does nothing to enhance the stature of the troubled series.

October 11 The annual league meeting gets underway in Chicago. Brooklyn owner Ferdinand H. Abell proposes to make all players free agents between January 1 and March 1 and allow all teams to bid on them, subject to a salary limit. The plan is ignored.

November 13 The NL votes to award British-born journalist Henry Chadwick $50 per month for life in recognition of his past services to the game.

BALTIMORE		BOSTON		BROOKLYN		CHICAGO		CINCINNATI		CLEVELAND	
M	N.Hanlon	M	F.Selee	M	D.Foutz	M	C.Anson	M	B.Ewing	M	P.Tebeau
1B	J.Doyle	1B	T.Tucker	1B	C.LaChance	1B	C.Anson	1B	B.Ewing	1B	P.Tebeau
2B	H.Reitz	2B	B.Lowe	2B	T.Daly	2B	F.Pfeffer	2B	B.McPhee	2B	C.Childs
SS	H.Jennings	SS	H.Long	SS	T.Corcoran	SS	B.Dahlen	SS	G.Smith	SS	E.McKean
3B	J.Donnelly	3B	J.Collins	3B	B.Shindle	3B	B.Everitt	3B	C.Irwin	3B	C.McGarr
LF	J.Kelley	LF	H.Duffy	LF	T.McCarthy	LF	G.Decker	LF	E.Burke	LF	J.Burkett
CF	S.Brodie	CF	B.Hamilton	CF	M.Griffin	CF	B.Lange	CF	D.Hoy	CF	J.McAleer
RF	W.Keeler	RF	J.Bannon	RF	F.Jones	RF	J.Ryan	RF	D.Miller	RF	H.Blake
C	W.Robinson	C	M.Bergen	C	J.Grim	C	M.Kittridge	C	H.Peitz	C	C.Zimmer
C1	B.Clarke	OC	F.Tenney	O1	J.Anderson	C	T.Donahue	1C	F.Vaughn	C1	J.O'Connor
/2	J.Quinn	3	J.Harrington	2O	G.Shoch	3	B.McCormick	2C	B.Grey	OP	B.Wallace
3	J.McGraw	C	C.Ganzel	C	B.Burrell	2	H.Truby	O	B.Holliday	O	J.Shearon
		2	D.McGann			O	G.Flynn				
P	B.Hoffer	P	K.Nichols	P	B.Kennedy	P	C.Griffith	P	F.Dwyer	P	C.Young
P	A.Pond	P	J.Stivetts	P	H.Payne	P	D.Friend	P	R.Ehret	P	N.Cuppy
P	G.Hemming	P	J.Sullivan	P	D.Daub	P	A.Terry	P	F.Foreman	P	Z.Wilson
P	S.McMahon	P	F.Klobedanz	P	B.Abbey	P	B.Briggs	P	C.Fisher	/P	D.Gear
P	D.Esper	/P	W.Mains	P	E.Stein	/P	D.Parker	P	B.Rhines		
/P	D.Clarkson	/P	T.Lewis	P	G.Harper	/P	M.McFarland	/P	B.Foreman		
/P	J.Corbett	/P	C.Dolan	/P	A.Gumbert	/P	W.Thornton	/P	B.Inks		
/P	J.Nops	/P	B.Banks								

LOUISVILLE		NEW YORK		PHILADELPHIA		PITTSBURGH		ST.LOUIS		WASHINGTON	
M	J.McCloskey	M	A.Irwin	M	B.Nash	M	C.Mack	M	H.Diddlebock	M	G.Schmelz
M	B.McGunnigle	M	B.Joyce	1B	D.Brouthers	1B	J.Beckley	M	A.Latham	1B	E.Cartwright
1B	J.Rogers	1B	W.Clark	2B	B.Hallman	2B	D.Padden	M	C.Von Der Ahe	2B	J.O'Brien
2B	J.O'Brien	2B	K.Gleason	SS	B.Hulen	SS	B.Ely	M	R.Connor	SS	G.DeMontreville
SS	J.Dolan	SS	F.Connaughton	3B	B.Nash	3B	D.Lyons	M	T.Dowd	3B	B.Joyce
3B	B.Clingman	3B	G.Davis	LF	E.Delahanty	LF	E.Smith	1B	R.Connor	LF	K.Selbach
LF	F.Clarke	LF	G.Stafford	CF	D.Cooley	CF	J.Stenzel	2B	T.Dowd	CF	T.Brown
CF	C.Dexter	CF	G.Van Haltren	RF	S.Thompson	RF	P.Donovan	SS	M.Cross	RF	B.Lush
RF	T.McCreery	RF	M.Tiernan	C	M.Grady	C	J.Sugden	3B	B.Myers	C	D.McGuire
C	D.Miller	C	P.Wilson			C	B.Merritt	LF	J.Sullivan		
				3S	L.Cross	2	L.Bierbauer	CF	T.Parrott	O	C.Abbey
1S	P.Cassidy	O1	H.Davis	O	J.Sullivan	1O	H.Davis	RF	K.Douglass	3	J.Rogers
O	O.Pickering	CS	D.Farrell	C	J.Clements	1	C.Mack	C	E.McFarland	3	H.Smith
O	D.Holmes	1	J.Beckley	1	N.Lajoie			O	T.Turner	C3	D.Farrell
2	J.Crooks	3	B.Joyce	C1	J.Boyle			2	J.Quinn	2	J.Crooks
S	F.Shannon	S	S.Fuller	O	S.Mertes			C	M.Murphy	C	P.McCauley
O	H.McFarland	C	D.Zearfoss					O	D.Cooley		
C	J.Warner			P	J.Taylor	P	F.Killen	O	T.Niland	P	W.Mercer
1	B.Hassamaer	P	D.Clarke	P	A.Orth	P	P.Hawley			P	D.McJames
S	F.Eustace	P	J.Meekin	P	K.Carsey	P	J.Hughey	P	T.Breitenstein	P	L.German
2	A.Johnson	P	M.Sullivan	P	H.Keener	P	C.Hastings	P	B.Hart	P	S.King
P	C.Fraser	P	E.Doheny	P	W.McGill	/P	B.Foreman	P	R.Donahue		
P	B.Hill					/P	E.Horton	P	B.Kissinger	/P	A.Maul
P	B.Cunningham	P	C.Seymour	P	A.Gumbert					/P	E.Norton
P	A.Herman	/P	S.Campfield	/P	C.Lucid					/P	J.Boyd
P	M.McDermott			/P	G.Wheeler					/P	C.Flynn
P	T.Smith										
/P	G.Weyhing										

TEAM	G	W	L	PCT	GB	R	OR	AB	H	2B	3B	HR	BB	SO	AVG	OBP	SLG	PRO	PRO+	BR	/A	PF	CHI	RC	SB	CS	SBA	SBR
BAL	132	90	39	.698		995	662	4719	1548	207	100	23	386	201	.328	.393	.429	.822	120	151	137	101	103	1003	441			
CLE	135	80	48	.625	9.5	840	650	4856	1463	207	72	28	436	316	.301	.363	.391	.754	97	26	-23	106	98	785	175			
CIN	128	77	50	.606	12	783	620	4360	1283	204	73	20	382	226	.294	.357	.388	.745	95	7	-43	107	103	761	350			
BOS	132	74	57	.565	17	860	761	4717	1416	175	74	36	414	274	.300	.363	.392	.755	98	26	-23	106	102	791	241			
CHI	132	71	57	.555	18.5	815	799	4582	1311	182	97	34	409	290	.286	.349	.390	.739	95	-7	-37	104	105	769	332			
PIT	131	66	63	.512	24	787	741	4701	1371	169	94	27	387	286	.292	.353	.385	.738	103	-7	25	96	98	746	217			
NY	133	64	67	.489	27	829	821	4661	1383	159	87	40	439	271	.297	.364	.394	.758	108	32	55	97	99	795	274			
PHI	130	62	68	.477	28.5	890	891	4680	1382	234	84	49	438	297	.295	.363	.413	.776	110	58	68	99	103	801	191			
WAS	133	58	73	.443	33	818	920	4639	1328	179	79	45	516	365	.286	.365	.383	.753	103	29	30	100	97	783	258			
BRO	133	58	73	.443	33	692	764	4548	1292	174	87	28	344	269	.284	.340	.379	.719	100	-45	-4	94	95	680	198			
STL	131	40	90	.308	50.5	593	929	4520	1162	134	78	37	332	300	.257	.313	.346	.659	81	-149	-125	96	96	572	185			
LOU	134	38	93	.290	53	653	997	4588	1197	142	80	37	371	427	.261	.322	.351	.673	85	-123	-98	96	100	603	195			
TOT	792					9555		55571	16136	2166	1005	404	4854	3522	.290	.354	.387	.741							3057			

TEAM	CG	SH	SV	IP	H	H/G	HR	BB	SO	RAT	ERA	ERA+	OAV	OOB	PR	/A	PF	CPI	FA	E	DP	FW	PW	BW	SBW	DIF
BAL	115	9	1	1168¹	1281	9.9	22	339	302	12.7	3.67	116	.277	.331	89	77	98	100	.945	296	114	2.6	6.5	11.6		4.7
CLE	113	9	5	1195²	1363	10.3	27	280	336	12.6	3.46	131	.285	.329	119	141	104	109	.949	288	117	3.6	12.0	-2.0		2.4
CIN	105	12	4	1108	1240	10.1	27	310	219	13.0	3.67	125	.281	.335	84	114	106	105	.951	252	107	4.7	9.7	-3.6		2.8
BOS	110	6	3	1155²	1254	9.8	31	397	277	13.1	3.78	120	.275	.357	74	97	104	106	.934	368	94	-1.7	8.2	-2.0		3.9
CHI	118	2	1	1161	1302	10.1	30	467	353	14.3	4.41	103	.282	.358	-7	15	104	94	.934	366	115	-1.6	1.3	-3.1		10.4
PIT	108	8	1	1159¹	1286	10.0	18	439	362	13.9	4.30	98	.280	.351	7	-15	96	94	.941	317	103	1.2	-1.3	2.1		-.6
NY	104	1	2	1136²	1303	10.3	33	403	312	14.0	4.54	92	.286	.352	-24	-45	96	94	.933	365	90	-1.3	-3.8	4.7		-1.0
PHI	107	1	2	1117	1473	11.9	39	387	243	15.4	5.20	83	.316	.375	-104	-112	99	99	.941	313	112	1.3	-9.5	5.8		-.6
WAS	106	2	3	1136²	1435	11.4	24	435	292	15.2	4.61	95	.306	.372	-32	-28	101	105	.927	398	99	-3.3	-2.4	2.5		-4.3
BRO	97	3	1	1144	1353	10.6	39	400	259	14.1	4.25	97	.292	.354	14	-17	95	104	.945	297	104	2.7	-1.4	-.3		-8.5
STL	115	1	1	1130²	1448	11.5	40	456	279	15.5	5.33	82	.309	.376	-122	-124	100	95	.936	345	73	-.5	-10.5	-10.6		-3.4
LOU	108	1	1	1148²	1398	11.0	48	541	288	15.9	5.12	84	.298	.381	-98	-103	96	99	.916	475	110	-7.8	-8.7	-8.3		-2.6
TOT	1306	57	28	13761²		10.6				14.1	4.36		.290	.354					.938	4080	1238					

Runs		**Hits**		**Doubles**		**Triples**		**Home Runs**		**Total Bases**	
Burkett-Cle	160	Burkett-Cle	240	Delahanty-Phi	44	VanHaltren-NY	21	Joyce-Was-NY	13	Burkett-Cle	317
Keeler-Bal	153	Keeler-Bal	210	Miller-Cin	38	McCreery-Lou	21	Delahanty-Phi	13	Delahanty-Phi	315
Hamilton-Bos	152	Jennings-Bal	209	Kelley-Bal	31	Kelley-Bal	19	Thompson-Phi	12	Kelley-Bal	282
Kelley-Bal	148	Delahanty-Phi	198	Dahlen-Chi	30	Dahlen-Chi	19	Connor-StL	11	VanHaltren-NY	272
Dahlen-Chi	137	VanHaltren-NY	197			Clarke-Lou	18			Keeler-Bal	270

Runs Batted In		**Runs Produced**		**Bases On Balls**		**Batting Average**		**On Base Percentage**		**Slugging Average**	
Delahanty-Phi	126	Jennings-Bal	246	Hamilton-Bos	110	Burkett-Cle	.410	Hamilton-Bos	.477	Delahanty-Phi	.631
Jennings-Bal	121	Delahanty-Phi	244	Joyce-Was-NY	101	Jennings-Bal	.401	Jennings-Bal	.472	Dahlen-Chi	.553
Duffy-Bos	113	Kelley-Bal	240	Childs-Cle	100	Delahanty-Phi	.397	Delahanty-Phi	.472	McCreery-Lou	.546
McKean-Cle	112	Keeler-Bal	231	Kelley-Bal	91	Keeler-Bal	.386	Joyce-Was-NY	.470	Kelley-Bal	.543
		Burkett-Cle	226	Tiernan-NY	77	Tiernan-NY	.369	Kelley-Bal	.469	Burkett-Cle	.541

Production		**Adjusted Production**		**Batter Runs**		**Adjusted Batter Runs**		**Clutch Hitting Index**		**Runs Created**	
Delahanty-Phi	1.103	Delahanty-Phi	192	Delahanty-Phi	64.7	Delahanty-Phi	66.6	Reitz-Bal	151	Kelley-Bal	178
Kelley-Bal	1.013	Kelley-Bal	164	Kelley-Bal	54.6	Kelley-Bal	52.5	Duffy-Bos	148	Delahanty-Phi	170
Burkett-Cle	1.002	Joyce-Was-NY	162	Burkett-Cle	54.5	Joyce-Was-NY	50.0	Anson-Chi	141	Burkett-Cle	166
Dahlen-Chi	.990	Tiernan-NY	159	Joyce-Was-NY	48.4	Tiernan-NY	47.8	Doyle-Bal	140	Hamilton-Bos	160
Joyce-Was-NY	.988	E.Smith-Pit	158	Hamilton-Bos	44.8	Burkett-Cle	45.9	Cross-Phi	139	Jennings-Bal	158

Total Average		**Stolen Bases**		**Stolen Base Average**		**Stolen Base Runs**		**Fielding Runs**		**Total Player Rating**	
Kelley-Bal	1.430	Kelley-Bal	87					Childs-Cle	42.4	Jennings-Bal	6.7
Delahanty-Phi	1.405	Lange-Chi	84					Jennings-Bal	34.2	Childs-Cle	6.6
Hamilton-Bos	1.316	Hamilton-Bos	83					Dahlen-Chi	24.5	Delahanty-Phi	6.0
Joyce-Was-NY	1.306	Miller-Cin	76					Clingman-Lou	23.7	Dahlen-Chi	5.5
Jennings-Bal	1.263	Doyle-Bal	73					Corcoran-Bro	23.5	Joyce-Was-NY	4.0

Wins		**Win Percentage**		**Games**		**Complete Games**		**Shutouts**		**Saves**	
Nichols-Bos	30	Hoffer-Bal	.781	Killen-Pit	52	Killen-Pit	44	Young-Cle	5	Young-Cle	3
Killen-Pit	30	Hemming-Bal	.714	Young-Cle	51	Young-Cle	42	Killen-Pit	5	Hill-Lou	2
Young-Cle	28	Dwyer-Cin	.686	Nichols-Bos	49	Mercer-Was	38			Fisher-Cin	2
Meekin-NY	26	Nichols-Bos	.682	Hawley-Pit	49						
		Griffith-Chi	.676	Clarke-NY	48						

Innings Pitched		**Fewest Hits/Game**		**Fewest BB/Game**		**Strikeouts**		**Strikeouts/Game**		**Ratio**	
Killen-Pit	432.1	Rhines-Cin	8.06	Young-Cle	1.35	Young-Cle	140	Briggs-Chi	3.90	Rhines-Cin	11.64
Young-Cle	414.1	Hawley-Pit	9.10	Clarke-NY	1.54	Hawley-Pit	137	Pond-Bal	3.36	Cuppy-Cle	11.82
Hawley-Pit	378.0	Sullivan-NY	9.13	Dwyer-Cin	1.87	Killen-Pit	134	McJames-Was	3.31	Young-Cle	11.95
Nichols-Bos	372.1	Friend-Chi	9.23	Cuppy-Cle	1.89	Breitenstein-StL	114	Hawley-Pit	3.26	Nichols-Bos	11.97
Mercer-Was	366.1	Hoffer-Bal	9.23	Griffith-Chi	1.98	Meekin-NY	110	Young-Cle	3.04	Esper-Bal	12.08

Earned Run Average		**Adjusted ERA**		**Opponents' Batting Avg.**		**Opponents' On Base Pct.**		**Starter Runs**		**Adjusted Starter Runs**	
Rhines-Cin	2.45	Rhines-Cin	188	Rhines-Cin	.238	Rhines-Cin	.311	Nichols-Bos	63.2	Nichols-Bos	70.6
Nichols-Bos	2.83	Nichols-Bos	160	Hawley-Pit	.261	Cuppy-Cle	.314	Young-Cle	51.5	Young-Cle	59.6
Cuppy-Cle	3.12	Dwyer-Cin	146	Sullivan-NY	.261	Young-Cle	.317	Cuppy-Cle	49.3	Cuppy-Cle	56.2
Dwyer-Cin	3.15	Cuppy-Cle	145	Friend-Chi	.264	Nichols-Bos	.317	Killen-Pit	45.3	Dwyer-Cin	46.7
Young-Cle	3.24	Young-Cle	140	Hoffer-Bal	.264	Esper-Bal	.319	Dwyer-Cin	38.7	Killen-Pit	37.5

Clutch Pitching Index		**Relief Runs**		**Adjusted Relief Runs**		**Relief Ranking**		**Total Pitcher Index**		**Total Baseball Ranking**	
Nichols-Bos	122							Nichols-Bos	6.6	Jennings-Bal	6.7
Wallace-Cle	120							Young-Cle	6.4	Childs-Cle	6.6
Payne-Bro	116							Cuppy-Cle	5.8	Nichols-Bos	6.5
Dwyer-Cin	115							Dwyer-Cin	4.7	Young-Cle	6.4
Rhines-Cin	114							Killen-Pit	4.2	Delahanty-Phi	6.0

March 9 Cleveland signs Holy Cross star Louis Sockalexis to a contract. Sockalexis, a full-blooded Penobscot Indian, soon earns the admiration of Spiders fans with his phenomenal all-around skills. Before long, baseball fans start referring to the Cleveland team as the "Indians." Although Sockalexis will only play parts of three seasons due to acute alcoholism, the nickname will be revived in 1915 and become the club's official name.

March 27 Cleveland president Frank DeHaas Robison proposes that NL teams chip in to pay the 1896 salary of New York star Amos Rusie, who had refused to play due to a contract dispute. Robison and other NL officials want to avoid Rusie's lawsuit, in which he seeks free agency. Although New York president Andrew Freeman vehemently opposes the NL plan, the $3,000 payment is made and Rusie rejoins the Giants.

April 22 Willie Keeler's single and double in the Orioles' first game begins a streak of safe hits in 44 consecutive games.

May 11 Charles "Duke" Farrell, Washington catcher, sets a major league record by throwing out eight Orioles trying to steal second base, but the Senators lose anyway 6-3.

May 23 A "shoot the chutes" waterslide opens at Sportsman's Park, St. Louis. With the Browns in last place, owner Von der Ahe is trying to draw customers with a variety of amusement park attractions.

May 31 Using mechanical dummies, "an electrical baseball machine" reproduces the Louisville doubleheader on stage at Philadelphia's McCauley Theater, which has been fitted out like a ballpark. Messages transmitted from the field are translated by "skillful manipulation" of the machine's keyboard into a reenactment.

June 29 Chicago scores in every inning to demolish Louisville 36-7 to set the NL record for runs scored.

July 16* A game is played under electric lights at Clyde Park in San Antonio, Texas. Dallas wins the exhibition 10–5.

July 18 Cap Anson makes his career 3,000th hit, a fourth-inning single, as Clark Griffith and the Colts defeat Baltimore, 6-3. The feat fails, however, to make the Chicago papers. Included in Cap's 3,000 hit total are 60 walks, officially counted as hits in 1887. In the eighth inning of the game, the O's John McGraw twice steps in front of pitches from Chicago's Clark Griffith, and, each time, umpire Jim McDonald refuses to award first base to McGraw.

July 31 Brooklyn pitcher Bill Kennedy becomes so upset at umpire Hank O'Day that he throws a ball at him. The ball misses O'Day, who has his back turned, allowing George Davis to score the winning run for the Giants.

October 11 Baltimore wins the Temple Cup and $310 for each player by defeating Boston 9-3. W. C. Temple of Pittsburgh, whose trophy has been contested for the last four baseball seasons, is extremely dissatisfied with this year's contest and later asks that the Cup be returned to him.

November 13 At the NL meetings, President Young announces that the Temple Cup Series has been discontinued, and adds that there will be two umpires per game next year.

BALTIMORE		BOSTON		BROOKLYN		CHICAGO		CINCINNATI		CLEVELAND	
M	N.Hanlon	M	F.Selee	M	B.Barnie	M	C.Anson	M	B.Ewing	M	P.Tebeau
1B	J.Doyle	1B	F.Tenney	1B	C.LaChance	1B	C.Anson	1B	J.Beckley	1B	P.Tebeau
2B	H.Reitz	2B	B.Lowe	2B	G.Shoch	2B	J.Connor	2B	B.McPhee	2B	C.Childs
SS	H.Jennings	SS	H.Long	SS	G.Smith	SS	B.Dahlen	SS	C.Ritchey	SS	E.McKean
3B	J.McGraw	3B	J.Collins	3B	B.Shindle	3B	B.Everitt	3B	C.Irwin	3B	B.Wallace
LF	J.Kelley	LF	H.Duffy	LF	J.Anderson	LF	G.Decker	LF	E.Burke	LF	J.Burkett
CF	J.Stenzel	CF	B.Hamilton	CF	M.Griffin	CF	B.Lange	CF	D.Hoy	CF	J.O'Connor
RF	W.Keeler	RF	C.Stahl	RF	F.Jones	RF	J.Ryan	RF	D.Miller	RF	C.Sockalexis
C	B.Clarke	C	M.Bergen	C	J.Grim	C	M.Kittridge	C	H.Peitz	C	C.Zimmer
3S	J.Quinn	OP	J.Stivetts	2	J.Canavan	2P	N.Callahan	S2	T.Corcoran	O	O.Pickering
C	W.Robinson	S	B.Allen	CO	A.Smith	3S	B.McCormick	1C	F.Vaughn	C	L.Criger
1O	T.O'Brien	C	C.Ganzel	C	B.Burrell	OP	W.Thornton	O	B.Holliday	O	S.McAllister
C	F.Bowerman	CO	G.Yeager			C	T.Donahue	C	P.Schriver	O	H.Blake
		C	F.Lake			2	F.Pfeffer			O	J.McAleer
P	J.Corbett			P	B.Kennedy			P	T.Breitenstein		
P	B.Hoffer	P	K.Nichols	P	H.Payne	P	C.Griffith	P	B.Rhines	P	C.Young
P	A.Pond	P	F.Klobedanz	P	J.Dunn	P	D.Friend	P	F.Dwyer	P	Z.Wilson
P	J.Nops	P	T.Lewis	P	C.Fisher	P	B.Briggs	P	R.Ehret	P	J.Powell
		P	J.Sullivan	P	D.Daub	P	R.Denzer	P	B.Dammann	P	N.Cuppy
P	D.Amole	/P	S.McMahon							/P	M.McDermott
/P	G.Blackburn					/P	J.Korwan			/P	H.Clarke
										/P	C.Brown

LOUISVILLE		NEW YORK		PHILADELPHIA		PITTSBURGH		ST.LOUIS		WASHINGTON	
M	J.Rogers	M	B.Joyce	M	G.Stallings	M	P.Donovan	M	T.Dowd	M	G.Schmelz
M	F.Clarke	1B	W.Clark	1B	N.Lajoie	1B	H.Davis	M	H.Nicol	M	T.Brown
1B	P.Werden	2B	K.Gleason	2B	L.Cross	2B	D.Padden	M	B.Hallman	1B	T.Tucker
2B	J.Rogers	SS	G.Davis	SS	S.Gillen	SS	B.Ely	M	C.Von Der Ahe	2B	J.O'Brien
SS	G.Stafford	3B	B.Joyce	3B	B.Nash	3B	J.Hoffmeister	1B	M.Grady	SS	G.DeMontreville
3B	B.Clingman	LF	D.Holmes	LF	E.Delahanty	LF	E.Smith	2B	B.Hallman	3B	C.Reilly
LF	F.Clarke	CF	G.Van Haltren	CF	D.Cooley	CF	S.Brodie	SS	M.Cross	LF	K.Selbach
CF	O.Pickering	RF	M.Tiernan	RF	T.Dowd	RF	P.Donovan	3B	F.Hartman	CF	T.Brown
RF	T.McCreery	C	J.Warner	C	J.Boyle	C	J.Sugden	LF	D.Lally	RF	C.Abbey
C	B.Wilson							CF	D.Harley	C	D.McGuire
		O	T.McCreery	O2	P.Geier	C	B.Merritt	RF	T.Turner		
OC	C.Dexter	C1	P.Wilson	C	J.Clements	OP	J.Tannehill	C	K.Douglass	OS	Z.Wrigley
O	H.Wagner	3	J.Donnelly	S	F.Shugart	3	J.Donnelly			C	D.Farrell
2S	A.Johnson	/3	C.Gettig	C	E.McFarland	1	D.Lyons	2O	J.Houseman	O	J.Gettman
S2	J.Dolan	1	J.Beckley	2	B.Hallman	1	J.Rothfuss	C	M.Murphy	1	E.Cartwright
O	D.Nance					O	T.Leahy	O	T.Dowd		
2	H.Smith	P	A.Rusie	P	J.Taylor			C	E.McFarland	P	W.Mercer
		P	J.Meekin	P	A.Orth	P	F.Killen	1	R.Connor	P	D.McJames
P	C.Fraser	P	C.Seymour	P	J.Fifield	P	P.Hawley			P	C.Swaim
P	B.Cunningham	P	M.Sullivan	P	G.Wheeler	P	J.Hughey	P	R.Donahue	P	S.King
P	B.Hill	P	E.Doheny			C	C.Hastings	P	B.Hart	P	L.German
P	B.Magee			/P	D.Dunkle	P	J.Gardner	P	K.Carsey		
		/P	D.Clarke	/P	Y.Johnson			P	W.Sudhoff	/P	R.Bresnahan
/P	G.Hemming			/P	K.Carsey					/P	E.Norton
/P	R.Evans			/P	B.Becker			/P	D.Esper		
/P	D.Clarke							P	P.Coleman		
/P	P.Dowling							P	C.Lucid		
/P	A.Herman							/P	B.Hutchison		
/P	B.Miller							/P	M.McDermott		
								/P	J.Grimes		

TEAM	G	W	L	PCT	GB	R	OR	AB	H	2B	3B	HR	BB	SO	AVG	OBP	SLG	PRO	PRO+	BR	/A	PF	CHI	RC	SB	CS	SBA	SBR
BOS	135	93	39	.705		1025	665	4937	1574	230	83	45	423	262	.319	.378	.426	.804	110	117	59	106	108	919	233			
BAL	136	90	40	.692	2	964	674	4872	1584	243	66	19	437	256	.325	.394	.414	.808	118	138	138	100	100	984	401			
NY	137	83	48	.634	9.5	895	695	4844	1449	188	84	31	404	327	.299	.361	.392	.753	106	25	48	97	107	829	328			
CIN	134	76	56	.576	17	763	705	4524	1311	219	69	22	380	218	.290	.353	.383	.736	93	-6	-56	107	100	715	194			
CLE	132	69	62	.527	23.5	773	680	4604	1374	192	88	16	435	344	.298	.364	.389	.753	98	25	-18	105	96	747	181			
WAS	135	61	71	.462	32	781	793	4636	1376	194	77	36	430	348	.297	.357	.395	.752	104	18	22	100	98	755	208			
BRO	136	61	71	.462	32	802	845	4810	1343	202	72	24	351	255	.279	.336	.366	.702	95	-74	-34	95	110	684	187			
PIT	135	60	71	.458	32.5	676	835	4590	1266	140	108	25	359	334	.276	.337	.370	.707	95	-61	-34	96	95	657	170			
CHI	138	59	73	.447	34	832	894	4803	1356	189	97	38	430	317	.282	.347	.386	.733	94	-16	-46	104	105	766	264			
PHI	134	55	77	.417	38	752	792	4756	1392	213	83	40	399	299	.293	.353	.398	.751	89	13	34	97	93	754	163			
LOU	134	52	78	.400	40	669	859	4520	1197	160	70	40	370	453	.265	.329	.358	.687	89	-94	-71	97	100	624	195			
STL	132	29	102	.221	63.5	588	1083	4642	1277	149	67	31	354	314	.275	.336	.356	.692	89	-84	-70	98	85	639	172			
TOT	809					9520		56538	16499	2319	964	367	4716	3727	.292	.354	.386	.741							2696			

TEAM	CG	SH	SV	IP	H	H/G	HR	BB	SO	RAT	ERA	ERA+	OAV	OOB	PR	/A	PF	CPI	FA	E	DP	FW	PW	BW	SBW	DIF
BOS	115	8	7	1194¹	1273	9.6	39	393	329	12.9	3.65	122	.271	.333	87	107	104	102	.951	272	80	3.9	9.2	5.1		8.8
BAL	118	3	0	1197²	1296	9.7	18	382	361	13.2	3.55	117	.274	.338	100	81	97	104	.951	277	110	3.8	6.9	11.8		2.4
NY	118	8	3	1187¹	1214	9.2	26	486	456	13.4	3.47	120	.263	.342	110	89	96	106	.930	397	109	-3.3	7.6	4.1		9.1
CIN	100	4	2	1156²	1375	10.7	18	329	270	13.7	4.09	111	.294	.347	29	58	106	101	.948	273	100	3.7	5.0	-4.8		6.1
CLE	111	6	0	1119¹	1297	10.4	32	289	277	13.1	3.95	114	.288	.337	45	67	104	100	.950	261	74	4.2	5.7	-1.5		-4.9
WAS	102	7	6	1148	1383	10.8	27	400	348	14.6	4.01	108	.296	.362	37	40	101	112	.933	369	103	-1.9	3.4	1.9		-8.4
BRO	114	4	2	1194²	1417	10.7	34	410	256	14.2	4.60	89	.293	.355	-39	-68	95	94	.936	364	99	-1.5	-5.8	-2.9		5.2
PIT	112	2	2	1153¹	1397	10.9	22	318	342	13.9	4.67	89	.297	.350	-47	-66	97	91	.936	346	70	-.5	-5.7	-2.9		3.6
CHI	131	2	1	1197	1485	11.2	30	433	361	14.9	4.53	98	.303	.367	-30	-12	104	103	.932	393	111	-2.9	-1.0	-3.9		.9
PHI	115	4	2	1155¹	1415	11.0	28	364	253	14.3	4.60	91	.300	.356	-38	-53	97	96	.944	296	72	2.3	-4.5	2.9		-11.7
LOU	114	2	0	1138	1363	10.8	39	459	267	15.1	4.42	96	.295	.369	-14	-22	99	106	.929	395	84	-3.6	-1.9	-6.1		-1.4
STL	109	1	1	1127¹	1584	12.6	54	453	207	16.8	6.21	71	.329	.395	-239	-228	102	93	.933	375	84	-2.7	-19.5	-6.0		-8.2
TOT	1359	51	26	13969		10.6				14.1	4.31		.292	.354					.939	4018	1096					

Runs		Hits		Doubles		Triples		Home Runs		Total Bases	
Hamilton-Bos	152	Keeler-Bal	239	Stenzel-Bal	43	Davis-Pit	28	Duffy-Bos	11	Lajoie-Phi	310
Keeler-Bal	145	F.Clarke-Lou	202	Lajoie-Phi	40	Lajoie-Phi	23	Davis-NY	10	Keeler-Bal	304
Griffin-Bro	136	Delahanty-Phi	200	Delahanty-Phi	40	Wallace-Cle	21	Lajoie-Phi	9	Delahanty-Phi	285
Jones-Bro	134	Burkett-Cle	198	Wallace-Cle	33	Keeler-Bal	19	Beckley-NY-Cin	8	F.Clarke-Lou	276
Jennings-Bal	133	Lajoie-Phi	197	Ryan-Chi	33					Duffy-Bos	265

Runs Batted In		Runs Produced		Bases On Balls		Batting Average		On Base Percentage		Slugging Average	
Davis-NY	136	Duffy-Bos	248	Hamilton-Bos	105	Keeler-Bal	.424	McGraw-Bal	.471	Lajoie-Phi	.569
Collins-Bos	132	Davis-NY	238	McGraw-Bal	99	F.Clarke-Lou	.390	Burkett-Cle	.468	Keeler-Bal	.539
Duffy-Bos	129	Collins-Bos	229	Griffin-Bro	81	Burkett-Cle	.383	Keeler-Bal	.464	Delahanty-Phi	.538
Lajoie-Phi	127	Kelley-Bal	226	Selbach-Was	80	Delahanty-Phi	.377	Jennings-Bal	.463	F.Clarke-Lou	.533
Kelley-Bal	118			Joyce-NY	78	Kelley-Bal	.362	F.Clarke-Lou	.462	Davis-NY	.509

Production		Adjusted Production		Batter Runs		Adjusted Batter Runs		Clutch Hitting Index		Runs Created	
Keeler-Bal	1.003	F.Clarke-Lou	168	Keeler-Bal	52.1	F.Clarke-Lou	53.2	Gleason-NY	139	Keeler-Bal	176
F.Clarke-Lou	.994	Keeler-Bal	164	F.Clarke-Lou	48.5	Keeler-Bal	52.1	Shindle-Bro	138	F.Clarke-Lou	158
Delahanty-Phi	.981	Delahanty-Phi	162	Delahanty-Phi	45.1	Delahanty-Phi	48.6	Collins-Bos	133	Delahanty-Phi	142
Lajoie-Phi	.960	Lajoie-Phi	156	Burkett-Cle	42.0	Lajoie-Phi	39.3	Reitz-Bal	131	Davis-NY	138
Burkett-Cle	.944	Kelley-Bal	147	Kelley-Bal	37.2	Kelley-Bal	37.2	Tenney-Bos	128	Stenzel-Bal	136

Total Average		Stolen Bases		Stolen Base Average		Stolen Base Runs		Fielding Runs		Total Player Rating	
F.Clarke-Lou	1.272	Lange-Chi	73					Clingman-Lou	28.6	Jennings-Bal	5.4
Keeler-Bal	1.262	Stenzel-Bal	69					Cross-StL	27.8	Davis-NY	4.8
Jennings-Bal	1.251	Hamilton-Bos	66					Jennings-Bal	27.1	F.Clarke-Lou	4.2
Hamilton-Bos	1.162	Davis-NY	65					Davis-NY	21.7	Delahanty-Phi	4.0
Kelley-Bal	1.143	Keeler-Bal	64					Reitz-Bal	21.5	Collins-Bos	3.5

Wins		Win Percentage		Games		Complete Games		Shutouts		Saves	
Nichols-Bos	31	Klobedanz-Bos	.788	Mercer-Was	47	Killen-Pit	38	Mercer-Was	3	Nichols-Bos	3
Rusie-NY	28	Nops-Bal	.769	Young-Cle	46	Griffith-Chi	38	McJames-Was	3	Mercer-Was	3
Klobedanz-Bos	26	Corbett-Bal	.750	Nichols-Bos	46	Donahue-StL	38				
Corbett-Bal	24	Nichols-Bos	.738	Donahue-StL	46	Nichols-Bos	37				
Breitenstein-Cin	23	Rusie-NY	.737			Kennedy-Bro	36				

Innings Pitched		Fewest Hits/Game		Fewest BB/Game		Strikeouts		Strikeouts/Game		Ratio	
Nichols-Bos	368.0	Seymour-NY	8.23	Young-Cle	1.31	McJames-Was	156	Seymour-NY	4.83	Nichols-Bos	10.59
Donahue-StL	348.0	Rusie-NY	8.77	Tannehill-Pit	1.52	Seymour-NY	149	McJames-Was	4.34	Rusie-NY	11.48
Griffith-Chi	343.2	Nichols-Bos	8.85	Nichols-Bos	1.66	Corbett-Bal	149	Corbett-Bal	4.28	Cuppy-Cle	11.80
Kennedy-Bro	343.1	Hill-Lou	9.45	Cuppy-Cle	1.70	Rusie-NY	135	Rusie-NY	3.77	Young-Cle	12.04
Mercer-Was	342.0	Corbett-Bal	9.49	Killen-Pit	2.03	Nichols-Bos	127	Nichols-Bos	3.11	Nops-Bal	12.07

Earned Run Average		Adjusted ERA		Opponents' Batting Avg.		Opponents' On Base Pct.		Starter Runs		Adjusted Starter Runs	
Rusie-NY	2.54	Nichols-Bos	169	Seymour-NY	.242	Nichols-Bos	.291	Nichols-Bos	68.1	Nichols-Bos	74.6
Nichols-Bos	2.64	Rusie-NY	163	Rusie-NY	.254	Rusie-NY	.308	Rusie-NY	63.3	Rusie-NY	57.7
Nops-Bal	2.81	Nops-Bal	148	Nichols-Bos	.256	Cuppy-Cle	.314	Mercer-Was	42.7	Mercer-Was	43.8
Corbett-Bal	3.11	Powell-Cle	142	Hill-Lou	.268	Young-Cle	.318	Corbett-Bal	41.8	Corbett-Bal	36.8
Powell-Cle	3.16	Cuppy-Cle	140	Corbett-Bal	.269	Nops-Bal	.319	Nops-Bal	36.6	Powell-Cle	33.2

Clutch Pitching Index		Relief Runs		Adjusted Relief Runs		Relief Ranking		Total Pitcher Index		Total Baseball Ranking	
Mercer-Was	132							Nichols-Bos	7.3	Nichols-Bos	7.3
Nops-Bal	120							Rusie-NY	6.1	Rusie-NY	6.1
Corbett-Bal	117							Mercer-Was	5.0	Jennings-Bal	5.4
Rusie-NY	117							Corbett-Bal	3.1	Mercer-Was	5.0
McJames-Was	117							Breitenstein-Cin	3.1	Davis-NY	4.8

January 31 Cap Anson is fired after 19 years as player-manager of Chicago. Strong-minded Cap, with a record of 1,288 victories and five pennants, was enormously popular in Chicago. Former infielder Tom Burns takes over for Chicago, who are now called the Orphans.

April 2* Famed heavyweight boxer Jim Corbett, whose brother Joe pitches for Baltimore, claims he made $17,000 last year by playing in well-advertised minor league games for a sizable cut of the gate.

April 16 The league urges official scorers to award hits, rather than automatic errors, on hard-hit balls that handcuff infielders; to be scrupulous in awarding assists to all players handling balls in rundowns; and to cease awarding hits to batters on fielder's-choice plays.

April 21 Phillies pitcher Bill Duggleby hits a bases-full home run in his first major league at bat against Cy Seymour, an event never duplicated. The Phillies win 13-4.

April 22 Two no-hitters are pitched on the same day. Baltimore's Jim Hughes beats Boston in his second major league start, and Cincinnati's Ted Breitenstein no-hits Pittsburgh.

May 11 With the bases full and one out, Oriole right fielder Tommy O'Brien muffs Bobby Lowe's short fly, recovers the ball, runs in, tags Jimmy Collins at second base, and steps on the bag to force Chick Stahl and complete an unassisted double play.

June 10 A hard week for managers: Tom Brown is replaced at Washington by "Dirty Jack" Doyle, Billy Barnie is fired by ninth-place Brooklyn. Barnie's successor, center field Mike Griffin, resigns after four games; President Charlie Ebbets fills in. "Scrappy" Bill Joyce is dropped by the New York Giants in favor of Cap Anson, who takes over on the eleventh.

June 13* Former pitcher Charles Swee-ney, recently released from San Quentin penitentiary where he served time for manslaughter, officiates in the San Francisco–San Jose game as a California League umpire.

July 5* With the agreement of Atlantic League president Ed Barrow, Lizzie (Stroud) Arlington pitches an inning for Reading against Allentown. The lady hurler gives up two hits but no runs in the first appearance of a woman in Organized Baseball.

July 7 Criticized for being unable "to handle men in the up-to-day style," Cap Anson resigns as Giants manager with a 9-13 record. Bill Joyce is reappointed on the same day.

August 26 Cleveland plays its final home game of the season and only their fourth in Cleveland since July ninth. With 83 of their final 87 games on the road, the team has earned nicknames such as the Nomads, Exiles, Misfits, and Wanderers.

BALTIMORE		BOSTON		BROOKLYN		CHICAGO		CINCINNATI		CLEVELAND	
M	N.Hanlon	M	F.Selee	M	B.Barnie	M	T.Burns	M	B.Ewing	M	P.Tebeau
1B	D.McGann	1B	F.Tenney	M	M.Griffin	1B	B.Everitt	1B	J.Beckley	1B	P.Tebeau
2B	G.DeMontreville	2B	B.Lowe	M	C.Ebbets	2B	J.Connor	2B	B.McPhee	2B	C.Childs
SS	H.Jennings	SS	H.Long	1B	C.LaChance	SS	B.Dahlen	SS	T.Corcoran	SS	E.McKean
3B	J.McGraw	3B	J.Collins	2B	B.Hallman	3B	B.McCormick	3B	C.Irwin	3B	B.Wallace
LF	D.Holmes	LF	H.Duffy	SS	G.Magoon	LF	J.Ryan	LF	E.Smith	LF	J.Burkett
CF	J.Kelley	CF	B.Hamilton	3B	B.Shindle	CF	B.Lange	CF	A.McBride	CF	J.McAleer
RF	W.Keeler	RF	C.Stahl	LF	J.Sheckard	RF	S.Mertes	RF	D.Miller	RF	H.Blake
C	W.Robinson	C	M.Bergen	CF	M.Griffin	C	T.Donahue	C	H.Peitz	C	L.Criger
				RF	F.Jones						
C1	B.Clarke	C1	G.Yeager	C	J.Ryan	OP	W.Thornton	2O	H.Steinfeldt	1C	J.O'Connor
O	J.Stenzel	O	G.Stafford			O	D.Green	1C	F.Vaughn	O	E.Heidrick
3S	S.Brodie	O1	J.Stivetts	1	T.Tucker	OP	F.Isbell	C	B.Wood	O	C.Sockalexis
3S	A.Ball			OC	A.Smith	CO	F.Chance	O	B.Holliday	C	C.Zimmer
O	T.O'Brien	P	K.Nichols	C	J.Grim			O	H.McFarland		
		P	T.Lewis	/O	J.Anderson	P	C.Griffith			P	C.Young
P	D.McJames	P	V.Willis	2	T.Daly	P	N.Callahan	P	P.Hawley	P	J.Powell
P	J.Hughes	P	F.Klobedanz			P	W.Woods	P	T.Breitenstein	P	Z.Wilson
P	A.Maul			P	B.Kennedy	P	M.Kilroy	P	B.Hill	P	N.Cuppy
P	J.Nops			P	J.Dunn			P	F.Dwyer		
P	F.Kitson			P	J.Yeager	/P	J.Taylor	P	B.Dammann	/P	C.Jones
				P	R.Miller	/P	B.Briggs			/P	S.McAllister
/P	B.Hoffer			P	K.McKenna	/P	B.Phyle			/P	C.Fraser
/P	A.Pond					/P	D.Friend			/P	F.Bates
				/P	E.Stein					/P	G.Kelb
				/P	H.Howell						
				/P	W.Gaston						

LOUISVILLE		NEW YORK		PHILADELPHIA		PITTSBURGH		ST.LOUIS		WASHINGTON	
M	F.Clarke	M	B.Joyce	M	G.Stallings	M	B.Watkins	M	T.Hurst	M	T.Brown
1B	H.Wagner	M	C.Anson	M	B.Shettsline	1B	W.Clark	1B	G.Decker	M	J.Doyle
2B	H.Smith	M	B.Joyce	1B	K.Douglass	2B	D.Padden	2B	J.Crooks	M	D.McGuire
SS	C.Ritchey	1B	B.Joyce	2B	N.Lajoie	SS	B.Ely	SS	G.Smith	M	A.Irwin
3B	B.Clingman	2B	K.Gleason	SS	M.Cross	3B	B.Grey	3B	L.Cross	3B	J.Doyle
LF	F.Clarke	SS	G.Davis	3B	B.Lauder	LF	J.McCarthy	LF	D.Harley	2B	H.Reitz
CF	D.Hoy	3B	F.Hartman	LF	E.Delahanty	CF	T.O'Brien	CF	J.Stenzel	SS	Z.Wrigley
RF	C.Dexter	LF	M.Tiernan	CF	D.Cooley	RF	P.Donovan	RF	T.Dowd	3B	J.Smith
C	M.Kittridge	CF	G.Van Haltren	RF	E.Flick	C	P.Schriver	C	J.Clements	LF	K.Selbach
		RF	J.Doyle	C	E.McFarland					CF	J.Anderson
2O	G.Stafford	C	J.Warner			C	F.Bowerman	2S	J.Quinn	RF	J.Gettman
1	G.Decker			3	E.Abbaticchio	1	H.Davis	CO	J.Sugden	C	D.McGuire
1	H.Davis	CO	M.Grady	C	M.Murphy	O	T.McCreery	1	T.Tucker		
C	B.Wilson	OP	C.Gettig	3	B.Nash	O	S.Brodie	SO	S.Sullivan	C1	D.Farrell
C	D.Powers	O	W.Wilmot	O	S.Thompson	2	B.Eagan	S	R.Hall	3O	B.Wagner
O	D.Nance	O	T.McCreery					O	T.Turner	3	D.Casey
O	T.Hartsel	O3	P.Foster	P	W.Piatt	P	J.Tannehill	O	D.Holmes	3	B.Myers
C	C.Snyder			P	R.Donahue	P	B.Rhines			O	B.Freeman
		P	C.Seymour	P	A.Orth	P	J.Gardner	P	J.Taylor	OP	B.Donovan
P	B.Cunningham	P	J.Meekin	P	J.Fifield	P	F.Killen	P	W.Sudhoff	1	C.Carr
P	B.Magee	P	A.Rusie	P	G.Wheeler	P	C.Hastings	P	J.Hughey		
P	P.Dowling	P	E.Doheny					P	K.Carsey	P	G.Weyhing
P	C.Fraser			P	D.Dunkle	P	B.Hart			P	W.Mercer
		/P	B.Carrick	/P	B.Duggleby	/P	S.Leever	P	D.Esper	P	B.Dinneen
P	R.Ehret			/P	E.Murphy	/P	B.Hoffer	P	P.Daniels	P	F.Killen
P	N.Altrock					/P	J.Cronin	/P	G.Gillpatrick	P	C.Swaim
						/P	Z.Rosebraugh	/P	H.Maupin		
										/P	R.Evans
										/P	D.Amole
										/P	K.Baker
										/P	P.Williams

TEAM	G	W	L	PCT	GB	R	OR	AB	H	2B	3B	HR	BB	SO	AVG	OBP	SLG	PRO	PRO+	BR	/A	PF	CHI	RC	SB	CS	SBA	SBR
BOS	152	102	47	.685		872	614	5276	1531	190	55	53	405	303	.290	.344	.377	.721	106	72	28	105	104	780	172			
BAL	154	96	53	.644	6	933	623	5242	1584	154	77	12	519	316	.302	.382	.368	.750	118	157	140	102	99	864	250			
CIN	157	92	60	.605	11.5	831	740	5334	1448	207	101	19	455	300	.271	.335	.359	.694	97	24	-31	107	103	732	165			
CHI	152	85	65	.567	17.5	828	679	5219	1431	175	84	18	476	394	.274	.343	.350	.693	104	29	31	100	104	735	220			
CLE	156	81	68	.544	21	730	683	5246	1379	162	56	18	545	306	.263	.338	.325	.663	96	-23	-13	99	97	641	93			
PHI	150	78	71	.523	24	823	784	5118	1431	238	81	33	432	382	.280	.348	.377	.725	118	84	120	96	98	769	182			
NY	157	77	73	.513	25.5	837	800	5349	1422	190	86	34	428	372	.266	.328	.353	.681	103	-5	19	97	109	714	214			
PIT	152	72	76	.486	29.5	634	694	5087	1313	140	88	14	336	343	.258	.313	.328	.641	90	-78	-65	98	96	589	107			
LOU	154	70	81	.464	30	728	833	5193	1389	150	71	32	375	429	.267	.325	.342	.667	98	-31	-19	98	101	687	235			
BRO	149	54	91	.372	46	638	811	5126	1314	156	66	17	328	314	.256	.309	.322	.631	85	-98	-95	100	101	577	130			
WAS	155	51	101	.336	52.5	704	939	5257	1423	177	80	36	370	386	.271	.327	.355	.682	100	-5	-3	100	94	703	197			
STL	154	39	111	.260	63.5	571	929	5214	1290	149	55	13	383	402	.247	.309	.305	.614	78	-127	-142	102	91	552	104			
TOT	921					9129		62661	16955	2088	900	299	5092	4247	.271	.334	.347	.681						2069				

TEAM	CG	SH	SV	IP	H	H/G	HR	BB	SO	RAT	ERA	ERA+	OAV	OOB	PR	/A	PF	CPI	FA	E	DP	FW	PW	BW	SBW	DIF
BOS	127	9	8	1340	1186	8.0	37	470	432	11.6	2.98	124	.236	.310	93	105	102	97	.950	310	102	3.1	9.8	2.6		12.0
BAL	138	12	0	1323	1236	8.4	17	400	422	11.5	2.90	123	.246	.310	104	98	99	99	.947	326	105	2.5	9.2	13.1		-3.2
CIN	131	10	2	1385¹	1484	9.6	16	449	294	13.0	3.50	110	.272	.336	17	51	106	103	.950	325	128	2.9	4.8	-2.9		11.2
CHI	137	13	0	1342²	1357	9.1	17	364	323	12.1	2.83	126	.261	.319	115	111	99	113	.936	412	149	-2.9	10.4	-2.9		-.4
CLE	142	9	0	1334	1429	9.6	26	309	339	12.1	3.20	113	.272	.320	59	60	100	105	.952	301	95	4.2	5.6	-1.2		-2.1
PHI	129	10	0	1288¹	1440	10.1	23	399	325	13.4	3.72	92	.281	.342	-17	-42	95	104	.937	379	102	-1.2	-3.9	11.2		-2.6
NY	141	9	1	1353²	1359	9.0	21	587	558	13.5	3.44	101	.260	.344	25	4	96	106	.932	447	113	-4.2	.4	-1.8		4.0
PIT	131	10	3	1323²	1400	9.5	14	346	330	12.3	3.41	104	.270	.323	29	21	99	98	.946	340	105	1.4	2.0	-6.1		.8
LOU	137	4	0	1334	1457	9.8	33	470	271	13.6	4.24	84	.276	.346	-95	-101	99	93	.939	382	114	-.8	-9.4	-1.8		6.5
BRO	134	1	0	1298²	1446	10.0	34	476	294	13.7	4.01	89	.280	.348	-59	-63	99	100	.947	334	125	1.3	-5.9	-8.9		-5.0
WAS	129	0	1	1307	1577	10.9	29	450	371	14.5	4.52	81	.297	.360	-134	-127	102	98	.929	443	119	-4.2	-11.9	-.3		-8.6
STL	133	0	2	1324¹	1584	10.9	32	372	288	13.9	4.53	83	.295	.350	-137	-111	105	93	.939	388	97	-1.2	-10.4	-13.3		-11.2
TOT	1609	87	17	15954²		9.6				12.9	3.60		.271	.334					.942	4387	1354					

Runs
McGraw-Bal	143
Jennings-Bal	135
VanHaltren-NY	129
Keeler-Bal	126
Cooley-Phi	123

Hits
Keeler-Bal	216
Burkett-Cle	213
VanHaltren-NY	204
Lajoie-Phi	197

Doubles
Lajoie-Phi	43
Delahanty-Phi	36
Dahlen-Chi	35
Collins-Bos	35
Anderson-Br-Ws-Br	33

Triples
Anderson-Br-Ws-Br	22
VanHaltren-NY	16
Hoy-Lou	16

Home Runs
Collins-Bos	15
Wagner-Lou	10
Joyce-NY	10
Anderson-Br-Ws-Br	9
McKean-Cle	9

Total Bases
Collins-Bos	286
Lajoie-Phi	280
VanHaltren-NY	270
Anderson-Br-Ws-Br	257
Cooley-Phi	256

Runs Batted In
Lajoie-Phi	127
Collins-Bos	111
Kelley-Bal	110
Duffy-Bos	108
McGann-Bal	106

Runs Produced
Lajoie-Phi	234
Jennings-Bal	221
Delahanty-Phi	203
Collins-Bos	203
McGann-Bal	200

Bases On Balls
McGraw-Bal	112
Joyce-NY	88
Hamilton-Bos	87
Flick-Phi	86
Jennings-Bal	78

Batting Average
Keeler-Bal	.385
Hamilton-Bos	.369
McGraw-Bal	.342
Smith-Cin	.342
Burkett-Cle	.341

On Base Percentage
Hamilton-Bos	.480
McGraw-Bal	.475
Jennings-Bal	.454
Flick-Phi	.430
Delahanty-Phi	.426

Slugging Average
Anderson-Br-Ws-Br	.494
Collins-Bos	.479
Lajoie-Phi	.461
Delahanty-Phi	.454
Hamilton-Bos	.453

Production
Hamilton-Bos	.933
Delahanty-Phi	.880
Flick-Phi	.878
Jennings-Bal	.876
McGraw-Bal	.871

Adjusted Production
Hamilton-Bos	159
Delahanty-Phi	159
Flick-Phi	158
Jennings-Bal	149
McGraw-Bal	148

Batter Runs
McGraw-Bal	45.1
Jennings-Bal	44.2
Hamilton-Bos	43.4
Delahanty-Phi	40.2
Flick-Phi	35.2

Adjusted Batter Runs
Delahanty-Phi	45.6
McGraw-Bal	42.8
Jennings-Bal	41.9
Flick-Phi	39.9
Hamilton-Bos	37.7

Clutch Hitting Index
Kelley-Bal	145
Grey-Pit	137
Davis-NY	136
Connor-Chi	136
Hartman-NY	135

Runs Created
Delahanty-Phi	135
McGraw-Bal	121
Hamilton-Bos	120
Jennings-Bal	119
Ryan-Chi	119

Total Average
Hamilton-Bos	1.262
McGraw-Bal	1.115
Delahanty-Phi	1.082
Jennings-Bal	1.050
Flick-Phi	1.035

Stolen Bases
Delahanty-Phi	58
Hamilton-Bos	54
DeMontreville-Bal	49
Dexter-Lou	44
McGraw-Bal	43

Stolen Base Average

Stolen Base Runs

Fielding Runs
Davis-NY	34.6
Dahlen-Chi	25.5
Gleason-NY	20.5
Selbach-Was	19.9
Cross-StL	18.4

Total Player Rating
Dahlen-Chi	4.6
Jennings-Bal	4.5
Davis-NY	4.4
Collins-Bos	3.8
Delahanty-Phi	3.7

Wins
Nichols-Bos	31
Cunningham-Lou	28
McJames-Bal	27
Hawley-Cin	27
Lewis-Bos	26

Win Percentage
Lewis-Bos	.765
Maul-Bal	.741
Nichols-Bos	.721
Hawley-Cin	.711
Griffith-Chi	.706

Games
Taylor-StL	50
Nichols-Bos	50
Young-Cle	46

Complete Games
Taylor-StL	42
Cunningham-Lou	41
Young-Cle	40
Nichols-Bos	40
McJames-Bal	40

Shutouts
Powell-Cle	6
Piatt-Phi	6
Tannehill-Pit	5
Nichols-Bos	5
Hughes-Bal	5

Saves
Nichols-Bos	4
Tannehill-Pit	2
Lewis-Bos	2
Hickman-Bos	2
Dammann-Cin	2

Innings Pitched
Taylor-StL	397.1
Nichols-Bos	388.0
Young-Cle	377.2
McJames-Bal	374.0
Cunningham-Lou	362.0

Fewest Hits/Game
Nichols-Bos	7.33
Willis-Bos	7.64
Lewis-Bos	7.67
Maul-Bal	7.77
McJames-Bal	7.87

Fewest BB/Game
Young-Cle	.98
Dwyer-Cin	1.58
Cunningham-Lou	1.62
Tannehill-Pit	1.74
Griffith-Chi	1.77

Strikeouts
Seymour-NY	239
McJames-Bal	178
Willis-Bos	160
Nichols-Bos	138
Piatt-Phi	121

Strikeouts/Game
Seymour-NY	6.03
Willis-Bos	4.63
McJames-Bal	4.28
Doheny-NY	4.06
Piatt-Phi	3.56

Ratio
Nichols-Bos	9.63
Maul-Bal	9.76
Young-Cle	10.41
Griffith-Chi	10.75
McJames-Bal	10.88

Earned Run Average
Griffith-Chi	1.88
Maul-Bal	2.10
Nichols-Bos	2.13
McJames-Bal	2.36
Callahan-Chi	2.46

Adjusted ERA
Griffith-Chi	190
Nichols-Bos	173
Maul-Bal	170
McJames-Bal	152
Callahan-Chi	145

Opponents' Batting Avg.
Nichols-Bos	.221
Willis-Bos	.229
Lewis-Bos	.229
Maul-Bal	.232
McJames-Bal	.234

Opponents' On Base Pct.
Nichols-Bos	.272
Maul-Bal	.275
Young-Cle	.288
Griffith-Chi	.294
McJames-Bal	.297

Starter Runs
Nichols-Bos	63.3
Griffith-Chi	62.4
McJames-Bal	51.7
Young-Cle	45.2
Maul-Bal	39.9

Adjusted Starter Runs
Nichols-Bos	67.1
Griffith-Chi	61.5
McJames-Bal	50.5
Young-Cle	45.6
Maul-Bal	39.2

Clutch Pitching Index
Griffith-Chi	135
Orth-Phi	120
Dammann-Cin	118
Doheny-NY	117
Callahan-Chi	116

Relief Runs

Adjusted Relief Runs

Relief Ranking

Total Pitcher Index
Nichols-Bos	6.9
Griffith-Chi	5.8
Young-Cle	5.3
McJames-Bal	4.3
Callahan-Chi	3.9

Total Baseball Ranking
Nichols-Bos	6.9
Griffith-Chi	5.8
Young-Cle	5.3
Dahlen-Chi	4.6
Jennings-Bal	4.5

February 7 Under a joint ownership arrangement, several Baltimore players are shifted to Brooklyn, and that club transfers several to the Orioles. Manager Ned Hanlon takes Willie Keeler, Joe Kelley, Hughie Jennings, and others with him while John McGraw and Wilbert Robinson remain in Baltimore. The powerful new Brooklyn team is nicknamed the Superbas.

April 3 The Robison brothers, owners of the Cleveland franchise, gain control of the St. Louis franchise as well, and redistribute players. St. Louis, which finished 12th in 1898, is enhanced with Cy Young, Jesse Burkett, Bobby Wallace, and manager-first baseman Patsy Tebeau. Cleveland is greatly weakened by the transfers. The new St. Louis owners change the name of Sportsman's Park to League Park and the color of the team socks from brown to red.

April 30 A new major league attendance record is set at Chicago as 27,000 fans watch Nixey Callahan shut out St. Louis 4–0. The crowd spills into the field causing any hit into the crowd to count for only one base.

July 1 Cleveland, which has averaged under 200 fans a game at home, splits a twin bill with Boston and decides to spend the rest of the season on the road. The club's record is 12-49. They will play just seven more home games and finish the year with a total attendance of 6,088, the lowest in major league history.

September 4 The Superbas, already famous for their late rallies, stage "Brooklyn Finishes" in two different boroughs, winning the morning game in Brooklyn with two in the ninth, and then taking the afternoon game in Manhattan with four in the eighth.

September 18 After losing 24 games in a row, Cleveland defeats Washington 5-4. The Spiders will go on to lose their next 16 games. They wind up with a record of 20-134.

October 11* The Western League holds its annual meeting in Chicago and changes its name to the American Baseball League. The AL considers putting clubs in Cleveland and Chicago.

December 8 Louisville president Barney Dreyfuss transfers to Pittsburgh (of which he is part owner) his top stars, including player-manager Fred Clarke, Hans Wagner, Tommy Leach, and Deacon Phillippe. Louisville is a likely candidate in the reduction of NL franchises from twelve to eight.

December 15 The NL rules Brooklyn's purchase of Zeke Wrigley in September is illegal and nullifies the 16 games he played for Brooklyn. But Brooklyn still wins the pennant.

BALTIMORE		BOSTON		BROOKLYN		CHICAGO		CINCINNATI		CLEVELAND	
M	J.McGraw	M	F.Selee	M	N.Hanlon	M	T.Burns	M	B.Ewing	M	L.Cross
1B	C.LaChance	1B	F.Tenney	1B	D.McGann	1B	B.Everitt	1B	J.Beckley	M	J.Quinn
2B	G.DeMontreville	2B	B.Lowe	2B	T.Daly	2B	B.McCormick	2B	B.McPhee	1B	T.Tucker
SS	B.Keister	SS	H.Long	SS	B.Dahlen	SS	G.DeMontreville	SS	T.Corcoran	2B	J.Quinn
3B	J.McGraw	3B	J.Collins	3B	D.Casey	3B	H.Wolverton	3B	C.Irwin	SS	H.Lochhead
LF	D.Holmes	LF	H.Duffy	LF	J.Kelley	LF	J.Ryan	LF	E.Smith	3B	S.Sullivan
CF	S.Brodie	CF	B.Hamilton	CF	F.Jones	CF	S.Mertes	CF	K.Selbach	LF	D.Harley
RF	J.Sheckard	RF	C.Stahl	RF	W.Keeler	RF	D.Green	RF	D.Miller	CF	T.Dowd
C	W.Robinson	C	M.Bergen	C	D.Farrell	C	T.Donahue	C	H.Peitz	RF	S.McAllister
										C	J.Sugden
O3	D.Fultz	C	B.Clarke	O1	J.Anderson	O1	B.Lange	32	H.Steinfeldt		
S	G.Magoon	O	G.Stafford	S	H.Jennings	23	J.Connor	O	A.McBride	O	C.Hemphill
1C	P.Crisham	O	C.Frisbee	C	D.McGuire	C	F.Chance	C	B.Wood	3	L.Cross
2	J.O'Brien	C	B.Sullivan	C	A.Smith	S	G.Magoon	S3	K.Elberfeld	C	O.Schreckengost
C	A.Smith					3	B.Bradley	O	S.Crawford	1C	J.Duncan
3	C.Harris	P	V.Willis	P	J.Dunn			1	F.Vaughn	C	C.Zimmer
		P	K.Nichols	P	J.Hughes	P	J.Taylor	O	J.Barrett		
P	J.McGinnity	P	T.Lewis	P	B.Kennedy	P	C.Griffith	O	S.Seybold	P	J.Hughey
P	F.Kitson	P	J.Meekin	P	D.McJames	P	N.Callahan			P	C.Knepper
P	J.Nops	P	F.Killen			P	N.Garvin	P	N.Hahn	P	F.Bates
P	H.Howell			/P	A.Maul			P	P.Hawley	P	C.Schmit
		P	H.Bailey	/P	B.Donovan	P	B.Phyle	P	B.Phillips	P	H.Colliflower
/P	B.Hill	P	C.Hickman			/P	D.Cogan	P	T.Breitenstein		
/P	K.McKenna	/P	F.Klobedanz			/P	J.Katoll	P	J.Taylor	P	W.Sudhoff
/P	R.Miller	/P	O.Streit							P	K.Carsey
								/P	E.Frisk	P	B.Hill
								/P	B.Dammann	/P	J.Harper
								/P	J.Cronin	/P	H.Maupin
								/P	F.Dwyer		

LOUISVILLE		NEW YORK		PHILADELPHIA		PITTSBURGH		ST.LOUIS		WASHINGTON	
M	F.Clarke	M	J.Day	M	B.Shettsline	M	B.Watkins	M	P.Tebeau	M	A.Irwin
1B	M.Kelley	M	F.Hoey	1B	D.Cooley	M	P.Donovan	1B	P.Tebeau	1B	D.McGann
2B	C.Ritchey	1B	J.Doyle	2B	N.Lajoie	1B	W.Clark	2B	C.Childs	2B	F.Bonner
SS	B.Clingman	2B	K.Gleason	SS	M.Cross	2B	J.O'Brien	SS	B.Wallace	SS	D.Padden
3B	T.Leach	SS	G.Davis	3B	B.Lauder	SS	B.Ely	3B	L.Cross	3B	C.Atherton
LF	F.Clarke	3B	F.Hartman	LF	E.Delahanty	3B	J.Williams	LF	J.Burkett	LF	J.O'Brien
CF	D.Hoy	LF	T.O'Brien	CF	R.Thomas	LF	J.McCarthy	CF	H.Blake	CF	J.Slagle
RF	C.Dexter	CF	G.Van Haltren	RF	E.Flick	CF	G.Beaumont	RF	E.Heidrick	RF	B.Freeman
C	C.Zimmer	RF	P.Foster	C	E.McFarland	RF	P.Donovan	C	L.Criger	C	D.McGuire
		C	J.Warner			C	F.Bowerman				
3O	H.Wagner			O1	P.Chiles			C1	J.O'Connor	3P	W.Mercer
C	D.Powers	C1	P.Wilson	C	K.Douglass	O	T.McCreery	S1	E.McKean	O1	S.Barry
1	G.Decker	C3	M.Grady	2	J.Dolan	C	P.Schriver	/1	O.Schreckengost	1	P.Cassidy
C	M.Kittridge	O	M.Tiernan	1	B.Goeckel	2	H.Reitz	O1	M.Donlin	C	M.Kittridge
1	D.Wills	O	T.Fleming			1	P.Dillon	O	J.Stenzel	2S	G.Stafford
O	T.Hartsel	S	H.Hardesty	P	W.Piatt	2S	A.Madison			S	F.Scheibeck
O	F.Ketchum	O	P.Woodruff	P	R.Donahue			P	J.Powell	C	M.Roach
				P	C.Fraser	P	S.Leever	P	C.Young	S	B.Hulen
P	B.Cunningham	P	B.Carrick	P	A.Orth	P	J.Tannehill	P	W.Sudhoff	1	H.Davis
P	D.Phillippe	P	C.Seymour	P	B.Bernhard	P	T.Sparks	P	N.Cuppy	O	J.Gettman
P	P.Dowling	P	E.Doheny			P	B.Hoffer				
P	W.Woods	P	J.Meekin	P	J.Fifield	P	J.Chesbro	P	C.Jones	P	G.Weyhing
		P	C.Gettig	/P	B.Magee			P	P.McBride	P	B.Dinneen
P	R.Waddell	P	T.Colcolough	/P	G.Wheeler	/P	C.Gray	/P	Z.Wilson	P	D.McFarlan
P	B.Magee					/P	B.Rhines	/P	T.Thomas		
/P	P.Flaherty					/P	J.Gardner	/P	J.Sutthoff	P	K.Baker
/P	H.Wilhelm					/P	H.Payne			/P	R.Evans
										/P	J.Fifield
										/P	B.Magee
										/P	K.Carsey
										/P	D.Dunkle

TEAM	G	W	L	PCT	GB	R	OR	AB	H	2B	3B	HR	BB	SO	AVG	OBP	SLG	PRO	PRO+	BR	/A	PF	CHI	RC	SB	CS	SBA	SBR
BRO	150	101	47	.682		892	658	4937	1436	178	97	27	477	263	.291	.368	.383	.751	110	87	68	102	103	824	271			
BOS	153	95	57	.625	8	858	645	5290	1517	178	90	39	431	269	.287	.345	.377	.722	94	21	-59	110	103	787	185			
PHI	154	94	58	.618	9	916	743	5353	1613	241	83	31	441	341	.301	.363	.395	.758	118	96	128	97	99	879	212			
BAL	152	86	62	.581	15	827	691	5073	1509	204	71	17	418	383	.297	.365	.376	.741	104	68	24	105	97	861	364			
STL	155	84	67	.556	18.5	819	739	5304	1514	172	88	47	468	262	.285	.347	.378	.725	102	28	9	102	97	801	210			
CIN	156	83	67	.553	19	856	770	5225	1439	194	105	13	485	295	.275	.345	.360	.705	97	-5	-20	102	106	762	228			
PIT	154	76	73	.510	25.5	834	765	5450	1574	196	121	27	384	345	.289	.343	.384	.727	105	26	29	100	97	815	179			
CHI	152	75	73	.507	26	812	763	5148	1428	173	82	27	406	342	.277	.338	.359	.697	99	-26	-5	97	105	743	247			
LOU	155	75	77	.493	28	827	775	5307	1484	192	68	40	436	375	.280	.343	.364	.707	99	-3	-2	100	101	781	233			
NY	152	60	90	.400	42	734	863	5092	1431	161	65	23	387	360	.281	.337	.352	.689	97	-39	-13	97	100	708	234			
WAS	155	54	98	.355	49	743	983	5256	1429	162	87	47	350	341	.272	.328	.363	.691	96	-45	-37	99	99	710	176			
CLE	154	20	134	.130	84	529	1252	5279	1333	142	50	12	289	280	.253	.299	.305	.604	76	-209	-168	93	92	541	127			
TOT	921					9647		62714	17707	2193	1007	350	4972	3856	.282	.343	.366	.710							2666			

TEAM	CG	SH	SV	IP	H	H/G	HR	BB	SO	RAT	ERA	ERA+	OAV	OOB	PR	/A	PF	CPI	FA	E	DP	FW	PW	BW	SBW	DIF
BRO	121	9	9	1269¹	1320	9.4	32	463	331	13.0	3.25	120	.268	.337	85	92	102	111	.948	314	125	2.9	8.3	6.2		9.6
BOS	138	13	4	1348	1273	8.5	44	432	385	11.8	3.26	127	.250	.317	88	133	108	95	.952	303	124	4.0	12.1	-5.3		8.3
PHI	129	15	2	1333¹	1398	9.4	17	370	281	12.5	3.47	106	.275	.328	56	30	96	97	.940	379	110	-.4	2.7	11.6		4.0
BAL	132	10	4	1304¹	1403	9.7	13	349	294	12.5	3.31	119	.275	.330	78	93	103	103	.949	308	96	3.5	8.4	2.2		-2.1
STL	134	7	1	1340²	1476	9.9	41	321	331	12.4	3.36	118	.280	.327	73	91	103	107	.939	397	117	-1.3	8.2	.8		.7
CIN	130	8	5	1361	1484	9.8	26	370	360	12.8	3.70	106	.278	.333	23	32	102	97	.947	339	111	2.3	2.9	-1.8		4.6
PIT	117	9	4	1364	1464	9.7	27	437	334	13.0	3.60	106	.274	.337	38	32	99	101	.945	361	98	.7	2.9	2.6		-4.7
CHI	147	8	1	1331¹	1433	9.7	20	330	313	12.5	3.37	111	.275	.328	71	55	97	102	.935	428	145	-3.5	5.0	-.5		-.0
LOU	134	5	2	1351²	1509	10.0	33	323	287	12.6	3.45	112	.282	.331	60	60	100	106	.939	394	101	-1.1	5.4	-.2		-5.2
NY	138	4	0	1278¹	1454	10.2	19	628	397	15.3	4.29	87	.286	.375	-63	-78	97	103	.932	433	140	-3.8	-7.1	-1.2		-3.0
WAS	131	3	0	1300¹	1649	11.4	35	422	328	14.9	4.93	79	.309	.368	-157	-149	102	95	.935	403	99	-1.6	-13.5	-3.4		-3.5
CLE	138	0	0	1264	1844	13.1	43	527	215	17.7	6.37	58	.340	.409	-353	-378	96	94	.937	388	121	-.9	-34.3	-15.2		-6.6
TOT	1589	91	32	15846¹		10.1				13.4	3.85		.282	.343					.942	4447	1387					

Runs
- McGraw-Bal 140
- Keeler-Bro 140
- Thomas-Phi 137
- Delahanty-Phi 135
- Williams-Pit 126

Hits
- Delahanty-Phi 238
- Burkett-StL 221
- Williams-Pit 219
- Keeler-Bro 216
- Tenney-Bos 209

Doubles
- Delahanty-Phi 55
- Wagner-Lou 43
- Holmes-Bal 31
- Long-Bos 30
- Duffy-Bos 29

Triples
- Williams-Pit 27
- Freeman-Was 25
- Stahl-Bos 19
- Tenney-Bos 17
- McCarthy-Pit 17

Home Runs
- Freeman-Was 25
- Wallace-StL 12
- Williams-Pit 9
- Mertes-Chi 9
- Delahanty-Phi 9

Total Bases
- Delahanty-Phi 338
- Freeman-Was 331
- Williams-Pit 328
- Stahl-Bos 284
- Wagner-Lou 282

Runs Batted In
- Delahanty-Phi 137
- Freeman-Was 122
- Williams-Pit 116
- Wagner-Lou 113
- Wallace-StL 108

Runs Produced
- Delahanty-Phi 263
- Williams-Pit 233
- Wagner-Lou 204
- Freeman-Was 204

Bases On Balls
- McGraw-Bal 124
- Thomas-Phi 115
- VanHaltren-NY 74
- Childs-StL 74

Batting Average
- Delahanty-Phi ...... .410
- Burkett-StL ...... .396
- McGraw-Bal ...... .391
- Keeler-Bro ...... .379
- Williams-Pit ...... .355

On Base Percentage
- McGraw-Bal ...... .547
- Delahanty-Phi ...... .464
- Burkett-StL ...... .463
- Thomas-Phi ...... .457
- Stahl-Bos ...... .426

Slugging Average
- Delahanty-Phi ...... .582
- Freeman-Was ...... .563
- Williams-Pit ...... .532
- Burkett-StL ...... .500
- Wagner-Lou ...... .494

Production
- Delahanty-Phi ...1.046
- McGraw-Bal ...... .994
- Burkett-StL ...... .963
- Williams-Pit ...... .949
- Freeman-Was ...... .925

Adjusted Production
- Delahanty-Phi 193
- McGraw-Bal 165
- Burkett-StL 160
- Williams-Pit 160
- Freeman-Was 154

Batter Runs
- Delahanty-Phi 67.9
- McGraw-Bal 56.8
- Burkett-StL 51.6
- Williams-Pit 49.0
- Stahl-Bos 42.2

Adjusted Batter Runs
- Delahanty-Phi 73.5
- McGraw-Bal 50.2
- Williams-Pit 49.5
- Burkett-StL 48.4
- Freeman-Was 37.6

Clutch Hitting Index
- Brodie-Bal 139
- Long-Bos 131
- Magoon-Bal-Chi ... 129
- Lauder-Phi 128
- Corcoran-Cin 128

Runs Created
- Delahanty-Phi 175
- Williams-Pit 152
- Burkett-StL 145
- McGraw-Bal 141
- Stahl-Bos 139

Total Average
- McGraw-Bal 1.601
- Delahanty-Phi ... 1.245
- Burkett-StL 1.107
- Williams-Pit 1.055
- Stahl-Bos 1.051

Stolen Bases
- Sheckard-Bal 77
- McGraw-Bal 73
- Heidrick-StL 55
- Holmes-Bal 50
- Clarke-Lou 49

Fielding Runs
- G.Davis-NY 46.3
- Wallace-StL 38.8
- Cross-Cle-StL 32.7
- Gleason-NY 25.7
- Collins-Bos 20.9

Total Player Rating
- G.Davis-NY 6.2
- Delahanty-Phi 5.6
- Wallace-StL 5.3
- Williams-Pit 5.2
- Lajoie-Phi 4.9

Wins
- McGinnity-Bal 28
- Hughes-Bro 28
- Willis-Bos 27
- Young-StL 26
- Tannehill-Pit 24

Win Percentage
- Hughes-Bro ...... .824
- Willis-Bos ...... .771
- Hahn-Cin ...... .742
- Donahue-Phi ...... .724
- Kennedy-Bro ...... .710

Games
- Leever-Pit 51
- Powell-StL 48
- McGinnity-Bal 48
- Young-StL 44
- Carrick-NY 44

Complete Games
- Young-StL 40
- Powell-StL 40
- Carrick-NY 40
- Taylor-Chi 39
- McGinnity-Bal 38

Shutouts
- Willis-Bos 5

Saves
- Leever-Pit 3

Innings Pitched
- Leever-Pit 379.0
- Powell-StL 373.0
- Young-StL 369.1
- McGinnity-Bal 366.1
- Carrick-NY 361.2

Fewest Hits/Game
- Willis-Bos 7.28
- Hughes-Bro 7.71
- Hahn-Cin 8.16
- Seymour-NY 8.28
- Leever-Pit 8.38

Fewest BB/Game
- Young-StL 1.07
- Cuppy-StL 1.36
- Tannehill-Pit 1.47
- Kitson-Bal 1.79
- Woods-Lou 1.79

Strikeouts
- Hahn-Cin 145
- Seymour-NY 142
- Leever-Pit 121
- Willis-Bos 120
- Doheny-NY 115

Strikeouts/Game
- Seymour-NY 4.76
- Hahn-Cin 4.22
- Doheny-NY 3.90
- McJames-Bro 3.43
- Willis-Bos 3.15

Ratio
- Young-StL 10.19
- Hahn-Cin 10.43
- Nichols-Bos 10.85
- Willis-Bos 11.14
- Kitson-Bal 11.15

Earned Run Average
- Willis-Bos 2.50
- Young-StL 2.58
- McGinnity-Bal 2.68
- Hahn-Cin 2.68
- Hughes-Bro 2.68

Adjusted ERA
- Willis-Bos 166
- Young-StL 154
- McGinnity-Bal 148
- Hahn-Cin 146
- Hughes-Bro 146

Opponents' Batting Avg.
- Willis-Bos ...... .222
- Hughes-Bro ...... .232
- Hahn-Cin ...... .242
- Seymour-NY ...... .245
- Leever-Pit ...... .247

Opponents' On Base Pct.
- Young-StL ...... .285
- Hahn-Cin ...... .290
- Nichols-Bos ...... .298
- Willis-Bos ...... .303
- Kitson-Bal ...... .304

Starter Runs
- Young-StL 52.0
- Willis-Bos 51.6
- McGinnity-Bal 47.7
- Hahn-Cin 40.2
- Kitson-Bal 39.2

Adjusted Starter Runs
- Willis-Bos 63.1
- Young-StL 57.2
- McGinnity-Bal 52.1
- Nichols-Bos 44.5
- Kitson-Bal 43.1

Clutch Pitching Index
- Kennedy-Bro 130
- Tannehill-Pit 124
- Dowling-Lou 121
- Callahan-Chi 121
- Woods-Lou 118

Relief Runs

Adjusted Relief Runs

Relief Ranking

Total Pitcher Index
- Young-StL 6.2
- Willis-Bos 5.3
- McGinnity-Bal 5.0
- Tannehill-Pit 4.8
- Hughes-Bro 4.7

Total Baseball Ranking
- G.Davis-NY 6.2
- Young-StL 6.2
- Delahanty-Phi 5.6
- Willis-Bos 5.3
- Wallace-StL 5.3

January 24 The NL Reduction Committee has a secret meeting in Cleveland, supposedly to discuss dropping Louisville, Baltimore, Washington, and Cleveland from the league roster.

February 17 Mary Hamilton Von Derbeck becomes owner of the Detroit AL franchise and Bennett Park in lieu of unpaid alimony. However, her ex-husband George Von Derbeck files the required bond with a Michigan court to cover the due alimony, regains ownership of the club, and sells it to Tiger manager George Stallings on March 6.

March 8 In New York, the NL meets and votes to go with eight teams. The league pays the Baltimore owners $30,000 for their franchise, with Ebbets and Hanlon reserving the right to sell the players. Cleveland, Louisville, and Washington receive $10,000 each, and Louisville owner Barney Dreyfuss sends most of his players to his Pittsburgh team. The circuit will remain the same for 53 years, until the Boston Braves move to Milwaukee in 1953.

March 16 At an AL meeting in Chicago Ban Johnson announces that an AL team will be placed in the Windy City, ensuring the stability of the league. Other franchises are in Kansas City, Minneapolis, Milwaukee, Indianapolis, Detroit, Cleveland, and Buffalo. In an agreement with Chicago NL officials the AL club will be situated on the south side of the city and will be permitted to use the nickname "White Stockings," formerly used by the NL team. However, the White Stockings will not be able to use the word "Chicago" in their official name.

April 30* Brothers Joe, Jim, and Tom Delahanty, playing their third year together with Allentown, open the Atlantic League season by banging out a family total of 11 hits good for 20 bases.

May 28 A fire in Cincinnati nearly destroys the grandstand. The new grandstand will not be built until 1902, and the Reds are forced to play on the road for a month.

June 9 A forerunner of today's players' union is organized in New York. Three delegates from each NL team launch the Players Protective Association (PPA) and elect Chief Zimmer president. Their goal is to negotiate contracts and rules changes.

July 7 Boston hurler Kid Nichols notches his 300th career victory, beating Chicago 11-4. The win comes two months before his thirty-first birthday, making him the youngest ever to reach that magic figure.

July 17 At Brooklyn's Washington Park, the Superbas tie the score against the Giants in the fifth. With two men on base, New York captain George Davis takes out pitcher Ed Doheny and brings in rookie Christy Mathewson, just brought up from Norfolk. He hits three batters, walks two, and gives up six runs in a 13-7 loss.

September 17 Reds shortstop Tommy Corcoran, coaching at third in a game at Philadelphia, uncovers a wire in the coaching box that leads across the outfield to the Phils' locker room, where reserve catcher Morgan Murphy is reading the opposing catcher's signs and relaying them to the Phils' coach using a buzzer hidden in the dirt.

October 13 Ban Johnson promises to put the following provisions in all player contracts in the AL: no suspensions for more than 10 days; clubs to pay doctor bills for injuries occurring during a game; if a club abandons the league, its players become free agents after 10 days; no farming or selling without the player's written consent; no reserve clause for more than three years or for less salary than the current year; and binding arbitration for disputes.

October 15 The Pittsburgh *Chronicle-Telegraph* World Title series between first-place Brooklyn and second-place Pittsburgh begins with a 5-2 win for Joe McGinnity over Rube Waddell. The Superbas win the series, the Cup given by the newspaper, and half the gate receipts. For his efforts, which include a league-leading 29 wins and 347 innings pitched, McGinnity is given permanent possession of the trophy and a $100 bonus.

November 14 The NL rejects the AL as an equal, declaring it an outlaw league outside of the National Agreement, thus inaugurating a state of war.

December 14 Suffering from a drop in attendance, NL owners vote to cut costs with a 16-player limit after May 1. The Players Protective Association claims the move is aimed at pressuring players into signing by shrinking the number of jobs.

December 15 Amos Rusie, a holdout for two years, is traded to the Reds by the Giants for Mathewson. Though only 30, Rusie, a future Hall of Fame pitcher, will not add to the 245 wins he collected in nine seasons. Appearing in just three games in 1901, he will finish with an 0-1 record.

	BOSTON		BROOKLYN		CHICAGO		CINCINNATI		NEW YORK		PHILADELPHIA		PITTSBURGH		ST.LOUIS
M	F.Selee	M	N.Hanlon	M	T.Loftus	M	B.Allen	M	B.Ewing	M	B.Shettsline	M	F.Clarke	M	P.Tebeau
1B	F.Tenney	1B	H.Jennings	1B	J.Ganzel	1B	J.Beckley	M	G.Davis	1B	E.Delahanty	1B	D.Cooley	M	L.Heilbroner
2B	B.Lowe	2B	T.Daly	2B	C.Childs	2B	J.Quinn	1B	J.Doyle	2B	N.Lajoie	2B	C.Ritchey	1B	D.McGann
SS	H.Long	SS	B.Dahlen	SS	B.McCormick	SS	T.Corcoran	2B	K.Gleason	SS	M.Cross	SS	B.Ely	2B	B.Keister
3B	J.Collins	3B	L.Cross	3B	B.Bradley	3B	H.Steinfeldt	SS	G.Davis	3B	H.Wolverton	3B	J.Williams	SS	B.Wallace
LF	C.Stahl	LF	J.Sheckard	LF	J.McCarthy	LF	S.Crawford	3B	C.Hickman	LF	J.Slagle	LF	F.Clarke	3B	J.McGraw
CF	B.Hamilton	CF	F.Jones	CF	D.Green	CF	J.Barrett	LF	K.Selbach	CF	R.Thomas	CF	G.Beaumont	LF	J.Burkett
RF	B.Freeman	RF	W.Keeler	RF	J.Ryan	RF	A.McBride	CF	G.Van Haltren	RF	E.Flick	RF	H.Wagner	CF	E.Heidrick
C	B.Clarke	C	D.Farrell	C	T.Donahue	C	H.Peitz	RF	E.Smith	C	E.McFarland	C	C.Zimmer	RF	P.Donovan
								C	F.Bowerman					C	L.Criger
OS	S.Barry	O1	J.Kelley	O1	S.Mertes	3S	C.Irwin	32	J.Dolan	1O	T.O'Brien				
C	B.Sullivan	C	D.McGuire	S	B.Clingman	C	M.Kahoe	C1	M.Grady	C	K.Douglass	3	T.Leach	O1	M.Donlin
O	H.Duffy	2S	G.DeMontreville	C	F.Chance	C3	B.Wood	C	J.Warner	12	P.Chiles	C	J.O'Connor	C	W.Robinson
C	J.Clements	/3	A.Smith	CO	C.Dexter	O	P.Geier	O	P.Foster	C	M.Murphy	C	T.McCreery	O3	P.Dillard
/C	J.Connor	/C	F.Steelman	3	S.Strang	O	E.Smith	2	D.Murphy	/3	B.Myers	C	P.Schriver	2	J.Quinn
		/3	D.Casey	1	B.Everitt	O	T.Hartsel	O	C.Bernard	/C	F.Jacklitsch	/1	P.Dillon	3	L.Cross
P	B.Dinneen			C	J.Kling	/O	D.Harley	/O	C.Frisbee	/3	C.Ziegler	/C	T.Latimer	2	O.Krueger
P	V.Willis	P	J.McGinnity	O	C.Dolan	/S	B.Allen	/S	T.Sheehan			/C	J.Donahue	C	J.O'Connor
P	K.Nichols	P	B.Kennedy	/C	A.Nichols					P	A.Orth	/O	E.Poole	/C	F.Buelow
P	T.Lewis	P	F.Kitson	/O	S.Dungan	P	E.Scott	P	B.Carrick	P	R.Donahue			/S	P.Tebeau
P	T.Pittinger	P	H.Howell	/3	H.Wolverton	P	N.Hahn	P	P.Hawley	P	C.Fraser	P	D.Phillippe	/C	H.Stanton
				/C	R.Bresnahan	P	D.Newton	P	W.Mercer	P	B.Bernhard	P	J.Tannehill		
P	N.Cuppy	/P	J.Nops			P	B.Phillips	P	E.Doheny	P	W.Piatt	P	S.Leever	P	C.Young
/P	H.Bailey	P	J.Dunn	P	N.Callahan	P	T.Breitenstein					P	J.Chesbro	P	C.Jones
/P	R.Chambers	/P	G.Weyhing	P	C.Griffith			P	D.Taylor	P	J.Dunn	P	R.Waddell	P	J.Powell
		/P	B.Donovan	P	N.Garvin	/P	A.Stimmel	P	C.Seymour	/P	A.Maul			P	W.Sudhoff
		/P	J.Yeager	P	J.Taylor			/P	C.Mathewson	P	B.Conn	/P	P.Flaherty	P	J.Hughey
				P	J.Menefee			/P	D.Cogan	/P	W.McLaughlin	/P	J.Meekin		
				/P	B.Cunningham							P	B.Husting	/P	G.Weyhing
				/P	F.Killen							/P	W.Woods	/P	T.Thomas
				/P	T.Hughes									/P	J.Harper
				/P	M.Eason										
				/P	E.Harvey										

TEAM	G	W	L	PCT	GB	R	OR	AB	H	2B	3B	HR	BB	SO	AVG	OBP	SLG	PRO	PRO+	BR	/A	PF	CHI	RC	SB	CS	SBA	SBR
BRO	142	82	54	.603		816	722	4860	1423	199	81	26	421	272	.293	.359	.383	.742	104	72	23	106	100	795	274			
PIT	140	79	60	.568	4.5	733	612	4817	1312	185	100	26	327	321	.272	.327	.368	.695	96	-25	-30	101	105	666	174			
PHI	141	75	63	.543	8	810	792	4969	1439	187	82	29	440	374	.290	.356	.378	.734	109	58	65	99	99	774	205			
BOS	142	66	72	.478	17	778	739	4952	1403	163	68	48	395	278	.283	.342	.373	.715	92	16	-78	112	102	724	182			
STL	142	65	75	.464	19	744	748	4877	1420	141	81	36	406	318	.291	.346	.375	.731	108	52	58	99	94	766	243			
CHI	146	65	75	.464	19	635	751	4907	1276	202	51	33	343	383	.260	.317	.342	.659	90	-87	-63	96	97	651	189			
CIN	144	62	77	.446	21.5	703	745	5026	1335	178	83	33	333	408	.266	.318	.354	.672	92	-71	-54	98	103	651	183			
NY	141	60	78	.435	23	713	823	4724	1317	177	61	23	369	343	.279	.338	.357	.695	102	-16	16	95	102	676	236			
TOT	569					5932		39132	10925	1432	607	254	3034	2697	.279	.339	.366	.705						1686				

TEAM	CG	SH	SV	IP	H	H/G	HR	BB	SO	RAT	ERA	ERA+	OAV	OOB	PR	/A	PF	CPI	FA	E	DP	FW	PW	BW	SBW	DIF
BRO	104	8	4	1225²	1370	10.1	30	405	300	13.6	3.89	99	.282	.346	-27	-8	104	99	.948	303	102	2.6	-.7	2.1		10.1
PIT	114	11	1	1229	1232	9.0	24	295	415	11.7	3.06	119	.261	.313	87	77	98	97	.945	322	106	1.1	7.0	-2.7		4.1
PHI	116	7	3	1248²	1506	10.9	29	402	284	14.2	4.12	88	.298	.357	-59	-71	98	103	.945	330	125	.8	-6.5	5.9		5.8
BOS	116	8	2	1240¹	1263	9.2	59	463	340	12.9	3.72	111	.264	.335	-4	55	112	97	.953	273	86	4.4	5.0	-7.1		-5.3
STL	117	12	0	1217¹	1373	10.2	37	299	325	12.7	3.75	97	.284	.331	-7	-16	98	98	.943	331	73	.8	-1.5	5.3		-9.7
CHI	137	9	1	1271	1375	9.7	21	324	357	12.6	3.23	112	.276	.330	66	52	98	106	.933	418	98	-3.9	4.8	-5.8		-.0
CIN	118	9	1	1274²	1383	9.8	28	404	399	13.0	3.96	96	.276	.338	-20	-24	99	94	.945	341	120	.5	-2.2	-4.9		-.9
NY	113	4	0	1207¹	1423	10.6	26	442	277	14.6	3.96	91	.293	.363	-35	-47	98	108	.928	439	124	-6.0	-4.3	1.5		-.2
TOT	935	68	12	9914		9.9				13.2	3.69		.279	.339					.942	2757	834					

Runs		Hits		Doubles		Triples		Home Runs		Total Bases	
Thomas-Phi	132	Keeler-Bro	204	Wagner-Pit	45	Wagner-Pit	22	Long-Bos	12	Wagner-Pit	302
Slagle-Phi	115	Burkett-StL	203	Lajoie-Phi	33	Kelley-Bro	17	Flick-Phi	11	Flick-Phi	297
VanHaltren-NY	114	Wagner-Pit	201	Flick-Phi	32	Hickman-NY	17	Donlin-StL	10	Burkett-StL	265
Barrett-Cin	114	Flick-Phi	200	Delahanty-Phi	32	Stahl-Bos	16	Hickman-NY	9	Keeler-Bro	253
Wagner-Pit	107	Beckley-Cin	190	VanHaltren-NY	30	Flick-Phi	16	Sullivan-Bos	8	Beckley-Cin	242

Runs Batted In		Runs Produced		Bases On Balls		Batting Average		On Base Percentage		Slugging Average	
Flick-Phi	110	Flick-Phi	205	Thomas-Phi	115	Wagner-Pit	.381	McGraw-StL	.505	Wagner-Pit	.573
Delahanty-Phi	109	Wagner-Pit	203	Hamilton-Bos	107	Flick-Phi	.367	Thomas-Phi	.451	Flick-Phi	.545
Wagner-Pit	100	Collins-Bos	193	McGraw-StL	85	Burkett-StL	.363	Hamilton-Bos	.449	Lajoie-Phi	.510
Collins-Bos	95	Beckley-Cin	190	Dahlen-Bro	73	Keeler-Bro	.362	Flick-Phi	.441	Kelley-Bro	.485
Beckley-Cin	94	Delahanty-Phi	189			McGraw-StL	.344	Wagner-Pit	.434	Hickman-NY	.482

Production		Adjusted Production		Batter Runs		Adjusted Batter Runs		Clutch Hitting Index		Runs Created	
Wagner-Pit	1.007	Wagner-Pit	175	Flick-Phi	53.5	Flick-Phi	54.7	Delahanty-Phi	143	Wagner-Pit	152
Flick-Phi	.986	Flick-Phi	172	Wagner-Pit	53.2	Wagner-Pit	52.3	Cross-Phi	142	Flick-Phi	151
McGraw-StL	.921	McGraw-StL	157	Burkett-StL	39.0	Burkett-StL	40.0	Jennings-Bro	138	Burkett-StL	133
Burkett-StL	.904	Selbach-NY	151	McGraw-StL	36.0	Selbach-NY	39.8	Lowe-Bos	122	Keeler-Bro	123
Selbach-NY	.885	Burkett-StL	150	Selbach-NY	34.3	McGraw-StL	36.8	Collins-Bos	119	Selbach-NY	121

Total Average		Stolen Bases		Stolen Base Average		Stolen Base Runs		Fielding Runs		Total Player Rating	
McGraw-StL	1.260	VanHaltren-NY	45					Steinfeldt-Cin	35.6	Lajoie-Phi	5.0
Wagner-Pit	1.193	Donovan-StL	45					Lajoie-Phi	29.5	Davis-NY	4.6
Flick-Phi	1.171	Barrett-Cin	44					Davis-NY	29.3	Flick-Phi	4.3
Selbach-NY	1.029	Keeler-Bro	41					Dahlen-Bro	19.8	Selbach-NY	3.5
Burkett-StL	1.017							Bradley-Chi	16.8	Wagner-Pit	3.3

Wins		Win Percentage		Games		Complete Games		Shutouts		Saves	
McGinnity-Bro	28	McGinnity-Bro	.778	Carrick-NY	45	Hawley-NY	34	Young-StL	4	Kitson-Bro	4
Tannehill-Pit	20	Tannehill-Pit	.769	McGinnity-Bro	44	Dinneen-Bos	33	Nichols-Bos	4	Bernhard-Phi	2
Phillippe-Pit	20	Fraser-Phi	.625	Scott-Cin	42			Hahn-Cin	4		
Kennedy-Bro	20	Phillippe-Pit	.606	Kennedy-Bro	42			Griffith-Chi	4		
Dinneen-Bos	20	Kennedy-Bro	.606								

Innings Pitched		Fewest Hits/Game		Fewest BB/Game		Strikeouts		Strikeouts/Game		Ratio	
McGinnity-Bro	343.0	Waddell-Pit	7.59	Young-StL	1.01	Hahn-Cin	132	Waddell-Pit	5.61	Phillippe-Pit	10.42
Carrick-NY	341.2	Garvin-Chi	8.22	Phillippe-Pit	1.35	Waddell-Pit	130	Garvin-Chi	3.91	Waddell-Pit	10.52
Hawley-NY	329.1	Nichols-Bos	8.36	Tannehill-Pit	1.65	Young-StL	115	Hahn-Cin	3.82	Young-StL	10.53
Young-StL	321.1	Dinneen-Bos	8.53	Griffith-Chi	1.85	Garvin-Chi	107	Newton-Cin	3.38	Garvin-Chi	11.18
Dinneen-Bos	320.2	Phillippe-Pit	8.84	Leever-Pit	1.86	Dinneen-Bos	107	Leever-Pit	3.25	Leever-Pit	11.30

Earned Run Average		Adjusted ERA		Opponents' Batting Avg.		Opponents' On Base Pct.		Starter Runs		Adjusted Starter Runs	
Waddell-Pit	2.37	Waddell-Pit	153	Waddell-Pit	.229	Phillippe-Pit	.289	Garvin-Chi	35.1	Dinneen-Bos	35.9
Garvin-Chi	2.41	Garvin-Chi	149	Garvin-Chi	.243	Waddell-Pit	.291	Waddell-Pit	30.7	McGinnity-Bro	34.2
Taylor-Chi	2.55	Taylor-Chi	141	Nichols-Bos	.246	Young-StL	.291	McGinnity-Bro	28.8	Garvin-Chi	32.6
Leever-Pit	2.71	Nichols-Bos	134	Dinneen-Bos	.250	Garvin-Chi	.304	Taylor-Chi	28.3	Waddell-Pit	29.1
Sudhoff-StL	2.76	Leever-Pit	134	Phillippe-Pit	.257	Leever-Pit	.306	Phillippe-Pit	26.5	Nichols-Bos	27.0

Clutch Pitching Index		Relief Runs		Adjusted Relief Runs		Relief Ranking		Total Pitcher Index		Total Baseball Ranking	
Fraser-Phi	131							Dinneen-Bos	3.6	Lajoie-Phi	5.0
Taylor-Chi	119							Garvin-Chi	3.1	Davis-NY	4.6
McGinnity-Bro	118							Taylor-Chi	2.7	Flick-Phi	4.3
Carrick-NY	115							Tannehill-Pit	2.7	Dinneen-Bos	3.6
Donahue-Phi	113							Nichols-Bos	2.6	Selbach-NY	3.5

February 8 News leaks out that Napoleon Lajoie, the Phillies second baseman and leading NL hitter, has jumped to the new Philadelphia AL club, along with pitchers Chick Fraser and Bill Bernhard.

February 27 The NL Rules Committee decrees that all fouls are to count as strikes, except after two strikes. To cut the cost of balls fouled and unrecovered, the committee urges that "batsmen who foul off good strikes are to be disciplined." Other new rules: a ball will be called if the pitcher does not throw to a ready and waiting batter within 20 seconds, or, when a batter is hit by a pitch.

March 2 Jimmy Collins, Connie Mack's choice for the all-time best third baseman, leaves the Boston NL club to manage the AL's new Boston Somersets. The Beaneaters also lose outfielder Hugh Duffy, who will manage Milwaukee (AL), and catcher Billy Sullivan, who signs with the Chicago White Stockings.

March 28 Phillies owner John Rogers files for an injunction prohibiting Nap Lajoie, Bill Bernhard, and Chick Fraser from playing for any other team—the most serious legal test of the reserve clause to date.

April 8 Amos Rusie, the "Hoosier Thunderbolt," makes his first start for the Cincinnati Reds after a two-year layoff and is bombed 14–3. After two more appearances, he goes back to digging ditches, having won 245 games.

April 26 After six postponements, the Giants finally get the season going. New York defeats the Brooklyn Superbas 5-3. It is Christy Mathewson's first of an NL-record 373 career victories.

May 21 Giants fractious owner Andrew Freedman accuses umpire Billy Nash of incompetence and bars him from the Polo Grounds. One Pirate and one Giant are forced to officiate.

May 30 An NL record crowd of 28,500 sees St. Louis beat the Giants 6–5 in 10 innings in the afternoon game of a split holiday doubleheader at New York.

June 9 Overflow crowds ringing the outfields of small parks is a frequent occurrence. At Cincinnati on this Sunday afternoon, the first-place Giants lead 15–4 after six innings before 17,000 fans. Ground-rule doubles multiply, and 19 more runs score in the next 2½ innings. When the crowd edges onto the infield, with the Giants leading 25–13, umpire Bob Emslie forfeits the game to New York. The game registers a record 31 hits and 13 doubles. Only one Giant will return to the team in 1902: five will go to the AL, and three will retire.

June 18 The Boston NL club lowers its admission price of 50 cents to the AL's 25 cents. The Somersets will still draw 200,000 more than the NL team.

June 20 Pittsburgh's Honus Wagner steals home twice in a single game, as Jack Chesbro blanks the Giants 7–0.

July 15 Christy Mathewson (22 years old) of the Giants pitches a no-hitter, blanking St. Louis 5–0 at League Park. Matty saves his own no-hitter in the sixth when an Otto Krueger hit caroms off first baseman John Ganzel's glove to Mathewson, who throws back to first base for a 3–1–3 putout.

August 4 Cincinnati and Pittsburgh players are clocked while running from home plate to first base. The fastest time for the 90-foot sprint is three seconds flat, by Pirates outfielder Ginger Beaumont.

August 6* The National Association of Professional Baseball Leagues is formed to help the minor leagues protect their interests.

September 19 All games are canceled out of respect for the funeral of President William McKinley, who died September 14 from gunshot wounds.

September 24 Jimmy Sheckard hits grand slams in two consecutive games, as Brooklyn beats Cincinnati 16–2 the day after a 25–6 win.

BOSTON	BROOKLYN	CHICAGO	CINCINNATI	NEW YORK	PHILADELPHIA	PITTSBURGH	ST.LOUIS
M F.Selee	M N.Hanlon	M T.Loftus	M B.McPhee	M G.Davis	M B.Shettsline	M F.Clarke	M P.Donovan
1B F.Tenney	1B J.Kelley	1B J.Doyle	1B J.Beckley	1B J.Ganzel	1B H.Jennings	1B K.Bransfield	1B D.McGann
2B G.DeMontreville	2B T.Daly	2B C.Childs	2B H.Steinfeldt	2B R.Nelson	2B B.Hallman	2B C.Ritchey	2B D.Padden
SS H.Long	SS B.Dahlen	SS B.McCormick	SS G.Magoon	SS G.Davis	SS M.Cross	SS B.Ely	SS B.Wallace
3B B.Lowe	3B C.Irwin	3B F.Raymer	3B C.Irwin	3B S.Strang	3B H.Wolverton	3B T.Leach	3B O.Krueger
LF D.Cooley	LF J.Sheckard	LF T.Hartsel	LF D.Harley	LF K.Selbach	LF E.Delahanty	LF F.Clarke	LF J.Burkett
CF B.Hamilton	CF T.McCreery	CF D.Green	CF J.Dobbs	CF G.Van Haltren	CF R.Thomas	CF G.Beaumont	CF E.Heidrick
RF J.Slagle	RF W.Keeler	RF F.Chance	RF S.Crawford	RF A.McBride	RF E.Flick	RF L.Davis	RF P.Donovan
C M.Kittridge	C D.McGuire	C J.Kling	C B.Bergen	C J.Warner	C E.McFarland	C C.Zimmer	C J.Ryan
O F.Crolius	C1 D.Farrell	13 C.Dexter	C2 H.Peitz	OS C.Hickman	23 S.Barry	SO H.Wagner	CO A.Nichols
C1 P.Moran	O C.Dolan	C M.Kahoe	2 B.Fox	C F.Bowerman	O J.Slagle	C J.O'Connor	C1 P.Schriver
O F.Murphy	3 F.Gatins	2 P.Childs	O H.Bay	2O F.Murphy	O K.Douglass	C G.Yeager	C P.Childs
O D.Gammons	O L.Davis	O C.Dolan	O A.McBride	O J.Jones	C F.Jacklitsch	3 J.Burke	1 B.Richardson
O J.Rickert	/S J.Gochnauer	OP J.Menefee	S T.Corcoran	C A.Smith	2 J.Dolan	/S L.Carr	C M.Heydon
O E.Smith	/C H.Hearne	3 J.Delahanty	2 P.O'Brien	O C.Bernard	/O G.Browne	/3 J.Smith	
O P.Carney	/C F.Steelman	O B.Gannon	3 J.Hurley	C C.Buelow	/2 B.Conn	/S T.Eagan	P J.Powell
O S.Barry		3 E.Hickey	/3 E.Haberer	2 J.Miller		/3 T.Turner	P J.Harper
/O B.Lush	P B.Donovan	/3 L.Hoffman	/3 C.Heileman	/2 H.Smith	P R.Donahue	/O E.Smith	P W.Sudhoff
/O G.Grossart	P F.Kitson	/O H.Croft	/2 M.Kahoe	/2 D.Murphy	P B.Duggleby	/C J.Donahue	P E.Murphy
/O F.Brown	P J.Hughes	/2 G.Schaefer	/2 C.Krause	/C J.Wall	P A.Orth		
/3 J.Hinton	P D.Newton				P D.White	P D.Phillippe	P C.Jones
	P D.McJames	P T.Hughes	P N.Hahn	P D.Taylor	P H.Townsend	P J.Chesbro	/P M.O'Neill
P K.Nichols	P J.Taylor	P J.Taylor	P B.Phillips	P C.Mathewson		P J.Tannehill	/P S.Yerkes
P B.Dinneen	P B.Kennedy	P R.Waddell	P D.Newton	P B.Phyle	/P J.Dunn	P S.Leever	/P T.Breitenstein
P V.Willis	/P G.McCann	P M.Eason	P A.Stimmel	P E.Doheny		PO E.Poole	/P B.Magee
P T.Pittinger	/P G.Wright	/P B.Cunningham	/P J.Sutthoff	P R.Denzer		P E.Doheny	/P C.Fisher
/P B.Lawson	/P K.Carsey	/P C.Ferguson	/P B.McFadden	/P B.Magee		/P S.Wiltse	/P B.Wicker
			/P W.Guese	/P A.Maul		/P G.Merritt	/P F.Burns
			/P C.Case	/P D.Leitner		/P R.Waddell	
			/P L.Swormstedt	/P D.Deegan			
			/P A.Rusie	/P W.Mills			
			/P D.Scott	/P I.Van Zandt			
			/P C.Heismann	/P J.Livingstone			
			/P G.Weyhing	/P L.Hesterfer			
			/P D.Parker	/P C.Fisher			
				/P H.Felix			

TEAM	G	W	L	PCT	GB	R	OR	AB	H	2B	3B	HR	BB	SO	AVG	OBP	SLG	PRO	PRO+	BR	/A	PF	CHI	RC	SB	CS	SBA	SBR
PIT	140	90	49	.647		776	**534**	4913	1407	182	92	29	386	493	.286	**.345**	.379	**.724**	113	**99**	76	103	102	743	203			
PHI	140	83	57	.593	7.5	668	543	4793	1275	194	58	24	**430**	549	.266	.334	.346	.680	101	29	15	102	98	652	199			
BRO	137	79	57	.581	9.5	744	600	4879	1399	**206**	93	32	312	**449**	.287	.335	.387	.722	112	86	66	103	102	718	178			
STL	142	76	64	.543	14.5	792	689	5039	**1430**	187	**94**	**39**	314	540	.284	.337	.381	.718	120	87	125	95	**104**	744	190			
BOS	140	69	69	.500	20.5	531	556	4746	1180	135	36	28	303	519	.249	.298	.310	.608	75	-104	-153	109	101	515	158			
CHI	140	53	86	.381	37	578	699	4844	1250	153	61	19	314	532	.258	.310	.326	.636	94	-57	-35	96	99	575	**204**			
NY	141	52	85	.380	37	544	755	4839	1225	167	46	19	303	575	.253	.303	.318	.621	89	-83	-62	96	98	529	133			
CIN	142	52	87	.374	38	561	818	4914	1232	173	70	38	323	584	.251	.303	.338	.641	97	-56	-17	93	94	570	137			
TOT	561					5194		38967	10398	1397	550	227	2685	4241	.267	.321	.348	.669							1402			

TEAM	CG	SH	SV	IP	H	H/G	HR	BB	SO	RAT	ERA	ERA+	OAV	OOB	PR	/A	PF	CPI	FA	E	DP	FW	PW	BW	SBW	DIF
PIT	119	**15**	4	1244²	1198	8.7	20	**244**	505	**10.9**	2.58	126	.252	.297	**102**	94	98	104	.950	287	97	1.2	9.2	7.4		2.6
PHI	125	**15**	2	1246²	1221	8.8	19	259	480	11.0	2.87	119	.255	.300	63	73	102	97	**.954**	**262**	65	**2.7**	7.2	1.5		1.7
BRO	111	7	**5**	1213²	1244	9.2	**18**	435	583	12.8	3.14	107	.264	.333	24	27	101	109	.950	281	99	1.2	2.6	6.5		.7
STL	118	5	**5**	1269²	1333	9.4	39	332	445	12.2	3.68	96	.268	.321	-51	-71	96	93	.949	305	**108**	.4	-7.0	**12.3**		.3
BOS	128	11	0	1263	**1196**	8.5	29	349	558	11.3	2.90	125	**.249**	.305	59	**99**	109	98	.952	282	89	1.5	**9.7**	-15.0		3.8
CHI	**131**	2	0	1241²	1348	9.8	27	324	**586**	12.5	3.33	97	.275	.327	-2	-14	97	105	.943	336	87	-1.8	-1.4	-3.4		-9.9
NY	118	11	1	1232	1389	10.1	24	377	542	13.4	3.87	85	.283	.342	-75	-78	100	99	.941	348	81	-2.3	-7.6	-6.1		-.4
CIN	126	4	0	1265²	1469	10.4	51	365	542	13.5	4.17	77	.289	.345	-120	-138	96	99	.940	355	102	-2.6	-13.5	-1.7		.3
TOT	976	70	17	9977		9.4				12.2	3.32		.267	.321					.947	2456	728					

Runs
Burkett-StL 142
Keeler-Bro 123
Beaumont-Pit 120
Clarke-Pit 118
Sheckard-Bro 116

Hits
Burkett-StL 226
Keeler-Bro 202
Sheckard-Bro 196
Wagner-Pit 194
Delahanty-Phi 192

Doubles
Delahanty-Phi 38
Daly-Bro 38
Wagner-Pit 37
Beckley-Cin 36
Wallace-StL 34

Triples
Sheckard-Bro 19
Flick-Phi 17

Home Runs
Crawford-Cin 16
Sheckard-Bro 11
Burkett-StL 10

Total Bases
Burkett-StL 306
Sheckard-Bro 296
Delahanty-Phi 286
Wagner-Pit 271

Runs Batted In
Wagner-Pit 126
Delahanty-Phi 108
Sheckard-Bro 104
Crawford-Cin 104

Runs Produced
Wagner-Pit 221
Sheckard-Bro 209
Burkett-StL 207
Delahanty-Phi 206
Flick-Phi 192

Bases On Balls
Thomas-Phi 100
Hartsel-Chi 74
Davis-Bro-Pit 66
Delahanty-Phi 65
Hamilton-Bos 64

Batting Average
Burkett-StL 376
Delahanty-Phi 354
Sheckard-Bro 354
Wagner-Pit 353
Keeler-Bro 339

On Base Percentage
Burkett-StL 440
Thomas-Phi 437
Delahanty-Phi 427
Wagner-Pit 417
Hartsel-Chi 414

Slugging Average
Sheckard-Bro 534
Delahanty-Phi 528
Crawford-Cin 524
Burkett-StL 509
Flick-Phi 500

Production
Delahanty-Phi 955
Burkett-StL 949
Sheckard-Bro 944
Wagner-Pit 911
Crawford-Cin 903

Adjusted Production
Burkett-StL 184
Delahanty-Phi 173
Crawford-Cin 172
Sheckard-Bro 168
Hartsel-Chi 163

Batter Runs
Burkett-StL 58.7
Delahanty-Phi 53.3
Sheckard-Bro 49.8
Wagner-Pit 44.9
Hartsel-Chi 42.6

Adjusted Batter Runs
Burkett-StL 65.9
Delahanty-Phi 50.7
Hartsel-Chi 47.2
Sheckard-Bro 46.5
Crawford-Cin 44.2

Clutch Hitting Index
Ganzel-NY 139
Dexter-Chi 136
Wagner-Pit 133
Long-Bos 133
Krueger-StL 128

Runs Created
Burkett-StL 151
Sheckard-Bro 139
Delahanty-Phi 139
Wagner-Pit 138
Hartsel-Chi 130

Total Average
Delahanty-Phi 1.097
Burkett-StL 1.072
Wagner-Pit 1.070
Sheckard-Bro 1.070
Hartsel-Chi 1.027

Stolen Bases
Wagner-Pit 49
Hartsel-Chi 41
Strang-NY 40
Harley-Cin 37
Beaumont-Pit 36

Stolen Base Average

Stolen Base Runs

Fielding Runs
Wallace-StL 29.6
Davis-NY 23.1
Flick-Phi 14.9
Dahlen-Bro 13.7
Kittridge-Bos 12.0

Total Player Rating
Wallace-StL 6.2
Burkett-StL 5.2
Wagner-Pit 5.1
Davis-NY 4.9
Sheckard-Bro 4.3

Wins
Donovan-Bro 25
Harper-StL 23
Phillippe-Pit 22
Hahn-Cin 22
Chesbro-Pit 21

Win Percentage
Chesbro-Pit 677
Phillippe-Pit 647
Tannehill-Pit 643
Harper-StL 639
Kitson-Bro 633

Games
Taylor-NY 45
Powell-StL 45
Donovan-Bro 45
Hahn-Cin 42
Mathewson-NY 40

Complete Games
Hahn-Cin 41
Taylor-NY 37
Mathewson-NY 36
Donovan-Bro 36

Shutouts
Willis-Bos 6
Orth-Phi 6
Chesbro-Pit 6

Saves
Powell-StL 3
Donovan-Bro 3
Sudhoff-StL 2
Phillippe-Pit 2
Kitson-Bro 2

Innings Pitched
Hahn-Cin 375.1
Taylor-NY 353.1
Donovan-Bro . . . 351.0
Powell-StL 338.1
Mathewson-NY . . . 336.0

Fewest Hits/Game
Townsend-Phi 7.39
Mathewson-NY . . . 7.71
Willis-Bos 7.72
Orth-Phi 7.99
Chesbro-Pit 8.17

Fewest BB/Game
Orth-Phi 1.02
Phillippe-Pit 1.16
Tannehill-Pit 1.28
Duggleby-Phi 1.30
Powell-StL 1.33

Strikeouts
Hahn-Cin 239
Donovan-Bro 226
Hughes-Chi 225
Mathewson-NY . . . 221
Waddell-Pit-Chi . . . 172

Strikeouts/Game
Hughes-Chi 6.57
Waddell-Pit-Chi . . . 6.16
Mathewson-NY . . . 5.92
Donovan-Bro 5.79
Hahn-Cin 5.73

Ratio
Orth-Phi 9.27
Phillippe-Pit 9.79
Tannehill-Pit 10.20
Chesbro-Pit 10.23
Willis-Bos 10.35

Earned Run Average
Tannehill-Pit 2.18
Phillippe-Pit 2.22
Orth-Phi 2.27
Willis-Bos 2.36
Chesbro-Pit 2.38

Adjusted ERA
Willis-Bos 153
Tannehill-Pit 150
Orth-Phi 150
Phillippe-Pit 147
Chesbro-Pit 137

Opponents' Batting Avg.
Townsend-Phi 223
Mathewson-NY 230
Willis-Bos 231
Orth-Phi 237
Chesbro-Pit 241

Opponents' On Base Pct.
Orth-Phi 264
Phillippe-Pit 275
Tannehill-Pit 284
Chesbro-Pit 284
Willis-Bos 286

Starter Runs
Phillippe-Pit 36.2
Mathewson-NY . . . 34.0
Orth-Phi 32.9
Willis-Bos 32.7
Tannehill-Pit 32.1

Adjusted Starter Runs
Willis-Bos 42.6
Orth-Phi 35.3
Phillippe-Pit 34.4
Mathewson-NY . . . 33.3
Tannehill-Pit 30.5

Clutch Pitching Index
Kitson-Bro 122
Taylor-Chi 116
Hughes-Bro 114
Taylor-NY 113
Donahue-Phi 109

Relief Runs

Adjusted Relief Runs

Relief Ranking

Total Pitcher Index
Orth-Phi 4.8
Willis-Bos 4.6
Phillippe-Pit 4.4
Mathewson-NY . . . 4.1
Tannehill-Pit 3.2

Total Baseball Ranking
Wallace-StL 6.2
Burkett-StL 5.2
Wagner-Pit 5.1
Davis-NY 4.9
Willis-Bos 4.6

January 4 The Baltimore AL club incorporates, with John McGraw as manager and part owner.

January 22 Connie Mack, Philadelphia A's manager/general manager, signs a 10-year lease on grounds at 29th and Columbia to be called Columbia Park. A contract is set for construction of single-deck stands to hold 7,500.

January 28 The AL formally organizes. The Baltimore Orioles, Philadelphia Athletics, and Boston Somersets are admitted to join the Washington Senators, Cleveland Blues, Detroit Tigers, Milwaukee Brewers, and Chicago White Stockings. Three of the original clubs—Indianapolis, Minneapolis, and Buffalo—are dropped. League power aggregates in president Ban Johnson as trustee for all ballpark leases and majority stockholdings, and with authority to buy out franchises. Player limit is 14 per team; schedule will be 140 games.

March 11 The *Cincinnati Enquirer* reports that Baltimore manager John McGraw has signed a Cherokee Indian named Tokohoma. It is really black second baseman Charlie Grant, who McGraw is trying to pass off as an Indian, but the ruse does not work.

April 3 Connie Mack accuses Christy Mathewson of reneging on a Philadel-phia contact signed in January. The young pitcher had accepted advance money from Mack, but jumped back to the Giants in March. Mack considers going to court, but eventually accepts the loss of the pitcher.

April 24 Chicago hosts the first game of the new AL. Roy Patterson's first of 20 wins in 1901, an 8-2 win over the Cleveland Blues, puts the White Stockings on their way to winning the AL's first pennant.

April 25 Detroit scores the greatest Opening Day rally in its AL debut. Trailing 13-4 in the bottom of the ninth, the Tigers score 10 runs for a 14-13 victory over the Milwaukee Brewers.

April 29 Admiral George Dewey and other prominent guests watch Washington defeat Baltimore 5–2 in the AL opener in the nation's capital.

May 8 In their long-delayed AL home opener, Boston defeats Philadelphia 12-4 behind Cy Young, who has jumped from the St. Louis NL team. He will lead the AL with his 1.62 ERA and 33 wins, 41.8 percent of his team's 79 victories. This post-1900 record will stand until Steve Carlton wins 45.8 percent of the Phils' 59 wins in 1972.

May 17 The Philadelphia Common Pleas Court rejects the Phillies' suit against Lajoie, Fraser, and Bernhard. The decision is appealed to the State Supreme Court, but the trio remains with the Athletics all season. Lajoie will hit .422, while Fraser wins 22 and Bernhard 17 for the fourth-place Athletics.

May 23 Philadelphia's Nap Lajoie is intentionally walked with the bases loaded by the White Stockings.

May 27 Third baseman Jimmy Burke of Milwaukee makes four errors in one inning, a record tied by Cleveland's Ray Chapman in 1914 and the Cubs' Len Merullo in 1942.

August 10 The Washington Senators' Dale Gear gives up an AL record 41 total bases in losing 13–0 to the Athletics. The 23 hits include four doubles, four triples, and two homers. Philadelphia A's pitcher Snake Wiltse has two doubles and two triples, becoming only the third hurler to collect four extra-base hits in a game.

September 3 Baltimore pitcher Joe McGinnity hurls two complete games against Milwaukee, winning 10–0 and losing 6–1.

November 5 Sportsman's Park in St. Louis is leased for five years by Ban Johnson and Charles Comiskey for an AL team; two weeks later the Milwaukee franchise is officially transferred.

BALTIMORE		BOSTON		CHICAGO		CLEVELAND		DETROIT		MILWAUKEE		PHILADELPHIA		WASHINGTON	
M	J.McGraw	M	J.Collins	M	C.Griffith	M	J.McAleer	M	G.Stallings	M	H.Duffy	M	C.Mack	M	J.Manning
1B	B.Hart	1B	B.Freeman	1B	F.Isbell	1B	C.LaChance	1B	P.Dillon	1B	J.Anderson	1B	H.Davis	1B	M.Grady
2B	J.Williams	2B	H.Ferris	2B	S.Mertes	2B	E.Beck	2B	K.Gleason	2B	N.Lajoie	2B	N.Lajoie	2B	J.Farrell
SS	B.Keister	SS	F.Parent	SS	F.Shugart	SS	F.Scheibeck	SS	K.Elberfeld	SS	W.Conroy	SS	J.Dolan	SS	B.Clingman
3B	J.McGraw	3B	J.Collins	3B	F.Hartman	3B	B.Bradley	3B	D.Casey	3B	J.Burke	3B	L.Cross	3B	B.Coughlin
LF	J.Jackson	LF	T.Dowd	LF	H.McFarland	LF	J.McCarthy	LF	D.Nance	LF	B.Hallman	LF	M.McIntyre	LF	P.Foster
CF	S.Brodie	CF	C.Stahl	CF	D.Hoy	CF	O.Pickering	CF	J.Barrett	CF	H.Duffy	CF	D.Fultz	CF	I.Waldron
RF	C.Seymour	RF	C.Hemphill	RF	F.Jones	RF	J.O'Brien	RF	D.Holmes	RF	I.Waldron	RF	S.Seybold	RF	S.Dungan
C	R.Bresnahan	C	O.Schreckengost	C	B.Sullivan	C	B.Wood	C	F.Buelow	C	B.Maloney	C	D.Powers	C	B.Clarke
O1	M.Donlin	C	L.Criger	C	J.Sugden	O	E.Harvey	C1	S.McAllister	3O	B.Friel	O	P.Geier	2	J.Quinn
3S	J.Dunn	O	C.Jones	S3	J.Burke	C	G.Yeager	C	A.Shaw	O	G.Hogriever	O	J.Hayden	OP	D.Gear
C	W.Robinson	/1	L.McLean	/O	P.Foster	C	J.Connor	C1	D.Crockett	C	J.Donahue	S	B.Ely	1	B.Everitt
1	F.Foutz	/C	J.Slattery	/2	D.Brain	O	F.Genins	/S	H.Lochhead	O	J.Connor	CO	F.Steelman	O	J.O'Brien
/1	G.Rohe	/3	H.Gleason			S	D.Shay			C	T.Leahy	/S	H.Lochhead	/O	C.Luskey
/O	C.Snodgrass			P	R.Patterson	O	T.Donovan	P	R.Miller	O	E.Bruyette	/C	H.Smith	/1	T.Jordan
/C	T.Latimer	P	C.Young	P	C.Griffith	S	J.McGuire	P	E.Siever	O	D.Jones	/C	M.Murphy	/O	B.Harrison
/1	S.Jordan	P	T.Lewis	P	N.Callahan	/S	B.Hallman	P	J.Cronin	S	G.Bone	/O	F.Ketchum		
		P	G.Winter	P	J.Katoll	/2	T.Eagan	P	J.Yeager	/O	P.Geier	/O	T.Leahy	P	B.Carrick
P	J.McGinnity	P	F.Mitchell	P	E.Harvey	/O	J.McAleer			/S	G.McBride	/O	B.Lindemann	P	W.Lee
P	H.Howell	P	N.Cuppy			/O	F.Cross	P	E.Frisk	/C	J.Butler	/1	C.Carr	P	C.Patten
P	F.Foreman					/O	E.Cermak	/O	F.Owen	/O	L.Gertenrich	/3	B.Lauder	P	W.Mercer
P	J.Nops	/P	W.Kellum	/P	J.Skopec	/O	S.Gallagher	/P	E.High			/2	B.McKinney		
		/P	G.Prentiss	/P	W.Piatt	/S	R.Hall			P	B.Reidy				
/P	C.Schmit	/P	B.Beville	/P	F.Dupee	/O	H.Hogan			P	N.Garvin	P	C.Fraser		
/P	B.Karns	/P	F.Foreman			/C	P.Livingston			P	B.Husting	P	E.Plank		
/P	S.Yerkes	/P	J.Volz							P	T.Sparks	P	B.Bernhard		
		/P	F.Morrissey			P	P.Dowling			P	P.Hawley	P	S.Wiltse		
						P	E.Moore					P	W.Piatt		
						P	B.Hart			P	P.Dowling				
						P	E.Scott					/P	B.Milligan		
						P	J.Bracken					/P	B.Baker		
												/P	J.McPherson		
						P	B.Hoffer					/P	D.Leitner		
						P	H.McNeal					/P	P.Loos		
						/P	B.Cristall								
						/P	D.Braggins								
						/P	G.Weyhing								
						/P	B.Baker								

TEAM	G	W	L	PCT	GB	R	OR	AB	H	2B	3B	HR	BB	SO	AVG	OBP	SLG	PRO	PRO+	BR	/A	PF	CHI	RC	SB	CS	SBA	SBR
CHI	137	83	53	.610		819	631	4725	1303	173	89	32	475	337	.276	.350	.370	.720	108	41	62	97	103	744	280			
BOS	138	79	57	.581	4	759	608	4866	1353	183	104	37	331	282	.278	.330	.381	.711	104	9	23	98	101	693	157			
DET	136	74	61	.548	8.5	741	694	4676	1303	180	80	29	380	346	.279	.340	.370	.710	98	15	-19	105	99	690	204			
PHI	137	74	62	.544	9	805	761	4882	1409	239	87	35	301	344	.289	.337	.395	.732	103	42	8	104	103	734	173			
BAL	135	68	65	.511	13.5	760	750	4589	1348	179	111	24	369	377	.294	.353	.397	.750	108	80	45	104	96	746	207			
WAS	138	61	72	.459	20.5	682	771	4772	1282	191	83	33	356	340	.269	.326	.364	.690	97	-24	-13	99	96	633	127			
CLE	138	54	82	.397	29	667	831	4833	1311	197	68	12	243	326	.271	.313	.348	.661	92	-82	-56	96	104	588	125			
MIL	139	48	89	.350	35.5	641	828	4795	1250	192	66	26	325	384	.261	.314	.345	.659	91	-81	-49	95	98	602	176			
TOT	549					5874		38138	10559	1534	688	228	2780	2736	.277	.333	.371	.704						1449				

TEAM	CG	SH	SV	IP	H	H/G	HR	BB	SO	RAT	ERA	ERA+	OAV	OOB	PR	/A	PF	CPI	FA	E	DP	FW	PW	BW	SBW	DIF
CHI	110	11	2	1218¹	1250	9.2	27	312	394	11.9	2.98	117	.263	.315	93	68	95	106	.941	345	100	.9	6.1	5.6		2.4
BOS	123	7	1	1217	1178	8.7	33	294	396	11.2	3.04	116	.251	.301	84	66	96	93	.943	337	104	1.6	6.0	2.1		1.4
DET	118	8	2	1188²	1328	10.1	22	313	307	12.8	3.30	116	.280	.330	48	71	105	109	.930	410	127	-3.3	6.4	-1.7		5.1
PHI	124	6	1	1200²	1346	10.1	20	374	350	13.3	4.00	94	.280	.339	-45	-32	103	94	.942	337	93	1.4	-2.9	.7		6.8
BAL	115	4	3	1158	1313	10.2	21	344	271	13.3	3.73	104	.282	.338	-9	17	106	101	.926	401	76	-2.9	1.5	4.1		-1.2
WAS	118	8	2	1183	1396	10.6	51	284	308	13.3	4.09	89	.291	.339	-57	-58	100	100	.943	323	97	2.4	-5.2	-1.2		-1.5
CLE	122	7	4	1182¹	1365	10.4	22	464	334	14.5	4.12	86	.286	.358	-60	-75	97	102	.942	329	99	2.1	-6.8	-5.1		-4.2
MIL	107	3	4	1218	1383	10.2	32	395	376	13.6	4.06	89	.283	.344	-53	-63	98	98	.934	393	106	-1.8	-5.7	-4.4		-8.6
TOT	937	54	19	9566		9.9				13.0	3.66		.277	.333					.938	2875	802					

Runs
Lajoie-Phi 145
Jones-Chi 120
Williams-Bal 113
Hoy-Chi 112
Barrett-Det 110

Hits
Lajoie-Phi 232
Anderson-Mil 190
Collins-Bos 187
Waldron-Mil-Was . . . 186
Dungan-Was 179

Doubles
Lajoie-Phi 48
Anderson-Mil 46
Collins-Bos 42
Farrell-Was 32

Triples
Williams-Bal 21
Keister-Bal 21
Mertes-Chi 17
Stahl-Bos 16
Collins-Bos 16

Home Runs
Lajoie-Phi 14
Freeman-Bos 12
Grady-Was 9

Total Bases
Lajoie-Phi 350
Collins-Bos 279
Anderson-Mil 274
Freeman-Bos 255
Williams-Bal 248

Runs Batted In
Lajoie-Phi 125
Freeman-Bos 114
Anderson-Mil 99
Mertes-Chi 98
Williams-Bal 96

Runs Produced
Lajoie-Phi 256
Williams-Bal 202
Collins-Bos 196
Freeman-Bos 190
Mertes-Chi 187

Bases On Balls
Hoy-Chi 86
Jones-Chi 84
Barrett-Det 76
McFarland-Chi 75
McGraw-Bal 61

Batting Average
Lajoie-Phi 426
Donlin-Bal 340
Freeman-Bos 339
Seybold-Phi 334
Collins-Bos 332

On Base Percentage
Lajoie-Phi 463
Jones-Chi 412
Donlin-Bal 409
Hoy-Chi 407
Freeman-Bos 400

Slugging Average
Lajoie-Phi 643
Freeman-Bos 520
Seybold-Phi 503
Williams-Bal 495
Collins-Bos 495

Production
Lajoie-Phi 1.106
Freeman-Bos 920
Seybold-Phi 901
Donlin-Bal 883
Williams-Bal 883

Adjusted Production
Lajoie-Phi 196
Freeman-Bos 157
Seybold-Phi 142
Collins-Bos 142
Donlin-Bal 138

Batter Runs
Lajoie-Phi 74.1
Freeman-Bos 34.9
McGraw-Bal 31.1
Donlin-Bal 29.5
Williams-Bal 29.3

Adjusted Batter Runs
Lajoie-Phi 67.4
Freeman-Bos 36.9
Collins-Bos 30.3
McGraw-Bal 27.9
Anderson-Mil 26.3

Clutch Hitting Index
Burke-Mil-Chi 140
Mertes-Chi 134
Keister-Bal 122
Hartman-Chi 120
Seymour-Bal 117

Runs Created
Lajoie-Phi 179
Collins-Bos 116
Anderson-Mil 114
Freeman-Bos 112
Donlin-Bal 109

Total Average
Lajoie-Phi 1.327
Donlin-Bal 1.000
Freeman-Bos 994
Seybold-Phi 963
Williams-Bal 956

Stolen Bases
Isbell-Chi 52
Mertes-Chi 46
Seymour-Bal 38
Jones-Chi 38

Stolen Base Average

Stolen Base Runs

Fielding Runs
Lajoie-Phi 28.7
Elberfeld-Det 22.0
Conroy-Mil 19.4
Clingman-Was 17.8
Farrell-Was 16.6

Total Player Rating
Lajoie-Phi 8.9
Elberfeld-Det 4.2
Collins-Bos 4.0
Freeman-Bos 2.7
Anderson-Mil 2.6

Wins
Young-Bos 33
McGinnity-Bal 26
Griffith-Chi 24
Miller-Det 23
Fraser-Phi 22

Win Percentage
Griffith-Chi 774
Young-Bos 767
Callahan-Chi 652
Patten-Was 643
Miller-Det 639

Games
McGinnity-Bal 48
Dowling-Mil-Cle . . . 43
Young-Bos 43
Carrick-Was 42
Patterson-Chi 41

Complete Games
McGinnity-Bal 39
Young-Bos 38
Miller-Det 35
Fraser-Phi 35
Carrick-Was 34

Shutouts
Young-Bos 5
Griffith-Chi 5
Patterson-Chi 4
Patten-Was 4
Moore-Cle 4

Saves
Hoffer-Cle 3
Garvin-Mil 2

Innings Pitched
McGinnity-Bal 382.0
Young-Bos 371.1
Miller-Det 332.0
Fraser-Phi 331.0
Carrick-Was 324.0

Fewest Hits/Game
Young-Bos 7.85
Callahan-Chi 8.15
Moore-Cle 8.38
Lewis-Bos 8.51
Winter-Bos 8.74

Fewest BB/Game
Young-Bos 90
Gear-Was 1.21
Lee-Was 1.55
Griffith-Chi 1.69
Cronin-Det 1.72

Strikeouts
Young-Bos 158
Patterson-Chi 127
Dowling-Mil-Cle . . . 124
Garvin-Mil 122
Fraser-Phi 110

Strikeouts/Game
Garvin-Mil 4.27
Patten-Was 3.86
Young-Bos 3.83
Patterson-Chi 3.66
Dowling-Mil-Cle . . . 3.65

Ratio
Young-Bos 8.92
Callahan-Chi 10.62
Griffith-Chi 11.10
Lewis-Bos 11.32
Winter-Bos 11.35

Earned Run Average
Young-Bos 1.62
Callahan-Chi 2.42
Yeager-Det 2.61
Griffith-Chi 2.67
Winter-Bos 2.80

Adjusted ERA
Young-Bos 217
Yeager-Det 147
Callahan-Chi 143
Griffith-Chi 130
Miller-Det 130

Opponents' Batting Avg.
Young-Bos 232
Callahan-Chi 239
Moore-Cle 244
Lewis-Bos 247
Winter-Bos 252

Opponents' On Base Pct.
Young-Bos 256
Callahan-Chi 290
Griffith-Chi 300
Lewis-Bos 304
Winter-Bos 304

Starter Runs
Young-Bos 84.1
Callahan-Chi 29.6
Griffith-Chi 29.5
Miller-Det 26.1
Yeager-Det 23.2

Adjusted Starter Runs
Young-Bos 78.5
Miller-Det 32.8
Yeager-Det 27.3
Callahan-Chi 25.2
Griffith-Chi 24.1

Clutch Pitching Index
Katoll-Chi 126
Yeager-Det 121
Siever-Det 116
Sparks-Mil 116
Young-Bos 113

Relief Runs

Adjusted Relief Runs

Relief Ranking

Total Pitcher Index
Young-Bos 8.3
Callahan-Chi 3.9
Griffith-Chi 3.7
Yeager-Det 3.5
Miller-Det 3.5

Total Baseball Ranking
Lajoie-Phi 8.9
Young-Bos 8.3
Elberfeld-Det 4.2
Collins-Bos 4.0
Callahan-Chi 3.9

January 30* Dashing Tony Mullane, the first player to have jumped the reserve rule by signing with the St. Louis Unions of the Union Association in 1883, signs a contract with Toledo, of the new American Association (AAA).

February 20 Nick Young remains as NL president when A. G. Spalding bows out of the battle, but the league will have no effective leadership until 1903.

April 21 The Pennsylvania Supreme Court, reversing a lower court's decision, grants a permanent injunction (effective only in Pennsylvania) barring jumpers Nap Lajoie, Chick Fraser, and Bill Bernhard from playing for the A's, or any team but the Phillies.

April 23 St. Louis Cardinals owner Frank DeHaas Robison offers to put up $10,000 that the Pirates will not repeat as NL champions. Pittsburgh players accept the challenge with a matching pool, and go on to win the pennant by 27½ games.

April 27 Cubs rookie RH pitcher Jim St. Vrain, sent up to pinch hit lefthanded, grounds to Pittsburgh shortstop Honus Wagner. The confused St. Vrain runs toward third base as the astonished Wagner throws him out. Pittsburgh wins 2–0.

May 7 The Cubs' Jack Taylor beats Christy Mathewson 4–0 at Chicago. Cubs manager Frank Selee comments that the distance from the pitcher's mound to the plate looks short. Horace Fogel, the Giants manager, measures the distance and finds the lane is 15 inches short. The subsequent New York protest is upheld, and two games are ordered replayed.

May 16 Two deaf mutes face each other for the first time when William "Dummy" Hoy leads off for the Reds against Luther "Dummy" Taylor of the Giants. The Reds win 5-3 with a 5-run rally in the ninth. Hoy goes 2-for-4.

June 3 The Cardinals' Mike O'Neill, a pitcher and one of four major league brothers, hits the first pinch grand slam ever, against Boston Beaneater Togie Pittinger. It is an inside-the-park homer at Boston and scores his brother Jack.

June 15* Corsicana (Texas League) beats Texarkana, 51–3, as Nig Clarke hits eight homers. The team's 53 hits include 21 homers, mostly over a short outfield fence.

July 8 John McGraw negotiates his release from Baltimore and signs to manage the New York Giants, although he'd secretly signed a contract several days earlier. McGraw also conspires to swing the sale of Orioles to the NL teams that helped him. McGraw enables the Orioles to release Dan McGann, Roger Bresna- han, Joe McGinnity and Jack Cronin to sign with the Giants. Joe Kelley and Cy Seymour go the Reds.

July 14 Little Tommy Leach of Pittsburgh, never considered a long-ball threat, hits two homers over the fence at Boston. He will close out the season with only six, but it's enough to give him sole leadership of the NL, which totals only 99. Leach's leading number is the lowest since Paul Hines hit four in a 60-game schedule in 1878.

September 1 Tinker, Evers, and Chance appear together in the Chicago Cubs lineup for the first time, but not in the positions that will earn them immortality. Johnny Evers, a New York State League rookie, starts at shortstop, with Joe Tinker at third, Frank Chance at first, and Bobby Lowe at second.

October 4 When Pirates owner Barney Dreyfuss demands a game be played despite a rain-soaked field, Cincinnati plays most of its team out of their normal positions. pitcher Rube Vickers, catching, sets a modern major league record with six passed balls. Pittsburgh wins 11–2, but Dreyfuss refunds fans' money, and the Reds return their share of the gate.

December 12 Harry Pulliam is elected president of the NL.

	BOSTON		BROOKLYN		CHICAGO		CINCINNATI		NEW YORK		PHILADELPHIA		PITTSBURGH		ST.LOUIS
M	A.Buckenberger	M	N.Hanlon	M	F.Selee	M	B.McPhee	M	H.Fogel	M	B.Shettsline	M	F.Clarke	M	P.Donovan
1B	F.Tenney	1B	T.McCreery	1B	F.Chance	M	F.Bancroft	M	H.Smith	1B	H.Jennings	1B	K.Bransfield	1B	R.Brashear
2B	G.DeMontreville	2B	T.Flood	2B	B.Lowe	M	J.Kelley	2B	J.McGraw	2B	P.Childs	2B	C.Ritchey	2B	J.Farrell
SS	H.Long	SS	B.Dahlen	SS	J.Tinker	1B	J.Beckley	1B	D.McGann	SS	R.Hulswitt	SS	W.Conroy	SS	O.Krueger
3B	E.Gremminger	3B	C.Irwin	3B	G.Schaefer	2B	H.Peitz	2B	H.Smith	3B	B.Hallman	3B	T.Leach	3B	F.Hartman
LF	D.Cooley	LF	J.Sheckard	LF	J.Slagle	SS	T.Corcoran	SS	J.Bean	LF	G.Browne	LF	F.Clarke	LF	G.Barclay
CF	B.Lush	CF	C.Dolan	CF	J.Dobbs	3B	H.Steinfeldt	3B	B.Lauder	CF	R.Thomas	CF	G.Beaumont	CF	H.Smoot
RF	P.Carney	RF	W.Keeler	RF	D.Jones	LF	J.Dobbs	LF	J.Jones	RF	S.Barry	RF	H.Wagner	RF	P.Donovan
C	M.Kittridge	C	H.Hearne	C	J.Kling	CF	D.Hoy	CF	S.Brodie	C	R.Dooin	C	H.Smith	C	J.Ryan
						RF	S.Crawford	RF	J.Dunn						
C	P.Moran	C1	D.Farrell	31	C.Dexter	C	B.Bergen	C	F.Bowerman	1C	K.Douglass	O	L.Davis	1C	A.Nichols
S2	C.Dexter	32	E.Wheeler	OP	J.Menefee					O2	H.Krug	2O	J.Burke	C	J.O'Neill
O	E.Courtney	C	L.Ritter	O	D.Miller	O	C.Seymour	O	G.Browne	3	H.Wolverton	3	J.O'Connor	3	J.Calhoun
/O	F.Brown	O	G.Hildebrand	O	B.Congalton	2	E.Beck	1	J.Doyle	C	F.Jacklitsch	C	C.Zimmer	A	A.Weaver
		O	R.Ward	O1	A.Williams	2	G.Magoon	OC	R.Bresnahan	3	P.Greene	C	J.Sebring	/1	D.Hazleton
P	V.Willis	/C	T.Latimer	1	H.O'Hagen	O2	J.Kelley	O	J.Jackson	C	B.Thomas	C	E.Phelps	/S	R.Kling
P	T.Pittinger	/C	J.Wall	2	J.Evers	O	M.Donlin	C	G.Yeager	/O	T.Fleming	/O	F.Crolius	/S	O.Williams
P	M.Eason	/C	N.Fuller	O	J.Murray	O	B.Maloney	S	J.McGraw	/O	B.Clay	/O	G.Merritt	/3	J.Murphy
P	J.Malarkey	/C	P.Deisel	1	D.Clark	2	J.Morrissey	O	G.Van Haltren	/O	N.Shea	/O	B.Miller		
				/O	L.Schlafly	/O	H.Bay	/O	H.O'Hagen	/C	J.Berry	/C	L.Fohl	P	M.O'Neill
/P	D.Hale	P	B.Donovan	/O	M.Lynch			O	R.Clark	/O	E.Watkins	/C	M.Hopkins	P	S.Yerkes
/P	B.Dresser	P	F.Kitson	/S	M.Jacobs	P	N.Hahn	S	H.Wagner	R	F.Mahar			P	E.Murphy
/P	F.Klobedanz	P	D.Newton	/C	M.Kahoe	P	B.Phillips	/O	J.Delahanty	R	T.Maher	P	J.Chesbro	P	B.Wicker
/P	R.Long	/2	J.Hughes	/2	S.Strang	P	H.Thielman	/O	J.Hendricks			P	D.Phillippe	P	C.Currie
/P	S.Curran	P	R.Evans	/C	P.Lamer	P	E.Poole	/O	J.Wall	P	D.White	P	J.Tannehill		
				/S	E.Glenn	P	B.Ewing	/O	J.McDonald	P	B.Duggleby	P	S.Leever	P	A.Pearson
		/P	J.McMakin	/O	J.Hendricks			/C	J.Robinson	P	H.Iburg	P	E.Doheny	/P	B.Popp
		/P	G.McCann	/O	C.Pedroes	P	C.Currie	/O	L.Washburn	P	C.Fraser			/P	W.Dunham
		/P	N.Garvin	/O	S.Kennedy	/P	C.Heismann	/C	J.O'Neill			/P	H.Cushman	/P	J.Hackett
		/P	L.Winham	/O	R.Hildebrand	/P	A.Stimmel	/O	J.Callahan	/P	B.Magee	/P	W.McLaughlin	/P	C.McFarland
				/O	J.Hughes	/P	R.Vickers	/O	C.Hartley	P	C.Vorhees	/P	E.Poole	/P	J.Adams
				/P	L.Swormstedt			/P	H.Felix						
				P	J.Hooker	/P	B.Hooker	P	C.Mathewson	/P	B.McFadden				
				P	P.Williams	/P	M.Glendon	P	D.Taylor	/P	J.Whiting				
				P	C.Lundgren			P	R.Evans	/P	B.Wolfe				
				P	B.Rhoads			P	J.McGinnity	/P	B.Salisbury				
				P	J.St.Vrain			P	T.Sparks	/P	H.Fox				
				/P	F.Morrissey			P	J.Cronin						
				/P	A.Hardy			P	R.Miller						
				/P	J.Gardner			/P	B.Kennedy						
				/P	M.Eason			/P	B.Blewett						
				/P	F.Glade			/P	J.Burke						
								/P	H.Thielman						
								/P	B.Magee						

TEAM	G	W	L	PCT	GB	R	OR	AB	H	2B	3B	HR	BB	SO	AVG	OBP	SLG	PRO	PRO+	BR	/A	PF	CHI	RC	SB	CS	SBA	SBR
PIT	142	103	36	.741		775	440	4926	1410	189	95	18	372	446	.286	.344	.374	.718	123	152	126	104	105	743	222			
BRO	141	75	63	.543	27.5	564	519	4845	1242	147	49	19	319	489	.256	.311	.319	.630	99	-4	-8	101	100	553	145			
BOS	142	73	64	.533	29	572	516	4728	1178	142	39	14	398	481	.249	.313	.305	.618	95	-16	-21	101	104	540	189			
CIN	141	70	70	.500	33.5	633	566	4908	1383	188	77	18	297	465	.282	.328	.362	.690	109	95	33	110	95	654	131			
CHI	141	68	69	.496	34	530	501	4802	1200	131	40	6	353	565	.250	.307	.304	.610	97	-41	-26	97	100	539	222			
STL	140	56	78	.418	44.5	517	695	4751	1226	116	37	10	273	438	.258	.306	.304	.610	97	-37	-16	96	101	516	158			
PHI	138	56	81	.409	46	484	649	4615	1139	110	43	5	356	481	.247	.305	.293	.598	90	-50	-50	100	98	473	108			
NY	139	48	88	.353	53.5	401	590	4571	1088	147	34	8	252	530	.238	.283	.290	.573	83	-98	-95	99	93	452	187			
TOT	562					4476		38146	9866	1170	414	98	2620	3895	.259	.313	.319	.631							1362			

TEAM	CG	SH	SV	IP	H	H/G	HR	BB	SO	RAT	ERA	ERA+	OAV	OOB	PR	/A	PF	CPI	FA	E	DP	FW	PW	BW	SBW	DIF
PIT	131	21	3	1264²	1142	8.1	4	250	564	10.3	2.30	119	.241	.288	67	61	98	94	.958	247	87	3.4	6.4	13.3		10.4
BRO	131	14	3	1256	1113	8.0	10	363	536	10.8	2.69	102	.238	.298	12	9	99	86	.952	275	79	1.5	.9	-.8		4.4
BOS	124	14	4	1259²	1233	8.8	16	372	523	11.8	2.61	108	.257	.316	24	29	102	109	.959	240	90	3.8	3.1	-2.2		-.2
CIN	130	9	1	1239	1228	8.9	15	352	430	11.9	2.67	112	.259	.318	14	43	108	108	.945	322	118	-1.4	4.5	3.5		-6.6
CHI	132	17	2	1275¹	1235	8.7	9	279	437	11.0	2.21	122	.254	.301	81	69	97	114	.946	327	111	-1.7	7.3	-2.7		-3.4
STL	112	7	4	1227²	1399	10.3	16	338	400	13.0	3.47	79	.287	.338	-95	-101	99	102	.944	336	107	-2.4	-10.7	-1.7		3.7
PHI	118	8	3	1211	1323	9.8	12	334	504	12.7	3.50	80	.278	.333	-97	-93	101	95	.946	305	81	-.7	-9.8	-5.3		3.3
NY	118	11	1	1226¹	1193	8.8	16	332	501	11.6	2.82	99	.255	.312	-5	-3	101	98	.943	330	104	-2.1	-.3	-10.0		-7.5
TOT	996	101	21	9959²		8.9				11.6	2.78		.259	.313					.949	2382	777					

Runs		Hits		Doubles		Triples		Home Runs		Total Bases	
Wagner-Pit	105	Beaumont-Pit	193	Wagner-Pit	30	Leach-Pit	22	Leach-Pit	6	Crawford-Cin	256
Clarke-Pit	103	Keeler-Bro	186	Clarke-Pit	27	Crawford-Cin	22	Beckley-Cin	5	Wagner-Pit	247
Beaumont-Pit	100	Crawford-Cin	185	Cooley-Bos	26	Wagner-Pit	16	Sheckard-Bro	4	Beckley-Cin	227
Leach-Pit	97	Wagner-Pit	176	Dahlen-Bro	25	Clarke-Pit	14	McCreery-Bro	4	Beaumont-Pit	226
Crawford-Cin	92	Beckley-Cin	175	Beckley-Cin	23	Gremminger-Bos	12			Leach-Pit	219

Runs Batted In		Runs Produced		Bases On Balls		Batting Average		On Base Percentage		Slugging Average	
Wagner-Pit	91	Wagner-Pit	193	R.Thomas-Phi	107	Beaumont-Pit	.357	R.Thomas-Phi	.414	Wagner-Pit	.463
Leach-Pit	85	Leach-Pit	176	Lush-Bos	76	Crawford-Cin	.333	Tenney-Bos	.409	Crawford-Cin	.461
Crawford-Cin	78	Crawford-Cin	167	Tenney-Bos	73	Keeler-Bro	.333	Beaumont-Pit	.404	Clarke-Pit	.449
Dahlen-Bro	74	Beaumont-Pit	167	Sheckard-Bro	57	Wagner-Pit	.330	Clarke-Pit	.401	Beckley-Cin	.427
		Clarke-Pit	154			Beckley-Cin	.330	Wagner-Pit	.394	Leach-Pit	.426

Production		Adjusted Production		Batter Runs		Adjusted Batter Runs		Clutch Hitting Index		Runs Created	
Wagner-Pit	.857	Wagner-Pit	159	Wagner-Pit	39.9	Wagner-Pit	36.3	Hartman-StL	160	Wagner-Pit	118
Clarke-Pit	.850	Clarke-Pit	156	Crawford-Cin	38.6	Clarke-Pit	31.7	Bransfield-Pit	133	Beaumont-Pit	109
Crawford-Cin	.848	Beaumont-Pit	148	Clarke-Pit	34.9	Beaumont-Pit	30.7	Ritchey-Pit	124	Crawford-Cin	108
Beaumont-Pit	.822	Crawford-Cin	147	Beaumont-Pit	34.1	Crawford-Cin	29.1	McCreery-Bro	124	Clarke-Pit	97
Beckley-Cin	.804	Tenney-Bos	141	Beckley-Cin	28.7	Tenney-Bos	27.8	Wagner-Pit	123	Beckley-Cin	94

Total Average		Stolen Bases		Stolen Base Average		Stolen Base Runs		Fielding Runs		Total Player Rating	
Wagner-Pit	.966	Wagner-Pit	42					Farrell-StL	33.5	Wagner-Pit	4.4
Clarke-Pit	.955	Slagle-Chi	40					Lowe-Chi	26.0	Tenney-Bos	3.9
Beaumont-Pit	.868	Donovan-StL	34					H.Long-Bos	22.9	Farrell-StL	3.3
Crawford-Cin	.865	Beaumont-Pit	33					Steinfeldt-Cin	21.8	Leach-Pit	3.3
Tenney-Bos	.845	Smith-NY	32					Leach-Pit	12.7	Crawford-Cin	2.5

Wins		Win Percentage		Games		Complete Games		Shutouts		Saves	
Chesbro-Pit	28	Chesbro-Pit	.824	Willis-Bos	51	Willis-Bos	45	Mathewson-NY	8	Willis-Bos	3
Willis-Bos	27	Doheny-Pit	.800	Pittinger-Bos	46	Pittinger-Bos	36	Chesbro-Pit	8	M.O'Neill-StL	2
Pittinger-Bos	27	Tannehill-Pit	.769	Yerkes-StL	39	Hahn-Cin	35	Taylor-Chi	7	Newton-Bro	2
Taylor-Chi	23	Phillippe-Pit	.690			White-Phi	34	Pittinger-Bos	7	Leever-Pit	2
Hahn-Cin	23	Leever-Pit	.682			Taylor-Chi	33	Hahn-Cin	6		

Innings Pitched		Fewest Hits/Game		Fewest BB/Game		Strikeouts		Strikeouts/Game		Ratio	
Willis-Bos	410.0	Newton-Bro	7.08	Phillippe-Pit	.86	Willis-Bos	225	White-Phi	5.44	Taylor-Chi	8.98
Pittinger-Bos	389.1	McGinnity-NY	7.18	Tannehill-Pit	.97	White-Phi	185	Mathewson-NY	5.17	Tannehill-Pit	9.27
Taylor-Chi	324.2	Taylor-Chi	7.51	Menefee-Chi	1.19	Pittinger-Bos	174	Donovan-Bro	5.14	McGinnity-NY	9.59
Hahn-Cin	321.0	Donovan-Bro	7.56	Taylor-Chi	1.19	Donovan-Bro	170	Willis-Bos	4.94	Hahn-Cin	9.70
White-Phi	306.0	Chesbro-Pit	7.61	Leever-Pit	1.26	Mathewson-NY	159	Wicker-StL	4.61	Phillippe-Pit	9.76

Earned Run Average		Adjusted ERA		Opponents' Batting Avg.		Opponents' On Base Pct.		Starter Runs		Adjusted Starter Runs	
Taylor-Chi	1.33	Taylor-Chi	203	Newton-Bro	.217	Taylor-Chi	.260	Taylor-Chi	52.2	Taylor-Chi	49.3
Hahn-Cin	1.77	Hahn-Cin	169	McGinnity-NY	.219	Tannehill-Pit	.266	Hahn-Cin	36.1	Hahn-Cin	43.7
Tannehill-Pit	1.95	Poole-Pit-Cin	142	Taylor-Chi	.227	McGinnity-NY	.273	Willis-Bos	26.5	Willis-Bos	28.4
Lundgren-Chi	1.97	Tannehill-Pit	140	Donovan-Bro	.228	Hahn-Cin	.275	Phillippe-Pit	22.0	Mathewson-NY	21.2
Phillippe-Pit	2.05	Lundgren-Chi	137	Chesbro-Pit	.229	Phillippe-Pit	.276	Tannehill-Pit	21.3	Phillippe-Pit	20.6

Clutch Pitching Index		Relief Runs		Adjusted Relief Runs		Relief Ranking		Total Pitcher Index		Total Baseball Ranking	
Lundgren-Chi	144							Taylor-Chi	6.3	Taylor-Chi	6.0
Poole-Pit-Cin	140							Hahn-Cin	4.6	Hahn-Cin	4.5
Eason-Chi-Bos	136							Tannehill-Pit	3.1	Wagner-Pit	4.4
Taylor-NY	126							Willis-Bos	3.1	Tenney-Bos	3.9
Taylor-Chi	122							Phillips-Cin	3.1	Farrell-StL	3.3

January 4 Bill Dinneen, winner of 36 games for the Beaneaters (NL) in the past two years, signs with the rival Boston Somersets (AL), for whom he will win 20 or more in each of the next three years.

April 26 In his major league debut, Cleveland's Addie Joss hurls a one-hitter against the Browns to win 3–0. The only hit is a scratch single by Jesse Burkett.

May 23 Cleveland financier Charles Somers, who is also the president of the Boston club, meets with Lajoie in Philadelphia and guarantees him a four-year contract at $7,000 per year no matter what the legal outcome of his case. Lajoie had played one game for the A's, then sat in the stands for two months. Even after joining Cleveland, for the rest of the season Lajoie stayed clear of Pennsylvania, where an injunction remained in force. In 1903, Cleveland fans will vote to rename the club the Naps in honor of Lajoie.

May 24 Bill Bradley, Cleveland third baseman, is the AL's first player to hit a home run in each of four consecutive games, a record not matched until Babe Ruth does it June 25, 1918.

June 10 Bobby Wallace, slick-fielding St. Louis shortstop, handles an AL record 17 chances in a 9-inning game while losing 5–4 to Boston.

June 11 Connie Mack signs Rube Waddell, who was pitching in the Pacific Coast League. He will go 24-7 for the remainder of 1902 for Philadelphia to finish second in the league in wins behind Cy Young's 32 for Boston.

June 30 Cleveland is the first AL team to hit three consecutive home runs in one inning as Napoleon Lajoie, Piano Legs Hickman, and Bill Bradley connect in the first inning off St. Louis. Two days later, Ed Delahanty, Bill Coughlin, and Boileryard Clarke will duplicate the feat for Washington against the White Stockings.

July 13 In the sixth inning of a game with the Tigers, Harry Davis of the A's attempts a double steal with Dave Fultz, who is on third base. But Davis does not draw a throw as he goes into second base. On the next pitch he "steals" first base. The next time he steals second base he does draw a throw and Fultz scores from third base. This double steal maneuver will be attempted in later years by Fred Tenney (July 31, 1908), and Germany Schaefer (September 4, 1908).

July 17 Left with only five players available to play, the Orioles forfeit a game to St. Louis and their franchise to the league, which borrows players from other teams and operates the club for the balance of the season.

August 18* The first unassisted triple play ever in a professional game is executed by first base Hal O'Hagan, of the Rochester Broncos (IL) against Jersey City.

August 25 Ban Johnson announces the AL's intention to have a New York team in 1903, with Clark Griffith as manager.

September 28 The AL season ends with the Athletics five games in front of the St. Louis Browns. Philadelphia's Socks Seybold hits 16 homers for the highest total to lead the AL until Babe Ruth's 29 in 1919.

December 9 The AL announces the purchase of grounds for a ballpark in New York, and the next day the NL declares its readiness to make peace.

	BALTIMORE		BOSTON		CHICAGO		CLEVELAND		DETROIT		PHILADELPHIA		ST.LOUIS		WASHINGTON
M	J.McGraw	M	J.Collins	M	C.Griffith	M	B.Armour	M	F.Dwyer	M	C.Mack	M	J.McAleer	M	T.Loftus
M	W.Robinson	1B	C.LaChance	1B	F.Isbell	1B	C.Hickman	1B	P.Dillon	1B	H.Davis	1B	J.Anderson	1B	S.Carey
1B	D.McGann	2B	H.Ferris	2B	T.Daly	2B	N.Lajoie	2B	K.Gleason	2B	D.Murphy	2B	D.Padden	2B	J.Doyle
2B	J.Williams	SS	F.Parent	SS	G.Davis	SS	J.Gochnauer	SS	K.Elberfeld	SS	M.Cross	SS	B.Wallace	SS	B.Ely
SS	B.Gilbert	3B	J.Collins	3B	S.Strang	3B	B.Bradley	3B	D.Casey	3B	L.Cross	3B	B.McCormick	3B	B.Coughlin
3B	R.Bresnahan	LF	P.Dougherty	LF	S.Mertes	LF	J.McCarthy	LF	D.Harley	LF	T.Hartsel	LF	J.Burkett	LF	E.Delahanty
LF	K.Selbach	CF	C.Stahl	CF	F.Jones	CF	H.Bay	CF	J.Barrett	CF	E.Heidrick	CF	J.Ryan
CF	H.McFarland	RF	B.Freeman	RF	D.Green	RF	E.Flick	RF	D.Holmes	RF	S.Seybold	RF	C.Hemphill	RF	W.Lee
RF	C.Seymour	C	L.Criger	C	B.Sullivan	C	H.Bemis	C	D.McGuire	C	O.Schreck't	C	J.Sugden	C	B.Clarke
C	W.Robinson														
		3O	H.Gleason	C	E.McFarland	O	O.Pickering	/1	S.McAllister	C	D.Powers	O2	B.Friel	O2	B.Keister
O	H.Arndt	C	J.Warner	/O	H.McFarland	C1	B.Wood	C	F.Buelow	2	L.Castro	C	M.Kahoe	3	H.Wolverton
O	J.Kelley	O	C.Hickman	/C	E.Hughes	2	E.Beck	2	F.Bonner	O	B.Maloney	/O	J.Stanley
1	T.Jones	/2	G.Wilson			2S	J.Thoney	O	P.LePine	O	E.Flick	O	J.Donahue	/2	J.Atz
C	A.Smith			P	N.Callahan	O	C.Hemphill	O	H.Arndt	/C	F.Steelman	O	D.Jones	/C	T.Donahue
3	J.Mathison	P	C.Young	P	R.Patterson	1	O.Schreck't	/2	J.O'Connell	/2	N.Lajoie	/O	J.McAleer		
3	A.Oyler	P	B.Dinneen	P	W.Piatt	O	E.Harvey	/O	L.Post						
3	J.McGraw	P	G.Winter	P	C.Griffith	/1	H.O'Hagen	/O	L.Schiappa'e	P	E.Plank	P	J.Powell	P	A.Orth
C	G.Yeager	P	T.Sparks	P	N.Garvin	/2	P.Graham			P	R.Waddell	P	R.Donahue	P	C.Patten
1	B.Mellor					/C	G.Starnagle	P	W.Mercer	P	B.Husting	P	J.Harper	P	B.Carrick
/O	J.Sheckard	/P	T.Hughes	/P	J.Durham			P	G.Mullin	P	S.Wiltse	P	W.Sudhoff	P	H.Townsend
/2	S.McAllister	/P	G.Prentiss	/P	D.Leitner	P	E.Moore	P	E.Siever	P	F.Mitchell	P	B.Reidy		
/3	J.Thoney	/P	D.Adkins	/P	S.McMackin	P	A.Joss	P	R.Miller					/P	C.Vorhees
/C	L.Drill	/P	D.Williams	/P	J.Katoll	P	B.Bernhard	P	J.Yeager	P	H.Wilson	/P	C.Shields		
/1	P.Dillon	/P	N.Altrock			P	G.Wright			/P	A.Coakley	/P	H.Kane		
/3	E.Courtney	/P	P.Deininger					P	A.McCarthy	B.Duggleby					
/O	S.Jordan	/P	B.Husting			/P	O.Streit	/P	R.Kisinger	/P	E.Kenna				
H	C.Burns	/P	F.Mitchell			/P	O.Hess	/P	W.Egan	/P	B.Bernhard				
						/P	G.Dorner	/P	J.Cronin	/P	O.Porter				
P	J.McGinnity					/P	J.Lundbom	/P	S.McMackin	/P	T.Quinn				
P	H.Howell					/P	D.Taylor	/P	J.Terry	/P	T.Walker				
P	S.Wiltse					/P	C.Smith	/P	E.Fisher						
P	C.Shields					/P	D.Varney								
P	J.Katoll					/P	D.Leitner								
						/P	L.Polchow								
P	I.Butler					/P	E.Walker								
P	T.Hughes					/P	G.Clark								
P	J.Cronin					/P	C.Vasbinder								
/P	E.Ross														
/P	F.Foreman														
/P	C.Heismann														
/P	D.Hale														
/P	B.Lawson														
/P	G.Prentiss														

TEAM	G	W	L	PCT	GB	R	OR	AB	H	2B	3B	HR	BB	SO	AVG	OBP	SLG	PRO	PRO+	BR	/A	PF	CHI	RC	SB	CS	SBA	SBR
PHI	137	83	53	.610		775	636	4762	1369	235	67	38	343	293	.287	.340	.389	.729	104	50	20	104	107	729	201			
STL	140	78	58	.574	5	619	607	4736	1254	208	61	29	373	327	.265	.323	.353	.676	94	-38	-29	99	97	612	137			
BOS	138	77	60	.562	6.5	664	600	4875	1356	195	95	42	275	375	.278	.322	.383	.705	98	0	-19	103	98	671	132			
CHI	138	74	60	.552	8	675	602	4654	1248	170	50	14	411	381	.268	.332	.335	.667	95	-43	-15	96	107	641	265			
CLE	137	69	67	.507	14	686	640	4840	1401	248	68	33	308	356	.289	.336	.389	.725	107	41	70	96	95	712	140			
WAS	138	61	75	.449	22	707	790	4734	1338	261	66	47	329	296	.283	.335	.395	.730	107	48	42	101	99	694	121			
DET	137	52	83	.385	30.5	566	657	4644	1167	141	55	22	359	287	.251	.312	.320	.632	79	-109	-120	102	103	527	130			
BAL	141	50	88	.362	34	715	848	4760	1318	202	107	33	417	429	.277	.342	.385	.727	103	51	19	104	97	723	189			
TOT	553					5407		38005	10451	1660	569	258	2815	2744	.275	.331	.369	.700						1315				

TEAM	CG	SH	SV	IP	H	H/G	HR	BB	SO	RAT	ERA	ERA+	OAV	OOB	PR	/A	PF	CPI	FA	E	DP	FW	PW	BW	SBW	DIF
PHI	114	5	2	1216¹	1292	9.6	33	368	455	12.7	3.29	111	.273	.334	39	51	103	110	.953	270	75	1.4	4.8	1.9		6.9
STL	120	7	2	1244	1273	9.2	36	343	348	12.0	3.34	106	.266	.321	32	26	99	99	.953	274	122	1.5	2.5	-2.8		8.7
BOS	123	6	1	1238	1217	8.8	27	326	431	11.5	3.02	118	.258	.311	75	75	100	99	.955	263	101	2.0	7.1	-1.8		1.2
CHI	116	11	0	1221²	1269	9.3	30	331	346	12.1	3.41	99	.269	.323	22	-5	95	98	.955	257	125	2.3	-.5	-1.4		6.6
CLE	116	16	3	1204¹	1199	9.0	26	411	361	12.4	3.28	105	.260	.327	39	21	96	101	.950	287	96	.3	2.0	6.6		-8.0
WAS	130	2	1	1207²	1403	10.5	56	312	300	13.2	4.36	85	.291	.341	-106	-88	104	94	.945	316	70	-1.3	-8.3	4.0		-1.3
DET	116	9	3	1190²	1267	9.6	20	370	245	12.6	3.56	102	.274	.333	1	10	102	99	.943	332	111	-2.5	.9	-11.4		-2.6
BAL	119	1	3	1210¹	1531	11.4	30	354	258	14.3	4.33	87	.309	.360	-102	-77	106	104	.938	357	109	-3.5	-7.3	1.8		-10.0
TOT	954	59	13	9733		9.7				12.6	3.57		.275	.331					.949	2356	809					

Runs
Hartsel-Phi 109
Fultz-Phi 109
Strang-Chi 108
Bradley-Cle 104
Delahanty-Was 103

Hits
Hickman-Bos-Cle .. 193
L.Cross-Phi 191
Bradley-Cle 187
Delahanty-Was 178
Freeman-Bos 174

Doubles
Delahanty-Was 43
Davis-Phi 43
L.Cross-Phi 39
Bradley-Cle 39
Freeman-Bos 38

Triples
Williams-Bal 21
Freeman-Bos 19
Ferris-Bos 14
Delahanty-Was 14
Hickman-Bos-Cle .. 13

Home Runs
Seybold-Phi 16
Hickman-Bos-Cle .. 11
Freeman-Bos 11
Bradley-Cle 11
Delahanty-Was 10

Total Bases
Hickman-Bos-Cle .. 288
Freeman-Bos 283
Bradley-Cle 283
Delahanty-Was 279
Seybold-Phi 264

Runs Batted In
Freeman-Bos 121
Hickman-Bos-Cle .. 110
L.Cross-Phi 108
Seybold-Phi 97

Runs Produced
L.Cross-Phi 198
Delahanty-Was 186
Freeman-Bos 185
Davis-Phi 175
Hickman-Bos-Cle .. 173

Bases On Balls
Hartsel-Phi 87
Strang-Chi 76
Barrett-Det 74
Burkett-StL 71
Davis-Chi 65

Batting Average
Lajoie-Phi-Cle .... .378
Delahanty-Was .... .376
Hickman-Bos-Cle ... .361
Dougherty-Bos .... .342
L.Cross-Phi ...... .342

On Base Percentage
Delahanty-Was .... .453
Dougherty-Bos .... .407
Barrett-Det ...... .397
Selbach-Bal ...... .393
Jones-Chi .... .390

Slugging Average
Delahanty-Was .... .590
Lajoie-Phi-Cle .... .565
Hickman-Bos-Cle ... .539
Bradley-Cle ...... .515
Seybold-Phi ...... .506

Production
Delahanty-Was 1.043
Hickman-Bos-Cle .. .926
Bradley-Cle ...... .890
Seybold-Phi ...... .881
Williams-Bal ..... .861

Adjusted Production
Delahanty-Was 186
Hickman-Bos-Cle .. 159
Bradley-Cle 151
Seybold-Phi 137
Freeman-Bos 131

Batter Runs
Delahanty-Was ... 57.0
Hickman-Bos-Cle .. 36.3
Lajoie-Phi-Cle ... 32.5
Bradley-Cle 30.7
Seybold-Phi 28.5

Adjusted Batter Runs
Delahanty-Was 56.0
Hickman-Bos-Cle .. 39.1
Lajoie-Phi-Cle ... 35.7
Bradley-Cle 35.1
Seybold-Phi 24.2

Clutch Hitting Index
Davis-Chi 136
L.Cross-Phi 131
Anderson-StL 131
Elberfeld-Det 130
Mertes-Chi 129

Runs Created
Delahanty-Was 137
Hickman-Bos-Cle .. 118
Bradley-Cle 114
Freeman-Bos 109
L.Cross-Phi 105

Total Average
Delahanty-Was 1.224
Hickman-Bos-Cle .. .935
Bradley-Cle ...... .895
Seybold-Phi ...... .894
Hartsel-Phi ...... .893

Stolen Bases
Hartsel-Phi 47
Mertes-Chi 46
Fultz-Phi 44

Stolen Base Average

Stolen Base Runs

Fielding Runs
Ferris-Bos 26.5
Schreck-Phi 20.9
Padden-StL 18.2
Jones-Chi 12.5
Coughlin-Was 11.8

Total Player Rating
Lajoie-Phi-Cle 6.2
Delahanty-Was 4.7
Bradley-Cle 4.4
Hickman-Bos-Cle .. 2.7
Schreck-Cle-Phi .. 2.7

Wins
Young-Bos 32
Waddell-Phi 24
Powell-StL 22
R.Donahue-StL ... 22
Dinneen-Bos 21

Win Percentage
Bernhard-Phi-Cle . .783
Waddell-Phi ..... .774
Young-Bos .... .744
R.Donahue-StL ... .667
Griffith-Chi .... .625

Games
Young-Bos 45
Powell-StL 42
Dinneen-Bos 42
Wiltse-Phi-Bal .. 38
Orth-Was 38

Complete Games
Young-Bos 41
Dinneen-Bos 39
Powell-StL 36
Orth-Was 36

Shutouts
Joss-Cle 5
Siever-Det 4
Moore-Cle 4
Mercer-Det 4

Saves
Powell-StL 2

Innings Pitched
Young-Bos 384.2
Dinneen-Bos 371.1
Powell-StL 328.1
Orth-Was 324.0
R.Donahue-StL .. 316.1

Fewest Hits/Game
Bernhard-Phi-Cle . 7.01
Waddell-Phi 7.30
Joss-Cle 7.52
Siever-Det 7.93
Winter-Bos 7.97

Fewest BB/Game
Orth-Was 1.11
Young-Bos 1.24
Bernhard-Phi-Cle . 1.47
Siever-Det 1.53
Plank-Phi 1.83

Strikeouts
Waddell-Phi 210
Young-Bos 160
Powell-StL 137
Dinneen-Bos 136
Plank-Phi 107

Strikeouts/Game
Waddell-Phi 6.84
Powell-StL 3.76
Young-Bos 3.74
Joss-Cle 3.54
Piatt-Chi 3.51

Ratio
Bernhard-Phi-Cle . 8.68
Siever-Det 9.56
Waddell-Phi 9.71
Young-Bos 9.73
Joss-Cle 10.46

Earned Run Average
Siever-Det 1.91
Waddell-Phi 2.05
Bernhard-Phi-Cle . 2.15
Young-Bos 2.15
Garvin-Chi 2.21

Adjusted ERA
Siever-Det 191
Waddell-Phi 179
Young-Bos 166
Bernhard-Phi-Cle . 160
Garvin-Chi 153

Opponents' Batting Avg.
Bernhard-Phi-Cle . .216
Waddell-Phi ..... .223
Joss-Cle .... .228
Siever-Det ...... .237
Winter-Bos ...... .238

Opponents' On Base Pct.
Bernhard-Phi-Cle . .254
Siever-Det ...... .273
Waddell-Phi ..... .276
Young-Bos .... .276
Joss-Cle .... .291

Starter Runs
Young-Bos 60.6
Waddell-Phi 46.6
Bernhard-Phi-Cle . 35.7
Siever-Det 34.7
R.Donahue-StL ... 28.5

Adjusted Starter Runs
Young-Bos 60.6
Waddell-Phi 49.5
Siever-Det 36.2
Bernhard-Phi-Cle . 32.6
R.Donahue-StL ... 26.9

Clutch Pitching Index
Garvin-Chi 129
Shields-Bal-StL .. 123
Husting-Bos-Phi .. 120
Moore-Cle 119
Sudhoff-StL 110

Relief Runs

Adjusted Relief Runs

Relief Ranking

Total Pitcher Index
Waddell-Phi 5.9
Young-Bos 5.8
Bernhard-Phi-Cle . 2.9
Siever-Det 2.6
Garvin-Chi 2.4

Total Baseball Ranking
Lajoie-Phi-Cle ... 6.2
Waddell-Phi 5.9
Young-Bos 5.8
Delahanty-Was ... 4.7
Bradley-Cle 4.4

January 9 At Cincinnati peace talks, the NL proposes a consolidated 12-team league, which the AL rejects. An agreement is reached to coexist peacefully if the AL promises to stay out of Pittsburgh. In the awarding of disputed contracts, the most hotly contested case is that of Sam Crawford, Reds outfielder who batted .333 and led the NL with 23 triples in 1902. The future Hall of Famer, signed by both Detroit and the Reds, is awarded to the Tigers, having signed with them first. Despite attempts by John Brush and Andrew Freedman to prevent the AL from finding suitable grounds in New York, AL president Ban Johnson finds a ballpark site at 165th Street and Broadway that will become Hilltop Park. Frank Farrell and Bill Devery pay $18,000 for the Baltimore franchise and will build a wooden grandstand seating 15,000 on the highest point of Manhattan. The team, logically, will be called the Highlanders.

February 28 A syndicate headed by Pittsburgh owner Barney Dreyfuss and James Potter buys the Philadelphia Phillies from John Rogers and A. J. Reach for $170,000. It will be another seven years before ownership interest in more than one team is prohibited.

March 7 In the first trade under the peace treaty, the Giants send their 1902 part-time manager Heinie Smith to Detroit for second baseman Kid Gleason, who is immediately moved to the Phils

where he will end a 20-year playing career.

May 6 The Pirates' Deacon Phillippe, en route to 25 wins, lets one get away when the Cubs score nine in the ninth for an 11–4 triumph.

May 16 A record 31,500 at the Polo Grounds see the first-place Giants beat Pittsburgh.

June 9 The Phils score, breaking the Pirates' record run of six straight shutouts and 56 scoreless innings. The Giants were blanked twice, Boston three times, and the Phils once during the run.

June 25 Boston Beaneater Wiley Piatt loses two complete games in one day, falling to Pittsburgh 1-0 and 5-3.

July 2 Pitcher Jack Doscher, making his debut with the Chicago Cubs, becomes the first son of a former major league player to also play in the major league. Father Herm was a third baseman with Troy, Chicago, and Cleveland before the turn of the century.

August 8 The Giants "Iron Man" Joe McGinnity pitches one of three doubleheaders he will win this month, beating Brooklyn 6-1 and 4-3; he also steals home in the second game. On August 1, he won two from Boston 4-1 and 5-2. On August 31, he will beat the Phillies twice. He has now done double work five times, including two losses on each of the two occasions at Baltimore in 1901. The combination of his 434 innings pitched and 31 wins, with Mathew-

son's 366 innings pitched and 30 wins, will make them the century's most productive one-season duo.

September 11* A new National Agreement signed by the National Association of minor league clubs officially organizes professional baseball under one comprehensive set of rules.

October 1 The first modern World Series game, also called "Championship of the United States," is played at Boston's Huntington Avenue Grounds before 16,242. Deacon Phillippe pitches Pittsburgh to a 7-3 win over Cy Young. Pittsburgh right fielder Jimmy Sebring hits the first home run. Third baseman Tommy Leach hits two triples for the Pirates and winds up with four, a Series record.

October 13 Pittsburgh's Deacon Phillippe pitches his fifth complete game of the Series, losing to Bill Dinneen, 3-0. Only 7,455, the smallest crowd of the Series, see Boston win the championship. Deacon's five decisions and 44 innings pitched are still World Series records.

October 15 With Pirates owner Dreyfuss putting his club's $6,699.56 gate receipts into the players' pool, the 16 Pirates receive $1,316 each, more than the victorious Boston players' $1,182. Deacon Phillippe receives a bonus and 10 shares of stock in the Pirates for his heroic efforts.

BOSTON	BROOKLYN	CHICAGO	CINCINNATI	NEW YORK	PHILADELPHIA	PITTSBURGH	ST.LOUIS
M A.Buckenberger	M N.Hanlon	M F.Selee	M J.Kelley	M J.McGraw	M C.Zimmer	M F.Clarke	M P.Donovan
1B F.Tenney	1B J.Doyle	1B F.Chance	1B J.Beckley	1B D.McGann	1B K.Douglass	1B K.Bransfield	1B J.Hackett
2B E.Abbaticchio	2B T.Flood	2B J.Evers	2B T.Daly	2B B.Gilbert	2B K.Gleason	2B C.Ritchey	2B J.Farrell
SS H.Aubrey	SS B.Dahlen	SS J.Tinker	SS T.Corcoran	SS C.Babb	SS R.Hulswitt	SS H.Wagner	SS D.Brain
3B E.Gremminger	3B S.Strang	3B D.Casey	3B H.Steinfeldt	3B B.Lauder	3B H.Wolverton	3B T.Leach	3B J.Burke
LF D.Cooley	LF J.Sheckard	LF J.Slagle	LF M.Donlin	LF S.Mertes	LF S.Barry	LF F.Clarke	LF G.Barclay
CF C.Dexter	CF J.Dobbs	CF D.Jones	CF C.Seymour	CF R.Bresnahan	CF R.Thomas	CF G.Beaumont	CF H.Smoot
RF P.Carney	RF J.McCredie	RF D.Harley	RF C.Dolan	RF G.Browne	RF B.Keister	RF J.Sebring	RF P.Donovan
C P.Moran	C L.Ritter	C J.Kling	C H.Peitz	C J.Warner	C F.Roth	C E.Phelps	C J.O'Neill
O J.Stanley	23 D.Jordan	S O.Williams	OS J.Kelley	O G.Van Haltren	J.Titus	SO O.Krueger	C1 J.Ryan
2S F.Bonner	C F.Jacklitsch	2 B.Lowe	C B.Bergen	S3 J.Dunn	23 B.Hallman	C H.Smith	OP J.Dunleavy
C M.Kittridge	O D.Gessler	O J.McCarthy	2 G.Magoon	C F.Bowerman	C R.Dooin	C A.Weaver	S O.Williams
O T.McCreery	O T.McCreery	2 T.Raub	2 J.Morrissey	/S G.Davis	C.Zimmer	/O G.Merritt	1 A.Nichols
C	C H.Hearne	O J.Dobbs	3 C.DeArmond	/2 J.McGraw	R.Brashear	/S J.Marshall	S L.DeMontreville
P T.Pittinger	O E.Householder	/O J.Cook	/O P.Cregan	P J.McGinnity	/3 J.Walsh	/O G.Curtis	C A.Weaver
P V.Willis	/O H.Thielman	/1 B.Hanlon	/C L.Fohl	C.Mathewson	H D.Rudolph	/C F.Carisch	/2 H.Berte
P J.Malarkey	/O H.Jennings	/3 G.Moriarty	/C E.Haberer	P D.Taylor	P B.Duggleby	/3 H.Lobert	/C J.Coveney
P W.Piatt	/C F.McManus	/C L.McLean	/O D.Kerwin	P J.Cronin	P C.Fraser	/O E.Diehl	/1 L.Ury
/2	/2 M.Broderick	P J.Taylor	/O H.Wood	P R.Miller	P T.Sparks	/O L.Gertenrich	P C.McFarland
P P.Williams	/C E.Hug	P J.Weimer	/C P.Deisel	/P R.Ames	P F.Mitchell	/O R.Grey	P M.Brown
	P O.Jones	P B.Wicker	P N.Hahn	/P B.Bartley	P J.McFetridge	/O S.Hofman	P C.Currie
	P H.Schmidt	P C.Lundgren	P B.Ewing		/P F.Burchell	P D.Phillippe	P M.O'Neill
	P N.Garvin	P J.Menefee	P J.Sutthoff		/P L.Washburn	P S.Leever	P B.Rhoads
	P R.Evans	/P C.Currie	P E.Poole		/P W.McLaughlin	P E.Doheny	P E.Murphy
	P B.Reidy	/P A.Hardy	P J.Harper		P P.Williams	P B.Kennedy	/P W.Sanders
	/P G.Thatcher	/P P.Graham	P B.Phillips			P K.Wilhelm	/P C.Moran
	/P R.Vickers	/P P.Williams	/P R.Reagan			P B.Veil	/P H.Betts
	/P J.Doscher	/P J.Doscher	/P J.Wiggs			P C.Falkenberg	/P P.Hynes
	/P B.Pounds		/P B.Hooker			/P G.Thompson	/P J.Lovett
						/P L.Winham	/P B.Wicker
						/P J.Pfiester	/P S.Yerkes
						/P D.Scanlan	/P L.Milton
						/P L.Moren	/P E.Taylor

TEAM	G	W	L	PCT	GB	R	OR	AB	H	2B	3B	HR	BB	SO	AVG	OBP	SLG	PRO	PRO+	BR	/A	PF	CHI	RC	SB	CS	SBA	SBR
PIT	141	91	49	.650		793	613	4988	1429	208	110	34	364		.286	.341	.393	.734	113	89	65	103	101	758	172			
NY	142	84	55	.604	6.5	729	567	4741	1290	181	49	20	379		.272	.338	.344	.682	97	9	-17	104	106	678	264			
CHI	139	82	56	.594	8	695	599	4733	1300	191	62	9	422		.275	.340	.347	.687	105	19	38	97	101	678	259			
CIN	141	74	65	.532	16.5	765	656	4857	1399	228	92	28	403		.288	.346	.390	.736	104	95	10	111	99	735	144			
BRO	139	70	66	.515	19	667	682	4534	1201	177	56	15	522		.265	.348	.339	.687	105	-27	47	97	97	661	273			
BOS	140	58	80	.420	32	578	699	4682	1145	176	47	25	398		.245	.312	.318	.630	90	-83	-60	96	100	540	159			
PHI	139	49	86	.363	39.5	617	738	4781	1283	186	62	12	338		.268	.322	.341	.663	98	-33	-12	97	97	596	120			
STL	139	43	94	.314	46.5	505	795	4689	1176	138	65	8	277		.251	.297	.313	.610	83	-124	-108	97	98	511	171			
TOT	560					5349		38005	10223	1485	543	151	3103	3767	.269	.331	.349	.679							1562			

TEAM	CG	SH	SV	IP	H	H/G	HR	BB	SO	RAT	ERA	ERA+	OAV	OOB	PR	/A	PF	CPI	FA	E	DP	FW	PW	BW	SBW	DIF
PIT	117	16	5	1251¹	1215	8.7	9	384	454	11.8	2.91	111	.255	.316	48	44	99	95	.951	295	100	1.6	4.2	6.2		8.9
NY	115	8	8	1262²	1257	9.0	20	371	628	11.9	2.95	113	.258	.316	43	56	102	98	.951	287	87	2.3	5.4	-1.6		8.5
CHI	117	6	6	1240¹	1182	8.6	14	354	451	11.4	2.77	113	.250	.307	67	46	96	93	.942	338	78	-1.6	4.4	3.6		6.5
CIN	126	11	1	1230	1277	9.3	14	378	480	12.6	3.07	116	.268	.331	26	65	109	105	.946	312	84	.4	6.2	1.0		-3.1
BRO	118	11	4	1221¹	1276	9.4	18	377	438	12.7	3.44	92	.275	.339	-25	-38	97	98	.951	284	98	2.0	-3.6	4.5		-.9
BOS	125	8	1	1228²	1310	9.6	30	460	516	13.4	3.34	96	.278	.348	-11	-21	98	112	.939	361	89	-3.0	-2.0	-5.8		-.2
PHI	126	5	3	1212¹	1347	10.0	21	425	381	13.6	3.96	82	.285	.352	-95	-97	100	97	.947	300	76	1.0	-9.3	-1.2		-9.0
STL	111	4	2	1212¹	1353	10.0	25	430	419	13.6	3.67	89	.284	.350	-55	-56	100	104	.940	354	111	-2.7	-5.4	-10.4		-7.1
TOT	955	69	30	9859		9.3				12.6	3.26		.269	.331					.946	2531	723					

Runs
Beaumont-Pit 137
Donlin-Cin 110
Browne-NY 105
Slagle-Chi 104
Strang-Bro 101

Hits
Beaumont-Pit 209
Seymour-Cin 191
Browne-NY 185
Wagner-Pit 182
Donlin-Cin 174

Doubles
Steinfeldt-Cin 32
Mertes-NY 32
Clarke-NY 32

Triples
Wagner-Pit 19
Donlin-Cin 18
Leach-Pit 17

Home Runs
Sheckard-Bro 9

Total Bases
Beaumont-Pit 272
Seymour-Cin 267
Wagner-Pit 265
Donlin-Cin 256
Sheckard-Bro 245

Runs Batted In
Mertes-NY 104
Wagner-Pit 101
Doyle-Bro 91
Leach-Pit 87
Steinfeldt-Cin 83

Runs Produced
Beaumont-Pit 198
Mertes-NY 197
Wagner-Pit 193
Leach-Pit 177
Doyle-Bro 175

Bases On Balls
Thomas-Phi 107
Dahlen-Bro 82
Slagle-Chi 81
Chance-Chi 78

Batting Average
Wagner-Pit 355
Clarke-Pit 351
Donlin-Cin 351
Bresnahan-NY 350
Seymour-Cin 342

On Base Percentage
Thomas-Phi 453
Bresnahan-NY 443
Chance-Chi 439
Sheckard-Bro 423
Donlin-Cin 420

Slugging Average
Clarke-Pit 532
Wagner-Pit 518
Donlin-Cin 516
Bresnahan-NY 493
Steinfeldt-Cin 481

Production
Clarke-Pit 946
Donlin-Cin 936
Bresnahan-NY 936
Wagner-Pit 931
Sheckard-Bro 899

Adjusted Production
Clarke-Pit 164
Sheckard-Bro 160
Bresnahan-NY 160
Wagner-Pit 160
Chance-Chi 155

Batter Runs
Donlin-Cin 42.6
Wagner-Pit 42.1
Sheckard-Bro 39.8
Bresnahan-NY 37.8
Clarke-Pit 37.3

Adjusted Batter Runs
Sheckard-Bro 43.3
Wagner-Pit 38.6
Chance-Chi 36.8
Clarke-Pit 34.3
Bresnahan-NY 34.1

Clutch Hitting Index
Corcoran-Cin 141
Doyle-Bro 131
Mertes-NY 123
Chance-Chi 118
Dobbs-Chi-Bro 118

Runs Created
Sheckard-Bro 137
Wagner-Pit 133
Donlin-Cin 122
Beaumont-Pit 119
Chance-Chi 118

Total Average
Chance-Chi . . . 1.175
Bresnahan-NY . . 1.144
Sheckard-Bro . . 1.142
Wagner-Pit 1.097
Clarke-Pit 1.061

Stolen Bases
Sheckard-Bro 67
Chance-Chi 67
Wagner-Pit 46
Strang-Bro 46
Mertes-NY 45

Stolen Base Average

Stolen Base Runs

Fielding Runs
Farrell-StL 28.1
Wagner-Pit 24.6
Sheckard-Bro 23.4
Moran-Bos 19.3
Ritchey-Pit 19.0

Total Player Rating
Wagner-Pit 6.3
Sheckard-Bro 5.5
Thomas-Phi 3.8
Moran-Bos 3.5
Tenney-Bos 3.1

Wins
McGinnity-NY 31
Mathewson-NY 30
Phillippe-Pit 25
Leever-Pit 25

Win Percentage
Leever-Pit 781
Phillippe-Pit 735
Weimer-Chi 714
Mathewson-NY 698
Wicker-StL-Chi 690

Games
McGinnity-NY 55
Mathewson-NY 45
Pittinger-Bos 44
Schmidt-Bro 40

Complete Games
McGinnity-NY 44
Mathewson-NY 37
Pittinger-Bos 35
Hahn-Cin 34
Taylor-Chi 33

Shutouts
Leever-Pit 7
Schmidt-Bro 5
Hahn-Cin 5
Phillippe-Pit 4
Jones-Bro 4

Saves
Miller-NY 3
Lundgren-Chi 3

Innings Pitched
McGinnity-NY . . . 434.0
Mathewson-NY . 366.1
Pittinger-Bos . . . 351.2
Jones-Bro 324.1
Taylor-Chi 312.1

Fewest Hits/Game
Weimer-Chi 7.69
Mathewson-NY . . 7.89
Taylor-Chi 7.98
Leever-Pit 8.07
McGinnity-NY . . . 8.11

Fewest BB/Game
Phillippe-Pit 90
Hahn-Cin 1.43
Taylor-Chi 1.64
McFarland-StL . . . 1.89
Leever-Pit 1.90

Strikeouts
Mathewson-NY 267
McGinnity-NY 171
Garvin-Bro 154
Pittinger-Bos 140
Weimer-Chi 128

Strikeouts/Game
Mathewson-NY 6.56
Piatt-Bos 4.97
Garvin-Bro 4.65
Weimer-Chi 4.09
Willis-Bos 4.05

Ratio
Phillippe-Pit 9.39
Taylor-Chi 9.77
Leever-Pit 10.13
Mathewson-NY . . 10.59
Hahn-Cin 10.70

Earned Run Average
Leever-Pit 2.06
Mathewson-NY . . . 2.26
Weimer-Chi 2.30
Phillippe-Pit 2.43
McGinnity-NY 2.43

Adjusted ERA
Leever-Pit 157
Mathewson-NY 148
Hahn-Cin 141
McGinnity-NY 138
Weimer-Chi 136

Opponents' Batting Avg.
Weimer-Chi 225
Mathewson-NY 231
Taylor-Chi 235
McGinnity-NY 236
Leever-Pit 238

Opponents' On Base Pct.
Phillippe-Pit 263
Taylor-Chi 273
Leever-Pit 282
Mathewson-NY 287
McGinnity-NY 291

Starter Runs
Mathewson-NY . . . 40.7
McGinnity-NY 40.2
Leever-Pit 38.0
Weimer-Chi 30.2
Taylor-Chi 28.2

Adjusted Starter Runs
McGinnity-NY 44.0
Mathewson-NY . . . 43.9
Leever-Pit 37.0
Hahn-Cin 33.8
Weimer-Chi 26.0

Clutch Pitching Index
Brown-StL 153
Pittinger-Bos 126
Malarkey-Bos 115
Piatt-Bos 115
Poole-Cin 113

Relief Runs

Adjusted Relief Runs

Relief Ranking

Total Pitcher Index
Mathewson-NY 5.3
McGinnity-NY 4.0
Leever-Pit 3.4
Hahn-Cin 3.2
Taylor-Chi 2.9

Total Baseball Ranking
Wagner-Pit 6.3
Sheckard-Bro 5.5
Mathewson-NY 5.3
McGinnity-NY 4.0
Thomas-Phi 3.8

January 9 Despite attempts by John Brush and Andrew Freedman to use their political influence to prevent the AL from finding suitable grounds in New York, Ban Johnson, aided by baseball writer Joe Vila, finds backers. He also finds a ballpark site at 165th Street and Broadway. Frank Farrell and Bill Devery pay $18,000 for the Baltimore franchise and will build a wooden grandstand seating 15,000 on the highest point of Manhattan. The team, logically, will be called the Highlanders.

January 12 Detroit pitcher Win Mercer, winner of 15 games in 1902, commits suicide by inhaling gas in San Francisco's Occidental Hotel. Mercer had recently been named Tigers manager.

April 14 Ed Delahanty, one of five major league brothers, and the greatest natural hitter of his time, rejoins the Washington Nationals in accordance with the peace terms. A three-year contract with the Giants at $8,000 a year, signed during the winter, is canceled. The Nationals reimburse the Giants for the $3,000 advanced to Big Ed.

April 30 Hilltop Park, the new AL park, opens in New York with an estimated crowd of 16,000 watching the home team beat Washington 6-2.

May 17 With Sunday baseball banned in Cleveland, the Blues (Indians) and Highlanders (Yankees) play at Columbus, Ohio. Cleveland's Addie Joss defeats Clark Griffith 9–2.

June 26 Veteran shortstop George Davis, who played for the White Stockings in 1902 and was awarded to them as part of the peace treaty, gets the approval of NL president Harry Pulliam to play for the Giants. After Davis plays in four games for the Giants, Chicago's owner Charles Comiskey gets an injunction preventing Davis from playing. On July 20, the NL directors vote that Davis cannot play for any team except the White Stockings. Davis sits out the rest of the season, rejoins Chicago in 1904, and finishes a 20-year career with them in 1909.

July 2 Seeing that fellow former American Leaguer George Davis is playing for the Giants, Ed Delahanty decides to jump to New York too. Leaving the AL Washington team in Detroit, he boards an eastbound train. He is put off the train for rowdy, and possibly drunken, behavior. When he tries to walk across the railroad bridge over the Niagara River, he falls to his death.

July 17* Dan McClelland of the Cuban X-Giants spins the first perfect game in black baseball history, blanking the Penn Park Athletic Club of York, Pennsylvania, 5–0.

August 4 Nap Lajoie is so furious that umpire Tommy Connolly has put an old black ball into play that he hurls the ball over the grandstand. His act results in Cleveland forfeiting the game to Detroit.

August 17 Ban Johnson orders betting suppressed at all AL parks, a noble but futile gesture.

September 3 Jesse Stovall of Cleveland pitches an 11-inning shutout in his major league debut. The 1-0 win over Detroit is the longest shutout ever in a debut.

September 17 The Boston Pilgrims clinch the AL pennant, beating Cleveland 14-3.

October 13 Bill Dinneen beats the Pirates, 3–0, to make Boston the first world champions.

December 18 Ban Johnson is reelected AL president and given a raise to $10,000.

	BOSTON		CHICAGO		CLEVELAND		DETROIT		NEW YORK		PHILADELPHIA		ST.LOUIS		WASHINGTON
M	J.Collins	M	J.Callahan	M	B.Armour	M	E.Barrow	M	C.Griffith	M	C.Mack	M	J.McAleer	M	T.Loftus
1B	C.LaChance	1B	F.Isbell	1B	C.Hickman	1B	C.Carr	1B	J.Ganzel	1B	H.Davis	1B	J.Anderson	1B	B.Clarke
2B	H.Ferris	2B	G.Magoon	2B	N.Lajoie	2B	H.Smith	2B	J.Williams	2B	D.Murphy	2B	B.Friel	2B	B.McCormick
SS	F.Parent	SS	L.Tannehill	SS	J.Gochnauer	SS	S.McAllister	SS	K.Elberfeld	SS	M.Cross	SS	B.Wallace	SS	C.Moran
3B	J.Collins	3B	N.Callahan	3B	B.Bradley	3B	J.Yeager	3B	W.Conroy	3B	L.Cross	3B	H.Hill	3B	B.Coughlin
LF	P.Dougherty	LF	D.Holmes	LF	J.McCarthy	LF	B.Lush	LF	L.Davis	LF	T.Hartsel	LF	J.Burkett	LF	K.Selbach
CF	C.Stahl	CF	F.Jones	CF	H.Bay	CF	J.Barrett	CF	H.McFarland	CF	O.Pickering	CF	E.Heidrick	CF	J.Ryan
RF	B.Freeman	RF	D.Green	RF	E.Flick	RF	S.Crawford	RF	W.Keeler	RF	S.Seybold	RF	C.Hemphill	RF	W.Lee
C	L.Criger	C	J.Slattery	C	H.Bemis	C	D.McGuire	C	M.Beville	C	O.Schreck't	C	M.Kahoe	C	M.Kittridge
O3	J.O'Brien	O	B.Hallman	C	F.Abbott	S2	H.Long	O	D.Fultz	O	D.Hoffman	C	J.Sugden	2O	R.Robinson
C	J.Stahl	C	E.McFarland	O	J.Thoney	C	F.Buelow	C	J.O'Connor	C	D.Powers	23	B.McCormick	1	S.Carey
C	D.Farrell	2	T.Daly	2	B.Clingman	S	K.Elberfeld	S	H.Long	/2	B.Daly	O	J.Martin	O	E.Delahanty
C	A.Smith	C	B.Sullivan	/O	J.Hardy	O	D.Gessler	S	E.Courtney	/C	J.Kalahan	2	D.Padden	C	L.Drill
/3	H.Gleason	1	C.Dolan	/1	J.Slattery	3	E.Courtney	/C	P.McCauley	/3	E.Hilley	O	P.Swander	23	J.Martin
H	G.Stone	3	P.Clark	/O	H.Iott	2	J.Burns	/C	J.Zalusky			2	B.Bowcock	O	J.Hendricks
				H	H.Hill	/S	J.Murphy	/3	J.Greene	P	E.Plank	/C	O.Shannon	O	D.Holmes
						/S	S.Nicholls	/1	T.Jordan	P	R.Waddell	/2	C.Gouzzie	2	G.DeMontreville
P	C.Young	P	D.White	P	A.Joss	/3	P.Greene	/1	F.Holmes	P	C.Bender			S	C.Osteen
P	B.Dinneen	P	P.Flaherty	P	E.Moore					P	W.Henley	P	J.Powell		
P	T.Hughes	P	R.Patterson	P	B.Bernhard	P	G.Mullin	P	J.Chesbro			P	W.Sudhoff	P	C.Patten
P	N.Gibson	P	F.Owen	P	R.Donahue	P	B.Donovan	P	J.Tannehill	/P	A.Coakley	P	E.Siever	P	A.Orth
P	G.Winter			P	G.Wright	P	F.Kitson	P	C.Griffith	/P	J.Fairbank	P	R.Donahue	P	H.Wilson
		P	D.Dunkle			P	R.Kisinger	P	H.Howell	/P	C.McGeehan			P	H.Townsend
/P	N.Altrock	P	N.Altrock	P	G.Dorner			P	B.Wolfe	/P	T.Quinn	/P	G.Wright	P	D.Dunkle
				/P	E.Killian					/P	E.Pinnance	/P	R.Evans		
				/P	J.Stovall	/P	M.Eason	/P	J.Deering			/P	B.Pelty		
				P	B.Rhoads	/P	J.Skopec	/P	S.Wiltse			/P	B.Reidy		
				/P	A.Pearson	/P	H.Kane	/P	A.Puttmann			/P	J.Terry		
				/P	M.Glendon	/P	A.Jones	/P	D.Adkins			/P	C.Morgan		
				/P	E.Walker			/P	E.Bliss						
				/P	B.Pounds			/P	E.Quick						

TEAM	G	W	L	PCT	GB	R	OR	AB	H	2B	3B	HR	BB	SO	AVG	OBP	SLG	PRO	PRO+	BR	/A	PF	CHI	RC	SB	CS	SBA	SBR
BOS	141	91	47	.659		708	504	4919	1336	222	113	48	262	561	.272	.313	.392	.705	111	91	55	105	103	680	141			
PHI	137	75	60	.556	14.5	597	519	4673	1236	227	68	32	268	513	.264	.309	.363	.672	102	36	9	105	100	598	157			
CLE	140	77	63	.550	15	639	579	4773	1265	231	95	31	259	595	.265	.308	.373	.681	112	51	62	98	102	634	175			
NY	136	72	62	.537	17	579	573	4565	1136	193	62	18	332	465	.249	.309	.330	.639	92	-6	-41	106	104	544	160			
DET	137	65	71	.478	25	567	594	4582	1229	162	91	12	292	526	.268	.318	.351	.669	110	39	56	97	94	587	128			
STL	139	65	74	.468	26.5	500	525	4639	1133	166	68	12	271	539	.244	.290	.317	.607	90	-66	-33	97	102	480	101			
CHI	138	60	77	.438	30.5	516	613	4670	1152	176	49	14	325	537	.247	.301	.314	.615	94	-46	-23	96	98	526	180			
WAS	140	43	94	.314	47.5	437	691	4613	1066	172	72	17	257	463	.231	.277	.311	.588	80	-98	-107	102	96	454	131			
TOT	554					4543		37434	9553	1549	618	184	2266	4199	.255	.303	.344	.648						1173				

TEAM	CG	SH	SV	IP	H	H/G	HR	BB	SO	RAT	ERA	ERA+	OAV	OOB	PR	/A	PF	CPI	FA	E	DP	FW	PW	BW	SBW	DIF
BOS	123	20	4	1255	1142	8.2	23	269	579	10.4	2.57	118	.242	.288	55	64	102	100	.959	239	86	2.3	6.6	5.7		7.4
PHI	112	10	1	1207	1124	8.4	20	315	728	11.3	2.98	103	.246	.305	-2	10	103	97	.960	217	66	3.2	1.0	.9		2.4
CLE	125	20	1	1243²	1161	8.4	16	271	521	10.6	2.73	105	.247	.293	32	17	96	97	.946	322	99	-3.2	1.8	6.4		2.0
NY	111	7	2	1201¹	1171	8.8	19	245	463	10.9	3.08	101	.255	.299	-16	5	105	93	.953	264	87	.0	.5	-4.3		8.7
DET	123	15	2	1196	1169	8.8	19	336	554	11.5	2.75	106	.256	.310	28	20	98	111	.950	281	82	-.9	2.1	5.8		-10.0
STL	124	12	3	1222¹	1220	9.0	26	237	511	11.0	2.77	105	.260	.300	26	19	98	108	.953	268	94	.2	2.0	-5.5		-1.1
CHI	114	9	4	1235	1233	9.0	23	287	391	11.5	3.02	93	.260	.309	-8	-29	95	103	.949	297	85	-1.8	-3.0	-2.4		-1.3
WAS	122	6	3	1223²	1333	9.8	38	306	452	12.4	3.82	82	.277	.325	-116	-94	106	96	.954	260	86	.8	-9.8	-11.1		-5.4
TOT	954	99	20	9784		8.8				11.2	2.96		.255	.303					.953	2148	685					

Runs		Hits		Doubles		Triples		Home Runs		Total Bases	
Dougherty-Bos	107	Dougherty-Bos	195	Seybold-Phi	45	Crawford-Det	25	Freeman-Bos	13	Freeman-Bos	281
Bradley-Cle	101	Crawford-Det	184	Lajoie-Cle	41	Bradley-Cle	22	Hickman-Cle	12	Crawford-Det	269
Keeler-NY	95	Parent-Bos	170	Freeman-Bos	39	Freeman-Bos	20	Ferris-Bos	9	Bradley-Cle	266
Barrett-Det	95	Bay-Cle	169	Bradley-Cle	36	Parent-Bos	17	Seybold-Phi	8	Lajoie-Cle	251
Bay-Cle	94	Bradley-Cle	168	Anderson-StL	34	Collins-Bos	17			Dougherty-Bos	250

Runs Batted In		Runs Produced		Bases On Balls		Batting Average		On Base Percentage		Slugging Average	
Freeman-Bos	104	Lajoie-Cle	176	Barrett-Det	74	Lajoie-Cle	.344	Barrett-Det	.407	Lajoie-Cle	.518
Hickman-Cle	97	Crawford-Det	173	Lush-Det	70	Crawford-Det	.335	Hartsel-Phi	.391	Bradley-Cle	.496
Lajoie-Cle	93	Freeman-Bos	165	Pickering-Phi	53	Dougherty-Bos	.331	Lajoie-Cle	.379	Freeman-Bos	.496
L.Cross-Phi	90	Bradley-Cle	163	Burkett-StL	52	Barrett-Det	.315	Lush-Det	.379	Crawford-Det	.489
Crawford-Det	89	Dougherty-Bos	162	Flick-Cle	51	Bradley-Cle	.313	Green-Chi	.375	Hartsel-Phi	.477

Production		Adjusted Production		Batter Runs		Adjusted Batter Runs		Clutch Hitting Index		Runs Created	
Lajoie-Cle	.896	Lajoie-Cle	170	Lajoie-Cle	37.6	Lajoie-Cle	39.3	Gochnauer-Cle	155	Dougherty-Bos	111
Hartsel-Phi	.868	Crawford-Det	159	Crawford-Det	34.5	Crawford-Det	37.5	L.Cross-Phi	144	Crawford-Det	110
Crawford-Det	.855	Bradley-Cle	154	Bradley-Cle	30.8	Bradley-Cle	32.6	Carr-Det	135	Lajoie-Cle	107
Bradley-Cle	.844	Hartsel-Phi	152	Barrett-Det	29.6	Barrett-Det	32.5	Williams-NY	130	Bradley-Cle	104
Freeman-Bos	.823	Green-Chi	146	Hartsel-Phi	28.0	Green-Chi	29.0	Anderson-StL	129	Barrett-Det	98

Total Average		Stolen Bases		Stolen Base Average		Stolen Base Runs		Fielding Runs		Total Player Rating	
Lajoie-Cle	.940	Bay-Cle	45					Lajoie-Cle	40.1	Lajoie-Cle	8.4
Hartsel-Phi	.934	Pickering-Phi	40					Criger-Bos	22.8	Bradley-Cle	4.7
Barrett-Det	.873	Holmes-Was-Chi	35					Schreckengost-Phi	18.2	Crawford-Det	3.3
Crawford-Det	.858	Dougherty-Bos	35					Wallace-StL	17.9	Elberfeld-Det-NY	3.2
Bradley-Cle	.856	Conroy-NY	33					Williams-NY	15.6	Barrett-Det	3.2

Wins		Win Percentage		Games		Complete Games		Shutouts		Saves	
Young-Bos	28	Young-Bos	.757	Plank-Phi	43	Young-Bos	34	Young-Bos	7	Young-Bos	2
Plank-Phi	23	Hughes-Bos	.741	Mullin-Det	41	Waddell-Phi	34	Mullin-Det	6	Powell-StL	2
		Moore-Cle	.679	Young-Bos	40	Donovan-Det	34	Dinneen-Bos	6	Orth-Was	2
		Dinneen-Bos	.618	Flaherty-Chi	40			Sudhoff-StL	5	Mullin-Det	2
		Plank-Phi	.590	Chesbro-NY	40			Hughes-Bos	5	Dinneen-Bos	2

Innings Pitched		Fewest Hits/Game		Fewest BB/Game		Strikeouts		Strikeouts/Game		Ratio	
Young-Bos	341.2	Moore-Cle	7.12	Young-Bos	.97	Waddell-Phi	302	Waddell-Phi	8.39	Joss-Cle	8.82
Plank-Phi	336.0	Donovan-Det	7.24	Bernhard-Cle	1.14	Donovan-Det	187	Donovan-Det	5.48	Young-Bos	8.96
Chesbro-NY	324.2	Joss-Cle	7.36	Donahue-StL-Cle	1.14	Young-Bos	176	Moore-Cle	5.38	Bernhard-Cle	9.34
Waddell-Phi	324.0	Waddell-Phi	7.61	Joss-Cle	1.17	Plank-Phi	176	Powell-StL	4.97	Moore-Cle	9.56
Mullin-Det	320.2	Dinneen-Bos	7.68	Tannehill-NY	1.28	Mullin-Det	170	Mullin-Det	4.77	Dinneen-Bos	9.78

Earned Run Average		Adjusted ERA		Opponents' Batting Avg.		Opponents' On Base Pct.		Starter Runs		Adjusted Starter Runs	
Moore-Cle	1.74	Moore-Cle	164	Moore-Cle	.217	Joss-Cle	.256	Moore-Cle	33.5	Young-Bos	36.1
Young-Bos	2.08	Young-Bos	146	Donovan-Det	.220	Young-Bos	.259	Young-Bos	33.4	Moore-Cle	30.5
Bernhard-Cle	2.12	Bernhard-Cle	135	Joss-Cle	.223	Bernhard-Cle	.267	White-Chi	27.7	Dinneen-Bos	25.8
White-Chi	2.13	Dinneen-Bos	134	Waddell-Phi	.229	Moore-Cle	.271	Mullin-Det	25.5	Plank-Phi	24.9
Joss-Cle	2.19	White-Chi	132	Dinneen-Bos	.230	Dinneen-Bos	.276	Joss-Cle	24.4	Mullin-Det	23.6

Clutch Pitching Index		Relief Runs		Adjusted Relief Runs		Relief Ranking		Total Pitcher Index		Total Baseball Ranking	
Kitson-Det	127							Young-Bos	4.9	Lajoie-Cle	8.4
Mullin-Det	121							Mullin-Det	4.1	Young-Bos	4.9
Donahue-StL-Cle	119							White-Chi	3.3	Bradley-Cle	4.7
Plank-Phi	116							Sudhoff-StL	2.7	Mullin-Det	4.1
Hughes-Bos	112							Joss-Cle	2.7	Crawford-Det	3.3

February 1 The Cards purchase veteran first baseman Jack Beckley from the Cincinnati Reds. The future Hall of Famer will have four decreasingly productive years in St. Louis before retiring.

April 17 The Brooklyn Superbas play their first Sunday game at home, beating Boston 9-1. To circumvent Sunday Blue Laws, no admission is charged, but fans are required to buy scorecards to enter the grandstand and box seats.

May 14 Cubs outfielder Jack McCarthy sprains an ankle by stepping on an umpire's broom at home plate. NL president Pulliam orders arbiters henceforward to use pocket-size whisk brooms for housekeeping at home. The AL will comply next year.

May 27 The Giants' Dan McGann steals five bases in one game, a feat not duplicated in the NL until August 24, 1974, by Davey Lopes.

May 30 Frank Chance of the Cubs is hit with pitches three times in the first game of a doubleheader. He loses consciousness on one occasion and continues to play when he comes to. He is hit twice in the second game by Win Kellum for a record five times in one day. The Reds and Cubs split the holiday twinbill.

June 11 Bob Wicker pitches 9⅓ hitless innings for the Cubs before losing to the Giants in the 12th, 1-0.

June 16 Christy Mathewson beats the Cardinals to start a 24-game winning streak against them that will not end until 1908.

July 5 The Giants' 18-game winning streak ends when the Phillies prevail 6-5 in 10 innings. The Giants record is now 53-18, effectively ending the NL race. By September 1, they will lead the Cubs by 15 games. John McGraw and John T. Brush say they have no intention of playing a postseason series with the AL champions. "When we clinch the NL pennant, we'll be champions of the only real major league," says McGraw.

September 15 Giants rookie George "Hooks" Wiltse wins his twelfth straight game, setting a major league mark for consecutive games won at the start of a career. It will be tied by relief hurler Clarence "Butch" Metzger in 1976.

September 22 In the final game of his 19-year career as an outfielder/catcher, future Hall of Famer Jim O'Rourke, 52, is the Giants backstop in their 7–5 defeat of the Cincinnati Reds. It is O'Rourke's first major league game since 1893, and he singles and scores a run.

October 3 Christy Mathewson of the Giants strikes out a record 16 Cards in a 3-1 Giants victory, which lasts one hour and 15 minutes.

October 10 The Giants' .262 will lead the NL in team batting, 31 points below the 1900 leaders. Team batting averages have dropped since then, mainly due to: the foul-strike rule adopted in 1901; and the introduction of the spitball and other doctored pitches in 1903.

November 8* Umpire Francis "Silk" O'Loughlin runs for a state assembly seat as a Democrat and loses.

BOSTON		BROOKLYN		CHICAGO		CINCINNATI		NEW YORK		PHILADELPHIA		PITTSBURGH		ST.LOUIS	
M	A.Buckenberger	M	N.Hanlon	M	F.Selee	M	J.Kelley	M	J.McGraw	M	H.Duffy	M	F.Clarke	M	K.Nichols
1B	F.Tenney	1B	P.Dillon	1B	F.Chance	1B	J.Kelley	1B	D.McGann	1B	J.Doyle	1B	K.Bransfield	1B	J.Beckley
2B	F.Raymer	2B	D.Jordan	2B	J.Evers	2B	M.Huggins	2B	B.Gilbert	2B	K.Gleason	2B	C.Ritchey	2B	J.Farrell
SS	E.Abbaticchio	SS	C.Babb	SS	J.Tinker	SS	T.Corcoran	SS	B.Dahlen	SS	R.Hulswitt	SS	H.Wagner	SS	D.Shay
3B	J.Delahanty	3B	M.McCormick	3B	D.Casey	3B	H.Steinfeldt	3B	A.Devlin	3B	H.Wolverton	3B	T.Leach	3B	J.Burke
LF	D.Cooley	LF	J.Sheckard	LF	J.Slagle	LF	F.Odwell	LF	S.Mertes	LF	J.Titus	LF	F.Clarke	LF	G.Barclay
CF	P.Geier	CF	J.Dobbs	CF	J.McCarthy	CF	C.Seymour	CF	R.Bresnahan	CF	R.Thomas	CF	G.Beaumont	CF	H.Smoot
RF	R.Cannell	RF	H.Lumley	RF	D.Jones	RF	C.Dolan	RF	G.Browne	RF	S.Magee	RF	J.Sebring	RF	S.Shannon
C	T.Needham	C	B.Bergen	C	J.Kling	C	A.Schlei	C	J.Warner	C	R.Dooin	C	E.Phelps	C	M.Grady
C3	P.Moran	O	D.Gessler	O1	S.Barry	32	S.Woodruff	1O	F.Bowerman	1O	J.Lush	OS	O.Krueger	S3	D.Brain
O	P.Carney	23	S.Strang	O1	O.Williams	C1	H.Peitz	O	M.McCormick	C	M.McCormick	O	M.McCormick	O	J.Dunleavy
O	G.Barclay	C	L.Ritter	C	J.O'Neill	O	M.Donlin	3S	J.Dunn	S3	S.Donahue	C	H.Smith	O	H.Hill
2	B.Lauterborn	3	E.Batch	O	H.McChesney	O	J.Sebring	O	M.Donlin	3S	B.Hall	C1	F.Carisch	C	L.McLean
C	D.Marshall	1	F.Jacklitsch	O	F.Schulte	O	G.Street	O	D.Marshall	O	S.Barry	O	J.Gilbert	C	D.Zearfoss
/O	K.O'Hara	/1	J.Doyle	/O	A.Smith	/C	P.O'Neill	/2	J.McGraw	O	H.Duffy	O	H.Cassady	C	B.Byers
/O	J.Stanley	/2	C.Loudenslager		S.Hofman			/1	D.Brouthers	O	D.Van Buren	/O	B.Smith	/2	S.Murch
/O	J.White	H	D.Van Buren	/3	G.Moriarty	P	N.Hahn	/C	J.O'Rourke	/C	D.Marshall	/C	E.Diehl	C	J.Butler
/C	G.McAuliffe			/O	I.Van Zandt	P	J.Harper	/1	J.McGinnity	/3	J.Purnell	/C	J.Archer	/2	S.Donahue
/S	A.Sullivan	P	O.Jones	/O	B.Carney	P	W.Kellum	/C	C.Mathewson	/1	K.Douglass	/C	J.Rafter	/C	C.Swindells
		P	J.Cronin	/C	F.Holmes	P	T.Walker	/2	D.Taylor	O	T.Fleming	/S	T.Stankard		
P	V.Willis	P	N.Garvin	/O	D.Rudolph	P	B.Ewing	/C	H.Wiltse	H	H.Long	H	B.Lowe	P	J.Taylor
P	T.Pittinger	P	E.Poole	/C	T.Stanton			P	R.Ames		B.Rementer			P	K.Nichols
P	K.Wilhelm	P	D.Scanlan			P	J.Sutthoff					P	S.Leever	P	C.McFarland
P	T.Fisher			P	J.Weimer	/P	C.Elliott			P	C.Fraser	P	P.Flaherty	P	M.O'Neill
P	E.McNichol	/P	F.Mitchell	P	B.Briggs			/P	B.Milligan	P	B.Duggleby	P	M.Lynch	P	J.Corbett
		/P	D.Reisling	P	C.Lundgren			/P	C.Elliott	P	T.Sparks	P	D.Phillippe		
/P	J.Stewart	/P	B.Reidy	P	B.Wicker					P	J.Sutthoff	P	C.Case	/P	J.McGinley
		/P	B.Durham	P	M.Brown					P	J.McPherson	P	R.Miller	/P	W.Sanders
		/P	G.Thatcher									/P	C.Robitaille		
		/P	J.Koukalik	P	F.Corridon					P	F.Mitchell	/P	H.Camnitz		
		/P	J.Doscher	/P	E.Groth					P	F.Corridon	/P	W.Lee		
										/P	R.Caldwell	/P	D.Scanlan		
										/P	J.Brackenridge	/P	J.Pfiester		
										/P	T.Barry	/P	B.Veil		
												/P	L.Moren		

TEAM	G	W	L	PCT	GB	R	OR	AB	H	2B	3B	HR	BB	SO	AVG	OBP	SLG	PRO	PRO+	BR	/A	PF	CHI	RC	SB	CS	SBA	SBR
NY	158	106	47	.693		744	476	5150	1347	202	65	31	434		.262	.328	.344	.672	109	87	57	104	104	712	283			
CHI	156	93	60	.608	13	599	517	5210	1294	157	62	22	298		.248	.295	.315	.610	94	-38	-39	100	104	582	227			
CIN	157	88	65	.575	18	695	547	5231	1332	189	92	21	399		.255	.313	.338	.651	98	42	-17	109	104	642	179			
PIT	156	87	66	.569	19	675	592	5160	1333	164	102	15	391		.258	.316	.338	.654	105	48	30	103	102	639	178			
STL	155	75	79	.487	31.5	602	595	5104	1292	175	66	24	343		.253	.306	.327	.633	106	7	34	96	99	602	199			
BRO	154	56	97	.366	50	497	614	4917	1142	159	53	15	411		.232	.297	.295	.592	91	-57	-44	98	93	521	205			
BOS	155	55	98	.359	51	491	749	5135	1217	153	50	24	316		.237	.287	.300	.587	90	-78	-59	96	94	508	143			
PHI	155	52	100	.342	53.5	571	784	5103	1268	170	54	23	377		.248	.305	.316	.621	102	-11	10	96	96	570	159			
TOT	623					4874		41010	10225	1369	544	175	2969	4277	.249	.306	.322	.628							1573			

TEAM	CG	SH	SV	IP	H	H/G	HR	BB	SO	RAT	ERA	ERA+	OAV	OOB	PR	/A	PF	CPI	FA	E	DP	FW	PW	BW	SBW	DIF
NY	127	21	15	1396²	1151	7.4	36	349	707	9.9	2.17	125	.222	.276	86	83	100	93	.956	294	93	2.3	8.8	6.0		12.4
CHI	139	18	6	1383²	1150	7.5	16	402	618	10.3	2.30	115	.224	.285	65	53	97	90	.954	298	89	1.8	5.6	-4.1		13.2
CIN	142	12	2	1392²	1256	8.1	13	343	502	10.7	2.34	125	.241	.295	60	88	107	102	.954	301	81	1.7	9.3	-1.8		2.3
PIT	133	15	1	1348¹	1273	8.5	13	379	455	11.4	2.89	95	.248	.306	-24	-24	100	92	.955	291	93	2.2	-2.5	3.2		7.6
STL	146	7	2	1368	1286	8.5	23	319	529	10.8	2.64	102	.239	.286	13	5	99	85	.952	307	83	1.1	.5	3.6		-7.2
BRO	135	12	2	1337¹	1281	8.6	27	414	453	11.8	2.70	101	.255	.319	4	4	100	112	.945	343	87	-1.4	.4	-4.7		-14.9
BOS	136	13	0	1348¹	1405	9.4	25	500	544	13.1	3.43	80	.272	.343	-105	-105	101	105	.945	353	91	-1.9	-11.1	-6.2		-2.3
PHI	131	10	2	1339¹	1418	9.5	22	425	469	12.9	3.39	79	.270	.332	-99	-110	98	100	.937	403	93	-5.1	-11.6	1.1		-8.3
TOT	1089	108	30	10914¹		8.4				11.3	2.73		.249	.306					.950	2590	710					

Runs		Hits		Doubles		Triples		Home Runs		Total Bases	
Browne-NY	99	Beaumont-Pit	185	Wagner-Pit	44	Lumley-Bro	18	Lumley-Bro	9	Wagner-Pit	255
Wagner-Pit	97	Beckley-StL	179	Mertes-NY	28	Wagner-Pit	14	Brain-StL	7	Lumley-Bro	247
Beaumont-Pit	97	Wagner-Pit	171	Delahanty-Bos	27	Tinker-Chi	13			Seymour-Cin	233
Huggins-Cin	96	Browne-NY	169	Seymour-Cin	26	Seymour-Cin	13			Beaumont-Pit	230
		Seymour-Cin	166	Dahlen-NY	26	Kelley-Cin	13			Beckley-StL	222

Runs Batted In		Runs Produced		Bases On Balls		Batting Average		On Base Percentage		Slugging Average	
Dahlen-NY	80	Wagner-Pit	168	Thomas-Phi	102	Wagner-Pit	.349	Wagner-Pit	.423	Wagner-Pit	.520
Mertes-NY	78	Mertes-NY	157	Huggins-Cin	88	Donlin-Cin-NY	.329	Thomas-Phi	.416	Grady-StL	.474
Lumley-Bro	78	Lumley-Bro	148	Devlin-NY	62	Beckley-StL	.325	Chance-Chi	.382	Donlin-Cin-NY	.457
Wagner-Pit	75	Dahlen-NY	148	Wagner-Pit	59	Grady-StL	.313	Huggins-Cin	.377	Seymour-Cin	.439
Corcoran-Cin	74	Beaumont-Pit	148	Ritchey-Pit	59	Seymour-Cin	.313	Beckley-StL	.375	Chance-Chi	.430

Production		Adjusted Production		Batter Runs		Adjusted Batter Runs		Clutch Hitting Index		Runs Created	
Wagner-Pit	.944	Wagner-Pit	186	Wagner-Pit	52.7	Wagner-Pit	49.7	Devlin-NY	154	Wagner-Pit	134
Chance-Chi	.812	Chance-Chi	150	Thomas-Phi	28.4	Thomas-Phi	31.8	Dahlen-NY	146	Lumley-Bro	95
Seymour-Cin	.790	Beckley-StL	147	Chance-Chi	27.2	Beckley-StL	29.8	Corcoran-Cin	137	Beckley-StL	94
Beckley-StL	.778	Thomas-Phi	141	Beckley-StL	25.7	Chance-Chi	27.2	Bransfield-Pit	132	Chance-Chi	93
Thomas-Phi	.761	Lumley-Bro	137	Seymour-Cin	24.9	Grady-StL	25.7	Gilbert-NY	128	Mertes-NY	93

Total Average		Stolen Bases		Stolen Base Average	Stolen Base Runs	Fielding Runs		Total Player Rating	
Wagner-Pit	1.163	Wagner-Pit	53			Leach-Pit	35.8	Wagner-Pit	4.8
Chance-Chi	.926	Mertes-NY	47			Evers-Chi	31.3	Leach-Pit	4.1
Thomas-Phi	.869	Dahlen-NY	47			Dahlen-NY	27.6	Thomas-Phi	4.0
Mertes-NY	.813	McGann-NY	42			Tinker-Chi	19.3	Chance-Chi	3.7
McGann-NY	.802	Chance-Chi	42			Farrell-StL	16.3	Dahlen-NY	3.3

Wins		Win Percentage		Games		Complete Games		Shutouts		Saves	
McGinnity-NY	35	McGinnity-NY	.814	McGinnity-NY	51	Willis-Bos	39	McGinnity-NY	9	McGinnity-NY	5
Mathewson-NY	33	Mathewson-NY	.733	Mathewson-NY	48	Taylor-StL	39	Harper-Cin	6	Wiltse-NY	3
Harper-Cin	23	Harper-Cin	.719	Jones-Bro	46	McGinnity-NY	38			Briggs-Chi	3
Taylor-NY	21	Flaherty-Pit	.679	Willis-Bos	43	Jones-Bro	38			Ames-NY	3
Nichols-StL	21			Fraser-Phi	42						

Innings Pitched		Fewest Hits/Game		Fewest BB/Game		Strikeouts		Strikeouts/Game		Ratio	
McGinnity-NY	408.0	Brown-Chi	6.57	Hahn-Cin	1.06	Mathewson-NY	212	Wiltse-NY	5.74	Brown-Chi	8.94
Jones-Bro	377.0	Weimer-Chi	6.71	Phillippe-Pit	1.40	Willis-Bos	196	Mathewson-NY	5.19	McGinnity-NY	8.96
Mathewson-NY	367.2	McGinnity-NY	6.77	Nichols-StL	1.42	Weimer-Chi	177	Weimer-Chi	5.19	Hahn-Cin	9.07
Taylor-StL	352.0	Garvin-Bro	6.99	Kellum-Cin	1.84	Pittinger-Bos	146	Willis-Bos	5.04	Nichols-StL	9.17
Willis-Bos	350.0	Taylor-NY	7.02	McFarland-StL	1.87	McGinnity-NY	144	Phillippe-Pit	4.43	Mathewson-NY	9.50

Earned Run Average		Adjusted ERA		Opponents' Batting Avg.		Opponents' On Base Pct.		Starter Runs		Adjusted Starter Runs	
McGinnity-NY	1.61	McGinnity-NY	169	Brown-Chi	.199	Brown-Chi	.253	McGinnity-NY	50.6	McGinnity-NY	50.1
Garvin-Bro	1.68	Garvin-Bro	162	Weimer-Chi	.204	Nichols-StL	.256	Mathewson-NY	28.4	Hahn-Cin	28.5
Brown-Chi	1.86	Brown-Chi	142	McGinnity-NY	.206	McGinnity-NY	.256	Weimer-Chi	28.0	Mathewson-NY	28.0
Weimer-Chi	1.91	Hahn-Cin	142	Taylor-NY	.214	Hahn-Cin	.262	Nichols-StL	25.0	Weimer-Chi	25.6
Nichols-StL	2.02	Weimer-Chi	139	Garvin-Bro	.218	Mathewson-NY	.270	Hahn-Cin	22.2	Nichols-StL	23.6

Clutch Pitching Index		Relief Runs	Adjusted Relief Runs	Relief Ranking	Total Pitcher Index		Total Baseball Ranking	
Garvin-Bro	153				McGinnity-NY	5.6	McGinnity-NY	5.6
O'Neill-StL	131				Mathewson-NY	4.7	Wagner-Pit	4.8
Briggs-Chi	128				Flaherty-Pit	3.4	Mathewson-NY	4.7
Jones-Bro	117				Hahn-Cin	3.3	Leach-Pit	4.1
Mitchell-Phi-Bro	116				Weimer-Chi	2.9	Thomas-Phi	4.0

January 4 The Highlanders announce plans to play on Sundays at Ridgewood Park on Long Island, but the Brooklyn club objects.

January 22 William H. Yawkey, the 28-year-old heir to a lumber and mining fortune, buys the Detroit Tigers from S. F. Angus for $50,000. New money and Frank Navin's shrewd management will bring three straight pennants to the franchise within a few years.

April 21 Ty Cobb makes his professional debut for Augusta (South Atlantic League), hitting a double and a home run in an 8-7 loss to Columbus.

May 5 Boston Pilgrim Cy Young pitches the second of three no-hitters, a 3-0 perfect game against the Philadelphia Athletics and Rube Waddell. Eventually Young will go on to complete 24 straight hitless innings, still the record, and 45 shutout innings in a row, a record broken by Jack Coombs's 53 in 1910, Walter Johnson's 56 in 1913, and later by Don Drysdale and Orel Hershiser. For Waddell it is one of 18 losses, the most of his career, against 25 wins. He will strike out 349, a record until Sandy Koufax fans 382 in 1965.

July 4 Jack Chesbro, the New York Highlanders spitballer, wins his 14th in a row, an AL record until Walter Johnson wins 16 straight in 1912.

August 6 Prompt action by Boston Pilgrims players Bill Dinneen, Norwood Gibson, Freddy Parent, and Hobe Ferris prevents a tragedy in a Cleveland hotel. Returning to their rooms following the game, the four are confronted by a fire sweeping through the fifth floor. They extinguish the blaze and are cited as heroes.

August 6 Lefthander Nick Altrock of the White Sox (their new nickname), en route to the first of three 20-win seasons, handles 13 fielding chances—the modern major league record for pitchers—in an 8-1 victory over the Athletics. He will finish the year with 49 putouts, an AL record for pitchers.

August 10 Jack Chesbro is knocked out by the White Sox after pitching 30 complete games in a row. For the year he will win 41 games, pitching 48 complete games out of 51 starts for the Highlanders. All are post-1900 records.

August 17 Jesse Tannehill, a lefthander who will win 20 games or more six times, pitches a no-hitter for Boston against the White Sox.

August 24 Willie Keeler collects two homers against the St. Louis Browns—both inside the park—in a 9-1 win at New York.

September 3* Syracuse (Eastern League) beats Scranton three times in a tripleheader.

September 30 White Sox lefthander Guy "Doc" White pitches his fifth shutout in 18 days, defeating New York. Of his seven shutouts for the year, six come in September. His scoreless streak will end at 45 innings on October 2nd, when the New York Highlanders score in the first inning.

October 7 George Stovall of Cleveland hits his first homer, and it comes off his older brother Jesse, pitching for Detroit in his last game. It marks the first time one brother gives up a homer to another, a feat which will be duplicated by the Ferrells in 1933 and the Niekros in 1976.

October 10 A doubleheader split will give Boston the AL pennant over the Highlanders. With the score 2-2 in the top of the ninth and a man on third base, Chesbro has a spitball get away from him for a wild pitch, and Boston's winning run scores. New York wins the second game, but Boston triumphs by 1½ games. The Pilgrim pitchers achieve 148 complete games—an AL record—as George Winter goes the route in the nightcap, a 1-0 loss. Both leagues set marks for total complete games: AL 1,098, NL 1,089.

October 28 After a fourth-place finish, the Cleveland Blues release Bill Armour and name Nap Lajoie manager. Eventually, they will rename the team the Naps in his honor.

BOSTON	CHICAGO	CLEVELAND	DETROIT	NEW YORK	PHILADELPHIA	ST.LOUIS	WASHINGTON
M J.Collins	M J.Callahan	M B.Armour	M E.Barrow	M C.Griffith	M C.Mack	M J.McAleer	M M.Kittridge
1B C.LaChance	M F.Jones	1B C.Hickman	M B.Lowe	1B J.Ganzel	1B H.Davis	1B T.Jones	M P.Donovan
2B H.Ferris	1B J.Donahue	2B N.Lajoie	1B C.Carr	2B W.Williams	2B D.Murphy	2B D.Padden	1B J.Stahl
SS F.Parent	2B G.Dundon	SS T.Turner	2B B.Lowe	SS K.Elberfeld	SS M.Cross	SS B.Wallace	2B B.McCormick
3B J.Collins	SS G.Davis	3B B.Bradley	SS C.O'Leary	3B W.Conroy	3B L.Cross	3B C.Moran	SS J.Cassidy
LF K.Selbach	3B L.Tannehill	LF B.Lush	3B E.Gremminger	LF P.Dougherty	LF T.Hartsel	LF J.Burkett	3B H.Hill
CF C.Stahl	LF N.Callahan	CF H.Bay	LF M.McIntyre	CF J.Anderson	CF O.Pickering	CF E.Heidrick	LF F.Huelsman
RF B.Freeman	CF F.Jones	RF E.Flick	CF J.Barrett	RF W.Keeler	RF S.Seybold	RF C.Hemphill	CF B.O'Neill
C L.Criger	RF D.Green	C H.Bemis	RF S.Crawford	C D.McGuire	C O.Schreck't	C J.Sugden	RF P.Donovan
	C B.Sullivan		C L.Drill				C M.Kittridge
C D.Farrell		1 G.Stovall		O D.Fultz	O D.Hoffman	O P.Hynes	
O P.Dougherty	12 F.Isbell	O F.Abbott	S3 R.Robinson	C R.Kleinow	C D.Powers	C M.Kahoe	C1 B.Clarke
/O B.O'Neill	O D.Holmes	1 C.Carr	3 B.Coughlin	3O J.Thoney	C1 P.Noonan	3 H.Hill	3 B.Coughlin
C T.Doran	C E.McFarland	C F.Buelow	C B.Wood	3 C.Osteen	/1 J.Mullin	S3 H.Gleason	S C.Moran
/2 B.Unglaub	C J.Jones	1 B.Schwartz	C1 M.Beville	/1 M.Beville	O L.Bruce	O F.Huelsman	K.Selbach
	/C M.Heydon	O C.Rossman	1 C.Hickman	/3 B.Unglaub		C J.O'Connor	CO L.Drill
P C.Young	/O F.Huelsman	O R.Vinson	C F.Buelow	/O O.Collins	P R.Waddell	/2 G.DeMontreville	2 J.Mullin
P B.Dinneen	/C C.Berry	/C H.Ostdiek	/O F.Huelsman	/C F.McManus	P E.Plank	/O A.Bader	OP A.Orth
P J.Tannehill		/S M.Donovan	/2 J.Burns	/O E.Bliss	P W.Henley	H P.Swander	O J.Thoney
P N.Gibson	P F.Owen		/C F.McManus	/C F.McManus	P C.Bender	H H.Vahrenhorst	2 R.Nill
P G.Winter	P N.Altrock	P B.Bernhard					1 L.Herring
	P D.White	P R.Donahue	P G.Mullin	P J.Chesbro		P B.Pelty	/O I.Hoffman
	P F.Smith	P E.Moore	P E.Killian	P J.Powell	/P A.Coakley	P H.Howell	
	P R.Patterson	P A.Joss	P B.Donovan	P A.Orth	/P F.Applegate	P F.Glade	P C.Patten
		P B.Rhoads	P F.Kitson	P T.Hughes	/P J.Fairbank	P W.Sudhoff	H.Townsend
	P E.Walsh		P J.Stovall	P C.Griffith	/P J.Barthold	P E.Siever	P B.Jacobson
	/P P.Flaherty	PO O.Hess		W.Clarkson			P B.Wolfe
	/P E.Stricklett	/P J.Hickey	/P C.Jaeger	/P A.Puttmann		/P C.Morgan	P T.Hughes
	/P T.Dougherty		/P B.Raymond	/P B.Wolfe		/P G.Wright	
			/P C.Ferry	/P N.Garvin			P D.Dunkle
							/P D.Mason
							/P H.Wilson

TEAM	G	W	L	PCT	GB	R	OR	AB	H	2B	3B	HR	BB	SO	AVG	OBP	SLG	PRO	PRO+	BR	/A	PF	CHI	RC	SB	CS	SBA	SBR
BOS	157	95	59	.617		608	466	5231	1294	194	105	26	347	570	.247	.301	.340	.641	102	42	8	106	101	597	101			
NY	155	92	59	.609	1.5	598	526	5220	1354	195	91	27	312	548	.259	.308	.347	.655	107	69	40	105	96	640	163			
CHI	156	89	65	.578	6	600	482	5027	1217	193	68	14	373	586	.242	.300	.316	.616	104	4	26	96	109	578	216			
CLE	154	86	65	.570	7.5	647	482	5152	1340	225	90	27	307	714	.260	.308	.354	.662	116	78	84	99	103	650	178			
PHI	155	81	70	.536	12.5	557	503	5088	1266	197	77	31	313	605	.249	.298	.336	.634	101	28	-1	105	98	579	137			
STL	156	65	87	.428	29	481	604	5291	1266	153	53	10	332	609	.239	.291	.294	.585	96	-52	-20	94	94	526	150			
DET	162	62	90	.408	32	505	627	5321	1231	154	69	11	344	635	.231	.282	.292	.574	90	-75	-60	97	102	502	112			
WAS	157	38	113	.252	55.5	437	743	5149	1170	171	57	10	283	759	.227	.275	.288	.563	84	-94	-87	98	97	475	150			
TOT	626					4433		41479	10138	1482	610	156	2611	5026	.244	.295	.321	.616						1207				

TEAM	CG	SH	SV	IP	H	H/G	HR	BB	SO	RAT	ERA	ERA+	OAV	OOB	PR	/A	PF	CPI	FA	E	DP	FW	PW	BW	SBW	DIF
BOS	148	21	1	1406	1208	7.7	31	233	612	9.4	2.12	126	.233	.270	75	86	103	101	.962	242	83	1.6	9.6	.9		5.9
NY	123	15	1	1380²	1180	7.7	29	311	684	10.0	2.57	106	.232	.282	4	22	104	90	.958	275	90	-.8	2.5	4.5		10.4
CHI	134	26	3	1380	1161	7.6	13	303	550	9.8	2.30	107	.229	.279	45	23	95	93	.964	238	95	1.7	2.6	2.9		4.8
CLE	141	20	0	1356²	1273	8.4	10	285	627	10.6	2.22	114	.249	.294	56	47	98	116	.959	255	86	.4	5.3	9.4		-4.5
PHI	136	26	0	1361¹	1149	7.6	13	366	887	10.4	2.35	114	.230	.291	38	50	103	100	.959	250	67	.8	5.6	-.1		-.8
STL	135	13	1	1410	1335	8.5	25	333	577	11.0	2.83	88	.251	.303	-36	-55	96	100	.960	267	78	-.2	-6.1	-2.2		-2.4
DET	143	15	2	1430	1345	8.5	16	433	556	11.6	2.77	92	.250	.314	-27	-35	98	106	.959	273	92	.0	-3.9	-6.7		-3.5
WAS	137	7	4	1359²	1487	9.8	19	347	533	12.5	3.62	73	.279	.330	-155	-145	102	99	.951	314	97	-3.1	-16.2	-9.7		-8.4
TOT	1097143		12	11084¹		8.2				10.7	2.60		.244	.295					.959	2114	688					

Runs		Hits		Doubles		Triples		Home Runs		Total Bases	
Dougherty-Bos-NY	113	Lajoie-Cle	208	Lajoie-Cle	49	Stahl-Bos	19	Davis-Phi	10	Lajoie-Cle	305
Flick-Cle	97	Keeler-NY	186	Collins-Bos	33	Freeman-Bos	19	Murphy-Phi	7	Flick-Cle	260
Bradley-Cle	94	Bradley-Cle	183	Bradley-Cle	32	Cassidy-Was	19	Freeman-Bos	7	Freeman-Bos	246
Lajoie-Cle	92	Dougherty-Bos-NY	181			Murphy-Phi	17			Bradley-Cle	246
		Flick-Cle	177			Flick-Cle	17				

Runs Batted In		Runs Produced		Bases On Balls		Batting Average		On Base Percentage		Slugging Average	
Lajoie-Cle	102	Lajoie-Cle	188	Barrett-Det	79	Lajoie-Cle	.376	Lajoie-Cle	.413	Lajoie-Cle	.552
Freeman-Bos	84	Bradley-Cle	172	Burkett-StL	78	Keeler-NY	.343	Keeler-NY	.390	Davis-Phi	.490
Bradley-Cle	83	Parent-Bos	156	Hartsel-Phi	75	Davis-Phi	.309	Flick-Cle	.371	Flick-Cle	.449
Anderson-NY	82	Collins-Bos	149	Selbach-Was-Bos	72	Flick-Cle	.306	Stahl-Bos	.366	Murphy-Phi	.440
		Murphy-Phi	148	Lush-Cle	72	Bradley-Cle	.300	Burkett-StL	.363	Hickman-Cle-Det	.437

Production		Adjusted Production		Batter Runs		Adjusted Batter Runs		Clutch Hitting Index		Runs Created	
Lajoie-Cle	.965	Lajoie-Cle	205	Lajoie-Cle	62.4	Lajoie-Cle	63.5	Callahan-Chi	132	Lajoie-Cle	142
Flick-Cle	.820	Flick-Cle	160	Flick-Cle	38.7	Flick-Cle	39.6	Wallace-StL	130	Flick-Cle	115
Keeler-NY	.799	Keeler-NY	146	Keeler-NY	32.7	Keeler-NY	28.5	Bradley-Cle	129	Keeler-NY	100
Stahl-Bos	.782	Stahl-Bos	139	Stahl-Bos	32.7	Stahl-Bos	27.3	Tannehill-Chi	129	Stahl-Bos	99
Murphy-Phi	.760	Hickman-Cle-Det	137	Davis-Phi	27.5	Burkett-StL	24.4	Anderson-NY	124	Bradley-Cle	95

Total Average		Stolen Bases		Stolen Base Average		Stolen Base Runs		Fielding Runs		Total Player Rating	
Lajoie-Cle	1.070	Flick-Cle	38					Tannehill-Chi	27.8	Lajoie-Cle	7.2
Flick-Cle	.891	Bay-Cle	38					Davis-Chi	16.8	Flick-Cle	4.5
Keeler-NY	.798	Heidrick-StL	35					Williams-NY	16.8	Murphy-Phi	3.9
Stahl-Bos	.782	Davis-Chi	32					Carr-Det-Cle	15.8	Bradley-Cle	3.9
Murphy-Phi	.741	Conroy-NY	30					Elberfeld-NY	15.3	Davis-Chi	3.4

Wins		Win Percentage		Games		Complete Games		Shutouts		Saves	
Chesbro-NY	41	Chesbro-NY	.774	Chesbro-NY	55	Chesbro-NY	48	Young-Bos	10	Patten-Was	3
Young-Bos	26	Tannehill-Bos	.656	Powell-NY	47	Mullin-Det	42	Waddell-Phi	8		
Plank-Phi	26	Smith-Chi	.640	Waddell-Phi	46	Young-Bos	40	White-Chi	7		
Waddell-Phi	25	Bernhard-Cle	.639	Patten-Was	45	Waddell-Phi	39	Plank-Phi	7		
		Dinneen-Bos	.622	Mullin-Det	45	Powell-NY	38	Mullin-Det	7		

Innings Pitched		Fewest Hits/Game		Fewest BB/Game		Strikeouts		Strikeouts/Game		Ratio	
Chesbro-NY	454.2	Chesbro-NY	6.69	Young-Bos	.69	Waddell-Phi	349	Waddell-Phi	8.20	Young-Bos	8.53
Powell-NY	390.1	Owen-Chi	6.94	Tannehill-Bos	1.05	Chesbro-NY	239	Bender-Phi	6.58	Chesbro-NY	8.57
Waddell-Phi	383.0	Smith-Chi	6.98	Patterson-Chi	1.31	Powell-NY	202	Moore-Cle	5.49	Owen-Chi	9.00
Mullin-Det	382.1	Gibson-Bos	7.12	Joss-Cle	1.40	Plank-Phi	201	Plank-Phi	5.06	Joss-Cle	9.22
Young-Bos	380.0	Waddell-Phi	7.21	Altrock-Chi	1.41	Young-Bos	200	Glade-StL	4.86	Dinneen-Bos	9.33

Earned Run Average		Adjusted ERA		Opponents' Batting Avg.		Opponents' On Base Pct.		Starter Runs		Adjusted Starter Runs	
Joss-Cle	1.59	Waddell-Phi	165	Chesbro-NY	.208	Young-Bos	.251	Waddell-Phi	41.5	Chesbro-NY	45.0
Waddell-Phi	1.62	Joss-Cle	159	Owen-Chi	.214	Chesbro-NY	.252	Chesbro-NY	39.2	Waddell-Phi	44.9
Hess-Cle	1.67	Chesbro-NY	149	Smith-Chi	.215	Owen-Chi	.261	Young-Bos	26.6	Young-Bos	29.8
White-Chi	1.78	White-Chi	138	Gibson-Bos	.219	Joss-Cle	.266	Owen-Chi	22.9	Plank-Phi	20.3
Chesbro-NY	1.82	Young-Bos	136	Waddell-Phi	.221	Dinneen-Bos	.268	Joss-Cle	21.5	Joss-Cle	20.2

Clutch Pitching Index		Relief Runs		Adjusted Relief Runs		Relief Ranking		Total Pitcher Index		Total Baseball Ranking	
White-Chi	153							Chesbro-NY	6.9	Lajoie-Cle	7.2
Siever-StL	134							Waddell-Phi	4.9	Chesbro-NY	6.9
Bernhard-Cle	130							Owen-Chi	3.5	Waddell-Phi	4.9
Waddell-Phi	126							Mullin-Det	3.2	Flick-Cle	4.5
Donahue-Cle	118							Young-Bos	3.1	Murphy-Phi	3.9

January 14 Giants owner John T. Brush, who refused to play the AL pennant winners in 1904, proposes rules governing future World Series.

February 25 While most clubs go south or stay close to home, the Cubs go to Santa Monica, California, for spring training, foreshadowing their eventual move to Catalina Island.

April 10* A New York magistrate rules Sunday baseball legal, but the battle will continue in the courts.

April 14 Boston's Kaiser Wilhelm loses to the Giants 10-1 in the opener at the Polo Grounds before 40,000. He will finish the year 4-22, one of four Beaneaters who will lose 20 or more this year. The other three are Irv Young, Vic Willis, and Chick Fraser.

April 26 Jack McCarthy becomes the second outfielder to complete three double plays in one game when he throws out three Pirates at home, preserving the 2–1 Chicago Cubs victory.

April 30 Over 30,000 attend a Sunday game between the Giants and Superbas in Brooklyn. To get around the law, fans make "contributions" for admission.

May 17* Waseda University of Tokyo defeats Los Angeles High School 5–3 in the first game of an American tour. It is the first baseball game ever played by Japanese outside Japan. Waseda starts a powerhouse tradition at Japan's Big Six universities that continues today.

May 19 Banished yesterday for abusive behavior, John McGraw roams the Polo Grounds before today's game with the Pirates, shouting insults at Barney Dreyfuss. McGraw accuses him of controlling the NL umpires through league president Harry Pulliam and welshing on gambling debts. McGraw is again ejected during the game. Eight days later, Pulliam levies a $150 fine and a 15-day suspension. Dreyfuss demands an NL hearing. McGraw files for an injunction against the fine and suspension, which the judge eventually grants. On June 1, the NL board meets in Boston and clears McGraw of the Dreyfuss charges, then censures Dreyfuss for engaging in a public altercation with McGraw.

May 30 Both leagues post record attendance figures for the Memorial Day holiday. Thanks to morning-afternoon doubleheaders, 67,806 see seven NL games.

June 13 For eight innings, Christy Mathewson and the Cubs' Mordecai "Three Finger" Brown match no-hitters. The Giants get two hits in the ninth to win 1-0, and preserve Matty's second no-hitter.

July 31 Charles P. Taft, owner of the Cincinnati *Times-Star* and brother of future president Charles W. Murphy's purchase of the Chicago Cubs for $125,000.

August 1 The Giants win their twelfth in a row, and eleventh straight against Cincinnati 10–5. The Pirates will end the streak at 13 on August 3, but the Giants will win the pennant easily, nine games ahead of Pittsburgh.

August 8 Pittsburgh second baseman Dave Brain, who hit three triples in a game for St. Louis against Pittsburgh on May 29, repeats the performance for Pittsburgh against Boston. He is the only player to perform the feat twice in one season.

September 14 Joe Tinker and Johnny Evers engage in a fistfight on the field during an exhibition game in Washington, Indiana, because Evers took a taxi to the park, leaving his teammates in the hotel lobby. The pair will not speak to each other again for 33 years.

October 7 Beaneaters first baseman Fred Tenney has one assist in the season's final game, giving him an NL record of 152. The mark will be topped by Sid Bream of Pittsburgh, with 166 in 1986.

October 9 At Philadelphia, the Giants' Christy Mathewson outpitches 26-game-winner Eddie Plank 3-0 in the first game of the all-shutout Series.

October 14 Mathewson pitches his third shutout in six days, giving up six hits to Bender's five. The Giants win 2-0. The A's .161 team BA is the lowest ever for a World Series; the teams' combined .185 is also the lowest. Each winning share is worth $1,142. The A's receive $382 each, but the club owners donate their share of the gate, raising the players' checks to $832.22.

December 15 After losing a record 29 games this year, veteran righthander Vic Willis is traded by seventh-place Boston NL to Pittsburgh for three unimportant players.

BOSTON		BROOKLYN		CHICAGO		CINCINNATI		NEW YORK		PHILADELPHIA		PITTSBURGH		ST.LOUIS	
M	F.Tenney	M	N.Hanlon	M	F.Selee	M	J.Kelley	M	J.McGraw	M	H.Duffy	M	F.Clarke	M	K.Nichols
1B	F.Tenney	1B	D.Gessler	M	F.Chance	1B	S.Barry	1B	D.McGann	1B	K.Bransfield	1B	D.Howard	M	J.Burke
2B	F.Raymer	2B	C.Malay	1B	F.Chance	2B	M.Huggins	2B	B.Gilbert	2B	K.Gleason	2B	C.Ritchey	M	S.Robison
SS	E.Abbaticchio	SS	P.Lewis	2B	J.Evers	SS	T.Corcoran	SS	B.Dahlen	SS	M.Doolan	SS	H.Wagner	1B	J.Beckley
3B	H.Wolverton	3B	E.Batch	SS	J.Tinker	3B	H.Steinfeldt	3B	A.Devlin	3B	E.Courtney	3B	D.Brain	2B	H.Arndt
LF	J.Delahanty	LF	J.Sheckard	3B	D.Casey	LF	J.Kelley	LF	S.Mertes	LF	S.Magee	LF	F.Clarke	SS	G.McBride
CF	R.Cannell	CF	J.Dobbs	LF	F.Schulte	CF	C.Seymour	CF	M.Donlin	CF	R.Thomas	CF	G.Beaumont	3B	J.Burke
RF	C.Dolan	RF	H.Lumley	CF	J.Slagle	RF	F.Odwell	RF	G.Browne	RF	J.Titus	RF	O.Clymer	LF	S.Shannon
C	P.Moran	C	L.Ritter	RF	B.Maloney	C	A.Schlei	C	R.Bresnahan	C	R.Dooin	C	H.Peitz	CF	H.Smoot
				C	J.Kling									RF	J.Dunleavy
C	T.Needham	C	B.Bergen			3O	A.Bridwell	C1	F.Bowerman	C	F.Abbott	O3	T.Leach	C	M.Grady
32	B.Lauterborn	S1	C.Babb	2	S.Hofman	O	J.Sebring	2O	S.Strang	S	O.Krueger	1	B.Clancy	2S	D.Shay
O	B.Sharpe	O	B.Hall	C	J.O'Neill	C	E.Phelps	1C	B.Clarke	C	M.Kahoe	C	G.Gibson	O2	J.Clarke
O	G.Barclay	2	R.Owens	O	J.McCarthy	/C	G.Street	/3	O.Neal	/O	H.Duffy	O	G.Ganley	S	D.Brain
/3	A.Strobel	2	J.Hummel	1	S.Barry	1	C.Dolan	/O	B.Hall	/C	R.Munson	1P	H.Hillebrand	C	J.Warner
/C	G.Street	/1	E.MacGamwell	3	H.Lobert	1	C.Blankenship	/O	M.Graham	/O	J.Lush	C	F.Carisch	C	T.Leahy
/S	D.Murphy	/1	A.Yale			O	J.Harper	/O	J.McGraw			3	G.McBride	3	A.Hoelskoetter
/C	B.McCarthy	P	H.McIntire	P	E.Reulbach	O	B.Hinchman	P	C.Mathewson	P	T.Pittinger	/O	J.Wallace	O	R.DeGroff
		P	D.Scanlan	P	J.Weimer	/3	M.Mowrey	P	J.McGinnity	P	B.Duggleby	/O	S.Flanagan	O	D.Zearfoss
P	I.Young	P	E.Stricklett	P	M.Brown			P	R.Ames	P	T.Sparks	/3	O.Knabe	O	J.Himes
P	V.Willis	P	M.Eason	P	B.Wicker	P	O.Overall	P	D.Taylor	P	F.Corridon	/C	H.Smith	/2	J.Farrell
P	C.Fraser	P	O.Jones	P	C.Lundgren	P	B.Ewing	P	H.Wiltse	P	K.Nichols			/2	S.Murch
P	K.Wilhelm			P	B.Briggs	P	C.Chech	P	C.Elliott	P	J.Sutthoff	P	D.Phillippe	/C	G.Shea
		P	F.Mitchell	P	B.Pfeffer	P	J.Harper			/P	R.Caldwell	P	S.Leever		
/P	D.Harley	P	J.Doscher			P	T.Walker			/P	H.Kane		C.Case	P	J.Taylor
/P	J.Volz	/P	D.Reisling			P	N.Hahn			/P	K.Brady		M.Lynch	P	C.McFarland
/P	F.Hershey					/P	R.Vowinkel			/P	B.Washer		P.Flaherty	P	J.Thielman
						/P	O.Johns						C.Robitaille	P	B.Brown
						/P	E.Baker					/P	L.Leifield	P	W.Egan
												/P	E.Kinsella	P	W.Kellum
												/P	G.Moore	/P	K.Nichols
														/P	S.McDougal
														/P	B.Campbell
														/P	J.McGinley

TEAM	G	W	L	PCT	GB	R	OR	AB	H	2B	3B	HR	BB	SO	AVG	OBP	SLG	PRO	PRO+	BR	/A	PF	CHI	RC	SB	CS	SBA	SBR
NY	155	105	48	.686		780	505	5094	1392	191	88	39	517		.273	.351	.368	.719	119	143	126	102	99	796	291			
PIT	155	96	57	.627	9	692	570	5213	1385	190	91	22	382		.266	.320	.350	.670	104	38	21	103	102	683	202			
CHI	155	92	61	.601	13	667	442	5108	1249	157	82	12	448		.245	.313	.314	.627	90	-30	-54	104	109	625	267			
PHI	155	83	69	.546	21.5	708	602	5243	1362	187	82	16	406		.260	.318	.336	.654	106	13	38	96	107	655	180			
CIN	155	79	74	.516	26	735	698	5205	1401	160	101	27	434		.269	.332	.354	.686	101	74	-3	111	102	710	181			
STL	154	58	96	.377	47.5	535	734	5066	1254	140	85	20	391		.248	.307	.321	.628	97	-36	-18	97	92	576	162			
BOS	156	51	103	.331	54.5	468	733	5190	1217	148	52	17	302		.234	.284	.293	.577	80	-135	-124	98	96	491	132			
BRO	155	48	104	.316	56.5	506	807	5100	1255	154	60	29	327		.246	.297	.317	.614	97	-66	-25	93	91	564	186			
TOT	620					5091		41219	10515	1327	641	182	3207	4462	.255	.315	.332	.647						1601				

TEAM	CG	SH	SV	IP	H	H/G	HR	BB	SO	RAT	ERA	ERA+	OAV	OOB	PR	/A	PF	CPI	FA	E	DP	FW	PW	BW	SBW	DIF
NY	117	18	15	1370	1160	7.6	25	364	760	10.2	2.39	122	.229	.284	91	80	98	92	.960	258	93	2.3	8.3	13.1		4.8
PIT	113	12	6	1382²	1270	8.3	12	389	512	11.2	2.86	104	.248	.308	20	16	100	95	.961	255	112	2.5	1.7	2.2		13.2
CHI	133	23	2	1407¹	1135	7.3	14	385	627	10.0	2.04	146	.224	.286	149	144	99	105	.962	248	99	2.9	15.0	-5.6		3.2
PHI	119	12	5	1398²	1303	8.4	21	411	516	11.5	2.81	104	.252	.316	28	12	97	104	.957	275	99	1.2	1.2	4.0		.6
CIN	119	10	2	1365²	1409	9.3	22	439	547	12.5	3.01	109	.272	.335	-3	41	110	116	.953	310	122	-1.0	4.3	-.3		-.4
STL	135	10	2	1347²	1431	9.6	28	367	411	12.3	3.59	83	.276	.329	-89	-93	99	97	.957	274	83	1.2	-9.7	-1.9		-8.6
BOS	139	14	0	1383	1390	9.0	36	433	533	12.1	3.52	88	.265	.326	-81	-68	103	95	.951	325	89	-1.8	-7.1	-12.9		-4.2
BRO	125	7	3	1347	1416	9.5	24	476	556	13.1	3.76	77	.274	.343	-114	-132	101	98	.937	408	101	-7.2	-13.7	-2.6		-4.5
TOT	1000	106	35	11002		8.6				11.6	2.99		.255	.315					.954	2353	798					

Runs
Donlin-NY 124
Thomas-Phi 118
Huggins-Cin 117
Wagner-Pit 114

Hits
Seymour-Cin 219
Donlin-NY 216
Wagner-Pit 199
Barry-Chi-Cin 182
Magee-Phi 180

Doubles
Seymour-Cin 40
Titus-Phi 36
Wagner-Pit 32
Donlin-NY 31
Ritchey-Pit 29

Triples
Seymour-Cin 21
Mertes-NY 17
Magee-Phi 17
Smoot-StL 16
Donlin-NY 16

Home Runs
Odwell-Cin 9
Seymour-Cin 8
Lumley-Bro 7
Donlin-NY 7
Dahlen-NY 7

Total Bases
Seymour-Cin 325
Donlin-NY 300
Wagner-Pit 277
Magee-Phi 253
Titus-Phi 239

Runs Batted In
Seymour-Cin 121
Mertes-NY 108
Wagner-Pit 101
Magee-Phi 98
Titus-Phi 89

Runs Produced
Wagner-Pit 209
Seymour-Cin 208
Donlin-NY 197
Magee-Phi 193
Titus-Phi 186

Bases On Balls
Huggins-Cin 103
Slagle-Chi 97
Thomas-Phi 93
Chance-Chi 78
Titus-Phi 69

Batting Average
Seymour-Cin 377
Wagner-Pit 363
Donlin-NY 356
Beaumont-Pit 328
Thomas-Phi 317

On Base Percentage
Chance-Chi 450
Seymour-Cin 429
Wagner-Pit 427
Thomas-Phi 417
Donlin-NY 413

Slugging Average
Seymour-Cin 559
Wagner-Pit 505
Donlin-NY 495
Titus-Phi 436
Grady-StL 434

Production
Seymour-Cin 988
Wagner-Pit 932
Donlin-NY 908
Chance-Chi 883
Titus-Phi 834

Adjusted Production
Seymour-Cin 175
Wagner-Pit 173
Donlin-NY 166
Chance-Chi 157
Titus-Phi 154

Batter Runs
Seymour-Cin 64.8
Wagner-Pit 52.3
Donlin-NY 51.3
Chance-Chi 37.2
Titus-Phi 34.7

Adjusted Batter Runs
Seymour-Cin 50.8
Wagner-Pit 49.3
Donlin-NY 48.7
Titus-Phi 38.6
Chance-Chi 33.7

Clutch Hitting Index
Mertes-NY 139
Dahlen-NY 136
Wolverton-Bos 132
Corcoran-Cin 131
Courtney-Phi 131

Runs Created
Seymour-Cin 153
Wagner-Pit 147
Donlin-NY 142
Magee-Phi 111
Mertes-NY 103

Total Average
Wagner-Pit 1.132
Chance-Chi 1.131
Seymour-Cin 1.102
Donlin-NY 1.003
McGann-NY 898

Stolen Bases
Maloney-Chi 59
Devlin-NY 59
Wagner-Pit 57
Mertes-NY 52
Magee-Phi 48

Stolen Base Average

Stolen Base Runs

Fielding Runs
Huggins-Cin 36.2
Gilbert-NY 25.4
Tenney-Bos 22.2
Wagner-Pit 20.3
Dahlen-NY 19.8

Total Player Rating
Wagner-Pit 7.3
Seymour-Cin 5.7
Huggins-Cin 4.5
Thomas-Phi 4.5
Titus-Phi 4.1

Wins
Mathewson-NY 31
Pittinger-Phi 23
Ames-NY 22
McGinnity-NY 21

Win Percentage
Leever-Pit 800
Mathewson-NY 775
Ames-NY 733
Wiltse-NY 714
Lynch-Pit 680

Games
Pittinger-Phi 46
McGinnity-NY 46
Young-Bos 43
Mathewson-NY 43
Overall-Cin 42

Complete Games
Young-Bos 41
Willis-Bos 36
Fraser-Bos 35
Taylor-StL 34

Shutouts
Mathewson-NY 8
Young-Bos 7
Reulbach-Chi 5
Phillippe-Pit 5
Briggs-Chi 5

Saves
Elliott-NY 6
Wiltse-NY 4
McGinnity-NY 3

Innings Pitched
Young-Bos 378.0
Willis-Bos 342.0
Mathewson-NY . . . 338.2
Pittinger-Phi 337.1
Fraser-Bos 334.1

Fewest Hits/Game
Reulbach-Chi 6.42
Mathewson-NY . . . 6.70
Lundgren-Chi 7.02
Wicker-Chi 7.03
Wiltse-NY 7.22

Fewest BB/Game
Phillippe-Pit 1.55
Brown-Chi 1.59
Young-Bos 1.69
Mathewson-NY . . . 1.70
McGinnity-NY 1.99

Strikeouts
Mathewson-NY . . . 206
Ames-NY 198
Overall-Cin 173
Ewing-Cin 164
Young-Bos 156

Strikeouts/Game
Ames-NY 6.78
Wiltse-NY 5.48
Mathewson-NY . . . 5.47
Overall-Cin 4.90
Scanlan-Bro 4.87

Ratio
Mathewson-NY . . . 8.42
Reulbach-Chi 9.23
Phillippe-Pit 9.45
Wicker-Chi 9.46
Brown-Chi 9.54

Earned Run Average
Mathewson-NY . . . 1.28
Reulbach-Chi 1.42
Wicker-Chi 2.02
Briggs-Chi 2.14
Brown-Chi 2.17

Adjusted ERA
Mathewson-NY . . . 229
Reulbach-Chi 209
Wicker-Chi 147
Briggs-Chi 139
Brown-Chi 137

Opponents' Batting Avg.
Reulbach-Chi 201
Mathewson-NY 205
Wiltse-NY 219
Lundgren-Chi 220
Wicker-Chi 221

Opponents' On Base Pct.
Mathewson-NY 245
Reulbach-Chi 266
Brown-Chi 271
Phillippe-Pit 274
Wicker-Chi 276

Starter Runs
Mathewson-NY . . . 64.6
Reulbach-Chi 50.9
Phillippe-Pit 24.7
Sparks-Phi 23.3
Brown-Chi 22.8

Adjusted Starter Runs
Mathewson-NY . . . 61.9
Reulbach-Chi 50.3
Ewing-Cin 27.1
Phillippe-Pit 24.7
Brown-Chi 22.2

Clutch Pitching Index
Chech-Cin 133
Duggleby-Phi 126
Overall-Cin 119
Briggs-Chi 119
Case-Pit 115

Relief Runs

Adjusted Relief Runs

Relief Ranking

Total Pitcher Index
Mathewson-NY . . . 9.6
Reulbach-Chi 4.8
Ewing-Cin 2.7
Brown-Chi 2.4
Wiltse-NY 2.4

Total Baseball Ranking
Mathewson-NY . . . 9.6
Wagner-Pit 7.3
Seymour-Cin 5.7
Reulbach-Chi 4.8
Huggins-Cin 4.5

February 2* Hugh Jennings, now managing Baltimore in the Eastern League, is admitted to the Maryland bar after completing law studies at Cornell. Two weeks later Yankees outfielder Dave Fultz, a Columbia graduate, passes the New York bar exam. In 1912 he will organize and lead the Players' Fraternity.

February 7 In Lynn, MA, Rube Waddell prevents a fire by carrying a burning stove out of a store and throwing it into a snowbank. Three days later he flees nearby Peabody to escape charges of assaulting and injuring his wife's parents.

March 29 A committee of Washington writers votes for "Nationals" as the AL team nickname, but "Senators" continues as the general favorite.

April 12 The Washington owners offer the players a $1,000 bonus if they finish higher than eighth and $500 for each position higher. They finish seventh, eleven games above St. Louis.

April 22 Having failed to give out rain checks the day before when a storm stopped the game, the Highlanders open the gates for free admission, and 30,000 people jam the park for the clash with Washington.

April 30* At Evansville, Indiana, future major league umpire Cy Rigler begins the practice of raising his right arm to indicate strikes, so that friends in the bleachers can distinguish calls.

May 30 Both leagues post record attendance figures for the Memorial Day holiday. Thanks to morning-afternoon doubleheaders, 80,963 attend eight AL games.

July 1 White Sox pitcher Frank Owen narrowly misses becoming the first man to pitch a doubleheader shutout as the Browns score one run off him in the two games.

July 4 In the afternoon game of a doubleheader, Philadelphia's Rube Waddell bests Cy Young in a 20-inning marathon, as the Athletics down Boston 4-2. Philadelphia catcher Ossie Schreckengost works 28 innings in one day, a major league record.

August 9 Mistaking her husband for a burglar, Ty Cobb's mother shoots and kills him. The Georgia Peach will make his major league debut with the Tigers three weeks later.

August 30 Cobb makes his major league debut, doubling off Jack Chesbro, as Detroit defeats New York 5–3. The two-bagger is the first of his 4,189 hits, a record topped by Pete Rose in 1985.

September 16 The Highlanders find themselves a little short on infielders so right fielder Willie Keeler, who is left-handed, plays second base in both games of a twin bill.

September 20 Chicago President Charles Comiskey orders a houseboat built for the express purpose of transporting and housing the team during spring training.

September 28 In a game that helps decide the pennant, the A's beat the White Sox 3–2, as Topsy Hartsel scores from second base with the winning run in the seventh inning. Harry Davis's RBI single to short left hits Hartsel's mitt, which the left fielder had left in the outfield when he came off the field. The A's take the series two games to one, and will finish two games ahead of Chicago.

October 2 The Washington outfield has no putouts or assists in a 3-2 win over Chicago.

October 5 Athletics pitcher Chief Bender has three hits, including a triple with three on, in an 8–0 victory over Washington. He then relieves Andy Coakley in the second game and wins 9–7. Overall, he has two wins, six hits, and eight RBI for the day.

BOSTON	CHICAGO	CLEVELAND	DETROIT	NEW YORK	PHILADELPHIA	ST.LOUIS	WASHINGTON
M J.Collins	M F.Jones	M N.Lajoie	M B.Armour	M C.Griffith	M C.Mack	M J.McAleer	M J.Stahl
1B M.Grimshaw	1B J.Donahue	M B.Bradley	1B C.Lindsay	1B H.Chase	1B H.Davis	1B T.Jones	1B J.Stahl
2B H.Ferris	2B G.Dundon	M N.Lajoie	2B G.Schaefer	2B J.Williams	2B D.Murphy	2B I.Rockenfield	2B C.Hickman
SS F.Parent	SS G.Davis	1B C.Carr	SS C.O'Leary	SS K.Elberfeld	SS J.Knight	SS B.Wallace	SS J.Cassidy
3B J.Collins	3B L.Tannehill	2B N.Lajoie	3B B.Coughlin	3B J.Yeager	3B L.Cross	3B H.Gleason	3B H.Hill
LF J.Burkett	LF N.Callahan	SS T.Turner	LF M.McIntyre	LF P.Dougherty	LF T.Hartsel	LF G.Stone	LF F.Huelsman
CF C.Stahl	CF F.Jones	3B B.Bradley	CF D.Cooley	CF D.Fultz	CF B.Koehler		CF C.Jones
RF K.Selbach	RF D.Green	LF J.Jackson	RF S.Crawford	RF W.Keeler	RF S.Seybold	RF E.Frisk	RF J.Anderson
C L.Criger	C B.Sullivan	CF H.Bay	C L.Drill	C R.Kleinow	C O.Schreck't	C J.Sugden	C M.Heydon
		RF E.Flick					
1O B.Freeman	2O F.Isbell	C F.Buelow	O1 C.Hickman	3O W.Conroy	S M.Cross	O I.Van Zandt	32 R.Nill
3 B.Unglaub	O D.Holmes		O3 B.Lowe	C D.McGuire	O B.Lord	C T.Spencer	O P.Knoll
C C.Armbruster	C E.McFarland	12 G.Stovall	O T.Cobb	O E.Hahn	C D.Powers	C F.Roth	O M.Kittridge
C A.McGovern	23 G.Rohe	C H.Bemis	O J.Warner	O J.Anderson	C H.Barton	2 C.Starr	2 J.Mullin
/O J.Godwin	/C H.Hart	OP O.Hess	C T.Doran	2 F.LaPorte		C A.Weaver	O J.Stanley
1 C.LaChance		2 N.Kahl	O J.Barrett	3 J.Cockman	P E.Plank	2 C.Moran	/O H.Cassady
/O P.Rising	P F.Owen	O R.Vinson	C J.Sullivan	/1 D.Powers	P R.Waddell	2 D.Padden	/O C.Rothgeb
/C D.Farrell	P N.Altrock	/C N.Clarke	/C B.Wood	/S R.Oldring	P A.Coakley	/C C.Gibson	/O H.Tate
/C T.Doran	P F.Smith	O B.Congalton	/C N.Clarke	/1 F.Delahanty	P C.Bender	/C B.Rickey	/O D.Sullivan
/C F.Owens	P D.White	2 J.Barbeau		/C J.Connor	P W.Henley		/O S.Shaughnessy
	P E.Walsh	/C H.Wakefield	P G.Mullin	/1 F.Curtis	P H.Howell		
P C.Young		/2 E.Grant	P E.Killian	/3 P.Cooney	P F.Glade		P C.Patten
P J.Tannehill	P R.Patterson	/3 E.Leber	P B.Donovan	/1 J.Doyle	P J.Dygert		P T.Hughes
P G.Winter			P F.Kitson	/C F.Jacklitsch	P J.Myers		P H.Townsend
P B.Dinneen		P A.Joss		/C J.McCarthy			P B.Wolfe
P N.Gibson		P E.Moore	/P G.Disch	R C.Fallon			P B.Jacobson
		P B.Rhoads	/P J.Wiggs			P C.Morgan	
/P E.Barry		P B.Bernhard	/P G.Ford	P A.Orth		/P H.Ables	P C.Falkenberg
/P E.Hughes		P R.Donahue	/P E.Cicotte	P J.Chesbro		/P J.Powell	P R.Adams
/P H.Olmsted			/P J.Eubank	P B.Hogg			/P H.Hardy
/P J.Harris		/P H.West	/P C.Jackson	P J.Powell			/P M.Manuel
		/P J.Halla	/P F.Thomas	P C.Griffith			
		/P C.Ferry	/P W.Justis				
			/P A.Bruckmiller	P A.Puttmann			
				P D.Newton			
				/P W.Clarkson			
				/P L.LeRoy			
				/P W.Good			
				/P A.Goodwin			

TEAM	G	W	L	PCT	GB	R	OR	AB	H	2B	3B	HR	BB	SO	AVG	OBP	SLG	PRO	PRO+	BR	/A	PF	CHI	RC	SB	CS	SBA	SBR
PHI	152	92	56	.622		623	492	5146	1310	256	51	24	376	644	.255	.310	.338	.648	109	60	49	102	98	632	190			
CHI	158	92	60	.605	2	612	451	5114	1213	200	55	11	439	613	.237	.305	.304	.609	103	0	24	96	104	577	194			
DET	154	79	74	.516	15.5	512	602	4971	1209	190	54	13	375	583	.243	.302	.311	.613	99	1	-3	101	92	540	129			
BOS	153	78	74	.513	16	579	564	5049	1179	165	69	29	486	553	.234	.305	.311	.616	100	14	8	101	99	550	131			
CLE	155	76	78	.494	19	567	587	5166	1318	211	72	18	360	712	.255	.301	.334	.635	106	33	25	101	94	608	188			
NY	152	71	78	.477	21.5	586	622	4957	1228	163	61	23	360	537	.248	.307	.319	.626	93	26	-40	111	101	580	200			
WAS	154	64	87	.424	29.5	559	623	5015	1121	193	68	22	298	824	.224	.274	.302	.576	92	-70	-51	96	115	492	169			
STL	156	54	99	.353	40.5	511	608	5204	1205	153	49	16	362	639	.232	.288	.289	.577	93	-64	-37	95	99	502	130			
TOT	617					4549		40622	9783	1531	479	156	2982	5105	.241	.299	.314	.613							1331			

TEAM	CG	SH	SV	IP	H	H/G	HR	BB	SO	RAT	ERA	ERA+	OAV	OOB	PR	/A	PF	CPI	FA	E	DP	FW	PW	BW	SBW	DIF
PHI	117	19	0	1383¹	1137	7.4	21	409	895	10.5	2.19	121	.227	.294	70	68	100	110	.957	265	64	.3	7.5	5.4		4.8
CHI	131	15	0	1427	1163	7.3	11	329	613	9.6	1.99	124	.226	.277	105	72	93	105	.968	217	95	4.2	7.9	2.6		1.3
DET	124	17	1	1348	1226	8.2	11	474	578	11.7	2.83	96	.246	.318	-27	-19	103	104	.957	267	80	.4	-2.1	-.3		4.5
BOS	124	14	1	1356¹	1198	7.9	33	292	652	10.2	2.84	95	.238	.286	-29	-21	102	88	.953	296	75	-1.6	-2.3	.9		5.1
CLE	140	16	0	1363¹	1251	8.3	23	334	555	10.9	2.85	92	.245	.299	-30	-31	99	96	.963	233	84	2.8	-3.4	2.7		-3.1
NY	88	16	4	1353²	1235	8.2	26	396	642	11.1	2.93	100	.246	.307	-42	-2	111	97	.952	293	88	-1.6	-.2	-4.4		2.7
WAS	118	12	1	1362¹	1250	8.3	12	385	539	11.2	2.87	92	.247	.308	-33	-35	100	98	.951	318	76	-3.0	-3.8	-5.6		.9
STL	134	10	2	1384²	1245	8.1	19	389	633	11.0	2.74	93	.243	.304	-14	-33	96	100	.955	296	78	-1.3	-3.6	-4.1		-13.5
TOT	976	119	9	10978²		8.0				10.8	2.65		.241	.299					.957	2185	640					

Runs		Hits		Doubles		Triples		Home Runs		Total Bases	
Davis-Phi	93	Stone-StL	187	Davis-Phi	47	Flick-Cle	18	Davis-Phi	8	Stone-StL	259
Jones-Chi	91	Davis-Phi	173	Crawford-Det	38	Ferris-Bos	16	Stone-StL	7	Davis-Phi	256
Bay-Cle	90	Crawford-Det	171	Hickman-Det-Was	37	Turner-Cle	14			Crawford-Det	247
Hartsel-Phi	88	Keeler-NY	169	Seybold-Phi	37	Stone-StL	13			Hickman-Det-Was	232
Keeler-NY	81	Bay-Cle	166			Burkett-Bos	13			Flick-Cle	231

Runs Batted In		Runs Produced		Bases On Balls		Batting Average		On Base Percentage		Slugging Average	
Davis-Phi	83	Davis-Phi	168	Hartsel-Phi	121	Flick-Cle	.308	Hartsel-Phi	.409	Flick-Cle	.462
L.Cross-Phi	77	Donahue-Chi	146	Jones-Chi	73	Keeler-NY	.302	Flick-Cle	.383	Isbell-Chi	.440
Donahue-Chi	76	L.Cross-Phi	146	Selbach-Bos	67	Bay-Cle	.301	Keeler-NY	.357	Crawford-Det	.430
Crawford-Det	75	Crawford-Det	142	Burkett-Bos	67	Crawford-Det	.297	Crawford-Det	.357	Davis-Phi	.422
Turner-Cle	72	Murphy-Phi	136	Davis-Chi	60	Isbell-Chi	.296	Selbach-Bos	.355	Stone-StL	.410

Production		Adjusted Production		Batter Runs		Adjusted Batter Runs		Clutch Hitting Index		Runs Created	
Flick-Cle	.845	Flick-Cle	165	Flick-Cle	38.6	Flick-Cle	37.3	Gleason-StL	134	Flick-Cle	106
Crawford-Det	.786	Crawford-Det	148	Hartsel-Phi	32.9	Stone-StL	32.1	Donahue-Chi	131	Stone-StL	102
Stone-StL	.756	Stone-StL	147	Crawford-Det	31.0	Hartsel-Phi	31.2	L.Cross-Phi	128	Davis-Phi	101
Davis-Phi	.756	Hartsel-Phi	138	Stone-StL	26.9	Crawford-Det	30.3	Fultz-NY	121	Crawford-Det	99
Hartsel-Phi	.755	Davis-Phi	137	Davis-Phi	24.9	Davis-Phi	23.4	Collins-Bos	116	Hartsel-Phi	96

Total Average		Stolen Bases		Stolen Base Average		Stolen Base Runs		Fielding Runs		Total Player Rating	
Flick-Cle	.945	Hoffman-Phi	46					Cassidy-Was	33.9	Davis-Chi	4.1
Hartsel-Phi	.885	Fultz-NY	44					Tannehill-StL	28.1	Crawford-Det	3.9
Crawford-Det	.797	Stahl-Was	41					Wallace-StL	19.8	Wallace-StL	3.9
Davis-Phi	.776	Hartsel-Phi	37					Davis-Chi	16.7	Flick-Cle	3.4
Stone-StL	.751							McIntyre-Det	16.5	Stone-StL	2.9

Wins		Win Percentage		Games		Complete Games		Shutouts		Saves	
Waddell-Phi	27	Waddell-Phi	.730	Waddell-Phi	46	Plank-Phi	35	Killian-Det	8	Buchanan-StL	2
Plank-Phi	24	Tannehill-Bos	.710	Mullin-Det	44	Mullin-Det	35	Waddell-Phi	7		
Killian-Det	23	Coakley-Phi	.692	Patten-Was	42	Howell-StL	35	Tannehill-Bos	6		
Altrock-Chi	23	Plank-Phi	.667	Owen-Chi	42	Killian-Det	33	Orth-NY	6		
Tannehill-Bos	22	Altrock-Chi	.657			Owen-Chi	32	Hughes-Was	6		

Innings Pitched		Fewest Hits/Game		Fewest BB/Game		Strikeouts		Strikeouts/Game		Ratio	
Mullin-Det	347.2	Waddell-Phi	6.33	Young-Bos	.84	Waddell-Phi	287	Waddell-Phi	7.86	Young-Bos	8.03
Plank-Phi	346.2	Smith-Chi	6.63	Joss-Cle	1.45	Young-Bos	210	Young-Bos	5.89	Waddell-Phi	9.06
Owen-Chi	334.0	Young-Bos	6.96	Owen-Chi	1.51	Plank-Phi	210	Bender-Phi	5.58	Owen-Chi	9.19
Waddell-Phi	328.2	Howell-StL	7.02	Bernhard-Cle	1.76	Howell-StL	198	Howell-StL	5.52	White-Chi	9.37
Howell-StL	323.0	White-Chi	7.05	Altrock-Chi	1.80	Smith-Chi	171	Hogg-NY	5.49	Joss-Cle	9.53

Earned Run Average		Adjusted ERA		Opponents' Batting Avg.		Opponents' On Base Pct.		Starter Runs		Adjusted Starter Runs	
Waddell-Phi	1.48	Waddell-Phi	179	Waddell-Phi	.200	Young-Bos	.241	Waddell-Phi	42.7	Waddell-Phi	42.8
White-Chi	1.76	Young-Bos	147	Smith-Chi	.208	Waddell-Phi	.264	Young-Bos	29.3	Young-Bos	30.9
Young-Bos	1.82	Coakley-Phi	144	Young-Bos	.216	Owen-Chi	.267	Altrock-Chi	26.9	Chesbro-NY	24.6
Coakley-Phi	1.84	White-Chi	140	Howell-StL	.217	White-Chi	.270	White-Chi	25.6	Coakley-Phi	23.1
Altrock-Chi	1.88	Chesbro-NY	133	White-Chi	.218	Joss-Cle	.274	Howell-StL	24.0	Altrock-Chi	20.3

Clutch Pitching Index		Relief Runs		Adjusted Relief Runs		Relief Ranking		Total Pitcher Index		Total Baseball Ranking	
Coakley-Phi	142							Howell-StL	4.9	Waddell-Phi	4.9
Altrock-Chi	118							Waddell-Phi	4.9	Howell-StL	4.8
Waddell-Phi	116							Young-Bos	3.3	Davis-Chi	4.1
Townsend-Was	115							Chesbro-NY	3.0	Crawford-Det	3.9
Mullin-Det	113							Altrock-Chi	2.8	Wallace-StL	3.9

January 12 The owners of the Boston Beaneaters reject a $250,000 offer for the team, which is destined to finish last again.

March 6 Rookie owner Charles W. Murphy puts the last pieces of a Cubs dynasty in place, trading rookie infielder Hans Lobert and lefthander Jake Weimer to the Cincinnati Reds for third baseman Harry Steinfeldt. Not a heavy hitter, Steinfeldt completes the Tinker-Evers-Chance infield with more than adequate defense.

April 12 Boston outfielder Johnny Bates hits a homer in his first major league at bat, connecting in the second inning against the Brooklyn Superbas.

April 22 A new rule puts the umpire in sole charge of all game balls. The home team manager previously had some say as to when a new ball was introduced.

April 28 It's the only time two player-managers steal home on the same day, though not in the same game. Cubs pilot Frank Chance steals in the ninth to give Chicago a 1–0 win over the Reds, and Fred Clarke matches him in the Pirates' 10–1 win over the St. Louis Cardinals.

June 1 Women appear at the Polo Grounds ticket windows for the first time. New ticket-selling machines are also introduced.

June 9 A 19-game losing streak ends for the Boston Beaneaters with a 6–3 win over the Cardinals.

June 17 In another test of Sunday baseball in Brooklyn, the police arrest Superbas president Charles Ebbets and manager Ned Hanlon, the visiting Reds' manager Joe Kelley, and starting pitcher Mal Eason. The case is dismissed as no admission was charged, and the law does not apply to "voluntary contributions."

June 19 NL directors pass a resolution urging all clubs to provide dressing rooms for visiting teams. Even those that do, however, offer such primitive facilities that most teams on the road continue to dress at their hotels.

August 13 The Cubs' Jack Taylor is knocked out by Brooklyn in the third inning, ending a string of 187 complete games and 15 relief appearances in which he finished each game. The record run began June 20, 1901. In 10 years he will fail to finish only eight of 286 starts.

September 1 With the regular umpires sick from food poisoning, Cub pitcher Carl Lundgren and Cardinal catcher Pete Noonan umpire. The Cubs win 8-1 for the 14th win in a row at the West Side Grounds.

September 3* The Philadelphia Giants win the Negro Championship Cup on Labor Day in Philadelphia before 10,000 fans, black baseball's largest crowd to date. Andrew "Rube" Foster pitches them to a 3-2 victory over the Cuban X-Giants, who have John Henry Lloyd in the lineup.

September 26 Rookie outfielder John Cameron of Boston, after one relief appearance, gets a starting assignment against the Cardinals. Leadoff batter Tom O'Hara beats out an infield single. Al Burch's line drive hits Cameron in the head, and caroms back on a fly to catcher Jack O'Neill, who throws to Fred Tenney at first base, doubling off O'Hara. Cameron retires with one assist and a headache in his last major league game.

October 4 The Cubs score their record 116th win of the year, beating the Pirates 4-0 in Pittsburgh. The win gives them a 60-15 road record, an .800 percentage mark that has never been equaled.

October 5 The Giants give Christy Mathewson's brother Henry a starting chance against Boston. He establishes a modern NL record by walking 14, hits one batter, and completes the 7-1 loss for the only major league decision of his career.

October 9 Snow flies at the Cubs' West Side Park as the first one-city World Series opens with the Cubs heavy favorites over the AL's "Hitless Wonders." Neither West Side Park nor the Sox's South Side Park can accommodate the crowds, so the Chicago *Tribune* recreates the games on mechanical boards displayed at theaters. White Sox starter Nick Altrock and Cubs starter Mordecai "Three Finger" Brown give up four hits each, but Cubs errors produce two unearned runs for a 2-1 White Sox victory.

October 12 It's Three Finger Brown's turn to throw a 2-hit shutout, besting Altrock 1-0 and evening the Series.

BOSTON		BROOKLYN		CHICAGO		CINCINNATI		NEW YORK		PHILADELPHIA		PITTSBURGH		ST.LOUIS	
M	F.Tenney	M	P.Donovan	M	F.Chance	M	N.Hanlon	M	J.McGraw	M	H.Duffy	M	F.Clarke	M	J.McCloskey
1B	F.Tenney	1B	T.Jordan	1B	F.Chance	1B	S.Deal	1B	D.McGann	1B	K.Bransfield	1B	J.Nealon	1B	J.Beckley
2B	A.Strobel	2B	W.Alperman	2B	J.Evers	2B	M.Huggins	2B	B.Gilbert	2B	K.Gleason	2B	C.Ritchey	2B	P.Bennett
SS	A.Bridwell	SS	P.Lewis	SS	J.Tinker	SS	T.Corcoran	SS	B.Dahlen	SS	M.Doolan	SS	H.Wagner	SS	G.McBride
3B	D.Brain	3B	D.Casey	3B	H.Steinfeldt	3B	J.Delahanty	3B	A.Devlin	3B	E.Courtney	3B	T.Sheehan	3B	H.Arndt
LF	D.Howard	LF	J.McCarthy	LF	J.Sheckard	LF	J.Kelley	LF	S.Shannon	LF	S.Magee	LF	F.Clarke	LF	S.Shannon
CF	J.Bates	CF	B.Maloney	CF	J.Slagle	CF	C.Seymour	CF	C.Seymour	RF	J.Titus	CF	G.Beaumont	CF	H.Smoot
RF	C.Dolan	RF	H.Lumley	RF	F.Schulte	RF	F.Jude	RF	G.Browne	C	R.Dooin	RF	B.Ganley	RF	A.Burch
C	T.Needham	C	B.Bergen	C	J.Kling	C	A.Schlei	C	R.Bresnahan	32	P.Sentell	C	G.Gibson	C	M.Grady
CO	S.Brown	2O	J.Hummel	C	P.Moran	1O	S.Barry	C1	F.Bowerman	C	J.Donovan	3O	T.Leach	3S	A.Hoelskoetter
C	J.O'Neill	C	L.Ritter	O1	S.Hofman	3S	H.Lobert	2O	S.Strang	3	J.Ward	OS	D.Meier	O1	S.Barry
O	G.Good	O	E.Batch	O	D.Gessler	O	H.Smoot	O	M.Smoot	/C	C.Crist	C	H.Peitz	O	S.Mertes
O	J.Cameron	/1	D.Gessler	/1	P.Noonan	O	F.Odwell	O	M.Donlin	/C	H.Huston	C	E.Phelps	O	J.Himes
S	F.Connaughton	/O	P.Donovan	H	B.Smith	C	P.Livingston	OC	D.Marshall	H	H.Duffy	O	B.Hallman	S	F.Crawford
/O	C.Spencer	/C	J.Butler	/C	T.Walsh	1	C.Carr	/S	J.Hannifin			O	O.Clymer	O	R.Murray
/O	T.Madden					O	J.Siegle	/C	A.Smith			/2	B.Abstein	C1	P.Noonan
/O	E.Diehl	P	M.Brown			O	B.Hinchman	/O	F.Burke	P	T.Sparks	/C	F.Carisch	C	D.Marshall
/S	J.Schulte	P	J.Pfiester	P	M.Brown	3	M.Mowrey	/C	M.Fitzgerald	P	J.Lush	/3	A.Storke	C	J.Marshall
P	I.Young	P	D.Scanlan	P	J.Pfiester	C	E.Phelps	/3	J.McGraw	P	B.Duggleby	/C	H.Smith	O	T.Raub
P	V.Lindaman	P	H.McIntire	P	E.Reulbach	C	L.McLean			P	L.Richie			3	B.Phyle
P	B.Pfeffer	P	M.Eason	P	C.Lundgren	/O	J.Barrett	P	C.Mathewson	P	T.Pittinger	P	V.Willis	O	T.O'Hara
P	G.Dorner	P	J.Pastorius	P	J.Taylor	/3	E.Tiemeyer	P	H.Wiltse			P	S.Leever	O	J.McCarthy
						/C	O.Stanage	P	D.Taylor	/P	W.Moser	P	L.Leifield	S	E.Holly
/P	R.Witherup	/P	J.Whiting	P	O.Overall			P	R.Ames	/P	J.McCloskey	/C	D.Phillippe	/C	D.Holmes
/P	J.Moroney	/P	J.Doscher	P	B.Wicker	P	J.Weimer	RP	G.Ferguson	/P	H.Kane	P	M.Lynch	/3	E.Zimmerman
/P	B.McCarthy	/P	C.McFarland	P	F.Beebe	P	B.Ewing			/P	C.Roy			/C	J.Slattery
		/P	H.Knolls	/P	J.Harper	P	C.Fraser	/P	H.Mathewson	/P	K.Nichols	/P	H.Hillebrand	/O	R.DeGroff
						P	B.Wicker					/P	C.McFarland		
						P	C.Hall					/P	E.Karger	P	B.Brown
												/P	K.Brady	P	E.Karger
				P	O.Overall							/P	C.Case	P	F.Beebe
				P	C.Chech							/P	H.Camnitz	P	J.Taylor
				/P	B.Essick							/P	L.Manske	P	C.Druhot
				/P	J.Harper							/P	B.Maxwell		
				/P	C.Druhot							/P	I.McIlveen	P	G.Thompson
				/P	L.Hafford									P	W.Egan
				/P	G.Dorner									/P	S.McGlynn
				/P	D.Mason									/P	I.Higginbotham
														/P	C.Rhodes
														/P	C.McFarland
														/P	A.Fromme
														/P	A.Puttmann
														/P	J.Thielman
														/P	B.Adams

TEAM	G	W	L	PCT	GB	R	OR	AB	H	2B	3B	HR	BB	SO	AVG	OBP	SLG	PRO	PRO+	BR	/A	PF	CHI	RC	SB	CS	SBA	SBR
CHI	155	116	36	.763		705	381	5018	1316	181	71	20	448		.262	.328	.339	.667	109	83	46	106	109	695	283			
NY	153	96	56	.632	20	625	510	4768	1217	162	53	15	563		.255	.343	.321	.664	112	92	78	102	98	659	288			
PIT	154	93	60	.608	23.5	623	470	5030	1313	164	67	12	424		.261	.324	.327	.651	105	55	28	104	102	625	162			
PHI	154	71	82	.464	45.5	528	564	4911	1183	197	47	12	432		.241	.307	.307	.614	98	-10	-11	100	99	550	180			
BRO	153	66	86	.434	50	496	625	4897	1156	141	68	25	388		.236	.297	.308	.605	103	-31	8	92	98	532	175			
CIN	155	64	87	.424	51.5	533	582	5025	1198	140	71	16	395		.238	.301	.304	.605	91	-28	-51	104	101	545	170			
STL	154	52	98	.347	63	470	607	5075	1195	137	69	10	361		.235	.291	.296	.587	93	-66	-46	96	97	498	110			
BOS	152	49	102	.325	66.5	408	649	4925	1115	136	43	16	356		.226	.286	.281	.567	85	-96	-84	97	93	449	95			
TOT	615					4388		39649	9693	1258	489	126	3367	4537	.244	.310	.310	.620						1463				

TEAM	CG	SH	SV	IP	H	H/G	HR	BB	SO	RAT	ERA	ERA+	OAV	OOB	PR	/A	PF	CPI	FA	E	DP	FW	PW	BW	SBW	DIF
CHI	125	30	10	1388[1]	1018	6.6	12	446	702	9.8	1.75	150	.207	.280	135	135	100	100	.969	194	100	4.5	15.0	5.1		15.3
NY	105	19	18	1334[1]	1207	8.1	13	394	639	11.0	2.49	105	.241	.300	20	15	99	96	.963	233	84	1.8	1.7	8.7		7.9
PIT	116	27	2	1358	1234	8.2	13	309	532	10.5	2.21	120	.245	.294	62	70	102	107	.964	228	109	2.2	7.8	3.1		3.4
PHI	108	21	5	1354[1]	1201	8.0	18	436	500	11.3	2.58	101	.235	.304	7	0	99	94	.956	271	83	-.6	0	-1.2		-3.7
BRO	119	22	11	1348[2]	1255	8.4	15	453	476	11.7	3.13	80	.249	.316	-76	-93	96	96	.955	283	73	-1.5	-10.3	.9		1.0
CIN	126	12	5	1369[2]	1248	8.2	14	470	567	11.6	2.69	102	.250	.320	-10	6	105	105	.959	262	97	.0	.7	-5.7		-6.6
STL	118	4	2	1354	1246	8.3	17	479	559	11.9	3.04	86	.246	.318	-63	-65	100	91	.957	272	92	-.7	-7.2	-5.1		-10.0
BOS	137	10	0	1334[1]	1291	8.7	24	436	562	12.0	3.14	85	.261	.328	-76	-70	102	100	.947	337	102	-5.2	-7.8	-9.3		-4.2
TOT	954	145	53	10841[2]		8.1				11.2	2.62			.310					.959	2080	740					

Runs
Wagner-Pit 103
Chance-Chi 103
Sheckard-Chi 90
Nealon-Pit 82

Hits
Steinfeldt-Chi 176
Wagner-Pit 175
Seymour-Cin-NY 165
Magee-Phi 159
Huggins-Cin 159

Doubles
Wagner-Pit 38
Magee-Phi 36
Bransfield-Phi 28
Steinfeldt-Chi 27
Sheckard-Chi 27

Triples
Schulte-Chi 13
Clarke-Pit 13
Nealon-Pit 12
Lumley-Bro 12

Home Runs
Jordan-Bro 12
Lumley-Bro 9
Seymour-Cin-NY 8
Schulte-Chi 7

Total Bases
Wagner-Pit 237
Steinfeldt-Chi 232
Lumley-Bro 231
Magee-Phi 229
Schulte-Chi 223

Runs Batted In
Steinfeldt-Chi 83
Nealon-Pit 83
Seymour-Cin-NY 80
Jordan-Bro 78

Runs Produced
Wagner-Pit 172
Chance-Chi 171
Nealon-Pit 162
Steinfeldt-Chi 161
Seymour-Cin-NY ... 142

Bases On Balls
Thomas-Phi 107
Bresnahan-NY 81
Titus-Phi 78
Dahlen-NY 76
Devlin-NY 74

Batting Average
Wagner-Pit .... .339
Steinfeldt-Chi ...... .327
Lumley-Bro .... .324
Strang-NY .... .319
Chance-Chi .... .319

On Base Percentage
Bresnahan-NY ...... .419
Chance-Chi .... .419
Wagner-Pit .... .416
Devlin-NY .... .396
Steinfeldt-Chi ...... .395

Slugging Average
Lumley-Bro .... .477
Wagner-Pit .... .459
Strang-NY .... .435
Steinfeldt-Chi ...... .430
Chance-Chi .... .430

Production
Wagner-Pit 875
Lumley-Bro 864
Chance-Chi 849
Steinfeldt-Chi 825
Devlin-NY 786

Adjusted Production
Lumley-Bro 184
Wagner-Pit 166
Chance-Chi 156
Jordan-Bro 153
Steinfeldt-Chi 149

Batter Runs
Wagner-Pit 44.7
Chance-Chi 39.1
Lumley-Bro 37.2
Steinfeldt-Chi 36.1
Devlin-NY 29.1

Adjusted Batter Runs
Lumley-Bro 44.6
Wagner-Pit 40.2
Chance-Chi 33.6
Steinfeldt-Chi 30.6
Devlin-NY 27.2

Clutch Hitting Index
Tinker-Chi 138
Nealon-Pit 134
Ritchey-Pit 128
Kelley-Cin 126
Shannon-StL-NY ... 125

Runs Created
Wagner-Pit 124
Chance-Chi 114
Steinfeldt-Chi 109
Lumley-Bro 107
Magee-Phi 102

Total Average
Chance-Chi 1.062
Wagner-Pit 1.050
Lumley-Bro .... .963
Devlin-NY .... .940
Bresnahan-NY 911

Stolen Bases
Chance-Chi 57
Magee-Phi 55
Devlin-NY 54
Wagner-Pit 53
Evers-Chi........... 49

Fielding Runs
Devlin-NY 28.0
Brain-Bos 25.7
Wagner-Pit 23.8
Gilbert-NY 22.6
Huggins-Cin 21.5

Total Player Rating
Wagner-Pit 7.3
Devlin-NY 6.5
Lumley-Bro 4.3
Huggins-Cin 4.0
Bresnahan-NY 3.9

Wins
McGinnity-NY 27
Brown-Chi 26
Willis-Pit 23
Mathewson-NY 22
Leever-Pit 22

Win Percentage
Reulbach-Chi ...... .826
Brown-Chi .... .813
Leever-Pit .... .759
Lundgren-Chi ..... .739
Pfiester-Chi ...... .714

Games
McGinnity-NY 45
Young-Bos 43
Sparks-Phi 42
Duggleby-Phi 42

Complete Games
Young-Bos 37
Pfeffer-Bos 33

Shutouts
Brown-Chi 9
Leifield-Pit 8

Saves
Ferguson-NY 7
Wiltse-NY 6
Stricklett-Bro 5

Innings Pitched
Young-Bos 358.1
McGinnity-NY ... 339.2
Willis-Pit 322.0
Sparks-Phi 316.2
Lindaman-Bos ... 307.1

Fewest Hits/Game
Reulbach-Chi 5.33
Pfiester-Chi 6.21
Brown-Chi 6.43
Beebe-Chi-StL 6.67
Lundgren-Chi 6.93

Fewest BB/Game
Phillippe-Pit 1.07
Leever-Pit 1.66
Sparks-Phi 1.76
Ewing-Cin 1.88
McGinnity-NY 1.88

Strikeouts
Beebe-Chi-StL 171
Pfeffer-Bos 158
Ames-NY 156
Pfiester-Chi 153

Strikeouts/Game
Ames-NY 6.90
Beebe-Chi-StL 6.67
Pfiester-Chi 5.49
Overall-Cin-Chi ... 5.05
Lush-Phi 4.84

Ratio
Brown-Chi 8.53
Pfiester-Chi 8.94
Sparks-Phi 8.98
Reulbach-Chi 9.66
Ewing-Cin 9.70

Earned Run Average
Brown-Chi 1.04
Pfiester-Chi 1.51
Reulbach-Chi 1.65
Willis-Pit 1.73
Leifield-Pit 1.87

Adjusted ERA
Brown-Chi 253
Pfiester-Chi 174
Reulbach-Chi 159
Willis-Pit 154
Leifield-Pit 143

Opponents' Batting Avg.
Reulbach-Chi ...... .175
Pfiester-Chi .... .194
Brown-Chi .... .202
Beebe-Chi-StL .... .209
Sparks-Phi .... .211

Opponents' On Base Pct.
Brown-Chi .... .252
Sparks-Phi .... .257
Pfiester-Chi ...... .258
Phillippe-Pit ..... .276
Reulbach-Chi ..... .278

Starter Runs
Brown-Chi 48.9
Willis-Pit 31.9
Pfiester-Chi 31.1
Reulbach-Chi 23.6
Leifield-Pit 21.6

Adjusted Starter Runs
Brown-Chi 49.0
Willis-Pit 33.3
Pfiester-Chi 31.3
Reulbach-Chi 23.7
Leifield-Pit 22.7

Clutch Pitching Index
Willis-Pit 139
Lindaman-Bos 126
Brown-Chi 122
Leifield-Pit 120
Lush-Phi 114

Relief Runs
Ferguson-NY 3

Adjusted Relief Runs
Ferguson-NY 1

Relief Ranking
Ferguson-NY 0

Total Pitcher Index
Brown-Chi 6.8
Willis-Pit 4.5
Taylor-StL-Chi 2.9
Weimer-Cin 2.9
Reulbach-Chi 2.8

Total Baseball Ranking
Wagner-Pit 7.3
Brown-Chi 6.8
Devlin-NY 6.5
Willis-Pit 4.5
Lumley-Bro 4.3

May 8 With the A's shorthanded because of injuries, Connie Mack puts pitcher Alvin "Chief" Bender in left field in the sixth inning in a game against the Boston Pilgrims. Bender hits two home runs, both inside the park.

May 17 Ty Cobb's bunt single spoils Rube Waddell's no-hit bid. The Philadelphia A's win 5–0.

May 25 Jesse Tannehill snaps the Boston Pilgrims' 20-game losing streak with a 3–0 win over the White Sox. Both Boston teams will finish last, while both Chicago teams will finish first. It's the first time two cities have had two winners and two cellar-dwellers, and it won't happen again until 1921, when New York has the winners and Philadelphia the cellar-dwellers.

July 5 Jack Coombs, the A's rookie righthander from Colby College, makes his major league debut, blanking Washington 3–0 for the Athletics.

August 2 While the Athletics, crippled by injuries, falter, Doc White launches the White Sox on a 19-game winning streak (longest in AL history) with a 3–0 win over Boston. The streak, interrupted only by a 0–0 tie with New York, catapults Chicago from fourth place to first in 10 days.

August 3 Tom Hughes of the Washington Nationals and Fred Glade of the St. Louis Browns enter the 10th inning with a scoreless tie. Hughes hits a home run for a 1–0 victory, the first pitcher to win a 1–0 extra-inning game with his own home run.

August 18 "Wee Willie" Keeler is struck out for only the second time this season, both times by spitballer Ed Walsh of the White Sox.

August 30 After pitching a shutout in his major league debut, righthander Slow Joe Doyle of the Highlanders becomes the first player to start out with two shutouts when he beats the Nationals 5–0. Of his 23 lifetime victories, seven will be shutouts. He is nicknamed "Slow" because of his time-consuming pace on the mound.

August 31 Beset by injuries, the Tigers call 46-year-old Sam Thompson out of retirement; he drives in two runs in a 5–1 win over the Browns. Thompson last played in the majors in 1898. He appears in eight games and bats .226.

September 1 The Highlanders win their sixth game in three days from Washington, sweeping their third straight doubleheader for an AL record. Three days later, they'll move into first place, sweeping Boston 7–0 and 1–0 for their fifth straight doubleheader sweep, a major league record.

September 1 The AL's longest game on record takes place in Boston. Rookie Jack Coombs and 24-year-old Joe Harris go the route in a 24-inning struggle, ending with a 4–1 Athletics victory after four hours and 47 minutes. Philadelphia's Coombs strikes out 18 and gives up 14 hits. The Pilgrims' Harris fans 14 and yields 16 hits.

September 17 Playing as "Sullivan" to conserve his college eligibility, Columbia University junior Eddie Collins makes his debut at shortstop with the Athletics. He gets one hit off Ed Walsh and strikes out twice. Collins will play 25 years in the major league, bat .333, and become a member of the Hall of Fame.

September 26 The Athletics finally score after being shut out for a major league record 48 consecutive innings, dating back to September 22. Harry Davis breaks the long drought with a two-run double against Cleveland, but the A's still lose 5–3.

October 1 Hugh Jennings resigns as Baltimore manager to take over at Detroit for 1907. Infusing the Tigers with aggressive Baltimore spirit, he will win pennants the next three years, and stay at the helm for 14.

October 14 The Sox jump on Three Finger Brown for seven runs in the first two innings, and coast behind Doc White to a 7–1 Series-ending victory. The Cubs' losers' share is $439.50, the lowest ever. The unlikely hero is reserve third baseman George Rohe, who delivers key hits for the "Hitless Wonders."

BOSTON		CHICAGO		CLEVELAND		DETROIT		NEW YORK		PHILADELPHIA		ST.LOUIS		WASHINGTON	
M	J.Collins	M	F.Jones	M	N.Lajoie	M	B.Armour	M	C.Griffith	M	C.Mack	M	J.McAleer	M	J.Stahl
M	C.Stahl	1B	J.Donahue	1B	C.Rossman	1B	C.Lindsay	1B	H.Chase	1B	H.Davis	1B	T.Jones	1B	J.Stahl
1B	M.Grimshaw	2B	F.Isbell	2B	N.Lajoie	2B	G.Schaefer	2B	J.Williams	2B	D.Murphy	2B	P.O'Brien	2B	L.Schlafly
2B	H.Ferris	SS	G.Davis	SS	T.Turner	SS	C.O'Leary	SS	K.Elberfeld	SS	M.Cross	SS	B.Wallace	SS	D.Altizer
SS	F.Parent	3B	L.Tannehill	3B	B.Bradley	3B	B.Coughlin	3B	F.LaPorte	3B	J.Knight	3B	R.Hartzell	3B	L.Cross
3B	R.Morgan	LF	E.Hahn	LF	J.Jackson	LF	M.McIntyre	LF	W.Conroy	LF	T.Hartsel	LF	G.Stone	LF	J.Anderson
LF	J.Hoey	CF	F.Jones	CF	E.Flick	CF	T.Cobb	CF	D.Hoffman	CF	B.Lord	CF	C.Hemphill	CF	C.Jones
CF	C.Stahl	RF	B.O'Neill	RF	B.Congalton	RF	S.Crawford	RF	W.Keeler	RF	S.Seybold	RF	H.Niles	RF	C.Hickman
RF	J.Hayden	C	B.Sullivan	C	H.Bemis	C	B.Schmidt	C	R.Kleinow	C	O.Schreckengost	C	B.Rickey	C	H.Wakefield
C	C.Armbruster														
		O	P.Dougherty	13	G.Stovall	O	D.Jones	O	F.Delahanty	O	H.Armbruster	C	T.Spencer	S2	R.Nill
O1	B.Freeman	3	G.Rohe	O	H.Bay	CO	F.Payne	3O	D.McGuire	O	D.Powers	O	B.Koehler	O	J.Stanley
O	K.Selbach	2S	G.Dundon	C	N.Clarke	C	J.Warner	S2	J.Yeager	3	R.Oldring	C	J.O'Connor	M	M.Heydon
3S	J.Godwin	C	F.Roth	3	J.Barbeau	S2	B.Lowe	/O	I.Thomas	3	A.Brouthers	2	I.Rockenfield	C	J.Warner
3	J.Collins	O	F.Hemphill	O	B.Caffyn	/O	S.Thompson	S	P.Dougherty		D.Shean	1	L.Nordyke	/C	M.Kittridge
C	B.Peterson	C	H.Hart	C	F.Buelow	/2	F.Scheibeck	C	I.Thomas		S.Nicholls			/S	O.Williams
C	B.Carrigan		B.Towne	/O	J.Birmingham	/3	G.Hetling		E.Hahn		C.Berry			/3	W.Shannabrook
C	C.Graham	/O	R.Vinson		M.Kittridge					/C	J.Byrnes			H	P.Duff
2	C.Chadbourne	/C	E.McFarland	/2	B.Shipke	P	G.Mullin	/O	D.Hoffman						
/2	H.Wagner	/S	L.Quillen			P	R.Donahue	P	A.Orth	/3	E.Lennox	P	H.Howell	P	C.Falkenberg
/C	L.Criger			P	O.Hess	P	E.Siever	P	J.Chesbro	/S	E.Collins	P	F.Glade	P	C.Patten
/C	T.Doran	P	F.Owen	P	B.Rhoads	P	B.Donovan	P	B.Hogg		W.Fetzer	P	B.Pelty	P	C.Smith
		P	N.Altrock	P	A.Joss	P	E.Killian	P	W.Clarkson		J.Hannifin	P	J.Powell	P	T.Hughes
P	C.Young	P	E.Walsh	P	B.Bernhard			H	D.Newton			P	E.Smith	P	F.Kitson
P	J.Harris	P	D.White	P	H.Townsend	P	J.Eubank	C	C.Griffith	P	R.Waddell	P	B.Jacobson		
P	B.Dinneen	P	R.Patterson			/P	E.Willett	/P	S.Doyle	P	C.Bender			/P	C.Goodwin
P	G.Winter			P	H.Eells	/P	J.Wiggs	P	L.LeRoy	P	J.Dygert			/P	H.Hardy
P	J.Tannehill	P	F.Smith	/P	E.Moore	/P	J.Rowan	P	N.Hahn	P	E.Plank			/P	W.Sudhoff
		/P	L.Fiene	/P	G.Liebhardt			/P	T.Hughes	P	J.Coombs			/P	B.Wolfe
P	R.Glaze							/P	C.Barger					/P	B.Edmondson
/P	F.Oberlin									P	A.Coakley			/P	W.Wilson
/P	E.Barry									/P	M.Cunningham			/P	C.Starkel
/P	L.Swormstedt									/P	H.Schumann				
/P	N.Gibson									/P	B.Bartley				
/P	E.Hughes									/P	J.Holmes				
/P	R.Kroh														

TEAM	G	W	L	PCT	GB	R	OR	AB	H	2B	3B	HR	BB	SO	AVG	OBP	SLG	PRO	PRO+	BR	/A	PF	CHI	RC	SB	CS	SBA	SBR
CHI	154	93	58	.616		570	**460**	4925	1133	152	52	7	**453**		.230	.301	.286	.587	91	-47	-33	97	**110**	531	214			
NY	155	90	61	.596	3	644	543	5095	1354	166	**77**	17	331		.266	.316	.339	.655	101	58	-5	110	103	644	192			
CLE	157	89	64	.582	5	**663**	482	5425	**1514**	240	73	12	330		.279	.325	.357	.682	121	111	121	99	93	**735**	203			
PHI	149	78	67	.538	12	561	543	4883	1206	213	49	**32**	385		.247	.308	.330	.638	102	30	12	103	97	581	165			
STL	154	76	73	.510	16	558	498	5030	1244	145	60	20	366		.247	.304	.312	.616	102	-6	18	96	101	579	221			
DET	151	71	78	.477	21	518	599	4930	1195	154	64	10	333		.242	.295	.306	.601	91	-37	-51	103	103	539	206			
WAS	151	55	95	.367	37.5	518	664	4956	1180	144	65	26	306		.238	.289	.309	.598	97	-44	-20	95	103	539	**233**			
BOS	155	49	105	.318	45.5	463	706	5168	1223	160	75	13	298		.237	.284	.304	.588	89	-66	-65	100	93	503	99			
TOT	613						4495	40412	10049	1374	515	137	2802	4561	.249	.303	.318	.621							1533			

TEAM	CG	SH	SV	IP	H	H/G	HR	BB	SO	RAT	ERA	ERA+	OAV	OOB	PR	/A	PF	CPI	FA	E	DP	FW	PW	BW	SBW	DIF
CHI	117	32	3	1375¹	1212	7.9	11	**255**	543	9.8	2.13	119	.239	**.280**	85	63	94	103	.963	243	80	1.8	6.9	-3.6		12.4
NY	99	18	5	1357²	1236	8.2	21	351	605	10.8	2.78	107	.246	.301	-13	28	110	95	.957	272	69	.1	3.1	-.5		11.9
CLE	**133**	27	4	1412²	1197	7.6	16	365	530	10.3	**2.09**	125	.232	.289	94	85	97	110	**.967**	217	111	3.8	9.3	13.3		-14.0
PHI	107	19	4	1322	1135	7.7	**9**	425	749	11.0	2.60	105	.236	.305	13	17	101	98	.956	267	86	-.2	1.9	1.3		2.5
STL	**133**	17	5	1357²	**1132**	7.5	14	314	535	10.0	2.23	116	**.230**	.284	70	54	96	98	.954	290	80	-1.1	5.9	2.0		-5.3
DET	128	7	4	1334¹	1398	9.4	14	389	469	12.4	3.06	90	.272	.330	-55	-43	103	111	.959	260	86	.4	-4.7	-5.6		6.4
WAS	115	13	1	1322²	1331	9.1	15	451	558	12.4	3.25	81	.265	.331	-83	-91	98	102	.955	279	78	-.8	-10.0	-2.2		-7.0
BOS	124	6	**6**	1382	1360	8.9	37	285	549	11.0	3.41	81	.262	.302	-111	-106	102	87	.949	335	84	-3.9	-11.7	-7.1		-5.3
TOT	956	139	32	10864¹		8.3				11.0	2.69		.249	.303					.958	2163	674					

Runs
Flick-Cle 98
Keeler-NY 96
Hartsel-Phi 96
Davis-Phi 94
Stone-StL 91

Hits
Lajoie-Cle 214
Stone-StL 208
Flick-Cle 194
Chase-NY 193
Keeler-NY 180

Doubles
Lajoie-Cle 48
Davis-Phi 42
Flick-Cle 34
Murphy-Phi 28
Turner-Cle 27

Triples
Flick-Cle 22
Stone-StL 20
Crawford-Det 16
Ferris-Bos 13

Home Runs
Davis-Phi 12
Hickman-Was 9
Stone-StL 6
Seybold-Phi 5

Total Bases
Stone-StL 291
Lajoie-Cle 280
Flick-Cle 275
Davis-Phi 253
Chase-NY 236

Runs Batted In
Davis-Phi 96
Lajoie-Cle 91
Davis-Chi 80
Williams-NY 77
Chase-NY 76

Runs Produced
Lajoie-Cle 179
Davis-Phi 178
Chase-NY 160
Flick-Cle 159
Stone-StL 156

Bases On Balls
Hartsel-Phi 88
Jones-Chi 83
E.Hahn-NY-Chi . . . 72
Wallace-StL 58
McIntyre-Det 56

Batting Average
Stone-StL 358
Lajoie-Cle 355
Chase-NY 323
Congalton-Cle 320
Seybold-Phi 316

On Base Percentage
Stone-StL 417
Lajoie-Cle 392
Flick-Cle 372
Hartsel-Phi 363
Davis-Phi 355

Slugging Average
Stone-StL 501
Lajoie-Cle 465
Davis-Phi 459
Flick-Cle 441
Hickman-Was 421

Production
Stone-StL 918
Lajoie-Cle 857
Davis-Phi 815
Flick-Cle 813
Crawford-Det 747

Adjusted Production
Stone-StL 195
Lajoie-Cle 170
Flick-Cle 156
Davis-Phi 150
Hickman-Was 135

Batter Runs
Stone-StL 57.8
Lajoie-Cle 44.9
Flick-Cle 38.4
Davis-Phi 33.1
Seybold-Phi 21.1

Adjusted Batter Runs
Stone-StL 63.2
Lajoie-Cle 46.4
Flick-Cle 39.9
Davis-Phi 30.2
Hemphill-StL 19.7

Clutch Hitting Index
Davis-Chi 154
Coughlin-Det 134
Stahl-Was 133
Wallace-StL 131
Williams-NY 130

Runs Created
Stone-StL 141
Lajoie-Cle 122
Flick-Cle 121
Davis-Phi 101
Chase-NY 95

Total Average
Stone-StL 1.032
Flick-Cle 872
Lajoie-Cle 866
Davis-Phi 846
Hartsel-Phi 753

Stolen Bases
Flick-Cle 39
Anderson-Was 39
Isbell-Chi 37
Altizer-Was 37
Donahue-Chi 36

Stolen Base Average

Stolen Base Runs

Fielding Runs
Tannehill-Chi 39.3
Lajoie-Cle 30.9
Turner-Cle 22.6
Schlafly-Was 14.8
McIntyre-Det 11.9

Total Player Rating
Lajoie-Cle 8.4
Stone-StL 5.9
Turner-Cle 4.6
Schlafly-Was 2.9
Davis-Chi 2.8

Wins
Orth-NY 27
Chesbro-NY 23
Rhoads-Cle 22
Owen-Chi 22

Win Percentage
Plank-Phi 760
White-Chi 750
Joss-Cle 700
Rhoads-Cle 688
Owen-Chi 629

Games
Chesbro-NY 49
Orth-NY 45
Waddell-Phi 43
Hess-Cle 43
Owen-Chi 42

Complete Games
Orth-NY 36
Mullin-Det 35
Hess-Cle 33
Rhoads-Cle 31

Shutouts
Walsh-Chi 10
Joss-Cle 9
Waddell-Phi 8

Saves
Hess-Cle 3
Bender-Phi 3

Innings Pitched
Orth-NY 338.2
Hess-Cle 333.2
Mullin-Det 330.0
Chesbro-NY 325.0
Rhoads-Cle 315.0

Fewest Hits/Game
Pelty-StL 6.53
White-Chi 6.57
Walsh-Chi 6.95
Joss-Cle 7.02
Powell-StL 7.23

Fewest BB/Game
Young-Bos 78
Altrock-Chi 1.31
Joss-Cle 1.37
White-Chi 1.56
Jacobson-StL 1.57

Strikeouts
Waddell-Phi 196
Falkenberg-Was . . . 178
Walsh-Chi 171
Hess-Cle 167
Bender-Phi 159

Strikeouts/Game
Waddell-Phi 6.47
Bender-Phi 6.00
Walsh-Chi 5.53
Falkenberg-Was . . . 5.36
Powell-StL 4.87

Ratio
White-Chi 8.33
Joss-Cle 8.49
Walsh-Chi 9.05
Pelty-StL 9.18
Powell-StL 9.55

Earned Run Average
White-Chi 1.52
Pelty-StL 1.59
Joss-Cle 1.72
Powell-StL 1.77
Rhoads-Cle 1.80

Adjusted ERA
White-Chi 167
Pelty-StL 163
Joss-Cle 152
Powell-StL 146
Rhoads-Cle 145

Opponents' Batting Avg.
Pelty-StL 206
White-Chi 207
Walsh-Chi 217
Joss-Cle 218
Powell-StL 223

Opponents' On Base Pct.
White-Chi 249
Joss-Cle 252
Walsh-Chi 265
Pelty-StL 267
Powell-StL 275

Starter Runs
Pelty-StL 31.9
Hess-Cle 31.7
Rhoads-Cle 31.1
Joss-Cle 30.3
White-Chi 28.6

Adjusted Starter Runs
Hess-Cle 29.0
Pelty-StL 28.8
Rhoads-Cle 28.6
Joss-Cle 28.0
White-Chi 24.9

Clutch Pitching Index
Rhoads-Cle 126
Siever-Det 125
Hess-Cle 124
Smith-Was 121
Donahue-Det 121

Relief Runs

Adjusted Relief Runs

Relief Ranking

Total Pitcher Index
Orth-NY 3.7
Joss-Cle 3.7
White-Chi 3.6
Pelty-StL 3.3
Hess-Cle 3.3

Total Baseball Ranking
Lajoie-Cle 8.4
Stone-StL 5.9
Turner-Cle 4.6
Orth-NY 3.9
Joss-Cle 3.7

January 10 John McGraw stops a runaway team of horses in Los Angeles, saving two young women from injury.

January 28 In an effort to reduce playing-date conflicts between their leagues, presidents Pulliam and Johnson meet to plan schedules. Conflicting dates are reduced to 27.

March 4 A judgment of $52,000 is awarded to the Baltimore club from Brooklyn. When Baltimore left the NL in 1903, Brooklyn agreed to pay $40,000 for the franchise but never did. The award includes interest.

April 11 On a cold day in New York, the Giants open against the Phillies before 16,000. A late snowstorm has been cleared, but there are large piles of snow surrounding the field. Frank Corridon is in the eighth inning of a shutout for the Giants when fans, who have been pelting the players with snowballs, begin jumping from the stands and running around the outfield. There are no police on duty at the park, so umpire Bill Klem forfeits the game 9-0 to the Phils.

April 11 New York catcher Roger Bresnahan appears wearing shin guards for the first time in a major league game, although the Phils' Red Dooin had worn papier-mache guards under his stockings in 1906 while catching and at bat. It will be a few years before detachable guards are adopted by all catchers.

June 19 Miller Huggins, diminutive second baseman of the Reds, leads off a home game against New York with a homer off Christy Mathewson. The rare occurrence (he hits only nine in his career) astonishes the home town fans, and they celebrate by presenting him with a pair of shoes, a gold watch, a five-pound box of chocolates, a scarf pin, and a Morris chair.

July 8 Bombarded by pop bottles in Brooklyn, irate Cubs manager Frank Chance throws one back into the stands where it cuts a boy's leg. Chance is mobbed and leaves the park in an armored car with a police escort after the Cubs' 5–0 victory.

July 23* The Austin Senators (Texas League) steal 23 bases and beat San Antonio 44–0.

July 30 Cincinnati manager Ned Hanlon, whose managing days began in 1889 at Pittsburgh, announces this will be his last season. His record includes five pennants—four at Baltimore, one at Brooklyn.

August 11 In the second game of a doubleheader, shortened to seven innings by prior agreement, St. Louis Cardinal hurler Ed Karger pitches a perfect game, 4–0, against Boston.

September 1 Cubs pitcher Ed Reulbach, who will be 17–4 with a 1.69 ERA, goes into the ninth with a 2–0 lead over the Cardinals at Chicago. He gives up eight straight hits, seven runs, and loses the game.

September 30 Cardinals first baseman Ed Konetchy steals home twice in St. Louis's game against Boston. St. Louis sets a major league one-game record with three steals of home as Joe Delahanty also scores in the eighth.

October 12 Three Finger Brown shuts out the Tigers, 2–0, to give Chicago a world championship. Each side has seven hits, but the Cubs steal four bases, giving them a total of 18 for the five-game series. The Cubs' staff has an ERA for the Series of 0.75, and the Tigers' big guns, Ty Cobb and Sam Crawford, score only one run apiece.

	BOSTON		BROOKLYN		CHICAGO		CINCINNATI		NEW YORK		PHILADELPHIA		PITTSBURGH		ST.LOUIS
M	F.Tenney	M	P.Donovan	M	F.Chance	M	N.Hanlon	M	J.McGraw	M	B.Murray	M	F.Clarke	M	J.McCloskey
1B	F.Tenney	1B	T.Jordan	1B	F.Chance	1B	J.Ganzel	1B	D.McGann	1B	K.Bransfield	1B	J.Nealon	1B	E.Konetchy
2B	C.Ritchey	2B	W.Alperman	2B	J.Evers	2B	M.Huggins	2B	L.Doyle	2B	O.Knabe	2B	E.Abbaticchio	2B	P.Bennett
SS	A.Bridwell	SS	P.Lewis	SS	J.Tinker	SS	H.Lobert	SS	B.Dahlen	SS	M.Doolan	SS	H.Wagner	SS	E.Holly
3B	D.Brain	3B	D.Casey	3B	H.Steinfeldt	3B	M.Mowrey	3B	A.Devlin	3B	E.Courtney	3B	A.Storke	3B	B.Byrne
LF	N.Randall	LF	E.Batch	LF	J.Sheckard	LF	F.Odwell	LF	S.Shannon	LF	S.Magee	LF	F.Clarke	LF	R.Murray
CF	G.Beaumont	CF	B.Maloney	CF	J.Slagle	CF	A.Kruger	CF	C.Seymour	CF	R.Thomas	CF	T.Leach	CF	S.Barry
RF	J.Bates	RF	H.Lumley	RF	F.Schulte	RF	M.Mitchell	RF	G.Browne	RF	J.Titus	RF	G.Anderson	RF	S.Barry
C	T.Needham	C	L.Ritter	C	J.Kling	C	L.McLean	C	R.Bresnahan	C	R.Dooin	C	G.Gibson	C	D.Marshall
C	S.Brown	2O	J.Hummel	OS	S.Hofman	C1	L.Davis	F.Bowerman	3	E.Grant	O	B.Hallman	21	A.Hoelskoetter
3S	B.Sweeney	C	B.Bergen	C	P.Moran	O3	J.Kane	O2	S.Strang	C	F.Jacklitsch	3S	T.Sheehan	O	P.Noonan
O	D.Howard	O	A.Burch	1	D.Howard	C	A.Schlei	2	T.Corcoran	O	F.Osborn	C	E.Phelps	O	J.Kelly
O	F.Burke	O	J.McCarthy	O	N.Randall	O	D.Paskert	13	J.Hannifin	2	K.Gleason	1	H.Swacina	O	T.O'Hara
O	I.Hoffman	C	J.Butler	/C	M.Kahoe	/O	M.O'Neill	2	D.Shay	/S	P.Sentell	O	O.Clymer	O	A.Burch
C	J.Ball	/C	J.Hurley	/S	B.Sweeney	/O	C.Autry	1	F.Merkle			O	D.Moeller	1	J.Beckley
/C	J.Orndorff	/O	E.McLane	/2	H.Zimmerman	/O	H.Wolter	/C	M.Fitzgerald	P	F.Corridon	C	H.Smith	O	H.Wolter
/C	J.Knotts	/O	P.Donovan	/C	J.Hardy	/C	B.McCarthy	/C	H.Curtis	P	T.Sparks	/3	B.McKechnie	O	B.Hopkins
/S	O.Westerberg					/C	P.Lamer	/1	M.Pfyl	P	L.Moren	/O	H.Maggert	/1	H.Arndt
/C	T.Asmussen	P	N.Rucker	P	O.Overall	H	E.Tiemeyer	/O	H.Wade	P	B.Brown	/C	B.Kelsey	/O	A.Shaw
/1	B.Brush	P	G.Bell	P	M.Brown					P	L.Richie	/S	M.Campbell	/O	F.Crawford
		P	E.Stricklett	P	C.Lundgren	P	B.Ewing	P	C.Mathewson					/O	J.Delahanty
P	G.Dorner	P	J.Pastorius	P	J.Pfiester	P	A.Coakley	P	J.McGinnity	P	T.Pittinger	P	V.Willis	/1	J.Baxter
P	V.Lindaman	P	H.McIntire	P	E.Reulbach	P	J.Weimer	P	R.Ames	/P	J.Lush	P	L.Leifield		
P	I.Young					P	R.Hitt	P	H.Wiltse	/P	G.McQuillan	P	S.Leever	P	S.McGlynn
P	P.Flaherty	P	D.Scanlan	P	C.Fraser	P	D.Mason	P	D.Taylor	/P	B.Duggleby	P	D.Phillippe	P	E.Karger
P	B.Pfeffer	/P	W.Henley	P	J.Taylor					/P	H.Coveleski	P	H.Camnitz	P	F.Beebe
		/P	J.Whiting	/P	K.Durbin	P	F.Smith	P	M.Lynch	/P	J.McCloskey			P	A.Fromme
P	J.Boultes					P	C.Hall	P	G.Ferguson			/P	N.Maddox	P	J.Lush
/P	S.Frock					/P	B.Spade	/P	R.Beecher			/P	B.Duggleby		
/P	F.Barberich					/P	B.Essick	/P	H.Mathewson			/P	M.Lynch	/P	B.Raymond
/P	R.Dessau					/P	B.Campbell					/P	B.Adams	/P	B.Brown
/P	E.Lindemann					/P	C.Minahan					/P	B.Otey	/P	C.Shields
						/P	F.Leary					/P	K.Brady	/P	C.Druhot
												/P	H.Wolter		
												/P	C.Walsh		

TEAM	G	W	L	PCT	GB	R	OR	AB	H	2B	3B	HR	BB	SO	AVG	OBP	SLG	PRO	PRO+	BR	/A	PF	CHI	RC	SB	CS	SBA	SBR
CHI	155	107	45	.704		574	390	4892	1224	162	48	13	435		.250	.318	.311	.629	98	25	-10	106	104	596	235			
PIT	157	91	63	.591	17	634	510	4957	1261	133	78	19	469		.254	.325	.324	.649	109	62	54	101	106	645	264			
PHI	149	83	64	.565	21.5	512	476	4725	1113	162	65	12	424		.236	.304	.305	.609	99	-11	-4	99	104	514	154			
NY	155	82	71	.536	25.5	574	510	4874	1222	160	48	23	516		.251	.331	.317	.648	107	68	49	103	96	617	205			
BRO	153	65	83	.439	40	446	522	4895	1135	142	63	18	336		.232	.287	.298	.585	98	-62	-26	92	98	488	121			
CIN	156	66	87	.431	41.5	526	519	4966	1226	126	90	15	372		.247	.304	.318	.622	98	3	-19	104	99	564	158			
BOS	152	58	90	.392	47	502	652	5020	1222	142	61	22	413		.243	.308	.309	.617	100	2	4	100	94	545	118			
STL	155	52	101	.340	55.5	419	608	5008	1163	121	51	19	312		.232	.283	.288	.571	88	-87	-73	97	97	474	125			
TOT	616					4187		39337	9566	1148	504	141	3277	4217	.243	.308	.309	.616						1380				

TEAM	CG	SH	SV	IP	H	H/G	HR	BB	SO	RAT	ERA	ERA+	OAV	OOB	PR	/A	PF	CPI	FA	E	DP	FW	PW	BW	SBW	DIF
CHI	114	32	8	1373[1]	1054	6.9	11	402	586	9.8	1.73	144	.216	.281	112	115	101	101	.967	211	110	3.1	13.1	-1.1		16.0
PIT	111	24	5	1363	1207	8.0	12	368	497	10.7	2.30	106	.241	.299	25	19	99	99	.959	256	75	.2	2.2	6.1		5.5
PHI	110	21	4	1299[1]	1095	7.6	13	422	499	10.9	2.43	99	.233	.304	5	-3	98	94	.957	256	104	-.7	-.3	-.5		11.0
NY	109	22	13	1371	1219	8.0	25	369	655	10.7	2.45	101	.238	.294	2	1	100	90	.963	232	75	1.6	.1	5.6		-1.8
BRO	125	20	1	1356[1]	1218	8.1	16	463	479	11.4	2.38	98	.249	.319	12	-9	95	113	.959	262	94	-.7	-1.0	-3.0		-4.4
CIN	118	10	2	1351[1]	1223	8.1	16	444	481	11.5	2.41	107	.251	.322	8	25	105	114	.963	227	118	2.1	2.8	-2.2		-13.3
BOS	121	9	2	1338[2]	1324	8.9	28	426	426	12.4	3.33	76	.268	.339	-129	-119	103	98	.961	249	128	.1	-13.5	.5		-3.1
STL	127	19	2	1365[2]	1212	8.0	20	500	594	11.6	2.70	93	.243	.318	-35	-32	101	97	.948	340	105	-5.8	-3.6	-8.3		-6.8
TOT	935	157	37	10818[2]		7.9				11.1	2.46		.243	.308					.960	2033	809					

Runs
Shannon-NY 104
Leach-Pit 102
Wagner-Pit 98
Clarke-Pit 97
Tenney-Bos 83

Hits
Beaumont-Bos 187
Wagner-Pit 180
Leach-Pit 166
Magee-Phi 165
Mitchell-Cin 163

Doubles
Wagner-Pit 38
Magee-Phi 28
Steinfeldt-Chi 25
Seymour-NY 25
Brain-Bos 24

Triples
Ganzel-Cin 16
Alperman-Bro 16
Wagner-Pit 14
Beaumont-Bos 14
Clarke-Pit 13

Home Runs
Brain-Bos 10
Lumley-Bro 9
Murray-StL 7
Wagner-Pit 6
Browne-NY 5

Total Bases
Wagner-Pit 264
Beaumont-Bos 246
Magee-Phi 229
Leach-Pit 221
Brain-Bos 214

Runs Batted In
Magee-Phi 85
Wagner-Pit 82
Abbaticchio-Pit . . . 82
Seymour-NY 75
Steinfeldt-Chi 70

Runs Produced
Wagner-Pit 174
Magee-Phi 156
Clarke-Pit 154
Abbaticchio-Pit . . . 143
Leach-Pit 141

Bases On Balls
Thomas-Phi 83
Huggins-Cin 83
Tenney-Bos 82
Shannon-NY 82
Anderson-Pit 80

Batting Average
Wagner-Pit 350
Magee-Phi 328
Beaumont-Bos 322
Leach-Pit 303
Seymour-NY 294

On Base Percentage
Wagner-Pit 408
Magee-Phi 396
Clarke-Pit 383
Devlin-NY 376
Thomas-Phi 374

Slugging Average
Wagner-Pit 513
Magee-Phi 455
Lumley-Bro 425
Beaumont-Bos 424
Brain-Bos 420

Production
Wagner-Pit 921
Magee-Phi 852
Beaumont-Bos 790
Clarke-Pit 772
Leach-Pit 756

Adjusted Production
Wagner-Pit 186
Magee-Phi 169
Beaumont-Bos . . . 148
Lumley-Bro 144
Jordan-Bro 141

Batter Runs
Wagner-Pit 50.5
Magee-Phi 38.4
Beaumont-Bos . . 29.5
Clarke-Pit 26.5
Leach-Pit 21.4

Adjusted Batter Runs
Wagner-Pit 49.1
Magee-Phi 39.8
Beaumont-Bos . . 29.8
Clarke-Pit 25.4
Jordan-Bro 25.3

Clutch Hitting Index
Abbaticchio-Pit . . 166
Seymour-NY 130
Steinfeldt-Chi . . . 130
Devlin-NY 126
Magee-Phi 121

Runs Created
Wagner-Pit 137
Magee-Phi 113
Beaumont-Bos . . . 103
Leach-Pit 98
Clarke-Pit 93

Total Average
Wagner-Pit 1.122
Magee-Phi 982
Clarke-Pit 865
Leach-Pit 801
Beaumont-Bos . . .791

Stolen Bases
Wagner-Pit 61
Magee-Phi 46
Evers-Chi 46
Leach-Pit 43
Devlin-NY 38

Fielding Runs
Evers-Chi 27.7
Brain-Bos 24.8
Mitchell-Cin 22.2
Byrne-StL 22.1
Tinker-Chi 15.7

Total Player Rating
Wagner-Pit 6.3
Brain-Bos 5.0
Magee-Phi 4.6
Beaumont-Bos . . . 3.2
Mitchell-Cin 3.2

Wins
Mathewson-NY 24
Overall-Chi 23
Sparks-Phi 22
Willis-Pit 21

Win Percentage
Reulbach-Chi 810
Brown-Chi 769
Overall-Chi 767
Sparks-Phi 733
Lundgren-Chi 720

Games
McGinnity-NY 47
McGlynn-StL 45
Mathewson-NY . . . 41
Ewing-Cin 41

Complete Games
McGlynn-StL 33
Ewing-Cin 32
Mathewson-NY . . . 31
Karger-StL 29
Willis-Pit 27

Shutouts
Overall-Chi 8
Mathewson-NY . . . 8
Lundgren-Chi 7

Saves
McGinnity-NY 4
Overall-Chi 3
Brown-Chi 3

Innings Pitched
McGlynn-StL 352.1
Ewing-Cin 332.2
Mathewson-NY . . . 315.0
Karger-StL 314.0
McGinnity-NY 310.1

Fewest Hits/Game
Lundgren-Chi 5.65
Pfiester-Chi 6.60
Overall-Chi 6.74
Camnitz-Pit 6.75
Reulbach-Chi 6.89

Fewest BB/Game
Phillippe-Pit 1.51
Mathewson-NY . . . 1.51
Brown-Chi 1.55
McGinnity-NY 1.68
Sparks-Phi 1.73

Strikeouts
Mathewson-NY . . . 178
Ewing-Cin 147
Ames-NY 146
Overall-Chi 141
Beebe-StL 141

Strikeouts/Game
Ames-NY 5.63
Beebe-StL 5.32
Mathewson-NY . . . 5.09
Overall-Chi 4.73
Reulbach-Chi 4.50

Ratio
Mathewson-NY . . . 8.71
Brown-Chi 8.73
Pfiester-Chi 9.05
Overall-Chi 9.42
Sparks-Phi 9.48

Earned Run Average
Pfiester-Chi 1.15
Lundgren-Chi 1.17
Brown-Chi 1.39
Leever-Pit 1.66
Overall-Chi 1.68

Adjusted ERA
Pfiester-Chi 215
Lundgren-Chi 212
Brown-Chi 179
Ewing-Cin 149
Overall-Chi 148

Opponents' Batting Avg.
Lundgren-Chi 185
Pfiester-Chi 207
Overall-Chi 208
Camnitz-Pit 211
Mathewson-NY . . .212

Opponents' On Base Pct.
Mathewson-NY . . .247
Brown-Chi 262
Pfiester-Chi 263
Overall-Chi 268
Karger-StL 270

Starter Runs
Lundgren-Chi . . . 29.7
Pfiester-Chi 28.4
Brown-Chi 27.8
Ewing-Cin 27.1
Overall-Chi 23.5

Adjusted Starter Runs
Ewing-Cin 31.6
Lundgren-Chi . . . 30.2
Pfiester-Chi 28.9
Brown-Chi 28.4
Overall-Chi 24.1

Clutch Pitching Index
Coakley-Cin 133
Pastorius-Bro 129
Brown-StL-Phi . . . 126
McIntire-Bro 125
Leifield-Pit 122

Relief Runs

Adjusted Relief Runs

Relief Ranking

Total Pitcher Index
Brown-Chi 4.0
Lundgren-Chi 3.6
Overall-Chi 3.5
Pfiester-Chi 3.1
Ewing-Cin 2.9

Total Baseball Ranking
Wagner-Pit 6.3
Brain-Bos 5.0
Magee-Phi 4.6
Brown-Chi 3.9
Lundgren-Chi 3.6

March 28 Boston outfielder Chick Stahl, who replaced Jimmy Collins as manager of the newly renamed Red Sox at the end of the 1906 season, commits suicide at spring training. After breakfast he returned to his room and drank four ounces of carbolic acid. He left a note: "Boys, I just couldn't help it. You drove me to it." Cy Young starts the season as manager, but there will be three others during the year.

April 15 The Cleveland club takes out a $100,000 policy to insure its players against injury in railroad accidents.

April 19 Ed Walsh has his sinker working as he fields 11 assists and two putouts during a 1–0 win over the Browns. His total of 13 chances ties the mark Nick Altrock set in 1904.

May 14 The flagpole at the White Sox ballpark, South Side Park, breaks during the pennant-raising ceremonies celebrating the 1906 championship.

June 13 The Boston Red Sox play an exhibition game at Providence, raising $3,140.50 for Chick Stahl's widow.

June 28 Washington steals a record 13 bases off catcher Branch Rickey in the Nationals' 16-5 win over New York. Rickey will spend the rest of the season in the outfield or at first base for the Highlanders.

July 16 Ed Walsh sets another fielding record for pitchers, handling 12 assists and three putouts in a 13-inning game.

August 2 Walter Johnson, 19, debuts with Washington and loses 3-2 to Detroit. The first hit off him is a bunt single by Ty Cobb.

August 15 Chief Bender wins his eleventh straight for the Athletics 4–2 over Cleveland, to tighten the race with the Tigers.

September 4 For his 32nd birthday tomorrow, Cleveland fans give manager Nap Lajoie a wagonload of gifts, including a live black sheep. Addie Joss pitches a one-hitter against Detroit.

September 30 An overflow crowd lines the outfield at Philadelphia's Columbia Park for the showdown doubleheader between the A's and Tigers, who are neck-and-neck in the pennant race. In the first game, the home team gets off to a 7-1 lead against 25-game winner Bill Donovan. But Rube Waddell, who relieves in the second, fails to hold the lead. A two-run home run by Ty Cobb ties it 8-8 in the ninth. Both teams score once in the eleventh; an umpire's ruling costs Philadelphia the game in the fourteenth. Harry Davis hits a long fly into the crowd in left center field, ordinarily a ground rule double. As Tiger center fielder Sam Crawford goes to the crowd's edge, a policeman stands up and moves, either to interfere or to get out of the way. Home plate umpire Silk O'Loughlin says there is no interference, then reverses his ruling when base umpire Tom Connolly offers a different opinion. When play resumes, the Athletics' Danny Murphy hits a long single that would have scored Davis. The game is called because of darkness in the seventeenth, a 9-9 tie. The second game is never played. The Tigers, in first place, leave for Washington where they will win 4. They will finish 1½ games in front.

October 2 Ty Cobb's 200th hit earns him a $500 bonus; he will wind up with 212 for the year.

October 8 With two out in the bottom of the ninth and the Tigers leading the Cubs 3-2, Chicago pinch hitter Del Howard strikes out, but Detroit catcher Charlie "Boss" Schmidt drops the third strike, and the tying run scores. The game will eventually be called because of darkness, a 12-inning 3-3 tie.

BOSTON	CHICAGO	CLEVELAND	DETROIT	NEW YORK	PHILADELPHIA	ST.LOUIS	WASHINGTON
M C.Young	M F.Jones	M N.Lajoie	M H.Jennings	M C.Griffith	M C.Mack	M J.McAleer	M J.Cantillon
M G.Huff	1B J.Donahue	1B G.Stovall	1B C.Rossman	1B H.Chase	1B H.Davis	1B T.Jones	1B J.Anderson
M B.Unglaub	2B F.Isbell	2B N.Lajoie	2B R.Downs	2B J.Williams	2B D.Murphy	2B H.Niles	2B J.Delahanty
M D.McGuire	SS G.Davis	SS T.Turner	SS C.O'Leary	SS K.Elberfeld	SS S.Nicholls	SS B.Wallace	SS D.Altizer
1B B.Unglaub	3B G.Rohe	3B B.Bradley	3B B.Coughlin	3B G.Moriarty	3B J.Collins	3B J.Yeager	3B B.Shipke
2B H.Ferris	LF P.Dougherty	LF B.Hinchman	LF D.Jones	LF W.Conroy	LF T.Hartsel	LF G.Stone	LF O.Clymer
SS H.Wagner	CF F.Jones	CF J.Birmingham	CF S.Crawford	CF D.Hoffman	CF R.Oldring	CF C.Hemphill	CF C.Jones
3B J.Knight	RF E.Hahn	RF E.Flick	RF T.Cobb	RF W.Keeler	RF S.Seybold	RF O.Pickering	RF B.Ganley
LF J.Barrett	C B.Sullivan	C N.Clarke	C B.Schmidt	C R.Kleinow	C O.Schreckengost	C T.Spencer	C J.Warner
CF D.Sullivan							
RF B.Congalton	3 L.Quillen	C H.Bemis	2S G.Schaefer	3O F.LaPorte	S M.Cross	32 R.Hartzell	2O R.Nill
C L.Criger	C E.McFarland	23 P.O'Brien	C F.Payne	C I.Thomas	O B.Lord	C J.Stephens	1O C.Hickman
	3 L.Tannehill	O H.Bay	O M.McIntyre	OC B.Rickey	3 D.Powers	3 J.Delahanty	O C.Milan
OS F.Parent	C H.Hart	1 P.Lister	C J.Archer	O R.Bell	3 J.Knight	C J.O'Connor	C M.Heydon
C A.Shaw	O M.Welday	O F.Delahanty	3 B.Lowe	S N.Ball	/S E.Collins	3 F.Buelow	3 L.Cross
1O M.Grimshaw	/O C.Hickman	2 H.Hinchman	C T.Erwin	/C W.Blair	/C C.Berry	2 K.Butler	2S N.Perrine
3 J.Collins	/3 J.Atz	/3 R.Nill	/2 H.Jennings	/3 B.Louden		H E.Frisk	S T.Smith
O J.Hoey	/C C.Armbruster	C H.Wakefield	/O R.Killefer	/C D.McGuire		R J.McAleer	3S P.O'Brien
C C.Armbruster		/O B.Congalton			P E.Plank		C C.Blankenship
O C.Chadbourne	P E.Walsh	P A.Joss	P G.Mullin	P A.Orth	P R.Waddell	P H.Howell	2 L.Schlafly
3 H.Lord	P F.Smith	P G.Liebhardt	P E.Killian	P J.Chesbro	P J.Dygert	P B.Pelty	O B.Kay
/O T.Speaker	P D.White	P B.Rhoads	P E.Siever	P S.Doyle	P C.Bender	P J.Powell	C B.Block
/C B.Peterson	P N.Altrock	P J.Thielman	P B.Donovan	P B.Hogg	P J.Coombs	P F.Glade	C M.Kahoe
/O B.Freeman	P R.Patterson	P O.Hess	P J.Eubank	P D.Newton	P B.Bartley	P B.Dinneen	/C O.Shannon
/O G.Whiteman	P F.Owen	P W.Clarkson	P E.Willett	P E.Moore	P R.Vickers	/P B.Jacobson	P C.Smith
H D.McGuire	/P L.Fiene	P H.Berger	/P E.Jones	/P F.Kitson	/P C.Fritz	/P C.Morgan	P C.Patten
		/P B.Bernhard	/P H.Malloy	/P B.Keefe	/P G.Craig	/P B.Bailey	P C.Falkenberg
P C.Young		/P E.Moore		/P T.Neuer	/P S.Hope	/P B.McGill	P T.Hughes
P G.Winter				/P L.Brockett			P W.Johnson
P R.Glaze				/P T.Hughes			
P T.Pruiett				/P R.Tift			P O.Graham
P J.Tannehill				/P W.Clarkson			P H.Gehring
				/P R.Castleton			/P F.Oberlin
P C.Morgan				/P R.Manning			/P F.Kitson
P J.Harris				/C C.Griffith			/P S.Lanford
P F.Oberlin				/P C.Barger			/P J.McDonald
/P R.Kroh							/P B.Durham
/P B.Dinneen							/P S.Edmonston
/P E.Barry							/P D.Tonkin
/P E.Steele							
/P F.Burchell							
/P B.Jacobson							

TEAM	G	W	L	PCT	GB	R	OR	AB	H	2B	3B	HR	BB	SO	AVG	OBP	SLG	PRO	PRO+	BR	/A	PF	CHI	RC	SB	CS	SBA	SBR
DET	153	92	58	.613		694	532	5204	1383	179	75	11	315		.266	.313	.335	.648	108	63	40	104	110	641	192			
PHI	150	88	57	.607	1.5	582	511	5010	1276	220	44	22	384		.255	.311	.329	.640	106	51	36	102	96	592	137			
CHI	157	87	64	.576	5.5	588	474	5070	1205	149	33	5	421		.238	.302	.283	.585	95	-37	-19	97	111	523	175			
CLE	158	85	67	.559	8	530	525	5068	1221	182	68	11	335		.241	.295	.310	.605	97	-12	-16	101	97	555	193			
NY	152	70	78	.473	21	605	665	5044	1258	150	67	15	304		.249	.299	.315	.614	93	1	-44	108	110	565	206			
STL	155	69	83	.454	24	542	555	5224	1324	154	63	10	370		.253	.308	.313	.621	103	18	20	100	91	580	144			
BOS	155	59	90	.396	32.5	464	558	5235	1224	154	48	18	305		.234	.281	.292	.573	89	-76	-72	99	94	493	125			
WAS	154	49	102	.325	43.5	506	691	5112	1243	134	57	12	390		.243	.304	.299	.603	105	-9	34	92	91	563	223			
TOT	617					4511		40967	10134	1322	455	104	2824	4479	.247	.302	.309	.611						1395				

TEAM	CG	SH	SV	IP	H	H/G	HR	BB	SO	RAT	ERA	ERA+	OAV	OOB	PR	/A	PF	CPI	FA	E	DP	FW	PW	BW	SBW	DIF
DET	120	15	7	1370²	1281	8.4	8	380	512	11.2	2.33	112	.251	.309	32	40	102	114	.959	260	79	1.0	4.4	4.4		7.2
PHI	106	27	6	1354²	1106	7.3	13	378	789	10.3	2.35	111	.226	.290	29	38	102	91	.958	263	67	.4	4.2	4.0		7.0
CHI	112	17	9	1406¹	1279	8.2	13	305	604	10.3	2.22	108	.245	.290	50	26	94	105	.966	233	101	3.4	2.9	-2.1		7.4
CLE	127	20	5	1392²	1253	8.1	8	362	513	10.8	2.26	111	.244	.300	43	36	99	108	.960	264	137	1.3	4.0	-1.8		5.5
NY	93	10	5	1333²	1327	9.0	13	428	511	12.2	3.03	92	.262	.325	-73	-35	110	102	.947	334	79	-4.4	-3.9	-4.9		9.1
STL	129	15	9	1381¹	1254	8.2	17	352	463	10.8	2.61	96	.245	.300	-10	-16	99	96	.959	266	97	.8	-1.8	2.2		-8.2
BOS	100	17	7	1414	1222	7.8	22	337	517	10.2	2.45	105	.236	.288	14	18	101	92	.959	274	100	.2	2.0	-8.0		-9.8
WAS	106	12	5	1351¹	1383	9.2	10	344	570	11.8	3.11	78	.268	.320	-86	-106	95	97	.951	310	69	-2.4	-11.7	3.8		-16.1
TOT	893	133	53	11004²		8.3				10.9	2.54		.247	.302					.958	2204	729					

Runs
Crawford-Det 102
D.Jones-Det 101
Cobb-Det 97
Hartsel-Phi 93
Hahn-Chi 87

Hits
Cobb-Det 212
Stone-StL 191
Crawford-Det 188
Ganley-Was 167
Flick-Cle 166

Doubles
Davis-Phi 35
Crawford-Det 34
Lajoie-Cle 30
J.Collins-Bos-Phi 29
Seybold-Phi 29

Triples
Flick-Cle 18
Crawford-Det 17
Cobb-Det 14
Unglaub-Bos 13

Home Runs
Davis-Phi 8
Seybold-Phi 5
Hoffman-NY 5
Cobb-Det 5

Total Bases
Cobb-Det 283
Crawford-Det 268
Stone-StL 238
Davis-Phi 230
Flick-Cle 226

Runs Batted In
Cobb-Det 119
Seybold-Phi 92
Davis-Phi 87
Crawford-Det 81
Wallace-StL 70

Runs Produced
Cobb-Det 211
Crawford-Det 179
Davis-Phi 163
Seybold-Phi 145
Donahue-Chi 143

Bases On Balls
Hartsel-Phi 106
Hahn-Chi 84
Jones-Chi 67
Flick-Cle 64
D.Jones-Det 60

Batting Average
Cobb-Det 350
Crawford-Det 323
Stone-StL 320
Flick-Cle 302
Nicholls-Phi 302

On Base Percentage
Hartsel-Phi 405
Stone-StL 387
Flick-Cle 386
Cobb-Det 380
Crawford-Det 366

Slugging Average
Cobb-Det 468
Crawford-Det 460
Flick-Cle 412
Stone-StL 399
Davis-Phi 395

Production
Cobb-Det 848
Crawford-Det 826
Flick-Cle 798
Stone-StL 787
Hartsel-Phi 771

Adjusted Production
Cobb-Det 164
Crawford-Det 157
Flick-Cle 153
Stone-StL 151
Hartsel-Phi 143

Batter Runs
Cobb-Det 44.2
Crawford-Det 38.6
Flick-Cle 35.7
Stone-StL 35.4
Hartsel-Phi 33.0

Adjusted Batter Runs
Cobb-Det 40.4
Stone-StL 35.7
Crawford-Det 35.0
Flick-Cle 34.9
Hartsel-Phi 30.7

Clutch Hitting Index
Seybold-Phi 150
Cobb-Det 143
Donahue-Chi 134
Chase-NY 133
Wallace-StL 133

Runs Created
Cobb-Det 130
Crawford-Det 108
Flick-Cle 107
Stone-StL 105
Hartsel-Phi 87

Total Average
Cobb-Det 919
Flick-Cle 893
Hartsel-Phi 855
Crawford-Det 825
Stone-StL 805

Stolen Bases
Cobb-Det 49
Flick-Cle 41
Conroy-NY 41
Ganley-Was 40
Altizer-Was 38

Stolen Base Average

Stolen Base Runs

Fielding Runs
Lajoie-Cle 45.9
Donahue-Chi 20.6
Murphy-Phi 13.5
Ferris-Bos 13.4
D.Jones-Det 13.2

Total Player Rating
Lajoie-Cle 6.7
Cobb-Det 5.0
Crawford-Det 4.1
Flick-Cle 3.3
Stone-StL 2.9

Wins
White-Chi 27
Joss-Cle 27
Killian-Det 25
Donovan-Det 25

Win Percentage
Donovan-Det 862
Dygert-Phi 724
Joss-Cle 711
Smith-Chi 697
White-Chi 675

Games
Walsh-Chi 56
White-Chi 46
Mullin-Det 46
Waddell-Phi 44

Complete Games
Walsh-Chi 37
Mullin-Det 35
Joss-Cle 34
Young-Bos 33
Plank-Phi 33

Shutouts
Plank-Phi 8
Waddell-Phi 7
Young-Bos 6
White-Chi 6
Joss-Cle 6

Saves
Dinneen-Bos-StL 4
Walsh-Chi 4
Hughes-Was 4

Innings Pitched
Walsh-Chi 422.1
Mullin-Det 357.1
Plank-Phi 343.2
Young-Bos 343.1
Joss-Cle 338.2

Fewest Hits/Game
Dygert-Phi 6.88
Winter-Bos 6.94
Walsh-Chi 7.27
Howell-StL 7.34
Donovan-Det 7.37

Fewest BB/Game
White-Chi 1.18
Altrock-Chi 1.31
Young-Bos 1.34
Bender-Phi 1.40
Joss-Cle 1.44

Strikeouts
Waddell-Phi 232
Walsh-Chi 206
Plank-Phi 183
Dygert-Phi 151
Young-Bos 147

Strikeouts/Game
Waddell-Phi 7.33
Dygert-Phi 5.19
Plank-Phi 4.79
Bender-Phi 4.60
Walsh-Chi 4.39

Ratio
Young-Bos 9.02
Joss-Cle 9.04
Bender-Phi 9.11
Winter-Bos 9.19
Walsh-Chi 9.29

Earned Run Average
Walsh-Chi 1.60
Killian-Det 1.78
Joss-Cle 1.83
Howell-StL 1.93
Young-Bos 1.99

Adjusted ERA
Walsh-Chi 150
Killian-Det 146
Joss-Cle 136
Howell-StL 130
Young-Bos 129

Opponents' Batting Avg.
Dygert-Phi 214
Winter-Bos 216
Walsh-Chi 224
Howell-StL 225
Donovan-Det 226

Opponents' On Base Pct.
Young-Bos 263
Joss-Cle 264
Bender-Phi 265
Winter-Bos 267
Walsh-Chi 269

Starter Runs
Walsh-Chi 44.2
Killian-Det 26.6
Joss-Cle 26.6
Howell-StL 21.3
Young-Bos 20.9

Adjusted Starter Runs
Walsh-Chi 37.3
Killian-Det 28.8
Joss-Cle 25.2
Young-Bos 22.1
Howell-StL 20.2

Clutch Pitching Index
Killian-Det 144
Hogg-NY 125
Liebhardt-Cle 125
Rhoads-Cle 119
Walsh-Chi 112

Relief Runs

Adjusted Relief Runs

Relief Ranking

Total Pitcher Index
Walsh-Chi 6.4
Killian-Det 4.7
Howell-StL 3.7
Joss-Cle 3.4
Plank-Phi 1.9

Total Baseball Ranking
Lajoie-Cle 6.7
Walsh-Chi 6.4
Cobb-Det 5.0
Killian-Det 4.8
Crawford-Det 4.1

March 16 Pittsburgh's Honus Wagner, 34, announces his retirement. An annual rite of spring, it will not keep him from playing in 151 games, more than in any of the past 10 years, and leading the league in hitting (for the sixth time), hits, total bases, doubles, triples, RBI, and stolen bases. He will miss the Triple Crown by hitting two fewer homers than Tim Jordan's 12.

August 21 Nationals catcher Gabby Street stands at the base of the Washington Monument and catches the thirteenth ball dropped from the top, 555 feet up, duplicating the feat performed by Pop Schriver of the Chicago Colts on August 24, 1894.

September 4 In a game whose significance will not be recognized until three weeks later, the Pirates and Cubs are tied 0-0 in the last of the 10th at Pittsburgh. With two outs and the bases loaded, Pittsburgh's Owen Wilson singles to center field, scoring Fred Clarke with the winning run. Warren Gill, on first base, does not get to second base but stops short, turns, and heads for the dugout, a common practice. The Cubs' Johnny Evers calls for the ball from Jimmy Slagle, touches second base, and claims the run does not count as Gill has been forced. The lone umpire, Hank O'Day, has left the field. When queried, he rules that Clarke had already scored, so the run counts. The Cubs protest to league president Pulliam, but are denied. This is the first time the Cubs try this tactic, but not the last.

September 23 Giants pitcher Mathewson and Cubs pitcher Three Finger Brown battle in the most controversial game ever played. The score is 1-1, with two outs in the last of the ninth. The Giants' Harry McCormick is on third base, and Fred Merkle (19, who is subbing for the sore-legged veteran Fred Tenney) on first. Al Bridwell singles, scoring McCormick. Halfway to second base, Merkle turns and heads for the clubhouse in center field. Johnny Evers secures a ball (Joe McGinnity swears *he* picked up the ball that was in play and threw it into the stands) and touches second as the crowd overruns the field. Umpire O'Day at first base claims he didn't see the play, but that evening he rules the run does not count, and the game ended with a tie score. (Years later, in an interview, Merkle will describe it this way: "When Bridwell shot that long single, I started across the grass for the clubhouse. Matty was near me. When Evers began shouting for the ball, he noticed something was wrong. Matty caught me by the arm and told me to wait a minute. We walked over toward second base, and Matty spoke to Emslie. 'How about this, Bob, is there any trouble with the score of the play?' 'It's all right,' said Emslie. 'You've got the game. I don't see anything wrong with the play.' Matty then took me by the arm and we walked to the clubhouse confident that we had won the game.")

September 24 NL president Henry Pulliam upholds O'Day's delayed decision and declares the game a tie, a decision nobody likes. The Cubs demand the game be forfeited to them as the crowd prevented play from continuing, although darkness would have soon ended it. Both teams appeal. Pulliam sees no inconsistency with the September 4 incident and claims he has merely upheld his umpire on a question of fact in each case.

October 4 The Cubs and Pirates play their last game of the year before 30,247, the largest crowd ever at West Side Park. The Cubs win 5-2. Then they await the results of the three Giants games with Boston. In downtown Pittsburgh, 50,000 people watch the progress of the Cubs game on temporary scoreboards. Fans fill New York's Polo Grounds to watch the action in the same way. Men with megaphones announce each pitch.

October 8 Later admitting he had nothing on the ball, Christy Mathewson loses to the Cubs 4-2 in the playoff replay of the disputed September 23 game. Three Finger Brown, relieving Jack Pfiester in the first, gets the win. The Giants played to a record 910,000 in attendance for the year, a figure that will be unmatched until 1920.

October 10 In Game 1 of the World Series, a rematch between the Cubs and Tigers, Chicago's Ed Reulbach, coasting with a 5-1 lead, tires in the seventh, and the Tigers take a 6-5 lead into the last of the eighth. But the Cubs jump on reliever Ed Summers, a 24-game winner, for six straight hits and five runs in the ninth, and Three Finger Brown gets the win 10-6.

October 14 Before the smallest crowd in modern World Series history—6,210—the Tigers are tamed on three hits by Overall, who fans 10 in a 2-0 win. The Cubs win the series in five games. Upset over seating arrangements at the World Series, baseball reporters form a professional group that will become the Baseball Writers Association of America.

BOSTON		BROOKLYN		CHICAGO		CINCINNATI		NEW YORK		PHILADELPHIA		PITTSBURGH		ST.LOUIS	
M	J.Kelley	M	P.Donovan	M	F.Chance	M	J.Ganzel	M	J.McGraw	M	B.Murray	M	F.Clarke	M	J.McCloskey
1B	D.McGann	1B	T.Jordan	1B	F.Chance	1B	J.Ganzel	1B	F.Tenney	1B	K.Bransfield	1B	H.Swacina	1B	E.Konetchy
2B	C.Ritchey	2B	H.Pattee	2B	J.Evers	2B	M.Huggins	2B	L.Doyle	2B	O.Knabe	2B	E.Abbaticchio	2B	B.Gilbert
SS	B.Dahlen	SS	P.Lewis	SS	J.Tinker	SS	R.Hulswitt	SS	A.Bridwell	SS	M.Doolan	SS	H.Wagner	SS	P.O'Rourke
3B	B.Sweeney	3B	T.Sheehan	3B	H.Steinfeldt	3B	H.Lobert	3B	A.Devlin	3B	E.Grant	3B	T.Leach	3B	B.Byrne
LF	J.Bates	LF	A.Burch	LF	J.Sheckard	LF	D.Paskert	LF	S.Shannon	LF	S.Magee	LF	F.Clarke	LF	J.Delahanty
CF	G.Beaumont	CF	B.Maloney	CF	J.Slagle	CF	J.Kane	CF	C.Seymour	CF	F.Osborn	CF	R.Thomas	CF	A.Shaw
RF	G.Browne	RF	H.Lumley	RF	F.Schulte	RF	M.Mitchell	RF	M.Donlin	RF	J.Titus	RF	C.Wilson	RF	R.Murray
C	F.Bowerman	C	B.Bergen	C	J.Kling	C	A.Schlei	C	R.Bresnahan	C	R.Dooin	C	G.Gibson	C	B.Ludwig
32	J.Hannifin	O2	J.Hummel	O1	S.Hofman	C1	L.McLean	31	M.McCormick	1	E.Courtney	1	A.Storke	2S	C.Charles
O1	J.Kelley	2	W.Alperman	O	D.Howard	3	M.Mowrey	O	B.Herzog	1	F.Jacklitsch	1	J.Kane	O	S.Barry
C	P.Graham	SO	T.McMillan	C	P.Moran	C	B.Bescher	S	T.Needham	S	D.Shean	O	S.Shannon	O	A.Hoelskoetter
O	B.Becker	C	L.Ritter	2	H.Zimmerman	1	D.Hoblitzel	/O	S.Barry	/O	W.Clement	O	D.Moeller	C	J.Bliss
C	H.Smith	O	T.Catterson	O	J.Hayden	O	D.Bayless	/O	S.Strang	/O	R.Thomas	1	W.Gill	S3	C.Osteen
1	F.Stem	C	J.Dunn	/C	D.Marshall	O	D.Brain	1	F.Merkle		M.McCormick	O	B.Becker		T.Reilly
/O	H.Moran	C	A.Farmer	H	V.Campbell	/O	T.Daley	/2	D.Brain	/O	C.Johnson	S	E.Phelps	S	W.Morris
/C	J.Ball	/1	S.Murch			/O	B.Coulson	/O	J.Devore	/2	K.Gleason	2	C.Starr	C	C.Moran
/S	W.Thomas					H	B.McGilvray	/C	F.Snodgrass	/C	P.Deininger	/C	P.O'Connor	/O	W.Murdoch
		P	N.Rucker	P	M.Brown	/C	D.Pearce	/O	S.Evans			H	H.Shaw	/O	R.McLaurin
P	V.Lindaman	P	K.Wilhelm	P	E.Reulbach			R	A.Wilson	P	G.McQuillan	P	V.Willis	/C	D.Marshall
P	P.Flaherty	P	H.McIntire	P	J.Pfiester	P	B.Ewing	P	C.Mathewson	P	T.Sparks	P	N.Maddox	P	B.Raymond
P	G.Dorner	P	J.Pastorius	P	O.Overall	P	B.Spade	P	H.Wiltse	P	F.Corridon	P	H.Camnitz	P	J.Lush
P	G.Ferguson	P	G.Bell	P	C.Fraser	P	A.Coakley	P	D.Crandall	P	L.Richie	P	L.Leifield	P	F.Beebe
P	T.McCarthy	P	J.Holmes	P	C.Lundgren	P	B.Campbell	P	J.McGinnity	P	L.Moren	P	S.Leever	P	E.Karger
P	I.Young	/P	A.Kruger	/P	A.Coakley	P	J.Weimer	P	D.Taylor	P	B.Foxen	/P	I.Young	P	S.Sallee
P	J.Boultes	/P	P.Finlayson	/P	R.Kroh	P	J.Dubuc	/P	R.Ames	P	H.Coveleski	/P	H.Young	P	A.Fromme
/P	T.Tuckey			/P	C.Spongberg	/P	J.Rowan	/P	B.Malarkey	/P	H.Hoch	/P	C.Brandom	P	I.Higginbotham
P	B.Chappelle			/P	B.Mack	/P	J.Doscher	/P	R.Beecher	/P	E.Moore	/P	B.Vail	P	S.McGlynn
/P	A.Mattern					/P	J.Volz	/P	R.Marquard	/P	B.Brown	/P	D.Phillippe	/P	C.Rhodes
/P	H.Young					/P	R.Savidge	/P	B.Durham			/P	T.McCarthy	/P	O.Baldwin
/P	B.Pfeffer					/P	M.O'Toole					/P	H.Hillebrand	/P	F.Gaiser
/P	C.Maloney					/P	B.Tozer								
						/P	B.Sincock								
						/P	T.McCarthy								
						/P	C.Rhodes								

TEAM	G	W	L	PCT	GB	R	OR	AB	H	2B	3B	HR	BB	SO	AVG	OBP	SLG	PRO	PRO+	BR	/A	PF	CHI	RC	SB	CS	SBA	SBR
CHI	158	99	55	.643		624	461	5085	1267	196	56	19	418		.249	.311	.321	.632	105	49	25	104	107	584	212			
PIT	155	98	56	.636	1	585	469	5109	1263	162	98	25	420		.247	.309	.332	.641	112	63	63	100	99	582	186			
NY	157	98	56	.636	1	652	456	5006	1339	182	43	20	494		.267	.342	.333	.675	117	138	106	105	97	646	181			
PHI	155	83	71	.539	16	504	445	5012	1223	194	68	11	334		.244	.298	.316	.614	100	12	-6	103	96	535	200			
CIN	155	73	81	.474	26	489	544	4879	1108	129	77	14	372		.227	.288	.294	.582	95	-41	-28	97	105	474	196			
BOS	156	63	91	.409	36	537	622	5131	1228	137	43	17	414		.239	.303	.293	.596	99	-12	-4	98	104	501	134			
BRO	154	53	101	.344	46	377	516	4897	1044	110	60	28	323		.213	.266	.277	.543	82	-112	-97	96	98	391	113			
STL	154	49	105	.318	50	371	626	4959	1105	134	57	17	282		.223	.271	.283	.554	87	-96	-77	95	92	420	150			
TOT	622					4139		40078	9577	1244	502	151	3057	4180	.239	.299	.306	.605							1372			

TEAM	CG	SH	SV	IP	H	H/G	HR	BB	SO	RAT	ERA	ERA+	OAV	OOB	PR	/A	PF	CPI	FA	E	DP	FW	PW	BW	SBW	DIF
CHI	108	29	12	1433²	1137	7.1	20	437	668	10.1	2.14	109	.221	.287	33	30	100	93	.969	205	76	3.7	3.5	2.9		11.9
PIT	100	24	9	1402¹	1142	7.3	16	406	468	10.3	2.12	108	.223	.287	34	24	97	92	.964	226	74	1.9	2.8	7.3		9.0
NY	95	25	18	1411	1214	7.7	26	288	656	9.8	2.14	112	.233	.277	32	39	102	92	.962	250	79	.4	4.5	12.3		3.7
PHI	116	22	6	1393	1167	7.5	8	379	476	10.3	2.10	115	.234	.294	38	46	103	103	.963	238	75	1.0	5.3	-.7		.3
CIN	110	17	8	1384	1218	7.9	19	415	433	10.9	2.37	96	.243	.307	-4	-19	98	104	.959	255	72	-.2	-2.2	-3.3		1.6
BOS	92	14	1	1404²	1262	8.1	29	423	416	11.2	2.79	86	.245	.310	-70	-68	102	93	.962	253	90	.0	-7.9	-.5		-5.7
BRO	118	20	4	1369	1165	7.7	17	444	535	11.0	2.47	94	.235	.306	-18	-24	99	97	.961	247	66	.3	-2.8	-11.3		-10.2
STL	97	13	4	1368	1217	8.0	16	430	528	11.1	2.64	89	.232	.296	-44	-51	100	82	.946	348	68	-6.8	-5.9	-8.9		-6.3
TOT	836	164	62	11165²		7.7				10.6	2.35		.239	.299					.961	2022	600					

Runs
Tenney-NY 101
Wagner-Pit 100
Leach-Pit 93
Evers-Chi 83
Clarke-Pit 83

Hits
Wagner-Pit 201
Donlin-NY 198
Murray-StL 167
Lobert-Cin 167
Bransfield-Phi 160

Doubles
Wagner-Pit 39
Magee-Phi 30
Chance-Chi 27
Knabe-Phi 26
Donlin-NY 26

Triples
Wagner-Pit 19
Lobert-Cin 18
Magee-Phi 16
Leach-Pit 16

Home Runs
Jordan-Bro 12
Wagner-Pit 10
Murray-StL 7
Tinker-Chi 6
Donlin-NY 6

Total Bases
Wagner-Pit 308
Donlin-NY 268
Murray-StL 237
Lobert-Cin 232
Leach-Pit 222

Runs Batted In
Wagner-Pit 109
Donlin-NY 106
Seymour-NY 92
Bransfield-Phi 71
Tinker-Chi 68

Runs Produced
Wagner-Pit 199
Donlin-NY 171
Tenney-NY 148
Seymour-NY 147

Bases On Balls
Bresnahan-NY 83
Tenney-NY 72
Evers-Chi 66
Clarke-Pit 65

Batting Average
Wagner-Pit 354
Donlin-NY 334
Doyle-NY 308
Bransfield-Phi 304
Evers-Chi 300

On Base Percentage
Wagner-Pit 415
Evers-Chi 402
Bresnahan-NY 401
Titus-Phi 365
Donlin-NY 364

Slugging Average
Wagner-Pit 542
Donlin-NY 452
Magee-Phi 417
Lobert-Cin 407
Murray-StL 400

Production
Wagner-Pit 957
Donlin-NY 816
Evers-Chi 777
Magee-Phi 776
Bresnahan-NY 760

Adjusted Production
Wagner-Pit 205
Donlin-NY 153
Lobert-Cin 145
Magee-Phi 143
Evers-Chi 143

Batter Runs
Wagner-Pit 65.2
Donlin-NY 36.6
Magee-Phi 27.3
Bresnahan-NY 27.0
Evers-Chi 26.4

Adjusted Batter Runs
Wagner-Pit 65.2
Donlin-NY 32.0
Lobert-Cin 27.3
Magee-Phi 24.6
Murray-StL 24.3

Clutch Hitting Index
Seymour-NY 150
McGann-Bos 133
Abbaticchio-Pit . . 132
Donlin-NY 129
Steinfeldt-Chi 129

Runs Created
Wagner-Pit 148
Donlin-NY 108
Lobert-Cin 97
Murray-StL 92
Magee-Phi 90

Total Average
Wagner-Pit 1.144
Evers-Chi 904
Magee-Phi 857
Donlin-NY 825
Bresnahan-NY 820

Stolen Bases
Wagner-Pit 53
Murray-StL 48
Lobert-Cin 47
Magee-Phi 40
Evers-Chi 36

Stolen Base Average

Stolen Base Runs

Fielding Runs
Dahlen-Bos 37.5
Tinker-Chi 30.4
Ritchey-Bos 15.6
Devlin-NY 12.8
Burch-Bro 12.6

Total Player Rating
Wagner-Pit 7.0
Tinker-Chi 4.8
Dahlen-Bos 4.2
Ritchey-Bos 3.1
Donlin-NY 3.0

Wins
Mathewson-NY 37
Brown-Chi 29
Reulbach-Chi 24

Win Percentage
Reulbach-Chi 774
Mathewson-NY . . .771
Brown-Chi 763
Maddox-Pit 742
Leever-Pit 682

Games
Mathewson-NY . . . 56
Raymond-StL 48
McQuillan-Phi 48
Reulbach-Chi 46

Complete Games
Mathewson-NY . . . 34
Wilhelm-Bro 33
McQuillan-Phi 32
Wiltse-NY 30
Rucker-Bro 30

Shutouts
Mathewson-NY . . . 11
Brown-Chi 9

Saves
McGinnity-NY 5
Mathewson-NY 5
Brown-Chi 5
Overall-Chi 4
Ewing-Cin 3

Innings Pitched
Mathewson-NY . 390.2
McQuillan-Phi . . 359.2
Rucker-Bro 333.1
Wilhelm-Bro 332.0
Wiltse-NY 330.0

Fewest Hits/Game
Brown-Chi 6.17
Raymond-StL 6.55
Mathewson-NY . . . 6.57
McQuillan-Phi 6.58
Overall-Chi 6.60

Fewest BB/Game
Mathewson-NY 97
Brown-Chi 1.41
Sparks-Phi 1.74
Ewing-Cin 1.75
Campbell-Cin 1.79

Strikeouts
Mathewson-NY . . . 259
Rucker-Bro 199
Overall-Chi 167
Raymond-StL 145
Reulbach-Chi 133

Strikeouts/Game
Overall-Chi 6.68
Mathewson-NY . . . 5.97
Rucker-Bro 5.37
Camnitz-Pit 4.49
Ferguson-Bos 4.24

Ratio
Mathewson-NY . . . 7.60
Brown-Chi 7.72
McQuillan-Phi 9.01
Willis-Pit 9.28
Ewing-Cin 9.47

Earned Run Average
Mathewson-NY . . . 1.43
Brown-Chi 1.47
McQuillan-Phi 1.53
Camnitz-Pit 1.56
Coakley-Cin-Chi . . . 1.78

Adjusted ERA
Mathewson-NY 168
Brown-Chi 159
McQuillan-Phi 158
Camnitz-Pit 147
Richie-Phi 132

Opponents' Batting Avg.
Beebe-StL 193
Brown-Chi 195
Mathewson-NY 200
McQuillan-Phi 207
Raymond-StL 207

Opponents' On Base Pct.
Mathewson-NY 225
Brown-Chi 232
Willis-Pit 262
McQuillan-Phi 263
Beebe-StL 267

Starter Runs
Mathewson-NY . . . 39.8
McQuillan-Phi 32.7
Brown-Chi 30.4
Camnitz-Pit 20.7
Wilhelm-Bro 17.5

Adjusted Starter Runs
Mathewson-NY . . . 42.1
McQuillan-Phi 35.2
Brown-Chi 30.1
Camnitz-Pit 19.1
Wilhelm-Bro 16.8

Clutch Pitching Index
Coakley-Cin-Chi . . . 134
McGinnity-NY 134
Richie-Phi 126
Fraser-Chi 126
Rucker-Bro 118

Relief Runs

Adjusted Relief Runs

Relief Ranking

Total Pitcher Index
Mathewson-NY . . . 7.3
Brown-Chi 4.1
McQuillan-Phi 3.9
Raymond-StL 2.1
Wilhelm-Bro 1.9

Total Baseball Ranking
Mathewson-NY . . . 7.3
Wagner-Pit 7.0
Tinker-Chi 4.8
Dahlen-Bos 4.2
Brown-Chi 4.1

February 3 Chris Von der Ahe, flamboyant former owner of the Browns, files for bankruptcy, claiming $27,000 in debts, and $200 in assets.

February 27 The sacrifice fly rule is adopted. No time at bat is charged if a run scores after the catch of a fly ball. The rule will be repealed in 1931, then reinstated or changed several times before permanent acceptance in 1954.

April 2 After a two-year investigation, the Mills Commission, formed on the recommendation of Al Spalding and headed by the former NL president A. G. Mills, declares that baseball was invented by Abner Doubleday in Cooperstown, New York, in 1839. Overwhelming evidence to the contrary is ignored, but the designation makes James Fenimore Cooper's town the most likely site for a Hall of Fame and museum when these establishments are conceived some 30 years later.

April 20 "The Father of Baseball," Henry Chadwick, reporter, commentator, scorer, and indefatigable promoter of the game, dies in Brooklyn at age 85.

June 30 Cy Young's third career no-hitter is an 8-0 Boston win over New York. At 41 years and three months, he is the oldest pitcher to turn the no-hit trick. Nolan Ryan will beat him in 1990 at the age of 43.

August 13 Cy Young Day is celebrated by 20,000 at Huntington Avenue Grounds in Boston. He pitches briefly against an All-Star team that includes Jack Chesbro, Hal Chase, and Willie Keeler. The game is interrupted several times for presentations to the great hurler.

August 20 Rube Waddell strikes out 17 Washington Nationals in 10 innings.

September 4 With a runner on third base, Germany Schaefer attempts to draw a throw by stealing second base, but the Cleveland catcher, Nig Clarke, holds on to the ball. With runners on second and third, Schaefer takes off for first base and is credited with a stolen base. On the next pitch he takes off again for second base and arrives safely, this time drawing a throw and allowing Davy Jones to score from third. This is the second time in five weeks this prank has been run.

September 7 Nationals pitcher Walter Johnson shuts out the New York Highlanders for the third time in four days, 4–0. He will pitch 110 shutouts during his career, 20 more than runner-up Grover Alexander.

September 13* Lancaster (Ohio State League) pitcher Walt "Smoke" Justis hurls his fourth no-hitter of the season, defeating Marion 3–0. Justis had no record in two major league appearances with Detroit in 1905.

October 2 In a great pitching duel, Ed Walsh is almost perfect, giving up four hits and striking out 15 in eight innings, but Cleveland's Addie Joss is completely perfect, setting down 27 straight White Sox for a 1-0 victory. The only run scores on a passed ball by Ossie Schreckengost. It is the high point of Joss's career. He will finish 24-12 with a 1.16 ERA.

October 5 Ed Walsh of the White Sox tops Detroit 6-1 for his 40th victory and forces the AL pennant race to the final day. He also leads the league in games (66), innings pitched (464), strikeouts (269), complete games (42), saves (6), shutouts (11), and winning percentage (.727). His ERA is 1.42.

October 6 Having pitched in 13 of the last 16 games, Ed Walsh does not start the White Sox finale against Detroit. Doc White is hit hard in the 7-0 loss that gives the pennant to the Tigers.

October 6 Detroit outfielder Sam Crawford leads the AL with seven homers. Having led the NL with 16 in 1901, he becomes the first player to lead both leagues in that department.

BOSTON	CHICAGO	CLEVELAND	DETROIT	NEW YORK	PHILADELPHIA	ST.LOUIS	WASHINGTON
M D.McGuire	M F.Jones	M N.Lajoie	M H.Jennings	M C.Griffith	M C.Mack	M J.McAleer	M J.Cantillon
M F.Lake	1B J.Donahue	1B G.Stovall	1B C.Rossman	1B K.Elberfeld	1B H.Davis	1B T.Jones	1B J.Freeman
1B J.Stahl	2B G.Davis	2B N.Lajoie	2B R.Downs	1B H.Chase	2B E.Collins	2B J.Williams	2B J.Delahanty
2B A.McConnell	SS F.Parent	SS G.Perring	SS G.Schaefer	2B H.Niles	SS S.Nicholls	SS B.Wallace	SS G.McBride
SS H.Wagner	3B L.Tannehill	3B B.Bradley	3B B.Coughlin	SS N.Ball	3B J.Collins	3B H.Ferris	3B B.Shipke
3B H.Lord	LF P.Dougherty	LF J.Clarke	LF M.McIntyre	3B W.Conroy	LF T.Hartsel	LF G.Stone	LF B.Ganley
LF J.Thoney	CF F.Jones	CF J.Birmingham	CF S.Crawford	LF J.Stahl	CF R.Oldring	CF D.Hoffman	CF C.Milan
CF D.Sullivan	RF E.Hahn	RF B.Hinchman	RF T.Cobb	CF C.Hemphill	RF D.Murphy	RF R.Hartzell	RF O.Pickering
RF D.Gessler	C B.Sullivan	C N.Clarke	C B.Schmidt	RF W.Keeler	C O.Schreckengost	C T.Spencer	C G.Street
C L.Criger	O J.Anderson	C H.Bemis	S C.O'Leary	C R.Kleinow	OP J.Coombs	O C.Jones	O2 O.Clymer
O G.Cravath	12 F.Isbell	OS T.Turner	O D.Jones	13 G.Moriarty	C D.Powers	C A.Schweitzer	32 B.Unglaub
1 B.Unglaub	2S J.Atz	O1 C.Hickman	C I.Thomas	C W.Blair	C J.Barry	C J.Stephens	23 D.Altizer
23 F.LaPorte	3 B.Purtell	O W.Good	2 R.Killefer	O I.McIlveen	O S.Seybold	O E.Heidrick	C J.Warner
C B.Carrigan	C A.Shaw	O D.Altizer	S D.Bush	2O F.LaPorte	O S.Smith	O D.Criss	O B.Edmondson
O T.Speaker	C A.Weaver	/O E.Flick	C F.Payne	OS Q.O'Rourke	C F.Manush	C S.Smith	C M.Kahoe
C P.Donahue	/C O.Schreckengost	/S R.Nill	/3 C.Perry	2 J.Sweeney	/C H.Moran	/C B.Blue	P T.Hughes
O J.McHale	P E.Walsh	/C G.Land	P E.Summers	O B.Cree	2 S.Barr	/2 J.Yeager	P W.Johnson
C E.McFarland	P F.Smith	/O D.Sullivan	P G.Mullin	2 E.Gardner	C J.Lapp	P H.Howell	P C.Smith
O J.Hoey	P D.White	/C H.Davidson	P B.Donovan	S K.Elberfeld	C A.Strunk	P W.Waddell	P B.Keeley
/2 H.Niles	P F.Owen	/1 D.McGuire	P E.Willett	/3 M.Donovan	/3 F.Baker	P J.Powell	P B.Burns
/O W.Carlisle	P N.Altrock	R H.Bay	P E.Killian	P J.Chesbro	/O J.Fox	P B.Dinneen	P E.Cates
/3 L.Gardner	P M.Manuel	P A.Joss	P E.Siever	P J.Lake	/O S.Shaughnessy	P B.Pelty	P C.Falkenberg
/O J.Barrett	/P L.Fiene	P B.Rhoads	P G.Winter	P R.Manning	/O J.Jackson	P B.Grahame	P J.Tannehill
/C H.Ostdiek	/P A.Nelson	P G.Liebhardt	/P G.Suggs	P B.Hogg	/C B.Blue	P B.Bailey	P R.Witherup
H D.McGuire	/P F.Olmstead	P H.Berger	/P H.Malloy	P A.Orth	/C B.Egan		/P C.Patten
P C.Young		P C.Chech		P D.Newton	P R.Vickers		/P H.Gehring
P E.Cicotte		P J.Thielman		P S.Doyle	P E.Plank		
P C.Morgan		/P C.Falkenberg		/P P.Wilson	P J.Dygert		
P F.Burchell		/P J.Ryan		/P J.Warhop	P C.Bender		
P G.Winter		/P B.Lattimore		/P F.Glade	P B.Schlitzer		
P E.Steele		/P E.Foster		/P H.Billiard	P N.Carter		
F.Arellanes		/P O.Hess		/P A.O'Connor	/P J.Flater		
T.Pruiett		/P W.Clarkson		/P H.Vaughn	/P H.Krause		
R.Glaze		/P J.Graney			/P A.Kellogg		
/P J.Wood					/P G.Salve		
/P K.Brady					/P B.Maxwell		
/P D.McMahon					/P E.Files		
/P J.Tannehill					/P D.Martin		
/P C.Patten							
/P C.Hartman							
/P J.Thielman							

TEAM	G	W	L	PCT	GB	R	OR	AB	H	2B	3B	HR	BB	SO	AVG	OBP	SLG	PRO	PRO+	BR	/A	PF	CHI	RC	SB	CS	SBA	SBR
DET	154	90	63	.588		647	547	5115	1347	199	86	19	320		.263	.312	.347	.659	115	102	75	104	102	604	165			
CLE	157	90	64	.584	0.5	568	457	5108	1221	188	58	18	364		.239	.297	.309	.606	103	14	12	100	102	528	177			
CHI	156	88	64	.579	1.5	537	470	5027	1127	145	41	3	463		.224	.298	.271	.569	91	-37	-29	98	105	479	209			
STL	155	83	69	.546	6.5	544	483	5151	1261	173	52	20	343		.245	.296	.310	.606	102	13	10	101	98	514	126			
BOS	155	75	79	.487	15.5	564	513	5048	1239	117	88	14	289		.245	.295	.312	.607	100	13	-2	103	104	513	167			
PHI	157	68	85	.444	22	486	562	5065	1131	183	50	21	368		.223	.281	.292	.573	86	-46	-79	107	100	450	116			
WAS	155	67	85	.441	22.5	479	539	5041	1186	132	74	8	368		.235	.293	.296	.589	106	-15	28	92	92	490	170			
NY	155	51	103	.331	39.5	459	713	5047	1190	142	50	13	288		.236	.283	.291	.574	91	-45	-50	101	96	478	231			
TOT	622					4284		40602	9702	1279	499	116	2803	4930	.239	.294	.304	.598						1361				

TEAM	CG	SH	SV	IP	H	H/G	HR	BB	SO	RAT	ERA	ERA+	OAV	OOB	PR	/A	PF	CPI	FA	E	DP	FW	PW	BW	SBW	DIF
DET	119	15	5	1374¹	1313	8.6	12	318	553	11.1	2.40	100	.255	.306	-3	2	101	113	.953	305	95	-2.1	.2	8.6		6.8
CLE	108	18	5	1424¹	1172	7.4	16	328	548	9.7	2.02	118	.229	.280	59	56	100	102	.962	257	95	1.6	6.4	1.4		3.7
CHI	107	23	10	1414	1165	7.4	11	284	623	9.4	2.22	104	.225	.269	26	13	97	82	.966	232	82	3.2	1.5	-3.3		10.7
STL	107	15	5	1397	1151	7.4	7	387	607	10.3	2.15	111	.230	.294	37	36	100	105	.964	237	97	2.7	4.1	1.1		-1.0
BOS	102	12	7	1380¹	1200	7.8	18	364	624	10.5	2.28	108	.238	.295	17	27	103	105	.955	297	71	-1.4	3.1	-.2		-3.4
PHI	102	23	4	1400¹	1194	7.7	10	410	741	10.6	2.56	100	.235	.298	-27	-4	107	92	.957	272	68	.6	-.5	-9.0		.4
WAS	106	15	7	1391²	1236	8.0	16	348	649	10.5	2.34	97	.241	.294	7	-12	96	102	.958	275	89	.1	-1.4	3.2		-10.9
NY	90	11	3	1366	1293	8.5	26	458	585	12.0	3.16	97	.252	.322	-117	-106	104	96	.947	337	78	-4.1	-12.1	-5.7		-4.1
TOT	841	132	46	11148		7.9				10.5	2.39		.239	.294					.958	2212	675					

Runs		Hits		Doubles		Triples		Home Runs		Total Bases	
McIntyre-Det	105	Cobb-Det	188	Cobb-Det	36	Cobb-Det	20	Crawford-Det	7	Cobb-Det	276
Crawford-Det	102	Crawford-Det	184	Rossman-Det	33	Stahl-NY-Bos	16	Hinchman-Cle	6	Crawford-Det	270
Schaefer-Det	96	McIntyre-Det	168	Crawford-Det	33	Crawford-Det	16	Niles-NY-Bos	5	Rossman-Det	219
Jones-Chi	92	Lajoie-Cle	168	Lajoie-Cle	32	Gessler-Bos	14	Stone-StL	5	McIntyre-Det	218
Stone-StL	89	Stone-StL	165	Stovall-Cle	29			Davis-Phi	5	Lajoie-Cle	218

Runs Batted In		Runs Produced		Bases On Balls		Batting Average		On Base Percentage		Slugging Average	
Cobb-Det	108	Cobb-Det	192	Hartsel-Phi	93	Cobb-Det	.324	Gessler-Bos	.394	Cobb-Det	.475
Crawford-Det	80	Crawford-Det	175	Jones-Chi	86	Crawford-Det	.311	McIntyre-Det	.392	Crawford-Det	.457
Lajoie-Cle	74	Lajoie-Cle	149	McIntyre-Det	83	Gessler-Bos	.308	Hemphill-NY	.374	Gessler-Bos	.423
Ferris-StL	74	Schaefer-Det	145	J.Clarke-Cle	76	Hemphill-NY	.297	Hartsel-Phi	.371	Rossman-Det	.418
Rossman-Det	71	Jones-Chi	141	Davis-Phi	61	McIntyre-Det	.295	Dougherty-Chi	.367	McIntyre-Det	.383

Production		Adjusted Production		Batter Runs		Adjusted Batter Runs		Clutch Hitting Index		Runs Created	
Cobb-Det	.842	Cobb-Det	166	Cobb-Det	43.8	Cobb-Det	39.6	Cobb-Det	141	Cobb-Det	114
Gessler-Bos	.817	Gessler-Bos	161	Crawford-Det	38.3	Crawford-Det	34.2	Wallace-StL	127	Crawford-Det	100
Crawford-Det	.812	Crawford-Det	157	McIntyre-Det	36.5	McIntyre-Det	32.3	Ferris-StL	125	McIntyre-Det	93
McIntyre-Det	.775	McIntyre-Det	146	Gessler-Bos	33.2	Gessler-Bos	31.0	Lajoie-Cle	124	Lajoie-Cle	83
Rossman-Det	.748	Rossman-Det	137	Lajoie-Cle	23.3	Lajoie-Cle	23.0	Jones-Chi	124	Hemphill-NY	83

Total Average		Stolen Bases		Stolen Base Average		Stolen Base Runs		Fielding Runs		Total Player Rating	
Cobb-Det	.903	Dougherty-Chi	47					Lajoie-Cle	49.4	Lajoie-Cle	7.8
Gessler-Bos	.880	Hemphill-NY	42					McBride-Was	32.0	McIntyre-Det	4.7
McIntyre-Det	.818	Schaefer-Det	40					Wagner-Bos	31.8	Cobb-Det	4.2
Hemphill-NY	.800	Cobb-Det	39					Wallace-StL	18.1	McBride-Was	3.4
Crawford-Det	.799	J.Clarke-Cle	37					Tannehill-Chi	17.8	Wallace-StL	3.1

Wins		Win Percentage		Games		Complete Games		Shutouts		Saves	
Walsh-Chi	40	Walsh-Chi	.727	Walsh-Chi	66	Walsh-Chi	42	Walsh-Chi	11	Walsh-Chi	6
Summers-Det	24	Donovan-Det	.720	Vickers-Phi	53	Young-Bos	30	Joss-Cle	9	Hughes-Was	4
Joss-Cle	24	Joss-Cle	.686	Chesbro-NY	45	Joss-Cle	29	Vickers-Phi	6	Waddell-StL	3
Young-Bos	21	Summers-Det	.667	Waddell-StL	43	Howell-StL	27	Johnson-Was	6		
Waddell-StL	19	Young-Bos	.656	Hughes-Was	43	Mullin-Det	26	Donovan-Det	6		

Innings Pitched		Fewest Hits/Game		Fewest BB/Game		Strikeouts		Strikeouts/Game		Ratio	
Walsh-Chi	464.0	Joss-Cle	6.42	Joss-Cle	.83	Walsh-Chi	269	Waddell-StL	7.31	Joss-Cle	7.31
Joss-Cle	325.0	Smith-Chi	6.44	Burns-Was	.99	Waddell-StL	232	Dygert-Phi	6.18	Walsh-Chi	7.91
Howell-StL	324.1	Walsh-Chi	6.65	Hughes-Was	1.09	Hughes-Was	165	Johnson-Was	5.62	Young-Bos	8.07
Vickers-Phi	317.0	Johnson-Was	6.81	Young-Bos	1.11	Dygert-Phi	164	Hughes-Was	5.37	Burns-Was	8.62
Summers-Det	301.0	Berger-Cle	6.86	Summers-Det	1.64	Johnson-Was	160	Donovan-Det	5.23	Smith-Chi	8.71

Earned Run Average		Adjusted ERA		Opponents' Batting Avg.		Opponents' On Base Pct.		Starter Runs		Adjusted Starter Runs	
Joss-Cle	1.16	Joss-Cle	205	Joss-Cle	.197	Joss-Cle	.218	Walsh-Chi	50.0	Walsh-Chi	46.0
Young-Bos	1.26	Young-Bos	194	Smith-Chi	.203	Walsh-Chi	.232	Joss-Cle	44.2	Joss-Cle	44.0
Walsh-Chi	1.42	Walsh-Chi	163	Walsh-Chi	.203	Young-Bos	.240	Young-Bos	37.3	Young-Bos	39.5
Summers-Det	1.64	Summers-Det	147	Johnson-Was	.211	Smith-Chi	.256	Summers-Det	24.8	Summers-Det	25.6
Johnson-Was	1.65	Johnson-Was	138	Young-Bos	.213	Burns-Was	.257	Johnson-Was	21.0	Rhoads-Cle	18.4

Clutch Pitching Index		Relief Runs		Adjusted Relief Runs		Relief Ranking		Total Pitcher Index		Total Baseball Ranking	
Summers-Det	142							Walsh-Chi	8.1	Walsh-Chi	8.1
Willett-Det	140							Joss-Cle	5.9	Lajoie-Cle	7.8
Rhoads-Cle	137							Young-Bos	4.1	Joss-Cle	5.9
Howell-StL	122							Rhoads-Cle	2.9	McIntyre-Det	4.7
Chech-Cle	119							Summers-Det	2.4	Cobb-Det	4.2

January 11 The National Commission approves owner Charles Murphy's payment of a $10,000 bonus to his Cubs for their 1908 World Series triumph.

February 4 John Clarkson, a 326-game winner dies at Belmont, Massachusetts, at age 47.

February 17 The NL deprives umpires of the power to fine players and decrees that relief pitchers must retire at least one batter before being relieved.

February 27 Joe "Iron Man" McGinnity is released by the Giants. He will pitch in the minor leagues for another 13 years, winning 20 or more in six of them.

April 15 Before an Opening Day crowd of 30,000 at New York, Red Ames pitches a no-hitter for nine innings against the Brooklyn Superbas, ruins it with one out in the 10th, then loses the game 3-0 in the 13th.

April 23 In the sixth inning of the Reds-Pirates game in Pittsburgh, Honus Wagner steps across the plate to the other batter's box as Reds pitcher Harry Gaspar delivers the ball. Umpire Bill Klem refuses to call him out. The Pirates win 2–1, but Reds manager Clark Griffith protests. Acting NL president Heydler backs Klem. The league will override

Heydler and Klem and order the game replayed September 20. The Pirates will win 4–3.

May 2 Honus Wagner steals his way around the bases in the first inning of a game against the Cubs. It is the fourth time he has performed this feat, an NL record.

May 11* Fred Toney, later to pitch in the only double no-hitter, throws a 17-inning no-hitter for Winchester (Blue Grass League), winning 1–0. He fans 19 opponents and walks only one.

June 16* Jim Thorpe makes his baseball pitching debut for Rocky Mount (Eastern Carolina League) with a 4–2 win over Raleigh. It is this professional play which will cause him to lose the medals he won in the 1912 Olympics.

June 19 An exhibition night game featuring two amateur teams is played in the Reds' park before 3,000 spectators, including the Cincinnati and Philadelphia teams, which had played there earlier.

July 29 NL president Harry Pulliam, despondent over his inability to handle the problems and controversies of the league, dies of a self-inflicted pistol wound.

August 18 Giants player-coach Arlie

Latham steals second base in the Giants' 14–1 win over the Phillies. At 49, he is the oldest major leaguer ever to steal a base.

August 31 The A. J. Reach Company is granted a patent for a cork-centered baseball, which will replace the hard rubber-cored one. This change will be particularly apparent in the NL in 1910-11.

October 8 The World Series pits the two leagues' top offensive stars, Honus Wagner and Ty Cobb, against each other. Pittsburgh manager Fred Clarke starts 27-year-old rookie righthander Babe Adams against Tigers pitcher George Mullin. There are only 11 hits in the game, but one is a home run by Clarke, and the Pirates win 4-1.

October 16 Babe Adams comes through with a 6-hit 8-0 win. It is his third complete-game victory and gives the Pirates their first World Championship.

November 26 The Phils are sold for $350,000 to a group headed by sportswriter Horace Fogel. Because of his dual roles, Fogel will become the only executive barred from a league meeting.

	BOSTON		BROOKLYN		CHICAGO		CINCINNATI		NEW YORK		PHILADELPHIA		PITTSBURGH		ST.LOUIS
M	F.Bowerman	M	H.Lumley	M	F.Chance	M	C.Griffith	M	J.McGraw	M	B.Murray	M	F.Clarke		R.Bresnahan
M	H.Smith	1B	T.Jordan	1B	F.Chance	1B	D.Hoblitzel	1B	F.Tenney	1B	K.Bransfield	1B	B.Abstein	1B	E.Konetchy
1B	F.Stern	2B	W.Alperman	2B	J.Evers	2B	D.Egan	2B	L.Doyle	2B	O.Knabe	2B	D.Miller	2B	C.Charles
2B	D.Shean	SS	T.McMillan	SS	J.Tinker	SS	T.Downey	SS	A.Bridwell	SS	M.Doolan	SS	H.Wagner	SS	R.Hulswitt
SS	J.Coffey	3B	E.Lennox	3B	H.Steinfeldt	3B	H.Lobert	3B	A.Devlin	3B	E.Grant	3B	J.Barbeau	3B	B.Byrne
3B	B.Sweeney	LF	W.Clement	LF	J.Sheckard	LF	B.Bescher	LF	M.McCormick	LF	S.Magee	LF	F.Clarke	LF	R.Ellis
LF	R.Thomas	CF	A.Burch	CF	S.Hofman	CF	R.Oakes	CF	B.O'Hara	CF	J.Bates	CF	T.Leach	CF	A.Shaw
CF	G.Beaumont	RF	H.Lumley	RF	F.Schulte	RF	M.Mitchell	RF	R.Murray	RF	J.Titus	RF	C.Wilson	RF	S.Evans
RF	B.Becker	C	B.Bergen	C	J.Archer	C	L.McLean	C	A.Schlei	C	R.Dooin	C	G.Gibson	C	E.Phelps
C	P.Graham														
		12	J.Hummel	C	P.Moran	O	D.Paskert	O	C.Seymour	O	F.Osborn	3	B.Byrne	O2	J.Delahanty
O1	F.Beck	3O	P.McElveen	1	D.Howard	23	M.Huggins	1	F.Merkle	2	J.Ward	13	A.Storke	C	R.Bresnahan
O	J.Bates	O	J.Kustus	2S	H.Zimmerman	C	F.Roth	C	C.Meyers	O	P.Deininger	S	E.Abbaticchio	3	J.Barbeau
2	C.Starr	C	D.Marshall	O	J.Stanley	3S	M.Mowrey	O	B.Herzog	21	D.Shean	/O	H.Hyatt	S	A.Storke
1	C.Autry	OP	G.Hunter	/O	J.Kane	O	W.Miller	S	A.Fletcher	C	D.Martel	O	W.Miller	C	J.Bliss
S	B.Dahlen	O	Z.Wheat	1	G.Browne	C	T.Clarke	32	T.Shafer	C	F.Jacklitsch	/C	M.Simon	S	H.Murphy
3	G.Getz	O	J.Sebring	1	F.Luderus	2	C.Charles	O	F.Snodgrass	H	W.Clement	/C	P.O'Connor	S	C.Osteen
C	H.Smith	O	R.Downey	/C	T.Needham	/1	C.Autry	C	A.Wilson	H	C.Starr	R	K.Durbin	2	B.Gilbert
C	F.Bowerman	/C	J.Dunn	/O	B.Davidson	/S	R.Ellam	O	J.Devore	/C	B.Froelich			/2	M.Mowrey
2	C.Ritchey	/S	L.Meyer			/S	B.Moriarty	/2	A.Latham	/C	E.McDonough	P	V.Willis	/O	B.James
C	B.Rariden	/O	H.Myers	P	M.Brown	/C	E.Haberer					P	Ho.Camnitz	/S	C.Enwright
C	A.Shaw	/2	H.Redmond	P	O.Overall	/O	S.McCabe	P	C.Mathewson	P	E.Moore	P	N.Maddox	/S	T.Reilly
/O	H.Moran	/O	T.Catterson	P	E.Reulbach	/1	D.Johnston	P	B.Raymond	P	L.Moren	P	L.Leifield	C	C.Blank
/3	H.Siner			P	J.Pfiester	/O	C.Patterson	P	H.Wiltse	P	G.McQuillan	P	D.Phillippe		
/O	E.Diehl	P	N.Rucker	P	R.Kroh	/C	S.Pauxtis	P	R.Ames	P	F.Corridon			P	F.Beebe
/O	B.Dam	P	G.Bell			/O	D.Young	P	R.Marquard	P	T.Sparks	P	Ha.Camnitz	P	J.Lush
		P	H.McIntire	P	R.Hagerman	/3	C.Dolan					P	B.Adams	P	S.Sallee
P	A.Mattern	P	K.Wilhelm	H	I.Higginbotham	H	K.Durbin	P	D.Crandall	H	H.Coveleski	P	S.Leever	P	B.Harmon
P	G.Ferguson	P	D.Scanlan	/P	R.Brown	/C	M.Konnick	/P	A.Klawitter	P	B.Foxen	P	C.Brandom	P	L.Backman
P	K.White			/P	K.Cole	/3	E.Midkiff	/P	L.Drucke	P	L.Richie	/P	S.Frock	RP	S.Melter
P	L.Richie	P	J.Pastorius	/P	C.Lundgren	/C	D.Pearce	/P	G.Daly	P	B.Brown	/P	B.Powell		
P	B.Brown	/P	E.Dent	/P	P.Ragan			/P	B.Durham	/P	F.Scanlan	/P	G.Moore	P	J.Raleigh
		/P	E.Knetzer	/P	R.Schwenck	P	A.Fromme	/P	J.Weimer	/P	B.Van Dyke	/P	C.Wacker	P	E.Higgins
P	T.Tuckey	/P	S.Fletcher	/P	C.Fraser	P	H.Gaspar	/P	R.Waller					P	C.Rhodes
P	C.Curtis	/P	P.Finlayson	/P	A.Coakley	P	J.Rowan							P	F.More
P	V.Lindaman					P	B.Ewing							/P	G.Lowdermilk
P	F.More					P	B.Campbell							/P	I.Higginbotham
/P	T.McCarthy													/P	J.Bernard
/P	B.Chappelle					P	B.Spade							/P	H.Sullivan
/P	G.Dorner					P	J.Dubuc								
/P	C.Evans					/P	E.Karger								
/P	J.Boultes					/P	T.Cantwell								
/P	B.Cooney					/P	R.Castleton								
						/P	P.Ragan								
						/P	J.Bushelman								
						/P	C.Carmichael								
						/P	C.Griffith								
						/P	B.Chappelle								
						/P	R.Savidge								

TEAM	G	W	L	PCT	GB	R	OR	AB	H	2B	3B	HR	BB	SO	AVG	OBP	SLG	PRO	PRO+	BR	/A	PF	CHI	RC	SB	CS	SBA	SBR
PIT	154	110	42	.724		699	447	5129	1332	218	92	25	479		.260	.327	.353	.680	109	100	44	108	103	656	185			
CHI	155	104	49	.680	6.5	635	390	4999	1227	203	60	20	420		.245	.308	.322	.630	100	7	-7	102	112	562	187			
NY	158	92	61	.601	18.5	623	546	5218	1327	173	68	26	530		.254	.329	.328	.657	109	70	60	102	95	640	234			
CIN	157	77	76	.503	33.5	606	599	5088	1273	159	72	22	478		.250	.319	.323	.642	107	35	40	99	100	618	280			
PHI	154	74	79	.484	36.5	516	518	5034	1228	185	53	12	369		.244	.303	.309	.612	95	-26	-34	101	96	534	185			
BRO	155	55	98	.359	55.5	444	627	5056	1157	176	59	16	330		.229	.279	.296	.575	87	-98	-82	98	98	456	141			
STL	154	54	98	.355	56	583	731	5108	1242	148	56	15	568		.243	.326	.303	.629	109	25	62	94	97	556	161			
BOS	155	45	108	.294	65.5	435	683	5017	1121	125	43	14	400		.223	.285	.274	.559	76	-117	-137	105	99	435	135			
TOT	621					4541		40649	9907	1387	503	150	3574	4437	.244	.310	.314	.624							1508			

TEAM	CG	SH	SV	IP	H	H/G	HR	BB	SO	RAT	ERA	ERA+	OAV	OOB	PR	/A	PF	CPI	FA	E	DP	FW	PW	BW	SBW	DIF
PIT	93	21	11	1401²	1174	7.5	12	320	490	9.9	2.07	131	.232	.284	81	100	105	97	.964	228	100	3.5	11.1	4.9		14.5
CHI	111	32	11	1399¹	1094	7.0	6	364	680	9.6	1.75	145	.215	.272	131	124	98	94	.962	244	95	2.6	13.8	-.8		11.9
NY	105	17	15	1440²	1248	7.8	28	397	735	10.5	2.27	112	.238	.295	51	42	98	102	.954	307	99	-1.1	4.7	6.7		5.3
CIN	91	10	8	1407	1233	7.9	5	510	477	11.4	2.52	103	.240	.314	11	9	100	100	.952	309	120	-1.4	1.0	4.4		-3.6
PHI	89	17	6	1391	1190	7.7	23	472	612	11.0	2.44	106	.235	.304	23	20	100	99	.962	241	97	2.7	2.2	-3.3		-4.1
BRO	126	18	3	1384¹	1277	8.3	31	528	594	12.1	3.10	83	.256	.333	-79	-82	100	102	.955	282	86	.2	-9.1	-9.1		-3.5
STL	84	5	4	1379²	1368	8.9	22	483	435	12.4	3.41	74	.263	.331	-126	-139	97	92	.950	322	90	-2.5	-15.4	6.9		-10.9
BOS	98	13	6	1370²	1329	8.7	23	543	414	12.6	3.20	88	.263	.339	-93	-60	109	103	.948	342	101	-3.7	-6.7	-15.2		-5.9
TOT	797	133	64	11174¹		8.0				11.2	2.59		.244	.310					.956	2275	788					

Runs
Leach-Pit 126
Clarke-Pit 97
Byrne-StL-Pit 92
Wagner-Pit 92

Hits
Doyle-NY 172
Grant-Phi 170
Wagner-Pit 168
Konetchy-StL 165
Burch-Bro 163

Doubles
Wagner-Pit 39
Magee-Phi 33
D.Miller-Pit 31
Sheckard-Chi 29
Leach-Pit 29

Triples
Mitchell-Cin 17
Magee-Phi 14
Konetchy-StL 14
D.Miller-Pit 13

Home Runs
Murray-NY 7
Leach-Pit 6
Doyle-NY 6
Becker-Bos 6
Wagner-Pit 5

Total Bases
Wagner-Pit 242
Doyle-NY 239
Konetchy-StL 228
Mitchell-Cin 225
D.Miller-Pit 222

Runs Batted In
Wagner-Pit 100
Murray-NY 91
D.Miller-Pit 87
Mitchell-Cin 86
Konetchy-StL 80

Runs Produced
Wagner-Pit 187
Mitchell-Cin 165
Konetchy-StL 164
Leach-Pit 163
Clarke-Pit 162

Bases On Balls
Clarke-Pit 80
Byrne-StL-Pit 78
Evers-Chi 73
Sheckard-Chi 72
Bridwell-NY 67

Batting Average
Wagner-Pit 339
Mitchell-Cin 310
Hoblitzel-Cin 308
Doyle-NY 302
Bridwell-NY 294

On Base Percentage
Wagner-Pit 420
Bridwell-NY 386
Clarke-Pit 384
Mitchell-Cin 378
Evers-Chi 369

Slugging Average
Wagner-Pit 489
Mitchell-Cin 430
Doyle-NY 419
Hoblitzel-Cin 418
McCormick-NY 402

Production
Wagner-Pit 909
Mitchell-Cin 808
Hoblitzel-Cin 782
Doyle-NY 779
Konetchy-StL 762

Adjusted Production
Wagner-Pit 168
Mitchell-Cin 152
Konetchy-StL 145
Hoblitzel-Cin 144
Doyle-NY 140

Batter Runs
Wagner-Pit 48.1
Mitchell-Cin 30.4
Doyle-NY 26.2
Clarke-Pit 25.4
Konetchy-StL 24.9

Adjusted Batter Runs
Wagner-Pit 39.6
Mitchell-Cin 31.1
Konetchy-StL 30.6
Hoblitzel-Cin 25.0
Doyle-NY 24.9

Clutch Hitting Index
Murray-NY 130
Abstein-Pit 129
Wagner-Pit 128
Lobert-Cin 125
D.Miller-Pit 124

Runs Created
Wagner-Pit 117
Mitchell-Cin 98
Doyle-NY 96
Clarke-Pit 92
Konetchy-StL 92

Total Average
Wagner-Pit 1.058
Mitchell-Cin 884
Clarke-Pit 821
Doyle-NY 809
Konetchy-StL 791

Stolen Bases
Bescher-Cin 54
Murray-NY 48
Egan-Cin 39
Magee-Phi 38
Burch-Bro 38

Stolen Base Average

Stolen Base Runs

Fielding Runs
Doolan-Phi 24.6
Egan-Cin 24.1
Byrne-StL-Pit 22.8
Bergen-Bro 21.7
Tinker-Chi 19.7

Total Player Rating
Wagner-Pit 5.2
Konetchy-StL 3.7
Devlin-NY 3.7
Mitchell-Cin 3.4
Byrne-StL-Pit 2.9

Wins
M.Brown-Chi 27
Mathewson-NY 25
H.Camnitz-Pit 25
Willis-Pit 22

Win Percentage
Mathewson-NY 806
H.Camnitz-Pit 806
M.Brown-Chi 750
Pfiester-Chi 739
Leifield-Pit 704

Games
M.Brown-Chi 50
Mattern-Bos 47
Gaspar-Cin 44
Beebe-StL 44

Complete Games
M.Brown-Chi 32
Bell-Bro 29
Rucker-Bro 28
Mathewson-NY 26

Shutouts
Overall-Chi 9
Mathewson-NY 8
M.Brown-Chi 8

Saves
M.Brown-Chi 7
Crandall-NY 6

Innings Pitched
M.Brown-Chi 342.2
Mattern-Bos 316.1
Rucker-Bro 309.1
Moore-Phi 299.2
Willis-Pit 289.2

Fewest Hits/Game
Mathewson-NY . . . 6.28
Fromme-Cin 6.28
Overall-Chi 6.44
M.Brown-Chi 6.46
H.Camnitz-Pit 6.58

Fewest BB/Game
Mathewson-NY 1.18
M.Brown-Chi 1.39
Wiltse-NY 1.70
Maddox-Pit 1.73
McQuillan-Phi 1.96

Strikeouts
Overall-Chi 205
Rucker-Bro 201
Moore-Phi 173
M.Brown-Chi 172
Ames-NY 156

Strikeouts/Game
Overall-Chi 6.47
Rucker-Bro 5.85
Ames-NY 5.75
Marquard-NY 5.67
Moore-Phi 5.20

Ratio
Mathewson-NY 7.45
M.Brown-Chi 8.04
H.Camnitz-Pit 8.97
Overall-Chi 9.22
McQuillan-Phi 9.34

Earned Run Average
Mathewson-NY . . . 1.14
M.Brown-Chi 1.31
Overall-Chi 1.42
H.Camnitz-Pit 1.62
Kroh-Chi 1.65

Adjusted ERA
Mathewson-NY 223
M.Brown-Chi 193
Overall-Chi 178
H.Camnitz-Pit 167
Reulbach-Chi 142

Opponents' Batting Avg.
Overall-Chi 198
Mathewson-NY 200
Fromme-Cin 201
M.Brown-Chi 202
Moore-Phi 210

Opponents' On Base Pct.
Mathewson-NY 228
M.Brown-Chi 239
Overall-Chi 262
H.Camnitz-Pit 267
McQuillan-Phi 271

Starter Runs
M.Brown-Chi 48.6
Mathewson-NY 44.2
Overall-Chi 37.0
H.Camnitz-Pit 30.4
Reulbach-Chi 23.6

Adjusted Starter Runs
M.Brown-Chi 46.5
Mathewson-NY 43.0
Overall-Chi 35.2
H.Camnitz-Pit 34.3
Adams-Pit 23.2

Clutch Pitching Index
Richie-Phi-Bos 126
Corridon-Phi 123
Sallee-StL 119
Wilhelm-Bro 117
Marquard-NY 117

Relief Runs

Adjusted Relief Runs

Relief Ranking

Total Pitcher Index
Mathewson-NY 7.0
M.Brown-Chi 5.4
Overall-Chi 5.1
H.Camnitz-Pit 3.7
Fromme-Cin 3.1

Total Baseball Ranking
Mathewson-NY 7.0
M.Brown-Chi 5.4
Wagner-Pit 5.2
Overall-Chi 5.1
Konetchy-StL 3.7

February 18 The Boston Red Sox trade Cy Young, who won 21 games at age 41 last season, to the Cleveland Naps for pitchers Charlie Chech and Jack Ryan, and $12,500.

April 8 While at spring training, Hal Chase of the Highlanders contracts smallpox. The entire team is vaccinated and quarantined while traveling north.

April 12 Philadelphia's Shibe Park, the first original steel-and-concrete major league park, is dedicated as a record crowd of 31,160 sees 18-year-old John "Stuffy" McInnis make his major league debut at shortstop. Eddie Plank pitches the A's to an 8-1 win over Boston.

April 18 The Tigers announce plans to build a new concrete and steel stadium, and the Pirates name their million-dollar ballpark Forbes Field in honor of the Revolutionary War general who founded Pittsburgh.

May 31* Pitchers Otto Burns of Decatur and Ed Clarke of Bloomington (Three I League) both go the distance in a 26-inning game won by Decatur 2–1.

June 10 George Mullin's winning streak reaches 11 with a 2–1 win over New York. On the 15th, he will finally lose to the Athletics 5–4.

June 19 Walter Johnson has a strange day beating the New York Highlanders 7–4. He gives up just three hits, but is unusually wild, issuing seven walks, un-corking four wild pitches, and hitting one batter, while fanning 10.

July 2 The White Sox steal 12 bases in the course of a 15–3 win over St. Louis. Three are steals of home, including one by pitcher Ed Walsh in the sixth inning.

July 16 Detroit and Washington play the longest scoreless game in AL history—18 innings. Ed Summers pitches the complete game, holding the Nationals to seven hits. The Nationals' 30-year-old rookie, Bill "Dolly" Gray, allows only one hit before leaving with an injury in the ninth.

July 19 Cleveland shortstop Neal Ball executes the majors' first unassisted triple play in the new century in the top of the second against the Red Sox. With Heinie Wagner on second base and Jake Stahl on first base, Amby McConnell hits a line drive to Ball, who steps on second base and tags Stahl coming down from first base.

July 31 For the second time in two years—the first was on May 21,1908— Bill Burns has a no-hitter broken up with two outs in the ninth, when Washington's Otis Clymer singles. Burns is the only pitcher to suffer this fate twice, until Dave Stieb of Toronto does on September 24 and 30, 1988.

August 4 Umpire Tim Hurst instigates a riot by spitting at Athletics second baseman Eddie Collins, who had questioned a call. This incident eventually leads to Hurst's banishment from baseball two weeks later.

September 13 Ty Cobb clinches the AL home run title with his ninth round-tripper. It is an inside-the-park drive against the Browns. In fact, all his nine home runs this season are inside the park, including two in one game on July 15. He is the only player in this century to lead in home runs without hitting one out of the park.

September 18 Ty Cobb wins the Triple Crown with a .377 batting average, nine home runs, and 107 RBI. He also leads the AL with 216 hits, 116 runs, and 296 total bases.

October 9 The Tigers win the second game of the World Series behind Bill Donovan 7-2. Ty Cobb's steal of home highlights a 3-run third. Detroit has been defenseless against stolen bases in the past three World Series, giving up 16 in five games to the Cubs in 1907, 15 in five games to the Cubs in 1908, and 18 in seven games to the Pirates this year, for a total of 49 in 17 games, the highest stolen base totals in all of World Series history.

October 14 George Mullin outlasts three Pirates pitchers for a 5-4 win that sends the Series to a seventh game in Detroit, making this the first World Series to go the limit.

	BOSTON		CHICAGO		CLEVELAND		DETROIT		NEW YORK		PHILADELPHIA		ST.LOUIS		WASHINGTON
M	F.Lake	M	B.Sullivan	M	N.Lajoie	M	H.Jennings	M	G.Stallings	M	C.Mack	M	J.McAleer	M	J.Cantillon
1B	J.Stahl	1B	F.Isbell	M	D.McGuire	1B	C.Rossman	1B	H.Chase	1B	H.Davis	1B	T.Jones	1B	J.Donahue
2B	A.McConnell	2B	J.Atz	1B	G.Stovall	2B	G.Schaefer	2B	F.LaPorte	2B	E.Collins	2B	J.Williams	2B	J.Delahanty
SS	H.Wagner	SS	F.Parent	2B	N.Lajoie	SS	D.Bush	SS	J.Knight	SS	J.Barry	SS	B.Wallace	SS	G.McBride
3B	H.Lord	3B	L.Tannehill	SS	N.Ball	3B	G.Moriarty	3B	J.Austin	3B	F.Baker	3B	H.Ferris	3B	W.Conroy
LF	H.Niles	LF	P.Dougherty	LF	B.Bradley	LF	M.McIntyre	LF	C.Engle	LF	G.Stone	LF	G.Stone	LF	J.Lelivelt
CF	T.Speaker	CF	D.Altizer	LF	B.Hinchman	CF	S.Crawford	CF	R.Demmitt	CF	R.Oldring	CF	D.Hoffman	CF	C.Milan
RF	D.Gessler	RF	E.Hahn	CF	J.Birmingham	RF	T.Cobb	RF	W.Keeler	RF	D.Murphy	RF	R.Hartzell	RF	G.Browne
C	B.Carrigan	C	B.Sullivan	RF	W.Good	C	B.Schmidt	C	R.Kleinow	C	I.Thomas	C	L.Criger	C	G.Street
				C	T.Easterly										
O	H.Hooper	32	B.Purtell			32	C.O'Leary	O	B.Cree	O	B.Ganley	1O	A.Griggs	1O	B.Unglaub
C	P.Donahue	OP	D.White	3S	G.Perring	C	O.Stanage	S3	K.Elberfeld	O	H.Heitmuller	O	J.McAleese	O	O.Clymer
2S	C.French	C	F.Owens	O	B.Lord	O	D.Jones	O	C.Hemphill	O	P.Livingston	O	J.Stephens	2	G.Schaefer
1P	H.Wolter	O	W.Cole	O	E.Flick	1	T.Jones	C	J.Sweeney	S	S.Nicholls	O	A.Schweitzer	O	R.Killefer
C	T.Spencer	O	B.Messenger	2S	T.Turner	2	J.Delahanty	C	W.Blair	C	J.Lapp	O	W.Devoy	3	B.Yohe
O	J.Thoney	C	F.Payne	C	N.Clarke	2	R.Killefer	2	E.Gardner	O	S.Barr	O	N.Crompton	O	B.Ganley
/3	L.Gardner	O	M.Welday	C	H.Bemis	C	H.Beckendorf	1	G.McConnell	S	S.McInnis	O	B.Shotton	C	C.Blankenship
/C	B.Madden	1	G.Davis	O	D.Reilley	/C	J.Casey	/2	A.Orth	/O	A.Strunk	/1	H.Patterson	1	J.Slattery
/O	P.Howard	O	G.Cravath	S	D.Stark	/1	D.Gainer	/2	N.Ball	/S	M.Rath	C	W.Smith	/O	D.Gessler
/1	B.Danzig	2	B.Reilly	/3	M.Netzel	/1	H.Jennings	/2	J.Ward	/O	J.Jackson	C	B.Killefer	O	W.Miller
/S	S.Yerkes	/O	C.Barrows	/O	T.Raftery			/2	B.Vaughn	/C	E.Larkin	/O	C.Rossman	1	J.Freeman
		/1	J.Donahue	/C	B.Higgins			/1	E.Tiemeyer	/C	J.Curry			2	S.Kelly
P	F.Arellanes	/1	H.Patterson	/O	J.Clarke	P	G.Mullin	/S	J.Wanner	/C	D.Powers	P	J.Powell	/O	J.Tannehill
P	J.Wood			/O	W.Doane	P	E.Willett	H	I.McIlveen			P	R.Waddell	/C	J.Hardy
P	E.Cicotte	P	F.Smith	/C	G.Land	P	E.Summers			P	E.Plank	P	B.Pelty	/3	B.Shipke
P	C.Chech	P	J.Scott	/O	D.Sullivan	P	E.Killian			P	C.Bender	P	B.Bailey	/C	M.Kahoe
			E.Walsh			P	B.Donovan	P	J.Warhop	P	C.Morgan	P	B.Grahame	/O	O.Collins
								P	J.Lake	P	H.Krause			/1	T.Crooke
P	E.Steele	P	B.Burns	P	C.Young	P	K.Speer	P	R.Manning	P	J.Coombs	P	B.Dinneen	/O	G.Cravath
P	R.Collins			P	H.Berger	P	R.Works	P	L.Brockett			P	D.Criss	/O	F.Hemphill
P	B.Schlitzer	P	H.Suter	P	A.Joss	P	G.Suggs	P	S.Doyle			P	H.Howell	/O	J.Sebring
P	E.Karger	P	L.Fiene	P	C.Falkenberg	/P	B.Lelivelt			P	J.Dygert	P	R.Vickers		
P	C.Morgan	/P	F.Olmstead	P	B.Rhoads	/P	E.Lafitte	P	T.Hughes	P	R.Vickers	/P	C.Rose		
P	J.Ryan	/P	F.Owen			/P	E.Jones	P	J.Quinn	/P	B.Schlitzer	/P	E.Kusel	P	W.Johnson
P	C.Hall	/P	N.Altrock	P	G.Liebhardt			P	P.Wilson	/P	T.Atkins	/P	J.Gilligan	P	B.Groom
P	L.Pape			P	C.Sitton			/P	J.Chesbro	/P	J.Kull	/P	P.Stremmel	P	D.Gray
P	F.Burchell			/P	H.Ables			/P	D.Newton			/P	B.McCorry	P	C.Smith
/P	C.Smith			/P	L.Wright			/P	D.Carroll					P	T.Hughes
/P	W.Matthews			/P	J.Upp			/P	B.Schmidt						
/P	F.Anderson			/P	H.Otis			/P	R.Ford					P	R.Witherup
/P	J.Chesbro			/P	R.Booles									P	D.Reisling
/P	C.Nourse			/P	W.Mitchell									/P	F.Oberlin
				/P	F.Winchell									/P	N.Altrock
														/P	D.Walker
														/P	B.Burns
														/P	B.Forman
														/P	J.Ohl
														/P	B.Keeley
														/P	J.Hovlik

TEAM	G	W	L	PCT	GB	R	OR	AB	H	2B	3B	HR	BB	SO	AVG	OBP	SLG	PRO	PRO+	BR	/A	PF	CHI	RC	SB	CS	SBA	SBR
DET	158	98	54	.645		666	493	5095	1360	209	58	19	397		.267	.325	.342	.667	113	98	70	104	103	660	280			
PHI	153	95	58	.621	3.5	605	408	4906	1257	186	88	21	403		.256	.321	.343	.664	115	91	79	102	97	613	205			
BOS	152	88	63	.583	9.5	597	550	4979	1307	151	69	20	348		.263	.321	.333	.654	112	73	60	102	99	599	215			
CHI	159	78	74	.513	20	492	463	5018	1109	145	56	4	441		.221	.291	.275	.566	89	-73	-53	96	104	474	211			
NY	153	74	77	.490	23.5	590	587	4981	1234	143	61	16	407		.248	.313	.311	.624	103	25	21	101	105	547	187			
CLE	155	71	82	.464	27.5	493	532	5048	1216	173	81	10	283		.241	.288	.313	.601	93	-28	-48	104	99	501	174			
STL	154	61	89	.407	36	441	575	4964	1151	116	45	10	331		.232	.287	.279	.566	91	-79	-48	93	100	436	136			
WAS	156	42	110	.276	56	380	656	4983	1113	149	41	9	321		.223	.276	.275	.551	84	-108	-89	95	91	420	136			
TOT	620					4264		39974	9747	1272	499	109	2931	4918	.244	.303	.309	.611							1544			

TEAM	CG	SH	SV	IP	H	H/G	HR	BB	SO	RAT	ERA	ERA+	OAV	OOB	PR	/A	PF	CPI	FA	E	DP	FW	PW	BW	SBW	DIF
DET	117	17	12	1420¹	1254	7.9	16	359	528	10.6	2.26	111	.238	.293	33	40	102	100	.959	276	87	.4	4.5	8.0		9.1
PHI	110	27	3	1378	1069	7.0	9	386	728	9.9	1.93	124	.217	.282	82	72	97	96	.961	245	92	1.8	8.2	9.0		-.5
BOS	75	11	15	1360¹	1214	8.0	18	384	555	10.9	2.59	96	.243	.303	-19	-16	101	96	.955	292	95	-1.3	-1.8	6.8		8.8
CHI	115	26	4	1430¹	1182	7.4	8	340	669	9.9	2.05	114	.229	.283	67	44	95	96	.964	246	101	2.4	5.0	-6.0		.6
NY	94	18	3	1350¹	1223	8.2	21	422	597	11.4	2.65	95	.248	.316	-26	-21	102	104	.948	330	94	-3.6	-2.4	2.4		2.1
CLE	110	15	3	1361	1212	8.0	9	348	568	10.6	2.40	106	.250	.307	11	21	103	107	.957	278	110	-.0	2.4	-5.5		-2.4
STL	105	21	4	1354²	1287	8.6	16	383	620	11.4	2.88	84	.261	.319	-61	-72	98	101	.958	267	107	.5	-8.2	-5.5		-.9
WAS	99	11	2	1374²	1288	8.4	12	424	653	11.6	3.04	80	.248	.312	-87	-96	98	87	.957	280	100	-.0	-10.9	-10.1		-12.9
TOT	825	146	51	11029²		7.9				10.8	2.47		.244	.303					.957	2214	786					

Runs
Cobb-Det 116
Bush-Det 114
Collins-Phi 104
Lord-Bos 86
Crawford-Det 83

Hits
Cobb-Det 216
Collins-Phi 198
Crawford-Det 185
Speaker-Bos 168
Lord-Bos 166

Doubles
Crawford-Det 35
Lajoie-Cle 33
Cobb-Det 33
Collins-Phi 30
Murphy-Phi 28

Triples
Baker-Phi 19
Murphy-Phi 14
Crawford-Det 14

Home Runs
Cobb-Det 9
Speaker-Bos 7
Stahl-Bos 6
Crawford-Det 6
Murphy-Phi 5

Total Bases
Cobb-Det 296
Crawford-Det 266
Collins-Phi 257
Baker-Phi 242
Speaker-Bos 241

Runs Batted In
Cobb-Det 107
Crawford-Det 97
Baker-Phi 85
Speaker-Bos 77
Davis-Phi 75

Runs Produced
Cobb-Det 214
Crawford-Det 174
Collins-Phi 157
Baker-Phi 154
Bush-Det 147

Bases On Balls
Bush-Det 88
Collins-Phi 62
Demmitt-NY 55
McIntyre-Det 54

Batting Average
Cobb-Det .... .377
Collins-Phi ..... .347
Lajoie-Cle ...... .324
Crawford-Det .... .314
Lord-Bos .... .311

On Base Percentage
Cobb-Det .... .431
Collins-Phi ..... .416
Bush-Det .... .380
Lajoie-Cle ...... .378
Stahl-Bos .... .377

Slugging Average
Cobb-Det .... .517
Crawford-Det .... .452
Collins-Phi ..... .450
Baker-Phi .... .447
Speaker-Bos ..... .443

Production
Cobb-Det .... .947
Collins-Phi ..... .866
Crawford-Det .... .817
Stahl-Bos .... .812
Lajoie-Cle ...... .809

Adjusted Production
Cobb-Det 190
Collins-Phi 170
Stahl-Bos 153
Crawford-Det 151
Speaker-Bos 151

Batter Runs
Cobb-Det 63.3
Collins-Phi 49.1
Crawford-Det 36.7
Speaker-Bos 31.5
Lajoie-Cle 28.8

Adjusted Batter Runs
Cobb-Det 57.9
Collins-Phi 46.9
Crawford-Det 32.4
Speaker-Bos 29.6
Stahl-Bos 26.8

Clutch Hitting Index
Chase-NY 143
Engle-NY 132
Crawford-Det 129
Cobb-Det 125
Davis-Phi 122

Runs Created
Cobb-Det 159
Collins-Phi 134
Crawford-Det 108
Speaker-Bos 99
Baker-Phi 90

Total Average
Cobb-Det 1.193
Collins-Phi 1.051
Stahl-Bos .... .857
Speaker-Bos ..... .854
Crawford-Det .... .851

Stolen Bases
Cobb-Det 76
Collins-Phi 67
Bush-Det 53
Lord-Bos 36
Dougherty-Chi ... 36

Stolen Base Average

Stolen Base Runs

Fielding Runs
Speaker-Bos 23.0
Lajoie-Cle 18.6
Parent-Chi 16.6
McConnell-Bos ... 14.5
Wagner-Bos 14.0

Total Player Rating
Cobb-Det 6.1
Collins-Phi 5.7
Speaker-Bos 5.2
Lajoie-Cle 4.6
Baker-Phi 2.5

Wins
Mullin-Det 29
Smith-Chi 25
Willett-Det 21

Win Percentage
Mullin-Det ...... .784
Krause-Phi ...... .692
Bender-Phi ...... .692
Summers-Det ..... .679
Willett-Det ..... .677

Games
Smith-Chi 51
Arellanes-Bos ... 45
Groom-Was 44
Willett-Det 41

Complete Games
Smith-Chi 37
Young-Cle 30
Mullin-Det 29
Johnson-Was 27
Morgan-Bos-Phi .. 26

Shutouts
Walsh-Chi 8
Smith-Chi 7
Krause-Phi 7
Coombs-Phi 6

Saves
Arellanes-Bos ... 8
Powell-StL 3

Innings Pitched
Smith-Chi 365.0
Mullin-Det 303.2
Johnson-Was 296.1
Young-Cle 294.1
Morgan-Bos-Phi .. 293.1

Fewest Hits/Game
Morgan-Bos-Phi .. 6.26
Krause-Phi 6.38
Walsh-Chi 6.49
Cicotte-Bos 6.61
Wood-Bos 6.78

Fewest BB/Game
Joss-Cle 1.15
White-Chi 1.57
Powell-StL 1.58
Bender-Phi 1.62
Summers-Det 1.66

Strikeouts
Smith-Chi 177
Johnson-Was 164
Berger-Cle 162
Bender-Phi 161
Waddell-StL 141

Strikeouts/Game
Berger-Cle 5.90
Krause-Phi 5.87
Bender-Phi 5.80
Waddell-StL 5.76
Bailey-StL 5.16

Ratio
Walsh-Chi 8.60
Joss-Cle 8.64
Smith-Chi 8.73
Bender-Phi 8.86
Krause-Phi 9.00

Earned Run Average
Krause-Phi 1.39
Walsh-Chi 1.41
Bender-Phi 1.66
Joss-Cle 1.71
Killian-Det 1.71

Adjusted ERA
Krause-Phi 172
Walsh-Chi 166
Joss-Cle 149
Killian-Det 147
Bender-Phi 145

Opponents' Batting Avg.
Morgan-Bos-Phi .. .202
Walsh-Chi .... .203
Krause-Phi ...... .204
Wood-Bos .... .209
Cicotte-Bos ..... .210

Opponents' On Base Pct.
Walsh-Chi .... .253
Bender-Phi ...... .254
Joss-Cle .... .255
Smith-Chi .... .257
Krause-Phi ...... .266

Starter Runs
Walsh-Chi 27.2
Smith-Chi 27.2
Krause-Phi 25.5
Bender-Phi 22.6
Morgan-Bos-Phi .. 21.5

Adjusted Starter Runs
Krause-Phi 23.8
Walsh-Chi 23.8
Joss-Cle 22.8
Smith-Chi 21.7
Bender-Phi 20.6

Clutch Pitching Index
Burns-Was-Chi ... 142
Killian-Det 132
Brockett-NY 132
Waddell-StL 125
Bailey-StL 117

Relief Runs

Adjusted Relief Runs

Relief Ranking

Total Pitcher Index
Smith-Chi 4.6
Walsh-Chi 4.4
Bender-Phi 2.9
Lake-NY 2.7
Plank-Phi 2.7

Total Baseball Ranking
Cobb-Det 6.1
Collins-Phi 5.7
Speaker-Bos 5.2
Lajoie-Cle 4.6
Smith-Chi 4.6

March 25 Chalmers Auto Company of Detroit offers to award a new car to the batting champs of each league, and the National Commission accepts.

April 1 Johnny Kling, who played for a Chicago semipro team while holding out for the entire 1909 season, is reinstated, fined $700, and required to play for the Cubs at his 1908 salary of $4,500.

May 4 President Taft sees the Reds and the Cardinals at Robison Field in St. Louis. Reds pitchers will walk 16 in the 12–3 loss, but Taft doesn't stick around. He leaves for Sportsman's Park in hopes of seeing some good baseball and is rewarded by a 3–3, 14-inning battle between the Browns' Joe Lake and the Naps' Cy Young that ends in darkness.

May 23 The Reds' Dode Paskert steals second, third, and home in the last inning against Boston.

May 26 The Pirates' Honus Wagner and John Miller narrowly escape death when their car crashes into the safety gates of a railroad crossing in Carnegie, PA.

June 21 Brooklyn rookie Jack Dalton has five straight hits off Christy Mathewson. Dalton will finish 1910 hitting .227.

June 22 Congressman John K. Tener, former Chicago White Stockings and Pittsburgh Alleghenies pitcher, wins the Republican nomination for governor of Pennsylvania. He will be elected and will serve as president of the NL while governor.

August 3 St. Louis manager-catcher Roger Bresnahan pitches 3⅓ innings, giving up six hits and no runs against Brooklyn. He last pitched in 1901, and will end his career with a mark of 4–1 as a hurler.

August 13 In the most evenly matched game ever played, the Pirates and Superbas (Dodgers) each have eight runs, 13 hits, 38 at bats, five strikeouts, three walks, one hit batter, one passed ball, 13 assists, 27 putouts, two errors, and use two pitchers.

August 23 Fred Clarke makes a record four outfield assists for Pittsburgh against the Phils.

September 19* A game between Mobile and Atlanta (Southern Association) takes just 32 minutes to complete. The game is conducted as an experiment with batters swinging at every good pitch and little time taken between pitches. There are no strikeouts and one walk as Mobile wins 2–1.

October 9* The Leland Giants begin a 16-game series in Havana, Cuba. The black team will play a series against the AL champion Detroit Tigers.

October 18 The Reds beat the Indians 8–5 in the seventh game of the first Ohio championship series.

October 20 Cubs manager Frank Chance becomes the first player ejected from a World Series game. Umpire Tom Connolly tosses Chance for protesting a Danny Murphy home run that struck a sign over the right field bleachers in Chicago in decisive Game 5.

December 13 Former New York Giant Dan McGann, who ended his 13-year career in 1908, shoots himself in a Louisville hotel.

BOSTON	BROOKLYN	CHICAGO	CINCINNATI	NEW YORK	PHILADELPHIA	PITTSBURGH	ST.LOUIS
M F.Lake	M B.Dahlen	M F.Chance	M C.Griffith	M J.McGraw	M R.Dooin	M F.Clarke	M R.Bresnahan
1B B.Sharpe	1B J.Daubert	1B F.Chance	1B D.Hoblitzel	1B F.Merkle	1B K.Bransfield	1B J.Flynn	1B E.Konetchy
2B D.Shean	2B J.Hummel	2B J.Evers	2B D.Egan	2B L.Doyle	2B O.Knabe	2B D.Miller	2B M.Huggins
SS B.Sweeney	SS T.Smith	SS J.Tinker	SS T.McMillan	SS A.Bridwell	SS M.Doolan	SS H.Wagner	SS A.Hauser
3B B.Herzog	3B E.Lennox	3B H.Steinfeldt	3B H.Lobert	3B A.Devlin	3B E.Grant	3B B.Byrne	3B M.Mowrey
LF B.Collins	LF Z.Wheat	LF J.Sheckard	LF B.Bescher	LF J.Devore	LF S.Magee	LF F.Clarke	LF R.Ellis
CF F.Beck	CF B.Davidson	CF S.Hofman	CF D.Paskert	CF F.Snodgrass	CF J.Bates	CF T.Leach	CF R.Oakes
RF D.Miller	RF J.Dalton	RF F.Schulte	RF M.Mitchell	RF R.Murray	RF J.Titus	RF C.Wilson	RF S.Evans
C P.Graham	C B.Bergen	C J.Kling	C L.McLean	C C.Meyers	C R.Dooin	C G.Gibson	C E.Phelps
S E.Abbaticchio	O1 A.Burch	C1 J.Archer	S3 T.Downey	O C.Seymour	O J.Walsh	O V.Campbell	C R.Bresnahan
C H.Smith	3 P.McElveen	2S H.Zimmerman	C T.Clarke	O B.Becker	C P.Moran	2S B.McKechnie	S R.Hulswitt
32 G.Getz	C T.Erwin	O G.Beaumont	O W.Miller	S2 A.Fletcher	1 J.Ward	1 H.Hyatt	O E.Zacher
C B.Rariden	S D.Stark	C T.Needham	S S.Woodruff	C A.Schlei	C R.Thomas	C M.Simon	C F.Betcher
O W.Good	O B.Coulson	O J.Kane	2 M.Corcoran	C A.Wilson	1 F.Luderus	/1 J.Kading	O O.Abbott
O H.Moran	O H.Smith	1 F.Luderus	/3 A.Phelan	/3 T.Shafer	/C E.McDonough	P B.Sharpe	C J.Bliss
3 J.Burg	S T.McMillan	H D.Miller	/O S.McCabe	/1 H.Gowdy	/O J.Castle	/S A.McCarthy	/3 J.Barbeau
/O R.Sellers	C O.Miller	P M.Brown	/C F.Roth	/O W.Keeler	/C H.Cheek	/O M.Carey	/O B.O'Hara
1 D.Martel	/O H.Lumley	P K.Cole	/S C.Charles	/O E.Zacher	P E.Moore	/C P.O'Connor	/O E.Lush
/O B.Cooney	H T.Jordan	P H.McIntire	/3 J.Doyle	P C.Mathewson	P B.Ewing	/S E.Abbaticchio	/C B.Kelly
H F.Liese	H B.Dahlen	P E.Reulbach	/S D.Altizer	P H.Wiltse	P L.Moren	P H.Camnitz	P B.Harmon
/C R.Elliott	/O G.Hunter	P O.Overall	/3 R.Robinson	P L.Drucke	P G.McQuillan	P B.Adams	P J.Lush
H A.Kruger	P N.Rucker	P L.Richie	/O M.Konnick	P D.Crandall	P E.Stack	P L.Leifield	P V.Willis
H F.Lake	P G.Bell	P J.Pfiester	H G.Wheeler	P R.Ames	P L.Schettler	P K.White	P F.Corridon
/O J.Riley	P C.Barger	P B.Pfeffer	/O N.Crompton	P B.Raymond	P B.Foxen	P D.Phillippe	P L.Backman
P A.Mattern	P D.Scanlan	/P R.Kroh	P J.Burns	P R.Marquard	P A.Brennan	P S.Leever	P S.Sallee
P B.Brown	P E.Knetzer	/P O.Weaver	/S B.Meinke	P W.Dickson	P J.Moroney	P N.Maddox	/P B.Steele
P S.Frock	RP R.Dessau	/P A.Carson	R C.Griffith	/P E.Hendricks	/C C.Girard	/P B.Powell	/P R.Golden
P C.Curtis	P K.Wilhelm	/P B.Foxen	P H.Gaspar	/P D.Rudolph	/P G.Chalmers	/P J.Ferry	/P B.Hearn
P G.Ferguson	/P F.Miller		P G.Suggs	/P A.Klawitter	/P B.Slaughter	/P L.Webb	/P E.Zmich
P B.Burke	/P S.Burk		P J.Rowan		/P T.Sparks	/P E.Steele	P C.Alberts
P J.Parson	/P G.Crable		P F.Beebe		/P B.Humphries	/P G.Moore	P E.Rieger
P C.Evans	/P F.Schneiberg		P B.Burns		/P B.Culp	/P K.Dowd	P E.Higgins
/P K.White			P A.Fromme		/P P.Flaherty	/P S.Frock	/P C.Pickett
/P L.Richie			/P H.Coveleski			/P J.Mercer	/P J.Raleigh
/P L.Tyler			/P R.Benton				/P R.Geyer
/P R.Good			/P W.Anderson				/P H.Patton
			/P B.Spade				/P B.Chambers
			/P R.Castleton				
			/P S.Doyle				
			/P M.Walker				
			/P T.Cantwell				
			/P W.Slagle				

TEAM	G	W	L	PCT	GB	R	OR	AB	H	2B	3B	HR	BB	SO	AVG	OBP	SLG	PRO	PRO+	BR	/A	PF	CHI	RC	SB	CS	SBA	SBR
CHI	154	104	50	.675		712	**499**	4977	1333	219	**84**	34	542	501	.268	.344	**.366**	.710	114	81	87	99	101	696	173			
NY	155	91	63	.591	13	**715**	567	5061	**1391**	204	83	31	562	489	.275	.354	**.366**	**.720**	116	106	105	100	97	**759**	282			
PIT	154	86	67	.562	17.5	655	576	5125	1364	214	83	33	437	524	.266	.328	.360	.688	100	30	-8	100	100	655	148			
PHI	157	78	75	.510	25.5	674	639	5171	1319	**223**	71	22	506	559	.255	.327	.338	.665	97	-4	-25	103	**106**	641	199			
CIN	156	75	79	.487	29	620	684	5121	1326	150	79	23	529	515	.259	.332	.333	.665	105	0	28	96	98	669	**310**			
BRO	156	64	90	.416	40	497	623	5125	1174	166	73	25	434	599	.229	.294	.305	.599	82	-132	-117	97	101	506	151			
STL	153	63	90	.412	40.5	639	718	4912	1217	167	70	15	**655**	581	.248	.345	.319	.664	103	19	43	96	99	609	179			
BOS	157	53	100	.346	50.5	495	701	5123	1260	173	49	31	359	540	.246	.301	.317	.618	81	-99	-122	105	96	536	152			
TOT	621					5007		40615	10384	1516	592	214	4024	4415	.256	.328	.338	.666							1594			

TEAM	CG	SH	SV	IP	H	H/G	HR	BB	SO	RAT	ERA	ERA+	OAV	OOB	PR	/A	PF	CPI	FA	E	DP	FW	PW	BW	SBW	DIF
CHI	100	**25**	13	1378²	**1171**	**7.6**	18	474	609	11.0	**2.51**	115	**.235**	.307	79	**54**	95	95	.963	**230**	110	2.1	5.7	9.2		10.1
NY	96	9	10	1391²	1290	8.3	30	397	**717**	11.2	2.68	110	.250	.308	54	44	98	99	.955	291	117	-1.7	4.6	**11.1**		.0
PIT	73	13	12	1376	1254	8.2	20	**392**	479	11.1	2.83	109	.250	.311	29	38	102	93	.961	245	102	1.1	4.0	-.8		5.2
PHI	84	17	9	1411¹	1297	8.3	36	547	657	12.1	3.05	102	.253	.330	-5	9	103	101	.960	258	132	.6	.9	-2.6		2.6
CIN	86	16	11	1386²	1334	8.7	27	528	497	12.5	3.08	94	.261	.338	-9	-29	96	105	.955	291	103	-1.6	-3.1	2.9		-.3
BRO	**103**	15	5	1420¹	1331	8.4	17	545	555	12.0	3.07	99	.259	.335	-7	-9	100	101	**.964**	235	125	2.0	-.9	-12.3		-1.7
STL	81	4	**14**	1337¹	1396	9.4	30	541	466	13.3	3.78	79	.275	.350	-112	-120	98	96	.959	261	109	.0	-12.6	4.5		-5.4
BOS	72	12	9	1390¹	1328	8.6	36	599	531	12.8	3.22	103	.265	.349	-30	14	110	**110**	.954	305	**137**	-2.4	1.5	-12.8		-9.8
TOT	695	111	83	11092¹		8.4				12.0	3.02		.256	.328					.959	2116	935					

Runs		Hits		Doubles		Triples		Home Runs		Total Bases	
Magee-Phi	110	Wagner-Pit	178	Byrne-Pit	43	Mitchell-Cin	18	Schulte-Chi	10	Magee-Phi	263
Huggins-StL	101	Byrne-Pit	178	Magee-Phi	39	Magee-Phi	17	Beck-Bos	10	Schulte-Chi	257
Byrne-Pit	101	Wheat-Bro	172	Wheat-Bro	36	Konetchy-StL	16	Doyle-NY	8	Byrne-Pit	251
Doyle-NY	97	Magee-Phi	172	Merkle-NY	35	Hofman-Chi	16	Daubert-Bro	8	Wheat-Bro	244
Bescher-Cin	95	Hoblitzel-Cin	170	Wagner-Pit	34					Wagner-Pit	240

Runs Batted In		Runs Produced		Bases On Balls		Batting Average		On Base Percentage		Slugging Average	
Magee-Phi	123	Magee-Phi	227	Huggins-StL	116	Magee-Phi	.331	Magee-Phi	.445	Magee-Phi	.507
Mitchell-Cin	88	Wagner-Pit	167	Evers-Chi	108	Campbell-Pit	.326	Snodgrass-NY	.440	Hofman-Chi	.461
Murray-NY	87	Hofman-Chi	166	Magee-Phi	94	Hofman-Chi	.325	Evers-Chi	.413	Schulte-Chi	.460
Hofman-Chi	86	Mitchell-Cin	162	Titus-Phi	93	Snodgrass-NY	.321	Hofman-Chi	.406	Merkle-NY	.441
Wagner-Pit	81	Konetchy-StL	162	Sheckard-Chi	83	Wagner-Pit	.320	Huggins-StL	.399	Campbell-Pit	.436

Production		Adjusted Production		Batter Runs		Adjusted Batter Runs		Clutch Hitting Index		Runs Created	
Magee-Phi	.952	Magee-Phi	172	Magee-Phi	54.9	Magee-Phi	50.9	Magee-Phi	139	Magee-Phi	139
Snodgrass-NY	.871	Snodgrass-NY	154	Hofman-Chi	32.4	Hofman-Chi	33.2	Evans-StL	135	Byrne-Pit	104
Hofman-Chi	.867	Hofman-Chi	154	Snodgrass-NY	31.9	Snodgrass-NY	31.8	Devlin-NY	132	Wagner-Pit	103
Konetchy-StL	.822	Konetchy-StL	145	Konetchy-StL	28.0	Konetchy-StL	31.5	Murray-NY	125	Hofman-Chi	102
Wagner-Pit	.822	Schulte-Chi	137	Wagner-Pit	27.9	Wagner-Pit	22.4	Steinfeldt-Chi	124	Doyle-NY	101

Total Average		Stolen Bases		Stolen Base Average		Stolen Base Runs		Fielding Runs		Total Player Rating	
Magee-Phi	1.205	Bescher-Cin	70					Shean-Bos	42.5	Konetchy-StL	4.1
Snodgrass-NY	1.071	Murray-NY	57					Doolan-Phi	20.7	Hofman-Chi	3.4
Hofman-Chi	.975	Paskert-Cin	51					Tinker-Chi	15.5	Wagner-Pit	3.2
Konetchy-StL	.884	Magee-Phi	49					Paskert-Cin	14.1	Mowrey-StL	3.2
Paskert-Cin	.884	Devore-NY	43					Knabe-Phi	13.9	Magee-Phi	3.2

Wins		Win Percentage		Games		Complete Games		Shutouts		Saves	
Mathewson-NY	27	Cole-Chi	.833	Mattern-Bos	51	Rucker-Bro	27	Rucker-Bro	6	Gaspar-Cin	7
Brown-Chi	25	Crandall-NY	.810	Gaspar-Cin	48	Mathewson-NY	27	Moore-Phi	6	Brown-Chi	7
Moore-Phi	22	Mathewson-NY	.750			Brown-Chi	27	Mattern-Bos	6	Crandall-NY	5
Suggs-Cin	20	Adams-Pit	.667			Bell-Bro	25	Brown-Chi	6	Richie-Bos-Chi	4
Cole-Chi	20	Brown-Chi	.641			Barger-Bro	25			Phillippe-Pit	4

Innings Pitched		Fewest Hits/Game		Fewest BB/Game		Strikeouts		Strikeouts/Game		Ratio	
Rucker-Bro	320.1	Cole-Chi	6.53	Suggs-Cin	1.62	Moore-Phi	185	Drucke-NY	6.31	Brown-Chi	9.87
Mathewson-NY	318.1	Scanlan-Bro	7.25	Mathewson-NY	1.70	Mathewson-NY	184	Frock-Pit-Bos	5.98	Mathewson-NY	10.04
Bell-Bro	310.0	Moore-Phi	7.25	Crandall-NY	1.86	Frock-Pit-Bos	171	Moore-Phi	5.88	Bell-Bro	10.25
Mattern-Bos	305.0	Drucke-NY	7.27	Brown-Chi	1.95	Drucke-NY	151	Mathewson-NY	5.20	Adams-Pit	10.40
Brown-Chi	295.1	Ames-NY	7.61	Wiltse-NY	1.99	Rucker-Bro	147	Ames-NY	4.44	Crandall-NY	10.44

Earned Run Average		Adjusted ERA		Opponents' Batting Avg.		Opponents' On Base Pct.		Starter Runs		Adjusted Starter Runs	
McQuillan-Phi	1.60	Cole-Chi	159	Cole-Chi	.211	Brown-Chi	.277	Mathewson-NY	40.0	Mathewson-NY	37.6
Cole-Chi	1.80	Mathewson-NY	156	Drucke-NY	.228	Mathewson-NY	.286	Brown-Chi	38.2	Brown-Chi	33.3
Brown-Chi	1.86	Brown-Chi	155	Moore-Phi	.228	Crandall-NY	.289	Cole-Chi	32.5	Cole-Chi	28.5
Mathewson-NY	1.89	Adams-Pit	138	Brown-Chi	.232	Adams-Pit	.291	McQuillan-Phi	24.2	McQuillan-Phi	25.8
Ames-NY	2.22	Ames-NY	133	Scanlan-Bro	.234	Bell-Bro	.296	Adams-Pit	21.3	Adams-Pit	23.1

Clutch Pitching Index		Relief Runs		Adjusted Relief Runs		Relief Ranking		Total Pitcher Index		Total Baseball Ranking	
Cole-Chi	136							Mathewson-NY	6.0	Mathewson-NY	6.0
Brown-Bos	122							Brown-Chi	4.9	Brown-Chi	4.9
Barger-Bro	122							Cole-Chi	3.0	Konetchy-StL	4.1
Mathewson-NY	117							Brown-Bos	2.5	Hofman-Chi	3.4
Curtis-Bos	116							McQuillan-Phi	2.4	Wagner-Pit	3.2

April 14 William Howard Taft becomes the first president to throw out the first ball at an Opening Day game in Washington. Walter Johnson catches it, then pitches the first of his 14 openers. An easy fly hit into the overflow crowd—a ground-rule double—mars his pitching gem, and he emerges with a 3-0 one-hitter.

May 12 The Athletics' Chief Bender pitches a 4–0 no-hitter against the Naps, missing a perfect game with one walk. Bender will be 23–5, one of only two 20-game-win seasons the future Hall of Famer will have in 15 years.

July 1 White Sox Park opens with a 2-0 loss to the Browns. The stadium, later called Comiskey Park, is baseball's biggest at the time and will cost $750,000. The stadium will be the oldest in baseball when it is closed in 1990, to be replaced by a structure called New Comiskey Park.

July 19 Cleveland's Cy Young, 43, wins his 500th game 5-4, over Washington in 11 innings.

August 4 Athletics' Jack Coombs and Chicago's Ed Walsh duel 16 innings to a 0–0 tie. Coombs gives up just three hits in what he calls his best game. (Working with little rest, he wins 18 of 19 starts in July, August, and September, finishing 30–9 with a 1.30 ERA. His 13 shutouts are the AL record; in 12 other games he gives up just one run.)

August 27* Using twenty 137,000 candlepower arc lights, two amateur teams play a night game at White Sox Park before 20,000. It's first AL night game will be played there in 1939.

September 5 Athletics pitcher Jack Coombs begins a streak of 53 shutout innings, topping Doc White's 45 of 1904. Three years later, Walter Johnson will top Coombs.

October 9 The battle for the AL batting title is decided on the final day, when Detroit's Ty Cobb edges Cleveland's Nap Lajoie .3850687 to .3840947. Neither man covers himself with glory. Lajoie goes 8-for-8 in a doubleheader with the Browns, accepting six "gift" hits on bunt singles on which Browns rookie third baseman Red Corriden is purposely stationed too deep to field. The prejudiced St. Louis scorer also credits popular Nap with a "hit" on the Brownie shortstop's wild throw to first base. Cobb, meanwhile, rather than risk his average, sits out the last two games. Ban Johnson investigates and clears everyone concerned, enabling Cobb to win the third of nine straight batting crowns. The embarrassed Chalmers Auto Company awards cars to both Ty and Nap. In 1981 Pete Palmer and Paul Mac Farlane uncover an error that, if corrected, would give the championship to Lajoie. The commissioner's committee votes unanimously to leave history unchanged.

October 17 With sore-armed Eddie Plank unavailable, Connie Mack will squeeze five complete games out of two pitchers in the World Series. Chief Bender's 4-1 three-hitter wins Game 1 for the Athletics at Philadelphia. Frank Baker's three hits drive in all the runs needed to beat the Cubs' Orval Overall.

October 18 Jack Coombs struggles for a 9-3 win, walking nine and giving up eight hits, but strands 14 Cubs, while a six-run seventh inning off Three Finger Brown blows open the game for the A's. Eddie Collins has two doubles and two stolen bases.

October 20 The A's dispose of Ed Reulbach in two innings, and Coombs coasts on one day's rest 12-5. He helps himself with three hits.

October 23 Three Finger Brown comes back to face Coombs, who takes a 2–1 lead into the seventh. The A's get to Brown for five runs in the eighth and post a 7–2 win to take the championship. The crowd of 27,374 is the Series largest. The A's .316 BA is a World Series record.

BOSTON	CHICAGO	CLEVELAND	DETROIT	NEW YORK	PHILADELPHIA	ST.LOUIS	WASHINGTON
M P.Donovan	M H.Duffy	M D.McGuire	M H.Jennings	M G.Stallings	M C.Mack	M J.O'Connor	M J.McAleer
1B J.Stahl	1B C.Gandil	1B G.Stovall	1B T.Jones	1B H.Chase	1B H.Davis	1B P.Newnam	1B B.Unglaub
2B L.Gardner	2B R.Zeider	2B N.Lajoie	2B J.Delahanty	1B H.Chase	2B E.Collins	2B F.Truesdale	2B R.Killefer
SS H.Wagner	SS L.Blackburne	SS T.Turner	SS D.Bush	2B F.LaPorte	SS J.Barry	SS B.Wallace	SS G.McBride
3B H.Lord	3B B.Purtell	3B B.Bradley	3B G.Moriarty	SS J.Knight	3B F.Baker	3B R.Hartzell	3B K.Elberfeld
LF D.Lewis	LF P.Dougherty	LF J.Graney	LF D.Jones	3B J.Austin	LF T.Hartsel	LF G.Stone	LF J.Lelivelt
CF T.Speaker	CF F.Parent	CF J.Birmingham	CF T.Cobb	LF B.Cree	CF R.Oldring	CF D.Hoffman	CF C.Milan
RF H.Hooper	RF S.Collins	RF B.Lord	RF S.Crawford	CF C.Hemphill	RF D.Murphy	RF A.Schweitzer	RF G.Dessler
C B.Carrigan	C F.Payne	C T.Easterly	C O.Stanage	RF H.Wolter	C J.Lapp	C J.Stephens	C G.Street
				C J.Sweeney			
32 C.Engle	S1 L.Tannehill	O H.Niles	O M.McIntyre	O B.Daniels	O B.Lord	O2 A.Griggs	3O W.Conroy
3 B.Purtell	O P.Meloan	O A.Kruger	2S C.O'Leary	C E.Gardner	C I.Thomas	C B.Killefer	2O G.Schaefer
C R.Kleinow	2O C.French	C H.Bemis	C B.Schmidt	2 R.Roach	C P.Livingston	O N.Northen	C E.Ainsmith
1 H.Bradley	3 H.Lord	3 G.Perring	1 H.Simmons	C F.Mitchell	1 H.Heitmuller	1 D.Criss	1 H.Beckendorf
O H.Niles	C B.Block	S N.Ball	3 C.Lathers	S E.Foster	S S.McInnis	1 B.Abstein	C1 J.Henry
/2 C.French	C B.Sullivan	C G.Land	C J.Casey	C L.Criger	1 B.Houser	S3 R.Corriden	2 B.Cunningham
C B.Madden	1 C.Mullen	O J.Jackson	/2 J.Kirke	/C W.Blair	O A.Strunk	O R.Fisher	O D.Ralston
2 A.McConnell	2 A.McConnell	/C H.Beckendorf	/C H.Beckendorf	/O L.Channell	C P.Donahue	3 J.McDonald	1 J.Somerlott
/S D.Lerchen	O G.Browne	O E.Flick	P G.Mullin	/O C.Engle	3 M.Rath	/1 B.Graham	/O G.Browne
/1 D.Moskiman	O D.Zwilling	3 M.Rath	P E.Willett	/C R.Kleinow	/1 E.Mack	C S.Allen	/1 T.Crooke
/O H.Myers	O F.Chouinard	1 E.Hohnhorst	P E.Summers	/S J.Walsh	/C C.Derrick	/O R.Demmitt	/C J.Hardy
/C P.Donahue	O W.Cole	S C.Knaupp	P B.Donovan	H T.Madden	P J.Coombs	C T.Mee	P W.Johnson
/O R.Pond	O E.Hahn	S N.Clarke	P S.Stroud	/O L.McClure	P C.Morgan	/3 R.Jansen	P B.Groom
/S E.Hearn	O R.Kelly	O D.Callahan	P R.Works	P R.Ford	P E.Plank	/C J.Crisp	P D.Gray
P E.Cicotte	/O B.Messenger	/O S.Smith	P E.Killian	P J.Warhop	P C.Bender	/C J.O'Connor	P D.Walker
P R.Collins	/O C.Barrows	/C B.Adams	P H.Pernoll	P J.Quinn	P H.Krause	P J.Lake	P D.Reisling
P J.Wood	/O R.Bowser	/3 H.Bronkie	P F.Browning	P H.Vaughn	P J.Dygert	P B.Bailey	/P F.Oberlin
P C.Hall	P E.Walsh	P P.Donahue	/P A.Loudell	P T.Hughes	P T.Atkins	P B.Pelty	/P B.Otey
P E.Karger	P D.White	/C D.McGuire	/C M.Peasley	R.Fisher	/P L.Russell	P F.Ray	/P E.Moyer
P C.Smith	P J.Scott	/O J.Rutherford	/P B.Lelivelt	P R.Manning		P J.Powell	/P D.Hinrichs
P F.Arellanes	P F.Olmstead	/S S.Nicholls	/P D.Skeels	P J.Frill		/P R.Nelson	/P J.Hovlik
/P B.Hunt	P I.Young	P C.Falkenberg		/P R.Caldwell		/P A.Malloy	/P B.Forman
/P F.Smith	P F.Lange	P W.Mitchell		/P S.Doyle		/P R.Mitchell	
/P M.McHale	P F.Smith	P C.Young				P E.Kinsella	
/P C.Mahoney	/P C.Chouneau	P E.Koestner				/P M.Hall	
/P F.Barberich	/P B.Burns	P S.Harkness				/P B.Grahame	
/P L.LeRoy		P F.Link				/P J.Gilligan	
		P A.Joss				/P B.Spade	
		P G.Kahler				/P R.Waddell	
		P H.Fanwell				/P P.Stremmel	
		P H.Berger				/P F.Link	
		/P F.Blanding				/P R.Boyd	
		/P B.DeMott				/P B.Crouch	
		/P W.Doane				/P H.Howell	
		/P H.Kirsch					

TEAM	G	W	L	PCT	GB	R	OR	AB	H	2B	3B	HR	BB	SO	AVG	OBP	SLG	PRO	PRO+	BR	/A	PF	CHI	RC	SB	CS	SBA	SBR
PHI	155	102	48	.680		673	441	5154	1373	191	105	19	409		.266	.326	.355	.681	120	105	112	99	99	665	207			
NY	156	88	63	.583	14.5	626	557	5051	1254	164	75	20	464		.248	.320	.322	.642	101	44	9	106	102	614	288			
DET	155	86	68	.558	18	679	582	5039	1317	190	72	28	459		.261	.329	.344	.673	110	96	52	107	102	655	249			
BOS	158	81	72	.529	22.5	638	564	5204	1350	175	87	43	430		.259	.323	.351	.674	114	93	77	102	94	656	194			
CLE	161	71	81	.467	32	548	657	5390	1316	188	64	9	366		.244	.297	.308	.605	94	-38	-45	101	99	548	189			
CHI	156	68	85	.444	35.5	457	479	5024	1058	115	58	7	403		.211	.275	.261	.536	76	-150	-133	96	112	415	183			
WAS	157	66	85	.437	36.5	501	550	4989	1175	145	47	9	449		.236	.309	.289	.598	98	-32	-7	95	94	508	192			
STL	158	47	107	.305	57	451	743	5077	1105	131	60	12	415		.218	.281	.274	.555	84	-117	-90	94	102	438	169			
TOT	628					4573		40928	9948	1299	568	147	3395	5278	.243	.308	.313	.621							1671			

TEAM	CG	SH	SV	IP	H	H/G	HR	BB	SO	RAT	ERA	ERA+	OAV	OOB	PR	/A	PF	CPI	FA	E	DP	FW	PW	BW	SBW	DIF
PHI	123	24	5	1421²	1103	7.0	8	450	789	10.2	1.79	133	.221	.292	116	91	94	111	.965	230	117	3.8	10.1	12.4		.6
NY	110	14	8	1399	1238	8.0	16	364	654	10.7	2.61	102	.243	.300	-15	4	106	91	.956	285	95	.2	-.1	1.0		10.8
DET	108	17	5	1380¹	1257	8.2	34	460	532	11.6	2.82	93	.248	.319	-47	-28	104	101	.956	288	79	-.0	-3.1	5.8		6.4
BOS	100	12	6	1430	1236	7.8	30	414	670	10.7	2.45	104	.235	.297	10	14	101	94	.954	309	80	-1.1	1.6	8.6		-4.5
CLE	92	13	5	1467	1392	8.5	10	488	617	11.9	2.88	90	.261	.330	-60	-50	103	104	.964	248	112	3.4	-5.6	-5.0		2.2
CHI	103	23	7	1421	1130	7.2	16	381	785	9.8	2.03	118	.222	.281	77	56	95	92	.954	314	100	-1.7	6.2	-14.8		1.8
WAS	119	19	3	1373¹	1215	8.0	19	375	674	10.8	2.46	101	.244	.304	8	5	99	101	.959	264	99	1.8	.6	-.8		-11.1
STL	101	9	3	1391	1356	8.8	14	532	557	12.6	3.09	80	.265	.341	-89	-95	102	106	.943	385	113	-6.3	-10.6	-10.0		-3.2
TOT	856	131	42	11283¹		7.9				11.0	2.52		.243	.308					.956	2323	795					

Runs
Cobb-Det 106
Lajoie-Cle 94
Speaker-Bos 92
Bush-Det 90
Milan-Was 89

Hits
Lajoie-Cle 227
Cobb-Det 194
Collins-Phi 188
Speaker-Bos 183
Crawford-Det 170

Doubles
Lajoie-Cle 51
Cobb-Det 35
Lewis-Bos 29
Murphy-Phi 28
Oldring-Phi 27

Triples
Crawford-Det 19
Lord-Cle-Phi 18
Murphy-Phi 18
Stahl-Bos 16
Cree-NY 16

Home Runs
Stahl-Bos 10
Lewis-Bos 8
Cobb-Det 8
Speaker-Bos 7
Crawford-Det 5

Total Bases
Lajoie-Cle 304
Cobb-Det 279
Speaker-Bos 252
Crawford-Det 249
Murphy-Phi 244

Runs Batted In
Crawford-Det 120
Cobb-Det 91
Collins-Phi 81
Stahl-Bos 77
Lajoie-Cle 76

Runs Produced
Crawford-Det 198
Cobb-Det 189
Lajoie-Cle 166
Collins-Phi 159
Baker-Phi 155

Bases On Balls
Bush-Det 78
Milan-Was 71
Wolter-NY 66
Cobb-Det 64

Batting Average
Cobb-Det 384
Lajoie-Cle 384
Speaker-Bos 340
Collins-Phi 324
Knight-NY 312

On Base Percentage
Cobb-Det 456
Lajoie-Cle 445
Speaker-Bos 404
Collins-Phi 382
Milan-Was 379

Slugging Average
Cobb-Det 551
Lajoie-Cle 514
Speaker-Bos 468
Murphy-Phi 436
Oldring-Phi 430

Production
Cobb-Det 1.008
Lajoie-Cle 960
Speaker-Bos 873
Collins-Phi 800
Cree-NY 775

Adjusted Production
Cobb-Det 202
Lajoie-Cle 198
Speaker-Bos 169
Collins-Phi 152
Murphy-Phi 143

Batter Runs
Lajoie-Cle 68.2
Cobb-Det 67.9
Speaker-Bos 44.9
Collins-Phi 33.4
Murphy-Phi 23.6

Adjusted Batter Runs
Lajoie-Cle 66.5
Cobb-Det 59.7
Speaker-Bos 42.4
Collins-Phi 34.4
Murphy-Phi 24.4

Clutch Hitting Index
LaPorte-NY 154
Crawford-Det 153
Chase-NY 135
Moriarty-Det 127
McBride-Was 122

Runs Created
Cobb-Det 156
Lajoie-Cle 147
Collins-Phi 123
Speaker-Bos 115
Crawford-Det 89

Total Average
Cobb-Det 1.321
Lajoie-Cle 1.085
Speaker-Bos 972
Collins-Phi 964
Cree-NY 820

Stolen Bases
Collins-Phi 81
Cobb-Det 65
Zeider-Chi 49
Bush-Det 49
Milan-Was 44

Fielding Runs
Collins-Phi 33.7
McBride-Was 26.6
Wallace-StL 21.9
Speaker-Bos 15.1
Lajoie-Cle 15.0

Total Player Rating
Lajoie-Cle 8.5
Collins-Phi 7.0
Cobb-Det 6.7
Speaker-Bos 5.5
Wallace-StL 3.6

Wins
Coombs-Phi 31
Ford-NY 26
Johnson-Was 25
Bender-Phi 23
Mullin-Det 21

Win Percentage
Bender-Phi 821
Ford-NY 813
Coombs-Phi 775
Donovan-Det 708
Mullin-Det 636

Games
Walsh-Chi 45
Johnson-Was 45
Coombs-Phi 45
Scott-Chi 41

Complete Games
Johnson-Was 38
Coombs-Phi 35
Walsh-Chi 33
Ford-NY 29
Mullin-Det 27

Shutouts
Coombs-Phi 13
Johnson-Was 8
Ford-NY 8
Walsh-Chi 7

Saves
Walsh-Chi 5
Browning-Det 3

Innings Pitched
Johnson-Was 370.0
Walsh-Chi 369.2
Coombs-Phi 353.0
Ford-NY 299.2
Morgan-Phi 290.2

Fewest Hits/Game
Ford-NY 5.83
Walsh-Chi 5.89
Coombs-Phi 6.32
Johnson-Was 6.37
Bender-Phi 6.55

Fewest BB/Game
Walsh-Chi 1.49
Young-Cle 1.49
Collins-Bos 1.51
Bender-Phi 1.69
Johnson-Was 1.85

Strikeouts
Johnson-Was 313
Walsh-Chi 258
Coombs-Phi 224
Ford-NY 209
Bender-Phi 155

Strikeouts/Game
Johnson-Was 7.61
Wood-Bos 6.64
Walsh-Chi 6.28
Ford-NY 6.28
Coombs-Phi 5.71

Ratio
Walsh-Chi 7.47
Ford-NY 8.17
Johnson-Was 8.54
Bender-Phi 8.60
Collins-Bos 9.09

Earned Run Average
Walsh-Chi 1.27
Coombs-Phi 1.30
Johnson-Was 1.36
Morgan-Phi 1.55
Bender-Phi 1.58

Adjusted ERA
Walsh-Chi 189
Johnson-Was 183
Coombs-Phi 182
Ford-NY 161
Collins-Bos 158

Opponents' Batting Avg.
Walsh-Chi 187
Ford-NY 188
Coombs-Phi 201
Johnson-Was 205
Hall-Bos 207

Opponents' On Base Pct.
Walsh-Chi 226
Ford-NY 245
Bender-Phi 255
Johnson-Was 257
Collins-Bos 264

Starter Runs
Walsh-Chi 51.4
Coombs-Phi 47.7
Johnson-Was 47.5
Morgan-Phi 31.3
Ford-NY 28.8

Adjusted Starter Runs
Johnson-Was 46.3
Walsh-Chi 46.3
Coombs-Phi 42.0
Ford-NY 33.4
Morgan-Phi 26.6

Clutch Pitching Index
Morgan-Phi 142
Olmstead-Chi 142
Vaughn-NY 122
Wood-Bos 116
Coombs-Phi 114

Relief Runs

Adjusted Relief Runs

Relief Ranking

Total Pitcher Index
Walsh-Chi 7.1
Johnson-Was 5.8
Coombs-Phi 4.8
Ford-NY 4.0
Bender-Phi 3.8

Total Baseball Ranking
Lajoie-Cle 8.5
Walsh-Chi 7.1
Collins-Phi 7.0
Cobb-Det 6.7
Johnson-Was 5.8

March 24 Matthew Stanley Robison, president of the Cardinals, dies unexpectedly. He leaves the club and the bulk of his estate to his niece, Mrs. Helene Hathaway Britton, who becomes the first female owner of a major league club.

April 4 The idea of selecting a Most Valuable Player is introduced. Hugh Chalmers, the automobile maker, offers a new car to the player in each league chosen MVP by a committee of baseball writers.

April 13 The night after the Giants' opener, the Polo Grounds grandstand and left field bleachers go up in flames. President Frank Farrell of the Highlanders invites the Giants to use the AL grounds; the offer is accepted, paving the way for the Giants' invitation for the AL team to use the Polo Grounds when the Hilltop Park lease expires after the 1912 season.

May 13 Fred Merkle has six RBI as the Giants tee off on three St. Louis pitchers for 13 runs in the first inning, including a major league record 10 before a single out is recorded. John McGraw decides to save starter Mathewson for another day. Rube Marquard works the last eight innings and strikes out 14, setting a record for strikeouts by a reliever. The Giants win 19-5.

June 3 Cub Frank "Wildfire" Schulte's grand slam beats the Giants. Schulte will hit four this season, a record number at the time but Schulte's only grand slams in his 11-year career.

July 11 The Federal Express of the New York, New Haven, and Hartford Railroad, carrying the St. Louis Cardinals to Boston, plunges down an 18-foot embankment outside Bridgeport, Connecticut, killing 14 passengers. The team's Pullmans were originally just behind the baggage coaches near the front. When noise prevented the players from sleeping, manager Bresnahan requested the car be changed. The day coach that replaced the players' car was crushed and splintered. The players help remove bodies and rescue the injured, then board a special train to Boston, where the day's game is postponed. The railroad pays each player $25 for his rescue work and for lost belongings.

July 22 The Pirates pay St. Paul of the American Association $22,500 for righthander Marty O'Toole, the highest purchase price to date for a player. In 1912, O'Toole will be 15–17 and lead the NL with 159 walks. He will last only two more years.

September 7 Grover Alexander (24 years old), winning a rookie record 28 games, pitches the Phils to a 1–0 win over Boston's 44-year-old Cy Young. Alexander's 31 complete games, 367 innings pitched, and seven shutouts lead the NL.

September 22 Cy Young, now with Boston's NL club, shuts out Pittsburgh 1-0 for his final career victory, number 511. His farewell appearance in a major league game on October 6 is a letdown, as he loses to Brooklyn 13-3 in his 906th game.

October 5 The National Commission sells motion picture rights to the World Series for $3,500. When the players demand a share of it, the Commission cancels the deal.

October 14 The World Series begins with the Giants dressed in the same black uniforms they wore in their 1905 conquest of the Mackmen, and this Series starts as their last meeting ended: with a Mathewson win. The largest crowd ever to watch a ballgame—38,281—is at the Polo Grounds. Gate receipts are $77,379.

December 14 Phillies owner Barney Dreyfuss proposes that each team in the World Series be required to turn over one-fourth of its share of the gate to the league, to be divided among the other teams. Until now, 10 percent of the gross went to the National Commission, 60 percent to the players, and the rest to the two pennant-winning clubs. The NL will pass the resolution and send it to the AL. It marks the beginning of changes that ultimately give players of the first four clubs a percentage of the World Series money.

	BOSTON		BROOKLYN		CHICAGO		CINCINNATI		NEW YORK		PHILADELPHIA		PITTSBURGH		ST.LOUIS
M	F.Tenney	M	B.Dahlen	M	F.Chance	M	C.Griffith	M	J.McGraw	M	R.Dooin	M	F.Clarke	M	R.Bresnahan
1B	F.Tenney	1B	J.Daubert	1B	V.Saier	1B	D.Hoblitzel	1B	F.Merkle	1B	F.Luderus	1B	N.Hunter	1B	E.Konetchy
2B	B.Sweeney	2B	J.Hummel	2B	H.Zimmerman	2B	D.Egan	2B	L.Doyle	2B	O.Knabe	2B	D.Miller	2B	M.Huggins
SS	B.Herzog	SS	B.Tooley	SS	J.Tinker	SS	T.Downey	SS	A.Bridwell	SS	M.Doolan	SS	H.Wagner	SS	A.Hauser
3B	S.Ingerton	3B	E.Zimmerman	3B	J.Doyle	3B	E.Grant	3B	A.Devlin	3B	H.Lobert	3B	B.Byrne	3B	M.Mowrey
LF	A.Kaiser	LF	Z.Wheat	LF	J.Sheckard	LF	B.Bescher	LF	J.Devore	LF	S.Magee	LF	F.Clarke	LF	R.Ellis
CF	M.Donlin	CF	B.Davidson	CF	S.Hofman	CF	J.Bates	CF	F.Snodgrass	CF	D.Paskert	CF	M.Carey	CF	R.Oakes
RF	D.Miller	RF	B.Coulson	RF	F.Schulte	RF	M.Mitchell	RF	R.Murray	RF	F.Beck	RF	C.Wilson	RF	S.Evans
C	J.Kling	C	B.Bergen	C	J.Archer	C	L.McLean	C	C.Meyers	C	R.Dooin	C	G.Gibson	C	J.Bliss
C	B.Rariden	C	T.Erwin	23	J.Evers	C	T.Clarke	S3	A.Fletcher	O2	J.Walsh	OS	T.Leach	C	R.Bresnahan
S	A.Bridwell	S2	D.Stark	O	W.Good	S3	J.Esmond	3	B.Herzog	O	J.Titus	12	B.McKechnie	3S	W.Smith
3	E.McDonald	3	A.Burch	2S	D.Shean	O	R.Marsans	O	B.Becker	C	P.Moran	C	M.Simon	2	L.Magee
O	W.Good	3	R.Smith	1	F.Chance	3	R.Almeida	O	A.Wilson	C	B.Madden	S2	A.McCarthy	O	M.McIvor
S	H.Spratt	O	H.Northen	O	A.Kaiser	O	F.Beck	O	G.Hartley	O	H.Welchonce	O	V.Campbell	C	I.Wingo
O	G.Jackson	O	J.Daley	C	J.Kling	S	D.Altizer	O	G.Burns	C	D.Cotter	1	J.Flynn	O	D.Wilie
J	J.Clarke	C	O.Miller	C	P.Graham	C	H.Severeid	/O	M.Donlin	/1	K.Bransfield	/O	B.Kelly	/O	J.Clark
1	H.Gowdy	O	H.Myers	C	T.Needham	/S	M.Balenti	/1	G.Paulette	C	T.Spencer	/1	B.Keen	/2	D.McGeehan
O	P.Flaherty	S	T.Smith	/1	K.Bransfield	P	D.Mahoney	/1	H.Gowdy	O	R.Thomas	/1	M.Keliher	/S	H.Morse
O	J.Kirke	/2	P.McElveen	/O	B.Collins	H	H.Northen	H	A.Schlei	/O	C.Lehr	/1	J.Dorsey	/3	E.Conwell
C	P.Graham	/O	A.Humphrey							/C	B.Killefer	H	J.Shovlin	H	M.Reed
1	B.Houser	/O	L.LeJeune	P	M.Brown	P	G.Suggs	P	C.Mathewson	R	R.Kleinow			/O	F.Gilhooley
3	A.Butler	/O	G.Browne	P	L.Richie	P	H.Gaspar	P	R.Marquard	/O	P.Mayes	P	L.Leifield		
3	H.Steinfeldt	/C	B.Higgins	P	E.Reulbach	P	B.Keefe	P	R.Ames	/C	J.Quinn	P	B.Adams	P	B.Harmon
O	B.Jones	/S	B.Dahlen	P	K.Cole	P	A.Fromme	P	D.Crandall	R	H.Miller	P	H.Camnitz	P	B.Steele
O	B.Collins			P	H.McIntire	P	F.Smith	P	H.Wiltse			P	E.Steele	P	S.Sallee
/3	H.Young	P	N.Rucker	RP	R.Richter							P	C.Hendrix	P	R.Golden
H	B.Weeden	P	C.Barger			P	G.McQuillan	P	B.Raymond	P	P.Alexander			P	R.Geyer
		P	E.Knetzer	P	F.Toney	P	B.Humphries	P	L.Drucke	P	E.Moore	P	J.Ferry		
P	B.Brown	P	B.Schardt	/P	O.Weaver	/P	R.Benton	/P	B.Maxwell	P	G.Chalmers	P	H.Gardner	P	L.Lowdermilk
P	A.Mattern	P	D.Scanlan	/P	C.Smith	/P	R.Boyd	/P	C.Faust	P	B.Burns	/P	M.O'Toole	P	G.Woodburn
P	L.Tyler			/P	J.Pfiester	/P	J.Compton	/P	D.Rudolph	P	E.Stack	/P	J.Nagle	P	G.Lowdermilk
P	H.Perdue	P	G.Bell	/P	C.Slapnicka	/P	B.Burns			P	F.Beebe	/P	H.Robinson	P	G.Dale
P	O.Weaver	P	P.Ragan	/P	B.Foxen	/P	B.Schreiber			P	J.Rowan	/P	D.Phillippe	P	J.Willis
		P	S.Burk	/P	L.Cheney	/P	H.Juul			P	C.Curtis	/P	K.White	/P	E.Zmich
P	B.Pfeffer	/P	E.Dent	/P	C.Curtis	/P	J.Tannehill			P	B.Humphries	/P	E.Cottrell	/P	J.McAdams
P	H.Griffin	/P	E.Steele	/P	E.Ovitz					P	T.Shultz	/P	S.Smith	/P	R.Radebaugh
P	C.Young	/P	W.Miller	/P	J.Rowan					P	B.Ewing			/P	J.Reis
P	C.Curtis	/P	J.Ryan	/P	H.Griffin					P	A.Brennan			/P	G.Zackert
/P	E.Donnelly	/P	R.Aitchison							P	B.Hall			/P	P.Standridge
/P	B.McTigue									P	B.Stanley			/P	B.Hearn
/P	B.Hogg									P	J.Smith			/P	H.Camnitz
/P	J.Parson									/P	T.Puckett				
/P	G.Ferguson														
/P	S.Frock														
/P	F.Thompson														
/P	B.Burke														

TEAM	G	W	L	PCT	GB	R	OR	AB	H	2B	3B	HR	BB	SO	AVG	OBP	SLG	PRO	PRO+	BR	/A	PF	CHI	RC	SB	CS	SBA	SBR
NY	154	99	54	.647		756	542	5006	1399	225	103	41	530	506	.279	.358	.390	.748	113	109	85	103	96	820	347			
CHI	157	92	62	.597	7.5	757	607	5130	1335	218	101	54	585	617	.260	.341	.374	.715	107	44	43	100	102	729	214			
PIT	155	85	69	.552	14.5	744	557	5137	1345	206	106	49	525	583	.262	.336	.372	.708	101	28	1	104	104	698	160			
PHI	153	79	73	.520	19.5	658	669	5044	1307	214	56	60	490	588	.259	.328	.359	.687	98	-11	-19	101	100	647	153			
STL	158	75	74	.503	22	671	745	5132	1295	199	86	26	592	650	.252	.337	.340	.677	99	-18	0	97	99	651	175			
CIN	159	70	83	.458	29	682	706	5291	1379	180	105	21	578	594	.261	.337	.346	.683	102	-10	15	96	97	716	289			
BRO	154	64	86	.427	33.5	539	659	5059	1198	151	71	28	425	593	.237	.301	.311	.612	80	-152	-131	96	106	528	184			
BOS	156	44	107	.291	54	699	1021	5308	1417	249	54	37	554	577	.267	.340	.355	.695	93	10	-48	108	98	696	169			
TOT	623					5506		41107	10675	1642	682	316	4279	4798	.260	.335	.356	.691							1691			

TEAM	CG	SH	SV	IP	H	H/G	HR	BB	SO	RAT	ERA	ERA+	OAV	OOB	PR	/A	PF	CPI	FA	E	DP	FW	PW	BW	SBW	DIF
NY	95	19	13	1368	1267	8.3	33	369	771	11.0	2.69	125	.246	.300	106	100	99	97	.959	256	86	.5	10.0	8.5		3.4
CHI	85	12	16	1411	1270	8.1	26	525	582	11.7	2.90	114	.245	.320	78	62	97	100	.960	260	114	.6	6.2	4.3		3.9
PIT	91	13	11	1380[1]	1249	8.1	36	375	605	10.8	2.84	121	.248	.306	85	87	101	97	.963	232	131	2.1	8.7	.1		-2.9
PHI	90	20	10	1373[1]	1285	8.4	43	598	697	12.7	3.30	104	.255	.340	14	19	101	104	.963	224	113	1.9	1.9	-1.9		1.1
STL	88	6	10	1402[1]	1296	8.3	39	701	561	13.2	3.68	91	.254	.350	-46	-52	99	97	.960	261	106	.6	-5.2	.0		5.1
CIN	77	4	12	1425	1410	8.9	36	476	557	12.3	3.26	101	.265	.332	21	5	97	103	.955	295	108	-1.4	.5	1.5		-7.1
BRO	81	13	10	1371[2]	1310	8.6	27	566	533	12.6	3.39	98	.263	.344	0	-12	98	103	.962	241	112	1.4	-1.2	-13.2		1.9
BOS	73	5	7	1374	1570	10.3	76	672	486	15.1	5.08	75	.296	.381	-258	-195	113	96	.947	347	110	-5.0	-19.6	-4.8		-2.1
TOT	680	92	89	11105[2]		8.6				12.4	3.39		.260	.335					.958	2123	880					

Runs		Hits		Doubles		Triples		Home Runs		Total Bases	
Sheckard-Chi	121	Miller-Bos	192	Konetchy-StL	38	Doyle-NY	25	Schulte-Chi	21	Schulte-Chi	308
Huggins-StL	106	Hoblitzel-Cin	180	Miller-Bos	36	Mitchell-Cin	22	Luderus-Phi	16	Doyle-NY	277
Bescher-Cin	106	Daubert-Bro	176	Wilson-Pit	34	Schulte-Chi	21	Magee-Phi	15	Luderus-Phi	260
Schulte-Chi	105	Schulte-Chi	173	Herzog-Bos-NY	33	Zimmerman-Chi	17	Doyle-NY	13	Hoblitzel-Cin	258
Doyle-NY	102	Luderus-Phi	166	Sweeney-Bos	33	Byrne-Pit	17			Wilson-Pit	257

Runs Batted In		Runs Produced		Bases On Balls		Batting Average		On Base Percentage		Slugging Average	
Wilson-Pit	107	Schulte-Chi	191	Sheckard-Chi	147	Wagner-Pit	.334	Sheckard-Chi	.434	Schulte-Chi	.534
Schulte-Chi	107	Konetchy-StL	172	Bates-Cin	103	Miller-Bos	.333	Wagner-Pit	.423	Doyle-NY	.527
Luderus-Phi	99	Wilson-Pit	167	Bescher-Cin	102	Meyers-NY	.332	Bates-Cin	.415	Wagner-Pit	.507
Magee-Phi	94	Wagner-Pit	167	Huggins-StL	96	Clarke-Pit	.324	Sweeney-Bos	.404	Clarke-Pit	.492
		Sheckard-Chi	167	Knabe-Phi	94	Fletcher-NY	.319	Doyle-NY	.397	Magee-Phi	.483

Production		Adjusted Production		Batter Runs		Adjusted Batter Runs		Clutch Hitting Index		Runs Created	
Wagner-Pit	.930	Schulte-Chi	155	Schulte-Chi	40.6	Schulte-Chi	40.3	Hofman-Chi	133	Schulte-Chi	127
Doyle-NY	.924	Wagner-Pit	154	Doyle-NY	39.3	Doyle-NY	35.9	Miller-Pit	128	Doyle-NY	124
Schulte-Chi	.918	Doyle-NY	153	Wagner-Pit	38.8	Wagner-Pit	35.0	Grant-Cin	126	Bescher-Cin	115
Magee-Phi	.849	Magee-Phi	135	Sheckard-Chi	31.7	Sheckard-Chi	31.5	Snodgrass-NY	124	Wagner-Pit	109
Wilson-Pit	.826	Konetchy-StL	132	Clarke-Pit	27.0	Bates-Cin	27.5	Wilson-Pit	117	Miller-Bos	107

Total Average		Stolen Bases		Stolen Base Average		Stolen Base Runs		Fielding Runs		Total Player Rating	
Doyle-NY	1.077	Bescher-Cin	81					Tinker-Chi	23.4	Wagner-Pit	4.5
Wagner-Pit	1.057	Devore-NY	61					Doolan-Phi	20.3	Sheckard-Chi	3.8
Schulte-Chi	1.015	Snodgrass-NY	51					Ingerton-Bos	18.2	Herzog-Bos-NY	3.2
Sheckard-Chi	1.003	Merkle-NY	49					Herzog-Bos-NY	17.8	Tinker-Chi	3.1
Bates-Cin	.943							Merkle-NY	15.3	Schulte-Chi	2.7

Wins		Win Percentage		Games		Complete Games		Shutouts		Saves	
Alexander-Phi	28	Marquard-NY	.774	Brown-Chi	53	Alexander-Phi	31	Alexander-Phi	7	Brown-Chi	13
Mathewson-NY	26	Crandall-NY	.750	Harmon-StL	51	Mathewson-NY	29	Adams-Pit	6	Crandall-NY	5
Marquard-NY	24	Cole-Chi	.720	Rucker-Bro	48	Harmon-StL	28				
Harmon-StL	23	Alexander-Phi	.683	Alexander-Phi	48	Leifield-Pit	26				
		Mathewson-NY	.667			Adams-Pit	24				

Innings Pitched		Fewest Hits/Game		Fewest BB/Game		Strikeouts		Strikeouts/Game		Ratio	
Alexander-Phi	367.0	Alexander-Phi	6.99	Mathewson-NY	1.11	Marquard-NY	237	Marquard-NY	7.68	Adams-Pit	9.30
Harmon-StL	348.0	Marquard-NY	7.16	Adams-Pit	1.29	Alexander-Phi	227	Alexander-Phi	5.57	Ames-NY	10.01
Leifield-Pit	318.0	Rucker-Bro	7.27	Steele-Pit-Bro	1.71	Rucker-Bro	190	Rucker-Bro	5.42	Mathewson-NY	10.03
Rucker-Bro	315.2	Ames-NY	7.46	Brown-Chi	1.83	Moore-Phi	174	Ames-NY	5.18	Steele-Pit-Bro	10.33
Moore-Phi	308.1	Harmon-StL	7.50	Wiltse-NY	1.87	Harmon-StL	144	Moore-Phi	5.08	Alexander-Phi	10.35

Earned Run Average		Adjusted ERA		Opponents' Batting Avg.		Opponents' On Base Pct.		Starter Runs		Adjusted Starter Runs	
Mathewson-NY	1.99	Mathewson-NY	168	Alexander-Phi	.219	Adams-Pit	.271	Mathewson-NY	47.7	Mathewson-NY	46.4
Richie-Chi	2.31	Adams-Pit	147	Marquard-NY	.219	Ames-NY	.277	Adams-Pit	34.5	Adams-Pit	35.5
Adams-Pit	2.33	Richie-Chi	143	Ames-NY	.223	Mathewson-NY	.283	Alexander-Phi	33.3	Alexander-Phi	34.9
Marquard-NY	2.50	Marquard-NY	134	Rucker-Bro	.226	Wiltse-NY	.292	Richie-Chi	30.3	Leifield-Pit	27.9
Alexander-Phi	2.57	Alexander-Phi	133	Keefe-Cin	.229	Alexander-Phi	.293	Marquard-NY	27.6	Richie-Chi	27.8

Clutch Pitching Index		Relief Runs		Adjusted Relief Runs		Relief Ranking		Total Pitcher Index		Total Baseball Ranking	
Moore-Phi	130	Richter-Chi	1.6	Richter-Chi	1.1	Richter-Chi	.8	Mathewson-NY	6.7	Mathewson-NY	6.7
Mathewson-NY	122							Alexander-Phi	3.6	Wagner-Pit	4.5
Richie-Chi	119							Adams-Pit	3.5	Sheckard-Chi	3.8
Leifield-Pit	117							Leifield-Pit	3.2	Alexander-Phi	3.6
Gaspar-Cin	115							Rucker-Bro	3.0	Adams-Pit	3.5

January 3 The National Commission adopts a rule that bars World Series winners from playing postseason exhibition games. This obscure rule will lead to a direct confrontation between Babe Ruth and Commissioner Kenesaw Mountain Landis in 1921.

January 14 Bobby Wallace, the era's outstanding AL shortstop, is named manager of the Browns. St. Louis will finish last, and he will be an infielder again by June 1912.

March 17 Plumbers at work on the drain pipes at Washington's ballpark start a fire that burns down the grandstand. Since the water has been shut off, firemen can do nothing. Stands will be rebuilt in time for the home opener.

April 17 Addie Joss's funeral is held at Toledo with Billy Sunday preaching the sermon. The funeral is the second largest in the city's history. His teammates insist on being there, forcing postponement of the season opener.

June 18 Down 13–1 after 5½ innings, the Tigers stage the biggest comeback in major league history to defeat Chicago by a score of 16–15.

July 4 In the morning game between Chicago and Detroit, Ed Walsh stops Ty Cobb's 40-game hitting streak, as the White Sox win 7-3. Cobb has batted .491 since the streak started on May 15.

July 19* While playing center field for Vernon (Pacific Coast League), Walter Carlisle executes an unassisted triple play in the sixth inning against Los Angeles. With men on first base and second base, he makes a spectacular diving catch of a short fly by batter Roy Akin, touches second base, and runs to first base to retire both runners.

October 10 The first game of the Ohio championship between Cleveland and the Reds is won by Cincinnati 4–0. The next day the St. Louis city series begins, and two days later the Chicago series. These postseason matches are popular with fans and players.

October 11 The first MVPs are announced. Using a point system—8 for a first-place vote, seven for second, and so on—the eight voting writers give outfielder Ty Cobb the maximum 64 points. pitcher Ed Walsh is second, and second baseman Eddie Collins third. The NL winner is the Cubs outfielder Frank "Wildfire" Schulte. Christy Mathewson is second. Winners receive Chalmers automobiles.

October 16 The World Series resumes today, Monday, and the pitchers continue to dominate. Rube Marquard and Eddie Plank are in command of a 1-1 game when Philadelphia's Eddie Collins doubles in the last of the sixth and Frank Baker hits one over the right field fence for a 3-1 victory.

October 17 After criticizing his teammate Marquard's pitching to Baker in his newspaper column, Christy Mathewson takes the mound for Game 3 against 29-game winner Jack Coombs. Matty takes a 1-0 lead into the ninth. With one out, Baker lines another drive over the right field fence to tie it. With that blow, he becomes "Home Run" Baker to future generations; the A's win 3-2.

October 24 After six days of rain, New York takes a 2-0 first-inning lead. But aided by an overflow crowd in the outfield, the A's collect seven doubles among their 11 hits, pick up three in the third and one in the fourth while Bender shuts down the Giants, and the A's take a 3-1 lead in games.

October 26 Chief Bender cruises to his second victory, a four-hit 13-2 breeze, capped by a seven-run seventh inning to give the A's a championship. Overall, the Giants manage just 13 runs and a .175 BA off Bender, Coombs, and Plank. Because of the NL's extended playing season, this is the latest ending ever for a World Series, until the "Earthquake Series" of 1989.

BOSTON	CHICAGO	CLEVELAND	DETROIT	NEW YORK	PHILADELPHIA	ST.LOUIS	WASHINGTON
M P.Donovan	M H.Duffy	M D.McGuire	M H.Jennings	M H.Chase	M C.Mack	M B.Wallace	M J.McAleer
1B C.Engle	1B S.Collins	M G.Stovall	1B J.Delahanty	1B H.Chase	1B S.McInnis	1B J.Black	1B G.Schaefer
2B H.Wagner	2B A.McConnell	1B G.Stovall	2B C.O'Leary	2B E.Gardner	2B E.Collins	2B F.LaPorte	2B B.Cunningham
SS S.Yerkes	SS L.Tannehill	2B N.Ball	SS D.Bush	SS J.Knight	SS J.Barry	SS B.Wallace	SS G.McBride
3B L.Gardner	3B H.Lord	SS I.Olson	3B G.Moriarty	3B R.Hartzell	3B F.Baker	3B J.Austin	3B W.Conroy
LF D.Lewis	LF N.Callahan	3B T.Turner	LF D.Jones	LF B.Cree	LF B.Lord	LF W.Hogan	LF T.Walker
CF T.Speaker	CF P.Bodie	LF J.Graney	CF T.Cobb	CF B.Daniels	CF R.Oldring	CF A.Shotton	CF C.Milan
RF H.Hooper	RF M.McIntyre	CF J.Birmingham	RF S.Crawford	RF H.Wolter	RF D.Murphy	RF A.Schweitzer	RF G.Gessler
C B.Carrigan	C B.Sullivan	RF J.Jackson	C O.Stanage	C W.Blair	C I.Thomas	C N.Clarke	C G.Street
1C R.Williams	1S R.Zeider	C G.Fisher	O D.Drake	C J.Sweeney	A.Strunk	C J.Stephens	23 K.Elberfeld
C L.Nunamaker	O P.Dougherty	O D.Drake	1 D.Gainer	S2 O.Johnson	1 H.Davis	O P.Meloan	C1 J.Henry
O J.Riggert	12 F.Payne	OC T.Easterly	2 P.Baumann	1 C.Hemphill	S2 J.Lapp	S2 E.Hallinan	O J.Lelivelt
O O.Henriksen	S R.Corhan	12 N.Lajoie	O B.Schaller	3 C.Dolan	2 C.Derrick	O P.Compton	O E.Ainsmith
3 B.Purtell	C B.Block	C S.Smith	/C B.Schmidt	C B.Williams	C P.Livingston	O J.Murray	3 R.Morgan
2 J.Lewis	C C.Mullen	O H.Butcher	/2 C.Lathers	/S R.Roach	/O T.Hartsel	C P.Krichell	O T.Long
1 H.Bradley	O C.Barrows	C G.Land	1 J.Ness	/O M.Fitzgerald	/O W.Hogan	O D.Hoffman	1 J.Somerlott
1 H.Myers	/1 T.Jones	2 A.Griggs	C J.Casey	/S S.Magner	/O C.Emerson	1 D.Rowan	/O W.Miller
/3 H.Janvrin	/2 F.Chouinard	3 B.Lindsay	/2 G.Tutwiler	/3 G.Zinn	/3 E.Mack	P.Newnam	/O C.Conway
/2 W.Lonergan	/C R.Kreitz	S C.Knaupp	/C S.Wilson	/2 J.Priest	P J.Coombs	H.Myers	R B.Smith
H J.Thoney	/O B.Messenger	/C S.O'Neill	P G.Mullin	/O M.Handiboe	P E.Plank	/O G.Williams	P W.Johnson
/C B.Madden	/2 F.Parent	/3 J.Mills	P E.Willett	/O G.Elliott	P C.Morgan	/2 A.Moulton	P B.Groom
/C R.Kleinow	/2 M.Berghammer	P V.Gregg	P E.Summers	/O E.Wilkinson	P C.Bender	/1 E.Gust	P T.Hughes
/1 H.Gunning	/C W.Mayer	P G.Krapp	P E.Lafitte	/2 J.Curry	P H.Krause	/C C.Southwick	P D.Walker
/O L.Wilson	/2 P.Meloan	P W.Mitchell	P B.Donovan	/O B.Bailey	P D.Martin	/3 A.Clancy	P D.Gray
/S S.Carlstrom	/O J.Johnston	P F.Blanding	P R.Works	/C J.Walsh	P D.Danforth	J.Duggan	P C.Becker
/C T.Tonneman	P E.Walsh	P G.Kahler	P J.Lively	P R.Ford	/P L.Russell	/H J.Crisp	P C.Cashion
/S J.Giannini	P J.Scott	/P W.Taylor	P T.Covington	P R.Caldwell	/P E.Leonard	R F.Truesdale	P F.Sherry
/1 T.Baker	P D.White	/P C.Mitchell	/P W.Taylor	P J.Warhop	P B.Brown	P J.Lake	P B.Otey
P J.Wood	P F.Lange	/P P.Cavet	/P C.Mitchell	P J.Quinn	P L.Long	P J.Powell	/P W.Herrell
P E.Cicotte	P F.Olmstead	P C.Falkenberg	/P P.Cavet	P R.Fisher	/P H.Armstrong	P B.Pelty	
P R.Collins	P J.Baker	P H.West		P H.Vaughn	/P A.Collamore	P E.Hamilton	
P L.Pape	P I.Young	P S.Harkness		P L.Brockett		P R.Mitchell	
P C.Hall	P J.Benz	/P B.James		/P R.Hoff		P L.George	
P E.Karger	P J.Hovlik	/P C.Young		/P A.Coakley		/P R.Nelson	
P J.Killilay	/P G.Mogridge	/P E.Yingling		/P H.Ables		/P E.Hawk	
/P B.O'Brien		/P J.Baskette		/P E.Klepfer		/P B.Bailey	
/P J.Nagle		/P J.Swindell				/P M.Allison	
/P W.Moser		/P P.Paige				/P C.Brown	
/P C.Hageman		/P B.Reisigl				/P E.Brown	
/P J.Bushelman		/P B.DeMott				/P G.Curry	
/P M.McHale						/P J.Pfeffer	
/P B.Thomas						/P B.Harper	
/P C.Smith						/P H.Gregory	
/P F.Smith						/P J.Willis	
						/P W.Moser	

TEAM	G	W	L	PCT	GB	R	OR	AB	H	2B	3B	HR	BB	SO	AVG	OBP	SLG	PRO	PRO+	BR	/A	PF	CHI	RC	SB	CS	SBA	SBR
PHI	152	101	50	.669		861	601	5199	1540	237	93	35	424		.296	.357	.398	.755	119	108	123	98	104	821	226			
DET	154	89	65	.578	13.5	831	776	5294	1544	230	96	30	471		.292	.355	.388	.743	108	91	50	105	102	825	276			
CLE	156	80	73	.523	22	691	712	5321	1501	238	81	20	354		.282	.333	.369	.702	101	1	-7	101	97	716	209			
CHI	154	77	74	.510	24	719	624	5213	1401	179	92	20	385		.269	.325	.350	.675	97	-46	-25	97	108	659	201			
BOS	153	78	75	.510	24	680	643	5014	1379	203	66	35	506		.275	.350	.363	.713	106	39	46	99	91	710	190			
NY	153	76	76	.500	25.5	684	724	5052	1374	190	96	25	493		.272	.344	.362	.706	97	24	-23	107	94	724	269			
WAS	154	64	90	.416	38.5	625	766	5065	1308	159	54	16	466		.258	.330	.320	.650	89	-75	-63	98	100	607	215			
STL	152	45	107	.296	56.5	567	812	4996	1192	187	63	17	460		.239	.307	.311	.618	81	-142	-121	96	105	515	125			
TOT	614					5658		41154	11239	1623	641	198	3559	5093	.273	.338	.358	.696						1711				

TEAM	CG	SH	SV	IP	H	H/G	HR	BB	SO	RAT	ERA	ERA+	OAV	OOB	PR	/A	PF	CPI	FA	E	DP	FW	PW	BW	SBW	DIF
PHI	97	13	13	1375²	1343	8.8	17	487	739	12.5	3.01	105	.264	.338	50	21	94	106	.964	225	100	4.9	2.1	12.1		6.5
DET	108	8	3	1387²	1514	9.8	28	460	538	13.3	3.73	93	.283	.348	-60	-45	104	97	.951	318	78	-1.0	-4.4	4.9		12.5
CLE	93	6	6	1390²	1382	8.9	17	552	675	12.9	3.36	101	.267	.345	-3	7	102	108	.954	302	108	.3	.7	-.7		3.2
CHI	85	17	11	1386¹	1349	8.8	22	384	752	11.5	2.97	108	.255	.310	57	38	96	88	.961	252	98	3.4	3.7	-2.5		-3.1
BOS	87	10	3	1351²	1309	8.7	21	473	711	12.2	2.74	119	.262	.332	89	78	98	113	.949	323	93	-1.4	7.7	4.5		-9.3
NY	90	5	3	1360²	1404	9.3	26	406	667	12.3	3.54	101	.270	.329	-30	9	108	89	.949	328	99	-1.7	.9	-2.3		3.1
WAS	106	13	3	1353¹	1471	9.8	39	410	628	12.8	3.52	93	.277	.334	-27	-38	98	96	.953	305	90	-.1	-3.7	-6.2		-3.0
STL	92	8	1	1332¹	1465	9.9	28	463	383	13.4	3.86	87	.278	.342	-77	-73	101	90	.945	358	104	-3.8	-7.2	-11.9		-8.1
TOT	758	80	48	10938¹		9.2				12.6	3.34		.273	.338					.953	2411	770					

Runs		Hits		Doubles		Triples		Home Runs		Total Bases	
Cobb-Det	147	Cobb-Det	248	Cobb-Det	47	Cobb-Det	24	Baker-Phi	11	Cobb-Det	367
Jackson-Cle	126	Jackson-Cle	233	Jackson-Cle	45	Cree-NY	22	Speaker-Bos	8	Jackson-Cle	337
Bush-Det	126	Crawford-Det	217	Baker-Phi	42	Jackson-Cle	19	Cobb-Det	8	Crawford-Det	302
Milan-Was	109	Baker-Phi	198	Lord-Phi	37	Lord-Chi	18			Baker-Phi	301
Crawford-Det	109	Milan-Was	194	LaPorte-StL	37	Wolter-NY	15			Cree-NY	267

Runs Batted In		Runs Produced		Bases On Balls		Batting Average		On Base Percentage		Slugging Average	
Cobb-Det	127	Cobb-Det	266	Bush-Det	98	Cobb-Det	.420	Jackson-Cle	.468	Cobb-Det	.621
Crawford-Det	115	Crawford-Det	217	Milan-Was	74	Jackson-Cle	.408	Cobb-Det	.467	Jackson-Cle	.590
Baker-Phi	115	Jackson-Cle	202	Gessler-Was	74	Crawford-Det	.378	Collins-Phi	.451	Crawford-Det	.526
Bodie-Chi	97	Baker-Phi	200	Hooper-Bos	73	Collins-Phi	.365	Crawford-Det	.438	Cree-NY	.513
Delahanty-Det	94			Austin-StL	69	Cree-NY	.348	Speaker-Bos	.418	Baker-Phi	.508

Production		Adjusted Production		Batter Runs		Adjusted Batter Runs		Clutch Hitting Index		Runs Created	
Cobb-Det	1.088	Cobb-Det	193	Cobb-Det	78.4	Cobb-Det	70.7	Stovall-Cle	163	Cobb-Det	207
Jackson-Cle	1.058	Jackson-Cle	192	Jackson-Cle	71.8	Jackson-Cle	70.1	Gessler-Was	147	Jackson-Cle	175
Crawford-Det	.964	Collins-Phi	163	Crawford-Det	52.4	Crawford-Det	45.9	Hartzell-NY	131	Crawford-Det	147
Collins-Phi	.932	Crawford-Det	160	Collins-Phi	43.0	Collins-Phi	45.0	Barry-Phi	130	Cree-NY	129
Cree-NY	.928	Speaker-Bos	158	Cree-NY	39.9	Speaker-Bos	39.3	Moriarty-Det	128	Baker-Phi	127

Total Average		Stolen Bases		Stolen Base Average		Stolen Base Runs		Fielding Runs		Total Player Rating	
Cobb-Det	1.464	Cobb-Det	83					Tannehill-Chi	42.5	Cobb-Det	7.1
Jackson-Cle	1.308	Milan-Was	58					Gardner-Bos	23.6	Jackson-Cle	6.8
Collins-Phi	1.125	Cree-NY	48					McBride-Was	23.5	Collins-Phi	4.4
Crawford-Det	1.120	Callahan-Chi	45					Bush-Det	16.7	Speaker-Bos	3.7
Cree-NY	1.103	Lord-Chi	43					Austin-StL	16.3	Baker-Phi	3.6

Wins		Win Percentage		Games		Complete Games		Shutouts		Saves	
Coombs-Phi	28	Bender-Phi	.773	Walsh-Chi	56	Johnson-Was	36	Plank-Phi	6	Walsh-Chi	4
Walsh-Chi	27	Gregg-Cle	.767	Coombs-Phi	47	Walsh-Chi	33	Johnson-Was	6	Plank-Phi	4
Johnson-Was	25	Plank-Phi	.742	Wood-Bos	44	Ford-NY	26	Wood-Bos	5	Hall-Bos	4
		Coombs-Phi	.700	Caldwell-NY	41	Coombs-Phi	26	Walsh-Chi	5	Wood-Bos	3
		Morgan-Phi	.682					Gregg-Cle	5	Bender-Phi	3

Innings Pitched		Fewest Hits/Game		Fewest BB/Game		Strikeouts		Strikeouts/Game		Ratio	
Walsh-Chi	368.2	Gregg-Cle	6.33	White-Chi	1.47	Walsh-Chi	255	Wood-Bos	7.54	Gregg-Cle	9.86
Coombs-Phi	336.2	Wood-Bos	7.38	Lake-StL	1.67	Wood-Bos	231	Walsh-Chi	6.23	Walsh-Chi	9.91
Johnson-Was	322.1	Krapp-Phi	7.62	Walsh-Chi	1.76	Johnson-Was	207	Lange-Chi	5.79	Wood-Bos	10.22
Ford-NY	281.1	Morgan-Phi	7.82	Warhop-NY	1.89	Coombs-Phi	185	Johnson-Was	5.78	Johnson-Was	10.33
Wood-Bos	275.2	Scott-Chi	7.91	Powell-StL	1.91	Ford-NY	158	Kahler-Cle	5.66	Ford-NY	10.59

Earned Run Average		Adjusted ERA		Opponents' Batting Avg.		Opponents' On Base Pct.		Starter Runs		Adjusted Starter Runs	
Gregg-Cle	1.80	Gregg-Cle	189	Gregg-Cle	.205	Walsh-Chi	.280	Johnson-Was	51.6	Johnson-Was	49.4
Johnson-Was	1.90	Johnson-Was	173	Wood-Bos	.223	Johnson-Was	.283	Walsh-Chi	45.8	Gregg-Cle	43.6
Wood-Bos	2.02	Wood-Bos	162	Krapp-Cle	.232	Wood-Bos	.284	Gregg-Cle	41.8	Ford-NY	41.2
Plank-Phi	2.10	Ford-NY	158	Ford-NY	.237	Gregg-Cle	.286	Wood-Bos	40.3	Walsh-Chi	40.8
Bender-Phi	2.16	Plank-Phi	150	Johnson-Was	.238	Ford-NY	.291	Plank-Phi	35.2	Wood-Bos	38.2

Clutch Pitching Index		Relief Runs		Adjusted Relief Runs		Relief Ranking		Total Pitcher Index		Total Baseball Ranking	
Plank-Phi	133							Wood-Bos	6.5	Cobb-Det	7.1
Pape-Bos	130							Johnson-Was	6.4	Jackson-Cle	6.8
Cicotte-Bos	122							Walsh-Chi	6.2	Wood-Bos	6.5
Bender-Phi	117							Gregg-Cle	4.7	Johnson-Was	6.4
Willett-Det	111							Ford-NY	4.3	Walsh-Chi	6.2

January 2 Brooklyn Dodgers president Charles Ebbets announces he has purchased grounds to build a new concrete-and-steel stadium to seat 30,000. During the year he will ease his pinched financial condition by selling half the team to Ed and Steve McKeever.

April 11 On Opening Day in Brooklyn, fans storm Washington Park hours before the 4:00 P.M. starting time, causing a near riot. An estimated 30,000 people crowd into the outfield and along foul lines. The Giants hit a record 13 ground-rule doubles and are leading 19–3 in the sixth when the game is called due to darkness.

April 12 The Tinker-Evers-Chance double play combination plays its final major league game together for the Cubs. Vic Saier will replace Chance at first base.

May 1* George Sisler, a University of Michigan freshman, strikes out 20 in seven innings.

May 30* Three doubleheader sweeps—Chicago Green Sox over Richmond, Virginia Rebels; Cincinnati over Reading, Pennsylvania, and Pittsburgh Filipinos over Cleveland—end a short, futile season of the would-be major league competitor, the United States League. Poorly organized and financed, the league began play May 1 and collapsed largely through the failure of the New York franchise to attract fans. The Filipinos, so named because old Pittsburgh favorite Deacon Phillippe was manager, had the best record: 16–8. Players and fields were barely above semipro level, but these promoters will be heard from again with the advent of the Federal League.

June 13 Christy Mathewson wins his 300th game 3-2 over the Cubs, in his 10th straight 20-win season.

July 3 The Giants Rube Marquard nips Nap Rucker 2-1 to capture his 19th straight game this season. With two end-of-year wins in 1911, he has 21 in a row in regular season play.

July 23* Iron Man McGinnity is *still* pitching doubleheaders, winning a pair of games for Newark against Rochester (International League) at age 41.

September 17 Center fielder Casey Stengel breaks in with Brooklyn and has four singles, a walk, two stolen bases, and two RBI in the 7-3 win over Pittsburgh.

October 6 Pirates outfielder Owen "Chief" Wilson hits his 36th triple, a major league season record that still stands.

October 9 Three errors by Giants shortstop Art Fletcher help put Christy Mathewson behind 4–2 until the team rallies for three in the eighth when Duffy Lewis muffs a fly ball by Fred Snodgrass. Boston ties it in the last of the eighth. The Giants push across a run in the tenth off reliever "Sea Lion" Hall, but Tris Speaker blasts a triple to deep center. Apparently out at home trying to stretch it into a homer, he is safe when catcher Art Wilson, who has just entered the game, drops the throw for New York's fifth error. Darkness ends the game at 6–6 after 11 innings.

October 15 In Game 7 on a cold day in Boston, the Giants catch up with Joe Wood's smoke, teeing off for six runs on seven hits before the 32,694 fans have settled down. Jeff Tesreau wobbles to an 11-4 win and the Series is tied at three all. The only Boston bright spot is Tris Speaker's unassisted double play in the eighth, the only one completed by an outfielder in World Series play.

BOSTON	BROOKLYN	CHICAGO	CINCINNATI	NEW YORK	PHILADELPHIA	PITTSBURGH	ST.LOUIS
M J.Kling	M B.Dahlen	M F.Chance	M H.O'Day	M J.McGraw	M R.Dooin	M F.Clarke	M R.Bresnahan
1B B.Houser	1B J.Daubert	1B V.Saier	1B D.Hoblitzel	1B F.Merkle	1B F.Luderus	1B D.Miller	1B E.Konetchy
2B B.Sweeney	2B G.Cutshaw	2B J.Evers	2B D.Egan	2B L.Doyle	2B O.Knabe	2B A.McCarthy	2B M.Huggins
SS F.O'Rourke	SS B.Tooley	SS J.Tinker	SS J.Esmond	SS A.Fletcher	SS M.Doolan	SS H.Wagner	SS A.Hauser
3B E.McDonald	3B R.Smith	3B H.Zimmerman	3B A.Phelan	3B B.Herzog	3B H.Lobert	3B B.Byrne	3B M.Mowrey
LF G.Jackson	LF Z.Wheat	LF J.Sheckard	LF B.Bescher	LF F.Snodgrass	LF S.Magee	LF M.Carey	LF L.Magee
CF V.Campbell	CF H.Moran	CF T.Leach	CF A.Marsans	CF B.Becker	CF D.Paskert	CF C.Wilson	CF R.Oakes
RF J.Titus	RF H.Northen	RF F.Schulte	RF M.Mitchell	RF R.Murray	RF G.Cravath	RF M.Donlin	RF S.Evans
C J.Kling	C O.Miller	C J.Archer	C L.McLean	C C.Meyers	C B.Killefer	C G.Gibson	C I.Wingo
1S A.Devlin	2O J.Hummel	O W.Miller	S3 E.Grant	O J.Devore	C R.Dooin	2 A.Butler	O R.Ellis
O3 J.Kirke	S B.Fisher	O S.Hofman	O J.Bates	S3 T.Shafer	O D.Miller	C B.Kelly	3S W.Smith
C B.Rariden	O J.Daley	2 R.Downs	C T.Clarke	C A.Wilson	3 T.Downey	C M.Simon	J.Bliss
O D.Miller	C T.Erwin	S T.Needham	S T.McDonald	O G.Burns	O J.Titus	O E.Mensor	R.Bresnahan
S A.Bridwell	C E.Phelps	O E.Lennox	O H.Severeid	2 H.Groh	23 J.Walsh	O H.Hyatt	2 J.Galloway
C H.Gowdy	3 E.Kirkpatrick	O C.Williams	O P.Knisely	/O M.McCormick	J.Dodge	O T.Leach	O F.Gilhooley
S H.Spratt	O C.Stengel	O D.Cotter	3 R.Almeida	C G.Hartley	P.Graham	3 B.McKechnie	O D.Wilie
S R.Maranville	/2 R.Downs	/O W.Good	/O A.Kyle	/1 D.Robertson	C.Dolan	3 J.Viox	3 P.Whitted
/O A.Kaiser	/S D.Stark	/S T.Downey	/C E.Blackburn	/C M.Loan	P.Moran	O S.Hofman	/O E.Miller
/2 J.Schultz	/C B.Higgins	/S C.Moore	P B.Keefe	P C.Mathewson	/3 J.Boyle	/1 S.Gray	/O T.Cather
/S D.Shean	P N.Rucker	/1 F.Chance	P G.Suggs	P R.Marquard	/O G.Mangus	/O O.Nicholson	C F.Snyder
/C G.Whitehouse	P E.Yingling	/C H.Chapman	P R.Benton	P J.Tesreau	/3 B.Brinker	/3 O.Dodd	/2 R.Rolling
/C M.Gonzalez	P E.Stack	/C M.Hechinger	P A.Fromme	P R.Ames	/3 G.Steinbrenner	O W.Rehg	/3 J.Kelleher
H B.Jones	P E.Knetzer	/C G.Yantz	P B.Humphries	P D.Crandall	H G.Browne	H R.Bisland	/C E.Burns
/3 A.Schwind	P F.Allen	P L.Cheney	/P H.Gaspar	P H.Wiltse	/2 J.Savage	/C E.Blackburn	H J.Clark
P L.Tyler	P C.Barger	P J.Lavender	/P F.Harter	/P A.Demaree	P P.Alexander	R R.Capron	/1 J.Mercer
P O.Hess	P M.Kent	P L.Richie	/P D.Davis	/P L.Kirby	P T.Seaton	R M.Keliher	/C M.Murphy
P H.Perdue	P C.Curtis	P E.Reulbach	/P F.Smith	/P L.Bader	P E.Moore	P C.Hendrix	P S.Sallee
P W.Dickson	/P B.Schardt	P C.Smith	/P H.McGraner	/P T.Goulait	P A.Brennan	P H.Camnitz	P B.Harmon
P E.Donnelly	/P S.Burk	P M.Brown	/P J.Bagby	/P L.Drucke	P E.Rixey	P M.O'Toole	P B.Steele
P B.Brown	/P E.Dent	P L.Leifield	/P F.Gregory	/P E.Shore	RP T.Shultz	P H.Robinson	P R.Geyer
P B.McTigue		/P H.McIntire	/P J.Frill		P G.Chalmers	P B.Adams	P J.Willis
P B.Hogg		/P J.Moroney	/P G.Moore		P C.Curtis	P K.Cole	RP G.Woodburn
/P R.Kroh		/P F.Toney	/P S.Fletcher		P H.Finneran	P E.Warner	P G.Dale
/P A.Mattern		/P K.Cole	/P R.Works		/P E.Mayer	/P J.Ferry	P D.Griner
/P S.White		/P G.Pearce	/P G.Packard		P R.Nelson	/P W.Cooper	/P S.Burk
/P K.Brady		/P G.Lowdermilk	/P B.Taylor		/P H.Ritter	/P L.Leifield	/P P.Perritt
/P H.Griffin		/P L.Madden	/P E.Donalds		/P H.Wallace	/P S.Smith	/P P.Redding
/P B.Brady		/P E.Cottrell	/P H.Horsey		/P F.Nicholson	/P H.Gardner	/P L.Lowdermilk
		/P J.Vernon	/P B.Prough		/P R.Marshall		/P W.Dell
		/P R.Sommers	/P C.Tompkins				/P R.Howell
		/P B.Powell	/P B.Cramer				/P B.Ewing
			/P B.Doak				/P G.Zackert

TEAM	G	W	L	PCT	GB	R	OR	AB	H	2B	3B	HR	BB	SO	AVG	OBP	SLG	PRO	PRO+	BR	/A	PF	CHI	RC	SB	CS	SBA	SBR
NY	154	103	48	.682		823	571	5067	1451	231	89	47	514	497	.286	.360	.395	.755	110	89	65	103	104	830	319			
PIT	152	93	58	.616	10	751	565	5252	1493	222	129	39	420	514	.284	.340	.398	.738	110	44	56	98	99	767	177			
CHI	152	91	59	.607	11.5	756	668	5048	1398	245	90	43	560	615	.277	.354	.387	.741	109	62	64	100	98	750	164			
CIN	155	75	78	.490	29	656	722	5115	1310	183	89	21	479	492	.256	.323	.339	.662	90	-90	-72	97	107	639	248			
PHI	152	73	79	.480	30.5	670	688	5077	1354	244	68	43	464	615	.267	.332	.367	.699	91	-23	-68	107	99	671	159			
STL	153	63	90	.412	41	659	830	5092	1366	190	77	27	508	620	.268	.340	.352	.692	97	-27	-11	98	97	675	193			
BRO	153	58	95	.379	46	651	754	5141	1377	220	73	32	490	584	.268	.336	.358	.694	100	-28	-2	96	96	677	179			
BOS	155	52	101	.340	52	693	861	5361	1465	227	68	35	454	690	.273	.335	.361	.696	94	-28	-40	102	99	693	137			
TOT	613					5659		41153	11214	1762	683	287	3889	4627	.272	.340	.369	.710						1576				

TEAM	CG	SH	SV	IP	H	H/G	HR	BB	SO	RAT	ERA	ERA+	OAV	OOB	PR	/A	PF	CPI	FA	E	DP	FW	PW	BW	SBW	DIF
NY	93	8	15	1369²	1352	8.9	36	338	652	11.3	2.58	130	.259	.307	124	118	99	103	.956	280	123	-2.1	11.6	6.4		11.6
PIT	94	18	7	1385	1268	8.2	28	497	664	11.8	2.85	114	.251	.324	84	60	96	99	.972	169	125	6.0	5.9	5.5		.1
CHI	80	15	9	1358²	1307	8.7	33	493	554	12.2	3.42	97	.259	.331	-4	-19	98	89	.960	249	125	-.0	-1.9	6.3		11.6
CIN	86	13	10	1377²	1455	9.5	28	452	561	12.9	3.42	98	.279	.344	-4	-14	99	102	.960	249	102	.4	-1.4	-7.1		6.6
PHI	81	10	9	1355	1381	9.2	43	515	616	12.9	3.25	111	.272	.344	23	54	106	107	.963	231	98	1.3	5.3	-6.7		-3.0
STL	61	6	12	1353	1466	9.8	31	560	487	13.7	3.85	89	.286	.361	-68	-63	101	102	.957	274	113	-1.8	-6.2	-1.1		-4.5
BRO	71	10	8	1357	1399	9.3	45	510	553	12.9	3.64	92	.273	.343	-37	-49	98	96	.959	255	96	-.3	-4.8	-.2		-13.1
BOS	88	5	5	1390²	1544	10.0	43	521	542	13.6	4.17	86	.291	.359	-119	-98	105	95	.954	297	129	-3.2	-9.6	-3.9		-7.7
TOT	654	85	75	10946²		9.2				12.7	3.40		.272	.340					.960	2004	911					

Runs
Bescher-Cin ... 120
Carey-Pit ... 114
Paskert-Phi ... 102
Campbell-Bos ... 102

Hits
Zimmerman-Chi ... 207
Sweeney-Bos ... 204
Campbell-Bos ... 185
Doyle-NY ... 184
Wagner-Pit ... 181

Doubles
Zimmerman-Chi ... 41
Paskert-Phi ... 37
Wagner-Pit ... 35
Miller-Pit ... 33
Doyle-NY ... 33

Triples
Wilson-Pit ... 36
Wagner-Pit ... 20
Murray-NY ... 20
Daubert-Bro ... 16

Home Runs
Zimmerman-Chi ... 14
Schulte-Chi ... 12
Wilson-Pit ... 11
Merkle-NY ... 11
Cravath-Phi ... 11

Total Bases
Zimmerman-Chi ... 318
Wilson-Pit ... 299
Wagner-Pit ... 277
Sweeney-Bos ... 264
Doyle-NY ... 263

Runs Batted In
Wagner-Pit ... 102
Sweeney-Bos ... 100
Zimmerman-Chi ... 99
Wilson-Pit ... 95
Murray-NY ... 92

Runs Produced
Wagner-Pit ... 186
Sweeney-Bos ... 183
Zimmerman-Chi ... 180
Doyle-NY ... 178
Carey-Pit ... 175

Bases On Balls
Sheckard-Chi ... 122
Paskert-Phi ... 91
Huggins-StL ... 87
Bescher-Cin ... 83
Titus-Phi-Bos ... 82

Batting Average
Zimmerman-Chi ... .372
Meyers-NY ... .358
Sweeney-Bos ... .344
Evers-Chi ... .341
Doyle-NY ... .330

On Base Percentage
Evers-Chi ... .431
Huggins-StL ... .422
Paskert-Phi ... .420
Zimmerman-Chi ... .418
Sweeney-Bos ... .416

Slugging Average
Zimmerman-Chi ... .571
Wilson-Pit ... .513
Wagner-Pit ... .496
Meyers-NY ... .477
Doyle-NY ... .471

Production
Zimmerman-Chi ... .989
Wagner-Pit ... .891
Evers-Chi ... .873
Doyle-NY ... .864
Titus-Phi-Bos ... .862

Adjusted Production
Zimmerman-Chi ... 169
Wagner-Pit ... 145
Evers-Chi ... 139
Wilson-Pit ... 134
Konetchy-StL ... 134

Batter Runs
Zimmerman-Chi ... 49.8
Wagner-Pit ... 32.1
Sweeney-Bos ... 30.9
Evers-Chi ... 29.1
Meyers-NY ... 28.2

Adjusted Batter Runs
Zimmerman-Chi ... 50.2
Wagner-Pit ... 33.8
Evers-Chi ... 29.4
Sweeney-Bos ... 29.0
Meyers-NY ... 25.8

Clutch Hitting Index
Sweeney-Bos ... 138
Tinker-Chi ... 131
Hoblitzel-Cin ... 124
Murray-NY ... 119
Snodgrass-NY ... 114

Runs Created
Zimmerman-Chi ... 141
Sweeney-Bos ... 123
Wagner-Pit ... 118
Doyle-NY ... 116
Paskert-Phi ... 108

Total Average
Zimmerman-Chi ... 1.100
Wagner-Pit ... .976
Paskert-Phi ... .965
Evers-Chi ... .962
Doyle-NY ... .955

Stolen Bases
Bescher-Cin ... 67
Carey-Pit ... 45
Snodgrass-NY ... 43
Murray-NY ... 38

Stolen Base Average

Stolen Base Runs

Fielding Runs
Sweeney-Bos ... 26.9
Tinker-Chi ... 24.7
Wagner-Pit ... 22.9
Herzog-NY ... 19.2
Fletcher-NY ... 15.8

Total Player Rating
Wagner-Pit ... 6.6
Zimmerman-Chi ... 5.1
Sweeney-Bos ... 5.0
Evers-Chi ... 3.1
Konetchy-StL ... 2.8

Wins
Marquard-NY ... 26
Cheney-Chi ... 26
Hendrix-Pit ... 24
Mathewson-NY ... 23
Camnitz-Pit ... 22

Win Percentage
Hendrix-Pit ... .727
Cheney-Chi ... .722
Tesreau-NY ... .708
Marquard-NY ... .703
Richie-Chi ... .667

Games
Benton-Cin ... 50
Sallee-StL ... 48
Alexander-Phi ... 46
Rucker-Bro ... 45
Seaton-Phi ... 44

Complete Games
Cheney-Chi ... 28
Mathewson-NY ... 27
Suggs-Cin ... 25
Hendrix-Pit ... 25
Alexander-Phi ... 25

Shutouts
Rucker-Bro ... 6
Suggs-Cin ... 5
O'Toole-Pit ... 5

Saves
Sallee-StL ... 6
Rucker-Bro ... 4
Reulbach-Chi ... 4
Mathewson-NY ... 4

Innings Pitched
Alexander-Phi ... 310.1
Mathewson-NY ... 310.0
Cheney-Chi ... 303.1
Suggs-Cin ... 303.0
Benton-Cin ... 302.0

Fewest Hits/Game
Tesreau-NY ... 6.56
Robinson-Pit ... 7.51
O'Toole-Pit ... 7.75
Cheney-Chi ... 7.77
Brown-Bos ... 7.81

Fewest BB/Game
Mathewson-NY ... .99
Robinson-Pit ... 1.54
Suggs-Cin ... 1.66
Ames-NY ... 1.76
Adams-Pit ... 1.85

Strikeouts
Alexander-Phi ... 195
Hendrix-Pit ... 176
Marquard-NY ... 175
Benton-Cin ... 162
Rucker-Bro ... 151

Strikeouts/Game
Alexander-Phi ... 5.66
Hendrix-Pit ... 5.49
Marquard-NY ... 5.35
Tyler-Bos ... 5.06
O'Toole-Pit ... 4.90

Ratio
Robinson-Pit ... 9.57
Mathewson-NY ... 10.07
Rucker-Bro ... 10.49
Tesreau-NY ... 10.85
Adams-Pit ... 10.94

Earned Run Average
Tesreau-NY ... 1.96
Mathewson-NY ... 2.12
Rucker-Bro ... 2.21
Robinson-Pit ... 2.26
Ames-NY ... 2.46

Adjusted ERA
Tesreau-NY ... 172
Mathewson-NY ... 159
Rucker-Bro ... 151
Rixey-Phi ... 145
Robinson-Pit ... 144

Opponents' Batting Avg.
Tesreau-NY ... .204
Cheney-Chi ... .234
Robinson-Pit ... .237
Brown-Bos ... .239
O'Toole-Pit ... .241

Opponents' On Base Pct.
Mathewson-NY ... .281
Robinson-Pit ... .284
Tesreau-NY ... .298
Tesreau-NY ... .298
Adams-Pit ... .303

Starter Runs
Mathewson-NY ... 44.1
Rucker-Bro ... 39.4
Tesreau-NY ... 38.8
Marquard-NY ... 27.3
Sallee-StL ... 26.0

Adjusted Starter Runs
Mathewson-NY ... 43.0
Tesreau-NY ... 37.9
Rucker-Bro ... 37.4
Alexander-Phi ... 27.7
Sallee-StL ... 26.6

Clutch Pitching Index
Ames-NY ... 125
Geyer-StL ... 125
Benton-Cin ... 116
Dickson-Bos ... 116
Yingling-Bro ... 114

Relief Runs

Adjusted Relief Runs

Relief Ranking

Total Pitcher Index
Rucker-Bro ... 5.2
Mathewson-NY ... 5.2
Hendrix-Pit ... 4.3
Tesreau-NY ... 3.3
Alexander-Phi ... 3.1

Total Baseball Ranking
Wagner-Pit ... 6.6
Rucker-Bro ... 5.2
Mathewson-NY ... 5.2
Zimmerman-Chi ... 5.1
Sweeney-Bos ... 5.0

April 20 The Boston Red Sox open in the new Fenway Park with a 7-6 11-inning win over the New York Highlanders before 27,000.

April 20 Detroit opens remodeled Navin Park (now Tiger Stadium) and beats Cleveland 6–5 in 11 innings before 24,384.

May 15 Ty Cobb charges into the stands in New York and attacks heckler Claude Lueker. Other fans and Tigers mix it up before order is restored. Ban Johnson suspends Cobb indefinitely for the incident.

May 18 The Tiger players protest Cobb's suspension and vote to strike. Faced with a $5,000 fine for failing to field a team, club owner Frank Navin orders manager Hugh Jennings to sign up some local amateurs. Aloysius Travers, Bill Leinhauser, Dan McGarvey, Billy Maharg (whose real name was Graham, "Maharg" reversed), Jim McGarr, Pat Meany, Jack Coffey, Hap Ward, and Ed Irvin put on Tiger uniforms. Two Detroit coaches, Joe Sugden, 41, and Jim McGuire, 48, complete the lineup. The Athletics win 24–2, as Travers goes all the way for Detroit, giving up 26 hits and 24 runs in eight innings. Irvin hits two triples in three at bats and closes his major league career with a 2.000 slugging average. Only one ever plays another major league game: Maharg will bat once for the Phils in 1916. He will also be involved as a conspirator in the Black Sox scandal of 1919. The Tigers return to the field two days later.

July 15* A U.S. team defeats the Swedish Vesteras Club 13–3 in a one-game Olympic exhibition in Stockholm, Sweden.

August 26 Walter Johnson's 16-game winning streak ends under rules that have since been changed. In the second game of a doubleheader against the Browns, he relieves Tom Hughes with one out and two on in the seventh inning of a 2-2 game. The two runners score and the Nationals lose 4-3. The two runs are charged to Johnson, not Hughes.

September 6 In one of the more dramatic matchups in history, Walter Johnson, who had won 16 straight games before losing, takes the mound in a doubleheader nightcap against Joe Wood, who is seeking his 14th straight win. Wood strikes out nine and beats the visiting Senators, 1–0.

September 7 Eddie Collins steals six bases in the Athletics' 9-7 defeat of Detroit, a post-1900 record that is still unmatched. Remarkably, on the 22nd, he will repeat with six against the Browns.

October 16 In the Series finale, in the last of the 10th, pinch hitter Clyde Engle lifts a can of corn to center fielder Snodgrass, who drops the ball. Snodgrass then makes a great catch of a long drive by Harry Hooper. Steve Yerkes walks, bringing up Tris Speaker, who pops a high foul along the first baseman line. Catcher John "Chief" Meyers chases it, but it drops a few feet from first baseman Merkle, who could have taken it easily. Reprieved, Speaker then singles in the tying run and sends Yerkes to third. Larry Gardner hits a long fly that scores Yerkes with the winning run.

BOSTON	CHICAGO	CLEVELAND	DETROIT	NEW YORK	PHILADELPHIA	ST.LOUIS	WASHINGTON
M J.Stahl	M J.Callahan	M H.Davis	M H.Jennings	M H.Wolverton	M C.Mack	M B.Wallace	M C.Griffith
1B J.Stahl	1B R.Zeider	M J.Birmingham	1B G.Moriarty	1B H.Chase	1B S.McInnis	M G.Stovall	1B C.Gandil
2B S.Yerkes	2B M.Rath	1B A.Griggs	2B B.Louden	2B H.Simmons	2B E.Collins	1B G.Stovall	2B R.Morgan
SS H.Wagner	SS B.Weaver	2B N.Lajoie	SS D.Bush	SS J.Martin	SS J.Barry	2B D.Pratt	SS G.McBride
3B L.Gardner	3B H.Lord	SS R.Peckinpaugh	3B C.Deal	3B R.Hartzell	3B F.Baker	SS B.Wallace	3B E.Foster
LF D.Lewis	LF N.Callahan	3B T.Turner	LF D.Jones	LF B.Daniels	LF A.Strunk	3B J.Austin	LF H.Shanks
CF T.Speaker	CF P.Bodie	LF B.Ryan	CF T.Cobb	CF D.Sterrett	CF R.Oldring	LF W.Hogan	CF C.Milan
RF H.Hooper	RF S.Collins	CF J.Birmingham	RF S.Crawford	RF G.Zinn	RF B.Lord	CF B.Shotton	RF D.Moeller
C B.Carrigan	C W.Kuhn	RF J.Jackson	C O.Stanage	C J.Sweeney	C J.Lapp	RF G.Williams	C J.Henry
12 C.Engle	O W.Mattick	C S.O'Neill	O3 O.Vitt	O B.Cree	O H.Maggert	C J.Stephens	C E.Ainsmith
1 H.Bradley	C B.Block	S3 I.Olson	2O J.Delahanty	2 E.Gardner	O E.Murphy	O P.Compton	O1 G.Schaefer
C H.Cady	1 B.Borton	O J.Graney	1 D.Gainer	3 D.Paddock	C I.Thomas	2O F.LaPorte	C R.Williams
C L.Nunamaker	C B.Sullivan	3 T.Easterly	3 R.Corriden	O J.Lelivelt	B.Egan	1 J.Kutina	2 F.LaPorte
O O.Henriksen	M M.McIntyre	1 D.Johnston	1 E.Onslow	S T.McMillan	D.Murphy	C P.Krichell	O T.Walker
2 N.Ball	1 J.Fournier	2 N.Ball	O B.Veach	S B.Stumpf	O J.Walsh	O H.Jantzen	2 J.Knight
/S M.Krug	C R.Schalk	S R.Chapman	C J.Onslow	C G.Street	C S.Derrick	C W.Alexander	1 J.Flynn
/C P.Thomas	C T.Easterly	O H.Butcher	C B.Kocher	3 E.Midkiff	/3 J.Mathes	S E.Hallinan	C B.Kenworthy
	S E.Johnson	O T.Hendryx	/3 P.Baumann	O P.Maloney	/3 H.Fahey	C J.Daley	/2 B.Cunningham
P J.Wood	/O C.Barrows	O F.Carisch	/O H.Perry	3 C.Dolan	H C.Emerson	/1 E.Miller	/O R.Moran
P B.O'Brien	/C W.Mayer	O B.Hunter	/O R.McDermott	/3 H.Wolverton	P J.Coombs	/O B.Brief	/S R.Roach
P H.Bedient	/1 M.Ens	O B.Adams	/O A.Bashang	B.Williams	E.Plank	/C F.Crossin	/1 J.Agler
P R.Collins	/O D.Berran	1 E.Hohnhorst	/2 C.O'Leary	3 C.Coleman	P B.Brown	/O B.Brown	H T.Long
P C.Hall	/3 L.Tannehill	C P.Livingston	/O B.Leinhauser	/O H.Wolter	P B.Houck	/C C.Snell	/3 J.Ryan
P L.Pape	/2 K.Gleason	3 H.Baker	/2 J.McGarr	S J.Dowd	C B.Bender	G.Aiton	R D.Howard
/P E.Cicotte	H P.McLarry	S K.Nash	/S O.O'Mara	/O K.Smith	RP H.Pennock	/S H.Smoyer	P W.Johnson
/P B.Van Dyke	/S L.Blackburne	/O A.Hauger	/1 J.Sugden	/O B.Otis	C C.Morgan	/S D.Shanley	P B.Groom
/P J.Bushelman	/C D.Paddock	/3 H.Bronkie	/3 E.Irvin	/O J.Little	/P R.Crabb	/C P.Ketter	P T.Hughes
/P D.Smith	H P.Wolfe	/O J.Kibble	/O D.McGarvey	/O B.Kauff	/S S.Coveleski	/C L.Criger	P C.Cashion
/P C.Hageman	/1 H.Davis	/O H.Eibel	/C D.McGuire	/C G.Fisher	/P D.Danforth	/S C.Miller	P H.Vaughn
	P E.Walsh	/C L.Nagelsen	/S P.Meaney	/O G.Batten	/P L.Russell	H T.Tennant	P J.Engel
	P J.Benz	/O M.Meixell	/O R.Ward	H J.Priest	/P H.Barry	F.Walden	/P D.Walker
	P D.White	/3 H.Grubb	/C H.Jennings	/C H.Thompson	/P J.Bush	P J.Powell	/P P.Musser
	P F.Lange	P V.Gregg	/3 B.Maharg	P R.Ford	/P H.Krause	P G.Baumgardner	/P J.Akers
	P E.Cicotte	P F.Blanding	/3 J.Smith	P J.Warhop	P R.Salmon	M.Allison	/P C.Becker
	P R.Peters	P G.Kahler	P E.Willett	P R.Caldwell	D.Martin	E.Brown	/P J.Boehling
	P G.Mogridge	P W.Mitchell	P J.Dubuc	P G.McConnell	S.Harrell	C.Brown	/P L.Schegg
	/P J.Scott	P B.Steen	P G.Mullin	P J.Quinn		R.Mitchell	/P B.Gallia
	/P W.Taylor	P R.Works	P J.Lake	R.Fisher		J.Lake	/P N.Altrock
	/P P.Douglas	P J.Baskette	P T.Covington	H.Vaughn		C.Weilman	/P H.Herring
	/P W.Johnson	P G.Krapp	/P B.Burns	G.Davis		W.Adams	/P S.White
	/P R.Jordan	P L.George	/P C.Wheatley	R.Keating		B.Pelty	/P C.Griffith
	/P R.Crabb	/P B.James	/P W.Jensen	T.Thompson		B.Napier	
	/P R.Bell	/P B.Brenner	/P G.Boehler	R.Hoff		R.Nelson	
	/P H.Smith	/P L.James	/P H.Dauss	A.Schulz		B.Bailey	
	/P F.Delhi	/P E.Wolf	E.Summers	G.Shears		J.Frill	
	/P F.Lamline	/P H.Krause	H.Moran			H.Spencer	
		/P R.Walker	B.Donovan				
		/P J.Neher	H.Pernoll				
		/P M.Walker	A.Travers				
			B.Troy				
			E.Lafitte				
			A.Remneas				
			P.McGehee				

TEAM	G	W	L	PCT	GB	R	OR	AB	H	2B	3B	HR	BB	SO	AVG	OBP	SLG	PRO	PRO+	BR	/A	PF	CHI	RC	SB	CS	SBA	SBR
BOS	154	105	47	.691		799	544	5071	1404	269	84	29	565		.277	.355	.380	.735	110	104	64	105	100	752	185			
WAS	154	91	61	.599	14	699	581	5075	1298	202	86	20	472		.256	.324	.341	.665	94	-32	-37	101	108	645	274			
PHI	153	90	62	.592	15	779	658	5111	1442	204	108	22	485		.282	.349	.377	.726	117	83	111	96	101	763	258			
CHI	158	78	76	.506	28	639	648	5182	1321	174	80	17	423		.255	.317	.329	.646	93	-68	-48	97	102	610	205			
CLE	155	75	78	.490	30.5	677	681	5132	1403	219	77	12	407		.273	.333	.353	.686	98	5	-16	103	98	671	194			
DET	154	69	84	.451	36.5	720	777	5143	1376	189	86	19	530		.268	.343	.349	.692	106	26	49	97	100	705	270			
STL	157	53	101	.344	53	552	764	5080	1262	166	71	19	449		.248	.315	.320	.635	90	-86	-65	96	94	565	176			
NY	153	50	102	.329	55	630	842	5092	1320	168	79	18	463		.259	.329	.334	.663	90	-31	-70	106	97	638	247			
TOT	619					5495		40886	10826	1591	671	156	3794	5157	.265	.333	.348	.681						1809				

TEAM	CG	SH	SV	IP	H	H/G	HR	BB	SO	RAT	ERA	ERA+	OAV	OOB	PR	/A	PF	CPI	FA	E	DP	FW	PW	BW	SBW	DIF
BOS	108	18	6	1362	1243	8.2	18	385	712	11.0	2.76	124	.248	.306	88	104	103	98	.957	267	88	2.4	10.4	6.4		9.8
WAS	98	11	7	1376²	1219	8.0	24	525	828	11.8	2.69	125	.242	.320	99	105	101	108	.954	297	92	.7	10.5	-3.7		7.6
PHI	95	11	9	1357	1273	8.4	12	518	601	12.3	3.32	93	.258	.336	2	-31	93	99	.959	263	115	2.5	-3.1	11.1		3.5
CHI	85	14	16	1413	1398	8.9	26	426	698	11.8	3.06	105	.264	.322	44	26	96	104	.956	291	102	1.5	2.6	-4.8		1.7
CLE	94	7	7	1352²	1367	9.1	15	523	622	12.9	3.30	104	.272	.346	6	21	103	110	.954	287	124	1.4	2.1	-1.6		-3.4
DET	107	7	5	1367¹	1438	9.5	16	521	512	13.3	3.77	87	.277	.350	-66	-71	98	100	.950	338	91	-1.7	-7.1	4.9		-3.6
STL	85	8	5	1369²	1433	9.4	17	442	547	12.7	3.71	90	.277	.341	-56	-55	100	97	.947	341	127	-1.6	-5.5	-6.5		-10.5
NY	105	5	3	1335	1448	9.8	28	436	637	13.0	4.13	88	.282	.344	-117	-71	108	92	.940	382	77	-4.4	-7.1	-7.0		-7.5
TOT	777	81	58	10933¹		8.9				12.3	3.34		.265	.333					.952	2466	816					

Runs		Hits		Doubles		Triples		Home Runs		Total Bases	
Collins-Phi	137	Jackson-Cle	226	Speaker-Bos	53	Jackson-Cle	26	Speaker-Bos	10	Jackson-Cle	331
Speaker-Bos	136	Cobb-Det	226	Jackson-Cle	44	Cobb-Det	23	Baker-Phi	10	Speaker-Bos	329
Jackson-Cle	121	Speaker-Bos	222	Baker-Phi	40	Crawford-Det	21	Cobb-Det	7	Cobb-Det	323
Cobb-Det	120	Baker-Phi	200	Lewis-Bos	36	Baker-Phi	21			Baker-Phi	312
Baker-Phi	116					Gardner-Bos	18			Crawford-Det	273

Runs Batted In		Runs Produced		Bases On Balls		Batting Average		On Base Percentage		Slugging Average	
Baker-Phi	130	Baker-Phi	236	Bush-Det	117	Cobb-Det	.409	Speaker-Bos	.464	Cobb-Det	.584
Lewis-Bos	109	Speaker-Bos	216	Collins-Phi	101	Jackson-Cle	.395	Jackson-Cle	.458	Jackson-Cle	.579
Crawford-Det	109	Jackson-Cle	208	Rath-Cle	95	Speaker-Bos	.383	Cobb-Det	.456	Speaker-Bos	.567
McInnis-Phi	101	Collins-Phi	201	Shotton-StL	86	Lajoie-Cle	.368	Collins-Phi	.450	Baker-Phi	.541
		Cobb-Det	196	Speaker-Bos	82	Collins-Phi	.348	Lajoie-Cle	.414	Crawford-Det	.470

Production		Adjusted Production		Batter Runs		Adjusted Batter Runs		Clutch Hitting Index		Runs Created	
Cobb-Det	1.040	Cobb-Det	203	Speaker-Bos	72.8	Cobb-Det	71.7	Lajoie-Cle	145	Speaker-Bos	175
Jackson-Cle	1.036	Jackson-Cle	190	Jackson-Cle	70.3	Jackson-Cle	65.8	Lewis-Bos	130	Cobb-Det	173
Speaker-Bos	1.031	Speaker-Bos	185	Cobb-Det	67.1	Speaker-Bos	65.3	Gandil-Was	125	Jackson-Cle	166
Baker-Phi	.945	Baker-Phi	176	Baker-Phi	49.2	Baker-Phi	53.8	Milan-Was	124	Baker-Phi	140
Collins-Phi	.885	Collins-Phi	159	Collins-Phi	43.7	Collins-Phi	48.2	McInnis-Phi	120	Collins-Phi	136

Total Average		Stolen Bases		Stolen Base Average	Stolen Base Runs	Fielding Runs		Total Player Rating	
Cobb-Det	1.321	Milan-Was	88			McBride-Was	31.1	Speaker-Bos	7.7
Speaker-Bos	1.310	Collins-Phi	63			Bush-Det	29.4	Jackson-Cle	6.9
Jackson-Cle	1.249	Cobb-Det	61			Louden-Det	22.8	Cobb-Det	6.4
Collins-Phi	1.130	Speaker-Bos	52			Speaker-Bos	21.6	Baker-Phi	6.3
Baker-Phi	1.082	Zeider-Chi	47			Rath-Chi	18.3	Collins-Phi	5.8

Wins		Win Percentage		Games		Complete Games		Shutouts		Saves	
Wood-Bos	34	Wood-Bos	.872	Walsh-Chi	62	Wood-Bos	35	Wood-Bos	10	Walsh-Chi	10
Johnson-Was	33	Plank-Phi	.813	Johnson-Was	50	Johnson-Was	34	Johnson-Was	7	Warhop-NY	3
Walsh-Chi	27	Johnson-Was	.733	Wood-Bos	43	Walsh-Chi	32	Walsh-Chi	6	Mogridge-Chi	3
Plank-Phi	26	Bedient-Bos	.690	Groom-Was	43	Ford-NY	30	Plank-Phi	5	Lange-Chi	3
Groom-Was	24	Coombs-Phi	.677	Benz-Chi	42			Collins-Bos	4	Dubuc-Det	3

Innings Pitched		Fewest Hits/Game		Fewest BB/Game		Strikeouts		Strikeouts/Game		Ratio	
Walsh-Chi	393.0	Johnson-Was	6.32	Bender-Phi	1.74	Johnson-Was	303	Johnson-Was	7.39	Johnson-Was	8.56
Johnson-Was	369.0	Wood-Bos	6.99	Johnson-Was	1.85	Wood-Bos	258	Wood-Bos	6.75	Wood-Bos	9.44
Wood-Bos	344.0	Houck-Phi	7.37	Collins-Bos	1.90	Walsh-Chi	254	Gregg-Cle	6.10	Walsh-Chi	9.78
Groom-Was	316.0	Walsh-Chi	7.60	Powell-StL	1.99	Gregg-Cle	184	Walsh-Chi	5.82	Bedient-Bos	10.29
Ford-NY	291.2	O'Brien-Bos	7.74	Warhop-NY	2.06	Groom-Was	179	Lange-Chi	5.23	Collins-Bos	10.66

Earned Run Average		Adjusted ERA		Opponents' Batting Avg.		Opponents' On Base Pct.		Starter Runs		Adjusted Starter Runs	
Johnson-Was	1.39	Johnson-Was	241	Johnson-Was	.196	Johnson-Was	.248	Johnson-Was	79.9	Johnson-Was	80.5
Wood-Bos	1.91	Wood-Bos	179	Wood-Bos	.216	Wood-Bos	.272	Wood-Bos	54.6	Wood-Bos	57.8
Walsh-Chi	2.15	Walsh-Chi	149	Walsh-Chi	.231	Walsh-Chi	.279	Walsh-Chi	51.8	Walsh-Chi	46.5
Plank-Phi	2.22	Plank-Phi	140	Houck-Phi	.234	Bedient-Bos	.288	Plank-Phi	32.3	O'Brien-Bos	25.8
Collins-Bos	2.53	Collins-Bos	135	Dubuc-Det	.235	Collins-Bos	.297	Groom-Was	25.2	Groom-Was	25.8

Clutch Pitching Index		Relief Runs	Adjusted Relief Runs	Relief Ranking	Total Pitcher Index		Total Baseball Ranking	
Hughes-Was	129				Johnson-Was	11.2	Johnson-Was	11.2
McConnell-NY	121				Wood-Bos	8.6	Wood-Bos	8.6
Cashion-Was	120				Walsh-Chi	6.6	Speaker-Bos	7.7
Kahler-Cle	120				Plank-Phi	3.2	Jackson-Cle	6.9
Plank-Phi	119				McConnell-NY	2.9	Walsh-Chi	6.6

February 1 Jim Thorpe signs with the New York Giants, but the Olympic medal winner will be more of a gate attraction than a threat at the plate.

March 8* 1913 The Federal League is organized as a six-team "outlaw" circuit and elects John T. Powers president. It will play 120 games at a level equivalent to the lower minor leagues, but will enhance its status considerably in 1914 to challenge the major leagues.

April 5 An exhibition game with the newly christened Yankees opens the equally new Ebbets Field; 25,000 are on hand to watch Nap Rucker beat the New Yorkers 3–2. The first homer is hit by Brooklyn's Casey Stengel, who legs out an inside-the-park homer.

April 9 With league approval, the Dodgers play their opener—and first regular-season game at Ebbets Field—a day ahead of the rest of the league. Cold weather keeps the crowd down to about 12,000, and the Phils' Tom Seaton beats Nap Rucker 1-0.

May 22 Ruling that a ballplayer on the field is a "public person," a New York judge throws out cases brought by New York and Boston players against a motion picture company that took movies of the 1912 World Series.

May 30 John McGraw joins Fred Clarke, Cap Anson, Frank Selee, and Connie Mack as managers who have won 1,000 games.

July 18 In blanking the Cards 5–0, Christy Mathewson yields a base on balls, ending a record string of 68 innings pitched without a walk.

August 10 Honus Wagner is given a souvenir bat carved from a piece of wood taken from naval hero Oliver Perry's flagship *Niagara,* which was sunk in Lake Erie 100 years before.

September 14 Cubs hurler Larry Cheney hurls a 14-hit shutout against the Giants, defeating them 7-0 while setting a major league record for most hits allowed in a whitewashing. Milt Gaston of Washington will duplicate the feat on July 10, 1928.

October 4 Despite the Dodgers' sixth-place finish, first baseman Jake Daubert earns a new Chalmers automobile as the NL MVP. Daubert led the NL at .350 and will repeat his batting title in 1914.

October 8 Christy Mathewson ties the Series, shutting the Athletics out for 10 innings to beat Eddie Plank 3-0. Mathewson also knocks in the winning run with a double in the tenth.

October 12 John McGraw hosts a reunion for Hugh Jennings and the old Orioles. After a night of heavy drinking, he blames his longtime friend, business partner, and teammate Wilbert Robinson for too many coaching mistakes in the Series. Robbie replies that McGraw made more mistakes than anybody. McGraw fires him. Eyewitnesses say Robbie douses McGraw with a glass of beer and leaves. They won't speak to each other for 17 years. Six days later Robbie will begin a legendary 18 years as Brooklyn manager. The team will carry the nickname Robins, as well as Dodgers, during his tenure.

BOSTON	BROOKLYN	CHICAGO	CINCINNATI	NEW YORK	PHILADELPHIA	PITTSBURGH	ST.LOUIS
M G.Stallings	M B.Dahlen	M J.Evers	M J.Tinker	M J.McGraw	M R.Dooin	M F.Clarke	M M.Huggins
1B H.Myers	1B J.Daubert	1B V.Saier	1B D.Hoblitzel	1B F.Merkle	1B F.Luderus	1B D.Miller	1B E.Konetchy
2B B.Sweeney	2B G.Cutshaw	2B J.Evers	2B H.Groh	2B L.Doyle	2B O.Knabe	2B J.Viox	2B M.Huggins
SS R.Maranville	SS B.Fisher	SS A.Bridwell	SS J.Tinker	SS A.Fletcher	SS M.Doolan	SS H.Wagner	SS C.O'Leary
3B A.Devlin	3B R.Smith	3B H.Zimmerman	3B J.Dodge	3B B.Herzog	3B H.Lobert	3B B.Byrne	3B M.Mowrey
LF J.Connolly	LF Z.Wheat	LF M.Mitchell	LF B.Bescher	LF G.Burns	LF S.Magee	LF M.Carey	LF L.Magee
CF L.Mann	CF C.Stengel	CF T.Leach	CF A.Marsans	CF F.Snodgrass	CF D.Paskert	CF M.Mitchell	CF R.Oakes
RF J.Titus	RF H.Moran	RF F.Schulte	RF J.Bates	RF R.Murray	RF G.Cravath	RF C.Wilson	RF S.Evans
C B.Rariden	C O.Miller	C J.Archer	C T.Clarke	C C.Meyers	C B.Killefer	C M.Simon	C I.Wingo
32 F.Smith	OS J.Hummel	23 A.Phelan	O J.Devore	32 T.Shafer	O B.Becker	2S A.Butler	OS P.Whitted
O B.Lord	C W.Fischer	O W.Miller	C J.Kling	O M.McCormick	O R.Dooin	O F.Kommers	O T.Cather
C B.Whaling	O B.Collins	O R.Bresnahan	2S D.Egan	OS A.Wilson	OS C.Dolan	3 C.Dolan	O L.McLean
3 T.McDonald	S E.Kirkpatrick	S2 C.Williams	S2 M.Berghammer	C L.McLean	O D.Miller	C G.Gibson	O J.Sheckard
O G.Zinn	O B.Meyer	3 O.Clymer	3 R.Almeida	O J.Thorpe	O B.Byrne	O S.Hofman	C P.Hildebrand
O T.Griffith	O L.Callahan	O R.Corriden	O J.Sheckard	O C.Cooper	O J.Devore	C B.Kelly	O F.Quinlan
1 B.Schmidt	C T.Erwin	O W.Good	O B.Becker	/O J.Devore	C D.Howley	O E.Booe	/S A.Hauser
O C.Seymour	/C L.McCarty	3 T.Needham	3 E.Grant	/3 E.Grant	C E.Burns	S3 A.McCarthy	C S.Roberts
O J.Kirke	/O A.Scheer	/O T.Stewart	O A.Wickland	/2 G.Hartley	/2 J.Walsh	O E.Mensor	/S Z.Beck
O O.Clymer	/C E.Phelps	/1 F.Mollwitz	S E.Blackburn	/S M.Stock	/S M.Reed	C B.Coleman	/C F.Snyder
2 C.Deal	/C M.Hechinger	/O M.Allison	/S T.McDonald	/O H.Groh	/O V.Duncan	/O R.Wood	/S W.Callahan
C D.Brown	/S R.Mowe	/3 C.Keating	/3 B.Niehoff	/S J.Evers	/S J.Dodge	/O F.Clarke	/C C.Miller
/O J.Schultz		/C B.Hargrave	R K.Meister	/O J.Merritt	/O R.Capron	/C G.Britton	/C H.Peitz
/1 B.Calhoun	P P.Ragan	/C M.Hechinger	/O H.Severeid	H H.Severeid	H P.Moran	/C J.Kafora	/S A.Cabrera
/O G.Jackson	P N.Rucker	R E.McDonald	/2 B.Hobbs	P C.Mathewson			H D.Crandall
/3 O.Dugey	P F.Allen		H H.Chapman	P R.Marquard	P T.Seaton	P B.Adams	H J.Vann
/C R.DeVogt	P C.Curtis		/C M.Stewart	P J.Tesreau	P P.Alexander	P C.Hendrix	H J.Whelan
/C H.Gowdy	P E.Yingling	P L.Cheney		P A.Demaree	P A.Brennan	P H.Robinson	
/O B.McKechnie		P J.Lavender	P C.Johnson	P A.Fromme	P E.Mayer	P H.Camnitz	
/O W.Collins	P E.Reulbach	P B.Humphries	P G.Suggs	RP D.Crandall	P E.Rixey	P M.O'Toole	P S.Sallee
/3 J.McCleskey	P E.Stack	P G.Pearce	P G.Packard	P H.Wiltse	P G.Chalmers	P G.McQuillan	P B.Harmon
H F.Mitchell	P B.Wagner	P C.Smith	P R.Ames	/P R.Ames	P E.Moore	P W.Cooper	P D.Griner
/2 A.Bues	P M.Walker	P O.Overall	P M.Brown	/P B.Hearn	/P H.Camnitz	P W.Luhrsen	P P.Perritt
R B.McTigue	/P J.Pfeffer	P L.Richie	RP F.Harter	/P R.Schauer	P R.Marshall	/P J.Conzelman	P B.Doak
/C W.Tragesser	P E.Brown	P H.Vaughn	P R.Benton	/P F.Schupp	/P D.Imlay	/P B.Duffy	RP B.Geyer
P L.Tyler	/P M.Kent	P E.Stack	/P A.Fromme		/P R.Nelson	/P E.Eayrs	P S.Burk
P D.Rudolph	/P B.Hall	P E.Reulbach	/P J.Rowan		/P H.Finneran	/P J.Scheneberg	P B.Steele
P O.Hess		/P F.Toney	/P C.Smith		/P J.Haislip	/P J.Ferry	/P H.Trekell
P H.Perdue		/P E.Moore	/P E.Herbert		/P R.Hartranft	/P A.Mamaux	/P B.Hopper
P B.James		/P L.Leifield	/P R.Works				/P D.Niehaus
P W.Dickson		/P D.Watson	/P D.Robertson				/P J.Willis
/P J.Quinn		/P Z.Zabel	/P A.Harrington				/P B.Hunt
P W.Noyes			P H.Betts				/P W.Marbet
/P P.Strand			/P J.McManus				/P P.Redding
/P L.Gervais			/P C.Morgan				
/P B.Brown			P R.Nelson				
/P G.Cocreham			/P H.McIntire				
/P G.Davis			/P B.Powell				

TEAM	G	W	L	PCT	GB	R	OR	AB	H	2B	3B	HR	BB	SO	AVG	OBP	SLG	PRO	PRO+	BR	/A	PF	CHI	RC	SB	CS	SBA	SBR
NY	156	101	51	.664		684	515	5218	1427	226	71	30	444	501	.273	.338	.361	.699	105	43	38	101	99	700	296			
PHI	159	88	63	.583	12.5	693	636	5400	1433	257	78	73	383	578	.265	.318	.382	.700	102	29	1	104	100	683	156			
CHI	155	88	65	.575	13.5	720	630	5022	1289	195	96	59	554	634	.257	.335	.369	.704	107	52	51	100	104	661	181			
PIT	155	78	71	.523	21.5	673	585	5252	1383	210	86	35	391	545	.263	.319	.356	.675	104	-13	15	96	106	629	181			
BOS	154	69	82	.457	31.5	641	690	5145	1318	191	60	32	488	640	.256	.326	.335	.661	93	-26	-38	102	103	603	177			
BRO	152	65	84	.436	34.5	595	613	5165	1394	193	86	39	361	555	.270	.321	.363	.684	98	4	-13	103	94	637	188			
CIN	156	64	89	.418	37.5	607	717	5132	1339	170	96	27	458	579	.261	.325	.347	.672	98	-10	-7	100	96	630	226			
STL	153	51	99	.340	49	528	755	4967	1229	152	72	15	451	573	.247	.316	.316	.632	88	-78	-70	99	97	534	171			
TOT	620					5141		41301	10812	1594	645	310	3530	4605	.262	.325	.354	.679							1576			

TEAM	CG	SH	SV	IP	H	H/G	HR	BB	SO	RAT	ERA	ERA+	OAV	OOB	PR	/A	PF	CPI	FA	E	DP	FW	PW	BW	SBW	DIF
NY	82	12	17	1422	1276	8.1	38	315	651	10.2	2.42	128	.243	.289	122	107	97	99	.961	254	107	-.6	11.1	4.0		10.5
PHI	77	20	11	1455¹	1407	8.7	40	512	667	12.1	3.15	106	.261	.330	7	27	104	103	.968	214	112	2.2	2.8	.1		7.4
CHI	89	12	15	1372¹	1330	8.7	39	478	556	12.1	3.13	101	.260	.328	9	6	99	103	.959	260	106	-1.1	.6	5.3		6.7
PIT	74	9	7	1400	1344	8.6	26	434	590	11.6	2.90	104	.260	.320	46	16	94	104	.964	226	94	1.1	1.7	1.6		-.8
BOS	105	13	3	1373¹	1343	8.8	37	419	597	11.8	3.19	103	.263	.324	1	12	103	100	.957	273	82	-2.0	1.2	-4.0		-1.8
BRO	71	9	9	1373	1287	8.4	33	439	548	11.6	3.13	105	.255	.321	11	23	103	97	.961	243	125	-.3	2.4	-1.4		-10.2
CIN	71	10	10	1380	1398	9.1	40	456	522	12.4	3.46	94	.273	.338	-40	-36	101	102	.961	251	104	-.4	-3.7	-.7		-7.6
STL	74	6	11	1351²	1426	9.5	57	477	465	13.0	4.23	76	.280	.348	-156	-152	101	92	.965	219	113	1.3	-15.8	-7.3		-2.2
TOT	643	91	81	11127²		8.7				11.9	3.20		.262	.325					.962	1940	843					

Runs		Hits		Doubles		Triples		Home Runs		Total Bases	
Leach-Chi	99	Cravath-Phi	179	Smith-Bro	40	Saier-Chi	21	Cravath-Phi	19	Cravath-Phi	298
Carey-Pit	99	Daubert-Bro	178	Burns-NY	37	Miller-Pit	20	Luderus-Phi	18	Luderus-Phi	254
Lobert-Phi	98	Burns-NY	173	Magee-Phi	36	Konetchy-StL	17	Saier-Chi	14	Saier-Chi	249
Saier-Chi	94	Lobert-Phi	172	Cravath-Phi	34	Wilson-Pit	14	Magee-Phi	11	Miller-Pit	243
Magee-Phi	92	Carey-Pit	172			Cravath-Phi	14	Wilson-Pit	10	Lobert-Phi	243

Runs Batted In		Runs Produced		Bases On Balls		Batting Average		On Base Percentage		Slugging Average	
Cravath-Phi	128	Cravath-Phi	187	Bescher-Cin	94	Daubert-Bro	.350	Huggins-StL	.432	Cravath-Phi	.568
Zimmerman-Chi	95	Saier-Chi	172	Huggins-StL	92	Cravath-Phi	.341	Cravath-Phi	.407	Becker-Cin-Phi	.502
Saier-Chi	92	Miller-Pit	158	Leach-Chi	77	Viox-Pit	.317	Daubert-Bro	.405	Zimmerman-Chi	.490
Miller-Pit	90	Zimmerman-Chi	155	Bridwell-Chi	74	Tinker-Cin	.317	Viox-Pit	.399	Saier-Chi	.480
Luderus-Phi	86	Magee-Phi	151			Becker-Cin-Phi	.316	Leach-Chi	.391	Magee-Phi	.479

Production		Adjusted Production		Batter Runs		Adjusted Batter Runs		Clutch Hitting Index		Runs Created	
Cravath-Phi	.974	Cravath-Phi	169	Cravath-Phi	50.5	Cravath-Phi	45.8	Zimmerman-Chi	132	Cravath-Phi	120
Zimmerman-Chi	.868	Zimmerman-Chi	147	Saier-Chi	27.5	Viox-Pit	28.8	Cutshaw-Bro	127	Saier-Chi	97
Saier-Chi	.850	Viox-Pit	142	Zimmerman-Chi	26.3	Saier-Chi	27.3	Saier-Chi	123	Lobert-Phi	96
Magee-Phi	.848	Saier-Chi	141	Daubert-Bro	25.2	Zimmerman-Chi	26.1	Doyle-NY	119	Daubert-Bro	94
Daubert-Bro	.829	Magee-Phi	136	Viox-Pit	24.8	Daubert-Bro	22.9	Fletcher-NY	116	Carey-Pit	92

Total Average		Stolen Bases		Stolen Base Average		Stolen Base Runs		Fielding Runs		Total Player Rating	
Cravath-Phi	1.058	Carey-Pit	61					Evers-Chi	29.9	Tinker-Cin	3.9
Saier-Chi	.927	Myers-Bos	57					Paskert-Phi	17.7	Cravath-Phi	3.7
Zimmerman-Chi	.925	Lobert-Phi	41					Cutshaw-Bro	17.5	Evers-Chi	3.5
Magee-Phi	.905	Burns-NY	40					Tinker-Cin	17.3	Zimmerman-Chi	3.4
Leach-Chi	.895	Cutshaw-Bro	39					Doolan-Phi	17.2	Wagner-Pit	3.1

Wins		Win Percentage		Games		Complete Games		Shutouts		Saves	
Seaton-Phi	27	Humphries-Chi	.800	Cheney-Chi	54	Tyler-Bos	28	Alexander-Phi	9	Cheney-Chi	11
Mathewson-NY	25	Alexander-Phi	.733	Seaton-Phi	52	Mathewson-NY	25	Seaton-Phi	5	Crandall-NY	6
Marquard-NY	23	Marquard-NY	.697	Sallee-StL	50	Cheney-Chi	25			Brown-Cin	6
Tesreau-NY	22	Mathewson-NY	.694	Alexander-Phi	47	Adams-Pit	24			Sallee-StL	5
Alexander-Phi	22	Seaton-Phi	.692	Camnitz-Pit-Phi	45	Alexander-Phi	23				

Innings Pitched		Fewest Hits/Game		Fewest BB/Game		Strikeouts		Strikeouts/Game		Ratio	
Seaton-Phi	322.1	Tesreau-NY	7.09	Mathewson-NY	.62	Seaton-Phi	168	Tesreau-NY	5.33	Mathewson-NY	9.18
Adams-Pit	313.2	Seaton-Phi	7.32	Humphries-Chi	1.19	Tesreau-NY	167	Hendrix-Pit	5.15	Adams-Pit	9.18
Alexander-Phi	306.1	Allen-Bro	7.42	Adams-Pit	1.41	Alexander-Phi	159	Marquard-NY	4.72	Marquard-NY	9.38
Mathewson-NY	306.0	Pearce-Chi	7.55	Marquard-NY	1.53	Marquard-NY	151	Seaton-Phi	4.69	Humphries-Chi	9.70
Cheney-Chi	305.0	Tyler-Bos	7.59	Suggs-Cin	1.58	Adams-Pit	144	Alexander-Phi	4.67	Demaree-NY	9.87

Earned Run Average		Adjusted ERA		Opponents' Batting Avg.		Opponents' On Base Pct.		Starter Runs		Adjusted Starter Runs	
Mathewson-NY	2.06	Mathewson-NY	151	Tesreau-NY	.220	Mathewson-NY	.266	Mathewson-NY	38.7	Mathewson-NY	35.9
Adams-Pit	2.15	Tesreau-NY	143	Seaton-Phi	.226	Adams-Pit	.267	Adams-Pit	36.4	Adams-Pit	29.8
Tesreau-NY	2.17	Demaree-NY	141	Allen-Bro	.231	Marquard-NY	.273	Tesreau-NY	32.2	Tesreau-NY	29.5
Demaree-NY	2.21	Adams-Pit	140	Pearce-Chi	.234	Humphries-Chi	.277	Marquard-NY	22.3	Seaton-Phi	26.2
Pearce-Chi	2.31	Brennan-Phi	139	Tyler-Bos	.235	Demaree-NY	.286	Demaree-NY	21.9	Brennan-Phi	21.5

Clutch Pitching Index		Relief Runs		Adjusted Relief Runs		Relief Ranking		Total Pitcher Index		Total Baseball Ranking	
Brennan-Phi	128	Crandall-NY	3.7	Crandall-NY	2.8	Crandall-NY	2.4	Mathewson-NY	4.6	Mathewson-NY	4.6
Packard-Cin	127							Tesreau-NY	3.9	Tinker-Cin	3.9
Brown-Cin	119							Adams-Pit	3.7	Tesreau-NY	3.9
Ames-NY-Cin	119							Tyler-Bos	2.9	Adams-Pit	3.7
Pearce-Chi	112							Seaton-Phi	2.7	Cravath-Phi	3.7

January 8 Frank Chance inherits Hal Chase and the weakest lineup the New York Yankees will ever have when he signs to manage the team.

January 22 The Giants give the Yankees permission to use the Polo Grounds for the season only, as the lease on the Hilltop grounds has expired. The Yankees will remain as tenants through 1922.

March 4 The Yankees become the first team to train outside the U.S. when they travel to Bermuda for spring practice.

April 10 President Woodrow Wilson, who receives a gold pass from Ban Johnson, throws out the first ball at Washington's home opener. In their first official game as Yankees, New York loses to Walter Johnson 2–1. After giving up an unearned run in the first, Johnson begins a string of shutout innings that will reach a record 56 before the St. Louis Browns score in the fourth on May 14.

May 6* Better organized and financed than other aspiring circuits, the Federal League opens modestly and quietly, with clubs in Chicago, Cleveland, Pittsburgh, Indianapolis, St. Louis, Kansas City, and Covington, KY. No attempt is made to sign established major league players. Cy Young manages Cleveland, Deacon Phillippe manages Pittsburgh. After a six-week season, the pennant winner is Indianapolis.

August 13* Petersburg pitcher Harry Hedgpeth (Virginia League) blanks Richmond twice, by scores of 1–0 and 10–0, both in nine innings. He gives up only one hit in the opener, while hurling a no-hitter in the second game.

September 22 Herb Pennock, 19, aided by Eddie Plank, blanks the Tigers 1–0 to clinch the AL pennant for the A's.

October 7 Rube Marquard gets the call for the Giants against Philadelphia's Chief Bender in Game 1 of the World Series. Bender yields 11 hits, but Frank Baker's home run and three RBI pace a 6-4 win over the New Yorkers.

October 11 John McGraw and the Giants lose to the AL for the third straight World Series. In Game 5, Mathewson is good, but Plank is better; his 2-hitter wins the 3-1 finale. Frank Baker at .450 and Eddie Collins at .421 lead a strong A's offense.

October 19* The Giants and White Sox, fortified with other players, start their world tour in Cincinnati. After a 31-game tour to Seattle, they will head for the Philippines, Australia, China, and Japan.

November 2* St. Louis Browns manager George Stovall is the first major league player to jump to the Federal League, signing to manage Kansas City. With glib salesman Jim Gilmore as its president, and backed by several millionaires, including oil magnate Harry Sinclair and Brooklyn baker Robert Ward, the Feds declare open war two weeks later by announcing they will not honor the major leagues' reserve clause. It will prove a long, costly struggle, similar to the AL's beginnings, but with more losers than winners.

	BOSTON		CHICAGO		CLEVELAND		DETROIT		NEW YORK		PHILADELPHIA		ST.LOUIS		WASHINGTON
M	J.Stahl	M	J.Callahan	M	J.Birmingham	M	H.Jennings	M	F.Chance	M	C.Mack	M	G.Stovall	M	C.Griffith
M	B.Carrigan	1B	H.Chase	1B	D.Johnston	1B	D.Gainer	1B	J.Knight	1B	S.McInnis	M	J.Austin	1B	C.Gandil
1B	C.Engle	2B	M.Rath	2B	N.Lajoie	2B	O.Vitt	2B	R.Hartzell	2B	E.Collins	M	B.Rickey	2B	R.Morgan
2B	S.Yerkes	SS	B.Weaver	SS	R.Chapman	SS	D.Bush	SS	R.Peckinpaugh	SS	J.Barry	1B	G.Stovall	SS	G.McBride
SS	H.Wagner	3B	H.Lord	3B	I.Olson	3B	G.Moriarty	3B	E.Midkiff	3B	F.Baker	2B	D.Pratt	3B	E.Foster
3B	L.Gardner	LF	P.Bodie	LF	J.Graney	LF	B.Veach	LF	B.Cree	LF	R.Oldring	SS	M.Balenti	LF	H.Shanks
LF	D.Lewis	CF	W.Mattick	CF	N.Leibold	CF	T.Cobb	CF	H.Wolter	CF	J.Walsh	3B	J.Austin	CF	C.Milan
CF	T.Speaker	RF	S.Collins	RF	J.Jackson	RF	S.Crawford	RF	B.Daniels	RF	E.Murphy	LF	J.Johnston	RF	D.Moeller
RF	H.Hooper	C	R.Schalk	C	S.O'Neill	C	O.Stanage	C	J.Sweeney	C	J.Lapp	CF	B.Shotton	C	J.Henry
C	B.Carrigan											RF	G.Williams		
		2	J.Berger	32	T.Turner	2	P.Baumann	3	F.Maisel	O	A.Strunk	C	S.Agnew	32	F.LaPorte
S3	H.Janvrin	O	L.Chappell	O	B.Ryan	23	B.Louden	S2	R.Zeider	C	W.Schang	O	S.Agnew	O	E.Ainsmith
O	W.Rehg	1O	J.Fournier	C	F.Carisch	C	R.McKee	1	H.Chase	O	T.Daley	1	B.Brief	C	R.Williams
C	H.Cady	C	T.Easterly	O	J.Birmingham	O	H.High	S	B.McKechnie	S	B.Orr	S	D.Lavan	2	G.Schaefer
C	P.Thomas	C	B.Schaller	C	G.Land	1	H.Rondeau	1	B.Borton	O	D.Murphy	S	B.Wallace	O	J.Gedeon
C	L.Nunamaker	1	B.Borton	3	R.Bates	C	F.Gibson	C	D.Gossett	C	I.Thomas	C	W.Alexander	O	J.Calvo
2	N.Ball	O	J.Beall	/O	J.Lelivelt	1	E.Onslow	O	F.Gilhooley	/1	H.Davis	O	P.Compton	/O	B.Spencer
1	B.Mundy	C	W.Kuhn	/S	G.Dunlop	3	C.Deal	1	H.Williams	/S	D.Lavan	O	B.McAllester	/O	M.Acosta
/O	O.Henriksen	/S	J.Breton	/2	L.Kopf	1	G.Tutwiler	O	D.Cook	/3	H.Fritz	O	T.Walker	/2	B.Morley
/C	W.Snell	/O	D.Jones	H	J.Beall	1	W.Pipp	S	C.Derrick	/O	G.Brickley	1	S.Covington	/C	J.Ryan
H	J.Stahl	/3	R.Zeider	/C	E.Krueger	2	L.Hennessey	O	B.Holden	P	P.Cruthers	O	D.Walsh		
		/O	E.Roush	/1	E.Edmonson	/O	A.Platte	/1	D.Sterrett	/C	W.McAvoy	S	R.Bisland	P	W.Johnson
P	D.Leonard	/O	N.Callahan	/O	J.Billings	/O	J.Burns	C	J.Smith	/C	J.Giebel	/2	B.Wares	P	B.Groom
P	H.Bedient	/C	T.Daly	/C	J.Bassler	/3	P.Peploski	O	G.Whiteman	/S	M.Peffer	/O	T.Sloan	P	J.Boehling
P	R.Collins	/3	D.Rader	H	G.Young	/3	S.Partenheimer	/S	B.Stumpf			/O	G.Maisel	P	J.Engel
P	J.Wood	/C	B.Meyer	H	R.Peckinpaugh	/O	R.Powell	/O	J.Lelivelt	P	E.Plank	/O	E.Walker	P	T.Hughes
P	E.Moseley			/O	B.Southworth			/1	F.Chance	P	C.Bender	/O	W.Meinert		
		P	R.Russell	R	J.Swindell	P	J.Dubuc	/C	B.Williams	P	B.Brown	/3	F.Graff	P	B.Gallia
P	C.Hall	P	J.Scott			P	E.Willett	/S	R.Young	P	J.Bush	/C	F.Crossin	P	G.Mullin
P	B.O'Brien	P	E.Cicotte	P	V.Gregg	P	H.Dauss	/S	L.Boone	P	B.Houck	/3	C.Flanagan	P	D.Ayers
P	R.Foster	P	J.Benz	P	C.Falkenberg	P	M.Hall	/C	B.Reynolds			H	L.Bonin	/P	S.Love
P	F.Anderson	P	D.White	P	W.Mitchell	P	J.Lake	/C	D.Costello	P	B.Shawkey	H	G.Tomer	/P	H.Harper
/P	P.Maloy			P	F.Blanding	RP	F.House	/C	H.Hanson	P	W.Wyckoff			/P	J.Shaw
/P	E.Chaney	P	E.Walsh	P	B.Steen					P	H.Pennock	P	G.Baumgardner	/P	J.Bentley
		P	F.Lange			P	C.Zamloch	P	R.Fisher	/P	J.Taff	P	C.Weilman	/P	N.Altrock
		P	P.Smith	P	G.Kahler	P	R.Comstock	P	R.Ford	/P	E.Cottrell	P	R.Mitchell	/P	C.Cashion
		/P	B.O'Brien	P	N.Cullop	/P	G.Mullin	P	A.Schulz	P	C.Boardman	P	E.Hamilton	/P	M.Williams
		/P	B.Lathrop	P	L.James	P	A.Klawitter	P	G.McConnell	P	P.Bohen	W.Leverenz	/P	J.Wilson
		/P	F.Miller	/P	J.Baskette	P	L.Williams	P	R.Caldwell	J.Coombs		/P	T.Drohan
		/P	B.Smith	/P	L.Brenton	P	A.Clauss			/P	D.Morey	P	D.Stone	/P	R.Dawson
		/P	J.Scoggins	/P	L.Dashner	P	C.Grover	P	R.Keating			/P	M.Allison	/P	C.Griffith
				/P	L.Glavenich	P	G.Boehler	P	J.Warhop			/P	W.Taylor	/P	H.Hedgpeth
				/P	D.Gregg	P	L.North	/P	M.McHale			/P	C.Brown		
						P	E.Renfer	P	E.Klepfer			/P	H.Schwenk		
						H	H.Elder	P	G.Clark			/P	W.Adams		
						/P	C.Harding	/P	C.Pieh			/P	J.Powell		
						/P	L.Lorenzen	/P	J.Hanley			/P	P.Schmidt		
								/P	R.Hoff						

TEAM	G	W	L	PCT	GB	R	OR	AB	H	2B	3B	HR	BB	SO	AVG	OBP	SLG	PRO	PRO+	BR	/A	PF	CHI	RC	SB	CS	SBA	SBR
PHI	153	96	57	.627		794	592	5044	1412	223	80	33	534	547	.280	.356	.375	.731	124	135	152	98	105	732	221			
WAS	155	90	64	.584	6.5	596	561	5074	1281	156	81	19	440	595	.252	.317	.326	.643	92	-35	-47	102	105	585	287			
CLE	155	86	66	.566	9.5	633	536	5031	1349	206	74	16	420	557	.268	.331	.348	.679	102	29	11	103	99	630	191			
BOS	151	79	71	.527	15.5	631	610	4965	1334	220	101	17	466	534	.269	.336	.364	.700	109	66	49	103	95	652	189			
CHI	153	78	74	.513	17.5	488	498	4822	1139	157	66	24	398	550	.236	.299	.311	.610	85	-94	-89	99	100	487	156			
DET	153	66	87	.431	30	624	716	5064	1344	180	101	24	496	501	.265	.336	.355	.691	111	56	66	99	93	655	218			
NY	153	57	94	.377	38	529	668	4880	1157	155	45	19	534	617	.237	.320	.292	.612	85	-75	-77	100	101	505	203			
STL	155	57	96	.373	39	528	642	5031	1193	179	73	18	455	769	.237	.306	.312	.618	90	-80	-65	97	101	524	209			
TOT	614					4823		39911	10209	1476	621	159	3743	4670	.256	.325	.336	.661						1674				

TEAM	CG	SH	SV	IP	H	H/G	HR	BB	SO	RAT	ERA	ERA+	OAV	OOB	PR	/A	PF	CPI	FA	E	DP	FW	PW	BW	SBW	DIF
PHI	69	17	22	1351¹	1200	8.0	24	532	630	11.8	3.19	87	.229	.304	-39	-65	94	70	.966	212	108	3.2	-6.9	16.2		7.0
WAS	78	23	20	1396¹	1177	7.6	35	465	758	11.0	2.73	108	.225	.297	31	34	101	80	.960	261	122	.3	3.6	-5.0		14.1
CLE	93	18	5	1386²	1278	8.3	19	502	689	11.8	2.54	119	.249	.321	59	74	104	108	.962	242	124	1.5	7.9	1.2		-.6
BOS	83	12	10	1358¹	1323	8.8	6	442	710	11.9	2.94	100	.260	.323	-2	-3	100	96	.961	237	84	1.4	-.3	5.2		-2.3
CHI	84	17	8	1360¹	1190	7.9	10	438	602	11.0	2.33	125	.237	.302	91	89	100	97	.960	255	104	.5	9.5	-9.5		1.5
DET	90	4	7	1360	1359	9.0	13	504	468	12.6	3.38	86	.265	.336	-68	-71	100	94	.954	300	105	-2.4	-7.6	7.0		-7.6
NY	75	8	7	1344	1318	8.8	31	455	530	12.2	3.27	91	.260	.327	-51	-42	102	94	.954	293	94	-1.9	-4.5	-8.2		-3.9
STL	104	14	5	1382²	1369	8.9	21	454	476	12.2	3.06	96	.266	.332	-20	-22	100	103	.954	301	125	-2.2	-2.3	-6.9		-8.0
TOT	676	113	84	10939¹		8.4				11.8	2.93		.256	.325					.959	2101	866					

Runs		Hits		Doubles		Triples		Home Runs		Total Bases	
Collins-Phi	125	Jackson-Cle	197	Jackson-Cle	39	Crawford-Det	23	Baker-Phi	12	Crawford-Det	298
Baker-Phi	116	Crawford-Det	193	Speaker-Bos	35	Speaker-Bos	22	Crawford-Det	9	Jackson-Cle	291
Jackson-Cle	109	Baker-Phi	190	Baker-Phi	34	Jackson-Cle	17	Bodie-Chi	8	Baker-Phi	278
Shotton-StL	105	Speaker-Bos	189	Crawford-Det	32	Williams-StL	16	Jackson-Cle	7	Speaker-Bos	277
E.Murphy-Phi	105	Collins-Phi	184			Cobb-Det	16			Collins-Phi	242

Runs Batted In		Runs Produced		Bases On Balls		Batting Average		On Base Percentage		Slugging Average	
Baker-Phi	117	Baker-Phi	221	Shotton-StL	99	Cobb-Det	.390	Cobb-Det	.467	Jackson-Cle	.551
McInnis-Phi	90	Collins-Phi	195	Collins-Phi	85	Jackson-Cle	.373	Jackson-Cle	.460	Cobb-Det	.535
Lewis-Bos	90	Jackson-Cle	173	Wolter-NY	80	Speaker-Bos	.363	Collins-Phi	.441	Speaker-Bos	.533
Pratt-StL	87	Oldring-Phi	167	Jackson-Cle	80	Collins-Phi	.345	Speaker-Bos	.441	Baker-Phi	.493
Barry-Phi	85	McInnis-Phi	165	Bush-Det	80	Baker-Phi	.337	Baker-Phi	.413	Crawford-Det	.489

Production		Adjusted Production		Batter Runs		Adjusted Batter Runs		Clutch Hitting Index		Runs Created	
Jackson-Cle	1.011	Cobb-Det	196	Jackson-Cle	65.5	Jackson-Cle	61.8	Barry-Phi	163	Jackson-Cle	140
Cobb-Det	1.002	Jackson-Cle	190	Speaker-Bos	55.9	Cobb-Det	53.4	Lewis-Bos	133	Speaker-Bos	136
Speaker-Bos	.974	Speaker-Bos	180	Cobb-Det	51.8	Speaker-Bos	52.9	Pratt-StL	127	Collins-Phi	126
Baker-Phi	.906	Baker-Phi	168	Baker-Phi	45.9	Baker-Phi	48.5	McInnis-Phi	122	Cobb-Det	124
Collins-Phi	.894	Collins-Phi	165	Collins-Phi	45.7	Collins-Phi	48.3	Turner-Cle	121	Baker-Phi	122

Total Average		Stolen Bases		Stolen Base Average		Stolen Base Runs		Fielding Runs		Total Player Rating	
Cobb-Det	1.310	Milan-Was	75					Weaver-Chi	33.6	Speaker-Bos	7.3
Jackson-Cle	1.215	Moeller-Was	62					Speaker-Bos	23.7	Collins-Phi	6.4
Speaker-Bos	1.193	Collins-Phi	55					Turner-Cle	16.3	Baker-Phi	6.1
Collins-Phi	1.111	Cobb-Det	51					Collins-Phi	15.6	Jackson-Cle	6.0
Baker-Phi	1.029	Speaker-Bos	46					Shotton-StL	12.8	Cobb-Det	5.3

Wins		Win Percentage		Games		Complete Games		Shutouts		Saves	
Johnson-Was	36	Johnson-Was	.837	Russell-Chi	52	Johnson-Was	29	Johnson-Was	11	Bender-Phi	13
Falkenberg-Cle	23	Bush-Phi	.714	Scott-Chi	48	Russell-Chi	26	Russell-Chi	8	Hughes-Was	6
Russell-Chi	22	Boehling-Was	.708	Johnson-Was	48	Scott-Chi	25	Plank-Phi	7	Bedient-Bos	5
Bender-Phi	21	Collins-Bos	.704	Bender-Phi	48			Falkenberg-Cle	6		
		Falkenberg-Cle	.697	V.Gregg-Cle	44						

Innings Pitched		Fewest Hits/Game		Fewest BB/Game		Strikeouts		Strikeouts/Game		Ratio	
Johnson-Was	346.0	Johnson-Was	6.03	Johnson-Was	.99	Johnson-Was	243	Johnson-Was	6.32	Johnson-Was	7.26
Russell-Chi	316.2	Mitchell-Cle	6.35	Collins-Bos	1.35	V.Gregg-Cle	166	Mitchell-Cle	5.85	Russell-Chi	9.55
Scott-Chi	312.1	Engel-Was	6.78	Mitchell-StL	1.72	Falkenberg-Cle	166	Plank-Phi	5.60	Scott-Chi	10.00
V.Gregg-Cle	285.2	Leverenz-StL	7.06	Plank-Phi	2.11	Scott-Chi	158	Falkenberg-Cle	5.41	Cicotte-Chi	10.07
Falkenberg-Cle	276.0	Russell-Chi	7.11	Weilman-StL	2.15	Groom-Was	156	Groom-Was	5.31	Plank-Phi	10.13

Earned Run Average		Adjusted ERA		Opponents' Batting Avg.		Opponents' On Base Pct.		Starter Runs		Adjusted Starter Runs	
Johnson-Was	1.14	Johnson-Was	258	Johnson-Was	.187	Johnson-Was	.217	Johnson-Was	68.6	Johnson-Was	69.4
Cicotte-Chi	1.58	Cicotte-Chi	185	Mitchell-Cle	.199	Russell-Chi	.273	Cicotte-Chi	40.2	Cicotte-Chi	40.0
Scott-Chi	1.90	Mitchell-Cle	159	Engel-Was	.207	Bender-Phi	.277	Russell-Chi	36.1	Russell-Chi	35.8
Russell-Chi	1.90	Scott-Chi	154	Houck-Phi	.214	Cicotte-Chi	.281	Scott-Chi	35.7	Scott-Chi	35.4
Mitchell-Cle	1.91	Russell-Chi	153	Russell-Chi	.219	Scott-Chi	.281	Mitchell-Cle	24.6	Mitchell-Cle	27.1

Clutch Pitching Index		Relief Runs		Adjusted Relief Runs		Relief Ranking		Total Pitcher Index		Total Baseball Ranking	
Blanding-Cle	141							Johnson-Was	10.9	Johnson-Was	10.9
V.Gregg-Cle	130							Cicotte-Chi	5.2	Speaker-Bos	7.3
Ford-NY	123							Russell-Chi	4.2	Collins-Phi	6.4
Baumgardner-StL	118							Scott-Chi	3.8	Baker-Phi	6.1
Cicotte-Chi	114							Boehling-Was	2.6	Jackson-Cle	6.0

February 1 The White Sox and Giants play a 3–3 tie in Cairo. The next day a triple play will be made in the shadow of the Pyramids.

February 3 A joint NL-AL rules committee decrees that: a runner touched or held by a coach while rounding third base is out; coaches may now assist other members of their team, not just base runners; the frequently violated rule requiring pitchers to stand behind the rubber until ready to pitch is rescinded—they may now stand on the rubber; base runners are now not permitted to run on an infield fly. A move to eliminate the intentional walk is defeated.

March 21 Charles W. Murphy sells the Cubs to Charles P. Taft of Cincinnati.

April 20 The 25-player limit is suspended in the AL and NL. With uncertainty over who has signed with what teams, it is almost impossible to know how many players may be on the roster at any one time.

July 17 Giants outfielder John "Red" Murray is knocked unconscious by lightning after catching a fly ball that ends a 21-inning victory over Pittsburgh. Murray is uninjured. Pittsburgh's Babe Adams pitches all 21 innings without yielding a single walk, the longest non-walk game in major league history.

September 7 The Braves and Giants play a morning-afternoon twinbill in Boston on Labor Day. To accommodate the crowds, the Braves move their home games to Fenway Park. The contenders draw 74,163 on the day.

September 23 After dropping their 19th straight in the first of two at Boston, the Reds break the longest losing streak in the club's history (and third longest in the NL) when Charles "King" Lear wins his only game of the year and only shutout ever, 3-0.

September 29 The Boston Braves, who were in last place in mid-July, clinch the pennant with a sensational second-half drive.

October 1 Phillies outfielder Gavvy Cravath hits homer No. 19 to lead the NL. He also leads NL outfielders with 34 assists in right field.

October 9 The Boston Braves go into the World Series as underdogs, despite their strong finish. Only one regular, left fielder Joe Connolly, hit .300. Their strengths are pitchers Dick Rudolph, George "Lefty" Tyler, and "Seattle Bill" James, second baseman Johnny Evers, who wins Chalmers's final MVP automobile, and shortstop Rabbit Maranville, their cleanup hitter. The Philadelphia A's Eddie Collins, with a .344 BA, wins the Chalmers AL award with 63 of 64 possible points. The A's have seven pitchers with 10 or more wins, led by Chief Bender's 17–3. Bender's World Series magic is quickly dispelled as the Braves knock him out in the sixth. Rudolph coasts to a 5-hit 7–1 victory. Hank Gowdy has a single, double, and triple. He will hit a World Series record .545, and Evers, .438. Bender makes his last World Series appearance, finishing with a record 59 strikeouts.

October 13 The first World Series sweep in history belongs to the Boston Braves—the only World Series the franchise will ever win in Boston. Bob Shawkey and Herb Pennock allow just six hits, but one is a two-run single by Evers, as Rudolph wins 3-1.

	BOSTON		BROOKLYN		CHICAGO		CINCINNATI		NEW YORK		PHILADELPHIA		PITTSBURGH		ST.LOUIS
M	G.Stallings	M	W.Robinson	M	H.O'Day	M	B.Herzog	M	J.McGraw	M	R.Dooin	M	F.Clarke	M	M.Huggins
1B	B.Schmidt	1B	J.Daubert	1B	V.Saier	1B	D.Hoblitzel	1B	F.Merkle	1B	F.Luderus	1B	E.Konetchy	1B	D.Miller
2B	J.Evers	2B	G.Cutshaw	2B	B.Sweeney	2B	H.Groh	2B	L.Doyle	2B	B.Byrne	2B	J.Viox	2B	M.Huggins
SS	R.Maranville	SS	D.Egan	SS	R.Corriden	SS	B.Herzog	SS	A.Fletcher	SS	J.Martin	SS	H.Wagner	SS	A.Butler
3B	C.Deal	3B	R.Smith	3B	H.Zimmerman	3B	B.Niehoff	3B	M.Stock	3B	H.Lobert	3B	M.Mowrey	3B	Z.Beck
LF	J.Connolly	LF	Z.Wheat	LF	F.Schulte	LF	G.Twombly	LF	G.Burns	LF	B.Becker	LF	M.Carey	LF	C.Dolan
CF	L.Mann	CF	J.Dalton	CF	T.Leach	CF	B.Daniels	CF	B.Bescher	CF	D.Paskert	CF	Jo.Kelly	CF	L.Magee
RF	L.Gilbert	RF	C.Stengel	RF	W.Good	RF	H.Moran	RF	F.Snodgrass	RF	G.Cravath	RF	M.Mitchell	RF	C.Wilson
C	H.Gowdy	C	L.McCarty	C	R.Bresnahan	C	T.Clarke	C	C.Meyers	C	B.Killefer	C	G.Gibson	C	F.Snyder
O2	P.Whitted	S	O.O'Mara	C	J.Archer	C	M.Gonzalez	3S	E.Grant	OS	S.Magee	O	Ji.Kelly	O	W.Cruise
3	R.Smith	O	H.Myers	O	J.Johnston	O	D.Miller	2	D.Robertson	2	H.Irelan	O	Z.Collins	O	I.Wingo
C	B.Whaling	3	G.Getz	/S	C.Derrick	O	J.Bates	C	L.McLean	C	E.Burns	32	A.McCarthy	1	L.Dressen
O	H.Moran	10	J.Hummel	O	C.Williams	O	R.Killefer	C	R.Murray	C	R.Dooin	O	B.Coleman	O	T.Cather
O	T.Cather	C	O.Miller	O	P.Knisely	12	B.Kellogg	H	M.Donlin	S2	M.Reed	3	J.Leonard	O	J.Riggert
O	J.Devore	C	W.Fischer	S	B.Fisher	O	A.Marsans	/O	J.Thorpe		J.Devore	O	E.Mensor	3	K.Nash
O	J.Murray	O	J.Riggert	/3	A.Phelan	S2	M.Berghammer	C	E.Johnson	/S	D.Murphy	/1	H.Hyatt	O	C.Miller
O2	O.Dugey	S	K.Elberfeld	3	A.Bues	1	F.Mollwitz	/O	S.Piez	/O	P.Hilly	O	D.Costello	/3	P.Whitted
3	J.Martin	/C	T.Erwin	C	B.Hargrave	30	F.Von Kolnitz	/C	H.Smith	/1	F.Mollenkamp	S	W.Gerber	/2	B.Betzel
O	T.Griffith			S	C.Keating	1	T.Graham	/1	W.Holke	H	F.Fletcher	2	P.Siglin	/C	P.O'Connor
O	W.Collins	P	J.Pfeffer	/1	F.Mollwitz	3	J.Rawlings	/2	F.Brainerd	H	G.McAvoy	/C	B.Schang	/C	J.Roche
/C	F.Tyler	P	E.Reulbach	/O	J.Bates	O	M.Uhler	/S	B.Dyer	/C	P.Moran	O	F.Scheeren	/S	R.Daringer
/1	C.Kraft	P	R.Ragan	O	E.Tyree	O	H.LaRoss	/S	D.Beatty			/S	I.McAuley		
/S	B.Martin	P	R.Aitchison	H	M.Allison	O	H.Lohr			P	P.Alexander	P	J.Kafora	P	P.Perritt
		P	F.Allen	/3	H.Bronkie	C	T.Erwin	P	J.Tesreau	P	E.Mayer	/O	C.Berger	P	S.Sallee
P	D.Rudolph			H	T.Stewart	O	B.Holden	P	C.Mathewson	P	B.Tincup	P	C.Smith	P	B.Doak
P	B.James	P	N.Rucker			/C	N.Glockson	P	R.Marquard	P	R.Marshall	H	F.Clarke	P	D.Griner
P	L.Tyler	P	C.Schmutz	P	L.Cheney	/S	C.Derrick	P	A.Demaree	P	J.Oeschger	H	P.Falsey	P	H.Perdue
P	D.Crutcher	P	E.Brown	/O	H.Vaughn	/O	E.Kippert	P	A.Fromme			/C	P.Kilhullen		
		/P	J.Enzmann	P	J.Lavender	/O	K.McLaughlin			P	E.Rixey	/C	B.Wagner	P	H.Robinson
		/P	B.Steele	P	B.Humphries			P	H.Wiltse	P	S.Baumgartner	/C	S.Brenegan	P	C.Hageman
P	O.Hess	/P	B.Wagner	P	G.Pearce	P	R.Ames	P	M.O'Toole	P	E.Matteson	H	R.Shafer	P	B.Steele
/P	G.Davis			RP	C.Hageman	P	R.Benton	/P	R.Schauer	P	E.Jacobs			/P	D.Niehaus
P	P.Strand			P	Z.Zabel	P	P.Douglas	/P	F.Schupp	/P	G.Chalmers	P	B.Adams	/P	S.Williams
/P	H.Perdue			P	C.Smith	P	E.Yingling	/P	H.Ritter			P	W.Cooper	/P	B.Hopper
P	G.Cocreham			/P	E.Stack	P	P.Schneider	/P	E.Erickson			P	G.McQuillan		
/P	T.Hughes			/P	G.McConnell	P	K.Lear	/P	A.Huenke			P	B.Harmon		
/P	D.Luque			/P	E.Koestner	P	D.Davenport					P	J.Conzelman		
/P	E.Cottrell					/P	P.Fittery								
						P	J.Rowan					P	M.O'Toole		
						/P	E.Koestner					P	E.Kantlehner		
						/P	K.Adams					P	A.Mamaux		
						/P	P.Fahrer					/P	H.Kelly		
						/P	B.Ingersoll					P	P.Bohen		
						/P	C.Johnson					/P	D.McArthur		
						/P	P.Griffin								

TEAM	G	W	L	PCT	GB	R	OR	AB	H	2B	3B	HR	BB	SO	AVG	OBP	SLG	PRO	PRO+	BR	/A	PF	CHI	RC	SB	CS	SBA	SBR
BOS	158	94	59	.614		657	548	5206	1307	213	60	35	**502**	617	.251	.323	.335	.658	103	17	21	99	103	602	139			
NY	156	84	70	.545	10.5	**672**	576	5146	1363	**222**	59	30	447	479	.265	**.330**	.348	.678	112	53	**75**	99	103	**644**	**239**			
STL	157	81	72	.529	13	558	**540**	5046	1249	203	65	33	445	618	.248	.314	.333	.647	100	-9	-2	99	95	576	204			
CHI	156	78	76	.506	16.5	605	638	5050	1229	199	74	42	501	577	.243	.317	.337	.654	101	7	9	100	100	579	164			
BRO	154	75	79	.487	19.5	622	618	5152	**1386**	172	**90**	31	376	559	**.269**	.323	.355	.678	106	43	29	102	97	629	173			
PHI	154	74	80	.481	20.5	651	687	5110	1345	211	52	**62**	472	570	.263	.329	**.361**	**.690**	105	69	26	107	97	636	145			
PIT	158	69	85	.448	25.5	503	**540**	5145	1197	148	79	18	416	608	.233	.295	.303	.598	88	-101	-80	96	101	488	147			
CIN	157	60	94	.390	34.5	530	651	4991	1178	142	64	16	441	627	.236	.305	.300	.605	83	-79	-94	103	**105**	506	224			
TOT	625					4798		40846	10254	1510	543	267	3600	4655	.251	.317	.334	.651						1435				

TEAM	CG	SH	SV	IP	H	H/G	HR	BB	SO	RAT	ERA	ERA+	OAV	OOB	PR	/A	PF	CPI	FA	E	DP	FW	PW	BW	SBW	DIF
BOS	**104**	19	6	1421	1272	8.1	38	477	606	11.4	2.74	100	.249	.319	7	1	99	102	.963	246	**143**	1.8	.1	2.3		13.3
NY	88	**20**	9	1390²	1298	8.4	47	**367**	563	11.0	2.94	90	.253	**.306**	-25	-46	95	92	.961	254	119	1.1	-5.0	**8.1**		2.8
STL	84	16	12	1424²	1279	8.1	26	422	531	11.1	**2.38**	117	.250	.313	**64**	**64**	100	**112**	.964	239	109	2.2	**6.9**	-.2		-4.4
CHI	70	14	11	1389¹	**1169**	7.6	37	528	**651**	11.2	2.71	103	**.233**	.311	12	9	100	92	.951	310	87	-2.7	1.0	1.0		1.8
BRO	80	11	11	1368¹	1282	8.4	36	466	605	11.8	2.82	101	.255	.323	-5	7	103	105	.961	248	112	1.2	.8	3.1		-7.1
PHI	85	14	7	1379¹	1403	9.2	26	452	650	12.4	3.06	96	.270	.335	-42	-21	105	106	.950	324	81	-3.9	-2.3	2.8		.3
PIT	86	10	11	1405	1272	8.1	27	392	488	**10.9**	2.70	98	.249	.308	13	-9	95	95	**.966**	**223**	96	**3.4**	-1.0	-8.6		-1.8
CIN	74	15	**15**	1387¹	1259	8.2	30	489	607	11.7	2.94	100	.248	.320	-24	-3	105	95	.952	314	113	-2.9	-.3	-10.1		-3.7
TOT	671	119	82	11165²		8.2				11.4	2.78		.251	.317					.958	2158	860					

Runs
Burns-NY	100
Magee-Phi	96
Daubert-Bro	89
Saier-Chi	87
Doyle-NY	87

Hits
Magee-Phi	171
Wheat-Bro	170
Burns-NY	170
Zimmerman-Chi	167
Becker-Phi	167

Doubles
Magee-Phi	39
Zimmerman-Chi	36
Burns-NY	35
Connolly-Bos	28

Triples
Carey-Pit	17
Zimmerman-Chi	12
Wilson-StL	12
Cutshaw-Bro	12

Home Runs
Cravath-Phi	19
Saier-Chi	18
Magee-Phi	15
Luderus-Phi	12

Total Bases
Magee-Phi	277
Cravath-Phi	249
Wheat-Bro	241
Zimmerman-Chi	239
Burns-NY	234

Runs Batted In
Magee-Phi	103
Cravath-Phi	100
Wheat-Bro	89
D.Miller-StL	88
Zimmerman-Chi	87

Runs Produced
Magee-Phi	184
Zimmerman-Chi	158
Cravath-Phi	157
Burns-NY	157
D.Miller-StL	151

Bases On Balls
Huggins-StL	105
Saier-Chi	94
Burns-NY	87
Evers-Bos	87
Cravath-Phi	83

Batting Average
Daubert-Bro	.329
Becker-Phi	.325
Dalton-Bro	.319
Wheat-Bro	.319
Stengel-Bro	.316

On Base Percentage
Stengel-Bro	.404
Burns-NY	.403
Cravath-Phi	.402
Huggins-StL	.396
Dalton-Bro	.396

Slugging Average
Magee-Phi	.509
Cravath-Phi	.499
Connolly-Bos	.494
Wheat-Bro	.452
Becker-Phi	.446

Production
Cravath-Phi	.901
Magee-Phi	.890
Wheat-Bro	.830
Stengel-Bro	.829
Burns-NY	.820

Adjusted Production
Cravath-Phi	157
Magee-Phi	154
Burns-NY	149
Stengel-Bro	143
Wheat-Bro	143

Batter Runs
Cravath-Phi	42.7
Magee-Phi	40.7
Burns-NY	34.0
Connolly-Bos	31.0
Wheat-Bro	29.3

Adjusted Batter Runs
Burns-NY	37.5
Cravath-Phi	36.0
Magee-Phi	34.0
Connolly-Bos	31.5
Wheat-Bro	27.3

Clutch Hitting Index
Fletcher-NY	129
Maranville-Bos	127
Cutshaw-Bro	123
D.Miller-StL	122
Schmidt-Bos	121

Runs Created
Burns-NY	113
Magee-Phi	110
Cravath-Phi	103
Wheat-Bro	95
Becker-Phi	87

Total Average
Burns-NY	.997
Cravath-Phi	.997
Magee-Phi	.965
Stengel-Bro	.904
Wheat-Bro	.857

Stolen Bases
Burns-NY	62
Herzog-Cin	46
Dolan-StL	42
Carey-Pit	38

Stolen Base Average

Stolen Base Runs

Fielding Runs
Maranville-Bos	51.8
Herzog-Cin	30.6
Cutshaw-Bro	27.5
Smith-Bro-Bos	22.6
Wheat-Bro	18.2

Total Player Rating
Maranville-Bos	5.9
Herzog-Cin	4.7
Magee-Phi	4.5
Smith-Bro-Bos	4.2
Wheat-Bro	4.1

Wins
Alexander-Phi	27
Tesreau-NY	26
Rudolph-Bos	26
James-Bos	26
Mathewson-NY	24

Win Percentage
James-Bos	.788
Doak-StL	.760
Tesreau-NY	.722
Rudolph-Bos	.722
Pfeffer-Bro	.657

Games
Cheney-Chi	50
Mayer-Phi	48
Ames-Cin	47

Complete Games
Alexander-Phi	32
Rudolph-Bos	31
James-Bos	30
Mathewson-NY	29
Pfeffer-Bro	27

Shutouts
Tesreau-NY	8
Doak-StL	7
Rudolph-Bos	6
Cheney-Chi	6
Alexander-Phi	6

Saves
Sallee-StL	6
Ames-Cin	6
Cheney-Chi	5
Pfeffer-Bro	4
McQuillan-Pit	4

Innings Pitched
Alexander-Phi	355.0
Rudolph-Bos	336.1
James-Bos	332.1
Tesreau-NY	322.1
Mayer-Phi	321.0

Fewest Hits/Game
Tesreau-NY	6.65
Doak-StL	6.79
Cheney-Chi	6.91
Douglas-Cin	6.99
James-Bos	7.07

Fewest BB/Game
Mathewson-NY	.66
Adams-Pit	1.24
Marquard-NY	1.58
Rudolph-Bos	1.63
Alexander-Phi	1.93

Strikeouts
Alexander-Phi	214
Tesreau-NY	189
Vaughn-Chi	165
Cheney-Chi	157
James-Bos	156

Strikeouts/Game
Alexander-Phi	5.43
Tesreau-NY	5.28
Vaughn-Chi	5.06
L.Tyler-Bos	4.64
Ragan-Bro	4.58

Ratio
Rudolph-Bos	9.45
Adams-Pit	9.51
Mathewson-NY	9.78
Doak-StL	10.09
Pfeffer-Bro	10.34

Earned Run Average
Doak-StL	1.72
James-Bos	1.90
Pfeffer-Bro	1.97
Vaughn-Chi	2.05
Sallee-StL	2.10

Adjusted ERA
Doak-StL	162
James-Bos	145
Pfeffer-Bro	145
Vaughn-Chi	135
Sallee-StL	133

Opponents' Batting Avg.
Tesreau-NY	.209
Cheney-Chi	.215
Doak-StL	.216
Vaughn-Chi	.222
Douglas-Cin	.223

Opponents' On Base Pct.
Adams-Pit	.276
Rudolph-Bos	.276
Mathewson-NY	.278
Alexander-Phi	.290
Doak-StL	.290

Starter Runs
James-Bos	32.8
Doak-StL	30.2
Pfeffer-Bro	28.5
Vaughn-Chi	23.9
Sallee-StL	21.4

Adjusted Starter Runs
James-Bos	31.6
Pfeffer-Bro	30.9
Doak-StL	30.4
Vaughn-Chi	23.6
Alexander-Phi	21.8

Clutch Pitching Index
Cooper-Pit	126
James-Bos	121
Crutcher-Bos	120
Perritt-StL	116
Sallee-StL	116

Relief Runs

Adjusted Relief Runs

Relief Ranking

Total Pitcher Index
James-Bos	3.6
Alexander-Phi	3.3
Doak-StL	3.2
Pfeffer-Bro	3.1
Sallee-StL	2.9

Total Baseball Ranking
Maranville-Bos	5.9
Herzog-Cin	4.7
Magee-Phi	4.5
Smith-Bro-Bos	4.2
Wheat-Bro	4.1

January 6 The National Commission grants some demands of the Players' Fraternity: players will be notified in writing of their transfer or release and receive a copy of their contract; players with 10 years in the major league are eligible to become free agents; clubs will pay traveling expenses to spring training and furnish all uniforms; all parks will have a blank green wall behind the pitcher in center field.

April 1 Future Hall of Famer Rube Waddell, weakened by a heroic effort to help contain a winter flood in Kentucky, dies at 37 of tuberculosis in a San Antonio sanitarium. Waddell won 20 games for four straight years with the Athletics and struck out 349 batters in 1904, still an AL record for lefthanders and the AL standard until Nolan Ryan eclipsed it in 1974.

April 22 At age 19, Babe Ruth's first professional game (as a pitcher) is a 6-hit 6-0 win for Baltimore (International League) over Buffalo. The second batter he faces is Joe McCarthy, the manager he will play for 17 years later with New York.

May 14 The White Sox' Jim Scott pitches a no-hitter for nine innings, then loses to Washington 1-0 in the tenth. It is the first of a record four no-hitters that White Sox rookie catcher Ray Schalk will catch in his 17 years with the team.

July 11 Babe Ruth breaks in with Boston, pitching a 4-3 win over Cleveland. In his first major league time at bat, Ruth strikes out. He will be 2-1 with Boston, spending most of the year at Providence (IL).

August 11 After missing six weeks, first with broken ribs, then a broken thumb, Ty Cobb signs a new three-year contract and returns to the lineup. Cobb will get into just 97 games, but he will win another batting crown at .368. Under existing rules his 345 at bats are enough to qualify.

August 31 Jack Fournier, first baseman of the White Sox, hits two homers off Walter Johnson, both inside the park. The second comes in the tenth to give Chicago a 4–3 victory. He will be the only player to hit two homers off the Big Train in one game until August 13, 1926, when Lou Gehrig will connect twice.

September 12 Yankee shortstop Roger Peckinpaugh, 23, replaces Frank Chance and becomes the youngest major league manager of all time and the seventh in the club's 12-year existence.

September 27 Cleveland second baseman Nap Lajoie collects his 3,000th major league hit, as the Indians defeat the Yankees 5-3.

November 1 Connie Mack begins cleaning house, asks waivers on Jack Coombs, Eddie Plank, and Chief Bender. Colby Jack goes to Brooklyn (NL). Plank and Bender escape Mack's maneuvering by jumping to the Federal League. Even though the A's won the pennant, Philadelphia fans did not support them, and the club lost $50,000.

December 8 After weeks of rumors, Connie Mack sells Eddie Collins, generally regarded as the game's finest position player, to the White Sox for $50,000. Collins signs a 5-year contract worth $75,000 and gets $15,000 as a signing bonus. The deal breaks up the A's "$100,000 Infield" and raises conjecture that Mack will leave to manage the Yankees.

December 31 Ban Johnson's efforts to strengthen the New York Yankees succeed when he arranges the purchase of the team by Colonel Jacob Ruppert and Cap Huston for $460,000. The new owners will name longtime Detroit pitcher Bill Donovan as manager.

BOSTON		CHICAGO		CLEVELAND		DETROIT		NEW YORK		PHILADELPHIA		ST.LOUIS		WASHINGTON	
M	B.Carrigan	M	J.Callahan	M	J.Birmingham	M	H.Jennings	M	F.Chance	M	C.Mack	M	B.Rickey	M	C.Griffith
1B	D.Hoblitzel	1B	J.Fournier	1B	D.Johnston	1B	G.Burns	M	R.Peckinpaugh	1B	S.McInnis	1B	J.Leary	1B	C.Gandil
2B	S.Yerkes	2B	L.Blackburne	2B	N.Lajoie	2B	M.Kavanagh	1B	C.Mullen	2B	E.Collins	2B	D.Pratt	2B	R.Morgan
SS	E.Scott	SS	B.Weaver	SS	R.Chapman	SS	D.Bush	2B	L.Boone	SS	J.Barry	SS	D.Lavan	SS	G.McBride
3B	L.Gardner	3B	J.Breton	3B	T.Turner	3B	G.Moriarty	SS	R.Peckinpaugh	3B	F.Baker	3B	J.Austin	3B	E.Foster
LF	D.Lewis	LF	R.Demmitt	LF	J.Graney	LF	B.Veach	3B	F.Maisel	LF	R.Oldring	LF	T.Walker	LF	H.Shanks
CF	T.Speaker	CF	P.Bodie	CF	N.Leibold	CF	T.Cobb	LF	R.Hartzell	CF	A.Strunk	CF	B.Shotton	CF	C.Milan
RF	H.Hooper	RF	S.Collins	RF	J.Jackson	RF	S.Crawford	CF	B.Cree	RF	E.Murphy	RF	G.Williams	RF	D.Moeller
C	B.Carrigan	C	R.Schalk	C	S.O'Neill	C	O.Stanage	RF	D.Cook	C	W.Schang	C	S.Agnew	C	J.Henry
								C	J.Sweeney						
21	H.Janvrin	1	H.Chase	S2	I.Olson	23	O.Vitt	O	L.Nunamaker	O	J.Walsh	S	B.Wares	O	M.Mitchell
C	H.Cady	3	S.Alcock	O1	J.Kirke	O	H.High	2	F.Truesdale	C	J.Lapp	31	I.Howard	C	R.Williams
O	W.Rehg	S2	J.Berger	O1	R.Wood	O	H.Heilmann	O	T.Daley	O	T.Daley	O	E.Walker	C	E.Ainsmith
1	C.Engle	O	T.Daly	S	B.Wambsganss	3	B.Purtell	1	H.Williams	O	L.Kopf	/1	F.Crossin	2	W.Smith
C	P.Thomas	C	B.Roth	C	F.Carisch	C	D.Baker	O	J.Walsh	O	C.Davies	S	B.Wallace	O	M.Acosta
O	O.Henriksen	O	W.Mayer	C	B.Egan	C	R.McKee	C	D.Gossett	/O	S.Thompson	/1	E.Miller	/2	G.Schaefer
12	D.Gainer	3	H.Lord	C	J.Bassler	/2	P.Baumann	/C	J.Rogers	/O	B.Orr	C	W.Rumler	C	C.Pick
/2	B.Swanson	3	H.Baker	3	L.Pezold	/S	F.McMullin	/O	A.Aragon	/C	W.McAvoy	/C	J.Jenkins	/O	J.Gedeon
/C	L.Nunamaker	O	W.Kuhn	S	J.Lelivelt	R	R.Demmitt	/O	C.Meara	/2	J.Rogers	/S	D.Walsh	/O	I.Meusel
/C	L.Pratt	/O	L.Chappell	S	R.Bisland	/1	D.Gainer	/O	B.Reynolds	/1	E.Mack	/1	D.Kauffman	/C	D.Neff
/1	S.Wilson	/O	P.Wolfe	O	E.Smith	P	H.Coveleski	/C	P.Schwert	/1	H.Davis	/O	B.Clemens	/C	T.Wilson
P	R.Collins	/O	C.Coombs	3	W.Barbare	P	H.Dauss	/O	F.Gilhooley	/S	S.Crane	/C	G.Hale	P	W.Johnson
P	D.Leonard	/2	C.Manda	O	J.Birmingham	P	J.Dubuc	/1	H.Kingman	/C	G.Hale	/O	T.Bowden	P	D.Ayers
P	H.Foster	H	C.Kavanagh	/S	B.Hartford	P	P.Cavet	H	L.Channell	P	F.Moore	/C	J.Enzenroth	P	J.Shaw
P	H.Bedient	/O	I.Porter	/C	J.Billings	P	A.Main	/1	J.Harris	/C	D.Sturgis	/3	E.Hemingway	P	J.Boehling
P	E.Shore	/O	H.Schreiber	/C	F.Mills	P	M.Hall	/O	A.Burr	/C	I.Thomas	/O	B.Messenger	P	J.Bentley
P	J.Wood	H	D.Brown	/S	G.Dunlop	P	R.Reynolds	/1	F.Chance	/O	T.Coyne	H	B.Rickey	RP	H.Harper
P	R.Johnson	/C	B.Sullivan	/3	A.Cypert	P	G.Boehler	P	J.Warhop	/1	B.Rochefort	/1	C.Bold	P	J.Engel
P	V.Gregg	P	J.Benz	/O	T.Ginn	/P	R.Oldham	P	R.Caldwell	/O	B.Sweeney	H	D.Schirick	P	M.Williams
P	F.Coumbe	H	E.Cicotte	H	T.Reilly	P	J.Williams	P	R.Keating	P	B.Shawkey	P	E.Hamilton	P	B.Gallia
/P	B.Ruth	P	J.Scott	P	W.Mitchell	/P	E.McCreery	P	R.Fisher	P	J.Bush	P	C.Weilman	P	C.Cashion
/P	G.Cooper	P	R.Faber	P	B.Steen	/P	L.Williams	P	M.McHale	P	W.Wyckoff	P	B.James	/P	J.Stevens
/P	M.Zeiser	P	B.Russell	P	R.Hagerman			P	K.Cole	P	E.Plank	P	G.Baumgardner	/P	N.Altrock
/P	E.Kelly	RP	B.Lathrop	P	G.Morton			P	B.Brown	P	C.Bender	P	W.Leverenz	/P	F.Barron
		P	M.Wolfgang	P	F.Blanding			/P	A.Schulz	P	H.Pennock	P	R.Mitchell	/P	C.Griffith
		/P	E.Walsh	P	A.Collamore			/P	G.Cooper	P	R.Bressler	P	H.Hoch		
		P	H.Jasper	P	V.Gregg					P	B.Brown	P	W.Taylor		
				P	A.Bowman					/P	B.Houck	/P	E.Manning		
				P	F.Coumbe					/P	W.Jensen	/P	G.Baichley		
				P	L.James					/P	J.Coombs	/P	A.Sothoron		
				P	H.Dillinger					/P	C.Boardman				
				/P	P.Carter					/P	F.Worden				
				/P	A.Tedrow										
				/P	G.Kahler										
				/P	L.Bishop										
				/P	N.Cullop										
				/P	S.Jones										
				/P	G.Beck										
				/P	H.Benn										

TEAM	G	W	L	PCT	GB	R	OR	AB	H	2B	3B	HR	BB	SO	AVG	OBP	SLG	PRO	PRO+	BR	/A	PF	CHI	RC	SB	CS	SBA	SBR
PHI	158	99	53	.651		749	529	5126	1392	165	80	29	545	517	.272	.348	.352	.700	123	112	140	96	107	662	231	188	55	-44
BOS	159	91	62	.595	8.5	589	510	5117	1278	226	85	18	490	549	.250	.320	.338	.658	105	26	26	100	98	567	177	176	50	-53
WAS	158	81	73	.526	19	572	519	5108	1245	176	81	18	470	640	.244	.313	.320	.633	93	-17	-39	104	102	544	220	163	57	-32
DET	157	80	73	.523	19.5	615	618	5102	1318	195	84	25	557	537	.258	.336	.344	.680	109	76	56	103	93	630	211	154	58	-29
STL	159	71	82	.464	28.5	523	615	5101	1241	185	75	17	423	863	.243	.306	.319	.625	99	-38	-17	96	99	516	233	189	55	-44
NY	157	70	84	.455	30	537	550	4992	1144	149	52	12	577	711	.229	.315	.287	.602	88	-60	-58	100	105	484	251	191	57	-39
CHI	157	70	84	.455	30	487	560	5040	1205	161	71	19	408	609	.239	.302	.311	.613	90	-59	-52	99	96	497	167	152	52	-41
CLE	157	51	102	.333	48.5	538	709	5157	1262	178	70	10	450	685	.245	.310	.312	.622	90	-39	-60	104	100	517	167	157	52	-44
TOT	631					4610		40743	10085	1435	598	148	3920	5111	.248	.319	.323	.642							1657	1370	55	-325

TEAM	CG	SH	SV	IP	H	H/G	HR	BB	SO	RAT	ERA	ERA+	OAV	OOB	PR	/A	PF	CPI	FA	E	DP	FW	PW	BW	SBW	DIF
PHI	89	24	17	1404	1264	8.1	18	521	720	11.6	2.78	94	.249	.322	-6	-27	95	100	.966	213	116	3.5	-3.0	15.5	-.4	7.4
BOS	88	24	8	1427¹	1207	7.6	18	393	602	10.3	2.36	114	.236	.295	59	50	98	94	.963	242	99	1.8	5.5	2.9	-1.4	5.6
WAS	75	25	20	1420²	1170	7.4	20	520	784	11.0	2.54	111	.233	.311	31	41	103	97	.961	254	116	1.0	4.5	-4.3	1.0	1.8
DET	81	14	12	1412	1285	8.2	17	498	567	11.8	2.86	98	.249	.322	-19	-10	103	97	.958	286	101	-1.1	-1.1	6.2	1.3	-1.8
STL	81	15	11	1410²	1309	8.4	20	540	553	12.1	2.85	95	.251	.327	-17	-22	99	103	.952	317	114	-2.7	-2.4	-1.9	-.4	1.9
NY	98	9	5	1397¹	1277	8.2	30	390	563	10.9	2.81	99	.250	.308	-12	-10	101	94	.963	238	93	1.9	-1.1	-6.4	.2	-1.5
CHI	74	17	11	1398²	1207	7.8	15	401	660	10.5	2.48	108	.239	.298	40	30	98	92	.955	299	90	-1.9	3.3	-5.7	-.0	-2.7
CLE	69	9	3	1391²	1365	8.8	10	666	688	13.4	3.21	90	.267	.357	-74	-55	105	110	.953	300	119	-1.9	-6.1	-6.6	-.4	-10.5
TOT	655	137	87	11262¹		8.1				11.5	2.73		.248	.319					.959	2149	848					

Runs		Hits		Doubles		Triples		Home Runs		Total Bases	
Collins-Phi	122	Speaker-Bos	193	Speaker-Bos	46	Crawford-Det	26	Baker-Phi	9	Speaker-Bos	287
Speaker-Bos	101	Crawford-Det	183	Lewis-Bos	37	Gardner-Bos	19	Crawford-Det	8	Crawford-Det	281
Murphy-Phi	101	Baker-Phi	182	Pratt-StL	34	Speaker-Bos	18	T.Walker-StL	6	Baker-Phi	252
Bush-Det	97	McInnis-Phi	181	Collins-Chi	34	T.Walker-StL	16	Fournier-Chi	6	Pratt-StL	240
		Collins-Phi	181	Leary-StL	28	Hooper-Bos	15			Collins-Phi	238

Runs Batted In		Runs Produced		Bases On Balls		Batting Average		On Base Percentage		Slugging Average	
Crawford-Det	104	Collins-Phi	205	Bush-Det	112	Cobb-Det	.368	Collins-Phi	.452	Cobb-Det	.513
McInnis-Phi	95	Speaker-Bos	187	Collins-Phi	97	Collins-Phi	.344	Speaker-Bos	.423	Speaker-Bos	.503
Speaker-Bos	90	Crawford-Det	170	Murphy-Phi	87	Speaker-Bos	.338	Jackson-Cle	.399	Crawford-Det	.483
Baker-Phi	89	McInnis-Phi	168	Speaker-Bos	77	Jackson-Cle	.338	Crawford-Det	.388	Jackson-Cle	.464
Collins-Phi	85	Baker-Phi	164	Maisel-NY	76	Baker-Phi	.319	Baker-Phi	.380	Collins-Phi	.452

Production		Adjusted Production		Batter Runs		Adjusted Batter Runs		Clutch Hitting Index		Runs Created	
Speaker-Bos	.926	Collins-Phi	179	Speaker-Bos	54.9	Collins-Phi	56.4	McInnis-Phi	147	Speaker-Bos	124
Collins-Phi	.904	Speaker-Bos	178	Collins-Phi	51.6	Speaker-Bos	54.9	Gandil-Was	138	Collins-Phi	120
Crawford-Det	.871	Crawford-Det	157	Cobb-Det	42.3	Cobb-Det	39.7	Collins-Phi	127	Crawford-Det	113
Jackson-Cle	.862	Baker-Phi	153	Crawford-Det	42.1	Crawford-Det	38.7	Lewis-Bos	125	Baker-Phi	95
Baker-Phi	.822	Jackson-Cle	153	Jackson-Cle	31.6	Baker-Phi	35.0	Crawford-Det	125	Cobb-Det	89

Total Average		Stolen Bases		Stolen Base Average		Stolen Base Runs		Fielding Runs		Total Player Rating	
Collins-Phi	.984	Maisel-NY	74	Maisel-NY	81.3	Maisel-NY	12.0	Bush-Det	33.5	Speaker-Bos	7.6
Speaker-Bos	.943	Collins-Phi	58	Sweeney-NY	76.0	Sweeney-NY	2.1	Speaker-Bos	27.7	Collins-Phi	5.9
Crawford-Det	.867	Speaker-Bos	42	Chapman-Cle	72.7	Kopf-Phi	1.8	Gandil-Was	23.7	Bush-Det	5.0
Jackson-Cle	.835	Shotton-StL	40	Moriarty-Det	69.4	Chapman-Cle	1.8	Boone-NY	22.7	Baker-Phi	4.7
T.Walker-StL	.776			Peckinpaugh-NY	69.1			Turner-Cle	21.3	T.Walker-StL	3.9

Wins		Win Percentage		Games		Complete Games		Shutouts		Saves	
Johnson-Was	28	Bender-Phi	.850	Johnson-Was	51	Johnson-Was	33	Johnson-Was	9	Shaw-Was	4
Coveleski-Det	22	Leonard-Bos	.792	Ayers-Was	49	Coveleski-Det	23	Leonard-Bos	7	Mitchell-StL	4
Collins-Bos	20	Plank-Phi	.682	Shaw-Was	48	Dauss-Det	22	Bender-Phi	7	Faber-Chi	4
Leonard-Bos	19	Shawkey-Phi	.667	Benz-Chi	48	Caldwell-NY	22	Collins-Bos	6	Dauss-Det	4
		Caldwell-NY	.654							Bentley-Was	4

Innings Pitched		Fewest Hits/Game		Fewest BB/Game		Strikeouts		Strikeouts/Game		Ratio	
Johnson-Was	371.2	Leonard-Bos	5.57	McHale-NY	1.55	Johnson-Was	225	Leonard-Bos	7.05	Leonard-Bos	8.29
Coveleski-Det	303.1	Caldwell-NY	6.46	Russell-Chi	1.77	Mitchell-Cle	179	Mitchell-Cle	6.27	Caldwell-NY	8.79
Hamilton-StL	302.1	Shaw-Was	6.93	Johnson-Was	1.79	Leonard-Bos	176	Shaw-Was	5.74	Johnson-Was	9.01
Dauss-Det	302.0	Johnson-Was	6.95	Warhop-NY	1.83	Shaw-Was	164	Johnson-Was	5.45	Foster-Bos	9.48
Weilman-StL	299.0	Foster-Bos	6.97	Ayers-Was	1.83	Dauss-Det	150	Bender-Phi	5.38	Ayers-Was	9.60

Earned Run Average		Adjusted ERA		Opponents' Batting Avg.		Opponents' On Base Pct.		Starter Runs		Adjusted Starter Runs	
Leonard-Bos	.96	Leonard-Bos	279	Leonard-Bos	.180	Leonard-Bos	.246	Leonard-Bos	44.3	Johnson-Was	45.0
Foster-Bos	1.70	Johnson-Was	163	Caldwell-NY	.205	Caldwell-NY	.260	Johnson-Was	41.9	Leonard-Bos	43.0
Johnson-Was	1.72	Foster-Bos	158	Shaw-Was	.216	Johnson-Was	.265	Foster-Bos	24.3	Foster-Bos	23.2
Caldwell-NY	1.94	Caldwell-NY	142	Johnson-Was	.217	Foster-Bos	.274	Weilman-StL	21.8	Weilman-StL	20.6
Shore-Bos	2.00	Cicotte-Chi	131	Foster-Bos	.218	Benz-Chi	.282	Cicotte-Chi	20.8	Caldwell-NY	19.2

Clutch Pitching Index		Relief Runs	Adjusted Relief Runs	Relief Ranking	Total Pitcher Index		Total Baseball Ranking	
Hagerman-Cle	126				Johnson-Was	7.3	Speaker-Bos	7.6
Steen-Cle	123				Leonard-Bos	4.6	Johnson-Was	7.2
Shawkey-Phi	109				Cicotte-Chi	2.7	Collins-Phi	5.9
James-StL	106				Foster-Bos	2.6	Bush-Det	5.0
Bender-Phi	106				Caldwell-NY	2.5	Baker-Phi	4.7

January 17 A report out of Chicago has FL president Gilmore offering Ty Cobb a five-year $75,000 contract. Cobb had replied he had already signed with the Tigers and could not sign with the Feds.

April 13 After building eight new ballparks in three months, the Federal League opens with the Baltimore Terrapins knocking off Buffalo in front of 27,140. Jack Quinn gets the first of his 26 wins, second in the league to ex-Pirate Claude Hendrix of the Chicago Whales. The Whales will finish second and the Terrapins third to Indianapolis.

June 3 Pitcher Chief Johnson jumps from Cincinnati to Kansas City (FL); a judge grants a permanent injunction against him playing for KC, but he pitches for the Packers through 1915.

June 5* Pitcher John Cantley of Opelika (Georgia-Alabama League) slugs three grand slams and a single for 15 RBI in a game against Talladega, winning the contest 19–1.

June 15 First baseman Hal Chase jumps from the White Sox to the FL's Buffalo franchise after giving owner Charles Comiskey ten days notice of his intent to do so.

July 7 Suffering heavy losses from Federal League competition in Baltimore, the Orioles' (IL) owner Jack Dunn offers Babe Ruth (plus Ernie Shore and C Ben Egan) for $10,000 to old friend Connie Mack, who refuses, pleading poverty. Cincinnati, which has a working agreement giving them the choice of two players, takes outfielder George Twombley and shortstop Claud Derrick. Dunn finally peddles his threesome to new owner Joe Lannin of the Red Sox for a reported $25,000.

September 5* Pitching for Providence in the IL, 19-year-old Babe Ruth beats Toronto 9–0 with a one-hitter, and hits his only minor league homer.

September 7 Floods severely damage the Kansas City Packers' (FL) ballpark, washing away fences and demolishing the clubhouse.

September 19 Ed Lafitte pitches a 6–2 no-hitter for the Brooklyn Tip-Tops (FL) over the Kansas City Packers. Wildness costs him the two runs. He will lead the FL with 127 walks.

October 6 The Chicago Whales lose to Kansas City while the Indianapolis Hoosiers beat St. Louis, giving Indianapolis a 1½ game pennant margin. Five .300 hitters, led by Benny Kauff's .370, pace the winners. Claude Hendrix of the Whales is the FL's top pitcher, 29–11.

December 4 Walter Johnson accepts an advance from the FL Chicago Whales. Clark Griffith threatens to take Johnson to court, claiming he has paid Johnson for the reserve option in his contract. Ban Johnson says Johnson was on the market and is "damaged goods," worth getting rid of. Griffith travels to Coffeyville, KS, to persuade his franchise player that the option clause is legal and binding. Whales manager Joe Tinker says he has signed Johnson for $16,000 and given him a $6,000 bonus. Two weeks later Griffith signs Johnson for three years at $12,500 per year and Johnson returns the bonus to the Feds.

December 7 Chief Bender signs a two-year deal with the Federal League; he will be assigned to Baltimore.

BALTIMORE	BROOKLYN	BUFFALO	CHICAGO	INDIANAPOLIS	KANSAS CITY	PITTSBURGH	ST.LOUIS
M O.Knabe	M B.Bradley	M L.Schlafly	M J.Tinker	M B.Phillips	M G.Stovall	M D.Gessler	M M.Brown
1B H.Swacina	1B H.Myers	1B J.Agler	1B F.Beck	1B C.Carr	1B G.Stovall	1B R.Oakes	1B H.Miller
2B O.Knabe	2B S.Hofman	2B T.Downey	2B J.Farrell	2B F.LaPorte	2B B.Kenworthy	1B H.Bradley	2B D.Crandall
SS M.Doolan	SS E.Gagnier	SS B.Louden	SS J.Tinker	SS J.Esmond	SS P.Goodwin	2B J.Lewis	SS A.Bridwell
3B J.Walsh	3B T.Wisterzil	3B F.Smith	3B R.Zeider	3B B.McKechnie	3B G.Perring	SS E.Holly	3B A.Boucher
LF H.Simmons	LF C.Cooper	LF F.Delahanty	LF M.Flack	LF A.Scheer	LF C.Chadbourne	3B E.Lennox	LF W.Miller
CF V.Duncan	CF A.Shaw	CF C.Hanford	CF D.Zwilling	CF V.Campbell	CF A.Kruger	LF D.Jones	CF D.Drake
RF B.Meyer	RF S.Evans	RF T.McDonald	RF A.Wickland	RF B.Kauff	RF G.Gilmore	CF R.Oakes	RF J.Tobin
C F.Jacklitsch	C G.Land	C W.Blair	C A.Wilson	C B.Rariden	C T.Easterly	RF J.Savage	C M.Simon
						C C.Berry	
O G.Zinn	O G.Anderson	1 H.Chase	3 H.Fritz	O A.Kaiser	O C.Coles	O2 T.McDonald	2S J.Misse
O J.Bates	S A.Halt	O E.Booe	O A.Walsh	O E.Roush	S J.Rawlings	13 C.Rheam	O F.Kommers
3S E.Kirkpatrick	2 J.Delahanty	O D.Young	23 B.Block	O B.Dolan	S3 C.Daringer	O F.Delahanty	C2 G.Hartley
C H.Russell	C F.Owens	2 L.Schlafly	1 J.Stanley	C G.Textor	O J.Potts	S S.Yerkes	O L.Kirby
O F.Kommers	C D.Murphy	3 C.Engle	/C C.Clemens	C B.Warren	C J.Enzenroth	S M.Menosky	C H.Chapman
C D.Kerr	1 A.Griggs	O A.LaVigne	/O B.Jackson	/1 F.Rooney	C D.Brown	C S.Roberts	2 J.Mathes
/O J.McCandless	O F.Chouinard	O L.Bonin	/S L.Kavanagh	/O E.Booe	/S W.Tappan	O R.Mattis	3 M.Cueto
/3 F.Lobert	C A.Watson	C N.Allen	/S J.Smith			D C.Kerr	/2 A.Marsans
/C M.Boucher	/3 R.Williams	O B.Collins	H J.Kading		P G.Packard	/2 B.Coulson	H F.Jones
/O F.Chouinard	H B.Bradley	H N.Pettigrew	H S.Roberts		P N.Cullop	/2 F.Chouinard	
		/C J.Snyder		P C.Falkenberg	P D.Stone	/S J.Scott	P B.Groom
	/S D.Wertz		P E.Moseley		/2 F.Madden		
P J.Quinn	P T.Seaton		P C.Hendrix	P G.Kaiserling	P B.Harris	/C F.Madden	P B.Groom
P G.Suggs	P E.Lafitte		P M.Fiske	P G.Mullin	P P.Henning	H M.Boucher	P D.Davenport
P K.Wilhelm	P H.Finneran	P F.Anderson	P E.Lange	P H.Billiard	P D.Adams		P H.Keupper
P F.Smith		P G.Krapp	P D.Watson	/P R.McConnaughey	C.Johnson		P E.Willett
P B.Bailey	P B.Houck	P R.Ford	P M.Prendergast	/P C.Whitehouse	G.Hogan	P E.Knetzer	P M.Brown
	P D.Marion	P E.Moore		/P F.Harter	D.Swan	P H.Camnitz	RP E.Herbert
P S.Conley	P R.Sommers	P A.Schulz	P T.McGuire	/P F.Harter		P W.Dickson	
P D.Yount	P B.Chappelle		P R.Johnson	/P E.Henderson		C.Barger	/P D.Watson
/P J.Ridgway	P B.Maxwell	P H.Moran	P A.Brennan	K.Keifer		M.Walker	/P T.Welch
/P V.Hughes	P J.Bluejacket	P B.Smith	/P D.Black	F.Ostendorf			
/P J.Allen	P M.Brown	P D.Woodman	/P D.Sherman	/P C.Woods		P G.LaClaire	
	P R.Peters	/P J.Houser				P W.Adams	
	/P H.Juul	/P E.Porray				/P E.Henderson	
	/P F.Wilson	/P B.Schlitzer				/P F.Allen	
	/P E.Chaney						
	/P J.Vernon						
	P J.McGraw						

TEAM	G	W	L	PCT	GB	R	OR	AB	H	2B	3B	HR	BB	SO	AVG	OBP	SLG	PRO	PRO+	BR	/A	PF	CHI	RC	SB	CS	SBA	SBR
IND	157	88	65	.575		762	622	5176	**1474**	230	90	33	470	668	**.285**	.349	.383	.732	95	-36	-103	111	100	765	273			
CHI	157	87	67	.565	1.5	621	**517**	5098	1314	227	50	**52**	520	645	.258	.331	.352	.683	98	-125	**-95**	94	94	634	171			
BAL	160	84	70	.545	4.5	645	628	5120	1374	222	67	32	487	589	.268	.337	.357	.694	92	-105	-122	103	94	652	152			
BUF	155	80	71	.530	7	620	602	5064	1264	177	74	37	430	761	.250	.311	.336	.647	80	-202	-211	102	**109**	574	228			
BRO	157	77	77	.500	11.5	662	677	5221	1402	225	85	42	404	665	.269	.326	.368	.694	96	-117	-113	99	99	669	220			
KC	154	67	84	.444	20	644	683	5127	1369	226	77	39	399	621	.267	.324	.364	.688	97	-127	-106	96	99	637	171			
PIT	154	64	86	.427	22.5	605	698	5114	1339	180	**90**	34	410	575	.262	.321	.352	.673	90	-152	-148	99	96	613	153			
STL	154	62	89	.411	25	565	697	5078	1254	193	65	26	503	662	.247	.319	.326	.645	77	-198	-222	105	96	554	113			
TOT	624					5124		40998	10790	1680	598	295	3623	5186	.263	.323	.355	.678							1481			

TEAM	CG	SH	SV	IP	H	H/G	HR	BB	SO	RAT	ERA	ERA+	OAV	OOB	PR	/A	PF	CPI	FA	E	DP	FW	PW	BW	SBW	DIF
IND	104	15	9	1397²	1352	8.7	**29**	476	664	12.1	3.06	102	.258	.325	-27	9	108	100	.956	289	113	-1.2	.9	-10.7		22.5
CHI	93	**17**	8	1420¹	**1204**	**7.6**	43	393	650	**10.3**	**2.44**	109	**.233**	.291	70	33	92	94	**.962**	249	114	1.1	**3.4**	-9.9		15.4
BAL	88	15	13	1392	1389	9.0	34	**392**	732	11.7	3.13	97	.268	.323	-38	-16	105	101	.960	263	105	.6	-1.7	-12.7		20.8
BUF	89	15	**16**	1387	1249	8.1	45	505	662	11.7	3.16	94	.245	.318	-42	-31	103	91	**.962**	242	109	**1.3**	-3.2	-21.9		28.4
BRO	91	11	9	1385¹	1375	8.9	31	559	636	12.9	3.33	86	.264	.341	-69	-71	100	102	.956	283	120	-.9	-7.4	-11.8		20.0
KC	82	10	12	1361	1387	9.2	37	445	600	12.4	3.41	82	.268	.331	-79	-95	96	98	.957	279	**135**	-.9	-9.9	-11.0		13.3
PIT	97	9	6	1370	1416	9.3	38	444	510	12.4	3.56	80	.273	.333	-103	-107	99	96	.960	253	92	.6	-11.1	-15.4		14.9
STL	97	9	6	1367²	1418	9.3	38	409	661	12.3	3.59	85	.267	.324	-107	-83	105	89	.957	273	94	-.6	-8.6	-23.1		18.8
TOT	741	101	79	11081		8.8				12.0	3.20		.263	.323					.959	2131	882					

Runs		Hits		Doubles		Triples		Home Runs		Total Bases	
Kauff-Ind	120	Kauff-Ind	211	Kauff-Ind	44	Evans-Bro	15	Zwilling-Chi	16	Kauff-Ind	305
McKechnie-Ind	107	Zwilling-Chi	185	Evans-Bro	41	Esmond-Ind	15	Kenworthy-KC	15	Zwilling-Chi	287
Duncan-Bal	99	Evans-Bro	179	Kenworthy-KC	40	Kenworthy-KC	14	Hanford-Buf	12	Kenworthy-KC	286
Kenworthy-KC	93	Oakes-Pit	178	Zwilling-Chi	38			Evans-Bro	12	Evans-Bro	286
Evans-Bro	93	Hanford-Buf	174							Hanford-Buf	264

Runs Batted In		Runs Produced		Bases On Balls		Batting Average		On Base Percentage		Slugging Average	
LaPorte-Ind	107	Kauff-Ind	207	Wickland-Chi	81	Kauff-Ind	.370	Kauff-Ind	.447	Evans-Bro	.556
Evans-Bro	96	LaPorte-Ind	189	Agler-Buf	77	Evans-Bro	.348	Evans-Bro	.416	Kauff-Ind	.534
Zwilling-Chi	95	Evans-Bro	177	Kauff-Ind	72	Easterly-KC	.335	Lennox-Pit	.414	Kenworthy-KC	.525
Kauff-Ind	95	Zwilling-Chi	170			Shaw-Bro	.324	Meyer-Bal	.395	Lennox-Pit	.493
Kenworthy-KC	91	Kenworthy-KC	169			Campbell-Ind	.318	Wilson-Chi	.394	Zwilling-Chi	.485

Production		Adjusted Production		Batter Runs		Adjusted Batter Runs		Clutch Hitting Index		Runs Created	
Kauff-Ind	.981	Evans-Bro	165	Kauff-Ind	47.0	Evans-Bro	38.0	LaPorte-Ind	151	Kauff-Ind	160
Evans-Bro	.973	Kauff-Ind	150	Evans-Bro	37.2	Kauff-Ind	34.5	Swacina-Bal	137	Evans-Bro	121
Lennox-Pit	.907	Kenworthy-KC	148	Lennox-Pit	23.2	Kenworthy-KC	25.0	Wisterzil-Bro	128	Kenworthy-KC	114
Kenworthy-KC	.896	Lennox-Pit	148	Kenworthy-KC	21.3	Lennox-Pit	23.9	Stovall-KC	128	Zwilling-Chi	106
Wilson-Chi	.860	Wilson-Chi	142	Wilson-Chi	15.3	Wilson-Chi	19.8	Carr-Ind	127	McKechnie-Ind	94

Total Average		Stolen Bases		Stolen Base Average		Stolen Base Runs		Fielding Runs		Total Player Rating	
Kauff-Ind	1.278	Kauff-Ind	75					Doolan-Bal	29.3	Wilson-Chi	4.6
Evans-Bro	1.087	McKechnie-Ind	47					McKechnie-Ind	22.9	Kenworthy-KC	4.5
Lennox-Pit	1.034	Myers-Bro	43					Kenworthy-KC	20.8	Kauff-Ind	4.4
Kenworthy-KC	.995	Chadbourne-KC	42					Rariden-Ind	20.1	Evans-Bro	2.9
Wilson-Chi	.939							Tinker-Chi	19.1	Yerkes-Pit	1.6

Wins		Win Percentage		Games		Complete Games		Shutouts		Saves	
Hendrix-Chi	29	Ford-Buf	.778	Hendrix-Chi	49	Hendrix-Chi	34	Falkenberg-Ind	9	Ford-Buf	6
Quinn-Bal	26	Hendrix-Chi	.744	Falkenberg-Ind	49	Falkenberg-Ind	33	Seaton-Bro	7	Wilhelm-Bal	5
Seaton-Bro	25	Quinn-Bal	.650	Wilhelm-Bal	47	Moseley-Ind	29	Suggs-Bal	6	Packard-KC	5
Falkenberg-Ind	25	Seaton-Bro	.641	Suggs-Bal	46	Quinn-Bal	27	Hendrix-Chi	6	Hendrix-Chi	5
Suggs-Bal	24	Suggs-Bal	.632	Quinn-Bal	46						

Innings Pitched		Fewest Hits/Game		Fewest BB/Game		Strikeouts		Strikeouts/Game		Ratio	
Falkenberg-Ind	377.1	Hendrix-Chi	6.51	Ford-Buf	1.49	Falkenberg-Ind	236	Davenport-StL	5.93	Hendrix-Chi	8.55
Hendrix-Chi	362.0	Ford-Buf	6.91	Suggs-Bal	1.61	Moseley-Ind	205	Moseley-Ind	5.83	Ford-Buf	8.66
Quinn-Bal	342.2	Krapp-Buf	7.05	Quinn-Bal	1.71	Hendrix-Chi	189	Falkenberg-Ind	5.63	Falkenberg-Ind	10.16
Suggs-Bal	319.1	Fiske-Chi	7.32	Hendrix-Chi	1.91	Seaton-Bro	172	Groom-StL	5.36	Fiske-Chi	10.32
Moseley-Ind	316.2	Watson-Chi-StL	7.34	Keupper-StL	2.07	Groom-StL	167	Seaton-Bro	5.11	Lange-Chi	10.42

Earned Run Average		Adjusted ERA		Opponents' Batting Avg.		Opponents' On Base Pct.		Starter Runs		Adjusted Starter Runs	
Johnson-Chi	1.57	Ford-Buf	163	Hendrix-Chi	.203	Hendrix-Chi	.251	Hendrix-Chi	48.0	Hendrix-Chi	38.7
Hendrix-Chi	1.69	Hendrix-Chi	157	Krapp-Buf	.210	Ford-Buf	.254	Ford-Buf	29.3	Falkenberg-Ind	37.7
Ford-Buf	1.82	Falkenberg-Ind	141	Ford-Buf	.214	Lange-Chi	.282	Falkenberg-Ind	27.9	Ford-Buf	31.3
Watson-Chi-StL	2.01	Watson-Chi-StL	137	Lange-Chi	.224	Falkenberg-Ind	.284	Watson-Chi-StL	22.1	Watson-Chi-StL	18.6
Falkenberg-Ind	2.22	Lange-Chi	119	Watson-Chi-StL	.230	Anderson-Buf	.297	Cullop-KC	17.8	Quinn-Bal	16.4

Clutch Pitching Index		Relief Runs	Adjusted Relief Runs	Relief Ranking	Total Pitcher Index		Total Baseball Ranking	
Mullin-Ind	128				Hendrix-Chi	5.4	Hendrix-Chi	5.4
Lafitte-Bro	122				Falkenberg-Ind	3.8	Wilson-Chi	4.6
Watson-Chi-StL	114				Ford-Buf	3.1	Kenworthy-KC	4.5
Kaiserling-Ind	109				Quinn-Bal	2.7	Kauff-Ind	4.4
Quinn-Bal	106				Krapp-Buf	1.8	Falkenberg-Ind	3.8

February 11* The International League tries to put a team in the Bronx, but Giants president Hempstead objects.

April 19 St. Louis Cardinals right-hander Lee Meadows makes his NL debut and becomes the first player to wear glasses regularly on the field since pitcher Will White in 1886.

April 29 Benny Kauff of the Brooklyn Brookfeds causes quite a stir when he jumps from the FL to the NL. Boston refuses to play New York if Kauff is in the lineup and the game is forfeited to New York. NL president John Tener, who was called from the ballpark by the other umpire, declares Kauff ineligible until reinstated and orders the game forfeited to Boston. The Braves win the exhibition game 13-8 and that score stands up when Tener rules it an official game and cancels both forfeits. Kauff returns to Brooklyn and leads the FL with a .342 average. John McGraw will have to wait until 1916 to sign him.

June 9 The Phils move into first place, as Grover Cleveland Alexander holds the Cubs hitless until the seventh. Alexander will be 31-10 and lead the NL with a 1.55 ERA, 36 CG, 376 IP, 241 strikeouts, and 12 shutouts.

June 17 George "Zip" Zabel comes out of the Cubs bullpen with two outs in the first and winds up with a 4-3 19-inning win over Brooklyn in the longest relief job ever.

June 18 Former Giants mascot Charley "Victory" Faust, 34, dies of pulmonary tuberculosis while confined to the Western Hospital for the Insane in Washington State.

July 23* Jack Ness of Oakland (Pacific Coast League) has his 49-game hitting streak stopped. He bats .440 in the longest streak thus far in Organized Baseball.

July 29 At 41, Honus Wagner becomes the oldest player in this century to hit a grand slam, an inside-the-park job against Jeff Pfeffer of Brooklyn. The record will stand until Tony Perez hits a grand slam on May 13, 1985, one day short of his 43rd birthday.

August 8 Hank O'Day, who managed the Cubs in 1914, returns to umpiring.

August 18 The new Braves Field opens in Boston. An estimated 46,500 jam the park to see the Braves beat the Cards 3-1.

August 18* *Asahi Shimbun,* the Japanese newspaper, sponsors the first National High School baseball tournament. It is an instant success and will continue every August (except during WW II) to the present. It will often be called the Koshien Tournament, after the stadium near Osaka where the games will be played, starting in 1924.

September 8 Fred Clarke resigns as Pirates manager, having won four pennants in 19 years.

September 29 The Phils clinch their first pennant on Grover Alexander's fourth one-hitter and 12th shutout of the year, 5-0 over the defending champion Braves.

October 9 President Wilson becomes the first President to attend a World Series game, at Game 2 in Philadelphia. Boston's 19-game winner Rube Foster allows the Phils three hits and drives in the winning run to break a 1–1 tie in the ninth against Erskine Mayer.

BOSTON	BROOKLYN	CHICAGO	CINCINNATI	NEW YORK	PHILADELPHIA	PITTSBURGH	ST.LOUIS
M G.Stallings	M W.Robinson	M R.Bresnahan	M B.Herzog	M J.McGraw	M P.Moran	M F.Clarke	M M.Huggins
1B B.Schmidt	1B J.Daubert	1B V.Saier	1B F.Mollwitz	1B F.Merkle	1B F.Luderus	1B D.Johnston	1B D.Miller
2B J.Evers	2B G.Cutshaw	2B H.Zimmerman	2B B.Rodgers	2B L.Doyle	2B B.Niehoff	2B J.Viox	2B M.Huggins
SS R.Maranville	SS O.O'Mara	SS B.Fisher	SS B.Herzog	SS A.Fletcher	SS D.Bancroft	SS H.Wagner	SS A.Butler
3B R.Smith	3B G.Getz	3B A.Phelan	3B H.Groh	3B H.Lobert	3B B.Byrne	3B D.Baird	3B B.Betzel
LF J.Connolly	LF Z.Wheat	LF F.Schulte	LF R.Killefer	LF G.Burns	LF B.Becker	LF M.Carey	LF B.Bescher
CF S.Magee	CF H.Myers	CF C.Williams	CF T.Leach	CF F.Snodgrass	CF P.Whitted	CF Z.Collins	CF C.Wilson
RF H.Moran	RF C.Stengel	RF W.Good	RF T.Griffith	RF D.Robertson	RF G.Cravath	RF B.Hinchman	RF T.Long
C H.Gowdy	C O.Miller	C J.Archer	C I.Wingo	C C.Meyers	C B.Killefer	C G.Gibson	C F.Snyder
2O E.Fitzpatrick	C L.McCarty	C R.Bresnahan	C T.Clarke	13 F.Brainerd	O D.Paskert	3S W.Gerber	O C.Dolan
O2 D.Egan	3 J.Schultz	3 R.Murray	O K.Williams	3 E.Grant	3 M.Stock	O D.Costello	1O H.Hyatt
C B.Whaling	O1 J.Hummel	O P.Knisely	23 I.Olson	O R.Murray	O E.Burns	O E.Barney	3 Z.Beck
O P.Compton	O B.Zimmerman	21 P.McLarry	2S J.Wagner	O R.Dooin	O B.Weiser	C B.Schang	C M.Gonzalez
O L.Gilbert	O A.Nixon	23 A.McCarthy	3 F.Von Kolnitz	C L.Wendell	2 O.Dugey	O L.LeJeune	S R.Hornsby
O T.Cather	/S I.Olson	S E.Mulligan	O G.Twombly	O C.Babington	O B.Adams	/2 A.McCarthy	/O J.Roche
O F.Snodgrass	/O R.Smyth	/C B.Hargrave	O J.Beall	C L.McLean	P P.Alexander	C L.Murphy	S R.Daringer
/O Z.Collins	/C M.Wheat	/S J.Schultz	C R.Dooin	C H.Smith	P E.Mayer	/S I.McAuley	/O H.Glenn
/O J.Shannon	H D.Egan	/2 J.Wallace	P G.Dale	/1 G.Kelly	P A.Demaree	/2 P.Siglin	/O J.Smith
/C W.Tragesser	/3 J.Karst	/O J.Fluhrer	P P.Schneider	/O M.Jacobson	P E.Rixey	/O P.Duncan	/O J.Brown
/C E.Blackburn	P J.Pfeffer	/3 R.Corriden	P F.Toney	/C B.Schang	P G.Chalmers	/C B.Wagner	P B.Doak
/3 F.Low	P W.Dell	/C B.O'Farrell	P R.Benton	/3 B.Dyer	/P G.McQuillan	/O P.Scheeren	P S.Sallee
/2 R.Shannon	P J.Coombs	P H.Vaughn	P K.Lear	/C B.Kocher	H S.Baumgartner	/O F.Clarke	P L.Meadows
P D.Rudolph	P S.Smith	P J.Lavender	P L.McKenry	/3 H.Baker	P B.Tincup	/P H.Daubert	P D.Griner
P T.Hughes	P E.Appleton	P G.Pearce	P R.Ames	P J.Tesreau	/P J.Oeschger	H S.Smith	P H.Robinson
P P.Ragan	P N.Rucker	P B.Humphries	P P.Douglas	P P.Perritt		P B.Harmon	P H.Perdue
P L.Tyler	P P.Douglas	P Z.Zabel	/P L.George	P C.Mathewson		P A.Mamaux	P R.Ames
P A.Nehf	/P R.Aitchison	P L.Cheney	/P C.Brown	P S.Stroud		P B.Adams	P D.Niehaus
P G.Davis	/P L.Cheney	P P.Standridge	/P R.Callahan	P R.Marquard		P W.Cooper	/P C.Boardman
P B.James	/P R.Marquard	P K.Adams	/P H.McCluskey	RP H.Ritter		P E.Kantlehner	/P F.Lamline
/P J.Barnes	/P L.Cadore	/P P.Douglas	/P G.Cochran	RP F.Schupp		RP J.Conzelman	
P D.Crutcher	/P P.Ragan	/P B.Hogg		P R.Schauer		P G.McQuillan	
P P.Strand	/P D.Mails	/P E.Schorr		P R.Benton		/P C.Hill	
/P O.Hess	/P C.Schmutz	/P B.Wright		/P F.Herbert		/P H.Kelly	
/P D.Luque	/P E.Brown			/P A.Fromme		/P P.Slattery	
/P G.Cocreham				/P E.Palmero		/P D.Vance	

TEAM	G	W	L	PCT	GB	R	OR	AB	H	2B	3B	HR	BB	SO	AVG	OBP	SLG	PRO	PRO+	BR	/A	PF	CHI	RC	SB	CS	SBA	SBR
PHI	153	90	62	.592		589	**463**	4916	1216	202	39	**58**	460	600	.247	.316	.340	**.656**	104	31	25	101	101	550	121	113	52	-32
BOS	157	83	69	.546	7	582	545	5070	1219	**231**	57	17	**549**	620	.240	**.321**	.319	.640	**105**	15	**42**	96	98	554	121	98	55	-23
BRO	154	80	72	.526	10	536	560	5120	1268	165	75	14	313	496	.248	.295	.317	.612	89	-56	-65	102	107	496	131	126	51	-36
CHI	156	73	80	.477	17.5	570	620	5114	1246	212	66	53	393	639	.244	.303	**.342**	.645	102	4	3	100	100	555	166	124	57	-25
PIT	156	73	81	.474	18	557	520	5113	1259	197	91	24	419	656	.246	.309	.334	.643	102	8	16	99	97	563	**182**	111	**62**	**-12**
STL	157	72	81	.471	18.5	**590**	601	5106	1297	159	**92**	20	457	658	**.254**	.320	.333	.653	104	30	29	100	98	**568**	162	144	53	-38
CIN	160	71	83	.461	20	516	585	5231	**1323**	194	84	21	360	512	.253	.308	.331	.639	98	-5	-15	102	91	553	156	142	52	-38
NY	155	69	83	.454	21	582	628	5218	1312	195	68	24	315	547	.251	.300	.329	.629	103	-27	4	94	**109**	526	155	137	53	-36
TOT	624					4522		40888	10140	1555	572	225	3266	4728	.248	.309	.331	.640							1194	995	55	-239

TEAM	CG	SH	SV	IP	H	H/G	HR	BB	SO	RAT	ERA	ERA+	OAV	OOB	PR	/A	PF	CPI	FA	E	DP	FW	PW	BW	SBW	DIF
PHI	98	20	8	1374¹	1161	**7.6**	26	342	652	10.0	2.17	126	.234	.288	87	85	100	103	.966	216	99	.8	9.4	2.8	-.2	1.2
BOS	95	17	**13**	1405²	1257	8.0	23	366	630	10.7	2.57	100	.246	.302	27	1	94	100	.966	213	115	1.4	.1	4.7	.8	.0
BRO	87	16	8	1389²	1252	8.1	29	473	499	11.6	2.66	104	.245	.318	14	17	101	**108**	.963	238	96	-.5	1.9	-7.2	-.7	10.6
CHI	71	18	8	1399	1272	8.2	28	480	**657**	11.6	3.11	89	.247	.316	-57	-54	101	91	.958	268	94	-2.3	-6.0	-.3	.5	4.0
PIT	91	18	11	1380	1229	8.0	**21**	384	544	10.8	2.60	105	.246	.304	23	19	99	100	.966	214	100	1.2	2.1	1.8	**2.0**	-11.1
STL	79	13	9	1400²	1320	8.5	30	402	538	11.3	2.89	96	.256	.314	-22	-17	101	101	.964	235	109	-.0	-1.9	3.2	-.9	-4.9
CIN	80	19	12	1432¹	1304	8.2	28	497	572	11.6	2.84	101	.250	.321	-15	2	104	104	.966	222	**148**	1.1	.2	-1.7	-.9	-4.8
NY	78	15	9	1385	1350	8.8	40	**325**	637	11.2	3.11	82	.260	.308	-57	-86	93	94	.960	256	119	-1.6	-9.6	.4	-.7	4.4
TOT	679	136	78	11166²		8.2				11.1	2.75		.248	.309					.964	1862	880					

Runs		Hits		Doubles		Triples		Home Runs		Total Bases	
Cravath-Phi	89	Doyle-NY	189	Doyle-NY	40	Long-StL	25	Cravath-Phi	24	Cravath-Phi	266
Doyle-NY	86	Griffith-Cin	179	Luderus-Phi	36	H.Wagner-Pit	17	Williams-Chi	13	Doyle-NY	261
Bancroft-Phi	85	Hinchman-Pit	177	Saier-Phi	35	Griffith-Cin	16	Schulte-Chi	12	Griffith-Cin	254
Burns-NY	83	Groh-Cin	170	Smith-Bos	34	Hinchman-Pit	14	Saier-Chi	11	Hinchman-Pit	253
O'Mara-Bro	77	Burns-NY	169	Magee-Bos	34	Burns-NY	14	Becker-Phi	11	H.Wagner-Pit	239

Runs Batted In		Runs Produced		Bases On Balls		Batting Average		On Base Percentage		Slugging Average	
Cravath-Phi	115	Cravath-Phi	180	Cravath-Phi	86	Doyle-NY	.320	Cravath-Phi	.393	Cravath-Phi	.510
Magee-Bos	87	Magee-Bos	157	Bancroft-Phi	77	Luderus-Phi	.315	Luderus-Phi	.376	Luderus-Phi	.457
Griffith-Cin	85	Doyle-NY	152	Viox-Pit	75	Griffith-Cin	.307	Daubert-Phi	.369	Long-StL	.446
H.Wagner-Pit	78	Hinchman-Pit	144	Huggins-StL	74	Hinchman-Pit	.307	Hinchman-Pit	.368	Saier-Chi	.445
Hinchman-Pit	77	Miller-StL	143	Smith-Bos	67	Daubert-Bro	.301	Doyle-NY	.358	Doyle-NY	.442

Production		Adjusted Production		Batter Runs		Adjusted Batter Runs		Clutch Hitting Index		Runs Created	
Cravath-Phi	.902	Cravath-Phi	170	Cravath-Phi	46.8	Cravath-Phi	45.6	Fletcher-NY	134	Cravath-Phi	105
Luderus-Phi	.833	Doyle-NY	150	Luderus-Phi	30.3	Doyle-NY	32.5	Magee-Bos	131	Doyle-NY	94
Hinchman-Pit	.807	Luderus-Phi	150	Hinchman-Pit	29.7	Hinchman-Pit	31.0	Miller-StL	128	Hinchman-Pit	94
Doyle-NY	.799	Hinchman-Pit	146	Doyle-NY	27.1	Luderus-Phi	29.3	Schmidt-Bos	125	Luderus-Phi	87
Saier-Chi	.795	Saier-Chi	140	Griffith-Cin	25.4	Griffith-Cin	23.8	Cutshaw-Bro	123	Griffith-Cin	85

Total Average		Stolen Bases		Stolen Base Average		Stolen Base Runs		Fielding Runs		Total Player Rating	
Cravath-Phi	.942	Carey-Pit	36	Bresnahan-Chi	86.4	Bresnahan-Chi	3.9	Fletcher-NY	34.1	Cravath-Phi	4.9
Saier-Chi	.819	Herzog-Cin	35	Saier-Chi	76.3	Saier-Chi	3.3	Herzog-Cin	30.9	Herzog-Cin	4.2
Luderus-Phi	.799	Saier-Chi	29	Baird-Pit	70.7	Costello-Pit	1.5	Maranville-Bro	20.9	Luderus-Phi	3.7
Hinchman-Pit	.741	Baird-Pit	29	Robertson-NY	68.8	Baird-Pit	1.5	Cutshaw-Bro	16.8	Snyder-StL	3.1
Doyle-NY	.714	Cutshaw-Bro	28	Herzog-Cin	68.6	Gerber-Pit	1.2	Magee-Bos	15.4	Fletcher-NY	3.0

Wins		Win Percentage		Games		Complete Games		Shutouts		Saves	
Alexander-Phi	31	Alexander-Phi	.756	Hughes-Bos	50	Alexander-Phi	36	Alexander-Phi	12	Hughes-Bos	9
Rudolph-Bos	22	Toney-Cin	.739	Dale-Cin	49	Rudolph-Bos	30	Tesreau-NY	8	Benton-Cin-NY	5
Mayer-Phi	21	Mamaux-Pit	.724	Alexander-Phi	49	Pfeffer-Bro	26	Toney-Cin	6	Lavender-Chi	4
Mamaux-Pit	21	Vaughn-Chi	.625	Schneider-Cin	48	Harmon-Pit	25	Pfeffer-Bro	6	Cooper-Pit	4
Vaughn-Chi	20	Coombs-Bro	.600	Sallee-StL	46	Tesreau-NY	24				

Innings Pitched		Fewest Hits/Game		Fewest BB/Game		Strikeouts		Strikeouts/Game		Ratio	
Alexander-Phi	376.1	Alexander-Phi	6.05	Mathewson-NY	.97	Alexander-Phi	241	Alexander-Phi	5.76	Alexander-Phi	7.82
Rudolph-Bos	341.1	Toney-Cin	6.47	Humphries-Chi	1.21	Tesreau-NY	176	Hughes-Bos	5.49	Hughes-Bos	8.89
Tesreau-NY	306.0	Mamaux-Pit	6.51	Adams-Pit	1.25	Hughes-Bos	171	Mamaux-Pit	5.44	Tesreau-NY	9.26
Dale-Cin	296.2	Hughes-Bos	6.68	Alexander-Phi	1.53	Mamaux-Pit	152	Douglas-Cin-Br-Chi	5.26	Toney-Cin	9.54
Pfeffer-Bro	291.2	Zabel-Chi	6.85	Rudolph-Bos	1.69	Vaughn-Chi	148	Tesreau-NY	5.18	Adams-Pit	9.73

Earned Run Average		Adjusted ERA		Opponents' Batting Avg.		Opponents' On Base Pct.		Starter Runs		Adjusted Starter Runs	
Alexander-Phi	1.22	Alexander-Phi	224	Alexander-Phi	.191	Alexander-Phi	.234	Alexander-Phi	63.8	Alexander-Phi	63.4
Toney-Cin	1.58	Toney-Cin	181	Toney-Cin	.207	Hughes-Bos	.265	Toney-Cin	28.9	Toney-Cin	31.6
Mamaux-Pit	2.04	Mamaux-Pit	134	Mamaux-Pit	.208	Tesreau-NY	.269	Pfeffer-Bro	21.0	Pfeffer-Bro	21.9
Pfeffer-Bro	2.10	Pfeffer-Bro	132	Hughes-Bos	.213	Toney-Cin	.278	Mamaux-Pit	19.8	Mamaux-Pit	19.2
Hughes-Bos	2.12	Hughes-Bos	122	Tesreau-NY	.215	Adams-Pit	.280	Hughes-Bos	19.5	Hughes-Bos	14.5

Clutch Pitching Index		Relief Runs	Adjusted Relief Runs	Relief Ranking	Total Pitcher Index		Total Baseball Ranking	
Humphries-Chi	139				Alexander-Phi	8.6	Alexander-Phi	8.6
Perritt-NY	122				Toney-Cin	3.1	Cravath-Phi	4.9
Schneider-Cin	121				Pfeffer-Bro	2.6	Herzog-Cin	4.2
Rixey-Phi	120				Mayer-Phi	2.2	Luderus-Phi	3.7
Stroud-NY	118				Schneider-Cin	2.0	Snyder-StL	3.1

January 5 Thirteen years after a Pennsylvania Supreme Court decision effectively banned him from playing for the Athletics, Nap Lajoie rejoins the team. With Lajoie out of Cleveland, a local newspaper runs a contest to rename the Naps. The winning nickname will be the Indians, after the late Lou Sockalexis, a Penobscot Indian who was a popular Cleveland player in the late 1890s.

January 9* The National Commission declares University of Michigan senior George Sisler a free agent after a two-year fight. After graduating, Sisler will sign with the St. Louis Browns, managed by his former college coach, Branch Rickey.

February 3 The AL bans the emery ball, a pitch introduced by Russ Ford in 1910.

April 14 The A's Herb Pennock comes within one out of pitching the first Opening Day no-hitter. A scratch single by Harry Hooper is the Red Sox' only hit in a 5-0 loss.

May 6 Babe Ruth hits his first major league home run off the Yankees' Jack Warhop in the third inning at New York's Polo Grounds. Ruth has two other hits but loses the game in the 13th.

June 18 Ty Cobb steals home twice in a game against Washington, on the front end of double and triple steals.

July 2 The A's sell Jack Barry for $8,000 to Boston. Five days later, they will sell Bob Shawkey to the Yankees for $18,000. Shawkey will win 168 games while wearing the Yankees' new pinstripes.

July 14 White Sox pitcher Red Faber steals three bases in the fourth inning against the A's. With the White Sox leading 4–2 in the fourth and rain threatening, the A's try to delay the game. Joe Bush purposely hits Faber with a pitch, and Faber, trying to speed up the game, tries to get thrown out by stealing. Little effort is made to retire him, and he scores Chicago's fifth run. His "steal" of home turns out to be the winning run, as rain never materializes, and Chicago wins 6–4.

August 29 George Sisler pitches against Walter Johnson and wins 2–1. He will be 4–4 for the Browns and 1–2 next year before moving permanently to first base.

September 22 Having loaned the Braves the use of their larger park in 1914, the Boston Red Sox request the use of the new, larger NL park for this year's World Series.

September 30 The Red Sox clinch the AL pennant by beating Detroit, giving them a 2½-game margin. The Tigers will win 100 games, the first time a runner-up has reached that mark.

October 13 The Phils get four runs early off Rube Foster, but the Red Sox break a tie in the ninth for the third time; reliever Eppa Rixey gives up Harry Hooper's second home run of the game, and Boston wins the game 5-4 and the Series four games to one.

Pos	BOSTON	CHICAGO	CLEVELAND	DETROIT	NEW YORK	PHILADELPHIA	ST.LOUIS	WASHINGTON
M	B.Carrigan	P.Rowland	J.Birmingham	H.Jennings	B.Donovan	C.Mack	B.Rickey	C.Griffith
1B	D.Hoblitzel	J.Fournier	J.Kirke	G.Burns	W.Pipp	S.McInnis	J.Leary	C.Gandil
2B	H.Wagner	E.Collins	B.Wambsganss	R.Young	L.Boone	N.Lajoie	D.Pratt	R.Morgan
SS	E.Scott	B.Weaver	R.Chapman	D.Bush	R.Peckinpaugh	L.Kopf	D.Lavan	G.McBride
3B	L.Gardner	L.Blackburne	W.Barbare	O.Vitt	F.Maisel	W.Schang	J.Austin	E.Foster
LF	D.Lewis	S.Collins	J.Graney	B.Veach	R.Hartzell	R.Oldring	B.Shotton	H.Shanks
CF	T.Speaker	H.Felsch	N.Leibold	T.Cobb	H.High	J.Walsh	T.Walker	C.Milan
RF	H.Hooper	E.Murphy	E.Smith	S.Crawford	D.Cook	A.Strunk	D.Walsh	D.Moeller
C	P.Thomas	R.Schalk	S.O'Neill	O.Stanage	L.Nunamaker	J.Lapp	S.Agnew	J.Henry

BOSTON	CHICAGO	CLEVELAND	DETROIT	NEW YORK	PHILADELPHIA	ST.LOUIS	WASHINGTON
S3 H.Janvrin	3O B.Roth	O1 J.Jackson	12 M.Kavanagh	23 P.Baumann	O E.Murphy	13 I.Howard	C1 R.Williams
2 J.Barry	O J.Jackson	23 T.Turner	C D.Baker	O B.Cree	23 E.Malone	1O G.Sisler	O M.Acosta
C H.Cady	1 B.Brief	O B.Southworth	C R.McKee	S J.Sweeney	S J.Barry	C H.Severeid	3O T.Connolly
1 D.Gainer	O F.Quinlan	3 B.Roth	1 B.Jacobson	1 C.Mullen	C W.McAvoy	1 D.Kauffman	C E.Ainsmith
C B.Carrigan	3 P.Johns	O D.Wile	3 G.Moriarty	O E.Miller	C C.Davies	O G.Williams	O C.Jamieson
O O.Henriksen	O N.Leibold	C B.Egan	/2 F.Fuller	C W.Alexander	3 T.Healy	O B.Jacobson	32 D.Neff
3 M.McNally	C W.Mayer	3 J.Evans	/C J.Peters	3 T.Hendryx	3 H.Damrau	O E.Walker	O T.Barber
/O C.Shorten	C T.Daly	2 J.Hammond	P H.Coveleski	O S.Shelton	/O E.Bankston	O B.Lee	1 J.Judge
/C R.Haley	3 J.Breton	P R.Wood	P H.Dauss	/O E.Barney	/O S.Thompson	/C M.Ruel	O H.Rondeau
/2 B.Rodgers	/O R.Demmitt	P P.Shields	P J.Dubuc	/C E.Krueger	/S S.Seibold	/S B.Wallace	/O M.Kopp
/O W.Rehg	H H.Baker	2 B.Rodgers	P B.Boland	/S P.Schwert	/S S.Crane	/C G.O'Brien	/2 C.Sawyer
P R.Foster	H L.Chappell	O J.Eschen	P B.Steen	/C T.Daley	/C C.Perkins	/O P.Parker	/O S.Mayer
P E.Shore	H C.Jackson	/C J.Billings	P P.Cavet	/O G.Layden	/3 O.Conway	/1 R.Schmandt	H C.Pick
P B.Ruth	P R.Faber	/3 T.Hoffman	P B.James	/O F.Gilhooley	/S S.Danner	/S S.Dee	P W.Johnson
P D.Leonard	P J.Scott	H B.Paschal	P R.Oldham	/C R.Walters	/3 S.McConnell	/3 B.Dalrymple	P B.Gallia
P J.Wood	P J.Benz	/C H.Haworth	/P G.Lowdermilk	P R.Caldwell	/C H.Bostick	H C.Burkam	P J.Boehling
P C.Mays	P R.Russell	H L.Gooch	/P G.Boehler	P R.Fisher	/2 R.Edwards	P C.Weilman	P A.Ayers
P R.Collins	P E.Cicotte	P G.Morton	/P B.Reynolds	P J.Warhop	/3 A.Corcoran	P G.Lowdermilk	P J.Shaw
P V.Gregg	P M.Wolfgang	P W.Mitchell	/P R.Ledbetter	P B.Brown	/C B.Haeffner	P E.Hamilton	P H.Harper
/P H.Pennock	/P E.Walsh	P R.Hagerman		P C.Pieh	/1 H.Davis	P B.James	/P G.Dumont
/P R.Comstock	/P H.Jasper	P S.Jones		P B.Shawkey	/3 F.Lear	P E.Koob	/P J.Engel
/P G.Cooper	/P E.Klepfer	P R.Walker		P R.Keating	/C I.Thomas	RP P.Perryman	P B.Hopper
	/P D.Davis	RP O.Harstad		P M.McHale	P W.Wyckoff	P R.Hoff	P S.Rice
	/P W.Johnson	P F.Coumbe		P K.Cole	P R.Bressler	/P T.McCabe	/P J.Bentley
		P A.Collamore		/P G.Mogridge	P J.Bush	/P H.Hoch	/P N.Altrock
		P L.Brenton		/P B.Donovan	P T.Sheehan	/P T.Phillips	
		P B.Steen		/P D.Vance	P T.Knowlson	/P J.Park	
		/P E.Klepfer		/P A.Russell	P B.Shawkey	/P G.Baumgardner	
		P P.Carter		/P C.Markle	P B.Davis	/P R.Cook	
		/P C.Garrett		/P E.Cottrell	P C.Crowell	/P J.Tillman	
		/P H.Hill		/P D.Tipple	P J.Nabors	/P W.Leverenz	
		/P A.Bowman		/P N.Brady	P H.Pennock	/P P.Sims	
					P D.Fillingim	/P A.Remneas	
					/P J.Richardson	/P A.Sothoron	
					/P H.Eccles	/P C.East	
					/P B.Morrisette	/P S.Perry	
					/P W.Ancker	/P R.McKay	
					/P H.Weaver		
					/P J.Sherman		
					/P B.Haas		
					/P J.Harper		
					/P E.Myers		
					/P C.Ray		
					/P B.Pepper		
					/P S.Pillion		
					/P B.Meehan		
					/P T.Turner		
					/P B.Cone		

TEAM	G	W	L	PCT	GB	R	OR	AB	H	2B	3B	HR	BB	SO	AVG	OBP	SLG	PRO	PRO+	BR	/A	PF	CHI	RC	SB	CS	SBA	SBR
BOS	155	101	50	.669		669	499	5024	1308	202	76	14	527	476	.260	.336	.339	.675	110	46	67	97	100	611	118	117	50	-35
DET	156	100	54	.649	2.5	778	597	5128	1372	207	94	23	681	527	.268	.357	.358	.715	114	131	93	105	101	711	241	146	62	-15
CHI	155	93	61	.604	9.5	717	509	4914	1269	163	102	25	583	575	.258	.345	.348	.693	110	83	62	103	102	637	233	183	56	-40
WAS	155	85	68	.556	17	569	491	5029	1225	152	79	12	458	541	.244	.312	.312	.624	90	-52	-63	102	103	535	186	106	64	-8
NY	154	69	83	.454	32.5	584	588	4982	1162	167	50	31	570	669	.233	.317	.305	.622	91	-46	-45	100	103	523	198	133	60	-20
STL	159	63	91	.409	39.5	521	680	5112	1255	166	65	19	472	765	.246	.315	.315	.630	98	-44	-22	96	91	535	202	160	56	-35
CLE	154	57	95	.375	44.5	539	670	5034	1210	169	79	20	490	681	.240	.312	.317	.629	91	-43	-54	102	95	526	138	117	54	-29
PHI	154	43	109	.283	58.5	545	888	5081	1204	183	72	16	436	634	.237	.304	.311	.615	92	-74	-56	97	103	507	127	89	59	-15
TOT	621					4922		40304	10005	1409	617	160	4217	4868	.248	.325	.326	.651						1443	1051	58	-198

TEAM	CG	SH	SV	IP	H	H/G	HR	BB	SO	RAT	ERA	ERA+	OAV	OOB	PR	/A	PF	CPI	FA	E	DP	FW	PW	BW	SBW	DIF
BOS	81	19	15	1397	1164	7.5	18	446	634	10.7	2.39	116	.231	.300	84	59	95	97	.964	226	95	2.5	6.3	7.1	-1.1	10.8
DET	86	10	19	1413¹	1259	8.0	14	492	550	11.5	2.86	106	.243	.316	11	25	103	94	.961	258	107	.5	2.7	9.9	1.0	9.0
CHI	91	16	9	1401	1242	8.0	14	350	635	10.4	2.43	122	.241	.294	78	84	101	95	.965	222	95	2.7	8.9	6.6	-1.6	-.6
WAS	87	21	13	1393²	1161	7.5	12	455	715	10.7	2.31	129	.232	.302	97	102	101	102	.964	230	101	2.2	10.8	-6.7	1.8	.4
NY	101	12	2	1382²	1272	8.3	41	517	559	12.0	3.06	96	.254	.329	-20	-20	100	104	.966	217	118	2.9	-2.1	-4.8	.5	-3.5
STL	76	6	7	1403	1256	8.1	21	612	566	12.4	3.04	94	.249	.338	-17	-31	98	103	.949	336	144	-4.3	-3.3	-2.3	-1.1	-3.0
CLE	62	11	10	1372	1287	8.4	18	518	610	12.0	3.13	97	.256	.329	-30	-13	104	98	.957	280	82	-1.2	-1.4	-5.7	-.5	-10.2
PHI	78	6	2	1348¹	1358	9.1	22	827	588	15.0	4.29	68	.278	.388	-204	-206	100	102	.947	338	118	-5.0	-21.9	-5.9	1.0	-1.2
TOT	662	101	77	11111		8.1				11.8	2.93		.248	.325					.959	2107	860					

Runs		Hits		Doubles		Triples		Home Runs		Total Bases	
Cobb-Det	144	Cobb-Det	208	Veach-Det	40	Crawford-Det	19	Roth-Chi-Cle	7	Cobb-Det	274
E.Collins-Chi	118	Crawford-Det	183	Pratt-StL	31	Fournier-Chi	18	Oldring-Phi	6	Crawford-Det	264
Vitt-Det	116	Veach-Det	178	Lewis-Bos	31	Roth-Chi-Cle	17			Veach-Det	247
Speaker-Bos	108	Speaker-Bos	176	Crawford-Det	31	S.Collins-Chi	17			Pratt-StL	237
Chapman-Cle	101	Pratt-StL	175	Cobb-Det	31	Chapman-Cle	17			E.Collins-Chi	227

Runs Batted In		Runs Produced		Bases On Balls		Batting Average		On Base Percentage		Slugging Average	
Veach-Det	112	Cobb-Det	240	E.Collins-Chi	119	Cobb-Det	.369	Cobb-Det	.486	Fournier-Chi	.491
Crawford-Det	112	E.Collins-Chi	191	Shotton-StL	118	E.Collins-Chi	.332	E.Collins-Chi	.460	Cobb-Det	.487
Cobb-Det	99	Veach-Det	190	Cobb-Det	118	Fournier-Chi	.322	Fournier-Chi	.429	Kavanagh-Det	.452
S.Collins-Chi	85	Crawford-Det	189	Bush-Det	118	Speaker-Bos	.322	Speaker-Bos	.416	J.Jackson-Cle-Chi	.445
J.Jackson-Cle-Chi	81	Speaker-Bos	177	Hooper-Bos	89	McInnis-Phi	.314	Shotton-StL	.409	Roth-Chi-Cle	.438

Production		Adjusted Production		Batter Runs		Adjusted Batter Runs		Clutch Hitting Index		Runs Created	
Cobb-Det	.973	Cobb-Det	182	Cobb-Det	71.6	Cobb-Det	64.5	Crawford-Det	138	Cobb-Det	155
Fournier-Chi	.920	Fournier-Chi	170	E.Collins-Chi	51.9	E.Collins-Chi	48.2	Veach-Det	135	E.Collins-Chi	116
E.Collins-Chi	.896	E.Collins-Chi	163	Fournier-Chi	40.9	Speaker-Bos	38.3	Schalk-Chi	128	Crawford-Det	101
J.Jackson-Cle-Chi	.830	Speaker-Bos	152	Speaker-Bos	35.0	Fournier-Chi	38.1	Gardner-Bos	123	Speaker-Bos	97
Speaker-Bos	.827	J.Jackson-Cle-Chi	145	Veach-Det	32.3	Shotton-StL	31.3	S.Collins-Chi	120	Veach-Det	97

Total Average		Stolen Bases		Stolen Base Average		Stolen Base Runs		Fielding Runs		Total Player Rating	
Cobb-Det	1.170	Cobb-Det	96	Schang-Phi	85.7	Maisel-NY	8.1	Boone-NY	20.8	Cobb-Det	6.2
E.Collins-Chi	.971	Maisel-NY	51	Maisel-NY	81.0	Cobb-Det	6.0	T.Walker-StL	14.8	E.Collins-Chi	6.1
Fournier-Chi	.964	E.Collins-Chi	46	Foster-Was	76.9	Schang-Phi	3.6	Vitt-Det	14.4	Speaker-Bos	4.0
Speaker-Bos	.801	Shotton-StL	43	Moeller-Was	76.2	Moeller-Was	3.6	Lajoie-Phi	14.1	Fournier-Chi	3.5
Veach-Det	.771	C.Milan-Was	40	Roth-Chi-Cle	72.2	Williams-StL	2.7	Speaker-Bos	13.4	Chapman-Cle	3.4

Wins		Win Percentage		Games		Complete Games		Shutouts		Saves	
Johnson-Was	27	Wood-Bos	.750	Faber-Chi	50	Johnson-Was	35	Scott-Chi	7	Mays-Bos	7
Scott-Chi	24	Shore-Bos	.704	Coveleski-Det	50	Caldwell-NY	31	Johnson-Was	7		
Faber-Chi	24	Foster-Bos	.704	Scott-Chi	48	Dauss-Det	27	Morton-Cle	6		
Dauss-Det	24	Ruth-Bos	.692	Jones-Cle	48	Scott-Chi	23	Foster-Bos	5		
Coveleski-Det	22	Scott-Chi	.686			Dubuc-Det	22	Dubuc-Det	5		

Innings Pitched		Fewest Hits/Game		Fewest BB/Game		Strikeouts		Strikeouts/Game		Ratio	
Johnson-Was	336.2	Leonard-Bos	6.38	Johnson-Was	1.50	Johnson-Was	203	Leonard-Bos	5.69	Johnson-Was	8.90
Coveleski-Det	312.2	Ruth-Bos	6.86	Ayers-Was	1.62	Faber-Chi	182	Mitchell-Cle	5.68	Morton-Cle	9.41
Dauss-Det	309.2	Wood-Bos	6.86	Benz-Chi	1.62	Wyckoff-Phi	157	Faber-Chi	5.47	Wood-Bos	9.44
Caldwell-NY	305.0	Johnson-Was	6.90	Russell-Chi	1.84	Coveleski-Det	150	Johnson-Was	5.43	Ayers-Was	9.50
Faber-Chi	299.2	Morton-Cle	7.09	Cicotte-Chi	1.93	Mitchell-Cle	149	Lowdermilk-StL-Det	5.32	Benz-Chi	9.63

Earned Run Average		Adjusted ERA		Opponents' Batting Avg.		Opponents' On Base Pct.		Starter Runs		Adjusted Starter Runs	
Wood-Bos	1.49	Johnson-Was	191	Leonard-Bos	.208	Johnson-Was	.260	Johnson-Was	51.7	Johnson-Was	52.9
Johnson-Was	1.55	Wood-Bos	186	Ruth-Bos	.212	Morton-Cle	.268	Shore-Bos	35.5	Shore-Bos	31.1
Shore-Bos	1.64	Shore-Bos	169	Johnson-Was	.214	Wood-Bos	.275	Scott-Chi	29.5	Scott-Chi	30.9
Scott-Chi	2.03	Scott-Chi	146	Morton-Cle	.216	Benz-Chi	.276	Wood-Bos	25.2	Morton-Cle	24.1
Fisher-NY	2.11	Morton-Cle	142	Wood-Bos	.216	Ayers-Was	.276	Foster-Bos	23.2	Benz-Chi	22.7

Clutch Pitching Index		Relief Runs	Adjusted Relief Runs	Relief Ranking	Total Pitcher Index		Total Baseball Ranking	
Hamilton-StL	125				Johnson-Was	7.7	Johnson-Was	7.6
Shore-Bos	122				Wood-Bos	3.6	Cobb-Det	6.2
Foster-Bos	121				Shore-Bos	3.5	E.Collins-Chi	6.1
Fisher-NY	119				Scott-Chi	3.4	Speaker-Bos	4.0
Wood-Bos	118				Dauss-Det	3.2	Wood-Bos	3.6

January 2 The Cardinals try to prevent outfielder Lee Magee, 25, from playing for the Brooklyn Tip-Tops. Like most such suits, it will fail. Magee will play and manage in the Federal League.

January 5 The Federal League sues Organized Baseball, claiming that it is an illegal trust and asking that it be dissolved and all contracts voided. The case is filed in U.S. court in Chicago, before Judge Kenesaw Mountain Landis. He will stall his decision, and peace is declared at the end of the year. The league shifts players to beef up teams in key cities. Benny Kauff, the FL's answer to Ty Cobb, is moved from Indianapolis to Brooklyn.

January 24 In a retreat from the FL competition, the Baltimore Orioles of the International League move to Richmond, VA. With the demise of the FL, the Orioles will return to Baltimore.

April 24 Frank Allen, Pittsburgh lefty, pitches a 2–0 no-hitter against the St. Louis Terriers. Allen will win 23 for Pittsburgh, who will finish third just a half game back of the first-place Chicago Whales and the second-place Terriers.

August 22 Newark takes two from Pittsburgh and leads by one percentage point over Kansas City, with Pittsburgh third and Chicago fourth, only 1½ games separating the teams. The race is so close by season's end Newark will be fifth, six games out. There will be nine 20-game winners, led by George McConnell's 25-10 for the Whales, the only year McConnell wins more than eight games.

September 7 The St. Louis Terriers' Dave Davenport, strikeout leader of the FL, pitches a 3–0 no-hitter over the Whales, one of his 10 shutouts and 22 wins. St. Louis will play two more games than Chicago and split them, thus trailing the Whales at season's end by one percentage point. Chicago will be 86–66; St. Louis, 87–67, and the Pittsburgh Rebels, 86–67. A percentage difference of .004, it is the closest bunching of the top three teams in any major league race.

October 9 FL officials meet secretly with the National Commission at Philadelphia's Bellevue-Stratford Hotel.

October 19 Brookfed owner Robert Ward dies at his New Rochelle, New York mansion. Ward's death increases pressure on the FL to make peace with Organized Baseball.

December 17 Baltimore FL officials unsuccessfully try to buy their way into the major leagues for $250,000. They then try to gain entrance into the IL but fail again.

December 22 Organized Baseball and the Federal League sign a peace treaty at Cincinnati, ending their two-year war. The Feds agree to go out of existence, but the major leagues pay an enormous price: $600,000 for distribution to FL owners; amalgamation of two Fed franchises, one each into NL and AL; recognition of Fed players' eligibility, and agreement to bid for them in a Fed-controlled auction. Baltimore gets short shrift and balks, but conferees, eager for settlement, defer its claims—a decision they will later repent.

BALTIMORE		BROOKLYN		BUFFALO		CHICAGO		KANSAS CITY		NEWARK		PITTSBURGH		ST.LOUIS	
M	O.Knabe	M	L.Magee	M	L.Schlafly	M	J.Tinker	M	G.Stovall	M	B.Phillips	M	R.Oakes	M	F.Jones
1B	H.Swacina	M	J.Ganzel	M	W.Blair	1B	F.Beck	1B	G.Stovall	1B	B.McKechnie	1B	E.Konetchy	1B	B.Borton
2B	O.Knabe	1B	H.Myers	M	H.Lord	2B	R.Zeider	2B	B.Kenworthy	1B	E.Huhn	2B	S.Yerkes	2B	B.Vaughn
SS	M.Doolan	2B	L.Magee	1B	H.Chase	SS	J.Smith	SS	J.Rawlings	2B	F.LaPorte	SS	M.Berghammer	SS	E.Johnson
3B	J.Walsh	SS	Fd.Smith	2B	B.Louden	3B	H.Fritz	SS	G.Perring	SS	J.Esmond	3B	M.Mowrey	3B	C.Deal
LF	V.Duncan	3B	A.Halt	SS	R.Roach	LF	L.Mann	LF	A.Shaw	3B	B.McKechnie	LF	A.Wickland	LF	W.Miller
CF	J.McCandless	LF	C.Cooper	3B	H.Lord	CF	D.Zwilling	CF	C.Chadbourne	LF	A.Scheer	CF	R.Oakes	CF	D.Drake
RF	S.Evans	CF	B.Kauff	CF	C.Engle	RF	M.Flack	RF	G.Gilmore	CF	E.Roush	RF	J.Kelly	RF	J.Tobin
C	F.Owens	RF	G.Anderson	RF	J.Dalton	C	A.Wilson	C	T.Easterly	RF	V.Campbell	C	C.Berry	C	G.Hartley
O	G.Zinn	C	G.Land	2	J.Farrell	C	W.Fischer	O	A.Kruger	C	B.Rariden	2S	J.Lewis	3	A.Kores
1	J.Agler	C	W.Blair	O1	S.Hofman	2	J.Farrell	S2	P.Goodwin	O1	G.Schaefer	C	P.O'Connor	C	H.Chapman
32	E.Kirkpatrick	O	S.Evans	/3	T.Downey	O	C.Hanford	C	D.Brown	1	R.Mills	O	C.Rheam	O	L.Kirby
C	F.Jacklitsch	C	M.Simon	O	T.McDonald	/3	T.Wisterzil	3	B.Bradley	O	G.Whitehouse		H.Bradley	23	A.Bridwell
2	J.Gallagher	1	H.Bradley	C	N.Allen	1	B.Jackson	/C	J.Enzenroth	3	T.Reed	/3	E.Lennox	O	A.Marsans
O	B.Meyer	3	T.Wisterzil	S	F.Smith	S	M.Doolan	P	N.Cullop		L.Strands	O	D.Jones	/3	J.Walsh
S	J.Smith	2	T.Helfrich	O	J.Agler	O	A.Wickland	P	G.Packard	/1	H.Bradley	O	F.Delahanty	/3	T.Wisterzil
2O	H.Simmons	C	H.Smith	/C	A.Watson	1	J.Weiss	P	C.Johnson	/C	G.Textor	S	E.Holly	/O	P.Compton
1	K.Crawford	S	E.Gagnier	/O	D.Young	S	J.Tinker	P	A.Main	/C	L.Pratt	/O	M.Menosky	/O	F.Jones
O	J.Hickman	C	L.Pratt	/2	E.Gagnier	S	A.Hauser	P	P.Henning	/C	B.Warren	/O	J.Savage	/1	J.Tobin
C	H.Russell	/1	A.Griggs	P	A.Schulz	3	C.Pechous	P	D.Adams		E.Reulbach	/C	O.Kerlin	/1	H.Miller
/1	K.Kolseth	2	D.Howard	P	H.Bedient	/C	C.Clemens	/P	C.Blackburn		E.Moseley	P	F.Allen	P	D.Davenport
/3	W.Reinecker	S	M.Reed	P	F.Anderson	P	G.McConnell	/P	J.Gingras		G.Kaiserling	P	E.Knetzer	P	D.Crandall
/2	C.Eakle	/2	J.Delahanty	P	G.Krapp	P	C.Hendrix	/P	B.Harris		H.Moran	P	C.Rogge	P	E.Plank
/C	D.Kerr	/C	A.Watson	P	R.Ford	P	M.Prendergast				C.Falkenberg	P	B.Hearn	P	B.Groom
/C	C.Maisel	/O	F.Kane	RP	R.Marshall	P	M.Brown				T.Seaton	P	C.Barger	P	D.Watson
/3	E.Forsythe	/2	A.Tesch	P	H.Ehmke	P	D.Black				C.Brandom	P	W.Dickson	P	E.Willett
H	C.Miller	/2	D.Murphy	P	E.Lafitte	P	A.Brennan				C.Whitehouse	P	R.Comstock	P	E.Herbert
P	J.Quinn	/C	D.Wright	/P	D.Woodman	P	R.Johnson				G.Mullin	P	G.LaClaire		
P	G.Suggs	/O	F.Chouinard	/P	G.LaClaire	/P	D.Woodman				H.Billiard	/P	H.Camnitz		
P	B.Bailey	P	A.Schulz	/P	B.Smith	/P	H.Rasmussen				F.Trautman	/P	S.Burk		
P	C.Bender	P	H.Finneran									/P	A.Braithwood		
P	R.Johnson	P	D.Marion									/P	J.Miljus		
P	F.Smith	P	T.Seaton												
P	S.Conley	P	J.Bluejacket												
P	G.LaClaire	P	B.Upham												
/P	C.Young	P	E.Lafitte												
/P	D.Black	P	Fk.Smith												
/P	L.Douglas	P	F.Wilson												
/P	T.Vereker	P	M.Walker												
/P	K.Wilhelm	P	H.Wiltse												
		/P	C.Falkenberg												
		/P	B.Herring												

TEAM	G	W	L	PCT	GB	R	OR	AB	H	2B	3B	HR	BB	SO	AVG	OBP	SLG	PRO	PRO+	BR	/A	PF	CHI	RC	SB	CS	SBA	SBR
CHI	155	86	66	.566		640	538	5133	1320	185	77	**50**	444	590	.257	.320	.352	.672	101	-110	-81	94	102	650	161			
STL	159	87	67	.565	0.5	634	527	5145	1344	199	**81**	23	576	**502**	.261	**.340**	.345	.685	94	-71	-100	105	92	698	195			
PIT	156	86	67	.562	0.5	592	**524**	5040	1318	180	80	20	448	561	.262	.326	.341	.667	94	-110	-106	99	95	655	224			
KC	153	81	72	.529	5.5	547	551	4937	1206	200	66	28	368	503	.244	.303	.329	.632	87	-182	-166	96	**103**	559	144			
NEW	155	80	72	.526	6	585	562	5097	1283	**210**	80	17	438	550	.252	.315	.334	.649	93	-148	-122	94	99	618	184			
BUF	153	74	78	.487	12	574	634	5065	1261	193	68	40	420	587	.249	.309	.334	.647	85	-158	-167	102	102	594	184			
BRO	153	70	82	.461	16	**647**	673	5035	**1348**	205	75	36	473	654	**.268**	.336	**.360**	**.696**	103	-56	-52	99	97	**704**	249			
BAL	154	47	107	.305	40	550	760	5060	1235	196	53	36	470	641	.244	.313	.325	.638	82	-167	-180	103	97	578	128			
TOT	619					4769		40512	10315	1568	580	250	3637	4588	.255	.316	.340	.656						1469				

TEAM	CG	SH	SV	IP	H	H/G	HR	BB	SO	RAT	ERA	ERA+	OAV	OOB	PR	/A	PF	CPI	FA	E	DP	FW	PW	BW	SBW	DIF
CHI	97	21	10	1397²	1232	**7.9**	33	402	576	**10.7**	2.64	95	**.240**	**.299**	14	-21	92	95	.964	233	102	.4	-2.3	-8.7		20.6
STL	94	**24**	9	1426	1267	8.0	22	396	**698**	**10.7**	2.73	**105**	.243	.300	-1	**22**	105	92	**.967**	212	111	2.0	**2.4**	-10.8		16.4
PIT	88	16	12	1382¹	1273	8.3	37	441	517	11.4	2.79	97	.253	.317	-10	-13	99	107	**.971**	**182**	98	**3.5**	-1.4	-11.4		18.8
KC	95	16	11	1359	**1210**	8.0	29	**390**	526	10.8	2.82	93	.242	.301	-14	-30	96	91	.962	246	96	-.5	-3.2	-17.9		26.1
NEW	**100**	16	7	1406²	1308	8.4	**15**	453	581	11.6	**2.60**	98	.253	.319	**19**	-7	94	**111**	.963	239	124	.0	-.8	-13.1		17.8
BUF	79	14	11	1360	1271	8.4	35	553	594	12.3	3.38	83	.254	.331	-99	-88	103	95	.964	232	112	.3	-9.5	-18.0		25.2
BRO	78	10	**16**	1355²	1299	8.6	27	536	467	12.3	3.37	81	.258	.332	-96	-98	100	97	.955	290	103	-3.1	-10.5	-5.6		13.3
BAL	85	5	7	1360¹	1455	9.6	52	466	570	13.0	3.96	72	.284	.349	-186	-165	105	100	.957	273	**140**	-2.0	-17.8	-19.4		9.2
TOT	716	122	83	11047²		8.4				11.6	3.03		.255	.316					.963	1907	886					

Runs
Borton-StL	97
Berghammer-Pit	96
Evans-Bro-Bal	94
Tobin-StL	92
Kauff-Bro	92

Hits
Tobin-StL	184
Konetchy-Pit	181
Evans-Bro-Bal	171
Kauff-Bro	165
Chase-Buf	165

Doubles
Evans-Bro-Bal	34
Zwilling-Chi	32
Konetchy-Pit	31
Chase-Buf	31

Triples
Mann-Chi	19
Konetchy-Pit	18
Kelly-Pit	17
Gilmore-KC	15

Home Runs
Chase-Buf	17
Zwilling-Chi	13
Kauff-Bro	12
Konetchy-Pit	10
Walsh-Bal-StL	9

Total Bases
Konetchy-Pit	278
Chase-Buf	267
Tobin-StL	254
Kauff-Bro	246
Zwilling-Chi	242

Runs Batted In
Zwilling-Chi	94
Konetchy-Pit	93
Chase-Buf	89
Kauff-Bro	83
Borton-StL	83

Runs Produced
Borton-StL	177
Kauff-Bro	163
Konetchy-Pit	162
Evans-Bro-Bal	157
Chase-Buf	157

Bases On Balls
Borton-StL	92
Kauff-Bro	85
Berghammer-Pit	83
W.Miller-StL	79

Batting Average
Kauff-Bro	.342
Fischer-Chi	.329
Magee-Bro	.323
Konetchy-Pit	.314
Flack-Chi	.314

On Base Percentage
Kauff-Bro	.446
W.Miller-StL	.400
Borton-StL	.395
Evans-Bro-Bal	.392
Cooper-Bro	.388

Slugging Average
Kauff-Bro	.509
Konetchy-Pit	.483
Chase-Buf	.471
Fischer-Chi	.449
Zwilling-Chi	.442

Production
Kauff-Bro	.955
Konetchy-Pit	.846
Evans-Bro-Bal	.818
Zwilling-Chi	.808
Mann-Chi	.795

Adjusted Production
Kauff-Bro	170
Konetchy-Pit	138
Zwilling-Chi	135
Mann-Chi	131
Flack-Chi	129

Batter Runs
Kauff-Bro	41.3
Konetchy-Pit	17.5
Wilson-Chi	17.5
Evans-Bro-Bal	16.3
Crandall-StL	13.9

Adjusted Batter Runs
Kauff-Bro	42.1
Wilson-Chi	20.7
Konetchy-Pit	18.3
Zwilling-Chi	16.0
Evans-Bro-Bal	15.1

Clutch Hitting Index
Oakes-Pit	152
Engle-Buf	129
F.Smith-Buf-Bro	123
Borton-StL	122
Halt-Bro	118

Runs Created
Kauff-Bro	132
Konetchy-Pit	111
Tobin-StL	106
Zwilling-Chi	99
Evans-Bro-Bal	99

Total Average
Kauff-Bro	1.233
Konetchy-Pit	.884
Cooper-Bro	.868
W.Miller-StL	.863
Zwilling-Chi	.857

Stolen Bases
Kauff-Bro	55
Mowrey-Pit	40
Kelly-Pit	38
Flack-Chi	37
Magee-Bro	34

Stolen Base Average

Stolen Base Runs

Fielding Runs
Doolan-Bal-Chi	33.0
Rariden-New	23.0
Cooper-Bro	18.3
Johnson-StL	17.7
Perring-KC	14.8

Total Player Rating
Kauff-Bro	5.3
Rariden-New	3.8
Cooper-Bro	2.4
Wilson-Chi	2.0
Zwilling-Chi	1.8

Wins
McConnell-Chi	25
Allen-Pit	23
Davenport-StL	22
Cullop-KC	22

Win Percentage
McConnell-Chi	.714
Brown-Chi	.680
Reulbach-New	.677
Cullop-KC	.667
Plank-StL	.656

Games
Davenport-StL	55
Bedient-Buf	53
Crandall-StL	51
Johnson-KC	46

Complete Games
Davenport-StL	30
Hendrix-Chi	26
Schulz-Buf	25
Allen-Pit	24

Shutouts
Davenport-StL	10
Plank-StL	6
Allen-Pit	6

Saves
Bedient-Buf	10
Barger-Pit	6
Wiltse-Bro	5
Upham-Bro	5

Innings Pitched
Davenport-StL	392.2
Crandall-StL	312.2
Schulz-Buf	309.2
McConnell-Chi	303.0
Cullop-KC	302.1

Fewest Hits/Game
Davenport-StL	6.88
Main-KC	7.08
Plank-StL	7.11
Brown-Chi	7.20
Anderson-Buf	7.20

Fewest BB/Game
Plank-StL	1.81
Bender-Bal	1.87
Hearn-Pit	1.90
Cullop-KC	1.99
Quinn-Bal	2.07

Strikeouts
Davenport-StL	229
Schulz-Buf	160
McConnell-Chi	151
Plank-StL	147

Strikeouts/Game
Anderson-Buf	5.33
Davenport-StL	5.25
Plank-StL	4.93
Bailey-Bal-Chi	4.91
Groom-StL	4.78

Ratio
Plank-StL	9.02
Davenport-StL	9.19
Brown-Chi	9.90
Anderson-Buf	10.01
Reulbach-New	10.17

Earned Run Average
Moseley-New	1.91
Plank-StL	2.08
Brown-Chi	2.09
McConnell-Chi	2.20
Davenport-StL	2.20

Adjusted ERA
Plank-StL	138
Moseley-New	134
Davenport-StL	131
Brown-Chi	120
Reulbach-New	115

Opponents' Batting Avg.
Davenport-StL	.215
Plank-StL	.218
Brown-Chi	.220
Main-KC	.222
Anderson-Buf	.222

Opponents' On Base Pct.
Plank-StL	.262
Davenport-StL	.268
Brown-Chi	.279
Anderson-Buf	.285
Reulbach-New	.287

Starter Runs
Moseley-New	24.2
Davenport-StL	23.0
Plank-StL	19.3
McConnell-Chi	17.8
Brown-Chi	16.6

Adjusted Starter Runs
Davenport-StL	29.5
Plank-StL	23.7
Moseley-New	19.2
Brown-Chi	10.9
McConnell-Chi	10.5

Clutch Pitching Index
Moran-New	129
Kaiserling-New	127
Rogge-Pit	127
Moseley-New	122
Suggs-Bal	117

Relief Runs

Adjusted Relief Runs

Relief Ranking

Total Pitcher Index
Plank-StL	2.9
Crandall-StL	2.6
McConnell-Chi	2.0
Brown-Chi	2.0
Moseley-New	1.3

Total Baseball Ranking
Kauff-Bro	5.3
Rariden-New	3.8
Plank-StL	2.9
Crandall-StL	2.6
Cooper-Bro	2.4

January 5 Happy to be rid of fractious Cubs owner Charles W. Murphy, the NL allows Charles H. Weeghman, president of the Federal League Chicago Whales, to buy the Cubs for $500,000. The Cubs will play in the FL's recently-built stadium, which will later become known as Wrigley Field.

January 8 Profiting handsomely on his 1913 investment of $187,000, owner James E. Gaffney sells his Boston Braves for $500,000 to Harvard's famous football coach, Percy Haughton, and a banking associate.

January 17 John McGraw's Giants buy the Feds' top star, Benny Kauff, from the Tip-Tops; their best catcher, Bill Rariden, from the Newark Peps; and spitballer Fred Anderson, from the Buffalo Buffeds (aka the Blues), for about $65,000.

February 7 The Federal League's year-old suit charging antitrust violations by Organized Baseball is dismissed by mutual consent in U.S. District Court in Chicago by Judge Kenesaw M. Landis.

February 8 The NL votes down a proposal by Charlie Ebbets of Brooklyn to limit the number of 25-cent seats clubs can sell to 2,000. Boston has 10,000 such seats; St. Louis, 9,000, Philadelphia, 6,500, and Cincinnati, 4,000.

March 3* Jack Dunn, owner of the IL Orioles, buys the park built by the FL Baltimore Terrapins.

April 29 Innovative owner Charles Weeghman allows Cub fans to keep balls hit into stands.

May 14 The Cardinals' rookie Rogers Hornsby hits his first homer. It is inside the park against the Brooklyn Dodgers at spacious Robison Field in St. Louis.

July 1 At age 42 years and four months, Honus Wagner is the oldest player to hit an inside-the-park home run. He connects for the Pirates in the fourth inning at Cincinnati.

September 4 To help draw a crowd, and because of their longtime rivalry, Christy Mathewson and Three Finger Brown close out their careers in the same game. Matty, now the manager of the Reds, wins 10-8 in his only game not pitched in a Giants uniform. Mathewson and Brown have dueled 25 times since 1903, with Brown, now back with the Cubs, winning 12 and losing 10; Matty was 12-13.

September 7 The Giants beat Brooklyn's Nap Rucker, 4-1, to launch New York's record 26-game winning streak.

October 10 Charles Ebbets becomes the first owner to raise the price of World Series grandstand seats to $5—up from $3.

October 16 Ebbets rewards manager Wilbert Robinson with a $5,000 bonus even though the Dodgers lost the Series.

December 2 Under pressure from the Players' Fraternity, the National Commission orders that injured players shall get full pay for the duration of their contracts. The injury clause previously let clubs suspend players after 15 days pay.

	BOSTON		BROOKLYN		CHICAGO		CINCINNATI		NEW YORK		PHILADELPHIA		PITTSBURGH		ST.LOUIS
M	G.Stallings	M	W.Robinson	M	J.Tinker	M	B.Herzog	M	J.McGraw	M	P.Moran	M	J.Callahan	M	M.Huggins
1B	E.Konetchy	1B	J.Daubert	M	V.Saier	M	I.Wingo	1B	F.Merkle	1B	F.Luderus	1B	D.Johnston	1B	D.Miller
2B	J.Evers	2B	G.Cutshaw	2B	O.Knabe	M	C.Mathewson	2B	L.Doyle	2B	B.Niehoff	2B	J.Farmer	2B	B.Betzel
SS	R.Maranville	SS	I.Olson	SS	C.Wortman	1B	H.Chase	SS	A.Fletcher	SS	D.Bancroft	SS	H.Wagner	SS	R.Corhan
3B	R.Smith	3B	M.Mowrey	3B	H.Zimmerman	2B	B.Louden	3B	B.McKechnie	3B	M.Stock	3B	D.Baird	3B	R.Hornsby
LF	S.Magee	LF	Z.Wheat	LF	L.Mann	SS	B.Herzog	LF	G.Burns	LF	P.Whitted	LF	F.Schulte	LF	B.Bescher
CF	F.Snodgrass	CF	H.Myers	CF	C.Williams	3B	H.Groh	CF	B.Kauff	CF	D.Paskert	CF	M.Carey	CF	J.Smith
RF	J.Wilhoit	RF	C.Stengel	RF	M.Flack	LF	G.Neale	RF	D.Robertson	RF	G.Cravath	RF	B.Hinchman	RF	C.Wilson
C	H.Gowdy	C	C.Meyers	C	J.Archer	CF	E.Roush	C	B.Rariden	C	B.Killefer	C	W.Schmidt	C	M.Gonzalez
						RF	T.Griffith								
O	Z.Collins	O	J.Johnston	32	R.Zeider	C	I.Wingo	23	B.Herzog	C	E.Burns	23	J.Schultz	O	T.Long
2S	D.Egan	C	O.Miller	O	F.Schulte			3	H.Zimmerman	3	B.Byrne	3	H.Warner	C1	F.Snyder
2O	E.Fitzpatrick	S	O.O'Mara	S	E.Mulligan	O	R.Killefer	1	W.Holke	O	W.Good	2O	C.Bigbee	3	Z.Beck
C	E.Blackburn	C1	L.McCarty	C	W.Fischer	1	F.Mollwitz	1O	G.Kelly	C	C.Cooper	O	D.Costello	O	A.Butler
O	J.Connolly	3	G.Getz	O	J.Kelly	C	T.Clarke	3	H.Lobert	2	O.Dugey	S	A.McCarthy	S	S.Bohne
O	P.Compton	1	F.Merkle	2	S.Yerkes	S	B.Fisher	O	E.Roush	C	B.Adams	O	E.Barney	C	T.Brottem
C	W.Tragesser	/O	J.Hickman	O	A.Wilson	3	B.McKechnie	C	L.McCarty	/O	B.Weiser	23	J.Viox	/2	S.Stewart
O	L.Chappell	/2	R.Smyth	2	A.McCarthy	C1	E.Huhn	O	B.Kocher	/O	B.Gandy	O	A.Wilson	/2	M.Huggins
/O	F.Bailey	/S	J.Kelleher	1	F.Mollwitz	S	F.Emmer	S	M.Doolan	/O	B.Maharg	C	W.Fischer	/O	W.Cruise
/C	A.Rico	/O	H.Miller	S	M.Doolan	O	P.Smith	/3	H.Hunter	H	B.Tincup	P	J.Smith	
/2	J.Mathes	/S	B.Fabrique	3	C.Pechous	S	L.Kopf	O	R.Dooin			2	O.Knabe	P	L.Meadows
		/O	A.Nixon	C	R.Elliott	O	K.Williams	/3	F.Brainerd	P	P.Alexander	C	G.Gibson	P	R.Ames
P	D.Rudolph	/C	M.Wheat	O	D.Zwilling	/O	J.Beall	H	L.Wendell	P	E.Rixey	O	R.O'Brien	P	B.Doak
P	L.Tyler	/C	A.Dede	/2	L.Doyle	/S	B.Hobbs	H	R.Killefer	P	A.Demaree	C	B.Wagner	P	B.Steele
P	P.Ragan			/O	E.Smith	/O	G.Twombly	H	H.Stafford	P	E.Mayer	/O	L.King	P	H.Jasper
P	J.Barnes	P	J.Pfeffer	/C	N.Allen	/S	B.Rodgers	/C	D.Kelleher	P	C.Bender	/O	P.Compton	RP	S.Williams
P	T.Hughes	P	L.Cheney	P	S.Hofman	R	J.Rodriguez	RP	G.McQuillan	/O	J.Altenburg		
		P	S.Smith	/C	C.Clemens	P	F.Toney					/S	F.Smykal	P	M.Watson
P	A.Nehf	P	R.Marquard	P	M.Jacobson	P	P.Schneider	P	J.Tesreau	P	G.Chalmers	/S	I.McAuley	P	S.Sallee
P	F.Allen	P	J.Coombs	/S	J.Tinker	P	A.Schulz	P	P.Perritt	P	J.Oeschger	/2	P.Siglin	P	C.Hall
P	E.Reulbach			/3	C.Deal	P	C.Mitchell	P	R.Benton	/P	G.Fortune	/2	B.Gleason	P	J.Lotz
/P	E.Knetzer	P	W.Dell	/S	M.Shay	P	E.Knetzer	P	F.Anderson	/P	S.Baumgartner	H	W.Fisher	/P	M.Currie
		P	E.Appleton	/3	H.Hunter			P	F.Schupp	/P	E.Kantlehner	/1	N.Halliday	/P	D.Griner
		/P	N.Rucker	H	E.Sicking	P	E.Moseley					H	G.Madden	/P	C.Warmoth
		P	D.Mails	/C	J.O'Connor	P	G.Dale	P	S.Sallee			H	B.Batsch	
		/P	L.Cadore	/C	B.O'Farrell	/P	L.McKenry	P	C.Mathewson					
						/P	C.Mathewson	P	S.Stroud			P	A.Mamaux	
				P	H.Vaughn	/P	J.Bluejacket	P	R.Schauer			P	W.Cooper	
				P	C.Hendrix	/P	T.Twining	/P	G.Smith			P	F.Miller	
				P	J.Lavender			/P	E.Palmero			P	B.Harmon	
				P	G.McConnell			/P	H.Ritter			P	E.Kantlehner	
				P	G.Packard									
												P	E.Jacobs	
				P	M.Prendergast							P	B.Adams	
				P	T.Seaton							P	B.Evans	
				P	M.Brown							/P	B.Grimes	
				/P	P.Carter							/P	P.Carpenter	
				/P	S.Perry							/P	C.Hill	
				/P	G.Pearce							/P	J.Scott	

TEAM	G	W	L	PCT	GB	R	OR	AB	H	2B	3B	HR	BB	SO	AVG	OBP	SLG	PRO	PRO+	BR	/A	PF	CHI	RC	SB	CS	SBA	SBR
BRO	156	94	60	.610		585	471	5234	1366	195	80	28	355	550	.261	.313	.345	.658	105	46	30	103	99	645	187			
PHI	154	91	62	.595	2.5	581	489	4985	1244	223	53	42	399	571	.250	.310	.341	.651	102	34	14	104	104	593	149			
BOS	158	89	63	.586	4	542	453	5075	1181	166	73	22	437	646	.233	.299	.307	.606	96	-38	-16	96	108	535	141			
NY	155	86	66	.566	7	597	504	5152	1305	188	74	42	356	558	.253	.307	.343	.650	112	31	61	95	106	617	206			
CHI	156	67	86	.438	26.5	520	541	5179	1237	194	56	46	399	662	.239	.298	.325	.623	88	-18	-74	111	99	559	133			
PIT	157	65	89	.422	29	484	586	5181	1246	147	91	20	372	618	.240	.298	.316	.614	94	-32	-37	101	95	556	173			
STL	153	60	93	.392	33.5	476	629	5030	1223	155	74	25	335	651	.243	.295	.318	.613	95	-35	-32	99	99	535	182			
CIN	155	60	93	.392	33.5	505	617	5254	1336	187	88	14	362	573	.254	.307	.331	.638	105	13	26	98	91	596	157			
TOT	622					4290		41090	10138	1455	589	239	3015	4829	.247	.303	.328	.632						1328				

TEAM	CG	SH	SV	IP	H	H/G	HR	BB	SO	RAT	ERA	ERA+	OAV	OOB	PR	/A	PF	CPI	FA	E	DP	FW	PW	BW	SBW	DIF
BRO	96	22	9	1427¹	1201	7.6	24	372	634	10.2	2.12	126	.232	.289	78	86	102	103	.965	224	90	1.2	9.8	3.4		2.5
PHI	97	25	9	1382¹	1238	8.1	28	295	601	10.3	2.36	112	.244	.292	39	44	101	101	.963	234	119	.4	5.0	1.6		7.5
BOS	97	23	11	1415²	1206	7.7	24	325	644	9.9	2.19	113	.235	.285	66	45	95	99	.967	212	124	2.1	5.1	-1.8		7.5
NY	88	22	12	1397¹	1267	8.2	41	310	638	10.4	2.60	93	.245	.293	2	-28	93	95	.966	217	108	1.5	-3.2	7.0		4.7
CHI	72	17	13	1416²	1265	8.0	32	365	616	10.6	2.65	110	.244	.298	-6	39	111	94	.957	286	104	-2.6	4.5	-8.5		-2.9
PIT	88	11	7	1419²	1277	8.1	24	443	596	11.1	2.76	97	.247	.311	-24	-14	103	97	.959	260	97	-.9	-1.6	-4.2		-5.3
STL	58	13	15	1355	1331	8.8	31	445	529	12.1	3.14	84	.265	.330	-80	-77	101	104	.957	278	124	-2.4	-8.8	-3.7		-1.7
CIN	86	7	6	1408	1356	8.7	35	461	569	11.9	3.10	84	.261	.326	-76	-82	99	102	.965	228	126	.9	-9.4	3.0		-11.0
TOT	682	140	82	11222		8.1				10.8	2.61		.247	.303					.963	1939	892					

Runs		Hits		Doubles		Triples		Home Runs		Total Bases	
Burns-NY	105	Chase-Cin	184	Niehoff-Phi	42	Hinchman-Pit	16	Williams-Chi	12	Z.Wheat-Bro	262
Carey-Pit	90	Robertson-NY	180	Z.Wheat-Bro	32	Roush-NY-Cin	15	Robertson-NY	12	Robertson-NY	250
Robertson-NY	88	Z.Wheat-Bro	177	Paskert-Phi	30	Kauff-NY	15	Cravath-Phi	11	Chase-Cin	249
Groh-Cin	85	Hinchman-Pit	175			Hornsby-StL	15	Z.Wheat-Bro	9	Hinchman-Pit	237
Paskert-Phi	82	Burns-NY	174					Kauff-NY	9	Burns-NY	229

Runs Batted In		Runs Produced		Bases On Balls		Batting Average		On Base Percentage		Slugging Average	
Zimmerman-Chi-NY	83	Zimmerman-Chi-NY	153	Groh-Cin	84	Chase-Cin	.339	Cravath-Phi	.379	Z.Wheat-Bro	.461
Chase-Cin	82	Robertson-NY	145	Saier-Chi	79	Daubert-Bro	.316	Hinchman-Pit	.378	Chase-Cin	.459
Hinchman-Pit	76	Chase-Cin	144	Bancroft-Phi	74	Hinchman-Pit	.315	Williams-Chi	.372	Williams-Chi	.459
Kauff-NY	74	Konetchy-Bos	143	Kauff-NY	68	Hornsby-StL	.313	Daubert-Bro	.371	Hornsby-StL	.444
Z.Wheat-Bro	73	Burns-NY	141	Cravath-Phi	64	Z.Wheat-Bro	.312	Groh-Cin	.370	Cravath-Phi	.440

Production		Adjusted Production		Batter Runs		Adjusted Batter Runs		Clutch Hitting Index		Runs Created	
Williams-Chi	.831	Chase-Cin	155	Z.Wheat-Bro	34.5	Chase-Cin	32.2	Mowrey-Bro	145	Z.Wheat-Bro	103
Z.Wheat-Bro	.828	Hornsby-StL	150	Hinchman-Pit	31.1	Z.Wheat-Bro	32.0	Zimmerman-Chi-NY	134	Hinchman-Pit	96
Chase-Cin	.822	Z.Wheat-Bro	149	Chase-Cin	30.2	Hinchman-Pit	30.3	Magee-Bos	133	Chase-Cin	93
Cravath-Phi	.819	Cravath-Phi	146	Cravath-Phi	28.7	Hornsby-StL	28.7	Smith-Bos	121	Hornsby-StL	88
Hornsby-StL	.814	Hinchman-Pit	146	Hornsby-StL	28.2	Cravath-Phi	25.9	Fletcher-NY	119	Carey-Pit	87

Total Average		Stolen Bases		Stolen Base Average		Stolen Base Runs		Fielding Runs		Total Player Rating	
Williams-Chi	.863	Carey-Pit	63	Carey-Pit	76.8	Carey-Pit	7.5	Carey-Pit	29.9	Groh-Cin	5.4
Cravath-Phi	.857	Kauff-NY	40	Bescher-StL	76.5	Bescher-StL	4.5	Betzel-StL	28.4	Carey-Pit	4.7
Z.Wheat-Bro	.844	Bescher-StL	39	Daubert-Bro	75.0	Daubert-Bro	2.1	Bancroft-Phi	24.5	Fletcher-NY	4.3
Hornsby-StL	.826	Burns-NY	37	Maranville-Bos	68.1	Maranville-Bos	6	Maranville-Bos	21.5	Doyle-NY-Chi	4.2
Hinchman-Pit	.797	Herzog-Cin-NY	34	Chase-Cin	66.7			Doyle-NY-Chi	20.0	Z.Wheat-Bro	3.7

Wins		Win Percentage		Games		Complete Games		Shutouts		Saves	
Alexander-Phi	33	Hughes-Bos	.842	Meadows-StL	51	Alexander-Phi	38	Alexander-Phi	16	Ames-StL	8
Pfeffer-Bro	25	Alexander-Phi	.733	Alexander-Phi	48	Pfeffer-Bro	30	Tyler-Bos	6	Packard-Chi	5
Rixey-Phi	22	Pfeffer-Bro	.694	Mamaux-Pit	45	Rudolph-Bos	27	Pfeffer-Bro	6	Marquard-Bro	5
Mamaux-Pit	21	Rixey-Phi	.688	Ames-StL	45	Mamaux-Pit	26			Hughes-Bos	5
		Benton-NY	.667			Demaree-Phi	25				

Innings Pitched		Fewest Hits/Game		Fewest BB/Game		Strikeouts		Strikeouts/Game		Ratio	
Alexander-Phi	389.0	Cheney-Bro	6.33	Rudolph-Bos	1.10	Alexander-Phi	167	Cheney-Bro	5.91	Rudolph-Bos	8.86
Pfeffer-Bro	328.2	Hughes-Bos	6.76	Alexander-Phi	1.16	Cheney-Bro	166	Hughes-Bos	5.42	Alexander-Phi	8.86
Rudolph-Bos	312.0	Cooper-Pit	6.91	Demaree-Phi	1.52	Mamaux-Pit	163	Hendrix-Chi	4.83	Marquard-Bro	9.09
Mamaux-Pit	310.0	Miller-Pit	7.02	Sallee-StL-NY	1.63	Toney-Cin	146	Mamaux-Pit	4.73	McConnell-Chi	9.30
Toney-Cin	300.0	Ragan-Bos	7.07	Marquard-Bro	1.67	Vaughn-Chi	144	Marquard-Bro	4.70	Ragan-Bos	9.40

Earned Run Average		Adjusted ERA		Opponents' Batting Avg.		Opponents' On Base Pct.		Starter Runs		Adjusted Starter Runs	
Alexander-Phi	1.55	Alexander-Phi	171	Cheney-Bro	.198	Rudolph-Bos	.261	Alexander-Phi	45.9	Alexander-Phi	47.4
Marquard-Bro	1.58	Marquard-Bro	169	Cooper-Pit	.215	Alexander-Phi	.262	Schupp-NY	26.7	Pfeffer-Bro	27.7
Rixey-Phi	1.85	Cooper-Pit	144	Hughes-Bos	.215	Marquard-Bro	.267	Pfeffer-Bro	25.4	Rixey-Phi	25.4
Cooper-Pit	1.87	Rixey-Phi	143	Ragan-Bos	.218	Ragan-Bos	.270	Rixey-Phi	24.3	Marquard-Bro	24.9
Pfeffer-Bro	1.92	Pfeffer-Bro	140	McConnell-Chi	.223	McConnell-Chi	.271	Marquard-Bro	23.5	Schupp-NY	23.8

Clutch Pitching Index		Relief Runs	Adjusted Relief Runs	Relief Ranking	Total Pitcher Index		Total Baseball Ranking	
Dell-Bro	124				Alexander-Phi	7.3	Alexander-Phi	7.3
Sallee-StL-NY	117				Pfeffer-Bro	3.6	Groh-Cin	5.4
Meadows-StL	116				Rixey-Phi	3.2	Carey-Pit	4.7
Schulz-Cin	114				Tyler-Bos	2.5	Fletcher-NY	4.3
Alexander-Phi	114				Cheney-Bro	2.3	Doyle-NY-Chi	4.2

January 4 The St. Louis Browns are the first of two major league franchises awarded to Federal League owners. Philip de Catesby Ball, ice manufacturing tycoon and principal stockholder of the Feds' St. Louis Terriers, pays a reported $525,000 for the Browns.

January 14 Lee Magee, player-manager of the Brooklyn Tip-Tops, is sold to the Yankees for about $25,000, and becomes the first Federal Leaguer welcomed back to Organized Baseball.

February 15 The Yankees buy Frank "Home Run" Baker from the Athletics for $37,500. He sat out the 1915 season.

April 12 On Opening Day, young Babe Ruth goes 8⅓ innings for a 2–1 win over the Athletics at Boston. A poor throw by Charlie Pick, A's third baseman, is the first of his 42 errors. This contributes to his overall .899 fielding average, a mark that Butch Hobson would equal in 1978.

April 15 White Sox catcher Ray Schalk steals twice against Detroit en route to a season total of 30, a record for catchers until 1982 when John Wathan swipes 36.

June 20 Tilly Walker's homer over the left field wall is the only homer the Red Sox will hit at Fenway this season. Boston shortstop Everett Scott starts a string of 1,307 consecutive games, all played at shortstop. He will complete the streak as a Yankee.

June 26 Cleveland players wear numbers on their sleeves in a game with the White Sox, marking the first time players are identified by numbers corresponding to those on the scorecard.

July 4 Joe Jackson goes 3-for-5 against the Athletics. In 30 games since May 31, he has gone 55-for-104, a .524 BA.

September 8 Switch hitter Wally Schang of the A's hits homers from both sides of the plate against the Yankees. Only a handful of people see the rare feat on a rainy day.

September 24 Marty Kavanaugh, Indians utility man, hits the AL's first pinch-hit grand slam for Cleveland in a 5-3 win over the Red Sox. The ball rolls through a hole in the fence and cannot be retrieved in time for a play at the plate.

September 26 Washington manager Griffith excuses several regulars for the remaining games of the season so he can use some new players. Included is Walter Johnson, who has already won 25 games for the seventh-place club. In a league-leading 371 innings pitched, he did not give up a home run, an all-time record.

October 7 Despite a four-run Brooklyn rally in the ninth, the Red Sox defeat Rube Marquard 6-5 to win Game 1 of the World Series at Braves Field. Ernie Shore gets the win, Carl Mays earns a save, and the Sox turn four double plays.

October 9 Babe Ruth outpitches Sherry Smith to win Game 2 of the World Series 2-1 in the 14th inning. This is the start of 29⅔ scoreless World Series innings pitched by Ruth.

October 12 Boston's 4-1 win in Game 5 ends the Series. The Red Sox players earn $3,826; The Dodgers get $2,834 per man.

November 1 Harry H. Frazee, New York theater owner and producer, buys the Red Sox for $675,000.

	BOSTON		CHICAGO		CLEVELAND		DETROIT		NEW YORK		PHILADELPHIA		ST.LOUIS		WASHINGTON
M	B.Carrigan	M	P.Rowland	M	L.Fohl	M	H.Jennings	M	B.Donovan	M	C.Mack	M	F.Jones	M	C.Griffith
1B	D.Hoblitzel	1B	J.Fournier	1B	C.Gandil	1B	G.Burns	1B	W.Pipp	1B	S.McInnis	1B	G.Sisler	1B	J.Judge
2B	J.Barry	2B	E.Collins	2B	I.Howard	2B	R.Young	2B	J.Gedeon	2B	N.Lajoie	2B	D.Pratt	2B	R.Morgan
SS	E.Scott	SS	Z.Terry	SS	B.Wambsganss	SS	D.Bush	SS	R.Peckinpaugh	SS	W.Witt	SS	D.Lavan	SS	G.McBride
3B	L.Gardner	3B	B.Weaver	3B	T.Turner	3B	O.Vitt	3B	F.Baker	3B	C.Pick	3B	J.Austin	3B	E.Foster
LF	D.Lewis	LF	J.Jackson	LF	J.Graney	LF	B.Veach	LF	H.High	LF	W.Schang	LF	B.Shotton	LF	H.Shanks
CF	T.Walker	CF	H.Felsch	CF	T.Speaker	CF	T.Cobb	CF	L.Magee	CF	A.Strunk	CF	A.Marsans	CF	C.Milan
RF	H.Hooper	RF	S.Collins	RF	B.Roth	RF	S.Crawford	RF	F.Gilhooley	RF	J.Walsh	RF	W.Miller	RF	D.Moeller
C	P.Thomas	C	R.Schalk	C	S.O'Neill	C	O.Stanage	C	L.Nunamaker	C	B.Meyer	C	H.Severeid	C	J.Henry
S2	H.Janvrin	1	J.Ness	S3	R.Chapman	O1	H.Heilmann	O3	P.Baumann	3	L.McElwee	S3	E.Johnson	1C	R.Williams
C	H.Cady	3	F.McMullin	C	E.Smith	C	D.Baker	O	R.Walters	O	R.Oldring	C	G.Hartley	O	S.Rice
1	D.Gainer	O	E.Murphy	3	J.Evans	O	M.Kavanagh	O3	F.Maisel	OS	L.King	O	J.Tobin	3	J.Leonard
23	M.McNally	C	J.Lapp	C	T.Daly	C	R.McKee	O	R.Oldring	2	O.Lawry	1	B.Borton	O	E.Smith
O	C.Shorten	O	N.Leibold	3	W.Barbare	O	G.Harper	C	E.Miller	C	V.Picinich	3	C.Deal	O	H.Rondeau
O	O.Henriksen	3	F.Von Kolnitz	/2	M.Kavanagh	O	T.Spencer	21	C.Mullen	O	R.Haley	/C	W.Rumler	O	C.Jamieson
C	S.Agnew	C	B.Lynn	C	H.DeBerry	/S	B.Dyer	3S	L.Boone	2	R.Grover	C	H.Chapman	C	E.Ainsmith
C	B.Carrigan	/S	C.Wright	C	J.Billings	/O	J.Dalton	C	W.Alexander	O	B.Stellbauer	/3	B.Wallace	C1	P.Gharrity
/O	J.Walsh	/1	Z.Hasbrook	/O	D.Moeller	/2	F.Fuller	O	R.Hartzell	O	J.Brown	O	B.Lee	/O	M.Menosky
/3	H.Wagner	/1	G.Moriarty	C	B.Coleman	/3	B.Ellison	O	T.Hendryx	/O	R.Mitterling	/C	V.Clemons	O	T.Barber
H	R.Haley	H	T.Jourdan	/3	C.Engle	/3	G.Maisel	/O	S.Hofman	/3	H.Rowe	H	G.Paulette	/2	C.Sawyer
		H	J.Fautsch	/1	L.Guisto	/C	B.Sullivan	/3	A.Aragon	/O	R.Lanning	/C	G.Hale	/O	M.Acosta
		R	R.Shook	/O	M.Allison			/O	D.Cook	/O	B.Thrasher	H	R.Kennedy		
P	B.Ruth			/2	A.Bergman	P	H.Coveleski	/O	G.Schaefer	C	M.Murphy			P	W.Johnson
P	D.Leonard			/O	H.Lohr	P	H.Dauss			/3	T.Healy	P	D.Davenport	P	B.Gallia
P	C.Mays	P	R.Russell	/C	J.Bradley	P	J.Dubuc	P	B.Shawkey	C	D.Carroll	P	C.Weilman	P	H.Harper
P	E.Shore	P	L.Williams	H	L.Chappell	P	B.James	P	G.Mogridge	/O	C.Grimm	P	E.Plank	P	D.Ayers
P	R.Foster	P	R.Faber	P	J.Leonard	P	G.Cunningham	P	R.Fisher	O	S.Thompson	P	B.Groom	P	J.Boehling
		P	E.Cicotte	R	O.Welf	RP	B.Boland	P	A.Russell	/O	B.Johnson	P	E.Koob		
P	V.Gregg	P	J.Scott					P	N.Cullop	/O	M.Divis			P	J.Shaw
P	S.Jones							RP	S.Love	/S	S.Crane	/P	E.Hamilton	P	G.Dumont
/P	H.Pennock	P	J.Benz	P	J.Bagby	P	W.Mitchell			/S	L.Malone	P	J.Park	/P	C.Thomas
/P	W.Wyckoff	P	M.Wolfgang	P	S.Coveleski	/P	H.Ehmke	P	R.Caldwell	H	H.Davis	P	T.McCabe	/P	M.Craft
/P	M.McHale	P	D.Danforth	P	G.Morton	/P	E.Hamilton	P	R.Keating			P	B.Fincher	/P	M.Goodwin
		/P	E.Walsh	P	E.Klepfer	/P	E.Erickson			P	E.Myers	/P	G.Baumgardner	/P	J.Bentley
				P	F.Coumbe	P	G.Boehler	P	U.Shocker	P	J.Bush	/P	D.Crandall		
				/P	D.Jones	P	C.Markle	P	J.Nabors						
		P	A.Gould	/P	B.McTigue	/P	J.Buckles	P	T.Sheehan						
		P	F.Beebe	/P	G.Lowdermilk	/P	M.Cantwell								
		P	O.Lambeth			/P	B.Donovan								
		P	J.Boehling					P	J.Johnson						
		P	G.Lowdermilk					P	M.Williams						
		P	W.Mitchell					/P	C.Crowell						
		/P	P.Smith					/P	G.Hesselbacher						
		/P	K.Penner					/P	R.Parnham						
		/P	M.McHale					/P	S.Seibold						
		/P	R.Hagerman					/P	W.Wyckoff						
		/P	S.DesJardien					/P	R.Bressler						
		/P	R.Gunkel					/P	C.Ray						
								/P	H.Weaver						
								/P	M.Driscoll						
								/P	A.Lindstrom						
								/P	B.Morrisette						
								/P	W.Whittaker						
								/P	J.Richardson						

TEAM	G	W	L	PCT	GB	R	OR	AB	H	2B	3B	HR	BB	SO	AVG	OBP	SLG	PRO	PRO+	BR	/A	PF	CHI	RC	SB	CS	SBA	SBR
BOS	156	91	63	.591		550	480	5018	1246	197	56	14	464	482	.248	.317	.318	.635	97	-20	-22	100	101	580	129			
CHI	155	89	65	.578	2	601	497	5081	1277	194	100	17	447	591	.251	.319	.339	.658	103	18	12	101	102	638	197			
DET	155	87	67	.565	4	670	595	5193	1371	202	96	17	545	529	.264	.337	.350	.687	109	78	55	104	101	700	190			
NY	156	80	74	.519	11	577	561	5198	1277	194	59	35	516	632	.246	.318	.326	.644	99	-4	-16	102	100	613	179			
STL	158	79	75	.513	12	588	545	5159	1262	181	50	14	627	640	.245	.331	.307	.638	103	2	30	95	99	620	234			
CLE	157	77	77	.500	14	630	602	5064	1264	205	66	16	522	605	.250	.324	.331	.655	97	17	-18	106	106	625	160			
WAS	159	76	77	.497	14.5	536	543	5114	1238	170	60	12	535	597	.242	.320	.306	.626	95	-30	-25	99	98	579	185			
PHI	154	36	117	.235	54.5	447	776	5010	1212	169	65	19	406	631	.242	.303	.313	.616	96	-61	-38	95	91	538	151			
TOT	625					4599		40837	10147	1540	552	144	4062	4707	.248	.321	.324	.645							1425			

TEAM	CG	SH	SV	IP	H	H/G	HR	BB	SO	RAT	ERA	ERA+	OAV	OOB	PR	/A	PF	CPI	FA	E	DP	FW	PW	BW	SBW	DIF
BOS	76	24	16	1410²	1221	7.8	10	463	584	11.0	2.48	112	.239	.307	55	44	98	99	.972	183	108	3.0	4.9	-2.4		8.5
CHI	73	20	15	1412¹	1189	7.6	14	405	644	10.3	2.36	117	.236	.296	72	61	98	96	.968	205	134	1.5	6.8	1.3		2.4
DET	81	8	13	1410	1254	8.0	12	578	531	12.1	2.97	96	.248	.333	-23	-18	101	100	.968	211	110	1.1	-2.0	6.1		4.8
NY	84	12	17	1428	1249	7.9	37	476	616	11.2	2.77	104	.244	.314	8	17	102	100	.967	219	119	.7	1.9	-1.8		2.2
STL	74	9	13	1443²	1292	8.1	15	478	505	11.3	2.58	106	.248	.316	39	26	97	105	.963	248	120	-.9	2.9	3.3		-3.3
CLE	65	9	16	1410	1383	8.8	16	467	537	12.0	2.90	103	.264	.328	-13	16	106	107	.965	232	130	.0	1.8	-2.0		.2
WAS	85	11	7	1430²	1271	8.0	14	490	706	11.3	2.67	104	.244	.314	25	17	99	99	.964	232	119	.2	1.9	-2.8		.2
PHI	94	11	3	1343²	1311	8.8	26	715	575	13.8	3.92	73	.267	.364	-163	-160	101	97	.951	314	126	-5.5	-17.7	-4.2		-13.1
TOT	632	104	100	11289		8.1				11.6	2.82		.248	.321					.965	1844	966					

Runs		Hits		Doubles		Triples		Home Runs		Total Bases	
Cobb-Det	113	Speaker-Cle	211	Speaker-Cle	41	Jackson-Chi	21	Pipp-NY	12	Jackson-Chi	293
Graney-Cle	106	Jackson-Chi	202	Graney-Cle	41	E.Collins-Chi	17	Baker-NY	10	Speaker-Cle	274
Speaker-Cle	102	Cobb-Det	201	Jackson-Chi	40	Witt-Phi	15	Schang-Phi	7	Cobb-Det	267
Shotton-StL	97	Sisler-StL	177	Pratt-StL	35	Veach-Det	15	Felsch-Chi	7	Veach-Det	245
Veach-Det	92	Shotton-StL	174	Veach-Det	33						

Runs Batted In		Runs Produced		Bases On Balls		Batting Average		On Base Percentage		Slugging Average	
Pratt-StL	103	Veach-Det	180	Shotton-StL	111	Speaker-Cle	.386	Speaker-Cle	.470	Speaker-Cle	.502
Pipp-NY	93	Speaker-Cle	179	Graney-Cle	102	Cobb-Det	.371	Cobb-Det	.452	Jackson-Chi	.495
Veach-Det	91	Cobb-Det	176	E.Collins-Chi	86	Jackson-Chi	.341	E.Collins-Chi	.405	Cobb-Det	.493
Speaker-Cle	79	Jackson-Chi	166	Speaker-Cle	82	Strunk-Phi	.316	Jackson-Chi	.393	Veach-Det	.433
Jackson-Chi	78	Pratt-StL	162	Hooper-Bos	80	Gardner-Bos	.308	Strunk-Phi	.393	Baker-NY	.428

Production		Adjusted Production		Batter Runs		Adjusted Batter Runs		Clutch Hitting Index		Runs Created	
Speaker-Cle	.972	Speaker-Cle	181	Speaker-Cle	64.6	Speaker-Cle	57.2	Pratt-StL	136	Cobb-Det	136
Cobb-Det	.944	Cobb-Det	177	Cobb-Det	57.5	Cobb-Det	53.4	Heilmann-Det	132	Speaker-Cle	132
Jackson-Chi	.888	Jackson-Chi	165	Jackson-Chi	44.9	Jackson-Chi	43.7	Marsans-StL	132	Jackson-Chi	119
Strunk-Phi	.814	Strunk-Phi	152	E.Collins-Chi	30.5	Strunk-Phi	34.7	Gandil-Cle	129	E.Collins-Chi	99
E.Collins-Chi	.802	E.Collins-Chi	139	Strunk-Phi	30.2	E.Collins-Chi	29.5	Burns-Det	127	Veach-Det	94

Total Average		Stolen Bases		Stolen Base Average		Stolen Base Runs		Fielding Runs		Total Player Rating	
Cobb-Det	1.071	Cobb-Det	68	Cobb-Det	73.9	Cobb-Det	6.0	Lavan-StL	34.2	Speaker-Cle	5.7
Speaker-Cle	1.017	Marsans-StL	46	Hooper-Bos	71.1	Hooper-Bos	1.5	Lajoie-Phi	30.4	Cobb-Det	5.4
Jackson-Chi	.876	Shotton-StL	41	Schalk-Chi	69.8	Schalk-Chi	1.2	Vitt-Det	27.6	Pratt-StL	4.2
E.Collins-Chi	.814	E.Collins-Chi	40	Roth-Cle	67.4	Roth-Cle	.3	Pratt-StL	22.4	Jackson-Chi	3.6
Graney-Cle	.761	Speaker-Cle	35	Shanks-Was	65.7			Milan-Was	16.5	Lavan-StL	3.4

Wins		Win Percentage		Games		Complete Games		Shutouts		Saves	
Johnson-Was	25	Cicotte-Chi	.682	Davenport-StL	59	Johnson-Was	36	Ruth-Bos	9	Shawkey-NY	8
Shawkey-NY	24	Ruth-Bos	.657	Russell-Chi	56	Myers-Phi	31	Bush-Phi	8	Russell-NY	6
Ruth-Bos	23	Coveleski-Det	.656	Shawkey-NY	53	Bush-Phi	25	Leonard-Bos	6	Leonard-Bos	6
Coveleski-Det	21	Faber-Chi	.654	Gallia-Was	49	Ruth-Bos	23	Russell-Chi	5	Cicotte-Chi	6
Dauss-Det	19	Shawkey-NY	.632			Coveleski-Det	22			Bagby-Cle	5

Innings Pitched		Fewest Hits/Game		Fewest BB/Game		Strikeouts		Strikeouts/Game		Ratio	
Johnson-Was	369.2	Ruth-Bos	6.40	Russell-Chi	1.43	Johnson-Was	228	Johnson-Was	5.55	Russell-Chi	8.51
Coveleski-Det	324.1	Shawkey-NY	6.64	Cullop-NY	1.72	Myers-Phi	182	Williams-Chi	5.54	Johnson-Was	9.28
Ruth-Bos	323.2	Cicotte-Chi	6.64	Coveleski-Det	1.75	Ruth-Bos	170	Russell-NY	5.46	Shawkey-NY	9.47
Myers-Phi	315.0	Bush-Phi	6.97	Shore-Bos	1.95	Bush-Phi	157	Harper-Was	5.37	Coveleski-Det	9.77
Davenport-StL	290.2	Russell-Chi	7.05	Johnson-Was	2.00	Harper-Was	149	Myers-Phi	5.20	Ruth-Bos	9.90

Earned Run Average		Adjusted ERA		Opponents' Batting Avg.		Opponents' On Base Pct.		Starter Runs		Adjusted Starter Runs	
Ruth-Bos	1.75	Ruth-Bos	158	Ruth-Bos	.201	Russell-Chi	.254	Ruth-Bos	38.6	Johnson-Was	36.5
Cicotte-Chi	1.78	Cicotte-Chi	155	Shawkey-NY	.209	Johnson-Was	.270	Johnson-Was	38.0	Ruth-Bos	36.4
Johnson-Was	1.90	Johnson-Was	147	Cicotte-Chi	.218	Shawkey-NY	.273	Coveleski-Det	30.8	Coveleski-Det	32.1
Coveleski-Det	1.97	Coveleski-Det	145	Bush-Phi	.219	Ruth-Bos	.280	Cicotte-Chi	21.7	Shawkey-NY	20.7
Faber-Chi	2.02	Cullop-NY	141	Johnson-Was	.220	Coveleski-Det	.282	Weilman-StL	20.6	Cicotte-Chi	20.3

Clutch Pitching Index		Relief Runs	Adjusted Relief Runs	Relief Ranking	Total Pitcher Index		Total Baseball Ranking	
Cicotte-Chi	117				Ruth-Bos	5.9	Ruth-Bos	5.9
Gallia-Was	117				Johnson-Was	5.1	Speaker-Cle	5.7
Mogridge-NY	113				Coveleski-Det	3.9	Cobb-Det	5.4
Fisher-NY	113				Mays-Bos	3.2	Johnson-Was	5.1
Weilman-StL	113				Shawkey-NY	2.9	Pratt-StL	4.2

April 10 The U.S. entry into World War I and a cold, wet spring put a damper on the start of the season; 48 NL games will be postponed in the first month. Half the major league clubs will show losses this year, and eight of the 20 existing minor leagues will fold before the season is over.

May 2 The Cubs' lefthander Hippo Vaughn and righthander Fred Toney of the Reds toe the mound in Chicago for a one-of-a-kind game. The Reds put up an all righthanded batting order, benching Edd Roush, who will lead the NL with a .341 BA. At the end of nine innings, both pitchers have no-hitters. With one out in the top of the tenth and men on second base and third base, Jim Thorpe hits a swinging bunt near the mound. Vaughn picks it up and throws home, but Art Wilson freezes; the ball hits his chest protector, and Larry Kopf slides in safe for the only run. Fred Toney sets the Cubs down in order and has the fourth 10-inning no-hitter to date. The run scored by the Reds is their first in 34 innings.

May 23 Grover Alexander of the Philadelphia Phils allows the Cincinnati Reds only two hits, collects three himself, including a homer, and wins 5–1.

June 1 Hank Gowdy of the Braves becomes the first major league player to enlist when he signs up in the Ohio National Guard. He will play until he reports for duty July 15.

June 8 After a game in Cincinnati, John McGraw takes a swing at umpire Bill "Lord" Byron as they are leaving the field, splitting Byron's lip. NL President John Tener fines McGraw $500 and suspends him for 16 days. McGraw sounds off to writer Sid Mercer about the general shortcomings of Tener and his umpires. When McGraw's quotes are published, he signs a statement denying he'd said what was printed. The Baseball Writers Association protests, forcing another NL meeting at which Tener finds McGraw guilty and fines him another $1,000. Mercer, a friend of McGraw's, quits the beat and never speaks to McGraw again.

July 1 Reds Fred Toney pitches a doubleheader, beating the Pirates 4-1 and 5-1. He walks one and allows three hits in each game, the fewest hits allowed by any pitcher winning two games in one day.

July 1 The Robins (Dodgers) play their first Sunday game in Brooklyn, charging regular admission and beating the Phils 3-2. Admission is charged for a pregame band concert and military drill exhibition before the game to benefit wartime charities. When the band concert ends, ticket sales stop to conform with the Sunday baseball laws.

August 21 Now with the Philadelphia Phils, Chief Bender, 34, pitches his third straight shutout, winning 6–0 over the Cubs. In his last active season, Bender will turn in four shutouts and win eight with two losses and a 1.67 ERA.

September 3 Trying to keep the Phils in the race, Grover Alexander does double duty, beating Brooklyn 6–0 and 9–3. He will win 30 for the third straight year, with a league-leading 1.86 ERA.

October 4 Braves southpaw Art Nehf's 40-inning scoreless streak is ended by the Robins in the eighth inning as Brooklyn beats Boston 5-1.

October 11 The Phils sell Grover Alexander and "Reindeer" Bill Killefer to the Cubs for righthander "Iron" Mike Prendergast, catcher Pickles Dillhoefer, and $55,000.

BOSTON	BROOKLYN	CHICAGO	CINCINNATI
M G.Stallings	M W.Robinson	M F.Mitchell	M C.Mathewson
1B E.Konetchy	1B J.Daubert	1B F.Merkle	1B H.Chase
2B J.Rawlings	2B G.Cutshaw	2B L.Doyle	2B D.Shean
SS R.Maranville	SS I.Olson	SS C.Wortman	SS L.Kopf
3B R.Smith	3B M.Mowrey	3B C.Deal	3B H.Groh
LF J.Kelly	LF Z.Wheat	LF L.Mann	LF G.Neale
CF R.Powell	CF J.Hickman	CF C.Williams	CF E.Roush
RF W.Rehg	RF C.Stengel	RF M.Flack	RF T.Griffith
C W.Tragesser	C O.Miller	C A.Wilson	C I.Wingo
O S.Magee	O1 J.Johnston	O H.Wolter	O J.Thorpe
O J.Wilhoit	O1 H.Myers	S3 R.Zeider	O M.Cueto
2O E.Fitzpatrick	3 F.O'Rourke	3 R.Elliott	O S.Magee
C H.Gowdy	C C.Meyers	S P.Kilduff	2S B.McKechnie
O F.Bailey	S B.Fabrique	C P.Dillhoefer	C T.Clarke
O G.Twombly	C E.Krueger	/3 C.Pechous	C E.Huhn
2 M.Massey	C M.Wheat	O M.Schick	/C H.Smith
2 J.Evers	/3 R.Smyth	/O T.Barber	/2 G.Getz
C C.Meyers	/C J.Snyder	/2 P.Driscoll	P F.Toney
1 S.Covington	/1 F.Merkle	/1 V.Saier	P P.Schneider
/O Z.Collins	/2 B.Leard	/1 R.Leslie	P M.Regan
C A.Rico	R L.Malone	/C B.O'Farrell	P C.Mitchell
/S H.Schreiber	P J.Pfeffer	/O W.Marriott	P H.Eller
/O L.Chappell	P L.Cadore	/O H.Wolfe	P J.Ring
/C F.Jacklitsch	P R.Marquard	H H.Hunter	/P D.Ruether
P J.Barnes	P S.Smith	H J.Archer	P E.Knetzer
P D.Rudolph	P L.Cheney	H E.Blackburn	P R.Sanders
P L.Tyler	P J.Coombs	P H.Vaughn	P S.Perry
P A.Nehf	P W.Dell	P P.Douglas	/P R.Bressler
P P.Ragan	/P J.Russell	P C.Hendrix	P J.Engel
P F.Allen	/P J.Miljus	P A.Demaree	/P H.Pillette
P T.Hughes	/P P.Wachtel	P P.Carter	
/P J.Scott	/P R.Durning	RP M.Prendergast	
/P E.Reulbach		P V.Aldridge	
/P E.Walsh		P T.Seaton	
/P C.Crum		P D.Ruether	
		/P H.Weaver	
		/P R.Walker	
		/P G.Packard	

NEW YORK	PHILADELPHIA	PITTSBURGH	ST.LOUIS
M J.McGraw	M P.Moran	M J.Callahan	M M.Huggins
1B W.Holke	1B F.Luderus	M H.Wagner	1B G.Paulette
2B B.Herzog	2B B.Niehoff	M H.Bezdek	2B D.Miller
SS A.Fletcher	SS D.Bancroft	1B H.Wagner	SS R.Hornsby
3B H.Zimmerman	3B M.Stock	2B J.Pitler	3B D.Baird
LF G.Burns	LF P.Whitted	SS C.Ward	LF W.Cruise
CF B.Kauff	CF D.Paskert	3B T.Boeckel	CF J.Smith
RF D.Robertson	RF G.Cravath	LF C.Bigbee	RF T.Long
C B.Rariden	C B.Killefer	CF M.Carey	C F.Snyder
C L.McCarty	2 J.Evers	RF L.King	2O B.Betzel
2 J.Smith	O F.Schulte	C W.Fischer	C1 M.Gonzalez
2 G.Gibson	O B.Adams	O1 B.Hinchman	3 F.Smith
2 P.Kilduff	O O.Dugey	C W.Schmidt	O B.Bescher
S J.Thorpe	S P.McGaffigan	32 A.McCarthy	O R.Smyth
O J.Wilhoit	C E.Burns	C1 B.Wagner	/C P.Livingston
/O R.Youngs	C C.Cooper	1 F.Mollwitz	/C J.Brock
/3 E.Hemingway	/3 H.Pearce	3 D.Baird	/3 T.DeFate
/2 A.Baird	/3 B.Byrne	S3 A.Debus	/3 B.Wallace
O R.Murray	P P.Alexander	O C.Jackson	O S.Stewart
/1 J.Rodriguez	P E.Rixey	1 B.Brief	/S I.McAuley
/C E.Krueger	P J.Oeschger	O F.Schulte	/C J.Roche
/C J.Onslow	P E.Mayer	S W.Caton	P B.Doak
/O G.Kelly	P J.Lavender	2 B.Gleason	P L.Meadows
P F.Schupp	P C.Bender	O D.Flinn	P R.Ames
P S.Sallee	P P.Fittery	/1 R.Miller	P M.Watson
P P.Perritt		/1 G.Kelly	P G.Packard
P R.Benton		/C R.Smith	P O.Horstmann
P J.Tesreau		/O J.Altenburg	P M.Goodwin
P F.Anderson		/2 B.Webb	P B.Steele
P A.Demaree		/C F.Blackwell	P J.May
P G.Smith		/O J.Wilhoit	/P L.North
P J.Middleton		/3 H.Warner	/P G.Pearce
/P A.Swigler		/2 H.Wolfe	/P B.Hitt
		H B.Shaw	/P T.Murchison
		/3 A.Reilly	
		P W.Cooper	
		P E.Jacobs	
		P F.Miller	
		P B.Grimes	
		P B.Steele	
		P H.Carlson	
		P A.Mamaux	
		/P B.Evans	
		/P E.Ponder	

TEAM	G	W	L	PCT	GB	R	OR	AB	H	2B	3B	HR	BB	SO	AVG	OBP	SLG	PRO	PRO+	BR	/A	PF	CHI	RC	SB	CS	SBA	SBR
NY	158	98	56	.636		**635**	457	5211	1360	170	71	**39**	373	533	.261	**.317**	.343	.660	113	**50**	69	97	105	597	**162**			
PHI	154	87	65	.572	10	578	500	5084	1262	**225**	60	38	**435**	533	.248	.310	.339	.649	101	29	5	104	100	556	109			
STL	154	82	70	.539	15	531	567	5083	1271	159	93	26	359	652	.250	.303	.333	.636	104	2	17	97	98	542	159			
CIN	157	78	76	.506	20	601	611	5251	**1385**	196	**100**	26	312	**477**	**.264**	.309	**.354**	**.663**	114	48	**73**	96	101	596	153			
CHI	157	74	80	.481	24	552	567	5135	1229	194	67	17	415	599	.239	.299	.313	.612	86	-35	-76	108	**107**	511	127			
BOS	157	72	81	.471	25.5	536	532	5201	1280	169	75	22	427	587	.246	.309	.320	.629	105	-2	30	94	96	549	155			
BRO	156	70	81	.464	26.5	511	559	5251	1299	159	78	25	334	527	.247	.296	.322	.618	93	-32	-46	103	98	522	130			
PIT	157	51	103	.331	47	464	595	5169	1230	160	61	9	399	580	.238	.298	.298	.596	86	-61	-78	103	94	493	150			
TOT	625					4408		41385	10316	1432	605	202	3054	4488	.249	.305	.328	.633						1145				

TEAM	CG	SH	SV	IP	H	H/G	HR	BB	SO	RAT	ERA	ERA+	OAV	OOB	PR	/A	PF	CPI	FA	E	DP	FW	PW	BW	SBW	DIF
NY	92	18	**14**	1426²	**1221**	7.7	29	327	551	9.9	2.27	112	**.234**	**.283**	**69**	43	94	97	**.968**	208	122	**1.8**	4.9	7.8		6.5
PHI	102	**22**	5	1389	1258	8.2	25	**325**	616	10.5	2.46	**114**	.246	.295	38	**53**	104	102	.967	212	112	1.2	**6.0**	.6		3.2
STL	66	16	10	1392²	1257	8.1	29	421	502	11.1	3.03	89	.248	.311	-51	-55	99	92	.967	221	**153**	.6	-6.2	1.9		9.7
CIN	94	12	6	1397¹	1358	8.7	20	442	488	11.5	2.70	97	.260	.317	1	-15	97	**110**	.962	247	120	-.7	-1.7	**8.3**		-4.9
CHI	79	16	9	1404	1303	8.4	34	374	**654**	10.9	2.62	110	.253	.307	14	40	107	108	.959	267	121	-1.9	4.5	-8.6		3.0
BOS	**105**	**22**	3	1424²	1309	8.3	19	371	593	10.8	2.77	92	.251	.304	-10	-38	94	96	.966	224	122	.7	-4.3	3.4		-4.3
BRO	99	8	9	1421¹	1288	8.2	32	405	582	11.0	2.78	100	.247	.307	-12	0	103	98	.962	245	102	-.7	.0	-5.2		.4
PIT	84	17	6	1417²	1318	8.4	**14**	432	509	11.3	3.01	94	.253	.314	-48	-29	105	94	.961	251	119	-.9	-3.3	-8.8		-13.0
TOT	721	131	62	11273¹		8.2				10.9	2.70		.249	.305					.964	1875	971					

Runs
Burns-NY 103
Groh-Cin 91
Kauff-NY 89
Hornsby-StL 86

Hits
Groh-Cin 182
Burns-NY 180
Roush-Cin 178
Zimmerman-NY . . . 174
Carey-Pit 174

Doubles
Groh-Cin 39
Merkle-Bro-Chi . . . 31
Smith-Bos 31
Cravath-Phi 29
Chase-Cin 28

Triples
Hornsby-StL 17
Cravath-Phi 16
Chase-Cin 15
Roush-Cin 14
Long-StL 14

Home Runs
Robertson-NY 12
Cravath-Phi 12
Hornsby-StL 8

Total Bases
Hornsby-StL 253
Groh-Cin 246
Burns-NY 246
Cravath-Phi 238

Runs Batted In
Zimmerman-NY . . . 102
Chase-Cin 86
Cravath-Phi 83
Stengel-Bro 73
Luderus-Phi 72

Runs Produced
Zimmerman-NY . . . 158
Chase-Cin 153
Kauff-NY 152
Roush-Cin 145
Hornsby-StL 144

Bases On Balls
Burns-NY 75
Groh-Cin 71
Cravath-Phi 70
Luderus-Phi 65
Paskert-Phi 62

Batting Average
Roush-Cin 341
Hornsby-StL 327
Z.Wheat-Bro 312
Kauff-NY 308
Groh-Cin 304

On Base Percentage
Groh-Cin 385
Hornsby-StL 385
Burns-NY 380
Roush-Cin 379
Kauff-NY 379

Slugging Average
Hornsby-StL 484
Cravath-Phi 473
Roush-Cin 454
Z.Wheat-Bro 423
Burns-NY 412

Production
Hornsby-StL 868
Cravath-Phi 842
Roush-Cin 833
Groh-Cin 796
Burns-NY 792

Adjusted Production
Hornsby-StL 170
Roush-Cin 162
Cravath-Phi 151
Groh-Cin 150
Burns-NY 148

Batter Runs
Hornsby-StL 39.6
Cravath-Phi 34.7
Groh-Cin 33.5
Roush-Cin 32.3
Burns-NY 32.2

Adjusted Batter Runs
Hornsby-StL 42.3
Groh-Cin 37.7
Roush-Cin 36.0
Burns-NY 35.4
Cravath-Phi 30.9

Clutch Hitting Index
Zimmerman-NY 146
Ward-NY 133
Luderus-Phi 132
Deal-Chi 130
Chase-Cin 121

Runs Created
Burns-NY 102
Hornsby-StL 100
Groh-Cin 96
Roush-Cin 94
Carey-Pit 94

Total Average
Hornsby-StL 906
Cravath-Phi 870
Burns-NY 868
Roush-Cin 843
Groh-Cin 815

Stolen Bases
Carey-Pit 46
Burns-NY 40
Kauff-NY 30
Maranville-Bos . . . 27
Baird-Pit-StL 26

Stolen Base Average

Stolen Base Runs

Fielding Runs
Bancroft-Phi 27.9
Fletcher-NY 27.4
Carey-Pit 24.5
Hornsby-StL 21.3
Miller-StL 18.6

Total Player Rating
Hornsby-StL 7.7
Groh-Cin 5.3
Fletcher-NY 4.1
Carey-Pit 3.9
Burns-NY 3.5

Wins
Alexander-Phi 30
Toney-Cin 24
Vaughn-Chi 23
Schupp-NY 21
Schneider-Cin 20

Win Percentage
Schupp-NY 750
Sallee-NY 720
Perritt-NY 708
Alexander-Phi 698
Nehf-Bos 680

Games
Douglas-Chi 51
Barnes-Bos 50
Schneider-Cin 46
Alexander-Phi 45
Doak-StL 44

Complete Games
Alexander-Phi 34
Toney-Cin 31
Vaughn-Chi 27
Barnes-Bos 27
Schupp-NY 25

Shutouts
Alexander-Phi 8
Toney-Cin 7
Cooper-Pit 7
Schupp-NY 6

Saves
Sallee-NY 4

Innings Pitched
Alexander-Phi . . . 388.0
Toney-Cin 339.2
Schneider-Cin . . . 333.2
Cooper-Pit 297.2
Vaughn-Chi 295.2

Fewest Hits/Game
Schupp-NY 6.68
Anderson-NY 6.78
Nehf-Bos 7.60
Pfeffer-Bro 7.61
Tyler-Bos 7.64

Fewest BB/Game
Alexander-Phi 1.30
Sallee-NY 1.42
Nehf-Bos 1.50
Barnes-Bos 1.53
Douglas-Chi 1.53

Strikeouts
Alexander-Phi 200
Vaughn-Chi 195
Douglas-Chi 151
Schupp-NY 147
Schneider-Cin 138

Strikeouts/Game
Vaughn-Chi 5.94
Schupp-NY 4.86
Alexander-Phi 4.64
Douglas-Chi 4.63
Marquard-Bro 4.53

Ratio
Anderson-NY 8.78
Schupp-NY 9.13
Alexander-Phi 9.23
Nehf-Bos 9.26
Barnes-Bos 9.58

Earned Run Average
Alexander-Phi 1.83
Anderson-NY 1.44
Perritt-NY 1.88
Schupp-NY 1.95
Vaughn-Chi 2.01

Adjusted ERA
Anderson-NY 176
Alexander-Phi 153
Vaughn-Chi 144
Perritt-NY 135
Schupp-NY 130

Opponents' Batting Avg.
Schupp-NY 209
Anderson-NY 209
Nehf-Bos 231
Marquard-Bro 232
Pfeffer-Bro 234

Opponents' On Base Pct.
Anderson-NY 255
Schupp-NY 265
Alexander-Phi 266
Nehf-Bos 268
Barnes-Bos 277

Starter Runs
Alexander-Phi 37.5
Vaughn-Chi 22.8
Schupp-NY 22.7
Anderson-NY 22.7
Schneider-Cin 22.2

Adjusted Starter Runs
Alexander-Phi 41.7
Vaughn-Chi 28.8
Anderson-NY 19.8
Schneider-Cin 18.7
Schupp-NY 17.9

Clutch Pitching Index
Schneider-Cin 145
Vaughn-Chi 120
Perritt-NY 118
Hendrix-Chi 117
Mayer-Phi 114

Relief Runs

Adjusted Relief Runs

Relief Ranking

Total Pitcher Index
Alexander-Phi 5.9
Vaughn-Chi 4.1
Rixey-Phi 2.6
Schneider-Cin 1.8
Anderson-NY 1.7

Total Baseball Ranking
Hornsby-StL 7.7
Alexander-Phi 5.9
Groh-Cin 5.3
Vaughn-Chi 4.1
Fletcher-NY 4.1

February 24 Smoky Joe Wood, his arm dead at 26, is sold by the Red Sox to Cleveland for $15,000. He will become an outfielder after one last, losing start on the mound, and will play five more years.

April 10 The AL gets the U.S. Army to assign drill sergeants to each team for daily pregame drills. A final contest will be held for a $500 prize. The St. Louis Browns will take the money.

April 11 Babe Ruth beats the Yankees, pitching a 3-hit 10–3 win for the Red Sox in the opener. By the end of May he will be 10-3 on the way to his best year (24–13) and a league-leading 35 complete games.

May 5 St. Louis Browns pitcher Ernie Koob pitches a 1–0 no-hitter over the White Sox' Ed Cicotte. A tainted first-inning hit by Buck Weaver is changed to an error after much discussion with umpires and players. The following day, the writers' association will take a mail vote on a resolution that a scorer's decision cannot be reversed.

May 6 No-hitters are thrown on consecutive days, as the Browns' Bob Groom no-hits the White Sox 3–0 in the second game of the doubleheader. This year, Groom will be the losingest pitcher in the AL for the third time. He lost a record-setting 19 straight games as a rookie with Washington in 1909.

June 23 In Boston, Babe Ruth starts against Washington. He walks leadoff man Eddie Foster, griping to plate umpire Brick Owens after each pitch. On ball four, Ruth plants a right to the umpire's jaw. He is ejected, and Ernie Shore relieves. Foster is caught stealing, and Shore retires all 26 men he faces in a 4-0 win, getting credit in the books for a perfect game. Ruth is not fined, but draws a 10-day suspension.

August 19 Coaching third in a 1-1 game against Washington, Detroit's Ty Cobb gives Tiger base runner "Tioga" George Burns a shove when Burns stops at third on a long hit; Burns keeps going and scores the winning run for the Tigers. Clark Griffith protests, and Ban Johnson upholds him, as the rules now ban coaches from touching a runner. The game is replayed, and Washington wins 2-0.

October 6 Happy Felsch's home run is the difference in Chicago, as Ed Cicotte beats the Giants' Slim Sallee 2-1 in the Series opener.

October 7 In Game 2 New York's Ferdie Schupp doesn't get out of the second inning, and reliever Fred Anderson is bombed in a 5-run fourth, as the 14 White Sox hits produce a 7-2 win for Red Faber. Faber's pitching is better than his baserunning; in the fifth inning, he tries to steal third, only to find teammate Buck Weaver occupying it.

October 15 After Red Faber and Rube Benton match three scoreless innings, Eddie Collins leads off the fourth and hits a grounder to Heinie Zimmerman at third base. Collins takes second when the throw goes past first baseman Walter Holke. Joe Jackson's fly to right field is dropped by Dave Robertson, and Collins goes to third. When Happy Felsch hits one back to the pitcher, Collins breaks for home. Benton throws to third to catch Collins, and catcher Bill Rariden comes up the line. But Collins keeps running and slides home safely with Zimmerman in pursuit. Zimmerman will be blamed for chasing the runner, but nobody was covering home plate for New York. Faber wins his third game of the Series 4-2.

October 26 Miller Huggins, who managed the Cardinals to a third-place finish, is signed to run the Yankees by owner Jake Ruppert. Co-owner Til Huston, who favored Wilbert Robinson for the job, has a falling out with partner Ruppert and will sell his half interest to Ruppert in 1923.

December 13 Connie Mack and the A's need money. He sells pitcher Joe Bush, catcher Wally Schang, and outfielder Amos Strunk to the Red Sox for sore–armed pitcher Vean Gregg, outfielder Merlin Kopp, catcher Pinch Thomas, and $60,000.

BOSTON	CHICAGO	CLEVELAND	DETROIT	NEW YORK	PHILADELPHIA	ST.LOUIS	WASHINGTON
M J.Barry	M P.Rowland	M L.Fohl	M H.Jennings	M B.Donovan	M C.Mack	M F.Jones	M C.Griffith
1B D.Hoblitzel	1B C.Gandil	1B J.Harris	1B G.Burns	1B W.Pipp	1B S.McInnis	1B G.Sisler	1B J.Judge
2B J.Barry	2B E.Collins	2B B.Wambsganss	2B R.Young	2B F.Maisel	2B R.Grover	2B D.Pratt	2B R.Morgan
SS E.Scott	SS S.Risberg	SS R.Chapman	SS D.Bush	SS R.Peckinpaugh	SS W.Witt	SS D.Lavan	SS H.Shanks
3B L.Gardner	3B B.Weaver	3B J.Evans	3B O.Vitt	3B F.Baker	3B R.Bates	3B J.Austin	3B E.Foster
LF D.Lewis	LF J.Jackson	LF J.Graney	LF B.Veach	LF H.High	LF P.Bodie	LF B.Shotton	LF M.Menosky
CF T.Walker	CF H.Felsch	CF T.Speaker	CF T.Cobb	CF E.Miller	CF A.Strunk	CF B.Jacobson	CF C.Milan
RF H.Hooper	RF N.Leibold	RF B.Roth	RF H.Heilmann	RF T.Hendryx	RF C.Jamieson	RF T.Sloan	RF S.Rice
C S.Agnew	C R.Schalk	C S.O'Neill	C O.Stanage	C L.Nunamaker	C W.Schang	C H.Severeid	C E.Ainsmith
C P.Thomas	O S.Collins	C L.Guisto	C T.Spencer	O L.Magee	O B.Meyer	O A.Marsans	31 J.Leonard
O J.Walsh	3 F.McMullin	32 T.Turner	O G.Harper	S R.Walters	S2 J.Dugan	S2 E.Johnson	1 P.Gharrity
1 D.Gainer	C B.Lynn	C E.Smith	1 S.Crawford	O F.Gilhooley	O B.Johnson	O E.Smith	C J.Henry
O C.Shorten	/O E.Murphy	C J.Billings	2 B.Jones	2 J.Gedeon	O R.Haley	/O W.Rumler	S G.McBride
2S H.Janvrin	1 T.Jourdan	/3 I.Howard	O B.Dyer	O A.Marsans	3 L.Magee	O W.Miller	S E.Smith
3 M.McNally	/C J.Jenkins	O M.Allison	C A.Yelle	C W.Alexander	/O W.McAvoy	C G.Hale	S S.Crane
C H.Cady	/2 B.Byrne	/C H.DeBerry	/1 B.Ellison	/O A.Aragon	/C C.Perkins	O R.Demmitt	O H.Milan
2 J.Cooney	H J.Fournier	/1 R.Miller	/O F.Nicholson	O B.Lamar	3 G.Bailey	S W.Gerber	/O C.Jamieson
H O.Henriksen	/2 Z.Hasbrook	/O M.Kavanagh	/O I.Flagstead	2 S.Fewster	H V.Picinich	/1 G.Paulette	/2 B.Murray
/C W.Mayer	/S Z.Terry	/3 F.Eunick	/2 T.DeFate	O S.Vick	/2 D.Bradshaw	/C G.Hartley	P W.Johnson
P B.Ruth	P E.Cicotte	P J.Bagby	H F.Walker	/S A.Ward	/R P.French	/2 B.Kenworthy	P J.Shaw
P D.Leonard	P R.Faber	P S.Coveleski	P H.Dauss	/O H.Camp	H H.Davis	/3 S.Moore	P B.Gallia
P C.Mays	P L.Williams	P E.Klepfer	P B.Boland	/C M.Ruel	P J.Bush	/S E.Murray	P D.Ayers
P E.Shore	P R.Russell	P G.Morton	P H.Ehmke	P B.Shawkey	P R.Schauer	H T.Richardson	P G.Dumont
P R.Foster	P D.Danforth	P F.Coumbe	P B.James	P R.Caldwell	P E.Myers	/R P.Bigler	P H.Harper
P H.Pennock	P J.Scott	P O.Lambeth	P W.Mitchell	P G.Mogridge	P J.Johnson	/S O.Neu	/P M.Craft
P L.Bader	P J.Benz	P A.Gould	P G.Cunningham	P N.Cullop	P W.Noyes	P D.Davenport	/P D.Waldbauer
/P S.Jones	/P M.Wolfgang	P J.Boehling	P D.Jones	P U.Shocker	P S.Seibold	P A.Sothoron	
/P W.Wyckoff		/P R.Torkelson	P H.Coveleski	P R.Fisher	P C.Falkenberg	P B.Groom	
		/P J.Wood	/P J.Couch	P S.Love	/P W.Anderson	P E.Koob	
		/P P.Smith		P A.Russell	/P R.Naylor	P E.Plank	
		/P G.Dickerson		/P E.Monroe	/P W.Johnson	P T.Rogers	
				/P B.McGraw	/P R.Parnham	P E.Hamilton	
				/P N.Brady	/P E.Bacon	P R.Wright	
				/P B.Piercy	/P D.Keefe	/P V.Molyneaux	
				/P H.Thormahlen	/P R.Hill	/P J.Park	
				/P J.Enright	/P J.Nabors	/P G.Lowdermilk	
				/P W.Smallwood		/P C.Weilman	
						/P S.Martin	
						/P T.McCabe	
						/P K.Pennington	

TEAM	G	W	L	PCT	GB	R	OR	AB	H	2B	3B	HR	BB	SO	AVG	OBP	SLG	PRO	PRO+	BR	/A	PF	CHI	RC	SB	CS	SBA	SBR
CHI	156	100	54	.649		656	464	5057	1281	152	81	18	522	479	.253	.329	.326	.655	103	36	23	102	108	607	219			
BOS	157	90	62	.592	9	555	454	5048	1243	198	64	14	466	473	.246	.314	.319	.633	100	-10	-4	99	99	550	105			
CLE	156	88	66	.571	12	584	543	4994	1224	218	64	13	549	596	.245	.324	.322	.646	96	21	-23	107	99	588	210			
DET	154	78	75	.510	21.5	639	577	5093	1317	204	77	25	483	476	.259	.328	.344	.672	111	61	64	100	102	615	163			
WAS	157	74	79	.484	25.5	543	566	5142	1238	173	70	4	500	574	.241	.313	.304	.617	95	-34	-28	99	101	531	166			
NY	155	71	82	.464	28.5	524	558	5136	1226	172	52	27	496	535	.239	.310	.308	.618	93	-34	-39	101	98	526	136			
STL	155	57	97	.370	43	510	687	5091	1250	183	63	15	405	540	.246	.305	.315	.620	98	-39	-20	96	99	523	157			
PHI	154	55	98	.359	44.5	529	691	5109	1296	177	62	17	435	519	.254	.316	.323	.639	101	-1	7	99	94	551	112			
TOT	622					4540		40670	10075	1477	533	133	3856	4192	.248	.318	.320	.638						1268				

TEAM	CG	SH	SV	IP	H	H/G	HR	BB	SO	RAT	ERA	ERA+	OAV	OOB	PR	/A	PF	CPI	FA	E	DP	FW	PW	BW	SBW	DIF
CHI	78	22	21	1424¹	1236	7.8	10	413	517	10.6	2.16	123	.238	.298	79	76	100	102	.967	204	117	2.3	8.5	2.6		9.7
BOS	115	15	7	1421¹	1197	7.6	12	413	509	10.5	2.20	117	.231	.295	73	60	97	95	.972	183	116	3.9	6.7	-.4		3.9
CLE	73	20	22	1412²	1270	8.1	17	438	451	11.1	2.52	112	.247	.310	22	48	106	101	.964	242	136	-.5	5.3	-2.6		8.7
DET	78	20	15	1396¹	1209	7.8	12	504	516	11.4	2.56	103	.240	.316	16	13	99	99	.964	234	95	-.1	1.4	7.1		-6.9
WAS	84	21	10	1413	1217	7.8	12	500	637	11.4	2.75	99	.239	.316	-14	-19	99	91	.961	251	127	-1.0	-2.1	-3.1		3.7
NY	87	10	6	1411¹	1280	8.2	28	427	571	11.1	2.66	101	.252	.314	0	3	101	102	.965	225	129	.6	.3	-4.3		-2.1
STL	66	12	12	1385¹	1320	8.6	19	537	429	12.3	3.20	81	.257	.332	-83	-96	98	94	.957	281	139	-3.4	-10.7	-2.2		-3.7
PHI	80	8	8	1365²	1310	8.6	23	562	516	12.5	3.27	84	.261	.338	-92	-79	103	97	.961	251	106	-1.4	-8.8	.8		-12.1
TOT	661	128	101	11230		8.0				11.4	2.66		.248	.318					.964	1871	965					

Runs		Hits		Doubles		Triples		Home Runs		Total Bases	
Bush-Det	112	Cobb-Det	225	Cobb-Det	44	Cobb-Det	24	Pipp-NY	9	Cobb-Det	335
Cobb-Det	107	Sisler-StL	190	Speaker-Cle	42	Jackson-Chi	17	Veach-Det	8	Veach-Det	261
Chapman-Cle	98	Speaker-Cle	184	Veach-Det	31	Judge-Was	15	Bodie-Phi	7	Speaker-Cle	254
Jackson-Chi	91	Veach-Det	182	Sisler-StL	30	Chapman-Cle	13			Sisler-StL	244
E.Collins-Chi	91			Roth-Cle	30					Bodie-Phi	233

Runs Batted In		Runs Produced		Bases On Balls		Batting Average		On Base Percentage		Slugging Average	
Veach-Det	103	Cobb-Det	203	Graney-Cle	94	Cobb-Det	.383	Cobb-Det	.444	Cobb-Det	.570
Felsch-Chi	102	Veach-Det	174	E.Collins-Chi	89	Sisler-StL	.353	Speaker-Cle	.432	Speaker-Cle	.486
Cobb-Det	102	Felsch-Chi	171	Hooper-Bos	80	Speaker-Cle	.352	Veach-Det	.393	Veach-Det	.457
Heilmann-Det	86	Jackson-Chi	161	Bush-Det	80	Veach-Det	.319	Sisler-StL	.390	Sisler-StL	.453
Jackson-Chi	75	E.Collins-Chi	158	Leibold-Chi	74	Felsch-Chi	.308	E.Collins-Chi	.389	Jackson-Chi	.429

Production		Adjusted Production		Batter Runs		Adjusted Batter Runs		Clutch Hitting Index		Runs Created	
Cobb-Det	1.014	Cobb-Det	210	Cobb-Det	74.4	Cobb-Det	75.0	Schalk-Chi	135	Cobb-Det	164
Speaker-Cle	.918	Speaker-Cle	168	Speaker-Cle	51.2	Speaker-Cle	43.3	Bates-Phi	134	Speaker-Cle	118
Veach-Det	.850	Sisler-StL	163	Veach-Det	40.1	Veach-Det	40.5	Felsch-Chi	133	Veach-Det	108
Sisler-StL	.843	Veach-Det	160	Sisler-StL	34.0	Sisler-StL	37.4	Veach-Det	130	Chapman-Cle	105
Jackson-Chi	.805	Jackson-Chi	142	Jackson-Chi	28.8	Jackson-Chi	26.9	E.Collins-Chi	128	Sisler-StL	104

Total Average		Stolen Bases		Stolen Base Average		Stolen Base Runs		Fielding Runs		Total Player Rating	
Cobb-Det	1.253	Cobb-Det	55					Chapman-Cle	24.4	Cobb-Det	8.5
Speaker-Cle	1.056	E.Collins-Chi	53					Felsch-Chi	18.9	Chapman-Cle	5.4
Veach-Det	.905	Chapman-Cle	52					Wambsganss-Cle	15.3	Speaker-Cle	4.7
Sisler-StL	.900	Roth-Cle	51					Ainsmith-Was	14.9	Veach-Det	4.0
E.Collins-Chi	.873	Sisler-StL	37					Pratt-StL	14.8	Sisler-StL	4.0

Wins		Win Percentage		Games		Complete Games		Shutouts		Saves	
Cicotte-Chi	28	Russell-Chi	.750	Danforth-Chi	50	Ruth-Bos	35	Coveleski-Cle	9	Danforth-Chi	9
Ruth-Bos	24	Mays-Bos	.710	Cicotte-Chi	49	Johnson-Was	30	Johnson-Was	8	Bagby-Cle	7
Johnson-Was	23	Cicotte-Chi	.700	Bagby-Cle	49	Cicotte-Chi	29	Bagby-Cle	8	Boland-Det	6
Bagby-Cle	23	Williams-Chi	.680	Sothoron-StL	48	Mays-Bos	27	Cicotte-Chi	7	Coumbe-Cle	5
Mays-Bos	22	Ruth-Bos	.649								

Innings Pitched		Fewest Hits/Game		Fewest BB/Game		Strikeouts		Strikeouts/Game		Ratio	
Cicotte-Chi	346.2	Coveleski-Cle	6.09	Russell-Chi	1.52	Johnson-Was	188	Johnson-Was	5.19	Cicotte-Chi	8.28
Ruth-Bos	326.1	Cicotte-Chi	6.39	Mogridge-NY	1.79	Cicotte-Chi	150	Harper-Was	4.97	Coveleski-Cle	8.96
Johnson-Was	326.0	Ruth-Bos	6.73	Cicotte-Chi	1.82	Leonard-Bos	144	Bush-Phi	4.67	Johnson-Was	9.11
Bagby-Cle	320.2	Johnson-Was	6.85	Johnson-Was	1.88	Coveleski-Cle	133	Leonard-Bos	4.40	Russell-Chi	9.65
Coveleski-Cle	298.1	Mays-Bos	7.16	Bagby-Cle	2.05	Ruth-Bos	128	Danforth-Chi	4.11	Mays-Bos	9.90

Earned Run Average		Adjusted ERA		Opponents' Batting Avg.		Opponents' On Base Pct.		Starter Runs		Adjusted Starter Runs	
Cicotte-Chi	1.53	Cicotte-Chi	173	Coveleski-Cle	.194	Cicotte-Chi	.248	Cicotte-Chi	43.5	Cicotte-Chi	43.3
Mays-Bos	1.74	Coveleski-Cle	156	Cicotte-Chi	.203	Coveleski-Cle	.261	Mays-Bos	29.4	Coveleski-Cle	33.8
Coveleski-Cle	1.81	Mays-Bos	148	Ruth-Bos	.211	Johnson-Was	.263	Coveleski-Cle	28.2	Bagby-Cle	30.9
Faber-Chi	1.92	Bagby-Cle	144	Johnson-Was	.211	Russell-Chi	.279	Bagby-Cle	24.8	Mays-Bos	26.8
Russell-Chi	1.95	Faber-Chi	138	Mays-Bos	.221	Mays-Bos	.282	Ruth-Bos	23.5	Ruth-Bos	20.5

Clutch Pitching Index		Relief Runs	Adjusted Relief Runs	Relief Ranking	Total Pitcher Index		Total Baseball Ranking	
Faber-Chi	136				Cicotte-Chi	5.4	Cobb-Det	8.5
Ayers-Was	128				Mays-Bos	4.8	Chapman-Cle	5.4
James-Det	127				Ruth-Bos	4.8	Cicotte-Chi	5.4
Morton-Cle	117				Bagby-Cle	3.8	Mays-Bos	4.8
Mitchell-Det	116				Coveleski-Cle	3.1	Ruth-Bos	4.8

January 2 Brooklyn sends outfielder Casey Stengel and infielder George Cutshaw to Pittsburgh for pitcher Burleigh Grimes, pitcher Al Mamaux, and infielder Chuck Ward.

February 23 Barney Dreyfuss of the Rules Committee launches a campaign to ban the spitter. He will succeed after the 1920 campaign.

April 4* Determined not to be a wartime casualty, the International League reorganizes. The Richmond, Montreal, and Providence franchises are replaced by Binghamton, Jersey City, and Syracuse. Expenses are slashed, causing the resignation of president Ed Barrow, who will go on to greater glory with the Boston Red Sox. The IL will be the only minor league to play its full schedule this year.

June 17 The National Commission rules that pitcher Scott Perry, who has been winning games for the Athletics, belongs to the Boston Braves. Although purchased by the Braves from Atlanta in 1917, the deal was not completed. While on Atlanta's ineligible list, he was sold to Connie Mack. Aroused by Perry's AL success, the Braves enter their proper claim. Mack breaks precedent, goes outside Organized Baseball to civil court, and gets an injunction against Boston. The NL, having sat still for the loss of George Sisler, is furious; President John K. Tener resigns. John Heydler succeeds him and arranges a compromise solution: Mack pays Boston $2,500 and keeps Perry (henceforth a loser). The clubs' anger at player-allocation decisions will ultimately topple the National Commission, making way for Judge K.M. Landis.

August 9 Reds manager Christy Mathewson suspects Hal Chase of taking bribes to fix games, and suspends him "for indifferent play." Chase will be reinstated and will play for the Giants in 1919.

August 24 Players in the World Series are granted an extended exemption from military service. The National Commission gets official approval to play three days later from General Enoch Crowder, providing that 10 percent of the revenue goes to war charities.

August 27 Christy Mathewson resigns as Reds manager to accept a commission as a captain in the chemical warfare branch of the Army.

September 10 Hippo Vaughn comes back with two days of rest and blanks the Red Sox 3–0 on five hits in Game 5. Players on both sides threaten to strike unless they are guaranteed $2,500 to the winners and $1,000 each for the losers. They back off, however, when told they will appear greedy while their countrymen are fighting a war. There are no fines, but no World Series rings or mementos are given out. Seventy-five years later, the oversight is rectified. Descendants of about two thirds of the players receive medallions created by Balfour, in the style in which they would have been crafted 75 years earlier, at a Fenway Park ceremony.

December 10 National League secretary John Heydler is elected president of the league.

BOSTON		BROOKLYN		CHICAGO		CINCINNATI		NEW YORK		PHILADELPHIA		PITTSBURGH		ST.LOUIS	
M	G.Stallings	M	W.Robinson	M	F.Mitchell	M	C.Mathewson	M	J.McGraw	M	P.Moran	M	H.Bezdek	M	J.Hendricks
1B	E.Konetchy	1B	J.Daubert	1B	F.Merkle	M	H.Groh	1B	W.Holke	1B	F.Luderus	1B	F.Mollwitz	1B	G.Paulette
2B	B.Herzog	2B	M.Doolan	2B	R.Zeider	1B	H.Chase	2B	L.Doyle	2B	P.McGaffigan	2B	G.Cutshaw	2B	B.Fisher
SS	J.Rawlings	SS	I.Olson	SS	C.Hollocher	2B	L.Magee	SS	A.Fletcher	SS	D.Bancroft	SS	H.Caton	SS	R.Hornsby
3B	R.Smith	3B	O.O'Mara	3B	C.Deal	SS	L.Blackburne	3B	H.Zimmerman	3B	M.Stock	3B	B.McKechnie	3B	D.Baird
LF	R.Massey	LF	Z.Wheat	LF	L.Mann	3B	H.Groh	LF	G.Burns	LF	I.Meusel	LF	C.Bigbee	LF	A.McHenry
CF	R.Powell	CF	H.Myers	CF	D.Paskert	LF	G.Neale	CF	B.Kauff	CF	C.Williams	CF	M.Carey	CF	C.Heathcote
RF	A.Wickland	RF	J.Johnston	RF	M.Flack	CF	E.Roush	RF	R.Youngs	RF	G.Cravath	RF	B.Southworth	RF	W.Cruise
C	A.Wilson	C	O.Miller	C	B.Killefer	RF	T.Griffith	C	L.McCarty	C	B.Adams	C	W.Schmidt	C	M.Gonzalez
O	Jo.Kelly	O	J.Hickman	O	T.Barber	C	I.Wingo	C	B.Rariden	C	E.Burns	O	C.Stengel	3O	B.Betzel
O	Ji.Kelly	C	M.Wheat	C	B.O'Farrell	1O	S.Magee	O	J.Wilhoit	2	H.Pearce	O	L.King	O	J.Smith
O	W.Rehg	2	R.Schmandt	2	P.Kilduff	O2	M.Cueto	32	E.Sicking	O	M.Fitzgerald	O	B.Hinchman	1	C.Grimm
S	Z.Terry	C	E.Krueger	2	C.Pick	C	N.Allen	2	J.Rodriguez	2	E.Hemingway	O	L.Boone	O	G.Anderson
O	C.Chadbourne	/O	C.Mitchell	2	B.McCabe	/C	H.Smith	O	J.Thorpe	O	P.Whitted	S	R.Ellam	O2	R.Smyth
C	J.Henry	/C	J.Archer	/2	C.Wortman	/C	J.Archer	O	P.Compton	/C	P.Dillhoefer	O	T.Leach	C	F.Snyder
2	J.Smith	/2	F.O'Rourke	/2	R.Elliott	P	H.Eller	1	J.Kirke	/C	M.Devine	C	J.Archer	2S	B.Wallace
C	B.Wagner	/O	A.Nixon	/C	T.Daly	P	P.Schneider	/2	B.Niehoff	/O	T.Pickup	/1	B.Shaw	2	B.Niehoff
S	R.Maranville	/3	C.Ward	H	F.Lear	P	J.Ring	/C	G.Gibson	P	M.Prendergast	C	R.Smith	3	H.Bronkie
/O	B.Murphy	/O	A.Bashang	/C	T.Clarke	P	F.Toney	P	P.Perritt	P	B.Hogg	P	F.Blackwell	O	J.Brock
/2	R.Conway	/2	R.Sheridan	P	H.Vaughn	P	R.Bressler	P	R.Causey	P	J.Oeschger	/3	G.Getz	O	J.Beall
H	F.Bailey	P	B.Grimes	P	L.Tyler	P	D.Luque	P	A.Demaree	P	E.Jacobs	/2	J.Pitler	/O	M.Kavanagh
H	S.Covington	P	R.Marquard	P	C.Hendrix	P	M.Regan	P	S.Sallee	P	M.Watson	P	W.Cooper	/2	D.Distel
H	T.Miller	P	L.Cheney	P	P.Douglas	P	G.Smith	P	F.Toney	RP	D.Davis	P	F.Miller	/O	W.Mattick
/H	D.Bass	P	J.Coombs	P	P.Carter	/P	R.Mitchell	/P	J.Tesreau		E.Mayer	P	R.Sanders	/S	B.Larmore
/C	W.Tragesser	P	D.Robertson	/P	S.Martin	/P	L.Jacobus	/P	F.Anderson	/P	A.Main	P	E.Mayer	/O	D.Wheeler
P	A.Nehf	P	D.Griner	P	R.Walker	/P	S.Conley	/P	B.Steele		G.Fortune	P	B.Harmon	/1	T.Brottem
P	P.Ragan	/P	G.Smith	/P	H.Weaver	/P	D.Ruether	/P	J.Barnes	P	B.Tincup	P	R.Comstock	/O	T.Menze
P	D.Rudolph	/P	L.Cadore	/P	P.Alexander	/P	J.Haines	P	F.Schupp	P	F.Woodward	/P	E.Hamilton	P	B.Doak
P	B.Hearn	/P	J.Pfeffer	/P	V.Aldridge			/P	G.Smith			P	C.Slapnicka	P	R.Ames
P	D.Fillingim	/P	A.Mamaux	/P	B.Napier			/P	R.Benton			P	B.Steele	P	B.Sherdel
/P	L.George	/P	R.Durning					/P	J.Ogden			/P	C.Hill	P	G.Packard
P	H.Canavan	/P	N.Plitt					/P	G.Ross			P	B.Adams	P	L.Meadows
/P	J.Northrop	/P	J.Hehl					/P	W.Hoyt			/P	E.Jacobs	P	J.May
/P	D.Crandall	/P	M.Herrmann									/P	H.Carlson	P	O.Tuero
/P	B.Upham	/P	J.Russell											P	O.Horstmann
/P	T.Hughes	/P	H.Heitmann											/P	R.Johnson
/P	H.McQuillan													/P	E.Howard
/P	C.Crum														

TEAM	G	W	L	PCT	GB	R	OR	AB	H	2B	3B	HR	BB	SO	AVG	OBP	SLG	PRO	PRO+	BR	/A	PF	CHI	RC	SB	CS	SBA	SBR
CHI	131	84	45	.651		538	393	4325	1147	164	53	21	358	343	.265	.325	.342	.667	106	48	35	102	102	524	159			
NY	124	71	53	.573	10.5	480	415	4164	1081	150	53	13	271	365	.260	.310	.330	.640	103	1	10	98	107	451	130			
CIN	129	68	60	.531	15.5	530	496	4265	1185	165	84	15	304	303	.278	.330	.366	.696	120	86	96	98	96	545	128			
PIT	126	65	60	.520	17	466	412	4091	1016	107	72	15	371	285	.248	.315	.321	.636	96	1	-15	104	102	466	200			
BRO	126	57	69	.452	25.5	360	463	4212	1052	121	62	10	212	326	.250	.291	.315	.606	90	-53	-51	100	91	405	113			
PHI	125	55	68	.447	26	430	507	4192	1022	158	28	25	346	400	.244	.305	.313	.618	88	-29	-58	107	101	417	97			
BOS	124	53	71	.427	28.5	424	469	4162	1014	107	59	13	350	438	.244	.307	.307	.614	97	-32	-14	96	100	412	83			
STL	131	51	78	.395	33	454	527	4369	1066	147	64	27	329	461	.244	.301	.325	.626	99	-21	-5	97	100	450	119			
TOT	508					3682		33780	8583	1119	475	139	2541	2921	.254	.311	.328	.638							1029			

TEAM	CG	SH	SV	IP	H	H/G	HR	BB	SO	RAT	ERA	ERA+	OAV	OOB	PR	/A	PF	CPI	FA	E	DP	FW	PW	BW	SBW	DIF
CHI	92	23	8	1197	1050	7.9	13	296	472	10.3	2.18	128	.239	.291	77	80	101	104	.966	188	91	.5	8.9	3.9		6.2
NY	74	18	11	1111²	1002	8.1	20	228	330	10.1	2.64	100	.243	.287	15	-1	95	87	.971	152	78	2.1	-.1	1.1		5.9
CIN	84	14	6	1142¹	1136	9.0	19	381	321	12.1	3.00	89	.268	.332	-30	-42	97	109	.964	192	127	.0	-4.7	10.7		-2.1
PIT	85	10	7	1140¹	1005	7.9	13	299	367	10.5	2.48	116	.243	.300	36	51	104	99	.966	179	108	.6	5.7	-1.7		-2.1
BRO	85	17	2	1131¹	1024	8.1	22	320	395	10.9	2.81	99	.248	.307	-6	-4	101	95	.963	193	74	-.3	-.4	-5.7		.4
PHI	78	10	6	1139²	1086	8.6	22	369	312	11.7	3.15	95	.258	.323	-49	-20	109	96	.961	211	91	-1.5	-2.2	-6.5		3.7
BOS	96	13	0	1117¹	1111	8.9	14	277	340	11.4	2.90	93	.266	.316	-17	-27	97	102	.965	184	89	.0	-3.0	-1.6		-4.5
STL	72	3	5	1193	1148	8.7	16	352	361	11.6	2.96	91	.261	.321	-27	-34	98	101	.962	220	116	-1.5	-3.8	-.6		-7.6
TOT	666	108	45	9172²		8.4				11.1	2.76		.254	.311					.965	1519	774					

Runs
Groh-Cin 86
Burns-NY 80
Flack-Chi 74
Hollocher-Chi 72

Hits
Hollocher-Chi 161
Groh-Cin 158
Roush-Cin 145
Youngs-NY 143
Merkle-Chi 143

Doubles
Groh-Cin 28
Mann-Chi 27
Cravath-Phi 27
Meusel-Phi 25
Merkle-Chi 25

Triples
Daubert-Bro 15
Wickland-Bos 13
S.Magee-Cin 13
L.Magee-Cin 13

Home Runs
Cravath-Phi 8
Williams-Phi 6
Cruise-StL 6

Total Bases
Hollocher-Chi 202
Roush-Cin 198
Groh-Cin 195
Mann-Chi 188
Merkle-Chi 187

Runs Batted In
S.Magee-Cin 76
Cutshaw-Pit 68
Luderus-Phi 67
R.Smith-Bos 65
Merkle-Chi 65

Runs Produced
Burns-NY 127
Paskert-Chi 125
Mann-Chi 122
Groh-Cin 122
S.Magee-Cin 120

Bases On Balls
Carey-Pit 62
Flack-Chi 56
Groh-Cin 54
Cravath-Phi 54
Bancroft-Phi 54

Batting Average
Z.Wheat-Bro ...... .335
Roush-Cin .... .333
Groh-Cin .... .320
Hollocher-Chi ..... .316
Daubert-Bro ...... .308

On Base Percentage
Groh-Cin .... .395
Hollocher-Chi ..... .379
R.Smith-Bos ...... .373
S.Magee-Cin ...... .370
Z.Wheat-Bro ...... .369

Slugging Average
Roush-Cin .... .455
Daubert-Bro ...... .429
Hornsby-StL ...... .416
S.Magee-Cin ...... .415
Wickland-Bos ..... .398

Production
Roush-Cin .... .823
Groh-Cin .... .791
Daubert-Bro ...... .789
S.Magee-Cin ...... .785
Hollocher-Chi .... .775

Adjusted Production
Roush-Cin 153
Groh-Cin 144
S.Magee-Cin 142
Daubert-Bro 141
Wickland-Bos 139

Batter Runs
Groh-Cin 26.4
Roush-Cin 24.3
Hollocher-Chi 23.0
S.Magee-Cin 19.2
Daubert-Bro 18.2

Adjusted Batter Runs
Groh-Cin 27.9
Roush-Cin 25.6
Hollocher-Chi 21.0
S.Magee-Cin 20.3
Daubert-Bro 18.4

Clutch Hitting Index
S.Magee-Cin 158
Konetchy-Bos 137
R.Smith-Bos 135
Z.Wheat-Bro 122
Paulette-StL 122

Runs Created
Hollocher-Chi 85
Roush-Cin 80
Groh-Cin 79
Carey-Pit 76
Burns-NY 74

Total Average
Roush-Cin .... .848
Carey-Pit .... .844
Wickland-Bos ..... .812
Burns-NY .... .809
S.Magee-Cin ...... .804

Stolen Bases
Carey-Pit 58
Burns-NY 40
Hollocher-Chi 26
Cutshaw-Pit 25
Baird-StL 25

Stolen Base Average

Stolen Base Runs

Fielding Runs
Fletcher-NY 22.3
Carey-Pit 18.6
Bancroft-Phi 17.9
Schmidt-Pit 15.8
Myers-Bro 13.0

Total Player Rating
Groh-Cin 3.6
Hornsby-StL 3.6
Fisher-StL 3.5
Roush-Cin 3.0
L.Magee-Cin 3.0

Wins
Vaughn-Chi 22
Hendrix-Chi 20
Tyler-Chi 19
Grimes-Bro 19
Cooper-Pit 19

Win Percentage
Hendrix-Chi ...... .741
Tyler-Chi .... .704
Mayer-Phi-Pit ... .696
Vaughn-Chi .... .688
Grimes-Bro .... .679

Games
Grimes-Bro 40
Cooper-Pit 38
Eller-Cin 37

Complete Games
Nehf-Bos 28
Vaughn-Chi 27
Cooper-Pit 26
Tyler-Chi 22
Hendrix-Chi 21

Shutouts
Vaughn-Chi 8
Grimes-Bro 7
Tyler-Chi 6
Perritt-NY 6

Saves
Toney-Cin-NY 3
Oeschger-Phi 3
Cooper-Pit 3
Anderson-NY 3

Innings Pitched
Vaughn-Chi 290.1
Nehf-Bos 284.1
Cooper-Pit 273.1
Grimes-Bro 269.2
Tyler-Chi 269.1

Fewest Hits/Game
Vaughn-Chi 6.70
Grimes-Bro 7.01
Cooper-Pit 7.21
Tyler-Chi 7.28
Jacobs-Pit-Phi ... 7.50

Fewest BB/Game
Sallee-NY .... .82
Perritt-NY 1.47
G.Smith-Cin-NY-Bro ... 1.50
Toney-Cin-NY 1.54
Demaree-NY 1.58

Strikeouts
Vaughn-Chi 148
Cooper-Pit 117
Grimes-Bro 113
Tyler-Chi 102
Nehf-Bos 96

Strikeouts/Game
Vaughn-Chi 4.59
Cooper-Pit 3.85
Grimes-Bro 3.77
Cheney-Bro 3.72
May-StL 3.60

Ratio
Sallee-NY 9.14
Vaughn-Chi 9.27
Grimes-Bro 9.68
Cooper-Pit 9.68
Tyler-Chi 9.69

Earned Run Average
Vaughn-Chi 1.74
Tyler-Chi 2.00
Cooper-Pit 2.11
Douglas-Chi 2.13
Grimes-Bro 2.14

Adjusted ERA
Vaughn-Chi 160
Tyler-Chi 139
Cooper-Pit 136
Douglas-Chi 131
Grimes-Bro 130

Opponents' Batting Avg.
Vaughn-Chi .... .208
Grimes-Bro .... .216
Cooper-Pit .... .223
Tyler-Chi .... .226
Jacobs-Pit-Phi ... .233

Opponents' On Base Pct.
Sallee-NY .... .259
Vaughn-Chi .... .266
Grimes-Bro .... .276
Perritt-NY .... .278
Cooper-Pit .... .279

Starter Runs
Vaughn-Chi 33.1
Tyler-Chi 22.7
Cooper-Pit 19.9
Grimes-Bro 18.8
Hamilton-Pit 11.6

Adjusted Starter Runs
Vaughn-Chi 33.8
Cooper-Pit 23.3
Tyler-Chi 23.3
Grimes-Bro 19.4
Hamilton-Pit 12.2

Clutch Pitching Index
Bressler-Cin 123
Mayer-Phi-Pit 117
Schneider-Cin 113
Eller-Cin 112
Demaree-NY 112

Relief Runs

Adjusted Relief Runs

Relief Ranking

Total Pitcher Index
Vaughn-Chi 4.4
Cooper-Pit 3.1
Tyler-Chi 3.0
Grimes-Bro 2.6
Hogg-Phi 2.0

Total Baseball Ranking
Vaughn-Chi 4.4
Groh-Cin 3.6
Hornsby-StL 3.6
Fisher-StL 3.5
Cooper-Pit 3.1

April 7* In the morning game of a doubleheader in Los Angeles, Doc Crandall's no-hit bid against Salt Lake City (Pacific Coast League) is spoiled with two outs in the ninth by Crandall's brother Karl, but Los Angeles wins 14–0.

April 15 The AL season opens with Babe Ruth pitching a 4-hit 7–1 victory over the A's. Red Sox manager Ed Barrow will start Ruth's conversion to slugger by working him into 72 games as outfielder-first baseman.

April 18 With two Tigers on base in the ninth, Cleveland center fielder Tris Speaker turns an unassisted double play. On April 29, he will do the same against Chicago, the fourth unassisted double play of his career, a record he will share with Cleveland teammate Elmer Smith.

May 14 Sunday baseball is made legal in Washington, D.C. District commissioners rescind the ban in view of the large increase in the city's wartime population and the need for recreation and amusement facilities. Five days later, the Senators beat Cleveland 1–0 in 18 innings in the first Sunday game as more than 15,000 fans attend.

June 1 Losing 5–4 against the Yankees, the White Sox load the bases in the ninth with no outs. Chick Gandil lines a shot to third baseman Frank Baker, who turns it into a game-ending triple play.

July 8 Babe Ruth's blast over the fence in Fenway scores Amos Strunk, as the Red Sox win 1–0 over Cleveland. Nevertheless, prevailing rules reduce Babe's home run to a triple because the winning run scored ahead of the home run. Ruth will tie for the AL title with 11 homers, even though he plays just 95 games.

July 19 Washington catcher Eddie Ainsmith applies for deferment from the draft. Secretary of War Newton D. Baker rules that baseball is not an essential occupation and all players of draft age are subject to the "work-in-essential-industries-or-fight" rule. The ruling sends many players to work in shipyards and other defense industries, where they can play part-time or semipro. Ban Johnson says the AL will close down July 21, but the next day both leagues vote to continue. A week later, Baker exempts players from the rule until September 1. Both leagues vote to cut the season short, and end on Labor Day, September 2.

July 25 Walter Johnson gives up one hit (a triple by George Sisler) in the first 11 innings of a 15-inning, four-hit 1–0 win.

September 1 Ty Cobb pitches two innings against the Browns while the Browns' George Sisler pitches one scoreless inning. The Browns win 6-2 as Sisler hits a double off Cobb.

September 5 In order to cut down on the use of trains, the first three games of the World Series are played in Chicago, the next three in Boston. The Cubs switch their home games to Comiskey Park with its larger seating capacity. Babe Ruth, having completed 13 scoreless innings in his first World Series two years ago, adds nine more in edging Hippo Vaughn 1-0 in the opener. During the seventh-inning stretch, a military band plays "The Star Spangled Banner." From then on, it is played at every World Series game, every season opener, and whenever a band is present to play it, though it is not yet adopted as the national anthem. The custom of playing it before every game will begin during World War II, after the installation of public address systems.

September 11 The Red Sox win the World Series in Game 6 on Carl Mays's second victory, a 2-1 three-hitter. With two on and two out in the third, utility outfielder George Whiteman lines a hard drive to right field. Max Flack drops it, allowing the only runs off Lefty Tyler. Cubs pitchers compile a 1.04 ERA, while Boston's .186 BA is the lowest ever for a World Series winner. The Red Sox will realize $1,102 each, the Cubs $671, the smallest winner's share ever earned.

BOSTON	CHICAGO	CLEVELAND	DETROIT	NEW YORK	PHILADELPHIA	ST.LOUIS	WASHINGTON
M E.Barrow	M P.Rowland	M L.Fohl	M H.Jennings	M M.Huggins	M C.Mack	M F.Jones	M C.Griffith
1B S.McInnis	1B C.Gandil	1B D.Johnston	1B H.Heilmann	1B W.Pipp	1B G.Burns	1B J.Austin	1B J.Judge
2B D.Shean	2B E.Collins	2B B.Wambsganss	2B R.Young	2B D.Pratt	2B J.Dykes	M J.Burke	2B R.Morgan
SS E.Scott	SS B.Weaver	SS R.Chapman	SS D.Bush	SS R.Peckinpaugh	1B J.Dugan	1B G.Sisler	SS D.Lavan
3B F.Thomas	3B F.McMullin	3B J.Evans	3B O.Vitt	3B F.Baker	3B L.Gardner	2B J.Gedeon	3B E.Foster
LF G.Whiteman	LF N.Leibold	LF J.Wood	LF B.Veach	LF P.Bodie	LF M.Kopp	SS J.Austin	LF B.Shotton
CF A.Strunk	CF S.Collins	CF T.Speaker	CF T.Cobb	CF E.Miller	CF T.Walker	3B F.Maisel	CF C.Milan
RF H.Hooper	RF E.Murphy	RF B.Roth	RF G.Harper	RF F.Gilhooley	RF C.Jamieson	LF E.Smith	RF F.Schulte
C S.Agnew	C R.Schalk	C S.O'Neill	C A.Yelle	C T.Hannah	C W.McAvoy	CF J.Tobin	C E.Ainsmith
OP B.Ruth	S3 S.Risberg	32 T.Turner	3 B.Jones	S2 R.Walters	S2 R.Shannon	RF R.Demmitt	O2 H.Shanks
CO W.Schang	O H.Felsch	O J.Graney	C O.Stanage	O H.Hyatt	C C.Perkins	S2 L.Nunamaker	C V.Picinich
1 D.Hoblitzel	O W.Good	1 E.Miller	O F.Walker	O A.Marsans	O M.Acosta	O T.Hendryx	S G.McBride
3 G.Cochran	3 B.Pinelli	O P.Thomas	O T.Spencer	O B.Lamar	O R.Oldring	S W.Gerber	O S.Rice
C W.Mayer	C O.Jacobs	1 R.Williams	1 L.Dressen	1 J.Fournier	2 C.Davidson	1 H.Severeid	/C J.Casey
3 J.Stansbury	O J.Jackson	3 A.Halt	1 A.Griggs	O J.Hummel	/O J.Munch	1 P.Johns	H P.Gharrity
3 J.Coffey	/2 J.Mostil	O B.Bescher	2 J.Coffey	S A.Ward	/O F.Fahey	S E.Johnson	/C M.Acosta
2 F.Truesdale	1 A.DeVormer	1 M.Kavanagh	1 M.Kavanagh	/O H.High		C G.Hale	/C B.Berman
3 W.Barbare	/1 T.Jourdan	/3 G.Getz	/O B.Ellison	/1 Z.Beck	P S.Perry	/3 K.Williams	P W.Johnson
O H.Miller	/O B.Lynn	/O J.Farmer	/2 J.Curry	/C M.Ruel	P V.Gregg	A.Sothoron	P H.Harper
/2 H.Wagner	H P.Hardgrove	/O E.Onslow	H J.Cobb	/O P.O'Connor	P W.Adams	D.Davenport	P J.Shaw
/S E.Gonzalez	H K.Willson	/2 G.Schaefer	/O H.Jennings	/O S.Vick	P M.Watson	T.Rogers	P D.Ayers
H R.Bluhm		/C J.Billings		/2 C.Fewster	P E.Myers	B.Gallia	P E.Matteson
		/C J.Peters					
P C.Mays	P E.Cicotte	P S.Coveleski	P H.Dauss	P G.Mogridge	P B.Geary	R.Wright	/P E.Yingling
P J.Bush	P F.Shellenback	P J.Bagby	P B.Boland	P S.Love	RP R.Johnson	RP B.Houck	/P E.Hovlik
P S.Jones	P J.Benz	P G.Morton	P R.Kallio	P R.Caldwell	P W.Pierson	U.Shocker	/P N.Altrock
P D.Leonard	P D.Danforth	P F.Coumbe	P G.Cunningham	P A.Russell	/P R.Shea	G.Lowdermilk	/P G.Dumont
/P L.Bader	P R.Russell	P J.Enzmann	P B.James	P H.Finneran	/P V.Keen	L.Leifield	/P R.Hansen
/P W.Kinney	/P L.Williams	P B.Groom	/P E.Erickson	/P H.Thormahlen	/P T.Zachary	B.Morris	/P M.Craft
/P J.Dubuc	/P R.Faber	/P G.McQuillan	/P D.Jones	/P R.Keating	/P C.Holmes	T.McCabe	/P A.Brennan
/P V.Molyneaux	/P J.Quinn	/P O.Lambeth	/P B.Bailey	/P H.Robinson	/P L.Bauer		/P G.Buckeye
/P D.McCabe	/P R.Mitchell	/P A.Brennan	/P H.Coveleski	/P R.Sanders			/P S.Rees
/P B.Pertica	/P M.Wolfgang	/P R.Wilkinson	/P H.Finneran	/P B.Shawkey			
/P W.Wyckoff	/P E.Corey		/P C.Hall	/P A.Ferguson			
			/P B.Donovan	/P E.Monroe			
			/P H.Hall	/P D.Vance			
			/P W.Mitchell	/P W.Bernhardt			
			/P B.Dyer	/P B.McGraw			

TEAM	G	W	L	PCT	GB	R	OR	AB	H	2B	3B	HR	BB	SO	AVG	OBP	SLG	PRO	PRO+	BR	/A	PF	CHI	RC	SB	CS	SBA	SBR
BOS	126	75	51	.595		474	**380**	3982	990	159	54	15	406	**324**	.249	.322	.327	.649	103	5	13	98	105	455	110			
CLE	129	73	54	.575	2.5	**504**	447	4166	1084	**176**	**67**	9	**491**	386	**.260**	**.344**	**.341**	**.685**	102	68	17	110	93	**537**	165			
WAS	130	72	56	.563	4	461	412	4472	**1144**	156	49	4	376	361	.256	.318	.315	.633	98	-21	-13	98	99	479	137			
NY	126	60	63	.488	13.5	493	475	4224	1085	160	45	20	367	370	.257	.320	.330	.650	99	2	-8	102	**106**	469	88			
STL	123	58	64	.475	15	426	448	4019	1040	152	40	5	397	340	.259	.331	.320	.651	105	11	**25**	97	93	467	138			
CHI	124	57	67	.460	17	457	446	4132	1057	136	55	8	375	358	.256	.322	.321	.643	98	-5	-9	101	102	458	116			
DET	128	55	71	.437	20	476	557	4262	1063	141	56	13	452	380	.249	.325	.318	.643	103	-2	17	96	101	470	123			
PHI	130	52	76	.406	24	412	538	4278	1039	124	44	**22**	343	485	.243	.303	.308	.611	88	-59	-63	101	102	415	83			
TOT	508					3703		33535	8502	1204	410	96	3207	3004	.254	.323	.322	.646							960			

TEAM	CG	SH	SV	IP	H	H/G	HR	BB	SO	RAT	ERA	ERA+	OAV	OOB	PR	/A	PF	CPI	FA	E	DP	FW	PW	BW	SBW	DIF
BOS	105	**26**	2	1120	**931**	7.5	**9**	380	392	10.8	2.31	116	**.231**	.302	58	47	97	95	**.971**	152	89	**2.5**	5.2	1.5		2.8
CLE	78	5	**13**	1161	1126	8.7	**9**	343	364	11.5	2.64	114	.262	.319	18	46	108	105	.962	207	82	-.7	5.1	1.9		3.1
WAS	75	19	8	1228	1021	**7.5**	10	395	**505**	10.6	**2.14**	**127**	**.231**	.298	**86**	**80**	98	99	.960	226	95	-1.8	**8.9**	-1.5		2.3
NY	59	8	**13**	1157¹	1103	8.6	25	463	370	12.5	3.00	94	.261	.340	-30	-24	102	**107**	.970	161	137	1.9	-2.7	-.9		.2
STL	67	8	8	1111¹	993	8.0	11	402	346	11.5	2.75	99	.246	.319	2	-2	99	98	.963	190	86	-.2	-.2	**2.8**		-5.4
CHI	76	9	8	1126	1092	8.7	**9**	**300**	349	11.3	2.73	100	.261	.314	5	-3	99	97	.967	169	98	1.2	-.3	-1.0		-4.9
DET	74	8	7	1160²	1130	8.8	10	437	374	12.4	3.40	78	.263	.335	-81	-99	96	89	.960	212	77	-1.1	-11.0	1.9		2.2
PHI	80	13	9	1156	1106	8.6	13	486	277	12.7	3.22	91	.266	.348	-58	-39	106	103	.959	228	136	-1.9	-4.4	-7.0		1.3
TOT	614	96	68	9220¹		8.3				11.7	2.77		.254	.323					.964	1545	800					

Runs		Hits		Doubles		Triples		Home Runs		Total Bases	
Chapman-Cle	84	Burns-Phi	178	Speaker-Cle	33	T.Cobb-Det	14	Walker-Phi	11	Burns-Phi	236
T.Cobb-Det	83	T.Cobb-Det	161	Ruth-Bos	26	Veach-Det	13	Ruth-Bos	11	T.Cobb-Det	217
Hooper-Bos	81	Sisler-StL	154	Hooper-Bos	26	Hooper-Bos	13	Burns-Phi	6	Baker-NY	206
Bush-Det	74	Baker-NY	154	Baker-NY	24	Roth-Cle	12	Baker-NY	6	Speaker-Cle	205
Speaker-Cle	73	Speaker-Cle	150							Sisler-StL	199

Runs Batted In		Runs Produced		Bases On Balls		Batting Average		On Base Percentage		Slugging Average	
Veach-Det	78	T.Cobb-Det	144	Chapman-Cle	84	T.Cobb-Det	.382	T.Cobb-Det	.440	Ruth-Bos	.555
Burns-Phi	70	Veach-Det	134	Bush-Det	79	Burns-Phi	.352	E.Collins-Chi	.407	T.Cobb-Det	.515
Wood-Cle	66	Speaker-Cle	134	Hooper-Bos	75	Sisler-StL	.341	Speaker-Cle	.403	Burns-Phi	.467
Ruth-Bos	66	Burns-Phi	125	E.Collins-Chi	73	Speaker-Cle	.318	Sisler-StL	.400	Sisler-StL	.440
T.Cobb-Det	64	Hooper-Bos	124	Shotton-Was	67	Baker-NY	.306	Hooper-Bos	.391	Speaker-Cle	.435

Production		Adjusted Production		Batter Runs		Adjusted Batter Runs		Clutch Hitting Index		Runs Created	
T.Cobb-Det	.955	T.Cobb-Det	196	T.Cobb-Det	44.0	T.Cobb-Det	47.8	Veach-Det	140	T.Cobb-Det	105
Burns-Phi	.857	Sisler-StL	159	Ruth-Bos	34.8	Ruth-Bos	36.0	Demmitt-StL	137	Sisler-StL	92
Sisler-StL	.841	Burns-Phi	157	Burns-Phi	32.8	Burns-Phi	31.9	McInnis-Phi	136	Burns-Phi	91
Speaker-Cle	.839	Hooper-Bos	142	Speaker-Cle	31.3	Sisler-StL	31.3	Shanks-Was	133	Speaker-Cle	90
Hooper-Bos	.796	Speaker-Cle	140	Sisler-StL	28.8	Hooper-Bos	26.5	S.Collins-Chi	132	Hooper-Bos	82

Total Average		Stolen Bases		Stolen Base Average		Stolen Base Runs		Fielding Runs		Total Player Rating	
T.Cobb-Det	1.131	Sisler-StL	45					Peckinpaugh-NY	25.0	T.Cobb-Det	4.8
Sisler-StL	.970	Roth-Cle	35					Scott-Bos	17.5	Sisler-StL	3.8
Speaker-Cle	.931	T.Cobb-Det	34					Dugan-Phi	17.0	Burns-Phi	3.6
Roth-Cle	.929	Chapman-Cle	30					Gedeon-StL	15.8	Baker-NY	3.2
Hooper-Bos	.875	Speaker-Cle	27					S.Collins-Chi	14.1	Speaker-Cle	3.0

Wins		Win Percentage		Games		Complete Games		Shutouts		Saves	
Johnson-Was	23	Jones-Bos	.762	Mogridge-NY	45	Perry-Phi	30	Mays-Bos	8	Mogridge-NY	7
Coveleski-Cle	22	Johnson-Was	.639	Bagby-Cle	45	Mays-Bos	30	Johnson-Was	8	Bagby-Cle	6
Mays-Bos	21	Coveleski-Cle	.629	Perry-Phi	44	Johnson-Was	29	Bush-Bos	7	Russell-NY	4
Perry-Phi	20	Mays-Bos	.618	Shaw-Was	41	Bush-Bos	26	Jones-Bos	5	Geary-Phi	4
Bagby-Cle	17	Shaw-Was	.571	Ayers-Was	40	Coveleski-Cle	25				

Innings Pitched		Fewest Hits/Game		Fewest BB/Game		Strikeouts		Strikeouts/Game		Ratio	
Perry-Phi	332.1	Sothoron-StL	6.55	Cicotte-Chi	1.35	Johnson-Was	162	Morton-Cle	5.16	Johnson-Was	8.81
Johnson-Was	326.0	Johnson-Was	6.65	Mogridge-NY	1.62	Shaw-Was	129	Shaw-Was	4.81	Ruth-Bos	9.52
Coveleski-Cle	311.0	Harper-Was	6.71	Benz-Chi	1.64	Bush-Bos	125	Johnson-Was	4.47	Sothoron-StL	9.56
Mays-Bos	293.1	Ruth-Bos	6.76	Enzmann-Cle	1.91	Morton-Cle	123	Bush-Bos	4.13	Coveleski-Cle	9.87
Bush-Bos	272.2	Mays-Bos	7.06	Johnson-Was	1.93	Mays-Bos	114	Love-NY	3.74	Mays-Bos	9.88

Earned Run Average		Adjusted ERA		Opponents' Batting Avg.		Opponents' On Base Pct.		Starter Runs		Adjusted Starter Runs	
Johnson-Was	1.27	Johnson-Was	214	Sothoron-StL	.205	Johnson-Was	.260	Johnson-Was	54.4	Johnson-Was	52.6
Coveleski-Cle	1.82	Coveleski-Cle	164	Johnson-Was	.210	Sothoron-StL	.274	Coveleski-Cle	32.8	Coveleski-Cle	40.6
Sothoron-StL	1.94	Perry-Phi	148	Harper-Was	.212	Ruth-Bos	.277	Perry-Phi	29.4	Perry-Phi	35.1
Perry-Phi	1.98	Sothoron-StL	141	Ruth-Bos	.214	Coveleski-Cle	.279	Bush-Bos	20.0	Sothoron-StL	18.5
Bush-Bos	2.11	Mogridge-NY	129	Mays-Bos	.221	Mays-Bos	.284	Sothoron-StL	19.4	Bush-Bos	17.1

Clutch Pitching Index		Relief Runs		Adjusted Relief Runs		Relief Ranking		Total Pitcher Index		Total Baseball Ranking	
Perry-Phi	124	Houck-StL	3.1	Houck-StL	2.8	Houck-StL	2.3	Johnson-Was	7.6	Johnson-Was	7.6
Mogridge-NY	123							Coveleski-Cle	4.6	Ruth-Bos	5.6
Coumbe-Cle	119							Mays-Bos	4.1	T.Cobb-Det	4.8
Russell-NY	119							Perry-Phi	3.9	Coveleski-Cle	4.6
Shellenback-Chi	116							Bush-Bos	3.1	Mays-Bos	4.1

January 14 John McGraw, Charles A. Stoneham, and Tammany politician Judge Francis X. McQuade buy controlling interest in the Giants from the John Brush estate.

January 30 When no word is received from manager Christy Mathewson, who is still in France, the Reds hire Pat Moran as manager.

February 1 After winning an out-of-court settlement of his suit against the Dodgers for the balance of his salary ($2,150) when the 1918 season ended a month early, former MVP Jake Daubert is traded to the Reds for outfielder Tommy Griffith.

February 5 Charges brought in 1918 by Reds owner Garry Herrmann and manager Mathewson against Hal Chase for betting against his team and throwing games in collusion with gamblers are dismissed by NL president John Heydler. Heydler decides Chase's sometimes indifferent play was due to "carelessness." Two weeks later John McGraw trades first baseman Walter Holke and catcher Bill Rariden to the Reds for Chase.

April 19 Pushed through the legislature by future New York City mayor Jimmy Walker, a bill legalizing Sunday baseball in the state is signed by Governor Al Smith.

April 23 Anticipating a poor season at the gate, the major leagues open a reduced 140-game season. Despite the lack of close races, attendance remains high all year and every club will show a profit.

May 4 The Giants play their first legal Sunday game at home, before 35,000 fans, losing to the Phils 4–3. More than 25,000 turn out in Brooklyn the same day.

May 25 Ever-popular Casey Stengel, now a Pirate, is good-naturedly applauded when he comes to bat in the seventh inning at Brooklyn, doffs his cap in response, and to everyone's delight releases an "irate but much relieved" sparrow he had hidden there.

June 15 A rain check dispute arises. Cincinnati rain checks read "not to be used after four and a half innings have been completed." But the game is called with the Reds at bat with one out in the bottom of the fifth and the game tied 1–1. The Reds honor the rain checks, but the Braves demand their share of the gate ($2,600), as a legal game has been played, based on the wording of the rain check. In a compromise, the Braves accept $1,300, and the other six clubs agree to share the cost. In future all rain checks will read "not good after five innings."

September 2 The National Commission recommends a best-of-9 World Series. The lengthier World Series is seen as a sign of greed and is abandoned after three years.

September 16 Dutch Ruether beats the Giants 4-3 to clinch the Reds' first pennant since American Association days.

October 1 Eddie Cicotte, a 29-game winner, is driven to cover in a 5-run fourth in the Series opener. Reds outfielder Greasy Neale, the only man to play in a World Series, coach a football team in the Rose Bowl, and become a pro football Hall of Fame coach, has three hits and will top the Reds with .357 for the Series.

October 9 Lefty Williams gets one man out in the first before departing. The Reds lead 4-0, and go on to give Hod Eller a 10-5 victory and the Reds the world title in eight games.

December 10 The NL proposes to ban the spitball's use by all new pitchers. The ban will be formally worked out by the Rules Committee in February.

BOSTON	BROOKLYN	CHICAGO	CINCINNATI	NEW YORK	PHILADELPHIA	PITTSBURGH	ST.LOUIS
M G.Stallings	M W.Robinson	M F.Mitchell	M P.Moran	M J.McGraw	M J.Coombs	M H.Bezdek	M B.Rickey
1B W.Holke	1B E.Konetchy	1B F.Merkle	1B J.Daubert	1B H.Chase	1B G.Cravath	1B F.Mollwitz	1B D.Miller
2B B.Herzog	2B J.Johnston	2B C.Pick	2B M.Rath	2B L.Doyle	1B F.Luderus	2B G.Cutshaw	2B M.Stock
SS R.Maranville	SS I.Olson	SS C.Hollocher	SS L.Kopf	SS A.Fletcher	2B G.Paulette	SS Z.Terry	SS D.Lavan
3B T.Boeckel	3B L.Malone	3B C.Deal	3B H.Groh	3B H.Zimmerman	SS D.Bancroft	3B W.Barbare	3B R.Hornsby
LF W.Cruise	LF Z.Wheat	LF L.Mann	LF R.Bressler	LF G.Burns	3B L.Blackburne	LF B.Southworth	LF A.McHenry
CF J.Riggert	CF H.Myers	CF M.Flack	CF E.Roush	CF B.Kauff	LF I.Meusel	CF C.Bigbee	CF C.Heathcote
RF R.Powell	RF T.Griffith		RF G.Neale	RF R.Youngs	CF C.Williams	RF C.Stengel	RF J.Smith
C H.Gowdy	C E.Krueger	C B.Killefer	C I.Wingo	C L.McCarty	RF L.Callahan	C W.Schmidt	C V.Clemons
O3 R.Smith	2 L.Magee	OS L.Magee	C B.Rariden	23 F.Frisch	C B.Adams	O M.Carey	O J.Schultz
2O J.Rawlings	C O.Miller	O T.Barber	O S.Magee	C M.Gonzalez	O2 P.Whitted	1 V.Saier	O B.Shotton
C A.Wilson	3 C.Ward	2 B.Herzog	O P.Duncan	1 G.Kelly	2S H.Pearce	3 T.Boeckel	C F.Snyder
O J.Thorpe	21 R.Schmandt	O B.O'Farrell	O M.Cueto	C F.Snyder	3 D.Baird	1 P.Whitted	1 G.Paulette
O L.Mann	C M.Wheat	O D.Robertson	3 H.Schreiber	2 A.Baird	O G.Cravath	C C.Lee	C P.Dilhoefer
2 C.Pick	O J.Hickman	3 P.Kilduff	/3 J.Smith	O J.Statz	S2 W.Tragesser	S3 H.Caton	1 F.Mollwitz
3 L.Blackburne	3 P.Kilduff	O B.McCabe	C N.Allen	C E.Smith	C H.Cady	O F.Nicholson	/3 D.Baird
O J.Kelly	3 D.Baird	/1 F.Lear	/O C.See	/O L.King	C B.LeBourveau	C F.Blackwell	/1 R.Leslie
O D.Nutter	/O H.Allen	C T.Daly	/O W.Rehg	/S E.Sicking	O N.Clarke	1 C.Grimm	/O W.Cruise
O D.Carroll	O O.O'Mara	/O W.Rehg	/O B.Zitzmann	/S J.Cooney	/S D.Wallace	/O J.Sweeney	/2 H.Janvrin
C W.Tragesser	/3 T.Fitzsimmons	/O B.Zitzmann	P H.Eller	/O B.Kinsella	/2 L.Raymond	/3 H.Warner	/2 B.Fisher
/O L.Christenbury	P J.Pfeffer	/O H.Reilly	P D.Ruether	/O C.Bowen	/3 J.Cavanaugh	P W.Cooper	/1 S.Fishburn
/S H.Ford	P L.Cadore	P H.Vaughn	P S.Sallee	/O J.Thorpe	H M.Pasquella	P B.Adams	/S W.Kimmick
C M.O'Neil	P A.Mamaux	P P.Alexander	P J.Ring	R D.Robertson	H B.Yeabsley	P F.Miller	H M.Pasquella
/O G.Bailey	P B.Grimes	P C.Hendrix	P R.Fisher	P J.Barnes	P G.Smith	P E.Hamilton	P B.Doak
H T.Miller	P S.Smith	P S.Martin	P D.Luque	P R.Benton	P L.Meadows	P H.Carlson	P M.Goodwin
H L.King	P C.Mitchell	P P.Douglas	/P R.Mitchell	P F.Toney	P E.Rixey	P E.Mayer	P O.Tuero
/C S.White	/P R.Marquard	P P.Carter	/P E.Gerner	P J.Dubuc	/P B.Hogg	P E.Ponder	P B.Sherdel
P D.Rudolph	/P L.Cheney	/P S.Bailey	/P M.Regan	P R.Causey	/P G.Packard	/P B.Evans	P J.May
P D.Fillingim	/P L.Henion	/P L.Tyler		P A.Nehf	P E.Jacobs	/P J.Wisner	P L.Meadows
P A.Nehf	/P J.Newkirk	/P H.Weaver		/P P.Douglas	P F.Woodward	/P C.Hill	P E.Jacobs
P R.Keating		/P J.Newkirk		/P F.Schupp	P L.Cheney		P F.Woodward
P A.Demaree				P J.Winters	P M.Watson		P R.Ames
P J.Scott				/P P.Ragan	P J.Oeschger		P F.Schupp
P R.Causey				/P P.Ryan	P P.Murray		/P O.Horstmann
P H.McQuillan				/P P.Perritt	P M.Cantwell		/P B.Bolden
/P J.Oeschger				/P B.Hubbell	P R.Ames		/P R.Parker
P J.Northrop				/P G.Smith	/P M.Prendergast		/P W.Koenigsmark
/P L.Cheney				/P C.Snover	/P L.Weinert		/P A.Reinhart
/P P.Ragan				/P J.Oeschger	/P R.Faircloth		
/P B.James				/P J.Jones			
				/P B.Steele			
				/P V.Barnes			

TEAM	G	W	L	PCT	GB	R	OR	AB	H	2B	3B	HR	BB	SO	AVG	OBP	SLG	PRO	PRO+	BR	/A	PF	CHI	RC	SB	CS	SBA	SBR
CIN	140	96	44	.686		577	401	4577	1204	135	**83**	20	405	368	.263	**.327**	.342	.669	110	43	57	97	104	552	143			
NY	140	87	53	.621	9	**605**	470	4664	1254	204	64	40	328	407	**.269**	.322	**.366**	**.688**	113	64	70	99	**106**	**576**	157			
CHI	140	75	65	.536	21	454	407	4581	1174	166	58	21	298	359	.256	.308	.332	.640	98	-14	-16	101	93	500	150			
PIT	139	71	68	.511	24.5	472	466	4538	1132	130	82	17	344	381	.249	.306	.325	.631	91	-25	-44	104	100	493	**196**			
BRO	141	69	71	.493	27	525	513	4844	**1272**	167	66	25	258	405	.263	.304	.340	.644	97	-13	-24	102	104	518	112			
BOS	140	57	82	.410	38.5	465	563	4746	1201	142	62	24	355	481	.253	.311	.324	.635	100	-17	4	96	92	509	145			
STL	138	54	83	.394	40.5	463	552	4588	1175	163	52	18	304	418	.256	.305	.326	.631	101	-28	1	94	99	485	148			
PHI	138	47	90	.343	47.5	510	699	4746	1191	**208**	50	**42**	323	469	.251	.303	.342	.645	92	-9	-45	107	101	506	114			
TOT	558					4071		37284	9603	1315	517	207	2615	3288	.258	.311	.337	.648							1165			

TEAM	CG	SH	SV	IP	H	H/G	HR	BB	SO	RAT	ERA	ERA+	OAV	OOB	PR	/A	PF	CPI	FA	E	DP	FW	PW	BW	SBW	DIF
CIN	89	**23**	9	1274	**1104**	**7.8**	21	298	407	10.0	2.23	124	**.239**	.288	96	75	95	104	**.974**	151	98	**2.7**	8.3	6.3		8.6
NY	72	11	**13**	1256	1153	8.3	34	305	340	10.6	2.70	104	.247	.296	29	14	96	96	.964	216	96	-1.0	1.6	**7.8**		8.7
CHI	80	21	5	1265	1127	8.0	**14**	294	**495**	10.3	2.21	130	.242	.291	98	93	99	106	.969	185	87	.7	**10.3**	-1.8		-4.3
PIT	91	17	4	1249	1113	8.0	23	**263**	391	10.2	2.88	105	.244	.290	4	19	104	84	.970	165	89	1.8	2.1	-4.9		2.5
BRO	**98**	12	1	1281	1256	8.8	21	292	476	11.1	2.73	109	.262	.309	25	33	102	106	.963	219	84	-1.1	3.7	-2.7		-.9
BOS	79	5	9	1270¹	1313	9.3	29	337	374	11.8	3.17	90	.276	.327	-36	-45	98	**107**	.966	204	111	-.4	-5.0	.4		-7.6
STL	55	6	8	1217¹	1146	8.5	25	415	414	11.9	3.23	86	.256	.326	-44	-60	96	97	.963	214	112	-1.1	-6.7	.1		-6.8
PHI	93	6	2	1252	1391	10.0	40	408	397	13.3	4.14	78	.294	.356	-171	-129	111	100	.963	218	112	-1.3	-14.3	-5.0		-.8
TOT	657	101	51	10064²		8.6				11.2	2.91		.258	.311					.967	1572	789					

Runs		Hits		Doubles		Triples		Home Runs		Total Bases	
Burns-NY	86	Olson-Bro	164	Youngs-NY	31	Southworth-Pit	14	Cravath-Phi	12	Myers-Bro	223
Groh-Cin	79	Hornsby-StL	163	Luderus-Phi	30	Myers-Bro	14	Kauff-NY	10	Hornsby-StL	220
Daubert-Cin	79	Roush-Cin	162	Burns-NY	30			Williams-Phi	9	Z.Wheat-Bro	219
Rath-Cin	77	Burns-NY	162	Kauff-NY	27			Hornsby-StL	8	Roush-Cin	217
				Meusel-Phi	26			Doyle-NY	7	Burns-NY	216

Runs Batted In		Runs Produced		Bases On Balls		Batting Average		On Base Percentage		Slugging Average	
Myers-Bro	73	Roush-Cin	140	Burns-NY	82	Roush-Cin	.321	Burns-NY	.396	Myers-Bro	.436
Roush-Cin	71	Groh-Cin	137	Rath-Cin	64	Hornsby-StL	.318	Groh-Cin	.392	Doyle-NY	.433
Hornsby-StL	71	Hornsby-StL	131	Groh-Cin	56	Youngs-NY	.311	Hornsby-StL	.384	Groh-Cin	.431
Kauff-NY	67			Luderus-Phi	54	Groh-Cin	.310	Youngs-NY	.384	Roush-Cin	.431
Groh-Cin	63			Boeckel-Pit-Bos	53	Stock-StL	.307	Roush-Cin	.380	Hornsby-StL	.430

Production		Adjusted Production		Batter Runs		Adjusted Batter Runs		Clutch Hitting Index		Runs Created	
Groh-Cin	.823	Hornsby-StL	154	Cravath-Phi	32.2	Hornsby-StL	33.8	Kopf-Cin	125	Burns-NY	96
Hornsby-StL	.814	Groh-Cin	151	Burns-NY	30.0	Burns-NY	31.1	Southworth-Pit	123	Roush-Cin	88
Roush-Cin	.811	Roush-Cin	147	Hornsby-StL	28.5	Groh-Cin	29.4	Zimmerman-NY	121	Hornsby-StL	87
Burns-NY	.801	Burns-NY	142	Groh-Cin	27.4	Roush-Cin	29.1	Roush-Cin	121	Youngs-NY	84
Youngs-NY	.799	Youngs-NY	142	Roush-Cin	26.9	Cravath-Phi	28.3	Merkle-Chi	120	Groh-Cin	81

Total Average		Stolen Bases		Stolen Base Average		Stolen Base Runs		Fielding Runs		Total Player Rating	
Burns-NY	.909	Burns-NY	40					Maranville-Bos	28.7	Maranville-Bos	4.7
Groh-Cin	.887	Cutshaw-Pit	36					Fletcher-NY	24.0	Hornsby-StL	4.5
Youngs-NY	.846	Bigbee-Pit	31					Bigbee-Pit	17.9	Stock-StL	4.3
Hornsby-StL	.837	Smith-StL	30					Killefer-Chi	17.4	Groh-Cin	3.5
Roush-Cin	.833							Stock-StL	16.8	Roush-Cin	3.3

Wins		Win Percentage		Games		Complete Games		Shutouts		Saves	
J.Barnes-NY	25	Ruether-Cin	.760	Tuero-StL	45	Cooper-Pit	27	Alexander-Chi	9	Tuero-StL	4
Vaughn-Chi	21	Sallee-Cin	.750	Meadows-StL-Phi	40	Pfeffer-Bro	26	Eller-Cin	7		
Sallee-Cin	21	J.Barnes-NY	.735	Vaughn-Chi	38	Vaughn-Chi	25	Adams-Pit	6		
		Eller-Cin	.679	Eller-Cin	38	Rudolph-Bos	24	Fisher-Cin	5		
		Adams-Pit	.630	J.Barnes-NY	38						

Innings Pitched		Fewest Hits/Game		Fewest BB/Game		Strikeouts		Strikeouts/Game		Ratio	
Vaughn-Chi	306.2	Alexander-Chi	6.89	Adams-Pit	.79	Vaughn-Chi	141	Eller-Cin	4.97	Adams-Pit	8.17
J.Barnes-NY	295.2	Cooper-Pit	7.19	Sallee-Cin	.79	Eller-Cin	137	Alexander-Chi	4.63	Alexander-Chi	8.35
Cooper-Pit	286.2	Ruether-Cin	7.23	J.Barnes-NY	1.07	Alexander-Chi	121	Meadows-StL-Phi	4.17	J.Barnes-NY	9.13
Rudolph-Bos	273.2	Carlson-Pit	7.28	Cadore-Bro	1.40	Meadows-StL-Phi	116	Vaughn-Chi	4.14	Fisher-Cin	9.29
Nehf-Bos-NY	270.2	Fisher-Cin	7.28	Alexander-Chi	1.46	Cooper-Pit	106	Grimes-Bro	4.07	Miller-Pit	9.33

Earned Run Average		Adjusted ERA		Opponents' Batting Avg.		Opponents' On Base Pct.		Starter Runs		Adjusted Starter Runs	
Alexander-Chi	1.72	Alexander-Chi	167	Alexander-Chi	.211	Adams-Pit	.241	Vaughn-Chi	38.1	Vaughn-Chi	37.0
Vaughn-Chi	1.79	Vaughn-Chi	161	Adams-Pit	.220	Alexander-Chi	.245	Alexander-Chi	31.0	Adams-Pit	30.3
Ruether-Cin	1.82	Ruether-Cin	152	Ruether-Cin	.223	J.Barnes-NY	.260	Ruether-Cin	29.4	Alexander-Chi	30.1
Toney-NY	1.84	Toney-NY	152	Cooper-Pit	.225	Fisher-Cin	.271	Adams-Pit	27.1	Ruether-Cin	25.7
Adams-Pit	1.98	Adams-Pit	152	Nehf-Bos-NY	.225	Miller-Pit	.272	Rudolph-Bos	22.5	Rudolph-Bos	20.8

Clutch Pitching Index		Relief Runs		Adjusted Relief Runs		Relief Ranking		Total Pitcher Index		Total Baseball Ranking	
Rudolph-Bos	141							Alexander-Chi	4.4	Maranville-Bos	4.7
Smith-Bro	141							Vaughn-Chi	4.2	Hornsby-StL	4.5
Martin-Chi	122							Ruether-Cin	3.1	Alexander-Chi	4.4
Jacobs-Phi-StL	122							Rudolph-Bos	2.9	Stock-StL	4.3
Toney-NY	120							Adams-Pit	2.7	Vaughn-Chi	4.2

March 1 Connie Mack makes one of his biggest player mistakes, trading third baseman Larry Gardner, outfielder Charlie Jamieson, and pitcher Elmer Myers to Cleveland for outfielder Braggo Roth. Roth will be shipped on to Boston by midseason. Gardner will put in six more .300 years, and Jamieson will be a top leadoff man and .303 hitter for the next 14 years.

July 13 Submarine pitcher Carl Mays quits the mound after two innings at Chicago, blaming his teammates for lack of support afield. In defiance of Ban Johnson's order that no action be taken until Mays is returned to good standing, Boston owner Harry Frazee trades Mays to the Yankees for pitchers Bob McGraw, Allen Russell and $40,000. Johnson suspends Mays indefinitely and orders umpires not to let him pitch for New York. The Yankees get a court order restraining Johnson from interfering, further eroding Johnson's authority and standing. The AL directors will reinstate Mays. In retaliation, on October 29 the National Commission will refuse to recognize the Yankees' third-place finish and will withhold the players' share of the pool. New York's owners will pay out of their own pockets.

August 14 Chicago White Sox center fielder Happy Felsch ties the major league record with four outfield assists in one game, but Boston beats the White Sox 15-6.

August 20* Wichita outfielder Joe Wilhoit (Western League) fails to get a hit, ending a 69-game streak in which he collected 155 hits in 299 at bats for a .505 batting average. The previous record was 49 by Oakland's Jack Ness (Pacific Coast League) in 1915.

August 24 Cleveland pitcher Ray Caldwell is flattened by a bolt of lightning in his debut with the team. He recovers to get the final out of the game, and defeats Philadelphia 2-1. Two weeks later he no-hits the Yankees.

September 20 Babe Ruth ties Ned Williamson's major league home run mark of 27 with a game-winner off Lefty Williams of the White Sox. Four days later he will hit No. 28 over the roof of the Polo Grounds.

October 1 Just before the start of the World Series, the highly favored White Sox became the betting underdogs. A year later the White Sox will become known as the Black Sox. Eight of them—pitchers Eddie Cicotte and Lefty Williams, outfielders Joe Jackson and Happy Felsch, first baseman Chick Gandil, shortstop Swede Risberg, third baseman Buck Weaver, and utility infielder Fred McMullin—will be barred from baseball for taking part in throwing the Series.

October 7 Happy Felsch's error and two boots by Swede Risberg help put Dickie Kerr in the hole 4-0, but Felsch, Weaver, and Jackson combine for seven hits as the Sox win 5-4. Dutch Ruether doesn't survive the sixth; Jimmy Ring is the loser, as Kerr wins his second game.

October 8 Ed Cicotte pitches Game 7, and the Sox play like they mean it. Joe Jackson and Felsch drive in two each for a 4-1 win.

December 26 Although it will not be officially announced until January, the Yankees buy Babe Ruth from financially pressed Harry Frazee, paying $100,000 (one-fourth cash, plus $25,000 a year at six percent) plus guaranteeing a $300,000 loan with Fenway Park as collateral.

	BOSTON		CHICAGO		CLEVELAND		DETROIT		NEW YORK		PHILADELPHIA		ST.LOUIS		WASHINGTON
M	E.Barrow	M	K.Gleason	M	L.Fohl	M	H.Jennings	M	M.Huggins	M	C.Mack	M	J.Burke	M	C.Griffith
1B	S.McInnis	1B	C.Gandil	M	T.Speaker	1B	H.Heilmann	1B	W.Pipp	1B	G.Burns	1B	G.Sisler	1B	J.Judge
2B	R.Shannon	2B	E.Collins	1B	D.Johnston	2B	R.Young	2B	D.Pratt	2B	W.Witt	2B	J.Gedeon	2B	H.Janvrin
SS	E.Scott	SS	S.Risberg	2B	B.Wambsganss	SS	D.Bush	SS	R.Peckinpaugh	SS	J.Dugan	SS	W.Gerber	SS	H.Shanks
3B	O.Vitt	3B	B.Weaver	SS	R.Chapman	3B	B.Jones	3B	F.Baker	3B	F.Thomas	3B	J.Austin	3B	E.Foster
LF	B.Ruth	LF	J.Jackson	3B	L.Gardner	LF	B.Veach	LF	D.Lewis	LF	M.Kopp	LF	J.Tobin	LF	M.Menosky
CF	B.Roth	CF	H.Felsch	LF	J.Graney	CF	T.Cobb	CF	P.Bodie	CF	T.Walker	CF	B.Jacobson	CF	C.Milan
RF	H.Hooper	RF	N.Leibold	CF	T.Speaker	RF	I.Flagstead	RF	S.Vick	RF	A.Strunk	RF	E.Smith	RF	S.Rice
C	W.Schang	C	R.Schalk	RF	E.Smith	C	E.Ainsmith	C	M.Ruel	C	C.Perkins	C	H.Severeid	C	V.Picinich
				C	S.O'Neill										
O	A.Strunk	O	S.Collins			O	C.Shorten	OS	C.Fewster	O	B.Roth	O	K.Williams	CO	P.Gharrity
O	B.Lamar	3	F.McMullin	O	J.Wood	2O	B.Ellison	C	T.Hannah	1O	D.Burrus	O	R.Demmitt	O	B.Murphy
C	R.Walters	C	B.Lynn	1	J.Harris	C	O.Stanage	O	A.Wickland	C	W.McAvoy	32	H.Bronkie	23	J.Leonard
1O	D.Gainer	/O	E.Murphy	S	H.Lunte	3S	B.Dyer	/1	A.Ward	2	R.Shannon	C	J.Billings	S	F.Ellerbe
O	F.Gilhooley	/C	J.Jenkins	C	L.Nunamaker	/C	A.Yelle	/O	G.Halas	S2	T.Turner	O	T.Sloan	O	S.Agnew
2	J.Barry	/3	H.McClellan	C	P.Thomas	R	S.Dowd	/O	B.Lamar	1	I.Griffin	C	W.Mayer	2	R.Grover
2	D.Shean			/S	J.Evans			/O	F.Gleich	S	C.Galloway	3	J.Schepner	S	G.McBride
S3	M.McNally	P	E.Cicotte			P	H.Dauss	/C	F.Hofmann	A	A.Wingo	/2	J.Shovlin	/2	B.Harris
/O	J.Wilhoit	P	L.Williams	P	S.Coveleski	P	H.Ehmke	H	F.Kane	2	R.Grover	/C	P.Collins	/S	I.Davis
/C	N.McNeil	P	D.Kerr	P	J.Bagby	P	B.Boland	H	C.Walker	/O	F.Welch	/S	G.Robertson	/3	C.Davidson
		P	R.Faber	P	G.Morton	P	D.Leonard			2	J.Dykes			P	D.Silva
P	S.Jones	P	G.Lowdermilk	P	E.Myers	P	D.Ayers	P	J.Quinn	/3	A.Ewoldt	P	A.Sothoron	/O	G.Twombly
P	H.Pennock	RP	D.Danforth	P	G.Uhle	RP	G.Cunningham	P	B.Shawkey	/O	C.High	P	B.Gallia	H	F.Kelliher
P	C.Mays			RP	T.Phillips			P	H.Thormahlen	P	B.Allen	P	U.Shocker	/S	J.Baker
P	A.Russell	/P	B.James					/C	G.Mogridge	/C	L.Styles	P	C.Weilman		
P	W.Hoyt	/P	F.Shellenback	P	H.Jasper	P	R.Kallio	P	C.Mays	/2	S.Dowd	P	D.Davenport	P	J.Shaw
		/P	E.Mayer	P	J.Enzmann	/P	E.Erickson			/C	J.Walker	RP	E.Koob	P	W.Johnson
P	R.Caldwell	/P	R.Wilkinson	/P	R.Caldwell	/P	W.Mitchell	P	E.Shore	/3	L.Groh	RP	R.Wright	P	H.Harper
P	B.James	/P	J.Sullivan	/P	F.Coumbe	/P	B.James	P	A.Russell					P	E.Erickson
P	G.Dumont	/P	W.Noyes	/P	T.Faeth			/P	P.Schneider	P	R.Naylor	/P	L.Leifield		
P	B.McGraw	/P	T.McGuire	/P	C.Jamieson			/P	L.Nelson	P	W.Kinney	/P	R.Mapel	P	T.Zachary
/P	P.Musser	/P	J.Benz	/P	E.Klepfer			/P	W.Smallwood	/P	J.Johnson	/P	E.Vangilder	P	M.Craft
/P	J.Bush	/P	C.Robertson	/P	J.Engel			/P	B.McGraw	P	S.Perry	/P	B.Bayne	P	D.Ayers
/P	G.Winn	/P	P.Ragan					/P	L.O'Doul	P	T.Rogers	/P	G.Lowdermilk	P	H.Thompson
		/P	R.Russell							/P	H.Haid	/P	T.Rogers	P	E.Gill
										P	W.Noyes			/P	D.Robertson
										P	S.Seibold			/P	H.Courtney
										/P	B.Geary			/P	A.Schacht
										/P	J.Zinn			/P	C.Whitehouse
										/P	C.Eckert			/P	B.Snyder
										/P	D.Boone			/P	E.Hovlik
										/P	W.Anderson			/P	C.Fisher
										/P	R.Roberts			/P	R.Jordan
										/P	M.Watson			/P	N.Altrock
										/P	B.Grevell				
										/P	B.Hasty				
										/P	H.Thompson				
										/P	P.Martin				
										/P	D.Keefe				
										/P	M.Kircher				
										/P	W.Pierson				
										/P	W.Adams				
										/P	L.York				

TEAM	G	W	L	PCT	GB	R	OR	AB	H	2B	3B	HR	BB	SO	AVG	OBP	SLG	PRO	PRO+	BR	/A	PF	CHI	RC	SB	CS	SBA	SBR
CHI	140	88	52	.629		667	534	4675	1343	218	70	25	427	358	.287	.351	.380	.731	111	69	66	100	103	668	150			
CLE	139	84	55	.604	3.5	636	537	4565	1268	254	72	24	498	367	.278	.354	.381	.735	107	78	39	106	98	651	113			
NY	141	80	59	.576	7.5	578	506	4775	1275	193	49	45	386	479	.267	.326	.356	.682	96	-20	-24	101	104	575	101			
DET	140	80	60	.571	8	618	578	4665	1319	222	84	23	429	427	.283	.346	.381	.727	113	60	75	98	97	649	121			
STL	140	67	72	.482	20.5	533	567	4672	1234	187	73	31	391	443	.264	.326	.355	.681	95	-22	-36	103	97	560	74			
BOS	138	66	71	.482	20.5	564	552	4548	1188	181	49	33	471	441	.261	.336	.344	.680	103	-11	21	94	102	559	108			
WAS	142	56	84	.400	32	533	570	4757	1238	177	63	24	416	511	.260	.325	.339	.664	93	-47	-42	99	100	558	142			
PHI	140	36	104	.257	52	457	742	4730	1156	175	71	35	349	565	.244	.300	.334	.634	82	-108	-113	101	100	487	103			
TOT	560					4586		37387	10021	1607	531	240	3367	3561	.268	.333	.359	.692						912				

TEAM	CG	SH	SV	IP	H	H/G	HR	BB	SO	RAT	ERA	ERA+	OAV	OOB	PR	/A	PF	CPI	FA	E	DP	FW	PW	BW	SBW	DIF
CHI	88	14	3	1265²	1245	8.9	24	342	468	11.5	3.04	105	.262	.315	26	19	99	99	.969	176	116	1.6	2.0	6.9		7.5
CLE	80	10	10	1245	1242	9.0	19	362	432	11.8	2.94	114	.264	.321	39	53	104	98	.965	201	102	-.0	5.5	4.1		4.9
NY	85	14	7	1287	1143	8.0	47	433	500	11.3	2.82	113	.240	.309	58	53	99	92	.968	193	108	.7	5.5	-2.5		6.8
DET	85	10	4	1256	1254	9.0	35	436	428	12.4	3.30	97	.266	.333	-11	-14	99	98	.964	205	81	-.2	-1.5	7.8		3.8
STL	78	14	4	1256	1255	9.0	35	421	415	12.3	3.13	106	.263	.328	13	24	103	99	.963	215	98	-.8	2.5	-3.8		-.4
BOS	89	15	8	1224¹	1251	9.2	16	421	381	12.5	3.31	91	.275	.341	-12	-41	99	101	.975	140	118	3.8	-4.3	2.2		-4.2
WAS	68	13	10	1274¹	1237	8.7	20	451	536	12.2	3.01	106	.259	.328	30	28	99	99	.960	227	86	-1.4	2.9	-4.4		-11.1
PHI	72	1	3	1239¹	1371	10.0	44	503	417	13.8	4.26	80	.292	.364	-143	-118	106	96	.956	257	96	-3.5	-12.4	-11.8		-6.3
TOT	645	91	49	10047²		9.0				12.2	3.22		.268	.333					.965	1614	805					

Runs		Hits		Doubles		Triples		Home Runs		Total Bases	
Ruth-Bos	103	Veach-Det	191	Veach-Det	45	Veach-Det	17	Ruth-Bos	29	Ruth-Bos	284
Sisler-StL	96	Cobb-Det	191	Speaker-Cle	38	Sisler-StL	15	T.Walker-Phi	10	Veach-Det	279
Cobb-Det	92	Jackson-Chi	181	Cobb-Det	36	Heilmann-Det	15	Sisler-StL	10	Sisler-StL	271
Weaver-Chi	89	Sisler-StL	180	O'Neill-Cle	35	Jackson-Chi	14	Baker-NY	10	Jackson-Chi	261
Peckinpaugh-NY	89	Rice-Was	179			Cobb-Det	13	Smith-Cle	9		

Runs Batted In		Runs Produced		Bases On Balls		Batting Average		On Base Percentage		Slugging Average	
Ruth-Bos	114	Ruth-Bos	188	Graney-Cle	105	Cobb-Det	.384	Ruth-Bos	.456	Ruth-Bos	.657
Veach-Det	101	Veach-Det	185	Ruth-Bos	101	Veach-Det	.355	Cobb-Det	.429	Sisler-StL	.530
Jackson-Chi	96	Sisler-StL	169	Judge-Was	81	Sisler-StL	.352	Jackson-Chi	.422	Veach-Det	.519
Heilmann-Det	93	Jackson-Chi	168	Hooper-Bos	79	Jackson-Chi	.351	Leibold-Chi	.404	Cobb-Det	.515
Lewis-NY	89	E.Collins-Chi	163	Bush-Det	75	Flagstead-Det	.331	E.Collins-Chi	.400	Jackson-Chi	.506

Production		Adjusted Production		Batter Runs		Adjusted Batter Runs		Clutch Hitting Index		Runs Created	
Ruth-Bos	1.114	Ruth-Bos	224	Ruth-Bos	66.5	Ruth-Bos	74.0	E.Collins-Chi	143	Ruth-Bos	128
Cobb-Det	.944	Cobb-Det	168	Jackson-Chi	41.7	Cobb-Det	44.0	Lewis-NY	131	Cobb-Det	116
Jackson-Chi	.928	Veach-Det	160	Cobb-Det	41.6	Jackson-Chi	41.3	Jones-Det	130	Veach-Det	115
Sisler-StL	.921	Jackson-Chi	159	Veach-Det	37.7	Veach-Det	40.1	Shanks-Was	123	Sisler-StL	112
Veach-Det	.916	Sisler-StL	153	Sisler-StL	35.8	Sisler-StL	33.4	Gardner-Cle	123	Jackson-Chi	111

Total Average		Stolen Bases		Stolen Base Average		Stolen Base Runs		Fielding Runs		Total Player Rating	
Ruth-Bos	1.358	E.Collins-Chi	33					Pratt-NY	28.0	Ruth-Bos	6.3
Cobb-Det	1.056	Sisler-StL	28					Peckinpaugh-NY	27.7	Peckinpaugh-NY	5.1
Sisler-StL	1.000	Cobb-Det	28					Felsch-Chi	21.4	Sisler-StL	4.3
Jackson-Chi	.997	Rice-Was	26					Speaker-Cle	19.1	Veach-Det	4.3
Veach-Det	.968							Young-Det	17.3	Pratt-NY	3.8

Wins		Win Percentage		Games		Complete Games		Shutouts		Saves	
Cicotte-Chi	29	Cicotte-Chi	.806	Shaw-Was	45	Cicotte-Chi	30	Johnson-Was	7	Russell-NY-Bos	5
Coveleski-Cle	24	Dauss-Det	.700	Russell-NY-Bos	44	Williams-Chi	27			Shawkey-NY	5
Williams-Chi	23	Williams-Chi	.676	Kinney-Phi	43	Johnson-Was	27			Shaw-Was	5
Dauss-Det	21	Pennock-Bos	.667	Coveleski-Cle	43	Mays-Bos-NY	26			Coveleski-Cle	4
		Coveleski-Cle	.667			Coveleski-Cle	24				

Innings Pitched		Fewest Hits/Game		Fewest BB/Game		Strikeouts		Strikeouts/Game		Ratio	
Shaw-Was	306.2	Johnson-Was	7.28	Cicotte-Chi	1.44	Johnson-Was	147	Erickson-Det-Was	5.52	Cicotte-Chi	9.01
Cicotte-Chi	306.2	Thormahlen-NY	7.39	Johnson-Was	1.58	Shaw-Was	128	Russell-NY-Bos	4.80	Johnson-Was	9.08
Williams-Chi	297.0	Shawkey-NY	7.51	Bagby-Cle	1.64	Williams-Chi	125	Johnson-Was	4.56	Williams-Chi	10.12
Johnson-Was	290.1	Cicotte-Chi	7.51	Williams-Chi	1.76	Shawkey-NY	122	Kinney-Phi	4.31	Thormahlen-NY	10.49
Coveleski-Cle	286.0	Mays-Bos-NY	7.68	Coveleski-Cle	1.89	Coveleski-Cle	118	Leonard-Det	4.22	Quinn-NY	10.59

Earned Run Average		Adjusted ERA		Opponents' Batting Avg.		Opponents' On Base Pct.		Starter Runs		Adjusted Starter Runs	
Johnson-Was	1.49	Johnson-Was	215	Johnson-Was	.219	Johnson-Was	.259	Johnson-Was	56.0	Johnson-Was	55.3
Cicotte-Chi	1.82	Cicotte-Chi	175	Cicotte-Chi	.228	Cicotte-Chi	.261	Cicotte-Chi	47.8	Cicotte-Chi	46.3
Weilman-StL	2.07	Weilman-StL	160	Thormahlen-NY	.228	Williams-Chi	.289	Mays-Bos-NY	33.3	Sothoron-StL	33.4
Mays-Bos-NY	2.10	Sothoron-StL	151	Shawkey-NY	.231	Morton-Cle	.293	Sothoron-StL	30.7	Mays-Bos-NY	29.4
Sothoron-StL	2.20	Mays-Bos-NY	147	Mays-Bos-NY	.233	Quinn-NY	.295	Coveleski-Cle	19.4	Coveleski-Cle	23.2

Clutch Pitching Index		Relief Runs		Adjusted Relief Runs		Relief Ranking		Total Pitcher Index		Total Baseball Ranking	
Weilman-StL	119	Phillips-Cle	1.7	Phillips-Cle	2.4	Phillips-Cle	2.0	Johnson-Was	7.2	Ruth-Bos	7.9
Sothoron-StL	114							Cicotte-Chi	5.2	Johnson-Was	7.1
Ehmke-Det	113							Mays-Bos-NY	3.8	Cicotte-Chi	5.2
Harper-Was	107							Coveleski-Cle	3.6	Peckinpaugh-NY	5.1
Pennock-Bos	107							Sothoron-StL	3.1	Sisler-StL	4.3

January 12 A plan developed by Charles Ebbets many years ago is finally adopted: the annual drafting of players from the minor leagues will be done in inverse order to the teams' final standings.

February 9 The Joint Rules Committee bans all foreign substances or other alterations to the ball by pitchers, including saliva, resin, talcum powder, paraffin, and the shine and emery ball. A pitcher caught cheating will be suspended for 10 days. The NL allows each club to name all its spitball pitchers. No pitchers other than those designated will be permitted to use it, and none at all after 1920. Other rules changes: the adoption of writer Fred Lieb's proposal that a game-winning homer with men on base be counted as a homer even if its run is not needed to win the game. Also, the intentional walk is banned, and everything that happens in a protested game will go in the records.

April 20 Phils' manager Gavvy Cravath inserts himself as a pinch hitter and hits a three-run home run, his last, to beat the Giants 3-0.

May 1 In Boston, Brooklyn's Leon Cadore and the Braves' Joe Oeschger duel 26 innings to a 1-1 tie in the longest game ever played in the major league. The Dodgers lose to the Phils at home in 13 innings the next day, then return to Boston for a Monday game where they lose again in 19. For 58 innings work in three days, they are 0-2.

September 17 The Cards set a record by cracking out 12 consecutive hits in the fourth and fifth innings against the Braves. Ten of the hits occur in the fourth inning when St. Louis scores eight runs. The last two outs come as Milt Stock tries to stretch a single into a double and Austin McHenry tries for an extra base on a double; both are thrown out. In the fifth inning, Doc Lavan opens with a double and Cliff Heathcote singles before a Redbird finally makes an out. St. Louis wins 9-4.

October 2 The Pirates and Reds, battling to determine second and third place, play a tripleheader in Pittsburgh. Starting at noon, the Reds win the first two 13-4 and 7-3, and the Pirates the finale 6-0.

October 6 When Wheeler Johnston pinch-hits for Cleveland in the ninth inning of Game 2, his brother Jimmy is playing third base for Brooklyn. They become the first brothers to take opposite sides in a World Series. Spitballer Burleigh Grimes (23-11) strands 10 Indians while the Robins chip away at Jim Bagby (31-12) for three single tallies and a 3-0 Series evener.

November 8 At a meeting to depose Ban Johnson, a new 12-team National League, made up of the dissenting 11 teams plus one of the five teams loyal to Johnson, is proposed and agreed to. John Heydler will be its president and Judge Landis the proposed chairman of the new commission. With no stomach for another war, four of the five AL clubs still backing Johnson agree to a joint meeting November 12 in Chicago.

November 12 With Johnson barred from the meeting, the 16 major league clubs settle their differences. The 12-team-league idea is discarded, and the two leagues will continue with their old identities. The owners unanimously elect Kenesaw Mountain Landis chairman for seven years. Judge Landis accepts, but only as sole commissioner with final authority over the players and owners, while remaining a federal judge (with his $7,500 federal salary deducted from the baseball salary of $50,000). The agreement will be signed on January 12, 1921, when he is to begin his duties.

December 6 A five-year-old lawsuit that awarded $264,000 damages to the Baltimore Federal League club on April 12, 1919, is reversed by a court of appeals, which upholds the reserve clause and holds that baseball is not interstate commerce nor subject to antitrust laws. The original suit was initiated because the Baltimore Feds were not included in the settlement of the Federal League war. They wanted a major league team in Baltimore and did not get it.

December 15 The NL reveals a most telling statistic, pointing out the changes in the game: the use of 27,924 baseballs during the season, an increase of 10,248 over 1919.

BOSTON	BROOKLYN	CHICAGO	CINCINNATI	NEW YORK	PHILADELPHIA	PITTSBURGH	ST.LOUIS
M G.Stallings	M W.Robinson	M F.Mitchell	M P.Moran	M J.McGraw	M G.Cravath	M M.Gibson	M B.Rickey
1B W.Holke	1B E.Konetchy	1B F.Merkle	1B J.Daubert	1B G.Kelly	1B G.Paulette	1B C.Grimm	1B J.Fournier
2B C.Pick	2B P.Kilduff	2B Z.Terry	2B M.Rath	2B L.Doyle	2B J.Rawlings	2B G.Cutshaw	2B R.Hornsby
SS R.Maranville	SS I.Olson	SS C.Hollocher	SS L.Kopf	SS D.Bancroft	SS A.Fletcher	SS H.Caton	SS D.Lavan
3B T.Boeckel	3B J.Johnston	3B C.Deal	3B H.Groh	3B F.Frisch	3B R.Miller	3B P.Whitted	3B M.Stock
LF L.Mann	LF Z.Wheat	LF D.Robertson	LF P.Duncan	LF G.Burns	LF I.Meusel	LF C.Bigbee	LF A.McHenry
CF R.Powell	CF H.Myers	CF D.Paskert	CF E.Roush	CF L.King	CF C.Williams	CF M.Carey	CF C.Heathcote
RF W.Cruise	RF T.Griffith	RF M.Flack	RF G.Neale	RF R.Youngs	RF C.Stengel	RF B.Southworth	C V.Clemons
C M.O'Neil	C O.Miller	C B.O'Farrell	C I.Wingo	C F.Snyder	C M.Wheat	C W.Schmidt	C J.Schultz
2S H.Ford	O B.Neis	1O T.Barber	S3 S.Crane	C S.Smith	23 D.Miller	O F.Nicholson	S1 H.Janvrin
O J.Sullivan	C E.Krueger	23 B.Herzog	2 E.Sicking	S3 A.Fletcher	O B.LeBourveau	S2 W.Barbare	C P.Dillhoefer
O E.Eayrs	C R.Elliott	C B.Killefer	C B.Rariden	O B.Kauff	3 R.Wrightstone	C B.Haeffner	C B.Shotton
C H.Gowdy	S C.Ward	O B.Twombly	C N.Allen	O V.Spencer	S W.Tragesser	3S B.McKechnie	/O M.Knode
O L.Christenbury	S B.McCabe	2O B.Friberg	O C.See	32 E.Sicking	S D.Bancroft	S C.Lee	/O H.Mueller
/O G.Bailey	1 R.Schmandt	C T.Daly	P J.Ring	3 F.Lear	C F.Withrow	S P.Traynor	/C L.McCarty
/3 A.Wilson	O B.Lamar	2 W.Marriott	P D.Ruether	2 R.Grimes	/O G.Cravath	3 C.Barnhart	/C G.Gilham
/1 R.Torphy	/O W.Hood	/S H.Leathers	P H.Eller	/C L.McCarty	/1 F.Luderus	2 C.Tierney	/C T.Griesenbeck
/2 J.Rawlings	/C Z.Taylor	/3 S.Clarke	P D.Luque	O J.Statz	R W.Walsh	/O H.Summa	/C B.Schindler
/1 T.Whelan	/3 D.Baird	H B.McCabe	P R.Fisher	/S A.Lefevre	P E.Rixey	H B.Hinchman	/O E.Hock
R O.Dugey	/S J.Sheehan	P P.Alexander	/P S.Sallee	/O C.Walker	P G.Smith	/C N.Clarke	P J.Haines
P J.Oeschger	/S R.Sheridan	P H.Vaughn	/P B.Napier	/C M.Gonzalez	P L.Meadows	H W.Hood	P B.Doak
P J.Scott	P B.Grimes	P C.Hendrix	/P R.Bressler	/C A.Gaston	P R.Causey	P W.Cooper	P F.Schupp
P D.Fillingim	P L.Cadore	P L.Tyler	/P L.Brenton	/3 D.Baird	P B.Hubbell	P B.Adams	P B.Sherdel
P H.McQuillan	P J.Pfeffer	P S.Martin	/P F.Coumbe	/O E.Brown	H.Betts	P H.Carlson	P M.Goodwin
P D.Rudolph	A.Mamaux	P P.Carter	/P M.Swartz	/O B.Kinsella	B.Gallia	P E.Hamilton	L.North
/P M.Watson	P R.Marquard	P S.Bailey	/P G.Lowe	P J.Barnes	P J.Enzmann	P E.Ponder	E.Jacobs
P B.Hearn	P S.Bailey	/P V.Cheeves	/P J.Theis	P A.Nehf	/P M.Cantwell	P J.Wisner	J.May
/P A.Pierotti	P S.Smith	/P C.Gaw		P F.Toney	/P L.Weinert	P J.Meador	/P M.Kircher
/P L.Townsend	P1 C.Mitchell	/P P.Jones		P P.Douglas	/P J.Keenan	/P J.Zinn	/P G.Lyons
/P J.Jones	P G.Mohart	/P J.Newkirk		P R.Benton		/P S.Blake	/P H.Kime
/P I.Townsend	/P J.Miljus	/P J.Jaeger		P J.Winters		/P M.Watson	/P W.Schulz
		/P T.Turner		P B.Hubbell		/P W.Glazner	/P G.Scott
				/P S.Sallee		/P J.Morrison	/P B.Glenn
				/P P.Perritt			/P O.Tuero
				/P R.Ryan			
				/P V.Barnes			
				/P T.Grubbs			
				/P C.Davenport			

TEAM	G	W	L	PCT	GB	R	OR	AB	H	2B	3B	HR	BB	SO	AVG	OBP	SLG	PRO	PRO+	BR	/A	PF	CHI	RC	SB	CS	SBA	SBR
BRO	155	93	61	.604		660	528	5399	1493	205	99	28	359	391	.277	.324	.367	.691	100	19	-2	103	103	637	70	80	47	-27
NY	155	86	68	.558	7	682	543	5309	1427	210	76	46	432	545	.269	.327	.363	.690	104	23	30	99	107	628	131	113	54	-29
CIN	154	82	71	.536	10.5	639	569	5176	1432	169	76	18	382	367	.277	.332	.349	.681	102	11	20	99	104	602	158	128	55	-29
PIT	155	79	75	.513	14	530	552	5219	1342	162	90	16	374	405	.257	.310	.332	.642	86	-67	-84	103	99	544	181	117	61	-16
STL	155	75	79	.487	18	675	682	5495	1589	238	96	32	373	484	.289	.337	.385	.722	117	83	110	96	94	704	126	114	53	-31
CHI	154	75	79	.487	18	619	635	5117	1350	223	67	34	428	421	.264	.326	.354	.680	98	7	-5	102	101	589	115	129	47	-43
BOS	153	62	90	.408	30	523	670	5218	1358	168	86	23	385	488	.260	.315	.339	.654	97	-45	-21	96	93	557	88	98	47	-32
PHI	153	62	91	.405	30.5	565	714	5264	1385	229	54	64	283	531	.263	.305	.364	.669	93	-30	-57	105	99	577	100	83	55	-20
TOT	617					4893		42197	11376	1604	644	261	3016	3632	.270	.322	.357	.679						969	862	53	-227

TEAM	CG	SH	SV	IP	H	H/G	HR	BB	SO	RAT	ERA	ERA+	OAV	OOB	PR	/A	PF	CPI	FA	E	DP	FW	PW	BW	SBW	DIF
BRO	89	17	10	1427¹	1381	8.7	25	327	553	10.9	2.62	122	.259	.304	81	91	102	102	.966	226	118	-.2	9.7	-.2	.1	6.5
NY	86	18	9	1408²	1379	8.8	44	297	380	10.8	2.80	107	.261	.303	51	30	96	99	.969	210	137	.8	3.2	3.2	-.0	1.9
CIN	90	12	9	1391²	1327	8.6	26	393	435	11.3	2.90	105	.256	.313	36	22	97	97	.968	200	125	1.3	2.4	2.1	-.0	-.2
PIT	92	17	10	1415¹	1389	8.8	25	280	444	10.8	2.89	111	.261	.301	39	51	103	91	.971	186	119	2.2	5.5	-9.0	1.3	2.0
STL	72	9	12	1426²	1488	9.4	30	479	529	12.8	3.43	87	.277	.343	-47	-72	95	103	.961	256	136	-2.0	-7.7	11.8	-.3	-3.8
CHI	95	13	9	1388²	1459	9.5	37	382	508	12.1	3.27	98	.276	.328	-21	-10	102	102	.965	225	112	-.2	-1.1	-.5	-1.6	1.4
BOS	93	14	6	1386¹	1464	9.5	39	415	368	12.4	3.54	86	.280	.337	-62	-75	97	100	.964	239	125	-1.1	-8.0	-2.2	-.4	-2.2
PHI	77	8	11	1380²	1480	9.6	35	444	419	12.8	3.63	94	.284	.345	-76	-35	109	102	.964	232	135	-.7	-3.7	-6.1	.9	-4.8
TOT	694	108	76	11225¹		9.1				11.7	3.13		.270	.322					.966	1774	1007					

Runs		Hits		Doubles		Triples		Home Runs		Total Bases	
Burns-NY	115	Hornsby-StL	218	Hornsby-StL	44	Myers-Bro	22	Williams-Phi	15	Hornsby-StL	329
Bancroft-Phi-NY	102	Youngs-NY	204	Bancroft-Phi-NY	36	Hornsby-StL	20	Meusel-Phi	14	Williams-Phi	293
Daubert-Cin	97	Stock-StL	204	Williams-Phi	36	Roush-Cin	16	Kelly-NY	11	Youngs-NY	277
Hornsby-StL	96	Roush-Cin	196	Myers-Bro	36	Maranville-Bos	15	Robertson-Chi	10	Wheat-Bro	270
Youngs-NY	92	Williams-Phi	192	Burns-NY	35	Bigbee-Pit	15	McHenry-StL	10	Myers-Bro	269

Runs Batted In		Runs Produced		Bases On Balls		Batting Average		On Base Percentage		Slugging Average	
Kelly-NY	94	Hornsby-StL	181	Burns-NY	76	Hornsby-StL	.370	Hornsby-StL	.431	Hornsby-StL	.559
Hornsby-StL	94	Roush-Cin	167	Youngs-NY	75	Nicholson-Pit	.360	Youngs-NY	.427	Nicholson-Pit	.530
Roush-Cin	90	Youngs-NY	164	Paskert-Chi	64	Youngs-NY	.351	Roush-Cin	.386	Williams-Phi	.497
Duncan-Cin	83	Stock-StL	161	Hornsby-StL	60	Roush-Cin	.339	Wheat-Bro	.385	Youngs-NY	.477
Myers-Bro	80	Myers-Bro	159	Groh-Cin	60	Wheat-Bro	.328	Groh-Cin	.375	Meusel-Phi	.473

Production		Adjusted Production		Batter Runs		Adjusted Batter Runs		Clutch Hitting Index		Runs Created	
Hornsby-StL	.990	Hornsby-StL	190	Hornsby-StL	62.6	Hornsby-StL	67.6	Whitted-Pit	151	Hornsby-StL	138
Youngs-NY	.904	Youngs-NY	161	Youngs-NY	47.1	Youngs-NY	48.4	Kopf-Cin	147	Youngs-NY	118
Williams-Phi	.861	Roush-Cin	142	Williams-Phi	32.1	Roush-Cin	31.1	Duncan-Cin	131	Williams-Phi	103
Wheat-Bro	.848	Williams-Phi	139	Wheat-Bro	31.9	Wheat-Bro	28.8	Roush-Cin	126	Wheat-Bro	102
Roush-Cin	.839	Wheat-Bro	138	Roush-Cin	29.7	Williams-Phi	27.5	Kelly-NY	122	Roush-Cin	98

Total Average		Stolen Bases		Stolen Base Average		Stolen Base Runs		Fielding Runs		Total Player Rating	
Hornsby-StL	1.008	Carey-Pit	52	Carey-Pit	83.9	Carey-Pit	9.6	Bancroft-Phi-NY	39.0	Hornsby-StL	8.1
Youngs-NY	.896	Roush-Cin	36	Frisch-NY	75.6	Frisch-NY	3.6	Lavan-StL	16.2	Bancroft-Phi-NY	5.7
Williams-Phi	.817	Frisch-NY	34	Neale-Cin	70.7	Neale-Cin	1.5	Roush-Cin	15.7	Youngs-NY	3.6
Wheat-Bro	.801	Bigbee-Pit	31	Bigbee-Pit	67.4	Tragesser-Phi	1.2	Maranville-Bos	14.3	Roush-Cin	3.4
Roush-Cin	.784	Neale-Cin	29	Meusel-Phi	60.7	Gowdy-Bos	1.2	Neale-Cin	14.3	Hollocher-Chi	2.7

Wins		Win Percentage		Games		Complete Games		Shutouts		Saves	
Alexander-Chi	27	Grimes-Bro	.676	Haines-StL	47	Alexander-Chi	33	Adams-Pit	8	Sherdel-StL	6
Cooper-Pit	24	Alexander-Chi	.659	Douglas-NY	46	Cooper-Pit	28	Alexander-Chi	7	McQuillan-Bos	5
Grimes-Bro	23	Toney-NY	.656	Alexander-Chi	46	Rixey-Phi	25			Alexander-Chi	5
Toney-NY	21	Pfeffer-Bro	.640	Scott-Bos	44	Grimes-Bro	25			Hubbell-NY-Phi	4
Nehf-NY	21	Nehf-NY	.636	Cooper-Pit	44	Vaughn-Chi	24			Mamaux-Bro	4

Innings Pitched		Fewest Hits/Game		Fewest BB/Game		Strikeouts		Strikeouts/Game		Ratio	
Alexander-Chi	363.1	Luque-Cin	7.28	Adams-Pit	.62	Alexander-Chi	173	Mamaux-Bro	4.77	Adams-Pit	8.86
Cooper-Pit	327.0	Ruether-Cin	7.96	Cooper-Pit	1.43	Vaughn-Chi	131	Alexander-Chi	4.29	Alexander-Chi	10.03
Grimes-Bro	303.2	Grimes-Bro	8.03	Nehf-NY	1.44	Grimes-Bro	131	Schupp-StL	4.27	Luque-Cin	10.05
Haines-StL	301.2	Mamaux-Bro	8.12	Benton-NY	1.44	Haines-StL	120	Marquard-Bro	4.22	J.Barnes-NY	10.12
Vaughn-Chi	301.0	Adams-Pit	8.21	Marquard-Bro	1.66	Schupp-StL	119	Sherdel-StL	3.92	Grimes-Bro	10.14

Earned Run Average		Adjusted ERA		Opponents' Batting Avg.		Opponents' On Base Pct.		Starter Runs		Adjusted Starter Runs	
Alexander-Chi	1.91	Alexander-Chi	168	Luque-Cin	.225	Adams-Pit	.259	Alexander-Chi	49.5	Alexander-Chi	52.4
Adams-Pit	2.16	Adams-Pit	149	Grimes-Bro	.238	Grimes-Bro	.282	Grimes-Bro	30.7	Grimes-Bro	33.0
Grimes-Bro	2.22	Grimes-Bro	144	Adams-Pit	.244	Alexander-Chi	.285	Adams-Pit	28.5	Adams-Pit	30.9
Cooper-Pit	2.39	Cooper-Pit	134	Ponder-Pit	.246	Luque-Cin	.286	Cooper-Pit	26.8	Cooper-Pit	29.8
Ruether-Cin	2.47	Vaughn-Chi	126	Ruether-Cin	.247	Ponder-Pit	.286	Vaughn-Chi	19.8	Vaughn-Chi	22.2

Clutch Pitching Index		Relief Runs		Adjusted Relief Runs		Relief Ranking		Total Pitcher Index		Total Baseball Ranking	
Meadows-Phi	121							Alexander-Chi	7.1	Hornsby-StL	8.1
Alexander-Chi	120							Grimes-Bro	5.4	Alexander-Chi	7.1
Vaughn-Chi	119							Smith-Bro	4.0	Bancroft-Phi-NY	5.7
Fillingim-Bos	118							Cooper-Pit	3.2	Grimes-Bro	5.4
Benton-NY	115							Adams-Pit	2.8	Smith-Bro	4.0

February 13* The Negro National League (chartered as the National Association of Colored Professional Baseball Clubs) is organized at a meeting at the YMCA in Kansas City, MO.

May 1 Babe Ruth's first home run as a Yankee clears the roof of the Polo Grounds in a 6-0 win over the Red Sox.

May 14 The Giants inform the Yankees that after the season, their lease will not be renewed. No reason is given but the recent signing of Babe Ruth appears to be the main cause.

June 26* Lou Gehrig gets his first national mention when, as a high school junior for New York City's School of Commerce, he steals the show in a high school championship game against Lane Tech in Chicago. His grand slam in the eighth gives the NY team a 12–8 victory. Scouts sit with open mouths as the ball sails out of Cubs Park (later known as Wrigley Field).

July 1 Walter Johnson pitches a no-hitter, his first, against the Red Sox at Fenway. An error by Bucky Harris costs him a perfect game. The next day Johnson comes up with the first sore arm of his life and is useless for the rest of the year.

July 10 After banging out 11 straight hits, Tris Speaker is stopped by Tom Zachary of Washington. It's the record until Michael "Pinky" Higgins of the Red Sox racks up 12 in a row in 1938.

August 16 At the Polo Grounds Cleveland shortstop Ray Chapman, 29, is beaned by a Carl Mays pitch. A right-handed batter who crowds the plate, Chapman freezes and fails to get out of the way of the submarine delivery. He is carried from the field and dies the next day from a fractured skull.

August 20 The Red Sox-Indians game in Boston is postponed to allow the Indian players to attend Ray Chapman's funeral in Cleveland.

September 28 A Chicago grand jury indicts the eight Chicago players in the 1919 World Series scandal. Charles Comiskey immediately suspends them. With the heart of the team sidelined, Chicago will lose two out of their final three games and the Indians win the pennant by two games. Had the grand jury come out with its findings a week later, the White Sox might have won, causing the cancellation of the World Series and the voiding of their pennant. For Cleveland it is their first pennant in any league after 39 years of trying.

September 29 Babe Ruth hits homer No. 54 in Philadelphia as the Yankees win 7–2. That is more than any other team total except the Phils. He is responsible for 241 of his team's 838 runs, even though he misses 12 games.

October 3 In the Browns' 16-7 win over Chicago, George Sisler gets his 257th hit of the season to set a major league record. He also hurls a scoreless ninth inning in relief.

October 10 In the bottom of the first of an event-filled game, Grimes gives up hits to Charlie Jamieson, Bill Wambsganss, and Speaker. Outfielder Elmer Smith then hits the first grand slam in World Series history. In the third inning, pitcher Jim Bagby comes up with two on and crashes another Grimes delivery for a three-run home run, the first ever by a pitcher in World Series play. Bagby is roughed for 13 hits, but he gets out of jams with the aid of three double plays and an unassisted triple play. In the fifth with Pete Kilduff on second base and Otto Miller on first base, relief pitcher Clarence Mitchell hits a line drive at shortstop Wambsganss, who steps on second base and tags the off-and-running Miller before he can retreat. Cleveland dominates 8-1.

October 12 Stan Coveleski wins his third game of the Series, and the Indians wrap it up, as Dodger bats are silent again. Burleigh Grimes is nicked for single scores in the fourth, fifth, and seventh, for a 3-0 loss.

October 23 The Chicago grand jury indictment adds the names of former featherweight boxing champ Abe Attell, Hal Chase, and Bill Burns as go-betweens in the World Series scandal. Confessions, later repudiated, are signed by Ed Cicotte, Joe Jackson, Lefty Williams, and Happy Felsch.

December 17 The AL votes to allow pitchers who used the spitball in 1920 to continue using it as long as they are in the league. The NL will do the same. There will be 17 in all.

	BOSTON		CHICAGO		CLEVELAND		DETROIT		NEW YORK		PHILADELPHIA		ST.LOUIS		WASHINGTON
M	E.Barrow	M	K.Gleason	M	T.Speaker	M	H.Jennings	M	M.Huggins	M	C.Mack	M	J.Burke	M	C.Griffith
1B	S.McInnis	1B	S.Collins	1B	D.Johnston	1B	H.Heilmann	1B	W.Pipp	1B	I.Griffin	1B	G.Sisler	1B	J.Judge
2B	M.McNally	2B	E.Collins	2B	B.Wambsganss	2B	R.Young	2B	D.Pratt	2B	J.Dykes	2B	J.Gedeon	2B	B.Harris
SS	E.Scott	SS	S.Risberg	SS	R.Chapman	SS	D.Bush	SS	R.Peckinpaugh	SS	C.Galloway	SS	W.Gerber	SS	J.O'Neill
3B	E.Foster	3B	B.Weaver	3B	L.Gardner	3B	B.Pinelli	3B	A.Ward	3B	F.Thomas	3B	J.Austin	3B	F.Ellerbe
LF	M.Menosky	LF	J.Jackson	LF	C.Jamieson	LF	B.Veach	LF	D.Lewis	LF	T.Walker	LF	K.Williams	LF	C.Milan
CF	T.Hendryx	CF	H.Felsch	CF	T.Speaker	CF	T.Cobb	CF	P.Bodie	CF	F.Welch	CF	B.Jacobson	CF	S.Rice
RF	H.Hooper	RF	N.Leibold	RF	E.Smith	RF	C.Shorten	RF	B.Ruth	RF	A.Strunk	RF	J.Tobin	RF	B.Roth
C	R.Walters	C	R.Schalk	C	S.O'Neill	C	O.Stanage	C	M.Ruel	C	C.Perkins	C	H.Severeid	C	P.Gharrity
CO	W.Schang	O	A.Strunk	O	J.Evans	O	I.Flagstead	O3	B.Meusel	3S	J.Dugan	3O	E.Smith	3O	H.Shanks
32	O.Vitt	1	T.Jourdan	O	J.Graney	C	B.Jones	C	T.Hannah	O2	W.Witt	3	J.Billings	S2	R.Shannon
2	C.Brady	3	F.McMullin	O	J.Wood	C	E.Ainsmith	O	S.Vick	OC	G.Myatt	3	F.Thompson	C	V.Picinich
O	G.Bailey	O	E.Murphy	O	H.Lunte	1	B.Ellison	O	F.Gleich	1	D.Burrus	/C	P.Collins	O	F.Brower
/O	H.Eibel	S	B.Lynn	S	J.Sewell	3	S.Hale	C	F.Hofmann	O	F.Walker	/O	L.Lamb	S	F.O'Rourke
/3	H.Hiller	/S	H.McClellan	1	G.Burns	C	C.Manion	/S	C.Fewster	S	R.Shannon	/O	D.Wetzel	S	G.McBride
/O	B.Paschal	/O	B.Falk	C	L.Nunamaker	/2	L.Woodall	/2	J.Lucey	/S	J.Shovlin	/1	R.Torres
/C	M.Devine	/C	B.Jonnard	/C	P.Thomas	3	C.Huber	/S	R.French	/2	B.Mullen	/O	J.Calvo
/O	H.Hunter					/S	D.Claire	H	T.Connelly	O	C.High	/3	M.McManus	/O	E.Johnson
/O	G.Orme	P	R.Faber	P	J.Bagby					O	C.Burns	/S	D.Lee	/O	D.Prothro
/C	E.Chaplin	P	E.Cicotte	P	S.Coveleski	P	H.Dauss	P	C.Mays	/C	L.Styles	/3	P.Speraw	/3	F.Thomas
/1	R.Grimes	P	L.Williams	P	R.Caldwell	P	H.Ehmke	S	B.Shawkey	S	E.McCann	H	J.Heving	/3	B.Hollahan
/O	J.Statz	P	D.Kerr	P	G.Morton	P	B.Oldham	P	J.Quinn	/C	J.Walker	/O	E.Pruess	/S	B.LaMotte
/C	P.Smith	P	R.Wilkinson			P	D.Ayers	P	R.Collins	/1	B.Kelly			H	E.Bowman
				P	G.Uhle	P	D.Leonard	P	H.Thormahlen	/C	E.Wingo			/2	A.Watt
		P	E.Myers	P	J.Bagby				H	T.Kearns	P	D.Davis	P	J.Leonard
P	S.Jones	P	G.Payne	P	J.Bagby	P	F.Okrie	P	G.Mogridge			P	U.Shocker		
P	J.Bush	/P	S.Hodge	/P	D.Mails	P	F.Okrie	P	E.Shore			P	A.Sothoron		
P	H.Pennock	/P	S.Heath	P	B.Clark	/P	B.Morrisette	P	B.McGraw	P	S.Perry	P	C.Weilman	P	T.Zachary
P	H.Harper	/P	J.Kiefer	P	D.Niehaus	/P	J.Bogart	/P	L.O'Doul	P	R.Naylor	P	B.Burwell	P	E.Erickson
P	W.Hoyt	/P	G.Lowdermilk	P	T.Faeth	/P	E.Alten			P	S.Harriss			P	J.Shaw
				/P	J.Boehling	/P	A.Conkwright			P	E.Rommel	P	E.Vangilder	P	H.Courtney
P	A.Russell			/P	T.Murchison	/P	H.Baumgartner			P	R.Moore	P	B.Bayne	P	W.Johnson
P	E.Myers			/P	G.Ellison	/P	B.Boland					P	J.DeBerry		
P	B.Karr					/P	J.Glaiser			P	D.Keefe	/P	A.Lynch	P	A.Schacht
P	G.Fortune					/P	R.Crumpler			P	B.Hasty	/P	R.Richmond	P	J.Acosta
/P	H.Deviney					/P	M.Wilson			P	W.Kinney	P	R.Sanders	P	B.Snyder
						/P	J.Coombs			/P	P.Martin	H	H.Leverette	/P	H.Biemiller
						/P	R.Cox			/P	C.Eckert	/P	L.Leifield	/P	G.Bono
						/P	S.Love			/P	B.Knowlton	/P	G.Boehler	/P	L.Carlson
						/P	C.Fried			/P	J.Slappey	/P	B.Gallia	/P	J.Gleason
						/P	L.Vedder			/P	F.Heimach	/P	J.Scheneberg	/P	C.Fisher
										/P	B.Shanner			/P	D.Shirey
														/P	J.Conway
														/P	J.Engel

TEAM	G	W	L	PCT	GB	R	OR	AB	H	2B	3B	HR	BB	SO	AVG	OBP	SLG	PRO	PRO+	BR	/A	PF	CHI	RC	SB	CS	SBA	SBR
CLE	154	98	56	.636		857	642	5196	1574	300	95	35	576	379	.303	.376	.417	.793	113	125	98	103	98	827	73	93	44	-34
CHI	154	96	58	.623	2	794	665	5328	1574	263	98	37	471	355	.295	.357	.402	.759	107	49	49	100	100	769	109	96	53	-25
NY	154	95	59	.617	3	838	629	5176	1448	268	71	115	539	626	.280	.350	.426	.776	107	71	43	104	105	773	64	82	44	-30
STL	154	76	77	.497	21.5	797	766	5358	1651	279	61	50	427	339	.308	.363	.419	.782	110	93	68	103	95	822	121	79	61	-11
BOS	154	72	81	.471	25.5	650	698	5199	1397	216	71	22	533	429	.269	.342	.350	.692	93	-70	-41	96	97	637	98	111	47	-37
WAS	153	68	84	.447	29	723	802	5251	1526	233	81	36	433	543	.291	.351	.386	.737	104	7	27	97	98	718	160	114	58	-20
DET	155	61	93	.396	37	652	833	5215	1408	228	72	30	479	391	.270	.334	.359	.693	91	-80	-64	98	100	639	76	68	53	-18
PHI	156	48	106	.312	50	558	834	5256	1324	220	49	44	353	593	.252	.305	.338	.643	74	-188	-193	101	106	543	50	67	43	-25
TOT	617					5869		41979	11902	2007	620	369	3811	3655	.284	.347	.387	.734							751	710	51	-201

TEAM	CG	SH	SV	IP	H	H/G	HR	BB	SO	RAT	ERA	ERA+	OAV	OOB	PR	/A	PF	CPI	FA	E	DP	FW	PW	BW	SBW	DIF
CLE	94	11	7	1377	1448	9.5	31	401	466	12.3	3.41	111	.276	.331	57	58	100	98	.971	184	124	2.1	5.6	9.5	-.9	4.6
CHI	109	9	10	1386²	1467	9.5	45	405	438	12.3	3.59	105	.280	.335	31	24	99	98	.968	198	142	1.2	2.3	4.8	.0	10.7
NY	88	15	11	1368	1414	9.3	48	420	480	12.3	3.32	115	.270	.328	72	75	101	99	.969	194	129	1.4	7.3	4.2	-.5	5.6
STL	84	9	14	1378²	1481	9.7	53	578	444	13.7	4.03	97	.283	.359	-38	-23	103	99	.963	233	119	-1.2	-2.2	6.6	1.4	-5.0
BOS	92	11	6	1395¹	1481	9.6	39	461	481	12.7	3.82	95	.279	.339	-5	-30	96	93	.972	183	131	2.2	-2.9	-4.0	-1.2	1.3
WAS	81	10	10	1367	1521	10.0	51	520	418	13.1	4.17	89	.288	.357	-58	-70	98	97	.963	232	95	-1.3	-6.8	2.6	.5	-3.1
DET	74	9	7	1385	1487	9.7	46	561	483	13.7	4.04	92	.284	.359	-38	-51	98	98	.964	230	95	-.9	-4.9	-6.2	.7	-4.6
PHI	79	6	2	1380¹	1612	10.5	56	461	423	13.8	3.93	102	.302	.362	-21	12	106	110	.959	266	125	-3.3	1.2	-18.7	.0	-8.1
TOT	701	80	67	11038		9.7				13.1	3.79		.284	.347					.966	1720	960					

Runs
Ruth-NY 158
Speaker-Cle 137
Sisler-StL 137
E.Collins-Chi 117

Hits
Sisler-StL 257
E.Collins-Chi 224
Jackson-Chi 218
Jacobson-StL 216
Speaker-Cle 214

Doubles
Speaker-Cle 50
Sisler-StL 49
Jackson-Chi 42

Triples
Jackson-Chi 20
Sisler-StL 18
Hooper-Bos 17

Home Runs
Ruth-NY 54
Sisler-StL 19
T.Walker-Phi 17
Felsch-Chi 14

Total Bases
Sisler-StL 399
Ruth-NY 388
Jackson-Chi 336
Speaker-Cle 310
Jacobson-StL 305

Runs Batted In
Ruth-NY 137
Sisler-StL 122
Jacobson-StL 122
Jackson-Chi 121
Gardner-Cle 118

Runs Produced
Ruth-NY 241
Sisler-StL 240
Speaker-Cle 236
Jackson-Chi 214
Jacobson-StL 210

Bases On Balls
Ruth-NY 148
Speaker-Cle 97
Hooper-Bos 88
Young-Det 85
Roth-Was 75

Batting Average
Sisler-StL .... .407
Speaker-Cle ...... .388
Jackson-Chi ...... .382
Ruth-NY .... .376
E.Collins-Chi ..... .372

On Base Percentage
Ruth-NY .... .530
Speaker-Cle ...... .483
Sisler-StL .... .449
Jackson-Chi ...... .444
E.Collins-Chi ..... .438

Slugging Average
Ruth-NY .... .847
Sisler-StL .... .632
Jackson-Chi ...... .589
Speaker-Cle ...... .562
Felsch-Chi .... .540

Production
Ruth-NY 1.378
Sisler-StL 1.082
Speaker-Cle 1.045
Jackson-Chi 1.033
E.Collins-Chi ..... .932

Adjusted Production
Ruth-NY 252
Sisler-StL 179
Jackson-Chi 172
Speaker-Cle 171
E.Collins-Chi 146

Batter Runs
Ruth-NY 113.2
Sisler-StL 73.2
Speaker-Cle 65.7
Jackson-Chi 58.4
E.Collins-Chi 42.3

Adjusted Batter Runs
Ruth-NY 106.7
Sisler-StL 68.5
Speaker-Cle 61.2
Jackson-Chi 58.4
E.Collins-Chi 42.3

Clutch Hitting Index
Gardner-Cle 144
Roth-Was 131
Smith-Chi 123
Risberg-Chi 121
Pratt-NY 118

Runs Created
Ruth-NY 211
Sisler-StL 176
Speaker-Cle 152
Jackson-Chi 145
E.Collins-Chi 134

Total Average
Ruth-NY 1.797
Sisler-StL 1.207
Speaker-Cle 1.165
Jackson-Chi 1.088
E.Collins-Chi ..... .984

Stolen Bases
Rice-Was 63
Sisler-StL 42
Roth-Was 24
Menosky-Bos 23
Tobin-StL 21

Stolen Base Average
E.Collins-Chi 71.4
Sisler-StL 71.2
Williams-StL 69.2
Rice-Was 67.7
Roth-Was 66.7

Stolen Base Runs
Sisler-StL 2.4
Burns-Phi-Cle 1.5
E.Collins-Chi 1.2
Smith-StL 9
Rice-Was 9

Fielding Runs
Perkins-Phi 22.8
Ward-NY 21.8
Rice-Was 21.4
Pinelli-Det 19.9
Felsch-Chi 17.7

Total Player Rating
Ruth-NY 8.6
Sisler-StL 7.8
E.Collins-Chi 5.6
Speaker-Cle 5.2
Jackson-Chi 4.1

Wins
Bagby-Cle 31
Mays-NY 26
Coveleski-Cle 24
Faber-Chi 23
Williams-Chi 22

Win Percentage
Bagby-Cle .... .721
Mays-NY .... .703
Kerr-Chi .... .700
Cicotte-Chi ...... .677

Games
Bagby-Cle 48
Ayers-Det 46
Mays-NY 45
Kerr-Chi 45
Zachary-Was 44

Complete Games
Bagby-Cle 30
Faber-Chi 28
Cicotte-Chi 28
Mays-NY 26
Coveleski-Cle 26

Shutouts
Mays-NY 6
Shocker-StL 5
Shawkey-NY 5

Saves
Shocker-StL 5
Kerr-Chi 5
Burwell-StL 4

Innings Pitched
Bagby-Cle 339.2
Faber-Chi 319.0
Coveleski-Cle 315.0
Mays-NY 312.0
Cicotte-Chi 303.1

Fewest Hits/Game
Coveleski-Cle 8.11
Shocker-StL 8.21
Collins-NY 8.22
Shawkey-NY 8.27
Davis-StL 8.35

Fewest BB/Game
Quinn-NY 1.71
Coveleski-Cle 1.86
Bagby-Cle 2.09
Cicotte-Chi 2.20
Perry-Phi 2.22

Strikeouts
Coveleski-Cle 133
Williams-Chi 128
Shawkey-NY 126
Faber-Chi 108
Shocker-StL 107

Strikeouts/Game
Ayers-Det 4.44
Shawkey-NY 4.24
Harper-Bos 3.93
Shocker-StL 3.92
Williams-Chi 3.85

Ratio
Coveleski-Cle 10.09
Shocker-StL 10.92
Rommel-Phi 10.99
Shawkey-NY 11.16
Bagby-Cle 11.18

Earned Run Average
Shawkey-NY 2.45
Coveleski-Cle 2.49
Shocker-StL 2.71
Rommel-Phi 2.85
Bagby-Cle 2.89

Adjusted ERA
Shawkey-NY 155
Coveleski-Cle 153
Shocker-StL 144
Rommel-Phi 141
Bagby-Cle 131

Opponents' Batting Avg.
Coveleski-Cle ..... .243
Collins-NY .... .247
Shawkey-NY ..... .248
Shocker-StL ...... .248
Ehmke-Det .... .253

Opponents' On Base Pct.
Coveleski-Cle ..... .285
Shocker-StL ...... .305
Shawkey-NY ..... .308
Quinn-NY .... .308
Rommel-Phi ...... .309

Starter Runs
Coveleski-Cle 45.6
Shawkey-NY 39.6
Bagby-Cle 33.9
Shocker-StL 29.4
Faber-Chi 28.2

Adjusted Starter Runs
Coveleski-Cle 45.7
Shawkey-NY 40.3
Bagby-Cle 34.1
Shocker-StL 32.7
Faber-Chi 27.2

Clutch Pitching Index
Naylor-Phi 130
Harper-Bos 128
Davis-StL 117
Oldham-Det 116
Perry-Phi 113

Total Pitcher Index
Coveleski-Cle 5.9
Shawkey-NY 4.3
Shocker-StL 4.0
Bagby-Cle 3.8
Mays-NY 3.7

Total Baseball Ranking
Ruth-NY 8.5
Sisler-StL 7.9
Coveleski-Cle 5.9
E.Collins-Chi 5.6
Speaker-Cle 5.2

January 21 Judge Kenesaw Mountain Landis officially takes over as baseball's commissioner.

January 22 The Reds trade pitcher Jimmy Ring and outfielder Greasy Neale to the Phils for lefty Eppa Rixey, who led the NL with 22 losses in 1920. Rixey will pitch his way into the Hall of Fame over the next 13 years.

June 13 Umpires in both leagues begin the practice of rubbing mud into the balls before each game, using a special clay supplied by A's coach Lena Blackburne from his New Jersey farm.

July 1 Casey Stengel is traded from the last-place Phils to the second-place Giants, along with infielder Johnny Rawlings and pitcher Red Causey for infielder Goldie Rapp and outfielders Lance Richbourg and Lee King.

July 29 John McGraw buys outfielder Irish Meusel, who is hitting .353 but has been suspended by the Phillies for lackadaisical play. McGraw gives up three bench warmers and $30,000. The Giants take three from the Reds and go into the NL lead for the first time. They will fall back by seven games before coming on with a rush in September.

August 5 The first radio broadcast of a major league game is heard over KDKA in Pittsburgh. The Pirates-Phils game is announced by Harold Arlin. The Pirates score three runs in the eighth inning, beating the Phils 8-5. Arlin is the grandfather of future San Diego Padre Steve Arlin.

August 24 The Pirates, in front by seven ½ games, drop a doubleheader to the Giants in New York before 35,000. Art Nehf wins the opener, 10–2, and Phil Douglas takes the nightcap, 7–0.

September 29 The Bucs drop a doubleheader to the Cardinals allowing the idle Giants to clinch the NL pennant, their seventh under manager McGraw.

October 5 The World Series opener is broadcast on KDKA radio, with Grantland Rice announcing; it's the only game of the season's World Series to be aired.

October 13 Waite Hoyt and Art Nehf come back for Game 8 with two days rest. With two on and two outs in the first, Giants first baseman George Kelly hits a grounder to short that goes through Roger Peckinpaugh, and a run scores. Not another Giant reaches third base the rest of the day. After Aaron Ward walks in the ninth, Frank "Home Run" Baker hits a drive toward right, but second baseman Johnny Rawlings spears it and throws him out while on the ground. Ward heads for third base and is gunned down by a throw from Kelly to Frisch to end the Series. The Giants are the first team to lose the first two games and come back to win the Series.

October 16 Judge Landis outlaws gentleman's agreements and cover-ups of players optioned to the minors without proper paperwork. He declares six players free agents, including Heinie Manush, who will ride a 17-year .330 BA into the Hall of Fame in 1964.

BOSTON	BROOKLYN	CHICAGO	CINCINNATI	NEW YORK	PHILADELPHIA	PITTSBURGH	ST.LOUIS
M F.Mitchell	M W.Robinson	M J.Evers	M P.Moran	M J.McGraw	M B.Donovan	M M.Gibson	M B.Rickey
1B W.Holke	1B R.Schmandt	M B.Killefer	1B J.Daubert	1B G.Kelly	M K.Wilhelm	1B C.Grimm	1B J.Fournier
2B H.Ford	2B P.Kilduff	1B R.Grimes	2B S.Bohne	2B J.Rawlings	1B E.Konetchy	2B G.Cutshaw	2B R.Hornsby
SS W.Barbare	SS I.Olson	2B Z.Terry	SS L.Kopf	SS D.Bancroft	2B J.Smith	SS R.Maranville	SS D.Lavan
3B T.Boeckel	3B J.Johnston	SS C.Hollocher	3B H.Groh	3B F.Frisch	SS F.Parkinson	3B C.Barnhart	3B M.Stock
LF W.Cruise	LF Z.Wheat	3B C.Deal	LF P.Duncan	LF I.Meusel	3B R.Wrightstone	LF C.Bigbee	LF A.McHenry
CF R.Powell	CF H.Myers	LF T.Barber	CF E.Roush	CF G.Burns	LF I.Meusel	CF M.Carey	CF L.Mann
RF B.Southworth	RF T.Griffith	CF G.Maisel	RF R.Bressler	RF R.Youngs	CF C.Williams	RF P.Whitted	RF J.Smith
C M.O'Neil	C O.Miller	RF M.Flack	C I.Wingo	C F.Snyder	RF B.LeBourveau	C W.Schmidt	C V.Clemons
		C B.O'Farrell			C F.Bruggy		
O F.Nicholson	O B.Neis	32 J.Kelleher	21 L.Fonseca	C E.Smith	31 D.Miller	23 C.Tierney	O J.Schultz
C H.Gowdy	1 E.Konetchy	O J.Sullivan	C B.Hargrave	O G.Walker	1O C.Lee	O D.Robertson	O H.Mueller
O A.Nixon	C E.Krueger	O B.Twombly	O G.Neale	3 G.Rapp	2 J.Rawlings	C T.Brottem	P.Dillhoefer
2 L.Christenbury	C Z.Taylor	C T.Daly	S S.Crane	O E.Brown	C R.Miller	O J.Mokan	O C.Heathcote
C F.Gibson	S2 H.Janvrin	C B.Killefer	O C.See	O L.King	C J.Peters	C B.Skiff	E.Ainsmith
H J.Sullivan	O W.Hood	/2 W.Marriott	O D.Paskert	S3 R.Miller	2 J.Monroe	C R.Rohwer	2 S.Toporcer
	S C.Ward	3 H.Warner	/C A.Douglass	3 P.Patterson	C B.Henline	C J.Gooch	O B.Shotton
P J.Oeschger	/2 J.Sheehan	/O D.Robertson	/O D.Williams	/1 M.Gonzalez	O C.Walker	/3 P.Traynor	/1 H.Janvrin
P M.Watson	/O E.Eayrs	/O R.Thomas	/3 W.Kimmick	C A.Gaston	C C.Stengel	/C M.Wilson	/C C.Niebergall
P H.McQuillan	/O B.Lamar	S C.Elliott	/O K.Hogan	/O C.Stengel	G.Neale	/O K.Cuyler	/O H.Hunter
P D.Fillingim		/2 J.Klugmann		/2 J.Monroe	/S D.Rader	/C B.Warwick	/1 H.Jones
P J.Scott	P B.Grimes	/C K.Wirts	P D.Luque	O J.Berry	M.Wheat		/S R.Ewing
	P L.Cadore		P E.Rixey	/2 H.Schreiber	L.Richbourg	P W.Cooper	H G.Gilham
P G.Braxton	P D.Ruether	P P.Alexander	P R.Marquard	/O J.Connelly	H H.Betts	P W.Glazner	H W.Irwin
P C.Morgan	P C.Mitchell	P S.Martin	P P.Donohue	/3 W.Kopf	D.Sedgwick	P E.Hamilton	H L.McCarty
/P J.Cooney	P S.Smith	P B.Freeman	RP B.Napier	/2 B.Heine	S.Baumgartner	P B.Adams	
/P I.Townsend		P V.Cheeves	P F.Coumbe	H J.Mahady	/P R.Causey	P J.Morrison	P J.Haines
/P E.Eayrs	P J.Miljus	P L.York	P C.Markle	/2 J.Mahady	P J.Keenan		P B.Doak
/P A.Pierotti	P F.Schupp		P L.Brenton	P A.Nehf	/P L.Weinert	P J.Zinn	P B.Pertica
/P L.Townsend	P A.Mamaux	P H.Vaughn	P C.Rogge	P J.Barnes	P P.Behan	P H.Carlson	P B.Walker
	/P J.Pfeffer	P P.Jones	P H.Eller	P F.Toney	/P K.Wilhelm	P C.Yellowhorse	P B.Sherdel
	/P S.Bailey	P E.Ponder	P B.Geary	P P.Douglas	P J.Ring	/P E.Ponder	RP L.North
	/P R.Gordinier	P L.Tyler	P L.Clarke	P R.Ryan	P G.Smith	/P L.Bigbee	P J.Pfeffer
	/P G.Mohart	/P V.Keen		RP S.Sallee	P L.Meadows	/P R.Wheeler	P B.Bailey
		/P T.Kaufmann		P R.Benton	P J.Winters	/P B.Hughes	P T.Riviere
		/P G.Stueland		/P R.Shea		/P D.Rader	/P F.Schupp
		/P O.Hanson		/P R.Causey		/P P.Morrison	P M.Goodwin
		/P S.Bailey		/P P.Perritt			P J.May
		/P O.Fuhr		/P C.Jonnard			/P M.Kircher
				/P W.Zink			

TEAM	G	W	L	PCT	GB	R	OR	AB	H	2B	3B	HR	BB	SO	AVG	OBP	SLG	PRO	PRO+	BR	/A	PF	CHI	RC	SB	CS	SBA	SBR
NY	153	94	59	.614		840	637	5278	1575	237	93	75	469	390	.298	.359	.421	.780	112	94	92	100	104	795	137	114	55	-27
PIT	154	90	63	.588	4	692	595	5379	1533	231	104	37	341	371	.285	.330	.387	.717	93	-37	-55	103	102	684	134	93	59	-16
STL	154	87	66	.569	7	809	681	5309	1635	260	88	83	382	452	.308	.358	.437	.795	118	114	131	98	98	816	94	94	50	-28
BOS	153	79	74	.516	15	721	697	5385	1561	209	100	61	377	470	.290	.339	.400	.739	107	6	46	95	100	718	94	100	48	-32
BRO	152	77	75	.507	16.5	667	681	5263	1476	209	85	59	325	400	.280	.325	.386	.711	90	-52	-75	104	104	655	91	73	55	-17
CIN	153	70	83	.458	24	618	649	5112	1421	221	94	20	375	308	.278	.330	.370	.703	96	-56	-27	95	98	623	117	120	49	-37
CHI	153	64	89	.418	30	668	773	5321	1553	234	56	37	343	374	.292	.339	.378	.717	95	-31	-32	100	99	671	70	97	42	-37
PHI	154	51	103	.331	43.5	617	919	5329	1512	238	50	88	294	615	.284	.324	.397	.721	89	-37	-89	108	94	668	66	80	45	-28
TOT	613					5632		42376	12266	1839	670	460	2906	3380	.289	.338	.397	.736							803	771	51	-222

TEAM	CG	SH	SV	IP	H	H/G	HR	BB	SO	RAT	ERA	ERA+	OAV	OOB	PR	/A	PF	CPI	FA	E	DP	FW	PW	BW	SBW	DIF
NY	71	9	18	1372¹	1497	9.8	79	295	357	11.9	3.55	103	.286	.326	34	16	97	102	.971	187	155	1.3	1.6	9.1	.0	5.5
PIT	88	10	10	1415²	1448	9.2	37	322	500	11.5	3.17	121	.271	.316	96	104	101	96	.973	172	129	2.3	10.3	-5.4	1.2	5.3
STL	70	10	16	1371²	1486	9.8	61	399	464	12.6	3.62	101	.282	.337	24	5	97	102	.965	219	130	-.6	.5	12.9	-.0	-2.3
BOS	74	11	12	1385	1488	9.7	54	420	382	12.6	3.90	94	.280	.337	-18	-38	97	93	.969	199	122	.5	-3.8	4.5	-.4	1.6
BRO	82	8	12	1363¹	1556	10.3	46	361	471	12.9	3.70	105	.293	.342	13	28	103	103	.964	232	142	-1.5	2.8	-7.4	1.1	6.1
CIN	83	7	9	1363	1500	9.9	37	305	408	12.0	3.46	103	.287	.328	48	17	95	100	.969	193	139	.9	1.7	-2.7	-.9	-5.5
CHI	73	7	7	1363	1605	10.6	67	409	441	13.6	4.39	87	.303	.357	-93	-88	101	99	.974	166	129	2.5	-8.7	-3.2	-.9	-2.3
PHI	82	5	8	1348²	1665	11.1	79	371	333	13.8	4.48	94	.308	.356	-105	-39	112	99	.955	295	127	-5.2	-3.9	-8.8	-.0	-8.1
TOT	623	67	92	10982²		10.0				12.6	3.78		.289	.338					.967	1663	1073					

Runs		Hits		Doubles		Triples		Home Runs		Total Bases	
Hornsby-StL	131	Hornsby-StL	235	Hornsby-StL	44	Powell-Bos	18	Kelly-NY	23	Hornsby-StL	378
Frisch-NY	121	Frisch-NY	211	Kelly-NY	42	Hornsby-StL	18	Hornsby-StL	21	Kelly-NY	310
Bancroft-NY	121	C.Bigbee-Pit	204	Johnston-Bro	41	Grimm-Pit	17	Williams-Phi	18	McHenry-StL	305
Powell-Bos	114	Johnston-Bro	203	Grimes-Chi	38	Frisch-NY	17	McHenry-StL	17	Meusel-Phi-NY	302
Burns-NY	111			McHenry-StL	37	C.Bigbee-Pit	17	Fournier-StL	16	Frisch-NY	300

Runs Batted In		Runs Produced		Bases On Balls		Batting Average		On Base Percentage		Slugging Average	
Hornsby-StL	126	Hornsby-StL	236	Burns-NY	80	Hornsby-StL	.397	Hornsby-StL	.458	Hornsby-StL	.639
Kelly-NY	122	Frisch-NY	213	Youngs-NY	71	Roush-Cin	.352	Youngs-NY	.411	McHenry-StL	.531
Youngs-NY	102	Kelly-NY	194	Grimes-Chi	70	McHenry-StL	.350	Fournier-StL	.409	Kelly-NY	.528
McHenry-StL	102	Youngs-NY	189	Carey-Pit	70	Cruise-Bos	.346	Grimes-Chi	.406	Meusel-Phi-NY	.515
Frisch-NY	100	Bancroft-NY	182	Bancroft-NY	66	Fournier-StL	.343	Carey-Pit	.395	Mann-StL	.512

Production		Adjusted Production		Batter Runs		Adjusted Batter Runs		Clutch Hitting Index		Runs Created	
Hornsby-StL	1.097	Hornsby-StL	191	Hornsby-StL	74.4	Hornsby-StL	77.7	Youngs-NY	142	Hornsby-StL	169
McHenry-StL	.924	McHenry-StL	145	Fournier-StL	34.5	Fournier-StL	36.9	Stock-StL	142	Frisch-NY	118
Fournier-StL	.914	Fournier-StL	144	McHenry-StL	33.5	McHenry-StL	35.8	Lavan-StL	140	Fournier-StL	114
Meusel-Phi-NY	.895	Kelly-NY	131	Meusel-Phi-NY	27.6	Cruise-Bos	28.5	Barnhart-Pit	123	McHenry-StL	111
Kelly-NY	.884	Youngs-NY	129	Frisch-NY	24.8	Roush-Cin	26.7	Konetchy-Bro-Phi	115	Meusel-Phi-NY	110

Total Average		Stolen Bases		Stolen Base Average		Stolen Base Runs		Fielding Runs		Total Player Rating	
Hornsby-StL	1.203	Frisch-NY	49	Frisch-NY	79.0	Frisch-NY	6.9	Lavan-StL	18.5	Hornsby-StL	7.1
Frisch-NY	.902	Carey-Pit	37	Carey-Pit	75.5	Carey-Pit	3.9	Bancroft-NY	17.4	Bancroft-NY	4.8
Fournier-StL	.882	Johnston-Bro	28	Maisel-Chi	70.8	Stock-StL	1.5	Williams-Phi	16.3	Frisch-NY	4.3
Carey-Pit	.868	Bohne-Cin	26	Maranville-Pit	67.6	Cutshaw-Pit	1.2	C.Bigbee-Pit	16.2	Johnston-Bro	3.0
Youngs-NY	.860	Maranville-Pit	25	Johnston-Bro	63.6			Carey-Pit	16.1	Kelly-NY	2.5

Wins		Win Percentage		Games		Complete Games		Shutouts		Saves	
Grimes-Bro	22	Doak-StL	.714	Scott-Bos	47	Grimes-Bro	30	Oeschger-Bos	3	North-StL	7
Cooper-Pit	22	Nehf-NY	.667	Oeschger-Bos	46	Cooper-Pit	29	J.Morrison-Pit	3	Barnes-NY	6
Oeschger-Bos	20	Grimes-Bro	.629	McQuillan-Bos	45	Luque-Cin	25	Mitchell-Bro	3	McQuillan-Bos	5
Nehf-NY	20	Barnes-NY	.625	Watson-Bos	44			Luque-Cin	3		
Rixey-Cin	19	Toney-NY	.621	Fillingim-Bos	44			Haines-StL	3		
								Fillingim-Bos	3		
								Douglas-NY	3		
								Alexander-Chi	3		

Innings Pitched		Fewest Hits/Game		Fewest BB/Game		Strikeouts		Strikeouts/Game		Ratio	
Cooper-Pit	327.0	Glazner-Pit	8.23	Adams-Pit	1.01	Grimes-Bro	136	Grimes-Bro	4.05	Adams-Pit	9.73
Luque-Cin	304.0	Adams-Pit	8.72	Alexander-Chi	1.18	Cooper-Pit	134	Cooper-Pit	3.69	Glazner-Pit	10.92
Grimes-Bro	302.1	Oeschger-Bos	9.12	Barnes-NY	1.53	Luque-Cin	102	Doak-StL	3.58	Nehf-NY	11.15
Rixey-Cin	301.0	Pertica-StL	9.16	Hubbell-Phi	1.55	McQuillan-Bos	94	Martin-Chi	3.56	Luque-Cin	11.34
Oeschger-Bos	299.0	Nehf-NY	9.18	Doak-StL	1.60			Glazner-Pit	3.38	Alexander-Chi	11.43

Earned Run Average		Adjusted ERA		Opponents' Batting Avg.		Opponents' On Base Pct.		Starter Runs		Adjusted Starter Runs	
Doak-StL	2.59	Adams-Pit	145	Glazner-Pit	.250	Adams-Pit	.272	Rixey-Cin	33.4	Grimes-Bro	35.5
Adams-Pit	2.64	Doak-StL	142	Adams-Pit	.251	Glazner-Pit	.306	Grimes-Bro	32.0	Glazner-Pit	27.6
Glazner-Pit	2.77	Glazner-Pit	138	Pertica-StL	.267	Nehf-NY	.311	Doak-StL	27.6	Rixey-Cin	26.6
Rixey-Cin	2.78	Grimes-Bro	137	Watson-Bos	.270	Luque-Cin	.312	Glazner-Pit	26.3	Doak-StL	24.9
Grimes-Bro	2.83	Mitchell-Bro	134	Nehf-NY	.271	Doak-StL	.313	Adams-Pit	20.2	Cooper-Pit	21.2

Clutch Pitching Index		Relief Runs		Adjusted Relief Runs		Relief Ranking		Total Pitcher Index		Total Baseball Ranking	
Barnes-NY	124	North-StL	2.3	North-StL	1.1	North-StL	1.1	Grimes-Bro	4.5	Hornsby-StL	7.1
Mitchell-Bro	118	Sallee-NY	1.5	Sallee-NY	.2	Sallee-NY	.2	Rixey-Cin	2.8	Bancroft-NY	4.8
Doak-StL	116							Mitchell-Bro	2.8	Grimes-Bro	4.5
Rixey-Cin	113							Adams-Pit	2.5	Frisch-NY	4.3
Grimes-Bro	112							Doak-StL	2.2	Johnston-Bro	3.0

April 13 With former president Woodrow Wilson, new president Warren G. Harding, and VP Calvin Coolidge watching, the Senators lose their home opener 6-3 to the Red Sox. Walter Johnson leaves after four innings, the first time he has failed to finish an opening game.

June 6* The Detroit Stars' Bill Gatewood pitches the first no-hitter in Negro League history, defeating the Cuban Stars 4-0.

June 7* The only Organized Baseball game canceled because of a murder occurs at Kingsport, Tennessee (Appalachian League), when the body of a slain girl is found at the ballpark. To keep the trail fresh, for bloodhounds, police close the park and cancel the scheduled game against Knoxville.

July 12 Babe Ruth hits his 137th career home run, passing nineteenth century star Roger Connor's career record of 136.

August 2 A Chicago jury brings in a verdict of not guilty against the Black Sox. That night, jurors and defendants celebrate with a party in an Italian restaurant. Ignoring the verdict, Judge Landis bans all eight defendants from baseball for life.

August 19 Ty Cobb gets hit No. 3,000 off Boston pitcher Elmer Myers. At 34, he's the youngest ever to turn the trick.

September 5 Walter Johnson breaks Cy Young's career strikeout mark by fanning seven Yankees to run his total to 2,287.

September 29 The Bucs drop a doubleheader to the Cardinals allowing the idle Giants to clinch the NL pennant, their seventh under manager McGraw.

October 1 White Sox catcher Ray Schalk makes a putout at first base. When the Indians' speedy Charlie Jamieson singles to right field, Schalk jogs toward first base in case Jamieson takes too wide a turn toward second, which he does. Schalk takes a throw from the outfielder and makes the putout. Schalk is the only catcher to make a putout at every base.

October 1 After clinching the pennant with a 5-3 win in the opener, the Yankees bring Babe Ruth in to pitch in relief in the nightcap. Ruth, with just one other pitching appearance all season, takes over in the eighth with New York in the lead, 6-0. He quickly allows the A's six runs to tie the score but then knuckles down to hold them scoreless through the eleventh when New York scores a run to win, 7-6. The stunt still costs Waite Hoyt a 20-win season.

October 5 In the first one-city World Series since 1906, the Polo Grounds will be the site for all nine games. Carl Mays (27-9) is at his best, needing 86 pitches to set the Giants down with five hits in this 3-0 Yankee win.

October 16 In defiance of a Landis ban on World Series participants playing postseason exhibitions, Ruth, Bob Meusel, and pitcher Bill Piercy launch a barnstorming tour in Buffalo. Five days later, they cut it short in Scranton. In the meantime Ruth openly challenges Landis to act. The judge does, fining the players their World Series shares—$3,362.26—and suspending them until May 20 of the following season.

	BOSTON		CHICAGO		CLEVELAND		DETROIT		NEW YORK		PHILADELPHIA		ST.LOUIS		WASHINGTON
M	H.Duffy	M	K.Gleason	M	T.Speaker	M	T.Cobb	M	M.Huggins	M	C.Mack	M	L.Fohl	M	G.McBride
1B	S.McInnis	1B	E.Sheely	1B	D.Johnston	1B	L.Blue	1B	W.Pipp	1B	J.Walker	1B	G.Sisler	1B	J.Judge
2B	D.Pratt	2B	E.Collins	2B	B.Wambsganss	2B	R.Young	2B	A.Ward	2B	J.Dykes	2B	M.McManus	2B	B.Harris
SS	E.Scott	SS	E.Johnson	SS	J.Sewell	SS	D.Bush	SS	R.Peckinpaugh	SS	C.Galloway	SS	W.Gerber	SS	F.O'Rourke
3B	E.Foster	3B	E.Mulligan	3B	L.Gardner	3B	B.Jones	3B	F.Baker	3B	J.Dugan	3B	F.Ellerbe	3B	H.Shanks
LF	M.Menosky	LF	B.Falk	LF	C.Jamieson	LF	B.Veach	LF	B.Ruth	LF	T.Walker	LF	K.Williams	LF	B.Miller
CF	N.Leibold	CF	A.Strunk	CF	T.Speaker	CF	T.Cobb	CF	E.Miller	CF	F.Welch	CF	B.Jacobson	CF	S.Rice
RF	S.Collins	RF	H.Hooper	RF	E.Smith	RF	H.Heilmann	RF	B.Meusel	RF	W.Witt	RF	J.Tobin	RF	C.Milan
C	M.Ruel	C	R.Schalk	C	S.O'Neill	C	J.Bassler	C	W.Schang	C	C.Perkins	C	H.Severeid	C	P.Gharrity
3	O.Vitt	O	J.Mostil	1	G.Burns	SO	I.Flagstead	32	M.McNally	1	F.Brazill	S2	D.Lee	O	F.Brower
C	R.Walters	2S	H.McClellan	2	R.Stephenson	O	C.Shorten	O2	C.Fewster	S	E.McCann	3	L.Lamb	O	E.Smith
O	T.Hendryx	C	Y.Yaryan	O	J.Wood	23	J.Sargent	O	B.Roth	O	P.Johnson	O	D.Wetzel	O	V.Picinich
O	P.Pittinger	C	G.Lees	O	J.Evans	C	E.Ainsmith	O	P.Bodie	1	I.Griffin	C	P.Collins	O	D.Lewis
O	S.Vick	/O	F.Bratschi	C	L.Nunamaker	C	L.Woodall	O	C.Hawks	3	Z.Collins	3	E.Smith	S	D.Bush
/O	E.Neitzke	H	R.Ostergard	O	J.Graney	O	H.Merritt	C	F.Hofmann	C	G.Myatt	2	B.Gleason	O	G.Goslin
/O	J.Perrin	/3	E.Leifer	C	P.Thomas	/2	S.Barnes	C	A.DeVormer	O	F.Walker	S	J.Austin	S	B.LaMotte
/C	E.Chaplin	H	E.Murphy	C	G.Shinault	/C	C.Manion	/S	J.Mitchell	C	F.Callaway	C	J.Billings	H	F.Ellerbe
H	H.Hiller	H	F.Pratt	/C	L.Sewell	/S	J.Tavener	/O	T.Connelly	/S	B.Barrett	/2	J.Riley	/C	T.Brottem
				/O	T.Jeanes	H	S.Hale			/O	B.Mallonee	/3	B.Mullen	/3	G.Foss
P	S.Jones	P	R.Faber	/1	L.Guisto	/O	G.Cunningham	P	C.Mays	/C	L.Styles	/2	L.Stuart	/C	R.Torres
P	J.Bush	P	D.Kerr	/C	A.Wilson	/3	C.Huber	P	W.Hoyt	/S	E.Yoter				
P	H.Pennock	P	R.Wilkinson					P	B.Shawkey	/S	D.Fulghum	P	U.Shocker	P	G.Mogridge
P	A.Russell	P	S.Hodge	P	S.Coveleski	P	D.Leonard	P	R.Collins	H	R.Shannon	P	D.Davis	P	W.Johnson
P	E.Myers	P	D.McWeeny	P	G.Uhle	P	H.Dauss	P	J.Quinn			P	E.Vangilder	P	T.Zachary
				P	D.Mails	P	R.Oldham			P	E.Rommel	P	R.Kolp	P	E.Erickson
P	B.Karr	P	J.Russell	P	J.Bagby	P	H.Ehmke	P	B.Piercy	P	S.Harriss	P	B.Bayne	P	H.Courtney
P	H.Thormahlen	P	D.Mulrenan	P	R.Caldwell	P	C.Holling	P	A.Ferguson	RP	R.Moore	RP	B.Burwell	RP	A.Schacht
/P	C.Fullerton	P	L.Davenport					/P	H.Harper	P	B.Hasty				
/P	A.Sothoron	/P	C.Twombly	P	A.Sothoron	P	J.Middleton	P	T.Sheehan	P	D.Keefe	P	E.Palmero	P	J.Acosta
/P	S.Dodge	P	J.Wieneke	P	G.Morton	P	B.Cole	/P	T.Rogers	RP	H.Freeman	/P	A.Sothoron	/P	J.Shaw
		/P	S.Connally	P	T.Odenwald	P	S.Sutherland					/P	B.Boland	/P	F.Woodward
		/P	L.Thompson	/P	B.Clark	P	S.Parks			P	R.Naylor	/P	R.Richmond	/P	T.Phillips
		/P	B.Morris	P	J.Petty	P	P.Perritt			P	S.Perry	/P	N.Cullop	/P	R.Bird
		/P	H.Fenner	/P	B.Henderson	/P	L.Stewart			/P	J.Sullivan	P	J.DeBerry	/P	N.Gaines
		/P	R.Pence			/P	D.Ayers			/P	L.Wolf	/P	B.Morris	/P	V.McIlree
		/P	J.Michaelson			/P	J.Walsh			/P	F.Heimach	/P	D.Henry	/P	R.Miller
		/P	C.Blackburn			/P	D.Boone			/P	B.Bishop	/P	G.Boehler		
										/P	A.Taylor				
										/P	R.Miner				

TEAM	G	W	L	PCT	GB	R	OR	AB	H	2B	3B	HR	BB	SO	AVG	OBP	SLG	PRO	PRO+	BR	/A	PF	CHI	RC	SB	CS	SBA	SBR
NY	153	98	55	.641		948	708	5249	1576	285	87	134	588	569	.300	.375	.464	.839	116	142	122	102	102	929	89	64	58	-12
CLE	154	94	60	.610	4.5	925	712	5383	1656	355	90	42	623	376	.308	.383	.430	.813	111	112	98	102	100	916	51	42	55	-10
STL	154	81	73	.526	17.5	835	845	5442	1655	246	106	67	413	407	.304	.357	.425	.782	98	28	-20	106	102	827	91	71	56	-15
WAS	154	80	73	.523	18	704	738	5294	1468	240	96	42	462	472	.277	.342	.383	.725	95	-80	-47	95	101	712	112	66	63	-6
BOS	154	75	79	.487	23.5	668	696	5206	1440	248	69	17	428	344	.277	.335	.361	.696	84	-133	-116	97	107	642	83	65	56	-14
DET	154	71	82	.464	27	883	852	5461	1724	268	100	58	582	376	.316	.385	.433	.818	115	120	129	99	94	921	95	89	52	-25
CHI	154	62	92	.403	36.5	683	858	5329	1509	242	82	35	445	474	.283	.343	.379	.722	90	-86	-77	99	99	695	94	93	50	-28
PHI	155	53	100	.346	45	657	894	5465	1497	256	64	82	424	565	.274	.331	.389	.720	88	-102	-105	101	96	710	69	56	55	-13
TOT	616					6303		42829	12525	2140	694	477	3965	3583	.292	.356	.408	.765							684	546	56	-122

TEAM	CG	SH	SV	IP	H	H/G	HR	BB	SO	RAT	ERA	ERA+	OAV	OOB	PR	/A	PF	CPI	FA	E	DP	FW	PW	BW	SBW	DIF
NY	92	8	15	1364	1461	9.6	51	470	481	13.1	3.82	111	.277	.342	70	62	99	99	.965	222	138	-.3	5.8	11.4	.3	4.3
CLE	81	11	14	1377	1534	10.0	43	431	475	13.0	3.90	109	.288	.344	58	55	100	100	.967	204	124	.8	5.1	9.2	.5	1.4
STL	77	9	9	1379	1541	10.1	71	556	477	13.9	4.61	97	.288	.360	-51	-22	105	94	.964	224	127	-.3	-2.1	-1.9	.0	8.2
WAS	80	10	10	1383²	1568	10.2	51	442	452	13.3	3.97	104	.291	.349	47	22	96	102	.963	235	153	-.9	2.1	-4.4	.9	5.9
BOS	88	9	5	1364¹	1521	10.0	53	452	446	13.3	3.98	106	.291	.352	45	37	99	104	.975	157	151	3.5	3.5	-10.8	.1	1.8
DET	73	4	16	1386¹	1634	10.6	71	495	452	14.2	4.40	97	.297	.361	-18	-20	100	102	.963	232	107	-.8	-1.9	12.1	-.9	-14.0
CHI	84	7	9	1365¹	1603	10.6	52	549	392	14.4	4.94	86	.303	.372	-99	-107	99	94	.969	200	155	1.0	-10.0	-7.2	-1.2	2.3
PHI	75	2	7	1400¹	1645	10.6	85	548	431	14.3	4.61	97	.300	.367	-52	-25	104	102	.958	274	144	-3.1	-2.3	-9.8	.2	-8.5
TOT	650	60	85	11020		10.2				13.7	4.28		.292	.356					.965	1748	1099					

Runs
Ruth-NY 177
Tobin-StL 132
Peckinpaugh-NY .. 128
Sisler-StL 125
Cobb-Det 124

Hits
Heilmann-Det 237
Tobin-StL 236
Sisler-StL 216
Jacobson-StL 211
Veach-Det 207

Doubles
Speaker-Cle 52
Ruth-NY 44
Veach-Det 43
Heilmann-Det 43
Meusel-NY 40

Triples
Tobin-StL 18
Sisler-StL 18
Shanks-Was 18

Home Runs
Ruth-NY 59
Williams-StL 24
Meusel-NY 24
T.Walker-Phi 23
Heilmann-Det 19

Total Bases
Ruth-NY 457
Heilmann-Det 365
Meusel-NY 334
Tobin-StL 327
Sisler-StL 326

Runs Batted In
Ruth-NY 171
Heilmann-Det 139
Meusel-NY 135
Veach-Det 128
Gardner-Cle 120

Runs Produced
Ruth-NY 289
Heilmann-Det 234
Veach-Det 222
Gardner-Cle 218
Sisler-StL 217

Bases On Balls
Ruth-NY 144
Blue-Det 103
Peckinpaugh-NY ... 84
J.Sewell-Cle 80
Schang-NY 78

Batting Average
Heilmann-Det .... .394
Cobb-Det .... .389
Ruth-NY .... .378
Sisler-StL .... .371
Speaker-Cle ..... .362

On Base Percentage
Ruth-NY .... .512
Cobb-Det .... .452
Heilmann-Det .... .444
Speaker-Cle ..... .439
Williams-StL ..... .429

Slugging Average
Ruth-NY .... .846
Heilmann-Det .... .606
Cobb-Det .... .596
Williams-StL ..... .561
Sisler-StL .... .560

Production
Ruth-NY 1.358
Heilmann-Det ... 1.051
Cobb-Det 1.048
Williams-StL .... .990
Speaker-Cle .... .977

Adjusted Production
Ruth-NY 236
Heilmann-Det 167
Cobb-Det 167
Speaker-Cle 146
Williams-StL 142

Batter Runs
Ruth-NY 119.2
Heilmann-Det ... 58.4
Cobb-Det 50.3
Williams-StL 42.5
Speaker-Cle 38.2

Adjusted Batter Runs
Ruth-NY 114.7
Heilmann-Det ... 59.9
Cobb-Det 51.5
Speaker-Cle 36.5
Williams-StL 35.2

Clutch Hitting Index
Gardner-Cle 141
Severeid-StL 127
Pratt-Bos 124
O'Rourke-Was 113
Sheely-Chi 112

Runs Created
Ruth-NY 238
Heilmann-Det 159
Cobb-Det 134
Sisler-StL 133
Williams-StL 130

Total Average
Ruth-NY 1.745
Cobb-Det 1.132
Heilmann-Det .. 1.121
Speaker-Cle ... 1.040
Williams-StL ... 1.037

Stolen Bases
Sisler-StL 35
Harris-Was 29
Rice-Was 26
Johnson-Chi 22
Cobb-Det 22

Stolen Base Average
Judge-Was 77.8
Harris-Was 76.3
Sisler-StL 76.1
Meusel-NY 73.9
Rice-Was 68.4

Stolen Base Runs
Sisler-StL 3.9
Harris-Was 3.3
Judge-Was 2.7
Welch-Phi 1.8

Fielding Runs
Scott-Bos 38.1
Collins-Chi 27.1
Dykes-Phi 25.0
Ward-NY 18.8
Johnson-Chi 18.0

Total Player Rating
Ruth-NY 9.4
Cobb-Det 4.9
Collins-Chi 4.0
Sisler-StL 3.6
Speaker-Cle 3.3

Wins
Shocker-StL 27
Mays-NY 27
Faber-Chi 25
Jones-Bos 23
Coveleski-Cle 23

Win Percentage
Mays-NY .... .750
Shocker-StL ..... .692
Bush-Bos .... .640
Coveleski-Cle .... .639
Faber-Chi .... .625

Games
Mays-NY 49
Shocker-StL 47
Bayne-StL 47
Rommel-Phi 46

Complete Games
Faber-Chi 32
Shocker-StL 30
Mays-NY 30
Coveleski-Cle 28

Shutouts
Jones-Bos 5
Shocker-StL 4
Mogridge-Was 4
Faber-Chi 4

Saves
Middleton-Det 7
Mays-NY 7

Innings Pitched
Mays-NY 336.2
Faber-Chi 330.2
Shocker-StL 326.2
Coveleski-Cle ... 315.0
Kerr-Chi 308.2

Fewest Hits/Game
Faber-Chi 7.97
Bush-Bos 8.63
Mays-NY 8.88
Shawkey-NY 9.00
Johnson-Was 9.03

Fewest BB/Game
Hasty-Phi 2.01
Mays-NY 2.03
Mogridge-Was ... 2.06
Bagby-Cle 2.07
Zachary-Was 2.12

Strikeouts
Johnson-Was 143
Shocker-StL 132
Shawkey-NY 126
Faber-Chi 124
Leonard-Det 120

Strikeouts/Game
Johnson-Was 4.88
Shawkey-NY 4.63
Bayne-StL 4.50
Leonard-Det 4.41
Mails-Cle 4.03

Ratio
Faber-Chi 10.53
Mays-NY 11.15
Mogridge-Was .. 11.69
Shocker-StL 12.04
Jones-Bos 12.11

Earned Run Average
Faber-Chi 2.48
Mogridge-Was ... 3.00
Mays-NY 3.05
Hoyt-NY 3.09
Jones-Bos 3.22

Adjusted ERA
Faber-Chi 171
Mays-NY 139
Mogridge-Was 137
Hoyt-NY 137
Jones-Bos 131

Opponents' Batting Avg.
Faber-Chi .... .242
Mays-NY .... .257
Bush-Bos .... .260
Shawkey-NY ..... .263
Johnson-Was .... .263

Opponents' On Base Pct.
Faber-Chi .... .297
Mays-NY .... .303
Mogridge-Was ... .313
Shocker-StL ..... .319
Johnson-Was .... .326

Starter Runs
Faber-Chi 66.3
Mays-NY 46.2
Mogridge-Was ... 41.0
Hoyt-NY 37.3
Jones-Bos 35.1

Adjusted Starter Runs
Faber-Chi 64.6
Mays-NY 44.4
Hoyt-NY 35.8
Mogridge-Was ... 35.7
Shocker-StL 33.6

Clutch Pitching Index
Russell-Bos 122
Zachary-Was 118
Keefe-Phi 114
Uhle-Cle 108
Sothoron-SL-Bs-Cle .. 108

Relief Runs

Adjusted Relief Runs

Relief Ranking

Total Pitcher Index
Faber-Chi 7.0
Mays-NY 5.8
Shocker-StL 4.3
Jones-Bos 4.0
Hoyt-NY 3.3

Total Baseball Ranking
Ruth-NY 8.7
Faber-Chi 7.0
Mays-NY 5.8
Cobb-Det 4.9
Shocker-StL 4.3

February 18 Judge Landis resigns his Federal judgeship, claiming the two jobs (judge and commissioner) take up too much time.

April 12 For the first time since 1900, there are no playing managers in the NL. Long considered an economic necessity, the dual role is no longer essential. It won't be until 1930 that the AL has all bench managers.

April 13 Dazzy Vance, 31, makes his Brooklyn debut and loses to the Giants' Phil Douglas, 4–3. In 1915 when Vance made one start for the Pirates, it was Douglas who beat him. Since then Vance has been in the minors. Despite his late start, the righthander will win 197 in 14 years and a place in the Hall of Fame in 1955.

April 29 The NY Giants hit four inside-the-park homers in one windswept game in spacious Braves Field in Boston. George Kelly hits two, and Ross Youngs and Dave Bancroft hit the others.

May 29 The U.S. Supreme Court rules baseball is not interstate commerce, and the Baltimore Feds lose their case. The request for a rehearing will be denied.

June 12 The Cards get 10 straight hits in the sixth to beat the Phils, 14–8, tying their own record of September 17, 1920. One of the hits would have been a homer by shortstop George "Specs" Toporcer, the first non-pitcher to wear glasses. Unfortunately, Toporcer's first major league homer is negated when he passes base runner Doc Lavan, and he is credited with only a single.

July 7 Pirates outfielder Max Carey is the busiest man on the field in an 18-inning 9-8 loss to the Giants. He gets six hits, draws three walks, has three stolen bases, including one of home, and catches seven fly balls.

July 22 When the Cards go into first place by beating Boston while the Reds are downing the Giants, it marks the first time both St. Louis teams are ever in first place at the same time.

August 25 In one of the most poorly pitched major league games ever played, the Cubs edge the Phils 26–23 in Chicago. There are 51 hits, 23 walks, and 10 errors. The Phils have the bases loaded in the ninth when the game ends, making a total of 16 left on base; the Cubs leave nine. When the Cubs score 14 in the fourth to take a 25–6 lead, outfielder Marty Callaghan bats three times, getting two hits and striking out. Time of game: 3:01.

September 20 Rogers Hornsby is stopped by Burleigh Grimes of Brooklyn after hitting in 33 straight games.

September 25 The Giants beat St. Louis 5-4 in 10 innings to clinch John McGraw's eighth pennant and the Giants' 10th in 41 years in the NL.

October 1 Rogers Hornsby's 3-for-5 on the last day puts him at .401, the first .400-hitter in the NL since Ed Delahanty in 1899. His NL-record 250 hits top Willie Keeler's 243 in 1897, and he wins the Triple Crown with 152 RBI and 42 home runs.

October 4 For the first time, the entire

World Series will be broadcast over the radio. Writer Grantland Rice does the announcing for station WJZ, Newark; it is relayed to WGY in Schenectady. For the first time since 1908, two repeaters meet in the World Series. In a return to the seven-game format, the Giants will win four games while scoring in only five innings. The Yankees' Joe Bush (26-7) leads Art Nehf (19-13) 2-0 when Irish Meusel's two-run single and Pep Young's sacrifice fly score three in the eighth to give the Giants a 3-2 win in Game 1.

October 5 Bob Shawkey (20-12) goes the route, with the Giants scoring three in the first and the Yanks getting single tallies in the first, fourth, and eighth. A near-riot erupts among the 36,514 fans when umpire George Hildebrand, acting on umpire Bill Klem's advice, calls the game, a 3-3 tie, due to darkness after 10 innings. The fans think there's light enough to continue. It takes a police escort to get Judge Landis out of the park and away from the unruly mob. That night he bends over backwards to negate the public's opinion that the game might have been called to provide an extra day's gate by donating the $120,554 receipts to charities. Half will go to New York charities, and half to disabled soldiers.

October 8 The Yanks score first, but the Giants score two in the third and three in the eighth to win the finale 5-3, as Art Nehf hands Joe Bush his second loss, and the Giants win the Series.

	BOSTON		BROOKLYN		CHICAGO		CINCINNATI		NEW YORK		PHILADELPHIA		PITTSBURGH		ST.LOUIS
M	F.Mitchell	M	W.Robinson	M	B.Killefer	M	P.Moran	M	J.McGraw	M	K.Wilhelm	M	M.Gibson	M	B.Rickey
1B	W.Holke	1B	R.Schmandt	1B	R.Grimes	1B	J.Daubert	1B	G.Kelly	1B	R.Leslie	M	B.McKechnie	1B	J.Fournier
2B	L.Kopf	2B	J.Johnston	2B	Z.Terry	2B	S.Bohne	2B	F.Frisch	2B	F.Parkinson	1B	C.Grimm	2B	R.Hornsby
SS	H.Ford	SS	I.Olson	SS	C.Hollocher	SS	I.Caveney	SS	D.Bancroft	SS	A.Fletcher	2B	C.Tierney	SS	S.Toporcer
3B	T.Boeckel	3B	A.High	3B	M.Krug	3B	B.Pinelli	3B	H.Groh	3B	G.Rapp	SS	R.Maranville	3B	M.Stock
LF	A.Nixon	LF	Z.Wheat	LF	H.Miller	LF	P.Duncan	LF	I.Meusel	LF	C.Lee	3B	P.Traynor	LF	J.Schultz
CF	R.Powell	CF	H.Myers	CF	J.Statz	CF	G.Burns	CF	C.Stengel	CF	C.Williams	LF	C.Bigbee	CF	J.Smith
RF	W.Cruise	RF	T.Griffith	RF	B.Friberg	RF	G.Harper	RF	R.Youngs	RF	C.Walker	CF	M.Carey	RF	M.Flack
C	M.O'Neil	C	H.DeBerry	C	B.O'Farrell	C	B.Hargrave	C	F.Snyder	C	B.Henline	RF	R.Russell	C	E.Ainsmith
												C	J.Gooch		
23	W.Barbare	O	B.Griffith	O	C.Heathcote	2	L.Fonseca	2	J.Rawlings	3S	R.Wrightstone	O	C.Barnhart	S	D.Lavan
O	F.Nicholson	C	O.Miller	O1	T.Barber	C	I.Wingo	C	E.Smith	O	B.LeBourveau	3O	W.Schmidt	O	A.McHenry
C	H.Gowdy	1	C.Mitchell	3	J.Kelleher	O	E.Roush	O	B.Cunningham	C	J.Mokan	C	J.Ens	O	V.Clemons
C1	F.Gibson	C	B.Hungling	O	M.Callaghan	S	W.Kimmick	O	R.Shinners	O	J.Peters	2	R.Rohwer	O	H.Mueller
O	B.Southworth	S	C.Ward	O	G.Maisel	/1	D.Robertson	/O	J.Smith	O	L.King	1	W.Mueller	1	J.Bottomley
O	L.Christenbury	O	B.Neis	C	G.Hartnett	O	G.Neale	/1	L.King	C	F.Withrow	O	J.Mokan	O	L.Mann
O	B.Roser	2	H.Janvrin	C	K.Wirts	/C	R.Lutz	C	A.Gaston	/C	R.Benton	P	J.Mattox	O	R.Blades
1	S.Henry	/1	S.Post	O	M.Flack			/2	F.Maguire	/2		C	B.Jonnard	C	C.Heathcote
/S	G.Gallagher	/C	Z.Taylor	2	S.Adams	P	E.Rixey	/O	M.Higbee			/2	S.Stewart	1O	D.Gainer
		/S	S.Crane	/O	H.Fitzgerald	/S	T.Jackson	P	J.Ring			/2	J.Hammond	/C	H.McCurdy
P	M.Watson	H	P.Whitted	/3	G.Grantham	P	D.Luque	/3	W.MacPhee	P	L.Meadows	/O	J.Miller	P	E.Vick
P	F.Miller	R	W.Hood	/1	W.Golvin	P	P.Donohue	H	I.Boone	P	G.Smith	H	T.Lovelace	/S	H.Freigau
P	R.Marquard			/2	J.Klugmann	P	C.Keck	R	J.Berry	P	B.Hubbell	P	T.McNamara		
P	J.Oeschger	P	D.Ruether	P	B.Weis	RP	J.Gillespie	R	C.Dolan	P	L.Weinert	H	A.Merewether	P	J.Pfeffer
P	H.McQuillan	P	B.Grimes	H	H.Cotter			P				R	K.Cuyler	P	B.Sherdel
RP	T.McNamara	P	D.Vance			P	C.Markle	P	A.Nehf	P	J.Winters			P	J.Haines
RP	G.Braxton	P	L.Cadore			P	K.Schnell	P	J.Barnes	P	J.Singleton	P	W.Cooper	P	B.Doak
		P	S.Smith	P	V.Aldridge	/P	J.Scott	P	R.Ryan	/P	P.Behan	P	J.Morrison	P	B.Pertica
P	D.Fillingim	RP	A.Mamaux	P	P.Alexander			P	P.Douglas	/P	L.Pinto	P	W.Glazner	RP	L.North
P	G.Lansing			P	T.Osborne			H	H.McQuillan	/P	H.Betts	H	B.Adams	RP	G.Barfoot
/P	H.Hulihan	P	H.Shriver	P	V.Cheeves			RP	C.Jonnard	/P	S.Baumgartner	P	E.Hamilton		
/P	J.Cooney	P	A.Decatur	P	P.Jones			RP	R.Causey	/P	T.Sullivan			P	J.Pfeffer
/P	J.Genewich	/P	R.Gordinier	P	T.Kaufmann			RP	V.Barnes			RP	C.Yellowhorse	/P	E.Sell
/P	D.Rudolph	/P	J.Murray	P	G.Stueland										B.Bailey
/P	J.Matthews	/P	P.Schreiber	/P	V.Keen			P	F.Toney			P	H.Carlson	P	R.Walker
/P	A.Yeargin			P	B.Freeman			P	J.Scott			/P	M.Brown	P	E.Dyer
/P	C.Morgan			/P	F.Fussell			/P	C.Hill			/P	B.Hollingsworth	/P	M.Goodwin
				/P	E.Morris			P	R.Shea			/P	J.Zinn	/P	J.Knight
				/P	S.Martin			/P	F.Johnson			/P	R.Wheeler	/P	J.Stuart
				/P	U.Eubanks			/P	C.Blume					/P	S.Benton
								/P	M.Cvengros						

TEAM	G	W	L	PCT	GB	R	OR	AB	H	2B	3B	HR	BB	SO	AVG	OBP	SLG	PRO	PRO+	BR	/A	PF	CHI	RC	SB	CS	SBA	SBR
NY	156	93	61	.604		852	**658**	5454	1661	253	90	80	448	421	.305	**.363**	.428	.791	109	77	70	101	99	848	116	83	58	-15
CIN	156	86	68	.558	7	766	677	5282	1561	226	99	45	436	381	.296	.353	.401	.754	102	8	23	98	99	737	130	136	49	-43
STL	154	85	69	.552	8	863	819	5425	1634	**280**	88	107	447	425	.301	.357	**.444**	**.801**	**118**	**91**	**132**	95	99	**860**	73	63	54	-16
PIT	155	85	69	.552	8	**865**	736	5521	**1698**	239	**110**	52	423	326	**.308**	.360	.419	.779	106	56	46	101	102	848	**145**	59	**71**	**8**
CHI	156	80	74	.519	13	771	808	5335	1564	248	71	42	**525**	447	.293	.359	.390	.749	97	7	-8	102	98	752	97	108	47	-36
BRO	155	76	78	.494	17	743	754	5413	1569	235	76	56	339	**318**	.290	.335	.392	.727	94	-58	-52	99	105	709	79	60	57	-12
PHI	154	57	96	.373	35.5	738	920	5459	1537	268	55	**116**	450	611	.282	.341	.415	.756	92	-3	-77	110	95	771	48	60	44	-22
BOS	154	53	100	.346	39.5	596	822	5161	1355	162	73	32	387	451	.263	.317	.341	.658	78	-179	-155	96	**106**	566	67	65	51	-19
TOT	620					6194		43050	12579	1911	662	530	3455	3380	.292	.348	.404	.753							755	634	54	-154

TEAM	CG	SH	SV	IP	H	H/G	HR	BB	SO	RAT	ERA	ERA+	OAV	OOB	PR	/A	PF	CPI	FA	E	DP	FW	PW	BW	SBW	DIF
NY	76	7	**15**	1396[1]	1454	9.4	71	393	388	12.0	**3.45**	116	**.272**	.324	100	83	98	99	**.970**	194	145	1.1	**7.8**	6.6	.4	.0
CIN	**88**	8	3	1385[2]	1481	9.6	49	**326**	357	11.0	3.53	113	.278	**.322**	87	69	97	95	.968	205	147	.4	6.5	2.2	-2.2	2.2
STL	60	8	12	1362[2]	1609	10.6	61	447	465	13.9	4.44	87	.299	.358	-52	-87	94	98	.961	239	122	-2.0	-8.2	**12.5**	.3	5.5
PIT	**88**	**15**	7	1387[1]	1613	10.5	52	358	490	13.0	3.98	102	.296	.343	18	13	99	99	**.970**	**187**	126	**1.5**	1.2	4.3	**2.6**	-1.6
CHI	74	8	12	1397[2]	1579	10.2	77	475	402	13.6	4.34	97	.292	.356	-38	-24	102	99	.968	204	154	.5	-2.3	-.8	-1.6	7.1
BRO	82	12	8	1385[2]	1574	10.2	74	490	**499**	13.6	4.05	100	.293	.356	8	2	99	**106**	.967	208	139	.1	.2	-4.9	.7	2.9
PHI	73	6	5	1372	1692	11.1	89	460	394	14.4	4.64	101	.307	.365	-82	7	114	102	.965	225	152	-1.1	.7	-7.3	-.3	-11.5
BOS	63	7	6	1348	1565	10.4	57	489	360	13.9	4.37	91	.298	.361	-41	-57	98	100	.965	215	121	-.4	-5.4	-14.6	.0	-3.1
TOT	604	71	68	11035[1]		10.2				13.3	4.10		.292	.348					.967	1677	1106					

Runs		Hits		Doubles		Triples		Home Runs		Total Bases	
Hornsby-StL	141	Hornsby-StL	250	Hornsby-StL	46	Daubert-Cin	22	Hornsby-StL	42	Hornsby-StL	450
Carey-Pit	140	Bigbee-Pit	215	Grimes-Chi	45	Meusel-NY	17	Williams-Phi	26	Meusel-NY	314
Smith-StL	117	Bancroft-NY	209	Duncan-Cin	44	Maranville-Pit	15	Lee-Phi	17	Wheat-Bro	302
Bancroft-NY	117	Carey-Pit	207	Bancroft-NY	41	Bigbee-Pit	15	Kelly-Phi	17	Williams-Phi	300
Maranville-Pit	115	Daubert-Cin	205	Hollocher-Chi	37					Daubert-Cin	300

Runs Batted In		Runs Produced		Bases On Balls		Batting Average		On Base Percentage		Slugging Average	
Hornsby-StL	152	Hornsby-StL	251	Carey-Pit	80	Hornsby-StL	.401	Hornsby-StL	.459	Hornsby-StL	.722
Meusel-NY	132	Meusel-NY	216	O'Farrell-Chi	79	Grimes-Chi	.354	Grimes-Chi	.442	Grimes-Chi	.572
Wheat-Bro	112	Bigbee-Pit	207	Bancroft-NY	79	Miller-Chi	.352	O'Farrell-Chi	.439	Lee-Phi	.540
Kelly-NY	107	Carey-Pit	200	Burns-Cin	78	Bigbee-Pit	.350	Carey-Pit	.408	Tierney-Pit	.515
		Wheat-Bro	188	Grimes-Chi	75	Tierney-Pit	.345	Bigbee-Pit	.405	Williams-Phi	.514

Production		Adjusted Production		Batter Runs		Adjusted Batter Runs		Clutch Hitting Index		Runs Created	
Hornsby-StL	1.181	Hornsby-StL	210	Hornsby-StL	90.0	Hornsby-StL	98.7	Terry-Chi	125	Hornsby-StL	200
Grimes-Chi	1.014	Grimes-Chi	157	Grimes-Chi	47.1	Grimes-Chi	44.8	Harper-Cin	117	Carey-Pit	131
Williams-Phi	.905	Daubert-Cin	130	Williams-Phi	27.5	Daubert-Cin	26.8	Meusel-NY	116	Grimes-Chi	130
Miller-Chi	.899	Wheat-Bro	129	Walker-Phi	26.3	Wheat-Bro	25.2	Pinelli-Cin	115	Walker-Phi	118
Walker-Phi	.899	Miller-Chi	128	Daubert-Cin	24.7	Russell-Pit	23.4	Tierney-Pit	114	Bigbee-Pit	116

Total Average		Stolen Bases		Stolen Base Average		Stolen Base Runs		Fielding Runs		Total Player Rating	
Hornsby-StL	1.353	Carey-Pit	51	Carey-Pit	96.2	Carey-Pit	14.1	Parkinson-Phi	31.0	Hornsby-StL	8.5
Grimes-Chi	1.107	Frisch-NY	31	Traynor-Pit	85.0	Traynor-Pit	3.3	Bancroft-NY	21.9	Bancroft-NY	4.5
Carey-Pit	.995	Burns-Cin	30	Smith-StL	72.0	Kelly-NY	1.8	Pinelli-Cin	21.1	Carey-Pit	4.1
O'Farrell-Chi	.951	Maranville-Pit	24	Johnston-Bro	66.7	T.Griffith-Bro	1.5	Carey-Pit	18.5	O'Farrell-Chi	3.8
Walker-Phi	.918	Bigbee-Pit	24	Youngs-NY	65.4	Smith-StL	1.2	Bigbee-Pit	16.6	Grimes-Chi	3.3

Wins		Win Percentage		Games		Complete Games		Shutouts		Saves	
Rixey-Cin	25	Donohue-Cin	.667	North-StL	53	Ruether-Bro	27	Vance-Bro	5	Jonnard-NY	5
Cooper-Pit	23	Rixey-Cin	.658	Sherdel-StL	47	Ruether-Bro	26	Morrison-Pit	5	North-StL	4
Ruether-Bro	21	Couch-Cin	.640	Ryan-NY	46	Rixey-Cin	26	Cooper-Pit	4		
Pfeffer-StL	19	Ruether-Bro	.636	Oeschger-Bos	46			Adams-Pit	4		
Nehf-NY	19	Cooper-Pit	.622	Morrison-Pit	45			Sherdel-StL	3		

Innings Pitched		Fewest Hits/Game		Fewest BB/Game		Strikeouts		Strikeouts/Game		Ratio	
Rixey-Cin	313.1	Douglas-NY	8.79	Adams-Pit	.79	Vance-Bro	134	Vance-Bro	4.91	Douglas-NY	11.02
Cooper-Pit	294.2	Osborne-Chi	8.95	Alexander-Chi	1.25	Cooper-Pit	129	Ring-Phi	4.19	Adams-Pit	11.03
Morrison-Pit	286.1	Ryan-NY	9.11	Rixey-Cin	1.29	Ring-Phi	116	Osborne-Chi	3.96	Rixey-Cin	11.09
Nehf-NY	268.1	Luque-Cin	9.17	Donohue-Cin	1.60	Morrison-Pit	104	Cooper-Pit	3.94	Donohue-Cin	11.34
Ruether-Bro	267.1	Vance-Bro	9.49	J.Barnes-NY	1.61	Grimes-Bro	99	Doak-StL	3.64	Luque-Cin	11.69

Earned Run Average		Adjusted ERA		Opponents' Batting Avg.		Opponents' On Base Pct.		Starter Runs		Adjusted Starter Runs	
Douglas-NY	2.63	Douglas-NY	152	Douglas-NY	.257	Douglas-NY	.302	Cooper-Pit	30.2	Cooper-Pit	29.4
Ryan-NY	3.01	Weinert-Phi	137	Luque-Cin	.268	Rixey-Cin	.303	Donohue-Cin	26.2	Douglas-NY	24.1
Donohue-Cin	3.12	Ryan-NY	133	Ryan-NY	.269	Adams-Pit	.307	Douglas-NY	25.8	Weinert-Phi	23.4
Cooper-Pit	3.18	Cooper-Pit	128	Osborne-Chi	.271	J.Barnes-NY	.311	Nehf-NY	24.2	Donohue-Cin	23.2
Nehf-NY	3.29	Donohue-Cin	128	Rixey-Cin	.275	Donohue-Cin	.312	Ryan-NY	23.3	Nehf-NY	21.3

Clutch Pitching Index		Relief Runs		Adjusted Relief Runs		Relief Ranking		Total Pitcher Index		Total Baseball Ranking	
Weinert-Phi	129	McNamara-Bos	13.2	McNamara-Bos	12.4	McNamara-Bos	11.0	Cooper-Pit	4.0	Hornsby-StL	8.5
Ryan-NY	116	Causey-NY	7.2	Causey-NY	6.4	Causey-NY	5.9	Ryan-NY	2.8	Bancroft-NY	4.5
Cooper-Pit	113	Braxton-Bos	5.4	Braxton-Bos	4.6	Mamaux-Bro	2.1	Meadows-Phi	2.6	Carey-Pit	4.1
Morrison-Pit	111	Mamaux-Bro	3.9	Mamaux-Bro	3.6	Braxton-Bos	1.9	Luque-Cin	2.6	Cooper-Pit	4.0
McQuillan-Bos-NY	110	V.Barnes-NY	3.5	V.Barnes-NY	3.0	Jonnard-NY	1.3	Nehf-NY	2.5	O'Farrell-Chi	3.8

January 10 The following round-robin deal benefits everyone: Roger Peckinpaugh goes from Boston to Washington; Joe Dugan, from the Athletics to Boston; and outfielder Bing Miller and pitcher Jose Acosta, from Washington to Philadelphia. Acosta will be sold to Chicago on February 4.

April 18 Willie Kamm doubles in his debut for the White Sox in a 6–5 loss at Cleveland. The first $100,000 minor leaguer (bought from the San Francisco Seals), Kamm will later be voted by Chicago fans the all-time White Sox third baseman.

April 22 The Browns' Ken Williams hits three home runs against the White Sox, each time with George Sisler on base. Williams will take the home run and RBI titles and become the first 30-30 man, with 39 home runs and 37 stolen bases.

April 30 Johnny Mostil, fleet-footed White Sox center fielder, moves over to left and makes two outstanding catches to save Charlie Robertson's 2–0 perfect game over Detroit. It's the only game Mostil ever plays in left field.

May 5 The Giants evict their AL tenants as of the end of the year, so the Yankees sign a contract to build their own $750,000 stadium on a site they had held an option on since 1920.

May 15 In a game at New York, Ty Cobb beats out a grounder to shortstop Everett Scott. Veteran writer Fred Lieb scores it a hit in the box score he files with the Associated Press. But official scorer John Kieran of the *Times* gives an error to Scott. At the season's end, the AL official records, based on Associated Press box scores, list Cobb at .401. New York writers complain unsuccessfully, claiming it should be .399, based on the official scorer's stats.

May 20 Babe Ruth and Bob Meusel, suspended on October 16, 1921, by Judge Landis, return to the New York lineup and go hitless. Ruth will hit his first home run of the year two days later.

July 17 Ty Cobb gets five hits in a game for the fourth time this year, setting an AL mark. His previous five-hit games were on May 7, July 7, and July 12.

July 22 The Yankees pick up third baseman Joe Dugan and one-time World Series hero Elmer Smith from Boston, giving up outfielder Elmer Miller, shortstop Chick Fewster, shortstop John Mitchell, and pitcher Lefty O'Doul. This deal leads to a rule barring non-waiver trades after June 15.

August 13 The New York Yankees' Everett Scott nears 1,000 consecutive games played, but it takes extra effort to keep the streak alive. After a train he is on is wrecked, he spends $40 to hire a car to get to Chicago in time for the game.

August 14 Lizzie Murphy plays first base for an AL all-star team in an exhibition game against the Boston Red Sox, making her the first female to play for a major league team.

September 18 George Sisler's 41-game hit streak is stopped by New York's Joe Bush, the same pitcher he'd started the streak against on July 27.

September 21 The AL reinstates the MVP award, last given in 1914, appointing a committee of one writer from each city, headed by I. E. Sanborn of the Chicago *Tribune*. The trophy goes to George Sisler. The NL will pick up the idea two years later.

September 30 The Yankees clinch their second pennant by beating Boston 3-1 behind Waite Hoyt and Joe Bush.

December 13 Alarmed at the increase in home run hitting (1,054 in the major leagues, up from 936), some AL owners back a zoning system setting a minimum of 300 feet for a ball to be called a home run. The motion dies.

December 16 The Eastern Colored League (chartered as the Mutual Association of Eastern Colored Baseball Clubs) is formally organized. The league will complete five seasons before folding in midsummer of 1928.

	BOSTON		CHICAGO		CLEVELAND		DETROIT		NEW YORK		PHILADELPHIA		ST.LOUIS		WASHINGTON
M	H.Duffy	M	K.Gleason	M	T.Speaker	M	T.Cobb	M	M.Huggins	M	C.Mack	M	L.Fohl	M	C.Milan
1B	G.Burns	1B	E.Sheely	1B	S.McInnis	1B	L.Blue	1B	W.Pipp	1B	J.Hauser	1B	G.Sisler	1B	J.Judge
2B	D.Pratt	2B	E.Collins	2B	B.Wambsganss	2B	G.Cutshaw	2B	A.Ward	2B	R.Young	2B	M.McManus	2B	B.Harris
SS	J.Mitchell	SS	E.Johnson	SS	J.Sewell	SS	T.Rigney	SS	E.Scott	SS	C.Galloway	SS	W.Gerber	SS	R.Peckinpaugh
3B	J.Dugan	3B	E.Mulligan	3B	L.Gardner	3B	B.Jones	3B	J.Dugan	3B	J.Dykes	3B	F.Ellerbe	3B	B.LaMotte
LF	M.Menosky	LF	B.Falk	LF	C.Jamieson	LF	B.Veach	LF	B.Ruth	LF	T.Walker	LF	K.Williams	LF	G.Goslin
CF	N.Leibold	CF	J.Mostil	CF	T.Speaker	CF	T.Cobb	CF	W.Witt	CF	B.Miller	CF	B.Jacobson	CF	S.Rice
RF	S.Collins	RF	H.Hooper	RF	J.Wood	RF	H.Heilmann	RF	B.Meusel	RF	F.Welch	RF	J.Tobin	RF	F.Brower
C	M.Ruel	C	R.Schalk	C	S.O'Neill	C	J.Bassler	C	W.Schang	C	C.Perkins	C	H.Severeid	C	P.Gharrity
O1	J.Harris	O	A.Strunk	32	R.Stephenson	31	F.Haney	3	F.Baker	O	E.Foster	3O	H.Shanks		
O	E.Smith	3	H.McClellan	O	J.Evans	2	D.Clark	O	E.Miller	1	D.Johnston	O	C.Shorten	O	V.Picinich
S3	F.O'Rourke	C	Y.Yaryan	C	L.Sewell	O	B.Fothergill	3	M.McNally	23	H.Scheer	C	P.Collins	O	E.Smith
3S	P.Pittinger	H	H.Bubser	1	L.Guisto	C	L.Woodall	O	C.Fewster	C	F.Bruggy	3	H.Bronkie	3	D.Bush
O	E.Miller	/2	J.Evers	O	P.McNulty	O	I.Flagstead	2	F.Hofmann	F.Callaway	/3	J.Austin	O	C.Milan
3	E.Foster	/C	R.Graham	O	J.Graney	C	C.Manion	O	N.McMillan	/3	F.Brazill	/3	G.Robertson	3	O.Bluege
C	R.Walters	/2	J.Jenkins	O	H.Summa	/S	C.Gagnon	C	A.DeVormer	/C	O.Fuhrman	/O	C.Durst	O	E.Goebel
3	C.Fewster	/C	J.Long	O	J.Connolly	/O	J.Mohardt	/O	C.Skinner	/3	F.McCue	/C	J.Billings	O	P.Lapan
C	E.Chaplin	H	A.Swentor	C	L.Nunamaker			O	E.Smith	/C	J.Berger			/O	G.McNamara
S	C.Maynard	/O	E.Pence	C	G.Shinault	P	H.Ehmke	/S	J.Mitchell			P	U.Shocker	/C	R.Torres
/O	D.Reichle			/2	J.Hammond	P	H.Pillette			P	E.Rommel	P	E.Vangilder		
/C	W.Lynch	P	R.Faber	/O	J.Rabbitt	P	H.Dauss	P	B.Shawkey	P	S.Harriss	P	D.Davis	P	W.Johnson
		P	C.Robertson	/3	B.Doran	P	R.Oldham	P	W.Hoyt	P	B.Hasty	P	R.Kolp	P	G.Mogridge
P	J.Quinn	P	D.Leverett	/3	I.Kahdot	P	O.Olsen	P	S.Jones	P	F.Heimach	P	R.Wright	P	R.Francis
P	R.Collins	P	S.Hodge	/1	U.Clanton			P	J.Bush	P	R.Naylor			P	T.Zachary
P	H.Pennock	P	T.Blankenship	/S	C.Sorrells	P	S.Johnson	P	C.Mays	RP	J.Sullivan	P	H.Pruett	P	E.Erickson
P	A.Ferguson					P	B.Cole	RP	G.Murray	RP	R.Eckert	P	B.Bayne		
P	B.Karr	P	H.Courtney	P	G.Uhle	P	L.Stoner					P	D.Danforth	P	J.Brillheart
RP	C.Fullerton	P	F.Schupp	P	S.Coveleski	/P	R.Moore	/P	L.O'Doul	/P	C.Ogden	/P	D.Henry	/P	T.Phillips
		/P	F.Mack	P	G.Morton	/P	C.Holling	/P	C.Llewellyn	/P	R.Moore	/P	H.Meine	/P	J.Gleason
P	A.Russell	/P	L.Davenport	P	D.Mails	/P	K.Holloway			P	R.Yarrison			/P	C.Warmoth
P	B.Piercy	/P	J.Acosta	P	J.Bagby					/P	O.Rettig			/P	L.Turk
/P	S.Dodge	/P	R.Wilkinson	RP	J.Lindsey					/P	G.Ketchum			/P	H.Courtney
/P	E.Myers	P	H.Blankenship							/P	R.Schillings			/P	C.Youngblood
		/P	L.Duff	P	J.Edwards					/P	H.O'Neill			/P	S.McGrew
		/P	D.McWeeny	P	D.Boone									/P	F.Woodward
		/P	J.Russell	P	D.Keefe										
		/P	D.McCabe	/P	G.Winn										
		/P	E.Bowles	/P	A.Sothoron										
		/P	E.Cox	/P	D.Metivier										
				/P	S.Smith										
				/P	P.Bedgood										
				/P	J.Middleton										
				/P	J.Shaute										
				/P	L.Drake										
				/P	G.Edmondson										
				/P	N.Pott										
				/P	T.Odenwald										
				/P	D.Hamann										
				/P	T.Jeanes										

TEAM	G	W	L	PCT	GB	R	OR	AB	H	2B	3B	HR	BB	SO	AVG	OBP	SLG	PRO	PRO+	BR	/A	PF	CHI	RC	SB	CS	SBA	SBR
NY	154	94	60	.610		758	618	5245	1504	220	75	95	497	532	.287	.353	.412	.765	103	36	19	102	99	774	62	59	51	-17
STL	154	93	61	.604	1	867	643	5416	1693	291	94	98	473	381	.313	.372	.455	.827	117	157	125	104	96	923	136	76	64	-5
DET	155	79	75	.513	15	828	791	5360	1641	250	87	54	530	378	.306	.372	.415	.787	115	44	121	97	98	847	78	62	56	-14
CLE	155	78	76	.506	16	768	817	5293	1544	320	73	32	554	331	.292	.364	.398	.762	104	43	37	101	97	792	90	58	61	-8
CHI	155	77	77	.500	17	691	691	5267	1463	243	62	45	482	463	.278	.343	.373	.716	92	-52	-49	100	101	690	109	84	56	-18
WAS	154	69	85	.448	25	650	706	5201	1395	229	76	45	458	442	.268	.334	.367	.701	93	-84	-53	95	103	656	97	63	61	-9
PHI	155	65	89	.422	29	705	830	5211	1409	229	63	111	437	591	.270	.331	.402	.733	94	-36	-54	103	104	849	60	69	47	-23
BOS	154	61	93	.396	33	598	769	5288	1392	250	55	45	366	455	.263	.316	.357	.673	82	-149	-144	99	105	599	64	67	49	-21
TOT	618					5865		42281	12041	2032	585	525	3797	3573	.285	.348	.398	.746							696	538	56	-114

TEAM	CG	SH	SV	IP	H	H/G	HR	BB	SO	RAT	ERA	ERA+	OAV	OOB	PR	/A	PF	CPI	FA	E	DP	FW	PW	BW	SBW	DIF
NY	100	7	14	1393²	1402	9.1	73	423	458	11.9	3.39	118	.268	.325	99	91	99	101	.975	157	124	2.0	8.8	1.8	-.3	4.5
STL	79	8	22	1392	1412	9.1	71	419	534	12.1	3.38	122	.268	.327	101	115	103	103	.968	201	158	-.5	11.2	12.1	.9	-7.7
DET	67	7	15	1391	1554	10.1	62	473	461	13.7	4.27	91	.288	.354	-37	-64	96	97	.970	191	133	.2	-6.2	11.8	.0	-3.7
CLE	76	14	7	1383²	1605	10.4	58	464	489	13.7	4.59	87	.296	.356	-85	-92	99	93	.968	202	147	-.5	-8.9	3.6	.6	6.2
CHI	86	13	8	1403²	1472	9.4	57	529	484	13.0	3.94	103	.278	.346	15	15	101	98	.975	155	143	2.2	1.5	-4.8	-.4	1.4
WAS	84	13	10	1362¹	1485	9.8	49	500	422	13.1	3.81	101	.286	.354	33	5	96	107	.969	196	168	-.2	.5	-5.1	.5	-3.7
PHI	73	4	6	1362¹	1573	10.4	107	469	373	13.7	4.59	87	.297	.357	-85	-55	105	99	.966	215	118	-1.2	-5.3	-5.2	-.8	.6
BOS	71	10	6	1373¹	1508	9.9	48	503	359	13.5	4.30	95	.287	.354	-41	-32	102	94	.965	224	145	-1.8	-3.1	-14.0	-.7	3.5
TOT	636	76	88	11062		9.8				13.1	4.03		.285	.348					.969	1541	1136					

Runs
Sisler-StL	134
Blue-Det	131
Williams-StL	128
Tobin-StL	122

Hits
Sisler-StL	246
Cobb-Det	211
Tobin-StL	207
Veach-Det	202

Doubles
Speaker-Cle	48
Pratt-Bos	44
Sisler-StL	42
Cobb-Det	42

Triples
Sisler-StL	18
Jacobson-StL	16
Cobb-Det	16
Judge-Was	15
Mostil-Chi	14

Home Runs
Williams-StL	39
Walker-Phi	37
Ruth-NY	35
Miller-Phi	21
Heilmann-Det	21

Total Bases
Williams-StL	367
Sisler-StL	348
Walker-Phi	310
Cobb-Det	297
Tobin-StL	296

Runs Batted In
Williams-StL	155
Veach-Det	126
McManus-StL	109
Sisler-StL	105
Jacobson-StL	102

Runs Produced
Williams-StL	244
Sisler-StL	231
Veach-Det	213
Cobb-Det	194
McManus-StL	186

Bases On Balls
Witt-NY	89
Ruth-NY	84
Blue-Det	82
Speaker-Cle	77
Williams-StL	74

Batting Average
Sisler-StL	.420
Cobb-Det	.401
Speaker-Cle	.378
Heilmann-Det	.356
Miller-Phi	.335

On Base Percentage
Speaker-Cle	.474
Sisler-StL	.467
Cobb-Det	.462
Ruth-NY	.434
Heilmann-Det	.432

Slugging Average
Ruth-NY	.672
Williams-StL	.627
Speaker-Cle	.606
Heilmann-Det	.598
Sisler-StL	.594

Production
Ruth-NY	1.106
Speaker-Cle	1.080
Sisler-StL	1.061
Williams-StL	1.040
Heilmann-Det	1.030

Adjusted Production
Ruth-NY	181
Speaker-Cle	178
Cobb-Det	172
Heilmann-Det	172
Sisler-StL	169

Batter Runs
Sisler-StL	64.4
Williams-StL	56.1
Speaker-Cle	52.8
Cobb-Det	52.4
Ruth-NY	50.5

Adjusted Batter Runs
Sisler-StL	59.4
Cobb-Det	56.5
Speaker-Cle	52.0
Williams-StL	51.3
Ruth-NY	48.1

Clutch Hitting Index
Veach-Det	143
O'Neill-Cle	132
Johnson-Chi	127
Wood-Cle	126
Gardner-Cle	125

Runs Created
Sisler-StL	162
Williams-StL	149
Cobb-Det	133
Speaker-Cle	127
Ruth-NY	120

Total Average
Speaker-Cle	1.272
Ruth-NY	1.254
Sisler-StL	1.203
Heilmann-Det	1.135
Williams-StL	1.131

Stolen Bases
Sisler-StL	51
Williams-StL	37
Harris-Was	25
Johnson-Chi	21

Stolen Base Average
Jacobson-StL	76.0
Sisler-StL	72.9
Harris-Was	69.4
Rice-Was	69.0
Rigney-Det	68.0

Stolen Base Runs
Sisler-StL	3.9
Veach-Det	2.1
Jacobson-StL	2.1
Evans-Cle	2.1
Shanks-Was	1.8

Fielding Runs
Harris-Was	26.4
Peckinpaugh-Was	20.4
Schalk-Chi	20.2
Scott-NY	17.3
Sisler-StL	12.1

Total Player Rating
Sisler-StL	6.6
Speaker-Cle	5.0
Williams-StL	4.4
Cobb-Det	4.3
Ruth-NY	3.7

Wins
Rommel-Phi	27
Bush-NY	26
Shocker-StL	24
Uhle-Cle	22
Faber-Chi	21

Win Percentage
Bush-NY	.788
Rommel-Phi	.675
Shawkey-NY	.625
Pillette-Det	.613
Hoyt-NY	.613

Games
Rommel-Phi	51
Uhle-Cle	50
Shocker-StL	48
Harriss-Phi	47

Complete Games
Faber-Chi	31
Shocker-StL	29
Uhle-Cle	23
Johnson-Was	23

Shutouts
Uhle-Cle	5

Saves
Jones-NY	8
Pruett-StL	7
Wright-StL	5

Innings Pitched
Faber-Chi	352.0
Shocker-StL	348.0
Shawkey-NY	299.2
Rommel-Phi	294.0
Uhle-Cle	287.1

Fewest Hits/Game
Davis-StL	8.36
Bush-NY	8.46
Faber-Chi	8.54
Shawkey-NY	8.59
Wright-StL	8.65

Fewest BB/Game
Shocker-StL	1.47
Vangilder-StL	1.76
Mays-NY	1.88
Kolp-StL	1.91
Hasty-Phi	1.92

Strikeouts
Shocker-StL	149
Faber-Chi	148
Shawkey-NY	130
Ehmke-Det	108
Johnson-Was	105

Strikeouts/Game
Morton-Cle	4.53
Harriss-Phi	4.00
Shawkey-NY	3.90
Shocker-StL	3.85
Faber-Chi	3.78

Ratio
Faber-Chi	10.82
Shocker-StL	11.02
Rommel-Phi	11.08
Vangilder-StL	11.09
Quinn-Bos	11.43

Earned Run Average
Faber-Chi	2.81
Pillette-Det	2.85
Shawkey-NY	2.91
Wright-StL	2.92
Shocker-StL	2.97

Adjusted ERA
Faber-Chi	144
Wright-StL	141
Shocker-StL	139
Shawkey-NY	137
Pillette-Det	136

Opponents' Batting Avg.
Davis-StL	.250
Bush-NY	.252
Faber-Chi	.252
Shawkey-NY	.256
Pillette-Det	.258

Opponents' On Base Pct.
Faber-Chi	.299
Shocker-StL	.304
Rommel-Phi	.309
Vangilder-StL	.310
Quinn-Bos	.311

Starter Runs
Faber-Chi	47.7
Shocker-StL	40.9
Shawkey-NY	37.2
Pillette-Det	36.0
Johnson-Was	32.4

Adjusted Starter Runs
Faber-Chi	48.8
Shocker-StL	44.8
Shawkey-NY	36.0
Rommel-Phi	31.5
Pillette-Det	31.1

Clutch Pitching Index
Mogridge-Was	124
Wright-StL	118
Johnson-Was	114
Pillette-Det	110
Shawkey-NY	109

Relief Runs
Murray-NY	4

Adjusted Relief Runs
Murray-NY	2

Relief Ranking
Murray-NY	1

Total Pitcher Index
Faber-Chi	4.9
Shocker-StL	4.8
Rommel-Phi	4.0
Vangilder-StL	3.4
Pillette-Det	3.2

Total Baseball Ranking
Sisler-StL	6.6
Speaker-Cle	5.0
Faber-Chi	4.9
Shocker-StL	4.8
Williams-StL	4.4

February 11 Jack Fournier comes to the Brooklyn Robins in a trade that sends catcher Hy Myers to St. Louis. Fournier, a Cardinal first baseman for years, says he'll quit if he has to move, but he gives in and plays another five years. With 22 homers, Fournier will finish second in the NL.

February 20 Christy Mathewson becomes president of the Boston Braves after buying the club for $300,000 with New York attorney Judge Emil Fuchs and Bostonian James McDonough. The deal does not include Braves Field, which still belongs to James Gaffney.

March 6 The Cardinals announce that their players will wear numerals on their uniforms and number them according to the batting order.

April 30 Phils outfielder Fred "Cy" Williams starts an unprecedented slugging spree, going 2-for-4 in a 12–3 loss to the Braves. In 15 games in the Baker Bowl, he will accumulate 65 total bases on 11 singles, 5 doubles, 11 home runs, and 29 RBI. He will lead the NL with 41 homers.

May 30 After playing before the NL's biggest crowd (41,000) in the afternoon game of the holiday twin bill against Brooklyn, the Giants head west with a four-game lead over the Pirates. With five future Hall of Famers in the lineup and eight on the roster during the season, the Giants will be the first team to hold first place from opening to closing day in a given season.

August 17 The Giants' George Kelly homers in the third, fourth, and fifth against the Cubs. New York wins, 13–6. Kelly adds a single and double to run his total bases to 15 for the game.

September 15* Paul Strand, right fielder for Salt Lake City (PCL), makes his 290th hit, a pro baseball record. He will play in 194 games, make 325 hits, including 66 doubles, 13 triples, and 43 homers, for a .394 BA, with 180 runs and 187 RBI. He also has 612 total chances in the outfield. Strand, 30, had come up to the Braves as a pitcher in 1913 and was 6-2 for the 1914 pennant winners, mostly in relief. The Athletics will pay a reported $100,000 (which Mack later says was really $40,000) for him, but he will hit just .167.

September 24 Bill Terry takes his first swings in a Giants uniform as a pinch hitter.

October 10 It's an all-New York World Series for the third time. In the first World Series game at Yankee Stadium, the home team takes a quick 3-0 lead, but Heinie Groh triples in two runs in a 4-run third that drives Waite Hoyt (17-9) to cover. A 4-4 tie is broken in the top of the ninth by the Giants when Casey Stengel's blast rolls to the outfield wall. The sore-legged veteran hobbles around the bases to score the winning run against reliever Joe Bush (19-15) before 55,307 spectators. This is also the first World Series to be broadcast on a nationwide radio network. Graham McNamee, aided by baseball writers taking turns, is at the mike.

December 6 While in Paris, John McGraw announces plans for a tour of Europe by the Giants and White Sox in 1924, as world interest in baseball grows. In Romania, Queen Marie will throw out the first ball to mark the game's debut in July.

BOSTON	BROOKLYN	CHICAGO	CINCINNATI	NEW YORK	PHILADELPHIA	PITTSBURGH	ST.LOUIS
M F.Mitchell	M W.Robinson	M B.Killefer	M P.Moran	M J.McGraw	M A.Fletcher	M B.McKechnie	M B.Rickey
1B S.McInnis	1B J.Fournier	1B R.Grimes	1B J.Daubert	1B G.Kelly	1B W.Holke	1B C.Grimm	1B J.Bottomley
2B H.Ford	2B I.Olson	2B G.Grantham	2B S.Bohne	2B F.Frisch	2B C.Tierney	2B J.Rawlings	2B R.Hornsby
SS B.Smith	SS J.Johnston	SS S.Adams	SS I.Caveney	SS D.Bancroft	SS H.Sand	SS R.Maranville	SS H.Freigau
3B T.Boeckel	3B A.High	3B B.Friberg	3B B.Pinelli	3B H.Groh	3B R.Wrightstone	3B P.Traynor	3B M.Stock
LF G.Felix	LF Z.Wheat	LF H.Miller	LF P.Duncan	LF I.Meusel	LF J.Mokan	LF C.Bigbee	LF J.Smith
CF R.Powell	CF B.Neis	CF J.Statz	CF E.Roush	CF B.Cunningham	CF C.Williams	CF M.Carey	CF H.Myers
RF B.Southworth	RF T.Griffith	RF C.Heathcote	RF G.Burns	RF R.Youngs	RF C.Walker	RF C.Barnhart	RF M.Flack
C M.O'Neil	C Z.Taylor	C B.O'Farrell	C B.Hargrave	C F.Snyder	C B.Henline	C W.Schmidt	C E.Ainsmith
O A.Nixon	O G.Bailey	S C.Hollocher	21 L.Fonseca	S3 T.Jackson	O1 C.Lee	O R.Russell	O R.Blades
O E.Smith	O B.Griffith	C1 G.Hartnett	C I.Wingo	O J.O'Connell	O J.Wilson	C J.Gooch	2S S.Toporcer
2 J.Conlon	1S H.DeBerry	1S J.Kelleher	O G.Harper	2S C.Stengel	2S F.Parkinson	2 C.Tierney	C H.Mueller
S L.Kopf	3 B.McCarren	1 A.Elliott	1 R.Bressler	C H.Gowdy	3 G.Rapp	O W.Mueller	C H.McCurdy
O B.Bagwell	S M.Berg	O M.Callaghan	2 W.Kimmick	C A.Gaston	C F.Leach	2 S.Adams	S V.Clemons
2 A.Hermann	1 D.Schliebner	O O.Vogel	S B.Fowler	C E.Smith	3 C.Lord	O K.Cuyler	S D.Lavan
C F.Gibson	C R.French	/C D.Grigsby	/C G.Sanberg	2 F.Maguire	3 A.Woehr	/C J.Mattox	O L.Mann
C H.Gowdy	C C.Hargreaves	/O B.Weis	/O E.Pick	/O R.Shinners	/2 J.Metz	/1 J.Ens	S L.Bell
/O W.Cruise	O T.Barber	/S P.Turgeon	H L.Mann	/O H.Wilson	/O T.Dennehey	/S E.Moore	/O E.Dyer
/O B.Emmerich	/3 B.Mullen	/C K.Wirts	R E.Hock	/O M.Solomon	/O M.O'Brien	/O F.Luce	/S J.Flowers
/S E.Padgett	/2 S.Stewart	H T.Murray	P D.Luque	/1 B.Terry	/C D.Parker	/1 E.Barnes	/C C.Niebergall
H S.Henry	/C E.Ainsmith	H B.Barrett	P E.Rixey	P H.McQuillan	/3 J.Bennett	P J.Morrison	/O T.Douthit
/C D.Cousineau	/C B.Hungling	P P.Alexander	P P.Donohue	P J.Scott	P J.Ring	P W.Cooper	/1 J.Hudgens
P R.Marquard	P B.Grimes	P V.Aldridge	P R.Benton	P A.Nehf	P W.Glazner	P L.Meadows	/O J.Schultz
P J.Genewich	P D.Vance	P T.Kaufmann	RP C.Keck	P J.Bentley	P L.Weinert	P B.Adams	/1 S.Walker
P J.Barnes	P D.Ruether	P T.Osborne	P B.Harris	P R.Ryan	P C.Mitchell	P E.Hamilton	/C G.Kopshaw
P J.Oeschger	P L.Dickerman	P V.Keen	P J.Couch	RP C.Jonnard	P R.Head	P J.Bagby	/O T.Stone
P T.McNamara	P D.Henry	RP F.Fussell	P H.McQuaid	RP V.Barnes	RP B.Hubbell	P R.Steineder	R B.Shotton
RP D.Fillingim	RP A.Decatur	P N.Dumovich	P G.Abrams	P M.Watson	P P.Behan	P E.Kunz	P J.Haines
P L.Benton	P G.Smith	/P V.Cheeves	/P H.Gill	P J.Barnes	P H.Betts	/P W.Glazner	P B.Sherdel
PO J.Cooney	/P L.Cadore	/P R.Wheeler	/P K.Schnell	P D.Gearin	P J.Winters	/P G.Boehler	P F.Toney
/P F.Miller	/P P.Schreiber	/P G.Stueland		/P F.Johnson	/P J.Couch	/P H.Carlson	P B.Doak
P M.Watson	/P A.Mamaux	/P P.Collins		/P W.Huntzinger	/P J.Bishop	/P A.Stone	P J.Pfeffer
/P D.Rudolph	/P H.Harper	/P E.Stauffer		/P R.Lucas	/P L.Meadows		RP L.North
/P J.Batchelder	/P H.Shriver	/P G.Bush		/P R.Walberg	/P B.Jones		P J.Stuart
					/P J.Grant		P C.Barfoot
					/P P.Ragan		/P E.Sell
					/P R.Miller		/P F.Wigington
					/P A.Gardiner		/P B.Pertica

TEAM	G	W	L	PCT	GB	R	OR	AB	H	2B	3B	HR	BB	SO	AVG	OBP	SLG	PRO	PRO+	BR	/A	PF	CHI	RC	SB	CS	SBA	SBR
NY	153	95	58	.621		854	679	5452	1610	248	76	85	487	406	.295	.356	.415	.771	110	72	83	99	103	816	106	70	60	-10
CIN	154	91	63	.591	4.5	708	629	5278	1506	237	95	45	439	367	.285	.344	.392	.736	102	-1	14	98	96	707	96	105	48	-34
PIT	154	87	67	.565	8.5	786	696	5405	1592	224	111	49	407	362	.295	.347	.404	.751	102	26	9	102	103	766	154	75	67	1
CHI	154	83	71	.539	12.5	756	704	5259	1516	243	52	90	455	485	.288	.348	.406	.754	104	33	32	100	99	735	181	143	56	-32
STL	154	79	74	.516	16	746	732	5526	1582	274	76	63	438	446	.286	.343	.398	.741	103	5	21	98	97	761	89	61	59	-10
BRO	155	76	78	.494	19.5	753	741	5476	1559	214	81	62	425	382	.285	.340	.387	.727	100	-20	1	97	102	730	71	50	59	-9
BOS	155	54	100	.351	41.5	636	798	5329	1455	213	58	32	429	404	.273	.331	.353	.684	90	-99	-73	96	99	625	57	80	42	-31
PHI	155	50	104	.325	45.5	748	1008	5491	1528	259	39	112	414	556	.278	.333	.401	.734	89	-15	-100	112	101	729	70	73	49	-23
TOT	617					5987		43216	12348	1912	588	538	3494	3408	.286	.343	.395	.737							824	657	56	-147

TEAM	CG	SH	SV	IP	H	H/G	HR	BB	SO	RAT	ERA	ERA+	OAV	OOB	PR	/A	PF	CPI	FA	E	DP	FW	PW	BW	SBW	DIF
NY	62	10	18	1378	1440	9.4	82	424	453	12.3	3.90	98	.271	.328	15	-13	96	93	.972	176	141	2.4	-1.3	8.0	.8	8.6
CIN	88	11	9	1391¹	1465	9.5	28	359	450	12.0	3.21	120	.273	.322	121	99	97	101	.969	202	144	.9	9.5	1.3	-1.5	3.7
PIT	92	5	9	1376¹	1513	9.9	53	402	414	12.7	3.87	103	.284	.337	19	19	100	98	.971	179	157	2.3	1.8	.9	1.9	3.2
CHI	80	8	11	1366²	1419	9.3	86	435	408	12.4	3.82	105	.269	.329	27	25	100	96	.967	208	144	.5	2.4	3.1	-1.3	1.3
STL	77	9	7	1398¹	1539	9.9	70	456	398	13.1	3.87	101	.284	.344	20	5	98	104	.963	232	141	-.9	.5	2.0	.8	.0
BRO	94	8	5	1396²	1503	9.7	55	476	548	13.0	3.74	103	.277	.340	39	20	97	100	.955	293	137	-4.4	1.9	.0	.9	.5
BOS	54	13	7	1392²	1662	10.7	64	394	351	13.5	4.21	94	.302	.352	-34	-41	100	102	.964	230	157	-.7	-3.9	-7.0	-1.2	-10.1
PHI	68	3	8	1376¹	1801	11.8	100	549	384	15.6	5.34	86	.322	.386	-205	-115	115	102	.966	217	172	.0	-11.1	-9.6	-.4	-6.0
TOT	615	67	74	11076¹		10.0				13.1	3.99		.286	.343					.966	1737	1193					

Runs		Hits		Doubles		Triples		Home Runs		Total Bases	
Youngs-NY	121	Frisch-NY	223	Roush-Cin	41	Traynor-Pit	19	Williams-Phi	41	Frisch-NY	311
Carey-Pit	120	Statz-Chi	209	Tierney-Pit-Phi	36	Carey-Pit	19	Fournier-Bro	22	Williams-Phi	308
Frisch-NY	116	Traynor-Pit	208	Grantham-Chi	36	Roush-Cin	18	Miller-Chi	20	Fournier-Bro	303
Johnston-Bro	111	Johnston-Bro	203	Bottomley-StL	34	Southworth-Bos	16	Meusel-NY	19	Traynor-Pit	301
Statz-Chi	110	Youngs-NY	200					Hornsby-StL	17	Statz-Chi	288

Runs Batted In		Runs Produced		Bases On Balls		Batting Average		On Base Percentage		Slugging Average	
Meusel-NY	125	Frisch-NY	215	Burns-Cin	101	Hornsby-StL	.384	Hornsby-StL	.459	Hornsby-StL	.627
Williams-Phi	114	Meusel-NY	208	Sand-Phi	82	Wheat-Bro	.375	Bottomley-StL	.425	Fournier-Bro	.588
Frisch-NY	111	Youngs-NY	205	Youngs-NY	73	Bottomley-StL	.371	Youngs-NY	.412	Williams-Phi	.576
Kelly-NY	103	Traynor-Pit	197	Carey-Pit	73	Fournier-Bro	.351	Fournier-Bro	.411	Barnhart-Pit	.563
Fournier-Bro	102	Carey-Pit	177	Grantham-Chi	71	Roush-Cin	.351	O'Farrell-Chi	.408	Bottomley-StL	.535

Production		Adjusted Production		Batter Runs		Adjusted Batter Runs		Clutch Hitting Index		Runs Created	
Hornsby-StL	1.086	Hornsby-StL	188	Hornsby-StL	52.1	Hornsby-StL	54.4	Stock-StL	136	Fournier-Bro	125
Fournier-Bro	.999	Fournier-Bro	165	Fournier-Bro	43.7	Fournier-Bro	47.0	McInnis-Bos	124	Frisch-NY	123
Bottomley-StL	.960	Bottomley-StL	155	Bottomley-StL	39.2	Bottomley-StL	41.5	Frisch-NY	123	Hornsby-StL	120
Williams-Phi	.947	Roush-Cin	149	Roush-Cin	34.0	Roush-Cin	36.2	Meusel-NY	117	Bottomley-StL	117
Roush-Cin	.938	Frisch-NY	133	Williams-Phi	33.2	Frisch-NY	29.8	Bigbee-Pit	114	Carey-Pit	117

Total Average		Stolen Bases		Stolen Base Average		Stolen Base Runs		Fielding Runs		Total Player Rating	
Hornsby-StL	1.194	Carey-Pit	51	Carey-Pit	86.4	Carey-Pit	10.5	Bancroft-NY	21.3	Fournier-Bro	4.3
Fournier-Bro	1.071	Grantham-Chi	43	Smith-StL	74.4	Smith-StL	3.0	Carey-Pit	19.7	Traynor-Pit	4.0
Bottomley-StL	.976	Smith-StL	32	Frisch-NY	70.7	Rawlings-Pit	2.7	Johnston-Bro	19.4	Carey-Pit	3.6
Williams-Phi	.966	Heathcote-Chi	32	Traynor-Pit	68.3			Statz-Chi	17.7	Bancroft-NY	3.6
Carey-Pit	.928			Heathcote-Chi	65.3			Tierney-Pit-Phi	14.4	Johnston-Bro	3.6

Wins		Win Percentage		Games		Complete Games		Shutouts		Saves	
Luque-Cin	27	Luque-Cin	.771	Ryan-NY	45	Grimes-Bro	33	Luque-Cin	6	Jonnard-NY	5
Morrison-Pit	25	Ryan-NY	.762	Jonnard-NY	45	Luque-Cin	28	J.Barnes-NY-Bos	5	Ryan-NY	4
Alexander-Chi	22	Scott-NY	.696	Oeschger-Bos	44	Morrison-Pit	27	McQuillan-NY	5		
Grimes-Bro	21	Morrison-Pit	.658	J.Barnes-NY-Bos	43	Cooper-Pit	26				
Donohue-Cin	21	Alexander-Chi	.647	Genewich-Bos	43	Alexander-Chi	26				

Innings Pitched		Fewest Hits/Game		Fewest BB/Game		Strikeouts		Strikeouts/Game		Ratio	
Grimes-Bro	327.0	Luque-Cin	7.80	Alexander-Chi	.89	Vance-Bro	197	Vance-Bro	6.32	Alexander-Chi	9.97
Luque-Cin	322.0	Vance-Bro	8.44	B.Adams-Pit	1.42	Luque-Cin	151	Luque-Cin	4.22	Luque-Cin	10.40
Rixey-Cin	309.0	Morrison-Pit	8.56	Genewich-Bos	1.82	Grimes-Bro	119	Bentley-NY	3.93	Ryan-NY	11.31
Alexander-Chi	305.0	Keen-Chi	8.59	Rixey-Cin	1.89	Morrison-Pit	114	Osborne-Chi	3.46	Aldridge-Chi	11.49
Ring-Phi	304.1	Aldridge-Chi	8.67	Meadows-Phi-Pit	2.15	Ring-Phi	112	Morrison-Pit	3.40	McQuillan-NY	11.56

Earned Run Average		Adjusted ERA		Opponents' Batting Avg.		Opponents' On Base Pct.		Starter Runs		Adjusted Starter Runs	
Luque-Cin	1.93	Luque-Cin	200	Luque-Cin	.235	Alexander-Chi	.277	Luque-Cin	73.9	Luque-Cin	69.1
Rixey-Cin	2.80	Rixey-Cin	138	Vance-Bro	.250	Luque-Cin	.291	Rixey-Cin	41.1	Rixey-Cin	36.5
Keen-Chi	3.00	Keen-Chi	133	Aldridge-Chi	.251	Aldridge-Chi	.307	Alexander-Chi	27.4	Alexander-Chi	27.4
Kaufmann-Chi	3.10	Kaufmann-Chi	129	Morrison-Pit	.253	Ryan-NY	.308	Haines-StL	26.1	Ring-Phi	24.3
Haines-StL	3.11	Alexander-Chi	125	Osborne-Chi	.255	McQuillan-NY	.315	Kaufmann-Chi	20.6	Haines-StL	23.2

Clutch Pitching Index		Relief Runs		Adjusted Relief Runs		Relief Ranking		Total Pitcher Index		Total Baseball Ranking	
Kaufmann-Chi	118	Decatur-Bro	15.3	Decatur-Bro	14.0	Decatur-Bro	8.7	Luque-Cin	7.4	Luque-Cin	7.4
Rixey-Cin	116	Jonnard-NY	7.6	Jonnard-NY	5.7	Jonnard-NY	4.4	Rixey-Cin	3.4	Fournier-Bro	4.3
Genewich-Bos	116	Keck-Cin	2.6	Keck-Cin	1.3	Keck-Cin	1.3	Alexander-Chi	3.2	Traynor-Pit	4.0
Doak-StL	116	V.Barnes-NY	.5					Kaufmann-Chi	2.4	Carey-Pit	3.6
Luque-Cin	115							Haines-StL	2.4	Bancroft-NY	3.6

April 3 Two "Black Sox" sue the White Sox. Swede Risberg and Happy Felsch seek $400,000 damages and $6,750 back salary for conspiracy and injury to reputation, but their suit will be unsuccessful.

April 18 The debut of Yankee Stadium is a huge success with an announced attendance of 74,217. Bob Shawkey, aided by Babe Ruth's 3-run home run, beats Howard Ehmke and the Red Sox 4-1.

May 13 Washington rookie Wally Warmoth strikes out Cleveland shortstop Joe Sewell twice. It's the first of only two times in his 14-year career that Sewell will fan twice in the same contest.

May 21 Formal transfer of T. L. Huston's interest in the Yankees to Jake Ruppert is completed for $1.5 million. Ten days later Ruppert buys two more sets of uniforms so his players can wear a clean outfit every day, an unprecedented move.

July 7 Cleveland scores in every inning against the Red Sox, but playing at home, the team does not bat in the ninth. In the eight innings, they run up a then AL-record 27 runs, including 13 in the sixth, for a 27-3 win. In three innings, Lefty O'Doul gives up 16 runs on 11 hits and eight walks. This is his last season as a major league pitcher, but he will return to the major leagues in 1928 as an outfielder.

July 11 Harry Frazee, owner of the Red Sox since 1916, sells out for over $1 million to a group of Ohio businessmen, who bring in veteran front office man Bob Quinn from St. Louis to run the club. Frazee's departure is welcomed by Boston fans who are fed up with the sale of Frazee's best players over the years.

August 11 Babe Ruth goes three for eight against the Tigers, while Harry Heilmann is five for 10 against the Yanks. The two are neck and neck at .390 for the year. After the game, AL President Ban Johnson rules that Ruth must give up his Sam Crawford bat, made for him by the future Hall of Famer. The bat is "four pieces of seasoned wood, carefully glued together." On August 21, Johnson rules that only one-piece bats will be allowed, a rule that also affects Ken Williams, who is using a plugged bat.

September 11 After leadoff hitter Whitey Witt reaches first on a controversial single, Boston pitcher Howard Ehmke retires the next 27 batters for a 3-0 win. The Boston crowd exhorted the scorer Fred Lieb to reverse his call on the hard grounder that third baseman Howard Shanks booted, but the one hit stood. Ehmke has now given up just one hit in his last two games.

September 14 George Burns, first baseman for the Boston Red Sox, makes an unassisted triple play on a line drive hit by Cleveland's Frank Brower. He tags out Rube Lutzke and rushes to second base for the third out before Riggs Stephenson returns.

October 2 Harry Heilmann goes 2-for-2 to put his average over .400. He will sit for the rest of the season, except for a pinch single on the final day, and will win the batting title with a .403 average.

October 15 After Babe Ruth's first-inning home run, the Giants peck away at Herb Pennock for four runs and take a 4-1 lead into the eighth. With one out, Art Nehf loads the bases on two singles and a walk, then walks in a run. Reliever Rosy Ryan forces in another run with a walk to Joe Dugan. Ruth strikes out, but Bob Meusel raps a single that scores the go-ahead runs. Sam Jones holds off the Giants, and the Yankees have their first World Championship.

October 19 Citing the unsavory characters associated with the sport, AL president Ban Johnson persuades AL owners to prohibit boxing matches in their parks. The NL declines to go along with it.

October 26 Frank Chance signs to manage the White Sox, replacing Kid Gleason, but he will resign February 17, 1924, because of illness. Coach Johnny Evers, named acting manager, will fill the job the entire season.

December 10 Traveling to Chicago for the major league meetings, Wild Bill Donovan, New Haven manager, is killed in a train wreck. Donovan was a pitcher for Detroit and managed the Yankees and Phils. New Haven president George Weiss, future general manager of the Yankees and Mets, had swapped berths with Donovan and escapes with only a minor injury.

	BOSTON		CHICAGO		CLEVELAND		DETROIT		NEW YORK		PHILADELPHIA		ST.LOUIS		WASHINGTON
M	F.Chance	M	K.Gleason	M	T.Speaker	M	T.Cobb	M	M.Huggins	M	C.Mack	M	L.Fohl	M	D.Bush
1B	G.Burns	1B	E.Sheely	1B	F.Brower	1B	L.Blue	1B	W.Pipp	1B	J.Hauser	M	J.Austin	1B	J.Judge
2B	C.Fewster	2B	E.Collins	2B	B.Wambsganss	2B	F.Haney	2B	A.Ward	2B	J.Dykes	1B	D.Schliebner	2B	B.Harris
SS	J.Mitchell	SS	H.McClellan	SS	J.Sewell	SS	T.Rigney	SS	E.Scott	SS	C.Galloway	2B	M.McManus	SS	R.Peckinpaugh
3B	H.Shanks	3B	W.Kamm	3B	R.Lutzke	3B	B.Jones	3B	J.Dugan	3B	S.Hale	SS	W.Gerber	3B	O.Bluege
LF	J.Harris	LF	B.Falk	LF	C.Jamieson	LF	B.Veach	LF	B.Meusel	LF	B.Miller	3B	G.Robertson	LF	G.Goslin
CF	D.Reichle	CF	J.Mostil	CF	T.Speaker	CF	T.Cobb	CF	W.Witt	CF	W.Matthews	LF	K.Williams	CF	N.Leibold
RF	I.Flagstead	RF	H.Hooper	RF	H.Summa	RF	H.Heilmann	RF	B.Ruth	RF	F.Welch	CF	B.Jacobson	RF	S.Rice
C	V.Picinich	C	R.Schalk	C	S.O'Neill	C	J.Bassler	C	W.Schang	C	C.Perkins	RF	J.Tobin	C	M.Ruel
												C	H.Severeid		
O	S.Collins	O	R.Elsh	2	R.Stephenson	O	B.Fothergill	C	F.Hofmann	O	B.McGowan			O3	J.Evans
32	N.McMillan	O	B.Barrett	O	G.Myatt	O	H.Manush	O	E.Smith	2	H.Scheer	3	H.Ezzell	C1	P.Gharrity
C	A.DeVormer	O	M.Archdeacon	1	L.Guisto	21	D.Pratt	O	H.Hendrick	O	H.Riconda	C	P.Collins	O	R.Wade
O	M.Menosky	2	J.Happenny	O	J.Connolly	C	L.Woodall	O	B.Bengough	O	T.Walker	2	E.Foster	3	B.Conroy
2S	P.Pittinger	C	R.Graham	3	L.Gardner	2	G.Cutshaw	C	B.Johnson	O	F.Bruggy	O	C.Durst	/3	P.Hargrave
C	R.Walters	C	B.Crouse	1	R.Knode	S	J.Kerr	S	M.McNally	O	W.French	O	B.Whaley	3	B.Murray
/O	J.Donahue	/O	A.Strunk	/C	L.Sewell	O	C.Manion	/1	L.Gehrig	/C	C.Rowland	3	F.Ellerbe	/2	J.O'Neill
/2	F.Fuller	S	E.Johnson	/3	W.Shaner	/3	L.Burke	O	H.Haines	/O	J.Jones	/C	J.Billings	/3	S.Fisher
O	N.Leibold	/2	L.Rosenberg	/O	S.Clarke	H	I.Flagstead	/S	M.Gazella	/O	D.Wood	/O	H.Bennett	/O	D.Bush
/O	I.Boone	/C	C.Dorman	/O	T.Gulley	/C	F.Carisch					H	H.Rice	/O	C.Smith
/O	C.Skinner	H	J.Cortazzo	/O	J.Gallagher			P	J.Bush	P	E.Rommel	/C	J.Schulte	/3	D.Prothro
		R	R.Snipes	R	K.Hogan			P	B.Shawkey	P	B.Hasty	H	B.Mizeur	/1	J.Riley
P	H.Ehmke	R	L.Taylor			P	H.Dauss	P	S.Jones	P	S.Harriss	H	S.Simon	H	P.Lapan
P	J.Quinn			P	G.Uhle	P	H.Pillette	P	W.Hoyt	P	F.Heimach	/M	J.Austin	H	J.Propst
P	A.Ferguson	P	C.Robertson	P	S.Coveleski	P	K.Holloway	P	H.Pennock	P	R.Naylor				
P	B.Piercy	P	R.Faber	P	J.Edwards	P	S.Johnson					P	E.Vangilder	P	W.Johnson
P	G.Murray	P	M.Cvengros	P	J.Shaute	P	B.Cole	RP	R.Francis	P	R.Walberg	P	U.Shocker	P	G.Mogridge
RP	L.O'Doul	P	T.Blankenship	P	G.Morton					/P	G.Pipgras	P	D.Danforth	P	T.Zachary
		P	D.Leverett	RP	D.Metivier	P	R.Collins	/P	O.Roettger	P	C.Ogden	P	R.Kolp	P	A.Russell
P	C.Fullerton			RP	D.Boone	P	O.Olsen			/P	D.Burns	P	D.Davis	P	P.Zahniser
P	L.Howe					/P	E.Whitehill			/P	R.Meeker	RP	C.Root		
/P	C.Blethen	/P	T.Lyons	P	S.Smith	/P	R.Moore			/P	W.Kinney			P	C.Warmoth
/P	C.Stimson	P	F.Mack	/P	P.Bedgood	/P	E.Wells			/P	A.Kellett			P	B.Hollingsworth
/P	D.Black	/P	C.Gillenwater	/P	J.Sullivan	/P	R.Clarke			/P	C.Wolfe	P	H.Pruett	P	F.Marberry
		/P	P.Castner	P	L.Drake					/P	H.Hulvey	P	R.Wright	P	M.Mitchell
		/P	S.Connally	P	G.Edmondson					/P	R.Kelly	P	B.Bayne	P	S.Friday
		/P	H.Blankenship	/P	J.Fry					/P	H.O'Neill	/P	G.Grant	/P	J.Brillheart
		/P	L.Davenport	/P	D.Levsen					/P	D.Ozmer	/P	S.Thurston	/P	D.Sedgwick
		/P	R.Proctor	/P	G.Winn							/P	J.Elliott	/P	S.McGrew
		P	S.Embrey											/P	S.Potter
		/P	L.Cadore											P	C.Roe
		/P	F.Woodward											/P	F.Schemanske
														/P	T.Wingfield

TEAM	G	W	L	PCT	GB	R	OR	AB	H	2B	3B	HR	BB	SO	AVG	OBP	SLG	PRO	PRO+	BR	/A	PF	CHI	RC	SB	CS	SBA	SBR
NY	152	98	54	.645		823	622	5347	1554	231	79	105	521	516	.291	.357	.422	.779	108	73	59	102	101	811	69	74	48	-24
DET	155	83	71	.539	16	831	741	5266	1579	270	69	41	596	385	.300	.377	.401	.778	113	91	108	98	98	827	87	62	58	-11
CLE	153	82	71	.536	16.5	888	746	5290	1594	301	75	59	633	384	.301	.381	.420	.801	117	135	137	100	100	868	79	79	50	-24
WAS	155	75	78	.490	23.5	720	747	5244	1436	224	93	26	532	448	.274	.346	.367	.713	95	-46	-11	95	104	693	102	68	60	-10
STL	154	74	78	.487	24	688	720	5298	1489	248	62	82	442	423	.281	.339	.398	.737	94	-15	-55	106	96	724	64	54	54	-13
PHI	153	69	83	.454	29	661	661	5196	1407	229	64	53	445	517	.271	.333	.370	.703	89	-74	-82	101	103	653	72	62	54	-16
CHI	156	69	85	.448	30	692	741	5246	1463	254	57	42	532	458	.279	.350	.373	.723	97	-26	-17	99	97	707	191	118	62	-14
BOS	154	61	91	.401	37	584	809	5181	1354	253	54	34	391	480	.261	.318	.351	.669	81	-143	-146	101	104	579	79	91	46	-31
TOT	616					5887		42068	11876	2010	553	442	4092	3611	.282	.351	.388	.739						743	608	55	-142

TEAM	CG	SH	SV	IP	H	H/G	HR	BB	SO	RAT	ERA	ERA+	OAV	OOB	PR	/A	PF	CPI	FA	E	DP	FW	PW	BW	SBW	DIF
NY	101	9	10	1380²	1365	8.9	68	491	506	12.3	3.62	109	.263	.330	55	49	99	96	.977	144	131	3.3	4.7	5.7	-.6	-3.9
DET	61	9	12	1373²	1502	9.8	58	449	447	13.1	4.09	94	.283	.345	-16	-34	97	96	.968	200	103	-3.3	10.4	.7	-1.9	
CLE	77	10	11	1376	1517	9.9	36	465	407	13.2	3.91	101	.285	.346	11	4	100	97	.964	226	143	-1.7	.4	13.2	-.6	-5.9
WAS	71	8	16	1374¹	1527	10.0	56	563	474	14.0	3.98	95	.291	.364	0	-30	95	109	.966	216	182	-.9	-2.9	-1.1	.7	2.6
STL	83	10	11	1373¹	1430	9.4	59	528	488	13.2	3.93	106	.275	.348	9	37	105	98	.971	177	145	1.4	3.6	-5.3	.5	-2.1
PHI	65	7	12	1364²	1465	9.7	68	550	400	13.5	4.08	101	.280	.352	-15	1	103	103	.965	221	127	-1.4	.0	-7.9	.2	-3.0
CHI	74	5	11	1397	1512	9.7	49	534	467	13.4	4.05	98	.283	.353	-10	-13	99	99	.971	184	138	1.1	-1.3	-1.6	.4	-6.6
BOS	77	3	11	1372	1534	10.1	48	520	412	13.9	4.20	98	.294	.366	-33	-15	103	104	.963	232	126	-2.0	-1.5	-14.1	-1.3	3.8
TOT	609	61	93	11011²		9.7				13.3	3.98		.282	.351					.968	1600	1095					

Runs
Ruth-NY 151
Speaker-Cle 133
Jamieson-Cle 130
Heilmann-Det 121
Rice-Was 117

Hits
Jamieson-Cle 222
Speaker-Cle 218
Heilmann-Det 211
Ruth-NY 205
Tobin-StL 202

Doubles
Speaker-Cle 59
Burns-Bos 47
Ruth-NY 45
Heilmann-Det 44
J.Sewell-Cle 41

Triples
Rice-Was 18
Goslin-Was 18
Tobin-StL 15
Mostil-Chi 15

Home Runs
Ruth-NY 41
Williams-StL 29
Heilmann-Det 18
Speaker-Cle 17
Hauser-Phi 17

Total Bases
Ruth-NY 399
Speaker-Cle 350
Williams-StL 346
Heilmann-Det 331
Tobin-StL 303

Runs Batted In
Ruth-NY 131
Speaker-Cle 130
Heilmann-Det 115
J.Sewell-Cle 109
Pipp-NY 108

Runs Produced
Speaker-Cle 246
Ruth-NY 241
Heilmann-Det 218
J.Sewell-Cle 204
Rice-Was 189

Bases On Balls
Ruth-NY 170
J.Sewell-Cle 98
Blue-Det 96
Speaker-Cle 93
Collins-Chi 84

Batting Average
Heilmann-Det 403
Ruth-NY 393
Speaker-Cle 380
Collins-Chi 360
Williams-StL 357

On Base Percentage
Ruth-NY 545
Heilmann-Det 481
Speaker-Cle 469
J.Sewell-Cle 456
Collins-Chi 455

Slugging Average
Ruth-NY 764
Heilmann-Det 632
Williams-StL 623
Speaker-Cle 610
Harris-Bos 520

Production
Ruth-NY 1.309
Heilmann-Det 1.113
Speaker-Cle 1.079
Williams-StL 1.062
J.Sewell-Cle 935

Adjusted Production
Ruth-NY 238
Heilmann-Det 195
Speaker-Cle 183
Williams-StL 168
J.Sewell-Cle 147

Batter Runs
Ruth-NY 119.1
Speaker-Cle 70.9
Heilmann-Det 70.7
Williams-StL 61.2
J.Sewell-Cle 42.8

Adjusted Batter Runs
Ruth-NY 115.7
Heilmann-Det 73.7
Speaker-Cle 71.2
Williams-StL 53.5
J.Sewell-Cle 43.0

Clutch Hitting Index
Pipp-NY 137
J.Sewell-Cle 123
Bassler-Det 122
Sheely-Chi 122
Meusel-NY 121

Runs Created
Ruth-NY 223
Speaker-Cle 166
Heilmann-Det 160
Williams-StL 148
J.Sewell-Cle 128

Total Average
Ruth-NY 1.683
Heilmann-Det 1.288
Speaker-Cle 1.222
Williams-StL 1.144
J.Sewell-Cle 1.025

Stolen Bases
Collins-Chi 48
Mostil-Chi 41
Harris-Was 23
Rice-Was 20

Stolen Base Average
Mostil-Chi 71.9
Rice-Was 71.4
Elsh-Chi 66.7
Collins-Chi 62.3
Harris-Was 59.0

Stolen Base Runs
Mostil-Chi 2.7
Barrett-Chi 1.8
Veach-Det 1.2
Rice-Was 1.2
Pratt-Det 1.2

Fielding Runs
Peckinpaugh-Was . . 22.8
Mostil-Chi 21.8
Harris-Was 19.4
Ruel-Was 18.5
Flagstead-Det-Bos 18.5

Total Player Rating
Ruth-NY 10.6
Speaker-Cle 6.4
Heilmann-Det 6.2
J.Sewell-Cle 6.0
Williams-StL 4.8

Wins
Uhle-Cle 26
Jones-NY 21
Dauss-Det 21
Shocker-StL 20
Ehmke-Bos 20

Win Percentage
Pennock-NY 760
Jones-NY 724
Hoyt-NY 654
Shocker-StL 625
Uhle-Cle 619

Games
Rommel-Phi 56
Uhle-Cle 54
Russell-Was 52
Cole-Det 52
Dauss-Det 50

Complete Games
Uhle-Cle 29
Ehmke-Bos 28
Shocker-StL 24
Dauss-Det 22
Bush-NY 22

Shutouts
Coveleski-Cle 5
Vangilder-StL 4
Dauss-Det 4

Saves
Russell-Was 9
Quinn-Bos 7
Harriss-Phi 6

Innings Pitched
Uhle-Cle 357.2
Ehmke-Bos 316.2
Dauss-Det 316.0
Rommel-Phi 297.2
Vangilder-StL 282.1

Fewest Hits/Game
Shawkey-NY 8.07
Hoyt-NY 8.56
Bush-NY 8.59
Russell-Was 8.78
Danforth-StL 8.79

Fewest BB/Game
Shocker-StL 1.59
Coveleski-Cle 1.66
Thurston-StL-Chi . . 1.75
Quinn-Bos 1.96
Dauss-Det 2.22

Strikeouts
Johnson-Was 130
Shawkey-NY 125
Bush-NY 125
Ehmke-Bos 121

Strikeouts/Game
Johnson-Det 4.75
Johnson-Was 4.48
Shawkey-NY 4.35
Bush-NY 4.08
Harriss-Phi 3.83

Ratio
Shocker-StL 11.16
Hoyt-NY 11.20
Pennock-NY 11.52
Jones-NY 11.63
Coveleski-Cle 11.64

Earned Run Average
Coveleski-Cle 2.76
Hoyt-NY 3.02
Russell-Was 3.03
Vangilder-StL 3.06
Mogridge-Was 3.11

Adjusted ERA
Coveleski-Cle 143
Vangilder-StL 136
Hoyt-NY 131
Thurston-StL-Chi . . 127
Rommel-Phi 126

Opponents' Batting Avg.
Shawkey-NY 246
Hoyt-NY 253
Jones-NY 257
Faber-Chi 259
Bush-NY 260

Opponents' On Base Pct.
Shocker-StL 306
Hoyt-NY 307
Faber-Chi 311
Jones-NY 312
Pennock-NY 314

Starter Runs
Coveleski-Cle 30.9
Vangilder-StL 28.9
Hoyt-NY 25.6
Rommel-Phi 23.7
Pennock-NY 22.4

Adjusted Starter Runs
Vangilder-StL 34.8
Coveleski-Cle 30.4
Rommel-Phi 27.8
Hoyt-NY 24.4
Shocker-StL 23.5

Clutch Pitching Index
Thurston-StL-Chi . . 139
Russell-Was 128
Mogridge-Was 122
Vangilder-StL 121
Coveleski-Cle 121

Relief Runs

Adjusted Relief Runs

Relief Ranking

Total Pitcher Index
Rommel-Phi 4.0
Vangilder-StL 3.4
Coveleski-Cle 2.9
Bush-NY 2.6
Uhle-Cle 2.4

Total Baseball Ranking
Ruth-NY 10.6
Speaker-Cle 6.4
Heilmann-Det 6.2
J.Sewell-Cle 6.0
Williams-StL 4.8

February 12 The NL decides to go along with the AL in offering a $1,000 prize to the player named MVP by a committee of writers.

April 15 The Cards' Rogers Hornsby is the only batter who ever goes 2-for-5 on Opening Day and improves on his batting average the rest of the year. His .424 will be the highest major league batting average in the century.

July 8 The Phils play a 25-inning doubleheader at Cincinnati without making an error.

July 16 Giants first baseman George Kelly hits his seventh homer and becomes the first to hit homers in six consecutive games. He will finish with 21 for the year.

September 4 Dazzy Vance chalks up his twelfth straight win, and 24th on the year; it's also the Dodgers' twelfth straight win. Two days later, spitballer Bill Doak pitches the Dodgers into first place with a 1–0 win over Boston, Brooklyn's 15th win in a row.

September 7 The Giants bring a half-game lead into Ebbets Field. With the park already packed, some 7,000 fans batter down the left field exit gate with a telephone pole and break into the field. The Giants win 8-7 despite three Dodger runs in the ninth.

September 10 The Giants rip the Braves 22-1 in the opener of a doubleheader at the Polo Grounds.

Frankie Frisch goes 6-for-6 before grounding out.

September 16 Cards first baseman Jim Bottomley's three singles, double, and two home runs produce a major league record 12 RBI in the St. Louis 17-3 win over Brooklyn.

September 20 Carl Mays wins his 20th for the Reds 9-6 over the Phils, becoming the first pitcher to win 20 for three different teams in his career. (Grover Alexander's 21 wins for the Cards in 1927 makes him the second; Gaylord Perry will be the third in 1978.)

September 27 The Giants clinch their fourth straight pennant, beating the Phils 5-1, while Brooklyn is losing 3-2 to Boston.

October 1 Another bribery scandal clouds the World Series. Judge Landis bans Giants outfielder Jimmy O'Connell and coach Cozy Dolan from the Series after they admit an attempt to bribe Phils shortstop Heinie Sand to "go easy" in their season-ending series against the Giants. O'Connell implicates Frank Frisch, George Kelly, and Ross Youngs, who deny everything and are cleared by Landis. O'Connell is out of baseball at 23.

October 4 For the fourth straight year, the Giants are in the Fall Classic. At third base is Fred Lindstrom, at 18 years, 10 months, the youngest ever to play in a World Series to date. President Calvin Coolidge is among 35,760 who jam the

D.C. stands in Game 1. George Kelly drops a home run into the bleachers in the second, and Terry does the same in the fourth for a 2-0 New York lead. Art Nehf (14-4) gives up one in the sixth. In the last of the ninth, the Senators score to send the game into extra innings. The Giants net two runs in the 12th. In the last of the 12th, Washington scores one, but the rally falls a run short, and Walter Johnson (23-7) loses his World Series debut. Nehf becomes the fifth pitcher to get three hits in a World Series game, a feat that will not be repeated until Orel Hershiser does it in 1988.

October 27 The Cubs trade pitcher Vic Aldridge, first baseman George Grantham, and first baseman Al Niehaus to Pittsburgh for first baseman Charlie Grimm, shortstop Rabbit Maranville, and pitcher Wilbur Cooper. Grantham will hit .300 for six seasons with the Bucs, while Grimm will play 11 seasons with Chicago, eventually becoming player-manager. In 1925, Maranville will be named a player-manager as well.

December 10 The two leagues agree on a permanent rotation for World Series play proposed by Charles Ebbets: first two games at one league's park, next three at the other league's park, last two if needed back at the first league's park, with openers to alternate between leagues. Next year's World Series will commence at the NL city.

	BOSTON		BROOKLYN		CHICAGO		CINCINNATI		NEW YORK		PHILADELPHIA		PITTSBURGH		ST.LOUIS
M	D.Bancroft	M	W.Robinson	M	B.Killefer	M	J.Hendricks	M	J.McGraw	M	A.Fletcher	M	B.McKechnie	M	B.Rickey
1B	S.McInnis	1B	J.Fournier	1B	H.Cotter	1B	J.Daubert	M	W.Holke	1B	C.Grimm	1B	J.Bottomley
2B	C.Tierney	2B	A.High	2B	G.Grantham	2B	H.Critz	M	J.McGraw	2B	H.Ford	2B	R.Maranville	2B	R.Hornsby
SS	B.Smith	SS	J.Mitchell	SS	S.Adams	SS	I.Caveney	1B	G.Kelly	SS	H.Sand	SS	G.Wright	SS	J.Cooney
3B	E.Padgett	3B	M.Stock	3B	B.Friberg	3B	B.Pinelli	2B	F.Frisch	3B	R.Wrightstone	3B	P.Traynor	3B	H.Freigau
LF	B.Cunningham	LF	Z.Wheat	LF	D.Grigsby	LF	P.Duncan	SS	T.Jackson	LF	J.Mokan	LF	K.Cuyler	LF	R.Blades
CF	G.Felix	CF	E.Brown	CF	J.Statz	CF	E.Roush	3B	H.Groh	CF	C.Williams	CF	M.Carey	CF	W.Holm
RF	C.Stengel	RF	T.Griffith	RF	C.Heathcote	RF	C.Walker	LF	I.Meusel	RF	G.Harper	RF	C.Barnhart	RF	J.Smith
C	M.O'Neil	C	Z.Taylor	C	G.Hartnett	C	B.Hargrave	CF	H.Wilson	C	B.Henline	C	J.Gooch	C	M.Gonzalez
								RF	R.Youngs						
S	D.Bancroft	S3	J.Johnston	S	C.Hollocher	2S	S.Bohne	C	F.Snyder	C	J.Wilson	O	C.Bigbee	O1	H.Mueller
C1	F.Gibson	C	H.DeBerry	C	B.O'Farrell	1O	R.Bressler			O	J.Schultz	O3	E.Moore	O	M.Flack
O	F.Wilson	O	B.Neis	1	R.Grimes	O	G.Burns	O	B.Southworth	3S	F.Parkinson	C	W.Schmidt	3S	S.Toporcer
O	R.Powell	O	D.Loftus	O	O.Vogel	O	I.Wingo	C	H.Gowdy	3	A.Woehr	C	E.Smith	O	T.Douthit
O	H.Thomas	2	J.Klugmann	21	B.Barrett	S	B.Fowler	1	B.Terry	O	F.Henrich	O	W.Mueller	O3	H.Myers
L	L.Mann	O	G.Bailey	O	B.Weis	O	G.Harper	O	J.O'Connell	O	C.Walker	/C	C.Knox	O	C.Hafey
2	M.Shay	S	B.Jones	O	H.Miller	O	C.Shorten	23	F.Lindstrom	O	C.Lee	/1	J.Ens	S	T.Thevenow
C	E.Smith	/C	C.Hargreaves	/O	H.Fitzgerald	2	L.Fonseca	/C	G.Hartley	C	L.Wendell	/1	E.Barnes	C	C.Niebergall
O	E.Sperber	/S	I.Olson	/1	T.Kearns	C	G.Sanberg	/O	E.Ainsmith	/O	F.Leach	H	J.Rawlings	S	L.Bell
/3	H.Lane	/2	F.Johnston	1	A.Elliott	/O	E.Hock	/O	B.Crump	/S	L.Metz			C	V.Clemons
H	W.Cruise			/S	R.Michaels	/O	C.Lee			/O	S.Emery	P	W.Cooper	C	E.Vick
/C	E.Phillips	C	B.Grimes	/C	J.Churry	/2	J.Begley	P	V.Barnes			P	R.Kremer	/O	E.Clough
/C	D.Cousineau	P	D.Vance			/O	G.Neale	P	J.Bentley	P	J.Ring	P	J.Morrison	/O	J.Schultz
H	A.Hermann	P	D.Ruether	P	V.Aldridge	/O	E.Pick	P	H.McQuillan	P	H.Carlson	P	L.Meadows	/2	D.Lavan
H	J.Kelleher	P	B.Doak	P	V.Keen	/C	J.Blott	P	A.Nehf	P	B.Hubbell	P	E.Yde	/C	R.Shepardson
H	W.Lefler	P	A.Decatur	P	T.Kaufmann			P	W.Dean	P	C.Mitchell	RP	A.Stone	/O	J.Bratcher
		P			E.Jacobs	P	E.Rixey	RP	C.Jonnard	P	W.Glazner				
P	J.Barnes	P	T.Osborne	P	P.Alexander	P	C.Mays					P	J.Pfeffer	P	J.Haines
P	J.Genewich	P	R.Ehrhardt			P	P.Donohue	P	R.Ryan	P	H.Betts	/P	B.Adams	P	A.Sothoron
P	J.Cooney	P	D.Henry	P	S.Blake	P	D.Luque	P	M.Watson	P	J.Couch	/P	D.Lundgren	P	B.Sherdel
P	T.McNamara	P	J.Roberts	P	R.Wheeler	P	T.Sheehan	P	E.Maun	P	J.Oeschger	/P	D.Songer	P	J.Stuart
P	A.Yeargin	/P	L.Dickerman	P	G.Bush	RP	J.May	P	H.Baldwin	/P	R.Steineder	/P	R.Steineder	P	E.Dyer
		/P	R.Yarrison	P	G.Milstead			P	W.Huntzinger	/P	B.Lewis	/P	B.May		
P	L.Benton	/P	N.Greene	/P	R.Pierce	P	R.Benton	/P	D.Gearin	/P	J.Bishop	/P	F.Sale	P	L.Dickerman
P	R.Lucas	/P	B.Hollingsworth	/P	H.Brett	/P	P.Dibut	/P	J.Oeschger	/P	L.Weinert			P	H.Bell
P	D.Stryker	/P	T.Wilson	/P	T.Osborne	/P	B.Harris	/P	L.Cadore	/P	E.Hamilton			P	J.Pfeffer
/P	R.Marquard	/P	T.Long					/P	K.Greenfield	/P	L.Pinto			P	J.Fowler
/P	L.North													/P	F.Rhem
/P	S.Graham													P	B.Doak
/P	J.Muich													/P	A.Delaney
/P	I.Kamp													/P	P.Day
/P	J.Batchelder													/P	L.North
/P	D.Gearin													/P	V.Shields
														/P	B.Vines
														/P	J.Berly

TEAM	G	W	L	PCT	GB	R	OR	AB	H	2B	3B	HR	BB	SO	AVG	OBP	SLG	PRO	PRO+	BR	/A	PF	CHI	RC	SB	CS	SBA	SBR
NY	154	93	60	.608		**857**	641	5445	**1634**	269	81	**95**	467	479	**.300**	**.358**	**.432**	**.790**	120	124	148	97	102	**849**	82	53	61	-7
BRO	154	92	62	.597	1.5	717	675	5339	1534	227	54	72	447	357	.287	.345	.391	.736	105	19	42	97	99	725	34	46	43	-17
PIT	153	90	63	.588	3	724	588	5288	1517	222	**122**	44	366	396	.287	.336	.400	.736	100	11	0	102	99	715	**181**	92	**66**	**-1**
CIN	153	83	70	.542	10	649	**579**	5301	1539	236	111	36	349	334	.290	.337	.397	.734	103	8	19	99	93	698	103	98	51	-28
CHI	154	81	72	.529	12	698	699	5134	1419	207	59	66	**469**	521	.276	.340	.378	.718	96	-10	-16	101	**103**	652	137	149	48	-48
STL	154	65	89	.422	28.5	740	750	5349	1552	**270**	47	67	382	418	.290	.341	.411	.752	108	42	55	98	100	740	86	86	50	-26
PHI	152	55	96	.364	37	676	849	5306	1459	256	56	94	382	452	.275	.328	.397	.725	88	-13	-96	112	99	687	57	67	46	-23
BOS	154	53	100	.346	40	520	800	5283	1355	194	52	25	354	451	.256	.306	.327	.633	77	-181	-160	96	**103**	532	74	68	52	-19
TOT	614					5581		42445	12009	1881	622	499	3216	3408	.283	.337	.392	.729							754	659	53	-169

TEAM	CG	SH	SV	IP	H	H/G	HR	BB	SO	RAT	ERA	ERA+	OAV	OOB	PR	/A	PF	CPI	FA	E	DP	FW	PW	BW	SBW	DIF
NY	71	4	**21**	1378²	1464	9.6	77	392	406	12.2	3.62	101	.274	.326	38	7	95	100	.971	186	160	.4	.7	**14.7**	1.4	-.7
BRO	**97**	10	5	1376¹	1432	9.4	58	403	**638**	12.2	3.64	103	.270	.326	35	16	97	96	.968	196	121	-.2	1.6	4.2	.4	9.0
PIT	85	**15**	5	1382	**1387**	**9.0**	42	323	364	**11.3**	3.27	117	**.267**	.313	92	88	99	97	.971	183	161	.5	8.7	.0	**2.0**	2.3
CIN	77	14	9	1378	1408	9.2	**30**	293	451	**11.3**	**3.12**	**121**	**.267**	**.309**	**115**	**99**	97	97	.966	217	142	-1.4	**9.8**	1.9	-.7	-3.1
CHI	85	4	6	1380²	1459	9.5	89	438	416	12.5	3.83	102	.275	.333	6	11	101	101	.966	218	153	-1.4	1.1	-1.6	-2.7	9.1
STL	79	7	6	1364²	1528	10.1	70	486	393	13.5	4.15	91	.290	.354	-43	-57	98	**104**	.969	188	162	.3	-5.7	5.5	-.5	-11.6
PHI	59	7	10	1354¹	1689	11.2	84	469	349	14.5	4.87	92	.313	.372	-151	-60	115	103	.972	175	**168**	.8	-6.0	-9.5	-.2	-5.7
BOS	66	10	4	1379¹	1607	10.5	49	402	364	13.3	4.46	86	.301	.353	-92	-100	99	96	**.973**	168	154	**1.4**	-9.9	-15.9	.2	.7
TOT	619	71	66	10994		9.8				12.6	3.87		.283	.337					.970	1531	1221					

Runs		Hits		Doubles		Triples		Home Runs		Total Bases	
Hornsby-StL	121	Hornsby-StL	227	Hornsby-StL	43	Roush-Cin	21	Fournier-Bro	27	Hornsby-StL	373
Frisch-NY	121	Wheat-Bro	212	Wheat-Bro	41	Maranville-Pit	20	Hornsby-StL	25	Wheat-Bro	311
Carey-Pit	113	Frisch-NY	198	Kelly-NY	37	Wright-Pit	18	Williams-Phi	24	Williams-Phi	308
Youngs-NY	112	High-Bro	191			Cuyler-Pit	16	Kelly-NY	21	Kelly-NY	303
Williams-Phi	101	Fournier-Bro	188			Frisch-NY	15			Fournier-Bro	302

Runs Batted In		Runs Produced		Bases On Balls		Batting Average		On Base Percentage		Slugging Average	
Kelly-NY	136	Kelly-NY	206	Hornsby-StL	89	Hornsby-StL	.424	Hornsby-StL	.507	Hornsby-StL	.696
Fournier-Bro	116	Hornsby-StL	190	Fournier-Bro	83	Wheat-Bro	.375	Youngs-NY	.441	Williams-Phi	.552
Wright-Pit	111	Wright-Pit	184	Youngs-NY	77	Youngs-NY	.356	Fournier-Bro	.428	Wheat-Bro	.549
Bottomley-StL	111	Bottomley-StL	184	Williams-Phi	67	Cuyler-Pit	.354	Wheat-Bro	.428	Cuyler-Pit	.539
Meusel-NY	102	Frisch-NY	183	Friberg-Chi	66	Roush-Cin	.348	Williams-Phi	.403	Fournier-Bro	.536

Production		Adjusted Production		Batter Runs		Adjusted Batter Runs		Clutch Hitting Index		Runs Created	
Hornsby-StL	1.203	Hornsby-StL	223	Hornsby-StL	94.1	Hornsby-StL	97.2	Friberg-Chi	141	Hornsby-StL	186
Wheat-Bro	.978	Wheat-Bro	165	Wheat-Bro	48.2	Fournier-Bro	52.2	Griffith-Bro	140	Fournier-Bro	133
Fournier-Bro	.965	Fournier-Bro	162	Fournier-Bro	48.1	Wheat-Bro	52.1	Meusel-NY	135	Wheat-Bro	132
Youngs-NY	.962	Youngs-NY	161	Youngs-NY	45.3	Youngs-NY	48.6	Wright-Pit	130	Youngs-NY	123
Williams-Phi	.955	Cuyler-Pit	147	Williams-Phi	42.0	Kelly-NY	32.3	Pinelli-Cin	129	Williams-Phi	121

Total Average		Stolen Bases		Stolen Base Average		Stolen Base Runs		Fielding Runs		Total Player Rating	
Hornsby-StL	1.424	Carey-Pit	49	Carey-Pit	79.0	Carey-Pit	6.9	Pinelli-Cin	26.7	Hornsby-StL	8.5
Fournier-Bro	1.045	Cuyler-Pit	32	Cuyler-Pit	74.4	Cuyler-Pit	3.0	Frisch-NY	24.9	Frisch-NY	5.4
Youngs-NY	1.023	Heathcote-Chi	26	Frisch-NY	71.0	Hartnett-Chi	1.8	Statz-Chi	14.5	Fournier-Bro	4.7
Wheat-Bro	1.014	Traynor-Pit	24	Critz-Cin	63.3			Ford-Phi	11.9	Wheat-Bro	4.5
Cuyler-Pit	.990	Smith-StL	24	Smith-StL	60.0			Wright-Pit	10.7	Youngs-NY	3.6

Wins		Win Percentage		Games		Complete Games		Shutouts		Saves	
Vance-Bro	28	Yde-Pit	.842	Morrison-Pit	41	Vance-Bro	30	Yde-Pit	4	May-Cin	6
Grimes-Bro	22	Vance-Bro	.824	Kremer-Pit	41	Grimes-Bro	30	Sothoron-StL	4	Ryan-NY	5
Mays-Cin	20	Bentley-NY	.762	Keen-Chi	40	Cooper-Pit	25	Rixey-Cin	4	Jonnard-NY	5
Cooper-Pit	20	Mays-Cin	.690	Sheehan-Cin	39	Barnes-Bos	21	Kremer-Pit	4		
Kremer-Pit	18	Kremer-Pit	.643			Aldridge-Chi	20	Cooper-Pit	4		
								Barnes-Bos	4		

Innings Pitched		Fewest Hits/Game		Fewest BB/Game		Strikeouts		Strikeouts/Game		Ratio	
Grimes-Bro	310.2	Vance-Bro	6.95	Benton-Cin	1.33	Vance-Bro	262	Vance-Bro	7.65	Vance-Bro	9.46
Vance-Bro	308.1	Yde-Pit	7.93	Alexander-Chi	1.33	Grimes-Bro	135	Grimes-Bro	3.91	Rixey-Cin	10.12
Cooper-Pit	268.2	Morrison-Pit	8.07	Cooper-Pit	1.34	Luque-Cin	86	Nehf-NY	3.77	Benton-Cin	10.73
Barnes-Bos	267.2	Doak-StL-Bro	8.14	Mays-Cin	1.43	Morrison-Pit	85	Luque-Cin	3.53	Doak-StL-Bro	10.87
Kremer-Pit	259.1	Rixey-Cin	8.27	Donohue-Cin	1.46	Kaufmann-Chi	79	Kaufmann-Chi	3.41	McQuillan-NY	10.96

Earned Run Average		Adjusted ERA		Opponents' Batting Avg.		Opponents' On Base Pct.		Starter Runs		Adjusted Starter Runs	
Vance-Bro	2.16	Vance-Bro	173	Vance-Bro	.213	Vance-Bro	.269	Vance-Bro	58.4	Vance-Bro	54.3
McQuillan-NY	2.69	Rixey-Cin	137	Yde-Pit	.244	Rixey-Cin	.285	Rixey-Cin	29.4	Rixey-Cin	26.7
Rixey-Cin	2.76	McQuillan-NY	136	Morrison-Pit	.245	Benton-Cin	.297	McQuillan-NY	24.0	Yde-Pit	21.7
Benton-Cin	2.77	Benton-Cin	136	Rixey-Cin	.246	Alexander-Chi	.299	Yde-Pit	22.3	McQuillan-NY	19.9
Yde-Pit	2.83	Yde-Pit	136	Doak-StL-Bro	.249	Nehf-NY	.301	Barnes-NY	20.5	Kremer-Pit	18.6

Clutch Pitching Index		Relief Runs		Adjusted Relief Runs		Relief Ranking		Total Pitcher Index		Total Baseball Ranking	
Sherdel-StL	117	Jonnard-NY	14.5	Jonnard-NY	12.5	Jonnard-NY	12.9	Vance-Bro	5.7	Hornsby-StL	8.5
Sothoron-StL	115	May-Cin	9.5	May-Cin	8.4	May-Cin	5.7	Mays-Cin	3.4	Vance-Bro	5.7
Ring-Phi	113	Stone-Pit	6.5	Stone-Pit	6.3	Stone-Pit	5.3	Rixey-Cin	3.1	Frisch-NY	5.4
McQuillan-NY	113							Cooper-Pit	2.5	Fournier-Bro	4.7
Aldridge-Chi	110							Yde-Pit	2.3	Wheat-Bro	4.5

February 10 Clark Griffith picks 27-year-old second baseman Bucky Harris to manage the Senators.

April 15 George Sisler returns after missing a full year due to impaired vision caused by severe sinusitis. He is 2-for-4 in the Browns' 7–3 win over the White Sox.

May 23 Walter Johnson strikes out 14 in a 4-0 one-hitter over the White Sox for his 103rd shutout. Johnson will have his best season in five years, going 23-7.

June 13 The first place Yankees come to Detroit with the Tigers close on their heels. New York leads 10-6 in the top of the ninth. Bob Meusel takes a pitch in his back, hurls his bat at pitcher Bert Cole, and charges the mound. Players from both teams start swinging. Fans rush out of the stands, eager to mix it up with players, police, and each other. the fight goes on for nearly 30 minutes while umpire Billy Evans, unable to clear the field, forfeits the game to New York. Cole and Meusel are suspended for 10 days.

August 2 A's first basemann Joe Hauser sets an AL record when he hits three homers and a double for 14 total bases. It'll be broken by Ty Cobb's 16 total bases on May 5, 1925.

August 13 Howard Ehmke has the White Sox popping up all day in his 6-0 win. Only one assist is made by Boston.

August 25 Walter Johnson hurls a seven-inning rain-shortened no-hitter against the Browns, winning by a score of 2-0.

August 28 Despite Babe Ruth's two home runs, the Senators beat the Yankees 11-6 and move into first place. The Yankees will tie them for two days in September, but otherwise the Senators stay on top till the end.

September 6 Urban Shocker of the Browns hurls two complete-game victories over the White Sox, winning each contest by a score of 6-2; he fans only one batter in the two games.

September 14 Walter Johnson is elected AL MVP with 55 points. White Sox second baseman Eddie Collins is second. He was runner-up to Ruth last year.

September 29 The Senators clinch the pennant in Boston, finishing two games in front of the Yankees.

October 10 President and Mrs. Coolidge and 31,665 others thrill to the second 3-hour battle of the Series. Bucky Harris starts 23-year-old righthander Curly Ogden (9-8) against Virgil Barnes (16-10), then pulls him after he fans Fred Lindstrom and walks Frisch. In comes lefty George Mogridge (16-11). Bucky Harris lifts one into the temporary seats in left field for a 1-0 lead. In the sixth a single ties it at 1-1, and Harris brings in Firpo Marberry for his fourth appearance. A base hit and two costly errors give the Giants a 3-1 lead. In the eighth, pinch-hitter Nemo Liebold doubles and catcher Muddy Ruel singles. A walk loads the bases and up comes Harris, who hits a hard bounder to third base that strikes a pebble and skips over Lindstrom's head and down the left field line as the tying runs score. With one out in the last of the 12th, Giants reliever Jack Bentley gets Muddy Ruel to pop up near home plate, but veteran catcher Hank Gowdy trips on his discarded mask, and the ball falls to the ground. Ruel then gets his second hit, a double. Walter Johnson reaches first base on shortstop Travis Jackson's error. Earl McNeely hits a grounder at Lindstrom, and again the ball takes a bounce over his head. Ruel tears home with the run that gives Washington its World Series championship.

October 20* Kansas City Monarchs manager Jose Mendez takes the mound to spin a 3-hit, 5–0 shutout over the Hilldales to win the final game of the first Negro League World Series. Nip Winters had pitched the first three Hilldale wins.

December 11 Eddie Collins signs as player-manager of the White Sox.

	BOSTON		CHICAGO		CLEVELAND		DETROIT		NEW YORK		PHILADELPHIA		ST.LOUIS		WASHINGTON
M	L.Fohl	M	E.Collins	M	T.Speaker	M	T.Cobb	M	M.Huggins	M	C.Mack	M	G.Sisler	M	B.Harris
1B	J.Harris	M	E.Sheely	1B	G.Burns	1B	L.Blue	1B	W.Pipp	1B	J.Hauser	1B	G.Sisler	1B	J.Judge
2B	B.Wambsganss	M	E.Collins	2B	C.Fewster	2B	D.Pratt	2B	A.Ward	2B	M.Bishop	2B	M.McManus	2B	B.Harris
SS	D.Lee	M	B.Barrett	SS	J.Sewell	SS	T.Rigney	SS	E.Scott	SS	C.Galloway	SS	W.Gerber	SS	R.Peckinpaugh
3B	D.Clark	1B	W.Kamm	3B	R.Lutzke	3B	B.Jones	3B	J.Dugan	3B	H.Riconda	3B	G.Robertson	3B	O.Bluege
LF	B.Veach	2B	B.Falk	LF	C.Jamieson	LF	H.Manush	LF	B.Meusel	LF	B.Lamar	LF	K.Williams	LF	G.Goslin
CF	I.Flagstead	SS	J.Mostil	CF	T.Speaker	CF	T.Cobb	CF	W.Witt	CF	A.Simmons	CF	B.Jacobson	CF	N.Leibold
RF	I.Boone	3B	H.Hooper	RF	H.Summa	RF	H.Heilmann	RF	B.Ruth	RF	B.Miller	RF	J.Tobin	RF	S.Rice
C	S.O'Neill	LF	B.Crouse	C	G.Myatt	C	J.Bassler	C	W.Schang	C	C.Perkins	C	H.Severeid	C	M.Ruel
3S	H.Ezzell	RF			P.McNulty	3	F.Haney	C	F.Hofmann	23	J.Dykes	O	J.Evans	O	E.McNeely
O1	S.Collins	C			R.Stephenson	2	L.Burke	2	E.Johnson	O	F.Welch	23	N.McMillan	O	W.Matthews
S3	H.Shanks				L.Sewell	2	F.O'Rourke	O	H.Hendrick	3	S.Hale	O	H.Bennett	3	D.Prothro
C	V.Picinich	O	M.Archdeacon	3	F.Ellerbe	O	B.Fothergill	23	M.McNally	O	P.Strand	3	H.Rice	3	M.Shirley
C	J.Heving	C	R.Schalk	C	F.Brower	O	L.Woodall	O	E.Combs	3	F.Bruggy	3	F.Ellerbe	3	T.Taylor
1	P.Todt	O	R.Elsh	O	S.Clarke	O	A.Wingo	/2	C.Gehringer	S	J.Chapman	C	T.Rego	C	B.Tate
O	D.Williams	S	R.French	S	R.Walters	/2	C.Manion	C	B.Bengough	/O	A.Strunk	C	P.Collins	O	S.Fisher
S	C.Geygan	S	R.Morehart	3	E.Yoter	/C	J.Kerr	/1	L.Gehrig	S	C.Gibson	/3	S.Simon	/C	P.Hargrave
/O	J.Connolly	S	H.McClellan	/3	L.Gardner	/3	J.Kerr	/O	B.Paschal	H	E.Sherling	/O	V.Elmore	/O	L.Richbourg
		C	J.Grabowski	1	R.Knode			/2	M.Hillis	H	J.Green	/3	P.Burke	/2	R.Miller
P	H.Ehmke	/1	B.Clancy	/O	T.Gulley	P	E.Whitehill	/C	C.Autry			H	B.Mizeur	/O	C.Smith
P	A.Ferguson	S	I.Davis	/O	J.Wyatt	P	L.Stoner			P	E.Rommel			/O	B.Griffith
P	J.Quinn	/C	J.Burns	/2	F.Spurgeon	P	R.Collins	P	H.Pennock	P	F.Heimach	P	U.Shocker	/O	W.Lefler
P	C.Fullerton	/C	K.Wirts	H	K.Hogan	P	K.Holloway	P	J.Bush	P	S.Baumgartner	P	D.Danforth	/O	C.East
P	B.Piercy	/2	B.Black			P	H.Dauss	P	W.Hoyt	P	D.Burns	P	E.Wingard	/S	C.Gagnon
RP	G.Murray	/S	W.Dashiell	P	J.Shaute			P	B.Shawkey	S	G.Gray	P	D.Davis		
		/S	F.Naleway	P	S.Smith	P	B.Cole	P	S.Jones	RP	B.Hasty	P	E.Vangilder	P	W.Johnson
P	B.Ross	/S	B.DeViveiros	P	S.Coveleski	P	S.Johnson	RP	M.Gaston			RP	H.Pruett	P	G.Mogridge
P	O.Fuhr	H	A.Strunk	P	G.Uhle	P	E.Wells			P	R.Meeker	RP	G.Grant	P	T.Zachary
/P	T.Wingfield			RP	D.Metivier	/O	D.Leonard	P	A.Mamaux	P	S.Harriss	RP	B.Bayne	P	F.Marberry
/P	R.Ruffing	P	S.Thurston			/P	H.Pillette	/P	W.Beall	P	R.Naylor			P	J.Martina
/P	H.Workman	P	T.Lyons	P	J.Edwards	/P	W.Ludolph	/P	C.Markle	/C	C.Ogden	P	R.Kolp	RP	A.Russell
/P	L.Howe	P	R.Faber	P	L.Roy	/P	R.Clarke	/P	G.Pipgras	/P	R.Walberg	P	G.Lyons	RP	B.Speece
/P	C.Winters	P	S.Connally	/P	C.Yowell	/P	K.Jones	/P	B.Shields	/P	W.Pierson	/P	O.Voigt		
/P	I.Jamerson	P	T.Blankenship	P	W.Clark			/P	O.Roettger			/P	B.Lasley	P	C.Ogden
/P	J.Woods			/P	B.Messenger							/P	E.Barnhart	P	P.Zahniser
/P	A.Kellett	P	M.Cvengros	/P	J.Dawson							/P	B.Beck	/P	S.McGrew
		P	D.Leverett	/P	V.Cheeves									/P	T.Wingfield
		P	C.Robertson	/P	D.Levsen									/P	N.Altrock
		P	L.Mangum	/P	J.Miller										
		P	D.McWeeny	/P	G.Morton										
		/P	M.Steengrafe	/P	L.Drake										
		/P	B.Barnes	/P	G.Edmonson										
		/P	H.Foreman	/P	F.Wayenberg										
		/P	L.Davenport	/P	P.Fitzke										
		/P	J.Dobb	/P	J.Lindsey										
		/P	B.Lawrence	/P	B.Kuhn										
		/P	W.Schultz												

TEAM	G	W	L	PCT	GB	R	OR	AB	H	2B	3B	HR	BB	SO	AVG	OBP	SLG	PRO	PRO+	BR	/A	PF	CHI	RC	SB	CS	SBA	SBR
WAS	156	92	62	.597		755	613	5304	1558	255	88	22	513	392	.294	.361	.387	.748	101	-8	16	97	98	762	116	85	58	-16
NY	153	89	63	.586	2	798	667	5240	1516	248	86	98	478	420	.289	.352	.426	.778	106	29	31	100	102	789	69	67	51	-20
DET	156	86	68	.558	6	849	796	5389	1604	315	76	35	607	400	.298	.373	.404	.777	108	53	67	98	100	837	100	77	56	-16
STL	153	74	78	.487	17	769	809	5236	1543	266	62	67	465	349	.295	.356	.408	.764	96	9	-38	106	101	762	85	85	50	-26
PHI	152	71	81	.467	20	685	778	5184	1459	251	59	63	374	484	.281	.334	.389	.723	90	-77	-83	101	105	674	77	68	53	-18
CLE	153	67	86	.438	24.5	755	814	5332	1580	306	59	41	492	371	.296	.361	.399	.760	100	8	-2	101	97	784	85	57	60	-9
BOS	157	67	87	.435	25	737	806	5340	1481	302	63	30	603	417	.277	.356	.374	.730	94	-42	-43	100	99	741	78	61	56	-13
CHI	154	66	87	.431	25.5	793	858	5255	1512	254	58	41	604	421	.288	.365	.382	.747	101	-6	18	97	103	761	137	92	60	-14
TOT	617					6141		42280	12253	2197	551	397	4136	3254	.290	.358	.397	.755							747	592	56	-131

TEAM	CG	SH	SV	IP	H	H/G	HR	BB	SO	RAT	ERA	ERA+	OAV	OOB	PR	/A	PF	CPI	FA	E	DP	FW	PW	BW	SBW	DIF
WAS	74	13	25	1383	1329	8.6	34	505	469	12.2	3.34	121	.259	.330	136	106	95	99	.972	171	149	1.3	10.0	1.5	.0	2.1
NY	76	13	13	1359¹	1483	9.8	59	522	487	13.4	3.86	108	.284	.353	56	44	98	107	.974	156	131	2.0	4.2	2.9	-.3	4.2
DET	60	5	20	1394²	1586	10.2	55	467	441	13.5	4.19	98	.293	.354	5	-12	97	101	.971	187	142	.4	-1.1	6.3	.0	3.4
STL	65	11	7	1353¹	1511	10.0	68	517	386	13.8	4.57	99	.289	.358	-51	-9	107	95	.969	184	142	.3	-.8	-3.6	-.9	3.0
PHI	68	8	10	1345	1527	10.2	43	597	371	14.4	4.39	98	.292	.368	-24	-15	101	101	.971	180	157	.5	-1.4	-7.8	-.2	3.9
CLE	87	7	7	1349	1603	10.7	43	503	315	14.3	4.40	97	.300	.365	-25	-20	101	101	.967	205	130	-1.0	-1.9	-.2	.7	-7.1
BOS	73	8	16	1391¹	1563	10.1	43	523	414	13.9	4.35	100	.290	.359	-19	2	103	97	.967	210	126	-1.0	.2	-4.1	.3	-5.5
CHI	76	1	11	1370²	1635	10.7	52	512	360	14.3	4.74	87	.305	.368	-78	-95	97	98	.963	229	136	-2.4	-9.0	1.7	.2	-1.1
TOT	579	66	109	10946¹		10.1				13.7	4.23		.290	.358					.969	1522	1113					

Runs		Hits		Doubles		Triples		Home Runs		Total Bases	
Ruth-NY	143	Rice-Was	216	J.Sewell-Cle	45	Pipp-NY	19	Ruth-NY	46	Ruth-NY	391
Cobb-Det	115	Jamieson-Cle	213	Heilmann-Det	45	Goslin-Was	17	Hauser-Phi	27	Jacobson-StL	306
Collins-Chi	108	Cobb-Det	211	Wambsganss-Bos	41	Heilmann-Det	16	Jacobson-StL	19	Heilmann-Det	304
Hooper-Chi	107	Ruth-NY	200	Jacobson-StL	41	Rice-Was	14	Williams-StL	18	Goslin-Was	299
Heilmann-Det	107	Goslin-Was	199	Meusel-NY	40	Jacobson-StL	12	Boone-Bos	13	Hauser-Phi	290

Runs Batted In		Runs Produced		Bases On Balls		Batting Average		On Base Percentage		Slugging Average	
Goslin-Was	129	Ruth-NY	218	Ruth-NY	142	Ruth-NY	.378	Ruth-NY	.513	Ruth-NY	.739
Ruth-NY	121	Goslin-Was	217	Rigney-Det	102	Jamieson-Cle	.359	Collins-Chi	.441	Heilmann-Det	.533
Meusel-NY	120	Heilmann-Det	211	Sheely-Chi	95	Falk-Chi	.352	Speaker-Cle	.432	Williams-StL	.533
Hauser-Phi	115	J.Sewell-Cle	201	Collins-Chi	89	Collins-Chi	.349	Heilmann-Det	.428	Jacobson-StL	.528
		Meusel-NY	201	Cobb-Det	85	Bassler-Det	.346	Sheely-Chi	.426	Myatt-Cle	.518

Production		Adjusted Production		Batter Runs		Adjusted Batter Runs		Clutch Hitting Index		Runs Created	
Ruth-NY	1.252	Ruth-NY	221	Ruth-NY	100.8	Ruth-NY	101.1	Sheely-Chi	149	Ruth-NY	205
Heilmann-Det	.961	Heilmann-Det	149	Heilmann-Det	40.4	Heilmann-Det	42.4	Kamm-Chi	138	Heilmann-Det	134
Williams-StL	.958	Goslin-Was	145	Goslin-Was	35.6	Goslin-Was	39.3	Pratt-Det	138	Goslin-Was	125
Speaker-Cle	.943	Speaker-Cle	141	Speaker-Cle	32.4	Collins-Chi	34.1	Rigney-Det	137	Cobb-Det	121
Goslin-Was	.937	Williams-StL	137	Collins-Chi	30.5	Speaker-Cle	31.1	Veach-Bos	131	Collins-Chi	119

Total Average		Stolen Bases		Stolen Base Average		Stolen Base Runs		Fielding Runs		Total Player Rating	
Ruth-NY	1.558	Collins-Chi	42	Collins-Chi	71.2	Collins-Chi	2.4	J.Sewell-Cle	21.4	Ruth-NY	8.5
Heilmann-Det	1.042	Meusel-NY	26	Harris-Was	66.7			Lutzke-Cle	19.4	J.Sewell-Cle	4.3
Williams-StL	1.039	Rice-Was	24	Meusel-NY	65.0			Dykes-Phi	15.9	Heilmann-Det	3.9
Speaker-Cle	.988	Cobb-Det	23	Rice-Was	64.9			Jacobson-StL	15.8	Rigney-Det	3.4
Collins-Chi	.976	Jamieson-Cle	21	Williams-StL	64.5			Wambsganss-Bos	14.4	Collins-Chi	2.9

Wins		Win Percentage		Games		Complete Games		Shutouts		Saves	
Johnson-Was	23	Johnson-Was	.767	Marberry-Was	50	Thurston-Chi	28	Johnson-Was	6	Marberry-Was	15
Pennock-NY	21	Pennock-NY	.700	Holloway-Det	49	Ehmke-Bos	26	Davis-StL	5	Russell-Was	8
Thurston-Chi	20	Whitehill-Det	.654	Shaute-Cle	46	Pennock-NY	25	Shocker-StL	4	Quinn-Bos	7
Shaute-Cle	20	Zachary-Was	.625	Hoyt-NY	46	Shaute-Cle	21	Pennock-NY	4	Dauss-Det	6
Ehmke-Bos	19			Ehmke-Bos	45	Rommel-Phi	21	Ehmke-Bos	4	Connally-Chi	6

Innings Pitched		Fewest Hits/Game		Fewest BB/Game		Strikeouts		Strikeouts/Game		Ratio	
Ehmke-Bos	315.0	Johnson-Was	7.55	Smith-Cle	1.53	Johnson-Was	158	Johnson-Was	5.12	Johnson-Was	10.37
Thurston-Chi	291.0	Collins-Det	8.29	Thurston-Chi	1.86	Ehmke-Bos	119	Shawkey-NY	4.94	Collins-Det	11.08
Pennock-NY	286.1	Marberry-Was	8.75	Shocker-StL	1.90	Shawkey-NY	114	Ehmke-Bos	3.40	Zachary-Was	11.28
Shaute-Cle	283.0	Zachary-Was	8.79	Pennock-NY	2.01	Pennock-NY	101	Shocker-StL	3.22	Smith-Cle	11.48
Rommel-Phi	278.0	Wingard-StL	8.88	Quinn-Bos	2.05	Shocker-StL	88	Pennock-NY	3.17	Pennock-NY	11.54

Earned Run Average		Adjusted ERA		Opponents' Batting Avg.		Opponents' On Base Pct.		Starter Runs		Adjusted Starter Runs	
Johnson-Was	2.72	Baumgartner-Phi	149	Johnson-Was	.224	Johnson-Was	.284	Johnson-Was	46.5	Pennock-NY	42.3
Zachary-Was	2.75	Johnson-Was	148	Collins-Det	.249	Collins-Det	.307	Pennock-NY	44.6	Johnson-Was	40.5
Pennock-NY	2.83	Pennock-NY	147	Marberry-Was	.262	Smith-Cle	.312	Smith-Cle	33.4	Smith-Cle	34.5
Baumgartner-Phi	2.88	Zachary-Was	147	Wingard-StL	.262	Pennock-NY	.314	Zachary-Was	33.2	Ehmke-Bos	31.9
Smith-Cle	3.02	Smith-Cle	142	Davis-StL	.263	Zachary-Was	.315	Baumgartner-Phi	27.1	Zachary-Was	28.9

Clutch Pitching Index		Relief Runs		Adjusted Relief Runs		Relief Ranking		Total Pitcher Index		Total Baseball Ranking	
Baumgartner-Phi	132	Speece-Was	9.5	Speece-Was	8.4	Speece-Was	4.2	Johnson-Was	4.5	Ruth-NY	8.5
Pennock-NY	117							Pennock-NY	3.8	Johnson-Was	4.5
Zachary-Was	113							Zachary-Was	3.7	J.Sewell-Cle	4.3
Ferguson-Bos	113							Bush-NY	3.4	Heilmann-Det	3.9
Hoyt-NY	112							Smith-Cle	3.4	Pennock-NY	3.8

January 5 During the White Sox' and Giants' tour of Europe, the French Baseball Federation awards silver medals to John McGraw, Charlie Comiskey, and Hugh Jennings for their efforts to advance the game in France.

February 2 The NL inaugurates its Golden Jubilee Year by holding its spring meeting in the same room in New York's Broadway Central Hotel where the league was organized on February 2, 1876.

February 25 John McGraw arrives in Florida and is installed as president of a real estate development near Bradenton called Pennant Park. With streets named for early Giants heroes, and lots offered for $2,500 to $5,000, McGraw hires a fleet of salesmen and heads north. A year later, the boom will go bust, washed away by two hurricanes. McGraw will incur a loss of $100,000 after paying off close friends, players, and other investors.

April 14 In the first regular-season Cubs game to be broadcast on the radio, Quin Ryan announces the contest from the grandstand roof for WGN. Grover Alexander wins for the Cubs 8-2 over the Pirates and adds a single, double, and home run.

April 18 Charles Ebbets, Dodgers president, dies on the morning of the opener at Ebbets Field, won by New York 7-1. No NL games will be played on the 21st, the day of his funeral. Ed McKeever, the new club president, will catch a cold that turns into pneumonia and will die May 27.

May 7 Pirates shortstop Glenn Wright pulls a solo triple play at second base in the ninth, grabbing Jim Bottomley's liner, stepping on the bag before Johnny Cooney can get back, and tagging Hornsby coming down from first base to end the game. The Pirates win, 10–9, after scoring six runs in the eighth.

May 8 Every NL city will have a Golden Jubilee Day. The first, between two of the original teams left from the 1876 season, at Boston, sees former Boston players from 1876 on hand. The Braves beat Chicago, 5–2.

May 30 Rogers Hornsby is named manager of the Cardinals, replacing Branch Rickey, who remains as general manager. Hornsby will be the only player-manager to win the triple crown, which he does by topping .400 for the third time in four years, hitting .403 with 39 home runs and 143 RBI. His .756 slugging average is still the NL's best.

September 23 Rogers Hornsby will win the MVP honor in the NL, rewriting the offensive record book while bringing the Cards home fourth. Other strong contenders are Kiki Cuyler, the Pirates top hitter at .357; the Giants' George Kelly; Pirates' shortstop Glenn Wright; Brooklyn's Dazzy Vance; and Dave Bancroft, who hit .319 and topped NL shortstops in fielding average while managing the fifth-place Braves.

October 7 Christy Mathewson dies of tuberculosis at Saranac Lake, New York, at the age of 45. At the time of his death he was part owner and president of the Boston Braves.

October 15 A steady downpour the day before has left the field a muddy mess. It's a short day for Vic Aldridge: three walks and two hits, and he's out of there with one out in the first. Walter Johnson takes a 4-0 lead to the mound. The Bucs clobber him for 15 hits, good for 24 total bases. The Senators make the most of seven hits, scoring seven runs, including Roger Peckinpaugh's home run, the 12th of the Series, a World Series record. Johnson would have fared better but for two more errors by shortstop Peckinpaugh, the MVP's seventh and eighth, still the World Series record for any position. Ray Kremer picks up his second win with a four-inning relief effort, as the Senators lose 9-7. The Series breaks all financial records, grossing almost $1.2 million. Winning shares are $5,332.72; losers' $3,734.60.

BOSTON		BROOKLYN		CHICAGO		CINCINNATI		NEW YORK		PHILADELPHIA		PITTSBURGH		ST.LOUIS	
M	D.Bancroft	M	W.Robinson	M	B.Killefer	M	J.Hendricks	M	J.McGraw	M	A.Fletcher	M	B.McKechnie	M	B.Rickey
1B	D.Burrus	1B	J.Fournier	M	W.Maranville	1B	W.Holke	M	H.Jennings	1B	C.Hawks	1B	G.Grantham	M	R.Hornsby
2B	D.Gautreau	2B	M.Stock	2B	M.Gibson	2B	H.Critz	M	J.McGraw	2B	B.Friberg	2B	E.Moore	1B	J.Bottomley
SS	D.Bancroft	SS	J.Mitchell	1B	C.Grimm	SS	I.Caveney	1B	B.Terry	SS	H.Sand	SS	G.Wright	2B	R.Hornsby
3B	W.Marriott	3B	J.Johnston	2B	S.Adams	3B	B.Pinelli	2B	G.Kelly	3B	C.Huber	3B	P.Traynor	SS	S.Toporcer
LF	D.Harris	LF	Z.Wheat	SS	R.Maranville	LF	B.Zitzmann	SS	T.Jackson	LF	G.Burns	LF	C.Barnhart	3B	L.Bell
CF	G.Felix	CF	E.Brown	3B	H.Freigau	CF	E.Roush	3B	F.Lindstrom	CF	G.Harper	CF	M.Carey	LF	R.Blades
RF	J.Welsh	RF	D.Cox	LF	A.Jahn	RF	C.Walker	LF	I.Meusel	RF	C.Williams	RF	K.Cuyler	CF	H.Mueller
C	F.Gibson	C	Z.Taylor	CF	M.Brooks	C	B.Hargrave	CF	B.Southworth	C	J.Wilson	C	E.Smith	RF	C.Hafey
				RF	C.Heathcote			RF	R.Youngs					C	B.O'Farrell
O	B.Neis	3	C.Tierney	C	G.Hartnett	1O	R.Bressler	C	F.Snyder	21	L.Fonseca	C	J.Gooch	O	R.Shinners
2S	E.Padgett	S	H.Ford			O	E.Smith			O	F.Leach	1	S.McInnis	O	J.Smith
C	M.O'Neil	C	H.DeBerry	O	T.Griffith	3	C.Dressen	32	F.Frisch	OS	R.Wrightstone	O	C.Bigbee	O	M.Flack
3	A.High	O	D.Loftus	C	M.Gonzalez	S2	S.Bohne	O	H.Wilson	2	B.Henline	2	J.Rawlings	S2	J.Cooney
O	L.Mann	23	A.High	1	B.Weis	1	A.Niehaus	C	H.Gowdy	O	J.Mokan	1	A.Niehaus	S	T.Thevenow
S2	B.Smith	C	C.Hargreaves	S3	P.Pittinger	C	I.Wingo	C	G.Hartley	S3	W.Kimmick	2	F.Thompson	C	W.Schmidt
C	O.Siemer	S	C.Corgan	3O	B.Friberg	C	E.Krueger	O	F.Walker	1	W.Holke	C	R.Spencer	O	T.Douthit
/2	H.Kibbie	/O	R.Hutson	C	J.Statz	O	J.Schultz	3	H.Groh	O	J.Schultz	/1	J.Ens	O	M.Gonzalez
O	F.Wilson	/O	T.Griffith	O	D.Grigsby	/C	A.Douglass	S	D.Farrell	/C	L.Wendell	/O	M.Haas	O	W.Holm
/O	S.Hogan	H	B.Barrett	S	I.McAuley	/C	F.Bruggy	C	M.Devine	/O	G.Durning			C	B.Warwick
/2	A.Hood	H	J.Standaert	/1	H.Miller	/1	J.Hudgens	/C	H.McMullen	/S	L.Metz	P	L.Meadows	/C	E.Vick
/2	R.Lucas			3	R.Michaels	/O	H.Myers	/O	A.Moore	/2	B.Meyer	P	R.Kremer	/S	H.Freigau
/2	H.Thomas	P	D.Vance	/O	A.Metzler	H	B.Fowler	/O	B.Carter			P	V.Aldridge	H	H.Myers
/O	C.Stengel	P	B.Grimes	/O	A.Munson	/O	O.Klee	H	E.Webb	P	J.Ring	P	J.Morrison	P	J.Haines
H	E.Sperber	P	R.Ehrhardt	/3	B.Barrett	/C	T.Sullivan	/O	P.Koehler	P	H.Carlson	P	E.Yde	P	B.Sherdel
/C	D.Cousineau	P	T.Osborne	/2	G.Staley					P	C.Mitchell	RP	T.Sheehan	P	F.Rhem
		P	J.Petty	/C	B.O'Farrell	P	P.Donohue	P	J.Scott	P	A.Decatur			P	A.Sothoron
P	J.Cooney	RP	B.Hubbell	/C	J.Churry	P	D.Luque	P	V.Barnes	P	J.Knight	P	B.Adams	P	A.Reinhart
P	J.Barnes			/O	C.Taylor	P	E.Rixey	RP	K.Greenfield	RP	H.Betts	P	R.Oldham		
P	L.Benton	P	L.Brown	/1	T.Kearns	P	R.Benton	P	J.Bentley	RP	J.Couch	P	B.Culloton	P	D.Songer
P	J.Genewich	P	J.Oeschger	P	M.Kerr	P	J.May	P	A.Nehf			/P	D.Songer	P	L.Dickerman
P	S.Graham	P	G.Cantrell			RP	H.Biemiller	RP	W.Huntzinger	R.Pierce		/P	L.Koupal	P	D.Mails
RP	R.Marquard	P	N.Greene	P	P.Alexander					P	D.Ulrich			P	E.Dyer
RP	I.Kamp	/P	B.McGraw	P	S.Blake			N.Brady	P	C.Willoughby			P	J.Stuart
		/P	H.Thormahlen	P	W.Cooper	P	C.Mays	P	F.Fitzsimmons	S.O'Neal			P	P.Day
P	R.Ryan	/P	J.Elliott	P	T.Kaufmann	P	T.Sheehan	P	H.McQuillan	D.Fillingim			/P	B.Hallahan
P	B.Vargus	/P	A.Rush	P	G.Bush	/P	M.Goodwin	P	J.Wisner	R.Crumpler			/P	E.Clough
/P	J.Batchelder	/P	J.Roberts	RP	V.Keen	/P	P.Dibut	/P	C.Davies	B.Vines			/P	G.Paulsen
/P	B.Anderson							/P	H.Baldwin	/P	B.Hubbell			
/P	F.Edwards			P	P.Jones									
/P	T.McNamara			P	E.Jacobs									
/P	J.Ogrodowski			/P	G.Milstead									
				P	H.Brett									
				/P	J.Brown									
				/P	G.Stueland									
				/P	B.Osborn									

TEAM	G	W	L	PCT	GB	R	OR	AB	H	2B	3B	HR	BB	SO	AVG	OBP	SLG	PRO	PRO+	BR	/A	PF	CHI	RC	SB	CS	SBA	SBR
PIT	153	95	58	.621		912	715	5372	1651	316	105	78	499	363	.307	.369	.449	.818	108	116	55	107	101	909	159	63	72	10
NY	152	86	66	.566	8.5	736	702	5327	1507	239	61	114	411	494	.283	.337	.415	.752	101	-26	3	96	100	742	79	65	55	-15
CIN	153	80	73	.523	15	690	643	5233	1490	221	90	44	409	327	.285	.339	.387	.726	93	-66	-49	98	100	680	108	107	50	-32
STL	153	77	76	.503	18	828	764	5329	1592	292	80	109	446	414	.299	.356	.445	.801	108	72	53	102	98	846	70	51	58	-10
BOS	153	70	83	.458	25	708	802	5365	1567	260	70	41	405	380	.292	.345	.390	.735	102	48	15	98	98	722	77	72	52	-20
PHI	153	68	85	.444	27	812	930	5412	1598	288	58	100	456	542	.295	.354	.425	.779	96	35	-37	109	99	814	48	59	45	-21
BRO	153	68	85	.444	27	786	866	5468	1617	250	86	64	437	383	.296	.351	.406	.757	102	-6	15	97	101	787	37	30	55	-7
CHI	154	68	86	.442	27.5	723	773	5353	1473	254	70	86	397	470	.275	.329	.397	.726	89	-77	-87	102	104	700	94	70	57	-14
TOT	612					6195		42859	12495	2120	614	636	3460	3373	.292	.348	.414	.762							672	517	57	-109

TEAM	CG	SH	SV	IP	H	H/G	HR	BB	SO	RAT	ERA	ERA+	OAV	OOB	PR	/A	PF	CPI	FA	E	DP	FW	PW	BW	SBW	DIF
PIT	77	2	13	1354²	1526	10.1	81	387	386	12.9	3.87	115	.287	.339	59	88	105	105	.964	224	171	-.9	8.2	5.1	2.2	3.8
NY	80	6	8	1354	1532	10.2	73	408	446	13.0	3.94	102	.289	.342	49	17	95	104	.968	199	129	.5	1.6	.3	-.1	7.8
CIN	92	11	12	1375¹	1447	9.5	35	324	437	11.8	3.38	121	.272	.317	135	110	96	95	.968	203	161	.3	10.3	-4.6	-1.7	-.8
STL	82	8	7	1335²	1480	10.0	86	470	428	13.4	4.36	99	.283	.347	-14	-7	101	96	.964	204	156	.3	-.7	5.0	.3	-4.4
BOS	77	5	4	1366²	1567	10.3	67	458	351	13.4	4.39	91	.291	.348	-19	-58	94	96	.964	221	145	-.7	-5.4	1.4	-.6	-1.2
PHI	69	8	9	1350²	1753	11.7	117	444	371	14.8	5.02	95	.315	.368	-114	-39	112	103	.966	211	147	-.1	-3.7	-3.5	-.7	-.6
BRO	82	4	4	1350²	1608	10.7	75	477	518	14.1	4.77	88	.301	.362	-76	-90	98	97	.966	210	130	-.0	-8.4	1.4	.6	-2.0
CHI	75	5	10	1370	1575	10.3	102	485	435	13.7	4.41	98	.292	.353	-21	-14	101	102	.969	198	161	.7	-1.3	-8.1	-.0	-.2
TOT	634	49	67	10857²		10.4				13.4	4.27		.292	.348					.966	1670	1200					

Runs
Cuyler-Pit 144
Hornsby-StL 133
Wheat-Bro 125
Traynor-Pit 114
Blades-StL 112

Hits
Bottomley-StL 227
Wheat-Bro 221
Cuyler-Pit 220
Hornsby-StL 203
Stock-Bro 202

Doubles
Bottomley-StL 44
Cuyler-Pit 43
Wheat-Bro 42
Hornsby-StL 41
Burrus-Bos 41

Triples
Cuyler-Pit 26
Walker-Cin 16
Roush-Cin 16
Fournier-Bro 16

Home Runs
Hornsby-StL 39
Hartnett-Chi 24
Fournier-Bro 22
Meusel-NY 21
Bottomley-StL 21

Total Bases
Hornsby-StL 381
Cuyler-Pit 369
Bottomley-StL 358
Wheat-Bro 333
Fournier-Bro 310

Runs Batted In
Hornsby-StL 143
Fournier-Bro 130
Bottomley-StL 128
Wright-Pit 121
Barnhart-Pit 114

Runs Produced
Hornsby-StL 237
Cuyler-Pit 228
Wheat-Bro 214
Traynor-Pit 214
Fournier-Bro 207

Bases On Balls
Fournier-Bro 86
Hornsby-StL 83
Moore-Pit 73
Youngs-NY 66
Carey-Pit 66

Batting Average
Hornsby-StL ...... .403
Bottomley-StL ...... .367
Wheat-Bro ...... .359
Cuyler-Pit ...... .357
Fournier-Bro ...... .350

On Base Percentage
Hornsby-StL ...... .489
Fournier-Bro ...... .446
Blades-StL ...... .423
Cuyler-Pit ...... .423
Carey-Pit ...... .418

Slugging Average
Hornsby-StL ...... .756
Cuyler-Pit ...... .598
Wrightstone-Phi ...... .591
Bottomley-StL ...... .578
Fournier-Bro ...... .569

Production
Hornsby-StL 1.245
Cuyler-Pit 1.021
Fournier-Bro 1.015
Bottomley-StL ...... .992
Blades-StL ...... .958

Adjusted Production
Hornsby-StL 208
Fournier-Bro 162
Cuyler-Pit 148
Bottomley-StL 147
Wheat-Bro 143

Batter Runs
Hornsby-StL 87.1
Cuyler-Pit 53.1
Fournier-Bro 50.1
Bottomley-StL 45.5
Wheat-Bro 35.0

Adjusted Batter Runs
Hornsby-StL 83.3
Fournier-Bro 53.8
Cuyler-Pit 43.5
Bottomley-StL 42.4
Wheat-Bro 38.3

Clutch Hitting Index
Barnhart-Pit 146
Traynor-Pit 117
Felix-Bos 115
E.Brown-Bro 114
Moore-Pit 112

Runs Created
Hornsby-StL 187
Cuyler-Pit 158
Bottomley-StL 145
Fournier-Bro 141
Wheat-Bro 134

Total Average
Hornsby-StL 1.539
Cuyler-Pit 1.141
Fournier-Bro 1.117
Bottomley-StL 1.025
Carey-Pit 1.011

Stolen Bases
Carey-Pit 46
Cuyler-Pit 41
Adams-Chi 26
Roush-Cin 22
Frisch-NY 21

Stolen Base Average
Smith-StL 90.9
Carey-Pit 80.7
Cuyler-Pit 75.9
Moore-Pit 73.1
Adams-Chi 68.4

Stolen Base Runs
Carey-Pit 7.2
Smith-StL 4.8
Cuyler-Pit 4.5
Stock-Bro 1.8
Grantham-Pit 1.8

Fielding Runs
Adams-Chi 28.1
Traynor-Pit 22.9
Critz-Cin 21.6
Pinelli-Cin 20.8
Kelly-NY 16.4

Total Player Rating
Hornsby-StL 6.0
Fournier-Bro 4.2
Cuyler-Pit 4.1
Bancroft-Bos 3.8
Traynor-Pit 3.5

Wins
Vance-Bro 22
Rixey-Cin 21
Donohue-Cin 21
Meadows-Pit 19

Win Percentage
Sherdel-StL ...... .714
Vance-Bro ...... .710
Aldridge-Pit ...... .682
Kremer-Pit ...... .680
Rixey-Cin ...... .656

Games
Morrison-Pit 44
Donohue-Cin 42
Bush-Chi 42
Osborne-Bro 41
Ring-Phi 21

Complete Games
Donohue-Cin 27
Vance-Bro 26
Rixey-Cin 22
Luque-Cin 22
Ring-Phi 21

Shutouts
Vance-Bro 4
Luque-Cin 4
Carlson-Phi 4
Donohue-Cin 3

Saves
Morrison-Pit 4
Bush-Chi 4

Innings Pitched
Donohue-Cin 301.0
Luque-Cin 291.0
Rixey-Cin 287.1
Ring-Phi 270.0
Vance-Bro 265.1

Fewest Hits/Game
Luque-Cin 8.13
Benton-Bos 8.35
Vance-Bro 8.38
Aldridge-Pit 9.20
Donohue-Cin 9.27

Fewest BB/Game
Alexander-Chi 1.11
Donohue-Cin 1.47
Rixey-Cin 1.47
Cooney-Bos 1.83
Sherdel-StL 1.89

Strikeouts
Vance-Bro 221
Luque-Cin 140
Ring-Phi 93
Blake-Chi 93
Aldridge-Pit 88

Strikeouts/Game
Vance-Bro 7.50
Luque-Cin 4.33
Sothoron-StL 3.87
Bush-Chi 3.76
Aldridge-Pit 3.71

Ratio
Luque-Cin 10.61
Donohue-Cin 10.79
Vance-Bro 10.96
Rixey-Cin 11.15
Alexander-Chi 11.52

Earned Run Average
Luque-Cin 2.63
Rixey-Cin 2.88
Reinhart-StL 3.05
Donohue-Cin 3.08
Benton-Bos 3.09

Adjusted ERA
Luque-Cin 156
Rixey-Cin 143
Sherdel-StL 139
Donohue-Cin 133
Benton-Bos 130

Opponents' Batting Avg.
Luque-Cin ...... .239
Benton-Bos ...... .249
Vance-Bro ...... .250
Donohue-Cin ...... .268
Scott-NY ...... .269

Opponents' On Base Pct.
Luque-Cin ...... .291
Donohue-Cin ...... .299
Vance-Bro ...... .304
Rixey-Cin ...... .307
Cooney-Bos ...... .312

Starter Runs
Luque-Cin 53.0
Rixey-Cin 44.2
Donohue-Cin 39.7
Scott-NY 29.6
Sherdel-StL 25.8

Adjusted Starter Runs
Luque-Cin 47.9
Rixey-Cin 39.2
Donohue-Cin 34.4
Sherdel-StL 27.0
Alexander-Chi 24.4

Clutch Pitching Index
Nehf-NY 122
Yde-Pit 117
Sherdel-StL 109
Rixey-Cin 108
Morrison-Pit 107

Relief Runs
Huntzinger-NY 5.5

Adjusted Relief Runs
Huntzinger-NY 3.9

Relief Ranking
Huntzinger-NY 3.2

Total Pitcher Index
Luque-Cin 6.1
Donohue-Cin 4.0
Rixey-Cin 3.6
Scott-NY 3.3
Sherdel-StL 2.6

Total Baseball Ranking
Luque-Cin 6.1
Hornsby-StL 6.0
Fournier-Bro 4.2
Cuyler-Pit 4.1
Donohue-Cin 4.0

February 10 At the AL meeting, a plan is adopted to alternate the site of future World Series openers by league rather than deciding it by a coin toss, with Games 1, 2, 6, and 7 in one park and 3, 4, 5 in the other, unless a ban on Sunday baseball interferes in one city.

April 14 Two future Hall of Famers make their major league debuts for the A's in the same game. Lefty Grove starts against Boston and leaves in the fourth after walking four and striking out nobody. He gives up five runs on six hits. In the eighth, Mickey Cochrane pinch-hits for catcher Cy Perkins, singles and stays in behind the plate while the A's go on to score nine runs in the last four innings to win 9-8 in 10 innings.

May 1 The A's introduce another future Hall of Famer, 17-year-old catcher Jimmie Foxx, who pinch hits and singles against Washington.

May 5 Ty Cobb is 6-for-6, including three home runs, in Detroit's 14-8 win over the Browns.

May 5 Everett Scott is benched by New York manager Miller Huggins, ending his 1,307-game playing streak. Pee Wee Wanninger replaces him at shortstop.

June 1 Lou Gehrig begins a consecutive-game streak that will surpass Everett Scott's mark by pinch-hitting for Pee Wee Wanninger, the shortstop who replaced Scott in the Yankees lineup. The next day, first baseman Wally Pipp shows up with a headache, and Gehrig takes over.

June 3 White Sox manager Eddie Collins makes hit No. 3,000 versus Detroit.

August 15 Little Dickie Kerr, the southpaw who won two games for the White Sox in the 1919 World Series, makes his first major league appearance since 1921. He has been playing semipro ball rather than accept Charles Comiskey's salary offer. When he relieves Red Faber in the third inning against the Tigers, play is stopped while admirers present him with a floral horseshoe.

August 29 After a night on the town, Babe Ruth shows up late for batting practice. Miller Huggins suspends Ruth and slaps a $5,000 fine on him for disobeying orders on the field and team rules off the field. In the showdown between the Bambino and the tiny manager, Jake Ruppert backs up his manager. Ruth is forced to apologize before he's reinstated nine days later. The day after his return to the lineup, Ruth hits home run number 300.

September 23 Washington shortstop Roger Peckinpaugh, a .294 hitter, is named the AL MVP with 45 points; A's outfielder Al Simmons is second with 41.

October 4 Harry Heilmann gets six hits in Detroit's doubleheader win over the Browns to edge out teammate Cobb for the batting crown, .393 to .389. Ty Cobb bats over .300 for the 20th time.

October 7 Walter Johnson (20-7) opens the World Series in Pittsburgh. A fifth-inning home run by Pie Traynor is the only damaging blow, as Johnson fans 10 of the heavy-hitting Bucs for a 4-1 win over Lee Meadows (19-10). Sam Rice, Joe Harris, and Ossie Bluege, with two hits each, drive in the Senators' runs.

October 10 For Game 3 it's clear but bitterly cold in Washington following a rainstorm that caused the game to be rescheduled. President Coolidge throws out the first ball. The Pirates hold a slim 3-2 lead after six. A walk and two singles score two in the eighth for Washington, and Firpo Marberry (8-6) closes it. Joe Harris has two hits for the third time; he'll lead the Senators with .440. Sam Rice makes a controversial game-saving play in the 8th, tumbling into the stands in the right corner to spear a long drive by Earl Smith. About 15 seconds later he emerges with the ball. Despite the Pirates' arguments that a fan might have given it to him, ump Cy Rigler calls Smith out. Questioned about it for the rest of his life, Rice leaves a letter, to be opened after his death (in 1974), in which he states: "At no time did I lose possession of the ball."

BOSTON	CHICAGO	CLEVELAND	DETROIT	NEW YORK	PHILADELPHIA	ST.LOUIS	WASHINGTON
M L.Fohl	M E.Collins	M T.Speaker	M T.Cobb	M M.Huggins	M C.Mack	M G.Sisler	M B.Harris
1B P.Todt	1B E.Sheely	1B G.Burns	1B L.Blue	1B L.Gehrig	1B J.Poole	1B G.Sisler	1B J.Judge
2B B.Wambsganss	2B E.Collins	2B C.Fewster	2B F.O'Rourke	2B A.Ward	2B M.Bishop	2B M.McManus	2B B.Harris
SS D.Lee	SS I.Davis	SS J.Sewell	SS J.Tavener	SS P.Wanninger	SS C.Galloway	SS B.LaMotte	SS R.Peckinpaugh
3B D.Prothro	3B W.Kamm	3B R.Lutzke	3B F.Haney	3B J.Dugan	3B S.Hale	3B G.Robertson	3B O.Bluege
LF R.Carlyle	LF B.Falk	LF C.Jamieson	LF A.Wingo	LF B.Meusel	LF B.Lamar	LF K.Williams	LF G.Goslin
CF I.Flagstead	CF J.Mostil	CF T.Speaker	CF T.Cobb	CF E.Combs	CF A.Simmons	CF B.Jacobson	CF E.McNeely
RF I.Boone	RF H.Hooper	RF P.McNulty	RF H.Heilmann	RF B.Ruth	RF B.Miller	RF H.Rice	RF S.Rice
C V.Picinich	C R.Schalk	C G.Myatt	C J.Bassler	C B.Bengough	C M.Cochrane	C L.Dixon	C M.Ruel
O T.Vache	2O B.Barrett	32 F.Spurgeon	O H.Manush	1 W.Pipp	32 J.Dykes	O W.Gerber	1O J.Harris
O D.Williams	C B.Crouse	O C.Lee	O B.Fothergill	2S E.Johnson	C F.Welch	S P.Hargrave	C H.Severeid
3 H.Ezzell	O S.Harris	C H.Summa	2 L.Burke	C W.Schang	C C.Perkins	O J.Tobin	S E.Scott
2 B.Rogell	/S J.Kane	C L.Sewell	C L.Woodall	32 S.Shanks	C W.French	O J.Evans	O N.Leibold
C J.Bischoff	O R.Elsh	3 J.Hodapp	32 B.Jones	O B.Veach	1 R.Holt	C H.Severeid	O S.Adams
C J.Heving	C J.Grabowski	R.Knode	S T.Rigney	S M.Koenig	/O B.Bagwell	C T.Rego	O B.Veach
S B.Connolly	C J.Bischoff	J.Klugmann	1 J.Neun	C S.O'Neill	/S C.Husta	/3 J.Austin	S B.Tate
O S.Rosenthal	/C M.Archdeacon	R.Stephenson	3 J.Warner	S E.Scott	/C C.Berry		/1 M.Shirley
O T.Jenkins	H B.Clancy	I.Eichrodt	/2 C.Gehringer	O W.Witt	S R.Smith		/3 M.McNally
S J.Rothrock	/O J.Mallonee	H.Hendrick	/C O.Stanage	/C R.Luebbe	C J.Foxx		O T.Jeanes
C A.Stokes	/C L.Tankersley	R.Walters	H A.Harrington	/1 F.Merkle	/2 D.Gautreau		S S.Stewart
2 M.Herrera	/1 C.Tolson	/1 C.Tolson	/C F.Hofmann	/1 J.Keesey		/O W.Matthews
S H.Welch		/C F.McCrea		H L.Durocher	/S C.Engle		/S B.Myer
/S T.Gross	P T.Lyons	/2 G.Bedford	P E.Whitehill	/3 H.Odom	P E.Rommel		/C P.Hargrave
/1 J.Harris	P R.Faber	/2 D.Ussat	P H.Dauss	P H.Pennock	P S.Harriss		/1 F.McGee
/S C.Geygan	P T.Blankenship	P S.Smith	P K.Holloway	P S.Jones	P S.Gray		H R.Carlyle
/O B.Veach	P S.Thurston	P G.Uhle	P L.Stoner	P U.Shocker	P L.Grove		P S.Coveleski
/O S.Collins	P C.Robertson	P B.Karr	P R.Collins	P W.Hoyt	P R.Walberg		P W.Johnson
P H.Ehmke	RP S.Connally	P J.Miller	RP J.Doyle	P B.Shawkey	P S.Baumgartner		P D.Ruether
P T.Wingfield	P M.Cvengros	P J.Shaute	P E.Wells	RP H.Johnson	/P J.Quinn		P T.Zachary
P R.Ruffing	/P J.Edwards	P B.Speece	P D.Leonard	RP A.Ferguson	/P A.Stokes		RP F.Marberry
P P.Zahniser	/P D.Kerr	P B.Cole	RP O.Carroll	/P B.Shields	P F.Heimach		RP V.Gregg
P J.Quinn	/P L.Mangum	P J.Edwards	/P S.Johnson	/P G.Braxton	/P E.Andrews		RP A.Russell
RP B.Ross	/P F.Mack	P C.Yowell	/P B.Moore	/P W.Beall	/P T.Glass		/P A.Ferguson
RP O.Fuhr	/P T.Riviere	/P D.Levsen		/P J.Marquis	/P L.Willis		P G.Mogridge
/P R.Francis	/P K.Ash	/P R.Benge		/P R.Francis			P C.Ogden
/P C.Fullerton	/P J.Freeze	/P L.Roy		/P C.Caldwell			P W.Ballou
/P R.Kallio	/P C.Bender						/P H.Kelley
/P A.Ferguson							/P L.Thomas
/P J.Kiefer							/P J.Lyle
/P J.Lucey							/P S.Pumpelly
/P H.Neubauer							
/P B.Adams							

TEAM	G	W	L	PCT	GB	R	OR	AB	H	2B	3B	HR	BB	SO	AVG	OBP	SLG	PRO	PRO+	BR	/A	PF	CHI	RC	SB	CS	SBA	SBR
WAS	152	96	55	.636		829	670	5206	1577	251	71	56	533	427	.303	.373	.411	.784	106	39	56	98	100	815	135	92	59	-15
PHI	153	88	64	.579	8.5	831	713	5399	1659	298	79	76	453	432	.307	.364	.434	.798	101	54	-2	107	97	856	67	60	53	-16
STL	154	82	71	.536	15	900	906	5440	1620	304	64	110	498	375	.298	.360	.439	.799		52	8	105	105	859	85	78	52	-21
DET	156	81	73	.526	16.5	903	829	5371	1621	277	84	50	640	386	.302	.379	.413	.792	109	63	76	99	102	872	97	63	61	-9
CHI	154	79	75	.513	18.5	811	770	5224	1482	299	59	38	662	405	.284	.370	.385	.755	102	-7	-36	95	101	782	131	87	60	-13
CLE	155	70	84	.455	27.5	782	817	5436	1613	285	58	52	520	379	.297	.361	.399	.760	97	-12	-18	101	98	795	90	77	54	-19
NY	156	69	85	.448	28.5	706	774	5353	1471	247	74	110	470	482	.275	.336	.410	.746	96	-61	-48	98	97	739	69	73	49	-23
BOS	152	47	105	.309	49.5	639	922	5166	1375	257	64	41	513	422	.266	.336	.364	.700	83	-131	-130	100	100	647	42	56	43	-21
TOT	616					6401		42595	12418	2218	557	533	4289	3308	.292	.360	.408	.768							716	586	55	-137

TEAM	CG	SH	SV	IP	H	H/G	HR	BB	SO	RAT	ERA	ERA+	OAV	OOB	PR	/A	PF	CPI	FA	E	DP	FW	PW	BW	SBW	DIF
WAS	69	10	21	1358¹	1434	9.5	49	543	463	13.3	3.70	114	.278	.351	105	79	96	107	.972	170	166	1.8	7.3	5.2	.2	6.0
PHI	61	8	18	1381²	1468	9.6	60	544	495	13.3	3.87	120	.276	.347	81	119	106	101	.966	211	148	-.6	11.0	-.2	.1	1.6
STL	67	7	10	1379²	1588	10.4	99	675	419	15.0	4.92	95	.298	.380	-80	-39	106	102	.964	226	164	-1.4	-3.6	.7	-.4	10.1
DET	66	2	18	1383²	1582	10.3	70	556	419	14.2	4.61	94	.296	.366	-32	-46	98	99	.972	173	143	1.9	-4.3	7.0	.8	-1.4
CHI	71	12	13	1385²	1579	10.3	69	489	374	13.6	4.29	97	.295	.356	17	-21	95	102	.968	200	162	.2	-1.9	3.3	.4	.0
CLE	93	6	9	1372¹	1604	10.5	41	493	345	14.0	4.49	98	.296	.359	-15	-9	101	95	.967	210	146	-.4	-.8	-1.7	-.2	-4.0
NY	80	8	13	1387²	1560	10.1	78	505	492	13.6	4.33	98	.289	.353	10	-11	97	99	.974	160	150	2.7	-1.0	-4.4	-.5	-4.7
BOS	68	6	6	1326²	1615	11.0	67	510	310	14.7	4.97	92	.308	.374	-84	-62	103	98	.957	271	150	-4.2	-5.7	-12.0	-.4	-6.6
TOT	575	59	108	10975²		10.2				14.0	4.39		.292	.360					.968	1621	1229					

Runs		Hits		Doubles		Triples		Home Runs		Total Bases	
Mostil-Chi	135	Simmons-Phi	253	McManus-StL	44	Goslin-Was	20	Meusel-NY	33	Simmons-Phi	392
Simmons-Phi	122	Rice-Was	227	Simmons-Phi	43	Mostil-Chi	16	Williams-StL	25	Meusel-NY	338
Combs-NY	117	Heilmann-Det	225	Sheely-Chi	43	Sisler-StL	15	Ruth-NY	25	Goslin-Was	329
Goslin-Was	116	Sisler-StL	224	Burns-Cle	41			Simmons-Phi	24	Heilmann-Det	326
Rice-Was	111	J.Sewell-Cle	204					Gehrig-NY	20	Sisler-StL	311

Runs Batted In		Runs Produced		Bases On Balls		Batting Average		On Base Percentage		Slugging Average	
Meusel-NY	138	Simmons-Phi	227	Mostil-Chi	90	Heilmann-Det	.393	Speaker-Cle	.479	Williams-StL	.613
Heilmann-Det	134	Heilmann-Det	218	Kamm-Chi	90	Speaker-Cle	.389	Cobb-Det	.468	Simmons-Phi	.599
Simmons-Phi	129	Goslin-Was	211	Collins-Chi	87	Simmons-Phi	.387	Collins-Chi	.461	Cobb-Det	.598
Goslin-Was	113	Meusel-NY	206	Bishop-Phi	87	Cobb-Det	.378	Heilmann-Det	.457	Speaker-Cle	.578
Sheely-Chi	111	Rice-Was	197	Blue-Det	83	Wingo-Det	.370	Wingo-Det	.456	Heilmann-Det	.569

Production		Adjusted Production		Batter Runs		Adjusted Batter Runs		Clutch Hitting Index		Runs Created	
Cobb-Det	1.066	Cobb-Det	171	Heilmann-Det	52.5	Heilmann-Det	54.6	Galloway-Phi	149	Simmons-Phi	155
Speaker-Cle	1.057	Speaker-Cle	166	Simmons-Phi	51.4	Cobb-Det	47.0	Blue-Det	136	Heilmann-Det	149
Heilmann-Det	1.026	Heilmann-Det	161	Speaker-Cle	47.0	Speaker-Cle	46.1	Sheely-Chi	127	Goslin-Was	131
Simmons-Phi	1.018	Wingo-Det	151	Cobb-Det	45.3	Simmons-Phi	42.1	Collins-Chi	123	Speaker-Cle	123
Wingo-Det	.983	Simmons-Phi	146	Wingo-Det	35.3	Wingo-Det	36.8	B.Harris-Was	120	Cobb-Det	118

Total Average		Stolen Bases		Stolen Base Average		Stolen Base Runs		Fielding Runs		Total Player Rating	
Speaker-Cle	1.231	Mostil-Chi	43	Blue-Det	79.2	Goslin-Was	3.3	Flagstead-Bos	19.9	Speaker-Cle	4.5
Cobb-Det	1.206	Goslin-Was	27	Goslin-Was	77.1	Haney-Det	2.7	J.Sewell-Cle	16.3	J.Sewell-Cle	3.8
Heilmann-Det	1.113	Rice-Was	26	Collins-Chi	76.0	Blue-Det	2.7	O'Rourke-Det	14.6	Heilmann-Det	3.7
Wingo-Det	1.041			Rice-Was	70.3	Collins-Chi	2.1	Goslin-Was	13.6	Goslin-Was	3.7
Collins-Chi	1.028			Mostil-Chi	68.3	Peckinpaugh-Was	1.5	Ruel-Was	11.5	Cobb-Det	3.3

Wins		Win Percentage		Games		Complete Games		Shutouts		Saves	
Rommel-Phi	21	Coveleski-Was	.800	Marberry-Was	55	Smith-Cle	22	Lyons-Chi	5	Marberry-Was	15
Lyons-Chi	21	Johnson-Was	.741	Walberg-Phi	53	Ehmke-Bos	22	Gray-Phi	4	Doyle-Det	8
Johnson-Was	20	Ruether-Was	.720	Vangilder-StL	52	Pennock-NY	21	Giard-StL	4	Connally-Chi	8
Coveleski-Was	20	Blankenship-Chi	.680	Rommel-Phi	52	Lyons-Chi	19			Walberg-Phi	7
Harriss-Phi	19	Rommel-Phi	.677	Pennock-NY	47	Wingfield-Bos	18				

Innings Pitched		Fewest Hits/Game		Fewest BB/Game		Strikeouts		Strikeouts/Game		Ratio	
Pennock-NY	277.0	Blankenship-Chi	8.46	Smith-Cle	1.82	Grove-Phi	116	Grove-Phi	5.30	Pennock-NY	11.05
Lyons-Chi	262.2	Johnson-Was	8.53	Quinn-Bos-Phi	1.85	Johnson-Was	108	Johnson-Was	4.24	Blankenship-Chi	11.13
Rommel-Phi	261.0	Coveleski-Was	8.59	Shocker-NY	2.14	Harriss-Phi	95	Shawkey-NY	3.92	Coveleski-Was	11.39
Ehmke-Bos	260.2	Pennock-NY	8.68	Faber-Chi	2.23	Ehmke-Bos	95	Walberg-Phi	3.85	Gray-Phi	11.71
Wingfield-Bos	254.1	Gray-Phi	8.79	Pennock-NY	2.31	Jones-NY	92	Gray-Phi	3.54	Johnson-Was	11.87

Earned Run Average		Adjusted ERA		Opponents' Batting Avg.		Opponents' On Base Pct.		Starter Runs		Adjusted Starter Runs	
Coveleski-Was	2.84	Coveleski-Was	149	Johnson-Was	.250	Pennock-NY	.303	Pennock-NY	44.2	Pennock-NY	40.2
Pennock-NY	2.96	Pennock-NY	144	Blankenship-Chi	.253	Blankenship-Chi	.308	Coveleski-Was	41.7	Coveleski-Was	37.2
Blankenship-Chi	3.03	Gray-Phi	142	Pennock-NY	.254	Coveleski-Was	.312	Blankenship-Chi	35.3	Harriss-Phi	32.5
Johnson-Was	3.07	Johnson-Was	138	Coveleski-Was	.255	Johnson-Was	.317	Johnson-Was	33.8	Gray-Phi	31.2
Dauss-Det	3.16	Blankenship-Chi	137	Gray-Phi	.260	Gray-Phi	.319	Lyons-Chi	33.3	Johnson-Was	29.6

Clutch Pitching Index		Relief Runs		Adjusted Relief Runs		Relief Ranking		Total Pitcher Index		Total Baseball Ranking	
Dauss-Det	119	Marberry-Was	9.6	Marberry-Was	7.8	Marberry-Was	13.4	Johnson-Was	4.3	Speaker-Cle	4.5
Shocker-NY	114	Gregg-Was	2.3	Gregg-Was	.9	Gregg-Was	.5	Pennock-NY	3.6	Johnson-Was	4.3
Zachary-Was	113							Harriss-Phi	3.6	J.Sewell-Cle	3.8
Lyons-Chi	111							Rommel-Phi	3.3	Heilmann-Det	3.7
Shawkey-NY	110							Dauss-Det	3.0	Goslin-Was	3.7

January 30 The major league Rules Committee agrees that pitchers may have access to a resin bag. On February 8 the AL will refuse to permit its use but changes its policy in April.

April 27 In the Giants' 9-8 win over the Phillies, 17-year-old Mel Ott makes his first appearance pinch-hitting for Jimmy Ring. He strikes out. Ott won't play regularly till 1927.

May 1* Satchel Paige, 19 years old, makes his debut in the Negro Southern League, pitching Chattanooga to a 5-4 win over Birmingham.

May 23 Hack Wilson becomes the first player to hit a ball off the Wrigley Field scoreboard, smacking a fifth-inning home run to start a route of the Braves. The Cubs score seven runs in the eighth inning to win 14–8.

June 22 The Cardinals pick up 39-year-old Grover Alexander on waivers from the Cubs to help in the pennant chase. He'll be 9-7 down the stretch.

July 22 The Reds pound four triples in the second inning, including two by Curt Walker, against the Braves, tying a major league record, and go on to win, 13-3. Walker's feat, the first since 1900, won't be repeated until Al Zarilla does it in 1946.

August 15 The Braves are at Ebbets Field with Brooklyn's Hank DeBerry on third base, Dazzy Vance on second base, and Chick Fewster on first base. Babe Herman drives the ball against the right field wall, and DeBerry scores. Vance holds up, then rounds third base headed for home. Fewster stops at third base. The right fielder throws home and traps Vance, who heads back to third base. Herman slides into third base as Fewster steps off. Herman is out for passing a base runner. Fewster, thinking he's out, too, walks off with Babe, and gets tagged out. Vance, still on third base, later admits it was his fault, but Herman, who doubles into a double play, gets the blame.

October 9 Grover Alexander scatters eight hits in Game 6 while the Cards tee off on Bob Shawkey (8-6), Urban Shocker, and Myles Thomas for 10 runs and 13 hits in a 10-2 romp.

October 10 Only 38,093 show up at the Stadium for the deciding World Series contest. Grover Alexander, possibly sleeping off a hangover in the bullpen, barely notices as Jess Haines take a 3-2 lead over Waite Hoyt. Haines weakens in the last of the seventh; three walks put Earle Combs, Bob Meusel, and Lou Gehrig on base with two out and Tony Lazzeri at the plate. Hornsby waves in Alexander. On a 1-1 count Lazzeri hits a line drive into the left-field seats, a few feet to the foul side of the pole, then swings and misses for strike three. Alexander sets the Yanks down in order until Babe Ruth draws his 11th walk with two out in the ninth, and is thrown out trying to steal second base. The Cards have their first World Championship.

December 5 Cardinals catcher Bob O'Farrell is named NL MVP. O'Farrell caught 146 games and batted .293. He polls 79 points. Reds second baseman Hughie Critz is runner-up with 60. Critz set a major league record with 588 assists, which will be topped by Frank Frisch with 643 in 1927.

December 20 Rogers Hornsby is traded from the Cardinals to the New York Giants for Frankie Frisch and pitcher Jimmy Ring.

BOSTON		BROOKLYN		CHICAGO		CINCINNATI		NEW YORK		PHILADELPHIA		PITTSBURGH		ST. LOUIS	
M	D.Bancroft	M	W.Robinson	M	J.McCarthy	M	J.Hendricks	M	J.McGraw	M	A.Fletcher	M	B.McKechnie	M	R.Hornsby
1B	D.Burrus	1B	B.Herman	1B	C.Grimm	1B	W.Pipp	1B	G.Kelly	1B	J.Bentley	1B	G.Grantham	1B	J.Bottomley
2B	D.Gautreau	2B	C.Fewster	2B	S.Adams	2B	H.Critz	2B	F.Frisch	2B	B.Friberg	2B	H.Rhyne	2B	R.Hornsby
SS	D.Bancroft	SS	J.Butler	SS	J.Cooney	SS	F.Emmer	SS	T.Jackson	SS	H.Sand	SS	G.Wright	SS	T.Thevenow
3B	A.High	3B	W.Marriott	3B	H.Freigau	3B	C.Dressen	3B	F.Lindstrom	3B	C.Huber	3B	P.Traynor	3B	L.Bell
LF	E.Brown	LF	Z.Wheat	LF	R.Stephenson	LF	C.Christensen	LF	I.Meusel	LF	J.Mokan	LF	K.Cuyler	LF	R.Blades
CF	J.Smith	CF	G.Felix	CF	H.Wilson	CF	E.Roush	CF	T.Tyson	CF	F.Leach	CF	M.Carey	CF	T.Douthit
RF	J.Welsh	RF	D.Cox	RF	C.Heathcote	RF	C.Walker	RF	R.Youngs	RF	C.Williams	RF	P.Waner	RF	B.Southworth
C	Z.Taylor	C	M.O'Neil	C	G.Hartnett	C	B.Hargrave	C	P.Florence	C	J.Wilson	C	E.Smith	C	B.O'Farrell
3S	E.Taylor	O	M.Jacobson	O	M.Gonzalez	1O	R.Bressler	1O	B.Terry	O	A.Nixon	O	J.Gooch	O	C.Hafey
O	F.Wilson	1	J.Fournier	O	P.Scott	O	V.Picinich	S	D.Farrell	13	R.Wrightstone	O	C.Barnhart	O	H.Mueller
2S	E.Moore	S2	R.Maranville	O	J.Kelly	3S	B.Pinelli	C	F.Snyder	2	G.Harper	2	J.Rawlings	O	W.Holm
O	L.Mann	C	C.Hargreaves	O	J.Munson	S	H.Ford	O	H.McMullen	1	R.Grimes	2	E.Moore	2	S.Toporcer
1P	J.Cooney	23	S.Bohne	2	C.Beck	O	B.Zitzmann	3	A.Moore	1	D.Attreau	1	S.McInnis	2	J.Flowers
O	B.Neis	C	H.DeBerry	1	C.Tolson	O	S.Bohne	O	J.Johnston	3	B.Rice	2	J.Cronin	C	E.Vick
C	O.Siemer	23	J.Standaert	S	R.Shannon	/1	J.Hudgens	O	M.Ott	O	D.Sothern	O	C.Bigbee	/C	B.Warwick
3	J.Johnston	O	M.Carey	O	M.Brooks	O	E.Allen	2S	A.Cohen	C	B.Jonnard	O	W.Mueller	H	J.Smith
C	F.Gibson	O	W.Witt	/S	H.Schreiber	/C	I.Wingo	/3	H.Groh	/1	W.Kimmick	O	F.Brickell	P	F.Rhem
/C	S.Hogan	/O	M.Clabaugh	/3	J.Graves	/S	E.Scott	C	G.Hartley	/3	E.Cotter	C	R.Spencer	P	B.Sherdel
/3	H.Riconda	/2	S.Dowd	/3	J.Churry	/3	D.Prothro	/O	B.Carter	/S	G.Stutz	/O	E.Murphy	P	J.Haines
/C	S.Womack	/2	M.Stock	/2	R.Michaels	/2	H.Carter	/C	J.Cummings	/S	J.Buskey	/O	A.Comorosky	P	V.Keen
P	L.Benton	P	J.Petty	P	C.Root	H	C.Sukeforth	/2	S.Slayback	/1	L.Dunham	P	R.Kremer	P	P.Alexander
P	J.Genewich	P	B.Grimes	P	S.Blake	P	P.Donohue	/2	F.Thompson	/2	L.Wendell	P	L.Meadows	RP	S.Johnson
P	B.Smith	P	D.McWeeny	P	T.Kaufmann	P	C.Mays	/O	M.Smith	/2	C.Keating	P	V.Aldridge	P	A.Reinhart
P	J.Werts	P	B.McGraw	P	P.Jones	P	D.Luque	/C	J.Hamby	P	H.Carlson	P	E.Yde	P	H.Bell
P	G.Mogridge	P	D.Vance	P	G.Bush	P	E.Rixey	H	J.Connell	P	W.Dean	P	D.Songer	P	B.Hallahan
P	B.Hearn	RP	R.Ehrhardt	P	B.Osborn	P	J.May	/C	J.Boyle	P	C.Mitchell	P	J.Morrison	P	A.Sothoron
P	H.Goldsmith	P	J.Barnes	P	B.Piercy	P	R.Lucas	P	J.Scott	P	C.Willoughby	P	J.Bush	/P	W.Huntzinger
P	S.Graham	P	G.Boehler	/P	W.Cooper	/P	R.Meeker	P	K.Greenfield	P	D.Ulrich	P	R.Oldham	/P	E.Dyer
/P	F.Edwards	/P	L.Williams	/P	G.Milstead	/P	A.Nehf	P	F.Fitzsimmons	RP	R.Pierce	/P	C.Hill	/P	E.Clough
/P	R.Ryan	/P	D.Stryker	/P	P.Alexander	/P	P.Day	P	V.Barnes	RP	E.Baecht	P	B.Adams	/P	D.Mails
/P	B.Vargus	/P	R.Moss	/P	W.Huntzinger	/P	M.Holland	P	J.Ring	/P	J.Knight	/P	T.Sheehan		
				/P	J.Welch	H	B.Springer	RP	C.Davies	P	E.Maun	/P	L.Koupal		
						P	R.Meadows	P	H.McQuillan	/P	L.Taber	/P	C.Nichols		
								/P	J.Wisner	/P	M.Kelly	/P	R.Mahaffey		
								/P	J.Poetz	/P	P.Rambo	/P	B.Culloton		
								/P	T.McNamara	/P	A.Decatur				
								/P	J.Bentley	/P	R.Yarnall				
								/P	A.Nehf						
								/P	N.Porter						
								/P	A.Smith						

TEAM	G	W	L	PCT	GB	R	OR	AB	H	2B	3B	HR	BB	SO	AVG	OBP	SLG	PRO	PRO+	BR	/A	PF	CHI	RC	SB	CS	SBA	SBR
STL	156	89	65	.578		817	678	5381	1541	259	82	90	478	518	.286	.348	.415	.763	107	76	46	104	102	770	83			
CIN	157	87	67	.565	2	747	651	5320	1541	242	120	35	454	333	.290	.349	.400	.749	110	52	72	97	97	738	51			
PIT	157	84	69	.549	4.5	769	689	5312	1514	243	106	44	434	350	.285	.343	.396	.739	99	28	-11	105	104	713	91			
CHI	155	82	72	.532	7	682	602	5229	1453	291	49	66	445	447	.278	.338	.390	.728	100	7	-2	101	96	685	85			
NY	151	74	77	.490	13.5	663	668	5167	1435	214	58	73	339	420	.278	.325	.384	.709	97	-36	-28	99	104	631	94			
BRO	155	71	82	.464	17.5	623	705	5130	1348	246	62	40	475	464	.263	.328	.358	.686	91	-65	-56	99	100	607	76			
BOS	153	66	86	.434	22	624	719	5216	1444	209	62	16	426	348	.277	.335	.350	.685	99	-66	-10	91	99	612	81			
PHI	152	58	93	.384	29.5	687	900	5254	1479	244	50	75	422	479	.281	.337	.390	.727	96	5	-31	105	98	683	47			
TOT	618					5612		42009	11755	1948	589	439	3473	3359	.280	.338	.386	.724							608			

TEAM	CG	SH	SV	IP	H	H/G	HR	BB	SO	RAT	ERA	ERA+	OAV	OOB	PR	/A	PF	CPI	FA	E	DP	FW	PW	BW	SBW	DIF
STL	90	10	6	1398²	1423	9.2	76	397	365	11.8	3.67	106	.269	.322	24	36	102	96	.969	198	141	.3	3.6	4.5		3.6
CIN	88	14	8	1408²	1449	9.3	40	324	424	11.5	3.42	108	.271	.316	64	42	97	95	.972	183	160	1.3	4.2	7.1		-2.6
PIT	83	12	18	1379¹	1422	9.3	50	455	387	12.5	3.67	107	.272	.334	24	42	103	99	.965	220	161	-.9	4.2	-1.1		5.3
CHI	77	13	14	1378¹	1407	9.2	39	486	508	12.6	3.26	118	.273	.340	87	89	101	113	.974	162	174	2.4	8.8	-.2		-6.0
NY	61	4	15	1341²	1370	9.2	70	427	419	12.2	3.77	100	.269	.328	8	-3	98	96	.970	186	150	.7	-.3	-2.8		.9
BRO	83	5	9	1361²	1440	9.5	50	472	517	12.8	3.82	100	.276	.339	1	0	100	98	.963	229	95	-1.5	.0	-5.5		1.6
BOS	60	9	9	1365¹	1536	10.1	46	455	408	13.4	4.01	88	.294	.354	-28	-71	93	100	.967	208	150	-.5	-7.0	-1.0		-1.5
PHI	68	5	5	1334¹	1699	11.5	68	454	331	14.7	5.03	82	.315	.371	-179	-133	108	98	.964	224	153	-1.5	-13.1	-3.1		.2
TOT	610	72	84	10968		9.6				12.7	3.82		.280	.338					.968	1610	1184					

Runs		Hits		Doubles		Triples		Home Runs		Total Bases	
Cuyler-Pit	113	Brown-Bos	201	Bottomley-StL	40	Waner-Pit	22	Wilson-Chi	21	Bottomley-StL	305
Waner-Pit	101	Cuyler-Pit	197	Roush-Cin	37	Walker-Cin	20	Bottomley-StL	19	L.Bell-StL	301
Southworth-NY-StL	99	Adams-Chi	193	Wilson-Chi	36	Traynor-Pit	17	Williams-Phi	18	Wilson-Chi	285
Sand-Phi	99	L.Bell-StL	189					L.Bell-StL	17	Waner-Pit	283
								Southworth-NY-StL	16	Cuyler-Pit	282

Runs Batted In		Runs Produced		Bases On Balls		Batting Average		On Base Percentage		Slugging Average	
Bottomley-StL	120	Bottomley-StL	199	Wilson-Chi	69	Hargrave-Cin	353	Waner-Pit	.413	Williams-Phi	.568
Wilson-Chi	109	Cuyler-Pit	197	Waner-Pit	66	Christensen-Cin	350	Blades-StL	.409	Wilson-Chi	.539
L.Bell-StL	100	Wilson-Chi	185	Sand-Phi	66	Smith-Pit	346	Wilson-Chi	.406	Waner-Pit	.528
Southworth-NY-StL	99	Southworth-NY-StL	182	Bancroft-Bos	64	Williams-Phi	345	Grantham-Pit	.400	Hargrave-Cin	.525
Pipp-Cin	99	Hornsby-StL	178	Blades-StL	62	Waner-Pit	336	Bancroft-Bos	.399	L.Bell-StL	.518

Production		Adjusted Production		Batter Runs		Adjusted Batter Runs		Clutch Hitting Index		Runs Created	
Wilson-Chi	.944	Wilson-Chi	150	Waner-Pit	39.5	Wilson-Chi	37.9	Butler-Bro	125	Waner-Pit	115
Waner-Pit	.941	Waner-Pit	144	Wilson-Chi	39.2	Waner-Pit	33.6	Pipp-Cin	122	Wilson-Chi	115
L.Bell-StL	.901	Herman-Bro	136	L.Bell-StL	31.6	L.Bell-StL	27.4	Hornsby-StL	116	L.Bell-StL	112
Grantham-Pit	.890	L.Bell-StL	135	Williams-Phi	29.8	Williams-Phi	26.0	Thevenow-StL	116	Bottomley-StL	109
Herman-Bro	.875	Grantham-Pit	131	Bottomley-StL	25.2	Herman-Bro	23.7	Burrus-Bos	116	Cuyler-Pit	105

Total Average		Stolen Bases		Stolen Base Average		Stolen Base Runs		Fielding Runs		Total Player Rating	
Wilson-Chi	1.031	Cuyler-Pit	35					Critz-Cin	24.0	Waner-Pit	3.1
Waner-Pit	1.022	Adams-Chi	27					Friberg-Phi	22.4	Wilson-Chi	3.0
Grantham-Pit	.938	Frisch-NY	23					Cooney-Chi	19.4	Bancroft-Bos	2.7
Blades-StL	.938	Douthit-StL	23					Thevenow-StL	18.4	O'Farrell-StL	2.7
L.Bell-StL	.929	Youngs-NY	21					Douthit-StL	17.8	Jackson-NY	2.6

Wins		Win Percentage		Games		Complete Games		Shutouts		Saves	
Rhem-StL	20	Kremer-Pit	.769	Scott-NY	50	Mays-Cin	24	Donohue-Cin	5	Davies-NY	6
Meadows-Pit	20	Rhem-StL	.741	Willoughby-Phi	47	Petty-Bro	23	B.Smith-Bos	4	Scott-NY	5
Kremer-Pit	20	Meadows-Pit	.690	Donohue-Cin	47	Root-Chi	21	Blake-Chi	4	Kremer-Pit	5
Donohue-Cin	20	Mays-Cin	.613	Ulrich-Phi	45	Rhem-StL	20			Ehrhardt-Bro	4
Mays-Cin	19	Donohue-Cin	.588	May-Cin	45	Carlson-Phi	20				

Innings Pitched		Fewest Hits/Game		Fewest BB/Game		Strikeouts		Strikeouts/Game		Ratio	
										Alexander-Chi-StL	
Donohue-Cin	285.2	Petty-Bro	8.03	Donohue-Cin	1.23	Vance-Bro	140	Vance-Bro	7.46		10.06
Mays-Cin	281.0	Greenfield-NY	8.33	Alexander-Chi-StL	1.39	Root-Chi	127	May-Cin	5.53	Petty-Bro	10.71
Petty-Bro	275.2	Rhem-StL	8.41	Carlson-Phi	1.58	May-Cin	103	Jones-Chi	4.49	Kremer-Pit	10.74
Root-Chi	271.1	Jones-Chi	8.48	Mays-Cin	1.70	Benton-Bos	103	Blake-Chi	4.33	Donohue-Cin	10.90
Carlson-Phi	267.1	Bush-Chi	8.52	Lucas-Cin	1.75	Petty-Bro	101	Root-Chi	4.21	Mays-Cin	10.99

Earned Run Average		Adjusted ERA		Opponents' Batting Avg.		Opponents' On Base Pct.		Starter Runs		Adjusted Starter Runs	
Kremer-Pit	2.61	Kremer-Pit	151	Petty-Bro	.240	Alexander-Chi-StL	.281	Kremer-Pit	31.3	Kremer-Pit	34.1
Root-Chi	2.82	Root-Chi	136	Alexander-Chi-StL	.250	Petty-Bro	.296	Root-Chi	30.3	Root-Chi	30.9
Petty-Bro	2.84	Petty-Bro	134	Rhem-StL	.250	Kremer-Pit	.296	Petty-Bro	30.1	Petty-Bro	30.0
Bush-Chi	2.86	Bush-Chi	134	Greenfield-NY	.251	Donohue-Cin	.298	Fitzsimmons-NY	23.0	Carlson-Phi	27.0
Barnes-NY	2.87	Barnes-NY	131	Kremer-Pit	.252	Rhem-StL	.305	Mays-Cin	21.4	Fitzsimmons-NY	21.3

Clutch Pitching Index		Relief Runs		Adjusted Relief Runs		Relief Ranking		Total Pitcher Index		Total Baseball Ranking	
Jones-Chi	122	Hallahan-StL	1.1	Hallahan-StL	1.6	Hallahan-StL	1.3	Kremer-Pit	3.7	Kremer-Pit	3.7
Blake-Chi	119							Root-Chi	3.2	Root-Chi	3.2
Fitzsimmons-NY	118							Mays-Cin	3.1	Waner-Pit	3.1
Werts-Bos	117							Petty-Bro	2.7	Mays-Cin	3.1
Root-Chi	111							Carlson-Phi	2.6	Wilson-Chi	3.0

April 13 Walter Johnson takes on A's knuckleballer Eddie Rommel in baseball's greatest opening-day pitchers' duel, a 15-inning battle won by the Senators, 1–0. Johnson gives up six walks and fans 12.

June 8 In Detroit, Babe Ruth slugs a homer reported to carry 626 feet. The hit, off Tiger pitcher Lil Stoner, lands at the intersection of Cherry Street and Brooklyn Avenue, two blocks from Navin Field.

August 4 Star Stanford fullback Ernie Nevers pitches his first complete game for the St. Louis Browns, beating the A's, 3-1.

August 22 After three games with the Tigers are rained out at home, Connie Mack and Tom Shibe decide that Sunday baseball is entitled to be played. Armed with a court injunction preventing police from interfering, they play the first Sunday game ever seen in Philadelphia. A light rain holds the crowd to 10,000, but Lefty Grove sets down the White Sox, 3–2, without incident. A court later rules Sunday baseball still illegal; it will be 1934 before that law changes in Philadelphia.

August 28 Emil Levsen of the pitches the Indians to a 6–1, 5–1 sweep of the Red Sox, making him the last major league pitcher to throw two complete games in a day.

September 25 The Yankees take two from the Browns to nail down the AL flag.

September 26 Browns coach Jimmie Austin, 46 years old, participates in the last game of the season against the Yankees. He contributes to the win by knocking in a run with a double and then stealing home; he's the oldest major leaguer to accomplish that feat.

October 2 Game 1 of the World Series before 61,658 at New York belongs to southpaws Herb Pennock (25-11) and Bill Sherdel (16-12). Two hits give the Cards a quick first-inning run. Sherdel issues three walks for a New York run without a hit. In the sixth, Babe Ruth slaps a single to left, moves to second base on a sacrifice, and scores on a Lou Gehrig single for a 2-1 win.

October 6 In Game 4, the Yankees tee off on Flint Rhem (20-7) and four other Cardinal hurlers for 10 runs and 14 hits, while Waite Hoyt (16-12) strands 10 Cardinal runners for a 10-5 win. Babe Ruth hits three home runs. Ruth's third clout, in the sixth, is the longest blast ever seen in St. Louis. It clears the park and goes through the window of an auto dealer across the street.

November 29 Tris Speaker resigns as Indians manager. Stories of a thrown game and betting on games by Ty Cobb and Speaker gain momentum when Judge Landis holds a secret hearing with the two stars and former pitcher-outfielder Smoky Joe Wood. The story and testimony will not be released until December 21. Former Tiger pitcher Dutch Leonard wrote to Harry Heilmann that he had turned over letters written to him by Joe Wood and Ty Cobb to AL president Ban Johnson, implicating Wood and Cobb in betting on a Tiger-Cleveland game played in Detroit, September 25, 1919. He charged that Cobb and Speaker conspired to let Detroit win to help them gain third-place money. At a secret meeting of AL directors, it was decided to let Cobb and Speaker resign with no publicity. But, as rumors spread, Judge Landis takes charge of the matter and holds the hearings, at which Leonard refuses to appear. Cobb and Wood admit to the letters and say Leonard is angry for having been released to the Pacific Coast League by Cobb. Speaker, not named in the letters, denies everything. Public sympathy is with the stars, but the matter will remain unresolved until January of next year.

	BOSTON		CHICAGO		CLEVELAND		DETROIT		NEW YORK		PHILADELPHIA		ST.LOUIS		WASHINGTON
M	L.Fohl	M	E.Collins	M	T.Speaker	M	T.Cobb	M	M.Huggins	M	C.Mack	M	G.Sisler	M	B.Harris
1B	P.Todt	1B	E.Sheely	1B	G.Burns	1B	L.Blue	1B	L.Gehrig	1B	J.Poole	1B	G.Sisler	1B	J.Judge
2B	B.Regan	2B	E.Collins	2B	F.Spurgeon	2B	C.Gehringer	2B	T.Lazzeri	2B	M.Bishop	2B	S.Melillo	2B	B.Harris
SS	T.Rigney	SS	B.Hunnefield	SS	J.Sewell	SS	J.Tavener	SS	M.Koenig	SS	C.Galloway	SS	W.Gerber	SS	B.Myer
3B	F.Haney	3B	W.Kamm	3B	R.Lutzke	3B	J.Warner	3B	J.Dugan	3B	J.Dykes	3B	M.McManus	3B	O.Bluege
LF	S.Rosenthal	LF	B.Falk	LF	C.Jamieson	LF	B.Fothergill	LF	B.Meusel	LF	B.Lamar	LF	K.Williams	LF	E.McNeely
CF	I.Flagstead	CF	J.Mostil	CF	T.Speaker	CF	H.Manush	CF	E.Combs	CF	A.Simmons	CF	H.Rice	CF	G.Goslin
RF	B.Jacobson	RF	B.Barrett	RF	H.Summa	RF	H.Heilmann	RF	B.Ruth	RF	W.French	RF	B.Miller	RF	S.Rice
C	A.Gaston	C	R.Schalk	C	L.Sewell	C	C.Manion	C	P.Collins	C	M.Cochrane	C	W.Schang	C	M.Ruel
23	M.Herrera	O	S.Harris	C	G.Myatt	1	J.Neun	O	B.Paschal	3	S.Hale	3S	G.Robertson	1O	J.Harris
O	J.Tobin	2	R.Morehart	O	I.Eichrodt	32	F.O'Rourke	3S	M.Gazella	1	J.Hauser	C	P.Hargrave	S	R.Peckinpaugh
O	W.Shaner	S	E.Scott	3	E.Padgett	O	A.Wingo	C	H.Severeid	O	F.Welch	O	H.Bennett	C	B.Tate
O	F.Bratschi	C	B.Crouse	/O	P.McNulty	O	T.Cobb	O	C.Perkins	O	C.Durst	2	S.Stewart
O	R.Carlyle	/O	J.Grabowski	/O	C.Lee	C	J.Bassler	O	R.Carlyle	O	B.Miller	O	B.Jacobson	O	D.Taylor
C	J.Bischoff	S	M.Berg	1	R.Knode	C	L.Woodall	/2	A.Ward	C	A.Metzler	C	L.Dixon	3	B.Reeves
O	H.Fitzgerald	C	H.McCurdy	2	G.Lacy	2	L.Burke	/2	S.Adams	S	B.Wambsganss	S	B.LaMotte	C	H.Severeid
C	A.Stokes	1	B.Clancy	/C	C.Autry	/3	B.Mullen	/C	B.Skiff	O	D.Barbee	/3	J.Austin	/O	J.Tobin
O	T.Jenkins	O	T.Gulley	/3	J.Hodapp	/C	R.Hayworth	H	N.Cullop	S	F.Sigafoos	O	T.Jeanes
/C	B.Moore	/O	P.Purdy					/1	F.Merkle	C	J.Foxx	P	T.Zachary	/C	R.Ennis
/S	J.Rothrock	/S	P.Veltman	P	G.Uhle	P	E.Whitehill	/C	H.Barnes	/O	T.Jenkins	P	M.Gaston
/3	C.Geygan			P	D.Levsen	P	S.Gibson	/O	K.Davis	S	C.Engle	P	E.Vangilder	P	W.Johnson
/3	B.Fowler	P	T.Lyons	P	J.Shaute	P	E.Wells					P	E.Wingard	P	S.Coveleski
/S	D.Lee	P	T.Thomas	P	S.Smith	P	L.Stoner	P	H.Pennock	P	L.Grove	P	W.Ballou	P	D.Ruether
/S	E.McCann	P	T.Blankenship	P	G.Buckeye	P	K.Holloway	P	U.Shocker	P	E.Rommel			P	A.Crowder
H	S.Langford	P	R.Faber					P	W.Hoyt	P	J.Quinn			P	C.Ogden
		P	J.Edwards	P	B.Karr	P	H.Dauss	P	S.Jones	P	R.Walberg	P	J.Giard	RP	F.Marberry
P	H.Wiltse			P	J.Miller	P	R.Collins	P	M.Thomas	P	S.Gray	P	D.Davis	RP	B.Morrell
P	T.Wingfield	P	S.Thurston	/P	W.Hudlin	P	A.Johns	RP	G.Braxton	RP	J.Pate	P	E.Nevers	RP	A.Ferguson
P	P.Zahniser	P	S.Connally	/P	N.Lehr	P	G.Smith					P	C.Falk
P	R.Ruffing	P	M.Steengrafe	/P	R.Benge	P	C.Barfoot					P	C.Jonnard
P	T.Welzer	P	D.Leverett	/P	B.Speece	P	R.Kneisch	P	H.Ehmke	/P	C.Robertson	P	G.Murray
RP	J.Russell	/P	L.Cox			P	W.Cooper	P	W.Beall	P	S.Harriss	/P	S.Bolen	P	J.Bush
		/P	P.McBee			/P	J.Doyle	P	H.McQuaid	P	F.Heimach			/P	D.Jones
P	S.Harriss							/P	D.Ruether	P	L.Willis			/P	E.Palmero
P	F.Heimach							/P	H.Johnson	P	S.Baumgartner			/P	H.Kelley
P	H.Ehmke													/P	L.Thomas
P	D.Lundgren													/P	J.Uchrinscko
P	J.Kiefer													/P	B.Hadley
/P	D.MacFayden													/P	F.Loftus
/P	H.Foreman														
/P	B.Ross														
/P	B.Clowers														
/P	R.Sommers														

TEAM	G	W	L	PCT	GB	R	OR	AB	H	2B	3B	HR	BB	SO	AVG	OBP	SLG	PRO	PRO+	BR	/A	PF	CHI	RC	SB	CS	SBA	SBR
NY	155	91	63	.591		847	713	5221	1508	262	75	121	642	580	.289	.369	.437	.806	119	123	137	98	98	866	79	62	56	-14
CLE	154	88	66	.571	3	738	612	5293	1529	333	49	27	455	332	.289	.349	.386	.735	97	-17	-23	101	103	735	88	42	68	1
PHI	150	83	67	.553	6	677	570	5046	1359	259	65	61	523	452	.269	.341	.383	.724	90	-39	-77	106	101	682	56	45	55	-10
WAS	152	81	69	.540	8	802	761	5223	1525	244	97	43	555	369	.292	.364	.401	.765	109	48	68	98	103	779	117	91	56	-20
CHI	155	81	72	.529	9.5	730	665	5220	1508	314	60	32	556	381	.289	.361	.390	.751	106	24	51	96	96	761	123	78	61	-10
DET	157	79	75	.513	12	793	830	5315	1547	281	90	36	599	423	.291	.367	.398	.765	105	52	42	101	99	801	88	71	55	-16
STL	155	62	92	.403	29	682	845	5259	1449	253	78	72	437	472	.276	.335	.394	.729	92	-38	-70	105	100	700	64	66	49	-20
BOS	154	46	107	.301	44.5	562	835	5185	1325	249	54	32	465	454	.256	.321	.343	.664	82	-156	-138	97	101	588	52	48	52	-13
TOT	616					5831		41762	11750	2195	568	424	4232	3463	.281	.351	.392	.743							667	503	57	-102

TEAM	CG	SH	SV	IP	H	H/G	HR	BB	SO	RAT	ERA	ERA+	OAV	OOB	PR	/A	PF	CPI	FA	E	DP	FW	PW	BW	SBW	DIF
NY	63	4	20	1372¹	1442	9.5	56	478	486	12.8	3.86	100	.274	.337	24	-1	96	96	.966	210	117	-1.1	-.0	13.3	-.1	2.0
CLE	96	11	4	1374	1412	9.2	49	450	381	12.5	3.40	119	.271	.334	94	101	101	105	.972	173	153	1.1	9.8	-2.2	1.3	1.1
PHI	62	10	16	1346	1362	9.1	38	451	571	12.3	3.00	139	.268	.331	153	174	104	114	.972	171	131	.9	16.9	-7.5	.3	-2.5
WAS	65	5	26	1348¹	1489	9.9	45	566	418	14.0	4.34	89	.287	.361	-48	-71	96	98	.969	184	129	.2	-6.9	6.4	-.7	6.8
CHI	85	11	12	1380	1426	9.3	47	506	458	12.7	3.74	103	.271	.336	43	16	96	96	.973	165	122	1.6	1.6	4.9	.3	-3.9
DET	57	10	18	1394²	1570	10.1	58	555	469	14.0	4.41	92	.292	.363	-61	-54	101	99	.969	193	151	.0	-5.2	4.1	-.3	3.4
STL	64	5	9	1368	1549	10.2	86	654	337	14.7	4.66	92	.297	.379	-98	-59	107	105	.963	235	167	-2.6	-5.7	-6.8	-.7	.8
BOS	53	6	5	1362	1520	10.0	45	546	336	13.9	4.72	86	.294	.365	-107	-101	101	92	.970	193	143	-.2	-9.8	-13.4	-.0	-7.2
TOT	545	62	110	10945¹		9.7				13.3	4.02		.281	.351					.969	1524	1113					

Runs		Hits		Doubles		Triples		Home Runs		Total Bases	
Ruth-NY	139	Rice-Was	216	Burns-Cle	64	Gehrig-NY	20	Ruth-NY	47	Ruth-NY	365
Gehrig-NY	135	Burns-Cle	216	Simmons-Phi	53	Gehringer-Det	17	Simmons-Phi	19	Simmons-Phi	329
Mostil-Chi	120	Goslin-Was	201	Speaker-Cle	52	Mostil-Chi	15	Lazzeri-NY	18	Gehrig-NY	314
Combs-NY	113	Simmons-Phi	199	Jacobson-StL-Bos	51	Goslin-Was	15	Williams-StL	17	Goslin-Was	308
Goslin-Was	105	Mostil-Chi	197	Gehrig-NY	47			Goslin-Was	17	Burns-Cle	298

Runs Batted In		Runs Produced		Bases On Balls		Batting Average		On Base Percentage		Slugging Average	
Ruth-NY	146	Ruth-NY	238	Ruth-NY	144	Manush-Det	.378	Ruth-NY	.516	Ruth-NY	.737
Lazzeri-NY	114	Gehrig-NY	231	Bishop-Phi	116	Ruth-NY	.372	Heilmann-Det	.445	Simmons-Phi	.564
Burns-Cle	114	Burns-Cle	207	Rigney-Bos	108	Fothergill-Det	.367	Bishop-Phi	.431	Manush-Det	.564
Gehrig-NY	112	Goslin-Was	196	Gehrig-NY	105	Heilmann-Det	.367	Goslin-Was	.425	Gehrig-NY	.549
Simmons-Phi	109	Falk-Chi	186	Speaker-Cle	94	Burns-Cle	.358	Manush-Det	.421	Goslin-Was	.542

Production		Adjusted Production		Batter Runs		Adjusted Batter Runs		Clutch Hitting Index		Runs Created	
Ruth-NY	1.253	Ruth-NY	228	Ruth-NY	97.4	Ruth-NY	100.3	Judge-Was	134	Ruth-NY	196
Manush-Det	.985	Goslin-Was	155	Gehrig-NY	44.2	Gehrig-NY	46.2	Dugan-NY	131	Gehrig-NY	137
Heilmann-Det	.979	Gehrig-NY	154	Goslin-Was	42.3	Goslin-Was	45.3	Haney-Bos	127	Goslin-Was	131
Gehrig-NY	.969	Manush-Det	153	Heilmann-Det	41.7	Heilmann-Det	40.3	Myer-Was	121	Simmons-Phi	129
Goslin-Was	.967	Heilmann-Det	152	Manush-Det	38.2	Manush-Det	36.8	Lutzke-Cle	118	Mostil-Chi	122

Total Average		Stolen Bases		Stolen Base Average		Stolen Base Runs		Fielding Runs		Total Player Rating	
Ruth-NY	1.606	Mostil-Chi	35	McNeely-Was	75.0	Mostil-Chi	2.1	Dykes-Phi	26.4	Ruth-NY	8.4
Gehrig-NY	1.058	Rice-Was	24	Hunnefield-Chi	72.7	McNeely-Was	1.8	Rigney-Bos	19.6	Goslin-Was	4.9
Heilmann-Det	1.040	Hunnefield-Chi	24	Mostil-Chi	71.4	Hunnefield-Chi	1.8	Goslin-Was	18.5	Mostil-Chi	4.0
Manush-Det	1.029	McNeely-Was	18	J.Sewell-Cle	70.8	Simmons-Phi	1.5	Regan-Bos	17.4	Rigney-Bos	3.9
Goslin-Was	1.008	J.Sewell-Cle	17	Lazzeri-NY	69.6			Mostil-Chi	17.1	J.Sewell-Cle	3.3

Wins		Win Percentage		Games		Complete Games		Shutouts		Saves	
Uhle-Cle	27	Uhle-Cle	.711	Marberry-Was	64	Uhle-Cle	32	Wells-Det	4	Marberry-Was	22
Pennock-NY	23	Pennock-NY	.676	Pate-Phi	47	Lyons-Chi	24			Dauss-Det	9
Shocker-NY	19	Shocker-NY	.633	Grove-Phi	45	Johnson-Was	22			Pate-Phi	6
Lyons-Chi	18	Faber-Chi	.625	Thomas-Chi	44	Grove-Phi	20			Grove-Phi	6
		Hoyt-NY	.571			Pennock-NY	19			Jones-NY	5

Innings Pitched		Fewest Hits/Game		Fewest BB/Game		Strikeouts		Strikeouts/Game		Ratio	
Uhle-Cle	318.1	Grove-Phi	7.92	Pennock-NY	1.45	Grove-Phi	194	Grove-Phi	6.77	Pennock-NY	11.52
Lyons-Chi	283.2	Thomas-Chi	8.13	Smith-Cle	1.48	Uhle-Cle	159	Thomas-Chi	4.59	Rommel-Phi	11.55
Pennock-NY	266.1	Lyons-Chi	8.48	Quinn-Phi	1.98	Thomas-Chi	127	Uhle-Cle	4.50	Johnson-Was	11.64
Johnson-Was	260.2	Lyons-Chi	8.50	Rommel-Phi	2.22	Johnson-Was	125	Johnson-Was	4.32	Grove-Phi	11.65
Shocker-NY	258.1	Buckeye-Cle	8.69	Wingfield-Bos	2.36	Whitehill-Det	109	Whitehill-Det	3.89	Lyons-Chi	11.90

Earned Run Average		Adjusted ERA		Opponents' Batting Avg.		Opponents' On Base Pct.		Starter Runs		Adjusted Starter Runs	
Grove-Phi	2.51	Grove-Phi	166	Thomas-Chi	.244	Pennock-NY	.313	Grove-Phi	43.1	Grove-Phi	47.4
Uhle-Cle	2.83	Uhle-Cle	143	Grove-Phi	.244	Rommel-Phi	.314	Uhle-Cle	42.1	Uhle-Cle	43.4
Lyons-Chi	3.01	Rommel-Phi	135	Lyons-Chi	.252	Hoyt-NY	.316	Lyons-Chi	31.6	Lyons-Chi	26.7
Rommel-Phi	3.08	Buckeye-Cle	131	Uhle-Cle	.253	Johnson-Was	.317	Coveleski-Was	24.5	Rommel-Phi	26.4
Buckeye-Cle	3.10	Lyons-Chi	128	Levsen-Cle	.261	Shocker-NY	.318	Rommel-Phi	22.7	Walberg-Phi	22.9

Clutch Pitching Index		Relief Runs		Adjusted Relief Runs		Relief Ranking		Total Pitcher Index		Total Baseball Ranking	
Wingard-StL	128	Pate-Phi	16.4	Pate-Phi	18.3	Marberry-Was	21.2	Uhle-Cle	5.2	Ruth-NY	8.4
Zachary-StL	122	Marberry-Was	15.6	Marberry-Was	13.3	Pate-Phi	15.3	Grove-Phi	4.0	Uhle-Cle	5.2
Grove-Phi	119	Braxton-NY	10.1	Braxton-NY	8.8	Braxton-NY	7.7	Lyons-Chi	3.3	Goslin-Was	4.9
Coveleski-Was	117	Russell-Bos	4.7	Russell-Bos	5.3	Russell-Bos	2.4	Walberg-Phi	2.8	Grove-Phi	4.0
Buckeye-Cle	114							Zachary-StL	2.7	Mostil-Chi	4.0

January 9 In a three-way deal, pitcher Burleigh Grimes goes from Brooklyn to the Giants, catcher Butch Henline goes from Philadelphia to Brooklyn, and Giants second baseman Fresco Thompson and pitcher Jack Scott wind up with the Phils.

January 31 NL President John Heydler rules that Rogers Hornsby cannot continue to hold stock in the Cardinals and play for the Giants.

February 9 The Giants send versatile George Kelly, along with cash, to the Reds for truculent holdout outfielder and former batting champ Edd Roush.

April 8 Four days before the season opens, recently traded Rogers Hornsby breaks the impasse caused by his trade, selling his stock in the Cardinals for $112,000. He receives $86,000 from Sam Breadon, $2,000 from each of the other seven NL clubs, and an extra $12,000 from the Giants.

May 14 During a game between the Phils and Cards, a section of right field at Baker Bowl collapses from the weight of the crowd and thousands of fans fall on those below. There are many injuries, but the one death that occurs is because of the crowd stampede, not the stands collapsing. Philadelphia was leading, 12–4, in the seventh when the tragedy occurs, and the game is called. The Phils' 12 remaining home games in May will be played at Shibe Park.

May 30 Shortstop Jimmy Cooney makes an unassisted triple play for the Cubs against Pittsburgh as he catches Paul Waner's line drive, steps on second base to retire Lloyd Waner, and tags Clyde Barnhart going back to first base.

June 18 It's Charles Lindbergh Day in St. Louis as the transatlantic flyer helps raise the Cardinals NL pennant before a 6–4 win over the Giants.

July 19 It's John McGraw Day at the Polo Grounds, in honor of his 25 years as Giants manager. The Cubs spoil the day with an 8–5 win.

July 27 Mel Ott, 18 years old, hits his first major league home run, an inside-the-park round-tripper. It is the only inside-the-park job of his 511 career homers.

September 4 Paul and Lloyd Waner hit homers for Pittsburgh in the same inning at Cincinnati's Redland Field, and both are "bounce home runs." Fair balls that bounce into the stands will be considered homers in the NL until 1930.

October 1 The Pirates clinch the NL flag, beating the Reds 9-6. They will finish 1½ games ahead of the Cards and two in front of New York.

October 22 Future Hall of Famer Ross Youngs, one of John McGraw's favorite players, dies of Bright's disease at age 30, cutting short a 10-year career in which he batted .322. Youngs had been accompanied by a specialist as early as 1924, and after the illness had been identified, the Giants hired a nurse to travel with Youngs. He was bedridden in 1927, after appearing in just 95 games in 1926.

December 4 Pirates outfielder Paul Waner noses out Frank Frisch for NL MVP honors with 72 points to 66.

BOSTON		BROOKLYN		CHICAGO		CINCINNATI		NEW YORK		PHILADELPHIA		PITTSBURGH		ST.LOUIS	
M	D.Bancroft	M	W.Robinson	M	J.McCarthy	M	J.Hendricks	M	J.McGraw	M	S.McInnis	M	D.Bush	M	B.O'Farrell
1B	J.Fournier	1B	B.Herman	1B	C.Grimm	1B	W.Pipp	M	R.Hornsby	1B	R.Wrightstone	1B	J.Harris	1B	J.Bottomley
2B	D.Gautreau	2B	J.Partridge	2B	C.Beck	2B	H.Critz	1B	B.Terry	2B	F.Thompson	2B	G.Grantham	2B	F.Frisch
SS	D.Bancroft	SS	J.Butler	SS	W.English	SS	H.Ford	2B	R.Hornsby	SS	H.Sand	SS	G.Wright	SS	H.Schuble
3B	A.High	3B	B.Barrett	3B	S.Adams	3B	C.Dressen	SS	T.Jackson	3B	B.Friberg	3B	P.Traynor	3B	L.Bell
LF	E.Brown	LF	G.Felix	LF	R.Stephenson	LF	R.Bressler	3B	F.Lindstrom	LF	D.Spalding	LF	C.Barnhart	LF	C.Hafey
CF	J.Welsh	CF	H.Wilson	CF	J.Statz	CF	E.Allen	LF	H.Mueller	CF	F.Leach	CF	L.Waner	CF	T.Douthit
RF	L.Richbourg	RF	M.Carey	RF	E.Webb	RF	C.Walker	CF	E.Roush	RF	C.Williams	RF	P.Waner	RF	B.Southworth
C	S.Hogan	C	H.DeBerry	C	G.Hartnett	C	B.Hargrave	RF	G.Harper	C	J.Wilson	C	J.Gooch	C	F.Snyder
								C	Z.Taylor						
S2	D.Farrell	O1	H.Hendrick	O	C.Heathcote	O	B.Zitzmann	3O	R.Reese	S	J.Cooney	O	K.Cuyler	O	W.Holm
32	E.Moore	S	J.Flowers	3	E.Pick	12	G.Kelly	O	M.Ott	O	J.Mokan	C	E.Smith	3S	S.Toporcer
1	D.Burrus	C	B.Henline	O	P.Scott	O	C.Christensen	O	T.Tyson	O	A.Nixon	23	H.Rhyne	S	T.Thevenow
O	J.Smith	C	C.Hargreaves	S	J.Cooney	S	V.Picinich	S	D.Farrell	C	B.Jonnard	C	R.Spencer	O	R.Blades
C	F.Gibson	O	I.Meusel	C	M.Gonzalez	S	P.Wanninger	C	A.DeVormer	O	D.Attreau	O	A.Comorosky	C	B.O'Farrell
C	L.Urban	O	O.Tremper	3	H.Freigau	2	P.Pittinger	C	J.Cummings	O	B.Hohman	3	H.Groh	C	J.Schulte
C	Z.Taylor	2	C.Corgan	/1	C.Tolson	C	B.Pinelli	O	L.Mann	/S	H.Baldwin	/2	J.Cronin	O	E.Orsatti
2	H.Thomas	/3	W.Marriott	3	E.Yoter	3	J.White	C	M.O'Neil	C	H.O'Donnell	/O	F.Brickell	/O	D.Clark
O	L.Mann	/O	M.Jacobson	C	H.Wilke	O	P.Purdy	/O	T.Jeanes	/2	B.Deitrick	/2	E.Sicking	/S	R.Maranville
O	E.Clark	/O	O.Roettger	H	F.Haney	C	C.Sukeforth	/O	H.Thomas	/1	S.McInnis	/O	H.Layne	/O	B.Schang
/O	S.Graves	H	C.Fewster	/C	J.Churry	/1	R.Wolf	H	B.Jordan			/S	D.Bartell	/O	H.Peel
/O	D.McNamara			H	T.Sewell			/O	J.Klinger					/O	W.Roettger
H	J.Cooney							/C	R.Smith						
P	B.Smith	P	D.Vance	P	C.Root	P	R.Lucas	P	B.Grimes	P	J.Scott	P	L.Meadows	P	J.Haines
P	K.Greenfield	P	J.Petty	P	S.Blake	P	J.May	P	F.Fitzsimmons	P	A.Ferguson	P	C.Hill	P	P.Alexander
P	J.Genewich	P	J.Elliott	P	G.Bush	P	D.Luque	P	V.Barnes	P	D.Ulrich	P	V.Aldridge	P	B.Sherdel
P	J.Werts	P	D.McWeeny	P	H.Carlson	P	E.Rixey	P	L.Benton	P	H.Pruett	P	R.Kremer	P	F.Rhem
P	C.Robertson	P	B.Doak	P	J.Brillheart	P	P.Donohue	P	D.Henry	P	L.Sweetland	RP	J.Morrison	P	B.McGraw
RP	G.Mogridge	RP	R.Ehrhardt	P	P.Jones	P	R.Kolp	RP	D.Songer	P	C.Willoughby	RP	M.Cvengros	RP	H.Bell
P	F.Edwards	RP	W.Clark	/P	T.Kaufmann	P	C.Mays	P	B.Clarkson	P	A.Decatur	P	J.Dawson	P	A.Reinhart
P	H.McQuillan	P	J.Barnes	/P	A.Nehf	P	A.Nehf	P	H.McQuillan	P	C.Mitchell	/P	J.Miljus	/P	F.Frankhouse
P	H.Goldsmith	P	N.Plitt	P	L.Roy	/P	P.Appleton	P	B.Cantwell	P	H.Carlson	/P	E.Yde	P	C.Littlejohn
P	L.Benton	/P	G.Cantrell	/P	L.Weinert	/P	J.Beckman	P	K.Greenfield	/P	T.Kaufmann	/P	C.Nichols	P	V.Keen
P	A.Mills	P	R.Moss	/P	H.Grampp			/P	F.Thomas	/P	R.Miller	/P	R.Mahaffey	P	J.Ring
P	G.Morrison	/P	B.McGraw	/P	W.Dean			/P	J.Bush	P	B.Clarkson	/P	J.Bush	/P	S.Johnson
/P	B.Hearn			/P	J.Welch			/P	J.Bentley	P	H.McQuillan	/P	D.Songer	/P	E.Dyer
/P	J.Knight							/P	J.Faulkner	/P	E.Baecht	/P	R.Peery	/P	T.Kaufmann
/P	D.Rudolph							/P	N.Plitt	/P	S.O'Neal				
								/P	V.Cheeves	/P	W.Dean				
								/P	H.Boney	/P	L.Taber				
								/P	B.Walker						
								/P	A.Johnson						
								/P	M.Holland						
								/P	N.Porter						

TEAM	G	W	L	PCT	GB	R	OR	AB	H	2B	3B	HR	BB	SO	AVG	OBP	SLG	PRO	PRO+	BR	/A	PF	CHI	RC	SB	CS	SBA	SBR
PIT	156	94	60	.610		**817**	659	5397	**1648**	258	78	54	437	355	**.305**	**.361**	.412	.773	106	99	42	107	99	791	65			
STL	153	92	61	.601	1.5	754	665	5207	1450	264	**79**	84	**484**	511	.278	.343	.408	.751	104	47	24	103	101	723	**110**			
NY	155	92	62	.597	2	**817**	720	5372	1594	251	62	**109**	461	462	.297	.356	**.427**	**.783**	116	113	115	100	98	**805**	73			
CHI	153	85	68	.556	8.5	750	661	5303	1505	**266**	63	74	481	492	.284	.346	.400	.746	106	43	41	100	99	730	65			
CIN	153	75	78	.490	18.5	643	653	5185	1439	222	77	29	402	332	.278	.332	.367	.699	96	-47	-27	97	100	628	62			
BRO	154	65	88	.425	28.5	541	**619**	5193	1314	195	74	39	368	494	.253	.306	.342	.648	79	-152	-154	100	102	539	106			
BOS	155	60	94	.390	34	651	771	5370	1498	216	61	37	346	363	.279	.326	.363	.689	98	-73	-24	92	**103**	626	100			
PHI	155	51	103	.331	43	678	903	5317	1487	216	46	57	434	482	.280	.337	.370	.707	94	-30	-39	101	100	660	68			
TOT	617					5651		42344	11935	1888	540	483	3413	3491	.282	.339	.386	.725							649			

TEAM	CG	SH	SV	IP	H	H/G	HR	BB	SO	RAT	ERA	ERA+	OAV	OOB	PR	/A	PF	CPI	FA	E	DP	FW	PW	BW	SBW	DIF
PIT	**90**	10	10	1385	1400	9.1	58	418	435	12.0	3.66	112	.267	.324	39	68	105	95	.969	187	130	.6	6.7	4.1		5.5
STL	89	**14**	11	1367[1]	1416	9.3	72	363	394	**11.8**	3.57	110	.271	**.320**	52	57	101	99	.966	213	**170**	-1.0	5.6	2.4		8.5
NY	65	7	**16**	1381[2]	1520	9.9	77	453	442	13.0	3.97	97	.283	.341	-8	-17	98	102	.969	195	160	.1	-1.7	**11.3**		5.2
CHI	75	11	5	1385	1439	9.4	50	514	465	12.9	3.65	106	.273	.342	40	31	99	**104**	**.971**	181	152	.8	3.1	4.0		.6
CIN	87	12	12	1368	1472	9.7	**36**	316	407	11.9	3.54	107	.281	.325	57	36	97	100	**.973**	165	160	1.6	3.6	-2.7		-4.0
BRO	74	7	10	1375[1]	**1382**	**9.0**	63	418	**574**	11.9	**3.36**	118	**.265**	.323	85	90	101	103	.963	229	117	-1.8	**8.9**	-15.2		-3.4
BOS	52	3	11	1390	1602	10.4	43	468	402	13.6	4.22	88	.296	.356	-48	-79	95	102	.963	231	130	-1.8	-7.8	-2.4		-5.0
PHI	81	5	6	1355[1]	1710	11.4	84	462	377	14.7	5.36	77	.317	.374	-218	-187	106	96	.972	169	152	1.5	-18.5	-3.8		-5.2
TOT	613	69	81	11007[2]		9.8				12.7	3.91		.282	.339					.969	1570	1171					

Runs		Hits		Doubles		Triples		Home Runs		Total Bases	
L.Waner-Pit	133	P.Waner-Pit	237	Stephenson-Chi	46	P.Waner-Pit	18	Wilson-Chi	30	P.Waner-Pit	342
Hornsby-NY	133	L.Waner-Pit	223	P.Waner-Pit	42	Bottomley-StL	15	Williams-Phi	30	Hornsby-NY	333
Wilson-Chi	119	Frisch-StL	208	Lindstrom-NY	36	Thompson-Phi	14	Hornsby-NY	26	Wilson-Chi	319
P.Waner-Pit	114	Hornsby-NY	205	Dressen-Cin	36	Terry-NY	13	Terry-NY	20	Terry-NY	307
Frisch-StL	112	Stephenson-Chi	199	Brown-Bos	35	Wilson-Chi	12	Bottomley-StL	19	Bottomley-StL	292

Runs Batted In		Runs Produced		Bases On Balls		Batting Average		On Base Percentage		Slugging Average	
P.Waner-Pit	131	P.Waner-Pit	236	Hornsby-NY	86	P.Waner-Pit	.380	Hornsby-NY	.448	Hafey-StL	.590
Wilson-Chi	129	Hornsby-NY	232	Harper-NY	84	Hornsby-NY	.361	P.Waner-Pit	.437	Hornsby-NY	.586
Hornsby-NY	125	Wilson-Chi	218	Grantham-Pit	74	L.Waner-Pit	.355	Harper-NY	.435	Wilson-Chi	.579
Bottomley-StL	124	Terry-NY	202	Bottomley-StL	74	Stephenson-Chi	.344	Stephenson-Chi	.415	P.Waner-Pit	.549
Terry-NY	121	Bottomley-StL	200			Traynor-Pit	.342	Harris-Pit	.402	Terry-NY	.529

Production		Adjusted Production		Batter Runs		Adjusted Batter Runs		Clutch Hitting Index		Runs Created	
Hornsby-NY	1.035	Hornsby-NY	175	Hornsby-NY	62.5	Hornsby-NY	62.8	P.Waner-Pit	135	Hornsby-NY	148
P.Waner-Pit	.986	Wilson-Chi	159	P.Waner-Pit	55.6	P.Waner-Pit	46.1	Wright-NY	134	P.Waner-Pit	145
Wilson-Chi	.980	P.Waner-Pit	152	Wilson-Chi	45.7	Wilson-Chi	45.5	Bressler-Cin	133	Wilson-Chi	126
Harper-NY	.930	Harper-NY	149	Harper-NY	37.1	Harper-NY	37.3	Farrell-NY-Bos	131	Stephenson-Chi	117
Terry-NY	.907	Stephenson-Chi	141	Stephenson-Chi	35.7	Stephenson-Chi	35.5	Bottomley-StL	124	Bottomley-StL	112

Total Average		Stolen Bases		Stolen Base Average		Stolen Base Runs		Fielding Runs		Total Player Rating	
Hornsby-NY	1.190	Frisch-StL	48					Frisch-StL	48.6	Frisch-StL	7.3
Wilson-Chi	1.088	Carey-Bro	32					Jackson-NY	27.9	Hornsby-NY	6.9
P.Waner-Pit	1.062	Hendrick-Bro	29					Friberg-Phi	25.3	Jackson-NY	5.4
Harper-NY	1.037	Adams-Chi	26					Beck-Chi	22.0	P.Waner-Pit	4.2
Stephenson-Chi	.955	Richbourg-Bos	24					Statz-Bro	15.2	Wilson-Chi	3.5

Wins		Win Percentage		Games		Complete Games		Shutouts		Saves	
Root-Chi	26	Benton-Bos-NY	.708	Scott-Phi	48	Vance-Bro	25	Haines-StL	6	Sherdel-StL	6
Haines-StL	24	Haines-StL	.706	Root-Chi	48	Meadows-Pit	25	Root-Chi	4	Nehf-Cin-Chi	5
Hill-Pit	22	Kremer-Pit	.704	Ehrhardt-Bro	46	Haines-StL	25	Lucas-Cin	4	Mogridge-Bos	5
Alexander-StL	21	Grimes-NY	.704	Henry-NY	45	Hill-Pit	22	Kremer-Pit	3	Henry-NY	4
		Alexander-StL	.677	May-Cin	44	Alexander-StL	22				

Innings Pitched		Fewest Hits/Game		Fewest BB/Game		Strikeouts		Strikeouts/Game		Ratio	
Root-Chi	309.0	Vance-Bro	7.97	Alexander-StL	1.28	Vance-Bro	184	Vance-Bro	6.06	Alexander-StL	10.07
Haines-StL	300.2	Kremer-Pit	8.16	Lucas-Cin	1.46	Root-Chi	145	Elliott-Bro	4.73	Lucas-Cin	10.14
Meadows-Pit	299.1	Haines-StL	8.17	Donohue-Cin	1.51	May-Cin	121	May-Cin	4.62	Kremer-Pit	10.27
Hill-Pit	277.2	Bush-Chi	8.24	Carlson-Phi-Chi	1.63	Grimes-NY	102	Pruett-Phi	4.35	Vance-Bro	10.44
Vance-Bro	273.1	Hill-Pit	8.43	Henry-NY	1.70	Petty-Bro	101	Root-Chi	4.22	Petty-Bro	10.60

Earned Run Average		Adjusted ERA		Opponents' Batting Avg.		Opponents' On Base Pct.		Starter Runs		Adjusted Starter Runs	
Kremer-Pit	2.47	Kremer-Pit	166	Vance-Bro	.239	Alexander-StL	.286	Alexander-StL	41.5	Alexander-StL	42.5
Alexander-StL	2.52	Alexander-StL	157	Kremer-Pit	.244	Lucas-Cin	.287	Haines-StL	39.8	Kremer-Pit	41.1
Vance-Bro	2.70	Vance-Bro	147	Haines-StL	.245	Kremer-Pit	.289	Vance-Bro	36.9	Haines-StL	40.8
Haines-StL	2.72	Haines-StL	145	Hill-Pit	.249	Vance-Bro	.291	Kremer-Pit	36.3	Vance-Bro	38.2
Petty-Bro	2.98	Petty-Bro	133	Bush-Chi	.250	Petty-Bro	.293	Petty-Bro	28.1	Petty-Bro	29.4

Clutch Pitching Index		Relief Runs		Adjusted Relief Runs		Relief Ranking		Total Pitcher Index		Total Baseball Ranking	
Blake-Chi	117	Clark-Bro	13.0	Clark-Bro	13.4	Clark-Bro	15.5	Alexander-StL	5.2	Frisch-StL	7.3
McWeeny-Bro	116	Ehrhardt-Bro	3.6	Cvengros-Pit	4.5	Ehrhardt-Bro	4.0	Haines-StL	4.3	Hornsby-NY	6.9
B.Smith-Bos	114	Cvengros-Pit	3.3	Ehrhardt-Bro	4.1	Cvengros-Pit	2.4	Kremer-Pit	4.3	Jackson-NY	5.4
Donohue-Cin	111	Songer-Pit-NY	1.9	Songer-Pit-NY	1.7	Songer-Pit-NY	2.3	Vance-Bro	3.8	Alexander-StL	5.2
Alexander-StL	109			H.Bell-StL	.1	H.Bell-StL	.0	Hill-Pit	3.2	Haines-StL	4.3

January 27 Citing accuser Dutch Leonard's refusal to appear at the hearings of January 5, Judge Landis issues a lengthy decision clearing Ty Cobb and Tris Speaker of any wrongdoing and ordering them reinstated by their teams. Both are made free agents; Connie Mack will sign Cobb on February 8; Speaker will sign with Washington on January 31.

April 26 Forty-year-old Ty Cobb has three hits, drives in the winning run, and steals home in the seventh inning. He tops that off with a ninth-inning shoe-string catch in shallow right field and then traps the runner off first for an unassisted double play to end the game as the A's win a 9–8 squeaker over Boston.

May 30* The Reading, Pennsylvania, team managed by Fred "Bonehead" Merkle, defeats Baltimore in the International League to break its 32-game losing streak.

May 31 Detroit first baseman Johnny Neun pulls the second unassisted triple play in two days. It happens in the ninth against Cleveland to end the game when Neun catches Homer Summa's line drive, touches Charlie Jamieson in the baseline and runs to second base where he tags the base Glenn Myatt has vacated. Detroit wins 1–0.

June 11 For the ninth inning, the Philadelphia Athletics field a team of seven Hall of Famers. The outfield consists of Ty Cobb in right, Al Simmons in center and Zack Wheat in left. At first base is Jimmie Foxx, at second is Eddie Collins, and Lefty Grove pitches in relief. Cy Perkins started as the catcher, but, when Mickey Cochrane pinch hit for him in the last inning, seven Cooperstown-bound players were in the lineup.

August 2 Washington celebrates Walter Johnson Day on the 20th anniversary of his joining the team. He receives $14,764.05, a silver service, and a Distinguished Service Cross made of gold with 20 diamonds. But the Tigers kayo him in a three-run ninth to win 7–6.

August 16 Babe Ruth christens the newly constructed Comiskey Park grandstand roof by cranking a Tommy Thomas pitch over the addition.

September 13 Babe Ruth hits two (52), and the Yankees win a pair from Cleveland to clinch the AL pennant with a 98-41 record.

September 30 With the score 2-2 in the eighth, Mark Koenig triples and Ruth hits home run number 60 off Tom Zachary for a 4-2 win. In the ninth Walter Johnson makes his final appearance as a player. He pinch hits for Zachary and flies out to Ruth.

October 5 Pittsburgh's Ray Kremer (19-8) opens Game 1 against Waite Hoyt (22-7). In the third, two walks and two Pirates errors help the Yankees to three runs and a 4-1 lead. Final: 5-4, New York.

October 7 The 60,695 on hand for Game 3 see the Yankees' Herb Pennock (19-8) take an 8-0 lead and a perfect game into the eighth. He retires Glenn Wright, but Pie Traynor breaks the spell with a single, and Clyde Barnhart doubles him home. Pennock settles for a 3-hit 8-1 victory.

October 8 Down three games to none, the Pirates give the ball to their biggest winner, Carmen Hill (22-11). In the fifth, Ruth's second home run of the Series scores Earle Combs ahead of him for a 3-1 lead. The Pirates tie it in the seventh. In the last of the ninth, Combs walks, Mark Koenig beats out a bunt, and Ruth walks to fill the bases. Reliever Johnny Miljus strikes out Lou Gehrig and Bob Meusel. With two strikes on Tony Lazzeri, a wild pitch rolls far enough away for Combs to score the winning run.

October 11 Lou Gehrig, who established a new major league record with 175 RBI, is named AL MVP. With 56 points, Gehrig wins over Harry Heilmann's 35 and Ted Lyons's 34. Ruth is not considered because former winners are not eligible.

December 11 The Browns sell George Sisler to Washington for $25,000.

December 13 Senators president Clark Griffith gains approval to have Washington open the AL season one day before the rest of the league, to celebrate a "National Day" with the U.S. President throwing out the first ball. The AL also installs Ernest S. Barnard as its president.

BOSTON	CHICAGO	CLEVELAND	DETROIT	NEW YORK	PHILADELPHIA	ST.LOUIS	WASHINGTON
M B.Carrigan	M R.Schalk	M J.McCallister	M G.Moriarty	M M.Huggins	M C.Mack	M D.Howley	M B.Harris
1B P.Todt	1B B.Clancy	1B G.Burns	1B L.Blue	1B L.Gehrig	1B J.Dykes	1B G.Sisler	1B J.Judge
2B B.Regan	2B A.Ward	2B L.Fonseca	2B C.Gehringer	2B T.Lazzeri	2B M.Bishop	2B S.Melillo	2B B.Harris
SS B.Myer	SS B.Hunnefield	SS J.Sewell	SS J.Tavener	SS M.Koenig	SS J.Boley	SS W.Gerber	SS B.Reeves
3B B.Rogell	3B W.Kamm	3B R.Lutzke	3B J.Warner	3B J.Dugan	3B S.Hale	3B F.O'Rourke	3B O.Bluege
LF W.Shaner	LF B.Falk	LF C.Jamieson	LF B.Fothergill	LF B.Meusel	LF B.Lamar	LF K.Williams	LF G.Goslin
CF I.Flagstead	CF A.Metzler	CF I.Eichrodt	CF H.Manush	CF E.Combs	CF A.Simmons	CF B.Miller	CF T.Speaker
RF J.Tobin	RF B.Barrett	RF H.Summa	RF H.Heilmann	RF B.Ruth	RF T.Cobb	RF H.Rice	RF S.Rice
C G.Hartley	C H.McCurdy	C L.Sewell	C J.Woodall	C P.Collins	C M.Cochrane	C W.Schang	C M.Ruel
O C.Carlyle	C B.Crouse	3 J.Hodapp	S2 M.McManus	C J.Grabowski	23 E.Collins	23 S.Adams	O E.McNeely
S2 J.Rothrock	2 R.Peckinpaugh	2 F.Spurgeon	1 J.Neun	2 R.Morehart	O W.French	O H.Bennett	S T.Rigney
C F.Hofmann	1 E.Sheely	O G.Myatt	2 J.Bassler	O R.Durst	S Z.Wheat	C S.O'Neill	C B.Tate
31 R.Rollings	S R.Flaskamper	O N.Cullop	O A.Wingo	O M.Gazella	C C.Perkins	S C.Galloway	2 S.Stewart
O B.Jacobson	O B.Neis	O S.Langford	O A.Ruble	C B.Bengough	1 J.Foxx	O F.Schulte	O S.West
3 F.Haney	2C M.Berg	O J.Gill	C M.Shea	1 J.Wera	1 D.Branom	C L.Dixon	O B.Myer
C B.Moore	O I.Boone	C C.Autry	3 B.DeVeiveiros		/O C.Bates	S3 O.Miller	O G.Ganzel
O A.Tarbert	O C.Reynolds	/O P.McNulty	H C.Manion		O B.Jacobson	/S R.Kress	S G.Gillis
S W.Wanninger	C R.Schalk	2 C.Lind	P E.Whitehill		/O R.Saunders	/1 G.Sturdy	/S J.Hayes
/O F.Welch	/O J.Mostil	/3 D.Ussat	P L.Stoner	P W.Hoyt	/3 J.Mellana	P M.Gaston	/O O.Tucker
/3 T.Rigney	2 R.Moore	/O G.Gerken	P S.Gibson	P W.Moore		P E.Vangilder	/O N.Cullop
/S M.Karow	/3 K.Willson	/2 J.Burnett	P K.Holloway	P H.Pennock		P S.Jones	/1 E.Onslow
/2 E.Eggert	/3 J.Battle	/2 E.Padgett	P O.Carroll	P U.Shocker		P E.Wingard	/C J.Berger
/O J.Freeman	/2 B.Way		P J.Billings	P D.Ruether		P L.Stewart	/C R.Barnes
H F.Bratschi	H L.Blackburne		P D.Hankins			/P J.Wright	/C M.O'Neil
P H.Wiltse	RP E.Jacobs	P W.Hudlin	/P E.Wells			P B.Beck	H B.Atkinson
P S.Harriss	RP B.Cole	P J.Shaute	/P J.Doyle			P S.Bolen	/2 B.Dear
P T.Welzer	P T.Thomas	P G.Buckeye	/P R.Smith		P L.Grove	P G.Blaeholder	P H.Lisenbee
P D.MacFayden	P T.Lyons	P J.Miller	/P J.Walkup		P R.Walberg	RP E.Nevers	P S.Thurston
P R.Ruffing	P T.Blankenship	P G.Uhle	/P A.Johns		P J.Quinn	RP W.Ballou	P B.Hadley
P J.Russell	P S.Connally	P D.Levsen		P G.Pipgras	P H.Ehmke	P T.Zachary	P W.Johnson
P D.Lundgren	P R.Faber	P B.Karr		P M.Thomas	P E.Rommel	/P A.Crowder	P T.Zachary
P T.Wingfield	/P C.Barnabe	P G.Grant		P B.Shawkey	RP J.Pate	/P C.Falk	P F.Marberry
/P J.Wilson	/P F.Stewart	P S.Smith		P J.Giard			RP G.Braxton
/P H.Bradley	/P J.Brown	/P J.Brown		/P W.Beall	P S.Gray		RP B.Burke
/P R.Sommers		/P H.McKain			P J.Johnson		P A.Crowder
/P F.Bennett		/P W.Underhill			P L.Willis		/P G.Murray
/P B.Cremins		/P H.Collard			P I.Powers		/P D.Coffman
/P F.Bushey		/P W.Ferrell			/P G.Cantrell		/P S.Coveleski
					/P N.Baker		/P P.Hopkins
					/P B.Wetzel		/P R.Judd
					/P C.Yerkes		/P D.Jones
							/P C.Van Alstyne

TEAM	G	W	L	PCT	GB	R	OR	AB	H	2B	3B	HR	BB	SO	AVG	OBP	SLG	PRO	PRO+	BR	/A	PF	CHI	RC	SB	CS	SBA	SBR
NY	155	110	44	.714		975	599	5347	1644	291	103	158	635	605	.307	.383	.489	.872	135	235	266	97	95	1016	90	64	58	-11
PHI	155	91	63	.591	19	841	726	5296	1606	281	70	56	551	326	.303	.372	.414	.786	103	79	32	106	99	839	101	63	62	-8
WAS	157	85	69	.552	25	782	730	5389	1549	268	87	29	498	359	.287	.351	.386	.737	97	-25	-16	99	104	758	133	52	72	9
DET	156	82	71	.536	27.5	845	805	5299	1533	282	100	51	587	420	.289	.363	.409	.772	105	47	35	101	103	813	139	73	66	-2
CHI	153	70	83	.458	39.5	662	708	5157	1433	285	61	36	493	389	.278	.344	.379	.722	94	-37	-37	98	95	685	89	75	54	-18
CLE	153	66	87	.431	43.5	668	766	5202	1471	321	52	26	381	366	.283	.337	.379	.716	90	-70	-75	101	100	669	65	72	47	-24
STL	155	59	94	.386	50.5	724	904	5220	1440	262	59	55	443	420	.276	.338	.380	.718	88	-68	-91	103	106	683	90	66	58	-13
BOS	154	51	103	.331	59	597	856	5207	1348	271	78	28	430	456	.259	.320	.357	.677	82	-149	-137	98	100	614	81	46	64	-3
TOT	619					6094		42117	12024	2261	610	439	4018	3341	.285	.352	.399	.751							788	511	61	-70

TEAM	CG	SH	SV	IP	H	H/G	HR	BB	SO	RAT	ERA	ERA+	OAV	OOB	PR	/A	PF	CPI	FA	E	DP	FW	PW	BW	SBW	DIF
NY	82	11	20	1389²	1403	9.1	42	409	431	11.9	3.20	120	.267	.323	145	100	93	104	.969	195	123	.7	9.5	25.3	-.2	-2.3
PHI	66	8	25	1384	1467	9.5	65	442	553	12.6	3.97	107	.278	.338	26	45	103	97	.970	190	124	1.0	4.3	3.0	.0	5.6
WAS	62	10	23	1402	1434	9.2	53	491	497	12.6	3.97	102	.269	.335	26	14	98	91	.969	195	125	.8	1.3	-1.5	1.7	5.7
DET	75	5	17	1387²	1542	10.0	52	577	421	14.0	4.14	102	.290	.364	0	9	102	106	.968	206	173	.1	.9	3.3	.6	.6
CHI	85	10	8	1367	1467	9.7	55	440	365	12.7	3.91	103	.283	.342	34	19	101	98	.971	178	131	1.6	1.8	-3.5	-.9	-5.5
CLE	72	5	8	1353¹	1542	10.3	37	508	366	13.9	4.27	98	.295	.361	-20	-11	102	102	.968	201	146	.2	-1.0	-7.1	-1.4	-1.0
STL	80	4	8	1353¹	1592	10.6	79	604	385	14.7	4.95	88	.304	.378	-122	-91	105	101	.960	248	166	-2.5	-8.6	-8.6	-.4	2.7
BOS	63	6	7	1366¹	1603	10.6	56	558	381	14.5	4.72	89	.305	.376	-88	-77	102	102	.964	228	167	-1.4	-7.3	-13.0	.5	-4.8
TOT	585	59	116	11003¹		9.9				13.4	4.14		.285	.352					.967	1641	1155					

Runs
Ruth-NY 158
Gehrig-NY 149
Combs-NY 137
Gehringer-Det 110
Heilmann-Det 106

Hits
Combs-NY 231
Gehrig-NY 218
Sisler-StL 201
Heilmann-Det 201
Goslin-Was 194

Doubles
Gehrig-NY 52
Burns-Cle 51
Heilmann-Det 50
J.Sewell-Cle 48
Meusel-NY 47

Triples
Combs-NY 23
Manush-Det 18
Gehrig-NY 18
Goslin-Was 15
Rice-Was 14

Home Runs
Ruth-NY 60
Gehrig-NY 47
Lazzeri-NY 18
Williams-StL 17
Simmons-Phi 15

Total Bases
Gehrig-NY 447
Ruth-NY 417
Combs-NY 331
Heilmann-Det 311
Goslin-Was 300

Runs Batted In
Gehrig-NY 175
Ruth-NY 164
Heilmann-Det 120
Goslin-Was 120
Fothergill-Det 114

Runs Produced
Gehrig-NY 277
Ruth-NY 262
Heilmann-Det 212
Goslin-Was 203
Fothergill-Det 198

Bases On Balls
Ruth-NY 138
Gehrig-NY 109
Bishop-Phi 105
Heilmann-Det 72
Blue-Det 71

Batting Average
Heilmann-Det 398
Simmons-Phi 392
Gehrig-NY 373
Fothergill-Det 359
Cobb-Phi 357

On Base Percentage
Ruth-NY 487
Heilmann-Det 475
Gehrig-NY 474
Bishop-Phi 442
Cobb-Phi 440

Slugging Average
Ruth-NY 772
Gehrig-NY 765
Simmons-Phi 645
Heilmann-Det 616
Williams-StL 525

Production
Ruth-NY 1.259
Gehrig-NY 1.240
Heilmann-Det 1.091
Fothergill-Det 929
Williams-StL 928

Adjusted Production
Ruth-NY 229
Gehrig-NY 224
Heilmann-Det 179
Combs-NY 143
Fothergill-Det 138

Batter Runs
Gehrig-NY 100.8
Ruth-NY 100.7
Heilmann-Det 62.3
Simmons-Phi 44.1
Combs-NY 37.1

Adjusted Batter Runs
Gehrig-NY 106.6
Ruth-NY 106.4
Heilmann-Det 60.4
Combs-NY 41.0
Simmons-Phi 38.5

Clutch Hitting Index
Fothergill-Det 119
Goslin-Was 118
Sisler-StL 116
Harris-Was 115
J.Sewell-Cle 114

Runs Created
Gehrig-NY 212
Ruth-NY 208
Heilmann-Det 150
Combs-NY 138
Goslin-Was 119

Total Average
Ruth-NY 1.571
Gehrig-NY 1.500
Heilmann-Det 1.265
Williams-StL 959
Combs-NY 955

Stolen Bases
Sisler-StL 27
Meusel-NY 24
Neun-Det 22
Lazzeri-NY 22
Cobb-Phi 22

Stolen Base Average
Harris-Was 85.7
Sisler-StL 79.4
Goslin-Was 77.8
Rice-Was 76.0
Neun-Det 75.9

Stolen Base Runs
Sisler-StL 3.9
Harris-Was 3.6
Goslin-Was 2.7

Fielding Runs
Gehringer-Det 19.8
Falk-Chi 18.2
Metzler-Chi 15.7
Bluege-Was 15.0
Koenig-NY 13.8

Total Player Rating
Ruth-NY 9.2
Gehrig-NY 8.1
Heilmann-Det 4.2
Simmons-Phi 3.4
Combs-NY 3.2

Wins
Lyons-Chi 22
Hoyt-NY 22
Grove-Phi 20

Win Percentage
Hoyt-NY 759
Shocker-NY 750
Moore-NY 731
Pennock-NY 704
Lisenbee-Was 667

Games
Braxton-Was 58
Marberry-Was 56
Grove-Phi 51
Moore-NY 50
Walberg-Phi 46

Complete Games
Lyons-Chi 30
Thomas-Chi 24
Hoyt-NY 23
Gaston-StL 21

Shutouts
Lisenbee-Was 4

Saves
Moore-NY 13
Braxton-Was 13
Marberry-Was 9
Grove-Phi 9

Innings Pitched
Thomas-Chi 307.2
Lyons-Chi 307.2
Hudlin-Cle 264.2
Grove-Phi 262.1
Hoyt-NY 256.1

Fewest Hits/Game
Moore-NY 7.82
Thomas-Chi 7.93
Pipgras-NY 8.01
Hadley-Was 8.02
Lisenbee-Was 8.22

Fewest BB/Game
Quinn-Phi 1.65
Shocker-NY 1.85
Hoyt-NY 1.90
Braxton-Was 1.91
Lyons-Chi 1.96

Strikeouts
Grove-Phi 174
Walberg-Phi 136
Thomas-Chi 107
Lisenbee-Was 105
Braxton-Was 96

Strikeouts/Game
Grove-Phi 5.97
Braxton-Was 5.56
Walberg-Phi 4.91
Pipgras-NY 4.38
Ruffing-Bos 4.38

Ratio
Moore-NY 10.35
Braxton-Was 10.37
Lyons-Chi 10.47
Hoyt-NY 10.53
Thomas-Chi 10.71

Earned Run Average
Moore-NY 2.28
Hoyt-NY 2.63
Shocker-NY 2.84
Lyons-Chi 2.84
Hadley-Was 2.85

Adjusted ERA
Moore-NY 169
Hoyt-NY 146
Lyons-Chi 143
Hadley-Was 142
Braxton-Was 137

Opponents' Batting Avg.
Moore-NY 234
Thomas-Chi 244
Hadley-Was 244
Lisenbee-Was 245
Braxton-Was 246

Opponents' On Base Pct.
Moore-NY 289
Braxton-Was 289
Lyons-Chi 292
Hoyt-NY 294
Thomas-Chi 303

Starter Runs
Lyons-Chi 44.4
Moore-NY 43.9
Hoyt-NY 42.8
Thomas-Chi 39.4
Shocker-NY 28.9

Adjusted Starter Runs
Lyons-Chi 41.3
Moore-NY 37.1
Thomas-Chi 36.3
Hoyt-NY 34.7
Grove-Phi 31.2

Clutch Pitching Index
Ruether-NY 119
Gibson-Det 119
Pennock-NY 118
Zachary-StL-Was . . 115
Stoner-Det 114

Relief Runs
Braxton-Was 20.4
Burke-Was 1.9
G.Smith-Det 1.8

Adjusted Relief Runs
Braxton-Was 19.1
G.Smith-Det 2.3
Burke-Was 1.1

Relief Ranking
Braxton-Was 24.6
G.Smith-Det 1.5
Burke-Was 5

Total Pitcher Index
Lyons-Chi 5.1
Moore-NY 4.8
Hoyt-NY 3.5
Grove-Phi 3.3
Thomas-Chi 2.9

Total Baseball Ranking
Ruth-NY 9.2
Gehrig-NY 8.1
Lyons-Chi 5.1
Moore-NY 4.8
Heilmann-Det 4.2

January 14 Alfred J. Reach, founder of the A. J. Reach sporting goods firm, dies at 87. He was one of the first to receive a salary when he signed as a catcher with the Philadelphia Athletics for $25 a week in 1865.

April 18 The Cubs set an NL Opening Day attendance record as a reported 46,000 jam Wrigley Field to see Cincinnati top the Cubs, 9–6. The two teams combine for 28 hits.

June 2 The Phillies defeat the Cardinals, 2–1, with all the runs scoring as the result of a record three pinch-hit homers.

June 25 The Giants' Fred Lindstrom strokes nine hits in a doubleheader against Philadelphia to tie the major league mark. The Giants sweep, 12-4 and 8-2.

July 12 Baseball's biggest battery is recorded, appropriately, with the New York Giants, as Garland "Gob" Buckeye, a 260 pound pro football lineman in the off-season, makes his NL pitching debut with 250-pound Frank "Shanty" Hogan behind the plate. In a more significant move, the Giants purchase 25-year-old lefty Carl Hubbell from Beaumont for an amount rumored to be the most ever paid for a Texas League player.

August 11 Carl Hubbell's first major league victory is a 4-0 shutout of the Phils. He'll be 10-6 down the stretch and will pitch 16 years with the Giants.

September 4 The Braves play a record nine consecutive doubleheaders between now and the 15th. They lose five of them in a row, including four to the Giants.

September 27 With the Giants just a half game behind the Cardinals, New York loses the first game of a doubleheader to the Cubs, 3–2. On a controversial play at the plate in the sixth inning, New York's Andy Reese bowled over catcher Gabby Hartnett who grabbed the runner to keep from falling. As Hartnett held him, Reese was tagged out by the Cubs third baseman, and the Giants bench erupted. The protest would be disallowed.

September 29 The Cardinals win the NL pennant with a 3-1 win at Boston while the Cubs are beating New York. The final margin is two games over the Giants, four over the Cubs.

November 3 Voters in Massachusetts approve Sunday baseball in Boston, provided that the ballpark is more than 1,000 feet from a church. This leaves Pennsylvania as the only state with no Sunday baseball in the major leagues.

December 2 Cardinals first baseman Jim Bottomley is voted NL MVP with 76 points to 70 for Giants third baseman Fred Lindstrom, whose .358 BA was third behind Hornsby and Paul Waner.

December 11 At the NL meeting, President John Heydler proposes the designated hitter for pitchers to improve and speed up the game. He contends fans are tired of seeing weak-hitting pitchers come to bat.

December 17 At a joint meeting, a rule is changed that ends the practice of minor league teams selling star prospects to friendly major league clubs for high prices, then getting the players back, forcing another major league club to pay the reputed price for the player. Another change bans the signing of players under the age of 17.

BOSTON	BROOKLYN	CHICAGO	CINCINNATI	NEW YORK	PHILADELPHIA	PITTSBURGH	ST.LOUIS
M J.Slattery	M W.Robinson	M J.McCarthy	M J.Hendricks	M J.McGraw	M B.Shotton	M D.Bush	M B.McKechnie
M R.Hornsby	1B D.Bissonette	1B C.Grimm	1B G.Kelly	1B B.Terry	1B D.Hurst	1B G.Grantham	1B J.Bottomley
1B G.Sisler	2B J.Flowers	2B F.Maguire	2B H.Critz	2B A.Cohen	2B F.Thompson	2B S.Adams	2B F.Frisch
2B R.Hornsby	SS D.Bancroft	SS W.English	SS H.Ford	SS T.Jackson	SS H.Sand	SS G.Wright	SS R.Maranville
SS D.Farrell	3B H.Hendrick	3B C.Beck	3B C.Dressen	3B F.Lindstrom	3B P.Whitney	3B P.Traynor	3B W.Holm
3B L.Bell	LF R.Bressler	LF R.Stephenson	LF B.Zitzmann	LF L.O'Doul	LF F.Leach	LF F.Brickell	LF C.Hafey
LF E.Brown	CF M.Carey	CF H.Wilson	CF C.Allen	CF W.Welsh	CF D.Sothern	CF L.Waner	CF T.Douthit
CF J.Smith	RF B.Herman	RF K.Cuyler	RF C.Walker	RF M.Ott	RF C.Williams	RF P.Waner	RF G.Harper
RF L.Richbourg	C H.DeBerry	C G.Hartnett	C V.Picinich	C S.Hogan	C W.Lerian	C C.Hargreaves	C J.Wilson
C Z.Taylor							
	23 H.Riconda	3 J.Butler	1 W.Pipp	O2 R.Reese	O C.Klein	2S D.Bartell	32 A.High
O E.Moore	O T.Tyson	C M.Gonzalez	O M.Callaghan	O L.Mann	C S.Davis	O C.Barnhart	O W.Roettger
O H.Mueller	O J.Statz	O E.Webb	O P.Purdy	O E.Roush	C J.Schulte	O P.Scott	S T.Thevenow
1 D.Burrus	3 W.Gilbert	O C.Heathcote	C B.Hargrave	C B.O'Farrell	O B.Deitrick	C A.Comorosky	O R.Blades
C A.Spohrer	C B.Henline	23 N.McMillan	O3 J.Stripp	S G.Harper	C B.Friberg	C R.Hemsley	O E.Orsatti
O E.Clark	C J.Gooch	1 J.Kelly	C C.Sukeforth	/O A.Jahn	O B.Kelly	C E.Smith	C E.Smith
S2 H.Freigau	O J.Harris	H J.Moore	S P.Pittinger	/C J.Cummings	/C A.Jahn	C J.Gooch	C B.O'Farrell
S Ji.Cooney	2 J.Partridge	H R.Jacobs	/2 J.White	/1 R.Wrightstone	1 R.Wrightstone	/3 E.Mulligan	G.Mancuso
/2 D.Gautreau	/3 C.Hargreaves	/3 E.Yoter		/O P.Veltman	/O P.Veltman	/2 M.Hillis	/1 S.Toporcer
/O D.Harris	H.Freigau		P E.Rixey	O A.Spohrer	O A.Nixon	/1 J.Harris	/O P.Martin
C L.Urban	/O O.Tremper	P P.Malone	P D.Luque	H R.Foley	/S H.MacDonald	C.Jones	H H.Williamson
H C.Fitzberger	M.West	P S.Blake	P R.Kolp	H C.Fullis	/C J.O'Connell	/C S.Davis	
/O D.McNamara	/C A.Lopez	P C.Root	P R.Lucas	/C B.Haeffner	/1 B.Windle		
/C B.Cronin		P G.Bush	P P.Donohue	/O J.Price	P R.Benge	J.Ring	
/C E.Williams	P D.Vance	P A.Nehf	RP P.Appleton		P L.Sweetland	P B.Grimes	P B.Sherdel
	P D.McWeeny	RP H.Carlson		P L.Benton	A.Ferguson	C.Hill	P.Alexander
P B.Smith	P J.Petty		P J.May	P F.Fitzsimmons	P C.Willoughby	R.Kremer	F.Rhem
P E.Brandt	P W.Clark	P P.Jones	P C.Mays	P J.Genewich	P F.Fussell	P J.Haines	
P A.Delaney	P J.Elliott	P E.Holley	/P K.Ash	P C.Hubbell	A.Walsh	J.Dawson	RP H.Haid
P K.Greenfield	RP R.Moss	P L.Weinert	P J.Edwards	P V.Aldridge	B.McGraw		
RP F.Edwards	RP R.Ehrhardt	/P B.Tincup	/P J.Beckman		P R.Miller	E.Brame	S.Johnson
		/P J.Welch	/P S.Johnson	P J.Faulkner	H.Pruett	J.Miljus	A.Reinhart
P B.Cantwell	P B.Doak		/P H.Pyle	P B.Walker	J.Milligan	W.Tauscher	C.Littlejohn
P Jo.Cooney	P L.Koupal			P D.Henry	/P E.Caldwell	L.Bartholomew	T.Kaufmann
P J.Genewich				/P V.Barnes	/P E.Baecht	H.Blankenship	
P V.Barnes				/P J.Scott	/P E.Lennon	B.Burwell	
P C.Robertson				/P T.Chaplin	/P C.Mitchell	L.Meadows	
P B.Clarkson				/P B.Cantwell	/P J.Greene	G.Spencer	
/P B.Hollingsworth				/P B.Clarkson	/P M.Walker	E.Tutwiler	
P J.Werts				/P G.Buckeye			
/P B.Hearn				/P L.Mangum			
/P H.Goldsmith				/P C.Nichols			
/P A.Mills							
/P C.Touchstone							
/P E.Palmero							
/P R.Boggs							
/P G.Morrison							

TEAM	G	W	L	PCT	GB	R	OR	AB	H	2B	3B	HR	BB	SO	AVG	OBP	SLG	PRO	PRO+	BR	/A	PF	CHI	RC	SB	CS	SBA	SBR
STL	154	95	59	.617		807	636	5357	1505	292	70	113	568	438	.281	.353	.425	.778	108	73	58	102	99	802	82			
NY	155	93	61	.604	2	807	653	5459	1600	276	59	118	444	376	.293	.349	.430	.779	110	68	65	100	100	805	62			
CHI	154	91	63	.591	4	714	615	5260	1460	251	64	92	508	517	.278	.345	.402	.747	103	11	21	99	97	728	83			
PIT	152	85	67	.559	9	837	704	5371	1659	246	100	52	435	352	.309	.364	.421	.785	108	89	56	104	103	809	64			
CIN	153	78	74	.513	16	648	686	5184	1449	229	67	32	386	330	.280	.333	.368	.701	91	-76	-66	98	104	630	83			
BRO	155	77	76	.503	17.5	665	640	5243	1393	229	70	66	557	510	.266	.340	.374	.714	94	-46	-37	99	98	673	81			
BOS	153	50	103	.327	44.5	631	878	5228	1439	241	41	52	447	377	.275	.335	.367	.702	95	-70	-37	95	99	643	60			
PHI	152	43	109	.283	51	660	957	5234	1396	257	47	85	503	510	.267	.333	.382	.715	90	-49	-72	103	99	667	53			
TOT	614					5769		42336	11901	2021	518	610	3848	3410	.281	.344	.397	.741							568			

TEAM	CG	SH	SV	IP	H	H/G	HR	BB	SO	RAT	ERA	ERA+	OAV	OOB	PR	/A	PF	CPI	FA	E	DP	FW	PW	BW	SBW	DIF
STL	83	4	21	1415¹	1470	9.3	86	399	422	12.1	3.38	118	.270	.323	96	98	100	105	.974	160	134	1.3	9.6	5.7		1.4
NY	79	7	16	1394	1454	9.4	77	405	399	12.1	3.67	107	.273	.327	50	37	98	98	.972	178	175	.3	3.6	6.4		5.7
CHI	75	12	14	1380²	1383	9.0	56	508	531	12.5	3.40	113	.267	.336	91	69	96	105	.975	156	176	1.6	6.7	2.1		3.6
PIT	82	8	11	1354	1422	9.5	66	446	385	12.6	3.95	100	.274	.335	6	16	102	123	.967	201	123	-1.3	1.6	5.5		3.2
CIN	68	11	11	1371²	1516	9.9	58	410	355	12.7	3.94	100	.289	.342	8	2	99	100	.974	162	194	1.1	.2	-6.5		7.1
BRO	75	16	15	1396	1378	8.9	59	468	551	12.1	3.25	122	.261	.324	114	112	100	101	.965	217	113	-2.0	10.9	-3.6		-4.8
BOS	54	1	6	1360	1596	10.6	100	524	343	14.2	4.83	81	.298	.363	-127	-140	98	97	.969	193	141	-.7	-13.7	-3.6		-8.5
PHI	42	4	11	1352²	1658	11.0	108	675	404	15.8	5.56	77	.314	.396	-237	-199	107	100	.971	181	171	-.0	-19.5	-7.0		-6.4
TOT	558	63	105	11024¹		9.7				13.0	3.99		.281	.344					.971	1448	1227					

Runs		Hits		Doubles		Triples		Home Runs		Total Bases	
P.Waner-Pit	142	Lindstrom-NY	231	P.Waner-Pit	50	Bottomley-StL	20	Wilson-Chi	31	Bottomley-StL	362
Bottomley-StL	123	P.Waner-Pit	223	Hafey-StL	46	P.Waner-Pit	19	Bottomley-StL	31	Lindstrom-NY	330
L.Waner-Pit	121	L.Waner-Pit	221	Hornsby-StL	42	L.Waner-Pit	14	Hafey-StL	27	P.Waner-Pit	329
Douthit-StL	111	Richbourg-Bos	206	Bottomley-StL	42	Bressler-Bro	13	Bissonette-Bro	25	Bissonette-Bro	319
Frisch-StL	107	Traynor-Pit	192	Lindstrom-NY	39	Bissonette-Bro	13	Hornsby-Bos	21	Hafey-StL	314

Runs Batted In		Runs Produced		Bases On Balls		Batting Average		On Base Percentage		Slugging Average	
Bottomley-StL	136	Bottomley-StL	228	Hornsby-Bos	107	Hornsby-Bos	.387	Hornsby-Bos	.498	Hornsby-Bos	.632
Traynor-Pit	124	P.Waner-Pit	222	Douthit-StL	84	P.Waner-Pit	.370	P.Waner-Pit	.446	Bottomley-StL	.628
Wilson-Chi	120	Traynor-Pit	212	Bressler-Bro	80	Lindstrom-NY	.358	Grantham-Pit	.408	Hafey-StL	.604
Hafey-StL	111	Lindstrom-NY	192	Wilson-Chi	77	Sisler-Bos	.340	Stephenson-Chi	.407	Wilson-Chi	.588
Lindstrom-NY	107	Hafey-StL	185	P.Waner-Pit	77	Herman-Bro	.340	Wilson-Chi	.404	P.Waner-Pit	.547

Production		Adjusted Production		Batter Runs		Adjusted Batter Runs		Clutch Hitting Index		Runs Created	
Hornsby-Bos	1.130	Hornsby-Bos	204	Hornsby-Bos	72.5	Hornsby-Bos	80.3	Traynor-Pit	147	Hornsby-Bos	154
Bottomley-StL	1.030	Bottomley-StL	163	P.Waner-Pit	53.4	Bottomley-StL	50.1	Walker-Cin	126	P.Waner-Pit	145
Wilson-Chi	.992	Wilson-Chi	159	Bottomley-StL	52.5	P.Waner-Pit	48.0	Whitney-Phi	124	Bottomley-StL	142
P.Waner-Pit	.992	Hafey-StL	152	Wilson-Chi	42.1	Wilson-Chi	43.7	Ford-Cin	123	Bissonette-Bro	125
Hafey-StL	.990	P.Waner-Pit	152	Hafey-StL	38.5	Bissonette-Bro	38.1	Wilson-Phi-StL	121	Wilson-Chi	122

Total Average		Stolen Bases		Stolen Base Average		Stolen Base Runs		Fielding Runs		Total Player Rating	
Hornsby-Bos	1.409	Cuyler-Chi	37					Maguire-Chi	50.5	Hornsby-Bos	5.8
Bottomley-StL	1.147	Frisch-StL	29					Jackson-NY	28.3	Lindstrom-NY	4.8
P.Waner-Pit	1.100	Walker-Cin	19					Douthit-StL	24.3	Jackson-NY	4.3
Wilson-Chi	1.090	Thompson-Phi	19					Lindstrom-NY	15.1	Hartnett-Chi	4.2
Hafey-StL	1.055							Ford-Cin	11.9	P.Waner-Pit	4.0

Wins		Win Percentage		Games		Complete Games		Shutouts		Saves	
Grimes-Pit	25	Benton-NY	.735	Grimes-Pit	48	Grimes-Pit	28	Vance-Bro	4	Sherdel-StL	5
Benton-NY	25	Haines-StL	.714	Kolp-Cin	44	Benton-NY	28	McWeeny-Bro	4	Haid-StL	5
Vance-Bro	22	Bush-Chi	.714	Rixey-Cin	43	Vance-Bro	24	Lucas-Cin	4	Carlson-Chi	4
Sherdel-StL	21	Fitzsimmons-NY	.690			Sherdel-StL	20	Grimes-Pit	4	Benton-NY	4
		Vance-Bro	.688			Haines-StL	20	Blake-Chi	4		

Innings Pitched		Fewest Hits/Game		Fewest BB/Game		Strikeouts		Strikeouts/Game		Ratio	
Grimes-Pit	330.2	Vance-Bro	7.26	Alexander-StL	1.37	Vance-Bro	200	Vance-Bro	6.42	Vance-Bro	9.79
Benton-NY	310.1	Blake-Chi	7.82	Sherdel-StL	2.03	Malone-Chi	155	Malone-Chi	5.57	Benton-NY	10.73
Rixey-Cin	291.1	Malone-Chi	7.83	Benton-NY	2.06	Root-Chi	122	Root-Chi	4.63	Grimes-Pit	10.81
Vance-Bro	280.1	McWeeny-Bro	8.04	Rixey-Cin	2.07	Grimes-Pit	97	Clark-Bro	3.93	Lucas-Cin	11.08
Fitzsimmons-NY	261.1	Root-Chi	8.13	Grimes-Pit	2.10	Benton-NY	90	Ring-Phi	3.75	Alexander-StL	11.12

Earned Run Avg.		Adjusted ERA		Opponents' Batting Avg.		Opponents' On Base Pct.		Starter Runs		Adjusted Starter Runs	
Vance-Bro	2.09	Vance-Bro	190	Vance-Bro	.221	Vance-Bro	.277	Vance-Bro	59.2	Vance-Bro	58.7
Blake-Chi	2.47	Blake-Chi	156	McWeeny-Bro	.235	Grimes-Pit	.297	Benton-NY	43.5	Benton-NY	40.7
Nehf-Chi	2.65	Clark-Bro	148	Malone-Chi	.236	Benton-NY	.300	Blake-Chi	40.6	Grimes-Pit	39.0
Clark-Bro	2.68	Nehf-Chi	145	Blake-Chi	.240	Sherdel-StL	.303	Grimes-Pit	36.5	Blake-Chi	36.8
Benton-NY	2.73	Benton-NY	143	Root-Chi	.242	Lucas-Cin	.304	Malone-Chi	32.1	Sherdel-StL	31.4

Clutch Pitching Index		Relief Runs		Adjusted Relief Runs		Relief Ranking		Total Pitcher Index		Total Baseball Ranking	
Nehf-Chi	133							Vance-Bro	7.0	Vance-Bro	7.0
Bush-Chi	117							Grimes-Pit	6.1	Grimes-Pit	6.1
Blake-Chi	115							Benton-NY	3.9	Hornsby-Bos	5.8
Kolp-Cin	114							Blake-Chi	3.8	Lindstrom-NY	4.8
Rhem-StL	114							Sherdel-StL	3.7	Jackson-NY	4.3

June 2 St. Mary's College football star Larry Bettencourt breaks in at third base with the Browns. A future member of the College Football Hall of Fame, Bettencourt was an All-American center who will later play for the Green Bay Packers. The $6,000 bonus he receives is a record for a rookie just out of school.

June 15 Ty Cobb, 41 years old, steals home for the 50th and final time in his 24-year career to extend his major league record. It comes in the eighth against the Indians.

July 14 At Boston, White Sox pitcher Ed Walsh, Jr. picks up his first win, topping the Red Sox, 11–4. Junior will only win 11 games to his father's 195: all 206 Walsh victories are for the White Sox.

July 22 Pitcher Red Faber of the White Sox comes up to bat in the eighth with two runners on base and the game with the Yankees tied, 4–4. He swings twice righthanded against righty Wilcy Moore and misses. He then switches to the left side and knocks in the winning runs with a single to center.

July 29 The Indians score eight in the first and nine in the second in a 24–6 win over the Yankees at home. Johnny Hodapp of the Indians becomes the first AL player to get two hits in an inning twice in a game. He strokes two singles in both the second and sixth innings of the game. The Yankees' lead shrinks from 11½ games to six in one week.

September 3 Ty Cobb makes the last of his 4,189 hits, the 724th double of his career, as a pinch hitter in the ninth inning of the first game at Washington. The hit is off Bump Hadley.

September 8 The Yankees sweep two from the A's, 3–0 and 7–3, to move back into first place to stay. The A's, in first place at the end of August, will run out of gas.

September 30 In Washington's 9-1 win over the Browns, Washington outfielder Leon "Goose" Goslin gets two hits for the third day in a row to edge Browns outfielder Heinie Manush .379 to .378 for his only batting title in his 18-year career. Nats' ace Sam Jones volunteered to pitch to stop Manush, while Blaeholder tried the same for St. Louis. Blaeholder got Goslin in his first two at bats, but Goose then hit a fifth inning home run.

October 4 The first Series game is a swift execution before 61,425 at New York. Babe Ruth has a single and double and scores twice, once on Bob Meusel's fourth-inning home run, and Lou Gehrig is 2-for-4 with two RBI off Bill Sherdel (21-10). Waite Hoyt (23-7) sets the Cards down with three hits, one a solo home run by Bottomley in the 7th, for a 4-1 win.

October 9 After a rainout, Waite Hoyt and Bill Sherdel are back on the mound for Game 4. After six innings, the Cards hold a 2-1 lead. With one out in the seventh, Ruth hits a home run, his second of the game, and Gehrig follows suit. When Meusel singles, in comes Alexander to face Tony Lazzeri, a replay of their confrontation two years earlier. Lazzeri doubles this time and later scores the fourth run of the inning. In the eighth, Cedric Durst, subbing for Earle Combs, hits one out of the park, and Ruth follows with his third home run of the game. The final score is 7-3, and the Yanks sweep their second straight World Series. Ruth's World Series BA of .625 is still unmatched; with Gehrig's .545 and a record nine RBI, they also set individual and team offensive records for hits, home runs, total bases, and at bats in a game.

October 15 Walter Johnson signs a three-year contract to manage the Senators.

October 16 Gordon "Mickey" Cochrane wins AL MVP honors, edging Heinie Manush by two points. Neither Ruth nor Gehrig is eligible, having won before.

November 3 Voters in Cleveland approve a bond issue to build a giant municipal stadium near the lakefront to attract events for the 1932 Olympics.

November 19 The Indians send $50,000 and two players to San Francisco (PCL) for outfielder Earl Averill.

BOSTON
M	B.Carrigan
1B	P.Todt
2B	B.Regan
SS	W.Gerber
3B	B.Myer
LF	K.Williams
CF	I.Flagstead
RF	D.Taitt
C	F.Hofmann
S2	B.Rogell
O3	J.Rothrock
C	C.Berry
C	J.Heving
O	G.Loepp
/1	R.Rollings
O	C.Sumner
/O	D.Williams
/O	A.Tarbert
/C	C.Asbjornson
/S	F.Moncewicz
R	P.Hinson
P	R.Ruffing
P	E.Morris
P	J.Russell
P	D.MacFayden
P	S.Harriss
RP	M.Settlemire
RP	P.Simmons
P	H.Bradley
P	M.Griffin
/P	C.Garrison
/P	H.Wiltse
/P	S.Slayton
/P	J.Wilson
/P	F.Bennett
/P	J.Shea

CHICAGO
M	R.Schalk
M	L.Blackburne
1B	B.Clancy
2B	B.Hunnefield
SS	B.Cissell
3B	W.Kamm
LF	B.Falk
CF	J.Mostil
RF	A.Metzler
C	B.Crouse
O	C.Reynolds
2S	B.Redfern
O2	B.Barrett
C	M.Berg
1	A.Shires
C	H.McCurdy
O	G.Blackerby
2	K.Swanson
O	R.Moore
/3	J.Mann
/C	R.Schalk
P	T.Thomas
P	T.Lyons
P	R.Faber
P	R.Blankenship
RP	S.Connally
P	G.Cox
P	E.Walsh
/P	C.Barnabe
/P	B.Weiland
/P	J.Goodell
/P	R.Wilson
/P	R.Leopold
/P	A.Williamson
/P	D.Dugan

CLEVELAND
M	R.Peckinpaugh
1B	L.Fonseca
2B	C.Lind
SS	J.Sewell
3B	J.Hodapp
LF	C.Jamieson
CF	S.Langford
RF	H.Summa
C	L.Sewell
1O	E.Morgan
3	G.Burns
O	L.Harvel
C	G.Myatt
O	G.Gerken
O	R.Dorman
C	C.Autry
S	E.Montague
O	O.Tucker
	B.Caldwell
/S	J.Goldman
/1	A.Van Camp
/1	C.Bolton
/S	J.Burnett
/3	A.Ward
/3	A.Reinholz
H	J.Gill
H	F.Wilson
P	J.Shaute
P	W.Hudlin
P	G.Uhle
P	J.Miller
P	G.Grant
RP	B.Bayne
RP	M.Harder
P	J.Miljus
P	D.Levsen
/P	G.Buckeye
P	W.Underhill
/P	W.Ferrell
/P	J.Brown
/P	C.Brown
/P	L.Barnhart
/P	J.Moore
/P	H.Collard

DETROIT
M	G.Moriarty
1B	B.Sweeney
2B	C.Gehringer
SS	J.Tavener
3B	M.McManus
LF	B.Fothergill
CF	H.Rice
RF	H.Heilmann
C	P.Hargrave
O	A.Wingo
3	J.Warner
C	L.Woodall
S3	C.Galloway
O	P.Easterling
O	J.Stone
1	J.Neun
C	M.Shea
P	O.Carroll
P	E.Whitehill
P	V.Sorrell
P	E.Vangilder
P	L.Stoner
RP	G.Smith
P	S.Gibson
P	K.Holloway
P	J.Billings
/P	P.Page
/P	C.Sullivan

NEW YORK
M	M.Huggins
1B	L.Gehrig
2B	T.Lazzeri
SS	M.Koenig
3B	J.Dugan
LF	B.Meusel
CF	E.Combs
RF	B.Ruth
C	J.Grabowski
2S	L.Durocher
3	G.Robertson
C	B.Bengough
C	P.Collins
O	C.Durst
O	B.Paschal
3	M.Gazella
/C	B.Burns
/1	G.Burns
P	G.Pipgras
P	W.Hoyt
P	H.Pennock
P	H.Johnson
P	A.Shealy
RP	W.Moore
P	F.Heimach
P	J.Bush
P	S.Coveleski
/P	T.Zachary
/P	M.Thomas
P	A.Campbell
/P	R.Ryan
/P	U.Shocker

PHILADELPHIA
M	C.Mack
1B	J.Hauser
2B	M.Bishop
SS	J.Boley
3B	S.Hale
LF	A.Simmons
CF	B.Miller
RF	T.Cobb
C	M.Cochrane
31	J.Foxx
O	M.Haas
2S	J.Dykes
O	T.Speaker
1P	O.Orwoll
O	W.French
S	J.Hassler
/2	E.Collins
C	C.Perkins
P	L.Grove
P	R.Walberg
P	J.Quinn
P	E.Rommel
P	G.Earnshaw
P	H.Ehmke
P	J.Bush
RP	B.Shores
/P	I.Powers
/P	J.Johnson
/P	C.Yerkes
/P	A.Daney

ST.LOUIS
M	D.Howley
1B	L.Blue
2B	O.Brannan
SS	R.Kress
3B	F.O'Rourke
LF	H.Manush
CF	F.Schulte
RF	E.McNeely
C	W.Schang
C	C.Manion
O	B.McGowan
3	L.Bettencourt
23	S.Melillo
/1	G.Sturdy
S	S.O'Neill
/3	B.Mullen
/3	O.Sax
/O	F.Bennett
/C	I.Danning
/O	F.Wilson
P	S.Gray
P	A.Crowder
P	J.Ogden
P	G.Blaeholder
P	L.Stewart
RP	D.Coffman
RP	H.Wiltse
RP	E.Strelecki
P	B.Beck
/P	E.Nevers
/P	J.Wright

WASHINGTON
M	B.Harris
1B	J.Judge
2B	B.Harris
SS	B.Reeves
3B	O.Bluege
LF	G.Goslin
CF	S.West
RF	S.Rice
C	M.Ruel
O	R.Barnes
S	J.Cronin
2S	J.Hayes
C	B.Tate
C	E.Kenna
S	G.Gillis
/1	G.Sisler
/O	D.Ganzel
O	D.Spalding
/1	H.Boss
/3	P.Ballenger
/C	A.Bool
/3	E.Crowley
H	H.McMullen
P	B.Hadley
P	S.Jones
P	G.Braxton
P	F.Marberry
P	M.Gaston
P	L.Brown
P	T.Zachary
P	B.Burke
P	H.Lisenbee
/P	C.Van Alstyne
/P	J.Weaver

TEAM	G	W	L	PCT	GB	R	OR	AB	H	2B	3B	HR	BB	SO	AVG	OBP	SLG	PRO	PRO+	BR	/A	PF	CHI	RC	SB	CS	SBA	SBR
NY	154	101	53	.656		894	685	5337	1578	269	79	133	562	544	.296	.365	.450	.815	124	146	175	97	100	888	51	51	50	-15
PHI	153	98	55	.641	2.5	829	615	5226	1540	276	75	89	533	442	.295	.363	.436	.799	112	115	92	103	97	843	59	48	55	-11
STL	154	82	72	.532	19	772	742	5217	1431	276	76	63	548	479	.274	.346	.393	.739	97	2	-21	103	104	736	76	43	64	-3
WAS	155	75	79	.487	26	718	705	5320	1510	277	93	40	481	390	.284	.346	.393	.739	101	1	6	99	97	743	110	59	65	-2
CHI	155	72	82	.468	33	656	725	5207	1405	231	77	24	469	488	.270	.334	.358	.692	88	-88	-79	99	102	641	139	82	63	-8
DET	154	68	86	.442	33	744	804	5292	1476	265	97	62	469	438	.279	.340	.401	.741	99	-2	-13	102	102	730	113	77	59	-12
CLE	155	62	92	.403	39	674	830	5386	1535	299	61	34	377	426	.285	.335	.382	.717	93	-49	-56	101	98	693	50	52	49	-16
BOS	154	57	96	.373	43.5	589	770	5132	1356	260	62	38	389	512	.264	.319	.361	.680	86	-119	-108	98	100	602	99	64	61	-9
TOT	617					5876		42117	11831	2200	620	483	3828	3719	.281	.344	.397	.741							697	476	59	-77

TEAM	CG	SH	SV	IP	H	H/G	HR	BB	SO	RAT	ERA	ERA+	OAV	OOB	PR	/A	PF	CPI	FA	E	DP	FW	PW	BW	SBW	DIF
NY	82	13	21	1375¹	1466	9.6	59	452	487	12.7	3.74	101	.276	.335	46	3	93	102	.968	194	136	-.0	.3	16.9	-.5	7.4
PHI	81	15	16	1367²	1349	8.9	66	424	607	11.8	3.36	119	.259	.318	103	97	99	99	.970	181	124	.6	9.4	8.9	-.1	2.7
STL	80	6	15	1374¹	1487	9.7	93	454	456	12.8	4.17	101	.282	.340	-20	3	104	100	.969	189	146	.2	-.3	-2.0	.6	5.9
WAS	77	15	10	1384	1420	9.2	40	466	462	12.5	3.88	103	.272	.335	25	19	99	94	.972	178	146	1.0	1.8	.6	.7	-6.1
CHI	88	6	11	1378	1518	9.9	66	501	418	13.4	3.98	102	.287	.352	8	8	100	108	.970	186	149	.5	.8	-7.6	.2	1.2
DET	65	5	16	1372	1481	9.7	58	567	451	13.7	4.32	95	.281	.355	-42	-34	102	97	.965	218	140	-1.5	-3.3	-1.3	-.2	-2.7
CLE	71	4	15	1378	1615	10.5	52	511	416	14.2	4.47	93	.303	.369	-66	-52	103	105	.965	221	187	-1.6	-5.0	-5.4	-.6	-2.4
BOS	70	5	9	1352	1492	9.9	49	452	407	13.2	4.39	93	.288	.349	-53	-44	102	94	.971	178	139	.9	-4.3	-10.4	.9	-5.8
TOT	614	69	113	10981¹		9.7				13.0	4.04		.281	.344					.969	1545	1167					

Runs		Hits		Doubles		Triples		Home Runs		Total Bases	
Ruth-NY	163	Manush-StL	241	Manush-StL	47	Combs-NY	21	Ruth-NY	54	Ruth-NY	380
Gehrig-NY	139	Gehrig-NY	210	Gehrig-NY	47	Manush-StL	20	Gehrig-NY	27	Manush-StL	367
Combs-NY	118	Rice-Was	202	Meusel-NY	45	Gehringer-Det	16	Goslin-Was	17	Gehrig-NY	364
Blue-StL	116	Combs-NY	194	Schulte-StL	44			Hauser-Phi	16	Combs-NY	290
Gehringer-Det	108	Gehringer-Det	193	Lind-Cle	42			Simmons-Phi	15	Heilmann-Det	283

Runs Batted In		Runs Produced		Bases On Balls		Batting Average		On Base Percentage		Slugging Average	
Ruth-NY	142	Gehrig-NY	254	Ruth-NY	135	Goslin-Was	.379	Gehrig-NY	.467	Ruth-NY	.709
Gehrig-NY	142	Ruth-NY	251	Blue-StL	105	Manush-StL	.378	Ruth-NY	.461	Gehrig-NY	.648
Meusel-NY	113	Manush-StL	199	Bishop-Phi	97	Gehringer-Det	.374	Goslin-Was	.442	Goslin-Was	.614
Manush-StL	108	Blue-StL	182	Gehrig-NY	95	Simmons-Phi	.351	Bishop-Phi	.435	Manush-StL	.575
		Meusel-NY	179	Judge-Was	80	Lazzeri-NY	.332	Manush-StL	.414	Simmons-Phi	.558

Production		Adjusted Production		Batter Runs		Adjusted Batter Runs		Clutch Hitting Index		Runs Created	
Ruth-NY	1.170	Ruth-NY	210	Ruth-NY	83.9	Ruth-NY	89.4	Cissell-Chi	130	Ruth-NY	182
Gehrig-NY	1.115	Gehrig-NY	196	Gehrig-NY	76.0	Gehrig-NY	81.2	Meusel-NY	128	Gehrig-NY	169
Goslin-Was	1.056	Goslin-Was	176	Manush-StL	50.3	Goslin-Was	49.8	Judge-Was	123	Manush-StL	150
Manush-StL	.989	Manush-StL	153	Goslin-Was	49.0	Manush-StL	46.2	Hodapp-Cle	118	Goslin-Was	125
Simmons-Phi	.954	Simmons-Phi	144	Foxx-Phi	30.5	Foxx-Phi	28.1	Boley-Phi	117	Combs-NY	114

Total Average		Stolen Bases		Stolen Base Average		Stolen Base Runs		Fielding Runs		Total Player Rating	
Ruth-NY	1.405	Myer-Bos	30	Rice-Was	84.2	Rice-Was	3.0	Gerber-StL-Bos	32.0	Ruth-NY	7.0
Gehrig-NY	1.256	Mostil-Chi	23	Goslin-Was	84.2	Goslin-Was	3.0	J.Sewell-Cle	27.0	J.Sewell-Cle	5.4
Goslin-Was	1.203	Rice-Det	20	Judge-Was	80.0	Reynolds-Chi	2.7	Jamieson-Cle	19.9	Gehrig-NY	5.1
Manush-StL	1.040	Cissell-Chi	18	Manush-StL	77.3	Judge-Was	2.4	Mostil-Chi	17.8	Goslin-Was	4.5
Simmons-Phi	.951	Bluege-Was	18			Manush-StL	2.1	Schulte-StL	17.3	Manush-StL	3.8

Wins		Win Percentage		Games		Complete Games		Shutouts		Saves	
Pipgras-NY	24	Crowder-StL	.808	Marberry-Was	48	Ruffing-Bos	25	Pennock-NY	5	Hoyt-NY	8
Grove-Phi	24	Hoyt-NY	.767	Morris-Bos	47	Thomas-Chi	24	Quinn-Phi	4	Hudlin-Cle	7
Hoyt-NY	23	Grove-Phi	.750	Pipgras-NY	46	Grove-Phi	24	Pipgras-NY	4	Lyons-Chi	6
Crowder-StL	21	Pennock-NY	.739	Rommel-Phi	43	Pipgras-NY	22	Jones-Was	4	Braxton-Was	6
Gray-StL	20	Quinn-Phi	.720					Grove-Phi	4		

Innings Pitched		Fewest Hits/Game		Fewest BB/Game		Strikeouts		Strikeouts/Game		Ratio	
Pipgras-NY	300.2	Braxton-Was	7.30	Rommel-Phi	1.35	Grove-Phi	183	Earnshaw-Phi	6.65	Braxton-Was	9.32
Ruffing-Bos	289.1	Grove-Phi	7.84	Quinn-Phi	1.45	Pipgras-NY	139	Grove-Phi	6.29	Grove-Phi	10.08
Thomas-Chi	283.0	Earnshaw-Phi	8.13	Pennock-NY	1.71	Thomas-Chi	129	Johnson-NY	4.97	Rommel-Phi	10.62
Hoyt-NY	273.0	Jones-Was	8.37	Braxton-Was	1.81	Ruffing-Bos	118	Walberg-Phi	4.28	Pennock-NY	10.88
Gray-StL	262.2	Johnson-NY	8.50	Russell-Bos	1.83	Earnshaw-Phi	117	Whitehill-Det	4.26	Hoyt-NY	11.21

Earned Run Average		Adjusted ERA		Opponents' Batting Avg.		Opponents' On Base Pct.		Starter Runs		Adjusted Starter Runs	
Braxton-Was	2.51	Braxton-Was	159	Braxton-Was	.222	Braxton-Was	.267	Grove-Phi	42.4	Grove-Phi	41.5
Pennock-NY	2.56	Grove-Phi	155	Grove-Phi	.229	Grove-Phi	.277	Braxton-Was	37.0	Braxton-Was	36.2
Grove-Phi	2.58	Pennock-NY	147	Earnshaw-Phi	.240	Rommel-Phi	.295	Pennock-NY	34.7	Thomas-Chi	30.2
Jones-Was	2.84	Jones-Was	141	Johnson-NY	.250	Pennock-NY	.302	Thomas-Chi	30.0	Gray-StL	29.4
Quinn-Phi	2.90	Quinn-Phi	138	Jones-Was	.252	Thomas-Chi	.310	Jones-Was	29.8	Jones-Was	29.0

Clutch Pitching Index		Relief Runs		Adjusted Relief Runs		Relief Ranking		Total Pitcher Index		Total Baseball Ranking	
Miller-Cle	119			Simmons-Bos	.5	Simmons-Bos	1	Grove-Phi	4.6	Ruth-NY	7.0
Quinn-Phi	119							Jones-Was	3.5	J.Sewell-Cle	5.4
Blankenship-Chi	114							Gray-StL	3.5	Gehrig-NY	5.1
Pennock-NY	113							Braxton-Was	3.5	Grove-Phi	4.6
Adkins-Chi	113							Thomas-Chi	3.3	Goslin-Was	4.5

January 1* Outfielder Jim Bell of Cienfuegos becomes the first man to connect for three homers in a game during professional league play in Cuba. Bell's feat occurs at Alda Park in a 15–11 victory over Club Havana.

April 16 The Cubs open at Wrigley Field before an estimated 50,000, the biggest Opening Day turnout they've ever had, and beat the Pirates 3–1.

May 8 The Giants' Carl Hubbell pitches an 11–0 no-hitter against the Pirates, allowing just one walk. In the ninth, the first two batters reached on errors before Hubbell recorded a strikeout and started the game-ending double play. It's the first no-hitter by a lefthander since Hub Leonard in 1918.

May 18 Brooklyn and Philadelphia score a major league-record 50 runs in a doubleheader at the Baker Bowl. The Robins (Dodgers) win the opener 20–16, and the Phils take the second game 8–6. Highlights include Brooklyn's Johnny Fredericks tallying five runs in the opener, which combined with his three yesterday, gives him a major league record eight in two games. The Dodgers pull off a triple play to keep some scoring down.

June 19 In their second straight doubleheader, The Giants sweep the Phillies, winning 15–14, in 11 innings, and 12–6. Mel Ott has two homers and four doubles for the day, while Edd Roush goes 8-for-12. In tomorrow's 11–6 win over the Phils, Ott will have three RBI, giving him 11 straight games with at least one ribbie. The 20-year-old will have 27 RBI in the 11 games and will finish the season with 151, second in the NL.

July 5 The Giants are the first team to use a public address system in a big league park, for a game against the Pirates.

July 18 Trying to curb the hitters, NL president Heydler orders umpires to rub up new balls before each game to remove the gloss.

August 10 Grover Cleveland Alexander beats the Phils 7-1 for his 373rd and last NL victory. He pitches four scoreless relief innings for the Cardinals and wins the game 11-9 in the 11th.

August 26 It's definitely the Cubs' year in the NL. In the eighth inning of a 5-5 tie with the Reds at Wrigley Field, Chicago's Norm McMillan hits a line drive down the left field line that Cincinnati left fielder Evar Swanson, shaded towards center, can't find. McMillan circles the bases as the Cubs take a four-run lead. Chicago relief pitcher Ken Penner picks up his jacket in the bullpen and finds the ball in his right sleeve.

September 27 Phils outfielder Chuck Klein hits homer No. 42, tying Mel Ott and equaling Hornsby's NL record. He'll hit one more to top the NL with 43.

October 5 Mel Ott of the Giants and Chuck Klein of the Phillies go into a season-ending doubleheader tied for the NL home run lead. In the opener, Ott gets a single, but Klein homers off Carl Hubbell to take the lead. Phillies pitchers proceed to walk Ott intentionally five straight times. The last walk comes with the bases loaded. Meanwhile, Phillie Lefty O'Doul gets six hits in the twinbill for an NL-record 254 hits.

	BOSTON		BROOKLYN		CHICAGO		CINCINNATI		NEW YORK		PHILADELPHIA		PITTSBURGH		ST.LOUIS
M	J.Fuchs	M	W.Robinson	M	J.McCarthy	M	J.Hendricks	M	J.McGraw	M	B.Shotton	M	D.Bush	M	B.Southworth
1B	G.Sisler	1B	D.Bissonette	1B	C.Grimm	1B	G.Kelly	1B	B.Terry	1B	D.Hurst	M	J.Ens	M	G.Street
2B	F.Maguire	2B	E.Moore	2B	R.Hornsby	2B	H.Critz	2B	A.Cohen	2B	F.Thompson	1B	E.Sheely	M	B.McKechnie
SS	R.Maranville	SS	D.Bancroft	SS	W.English	SS	H.Ford	SS	T.Jackson	SS	T.Thevenow	2B	G.Grantham	1B	J.Bottomley
3B	L.Bell	3B	W.Gilbert	3B	N.McMillan	3B	C.Dressen	3B	F.Lindstrom	3B	P.Whitney	SS	D.Bartell	2B	F.Frisch
LF	G.Harper	LF	R.Bressler	LF	R.Stephenson	LF	E.Swanson	LF	F.Leach	LF	L.O'Doul	3B	P.Traynor	SS	C.Gelbert
CF	E.Clark	CF	J.Frederick	CF	H.Wilson	CF	E.Allen	CF	E.Roush	CF	D.Sothern	LF	A.Comorosky	3B	A.High
RF	L.Richbourg	RF	B.Herman	RF	K.Cuyler	RF	C.Walker	RF	M.Ott	RF	C.Klein	CF	L.Waner	LF	C.Hafey
C	A.Spohrer	C	V.Picinich	C	Z.Taylor	C	J.Gooch	C	S.Hogan	C	W.Lerian	RF	P.Waner	CF	T.Douthit
												C	C.Hargreaves	RF	E.Orsatti
O	J.Welsh	O1	H.Hendrick	O	C.Heathcote	C	C.Sukeforth	C	B.O'Farrell	C	S.Davis			C	J.Wilson
3	J.Dugan	C	H.DeBerry	3S	C.Beck	S	P.Pittinger	O	C.Fullis	SO	B.Friberg	C	R.Hemsley		
2	B.James	2	B.Rhiel	C	M.Gonzalez	3	J.Stripp	2	R.Reese	O	H.Peel	S2	S.Adams	O	W.Roettger
C	Z.Taylor	2	J.Flowers	1	C.Tolson	O	P.Purdy	32	D.Farrell	O	C.Williams	S3	S.Clarke	C	W.Holm
O	H.Mueller	C	B.Henline	C	E.Grace	O	B.Zitzmann	O	J.Welsh	O	T.Sigman	O	F.Brickell	C	E.Smith
C	L.Legett	S	J.Warner	/3	F.Blair	/1	L.Dixon	/1	P.Crawford	O	G.Susce	S	C.Jones	/3	J.Butler
OP	J.Cooney	O	N.Cullop	C	J.Schulte	/1	W.Shaner	O	T.Kaufmann	H	J.O'Rourke	/O	I.Flagstead	2	C.Selph
O	P.Voyles	/S	G.Wright	O	J.Moore	H	E.Crabtree	/2	D.Marshall	/1	T.Lyons	/C	B.Linton	/O	E.Delker
O	B.Boyle	/O	M.Carey	/C	G.Hartnett	/C	H.McMullen	/C	J.Cummings			/S	H.Riconda	/O	B.Southworth
/O	B.Dunlap	/O	M.West	/C	T.Angley	/1	I.Wingo	/1	B.Jordan	P	C.Willoughby	/O	J.Mosolf	C	B.Jonnard
/3	G.Robertson	H	J.Gooch	/O	D.Taylor			/C	R.Schalk	P	L.Sweetland	/3	J.Stroner	/3	F.Haney
/O	R.Barron					P	R.Lucas	/O	S.Leslie	P	R.Benge	/C	J.O'Connell		
/O	J.Smith	P	W.Clark	P	C.Root	P	E.Rixey	/C	P.Veltman	P	P.Collins	/S	B.Sankey	P	B.Sherdel
/C	H.Gowdy	P	D.Vance	P	G.Bush	P	J.May			RP	H.Elliott	/1	B.Windle	P	S.Johnson
/3	H.Peploski	P	R.Moss	P	P.Malone	P	P.Donohue	P	C.Hubbell	RP	B.McGraw	R	M.Ingram	P	J.Haines
/C	B.Cronin	P	C.Dudley	P	S.Blake	P	D.Luque	P	L.Benton	RP	S.Dailey			P	C.Mitchell
/2	D.Farrell	P	D.McWeeny	P	A.Nehf	RP	K.Ash	P	F.Fitzsimmons			P	B.Grimes	P	H.Haid
/C	J.Cummings	RP	C.Moore	RP	M.Cvengros	RP	R.Ehrhardt	P	B.Walker	P	L.Roy	P	E.Brame		
/C	P.Collins	RP	W.Ballou					P	C.Mays	P	L.Koupal	P	R.Kremer	P	F.Frankhouse
H	A.Weston			P	H.Carlson	P	R.Kolp	RP	R.Judd	P	H.Smythe	P	J.Petty	P	P.Alexander
/2	J.Evers	P	J.Morrison	P	C.Jonnard	/P	M.Gudat			P	J.Greene	P	S.Swetonic	P	B.Hallahan
		P	L.Koupal	P	T.Horne	/P	B.Frey	P	D.Henry	/P	A.Ferguson	RP	C.Hill	/P	A.Grabowski
P	B.Smith	/P	J.Elliott	/P	K.Penner	/P	D.Kemner	P	J.Scott	/P	E.Miller			/P	J.Lindsey
P	S.Seibold	/P	J.Pattison	/P	B.Osborn	/P	S.Johnson	P	J.Genewich	/P	J.Milligan	P	L.French	/P	M.Holland
P	P.Jones	/P	K.Greenfield	/P	H.Grampp	/P	P.Zahniser	/P	R.Lucas	/P	J.Holloway	P	H.Meine	/P	H.Bell
P	E.Brandt	/P	B.Newsom					/P	R.Parmelee			P	F.Fussell	/P	B.Doak
P	B.Cantwell	/P	J.Bradshaw					/P	J.Tennant			P	J.Dawson	/P	C.Hill
		/P	L.Roy									/P	L.Chagnon	/P	H.Goldsmith
P	D.Leverett	/P	C.Blethen									/P	R.Erickson		
P	B.Cunningham	/P	A.Ferguson									/P	L.Meadows		
P	A.Delaney														
/P	R.Peery														
P	B.Hearn														
/P	K.Greenfield														
/P	B.Clarkson														
/P	J.Werts														
/P	C.Touchstone														

TEAM	G	W	L	PCT	GB	R	OR	AB	H	2B	3B	HR	BB	SO	AVG	OBP	SLG	PRO	PRO+	BR	/A	PF	CHI	RC	SB	CS	SBA	SBR
CHI	156	98	54	.645		982	758	5471	1655	310	46	139	589	567	.303	.373	.452	.825	111	92	90	100	104	916	103			
PIT	154	88	65	.575	10.5	904	780	5490	1663	285	116	60	503	335	.303	.364	.430	.794	101	28	7	102	104	850	94			
NY	152	84	67	.556	13.5	897	709	5388	1594	251	47	136	482	405	.296	.358	.436	.794	103	18	21	100	106	827	85			
STL	154	78	74	.513	20	831	806	5364	1569	310	84	100	490	455	.293	.354	.438	.792	101	12	4	101	100	819	72			
PHI	154	71	82	.464	27.5	897	1032	5484	1693	305	51	153	573	470	.309	.377	.467	.844	108	125	62	107	92	951	59			
BRO	153	70	83	.458	28.5	755	888	5273	1535	282	69	99	504	454	.291	.355	.427	.782	102	-1	15	98	93	792	80			
CIN	155	66	88	.429	33	686	760	5269	1478	258	79	34	412	347	.281	.336	.379	.715	87	-133	-102	95	103	664	134			
BOS	154	56	98	.364	43	657	876	5291	1481	252	77	33	408	432	.280	.335	.375	.710	85	-142	-116	96	99	659	65			
TOT	616					6609		43030	12668	2253	569	754	3961	3465	.294	.357	.426	.783							692			

TEAM	CG	SH	SV	IP	H	H/G	HR	BB	SO	RAT	ERA	ERA+	OAV	OOB	PR	/A	PF	CPI	FA	E	DP	FW	PW	BW	SBW	DIF
CHI	79	14	21	1398²	1542	9.9	77	537	548	13.5	4.16	111	.284	.350	86	70	98	104	.975	154	169	1.4	6.4	8.2		6.0
PIT	79	5	13	1379	1530	10.0	96	439	409	13.0	4.36	109	.284	.340	54	62	101	98	.970	181	136	-.2	5.6	.6		5.5
NY	68	9	13	1372	1536	10.1	102	387	431	12.7	3.97	115	.287	.337	113	93	97	109	.975	158	163	.9	8.5	1.9		-2.8
STL	83	6	8	1359²	1604	10.6	101	474	453	13.9	4.66	100	.297	.357	8	-1	99	102	.971	174	149	.2	-.0	.4		1.6
PHI	45	5	24	1348	1743	11.6	122	616	369	16.0	6.13	85	.319	.391	-212	-142	110	96	.969	191	153	-.8	-12.9	5.6		2.6
BRO	59	8	16	1358	1553	10.3	92	549	549	14.2	4.92	94	.290	.360	-32	-48	98	95	.968	192	113	-.9	-4.4	1.4		-2.6
CIN	75	5	8	1369¹	1558	10.2	61	413	347	13.1	4.41	103	.292	.345	46	22	97	97	.974	162	148	.9	2.0	-9.3		-4.6
BOS	78	4	12	1352²	1604	10.7	103	530	366	14.4	5.12	91	.302	.367	-62	-68	99	99	.967	204	146	-1.5	-6.2	-10.6		-2.7
TOT	566	56	115	10937¹		10.4				13.8	4.71		.294	.357					.971	1416	1177					

Runs
Hornsby-Chi 156
O'Doul-Phi 152
Ott-NY 138
Wilson-Chi 135
L.Waner-Pit 134

Hits
O'Doul-Phi 254
L.Waner-Pit 234
Hornsby-Chi 229
Terry-NY 226
Klein-Phi 219

Doubles
Frederick-Bro 52
Hornsby-Chi 47
Hafey-StL 47
Klein-Phi 45
Kelly-Cin 45

Triples
L.Waner-Pit 20
P.Waner-Pit 15
Walker-Cin 15
Whitney-Phi 14

Home Runs
Klein-Phi 43
Ott-NY 42
Wilson-Chi 39
Hornsby-Chi 39
O'Doul-Phi 32

Total Bases
Hornsby-Chi 409
Klein-Phi 405
O'Doul-Phi 397
Wilson-Chi 355
Herman-Bro 348

Runs Batted In
Wilson-Chi 159
Ott-NY 151
Hornsby-Chi 149
Klein-Phi 145
Bottomley-StL 137

Runs Produced
Hornsby-Chi 266
Wilson-Chi 255
Ott-NY 247
O'Doul-Phi 242
Klein-Phi 228

Bases On Balls
Ott-NY 113
Grantham-Pit 93
P.Waner-Pit 89
Hornsby-Chi 87
Walker-Cin 85

Batting Average
O'Doul-Phi 398
Herman-Bro 381
Hornsby-Chi 380
Terry-NY 372
Stephenson-Chi . . .362

On Base Percentage
O'Doul-Phi 465
Hornsby-Chi 459
Ott-NY 449
Stephenson-Chi . . .445
Cuyler-Chi 438

Slugging Average
Hornsby-Chi 679
Klein-Phi 657
Ott-NY 635
Hafey-StL 632
O'Doul-Phi 622

Production
Hornsby-Chi 1.139
O'Doul-Phi 1.087
Ott-NY 1.084
Klein-Phi 1.065
Herman-Bro 1.047

Adjusted Production
Hornsby-Chi 178
Ott-NY 166
Herman-Bro 160
O'Doul-Phi 157
Wilson-Chi 155

Batter Runs
Hornsby-Chi 74.1
O'Doul-Phi 68.5
Ott-NY 58.4
Klein-Phi 53.3
Herman-Bro 49.6

Adjusted Batter Runs
Hornsby-Chi 73.8
Ott-NY 58.9
O'Doul-Phi 57.8
Herman-Bro 52.4
Wilson-Chi 48.7

Clutch Hitting Index
Traynor-Pit 139
Sheely-Pit 137
Comorosky-Pit 133
Grimm-Chi 127
Kelly-Cin 122

Runs Created
Hornsby-Chi 183
O'Doul-Phi 180
Klein-Phi 158
Ott-NY 157
Wilson-Chi 148

Total Average
Hornsby-Chi 1.338
Ott-NY 1.287
O'Doul-Phi 1.247
Herman-Bro 1.205
Cuyler-Chi 1.181

Stolen Bases
Cuyler-Chi 43
Swanson-Cin 33
Frisch-StL 24
Herman-Bro 21
Allen-Cin 21

Stolen Base Average

Stolen Base Runs

Fielding Runs
Whitney-Phi 21.3
Maranville-Bos 19.5
Jackson-NY 19.2
L.Waner-Pit 15.7
English-Chi 15.4

Total Player Rating
Hornsby-Chi 7.2
Ott-NY 5.2
O'Doul-Phi 4.7
Jackson-NY 4.1
Wilson-Chi 3.2

Wins
Malone-Chi 22
Root-Chi 19
Lucas-Cin 19

Win Percentage
Root-Chi 760
Bush-Chi 720
Grimes-Pit 708
Malone-Chi 688
Kremer-Pit 643

Games
Bush-Chi 50
Willoughby-Phi 49
Sweetland-Phi 43
Root-Chi 43
Collins-Phi 43

Complete Games
Lucas-Cin 28

Shutouts
Malone-Chi 5
Root-Chi 4
Fitzsimmons-NY 4

Saves
Morrison-Bro 8
Bush-Chi 8
Koupal-Bro-Phi 6

Innings Pitched
Clark-Bro 279.0
Root-Chi 272.0
Bush-Chi 270.2
Lucas-Cin 270.0
Hubbell-NY 268.0

Fewest Hits/Game
Lucas-Cin 8.90
Hubbell-NY 9.17
Kremer-Pit 9.18
Johnson-StL 9.18
Bush-Chi 9.21

Fewest BB/Game
Vance-Bro 1.83
Lucas-Cin 1.93
Petty-Pit 2.05
Hubbell-NY 2.25
Clark-Bro 2.29

Strikeouts
Malone-Chi 166
Clark-Bro 140
Vance-Bro 126
Root-Chi 124
Hubbell-NY 106

Strikeouts/Game
Malone-Chi 5.60
Vance-Bro 4.90
Clark-Bro 4.52
May-Cin 4.16
Root-Chi 4.10

Ratio
Lucas-Cin 10.87
Hubbell-NY 11.62
Kremer-Pit 11.65
Petty-Pit 11.67
Vance-Bro 11.67

Earned Run Average
Walker-NY 3.09
Grimes-Pit 3.13
Root-Chi 3.47
Malone-Chi 3.57
Lucas-Cin 3.60

Adjusted ERA
Grimes-Pit 152
Walker-NY 148
Root-Chi 133
Johnson-StL 129
Malone-Chi 129

Opponents' Batting Avg.
Lucas-Cin 257
Johnson-StL 265
Hubbell-NY 265
Bush-Chi 265
Grimes-Pit 269

Opponents' On Base Pct.
Lucas-Cin 297
Hubbell-NY 313
Clark-Bro 316
Vance-Bro 316
Petty-Pit 317

Starter Runs
Grimes-Pit 40.8
Root-Chi 37.4
Malone-Chi 33.8
Lucas-Cin 33.3
Walker-NY 32.0

Adjusted Starter Runs
Grimes-Pit 42.2
Root-Chi 34.4
Malone-Chi 30.8
Walker-NY 29.4
Lucas-Cin 28.8

Clutch Pitching Index
Mitchell-StL 129
Walker-NY 129
Sweetland-Phi 116
Grimes-Pit 116
Malone-Chi 115

Relief Runs
Hill-Pit-StL 2.9
Cvengros-Chi 5

Adjusted Relief Runs
Hill-Pit-StL 3.3

Relief Ranking
Hill-Pit-StL 2.0

Total Pitcher Index
Grimes-Pit 4.7
Lucas-Cin 4.0
Malone-Chi 3.0
Clark-Bro 2.5
Root-Chi 2.4

Total Baseball Ranking
Hornsby-Chi 7.2
Ott-NY 5.2
Grimes-Pit 4.7
O'Doul-Phi 4.7
Jackson-NY 4.1

January 22 The Yankees announce they'll put numbers on the backs of their uniforms, becoming the first baseball team to start continuous use of the numbers. The first numbers are based on positions in the batting order; thus, Ruth will wear number three and Gehrig four. By 1931 all AL teams will use them; it will be 1933 before all NL players are numbered.

February 20 The Red Sox announce they'll play Sunday games, allowed for the first time in Boston, at Braves Field because Fenway Park is located too close to a church.

April 16 Cleveland outfielder Earl Averill becomes the first AL player to hit a home run on his first major league time at bat when he blasts an 0-and-2 pitch off Detroit's Earl Whitehill in the Indians' 5-4, 11-inning victory.

April 17 Babe Ruth and actress Claire Hodgson are married at five A.M. to avoid crowds. The Yankee opener with the Red Sox is rained out. The next day, in his first at bat against Red Ruffing, the Babe will hit a homer. Rounding second base, he doffs his cap to Claire in the stands. Gehrig adds a homer in the sixth, and New York wins 7–3.

April 28 The Red Sox play the first Sunday game in Boston history, but they do it at Braves Field losing to the A's, 7–3. Protests by a few members of a nearby church are the reason for the shift from Fenway. The Braves, rained out of their scheduled Sunday game on April 21, will play their first Sunday home game on May 5.

May 6 The AL announces that it will discontinue the MVP award. The NL will abandon it after this year; in 1931 the Baseball Writers Association will pick it up and conduct the balloting from then on.

July 6 After watching the Tigers belt eight homers on the second, third, and fourth, the Browns use the off day to erect a screen in front of the right field pavilion. The screen stretches 156 feet from the foul pole toward center field, 310 feet down the line from home. In the next day's game, Heinie Manush will hit three balls off the screen against the Yankees' Waite Hoyt, while Ruth will hit two off it in the series. This screen will remain in place into the 1940s, the only stadium with extended outfield seating where it is impossible to catch a home run ball.

August 14 It is Charlie Gehringer Day in Detroit, and the popular second baseman handles 10 chances in the field, hits three singles and a homer, and steals home in a 17–13 win over the Yankees.

August 17 The Yankees buy pitcher Lefty Gomez from San Francisco (PCL) for delivery in September 1930.

September 25 Three days after turning the team over to coach Art Fletcher, Yankee manager Miller Huggins dies from blood poisoning at New York's St. Vincent Hospital. He was 49. On the day of his funeral in Cincinnati, the AL will cancel all games.

October 8 Howard Ehmke (7-2), who has been scouting the Cubs for a week, is the Athletics' surprise starter in Game 1 of the World Series at Chicago. A crowd of 50,740 Cubs fans watches Ehmke strike out a World Series-record 13 that will stand until Brooklyn's Carl Erskine fans 14 Yankees in 1953. He holds the Cubs scoreless until the ninth for a 3-1 win. Charlie Root (19-6) yields just three hits, but one is a home run by Jimmie Foxx in the seventh.

October 12 At age 45, John Quinn (11-9) gets a start against Root. After giving up a home run to Charlie Grimm with a man on in the third, Quinn serves up four straight singles to open the sixth , and in comes Rube Walberg (18-11). The inning ends with the score 7-0. Trailing 8-0 in the seventh, the Athletics, in the greatest rally in World Series history, shake Chicago by scoring 10 runs for a 10-8 victory. The most damaging play is Hack Wilson's misjudgment of a fly from Mule Haas's bat, which goes for a three-run, inside-the-park home run.

October 14 After the teams take Sunday off, a special train from Washington brings President and Mrs. Hoover to Shibe Park to see if Howard Ehmke can wind up the Series against Pat Malone. They match zeros for three innings, but, with two outs in the fourth, a walk and three hits give the Cubs a 2-0 lead. Malone stifles the A's with two hits, and the 2-0 lead holds up into the ninth. The Athletics rally and come up with three runs, the winning run scoring on a Bing Miller double, and take the Series, four games to one.

	BOSTON		CHICAGO		CLEVELAND		DETROIT		NEW YORK		PHILADELPHIA		ST.LOUIS		WASHINGTON
M	B.Carrigan	M	L.Blackburne	M	R.Peckinpaugh	M	B.Harris	M	M.Huggins	M	C.Mack	M	D.Howley	M	W.Johnson
1B	P.Todt	1B	A.Shires	1B	L.Fonseca	1B	D.Alexander	M	A.Fletcher	1B	J.Foxx	1B	L.Blue	1B	J.Judge
2B	B.Regan	2B	J.Kerr	2B	J.Hodapp	2B	C.Gehringer	1B	L.Gehrig	2B	M.Bishop	2B	S.Melillo	2B	B.Myer
SS	H.Rhyne	SS	B.Cissell	SS	J.Tavener	SS	H.Schuble	2B	T.Lazzeri	SS	J.Boley	SS	R.Kress	SS	J.Cronin
3B	B.Reeves	3B	W.Kamm	3B	J.Sewell	3B	M.McManus	SS	L.Durocher	3B	S.Hale	3B	F.O'Rourke	3B	J.Hayes
LF	R.Scarritt	LF	A.Metzler	LF	C.Jamieson	LF	R.Johnson	3B	G.Robertson	LF	A.Simmons	LF	H.Manush	LF	G.Goslin
CF	J.Rothrock	CF	D.Hoffman	CF	E.Averill	CF	H.Rice	LF	B.Meusel	CF	M.Haas	CF	F.Schulte	CF	S.West
RF	Bi.Barrett	RF	C.Reynolds	RF	B.Falk	RF	H.Heilmann	CF	E.Combs	RF	B.Miller	RF	B.McGowan	RF	S.Rice
C	C.Berry	C	M.Berg	C	L.Sewell	C	E.Phillips	RF	B.Ruth	C	M.Cochrane	C	W.Schang	C	B.Tate
								C	B.Dickey						
O	E.Bigelow	1	B.Clancy	O	E.Morgan	O	B.Fothergill	O	J.Dykes	O	E.McNeely	32	O.Bluege
S2	B.Narleski	O	J.Watwood	S	R.Gardner	C	P.Hargrave	S3	M.Koenig	O	H.Summa	O	R.Badgro	C	M.Ruel
3	Bo.Barrett	2	B.Hunnefield	2	C.Lind	C	M.Shea	3S	L.Lary	C	C.Perkins	C	R.Ferrell	O	R.Barnes
C	J.Heving	O	D.Taitt	O2	D.Porter	O	J.Stone	O	C.Durst	2	J.Cronin	C	C.Manion	C	R.Spencer
O	K.Williams	C	B.Crouse	C	G.Myatt	S	Y.Wuestling	O	S.Byrd	1	G.Burns	2	O.Brannan	1	H.Boss
C	A.Gaston	C	C.Autry	/1	J.Hauser	S	B.Akers	O	B.Paschal	O	W.French	/S	E.Roetz	/1	C.Gooch
S2	W.Gerber	2	B.Redfern	S	J.Burnett	C	R.Hayworth	/2	B.Morse	3	L.Dondero	O	I.Flagstead
2	G.Gillis	O	J.Mostil	C	G.Hartley	/3	F.Sigafoos	C	J.Grabowski	/O	B.LeBourveau	/O	T.Jenkins	C	S.Harris
O	D.Taitt	/2	F.Sigafoos	R	D.Jessee	S	N.Richardson	/S	A.Jorgens	/3	E.McNair	/3	J.Austin	/2	S.Stewart
O	I.Flagstead	H	B.Barrett			/2	B.Harris	/3	J.Wera	H	E.Collins	/O	D.Land
/O	J.Cicero	H	K.Swanson	P	W.Hudlin	H	L.Woodall	H	G.Burns	/O	C.Mattox	P	S.Gray	P	P.Gharrity
C	C.Asbjornson			P	W.Ferrell			R	L.Funk	/C	C.Cramer	P	A.Crowder	/O	N.Altrock
1	J.Standaert	P	T.Thomas	P	J.Miller	P	G.Uhle			/S	J.Hassler	P	G.Blaeholder
/C	E.Connolly	P	T.Lyons	P	J.Shaute	P	E.Whitehill	P	G.Pipgras	/3	R.Miller	P	R.Collins	P	F.Marberry
/O	J.Ryan	P	R.Faber	P	J.Miljus	P	V.Sorrell	P	W.Hoyt			P	L.Stewart	P	B.Hadley
		P	H.McKain			P	O.Carroll	P	E.Wells	P	L.Grove	RP	C.Kimsey	P	G.Braxton
P	R.Ruffing	P	G.Adkins	P	K.Holloway	RP	A.Prudhomme	P	H.Pennock	P	R.Walberg	RP	D.Coffman	P	L.Brown
P	M.Gaston			P	J.Zinn	RP	L.Stoner	P	R.Sherid	P	G.Earnshaw			P	S.Jones
P	J.Russell	P	E.Walsh	P	M.Shoffner			RP	W.Moore	P	J.Quinn	P	J.Ogden
P	D.MacFayden	P	D.Dugan	P	G.Grant	P	E.Yde			P	B.Shores	/P	E.Strelecki	P	B.Burke
P	E.Morris	P	B.Weiland	P	M.Harder	P	S.Graham	P	F.Heimach			/P	F.Stiely	P	M.Thomas
RP	E.Carroll	/P	T.Blankenship	/P	C.Brown	/P	G.Smith	P	T.Zachary	P	E.Rommel	/P	P.Hopkins	P	A.Liska
		/P	D.Henry	/P	J.Moore	/P	A.Herring	P	H.Johnson	P	H.Ehmke	/P	H.Cobb	/P	P.Hopkins
P	B.Bayne	P	S.Connally			/P	C.Hogsett	P	G.Rhodes	P	C.Yerkes	/P	O.Estrada	P	W.Beall
P	R.Dobens	P	J.Byrne			P	P.Page	/P	B.Nekola	P	O.Orwoll			P	P.McCullough
P	E.Durham	/P	L.Blackburne			/P	W.Wyatt	/P	M.Thomas	P	B.Breckinridge			P	D.Savidge
/P	H.Lisenbee					/P	J.Billings							/P	A.Campbell
/P	P.Simmons					/P	E.Vangilder							/P	E.Wineapple
/P	H.Bradley					/P	F.Barnes								

TEAM	G	W	L	PCT	GB	R	OR	AB	H	2B	3B	HR	BB	SO	AVG	OBP	SLG	PRO	PRO+	BR	/A	PF	CHI	RC	SB	CS	SBA	SBR
PHI	151	104	46	.693	—	901	**615**	5204	1539	288	76	122	543	440	.296	**.365**	.451	**.816**	111	**113**	81	104	**102**	875	61	38	62	-5
NY	154	88	66	.571	18	899	775	5379	1587	262	74	**142**	554	518	.295	.364	.450	.814	**123**	111	**171**	93	101	892	51	44	54	-11
CLE	152	81	71	.533	24	717	736	5187	1525	294	79	62	453	363	.294	.354	.417	.771	100	26	-2	104	92	763	75	85	47	-29
STL	154	79	73	.520	26	733	713	5174	1426	277	64	46	**589**	431	.276	.352	.381	.733	91	-33	-61	104	100	723	72	46	61	-6
WAS	153	71	81	.467	34	730	776	5237	1445	244	66	48	556	400	.276	.347	.375	.722	90	-56	-61	101	**102**	706	86	61	59	-11
DET	155	70	84	.455	36	**926**	928	5592	**1671**	**339**	**97**	110	521	496	**.299**	.360	**.453**	.813	114	110	106	101	101	**914**	95	72	57	-15
CHI	152	59	93	.388	46	627	792	5248	1406	240	74	37	425	436	.268	.325	.363	.688	83	-134	-127	99	**102**	633	**109**	65	**63**	-6
BOS	155	58	96	.377	48	605	803	5160	1377	285	69	28	413	494	.267	.325	.365	.690	85	-130	-115	98	99	616	85	80	52	-23
TOT	613					6138		42181	11976	2229	599	595	4054	3578	.284	.349	.407	.756							634	491	56	-104

TEAM	CG	SH	SV	IP	H	H/G	HR	BB	SO	RAT	ERA	ERA+	OAV	OOB	PR	/A	PF	CPI	FA	E	DP	FW	PW	BW	SBW	DIF
PHI	70	9	**24**	1357	**1371**	9.1	73	487	**573**	12.4	**3.44**	123	**.264**	.329	121	119	100	105	**.975**	146	117	2.6	11.2	7.6	.8	6.8
NY	64	12	18	1366²	1475	9.7	83	485	484	13.1	4.19	92	.278	.341	7	-52	91	96	.971	178	153	.8	-4.9	**16.1**	.2	-1.2
CLE	80	8	10	1352	1570	10.5	56	488	389	13.9	4.05	109	.295	.357	28	57	105	**109**	.968	198	**162**	-.6	5.4	-.2	-1.5	1.9
STL	83	**15**	10	1371	1469	9.6	100	**462**	415	12.8	4.08	108	.279	.340	25	51	104	102	**.975**	156	148	2.2	4.8	-5.8	.7	1.1
WAS	62	8	17	1354²	1429	9.5	**48**	496	494	12.9	4.34	98	.276	.342	-15	-16	101	89	.968	195	156	-.3	-1.5	-5.8	-.2	2.4
DET	82	5	9	1390¹	1641	10.6	73	646	467	15.0	4.96	86	.301	.377	-111	-105	101	100	.961	242	149	-3.0	-9.9	10.0	-.2	-3.9
CHI	78	5	7	1357²	1481	9.8	84	505	328	13.4	4.41	97	.284	.351	-26	-22	101	98	.970	188	153	.0	-2.1	-12.0	.7	-3.7
BOS	**84**	9	5	1366²	1537	10.1	78	496	416	13.6	4.43	96	.291	.355	-28	-25	101	100	.965	218	159	-1.6	-2.4	-10.8	-.9	-3.3
TOT	603	66	100	10916		9.9				13.4	4.24		.284	.349					.969	1521	1197					

Runs
Gehringer-Det 131
Johnson-Det 128
Gehrig-NY 127
Foxx-Phi 123
Ruth-NY 121

Hits
Gehringer-Det 215
Alexander-Det 215
Simmons-Phi 212
Fonseca-Cle 209
Manush-StL 204

Doubles
Manush-StL 45
Johnson-Det 45
Gehringer-Det 45
Fonseca-Cle 44

Triples
Gehringer-Det 19
Scarritt-Bos 17
B.Miller-Phi 16

Home Runs
Ruth-NY 46
Gehrig-NY 35
Simmons-Phi 34
Foxx-Phi 33
Alexander-Det 25

Total Bases
Simmons-Phi 373
Alexander-Det 363
Ruth-NY 348
Gehringer-Det 337

Runs Batted In
Simmons-Phi 157
Ruth-NY 154
Alexander-Det 137
Gehrig-NY 126
Heilmann-Det 120

Runs Produced
Simmons-Phi 237
Ruth-NY 229
Gehringer-Det 224
Alexander-Det 222
Gehrig-NY 218

Bases On Balls
Bishop-Phi 128
Blue-StL 126
Gehrig-NY 122
Foxx-Phi 103
Cronin-Was 85

Batting Average
Fonseca-Cle 369
Simmons-Phi 365
Manush-StL 355
Lazzeri-NY 354
Foxx-Phi 354

On Base Percentage
Foxx-Phi ..... .463
Gehrig-NY ..... .431
Ruth-NY ..... .430
Lazzeri-NY ..... .429
Fonseca-Cle ..... .427

Slugging Average
Ruth-NY ..... .697
Simmons-Phi ..... .642
Foxx-Phi ..... .625
Gehrig-NY ..... .584
Alexander-Det ..... .580

Production
Ruth-NY 1.128
Foxx-Phi 1.088
Simmons-Phi 1.040
Gehrig-NY 1.015
Lazzeri-NY ..... .991

Adjusted Production
Ruth-NY 199
Foxx-Phi 171
Gehrig-NY 170
Lazzeri-NY 164
Simmons-Phi 158

Batter Runs
Foxx-Phi 63.1
Ruth-NY 61.9
Gehrig-NY 51.6
Simmons-Phi 50.3
Lazzeri-NY 43.9

Adjusted Batter Runs
Ruth-NY 71.2
Gehringer-Det 61.1
Foxx-Phi 58.0
Lazzeri-NY 52.4
Simmons-Phi 45.6

Clutch Hitting Index
West-Was 130
Heilmann-Det 129
Kress-StL 123
Myer-Was 119
Falk-Cle 118

Runs Created
Foxx-Phi 154
Ruth-NY 150
Gehrig-NY 146
Simmons-Phi 145
Alexander-Det 140

Total Average
Ruth-NY 1.288
Foxx-Phi 1.261
Gehrig-NY 1.151
Simmons-Phi 1.097
Lazzeri-NY 1.041

Stolen Bases
Gehringer-Det 27
Cissell-Chi 25
B.Miller-Phi 24
Rothrock-Bos 23
Johnson-Det 20

Stolen Base Average
Gehringer-Det 75.0
B.Miller-Phi 72.7
Myer-Was 72.0
Reynolds-Chi 67.9
Rice-Was 66.7

Stolen Base Runs
Gehringer-Det 2.7
B.Miller-Phi 1.8
Myer-Was 1.2
Goslin-Was 1.2
Berg-Chi 9

Fielding Runs
Durocher-NY 26.2
Kerr-Chi 24.0
Melillo-StL 22.5
Simmons-Phi 17.3
West-Was 15.0

Total Player Rating
Ruth-NY 5.0
Simmons-Phi 4.9
Lazzeri-NY 4.8
Gehringer-Det 3.9
Gehrig-NY 3.7

Wins
Earnshaw-Phi 24
Ferrell-Cle 21
Grove-Phi 20
Marberry-Was 19

Win Percentage
Grove-Phi ..... .769
Earnshaw-Phi ..... .750
Ferrell-Cle ..... .677
Walberg-Phi ..... .621
Marberry-Was ..... .613

Games
Marberry-Was 49
Earnshaw-Phi 44
Gray-StL 43
Ferrell-Cle 43

Complete Games
Thomas-Chi 24
Uhle-Det 23
Gray-StL 23
Hudlin-Cle 22
Lyons-Chi 21

Shutouts
MacFayden-Bos 4
Gray-StL 4
Crowder-StL 4
Blaeholder-StL 4

Saves
Marberry-Was 11
Moore-NY 8
Shores-Phi 7
Ferrell-Cle 5

Innings Pitched
Gray-StL 305.0
Hudlin-Cle 280.1
Grove-Phi 275.1
Walberg-Phi 267.2
Crowder-StL 266.2

Fewest Hits/Game
Earnshaw-Phi 8.23
Wells-NY 8.33
Marberry-Was 8.38
Walberg-Phi 8.61
McKain-Chi 9.00

Fewest BB/Game
Russell-Bos 1.58
Pennock-NY 1.60
Thomas-Chi 2.08
Uhle-Det 2.10
Quinn-Phi 2.18

Strikeouts
Grove-Phi 170
Earnshaw-Phi 149
Pipgras-NY 125
Marberry-Was 121

Strikeouts/Game
Grove-Phi 5.56
Earnshaw-Phi 5.27
Pipgras-NY 4.99
Hadley-Was 4.52
Marberry-Was 4.35

Ratio
Marberry-Was 11.07
Thomas-Chi 11.44
Grove-Phi 11.83
Walberg-Phi 11.94
Faber-Chi 11.96

Earned Run Average
Grove-Phi 2.81
Marberry-Was 3.06
Thomas-Chi 3.19
Earnshaw-Phi 3.29
Hudlin-Cle 3.34

Adjusted ERA
Grove-Phi 150
Marberry-Was 139
Thomas-Chi 134
Hudlin-Cle 133
Earnshaw-Phi 129

Opponents' Batting Avg.
Earnshaw-Phi ..... .241
Wells-NY ..... .248
Marberry-Was ..... .252
Walberg-Phi ..... .254
Grove-Phi ..... .262

Opponents' On Base Pct.
Marberry-Was ..... .308
Thomas-Chi ..... .310
Grove-Phi ..... .316
Hudlin-Cle ..... .318
Walberg-Phi ..... .320

Starter Runs
Grove-Phi 43.7
Marberry-Was 32.9
Thomas-Chi 30.3
Hudlin-Cle 28.1
Earnshaw-Phi 27.0

Adjusted Starter Runs
Grove-Phi 43.3
Hudlin-Cle 34.3
Marberry-Was 32.8
Thomas-Chi 31.4
Earnshaw-Phi 26.6

Clutch Pitching Index
McKain-Chi 130
M.Gaston-Bos 116
Shaute-Cle 116
Ferrell-Cle 116
Collins-StL 113

Relief Runs
Moore-NY 7

Adjusted Relief Runs

Relief Ranking

Total Pitcher Index
Hudlin-Cle 3.9
Marberry-Was 3.8
Grove-Phi 3.5
Thomas-Chi 3.4
Ferrell-Cle 3.4

Total Baseball Ranking
Ruth-NY 5.0
Simmons-Phi 4.9
Lazzeri-NY 4.8
Gehringer-Det 3.9
Hudlin-Cle 3.9

January 20 Commissioner Kennesaw Mountain Landis bans boxing for all players in baseball following the brief boxing career of Art Shires. "Whataman" Shires fought football players as well as baseball players, and his challenge to Hack Wilson purportedly prompts the ban.

April 28* The first night game in Organized Baseball—played with temporary lights—is played in the Class C Western Association with 1,000 fans on hand. Home team Independence loses to Muskogee 13-3.

April 29 Suspicions that the ball is the liveliest ever increase as 123 runs are scored in seven major league games. (The NL will hit .303 as a whole this year, and the AL hits .288.)

May 2* Des Moines (Western League) defeats Wichita 13-6 to open the first ballpark with permanently installed lights. The Demons' victory is the first night game to be broadcast nationally.

May 12 The wind is blowing out at Wrigley Field as Giants pitcher Larry Benton sets a modern major league record (since tied several times) by surrendering six home runs in a single game, but he still gets credit for the 14-12 victory. (Benton also hits a home run.)

June 3 Grover Cleveland Alexander is released by the Phillies after posting a 0-3 record. He ends his career thinking he has the NL record for most wins at 373, one more than Christy Mathewson. In 1946, a win disallowed in 1902 is restored to Mathewson's record, to leave the two pitchers in a tie.

August 26 Hack Wilson hits his 44th home run, breaking Chuck Klein's one-year-old NL record, as the Cubs defeat the Pirates 7-5.

September 12 Brooklyn catcher Al Lopez drives one over the head of Cincinnati left fielder Bob Meusel, and the ball bounces into the bleachers at Ebbets Field. It will be the major leagues' last recorded bounce home run, as the NL rules after the season that such a hit will henceforth be a double. The AL had made the change after the 1929 season.

September 16 At Ebbets Field, the Cards (82–60) and Brooklyn (84–60) square off before 30,000. St. Louis pitcher Bill Hallahan retires the first 20 batters, before he fumbles a grounder. A single in the eighth spoils his no-hitter. The Cards finally score in the 10th and hold on for a 1–0 win. The victory gives the Cards first place by a percentage point over Brooklyn, losers for the first time in 11 games.

September 20 Hack Wilson records his 176th RBI, passing Lou Gehrig's 1927 major league record.

September 27 Hack Wilson clubs two home runs to finish with a still-standing NL record of 56. The Cubs win 13-8 over the Reds at Wrigley as Pat Malone wins his 20th of the year.

September 27 Wally Berger hits his 38th home run for the Braves, at Ebbets Field, as Boston tops Brooklyn 7-1. It was a record for all rookies at the time and still stands as an NL record, later tied by Frank Robinson.

September 28 The Cubs bring down the season's curtain as Wilson has his 189th and 190th RBI in a 12-11 victory over the Reds. With Riggs Stephenson and Kiki Cuyler each driving in 100 runs, the Cubs have the only all-100 RBI outfield this century. (The Boston outfield in 1894 also had the same credentials.)

September 28 Bill Terry goes hitless as the Giants edge the Dodgers for third place with a 10-inning win over the Phillies at the Polo Grounds. He finishes at .401, the last NL player to hit over .400. The Giants set a twentieth century single season batting average record of .319. (The Phillies hit .349 in 1894.)

September 28 Dizzy Dean scatters three hits for a 3-1 victory in his major league debut. The 19-year-old rookie, fresh from the Texas League, pitches the final game of the season for the pennant-winning Cardinals.

December 13 The 15-year career of George Sisler ends as the Boston Braves release him. A lifetime .340 hitter who twice led the AL with averages above .400, Sisler would be among the first to be elected to the Baseball Hall of Fame and was enshrined in 1939.

	BOSTON		BROOKLYN		CHICAGO		CINCINNATI		NEW YORK		PHILADELPHIA		PITTSBURGH		ST.LOUIS
M	B.McKechnie	M	W.Robinson	M	J.McCarthy	M	D.Howley	M	J.McGraw	M	B.Shotton	M	J.Ens	M	G.Street
1B	G.Sisler	1B	D.Bissonette	M	R.Hornsby	1B	J.Stripp	1B	B.Terry	1B	D.Hurst	1B	G.Suhr	1B	J.Bottomley
2B	F.Maguire	2B	N.Finn	1B	C.Grimm	2B	H.Ford	2B	H.Critz	2B	F.Thompson	2B	G.Grantham	2B	F.Frisch
SS	R.Maranville	SS	G.Wright	2B	F.Blair	SS	L.Durocher	SS	T.Jackson	SS	T.Thevenow	SS	D.Bartell	SS	C.Gelbert
3B	B.Chatham	3B	W.Gilbert	SS	W.English	3B	T.Cuccinello	3B	F.Lindstrom	3B	P.Whitney	3B	P.Traynor	3B	S.Adams
LF	W.Berger	LF	R.Bressler	3B	L.Bell	LF	T.Walker	LF	F.Leach	LF	L.O'Doul	LF	A.Comorosky	LF	C.Hafey
CF	J.Welsh	CF	J.Frederick	LF	R.Stephenson	CF	B.Meusel	CF	W.Roettger	CF	D.Sothern	CF	L.Waner	CF	T.Douthit
RF	L.Richbourg	RF	B.Herman	CF	H.Wilson	RF	H.Heilmann	RF	M.Ott	RF	C.Klein	RF	P.Waner	RF	G.Watkins
C	A.Spohrer	C	A.Lopez	RF	K.Cuyler	C	C.Sukeforth	C	S.Hogan	C	S.Davis	C	R.Hemsley	C	J.Wilson
				C	G.Hartnett										
O	E.Clark	2	J.Flowers			O	E.Swanson	C	B.O'Farrell	2O	B.Friberg	O	F.Brickell	O	S.Fisher
1	J.Neun	2O	E.Moore	S2	C.Beck	C	J.Gooch	O	E.Allen	1	M.Sherlock	C	A.Bool	C	G.Mancuso
O3	R.Moore	O	H.Hendrick	O	D.Taylor	O	M.Callaghan	S2	D.Marshall		F.Brickell	3S	C.Engle	3	A.High
C	B.Cronin	O	I.Boone	1	G.Kelly	21	P.Crawford	O3	R.Reese	C	T.Rensa	O	I.Flagstead	1O	E.Orsatti
32	R.Rollings	C	H.DeBerry	C	C.Heathcote	1	G.Kelly	2	P.Crawford	O	H.McCurdy	O	J.Mosolf	O	R.Blades
3	G.Robertson	S	V.Picinich	S	D.Farrell	2	H.Critz	/S	D.Bancroft	O	T.Sigman	O	D.Sothern	O	H.Peel
3	B.Rhiel	O	H.Lee	2	R.Hornsby	O	E.Allen	/O	C.Fullis	/O	C.Williams	/O	G.Dugas	S	D.Farrell
/O	B.Dunlap	S	G.Slade	C	Z.Taylor	O	J.Cullop	/O	J.Moore	/C	J.Spotts	C	C.Hargreaves	/O	G.Puccinelli
C	H.Gowdy	/3	J.Warner	/1	C.Tolson	3	C.Dressen	/O	R.Rosenberg			/S	B.Sankey	O	E.Smith
/2	B.James					/C	L.Styles	/C	F.Healy	P	P.Collins	/2	S.Clarke	H	P.Martin
/O	B.Boyle	P	D.Vance	P	P.Malone	H	H.Riconda	H	S.Leslie	P	R.Benge	/S	H.Groskloss		
R	O.Kahn	P	W.Clark	P	G.Bush					P	L.Sweetland			P	B.Hallahan
		P	D.Luque	P	C.Root	P	B.Frey	P	B.Walker	P	C.Willoughby	P	R.Kremer	P	S.Johnson
P	S.Seibold	P	J.Elliott	P	S.Blake	P	R.Lucas	P	C.Hubbell	P	C.Collard	P	L.French	P	J.Haines
P	B.Smith	P	R.Phelps	P	B.Teachout	P	L.Benton	P	F.Fitzsimmons	RP	H.Elliott	P	E.Brame	P	B.Grimes
P	B.Cantwell			RP	L.Nelson	P	R.Kolp	P	H.Pruett	RP	H.Smythe	P	G.Spencer	P	F.Rhem
P	T.Zachary					P	E.Rixey	P	C.Mitchell			P	H.Meine	RP	H.Bell
P	E.Brandt	P	R.Moss			RP	S.Johnson	RP	J.Heving	P	S.Hansen			RP	J.Lindsey
RP	B.Cunningham	P	C.Dudley	P	B.Osborn	RP	A.Campbell			P	C.Nichols	S	S.Swetonic		
		P	J.Morrison	/P	H.Carlson					P	B.Phillips	O	L.Chagnon	P	A.Grabowski
				/P	J.Petty			P	P.Donohue	/P	L.Koupal	/P	S.Wood	/P	B.Sherdel
P	B.Sherdel	/P	F.Heimach	P	A.Shealy	P	J.May	P	T.Chaplin	P	J.Milligan	P	J.Petty	P	H.Haid
P	F.Frankhouse	P	B.Newsom	P	M.Moss	P	K.Ash	P	J.Genewich	/P	P.Alexander	P	P.Jones	/P	F.Frankhouse
P	B.Grimes	/P	J.Faulkner	/P	B.McAfee	/P	P.Donohue	P	L.Benton	/P	B.Speece	/P	R.Erickson	/P	C.Hill
/P	K.Jones	/P	C.Moore	/P	L.Warneke	P	D.McWeeny	P	R.Parmelee			/P	L.Stoner	/P	T.Kaufmann
/P	J.Cooney					/P	O.Carroll	P	R.Lucas			/P	M.Lang	/P	D.Dean
/P	B.Brown					/P	A.Eckert	/P	R.Judd			/P	A.Bednar	/P	C.Mitchell
						/P	B.Wysong	/P	B.Morrell			/P	B.Walter		

TEAM	G	W	L	PCT	GB	R	OR	AB	H	2B	3B	HR	BB	SO	AVG	OBP	SLG	PRO	PRO+	BR	/A	PF	CHI	RC	SB	CS	SBA	SBR
STL	154	92	62	.597		**1004**	784	5512	1732	**373**	89	104	479	496	.314	.372	.471	.843	105	72	40	103	104	944	72			
CHI	156	90	64	.584	2	998	870	5581	1722	305	72	**171**	**588**	635	.309	**.378**	**.481**	**.859**	111	**110**	**103**	101	98	**1001**	70			
NY	154	87	67	.565	5	959	814	5553	1769	264	83	143	422	**382**	**.319**	.369	.473	.842	110	67	87	98	101	941	59			
BRO	154	86	68	.558	6	871	**738**	5433	1654	303	73	122	481	541	.304	.364	.454	.818	103	21	32	99	97	881	53		**76**	
PIT	154	80	74	.519	12	891	928	5346	1622	285	**119**	86	494	449	.303	.365	.449	.814	101	15	12	100	101	862	76			
BOS	154	70	84	.455	22	693	835	5356	1503	246	78	66	332	397	.281	.326	.393	.719	81	-186	-164	97	**105**	669	69			
CIN	154	59	95	.383	33	665	857	5245	1475	265	67	74	445	489	.281	.339	.400	.739	87	-135	-100	95	94	703	48			
PHI	156	52	102	.338	40	944	1199	5667	**1783**	345	44	126	450	459	.315	.367	.458	.825	97	37	-31	107	100	929	34			
TOT	618					7025		43693	13260	2386	625	892	3691	3848	.303	.360	.448	.808							481			

TEAM	CG	SH	SV	IP	H	H/G	HR	BB	SO	RAT	ERA	ERA+	OAV	OOB	PR	/A	PF	CPI	FA	E	DP	FW	PW	BW	SBW	DIF
STL	63	5	**21**	1380²	1596	10.4	87	476	**639**	13.7	4.39	114	.294	.353	89	95	101	**104**	.970	183	176	.2	8.4	3.5		2.9
CHI	67	6	12	1403²	1642	10.5	111	528	601	14.1	4.80	102	.294	.357	26	14	98	99	.973	170	167	1.0	1.2	**9.1**		1.6
NY	64	6	19	1363¹	1546	10.2	117	439	522	13.3	4.61	103	.290	.348	54	18	95	99	**.974**	164	144	1.3	1.6	7.7		-.5
BRO	74	**13**	15	1372	1480	**9.7**	115	394	526	**12.4**	**4.03**	**122**	**.278**	**.330**	144	135	99	102	.972	174	167	.7	**11.9**	2.8		-6.4
PIT	**80**	7	13	1361¹	1730	11.4	128	438	393	14.5	5.24	95	.313	.367	-41	-40	100	101	.965	216	164	-1.8	-3.5	1.1		7.2
BOS	71	6	11	1361	1624	10.7	117	475	424	14.0	4.91	100	.302	.360	9	3	99	102	.971	178	167	.4	.3	-14.5		6.8
CIN	61	6	11	1335	1650	11.1	**75**	**394**	361	13.9	5.08	95	.310	.361	-15	-37	97	96	.973	**161**	164	**1.4**	-3.3	-8.8		-7.3
PHI	54	3	7	1372²	1993	13.1	142	543	384	16.8	6.71	81	.346	.405	-266	-189	110	99	.962	239	169	-3.0	-16.7	-2.7		-2.6
TOT	534	52	109	10949²		10.9				14.1	4.97		.303	.360					.970	1485	1318					

Runs		Hits		Doubles		Triples		Home Runs		Total Bases	
Klein-Phi	158	Terry-NY	254	Klein-Phi	59	Comorosky-Pit	23	Wilson-Chi	56	Klein-Phi	445
Cuyler-Chi	155	Klein-Phi	250	Cuyler-Chi	50	P.Waner-Pit	18	Klein-Phi	40	Wilson-Chi	423
English-Chi	152	Herman-Bro	241	Herman-Bro	48	English-Chi	17	Berger-Bos	38	Herman-Bro	416
Wilson-Chi	146	Lindstrom-NY	231	Comorosky-Pit	47	Cuyler-Chi	17	Hartnett-Chi	37	Terry-NY	392
Herman-Bro	143	Cuyler-Chi	228	Frisch-StL	46	Terry-NY	15	Herman-Bro	35	Cuyler-Chi	351

Runs Batted In		Runs Produced		Bases On Balls		Batting Average		On Base Percentage		Slugging Average	
Wilson-Chi	190	Klein-Phi	288	Wilson-Chi	105	Terry-NY	.401	Ott-NY	.458	Wilson-Chi	.723
Klein-Phi	170	Wilson-Chi	280	Ott-NY	103	Herman-Bro	.393	Herman-Bro	.455	Klein-Phi	.687
Cuyler-Chi	134	Cuyler-Chi	276	English-Chi	100	Klein-Phi	.386	Wilson-Chi	.454	Herman-Bro	.678
Herman-Bro	130	Terry-NY	245	Grantham-Pit	81	O'Doul-Phi	.383	O'Doul-Phi	.453	Hafey-StL	.652
Terry-NY	129	Herman-Bro	238	Suhr-Pit	80	Lindstrom-NY	.379	Terry-NY	.452	Hartnett-Chi	.630

Production		Adjusted Production		Batter Runs		Adjusted Batter Runs		Clutch Hitting Index		Runs Created	
Wilson-Chi	1.177	Wilson-Chi	177	Wilson-Chi	75.4	Wilson-Chi	74.2	Thevenow-Phi	138	Wilson-Chi	189
Herman-Bro	1.132	Herman-Bro	171	Herman-Bro	68.7	Herman-Bro	70.7	Traynor-Pit	133	Klein-Phi	186
Klein-Phi	1.123	Terry-NY	159	Klein-Phi	67.3	Terry-NY	61.0	Cuyler-Chi	129	Herman-Bro	183
Terry-NY	1.071	Klein-Phi	155	Terry-NY	57.6	Klein-Phi	55.3	Frisch-StL	126	Terry-NY	170
Hafey-StL	1.059	Ott-NY	152	O'Doul-Phi	46.9	Ott-NY	48.3	Whitney-Phi	120	Cuyler-Chi	148

Total Average		Stolen Bases		Stolen Base Average		Stolen Base Runs		Fielding Runs		Total Player Rating	
Wilson-Chi	1.411	Cuyler-Chi	37					Frisch-StL	27.5	Klein-Phi	5.8
Herman-Bro	1.351	P.Waner-Pit	18					Klein-Phi	23.0	Terry-NY	5.0
Klein-Phi	1.274	Herman-Bro	18					Whitney-Phi	20.3	Wilson-Chi	4.8
Ott-NY	1.224							Terry-NY	12.6	Lindstrom-NY	4.8
Terry-NY	1.208							Cuyler-Chi	12.2	Frisch-StL	4.4

Wins		Win Percentage		Games		Complete Games		Shutouts		Saves	
Malone-Chi	20	Fitzsimmons-NY	.731	Elliott-Phi	48	Malone-Chi	22	Vance-Bro	4	Bell-StL	8
Kremer-Pit	20	Malone-Chi	.690	Collins-Pit	47	Brame-Pit	22	Root-Chi	4	Heving-NY	6
Fitzsimmons-NY	19	Brame-Pit	.680	Bush-Chi	46	French-Pit	21	Hubbell-NY	3	Clark-Bro	6
		Kremer-Pit	.625	Pruett-NY	45	Vance-Bro	20	French-Pit	3		
		Hallahan-StL	.625	Malone-Chi	45	Seibold-Bos	20				

Innings Pitched		Fewest Hits/Game		Fewest BB/Game		Strikeouts		Strikeouts/Game		Ratio	
Kremer-Pit	276.0	Vance-Bro	8.39	Clark-Bro	1.71	Hallahan-StL	177	Hallahan-StL	6.71	Vance-Bro	10.47
French-Pit	274.2	Hallahan-StL	8.84	Kolp-Cin	1.82	Vance-Bro	173	Vance-Bro	6.02	Clark-Bro	11.11
Malone-Chi	271.2	Fitzsimmons-NY	9.23	Johnson-StL	1.82	Malone-Chi	142	Root-Chi	5.07	Kolp-Cin	11.44
Vance-Bro	258.2	Elliott-Bro	9.26	Lucas-Cin	1.88	Root-Chi	124	Malone-Chi	4.70	Fitzsimmons-NY	11.63
Seibold-Bos	251.0	Clark-Bro	9.41	Vance-Bro	1.91	Hubbell-NY	117	Johnson-StL	4.41	Johnson-StL	12.33

Earned Run Average		Adjusted ERA		Opponents' Batting Avg.		Opponents' On Base Pct.		Starter Runs		Adjusted Starter Runs	
Vance-Bro	2.61	Vance-Bro	188	Vance-Bro	.246	Vance-Bro	.289	Vance-Bro	67.9	Vance-Bro	66.2
Hubbell-NY	3.87	Elliott-Bro	124	Hallahan-StL	.260	Clark-Bro	.306	Malone-Chi	31.1	Malone-Chi	28.5
Walker-NY	3.93	Malone-Chi	124	Fitzsimmons-NY	.266	Fitzsimmons-NY	.314	Hubbell-NY	29.5	Hubbell-NY	23.1
Malone-Chi	3.94	Grimes-Bos-StL	123	Walker-NY	.268	Kolp-Cin	.314	Walker-NY	28.5	Seibold-Bos	22.7
Elliott-Bro	3.95	Hubbell-NY	122	Malone-Chi	.271	Hubbell-NY	.327	Seibold-Bos	23.7	Walker-NY	22.0

Clutch Pitching Index		Relief Runs		Adjusted Relief Runs		Relief Ranking		Total Pitcher Index		Total Baseball Ranking	
Grimes-Bos-StL	119	Bell-StL	13.7	Bell-StL	14.3	Bell-StL	10.0	Vance-Bro	6.6	Vance-Bro	6.6
Smith-Bos	117	Lindsey-StL	6.4	Lindsey-StL	6.9	Lindsey-StL	7.8	Malone-Chi	2.8	Klein-Phi	5.8
Haines-StL	109	Johnson-Cin	.3					Grimes-Bos-StL	2.6	Terry-NY	5.0
Vance-Bro	108							Fitzsimmons-NY	2.2	Wilson-Chi	4.8
Seibold-Bos	107							Walker-NY	2.1	Lindstrom-NY	4.8

February 12 Connie Mack is awarded the prestigious Edward W. Bok Prize given to the Philadelphian who has done the most for the city in the past year. Mack, the first sports figure to be so honored, led the Athletics to a World Championship in 1929.

March 8 Babe Ruth signs a two-year contract for $160,000 with New York to become, at $80,000 per year, the highest paid player of all time. When it is pointed out he is earning more money than the President of the United States, Ruth observes: "I had a better year than he did." Ed Barrow, Yankee GM, assures posterity, "No one will ever be paid more than Ruth."

May 21 Babe Ruth hits three consecutive home runs in the first game of a doubleheader against the A's, then batting against Jack Quinn in the ninth, Ruth decides to hit right-handed. After two strikes, he switches to lefty but strikes out.

May 26 Joe Sewell strikes out twice facing lefthander Pat Caraway of the White Sox. It is the last time the Indians third baseman will fan this season, striking out only three times in 353 at bats.

July 25 The Athletics pull off triple steals twice in one game against the Indians. Al Simmons, Bing Miller, and Dib Williams are the thieves in the first inning, and Cochrane, Simmons, and Foxx steal together in the fourth. This is the only time in major league history this has occurred.

September 18 The Philadelphia Athletics win the AL pennant for the second year in a row, defeating the White Sox 14-10.

September 28 Babe Ruth returns to the scene of his youthful fame, the pitcher's mound at Fenway Park. The Yankees slugger hurls a 9–3 complete game win over the Red Sox in the season finale. Lou Gehrig takes Ruth's spot in left field, ending his streak of 885 consecutive games at first base.

October 1 The World Series opens at Philadelphia's Shibe Park. The defending World Champion Athletics are held to five hits by Burleigh Grimes. Lefty Grove limits the Cards to a pair of runs, as the A's five hits include home runs by Mickey Cochrane and Al Simmons, two triples and a double, providing Philadelphia with a 5-2 victory.

October 8 George Earnshaw finishes off the Cardinals 7-1, pitching shutout ball until the ninth inning. He is clearly the pitching star of the World Series with two wins and seven shutout innings of a game in which reliever Lefty Grove got the decision. Despite the "lively" ball and the many outstanding hitters on both sides, it is a pitching-dominated Series. The Cards bat only .200 as a team and the A's .197.

October 10 With no MVP award for the second year in a row, the Associated Press polls its members and names Joe Cronin unofficial AL MVP. The Baseball Writers Association names Hack Wilson the MVP of the NL. The Cubs give Wilson a bonus of $1,000, the monetary reward which the MVP title had carried as an official league honor.

November 25 *The Sporting News,* also acting to fill the MVP void, announces its selection of Bill Terry as the Most Valuable Player in the NL and Joe Cronin in the AL.

December 11 The BBWAA votes to continue the custom of selecting an MVP for each league. Beginning in 1931 the annual vote of the BBWAA will designate a player for this honor in each league. Previous MVP winners will be able to repeat under the new rules, something that was prohibited by the AL in the 1920s.

December 12 The Rules Committee of baseball issues a greatly revised code, reducing the number of rules by combining many. The sacrifice fly rule is abolished as is the rule awarding home runs when the ball bounces into the stands. This rule had already been in effect in the AL but not in the NL.

BOSTON	CHICAGO	CLEVELAND	DETROIT	NEW YORK	PHILADELPHIA	ST.LOUIS	WASHINGTON
M H.Wagner	M D.Bush	M R.Peckinpaugh	M B.Harris	M B.Shawkey	M C.Mack	M B.Killefer	M W.Johnson
1B P.Todt	1B J.Watwood	1B E.Morgan	1B D.Alexander	1B L.Gehrig	1B J.Foxx	1B L.Blue	1B J.Judge
2B B.Regan	2B B.Cissell	2B J.Hodapp	2B C.Gehringer	2B T.Lazzeri	2B M.Bishop	2B S.Melillo	2B B.Myer
SS H.Rhyne	SS G.Mulleavy	SS J.Goldman	SS M.Koenig	SS L.Lary	SS J.Boley	SS R.Kress	SS J.Cronin
3B O.Miller	3B W.Kamm	3B J.Sewell	3B M.McManus	3B B.Chapman	3B J.Dykes	3B F.O'Rourke	3B O.Bluege
LF R.Scarritt	LF S.Jolley	LF C.Jamieson	LF J.Stone	LF E.Combs	LF A.Simmons	LF G.Goslin	LF H.Manush
CF T.Oliver	CF R.Barnes	CF E.Averill	CF L.Funk	CF H.Rice	CF M.Haas	CF F.Schulte	CF S.West
RF E.Webb	RF C.Reynolds	RF D.Porter	RF R.Johnson	RF B.Ruth	RF B.Miller	RF T.Gullic	RF S.Rice
C C.Berry	C B.Tate	C L.Sewell	C R.Hayworth	C B.Dickey	C M.Cochrane	C R.Ferrell	C R.Spencer
O C.Durst	2S J.Kerr	O B.Seeds	O B.Akers	O S.Byrd	O E.McNair	O1 E.McNeely	O D.Harris
3S B.Reeves	1 B.Clancy	C G.Myatt	S3 B.Rogell	O D.Cooke	2S D.Williams	O R.Badgro	C M.Ruel
1 B.Sweeney	O B.Fothergill	O B.Falk	O B.Fothergill	2 J.Reese	C W.Schang	O A.Metzler	O G.Goslin
C J.Heving	C A.Shires	S3 E.Montague	C P.Hargrave	C B.Bengough	O D.Cramer	3 S.Hale	2 J.Hayes
S R.Warstler	C B.Crouse	3S J.Burnett	O H.Rice	S M.Koenig	O H.Summa	C C.Manion	O G.Loepp
S3 B.Narleski	3S I.Jeffries	1 L.Fonseca	O G.Desautels	/S Y.Wuestling	O J.Moore	/S J.Levey	3 A.Shires
/O J.Rothrock	3 B.Ryan	S C.Lind	S P.Easterling	C A.Jorgens	S S.Harris	C B.Hungling	1 J.Kuhel
C E.Connolly	O D.Harris	C J.Sprinz	O F.Doljack	/O C.Durst	C Cy.Perkins	/1 J.Burns	3 J.McLeod
/O J.Cicero	S B.Hunnefield	/O J.Vosmik	O T.Hughes	/S B.Werber	/1 P.Higgins	/2 L.Storti	/C P.Hargrave
/O B.Barrett	O A.Metzler	C R.Winegarner	C T.Rensa	/O B.Karlon	/1 J.Burns	/C J.Crouch	/C B.Tate
/O C.Small	S E.Smith	S R.Gardner	1 J.Shevlin		/2 J.Keesey	/S J.Hassler	/3 R.Treadaway
H J.Galvin	C C.Autry	/3 G.DeTore	O J.Watson	P G.Pipgras	H E.Collins	/O T.Jenkins	H R.Barnes
H T.Winsett	C M.Berg	/C G.Hartley	/S Y.Wuestling	P R.Ruffing			/O B.Barrett
	C J.Riddle		/C H.Wise	P H.Johnson	P G.Earnshaw	P L.Stewart	/O J.Powell
P M.Gaston	O JW.Moore	P W.Ferrell	H H.Greenberg	P H.Pennock	P L.Grove	P D.Coffman	/1 H.Boss
P D.MacFayden	/S L.Appling	P W.Hudlin	P G.Uhle	RP L.McEvoy	P R.Walberg	P G.Blaeholder	/C P.Gharrity
P H.Lisenbee	/O B.Campbell	P C.Brown	P V.Sorrell	P E.Wells	P B.Shores	P R.Collins	P B.Hadley
P J.Russell	/C B.Henline	P M.Harder	P E.Whitehill	P W.Hoyt	P R.Mahaffey	P S.Gray	P A.Crowder
P E.Durham	C J.Klinger	P P.Appleton	P C.Hogsett	/P R.Sherid	P J.Quinn	RP C.Kimsey	P L.Brown
RP G.Smith	/2 H.Willingham		P W.Hoyt	/P O.Carroll	P E.Rommel	RP H.Holshouser	P F.Marberry
		P J.Miller	RP C.Sullivan	/P T.Zachary	/P Ch.Perkins	P R.Stiles	P S.Jones
P E.Morris	P T.Lyons	P M.Shoffner	P W.Wyatt	/P F.Barnes	/P H.Ehmke	P A.Crowder	
P F.Bushey	P P.Caraway	/P B.Bean	P A.Herring	/P B.Henderson	/P G.Liebhardt	/P F.Stiely	P A.Liska
/P R.Ruffing	P T.Thomas	/P R.Lawson	/P T.Bridges	/P S.Gibson	/P A.Mahon		P B.Burke
/P B.Shields	P R.Faber	/P K.Holloway	/P G.Cantrell	P F.Edwards			P M.Thomas
/P B.Bayne	P D.Henry	/P S.Gliatto	/P O.Carroll	/P G.Rhodes			/P C.Fischer
/P F.Mulroney	RP E.Walsh	/P L.Barnhart	P P.Page				P G.Braxton
/P B.Kline	RP H.McKain	/P J.Shaute	/P J.Samuels				/P C.Moore
	P G.Braxton						/P H.Child
	/P JS.Moore						
	P B.Weiland						
	/P T.Blankenship						
	/P B.Wehde						

TEAM	G	W	L	PCT	GB	R	OR	AB	H	2B	3B	HR	BB	SO	AVG	OBP	SLG	PRO	PRO+	BR	/A	PF	CHI	RC	SB	CS	SBA	SBR
PHI	154	102	52	.662		951	751	5345	1573	319	74	125	599	531	.294	.369	.452	.821	108	102	60	104	100	913	48	33	59	-5
WAS	154	94	60	.610	8	892	689	5370	1620	300	98	57	537	438	.302	.369	.426	.795	106	59	55	100	99	860	101	67	60	-10
NY	154	86	68	.558	16	1062	898	5448	1683	298	110	152	644	569	.309	.384	.488	.872	131	206	255	96	99	1035	91	60	60	-9
CLE	154	81	73	.526	21	890	915	5439	1654	358	59	72	490	461	.304	.364	.431	.795	102	54	20	104	99	863	51	47	52	-13
DET	154	75	79	.487	27	783	833	5297	1504	298	90	82	461	508	.284	.344	.421	.765	96	-18	-33	102	98	771	98	70	58	-13
STL	154	64	90	.416	38	751	886	5278	1415	289	67	75	497	550	.268	.333	.391	.724	85	-96	-121	103	104	696	93	71	57	-15
CHI	154	62	92	.403	40	729	884	5419	1496	256	90	63	389	479	.276	.328	.391	.719	89	-111	-87	97	102	706	74	40	65	-2
BOS	154	52	102	.338	50	612	814	5286	1393	257	68	47	358	552	.264	.313	.365	.678	79	-192	-169	96	100	608	42	35	55	-8
TOT	616					6670		42882	12338	2375	656	673	3975	4088	.288	.351	.421	.772							598	423	59	-74

TEAM	CG	SH	SV	IP	H	H/G	HR	BB	SO	RAT	ERA	ERA+	OAV	OOB	PR	/A	PF	CPI	FA	E	DP	FW	PW	BW	SBW	DIF
PHI	72	8	21	1371	1457	9.6	84	488	672	12.9	4.28	109	.274	.337	56	58	101	98	.975	145	121	3.0	5.2	5.4	.4	11.0
WAS	78	6	14	1369	1367	9.0	52	504	524	12.5	3.96	116	.264	.332	104	96	99	97	.974	157	150	2.3	8.7	5.0	-.0	1.1
NY	65	7	15	1367²	1566	10.3	93	524	572	13.9	4.88	88	.287	.352	-36	-90	93	96	.965	207	132	-.7	-8.1	23.1	.0	-5.2
CLE	68	5	14	1360	1663	11.0	85	528	442	14.6	4.88	88	.305	.368	-36	-9	104	107	.962	237	156	-2.5	-.8	1.8	-.3	5.9
DET	68	4	17	1351²	1507	10.0	86	570	574	14.0	4.70	102	.286	.359	-8	13	103	102	.967	192	156	.2	1.2	-3.0	-.3	-.0
STL	68	5	10	1371²	1639	10.8	124	449	470	13.9	5.07	96	.300	.356	-65	-31	105	101	.970	188	152	.4	-2.8	-10.9	-.5	.9
CHI	63	2	10	1361	1629	10.8	74	407	471	13.6	4.71	98	.300	.352	-10	-15	99	101	.962	235	136	-2.4	-1.4	-7.9	.7	-4.0
BOS	78	4	5	1360¹	1515	10.0	75	488	356	13.4	4.68	98	.286	.348	-6	-12	99	97	.968	196	161	-.0	-1.1	-15.3	.1	-8.7
TOT	560	41	106	10912¹		10.2				13.6	4.65		.288	.351					.968	1557	1164					

Runs		Hits		Doubles		Triples		Home Runs		Total Bases	
Simmons-Phi	152	Hodapp-Cle	225	Hodapp-Cle	51	Combs-NY	22	Ruth-NY	49	Gehrig-NY	419
Ruth-NY	150	Gehrig-NY	220	Manush-StL-Was	49	Reynolds-Chi	18	Gehrig-NY	41	Simmons-Phi	392
Gehringer-Det	144	Simmons-Phi	211	Morgan-Cle	47	Gehrig-NY	17	Goslin-Was-StL	37	Ruth-NY	379
Gehrig-NY	143	Rice-Was	207	Gehringer-Det	47	Simmons-Phi	16	Foxx-Phi	37	Foxx-Phi	358
Combs-NY	129	Morgan-Cle	204							Simmons-Phi	36		

Runs Batted In		Runs Produced		Bases On Balls		Batting Average		On Base Percentage		Slugging Average	
Gehrig-NY	174	Simmons-Phi	281	Ruth-NY	136	Simmons-Phi	.381	Ruth-NY	.493	Ruth-NY	.732
Simmons-Phi	165	Gehrig-NY	276	Bishop-Phi	128	Gehrig-NY	.379	Gehrig-NY	.473	Gehrig-NY	.721
Foxx-Phi	156	Ruth-NY	254	Gehrig-NY	101	Ruth-NY	.359	Foxx-Phi	.429	Simmons-Phi	.708
Ruth-NY	153	Foxx-Phi	246	Foxx-Phi	93	Reynolds-Chi	.359	Bishop-Phi	.426	Foxx-Phi	.637
Goslin-Was-StL	138	Cronin-Was	240	Blue-StL	81	Cochrane-Phi	.357	Combs-NY	.424		

Production		Adjusted Production		Batter Runs		Adjusted Batter Runs		Clutch Hitting Index		Runs Created	
Ruth-NY	1.225	Ruth-NY	216	Ruth-NY	89.5	Ruth-NY	97.9	Rice-Det-NY	137	Gehrig-NY	195
Gehrig-NY	1.194	Gehrig-NY	207	Gehrig-NY	88.4	Gehrig-NY	96.9	Lazzeri-NY	125	Ruth-NY	191
Simmons-Phi	1.130	Simmons-Phi	173	Simmons-Phi	64.2	Simmons-Phi	57.8	Dykes-Phi	113	Simmons-Phi	163
Foxx-Phi	1.066	Foxx-Phi	159	Foxx-Phi	57.0	Foxx-Phi	50.5	Cronin-Was	112	Foxx-Phi	154
Morgan-Cle	1.014	Morgan-Cle	148	Morgan-Cle	46.3	Morgan-Cle	41.1	Alexander-Det	112	Morgan-Cle	144

Total Average		Stolen Bases		Stolen Base Average		Stolen Base Runs		Fielding Runs		Total Player Rating	
Ruth-NY	1.509	McManus-Det	23	Reynolds-Chi	80.0	Lary-NY	3.0	Melillo-StL	26.8	Ruth-NY	7.3
Gehrig-NY	1.389	Gehringer-Det	19	McManus-Det	74.2	Reynolds-Chi	2.4	Cronin-Was	26.1	Gehrig-NY	6.9
Simmons-Phi	1.272	Goslin-Was-StL	17	Cissell-Chi	64.0	McManus-Det	2.1	Goldman-Cle	20.7	Cronin-Was	6.7
Foxx-Phi	1.184	Johnson-Det	17	Johnson-Det	63.0			Oliver-Bos	15.2	Simmons-Phi	4.9
Morgan-Cle	1.089	Cronin-Was	17	Cronin-Was	63.0			Kamm-Chi	14.9	Cochrane-Phi	4.0

Wins		Win Percentage		Games		Complete Games		Shutouts		Saves	
Grove-Phi	28	Grove-Phi	.848	Grove-Phi	50	Lyons-Chi	29	Pipgras-NY	3	Grove-Phi	9
Ferrell-Cle	25	Marberry-Was	.750	Earnshaw-Phi	49	Crowder-StL-Was	25	Earnshaw-Phi	3	Braxton-Was-Chi	6
Lyons-Chi	22	Jones-Was	.682	Pipgras-NY	44	Ferrell-Cle	25	Brown-Cle	3	Quinn-Phi	6
Earnshaw-Phi	22	Ferrell-Cle	.658	Johnson-NY	44	Stewart-StL	23			Sullivan-Det	5
Stewart-StL	20	Ruffing-Bos-NY	.652	Ferrell-Cle	43	Grove-Phi	22			McKain-Chi	5

Innings Pitched		Fewest Hits/Game		Fewest BB/Game		Strikeouts		Strikeouts/Game		Ratio	
Lyons-Chi	297.2	Hadley-Was	8.37	Pennock-NY	1.15	Grove-Phi	209	Grove-Phi	6.46	Grove-Phi	10.45
Ferrell-Cle	296.2	Grove-Phi	8.44	Lyons-Chi	1.72	Earnshaw-Phi	193	Johnson-NY	5.90	Stewart-StL	11.69
Earnshaw-Phi	296.0	Collins-StL	8.81	Grove-Phi	1.86	Hadley-Was	162	Earnshaw-Phi	5.87	Lyons-Chi	11.79
Grove-Phi	291.0	Crowder-StL-Was	8.88	Russell-Bos	2.08	Ferrell-Cle	143	Hadley-Was	5.60	Marberry-Was	11.82
Crowder-StL-Was	279.2	Gaston-Bos	8.97	Brown-Cle	2.15	Ruffing-Bos-NY	131	Ruffing-Bos-NY	5.32	Caraway-Chi	11.82

Earned Run Average		Adjusted ERA		Opponents' Batting Avg.		Opponents' On Base Pct.		Starter Runs		Adjusted Starter Runs	
Grove-Phi	2.54	Grove-Phi	184	Grove-Phi	.247	Grove-Phi	.288	Grove-Phi	68.3	Grove-Phi	69.0
Ferrell-Cle	3.31	Ferrell-Cle	146	Hadley-Was	.247	Stewart-StL	.315	Ferrell-Cle	44.2	Ferrell-Cle	50.0
Stewart-StL	3.45	Stewart-StL	141	Crowder-StL-Was	.259	Lyons-Chi	.319	Stewart-StL	35.9	Stewart-StL	42.7
Uhle-Det	3.65	Uhle-Det	131	Collins-StL	.259	Marberry-Was	.321	Lyons-Chi	28.7	Uhle-Det	30.4
Hadley-Was	3.73	Sorrell-Det	124	Gaston-Bos	.259	Crowder-StL-Was	.321	Hadley-Was	26.4	Lyons-Chi	27.8

Clutch Pitching Index		Relief Runs		Adjusted Relief Runs		Relief Ranking		Total Pitcher Index		Total Baseball Ranking	
Henry-Chi	122	Quinn-Phi	2.3	Quinn-Phi	2.5	Quinn-Phi	4.5	Grove-Phi	7.3	Ruth-NY	7.6
Harder-Cle	115							Ferrell-Cle	6.2	Grove-Phi	7.3
Sorrell-Det	115							Stewart-StL	4.7	Gehrig-NY	6.9
Hoyt-NY-Det	113							Lyons-Chi	4.1	Cronin-Was	6.7
Ferrell-Cle	113							Uhle-Det	3.2	Ferrell-Cle	6.2

January 5* Mrs. Lucille Thomas becomes the first woman to buy a professional baseball team, purchasing the Topeka franchise in the Western League.

June 27 The largest total crowd in Cubs history, 51,556, jams Wrigley Field to watch Kiki Cuyler crack a 10th inning home run to beat Brooklyn 7–5. The attendance includes 19,748 paying customers, 1,332 pass holders and 30,476 Ladies Day fans.

July 12 The largest crowd in the history of Sportsman's Park in St. Louis, 45,715 (in a ballpark with 35,000 seats), creates a travesty and permanently distorts the record for doubles hit in a game. Easy fly balls drop for ground-rule doubles among the fans encroaching on the field. There are 32 doubles hit in two games, 11 in the first and 21 in the second, for records both for the most doubles in one game and for a doubleheader.

August 20 Tony Freitas, who will win 342 minor league games, is let out of jail to pitch for Sacramento (PCL). He wins the game and then returns to finish a 5-day sentence for speeding.

September 16 World Series tickets can now be printed as the St. Louis Cardinals repeat as NL champions. They beat the Phillies 6-3 and prepare for a rematch of the 1930 World Series.

September 27 The most desperately contested battle for individual honors takes place in the race for the NL batting title. Chick Hafey, who reported late due to a contract dispute, goes into the final doubleheader with the Reds batting .353, four points over Bill Terry, last year's champ. Hafey gets only one hit in eight times at bat to drop to .349. Bill Terry's Giants are playing archenemy Brooklyn at Ebbets Field. Brooklyn, in their last game as the Robins, wins 12-3. Terry gets only one hit in four times at bat. The title goes to Hafey, who batted .3488 to Terry's .3486. Jim Bottomley, Hafey's Cardinal teammate, finishes at .3481.

October 2 The Cards even the World Series as Wild Bill Hallahan shuts out the A's 2-0 despite seven walks and a wild pitch. Pepper Martin continues to steal the Series, scoring from second base on a base hit in the second inning and sliding home in a cloud of dust on a squeeze play in the eighth. He has two stolen bases, but the game almost gets away on a bonehead play by the usually savvy Cardinal catcher Jimmy Wilson. With two on base in the ninth, and two outs, pinch hitter Johnny Moore swings at a ball in the dirt and misses. Wilson needs only to throw the ball to the first baseman. Instead, he throws it to third, and everyone is safe. Fortunately for Wilson's reputation, Jim Bottomley makes a sensational catch, leaning into the box seats to get the final out on a pop foul by Max Bishop.

October 7 Connie Mack, who surprised everyone in 1929 by starting veteran Howard Ehmke in the World Series opener, tries the ploy with Waite Hoyt. Pitching in his seventh World Series, Hoyt falls victim to Martin, who homers and drives in four runs with three hits. Hallahan wins for the Cards 5-1.

October 10 Burleigh Grimes carries a 4-0 lead into the ninth before he weakens. The A's score twice and have two on with two outs, when Bill Hallahan rescues Grimes. Max Bishop flies to Martin for the final out as the Cardinals take the Series four games to three.

October 20 Frankie Frisch, the Cardinals' fiery field leader, is named MVP of the NL. He led in stolen bases with 28, hit .313, and was chosen for his all-around excellence.

October 23 Brooklyn announces Wilbert Robinson is through as manager and the club will be called the Robins only in the past tense. Max Carey, a no-nonsense sort, will take over next year.

December 9 Baseball owners, fearful of the effects of the Depression, vote to cut squads from 25 players to 23. Both leagues will also stop awarding MVP trophies, and the NL continues to prohibit uniform numbers.

December 11 Despite two wins in the World Series, spitball veteran Burleigh Grimes is traded by the Cards to the Cubs for the fallen Hack Wilson.

BOSTON		BROOKLYN		CHICAGO		CINCINNATI		NEW YORK		PHILADELPHIA		PITTSBURGH		ST.LOUIS	
M	B.McKechnie	M	W.Robinson	M	R.Hornsby	M	D.Howley	M	J.McGraw	M	B.Shotton	M	J.Ens	M	G.Street
1B	E.Sheely	1B	D.Bissonette	1B	C.Grimm	1B	H.Hendrick	1B	B.Terry	1B	D.Hurst	1B	G.Suhr	1B	J.Bottomley
2B	F.Maguire	2B	N.Finn	2B	R.Hornsby	2B	T.Cuccinello	2B	B.Hunnefield	2B	L.Mallon	2B	G.Grantham	2B	F.Frisch
SS	R.Maranville	SS	G.Slade	SS	W.English	SS	L.Durocher	SS	T.Jackson	SS	D.Bartell	SS	T.Thevenow	SS	C.Gelbert
3B	B.Urbanski	3B	W.Gilbert	3B	L.Bell	3B	J.Stripp	3B	J.Vergez	3B	P.Whitney	3B	P.Traynor	3B	S.Adams
LF	R.Worthington	LF	L.O'Doul	LF	D.Taylor	LF	E.Roush	LF	F.Leach	LF	C.Klein	LF	A.Comorosky	LF	C.Hafey
CF	W.Berger	CF	J.Frederick	CF	H.Wilson	CF	T.Douthit	CF	E.Allen	CF	F.Brickell	CF	L.Waner	CF	P.Martin
RF	W.Schulmerich	RF	B.Herman	RF	K.Cuyler	RF	E.Crabtree	RF	M.Ott	RF	B.Arlett	RF	P.Waner	RF	G.Watkins
C	A.Spohrer	C	A.Lopez	C	G.Hartnett	C	C.Sukeforth	C	S.Hogan	C	S.Davis	C	E.Phillips	C	J.Wilson
O	L.Richbourg	S	G.Wright	32	B.Jurges	O	N.Cullop	23	F.Lindstrom	O	B.Friberg	O	W.Jensen	1	R.Collins
O3	R.Moore	C	E.Lombardi	O	H.Stephenson	O	C.Heathcote	O	C.Fullis	O	F.Koster	2	T.Piet	C	G.Mancuso
3	B.Dreesen	2S	F.Thompson	21	F.Blair	O	W.Roettger	O	H.Critz	2	T.Taitt	2	H.Groskloss	O	E.Orsatti
C	J.Neun	O	R.Bressler	O	V.Barton	S	H.Ford	2S	D.Marshall	2	H.McCurdy	S	E.Grace	O	W.Roettger
1	A.Bool	C	V.Picinich	3	R.Hemsley	3	C.Beck	O	B.O'Farrell	O	H.Lee	S	B.Sankey	S2	J.Flowers
C	C.Wilson	/2	J.Flowers	O	J.Moore	C	C.Asbjornson	S	S.Leslie	S	L.Stevens	2	B.Regan	2	J.Douthit
3	E.Clark	O	D.Sothern	2	B.Herman	O	L.Styles	/3	G.English	/S	H.Willingham	O	F.Bennett	32	A.High
/S	B.Chatham	/3	B.Reis	S	J.Adair	3	F.Sigafoos	/O	J.Moore	C	T.Rensa	/O	J.Mosolf	O	R.Blades
/3	B.Walters	/O	M.Rosenfeld	/O	M.Kreevich	/1	M.Heath	/C	F.Healy	/C	G.Connell	/C	R.Hemsley	C	M.Gonzalez
/3	B.Hunnefield	H	I.Boone	/C	E.Grace	/3	C.Dressen	P	F.Fitzsimmons	P	J.Elliott	/C	H.Finney	/S	J.Benes
H	J.Scalzi	/S	J.Warner	/C	Z.Taylor	/O	G.Moore	P	C.Hubbell	P	R.Benge	H	P.McClanahan	/3	R.Cunningham
H	P.Veltman	/O	A.Cohen	P	C.Root	H	R.Fitzgerald	P	B.Walker	P	P.Collins	/C	B.Steinecke	/3	E.Delker
P	E.Brandt	H	H.Hendrick	P	B.Smith	P	S.Johnson	P	C.Mitchell	P	C.Dudley	P	H.Meine	/O	J.Hunt
P	T.Zachary	P	W.Clark	P	P.Malone	P	R.Lucas	P	J.Berly	P	F.Watt	P	L.French	/C	G.Street
P	S.Seibold	P	D.Vance	P	G.Bush	P	L.Benton	P	J.Mooney	P	S.Bolen	P	R.Kremer	P	B.Hallahan
P	B.Cantwell	P	R.Phelps	RP	J.May	P	B.Frey	P	B.Morrell	P	S.Blake	P	G.Spencer	P	B.Grimes
P	B.Sherdel	P	S.Thurston	RP	B.Teachout	P	E.Rixey	P	R.Parmelee	RP	E.Fallenstein	P	E.Brame	P	P.Derringer
RP	H.Haid	P	F.Heimach	P	E.Baecht	P	O.Carroll	P	T.Chaplin	P	D.Schesler	RP	B.Osborn	P	F.Rhem
P	B.Cunningham	RP	J.Quinn	P	L.Warneke	P	R.Kolp	P	J.Heving		H.Elliott		S.Wood	P	S.Johnson
	F.Frankhouse	RP	C.Moore	P	S.Blake	P	J.Ogden	/P	H.Schumacher		L.Stoner		B.Harris	P	J.Lindsey
P	R.Moss	RP	P.Day	/P	J.Welch	/P	E.Strelecki	/P	P.Donohue	/P	J.Milligan		S.Swetonic	RP	A.Stout
P	B.McAfee	P	J.Shaute			P	B.Wysong	/P	E.Planeta	/P	B.Adams		C.Willoughby	P	J.Haines
/P	B.Brown	P	D.Luque			P	A.Eckert	/P	R.Lucas	P	C.Nichols		G.Grant	P	T.Kaufmann
		/P	V.Mungo			/P	W.Hilcher			/P	B.Shields		A.Bednar	P	T.Kaufmann
		/P	P.Gallivan							/P	H.Wiltse				
		/P	E.Mattingly												
		/P	R.Moss												

TEAM	G	W	L	PCT	GB	R	OR	AB	H	2B	3B	HR	BB	SO	AVG	OBP	SLG	PRO	PRO+	BR	/A	PF	CHI	RC	SB	CS	SBA	SBR
STL	154	101	53	.656		815	614	5435	1554	353	74	60	432	475	.286	.342	.411	.753	105	61	31	104	107	787	114			
NY	153	87	65	.572	13	768	599	5372	1554	251	64	101	383	395	.289	.340	.416	.756	112	61	80	98	103	776	83			
CHI	156	84	70	.545	17	828	710	5451	1578	340	66	84	577	641	.289	.360	.422	.782	115	131	117	102	97	865	49			
BRO	153	79	73	.520	21	681	673	5309	1464	240	77	71	409	512	.276	.331	.390	.721	101	-3	2	99	101	705	45			
PIT	155	75	79	.487	26	636	691	5360	1425	243	70	41	409	454	.266	.330	.360	.690	93	-54	-48	99	98	667	59			
PHI	155	66	88	.429	35	684	828	5375	1502	299	52	81	437	492	.279	.336	.400	.736	96	27	-30	108	95	745	42			
BOS	156	64	90	.416	37	533	680	5296	1367	221	59	34	368	430	.258	.309	.341	.650	84	-137	-118	96	98	580	46			
CIN	154	58	96	.377	43	592	742	5343	1439	241	70	21	403	463	.269	.323	.352	.675	94	-85	-49	94	99	631	24			
TOT	618					5537		42941	11883	2188	532	493	3502	3862	.277	.334	.387	.721							462			

TEAM	CG	SH	SV	IP	H	H/G	HR	BB	SO	RAT	ERA	ERA+	OAV	OOB	PR	/A	PF	CPI	FA	E	DP	FW	PW	BW	SBW	DIF
STL	80	17	20	1384²	1470	9.6	65	449	626	12.6	3.45	114	.273	.332	63	74	102	110	.974	160	169	1.0	7.4	3.1		12.6
NY	90	17	12	1360²	1341	8.9	71	422	570	11.8	3.30	112	.255	.313	85	58	96	100	.974	159	126	1.0	5.8	8.0		-3.7
CHI	80	8	8	1385²	1448	9.4	54	524	541	13.0	3.97	97	.268	.337	-17	-19	100	94	.973	169	141	.6	-1.9	11.6		-3.3
BRO	64	9	18	1356	1520	10.1	56	351	546	12.5	3.84	99	.283	.329	3	-5	99	100	.969	187	154	-.7	-.5	.2		4.0
PIT	89	9	5	1390	1489	9.6	55	442	345	12.6	3.66	105	.274	.331	32	28	100	102	.968	194	167	-.9	2.8	-4.8		.9
PHI	60	6	16	1360¹	1603	10.6	75	511	499	14.2	4.58	93	.293	.358	-108	-51	110	100	.966	210	149	-1.9	-5.1	-3.0		-1.1
BOS	78	12	9	1380¹	1465	9.6	66	406	419	12.3	3.90	97	.272	.325	-5	-18	98	94	.973	170	141	.5	-1.8	-11.7		.0
CIN	70	7	6	1345	1545	10.3	51	399	317	13.1	4.22	89	.294	.346	-53	-72	97	101	.973	165	194	.7	-7.2	-4.9		-7.6
TOT	611	85	94	10962²		9.8				12.8	3.86		.277	.334					.971	1414	1241					

Runs		Hits		Doubles		Triples		Home Runs		Total Bases	
Terry-NY	121	L.Waner-Pit	214	Adams-StL	46	Terry-NY	20	Klein-Phi	31	Klein-Phi	347
Klein-Phi	121	Terry-NY	213	Berger-Bos	44	Herman-Bro	16	Ott-NY	29	Terry-NY	323
English-Chi	117	English-Chi	202	Terry-NY	43	Traynor-Pit	15	Berger-Bos	19	Herman-Bro	320
Cuyler-Chi	110	Cuyler-Chi	202	Herman-Bro	43	Bissonette-Bro	14	Herman-Bro	18	Berger-Bos	316
Ott-NY	104	Klein-Phi	200	Bartell-Phi	43			Arlett-Phi	18	Cuyler-Chi	290

Runs Batted In		Runs Produced		Bases On Balls		Batting Average		On Base Percentage		Slugging Average	
Klein-Phi	121	Terry-NY	224	Ott-NY	80	Hafey-StL	.349	Hafey-StL	.404	Klein-Phi	.584
Ott-NY	115	Klein-Phi	211	P.Waner-Pit	73	Terry-NY	.349	Cuyler-Chi	.404	Hornsby-Chi	.574
Terry-NY	112	Ott-NY	190	Cuyler-Chi	72	Bottomley-StL	.348	P.Waner-Pit	.404	Hafey-StL	.569
Traynor-Pit	103	Cuyler-Chi	189	Grantham-Pit	71	Klein-Phi	.337	Grantham-Pit	.400	Ott-NY	.545
Herman-Bro	97	Traynor-Pit	182	English-Chi	68	O'Doul-Bro	.336	Klein-Phi	.398	Arlett-Phi	.538

Production		Adjusted Production		Batter Runs		Adjusted Batter Runs		Clutch Hitting Index		Runs Created	
Klein-Phi	.982	Ott-NY	153	Klein-Phi	48.9	Terry-NY	42.0	Sheely-Bos	150	Klein-Phi	140
Hafey-StL	.973	Hafey-StL	153	Terry-NY	39.0	Klein-Phi	39.3	Traynor-Pit	127	Terry-NY	130
Ott-NY	.937	Terry-NY	150	Hafey-StL	36.2	Ott-NY	37.6	Frisch-StL	122	Cuyler-Chi	122
Terry-NY	.926	Klein-Phi	149	Ott-NY	35.0	Berger-Bos	35.6	Gelbert-StL	122	Berger-Bos	122
Berger-Bos	.892	Berger-Bos	143	Hornsby-Chi	33.5	Hafey-StL	32.6	Hendrick-Bro-Cin	120	Herman-Bro	118

Total Average		Stolen Bases		Stolen Base Average		Stolen Base Runs		Fielding Runs		Total Player Rating	
Hafey-StL	1.055	Frisch-StL	28					L.Waner-Pit	18.3	Ott-NY	3.6
Klein-Phi	1.051	Herman-Bro	17					Frisch-StL	16.3	Terry-NY	3.6
Ott-NY	1.031	Martin-StL	16					P.Waner-Pit	14.6	Berger-Bos	3.5
Terry-NY	.955	Adams-StL	16					Gelbert-StL	12.9	Cuccinello-Cin	3.3
Cuyler-Chi	.925	Watkins-StL	15					Hurst-Phi	11.4	P.Waner-Pit	3.1

Wins		Win Percentage		Games		Complete Games		Shutouts		Saves	
Meine-Pit	19	Derringer-StL	.692	J.Elliott-Phi	52	Lucas-Cin	24	Walker-NY	6	Quinn-Bro	15
Hallahan-StL	19	Hallahan-StL	.679	Johnson-Cin	42	Brandt-Bos	23	Hubbell-NY	4	Lindsey-StL	7
J.Elliott-Phi	19	Bush-Chi	.667	Collins-Phi	42	Meine-Pit	22	Fitzsimmons-NY	4	J.Elliott-Phi	5
		Grimes-StL	.654			Hubbell-NY	21	Derringer-StL	4	Hallahan-StL	4
						French-Pit	20			Collins-Phi	4

Innings Pitched		Fewest Hits/Game		Fewest BB/Game		Strikeouts		Strikeouts/Game		Ratio	
Meine-Pit	284.0	Hubbell-NY	7.66	Johnson-StL	1.40	Hallahan-StL	159	Vance-Bro	6.17	Hubbell-NY	10.23
French-Pit	275.2	Walker-NY	7.97	Lucas-Cin	1.47	Hubbell-NY	155	Hallahan-StL	5.75	Walker-NY	10.49
Johnson-Cin	262.1	Brandt-Bos	8.21	Cantwell-Bos	1.96	Vance-Bro	150	Derringer-StL	5.70	Johnson-StL	10.50
Fitzsimmons-NY	253.2	Fitzsimmons-NY	8.59	Clark-Bro	2.01	Derringer-StL	134	Hubbell-NY	5.63	Fitzsimmons-NY	10.79
Root-Chi	251.0	Root-Chi	8.61	Zachary-Bos	2.08	Root-Chi	131	Root-Chi	4.70	Brandt-Bos	11.12

Earned Run Average		Adjusted ERA		Opponents' Batting Avg.		Opponents' On Base Pct.		Starter Runs		Adjusted Starter Runs	
Walker-NY	2.26	Walker-NY	164	Hubbell-NY	.227	Hubbell-NY	.282	Walker-NY	42.7	Walker-NY	38.1
Hubbell-NY	2.65	Hubbell-NY	139	Walker-NY	.231	Walker-NY	.283	Hubbell-NY	33.5	Benge-Phi	29.4
Brandt-Bos	2.92	Benge-Phi	134	Brandt-Bos	.244	Johnson-StL	.286	Meine-Pit	27.9	Hubbell-NY	28.7
Meine-Pit	2.98	Johnson-StL	131	Fitzsimmons-NY	.251	Fitzsimmons-NY	.296	Brandt-Bos	26.3	Meine-Pit	27.3
Johnson-StL	3.00	Brandt-Bos	130	Root-Chi	.252	Cantwell-Bos	.301	Fitzsimmons-NY	22.9	Brandt-Bos	24.2

Clutch Pitching Index		Relief Runs		Adjusted Relief Runs		Relief Ranking		Total Pitcher Index		Total Baseball Ranking	
Benton-Cin	125	Lindsey-StL	9.1	Lindsey-StL	9.6	Quinn-Bro	14.7	Fitzsimmons-NY	3.7	Fitzsimmons-NY	3.7
Dudley-Phi	120	Quinn-Bro	8.6	Quinn-Bro	8.2	Lindsey-StL	13.6	Brandt-Bos	3.6	Ott-NY	3.6
Grimes-StL	114	Moore-Bro	.5	Moore-Bro	1	Moore-Bro	0	Benge-Phi	3.3	Terry-NY	3.6
Hallahan-StL	113							Hubbell-NY	3.1	Brandt-Bos	3.6
Derringer-StL	112							Walker-NY	2.8	Berger-Bos	3.5

February 21 The White Sox and Giants become the first major league teams to meet in a night game. They collect 23 hits in a 10-inning exhibition game played in Houston, at Buffs Stadium.

February 27 E. S. Barnard, recently reappointed AL president, dies at 57. He had succeeded Ban Johnson in 1927.

February 28 Ban Johnson dies after a long illness. He had created the AL and been its dynamic, dictatorial leader until subdued by the advent of Judge Landis, who took office as the first commissioner in January 1921.

April 26 With Lyn Lary on base for the Yankees, Lou Gehrig's drive into the stands at Washington bounces back and is caught by center fielder Harry Rice. According to the rules, this is a home run, but when Lary sees Rice catching the ball, he thinks it's the final out of the inning. Lary heads for the dugout after crossing third base while Gehrig circles the bases. He is called out and gets credit for a triple instead of a home run and loses two RBI. As a result, Gehrig will end the season tied for the home run title with Babe Ruth.

April 29 Wes Ferrell pitches a 9–0 no-hit game for Cleveland against the St. Louis Browns. His brother, Rick, almost gets a hit for the Browns when he beats out a grounder that is ruled an error. Ferrell strikes out eight and bats in four runs with a home run and a double.

May 27 AL Secretary Will Harridge is elected to succeed E. S. Barnard as president of the league.

June 15 Cut-down day for major league rosters brings the retirement of Eddie Collins and Harry Heilmann. Collins becomes a coach for the A's. Heilmann will return briefly to the Reds in 1932.

August 21 Babe Ruth hits his 600th home run, off George Blaeholder of the Browns, as the Yankees win, 11–7. Lou Gehrig homers immediately after the Babe's historic blow. In their 10 years as teammates, they will homer in the same inning 19 times and in the same game 72 times.

August 23 Lefty Grove is frustrated in his effort to win a record-breaking 17th game in a row, as Johnny Moore misjudges a routine fly ball to allow the game's lone run. The volatile Grove is outraged that Al Simmons, the Athletics' regular outfielder, misses the game, which is won by Dick Coffman of the Browns 1-0.

September 15 The Philadelphia Athletics clinch the pennant, beating Cleveland at home. Eddie Rommel, veteran knuckleball pitcher for the A's, is the winning hurler, as Connie Mack wins his third successive pennant. It is Mack's ninth, and last, AL championship.

September 17 On his 32nd birthday, outfielder Earl Webb of the Red Sox sets the still-standing major league record for two-base hits at 65. He will finish the season with 67.

September 19 Lefty Grove wins his 30th game, beating the White Sox 2-1. He is the first to win 30 since Jim Bagby of Cleveland in 1920 and will be the last AL hurler to do so until Denny McLain in 1968.

September 20 Lou Gehrig drives in four runs to break his old RBI mark of 175, set in 1927. By the season's end he will have a total of 184.

September 24 A round-robin playoff among New York City's three major league teams, to raise money for the unemployed, concludes with Brooklyn losing to both the Giants and the Yankees at the Polo Grounds. A near capacity crowd turns out and adds $48,000 to bring the fund to $108,000. In field events held between games, Babe Ruth, normally a left-handed hitter, bats righty and wins the fungo hitting contest. Ruth's drive lands in deep center field, 421 feet away.

October 1 John "Pepper" Martin, an unheralded rookie, gets three hits, but the A's Lefty Grove coasts to an easy 6-2 victory in the World Series opener in St. Louis.

October 5 Because of a Pennsylvania law banning baseball on Sunday, an extra day is added as the Series moves to Philadelphia. Lefty Grove pitches the third game with three days rest. However, Burleigh Grimes, who had lost twice to Grove in 1930, has a no-hitter until the eighth inning, winning 5-2. Martin continues to excite the crowds with two more hits, scoring twice.

October 6 The A's George Earnshaw evens the World Series with a 3-0 shutout, giving up two hits to the red-hot Martin. Jimmie Foxx hits a ball over the left field stands, judged one of the longest drives ever at Shibe Park.

October 9 With the Series back in St. Louis, Lefty Grove evens matters by containing Pepper Martin and winning easily 8-1.

BOSTON

Pos	Player
M	S.Collins
1B	B.Sweeney
2B	R.Warstler
SS	H.Rhyne
3B	O.Miller
LF	J.Rothrock
CF	T.Oliver
RF	E.Webb
C	C.Berry
32	U.Pickering
O1	A.Van Camp
C	E.Connolly
2	B.Reeves
C	M.Ruel
/O	T.Winsett
3	M.McManus
2	M.Olson
2	O.Marquardt
O	G.Rye
/O	R.Scarritt
/O	G.Stumpf
/C	H.Storie
/1	J.Smith
/2	P.Creeden
/O	J.Lucas
H	B.McWilliams
R	B.Marshall
RP	J.Russell
RP	D.MacFayden
P	W.Moore
P	H.Lisenbee
P	E.Durham
P	E.Morris
P	M.Gaston
P	B.Kline
P	J.Brillheart
/P	J.McLaughlin
/P	W.Murphy

CHICAGO

Pos	Player
M	D.Bush
1B	L.Blue
2B	J.Kerr
SS	B.Cissell
3B	B.Sullivan
LF	L.Fonseca
CF	J.Watwood
RF	C.Reynolds
C	B.Tate
S	L.Appling
C	B.Fothergill
C	F.Grube
3	I.Jeffries
O	B.Seeds
1	L.Fonseca
O	M.Simons
O	I.Eichrodt
S	S.Jolley
O	W.Kamm
O	B.Norman
/O	B.Campbell
/C	B.Henline
/C	H.Garrity
P	V.Frasier
P	T.Thomas
P	P.Caraway
P	R.Faber
P	H.McKain
RP	J.Moore
RP	G.Braxton
P	T.Lyons
P	B.Weiland
P	G.Bowler
/P	L.Garland
/P	B.Wehde

CLEVELAND

Pos	Player
M	R.Peckinpaugh
1B	E.Morgan
2B	J.Hodapp
SS	E.Montague
3B	W.Kamm
LF	J.Vosmik
CF	E.Averill
RF	D.Porter
C	L.Sewell
S2	J.Burnett
C	G.Myatt
O	B.Falk
O	B.Seeds
3	L.Fonseca
32	O.Hale
S	B.Hunnefield
S	J.Goldman
3S	G.DeTore
1	B.Connatser
O	C.Jamieson
/C	M.Berg
/C	J.Sprinz
P	W.Ferrell
P	W.Hudlin
P	C.Brown
P	M.Harder
RP	P.Appleton
P	S.Connally
P	R.Lawson
P	F.Thomas
P	J.Miller
P	M.Shoffner
/P	O.Hildebrand
/P	B.Bean
/P	H.Craghead
/P	P.Donohue

DETROIT

Pos	Player
M	B.Harris
1B	D.Alexander
2B	C.Gehringer
SS	B.Rogell
3B	M.McManus
LF	J.Stone
CF	H.Walker
RF	R.Johnson
C	R.Hayworth
2S	M.Koenig
S3	M.Owen
O	G.Walker
O	F.Doljack
3	N.Richardson
O	J.Grabowski
O	W.Schang
S	B.Akers
S	L.Brower
O	G.Quellich
C	M.Ruel
/3	J.Dugan
/C	G.Desautels
/O	I.Shiver
/2	B.Harris
P	E.Whitehill
P	V.Sorrell
P	G.Uhle
P	T.Bridges
P	A.Herring
P	C.Hogsett
P	C.Sullivan
P	W.Hoyt
P	W.Wyatt
/P	O.Collier

NEW YORK

Pos	Player
M	J.McCarthy
1B	L.Gehrig
2B	T.Lazzeri
SS	L.Lary
3B	J.Sewell
LF	B.Chapman
CF	E.Combs
RF	B.Ruth
C	B.Dickey
O	S.Byrd
2	J.Reese
C	M.Owen
C	G.Walker
C	C.Perkins
C	D.Cooke
O	M.Hoag
/O	D.Walker
/S	R.Rolfe
P	L.Gomez
P	R.Ruffing
P	H.Johnson
P	H.Pennock
P	G.Pipgras
P	E.Wells
P	G.Rhodes
P	R.Sherid
P	G.Uhle
/P	I.Andrews
/P	L.Weinert
/P	L.McEvoy

PHILADELPHIA

Pos	Player
M	C.Mack
1B	J.Foxx
2B	M.Bishop
SS	D.Williams
3B	J.Dykes
LF	A.Simmons
CF	M.Haas
RF	B.Miller
C	M.Cochrane
32	E.McNair
3	L.Storti
O	L.Bettencourt
O	D.Cramer
1	P.Todt
O	J.Moore
C	J.Heving
C	J.Palmisano
/O	L.Finney
P	R.Walberg
P	L.Grove
	G.Earnshaw
	R.Mahaffey
	E.Rommel
P	W.Hoyt
P	H.McDonald
/P	B.Shores
/P	J.Peterson
/P	L.Krausse
/P	S.Carter

ST.LOUIS

Pos	Player
M	B.Killefer
1B	J.Burns
2B	S.Melillo
SS	J.Levey
3B	R.Kress
LF	G.Goslin
CF	F.Schulte
RF	T.Jenkins
C	R.Ferrell
3	L.Storti
O	L.Bettencourt
C	B.Bengough
O	E.McNeely
3	E.Grimes
C	R.Young
/O	F.Waddey
/O	B.Stanton
/C	J.Crouch
/S	F.O'Rourke
/O	N.Kloza
P	L.Stewart
P	S.Gray
P	G.Blaeholder
P	D.Coffman
P	R.Collins
RP	C.Kimsey
RP	R.Stiles
P	W.Hebert
P	B.Cooney
/P	G.Braxton
/P	F.Stiely
/P	J.Doyle

WASHINGTON

Pos	Player
M	W.Johnson
1B	J.Kuhel
2B	B.Myer
SS	J.Cronin
3B	O.Bluege
LF	H.Manush
CF	S.West
RF	S.Rice
C	R.Spencer
O	D.Harris
O	H.Rice
2	J.Hayes
O	P.Hargrave
1	J.Judge
O	C.Bolton
/O	J.Gill
/1	B.Jordan
/3	B.Andrus
H	B.Phelps
H	N.Altrock
P	L.Brown
P	A.Crowder
P	F.Marberry
P	C.Fischer
P	B.Hadley
P	S.Jones
P	B.Burke
/P	W.Tauscher
/P	M.Weaver
/P	W.Masters
/P	A.Liska

TEAM	G	W	L	PCT	GB	R	OR	AB	H	2B	3B	HR	BB	SO	AVG	OBP	SLG	PRO	PRO+	BR	/A	PF	CHI	RC	SB	CS	SBA	SBR
PHI	153	107	45	.704		858	626	5377	1544	311	64	118	528	543	.287	.355	.435	.790	107	93	40	106	98	843	25	23	52	-6
NY	155	94	59	.614	13.5	1067	760	5608	1667	277	78	155	748	554	.297	.383	.457	.840	135	220	280	94	100	1016	138	68	67	1
WAS	156	92	62	.597	16	843	691	5576	1588	308	93	49	481	459	.285	.345	.400	.745	100	8	4	101	103	774	72	64	53	-17
CLE	155	78	76	.506	30	885	833	5445	1612	321	69	71	555	433	.296	.363	.419	.782	105	91	41	106	100	840	63	60	51	-17
STL	154	63	91	.409	45	722	870	5374	1455	287	62	76	488	580	.271	.333	.390	.723	92	-40	-66	104	98	696	73	80	48	-26
BOS	153	62	90	.408	45	625	800	5379	1409	289	34	37	405	565	.262	.315	.349	.664	85	-154	-121	95	102	596	42	43	49	-13
DET	154	61	93	.396	47	651	836	5430	1456	292	69	43	480	468	.268	.330	.371	.701	87	-79	-103	103	93	675	117	75	61	-10
CHI	156	56	97	.366	51.5	704	939	5481	1423	238	69	27	483	445	.260	.323	.343	.666	86	-146	-108	94	108	632	94	39	71	5
TOT	618					6355		43670	12154	2323	538	576	4168	4047	.278	.344	.396	.740							624	452	58	-84

TEAM	CG	SH	SV	IP	H	H/G	HR	BB	SO	RAT	ERA	ERA+	OAV	OOB	PR	/A	PF	CPI	FA	E	DP	FW	PW	BW	SBW	DIF
PHI	97	12	16	1365¹	1342	8.8	73	457	574	11.9	3.47	130	.256	.316	138	155	103	105	.976	141	151	3.2	14.4	3.7	.4	9.3
NY	78	4	17	1410¹	1461	9.3	67	543	686	12.9	4.20	94	.263	.332	28	-37	91	94	.972	169	131	1.7	-3.4	26.1	1.1	-7.9
WAS	60	7	24	1394¹	1434	9.3	73	498	582	12.6	3.76	114	.264	.327	95	82	98	104	.976	142	148	3.3	7.6	.4	-.6	4.3
CLE	76	6	9	1354²	1577	10.5	64	561	470	14.4	4.63	100	.286	.355	-38	-2	106	100	.963	232	143	-2.0	-.2	3.8	-.6	.0
STL	65	4	10	1362	1623	10.7	84	444	436	13.8	4.76	97	.293	.348	-57	-18	106	99	.963	232	160	-2.1	-1.7	-6.1	-1.4	-2.6
BOS	61	5	10	1366²	1559	10.3	54	473	365	13.5	4.60	94	.285	.344	-33	-44	98	95	.970	188	127	.4	-4.1	-11.3	-.2	1.2
DET	86	5	6	1384¹	1549	10.1	79	597	511	14.1	4.59	100	.282	.355	-32	-1	105	102	.964	220	139	-1.4	-.0	-9.6	.0	-5.0
CHI	54	6	10	1390¹	1613	10.4	82	588	421	14.5	5.04	85	.287	.358	-101	-122	94	96	.961	245	131	-2.7	-11.4	-10.1	1.4	1.7
TOT	577	49	102	11028		9.9				13.5	4.38		.278	.344					.968	1569	1130					

Runs
Gehrig-NY 163
Ruth-NY 149
Averill-Cle 140
Combs-NY 120
Chapman-NY 120

Hits
Gehrig-NY 211
Averill-Cle 209
Simmons-Phi 200
Ruth-NY 199
Webb-Bos 196

Doubles
Webb-Bos 67
Alexander-Det ... 47
Kress-StL 46
Cronin-Was 44

Triples
Johnson-Det 19
Gehrig-NY 15
Blue-Chi 15
Vosmik-Cle 14
Reynolds-Chi 14

Home Runs
Ruth-NY 46
Gehrig-NY 46
Averill-Cle 32
Foxx-Phi 30
Goslin-StL 24

Total Bases
Gehrig-NY 410
Ruth-NY 374
Averill-Cle 361
Simmons-Phi 329
Goslin-StL 328

Runs Batted In
Gehrig-NY 184
Ruth-NY 163
Averill-Cle 143
Simmons-Phi 128
Cronin-Was 126

Runs Produced
Gehrig-NY 301
Ruth-NY 266
Averill-Cle 251
Chapman-NY 225
Cronin-Was 217

Bases On Balls
Ruth-NY 128
Blue-Chi 127
Gehrig-NY 117
Bishop-Phi 112
Lary-NY 88

Batting Average
Simmons-Phi 390
Ruth-NY 373
Morgan-Cle 351
Cochrane-Phi 349
Gehrig-NY 341

On Base Percentage
Ruth-NY 495
Morgan-Cle 451
Gehrig-NY 446
Simmons-Phi 444
Blue-Chi 430

Slugging Average
Ruth-NY 700
Gehrig-NY 662
Simmons-Phi 641
Averill-Cle 576
Foxx-Phi 567

Production
Ruth-NY 1.195
Gehrig-NY 1.108
Simmons-Phi 1.085
Averill-Cle 979
Cochrane-Phi 976

Adjusted Production
Ruth-NY 223
Gehrig-NY 199
Simmons-Phi 172
Webb-Bos 151
Goslin-StL 147

Batter Runs
Ruth-NY 91.5
Gehrig-NY 79.9
Simmons-Phi 59.6
Averill-Cle 48.2
Goslin-StL 44.7

Adjusted Batter Runs
Ruth-NY 101.8
Gehrig-NY 90.0
Simmons-Phi 51.6
Webb-Bos 43.4
Averill-Cle 40.5

Clutch Hitting Index
Bluege-Was 126
Kamm-Chi-Cle ... 124
Vosmik-Cle 119
Lazzeri-NY 118
Spencer-Was 118

Runs Created
Ruth-NY 192
Gehrig-NY 185
Simmons-Phi 145
Averill-Cle 144
Goslin-StL 137

Total Average
Ruth-NY 1.487
Gehrig-NY 1.267
Simmons-Phi 1.199
Morgan-Cle 1.046
Cochrane-Phi ...1.033

Stolen Bases
Chapman-NY 61
Johnson-Det 33
Burns-StL 19
Lazzeri-NY 18
Cissell-Chi 18

Stolen Base Average
Cissell-Chi 75.0
Reynolds-Chi 73.9
Chapman-NY 72.6
Lazzeri-NY 66.7
Bluege-Was 61.5

Stolen Base Runs
Chapman-NY 4.5
H.Walker-Det 2.4
Blue-Chi 2.1
Cissell-Chi 1.8

Fielding Runs
Melillo-StL 33.1
McManus-Det-Bos 21.1
West-Was 21.0
Burns-StL 18.4
Rhyne-Bos 16.9

Total Player Rating
Ruth-NY 7.3
Gehrig-NY 5.8
Cronin-Was 4.6
Simmons-Phi 4.6
Cochrane-Phi 4.3

Wins
Grove-Phi 31
Ferrell-Cle 22
Gomez-NY 21
Earnshaw-Phi 21
Walberg-Phi 20

Win Percentage
Grove-Phi 886
Marberry-Was 800
Mahaffey-Phi 789
Earnshaw-Phi 750
Gomez-NY 700

Games
Hadley-Was 55
Moore-Bos 53
Caraway-Chi 51
Frasier-Chi 46
Fischer-Was 46

Complete Games
Grove-Phi 27
Ferrell-Cle 27
Earnshaw-Phi 23
Whitehill-Det 22
Stewart-StL 20

Shutouts
Grove-Phi 4
Earnshaw-Phi 3

Saves
Moore-Bos 10
Hadley-Was 8
Marberry-Was 7
Kimsey-StL 7
Earnshaw-Phi 6

Innings Pitched
Walberg-Phi 291.0
Grove-Phi 288.2
Earnshaw-Phi 281.2
Ferrell-Cle 276.1
Whitehill-Det ...271.1

Fewest Hits/Game
Hadley-Was 7.26
Gomez-NY 7.63
Grove-Phi 7.76
Johnson-NY 8.07
Earnshaw-Phi 8.15

Fewest BB/Game
Pennock-NY 1.43
Gray-StL 1.88
Grove-Phi 1.93
Brown-Cle 2.12
Blaeholder-StL .. 2.23

Strikeouts
Grove-Phi 175
Earnshaw-Phi 152
Gomez-NY 150
Ruffing-NY 132
Hadley-Was 124

Strikeouts/Game
Hadley-Was 6.21
Gomez-NY 5.56
Bridges-Det 5.46
Grove-Phi 5.46
Ruffing-NY 5.01

Ratio
Grove-Phi 9.73
Earnshaw-Phi ... 10.64
Gomez-NY 10.93
Coffman-StL 11.27
Uhle-Det 11.33

Earned Run Average
Grove-Phi 2.06
Gomez-NY 2.67
Hadley-Was 3.06
Brown-Was 3.20
Marberry-Was 3.45

Adjusted ERA
Grove-Phi 218
Gomez-NY 149
Hadley-Was 140
Brown-Was 134
Uhle-Det 131

Opponents' Batting Avg.
Hadley-Was 218
Gomez-NY 226
Grove-Phi 229
Johnson-NY 234
Earnshaw-Phi 236

Opponents' On Base Pct.
Grove-Phi 271
Earnshaw-Phi 288
Gomez-NY 295
Coffman-StL 298
Uhle-Det 304

Starter Runs
Grove-Phi 74.5
Gomez-NY 46.2
Brown-Was 33.9
Hadley-Was 26.4
Marberry-Was 22.6

Adjusted Starter Runs
Grove-Phi 78.1
Gomez-NY 35.1
Brown-Was 31.3
Ferrell-Cle 26.9
Earnshaw-Phi 25.6

Clutch Pitching Index
Grove-Phi 118
Faber-Chi 116
Whitehill-Det ... 115
Pennock-NY 110
Brown-Was 110

Relief Runs

Adjusted Relief Runs
Kimsey-StL 2.6

Relief Ranking
Kimsey-StL 2.9

Total Pitcher Index
Grove-Phi 8.7
Ferrell-Cle 5.2
Gomez-NY 3.5
Brown-Was 3.4
Earnshaw-Phi 2.9

Total Baseball Ranking
Grove-Phi 8.7
Ruth-NY 7.3
Gehrig-NY 5.8
Ferrell-Cle 5.2
Cronin-Was 4.6

January 26 William K. Wrigley, owner of the Cubs since 1919, dies and is buried on Catalina Island. His only son, Philip K. Wrigley, inherits the Cubs and the minor league Los Angeles Angels.

May 11 Cardinals hurler Wild Bill Hallahan lives up to his name with three wild pitches in the 12th inning in a game that Brooklyn wins at St. Louis 6–3. He ties the record set by Jake Weimer of the Cubs on May 10, 1903.

June 3 John McGraw, who came to New York in 1902, resigns as manager of the Giants and is replaced by Bill Terry, the team's star first baseman.

June 7 Pitcher John Quinn, at 48, becomes the oldest player to have an extra-base hit (a double) and bat in a run, as the Dodgers beat the Cubs 9–2.

June 22 The NL, at a meeting of club presidents, finally approves players wearing numbers. The AL had started the practice in 1929.

July 6 Cubs shortstop Bill Jurges is shot twice in his Chicago hotel room by a spurned girlfriend, Violet Popovich Valli. In a scuffle for the gun, Jurges is hit in the shoulder and hand. Jurges fails to

prosecute, and Valli will be signed to a 22-week contract to sing in local nightclubs and theaters. She is billed as "Violet (What I Did for Love) Valli—the Most Talked About Girl in Chicago."

August 13 Commissioner Kenesaw Mountain Landis clears Rogers Hornsby of charges of fraudulently "borrowing" money from Cubs players. The Chicago papers said Hornsby had obtained money from players, either loaned to him to bet on horse races, or to share in joint ventures. When Hornsby is fined, the players want refunds. Hornsby wants a lump payoff by the Cubs, who refuse. Landis holds several hearings, and as he doesn't punish anyone, it is taken as exoneration.

August 14 John Quinn becomes, at 49, the oldest pitcher to win a major league game. He relieves Van Mungo in the ninth with the game between Brooklyn and New York tied at 1–1. The Dodgers win in the 10th after Johnny Frederick hits a pinch-hit home run off Carl Hubbell in the ninth to tie. It is Frederick's fourth pinch-hit homer of the year, for a new major league record. He will have six by the season's end.

September 7 Pirates catcher Earl Grace makes a wild throw to end a streak of 110 consecutive errorless games. It is Grace's only error of the season for a still-standing NL record.

September 20 The Chicago Cubs clinch the NL pennant when Kiki Cuyler hits a triple with the bases loaded for a 5-2 win over Pittsburgh.

September 22 The Cubs announce World Series shares and snub former manager Rogers Hornsby. Late-season arrival Mark Koenig gets just a half share.

September 26 Chuck Klein closes the season with 38 home runs and 20 stolen bases and becomes the only player of the lively ball era (1920 and after) to lead his league in these two departments.

October 19 The BBWAA MVP awards are announced, with Jimmie Foxx winning in the AL and Chuck Klein in the NL.

December 15 A joint meeting of AL and NL owners approves the concept of "chain store" baseball, developed as the St. Louis Cardinal farm system, despite strenuous objections by Judge Landis.

	BOSTON		BROOKLYN		CHICAGO		CINCINNATI		NEW YORK		PHILADELPHIA		PITTSBURGH		ST.LOUIS
M	B.McKechnie	M	M.Carey	M	R.Hornsby	M	D.Howley	M	J.McGraw	M	B.Shotton	M	M.Gibson	M	G.Street
1B	A.Shires	1B	G.Kelly	M	C.Grimm	1B	H.Hendrick	1B	B.Terry	1B	D.Hurst	1B	G.Suhr	1B	R.Collins
2B	R.Maranville	2B	T.Cuccinello	1B	C.Grimm	2B	G.Grantham	2B	H.Critz	2B	L.Mallon	2B	T.Piet	2B	J.Reese
SS	B.Urbanski	SS	G.Wright	2B	B.Herman	SS	L.Durocher	SS	D.Bartell	SS	D.Bartell	SS	A.Vaughan	SS	C.Gelbert
3B	F.Knothe	3B	J.Stripp	SS	B.Jurges	3B	W.Gilbert	3B	D.Marshall	3B	P.Whitney	3B	P.Traynor	3B	J.Flowers
LF	R.Worthington	LF	L.O'Doul	3B	W.English	LF	W.Roettger	3B	J.Vergez	LF	H.Lee	LF	A.Comorosky	LF	E.Orsatti
CF	W.Berger	CF	D.Taylor	LF	R.Stephenson	CF	E.Crabtree	LF	J.Moore	CF	K.Davis	CF	L.Waner	CF	P.Martin
RF	W.Schulmerich	RF	H.Wilson	CF	J.Moore	RF	B.Herman	CF	F.Lindstrom	RF	C.Klein	RF	P.Waner	RF	G.Watkins
C	A.Spohrer	C	A.Lopez	RF	K.Cuyler	C	E.Lombardi	RF	M.Ott	C	S.Davis	C	E.Grace	C	G.Mancuso
				C	G.Hartnett			C	S.Hogan						
O3	R.Moore	O	J.Frederick			O	T.Douthit			2	B.Friberg	O	D.Barbee	23	F.Frisch
O	F.Leach	S3	G.Slade	3	S.Hack	S2	J.Morrissey	O	C.Fullis	C	H.McCurdy	S3	T.Thevenow	1	J.Bottomley
C	P.Hargrave	1	B.Clancy	O	R.Hemsley	O	C.Hafey	3S	G.English	O	R.Bressler	C	T.Padden	C	J.Wilson
1	B.Jordan	3	N.Finn	O	L.Richbourg	32	A.High	S	T.Jackson	O	A.Todd	O	G.Dugas	O	R.Blades
O	D.Holland	C	C.Sukeforth	O	V.Barton	C	C.Manion	O	L.Koenecke	O	F.Brickell	O	H.Finney	3	S.Adams
2S	H.Ford	S	V.Picinich	S	M.Koenig	1	M.Heath	2	E.Allen	/C	E.Delker	/C	B.Brenzel	O	G.Puccinelli
3	B.Akers	O	M.Rosenfeld	O	M.Gudat	O	C.Asbjornson	S	E.Moore	/1	C.Heathcote	/3	B.Brubaker	O	J.Medwick
3	B.Walters	/O	A.Cohen	O	R.Hornsby	/1	H.Heilmann	/1	S.Leslie	/2	G.Knothe	/S	H.Groskloss	S	C.Wilson
O	E.Clark	/O	I.Boone	O	F.Demaree	/1	J.Shevlin	C	B.O'Farrell	/O	R.Scarritt	O	W.Jensen	3	H.Hendrick
C	J.Schulte	/1	B.Caldwell	C	Z.Taylor	C	C.Heathcote	C	F.Healy	H	D.Taitt			O	R.Pepper
H	O.Eckhardt	/C	P.Richards	/O	D.Taylor	R	O.Bluege	/S	A.McLarney	H	H.Willingham	P	L.French	2	E.Delker
		/1	D.Siebert	/1	H.Taylor			H	J.Tobin			P	B.Swift	/C	B.DeLancey
P	E.Brandt	/3	B.Reis			P	R.Lucas	H	P.Veltman	P	E.Holley	/3	H.Meine	/3	R.Cunningham
P	H.Betts	H	F.Thompson	P	L.Warneke	P	S.Johnson			P	R.Benge	/O	B.Harris	/O	J.Hunt
P	B.Brown			P	G.Bush	P	O.Carroll	P	C.Hubbell	P	S.Hansen	/O	S.Swetonic	/O	R.Bressler
P	T.Zachary	P	W.Clark	P	P.Malone	P	L.Benton	P	F.Fitzsimmons	P	P.Collins	RP	E.Brame	/O	W.Holm
P	B.Cantwell	P	V.Mungo	P	C.Root	P	R.Kolp	P	B.Walker	P	F.Rhem			/C	M.Gonzalez
RP	F.Frankhouse	P	D.Vance	P	B.Grimes	RP	J.Ogden	P	J.Mooney			P	G.Spencer	/S	H.Ford
RP	B.Cunningham	P	F.Heimach	RP	J.May			P	H.Bell	J.Elliott	P	L.Chagnon	/S	S.Webb
		P	S.Thurston					P	B.Frey	RP	D.Luque	P	H.Elliott	P	R.Kremer
P	S.Seibold	RP	J.Quinn	P	B.Smith	P	E.Rixey	RP	S.Gibson	P	J.Berly	/P	H.Smith	P	D.Dean
P	H.Pruett	RP	C.Moore	P	B.Tinning	P	W.Hilcher			P	R.Grabowski			P	P.Derringer
/P	L.Mangum			/P	L.Herrmann	/P	B.Wysong	P	H.Schumacher	/P	A.Liska			P	T.Carleton
/P	B.Sherdel	P	J.Shaute	/P	C.Yerkes			P	W.Hoyt	P	C.Nichols			P	B.Hallahan
		P	R.Phelps	/P	E.Baecht			/P	C.Mitchell	/P	C.Dudley			P	S.Johnson
		/P	W.Hoyt	/P	B.Newsom			/P	R.Parmelee	/P	S.Bolen			RP	J.Lindsey
		/P	F.Thomas							/P	B.Adams			RP	A.Stout
		/P	E.Pipgras												
		/P	A.Jones											P	J.Haines
														/P	F.Rhem
														/P	R.Starr
														/P	J.Winford
														/P	B.Sherdel
														/P	B.Frey
														/P	D.Terwilliger
														/P	B.Teachout

TEAM	G	W	L	PCT	GB	R	OR	AB	H	2B	3B	HR	BB	SO	AVG	OBP	SLG	PRO	PRO+	BR	/A	PF	CHI	RC	SB	CS	SBA	SBR
CHI	154	90	64	.584		720	633	5462	1519	296	60	69	398	514	.278	.330	.392	.722	101	0	7	99	101	728	48			
PIT	154	86	68	.558	4	701	711	5421	1543	274	90	48	358	385	.285	.333	.395	.728	103	9	22	98	99	729	71			
BRO	154	81	73	.526	9	752	747	5433	1538	296	59	110	388	574	.283	.334	.420	.754	110	55	71	98	99	778	61			
PHI	154	78	76	.506	12	844	796	5510	1608	330	67	122	446	547	.292	.348	.442	.790	105	132	32	112	98	870	71			
BOS	155	77	77	.500	13	649	655	5506	1460	262	53	63	347	496	.265	.311	.366	.677	90	-94	-71	96	105	643	36			
STL	156	72	82	.468	18	684	717	5458	1467	307	51	76	420	514	.269	.324	.385	.709	93	-27	-47	103	100	702	92			
NY	154	72	82	.468	18	755	706	5530	1527	263	54	116	348	391	.276	.322	.406	.728	103	1	16	98	107	735	31			
CIN	155	60	94	.390	30	575	715	5443	1429	265	68	47	436	436	.263	.320	.362	.682	92	-77	-56	97	91	654	35			
TOT	618					5680		43763	12091	2293	502	651	3141	3857	.276	.328	.396	.724							445			

TEAM	CG	SH	SV	IP	H	H/G	HR	BB	SO	RAT	ERA	ERA+	OAV	OOB	PR	/A	PF	CPI	FA	E	DP	FW	PW	BW	SBW	DIF
CHI	79	9	7	1401	1444	9.3	68	409	527	12.1	3.44	109	.264	.319	68	50	97	102	.973	173	146	.4	4.9	.7		7.0
PIT	71	12	12	1377	1472	9.6	86	338	377	11.9	3.75	102	.270	.314	20	10	98	96	.969	185	124	-.4	1.0	2.2		6.2
BRO	61	7	16	1379²	1538	10.0	72	410	497	12.8	4.27	89	.282	.334	-60	-68	98	94	.971	183	169	-.3	-6.7	7.0		4.0
PHI	59	4	17	1384	1589	10.3	107	450	459	13.5	4.47	99	.287	.344	-91	-9	114	100	.968	194	133	-.9	-.9	3.2		-.3
BOS	72	8	8	1414	1483	9.4	61	420	440	12.3	3.53	107	.272	.328	55	36	97	105	.976	152	145	1.7	3.6	-7.0		1.7
STL	70	13	9	1396	1533	9.9	76	455	681	13.0	3.97	99	.282	.340	-14	-4	101	104	.971	175	155	.4	-.6	-4.7		-.1
NY	57	3	16	1375¹	1533	10.0	112	387	506	12.7	3.83	97	.280	.330	8	-18	96	108	.969	191	143	-.7	-1.8	1.6		-4.1
CIN	83	6	6	1394²	1505	9.7	69	276	359	11.6	3.79	102	.274	.311	14	10	99	92	.971	178	129	.1	1.0	-5.5		-12.6
TOT	552	62	91	11121²		9.8				12.5	3.88		.276	.328					.971	1431	1144					

Runs
Klein-Phi	152
Terry-NY	124
O'Doul-Bro	120
Ott-NY	119
Bartell-Phi	118

Hits
Klein-Phi	226
Terry-NY	225
O'Doul-Bro	219
P.Waner-Pit	215
Herman-Chi	206

Doubles
P.Waner-Pit	62
Klein-Phi	50
Stephenson-Chi	49
Bartell-Phi	48

Triples
Herman-Cin	19
Suhr-Pit	16
Klein-Phi	15

Home Runs
Ott-NY	38
Klein-Phi	38
Terry-NY	28
Hurst-Phi	24
Wilson-Bro	23

Total Bases
Klein-Phi	420
Terry-NY	373
Ott-NY	340
O'Doul-Bro	330
P.Waner-Pit	321

Runs Batted In
Hurst-Phi	143
Klein-Phi	137
Whitney-Phi	124
Wilson-Bro	123
Ott-NY	123

Runs Produced
Klein-Phi	251
Hurst-Phi	228
Terry-NY	213
Whitney-Phi	204
Ott-NY	204

Bases On Balls
Ott-NY	100
Hurst-Phi	65
Bartell-Phi	64
Suhr-Pit	63

Batting Average
O'Doul-Bro	.368
Terry-NY	.350
Klein-Phi	.348
P.Waner-Pit	.341
Hurst-Phi	.339

On Base Percentage
Ott-NY	.424
O'Doul-Bro	.423
Hurst-Phi	.412
Klein-Phi	.404
P.Waner-Pit	.397

Slugging Average
Klein-Phi	.646
Ott-NY	.601
Terry-NY	.580
O'Doul-Bro	.555
Hurst-Phi	.547

Production
Klein-Phi	1.050
Ott-NY	1.025
O'Doul-Bro	.978
Terry-NY	.962
Hurst-Phi	.959

Adjusted Production
Ott-NY	175
O'Doul-Bro	164
Klein-Phi	158
Terry-NY	158
Herman-Cin	152

Batter Runs
Klein-Phi	68.2
Ott-NY	59.8
O'Doul-Bro	51.2
Terry-NY	46.4
Hurst-Phi	46.2

Adjusted Batter Runs
Ott-NY	62.8
O'Doul-Bro	53.9
Klein-Phi	50.9
Terry-NY	49.1
Herman-Cin	41.8

Clutch Hitting Index
Wilson-Bro	132
Whitney-Phi	131
Hogan-NY	129
Cuyler-Chi	126
Hurst-Phi	124

Runs Created
Klein-Phi	171
Ott-NY	151
O'Doul-Bro	142
Terry-NY	142
Hurst-Phi	134

Total Average
Klein-Phi	1.182
Ott-NY	1.166
O'Doul-Bro	1.059
Hurst-Phi	1.042
Terry-NY	.981

Stolen Bases
Klein-Phi	20
Piet-Pit	19
Watkins-StL	18
Frisch-StL	18
K.Davis-Phi	16

Stolen Base Average

Stolen Base Runs

Fielding Runs
Jurges-NY	31.7
Cuccinello-Bro	19.0
Herman-Chi	16.8
Frisch-StL	16.4
Stripp-Bro	15.9

Total Player Rating
Ott-NY	5.3
Klein-Phi	4.9
Terry-NY	4.9
Herman-Cin	4.7
O'Doul-Bro	3.9

Wins
Warneke-Chi	22
Clark-Bro	20
Bush-Chi	19

Win Percentage
Warneke-Chi	.786
Bush-Chi	.633
Rhem-StL-Phi	.625
Clark-Bro	.625
Hubbell-NY	.621

Games
French-Pit	47
Dean-StL	46
Carleton-StL	44
Collins-Phi	43

Complete Games
Lucas-Cin	28
Warneke-Chi	25
Hubbell-NY	22

Shutouts
Warneke-Chi	4
Swetonic-Pit	4
Dean-StL	4

Saves
Quinn-Bro	8
Benge-Phi	6
Luque-NY	5
Cantwell-Bos	5

Innings Pitched
Dean-StL	286.0
Hubbell-NY	284.0
Warneke-Chi	277.0
French-Pit	274.1
Clark-Bro	273.0

Fewest Hits/Game
Swetonic-Pit	7.41
Brown-Bos	7.90
Warneke-Chi	8.03
Hubbell-NY	8.24
Malone-Chi	8.43

Fewest BB/Game
Swift-Pit	1.09
Lucas-Cin	1.17
Hubbell-NY	1.27
Benton-Cin	1.35
Betts-Bos	1.42

Strikeouts
Dean-StL	191
Hubbell-NY	137
Malone-Chi	120
Carleton-StL	113
Brown-Bos	110

Strikeouts/Game
Dean-StL	6.01
Hallahan-StL	5.51
Vance-Bro	5.28
Carleton-StL	5.18
Brown-Bos	4.65

Ratio
Hubbell-NY	9.63
Swift-Pit	9.78
Lucas-Cin	9.92
Warneke-Chi	10.17
Swetonic-Pit	10.46

Earned Run Average
Warneke-Chi	2.37
Hubbell-NY	2.50
Betts-Bos	2.80
Swetonic-Pit	2.82
Lucas-Cin	2.94

Adjusted ERA
Warneke-Chi	159
Hubbell-NY	148
Swetonic-Pit	135
Betts-Bos	134
Lucas-Cin	131

Opponents' Batting Avg.
Swetonic-Pit	.221
Warneke-Chi	.237
Hubbell-NY	.238
Brown-Bos	.238
Malone-Chi	.244

Opponents' On Base Pct.
Hubbell-NY	.268
Swift-Pit	.272
Lucas-Cin	.274
Warneke-Chi	.283
Swetonic-Pit	.286

Starter Runs
Warneke-Chi	46.4
Hubbell-NY	43.4
Lucas-Cin	28.1
Betts-Bos	26.5
French-Pit	26.2

Adjusted Starter Runs
Warneke-Chi	42.9
Hubbell-NY	38.1
Lucas-Cin	27.4
French-Pit	24.2
Betts-Bos	23.6

Clutch Pitching Index
Bush-Chi	123
French-Pit	123
Zachary-Bos	117
Hallahan-StL	113
Derringer-StL	113

Relief Runs
Quinn-Bro	5.6
Frankhouse-Bos	3.8

Adjusted Relief Runs
Quinn-Bro	5.0
Frankhouse-Bos	2.4

Relief Ranking
Quinn-Bro	6.2
Frankhouse-Bos	2.0

Total Pitcher Index
Hubbell-NY	4.8
Lucas-Cin	4.4
Warneke-Chi	4.1
Cantwell-Bos	2.6
French-Pit	2.5

Total Baseball Ranking
Ott-NY	5.3
Klein-Phi	4.9
Terry-NY	4.9
Hubbell-NY	4.8
Herman-Cin	4.7

May 30 A plaque in memory of Miller Huggins, former Yankee manager, is dedicated at Yankee Stadium. It is the first of an array of monuments erected in the ballpark.

June 3 Lou Gehrig hits four consecutive home runs and narrowly misses a fifth in the Yankees-Athletics slugfest won by New York 20-13. But the bigger headlines go to John McGraw, who resigns after 30 years as manager of the Giants and is replaced by Bill Terry.

June 20 Roger Cramer of the A's has six hits in consecutive times at bat in a nine-inning game. Cramer will do this again in 1935, the only AL player to repeat the feat.

June 23 Lou Gehrig plays his 1,103rd successive game in a New York uniform, equaling Joe Sewell's record with one team (Cleveland).

July 10 An extraordinary 18-inning game is won by the Athletics at Cleveland, 18–17. To save train fare for the single-date appearance, Connie Mack takes along just two pitchers. Lew Krausse, Sr. the A's starting pitcher, gives up four hits in the first inning and his replacement, Eddie Rommel pitches 17 innings in relief, giving up a record 29 hits, but still wins. Cleveland's Johnny Burnett sets a major league record by collecting nine hits in eleven at bats, while the A's Jimmie Foxx strokes six hits, including three home runs. Foxx totals 16 bases in the game, the third AL player to do it.

July 31 Cleveland plays its first game in new Municipal Stadium before a crowd in excess of 80,000 (paid attendance of 76,979), but Mel Harder loses to the A's Lefty Grove 1–0 on Cochrane's RBI single.

August 21 Cleveland's Wes Ferrell becomes the century's first pitcher to win 20 or more games in each of his first four seasons, beating Washington 11-5.

September 3 Jimmie Foxx of the A's poles his 50th and 51st home runs to become the third player to reach 50 in a season, joining Babe Ruth and Hack Wilson.

September 25 Jimmie Foxx hits his 58th home run in the last game of the season to finish two short of Ruth's 1927 record of 60.

September 28 In the opening game of the World Series, Lou Gehrig's home run leads the Yankees to a 12-6 win over the Cubs.

September 29 Lefty Gomez breezes to a 5-2 win over the Cubs, and Gehrig gets three hits for the Yankees' second victory.

October 1 The World Series moves to Chicago, and the Yankees continue to torment the Cubs. In the fifth inning, Babe Ruth waits until he has two strikes and then gestures to pitcher Charlie Root. He belts the next pitch into the center fielder bleachers. It is Ruth's second home run of the game, the "Called Shot." Gehrig also hammers out two round-trippers.

October 2 Tony Lazzeri hits two home runs, and the Yankees sweep the Series, beating the demoralized Chicago Cubs 13-6.

	BOSTON		CHICAGO		CLEVELAND		DETROIT		NEW YORK		PHILADELPHIA		ST.LOUIS		WASHINGTON
M	S.Collins	M	L.Fonseca	M	R.Peckinpaugh	M	B.Harris	M	J.McCarthy	M	C.Mack	M	B.Killefer	M	W.Johnson
M	M.McManus	1B	L.Blue	1B	E.Morgan	1B	H.Davis	1B	L.Gehrig	1B	J.Foxx	1B	J.Burns	1B	J.Kuhel
1B	D.Alexander	2B	J.Hayes	2B	B.Cissell	2B	C.Gehringer	2B	T.Lazzeri	2B	M.Bishop	2B	S.Melillo	2B	B.Myer
2B	M.Olson	SS	L.Appling	SS	J.Burnett	SS	B.Rogell	SS	F.Crosetti	SS	E.McNair	SS	J.Levey	SS	J.Cronin
SS	R.Warstler	3B	C.Selph	3B	W.Kamm	3B	H.Schuble	3B	J.Sewell	3B	J.Dykes	3B	A.Scharein	3B	O.Bluege
3B	U.Pickering	LF	B.Fothergill	LF	J.Vosmik	LF	J.Stone	LF	B.Chapman	LF	A.Simmons	LF	G.Goslin	LF	H.Manush
LF	S.Jolley	CF	L.Funk	CF	E.Averill	CF	G.Walker	CF	E.Combs	CF	M.Haas	CF	F.Schulte	CF	S.West
CF	T.Oliver	RF	B.Seeds	RF	D.Porter	RF	E.Webb	RF	B.Ruth	RF	D.Cramer	RF	B.Campbell	RF	C.Reynolds
RF	R.Johnson	C	F.Grube	C	L.Sewell	C	R.Hayworth	C	B.Dickey	C	M.Cochrane	C	R.Ferrell	C	R.Spencer
C	B.Tate														
		OS	R.Kress	C	G.Myatt	31	B.Rhiel	O	S.Byrd	O	B.Miller	3	L.Storti	O	S.Rice
O1	J.Watwood	13	B.Sullivan	S3	E.Montague	O	J.White	S	L.Lary	2	D.Williams	C	B.Bengough	1	J.Judge
23	M.McManus	C	C.Berry	1	B.Connatser	O	R.Johnson	2	A.Jorgens	O	D.Garms	O	D.Garms	C	M.Berg
C	E.Connolly	O	J.Hodapp	/O	M.Powers	3	N.Richardson	2	D.Farrell	O	E.Coleman	3	E.Grimes	O	D.Harris
S	H.Rhyne	O	J.Rothrock	C	F.Pytlak	C	M.Ruel	O	M.Hoag	1	O.Roettger	O	T.Jenkins	2S	J.Kerr
O	E.Webb	3	C.English	/2	J.Hodapp	O	G.Desautels	2	J.Saltzgaver	/C	E.Madjeski	3	R.Kress	C	H.Maple
O	G.Stumpf	O	E.Swanson	/O	C.Jamieson	O	B.Lawrence	/C	E.Phillips	S	J.Boley	/O	L.Bettencourt	/3	W.Kingdon
1	A.Van Camp	1	J.Watwood	/S	J.Boley	/O	F.Doljack	/C	J.Glenn	/O	J.Jones	/C	J.Schulte	/3	D.Musser
O	J.Rothrock	O	B.Norman	/1	B.Seeds	/1	D.Alexander	/2	R.Schalk	/S	A.Reiss	/O	S.Fisher	/S	J.McLeod
1	J.Reder	S	B.Cissell	/S	B.Berger	/C	G.Susce	H	D.Cooke	H	E.Cihocki	/O	N.Kloza		
/2	A.Spognardi	O	S.Jolley									/3	J.McLaughlin		
C	C.Berry	/O	L.Fonseca	P	W.Ferrell	P	E.Whitehill	P	L.Gomez	P	L.Grove			P	A.Crowder
/C	H.Storie	/O	H.Anderson	P	C.Brown	P	V.Sorrell	P	R.Ruffing	P	R.Walberg	P	L.Stewart	P	M.Weaver
H	O.Miller	/O	B.Campbell	P	M.Harder	P	W.Wyatt	P	G.Pipgras	P	G.Earnshaw	P	G.Blaeholder	P	L.Brown
H	J.Lucas	/C	B.Tate	P	W.Hudlin	P	T.Bridges	P	J.Allen	P	R.Mahaffey	P	B.Hadley	P	F.Marberry
/C	H.Patterson	/O	M.Simons	P	O.Hildebrand	P	C.Hogsett	P	H.Pennock	P	T.Freitas	P	S.Gray	P	T.Thomas
		/2	G.Mulleavy					RP	J.Brown	RP	L.Krausse	P	W.Hebert	P	B.Burke
P	B.Weiland			P	J.Russell	P	G.Uhle					RP	C.Kimsey	P	D.Coffman
P	E.Durham	P	T.Lyons	P	S.Connally	P	B.Marrow	P	D.MacFayden	P	E.Rommel			P	C.Fischer
P	B.Kline	P	S.Jones	/P	R.Winegarner	P	I.Goldstein	P	E.Wells	P	S.Cain	P	C.Fischer	/P	B.McAfee
P	I.Andrews	P	M.Gaston	/P	M.Pearson	P	A.Herring	/P	H.Johnson	/P	T.McKeithan	P	B.Cooney	/P	F.Ragland
RP	W.Moore	P	V.Frasier	/P	L.Moon	/P	R.Sewell	/P	I.Andrews	/P	J.Bowman	/P	D.Coffman	/P	B.Friedrichs
RP	J.Michaels	P	P.Gregory	/P	P.Appleton			P	W.Moore	/P	J.DeShong	/P	L.Polli	/P	B.Thomas
RP	L.Boerner	RP	R.Faber					P	G.Rhodes	/P	I.Stein			/P	E.Edelen
								/P	C.Devens						
P	G.Rhodes	P	P.Caraway					/P	J.Murphy						
P	D.MacFayden	P	P.Daglia												
P	H.Lisenbee	P	T.Thomas												
P	J.Welch	P	B.Chamberlain												
P	P.Appleton	P	P.Gallivan												
P	J.Russell	/P	C.Biggs												
/P	E.Gallagher	/P	E.Walsh												
/P	G.McNaughton	/P	B.Hadley												
/P	P.Donohue	/P	A.Evans												
/P	R.Leheny	/P	C.Kimsey												
/P	J.McLaughlin	/P	H.McKain												
		/P	F.Kowalik												
		/P	A.Smith												
		/P	A.Wise												
		/P	G.Bowler												
		/P	L.Bartholomew												
		/P	C.Fieber												
		/P	J.Moore												
		/P	B.Poser												

TEAM	G	W	L	PCT	GB	R	OR	AB	H	2B	3B	HR	BB	SO	AVG	OBP	SLG	PRO	PRO+	BR	/A	PF	CHI	RC	SB	CS	SBA	SBR
NY	156	107	47	.695		1002	724	5477	1564	279	82	160	766	527	.286	.376	.454	.830	128	172	225	95	99	961	77	66	54	-17
PHI	154	94	60	.610	13	981	752	5537	1606	303	52	172	647	630	.290	.366	.457	.823	115	148	113	104	100	951	38	23	62	-2
WAS	154	93	61	.604	14	840	716	5515	1565	303	100	61	505	442	.284	.347	.408	.755	102	8	19	99	103	793	70	47	60	-17
CLE	153	87	65	.572	19	845	747	5412	1544	310	74	78	566	454	.285	.357	.413	.770	99	44	-11	107	99	811	52	54	49	-17
DET	153	76	75	.503	29.5	799	787	5409	1479	291	80	80	486	523	.273	.335	.401	.736	92	-35	-65	104	106	741	103	63	68	2
STL	154	63	91	.409	44	736	898	5449	1502	274	69	67	507	528	.276	.339	.388	.727	89	-45	-88	106	97	726	69	62	53	-17
CHI	152	49	102	.325	56.5	667	897	5336	1426	274	56	36	459	386	.267	.327	.360	.687	90	-122	-80	94	101	642	89	58	61	-8
BOS	154	43	111	.279	64	566	915	5295	1331	253	57	53	469	539	.251	.314	.351	.665	80	-171	-154	97	94	593	46	46	50	-14
TOT	615					6436		43430	12017	2287	570	707	4405	4029	.277	.346	.404	.750							544	405	57	-80

TEAM	CG	SH	SV	IP	H	H/G	HR	BB	SO	RAT	ERA	ERA+	OAV	OOB	PR	/A	PF	CPI	FA	E	DP	FW	PW	BW	SBW	DIF
NY	96	11	15	1408	1425	9.1	93	561	780	12.8	3.98	102	.260	.331	78	15	91	101	.969	188	124	.2	1.4	20.8	-.6	8.3
PHI	95	10	10	1386	1477	9.6	112	511	595	13.0	4.45	102	.271	.336	4	11	101	98	.979	124	142	3.8	1.0	10.4	.7	1.0
WAS	66	11	22	1383[1]	1463	9.5	73	526	437	13.0	4.16	104	.271	.337	49	24	96	100	.979	125	157	3.8	2.2	1.8	.3	8.0
CLE	94	6	8	1377[1]	1506	9.8	70	446	439	12.8	4.12	115	.273	.329	55	96	106	98	.969	191	129	-.2	8.9	-1.0	-.6	4.0
DET	67	9	17	1362[2]	1421	9.4	89	592	521	13.5	4.30	109	.269	.346	27	61	105	102	.969	187	154	.0	5.6	-6.0	1.1	-.3
STL	63	7	11	1376[2]	1592	10.4	103	574	496	14.3	5.01	97	.290	.359	-81	-24	108	100	.969	188	156	.0	-2.2	-8.1	-.6	-3.0
CHI	50	2	12	1348[2]	1551	10.4	88	580	379	14.4	4.82	90	.287	.359	-52	-75	97	101	.958	264	170	-4.6	-6.9	-7.4	.2	-7.8
BOS	42	3	7	1362	1574	10.4	79	612	365	14.6	5.02	90	.289	.364	-81	-79	100	99	.963	233	165	-2.6	-7.3	-14.2	-.4	-9.5
TOT	573	59	102	11004[2]		9.8				13.6	4.48		.277	.346					.969	1500	1197					

Runs
Foxx-Phi 151
Simmons-Phi 144
Combs-NY 143
Gehrig-NY 138
Manush-Was 121

Hits
Simmons-Phi 216
Manush-Was 214
Foxx-Phi 213
Gehrig-NY 208
Averill-Cle 198

Doubles
McNair-Phi 47
Gehringer-Det ... 44
Cronin-Was 43

Triples
Cronin-Was 18
Myer-Was 16
Lazzeri-NY 16
Chapman-NY 15

Home Runs
Foxx-Phi 58
Ruth-NY 41
Simmons-Phi 35
Gehrig-NY 34
Averill-Cle 32

Total Bases
Foxx-Phi 438
Gehrig-NY 370
Simmons-Phi 367
Averill-Cle 359
Manush-Was 325

Runs Batted In
Foxx-Phi 169
Simmons-Phi 151
Gehrig-NY 151
Ruth-NY 137
Averill-Cle 124

Runs Produced
Foxx-Phi 262
Simmons-Phi 260
Gehrig-NY 255
Manush-Was 223
Ruth-NY 216

Bases On Balls
Ruth-NY 130
Foxx-Phi 116
Bishop-Phi 110
Gehrig-NY 108
Cochrane-Phi 100

Batting Average
Alexander-Det-Bos ... .367
Foxx-Phi .... .364
Gehrig-NY .... .349
Manush-Was ...... .342
Ruth-NY .... .341

On Base Percentage
Ruth-NY .... .489
Foxx-Phi .... .469
Gehrig-NY .... .451
Bishop-Phi ...... .412
Cochrane-Phi .... .412

Slugging Average
Foxx-Phi .... .749
Ruth-NY .... .661
Gehrig-NY .... .621
Averill-Cle ..... .569
Simmons-Phi ..... .548

Production
Foxx-Phi 1.218
Ruth-NY 1.150
Gehrig-NY 1.072
Averill-Cle ..... .961
Cochrane-Phi .... .921

Adjusted Production
Ruth-NY 206
Foxx-Phi 203
Gehrig-NY 184
Lazzeri-NY 140
Averill-Cle 137

Batter Runs
Foxx-Phi 96.7
Ruth-NY 71.2
Gehrig-NY 68.6
Averill-Cle 41.1
Alexander-Det-Bos ... 31.8

Adjusted Batter Runs
Foxx-Phi 90.0
Ruth-NY 79.2
Gehrig-NY 77.2
Alexander-Det-Bos ... 33.3
Averill-Cle 32.5

Clutch Hitting Index
Dykes-Phi 124
Cronin-Was 121
Kamm-Cle 119
Lazzeri-NY 118
Davis-Det 114

Runs Created
Foxx-Phi 207
Gehrig-NY 168
Ruth-NY 157
Averill-Cle 140
Simmons-Phi 134

Total Average
Foxx-Phi 1.451
Ruth-NY 1.432
Gehrig-NY 1.188
Cochrane-Phi 1.000
Averill-Cle ..... .991

Stolen Bases
Chapman-NY 38
Walker-Det 30
Johnson-Det-Bos . 20
Cissell-Chi-Cle . 18

Stolen Base Average
Walker-Det 83.3
Johnson-Det-Bos . 76.9
Blue-Chi 73.9
Chapman-NY 67.9
Burns-StL 60.7

Stolen Base Runs
Walker-Det 5.4
Johnson-Det-Bos . 2.4
Blue-Chi 1.5

Fielding Runs
Warstler-Bos 27.9
Vosmik-Cle 23.8
West-Was 19.3
Appling-Chi 18.1
Kress-StL-Chi ... 12.8

Total Player Rating
Foxx-Phi 6.5
Ruth-NY 5.8
Gehrig-NY 4.9
Cochrane-Phi 4.1
Cronin-Was 3.9

Wins
Crowder-Was 26
Grove-Phi 25
Gomez-NY 24
Ferrell-Cle 23
Weaver-Was 22

Win Percentage
Allen-NY .... .810
Gomez-NY .... .774
Ruffing-NY ...... .720
Grove-Phi .... .714
Weaver-Was ...... .688

Games
Marberry-Was 54
Gray-StL 52
Crowder-Was 50

Complete Games
Grove-Phi 27
Ferrell-Cle 26
Ruffing-NY 22

Shutouts
Grove-Phi 4
Bridges-Det 4

Saves
Marberry-Was 13
Moore-Bos-NY 8
Hogsett-Det 7
Grove-Phi 7
Faber-Chi 6

Innings Pitched
Crowder-Was 327.0
Grove-Phi 291.2
Ferrell-Cle 287.2
Walberg-Phi 272.0
Gomez-NY 265.1

Fewest Hits/Game
Allen-NY 7.59
Ruffing-NY 7.61
Bridges-Det 7.79
Grove-Phi 8.30
Crowder-Was 8.78

Fewest BB/Game
Brown-Cle 1.71
Crowder-Was 2.12
Gray-StL 2.31
Harder-Cle 2.40
Grove-Phi 2.44

Strikeouts
Ruffing-NY 190
Grove-Phi 188
Gomez-NY 176
Hadley-Chi-StL .. 145
Pipgras-NY 111

Strikeouts/Game
Ruffing-NY 6.60
Gomez-NY 5.97
Grove-Phi 5.80
Hadley-Chi-StL .. 5.26
Allen-NY 5.11

Ratio
Grove-Phi 10.77
Crowder-Was 10.90
Allen-NY 11.39
Ruffing-NY 11.71
Sorrell-Det 12.06

Earned Run Average
Grove-Phi 2.84
Ruffing-NY 3.09
Lyons-Chi 3.28
Crowder-Was 3.33
Bridges-Det 3.36

Adjusted ERA
Grove-Phi 159
Bridges-Det 140
Hogsett-Det 133
Lyons-Chi 132
Ruffing-NY 132

Opponents' Batting Avg.
Ruffing-NY ...... .226
Allen-NY .... .228
Bridges-Det ..... .233
Grove-Phi .... .241
Crowder-Was ..... .252

Opponents' On Base Pct.
Grove-Phi .... .292
Crowder-Was ..... .295
Allen-NY .... .306
Ruffing-NY ...... .311
Brown-Cle .... .314

Starter Runs
Grove-Phi 53.2
Crowder-Was 41.7
Ruffing-NY 39.9
Lyons-Chi 30.8
Ferrell-Cle 26.2

Adjusted Starter Runs
Grove-Phi 54.6
Crowder-Was 35.7
Ferrell-Cle 34.6
Bridges-Det 30.0
Ruffing-NY 28.3

Clutch Pitching Index
Hogsett-Det 129
Lyons-Chi 120
Weiland-Bos 117
Bridges-Det 116
Gaston-Chi 115

Relief Runs
Faber-Chi 8.8
Kimsey-StL-Chi .. 6.5

Adjusted Relief Runs
Kimsey-StL-Chi .. 9.5
Faber-Chi 7.0

Relief Ranking
Kimsey-StL-Chi .. 8.9
Faber-Chi 8.6

Total Pitcher Index
Grove-Phi 5.9
Ferrell-Cle 4.3
Ruffing-NY 3.5
Crowder-Was 3.5
Bridges-Det 3.2

Total Baseball Ranking
Foxx-Phi 6.5
Grove-Phi 5.9
Ruth-NY 5.8
Gehrig-NY 4.9
Ferrell-Cle 4.3

January 7 Baseball Commissioner Kenesaw Mountain Landis voluntarily cuts his salary by 40 percent as a signal that all salaries are to be trimmed because of the Depression.

May 14 With rain pelting down at Ebbets Field, Hack Wilson pounds a ninth-inning pinch grand slam, the first in Dodger history, to beat the Phils' Ad Liska, 8–6.

August 1 Carl Hubbell breaks Ed Reulbach's 1908 NL record for consecutive scoreless innings, with 45⅓, although the Giants lose to Boston 3-1.

September 17 The Giants spoil Dizzy Dean Day at Sportsman's Park, 4–3, but the popular pitcher drives home in a new Buick, given to him by St. Louis fans.

September 19 Although they lose to St. Louis 12-3, the Giants clinch the pennant when runner-up Pittsburgh splits a pair in Philadelphia.

September 21 With Lefty Walter Stewart pitching, Washington eliminates the Yankees and clinches the AL pennant in a 2-1 home win over St. Louis.

October 3 The Giants take the opener of the World Series at the Polo Grounds, as Carl Hubbell holds the Senators to five hits and three unearned runs. Washington unravels when Buddy Myer makes a

July 2 Carl Hubbell pitches an entire 18-inning shutout for the Giants over the Cardinals to tie a record for the longest 1–0 game. In the first game of a doubleheader, Hubbell strikes out 12 and walks none, allowing only six hits in a duel with Tex Carleton, who goes the first 16 innings. Jess Haines relieves in the 17th and in the 18th gives up a single to Joe Moore, a sacrifice bunt to Gus record-tying three errors. Mel Ott is the hitting star, tying a World Series record by going 4-for-4.

October 3 The Giants take Game 1 of the World Series at the Polo Grounds, as Carl Hubbell holds the Senators to five hits and three unearned runs. Washington unravels when Buddy Myer makes a record-tying three errors. Mel Ott is the hitting star, tying a World Series record by going 4-for-4.

October 6 Carl Hubbell wins for the second time, going 11 innings for the 2–1 victory in a pitching duel with Monte Weaver. Heinie Manush is thrown out of the game for brushing umpire Charlie Moran in the sixth inning. Travis Jackson beats out a surprise bunt to open the 11th inning, is sacrificed to second base on a close play, and scores on a single by Blondy Ryan.

Mancuso, and an intentional pass to Travis Jackson. Hubbell then forces at second, and a single by Hughie Critz ends it. In the second game of the day, played in semidarkness, Roy Parmelee wins 1–0 on a Johnny Vergez home run. The notoriously wild Giants' pitcher does not issue a walk and strikes out 13 to beat Dizzy Dean, who is pitching on one day's rest.

October 7 The World Series comes to a close when Mel Ott homers in the 10th inning for a 4-3 Giants victory. Dolf Luque gets the win in relief.

October 12 Jimmie Foxx (AL) and Carl Hubbell (NL) are named MVPs by the baseball writers.

November 21 Chuck Klein, who won the Triple Crown with the Phillies, is sold to the Chicago Cubs for $125,000 and veterans Mark Koenig, Harvey Hendrick, and rookie Ted Kleinhans. Klein, the only player to be traded after a Triple Crown season, will have two solid years at Wrigley before returning to the Phils.

December 15 The major leagues agree on a uniform ball to be livelier than the NL ball of recent seasons, to match the AL balls. Owners also agree to ban Sunday doubleheaders until after June 15.

BOSTON		BROOKLYN		CHICAGO		CINCINNATI		NEW YORK		PHILADELPHIA		PITTSBURGH		ST.LOUIS	
M	B.McKechnie	M	M.Carey	M	C.Grimm	M	D.Bush	M	B.Terry	M	B.Shotton	M	M.Gibson	M	G.Street
1B	B.Jordan	1B	S.Leslie	1B	C.Grimm	1B	J.Bottomley	1B	B.Terry	1B	D.Hurst	1B	G.Suhr	M	F.Frisch
2B	R.Maranville	2B	T.Cuccinello	2B	Bi.Herman	2B	J.Morrissey	2B	H.Critz	2B	J.Warner	2B	T.Piet	1B	R.Collins
SS	B.Urbanski	SS	G.Wright	SS	B.Jurges	SS	O.Bluege	SS	B.Ryan	SS	D.Bartell	SS	A.Vaughan	2B	F.Frisch
3B	P.Whitney	3B	J.Stripp	3B	W.English	3B	S.Adams	3B	J.Vergez	3B	J.McLeod	3B	P.Traynor	SS	L.Durocher
LF	H.Lee	LF	H.Wilson	LF	R.Stephenson	LF	J.Moore	LF	J.Moore	LF	W.Schulmerich	LF	L.Waner	3B	P.Martin
CF	W.Berger	CF	D.Taylor	CF	F.Demaree	CF	C.Hafey	CF	K.Davis	CF	F.Lindstrom	CF	F.Lindstrom	LF	J.Medwick
RF	R.Moore	RF	J.Frederick	RF	Ba.Herman	RF	H.Rice	RF	M.Ott	RF	C.Klein	RF	P.Waner	CF	E.Orsatti
C	S.Hogan	C	A.Lopez	C	G.Hartnett	C	E.Lombardi	C	G.Mancuso	C	S.Davis	C	E.Grace	RF	G.Watkins
														C	J.Wilson
O	J.Mowry	O	B.Boyle	O	K.Cuyler	21	G.Grantham	O	L.O'Doul	2	N.Finn	2	T.Thevenow		
C	A.Spohrer	S2	J.Jordan	3S	M.Koenig	O	W.Roettger	O	H.Peel	O	H.Lee	O	W.Jensen	O	E.Allen
3	F.Knothe	S2	J.Flowers	1	H.Hendrick	C	R.Hemsley	1	S.Leslie	O	A.Todd	O	A.Comorosky	12	P.Crawford
3	D.Gyselman	O	J.Hutcheson	C	G.Campbell	C	C.Manion	2	B.James	3	P.Whitney	C	H.Finney		B.O'Farrell
O	T.Thompson	O	L.O'Doul	O	J.Mosolf	S	L.Durocher	S3	T.Jackson	C	F.Knothe	C	T.Padden	2	R.Hornsby
O	W.Schulmerich	C	C.Outen	O	T.Douthit	3	A.High	C	P.Richards	C	M.Haslin	C	V.Picinich	S	G.Slade
C	P.Hargrave	S	L.Frey	3	S.Hack	2	T.Robello	3	C.Dressen	/C	H.McCurdy	/2	P.Young	O	G.Moore
O	R.Worthington	1	D.Bissonette	C	D.Camilli	/C	J.Crouch	/1	J.Malay	2	E.Delker	/3	B.Brubaker	/C	B.Lewis
/O	D.Holland	1	J.Judge	C	Z.Taylor	R	T.Douthit	/O	P.Weintraub	H	A.Cohen	H	R.Nonnenkamp	C	E.Crabtree
/O	E.Clark	C	C.Sukeforth	/C	B.Phelps	/3	E.Hunter	/O	H.Leiber	/O	F.Brickell				S.Adams
/S	H.Ford	2	B.Delmas					/C	H.Danning	H	H.Willingham	P	L.French	/O	R.Pepper
/2	A.Wright	/O	M.Rosenfeld	P	L.Warneke	P	P.Derringer					P	B.Swift	/S	B.Whitehead
		/C	V.Picinich	P	G.Bush	P	R.Lucas					P	H.Meine	/S	J.Sprinz
		/1	L.Blue	P	C.Root	P	S.Johnson	P	C.Hubbell	P	E.Holley	P	S.Swetonic	/S	C.Wilson
P	E.Brandt			P	P.Malone	P	L.Benton	P	H.Schumacher	P	S.Hansen	P	H.Smith		
P	B.Cantwell			P	B.Tinning	P	R.Kolp	P	F.Fitzsimmons	P	J.Elliott	RP	L.Chagnon	P	D.Dean
P	F.Frankhouse	P	B.Beck					P	R.Parmelee	P	C.Moore	RP	B.Harris	P	T.Carleton
P	H.Betts	P	V.Mungo	P	L.Nelson	P	B.Frey	RP	H.Bell	P	P.Collins			P	B.Hallahan
P	T.Zachary	P	R.Benge	P	E.Rixey	B.Smith		RP	D.Luque	RP	A.Liska	P	W.Hoyt	P	B.Walker
		P	O.Carroll	P	R.Henshaw	B.Smith		RP	G.Spencer			/P	R.Birkofer	P	J.Haines
August 1		P	S.Thurston	/P	L.Herrmann	A.Stout				F		/P	R.Kremer	RP	S.Johnson
P	B.Smith	RP	J.Shaute	/P	B.Richmond	P	J.Quinn	P	W.Clark	F.Rhem	/P	C.Dudley		
P	S.Seibold	RP	R.Ryan	/P	C.Yerkes			/P	B.Shores	F.Pearce			P	D.Vance
/P	E.Fallenstein	P	W.Clark					/P	J.Salveson	J.Jackson			P	J.Mooney
/P	R.Starr	P	D.Leonard					/P	G.Uhle	J.Berly			/P	P.Derringer
/P	B.Brown	P	F.Heimach					/P	R.Starr	R.Grabowski			/P	B.Grimes
		/P	R.Lucas							F.Ragland			/P	J.Lindsey
										/P	C.Pickrel			/P	A.Stout
										/P	C.Butler				

TEAM	G	W	L	PCT	GB	R	OR	AB	H	2B	3B	HR	BB	SO	AVG	OBP	SLG	PRO	PRO+	BR	/A	PF	CHI	RC	SB	CS	SBA	SBR
NY	156	91	61	.599		636	**515**	5461	1437	204	41	**82**	377	477	.263	.312	.361	.673	100	-14	-4	98	**104**	617	31			
PIT	154	87	67	.565	5	667	619	5429	**1548**	249	**84**	39	366	334	**.285**	**.333**	**.383**	**.716**	111	71	72	100	96	**709**	34			
CHI	154	86	68	.558	6	646	536	5255	1422	**256**	51	72	392	475	.271	.325	.380	.705	107	47	49	100	99	643	52			
BOS	156	83	71	.539	9	552	531	5243	1320	217	56	54	326	428	.252	.299	.345	.644	98	-70	-27	92	**104**	538	25			
STL	154	82	71	.536	9.5	**687**	609	5387	1486	**256**	61	57	391	528	.276	.329	.378	.707	103	53	18	105	102	676	**99**			
BRO	157	65	88	.425	26.5	617	695	5367	1413	224	51	62	**397**	453	.263	.316	.359	.675	103	-8	18	96	101	612	82			
PHI	152	60	92	.395	31	607	760	5261	1439	240	41	60	381	479	.274	.326	.369	.695	93	32	-49	113	95	642	55			
CIN	153	58	94	.382	33	496	643	5156	1267	208	37	34	349	354	.246	.298	.320	.618	83	-111	-104	99	103	487	30			
TOT	618					4908		42559	11332	1854	422	460	2979	3528	.266	.317	.362	.679							408			

TEAM	CG	SH	SV	IP	H	H/G	HR	BB	SO	RAT	ERA	ERA+	OAV	OOB	PR	/A	PF	CPI	FA	E	DP	FW	PW	BW	SBW	DIF
NY	75	**23**	15	1408²	**1280**	8.2	61	400	555	10.9	2.71	118	**.242**	**.299**	98	78	96	102	.973	178	156	-.5	8.3	-.4		7.6
PIT	70	16	12	1373¹	1417	9.3	54	313	401	11.5	3.27	101	.264	.308	10	7	99	95	.972	166	133	.2	.7	**7.6**		1.5
CHI	**95**	16	9	1362	1316	8.7	51	413	488	11.6	2.93	112	.254	.312	62	52	98	105	.973	168	**163**	.0	5.5	5.2		-1.7
BOS	85	15	**16**	1403	1391	8.9	54	355	383	11.3	2.96	103	.261	.309	58	14	92	105	**.978**	138	148	2.1	1.5	-2.9		5.2
STL	73	11	**16**	1382²	1391	9.1	55	452	**635**	12.1	3.37	103	.261	.321	-5	16	104	105	.973	162	119	.4	1.7	1.9		1.5
BRO	71	9	10	1386¹	1502	9.8	51	374	415	12.4	3.73	86	.275	.326	-60	-79	96	95	.971	177	120	-.3	-8.4	1.9		-4.7
PHI	52	10	13	1336²	1563	10.5	87	410	341	13.6	4.34	88	.293	.348	-150	-79	114	101	.970	183	156	-1.1	-8.4	-5.2		-1.4
CIN	74	13	8	1352	1470	9.8	**47**	**257**	310	11.6	3.42	99	.279	.314	-13	-5	102	99	.971	177	139	-.6	-.5	-11.0		-5.8
TOT	595	113	99	11004²		9.3				11.9	3.34		.266	.317					.973	1349	1134					

Runs
Martin-StL 122
P.Waner-Pit 101
Klein-Phi 101
Ott-NY 98
Medwick-StL 92

Hits
Klein-Phi 223
Fullis-Phi 200
P.Waner-Pit 191
Traynor-Pit 190
Martin-StL 189

Doubles
Klein-Phi 44
Medwick-StL 40
Lindstrom-Pit 39
P.Waner-Pit 38
Berger-Bos 37

Triples
Vaughan-Pit 19
P.Waner-Pit 16
Martin-StL 12
B.Herman-Chi 12

Home Runs
Klein-Phi 28
Berger-Bos 27
Ott-NY 23
Medwick-StL 18

Total Bases
Klein-Phi 365
Berger-Bos 299
Medwick-StL 296
P.Waner-Pit 282
Vaughan-Pit 274

Runs Batted In
Klein-Phi 120
Berger-Bos 106
Ott-NY 103
Medwick-StL 98
Vaughan-Pit 97

Runs Produced
Klein-Phi 193
Ott-NY 178
Vaughan-Pit 173
Medwick-StL 172
Martin-StL 171

Bases On Balls
Ott-NY 75
Suhr-Pit 72
Martin-StL 67
Vaughan-Pit 64
P.Waner-Pit 60

Batting Average
Klein-Phi .... .368
Davis-Phi .... .349
Stephenson-Chi ... .329
Piet-Pit .... .323
Terry-NY .... .322

On Base Percentage
Klein-Phi .... .422
Berger-Bos .... .395
Vaughan-Pit ...... .388
Martin-StL .... .387
Terry-NY .... .375

Slugging Average
Klein-Phi .... .602
Berger-Bos .... .566
B.Herman-Chi ..... .502
Medwick-StL ...... .497
Vaughan-Pit ...... .478

Production
Klein-Phi 1.025
Berger-Bos .... .932
Davis-Phi .... .867
Vaughan-Pit ...... .866
B.Herman-Chi ..... .855

Adjusted Production
Berger-Bos 177
Klein-Phi 168
Vaughan-Pit 146
B.Herman-Chi 142
Ott-NY 139

Batter Runs
Klein-Phi 69.1
Berger-Bos 40.5
Vaughan-Pit 35.2
Martin-StL 32.3
Davis-Phi 29.8

Adjusted Batter Runs
Klein-Phi 52.4
Berger-Bos 49.0
Vaughan-Pit 35.4
Ott-NY 29.9
P.Waner-Pit 28.9

Clutch Hitting Index
Hartnett-Chi 120
Traynor-Pit 119
Rice-Cin 117
Ott-NY 114
Bottomley-Cin 111

Runs Created
Klein-Phi 162
Berger-Bos 113
Vaughan-Pit 112
Martin-StL 111
P.Waner-Pit 109

Total Average
Klein-Phi 1.132
Berger-Bos .... .935
Martin-StL .... .881
Vaughan-Pit ...... .861
B.Herman-Chi ..... .827

Stolen Bases
Martin-StL 26
Fullis-Phi 18
Frisch-StL 18
Klein-Phi 15
Orsatti-StL 14

Stolen Base Average

Stolen Base Runs

Fielding Runs
Critz-NY 46.5
B.Herman-Chi 29.1
Jurges-Chi 20.1
Lopez-Bro 18.4
Ryan-NY 17.4

Total Player Rating
Klein-Phi 5.5
Berger-Bos 4.7
Vaughan-Pit 3.8
B.Herman-Chi 3.5
Martin-StL 3.5

Wins
Hubbell-NY 23
Dean-StL 20
Cantwell-Bos 20
Bush-Chi 20
Schumacher-NY ... 19

Win Percentage
Cantwell-Bos ..... .667
Hubbell-NY .... .657
Meine-Pit .... .652
Bush-Chi .... .625
Schumacher-NY .. .613

Games
Dean-StL 48
French-Pit 47
Liska-Phi 45
Hubbell-NY 45
Carleton-StL 44

Complete Games
Warneke-Chi 26
Dean-StL 26
Brandt-Bos 23
Hubbell-NY 22

Shutouts
Hubbell-NY 10
Schumacher-NY ... 7
French-Pit 5

Saves
Collins-Phi 6
Hubbell-NY 5
Harris-Pit 5
Bell-NY 5

Innings Pitched
Hubbell-NY 308.2
Dean-StL 293.0
French-Pit 291.1
Brandt-Bos 287.2
Warneke-Chi 287.1

Fewest Hits/Game
Schumacher-NY .. 6.92
Hubbell-NY 7.46
Parmelee-NY 7.87
Brandt-Bos 8.01
Mungo-Bro 8.09

Fewest BB/Game
Lucas-Cin .... .74
Hubbell-NY 1.37
Swift-Pit 1.48
Hansen-Phi 1.60
French-Pit 1.70

Strikeouts
Dean-StL 199
Hubbell-NY 156
Carleton-StL 147
Warneke-Chi 133
Parmelee-NY 132

Strikeouts/Game
Dean-StL 6.11
Parmelee-NY 5.44
Carleton-StL 4.78
Hubbell-NY 4.55
Warneke-Chi 4.17

Ratio
Hubbell-NY 8.92
Schumacher-NY ... 9.88
Betts-Bos 10.41
Swift-Pit 10.47
Brandt-Bos 10.51

Earned Run Average
Hubbell-NY 1.66
Warneke-Chi 2.00
Schumacher-NY .. 2.16
Brandt-Bos 2.60
Root-Chi 2.60

Adjusted ERA
Hubbell-NY 193
Warneke-Chi 163
Schumacher-NY ... 149
Root-Chi 126
French-Pit 122

Opponents' Batting Avg.
Schumacher-NY .. .214
Hubbell-NY ...... .227
Parmelee-NY ..... .232
Mungo-Bro .... .236
Warneke-Chi ..... .244

Opponents' On Base Pct.
Hubbell-NY ...... .260
Schumacher-NY .. .280
Swift-Pit .... .285
Betts-Bos .... .290
Cantwell-Bos .... .291

Starter Runs
Hubbell-NY 57.4
Warneke-Chi 42.5
Schumacher-NY .. 33.9
Brandt-Bos 23.6
Cantwell-Bos 20.4

Adjusted Starter Runs
Hubbell-NY 53.1
Warneke-Chi 40.4
Schumacher-NY .. 30.2
French-Pit 19.3
Root-Chi 18.0

Clutch Pitching Index
Warneke-Chi 131
Root-Chi 120
Walker-StL 117
Holley-Phi 115
Hubbell-NY 112

Relief Runs
Bell-NY 15.0
Luque-NY 5.8
Harris-Pit 7

Adjusted Relief Runs
Bell-NY 13.6
Luque-NY 4.6
Harris-Pit 6

Relief Ranking
Bell-NY 14.2
Luque-NY 5.7
Harris-Pit 9

Total Pitcher Index
Hubbell-NY 7.5
Warneke-Chi 6.2
Schumacher-NY ... 4.2
Brandt-Bos 2.7
Bush-Chi 2.1

Total Baseball Ranking
Hubbell-NY 7.5
Warneke-Chi 6.2
Klein-Phi 5.5
Berger-Bos 4.7
Schumacher-NY ... 4.2

February 25 Multimillionaire sportsman Tom Yawkey and former star player Eddie Collins buy the Boston Red Sox from Robert Quinn.

April 23 Lou Gehrig's consecutive-game streak is threatened when he is knocked unconscious by an Earl Whitehill pitch in the New York–Washington game. He recovers and finishes the game.

May 18 The first major league All-Star Game is announced for July 6 at Comiskey Park. It will be played as part of the Chicago World's Fair celebration and is sponsored by the Chicago *Tribune*.

June 8 Jimmie Foxx homers in his first three at bats, as the A's outscore the Yankees 14–10. He had homered his last time up the previous day to give him four consecutive home runs.

June 9 Walter Johnson takes over as Cleveland manager.

June 14 Lou Gehrig's consecutive-game streak of 1,249 survives, even though he and manager Joe McCarthy are thrown out of a game.

July 6 Babe Ruth is the star of the first All-Star Game. His two-run home run at Comiskey Park is the deciding blow as the AL is a 4-2 winner over the NL. John McGraw comes out of retirement to manage the National Leaguers.

July 19 For the first time, brothers on opposite teams homer in the same game. Red Sox catcher Rick Ferrell hits his home run off brother Wes of Cleveland. Wes hits his off Hank Johnson in the third inning. He will wind up his career with 38 home runs (not all of them hit as a pitcher) in 548 games. Rick will hit only 28 in 1,884 games.

August 3 The Yankees are shut out by the A's and Lefty Grove, 7-0, their first scoreless game since August 2, 1931. They had tallied in 308 games in a row, during which they scored 1,986 runs (6.5 per game) to 1,434 for the opposition.

August 14 Jimmie Foxx hits for the cycle and drives in nine runs to break the AL record, as the A's beat the Indians 11–5. A record eight players will hit for the cycle this year.

August 22 William Veeck, president of the Chicago Cubs, urges a midsummer series of inter-league games. He also proposes a split season. While some owners are in agreement on interleague play, Washington owner Clark Griffith is opposed. "We're not going for any Hippodrome stuff. The American League is a big league."

September 10* The first Negro League East-West All-Star Game is played at Comiskey Park. Willie Foster goes the distance in the West's 11-7 victory.

December 3 Connie Mack sells catcher Mickey Cochrane to Detroit for $100,000. Cochrane is named manager. Nine days later Mack sells Lefty Grove, Max Bishop, and George Walberg to the Boston Red Sox for $125,000. George Earnshaw goes to the White Sox for $20,000 and another player.

December 29 Yankees owner Jake Ruppert refuses to release Babe Ruth so he can become manager of the Cincinnati Reds.

BOSTON	CHICAGO	CLEVELAND	DETROIT	NEW YORK	PHILADELPHIA	ST.LOUIS	WASHINGTON
M M.McManus	M L.Fonseca	M R.Peckinpaugh	M B.Harris	M J.McCarthy	M C.Mack	M B.Killefer	M J.Cronin
1B D.Alexander	1B R.Kress	M B.Falk	M D.Baker	1B L.Gehrig	1B J.Foxx	M A.Sothoron	1B J.Kuhel
2B J.Hodapp	2B J.Hayes	M W.Johnson	1B H.Greenberg	2B T.Lazzeri	2B M.Bishop	M R.Hornsby	2B B.Myer
SS R.Warstler	SS L.Appling	1B H.Boss	2B C.Gehringer	SS F.Crosetti	SS D.Williams	1B J.Burns	SS J.Cronin
3B M.McManus	3B J.Dykes	2B O.Hale	SS B.Rogell	3B J.Sewell	3B P.Higgins	2B S.Melillo	3B O.Bluege
LF S.Jolley	LF A.Simmons	SS B.Knickerb'r	3B M.Owen	LF B.Chapman	LF B.Johnson	SS J.Levey	LF H.Manush
CF D.Cooke	CF M.Haas	3B W.Kamm	LF G.Walker	CF E.Combs	CF D.Cramer	3B A.Scharein	CF F.Schulte
RF R.Johnson	RF E.Swanson	LF J.Vosmik	CF P.Fox	RF B.Ruth	RF E.Coleman	LF C.Reynolds	RF G.Goslin
C R.Ferrell	C F.Grube	CF E.Averill	RF J.Stone	C B.Dickey	C M.Cochrane	CF S.West	C L.Sewell
		RF D.Porter	C R.Hayworth			RF B.Campbell	
S3 B.Werber	C C.Berry	C R.Spencer		O D.Walker	S2 E.McNair	C M.Shea	O D.Harris
O T.Oliver	1 B.Sullivan		O J.White	3S L.Lary	O L.Finney		23 B.Boken
1O B.Seeds	O1 E.Webb	2S B.Cissell	1 H.Davis	O S.Byrd	C E.Madjeski	O3 T.Gullic	O S.Rice
3 B.Walters	23 H.Rhyne	S2 J.Burnett	O F.Doljack	S2 D.Farrell	O B.Miller	32 L.Storti	C M.Berg
1 J.Judge	1 L.Fonseca	C F.Pytlak	3 H.Schuble	C A.Jorgens	S C.Cihocki	C D.Garms	3 C.Travis
C J.Gooch	/O J.Stoneham	O M.Galatzer	C J.Pasek	/C T.Rensa	C F.Hayes	C R.Hemsley	2 J.Kerr
C M.Shea	O M.Bocek	1 E.Morgan	C G.Desautels	/C J.Glenn	/O J.Zapustas	C R.Ferrell	/C C.Bolton
2 F.Muller	/2 C.English	C G.Myatt	/C F.Reiber	/3 B.Werber		C M.Ruel	H N.Altrock
O M.Almada	/O L.Funk	O J.Oulliber	/O B.Rhiel	P R.Ruffing	P L.Grove	/C J.Crouch	
/2 B.Friberg	H M.Lovett	O M.Powers	/O E.Webb	P L.Gomez	P S.Cain	H R.Hornsby	P A.Crowder
O G.Stumpf		1 H.Trosky		P J.Allen	P R.Walberg		P E.Whitehill
/O B.Fothergill	P T.Lyons		P F.Marberry	P R.Van Atta	P R.Mahaffey	P B.Hadley	P L.Stewart
/O J.Watwood	P S.Jones	P M.Harder	P V.Sorrell	P D.MacFayden	P G.Earnshaw	P G.Blaeholder	P M.Weaver
/O T.Winsett	P M.Gaston	P O.Hildebrand	P T.Bridges	RP H.Pennock	P J.Peterson	P E.Wells	P T.Thomas
/C L.Legett	P E.Durham	P W.Ferrell	P C.Fischer	RP W.Moore		P R.Stiles	RP J.Russell
/2 M.Olson	P J.Miller	P C.Brown	P S.Rowe			RP S.Gray	RP B.McAfee
R G.Mulleavy	P J.Heving	P W.Hudlin	RP C.Hogsett	P D.Brennan	P D.Barrett	RP W.Hebert	
	RP R.Faber	RP S.Connally	RP A.Herring	P J.Brown	P T.Freitas	RP H.McDonald	
		RP B.Bean			P B.Coombs		
P G.Rhodes	P P.Gregory		P V.Frasier	P C.Devens	P B.Dietrich		/P A.McColl
P B.Weiland	P C.Kimsey	P M.Pearson	P E.Auker	P G.Uhle	P H.McDonald	P J.Knott	/P E.Linke
P L.Brown	P W.Wyatt	P H.Craghead	/P L.Hamlin	/P G.Pipgras	P G.Claset	P D.Coffman	/P R.Prim
P H.Johnson	/P L.Tietje	/P T.Lee	/P W.Wyatt	/P P.Appleton	P T.McKeithan	P L.Brown	/P E.Chapman
P I.Andrews	P V.Frasier		/P R.Lawson		P H.Winston	P G.Braxton	/P B.Thomas
RP J.Welch	P H.Haid		/P B.Nekola		P E.Roy		/P J.Campbell
RP B.Kline	/P I.Hutchinson		/P G.Uhle				
	/P G.Murray						
P G.Pipgras							
/P C.Fullerton							
/P J.McLaughlin							
/P M.Meola							

TEAM	G	W	L	PCT	GB	R	OR	AB	H	2B	3B	HR	BB	SO	AVG	OBP	SLG	PRO	PRO+	BR	/A	PF	CHI	RC	SB	CS	SBA	SBR
WAS	153	99	53	.651		850	**665**	5524	**1586**	281	**86**	60	539	395	**.287**	.353	.402	.755	107	47	56	99	102	798	65	50	57	-11
NY	152	91	59	.607	7	**927**	768	5274	1495	241	75	**144**	**700**	506	.283	**.369**	**.440**	**.809**	**129**	**155**	**211**	94	100	**880**	**76**	59	56	-13
PHI	152	79	72	.523	19.5	875	853	5330	1519	**297**	57	139	625	618	.285	.362	.440	.802	118	135	126	101	97	868	34	34	50	-10
CLE	151	75	76	.497	23.5	654	669	5240	1366	218	77	50	448	426	.261	.321	.360	.681	82	-103	-132	105	**103**	616	36	40	47	-13
DET	155	75	79	.487	25	722	733	5502	1479	283	78	57	475	523	.269	.329	.380	.709	92	-54	-68	102	101	698	68	50	58	-10
CHI	151	67	83	.447	31	683	814	5318	1448	231	53	43	538	416	.272	.342	.360	.702	96	-50	-20	96	96	674	43	46	48	-15
BOS	149	63	86	.423	34.5	700	758	5201	1407	294	56	50	525	464	.271	.339	.377	.716	97	-29	-22	99	98	687	58	37	**61**	**-5**
STL	153	55	96	.364	43.5	669	820	5285	1337	244	64	64	520	556	.253	.322	.360	.682	81	-102	-143	106	**103**	625	72	60	55	-14
TOT	608					6080		42674	11637	2089	546	607	4370	3904	.273	.342	.390	.732							452	376	55	-90

TEAM	CG	SH	SV	IP	H	H/G	HR	BB	SO	RAT	ERA	ERA+	OAV	OOB	PR	/A	PF	CPI	FA	E	DP	FW	PW	BW	SBW	DIF
WAS	68	5	**26**	1389²	1415	9.2	64	**452**	447	**12.2**	3.82	109	**.263**	.322	71	56	98	98	**.979**	**131**	149	**2.6**	5.3	5.3	.0	9.8
NY	70	8	22	1354²	1426	9.5	66	612	**711**	13.6	4.36	89	.267	.344	-13	-72	91	96	.972	165	122	.4	-6.8	**20.0**	-.2	2.6
PHI	69	6	14	1343²	1523	10.2	77	644	423	14.6	4.81	89	.283	.361	-79	-78	100	99	.966	203	121	-1.9	-7.4	11.9	.1	.8
CLE	**74**	**12**	7	1350	**1382**	9.2	60	465	437	12.4	**3.71**	**111**	104	.264	.325	86	111	104	102	.974	156	127	.9	**10.5**	-12.5	-.2	.8
DET	69	6	17	1398	1415	**9.1**	84	561	575	12.9	3.95	109	**.263**	.335	52	57	101	**103**	.971	178	**167**	.2	5.4	-6.4	.1	-.9
CHI	53	8	13	1371¹	1505	9.9	85	519	423	13.5	4.45	95	.277	.343	-26	-32	99	99	.970	186	143	-1.0	-3.0	-1.9	-.4	-1.8
BOS	60	4	14	1327²	1396	9.5	75	591	467	13.6	4.35	101	.271	.348	-10	4	102	100	.966	204	133	-2.2	.4	-2.1	**.6**	-8.2
STL	55	7	10	1360²	1574	10.4	96	531	426	14.0	4.82	97	.289	.354	-82	-25	109	100	.976	149	162	1.5	-2.4	-13.5	-.3	-5.8
TOT	518	56	123	10895²		9.6				13.3	4.28		.273	.342					.972	1372	1124					

Runs		Hits		Doubles		Triples		Home Runs		Total Bases	
Gehrig-NY	138	Manush-Was	221	Cronin-Was	45	Manush-Was	17	Foxx-Phi	48	Foxx-Phi	403
Foxx-Phi	125	Gehringer-Det	204	Johnson-Phi	44	Combs-NY	16	Ruth-NY	34	Gehrig-NY	359
Manush-Was	115	Foxx-Phi	204	Burns-StL	43	Averill-Cle	16	Gehrig-NY	32	Manush-Was	302
Chapman-NY	112	Simmons-Chi	200	Rogell-Det	42	Myer-Was	15	Johnson-Phi	21	Gehringer-Det	294
Cramer-Phi	109	Gehrig-NY	198	Gehringer-Det	42	Reynolds-StL	14	Lazzeri-NY	18	Simmons-Chi	291

Runs Batted In		Runs Produced		Bases On Balls		Batting Average		On Base Percentage		Slugging Average	
Foxx-Phi	163	Gehrig-NY	245	Ruth-NY	114	Foxx-Phi	.356	Cochrane-Phi	.459	Foxx-Phi	.703
Gehrig-NY	139	Foxx-Phi	240	Cochrane-Phi	106	Manush-Was	.336	Foxx-Phi	.449	Gehrig-NY	.605
Simmons-Chi	119	Manush-Was	205	Bishop-Phi	106	Gehrig-NY	.334	Bishop-Phi	.446	Ruth-NY	.582
Cronin-Was	118	Cronin-Was	202	Foxx-Phi	96	Simmons-Chi	.331	Ruth-NY	.442	Cochrane-Phi	.515
Kuhel-Was	107	Chapman-NY	201	Swanson-Chi	93	Gehringer-Det	.325	Gehrig-NY	.424	Johnson-Phi	.505

Production		Adjusted Production		Batter Runs		Adjusted Batter Runs		Clutch Hitting Index		Runs Created	
Foxx-Phi	1.153	Foxx-Phi	199	Foxx-Phi	82.7	Foxx-Phi	81.0	Cronin-Was	126	Foxx-Phi	184
Gehrig-NY	1.030	Gehrig-NY	181	Gehrig-NY	59.5	Gehrig-NY	68.5	Melillo-StL	125	Gehrig-NY	151
Ruth-NY	1.023	Ruth-NY	180	Ruth-NY	49.5	Ruth-NY	57.1	Ferrell-StL-Bos	124	Ruth-NY	124
Cochrane-Phi	.974	Cochrane-Phi	156	Cochrane-Phi	41.6	Cochrane-Phi	40.5	Bluege-Was	123	Gehringer-Det	117
Johnson-Phi	.892	Dickey-NY	138	Johnson-Phi	26.8	Lazzeri-NY	27.7	Kress-Chi	121	Manush-Was	111

Total Average		Stolen Bases		Stolen Base Average		Stolen Base Runs		Fielding Runs		Total Player Rating	
Foxx-Phi	1.348	Chapman-NY	27	Walker-Det	74.3	Walker-Det	2.4	Melillo-StL	23.3	Foxx-Phi	6.7
Ruth-NY	1.172	Walker-Det	26	Kuhel-Was	68.0	Werber-NY-Bos	1.5	Rogell-Det	19.5	Gehrig-NY	4.3
Cochrane-Phi	1.118	Swanson-Chi	19	Swanson-Chi	63.3	Stumpf-Bos	1.2	Schulte-Was	15.8	Cronin-Was	4.0
Gehrig-NY	1.098	Kuhel-Was	17	Chapman-NY	60.0			Simmons-Chi	14.3	Ruth-NY	3.8
Johnson-Phi	.940							Scharein-StL	14.0	Cochrane-Phi	3.7

Wins		Win Percentage		Games		Complete Games		Shutouts		Saves	
Grove-Phi	24	Grove-Phi	.750	Crowder-Was	52	Grove-Phi	21	Hildebrand-Cle	6	Russell-Was	13
Crowder-Was	24	Whitehill-Was	.733	Russell-Was	50	Whitehill-Was	19	Gomez-NY	4	Hogsett-Det	9
Whitehill-Was	22	Stewart-Was	.714	Welch-Bos	47	Hadley-StL	19	Blaeholder-StL	3	Moore-NY	8
		Allen-NY	.682	Kline-Bos	46	Ruffing-NY	18			Heving-Chi	6
										Grove-Phi	6

Innings Pitched		Fewest Hits/Game		Fewest BB/Game		Strikeouts		Strikeouts/Game		Ratio	
Hadley-StL	316.2	Bridges-Det	7.42	Brown-Cle	1.65	Gomez-NY	163	Gomez-NY	6.25	Marberry-Det	11.10
Crowder-Was	299.1	Weiland-Bos	8.20	Marberry-Det	2.30	Hadley-StL	149	Allen-NY	5.80	Stewart-Was	11.24
Grove-Phi	275.1	Allen-NY	8.33	Stewart-Was	2.34	Ruffing-NY	122	Ruffing-NY	4.67	Harder-Cle	11.53
Whitehill-Was	270.0	Gomez-NY	8.36	Harder-Cle	2.38	Bridges-Det	120	Bridges-Det	4.64	Brown-Cle	11.58
Blaeholder-StL	255.2	Hildebrand-Cle	8.37	Blaeholder-StL	2.43	Allen-NY	119	Fischer-Det	4.58	Weaver-Was	11.88

Earned Run Average		Adjusted ERA		Opponents' Batting Avg.		Opponents' On Base Pct.		Starter Runs		Adjusted Starter Runs	
Pearson-Cle	2.33	Harder-Cle	151	Bridges-Det	.226	Marberry-Det	.302	Harder-Cle	37.4	Harder-Cle	41.9
Harder-Cle	2.95	Bridges-Det	140	Gomez-NY	.240	Stewart-Was	.304	Grove-Phi	33.0	Grove-Phi	33.1
Bridges-Det	3.09	Grove-Phi	134	Allen-NY	.242	Harder-Cle	.309	Bridges-Det	30.8	Pearson-Cle	31.8
Gomez-NY	3.18	Marberry-Det	131	Weiland-Bos	.244	Brown-Cle	.310	Pearson-Cle	29.4	Bridges-Det	31.6
Grove-Phi	3.20	Brown-Cle	130	Hildebrand-Cle	.245	Grove-Phi	.316	Gomez-NY	28.6	Marberry-Det	27.2

Clutch Pitching Index		Relief Runs		Adjusted Relief Runs		Relief Ranking		Total Pitcher Index		Total Baseball Ranking	
Cain-Phi	125	Russell-Was	22.0	Russell-Was	20.6	Russell-Was	31.8	Harder-Cle	5.7	Foxx-Phi	6.7
Jones-Chi	124	Heving-Chi	21.1	Heving-Chi	20.6	Heving-Chi	21.2	Bridges-Det	3.5	Harder-Cle	5.7
Harder-Cle	115	Faber-Chi	8.1	Faber-Chi	7.7	Gray-StL	6.7	Russell-Was	3.4	Gehrig-NY	4.3
Whitehill-Was	112	Burke-Was	7.4	Gray-StL	6.9	Burke-Was	6.6	Pearson-Cle	3.3	Cronin-Was	4.0
Grove-Phi	111	Herring-Det	3.0	Burke-Was	6.7	Faber-Chi	6.6	Grove-Phi	2.9	Ruth-NY	3.8

February 25 John McGraw, in ill health since his retirement as Giants manager early in the 1932 season, dies at his home in New Rochelle, New York, at age 60. His last public appearance had been the 1933 All-Star Game as the NL manager.

April 17 At Ebbets Field, Casey Stengel makes his managerial debut, but his Dodgers lose, 8–7, to the Braves.

April 29 With Pennsylvania's Blue Law repealed, Pittsburgh becomes the last major league city to play a home game on a Sunday, beating the Reds 9-5.

July 4 When Dodgers manager Casey Stengel comes out to the mound to remove pitcher Walter "Boom Boom" Beck from the game in Philadelphia's Baker Bowl, the frustrated Beck turns and fires the ball at the tin wall in right field. Dodgers outfielder Hack Wilson, not paying attention to the happenings, hears the ball, hurries to retrieve it, and fires a strike to second base.

July 10 The second annual All-Star Game produces Carl Hubbell's amazing feat of striking out five future Hall of Famers in a row. Off to a shaky start with two on base in the first inning, Hubbell uses his screwball to fan Ruth, Gehrig, and Foxx. He adds Al Simmons and Joe Cronin to start the second. After three scoreless innings he leaves with the NL ahead 4-0. The AL rallies, scoring nine runs off Warneke, Mungo, and Dean, while Mel Harder pitches five shutout innings in relief of Red Ruffing to hold the lead. Frisch and Medwick hit home runs. Earl Averill's three RBI are decisive for the AL 9-7 victory.

August 8 Wilbert Robinson dies in Atlanta. Beloved as "Uncle Robbie," the jovial and bemused manager of the Dodgers for 18 seasons, his 7-for-7 day with Baltimore still stands as a major league record, though it's been tied by several players since.

September 13 Commissioner Kenesaw Mountain Landis sells the World Series broadcast rights to the Ford Motor Company for $100,000. Previously no fee had been charged.

September 16 The largest turnout in Polo Grounds history, 62,573, suffers as the Deans take two from the Giants. Diz needs relief from Tex Carleton in the 5–3 opener, but Paul goes 11 innings for a 3–1 win. The Cardinals leave New York 3½ games behind the league-leading Giants.

October 3 Dizzy Dean wins the opening game of the World Series 8-3, as Detroit manager Mickey Cochrane holds back his ace, Schoolboy Rowe. Veteran Al Crowder is ineffective as the Cardinals romp. Joe Medwick homers in a 4-for-4 day while the Tigers make five errors.

October 9 Dizzy Dean makes good his boast that "me and Paul will win all four games." He humbles Detroit 11-0, as the Tigers go to pieces. When Joe Medwick slides roughly into third base in the sixth inning, he tangles with Marv Owen. Irate Tigers fans in the temporary left field stands then launch a barrage of fruit at Medwick, halting the game. With the score at 9-0, Commissioner Landis removes Medwick from the game "for his own safety."

November 8 Ford Frick, NL publicity director, is named league president. He will eventually become commissioner.

December 11 The NL votes to permit night baseball, authorizing a maximum of seven games by any team installing lights. The AL does not grant permission for night games until 1937.

December 26* Matsutaro Shoriki, head of Yomiuri Newspapers, announces the official formation of Japan's first professional team, the Tokyo-based Yomiuri Giants. The team is made up of players signed to compete against the American all-star team. Professional league play, with six teams, does not begin until 1936.

BOSTON	BROOKLYN	CHICAGO	CINCINNATI	NEW YORK	PHILADELPHIA	PITTSBURGH	ST.LOUIS
M B.McKechnie	M C.Stengel	M C.Grimm	M B.O'Farrell	M B.Terry	M J.Wilson	M M.Gibson	M F.Frisch
1B B.Jordan	1B S.Leslie	1B C.Grimm	1B B.Shotton	1B B.Terry	1B D.Camilli	M P.Traynor	1B R.Collins
2B M.McManus	2B T.Cuccinello	2B Bi.Herman	M C.Dressen	2B B.Critz	2B L.Chiozza	1B G.Suhr	2B F.Frisch
SS B.Urbanski	SS L.Frey	SS B.Jurges	1B J.Bottomley	SS T.Jackson	SS D.Bartell	2B C.Lavagetto	SS L.Durocher
3B P.Whitney	3B J.Stripp	3B S.Hack	2B T.Piet	3B J.Vergez	3B B.Walters	SS A.Vaughan	3B P.Martin
LF H.Lee	LF D.Taylor	LF C.Klein	SS G.Slade	LF J.Moore	LF E.Allen	3B P.Traynor	LF J.Medwick
CF W.Berger	CF L.Koenecke	CF K.Cuyler	3B M.Koenig	CF G.Watkins	CF K.Davis	LF F.Lindstrom	CF E.Orsatti
RF T.Thompson	RF B.Boyle	RF Ba.Herman	LF H.Pool	RF M.Ott	RF J.Moore	CF L.Waner	RF I.Rothrock
C A.Spohrer	C A.Lopez	C G.Hartnett	CF C.Hafey	C G.Mancuso	C A.Todd	RF P.Waner	C S.Davis
C S.Hogan	O J.Frederick	S3 W.English	RF A.Comorosky	3S B.Ryan	C J.Wilson	C E.Grace	2S B.Whitehead
O1 R.Moore	S2 J.Jordan	O T.Stainback	C E.Lombardi	O H.Leiber	2 I.Jeffries	23 T.Thevenow	C B.DeLancey
2 L.Mallon	O H.Wilson	1 D.Hurst	32 S.Adams	2 L.O'Doul	32 M.Haslin	O W.Jensen	O C.Fullis
O J.Mowry	O2 G.Chapman	O D.Camilli	O W.Schulmerich	C H.Danning	O D.Hurst	O T.Padden	O B.Mills
O R.Worthington	2 J.Bucher	O R.Stephenson	C B.O'Farrell	O P.Richards	O H.Hendrick	O W.Roettger	/3 P.Crawford
3 D.Gyselman	C R.Berres	2 B.Phelps	O L.Blakely	O P.Weintraub	C C.Fullis	C P.Veltman	/O K.Davis
/S D.McGee	C C.Sukeforth	C B.O'Farrell	2 A.Kampouris	3 H.Peel	O A.High	/2 P.Young	/O G.Moore
/O J.Tyler	C J.McCarthy	C B.Tate	O I.Shiver	/1 G.Grantham	/3 A.Ruble	/3 B.Brubaker	/C F.Healy
/1 E.Fletcher	/O N.Tremark	/1 P.Cavarretta	C C.Manion	H F.Thompson	/C W.Schulmerich	/C H.Finney	H L.Riggs
P E.Brandt	/C W.Millies	P L.Warneke	O J.Moore	P C.Hubbell	1 B.Clancy	P L.French	H R.Worthington
P F.Frankhouse	/3 B.Hogg	P B.Lee	1 J.Shevlin	P H.Schumacher	P E.Boland	P B.Swift	P D.Dean
P H.Betts	P V.Mungo	P G.Bush	/1 F.McCormick	P F.Fitzsimmons	/3 M.Hopkins	P R.Birkofer	P T.Carleton
P F.Rhem	P R.Benge	P P.Malone	H J.Flowers	P R.Parmelee	/O P.Oana	P W.Hoyt	P P.Dean
P B.Cantwell	P D.Leonard	P J.Weaver	/2 B.Marshall	P J.Bowman	/O H.Wilson	P R.Lucas	P B.Hallahan
P B.Smith	P J.Babich	P B.Tinning	/O T.Petoskey	RP A.Smith	/C J.Holden	RP L.Chagnon	P B.Walker
RP L.Mangum	P T.Zachary	P C.Root	/1 H.McCurdy	RP H.Bell	/O F.Frink	RP H.Smith	RP J.Haines
RP B.Brown	RP O.Carroll	P R.Joiner	H T.Robello	P D.Luque	P C.Davis	P H.Meine	RP J.Mooney
P D.Barrett	RP B.Beck	/P C.Wiedemeyer	P P.Derringer	P J.Salveson	P P.Collins	/P B.Grimes	P D.Vance
/P T.Zachary	P L.Munns	/P D.Ward	P B.Frey	/P W.Clark	P S.Hansen	/P B.Harris	/P R.Rhem
P C.Pickrel	P A.Herring	/P L.Nelson	/P Si.Johnson	/P S.Castleman	P S.Johnson	/P E.Holley	/P J.Lindsey
/P J.Elliott	P R.Lucas		P T.Freitas		P C.Moore	/P C.Blanton	/P J.Winford
	P W.Clark		P A.Stout		RP R.Grabowski	/P S.Struss	/P B.Grimes
	P C.Perkins		RP D.Brennan		RP G.Darrow	/P L.Johnson	/P C.Heise
	/P H.Smythe		RP R.Kolp		P E.Moore		
	/P P.Page		P T.Kleinhans		P E.Holley		
			P L.Benton		/P F.Pearce		
			/P B.Richmond		/P T.Kleinhans		
			/P D.Vance		/P B.Lohrman		
			/P J.Shaute		/P J.Elliott		
			/P W.Wistert		/P C.Malis		
			/P L.Grissom				
			/P Sy.Johnson				
			/P J.Lindsey				
			/P S.Edwards				
			/P J.Barnes				

TEAM	G	W	L	PCT	GB	R	OR	AB	H	2B	3B	HR	BB	SO	AVG	OBP	SLG	PRO	PRO+	BR	/A	PF	CHI	RC	SB	CS	SBA	SBR
STL	154	95	58	.621		**799**	656	5502	**1582**	**294**	75	104	392	535	**.288**	.337	**.425**	**.762**	102	63	12	107	101	**796**	69			
NY	153	93	60	.608	2	760	**583**	5396	1485	240	41	**126**	406	526	.275	.329	.405	.734	105	8	25	98	**105**	742	19			
CHI	152	86	65	.570	8	705	639	5347	1494	263	44	101	375	630	.279	.330	.402	.732	103	5	19	98	99	719	59			
BOS	152	78	73	.517	16	683	714	5370	1460	233	44	83	375	440	.272	.323	.378	.701	101	-52	-3	93	104	660	30			
PIT	151	74	76	.493	19.5	735	713	5361	1541	281	**77**	52	440	398	.287	.344	.398	.742	102	34	17	102	99	742	44			
BRO	153	71	81	.467	23.5	748	795	5427	1526	284	52	79	**548**	555	.281	**.350**	.396	.746	**112**	51	**90**	95	95	782	55			
PHI	149	56	93	.376	37	675	794	5218	1480	286	35	56	398	534	.284	.338	.384	.722	87	-3	-95	113	98	685	52			
CIN	152	52	99	.344	42	590	801	5361	1428	227	65	55	313	532	.266	.311	.364	.675	88	-105	-91	98	99	603	34			
TOT	608					5695		42982	11996	2108	433	656	3247	4150	.279	.333	.394	.727							362			

TEAM	CG	SH	SV	IP	H	H/G	HR	BB	SO	RAT	ERA	ERA+	OAV	OOB	PR	/A	PF	CPI	FA	E	DP	FW	PW	BW	SBW	DIF
STL	**78**	**15**	16	1386²	1463	9.5	77	411	**689**	12.4	3.69	115	.268	.323	58	83	104	101	.972	166	141	.3	8.1	1.2		8.9
NY	68	13	**30**	1370	**1384**	**9.1**	75	**351**	499	**11.5**	**3.19**	121	**.260**	.308	132	102	95	105	.972	179	**141**	-.5	**9.9**	2.4		4.6
CHI	73	11	9	1361¹	1432	9.5	80	417	633	12.3	3.76	103	.269	.325	46	18	95	101	**.977**	137	135	**1.9**	1.8	1.9		5.0
BOS	62	12	20	1359²	1512	10.0	78	405	462	12.8	4.11	93	.279	.331	-7	-44	94	97	.972	169	120	.0	-4.3	-.3		7.1
PIT	63	8	8	1329²	1523	10.3	78	354	487	12.9	4.20	98	.284	.332	-20	-13	101	98	.975	145	118	1.4	-1.3	1.7		-2.8
BRO	66	6	12	1354¹	1540	10.2	81	475	520	13.6	4.48	87	.285	.346	-63	-87	96	97	.970	180	**141**	-.6	-8.5	**8.8**		-4.7
PHI	52	8	15	1297	1501	10.4	126	437	416	13.6	4.76	99	.288	.347	-101	-4	116	99	.966	197	140	-1.8	-.4	-9.3		-7.0
CIN	51	3	19	1347²	1645	11.0	**61**	389	438	13.8	4.37	93	.299	.348	-46	-43	101	102	.970	181	136	-.7	-4.2	-8.9		-9.9
TOT	513	76	129	10806¹		10.0				12.9	4.06		.279	.333					.972	1354	1072					

Runs		Hits		Doubles		Triples		Home Runs		Total Bases	
P.Waner-Pit	122	P.Waner-Pit	217	Cuyler-Chi	42	Medwick-StL	18	Ott-NY	35	Collins-StL	369
Ott-NY	119	Terry-NY	213	Allen-Phi	42	P.Waner-Pit	16	Collins-StL	35	Ott-NY	344
Collins-StL	116	Collins-StL	200	Vaughan-Pit	41	Suhr-Pit	13	Berger-Bos	34	Berger-Bos	336
Vaughan-Pit	115	Medwick-StL	198	Medwick-StL	40	Collins-StL	12	Hartnett-Chi	22	Medwick-StL	328
Medwick-StL	110			Collins-StL	40			Klein-Chi	20	P.Waner-Pit	323

Runs Batted In		Runs Produced		Bases On Balls		Batting Average		On Base Percentage		Slugging Average	
Ott-NY	135	Ott-NY	219	Vaughan-Pit	94	P.Waner-Pit	.362	Vaughan-Pit	.431	Collins-StL	.615
Collins-StL	128	Collins-StL	209	Ott-NY	85	Terry-NY	.354	P.Waner-Pit	.429	Ott-NY	.591
Berger-Bos	121	P.Waner-Pit	198	Koenecke-Bro	70	Cuyler-Chi	.338	Ott-NY	.415	DeLancey-StL	.565
Medwick-StL	106	Medwick-StL	198	Leslie-Bro	69	Vaughan-Pit	.333	Terry-NY	.414	Berger-Bos	.546
Suhr-Pit	103	Vaughan-Pit	197	P.Waner-Pit	68	Collins-StL	.333	Koenecke-Bro	.411	P.Waner-Pit	.539

Production		Adjusted Production		Batter Runs		Adjusted Batter Runs		Clutch Hitting Index		Runs Created	
Collins-StL	1.008	Ott-NY	170	Ott-NY	55.2	Ott-NY	58.5	Thevenow-Pit	133	Ott-NY	150
Ott-NY	1.006	Collins-StL	155	Collins-StL	53.3	P.Waner-Pit	47.2	Durocher-StL	132	Collins-StL	148
P.Waner-Pit	.968	P.Waner-Pit	154	P.Waner-Pit	50.2	Collins-StL	44.9	Leslie-Bro	126	P.Waner-Pit	142
Vaughan-Pit	.942	Koenecke-Bro	152	Vaughan-Pit	44.3	Vaughan-Pit	41.5	Jackson-NY	124	Vaughan-Pit	135
Koenecke-Bro	.919	Berger-Bos	148	Terry-NY	31.5	Berger-Bos	37.7	Cuccinello-Bro	124	Terry-NY	122

Total Average		Stolen Bases		Stolen Base Average		Stolen Base Runs		Fielding Runs		Total Player Rating	
Ott-NY	1.075	Martin-StL	23					Critz-NY	25.0	Vaughan-Pit	5.1
Collins-StL	1.046	Cuyler-Chi	15					K.Davis-StL-Phi	17.8	P.Waner-Pit	4.6
Vaughan-Pit	1.043	Bartell-Phi	13					B.Herman-Chi	15.6	Ott-NY	4.1
P.Waner-Pit	1.010	Taylor-Bro	12					Bartell-Phi	13.5	Collins-StL	3.8
Koenecke-Bro	.981							Hartnett-Chi	13.5	Hartnett-Chi	3.5

Wins		Win Percentage		Games		Complete Games		Shutouts		Saves	
D.Dean-StL	30	D.Dean-StL	.811	C.Davis-Phi	51	Hubbell-NY	25	D.Dean-StL	7	Hubbell-NY	8
Schumacher-NY	23	Hoyt-Pit	.714	Hansen-Phi	50	D.Dean-StL	24	Hubbell-NY	5	Luque-NY	7
Warneke-Chi	22	Schumacher-NY	.697	D.Dean-StL	50	Warneke-Chi	23	P.Dean-StL	5	D.Dean-StL	7
Hubbell-NY	21	Warneke-Chi	.688	Hubbell-NY	49	Mungo-Bro	22	Lee-Chi	4	Bell-NY	6
		Frankhouse-Bos	.654	French-Pit	49	Brandt-Bos	20				

Innings Pitched		Fewest Hits/Game		Fewest BB/Game		Strikeouts		Strikeouts/Game		Ratio	
Mungo-Bro	315.1	Parmelee-NY	7.90	Hubbell-NY	1.06	D.Dean-StL	195	P.Dean-StL	5.79	Hubbell-NY	9.35
Hubbell-NY	313.0	Hubbell-NY	8.22	Freitas-Cin	1.47	Mungo-Bro	184	D.Dean-StL	5.63	Warneke-Chi	10.53
D.Dean-StL	311.2	D.Dean-StL	8.32	Frey-Cin	1.54	P.Dean-StL	150	Weaver-Chi	5.55	D.Dean-StL	10.66
Schumacher-NY	297.0	Warneke-Chi	8.43	Leonard-Bro	1.62	Warneke-Chi	143	Mungo-Bro	5.25	Hoyt-Pit	10.81
Warneke-Chi	291.1	Mungo-Bro	8.56	Fitzsimmons-NY	1.74	Derringer-Cin	122	Malone-Chi	5.23	Fitzsimmons-NY	10.87

Earned Run Average		Adjusted ERA		Opponents' Batting Avg.		Opponents' On Base Pct.		Starter Runs		Adjusted Starter Runs	
Hubbell-NY	2.30	Hubbell-NY	168	Parmelee-NY	.238	Hubbell-NY	.263	Hubbell-NY	61.3	Hubbell-NY	54.5
D.Dean-StL	2.66	C.Davis-Phi	160	Hubbell-NY	.239	Warneke-Chi	.287	D.Dean-StL	48.7	D.Dean-StL	54.3
Hoyt-Pit	2.93	D.Dean-StL	159	D.Dean-StL	.241	D.Dean-StL	.289	C.Davis-Phi	33.8	C.Davis-Phi	54.0
C.Davis-Phi	2.95	Hoyt-Pit	141	Warneke-Chi	.244	P.Dean-StL	.292	Fitzsimmons-NY	29.8	Hoyt-Pit	25.2
Fitzsimmons-NY	3.04	Walker-StL	135	P.Dean-StL	.248	Hoyt-Pit	.296	Schumacher-NY	29.0	Fitzsimmons-NY	24.1

Clutch Pitching Index		Relief Runs		Adjusted Relief Runs		Relief Ranking		Total Pitcher Index		Total Baseball Ranking	
Walker-StL	137	Haines-StL	5.6	Haines-StL	7.2	Haines-StL	6.0	C.Davis-Phi	7.8	C.Davis-Phi	7.8
Leonard-Bro	121	Bell-NY	2.4	Brennan-Cin	2.4	Brennan-Cin	2.1	D.Dean-StL	6.4	D.Dean-StL	6.4
C.Davis-Phi	120	Brennan-Cin	2.2	Bell-NY	1.2	Bell-NY	1.7	Hubbell-NY	6.0	Hubbell-NY	6.0
Freitas-Cin	111							Fitzsimmons-NY	3.7	Vaughan-Pit	5.1
Frankhouse-Bos	110							Schumacher-NY	3.5	P.Waner-Pit	4.6

January 15 Babe Ruth accepts a cut of $17,000 and signs a contract for $35,000.

January 19 Judge Landis denies Shoeless Joe Jackson's appeal for reinstatement.

March 20 All-around athlete Mildred "Babe" Didrickson pitches the first inning for the Philadelphia Athletics in a spring training exhibition game against the Brooklyn Dodgers. She gives up one walk but no hits.

April 21 Moe Berg, little-used Senators catcher, plays his 117th consecutive errorless game, dating back to 1931, an AL record.

May 6 The Red Sox score 12 runs in the fourth inning, helped along by a record four consecutive triples hit by Carl Reynolds, Moose Solters, Rick Ferrell, and Bucky Walters, to beat Detroit, 14–4. The record is five, set in the AL's inaugural year of 1901.

May 18 At Comiskey Park, Jimmie Foxx tees off against Ted Lyons and hits the first home run ever to land in the center field bleachers. Hank Greenberg will match Double X in 1938, then no one will reach the bleachers until Alex Johnson in 1970.

July 5 Lou Gehrig hits an inside-the-park grand slam, as the Yankees beat the Senators, 8–3. It is his fourth of the season and 17th overall, passing Babe Ruth's career total. Gehrig will eventually set a career record of 23 grand slams.

July 13 Babe Ruth hits his 700th home run to win the game at Detroit's Navin Field and put the Yankees back in first place. Lou Gehrig has a lumbago seizure and is helped off the field.

July 14 Lou Gehrig's consecutive-game string is extended by having him lead off, listed in the lineup as shortstop. He singles and leaves the game.

July 17 Babe Ruth draws his 2,000th base on balls at Cleveland. He will retire with a still untopped walk record of 2,056.

August 12 Making a farewell appearance in Boston, Babe Ruth draws a record 46,766 fans, with an estimated 20,000 turned away at Fenway Park where he began his career as a pitcher 20 years ago. Ruth singles and doubles in the first game, but the Yankees lose to Wes Ferrell 6–4. Walks hold him to one official at bat in the second game, which the Yankees win, and he leaves the field to standing cheers in the eighth inning.

August 25 Schoolboy Rowe, Detroit's sensational rookie pitcher, defeats the Senators 4–2 for his 16th win in a row, tying the AL record held by Walter Johnson, Joe Wood, and Lefty Grove.

September 24 Idle Detroit wins the pennant, as the Red Sox beat the Yankees 5–0 in the season's finale at Yankee Stadium. Ruth walks in the first inning, limps to first base, and leaves for a pinch runner in his last home game.

September 30 Coach Charley O'Leary scores a run as a pinch hitter for the Browns at age 52—the oldest major league player ever to do so.

November 3 Although Lou Gehrig wins the Triple Crown with 49 home runs, 165 RBI, and a .363 BA, Mickey Cochrane, with two home runs, 76 RBI, and a .320 BA, is named AL MVP. Dizzy Dean, with a 30-7 record, is chosen as NL MVP.

	BOSTON		CHICAGO		CLEVELAND		DETROIT		NEW YORK		PHILADELPHIA		ST.LOUIS		WASHINGTON
M	B.Harris	M	L.Fonseca	M	W.Johnson	M	M.Cochrane	M	J.McCarthy	M	C.Mack	M	R.Hornsby	M	J.Cronin
1B	E.Morgan	M	J.Dykes	1B	H.Trosky	1B	H.Greenberg	1B	L.Gehrig	1B	J.Foxx	1B	J.Burns	1B	J.Kuhel
2B	B.Cissell	1B	Z.Bonura	2B	O.Hale	2B	C.Gehringer	2B	T.Lazzeri	2B	R.Warstler	2B	S.Melillo	2B	B.Myer
SS	L.Lary	2B	J.Hayes	SS	B.Knickerb'r	SS	B.Rogell	SS	F.Crosetti	SS	E.McNair	SS	A.Strange	SS	J.Cronin
3B	B.Werber	SS	L.Appling	3B	W.Kamm	3B	M.Owen	3B	J.Saltzgaver	3B	P.Higgins	3B	H.Clift	3B	C.Travis
LF	R.Johnson	3B	J.Dykes	LF	J.Vosmik	LF	G.Goslin	LF	M.Hoag	LF	B.Johnson	LF	R.Pepper	LF	H.Manush
CF	C.Reynolds	LF	A.Simmons	CF	E.Averill	CF	J.White	CF	B.Chapman	CF	D.Cramer	CF	S.West	CF	F.Schulte
RF	D.Porter	CF	M.Haas	RF	S.Rice	RF	P.Fox	RF	B.Ruth	RF	E.Coleman	RF	B.Campbell	RF	J.Stone
C	R.Ferrell	RF	E.Swanson	C	F.Pytlak	C	M.Cochrane	C	B.Dickey	C	C.Berry	C	R.Hemsley	C	E.Phillips
		C	E.Madjeski												
21	M.Bishop			3	J.Burnett	O	G.Walker	O	S.Byrd	O1	L.Finney	S2	O.Bejma	3S	O.Bluege
O	M.Solters	2S	B.Boken	O	M.Galatzer	C	R.Hayworth	S3	R.Rolfe	C	F.Hayes	O	D.Garms	O	D.Harris
O	D.Cooke	O	J.Conlan	O	B.Seeds	O	F.Doljack	C	E.Combs	2	D.Williams	O	F.Grube	1	P.Susko
O	M.Almada	3	M.Hopkins	O	D.Holland	/3	F.Clifton	2	D.Heffner	O	B.Miller	/O	E.Clark	C	L.Sewell
3	B.Walters	C	M.Shea	C	G.Myatt	/S	H.Schuble	C	A.Jorgens	/O	J.McQuaig	/O	G.Puccinelli	1O	R.Kress
C	G.Hinkle	O	F.Uhalt	C	M.Berg	/C	R.York	O	G.Selkirk	/C	C.Moss	/3	R.Hornsby	C	C.Bolton
O	S.Graham	S3	J.Chamberlain	2	E.Moore	H	C.Perkins	/O	D.Walker	/C	E.Madjeski	/O	G.Hartley	32	J.Kerr
C	L.Legett	O	F.Bordagaray	C	B.Brenzel	H	F.Reiber	/C	Z.Taylor			H	A.Scharein	C	M.Berg
/2	A.Niemiec	C	M.Ruel	O	D.Porter	H	I.Wilson	/1	L.Lary	P	J.Marcum	H	C.O'Leary	O	J.Gill
/1	J.Judge	O	R.Radcliff	O	K.Carson					P	S.Cain			/O	J.Powell
/S	R.Kellett	O	M.Bocek	/C	B.Garbark	P	T.Bridges	P	L.Gomez	P	B.Dietrich	P	B.Newsom	/O	F.Sington
/O	B.Seeds	3	M.Mauldin	/C	R.Spencer	P	S.Rowe	P	R.Ruffing	P	J.Cascarella	P	G.Blaeholder	/3	B.Boken
/2	F.Muller	/O	C.Uhlir			P	E.Auker	P	J.Murphy	P	A.Benton	P	B.Hadley	/O	G.Dugas
		/C	G.Caithamer			P	M.Pearson	P	J.Broaca			P	D.Coffman	C	E.Klumpp
P	G.Rhodes	/2	R.Kress	P	M.Harder	P	V.Sorrell	P	J.DeShong	P	R.Mahaffey	P	I.Andrews		
P	J.Welch	/C	J.Pasek	P	O.Hildebrand	RP	C.Hogsett			P	B.Kline	RP	E.Wells	P	E.Whitehill
P	F.Ostermueller	/C	B.Fehring	P	W.Hudlin			/P	D.MacFayden	/P	G.Caster	RP	B.McAfee	P	M.Weaver
P	W.Ferrell			P	L.Brown	P	C.Fischer	P	R.Van Atta	P	M.Flohr			P	B.Burke
P	H.Johnson	P	G.Earnshaw	RP	B.Bean	P	L.Hamlin	P	J.Allen	/P	H.Matuzak	P	J.Knott	P	L.Stewart
RP	H.Pennock	P	T.Lyons	RP	C.Brown	/P	A.Crowder	P	B.Grimes	/P	W.Wilshere	/P	J.Weaver	P	T.Thomas
		P	M.Gaston			/P	V.Frasier	P	G.Uhle	/P	E.Lagger	/P	L.Mills	RP	J.Russell
P	L.Grove	P	S.Jones	P	T.Lee	/P	R.Phillips	/P	H.Smythe	P	J.Wilson	/P	J.Walkup	RP	A.McColl
P	R.Walberg	P	L.Tietje	P	R.Winegarner	/P	S.Larkin	/P	C.Devens	P	T.McKeithan				
P	B.Weiland	RP	J.Heving	P	B.Weiland			/P	V.Tamulis	P	R.Vaughn			P	A.Crowder
P	J.Mulligan	RP	W.Wyatt	/P	S.Connally			/P	F.Newkirk					P	E.Linke
/P	G.Hockette			/P	B.Perrin									/P	R.Diggs
/P	S.Merena	P	P.Gallivan	/P	D.Galehouse									/P	S.Cohen
/P	G.Pipgras	P	H.Kinzy											/P	R.Prim
		/P	V.Kennedy											/P	O.Armbrust
		/P	H.Klaerner											/P	A.Benson
		/P	L.Stine											/P	B.Kline
		/P	M.Stratton											/P	J.Milligan
		/P	J.Pomorski											/P	M.Filley

TEAM	G	W	L	PCT	GB	R	OR	AB	H	2B	3B	HR	BB	SO	AVG	OBP	SLG	PRO	PRO+	BR	/A	PF	CHI	RC	SB	CS	SBA	SBR
DET	154	101	53	.656		958	708	5475	1644	349	53	74	639	528	.300	.376	.424	.800	113	112	110	100	104	905	125	55	69	5
NY	154	94	60	.610	7	842	669	5368	1494	226	61	135	700	597	.278	.364	.419	.783	117	70	130	93	96	848	71	46	61	-6
CLE	154	85	69	.552	16	814	763	5396	1550	340	46	100	526	433	.287	.353	.423	.776	105	44	32	102	98	820	52	32	62	-4
BOS	153	76	76	.500	24	820	775	5339	1465	287	70	51	610	535	.274	.350	.383	.733	90	-28	-82	107	108	748	116	47	71	7
PHI	153	68	82	.453	31	764	838	5317	1491	236	50	144	491	584	.280	.343	.425	.768	108	20	49	96	97	785	57	35	62	-4
STL	154	67	85	.441	33	674	800	5288	1417	252	59	62	514	631	.268	.335	.373	.708	82	-84	-142	108	98	680	43	31	58	-6
WAS	155	66	86	.434	34	729	806	5448	1512	278	70	51	570	447	.278	.348	.382	.730	99	-35	-6	96	95	747	47	42	53	-11
CHI	153	53	99	.349	47	704	946	5301	1395	237	40	71	565	524	.263	.336	.363	.699	84	-97	-118	103	103	672	36	27	57	-5
TOT	615					6305		42932	11968	2205	449	688	4615	4279	.279	.351	.399	.750							547	315	63	-25

TEAM	CG	SH	SV	IP	H	H/G	HR	BB	SO	RAT	ERA	ERA+	OAV	OOB	PR	/A	PF	CPI	FA	E	DP	FW	PW	BW	SBW	DIF
DET	74	13	14	1370²	1467	9.6	86	488	640	12.9	4.06	108	.273	.335	67	50	98	102	.974	159	150	1.2	4.6	10.2	.8	7.2
NY	83	13	10	1382²	1349	8.8	71	542	656	12.4	3.76	108	.254	.324	114	48	90	97	.973	157	151	1.3	4.5	12.1	-.3	-.5
CLE	72	8	19	1367	1476	9.7	70	582	554	13.7	4.28	106	.275	.349	33	40	101	101	.972	172	164	.4	3.7	3.0	-.0	1.0
BOS	68	9	9	1361	1527	10.1	70	543	538	13.8	4.32	111	.283	.363	27	73	107	103	.969	188	141	-.5	6.8	-7.6	.9	.4
PHI	68	8	8	1337	1429	9.6	84	693	480	14.4	5.01	87	.275	.363	-77	-94	97	94	.967	196	166	-1.0	-8.7	4.6	-.0	-1.8
STL	50	6	20	1350	1499	10.0	94	632	499	14.3	4.49	111	.283	.361	1	75	111	107	.969	187	160	-.4	7.0	-13.2	-.3	-2.1
WAS	61	4	12	1381¹	1622	10.6	74	503	412	13.9	4.68	92	.295	.355	-28	-55	96	101	.974	162	167	1.0	-5.1	-.6	-.7	-4.6
CHI	72	5	8	1355	1599	10.6	139	628	506	14.9	5.41	88	.292	.367	-137	-101	105	97	.966	207	126	-1.6	-9.4	-11.0	-.2	-.9
TOT	548	66	100	10904²		9.9				13.8	4.50		.279	.351					.970	1428	1225					

Runs		Hits		Doubles		Triples		Home Runs		Total Bases	
Gehringer-Det	134	Gehringer-Det	214	Greenberg-Det	63	Chapman-NY	13	Gehrig-NY	49	Gehrig-NY	409
Werber-Bos	129	Gehrig-NY	210	Gehringer-Det	50	Manush-Was	11	Foxx-Phi	44	Trosky-Cle	374
Gehrig-NY	128	Trosky-Cle	206	Averill-Cle	48			Trosky-Cle	35	Greenberg-Det	356
Averill-Cle	128	Cramer-Phi	202	Trosky-Cle	45			Johnson-Phi	34	Foxx-Phi	352
Foxx-Phi	120	Greenberg-Det	201	Hale-Cle	44			Averill-Cle	31	Averill-Cle	340

Runs Batted In		Runs Produced		Bases On Balls		Batting Average		On Base Percentage		Slugging Average	
Gehrig-NY	165	Gehringer-Det	250	Foxx-Phi	111	Gehrig-NY	.363	Gehrig-NY	.465	Gehrig-NY	.706
Trosky-Cle	142	Gehrig-NY	244	Gehrig-NY	109	Gehringer-Det	.356	Gehringer-Det	.450	Foxx-Phi	.653
Greenberg-Det	139	Greenberg-Det	231	Ruth-NY	103	Manush-Was	.349	Foxx-Phi	.449	Greenberg-Det	.600
Foxx-Phi	130	Trosky-Cle	224	Myer-Was	102	Simmons-Chi	.344	Cochrane-Det	.428	Trosky-Cle	.598
Gehringer-Det	127	Rogell-Det	211			Vosmik-Cle	.341	Myer-Was	.419	Averill-Cle	.569

Production		Adjusted Production		Batter Runs		Adjusted Batter Runs		Clutch Hitting Index		Runs Created	
Gehrig-NY	1.172	Gehrig-NY	213	Gehrig-NY	85.6	Gehrig-NY	98.0	Dykes-Chi	137	Gehrig-NY	195
Foxx-Phi	1.102	Foxx-Phi	188	Foxx-Phi	66.4	Foxx-Phi	72.1	Cronin-Was	131	Foxx-Phi	165
Greenberg-Det	1.005	Greenberg-Det	156	Gehringer-Det	47.8	Greenberg-Det	47.5	Pepper-StL	129	Averill-Cle	145
Trosky-Cle	.987	Trosky-Cle	149	Greenberg-Det	46.7	Greenberg-Det	46.4	Cochrane-Det	129	Trosky-Cle	145
Averill-Cle	.982	Averill-Cle	149	Averill-Cle	45.6	Averill-Cle	43.6	Rogell-Det	126	Gehringer-Det	144

Total Average		Stolen Bases		Stolen Base Average		Stolen Base Runs		Fielding Runs		Total Player Rating	
Gehrig-NY	1.401	Werber-Bos	40	White-Det	82.4	White-Det	4.8	Hale-Cle	25.7	Gehrig-NY	7.8
Foxx-Phi	1.310	White-Det	28	Werber-Bos	72.7	Werber-Bos	3.0	Hemsley-StL	23.3	Foxx-Phi	6.1
Averill-Cle	1.075	Chapman-NY	26	Fox-Det	71.4	Lazzeri-NY	2.7	Werber-Bos	20.3	Gehringer-Det	5.7
Greenberg-Det	1.071	Fox-Det	25	Walker-Det	69.0	Cronin-Was	2.4	Cronin-Was	18.4	Averill-Cle	4.2
Gehringer-Det	1.053	Walker-Det	20	Chapman-NY	61.9			Melillo-StL	18.1	Werber-Bos	4.1

Wins		Win Percentage		Games		Complete Games		Shutouts		Saves	
Gomez-NY	26	Gomez-NY	.839	Russell-Was	54	Gomez-NY	25	Harder-Cle	6	Russell-Was	7
Rowe-Det	24	Rowe-Det	.750	Newsom-StL	47	Bridges-Det	23	Gomez-NY	6	L.Brown-Cle	6
Bridges-Det	22	Marberry-Det	.750	Rowe-Det	45	Lyons-Chi	21	Ruffing-NY	5	Newsom-StL	5
Harder-Cle	20	Auker-Det	.682	Knott-StL	45	Rowe-Det	20	Dietrich-Phi	4		
Ruffing-NY	19	Bridges-Det	.667								

Innings Pitched		Fewest Hits/Game		Fewest BB/Game		Strikeouts		Strikeouts/Game		Ratio	
Gomez-NY	281.2	Gomez-NY	7.13	W.Ferrell-Bos	2.44	Gomez-NY	158	Ruffing-NY	5.23	Gomez-NY	10.19
Bridges-Det	275.0	Ruffing-NY	8.15	Auker-Det	2.46	Bridges-Det	151	Gomez-NY	5.05	Rowe-Det	11.54
Rowe-Det	266.0	Bridges-Det	8.15	Blaeholder-StL	2.61	Ruffing-NY	149	Rowe-Det	5.04	Bridges-Det	11.65
Newsom-StL	262.1	Burke-Was	8.30	Rowe-Det	2.74	Rowe-Det	149	Pearson-Cle	4.95	Murphy-NY	11.66
Ruffing-NY	256.1	Murphy-NY	8.36	Weaver-Was	2.77	Pearson-Cle	140	Bridges-Det	4.94	Harder-Cle	11.77

Earned Run Average		Adjusted ERA		Opponents' Batting Avg.		Opponents' On Base Pct.		Starter Runs		Adjusted Starter Runs	
Gomez-NY	2.33	Harder-Cle	174	Gomez-NY	.215	Gomez-NY	.282	Gomez-NY	67.7	Harder-Cle	55.0
Harder-Cle	2.61	Gomez-NY	174	Ruffing-NY	.236	Ruffing-NY	.310	Harder-Cle	53.6	Gomez-NY	54.2
Murphy-NY	3.12	Ostermueller-Bos	138	Bridges-Det	.241	Rowe-Det	.312	Murphy-NY	31.8	Ostermueller-Bos	29.0
Burke-Was	3.21	Burke-Was	134	Burke-Was	.245	Bridges-Det	.312	Rowe-Det	30.9	Newsom-StL	28.6
Auker-Det	3.42	W.Ferrell-Bos	132	Benton-Phi	.249	Harder-Cle	.316	Bridges-Det	25.4	Rowe-Det	27.7

Clutch Pitching Index		Relief Runs		Adjusted Relief Runs		Relief Ranking		Total Pitcher Index		Total Baseball Ranking	
Harder-Cle	127	Pennock-Bos	10.0	Pennock-Bos	12.1	Bean-Cle	4.1	Harder-Cle	6.4	Gehrig-NY	7.8
Auker-Det	123	McColl-Was	8.0	McColl-Was	5.7	Pennock-Bos	3.9	Gomez-NY	4.8	Harder-Cle	6.4
Ostermueller-Bos	116	Russell-Was	5.8	Bean-Cle	3.9	McColl-Was	3.3	Rowe-Det	4.0	Foxx-Phi	6.1
Murphy-NY	113	Bean-Cle	3.7	Russell-Was	2.6	Russell-Was	2.5	Newsom-StL	3.2	Gehringer-Det	5.7
Coffman-StL	109			Wells-StL	2.1	Wells-StL	1.7	Ostermueller-Bos	3.1	Gomez-NY	4.8

April 16 Babe Ruth, released by the Yankees to sign with the Boston Braves for $20,000 and a share in the team's profits, draws the largest Opening Day crowd, 25,000, in Braves' history in his NL debut. It includes a 430-foot home run off Carl Hubbell, as Boston beats New York 4-2.

April 28 Trade unions direct their attention at the Cardinals, voting to boycott their games because team captain Leo Durocher made an anti-union statement in behalf of his wife's dress business. The ballpark is eventually picketed to protest non-union ushers, gate men, and vendors.

May 8 Reds backstop Ernie Lombardi equals the major league record with four doubles in consecutive innings, each off a different pitcher. The slow-footed Lombardi also has a "long single" in the 23-hit, 15–4 win over the Phillies.

May 9 The Braves' Rabbit Maranville sets a new record for NL service by appearing in his 23rd season. It is his first appearance since breaking his ankle in last year's spring training.

May 24 The Cincinnati Reds host the Philadelphia Phillies in the first major league night game, winning 2-1. On the initiative of Larry MacPhail, President Franklin Delano Roosevelt throws the switch at the White House to turn on the lights. The Reds will play seven night games, one each against the other NL teams.

May 25 Babe Ruth has a last hurrah, hitting three home runs at Pittsburgh. The final one, the last of his 714 career home runs, is the first to clear the right field grandstand at Forbes Field and is measured at 600 feet. He will announce his retirement June 2.

May 30 The Memorial Day twin bill at the Polo Grounds breaks all NL attendance records when 63,943 see the Giants take a pair from the Dodgers.

July 31 The Reds oversell their night game, and 30,000 jam in for the match against the Cards. Kitty Burke, a female fan, slips under the ropes around the infield and grabs a bat. Paul Dean lobs a pitch and she grounds out. Manager Frisch demands it count as an at bat.

September 22 The Boston Braves lose their 110th game and will lose 115, the most since 1900 until the 1962 expansion New York Mets lose 120 in a 162-game schedule. The Braves' winning percentage is .248.

September 27 The Cubs clinch the NL pennant in the first game of a doubleheader with the Cardinals 6-2, besting Dizzy Dean, as Bill Lee wins his 20th. By winning the second game 5-3, the Cubs extend their win streak to 21 games.

October 23 Gabby Hartnett is selected by the BBWAA as the NL MVP, with Dizzy Dean the runner-up.

October 24 Judge Kenesaw Mountain Landis levies $200 fines on umpire George Moriarty, Cubs manager Charlie Grimm, and Chicago players Woody English, Billy Jurges, and Billy Herman for their conduct in the World Series.

November 26 The NL takes over the bankrupt, last-place Boston Braves franchise after several failed attempts to buy the club, ultimately accepting Bob Quinn, who had been GM of the Brooklyn Dodgers, as president.

	BOSTON		BROOKLYN		CHICAGO		CINCINNATI		NEW YORK		PHILADELPHIA		PITTSBURGH		ST.LOUIS
M	B.McKechnie	M	C.Stengel	M	C.Grimm	M	C.Dressen	M	B.Terry	M	J.Wilson	M	P.Traynor	M	F.Frisch
1B	B.Jordan	1B	S.Leslie	1B	P.Cavarretta	1B	J.Bottomley	1B	B.Terry	1B	D.Camilli	1B	G.Suhr	1B	R.Collins
2B	L.Mallon	2B	T.Cuccinello	2B	B.Herman	2B	A.Kampouris	2B	M.Koenig	2B	L.Chiozza	2B	P.Young	2B	F.Frisch
SS	B.Urbanski	SS	L.Frey	SS	B.Jurges	SS	B.Myers	SS	D.Bartell	SS	M.Haslin	SS	A.Vaughan	SS	L.Durocher
3B	P.Whitney	3B	J.Stripp	3B	S.Hack	3B	L.Riggs	3B	T.Jackson	3B	J.Vergez	3B	T.Thevenow	3B	P.Martin
LF	H.Lee	LF	D.Taylor	LF	A.Galan	LF	B.Herman	LF	J.Moore	LF	G.Watkins	LF	W.Jensen	LF	J.Medwick
CF	W.Berger	CF	F.Bordagaray	CF	F.Demaree	CF	S.Byrd	CF	H.Leiber	CF	E.Allen	CF	L.Waner	CF	T.Moore
RF	T.Thompson	RF	B.Boyle	RF	C.Klein	RF	I.Goodman	RF	M.Ott	RF	J.Moore	RF	P.Waner	RF	J.Rothrock
C	A.Spohrer	C	A.Lopez	C	G.Hartnett	C	E.Lombardi	C	G.Mancuso	C	A.Todd	C	T.Padden	C	B.DeLancey
O1	R.Moore	23	J.Bucher	O3	F.Lindstrom	13	B.Sullivan	2	H.Critz	23	J.Wilson	23	C.Lavagetto	C	S.Davis
3S	J.Coscarart	2S	J.Jordan	C	K.O'Dea	O	K.Cuyler	2	A.Cuccinello	S2	C.Gomez	C	E.Grace	2	B.Whitehead
C	S.Hogan	O	L.Koenecke	O	K.Cuyler	C	G.Campbell	S	B.Ryan	3	P.Traynor	O	E.Orsatti
1	E.Fletcher	O	B.Phelps	O	T.Stainback	S2	G.Slade	1	P.Weintraub	O	E.Boland	O	B.Hafey	3S	C.Gelbert
O	J.Mowry	OP	B.Reis	3S	W.English	O	A.Comorosky	O	K.Davis	O	F.Lucas	O	B.Herman	/3	C.Wilson
C	R.Mueller	O	B.Mills	/C	W.Stephenson	C	H.Erickson	/C	G.Myatt	/C	J.Holden	/1	E.Browne	/O	L.King
O	B.Ruth	O	Z.Taylor	/1	C.Grimm	O	H.Pool	/C	P.Richards	/S	A.Bramhall	/3	B.Brubaker	/O	T.Winsett
2	R.Maranville	1	J.McCarthy	H	J.Gill	O	C.Hafey	H	J.Malay	/C	B.Jonnard	/C	A.Epps	/2	L.Judy
O	J.Tyler	O	J.Cooney			S	C.Chapman			/S	D.Chiozza	R	S.Swetonic	/C	B.O'Farrell
/2	E.Moriarty	/2	V.Sherlock	P	L.Warneke	/1	L.Scarsella	P	C.Hubbell					/C	S.Narron
/C	A.Doll	/O	N.Tremark	P	B.Lee	/O	T.Petoskey	P	H.Schumacher	P	C.Davis	P	C.Blanton	H	G.Moore
/C	B.Lewis	/3	F.Skaff	P	L.French	/O	T.Piet	P	R.Parmelee	P	O.Jorgens	P	B.Swift
		/S	R.Dedeaux	P	C.Root	/O	L.Gamble	P	S.Castleman	P	S.Johnson	P	G.Bush	P	D.Dean
P	F.Frankhouse	/C	W.Ock	RP	T.Carleton			P	A.Smith	P	J.Bivin	P	J.Weaver	P	P.Dean
P	B.Cantwell	/C	R.Onis	RP	F.Kowalik	P	P.Derringer	RP	A.Stout	RP	B.Walters	P	W.Hoyt	P	B.Walker
P	B.Smith					P	A.Hollingsworth	RP	F.Gabler	RP	P.Pezzullo			P	B.Hallahan
P	E.Brandt	P	V.Mungo	P	R.Henshaw	P	G.Schott			RP	R.Prim	P	R.Birkofer	P	E.Heusser
P	H.Betts	P	W.Clark	P	H.Casey	P	T.Freitas	P	F.Fitzsimmons	RP	H.Mulcahy	P	R.Lucas
RP	L.Benton	P	G.Earnshaw	/P	C.Bryant	P	S.Johnson	P	L.Chagnon			P	M.Brown	P	J.Haines
		P	T.Zachary	/P	C.Shoun			/P	H.Gumbert	P	J.Bowman	/P	J.Salveson	P	P.Collins
P	D.MacFayden	P	J.Babich	/P	R.Joiner	P	D.Brennan	/P	E.Moore	P	E.Moore	/P	C.Passeau	P	R.Harrell
P	B.Brown	RP	L.Munns			P	B.Frey	/P	D.Luque	/P	H.Kelleher	/P	H.Smith	/P	M.Ryba
P	F.Rhem	RP	D.Vance			P	L.Herrmann			/P	P.Collins	/P	W.Osborne	/P	N.Kleinke
/P	A.Blanche					P	E.Nelson			/P	F.Pearce			/P	J.Winford
/P	L.Mangum	P	D.Leonard			/P	D.MacFayden			/P	T.Thomas			/P	B.McGee
		P	R.Benge			/P	L.Grissom			/P	S.Hansen			/P	B.Tinning
		P	T.Baker			/P	W.Hilcher							/P	T.Kaufmann
		/P	H.Eisenstat											/P	A.Eckert
		/P	F.Lamanske											/P	M.Copeland
		/P	B.Logan											/P	D.Ward
		/P	B.Barr
		/P	H.Green

TEAM	G	W	L	PCT	GB	R	OR	AB	H	2B	3B	HR	BB	SO	AVG	OBP	SLG	PRO	PRO+	BR	/A	PF	CHI	RC	SB	CS	SBA	SBR
CHI	154	100	54	.649		847	597	5486	1581	303	62	88	464	471	.288	.347	.414	.761	110	81	76	101	102	812	66			
STL	154	96	58	.623	4	829	625	5457	1548	286	59	86	404	521	.284	.335	.405	.740	101	33	3	104	109	759	71			
NY	156	91	62	.595	8.5	770	675	5623	1608	248	56	123	392	479	.286	.336	.416	.752	110	54	68	98	96	797	32			
PIT	153	86	67	.562	13.5	743	647	5415	1543	255	90	66	457	437	.285	.343	.402	.745	103	49	24	103	96	758	30			
BRO	154	70	83	.458	29.5	711	767	5410	1496	235	62	59	430	520	.277	.333	.376	.709	99	-21	-6	98	101	691	60			
CIN	154	68	85	.444	31.5	646	772	5296	1403	244	68	73	392	547	.265	.319	.378	.697	96	-51	-31	97	99	658	72			
PHI	156	64	89	.418	35.5	685	871	5442	1466	249	32	92	392	661	.269	.322	.378	.700	85	-47	-116	110	101	681	52			
BOS	153	38	115	.248	61.5	575	852	5309	1396	233	33	75	353	436	.263	.311	.362	.673	93	-98	-50	92	95	596	20			
TOT	617					5806		43438	12041	2053	462	662	3284	4072	.277	.331	.391	.722							403			

TEAM	CG	SH	SV	IP	H	H/G	HR	BB	SO	RAT	ERA	ERA+	OAV	OOB	PR	/A	PF	CPI	FA	E	DP	FW	PW	BW	SBW	DIF
CHI	81	12	14	1394[1]	1417	9.1	85	400	589	11.9	3.26	121	.263	.317	118	103	98	111	.970	186	163	.3	10.0	7.4		5.3
STL	73	10	18	1384[2]	1445	9.4	68	377	602	12.0	3.52	116	.267	.318	76	89	102	101	.972	164	133	1.6	8.6	.3		8.5
NY	76	10	11	1403[2]	1433	9.2	106	411	524	12.0	3.78	102	.262	.318	37	11	96	98	.972	174	129	1.1	1.1	6.6		5.7
PIT	76	15	11	1365[2]	1428	9.4	63	312	549	11.6	3.42	120	.265	.307	91	103	102	98	.968	190	94	.0	10.0	2.3		-2.8
BRO	62	11	20	1358	1519	10.1	88	436	480	13.1	4.22	94	.281	.337	-31	-37	99	100	.969	188	146	.2	-3.6	-.6		-2.5
CIN	59	9	13	1356	1490	9.9	65	438	500	13.0	4.30	93	.278	.336	-43	-49	99	94	.966	204	139	-.7	-4.8	-3.0		.0
PHI	53	8	15	1374[2]	1652	10.8	106	505	475	14.4	4.76	95	.295	.358	-113	-35	113	102	.963	228	145	-2.0	-3.4	-11.3		4.1
BOS	54	6	5	1330	1645	11.1	81	404	355	14.0	4.93	77	.303	.354	-135	-169	94	96	.967	197	101	-.4	-16.4	-4.9		-16.8
TOT	534	81	107	10967		9.9				12.7	4.02		.277	.331					.968	1531	1050					

Runs		Hits		Doubles		Triples		Home Runs		Total Bases	
Galan-Chi	133	Herman-Chi	227	Herman-Chi	57	Goodman-Cin	18	Berger-Bos	34	Medwick-StL	365
Medwick-StL	132	Medwick-StL	224	Medwick-StL	46	L.Waner-Pit	14	Ott-NY	31	Ott-NY	329
Martin-StL	121			Allen-Phi	46	Medwick-StL	13	Camilli-Phi	25	Berger-Bos	323
Ott-NY	113			Martin-StL	41			Medwick-StL	23	Herman-Chi	317
Herman-Chi	113			Galan-Chi	41			R.Collins-StL	23	Leiber-NY	314

Runs Batted In		Runs Produced		Bases On Balls		Batting Average		On Base Percentage		Slugging Average	
Berger-Bos	130	Medwick-StL	235	Vaughan-Pit	97	Vaughan-Pit	.385	Vaughan-Pit	.491	Vaughan-Pit	.607
Medwick-StL	126	R.Collins-StL	208	Galan-Chi	87	Medwick-StL	.353	Ott-NY	.407	Medwick-StL	.576
R.Collins-StL	122	Galan-Chi	200	Ott-NY	82	Hartnett-Chi	.344	Hack-Chi	.406	Ott-NY	.555
Ott-NY	114	Ott-NY	196	Suhr-Pit	70	Lombardi-Cin	.343	Galan-Chi	.399	Berger-Bos	.548
Leiber-NY	107	Leiber-NY	195	Frey-Bro	66	Herman-Chi	.341	P.Waner-Pit	.392	Hartnett-Chi	.545

Production		Adjusted Production		Batter Runs		Adjusted Batter Runs		Clutch Hitting Index		Runs Created	
Vaughan-Pit	1.098	Vaughan-Pit	187	Vaughan-Pit	71.9	Vaughan-Pit	67.3	Leslie-Bro	135	Vaughan-Pit	163
Medwick-StL	.962	Ott-NY	159	Ott-NY	47.6	Ott-NY	50.0	Young-Pit	128	Ott-NY	144
Ott-NY	.962	Berger-Bos	151	Medwick-StL	46.0	Medwick-StL	41.0	Durocher-StL	125	Medwick-StL	139
R.Collins-StL	.915	Medwick-StL	149	R.Collins-StL	35.0	Berger-Bos	38.7	Jurges-Chi	121	Galan-Chi	133
Berger-Bos	.903	Leiber-NY	143	Leiber-NY	34.3	Leiber-NY	36.4	Whitney-Bos	113	R.Collins-StL	125

Total Average		Stolen Bases		Stolen Base Average		Stolen Base Runs		Fielding Runs		Total Player Rating	
Vaughan-Pit	1.317	Galan-Chi	22					Jurges-Chi	30.2	Vaughan-Pit	6.1
Ott-NY	1.037	Martin-StL	20					Herman-Chi	18.9	Herman-Chi	5.4
Medwick-StL	.948	Bordagaray-Bro	18					Allen-Phi	16.5	Ott-NY	4.9
Galan-Chi	.937	Hack-Chi	14					Hartnett-Chi	14.5	Hartnett-Chi	4.8
R.Collins-StL	.930	Goodman-Cin	14					T.Moore-StL	13.8	Berger-Bos	4.0

Wins		Win Percentage		Games		Complete Games		Shutouts		Saves	
D.Dean-StL	28	Lee-Chi	.769	Jorgens-Phi	53	D.Dean-StL	29	Weaver-Pit	4	Leonard-Bro	8
Hubbell-NY	23	Castleman-NY	.714	D.Dean-StL	50	Hubbell-NY	24	Mungo-Bro	4	Johnson-Phi	6
Derringer-Cin	22	D.Dean-StL	.700	Bivin-Phi	47	Blanton-Pit	23	French-Chi	4	Hoyt-Pit	6
Warneke-Chi	20	Schumacher-NY	.679	Smith-Bos	46	Warneke-Chi	20	Fitzsimmons-NY	4		
Lee-Chi	20	Hubbell-NY	.657	P.Dean-StL	46	Derringer-Cin	20	Blanton-Pit	4		

Innings Pitched		Fewest Hits/Game		Fewest BB/Game		Strikeouts		Strikeouts/Game		Ratio	
D.Dean-StL	325.1	Blanton-Pit	7.79	Clark-Bro	1.22	D.Dean-StL	190	Mungo-Bro	6.00	Blanton-Pit	9.80
Hubbell-NY	302.2	Schumacher-NY	8.08	Hubbell-NY	1.46	Hubbell-NY	150	D.Dean-StL	5.26	Swift-Pit	10.21
Derringer-Cin	276.2	Parmelee-NY	8.52	Hoyt-Pit	1.48	Mungo-Bro	143	Blanton-Pit	5.02	Clark-Bro	10.61
P.Dean-StL	269.2	Swift-Pit	8.53	Derringer-Cin	1.59	P.Dean-StL	143	P.Dean-StL	4.77	Warneke-Chi	10.66
		Hollingsworth-Cin	8.57	Johnson-Phi	1.60	Blanton-Pit	142	Hollingsworth-Cin	4.62	Schumacher-NY	10.66

Earned Run Average		Adjusted ERA		Opponents' Batting Avg.		Opponents' On Base Pct.		Starter Runs		Adjusted Starter Runs	
Blanton-Pit	2.58	Blanton-Pit	159	Blanton-Pit	.229	Blanton-Pit	.272	Blanton-Pit	40.6	Blanton-Pit	43.0
Swift-Pit	2.70	Swift-Pit	152	Schumacher-NY	.238	Swift-Pit	.282	D.Dean-StL	35.3	D.Dean-StL	38.2
Schumacher-NY	2.89	D.Dean-StL	135	Hollingsworth-Cin	.243	Clark-Bro	.289	Schumacher-NY	32.8	Swift-Pit	31.9
French-Chi	2.96	Schumacher-NY	133	Swift-Pit	.247	Schumacher-NY	.292	Swift-Pit	29.9	Schumacher-NY	28.0
Lee-Chi	2.96	French-Chi	133	P.Dean-StL	.249	P.Dean-StL	.292	Lee-Chi	29.5	Lee-Chi	27.0

Clutch Pitching Index		Relief Runs		Adjusted Relief Runs		Relief Ranking		Total Pitcher Index		Total Baseball Ranking	
French-Chi	126							Blanton-Pit	4.7	Vaughan-Pit	6.1
Zachary-Bro	121							D.Dean-StL	4.3	Herman-Chi	5.4
Walker-StL	116							Schumacher-NY	3.7	Ott-NY	4.9
Lee-Chi	111							Swift-Pit	3.2	Hartnett-Chi	4.8
Hallahan-StL	111							Warneke-Chi	3.0	Blanton-Pit	4.7

April 18 Detroit's Jo Jo White ties an AL record with 5 walks.

May 15 Lou Gehrig steals home in a 4-0 Yankee win over the Tigers. It is his fifteenth and last steal of home, all of which were double steals.

May 21 Buck Newsom is sold by the Browns to the Senators for $40,000.

May 22* The Albany Senators (IL) sign Alabama Pitts, legendary athletic star and parolee from Sing Sing prison.

June 1 At Yankee Stadium, the Bombers hit a record six solo home runs in beating Boston, 7–2. Bill Dickey (2), Frank Crosetti, Ben Chapman, George Selkirk, and Red Rolfe are the sluggers.

June 28 Earl Averill's consecutive-game streak ends at 673 for the Indians when he is injured in a pre-Fourth of July fireworks accident.

July 8 The AL continues its All-Star Game reign, winning the third event, at Cleveland's Municipal Stadium 4-1. Jimmie Foxx is the hitting star with a homer and three RBI.

July 31 Two AL pitchers each hit two homers in a game. Wes Ferrell clouts a couple against Buck Newsom of the Browns and knocks in four runs in a 6-4 win for Boston. Mel Harder hits two for Cleveland but loses 6-4 to the White Sox.

August 4 Walter Johnson resigns as Cleveland manager and is replaced by Steve O'Neill.

August 31 Vern Kennedy pitches the first AL no-hitter since 1931, and the first ever in Comiskey Park, blanking Cleveland, 5–0. He also is the batting star with a bases-loaded triple.

September 7 With no outs and the bases loaded, and the Indians leading, 5–3, in the ninth, Boston's Joe Cronin lines a drive off the head of Cleveland third baseman Odell Hale. The ball caroms to shortstop Bill Knickerbocker, who starts a triple play that ends the game.

September 20* The Pittsburgh Crawfords beat the New York Cubans to win the Negro National League Championship 3-0 behind the pitching of Leroy Matlock and the extra base hits of Josh Gibson, Cool Papa Bell, and Oscar Charleston.

September 21 The Detroit Tigers clinch the pennant with a double win over the St. Louis Browns.

October 3 The Tigers even the Series behind Tommy Bridges 8–3, but lose Hank Greenberg who injures his wrist trying to score from first on a single.

October 7 The Tigers end the Series in six games behind Tommy Bridges' second complete game 4-3. Goose Goslin's single, with two out in the bottom of the ninth, wins the game.

October 20 Hank Greenberg is named AL MVP by the BBWAA; Wes Ferrell is runner-up.

December 10 Jimmie Foxx, with Johnny Marcum, is sold by the A's to the Red Sox for $150,000; Al Simmons is sold by the White Sox to the Tigers for $75,000.

BOSTON		CHICAGO		CLEVELAND		DETROIT		NEW YORK		PHILADELPHIA		ST.LOUIS		WASHINGTON	
M	J.Cronin	M	J.Dykes	M	W.Johnson	M	M.Cochrane	M	J.McCarthy	M	C.Mack	M	R.Hornsby	M	B.Harris
1B	B.Dahlgren	1B	Z.Bonura	M	S.O'Neill	1B	H.Greenberg	1B	L.Gehrig	1B	J.Foxx	1B	J.Burns	1B	J.Kuhel
2B	S.Melillo	2B	J.Hayes	1B	H.Trosky	2B	C.Gehringer	2B	T.Lazzeri	2B	R.Warstler	2B	T.Carey	2B	B.Myer
SS	J.Cronin	SS	L.Appling	2B	B.Berger	SS	B.Rogell	SS	F.Crosetti	SS	E.McNair	SS	L.Lary	SS	O.Bluege
3B	B.Werber	3B	J.Dykes	SS	B.Knickerb'r	3B	M.Owen	3B	R.Rolfe	3B	P.Higgins	3B	H.Clift	3B	C.Travis
LF	R.Johnson	LF	R.Radcliff	3B	O.Hale	LF	G.Goslin	LF	J.Hill	LF	B.Johnson	LF	M.Solters	LF	H.Manush
CF	M.Almada	CF	A.Simmons	LF	J.Vosmik	CF	J.White	CF	B.Chapman	CF	D.Cramer	CF	S.West	CF	J.Powell
RF	D.Cooke	RF	M.Haas	CF	E.Averill	RF	P.Fox	RF	G.Selkirk	RF	W.Moses	RF	E.Coleman	RF	J.Stone
C	R.Ferrell	C	L.Sewell	RF	M.Galatzer	C	M.Cochrane	C	B.Dickey	C	P.Richards	C	R.Hemsley	C	C.Bolton
				C	E.Phillips										
32	D.Williams	O	G.Washington			O	G.Walker	O	E.Combs	O1	L.Finney	O	R.Pepper	S	R.Kress
O	C.Reynolds	23	T.Piet	O	B.Campbell	C	R.Hayworth	23	J.Saltzgaver	C	B.Berry	O1	B.Bell	O	F.Schulte
O	B.Miller	3	M.Hopkins	2S	R.Hughes	3	F.Clifton	O	M.Hoag	S2	S.Newsome	3S	J.Burnett	O	D.Miles
21	M.Bishop	O	J.Conlan	O	A.Wright	/O	H.Walker	S	B.Ryan	1	A.Hooks	2	O.Bejma	C	S.Holbrook
C	M.Berg	C	M.Shea	C	F.Pytlak	/O	C.Morgan	C	A.Jorgens	/2	B.Snyder	S	A.Strange	S	L.Lary
O	M.Solters	/O	F.Tauby	/C	B.Brenzel	/C	F.Reiber	S	N.Richardson	/S	J.Peerson	C	T.Heath	S	A.Strange
/C	G.Dickey	/2	G.Wright	C	G.Myatt	/3	H.Schuble	C	J.Glenn	/O	E.Coleman	2	S.Melillo	3	B.Estalella
/O	S.Graham	/3	M.Kreevich	/O	K.Carson	/O	H.Shelley	2	D.Heffner	/C	B.Patton	O	M.Mazzera	/3	J.Redmond
/2	D.Farrell	/C	F.Grube	/C	B.Garbark			/O	D.Walker	/2	D.Williams	/1	H.Mueller	/3	B.Lewis
/3	J.Kroner	R	B.Hafey	/3	H.Kamm	P	S.Rowe	P	L.Gomez	/C	J.Owens	/1	R.Hornsby	C	C.Starr
R	L.Legett			/C	G.George	P	T.Bridges	P	R.Ruffing	/C	C.Conroy	/O	D.Garms	/S	J.Mihalic
		P	J.Whitehead			P	A.Crowder	P	J.Broaca	/C	C.Moss	/O	H.Warnock	/O	F.Sington
P	W.Ferrell	P	V.Kennedy	P	M.Harder	P	E.Auker	P	J.Allen	P	J.Marcum	/C	F.Grube	/O	R.Marion
P	L.Grove	P	T.Lyons	P	W.Hudlin	P	J.Sullivan	RP	V.Tamulis	P	B.Dietrich	P	I.Andrews	P	E.Whitehill
P	G.Rhodes	P	L.Tietje	P	M.Pearson	RP	C.Hogsett	RP	J.Murphy	P	G.Blaeholder	P	J.Knott	P	B.Hadley
P	J.Welch	P	S.Jones	P	T.Lee	P	V.Sorrell	RP	J.DeShong	P	W.Wilshere	P	J.Walkup	P	B.Newsom
P	R.Walberg	RP	W.Wyatt	P	O.Hildebrand	/P	R.Lawson	RP	P.Malone	P	R.Mahaffey	P	R.Van Atta	P	E.Linke
RP	J.Wilson	P	R.Phelps	RP	L.Brown	/P	C.Hatter	P	J.Brown	RP	A.Benton	P	S.Cain	RP	J.Russell
RP	G.Hockette	P	C.Fischer	RP	R.Winegarner	/P	F.Marberry	/P	R.Van Atta	RP	B.Caster	/P	B.Newsom	RP	L.Pettit
		P	J.Salveson	RP	C.Brown	/P	C.Fischer			RP	D.Lieber	/P	E.Caldwell	P	B.Burke
P	F.Ostermueller	/P	M.Stratton	P	L.Stewart					P	C.Doyle	/P	B.Weiland	P	H.Coppola
P	H.Johnson	P	J.Vance	/P	D.Galehouse					P	G.Turbeville	/P	S.Hansen	P	B.Bean
P	S.Bowers	/P	G.Earnshaw	/P	B.Bean					/P	J.Cascarella	/P	G.Blaeholder	/P	J.Hayes
/P	J.Cascarella	/P	I.Chelini							P	S.Cain	/P	B.Poser	/P	D.Lanahan
/P	G.Pipgras	/P	L.Stine							/P	W.Upchurch			/P	P.Hensiek
/P	H.Vandenberg									/P	H.Fink			/P	M.Weaver
/P	W.Ripley									/P	V.Eaves			/P	B.Rogers
										/P	A.Veach			/P	A.McLean
										/P	B.Ferrazzi			/P	L.Stewart
										/P	E.Huckleberry			/P	T.Thomas
										/P	W.Martini				

TEAM	G	W	L	PCT	GB	R	OR	AB	H	2B	3B	HR	BB	SO	AVG	OBP	SLG	PRO	PRO+	BR	/A	PF	CHI	RC	SB	CS	SBA	SBR
DET	152	93	58	.616		**919**	665	5423	1573	301	83	106	**627**	456	**.290**	**.366**	**.435**	**.801**	116	95	126	97	104	885	70	45	61	-6
NY	149	89	60	.597	3	818	**632**	5214	1462	255	70	104	604	469	.280	.358	.416	.774	111	42	87	94	102	799	68	46	60	-7
CLE	156	82	71	.536	12	776	739	5534	1573	**324**	77	93	460	567	.284	.341	.421	.762	100	3	-11	102	99	796	63	54	54	-14
BOS	154	78	75	.510	16	718	732	5288	1458	281	63	69	609	470	.276	.353	.392	.745	92	-11	-62	107	94	757	**91**	59	61	-8
CHI	153	74	78	.487	19.5	738	750	5314	1460	262	42	74	580	**405**	.275	.348	.382	.730	92	-41	-59	103	101	733	46	28	62	-3
WAS	154	67	86	.438	27	823	903	5592	**1591**	255	95	32	596	406	.285	.357	.381	.738	99	-18	8	97	**104**	788	54	37	59	-6
STL	155	65	87	.428	28.5	718	930	5365	1446	291	51	73	593	561	.270	.344	.384	.728	90	-49	-83	105	98	735	45	25	**64**	**-2**
PHI	149	58	91	.389	34	710	869	5269	1470	243	44	**112**	475	602	.279	.341	.406	.747	99	-23	-17	99	98	738	43	35	55	-8
TOT	611					6220		42999	12033	2212	525	663	4544	3936	.280	.351	.402	.753							480	329	59	-53

TEAM	CG	SH	SV	IP	H	H/G	HR	BB	SO	RAT	ERA	ERA+	OAV	OOB	PR	/A	PF	CPI	FA	E	DP	FW	PW	BW	SBW	DIF
DET	**87**	**16**	11	1364	1440	9.5	78	522	584	13.1	3.82	109	.271	.339	96	53	94	107	.978	128	154	2.3	5.0	11.8	.0	-1.6
NY	76	12	13	1331	**1276**	8.6	91	516	**594**	12.2	3.60	112	**.251**	.321	**126**	66	91	101	.974	151	114	.8	6.2	8.1	-.0	-.6
CLE	67	12	**21**	1396	1527	9.8	68	**457**	498	12.9	4.15	108	.278	.335	47	55	101	97	.972	177	147	-.3	5.2	-1.0	-.7	2.3
BOS	82	6	11	1376	1520	9.9	**67**	520	470	13.5	4.05	**106**	.280	.346	62	**106**	107	105	.969	194	136	-1.4	**9.9**	-5.8	-.1	-1.1
CHI	80	8	8	1360²	1443	9.5	105	574	436	13.5	4.38	106	.272	.346	12	36	104	104	.976	146	133	1.3	3.4	-5.5	.3	-1.5
WAS	67	5	12	1378²	1672	10.9	89	613	456	15.1	5.25	82	.302	.374	-122	-142	97	99	.972	171	**186**	-.0	-13.3	.7	.0	3.0
STL	42	4	15	1380¹	1667	10.9	92	641	435	15.2	5.26	91	.297	.371	-124	-72	108	97	.970	187	138	-.9	-6.7	-7.8	**.4**	4.0
PHI	58	7	10	1326¹	1486	10.1	73	704	469	15.0	5.12	89	.285	.372	-97	-84	102	96	.968	190	150	-1.4	-7.9	-1.6	-.1	-5.5
TOT	559	70	101	10913		9.9				13.8	4.46		.280	.351					.972	1344	1158					

Runs
Gehrig-NY 125
Gehringer-Det 123
Greenberg-Det 121
Foxx-Phi 118
Chapman-NY 118

Hits
Vosmik-Cle 216
Myer-Was 215
Cramer-Phi 214
Greenberg-Det 203

Doubles
Vosmik-Cle 47
Greenberg-Det 46
Solters-Bos-StL ... 45
Fox-Det 38
Chapman-NY 38

Triples
Vosmik-Cle 20
Stone-Was 18
Greenberg-Det 16
Cronin-Bos 14
Averill-Cle 13

Home Runs
Greenberg-Det 36
Foxx-Phi 36
Gehrig-NY 30
Johnson-Phi 28
Trosky-Cle 26

Total Bases
Greenberg-Det 389
Foxx-Phi 340
Vosmik-Cle 333
Solters-Bos-StL ... 314
Gehrig-NY 312

Runs Batted In
Greenberg-Det 170
Gehrig-NY 119
Foxx-Phi 115
Trosky-Cle 113
Solters-Bos-StL ... 112

Runs Produced
Greenberg-Det 255
Gehrig-NY 214
Gehringer-Det 212
Myer-Was 210
Foxx-Phi 197

Bases On Balls
Gehrig-NY 132
Appling-Chi 122
Foxx-Phi 114
Myer-Was 96
Cochrane-Det 96

Batting Average
Myer-Was .... .349
Vosmik-Cle .... .348
Foxx-Phi .... .346
Cramer-Phi .... .332
Gehringer-Det ..... .330

On Base Percentage
Gehrig-NY .... .466
Foxx-Phi .... .461
Cochrane-Det ...... .452
Myer-Was .... .440
Appling-Chi .... .437

Slugging Average
Foxx-Phi .... .636
Greenberg-Det ..... .628
Gehrig-NY .... .583
Vosmik-Cle .... .537
Fox-Det .... .513

Production
Foxx-Phi 1.096
Gehrig-NY 1.049
Greenberg-Det 1.039
Vosmik-Cle .... .946
Gehringer-Det ..... .911

Adjusted Production
Foxx-Phi 182
Gehrig-NY 180
Greenberg-Det 171
Vosmik-Cle 140
Myer-Was 139

Batter Runs
Foxx-Phi 67.2
Gehrig-NY 61.6
Greenberg-Det 57.5
Vosmik-Cle 38.3
Myer-Was 36.5

Adjusted Batter Runs
Gehrig-NY 70.1
Foxx-Phi 68.4
Greenberg-Det 62.7
Myer-Was 40.8
Gehringer-Det 36.3

Clutch Hitting Index
Owen-Det 134
Kuhel-Was 124
Goslin-Det 124
Powell-Was 124
Myer-Was 122

Runs Created
Foxx-Phi 163
Greenberg-Det 161
Gehrig-NY 154
Vosmik-Cle 137
Myer-Was 132

Total Average
Foxx-Phi 1.288
Gehrig-NY 1.230
Greenberg-Det 1.138
Cochrane-Det 1.000
Vosmik-Cle .... .980

Stolen Bases
Werber-Bos 29
Lary-Was-StL 28
Almada-Bos 20
White-Det 19
Chapman-NY 17

Stolen Base Average
Lary-Was-StL 87.5
Werber-Bos 80.6
Almada-Bos 69.0
White-Det 65.5
Chapman-NY 63.0

Stolen Base Runs
Lary-Was-StL 6.0
Werber-Bos 4.5
Solters-Bos-StL ... 2.1
Hughes-Cle 2.1

Fielding Runs
Appling-Chi 21.3
Travis-Was 21.3
Solters-Bos-StL ... 18.6
Melillo-StL-Bos ... 18.6
Werber-Bos 17.2

Total Player Rating
Foxx-Phi 5.7
Myer-Was 5.4
Gehrig-NY 4.8
Greenberg-Det 4.7
Gehringer-Det 4.7

Wins
W.Ferrell-Bos 25
Harder-Cle 22
Bridges-Det 21
Grove-Bos 20
Rowe-Det 19

Win Percentage
Auker-Det .... .720
Broaca-NY .... .682
Bridges-Det .... .677
Harder-Cle .... .667
Lyons-Chi .... .652

Games
VanAtta-NY-StL 58
Walkup-StL 55
Andrews-StL 50
Thomas-StL 49
Knott-StL 48

Complete Games
W.Ferrell-Bos 31
Grove-Bos 23
Bridges-Det 23
Rowe-Det 21

Shutouts
Rowe-Det 6
Harder-Cle 4
Bridges-Det 4

Saves
Knott-StL 7

Innings Pitched
W.Ferrell-Bos 322.1
Harder-Cle 287.1
Whitehill-Was 279.1
Rowe-Det 275.2
Bridges-Det 274.1

Fewest Hits/Game
Allen-NY 8.03
Ruffing-NY 8.15
Gomez-NY 8.16
Whitehead-Chi 8.46
Grove-Bos 8.87

Fewest BB/Game
Harder-Cle 1.66
Grove-Bos 2.14
Rowe-Det 2.22
Andrews-StL 2.24
Hudlin-Cle 2.37

Strikeouts
Bridges-Det 163
Rowe-Det 140
Gomez-NY 138
Grove-Bos 121
Allen-NY 113

Strikeouts/Game
Allen-NY 6.09
Bridges-Det 5.35
Gomez-NY 5.05
VanAtta-NY-StL 4.63
Rowe-Det 4.57

Ratio
Grove-Bos 11.11
Rowe-Det 11.17
Ruffing-NY 11.27
Allen-NY 11.37
Gomez-NY 11.38

Earned Run Average
Grove-Bos 2.70
Lyons-Chi 3.02
Ruffing-NY 3.12
Gomez-NY 3.18
Harder-Cle 3.29

Adjusted ERA
Grove-Bos 176
Lyons-Chi 153
Harder-Cle 137
Andrews-StL 135
W.Ferrell-Bos 135

Opponents' Batting Avg.
Allen-NY .... .238
Ruffing-NY .... .239
Gomez-NY .... .242
Whitehead-Chi ..... .250
Broaca-NY .... .254

Opponents' On Base Pct.
Rowe-Det .... .301
Grove-Bos .... .302
Ruffing-NY .... .303
Allen-NY .... .307
Harder-Cle .... .307

Starter Runs
Grove-Bos 53.1
Harder-Cle 37.2
Gomez-NY 34.8
W.Ferrell-Bos 33.6
Ruffing-NY 32.9

Adjusted Starter Runs
Grove-Bos 61.9
W.Ferrell-Bos 43.9
Harder-Cle 38.8
Lyons-Chi 33.9
Andrews-StL 29.6

Clutch Pitching Index
Lyons-Chi 124
Bridges-Det 113
Auker-Det 112
Grove-Bos 112
Tietje-Chi 110

Relief Runs
L.Brown-Cle 11.4
Hogsett-Det 9.9
DeShong-NY 9.2
Murphy-NY 4.9
Wilson-Bos 1.7

Adjusted Relief Runs
L.Brown-Cle 12.1
Hogsett-Det 6.8
DeShong-NY 6.0
Wilson-Bos 3.7

Relief Ranking
L.Brown-Cle 14.2
Hogsett-Det 8.4
DeShong-NY 4.5
Wilson-Bos 3.8

Total Pitcher Index
W.Ferrell-Bos 7.2
Grove-Bos 6.4
Harder-Cle 4.4
Lyons-Chi 3.6
Ruffing-NY 3.5

Total Baseball Ranking
W.Ferrell-Bos 7.2
Grove-Bos 6.4
Foxx-Phi 5.7
Myer-Was 5.4
Gehrig-NY 4.8

January 15 IRS figures for 1934 show Branch Rickey as the highest paid man in baseball at $49,470. Commissioner Landis had voluntarily taken a cut in 1933 from $65,000 to $40,000 because of the Depression.

January 30 The new owners of the Boston Braves ask newspapermen to pick a new nickname for the team from suggestions made by fans. They choose the Bees, but the name will not catch on. It will be scrapped after the 1940 season.

April 14 In a 12-7 loss to the Cubs, Cardinals rookie Eddie Morgan becomes the first player to pinch hit a home run in his first major league at bat. It is the only one he'll hit in a 39-game career.

July 7 The NL, having lost the first three All-Star Games, wins 4–3 at Fenway Park. After Dizzy Dean and Carl Hubbell each pitch scoreless three-inning stints, Curt Davis is hammered by the AL, including Lou Gehrig's home run, but Lon Warneke shuts the door. Meanwhile, the NL is helped by Joe DiMaggio's loose fielding and error and Augie Galan's home run. The NL plays its starting lineup except for two late-inning pinch hitters.

July 10 Philadelphia's Chuck Klein hits four home runs in five at bats in a 10-inning game at Forbes Field. His final home run beats the Pirates 9-6

July 15 Cincinnati plays the first Ladies Night game, beating Brooklyn 5–3.

July 21 Cardinals slugger Joe Medwick has 10 hits in succession to equal the NL record. He had seven hits in his last seven times at bat in a doubleheader on July 19, and he hit safely in his first three today before being stopped by the Giants' Carl Hubbell.

August 12 The largest crowd ever to watch a baseball game, estimated at between 90,000 and 125,000, sees a "demonstration game" as an event of the Olympics in Berlin. The world amateurs beat the U.S. amateurs 6-5.

September 14 Pittsburgh's Paul Waner ties Rogers Hornsby's modern NL record, reaching 200 hits for the seventh time.

September 23 Carl Hubbell notches his 16th consecutive victory, his 26th of the year, beating the Phils 5-4. He resumes the streak next year to reach a record 24 wins in a row.

September 24 The Giants clinch the pennant, winning 2-1 in the 10th of the opening game of a doubleheader with the Boston Bees. Pitcher Hal Schumacher singles in the winning run.

September 25 Joe Medwick sets a still-standing NL record with his 64th double.

September 27 When Johnny Mize is thrown out in the seventh inning for arguing, Cardinal rookie first baseman Walt Alston subs. In his only major league game, the future Hall of Fame manager makes one error in two chances and is fanned by Lon Warneke in his only at bat.

September 30 In the World Series opener, Carl Hubbell scatters seven hits in a 6-1 win and limits the Yankees to just a solo home run by George Selkirk.

October 20 Carl Hubbell, 26-6, edges out Dizzy Dean, 24-13, for MVP honors in the NL.

	BOSTON		BROOKLYN		CHICAGO		CINCINNATI		NEW YORK		PHILADELPHIA		PITTSBURGH		ST.LOUIS
M	B.McKechnie	M	C.Stengel	M	C.Grimm	M	C.Dressen	M	B.Terry	M	J.Wilson	M	P.Traynor	M	F.Frisch
1B	B.Jordan	1B	B.Hassett	1B	P.Cavarretta	1B	L.Scarsella	1B	S.Leslie	1B	D.Camilli	1B	G.Suhr	1B	J.Mize
2B	T.Cuccinello	2B	J.Jordan	2B	B.Herman	2B	A.Kampouris	2B	B.Whitehead	2B	C.Gomez	2B	P.Young	2B	S.Martin
SS	B.Urbanski	SS	L.Frey	SS	B.Jurges	SS	B.Myers	SS	D.Bartell	SS	L.Norris	SS	A.Vaughan	SS	L.Durocher
3B	J.Coscarart	3B	J.Stripp	3B	S.Hack	3B	L.Riggs	3B	T.Jackson	3B	P.Whitney	3B	B.Brubaker	3B	C.Gelbert
LF	H.Lee	LF	G.Watkins	LF	E.Allen	LF	B.Herman	LF	J.Moore	LF	J.Moore	LF	W.Jensen	LF	J.Medwick
CF	W.Berger	CF	J.Cooney	CF	A.Galan	CF	K.Cuyler	CF	H.Leiber	CF	E.Sulik	CF	L.Waner	CF	T.Moore
RF	G.Moore	RF	F.Bordagaray	RF	F.Demaree	RF	I.Goodman	RF	M.Ott	RF	C.Klein	RF	P.Waner	RF	P.Martin
C	A.Lopez	C	R.Berres	C	G.Hartnett	C	E.Lombardi	C	G.Mancuso	C	E.Grace	C	T.Padden	C	S.Davis
O1	T.Thompson	32	J.Bucher	C	K.O'Dea	O2	C.Chapman	O	J.Ripple	O2	L.Chiozza	C	A.Todd	1	R.Collins
S	R.Warstler	C	B.Phelps	S3	W.English	S2	T.Thevenow	C	B.Terry	C	J.Wilson	O	F.Schulte	C	R.Ogrodowski
3	M.Haslin	O	E.Wilson	O	J.Gill	O	H.Walker	3	E.Mayo	C	B.Atwood	23	C.Lavagetto	23	F.Frisch
C	R.Mueller	S	B.Geraghty	1	C.Grimm	C	G.Campbell	C	H.Danning	O	E.Allen	O	B.Hafey	32	A.Garibaldi
C	B.Lewis	O	D.Taylor	O	C.Klein	C	S.Byrd	23	K.Davis	C	C.Sheerin	O	H.Finney	O	L.King
3	P.Whitney	O	F.Lindstrom	O	T.Stainback	1	G.McQuinn	S	M.Koenig	O	G.Watkins	3	E.Browne	3	D.Gutteridge
H	E.Moriarty	O	R.Moore	/S	G.Lillard	2	L.Handley	O	G.Watkins	2	M.Haslin	/O	J.Dickshot	O	C.Fullis
H	A.Pilney	O	T.Winsett	/C	W.Stephenson	/S	E.Joost	/1	J.McCarthy	O	M.Arnovich			/O	E.Morgan
/2	S.Larsen	C	S.Gautreaux			/S	E.Miller	/3	J.Martin	3	J.Vergez	P	B.Swift	/3	J.Vergez
		O	O.Eckhardt					/C	J.Sheehan	2	S.Sperry	P	C.Blanton	/O	L.Scoffic
P	D.MacFayden	/O	N.Tremark	P	B.Lee	P	P.Derringer	/2	C.English	/1	G.Corbett	P	J.Weaver	/S	P.Ankenman
P	T.Chaplin	2	J.Radtke	P	L.Warneke	P	A.Hollingsworth	H	B.Young	/O	W.Bashore	P	R.Lucas	/1	W.Alston
P	J.Lanning	/S	J.Hudson	P	T.Carleton	P	G.Schott			H	J.Holden	P	M.Brown	/3	H.Schuble
P	B.Reis	/O	D.Siebert	P	B.Hallahan	P	C.Hubbell								
P	B.Smith			RP	C.Root	P	B.Frey	P	H.Schumacher	P	B.Walters	P	W.Hoyt	P	D.Dean
		P	V.Mungo	RP	C.Bryant	RP	D.Brennan	P	A.Smith	P	C.Passeau	P	R.Birkofer	P	R.Parmelee
P	B.Cantwell	P	F.Frankhouse					P	F.Gabler	P	J.Bowman	P	J.Tising	P	J.Winford
P	R.Benge	P	E.Brandt	P	R.Henshaw	P	P.Davis	P	H.Gumbert	O	O.Jorgens	P	G.Bush	P	J.Haines
P	G.Bush	P	M.Butcher	/P	F.Kowalik	P	L.Stine	RP	D.Coffman	RP	S.Johnson	/P	J.Welch	RP	E.Heusser
P	R.Weir	P	W.Clark	/P	C.Shoun	P	W.Hilcher			RP	E.Moore	/P	R.Bauers	RP	G.Earnshaw
/P	W.Osborne	RP	G.Jeffcoat			/P	L.Grissom	P	F.Fitzsimmons						
P	A.Blanche	RP	T.Baker			/P	E.Nelson	P	S.Castleman	P	F.Kowalik			P	P.Dean
/P	A.Murray					/P	J.Mooty	/P	F.Marberry	P	P.Sivess			P	B.Walker
/P	F.Kowalik	P	G.Earnshaw			/P	T.Freitas			P	C.Davis			P	S.Johnson
/P	B.Brown	P	D.Leonard			/P	D.Moore			P	R.Benge			P	M.Ryba
/P	A.Doll	P	H.Winston			/P	W.Moore			P	H.Kelleher			/P	B.Hallahan
/P	J.McCloskey	/P	H.Eisenstat			/P	S.Johnson			P	H.Mulcahy			P	F.Rhem
/P	J.Babich	/P	T.Zachary							/P	T.Zachary			/P	L.Munns
/P	K.Weafer									/P	E.Burkart			/P	C.Pippen
/P	G.Ford									/P	H.Harris			/P	B.McGee
										/P	L.Bertrand			/P	B.Cox
										/P	P.Pezzullo			/P	N.Potter

TEAM	G	W	L	PCT	GB	R	OR	AB	H	2B	3B	HR	BB	SO	AVG	OBP	SLG	PRO	PRO+	BR	/A	PF	CHI	RC	SB	CS	SBA	SBR
NY	154	92	62	.597		742	621	5449	1529	237	48	97	431	452	.281	.337	.395	.732	104	19	27	99	99	744	31			
STL	155	87	67	.565	5	795	794	5537	1554	332	60	88	442	577	.281	.336	.410	.746	106	40	43	100	103	772	69			
CHI	154	87	67	.565	5	755	603	5409	1545	275	36	76	491	462	.286	.349	.392	.741	104	44	27	102	97	757	68			
PIT	156	84	70	.545	8	804	718	5586	1596	283	80	60	517	502	.286	.349	.397	.746	105	56	38	102	100	798	37			
CIN	154	74	80	.481	18	722	760	5393	1476	224	73	82	410	584	.274	.329	.388	.717	106	-14	-30	94	104	699	68			
BOS	157	71	83	.461	21	631	715	5478	1450	207	45	67	433	582	.265	.322	.356	.678	94	-86	-45	94	98	635	23			
BRO	156	67	87	.435	25	662	752	5574	1518	263	43	33	390	458	.272	.323	.353	.676	87	-92	-98	101	104	649	55			
PHI	154	54	100	.351	38	726	874	5465	1538	250	46	103	451	586	.281	.339	.401	.740	95	32	-44	110	96	757	50			
TOT	620					5837		43891	12206	2071	431	606	3565	4203	.278	.335	.386	.722							401			

TEAM	CG	SH	SV	IP	H	H/G	HR	BB	SO	RAT	ERA	ERA+	OAV	OOB	PR	/A	PF	CPI	FA	E	DP	FW	PW	BW	SBW	DIF
NY	60	12	22	1385²	1458	9.5	75	401	500	12.2	3.46	113	.273	.327	86	67	97	110	.974	168	164	1.1	6.5	2.6		4.7
STL	65	5	24	1398	1610	10.4	89	434	559	13.4	4.47	88	.289	.344	-71	-84	98	98	.974	156	134	1.9	-8.2	4.2		12.1
CHI	77	18	10	1382¹	1413	9.2	77	434	597	12.2	3.54	113	.265	.324	74	68	99	104	.976	146	156	2.4	6.6	2.6		-1.6
PIT	67	5	12	1395¹	1475	9.5	74	379	559	12.1	3.89	104	.269	.319	20	25	101	92	.967	199	113	-.5	2.4	3.7		1.4
CIN	50	6	23	1367¹	1576	10.4	51	418	459	13.3	4.22	91	.287	.341	-31	-61	95	97	.969	191	150	-.2	-6.0	2.9		.2
BOS	61	7	13	1413¹	1566	10.0	69	451	421	13.0	3.94	97	.281	.337	12	-18	95	103	.971	189	175	.1	-1.8	-4.4		.0
BRO	59	7	18	1403	1466	9.4	84	528	651	13.0	3.98	104	.266	.333	5	22	103	97	.966	208	107	-1.0	2.1	-9.6		-1.6
PHI	51	7	14	1365¹	1630	10.7	87	515	454	14.4	4.64	98	.292	.356	-95	-17	113	100	.959	252	144	-3.7	-1.7	-4.3		-13.4
TOT	490	67	136	11110¹		9.9				12.9	4.02		.278	.335					.969	1509	1143					

Runs
Vaughan-Pit 122
P.Martin-StL 121
Ott-NY 120
Medwick-StL 115
Suhr-Pit 111

Hits
Medwick-StL 223
P.Waner-Pit 218
Demaree-Chi 212
Herman-Chi 211
Moore-NY 205

Doubles
Medwick-StL 64
Herman-Chi 57
P.Waner-Pit 53
Moore-StL 39
Moore-Bos 38

Triples
Goodman-Cin 14
Medwick-StL 13
Camilli-Phi 13

Home Runs
Ott-NY 33
Camilli-Phi 28
Klein-Chi-Phi 25
Berger-Bos 25
Mize-StL 19

Total Bases
Medwick-StL 367
Ott-NY 314
Klein-Chi-Phi 308
Camilli-Phi 306
P.Waner-Pit 304

Runs Batted In
Medwick-StL 138
Ott-NY 135
Suhr-Pit 118
Klein-Chi-Phi 104

Runs Produced
Medwick-StL 235
Ott-NY 222
Suhr-Pit 218
P.Waner-Pit 196
Vaughan-Pit 191

Bases On Balls
Vaughan-Pit 118
Camilli-Phi 116
Ott-NY 111
Suhr-Pit 95
Hack-Chi 89

Batting Average
P.Waner-Pit .... .373
Phelps-Bro .... .367
Medwick-StL ...... .351
Demaree-Chi ...... .350
Vaughan-Pit ...... .335

On Base Percentage
Vaughan-Pit ...... .453
Ott-NY .... .448
P.Waner-Pit ...... .446
Camilli-Phi .... .441
Suhr-Pit .... .410

Slugging Average
Ott-NY .... .588
Camilli-Phi .... .577
Mize-StL .... .577
Medwick-StL ...... .577
P.Waner-Pit ...... .520

Production
Ott-NY 1.036
Camilli-Phi 1.018
P.Waner-Pit ...... .965
Medwick-StL ...... .964
Vaughan-Pit ...... .927

Adjusted Production
Ott-NY 179
Medwick-StL 157
Camilli-Phi 156
P.Waner-Pit 156
Vaughan-Pit 146

Batter Runs
Ott-NY 61.9
Camilli-Phi 58.0
P.Waner-Pit 51.4
Vaughan-Pit 47.3
Medwick-StL 46.9

Adjusted Batter Runs
Ott-NY 63.5
P.Waner-Pit 48.4
Medwick-StL 47.4
Camilli-Phi 44.9
Vaughan-Pit 44.3

Clutch Hitting Index
Brubaker-Pit 147
Young-Pit 131
Suhr-Pit 124
Herman-Chi 115
Whitney-Bos-Phi .. 114

Runs Created
Ott-NY 153
Camilli-Phi 148
Medwick-StL 141
P.Waner-Pit 140
Vaughan-Pit 137

Total Average
Ott-NY 1.188
Camilli-Phi 1.162
Vaughan-Pit 1.034
P.Waner-Pit 1.016
Medwick-StL ...... .956

Stolen Bases
P.Martin-StL 23
S.Martin-StL 17
Hack-Chi 17
Chiozza-Phi 17

Stolen Base Average

Stolen Base Runs

Fielding Runs
Bartell-NY 44.8
Whitehead-NY 29.2
Kampouris-Cin ... 28.0
Berres-Bro 23.0

Total Player Rating
Bartell-NY 5.7
Medwick-StL 5.3
Ott-NY 5.2
Herman-Chi 5.0
P.Waner-Pit 4.9

Wins
Hubbell-NY 26
D.Dean-StL 24
Derringer-Cin 19

Win Percentage
Hubbell-NY ...... .813
Lucas-Pit .... .789
French-Chi .... .667
D.Dean-StL ...... .649
Lee-Chi .... .621

Games
Derringer-Cin 51
D.Dean-StL 51
Passeau-Phi 49
Brown-Pit 47

Complete Games
D.Dean-StL 28
Hubbell-NY 25
Mungo-Bro 22
MacFayden-Bos ... 21
Lee-Chi 20

Shutouts
Warneke-Chi 4
Walters-Phi 4
Smith-NY 4
Lee-Chi 4
French-Chi 4
Carleton-Chi 4
Blanton-Pit 4

Saves
D.Dean-StL 11
Brennan-Cin 9
Smith-Bos 8
Johnson-Phi 7
Coffman-NY 7

Innings Pitched
D.Dean-StL 315.0
Mungo-Bro 311.2
Hubbell-NY 304.0
Derringer-Cin 282.1
MacFayden-Bos ..266.2

Fewest Hits/Game
Hubbell-NY 7.85
Mungo-Bro 7.94
Lee-Chi 8.28
D.Dean-StL 8.86
Blanton-Pit 8.97

Fewest BB/Game
Lucas-Pit 1.33
Derringer-Cin 1.34
D.Dean-StL 1.51
Hubbell-NY 1.69
Gabler-NY 1.89

Strikeouts
Mungo-Bro 238
D.Dean-StL 195
Blanton-Pit 127
Hubbell-NY 123
Derringer-Cin 121

Strikeouts/Game
Mungo-Bro 6.87
D.Dean-StL 5.57
Blanton-Pit 4.85
Weaver-Pit 4.31
Warneke-Chi 4.23

Ratio
Hubbell-NY 9.68
D.Dean-StL 10.46
Lucas-Pit 10.61
Blanton-Pit 11.19
Davis-Phi-Chi 11.35

Earned Run Average
Hubbell-NY 2.31
MacFayden-Bos ..2.87
Gabler-NY 3.12
D.Dean-StL 3.17
Lucas-Pit 3.18

Adjusted ERA
Hubbell-NY 169
MacFayden-Bos .. 134
Passeau-Phi 130
Lucas-Pit 128
Gabler-NY 125

Opponents' Batting Avg.
Mungo-Bro .... .234
Hubbell-NY ...... .236
Lee-Chi........... .246
D.Dean-StL ...... .253
Blanton-Pit .... .257

Opponents' On Base Pct.
Hubbell-NY ...... .276
D.Dean-StL ...... .285
Lucas-Pit .... .287
Blanton-Pit .... .301
Mungo-Bro .... .305

Starter Runs
Hubbell-NY 57.7
MacFayden-Bos .. 34.0
D.Dean-StL 29.6
Mungo-Bro 23.1
Lee-Chi 20.4

Adjusted Starter Runs
Hubbell-NY 53.5
MacFayden-Bos .. 28.5
Mungo-Bro 27.0
D.Dean-StL 26.9
Passeau-Phi 25.4

Clutch Pitching Index
Schumacher-NY .. 120
Gabler-NY 119
Chaplin-Bos 111
Smith-NY 110
Carleton-Chi 109

Relief Runs
Bryant-Chi 4.6
Coffman-NY 1.4

Adjusted Relief Runs
Bryant-Chi 4.4
Johnson-Phi 2.9

Relief Ranking
Johnson-Phi 3.2
Bryant-Chi 2.1

Total Pitcher Index
Hubbell-NY 5.5
Passeau-Phi 3.3
D.Dean-StL 2.8
Mungo-Bro 2.8
MacFayden-Bos ... 2.7

Total Baseball Ranking
Bartell-NY 5.7
Hubbell-NY 5.5
Medwick-StL 5.3
Ott-NY 5.2
Herman-Chi 5.0

February 2 The baseball writers vote for the first players to be named to the new Baseball Hall of Fame. Ty Cobb, Babe Ruth, Honus Wagner, Christy Mathewson, and Walter Johnson each receive the requisite 75 percent of ballots cast. Active players also are eligible in this first election, with Hornsby finishing 9th, Cochrane 10th, Gehrig 15th, and Foxx 19th. Tainted former star Hal Chase receives 11 votes for 25th place, and Joe Jackson gets two votes to tie for 36th place.

April 29* Nagoya defeats Daitokyo 8–5 in the first professional baseball game played in Japan.

May 3 Joe DiMaggio makes his regular-season debut with the Yankees and has three hits, one a triple, as New York routs St. Louis 14–5.

May 24 Yankees second baseman Tony Lazzeri sets several slugging marks with two grand slams, a third home run, and a triple for 15 total bases in a 25–2 slaughter of the Athletics at Shibe Park. He has hit seven home runs in four games and six in three games. He also sets a new AL mark of 11 RBI in one game.

June 19 Joe McCarthy is named to manage the AL All-Stars, rather than the high-strung Mickey Cochrane, who is very close to a nervous breakdown.

June 24 Joe DiMaggio ties three major league records in New York's 10-run fifth inning against the White Sox, hitting two home runs for eight total bases. With two doubles, he equals the modern record of four long hits in a game. New York wins 18-11.

July 19 Bob Feller makes his major league debut in relief. He pitches the eighth inning at Washington, giving up no hits and fanning one.

August 21 Wes Ferrell, in a tantrum for what he considers shabby support, walks off the mound during a Yankee rally and is suspended and fined $1,000 by Boston manager Joe Cronin. It is the second time in five days he has walked off the mound, having done it in Boston last Sunday in a game against the Senators. Ferrell, furious when he hears about the fine, says he will not pay it. "They can suspend me or trade me, but they're not getting any dough from me." The Red Sox lift the suspension in four days and will trade Ferrell after the season.

August 23 Seventeen-year-old Bob Feller makes his first start and strikes out 15, one less than the AL record, as Cleveland beats St. Louis 4-1. He'll break the AL mark and ties the major league standard on September 13 with 17 strikeouts.

October 2 The Yankees score a still-standing World Series record 18 runs, as they demolish the Giants 18-4.

October 6 The Yankees roll to a 13-5 Series-ending victory. Lefty Gomez is the winning pitcher. In the six games the Yankees score 43 runs to the Giants' 23.

October 16 Lou Gehrig, who hit 49 home runs, scored 167 runs, knocked in 152, and batted .354, is voted AL MVP by the BBWAA.

December 9 The AL okays night baseball for St. Louis. The NL adopts a new design for home plate. It will have beveled edges, the first change in 50 years. The AL adopts a rule stating that no batter can be batting champion unless he has 400 or more at bats.

BOSTON	CHICAGO	CLEVELAND	DETROIT	NEW YORK	PHILADELPHIA	ST.LOUIS	WASHINGTON
M J.Cronin	M J.Dykes	M S.O'Neill	M M.Cochrane	M J.McCarthy	M C.Mack	M R.Hornsby	M B.Harris
1B J.Foxx	1B Z.Bonura	1B H.Trosky	M D.Baker	1B L.Gehrig	1B L.Finney	1B J.Bottomley	1B J.Kuhel
2B S.Melillo	2B J.Hayes	2B R.Hughes	M M.Cochrane	2B T.Lazzeri	2B R.Warstler	2B T.Carey	2B O.Bluege
SS E.McNair	SS L.Appling	SS B.Knickerb'r	1B J.Burns	SS F.Crosetti	SS S.Newsome	SS L.Lary	SS C.Travis
3B B.Werber	3B J.Dykes	3B O.Hale	2B C.Gehringer	3B R.Rolfe	3B P.Higgins	3B H.Clift	3B B.Lewis
LF H.Manush	LF R.Radcliff	LF J.Vosmik	SS B.Rogell	LF J.DiMaggio	LF B.Johnson	LF M.Solters	LF J.Stone
CF D.Cramer	CF M.Kreevich	CF E.Averill	3B M.Owen	CF J.Powell	CF W.Moses	CF S.West	CF B.Chapman
RF D.Cooke	RF M.Haas	RF R.Weatherly	LF G.Goslin	RF G.Selkirk	RF G.Puccinelli	RF B.Bell	RF C.Reynolds
C R.Ferrell	C L.Sewell	C B.Sullivan	CF A.Simmons	C B.Dickey	C F.Hayes	C R.Hemsley	C C.Bolton
			RF G.Walker				
O M.Almada	23 T.Piet	C F.Pytlak	C R.Hayworth	O M.Hoag	1 C.Dean	C T.Giuliani	S2 R.Kress
23 J.Kroner	O L.Rosenthal	O B.Campbell		O R.Johnson	2 A.Niemiec	2 O.Bejma	O J.Hill
S3 J.Cronin	C F.Grube	O J.Gleeson	O P.Fox	O B.Chapman	S3 R.Peters	O E.Coleman	C W.Millies
C M.Berg	O D.Walker	C M.Galatzer	C M.Cochrane	C J.Glenn	C C.Moss	O R.Pepper	O J.Powell
1 B.Dahlgren	O G.Washington	C G.George	C G.Myatt	3 J.Saltzgaver	/2 D.Culler	/1 J.Burns	2 B.Myer
O F.Gaffke	/3 J.Morrissey	C B.Berger	C F.Reiber	C A.Jorgens	/2 H.Luby	/1 R.Hornsby	O F.Sington
O B.Miller	C M.Shea	C J.Becker	O J.White	/3 D.Heffner	/S J.Peerson		2 J.Mihalic
C G.Dickey	/O G.Stumpf	O J.Heath	1 H.Greenberg	/O B.Seeds	/O E.Mailho	P C.Hogsett	C S.Hogan
	/1 L.Rock		C B.Tebbetts	/O D.Walker	C C.Berry	P J.Knott	O D.Miles
P W.Ferrell		P J.Allen	/S F.Clifton		/O B.Nicholson	P I.Andrews	H B.Estalella
P L.Grove	P V.Kennedy	P M.Harder	/S S.Parker	P R.Ruffing	/1 J.Oglesby	P E.Caldwell	/C A.Sabo
P F.Ostermueller	P J.Whitehead	P O.Hildebrand	/3 G.English	P M.Pearson	/C B.Conroy	P T.Thomas	/C C.Starr
P J.Marcum	P S.Cain	P D.Galehouse		P J.Broaca		RP R.Van Atta	
P J.Wilson	P T.Lyons	P L.Brown	P T.Bridges	P L.Gomez	P H.Kelley	RP R.Mahaffey	P B.Newsom
	P M.Stratton	RP T.Lee	P S.Rowe	P B.Hadley	P G.Rhodes	RP G.Liebhardt	P J.DeShong
P R.Walberg	RP C.Brown	RP W.Hudlin	P E.Auker		P B.Ross		E.Whitehill
P J.Henry	RP R.Evans		P V.Sorrell	P P.Malone	P H.Fink	P L.Tietje	P P.Appleton
P J.Russell		P G.Blaeholder	P R.Lawson	P J.Murphy	P R.Gumpert	/P S.Jakucki	J.Cascarella
/P J.Welch	P I.Chelini	RP B.Feller	RP C.Kimsey	RP J.Brown		/P H.Kimberlin	RP J.Russell
P J.Cascarella	P B.Dietrich	/P A.Milnar	P T.Kleinhans		H.Lisenbee	/P M.Meola	P M.Weaver
/P M.Meola	P R.Phelps	/P R.Winegarner	R.Phillips	/P K.Wicker	B.Dietrich	/P S.Cain	E.Linke
/P T.Olson	/P B.Shores	/P B.Zuber	P J.Sullivan	/P S.Sundra	G.Turveville	/P J.Walkup	S.Cohen
/P J.Poindexter	/P W.Wyatt	/P G.Uhle	P J.Wade		/P C.Doyle		/P H.Coppola
/P S.Bowers	/P L.Tietje	/P P.Kardow	/P A.Crowder		P S.Flythe		/P F.Marberry
/P E.Dickman			C.Hogsett		/O F.Archer		/P J.Bokina
					/P W.Upchurch		/P B.Dietrich
					/P P.Naktenis		/P B.Phebus
					/P E.Smith		/P K.Chase
					/P W.Wilshere		
					P R.Bullock		
					/P H.Matuzak		
					/P H.Johnson		
					/P D.Lieber		

TEAM	G	W	L	PCT	GB	R	OR	AB	H	2B	3B	HR	BB	SO	AVG	OBP	SLG	PRO	PRO+	BR	/A	PF	CHI	RC	SB	CS	SBA	SBR
NY	155	102	51	.667		1065	731	5591	1676	315	83	182	700	594	.300	.381	.483	.864	124	162	200	97	100	1056	77	40	66	-1
DET	154	83	71	.539	19.5	921	871	5464	1638	326	55	94	640	462	.300	.377	.431	.808	106	57	54	100	98	912	73	49	60	-8
CHI	153	81	70	.536	20	920	873	5466	1597	282	56	60	684	417	.292	.374	.397	.771	94	-9	-41	104	104	851	66	29	69	2
WAS	153	82	71	.536	20	889	799	5433	1601	293	84	62	576	398	.295	.365	.414	.779	105	-7	41	94	104	847	104	42	71	6
CLE	157	80	74	.519	22.5	921	862	5646	1715	357	82	123	514	470	.304	.364	.461	.825	109	70	62	101	96	948	66	53	55	-12
BOS	155	74	80	.481	28.5	775	764	5383	1485	288	62	86	584	465	.276	.349	.400	.749	86	-72	-117	106	98	773	55	44	56	-10
STL	155	57	95	.375	44.5	804	1064	5391	1502	299	66	79	625	627	.279	.356	.403	.759	91	-51	-74	103	99	804	62	20	76	7
PHI	154	53	100	.346	49	714	1045	5373	1443	240	60	72	524	590	.269	.336	.376	.712	84	-151	-137	98	102	694	59	43	58	-8
TOT	618					7009		43747	12657	2400	548	758	4847	4023	.289	.363	.421	.784							562	320	64	-23

TEAM	CG	SH	SV	IP	H	H/G	HR	BB	SO	RAT	ERA	ERA+	OAV	OOB	PR	/A	PF	CPI	FA	E	DP	FW	PW	BW	SBW	DIF
NY	77	6	21	1400¹	1474	9.5	84	663	624	13.8	4.17	112	.271	.351	135	75	92	108	.973	163	148	.8	6.6	17.7	.2	.3
DET	76	13	13	1360	1568	10.4	100	562	526	14.2	5.00	99	.289	.358	6	-7	98	100	.975	153	159	1.3	-.6	4.8	-.4	1.0
CHI	80	5	8	1365	1603	10.6	104	578	414	14.5	5.06	103	.293	.363	-4	21	103	102	.973	168	174	.4	1.9	-3.6	.4	6.5
WAS	78	8	14	1345²	1484	9.9	73	588	462	14.0	4.58	104	.279	.363	68	29	95	101	.970	182	163	-.4	2.6	3.6	.8	-1.1
CLE	74	6	12	1389¹	1604	10.4	73	607	619	14.5	4.83	104	.289	.362	32	32	100	102	.971	178	154	.0	5.8	5.5	-.8	-4.6
BOS	78	11	9	1372¹	1501	9.8	78	552	584	13.6	4.39	121	.277	.346	99	142	106	102	.972	165	139	.7	12.5	-10.3	-.6	-5.2
STL	54	3	13	1348¹	1776	11.9	115	609	399	16.2	6.24	86	.314	.385	-180	-130	107	95	.969	188	143	-.6	-11.5	-6.5	.9	-1.2
PHI	68	3	12	1352¹	1645	10.9	131	696	405	15.7	6.08	84	.300	.381	-156	-146	101	94	.965	209	152	-1.9	-12.9	-12.1	-.4	3.8
TOT	585	55	102	10933¹		10.4				14.6	5.04		.289	.363					.971	1406	1232					

Runs		Hits		Doubles		Triples		Home Runs		Total Bases	
Gehrig-NY	167	Averill-Cle	232	Gehringer-Det	60	Rolfe-NY	15	Gehrig-NY	49	Trosky-Cle	405
Clift-StL	145	Gehringer-Det	227	Walker-Det	55	DiMaggio-NY	15	Trosky-Cle	42	Gehrig-NY	403
Gehringer-Det	144	Trosky-Cle	216	Chapman-NY-Was	50	Averill-Cle	15	Foxx-Bos	41	Averill-Cle	385
Crosetti-NY	137	Bell-StL	212	Hale-Cle	50	B.Johnson-Phi	14	DiMaggio-NY	29	Foxx-Bos	369
Averill-Cle	136	Radcliff-Chi	207					Averill-Cle	28	DiMaggio-NY	367

Runs Batted In		Runs Produced		Bases On Balls		Batting Average		On Base Percentage		Slugging Average	
Trosky-Cle	162	Gehrig-NY	270	Gehrig-NY	130	Appling-Chi	.388	Gehrig-NY	.478	Gehrig-NY	.696
Gehrig-NY	152	Bonura-Chi	246	Lary-StL	117	Averill-Cle	.378	Appling-Chi	.474	Trosky-Cle	.644
Foxx-Bos	143	Gehringer-Det	245	Clift-StL	115	Dickey-NY	.362	Foxx-Bos	.440	Foxx-Bos	.631
Bonura-Chi	138	Trosky-Cle	244	Foxx-Bos	105	Gehringer-Det	.354	Averill-Cle	.438	Averill-Cle	.627
Solters-StL	134	Averill-Cle	234	Lazzeri-NY	97	Gehrig-NY	.354	Gehringer-Det	.431	Dickey-NY	.617

Production		Adjusted Production		Batter Runs		Adjusted Batter Runs		Clutch Hitting Index		Runs Created	
Gehrig-NY	1.174	Gehrig-NY	193	Gehrig-NY	82.2	Gehrig-NY	88.8	Appling-Chi	132	Gehrig-NY	199
Foxx-Bos	1.071	Averill-Cle	159	Foxx-Bos	56.8	Averill-Cle	55.2	Sewell-Chi	131	Averill-Cle	168
Averill-Cle	1.065	Foxx-Bos	153	Averill-Cle	56.4	Foxx-Bos	48.2	Bonura-Chi	127	Foxx-Bos	168
Trosky-Cle	1.026	Trosky-Cle	148	Gehringer-Det	43.0	Gehringer-Det	42.6	Owen-Det	126	Gehringer-Det	157
Gehringer-Det	.987	Stone-Was	145	Trosky-Cle	41.9	Trosky-Cle	40.8	Vosmik-Cle	125	Trosky-Cle	150

Total Average		Stolen Bases		Stolen Base Average		Stolen Base Runs		Fielding Runs		Total Player Rating	
Gehrig-NY	1.426	Lary-StL	37	Lary-StL	80.4	Lary-StL	5.7	Hayes-Chi	17.1	Gehrig-NY	6.4
Foxx-Bos	1.238	Powell-Was-NY	26	Crosetti-NY	72.0	Hill-Was	3.3	Hale-Cle	16.5	Gehringer-Det	6.1
Averill-Cle	1.171	Werber-Bos	23	Powell-Was-NY	70.3	Stone-Was	2.4	Cramer-Bos	16.3	Appling-Chi	5.1
Appling-Chi	1.088	Chapman-NY-Was	20	Chapman-NY-Was	69.0	Sewell-Chi	2.1	Gehringer-Det	15.7	Averill-Cle	3.9
Gehringer-Det	1.075	Hughes-Cle	20	Hughes-Cle	69.0			Appling-Chi	15.2	Dickey-NY	3.8

Wins		Win Percentage		Games		Complete Games		Shutouts		Saves	
Bridges-Det	23	Pearson-NY	.731	VanAtta-StL	52	W.Ferrell-Bos	28	Grove-Bos	6	Malone-NY	9
Kennedy-Chi	21	Kennedy-Chi	.700	Knott-StL	47	Bridges-Det	26	Bridges-Det	5	Knott-StL	6
Ruffing-NY	20	Bridges-Det	.676			Ruffing-NY	25	Rowe-Det	4	Murphy-NY	5
W.Ferrell-Bos	20	Allen-Cle	.667			Newsom-Was	24	Newsom-Was	4	Brown-Chi	5
Allen-Cle	20	Rowe-Det	.655			Grove-Bos	22	Allen-Cle	4	Hildebrand-Cle	4

Innings Pitched		Fewest Hits/Game		Fewest BB/Game		Strikeouts		Strikeouts/Game		Ratio	
W.Ferrell-Bos	301.0	Pearson-NY	7.71	Lyons-Chi	2.23	Bridges-Det	175	Allen-Cle	6.11	Grove-Bos	10.87
Bridges-Det	294.2	Grove-Bos	8.42	Grove-Bos	2.31	Allen-Cle	165	Bridges-Det	5.35	Rowe-Det	12.18
Newsom-Was	285.2	Rowe-Det	8.67	Rowe-Det	2.35	Newsom-Was	156	Gomez-NY	5.01	Ruffing-NY	12.19
Kennedy-Chi	274.1	Gomez-NY	8.78	Andrews-StL	2.35	Grove-Bos	130	Newsom-Was	4.91	Allen-Cle	12.30
Ruffing-NY	271.0	Bridges-Det	8.83	Marcum-Bos	2.69	Pearson-NY	118	Pearson-NY	4.76	Appleton-Was	12.45

Earned Run Average		Adjusted ERA		Opponents' Batting Avg.		Opponents' On Base Pct.		Starter Runs		Adjusted Starter Runs	
Grove-Bos	2.81	Grove-Bos	189	Pearson-NY	.233	Grove-Bos	.297	Grove-Bos	62.8	Grove-Bos	70.6
Allen-Cle	3.44	Allen-Cle	146	Grove-Bos	.246	Rowe-Det	.321	Bridges-Det	46.9	Bridges-Det	44.1
Appleton-Was	3.53	Bridges-Det	137	Gomez-NY	.254	Ruffing-NY	.323	Allen-Cle	43.0	Allen-Cle	43.0
Bridges-Det	3.60	Appleton-Was	135	Appleton-Was	.254	Appleton-Was	.324	Ruffing-NY	35.7	W.Ferrell-Bos	37.8
Pearson-NY	3.71	Kelley-Phi	132	Bridges-Det	.255	Bridges-Det	.326	Appleton-Was	33.9	Kelley-Phi	32.4

Clutch Pitching Index		Relief Runs		Adjusted Relief Runs		Relief Ranking		Total Pitcher Index		Total Baseball Ranking	
Hadley-NY	116	Lee-Cle	2.1	Gumpert-Phi	2.3	Brown-Chi	2.0	Grove-Bos	7.0	Grove-Bos	7.0
Kelley-Phi	115	Gumpert-Phi	1.9	Lee-Cle	2.1	Lee-Cle	1.3	W.Ferrell-Bos	4.5	Gehrig-NY	6.4
Grove-Bos	115	Kimsey-Det	1.1	Brown-Chi	1.9	Gumpert-Phi	1.2	Allen-Cle	4.5	Gehringer-Det	6.1
Bridges-Det	109	Brown-Chi	.5	Kimsey-Det	.6	Kimsey-Det	.6	Bridges-Det	4.4	Appling-Chi	5.1
Thomas-StL	107							Ruffing-NY	3.9	W.Ferrell-Bos	4.5

March 20* Josh Gibson and Judy Johnson, two future Hall of Famers, are traded to the Homestead Grays for two journeymen players and $2,500. The transaction is called the biggest deal in Negro baseball history.

April 2 Dizzy Dean, Paul Dean, and Joe Medwick have a scuffle in a Tampa hotel lobby with New York *News* reporter Jack Miley and Chicago *Tribune* writer Irv Kupcinet.

April 22* Satchel Paige and Josh Gibson are among 18 black players who jump to the Dominican Republic league. Negro League owners regard this as desertion and plan to ban the players from the league. In May, Paige will be banned for life.

April 23 Carl Hubbell's first start of the season is a three-hitter against the Boston Bees. For the Giants ace, it is his 17th straight win, dating back to July 17 of last year.

April 25 Giants rookie pitcher Cliff Melton strikes out 13 in his first ML game but loses to the Boston Bees 3-1.

May 31 A Memorial Day crowd of 61,756, the second-largest crowd in Polo Grounds history, sees the Dodgers end Carl Hubbell's consecutive-game winning streak at 24 over two seasons. Brooklyn routs King Carl in the fourth inning and wins 10-3.

June 5 Gus Suhr's NL record of 822 consecutive games, started on September 11, 1931, ends when he attends his mother's funeral in San Francisco.

June 6 One of baseball's rarest feats takes place when Woody English of the Dodgers wins a suit by hitting the sign of clothier Abe Stark at the base of the Ebbets Field scoreboard.

June 27 Backed by two Mel Ott home runs, Carl Hubbell outpitches Dizzy Dean to give the Giants an 8–1 win over the Cards. This is the last time the two Hall of Famers will face each other; Hubbell has won 8 of the 11 matches.

August 6 For the first time in the century, the first two batters in a game—Roy Johnson and Rabbit Warstler of the Boston Bees—lead off with home runs. They do it off Cubs pitcher Tex Carleton.

September 18 Pittsburgh outfielder Paul Waner records his eighth year of 200 or more hits.

September 29 New York rookie Cliff Melton wins his 20th game in the opening game of a doubleheader, but the Phillies beat the Giants in the second game, preventing New York from clinching the flag, which they do the following day.

October 9 Carl Hubbell staves off a Yankee sweep with a 6-hit, 7-3 victory. The Giants score six runs in the second inning.

October 25 Casey Stengel signs to manage the Boston Bees.

November 9 St. Louis Cardinals Triple Crown winner Joe Medwick is named NL MVP by the BBWAA.

BOSTON		BROOKLYN		CHICAGO		CINCINNATI		NEW YORK		PHILADELPHIA		PITTSBURGH		ST.LOUIS	
M	B.McKechnie	M	B.Grimes	M	C.Grimm	M	C.Dressen	M	B.Terry	M	J.Wilson	M	P.Traynor	M	F.Frisch
1B	E.Fletcher	1B	B.Hassett	1B	R.Collins	1B	B.Jordan	1B	J.McCarthy	1B	D.Camilli	1B	G.Suhr	1B	J.Mize
2B	T.Cuccinello	2B	C.Lavagetto	2B	B.Herman	2B	A.Kampouris	2B	B.Whitehead	2B	D.Young	2B	L.Handley	2B	J.Brown
SS	R.Warstler	SS	W.English	SS	B.Jurges	SS	B.Myers	SS	D.Bartell	SS	G.Scharein	SS	A.Vaughan	SS	L.Durocher
3B	G.English	3B	J.Stripp	3B	S.Hack	3B	L.Riggs	3B	L.Chiozza	3B	P.Whitney	3B	B.Brubaker	3B	D.Gutteridge
LF	D.Garms	LF	T.Winsett	LF	A.Galan	LF	K.Cuyler	LF	J.Moore	LF	M.Arnovich	LF	W.Jensen	LF	J.Medwick
CF	V.DiMaggio	CF	J.Cooney	CF	J.Marty	CF	C.Hafey	CF	J.Ripple	CF	H.Martin	CF	L.Waner	CF	T.Moore
RF	G.Moore	RF	H.Manush	RF	F.Demaree	RF	I.Goodman	RF	M.Ott	RF	C.Klein	RF	P.Waner	RF	D.Padgett
C	A.Lopez	C	B.Phelps	C	G.Hartnett	C	E.Lombardi	C	H.Danning	C	A.Atwood	C	A.Todd	C	B.Ogrodowski
O	R.Johnson	O	G.Brack	O1	P.Cavarretta	1O	L.Scarsella	C	G.Mancuso	O1	E.Browne	S3	P.Young	3O	F.Bordagaray
C	R.Mueller	23	J.Bucher	C	K.O'Dea	O	H.Walker	O	W.Berger	O	J.Moore	O	J.Dickshot		P.Martin
3	E.Mayo	C	R.Spencer	S2	L.Frey	C	S.Davis	1	S.Leslie	23	L.Norris	C	T.Padden	C	M.Owen
O	W.Berger	S	L.Brown	O	T.Stainback	O	P.Weintraub	C	H.Leiber	/O	E.Grace	/O	F.Schulte	2	S.Martin
O	B.Reis	O	G.Rosen	C	S.Davis	3	J.Outlaw	O	K.Davis	/3	J.Wilson	/3	P.Traynor	/1	D.Siebert
S	T.Thevenow	O	E.Wilson	O	P.Weintraub	O	K.Davis	S	B.Ryan	/C	W.Stephenson	/C	R.Berres	C	H.Bremer
/O	B.McGowan	/1	E.Morgan	/O	C.Reynolds	S	C.Gelbert	/S	M.Haslin	/O	F.Tauby	/S	B.Schuster	/2	F.Frisch
H	B.Jordan	O	G.Cisar	H	B.Garbark	1	F.McCormick	/O	E.Madjeski	/O	H.Gorman	P	C.Blanton	/O	R.Moore
/C	J.Riddle	S	J.Daniel		D.Meyer	3	C.English	/O	P.Weintraub	/3	G.Corbett	P	R.Bauers	P	B.Weiland
H	B.Urbanski		J.Hudson	P	B.Lee	S	E.Miller	P	C.Hubbell	/3	B.Andrus	P	E.Brandt	P	L.Warneke
/C	L.Wasem	/O	B.Haas	P	L.French	O	H.Craft	P	C.Melton	P	C.Passeau	P	B.Swift	P	D.Dean
P	L.Fette	C	R.Moore	P	T.Carleton	C	G.Campbell	P	H.Schumacher	P	B.Walters	P	J.Bowman	P	S.Johnson
P	J.Turner	/3	N.Polly	P	C.Root	/O	P.Jorgensen	P	H.Gumbert	P	W.LaMaster	RP	M.Brown	P	M.Ryba
P	D.MacFayden		A.Parks	P	R.Parmelee	/O	D.Mele	P	S.Castleman	P	H.Mulcahy		R.Lucas	RP	R.Harrell
P	G.Bush	/C	E.Klumpp	RP	C.Shoun	/C	D.Moore	RP	A.Smith	P	S.Johnson	P	J.Weaver	P	J.Haines
P	J.Lanning	H	S.Gautreaux	P	C.Bryant	/2	E.Joost	RP	D.Coffman	RP	J.Jorgens	P	J.Tobin	P	J.Winford
RP	I.Hutchinson	/2	G.Fallon	P	C.Davis	H	D.Dwyer	P	T.Baker	RP	H.Kelleher	P	W.Hoyt	S	S.Blake
P	F.Gabler	P	M.Butcher	/P	B.Logan	/C	G.Brittain	/P	F.Fitzsimmons	P	P.Sivess	/P	K.Heintzelman	/P	T.Sunkel
P	B.Smith	P	L.Hamlin	/P	K.Higbe	H	A.Moser	/P	B.Lohrman	/P	E.Burkart			/P	H.Krist
/P	M.Shoffner	P	F.Frankhouse	/P	N.Kimball	/C	H.Chozen	/P	D.Brennan	/P	B.Allen			/P	N.Kleinke
P	R.Weir	P	W.Hoyt			P	L.Grissom	/P	J.Brown	/P	L.Crawford			/P	B.McGee
/P	V.Frasier	P	V.Mungo			P	P.Derringer	/P	F.Gabler	/P	L.Pettit			/P	N.Andrews
		RP	G.Jeffcoat			P	P.Davis	/P	H.Vandenberg	/P	W.Masters			/P	A.White
		P	R.Henshaw			P	A.Hollingsworth	/P	B.Cantwell	/P	B.Burke			/P	J.Chambers
		P	F.Fitzsimmons			P	G.Schott							/P	P.Dean
		P	H.Eisenstat			P	J.Vander Meer								
		P	J.Lindsey			P	B.Hallahan								
		P	R.Birkofer			P	J.Cascarella								
		P	B.Cantwell			P	W.Moore								
		/P	B.Marrow			P	J.Mooty								
		/P	T.Baker			/P	T.Kleinhans								
		/P	J.Peterson			P	D.Brennan								
		/P	W.Clark			/P	J.Brown								
						/P	P.Gehrman								
						/P	R.Barrett								

TEAM	G	W	L	PCT	GB	R	OR	AB	H	2B	3B	HR	BB	SO	AVG	OBP	SLG	PRO	PRO+	BR	/A	PF	CHI	RC	SB	CS	SBA	SBR
NY	152	95	57	.625		732	602	5329	1484	251	41	**111**	412	492	.278	.334	.403	.737	105	40	31	101	100	734	45			
CHI	154	93	61	.604	1	**811**	682	5349	1537	253	74	96	**538**	496	**.287**	**.355**	**.416**	**.771**	111	117	83	104	98	734	71			
PIT	154	86	68	.558	10	704	646	5433	**1550**	223	**86**	47	463	480	.285	.343	.384	.727	104	30	30	100	96	734	32			
STL	157	81	73	.526	15	789	733	5476	1543	**264**	67	94	385	569	.282	.331	.406	.737	104	36	21	102	**107**	744	**78**			
BOS	152	79	73	.520	16	579	**556**	5124	1265	200	41	63	465	707	.247	.314	.339	.653	91	-109	-59	91	102	565	45			
BRO	155	62	91	.405	33.5	616	772	5295	1401	258	53	37	469	583	.265	.327	.354	.681	90	-57	-67	102	97	629	69			
PHI	155	61	92	.399	34.5	724	869	5424	1482	258	37	103	478	640	.273	.334	.391	.725	95	21	-38	108	100	730	66			
CIN	155	56	98	.364	40	612	707	5230	1329	215	59	73	437	586	.254	.315	.360	.675	94	-78	-49	95	102	599	53			
TOT	617					5567		42660	11591	1922	458	624	3667	4553	.272	.332	.382	.714							459			

TEAM	CG	SH	SV	IP	H	H/G	HR	BB	SO	RAT	ERA	ERA+	OAV	OOB	PR	/A	PF	CPI	FA	E	DP	FW	PW	BW	SBW	DIF
NY	67	11	17	1361	**1341**	8.9	85	404	**653**	11.7	3.43	113	**.258**	.314	73	69	99	102	.974	159	143	.9	**6.8**	3.1		8.2
CHI	73	11	13	1381¹	1434	9.3	91	502	596	12.8	3.97	100	.267	.332	-10	0	102	99	**.975**	151	141	1.5	.0	**8.2**		6.3
PIT	67	12	17	1366¹	1398	9.2	71	428	643	12.2	3.56	108	.264	.321	53	45	99	101	.970	181	135	-.2	4.5	3.0		1.8
STL	81	10	4	1392	1546	10.0	95	448	571	13.0	3.98	100	.281	.337	-10	-1	102	**105**	.973	164	127	1.0	-.0	2.1		1.1
BOS	**85**	**16**	10	1359¹	1344	8.9	60	**372**	387	**11.4**	**3.22**	111	.259	**.310**	105	55	92	103	**.975**	157	128	1.0	5.5	-5.9		2.4
BRO	63	5	8	1362²	1470	9.7	68	476	592	13.0	4.13	98	.274	.336	-33	-14	103	96	.964	217	127	-2.2	-1.4	-6.6		-4.3
PHI	59	6	15	1373²	1629	10.7	116	501	529	14.2	5.05	86	.297	.359	-174	-114	111	97	.970	184	**157**	-.3	-11.3	-3.8		-.1
CIN	64	10	**18**	1358¹	1428	9.5	**38**	533	581	13.1	3.94	95	.270	.339	-4	-32	95	97	.966	208	139	-1.6	-3.2	-4.9		-11.3
TOT	559	81	102	10954²		9.5				12.7	3.91		.272	.332					.971	1421	1097					

Runs
Medwick-StL 111
Herman-Chi 106
Hack-Chi 106
Galan-Chi 104
Demaree-Chi 104

Hits
Medwick-StL 237
P.Waner-Pit 219
Mize-StL 204
Demaree-Chi 199
Herman-Chi 189

Doubles
Medwick-StL 56
Mize-StL 40
Bartell-NY 38
Phelps-Bro 37
Moore-NY 37

Triples
Vaughan-Pit 17
Suhr-Pit 14
Handley-Pit 12
Goodman-Cin 12
Herman-Chi 11

Home Runs
Ott-NY 31
Medwick-StL 31
Camilli-Phi 27
Mize-StL 25
Galan-Chi 18

Total Bases
Medwick-StL 406
Mize-StL 333
Demaree-Chi 298
Ott-NY 285
Camilli-Phi 279

Runs Batted In
Medwick-StL 154
Demaree-Chi 115
Mize-StL 113
Suhr-Pit 97
Ott-NY 95

Runs Produced
Medwick-StL 234
Demaree-Chi 202
Mize-StL 191
Hack-Chi 167
P.Waner-Pit 166

Bases On Balls
Ott-NY 102
Camilli-Phi 90
Suhr-Pit 83
Hack-Chi 83
Galan-Chi 79

Batting Average
Medwick-StL ..... .374
Mize-StL ..... .364
Hartnett-Chi ..... .354
P.Waner-Pit ..... .354
Whitney-Phi ..... .341

On Base Percentage
Camilli-Phi ..... .446
Mize-StL ..... .427
Medwick-StL ..... .414
P.Waner-Pit ..... .413
Ott-NY ..... .408

Slugging Average
Medwick-StL ..... .641
Mize-StL ..... .595
Camilli-Phi ..... .587
Hartnett-Chi ..... .548
Ott-NY ..... .523

Production
Medwick-StL 1.056
Camilli-Phi 1.034
Mize-StL 1.021
Ott-NY ..... .931
Herman-Chi ..... .875

Adjusted Production
Medwick-StL 179
Mize-StL 171
Camilli-Phi 165
Ott-NY 149
P.Waner-Pit 132

Batter Runs
Medwick-StL 68.8
Mize-StL 57.4
Camilli-Phi 54.9
Ott-NY 41.2
Hartnett-Chi 31.1

Adjusted Batter Runs
Medwick-StL 65.9
Mize-StL 54.9
Camilli-Phi 45.4
Ott-NY 39.8
P.Waner-Pit 29.8

Clutch Hitting Index
Scharein-Phi 136
Durocher-StL 133
Suhr-Pit 129
Jurges-Chi 124
Todd-Pit 120

Runs Created
Medwick-StL 170
Mize-StL 150
Camilli-Phi 137
Ott-NY 128
P.Waner-Pit 118

Total Average
Camilli-Phi 1.189
Medwick-StL 1.113
Mize-StL 1.097
Ott-NY 1.021
Vaughan-Pit ..... .864

Stolen Bases
Galan-Chi 23
Hack-Chi 16

Fielding Runs
Bartell-NY 37.5
Whitehead-NY 26.1
Riggs-Cin 19.5
Herman-Chi 18.6
Young-Pit 18.1

Total Player Rating
Medwick-StL 6.2
Bartell-NY 6.1
Herman-Chi 5.2
Ott-NY 3.7
Camilli-Phi 3.3

Wins
Hubbell-NY 22
Turner-Bos 20
Melton-NY 20
Fette-Bos 20
Warneke-StL 18

Win Percentage
Hubbell-NY ..... .733
Melton-NY ..... .690
Fette-Bos ..... .667
Carleton-Chi ..... .667
Turner-Bos ..... .645

Games
Mulcahy-Phi 56
Jorgens-Phi 52

Complete Games
Turner-Bos 24
Fette-Bos 23
Weiland-StL 21

Shutouts
Turner-Bos 5
Grissom-Cin 5
Fette-Bos 5

Saves
Melton-NY 7
Brown-Pit 7
Grissom-Cin 6
Root-Chi 5
Hollingsworth-Cin 5

Innings Pitched
Passeau-Phi 292.1
Lee-Chi 272.1
Weiland-StL 264.1
Hubbell-NY 261.2
Fette-Bos 259.0

Fewest Hits/Game
Mungo-Bro 7.60
Grissom-Cin 7.77
Melton-NY 7.84
Carleton-Chi 7.91
Turner-Bos 7.99

Fewest BB/Game
D.Dean-StL 1.51
Root-Chi 1.61
Hoyt-Pit-Bro 1.66
Turner-Bos 1.82
Castleman-NY 1.85

Strikeouts
Hubbell-NY 159
Grissom-Cin 149
Blanton-Pit 143
Melton-NY 142

Strikeouts/Game
Mungo-Bro 6.82
Grissom-Cin 6.00
Bauers-Pit 5.66
Henshaw-Bro 5.64
LaMaster-Phi 5.51

Ratio
Turner-Bos 9.82
Melton-NY 10.05
Castleman-NY 10.16
Root-Chi 10.53
D.Dean-StL 10.72

Earned Run Average
Turner-Bos 2.38
Melton-NY 2.61
D.Dean-StL 2.69
Bauers-Pit 2.88
Fette-Bos 2.88

Adjusted ERA
Turner-Bos 150
Melton-NY 149
D.Dean-StL 148
Mungo-Bro 139
Bauers-Pit 134

Opponents' Batting Avg.
Mungo-Bro ..... .229
Grissom-Cin ..... .232
Melton-NY ..... .233
Turner-Bos ..... .235
Carleton-Chi ..... .236

Opponents' On Base Pct.
Turner-Bos ..... .274
Melton-NY ..... .280
Castleman-NY ..... .287
Root-Chi ..... .290
D.Dean-StL ..... .291

Starter Runs
Turner-Bos 43.5
Melton-NY 35.8
Fette-Bos 29.5
MacFayden-Bos 26.9
D.Dean-StL 26.7

Adjusted Starter Runs
Melton-NY 35.0
Turner-Bos 34.2
D.Dean-StL 28.2
Bauers-Pit 20.5
Mungo-Bro 20.1

Clutch Pitching Index
Johnson-StL 128
Brandt-Pit 124
Weiland-StL 115
Frankhouse-Bro 113
MacFayden-Bos 112

Relief Runs
Coffman-NY 7.8
Hutchinson-Bos 1.8

Adjusted Relief Runs
Coffman-NY 7.5

Relief Ranking
Coffman-NY 9.9

Total Pitcher Index
Turner-Bos 4.5
Melton-NY 3.9
Mungo-Bro 3.0
D.Dean-StL 3.0
Fette-Bos 2.5

Total Baseball Ranking
Medwick-StL 6.2
Bartell-NY 6.1
Herman-Chi 5.2
Turner-Bos 4.5
Melton-NY 3.9

January 19 Nap Lajoie, Tris Speaker, and Cy Young are voted into the Baseball Hall of Fame by the BBWAA.

May 25 After hitting a home run against the Yankees in his prior at bat, Mickey Cochrane suffers a skull fracture from a Bump Hadley pitch and will never return to active play.

June 1 White Sox hurler Bill Dietrich pitches an 8–0 no-hitter against the Browns. It is the third no-hitter Luke Sewell has caught, having previously been behind the plate for Wes Ferrell in 1931 and Vern Kennedy in 1935.

June 3 Josh Gibson is credited with a drive that hits just two feet below the rim of Yankee Stadium, about 580 feet from home plate. It is estimated that the ball would have traveled nearly 700 feet.

July 7 Lou Gehrig leads the AL All-Stars over the NL 8-3 with a home run, double, and four RBI. FDR attends the game in Washington. Dizzy Dean's toe is fractured by a drive off the bat of Earl Averill. After the injury Dean is unable to pitch with the same delivery. He uses an unnatural motion, causing an arm injury from which he never recovers.

August 29 The A's set a new AL record in the opener of a doubleheader with the White Sox by scoring 12 runs in the first inning, six of which are driven in by Bob Johnson.

August 31 Detroit's rookie Rudy York sets a new record for home runs in a month, hitting his 17th and 18th to eclipse Babe Ruth's mark set in September 1927. He knocks in seven runs against Pete Appleton, as Detroit beats Washington 12-3.

September 2 The first two batters in a game—the White Sox Boze Berger and Mike Kreevich—hit home runs, victimizing Boston's Johnny Marcum. This is the first time two AL batters have opened with home runs.

September 17 Cleveland's Johnny Allen wins his 12th straight without a loss, equaling Tom Zachary's 1929 record of 12-0.

September 19 Hank Greenberg's home run in Detroit's 8–1 win over New York is the first ever hit into the center field stands at Yankee Stadium.

September 23 The Yankees lose 9–5 but clinch the pennant when the Red Sox beat Detroit.

October 6 Carl Hubbell and Lefty Gomez duel in the opening game of the World Series, a rematch of last year's teams. The Yankees score seven runs in the sixth inning on five singles, three walks, and two errors. Tony Lazzeri homers in the bottom of the eighth to make the final score 8-1.

October 10 Lefty Gomez wins again, and the Yankees wrap up the Series. Gomez himself knocks in the winning run in the 4-2 clincher. It is a record fifth World Series win, without a loss, for Gomez.

November 2 AL batting champ Charlie Gehringer is named MVP by the BBWAA.

	BOSTON		CHICAGO		CLEVELAND		DETROIT		NEW YORK		PHILADELPHIA		ST.LOUIS		WASHINGTON
M	J.Cronin	M	J.Dykes	M	S.O'Neill	M	M.Cochrane	M	J.McCarthy	M	C.Mack	M	R.Hornsby	M	B.Harris
1B	J.Foxx	1B	Z.Bonura	1B	H.Trosky	M	D.Baker	1B	L.Gehrig	M	E.Mack	1B	J.Bottomley	1B	J.Kuhel
2B	E.McNair	2B	J.Hayes	2B	J.Kroner	M	M.Cochrane	2B	T.Lazzeri	1B	C.Dean	1B	H.Davis	2B	B.Myer
SS	J.Cronin	SS	L.Appling	SS	L.Lary	M	D.Baker	SS	F.Crosetti	2B	R.Peters	2B	T.Carey	SS	C.Travis
3B	P.Higgins	3B	T.Piet	3B	O.Hale	M	C.Perkins	3B	R.Rolfe	SS	S.Newsome	SS	B.Knickerb'r	3B	B.Lewis
LF	B.Mills	LF	R.Radcliff	LF	M.Solters	1B	H.Greenberg	LF	J.Powell	3B	B.Werber	3B	H.Clift	LF	A.Simmons
CF	D.Cramer	CF	M.Kreevich	CF	E.Averill	2B	C.Gehringer	CF	J.DiMaggio	LF	B.Johnson	LF	J.Vosmik	CF	M.Almada
RF	B.Chapman	RF	D.Walker	RF	B.Campbell	SS	B.Rogell	RF	M.Hoag	CF	J.Hill	CF	S.West	RF	J.Stone
C	G.Desautels	C	L.Sewell	C	F.Pytlak	3B	M.Owen	C	B.Dickey	RF	W.Moses	RF	B.Bell	C	R.Ferrell
						LF	G.Walker			C	E.Brucker	C	R.Hemsley		
O	F.Gaffke	3	B.Berger	32	R.Hughes	CF	J.White	O	G.Selkirk					O	F.Sington
O	D.Dallessandro	1	M.Haas	C	B.Sullivan	RF	P.Fox	O	T.Henrich	1O	L.Finney	O	E.Allen	C	W.Millies
2	B.Doerr	3	M.Connors	O	R.Weatherly	C	R.York	2S	D.Heffner	O	J.Rothrock	C	B.Huffman	C	B.Chapman
C	M.Berg	O	L.Rosenthal	O	J.Heath			C	J.Glenn	C	F.Hayes	1	J.Bottomley	S	O.Bluege
O	M.Almada	13	J.Dykes	C	J.Becker	O	C.Laabs	O	R.Johnson	2	W.Ambler	2	R.Barkley	1	J.Wasdell
C	R.Ferrell	O	H.Steinbacher	/O	H.Alexander	O	G.Goslin	2	A.Jorgens	C	B.Cissell	2	N.Lipscomb	2	J.Mihalic
2	S.Melillo	C	M.Shea	/2	B.Monaco	C	B.Tebbetts	/1	J.Saltzgaver	1	G.Hasson	O	E.Silber	O	J.Hill
/C	J.Peacock	C	T.Rensa	/3	K.Keltner	H	M.Cochrane	S	A.Parker	C	B.Conroy	2	R.Hornsby	O	G.Case
R	S.Bowers			H	B.Sodd	C	B.Hayworth			2S	W.Huston	C	T.Giuliani	C	S.Hogan
R	B.Daughters	P	V.Kennedy			2	G.English	P	L.Gomez	/O	B.Barna	C	T.Heath	2	J.Bloodworth
		P	T.Lee	P	M.Harder	C	C.Bolton	P	R.Ruffing	H	D.Morris	/C	S.Harshany	/C	J.Riddle
P	L.Grove	P	T.Lyons	P	D.Galehouse	C	C.Gelbert	/O	B.Hadley	/O	E.Yount	H	M.Mazzera	/C	M.Gray
P	J.Wilson	P	J.Whitehead	P	W.Hudlin	/3	F.Clifton	/O	M.Pearson	/C	H.Wagner	/O	T.Cafego	/S	F.Trechock
P	B.Newsom	P	M.Stratton	P	J.Allen	/O	B.Herman	RP	J.Murphy					/C	H.Crompton
P	J.Marcum	RP	C.Brown	RP	B.Feller			RP	F.Makosky			P	O.Hildebrand	/C	M.Guerra
P	A.McKain			RP	L.Brown	P	E.Auker			P	G.Caster	P	J.Knott	/2	J.Lynn
		P	B.Dietrich	RP	W.Wyatt	P	T.Bridges	P	P.Malone	P	H.Kelley	P	C.Hogsett	/C	A.Sabo
P	R.Walberg	P	J.Rigney	RP	J.Heving	P	R.Lawson	P	K.Wicker	P	E.Smith	P	J.Walkup		
P	F.Ostermueller	P	S.Cain			P	J.Wade	P	S.Chandler	P	B.Thomas	P	J.Bonetti	P	J.DeShong
P	W.Ferrell	/P	B.Cox	P	E.Whitehill	P	B.Poffenberger	P	I.Andrews	P	B.Ross			P	W.Ferrell
P	T.Olson	/P	I.Chelini	P	I.Andrews			/P	J.Broaca	RP	H.Fink	P	B.Trotter	P	M.Weaver
/P	J.Gonzales	/P	G.Gick	/P	K.Jungels	P	G.Gill	/P	J.Vance	RP	G.Turbeville	P	L.Koupal	P	P.Appleton
/P	J.Henry			/P	C.Fischer	P	S.Coffman					P	R.Van Atta	P	E.Linke
/P	T.Thomas					P	J.Russell			P	L.Nelson	P	S.Blake	RP	S.Cohen
						P	P.McLaughlin			P	A.Williams	P	T.Thomas		
						P	S.Rowe			P	R.Gumpert	/P	L.Tietje	P	K.Chase
						/P	V.Sorrell			/P	B.Kalfass	/P	E.Caldwell		C.Fischer
						/P	C.Hatter			/P	F.Archer	/P	B.Strickland	P	B.Newsom
						/P	B.Logan					/P	H.Kimberlin	/P	B.Phebus
												/P	L.Mills	/P	J.Krakauskas
												/P	E.Bildilli	/P	J.Cascarella
												/P	G.Hennessey	P	B.Jacobs
												/P	E.Baecht	/P	J.Kohlman
												/P	B.Miller	P	R.Anderson
												/P	B.Muncrief	/P	D.Lanahan

TEAM	G	W	L	PCT	GB	R	OR	AB	H	2B	3B	HR	BB	SO	AVG	OBP	SLG	PRO	PRO+	BR	/A	PF	CHI	RC	SB	CS	SBA	SBR
NY	157	102	52	.662		979	671	5487	1554	282	73	174	709	607	.283	.369	.456	.825	113	112	106	101	103	952	60	36	63	-4
DET	155	89	65	.578	13	935	841	5516	1611	309	62	150	656	711	.292	.370	.452	.822	111	106	85	102	100	947	89	45	66	0
CHI	154	86	68	.558	16	780	730	5277	1478	280	76	67	549	447	.280	.350	.400	.750	95	-38	-37	100	103	763	70	34	67	1
CLE	156	83	71	.539	19	817	768	5353	1499	304	76	103	570	551	.280	.352	.423	.775	100	4	-1	101	101	813	78	51	60	-7
BOS	154	80	72	.526	21	821	775	5354	1506	269	64	100	601	557	.281	.357	.411	.768	96	-1	-32	104	102	804	79	61	56	-13
WAS	158	73	80	.477	28.5	757	841	5578	1559	245	84	47	591	503	.279	.351	.379	.730	94	-74	-40	96	100	767	61	35	64	-3
PHI	154	54	97	.358	46.5	699	854	5228	1398	278	60	94	583	557	.267	.341	.397	.738	93	-63	-52	98	97	732	95	48	66	0
STL	156	46	108	.299	56	715	1023	5510	1573	327	44	71	514	510	.285	.348	.399	.747	93	-47	-52	101	93	780	30	27	53	-7
TOT	622					6503		43303	12178	2294	539	806	4773	4443	.281	.355	.415	.770							562	337	63	-34

TEAM	CG	SH	SV	IP	H	H/G	HR	BB	SO	RAT	ERA	ERA+	OAV	OOB	PR	/A	PF	CPI	FA	E	DP	FW	PW	BW	SBW	DIF
NY	82	15	21	1396	1417	9.1	92	506	652	12.5	3.65	122	.261	.325	151	124	96	103	.972	170	134	.2	11.4	9.7	.0	3.7
DET	70	6	11	1378	1521	9.9	102	635	485	14.2	4.87	96	.279	.357	-38	-30	101	95	.976	147	149	1.4	-2.8	7.8	.4	5.2
CHI	70	15	21	1351¹	1435	9.6	115	532	533	13.2	4.17	110	.273	.341	68	65	100	104	.971	174	173	-.2	6.0	-3.4	.5	6.2
CLE	64	4	15	1364²	1529	10.1	61	566	630	14.0	4.39	105	.285	.356	35	33	100	102	.974	159	153	.8	3.0	-.0	-.3	2.5
BOS	74	6	14	1366	1518	10.0	92	597	682	14.0	4.48	106	.279	.352	21	41	103	100	.970	177	139	-.4	3.8	-2.9	-.8	4.4
WAS	75	5	14	1398²	1498	9.6	96	671	524	14.1	4.58	97	.275	.357	7	-23	96	99	.972	170	181	.3	-2.1	-3.7	.1	1.9
PHI	65	6	9	1335	1490	10.0	105	613	469	14.3	4.85	97	.281	.358	-35	-21	102	97	.967	198	150	-1.7	-1.9	-4.8	.4	-13.5
STL	55	2	8	1363	1768	11.7	143	653	468	16.2	6.00	80	.315	.390	-209	-178	105	100	.972	173	166	-.0	-16.3	-4.8	-.3	-9.6
TOT	555	59	113	10952²		10.0				14.1	4.62		.281	.355					.972	1368	1245					

Runs		Hits		Doubles		Triples		Home Runs		Total Bases	
DiMaggio-NY	151	Bell-StL	218	Bell-StL	51	Walker-Chi	16	DiMaggio-NY	46	DiMaggio-NY	418
Rolfe-NY	143	DiMaggio-NY	215	Greenberg-Det	49	Kreevich-Chi	16	Greenberg-Det	40	Greenberg-Det	397
Gehrig-NY	138	Walker-Det	213	Moses-Phi	48	Stone-Was	15	Gehrig-NY	37	Gehrig-NY	366
Greenberg-Det	137	Lewis-Was	210	Vosmik-StL	47	DiMaggio-NY	15	Foxx-Bos	36	Moses-Phi	357
Gehringer-Det	133	Gehringer-Det	209	Lary-Cle	46	Greenberg-Det	14	York-Det	35	Trosky-Cle	329

Runs Batted In		Runs Produced		Bases On Balls		Batting Average		On Base Percentage		Slugging Average	
Greenberg-Det	183	Greenberg-Det	280	Gehrig-NY	127	Gehringer-Det	.371	Gehrig-NY	.473	DiMaggio-NY	.673
DiMaggio-NY	167	DiMaggio-NY	272	Greenberg-Det	102	Gehrig-NY	.351	Gehringer-Det	.458	Greenberg-Det	.668
Gehrig-NY	159	Gehrig-NY	260	Foxx-Bos	99	DiMaggio-NY	.346	Greenberg-Det	.436	York-Det	.651
Dickey-NY	133	Gehringer-Det	215	Johnson-Phi	98	Bonura-Chi	.345	Johnson-Phi	.425	Gehrig-NY	.643
Trosky-Cle	128	Foxx-Bos	202	Clift-StL	98	Travis-Was	.344	Dickey-NY	.417	Bonura-Chi	.573

Production		Adjusted Production		Batter Runs		Adjusted Batter Runs		Clutch Hitting Index		Runs Created	
Gehrig-NY	1.116	Gehrig-NY	177	Gehrig-NY	73.3	Gehrig-NY	72.3	Hayes-Chi	152	Gehrig-NY	181
Greenberg-Det	1.105	Greenberg-Det	171	Greenberg-Det	67.2	Greenberg-Det	63.7	Higgins-Bos	127	Greenberg-Det	178
DiMaggio-NY	1.085	DiMaggio-NY	168	DiMaggio-NY	61.3	DiMaggio-NY	60.4	Myer-Was	125	DiMaggio-NY	173
Dickey-NY	.987	Johnson-Phi	147	Gehringer-Det	44.0	Gehringer-Det	41.1	Hale-Cle	117	Gehringer-Det	140
Bonura-Chi	.984	Bonura-Chi	146	Dickey-NY	37.5	Johnson-Phi	36.8	Werber-Phi	116	Clift-StL	134

Total Average		Stolen Bases		Stolen Base Average		Stolen Base Runs		Fielding Runs		Total Player Rating	
Gehrig-NY	1.339	Chapman-Was-Bos	35	Hill-Was-Phi	81.8	Chapman-Was-Bos	3.3	Clift-StL	41.0	Clift-StL	7.2
Greenberg-Det	1.277	Werber-Phi	35	Walker-Det	76.7	Hill-Was-Phi	3.0	Hale-Cle	25.9	DiMaggio-NY	6.0
DiMaggio-NY	1.207	Walker-Det	23	Pytlak-Cle	76.2	Werber-Phi	2.7	Hayes-Chi	20.5	Gehringer-Det	5.2
Gehringer-Det	1.089			Chapman-Was-Bos	74.5	Walker-Det	2.7	Appling-Chi	13.8	Dickey-NY	5.1
Johnson-Phi	1.083			Werber-Phi	72.9	Kreevich-Chi	2.4	Dickey-NY	12.3	Greenberg-Det	4.7

Wins		Win Percentage		Games		Complete Games		Shutouts		Saves	
Gomez-NY	21	Allen-Cle	.938	Brown-Chi	53	W.Ferrell-Bos-Was	26	Gomez-NY	6	Brown-Chi	18
Ruffing-NY	20	Stratton-Chi	.750	Wilson-Bos	51	Gomez-NY	25	Stratton-Chi	5	Murphy-NY	10
Lawson-Det	18	Ruffing-NY	.741	Newsom-Was-Bos	41	Ruffing-NY	22	Whitehead-Chi	4	Wilson-Bos	7
Grove-Bos	17	Lawson-Det	.720	Kelley-Phi	41	Grove-Bos	21	Ruffing-NY	4	Malone-NY	6
Auker-Det	17	Gomez-NY	.656	Heving-Cle	40	DeShong-Was	20	Appleton-Was	4		

Innings Pitched		Fewest Hits/Game		Fewest BB/Game		Strikeouts		Strikeouts/Game		Ratio	
W.Ferrell-Bos-Was	281.0	Gomez-NY	7.53	Stratton-Chi	2.02	Gomez-NY	194	Gomez-NY	6.27	Stratton-Chi	9.89
Gomez-NY	278.1	Stratton-Chi	7.76	Hudlin-Cle	2.20	Newsom-Was-Bos	166	Wilson-Bos	5.57	Gomez-NY	10.57
Newsom-Was-Bos	275.1	Smith-Phi	8.15	Marcum-Bos	2.30	Grove-Bos	153	Newsom-Was-Bos	5.43	Ruffing-NY	10.92
DeShong-Was	264.1	Allen-Cle	8.17	Ruffing-NY	2.39	Feller-Cle	150	Grove-Bos	5.26	Allen-Cle	11.55
Grove-Bos	262.0	Ruffing-NY	8.50	Lyons-Chi	2.39	Bridges-Det	138	Bridges-Det	5.06	Lee-Chi	11.87

Earned Run Average		Adjusted ERA		Opponents' Batting Avg.		Opponents' On Base Pct.		Starter Runs		Adjusted Starter Runs	
Gomez-NY	2.33	Stratton-Chi	191	Gomez-NY	.223	Stratton-Chi	.280	Gomez-NY	70.9	Gomez-NY	65.5
Stratton-Chi	2.40	Gomez-NY	191	Stratton-Chi	.234	Gomez-NY	.287	Ruffing-NY	46.6	Grove-Bos	50.2
Allen-Cle	2.55	Allen-Cle	181	Smith-Phi	.242	Ruffing-NY	.296	Grove-Bos	46.5	Ruffing-NY	41.6
Ruffing-NY	2.98	Grove-Bos	157	Allen-Cle	.244	Lee-Chi	.312	Stratton-Chi	40.6	Stratton-Chi	40.2
Grove-Bos	3.02	Ruffing-NY	149	Ruffing-NY	.247	Allen-Cle	.313	Allen-Cle	39.8	Allen-Cle	39.6

Clutch Pitching Index		Relief Runs		Adjusted Relief Runs		Relief Ranking		Total Pitcher Index		Total Baseball Ranking	
Allen-Cle	120	Brown-Chi	13.3	Brown-Chi	13.1	Brown-Chi	21.9	Gomez-NY	6.5	Clift-StL	7.2
Whitehead-Chi	119	Cohen-Was	9.2	Cohen-Was	9.2	Cohen-Was	9.2	Stratton-Chi	4.5	Gomez-NY	6.5
Knott-StL	112	Murphy-NY	5.5	Fink-Phi	5.9	Murphy-NY	5.3	Grove-Bos	4.0	DiMaggio-NY	6.0
Grove-Bos	111	Fink-Phi	5.1	Murphy-NY	3.3	Fink-Phi	2.2	Ruffing-NY	3.7	Gehringer-Det	5.2
Galehouse-Cle	110	Wyatt-Cle	1.5	Wyatt-Cle	1.4	Wyatt-Cle	.8	Auker-Det	2.9	Dickey-NY	5.1

January 18 Grover Cleveland Alexander is elected to the Baseball Hall of Fame, the only player to get the required 75 percent of the BBWAA votes.

March 23 Judge Landis frees 74 Cardinal minor leaguers, among them Pete Reiser, in yet another attempt to halt the farm system "cover-up." Dodger GM Larry MacPhail makes a pact with Branch Rickey to take the unknown player and swap him back in the future, but Reiser's ability is too great to hide.

April 16 Dizzy Dean is sold by the Cardinals to the Chicago Cubs. The Cubs pay $200,000 and send pitcher Curt Davis and Clyde Shoun to St. Louis. The Cardinals also buy Tuck Stainback from the Cubs for $15,000.

April 19 In the top of the first inning at Philadelphia, Dodger Ernie Koy homers in his first major league at bat. In the bottom of the inning, leadoff man Emmett Mueller also hits a home run in his first time up in the major leagues.

May 5 Harold Kelleher of the Phillies faces 16 batters in the sixth inning, as the Cubs score 12 runs. Both marks are NL records off one hurler in a single inning. The Cubs win 21–2 with Joe Marty tallying four runs, four RBI, and four hits. The loss goes to Wayne LeMaster who threw just three pitches to leadoff batter Stan Hack before leaving the game with an injury.

June 15 Johnny Vander Meer stuns baseball by pitching his second successive no-hitter, defeating the Dodgers 6-0, as Brooklyn plays the first night game ever at Ebbets Field. In front of 38,748 fans, Vandy strikes out seven and walks eight, including three walks in the ninth. A force at home and a fly ball end the game. In a pregame event, Ernie Koy, with a 10-yard start, beats Olympic champion Jesse Owens in the 100-yard dash.

June 18 Babe Ruth is signed as a Dodgers coach for the rest of the season. He is in uniform for batting demonstrations the following day.

July 6 The NL wins the sixth All-Star Game 4–1, with the aid of fine pitching and four AL errors. Starter Johnny Vander Meer gets the win.

August 2 Larry MacPhail has official baseballs dyed dandelion yellow, and they are used in the first game of a doubleheader between the Dodgers and Cardinals at Ebbets Field. The Dodgers win 6-2, but Johnny Mize hits a Freddie Fitzsimmons knuckleball for the first "yellow" home run. The Dodgers will use up their yellow balls in three more games in 1939.

September 28 Cubs manager Gabby Hartnett hits the homer in the gloamin' against Mace Brown in the bottom of the ninth to break a 5-5 tie and put the Cubs in first place ahead of the Pirates. With two outs and none on base, the umpires intended to call the game because of darkness after Hartnett's turn at bat.

October 1 The Cubs clinch the pennant, beating the Cards in the second game of a twin bill while the Reds beat the Pirates.

November 1 NL batting champ Ernie Lombardi is named MVP by the BBWAA. Chicago pitcher Bill Lee is runner-up.

	BOSTON		BROOKLYN		CHICAGO		CINCINNATI		NEW YORK		PHILADELPHIA		PITTSBURGH		ST.LOUIS
M	C.Stengel	M	B.Grimes	M	C.Grimm	M	B.McKechnie	M	B.Terry	M	J.Wilson	M	P.Traynor	M	F.Frisch
1B	E.Fletcher	1B	D.Camilli	1B	G.Hartnett	1B	F.McCormick	1B	J.McCarthy	1B	H.Lobert	1B	G.Suhr	M	M.Gonzalez
2B	T.Cuccinello	2B	J.Hudson	1B	R.Collins	2B	L.Frey	2B	A.Kampouris	1B	P.Weintraub	2B	P.Young	1B	J.Mize
SS	R.Warstler	SS	L.Durocher	2B	B.Herman	SS	B.Myers	SS	D.Bartell	2B	H.Mueller	SS	A.Vaughan	2B	S.Martin
3B	J.Stripp	3B	C.Lavagetto	SS	B.Jurges	3B	L.Riggs	3B	M.Ott	SS	D.Young	3B	L.Handley	SS	L.Myers
LF	M.West	LF	B.Hassett	3B	S.Hack	LF	W.Berger	LF	J.Moore	3B	P.Whitney	LF	J.Rizzo	3B	D.Gutteridge
CF	V.DiMaggio	CF	E.Koy	LF	A.Galan	CF	H.Craft	CF	H.Leiber	LF	M.Arnovich	CF	L.Waner	LF	J.Medwick
RF	J.Cooney	RF	G.Rosen	CF	C.Reynolds	RF	I.Goodman	RF	J.Ripple	CF	H.Martin	RF	P.Waner	CF	T.Moore
C	R.Mueller	C	B.Phelps	RF	F.Demaree	C	E.Lombardi	C	H.Danning	RF	C.Klein	C	A.Todd	RF	E.Slaughter
				C	G.Hartnett					C	B.Atwood			C	M.Owen
O3	D.Garms	O	K.Cuyler			O	D.Cooke	O	B.Seeds			O	W.Jensen		
C	A.Lopez	C	G.Campbell	O1	P.Cavarretta	C	W.Hershberger	2O	L.Chiozza	S2	G.Scharein	3	B.Brubaker	2S	J.Brown
O	G.Moore	C	M.Shea	C	K.O'Dea	S	N.Richardson	S3	G.Myatt	31	B.Jordan	C	R.Berres	O1	D.Padgett
3	G.English	O	T.Stainback	O	J.Marty	/O	L.Gamble	O	G.Mancuso	O	G.Brack	O	J.Dickshot	O	P.Martin
O	H.Maggert	2	P.Coscarart	S	T.Lazzeri	2	A.Kampouris	1	S.Leslie	O	S.Davis	/2	T.Thevenow	3	J.Stripp
S	J.Hitchcock	3	W.English	C	B.Garbark	3	D.Lang	2	B.Cissell	O	T.Stainback	H	H.Manush	O	F.Bordagaray
C	J.Riddle	O	O.Hockett	O	C.Triplett	C	S.Davis	32	M.Haslin	1	G.Corbett			C	H.Bremer
/O	R.Johnson	O	G.Brack	O	J.Asbell	/O	K.Davis	/O	W.Berger	1	E.Browne	P	R.Bauers	2	J.Bucher
/3	E.Mayo	/S	F.Sington	/S	S.Mesner	/S	J.Stein	/2	B.Ryan	C	C.Clark	P	J.Tobin	O	H.Epps
/S	J.Walsh	O	H.Manush	/S	B.Mattick	/O	N.Bongiovanni	H	L.Powers	/3	J.Stein	P	C.Blanton	/S	C.Crespi
/O	R.McLeod	S	W.Williams			H	B.Jordan			/S	E.Feinberg	P	B.Klinger	/O	T.Stainback
/C	B.Sutcliffe	C	R.Spencer	P	B.Lee	H	D.West	P	C.Melton	/O	A.Pitko	P	B.Swift	H	D.Siebert
H	B.Kahle	/S	P.Rogers	P	C.Bryant	R	J.Outlaw	P	H.Gumbert	/O	R.Stoviak	RP	M.Brown		
/2	T.Kane	/O	T.Winsett	P	L.French			P	H.Schumacher	/O	A.Rebel			P	B.Weiland
		C	P.Chervinko	P	T.Carleton	P	P.Derringer	P	C.Hubbell	/C	J.Wilson	P	E.Brandt	P	B.McGee
P	J.Turner	/C	G.George	P	C.Root	P	J.Vander Meer	P	B.Lohrman	H	H.Gorman	P	R.Lucas	P	L.Warneke
P	L.Fette	/C	R.Hayworth	RP	J.Russell	P	B.Walters	RP	D.Coffman			P	J.Bowman	P	C.Davis
P	D.MacFayden	/C	R.Thomas			P	P.Davis	RP	J.Brown	P	H.Mulcahy	P	R.Sewell	P	R.Henshaw
P	I.Hutchinson	H	B.Haas			P	J.Weaver			P	C.Passeau	/P	K.Heintzelman	RP	C.Shoun
P	M.Shoffner			P	V.Page	RP	G.Schott	P	S.Castleman	P	A.Hollingsworth			RP	R.Harrell
		P	L.Hamlin	/P	A.Epperly	RP	J.Cascarella	P	J.Wittig	M.Butcher					
		P	F.Fitzsimmons	P	B.Logan			/P	H.Vandenberg	RP	B.Sivess			P	M.Macon
P	J.Lanning	P	T.Pressnell	/P	K.Higbe	P	W.Moore	/P	T.Baker	RP	A.Smith			P	M.Lanier
P	D.Errickson	P	V.Tamulis	/P	N.Kimball	P	L.Grissom	/P	O.Georgy			B.Hallahan	/P	P.Dean
PO	B.Reis	P	B.Posedel			/P	A.Hollingsworth			P	S.Johnson	/P	M.Cooper	
/P	R.Weir					/P	R.Barrett			P	B.Walters	/P	S.Johnson	
/P	T.Earley	P	V.Mungo			/P	R.Benge			P	W.LaMaster	/P	G.Bush	
/P	T.Reis	P	F.Frankhouse			/P	T.Kleinhans			/P	E.Burkart	/P	M.Ryba	
/P	A.Doll	P	M.Butcher							/P	H.Kelleher	/P	P.Roe	
/P	H.Moran	P	L.Rogers							/P	T.Lanning	/P	H.Krist	
/P	A.Kenney	P	B.Marrow							/P	T.Reis			
/P	J.Niggeling	P	W.Hoyt							/P	E.Heusser			
/P	M.Balas	/P	J.Gaddy											
/P	F.Gabler	/P	W.LaMaster											
		/P	S.Nahem											
		/P	J.Winford											
		/P	D.Potter											

TEAM	G	W	L	PCT	GB	R	OR	AB	H	2B	3B	HR	BB	SO	AVG	OBP	SLG	PRO	PRO+	BR	/A	PF	CHI	RC	SB	CS	SBA	SBR
CHI	154	89	63	.586		713	598	5333	1435	242	70	65	522	476	.269	.338	.377	.715	100	25	6	103	101	689	49			
PIT	152	86	64	.573	2	707	630	5422	1511	265	66	65	485	409	.279	.340	.388	.728	106	48	43	101	96	727	47			
NY	152	83	67	.553	5	705	637	5255	1424	210	36	125	465	528	.271	.334	.396	.730	106	45	39	101	99	715	31			
CIN	151	82	68	.547	6	723	634	5391	1495	251	57	110	366	518	.277	.327	.406	.733	110	43	62	97	101	720	19			
BOS	153	77	75	.507	12	561	618	5250	1311	199	39	54	424	548	.250	.309	.333	.642	91	-119	-66	90	104	549	49			
STL	156	71	80	.470	17.5	725	721	5528	1542	288	74	91	412	492	.279	.331	.407	.738	103	56	14	106	97	752	55			
BRO	151	69	80	.463	18.5	704	710	5142	1322	225	79	61	611	615	.257	.338	.367	.705	98	13	-3	102	103	671	66			
PHI	151	45	105	.300	43	550	840	5192	1318	233	29	40	423	507	.254	.312	.333	.645	85	-111	-96	97	101	549	38			
TOT	610					5388		42513	11358	1913	450	611	3708	4093	.267	.329	.376	.705							354			

TEAM	CG	SH	SV	IP	H	H/G	HR	BB	SO	RAT	ERA	ERA+	OAV	OOB	PR	/A	PF	CPI	FA	E	DP	FW	PW	BW	SBW	DIF
CHI	67	16	18	1396²	1414	9.1	71	454	583	12.1	3.37	113	.262	.322	64	66	101	105	.978	135	151	2.3	6.6	.6		3.5
PIT	57	8	15	1379¹	1406	9.2	71	432	557	12.2	3.46	109	.266	.324	49	50	100	106	.974	163	168	.5	5.0	4.3		1.2
NY	59	8	18	1349	1370	9.1	87	389	497	11.9	3.62	104	.261	.314	24	20	99	97	.973	168	147	.2	2.0	3.9		1.9
CIN	72	11	16	1362	1329	8.8	75	463	542	11.9	3.62	101	.254	.316	25	3	96	94	.971	172	133	-.1	.3	6.2		.6
BOS	83	15	12	1380	1375	9.0	66	465	413	12.2	3.40	101	.258	.322	58	3	91	103	.972	173	136	-.0	.3	-6.6		7.4
STL	58	10	16	1384²	1482	9.6	77	474	534	12.8	3.84	103	.272	.333	-9	17	104	102	.967	199	145	-1.4	1.7	1.4		-6.2
BRO	56	12	14	1332	1464	9.9	88	446	469	13.1	4.07	96	.278	.338	-42	-26	103	102	.973	157	148	.8	-2.6	-.3		-3.3
PHI	68	3	6	1329¹	1516	10.3	76	582	492	14.4	4.93	79	.285	.358	-169	-155	103	92	.966	201	135	-1.8	-15.6	-9.7		-2.9
TOT	520	83	115	10913¹		9.4				12.6	3.78		.267	.329					.972	1368	1163					

Runs		Hits		Doubles		Triples		Home Runs		Total Bases	
Ott-NY	116	McCormick-Cin	209	Medwick-StL	47	Mize-StL	16	Ott-NY	36	Mize-StL	326
Hack-Chi	109	Hack-Chi	195	McCormick-Cin	40	Gutteridge-StL	15	Goodman-Cin	30	Medwick-StL	316
Camilli-Bro	106	L.Waner-Pit	194	Young-Pit	36	Suhr-Pit	14	Mize-StL	27	Ott-NY	307
Goodman-Cin	103	Medwick-StL	190	Martin-Phi	36	Riggs-Cin	13	Camilli-Bro	24	Goodman-Cin	303
Medwick-StL	100	Mize-StL	179			Koy-Bro	13	Rizzo-Pit	23	Rizzo-Pit	285

Runs Batted In		Runs Produced		Bases On Balls		Batting Average		On Base Percentage		Slugging Average	
Medwick-StL	122	Medwick-StL	201	Camilli-Bro	119	Lombardi-Cin	.342	Ott-NY	.442	Mize-StL	.614
Ott-NY	116	Ott-NY	196	Ott-NY	118	Mize-StL	.337	Vaughan-Pit	.433	Ott-NY	.583
Rizzo-Pit	111	McCormick-Cin	190	Vaughan-Pit	104	McCormick-Cin	.327	Mize-StL	.422	Medwick-StL	.536
McCormick-Cin	106	Rizzo-Pit	185	Hack-Chi	94	Medwick-StL	.322	Hack-Chi	.411	Goodman-Cin	.533
Mize-StL	102	Camilli-Bro	182	Suhr-Pit	87	Vaughan-Pit	.322	Suhr-Pit	.394	Lombardi-Cin	.524

Production		Adjusted Production		Batter Runs		Adjusted Batter Runs		Clutch Hitting Index		Runs Created	
Mize-StL	1.036	Ott-NY	178	Ott-NY	61.9	Ott-NY	60.8	Durocher-Bro	140	Ott-NY	149
Ott-NY	1.024	Mize-StL	172	Mize-StL	59.2	Mize-StL	52.2	McCormick-Cin	134	Mize-StL	141
Lombardi-Cin	.915	Lombardi-Cin	154	Vaughan-Pit	36.4	Goodman-Cin	36.4	Arnovich-Phi	128	Hack-Chi	119
Medwick-StL	.905	Goodman-Cin	149	Medwick-StL	34.4	Vaughan-Pit	35.6	Todd-Pit	127	Goodman-Cin	116
Goodman-Cin	.901	Vaughan-Pit	140	Goodman-Cin	33.5	Lombardi-Cin	34.4	Lavagetto-Bro	125	Vaughan-Pit	115

Total Average		Stolen Bases		Stolen Base Average		Stolen Base Runs		Fielding Runs		Total Player Rating	
Ott-NY	1.164	Hack-Chi	16					Young-Pit	31.8	Vaughan-Pit	6.4
Mize-StL	1.104	Lavagetto-Bro	15					Herman-Chi	24.8	Ott-NY	6.1
Camilli-Bro	.964	Koy-Bro	15					Bartell-NY	22.4	Lombardi-Cin	3.8
Vaughan-Pit	.960	Vaughan-Pit	14					Vaughan-Pit	18.3	Goodman-Cin	3.7
Goodman-Cin	.908	Gutteridge-StL	14					Arnovich-Phi	16.7	Hack-Chi	3.6

Wins		Win Percentage		Games		Complete Games		Shutouts		Saves	
Lee-Chi	22	Lee-Chi	.710	Coffman-NY	51	Derringer-Cin	26	Lee-Chi	9	Coffman-NY	12
Derringer-Cin	21	Bryant-Chi	.633	Brown-Pit	51	Turner-Bos	22	MacFayden-Bos	5	Root-Chi	8
Bryant-Chi	19	Brown-Pit	.625	McGee-StL	47	Walters-Phi-Cin	20	Warneke-StL	4	Hamlin-Bro	6
Weiland-StL	16	VanderMeer-Cin	.600	Mulcahy-Phi	46	MacFayden-Bos	19	Derringer-Cin	4	Errickson-Bos	6
		Derringer-Cin	.600			Lee-Chi	19				

Innings Pitched		Fewest Hits/Game		Fewest BB/Game		Strikeouts		Strikeouts/Game		Ratio	
Derringer-Cin	307.0	VanderMeer-Cin	7.07	Davis-StL	1.40	Bryant-Chi	135	Hubbell-NY	5.23	Hubbell-NY	10.36
Lee-Chi	291.0	Bauers-Pit	7.67	Derringer-Cin	1.44	Derringer-Cin	132	VanderMeer-Cin	4.99	Derringer-Cin	10.67
Bryant-Chi	270.1	Bryant-Chi	7.82	Hubbell-NY	1.66	VanderMeer-Cin	125	Weiland-StL	4.61	Root-Chi	10.92
Turner-Bos	268.0	MacFayden-Bos	8.52	Root-Chi	1.68	Lee-Chi	121	Bryant-Chi	4.49	Turner-Bos	10.95
Mulcahy-Phi	267.1	Klinger-Pit	8.59	Turner-Bos	1.81					Lee-Chi	11.04

Earned Run Average		Adjusted ERA		Opponents' Batting Avg.		Opponents' On Base Pct.		Starter Runs		Adjusted Starter Runs	
Lee-Chi	2.66	Lee-Chi	144	VanderMeer-Cin	.213	Hubbell-NY	.285	Lee-Chi	36.3	Lee-Chi	37.6
Root-Chi	2.86	Root-Chi	134	Bauers-Pit	.233	Derringer-Cin	.291	Derringer-Cin	29.1	Derringer-Cin	24.3
Derringer-Cin	2.93	Fitzsimmons-Bro	129	Bryant-Chi	.235	Root-Chi	.294	Bryant-Chi	20.6	Bryant-Chi	21.8
MacFayden-Bos	2.95	Klinger-Pit	127	MacFayden-Bos	.247	Lohrman-NY	.294	MacFayden-Bos	20.3	Fitzsimmons-Bro	19.8
Klinger-Pit	2.99	Derringer-Cin	124	Schumacher-NY	.248	Schumacher-NY	.299	Bauers-Pit	19.2	Bauers-Pit	19.4

Clutch Pitching Index		Relief Runs		Adjusted Relief Runs		Relief Ranking		Total Pitcher Index		Total Baseball Ranking	
Lee-Chi	119	Brown-NY	19.8	Brown-NY	19.6	Brown-NY	18.1	Lee-Chi	4.0	Vaughan-Pit	6.4
Pressnell-Bro	111	Russell-Chi	5.0	Russell-Chi	5.5	Coffman-NY	4.3	Bryant-Chi	2.4	Ott-NY	6.1
Blanton-Pit	111	Coffman-NY	3.8	Coffman-NY	3.5	Russell-Chi	3.7	Derringer-Cin	2.4	Lee-Chi	4.0
Tamulis-Bro	110							Fitzsimmons-Bro	2.3	Lombardi-Cin	3.8
Fette-Bos	110							Bauers-Pit	2.1	Goodman-Cin	3.7

April 24 Goose Goslin's pinch-hit home run is the fifth of his career, for a new AL record, but the Yankees beat the Senators 4–3.

May 3 Lefty Grove defeats the Tigers 4-3 in 10 innings for the first of a record 20 consecutive victories at his new home field, Fenway Park in Boston. He will not lose there until May 12, 1941.

May 30 The largest crowd in Yankee Stadium history, 83,533, sees Red Ruffing end Lefty Grove's eight-game winning streak in a 10–0 victory over the Red Sox. Six thousand fans are turned away, and 511 are given refunds because there is no place to sit. The Yankees also take the second game of the doubleheader, 5–4, in a game made famous for a fight between Yankee outfielder Jake Powell and Boston player-manager Joe Cronin.

June 16 Jimmie Foxx is walked a record six consecutive times by Browns pitchers, as the Red Sox win 12–8.

August 20 Lou Gehrig hits a first inning grand slam, the 23rd and last of his career for a still-standing record. It comes off Buck Ross of the A's.

August 24* Virgil Trucks strikes out his 418th batter—the highest season total in organized ball—for Andalusia in the Alabama-Florida League game.

August 27 Yankees pitcher Monte Pearson tosses a no-hitter in the second game of a doubleheader with Cleveland, winning his 10th straight game, 13–0. Joe DiMaggio knocks three triples in the first game of a doubleheader, an 8-7 win in New York. The Yankees, playing their sixth successive doubleheader, increase their AL lead to 12 games.

September 10 Jimmie Foxx of the Red Sox hits two home runs in a game for the ninth time this season, breaking a record held by Babe Ruth and Hack Wilson.

September 13 A special committee names Alexander Cartwright to Baseball's Hall of Fame for originating the sport's basic concepts. Henry Chadwick, inventor of the box score and the first baseball writer, is also honored.

October 2 Bob Feller sets a major league strikeout record by fanning 18 Tigers. At one point Feller has six straight strikeouts, yet loses 4-1 to Harry Eisenstat's four-hitter.

October 5 Bill Dickey ties a World Series record with four hits, as Red Ruffing pitches the Yankees to a 3-1 win in the Series opener at Wrigley Field.

October 9 The Yankees become the first team to win three successive World Championships, defeating the Cubs by a score of 8-3, as Red Ruffing wins his second game and the Yankees sweep.

November 2 Jimmie Foxx is voted MVP of the AL for the third time, with Yankees catcher Bill Dickey second in the voting.

November 6 The three DiMaggio brothers play together for the first time, making up an outfield for an all-star team in a West Coast charity game.

December 14 The major leagues agree on a standard ball. The NL grants Cincinnati its season opener a day before the rest of the league in recognition of baseball's 100th anniversary and the 1869 Red Stockings being the first professional team. The AL permits Cleveland and Philadelphia to play night games.

BOSTON		CHICAGO		CLEVELAND		DETROIT		NEW YORK		PHILADELPHIA		ST.LOUIS		WASHINGTON	
M	J.Cronin	M	J.Dykes	M	O.Vitt	M	M.Cochrane	M	J.McCarthy	M	C.Mack	M	G.Street	M	B.Harris
1B	J.Foxx	1B	J.Kuhel	1B	H.Trosky	M	D.Baker	1B	L.Gehrig	M	L.Finney	M	S.Melillo	1B	Z.Bonura
2B	B.Doerr	2B	J.Hayes	2B	O.Hale	1B	H.Greenberg	2B	J.Gordon	1B	D.Lodigiani	1B	G.McQuinn	2B	B.Myer
SS	J.Cronin	SS	L.Appling	SS	L.Lary	2B	C.Gehringer	SS	F.Crosetti	SS	W.Ambler	2B	D.Heffner	SS	C.Travis
3B	P.Higgins	3B	M.Owen	3B	K.Keltner	SS	B.Rogell	3B	R.Rolfe	SS	B.Werber	SS	R.Kress	3B	B.Lewis
LF	J.Vosmik	LF	G.Walker	LF	J.Heath	3B	D.Ross	LF	S.Selkirk	3B	S.Chapman	3B	H.Clift	LF	A.Simmons
CF	D.Cramer	CF	M.Kreevich	CF	E.Averill	LF	D.Walker	CF	J.DiMaggio	LF	B.Johnson	LF	B.Mills	CF	S.West
RF	B.Chapman	RF	H.Steinbacher	RF	B.Campbell	CF	C.Morgan	RF	T.Henrich	RF	W.Moses	CF	M.Almada	RF	G.Case
C	G.Desautels	C	L.Sewell	C	F.Pytlak	RF	P.Fox	C	B.Dickey	RF	F.Hayes	RF	B.Bell	C	R.Ferrell
						C	R.York					C	B.Sullivan		
C	J.Peacock	S2	B.Berger	O	R.Weatherly			O	M.Hoag	2	S.Sperry			O	T.Wright
O	R.Nonnenkamp	O1	R.Radcliff	O	R.Hemsley	3S	M.Christman	O	J.Powell	1	D.Siebert	O	M.Mazzera	O	J.Stone
S2	E.McNair	C	T.Rensa	O	M.Solters	O	C.Laabs	2	B.Knickerb'r	C	E.Brucker	C	T.Heath	O	M.Almada
3	J.Tabor	C	N.Schlueter	2	J.Kroner	O	J.White	S	J.Glenn	S	A.Parker	O	S.West	2S	O.Bluege
/C	M.Berg	O	L.Rosenthal	C	S.Webb	C	B.Tebbetts	/3	B.Dahlgren	O	H.Wagner	O	G.McQuillen	1	J.Wasdell
/O	F.Gaffke	2	J.Dykes	/C	H.Helf	3	T.Piet	/C	A.Jorgens	1	N.Etten	2	R.Hughes	O	T.Giuliani
		2	G.Meyer	/2	O.Grimes	O	R.Cullenbine			O	M.Haas	O	J.Grace	O	G.Goslin
P	J.Bagby	1	M.Connors	/S	T.Irwin	/C	R.Hayworth	P	R.Ruffing	1	G.Hasson	/O	E.Allen	/C	M.Livingston
P	J.Wilson	C	M.Tresh	/2	R.Mack	/2	B.McCoy	P	L.Gomez	S	S.Newsome	C	S.Harshany		
P	F.Ostermueller	/S	J.Gerlach	/O	C.Workman	H	G.Archie	P	M.Pearson	S	I.Bartling	/S	S.Gryska	P	D.Leonard
P	L.Grove	/1	T.Thompson	/3	L.Boudreau			P	S.Chandler	/O	B.Barna	/3	J.Lucadello	P	P.Appleton
P	E.Dickman	/2	J.Landrum	R	L.Russell	P	V.Kennedy	P	B.Hadley	/O	P.Easterling			P	K.Chase
RP	A.McKain	R	J.Martin			P	G.Gill	RP	J.Murphy	/S	R.Peters	P	B.Newsom	P	W.Ferrell
				P	B.Feller	P	E.Auker	RP	I.Andrews	/C	C.Berry	P	L.Mills	P	H.Kelley
P	J.Marcum	P	T.Lee	P	M.Harder	P	T.Bridges					P	O.Hildebrand	RP	C.Hogsett
P	J.Heving	P	T.Lyons	P	J.Allen	P	R.Lawson	P	S.Sundra	P	G.Caster	P	R.Van Atta		
P	B.Harris	P	M.Stratton	P	E.Whitehill	RP	S.Coffman	P	J.Beggs	P	B.Thomas	P	J.Walkup	P	M.Weaver
P	C.Wagner	P	J.Whitehead	P	W.Hudlin	RP	J.Wade	/P	W.Ferrell	P	L.Nelson	RP	E.Cole	P	J.DeShong
P	D.Midkiff	P	J.Rigney	RP	J.Humphries			/P	A.Donald	P	B.Ross	RP	B.Cox	P	K.Krakauskas
P	L.Rogers			RP	A.Milnar	P	H.Eisenstat	/P	J.Vance	P	E.Smith			/P	R.Monteagudo
/P	A.Baker	P	J.Knott			P	B.Poffenberger	/P	L.Stine	P	F.Johnson			/P	J.Kohlman
/P	T.Olson	P	F.Gabler	P	D.Galehouse	P	A.Benton	/P	K.Wicker	P	L.Tietje			/P	B.Phebus
/P	B.Lefebvre	/P	B.Dietrich	P	B.Zuber	/P	S.Rowe			P	N.Potter	P	E.Linke		
/P	B.Humphrey	/P	H.Boyles	/P	K.Jungels	/P	B.Harris			P	A.Williams	P	J.Bonetti		
		/P	S.Cain	/P	C.Smith	/P	J.Rogalski			P	D.Smith	/P	E.Bildilli		
		/P	C.Brown	/P	J.Heving	/P	W.Davis			/P	C.Dean	/P	V.Tamulis		
		/P	G.Ford	/P	C.Suche					/P	J.Reninger	/P	H.Kimberlin		
		/P	B.Cox							/P	R.Gumpert	/P	B.Trotter		
		/P	B.Uhl							/P	R.Buxton	/P	J.Weaver		
		/P	G.Gick							/P	H.Kelley	/P	G.Liebhardt		

TEAM	G	W	L	PCT	GB	R	OR	AB	H	2B	3B	HR	BB	SO	AVG	OBP	SLG	PRO	PRO+	BR	/A	PF	CHI	RC	SB	CS	SBA	SBR
NY	157	99	53	.651		966	710	5410	1480	283	63	174	749	616	.274	.366	.446	.812	111	77	82	100	104	926	91	28	76	11
BOS	150	88	61	.591	9.5	902	751	5229	1566	298	56	98	650	463	.299	.378	.434	.812	105	87	46	105	100	881	55	51	52	-14
CLE	153	86	66	.566	13	847	782	5356	1506	300	89	113	550	605	.281	.350	.434	.784	104	9	26	98	102	832	83	36	70	3
DET	155	84	70	.545	16	862	795	5270	1434	219	52	137	693	581	.272	.359	.411	.770	94	0	-47	106	104	812	76	41	65	-2
WAS	152	75	76	.497	23.5	814	873	5474	1602	278	72	85	573	379	.293	.362	.416	.778	108	12	71	93	96	845	65	37	64	-3
CHI	149	65	83	.439	32	709	752	5199	1439	239	55	67	514	489	.277	.343	.383	.726	86	-91	-107	102	101	700	56	39	59	-7
STL	156	55	97	.362	44	755	962	5333	1498	273	36	92	590	528	.281	.355	.397	.752	95	-38	-36	100	96	774	51	40	56	-9
PHI	154	53	99	.349	46	726	956	5229	1410	243	62	98	605	590	.270	.348	.396	.744	95	-57	-37	97	97	741	65	53	55	-12
TOT	613					6581		42500	11935	2133	485	864	4924	4251	.281	.358	.415	.773							542	325	63	-32

TEAM	CG	SH	SV	IP	H	H/G	HR	BB	SO	RAT	ERA	ERA+	OAV	OOB	PR	/A	PF	CPI	FA	E	DP	FW	PW	BW	SBW	DIF
NY	91	11	13	1382	1436	9.4	85	566	567	13.1	3.91	116	.268	.339	134	95	95	106	.973	169	177	.5	8.6	7.4	1.4	5.2
BOS	67	10	15	1316¹	1472	10.1	102	528	484	13.8	4.46	111	.281	.349	48	70	103	103	.968	190	172	-1.1	6.3	4.2	-.9	5.1
CLE	68	5	17	1353	1416	9.4	100	681	717	14.1	4.60	101	.268	.355	29	7	97	99	.974	151	145	1.2	.6	2.3	.6	5.1
DET	75	3	11	1348¹	1532	10.2	110	608	435	14.4	4.79	104	.287	.361	1	32	104	103	.976	147	172	1.6	2.9	-4.2	.2	6.6
WAS	59	6	11	1360¹	1472	9.7	92	655	515	14.3	4.94	91	.276	.358	-22	-64	94	94	.970	180	179	-.5	-5.8	6.4	.0	-.8
CHI	83	5	9	1316¹	1449	9.9	101	550	432	13.8	4.36	112	.279	.350	62	78	102	106	.967	196	155	-1.6	7.0	-9.7	-.3	-4.6
STL	71	3	7	1344²	1584	10.6	132	737	632	15.7	5.80	86	.295	.382	-151	-124	104	96	.975	145	163	1.8	-11.2	-3.3	-.4	-7.9
PHI	56	4	12	1324	1573	10.7	142	599	473	14.9	5.48	88	.292	.365	-101	-95	101	96	.965	206	119	-1.8	-8.6	-3.3	-.7	-8.6
TOT	570	47	95	10745		10.0				14.3	4.79		.281	.358					.971	1384	1282					

Runs
Greenberg-Det 144
Foxx-Bos 139
Gehringer-Det 133
Rolfe-NY 132
DiMaggio-NY 129

Hits
Vosmik-Bos 201
Cramer-Bos 198
Almada-Was-StL . . . 197
Foxx-Bos 197
Rolfe-NY 196

Doubles
Cronin-Bos 51
McQuinn-StL 42
Trosky-Cle 40
Chapman-Bos 40
Vosmik-Bos 37

Triples
Heath-Cle 18
Averill-Cle 15
DiMaggio-NY 13

Home Runs
Greenberg-Det 58
Foxx-Bos 50
Clift-StL 34
York-Det 33
DiMaggio-NY 32

Total Bases
Foxx-Bos 398
Greenberg-Det 380
DiMaggio-NY 348
Johnson-Phi 311
Heath-Cle 302

Runs Batted In
Foxx-Bos 175
Greenberg-Det 146
DiMaggio-NY 140
York-Det 127
Clift-StL 118

Runs Produced
Foxx-Bos 264
DiMaggio-NY 237
Greenberg-Det 232
Gehringer-Det 220
Clift-StL 203

Bases On Balls
Greenberg-Det 119
Foxx-Bos 119
Clift-StL 118
Gehringer-Det 113
Gehrig-NY 107

Batting Average
Foxx-Bos 349
Heath-Cle 343
Chapman-Bos 340
Myer-Was 336
Travis-Was 335

On Base Percentage
Foxx-Bos 462
Myer-Was 454
Greenberg-Det 438
Averill-Cle 429
Cronin-Bos 428

Slugging Average
Foxx-Bos 704
Greenberg-Det 683
Heath-Cle 602
DiMaggio-NY 581
York-Det 579

Production
Foxx-Bos 1.166
Greenberg-Det . . . 1.122
York-Det 995
Heath-Cle 985
Dickey-NY 981

Adjusted Production
Foxx-Bos 180
Greenberg-Det . . . 167
Heath-Cle 146
Dickey-NY 144
Clift-StL 143

Batter Runs
Foxx-Bos 78.2
Greenberg-Det . . . 66.0
Clift-StL 37.7
Cronin-Bos 34.8
York-Det 33.9

Adjusted Batter Runs
Foxx-Bos 70.4
Greenberg-Det . . . 57.1
Clift-StL 38.0
Johnson-Phi 35.8
Averill-Cle 33.9

Clutch Hitting Index
Higgins-Bos 140
Heffner-StL 138
R.Ferrell-Was 116
Doerr-Bos 116
Bonura-Was 111

Runs Created
Foxx-Bos 189
Greenberg-Det . . . 172
DiMaggio-NY . . . 136
Clift-StL 133
Gehrig-NY 131

Total Average
Foxx-Bos 1.392
Greenberg-Det . . . 1.306
Clift-StL 1.104
York-Det 1.104
Dickey-NY 1.083

Stolen Bases
Crosetti-NY 27
Lary-Cle 23
Werber-Phi 19
Lewis-Was 17
Fox-Det 16

Stolen Base Average
Lary-Cle 79.3
Fox-Det 69.6
Crosetti-NY 69.2
Lewis-Was 65.4
Werber-Phi 55.9

Stolen Base Runs
Gehringer-Det 3.6
Rolfe-NY 3.3
Lary-Cle 3.3
Hale-Cle 1.8

Fielding Runs
Gordon-NY 23.7
Crosetti-NY 17.6
Clift-StL 14.0
Johnson-Phi 10.3
Cramer-Bos 8.7

Total Player Rating
Foxx-Bos 5.2
Clift-StL 4.8
Cronin-Bos 4.2
Greenberg-Det 4.0
Dickey-NY 3.7

Wins
Ruffing-NY 21
Newsom-StL 20
Gomez-NY 18
Harder-Cle 17
Feller-Cle 17

Win Percentage
Ruffing-NY 750
Pearson-NY 696
Harder-Cle 630
Stratton-Chi 625
Feller-Cle 607

Games
Humphries-Cle 45
Newsom-StL 44
E.Smith-Phi 43
Bagby-Bos 43
Appleton-Was 43

Complete Games
Newsom-StL 31
Ruffing-NY 22
Gomez-NY 20
Feller-Cle 20
Caster-Phi 20

Shutouts
Gomez-NY 4
Wilson-Bos 3
Ruffing-NY 3
Leonard-Was 3

Saves
Murphy-NY 11
McKain-Bos 6
Humphries-Cle 6
Potter-Phi 5
Appleton-Was 5

Innings Pitched
Newsom-StL . . . 329.2
Caster-Phi 281.1
Feller-Cle 277.2
Ruffing-NY 247.1
Lee-Chi 245.1

Fewest Hits/Game
Feller-Cle 7.29
Allen-Cle 8.51
Pearson-NY 8.82
Rigney-Chi 8.84
Hadley-NY 8.87

Fewest BB/Game
Leonard-Was 2.14
Harder-Cle 2.33
Lyons-Chi 2.40
Chandler-NY 2.46
Thomas-Phi 2.63

Strikeouts
Feller-Cle 240
Newsom-StL 226
L.Mills-StL 134
Gomez-NY 129
Ruffing-NY 127

Strikeouts/Game
Feller-Cle 7.78
Newsom-StL 6.17
L.Mills-StL 5.73
Grove-Bos 5.44
Allen-Cle 5.04

Ratio
Leonard-Was 11.32
Ruffing-NY 11.94
Stratton-Chi 12.03
Chandler-NY 12.14
Harder-Cle 12.15

Earned Run Average
Grove-Bos 3.08
Ruffing-NY 3.31
Gomez-NY 3.35
Leonard-Was 3.43
Lee-Chi 3.49

Adjusted ERA
Grove-Bos 160
Lee-Chi 140
Rigney-Chi 138
Ruffing-NY 137
Gomez-NY 135

Opponents' Batting Avg.
Feller-Cle 220
Allen-Cle 246
Hadley-NY 254
Stratton-Chi 255
Rigney-Chi 256

Opponents' On Base Pct.
Leonard-Was 305
Stratton-Chi 315
Ruffing-NY 317
Harder-Cle 319
Grove-Bos 319

Starter Runs
Ruffing-NY 40.6
Gomez-NY 38.2
Lee-Chi 35.6
Leonard-Was 33.8
Grove-Bos 31.1

Adjusted Starter Runs
Lee-Chi 38.4
Grove-Bos 33.7
Ruffing-NY 33.6
Gomez-NY 31.4
Leonard-Was 27.0

Clutch Pitching Index
Lyons-Chi 125
Gill-Det 119
Grove-Bos 118
Rigney-Chi 117
Ruffing-NY 110

Relief Runs
Murphy-NY 5.6
McKain-Bos 3.0

Adjusted Relief Runs
McKain-Bos 4.6
Murphy-NY 3.0

Relief Ranking
McKain-Bos 4.4
Murphy-NY 3.8

Total Pitcher Index
Ruffing-NY 4.0
Lee-Chi 3.8
Gomez-NY 3.3
Leonard-Was 3.1
Grove-Bos 3.1

Total Baseball Ranking
Foxx-Bos 5.2
Clift-StL 4.8
Cronin-Bos 4.2
Greenberg-Det 4.0
Ruffing-NY 4.0

January 24 George Sisler, Eddie Collins, and Willie Keeler are elected to the Baseball Hall of Fame by the BBWAA.

May 14 Making his first appearance since elbow surgery in August 1938, Carl Hubbell pitches New York to a 2–1 win over the Phillies. Catcher Ken O'Dea hits a 10th inning home run to win it for King Carl.

May 17 The first baseball game ever televised, Princeton against Columbia at Baker Field, Columbia's home field, is seen by a handful of viewers via W2XBS in New York City. Bill Stern announces, as Princeton wins 2-1 in 10 innings. The second game of the doubleheader is not televised. Reviewing the game the next day, the New York *Times* sniffs, "it is difficult to see how this sort of thing can catch the public fancy."

June 6 At the Polo Grounds, the Giants unload on the Reds with five home runs in the fourth inning. Harry Danning and Frank Demaree hit homers, and then, with two out, Burgess Meredith, pitcher Frank Salvo and Joe Moore hit successive shots. Clouts by Mel Ott and another by Moore give New York seven home runs for the day, as they coast to a 17–3 win.

June 12 The greatest gathering of members and future inductees of the Baseball Hall of Fame assembles in Cooperstown, NY, for the dedication of the museum. A six-inning game at Doubleday Field presents lineups studded with players who will be elected in the future, as Babe Ruth, Ty Cobb, Honus Wagner, Walter Johnson, Grover Alexander, Nap Lajoie, George Sisler, Eddie Collins, Tris Speaker, Cy Young, and Connie Mack accept their plaques.

July 15 A disputed call on a fly ball down the left field foul line at the Polo Grounds touches off a melee in which the Giants Billy Jurges and umpire George Magerkurth spit at each other. Both will be fined $150 and suspended for 10 days. NL President Ford Frick announces that two-foot screens are to be installed inside all foul poles to prevent future arguments. The AL eventually also adopts the rule.

August 13 The Giants hit three successive home runs in the fourth inning, with Joe Moore, Alex Kampouris, and pitcher Bill Lohrman connecting. The Giants add four more home runs in the game to beat the Phils, 11–2. Pitcher Bill Kersieck gives up six of the 11 runs, including all of the runs scored in the fourth.

August 16 The Giants suspend second baseman Burgess Whitehead, who will show up the next day in full uniform at Yankee Stadium and ask to work out. Yankee manager Joe McCarthy refuses. Whitehead rejoins the Giants a few days later, but he will be suspended again in mid-September after leaving the team.

August 26 The first major league baseball game is telecast from Ebbets Field as the Reds play the Dodgers in a doubleheader. Red Barber broadcasts the game over W2XBS. The Dodgers take the first game 6-2, and the Reds take the second 5-1.

September 21 The NL announces that for the first time in the twentieth century, games will be transferred from one city to another. The Dodgers' doubleheader in Philadelphia will be moved to Brooklyn in an effort to top one million paid attendance.

September 28 Cincinnati clinches the pennant with Paul Derringer defeating second-place St. Louis 5-3.

October 17 Bucky Walters is voted NL MVP by the BBWAA, with Johnny Mize second.

BOSTON	BROOKLYN	CHICAGO	CINCINNATI	NEW YORK	PHILADELPHIA	PITTSBURGH	ST.LOUIS
M C.Stengel	M L.Durocher	M G.Hartnett	M B.McKechnie	M B.Terry	M D.Prothro	M P.Traynor	M R.Blades
1B B.Hassett	1B D.Camilli	1B R.Russell	1B F.McCormick	1B Z.Bonura	1B G.Suhr	1B E.Fletcher	1B J.Mize
2B T.Cuccinello	2B P.Coscarart	2B B.Herman	2B L.Frey	2B B.Whitehead	2B R.Hughes	2B P.Young	2B S.Martin
SS E.Miller	SS L.Durocher	SS D.Bartell	SS B.Myers	SS B.Jurges	SS G.Scharein	SS A.Vaughan	SS J.Brown
3B H.Majeski	3B C.Lavagetto	3B S.Hack	3B B.Werber	3B T.Hafey	3B P.May	3B L.Handley	3B J.Gutteridge
LF M.West	LF E.Koy	LF A.Galan	LF W.Berger	LF J.Moore	LF M.Arnovich	LF J.Rizzo	LF J.Medwick
CF J.Cooney	CF D.Walker	CF H.Leiber	CF H.Craft	CF F.Demaree	CF H.Martin	CF L.Waner	CF T.Moore
RF D.Garms	RF G.Moore	RF J.Gleeson	RF I.Goodman	RF M.Ott	RF L.Scott	RF P.Waner	RF E.Slaughter
C A.Lopez	C B.Phelps	C G.Hartnett	C E.Lombardi	C H.Danning	C S.Davis	C R.Mueller	C M.Owen
O A.Simmons	S2 J.Hudson	O C.Reynolds	O L.Gamble	O1 A.Kampouris	O1 G.Brack	23 B.Brubaker	O3 P.Martin
S2 R.Warstler	C A.Todd	O G.Mancuso	C W.Hershberger	23 B.Seeds	23 H.Mueller	O C.Klein	C D.Padgett
23 S.Sisti	O A.Parks	O B.Nicholson	O N.Bongiovanni	3 L.Chiozza	O J.Marty	O F.Bell	S3 L.Myers
O J.Outlaw	O T.Stainback	S B.Mattick	2 E.Joost	S2 J.Ripple	S2 D.Young	C R.Berres	O L.King
C P.Masi	O G.Rosen	O J.Marty	O F.Bordagaray	1 J.McCarthy	1 J.Bolling	1 G.Suhr	S L.Lary
1 E.Fletcher	O M.Almada	1 P.Cavarretta	3 L.Riggs	1 B.Young	O W.Millies	O B.Elliott	/2 C.Crespi
S W.Wietelmann	O J.Ripple	S S.Mesner	/O A.Simmons	O G.Myatt	P P.Whitney	C M.Van Robays	C H.Franks
O B.Rowell	O F.Sington	C B.Garbark	3 D.West	C T.Lazzeri	O B.Bates	C G.Susce	/C H.Bremer
/O R.Hodgin	2 T.Lazzeri	P B.Lee	/O V.DiMaggio	1 J.Dickshot	O B.Warren	3 F.Gustine	/2 B.Repass
/O C.Ross	S L.Lary	P C.Passeau	H L.Scarsella	/S S.Scalzi	P L.Powers	2 R.Juelich	/1 J.Hopp
C S.Andrews	C R.Hayworth	P L.French	/O B.Hafey	/C R.Hayworth	/S S.Benjamin	/O J.Schultz	/1 E.Lake
/O C.Clemens	/C C.Hartje	P C.Root	/1 M.Galatzer	P H.Gumbert	O C.Klein	/O W.Jensen	/S J.Orengo
/2 O.Huber	/O O.Hockett	P V.Page	/S N.Richardson	P C.Melton	2 C.Letchas	/O H.Manush	H B.Adams
/S R.Barkley	/O L.Deal	RP J.Russell	/C J.Wilson	P B.Lohrman	C D.Coble	H E.Yount	R J.Echols
/S B.Schuster	R G.Schott	RP G.Lillard	P B.Walters	P H.Schumacher	/2 E.Feinberg	P B.Klinger	P C.Davis
H O.Hill	RP G.Lillard	P D.Dean	P P.Derringer	P C.Hubbell	P L.Gabrielson	P M.Brown	P M.Cooper
P B.Posedel	P L.Hamlin	P E.Whitehill	P W.Moore	RP J.Brown	P B.Atwood	P J.Bowman	P B.Bowman
P D.MacFayden	P H.Casey	/P C.Bryant	P J.Thompson	RP R.Lynn	P J.Watwood	P R.Sewell	P L.Warneke
P J.Turner	P V.Tamulis	/P K.Higbe	P J.Vander Meer	P M.Salvo	P H.Mulcahy	P J.Tobin	P B.McGee
P L.Fette	P T.Pressnell	/P R.Harrell	P J.Niggeling	P D.Coffman	P K.Higbe	P B.Swift	RP C.Shoun
P M.Shoffner	P F.Fitzsimmons	/P V.Olsen	P M.Shoffner	P S.Castleman	P B.Beck	P M.Butcher	P B.Weiland
P J.Lanning	RP I.Hutchinson		P P.Davis	/P J.Wittig	P I.Pearson	P R.Bauers	P T.Sunkel
P D.Errickson	RP R.Evans		P H.Johnson	/P H.Vandenberg	P S.Johnson	P C.Blanton	P P.Dean
P J.Sullivan	P W.Wyatt		/P W.Livengood	RP T.Gorman	RP B.Kerksieck	P K.Heintzelman	P M.Lanier
P T.Earley	P V.Mungo		/P R.Barrett		P M.Butcher	P B.Clemensen	/P N.Andrews
P F.Frankhouse	/P B.Crouch		/P P.Naktenis		P R.Harrell	/P O.Swigart	/P M.Dickson
/P H.Moran	/P A.Hollingsworth		/P J.Weaver		P A.Hollingsworth	/P J.Gee	/P F.Barrett
/P G.Barnicle	/P C.Doyle		/P E.Riddle		/P C.Passeau	/P P.Rambert	/P K.Raffensberger
/P J.Callahan	/P B.Poffenberger		/P A.Jacobs		/P J.Poindexter		
/P A.Veigel	/P G.Jeffcoat				/P R.Bruner		
/P R.Weir					/P J.Henry		
					/P G.Schott		
					/P A.Smith		
					/P E.Burkart		
					/P B.Hoffman		

TEAM	G	W	L	PCT	GB	R	OR	AB	H	2B	3B	HR	BB	SO	AVG	OBP	SLG	PRO	PRO+	BR	/A	PF	CHI	RC	SB	CS	SBA	SBR
CIN	156	97	57	.630		767	595	5378	1493	269	60	98	500	538	.278	.343	.405	.748	106	51	47	101	102	759	46			
STL	155	92	61	.601	4.5	779	633	5447	1601	332	62	98	475	566	.294	.354	.432	.786	110	122	72	106	94	834	44			
BRO	157	84	69	.549	12.5	708	645	5350	1420	265	57	78	564	639	.265	.338	.380	.718	96	0	-25	104	102	697	59			
CHI	156	84	70	.545	13	724	678	5293	1407	263	62	91	523	553	.266	.336	.391	.727	99	10	-2	102	103	702	61			
NY	151	77	74	.510	18.5	703	685	5129	1395	211	38	116	477	499	.272	.340	.396	.736	103	28	22	101	101	683	26			
PIT	153	68	85	.444	28.5	666	721	5269	1453	261	60	63	477	420	.276	.338	.384	.722	102	4	15	98	97	687	44			
BOS	152	63	88	.417	32.5	572	659	5286	1395	199	39	56	366	494	.264	.314	.348	.662	91	-117	-78	93	104	575	41			
PHI	152	45	106	.298	50.5	553	856	5133	1341	232	40	49	421	486	.261	.318	.351	.669	89	-98	-82	97	99	570	47			
TOT	616					5472		42285	11505	2032	418	649	3824	4195	.272	.335	.386	.721							368			

TEAM	CG	SH	SV	IP	H	H/G	HR	BB	SO	RAT	ERA	ERA+	OAV	OOB	PR	/A	PF	CPI	FA	E	DP	FW	PW	BW	SBW	DIF
CIN	86	13	9	1403²	1340	8.6	81	499	637	12.0	3.27	117	.255	.322	101	87	98	107	.974	162	170	.6	8.7	4.7		6.0
STL	45	18	32	1384²	1377	9.0	76	498	603	12.3	3.59	115	.260	.326	50	80	105	100	.971	177	140	-.2	8.0	7.2		.5
BRO	69	9	13	1410¹	1431	9.1	93	399	528	11.9	3.64	110	.263	.317	43	60	103	97	.972	176	157	-.0	6.0	-2.5		4.0
CHI	72	8	13	1392¹	1504	9.7	74	430	584	12.6	3.80	104	.276	.331	18	21	101	100	.970	186	126	-.6	2.1	-.2		5.7
NY	55	6	20	1319	1412	9.6	86	477	505	13.1	4.07	96	.275	.340	-22	-20	102	100	.975	153	151	.8	-2.0	2.2		.5
PIT	53	10	15	1354	1537	10.2	70	423	464	13.2	4.15	92	.287	.342	-36	-49	98	100	.972	168	153	.1	-4.9	1.5		-5.2
BOS	68	11	15	1358¹	1400	9.3	63	513	430	12.8	3.71	100	.271	.339	31	-3	94	104	.971	181	178	-.6	-.3	-7.8		-3.8
PHI	67	3	12	1326²	1502	10.2	106	579	447	14.4	5.17	77	.289	.365	-185	-171	102	93	.970	171	136	-.0	-17.1	-8.2		-5.1
TOT	515	78	129	10949		9.5				12.8	3.92		.272	.335					.972	1374	1211					

Runs		Hits		Doubles		Triples		Home Runs		Total Bases	
Werber-Cin	115	McCormick-Cin	209	Slaughter-StL	52	Herman-Chi	18	Mize-StL	28	Mize-StL	353
Hack-Chi	112	Medwick-StL	201	Medwick-StL	48	Goodman-Cin	16	Ott-NY	27	McCormick-Cin	312
Herman-Chi	111	Mize-StL	197	Mize-StL	44	Mize-StL	14	Camilli-Bro	26	Medwick-StL	307
Camilli-Bro	105	Slaughter-StL	193	McCormick-Cin	41	Camilli-Bro	12	Leiber-Chi	24	Camilli-Bro	296
		Brown-StL	192					Lombardi-Cin	20	Slaughter-StL	291

Runs Batted In		Runs Produced		Bases On Balls		Batting Average		On Base Percentage		Slugging Average	
McCormick-Cin	128	McCormick-Cin	209	Camilli-Bro	110	Mize-StL	.349	Ott-NY	.449	Mize-StL	.626
Medwick-StL	117	Medwick-StL	201	Ott-NY	100	McCormick-Cin	.332	Mize-StL	.444	Ott-NY	.581
Mize-StL	108	Mize-StL	184	Mize-StL	92	Medwick-StL	.332	Camilli-Bro	.409	Leiber-Chi	.556
Camilli-Bro	104	Camilli-Bro	183	Werber-Cin	91	P.Waner-Pit	.328	Goodman-Cin	.401	Camilli-Bro	.524
Leiber-Chi	88	Herman-Chi	174	Lavagetto-Bro	78	Arnovich-Phi	.324	Arnovich-Phi	.397	Goodman-Cin	.515

Production		Adjusted Production		Batter Runs		Adjusted Batter Runs		Clutch Hitting Index		Runs Created	
Mize-StL	1.070	Mize-StL	174	Mize-StL	68.7	Mize-StL	60.0	May-Phi	120	Mize-StL	162
Ott-NY	1.030	Ott-NY	173	Ott-NY	45.9	Ott-NY	45.1	Lavagetto-Bro	116	Camilli-Bro	128
Camilli-Bro	.933	Camilli-Bro	144	Camilli-Bro	41.8	Camilli-Bro	37.6	McCormick-Cin	116	Medwick-StL	114
Goodman-Cin	.916	Goodman-Cin	144	Leiber-Chi	30.5	Goodman-Cin	29.4	R.Russell-Chi	116	Ott-NY	112
Medwick-StL	.886	West-Bos	139	Goodman-Cin	29.8	Leiber-Chi	29.1	Bonura-NY	113	McCormick-Cin	110

Total Average		Stolen Bases		Stolen Base Average		Stolen Base Runs		Fielding Runs		Total Player Rating	
Mize-StL	1.194	Handley-Pit	17					Slaughter-StL	15.8	Frey-Cin	4.0
Ott-NY	1.194	Hack-Chi	17					Frey-Cin	15.1	Mize-StL	3.9
Camilli-Bro	.995	Werber-Cin	15					Arnovich-Phi	14.9	Vaughan-Pit	3.9
Goodman-Cin	.941	Lavagetto-Bro	14					Jurges-NY	14.9	Ott-NY	3.6
Frey-Cin	.860	Hassett-Bos	13					Werber-Cin	12.6	Goodman-Cin	3.1

Wins		Win Percentage		Games		Complete Games		Shutouts		Saves	
Walters-Cin	27	Derringer-Cin	.781	Shoun-StL	53	Walters-Cin	31	Fette-Bos	6	Shoun-StL	9
Derringer-Cin	25	Walters-Cin	.711	Sewell-Pit	52	Derringer-Cin	28	Posedel-Bos	5	Bowman-StL	9
Davis-Chi	22	French-Chi	.652	Bowman-StL	51	Lee-Chi	20	Derringer-Cin	5	Davis-StL	7
Hamlin-Bro	20	Gumbert-NY	.621	Davis-StL	49	Hamlin-Bro	19	McGee-StL	4	Brown-NY	7
Lee-Chi	19	Hamlin-Bro	.606	Brown-Pit	47	Posedel-Bos	18			Brown-Pit	7

Innings Pitched		Fewest Hits/Game		Fewest BB/Game		Strikeouts		Strikeouts/Game		Ratio	
Walters-Cin	319.0	Walters-Cin	7.05	Derringer-Cin	1.05	Passeau-Phi-Chi	137	Cooper-StL	5.55	Hubbell-NY	10.29
Derringer-Cin	301.0	Bowman-StL	7.49	Hubbell-NY	1.40	Walters-Cin	137	Tamulis-Bro	4.71	Walters-Cin	10.30
Lee-Chi	282.1	Moore-Cin	8.49	Davis-StL	1.74	Cooper-StL	130	French-Chi	4.55	Hamlin-Bro	10.31
Passeau-Phi-Chi	274.1	Hamlin-Bro	8.51	Hamlin-Bro	1.80	Derringer-Cin	128	Passeau-Phi-Chi	4.49	Derringer-Cin	10.73
Hamlin-Bro	269.2	Hubbell-NY	8.77	Root-Chi	1.83	Lee-Chi	105	Bowman-StL	4.15	Bowman-StL	10.74

Earned Run Average		Adjusted ERA		Opponents' Batting Avg.		Opponents' On Base Pct.		Starter Runs		Adjusted Starter Runs	
Walters-Cin	2.29	Walters-Cin	168	Walters-Cin	.220	Hubbell-NY	.280	Walters-Cin	57.8	Walters-Cin	54.7
Bowman-StL	2.60	Bowman-StL	158	Bowman-StL	.232	Hamlin-Bro	.285	Derringer-Cin	33.0	Derringer-Cin	30.1
Hubbell-NY	2.75	Hubbell-NY	143	Hamlin-Bro	.248	Walters-Cin	.291	Casey-Bro	24.9	Bowman-StL	28.4
Casey-Bro	2.93	Casey-Bro	137	Hubbell-NY	.249	Derringer-Cin	.295	Bowman-StL	24.7	Casey-Bro	27.7
Derringer-Cin	2.93	Derringer-Cin	131	Moore-Cin	.254	Bowman-StL	.302	Thompson-Cin	23.3	Thompson-Cin	21.8

Clutch Pitching Index		Relief Runs		Adjusted Relief Runs		Relief Ranking		Total Pitcher Index		Total Baseball Ranking	
Brown-Pit	120	J.Russell-Chi	1.9	Shoun-StL	4.1	Shoun-StL	2.2	Walters-Cin	8.5	Walters-Cin	8.5
Shoffner-Bos-Cin	115	Shoun-StL	1.8	J.Russell-Chi	2.0	J.Russell-Chi	2.1	Davis-StL	3.3	Frey-Cin	4.0
Casey-Bro	113							Casey-Bro	3.1	Mize-StL	3.9
Cooper-StL	113							Bowman-StL	2.7	Vaughan-Pit	3.9
Moore-Cin	113							Derringer-Cin	2.7	Ott-NY	3.6

January 13 Yankee owner Colonel Jacob Ruppert dies. Ed Barrow will be elected president to succeed Colonel Ruppert on January 17.

April 20 The Red Sox show off rookie Ted Williams in the opener in New York. After striking out twice, he collects a double off Red Ruffing, who wins 2-0. Gehrig goes hitless in the only game featuring the two great sluggers. Other notables in what will become a historic box score include Joe DiMaggio, Bill Dickey, Jimmie Foxx, Joe Cronin, Bobby Doerr, and Lefty Grove.

May 2 Lou Gehrig voluntarily benches himself "for the good of the team." His consecutive-game string stops at 2,130. Babe Dahlgren, his replacement, has a home run and double, as the Yankees rout Detroit 22-2.

May 16 The first AL night game is played at Shibe Park, with Cleveland beating the A's 8-3 in 10 innings.

June 21 The New York Yankees announce Lou Gehrig's retirement, based on the report that he has amyotrophic lateral sclerosis. The 36-year-old star will remain with the team as captain.

June 28 The Yankees hit eight home runs in the first game of a doubleheader with the A's, and five more in the nightcap. Both are major league records, as is the 53 total bases in a doubleheader. Joe DiMaggio, Babe Dahlgren, and Joe Gordon each hit three home runs. The Yankees win the opener, 23–2, and take the nightcap, 10–0.

July 4 A tearful Lou Gehrig tells 61,808 fans at Yankee Stadium, "I consider myself the luckiest man on the face of the earth." Gehrig's uniform number 4 is retired, the first major league player so honored.

July 11 With another Yankee-dominated lineup, the AL defeats the NL 3–1 in the seventh All-Star Game, at Yankee Stadium. Cincinnati outfielder Ival Goodman fractures his shoulder diving for a ball.

September 16 The New York Yankees clinch their fourth successive pennant with a win over Detroit.

September 27 The hometown Chicago White Sox play the first "day-night" doubleheader against Cleveland, but lose both games 5-2 and 7-5. Fans are charged separate admissions for each game.

October 4 The World Series, with the Yankees as heavy favorites, begins in New York. The pitching of Red Ruffing for New York and Paul Derringer for Cincinnati produces a tense, low-scoring duel that is tied 1-1 until the last of the ninth, when Yankees catcher Bill Dickey singles home the winning run.

October 8 In the tenth inning of Game 4, the Reds make three errors and watch in shock as the Yankees run wild. The inning is climaxed by Joe DiMaggio's slide across the plate left unguarded by Ernie Lombardi, who was stunned by a kick in the groin by the preceding runner, Charlie Keller. The Yankees sweep the Reds and win their fourth straight World Championship.

October 24 The AL MVP is Joe DiMaggio, with Jimmie Foxx the runner-up, in the BBWAA poll.

December 7 Lou Gehrig, age 36, is elected to Baseball's Hall of Fame.

	BOSTON		CHICAGO		CLEVELAND		DETROIT		NEW YORK		PHILADELPHIA		ST.LOUIS		WASHINGTON
M	J.Cronin	M	J.Dykes	M	O.Vitt	M	D.Baker	M	J.McCarthy	M	C.Mack	M	F.Haney	M	B.Harris
1B	J.Foxx	1B	J.Kuhel	1B	H.Trosky	1B	H.Greenberg	1B	B.Dahlgren	1B	E.Mack	1B	G.McQuinn	1B	M.Vernon
2B	B.Doerr	2B	O.Bejma	2B	O.Hale	2B	C.Gehringer	2B	J.Gordon	1B	D.Siebert	2B	J.Berardino	2B	J.Bloodworth
SS	J.Cronin	SS	L.Appling	SS	S.Webb	SS	F.Croucher	SS	F.Crosetti	2B	J.Gantenbein	SS	D.Heffner	SS	C.Travis
3B	J.Tabor	3B	E.McNair	3B	K.Keltner	3B	P.Higgins	3B	R.Rolfe	SS	S.Newsome	3B	H.Clift	3B	B.Lewis
LF	J.Vosmik	LF	G.Walker	LF	J.Heath	LF	E.Averill	LF	G.Selkirk	3B	D.Lodigiani	LF	J.Gallagher	LF	T.Wright
CF	D.Cramer	CF	M.Kreevich	CF	B.Chapman	CF	B.McCosky	CF	J.DiMaggio	LF	B.Johnson	CF	C.Laabs	CF	S.West
RF	T.Williams	RF	L.Rosenthal	RF	B.Campbell	RF	P.Fox	RF	C.Keller	CF	S.Chapman	RF	M.Hoag	RF	G.Case
C	J.Peacock	C	M.Tresh	C	R.Hemsley	C	B.Tebbetts	C	B.Dickey	RF	W.Moses	C	J.Glenn	C	R.Ferrell
										C	F.Hayes				
1O	L.Finney	O1	R.Radcliff	21	O.Grimes	C1	R.York	O	T.Henrich			OC	B.Sullivan	O	B.Estalella
C	G.Desautels	2	J.Hayes	O	R.Weatherly	2S	B.McCoy	C	B.Rosar	S2	W.Ambler	S	M.Christman	2	B.Myer
2S	T.Carey	3	M.Owen	S	L.Boudreau	O	R.Cullenbine	O	J.Powell	O	D.Miles	O	J.Grace	O	J.Welaj
O	R.Nonnenkamp	O	H.Steinbacher	S3	F.Pytlak	S3	B.Rogell	O	J.Gallagher	23	B.Nagel	O	S.Harshany	S3	C.Gelbert
C	M.Berg	C	K.Silvestri	2	R.Mack	S2	R.Kress	/1	L.Gehrig	C	E.Brucker	O	M.Almada	C	T.Giuliani
S	B.Berger	C	N.Schlueter	O	M.Solters	O	D.Walker	/2	B.Knickerb'r	1	N.Etten	O	M.Solters	1	J.Wasdell
H	F.Gaffke	C	T.Rensa	2	J.Shilling	B	B.Bell	/C	A.Jorgens	C	E.Tipton	C	H.Spindel	1	B.Prichard
		/3	B.Kennedy	O	E.Averill	/3	M.Christman			3	A.Brancato	O	M.Mazzera	O	J.Early
P	L.Grove	/3	J.Gerlach	C	L.Sewell	/O	L.Fleming	S	R.Ruffing	S	F.Chapman	O	T.Thompson	1	O.Bluege
P	J.Wilson	/3	J.Dykes	/S	L.Lary	/O	C.Laabs	P	L.Gomez	/O	L.Finney	S	S.Gryska	S	H.Quick
P	F.Ostermueller	H	T.Thompson			/C	M.Shea	P	B.Hadley	/O	E.Collins	S	R.Kress	/2	E.Leip
P	E.Auker			P	B.Feller	/C	D.Parsons	P	A.Donald	/S	B.Lillard	C	B.Bell	/2	M.Aderholt
P	D.Galehouse	P	T.Lee	P	A.Milnar			P	M.Pearson	/3	B.McNamara	/2	J.Lucadello	/C	A.Evans
RP	E.Dickman	P	J.Rigney	P	M.Harder	P	B.Newsom	RP	J.Murphy	/C	H.Wagner	/2	R.Hughes	/O	E.Gedeon
RP	J.Heving	P	E.Smith	P	J.Allen	P	T.Bridges			/C	H.O'Neill	/S	B.Neighbors	/O	B.Loane
RP	J.Wade	P	T.Lyons	P	W.Hudlin	P	S.Rowe	P	O.Hildebrand			H	E.Silber	/O	A.Pitko
		P	J.Knott	RP	J.Dobson	P	D.Trout	P	S.Sundra	P	L.Nelson				
P	J.Bagby	RP	C.Brown			P	A.Benton	P	M.Russo	P	N.Potter	P	J.Kramer	P	D.Leonard
P	W.Rich					RP	B.Thomas	P	S.Chandler	P	B.Ross	P	V.Kennedy	P	K.Chase
/P	C.Wagner	P	B.Dietrich	P	H.Eisenstat			/P	W.Ferrell	P	B.Beckmann	P	B.Trotter	P	J.Krakauskas
/P	B.Lefebvre	P	J.Marcum	P	J.Broaca	P	A.McKain	/P	M.Breuer	P	G.Caster	P	R.Lawson	P	J.Haynes
/P	M.Weaver	/P	J.Whitehead	P	B.Zuber	P	F.Hutchinson			RP	C.Dean	P	L.Mills	P	A.Carrasquel
/P	B.Sayles	P	V.Frasier	/P	J.Humphries	P	S.Coffman					RP	J.Whitehead	RP	P.Appleton
		/P	A.Herring	/P	T.Drake	P	H.Eisenstat			P	C.Pippen			RP	W.Masterson
		/P	V.Eaves	/P	F.Stromme	P	V.Kennedy			P	B.Joyce	P	B.Harris		
		/P	H.Boyles	/P	L.Sullivan	P	B.Harris			P	R.Parmelee	P	G.Gill	P	H.Kelley
		/P	J.Dobernic	/P	M.Naymick	/P	F.Giebell			/P	L.McCrabb	P	J.Marcum	/P	J.DeShong
						/P	C.Pippen			/P	S.Page	/P	B.Newsom	/P	E.Wynn
						/P	J.Walkup			P	J.Reninger	P	H.Kimberlin	/P	B.Thomas
						/P	R.Lawson			/P	W.Masters	/P	E.Bildilli	/P	D.Bass
						/P	G.Gill			/P	E.Smith	/P	J.Wade	/P	B.Holland
						/P	R.Lynn			/P	B.Thomas	/P	F.Johnson	/P	L.Thuman
						/P	H.Newhouser			/P	J.Schelle	/P	L.Hanning	/P	B.Jacobs
										/P	D.Smith	/P	B.Cox	/P	M.Palagyi
												/P	E.Pyle		
												/P	R.Van Atta		
												/P	E.Cole		
												/P	B.Muncrief		
												/P	J.Walkup		

TEAM	G	W	L	PCT	GB	R	OR	AB	H	2B	3B	HR	BB	SO	AVG	OBP	SLG	PRO	PRO+	BR	/A	PF	CHI	RC	SB	CS	SBA	SBR
NY	152	106	45	.702		967	556	5300	1521	259	55	166	701	543	.287	.374	.451	.825	119	134	149	98	102	923	72	37	66	-1
BOS	152	89	62	.589	17	890	795	5308	1543	287	57	124	591	505	.291	.363	.436	.799	106	78	45	104	101	831	42	44	49	-14
CLE	154	87	67	.565	20.5	797	700	5316	1490	291	79	85	557	574	.280	.350	.413	.763	105	4	32	97	100	775	72	46	61	-6
CHI	155	85	69	.552	22.5	755	737	5279	1451	220	56	64	579	502	.275	.349	.374	.723	89	-62	-81	103	103	708	113	61	65	-3
DET	155	81	73	.526	26.5	849	762	5326	1487	277	67	124	620	592	.279	.346	.426	.782	99	43	-21	108	100	821	88	38	70	4
WAS	153	65	87	.428	41.5	702	797	5334	1483	249	79	44	547	460	.278	.346	.379	.725	98	-62	-8	93	96	718	94	47	67	0
PHI	153	55	97	.362	51.5	711	1022	5309	1438	282	55	98	503	532	.271	.336	.400	.736	96	-55	-40	98	97	713	60	34	64	-2
STL	156	43	111	.279	64.5	733	1035	5422	1453	242	50	91	559	606	.268	.339	.381	.720	88	-79	-94	102	100	706	48	38	56	-8
TOT	615					6404		42594	11866	2107	498	796	4657	4314	.279	.352	.407	.759							589	345	63	-30

TEAM	CG	SH	SV	IP	H	H/G	HR	BB	SO	RAT	ERA	ERA+	OAV	OOB	PR	/A	PF	CPI	FA	E	DP	FW	PW	BW	SBW	DIF
NY	87	15	26	1348²	1208	8.1	85	567	565	11.9	3.31	132	.241	.319	196	157	94	107	.978	126	159	2.9	14.5	13.7	.3	-.8
BOS	52	4	20	1350²	1533	10.2	77	543	539	14.0	4.56	104	.287	.355	9	25	102	102	.970	180	147	.0	2.3	4.1	-.9	7.9
CLE	69	10	13	1364²	1394	9.2	75	602	614	13.3	4.08	108	.267	.344	81	49	95	103	.970	180	148	.2	4.5	2.9	-.2	2.5
CHI	62	5	21	1377	1470	9.6	99	454	535	12.7	4.31	110	.275	.333	48	65	102	98	.972	167	140	1.0	6.0	-7.5	.0	8.4
DET	64	8	16	1367¹	1430	9.4	104	574	633	13.6	4.29	114	.268	.341	50	91	106	100	.967	198	147	-.6	8.4	-1.9	.7	-2.5
WAS	72	4	10	1354²	1420	9.4	75	602	521	13.6	4.60	94	.271	.348	2	-39	94	94	.966	205	167	-1.1	-3.6	-.7	.3	-5.9
PHI	50	6	12	1342²	1687	11.3	148	579	397	15.3	5.79	81	.307	.375	-175	-162	102	99	.964	210	131	-1.4	-14.9	-3.7	.2	-1.2
STL	56	3	3	1371¹	1724	11.3	133	739	516	16.4	6.01	81	.310	.393	-212	-175	105	100	.968	199	144	-.6	-16.1	-8.7	-.4	-8.2
TOT	512	55	121	10877		9.8				13.8	4.62		.279	.352					.969	1465	1183					

Runs		Hits		Doubles		Triples		Home Runs		Total Bases	
Rolfe-NY	139	Rolfe-NY	213	Rolfe-NY	46	Lewis-Was	16	Foxx-Bos	35	Williams-Bos	344
Williams-Bos	131	McQuinn-StL	195	Williams-Bos	44	McCosky-Det	14	Greenberg-Det	33	Foxx-Bos	324
Foxx-Bos	130	Keltner-Cle	191	Greenberg-Det	42	McQuinn-StL	13	Williams-Bos	31	Rolfe-NY	321
McCosky-Det	120	McCosky-Det	190	McQuinn-StL	37	Campbell-Cle	13	DiMaggio-NY	30	McQuinn-StL	318
Johnson-Phi	115	Williams-Bos	185	Keltner-Cle	35			Gordon-NY	28	Greenberg-Det	311

Runs Batted In		Runs Produced		Bases On Balls		Batting Average		On Base Percentage		Slugging Average	
Williams-Bos	145	Williams-Bos	245	Clift-StL	111	DiMaggio-NY	.381	Foxx-Bos	.464	Foxx-Bos	.694
DiMaggio-NY	126	Johnson-Phi	206	Williams-Bos	107	Foxx-Bos	.360	Selkirk-NY	.452	DiMaggio-NY	.671
Johnson-Phi	114	Rolfe-NY	205	Appling-Chi	105	Johnson-Phi	.338	DiMaggio-NY	.448	Greenberg-Det	.622
Greenberg-Det	112	DiMaggio-NY	204	Selkirk-NY	103	Trosky-Cle	.335	Keller-NY	.447	Williams-Bos	.609
		Foxx-Bos	200	Johnson-Phi	99	Rolfe-NY	.329	Johnson-Phi	.440	Trosky-Cle	.589

Production		Adjusted Production		Batter Runs		Adjusted Batter Runs		Clutch Hitting Index		Runs Created	
Foxx-Bos	1.158	DiMaggio-NY	185	Foxx-Bos	66.1	Foxx-Bos	60.8	Wright-Was	129	Williams-Bos	157
DiMaggio-NY	1.119	Foxx-Bos	185	Williams-Bos	56.3	DiMaggio-NY	58.1	McNair-Chi	116	Foxx-Bos	150
Williams-Bos	1.045	Williams-Bos	158	DiMaggio-NY	56.0	Williams-Bos	50.9	Dahlgren-NY	116	DiMaggio-NY	139
Greenberg-Det	1.042	Trosky-Cle	157	Greenberg-Det	47.3	Johnson-Phi	48.5	Selkirk-NY	115	Johnson-Phi	138
Trosky-Cle	.994	Johnson-Phi	156	Johnson-Phi	45.7	Greenberg-Det	38.0	Higgins-Det	115	Greenberg-Det	136

Total Average		Stolen Bases		Stolen Base Average		Stolen Base Runs		Fielding Runs		Total Player Rating	
Foxx-Bos	1.304	Case-Was	51	McCosky-Det	83.3	Case-Was	5.1	Doerr-Bos	27.3	DiMaggio-NY	5.7
DiMaggio-NY	1.242	Kreevich-Chi	23	Kuhel-Chi	78.3	McCosky-Det	3.6	Kreevich-Chi	16.1	Foxx-Bos	4.9
Williams-Bos	1.161	Fox-Det	23	Chapman-Cle	75.0	Welaj-Was	2.7	Tebbetts-Det	14.5	Johnson-Phi	4.7
Greenberg-Det	1.152	McCosky-Det	20	Case-Was	75.0	Kuhel-Chi	2.4	Lewis-Was	13.6	Williams-Bos	4.3
Selkirk-NY	1.121			Walker-Chi	73.9	Henrich-NY	2.1	Clift-StL	12.0	Dickey-NY	3.9

Wins		Win Percentage		Games		Complete Games		Shutouts		Saves	
Feller-Cle	24	Grove-Bos	.789	Brown-Chi	61	Newsom-StL-Det	24	Ruffing-NY	5	Murphy-NY	19
Ruffing-NY	21	Ruffing-NY	.750	Dean-Phi	54	Feller-Cle	24	Feller-Cle	4	Brown-Chi	18
Newsom-StL-Det	20	Feller-Cle	.727	Dickman-Bos	48	Ruffing-NY	22	Newsom-StL-Det	3	Heving-Bos	7
Leonard-Was	20	Leonard-Was	.714	Heving-Bos	46	Leonard-Was	21			Dean-Phi	7
Bridges-Det	17	Bridges-Det	.708			Grove-Bos	17			Appleton-Was	6

Innings Pitched		Fewest Hits/Game		Fewest BB/Game		Strikeouts		Strikeouts/Game		Ratio	
Feller-Cle	296.2	Feller-Cle	6.89	Lyons-Chi	1.36	Feller-Cle	246	Feller-Cle	7.46	Lyons-Chi	9.85
Newsom-StL-Det	291.2	Hadley-NY	7.71	Leonard-Was	1.97	Newsom-StL-Det	192	Newsom-StL-Det	5.92	Ruffing-NY	11.11
Leonard-Was	269.1	Gomez-NY	7.86	Beckmann-Phi	2.38	Bridges-Det	129	Bridges-Det	5.86	Leonard-Was	11.26
Lee-Chi	235.0	Ruffing-NY	8.14	Lee-Chi	2.68	Rigney-Chi	119	Rigney-Chi	4.90	Grove-Bos	11.26
Ruffing-NY	233.1	Chase-Was	8.34	Grove-Bos	2.73	Chase-Was	118	Gomez-NY	4.64	Feller-Cle	11.29

Earned Run Average		Adjusted ERA		Opponents' Batting Avg.		Opponents' On Base Pct.		Starter Runs		Adjusted Starter Runs	
Grove-Bos	2.54	Grove-Bos	186	Feller-Cle	.210	Lyons-Chi	.276	Feller-Cle	58.3	Feller-Cle	51.1
Lyons-Chi	2.76	Lyons-Chi	171	Gomez-NY	.235	Ruffing-NY	.301	Grove-Bos	44.0	Grove-Bos	46.3
Feller-Cle	2.85	Feller-Cle	154	Hadley-NY	.237	Feller-Cle	.303	Ruffing-NY	43.8	Newsom-StL-Det	42.3
Ruffing-NY	2.93	Ruffing-NY	149	Ruffing-NY	.240	Bridges-Det	.304	Lyons-Chi	35.6	Lyons-Chi	37.8
Hadley-NY	2.98	Hadley-NY	146	Bridges-Det	.243	Leonard-Was	.305	Newsom-StL-Det	33.7	Ruffing-NY	36.9

Clutch Pitching Index		Relief Runs		Adjusted Relief Runs		Relief Ranking		Total Pitcher Index		Total Baseball Ranking	
Hadley-NY	132	Heving-Bos	10.9	Heving-Bos	12.2	Brown-Chi	21.7	Feller-Cle	5.6	DiMaggio-NY	5.7
Grove-Bos	126	Brown-Chi	9.7	Brown-Chi	11.2	Heving-Bos	16.1	Ruffing-NY	4.7	Feller-Cle	5.6
Trout-Det	116	Dickman-Bos	2.3	Dickman-Bos	3.7	Dickman-Bos	3.6	Lyons-Chi	4.3	Foxx-Bos	4.9
Harder-Cle	116	Murphy-NY	1.5					Grove-Bos	3.7	Johnson-Phi	4.7
Milnar-Cle	110	Appleton-Was	.7					Newsom-StL-Det	3.5	Ruffing-NY	4.7

May 8 The Waner brothers, Lloyd and Paul, lose their places in the Pittsburgh outfield when new manager Frank Frisch acquires Vince DiMaggio for Johnny Rizzo. Vince takes over center field, flanked by Maurice Van Robays and Bob Elliott, each playing their first full season.

May 24 The New York Giants rip the Boston Bees, 8–1, in the first night game at the Polo Grounds before 22,260. Harry Gumbert is the winner.

June 4 The Pirates rout the Boston Bees, 14–2, in the first night game at Pittsburgh's Forbes Field as 20,319 look on.

August 3 With Ernie Lombardi hurt, Reds catcher Willard Hershberger is hitting .309 after taking over. However, depressed in recent weeks, Hershberger commits suicide by slashing his throat in Boston's Copley Plaza Hotel. Hershberger blamed himself for calling wrong pitches in the July 31 5-4 loss to New York. Leading 4-1, Bucky Walters retired the first two batters in the ninth and had two strikes on each of the next four batters. But Harry Danning and Burgess Whitehead each homered with a man on. Hershberger's father had also committed suicide, in 1928.

September 16 A rhubarb at Ebbets Field results in a suspension and fine for Dodger manager Leo Durocher for "inciting a riot." Perhaps better known from the game is the photo showing an obese Brooklyn fan astride George Magerkurth, pummeling the veteran umpire.

October 3 Jimmy Ripple's two-run home run in the third provides the winning margin as the Reds end the NL's 10-game World Series losing streak with a 5-3 win over the Detroit Tigers. Walters gives up only three hits, but he's lucky to escape a jittery first inning.

October 7 Back in Cincinnati, Bucky Walters evens the Series for the Reds with a 4-0 shutout, scattering five hits. Walters also becomes the first pitcher in 14 years to hit a home run in the Series.

October 8 With only one day's rest, Bobo Newsom comes back for the Tigers and nearly has enough to win Game 7. Detroit gets an unearned run off Paul Derringer in the third, and Newsom holds the Reds scoreless through six innings. In the seventh, however, Frank McCormick and Jimmy Ripple hit consecutive doubles, and Ripple later scores on Billy Myers's sac fly. Derringer gives up seven hits in the first six innings but sets the Tigers down in order in the final three frames for the 2-1 win. Old Jimmy Wilson catches six of the seven games, hits .353, and has the only stolen base of the Series. The Reds' share is $5,803 and the Tigers get $3,532.

BOSTON		BROOKLYN		CHICAGO		CINCINNATI		NEW YORK		PHILADELPHIA		PITTSBURGH		ST.LOUIS	
M	C.Stengel	M	L.Durocher	M	G.Hartnett	M	B.McKechnie	M	B.Terry	M	D.Prothro	M	F.Frisch	M	R.Blades
1B	B.Hassett	1B	D.Camilli	1B	P.Cavarretta	1B	F.McCormick	1B	B.Young	1B	A.Mahan	1B	E.Fletcher	M	M.Gonzalez
2B	B.Rowell	2B	P.Coscarart	2B	B.Herman	2B	L.Frey	2B	T.Cuccinello	2B	H.Schulte	2B	F.Gustine		B.Southworth
SS	E.Miller	SS	P.Reese	SS	B.Mattick	SS	B.Myers	SS	M.Witek	SS	B.Bragan	SS	A.Vaughan	1B	J.Mize
3B	S.Sisti	3B	C.Lavagetto	3B	S.Hack	3B	B.Werber	3B	B.Whitehead	3B	P.May	3B	L.Handley	2B	J.Orengo
LF	C.Ross	LF	J.Medwick	LF	B.Nicholson	LF	M.McCormick	LF	J.Moore	LF	J.Rizzo	LF	M.Van Robays	SS	M.Marion
CF	J.Cooney	CF	D.Walker	CF	J.Gleeson	CF	H.Craft	CF	F.Demaree	CF	J.Marty	CF	V.DiMaggio	3B	S.Martin
RF	M.West	RF	J.Vosmik	RF	H.Leiber	RF	I.Goodman	RF	M.Ott	RF	C.Klein	RF	B.Elliott	LF	E.Koy
C	R.Berres	C	B.Phelps	C	A.Todd	C	E.Lombardi	C	H.Danning	C	B.Warren	C	S.Davis	CF	T.Moore
														RF	E.Slaughter
O	G.Moore	O1	J.Wasdell	S	D.Dallessandro	S	E.Joost	2O	B.Rucker	3O	H.Mueller	3O	D.Garms	C	M.Owen
23	A.Glossop	3O	P.Reiser	1	R.Russell	S	M.Arnovich	S	B.Jurges	O	B.Atwood	O	P.Waner	23	J.Brown
C	P.Masi	S2	J.Hudson	O	A.Galan	C	W.Hershberger	O1	B.Seeds	O1	M.Mazzera	C	A.Lopez	C	D.Padgett
3	T.Cuccinello	S	L.Durocher	O	Z.Bonura	C	J.Rizzo	C	K.O'Dea	O	D.Litwhiler	2	L.Waner	C	P.Martin
C	A.Lopez	O	G.Mancuso	S2	R.Warstler	2	J.Ripple	/1	J.Glossop	O	M.Arnovich	2	P.Young	O	J.Medwick
1	L.Scarsella	C	C.Gilbert	C	R.Collins	3	L.Riggs	C	J.McCarthy	3	H.Martin	3	B.Brubaker	O1	J.Hopp
2	R.Warstler	C	H.Franks	C	G.Hartnett	C	B.Baker	/O	B.Maynard	C	W.Millies	C	J.Schultz	3	D.Gutteridge
2	W.Wietelmann	O	J.Gallagher	S	B.Rogell	C	L.Gamble	/3	G.Stewart	C	W.Berger	C	E.Fernandes	2	E.Lake
O	M.Preibisch	/C	R.Cullenbine	/C	C.McCullough	C	J.Wilson	/O	R.Tramback	S	G.Jumonville	C	R.Berres	/O	H.Walker
	S.Andrews	O	E.Koy	/S	B.Sturgeon	/C	D.West			/S	D.Young	/2	J.Rizzo	/O	C.Gillenwater
C	S.Broskie	3	D.Ross	P	C.Passeau	/O	M.Dejan	P	H.Gumbert	H	N.Stewart	/O	E.Leip	/C	W.Cooper
O	B.Loane	/O	G.Moore	P	L.French	/O	V.DiMaggio	P	H.Schumacher	/1	G.Suhr	/O	F.Bell	C	B.DeLancey
/1	B.Gremp	/O	J.Ripple	P	B.Lee	H	W.Berger	P	C.Hubbell	/O	G.Scharein	/O	F.Kalin	H	H.Epps
/O	D.Manno	/C	T.Giuliani	P	V.Olsen	P	B.Walters	P	B.Lohrman	/S	A.Monchak	/C	R.Mueller	/3	C.Crespi
/O	C.Wilborn			P	J.Mooty	P	P.Derringer	P	C.Melton	P	S.File	P	R.Sewell	/O	R.Jones
H	H.Majeski	P	W.Wyatt	RP	K.Raffensberger	RP	J.Thompson	/S	J.Brown	P	S.Benjamin	P	J.Bowman	P	L.Warneke
		P	L.Hamlin	RP	V.Page	P	J.Turner	/S	R.Joiner	P	E.Levy	P	M.Brown	P	M.Cooper
P	D.Errickson	P	V.Tamulis	P	C.Root	P	W.Moore	P	P.Dean	P	R.Hughes	P	K.Heintzelman	P	B.McGee
P	B.Posedel	P	H.Casey	P	D.Dean	RP	M.Shoffner	P	R.Lynn	P	H.Mulcahy	P	B.Klinger	P	C.Shoun
P	J.Sullivan	P	T.Carleton	/P	C.Bryant	RP	J.Hutchings	/P	H.Vandenberg	P	K.Higbe	RP	D.Lanahan	P	B.Bowman
P	M.Salvo	RP	T.Pressnell	/P	J.Bonetti	/P	B.Carpenter			P	I.Pearson	RP	D.MacFayden	RP	J.Russell
P	N.Strincevich	P	C.Davis			/P	W.Hudlin			P	Si.Johnson	/P	O.Swigart	P	M.Lanier
RP	A.Javery	P	F.Fitzsimmons			P	J.Vander Meer			P	B.Beck	/P	D.Dietz	P	C.Doyle
RP	A.Piechota	P	L.Grissom			P	E.Riddle			P	M.Butcher	/P	P.Rambert	P	I.Hutchinson
RP	D.Coffman	P	E.Head			P	L.Guise			P	J.Lanning	/P	R.Harrell	/P	C.Davis
		P	N.Kimball			/P	R.Barrett			P	R.Bauers			/P	E.White
P	J.Tobin	/P	V.Mungo							P	L.Smoll			/P	N.Kimball
P	G.Barnicle	/P	W.Flowers							/P	C.Blanton			/P	G.Lillard
/P	L.Fette	/P	S.Rachunok							/P	C.Frye			/P	H.Brecheen
/P	T.Earley	/P	C.Doyle							/P	Sy.Johnson			/P	M.Dickson
/P	J.Callahan	/P	W.Ferrell							/P	L.Brown			/P	B.Weiland
/P	F.LaManna	/P	L.Fette							/P	J.Podgajny				
/P	B.Swift	/P	M.Macon							/P	L.Hoerst				
/P	A.Williams									/P	M.Wilson				
/P	A.Johnson									/P	R.Bruner				
										/P	P.Masterson				

TEAM	G	W	L	PCT	GB	R	OR	AB	H	2B	3B	HR	BB	SO	AVG	OBP	SLG	PRO	PRO+	BR	/A	PF	CHI	RC	SB	CS	SBA	SBR
CIN	155	100	53	.654		707	528	5372	1427	264	38	89	453	503	.266	.327	.379	.706	100	6	-1	101	103	672	72			
BRO	156	88	65	.575	12	697	621	5470	1421	256	70	93	522	570	.260	.327	.383	.710	96	15	-28	106	98	692	56			
STL	156	84	69	.549	16	747	699	5499	1514	266	61	119	479	610	.275	.336	.411	.747	106	83	39	106	96	764	97			
PIT	156	78	76	.506	22.5	809	783	5466	1511	276	68	76	553	494	.276	.346	.394	.740	112	84	90	99	104	757	69			
CHI	154	75	79	.487	25.5	681	636	5389	1441	272	48	86	482	566	.267	.331	.384	.715	106	25	39	98	97	691	63			
NY	152	72	80	.474	27.5	663	659	5324	1423	201	46	91	453	478	.267	.329	.374	.703	99	3	-2	101	98	653	45			
BOS	152	65	87	.428	34.5	623	745	5329	1366	219	50	59	402	581	.256	.311	.349	.660	93	-83	-51	95	108	583	48			
PHI	153	50	103	.327	50	494	750	5137	1225	180	35	75	435	527	.238	.300	.331	.631	83	-133	-113	96	96	512	25			
TOT	617					5421		42986	11328	1934	416	688	3779	4329	.264	.326	.376	.702							475			

TEAM	CG	SH	SV	IP	H	H/G	HR	BB	SO	RAT	ERA	ERA+	OAV	OOB	PR	/A	PF	CPI	FA	E	DP	FW	PW	BW	SBW	DIF
CIN	91	10	11	1407²	1263	8.1	73	445	557	11.0	3.05	124	.240	.302	125	115	98	102	.981	117	158	2.9	11.6	-.1		9.1
BRO	65	17	14	1433	1366	8.6	101	393	639	11.2	3.50	114	.248	.302	56	79	104	95	.970	183	110	-.3	8.0	-2.8		6.7
STL	71	10	14	1396	1457	9.4	83	488	550	12.7	3.83	104	.266	.329	3	24	104	102	.971	174	134	.1	2.4	3.9		1.0
PIT	49	8	24	1388²	1569	10.2	72	492	491	13.6	4.36	87	.283	.345	-79	-85	99	99	.966	217	161	-2.0	-8.6	9.1		2.5
CHI	69	12	14	1392	1418	9.2	74	430	564	12.1	3.54	106	.262	.319	47	32	97	103	.968	199	143	-1.2	-1.6	-.2		-8.0
NY	57	11	18	1360¹	1383	9.1	110	473	606	12.4	3.79	102	.262	.325	9	14	101	104	.977	139	132	1.6	1.4	-.2		-6.8
BOS	76	9	12	1359	1444	9.6	83	573	435	13.6	4.36	85	.274	.349	-77	-97	97	100	.970	184	169	-.6	-9.8	-5.2		4.6
PHI	66	5	8	1357	1429	9.5	92	475	485	12.8	4.40	89	.270	.333	-83	-75	101	93	.970	181	136	-.4	-7.6	-11.4		-7.1
TOT	544	82	115	11093²		9.2				12.4	3.85		.264	.326					.972	1394	1143					

Runs
Vaughan-Pit 113
Mize-StL 111
Werber-Cin 105
Frey-Cin 102
Hack-Chi 101

Hits
F.McCormick-Cin . . 191
Hack-Chi 191
Mize-StL 182
Vaughan-Pit 178
Medwick-StL-Bro . . 175

Doubles
F.McCormick-Cin . . 44
Vaughan-Pit 40
Gleeson-Chi 39
Hack-Chi 38
Walker-Bro 37

Triples
Vaughan-Pit 15
Ross-Bos 14
Slaughter-StL 13
Mize-StL 13
Camilli-Bro 13

Home Runs
Mize-StL 43
Nicholson-Chi 25
Rizzo-Pit-Cin-Phi . . 24
Camilli-Bro 23

Total Bases
Mize-StL 368
F.McCormick-Cin . . 298
Medwick-StL-Bro . 280
Camilli-Bro 271
Vaughan-Pit 269

Runs Batted In
Mize-StL 137
F.McCormick-Cin . . 127
VanRobays-Pit 116
Fletcher-Pit 104
Young-NY 101

Runs Produced
Mize-StL 205
Vaughan-Pit 201
F.McCormick-Cin . . 201
VanRobays-Pit 187
Fletcher-Pit 182

Bases On Balls
Fletcher-Pit 119
Ott-NY 100
Camilli-Bro 89
Vaughan-Pit 88
Mize-StL 82

Batting Average
Garms-Pit 355
Davis-Pit 326
Lombardi-Cin 319
Cooney-Bos 318
Hack-Chi 317

On Base Percentage
Fletcher-Pit 418
Ott-NY 407
Mize-StL 404
Camilli-Bro 397
Hack-Chi 395

Slugging Average
Mize-StL 636
Nicholson-Chi 534
Camilli-Bro 529
DiMaggio-Cin-Pit . . .519
Slaughter-StL 504

Production
Mize-StL 1.039
Camilli-Bro 926
Nicholson-Chi 899
Slaughter-StL 874
Ott-NY 864

Adjusted Production
Mize-StL 173
Nicholson-Chi 148
Camilli-Bro 144
Gleeson-Chi 139
Fletcher-Pit 137

Batter Runs
Mize-StL 63.9
Camilli-Bro 38.7
Fletcher-Pit 31.8
Ott-NY 31.7
Vaughan-Pit 28.8

Adjusted Batter Runs
Mize-StL 56.2
Fletcher-Pit 32.6
Camilli-Bro 32.3
Ott-NY 30.8
Nicholson-Chi 30.5

Clutch Hitting Index
VanRobays-Pit 154
Fletcher-Pit 129
F.McCormick-Cin . . 121
Young-NY 115
Danning-NY 115

Runs Created
Mize-StL 152
Camilli-Bro 114
Vaughan-Pit 113
Hack-Chi 112
Ott-NY 107

Total Average
Mize-StL 1.135
Camilli-Bro 1.005
Fletcher-Pit 930
Ott-NY 915
Nicholson-Chi 901

Stolen Bases
Frey-Cin 22
Hack-Chi 21
Moore-StL 18
Werber-Cin 16
Reese-Bro 15

Stolen Base Average

Stolen Base Runs

Fielding Runs
Witek-NY 19.0
Herman-Chi 18.9
Frey-Cin 18.2
Moore-StL 16.8
Miller-Bos 14.7

Total Player Rating
Vaughan-Pit 5.1
Hack-Chi 4.5
Miller-Bos 3.5
Mize-StL 3.4
Frey-Cin 3.1

Wins
Walters-Cin 22
Passeau-Chi 20
Derringer-Cin 20

Win Percentage
Fitzsimmons-Bro . .889
Sewell-Pit 762
Walters-Cin 688
Thompson-Cin 640
Derringer-Cin 625

Games
Shoun-StL 54
Brown-Pit 48
Passeau-Chi 46
Casey-Bro 44
Raffensberger-Chi . . 43

Complete Games
Walters-Cin 29
Derringer-Cin 26
Mulcahy-Phi 21
Passeau-Chi 20
Higbe-Phi 20

Shutouts
Wyatt-Bro 5
Salvo-Bos 5

Saves
Brown-NY 7
Brown-Pit 7
Beggs-Cin 7
Shoun-StL 5
Passeau-Chi 5

Innings Pitched
Walters-Cin 305.0
Derringer-Cin . . . 296.2
Higbe-Phi 283.0
Passeau-Chi 280.2
Mulcahy-Phi 280.0

Fewest Hits/Game
Walters-Cin 7.11
Higbe-Phi 7.70
Thompson-Cin 7.87
Casey-Bro 7.95
Sullivan-Bos 7.97

Fewest BB/Game
Derringer-Cin 1.46
Turner-Cin 1.54
Hamlin-Bro 1.68
Davis-StL-Bro 1.79
Warneke-StL 1.82

Strikeouts
Higbe-Phi 137
Wyatt-Bro 124
Passeau-Chi 124
Schumacher-NY . . . 123

Strikeouts/Game
Melton-NY 4.91
Schumacher-NY . . . 4.88
Wyatt-Bro 4.66
Hamlin-Bro 4.49
Higbe-Phi 4.36

Ratio
Derringer-Cin 9.95
Walters-Cin 9.97
Passeau-Chi 10.33
Turner-Cin 10.54
Tamulis-Bro 10.73

Earned Run Average
Walters-Cin 2.48
Passeau-Chi 2.50
Sewell-Pit 2.80
Fitzsimmons-Bro . . 2.81
Turner-Cin 2.89

Adjusted ERA
Walters-Cin 153
Passeau-Chi 150
Sewell-Pit 136
Turner-Cin 131
Hamlin-Bro 131

Opponents' Batting Avg.
Walters-Cin 220
Higbe-Phi 232
Thompson-Cin 233
Passeau-Chi 237
Casey-Bro 237

Opponents' On Base Pct.
Derringer-Cin 276
Passeau-Chi 278
Walters-Cin 283
Tamulis-Bro 288
Hamlin-Bro 292

Starter Runs
Walters-Cin 46.4
Passeau-Chi 42.0
Derringer-Cin 25.8
Sewell-Pit 22.1
Turner-Cin 20.0

Adjusted Starter Runs
Walters-Cin 44.3
Passeau-Chi 38.9
Derringer-Cin 23.8
Warneke-StL 21.8
Sewell-Pit 21.3

Clutch Pitching Index
Errickson-Bos 124
Olsen-Chi 119
Schumacher-NY . . 113
Turner-Cin 113
Hamlin-Bro 111

Relief Runs
Beggs-Cin 15.8
Russell-StL 8.1
Raffensberger-Pit . . 6.0
MacFayden-Pit 3.0
Joiner-NY 2.7

Adjusted Relief Runs
Beggs-Cin 15.3
Russell-StL 8.9
Raffensberger-Chi . . 4.8
Brown-NY 2.9
Joiner-NY 2.9

Relief Ranking
Beggs-Cin 30.0
Russell-StL 10.8
Raffensberger-Chi . .6.2
Brown-NY 3.6
Pressnell-Bro 3.6

Total Pitcher Index
Passeau-Chi 5.3
Walters-Cin 4.7
Beggs-Cin 3.3
Sewell-Pit 2.7
Warneke-StL 2.6

Total Baseball Ranking
Passeau-Chi 5.3
Vaughan-Pit 5.1
Walters-Cin 4.7
Hack-Chi 4.5
Miller-Bos 3.5

January 14 Commissioner Kenesaw Landis gives free agency to 91 Detroit players and farm hands. Citing cover-ups of the movement of players within its organization, Landis hands freedom to Roy Cullenbine, Benny McCoy, Lloyd Dietz, and Steve Rachunok from the parent roster and orders $47,250 paid as compensation to 14 players. Johnny Sain is one of 23 players who will later make it to the major leagues. Landis's edict nullifies a deal which would have brought Wally Moses to the Tigers for Benny McCoy and George Coffman. McCoy is considered the plum of the 91 players, and several clubs bid for the second baseman. Connie Mack keeps Moses and signs McCoy for a $45,000 bonus and two-season contract at $10,000 a year.

April 16 Working in 47-degree weather, Bob Feller of the Cleveland Indians throws an Opening Day no-hitter against the Chicago White Sox winning, 1–0, at Comiskey Park. Rollie Hemsley has the only RBI, and Edgar Smith is the losing pitcher. It's the first Opening Day no-hitter since Leon "Red" Ames pitched one for the Giants in 1909.

May 14 Boston's Jimmie Foxx blasts a 10th inning home run off White Sox pitcher Johnny Rigney to give first-place Boston a 7-6 win. The ball goes over the left field roof and is considered the longest poke in the history of the original Comiskey Park .

May 24 The Cleveland Indians edge the St. Louis Browns, 3–2, in the first night game at Sportsman's Park in St. Louis before 24,827. Bob Feller beats Eldon Auker and helps his cause by hitting a home run.

July 14 In the aftermath of the beanball wars, Spalding advertises a batting helmet with ear flaps in *The Sporting News*. Players express no interest, but next year Brooklyn will introduce a cap liner, which some batters start to use.

August 24 Ted Williams of the Boston Red Sox pitches the last two innings in a 12-1 loss to the Detroit Tigers. Williams allows three hits and one run but strikes out Tiger slugger Rudy York on three pitches.

September 24 George Caster of the Philadelphia Athletics allows six home runs against the Boston Red Sox, four of them coming in the sixth inning as Ted Williams, Jimmie Foxx, Joe Cronin, and Jim Tabor connect. Foxx's home run is his 500th. Boston wins 10–9 in 10 innings, then wins the second game, 3–2.

September 27 The Yankees, winners of eight straight games, have their pennant hopes dashed by the A's, 6-2 winners over New York. New York is out of the World Series for the first time since 1935 as the Tigers become champs.

October 2 The Series opens in Cincinnati, and the Reds lose 7-2, the tenth straight World Series loss for a NL team. The Tigers bunch five singles, a walk, and an error in the second off Paul Derringer to score five runs. Bruce Campbell adds a two-run home run, and Bobo Newsom rations eight hits and only one walk. Bobo's father, visiting from South Carolina, dies in a Cincinnati hotel the next morning.

October 6 Detroit regains the advantage with Bobo Newsom pitching even better than he had in the first game. Newsom's 8-0 whitewash is the first Detroit shutout in the World Series since 1909.

November 5 Former Washington hurler Walter Johnson, who won 417 games for the Senators, goes down in defeat as a Republican candidate for the U.S. House of Representatives from Maryland.

December 20 Connie Mack acquires controlling interest in the Athletics from the Shibe family at the price of $42,000.

BOSTON		CHICAGO		CLEVELAND		DETROIT		NEW YORK		PHILADELPHIA		ST.LOUIS		WASHINGTON	
M	J.Cronin	M	J.Dykes	M	O.Vitt	M	D.Baker	M	J.McCarthy	M	C.Mack	M	F.Haney	M	B.Harris
1B	J.Foxx	1B	J.Kuhel	1B	H.Trosky	1B	R.York	1B	B.Dahlgren	1B	D.Siebert	1B	G.McQuinn	1B	Z.Bonura
2B	B.Doerr	2B	S.Webb	2B	R.Mack	2B	C.Gehringer	2B	J.Gordon	2B	B.McCoy	2B	D.Heffner	2B	J.Bloodworth
SS	J.Cronin	SS	L.Appling	SS	L.Boudreau	SS	D.Bartell	SS	F.Crosetti	SS	A.Brancato	SS	J.Berardino	SS	J.Pofahl
3B	J.Tabor	3B	B.Kennedy	3B	K.Keltner	3B	P.Higgins	3B	R.Rolfe	3B	A.Rubeling	3B	H.Clift	3B	C.Travis
LF	T.Williams	LF	M.Solters	LF	B.Chapman	LF	H.Greenberg	LF	G.Selkirk	LF	B.Johnson	LF	R.Radcliff	LF	G.Walker
CF	D.DiMaggio	CF	M.Kreevich	CF	R.Weatherly	CF	B.McCosky	CF	J.DiMaggio	CF	S.Chapman	CF	W.Judnich	CF	G.Case
RF	D.Cramer	RF	T.Wright	RF	B.Bell	RF	P.Fox	RF	C.Keller	RF	W.Moses	RF	R.Cullenbine	RF	B.Lewis
C	G.Desautels	C	M.Tresh	C	R.Hemsley	C	B.Tebbetts	C	B.Dickey	C	F.Hayes	C	B.Swift	C	R.Ferrell
O1	L.Finney	O	L.Rosenthal	O	J.Heath	O	B.Campbell	O	T.Henrich	O	D.Miles	O	C.Laabs	O	J.Welaj
C	J.Peacock	2	E.McNair	O	F.Pytlak	C	B.Sullivan	C	B.Rosar	C	B.Lillard	OC	J.Grace	2	B.Myer
3	C.Gelbert	C	T.Turner	/2	R.Peters	O	E.Averill	3	B.Knickerb'r	3	J.Gantenbein	O	M.Hoag	C	J.Early
O	S.Spence	2	J.Hayes	O	S.Campbell	3S	B.Kress	O	B.Mills	O	A.Simmons	O	A.Strange	1	J.Sanford
S	T.Carey	2	D.Kolloway	/3	O.Hale	2	D.Meyer	/O	J.Powell	C	H.Wagner	C	G.Susce	1	S.West
/3	M.Owen	/C	K.Silvestri	/1	O.Grimes	S	F.Croucher	S	M.Chartak	O	F.Chapman	O	J.Gallagher	S	C.Gelbert
C	J.Glenn	H	D.Short	/C	H.Helf	/O	T.Stainback			2	C.Davis	2	J.Lucadello	/1	J.Wasdell
/1	T.Lupien	P	J.Rigney	P	B.Feller	2	S.Metha	P	R.Ruffing	S	E.Brucker	S	L.Lary	S	S.Robertson
H	R.Nonnenkamp	P	T.Lee	P	A.Milnar	/O	P.Mullin	P	M.Russo	/O	E.Valo	H	F.White	/C	A.Evans
P	J.Bagby	P	E.Smith	P	M.Harder	H	F.Secory	P	S.Chandler	/S	J.Wallaesa	/C	S.Harshany	/1	M.Vernon
P	J.Wilson	P	T.Lyons	P	A.Smith	P	B.Newsom	P	M.Breuer	P	E.Tipton	P	E.Auker	/O	J.Mallory
P	L.Grove	P	J.Knott	P	J.Allen	P	T.Bridges	P	A.Donald	H	D.Lodigiani	P	V.Kennedy	/C	D.Hahn
P	F.Ostermueller	RP	C.Brown	RP	J.Dobson	P	S.Rowe	RP	J.Murphy	/C	B.Hancken	P	B.Harris	/2	M.Aderholt
P	H.Hash	RP	P.Appleton	RP	H.Eisenstat	P	J.Gorsica	P	M.Pearson	P	J.Babich	P	J.Niggeling	P	D.Leonard
RP	E.Dickman	P	B.Dietrich	P	J.Humphries	P	H.Newhouser	P	T.Bonham	P	N.Potter	P	E.Bildilli	P	K.Chase
P	D.Galehouse	/P	V.Eaves	P	M.Naymick	RP	A.Benton	P	S.Sundra	P	G.Caster	RP	B.Trotter	P	S.Hudson
P	J.Heving	/P	J.Hallett	/P	W.Hudlin	RP	T.Seats	P	B.Hadley	RP	C.Dean	RP	S.Coffman	P	W.Masterson
P	E.Johnson	/P	E.Weiland	P	B.Zuber	RP	A.McKain	/P	L.Gomez	RP	B.Ross	RP	R.Lawson	P	J.Krakauskas
P	M.Harris	/P	O.Grove	/P	N.Andrews	P	D.Trout	P	O.Hildebrand	P	E.Heusser	P	J.Kramer	RP	J.Haynes
P	B.Fleming			/P	D.Howell	P	F.Hutchinson	/P	L.Grissom	P	B.Beckmann	P	L.Mills	RP	A.Carrasquel
P	C.Wagner			/P	K.Jungels	P	C.Smith			P	P.Vaughan	P	J.Whitehead	P	R.Monteagudo
/P	B.Butland			/P	C.Dorsett	/P	C.Pippen			P	H.Besse	P	B.Cox	/P	W.Hudlin
/P	Y.Terry					/P	F.Giebell			/P	L.McCrabb	P	W.Hudlin	/P	A.Hollingsworth
/P	A.Mustaikis					/P	L.Nelson			/P	P.Marchildon	/P	M.Newlin	/P	B.Jacobs
/P	W.Rich					/P	B.Thomas			/P	C.Miles			/P	R.Anderson
						/P	D.Conger			/P	P.McLaughlin			/P	L.Thuman
						/P	B.Uhl							/P	G.Torres

TEAM	G	W	L	PCT	GB	R	OR	AB	H	2B	3B	HR	BB	SO	AVG	OBP	SLG	PRO	PRO+	BR	/A	PF	CHI	RC	SB	CS	SBA	SBR
DET	155	90	64	.584		888	717	5418	1549	312	65	134	664	556	.286	.366	.442	.808	105	124	38	110	97	913	66	39	63	-4
CLE	155	89	65	.578	1	710	637	5361	1422	287	61	101	519	597	.265	.332	.398	.730	98	-43	-22	97	99	724	53	36	60	-6
NY	155	88	66	.571	2	817	671	5286	1371	243	66	155	546	606	.259	.344	.418	.762	107	25	57	96	103	789	59	36	62	-4
CHI	155	82	72	.532	8	735	672	5386	1499	238	63	73	496	569	.278	.340	.387	.727	93	-41	-50	101	102	713	52	60	46	-20
BOS	154	82	72	.532	8	872	825	5481	1566	301	80	145	590	597	.286	.356	.449	.805	110	109	73	104	97	889	55	49	53	-13
STL	156	67	87	.435	23	757	882	5416	1423	278	58	118	556	642	.263	.333	.401	.734	94	-35	-50	102	103	744	51	40	56	-9
WAS	154	64	90	.416	26	665	811	5365	1453	266	67	52	468	504	.271	.331	.374	.705	95	-85	-42	94	100	690	94	40	70	4
PHI	154	54	100	.351	36	703	932	5304	1391	242	53	105	556	656	.262	.334	.387	.721	95	-53	-38	98	100	704	48	33	59	-5
TOT	619					6147		43017	11674	2167	513	883	4497	4727	.271	.342	.407	.750							478	333	59	-56

TEAM	CG	SH	SV	IP	H	H/G	HR	BB	SO	RAT	ERA	ERA+	OAV	OOB	PR	/A	PF	CPI	FA	E	DP	FW	PW	BW	SBW	DIF
DET	59	10	23	1375¹	1425	9.3	102	570	752	13.2	4.01	119	.266	.338	57	114	109	105	.968	194	116	-.7	10.8	3.6	.3	-1.0
CLE	72	13	22	1375	1328	8.7	86	512	686	12.2	3.63	116	.254	.324	115	89	96	102	.975	149	164	1.7	8.4	-2.1	.0	3.9
NY	76	10	14	1373	1389	9.1	119	511	559	12.6	3.89	104	.261	.328	76	22	92	104	.975	152	158	1.6	2.1	5.4	.3	1.7
CHI	83	10	18	1386²	1335	8.7	111	480	574	11.9	3.74	118	.250	.313	99	105	101	96	.969	185	125	-.2	9.9	-4.7	-1.2	1.2
BOS	51	4	16	1379²	1568	10.2	124	625	613	14.5	4.89	92	.284	.359	-77	-60	103	101	.972	173	156	.4	-5.7	6.9	-.6	3.9
STL	64	4	9	1373¹	1592	10.4	113	646	439	14.8	5.12	89	.290	.367	-113	-82	105	100	.974	158	179	1.3	-7.7	-4.7	-.2	1.3
WAS	74	6	7	1350	1494	10.0	93	618	618	14.2	4.59	91	.281	.359	-31	-64	95	103	.968	194	166	-.7	-6.0	-4.0	1.0	-3.3
PHI	72	4	12	1345	1543	10.3	135	534	488	14.0	5.22	85	.283	.348	-125	-116	101	91	.960	238	131	-3.1	-11.0	-3.6	.2	-5.6
TOT	551	61	121	10958		9.6				13.4	4.38		.271	.342					.970	1443	1195					

Runs		Hits		Doubles		Triples		Home Runs		Total Bases	
Williams-Bos	134	Radcliff-StL	200	Greenberg-Det	50	McCosky-Det	19	Greenberg-Det	41	Greenberg-Det	384
Greenberg-Det	129	McCosky-Det	200	York-Det	46	Keller-NY	15	Foxx-Bos	36	York-Det	343
McCosky-Det	123	Cramer-Bos	200	Boudreau-Cle	46	Finney-Bos	15	York-Det	33	Williams-Bos	333
Gordon-NY	112	Appling-Chi	197	Williams-Bos	43	Williams-Bos	14	Johnson-Phi	31	DiMaggio-NY	318
Kuhel-Chi	111	Wright-Chi	196	Moses-Phi	41	Appling-Chi	13	DiMaggio-NY	31	Gordon-NY	315

Runs Batted In		Runs Produced		Bases On Balls		Batting Average		On Base Percentage		Slugging Average	
Greenberg-Det	150	Greenberg-Det	238	Keller-NY	106	DiMaggio-NY	.352	Williams-Bos	.442	Greenberg-Det	.670
York-Det	134	Williams-Bos	224	Clift-StL	104	Appling-Chi	.348	Greenberg-Det	.433	DiMaggio-NY	.626
DiMaggio-NY	133	York-Det	206	Gehringer-Det	101	Williams-Bos	.344	Gehringer-Det	.428	Williams-Bos	.594
Foxx-Bos	119	DiMaggio-NY	195	Foxx-Bos	101	Radcliff-StL	.342	DiMaggio-NY	.425	York-Det	.583
Williams-Bos	113	Cronin-Bos	191	Williams-Bos	96	Greenberg-Det	.340	Appling-Chi	.420	Foxx-Bos	.581

Production		Adjusted Production		Batter Runs		Adjusted Batter Runs		Clutch Hitting Index		Runs Created	
Greenberg-Det	1.103	DiMaggio-NY	176	Greenberg-Det	68.8	DiMaggio-NY	55.9	Tresh-Chi	131	Greenberg-Det	171
DiMaggio-NY	1.051	Greenberg-Det	166	Williams-Bos	57.2	Greenberg-Det	54.7	Boudreau-Cle	130	Williams-Bos	154
Williams-Bos	1.036	Williams-Bos	159	DiMaggio-NY	50.8	Williams-Bos	51.6	Walker-Was	117	York-Det	147
York-Det	.993	Foxx-Bos	148	York-Det	47.3	Foxx-Bos	37.8	Bell-Cle	114	DiMaggio-NY	135
Foxx-Bos	.993	Keller-NY	142	Foxx-Bos	42.6	York-Det	34.9	Cronin-Bos	109	Foxx-Bos	124

Total Average		Stolen Bases		Stolen Base Average		Stolen Base Runs		Fielding Runs		Total Player Rating	
Greenberg-Det	1.215	Case-Was	35	Walker-Was	84.0	Case-Was	4.5	Heffner-StL	19.1	DiMaggio-NY	4.5
Williams-Bos	1.122	Walker-Was	21	Case-Was	77.8	Walker-Was	3.9	Doerr-Bos	18.3	Greenberg-Det	4.4
DiMaggio-NY	1.098	Gordon-NY	18	Gordon-NY	69.2	Gehringer-Det	3.0	Tebbetts-Det	18.2	Williams-Bos	4.0
York-Det	1.050	Lewis-Was	15			Bartell-Det	2.4	Travis-Was	15.7	Gordon-NY	3.9
Foxx-Bos	1.026	Kreevich-Chi	15			Rosar-NY	1.5	Gordon-NY	14.0	Doerr-Bos	3.6

Wins		Win Percentage		Games		Complete Games		Shutouts		Saves	
Feller-Cle	27	Rowe-Det	.842	Feller-Cle	43	Feller-Cle	31	Milnar-Cle	4	Benton-Det	17
Newsom-Det	21	Newsom-Det	.808	Benton-Det	42	Lee-Chi	24	Lyons-Chi	4	Brown-Chi	10
Milnar-Cle	18	Feller-Cle	.711	Wilson-Bos	41	Leonard-Was	23	Feller-Cle	4	Murphy-NY	9
Hudson-Was	17	Smith-Cle	.682	Heusser-Phi	41						
		Milnar-Cle	.643	Dobson-Cle	40						

Innings Pitched		Fewest Hits/Game		Fewest BB/Game		Strikeouts		Strikeouts/Game		Ratio	
Feller-Cle	320.1	Feller-Cle	6.88	Lyons-Chi	1.79	Feller-Cle	261	Feller-Cle	7.33	Feller-Cle	10.34
Leonard-Was	289.0	Rigney-Chi	7.70	Lee-Chi	2.21	Newsom-Det	164	Bridges-Det	6.06	Rigney-Chi	10.65
Rigney-Chi	280.2	Smith-Chi	7.77	Rowe-Det	2.29	Rigney-Chi	141	Wilson-Bos	5.82	Lyons-Chi	10.87
Newsom-Det	264.0	Bridges-Det	7.79	Leonard-Was	2.43	Bridges-Det	133	Newsom-Det	5.59	Lee-Chi	11.09
Auker-StL	263.2	Newsom-Det	8.01	Russo-NY	2.61	Chase-Was	129	Smith-Chi	5.17	Russo-NY	11.27

Earned Run Average		Adjusted ERA		Opponents' Batting Avg.		Opponents' On Base Pct.		Starter Runs		Adjusted Starter Runs	
Feller-Cle	2.61	Newsom-Det	168	Feller-Cle	.210	Feller-Cle	.285	Feller-Cle	63.0	Feller-Cle	57.1
Newsom-Det	2.83	Feller-Cle	161	Smith-Chi	.228	Lyons-Chi	.287	Newsom-Det	45.6	Newsom-Det	56.5
Rigney-Chi	3.11	Rigney-Chi	142	Bridges-Det	.229	Rigney-Chi	.292	Rigney-Chi	39.7	Rigney-Chi	40.9
Smith-Chi	3.21	Bridges-Det	141	Rigney-Chi	.230	Lee-Chi	.300	Chase-Was	33.4	Bridges-Det	30.5
Chase-Was	3.23	Smith-Chi	138	Newsom-Det	.238	Russo-NY	.303	Milnar-Cle	30.0	Smith-Chi	27.9

Clutch Pitching Index		Relief Runs		Adjusted Relief Runs		Relief Ranking		Total Pitcher Index		Total Baseball Ranking	
Chase-Was	134	Eisenstat-Cle	9.9	Trotter-StL	8.9	Trotter-StL	11.1	Feller-Cle	6.1	Feller-Cle	6.1
Leonard-Was	122	Trotter-StL	6.7	Eisenstat-Cle	8.6	Brown-Chi	9.3	Newsom-Det	4.6	Newsom-Det	4.6
Newsom-Det	119	Brown-Chi	5.1	Brown-Chi	5.4	Benton-Det	6.7	Rigney-Chi	4.2	DiMaggio-NY	4.5
Smith-Cle	117	Murphy-NY	4.8	Benton-Det	2.9	Eisenstat-Cle	6.5	Smith-Chi	2.9	Greenberg-Det	4.4
Milnar-Cle	115			Murphy-NY	2.4	Murphy-NY	4.8	Rowe-Det	2.9	Rigney-Chi	4.2

April 20 The Dodgers start to wear liners in their caps as a cautious response to the numerous beanball wars of 1940 that hospitalized Joe Medwick, Billy Jurges, and others. The liners are thin enough to be hardly noticeable, but most major league players continue to disdain the protection.

April 26 A baseball tradition is born at Wrigley Field. The Chicago ballpark is the first to install an organ, but the Cubs fall to the Cardinals 6-2 in Roy Nelson's debut at the keyboard.

May 3 Hank Gornicki of the St. Louis Cardinals pitches a one-hitter in his big-league debut, beating the Philadelphia Phillies, 6–0. Stan Benjamin's single is the lone hit.

June 1 Mel Ott's two-run homer, the 400th of his career and his 1,500th RBI, gives the Giants a 3–2 win over the Reds.

June 6 The Giants use plastic batting helmets for the first time against the Pirates but lose a doubleheader to the Bucs 5–4 and 4–3. In game two, Pittsburgh pitcher Rip Sewell sets an NL record by totaling 11 assists.

August 4 In the third inning, catcher Mickey Owens catches three foul flies, the first time in the major leagues that feat has been recorded. His Dodgers rally to whip the Giants 11–6.

August 19 Pittsburgh Pirates manager Frankie Frisch is ejected by umpire Jocko Conlan from the second game of a doubleheader when he appears on the field with an umbrella to protest the rainy conditions at Brooklyn's Ebbets Field. The argument is later portrayed in an oil painting by artist Norman Rockwell.

August 30 The Cardinals' Lon Warneke no-hits the Cincinnati Reds 2–0 with only three balls hit to the outfield. It is Warneke's 15th victory of the season and, with the Dodgers' doubleheader loss to the Giants, puts St. Louis in first place by two percentage points. The fifth place Giants beat Brooklyn, 4–3 and 5–1, at the Polo Grounds.

September 17 Stan Musial makes his major league debut, going 2-for-4 as the St. Louis Cardinals beat the Boston Braves. Musial, who started the season in the Western Association (Class C), will hit .426 in 12 games.

September 28 A jubilant crowd at Ebbets Field watches as the Dodgers beat the Phillies 6-1 to clinch the pennant. The crowd sets a new attendance record at 1,215,253.

October 5 With two out in the ninth inning, Dodger catcher Mickey Owen drops a third strike on Tommy Henrich, which would have given Brooklyn a 4-3 victory over New York and tied the Series at two games apiece. The Yankees then rally for a 7-4 win and clinch the next day behind pitcher Ernie "Tiny" Bonham.

December 2 The Giants name Mel Ott as player-manager replacing Bill Terry, who moves up to the general manager's spot.

BOSTON	BROOKLYN	CHICAGO	CINCINNATI	NEW YORK	PHILADELPHIA	PITTSBURGH	ST.LOUIS
M C.Stengel	M L.Durocher	M J.Wilson	M B.McKechnie	M B.Terry	M D.Prothro	M F.Frisch	M B.Southworth
1B B.Hassett	1B D.Camilli	1B B.Dahlgren	1B F.McCormick	1B B.Young	1B N.Etten	1B E.Fletcher	1B J.Mize
2B B.Rowell	2B B.Herman	2B L.Stringer	2B L.Frey	2B B.Whitehead	2B D.Murtaugh	2B F.Gustine	2B C.Crespi
SS E.Miller	SS P.Reese	SS B.Sturgeon	SS E.Joost	SS B.Jurges	SS B.Bragan	SS A.Vaughan	SS M.Marion
3B S.Sisti	3B C.Lavagetto	3B S.Hack	3B B.Werber	3B D.Bartell	3B P.May	3B L.Handley	3B J.Brown
LF M.West	LF J.Medwick	LF D.Dallessandro	LF M.McCormick	LF J.Moore	LF D.Litwhiler	LF M.Van Robays	LF J.Hopp
CF J.Cooney	CF P.Reiser	CF P.Cavarretta	CF H.Craft	CF J.Rucker	CF J.Marty	CF V.DiMaggio	CF T.Moore
RF G.Moore	RF D.Walker	RF B.Nicholson	RF J.Gleeson	RF M.Ott	RF S.Benjamin	RF B.Elliott	RF E.Slaughter
C R.Berres	C M.Owen	C C.McCullough	C E.Lombardi	C H.Danning	C B.Warren	C A.Lopez	C W.Cooper
O P.Waner	O1 J.Wasdell	O L.Novikoff	O E.Koy	3 J.Orengo	2 M.Livingston	2 S.Martin	OC D.Padgett
C P.Masi	3 L.Riggs	O1 H.Leiber	C D.West	O M.Arnovich	O J.Rizzo	S A.Anderson	C C.Triplett
2 S.Roberge	C H.Franks	3 B.Scheffing	3 C.Aleno	C G.Hartnett	2O H.Mueller	3O D.Garms	O E.Crabtree
1 B.Dahlgren	2 P.Coscarart	O A.Galan	O L.Waner	2 O.Hale	2S H.Marnie	O B.Stewart	S3 E.Lake
O F.Demaree	O J.Vosmik	S2 J.Hudson	O I.Goodman	C K.O'Dea	O C.Klein	C S.Davis	3 S.Mesner
1 B.Gremp	2 A.Kampouris	O C.Gilbert	O J.Ripple	2 M.Witek	2 B.Nagel	C B.Baker	1 S.Musial
3 H.Majeski	S L.Durocher	O B.Olsen	O E.Lukon	3 J.Davis	O J.Carlin	1 R.Collins	O E.Koy
C A.Montgomery	/O P.Waner	C G.George	S B.Mattick	O B.Barna	/O P.Busby	S B.Cox	/O H.Walker
O L.Waner	C B.Phelps	S B.Myers	/O B.Sauer	/1 J.McCarthy	/2 J.Jumonville	/O V.Smith	/O E.Dusak
O C.Ross	/O A.Galan	2 B.Herman	/2 B.Zientara	O F.Demaree	/C W.Millies	/2 E.Leip	/O W.Sessi
2 W.Wietelmann	/O T.Tatum	/1 E.Waitkus	/3 P.Young	/O S.Gordon		/O C.Rikard	/O W.Kurowski
/O D.Manno	/C T.Giuliani	/S L.Merullo	C J.Riddle	/C R.Blaemire	P J.Podgajny	/O L.Waner	H P.Young
/2 J.Dudra	/C G.Pfister	/1 R.Russell	C B.Baker	R J.Aragon	P T.Hughes	/C J.Schultz	/C C.Marshall
/O E.Averill		/O F.Jelincich	H E.Shokes		P C.Blanton		
/O B.Bray		H A.Todd	/C R.Lamanno	P H.Schumacher	P S.Johnson	P R.Sewell	
/O M.Preibisch				P C.Melton	P L.Grissom	P M.Butcher	P L.Warneke
	P K.Higbe	P C.Passeau	P B.Walters	P C.Hubbell	RP I.Pearson	P K.Heintzelman	P E.White
P J.Tobin	P C.Davis	P V.Olsen	P P.Derringer	RP B.Lohrman	RP B.Hoerst	P J.Lanning	P M.Cooper
P M.Salvo	P L.Hamlin	P B.Lee	P J.Vander Meer	RP B.Carpenter	RP B.Beck	P B.Klinger	P M.Lanier
P A.Johnson		P J.Mooty	P E.Riddle	RP B.Bowman			P H.Gumbert
P D.Errickson	P F.Fitzsimmons	P P.Erickson	P J.Turner	RP A.Adams	P R.Melton	P D.Dietz	RP C.Shoun
P A.Javery	P J.Allen	RP T.Pressnell	RP W.Moore	RP J.Brown	P B.Crouch	P L.Wilkie	RP I.Hutchinson
RP J.Hutchings	P N.Kimball	RP V.Page	RP J.Beggs		P R.Bruner	P J.Bowman	
RP F.LaManna	P M.Brown			P B.McGee	P B.Harman	P J.Sullivan	P H.Krist
	P K.Wicker			P J.Wittig	/P V.Tamulis	P R.Bauers	P S.Nahem
P T.Earley	P T.Drake	P C.Root	P J.Thompson	/P H.Gumbert	/P P.Masterson	/P N.Strincevich	/P H.Pollet
P B.Posedel	P B.Swift	P V.Eaves	/P R.Starr	/P D.Koslo	/P G.Lambert	/P B.Clemensen	/P B.Crouch
P J.Sullivan	P V.Tamulis	/P J.Schmitz	/P M.Pearson	/P H.Feldman	/P D.Jones	/P D.Lanahan	/P B.McGee
/P W.Ferrell	P L.French	P K.Raffensberger	/P J.Hutchings	/P B.Logan		/P B.Brandt	/P J.Grodzicki
/P G.Barnicle	/P E.Albosta	/P R.Meers		/P H.East		/P J.Gee	/P H.Gornicki
/P N.Strincevich	/P L.Grissom	/P W.Lanfranconi		/P T.Sunkel		/P D.Conger	/P J.Beazley
/P E.Carnett	/P B.Chipman	/P W.Quinn		/P B.Hadley		/P M.Brown	/P H.Lyons
/P A.Piechota	/P V.Mungo	/P E.Kush		/P R.Fischer			
		/P H.Gornicki		/P P.Dean			
		/P D.Dean					

TEAM	G	W	L	PCT	GB	R	OR	AB	H	2B	3B	HR	BB	SO	AVG	OBP	SLG	PRO	PRO+	BR	/A	PF	CHI	RC	SB	CS	SBA	SBR
BRO	157	100	54	.649		800	581	5485	1494	286	69	101	600	535	.272	.347	.405	.752	113	128	93	104	98	792	36			
STL	155	97	56	.634	2.5	734	589	5457	1482	254	56	70	540	543	.272	.340	.377	.717	102	62	13	107	99	719	47			
CIN	154	88	66	.571	12	616	564	5218	1288	213	33	64	477	428	.247	.313	.337	.650	89	-72	-74	100	108	556	68			
PIT	156	81	73	.526	19	690	643	5297	1417	233	65	56	547	516	.268	.338	.368	.706	105	39	42	100	99	670	59			
NY	156	74	79	.484	25.5	667	706	5395	1401	248	35	95	504	518	.260	.326	.371	.697	101	15	1	102	98	659	36			
CHI	155	70	84	.455	30	666	669	5230	1323	239	25	99	559	670	.253	.327	.365	.692	105	9	33	96	101	642	39			
BOS	156	62	92	.403	38	592	720	5414	1357	231	38	48	471	608	.251	.312	.334	.646	92	-82	-58	96	103	568	61			
PHI	155	43	111	.279	57	501	793	5233	1277	188	38	64	451	596	.244	.307	.331	.638	89	-97	-77	96	93	528	65			
TOT	622					5266		42729	11039	1892	359	597	4149	4414	.258	.326	.361	.688						411				

TEAM	CG	SH	SV	IP	H	H/G	HR	BB	SO	RAT	ERA	ERA+	OAV	OOB	PR	/A	PF	CPI	FA	E	DP	FW	PW	BW	SBW	DIF
BRO	66	17	22	1421	1236	7.8	81	495	603	11.1	3.14	117	.233	.300	78	83	101	93	.974	162	125	.9	8.5	9.6		4.0
STL	64	15	20	1416¹	1289	8.2	85	502	659	11.5	3.19	118	.242	.310	70	90	104	101	.973	172	146	.2	9.2	1.3		9.7
CIN	89	19	10	1386²	1300	8.4	61	510	627	11.9	3.17	114	.250	.319	72	66	99	106	.975	152	147	1.3	6.8	-7.6		10.6
PIT	71	8	12	1374¹	1392	9.1	66	492	410	12.4	3.48	104	.260	.323	23	19	99	102	.968	196	130	-1.1	2.0	4.3		-1.1
NY	55	12	18	1391²	1455	9.4	90	539	566	13.0	3.94	94	.269	.337	-48	-39	102	102	.974	160	144	.9	-4.0	.1		.5
CHI	74	8	9	1364²	1431	9.4	60	449	548	12.5	3.72	94	.267	.327	-13	-32	97	94	.970	180	139	-.3	-3.3	3.4		-6.8
BOS	62	10	9	1385²	1440	9.4	75	554	446	13.2	3.95	90	.269	.341	-49	-58	98	102	.969	191	174	-.9	-6.0	-6.0		-2.2
PHI	35	4	9	1372¹	1499	9.8	79	606	552	14.0	4.50	82	.279	.355	-132	-121	102	98	.969	187	147	-.7	-12.4	-7.9		-13.0
TOT	516	93	109	11112²		8.9				12.4	3.63		.258	.326					.972	1400	1152					

Runs
Reiser-Bro 117
Hack-Chi 111
Medwick-Bro 100
Rucker-NY 95
Fletcher-Pit 95

Hits
Hack-Chi 186
Reiser-Bro 184
Litwhiler-Phi 180
Rucker-NY 179
Medwick-Bro 171

Doubles
Reiser-Bro 39
Mize-StL 39
Rucker-NY 38
Dallessandro-Chi .. 36

Triples
Reiser-Bro 17
Fletcher-Pit 13
Hopp-StL 11
Medwick-Bro 10
Elliott-Pit 10

Home Runs
Camilli-Bro 34
Ott-NY 27
Nicholson-Chi 26
Young-NY 25
Dahlgren-Bos-Chi ... 23

Total Bases
Reiser-Bro 299
Camilli-Bro 294
Medwick-Bro 278
Litwhiler-Phi 275
Young-NY 265

Runs Batted In
Camilli-Bro 120
Young-NY 104
Mize-StL 100
DiMaggio-Pit 100
Nicholson-Chi 98

Runs Produced
Reiser-Bro 179
Camilli-Bro 178
Medwick-Bro 170
Young-NY 169
Fletcher-Pit 158

Bases On Balls
Fletcher-Pit 118
Camilli-Bro 104
Ott-NY 100
Hack-Chi 99

Batting Average
Reiser-Bro .... .343
Cooney-Bos ...... .319
Medwick-Bro .... .318
Hack-Chi .... .317
Mize-StL .... .317

On Base Percentage
Fletcher-Pit ...... .421
Hack-Chi .... .417
Camilli-Bro ...... .407
Reiser-Bro .... .406
Mize-StL .... .406

Slugging Average
Reiser-Bro .... .558
Camilli-Bro ...... .556
Mize-StL .... .535
Medwick-Bro .... .517
Slaughter-StL .... .496

Production
Reiser-Bro .... .964
Camilli-Bro ...... .962
Mize-StL .... .941
Ott-NY .... .898
Slaughter-StL .... .886

Adjusted Production
Reiser-Bro 163
Camilli-Bro 162
Mize-StL 153
Ott-NY 149
Fletcher-Pit 148

Batter Runs
Camilli-Bro 50.2
Reiser-Bro 48.0
Mize-StL 40.2
Ott-NY 38.7
Fletcher-Pit 38.2

Adjusted Batter Runs
Camilli-Bro 45.1
Reiser-Bro 43.1
Fletcher-Pit 38.6
Hack-Chi 37.9
Ott-NY 36.5

Clutch Hitting Index
Lavagetto-Bro 160
VanRobays-Pit 143
Dallessandro-Chi . 139
Bragan-Phi 124
Elliott-Pit 121

Runs Created
Camilli-Bro 128
Reiser-Bro 124
Ott-NY 115
Hack-Chi 114
Fletcher-Pit 111

Total Average
Camilli-Bro 1.057
Reiser-Bro 1.006
Mize-StL .... .991
Ott-NY .... .976
Fletcher-Pit ...... .965

Stolen Bases
Murtaugh-Phi 18
Benjamin-Phi 17
Handley-Pit 16
Frey-Cin 16
Hopp-StL 15

Stolen Base Average

Stolen Base Runs

Fielding Runs
May-Phi 25.2
Stringer-Chi 20.1
Litwhiler-Phi 17.1
Werber-Cin 12.5
Miller-Bos 12.2

Total Player Rating
Reiser-Bro 4.7
Camilli-Bro 3.7
Fletcher-Pit 3.7
Ott-NY 3.3
Litwhiler-Phi 3.2

Wins
Wyatt-Bro 22
Higbe-Bro 22
Walters-Cin 19
E.Riddle-Cin 19

Win Percentage
E.Riddle-Cin ...... .826
Higbe-Bro .... .710
White-StL .... .708
Wyatt-Bro .... .688
Warneke-StL ...... .654

Games
Higbe-Bro 48
Pearson-Phi 46
Casey-Bro 45
Hutchings-Cin-Bos . 44
Johnson-Bos 43

Complete Games
Walters-Cin 27
Wyatt-Bro 23
Tobin-Bos 20
Passeau-Chi 20

Shutouts
Wyatt-Bro 7
VanderMeer-Cin 6
Walters-Cin 5
Davis-Phi 5

Saves
Brown-NY 8
Crouch-Phi-StL 7
Casey-Bro 7
Pearson-Phi 6

Innings Pitched
Walters-Cin 302.0
Higbe-Bro 298.0
Wyatt-Bro 288.1
Sewell-Pit 249.0
Warneke-StL 246.0

Fewest Hits/Game
VanderMeer-Cin .. 6.84
Wyatt-Bro 6.96
White-StL 7.24
Higbe-Bro 7.37
E.Riddle-Cin 7.48

Fewest BB/Game
Passeau-Chi 2.03
Derringer-Cin 2.13
Lohrman-NY 2.26
Tobin-Bos 2.27
Lee-Chi 2.31

Strikeouts
VanderMeer-Cin ... 202
Wyatt-Bro 176
Walters-Cin 129
Higbe-Bro 121
M.Cooper-StL 118

Strikeouts/Game
VanderMeer-Cin .. 8.03
M.Cooper-StL 5.69
Wyatt-Bro 5.49
White-StL 5.01
Melton-NY 4.63

Ratio
Wyatt-Bro 9.58
E.Riddle-Cin 10.14
White-StL 10.50
Tobin-Bos 10.93
Sewell-Pit 11.28

Earned Run Average
E.Riddle-Cin 2.24
Wyatt-Bro 2.34
White-StL 2.40
VanderMeer-Cin ... 2.82
Walters-Cin 2.83

Adjusted ERA
E.Riddle-Cin 160
White-StL 157
Wyatt-Bro 157
VanderMeer-Cin ... 127
Walters-Cin 127

Opponents' Batting Avg.
Wyatt-Bro .... .212
VanderMeer-Cin .... .214
White-StL .... .217
Higbe-Bro .... .220
E.Riddle-Cin ...... .224

Opponents' On Base Pct.
Wyatt-Bro .... .270
E.Riddle-Cin ...... .282
White-StL .... .287
Sewell-Pit .... .299
Tobin-Bos .... .300

Starter Runs
Wyatt-Bro 41.4
E.Riddle-Cin 33.5
White-StL 28.8
Walters-Cin 26.9
VanderMeer-Cin ... 20.4

Adjusted Starter Runs
Wyatt-Bro 42.4
E.Riddle-Cin 32.6
White-StL 31.8
Walters-Cin 25.7
VanderMeer-Cin ... 19.5

Clutch Pitching Index
V.Olsen-Chi 120
Heintzelman-Pit ... 117
Butcher-Pit 112
Johnson-Bos 111
Walters-Cin 111

Relief Runs
Pressnell-Chi 4.3
Brown-NY 2.0
Pearson-Phi 9
Sullivan-Bos-Pit 0

Adjusted Relief Runs
Pressnell-Chi 3.3
Brown-NY 2.4
Pearson-Phi 1.9

Relief Ranking
Pressnell-Chi 3.5
Brown-NY 3.0
Pearson-Phi 2.5

Total Pitcher Index
Wyatt-Bro 5.3
E.Riddle-Cin 3.6
Walters-Cin 3.3
White-StL 3.3
Gumbert-NY-StL ... 2.3

Total Baseball Ranking
Wyatt-Bro 5.3
Reiser-Bro 4.7
Camilli-Bro 3.7
Fletcher-Pit 3.7
E.Riddle-Cin 3.6

May 6 Playing in his last game before induction into the Army, Hank Greenberg hits two home runs to lead Detroit to a 7-4 win over the Yankees. A few days later outfielder Joe Gallagher of the Dodgers is drafted, but no other regular major league player will be drafted during the season.

May 15 Joe DiMaggio gets a single in four at bats against Ed Smith of the Chicago White Sox to start his 56-game hitting streak.

May 25 Ted Williams raises his batting average over .400 for the first time during the season.

June 2 New York Yankees first baseman Lou Gehrig dies of amyotrophic lateral sclerosis at age 37 in New York. From that time on, the illness is known primarily as Lou Gehrig's Disease.

July 8 At the All-Star Game at Briggs Stadium, Ted Williams, hitting .405 at the break, homers off Chicago Cubs pitcher Claude Passeau with two out and two on in the ninth inning to give the AL a dramatic 7-5 victory. Williams's four RBI are matched by NL shortstop Arky Vaughan, who hits home runs in the seventh and eighth.

July 17 In front of more than 60,000 fans at Cleveland, Joe DiMaggio's hitting streak is ended at 56 games. Indian pitchers Al Smith and Jim Bagby, plus sensational plays by third baseman Ken Keltner, stop the Yankee Clipper, but New York edges the Indians 6-5.

July 25 Forty-one-year-old Lefty Grove wins his 300th game as the Boston Red Sox defeat the Cleveland Indians 10-6 before a Fenway Ladies Day crowd of 16,000. Though he will make six more starts, this will be Grove's last career win.

August 1 Lefty Gomez of the New York Yankees pitches a 9–0 shutout over the St. Louis Browns despite walking 11 batters, the most ever issued in a shutout. Fifteen base runners are left stranded by the Browns.

August 3 Browns pitcher Johnny Niggling gets Joe DiMaggio in four at bats to stop Joe DiMaggio's streak of reaching base in 74 consecutive games.

September 28 Ted Williams collects four hits in five at bats in the 12-11 first-game victory in Philadelphia to bring his average to .404. He goes 2-for-3 in game two against rookie Fred Caligiuri, who beats Lefty Grove 7-1. Williams will finish the season with a .406 batting average.

September 29 Overshadowed by the .406 mark of Ted Williams and the hitting streak of Joe DiMaggio, Jeff Heath of the Indians hits over 20 doubles, triples, and home runs during the season. The Canadian muscleman will finish with 32 doubles, 20 triples, and 24 home runs. It will be 38 years before George Brett duplicates the feat in the AL.

October 1 Red Ruffing pitches the Yankees to a 3-2 win over the Dodgers at Yankee Stadium in the opening game of the World Series. Joe Gordon chips in with a home run and RBI single.

October 4 In the seventh inning of a scoreless tie, Yankees pitcher Marius Russo breaks pitcher Fred Fitzsimmons's knee with a line drive. The Yankees score two in the eighth off Hugh Casey to win 2-1.

November 25 Lou Boudreau is named player-manager of the Cleveland Indians. At 24 years, four months, and eight days, Boudreau is the youngest manager appointed in this century. Scotland-born Jim McCormick managed Cleveland in 1879 at the age of 23.

November 27 Joe DiMaggio is named AL MVP. His 56-game hitting streak edges out Ted Williams and his .406 batting average for the award (291 votes for DiMaggio and 254 for Williams).

	BOSTON		CHICAGO		CLEVELAND		DETROIT		NEW YORK		PHILADELPHIA		ST.LOUIS		WASHINGTON
M	J.Cronin	M	J.Dykes	M	R.Peckinpaugh	M	D.Baker	M	J.McCarthy	M	C.Mack	M	F.Haney	M	B.Harris
1B	J.Foxx	1B	J.Kuhel	1B	H.Trosky	1B	R.York	1B	J.Sturm	1B	D.Siebert	M	L.Sewell	1B	M.Vernon
2B	B.Doerr	2B	B.Knickerb'r	2B	R.Mack	2B	C.Gehringer	2B	J.Gordon	2B	B.McCoy	1B	G.McQuinn	2B	J.Bloodworth
SS	J.Cronin	SS	L.Appling	SS	L.Boudreau	SS	F.Croucher	SS	P.Rizzuto	SS	A.Brancato	2B	D.Heffner	SS	C.Travis
3B	J.Tabor	3B	D.Lodigiani	3B	K.Keltner	3B	P.Higgins	3B	R.Rolfe	3B	P.Suder	SS	J.Berardino	3B	G.Archie
LF	T.Williams	LF	M.Hoag	LF	G.Walker	LF	R.Radcliff	LF	C.Keller	LF	B.Johnson	3B	H.Clift	LF	G.Case
CF	D.DiMaggio	CF	M.Kreevich	CF	R.Weatherly	CF	B.McCosky	CF	J.DiMaggio	CF	S.Chapman	LF	R.Cullenbine	CF	D.Cramer
RF	L.Finney	RF	T.Wright	RF	J.Heath	RF	B.Campbell	RF	T.Henrich	RF	W.Moses	CF	W.Judnich	RF	B.Lewis
C	F.Pytlak	C	M.Tresh	C	R.Hemsley	C	B.Tebbetts	C	B.Dickey	C	F.Hayes	RF	C.Laabs	C	J.Early
												C	R.Ferrell		
O	P.Fox	2	D.Kolloway	O	S.Campbell	O	T.Stainback	C	B.Rosar	O	E.Collins	O	J.Grace	O	A.Evans
C	J.Peacock	3	B.Kennedy	12	O.Grimes	C	B.Sullivan	23	J.Priddy	O	D.Miles			O	B.Chapman
S2	S.Newsome	O	M.Solters	C	G.Desautels	O	P.Mullin	O	G.Selkirk	C	H.Wagner	2S	J.Lucadello	2	B.Myer
O	S.Spence	O	B.Chapman	O1	B.Bell	2	D.Meyer	S3	F.Crosetti	21	C.Davis	C	B.Swift	O	J.Welaj
/1	A.Flair	C	T.Turner	O	L.Rosenthal	S2	B.Perry	O	F.Bordagaray	S	F.Chapman	S	A.Strange	O	R.Ortiz
/3	O.Hale	2	S.Webb	O	H.Edwards	O	H.Greenberg	C	K.Silvestri	O	E.Valo	O	B.Estalella	S	J.Pofahl
/2	T.Carey	O	L.Rosenthal	S	R.Peters	O	N.Harris	H	J.Lindell	/3	D.Richmond	C	B.Radcliff	/P	F.Ferrell
R	P.Campbell	C	G.Dickey	C	J.Hegan	3	E.McNair			/O	A.Simmons	C	F.Grube	3	H.Layne
		/1	J.Jones	/O	B.Frierson	/S	D.Bartell	P	M.Russo	/3	A.Rubeling	/1	G.Archie	/O	S.West
P	D.Newsome	/O	D.Philley	/1	L.Fleming	/S	M.Franklin	P	R.Ruffing	/O	F.Mackiewicz	/O	G.McQuillen	/2	M.Aderholt
P	M.Harris	/O	D.Short	/1	V.Freiburger	O	B.Patrick	P	S.Chandler	/1	E.Tipton	/1	C.Stevens	/O	C.Bolton
P	C.Wagner	H	S.Goletz	H	R.Howell	/O	D.Wakefield	P	A.Donald	/C	J.Leovich	/S	V.Stephens	/2	C.Letchas
P	L.Grove	H	C.Hajduk	/O	O.Hockett	/O	H.Evers	H	L.Gomez	H	R.Poole	H	M.Hoag	/1	J.Sanford
P	J.Dobson			/O	F.Gaffke	H	F.Hutchinson	RP	J.Murphy					/3	S.Robertson
		P	T.Lee	/3	B.Lemon			RP	C.Stanceu	P	P.Marchildon	P	E.Auker		
P	M.Ryba	P	E.Smith	H	C.Workman	P	B.Newsom	RP	N.Branch	P	J.Knott	P	B.Muncrief	P	D.Leonard
P	J.Wilson	P	J.Rigney	/S	J.Conway	P	H.Newhouser			P	L.McCrabb	P	D.Galehouse	P	S.Hudson
P	E.Johnson	P	T.Lyons	/C	G.Susce	P	J.Gorsica	P	M.Breuer	P	L.Harris	P	B.Harris	P	K.Chase
P	T.Hughson	P	B.Dietrich			P	A.Benton	P	T.Bonham	P	B.Beckmann	P	J.Niggeling	P	S.Sundra
P	B.Fleming			P	B.Feller	P	D.Trout	P	S.Peek			RP	J.Kramer	P	R.Anderson
/P	E.Dickman	P	B.Ross	P	A.Milnar	RP	B.Thomas	/P	G.Washburn	P	T.Ferrick	RP	B.Trotter	RP	A.Carrasquel
P	N.Potter	P	J.Hallett	P	A.Smith			P	B.Hadley					RP	B.Zuber
/P	O.Judd	P	J.Humphries	P	J.Bagby			P	T.Bridges	P	J.Babich	P	G.Caster	RP	W.Masterson
/P	H.Hash	/P	J.Haynes	RP	C.Brown	P	S.Rowe	P	C.Dean	P	J.Allen			
/P	W.Rich	P	P.Appleton	RP	J.Heving	P	A.McKain	/P	F.Caligiuri	P	F.Ostermueller	P	V.Kennedy	
		/P	O.Grove			P	F.Giebell	/P	D.Fowler	/P	V.Kennedy	/P	E.Wynn	
				P	M.Harder	/P	H.Manders	/P	N.Potter	P	M.Newlin	/P	D.Mulligan	
				/P	C.Dean	/P	L.Mueller	/P	P.Vaughan	/P	A.McKain	/P	D.MacFayden	
				P	J.Krakauskas	/P	H.White	/P	H.Besse	/P	E.Bildilli	/P	H.Dean	
				H	H.Eisenstat	/P	E.Cook	/P	R.Wolff	/P	H.Iott	/P	R.Miller	
				/P	S.Gromek	/P	V.Trucks	P	R.Johnson				
				/P	K.Jungels			/P	T.Shirley				
				C.Dorsett				/P	B.Ross				
				/P	R.Embree			/P	P.Tobin				
				/P	N.Andrews								

TEAM	G	W	L	PCT	GB	R	OR	AB	H	2B	3B	HR	BB	SO	AVG	OBP	SLG	PRO	PRO+	BR	/A	PF	CHI	RC	SB	CS	SBA	SBR
NY	156	101	53	.656		830	**631**	5444	1464	243	60	151	616	565	.269	.346	.419	.765	111	64	75	99	103	822	51	33	61	-5
BOS	155	84	70	.545	17	**865**	750	5359	**1517**	**304**	55	124	683	567	**.283**	**.366**	**.430**	**.796**	115	136	115	102	98	**872**	67	51	57	-11
CHI	156	77	77	.500	24	638	649	5404	1376	245	47	47	510	**476**	.255	.322	.343	.665	84	-128	-120	99	106	612	**91**	53	63	-5
DET	155	75	79	.487	26	686	743	5370	1412	247	55	81	602	584	.263	.340	.375	.715	87	-27	-98	110	97	713	43	28	61	-4
CLE	155	75	79	.487	26	677	668	5283	1350	249	**84**	103	512	605	.256	.323	.393	.716	101	-40	-7	95	100	691	63	47	57	-9
WAS	156	70	84	.455	31	728	798	5521	1502	257	80	52	470	488	.272	.331	.376	.707	99	-53	-21	95	**107**	702	79	36	**69**	**2**
STL	157	70	84	.455	31	765	823	5408	1440	281	58	91	**775**	552	.266	.360	.390	.750	103	56	29	103	93	804	50	39	56	-8
PHI	154	64	90	.416	37	713	840	5336	1431	240	69	85	574	588	.268	.340	.387	.727	102	-7	11	98	99	711	27	36	43	-14
TOT	622					5902		43125	11492	2066	508	734	4742	4425	.266	.341	.389	.730			471	323					59	-53

TEAM	CG	SH	SV	IP	H	H/G	HR	BB	SO	RAT	ERA	ERA+	OAV	OOB	PR	/A	PF	CPI	FA	E	DP	FW	PW	BW	SBW	DIF
NY	75	13	**26**	1396[1]	**1309**	8.4	81	598	589	12.4	3.53	112	**.248**	.325	96	63	95	102	.973	165	**196**	.5	6.1	7.3	.2	10.0
BOS	70	8	11	1372	1453	9.5	88	611	574	13.7	4.19	100	.270	.347	-6	-3	101	102	.972	172	139	.0	-.3	11.1	-.4	-3.5
CHI	**106**	14	4	1416	1362	8.7	89	**521**	564	12.1	3.52	116	.252	.320	99	91	99	102	.971	180	145	-.3	8.8	-11.6	.2	3.0
DET	52	8	16	1381[2]	1399	9.1	80	645	**697**	13.4	4.18	109	.260	.341	-4	57	110	96	.969	186	129	-.7	5.5	-9.5	.2	2.5
CLE	68	10	19	1377	1366	8.9	71	660	617	13.4	3.90	101	.259	.344	39	7	95	103	**.976**	142	158	**1.7**	.7	-.7	-.2	-3.5
WAS	69	8	7	1389[1]	1524	9.9	**69**	603	544	13.9	4.35	93	.279	.353	-32	-48	98	101	.969	187	169	-.7	-4.7	-2.0	**.8**	-.4
STL	65	7	10	1389	1563	10.1	120	549	454	13.8	4.72	91	.283	.350	-88	-64	104	99	.975	151	156	1.3	-6.2	2.8	-.1	-4.8
PHI	64	3	18	1365[1]	1516	10.0	136	557	386	13.8	4.83	87	.279	.348	-104	-98	101	97	.967	200	150	-1.6	-9.5	1.1	-.7	-2.3
TOT	569	71	111	11086[2]		9.3				13.3	4.15		.266	.341					.972	1383	1242					

Runs		Hits		Doubles		Triples		Home Runs		Total Bases	
Williams-Bos	135	Travis-Was	218	Boudreau-Cle	45	Heath-Cle	20	Williams-Bos	37	DiMaggio-NY	348
DiMaggio-NY	122	Heath-Cle	199	DiMaggio-NY	43	Travis-Was	19	Keller-NY	33	Heath-Cle	343
DiMaggio-Bos	117	DiMaggio-NY	193	Judnich-StL	40	Keltner-Cle	13	Henrich-NY	31	Williams-Bos	335
Clift-StL	108	Appling-Chi	186	Travis-Was	39			DiMaggio-NY	30	Travis-Was	316
		Williams-Bos	185	Kuhel-Chi	39			York-Det	27	S.Chapman-Phi	300

Runs Batted In		Runs Produced		Bases On Balls		Batting Average		On Base Percentage		Slugging Average	
DiMaggio-NY	125	Williams-Bos	218	Williams-Bos	145	Williams-Bos	.406	Williams-Bos	.551	Williams-Bos	.735
Heath-Cle	123	DiMaggio-NY	217	Cullenbine-StL	121	Travis-Was	.359	Cullenbine-StL	.452	DiMaggio-NY	.643
Keller-NY	122	Travis-Was	200	Clift-StL	113	DiMaggio-NY	.357	DiMaggio-NY	.440	Heath-Cle	.586
Williams-Bos	120	Keller-NY	191	Keller-NY	102	Heath-Cle	.340	Keller-NY	.416	Keller-NY	.580
York-Det	111	Heath-Cle	188			Siebert-Phi	.334	Foxx-Bos	.412	S.Chapman-Phi	.543

Production		Adjusted Production		Batter Runs		Adjusted Batter Runs		Clutch Hitting Index		Runs Created	
Williams-Bos	1.286	Williams-Bos	232	Williams-Bos	102.0	Williams-Bos	97.9	Berardino-StL	152	Williams-Bos	202
DiMaggio-NY	1.083	DiMaggio-NY	186	DiMaggio-NY	64.3	DiMaggio-NY	66.3	Cullenbine-StL	126	DiMaggio-NY	162
Keller-NY	.996	Heath-Cle	165	Keller-NY	45.7	Heath-Cle	51.0	Tabor-Bos	125	Heath-Cle	138
Heath-Cle	.982	Keller-NY	163	Heath-Cle	44.8	Keller-NY	47.4	Foxx-Bos	116	Keller-NY	134
Travis-Was	.930	Travis-Was	152	Cullenbine-StL	38.3	Travis-Was	43.7	Wright-Chi	116	Travis-Was	131

Total Average		Stolen Bases		Stolen Base Average		Stolen Base Runs		Fielding Runs		Total Player Rating	
Williams-Bos	1.688	Case-Was	33	Kuhel-Chi	80.0	Case-Was	4.5	Bloodworth-Was	34.7	Williams-Bos	7.9
DiMaggio-NY	1.208	Kuhel-Chi	20	Case-Was	78.6	Kuhel-Chi	3.0	Keltner-Cle	22.5	DiMaggio-NY	6.4
Keller-NY	1.099	Heath-Cle	18	Kreevich-Chi	77.3	Kreevich-Chi	2.1	Rizzuto-NY	15.6	Travis-Was	5.3
Cullenbine-StL	1.023	Tabor-Bos	17	Tabor-Bos	65.4	Fox-Bos	1.5	Case-Was	15.2	Keller-NY	4.1
Heath-Cle	1.000	Kreevich-Chi	17	Heath-Cle	60.0			S.Chapman-Phi	14.4	Keltner-Cle	3.5

Wins		Win Percentage		Games		Complete Games		Shutouts		Saves	
Feller-Cle	25	Gomez-NY	.750	Feller-Cle	44	Lee-Chi	30	Feller-Cle	6	Murphy-NY	15
Lee-Chi	22	Ruffing-NY	.714	Newsom-Det	43	Feller-Cle	28	Leonard-Was	4	Ferrick-Phi	7
D.Newsome-Bos	19	Benton-Det	.714	Brown-Chi	41	Smith-Chi	21	Humphries-Chi	4	Benton-Det	7
Leonard-Was	18	Lee-Chi	.667	Ryba-Bos	40	Lyons-Chi	19	Chandler-NY	4	Ryba-Bos	6
		Feller-Cle	.658	Benton-Det	38	Leonard-Was	19				

Innings Pitched		Fewest Hits/Game		Fewest BB/Game		Strikeouts		Strikeouts/Game		Ratio	
Feller-Cle	343.0	Benton-Det	7.42	Lyons-Chi	1.78	Feller-Cle	260	Feller-Cle	6.82	Lee-Chi	10.61
Lee-Chi	300.1	Feller-Cle	7.45	Leonard-Was	1.90	Newsom-Det	175	Newsom-Det	6.29	Ruffing-NY	11.25
Smith-Chi	263.1	Lee-Chi	7.73	Muncrief-StL	2.23	Lee-Chi	130	Newhouser-Det	5.51	Benton-Det	11.30
Leonard-Was	256.0	Donald-NY	7.98	Ruffing-NY	2.62	Rigney-Chi	119	Harris-Bos	5.15	Chandler-NY	11.33
Newsom-Det	250.1	Chandler-NY	8.03	Lee-Chi	2.76			Rigney-Chi	4.52	Lyons-Chi	11.53

Earned Run Average		Adjusted ERA		Opponents' Batting Avg.		Opponents' On Base Pct.		Starter Runs		Adjusted Starter Runs	
Lee-Chi	2.37	Lee-Chi	173	Benton-Det	.221	Lee-Chi	.293	Lee-Chi	59.4	Lee-Chi	57.7
Benton-Det	2.97	Benton-Det	153	Feller-Cle	.226	Benton-Det	.302	Feller-Cle	38.1	Feller-Cle	30.2
Wagner-Bos	3.07	Wagner-Bos	136	Lee-Chi	.232	Ruffing-NY	.306	Smith-Chi	28.4	Benton-Det	27.6
Russo-NY	3.09	Smith-Chi	129	Donald-NY	.237	Chandler-NY	.307	Russo-NY	24.6	Smith-Chi	26.9
Feller-Cle	3.15	Harris-Bos	128	Chandler-NY	.239	Lyons-Chi	.308	Wagner-Bos	22.3	Wagner-Bos	22.8

Clutch Pitching Index		Relief Runs		Adjusted Relief Runs		Relief Ranking		Total Pitcher Index		Total Baseball Ranking	
Lee-Chi	122	Murphy-NY	18.6	Murphy-NY	16.8	Murphy-NY	28.8	Lee-Chi	6.6	Williams-Bos	7.9
Wagner-Bos	120	Heving-Cle	14.6	Heving-Cle	12.9	Heving-Cle	13.6	Smith-Chi	3.2	Lee-Chi	6.6
Gomez-NY	115	Carrasquel-Was	7.5	Carrasquel-Was	6.4	Carrasquel-Was	5.1	Feller-Cle	3.2	DiMaggio-NY	6.4
Marchildon-Phi	115	Brown-Cle	7.3	Brown-Cle	5.5	Brown-Cle	4.9	Benton-Det	3.1	Travis-Was	5.3
Smith-Chi	112			Thomas-Det	2.7	Thomas-Det	1.5	Murphy-NY	2.7	Keller-NY	4.1

January 4 Rogers Hornsby becomes the 14th player selected to the Hall of Fame, getting 78 percent of the vote.

January 15 The Cubs, who had signed contracts to install lights at Wrigley Field, drop their plans because of the military's need for the material.

February 5 In one of their best trades ever, the Braves get Tommy Holmes from the Yankees for Buddy Hassett and Gene Moore. Hassett will hit .284, then join the Navy, and will not make it back to the ML. The much-traveled Moore will never play for the Yanks. Holmes, who couldn't break into New York's outfield, will hit over .300 in 10 seasons with the Braves and win the MVP award in 1948.

May 8 At Ebbets Field, in the first twilight game in 24 years, the Dodgers top the Giants 7-6. Nearly $60,000 is raised for the Navy Relief Fund, as all the proceeds are donated. Everyone, including the ball players, pay their way into the park.

May 13 Pitcher Jim Tobin of the Boston Braves slams three successive home runs to beat the Chicago Cubs at Braves Field.

May 19 Paul Waner, now with the Boston Braves, joins Cap Anson and Honus Wagner as the only NL players with 3,000 hits, with a single off Rip Sewell of the Pittsburgh Pirates. Two days earlier,

Waner's grounder bounced off an infielder's glove and had been ruled a hit. Waner, who did not want his 3000th hit to be a tainted one, signaled to the scorekeeper that it was an error, and the ruling was changed.

May 31 Before 22,000 at Griffith Stadium, Satchel Paige pitches five innings to defeat the Dizzy Dean All-Stars 8-1. Judge Landis will prohibit a scheduled July 4 matchup because the first two games outdrew major league games.

September 13 Chicago Cubs shortstop Lennie Merullo makes a major league record four errors in the second inning of the nightcap against the Boston Braves. Merullo's son is born today and is named, appropriately, Boots. The Cubs win, 12-8, after losing the first game, 10-6.

September 24 Mort Cooper tosses his 10th shutout of the year to give the Cardinals a 6-0 victory over the Reds. His 22nd win of the year clinches at least a tie for the pennant.

September 26 Youngsters, admitted free for bringing scrap metal to aid the war effort, get restless and invade the field at the Polo Grounds in the eighth inning of the second game with the Giants leading, 5-2. Umpire Ziggy Sears forfeits the game, 9-0, to the Braves. Boston pitcher Warren Spahn is not

charged with a loss, although he was losing at the time of the forfeit. But he is given credit for a complete game, his only one in four appearances for the year.

September 27 On the last day of the season, the Cardinals, winners of nine games out of ten, have a 1½ game lead over the Dodgers, winner of seven straight. The Cardinals clinch the NL pennant by winning the first game of a doubleheader from the Cubs by a score of 9-2. Billy Southworth benches his regulars in the nightcap, but the Cards still win, 4-1, giving Johnny Beasley his 21st win of the year. Kirby Higbe wins for the Dodgers, 4-3, at Shibe Park. Brooklyn finishes with 104 victories, the most for a runner-up team since the 1909 Cubs won that many.

September 30 Down 7-0 to Red Ruffing in the Series opener, the Cardinals storm back for four ninth-inning runs, not enough to win but enough to foretell the result.

October 5 Whitey Kurowski's two-run home run in the ninth inning gives St. Louis a 4-2 World Series triumph and enables the Cardinals to upset the New York Yankees in five games.

November 1 After two decades in St. Louis, Branch Rickey splits with owner Sam Breadon and signs to become GM at Brooklyn.

	BOSTON		BROOKLYN		CHICAGO		CINCINNATI		NEW YORK		PHILADELPHIA		PITTSBURGH		ST.LOUIS
M	C.Stengel	M	L.Durocher	M	J.Wilson	M	B.McKechnie	M	M.Ott	M	H.Lobert	M	F.Frisch	M	B.Southworth
1B	M.West	1B	D.Camilli	1B	P.Cavarretta	1B	F.McCormick	1B	J.Mize	1B	N.Etten	1B	E.Fletcher	1B	J.Hopp
2B	S.Sisti	2B	B.Herman	2B	L.Stringer	2B	L.Frey	2B	M.Witek	2B	A.Glossop	2B	F.Gustine	2B	C.Crespi
SS	E.Miller	SS	P.Reese	SS	L.Merullo	SS	E.Joost	SS	B.Jurges	SS	B.Bragan	SS	P.Coscarart	SS	M.Marion
3B	N.Fernandez	3B	A.Vaughan	3B	S.Hack	3B	B.Haas	3B	B.Werber	3B	P.May	3B	B.Elliott	3B	W.Kurowski
LF	C.Ross	LF	J.Medwick	LF	L.Novikoff	LF	E.Tipton	LF	B.Barna	LF	D.Litwhiler	LF	J.Wasdell	LF	S.Musial
CF	T.Holmes	CF	P.Reiser	CF	D.Dallessandro	CF	G.Walker	CF	W.Marshall	CF	E.Koy	CF	V.DiMaggio	CF	T.Moore
RF	P.Waner	RF	D.Walker	RF	B.Nicholson	RF	M.Marshall	RF	M.Ott	RF	R.Northey	RF	J.Barrett	RF	E.Slaughter
C	E.Lombardi	C	M.Owen	C	C.McCullough	C	R.Lamanno	C	H.Danning	C	B.Warren	C	A.Lopez	C	W.Cooper
C	C.Kluttz	O	J.Rizzo	12	R.Russell	O	I.Goodman	O1	B.Young	S3	D.Murtaugh	C	B.Phelps	23	J.Brown
1	B.Gremp	O	A.Galan	1	J.Foxx	O	M.McCormick	3S	D.Bartell	O	L.Waner	O	M.Van Robays	1	R.Sanders
O1	J.Cooney	3	L.Riggs	O	C.Gilbert	O3	R.Hemsley	O3	B.Maynard	O3	M.Livingston	O3	B.Stewart	O	K.O'Dea
O	F.Demaree	2S	B.Sullivan	2S	C.Hernandez	O	H.Craft	O	H.Leiber	O1	S.Benjamin	S	A.Anderson	O	H.Walker
23	S.Roberge	O	F.Bordagaray	C	C.Hernandez	C	F.Kelleher	O	G.Mancuso	OP	E.Naylor	2	S.Martin	O	C.Triplett
32	T.Cuccinello	/2	A.Kampouris	C	B.Scheffing	S	D.Phillips	C	R.Berres	S	B.Burich	O	C.Rikard	/O	E.Dusak
C	P.Masi	1	B.Dahlgren	O	P.Lowrey	C	D.West	2	C.Ryan	O	E.Freed	/O	F.Colman	S	B.Blattner
3	D.Detweiler	/C	C.Dapper	1	B.Dahlgren	O	C.Vollmer	/3	S.Gordon	2	H.Marnie	/O	J.Wyrostek	/C	G.Mancuso
S	W.Wietelmann	R	S.Rojek	/3	C.Block	C	A.Lakeman	/O	H.Moss	/1	E.Murphy	/S	H.Geary	/C	S.Narron
/O	F.McElyea			/O	M.Rickert	/3	J.Abreu	/C	C.Fox	H	C.Klein	C	B.Baker	H	E.Crabtree
/S	M.Sandlock	P	K.Higbe	P	P.Gillespie	/O	J.Gleeson			/3	B.Hodge	/O	J.Russell	/S	J.Cross
		P	W.Wyatt	/O	W.Platt	/1	H.Sauer	P	H.Schumacher	/C	B.Peterman	R	E.Leip		
P	J.Tobin	P	C.Davis	/C	M.Felderman	/3	C.Aleno	P	B.Carpenter	/C	B.Culp			P	M.Cooper
P	A.Javery	P	L.French			/S	B.Mattick	P	B.Lohrman			P	R.Sewell	P	J.Beazley
P	L.Tost	P	E.Head	P	C.Passeau	/O	F.Secory	P	C.Hubbell	P	T.Hughes	P	B.Klinger	P	H.Gumbert
P	M.Salvo	RP	H.Casey	P	B.Lee	H	E.Koy	P	C.Melton	P	R.Melton	P	M.Butcher	P	M.Lanier
P	T.Earley	RP	L.Webber	P	H.Bithorn			RP	A.Adams	P	S.Johnson	P	D.Dietz	P	E.White
RP	J.Sain			P	V.Olsen					P	J.Podgajny	P	K.Heintzelman		
RP	B.Donovan	P	J.Allen	P	B.Fleming	P	B.Walters	P	H.Feldman	P	L.Hoerst			P	M.Dickson
RP	D.Errickson	P	M.Macon			P	J.Vander Meer	P	B.McGee	RP	I.Pearson	P	J.Lanning	P	H.Krist
		/P	B.Newsom	P	L.Warneke	P	P.Derringer	P	D.Koslo	RP	S.Nahem	P	H.Gornicki	P	H.Pollet
P	J.Hutchings	/P	S.Rowe	P	J.Schmitz	P	E.Riddle	P	T.Sunkel	RP	B.Beck	P	L.Hamlin	P	L.Warneke
P	L.Wallace	/P	N.Kimball	P	J.Mooty	RP	J.Beggs	P	V.Mungo			P	L.Wilkie	P	B.Lohrman
/P	W.Spahn	/P	C.Kehn	P	P.Erickson	RP	C.Shoun	/P	B.Voiselle	P	C.Blanton	/P	J.Hallett	P	W.Moore
/P	F.LaManna	/P	F.Fitzsimmons	P	T.Pressnell			/P	H.East	/P	A.Lapihuska	/P	N.Strincevich	P	B.Beckmann
/P	A.Johnson	/P	B.Chipman	P	H.Wyse	P	J.Thompson			/P	G.Hennessey	/P	B.Brandt	/P	C.Shoun
/P	G.Diehl			P	D.Errickson	/P	E.Blackwell			/P	P.Masterson	/P	K.Jungels		
/P	J.Hickey			/P	E.Hanyzewski	/P	J.Turner			/P	H.Flitcraft	/P	D.Conger		
				/P	J.Flores	/P	W.Moore			/P	G.Lambert	/P	H.Shuman		
				/P	V.Eaves										
				/P	J.Berry										
				/P	E.Kush										
				/P	B.Bowman										

TEAM	G	W	L	PCT	GB	R	OR	AB	H	2B	3B	HR	BB	SO	AVG	OBP	SLG	PRO	PRO+	BR	/A	PF	CHI	RC	SB	CS	SBA	SBR
STL	156	106	48	.688		755	482	5421	1454	282	69	60	551	507	.268	.338	.379	.717	109	109	54	108	103	718	71			
BRO	155	104	50	.675	2	742	510	5285	1398	263	34	62	572	484	.265	.338	.362	.700	110	80	69	102	107	671	81			
NY	154	85	67	.559	20	675	600	5210	1323	162	35	109	558	511	.254	.330	.361	.691	108	59	56	101	102	627	39			
CIN	154	76	76	.500	29	527	545	5260	1216	198	39	66	483	549	.231	.299	.321	.620	88	-81	-80	100	102	519	42			
PIT	151	66	81	.449	36.5	585	631	5104	1250	173	49	54	537	536	.245	.320	.333	.650	95	-15	-29	103	102	556	41			
CHI	155	68	86	.442	38	591	665	5352	1360	224	41	75	509	607	.254	.321	.353	.674	108	23	47	96	93	619	63			
BOS	150	59	89	.399	44	515	645	5077	1216	210	19	68	474	507	.240	.307	.329	.636	94	-48	-37	98	97	520	49			
PHI	151	42	109	.278	62.5	394	706	5060	1174	168	37	44	392	488	.232	.289	.306	.595	84	-125	-103	95	89	451	37			
TOT	613					4784		41769	10391	1680	323	538	4076	4189	.249	.318	.343	.661						423				

TEAM	CG	SH	SV	IP	H	H/G	HR	BB	SO	RAT	ERA	ERA+	OAV	OOB	PR	/A	PF	CPI	FA	E	DP	FW	PW	BW	SBW	DIF
STL	70	18	15	1410[1]	1192	7.6	49	473	651	10.7	2.55	134	.228	.294	120	137	103	102	.972	169	137	-.1	14.7	5.8		8.6
BRO	67	16	24	1398[2]	1205	7.8	73	493	612	11.1	2.84	115	.231	.302	73	64	98	101	.977	138	150	1.7	6.9	7.4		11.1
NY	70	12	13	1370	1299	8.5	94	493	497	11.9	3.31	101	.250	.316	0	7	101	104	.977	138	128	1.6	.8	6.0		.6
CIN	80	12	8	1411[2]	1213	7.7	47	526	616	11.2	2.82	117	.230	.302	78	73	99	97	.971	177	158	-.7	7.8	-8.6		1.5
PIT	64	13	11	1351[1]	1376	9.2	62	435	426	12.1	3.58	94	.262	.320	-41	-30	102	97	.969	184	128	-1.3	-3.2	-3.1		.1
CHI	71	10	14	1400[2]	1447	9.3	70	525	507	12.8	3.60	89	.267	.334	-44	-62	97	105	.973	170	136	-.2	-6.7	5.0		-7.2
BOS	68	9	8	1334	1326	8.9	82	518	414	12.6	3.76	89	.260	.331	-66	-62	101	100	.976	142	138	1.1	-6.7	-4.0		-5.5
PHI	51	2	6	1341	1328	8.9	61	605	472	15.1	4.12	80	.260	.342	-120	-122	100	93	.968	194	147	-1.9	-13.1	-11.1		-7.4
TOT	541	92	99	11017[2]		8.5				11.9	3.31		.249	.318					.973	1312	1122					

Runs
Ott-NY 118
Slaughter-StL 100
Mize-NY 97
Hack-Chi 91

Hits
Slaughter-StL 188
Nicholson-Chi 173
Medwick-Bro 166
Hack-Chi 166
Elliott-Pit 166

Doubles
Marion-StL 38
Medwick-Bro 37
Hack-Chi 36
Herman-Bro 34
Reiser-Bro 33

Triples
Slaughter-StL 17
Nicholson-Chi 11
Musial-StL 10
Litwhiler-Phi 9

Home Runs
Ott-NY 30
Mize-NY 26
Camilli-Bro 26
Nicholson-Chi 21
West-Bos 16

Total Bases
Slaughter-StL 292
Mize-NY 282
Nicholson-Chi 280
Ott-NY 273
Camilli-Bro 247

Runs Batted In
Mize-NY 110
Camilli-Bro 109
Slaughter-StL 98
Medwick-Bro 96
Ott-NY 93

Runs Produced
Slaughter-StL 185
Ott-NY 181
Mize-NY 181
Camilli-Bro 172
Medwick-Bro 161

Bases On Balls
Ott-NY 109
Fletcher-Pit 105
Camilli-Bro 97
Hack-Chi 94
Slaughter-StL 88

Batting Average
Lombardi-Bos 330
Slaughter-StL 318
Musial-StL 315
Reiser-Bro 310
Mize-NY 305

On Base Percentage
Fletcher-Pit 417
Ott-NY 415
Slaughter-StL 412
Hack-Chi 402
Musial-StL 397

Slugging Average
Mize-NY 521
Ott-NY 497
Slaughter-StL 494
Musial-StL 490
Lombardi-Bos 482

Production
Ott-NY 912
Slaughter-StL 906
Mize-NY 901
Musial-StL 888
Nicholson-Chi 859

Adjusted Production
Ott-NY 165
Mize-NY 161
Nicholson-Chi 156
Slaughter-StL 153
Musial-StL 148

Batter Runs
Slaughter-StL 49.8
Ott-NY 49.3
Mize-NY 40.8
Nicholson-Chi 37.6
Musial-StL 35.0

Adjusted Batter Runs
Ott-NY 48.7
Nicholson-Chi 41.7
Slaughter-StL 41.1
Mize-NY 40.2
Hack-Chi 33.5

Clutch Hitting Index
Brown-StL 146
Medwick-Bro 143
Owen-Bro 120
Camilli-Bro 117
F.McCormick-Cin . . 116

Runs Created
Slaughter-StL 128
Ott-NY 122
Nicholson-Chi 112
Mize-NY 110
Hack-Chi 100

Total Average
Ott-NY 990
Slaughter-StL 966
Musial-StL 926
Mize-NY 911
Camilli-Bro 888

Stolen Bases
Reiser-Bro 20
Reese-Bro 15
Fernandez-Bos 15
Merullo-Chi 14
Hopp-StL 14

Stolen Base Average

Stolen Base Runs

Fielding Runs
DiMaggio-Pit 19.8
Reese-Bro 17.4
May-Phi 17.2
Holmes-Bos 14.8
Fletcher-Pit 11.5

Total Player Rating
Nicholson-Chi 4.8
Ott-NY 4.2
Slaughter-StL 3.9
Fletcher-Pit 3.2
Mize-NY 3.0

Wins
M.Cooper-StL 22
Beazley-StL 21
Wyatt-Bro 19
Passeau-Chi 19
VanderMeer-Cin 18

Win Percentage
French-Bro 789
Beazley-StL 778
M.Cooper-StL 759
Wyatt-Bro 731
Davis-Bro 714

Games
Adams-NY 61
Casey-Bro 50
Podgajny-Phi 43
Beazley-StL 43

Complete Games
Tobin-Bos 28
Passeau-Chi 24
M.Cooper-StL 22
Walters-Cin 21
VanderMeer-Cin 21

Shutouts
M.Cooper-StL 10
Sewell-Pit 5
Javery-Bos 5
Davis-Bro 5

Saves
Casey-Bro 13
Adams-NY 11
Beggs-Cin 8
Sain-Bos 6
Gumbert-StL 5

Innings Pitched
Tobin-Bos 287.2
M.Cooper-StL 278.2
Passeau-Chi 278.1
Starr-Cin 276.2
Javery-Bos 261.0

Fewest Hits/Game
M.Cooper-StL 6.69
VanderMeer-Cin 6.93
Higbe-Bro 7.31
Starr-Cin 7.42
Beazley-StL 7.57

Fewest BB/Game
Warneke-StL-Chi . . 1.79
Lohrman-StL-NY . . . 1.85
Hubbell-NY 1.94
Derringer-Cin 2.11
M.Cooper-StL 2.20

Strikeouts
VanderMeer-Cin 186
M.Cooper-StL 152
Higbe-Bro 115
Walters-Cin 109
Melton-Phi 107

Strikeouts/Game
VanderMeer-Cin 6.86
Lanier-StL 5.20
M.Cooper-StL 4.91
Higbe-Bro 4.67
Melton-Phi 4.60

Ratio
M.Cooper-StL 9.04
Lohrman-StL-NY . . 10.07
Davis-Bro 10.35
Warneke-StL-Chi . . 10.39
Wyatt-Bro 10.56

Earned Run Average
M.Cooper-StL 1.78
Beazley-StL 2.13
Davis-Bro 2.36
VanderMeer-Cin . . . 2.43
Lohrman-StL-NY . . 2.48

Adjusted ERA
M.Cooper-StL 193
Beazley-StL 161
Davis-Bro 138
Lohrman-StL-NY . . 136
VanderMeer-Cin . . . 135

Opponents' Batting Avg.
M.Cooper-StL 204
VanderMeer-Cin 208
Wyatt-Bro 223
Higbe-Bro 225
Starr-Cin 226

Opponents' On Base Pct.
M.Cooper-StL 258
Lohrman-StL-NY . . .281
Wyatt-Bro 286
Warneke-StL-Chi . . .286
Davis-Bro 287

Starter Runs
M.Cooper-StL 47.6
Beazley-StL 28.3
French-Bro 24.4
VanderMeer-Cin . . . 23.8
Davis-Bro 21.8

Adjusted Starter Runs
M.Cooper-StL 51.0
Beazley-StL 30.9
French-Bro 23.5
VanderMeer-Cin . . . 23.0
Davis-Bro 20.6

Clutch Pitching Index
Bithorn-Chi 130
Passeau-Chi 121
Beazley-StL 114
Schumacher-NY . . . 113
Carpenter-NY 112

Relief Runs
Adams-NY 14.4
Casey-Bro 13.2
Beggs-Cin 11.6
Shoun-StL-Cin 9.4
Webber-Bro 2.0

Adjusted Relief Runs
Adams-NY 14.8
Casey-Bro 12.6
Beggs-Cin 11.3
Shoun-StL-Cin 9.1
Webber-Bro 1.7

Relief Ranking
Adams-NY 20.9
Beggs-Cin 15.0
Casey-Bro 12.4
Shoun-StL-Cin 4.4
Webber-Bro 1.6

Total Pitcher Index
M.Cooper-StL 5.0
Beazley-StL 4.0
French-Bro 3.4
Walters-Cin 3.0
VanderMeer-Cin . . . 2.9

Total Baseball Ranking
M.Cooper-StL 5.0
Nicholson-Chi 4.8
Ott-NY 4.2
Beazley-StL 4.0
Slaughter-StL 3.9

January 6 Bob Feller, winner of 76 games for the Indians in three previous seasons, follows Hank Greenberg into the military. Feller, saying "I've always wanted to be on the winning side," enlists in the Navy and reports to Norfolk, Virginia, for duty.

January 15 President Roosevelt gives baseball the go-ahead to play despite World War II. In his famous "green light" letter FDR says, "I honestly think it would be best for the country to keep baseball going." He encourages more night baseball so that war workers may attend.

February 3 At a special meeting of owners to discuss wartime regulations, they decide to allow 14 night games for each club, with Washington allowed 21. Two All-Star Games will be played, one with a military All-Star team. Curfews are set for night games with no inning to start after 12:50 war time.

June 2 Red Sox star Ted Williams enlists as a Navy aviator. He will finish the season with his team as will many other players who enlist or await the draft. Among AL regulars of 1941 who are now in the service: Johnny Rigney, Joe Grace, John Berardino, Cecil Travis, Bob Feller, Pat Mullin, Buddy Lewis, Sam Chapman, and Johnny Sturm.

July 6 First-inning home runs by Lou Boudreau and Rudy York off Mort Cooper lead the AL to a 3–1 triumph over the NL in the All-Star Game at the Polo Grounds. Mickey Owen's pinch home run is the NL's only score. He does not hit a single homer during the regular schedule.

July 7 A military all-star team that includes Bob Feller, Cecil Travis, Sam Chapman, Benny McCoy, Johnny Sturm, and Frank Pytlak loses, 5–0, to AL stars in a game at Cleveland in front of more than 60,000 fans. Jim Bagby wins against his Indian teammate Feller. Military relief receives $160,000.

August 23 Walter Johnson pitching to Babe Ruth is the pregame attraction that draws 69,000 for the New York-Washington game at Yankee Stadium that provides $80,000 for Army-Navy relief. Ruth hits the fifth pitch into the right field stands.

September 14 The Yankees clinch the pennant against Cleveland 8-3. Ernie Bonham wins his 20th game, and DiMaggio strokes four hits.

September 14* Leon Day, pitching for the Homestead Grays in the Negro League World Series, fans 12 in beating Satchel Paige and the Kansas City

Monarchs 4-1 in Game 4. The Monarchs protest, contending that Day and three other players were picked up from other teams. Day's win is disallowed, and the Monarchs sweep the four games.

September 30 Down 7–0 to Yankees hurler Red Ruffing in the Series opener, the Cardinals storm back for four ninth-inning runs. It's not enough to win, but it is a sign of things to come in the World Series.

October 1 Behind 3–0, the Yankees tie it up in the top of the eighth, but rookie Stan Musial singles in Enos Slaughter in the bottom of the inning to forge a 4–3 Cardinal victory to even the World Series at one game apiece.

November 3 Ted Williams is the Triple Crown winner in both leagues, but the writers select second baseman Joe Gordon by 21 votes as AL MVP. Gordon of the Yankees leads the AL with 95 strikeouts, the most ground balls hit into double plays (22), and the most errors at his position (28). Pitcher Mort Cooper gets the MVP honor in the NL.

December 1 At major league meetings in Chicago, the owners decide that spring training in 1943 will be limited to locations north of the Potomac or Ohio rivers and east of the Mississippi.

	BOSTON		CHICAGO		CLEVELAND		DETROIT		NEW YORK		PHILADELPHIA		ST.LOUIS		WASHINGTON
M	J.Cronin	M	J.Dykes	M	L.Boudreau	M	D.Baker	M	J.McCarthy	M	C.Mack	M	L.Sewell	M	B.Harris
1B	T.Lupien	1B	J.Kuhel	1B	L.Fleming	1B	R.York	1B	B.Hassett	1B	D.Siebert	1B	G.McQuinn	1B	M.Vernon
2B	B.Doerr	2B	D.Kolloway	2B	R.Mack	2B	J.Bloodworth	2B	J.Gordon	2B	B.Knickerb'r	2B	D.Gutteridge	2B	E.Clary
SS	J.Pesky	SS	L.Appling	SS	L.Boudreau	SS	B.Hitchcock	SS	P.Rizzuto	SS	P.Suder	SS	V.Stephens	SS	J.Sullivan
3B	J.Tabor	3B	B.Kennedy	3B	K.Keltner	3B	P.Higgins	3B	F.Crosetti	3B	B.Blair	3B	H.Clift	3B	B.Estalella
LF	T.Williams	LF	T.Wright	LF	J.Heath	LF	B.McCosky	LF	C.Keller	LF	B.Johnson	LF	G.McQuillen	LF	G.Case
CF	D.DiMaggio	CF	M.Hoag	CF	R.Weatherly	CF	D.Cramer	CF	J.DiMaggio	CF	M.Kreevich	CF	W.Judnich	CF	S.Spence
RF	L.Finney	RF	W.Moses	RF	O.Hockett	RF	N.Harris	RF	T.Henrich	RF	E.Valo	RF	C.Laabs	RF	B.Campbell
C	B.Conroy	C	M.Tresh	C	O.Denning	C	B.Tebbetts	C	B.Dickey	C	H.Wagner	C	R.Ferrell	C	J.Early
C	J.Peacock	C	T.Turner	O	B.Mills	O3	D.Ross	3	B.Rolfe	O	D.Miles	S2	T.Criscola	S2	J.Pofahl
O	P.Fox	3	D.Lodigiani	C	J.Hegan	C	D.Parsons	C	B.Rosar	2S	C.Davis	O	M.Chartak	23	B.Repass
1	J.Foxx	O	S.West	C	G.Desautels	S	M.Franklin	31	J.Priddy	C	B.Swift	C	F.Hayes	O3	R.Cullenbine
32	S.Newsome	C	S.Dickey	O	R.Radcliff	O	R.Hemsley	S	J.Wallaesa	O	R.Cullenbine	O	B.Swift	O	A.Evans
3	J.Cronin	2	S.Webb	O	F.Gaffke	O	J.Lipon	O	G.Selkirk	E.McNair	C	B.Swift	O	M.Chartak
/O	P.Campbell	O	B.Mueller	S	R.Peters	S	E.McNair	C	R.Cullenbine	C	F.Hayes	/S	J.Berardino	2	C.Gomez
/O	A.Gilbert	S	L.Wells	O	H.Edwards	2	D.Meyer	1	E.Levy	/O	E.Collins	3	A.Strange	2	F.Croucher
/2	T.Carey	O	V.Heim	/2	T.Sepkowski	/2	C.Gehringer	C	E.Kearse	J.Castiglia	/2	D.Heffner	/3	R.Ortiz
		3	J.Grant	/1	E.Robinson	C	H.Riebe	/O	T.Stainback	/O	K.Richardson	/C	L.Sewell	/3	R.Hoffman
P	T.Hughson	O	B.Sketchley	/3	B.Lemon	/O	B.Patrick	/O	M.Chartak	/O	F.Mackiewicz	H	B.Dahlgren	/3	S.Galle
P	C.Wagner	/O	T.Tucker	/C	G.Susce	/C	A.Unser			G.Yankowski	H	R.Hayworth	/O	A.Kvasnak
P	J.Dobson	/1	J.Jones					P	T.Bonham	/S	L.Eschen			/O	G.Moore
P	D.Newsome			P	J.Bagby	P	A.Benton	P	S.Chandler	/1	B.Konopka	P	E.Auker		
P	O.Judd	P	J.Humphries	P	M.Harder	P	D.Trout	P	R.Ruffing	P	D.Adkins	P	J.Niggeling	P	S.Hudson
RP	M.Brown	P	E.Smith	P	C.Dean	P	H.White	P	H.Borowy			P	D.Galehouse	P	B.Newsom
		P	T.Lyons	P	A.Smith	P	H.Newhouser	P	M.Breuer	P	P.Marchildon	P	A.Hollingsworth	P	E.Wynn
P	B.Butland	P	B.Dietrich	P	A.Milnar	P	T.Bridges	RP	J.Murphy	P	R.Wolff	P	B.Muncrief	P	A.Carrasquel
P	Y.Terry	P	B.Ross	RP	T.Ferrick	RP	R.Henshaw	RP	J.Lindell	P	L.Harris	RP	G.Caster	P	W.Masterson
P	K.Chase	RP	J.Haynes	RP	H.Eisenstat	RP	J.Gorsica			P	R.Christopher				
P	M.Ryba							P	A.Donald	P	D.Fowler	P	S.Sundra	P	B.Zuber
		P	J.Wade	P	V.Kennedy	P	V.Trucks	P	L.Gomez			P	S.Ferens	P	R.Scarborough
		P	T.Lee	P	R.Embree	/P	C.Fuchs	/P	M.Russo	P	H.Besse	/P	F.Ostermueller	P	J.Wilson
		P	O.Grove	P	J.Heving	P	H.Manders	P	N.Branch	P	J.Knott	P	B.Harris	/P	B.Trotter
		/P	J.Rigney	P	S.Gromek	P	J.Wilson	/P	J.Turner	P	B.Harris	P	P.Appleton	/P	D.Leonard
		/P	L.Perme	/P	R.Poat	/P	S.Rowe	/P	M.Queen	P	F.Caligiuri	P	F.Biscan	/P	S.Sundra
		/P	E.Weiland	/P	C.Brown					P	T.Shirley	P	L.Hanning	/P	H.Cathey
		/P	P.Appleton	/P	J.Krakauskas					/P	B.Savage	/P	E.Pyle	/P	B.Kennedy
				/P	A.Reynolds					/P	B.Beckmann	/P	J.Whitehead	P	L.Bevil
				/P	P.Center					/P	J.Coleman	P	B.Trotter	/P	D.Adkins
				/P	P.Calvert					/P	L.McCrabb			/P	P.McCullough
										/P	T.Abernathy				
										/P	S.Lowry				

TEAM	G	W	L	PCT	GB	R	OR	AB	H	2B	3B	HR	BB	SO	AVG	OBP	SLG	PRO	PRO+	BR	/A	PF	CHI	RC	SB	CS	SBA	SBR
NY	154	103	51	.669		801	507	5305	1429	223	57	108	591	556	.269	.346	.394	.740	118	104	120	98	104	759	69	33	68	1
BOS	152	93	59	.612	9	761	594	5248	1451	244	55	103	591	508	.276	.352	.403	.755	116	132	105	103	96	774	68	61	53	-16
STL	151	82	69	.543	19.5	730	637	5229	1354	239	62	98	609	607	.259	.338	.385	.723	109	68	57	102	101	703	37	38	49	-12
CLE	156	75	79	.487	28	590	659	5317	1344	223	58	50	500	544	.253	.320	.345	.665	100	-43	-7	94	96	596	69	74	48	-24
DET	156	73	81	.474	30	589	587	5327	1313	217	37	76	509	476	.246	.314	.344	.658	85	-57	-106	108	98	582	39	40	49	-12
CHI	148	66	82	.446	34	538	609	4949	1215	214	36	25	497	427	.246	.316	.318	.634	87	-87	-75	98	102	520	114	70	62	-8
WAS	151	62	89	.411	39.5	653	817	5295	1364	224	49	40	581	536	.258	.333	.341	.674	98	-14	-8	99	101	641	98	29	77	12
PHI	154	55	99	.357	48	549	801	5285	1315	213	46	33	440	490	.249	.309	.325	.634	86	-101	-98	99	101	536	44	45	49	-14
TOT	611					5211		41955	10785	1797	400	533	4318	4144	.257	.329	.357	.686							538	390	58	-73

TEAM	CG	SH	SV	IP	H	H/G	HR	BB	SO	RAT	ERA	ERA+	OAV	OOB	PR	/A	PF	CPI	FA	E	DP	FW	PW	BW	SBW	DIF
NY	88	18	17	1375	1259	8.2	71	431	558	11.2	2.91	118	.244	.304	115	82	94	108	.976	142	190	2.0	8.4	12.3	1.0	2.3
BOS	84	11	17	1358²	1260	8.3	65	553	500	12.1	3.44	108	.247	.322	32	43	102	99	.974	157	156	1.0	4.4	10.8	-.7	1.5
STL	68	12	13	1363	1387	9.2	63	505	488	12.7	3.59	103	.262	.330	10	17	101	103	.972	167	143	.4	1.7	5.8	-.3	-1.2
CLE	61	12	11	1402²	1353	8.7	61	560	448	12.4	3.59	96	.254	.327	10	-23	94	99	.974	163	175	1.0	-2.4	-.7	-1.5	1.6
DET	65	12	14	1399¹	1321	8.5	60	598	671	12.5	3.13	126	.248	.326	82	127	108	111	.969	194	142	-.8	13.0	-10.9	-.3	-5.1
CHI	86	8	8	1314¹	1304	8.9	74	473	432	12.3	3.58	100	.258	.325	11	3	98	102	.970	173	144	-.1	.3	-7.7	.1	-.6
WAS	68	12	11	1346²	1496	10.0	50	558	496	13.8	4.58	80	.279	.349	-139	-139	100	91	.962	222	133	-2.7	-14.2	-.8	2.2	2.1
PHI	67	5	9	1374²	1404	9.2	89	639	546	13.5	4.45	85	.263	.344	-120	-102	103	93	.969	188	124	-.6	-10.4	-10.0	-.5	-.5
TOT	587	90	100	10934¹		8.9				12.6	3.66		.257	.329					.971	1406	1207					

Runs		Hits		Doubles		Triples		Home Runs		Total Bases	
Williams-Bos	141	Pesky-Bos	205	Kolloway-Chi	40	Spence-Was	15	Williams-Bos	36	Williams-Bos	338
DiMaggio-NY	123	Spence-Was	203	Clift-StL	39	Heath-Cle	13	Laabs-StL	27	DiMaggio-NY	304
DiMaggio-Bos	110	Williams-Bos	186	Heath-Cle	37	DiMaggio-NY	13	Keller-NY	26	Keller-NY	279
Clift-StL	108	DiMaggio-NY	186	DiMaggio-Bos	36	McQuillen-StL	12	York-Det	21	Spence-Was	272
Keller-NY	106	Keltner-Cle	179					DiMaggio-NY	21	DiMaggio-Bos	272

Runs Batted In		Runs Produced		Bases On Balls		Batting Average		On Base Percentage		Slugging Average	
Williams-Bos	137	Williams-Bos	242	Williams-Bos	145	Williams-Bos	.356	Williams-Bos	.499	Williams-Bos	.648
DiMaggio-NY	114	DiMaggio-NY	216	Keller-NY	114	Pesky-Bos	.331	Keller-NY	.417	Keller-NY	.513
Keller-NY	108	Keller-NY	188	Fleming-Cle	106	Spence-Was	.323	Judnich-StL	.413	Judnich-StL	.499
Gordon-NY	103	Gordon-NY	173	Clift-StL	106	Gordon-NY	.322	Fleming-Cle	.412	DiMaggio-NY	.498
Doerr-Bos	102	Spence-Was	169	Cullenbine-SL-W-NY	92	Case-Was	.320	Gordon-NY	.409	Laabs-StL	.498

Production		Adjusted Production		Batter Runs		Adjusted Batter Runs		Clutch Hitting Index		Runs Created	
Williams-Bos	1.147	Williams-Bos	214	Williams-Bos	92.6	Williams-Bos	87.0	Lupien-Bos	124	Williams-Bos	185
Keller-NY	.930	Keller-NY	164	Keller-NY	46.9	Keller-NY	49.4	Cullenbine-SL-W-NY	116	Keller-NY	131
Judnich-StL	.912	Gordon-NY	156	Gordon-NY	38.6	Gordon-NY	40.8	Vernon-Was	113	DiMaggio-NY	120
Gordon-NY	.900	Judnich-StL	153	Judnich-StL	35.4	Fleming-Cle	38.3	Siebert-Phi	113	Spence-Was	111
Laabs-StL	.878	DiMaggio-NY	148	DiMaggio-NY	34.5	DiMaggio-NY	36.8	Tabor-Bos	112	Gordon-NY	108

Total Average		Stolen Bases		Stolen Base Average		Stolen Base Runs		Fielding Runs		Total Player Rating	
Williams-Bos	1.394	Case-Was	44	Case-Was	88.0	Case-Was	9.6	Rizzuto-NY	25.0	Williams-Bos	8.1
Keller-NY	1.038	Vernon-Was	25	Vernon-Was	80.6	Vernon-Was	3.9	Pesky-Bos	17.7	Gordon-NY	5.4
Judnich-StL	.950	Rizzuto-NY	22	Rizzuto-NY	78.6	Rizzuto-NY	3.0	DiMaggio-Bos	16.9	Keller-NY	4.4
Gordon-NY	.891	Kuhel-Chi	22	Appling-Chi	77.3	Keller-NY	3.0	Keltner-Cle	15.6	Pesky-Bos	4.1
Laabs-StL	.878			Kuhel-Chi	71.0	Appling-Chi	2.1	York-Det	15.4	Rizzuto-NY	4.0

Wins		Win Percentage		Games		Complete Games		Shutouts		Saves	
Hughson-Bos	22	Bonham-NY	.808	Haynes-Chi	40	Hughson-Bos	22	Bonham-NY	6	Murphy-NY	11
Bonham-NY	21	Borowy-NY	.789	Caster-StL	39	Bonham-NY	22			Haynes-Chi	6
Marchildon-Phi	17	Hughson-Bos	.786			Lyons-Chi	20			Brown-Bos	6
Bagby-Cle	17	Chandler-NY	.762			Hudson-Was	19			Newhouser-Det	5
Chandler-NY	16	Bagby-Cle	.654							Caster-StL	5

Innings Pitched		Fewest Hits/Game		Fewest BB/Game		Strikeouts		Strikeouts/Game		Ratio	
Hughson-Bos	281.0	Newhouser-Det	6.71	Bonham-NY	.96	Newsom-Was	113	Newhouser-Det	5.05	Bonham-NY	8.92
Bagby-Cle	270.2	Niggeling-StL	7.55	Lyons-Chi	1.30	Hughson-Bos	113	Bridges-Det	5.02	Lyons-Chi	9.73
Auker-StL	249.0	Dobson-Bos	7.64	Ruffing-NY	1.91	Marchildon-Phi	110	Trucks-Det	4.88	Ruffing-NY	10.55
Marchildon-Phi	244.0	Trucks-Det	7.89	Breuer-NY	2.03	Benton-Det	110	Newsom-Was	4.76	Breuer-NY	10.68
Hudson-Was	239.1	Chandler-NY	7.89	Bagby-Cle	2.13	Niggeling-StL	107	Niggeling-StL	4.67	Hughson-Bos	10.70

Earned Run Average		Adjusted ERA		Opponents' Batting Avg.		Opponents' On Base Pct.		Starter Runs		Adjusted Starter Runs	
Lyons-Chi	2.10	Lyons-Chi	172	Newhouser-Det	.207	Bonham-NY	.259	Bonham-NY	34.8	Hughson-Bos	35.5
Bonham-NY	2.27	Newhouser-Det	161	Niggeling-StL	.226	Lyons-Chi	.275	Hughson-Bos	33.2	Newhouser-Det	30.6
Chandler-NY	2.38	Bonham-NY	152	Dobson-Bos	.231	Ruffing-NY	.292	Lyons-Chi	31.3	Lyons-Chi	30.1
Newhouser-Det	2.45	Chandler-NY	145	Trucks-Det	.231	Breuer-NY	.295	Chandler-NY	28.5	Bonham-NY	29.4
Borowy-NY	2.52	Trucks-Det	144	Borowy-NY	.233	Hughson-Bos	.296	Humphries-Chi	24.8	Benton-Det	26.5

Clutch Pitching Index		Relief Runs		Adjusted Relief Runs		Relief Ranking		Total Pitcher Index		Total Baseball Ranking	
Chandler-NY	136	Ferrick-Cle	15.0	Ferrick-Cle	13.2	Haynes-Chi	14.2	Lyons-Chi	4.0	Williams-Bos	8.1
Lyons-Chi	131	Haynes-Chi	11.9	Haynes-Chi	11.2	Caster-StL	10.0	Newhouser-Det	4.0	Gordon-NY	5.4
Hollingsworth-StL	123	Caster-StL	7.5	Caster-StL	7.9	Ferrick-Cle	8.4	Hughson-Bos	3.8	Keller-NY	4.4
Humphries-Chi	121	Murphy-NY	1.6	Brown-Bos	2.0	Brown-Bos	4.0	Chandler-NY	3.2	Pesky-Bos	4.1
Niggeling-StL	119	Brown-Bos	1.5	Murphy-NY	.2	Murphy-NY	.5	Humphries-Chi	2.7	Lyons-Chi	4.0

February 9 The NL is looking for a buyer for the Phillies, whose owner, Gerry Nugent, has fallen in arrears on rent and bank loans. The league pays $10 a share for 4,685 out of 5,000 outstanding shares in club and sells the club nine days later to William D. Cox of New York.

February 20 Phil Wrigley and Branch Rickey charter the All-American Girls Softball League. The league will operate around the Chicago area and is formed as a backup in case the government shuts down major league baseball. The league will later change its name, switch to hardball with a pitching distance of 40 feet and bases 68 feet apart, and inspire the movie, *A League of Their Own*.

April 20 Braves manager Casey Stengel is struck by a taxi, fractures a leg, and will miss much of the season. The cabdriver is nominated Sportsman of the Year in Boston by a local newspaper, weary of Stengel's humor in the face of the Braves' pitiful record

May 30 The Cubs play 32 games before hitting a home run. Bill Nicholson hits the first Cubs blast of the year against the Braves in the club's 1,120th at bat of the season.

June 1 Rip Sewell of the Pirates throws his dew-drop ball in a game. Sewell loops the ball 18 to 20 feet high on its way to the strike zone. Later it is called a blooper or "eephus" ball. The pitch is more than a gag, and Sewell is on his way to a 20-win season.

June 4 Mort Cooper of the St. Louis Cardinals pitches back-to-back one-hitters, beating the Brooklyn Dodgers on May 31 and the Philadelphia Phillies on June 4. Hits by Billy Herman on May 31 and by Jimmy Wasdell of the Phils deprive him of no-hitters.

July 18 Playing as if neither team wanted the win, the Giants and Phillies strand 30 baserunners, a major league record. New York wins, 10–6.

August 18 Carl Hubbell wins his 253rd and final game, all with the Giants, as he beats the Pirates 3-2. He will retire at the end of the year and take over the Giants' farm system.

September 18 The Cardinals clinch the NL pennant. St. Louis pitchers Howie Pollet, Max Lanier, and Mort Cooper will rank 1-2-3 in NL ERA, and Al Brazle at 1.53 and Harry Brecheen at 2.27 are near the same level. Stan Musial, in his second season, hits .357 and has 220 hits, 347 total bases, 48 doubles, 20 triples.

October 6 Robert Cooper, father of pitcher Mort Cooper and C Walker Cooper, dies at his home in Independence, Missouri, but both players decide to play in the World Series. Mort goes on to beat the New York Yankees 4-3, resurrecting memories of 1942 when the Yankees lost four straight after winning the opener. Marty Marion and Ray Sanders homer.

November 23 Commissioner Landis rules that Phils owner William D. Cox is permanently ineligible to hold office or be employed in baseball for having bet on his own team. The Carpenter family of Delaware will buy the Philadelphia club, and Bob Carpenter, age 28, will become president. The Phils, in an effort to change their image, will conduct a contest for a new name. The winning entry, the Blue Jays, submitted by a Mrs. John Crooks, will be the unofficial team name for 1944-45 until it's abandoned in 1946.

BOSTON	BROOKLYN	CHICAGO	CINCINNATI	NEW YORK	PHILADELPHIA	PITTSBURGH	ST.LOUIS
M B.Coleman	M L.Durocher	M J.Wilson	M B.McKechnie	M M.Ott	M B.Harris	M F.Frisch	M B.Southworth
M C.Stengel	1B D.Camilli	1B P.Cavarretta	1B F.McCormick	1B J.Orengo	M F.Fitzsimmons	1B E.Fletcher	1B R.Sanders
1B J.McCarthy	2B B.Herman	2B E.Stanky	2B L.Frey	2B M.Witek	1B J.Wasdell	2B P.Coscarart	2B L.Klein
2B C.Ryan	SS A.Glossop	SS L.Merullo	SS E.Miller	SS B.Jurges	2B D.Murtaugh	SS F.Gustine	SS M.Marion
SS W.Wietelmann	3B A.Vaughan	3B S.Hack	3B S.Mesner	3B B.Bartell	SS G.Stewart	3B B.Elliott	3B W.Kurowski
3B E.Joost	LF D.Walker	LF L.Novikoff	LF E.Tipton	LF J.Medwick	3B P.May	LF J.Russell	LF D.Litwhiler
LF B.Nieman	CF A.Galan	CF P.Lowrey	CF G.Walker	CF J.Rucker	CF C.Triplett	CF V.DiMaggio	CF H.Walker
CF T.Holmes	RF P.Waner	RF B.Nicholson	RF M.Marshall	RF M.Ott	RF B.Adams	RF J.Barrett	RF S.Musial
RF C.Workman	C M.Owen	C C.McCullough	C R.Mueller	C G.Mancuso	C R.Northey	C A.Lopez	C W.Cooper
C P.Masi					C M.Livingston		
	O3 F.Bordagaray	O I.Goodman	O E.Crabtree	31 S.Gordon		O M.Van Robays	O3 D.Garms
O C.Ross	O L.Olmo	13 D.Dallessandro	C B.Haas	C E.Lombardi	13 B.Dahlgren	O T.O'Brien	O1 J.Hopp
1 K.Farrell	C3 B.Bragan	O C.Hernandez	O D.Clay	O3 B.Maynard	2S R.Hamrick	C B.Baker	C K.O'Dea
C C.Kluttz	1 H.Schultz	2 S.Martin	2 W.Williams	O C.Mead	S C.Brewster	2 A.Rubeling	2 J.Brown
C H.Poland	C J.Medwick	C M.Livingston	1 A.Lakeman	1 N.Reyes	O D.Litwhiler	S H.Geary	O F.Demaree
3 J.Burns	C D.Moore	1 H.Becker	C T.DePhillips	O B.Barna	O E.Naylor	O J.Wyrostek	2 G.Fallon
3 H.Heltzel	O G.Hermanski	O A.Pafko	S M.McCormick	O B.Kerr	O D.Moore	O F.Colman	/O C.Triplett
/3 B.Brubaker	S R.Barkley	O E.Sauer	/O C.Aleno	/C J.Stephenson	C B.Finley	/S T.Ordenana	/O B.Adams
/3 T.Cuccinello	2 A.Kampouris	B.Schuster	/O F.Kelleher	C R.Berres	A.Seminick	/C H.Camelli	/C S.Narron
/1 B.Etchison	/1 J.Cooney	A.Todd	/2 C.Brewster	/O V.Bradford	T.Padden	H J.Wasdell	
H C.Creeden	/S B.Bartley	D.Johnson	/1 L.Goldstein		P.Busby		P M.Cooper
H S.Gentile	/2 A.Campanis	2 W.Platt	R D.West		B.Culp	P R.Sewell	P M.Lanier
/2 B.Geraghty	/3 B.Hart	/3 P.Elko	P J.Vander Meer	P C.Melton	/O C.Klein	P B.Klinger	P H.Krist
	/S L.Durocher	/O J.Ostrowski	P E.Riddle	P J.Wittig	/S G.DelSavio	P M.Butcher	P H.Brecheen
P A.Javery	/O C.Gillenwater	C.Gilbert	P B.Walters	P V.Mungo		P W.Hebert	P H.Gumbert
P N.Andrews	/3 J.Orengo	B.Holm	P R.Starr	P R.Fischer	P A.Gerheauser	P H.Gornicki	RP R.Munger
P R.Barrett	/S P.Ankenman	M.Kreitner	P C.Shoun	P K.Chase	P J.Kraus	RP B.Brandt	P H.Pollet
P J.Tobin	/3 G.Hodges	P C.Passeau	RP J.Beggs	RP A.Adams	P S.Rowe	P X.Rescigno	P M.Dickson
P M.Salvo	H H.Peck	P H.Bithorn	P E.Heusser	RP B.Sayles	P D.Barrett	P J.Gee	P A.Brazle
RP D.Odom	P K.Higbe	P P.Derringer	P R.Stone	P H.Feldman	P S.Johnson	/P J.Hallett	P E.White
	P W.Wyatt	P H.Wyse	/P B.Malloy	P B.Lohrman	RP N.Kimball	/P J.Podgajny	/P B.Byerly
P B.Cardoni	P E.Head	P E.Hanyzewski	/P J.Niemes	/P C.Hubbell	/P C.Fuchs	P J.Lanning	
P D.MacFayden	P B.Newsom	RP R.Prim		P K.Trinkle	P J.Podgajny	P H.Shuman	
/P G.Jeffcoat	RP L.Webber	P L.Warneke		P J.Allen	P B.Lee	/P D.Dietz	
P B.Donovan	P R.Melton	P B.Lee		P H.East	P D.Conger	/P C.Cuccurullo	
/P C.Lindquist	P M.Macon	/P D.Barrett		/P B.Voiselle	P D.Dietz		
/P J.Dagenhard	/P R.Barney	P P.Erickson		/P B.Coombs	/P A.Karl		
/P A.Stout	P F.Fitzsimmons	/P J.Burrows		/P F.Seward	/P D.Matthewson		
/P L.Tost	/P J.Allen	P B.Fleming		/P T.Sunkel	/P G.Eyrich		
/P G.Diehl	/P B.Lohrman	/P W.Signer			/P B.Beck		
/P R.Martin	/P F.Ostermueller	P D.Alderson			/P R.McKee		
/P R.Talcott	/P H.Gregg	/P J.Mooty			/P K.Raffensberger		
	/P B.Sayles				/P D.Donahue		
	/P N.Kimball				/P A.Lapihuska		
	/P C.Haughey				/P B.Webb		
	/P B.Chipman				/P M.Salvo		

TEAM	G	W	L	PCT	GB	R	OR	AB	H	2B	3B	HR	BB	SO	AVG	OBP	SLG	PRO	PRO+	BR	/A	PF	CHI	RC	SB	CS	SBA	SBR
STL	157	105	49	.682		679	475	5438	1515	259	72	70	428	438	.279	.333	.391	.724	110	92	61	104	95	720	40			
CIN	155	87	67	.565	18	608	543	5329	1362	229	47	43	445	476	.256	.315	.340	.655	96	-35	-27	99	106	581	49			
BRO	153	81	72	.529	23.5	716	674	5309	1444	263	35	39	580	422	.272	.346	.357	.703	110	70	69	100	104	675	58			
PIT	157	80	74	.519	25	669	605	5353	1401	240	73	42	573	566	.262	.335	.357	.692	103	45	22	103	100	657	64			
CHI	154	74	79	.484	30.5	632	600	5279	1380	207	56	52	574	522	.261	.336	.351	.687	107	38	48	99	97	641	53			
BOS	153	68	85	.444	36.5	465	612	5196	1213	202	36	39	469	609	.233	.299	.309	.608	82	-121	-114	99	98	491	56			
PHI	157	64	90	.416	41	571	676	5297	1321	186	36	66	499	556	.249	.316	.335	.651	98	-38	-15	96	100	565	29			
NY	156	55	98	.359	49.5	558	713	5290	1309	153	33	81	480	470	.247	.313	.335	.648	92	-48	-52	101	100	552	35			
TOT	621					4898		42491	10945	1739	388	432	4048	4059	.258	.324	.347	.672							384			

TEAM	CG	SH	SV	IP	H	H/G	HR	BB	SO	RAT	ERA	ERA+	OAV	OOB	PR	/A	PF	CPI	FA	E	DP	FW	PW	BW	SBW	DIF
STL	94	21	15	1427	1246	7.9	33	477	639	11.0	2.57	131	.237	.303	129	126	99	105	.976	151	183	.9	13.5	6.5		7.2
CIN	78	18	17	1404	1299	8.3	38	579	498	12.1	3.13	106	.251	.328	39	28	98	105	.980	125	193	2.2	3.0	-2.9		7.7
BRO	50	13	22	1369²	1326	8.7	59	637	588	13.1	3.88	86	.254	.338	-76	-80	99	93	.972	168	137	-.3	-8.5	7.4		6.0
PIT	74	11	12	1404	1424	9.1	44	422	396	11.9	3.31	101	.264	.319	47	60	103	107	.973	170	159	-.2	6.4	2.3		-5.5
CHI	67	13	14	1386	1379	9.0	53	394	513	11.6	3.31	101	.258	.311	11	3	99	95	.973	168	138	-.3	.3	5.1		-7.7
BOS	87	13	4	1397²	1361	8.8	66	441	409	11.8	3.25	105	.255	.314	20	25	101	100	.972	176	139	-.8	2.7	-12.2		1.8
PHI	66	10	14	1392²	1436	9.3	59	451	431	12.3	3.79	89	.267	.326	-62	-64	100	93	.969	189	143	-1.3	-6.8	-1.6		-3.3
NY	35	6	19	1394²	1474	9.5	80	626	588	13.7	4.08	84	.272	.350	-108	-99	102	101	.973	166	140	-.0	-10.6	-5.6		-5.3
TOT	551	105	117	11175²		8.8				12.2	3.38		.258	.324					.974	1313	1232					

Runs
Vaughan-Bro 112
Musial-StL 108
Nicholson-Chi 95
Cavarretta-Chi 93
Stanky-Chi 92

Hits
Musial-StL 220
Witek-NY 195
Herman-Bro 193
Nicholson-Chi 188
Vaughan-Bro 186

Doubles
Musial-StL 48
Herman-Bro 41
DiMaggio-Pit 41
Vaughan-Bro 39
Holmes-Bos 33

Triples
Musial-StL 20
Klein-StL 14
Lowrey-Chi 12
Elliott-Pit 12

Home Runs
Nicholson-Chi 29
Ott-NY 18
Northey-Phi 16
Triplett-StL-Phi ... 15
DiMaggio-Pit 15

Total Bases
Musial-StL 347
Nicholson-Chi 323
Elliott-Pit 258
Klein-StL 257

Runs Batted In
Nicholson-Chi 128
Elliott-Pit 101
Herman-Bro 100
DiMaggio-Pit 88

Runs Produced
Nicholson-Chi 194
Musial-StL 176
Elliott-Pit 176
Herman-Bro 174
Vaughan-Bro 173

Bases On Balls
Galan-Bro 103
Ott-NY 95
Fletcher-Pit 95
Stanky-Chi 92
Tipton-Cin 85

Batting Average
Musial-StL .... .357
Herman-Bro .... .330
W.Cooper-StL ..... .318
Elliott-Pit .... .315
Witek-NY .... .314

On Base Percentage
Musial-StL .... .425
Galan-Bro .... .412
Herman-Bro .... .398
Fletcher-Pit ..... .395
Tipton-Cin .... .395

Slugging Average
Musial-StL .... .562
Nicholson-Chi ..... .531
W.Cooper-StL ..... .463
Elliott-Pit .... .444
Triplett-StL-Phi ... .439

Production
Musial-StL .... .988
Nicholson-Chi .... .917
Elliott-Pit .... .820
Tipton-Cin .... .819
Galan-Bro .... .818

Adjusted Production
Musial-StL 176
Nicholson-Chi 166
Tipton-Cin 138
Galan-Bro 136
Herman-Bro 135

Batter Runs
Musial-StL 65.5
Nicholson-Chi 47.7
Galan-Bro 28.3
Herman-Bro 28.0
Elliott-Pit 26.5

Adjusted Batter Runs
Musial-StL 59.6
Nicholson-Chi 49.5
Galan-Bro 28.3
Herman-Bro 27.8
Tipton-Cin 27.1

Clutch Hitting Index
Miller-Cin 138
Herman-Bro 131
Elliott-Pit 123
Wasdell-Pit-Phi ... 121
Medwick-Bro-NY ... 117

Runs Created
Musial-StL 147
Nicholson-Chi 129
Herman-Bro 97
Vaughan-Bro 96
Elliott-Pit 96

Total Average
Musial-StL 1.039
Nicholson-Chi .... .944
Ott-NY .... .895
Galan-Bro .... .876
Tipton-Cin .... .825

Stolen Bases
Vaughan-Bro 20
Lowrey-Chi 13
Workman-Bos 12
Russell-Pit 12
Gustine-Pit 12

Stolen Base Average

Stolen Base Runs

Fielding Runs
Miller-Cin 26.6
Marion-StL 25.3
Mueller-Cin 20.2
Wietelmann-Bos ... 20.0
Galan-Bro 16.1

Total Player Rating
Musial-StL 6.4
Nicholson-Chi 4.9
Galan-Bro 3.9
Mueller-Cin 3.8
Witek-NY 3.3

Wins
Sewell-Pit 21
Riddle-Cin 21
M.Cooper-StL 21
Bithorn-Chi 18
Javery-Bos 17

Win Percentage
M.Cooper-StL ..... .724
Sewell-Pit .... .700
Lanier-StL .... .682
Riddle-Cin .... .656
Bithorn-Chi .... .600

Games
Adams-NY 70
Webber-Bro 54
Head-Bro 47
Shoun-Cin 45
Mungo-NY 45

Complete Games
Sewell-Pit 25
Tobin-Bos 24
M.Cooper-StL 24
Andrews-Bos 23

Shutouts
Bithorn-Chi 7
M.Cooper-StL 6

Saves
Webber-Bro 10
Adams-NY 9
Shoun-Cin 7
Head-Bro 6
Beggs-Cin 6

Innings Pitched
Javery-Bos 303.0
VanderMeer-Cin ... 289.0
Andrews-Bos 283.2
M.Cooper-StL 274.0
Sewell-Pit 265.1

Fewest Hits/Game
Wyatt-Bro 6.92
VanderMeer-Cin ... 7.10
M.Cooper-StL 7.49
Krist-StL 7.72
Barrett-Chi-Phi ... 7.94

Fewest BB/Game
Rowe-Phi 1.31
Wyse-Chi 1.96
Derringer-Chi 2.02
Davis-Phi 2.14
Wyatt-Bro 2.14

Strikeouts
VanderMeer-Cin ... 174
M.Cooper-StL 141
Javery-Bos 134
Lanier-StL 123
Higbe-Bro 108

Strikeouts/Game
VanderMeer-Cin ... 5.42
Higbe-Bro 5.25
Lanier-StL 5.19
M.Cooper-StL 4.63
Head-Bro 4.40

Ratio
Wyatt-Bro 9.07
M.Cooper-StL 10.25
Rowe-Phi 10.31
Andrews-Bos 10.60
Bithorn-Chi 10.60

Earned Run Average
Pollet-StL 1.75
Lanier-StL 1.90
M.Cooper-StL 2.30
Wyatt-Bro 2.49
Sewell-Pit 2.54

Adjusted ERA
Lanier-StL 177
M.Cooper-StL 146
Sewell-Pit 137
Wyatt-Bro 135
Butcher-Pit 134

Opponents' Batting Avg.
Wyatt-Bro .... .207
VanderMeer-Cin ... .224
M.Cooper-StL ..... .226
Krist-StL .... .233
Barrett-Chi-Phi ... .237

Opponents' On Base Pct.
Wyatt-Bro .... .255
Rowe-Phi .... .279
M.Cooper-StL ..... .286
Andrews-Bos ..... .291
Bithorn-Chi .... .294

Starter Runs
Lanier-StL 35.2
M.Cooper-StL 33.0
Andrews-Bos 25.6
Sewell-Pit 24.7
Riddle-Cin 21.9

Adjusted Starter Runs
Lanier-StL 34.7
M.Cooper-StL 32.4
Sewell-Pit 27.5
Andrews-Bos 26.6
Pollet-StL 21.2

Clutch Pitching Index
Lanier-StL 151
Butcher-Pit 122
Sewell-Pit 121
Riddle-Cin 118
Tobin-Bos 113

Relief Runs
Beggs-Cin 13.4
Adams-NY 8.8
Prim-Chi 5.6
Brandt-Pit 1.6

Adjusted Relief Runs
Beggs-Cin 12.5
Adams-NY 9.7
Prim-Chi 5.2
Brandt-Pit 2.2

Relief Ranking
Beggs-Cin 14.1
Adams-NY 12.6
Prim-Chi 5.7
Brandt-Pit 1.7

Total Pitcher Index
Sewell-Pit 4.0
Tobin-Bos 3.5
Lanier-StL 3.5
Andrews-Bos 3.4
M.Cooper-StL 3.2

Total Baseball Ranking
Musial-StL 6.4
Nicholson-Chi 4.9
Sewell-Pit 4.0
Galan-Bro 3.9
Mueller-Cin 3.8

January 5 Teams agree to start the season later than usual and train in northern areas. Resorts, armories, and university facilities are chosen for training sites. The Dodgers train at Bear Mountain, New York; the Cards prepare at Cape Girardeau, Missouri; the Yankees get ready in Atlantic City.

February 24 The Texas League announces it will quit for the duration of the war. Only nine minor leagues will start the season, and advertisements for players appear in *The Sporting News*.

March 13 The major leagues approve an official ball, which will be made from reclaimed cork and balata in the interior, materials not needed in the war effort. Officials insist the ball will have the resiliency of the 1939 ball, but the players will express dismay that they cannot drive the new ball and point out the dearth of runs and homers in 1942 even with the old ball.

April 24 A spokesman for A. G. Spalding defends the war-time baseball, saying the 11 shutouts in the first 29 games are the result of the weather being "too wet and too cold. In time the new ball will prove to be just as lively as the old one." A few days later the company admits that the balls contain an inferior grade of rubber cement, which has hardened. The teams agree to use up their stock of balls left over from the 1942 season while a new supply of higher-quality balls is made.

June 17 Player-manager Joe Cronin of the Red Sox hits two three-run pinch home runs, one in each game of a doubleheader, as Boston beats the St. Louis Browns, 5–4, and loses, 8–7. He had hit a three-run pinch home run two nights before against the A's, three home runs in his last four at bats. He will pinch hit 42 times this year with 18 hits, including an AL record five pinch-hit homers.

July 13 The AL edges the NL 5–3 at Shibe Park in the first All-Star Game played under the lights. Bobby Doerr of the Red Sox is the hitting hero with a three-run home run off Mort Cooper in the second inning.

August 24 The Philadelphia Athletics drop their 20th game in a row, losing to Chicago, 6–5. This ties the AL record. They dodge the bullet in the nightcap by scoring eight runs in the second inning to win, 8–1.

September 6 Pitcher Carl Scheib of the Philadelphia Athletics becomes the youngest player to appear in an AL game at age 16 years, 248 days. He gives up two hits in ⅓ of an inning.

October 2 The Yankees take two from the Browns 5–1 and 7–6 for their 14th sweep of a doubleheader, an AL mark. Arthur "Bud" Metheny hits a home run in the opener for the Yankees' 100th roundtripper of the season.

October 5 Many major league players have gone into the war, including several key Yankees and Cardinals players. Nevertheless, both these clubs are back in the Series. New York wins the opener at Yankee Stadium 4–2 behind Spud Chandler.

October 11 Bill Dickey's two-run home run off Mort Cooper in the sixth gives the Yanks the championship. Spud Chandler gives up 10 hits but strands 11 in the 2–0 victory. A full share is worth $6,139 to the New York players; the Cards get $4,321 each. The Series grosses $1.1 million at the gate, receives $100,000 for broadcast rights, and donates $308,000 to War Funds.

November 11 The MVPs for both leagues are named. Spud Chandler wins it in the AL; Stan Musial, in the NL.

BOSTON	CHICAGO	CLEVELAND	DETROIT	NEW YORK	PHILADELPHIA	ST.LOUIS	WASHINGTON
M J.Cronin	M J.Dykes	M L.Boudreau	M S.O'Neill	M J.McCarthy	M C.Mack	M L.Sewell	M O.Bluege
1B T.Lupien	1B J.Kuhel	1B M.Rocco	1B R.York	1B N.Etten	1B D.Siebert	1B G.McQuinn	1B M.Vernon
2B B.Doerr	2B D.Kolloway	2B R.Mack	2B J.Bloodworth	2B J.Gordon	2B P.Suder	2B D.Gutteridge	2B J.Priddy
SS S.Newsome	SS L.Appling	SS L.Boudreau	SS J.Hoover	SS F.Crosetti	SS I.Hall	SS V.Stephens	SS J.Sullivan
3B J.Tabor	3B R.Hodgin	3B K.Keltner	3B P.Higgins	3B B.Johnson	3B E.Mayo	3B H.Clift	3B E.Clary
LF L.Culberson	LF G.Curtright	LF J.Heath	LF D.Wakefield	LF C.Keller	LF B.Estalella	LF C.Laabs	LF B.Johnson
CF C.Metkovich	CF T.Tucker	CF O.Hockett	CF D.Cramer	CF J.Lindell	CF J.White	CF M.Byrnes	CF S.Spence
RF P.Fox	RF W.Moses	RF R.Cullenbine	RF N.Harris	RF B.Metheny	RF J.Welaj	RF M.Chartak	RF G.Case
C R.Partee	C M.Tresh	C B.Rosar	C P.Richards	C B.Dickey	C H.Wagner	C F.Hayes	C J.Early
S E.Lake	2 S.Webb	O H.Edwards	OS D.Ross	O R.Weatherly	O E.Valo	3S M.Christman	O G.Moore
O J.Lazor	3 J.Grant	3S R.Peters	23 J.Wood	S S.Stirnweiss	O B.Swift	O A.Zarilla	32 A.Kampouris
O A.Simmons	C T.Turner	C G.Desautels	O R.Radcliff	O T.Stainback	O D.Heffner	O R.Ferrell	C T.Giuliani
O F.Garrison	32 D.Culler	1 O.Denning	C D.Parsons	C K.Sears	O J.Tyack	O M.Kreevich	3 J.Powell
O D.Miles	O T.Cuccinello	O P.Seerey	C A.Unser	C R.Hemsley	O J.Ripple	C J.Schultz	3 S.Robertson
C J.Peacock	C V.Castino	/O G.Woodling	O J.Outlaw	O O.Grimes	3 G.Staller	3 E.Clary	2 G.Myatt
O B.Barna	O M.Solters	/3 J.Grant	O C.Metro	H A.Robinson	O B.Burgo	O T.Criscola	/3 H.Clift
O T.McBride	/1 D.Hanski	/3 E.Turchin	H J.McHale		1 F.Skaff	S F.Baker	/S R.Roberts
C B.Conroy	/3 C.Michaels	/O F.Doljack	P D.Trout	P S.Chandler	2 J.Rullo	/O H.Epps	/O R.Marion
3 J.Cronin	H F.Kalin	/C J.McDonnell	P V.Trucks	P T.Bonham	/O W.Wheaton	2 D.Heffner	/1 E.Butka
C D.Doyle	P O.Grove	/C G.Susce	P H.Newhouser	P H.Borowy	/S E.Busch	R H.Schmulbach	/O R.Ortiz
	P E.Smith	P J.Bagby	P T.Bridges	P A.Donald	/C T.Parisse	P D.Galehouse	/C T.Padden
P T.Hughson	P J.Humphries	P A.Smith	P H.White	RP J.Murphy	P F.Mackiewicz	P S.Sundra	H R.Barbary
P Y.Terry	P B.Dietrich	P A.Reynolds	RP J.Gorsica	H B.Zuber	P L.Flick	P B.Muncrief	P E.Wynn
P J.Dobson	P B.Ross	P V.Kennedy	RP R.Henshaw	H M.Russo	/3 G.Kell	P N.Potter	P D.Leonard
P O.Judd	RP G.Maltzberger	P M.Harder	P S.Overmire	H J.Turner	H V.Benson	P B.Hollingsworth	P M.Candini
P D.Newsome	RP B.Swift	RP J.Heving	P J.Oana	P T.Byrne	P B.Konopka	RP G.Caster	P M.Haefner
RP M.Brown	P T.Lee	RP M.Naymick	/P R.Gentry	/P M.Breuer	P E.Brucker	P J.Niggeling	P A.Carrasquel
P M.Ryba	P J.Haynes	P J.Salveson	P J.Orrell		P J.Flores	P B.Newsom	P J.Mertz
P P.Woods	P J.Wade	P C.Dean			P R.Wolff	P C.Fuchs	P R.Scarborough
P L.Lucier	/P F.Speer	P R.Poat			P L.Harris	P F.Ostermueller	P E.Pyle
P E.O'Neill		P P.Center			P D.Black	P A.McKain	/P J.Niggeling
/P K.Chase		P A.Milnar			P O.Arntzen	/P A.Milnar	/P B.Newsom
P A.Karl		/P E.Klieman			/P	/P P.Dean	/P B.Lefebvre
		/P P.Calvert			P R.Christopher	/P S.Peterson	/P D.Adkins
		/P S.Gromek			P L.Ciola	/P J.Kramer	/P O.Scheetz
					P E.Fagan	/P F.Sanford	/P O.Miller
					/P B.Kuczynski	/P O.Miller	/P L.Gomez
					/P C.Scheib	/P A.LaMacchia	/P V.Curtis
					/P C.Bowles		/P L.Carpenter
					/P S.Lowry		
					/P H.Besse		
					/P T.Abernathy		
					/P J.Burrows		
					/P J.Mains		
					/P N.Brown		
					/P T.Clyde		

TEAM	G	W	L	PCT	GB	R	OR	AB	H	2B	3B	HR	BB	SO	AVG	OBP	SLG	PRO	PRO+	BR	/A	PF	CHI	RC	SB	CS	SBA	SBR
NY	155	98	56	.636		**669**	542	5282	1350	218	**59**	**100**	624	562	.256	**.337**	**.376**	**.713**	114	97	92	101	95	683	46	60	43	-22
WAS	153	84	69	.549	13.5	666	595	5233	1328	245	50	47	605	579	.254	.336	.347	.683	110	45	69	96	103	656	142	55	**72**	10
CLE	153	82	71	.536	15.5	600	577	5269	1344	**246**	45	55	567	521	.255	.329	.350	.679	112	32	71	94	95	626	47	58	45	-21
CHI	155	82	72	.532	16	573	594	5254	1297	193	46	33	561	581	.247	.322	.320	.642	94	-33	-32	100	102	570	**173**	87	67	0
DET	155	78	76	.506	20	632	560	5364	**1401**	200	47	77	483	553	**.261**	.324	.359	.683	98	32	-17	108	99	620	40	43	48	-14
STL	153	72	80	.474	25	596	604	5175	1269	229	36	78	569	646	.245	.322	.349	.671	100	14	1	102	98	603	37	43	46	-15
BOS	155	68	84	.447	29	563	607	5392	1314	223	42	57	486	591	.244	.308	.332	.640	92	-48	-57	102	101	570	86	61	59	-11
PHI	155	49	105	.318	49	497	717	5244	1219	174	44	26	430	**465**	.232	.294	.297	.591	78	-137	-135	100	**111**	466	55	42	57	-9
TOT	617					4796		42213	10522	1728	369	473	4325	4498	.249	.322	.341	.663						626	449	58		-82

TEAM	CG	SH	SV	IP	H	H/G	HR	BB	SO	RAT	ERA	ERA+	OAV	OOB	PR	/A	PF	CPI	FA	E	DP	FW	PW	BW	SBW	DIF
NY	83	14	13	1415[1]	1229	**7.8**	60	489	653	11.0	**2.93**	110	**.234**	.301	58	46	98	95	.974	160	166	.2	5.0	**10.0**	-1.3	7.1
WAS	61	16	**21**	1388	1293	8.4	**48**	540	495	12.0	3.18	101	.246	.318	17	3	97	99	.971	179	145	-1.0	.3	7.5	**2.2**	-1.5
CLE	64	14	20	1406[1]	1234	7.9	52	606	585	11.9	3.15	99	.239	.322	23	-6	94	100	.975	157	**183**	.3	-.6	7.7	-1.2	-.7
CHI	70	12	19	1400[1]	1352	8.7	54	501	476	12.1	3.20	104	.255	.324	15	21	101	105	.973	160	167	-.0	2.3	-3.5	1.1	5.2
DET	67	**18**	20	1411[2]	**1226**	**7.8**	51	549	**706**	11.4	3.00	**117**	.234	.308	46	**81**	107	105	.971	177	130	-.7	**8.8**	-1.8	-.4	-4.8
STL	64	10	14	1385	1397	9.1	74	**488**	572	12.4	3.41	97	.263	.327	-18	-13	101	**106**	.975	152	127	**.6**	-1.4	.1	-.5	-2.8
BOS	62	13	16	1426[1]	1369	8.6	61	615	513	12.6	3.45	96	.257	.335	-25	-22	101	105	**.976**	153	179	**.6**	-2.4	-6.2	-.0	.0
PHI	73	5	13	1394	1421	9.2	73	536	503	12.9	4.05	84	.265	.336	-117	-101	103	94	.973	162	148	.1	-10.9	-14.6	.1	-2.7
TOT	544	102	136	11227		8.4				12.0	3.30		.249	.322					.973	1306	1245					

Runs		Hits		Doubles		Triples		Home Runs		Total Bases	
Case-Was	102	Wakefield-Det	200	Wakefield-Det	38	Moses-Chi	12	York-Det	34	York-Det	301
Keller-NY	97	Appling-Chi	192	Case-Was	36	Lindell-NY	12	Keller-NY	31	Wakefield-Det	275
Wakefield-Det	91	Cramer-Det	182	Gutteridge-StL	35	York-Det	11	Stephens-StL	22	Keller-NY	269
York-Det	90	Case-Was	180	Etten-NY	35	Keller-NY	11	Heath-Cle	18	Doerr-Bos	249
Vernon-Was	89					Spence-Was	10			Stephens-StL	247

Runs Batted In		Runs Produced		Bases On Balls		Batting Average		On Base Percentage		Slugging Average	
York-Det	118	York-Det	174	Keller-NY	106	Appling-Chi	.328	Appling-Chi	.419	York-Det	.527
Etten-NY	107	Etten-NY	171	Gordon-NY	98	Wakefield-Det	.316	Cullenbine-Cle	.407	Keller-NY	.525
Johnson-NY	94	Wakefield-Det	163	Cullenbine-Cle	96	Hodgin-Chi	.314	Keller-NY	.396	Stephens-StL	.482
Stephens-StL	91	Johnson-NY	159	Boudreau-Cle	90	Cramer-Det	.300	Boudreau-Cle	.388	Heath-Cle	.481
Spence-Was	88	Case-Was	153	Appling-Chi	90	Case-Was	.294	Curtright-Chi	.382	Wakefield-Det	.434

Production		Adjusted Production		Batter Runs		Adjusted Batter Runs		Clutch Hitting Index		Runs Created	
Keller-NY	.922	Keller-NY	167	Keller-NY	45.8	Keller-NY	45.0	Sullivan-Was	162	Keller-NY	116
York-Det	.893	Heath-Cle	157	York-Det	41.0	Appling-Chi	35.1	Johnson-NY	134	Appling-Chi	109
Heath-Cle	.850	York-Det	148	Appling-Chi	35.0	York-Det	33.0	Siebert-Phi	128	York-Det	108
Stephens-StL	.839	Cullenbine-Cle	146	Wakefield-Det	28.8	Cullenbine-Cle	32.9	Early-Was	125	Wakefield-Det	101
Appling-Chi	.825	Appling-Chi	142	Cullenbine-Cle	27.4	Heath-Cle	29.7	McQuinn-StL	125	Spence-Was	93

Total Average		Stolen Bases		Stolen Base Average		Stolen Base Runs		Fielding Runs		Total Player Rating	
Keller-NY	.979	Case-Was	61	Case-Was	81.3	Case-Was	9.9	Boudreau-Cle	28.4	Boudreau-Cle	6.7
York-Det	.871	Moses-Chi	56	Moses-Chi	80.0	Moses-Chi	8.4	Gordon-NY	25.7	Appling-Chi	6.0
Appling-Chi	.841	Tucker-Chi	29	Appling-Chi	77.1	Culberson-Bos	4.2	Clift-StL-Was	18.3	Gordon-NY	5.4
Heath-Cle	.828	Appling-Chi	27	Vernon-Was	75.0	Appling-Chi	3.3	York-Det	17.6	York-Det	4.3
Cullenbine-Cle	.816	Vernon-Was	24	Fox-Bos	73.3	Vernon-Was	2.4	Bloodworth-Det	17.2	Keller-NY	4.3

Wins		Win Percentage		Games		Complete Games		Shutouts		Saves	
Trout-Det	20	Chandler-NY	.833	Brown-Bos	49	Hughson-Bos	20	Trout-Det	5	Maltzberger-Chi	14
Chandler-NY	20	Smith-Cle	.708	Trout-Det	44	Chandler-NY	20	Chandler-NY	5	Heving-Cle	9
Wynn-Was	18	Bonham-NY	.652	Wolff-Phi	41	Wensloff-NY	18	Hughson-Bos	4	Brown-Bos	9
Smith-Cle	17	Trout-Det	.625	Ryba-Bos	40	Trout-Det	18	Bonham-NY	4	Murphy-NY	8
Bagby-Cle	17	Grove-Chi	.625	Carrasquel-Was	39	Grove-Chi	18			Caster-StL	8

Innings Pitched		Fewest Hits/Game		Fewest BB/Game		Strikeouts		Strikeouts/Game		Ratio	
Bagby-Cle	273.0	Reynolds-Cle	6.34	Leonard-Was	1.88	Reynolds-Cle	151	Reynolds-Cle	6.84	Chandler-NY	9.07
Hughson-Bos	266.0	Niggeling-StL-Was	6.66	Chandler-NY	1.92	Newhouser-Det	144	Newhouser-Det	6.62	Trucks-Det	9.90
Wynn-Was	256.2	Haefner-Was	6.86	Bonham-NY	2.07	Chandler-NY	134	Bridges-Det	5.82	Bonham-NY	9.97
Chandler-NY	253.0	Chandler-NY	7.01	Muncrief-StL	2.11	Bridges-Det	124	Trucks-Det	5.24	Wensloff-NY	10.07
Trout-Det	246.2	Wensloff-NY	7.21	Trucks-Det	2.31	Trucks-Det	118	Chandler-NY	4.77	Niggeling-StL-Was	10.24

Earned Run Average		Adjusted ERA		Opponents' Batting Avg.		Opponents' On Base Pct.		Starter Runs		Adjusted Starter Runs	
Chandler-NY	1.64	Chandler-NY	197	Reynolds-Cle	.202	Chandler-NY	.261	Chandler-NY	46.6	Chandler-NY	44.4
Bonham-NY	2.27	Bridges-Det	147	Niggeling-StL-Was	.204	Trucks-Det	.276	Bonham-NY	25.6	Trout-Det	28.5
Haefner-Was	2.29	Trout-Det	142	Haefner-Was	.208	Wensloff-NY	.282	Trout-Det	22.3	Bridges-Det	24.0
Bridges-Det	2.39	Bonham-NY	141	Chandler-NY	.215	Bonham-NY	.282	Hughson-Bos	19.4	Bonham-NY	23.6
Trout-Det	2.48	Haefner-Was	140	Wensloff-NY	.219	Niggeling-StL-Was	.282	Bridges-Det	19.2	Hughson-Bos	19.9

Clutch Pitching Index		Relief Runs		Adjusted Relief Runs		Relief Ranking		Total Pitcher Index		Total Baseball Ranking	
Hughson-Bos	124	Brown-Bos	12.2	Brown-Bos	12.3	Caster-StL	19.2	Chandler-NY	5.7	Boudreau-Cle	6.7
Muncrief-StL	120	Caster-StL	10.0	Caster-StL	10.2	Brown-Bos	17.0	Trout-Det	4.7	Appling-Chi	6.0
Bonham-NY	116	Maltzberger-Chi	9.1	Maltzberger-Chi	9.6	Maltzberger-Chi	12.7	Bridges-Det	2.6	Chandler-NY	5.7
Galehouse-StL	115	Naymick-Cle	6.9	Naymick-Cle	5.6	Murphy-NY	12.6	Caster-StL	2.1	Gordon-NY	5.4
Candini-Was	115	Murphy-NY	5.9	Murphy-NY	5.3	Naymick-Cle	6.9	Bonham-NY	2.0	Trout-Det	4.7

January 27 Lou Perini, Guido Rugo, and Joseph Maney, known as "the Three Little Steamshovels," buy the Braves and oust Casey Stengel as manager.

February 2 The leagues meet at New York to discuss postwar action. They decide players with war service will be guaranteed 30 days of trial at pay and restrictions on their release or assignment. Military service will count as playing time.

April 27 Boston knuckleballer Jim Tobin hits a home run and no-hits the Brooklyn Dodgers, 2–0, before a midweek crowd of 1,984 at Braves Field. Tobin walks Paul Waner to lead off the game, then retires 26 consecutive batters before walking Waner again with two outs in the ninth inning

May 15 Reds reliever Clyde Shoun, making his first start of the season, throws a no-hitter to nip the Boston Braves, 1–0. Only 1,014 see the 32-year-old lefty top Jim Tobin, who had thrown one in April.

May 23 Wartime restrictions are eased, and the Polo Grounds is the scene of the first night game in metropolitan New York City since 1941.

June 10 Pitcher Joe Nuxhall of the Cincinnati Reds becomes the youngest player in major league history. Nuxhall, only 15 years, 10 months old, pitches 2/3 of an inning in an 18-0 loss to the St. Louis Cardinals. He manages to give up five walks and two hits before Bill McKechnie takes him out.

July 11 Phil Cavarretta of the Cubs sets an All-Star Game record by reaching base five successive times on a triple, single, and three walks; NL romps 7-1.

August 3 Tommy Brown, just 16 years and eight months old, plays shortstop for Brooklyn in both games of a twin bill loss, 6-2 and 7-1, to the Cubs.

August 10 Red Barrett of the Boston Braves throws only 58 pitches and shuts out the Cincinnati Reds, 2–0. This is the ML record for fewest pitches in a nine-inning game. The game takes one hour, 15 minutes, the shortest night game ever.

September 21 The Cardinals finally clinch the NL flag with a 5-4 win over Boston. Twenty games ahead on September 1, the Cards then blew 15 of the next 20 games. They will finish with 105 victories and their third title under Billy Southworth, whose clubs win 316 games in three years.

October 9 Emil Verban drives in three runs as the Cardinals top the Browns 3-1 and win the Series in six games. Ted Wilks allows no one to reach base in 3⅔ innings of relief, fanning four pinch hitters. George McQuinn hits .438 for the Series. The winners get $4,626 each; the Browns take $2,743, the lowest player shares since 1933.

December 21 The NL MVP award goes to fielding wizard Marty Marion, who tallies one more vote than Cubs slugger Bill Nicholson.

BOSTON	BROOKLYN	CHICAGO	CINCINNATI	NEW YORK	PHILADELPHIA	PITTSBURGH	ST.LOUIS
M B.Coleman	M L.Durocher	M J.Wilson	M B.McKechnie	M M.Ott	M F.Fitzsimmons	M F.Frisch	M B.Southworth
1B B.Etchison	1B H.Schultz	M R.Johnson	1B F.McCormick	1B P.Weintraub	1B T.Lupien	1B B.Dahlgren	1B R.Sanders
2B C.Ryan	2B E.Stanky	M C.Grimm	2B W.Williams	2B G.Hausmann	2B M.Mullen	2B P.Coscarart	2B E.Verban
SS W.Wietelmann	SS B.Bragan	1B P.Cavarretta	SS E.Miller	SS B.Kerr	SS R.Hamrick	SS F.Gustine	SS M.Marion
3B D.Phillips	3B F.Bordagaray	2B D.Johnson	3B S.Mesner	3B H.Luby	3B G.Stewart	3B B.Elliott	3B W.Kurowski
LF B.Nieman	LF A.Galan	SS L.Merullo	LF E.Tipton	LF J.Medwick	LF J.Wasdell	LF J.Russell	LF D.Litwhiler
CF T.Holmes	CF G.Rosen	3B S.Hack	CF D.Clay	CF J.Rucker	CF B.Adams	CF V.DiMaggio	CF J.Hopp
RF C.Workman	RF D.Walker	LF D.Dallessandro	RF G.Walker	RF M.Ott	RF R.Northey	RF J.Barrett	RF S.Musial
C P.Masi	C M.Owen	CF A.Pafko	C R.Mueller	C E.Lombardi	C B.Finley	C A.Lopez	C W.Cooper
		RF B.Nicholson					
1O M.Macon	O2 L.Olmo	C D.Williams	O M.Marshall	13 N.Reyes	C C.Letchas	O F.Colman	C K.O'Dea
C C.Kluttz	S T.Brown	3S R.Hughes	O T.Criscola	3S B.Jurges	C J.Peacock	O2 A.Rubeling	O A.Bergamo
O A.Wright	O P.Waner	S B.Schuster	3 C.Aleno	C G.Mancuso	T.Cieslak	S F.Zak	O3 D.Garms
C S.Hofferth	1 J.Bolling	O I.Goodman	O E.Crabtree	O R.Treadway	O C.Triplett	O T.O'Brien	2S G.Fallon
O C.Ross	2 E.Basinski	O L.Novikoff	O J.White	O D.Gardella	S G.Hamner	O H.Camelli	/1 J.Antonelli
2 F.Drews	2 B.Koch	C B.Holm	/3 B.Fausett	O B.Sloan	C A.Seminick	C S.Davis	/C B.Keely
3 R.Gladu	3S E.Miksis	/O M.Kreitner	C J.Just	S C.Mead	H H.Heltzel	O L.Handley	/O L.Waner
3 W.Huston	S B.Hart	/C L.Rice	/O C.Ramos	/C S.Filipowicz	/C L.Riley	/O A.Gionfriddo	P M.Cooper
2 S.Shemo	C G.English	O E.Sauer	H A.Lakeman	/2 L.Rice	/O C.Klein	/O B.Rodgers	P M.Lanier
3 M.Sandlock	O M.Aderholt	S C.Brewster	/3 K.Wahl	/2 R.Nichols	/C J.Antolick	/S V.Barnhart	T.Wilks
/S D.Culler	/O R.Durrett	R R.Easterwood	R M.Kosman	P B.Voiselle	/1 P.Caballero	/1 H.Sweeney	H.Brecheen
/C H.Poland	2 P.Ankenman	/C P.Gillespie	/C J.Riddle	H.Feldman	/C B.Culp	P R.Sewell	A.Jurisich
/O C.Clemens	/2 L.Rochelli	/2 E.Stanky	P B.Walters	E.Pyle	H N.Goulish	P F.Ostermueller	RP B.Donnelly
/2 B.Geraghty	/S G.Mauch	/3 P.Elko	RP C.Shoun	R.Fischer	T.Tyson	P M.Butcher	P R.Munger
/2 P.Capri	/O L.Waner	/3 J.Foxx	P E.Heusser	RP B.Walters	K.Raffensberger	P N.Strincevich	P F.Schmidt
R G.Patton	/C R.Hayworth	O J.Ostrowski	P T.DeLa Cruz	RP A.Adams	C.Schanz	P P.Roe	H.Gumbert
P J.Tobin	/C S.Andrews	/C J.Stephenson	P H.Gumbert	A.Hansen	RP D.Barrett	P R.Starr	/P B.Byerly
P N.Andrews	/C F.Dantonio	R G.Mann	A.Carter	J.Allen	B.Lee	RP X.Rescigno	/P B.Trotter
P A.Javery	/C J.Cooney	P H.Wyse	J.Konstanty	F.Seward	A.Gerheauser	P C.Cuccurullo	/P M.Naymick
P R.Barrett	H C.Smyres	P C.Passeau	E.Riddle	C.Melton	RP A.Karl	/P J.Gee	
P I.Hutchinson	/C R.Jarvis	P P.Derringer	B.Malloy	RP J.Brewer	V.Kennedy	/P L.Gilmore	
P B.Cardoni	P H.Gregg	P B.Fleming	J.Beggs	L.Polli	C.Covington	/P J.Vitelli	
P J.Hutchings	P C.Davis	P B.Chipman	H.Fox	/P K.Brondell	D.Matthewson	R.Wise	
P S.Klopp	P R.Melton	P H.Vandenberg	B.Lohrman	/P B.Barthelson	H.Shuman		
/P W.Rich	RP L.Webber	P P.Erickson	J.Nuxhall	/P J.Gee	B.Mussill		
/P J.Hickey	P C.McLish	P R.Lynn	K.Peterson	/P W.Miller	D.Donahue		
/P C.Lindquist	P B.Chapman	P E.Hanyzewski	J.Eisenhart	/P F.Rosso	J.Fick		
/P G.Woodend	P T.Warren	P D.Alderson		/P W.Ockey	L.Lucier		
/P H.MacPherson	/P E.Head	/P C.Gassaway			R.McKee		
	P A.Herring	P M.Stewart			C.Ripple		
	P R.Branca	/P H.Miklos			A.Verdel		
	P C.King	/P J.Burrows					
	P F.Ostermueller						
	/P W.Wyatt						
	P B.Chipman						
	P T.Sunkel						
	P W.Flowers						
	/P C.Fuchs						
	/P J.Wells						
	/P C.Zachary						
	/P C.Crocker						
	/P B.Lohrman						
	/P C.Osgood						
	/P J.Franklin						
	/P F.Wurm						

TEAM	G	W	L	PCT	GB	R	OR	AB	H	2B	3B	HR	BB	SO	AVG	OBP	SLG	PRO	PRO+	BR	/A	PF	CHI	RC	SB	CS	SBA	SBR
STL	157	105	49	.682		772	490	5475	1507	274	59	100	544	473	.275	.344	.402	.746	114	110	96	102	98	775	37			
PIT	158	90	63	.588	14.5	744	662	5428	1441	248	80	70	573	616	.265	.338	.379	.717	104	58	27	104	102	707	87			
CIN	155	89	65	.578	16	573	537	5271	1340	229	31	51	423	391	.254	.313	.338	.651	92	-74	-53	96	101	558	51			
CHI	157	75	79	.487	30	702	669	5462	1425	236	46	71	520	521	.261	.328	.360	.688	101	-2	2	99	104	658	53			
NY	155	67	87	.435	38	682	773	5306	1398	191	47	93	512	480	.263	.331	.370	.701	103	22	24	100	100	656	39			
BOS	155	65	89	.422	40	593	674	5282	1299	250	39	79	456	509	.246	.308	.353	.661	88	-61	-85	104	101	586	37			
BRO	155	63	91	.409	42	690	832	5393	1450	255	51	56	486	451	.269	.331	.366	.697	104	16	28	98	101	664	45			
PHI	154	61	92	.399	43.5	539	658	5301	1331	199	42	55	470	500	.251	.316	.336	.652	92	-70	-51	97	92	571	32			
TOT	623					5295		42918	11191	1882	395	575	3984	3941	.261	.326	.363	.689						381				

TEAM	CG	SH	SV	IP	H	H/G	HR	BB	SO	RAT	ERA	ERA+	OAV	OOB	PR	/A	PF	CPI	FA	E	DP	FW	PW	BW	SBW	DIF
STL	89	26	12	1427	1228	7.7	55	468	637	10.8	2.67	132	.233	.298	148	134	98	103	.982	112	162	3.7	13.8	9.9		.7
PIT	77	10	19	1414[1]	1466	9.3	65	435	452	12.2	3.44	108	.265	.321	27	45	103	103	.970	191	122	-1.1	4.6	2.8		7.2
CIN	93	17	12	1398[1]	1292	8.3	60	390	369	10.9	2.97	117	.246	.300	99	80	97	99	.978	137	153	2.0	8.2	-5.4		7.2
CHI	70	11	13	1400[2]	1484	9.5	75	458	545	12.5	3.59	98	.274	.331	4	-8	98	108	.970	186	151	-.8	-.8	.2		-.5
NY	47	4	21	1363[2]	1413	9.3	116	587	499	13.4	4.29	85	.265	.342	-103	-94	102	98	.971	179	128	-.5	-9.6	2.5		-2.3
BOS	70	13	12	1388[1]	1430	9.3	80	527	454	12.8	3.67	104	.267	.335	-9	23	106	106	.971	182	160	-.7	2.4	-8.7		-4.9
BRO	50	4	13	1367[2]	1471	9.7	75	660	487	14.3	4.68	76	.274	.357	-162	-172	98	93	.966	197	112	-1.7	-17.7	2.9		2.4
PHI	66	11	6	1395[1]	1407	9.1	49	459	496	12.2	3.64	99	.261	.321	-4	-5	100	93	.972	177	138	-.5	-.5	-5.2		-9.3
TOT	562	96	108	11155[1]		9.0				12.4	3.61		.261	.326					.972	1361	1126					

Runs
Nicholson-Chi 116
Musial-StL 112
Russell-Pit 109
Hopp-StL 106
Cavarretta-Chi . . . 106

Hits
Musial-StL 197
Cavarretta-Chi 197
Holmes-Bos 195
Walker-Bro 191
Russell-Pit 181

Doubles
Musial-StL 51
Galan-Bro 43
Holmes-Bos 42

Triples
Barrett-Pit 19
Elliott-Pit 16
Cavarretta-Chi . . . 15
Russell-Pit 14
Musial-StL 14

Home Runs
Nicholson-Chi 33
Ott-NY 26
Northey-Phi 22
McCormick-Cin . . . 20
Kurowski-StL 20

Total Bases
Nicholson-Chi 317
Musial-StL 312
Holmes-Bos 288
Walker-Bro 283
Northey-Phi 283

Runs Batted In
Nicholson-Chi 122
Elliott-Pit 108
Northey-Phi 104
Sanders-StL 102
McCormick-Cin . . . 102

Runs Produced
Nicholson-Chi 205
Musial-StL 194
Elliott-Pit 183
Cavarretta-Chi . . . 183

Bases On Balls
Galan-Bro 101
Nicholson-Chi 93
Ott-NY 90
Musial-StL 90
Barrett-Pit 86

Batting Average
Walker-Bro 357
Musial-StL 347
Medwick-NY 337
Hopp-StL 336
Cavarretta-Chi 321

On Base Percentage
Musial-StL 440
Walker-Bro 434
Galan-Bro 426
Ott-NY 423
Hopp-StL 404

Slugging Average
Musial-StL 549
Nicholson-Chi 545
Ott-NY 544
Walker-Bro 529
Weintraub-NY 524

Production
Musial-StL 990
Ott-NY 967
Walker-Bro 963
Nicholson-Chi 935
Galan-Bro 922

Adjusted Production
Musial-StL 174
Walker-Bro 173
Ott-NY 171
Nicholson-Chi 162
Galan-Bro 162

Batter Runs
Musial-StL 60.9
Walker-Bro 51.2
Nicholson-Chi . . . 47.4
Galan-Bro 46.5
Ott-NY 40.4

Adjusted Batter Runs
Musial-StL 58.5
Walker-Bro 53.4
Galan-Bro 48.7
Nicholson-Chi . . . 48.2
Ott-NY 40.7

Clutch Hitting Index
Olmo-Bro 132
Elliott-Pit 126
Dahlgren-Pit 119
Schultz-Bro 118
Medwick-NY 117

Runs Created
Musial-StL 145
Nicholson-Chi 132
Walker-Bro 128
Galan-Bro 123
Russell-Pit 112

Total Average
Musial-StL 1.095
Ott-NY 1.087
Walker-Bro 1.034
Nicholson-Chi . . . 1.002
Galan-Bro 992

Stolen Bases
Barrett-Pit 28
Lupien-Phi 18
Hughes-Chi 16
Hopp-StL 15
Kerr-NY 14

Stolen Base Average

Stolen Base Runs

Fielding Runs
Kerr-NY 16.8
Luby-NY 16.4
Williams-Cin 15.0
Pafko-Chi 14.7
Russell-Pit 13.3

Total Player Rating
Musial-StL 5.4
Walker-Bro 4.4
Nicholson-Chi 4.2
Galan-Bro 4.0
McCormick-Cin . . . 3.7

Wins
Walters-Cin 23
M.Cooper-StL 22
Voiselle-NY 21
Sewell-Pit 21
Tobin-Bos 18

Win Percentage
Wilks-StL 810
Brecheen-StL 762
M.Cooper-StL 759
Walters-Cin 742
Sewell-Pit 636

Games
Adams-NY 65
Webber-Bro 48
Rescigno-Pit 48
Voiselle-NY 43
Tobin-Bos 43

Complete Games
Tobin-Bos 28
Walters-Cin 27
Voiselle-NY 25
Sewell-Pit 24
M.Cooper-StL 22

Shutouts
M.Cooper-StL 7
Walters-Cin 6
Tobin-Bos 5
Lanier-StL 5
Butcher-Pit 5

Saves
Adams-NY 13
Schmidt-StL 5
Rescigno-Pit 5
Davis-Bro 4
Cuccurullo-Pit . . . 4

Innings Pitched
Voiselle-NY 312.2
Tobin-Bos 299.1
Sewell-Pit 286.0
Walters-Cin 285.0
Raffensberger-Phi . 258.2

Fewest Hits/Game
Walters-Cin 7.36
Wilks-StL 7.50
Lanier-StL 7.70
Heusser-Cin 7.71
Voiselle-NY 7.94

Fewest BB/Game
Raffensberger-Phi . 1.57
Strincevich-Pit . . . 1.75
Davis-Bro 1.81
Shoun-Cin 1.87
Derringer-Chi 1.95

Strikeouts
Voiselle-NY 161
Lanier-StL 141
Javery-Bos 137
Raffensberger-Phi . 136

Strikeouts/Game
Lanier-StL 5.66
Javery-Bos 4.85
Raffensberger-Phi . 4.73
Voiselle-NY 4.63
Melton-Bro 4.37

Ratio
Wilks-StL 9.66
Heusser-Cin 9.72
De LaCruz-Cin . . . 10.16
Walters-Cin 10.23
M.Cooper-StL 10.41

Earned Run Average
Heusser-Cin 2.38
Walters-Cin 2.40
M.Cooper-StL 2.46
Wilks-StL 2.64
Lanier-StL 2.65

Adjusted ERA
Heusser-Cin 146
Walters-Cin 145
M.Cooper-StL 143
Wilks-StL 133
Lanier-StL 133

Opponents' Batting Avg.
Walters-Cin 219
Wilks-StL 227
Heusser-Cin 231
Voiselle-NY 232
Lanier-StL 234

Opponents' On Base Pct.
Wilks-StL 275
Heusser-Cin 275
Walters-Cin 281
De LaCruz-Cin 284
Raffensberger-Phi . .285

Starter Runs
Walters-Cin 38.3
M.Cooper-StL 32.2
Munger-StL 30.5
Heusser-Cin 26.3
Lanier-StL 24.0

Adjusted Starter Runs
Walters-Cin 34.4
M.Cooper-StL 29.8
Munger-StL 29.4
Tobin-Bos 27.0
Ostermueller-Br-Pt 23.9

Clutch Pitching Index
Fleming-Chi 121
Ostermueller-Br-Pt 120
Chipman-Bro-Chi . . 119
Wyse-Chi 113
Javery-Bos 111

Relief Runs
Karl-Phi 12.7
Donnelly-StL 12.6

Adjusted Relief Runs
Karl-Phi 12.7
Donnelly-StL 11.9

Relief Ranking
Karl-Phi 7.1
Donnelly-StL 4.9

Total Pitcher Index
Walters-Cin 4.7
Tobin-Bos 4.7
Munger-StL 3.6
M.Cooper-StL 3.0
Heusser-Cin 2.9

Total Baseball Ranking
Musial-StL 5.4
Walters-Cin 4.7
Tobin-Bos 4.7
Walker-Bro 4.4
Nicholson-Chi 4.2

April 29 Jack Kramer pitches the Browns' to their AL record ninth straight win to start the season. The 3–1 win over the Indians gives the first place Browns a 3½ game lead.

May 1 George Myatt of the Washington Senators collects six hits in six at bats, as the Nats pound out 20 hits to beat Boston, 11–4.

May 10 Mel Harder wins his 200th career game as Cleveland defeats the Red Sox 5–4. He is the 50th to reach this mark.

June 6 All major league games are canceled as the country's focus is turned toward Europe while allied forces invade occupied France.

June 26 More than 50,000 pack the Polo Grounds to watch the Yankees, Dodgers, and Giants play each other in a six-inning contest to raise money for war bonds. Each team plays successive innings against the other two teams, then sits out an inning. The final score is Dodgers 5, Yankees 1, Giants 0.

July 20 The Browns' Nelson Potter becomes the first pitcher suspended for throwing spitballs. He is banished for 10 days for allegedly "putting an illegal substance on the ball." Potter will return to win 19 games for St. Louis.

September 15 Radio announcer Bill Stern reports on a scandal involving the Browns. A Chicago newspaper attributes the Browns' recent slump to the fact that the league wants a larger park for the World Series. Four days later Stern repudiates the story.

October 1 The Browns have their first sellout in 20 years as 37,815 pack Sportsman's Park. St. Louis clinches the flag on the final day of the season by sweeping the Yankees and winning 5-2 on a pair of two-run home runs by Chet Laabs. Sig Jakucki is the winning pitcher.

October 4 The first all-St. Louis World Series, dubbed the Streetcar Series, opens with the Browns as the visiting team, beating the Cardinals 2-1 on George McQuinn's home run. Denny Galehouse is the winning pitcher and Mort Cooper loses despite allowing just two hits. It is the first Series in which all games are played west of the Mississippi River and is played with no days off.

November 23 Five groups totaling 23 players, managers, umpires, and writers visit war theaters as part of the USO program. Included are Mel Ott, Dutch Leonard, Frankie Frisch, Bucky Walters, Harry Heilmann, Carl Hubbell, Freddie Fitzsimmons, Bill Summers, Beans Reardon, Johnny Lindell, Tuck Stainback, Steve O'Neill, Leo Durocher, Joe Medwick, Nick Etten, Dixie Walker, Paul Waner, and Rip Sewell.

November 25 Kenesaw Mountain Landis, baseball's first commissioner, dies of a heart attack at age 78 in Chicago. The Commissioner had ruled over baseball since November 1920 in the wake of the Black Sox scandal, and wielded authority perhaps unparalleled in any other industry.

November 28 Hal Newhouser is named MVP in the AL gathering four more votes than teammate Dizzy Trout.

December 28 Former Washington third baseman Buddy Lewis wins the Distinguished Flying Cross for precision flying over the Burma War Theater.

BOSTON	CHICAGO	CLEVELAND	DETROIT	NEW YORK	PHILADELPHIA	ST.LOUIS	WASHINGTON
M J.Cronin	M J.Dykes	M L.Boudreau	M S.O'Neill	M J.McCarthy	M C.Mack	M L.Sewell	M O.Bluege
1B L.Finney	1B H.Trosky	1B M.Rocco	1B R.York	1B N.Etten	1B B.McGhee	1B G.McQuinn	1B J.Kuhel
2B B.Doerr	2B R.Schalk	2B R.Mack	2B E.Mayo	2B S.Stirnweiss	2B I.Hall	2B D.Gutteridge	2B G.Myatt
SS S.Newsome	SS S.Webb	SS L.Boudreau	SS J.Hoover	SS M.Milosevich	SS E.Busch	SS V.Stephens	SS J.Sullivan
3B J.Tabor	3B R.Hodgin	3B K.Keltner	3B P.Higgins	3B O.Grimes	3B G.Kell	3B M.Christman	3B G.Torres
LF B.Johnson	LF E.Carnett	LF P.Seerey	LF D.Wakefield	LF H.Martin	LF F.Garrison	LF M.Byrnes	LF G.Case
CF C.Metkovich	CF T.Tucker	CF O.Hockett	CF D.Cramer	CF J.Lindell	CF B.Estalella	CF M.Kreevich	CF S.Spence
RF P.Fox	RF W.Moses	RF R.Cullenbine	RF J.Outlaw	RF B.Metheny	RF J.White	RF G.Moore	RF R.Ortiz
C R.Partee	C M.Tresh	C B.Rosar	C P.Richards	C R.Hemsley	C F.Hayes	C F.Mancuso	C R.Ferrell
O L.Culberson	O G.Curtright	2S R.Peters	C C.Hostetler	1O D.Siebert	O H.Epps	O A.Zarilla	O J.Powell
32 J.Bucher	3 G.Clarke	O M.Hoag	C B.Swift	3 D.Savage	2 J.Rullo	C R.Hayworth	C M.Guerra
C H.Wagner	O J.Dickshot	O P.O'Dea	S D.Ross	2 F.Crosetti	O B.Burgo	O C.Laabs	2 F.Vaughn
O T.McBride	3 T.Cuccinello	O J.Heath	S3 J.Orengo	O E.Levy	3 J.Burns	2S F.Baker	3 H.Layne
1 J.Cronin	C T.Turner	O N.Schlueter	O C.Metro	O R.Derry	O L.Rosenthal	1 M.Chartak	O E.Boland
S E.Lake	C V.Castino	2 J.Grant	/2 A.Unser	O T.Stainback	O C.Metro	O H.Epps	H.Clift
O F.Garrison	S C.Michaels	C G.Susce	/2 D.Heffner	/O J.Cooney	/O L.Flick	O F.Demaree	1 E.Butka
C B.Conroy	O M.Hoag	C J.McDonnell	/2 R.Borom	/O L.Rosenthal	/O L.Rosenthal	/O T.Hafey	/O R.Monteagudo
/O J.Lazor	C T.Jordan	/C R.Lyon	/S B.Floyd	/C B.Drescher	/S B.Wilkins	/C J.Schultz	O J.Vosmik
/C J.Peacock	/2 W.Metzig	/C H.Ruszkowski	/C H.Miller	H P.Waner	C B.Garbark	/O B.Martin	/C A.Evans
		/2 S.Biras	/2 J.Sullivan	/C R.Collins	/O H.Peck	H L.Schulte	E.Yost
P T.Hughson	P B.Dietrich	/C J.Devlin	P D.Trout	P H.Borowy	/O A.Simmons	P J.Kramer	/O G.Binks
P P.Woods	P O.Grove	P S.Gromek	P H.Newhouser	P M.Dubiel	/O B.Mills	P N.Potter	/2 P.Gomez
P J.Bowman	P E.Lopat	P M.Harder	P R.Gentry	P T.Bonham	/C T.Parisse	P B.Muncrief	/3 L.Suarez
P E.O'Neill	P J.Humphries	P A.Smith	P S.Overmire	P A.Donald	/C J.Pruett	P S.Jakucki	H R.Valdes
P M.Ryba	P J.Haynes	P E.Klieman	P J.Gorsica	P B.Zuber	/C H.Wagner	P D.Galehouse	P D.Leonard
RP F.Barrett	RP G.Maltzberger	P A.Reynolds	RP B.Beck	P J.Page	P B.Newsom	RP G.Caster	P M.Haefner
P C.Hausmann	P T.Lee	RP J.Heving	P J.Mooty	P S.Roser	P R.Christopher	P A.Hollingsworth	P E.Wynn
P Y.Terry	P B.Ross	RP R.Poat	P J.Orrell	P M.Queen	P L.Hamlin	P T.Shirley	P J.Niggeling
P R.Cecil	P J.Wade	RP P.Calvert	/P Z.Eaton	/P B.Bevens	P J.Flores	P S.Zoldak	P R.Wolff
/P C.Dreisewerd	/P D.Hanski	P J.Bagby	/P R.Henshaw	P J.Turner	/P D.Black	P L.West	RP B.Lefebvre
/P O.Judd	/P F.Speer	P V.Kennedy	P B.Gillespie	P A.Lyons	RP J.Berry	/P S.Sundra	P A.Carrasquel
/P V.Johnson		P H.Kleine	/P C.Hogsett	P J.Johnson	P L.Harris	/P W.Hudlin	P M.Candini
/P J.Wood		/P E.Henry		/P S.Chandler	P W.Wheaton		/P B.Ortiz
/P L.Lucier		/P M.Naymick			P C.Scheib		/P J.Thesenga
/P S.Partenheimer		/P B.Bonness			/P T.Abernathy		/P V.Curtis
		/P R.Embree			/P J.McGillen		/P S.Ullrich
							/P W.Holborow
							/P B.Zinser

TEAM	G	W	L	PCT	GB	R	OR	AB	H	2B	3B	HR	BB	SO	AVG	OBP	SLG	PRO	PRO+	BR	/A	PF	CHI	RC	SB	CS	SBA	SBR
STL	154	89	65	.578		684	587	5269	1328	223	45	72	531	604	.252	.323	.352	.675	94	-4	-40	106	110	629	44	33	57	-7
DET	156	88	66	.571	1	658	581	5344	1405	220	44	60	532	500	.263	.332	.354	.686	97	21	-15	106	100	641	61	55	53	-15
NY	154	83	71	.539	6	674	617	5331	1410	216	74	96	523	627	.264	.333	.387	.720	108	75	52	103	95	707	91	31	75	9
BOS	156	77	77	.500	12	739	676	5400	1456	277	56	69	522	505	.270	.336	.380	.716	112	73	82	99	103	710	60	40	60	-6
PHI	155	72	82	.468	17	525	594	5312	1364	169	47	36	422	490	.257	.314	.327	.641	90	-73	-65	99	96	547	42	32	57	-7
CLE	155	72	82	.468	17	643	677	5481	1458	205	50	70	512	593	.266	.331	.372	.703	111	46	72	96	93	684	48	42	53	-11
CHI	154	71	83	.461	18	543	662	5292	1307	210	55	23	439	448	.247	.307	.320	.627	86	-97	-90	99	104	533	66	47	58	-8
WAS	154	64	90	.416	25	592	664	5319	1386	186	42	33	470	477	.261	.324	.330	.654	97	-41	-15	96	101	594	127	59	68	3
TOT	619					5058		42748	11114	1771	413	459	3951	4244	.260	.325	.353	.678							539	339	61	-42

TEAM	CG	SH	SV	IP	H	H/G	HR	BB	SO	RAT	ERA	ERA+	OAV	OOB	PR	/A	PF	CPI	FA	E	DP	FW	PW	BW	SBW	DIF
STL	71	16	17	1397¹	1392	9.0	58	469	581	12.1	3.17	114	.259	.320	41	66	105	105	.972	171	142	.5	6.9	-4.2	-.2	9.0
DET	87	20	8	1400	1373	8.8	39	452	568	11.9	3.09	116	.257	.318	54	75	104	103	.970	190	184	-.5	7.9	-1.6	-1.0	6.2
NY	78	9	13	1390¹	1351	8.7	82	532	529	12.3	3.39	103	.257	.326	7	15	102	105	.974	156	170	1.3	1.6	5.5	1.5	-3.9
BOS	58	7	17	1394¹	1404	9.1	66	592	524	13.0	3.82	89	.263	.339	-60	-65	99	98	.972	171	154	.6	-6.8	8.6	-.0	-2.3
PHI	72	10	14	1419¹	1345	8.7	58	390	534	11.4	3.26	107	.252	.307	27	35	102	93	.971	176	127	.2	3.7	-6.8	-.2	-1.9
CLE	48	7	18	1419¹	1428	9.1	40	621	524	13.2	3.65	90	.265	.344	-35	-56	96	102	.974	165	192	.9	-5.9	7.6	-.6	-6.9
CHI	64	5	17	1390²	1411	9.1	68	420	481	12.0	3.58	96	.264	.320	-23	-23	100	97	.970	183	154	-.2	-2.4	-9.5	-.3	6.4
WAS	83	13	11	1381	1410	9.2	48	475	503	12.4	3.49	93	.264	.327	-10	-36	95	99	.964	218	156	-2.3	-3.8	-1.6	.9	-6.2
TOT	561	87	115	11170¹		9.0				12.3	3.43		.260	.325					.971	1430	1279					

Runs		**Hits**		**Doubles**		**Triples**		**Home Runs**		**Total Bases**	
Stirnweiss-NY	125	Stirnweiss-NY	205	Boudreau-Cle	45	Stirnweiss-NY	16	Etten-NY	22	Lindell-NY	297
B.Johnson-Bos	106	Boudreau-Cle	191	Keltner-Cle	41	Lindell-NY	16	Stephens-StL	20	Stirnweiss-NY	296
Cullenbine-Cle	98	Spence-Was	187	B.Johnson-Bos	40	Gutteridge-StL	11	York-Det	18	Spence-Was	288
Doerr-Bos	95	Lindell-NY	178	Fox-Bos	37	Doerr-Bos	10	Spence-Was	18	B.Johnson-Bos	277
Metkovich-Bos	94	Rocco-Cle	174	Stirnweiss-NY	35			Lindell-NY	18		

Runs Batted In		**Runs Produced**		**Bases On Balls**		**Batting Average**		**On Base Percentage**		**Slugging Average**	
Stephens-StL	109	B.Johnson-Bos	195	Etten-NY	97	Boudreau-Cle	.327	B.Johnson-Bos	.431	Doerr-Bos	.528
B.Johnson-Bos	106	Stephens-StL	180	B.Johnson-Bos	95	Doerr-Bos	.325	Boudreau-Cle	.406	B.Johnson-Bos	.528
Lindell-NY	103	Lindell-NY	176	Cullenbine-Cle	87	B.Johnson-Bos	.324	Doerr-Bos	.399	Lindell-NY	.500
Spence-Was	100	Spence-Was	165	McQuinn-StL	85	Stirnweiss-NY	.319	Etten-NY	.399	Spence-Was	.486
York-Det	98	Cullenbine-Cle	162	Higgins-Det	81	Spence-Was	.316	Byrnes-StL	.396		

Production		**Adjusted Production**		**Batter Runs**		**Adjusted Batter Runs**		**Clutch Hitting Index**		**Runs Created**	
B.Johnson-Bos	.959	B.Johnson-Bos	175	B.Johnson-Bos	52.9	B.Johnson-Bos	54.4	Christman-StL	134	Stirnweiss-NY	128
Doerr-Bos	.927	Doerr-Bos	166	Spence-Was	38.1	Spence-Was	43.1	Carnett-Chi	123	B.Johnson-Bos	124
Spence-Was	.877	Spence-Was	157	Doerr-Bos	38.0	Doerr-Bos	39.2	Mayo-Det	121	Spence-Was	118
Etten-NY	.865	Boudreau-Cle	146	Etten-NY	37.3	Boudreau-Cle	37.2	Torres-Was	115	Etten-NY	114
Lindell-NY	.851	Etten-NY	142	Wakefield-Det	36.7	Etten-NY	33.7	Stephens-StL	112	Boudreau-Cle	112

Total Average		**Stolen Bases**		**Stolen Base Average**		**Stolen Base Runs**		**Fielding Runs**		**Total Player Rating**	
B.Johnson-Bos	.987	Stirnweiss-NY	55	Stirnweiss-NY	83.3	Stirnweiss-NY	9.9	Mayo-Det	29.4	Boudreau-Cle	7.8
Doerr-Bos	.945	Case-Was	49	Moses-Chi	75.0	Case-Was	3.9	Boudreau-Cle	25.8	Stirnweiss-NY	7.1
Stirnweiss-NY	.910	Myatt-Was	26	Case-Was	73.1	Moses-Chi	2.1	Stirnweiss-NY	18.9	Spence-Was	5.2
Etten-NY	.879	Moses-Chi	21	Myatt-Was	72.2	Myatt-Was	1.8	Spence-Was	18.6	Doerr-Bos	5.2
Spence-Was	.856	Gutteridge-StL	20	Gutteridge-StL	71.4	Grimes-NY	1.8	Tucker-Chi	17.7	B.Johnson-Bos	4.9

Wins		**Win Percentage**		**Games**		**Complete Games**		**Shutouts**		**Saves**	
Newhouser-Det	29	Hughson-Bos	.783	Heving-Cle	63	Trout-Det	33	Trout-Det	7	Maltzberger-Chi	12
Trout-Det	27	Newhouser-Det	.763	Berry-Phi	53	Newhouser-Det	25	Newhouser-Det	6	Caster-StL	12
Potter-StL	19	Potter-StL	.731	Trout-Det	49			Jakucki-StL	4	Berry-Phi	12
Hughson-Bos	18	Trout-Det	.659	Newhouser-Det	47					Heving-Cle	10
		Borowy-NY	.586	Klieman-Cle	47					Barrett-Bos	8

Innings Pitched		**Fewest Hits/Game**		**Fewest BB/Game**		**Strikeouts**		**Strikeouts/Game**		**Ratio**	
Trout-Det	352.1	Gromek-Cle	7.07	Harris-Phi	1.34	Newhouser-Det	187	Newhouser-Det	5.39	Hughson-Bos	9.52
Newhouser-Det	312.1	Niggeling-Was	7.17	Leonard-Was	1.45	Trout-Det	144	Niggeling-Was	5.29	Trout-Det	10.24
Newsom-Phi	265.0	Newhouser-Det	7.61	Bonham-NY	1.73	Newsom-Phi	142	Gromek-Cle	5.08	Leonard-Was	10.28
Kramer-StL	257.0	Hughson-Bos	7.61	Gorsica-Det	1.78	Kramer-StL	124	Hughson-Bos	4.96	Gromek-Cle	10.30
Borowy-NY	252.2	Borowy-NY	7.98	Hamlin-Phi	1.80	Niggeling-Was	121	Newsom-Phi	4.82	Newhouser-Det	10.58

Earned Run Average		**Adjusted ERA**		**Opponents' Batting Avg.**		**Opponents' On Base Pct.**		**Starter Runs**		**Adjusted Starter Runs**	
Trout-Det	2.12	Trout-Det	168	Gromek-Cle	.219	Hughson-Bos	.267	Trout-Det	51.3	Trout-Det	56.7
Newhouser-Det	2.22	Newhouser-Det	161	Niggeling-Was	.221	Leonard-Was	.284	Newhouser-Det	42.1	Newhouser-Det	46.8
Hughson-Bos	2.26	Hughson-Bos	151	Hughson-Bos	.225	Trout-Det	.284	Kramer-StL	27.0	Kramer-StL	31.8
Niggeling-Was	2.32	Kramer-StL	145	Newhouser-Det	.230	Gromek-Cle	.290	Hughson-Bos	26.5	Hughson-Bos	25.8
Kramer-StL	2.49	Niggeling-Was	141	Borowy-NY	.236	Newhouser-Det	.293	Niggeling-Was	25.5	Borowy-NY	23.9

Clutch Pitching Index		**Relief Runs**		**Adjusted Relief Runs**		**Relief Ranking**		**Total Pitcher Index**		**Total Baseball Ranking**	
Donald-NY	129	Heving-Cle	19.6	Berry-Phi	19.1	Berry-Phi	32.4	Trout-Det	9.1	Trout-Det	9.1
Woods-Bos	122	Berry-Phi	18.4	Heving-Cle	17.9	Heving-Cle	18.2	Newhouser-Det	6.5	Boudreau-Cle	7.8
Smith-Cle	116	Caster-StL	8.9	Caster-StL	10.4	Caster-StL	17.3	Kramer-StL	4.3	Stirnweiss-NY	7.1
Haynes-Chi	116	Maltzberger-Chi	4.8	Maltzberger-Chi	4.8	Maltzberger-Chi	8.5	Berry-Phi	3.6	Newhouser-Det	6.5
Bonham-NY	115							Hughson-Bos	3.0	Spence-Was	5.2

January 10 Baseball writers again fail to elect a new Hall of Famer. Frank Chance, Rube Waddell, and Ed Walsh come closest, but none gets the required three-fourths of the vote.

March 15 With war-time travel restrictions still in effect, the Dodgers open spring training at Bear Mountain, New York with 15 players in camp. Seven teams—the Browns, Tigers, Reds, Indians, Cubs, Pirates and White Sox—are training in Indiana, the most of any state. The Red Sox are at Tufts College while the Braves are prepping at the Choate School in Connecticut.

April 25 Baseball writers cannot seem to get any Hall of Fame candidates past the 75 percent requirement, but a committee selected to bring in some old-timers succeeds with these names: Jimmy Collins, Roger Bresnahan, Fred Clarke, Dan Brouthers, Ed Delahanty, Hugh Jennings, Mike Kelley, Jim O'Rourke, Wilbert Robinson and Hugh Duffy.

July 12 The Chicago Cubs stop Tommy Holmes's modern-day NL hitting streak at 37 games, beating the Boston Braves 6-1 behind Hank Wyse for their 11th victory in a row. Holmes hits .433 during the streak and will finish at .352, second in the NL. His 9 strikeouts coupled with 28 home runs and 47 doubles is unparalleled for making contact and hitting for average and power.

August 1 Mel Ott hits the 500th home run of his career. He will hit 10 more this season and one on Opening Day of 1946 to finish with 511. Of Ott's total, 324 will be hit in the Polo Grounds.

August 13 Branch Rickey becomes the principal stockholder of the Dodgers. He and associates Walter O'Malley and John Smith acquire the 50 percent interest of the Ebbets estate for a reported price of $750,000.

August 15 Commissioner Chandler sells World Series radio rights for $150,000 to Gillette. Ford had been the sponsor since 1934, paying $100,000 annually.

August 19 In game two of a doubleheader against the Reds, 37-year-old slugger Jimmie Foxx pitches the first seven innings for the Philadelphia Blue Jays. He leaves with a 4-1 lead, and Andy Karl saves Foxx's only major league decision. His ERA in 10 major league appearances is 1.52.

August 20 At the age of 17, shortstop Tommy Brown of the Brooklyn Dodgers is the youngest player to hit a major league home run. Brown homers off Pirates southpaw Preacher Roe.

September 29 The Cubs clinch the NL flag on Hank Borowy's 4-3 win over Pittsburgh in the first game of a doubleheader. The final margin for Chicago is three games over the Cardinals. In 1945, the Chicago Cubs win twenty doubleheaders.

October 3 The Tigers and Cubs meet in the World Series for the fourth time. Hank Borowy pitches a six-hitter and Hal Newhouser is roughed up for eight runs in three innings; Cubs win 9-0.

October 5 Claude Passeau of the Chicago Cubs pitches a one-hitter, beating the Detroit Tigers 3-0 in the third game of the World Series. Rudy York's second-inning single spoils Passeau's no-hit bid. Bill Nicholson drives in the first run.

October 23 Branch Rickey announces the signing of Jackie Robinson by the Dodger organization and, one week later, signs him to Montreal (IL) for 1946.

November 15 The rules are revised for election of modern players to the Hall of Fame. A runoff election is formulated as a way to qualify more players for selection, but it fails to meet its objective as no one reaches the 75 percent requirement in the runoff. Frank Chance, Johnny Evers, Miller Huggins, and Ed Walsh come closest.

BOSTON	BROOKLYN	CHICAGO	CINCINNATI	NEW YORK	PHILADELPHIA	PITTSBURGH	ST.LOUIS
M B.Coleman	M L.Durocher	M C.Grimm	M B.McKechnie	M M.Ott	M F.Fitzsimmons	M F.Frisch	M B.Southworth
M D.Bissonette	1B A.Galan	1B P.Cavarretta	1B F.McCormick	1B P.Weintraub	M B.Chapman	1B B.Dahlgren	1B R.Sanders
1B V.Shupe	2B E.Stanky	2B D.Johnson	2B W.Williams	2B G.Hausmann	1B J.Wasdell	2B P.Coscarart	2B E.Verban
2B W.Wietelmann	SS E.Basinski	SS L.Merullo	SS E.Miller	SS B.Kerr	2B T.Daniels	SS F.Gustine	SS M.Marion
SS D.Culler	3B F.Bordagaray	3B S.Hack	3B S.Mesner	3B N.Reyes	SS B.Mott	3B B.Elliott	3B W.Kurowski
3B C.Workman	LF L.Olmo	LF P.Lowrey	LF E.Tipton	LF D.Gardella	3B J.Antonelli	LF J.Russell	LF R.Schoendienst
LF B.Nieman	CF G.Rosen	CF A.Pafko	CF D.Clay	CF J.Rucker	LF C.Triplett	CF A.Gionfriddo	CF B.Adams
CF C.Gillenwater	RF D.Walker	RF B.Nicholson	RF A.Libke	RF M.Ott	CF V.DiMaggio	RF J.Barrett	RF J.Hopp
RF T.Holmes	C M.Sandlock	C M.Livingston	C A.Lakeman	C E.Lombardi	RF V.Dinges	C A.Lopez	C K.O'Dea
C P.Masi	1 E.Stevens	S2 R.Hughes	O G.Walker	O R.Treadway	C A.Seminick	3 L.Handley	O A.Bergamo
1 J.Mack	S T.Brown	C P.Gillespie	C A.Unser	C C.Kluttz	OP R.Monteagudo	C B.Salkeld	C D.Rice
O1 J.Medwick	3 B.Hart	1 H.Becker	2S K.Wahl	3 B.Jurges	OS G.Crawford	S V.Barnhart	3O D.Garms
C S.Hofferth	1 H.Schultz	C D.Williams	O D.Sipek	O W.Lockman	13 J.Foxx	O T.O'Brien	/O A.Rebel
2 F.Drews	C F.Dantonio	C L.Rice	O H.Sauer	O S.Filipowicz	O G.Mancuso	1O F.Colman	/S L.Klein
23 E.Joost	C J.Peacock	O E.Sauer	S W.Flager	1 M.Schemer	O J.Powell	2 J.Saltzgaver	S G.Fallon
O B.Ramsey	C M.Owen	C F.Secory	C J.Riddle	1 R.Zimmerman	O W.Flager	C S.Davis	O D.Bartosch
32 T.Nelson	/O M.Aderholt	S B.Schuster	C J.Just	2 J.Mallory	2 Ga.Hamner	S F.Zak	O P.Young
O M.Aderholt	C C.Sukeforth	/O C.Block	/O E.Lukon	3 J.Medwick	/O L.Waner	/O L.Waner	O J.Mallory
C C.Kluttz	S C.Andrews	H J.Moore	R R.Medeiros	C M.Mead	C H.Spindel	/C H.Camelli	/C W.Cooper
2 S.Shemo	O B.Herman	/O L.Christopher	P E.Heusser	C R.Berres	C J.Peacock	H B.Rodgers	/C G.Crumling
/O S.Wentzel	/O R.Durrett	P H.Wyse	P J.Bowman	/1 A.Gardella	2 E.Walczak	R J.Vitelli	/3 J.Antonelli
/C M.Ulisney	/1 J.Douglas	P C.Passeau	P B.Walters	/3 J.Hudson	O B.Adams	P P.Roe	/C G.Crawford
/3 N.Wallen	/2 L.Durocher	P P.Derringer	P H.Fox	/C B.DeKoning	1 T.Lupien	P N.Strincevich	/C B.Keely
P J.Tobin	/3 C.Corbitt	P R.Prim	P V.Kennedy	S B.Voiselle	O B.Chapman	P R.Sewell	P R.Barrett
P B.Logan	H D.Lund	P H.Borowy	RP H.Lisenbee	P H.Feldman	S Gr.Hamner	P M.Butcher	P K.Burkhart
P J.Hutchings	/C R.Hayworth	RP B.Chipman	P F.Dasso	P V.Mungo	S S.Andrews	RP A.Gerheauser	P B.Donnelly
P N.Andrews	/S B.White	P P.Erickson	P E.Harrist	P J.Brewer	P D.Hasenmayer	RP X.Rescigno	P H.Brecheen
P E.Wright	R E.Palica	P H.Vandenberg	P B.Beck	P S.Emmerich	P N.Goulish	RP C.Cuccurullo	P G.Dockins
RP D.Hendrickson	P H.Gregg	P M.Stewart	P A.Carter	RP A.Adams	RP P.Caballero		RP B.Byerly
P B.Lee	P V.Lombardi	/P L.Warneke	P M.Modak	RP R.Fischer	P D.Barrett		RP A.Jurisich
P M.Cooper	P C.Davis	/P R.Starr	/P J.Hetki	P A.Hansen	P C.Schanz		P T.Wilks
P A.Javery	P A.Herring	/P J.Comellas	/P E.Riddle	P S.Maglie	P C.Sproull		P J.Creel
P T.Earley	P T.Seats	/P W.Signer	/P M.Bosser	P A.Zabala	P D.Mauney		P G.Gardner
/P R.Barrett	RP C.King	/P E.Hanyzewski	/P H.Wehmeier	P R.Harrell	RP A.Karl		/P M.Lanier
/P E.Singleton	/P C.Buker	/P G.Hennessey	/P G.Bush	/P D.Fisher	P O.Judd		/P M.Cooper
P I.Hutchinson	P R.Branca			/P L.Bain	P J.Kraus		/P B.Crouch
/P L.Wallace	P L.Webber			/P R.Lee	P B.Lee		/P S.Partenheimer
/P B.Whitcher	P L.Pfund			/P E.Pyle	P W.Wyatt		/P A.Lopatka
/P H.Schacker	P B.Chapman			/P J.Phillips	P I.Leon		
/P E.Pyle	/P O.Nitcholas			/P J.Gee	P V.Kennedy		
/P L.Fette	/P R.Hathaway				/P H.Mulcahy		
/P C.Cozart	/P E.Rudolph				/P D.Coffman		
/P J.Heving	/P C.Crocker				/P K.Raffensberger		
/P B.Cardoni					/P L.Scott		
					P L.Lucier		
					/P D.Grate		
					/P C.Ripple		
					/P M.Chetkovich		

TEAM	G	W	L	PCT	GB	R	OR	AB	H	2B	3B	HR	BB	SO	AVG	OBP	SLG	PRO	PRO+	BR	/A	PF	CHI	RC	SB	CS	SBA	SBR
CHI	155	98	56	.636		735	532	5298	1465	229	52	57	554	462	**.277**	**.349**	.372	.721	109	53	69	98	99	714	69			
STL	155	95	59	.617	3	756	583	5487	**1498**	256	44	64	515	488	.273	.338	.371	.709	102	25	7	102	**103**	716	55			
BRO	155	87	67	.565	11	**795**	724	5418	1468	257	71	57	**629**	434	.271	.349	.376	**.725**	109	66	72	99	102	**746**	75			
PIT	155	82	72	.532	16	753	686	5343	1425	**259**	56	72	590	480	.267	.342	.377	.719	102	45	16	104	102	701	81			
NY	154	78	74	.513	19	668	700	5350	1439	175	35	**114**	501	457	.269	.336	**.379**	.715	103	33	22	102	93	692	38			
BOS	154	67	85	.441	30	721	728	5441	1453	229	25	101	520	510	.267	.334	.374	.708	102	20	16	101	100	692	**82**			
CIN	154	61	93	.396	37	536	694	5283	1317	221	26	56	392	532	.249	.304	.333	.637	85	-122	-110	98	99	537	71			
PHI	154	46	108	.299	52	548	865	5203	1278	197	27	56	449	501	.246	.307	.326	.633	84	-122	-107	97	102	527	54			
TOT	618					5512		42823	11343	1823	336	577	4150	3864	.265	.333	.364	.696							525			

TEAM	CG	SH	SV	IP	H	H/G	HR	BB	SO	RAT	ERA	ERA+	OAV	OOB	PR	/A	PF	CPI	FA	E	DP	FW	PW	BW	SBW	DIF
CHI	86	15	14	1366¹	1301	8.6	57	385	541	11.3	**2.98**	123	**.249**	.304	125	102	96	102	**.980**	121	124	3.4	10.2	6.9		.5
STL	77	**18**	9	1408²	1351	8.6	70	497	510	12.0	3.24	116	.253	.320	88	79	99	**106**	.977	137	150	2.4	7.9	.7		7.0
BRO	61	7	18	1392¹	1357	8.8	74	586	557	12.8	3.70	101	.253	.331	15	7	99	98	.962	230	144	-3.2	.7	**7.2**		5.3
PIT	73	8	16	1387¹	1477	9.6	61	455	518	12.7	3.76	105	.272	.331	6	27	104	100	.971	178	141	-.0	2.7	1.6		.8
NY	53	13	21	1374²	1401	9.4	85	528	530	12.8	4.06	96	.263	.332	-40	-23	103	95	.973	166	112	.6	-2.3	2.2		1.5
BOS	57	7	13	1391²	1474	9.5	99	557	404	13.3	4.04	95	.272	.342	-37	-32	101	104	.969	193	**160**	-1.1	-3.2	1.6		-6.3
CIN	77	11	6	1365²	1438	9.5	70	534	372	13.2	4.00	94	.271	.340	-31	-36	99	100	.976	146	138	1.8	-3.6	-11.0		-3.2
PHI	31	4	**26**	1352²	1544	10.3	61	608	432	14.5	4.64	83	.285	.360	-126	-123	101	97	.962	234	150	-3.5	-12.3	-10.7		-4.4
TOT	515	83	123	11039¹		9.2				12.8	3.80		.265	.333					.971	1405	1119					

Runs		Hits		Doubles		Triples		Home Runs		Total Bases	
Stanky-Bro	128	Holmes-Bos	224	Holmes-Bos	47	Olmo-Bro	13	Holmes-Bos	28	Holmes-Bos	367
Rosen-Bro	126	Rosen-Bro	197	Walker-Bro	42	Pafko-Chi	12	Workman-Bos	25	Adams-Phi-StL	279
Holmes-Bos	125	Hack-Chi	193	Galan-Bro	36	Rucker-NY	11	Adams-Phi-StL	22	Rosen-Bro	279
Galan-Bro	114	Clay-Cin	184	Elliott-Pit	36	Rosen-Bro	11	Ott-NY	21	Walker-Bro	266
Hack-Chi	110			Cavarretta-Chi	34	Cavarretta-Chi	10	Kurowski-StL	21	Kurowski-StL	261

Runs Batted In		Runs Produced		Bases On Balls		Batting Average		On Base Percentage		Slugging Average	
Walker-Bro	124	Walker-Bro	218	Stanky-Bro	148	Cavarretta-Chi	.355	Cavarretta-Chi	.449	Holmes-Bos	.577
Holmes-Bos	117	Holmes-Bos	214	Galan-Bro	114	Holmes-Bos	.352	Galan-Bro	.423	Kurowski-StL	.511
Pafko-Chi	110	Galan-Bro	197	Hack-Chi	99	Rosen-Bro	.325	Hack-Chi	.420	Cavarretta-Chi	.500
Olmo-Bro	110	Adams-Phi-StL	191	Nicholson-Chi	92	Hack-Chi	.323	Holmes-Bos	.420	Ott-NY	.499
Adams-Phi-StL	109	Rosen-Bro	189	Sanders-StL	83	Kurowski-StL	.323	Stanky-Bro	.417	Olmo-Bro	.462

Production		Adjusted Production		Batter Runs		Adjusted Batter Runs		Clutch Hitting Index		Runs Created	
Holmes-Bos	.997	Holmes-Bos	175	Holmes-Bos	62.9	Holmes-Bos	62.1	Walker-Bro	135	Holmes-Bos	156
Cavarretta-Chi	.949	Cavarretta-Chi	167	Cavarretta-Chi	46.4	Cavarretta-Chi	48.8	Elliott-Pit	135	Cavarretta-Chi	119
Ott-NY	.910	Ott-NY	150	Galan-Bro	36.8	Galan-Bro	37.7	Lowrey-Chi	129	Galan-Bro	116
Kurowski-StL	.894	Kurowski-StL	144	Ott-NY	33.4	Ott-NY	32.0	Cavarretta-Chi	126	Hack-Chi	111
Galan-Bro	.864	Galan-Bro	142	Kurowski-StL	30.7	Hack-Chi	31.7	Olmo-Bro	125	Rosen-Bro	110

Total Average		Stolen Bases		Stolen Base Average		Stolen Base Runs		Fielding Runs		Total Player Rating	
Holmes-Bos	1.078	Schoendienst-StL	26					Kerr-NY	28.3	Holmes-Bos	5.4
Cavarretta-Chi	1.037	Barrett-Pit	25					Gillenwater-Bos	23.8	Hack-Chi	5.2
Ott-NY	.959	Clay-Cin	19					Coscarart-Pit	21.1	Cavarretta-Chi	3.8
Galan-Bro	.936							Hack-Chi	18.0	Stanky-Bro	3.6
Kurowski-StL	.876							Walker-Bro	12.4	Kurowski-StL	3.3

Wins		Win Percentage		Games		Complete Games		Shutouts		Saves	
Barrett-Bos-StL	23	Brecheen-StL	.789	Karl-Phi	67	Barrett-Bos-StL	24	Passeau-Chi	5	Karl-Phi	15
Wyse-Chi	22	Burkhart-StL	.692	Adams-NY	65	Wyse-Chi	23	Voiselle-NY	4	Adams-NY	15
Gregg-Bro	18	Wyse-Chi	.688	Hutchings-Bos	57	Passeau-Chi	19	Heusser-Cin	4	Rescigno-Pit	9
Burkhart-StL	18	Barrett-Bos-StL	.657	Barrett-Bos-StL	45	Strincevich-Pit	18	Donnelly-StL	4		
Passeau-Chi	17	Passeau-Chi	.654	Fox-Cin	45	Heusser-Cin	18	Burkhart-StL	4		

Innings Pitched		Fewest Hits/Game		Fewest BB/Game		Strikeouts		Strikeouts/Game		Ratio	
Barrett-Bos-StL	284.2	Prim-Chi	7.73	Prim-Chi	1.25	Roe-Pit	148	Roe-Pit	5.67	Prim-Chi	9.04
Wyse-Chi	278.1	Brecheen-StL	7.78	Barrett-Bos-StL	1.71	Gregg-Bro	139	Mungo-NY	4.97	Roe-Pit	10.53
Gregg-Bro	254.1	Gregg-Bro	7.82	Roe-Pit	1.76	Voiselle-NY	115	Gregg-Bro	4.92	Passeau-Chi	10.55
Roe-Pit	235.0	Mungo-NY	7.92	Wyse-Chi	1.78	Mungo-NY	101	Hutchings-Bos	4.82	Brecheen-StL	10.58
Voiselle-NY	232.1	Passeau-Chi	8.13	Strincevich-Pit	1.93	Hutchings-Bos	99	Prim-Chi	4.79	Wyse-Chi	10.74

Earned Run Average		Adjusted ERA		Opponents' Batting Avg.		Opponents' On Base Pct.		Starter Runs		Adjusted Starter Runs	
Borowy-Chi	2.13	Prim-Chi	152	Prim-Chi	.228	Prim-Chi	.256	Wyse-Chi	34.5	Passeau-Chi	30.1
Prim-Chi	2.40	Brecheen-StL	149	Gregg-Bro	.232	Passeau-Chi	.289	Passeau-Chi	33.8	Wyse-Chi	29.9
Passeau-Chi	2.46	Passeau-Chi	149	Brecheen-StL	.238	Barrett-Bos-StL	.295	Prim-Chi	25.8	Roe-Pit	28.0
Brecheen-StL	2.52	Walters-Cin	140	Mungo-NY	.238	Wyse-Chi	.296	Barrett-Bos-StL	25.2	Barrett-Bos-StL	23.7
Walters-Cin	2.68	Roe-Pit	137	Passeau-Chi	.238	Roe-Pit	.296	Roe-Pit	24.2	Prim-Chi	23.1

Clutch Pitching Index		Relief Runs		Adjusted Relief Runs		Relief Ranking		Total Pitcher Index		Total Baseball Ranking	
Butcher-Pit	124	Karl-Phi	16.3	Karl-Phi	16.9	Karl-Phi	16.6	Passeau-Chi	3.8	Holmes-Bos	5.4
Logan-Bos	124	Buker-Bro	4.9	Adams-NY	6.1	Adams-NY	11.5	Wyse-Chi	3.2	Hack-Chi	5.2
Walters-Cin	124	Adams-NY	4.7	Buker-Bro	4.4	Buker-Bro	4.7	Prim-Chi	3.0	Cavarretta-Chi	3.8
Lee-Phi-Bos	123	Chipman-Chi	2.4	Chipman-Chi	1.2	Chipman-Chi	1.4	Walters-Cin	2.9	Passeau-Chi	3.8
Wyse-Chi	117							Roe-Pit	2.8	Stanky-Bro	3.6

January 25 The Yankees are sold by the Ruppert estate to Larry MacPhail, Dan Topping, and Del Webb for $2.8 million. For that price the trio obtains 400 players, 266 of them in military service, Yankee Stadium, parks in Newark and Kansas City, and leases on other minor league ballparks. Jake Ruppert, who died in 1939, paid more than the new purchase price for the ground on which Yankee Stadium was built in 1923.

March 15 Bert Shepard, a one-legged veteran of the war, tries out as a pitcher for the Senators (and subsequently appears in a league game). The symbol of wartime baseball, outfielder Pete Gray of the Browns, will field and bat with only one arm.

May 13 David "Boo" Ferriss reaches 22 shutout innings before allowing a run versus the Tigers in a 6-2 Red Sox win. This sets an AL record for scoreless innings at the start of a major league career. Ferriss strikes out first baseman Rudy York four times, all on called third strikes.

May 20 In St. Louis, Pete Gray stars, as the Browns sweep the Yankees 10-1 and 5-2. Gray has two RBI on three hits in the opener, and in the nightcap he scores the winning run and hauls in seven fly balls, three on spectacular catches.

July 1 The first of the superstars returns from the war. Hank Greenberg, gone for four years, homers in his first game following his release from the army. Charlie Gassaway of the Athletics gives up the blow before 47,700 in a Sunday game at Briggs Stadium. The Tigers win 9-5 to lead the Yankees by 3½ games with Chicago and Boston following.

July 10 The All-Star Game at Fenway Park is canceled because of travel restrictions. During the schedule break, seven inter-league games are played for war charity. Plans for a USO-sponsored all-star game in Europe do not materialize, although the war in Germany is over, and fighting in the Pacific will be over in six weeks.

August 24 Cleveland ace Bob Feller returns from the Navy and attracts a crowd of 46,477, who watch him strike out 12 and yield only four hits in a 4-2 win over Detroit's Hal Newhouser. He will get nine starts during the remainder of the year, and his five wins will include a one-hitter and two four-hitters. With the war now over, fans are clamoring for entertainment, and it is clear Feller is still baseball's number one ticket seller.

September 7 Joe Kuhel hits an inside-the-park home run, the only home run hit by a Senator all season at Washington's spacious Griffith Stadium. The Nats hit 26 on the road.

September 9 Dick Fowler of the Philadelphia Athletics returns from three years with the Canadian Army and pitches a no-hitter, walking four and beating the St. Louis Browns 1-0 in the second game of a doubleheader. It is Fowler's first start since his return, his first major league shutout, and the first no-hitter by an Athletic since 1916.

September 30 Hank Greenberg's grand-slam home run in the ninth inning on the final day of the season beats the St. Louis Browns 6-3 and clinches the AL pennant for the Detroit Tigers. Virgil Trucks, discharged three days earlier from the Navy, is the starter, with Newhouser relieving in the fifth .

October 6 Tavern owner "Billy Goat" Sianis buys a box seat for his goat for the fourth game of the World Series and is escorted out of Wrigley Field. In retaliation Sianis casts a "goat curse" over the Cubs, dooming them to never win a World Series. The Tigers tie the series on Dizzy Trout's 5-hit 4-1 win. Detroit scores all its runs in the fourth, with Hank Greenberg, Roy Cullenbine, Paul Richards, and a forceout scoring the runners.

October 10 The Tigers tally five runs in the first inning and rout the Chicago Cubs 9-3 behind Hal Newhouser, who strikes out 10. Total receipts of $1.6 million set a World Series record.

BOSTON	CHICAGO	CLEVELAND	DETROIT	NEW YORK	PHILADELPHIA	ST.LOUIS	WASHINGTON
M J.Cronin	M J.Dykes	M L.Boudreau	M S.O'Neill	M J.McCarthy	M C.Mack	M L.Sewell	M O.Bluege
1B C.Metkovich	1B K.Farrell	1B M.Rocco	1B R.York	1B N.Etten	1B D.Siebert	1B G.McQuinn	1B J.Kuhel
2B S.Newsome	2B R.Schalk	2B D.Meyer	2B E.Mayo	2B S.Stirnweiss	2B I.Hall	2B D.Gutteridge	2B G.Myatt
SS E.Lake	SS C.Michaels	SS L.Boudreau	SS S.Webb	SS F.Crosetti	SS E.Busch	SS V.Stephens	SS G.Torres
3B J.Tobin	3B T.Cuccinello	3B D.Ross	3B B.Maier	3B O.Grimes	3B G.Kell	3B M.Christman	3B H.Clift
LF B.Johnson	LF J.Dickshot	LF J.Heath	LF J.Outlaw	LF H.Martin	LF M.Smith	LF M.Byrnes	LF G.Case
CF L.Culberson	CF O.Hockett	CF F.Mackiewicz	CF D.Cramer	CF T.Stainback	CF B.Estalella	CF M.Kreevich	CF G.Binks
RF J.Lazor	RF W.Moses	RF P.Seerey	RF R.Cullenbine	RF B.Metheny	RF H.Peck	RF G.Moore	RF B.Lewis
C B.Garbark	C M.Tresh	C F.Hayes	C B.Swift	C M.Garbark	C B.Rosar	C F.Mancuso	C R.Ferrell
O1 T.McBride	O G.Curtright	S3 A.Cihocki	O H.Greenberg	O R.Derry	O B.McGhee	32 L.Schulte	2 F.Vaughn
2 B.Steiner	1 B.Nagel	O P.O'Dea	O P.Richards	O C.Keller	O C.Metro	O P.Gray	O M.Kreevich
O P.Fox	32 F.Baker	O L.Fleming	S J.Hoover	S A.Robinson	S B.Wilkins	O1 L.Finney	C A.Evans
3 T.LaForest	S2 D.Reynolds	O M.Hoag	2 R.Borom	C J.Lindell	C G.George	O B.Martin	3 H.Layne
1 D.Camilli	S L.Appling	O E.Carnett	/O C.Hostetler	C B.Drescher	C F.Hayes	O R.Hayworth	O M.Guerra
3 J.Bucher	C V.Castino	3S E.Wheeler	/3 D.Ross	C H.Crompton	O E.Kish	O C.Laabs	O J.Zardon
C B.Holm	/3 J.Orengo	C J.McDonnell	C M.Milosevich	C D.Ross	O J.Burns	/C J.Schultz	O J.Powell
C F.Walters	/O B.Mueller	/O H.Ruszkowski	/O E.Mierkowicz	S J.Buzas	/O L.Rosenthal	3 E.Clary	O V.Ventura
C R.Steiner	P T.Lee	S E.Weingartner	/1 J.McHale	3 D.Savage	S A.Brancato	P N.Potter	3 C.Travis
/C F.Pytlak	P O.Grove	/O S.Benjamin	/C H.Miller	H P.Waner	/O S.Chapman	P J.Kramer	S D.Kimble
/O L.Christopher	P E.Lopat	/C R.Steiner	/C M.Welch	P B.Bevens	/O F.Garrison	P S.Jakucki	O W.Chipple
/3 J.Cronin	P J.Humphries	/1 P.Williams	H R.Kerns	P T.Bonham	/O J.Cicero	P T.Shirley	/O H.McFarland
/3 N.Polly	P B.Dietrich	H R.Cullenbine	H C.McNabb	P A.Gettel	/C J.Astroth	P A.Hollingsworth	P R.Wolff
H L.Finney	RP J.Johnson	/3 B.Rothel	P H.Newhouser	P M.Dubiel	P J.Pruett	RP S.Zoldak	P M.Pieretti
P D.Ferriss	P E.Caldwell	C G.Desautels	P D.Trout	P H.Borowy	/O L.Drake	P B.Muncrief	P D.Leonard
P J.Wilson	P J.Haynes	P S.Gromek	P A.Benton	RP K.Holcombe	P B.Newsom	P L.West	P J.Niggeling
P E.O'Neill	P F.Papish	P A.Reynolds	RP S.Overmire	RP J.Turner	P R.Christopher	P E.Jones	RP S.Ullrich
P C.Hausmann	P B.Ross	P J.Bagby	P L.Mueller	P B.Zuber	P J.Flores	P G.Caster	P A.Carrasquel
P M.Ryba	/P C.Touchstone	P A.Smith	RP W.Wilson	P J.Page	P L.Knerr	/C C.Fannin	P W.Holborow
RP F.Barrett		P E.Klieman	RP G.Caster	P R.Ruffing	P D.Black	/P A.LaMacchia	P W.Masterson
P P.Woods		RP P.Center	P J.Tobin	/P A.Donald	RP J.Berry	/P P.Appleton	/P P.Appleton
P R.Heflin		RP J.Salveson	P Z.Eaton	/P S.Chandler	/P C.Gassaway	/P D.Sanders	/P A.Roche
P V.Johnson		P M.Harder	P J.Orrell	/P S.Roser	P S.Gerkin		/P B.Shepard
P O.Clark		/P B.Feller	/P A.Houtteman	/P P.Schreiber	/P D.Fowler		/P D.Stone
P Y.Terry		/P R.Embree	/P T.Bridges		/P C.Bowles		/P J.Cleary
/P R.Cecil		/P E.Henry	/P P.Oana		/P P.Marchildon		
/P J.Bowman		/P H.Kleine	/P B.Pierce		/P C.Scheib		
/P C.Dreisewerd		/P P.Calvert	/P V.Trucks		/P B.Connelly		
/P O.Judd			/P P.McLaughlin		/P W.Crowson		

TEAM	G	W	L	PCT	GB	R	OR	AB	H	2B	3B	HR	BB	SO	AVG	OBP	SLG	PRO	PRO+	BR	/A	PF	CHI	RC	SB	CS	SBA	SBR
DET	155	88	65	.575		633	565	5257	1345	227	47	77	517	533	.256	.324	.361	.685	98	20	-20	106	102	627	60	54	53	-14
WAS	156	87	67	.565	1.5	622	562	5326	1375	197	63	27	545	489	.258	.330	.334	.664	107	-8	43	92	103	612	110	65	63	-6
STL	154	81	70	.536	6	597	548	5227	1302	215	37	63	500	555	.249	.316	.341	.657	91	-29	-58	105	105	584	25	31	45	-11
NY	152	81	71	.533	6.5	676	606	5176	1343	189	61	93	618	567	.259	.343	.373	.716	108	90	58	105	97	698	64	43	60	-7
CLE	147	73	72	.503	11	557	548	4898	1249	216	48	65	505	578	.255	.326	.359	.685	109	23	48	96	95	588	19	31	38	-13
CHI	150	71	78	.477	15	596	653	5077	1330	204	55	22	470	467	.262	.326	.337	.663	100	-13	2	97	105	571	78	54	59	-9
BOS	157	71	83	.461	17.5	599	674	5367	1393	225	44	50	541	534	.260	.330	.346	.676	100	12	-2	102	96	634	72	50	59	-8
PHI	153	52	98	.347	34.5	494	638	5296	1297	201	37	33	449	463	.245	.306	.316	.622	86	-96	-94	100	98	523	25	45	36	-20
TOT	612					4774		41624	10634	1674	392	430	4145	4186	.255	.325	.346	.671							453	373	55	-88

TEAM	CG	SH	SV	IP	H	H/G	HR	BB	SO	RAT	ERA	ERA+	OAV	OOB	PR	/A	PF	CPI	FA	E	DP	FW	PW	BW	SBW	DIF
DET	78	19	16	1393²	1305	8.4	48	538	588	12.1	2.99	118	.250	.322	58	81	105	108	.975	158	173	.4	8.7	-2.1	-.3	4.9
WAS	82	19	11	1412¹	1307	8.3	42	440	550	11.2	2.92	106	.242	.301	69	28	92	93	.970	183	124	-1.0	3.0	4.6	.5	2.8
STL	91	10	8	1382²	1307	8.5	59	506	570	11.8	3.14	112	.249	.316	34	58	105	101	.976	143	123	1.2	6.2	-6.2	.0	4.3
NY	78	9	14	1355	1277	8.5	66	485	474	11.8	3.45	100	.250	.316	-13	1	103	93	.971	175	170	-.7	.1	6.2	.4	-1.0
CLE	76	14	12	1302²	1269	8.8	39	501	497	12.4	3.31	98	.257	.328	8	-9	97	102	.977	126	149	1.7	-1.0	5.1	-.2	-5.2
CHI	84	13	13	1330²	1400	9.5	63	448	486	12.7	3.69	90	.270	.332	-49	-55	99	100	.970	180	139	-1.1	-5.9	.2	.2	3.1
BOS	71	15	13	1390²	1389	9.0	58	656	490	13.4	3.80	90	.264	.348	-67	-61	101	102	.973	169	198	-.1	-6.5	-.2	.3	.5
PHI	65	11	8	1381	1380	9.0	55	571	531	12.9	3.62	95	.262	.337	-40	-29	102	101	.973	168	160	-.3	-3.1	-10.1	-1.0	-8.6
TOT	625	110	95	10948¹		8.7				12.3	3.36		.255	.325					.973	1302	1236					

Runs
Stirnweiss-NY 107
Stephens-StL 90
Cullenbine-Cle-Det 83

Hits
Stirnweiss-NY 195
Moses-Chi 168
Stephens-StL 165
Hall-Phi 161
Etten-NY 161

Doubles
Moses-Chi 35
Stirnweiss-NY 32
Binks-Was 32
McQuinn-StL 31

Triples
Stirnweiss-NY 22
Moses-Chi 15
Kuhel-Was 13
Dickshot-Chi 10
Peck-Phi 9

Home Runs
Stephens-StL 24
Cullenbine-Cle-Det .. 18
York-Det 18
Etten-NY 18
Heath-Cle 15

Total Bases
Stirnweiss-NY 301
Stephens-StL 270
Etten-NY 247
York-Det 246
Moses-Chi 239

Runs Batted In
Etten-NY 111
Cullenbine-Cle-Det .. 93
Stephens-StL 89
York-Det 87
Binks-Was 81

Runs Produced
Etten-NY 170
Stirnweiss-NY 161
Cullenbine-Cle-Det 158
Stephens-StL 155
Kuhel-Was 146

Bases On Balls
Cullenbine-Cle-Det 113
Lake-Bos 106
Grimes-NY 97
Etten-NY 90
Kuhel-Was 79

Batting Average
Stirnweiss-NY .... .309
Cuccinello-Chi .... .308
Dickshot-Chi ...... .302
Estalella-Phi ...... .299
Myatt-Was .... .296

On Base Percentage
Lake-Bos .... .412
Cullenbine-Cle-Det .. .402
Estalella-Phi ...... .399
Grimes-NY .... .395
Etten-NY .... .387

Slugging Average
Stirnweiss-NY ...... .476
Stephens-StL ...... .473
Cullenbine-Cle-Det .. .444
Etten-NY .... .437
Estalella-Phi ...... .435

Production
Stirnweiss-NY 862
Cullenbine-Cle-Det 846
Estalella-Phi 834
Stephens-StL 825
Etten-NY 824

Adjusted Production
Stirnweiss-NY 143
Estalella-Phi 142
Kuhel-Was 137
Cullenbine-Cle-Det 137
Lake-Bos 136

Batter Runs
Stirnweiss-NY 39.1
Cullenbine-Cle-Det 35.1
Etten-NY 29.9
Heath-Cle 29.4
Lake-Bos 28.7

Adjusted Batter Runs
Stirnweiss-NY 34.0
Heath-Cle 32.6
Cullenbine-Cle-Det 29.2
Lake-Bos 26.7
Kuhel-Was 26.5

Clutch Hitting Index
Schalk-Chi 135
Michaels-Chi 132
Tresh-Chi 130
Etten-NY 121
Binks-Was 119

Runs Created
Stirnweiss-NY 121
Cullenbine-Cle-Det .. 106
Etten-NY 98
Stephens-StL 98
Moses-Chi 97

Total Average
Cullenbine-Cle-Det 888
Stirnweiss-NY 855
Lake-Bos 849
Etten-NY 794
Estalella-Phi 789

Stolen Bases
Stirnweiss-NY 33
Myatt-Was 30
Case-Was 30
Metkovich-Bos 19
Dickshot-Chi 18

Stolen Base Average
Dickshot-Chi 85.7
Metkovich-Bos 76.0
Myatt-Was 73.2
Stirnweiss-NY 66.0
Case-Was 65.2

Stolen Base Runs
Dickshot-Chi 3.6
Myatt-Was 2.4
Metkovich-Bos 2.1
Crosetti-NY 1.5
Richards-Det 1.2

Fielding Runs
Hall-Phi 26.1
Stirnweiss-NY 25.5
Webb-Det 23.0
Newsome-Bos 22.2
Kell-Phi 21.7

Total Player Rating
Stirnweiss-NY 7.2
Lake-Bos 5.7
Cullenbine-Cle-Det 3.4
Mayo-Det 3.1
Newsome-Bos 2.9

Wins
Newhouser-Det 25
Ferriss-Bos 21
Wolff-Was 20
Gromek-Cle 19

Win Percentage
Newhouser-Det .... .735
Leonard-Was ...... .708
Gromek-Cle ...... .679
Ferriss-Bos ...... .677
Wolff-Was .... .667

Games
Berry-Phi 52
Reynolds-Cle 44
Pieretti-Was 44
Trout-Det 41
Newhouser-Det 40

Complete Games
Newhouser-Det 29
Ferriss-Bos 26
Wolff-Was 21
Potter-StL 21
Gromek-Cle 21

Shutouts
Newhouser-Det 8
Ferriss-Bos 5
Benton-Det 5

Saves
Turner-NY 10
Berry-Phi 5

Innings Pitched
Newhouser-Det .. 313.1
Ferriss-Bos 264.2
Newsom-Phi 257.1
Potter-StL 255.1
Gromek-Cle 251.0

Fewest Hits/Game
Newhouser-Det ... 6.86
Wolff-Was 7.20
Potter-StL 7.47
Lee-Chi 8.20
Niggeling-Was 8.20

Fewest BB/Game
Bonham-NY 1.10
Leonard-Was 1.46
Wolff-Was 1.91
Overmire-Det 2.33
Gromek-Cle 2.37

Strikeouts
Newhouser-Det 212
Potter-StL 129
Newsom-Phi 127
Reynolds-Cle 112

Strikeouts/Game
Newhouser-Det 6.09
Kramer-StL 4.62
Niggeling-Was 4.58
Potter-StL 4.55
Newsom-Phi 4.44

Ratio
Wolff-Was 9.14
Potter-StL 9.90
Newhouser-Det 10.02
Leonard-Was 10.21
Bonham-NY 10.41

Earned Run Average
Newhouser-Det ... 1.81
Benton-Det 2.02
Wolff-Was 2.12
Leonard-Was 2.13
Lee-Chi 2.44

Adjusted ERA
Newhouser-Det 194
Benton-Det 174
Wolff-Was 146
Leonard-Was 146
Potter-StL 143

Opponents' Batting Avg.
Newhouser-Det ... .211
Wolff-Was .... .215
Potter-StL ...... .226
Niggeling-Was .... .240
Benton-Det ...... .241

Opponents' On Base Pct.
Wolff-Was .... .258
Potter-StL ...... .279
Leonard-Was ...... .279
Newhouser-Det .... .281
Bonham-NY ..... .288

Starter Runs
Newhouser-Det .. 54.1
Wolff-Was 34.5
Leonard-Was 29.8
Benton-Det 28.7
Potter-StL 25.5

Adjusted Starter Runs
Newhouser-Det 59.4
Benton-Det 31.9
Potter-StL 29.8
Wolff-Was 27.2
Leonard-Was 23.5

Clutch Pitching Index
Benton-Det 139
Lee-Chi 121
Shirley-StL 116
Hollingsworth-StL .. 116
Ferriss-Bos 114

Relief Runs
Berry-Phi 14.7
Holcombe-NY 9.7
Barrett-Bos 7.2
Zoldak-StL 0

Adjusted Relief Runs
Berry-Phi 15.7
Holcombe-NY 10.3
Barrett-Bos 7.5
Zoldak-StL 1.2

Relief Ranking
Berry-Phi 17.6
Holcombe-NY 10.0
Barrett-Bos 6.1
Zoldak-StL 8

Total Pitcher Index
Newhouser-Det 7.8
Potter-StL 3.5
Ferriss-Bos 3.3
Benton-Det 3.2
Leonard-Was 2.8

Total Baseball Ranking
Newhouser-Det 7.8
Stirnweiss-NY 7.2
Lake-Bos 5.7
Potter-StL 3.5
Cullenbine-Cle-Det 3.4

January 12* The first professional league game is played in Venezuela, launching the newly constituted four-team Liga de Beisbol Profesional de Venezuela. The game is won by Magallanes 5-2.

February 19 Giants outfielder Danny Gardella becomes the first major leaguer to announce he is jumping to the "outlaw" Mexican League. His attempt to return to the major leagues a few years later will initiate a major court battle.

April 14 Manager Mel Ott of the Giants hits his 511th and final home run on Opening Day, an 8–4 home victory over the Phils. The next day Ott will injure his knee diving for a ball and will play only occasionally thereafter.

April 18 Jackie Robinson debuts as a second baseman for the Montreal Royals (International League) and becomes the first black player in Organized Baseball in this century. A home run and three singles versus Jersey City start the season in which he will win the IL batting championship at .349.

April 24 Eleven former players—Joe Tinker, Johnny Evers, Frank Chance, Jess Burkett, Tom McCarthy, Rube Waddell, Eddie Plank, Ed Walsh, Jack Chesbro, Clark Griffith, and Joe McGinnity—are named to the Hall of Fame.

May 20 Claude Passeau of the Chicago Cubs makes his first error since September 21, 1941, ending his streak with an all-time fielding record for pitchers of 273 consecutive errorless chances.

May 30 In a play that anticipates a scene in *The Natural* by Brooklyn-native Bernard Malamud, the Braves' Bama Rowell smashes a home run in the second inning of the second game of a doubleheader at Ebbets Field. The ball shatters the Bulova clock high atop the right field scoreboard at 4:25 P.M., showering glass down on the Dodgers' right fielder Fred "Dixie" Walker. An hour later the clock stops.

July 22 Clubs approve a change to a 168-game schedule, but they will rescind the decision at another meeting September 16. Television is first recognized, with clubs given rights to their own games. Players jumping to outlaw leagues will not be allowed to apply for reinstatement for five years.

August 8 The Dreyfuss family, owners of the Pittsburgh Pirates since 1900, sell the club to a group headed by Frank McKinney and John Galbreath. Singer Bing Crosby is among investors who pay $2.5 million for the Bucs.

October 3 The St. Louis Cardinals wallop the Brooklyn Dodgers 8-4 at Ebbets Field to win the NL playoffs 2-0 and advance to the World Series. Erv Dusak and Enos Slaughter lead the attack. Losing pitcher is Ralph Branca.

October 15 Enos Slaughter sprints all the way from first base and slides home with the winning run in the eighth inning on Harry Walker's double, as the Cardinals edge the Boston Red Sox 4-3, giving St. Louis the World Series four games to three. Harry Brecheen wins three games for the Cardinals. Billed as the duel between the two best hitters in baseball, the Series sees Stan Musial go 6-for-27 and Ted Williams 5-for-25.

November 22 The NL names Stan Musial MVP.

	BOSTON		BROOKLYN		CHICAGO		CINCINNATI		NEW YORK		PHILADELPHIA		PITTSBURGH		ST.LOUIS
M	B.Southworth	M	L.Durocher	M	C.Grimm	M	B.McKechnie	M	M.Ott	M	B.Chapman	M	F.Frisch	M	E.Dyer
1B	R.Sanders	1B	E.Stevens	M	H.Gowdy	M	H.Gowdy	1B	J.Mize	1B	F.McCormick	1B	S.Davis	1B	S.Musial
2B	C.Ryan	2B	E.Stanky	2B	D.Johnson	1B	B.Haas	2B	B.Blattner	2B	E.Verban	1B	E.Fletcher	2B	R.Schoendienst
SS	D.Culler	SS	P.Reese	SS	B.Jurges	2B	B.Adams	SS	B.Kerr	SS	S.Newsome	2B	F.Gustine	SS	M.Marion
3B	N.Fernandez	3B	C.Lavagetto	3B	S.Hack	SS	E.Miller	3B	B.Rigney	3B	J.Tabor	SS	B.Cox	3B	W.Kurowski
LF	B.Rowell	LF	P.Reiser	LF	M.Rickert	3B	G.Hatton	LF	S.Gordon	LF	D.Ennis	3B	L.Handley	LF	E.Dusak
CF	C.Gillenwater	CF	C.Furillo	CF	P.Lowrey	LF	E.Lukon	CF	W.Marshall	CF	J.Wyrostek	LF	J.Russell	CF	H.Walker
RF	T.Holmes	RF	D.Walker	RF	P.Cavarretta	CF	D.Clay	RF	G.Rosen	RF	R.Northey	CF	R.Kiner	RF	E.Slaughter
C	P.Masi	C	B.Edwards	C	C.McCullough	RF	A.Libke	C	W.Cooper	C	A.Seminick	RF	B.Elliott	C	J.Garagiola
						C	R.Mueller					C	A.Lopez		
1O	J.Hopp	O3	A.Galan	O	B.Nicholson			O	J.Graham	S3	R.Hughes			O	T.Moore
21	B.Herman	O	D.Whitman	S2	B.Sturgeon	2O	L.Frey	O	J.Rucker	O	C.Gilbert	S2	J.Brown	1O	D.Sisler
O	D.Litwhiler	1	H.Schultz	O	A.Pafko	23	B.Zientara	1O	B.Young	C	R.Hemsley	C	B.Salkeld	O	B.Adams
3	S.Roberge	C	F.Anderson	2	L.Stringer	S	C.Corbitt	23	M.Witek	1	V.Dinges	O	M.Van Robays	O	D.Rice
O	M.McCormick	32	B.Herman	C	M.Livingston	C	R.Lamanno	C	E.Lombardi	S	J.O'Neil	O	C.Workman	2	C.Kluttz
C	D.Padgett	32	B.Ramazzotti	3	J.Ostrowski	O	M.West	O	B.Warren	O	J.Wasdell	2	B.Whitehead	S	J.Cross
S	W.Wietelmann	O	G.Hermanski	S	L.Merullo	O	M.Usher	/O	M.Ott	/O	K.Novikoff	O	B.Baker	C	K.O'Dea
C	S.Hofferth	C	J.Medwick	1	B.Scheffing	3	E.Shokes	/2	B.Thomson	O	K.Richardson	O	A.Gionfriddo	/O	B.Endicott
O	C.Workman	3	E.Miksis	O	D.Dallessandro	O	M.McCormick	/2	J.Pike	C	V.DiMaggio	C	H.Camelli	H	W.Sessi
O	T.Neill	S	S.Rojek	/C	F.Secory	/C	A.Lakeman	/2	V.DiMaggio	/2	D.Murtaugh	O	J.Barrett	/2	N.Jones
O	J.Barrett	C	M.Sandlock	/3	C.Block	/O	H.Moss	/C	M.Grasso	/2	G.Lawing	/O	F.Colman	H	D.Litwhiler
C	K.O'Dea	C	D.Padgett	/O	C.Gilbert	/O	C.Vollmer	/C	G.Lawing	/C	C.Letchas	/C	V.Smith	/C	D.Wilber
S	A.Dark	/1	J.Graham	/3	H.Schenz	H	L.Goldstein	/3	J.Gladd	/3	D.Moore	H	F.Zak	H	E.Verban
/1	J.McCarthy	/O	J.Tepsic	/2	A.Glossop	/O	G.Lawing	/2	D.Lajeskie	S	D.Hasenmayer	/C	R.Jarvis		
/C	H.Poland	/3	L.Riggs	H	H.Becker			/C	C.Kluttz	/S	G.Hamner	/O	B.Guintini		
/C	B.Brady	/O	G.Rosen	C	C.Garriott	P	J.Vander Meer	/3	B.Maynard	/3	H.Spindel	P	P.Coscarart	P	H.Pollet
H	D.Phillips	H	E.Naylor	/C	D.Williams	P	E.Blackwell	/O	M.Arnovich	H	B.Burich	H	A.Anderson	P	H.Brecheen
H	D.Detweiler	R	J.Corriden	/C	T.Pawelek	P	J.Beggs	/3	D.Bartell	H	G.Crawford	H	V.Barnhart	P	M.Dickson
/1	M.West	R	O.Davis	/O	C.Maddern	P	E.Heusser	H	M.Schemer					P	A.Brazle
/3	S.Sisti					P	B.Walters			P	K.Raffensberger			P	J.Beazley
		P	J.Hatten	P	J.Schmitz	RP	C.Shoun	RP	D.Koslo	P	O.Judd	P	F.Ostermueller	RP	T.Wilks
P	J.Sain	P	K.Higbe	P	H.Wyse	RP	B.Malloy	P	M.Kennedy	P	S.Rowe	P	N.Strincevich	RP	R.Barrett
P	M.Cooper	P	V.Lombardi	P	H.Borowy	RP	C.Lambert	P	B.Voiselle	P	C.Schanz	P	H.Sewell		
P	E.Wright	P	H.Behrman	P	P.Erickson			RP	K.Trinkle	P	T.Hughes	P	E.Bahr	P	K.Burkhart
P	B.Lee	P	H.Gregg	P	E.Kush	P	J.Hetki	P	H.Schumacher	RP	A.Karl	RP	A.Gerheauser	/P	M.Lanier
P	S.Johnson	RP	H.Casey			P	H.Gumbert	RP	M.Budnick	P	D.Mulligan			P	R.Munger
RP	L.Wallace	RP	A.Herring	P	C.Passeau	/P	N.Andrews	RP	J.Thompson	P	D.Mauney	P	J.Hallett	/P	F.Martin
		RP	R.Branca	P	B.Chipman	/P	H.Fox	P		P	B.Donnelly	P	K.Gables	/P	F.Schmidt
P	W.Spahn			P	H.Bithorn	/P	G.Burpo	P	B.Joyce	P	C.Stanceu	P	J.Lanning	/P	H.Krist
/P	J.Niggeling	P	R.Melton	P	R.Bauers	/P	F.Dasso	P	J.Gee	P	L.Hoerst	P	P.Roe	/P	B.Donnelly
P	F.Barrett	P	E.Head	P	B.Fleming			P	W.Abernathy	P	A.Jurisich	/P	E.Albosta	/P	J.Grodzicki
P	S.Roser	P	R.Barney	P	R.Prim			P	B.Carpenter	P	H.Mulcahy	/P	H.Gornicki		
P	E.Singleton	P	L.Webber	/P	R.Meyer			P	R.Fischer	P	J.Humphries	/P	L.Howard		
P	B.Posedel	/P	J.Roy	/P	D.Lade			/P	S.Jones	/P	I.Pearson	/P	J.Walsh		
P	E.White	/P	H.Taylor	/P	R.Adams			P	J.Kraus	/P	L.Possehl	/P	A.Tate		
P	J.Konstanty	/P	P.Minner	/P	R.Meers			/P	M.Grissom	/P	D.Grate	/P	L.Wilkie		
/P	D.Mulligan	/P	C.Davis	/P	V.Olsen			/P	N.Andrews	/P	A.Lopatka	/P	J.Hopper		
/P	J.Hutchings	/P	G.Moulder	/P	E.Hanyzewski			/P	S.Emmerich	/P	E.Hodkey	/P	B.Clemensen		
/P	A.Javery	/P	C.McLish	/P	H.Manders			/P	H.Feldman	/P	S.Johnson				
/P	E.Reid			/P	E.O'Neill			/P	R.Kress	/P	D.Koecher				
/P	D.Hendrickson							/P	A.Adams	/P	C.Ripple				
/P	A.Williams							/P	J.Brewer	/P	B.Chapman				
								/P	J.Carden	/P	A.Milnar				

TEAM	G	W	L	PCT	GB	R	OR	AB	H	2B	3B	HR	BB	SO	AVG	OBP	SLG	PRO	PRO+	BR	/A	PF	CHI	RC	SB	CS	SBA	SBR
STL	156	98	58	.628		712	545	5372	1426	265	56	81	530	537	.265	.334	.381	.715	105	54	25	104	105	702	58			
BRO	157	96	60	.615	2	701	570	5285	1376	233	66	55	691	575	.260	.348	.361	.709	106	60	53	101	101	699	100			
CHI	155	82	71	.536	14.5	626	581	5298	1344	223	50	56	586	599	.254	.331	.346	.677	100	-9	3	98	102	622	43			
BOS	154	81	72	.529	15.5	630	592	5225	1377	238	48	44	558	468	.264	.337	.353	.690	101	16	8	101	100	641	60			
PHI	155	69	85	.448	28	560	705	5233	1351	209	40	80	417	590	.258	.315	.359	.674	100	-30	-14	97	99	598	41			
CIN	156	67	87	.435	30	523	570	5291	1262	206	33	65	493	604	.239	.307	.327	.634	88	-101	-82	96	102	546	82			
PIT	155	63	91	.409	34	552	668	5199	1300	202	52	60	592	555	.250	.328	.344	.672	95	-18	-33	103	93	602	48			
NY	154	61	93	.396	36	612	685	5191	1326	176	37	121	532	546	.255	.328	.374	.702	104	27	23	101	97	644	46			
TOT	621					4916		42094	10762	1752	382	562	4399	4474	.256	.329	.355	.684							478			

TEAM	CG	SH	SV	IP	H	H/G	HR	BB	SO	RAT	ERA	ERA+	OAV	OOB	PR	/A	PF	CPI	FA	E	DP	FW	PW	BW	SBW	DIF
STL	75	18	15	1397	1326	8.5	63	493	607	11.9	3.01	115	.254	.322	63	70	101	108	.980	124	167	2.1	7.4	2.7		7.8
BRO	52	14	28	1418	1280	8.1	58	671	647	12.5	3.05	111	.243	.331	58	52	99	107	.972	174	154	-.9	5.5	5.6		7.7
CHI	59	15	11	1393	1370	8.9	58	527	619	12.4	3.24	102	.256	.325	26	15	97	102	.976	146	119	.7	1.6	.3		2.9
BOS	73	10	12	1371	1291	8.5	76	478	566	11.7	3.35	102	.249	.314	10	13	101	93	.972	169	129	-.8	1.4	.8		3.0
PHI	55	11	23	1369	1442	9.5	73	542	490	13.3	3.99	86	.273	.344	-88	-85	101	98	.975	148	144	.6	-9.0	-1.5		1.9
CIN	69	17	11	1413[1]	1334	8.5	70	467	506	11.6	3.08	109	.252	.314	53	42	98	101	.975	155	192	.2	4.5	-8.7		-6.0
PIT	61	10	6	1370	1406	9.2	50	561	458	13.1	3.72	95	.269	.342	-46	-29	103	99	.970	184	127	-1.6	-3.1	-3.5		-5.8
NY	47	8	13	1353[1]	1313	8.7	114	660	581	13.2	3.92	88	.256	.343	-76	-71	101	100	.973	159	121	-.2	-7.5	2.4		-10.7
TOT	491	103	119	11084[2]		8.7				12.5	3.41		.256	.329					.974	1259	1153					

Runs		Hits		Doubles		Triples		Home Runs		Total Bases	
Musial-StL	124	Musial-StL	228	Musial-StL	50	Musial-StL	20	Kiner-Pit	23	Musial-StL	366
Slaughter-StL	100	Walker-Bro	184	Holmes-Bos	35	Reese-Bro	10	Mize-NY	22	Slaughter-StL	283
Stanky-Bro	98	Slaughter-StL	183	Kurowski-StL	32	Cavarretta-Chi	10	Slaughter-StL	18	Ennis-Phi	262
Schoendienst-StL	94	Holmes-Bos	176	Herman-Bro-Bos	31	Walker-Bro	9	Ennis-Phi	17	Walker-Bro	258
Cavarretta-Chi	89	Schoendienst-StL	170							Holmes-Bos	241

Runs Batted In		Runs Produced		Bases On Balls		Batting Average		On Base Percentage		Slugging Average	
Slaughter-StL	130	Slaughter-StL	212	Stanky-Bro	137	Musial-StL	.365	Stanky-Bro	.436	Musial-StL	.587
Walker-Bro	116	Musial-StL	211	Fletcher-Pit	111	Hopp-Bos	.333	Musial-StL	.434	Ennis-Phi	.485
Musial-StL	103	Walker-Bro	187	Cavarretta-Chi	88	Walker-Bro	.319	Cavarretta-Chi	.401	Slaughter-StL	.465
Kurowski-StL	89	Cavarretta-Chi	159	Reese-Bro	87	Ennis-Phi	.313	Herman-Bro-Bos	.395	Kurowski-StL	.462
Kiner-Pit	81	Holmes-Bos	153	Hack-Chi	83	Holmes-Bos	.310	Walker-Bro	.391	Walker-Bro	.448

Production		Adjusted Production		Batter Runs		Adjusted Batter Runs		Clutch Hitting Index		Runs Created	
Musial-StL	1.021	Musial-StL	180	Musial-StL	70.9	Musial-StL	64.8	Walker-Bro	138	Musial-StL	164
Kurowski-StL	.853	Ennis-Phi	144	Mize-NY	43.6	Mize-NY	43.0	Slaughter-StL	131	Slaughter-StL	110
Ennis-Phi	.849	Cavarretta-Chi	140	Kurowski-StL	29.1	Cavarretta-Chi	29.5	Elliott-Pit	127	Walker-Bro	104
Walker-Bro	.839	Walker-Bro	136	Walker-Bro	28.9	Walker-Bro	27.9	Fletcher-Pit	123	Mize-NY	100
Slaughter-StL	.838	Kurowski-StL	136	Slaughter-StL	28.6	Ennis-Phi	27.9	Reiser-Bro	120	Kurowski-StL	97

Total Average		Stolen Bases		Stolen Base Average	Stolen Base Runs	Fielding Runs		Total Player Rating	
Musial-StL	1.114	Reiser-Bro	34			Marion-StL	18.8	Musial-StL	5.7
Stanky-Bro	.890	Haas-Cin	22			Wyrostek-Phi	17.2	Mize-NY	4.4
Reiser-Bro	.877	Hopp-Bos	21			Ennis-Phi	13.6	Ennis-Phi	3.7
Kurowski-StL	.855	Adams-Cin	16			Handley-Pit	13.2	Stanky-Bro	3.1
Walker-Bro	.848	Walker-Bro	14			Mueller-Cin	9.8	Kurowski-StL	2.9

Wins		Win Percentage		Games		Complete Games		Shutouts		Saves	
Pollet-StL	21	Dickson-StL	.714	Trinkle-NY	48	Sain-Bos	24	Brecheen-StL	5	Raffensberger-Phi	6
Sain-Bos	20	Higbe-Bro	.680	Dickson-StL	47	Pollet-StL	22	Blackwell-Cin	5	Pollet-StL	5
Higbe-Bro	17	Pollet-StL	.677	Behrman-Bro	47	Koslo-NY	17	VanderMeer-Cin	4	Karl-Phi	5
Dickson-StL	15	Sain-Bos	.588	Casey-Bro	46	Ostermueller-Pit	16	Pollet-StL	4	Herring-Bro	5
Brecheen-StL	15	Brecheen-StL	.500			Cooper-Bos	15	Cooper-Bos	4	Casey-Bro	5

Innings Pitched		Fewest Hits/Game		Fewest BB/Game		Strikeouts		Strikeouts/Game		Ratio	
Pollet-StL	266.0	Kennedy-NY	7.38	Cooper-Bos	1.76	Schmitz-Chi	135	Higbe-Bro	5.72	Cooper-Bos	9.95
Koslo-NY	265.1	Schmitz-Chi	7.38	Raffensberger-Phi	1.79	Higbe-Bro	134	Schmitz-Chi	5.42	Beggs-Cin	10.18
Sain-Bos	265.0	Blackwell-Cin	7.41	Beggs-Cin	1.85	Sain-Bos	129	Blackwell-Cin	4.63	Sain-Bos	10.66
Brecheen-StL	231.1	Higbe-Bro	7.60	Heusser-Cin	2.09	Koslo-NY	121	Brecheen-StL	4.55	Dickson-StL	10.74
Schmitz-Chi	224.1	Sain-Bos	7.64	Strincevich-Pit	2.25	Brecheen-StL	117	Voiselle-NY	4.50	Pollet-StL	10.79

Earned Run Average		Adjusted ERA		Opponents' Batting Avg.		Opponents' On Base Pct.		Starter Runs		Adjusted Starter Runs	
Pollet-StL	2.10	Pollet-StL	165	Schmitz-Chi	.221	Cooper-Bos	.276	Pollet-StL	38.9	Pollet-StL	40.1
Sain-Bos	2.21	Sain-Bos	155	Kennedy-NY	.224	Beggs-Cin	.287	Sain-Bos	35.5	Sain-Bos	36.0
Beggs-Cin	2.32	Beggs-Cin	144	Blackwell-Cin	.226	Sain-Bos	.294	Brecheen-StL	23.7	Brecheen-StL	24.8
Blackwell-Cin	2.45	Brecheen-StL	139	Higbe-Bro	.229	Dickson-StL	.295	Beggs-Cin	23.1	Beggs-Cin	21.6
Brecheen-StL	2.49	Blackwell-Cin	136	Sain-Bos	.230	Pollet-StL	.300	Blackwell-Cin	20.7	Rowe-Phi	19.9

Clutch Pitching Index		Relief Runs		Adjusted Relief Runs		Relief Ranking		Total Pitcher Index		Total Baseball Ranking	
Hatten-Bro	129	Casey-Bro	15.8	Casey-Bro	15.5	Casey-Bro	24.1	Sain-Bos	5.9	Sain-Bos	5.9
Pollet-StL	127	Thompson-NY	14.8	Thompson-NY	15.0	Thompson-NY	23.7	Pollet-StL	5.1	Musial-StL	5.7
Beggs-Cin	124	Malloy-Cin	5.3	Malloy-Cin	4.8	Malloy-Cin	4.5	Brecheen-StL	3.1	Pollet-StL	5.1
Wyse-Chi	117	Budnick-NY	2.5	Budnick-NY	2.8	Budnick-NY	1.6	Beggs-Cin	2.9	Mize-NY	4.4
Ostermueller-Pit	110	Herring-Bro	.6	Wilks-StL	.5	Wilks-StL	.4	Casey-Bro	2.9	Ennis-Phi	3.7

April 30 Dispelling the rumors that he had lost his fastball after nearly four years in the Navy, Bob Feller of the Cleveland Indians hurls his second no-hitter, beating the New York Yankees 1-0 on Frankie Hayes' home run in the ninth inning.

May 28 The Washington Senators edge the New York Yankees 2-1 before 49,917 fans in the first night game at Yankee Stadium.

June 21 A Federal judge rules that the Seattle club does not have to play returning serviceman Al Niemiec but it does have to pay him his $720 a month contract through the season. At mid-season 143 players who had major league contracts when they went to war had been released or sent to the minors. Former major league players Van Mungo, Lou Finney, Chubby Dean, Nate Andrews, and Max Butcher all play in Class D leagues.

June 22 Bill Veeck heads a syndicate which purchases the Cleveland Indians, launching Veeck on a long career as a lively promoter. A minor but typical change is the regular posting of NL scores on the Cleveland scoreboard, a departure from the long-standing practice of both leagues.

July 8 A special meeting of clubs deals with Mexican League defections and attempts by players to gain new rights. Some of the results include: $5,000 minimum salary, $25-per-week training-camp expenses, a fixed period for spring training, 25 days for postseason barnstorming, maximum pay cut of 25 percent. A pension fund aimed at providing $100 a month for retired 10-year players will be funded by World Series rights and net proceeds from All-Star Games. Each league will have a player rep to baseball councils. The first player reps named are Yankees pitcher Johnny Murphy and Dodgers outfielder Dixie Walker.

July 14 Player-manager Lou Boudreau of Cleveland hits four doubles and one home run, but Ted Williams wallops three home runs and drives in eight runs, as the Boston Red Sox top the Indians 11-10. Boudreau's five extra base hits is a major league record that Willie Stargell will tie August 1, 1970. In the second game, the famous Boudreau Shift is born. Boudreau shifts all his players, except the third baseman and left fielder, to the right side of the diamond in an effort to stop Williams. Ted grounds out and walks twice while ignoring the shift.

September 8 With the Red Sox running away with the AL race, attention closes in on Bob Feller's strikeout pace. He reaches 300 today, a number reached by Walter Johnson and Rube Waddell twice each. Can Feller beat Waddell's 346 of 1904? Boudreau finds plenty of innings for Feller to work as the season comes to an end, and statisticians discover an error in the August 24 box score that shorted the fireballer one strikeout against the A's. Counting that one, Feller ends with 348. Alas Waddell's old record of 346 was apparently based on the compilations of George Moreland, an early baseball historian. TSN researchers later revise Waddell's total to 349.

October 6 The World Series opens with a Red Sox 3-2 win as Rudy York hits a 10th-inning home run off Howie Pollet. The Sox tie the game in the ninth when an easy grounder to Marty Marion takes a freak bounce and goes through his legs.

November 15 Ted Williams is picked as the AL MVP.

BOSTON	CHICAGO	CLEVELAND	DETROIT	NEW YORK	PHILADELPHIA	ST.LOUIS	WASHINGTON
M J.Cronin	M J.Dykes	M L.Boudreau	M S.O'Neill	M J.McCarthy	M C.Mack	M L.Sewell	M O.Bluege
1B R.York	M T.Lyons	1B L.Fleming	1B H.Greenberg	M B.Dickey	1B G.McQuinn	M Z.Taylor	1B M.Vernon
2B B.Doerr	1B H.Trosky	2B D.Meyer	2B J.Bloodworth	M J.Neun	2B G.Handley	1B C.Stevens	2B J.Priddy
SS J.Pesky	2B D.Kolloway	SS L.Boudreau	SS E.Lake	1B N.Etten	SS P.Suder	2B J.Berardino	SS B.Hitchcock
3B R.Russell	SS L.Appling	3B K.Keltner	3B G.Kell	2B J.Gordon	3B H.Majeski	SS V.Stephens	3B C.Travis
LF T.Williams	3B D.Lodigiani	LF G.Case	LF D.Wakefield	SS P.Rizzuto	LF S.Chapman	3B M.Christman	LF J.Grace
CF D.DiMaggio	LF B.Kennedy	CF P.Seerey	CF H.Evers	3B S.Stirnweiss	CF B.McCosky	LF J.Heath	CF S.Spence
RF C.Metkovich	CF T.Tucker	RF H.Edwards	RF R.Cullenbine	LF C.Keller	RF E.Valo	CF W.Judnich	RF B.Lewis
C H.Wagner	RF T.Wright	C J.Hegan	C B.Tebbetts	CF J.DiMaggio	C B.Rosar	RF A.Zarilla	C A.Evans
	C M.Tresh			RF T.Henrich		C F.Mancuso	
3 P.Higgins	23 C.Michaels	2S J.Conway	O3 J.Outlaw	C A.Robinson	O T.Stainback	O C.Laabs	32 S.Robertson
O L.Culberson	O R.Hodgin	O F.Mackiewicz	O P.Mullin	O1 J.Lindell	S J.Wallaesa	3 B.Dillinger	S J.Early
O W.Moses	O W.Platt	2 R.Mack	2 D.Cramer	2 B.Johnson	2 O.Grimes	32 J.Lucadello	S3 G.Torres
O T.McBride	1 J.Kuhel	C F.Hayes	2 E.Mayo	C B.Dickey	32 I.Hall	O H.Helf	O J.Heath
C R.Partee	C F.Hayes	3 D.Ross	2 S.Webb	1 S.Souchock	O R.Derry	O G.McQuillen	O G.Binks
3 E.Pellagrini	O W.Moses	1 H.Becker	C P.Richards	S F.Crosetti	O H.Peck	O J.Grace	O G.Coan
/2 D.Gutteridge	3 L.Wells	C G.Woodling	C A.Moore	C G.Niarhos	C G.Desautels	1 B.Dahlgren	C G.Myatt
3 E.Andres	1 J.Jones	1 M.Rocco	C B.Swift	/S O.Grimes	/S J.Caulfield	1 J.Witte	/3 J.Sanford
C E.McGah	C G.Dickey	C S.Lollar	O B.McCosky	/S B.Brown	1 B.Konopka	C J.Schultz	/3 E.Yost
/O J.Lazor	O D.Philley	O D.Mitchell	3 P.Higgins	/S Y.Berra	1 G.Kell	O P.Lehner	/1 J.Kuhel
/1 P.Campbell	O G.Curtright	/1 J.Wasdell	/S J.Lipon	/C K.Silvestri	O D.Richmond	C L.Moss	/O R.Goolsby
/C F.Pytlak	C E.Fernandes	C T.Jordan	/O J.Groth	/O F.Colman	O F.Garrison	O L.Finney	P M.Haefner
/2 T.Carey	/3 F.Baker	/3 H.Moss	/2 J.Hitchcock	/3 B.Bockman	/C J.Astroth	/C K.Sears	P B.Newsom
/3 B.Steiner	/C F.Whitman	H E.Robinson	H N.Harris	/O H.Majeski	/O G.Armstrong	/O G.Bradley	P D.Leonard
/O A.Gilbert	/C T.Jordan	/O B.Mills	P H.Newhouser	/3 B.Drescher	/O V.Benson	/1 G.Archie	P R.Scarborough
P T.Hughson	/O J.Smaza	/S R.Peters	H D.Trout	P B.Metheny	P P.Marchildon	/C B.Martin	P S.Hudson
P D.Ferriss	P E.Lopat	/S J.Price	H V.Trucks	H R.Weatherly	P D.Fowler	/2 L.Schulte	RP M.Pieretti
P M.Harris	O O.Grove	/C R.Weigel	P F.Hutchinson	P S.Chandler	P B.Savage	P J.Kramer	P R.Wolff
P J.Dobson	P J.Haynes	/3 T.Sepkowski	P A.Benton	P B.Bevens	P J.Flores	P D.Galehouse	P E.Wynn
P J.Bagby	P E.Smith	H B.Monaco	P S.Overmire	P J.Page	P L.Knerr	P N.Potter	P W.Masterson
RP E.Johnson	P F.Papish	/S C.Brewster	P G.Caster	P R.Gumpert	P L.Harris	P T.Shirley	P B.Kennedy
RP B.Klinger	RP E.Caldwell	P B.Feller	P H.White	P T.Bonham	P R.Christopher	RP S.Ferens	/P J.Niggeling
RP C.Dreisewerd	RP R.Hamner	P R.Embree	P J.Gorsica	/P J.Wade	P B.Newsom	RP E.Kinder	/P M.Candini
P B.Zuber	RP A.Hollingsworth	P A.Reynolds	P T.Bridges	/P M.Queen	RP E.Fagan	P B.Muncrief	P V.Curtis
/P C.Wagner	P J.Rigney	P S.Gromek	P T.Gray	/P M.Russo	/P H.Besse	P C.Fannin	P M.Wilson
P M.Brown	P B.Dietrich	RP B.Lemon	/P L.Kretlow	/P V.Raschi	/P B.McCahan	P O.Miller	/P J.Wade
/P B.Butland	/P T.Lee	RP J.Krakauskas	/P A.Houtteman	/P F.Hiller	/P L.Griffith	/P T.Ferrick	/P A.LaMacchia
/P R.Heflin	/P T.Lyons	P M.Harder	/P H.Manders	/P T.Byrne	P J.Berry	/P F.Biscan	
/P M.Ryba	P G.Maltzberger	P C.Gassaway	/P R.Gentry	/P A.Lyons	P J.Coleman	/P F.Sanford	
/P M.Deutsch	P E.O'Neill	P D.Black		/P K.Drews	P N.Brown	/P C.Johnson	
/P J.Wilson	/P L.Perme	P J.Berry		/P B.Zuber	P J.Knott	/P A.LaMacchia	
		P P.Center		/P C.Stanceu	P P.Cooper	/P A.Milnar	
		/P T.Ferrick		/P S.Roser	P P.Vaughan	/P A.Hollingsworth	
		/P E.Klieman		/P H.Karpel		/P S.Sundra	
		/P V.Johnson				/P R.Shore	
		/P B.Kuzava					
		/P R.Flanigan					
		/P J.Podgajny					
		/P L.Webber					
		/P R.McCabe					

TEAM	G	W	L	PCT	GB	R	OR	AB	H	2B	3B	HR	BB	SO	AVG	OBP	SLG	PRO	PRO+	BR	/A	PF	CHI	RC	SB	CS	SBA	SBR
BOS	156	104	50	.675		792	594	5318	1441	268	50	109	687	661	.271	.356	.402	.758	113	136	92	106	101	790	45	36	56	-8
DET	155	92	62	.597	12	704	567	5318	1373	212	41	108	627	616	.258	.337	.374	.711	100	42	0	106	103	698	65	41	61	-5
NY	154	87	67	.565	17	684	547	5139	1275	208	50	136	627	706	.248	.334	.387	.721	107	55	46	101	101	695	48	35	58	-7
WAS	155	76	78	.494	28	608	706	5337	1388	260	63	60	511	641	.260	.327	.366	.693	106	1	39	94	96	653	51	50	50	-15
CHI	155	74	80	.481	30	562	595	5312	1364	206	44	37	500	600	.257	.323	.333	.656	99	-64	-43	96	100	579	78	64	51	-15
CLE	156	68	86	.442	36	537	638	5242	1285	233	56	79	506	697	.245	.313	.356	.669	99	-49	-12	94	94	596	57	49	54	-12
STL	156	66	88	.429	38	621	710	5373	1350	220	46	84	465	713	.251	.313	.356	.669	89	-53	-82	105	108	601	23	35	40	-14
PHI	155	49	105	.318	55	529	680	5200	1317	220	51	40	482	594	.253	.318	.338	.656	91	-68	-65	99	97	574	39	30	57	-6
TOT	621					5037		42239	10793	1827	401	653	4401	5228	.256	.328	.364	.692							406	340	54	-82

TEAM	CG	SH	SV	IP	H	H/G	HR	BB	SO	RAT	ERA	ERA+	OAV	OOB	PR	/A	PF	CPI	FA	E	DP	FW	PW	BW	SBW	DIF
BOS	79	15	20	1396²	1359	8.8	89	501	667	12.1	3.38	108	.254	.319	19	44	105	100	.977	139	163	1.5	4.6	9.6	.2	11.0
DET	94	18	15	1402	1277	8.2	97	497	896	11.5	3.22	114	.241	.307	45	68	104	95	.974	155	138	.5	7.1	.0	.6	6.9
NY	68	17	17	1361	1232	8.1	66	552	653	11.9	3.13	110	.243	.319	56	48	99	100	.975	150	174	.7	5.0	4.8	.3	-.9
WAS	71	8	10	1396¹	1459	9.4	81	547	537	13.1	3.74	90	.269	.339	-36	-61	96	100	.966	211	162	-2.8	-6.4	4.1	-.5	4.6
CHI	62	9	16	1392¹	1348	8.7	80	508	550	12.1	3.10	110	.255	.323	63	49	97	110	.972	175	170	-.7	5.1	-4.5	-.5	-2.4
CLE	63	16	13	1388²	1282	8.3	84	649	789	12.6	3.62	91	.245	.331	-17	-48	94	96	.975	147	147	1.0	-5.0	-1.3	-.2	-3.5
STL	63	13	12	1382¹	1465	9.5	73	573	574	13.3	3.95	94	.272	.343	-69	-34	107	99	.974	159	157	.3	-3.6	-8.6	-.4	1.3
PHI	61	10	5	1342¹	1371	9.2	83	577	562	13.2	3.90	91	.264	.340	-59	-10	99	98	.971	167	141	-.2	-5.6	-6.8	.4	-15.8
TOT	561	106	108	11062		8.8				12.5	3.50		.256	.328					.973	1303	1252					

Runs
Williams-Bos 142
Pesky-Bos 115
Lake-Det 105
Keller-NY 98
Doerr-Bos 95

Hits
Pesky-Bos 208
Vernon-Was 207
Appling-Chi 180
Williams-Bos 176
Lewis-Was 170

Doubles
Vernon-Was 51
Spence-Was 50
Pesky-Bos 43
Williams-Bos 37
Doerr-Bos 34

Triples
Edwards-Cle 16
Lewis-Was 13
Kell-Phi-Det 10
Spence-Was 10
Keller-NY 10

Home Runs
Greenberg-Det 44
Williams-Bos 38
Keller-NY 30
Seerey-Cle......... 26
DiMaggio-NY 25

Total Bases
Williams-Bos 343
Greenberg-Det 316
Vernon-Was 298
Spence-Was 287
Keller-NY 287

Runs Batted In
Greenberg-Det 127
Williams-Bos 123
York-Bos 119
Doerr-Bos 116
Keller-NY 101

Runs Produced
Williams-Bos 227
Doerr-Bos 193
York-Bos 180
Greenberg-Det 174
Keller-NY 169

Bases On Balls
Williams-Bos 156
Keller-NY 113
Lake-Det 103
Cullenbine-Det 88
Henrich-NY 87

Batting Average
Vernon-Was 353
Williams-Bos 342
Pesky-Bos 335
Kell-Phi-Det 322
DiMaggio-Bos 316

On Base Percentage
Williams-Bos 497
Keller-NY 405
Vernon-Was 403
Pesky-Bos 401
DiMaggio-Bos 393

Slugging Average
Williams-Bos 667
Greenberg-Det 604
Keller-NY 533
DiMaggio-NY 511
Edwards-Cle 509

Production
Williams-Bos ...1.164
Greenberg-Det 977
Keller-NY 938
Vernon-Was 910
DiMaggio-NY 878

Adjusted Production
Williams-Bos 211
Vernon-Was 163
Greenberg-Det 160
Keller-NY 158
Edwards-Cle 151

Batter Runs
Williams-Bos 94.2
Greenberg-Det 46.1
Keller-NY 45.9
Cullenbine-Det ... 42.2
Vernon-Was 40.3

Adjusted Batter Runs
Williams-Bos 85.2
Vernon-Was 46.9
Keller-NY 44.4
Greenberg-Det 39.6
Cullenbine-Det ... 37.0

Clutch Hitting Index
Travis-Was 136
York-Bos 135
Doerr-Bos 126
Henrich-NY 119
Heath-Was-StL 109

Runs Created
Williams-Bos 188
Keller-NY 127
Vernon-Was 120
Greenberg-Det 119
Pesky-Bos 111

Total Average
Williams-Bos ...1.431
Greenberg-Det ..1.010
Keller-NY 1.005
Vernon-Was 873
DiMaggio-NY 862

Stolen Bases
Case-Cle 28
Stirnweiss-NY 18
Lake-Det 15

Stolen Base Average
Stirnweiss-NY 75.0
Case-Cle 71.8

Stolen Base Runs
Stirnweiss-NY 1.8
Dillinger-StL 1.8
Case-Cle 1.8
Philley-Chi 1.5
Evers-Det 1.5

Fielding Runs
Doerr-Bos 26.8
Gordon-NY 21.5
Boudreau-Cle 16.2
Rizzuto-NY 13.1
Pesky-Bos 12.0

Total Player Rating
Williams-Bos 7.9
Doerr-Bos 4.8
Pesky-Bos 4.2
Vernon-Was 3.6
Greenberg-Det 3.5

Wins
Newhouser-Det 26
Feller-Cle 26
Ferriss-Bos 25
Hughson-Bos 20
Chandler-NY 20

Win Percentage
Ferriss-Bos 806
Newhouser-Det ...743
Chandler-NY 714
Harris-Bos 654
Hughson-Bos 645

Games
Feller-Cle 48
Savage-Phi 40
Ferriss-Bos 40
Hughson-Bos 39
Caldwell-Chi 39

Complete Games
Feller-Cle 36
Newhouser-Det 29
Ferriss-Bos 26
Trout-Det 23
Hughson-Bos 21

Shutouts
Feller-Cle 10
Newhouser-Det 6
Hughson-Bos 6
Ferriss-Bos 6
Chandler-NY 6

Saves
Klinger-Bos 9
Caldwell-Chi 8
Murphy-NY 7
Ferrick-Cle-StL ... 6

Innings Pitched
Feller-Cle 371.1
Newhouser-Det ..292.2
Hughson-Bos 278.0
Trout-Det 276.1
Ferriss-Bos 274.0

Fewest Hits/Game
Newhouser-Det ...6.61
Feller-Cle 6.71
Chandler-NY 6.99
Embree-Cle 7.65
Bevens-NY 7.68

Fewest BB/Game
Hughson-Bos 1.65
Lopat-Chi 1.87
Leonard-Was 2.00
Flores-Phi 2.21
Ferriss-Bos 2.33

Strikeouts
Feller-Cle 348
Newhouser-Det ... 275
Hughson-Bos 172
Trucks-Det 161
Trout-Det 151

Strikeouts/Game
Newhouser-Det ...8.46
Feller-Cle 8.43
Trucks-Det 6.12
Hutchinson-Det ...6.00
Hughson-Bos 5.57

Ratio
Newhouser-Det ...9.66
Hughson-Bos 9.87
Chandler-NY 10.18
Lopat-Chi 10.32
Feller-Cle 10.49

Earned Run Average
Newhouser-Det ...1.94
Chandler-NY 2.10
Feller-Cle 2.18
Bevens-NY 2.23
Flores-Phi 2.32

Adjusted ERA
Newhouser-Det ... 189
Chandler-NY 164
Trout-Det 156
Bevens-NY 154
Flores-Phi 153

Opponents' Batting Avg.
Newhouser-Det ...201
Feller-Cle 208
Chandler-NY 218
Embree-Cle 227
Bevens-NY 232

Opponents' On Base Pct.
Newhouser-Det ...269
Hughson-Bos 274
Chandler-NY 288
Lopat-Chi 288
Feller-Cle 291

Starter Runs
Feller-Cle 54.5
Newhouser-Det ... 50.9
Chandler-NY 40.2
Trout-Det 35.6
Bevens-NY 35.2

Adjusted Starter Runs
Newhouser-Det ... 55.8
Feller-Cle 46.5
Trout-Det 40.2
Chandler-NY 38.7
Bevens-NY 33.7

Clutch Pitching Index
Grove-Chi 126
Flores-Phi 121
Trout-Det 119
Haynes-Chi 118
Bevens-NY 115

Relief Runs
Caldwell-Chi 14.3
Lemon-Cle 10.6
Klinger-Bos 7.2
Kinder-StL 1.7

Adjusted Relief Runs
Caldwell-Chi 13.4
Lemon-Cle 8.5
Klinger-Bos 8.2
Kinder-StL 3.9

Relief Ranking
Caldwell-Chi 25.2
Klinger-Bos 9.4
Lemon-Cle 7.6
Kinder-StL 2.5

Total Pitcher Index
Newhouser-Det 7.1
Trout-Det 5.3
Feller-Cle 4.9
Chandler-NY 4.8
Bevens-NY 3.0

Total Baseball Ranking
Williams-Bos 7.9
Newhouser-Det 7.1
Trout-Det 5.3
Feller-Cle 4.9
Chandler-NY 4.8

January 18 The Pirates buy first baseman Hank Greenberg from the Tigers for a reported $25,000 to $35,000. Greenberg led the AL in home runs with 44 in 1946.

April 1 Branch Rickey deflects pressure on Jackie Robinson by keeping him in Montreal, although it is clear the contending Dodgers can use the 1946 International League batting king.

April 9 Commissioner Happy Chandler suspends manager Leo Durocher of the Brooklyn Dodgers for the entire season for incidents detrimental to baseball.

April 15 Jackie Robinson goes hitless in three trips in his Brooklyn debut but handles 11 chances at first base, a new position for him, in a 5-3 win over the Braves. Coach Clyde Sukeforth, interim manager and the man credited with first scouting Robinson, guides the team to two wins before stepping down.

April 18 Dodger scout Burt Shotton is the surprise choice to replace Leo Durocher on the third day of the season.

May 8 A movement among Cardinal players to protest its first meeting with Jackie Robinson and the Dodgers is aborted by a clubhouse talk from owner Sam Breadon, according to a story by league president Ford Frick. Breadon denies the story.

June 22 Ewell Blackwell just misses pitching back-to-back no-hitters when Eddie Stanky of the Brooklyn Dodgers singles with one out in the ninth inning. Blackwell then gets Al Gionfriddo before Jackie Robinson bangs out a second single. Blackwell wins 4-0, his ninth straight win to improve to 11-2. Stanky's hit ends Blackwell's hitless-inning skein at 19.

June 24 The Dodgers win 4-2 over the Pirates, as Jackie Robinson swipes home for the first of 19 times in his career.

July 30 The New York Giants edge the Cincinnati Reds 6-5 in 10 innings, ending Ewell Blackwell's winning streak at 16 games. All were complete games, and five were shutouts.

August 20 The Boston Braves hit a million in attendance for the first time.

August 21 The first Little League World Series tournament is held in Williamsport, Pennsylvania. The Maynard Midgets of Williamsport win the World Series 16-7.

September 12 Ralph Kiner hits his record eighth home run in four games to pass Johnny Mize in the home run race as Pittsburgh tops the Boston Braves 4-3.

September 17 Jackie Robinson is named Rookie of the Year by *The Sporting News* two weeks before the season is over. At year's end he has hit .297 and led the NL in stolen bases and sacrifices.

September 22 The Dodgers win the pennant while idle. The Cards lose to the Cubs to clinch the Dodgers' first title since 1941, this time with a 5-game margin.

September 29 Hitless the first four innings against Brooklyn's Ralph Branca, the Yankees score five runs in the fifth inning and win the World Series opener 5-3 before a record World Series crowd of 73,365 at Yankee Stadium.

October 2 The Dodgers squeak to a 9-8 win, jumping on Bobo Newsom and Vic Raschi in the second for six runs. Yogi Berra becomes the first player to hit a pinch home run in World Series history, against Brooklyn's Ralph Branca in the seventh inning.

October 3 Brooklyn pinch hitter Cookie Lavagetto doubles home two runs with two out in the bottom of the ninth to break up Floyd Bevens' no-hit bid and give the Dodgers a dramatic 3-2 victory over the Yankees in Game 4 at Ebbets Field.

October 5 Center fielder Al Gionfriddo's magnificent catch takes a home run away from Joe DiMaggio, which would have tied the sixth game of the World Series at Yankee Stadium. The Brooklyn Dodgers go on to win 8-6 before a record World Series crowd of 74,065.

BOSTON		BROOKLYN		CHICAGO		CINCINNATI		NEW YORK		PHILADELPHIA		PITTSBURGH		ST.LOUIS	
M	B.Southworth	M	C.Sukeforth	M	C.Grimm	M	J.Neun	M	M.Ott	M	B.Chapman	M	B.Herman	M	E.Dyer
1B	E.Torgeson	M	B.Shotton	1B	E.Waitkus	1B	B.Young	1B	J.Mize	1B	H.Schultz	M	B.Burwell	1B	S.Musial
2B	C.Ryan	1B	J.Robinson	2B	B.Zientara	2B	B.Rigney	2B	B.Kerr	2B	E.Verban	1B	H.Greenberg	2B	R.Schoendienst
SS	D.Culler	2B	E.Stanky	SS	L.Merullo	SS	E.Miller	SS	J.Lohrke	SS	S.Newsome	2B	J.Bloodworth	SS	M.Marion
3B	B.Elliott	SS	P.Reese	3B	P.Lowrey	3B	G.Hatton	3B	S.Gordon	3B	L.Handley	SS	B.Cox	3B	W.Kurowski
LF	B.Rowell	3B	S.Jorgensen	LF	P.Cavarretta	LF	A.Galan	LF	B.Thomson	LF	D.Ennis	3B	F.Gustine	LF	E.Slaughter
CF	J.Hopp	LF	P.Reiser	CF	A.Pafko	CF	B.Haas	CF	W.Marshall	CF	H.Walker	LF	R.Kiner	CF	T.Moore
RF	T.Holmes	CF	C.Furillo	RF	B.Nicholson	RF	F.Baumholtz	RF	W.Cooper	RF	J.Wyrostek	CF	J.Russell	RF	R.Northey
C	P.Masi	RF	D.Walker	C	B.Scheffing	C	R.Lamanno			C	A.Seminick	RF	W.Westlake	C	D.Rice
O	M.McCormick	C	B.Edwards	3	S.Hack	2	B.Adams	O	G.Gearhart	3	J.Tabor	C	D.Howell	O	C.Diering
O	D.Litwhiler	O	G.Hermanski	2	C.McCullough	O	E.Lukon	2	M.Witek	S	R.LaPointe	C	C.Rikard	O	E.Dusak
1	F.McCormick	O3	A.Vaughan	S2	B.Sturgeon	O	R.Mueller	23	B.Blattner	C	B.Adams	C	C.Kluttz	O	J.Garagiola
S	N.Fernandez	2O	E.Miksis	O	C.Aberson	O	T.Tatum	C	E.Lombardi	1C	A.Lakeman	2	E.Basinski	O	J.Medwick
S	S.Sisti	O	D.Snider	O	M.Rickert	O	C.Vollmer	1C	J.Lafata	C	D.Padgett	1	E.Fletcher	C	D.Wilber
C	H.Camelli	S	S.Rojek	3	D.Dallessandro	3	K.Wahl	/2	B.Rhawn	1	C.Gilbert	S2	W.Wietelmann	1	D.Sisler
/O	T.Neill	C	G.Hodges	2	R.Mack	/1	C.Kress	H	B.Young	S	J.Albright	C	G.Woodling	2	N.Jones
/2	D.Murtaugh	3	C.Lavagetto	/2	L.Frey	H	B.Young	/O	F.White	3	W.Jones	C	B.Salkeld	3S	J.Cross
H	B.Brady	O	A.Gionfriddo	S	B.Jurges	/O	H.Poland	3	W.Westrum	/C	R.Northey	O	P.Sullivan	O	H.Walker
P	W.Spahn	C	B.Bragan	/C	M.Livingston	/1	T.Kluszewski	/C	M.Livingston	1	N.Etten	S	P.Castiglione	C	B.Creger
P	J.Sain	/3	T.Brown	H	S.Madrid	H	A.Lakeman	1	B.Warren	2	F.McCormick	2	B.Herman	P	M.Dickson
P	R.Barrett	/O	D.Lund	/S	H.Schenz	/S	V.Stallcup	/O	S.Yvars	/O	J.Levan	C	R.Jarvis	P	R.Munger
P	B.Voiselle	/1	E.Stevens	/C	D.Williams	P	E.Blackwell	/C	M.Ott	/2	H.Poland	/2	G.Mauch	P	H.Brecheen
P	S.Johnson	/O	D.Whitman	P	J.Schmitz	P	J.Vander Meer	/2	W.Lockman	H	P.Caballero	H	A.Gionfriddo	P	H.Pollet
RP	C.Shoun	/O	M.Rackley	P	D.Lade	P	K.Peterson	P	L.Jansen	/S	G.Hamner	P	K.Higbe	P	A.Brazle
RP	E.Wright	/O	T.Tatum	P	H.Borowy	P	B.Lively	P	D.Koslo	H	L.Finney	P	F.Ostermueller	RP	K.Burkhart
RP	W.Lanfranconi	/1	H.Schultz	P	P.Erickson	P	B.Walters	P	M.Kennedy	/C	R.Hemsley	P	T.Bonham	RP	T.Wilks
P	M.Cooper	P	R.Branca	P	H.Wyse	RP	J.Hetki	/C	C.Hartung	P	D.Leonard	P	R.Roe	P	J.Hearn
P	A.Karl	P	J.Hatten	RP	E.Kush	RP	H.Gumbert	P	K.Trinkle	P	S.Rowe	RP	R.Sewell	P	G.Staley
/P	J.Beazley	P	V.Lombardi	RP	R.Meers	P	E.Erautt	RP	J.Beggs	P	O.Judd	RP	R.Strincevich	P	J.Grodzicki
/P	G.Elliott	P	H.Taylor	P	B.Chipman	P	K.Raffensberger	H	A.Hansen	P	K.Heintzelman	RP	E.Singleton	/P	K.Johnson
/P	R.Martin	RP	H.Gregg	P	C.Passeau	P	J.Beggs	RP	H.Iott	P	T.Hughes	P	J.Bagby	/P	F.Schmidt
/P	J.Lanning	RP	H.Behrman	P	R.Meyer	P	E.Riddle	/P	R.Poat	RP	F.Schmidt	P	E.Bahr		
/P	E.White	RP	R.Barney	/P	R.Hamner	P	C.Shoun	P	S.Jones	P	B.Donnelly	P	M.Queen		
/P	M.Macon	P	C.King	P	B.Lee	/P	H.Perkowski	P	B.Voiselle	P	A.Jurisich	P	R.Wolff		
/P	D.Mulligan	P	H.Casey	/P	O.Miller	/P	C.Lambert	P	M.Cooper	P	C.Schanz	P	A.Lyons		
		P	E.Chandler	/P	B.Carpenter	/P	K.Polivka	P	J.Thompson	P	K.Raffensberger	P	H.Behrman		
		/P	K.Higbe	/P	F.Schmidt	/P	M.Schultz	P	B.Ayers	/P	D.Koecher	P	S.Nagy		
		P	P.Haugstad			/P	B.Malloy	/P	M.Budnick	/P	D.Mauney	P	A.Herring		
		/P	D.Bankhead			/P	H.Wehmeier	/P	H.Andrews	/P	L.Hoerst	P	H.Mulcahy		
		/P	J.Banta					/P	M.Picone	/P	C.Simmons	P	K.Heintzelman		
		/P	G.Dockins					/P	B.Carpenter	/P	H.Spragins	P	L.Howard		
		/P	R.Melton					/P	W.Abernathy	/P	L.Possehl	P	C.McLish		
		/P	E.Palica									/P	L.Tost		
		/P	W.Ramsdell									/P	K.Gables		
		/P	J.Van Cuyk												

TEAM	G	W	L	PCT	GB	R	OR	AB	H	2B	3B	HR	BB	SO	AVG	OBP	SLG	PRO	PRO+	BR	/A	PF	CHI	RC	SB	CS	SBA	SBR
BRO	155	94	60	.610		774	668	5249	1428	241	50	83	732	561	.272	.364	.384	.748	102	62	32	104	98	781	88			
STL	156	89	65	.578	5	780	634	5422	1462	235	65	115	612	511	.270	.347	.401	.748	101	41	7	104	102	762	28			
BOS	154	86	68	.558	8	701	622	5253	1444	265	42	85	558	500	.275	.346	.390	.736	105	19	36	98	97	717	58			
NY	155	81	73	.526	13	830	761	5343	1446	220	48	221	494	568	.271	.335	.454	.789	114	95	90	101	104	809	29			
CIN	154	73	81	.474	21	681	755	5299	1372	242	43	95	539	530	.259	.330	.375	.705	95	-48	-43	99	103	672	46			
CHI	155	69	85	.448	25	567	722	5305	1373	231	48	71	471	578	.259	.321	.361	.682	91	-93	-69	96	96	620	22			
PIT	156	62	92	.403	32	744	817	5307	1385	216	44	156	607	687	.261	.340	.406	.746	102	31	10	103	100	738	30			
PHI	155	62	92	.403	32	589	687	5256	1354	210	52	60	464	594	.258	.321	.352	.673	88	-108	-87	96	101	597	60			
TOT	620					5666		42434	11264	1860	392	886	4477	4529	.265	.338	.390	.729							361			

TEAM	CG	SH	SV	IP	H	H/G	HR	BB	SO	RAT	ERA	ERA+	OAV	OOB	PR	/A	PF	CPI	FA	E	DP	FW	PW	BW	SBW	DIF
BRO	47	14	34	1375	1299	8.5	104	626	592	12.8	3.82	108	.251	.336	37	49	102	100	.978	129	169	.9	4.8	3.1		8.1
STL	65	12	20	1397²	1417	9.1	106	495	642	12.4	3.53	117	.266	.330	83	94	102	110	.979	128	169	1.1	9.2	.7		1.0
BOS	74	14	13	1362²	1342	8.9	93	453	494	11.9	3.62	108	.255	.330	67	41	96	95	.974	155	124	-.6	4.0	3.5		2.0
NY	58	6	14	1363¹	1428	9.4	102	590	553	13.4	4.44	92	.267	.342	-58	-56	100	98	.974	155	136	-.7	-5.5	8.9		1.3
CIN	54	13	13	1365¹	1442	9.5	102	589	633	13.5	4.41	93	.274	.349	-53	-46	101	98	.977	138	134	.3	-4.5	-4.2		4.4
CHI	46	8	15	1367	1449	9.5	106	618	571	13.7	4.04	98	.274	.353	4	-13	97	109	.975	150	159	-.4	-1.3	-6.8		.4
PIT	44	9	13	1374	1488	9.7	155	592	530	13.9	4.68	90	.278	.354	-95	-71	104	101	.975	149	131	-.2	-7.0	1.0		-8.8
PHI	70	14	8	1362	1399	9.2	98	513	514	12.8	3.96	101	.276	.346	15	7	99	108	.974	152	140	-.5	.7	-8.6		-6.7
TOT	458	84	136	10967¹		9.2				13.1	4.06		.265	.338					.976	1154	1162					

Runs
Mize-NY 137
Robinson-Bro 125
Kiner-Pit 118
Musial-StL 113
Kurowski-StL 108

Hits
Holmes-Bos 191
Walker-StL-Phi 186
Musial-StL 183
Gustine-Pit 183
Baumholtz-Cin 182

Doubles
Miller-Cin 38
B.Elliott-Bos 35
Ryan-Bos 33
Holmes-Bos 33
Baumholtz-Cin 32

Triples
Walker-StL-Phi 16
Slaughter-StL 13
Musial-StL 13
Schoendienst-StL .. 9
Baumholtz-Cin 9

Home Runs
Mize-NY 51
Kiner-Pit 51
Marshall-NY 36
W.Cooper-NY 35
Thomson-NY 29

Total Bases
Kiner-Pit 361
Mize-NY 360
Marshall-NY 310
W.Cooper-NY 302
Musial-StL 296

Runs Batted In
Mize-NY 138
Kiner-Pit 127
W.Cooper-NY 122
B.Elliott-Bos 113
Marshall-NY 107

Runs Produced
Mize-NY 224
Kiner-Pit 194
Musial-StL 189
Kurowski-StL 185
B.Elliott-Bos 184

Bases On Balls
Reese-Bro 104
Greenberg-Pit 104
Stanky-Bro 103
Kiner-Pit 98
Walker-Bro 97

Batting Average
Walker-StL-Phi .... .363
B.Elliott-Bos ..... .317
Cavarretta-Chi .... .314
Kiner-Pit .... .313
Musial-StL .... .312

On Base Percentage
Galan-Cin .... .449
Walker-StL-Phi .... .436
Kurowski-StL ..... .420
Kiner-Pit .... .417
Walker-Bro .... .415

Slugging Average
Kiner-Pit .... .639
Mize-NY .... .614
W.Cooper-NY ..... .586
Kurowski-StL ..... .544
Marshall-NY ...... .528

Production
Kiner-Pit 1.055
Mize-NY .... .998
Kurowski-StL ..... .964
B.Elliott-Bos ..... .927
W.Cooper-NY ..... .926

Adjusted Production
Kiner-Pit 172
Mize-NY 160
Walker-StL-Phi 150
B.Elliott-Bos 148
Kurowski-StL 148

Batter Runs
Kiner-Pit 61.4
Mize-NY 48.3
Kurowski-StL 41.8
B.Elliott-Bos 36.8
Walker-StL-Phi 35.4

Adjusted Batter Runs
Kiner-Pit 57.5
Mize-NY 47.5
B.Elliott-Bos 39.5
Walker-StL-Phi 38.8
Kurowski-StL 36.8

Clutch Hitting Index
Marion-StL 128
Haas-Cin 125
Walker-Bro 125
Edwards-Bro 125
Jorgensen-Bro 122

Runs Created
Kiner-Pit 154
Mize-NY 143
B.Elliott-Bos 120
Kurowski-StL 118
Musial-StL 118

Total Average
Kiner-Pit 1.155
Mize-NY 1.060
Kurowski-StL 1.019
Walker-StL-Phi .... .979
Torgeson-Bos ..... .973

Stolen Bases
Robinson-Bro 29
Reiser-Bro 14
Walker-StL-Phi 13
Hopp-Bos 13
Torgeson-Bos 11

Stolen Base Average

Stolen Base Runs

Fielding Runs
Marion-StL 20.1
Verban-Phi 16.9
Gustine-Pit 14.8
Kiner-Pit 13.2
Kerr-NY 12.1

Total Player Rating
Kiner-Pit 6.0
Mize-NY 4.9
Walker-StL-Phi 4.2
B.Elliott-Bos 3.7
Marshall-NY 2.9

Wins
Blackwell-Cin 22
Spahn-Bos 21
Sain-Bos 21
Jansen-NY 21
Branca-Bro 21

Win Percentage
Jansen-NY .... .808
Munger-StL ...... .762
Blackwell-Cin ..... .733
Hatten-Bro .... .680
Spahn-Bos .... .677

Games
Trinkle-NY 62
Higbe-Bro-Pit 50
Behrman-Bro-Pt-Bro 50
Kush-Chi 47
Dickson-StL 47

Complete Games
Blackwell-Cin 23
Spahn-Bos 22
Sain-Bos 22
Jansen-NY 20
Leonard-Phi 19

Shutouts
Spahn-Bos 7
Munger-StL 6
Blackwell-Cin 6
Dickson-StL 4
Branca-Bro 4

Saves
Casey-Bro 18
Trinkle-NY 10
Gumbert-Cin 10
Behrman-Bro-Pt-Bro 8

Innings Pitched
Spahn-Bos 289.2
Branca-Bro 280.0
Blackwell-Cin 273.0
Sain-Bos 266.0
Jansen-NY 248.0

Fewest Hits/Game
Taylor-Bro 7.22
Blackwell-Cin 7.48
Spahn-Bos 7.61
Lombardi-Bro 8.04
Branca-Bro 8.07

Fewest BB/Game
Jansen-NY 2.07
Rowe-Phi 2.07
Leonard-Phi 2.18
Barrett-Bos 2.26
Brazle-StL 2.57

Strikeouts
Blackwell-Cin 193
Branca-Bro 148
Sain-Bos 132
Spahn-Bos 123
Munger-StL 123

Strikeouts/Game
Blackwell-Cin 6.36
Munger-StL 4.93
Branca-Bro 4.76
Brazle-StL 4.55
Sain-Bos 4.47

Ratio
Spahn-Bos 10.25
Blackwell-Cin 10.75
Leonard-Phi 10.84
Jansen-NY 10.85
Barrett-Bos 10.89

Earned Run Average
Spahn-Bos 2.33
Blackwell-Cin 2.47
Branca-Bro 2.67
Leonard-Phi 2.68
Brazle-StL 2.84

Adjusted ERA
Spahn-Bos 167
Blackwell-Cin 166
Branca-Bro 155
Leonard-Phi 149
Brazle-StL 146

Opponents' Batting Avg.
Taylor-Bro .... .225
Spahn-Bos .... .226
Blackwell-Cin ..... .234
Branca-Bro .... .240
Lombardi-Bro ..... .241

Opponents' On Base Pct.
Spahn-Bos .... .283
Barrett-Bos ...... .292
Blackwell-Cin ..... .304
Leonard-Phi ...... .306
Jansen-NY .... .306

Starter Runs
Spahn-Bos 55.7
Blackwell-Cin 48.2
Branca-Bro 43.3
Leonard-Phi 36.0
Dickson-StL 25.5

Adjusted Starter Runs
Spahn-Bos 50.3
Blackwell-Cin 49.5
Branca-Bro 45.6
Leonard-Phi 34.6
Dickson-StL 27.4

Clutch Pitching Index
Brazle-StL 139
Leonard-Phi 123
Branca-Bro 122
Blackwell-Cin 115
Jansen-NY 114

Relief Runs
Lanfranconi-Bos ... 7.9
Kush-Chi 7.1
Trinkle-NY 3.3
Gumbert-Cin 1.8
Casey-Bro 6

Adjusted Relief Runs
Lanfranconi-Bos ... 6.7
Kush-Chi 5.9
Trinkle-NY 3.4
Gumbert-Cin 2.2
Casey-Bro 1.2

Relief Ranking
Lanfranconi-Bos ... 7.8
Kush-Chi 7.2
Gumbert-Cin 4.9
Trinkle-NY 4.7
Casey-Bro 2.6

Total Pitcher Index
Blackwell-Cin 5.2
Spahn-Bos 5.1
Branca-Bro 4.4
Leonard-Phi 4.3
Brazle-StL 3.4

Total Baseball Ranking
Kiner-Pit 6.0
Blackwell-Cin 5.2
Spahn-Bos 5.1
Mize-NY 4.9
Branca-Bro 4.4

January 20 Famed Negro League slugger Josh Gibson dies of a brain tumor at age 35.

January 21 A rule change that only allows voting for players after 1921 produces four new Hall of Famers: Carl Hubbell, Frank Frisch, Mickey Cochrane, and Lefty Grove. Pie Traynor misses selection by two votes.

March 1 In anticipation of the signing of the first black players, Bill Veeck, a resident of Phoenix, had set up a spring training camp there for the Cleveland Indians. Arizona was chosen because of its relatively tolerant racial climate.

May 1 For the first time Cleveland will play all its games at Municipal Stadium, abandoning League Park, where the club played most weekday games. Bill Veeck installs an inner fence to cut power alleys from 435 to 365 feet.

June 13 The Boston Red Sox beat the Chicago White Sox 5-3 before 34,510 "first nighters" in the first night game at Fenway Park.

July 5 Larry Doby of the Cleveland Indians becomes the first black to play in the AL. He strikes out as a pinch hitter, as the Chicago White Sox edge the Indians 6-5. Tomorrow he will go 1-for-5 in his first full game at first base.

July 8 Clutch pinch hits by Luke Appling and Stan Spence lead the AL to a 2–1 win over the NL in the All-Star Game at Wrigley Field. Schoolboy Rowe pinch hits for Johnny Sain, becoming the first player to appear for each side. Rowe pitched three innings for the AL in 1936.

September 15 Even though they're rained out, the Yankees clinch the pennant when the Red Sox lose. New York is 90-53 at the time.

September 28 On the season's last day, the Browns, desperate to attract fans, bring announcer Dizzy Dean in to pitch against the White Sox. Diz gives up only three hits in four innings and laces a clean single in his only at bat, but a pulled leg muscle forces his retirement. The White Sox score all their runs in the ninth to win 5-2. Even with Diz, the game draws less than 16,000, and the Browns finish the year with only 320,000 attendance, less than half that of 1946.

September 29 Joe McCarthy, who led the Yankees to nine pennants, is coaxed out of retirement and signs to manage the Red Sox. Joe Cronin will become general manager of Tom Yawkey's team.

October 1 New York's Allie Reynolds spaces nine hits and coasts to a 10–3 victory to give the Yankees a two games-to-none lead in the World Series. Tommy Henrich's solo home run in the fifth puts the game away for the Yankees.

October 6 The New York Yankees beat the Brooklyn Dodgers 5-2 to win the World Series in seven games. Relief pitcher Hugh Casey of the Dodgers appears in six games, winning two while notching an 0.87 ERA. Series heroes Bevens, Gionfriddo, and Lavagetto will never play another major league game.

October 7 Larry MacPhail resigns as Yankees general manager moments after the final game of the Series. Co-owners Dan Topping and Del Webb then buy out MacPhail's one-third interest in the club for $2 million. George Weiss will become GM.

October 20 Radio rights for the World Series sell for $475,000 for three years. Every franchise but Pittsburgh has sold 1948 TV rights. The Giants get $400,000 for radio-TV rights from Chesterfield.

November 27 Setting off a storm of controversy, Joe DiMaggio is named American League MVP by a single point over Ted Williams. Williams, the Triple Crown winner, receives 201 points, and is completely left off a Boston writer's ballot. Even a 10th-place vote would have given Williams the needed two points; however, Williams is selected *The Sporting News* Player of the Year.

BOSTON	CHICAGO	CLEVELAND	DETROIT	NEW YORK	PHILADELPHIA	ST.LOUIS	WASHINGTON
M J.Cronin	M T.Lyons	M L.Boudreau	M S.O'Neill	M B.Harris	M C.Mack	M M.Ruel	M O.Bluege
1B J.Jones	1B R.York	1B E.Robinson	1B R.Cullenbine	1B G.McQuinn	1B F.Fain	1B W.Judnich	1B M.Vernon
2B B.Doerr	2B D.Kolloway	2B J.Gordon	2B E.Mayo	2B S.Stirnweiss	2B P.Suder	2B J.Berardino	2B J.Priddy
SS J.Pesky	SS L.Appling	SS L.Boudreau	SS E.Lake	SS P.Rizzuto	SS E.Joost	SS V.Stephens	SS M.Christman
3B S.Dente	3B F.Baker	3B K.Keltner	3B G.Kell	3B B.Johnson	3B H.Majeski	3B B.Dillinger	3B E.Yost
LF T.Williams	LF T.Wright	LF D.Mitchell	LF D.Wakefield	LF J.Lindell	LF B.McCosky	LF J.Heath	LF J.Grace
CF D.DiMaggio	CF D.Philley	CF C.Metkovich	CF H.Evers	CF J.DiMaggio	CF S.Chapman	CF P.Lehner	CF S.Spence
RF S.Mele	RF B.Kennedy	RF H.Edwards	RF P.Mullin	RF T.Henrich	RF E.Valo	RF A.Zarilla	RF B.Lewis
C B.Tebbetts	C M.Tresh	C J.Hegan	C B.Swift	C A.Robinson	C B.Rosar	C L.Moss	C A.Evans
O W.Moses	23 C.Michaels	1 L.Fleming	O V.Wertz	O1 Y.Berra	O1 G.Binks	O1 R.Coleman	O3 S.Robertson
3S E.Pellagrini	O T.Tucker	O H.Peck	O H.Wagner	C C.Keller	C M.Guerra	23 B.Hitchcock	3S C.Travis
1 R.York	C G.Dickey	O P.Seerey	O D.Cramer	3S B.Brown	23 G.Handley	C J.Early	O T.McBride
C R.Partee	SO J.Wallaesa	O A.Lopez	O J.Outlaw	1 R.Houk	1 D.Adams	1 J.Witte	S J.Sullivan
23 D.Gutteridge	O R.Hodgin	3 E.Bockman	1 J.McHale	O A.Clark	O A.Knickerbocker	2 R.Peters	F.Mancuso
O L.Culberson	1 J.Jones	/2 L.Doby	2 S.Webb	1 J.Phillips	3 M.Rutner	/S P.Currin	C R.Ferrell
3 M.Combs	C J.Stephenson	C H.Ruszkowski	C B.Tebbetts	3 S.Lollar	/O C.Laabs	/C G.McQuillen	O G.Case
C H.Wagner	/O L.Christopher	/3 A.Rosen	O E.Mierkowicz	/O F.Colman	/3 D.Richmond	P J.Kramer	O G.Coan
3 R.Russell	H J.Kuhel	/O T.Sepkowski	/C H.Riebe	/2 L.Frey	/1 P.Cooper	P E.Kinder	/2 E.Lyons
/C M.Batts	P E.Lopat	/O F.Mackiewicz	/O J.Groth	/C J.Lucadello	/C H.Franks	P F.Sanford	/O J.Wooten
/C E.McGah	P F.Papish	H H.Becker	R B.Steiner	/C K.Silvestri	H R.Poole	P B.Muncrief	/2 G.Myatt
/C F.Hayes	P J.Haynes	H J.Wasdell	P H.Newhouser	/2 F.Crosetti	H N.Fox	RP S.Zoldak	/O F.Mackiewicz
/3 S.Shofner	P O.Grove	P B.Feller	R F.Hutchinson	H R.Mack	H T.Kirk	RP G.Moulder	/2 C.Ermer
/O B.Goodman	P B.Gillespie	P D.Black	P D.Trout	H T.Sepkowski	P P.Marchildon	P C.Fannin	P W.Masterson
/O T.McBride	RP E.Harrist	P B.Lemon	P V.Trucks	P A.Reynolds	P D.Fowler	P N.Potter	P E.Wynn
/C T.Aulds	RP P.Gebrian	P R.Embree	P S.Overmire	P S.Shea	RP B.McCahan	P Wa.Brown	P M.Haefner
P J.Dobson	RP G.Maltzberger	P A.Gettel	RP H.White	P B.Bevens	P J.Coleman	/P D.Galehouse	P R.Scarborough
P D.Ferriss	P T.Lee	RP B.Stephens	RP J.Gorsica	P S.Chandler	P J.Flores	/P H.Iott	P S.Hudson
P T.Hughson	P E.Caldwell	RP E.Klieman	/P R.Gentry	P B.Newsom	P R.Christopher	P B.Swartz	RP M.Candini
P D.Galehouse	P R.Ruffing	RP S.Gromek		RP J.Page	P B.Savage	P D.Dean	RP T.Ferrick
P E.Johnson	P J.Rigney	P M.Harder		RP R.Gumpert	P C.Scheib		RP S.Cary
RP J.Murphy	P E.Smith	P L.Willis		P V.Raschi	P B.Dietrich		P B.Newsom
RP B.Zuber	/P H.Bithorn	/P B.Kuzava		P K.Drews	/P L.Brissie		P M.Pieretti
P H.Dorish		/P R.Wolff		P D.Johnson			/P L.Knerr
P M.Harris		/P C.Dorsett		P B.Wensloff			/P B.Kennedy
P M.Parnell		/P E.Groth		/P D.Starr			/P H.Toenes
P B.Klinger		/P L.Linde		/P A.Lyons			/P L.Harris
/P T.Fine		/P G.Bearden		/P B.Wight			/P B.Dozier
/P E.Smith				/P M.Queen			
/P C.Deal				/P T.Byrne			
/P C.Stobbs				/P R.Ardizoia			
/P B.Butland							
/P A.Widmar							

TEAM	G	W	L	PCT	GB	R	OR	AB	H	2B	3B	HR	BB	SO	AVG	OBP	SLG	PRO	PRO+	BR	/A	PF	CHI	RC	SB	CS	SBA	SBR
NY	155	97	57	.630		794	568	5308	1439	230	72	115	610	581	.271	.349	.407	.756	117	110	118	99	104	780	27	23	54	-6
DET	158	85	69	.552	12	714	642	5276	1363	234	42	103	762	565	.258	.353	.377	.730	106	77	55	103	96	735	52	60	46	-20
BOS	157	83	71	.539	14	720	669	5322	1412	206	54	103	666	590	.265	.349	.382	.731	102	71	17	107	98	734	41	35	54	-9
CLE	157	80	74	.519	17	687	588	5367	1392	234	51	112	502	609	.259	.324	.385	.709	106	9	27	97	105	687	29	25	54	-6
PHI	156	78	76	.506	19	633	614	5198	1311	218	52	61	605	563	.252	.333	.349	.682	94	-24	-36	102	102	635	37	33	53	-9
CHI	155	70	84	.455	27	553	661	5274	1350	211	41	53	492	527	.256	.321	.342	.663	93	-69	-48	96	98	584	91	57	61	-7
WAS	154	64	90	.416	33	496	675	5112	1234	186	48	42	525	534	.241	.313	.321	.634	84	-118	-105	97	99	523	53	51	51	-15
STL	154	59	95	.383	38	564	744	5145	1238	189	52	90	583	664	.241	.320	.350	.670	90	-55	-66	102	98	596	69	49	58	-9
TOT	623					5161		42002	10739	1708	412	679	4745	4633	.256	.333	.364	.698							399	333	55	-80

TEAM	CG	SH	SV	IP	H	H/G	HR	BB	SO	RAT	ERA	ERA+	OAV	OOB	PR	/A	PF	CPI	FA	E	DP	FW	PW	BW	SBW	DIF
NY	73	14	21	1374¹	1221	8.0	95	628	691	12.2	3.39	104	.238	.323	48	22	95	100	.981	109	151	1.5	2.3	12.2	.4	3.6
DET	77	15	18	1398²	1382	8.9	79	531	648	12.4	3.57	106	.258	.326	21	31	102	100	.975	155	142	-1.0	3.2	5.7	-1.0	1.1
BOS	64	13	19	1391¹	1383	8.9	84	575	586	12.8	3.81	102	.261	.335	-16	12	105	100	.977	137	172	-.0	1.2	1.8	.1	2.9
CLE	55	13	29	1402¹	1244	8.0	94	628	590	12.2	3.44	101	.240	.325	41	7	94	100	.983	104	178	1.9	.7	2.8	.4	-2.8
PHI	70	12	15	1391¹	1291	8.4	85	597	493	12.3	3.51	109	.247	.326	30	46	103	99	.976	143	161	-.4	4.8	-3.7	.1	.3
CHI	47	11	27	1391	1384	9.0	76	603	522	13.0	3.64	100	.261	.339	11	3	99	105	.975	155	180	-1.2	.3	-5.0	.3	-1.5
WAS	67	15	12	1362	1408	9.3	63	579	551	13.2	3.97	94	.267	.342	-40	-37	101	98	.976	143	151	-.5	-3.8	-10.9	-.5	2.7
STL	50	7	13	1365	1426	9.4	103	604	552	13.4	4.33	90	.272	.348	-94	-68	105	98	.977	134	169	-.0	-7.0	-6.8	.1	-4.2
TOT	503	100	154	11076		8.7				12.7	3.71		.256	.333					.977	1080	1304					

Runs
Williams-Bos 125
Henrich-NY 109
Pesky-Bos 106
Stirnweiss-NY 102
DiMaggio-NY 97

Hits
Pesky-Bos 207
Kell-Det 188
Williams-Bos 181
McCosky-Phi 179

Doubles
Boudreau-Cle 45
Williams-Bos 40
Henrich-NY 35
DiMaggio-NY 31

Triples
Henrich-NY 13
Vernon-Was 12
Philley-Chi 11

Home Runs
Williams-Bos 32
Gordon-Cle 29
Heath-StL 27
Cullenbine-Det 24
York-Bos-Chi 21

Total Bases
Williams-Bos 335
Gordon-Cle 279
DiMaggio-NY 279
Henrich-NY 267
Pesky-Bos 250

Runs Batted In
Williams-Bos 114
Henrich-NY 98
DiMaggio-NY 97
Jones-Chi-Bos 96

Runs Produced
Williams-Bos 207
Henrich-NY 191
DiMaggio-NY 174
Kell-Det 163
Doerr-Bos 157

Bases On Balls
Williams-Bos 162
Cullenbine-Det 137
Lake-Det 120
Joost-Phi 114
Fain-Phi 95

Batting Average
Williams-Bos ..... .343
McCosky-Phi ..... .328
Pesky-Bos ..... .324
Wright-Chi ..... .324
Kell-Det ..... .320

On Base Percentage
Williams-Bos ..... .499
Fain-Phi ..... .414
Cullenbine-Det ..... .401
McCosky-Phi ..... .395
McQuinn-NY ..... .395

Slugging Average
Williams-Bos ..... .634
DiMaggio-NY ..... .522
Gordon-Cle ..... .496
Henrich-NY ..... .485
Heath-StL ..... .485

Production
Williams-Bos 1.133
DiMaggio-NY ..... .913
Henrich-NY ..... .857
Heath-StL ..... .850
Gordon-Cle ..... .842

Adjusted Production
Williams-Bos 199
DiMaggio-NY 154
Henrich-NY 139
Gordon-Cle 136
Heath-StL 133

Batter Runs
Williams-Bos 91.1
DiMaggio-NY 36.5
Henrich-NY 26.4
Fain-Phi 24.7
Cullenbine-Det 23.8

Adjusted Batter Runs
Williams-Bos 79.3
DiMaggio-NY 37.5
Henrich-NY 27.4
McQuinn-NY 24.2
Gordon-Cle 23.8

Clutch Hitting Index
B.Johnson-NY 140
Kell-Det 121
Jones-Chi-Bos 119
Joost-Phi 118
Majeski-Phi 115

Runs Created
Williams-Bos 186
DiMaggio-NY 112
Henrich-NY 104
Pesky-Bos 103
McQuinn-NY 97

Total Average
Williams-Bos 1.391
DiMaggio-NY ..... .918
Cullenbine-Det ..... .898
Heath-StL ..... .856
Henrich-NY ..... .849

Stolen Bases
Dillinger-StL 34
Philley-Chi 21
Vernon-Was 12
Pesky-Bos 12

Stolen Base Average
Dillinger-StL 72.3
Philley-Chi 56.8

Stolen Base Runs
Dillinger-StL 2.4
Valo-Phi 1.5
Binks-Phi 1.2

Fielding Runs
Doerr-Bos 23.8
DiMaggio-Bos 19.0
Baker-Chi 18.3
Kell-Det 17.9
Boudreau-Cle 16.7

Total Player Rating
Williams-Bos 7.2
Boudreau-Cle 4.8
Doerr-Bos 3.3
Cullenbine-Det 3.3
Gordon-Cle 3.1

Wins
Feller-Cle 20
Reynolds-NY 19
Marchildon-Phi 19
Hutchinson-Det 18
Dobson-Bos 18

Win Percentage
Reynolds-NY ..... .704
Dobson-Bos ..... .692
Marchildon-Phi ..... .679
Feller-Cle ..... .645
Hutchinson-Det ..... .643

Games
Klieman-Cle 58
Page-NY 56
Johnson-Bos 45
Savage-Phi 44
Christopher-Phi 44

Complete Games
Newhouser-Det 24
Wynn-Was 22
Lopat-Chi 22
Marchildon-Phi 21
Feller-Cle 20

Shutouts
Feller-Cle 5
Reynolds-NY 4
Masterson-Was 4
Haefner-Was 4

Saves
Page-NY 17
Klieman-Cle 17
Christopher-Phi 12
Ferrick-Was 9

Innings Pitched
Feller-Cle 299.0
Newhouser-Det 285.0
Marchildon-Phi 276.2
Masterson-Was 253.0
Lopat-Chi 252.2

Fewest Hits/Game
Shea-NY 6.40
Feller-Cle 6.92
Marchildon-Phi 7.42
Embree-Cle 7.58
Masterson-Was 7.65

Fewest BB/Game
Galehouse-StL-Bos 2.48
Hutchinson-Det 2.50
Lopat-Chi 2.60
Muncrief-StL 2.60
Dobson-Bos 2.87

Strikeouts
Feller-Cle 196
Newhouser-Det 176
Masterson-Was 135
Reynolds-NY 129
Marchildon-Phi 128

Strikeouts/Game
Feller-Cle 5.90
Hughson-Bos 5.66
Newhouser-Det 5.56
Trucks-Det 5.38
Kinder-StL 5.09

Ratio
Feller-Cle 10.87
Dobson-Bos 10.90
Shea-NY 11.08
Masterson-Was 11.17
Hutchinson-Det 11.23

Earned Run Average
Haynes-Chi 2.42
Chandler-NY 2.46
Feller-Cle 2.68
Fowler-Phi 2.81
Lopat-Chi 2.81

Adjusted ERA
Haynes-Chi 151
Fowler-Phi 136
Dobson-Bos 132
Newhouser-Det 131
Feller-Cle 130

Opponents' Batting Avg.
Shea-NY ..... .200
Feller-Cle ..... .215
Marchildon-Phi ..... .224
Reynolds-NY ..... .227
Embree-Cle ..... .233

Opponents' On Base Pct.
Dobson-Bos ..... .299
Feller-Cle ..... .300
Shea-NY ..... .303
Hutchinson-Det ..... .304
Lopat-Chi ..... .307

Starter Runs
Feller-Cle 34.1
Newhouser-Det 26.3
Haynes-Chi 25.9
Lopat-Chi 25.0
Fowler-Phi 22.6

Adjusted Starter Runs
Newhouser-Det 28.3
Feller-Cle 26.7
Fowler-Phi 25.3
Haynes-Chi 24.9
Dobson-Bos 23.8

Clutch Pitching Index
Haynes-Chi 124
Fowler-Phi 119
Lopat-Chi 116
Ferriss-Bos 114
Newsom-Was-NY 112

Relief Runs
Page-NY 19.2
Christopher-Phi 7.2
Klieman-Cle 6.9
Murphy-Bos 5.5
Ferrick-Was 3.7

Adjusted Relief Runs
Page-NY 16.5
Christopher-Phi 8.2
Murphy-Bos 6.6
Klieman-Cle 4.6
Ferrick-Was 3.8

Relief Ranking
Page-NY 27.6
Christopher-Phi 18.2
Klieman-Cle 6.0
Ferrick-Was 5.9
Maltzberger-Chi 1.6

Total Pitcher Index
Newhouser-Det 3.9
Hutchinson-Det 3.7
Christopher-Phi 3.1
Page-NY 3.0
Haynes-Chi 2.9

Total Baseball Ranking
Williams-Bos 7.2
Boudreau-Cle 4.8
Newhouser-Det 3.9
Hutchinson-Det 3.7
Doerr-Bos 3.3

February 27 Herb Pennock and Pie Traynor are elected to the Hall of Fame. With 91 votes needed for selection, Pennock, who died a month before, gets 94, Traynor 93.

April 21 Leo Durocher, back at the helm of the Dodgers after a one-year suspension, uses 24 men in one game, a 9–5 loss to the Giants.

May 8 An infield single by Johnny Blatnik of the Phillies in the seventh prevents a perfect game by Harry Brecheen of the Cardinals. The Cards win, 5–0. Brecheen will become the NL ERA leader with 2.24 and the winning percentage leader on a 20-7 record.

June 18 The Pirates spoil Robin Roberts' debut, beating the Phils' rookie 2-0. Roberts was called up after a 9-1 start at Wilmington (Interstate League).

July 1 Brooklyn's Roy Campanella makes his debut, catching Ralph Branca. Campy doubles in his first at-bat, adds two singles, but the Giants win 6-4.

July 16 There are three managerial changes in one day. The Giants remove Mel Ott and replace him with Leo Durocher, who obtains his release from Brooklyn. The Dodgers bring back Burt Shotton, and Eddie Sawyer replaces Ben Chapman with the Phillies.

July 26 Leo Durocher makes his first appearance at Ebbets Field since taking over the Giants, and a turnaway crowd delights in the Dodgers' 13–4 win.

September 12 Ralph Kiner sets a major league record with his eigth home run in four games, collecting his 37th and 38th of the year to take the lead. The Pirates beat the Braves in Pittsburgh, 4–3, to move four games back of first place Boston.

September 23 The Braves clinch the NL flag by defeating the Giants 3-2. Two days before the season is over they lose their best hitter, outfielder Jeff Heath, who breaks an ankle sliding home against Brooklyn.

October 3* Luke Easter's grand slam highlights the Homestead Grays' 19-hit assault on the Birmingham Black Barons in the fourth game of the final Negro League World Series; the Negro National League becomes a casualty of integration and folds during the winter.

October 6 In the World Series opener in Boston, Phil Masi is called safe at second base on a disputed call by umpire Bill Stewart on a pickoff attempt in the eighth. Masi then scores on a single by Tommy Holmes as Johnny Sain and the Boston Braves top the Cleveland Indians and Bob Feller 1-0.

October 10 A six-run seventh inning knocks out Bob Feller and two successors for the Braves' 11–5 victory to cut the World Series deficit to three games to two. Bob Elliott has two home runs. The World Series crowd is even larger than the day before, 86,288, and won't be exceeded until Game 3 in the LA Coliseum in 1959 (92,394).

October 11 In Boston, the Cleveland Indians nip the Braves 4-3 to take the World Series in six games. Rookie lefty Gene Bearden is the pitching hero in relief.

December 2 Stan Musial is picked MVP in the NL. Musial led the NL in batting at .365, runs (135), RBI (131), and in doubles and triples. His 39 home runs were one short of Mize and Kiner.

BOSTON		BROOKLYN		CHICAGO		CINCINNATI		NEW YORK		PHILADELPHIA		PITTSBURGH		ST.LOUIS	
M	B.Southworth	M	L.Durocher	M	C.Grimm	M	J.Neun	M	M.Ott	M	B.Chapman	M	B.Meyer	M	E.Dyer
1B	E.Torgeson	M	R.Blades	1B	E.Waitkus	M	B.Walters	M	L.Durocher	M	D.Cooke	1B	E.Stevens	1B	N.Jones
2B	E.Stanky	M	B.Shotton	2B	H.Schenz	1B	T.Kluszewski	1B	J.Mize	M	E.Sawyer	2B	D.Murtaugh	2B	R.Schoendienst
SS	A.Dark	1B	G.Hodges	SS	R.Smalley	2B	B.Adams	1B	B.Rigney	1B	D.Sisler	SS	S.Rojek	SS	M.Marion
3B	B.Elliott	2B	J.Robinson	3B	A.Pafko	SS	V.Stallcup	SS	B.Kerr	2B	G.Hamner	3B	F.Gustine	3B	D.Lang
LF	J.Heath	SS	P.Reese	LF	P.Lowrey	3B	G.Hatton	3B	S.Gordon	SS	E.Miller	LF	R.Kiner	LF	E.Slaughter
CF	J.Russell	3B	B.Cox	CF	H.Jeffcoat	LF	H.Sauer	LF	B.Thomson	3B	P.Caballero	CF	W.Westlake	CF	T.Moore
RF	T.Holmes	LF	M.Rackley	RF	B.Nicholson	CF	J.Wyrostek	CF	W.Lockman	LF	J.Blatnik	RF	D.Walker	RF	S.Musial
C	P.Masi	CF	C.Furillo	C	B.Scheffing	RF	F.Baumholtz	RF	W.Marshall	CF	R.Ashburn	C	E.Fitz Gerald	C	D.Rice
		RF	G.Hermanski			C	R.Lamanno	C	W.Cooper	RF	D.Ennis				
O	M.McCormick	C	R.Campanella	1O	P.Cavarretta					C	A.Seminick	O1	J.Hopp	O2	E.Dusak
O	C.Conatser			2	E.Verban	O3	D.Litwhiler	32	J.Lohrke			C	C.Kluttz	O	R.Northey
2S	S.Sisti	CO	B.Edwards	C	C.Maddern	23	C.Corbitt	C	W.Westrum	31	B.Haas	3	E.Bockman	2S	R.LaPointe
C	B.Salkeld	23	E.Miksis	C	C.McCullough	2	B.Zientara	O	M.Livingston	O	H.Walker	1O	M.West	3	W.Kurowski
1	F.McCormick	O	D.Whitman	C	R.Walker	1	B.Young	O	L.Layton	3O	B.Rowell	O	T.Beard	C	B.Baker
2	C.Ryan	O	D.Shuba	2S	G.Mauch	C	D.Williams	O	D.Mueller	2	E.Verban	2	M.Basgall	1	Ba.Young
2	B.Sturgeon	O	D.Snider	S	D.Culler	O	A.Galan	/1	J.McCarthy	C	D.Padgett	C	J.Riddle	C	D.Wilber
/O	D.Litwhiler	1	P.Ward	/O	C.Aberson	1	H.Schultz	2	L.Frey	C	A.Lakeman	/S	G.Wilson	C	J.Garagiola
/O	M.Rickert	3	T.Brown	/S	J.Cross	C	R.Mueller	2	J.Conway	3	W.Jones	/S	P.Castiglione	/O	H.Rice
/C	P.Burris	O	P.Reiser	/2	D.Johnson	/O	S.Filipowicz	S	B.Rhawn	O	J.Mayo	H	D.Gutteridge	/3	E.Kazak
H	R.Sanders	O	A.Vaughan	/2	D.Lynch	/O	C.Vollmer	C	S.Yvars	/C	S.Lopata	/C	E.Turner	/O	J.Medwick
		3	S.Jorgensen	/O	C.Mauro	H	M.Rickert	/O	P.Milne	/1	H.Schultz			/O	C.Diering
P	J.Sain	O	D.Lund	H	C.Sawatski	H	H.Poland	/2	B.Blattner	/C	H.Wagner	P	B.Chesnes	/C	J.Bucha
P	W.Spahn	/2	G.Mauch					/O	H.Bamberger			P	E.Riddle	H	L.Miggins
P	B.Voiselle	/C	B.Bragan	P	J.Schmitz	P	J.Vander Meer	/1	J.Harshman	P	D.Leonard	P	V.Lombardi	/3	Bo.Young
P	V.Bickford	/3	B.Ramazzotti	P	R.Meyer	H	K.RaffensbergerH		J.Lafata	P	C.Simmons	P	T.Bonham	R	J.Cross
P	R.Barrett			P	D.McCall	P	H.Fox			P	M.Dubiel	P	F.Ostermueller		
RP	B.Hogue	P	R.Barney	P	B.Rush	P	H.Wehmeier	P	L.Jansen	P	S.Rowe	RP	K.Higbe	P	M.Dickson
RP	C.Shoun	P	R.Branca	P	H.Borowy	P	E.Blackwell	P	S.Jones	P	R.Roberts	RP	E.Singleton	P	H.Brecheen
		P	J.Hatten	RP	J.Dobernic	RP	H.Gumbert	P	R.Poat	RP	E.Heusser	P	M.Queen	P	H.Pollet
P	N.Potter	P	P.Roe	RP	E.Kush	RP	W.Cress	RP	C.Hartung	RP	S.Nahem			P	R.Munger
P	E.White	P	E.Palica	RP	B.Chipman			P	D.Koslo			P	R.Sewell	P	A.Brazle
P	J.Prendergast	RP	H.Behrman			P	K.Peterson	RP	A.Hansen	P	B.Donnelly	P	H.Gregg	RP	T.Wilks
/P	J.Beazley	RP	P.Minner			P	K.Burkhart	RP	K.Trinkle	P	K.Heintzelman	P	W.Main	RP	J.Hearn
/P	A.Lyons	RP	W.Ramsdell	P	R.Hamner	/P	B.Walters			P	C.Bicknell	/P	C.McLish	RP	G.Staley
/P	E.Wright			P	C.Chambers	P	J.Blackburn	P	M.Kennedy	/P	P.Erickson	/P	N.Strincevich		
/P	J.Antonelli	P	H.Taylor	P	D.Lade	P	T.Hughes	P	A.Konikowski	/P	N.Strincevich	/P	J.Walsh	P	K.Johnson
/P	G.Elliott	P	C.Erskine	/P	P.Erickson	P	B.Lively	P	T.Lee	P	L.Possehl			P	K.Burkhart
/P	R.Martin	P	H.Casey	/P	B.Wade	/P	J.Hetki	P	R.Webb	/P	O.Judd			P	A.Papai
		/P	C.King	/P	W.Hacker	/P	E.Erautt	/P	B.Newsom	/P	J.Thompson			/P	C.Beers
		/P	L.Sloat	/P	T.Jacobs	/P	K.Holcombe	/P	C.Dreisewerd	/P	J.Konstanty			/P	R.Yochim
		/P	J.Van Cuyk	/P	D.Carlsen			/P	L.Lombardo	P	D.Koecher				
		/P	J.Hall					/P	J.Hallett	P	L.Grasmick				
		/P	J.Banta					/P	M.McGowan	P	A.Porto				
		/P	P.Haugstad					/P	H.Andrews						
		/P	E.Sexauer					/P	P.Erickson						
								/P	J.Beggs						

TEAM	G	W	L	PCT	GB	R	OR	AB	H	2B	3B	HR	BB	SO	AVG	OBP	SLG	PRO	PRO+	BR	/A	PF	CHI	RC	SB	CS	SBA	SBR
BOS	154	91	62	.595		739	584	5297	1458	272	49	95	671	536	.275	.359	.399	.758	114	95	109	98	92	784	43			
STL	155	85	69	.552	6.5	742	646	5302	1396	238	58	105	594	521	.263	.340	.389	.729	98	31	-10	106	103	713	24			
BRO	155	84	70	.545	7.5	744	667	5328	1393	256	54	91	601	684	.261	.338	.381	.719	99	13	-11	103	105	709	114			
PIT	156	83	71	.539	8.5	706	699	5286	1388	191	54	108	580	578	.263	.338	.380	.718	99	10	-4	102	101	698	68			
NY	155	78	76	.506	13.5	780	704	5277	1352	210	49	164	599	648	.256	.334	.408	.742	106	46	42	101	106	731	51			
PHI	155	66	88	.429	25.5	591	729	5287	1367	223	39	91	440	598	.259	.318	.368	.686	94	-63	-52	98	97	625	68			
CIN	153	64	89	.418	27	588	752	5127	1266	221	37	104	478	586	.247	.313	.365	.678	92	-76	-56	97	101	587	42			
CHI	155	64	90	.416	27.5	597	706	5352	1402	225	44	87	443	578	.262	.322	.369	.691	97	-52	-27	96	95	641	39			
TOT	619					5487		42256	11022	1840	384	845	4406	4729	.261	.333	.383	.715							449			

TEAM	CG	SH	SV	IP	H	H/G	HR	BB	SO	RAT	ERA	ERA+	OAV	OOB	PR	/A	PF	CPI	FA	E	DP	FW	PW	BW	SBW	DIF
BOS	70	10	17	1389^1	1354	8.8	93	430	579	11.6	3.37	114	.249	.306	89	71	97	96	.976	143	132	.7	7.1	10.9		-4.2
STL	60	13	18	1368	1392	9.2	103	476	625	12.4	3.91	105	.262	.324	7	28	103	97	.980	119	138	2.1	2.8	-1.0		4.1
BRO	52	9	22	1392^2	1328	8.6	119	633	670	12.9	3.75	106	.253	.337	31	37	101	107	.973	161	151	-.2	3.7	-1.1		4.6
PIT	65	5	19	1371^2	1373	9.0	120	564	543	12.9	4.15	98	.261	.335	-29	-12	103	98	.977	137	150	1.2	-1.2	-.4		6.4
NY	54	15	21	1373	1425	9.3	122	556	527	13.2	3.93	100	.269	.342	4	0	100	109	.974	156	134	.1	.0	4.2		-3.3
PHI	61	6	15	1362^1	1385	9.1	95	556	550	13.0	4.08	97	.262	.335	-18	-20	100	97	.964	210	126	-2.8	-2.0	-5.2		-1.0
CIN	40	8	20	1343^1	1410	9.4	104	572	599	13.4	4.47	87	.270	.344	-77	-85	99	95	.973	158	135	-.1	-8.5	-5.6		1.7
CHI	51	7	10	1355^1	1355	9.0	89	619	636	13.2	4.00	97	.261	.342	-7	-15	99	101	.972	172	152	-.7	-1.5	-2.7		-8.1
TOT	453	73	142	10955^2		9.1				12.8	3.95		.261	.333					.974	1256	1118					

Runs
Musial-StL 135
Lockman-NY 117
Mize-NY 110
Robinson-Bro 108
Kiner-Pit 104

Hits
Musial-StL 230
Holmes-Bos 190
Rojek-Pit 186
Slaughter-StL 176
Dark-Bos 175

Doubles
Musial-StL 46
Ennis-Phi 40
Dark-Bos 39
Robinson-Bro 38
Holmes-Bos 35

Triples
Musial-StL 18
Hopp-Pit 12
Slaughter-StL 11
Waitkus-Chi 10
Lockman-NY 10

Home Runs
Mize-NY 40
Kiner-Pit 40
Musial-StL 39
Sauer-Cin 35

Total Bases
Musial-StL 429
Mize-NY 316
Ennis-Phi 309
Kiner-Pit 296
Pafko-Chi 283

Runs Batted In
Musial-StL 131
Mize-NY 125
Kiner-Pit 123
Gordon-NY 107
Pafko-Chi 101

Runs Produced
Musial-StL 227
Mize-NY 195
Kiner-Pit 187
Robinson-Bro 181
Gordon-NY 177

Bases On Balls
B.Elliott-Bos 131
Kiner-Pit 112
Mize-NY 94

Batting Average
Musial-StL 376
Ashburn-Phi 333
Holmes-Bos 325
Dark-Bos 322
Slaughter-StL 321

On Base Percentage
Musial-StL 450
B.Elliott-Bos 423
Ashburn-Phi 410
Slaughter-StL 409
Mize-NY 395

Slugging Average
Musial-StL 702
Mize-NY 564
Gordon-NY 537
Kiner-Pit 533
Ennis-Phi 525

Production
Musial-StL 1.152
Mize-NY 959
Gordon-NY 927
Kiner-Pit 924
B.Elliott-Bos 897

Adjusted Production
Musial-StL 196
Mize-NY 156
Gordon-NY 148
Kiner-Pit 145
B.Elliott-Bos 145

Batter Runs
Musial-StL 90.2
Mize-NY 44.6
Kiner-Pit 38.5
B.Elliott-Bos 37.8
Gordon-NY 35.1

Adjusted Batter Runs
Musial-StL 80.8
Mize-NY 43.9
B.Elliott-Bos 39.8
Kiner-Pit 36.2
Gordon-NY 34.4

Clutch Hitting Index
Murtaugh-Pit 135
Jones-StL 129
Stallcup-Cin 128
Lowrey-Chi 123
Torgeson-Bos 118

Runs Created
Musial-StL 191
Mize-NY 131
Kiner-Pit 120
B.Elliott-Bos 117
Slaughter-StL 110

Total Average
Musial-StL 1.298
Mize-NY 1.032
B.Elliott-Bos 980
Kiner-Pit 974
Gordon-NY 953

Stolen Bases
Ashburn-Phi 32
Reese-Bro 25
Rojek-Pit 24
Robinson-Bro 22
Torgeson-Bos 19

Stolen Base Average

Stolen Base Runs

Fielding Runs
Ashburn-Phi 17.8
Pafko-Chi 12.8
Reese-Bro 10.3
Marion-StL 9.4
Gustine-Pit 9.0

Total Player Rating
Musial-StL 6.3
Mize-NY 4.6
Pafko-Chi 4.3
Kiner-Pit 3.4
B.Elliott-Bos 2.8

Wins
Sain-Bos 24
Brecheen-StL 20
Schmitz-Chi 18
Jansen-NY 18
VanderMeer-Cin . . . 17

Win Percentage
Brecheen-StL 741
Jones-NY 667
Sain-Bos 615
Jansen-NY 600
Schmitz-Chi 581

Games
Gumbert-Cin 61
Wilks-StL 57
Higbe-Pit 56
Jones-NY 55
Dobernic-Chi 54

Complete Games
Sain-Bos 28
Brecheen-StL 21
Schmitz-Chi 18
Spahn-Bos 16
Leonard-Phi 16

Shutouts
Brecheen-StL 7
Sain-Bos 4
Raffensberger-Cin . . . 4
Jansen-NY 4
Barney-Bro 4

Saves
Gumbert-Cin 17
Wilks-StL 13
Higbe-Pit 10
Trinkle-NY 7
Behrman-Bro 7

Innings Pitched
Sain-Bos 314.2
Jansen-NY 277.0
Spahn-Bos 257.0
Dickson-StL 252.1
Barney-Bro 246.2

Fewest Hits/Game
Schmitz-Chi 6.92
Barney-Bro 7.04
Brecheen-StL 7.44
Branca-Bro 7.89
Roe-Bro 7.90

Fewest BB/Game
Roe-Bro 1.67
Jansen-NY 1.75
Raffensberger-Cin . . 1.85
Brecheen-StL 1.89
Leonard-Phi 2.15

Strikeouts
Brecheen-StL 149
Barney-Bro 138
Sain-Bos 137
Jansen-NY 126
Branca-Bro 122

Strikeouts/Game
Brecheen-StL 5.75
Branca-Bro 5.09
Barney-Bro 5.04
Higbe-Pit 4.90
Meyer-Chi 4.86

Ratio
Brecheen-StL 9.41
Roe-Bro 9.68
Schmitz-Chi 10.60
Sain-Bos 11.01
Spahn-Bos 11.03

Earned Run Average
Brecheen-StL 2.24
Leonard-Phi 2.51
Sain-Bos 2.60
Roe-Bro 2.63
Schmitz-Chi 2.64

Adjusted ERA
Brecheen-StL 183
Leonard-Phi 157
Roe-Bro 152
Schmitz-Chi 148
Sain-Bos 147

Opponents' Batting Avg.
Schmitz-Chi 215
Barney-Bro 217
Brecheen-StL 222
Branca-Bro 232
Roe-Bro 233

Opponents' On Base Pct.
Brecheen-StL 265
Roe-Bro 271
Schmitz-Chi 295
Sain-Bos 296
Raffensberger-Cin . . .296

Starter Runs
Sain-Bos 47.3
Brecheen-StL 44.5
Leonard-Phi 36.2
Schmitz-Chi 35.3
Roe-Bro 26.1

Adjusted Starter Runs
Brecheen-StL 48.0
Sain-Bos 43.0
Leonard-Phi 35.9
Schmitz-Chi 34.0
Roe-Bro 26.8

Clutch Pitching Index
Leonard-Phi 134
Jones-NY 126
Hatten-Bro 124
Voiselle-Bos 120
Sain-Bos 115

Relief Runs
Wilks-StL 19.4
Hansen-NY 10.9
Minner-Bro 10.5
Higbe-Pit 10.4
Dobernic-Chi 7.6

Adjusted Relief Runs
Wilks-StL 21.4
Higbe-Pit 12.4
Minner-Bro 10.7
Hansen-NY 10.7
Dobernic-Chi 7.2

Relief Ranking
Wilks-StL 22.4
Higbe-Pit 12.4
Minner-Bro 11.3
Gumbert-Cin 9.7
Trinkle-NY 8.1

Total Pitcher Index
Brecheen-StL 5.5
Sain-Bos 5.3
Schmitz-Chi 4.6
Leonard-Phi 4.6
Roe-Bro 2.6

Total Baseball Ranking
Musial-StL 6.3
Brecheen-StL 5.5
Sain-Bos 5.3
Schmitz-Chi 4.6
Leonard-Phi 4.6

April 16 The White Sox beat the Cubs 4-1 at Wrigley Field with Jack Brickhouse at the WGN-TV mike, the first telecast in Chicago history.

May 20 In a 13–4 Cleveland win, the Indians collect 18 bases on balls in a game with the Red Sox to tie the AL record.

May 27 Recently retired slugger Hank Greenberg buys an interest in the Cleveland club, becoming the Indians' second-largest stockholder.

June 13 The Yankees retire Babe Ruth's No. 3 in the Babe's final appearance at Yankee Stadium. After the ceremonies the Yankees beat the Cleveland Indians 5-3.

June 15 The Detroit Tigers beat the Philadelphia Athletics 4–1 before a crowd of 54,480 in the first night game at Briggs Stadium. The Tigers are the last AL team to install lights.

June 20 Cleveland draws 82,781 for a doubleheader, a major league record for a regular season game that will be broken by the same club in 1954. The Indians will attract 2.6 million for the season, surpassing the Yankees' 1947 attendance.

July 4 Ted Williams of the Red Sox faces three pitchers in the seventh inning, a first in AL history as Boston scores 14 runs and beats the Philadelphia Athletics, 20–8. The 14 runs in one inning is also a record.

July 7 The Indians sign Satchel Paige, fabulous veteran Negro League pitcher. Although his signing is ridiculed as a Bill Veeck publicity stunt, the 42-year-old Paige will finish at 6-1.

July 18 Pat Seerey, chunky Sox outfielder, hits four home runs, his last in the 11th inning, to lead the Chicago White Sox to a 12-11 victory over the Athletics in Philadelphia. Seerey is the fifth major league player to accomplish the feat.

July 26 Babe Ruth makes his last public appearance, at the New York premiere of the film *The Babe Ruth Story*. He will die three weeks later.

August 13 The promise of Paige on the mound brings 51,013 to Comiskey Park to see "Ol' Satch" pitch; he throws his first major league shutout as Cleveland wins 5-0.

August 16 Babe Ruth dies of throat cancer at age 53 in New York.

August 17 Tom Henrich hits his fourth grand slam of the season, off the Senators' Sid Hudson. to tie Ruth, Gehrig, and Rudy York for the AL record.

August 21 Aaron Robinson homers in the ninth off Bob Lemon to help the White Sox beat the Indians 3-2. The run breaks the 47-inning scoreless streak by Indians pitchers. Satchel Paige, Gene Bearden, Sam Zoldak, and Bob Lemon had shutouts during the streak.

September 22 Stan Musial collects his fifth hit in a game for the fifth time in one season, tying Ty Cobb's all-time record. Musial hits a home run, a double, and three singles against the Boston Braves.

September 24 The Yankees whip the Red Sox 9-6 while Cleveland loses at Detroit, 4-3. New York, Boston and Cleveland are now tied for first place in the AL with identical 91-56 records.

October 4 In a one-game playoff for the AL pennant at Fenway Park, the Cleveland Indians beat the Boston Red Sox 8-3 behind rookie knuckleballer Gene Bearden, who wins his 20th game.

November 30 Player-manager Lou Boudreau is selected the AL MVP. Boudreau had almost been traded to the Browns earlier in the year, but protests by fans kept Lou in Cleveland. After the World Series win, owner Bill Veeck commented, "Sometimes the best trades are the ones you never make."

BOSTON		CHICAGO		CLEVELAND		DETROIT		NEW YORK		PHILADELPHIA		ST.LOUIS		WASHINGTON	
M	J.McCarthy	M	T.Lyons	M	L.Boudreau	M	S.O'Neill	M	B.Harris	M	C.Mack	M	Z.Taylor	M	J.Kuhel
1B	B.Goodman	1B	T.Lupien	1B	E.Robinson	1B	G.Vico	1B	G.McQuinn	1B	F.Fain	1B	C.Stevens	1B	M.Vernon
2B	B.Doerr	2B	D.Kolloway	2B	J.Gordon	2B	E.Mayo	2B	S.Stirnweiss	2B	P.Suder	2B	J.Priddy	2B	A.Kozar
SS	V.Stephens	SS	C.Michaels	SS	L.Boudreau	SS	J.Lipon	SS	P.Rizzuto	SS	E.Joost	SS	E.Pellagrini	SS	M.Christman
3B	J.Pesky	3B	L.Appling	3B	K.Keltner	3B	G.Kell	3B	B.Johnson	3B	H.Majeski	3B	B.Dillinger	3B	E.Yost
LF	T.Williams	LF	P.Seerey	LF	D.Mitchell	LF	V.Wertz	LF	J.Lindell	LF	B.McCosky	LF	W.Platt	LF	G.Coan
CF	D.DiMaggio	CF	D.Philley	CF	T.Tucker	CF	H.Evers	CF	J.DiMaggio	CF	S.Chapman	CF	P.Lehner	CF	J.Wooten
RF	S.Spence	RF	T.Wright	RF	L.Doby	RF	P.Mullin	RF	T.Henrich	RF	E.Valo	RF	A.Zarilla	RF	B.Stewart
C	B.Tebbetts	C	A.Robinson	C	J.Hegan	C	B.Swift	C	G.Niarhos	C	B.Rosar	C	L.Moss	C	J.Early
O	W.Moses	32	F.Baker	O	A.Clark	CO	D.Wakefield	CO	Y.Berra	O3	D.White	S	S.Dente	C	A.Evans
O	S.Mele	O1	R.Hodgin	O1	W.Judnich	S2	N.Berry	3S	B.Brown	O	R.Coleman	O	D.Kokos	O	C.Gillenwater
23	B.Hitchcock	C	R.Weigel	23	H.Edwards	23	E.Lake	O	C.Keller	C	M.Guerra	1	H.Arft	O	T.McBride
C	M.Batts	O	B.Kennedy	21	J.Berardino	30	J.Outlaw	1	S.Souchock	C	H.Franks	C	R.Partee	S	S.Robertson
1	J.Jones	C	M.Tresh	C	J.Tipton	1	H.Wagner	O	C.Mapes	/2	S.Webb	O	D.Lund	S	J.Sullivan
/2	L.Stringer	O	J.Delsing	Bo.Kennedy	1	P.Campbell	O	H.Bauer	1	R.York	O	P.Laydon	C	L.Okrie
/C	B.Martin	/S	J.Wallaesa	/O	H.Peck	C	H.Riebe	C	S.Lollar	O	G.Binks	2S	A.Anderson	O	S.Meeks
H	T.Wright	/O	H.Adams	/O	P.Seerey	C	J.Ginsberg	C	R.Houk	/S	B.DeMars	H	J.Schultz	O	L.Culberson
H	J.Ostrowski	/O	J.Scala	/S	R.Boone	/O	J.Groth	/2	F.Crosetti	/2	N.Fox	/O	R.Coleman	/S	A.Fleitas
H	N.Sheridan	/S	F.Whitman	/3	A.Rosen	/2	J.Bero	/1	C.Silvera	/1	B.Wellman	/O	K.Wood	/S	J.Clark
				H	R.Murray	/O	E.Mierkowicz	/C	J.Collins	/C	E.Brucker	/O	G.Binks	/O	L.Drake
						/O	D.Cramer	H	B.Stewart			/1	J.McCarthy	/O	C.Vollmer
P	J.Dobson	P	B.Wight			H	J.McHale	/1	J.Phillips	P	P.Marchildon	H	T.Jordan	H	J.Difani
P	M.Parnell	P	J.Haynes	P	B.Lemon			R	L.Frey	P	J.Coleman				
P	J.Kramer	P	A.Gettel	P	B.Feller	P	H.Newhouser			P	D.Fowler	P	F.Sanford	P	E.Wynn
P	E.Kinder	P	M.Pieretti	P	G.Bearden	P	F.Hutchinson	P	A.Reynolds	P	C.Scheib	P	C.Fannin	P	W.Masterson
P	D.Galehouse	P	R.Gumpert	P	S.Gromek	P	V.Trucks	P	E.Lopat	P	L.Brissie	P	N.Garver	P	R.Scarborough
RP	E.Johnson	RP	H.Judson	P	S.Zoldak	P	D.Trout	P	V.Raschi	RP	B.Harris	P	B.Kennedy	P	S.Hudson
		RP	F.Papish	RP	E.Klieman	P	A.Houtteman	P	S.Shea	RP	B.Savage	RP	B.Stephens	P	M.Haefner
P	D.Ferriss	RP	O.Grove	P	R.Christopher	RP	S.Overmire	P	T.Byrne	P	B.McCahan	RP	F.Biscan	RP	F.Thompson
P	M.Harris			RP	D.Black	RP	B.Pierce	RP	J.Page	P	A.Kellner	RP	A.Widmar	RP	M.Candini
/P	M.McDermott	P	G.Moulder					RP	F.Hiller					RP	T.Ferrick
P	T.Hughson	P	B.Gillespie	P	S.Paige					/P	N.Potter	P	J.Ostrowski		
/P	H.Dorish	P	I.Pearson	P	B.Muncrief	P	T.Gray			/P	W.Holborow	P	S.Zoldak	P	D.Welteroth
/P	E.Caldwell	P	E.Caldwell	/P	Bi.Kennedy	P	A.Benton	P	B.Porterfield	/P	B.Dietrich	P	K.Drews	H	E.Harrist
/P	C.Stobbs	P	E.Harrist	/P	L.Linde	P	H.White	/P	R.Embree			P	R.Shore	/P	D.Weik
/P	C.Deal	/P	M.Rotblatt	/P	A.Gettel	/P	L.Kretlow	P	K.Drews			P	B.Schwamb	/P	M.Pieretti
/P	M.Palm	/P	F.Bradley	/P	M.Garcia	/P	R.Gentry	P	R.Gumpert			P	A.Gerheauser	/P	R.Garcia
/P	W.McCall	/P	J.Goodwin	/P	B.Wensloff			/P	D.Starr			P	C.Dreisewerd	/P	C.Cooper
				/P	E.Groth			/P	C.Marshall			/P	N.Potter		
				/P	L.Webber							/P	J.Wilson		

TEAM	G	W	L	PCT	GB	R	OR	AB	H	2B	3B	HR	BB	SO	AVG	OBP	SLG	PRO	PRO+	BR	/A	PF	CHI	RC	SB	CS	SBA	SBR
CLE	156	97	58	.626		840	568	5446	1534	242	54	155	646	575	.282	.360	.431	.791	119	112	134	97	97	868	54	44	55	-10
BOS	155	96	59	.619	1	907	720	5363	1471	277	40	121	823	552	.274	.374	.409	.783	109	116	72	105	104	869	38	17	69	1
NY	154	94	60	.610	2.5	857	633	5324	1480	251	75	139	623	478	.278	.356	.432	.788	116	99	107	99	103	838	24	24	50	-7
PHI	154	84	70	.545	12.5	729	735	5181	1345	231	47	68	726	523	.260	.353	.362	.715	96	-20	-21	100	102	699	40	32	56	-7
DET	154	78	76	.506	18.5	700	726	5235	1396	219	58	78	671	504	.267	.353	.375	.728	96	0	-20	103	95	723	22	32	41	-13
STL	155	59	94	.386	37	671	849	5303	1438	251	62	63	585	572	.271	.345	.378	.723	96	-21	-39	103	95	711	63	46	59	-8
WAS	154	56	97	.366	40	578	796	5111	1245	203	75	31	568	572	.244	.322	.331	.653	81	-151	-135	97	105	566	76	48	61	-6
CHI	154	51	101	.336	44.5	559	814	5192	1303	172	39	55	595	528	.251	.329	.331	.660	84	-134	-115	97	97	588	46	47	49	-14
TOT	618					5841		42155	11212	1846	450	710	5230	4304	.266	.349	.382	.731							363	288	56	-64

TEAM	CG	SH	SV	IP	H	H/G	HR	BB	SO	RAT	ERA	ERA+	OAV	OOB	PR	/A	PF	CPI	FA	E	DP	FW	PW	BW	SBW	DIF
CLE	66	26	30	1409[1]	1246	8.0	82	625	593	12.1	3.22	126	.239	.323	167	130	95	108	.982	114	183	1.4	12.6	13.0	-.2	-7.3
BOS	70	11	13	1379[1]	1445	9.4	83	592	513	13.4	4.26	103	.270	.345	4	21	102	99	.981	116	174	1.2	2.0	7.0	.9	7.4
NY	62	16	24	1365[2]	1289	8.5	94	641	654	12.9	3.75	109	.250	.336	82	51	95	104	.979	120	161	.9	4.9	10.4	.0	.6
PHI	74	7	18	1368[2]	1456	9.6	86	638	486	13.4	4.43	97	.275	.355	-21	-20	100	101	.981	113	180	1.3	-1.9	-2.0	.0	9.6
DET	60	5	22	1377	1367	8.9	92	589	678	12.9	4.15	105	.259	.335	21	33	102	95	.974	155	143	-.9	3.2	-1.9	-.5	1.2
STL	35	4	20	1373[1]	1513	9.9	103	737	531	14.9	5.01	91	.281	.371	-109	-69	106	99	.972	168	190	-1.6	-6.7	-3.8	.0	-5.4
WAS	42	4	22	1357[1]	1439	9.5	81	734	446	14.6	4.65	93	.273	.364	-55	-47	101	99	.974	154	144	-.9	-4.6	-13.1	.2	-2.2
CHI	35	2	23	1345[2]	1454	9.7	89	673	403	14.4	4.89	87	.280	.365	-90	-94	99	97	.974	160	176	-1.2	-9.1	-11.1	-.6	-3.0
TOT	444	75	172	10976[1]		9.2				13.6	4.29		.266	.349					.977	1100	1351					

Runs
Henrich-NY 138
DiMaggio-Bos 127
Williams-Bos 124
Pesky-Bos 124
Boudreau-Cle 116

Hits
Dillinger-StL 207
Mitchell-Cle 204
Boudreau-Cle 199
DiMaggio-NY 190
Williams-Bos 188

Doubles
Williams-Bos 44
Henrich-NY 42
Majeski-Phi 41
Priddy-StL 40
DiMaggio-Bos 40

Triples
Henrich-NY 14
Stewart-NY-Was 13
Yost-Was 11
Mullin-Det 11
DiMaggio-NY 11

Home Runs
DiMaggio-NY 39
Gordon-Cle 32
Keltner-Cle 31
Stephens-Bos 29
Doerr-Bos 27

Total Bases
DiMaggio-NY 355
Henrich-NY 326
Williams-Bos 313
Stephens-Bos 299
Boudreau-Cle 299

Runs Batted In
DiMaggio-NY 155
Stephens-Bos 137
Williams-Bos 127
Gordon-Cle 124
Majeski-Phi 120

Runs Produced
Williams-Bos 226
DiMaggio-NY 226
Stephens-Bos 222
Henrich-NY 213
DiMaggio-Bos 205

Bases On Balls
Williams-Bos 126
Joost-Phi 119
Fain-Phi 113
DiMaggio-Bos 101
Pesky-Bos 99

Batting Average
Williams-Bos .... .369
Boudreau-Cle .... .355
Mitchell-Cle .... .336
Zarilla-StL .... .329
McCosky-Phi .... .326

On Base Percentage
Williams-Bos .... .497
Boudreau-Cle .... .453
Appling-Chi .... .423
Goodman-Bos .... .414
Fain-Phi .... .412

Slugging Average
Williams-Bos .... .615
DiMaggio-NY .... .598
Henrich-NY .... .554
Boudreau-Cle .... .534
Keltner-Cle .... .522

Production
Williams-Bos 1.112
DiMaggio-NY 994
Boudreau-Cle 987
Henrich-NY 945
Keltner-Cle 917

Adjusted Production
Williams-Bos 185
Boudreau-Cle 166
DiMaggio-NY 164
Henrich-NY 151
Keltner-Cle 146

Batter Runs
Williams-Bos 75.7
Boudreau-Cle 52.7
DiMaggio-NY 48.6
Henrich-NY 38.9
Keltner-Cle 33.0

Adjusted Batter Runs
Williams-Bos 68.2
Boudreau-Cle 56.2
DiMaggio-NY 49.9
Henrich-NY 40.1
Keltner-Cle 36.0

Clutch Hitting Index
Platt-StL 126
Majeski-Phi 121
Goodman-Bos 120
Stephens-Bos 120
Tebbetts-Bos 119

Runs Created
Williams-Bos 172
Boudreau-Cle 143
DiMaggio-NY 140
Henrich-NY 130
Keltner-Cle 116

Total Average
Williams-Bos 1.347
Boudreau-Cle 1.058
DiMaggio-NY 1.012
Henrich-NY 955
Keltner-Cle 918

Stolen Bases
Dillinger-StL 28
Coan-Was 23
Vernon-Was 15
Mitchell-Cle 13

Stolen Base Average
Coan-Was 71.9
Dillinger-StL 71.8

Stolen Base Runs
Robertson-Was 2.4
Tucker-Cle 2.1
DiMaggio-Bos 1.8
Dillinger-StL 1.8

Fielding Runs
Pellagrini-StL 24.0
Priddy-StL 23.5
Hegan-Cle 21.3
DiMaggio-Bos 15.8
Philley-Chi 15.1

Total Player Rating
Boudreau-Cle 6.9
Williams-Bos 5.8
Priddy-StL 4.4
DiMaggio-NY 4.3
Doerr-Bos 3.6

Wins
Newhouser-Det 21
Lemon-Cle 20
Bearden-Cle 20
Raschi-NY 19
Feller-Cle 19

Win Percentage
Kramer-Bos 783
Bearden-Cle 741
Raschi-NY 704
Reynolds-NY 696

Games
Page-NY 55
Widmar-StL 49
Biscan-StL 47
Thompson-Was 46

Complete Games
Lemon-Cle 20
Newhouser-Det 19
Raschi-NY 18
Feller-Cle 18

Shutouts
Lemon-Cle 10
Raschi-NY 6
Bearden-Cle 6
Dobson-Bos 5

Saves
Christopher-Cle 17
Page-NY 16
Houtteman-Det 10
Ferrick-Was 10
Judson-Chi......... 8

Innings Pitched
Lemon-Cle 293.2
Feller-Cle 280.1
Newhouser-Det ...272.1
Dobson-Bos 245.1
Reynolds-NY ...236.1

Fewest Hits/Game
Shea-NY 6.76
Lemon-Cle 7.08
Bearden-Cle 7.33
Scarborough-Was. 8.06
Trucks-Det 8.08

Fewest BB/Game
Hutchinson-Det ... 1.95
Zoldak-StL-Cle 2.42
Lopat-NY 2.62
Kramer-Bos 2.81
Houtteman-Det ... 2.85

Strikeouts
Feller-Cle 164
Lemon-Cle 147
Newhouser-Det 143
Brissie-Phi 127
Raschi-NY 124

Strikeouts/Game
Brissie-Phi 5.89
Feller-Cle 5.27
Trucks-Det 5.23
Raschi-NY 5.01
Newhouser-Det 4.73

Ratio
Hutchinson-Det ...11.08
Lemon-Cle 11.12
Raschi-NY 11.52
Newhouser-Det ...11.53
Bearden-Cle 11.60

Earned Run Average
Bearden-Cle 2.43
Scarborough-Was .2.82
Lemon-Cle 2.82
Newhouser-Det ...3.01
Parnell-Bos 3.14

Adjusted ERA
Bearden-Cle 167
Scarborough-Was .. 154
Newhouser-Det....145
Lemon-Cle 144
Parnell-Bos 140

Opponents' Batting Avg.
Shea-NY .... .208
Lemon-Cle .... .216
Bearden-Cle ...... .229
Scarborough-Was. .233
Trucks-Det .... .240

Opponents' On Base Pct.
Hutchinson-Det ...297
Lemon-Cle .... .302
Scarborough-Was. .307
Newhouser-Det ...309
Raschi-NY .... .310

Starter Runs
Lemon-Cle 48.0
Bearden-Cle 47.5
Newhouser-Det 38.8
Scarborough-Was. 30.3
Parnell-Bos 27.1

Adjusted Starter Runs
Bearden-Cle 41.6
Newhouser-Det .. 41.1
Lemon-Cle 40.4
Scarborough-Was. 31.5
Parnell-Bos....... 29.5

Clutch Pitching Index
Bearden-Cle 132
Garver-StL 129
Fowler-Phi 119
Lopat-NY 118
Reynolds-NY 117

Relief Runs
Klieman-Cle 15.0
Christopher-Cle 9.1
Thompson-Was 6.6
Hiller-NY 1.7
Harris-Phi 1.6

Adjusted Relief Runs
Klieman-Cle 12.9
Christopher-Cle 7.6
Thompson-Was 7.4
Harris-Phi 1.6
Ferrick-Was 1.6

Relief Ranking
Christopher-Cle ...10.7
Klieman-Cle 8.8
Thompson-Was 8.6
Ferrick-Was 1.8
Harris-Phi 1.3

Total Pitcher Index
Lemon-Cle 6.8
Bearden-Cle 5.5
Newhouser-Det 4.9
Scarborough-Was. 3.8
Garver-StL 2.7

Total Baseball Ranking
Boudreau-Cle 6.9
Lemon-Cle 6.8
Williams-Bos 5.8
Bearden-Cle 5.5
Newhouser-Det 4.9

April 28 A New York fan charges Leo Durocher with assault after the Giants lose, 15–2, to Brooklyn. Commissioner Chandler suspends Durocher, but he is absolved on May 3. Chandler criticizes teams for lax security that allows fans on the field.

April 30 Rocky Nelson hits an "inside-the-glove" two-run home run in short left field to turn a ninth inning 3–1 Cubs' lead into a 4–3 Cardinals' victory. Cubs center fielder Andy Pafko's catch is ruled a trap by umpire Al Barlick, as Pafko races in, holding the ball high as runners circle the bases.

May 22 In his first major league start, Don Newcombe shuts out Cincinnati on five hits to win 3-0.

June 15 Eddie Waitkus of the Phillies is shot by 19-year-old Ruth Steinhagen at Chicago's Edgewater Beach Hotel. She will later be placed in a mental hospital. Waitkus battles for his life and will come back to play the following season.

July 8 Monte Irvin and Hank Thompson, brought up from Jersey City three days earlier, are the first blacks to play for the Giants. Thompson, who was also the first black to play for the St. Louis Browns in 1947, starts at second, and Irvin pinch hits in the eighth for Clint Hartung. When Thompson steps in against Don Newcombe, it is the first time in major league history that a black pitcher and a black hitter have faced off. The Dodgers win the game, 4–3.

July 18 Jackie Robinson testifies in front of the House Un-American Activities Committee, then, that night, scores twice, once on a steal of home, to lead the Dodgers past the Cubs, 3–0.

August 21 A barrage of bottles from the Philadelphia stands to protest a decision by umpire George Barr over a line drive trapped by Richie Ashburn results in the first forfeiture in the major leagues in seven years.

September 15 Pirates pitcher Ernie Bonham dies following an appendectomy and stomach surgery, just 18 days after his last pitching performance, an 8–2 win over the Phillies. Mrs. Bonham will receive the first benefits under the players pension plan, $90 a month for 10 years.

September 30 Ralph Kiner hits his 54th homer and 16th in September, as the Pirates beat Herm Wehmeier and the Reds 3-2.

October 2 One game back on the final day, the Cards win 13-5 over the Cubs and await the progress of the Dodgers against the Phils. The Phillies shell Don Newcombe and tie the game 7-7 in the sixth. The game goes overtime before the Dodgers get two in the 10th to win the pennant.

October 6 Another 1-0 game, and Preacher Roe wins this one for Brooklyn to knot the Series. Gil Hodges' single drives in Jackie Robinson in the second for the winner.

November 18 NL batting leader (.342) Jackie Robinson is picked for the MVP award.

December 31 The 1940s ends as the only decade in Major League Baseball history in which no new stadiums are built. After Cleveland opened Municipal Stadium in 1932, no new ballpark will be opened until County Stadium in Milwaukee is unveiled in 1953.

BOSTON		BROOKLYN		CHICAGO		CINCINNATI		NEW YORK		PHILADELPHIA		PITTSBURGH		ST.LOUIS	
M	B.Southworth	M	B.Shotton	M	C.Grimm	M	B.Walters	M	L.Durocher	M	E.Sawyer	M	B.Meyer	M	E.Dyer
M	J.Cooney	1B	G.Hodges	M	F.Frisch	M	L.Sewell	1B	J.Mize	1B	D.Sisler	1B	J.Hopp	1B	N.Jones
1B	E.Fletcher	2B	J.Robinson	1B	H.Reich	1B	T.Kluszewski	2B	H.Thompson	2B	E.Miller	2B	M.Basgall	2B	R.Schoendienst
2B	E.Stanky	SS	P.Reese	2B	E.Verban	2B	J.Bloodworth	SS	B.Kerr	SS	G.Hamner	SS	S.Rojek	SS	M.Marion
SS	A.Dark	3B	B.Cox	SS	R.Smalley	SS	V.Stallcup	3B	S.Gordon	3B	W.Jones	3B	P.Castiglione	3B	E.Kazak
3B	B.Elliott	LF	G.Hermanski	3B	F.Gustine	3B	G.Hatton	LF	W.Lockman	LF	D.Ennis	LF	R.Kiner	LF	E.Slaughter
LF	M.Rickert	CF	D.Snider	LF	B.Sauer	LF	P.Lowrey	CF	B.Thomson	CF	R.Ashburn	CF	D.Restelli	CF	C.Diering
CF	J.Russell	RF	C.Furillo	CF	A.Pafko	CF	L.Merriman	RF	W.Marshall	RF	B.Nicholson	RF	W.Westlake	RF	S.Musial
RF	T.Holmes	C	R.Campanella	RF	H.Jeffcoat	RF	J.Wyrostek	C	W.Westrum	C	A.Seminick	C	C.McCullough	C	D.Rice
C	B.Salkeld			C	M.Owen	C	W.Cooper								
		/O	M.Rackley					S2	B.Rigney	O	S.Hollmig	2	D.Murtaugh		R.Northey
O2	S.Sisti	C	B.Edwards	1O	P.Cavarretta	23	B.Adams	23	J.Lohrke	C	S.Lopata	1	E.Stevens	3	T.Glaviano
C	D.Crandall	O	M.McCormick	3S	B.Ramazzotti	O	D.Litwhiler	C	R.Mueller	1	E.Waitkus	3	E.Bockman	1	R.Nelson
O	P.Reiser	3	S.Jorgensen	O	H.Edwards	O	H.Walker	C	W.Cooper	3	M.Goliat	O	T.Saffell		J.Garagiola
O	E.Sauer	3	E.Miksis	O	R.Walker	O	H.Howell	1	J.Lafata	23	B.Blattner	O	D.Walker	S	L.Klein
3S	C.Ryan	O	L.Olmo	O	F.Baumholtz	1	H.Sauer	13	B.Haas	2	P.Caballero	C	E.FitzGerald	O	H.Rice
O	C.Conatser	O	T.Brown	O	H.Walker	C	B.Mueller	C	M.Irvin	O	P.Mayo	C	P.Masi		E.Sauer
O	J.Heath	/O	C.Abrams	2S	G.Mauch	S2	C.Corbitt	O	M.Livingston	1	E.Sanicki	1	J.Phillips	2	S.Hemus
O	P.Masi	/O	J.Hopp	C	B.Scheffing	O	F.Baumholtz	/O	D.Mueller	/O	B.Glynn	/O	W.Judnich	C	B.Baker
1	E.Torgeson	H	B.Ramazzotti	2	W.Terwilliger	2	S.Meeks	2	D.Williams	/O	J.Blatnik	/O	M.Rackley	/1	S.Bilko
C	M.Livingston	/1	C.Connors	O	P.Lowrey	1	C.Kress	2	B.Hofman	/1	K.Silvestri	/1	L.Fleming	/3	W.Kurowski
/1	R.Sanders	H	G.Shuba	O	R.Novotney	C	J.Pramesa	2	G.Hausmann	O	H.Wagner	O	T.Beard	/O	B.Howerton
/O	D.Thompson	P	D.Newcombe	/C	S.Burgess	/O	W.Post	/O	P.Milne	/3	B.Haas	/3	B.Rhawn	/C	D.Wilber
/1	A.Lakeman	P	P.Roe	3	B.Serena			/2	B.Rhawn			R	J.Cassini	H	R.Derry
H	S.Kuczek	P	J.Hatten	/3	H.Schenz	P	K.Raffensberger		A.Galan	P	K.Heintzelman			R	E.Dusak
P	W.Spahn	P	R.Branca	/1	C.Maddern	P	H.Fox	/S	R.Rufer	P	R.Roberts	P	M.Dickson		
P	J.Sain	P	J.Banta	/O	C.Aberson	P	H.Wehmeier	/C	S.Yvars	P	R.Meyer	P	B.Werle	P	H.Pollet
P	V.Bickford	RP	E.Palica	H	J.Kirby	P	J.Vander Meer	/C	H.Franks	P	H.Borowy	P	C.Chambers	P	H.Brecheen
P	B.Voiselle	RP	P.Minner	P	J.Schmitz	P	B.Lively	/S	D.Culler	P	C.Simmons	P	B.Chesnes	P	A.Brazle
P	J.Antonelli	P	R.Barney	P	B.Rush	RP	E.Erautt	P	L.Jansen	RP	J.Konstanty	P	V.Lombardi	P	R.Munger
RP	N.Potter	P	C.Erskine	P	D.Leonard	RP	E.Blackwell	RP	M.Kennedy	RP	K.Trinkle	RP	R.Sewell	P	G.Staley
RP	B.Hall	P	M.Martin	P	M.Dubiel	RP	K.Peterson	P	D.Koslo	RP	S.Rowe			RP	T.Wilks
RP	B.Hogue	/P	P.McGlothin	P	D.Lade	P	F.Fanovich	P	S.Jones	P	B.Donnelly	P	T.Bonham		
		/P	B.Podbielan	RP	B.Chipman	P	H.Gumbert	P	C.Hartung	/P	J.Thompson	P	E.Riddle	P	M.Lanier
P	G.Elliott	/P	J.Van Cuyk	RP	D.Adkins	RP	K.Burkhart	/P	K.Higbe	P	C.Bicknell	/P	J.Walsh	P	F.Martin
P	R.Barrett			RP	B.Muncrief	/P	H.Perkowski	/P	H.Behrman	/P	B.Miller	/P	H.Casey	P	J.Hearn
/P	J.Beazley			P	W.Hacker	P	J.Dobernic	/P	A.Hansen			P	B.Muncrief	P	K.Johnson
/P	C.Shoun			P	E.Kush	/P	M.Howell	P	R.Webb			P	R.Poat	P	B.Reeder
				/P	C.McLish	/P	W.Cress	/P	A.Zabala			P	H.Gumbert	P	C.Boyer
				/P	R.Hamner			/P	R.Bowman			/P	H.Gregg	/P	R.Yochim
				/P	L.Sloat			/P	A.Tomasic			/P	K.Higbe	/P	K.Krieger
				/P	J.Dobernic			/P	R.Poat						
				/P	M.Cooper										

TEAM	G	W	L	PCT	GB	R	OR	AB	H	2B	3B	HR	BB	SO	AVG	OBP	SLG	PRO	PRO+	BR	/A	PF	CHI	RC	SB	CS	SBA	SBR
BRO	156	97	57	.630		879	651	5400	1477	236	47	152	638	570	.274	.354	.419	.773	110	103	69	104	106	815	117			
STL	157	96	58	.623	1	766	616	5463	1513	281	54	102	569	482	.277	.348	.404	.752	103	61	25	105	98	777	17			
PHI	154	81	73	.526	16	662	668	5307	1349	232	55	122	528	670	.254	.325	.388	.713	100	-27	-9	97	99	674	27			
BOS	157	75	79	.487	22	706	719	5336	1376	246	33	103	684	656	.258	.345	.374	.719	105	6	45	95	97	710	28			
NY	156	73	81	.474	24	736	693	5308	1383	203	52	147	613	523	.261	.340	.401	.741	105	36	37	100	99	735	43			
PIT	154	71	83	.461	26	681	760	5214	1350	191	41	126	548	554	.259	.332	.384	.716	96	-14	-32	103	101	682	48			
CIN	156	62	92	.403	35	627	770	5469	1423	264	35	86	429	559	.260	.316	.368	.684	88	-84	-91	101	101	636	31			
CHI	154	61	93	.396	36	593	773	5214	1336	212	53	97	396	573	.256	.312	.373	.685	91	-83	-67	97	100	601	53			
TOT	622					5650		42711	11207	1865	370	935	4405	4587	.262	.334	.389	.723							364			

TEAM	CG	SH	SV	IP	H	H/G	HR	BB	SO	RAT	ERA	ERA+	OAV	OOB	PR	/A	PF	CPI	FA	E	DP	FW	PW	BW	SBW	DIF
BRO	62	15	17	1408²	1306	8.3	132	582	743	12.2	3.80	108	.246	.324	37	46	102	99	.980	122	162	1.5	4.6	6.8		7.1
STL	64	13	19	1407²	1356	8.7	87	507	606	12.1	3.44	121	.252	.319	94	113	103	101	.976	146	149	.3	11.2	2.5		5.1
PHI	58	12	15	1391²	1389	9.0	104	502	495	12.4	3.89	101	.268	.335	23	8	98	105	.974	156	141	-.5	.8	-.9		4.6
BOS	68	12	11	1400	1466	9.4	110	520	589	12.9	3.99	96	.268	.334	8	-32	94	102	.976	148	144	.1	-3.2	4.5		-3.4
NY	68	10	9	1374¹	1328	8.7	132	544	516	12.4	3.82	104	.249	.321	33	24	98	97	.973	161	134	-.6	2.4	3.7		-9.4
PIT	53	9	15	1356	1452	9.6	142	535	556	13.4	4.57	92	.274	.344	-79	-55	104	99	.978	132	173	.9	-5.5	-3.2		1.7
CIN	55	10	6	1401²	1423	9.1	124	640	538	13.4	4.34	96	.264	.345	-47	-24	104	99	.977	138	150	.6	-2.4	-9.0		-4.2
CHI	44	8	17	1357²	1487	9.9	104	575	544	13.8	4.50	90	.279	.351	-70	-71	100	100	.970	186	160	-2.1	-7.0	-6.6		-.2
TOT	472	89	109	11097²		9.1				12.8	4.04		.262	.334					.975	1189	1213					

Runs		Hits		Doubles		Triples		Home Runs		Total Bases	
Reese-Bro	132	Musial-StL	207	Musial-StL	41	Slaughter-StL	13	Kiner-Pit	54	Musial-StL	382
Musial-StL	128	Robinson-Bro	203	Ennis-Phi	39	Musial-StL	13	Musial-StL	36	Kiner-Pit	361
Robinson-Bro	122	Thomson-NY	198	Robinson-Bro	38	Robinson-Bro	12	Sauer-Cin-Chi	31	Thomson-NY	332
Kiner-Pit	116	Slaughter-StL	191	Hatton-Cin	38	Ennis-Phi	11	Thomson-NY	27	Ennis-Phi	320
Schoendienst-StL	102	Schoendienst-StL	190			Ashburn-Phi	11	Gordon-NY	26	Robinson-Bro	313

Runs Batted In		Runs Produced		Bases On Balls		Batting Average		On Base Percentage		Slugging Average	
Kiner-Pit	127	Robinson-Bro	230	Kiner-Pit	117	Robinson-Bro	.342	Musial-StL	.438	Kiner-Pit	.658
Robinson-Bro	124	Musial-StL	215	Reese-Bro	116	Musial-StL	.338	Robinson-Bro	.432	Musial-StL	.624
Musial-StL	123	Reese-Bro	189	Stanky-Bos	113	Slaughter-StL	.336	Kiner-Pit	.432	Robinson-Bro	.528
Hodges-Bro	115	Kiner-Pit	189	Musial-StL	107	Furillo-Bro	.322	Slaughter-StL	.418	Ennis-Phi	.525
Ennis-Phi	110	Hodges-Bro	186	Gordon-NY	95	Kiner-Pit	.310	Stanky-Bos	.417	Thomson-NY	.518

Production		Adjusted Production		Batter Runs		Adjusted Batter Runs		Clutch Hitting Index		Runs Created	
Kiner-Pit	1.089	Kiner-Pit	183	Musial-StL	72.4	Kiner-Pit	66.2	Robinson-Bro	130	Musial-StL	173
Musial-StL	1.062	Musial-StL	174	Kiner-Pit	70.0	Musial-StL	65.3	Marion-StL	117	Kiner-Pit	163
Robinson-Bro	.960	Robinson-Bro	150	Robinson-Bro	49.9	Robinson-Bro	44.5	Russell-Bos	116	Robinson-Bro	135
Slaughter-StL	.929	Gordon-NY	142	Slaughter-StL	40.1	Slaughter-StL	34.8	Hodges-Bro	116	Slaughter-StL	127
Gordon-NY	.909	Slaughter-StL	141	Gordon-NY	31.6	Ennis-Phi	32.3	Cooper-NY-Cin	114	Ennis-Phi	118

Total Average		Stolen Bases		Stolen Base Average		Stolen Base Runs		Fielding Runs		Total Player Rating	
Kiner-Pit	1.247	Robinson-Bro	37					Ashburn-Phi	24.7	Kiner-Pit	5.6
Musial-StL	1.185	Reese-Bro	26					Schoendienst-StL	24.0	Robinson-Bro	4.9
Robinson-Bro	1.078							Thomson-NY	19.5	Musial-StL	3.8
Slaughter-StL	.971							Marion-StL	16.6	Thomson-NY	3.6
Gordon-NY	.925							Reich-Chi	14.1	B.Elliott-Bos	3.5

Wins		Win Percentage		Games		Complete Games		Shutouts		Saves	
Spahn-Bos	21	Roe-Bro	.714	Wilks-StL	59	Spahn-Bos	25	Raffensberger-Cin	5	Wilks-StL	9
Pollet-StL	20	Pollet-StL	.690	Konstanty-Phi	53	Raffensberger-Cin	20	Pollet-StL	5	Potter-Bos	7
Raffensberger-Cin	18	Newcombe-Bro	.680	Palica-Bro	49	Newcombe-Bro	19	Newcombe-Bro	5	Konstanty-Phi	7
		Meyer-Phi	.680	Banta-Bro	48	Pollet-StL	17	Heintzelman-Phi	5	Staley-StL	6
		Munger-StL	.652	Muncrief-Pit-Chi	47	Jansen-NY	17			Palica-Bro	6

Innings Pitched		Fewest Hits/Game		Fewest BB/Game		Strikeouts		Strikeouts/Game		Ratio	
Spahn-Bos	302.1	Staley-StL	8.09	Koslo-NY	1.83	Spahn-Bos	151	Newcombe-Bro	5.49	Koslo-NY	10.02
Raffensberger-Cin	284.0	Koslo-NY	8.19	Roe-Bro	1.86	Newcombe-Bro	149	Branca-Bro	5.26	Staley-StL	10.40
Jansen-NY	259.2	Newcombe-Bro	8.21	Werle-Pit	2.08	Jansen-NY	113	Chambers-Pit	4.72	Roe-Bro	10.45
Heintzelman-Phi	250.0	Kennedy-NY	8.38	Jansen-NY	2.15	Roe-Bro	109	Roe-Bro	4.61	Newcombe-Bro	11.01
Newcombe-Bro	244.1	Meyer-Phi	8.41	Leonard-Chi	2.15	Branca-Bro	109	Spahn-Bos	4.50	Spahn-Bos	11.07

Earned Run Average		Adjusted ERA		Opponents' Batting Avg.		Opponents' On Base Pct.		Starter Runs		Adjusted Starter Runs	
Koslo-NY	2.50	Koslo-NY	159	Staley-StL	.238	Koslo-NY	.278	Koslo-NY	36.2	Pollet-StL	35.7
Staley-StL	2.73	Staley-StL	152	Koslo-NY	.239	Staley-StL	.286	Spahn-Bos	32.7	Koslo-NY	34.8
Pollet-StL	2.77	Pollet-StL	150	Kennedy-NY	.242	Roe-Bro	.293	Pollet-StL	32.6	Roe-Bro	30.9
Roe-Bro	2.79	Roe-Bro	147	Newcombe-Bro	.243	Spahn-Bos	.299	Roe-Bro	29.5	Staley-StL	27.2
Heintzelman-Phi	3.02	Brazle-StL	131	Spahn-Bos	.245	Newcombe-Bro	.301	Heintzelman-Phi	28.2	Heintzelman-Phi	25.5

Clutch Pitching Index		Relief Runs		Adjusted Relief Runs		Relief Ranking		Total Pitcher Index		Total Baseball Ranking	
Roe-Bro	126	Erautt-Cin	8.6	Erautt-Cin	10.3	Erautt-Cin	12.6	Pollet-StL	4.2	Kiner-Pit	5.6
Heintzelman-Phi	123	Konstanty-Phi	8.5	Konstanty-Phi	7.5	Konstanty-Phi	11.0	Koslo-NY	4.2	Robinson-Bro	4.9
Brazle-StL	121	Hogue-Bos	7.3	Wilks-StL	5.7	Palica-Bro	8.9	Staley-StL	3.5	Pollet-StL	4.2
Jones-NY	116	Palica-Bro	4.5	Hogue-Bos	5.2	Wilks-StL	6.6	Dickson-Pit	3.0	Koslo-NY	4.2
Dickson-Pit	113	Wilks-StL	4.1	Palica-Bro	5.2	Hogue-Bos	3.1	Newcombe-Bro	2.8	Musial-StL	3.8

March 1 The Browns, owners of Sportsman's Park, move to evict the Cardinals in order to gain a rental increase.

April 19 At pregame ceremonies marking the season opener in Yankee Stadium, a granite monument to Babe Ruth is unveiled in center field. Plaques honoring Lou Gehrig and Miller Huggins are also presented.

May 5 Tigers second baseman Charlie Gehringer is picked for the Hall of Fame. Two days later, the Old-Timers Committee will select Kid Nichols and Three-Finger Brown.

May 6 Nine hitless innings in relief are thrown by A's rookie Bobby Shantz in a 13-inning, 5-4, Athletics' win over the Tigers. Shantz gives up a run in the 13th, but old-timer Wally Moses saves him with a two-run home run.

May 27 The Indians start so badly, 12-17, that owner Bill Veeck arranges a "Second Opening Day."

July 12 The NL commits five errors, allowing the AL to record an 11-7 triumph in the All-Star Game at Ebbets Field. The contest marks the first appearance of black players—Jackie Robinson, Roy Campanella, and Don Newcombe in the NL lineup and Larry Doby among the AL stars.

August 6 Luke Appling appears as shortstop in his 2,154th game, surpassing Rabbit Maranville's major league mark. Appling will finish his career with 2,218.

September 26 Before 67,434 at Yankee Stadium, the Red Sox survive a rhubarb-filled, 7-6 win when Johnny Pesky scores on a disputed squeeze play. Leading by one game, the Sox move on to Washington for a 3-game series before the last two games of the year with the Yankees.

October 2 The New York Yankees and the Boston Red Sox enter the final day of the season tied for first place. Nearly 70,000 pack Yankee Stadium to see the finale. Vic Raschi nurses a 1-0 lead into the eighth against Ellis Kinder before the Yankees score four against a tired Mel Parnell and an unlucky Tex Hughson. A Sox rally falls short, and the Yankees win the game and the pennant 5-3. Ted Williams is hitless in two official trips, while George Kell of the Tigers goes 2-for-3. Kell's final mark is .3429 and Williams's is .3427.

October 5 In the Series opener at the Stadium, the New York Yankees and Allie Reynolds beat the Brooklyn Dodgers 1-0 on Tommy Henrich's ninth-inning home run off Don Newcombe. Newcombe had struck out 11 and walked none before Henrich's blast.

October 9 The Yankees pound the Dodgers 10-6 to win the World Series in five games. Pinch hitter and third baseman Bobby Brown is the hitting hero, batting .500 and driving in five runs.

October 29 In arguably their best trade ever, the White Sox send catcher Joe Tipton, who hit .204 in his one season in Chicago, to the Athletics for young Nellie Fox.

November 21 Bill Veeck sells the Indians for $2.2 million to a local syndicate headed by Ellis Ryan. Hank Greenberg will be general manager.

November 25 Ted Williams, who lost the Triple Crown when his batting average was .0002 below that of George Kell, wins the MVP vote in a landslide. Phil Rizzuto and Joe Page finish second and third in the voting.

December 12 By a 7-1 vote, the AL rejects a proposal to bring back the legal spitball. The rules committee also alters the strike zone to the space between the armpits and the top of the knees.

BOSTON	CHICAGO	CLEVELAND	DETROIT	NEW YORK	PHILADELPHIA	ST.LOUIS	WASHINGTON
M J.McCarthy	M J.Onslow	M L.Boudreau	M R.Rolfe	M C.Stengel	M C.Mack	M Z.Taylor	M J.Kuhel
1B B.Goodman	1B C.Kress	1B M.Vernon	1B P.Campbell	1B T.Henrich	1B F.Fain	1B J.Graham	1B E.Robinson
2B B.Doerr	2B C.Michaels	2B J.Gordon	2B N.Berry	2B J.Coleman	2B P.Suder	2B J.Priddy	2B A.Kozar
SS V.Stephens	SS L.Appling	SS L.Boudreau	SS J.Lipon	SS P.Rizzuto	SS E.Joost	SS E.Pellagrini	SS S.Dente
3B J.Pesky	3B F.Baker	3B K.Keltner	3B G.Kell	3B B.Brown	3B H.Majeski	3B B.Dillinger	3B B.Yost
LF T.Williams	LF G.Zernial	LF D.Mitchell	LF H.Evers	LF G.Woodling	LF E.Valo	LF R.Sievers	LF B.Stewart
CF D.DiMaggio	CF C.Metkovich	CF L.Doby	CF J.Groth	CF C.Mapes	CF S.Chapman	CF S.Spence	CF C.Vollmer
RF A.Zarilla	RF D.Philley	RF B.Kennedy	RF V.Wertz	RF H.Bauer	RF W.Moses	RF D.Kokos	RF B.Lewis
C B.Tebbetts	C D.Wheeler	C J.Hegan	C A.Robinson	C Y.Berra	C M.Guerra	C S.Lollar	C A.Evans
C M.Batts	O1 S.Souchock	S R.Boone	21 D.Kolloway	31 B.Johnson	2 N.Fox	O1 P.Lehner	O G.Coan
1 B.Hitchcock	O H.Adams	O T.Tucker	S2 E.Lake	O J.DiMaggio	O D.White	C L.Moss	23 S.Robertson
O T.O'Brien	C J.Tipton	3 J.Berardino	O P.Mullin	O J.Lindell	O T.Wright	S3 J.Sullivan	O1 S.Mele
O S.Mele	C E.Malone	O A.Clark	C B.Swift	1 D.Kryhoski	C J.Astroth	S A.Anderson	C J.Early
1 W.Dropo	O J.Ostrowski	3 L.Easter	1 G.Vico	2 S.Stirnweiss	S3 T.Davis	O A.Zarilla	O R.Ortiz
/2 L.Stringer	1 G.Goldsberry	C M.Tresh	O D.Wakefield	C C.Silvera	/O A.Galan	O G.Elder	3 M.Christman
/3 M.Combs	O J.Scala	/O H.Peck	C H.Riebe	O J.Phillips	/1 H.Biasatti	/2 O.Friend	O J.Simmons
/O S.Spence	O B.Bowers	/O M.Minoso	H J.Outlaw	C G.Niarhos	/O B.Estalella	/S A.Naples	O R.Weigel
H T.Wright	3 B.Rhawn	/O H.Edwards	H D.Lund	/1 F.Mole	P A.Kellner	/O K.Wood	H H.Keller
/C B.Martin	3 R.Krsnich	/2 B.Avila	R B.Mavis	/1 J.Mize	P J.Coleman	H H.Arft	H H.Reich
P M.Parnell	O E.Rapp	/O M.Nielsen	H E.Rapp	/O J.Delsing	P L.Brissie	H F.Pack	/2 J.Difani
P E.Kinder	S F.Hancock	/O H.Reich	P H.Newhouser	/1 J.Collins	P D.Fowler	P N.Garver	P S.Hudson
P J.Dobson	O D.Lane	R F.Marsh	P V.Trucks	/C R.Houk	P C.Scheib	P B.Kennedy	P R.Scarborough
P C.Stobbs	/O B.Higdon	P B.Lemon	P A.Houtteman	H M.Witek	RP B.Harris	P C.Fannin	P P.Calvert
P J.Kramer	/C G.Yankowski	P B.Feller	P T.Gray	P V.Raschi	P B.Shantz	P A.Papai	P M.Harris
RP T.Hughson	/S J.Baumer	P M.Garcia	P F.Hutchinson	P E.Lopat	/P B.McCahan	P J.Ostrowski	P L.Hittle
RP E.Johnson	/3 D.Kolloway	P E.Wynn	RP D.Trout	P A.Reynolds	/P P.Marchildon	RP T.Ferrick	RP J.Haynes
P M.McDermott	/O P.Seerey	P A.Benton	P L.Kretlow	P T.Byrne	/P J.Wilson	RP D.Starr	RP D.Welteroth
P W.Masterson	P B.Wight	RP S.Paige	P M.Grissom	P F.Sanford	/P C.Hausmann	P K.Drews	P D.Weik
/P M.Harris	P R.Gumpert	RP F.Papish	P M.Stuart	RP J.Page		P R.Embree	P M.Haefner
/P F.Quinn	P B.Pierce	RP S.Zoldak	P S.Overmire	RP S.Shea		P R.Shore	P W.Masterson
/P W.McCall	P B.Kuzava	P G.Bearden	/P H.White	RP C.Marshall		P R.Winegarner	P A.Gettel
/P H.Dorish	P H.Judson	P S.Gromek	/P S.Rogovin	P B.Porterfield		/P R.Raney	P J.Gonzalez
/P D.Ferriss	RP M.Pieretti			P D.Pillette		/P B.Malloy	/P F.Thompson
P J.Robinson	RP M.Surkont			P R.Buxton		/P B.Savage	/P M.Candini
/P D.Galehouse	P M.Haefner			/P H.Casey		/P E.Albrecht	/P B.Dozier
/P J.Wittig	P A.Gettel			/P F.Hiller		/P I.Medlinger	/P J.Pearce
	P E.Klieman			/P W.Hood		/P J.Bilbrey	/P E.Klieman
	P C.Shoun						/P D.Sutherland
	/P B.Cain						
	/P J.Bruner						
	/P B.Evans						
	/P E.Groth						
	/P A.Carrasquel						
	/P F.Bradley						
	/P O.Grove						

TEAM	G	W	L	PCT	GB	R	OR	AB	H	2B	3B	HR	BB	SO	AVG	OBP	SLG	PRO	PRO+	BR	/A	PF	CHI	RC	SB	CS	SBA	SBR
NY	155	97	57	.630		829	637	5196	1396	215	60	115	731	539	.269	.362	.400	.762	108	58	58	100	**106**	790	58	30	**66**	-1
BOS	155	96	58	.623	1	**896**	667	5320	**1500**	272	36	**131**	**835**	510	**.282**	**.381**	**.420**	**.801**	111	147	83	107	100	**890**	43	25	63	-2
CLE	154	89	65	.578	8	675	**574**	5221	1358	194	58	112	601	534	.260	.339	.384	.723	99	-30	-16	98	99	696	44	40	52	-11
DET	155	87	67	.565	10	751	655	5259	1405	215	51	88	751	502	.267	.361	.384	.739	102	20	18	100	99	739	39	52	43	-20
PHI	154	81	73	.526	16	726	725	5123	1331	214	49	82	783	493	.260	.361	.369	.730	104	6	31	97	99	719	36	25	59	-4
CHI	154	63	91	.409	34	648	737	5204	1340	207	**66**	43	702	596	.257	.347	.347	.694	93	-66	-45	97	99	657	**62**	55	53	-14
STL	155	53	101	.344	44	667	913	5112	1301	213	30	117	631	700	.254	.339	.377	.716	92	-41	-69	104	101	670	38	39	49	-12
WAS	154	50	104	.325	47	584	868	5234	1330	207	41	81	593	495	.254	.333	.356	.689	90	-93	-80	98	95	640	46	33	58	-6
TOT	618					5776		41669	10961	1737	391	769	5627	4369	.263	.353	.379	.732							366	299	55	-70

TEAM	CG	SH	SV	IP	H	H/G	HR	BB	SO	RAT	ERA	ERA+	OAV	OOB	PR	/A	PF	CPI	FA	E	DP	FW	PW	BW	SBW	DIF
NY	59	12	**36**	1371.1	**1231**	8.1	98	812	671	13.6	3.69	110	**.242**	.351	77	54	96	**107**	.977	138	195	.0	5.3	5.6	**.7**	8.3
BOS	84	16	16	1377	1375	9.0	82	661	598	13.5	3.97	110	.262	.347	34	59	104	101	.980	120	207	1.1	5.7	**8.1**	**.7**	3.4
CLE	65	10	19	1383.2	1275	8.3	82	**611**	631	12.4	3.36	119	.247	.329	129	98	104		**.983**	103	192	2.1	**9.5**	-1.6	-.2	2.2
DET	70	19	12	1393.2	1338	8.6	102	628	631	12.8	3.77	110	.254	.335	66	60	99	100	.978	131	174	.4	5.8	1.8	-1.1	3.1
PHI	**85**	9	11	1365	1359	9.0	105	758	490	14.1	4.23	97	.263	.360	-5	-19	98	103	.976	140	**217**	-.1	-1.8	3.0	.5	2.5
CHI	57	10	17	1363.1	1362	9.0	108	693	502	13.7	4.30	97	.264	.353	-15	-19	99	99	.977	141	180	-.2	-1.8	-4.4	-.5	-7.0
STL	43	3	16	1341.1	1583	10.6	113	685	432	15.4	5.21	87	.294	.377	-151	-102	108	99	.971	166	154	-1.6	-9.9	-6.7	-.3	-5.4
WAS	44	9	9	1345.2	1438	9.6	**79**	779	451	15.0	5.10	84	.276	.373	-134	-126	101	91	.973	161	168	-1.4	-12.3	-7.8	.3	-5.8
TOT	507	88	136	10941		9.0				13.8	4.20		.263	.353					.977	1100	1487					

Runs
Williams-Bos 150
Joost-Phi 128
DiMaggio-Bos 126
Stephens-Bos 113
Pesky-Bos 111

Hits
Mitchell-Cle 203
Williams-Bos 194
DiMaggio-Bos 186
Wertz-Det 185
Pesky-Bos 185

Doubles
Williams-Bos 39
Kell-Det 38
DiMaggio-Bos 34
Zarilla-StL-Bos 33
Stephens-Bos 31

Triples
Mitchell-Cle 23
Dillinger-StL 13
Valo-Phi 12

Home Runs
Williams-Bos 43
Stephens-Bos 39

Total Bases
Williams-Bos 368
Stephens-Bos 329
Wertz-Det 283
Mitchell-Cle 274
Doerr-Bos 269

Runs Batted In
Williams-Bos 159
Stephens-Bos 159
Wertz-Det 133
Doerr-Bos 109
Chapman-Phi 108

Runs Produced
Williams-Bos 266
Stephens-Bos 233
Wertz-Det 209
Joost-Phi 186
Doerr-Bos 182

Bases On Balls
Williams-Bos 162
Joost-Phi 149
Fain-Phi 136
Appling-Chi 121
Valo-Phi 119

Batting Average
Kell-Det 343
Williams-Bos 343
Dillinger-StL 324
Mitchell-Cle 317
Doerr-Bos 309

On Base Percentage
Williams-Bos 490
Appling-Chi 439
Joost-Phi 429
Kell-Det 424
Michaels-Chi 417

Slugging Average
Williams-Bos 650
Stephens-Bos 539
Henrich-NY 526
Doerr-Bos 497
Berra-NY 480

Production
Williams-Bos 1.141
Henrich-NY 942
Stephens-Bos 930
Kell-Det 892
Doerr-Bos 890

Adjusted Production
Williams-Bos 187
Henrich-NY 148
Joost-Phi 138
Kell-Det 136
Stephens-Bos 135

Batter Runs
Williams-Bos 88.9
Stephens-Bos 36.9
Joost-Phi 31.9
DiMaggio-NY 31.7
Henrich-NY 29.7

Adjusted Batter Runs
Williams-Bos 76.6
Joost-Phi 35.8
DiMaggio-NY 31.7
Henrich-NY 29.7
Stephens-Bos 28.3

Clutch Hitting Index
Fain-Phi 143
Lipon-Det 124
Valo-Phi 124
Wertz-Det 121
Williams-Bos 120

Runs Created
Williams-Bos 193
Stephens-Bos 132
Joost-Phi 119
DiMaggio-Bos 110
Wertz-Det 110

Total Average
Williams-Bos 1.347
Henrich-NY 1.017
Joost-Phi 995
Stephens-Bos 947
Kell-Det 877

Stolen Bases
Dillinger-StL 20
Rizzuto-NY 18
Valo-Phi 14
Philley-Chi 13

Stolen Base Average
Rizzuto-NY 75.0
Dillinger-StL 58.8

Stolen Base Runs
Tebbetts-Bos 1.8
Rizzuto-NY 1.8
Mapes-NY 1.8
Fain-Phi 1.8
Philley-Chi 1.5

Fielding Runs
Doerr-Bos 27.8
Pesky-Bos 21.4
Vernon-Cle 18.8
DiMaggio-Bos 14.3
Baker-Chi 11.8

Total Player Rating
Williams-Bos 6.7
Joost-Phi 5.2
Doerr-Bos 5.0
Stephens-Bos 4.1
Michaels-Chi 3.9

Wins
Parnell-Bos 25
Kinder-Bos 23
Lemon-Cle 22
Raschi-NY 21
Kellner-Phi 20

Win Percentage
Kinder-Bos 793
Parnell-Bos 781
Reynolds-NY 739
Lemon-Cle 688

Games
Page-NY 60
Welteroth-Was 52
Ferrick-StL 50
Kennedy-StL 48
Surkont-Chi 44

Complete Games
Parnell-Bos 27
Newhouser-Det 22
Lemon-Cle 22
Raschi-NY 21

Shutouts
Trucks-Det 6
Kinder-Bos 6
Garcia-Cle 5

Saves
Page-NY 27
Benton-Cle 10
Ferrick-StL 6
Paige-Cle 5

Innings Pitched
Parnell-Bos 295.1
Newhouser-Det 292.0
Lemon-Cle 279.2
Trucks-Det 275.0
Raschi-NY 274.2

Fewest Hits/Game
Byrne-NY 5.74
Lemon-Cle 6.79
Trucks-Det 6.84
Gray-Det 7.52
Pierce-Chi 7.60

Fewest BB/Game
Hutchinson-Det . . . 2.48
Houtteman-Det 2.61
Lopat-NY 2.88
Garcia-Cle 3.07
Wynn-Cle 3.12

Strikeouts
Trucks-Det 153
Newhouser-Det 144
Lemon-Cle 138
Kinder-Bos 138
Byrne-NY 129

Strikeouts/Game
Byrne-NY 5.92
Trucks-Det 5.01
Pierce-Chi 4.98
Kinder-Bos 4.93
Garcia-Cle 4.82

Ratio
Hutchinson-Det . . . 10.49
Trucks-Det 11.03
Garcia-Cle 11.07
Lemon-Cle 11.39
Gumpert-Chi 11.81

Earned Run Average
Garcia-Cle 2.36
Parnell-Bos 2.77
Trucks-Det 2.81
Hutchinson-Det . . . 2.96
Lemon-Cle 2.99

Adjusted ERA
Garcia-Cle 169
Parnell-Bos 157
Trucks-Det 148
Hutchinson-Det 141
Lemon-Cle 133

Opponents' Batting Avg.
Byrne-NY 183
Lemon-Cle 211
Trucks-Det 211
Gray-Det 227
Pierce-Chi 228

Opponents' On Base Pct.
Hutchinson-Det 290
Trucks-Det 301
Garcia-Cle 308
Lemon-Cle 309
Gumpert-Chi 318

Starter Runs
Parnell-Bos 46.7
Trucks-Det 42.3
Lemon-Cle 37.4
Garcia-Cle 35.9
Benton-Cle 31.3

Adjusted Starter Runs
Parnell-Bos 52.1
Trucks-Det 41.1
Garcia-Cle 31.9
Lemon-Cle 31.0
Benton-Cle 28.2

Clutch Pitching Index
Garcia-Cle 123
Lopat-NY 122
Wight-Chi 118
Houtteman-Det 115
Kinder-Bos 114

Relief Runs
Page-NY 24.1
Paige-Cle 10.7
Papish-Cle 6.9
Ferrick-StL 3.7

Adjusted Relief Runs
Page-NY 21.8
Paige-Cle 8.8
Ferrick-StL 7.5
Papish-Cle 5.5
Starr-StL 1.9

Relief Ranking
Page-NY 40.3
Paige-Cle 11.7
Ferrick-StL 7.4
Starr-StL 1.7
Papish-Cle 1.0

Total Pitcher Index
Lemon-Cle 5.7
Parnell-Bos 5.5
Page-NY 3.8
Garcia-Cle 3.6
Hutchinson-Det 3.4

Total Baseball Ranking
Williams-Bos 6.7
Lemon-Cle 5.7
Parnell-Bos 5.5
Joost-Phi 5.2
Doerr-Bos 5.0

January 23 The Associated Press picks the "Miracle Braves" of 1914 as the greatest sports upset of the century.

April 18 The first Opening Day night game is played in St. Louis with the Cardinals defeating the Pirates 4-2.

July 4 Braves slugger Sid Gordon ties the major league season grand slam record with four when he hits one against the Phillies. Boston's 12–9 win in the second game of a twinbill means totals of 40 runs, 55 hits, and 90 total bases for the day.

July 11 Making a leaping, off-the-wall catch of a Ralph Kiner drive, Ted Williams fractures his left elbow in the All-Star game at Chicago. Remaining in the game, he puts the AL ahead, 3-2, with an RBI single. Kiner's ninth-inning home run evens up the game, and Red Schoendienst's blast in the 14th wins it.

July 26 Brooklyn beats the Cardinals 7-5 as the Dodgers' Jim Russell switch hits home runs, making him the first switch hitter in history to do it more than once.

August 16 Henry Thompson of the Giants hits two inside the park, against the Dodgers at the Polo Grounds. He's the first player to do this since Terry Moore hit two for the Cardinals at Forbes Field on this date in 1939.

August 19 The Gillette Safety Razor Co. pays $800,000 for TV rights to the World Series. Radio rights will add another $175,000 more.

September 26 Phils' relief ace Jim Konstanty makes his 71st appearance, a major league record, in the Phils' 8-7 win over the Braves in front of 1,987 Boston fans.

October 1 Dick Sisler's dramatic home run off Don Newcombe in the 10th clinches the pennant 4-1 for the Whiz Kids. It is the Phillies' first pennant in 35 years. In the play that sets the stage for Sisler's heroics, center fielder Richie Ashburn throws out Dodger runner Cal Abrams at the plate in the bottom of the ninth.

October 3 Baseball rules that Phils lefty Curt Simmons cannot play in the World Series despite his being on furlough from the Army.

October 4 Relief ace Jim Konstanty of the Phils starts and loses to Vic Raschi and the Yankees in Philadelphia 1-0 in Game 1 of the World Series. Bobby Brown doubles and comes around on two long flies to score the lone run.

October 16 The Brooklyn Dodgers fail to renew Branch Rickey's contract as president.

November 2 The baseball writers select Phillies relief pitcher Jim Konstanty as the NL's MVP.

November 6 After his contract as Dodger president is not renewed, Branch Rickey sells his 25 percent interest in the club for a reported $1.05 million and signs a five-year contract as executive vice president/GM with the Pittsburgh Pirates.

November 9 The baseball writers name Sam Jethroe of the Boston Braves as the NL Rookie of the Year.

December 11 At the winter meeting, held in St. Petersburg, Florida major league owners vote, 9-7, against renewing Commissioner Happy Chandler's contract for a new term, starting in 1951. The Cardinals' Fred Saigh led the opposition to Chandler, who had jeopardized the reserve clause and ordered investigations of the alleged gambling activities of several owners.

December 12 The owners vote to drop the four-year old bonus and high school rule. This rule, passed to prevent the wealthy clubs from buying up all the talent, required that "bonus" players must stay on the major league roster after just one season in the minors.

BOSTON	BROOKLYN	CHICAGO	CINCINNATI	NEW YORK	PHILADELPHIA	PITTSBURGH	ST.LOUIS
M B.Southworth	M B.Shotton	M F.Frisch	M L.Sewell	M L.Durocher	M E.Sawyer	M B.Meyer	M E.Dyer
1B E.Torgeson	1B G.Hodges	1B P.Ward	1B T.Kluszewski	1B T.Gilbert	1B E.Waitkus	1B J.Hopp	1B R.Nelson
2B R.Hartsfield	2B J.Robinson	2B W.Terwilliger	2B C.Ryan	2B E.Stanky	2B M.Goliat	2B D.Murtaugh	2B R.Schoendienst
SS B.Kerr	SS P.Reese	SS R.Smalley	SS V.Stallcup	SS A.Dark	SS G.Hamner	SS S.Rojek	SS M.Marion
3B B.Elliott	3B B.Cox	3B B.Serena	3B G.Hatton	3B H.Thompson	3B W.Jones	3B N.Fernandez	3B T.Glaviano
LF S.Gordon	LF G.Hermanski	LF H.Sauer	LF J.Adcock	LF W.Lockman	LF D.Sisler	LF R.Kiner	LF S.Musial
CF S.Jethroe	CF D.Snider	CF A.Pafko	CF B.Usher	CF B.Thomson	CF R.Ashburn	CF W.Westlake	CF B.Howerton
RF T.Holmes	RF C.Furillo	RF B.Borkowski	RF J.Wyrostek	RF D.Mueller	RF D.Ennis	RF G.Bell	RF E.Slaughter
C W.Cooper	C R.Campanella	C M.Owen	C D.Howell	C W.Westrum	C A.Seminick	C C.McCullough	C D.Rice
O W.Marshall	O J.Russell	1 P.Cavarretta	23 B.Adams	O M.Irvin	O D.Whitman	3S P.Castiglione	3 C.Diering
C D.Crandall	3S B.Morgan	23 R.Walker	O L.Merriman	1O B.Rigney	3S S.Lopata	S3 D.O'Connell	3 E.Kazak
O L.Olmo	C B.Edwards	O C.Mauro	O P.Lowrey	23 R.Weatherly	3 J.Bloodworth	3 B.Dillinger	S E.Miller
2 G.Mauch	O G.Shuba	O H.Jeffcoat	C J.Pramesa	O J.Lohrke	1 B.Nicholson	1 J.Phillips	O H.Walker
S2 S.Sisti	23 T.Brown	O B.Ramazzotti	O D.Litwhiler	S J.Maguire	O J.Mayo	O T.Saffell	O H.Rice
O P.Reiser	2S E.Miksis	O R.Northey	S S.Meeks	/O J.Jorgensen	P P.Caballero	O T.Beard	O J.Lindell
2 C.Ryan	O C.Abrams	O R.Jackson	O R.Northey	/3 S.Jorgensen	/C K.Silvestri	C R.Mueller	C J.Garagiola
/O B.Addis	/1 W.Belardi	O H.Edwards	C W.Cooper	/1 J.Harshman	2 S.Hollmig	2 J.Berardino	/P P.Lowrey
/C P.Burris	/C S.Lembo	C C.Sawatski	C B.Scheffing	/O S.Yvars	1 J.Blatnik	1 D.Coogan	C J.Bucha
/C W.Linden	/3 S.Jorgensen	O E.Verban	/2 J.Bloodworth	/C R.Mueller		23 H.Schenz	/1 S.Bilko
/2 E.Verban		/C B.Scheffing	/C H.Landrith	/S R.Rufer	P R.Roberts	C E.Turner	/1 N.Jones
	P D.Newcombe	/C H.Chiti	H T.Tappe	M M.McCormick	C C.Simmons	1 E.Stevens	/O J.Blatnik
	P P.Roe		H M.Rackley	H P.Milne	S B.Miller	S G.Strickland	/3 S.Hemus
P V.Bickford	P E.Palica	P B.Rush	/O J.Bolger	H M.Blaylock	P R.Meyer	/O M.Rickert	1 D.Bollweg
P W.Spahn	P R.Branca	P J.Schmitz		/1 N.Reyes	P B.Church	/C E.FitzGerald	/1 E.Mickelson
P J.Sain	P D.Bankhead	P P.Minner	P E.Blackwell		RP J.Konstanty		H D.Gardella
P B.Chipman		P F.Hiller	P K.Raffensberger	P L.Jansen		P C.Chambers	H E.Mierkowicz
RP B.Hogue	P C.Erskine	P M.Dubiel	P H.Wehmeier	S S.Maglie		P M.Dickson	
RP J.Antonelli	P B.Podbielan	RP J.Vander Meer	P H.Fox	S S.Jones	P K.Heintzelman	P B.Werle	P H.Pollet
RP B.Hall	P J.Hatten	RP D.Leonard	P W.Ramsdell	P D.Koslo	P K.Johnson	P B.Macdonald	P M.Lanier
	P J.Banta	RP B.Voiselle	RP F.Smith	P J.Hearn	P M.Candini	P V.Law	P G.Staley
P N.Roy	P R.Barney		RP E.Erautt	RP J.Kramer	P B.Donnelly	RP V.Lombardi	P A.Brazle
/P M.Surkont	P C.Van Cuyk	P D.Lade	RP J.Hetki	RP A.Hansen	P H.Borowy	RP J.Walsh	P H.Brecheen
P D.Donovan	P B.Loes	P J.Klippstein		/P J.Brittin	P P.Stuffel		RP F.Martin
/P M.Haefner	/P A.Epperly	/P W.Hacker	P H.Perkowski		/P J.Thompson	P M.Queen	
P E.Johnson	/P J.Landrum	/P A.Varga	/P K.Peterson	P M.Kennedy	/P S.Ridzik	/P B.Chesnes	P R.Munger
/P D.Cole	/P W.Ramsdell		P B.Byerly	P C.Hartung		P B.Pierro	P C.Boyer
/P M.Wall	/P J.Romano		P J.Avrea	P K.Higbe		P H.Borowy	P E.Dusak
/P B.Walters	/P C.Labine			P G.Spencer		P W.Main	P T.Wilks
/P D.Manville	/P P.McGlothin					/P W.McCall	P A.Papai
	/P M.Mallette					/P H.Gregg	P T.Poholsky
						/P F.Barrett	/P J.Hearn
						/P H.Gumbert	/P K.Johnson
						/P F.Papish	/P C.Deal

TEAM	G	W	L	PCT	GB	R	OR	AB	H	2B	3B	HR	BB	SO	AVG	OBP	SLG	PRO	PRO+	BR	/A	PF	CHI	RC	SB	CS	SBA	SBR
PHI	157	91	63	.591		722	**624**	5426	1440	225	55	125	535	569	.265	.334	.396	.730	100	-14	-2	98	101	714	33			
BRO	155	89	65	.578	2	**847**	724	5364	**1461**	247	46	**194**	607	632	**.272**	.349	.444	.793	113	**107**	**90**	102	101	**833**	77			
NY	154	86	68	.558	5	735	643	5238	1352	204	50	133	**627**	629	.258	.342	.392	.734	100	4	0	101	101	726	42			
BOS	156	83	71	.539	8	785	736	5363	1411	246	36	148	615	616	.263	.342	.405	.747	110	24	73	94	**104**	750	71			
STL	153	78	75	.510	12.5	693	670	5215	1353	255	50	102	606	604	.259	.339	.386	.725	93	-15	-49	105	99	696	23			
CIN	153	66	87	.431	24.5	654	734	5253	1366	**257**	27	99	504	**497**	.260	.327	.376	.703	91	-65	-67	100	100	643	37			
CHI	154	64	89	.418	26.5	643	772	5230	1298	224	47	161	479	767	.248	.315	.401	.716	95	-53	-45	99	100	658	46			
PIT	154	57	96	.373	33.5	681	857	5327	1404	227	**59**	138	564	693	.264	.338	.406	.744	99	13	-11	103	93	729	43			
TOT	618					5760		42416	11085	1885	370	1100	4537	5007	.261	.336	.401	.737							372			

TEAM	CG	SH	SV	IP	H	H/G	HR	BB	SO	RAT	ERA	ERA+	OAV	OOB	PR	/A	PF	CPI	FA	E	DP	FW	PW	BW	SBW	DIF
PHI	57	13	**27**	1406	1324	8.5	122	**530**	620	12.0	3.50	116	.250	.320	101	86	98	105	.975	151	155	.1	8.4	-.2		5.7
BRO	62	10	21	1389²	1397	9.0	163	591	**772**	13.0	4.28	96	.263	.339	-22	-29	99	102	**.979**	127	**183**	**1.4**	-2.8	**8.8**		4.7
NY	70	**19**	15	1375	**1268**	**8.3**	140	536	596	**12.0**	3.71	110	.246	.320	66	59	99	99	.970	182	146	-1.7	-4.4	7.1		4.9
BOS	**88**	7	10	1385¹	1411	9.2	129	554	615	13.0	4.14	93	.263	.336	0	-45	93	99	.978	130	172	1.1	4.8	-4.8		.4
STL	57	10	14	1356	1398	9.3	**119**	535	603	13.0	3.97	108	.268	.339	26	49	104	**105**	.978	130	172	.5	-1.3	-6.5		-3.2
CIN	67	7	13	1357²	1363	9.0	145	582	686	13.2	4.32	98	.259	.338	-26	-13	102	97	.976	140	132	.5	-1.1	-4.4		-4.2
CHI	55	9	19	1371¹	1452	9.5	130	593	559	13.6	4.28	98	.271	.347	-21	-11	101	103	.968	201	169	-2.8	-1.1	-4.4		-4.2
PIT	42	6	16	1368²	1472	9.7	152	616	556	13.9	4.96	88	.275	.353	-124	-88	106	95	.977	136	165	.8	-8.6	-1.1		-10.6
TOT	498	81	135	11009²		9.1				13.0	4.14		.261	.336					.975	1204	1303					

Runs		Hits		Doubles		Triples		Home Runs		Total Bases	
Torgeson-Bos	120	Snider-Bro	199	Schoendienst-StL	43	Ashburn-Phi	14	Kiner-Pit	47	Snider-Bro	343
Stanky-NY	115	Musial-StL	192	Musial-StL	41	Bell-Pit	11	Pafko-Chi	36	Musial-StL	331
Kiner-Pit	112	Furillo-Bro	189	Robinson-Bro	39	Snider-Bro	10	Sauer-Chi	32	Ennis-Phi	328
Snider-Bro	109	Ennis-Phi	185	Kluszewski-Cin	37	Smalley-Chi	9	Hodges-Bro	32	Kiner-Pit	323
Musial-StL	105	Waitkus-Phi	182	Dark-NY	36	Schoendienst-StL	9			Pafko-Chi	304

Runs Batted In		Runs Produced		Bases On Balls		Batting Average		On Base Percentage		Slugging Average	
Ennis-Phi	126	Furillo-Bro	187	Stanky-NY	144	Musial-StL	.346	Stanky-NY	.460	Musial-StL	.596
Kiner-Pit	118	Ennis-Phi	187	Robinson-Bro	122	Robinson-Bro	.328	Musial-StL	.437	Pafko-Chi	.591
Hodges-Bro	113	Musial-StL	186	Torgeson-Bos	119	Snider-Bro	.321	Robinson-Bro	.423	Kiner-Pit	.590
Kluszewski-Cin	111	Snider-Bro	185	Westrum-NY	92	Ennis-Phi	.311	Glaviano-StL	.421	Gordon-Bos	.557
Musial-StL	109	Torgeson-Bos	184	Reese-Bro	91	Kluszewski-Cin	.307	Torgeson-Bos	.412	Snider-Bro	.553

Production		Adjusted Production		Batter Runs		Adjusted Batter Runs		Clutch Hitting Index		Runs Created	
Musial-StL	1.034	Musial-StL	161	Musial-StL	57.3	Musial-StL	50.9	D.Mueller-NY	138	Musial-StL	149
Kiner-Pit	.998	Gordon-Bos	160	Kiner-Pit	48.7	Kiner-Pit	44.5	Slaughter-StL	136	Kiner-Pit	133
Pafko-Chi	.989	Pafko-Chi	158	Pafko-Chi	41.5	Pafko-Chi	42.8	Westlake-Pit	115	Snider-Bro	131
Gordon-Bos	.960	Kiner-Pit	154	Snider-Bro	35.6	Gordon-Bos	42.1	Wyrostek-Cin	112	Pafko-Chi	124
Snider-Bro	.932	Elliott-Bos	143	Gordon-Bos	35.3	Torgeson-Bos	38.7	Thompson-NY	111	Torgeson-Bos	121

Total Average		Stolen Bases		Stolen Base Average		Stolen Base Runs		Fielding Runs		Total Player Rating	
Musial-StL	1.139	Jethroe-Bos	35					Smalley-Chi	21.3	Robinson-Bro	4.7
Kiner-Pit	1.071	Reese-Bro	17					Cox-Bro	12.0	Stanky-NY	4.1
Pafko-Chi	1.057	Snider-Bro	16					Ryan-Bos-Cin	11.6	Gordon-Bos	4.1
Stanky-NY	1.013	Torgeson-Bos	15					Robinson-Bro	10.6	Pafko-Chi	3.5
Gordon-Bos	1.003	Ashburn-Phi	14					Westrum-NY	10.4	Seminick-Phi	3.5

Wins		Win Percentage		Games		Complete Games		Shutouts		Saves	
Spahn-Bos	21	Maglie-NY	.818	Konstanty-Phi	74	Bickford-Bos	27	Hearn-StL-NY	5	Konstanty-Phi	22
Sain-Bos	20	Konstanty-Phi	.696	Dickson-Pit	51	Spahn-Bos	25	Roberts-Phi	5	Werle-Pit	8
Roberts-Phi	20	Simmons-Phi	.680	Werle-Pit	48	Sain-Bos	25	Maglie-NY	5	Hogue-Bos	7
		Roberts-Phi	.645	Maglie-NY	47	Roberts-Phi	21	Jansen-NY	5	Branca-Bro	7
				Brazle-StL	46	Jansen-NY	21				

Innings Pitched		Fewest Hits/Game		Fewest BB/Game		Strikeouts		Strikeouts/Game		Ratio	
Bickford-Bos	311.2	Blackwell-Cin	7.00	Raffensberger-Cin	1.51	Spahn-Bos	191	Blackwell-Cin	6.48	Jansen-NY	9.62
Roberts-Phi	304.1	Maglie-NY	7.38	Jansen-NY	1.80	Blackwell-Cin	188	Simmons-Phi	6.12	Roberts-Phi	10.68
Spahn-Bos	293.0	Simmons-Phi	7.46	Sain-Bos	2.26	Jansen-NY	161	Spahn-Bos	5.87	Brecheen-StL	10.97
Sain-Bos	278.1	Spahn-Bos	7.62	Roberts-Phi	2.28	Simmons-Phi	146	Palica-Bro	5.86	Spahn-Bos	11.06
Jansen-NY	275.0	Jansen-NY	7.79	Roe-Bro	2.37	Roberts-Phi	146	Jansen-NY	5.27	Simmons-Phi	11.24

Earned Run Average		Adjusted ERA		Opponents' Batting Avg.		Opponents' On Base Pct.		Starter Runs		Adjusted Starter Runs	
Hearn-StL-NY	2.49	Maglie-NY	151	Blackwell-Cin	.210	Jansen-NY	.271	Roberts-Phi	38.0	Blackwell-Cin	36.7
Maglie-NY	2.71	Blackwell-Cin	143	Simmons-Phi	.223	Roberts-Phi	.297	Jansen-NY	34.5	Roberts-Phi	34.8
Blackwell-Cin	2.97	Lanier-StL	137	Maglie-NY	.226	Brecheen-StL	.298	Blackwell-Cin	34.1	Jansen-NY	33.1
Jansen-NY	3.01	Jansen-NY	136	Spahn-Bos	.227	Spahn-Bos	.299	Maglie-NY	32.8	Maglie-NY	31.7
Roberts-Phi	3.02	Roberts-Phi	134	Jansen-NY	.232	Blackwell-Cin	.301	Spahn-Bos	31.8	Pollet-StL	25.9

Clutch Pitching Index		Relief Runs		Adjusted Relief Runs		Relief Ranking		Total Pitcher Index		Total Baseball Ranking	
Brazle-StL	125	Konstanty-Phi	24.9	Konstanty-Phi	23.3	Konstanty-Phi	39.4	Blackwell-Cin	4.3	Robinson-Bro	4.7
Roe-Bro	118	Kramer-NY	5.9	Kramer-NY	5.4	Kramer-NY	5.2	Jansen-NY	3.8	Blackwell-Cin	4.3
Maglie-NY	116	Leonard-Chi	3.1	Smith-Cin	3.6	Smith-Cin	3.5	Konstanty-Phi	3.6	Stanky-NY	4.1
Ramsdell-Bro-Cin	115	VanderMeer-Chi	2.9	Leonard-Chi	3.5	Leonard-Chi	3.2	Maglie-NY	3.3	Gordon-Bos	4.1
Minner-Chi	113	Smith-Cin	2.7	VanderMeer-Chi	3.4	VanderMeer-Chi	3.0	Spahn-Bos	3.1	Jansen-NY	3.8

January 18 The Indians' Bob Feller, whose 1949 record was a lackluster 15-14, takes a $20,000 salary cut to $45,000 at his own suggestion.

February 7 Red Sox slugger Ted Williams becomes the highest paid player in history, by signing for $125,000.

April 18 President Harry Truman throws out two balls at the Washington opener—one left-handed and the other right-handed—then watches the Senators beat the A's 8-7.

May 26 The Athletics make some changes. Connie Mack's son, Earle, who had been assistant manager, assumes the duties of chief scout. Earle, who had hoped to succeed his father as manager, is replaced by Jimmie Dykes. Mickey Cochrane is named general manager.

June 2 St. Louis Browns pitcher Harry Dorish becomes the last AL pitcher to steal home, doing it on the front end of a double steal.

June 8 In the most lopsided score since 1900, the Boston Red Sox annihilate the St. Louis Browns at Fenway Park 29-4. Bobby Doerr has three home runs and eight RBI; Walt Dropo, two home runs and seven RBI, and Ted Williams, two home runs and five RBI.

June 12 Major League Baseball names Connie Mack as the Honorary Manager of the All-Star Game.

June 21 Joe DiMaggio gets his 2,000th

hit, a seventh-inning single off the Indians' Chick Pieretti, as the Yanks win, 8–2. DiMaggio joins Luke Appling and Wally Moses as the only active players with 2,000 or more hits.

July 2 Indians hurler Bob Feller wins his 200th major league game, 5–3, over Detroit in the second game of a doubleheader split.

July 3 With rookie Joe Collins not hitting and Tommy Henrich injured, Casey Stengel asks Joe DiMaggio to play first baseman in an experiment. In the 7-2 loss he handles 13 chances cleanly.

August 11 Hitting just .279, Yankee great Joe DiMaggio is benched for the first time in his career. He is currently languishing in a 4-for-38 slump.

August 28 Earle and Roy Mack, Connie's sons by his first marriage, purchase 54 percent interest in the Athletics from Connie Mack, Jr., their younger brother from a 2nd marriage. Earle, Roy and Connie Mack now own the club outright.

September 10 Joe DiMaggio becomes the first player to hit three home runs in one game at spacious Griffith Stadium, as the Yanks beat Washington 8-1.

September 15 For a record sixth time, Johnny Mize hits three home runs in one game, but the Yanks lose 9-7 at Detroit.

September 29 The idle Yankees clinch their second consecutive pennant under Casey Stengel, as Cleveland's Bob

Lemon sets down Detroit 12-2 for his 23rd win.

October 2 Dom DiMaggio of the Red Sox is the AL leader in steals with 15, the lowest league-leading figure ever.

October 7 Whitey Ford wins his first World Series game, 5-2 over Bob Miller at the Stadium. The four-game sweep gives the Yankees their 13th World Championship.

October 26 The Baseball Writers of America select Yankee shortstop Phil Rizzuto as the AL MVP.

November 8 The Baseball Writers Association of America announces that slugging first baseman Walt Dropo of the Boston Red Sox is the Rookie of the Year in the AL. Dropo led the league in RBI with 144.

November 9 The White Sox release Luke Appling, who has been with the Sox since 1930, so he can become the manager of the Memphis Chicks of the Southern Association.

November 10 After nine years at the helm, the Indians fire manager Lou Boudreau amid the howls of fan protest. Although Boudreau's overall winning percentage is a moderate .529, he won 92 games in a fourth-place finish, his best showing since his Tribe won 97 in the championship year of 1948. Al Lopez, who has piloted Minneapolis (AA) since 1948, takes over with a two-year contract.

	BOSTON		CHICAGO		CLEVELAND		DETROIT		NEW YORK		PHILADELPHIA		ST.LOUIS		WASHINGTON
M	J.McCarthy	M	J.Onslow	M	L.Boudreau	M	R.Rolfe	M	C.Stengel	M	C.Mack	M	Z.Taylor	M	B.Harris
M	S.O'Neill	M	R.Corriden	1B	L.Easter	1B	D.Kolloway	1B	J.Collins	1B	F.Fain	1B	D.Lenhardt	1B	M.Vernon
1B	W.Dropo	1B	E.Robinson	2B	J.Gordon	2B	J.Priddy	2B	J.Coleman	2B	B.Hitchcock	2B	O.Friend	2B	C.Michaels
2B	B.Doerr	2B	N.Fox	SS	R.Boone	SS	J.Lipon	SS	P.Rizzuto	SS	E.Joost	SS	T.Upton	SS	S.Dente
SS	V.Stephens	SS	C.Carrasquel	3B	A.Rosen	3B	G.Kell	3B	B.Johnson	3B	B.Dillinger	3B	B.Sommers	3B	E.Yost
3B	J.Pesky	3B	H.Majeski	LF	D.Mitchell	LF	H.Evers	LF	G.Woodling	LF	P.Lehner	LF	D.Kokos	LF	B.Stewart
LF	T.Williams	LF	G.Zernial	CF	L.Doby	CF	J.Groth	CF	J.DiMaggio	CF	S.Chapman	CF	R.Coleman	CF	I.Noren
CF	D.DiMaggio	CF	D.Philley	RF	B.Kennedy	RF	V.Wertz	RF	H.Bauer	RF	E.Valo	RF	K.Wood	RF	S.Mele
RF	A.Zarilla	RF	M.Rickert	C	J.Hegan	C	A.Robinson	C	Y.Berra	C	M.Guerra	C	S.Lollar	C	A.Evans
C	B.Tebbetts	C	P.Masi												
				S	L.Boudreau	1	D.Kryhoski	3	B.Brown	3S	K.Wahl	1	H.Arft	O	G.Coan
O3	B.Goodman	3	F.Baker	2	B.Avila	O	P.Mullin	O	C.Mapes	O	W.Moses	O3	R.Sievers	C	M.Grasso
C	M.Batts	O	M.McCormick	O	A.Clark	C	B.Swift	1	J.Mize	23	P.Suder	23	S.Stirnweiss	O	J.Ostrowski
O	C.Vollmer	2	C.Michaels	C	R.Murray	C	J.Ginsberg	T.Henrich		C	J.Tipton	C	L.Moss	1	E.Robinson
O	T.Wright	S1	L.Appling	O	T.Tucker	/O	C.Keller	O	J.Jensen	O	B.McCosky	O	J.Delsing	O2	S.Robertson
C	B.Rosar	1	G.Goldsberry	1	M.Vernon	S	N.Berry	2	B.Martin	C	J.Astroth	S	B.DeMars	M.Combs	
/O	T.O'Brien	O	H.Adams	O	J.Lemon	/S	E.Lake	1	J.Hopp	/O	B.Wellman	3	L.Thomas	O	R.Ortiz
/3	K.Keltner	C	G.Niarhos	/1	H.Conyers	/C	F.House	C	C.Silvera	/O	R.Ortiz	/3	F.Gustine	2	A.Kozar
/3	L.Stringer	C	E.Malone	/2	J.Berardino	H	P.Campbell	/O	J.Lindell	/2	G.Markland			/C	H.Keller
/3	F.Hatfield	/3	J.Scala					H	J.Delsing	/O	B.Guintini	P	N.Garver	C	L.Okrie
/O	C.Maxwell	O	J.Ostrowski	P	B.Lemon	P	A.Houtteman	/O	R.Houk	/C	B.Rinker	P	A.Widmar	/1	F.Taylor
/O	J.Piersall	O	J.Busby	P	B.Feller	P	F.Hutchinson	/1	H.Workman			P	S.Overmire	/O	C.Vollmer
H	M.Combs	/C	J.Erautt	P	E.Wynn	P	H.Newhouser	/2	S.Stirnweiss	P	L.Brissie	P	D.Starr	/O	T.O'Brien
/C	B.Scherbarth	/2	A.Kozar	P	M.Garcia	P	D.Trout	H	D.Wakefield	P	A.Kellner	P	H.Dorish	H	G.Genovese
		/1	C.Kress	P	S.Gromek	P	T.Gray	R	G.Niarhos	P	B.Shantz	RP	C.Marshall		
P	M.Parnell	/O	E.McGhee	RP	M.Pieretti	RP	H.White			P	H.Wyse			P	S.Hudson
P	E.Kinder	/O	B.Wilson	RP	A.Benton	RP	P.Calvert	P	V.Raschi	P	B.Hooper	P	C.Fannin	P	B.Kuzava
P	J.Dobson	/3	J.Kirrene	RP	J.Flores			P	A.Reynolds	RP	D.Scheib	P	D.Johnson	P	C.Marrero
P	C.Stobbs	/C	B.Salkeld			/P	V.Trucks	P	E.Lopat			P	D.Pillette	P	S.Consuegra
P	M.McDermott			P	M.Pieretti	P	M.Stuart	P	T.Byrne	P	D.Fowler	P	J.Ostrowski	P	J.Haynes
		P	B.Pierce	P	G.Bearden	P	S.Rogovin	P	F.Sanford	P	J.Coleman	P	T.Fine	RP	M.Harris
P	W.Masterson	P	B.Wight	P	D.Weik	P	H.Borowy	RP	T.Ferrick	P	J.Murray	P	J.Bruner	RP	J.Pearce
P	W.Nixon	P	B.Cain	P	D.Rozek	RP	R.Herbert	RP	J.Page	P	J.Kucab	P	T.Ferrick		
P	A.Papai	P	R.Gumpert	/P	A.Aber	/P	B.Connelly			P	M.Burtschy	/P	L.Kretlow	P	A.Sima
P	D.Littlefield	P	R.Scarborough					P	W.Ford	/P	H.Byrd	/P	S.Schacht	P	G.Bearden
P	C.Schanz	RP	H.Judson					P	J.Ostrowski	/P	E.Klieman	/P	E.Albrecht	/P	R.Scarborough
/P	J.McDonald	RP	L.Aloma					P	B.Porterfield	/P	L.McCrabb	/P	R.Bauers	P	S.Nagy
/P	H.Taylor	RP	M.Haefner					P	D.Johnson			/P	B.Kennedy	P	D.Weik
P	E.Johnson							/P	D.Pillette			/P	R.Raney	P	L.Hittle
/P	G.Mueller	P	K.Holcombe					/P	E.Nevel			/P	L.Sleater	P	E.Singleton
/P	J.Atkins	P	B.Kuzava					/P	D.Madison					/P	J.Moreno
/P	J.Suchecki	P	L.Kretlow					/P	L.Burdette					/P	C.Pascual
/P	F.Quinn	/P	J.Bruner											/P	B.Ross
/P	D.Ferriss	/P	M.Rotblatt											/P	D.Welteroth
/P	B.Gillespie	/P	J.Perkovich											/P	R.Martinez
/P	P.Marchildon	/P	B.Connelly												
		/P	G.Keriazakos												
		/P	C.Cuellar												

TEAM	G	W	L	PCT	GB	R	OR	AB	H	2B	3B	HR	BB	SO	AVG	OBP	SLG	PRO	PRO+	BR	/A	PF	CHI	RC	SB	CS	SBA	SBR
NY	155	98	56	.636		914	691	5361	1511	234	70	159	687	463	.282	.367	.441	.808	116	92	118	97	104	902	41	28	59	-5
DET	157	95	59	.617	3	837	713	5381	1518	285	50	114	722	480	.282	.369	.417	.786	104	60	33	103	97	846	23	40	37	-17
BOS	154	94	60	.610	4	1027	804	5516	1665	287	61	161	719	582	.302	.385	.464	.849	112	185	90	110	103	1014	32	17	65	-1
CLE	155	92	62	.597	6	806	654	5263	1417	222	46	164	693	624	.269	.358	.422	.780	109	39	66	97	98	820	40	34	54	-8
WAS	155	67	87	.435	31	690	813	5251	1365	190	53	76	671	606	.260	.347	.360	.707	91	-93	-61	95	101	690	42	25	63	-2
CHI	156	60	94	.390	38	625	749	5260	1368	172	47	93	551	566	.260	.333	.364	.697	86	-125	-107	97	98	648	19	22	46	-8
STL	154	58	96	.377	40	684	916	5163	1269	235	43	106	690	744	.246	.337	.370	.707	84	-102	-127	104	103	667	39	40	49	-12
PHI	154	52	102	.338	46	670	913	5212	1361	204	53	100	685	493	.261	.349	.378	.727	94	-56	-42	98	98	708	42	25	63	-2
TOT	620					6253		42407	11474	1829	423	973	5418	4558	.271	.356	.402	.759							278	231	55	-55

TEAM	CG	SH	SV	IP	H	H/G	HR	BB	SO	RAT	ERA	ERA+	OAV	OOB	PR	/A	PF	CPI	FA	E	DP	FW	PW	BW	SBW	DIF
NY	66	12	31	1372²	1322	8.7	118	708	712	13.5	4.15	103	.255	.348	65	22	94	102	.980	119	188	1.3	2.1	11.0	.2	6.4
DET	72	9	20	1407¹	1444	9.2	141	553	576	13.0	4.12	114	.267	.339	71	88	102	105	.981	120	194	1.3	8.2	3.1	-.9	6.3
BOS	66	6	28	1362¹	1413	9.3	121	748	630	14.4	4.88	100	.270	.364	-46	3	107	97	.981	111	181	1.7	.3	8.4	.6	6.1
CLE	69	11	16	1378²	1289	8.4	120	647	674	12.8	3.75	115	.248	.333	126	88	95	103	.978	129	160	.7	8.2	6.2	-.1	-.0
WAS	59	7	18	1364²	1479	9.8	99	648	486	14.2	4.66	96	.278	.359	-12	-25	98	99	.972	167	181	-1.4	-2.3	-5.7	.5	-1.0
CHI	62	7	9	1365²	1370	9.0	107	734	566	14.0	4.41	102	.263	.356	26	12	98	100	.977	140	181	.2	1.1	-10.0	-.1	-8.2
STL	56	7	14	1365¹	1629	10.7	129	651	448	15.2	5.20	95	.295	.372	-94	-38	108	100	.967	196	155	-3.1	-3.6	-11.9	-.5	-.0
PHI	50	3	18	1346¹	1528	10.2	138	729	466	15.3	5.49	87	.287	.376	-136	-140	99	96	.974	155	208	-.8	-13.1	-3.9	.5	-7.7
TOT	500	62	154	10963		9.4				14.0	4.58		.271	.356					.976	1137	1448					

Runs
DiMaggio-Bos 131
Stephens-Bos 125
Rizzuto-NY 125
Berra-NY 116

Hits
Kell-Det 218
Rizzuto-NY 200
DiMaggio-Bos 193
Berra-NY 192
Stephens-Bos 185

Doubles
Kell-Det 56
Wertz-Det 37
Rizzuto-NY 36
Evers-Det 35
Stephens-Bos 34

Triples
Evers-Det 11
Doerr-Bos 11
DiMaggio-Bos 11

Home Runs
Rosen-Cle 37
Dropo-Bos 34
DiMaggio-NY 32
Stephens-Bos 30
Zernial-Chi 29

Total Bases
Dropo-Bos 326
Stephens-Bos 321
Berra-NY 318
Kell-Det 310
DiMaggio-NY 307

Runs Batted In
Stephens-Bos 144
Dropo-Bos 144
Berra-NY 124
Wertz-Det 123
DiMaggio-NY 122

Runs Produced
Stephens-Bos 239
Berra-NY 212
Dropo-Bos 211
Kell-Det 207
DiMaggio-NY 204

Bases On Balls
Yost-Was 141
Fain-Phi 133
Pesky-Bos 104
Joost-Phi 103
Rosen-Cle 100

Batting Average
Goodman-Bos ..... .354
Kell-Det ..... .340
DiMaggio-Bos ..... .328
Doby-Cle ..... .326
Zarilla-Bos ..... .325

On Base Percentage
Doby-Cle ..... .442
Yost-Was ..... .440
Pesky-Bos ..... .437
Fain-Phi ..... .430
Goodman-Bos ..... .427

Slugging Average
DiMaggio-NY ..... .585
Dropo-Bos ..... .583
Evers-Det ..... .551
Doby-Cle ..... .545
Rosen-Cle ..... .543

Production
Doby-Cle ..... .986
DiMaggio-NY ..... .979
Dropo-Bos ..... .961
Evers-Det ..... .959
Rosen-Cle ..... .948

Adjusted Production
Doby-Cle 156
DiMaggio-NY 152
Rosen-Cle 146
Evers-Det 139
Berra-NY 136

Batter Runs
Doby-Cle 41.7
Williams-Bos 40.9
DiMaggio-NY 35.4
Rosen-Cle 34.3
Evers-Det 33.5

Adjusted Batter Runs
Doby-Cle 45.7
DiMaggio-NY 38.8
Rosen-Cle 38.3
Williams-Bos 32.1
Evers-Det 30.0

Clutch Hitting Index
Vernon-Cle-Was 126
Mele-Was 125
Noren-Was 116
Stephens-Bos 110
Fain-Phi 108

Runs Created
Doby-Cle 130
Wertz-Det 128
DiMaggio-NY 125
Berra-NY 125
Rizzuto-NY 124

Total Average
Doby-Cle 1.073
DiMaggio-NY 1.018
Wertz-Det ..... .978
Zarilla-Bos ..... .954
Rosen-Cle ..... .953

Stolen Bases
DiMaggio-Bos 15
Valo-Phi 12
Rizzuto-NY 12
Coan-Was 10
Lipon-Det 9

Stolen Base Average

Stolen Base Runs
DiMaggio-Bos 2.1
Vernon-Cle-Was 1.8
Collins-NY 1.5
Avila-Cle 1.5
Jensen-NY 1.2

Fielding Runs
Priddy-Det 31.3
Hegan-Cle 24.2
Pesky-Bos 21.5
Noren-Was 15.9
Carrasquel-Chi 11.2

Total Player Rating
Rizzuto-NY 4.1
Berra-NY 3.4
DiMaggio-NY 3.1
Rosen-Cle 3.1
Doby-Cle 3.1

Wins
B.Lemon-Cle 23
Raschi-NY 21
Houtteman-Det 19

Win Percentage
Raschi-NY ..... .724
Wynn-Cle ..... .692
Lopat-NY ..... .692
Hutchinson-Det ..... .680
B.Lemon-Cle ..... .676

Games
Harris-Was 53
Kinder-Bos 48
Ferrick-StL-NY 46
Judson-Chi 46
Brissie-Phi 46

Complete Games
B.Lemon-Cle 22
Garver-StL 22
Parnell-Bos 21
Houtteman-Det 21

Shutouts
Houtteman-Det 4

Saves
Harris-Was 15
Page-NY 13
Ferrick-StL-NY 11
Kinder-Bos 9
Brissie-Phi 8

Innings Pitched
B.Lemon-Cle 288.0
Houtteman-Det 274.2
Garver-StL 260.0
Raschi-NY 256.2
Parnell-Bos 249.0

Fewest Hits/Game
Wynn-Cle 6.99
Pierce-Chi 7.76
Cain-Chi 8.02
Reynolds-NY 8.04
Raschi-NY 8.14

Fewest BB/Game
Hutchinson-Det 1.86
Lopat-NY 2.48
Overmire-StL 2.52
Trout-Det 3.12
Houtteman-Det 3.24

Strikeouts
B.Lemon-Cle 170
Reynolds-NY 160
Raschi-NY 155
Wynn-Cle 143
Feller-Cle 119

Strikeouts/Game
Wynn-Cle 6.02
Reynolds-NY 5.98
Raschi-NY 5.44
B.Lemon-Cle 5.31
Byrne-NY 5.22

Ratio
Wynn-Cle 11.41
Lopat-NY 11.92
Houtteman-Det 11.93
Raschi-NY 12.31
Feller-Cle 12.32

Earned Run Average
Wynn-Cle 3.20
Garver-StL 3.39
Feller-Cle 3.43
Lopat-NY 3.47
Houtteman-Det 3.54

Adjusted ERA
Garver-StL 146
Parnell-Bos 136
Wynn-Cle 135
Houtteman-Det 132
Feller-Cle 126

Opponents' Batting Avg.
Wynn-Cle ..... .212
Pierce-Chi ..... .228
Reynolds-NY ..... .242
Raschi-NY ..... .243
Cain-Chi ..... .244

Opponents' On Base Pct.
Wynn-Cle ..... .305
Lopat-NY ..... .317
Houtteman-Det ..... .322
Feller-Cle ..... .325
Raschi-NY ..... .327

Starter Runs
Garver-StL 34.3
Wynn-Cle 32.7
Houtteman-Det 31.7
Feller-Cle 31.7
Lopat-NY 29.2

Adjusted Starter Runs
Garver-StL 45.0
Parnell-Bos 35.5
Houtteman-Det 35.1
Wynn-Cle 26.8
Feller-Cle 24.9

Clutch Pitching Index
Garver-StL 119
Hudson-Was 113
B.Lemon-Cle 111
Houtteman-Det 110
Parnell-Bos 110

Relief Runs
Judson-Chi 8.0
Aloma-Chi 7.6
Benton-Cle 7.0
Ferrick-StL-NY 6.2
Flores-Cle 5.0

Adjusted Relief Runs
Judson-Chi 6.8
Aloma-Chi 6.7
Ferrick-StL-NY 6.2
Benton-Cle 5.3
Flores-Cle 3.5

Relief Ranking
Ferrick-StL-NY 13.0
Aloma-Chi 6.9
Benton-Cle 5.3
Flores-Cle 4.2
Judson-Chi 2.7

Total Pitcher Index
Garver-StL 5.7
Parnell-Bos 3.9
B.Lemon-Cle 3.7
Wynn-Cle 3.6
Houtteman-Det 3.5

Total Baseball Ranking
Garver-StL 5.7
Rizzuto-NY 4.1
Parnell-Bos 3.9
B.Lemon-Cle 3.7
Wynn-Cle 3.6

January 26 The baseball writers vote Mel Ott and Jimmie Foxx into the Hall of Fame.

April 17 In pregame ceremonies at Wrigley Field, Sam Snead tees off from home plate and hits a golf ball off the center field scoreboard, the only ball ever to reach the structure. The Cubs follow up in their home opener by beating the Reds 8–3.

May 25 Giants rookie Willie Mays, who was hitting .477 with Minneapolis, goes 0-for-5 in his major league debut against the Phils.

May 28 After going 0-for-12, Willie Mays connects for his first major league hit, a home run off Braves pitcher Warren Spahn. The Giants lose the game, 4–1.

July 10 Exploding for a record four home runs, the NL trounces the AL 8–3 at the annual All-Star Game at Briggs Stadium in Detroit. Pittsburgh slugger Ralph Kiner homers for the third year in a row.

July 20 In a move that will aid their pennant drive, the Giants put outfielder Bobby Thomson at third baseman to replace Hank Thompson, out with an injury. Thomson, who's been riding the bench since losing his starting job to the rookie Mays, will hit .357 for the rest of the season.

September 13 The Cards split a rare doubleheader, with two different teams, defeating the Giants 6-4 in the first game in the afternoon and losing 2-0 to the Braves in the nightcap. It's the first time a team in the NL has played two different teams in the same day since the early years of the century.

September 20 The owners elect NL President Ford Frick as the third commissioner of baseball for a seven-year term at $65,000 per annum.

October 1 With both the Dodgers and Giants tied 96-58 at the end of the regular season, Brooklyn wins the coin toss and elects to play the first game of the playoffs at home. The next two games will be played at the Polo Grounds. In the NL's first best-of-three play-off since 1946, Ralph Branca of the Dodgers loses to Jim Hearn and the Giants 3-1. Branca serves up home runs to Bobby Thomson and Monte Irvin in the first game ever to be telecast live coast-to-coast.

October 2 The Dodgers bounce back as rookie Clem Labine evens the playoff with a 10-0 win, besting the Giants' Sheldon Jones. Home runs are smashed by Jackie Robinson, Gil Hodges, Andy Pafko, and Rube Walker. Willie Mays grounds into three double plays.

October 3 The Giants' Bobby Thomson hits the most famous home run in history, off Ralph Branca. His "shot heard 'round the world" with two on and the Giants trailing 4-2 in the bottom of the ninth defeats Brooklyn 5-4 and sends the jubilant Giants into the World Series.

October 4 In the opening game of the World Series, Monte Irvin steals home in the first inning and collects four hits. The Giants defeat Allie Reynolds and the Yankees 5-1 with Dave Koslo going all the way at Yankee Stadium.

October 6 Back at the Polo Grounds, the Giants win 6-2, as Whitey Lockman homers with two on in the fifth. The Giants score five in the inning after Eddie Stanky kicks the ball out of Phil Rizzuto's glove on a tag play at second baseman.

November 1 The NL votes Roy Campanella the league's MVP for what will be the first of three such awards.

BOSTON		BROOKLYN		CHICAGO		CINCINNATI		NEW YORK		PHILADELPHIA		PITTSBURGH		ST.LOUIS	
M	B.Southworth	M	C.Dressen	M	F.Frisch	M	L.Sewell	M	L.Durocher	M	E.Sawyer	M	B.Meyer	M	M.Marion
M	T.Holmes	1B	G.Hodges	M	P.Cavarretta	1B	T.Kluszewski	1B	W.Lockman	1B	E.Waitkus	1B	J.Phillips	1B	N.Jones
1B	E.Torgeson	2B	J.Robinson	1B	C.Connors	2B	C.Ryan	2B	E.Stanky	2B	P.Caballero	2B	D.Murtaugh	2B	R.Schoendienst
2B	R.Hartsfield	SS	P.Reese	2B	E.Miksis	SS	V.Stallcup	SS	A.Dark	SS	G.Hamner	SS	G.Strickland	SS	S.Hemus
SS	B.Kerr	3B	B.Cox	SS	R.Smalley	3B	G.Hatton	3B	H.Thompson	3B	W.Jones	3B	P.Castiglione	3B	B.Johnson
3B	B.Elliott	LF	A.Pafko	3B	R.Jackson	LF	J.Adcock	LF	M.Irvin	LF	D.Sisler	LF	R.Kiner	LF	S.Musial
LF	S.Gordon	CF	D.Snider	LF	H.Sauer	CF	L.Merriman	CF	W.Mays	CF	R.Ashburn	CF	C.Metkovich	CF	P.Lowrey
CF	S.Jethroe	RF	C.Furillo	CF	H.Jeffcoat	RF	J.Wyrostek	RF	D.Mueller	RF	D.Ennis	RF	G.Bell	RF	S.Slaughter
RF	W.Marshall	C	R.Campanella	RF	F.Baumholtz	C	D.Howell	C	W.Westrum	C	A.Seminick	C	C.McCullough	C	D.Rice
C	W.Cooper			C	S.Burgess										
		O	C.Abrams			32	B.Adams	O3	B.Thomson	C	D.Wilber	O	B.Howerton	O	W.Westlake
S2	S.Sisti	32	R.Bridges	O	G.Hermanski	O	B.Usher	C	R.Noble	C	E.Pellagrini		J.Garagiola		H.Rice
C	E.St.Claire	O	D.Thompson		P.Cavarretta	C	J.Pramesa	O2	B.Rigney	O2	T.Brown	1O	R.Nelson	S	S.Rojek
O	B.Addis	O	G.Hermanski	2	W.Terwilliger	S3	R.McMillan	2	D.Williams	2	B.Nicholson	3O	W.Westlake	O	T.Glaviano
S	J.Logan	C	R.Walker	O	A.Pafko	O	H.Edwards	O	S.Jorgensen	O	M.Goliat	2	M.Basgall	C	B.Sarni
O	L.Marquez	O	D.Williams	1	D.Fondy	C	B.Scheffing	2	C.Hartung	O	D.Young	2	F.Thomas	C	C.Diering
C	R.Mueller	2	W.Terwilliger	S	J.Cusick	O	B.McCosky	/2	S.Yvars	2	J.Bloodworth	O	P.Reiser	1	S.Bilko
O	L.Olmo	/C	B.Edwards	S	B.Ramazzotti	/O	W.Post	3	J.Lohrke	/O	M.Clark	O	D.Cole	C	J.Garagiola
/O	T.Holmes	H	H.Edwards	C	B.Edwards	/2	S.Meeks	/2	A.Wilson	/O	D.Whitman	O	E.FitzGerald	O	B.Howerton
S	G.Mauch	/O	T.Brown	/O	M.Owen	/O	D.Litwhiler	/O	J.Maguire	/C	K.Silvestri	O	T.Saffell	/3	W.Benson
H	B.Thorpe	/O	J.Russell	/C	R.Walker	/C	H.Landrith	/C	E.Rapp	/C	S.Lopata	2	J.Merson	2	D.Cole
P	W.Spahn	/3	E.Miksis	C	B.Borkowski	H	T.Tappe	H	H.Schenz	O	S.Sanicki	O	T.Beard	3	D.Richmond
P	M.Surkont	/C	M.Livingston	3	B.Serena	R	J.Bolger			H	S.Hollmig	3	D.Smith		E.Kazak
P	V.Bickford	H	W.Belardi	/C	H.Chiti			P	S.Maglie			3	B.Dillinger	/O	H.Walker
P	J.Sain	P	D.Newcombe	/O	C.Mauro	P	K.Raffensberger	P	L.Jansen	P	R.Roberts	O	D.Dusak	/1	R.Nelson
P	C.Nichols	P	P.Roe	/1	F.Richards	P	E.Blackwell	P	J.Hearn	P	B.Church	O	D.Restelli	C	B.Scheffing
RP	D.Cole	P	R.Branca	P	B.Rush	P	H.Fox	P	D.Koslo	P	R.Meyer	/S	S.Rojek	/1	D.Bollweg
RP	G.Estock	P	C.Erskine	P	P.Minner	P	W.Ramsdell	RP	G.Spencer	P	J.Thompson	/1	D.Long	/O	J.Van Noy
RP	B.Chipman	RP	C.King	P	C.McLish	RP	H.Wehmeier	RP	S.Jones	/2	K.Heintzelman	/1	J.Maguire	/O	L.Ciaffone
P	J.Wilson	RP	B.Podbielan	P	F.Hiller	RP	H.Perkowski	RP	M.Kennedy	RP	J.Konstanty	H	H.Fisher		
P	P.Paine	RP	E.Palica	P	T.Lown	RP	F.Smith							P	G.Staley
/P	D.Donovan	P	C.Labine	RP	D.Leonard	RP	B.Byerly	P	A.Corwin	P	K.Johnson	P	M.Dickson	P	T.Poholsky
/P	B.Donnelly	P	J.Schmitz	RP	M.Dubiel	/P	E.Erautt	P	A.Gettel	P	A.Hansen	P	M.Queen	P	M.Lanier
/P	B.Hogue	P	J.Hatten	P	B.Kelly	/P	K.Peterson	/P	R.Bowman	P	N.Jordan	P	B.Friend	P	H.Brecheen
/P	S.Schacht	P	P.Haugstad	P	J.Klippstein	/P	J.Blackburn	/P	J.Kramer	P	B.Miller	P	H.Pollet	P	C.Chambers
/P	L.Burdette	/P	C.Van Cuyk	P	B.Schultz	/P	E.Blake	/P	A.Konikowski	P	M.Candini	P	V.Law	RP	A.Brazle
		/P	D.Bankhead	/P	J.Hatten			/P	G.Bamberger	P	K.Drews	RP	B.Werle	RP	D.Bokelmann
		/P	E.Mossor	/P	J.Schmitz			/P	R.Hardy	P	L.Cristante	RP	T.Wilks	P	R.Munger
				/P	A.Varga					/P	L.Possehl	RP	J.Walsh	P	J.Presko
				/P	W.Hacker					/P	J.Brittin			P	C.Boyer
												P	C.Chambers	P	T.Wilks
												P	P.LaPalme	/P	J.Collum
												/P	D.Carlsen	/P	J.Crimian
												P	B.Koski	/P	H.Pollet
												/P	J.Muir	/P	E.Dusak
												/P	L.Yochim	/P	B.Habenicht
												/P	C.Dempsey	/P	K.Krieger
												/P	P.Pettit	/P	D.Lewandowski

TEAM	G	W	L	PCT	GB	R	OR	AB	H	2B	3B	HR	BB	SO	AVG	OBP	SLG	PRO	PRO+	BR	/A	PF	CHI	RC	SB	CS	SBA	SBR
NY	157	98	59	.624		781	641	5360	1396	201	53	179	671	624	.260	.347	.418	.765	111	91	85	101	97	812	55	34	62	-4
BRO	158	97	60	.618	1	855	672	5492	1511	249	37	184	603	649	.275	.352	.434	.786	116	130	113	102	101	843	89	70	56	-15
STL	155	81	73	.526	15.5	683	671	5317	1404	230	57	95	569	492	.264	.339	.382	.721	99	7	3	101	97	705	30	30	50	-9
BOS	155	76	78	.494	20.5	723	662	5293	1385	234	37	130	565	617	.262	.336	.394	.730	111	20	70	93	102	719	80	34	70	4
PHI	154	73	81	.474	23.5	648	644	5332	1384	199	47	108	505	525	.260	.336	.375	.701	96	-38	-28	99	99	676	63	28	69	2
CIN	155	68	86	.442	28.5	559	667	5285	1309	215	33	88	415	577	.248	.304	.351	.655	81	-134	-142	102	104	562	44	40	52	-11
PIT	155	64	90	.416	32.5	689	845	5318	1372	218	56	137	557	615	.258	.331	.397	.728	99	11	-9	103	98	712	29	27	52	-8
CHI	155	62	92	.403	34.5	614	750	5307	1327	200	47	103	477	647	.250	.315	.364	.679	86	-86	-97	102	103	613	63	30	68	1
TOT	622					5552		42704	11088	1746	367	1024	4362	4746	.260	.331	.390	.721							453	293	61	-40

TEAM	CG	SH	SV	IP	H	H/G	HR	BB	SO	RAT	ERA	ERA+	OAV	OOB	PR	/A	PF	CPI	FA	E	DP	FW	PW	BW	SBW	DIF
NY	64	9	18	1412^2	1334	8.5	148	482	625	11.7	3.48	113	.248	.313	75	69	99	104	.972	171	175	-1.0	6.9	8.5	.0	5.0
BRO	64	10	13	1423^1	1360	8.6	150	549	693	12.2	3.88	101	.253	.326	13	8	99	101	.979	129	192	1.3	.8	11.3	-1.0	6.1
STL	58	9	23	1387^2	1391	9.0	119	568	546	12.8	3.95	100	.264	.338	1	2	100	103	.980	125	187	1.3	.2	.3	-.4	2.6
BOS	73	16	12	1389	1378	8.9	96	595	604	13.0	3.75	98	.259	.337	33	-11	93	104	.976	145	157	.3	-1.1	7.0	.9	-3.1
PHI	57	19	15	1384^2	1373	8.9	110	497	570	12.4	3.81	100	.258	.324	23	6	97	98	.977	138	146	.6		-2.8	.7	-3.1
CIN	55	14	23	1390^2	1357	8.8	119	490	584	12.2	3.70	110	.255	.323	40	58	103	100	.977	140	141	.5	5.8	-14.2	-.6	-.5
PIT	40	9	22	1380^1	1479	9.6	157	609	580	13.8	4.79	88	.274	.350	-128	-88	107	97	.972	170	178	-1.1	-8.8	-.9	-.3	-1.9
CHI	48	10	10	1385^2	1416	9.2	125	572	544	13.1	4.34	94	.265	.340	-58	-38	103	96	.971	181	161	-1.7	-3.8	-9.7	.6	-.4
TOT	459	96	136	11154		8.9				12.6	3.96		.260	.331					.975	1199	1337					

Runs
Musial-StL 124
Kiner-Pit 124
Hodges-Bro 118
Dark-NY 114
Robinson-Bro 106

Hits
Ashburn-Phi 221
Musial-StL 205
Furillo-Bro 197
Dark-NY 196
Robinson-Bro 185

Doubles
Dark-NY 41
Kluszewski-Cin ... 35
Robinson-Bro 33
Campanella-Bro ... 33

Triples
Musial-StL 12
Bell-Pit 12
Irvin-NY 11
Jethroe-Bos 10
Baumholtz-Chi 10

Home Runs
Kiner-Pit 42
Hodges-Bro 40
Campanella-Bro ... 33
Thomson-NY 32
Musial-StL 32

Total Bases
Musial-StL 355
Kiner-Pit 333
Hodges-Bro 307
Campanella-Bro ... 298

Runs Batted In
Irvin-NY 121
Kiner-Pit 109
Gordon-Bos 109
Musial-StL 108
Campanella-Bro ... 108

Runs Produced
Musial-StL 200
Kiner-Pit 191
Irvin-NY 191
Hodges-Bro 181
Gordon-Bos 176

Bases On Balls
Kiner-Pit 137
Stanky-NY 127
Westrum-NY 104
Torgeson-Bos 102
Musial-StL 98

Batting Average
Musial-StL .... .355
Ashburn-Phi ...... .344
Robinson-Bro ..... .338
Campanella-Bro ... .325
Irvin-NY .... .312

On Base Percentage
Kiner-Pit .... .452
Musial-StL .... .449
Robinson-Bro ..... .429
Irvin-NY .... .415
Stanky-NY .... .401

Slugging Average
Kiner-Pit .... .627
Musial-StL .... .614
Campanella-Bro ... .590
Thomson-NY .... .562
Hodges-Bro .... .527

Production
Kiner-Pit 1.079
Musial-StL 1.063
Campanella-Bro ... .983
Robinson-Bro ..... .957
Thomson-NY .... .947

Adjusted Production
Musial-StL 182
Kiner-Pit 182
Campanella-Bro ... 158
Robinson-Bro 153
Thomson-NY 150

Batter Runs
Kiner-Pit 70.8
Musial-StL 70.1
Robinson-Bro 45.8
Campanella-Bro ... 41.7
Irvin-NY 40.7

Adjusted Batter Runs
Musial-StL 69.2
Kiner-Pit 66.5
Robinson-Bro 43.4
Irvin-NY 39.7
Campanella-Bro ... 39.6

Clutch Hitting Index
Slaughter-StL 136
Reese-Bro 130
Irvin-NY 118
Westlake-Pit-StL .. 112
Torgeson-Bos 109

Runs Created
Musial-StL 169
Kiner-Pit 165
Robinson-Bro 133
Irvin-NY 127
Hodges-Bro 119

Total Average
Kiner-Pit 1.251
Musial-StL 1.180
Robinson-Bro 1.034
Irvin-NY .... .985
Campanella-Bro ... .978

Stolen Bases
Jethroe-Bos 35
Ashburn-Phi 29
Robinson-Bro 25
Torgeson-Bos 20
Reese-Bro 20

Stolen Base Average
Jethroe-Bos 87.5
Ashburn-Phi 82.9
Robinson-Bro 75.8
Torgeson-Bos 64.5
Reese-Bro 58.8

Stolen Base Runs
Jethroe-Bos 7.5
Ashburn-Phi 5.1
Robinson-Bro 2.7
Jackson-Chi 2.4
Irvin-NY 2.4

Fielding Runs
Ashburn-Phi 32.3
Robinson-Bro 16.5
Furillo-Bro 16.1
Schoendienst-StL .. 15.5
Hemus-StL 13.4

Total Player Rating
Robinson-Bro 6.8
Musial-StL 6.4
Kiner-Pit 5.4
Campanella-Bro ... 5.2
Ashburn-Phi 5.2

Wins
Maglie-NY 23
Jansen-NY 23
Spahn-Bos 22
Roe-Bro 22
Roberts-Phi 21

Win Percentage
Roe-Bro .... .880
Maglie-NY .... .793
Newcombe-Bro ..... .690
Jansen-NY .... .676
Hearn-NY .... .654

Games
Wilks-StL-Pit 65
Werle-Pit 59
Konstanty-Phi 58
Spencer-NY 57
Brazle-StL 56

Complete Games
Spahn-Bos 26
Roberts-Phi 22
Maglie-NY 22
Roe-Bro 19
Dickson-Pit 19

Shutouts
Spahn-Bos 7
Roberts-Phi 6
Raffensberger-Cin . 5

Saves
Wilks-StL-Pit 13
Smith-Cin 11
Konstanty-Phi 9
Brazle-StL 7

Innings Pitched
Roberts-Phi 315.0
Spahn-Bos 310.2
Maglie-NY 298.0
Dickson-Pit 288.2
Jansen-NY 278.2

Fewest Hits/Game
Maglie-NY 7.67
Newcombe-Bro 7.78
Blackwell-Cin 7.89
Branca-Bro 7.94
Queen-Pit 7.97

Fewest BB/Game
Raffensberger-Cin . 1.38
Jansen-NY 1.81
Roberts-Phi 1.83
Roe-Bro 2.24
Sain-Bos 2.53

Strikeouts
Spahn-Bos 164
Newcombe-Bro 164
Maglie-NY 146
Jansen-NY 145
Rush-Chi 129

Strikeouts/Game
Queen-Pit 6.58
Rush-Chi 5.49
Newcombe-Bro 5.43
Branca-Bro 5.21
Spahn-Bos 4.75

Ratio
Raffensberger-Cin . 9.99
Roberts-Phi 10.03
Jansen-NY 10.11
Maglie-NY 10.45
Roe-Bro 10.86

Earned Run Average
Nichols-Bos 2.88
Maglie-NY 2.93
Spahn-Bos 2.98
Roberts-Phi 3.03
Jansen-NY 3.04

Adjusted ERA
Maglie-NY 134
Roe-Bro 129
Jansen-NY 129
Nichols-Bos 127
Roberts-Phi 127

Opponents' Batting Avg.
Maglie-NY .... .230
Newcombe-Bro ..... .230
Blackwell-Cin .... .233
Queen-Pit .... .233
Branca-Bro .... .237

Opponents' On Base Pct.
Roberts-Phi ...... .278
Jansen-NY .... .279
Raffensberger-Cin . .279
Maglie-NY .... .289
Newcombe-Bro ..... .297

Starter Runs
Maglie-NY 34.1
Spahn-Bos 33.7
Roberts-Phi 32.6
Jansen-NY 28.6
Roe-Bro 26.4

Adjusted Starter Runs
Maglie-NY 32.7
Roberts-Phi 28.7
Jansen-NY 27.2
Roe-Bro 25.3
Spahn-Bos 23.8

Clutch Pitching Index
Roe-Bro 122
Sain-Bos 113
Nichols-Bos 112
Minner-Chi 111
Bickford-Bos 108

Relief Runs
Brazle-StL 14.9
Kennedy-NY 12.9
Perkowski-Cin 12.9
Wilks-StL-Pit 12.3
Leonard-Chi 11.9

Adjusted Relief Runs
Brazle-StL 15.0
Wilks-StL-Pit 14.7
Perkowski-Cin 14.2
Leonard-Chi 13.1
Kennedy-NY 12.6

Relief Ranking
Leonard-Chi 24.3
Wilks-StL-Pit 14.8
Perkowski-Cin 11.6
Smith-Cin 11.2
Brazle-StL 11.1

Total Pitcher Index
Roberts-Phi 3.4
Maglie-NY 2.9
Blackwell-Cin 2.9
Jansen-NY 2.9
Spahn-Bos 2.9

Total Baseball Ranking
Robinson-Bro 6.8
Musial-StL 6.4
Kiner-Pit 5.4
Campanella-Bro ... 5.2
Ashburn-Phi 5.2

January 29 Baseball signs a six-year All-Star Game pact for TV-radio rights calling for $6 million.

February 9 The St. Louis Browns sign Satchel Paige, 45. He had been out of Major League Baseball since last pitching for the Indians in 1949.

February 21 The South Carolina House introduces a resolution urging that "Shoeless Joe" Jackson, who was banished from baseball because of his part in the Black Sox Scandal of 1919, be reinstated.

April 18 Mickey Mantle goes 1-for-4 in his first game as Eddie Lopat two-hits the Red Sox 6-1.

May 1 The Yankees' new phenom, Mickey Mantle, connects for his first major league home run, off Randy Gumpert of the White Sox. Minnie Minoso becomes the first black to play for the White Sox. He plays third base and, facing Vic Raschi in his first major league at bat, rips a home run to center field. The Yankees win 8–3.

July 1 Bob Feller pitches the third no-hitter of his career, tying the record of Cy Young and Larry Corcoran, as he beats Detroit's Bob Cain 2-1.

July 2 Bill Veeck gets the necessary 75 percent of outstanding stock on the last day of his option to buy the St. Louis Browns from Bill and Charlie DeWitt.

July 8 The feud between Joe DiMaggio and Casey Stengel reaches a head. After DiMag makes a misplay in the first inning, Stengel sends reserve Jackie Jensen out to center field to relieve the Yankee Clipper in the second.

August 19 Bill Veeck signs a 3'7" midget, Eddie Gaedel, who goes to bat wearing the number 1/8 in the first inning of the nightcap with the Tigers. Lefty Bob Cain walks him on four pitches. Jim Delsing then pinch runs or Gaedel. Two days later the major league commissioner bars Eddie Gaedel from appearing in any more games.

August 28 The Yankees make another late-season insurance measure buying Johnny Sain from the Braves for $50,000 and a young pitcher named Lew Burdette.

September 28 Allie Reynolds pitches his second no-hitter of the season, defeating the Red Sox in Yankee Stadium 8-0. With two outs in the ninth, Ted Williams hits a foul pop that catcher Yogi Berra drops. Williams then hits another foul fly that Berra grabs for the last out.

October 9 Gil McDougald becomes the first rookie to hit a grand slam in the World Series, as the Yankees win in a romp 13-1. Ed Lopat wins his second game.

October 10 Hank Bauer's bases-loaded triple propels the Yankees to a 4-3 win and their third straight championship.

November 8 Yogi Berra of the NY Yankees wins the first of his three MVP awards.

November 18 Former Cub first baseman and future star of *The Rifleman* Chuck Connors is the first player to oppose the major league draft. Currently the first baseman of the LA Angels (PCL), Connors wants to stay in California, instead of going to whatever team might draft him for the major leagues. The PCL views his refusal in a positive manner, allowing them to ask higher prices for players than what the major league usually offers.

December 11 Joe DiMaggio officially retires as a member of the New York Yankees with 361 home runs and an average of .325 after 13 seasons.

BOSTON	CHICAGO	CLEVELAND	DETROIT	NEW YORK	PHILADELPHIA	ST.LOUIS	WASHINGTON
M S.O'Neill	M P.Richards	M A.Lopez	M R.Rolfe	M C.Stengel	M J.Dykes	M Z.Taylor	M B.Harris
1B W.Dropo	1B E.Robinson	1B L.Easter	1B D.Kryhoski	1B J.Collins	1B F.Fain	1B H.Arft	1B M.Vernon
2B B.Doerr	2B N.Fox	2B B.Avila	2B J.Priddy	2B J.Coleman	2B P.Suder	2B B.Young	2B C.Michaels
SS J.Pesky	SS C.Carrasquel	SS R.Boone	SS J.Lipon	SS P.Rizzuto	SS E.Joost	SS B.Jennings	SS P.Runnels
3B V.Stephens	3B B.Dillinger	3B A.Rosen	3B G.Kell	3B B.Brown	3B H.Majeski	3B F.Marsh	3B B.Yost
LF T.Williams	LF M.Minoso	LF D.Mitchell	LF H.Evers	LF G.Woodling	LF G.Zernial	LF R.Coleman	LF G.Coan
CF D.DiMaggio	CF J.Busby	CF L.Doby	CF J.Groth	CF J.DiMaggio	CF D.Philley	CF J.Delsing	CF I.Noren
RF C.Vollmer	RF A.Zarilla	RF B.Kennedy	RF V.Wertz	RF H.Bauer	RF E.Valo	RF K.Wood	RF S.Mele
C L.Moss	C P.Masi	C J.Hegan	C J.Ginsberg	C Y.Berra	C J.Tipton	C S.Lollar	C M.Guerra
12 B.Goodman	O B.Stewart	O S.Chapman	O P.Mullin	O M.Mantle	1 L.Limmer	O M.Batts	S2 S.Dente
S3 L.Boudreau	O D.Lenhardt	O1 H.Simpson	1 D.Kolloway	32 G.McDougald	32 B.Hitchcock	O C.Mapes	O M.McCormick
C B.Rosar	O R.Coleman	C B.Tebbetts	O S.Souchock	1 J.Mize	C J.Astroth	O J.Bero	S2 G.Verble
3 F.Hatfield	3 G.Niarhos	2 S.Stirnweiss	S2 N.Berry	O J.Jensen	O3 A.Clark	S T.Upton	C M.Grasso
O C.Maxwell	O F.Baker	O B.McCosky	1 B.Swift	2 J.Hopp	2 L.Klein	O J.Maguire	C C.Kluttz
C A.Robinson	C B.Sheely	S M.Combs	C A.Robinson	2 B.Martin	3 W.Moses	3 J.Berardino	O S.Robertson
O T.Wright	S2 J.DeMaestri	/1 M.Minoso	/O C.Keller	O C.Mapes	1 R.Murray	O D.Long	/O F.Campos
C M.Guerra	/O P.Lehner	/O P.Lehner	C F.House	O C.Silvera	O S.Chapman	O D.Lenhardt	/O D.Porter
C M.Batts	/1 B.Haas	/O C.Maddern	/O R.Sullivan	3 B.Johnson	3 K.Wahl	O E.Rapp	/C F.Sacka
C A.Evans	/3 H.Majeski	/C A.Clark	/2 A.Federoff	/O B.Cerv	/O P.Lehner	1 B.Taylor	/1 F.Taylor
/2 M.Hoderlein	C J.Erautt	H H.Naragon	H D.Daugherty	/S J.Brideweser	1 B.McCosky	O R.Sievers	/S W.Miranda
/1 N.Zauchin	/O D.Philley	H M.Nielsen	P T.Gray	/C R.Houk	/2 T.Davis	O P.Lehner	/1 L.Okrie
/O B.DiPietro	/O G.Zernial	H L.Klein	P D.Trout	/O A.Wilson	/2 E.Samcoff	C L.Moss	/1 R.Hawes
/S A.Richter	/1 B.Boyd	/C R.Murray	P F.Hutchinson	/C C.Courtney	P A.Kellner	O B.Nieman	P C.Marrero
/C S.White	/1 G.Goldsberry	H T.Tucker	P V.Trucks	P V.Raschi	P B.Shantz	1 J.Lutz	P S.Consuegra
/O K.Olson	/C R.Wilson	R D.Hansen	P B.Cain	P E.Lopat	P B.Hooper	/3 K.Wahl	P J.Johnson
P M.Parnell	/C S.Hairston	P E.Wynn	RP G.Bearden	P A.Reynolds	P C.Scheib	S B.Thomas	P S.Hudson
P R.Scarborough	H R.Nelson	P B.Lemon	RP H.White	P T.Morgan	P M.Martin	/3 J.Dyck	P B.Porterfield
P M.McDermott	P B.Pierce	P M.Garcia	P M.Stuart	P S.Shea	RP J.Kucab	/O F.Saucier	RP M.Harris
P C.Stobbs	P S.Rogovin	P B.Feller	P H.Newhouser	RP J.Ostrowski	P S.Zoldak	/2 M.Goliat	RP J.Haynes
P W.Nixon	P K.Holcombe	P S.Gromek	P H.Borowy	P B.Kuzava	P D.Fowler	/S B.DeMars	P J.Moreno
RP E.Kinder	P J.Dobson	RP L.Brissie	/P S.Rogovin	P A.Schallock	P J.Coleman	/C C.Kluttz	P A.Sima
RP H.Taylor	P R.Gumpert	/P D.Rozek	/P R.Herbert	P S.Overmire	/P M.Burtschy	H E.Gaedel	P D.Starr
RP W.Masterson	RP L.Aloma	/P S.Jones	/P W.McLeland	/P J.Kramer	/P H.Wyse	P N.Garver	/P B.Kuzava
P B.Wight	RP M.Rotblatt	/P J.Fahr	/P E.Johnson	/P J.Sain	/P L.Brissie	P D.Pillette	P T.Ferrick
P L.Kiely	P L.Kretlow	/P B.Harris	/P D.Marlowe	/P F.Sanford	/P B.Harris	P T.Byrne	/P F.Sanford
/P B.Evans	P H.Judson	/P J.Vander Meer	/P P.Calvert	/P T.Byrne		P A.Widmar	/P B.Ross
/P H.Hisner	/P H.Dorish			/P T.Ferrick		RP B.Mahoney	/P A.Brown
/P B.Flowers	/P B.Cain			/P B.Wiesler		RP S.Paige	/P H.Wyse
/P P.Hinrichs	/P R.Grimsley			/P B.Hogue		RP B.Kennedy	/P G.Bearden
	/P D.Littlefield			/P E.Nevel		P J.Suchecki	
	/P H.Brown			/P B.Muncrief		P J.McDonald	
	/P B.Mahoney			/P B.Porterfield		P L.Sleater	
						P D.Starr	
						/P S.Overmire	
						/P B.Hogue	
						/P F.Sanford	
						/P D.Markell	
						/P C.Fannin	
						/P D.Johnson	
						/P I.Medlinger	
						/P B.Turley	
						/P S.Schacht	
						/P B.Herrera	

TEAM	G	W	L	PCT	GB	R	OR	AB	H	2B	3B	HR	BB	SO	AVG	OBP	SLG	PRO	PRO+	BR	/A	PF	CHI	RC	SB	CS	SBA	SBR
NY	154	98	56	.636		798	621	5194	1395	208	48	140	605	547	.269	.349	.408	.757	113	62	90	96	104	762	78	39	67	0
CLE	155	93	61	.604	5	696	594	5250	1346	208	35	140	606	632	.256	.336	.389	.725	106	0	40	94	98	710	52	35	60	-5
BOS	154	87	67	.565	11	804	725	5378	1428	233	32	127	756	594	.266	.358	.392	.750	98	64	-13	110	100	778	20	21	49	-7
CHI	155	81	73	.526	17	714	644	5378	1453	229	64	86	596	524	.270	.349	.385	.734	105	23	39	98	95	745	99	70	59	-12
DET	154	73	81	.474	25	685	741	5336	1413	231	35	104	568	525	.265	.338	.380	.718	99	-14	-17	100	98	697	37	34	52	-9
PHI	154	70	84	.455	28	736	745	5277	1381	262	43	102	677	565	.262	.338	.386	.735	101	29	13	102	98	745	47	36	57	-8
WAS	154	62	92	.403	36	672	764	5329	1399	242	45	54	560	515	.263	.336	.355	.691	93	-60	-48	98	103	648	45	38	54	-9
STL	154	52	102	.338	46	611	882	5219	1288	223	47	86	521	693	.247	.317	.357	.674	84	-102	-119	103	103	592	35	38	48	-12
TOT	617					5716		42361	11103	1836	349	839	4889	4595	.262	.342	.381	.723							413	311	57	-63

TEAM	CG	SH	SV	IP	H	H/G	HR	BB	SO	RAT	ERA	ERA+	OAV	OOB	PR	/A	PF	CPI	FA	E	DP	FW	PW	BW	SBW	DIF
NY	66	24	22	1367	1290	8.5	92	562	664	12.4	3.56	107	.250	.328	85	41	93	103	.975	144	190	.3	4.0	8.9	.8	7.0
CLE	76	10	19	1391¹	1287	8.3	86	577	642	12.2	3.38	112	.245	.323	114	63	92	103	.978	134	151	.9	6.2	3.9	.3	4.7
BOS	46	7	24	1399	1413	9.1	100	599	658	13.2	4.14	108	.264	.342	-2	50	108	100	.977	141	184	.5	4.9	-1.3	.0	5.8
CHI	74	11	14	1418¹	1353	8.6	109	549	572	12.2	3.50	115	.252	.323	97	84	98	105	.975	151	176	.0	8.3	3.8	-.4	-7.7
DET	51	8	17	1384	1385	9.0	102	602	597	13.2	4.29	97	.262	.342	-26	-18	101	96	.973	163	166	-.7	-1.8	-1.7	-.1	.2
PHI	52	7	22	1358	1421	9.4	109	569	437	13.4	4.47	96	.272	.347	-52	-29	104	98	.978	136	204	.8	-2.9	1.3	-.0	-6.2
WAS	58	6	13	1366¹	1429	9.4	110	630	475	13.7	4.49	91	.269	.348	-55	-59	99	97	.973	160	148	-.5	-5.8	-4.7	-.1	-3.8
STL	56	5	9	1370¹	1525	10.0	131	801	550	15.5	5.18	85	.282	.379	-160	-119	107	101	.971	172	179	-1.2	-11.7	-11.7	-.4	-.0
TOT	479	78	140	11054¹		9.0				13.2	4.12		.262	.342					.975	1201	1398					

Runs
DiMaggio-Bos 113
Minoso-Cle-Chi ... 112
Yost-Was 109
Williams-Bos 109
Joost-Phi 107

Hits
Kell-Det 191
Fox-Chi 189
DiMaggio-Bos 189
Minoso-Cle-Chi ... 173
Williams-Bos 169

Doubles
Yost-Was 36
Mele-Was 36
Kell-Det 36

Triples
Minoso-Cle-Chi ... 14
Coleman-StL-Chi ... 12
Fox-Chi 12
Young-StL 9

Home Runs
Zernial-Chi-Phi ... 33
Williams-Bos 30
Robinson-Chi 29

Total Bases
Williams-Bos 295
Zernial-Chi-Phi ... 292
Robinson-Chi 279
Berra-NY 269
DiMaggio-Bos 267

Runs Batted In
Zernial-Chi-Phi ... 129
Williams-Bos 126
Robinson-Chi 117
Easter-Cle 103
Rosen-Cle........ 102

Runs Produced
Williams-Bos 205
Zernial-Chi-Phi ... 188
Minoso-Cle-Chi ... 178
Robinson-Chi 173
DiMaggio-Bos 173

Bases On Balls
Williams-Bos 144
Yost-Was 126
Joost-Phi 106
Doby-Cle 101
Rosen-Cle 85

Batting Average
Fain-Phi 344
Minoso-Cle-Chi ...326
Kell-Det 319
Williams-Bos 318
Fox-Chi 313

On Base Percentage
Williams-Bos ..... .464
Fain-Phi .... .451
Doby-Cle .... .428
Yost-Was .... .423
Minoso-Cle-Chi ... .422

Slugging Average
Williams-Bos 556
Doby-Cle 512
Zernial-Chi-Phi ...511
Wertz-Det 511
Minoso-Cle-Chi ...500

Production
Williams-Bos 1.019
Doby-Cle 941
Minoso-Cle-Chi ...922
Fain-Phi 921
Wertz-Det 894

Adjusted Production
Doby-Cle 163
Williams-Bos 159
Minoso-Cle-Chi... 152
Fain-Phi 146
Wertz-Det 140

Batter Runs
Williams-Bos 62.8
Minoso-Cle-Chi .. 38.2
Doby-Cle 37.0
Fain-Phi 33.8
Joost-Phi 30.5

Adjusted Batter Runs
Williams-Bos 49.5
Doby-Cle 42.9
Minoso-Cle-Chi .. 40.8
Yost-Was 32.2
Fain-Phi 31.8

Clutch Hitting Index
Mele-Was......... 136
Busby-Chi 127
Noren-Was 120
Zernial-Chi-Phi .. 118
DiMaggio-NY 113

Runs Created
Williams-Bos 152
Minoso-Cle-Chi .. 120
Yost-Was 117
Joost-Phi 115
Doby-Cle 108

Total Average
Williams-Bos 1.177
Doby-Cle 1.031
Minoso-Cle-Chi ...987
Fain-Phi 959
Yost-Was 909

Stolen Bases
Minoso-Cle-Chi.... 31
Busby-Chi 26
Rizzuto-NY 18

Stolen Base Average
Rizzuto-NY 85.7
Minoso-Cle-Chi ... 75.6
Busby-Chi 70.3

Stolen Base Runs
Rizzuto-NY 3.6
Minoso-Cle-Chi .. 3.3
Carrasquel-Chi 1.8

Fielding Runs
Coan-Was 22.0
Noren-Was 21.1
Stephens-Bos 14.1
Fain-Phi 12.6
Carrasquel-Chi .. 12.5

Total Player Rating
Williams-Bos 4.5
Joost-Phi 3.9
Doby-Cle 3.6
Fain-Phi 3.6
Berra-NY 3.3

Wins
Feller-Cle 22
Raschi-NY 21
Lopat-NY 21

Win Percentage
Feller-Cle .... .733
Lopat-NY .... .700
Reynolds-NY ...... .680
Raschi-NY .... .677
Shantz-Phi........ .643

Games
Kinder-Bos 63
Brissie-Phi-Cle..... 56
Garcia-Cle 47
Scheib-Phi 46

Complete Games
Garver-StL 24
Wynn-Cle 21
Lopat-NY 20
Pierce-Chi 18

Shutouts
Reynolds-NY 7
Raschi-NY 4
Lopat-NY 4
Feller-Cle 4

Saves
Kinder-Bos 14
Scheib-Phi 10
Brissie-Phi-Cle ... 9
Reynolds-NY 7
Garcia-Cle 6

Innings Pitched
Wynn-Cle 274.1
Lemon-Cle 263.1
Raschi-NY 258.1
Garcia-Cle 254.0
Feller-Cle 249.2

Fewest Hits/Game
Reynolds-NY 6.96
McDermott-Bos ... 7.38
Wynn-Cle 7.45
Rogovin-Det-Chi .. 7.85
Lopat-NY 8.02

Fewest BB/Game
Hutchinson-Det ... 1.29
Lopat-NY 2.72
Pierce-Chi 2.73
Hooper-Phi 2.90
Garcia-Cle 2.91

Strikeouts
Raschi-NY 164
Wynn-Cle 133
Lemon-Cle 132
Gray-Det 131
McDermott-Bos ... 127

Strikeouts/Game
McDermott-Bos .. 6.65
Gray-Det 5.97
Raschi-NY 5.71
Reynolds-NY 5.13
Lemon-Cle 4.51

Ratio
Lopat-NY 10.85
Rogovin-Det-Chi ..10.97
Wynn-Cle 11.06
Hutchinson-Det ..11.13
Reynolds-NY 11.24

Earned Run Average
Rogovin-Det-Chi ..2.78
Lopat-NY 2.91
Wynn-Cle 3.02
Pierce-Chi 3.03
Reynolds-NY 3.05

Adjusted ERA
Rogovin-Det-Chi ... 146
Parnell-Bos 137
McDermott-Bos ... 133
Pierce-Chi 133
Lopat-NY 131

Opponents' Batting Avg.
Reynolds-NY 213
Wynn-Cle 225
McDermott-Bos ...226
Rogovin-Det-Chi ...235
Lopat-NY 239

Opponents' On Base Pct.
Lopat-NY 298
Rogovin-Det-Chi ...301
Wynn-Cle 301
Hutchinson-Det ...302
Reynolds-NY 304

Starter Runs
Wynn-Cle 33.6
Rogovin-Det-Chi .. 32.2
Lopat-NY 31.5
Pierce-Chi 29.1
Garcia-Cle 27.3

Adjusted Starter Runs
Rogovin-Det-Chi .. 30.5
Parnell-Bos 29.5
Pierce-Chi 26.7
Lopat-NY 23.8
Wynn-Cle 23.4

Clutch Pitching Index
Parnell-Bos 119
Pierce-Chi 113
Rogovin-Det-Chi . 111
Feller-Cle 109
Raschi-NY 108

Relief Runs
Kinder-Bos 22.2
Aloma-Chi 17.7
Brissie-Phi-Cle .. 7.5
Ostrowski-NY 6.7
Masterson-Bos ... 5.2

Adjusted Relief Runs
Kinder-Bos 26.9
Aloma-Chi 17.1
Masterson-Bos ... 7.4
Brissie-Phi-Cle .. 3.6
Ostrowski-NY 3.6

Relief Ranking
Kinder-Bos 31.5
Aloma-Chi 15.0
Harris-Was 4.3
Masterson-Bos ... 3.9
Ostrowski-NY 3.8

Total Pitcher Index
Parnell-Bos 4.1
Garver-StL 3.1
Pierce-Chi 2.9
Kinder-Bos 2.7

Total Baseball Ranking
Williams-Bos 4.5
Parnell-Bos 4.1
Joost-Phi 3.9
Doby-Cle 3.6
Fain-Phi 3.6

January 16 The U.S. Standardization Board clears the way for Stan Musial to get a salary increase to $85,000. Prior to this relaxation of the rules, there was a wage freeze in effect due to the Korean War.

January 31 Harry Heilmann with 203 votes and Paul Waner with 195 become the newest members of the Hall of Fame.

February 16 Hall of Famer Honus Wagner, 77, retires after 40 years as a major league player and coach. He receives a pension from the Pirates, with whom he spent most of those years.

April 15 In the last home opener in Braves Field in Boston, 4,694 fans watch Warren Spahn lose 3-2 to Brooklyn's Preacher Roe.

April 23 Future Hall of Famer Hoyt Wilhelm of the New York Giants wins his first major league game pitching five innings in relief in a 9-5 win. He homers in his first at bat against the Braves' Dick Hoover. It's Wilhelm's only major league home run in 1,070 games.

May 28 The Giants Willie Mays enters the army. Although Mays is hitting just .236, the Giants are 2½ games in first place. They will lose eight of their next ten games.

May 31 Charlie Grimm succeeds Tommy Holmes as manager of the Boston Braves. Holmes will sign on with the Dodgers as a pinch hitter, but hit just .111.

June 14 The Braves get a split. Warren Spahn ties the NL record of Jim Whitney with 18 strikeouts but loses to the Cubs 3-1 in 15 innings; however, on the same day, Braves scout Dewey Griggs signs Henry Aaron to a Braves contract.

July 8 The NL defeats the AL, 3–2 ,behind the pitching of the Phils' Curt Simmons and the Cubs' Bob Rush at the All-Star Game in Philadelphia. The game is ended after five innings because of rain. Cub Hank Sauer's homer with Stan Musial aboard in the fourth proves to be the deciding run.

July 30 Baseball Commissioner Ford Frick sets a waiver rule to bar interleague deals until all clubs bid, with the club lowest in the league to get the first pick. He sets the price at $10,000. He also bars all other deals after July 31.

September 15 The Braves play their last game in Boston's Braves Field before moving to Milwaukee, losing to Brooklyn's Joe Black 8-2. The crowd of 8,822 is the Braves' second largest of the season.

September 23 The Dodgers clinch the NL pennant, the first time in four years the NL winner is not determined by the outcome of the last game.

September 29 Stan Musial makes his only major league pitching appearance. With his sixth batting title wrapped up, he takes the mound against the Cubs Frank Baumholtz, the runner-up in the batting race. Baumholtz, batting right-handed, reaches base on an error, and Harvey Haddix relieves Musial. The Cubs win, 3–0, behind Paul Minner.

October 1 In Game 1 of the World Series, the Dodgers defeat the Yankees 4-2 at Ebbets Field behind relief ace Joe Black, who started only two games during the season.

November 20 The writers name Cubs slugger Hank Sauer as the NL MVP. The Cubs finished in fifth place, despite Sauer's 37 home runs and 121 RBI.

November 21 Dodgers pitcher Joe Black, who had a record of 15-4, is voted NL Rookie of the Year.

	BOSTON		BROOKLYN		CHICAGO		CINCINNATI		NEW YORK		PHILADELPHIA		PITTSBURGH		ST.LOUIS
M	T.Holmes	M	C.Dressen	M	P.Cavarretta	M	L.Sewell	M	L.Durocher	M	E.Sawyer	M	B.Meyer	M	E.Stanky
M	C.Grimm	1B	G.Hodges	1B	D.Fondy	1B	E.Brucker	1B	W.Lockman	1B	S.O'Neill	1B	T.Bartirome	1B	D.Sisler
1B	E.Torgeson	2B	J.Robinson	2B	E.Miksis	M	R.Hornsby	2B	D.Williams	1B	E.Waitkus	2B	J.Merson	2B	R.Schoendienst
2B	J.Dittmer	SS	P.Reese	SS	R.Smalley	1B	T.Kluszewski	SS	A.Dark	2B	C.Ryan	SS	D.Groat	SS	S.Hemus
SS	J.Logan	3B	B.Cox	3B	R.Jackson	2B	G.Hatton	3B	B.Thomson	SS	G.Hamner	3B	P.Castiglione	3B	B.Johnson
3B	E.Mathews	LF	A.Pafko	LF	H.Sauer	SS	R.McMillan	LF	B.Elliott	3B	W.Jones	LF	R.Kiner	LF	P.Lowrey
LF	S.Gordon	CF	D.Snider	CF	H.Jeffcoat	3B	B.Adams	CF	H.Thompson	LF	D.Ennis	CF	B.Del Greco	CF	S.Musial
CF	S.Jethroe	RF	C.Furillo	RF	F.Baumholtz	LF	J.Adcock	RF	D.Mueller	CF	R.Ashburn	RF	G.Bell	RF	E.Slaughter
RF	J.Daniels	C	R.Campanella	C	T.Atwell	CF	B.Borkowski	C	W.Westrum	RF	J.Wyrostek	C	J.Garagiola	C	D.Rice
C	W.Cooper					RF	W.Marshall			C	S.Burgess				
		O	G.Shuba	O	G.Hermanski	C	A.Seminick	O	D.Rhodes			S2	C.Koshorek	O	H.Rice
O	B.Thorpe	3	B.Morgan	32	B.Serena			C	S.Yvars	C	S.Lopata	1O	C.Metkovich	3	T.Glaviano
2O	S.Sisti	C	R.Walker	O	B.Addis	O	H.Edwards	O	W.Mays	O	M.Clark	2S	G.Strickland	O	L.Miggins
1	G.Crowe	O	D.Williams	S2	T.Brown	O	W.Westlake	O	M.Irvin	O	J.Mayo	C	C.McCullough	2	E.Stanky
C	P.Burris	2S	R.Bridges	2	B.Ramazzotti	O	C.Abrams	O	G.Wilson	3	B.Nicholson	O	S.Senerchia	O	W.Westlake
C	E.St.Claire	O	S.Amoros	C	H.Chiti	C	J.Rossi	3	B.Rigney	/S	P.Caballero	O	B.Davis	1	S.Bilko
2	R.Hartsfield	/1	R.Nelson	C	B.Edwards	O	J.Wyrostek	O	C.Hartung	/1	N.Jones	O	D.Hall	C	L.Fusselman
S	J.Cusick	/O	T.Holmes	1	P.Cavarretta	2	E.Pellagrini	2	B.Hofman	/S	J.Lohrke	O	L.Walls	3	V.Benson
O	W.Marshall	/O	C.Abrams	C	J.Pramesa	2	J.Temple	O	R.Katt	/1	T.Brown	C	E.FitzGerald	S	V.Stallcup
2	B.Reed	/C	S.Lembo	/S	L.Brinkopf	O	J.Greengrass	O	C.Diering	/2	D.Young	3	D.Smith	/1	N.Hertweck
O	P.Whisenant			/S	B.Hardin	O	W.Post	/S	D.Spencer	H	D.Wilber	2	J.Berardino	O	B.Sarni
/S	B.Clarkson	P	C.Erskine	H	R.Northey	C	H.Landrith	/O	B.Howerton			O	T.Beard	/S	G.Mauch
/S	B.Klaus	P	B.Loes	H	B.Usher	C	D.Howell	/C	R.Noble	P	R.Roberts	O	E.Dusak	/3	E.Kazak
		P	B.Wade			/O	D.Sisler	H	D.Wakefield	P	R.Meyer	/O	B.Howerton	H	H.Gorman
P	W.Spahn	P	P.Roe	P	B.Rush	/3	E.Kazak			P	K.Drews	/O	F.Thomas		
P	J.Wilson	P	C.Van Cuyk	P	J.Klippstein	/S	V.Stallcup	P	J.Hearn	P	C.Simmons	/C	J.Mangan	P	G.Staley
P	M.Surkont	RP	J.Black	P	W.Hacker			P	S.Maglie	P	S.Ridzik	/1	J.Phillips	P	V.Mizell
P	V.Bickford			P	P.Minner	P	K.RaffensbergerP		L.Jansen	RP	J.Konstanty			P	J.Presko
P	L.Burdette	P	J.Rutherford	P	T.Lown	P	H.Perkowski	P	D.Koslo	RP	A.Hansen	P	M.Dickson	P	C.Boyer
RP	S.Jones	P	C.Labine	RP	B.Schultz	P	H.Wehmeier	P	M.Lanier			P	H.Pollet	P	H.Brecheen
		P	R.Branca	RP	D.Leonard	RP	B.Church	RP	M.Wilhelm	P	H.Fox	P	B.Friend	RP	A.Brazle
P	E.Johnson	P	C.King			P	F.Hiller	RP	M.Kennedy	P	K.Heintzelman	P	W.Main	RP	E.Yuhas
P	V.Jester	/P	J.Landrum	P	B.Kelly	RP	F.Smith	/P	G.Spencer	L.Possehl	RP	R.Kline	P	C.Chambers
P	D.Cole	P	J.Schmitz	P	W.Ramsdell	RP	J.Nuxhall			/P	B.Miller	RP	T.Wilks	P	S.Miller
P	B.Chipman	P	R.Moore	P	J.Hatten			P	A.Corwin	RP	K.Peterson	RP	P.LaPalme	/P	H.Haddix
/P	G.Conley	/P	J.Hughes	P	D.Manville	P	E.Blackwell	P	H.Gregg	/P	P.Stuffel			P	B.Werle
/P	D.Donovan	/P	K.Lehman	/P	V.Fear	P	B.Podbielan	/P	B.Connelly	/P	B.Church	P	C.Hogue	P	W.Schmidt
/P	B.Thiel	/P	R.Negray	/P	C.Howe	/P	B.Byerly	/P	M.Picone			P	R.Necciai	P	M.Clark
/P	D.Hoover	/P	B.Podbielan	/P	M.Dubiel	P	P.Haugstad	/P	J.Harshman			P	J.Waugh	P	D.Bokelmann
						/P	N.Jordan	/P	G.Bamberger			P	J.Muir	/P	J.Crimian
						/P	J.Schmitz	/P	R.Bowman			/P	R.Munger	/P	B.Tiefenauer
						/P	E.Blake					/P	H.Fisher	/P	R.Munger
												/P	B.Bell	/P	J.Collum
												/P	D.Carlsen	/P	F.Hahn
												/P	J.Suchecki		
												/P	J.Dunn		
												/P	B.Werle		
												/P	E.Wolfe		
												/P	M.Queen		

TEAM	G	W	L	PCT	GB	R	OR	AB	H	2B	3B	HR	BB	SO	AVG	OBP	SLG	PRO	PRO+	BR	/A	PF	CHI	RC	SB	CS	SBA	SBR
BRO	155	96	57	.627		775	603	5266	1380	199	32	153	663	699	.262	.348	.399	.747	113	107	98	101	100	754	90	49	65	-2
NY	154	92	62	.597	4.5	722	639	5229	1337	186	56	151	536	672	.256	.329	.399	.728	107	56	51	101	103	712	30	31	49	-10
STL	154	88	66	.571	8.5	677	630	5200	1386	247	54	97	537	479	.267	.340	.391	.731	110	68	67	100	95	708	33	32	51	-9
PHI	154	87	67	.565	9.5	657	552	5205	1353	237	45	93	540	534	.260	.332	.376	.708	104	26	33	99	98	671	60	41	59	-7
CHI	155	77	77	.500	19.5	628	631	5330	1408	223	45	107	492	712	.264	.321	.383	.704	101	5	-3	101	97	652	50	40	56	-9
CIN	154	69	85	.448	27.5	615	659	5234	1303	212	45	104	480	709	.249	.314	.366	.680	95	-36	-34	100	101	610	32	42	43	-16
BOS	155	64	89	.418	32	569	651	5221	1214	187	31	110	483	711	.233	.301	.343	.644	88	-102	-83	97	106	555	58	34	63	-3
PIT	155	42	112	.273	54.5	515	793	5193	1201	181	30	92	486	724	.231	.300	.331	.631	79	-125	-139	103	101	530	43	41	51	-12
TOT	618					5158		41878	10582	1672	338	907	4147	5240	.253	.323	.374	.697							396	310	56	-67

TEAM	CG	SH	SV	IP	H	H/G	HR	BB	SO	RAT	ERA	ERA+	OAV	OOB	PR	/A	PF	CPI	FA	E	DP	FW	PW	BW	SBW	DIF
BRO	45	11	24	1399^1	1295	8.3	121	544	773	12.0	3.53	103	.247	.321	31	17	98	103	.982	106	169	2.0	1.8	10.1	.7	4.9
NY	49	12	31	1371	1282	8.4	121	538	655	12.2	3.59	103	.248	.323	22	17	99	103	.974	158	175	-.8	1.8	5.3	-.2	8.9
STL	49	12	27	1361^1	1274	8.4	119	501	712	11.9	3.66	101	.247	.317	11	8	100	98	.977	141	159	.1	.8	6.9	-.0	3.2
PHI	80	17	16	1386^2	1306	8.5	95	373	609	11.0	3.07	119	.249	.301	102	90	98	104	.975	150	145	-.4	9.3	3.4	.1	-2.5
CHI	59	15	15	1386^1	1265	8.2	101	534	661	11.9	3.58	107	.240	.314	23	41	103	103	.982	107	145	-.1	4.2	-.3	-.0	-3.8
CIN	56	11	12	1363^1	1377	9.1	111	517	579	12.8	4.01	94	.267	.338	-43	-36	101	103	.975	146	123	1.9	-3.7	-3.5	-.8	-1.9
BOS	63	11	13	1396	1388	8.9	106	525	687	12.5	3.78	96	.259	.329	-7	-26	97	102	.975	154	143	-.5	-2.7	-8.6	.6	-1.3
PIT	43	5	8	1363^2	1395	9.2	133	615	564	13.4	4.65	86	.265	.345	-139	-99	103	94	.970	182	167	-2.0	-10.2	-14.4	-.4	-8.0
TOT	444	94	146	11027^2		8.6				12.2	3.73		.253	.323					.976	1144	1226					

Runs		Hits		Doubles		Triples		Home Runs		Total Bases	
Musial-StL	105	Musial-StL	194	Musial-StL	42	Thomson-NY	14	Sauer-Chi	37	Musial-StL	311
Hemus-StL	105	Schoendienst-StL	188	Schoendienst-StL	40	Slaughter-StL	12	Kiner-Pit	37	Sauer-Chi	301
Robinson-Bro	104	Adams-Cin	180	McMillan-Cin	32	Kluszewski-Cin	11	Hodges-Bro	32	Thomson-NY	293
Lockman-NY	99	Dark-NY	177	Sauer-Chi	31	Ennis-Phi	10	Mathews-Bos	25	Ennis-Phi	281
Reese-Bro	94	Lockman-NY	176	Ashburn-Phi	31			Gordon-Bos	25	Snider-Bro	264

Runs Batted In		Runs Produced		Bases On Balls		Batting Average		On Base Percentage		Slugging Average	
Sauer-Chi	121	Ennis-Phi	177	Kiner-Pit	110	Musial-StL	.336	Robinson-Bro	.440	Musial-StL	.538
Thomson-NY	108	Musial-StL	175	Hodges-Bro	107	Baumholtz-Chi	.325	Musial-StL	.432	Sauer-Chi	.531
Ennis-Phi	107	Thomson-NY	173	Robinson-Bro	106	Kluszewski-Cin	.320	Hemus-StL	.392	Kluszewski-Cin	.509
Hodges-Bro	102	Sauer-Chi	173	Musial-StL	96	Robinson-Bro	.308	Hodges-Bro	.386	Kiner-Pit	.500
Slaughter-StL	101	Slaughter-StL	163	Hemus-StL	96	Snider-Bro	.303	Slaughter-StL	.386	Hodges-Bro	.500

Production		Adjusted Production		Batter Runs		Adjusted Batter Runs		Clutch Hitting Index		Runs Created	
Musial-StL	.970	Musial-StL	167	Musial-StL	55.7	Musial-StL	55.6	Slaughter-StL	138	Musial-StL	141
Robinson-Bro	.904	Robinson-Bro	149	Robinson-Bro	41.9	Robinson-Bro	40.7	Hatton-Cin	129	Robinson-Bro	116
Kluszewski-Cin	.892	Kluszewski-Cin	146	Sauer-Chi	32.8	Gordon-Bos	31.8	Campanella-Bro	128	Sauer-Chi	111
Sauer-Chi	.892	Gordon-Bos	144	Kiner-Pit	32.7	Sauer-Chi	31.5	Sauer-Chi	115	Kiner-Pit	111
Hodges-Bro	.886	Sauer-Chi	143	Hodges-Bro	32.4	Hodges-Bro	31.3	Wyrostek-Cin-Phi	112	Hodges-Bro	106

Total Average		Stolen Bases		Stolen Base Average		Stolen Base Runs		Fielding Runs		Total Player Rating	
Musial-StL	1.017	Reese-Bro	30	Reese-Bro	85.7	Reese-Bro	6.0	Schoendienst-StL	32.9	Robinson-Bro	5.6
Robinson-Bro	.995	Jethroe-Bos	28	Robinson-Bro	77.4	Robinson-Bro	3.0	Logan-Bos	17.6	Schoendienst-StL	4.9
Kiner-Pit	.955	Robinson-Bro	24	Jethroe-Bos	75.7	Jethroe-Bos	3.0	Sauer-Chi	16.6	Sauer-Chi	4.2
Hodges-Bro	.921	Ashburn-Phi	16	Ashburn-Phi	59.3	Davis-Pit	1.5	Ashburn-Phi	15.1	Musial-StL	4.2
Sauer-Chi	.886					Slaughter-StL	1.2	McMillan-Cin	10.6	Hemus-StL	3.8

Wins		Win Percentage		Games		Complete Games		Shutouts		Saves	
Roberts-Phi	28	Wilhelm-NY	.833	Wilhelm-NY	71	Roberts-Phi	30	Simmons-Phi	6	Brazle-StL	16
Maglie-NY	18	Roberts-Phi	.800	Black-Bro	56	Dickson-Pit	21	Raffensberger-Cin	6	Black-Bro	15
Staley-StL	17	Black-Bro	.789	Yuhas-StL	54	Spahn-Bos	19			Wilhelm-NY	11
Rush-Chi	17	Maglie-NY	.692	Smith-Cin	53	Raffensberger-Cin	18			Leonard-Chi	11
Raffensberger-Cin	17	Hacker-Chi	.625	Main-Pit	48	Rush-Chi	17				

Innings Pitched		Fewest Hits/Game		Fewest BB/Game		Strikeouts		Strikeouts/Game		Ratio	
Roberts-Phi	330.0	Hacker-Chi	7.01	Roberts-Phi	1.23	Spahn-Bos	183	Mizell-StL	6.92	Hacker-Chi	8.56
Spahn-Bos	290.0	Wilhelm-NY	7.17	Hacker-Chi	1.51	Rush-Chi	157	Simmons-Phi	6.30	Roberts-Phi	9.33
Dickson-Pit	277.2	Erskine-Bro	7.27	Raffensberger-Cin	1.64	Roberts-Phi	148	Wilhelm-NY	6.10	Erskine-Bro	10.45
Rush-Chi	250.1	Rush-Chi	7.37	Staley-StL	1.95	Mizell-StL	146	Wade-Bro	5.90	Rush-Chi	10.50
Raffensberger-Cin	247.0	Loes-Bro	7.40	Drews-Phi	2.05	Simmons-Phi	141	Erskine-Bro	5.70	Drews-Phi	10.59

Earned Run Average		Adjusted ERA		Opponents' Batting Avg.		Opponents' On Base Pct.		Starter Runs		Adjusted Starter Runs	
Wilhelm-NY	2.43	Wilhelm-NY	152	Hacker-Chi	.212	Hacker-Chi	.247	Roberts-Phi	41.8	Roberts-Phi	39.0
Hacker-Chi	2.58	Hacker-Chi	149	Rush-Chi	.216	Roberts-Phi	.263	Rush-Chi	28.8	Rush-Chi	32.1
Roberts-Phi	2.59	Rush-Chi	143	Wilhelm-NY	.220	Rush-Chi	.282	Drews-Phi	25.8	Raffensberger-Cin	26.6
Loes-Bro	2.69	Roberts-Phi	141	Erskine-Bro	.220	Erskine-Bro	.289	Raffensberger-Cin	25.4	Hacker-Chi	26.2
Rush-Chi	2.70	Loes-Bro	135	Loes-Bro	.224	Spahn-Bos	.291	Spahn-Bos	24.3	Drews-Phi	23.8

Clutch Pitching Index		Relief Runs		Adjusted Relief Runs		Relief Ranking		Total Pitcher Index		Total Baseball Ranking	
Roe-Bro	127	Black-Bro	25.0	Black-Bro	23.5	Black-Bro	33.9	Rush-Chi	5.0	Robinson-Bro	5.6
Church-Phi-Cin	119	Wilhelm-NY	23.1	Wilhelm-NY	22.5	Wilhelm-NY	26.4	Roberts-Phi	4.0	Rush-Chi	5.0
Wilhelm-NY	119	Brazle-StL	12.3	Leonard-Chi	12.5	Brazle-StL	20.9	Black-Bro	3.3	Schoendienst-StL	4.9
Raffensberger-Cin	117	Leonard-Chi	11.6	Brazle-StL	12.1	Yuhas-StL	15.4	Wilhelm-NY	2.9	Sauer-Chi	4.2
Maglie-NY	116	Yuhas-StL	11.2	Yuhas-StL	11.0	Leonard-Chi	11.4	Drews-Phi	2.8	Musial-StL	4.2

January 9 As the Korean War drags on, the Marines give notice that they will recall Ted Williams to active duty.

April 23 Bob Cain of the Browns and Bob Feller of the Indians each pitch a one-hitter, with the Browns prevailing 1-0. It ties a major league record for the fewest hits by two teams in a game. Bobby Young hits a triple in the first inning and scores on an Al Rosen error, as the Browns move into first place. The Indians only hit is a single by Luke Easter. For Feller, it is the fourth time he's one-hit the Browns.

April 28 The St. Louis Browns lend two black minor league players, third baseman John Britton and pitcher Jim Newberry, to the Hankyu Braves of the Japanese Pacific League, making them the first team to send players outside of the U.S. Abe Saperstein, owner and coach of the world-famous Harlem Globetrotters, negotiates this special example in "lend-lease"for both sides.

April 30 Before 24,767 at Ted Williams Day at Fenway Park, the Red Sox slugger plays in his final game before going to Korea as a marine fighter pilot. In his last at bat, Williams hits a game-winning two-run home run against Detroit's Dizzy Trout to give Boston a 5–3 win.

June 10 The St. Louis Browns fire manager Rogers Hornsby in Boston. The players present owner Bill Veeck with a trophy for freeing them from Rajah's tyranny. The stunt was actually the work of Veeck and team traveling secretary Bill Durney. The Browns name Marty Marion as their player-manager.

August 25 In a 1-0 win at Yankee Stadium, Virgil Trucks of the Detroit Tigers pitches his second no-hitter of the season. The no-hitter is in doubt for three innings when a play made by shortstop Johnny Pesky in the third inning is under debate. The official scorer, John Drebinger, records it as an error when Pesky has trouble getting a ball hit by Phil Rizzuto out of his glove. Dan Daniel of the New York *World Telegram* convinces Drebinger that it cannot be ruled an error because the ball was stuck in the fielder's glove, and Rizzuto is awarded a hit. In the sixth inning, Drebinger calls Pesky in the dugout from the press box, and the shortstop says that he should be given the error rather than Rizzuto the hit. The call is changed yet again, and Virgil Trucks' no-hitter is preserved.

September 7 Johnny Mize's pinch-hit grand slam gives the Yanks a 5–1 win at Washington. He has now homered in each one of the 15 major league parks, including Sportsman's Park in St. Louis while in each league.

September 25 Hal Newhouser of the Tigers wins his 200th game. It is his last win for Detroit, who will release him in early 1953.

September 26 The Yanks clinch their fourth straight pennant, an 11-inning 5-2 win at Philadelphia behind Ed Lopat and Johnny Sain.

October 6 At Ebbets Field, the Yankees even it up for the third time, as Raschi and Reynolds combine for a 3-2 win in Brooklyn. Right fielder Carl Furillo robs Johnny Mize of a home run in the ninth.

October 7 In Game 7 the Yankees take their fourth consecutive World Series championship, as Allie Reynolds, one of three relievers, defeats Joe Black 4-2. Billy Martin saves the day by snaring a two-out, bases-loaded infield pop off the bat of Jackie Robinson. Gil Hodges goes hitless again and is 0-for-21 in the Series.

November 12 The baseball writers name Philadelphia pitcher Bobby Shantz as the AL MVP. He was 24-7 for the 79-75 A's.

	BOSTON		CHICAGO		CLEVELAND		DETROIT		NEW YORK		PHILADELPHIA		ST.LOUIS		WASHINGTON
M	L.Boudreau	M	P.Richards	M	A.Lopez	M	R.Rolfe	M	C.Stengel	M	J.Dykes	M	R.Hornsby	M	B.Harris
1B	D.Gernert	1B	E.Robinson	1B	L.Easter	1B	F.Hutchinson	1B	J.Collins	1B	F.Fain	M	M.Marion	1B	M.Vernon
2B	B.Goodman	2B	N.Fox	2B	B.Avila	1B	W.Dropo	2B	B.Martin	2B	S.Kell	1B	D.Kryhoski	2B	F.Baker
SS	J.Lipon	SS	C.Carrasquel	2B	R.Boone	2B	J.Priddy	SS	P.Rizzuto	SS	E.Joost	2B	B.Young	SS	P.Runnels
3B	G.Kell	3B	H.Rodriguez	3B	A.Rosen	SS	N.Berry	3B	G.McDougald	3B	B.Hitchcock	SS	J.DeMaestri	3B	E.Yost
LF	H.Evers	LF	M.Minoso	LF	D.Mitchell	3B	F.Hatfield	LF	G.Woodling	LF	G.Zernial	3B	J.Dyck	LF	G.Coan
CF	D.DiMaggio	CF	R.Coleman	CF	L.Doby	LF	P.Mullin	CF	M.Mantle	CF	D.Philley	LF	J.Delsing	CF	J.Busby
RF	F.Throneberry	RF	S.Mele	RF	H.Simpson	CF	J.Groth	RF	H.Bauer	RF	E.Valo	CF	J.Rivera	RF	J.Jensen
C	S.White	C	S.Lollar	C	J.Hegan	RF	V.Wertz	C	Y.Berra	C	J.Astroth	RF	B.Nieman	C	M.Grasso
						C	J.Ginsberg					C	C.Courtney		
S3	V.Stephens	O	B.Stewart	O	J.Fridley			O1	I.Noren	2S	P.Suder			O	K.Wood
23	T.Lepcio	O	J.Rivera	S	M.Combs	O3	S.Souchock	1	J.Mize	2	C.Michaels	/2	F.Marsh	2	M.Hoderlein
O	C.Vollmer	/S	W.Miranda	C	J.Tipton	2	A.Federoff	3	B.Brown	O	A.Clark	1	G.Goldsberry	C	C.Kluttz
SO	J.Piersall	S3	S.Dente	C	B.Tebbetts	O	C.Mapes	O	B.Cerv	R	R.Murray	S	M.Marion	O	F.Campos
C	D.Wilber	O	T.Wright	1	B.Glynn	S2	J.Pesky	C	C.Silvera	3	H.Majeski	3	C.Michaels	O	A.Wilson
1	W.Dropo	O	A.Zarilla	G	G.Strickland	C	M.Batts	2	J.Coleman	O	K.Thomas	O	V.Wertz	2	C.Michaels
O	D.Lenhardt	3	R.Krsnich	O	B.McCosky	1	D.Kolloway	3	A.Carey	C	J.Tipton	O	A.Zarilla	O	E.Rapp
3	J.Pesky	C	B.Sheely	O	W.Westlake	3	G.Kell	S	J.Brideweser	/2	S.Robertson	3	L.Thomas	2	J.Snyder
O	G.Schmees	C	P.Masi	3	H.Majeski	O	D.Lenhardt	1	J.Hopp	/3	H.Bevan	C	L.Moss	O	I.Noren
O	A.Zarilla	O	J.Busby	O	P.Reiser	S	J.Lipon	2	K.Segrist	/1	T.Hamilton	O	J.Porter	O	S.Mele
C	G.Niarhos	C	D.Johnson	O	B.Kennedy	/3	J.Delsing	/3	L.Babe	/S	J.Littrell	C	T.Wright	/2	F.Marsh
O	G.Stephens	/3	L.Thomas	O	D.Pope	S	H.Kuenn	/O	J.Jensen			O	T.Wright	/C	G.Bradshaw
O	A.Wilson	/O	H.Edwards	/2	J.Berardino	O	B.Swift	/C	R.Houk	P	B.Shantz	O	G.Schmees	2	H.Keller
S	M.Bolling	/O	G.Wilson	/C	Q.Trouppe	O	R.Sullivan	H	A.Wilson	P	A.Kellner	/O	E.Rapp	/1	F.Taylor
3	F.Hatfield	/1	K.Landenberger	/3	S.Stirnweiss	/O	J.Hopp	/O	C.Keller	P	H.Byrd	O	D.Lenhardt	/S	T.Upton
O	K.Wood	/S	S.Esposito			O	G.Lerchen			P	C.Scheib	O	R.Coleman	O	B.Varner
/1	C.Maxwell	/C	R.Wilson	P	B.Lemon	/O	B.Tuttle	P	A.Reynolds	P	B.Hooper	/1	R.Sievers	R	S.Robertson
/O	T.Williams	H	D.Nicholas	P	M.Garcia	/O	D.Lund	P	V.Raschi	RP	J.Kucab	1	H.Arft		
/O	P.Lehner			P	E.Wynn	/1	B.Taylor	P	E.Lopat			/O	J.Crawford	P	B.Porterfield
/S	L.Boudreau	P	B.Pierce	P	B.Feller	P	C.Linhart	P	J.Sain	P	S.Zoldak	/S	W.Miranda	P	C.Marrero
/3	H.Bevan	P	S.Rogovin	P	S.Gromek	H	H.Evers			P	D.Fowler	/S	S.Rojek	P	S.Shea
/C	L.Okrie	P	J.Dobson	RP	L.Brissie	R	A.Garbowski	RP	J.McDonald	P	B.Newsom	/2	M.Goliat	P	W.Masterson
		P	M.Grissom	RP	M.Harris			RP	B.Hogue	P	E.Wright			P	J.Moreno
P	M.Parnell	P	C.Stobbs			P	T.Gray			/P	C.Bishop	P	D.Pillette	RP	S.Consuegra
P	M.McDermott	RP	H.Dorish			P	A.Houtteman	P	T.Morgan	/P	M.Martin	P	T.Byrne	RP	D.Johnson
P	D.Trout	RP	B.Kennedy	P	S.Jones	P	V.Trucks	P	B.Miller	/P	M.Fricano	P	B.Cain	RP	T.Ferrick
P	S.Hudson			P	D.Rozek	P	H.Newhouser	P	T.Gorman	/P	W.Kellner	P	G.Bearden		
P	D.Brodowski	P	L.Kretlow	/P	T.Wilks	P	B.Wight	P	J.Ostrowski	P	T.Hoyle	P	N.Garver	P	R.Gumpert
RP	I.Delock	P	H.Brown	/P	B.Abernathie	RP	H.White	/P	R.Scarborough	/P	L.Matarazzo	RP	D.Madison	P	J.Haynes
RP	R.Scarborough	P	L.Aloma	/P	G.Zuverink	RP	D.Littlefield	/P	H.Schaeffer					P	S.Hudson
		P	K.Holcombe					/P	E.Blackwell			P	S.Paige	/P	L.Sleater
P	W.Nixon	P	H.Judson			P	B.Hoeft	/P	J.Schmitz			E	E.Harrist	/P	M.Fornieles
P	E.Kinder	/P	H.Hudson			P	M.Stuart	/P	A.Schallock			/P	D.Littlefield	P	B.Newsom
P	B.Henry	/P	A.Widmar			P	F.Hutchinson					P	S.Overmire	/P	R.Sanchez
P	A.Benton					P	D.Trout					P	M.Stuart	/P	M.Harris
P	R.Brickner					P	D.Madison					P	K.Holcombe	/P	B.Stewart
P	B.Wight					/P	K.Johnson					P	C.Fannin	/P	H.Grossman
P	R.Gumpert					/P	D.Marlowe					/P	B.Hogue		
/P	H.Freeman					N	N.Garver					/P	J.Hetki		
/P	J.Atkins					/P	B.Black					/P	L.Sleater		
/P	H.Taylor					/P	W.McLeland					/P	H.Hudson		
/P	W.Masterson											/P	B.Mahoney		
												/P	P.Taylor		

TEAM	G	W	L	PCT	GB	R	OR	AB	H	2B	3B	HR	BB	SO	AVG	OBP	SLG	PRO	PRO+	BR	/A	PF	CHI	RC	SB	CS	SBA	SBR
NY	154	95	59	.617		727	557	5294	1411	221	56	129	566	652	.267	.341	.403	.744	121	89	134	94	99	758	52	42	55	-10
CLE	155	93	61	.604	2	763	606	5330	1399	211	49	148	626	749	.262	.342	.404	.746	122	95	144	94	102	759	46	39	54	-10
CHI	156	81	73	.526	14	610	568	5316	1337	199	38	80	541	521	.252	.327	.348	.675	93	-35	-40	101	99	633	61	38	62	-5
PHI	155	79	75	.513	16	664	723	5163	1305	212	35	89	683	561	.253	.343	.359	.702	96	26	-16	106	99	659	52	43	55	-10
WAS	157	78	76	.506	17	598	608	5357	1282	225	44	50	580	607	.239	.317	.326	.643	88	-98	-79	97	107	572	48	37	56	-8
BOS	154	76	78	.494	19	668	658	5246	1338	233	34	113	542	739	.255	.328	.377	.705	96	14	-37	108	103	659	59	47	56	-11
STL	155	64	90	.416	31	604	733	5353	1340	225	46	82	540	720	.250	.322	.356	.678	92	-39	-56	103	99	631	30	34	47	-11
DET	156	50	104	.325	45	557	738	5258	1278	190	37	103	553	605	.243	.318	.352	.670	92	-52	-57	101	95	594	27	38	42	-15
TOT	621					5191		42317	10690	1716	339	794	4631	5154	.253	.330	.365	.695							375	318	54	-78

TEAM	CG	SH	SV	IP	H	H/G	HR	BB	SO	RAT	ERA	ERA+	OAV	OOB	PR	/A	PF	CPI	FA	E	DP	FW	PW	BW	SBW	DIF
NY	72	21	27	1381	1240	8.1	94	581	666	12.1	3.14	106	.243	.324	82	28	90	110	.979	127	199	.8	2.9	13.9	-.0	.5
CLE	80	19	18	1407	1278	8.2	94	556	671	11.9	3.32	101	.241	.316	55	4	91	99	.975	155	141	-.8	.4	14.9	-.0	1.5
CHI	53	15	28	1416²	1251	7.9	86	578	774	11.7	3.25	112	.238	.316	66	62	99	98	.980	123	158	1.1	6.4	-4.2	.5	.1
PHI	73	11	16	1384¹	1402	9.1	113	526	562	12.4	4.15	95	.263	.333	-74	-30	108	94	.977	140	148	.0	-3.1	-1.7	-.0	6.7
WAS	75	10	15	1429²	1405	8.8	78	577	574	12.7	3.37	105	.258	.332	48	29	97	108	.976	132	152	.6	3.0	-8.2	.2	5.4
BOS	53	7	24	1372¹	1332	8.7	107	623	624	13.1	3.80	104	.256	.340	-20	21	107	104	.976	155	181	-.3	2.2	-3.8	-.1	1.1
STL	48	6	18	1399	1388	8.9	111	598	581	13.0	4.12	95	.260	.339	-69	-32	107	97	.974	155	176	-.8	-3.3	-5.8	-.1	-2.9
DET	51	10	14	1388¹	1394	9.0	111	591	702	13.0	4.25	90	.262	.338	-89	-69	104	94	.975	152	145	-.6	-7.2	-5.9	-.5	-12.8
TOT	505	99	160	11178¹		8.6				12.5	3.67		.253	.330					.977	1129	1300					

Runs		Hits		Doubles		Triples		Home Runs		Total Bases	
Doby-Cle	104	Fox-Chi	192	Fain-Phi	43	Avila-Cle	11	Doby-Cle	32	Rosen-Cle	297
Avila-Cle	102	Avila-Cle	179	Mantle-NY	37	Simpson-Cle	10	Easter-Cle	31	Mantle-NY	291
Rosen-Cle	101	Robinson-Chi	176	Vernon-Was	33	Rizzuto-NY	10	Berra-NY	30	Dropo-Bos-Det	282
Berra-NY	97	Fain-Phi	176	Robinson-Chi	33	Fox-Chi	10	Dropo-Bos-Det	29	Doby-Cle	281
Minoso-Chi	96							Zernial-Phi	29	Robinson-Chi	277

Runs Batted In		Runs Produced		Bases On Balls		Batting Average		On Base Percentage		Slugging Average	
Rosen-Cle	105	Rosen-Cle	178	Yost-Was	129	Fain-Phi	.327	Fain-Phi	.438	Doby-Cle	.541
Robinson-Chi	104	Doby-Cle	176	Joost-Phi	122	Mitchell-Cle	.323	Valo-Phi	.432	Mantle-NY	.530
Doby-Cle	104	Berra-NY	165	Fain-Phi	105	Mantle-NY	.311	Mantle-NY	.394	Rosen-Cle	.524
Zernial-Phi	100	Robinson-Chi	161	Valo-Phi	101	Kell-Det-Bos	.311	Joost-Phi	.388	Easter-Cle	.513
Berra-NY	98	Mantle-NY	158	Doby-Cle	90	Woodling-NY	.309	Rosen-Cle	.387	Wertz-Det-StL	.506

Production		Adjusted Production		Batter Runs		Adjusted Batter Runs		Clutch Hitting Index		Runs Created	
Mantle-NY	.924	Doby-Cle	166	Mantle-NY	40.3	Mantle-NY	46.9	Runnels-Was	120	Mantle-NY	123
Doby-Cle	.924	Mantle-NY	166	Rosen-Cle	38.6	Rosen-Cle	45.8	Philley-Phi	116	Doby-Cle	116
Rosen-Cle	.911	Rosen-Cle	162	Doby-Cle	37.9	Doby-Cle	44.8	McDougald-NY	115	Rosen-Cle	115
Wertz-Det-StL	.887	Easter-Cle	144	Fain-Phi	36.3	Fain-Phi	29.8	Easter-Cle	110	Robinson-Chi	113
Fain-Phi	.867	Wertz-Det-StL	143	Robinson-Chi	28.3	Woodling-NY	28.2	Joost-Phi	107	Fain-Phi	107

Total Average		Stolen Bases		Stolen Base Average		Stolen Base Runs		Fielding Runs		Total Player Rating	
Doby-Cle	.974	Minoso-Chi	22	Jensen-NY-Was	75.0	Jensen-NY-Was	1.8	Goodman-Bos	20.1	Doby-Cle	5.1
Mantle-NY	.961	Rivera-StL-Chi	21	Rizzuto-NY	73.9	Rizzuto-NY	1.5	Rizzuto-NY	18.9	Mantle-NY	4.6
Wertz-Det-StL	.912	Jensen-NY-Was	18	Rivera-StL-Chi	70.0	Michaels-Ws-SL-Phi	1.2	Martin-NY	18.3	Fain-Phi	3.9
Rosen-Cle	.900	Rizzuto-NY	17	Throneberry-Bos	69.6	Porter-StL	1.2	Hatfield-Bos-Det	17.8	Berra-NY	3.5
Valo-Phi	.873	Throneberry-Bos	16	Minoso-Chi	57.9	Goodman-Bos	1.2	Fain-Phi	16.0	Goodman-Bos	3.0

Wins		Win Percentage		Games		Complete Games		Shutouts		Saves	
Shantz-Phi	24	Shantz-Phi	.774	Kennedy-Chi	47	Lemon-Cle	28	Reynolds-NY	6	Dorish-Chi	11
Wynn-Cle	23	Raschi-NY	.727	Shantz-Phi	46	Shantz-Phi	27	Garcia-Cle	5	Paige-StL	10
Lemon-Cle	22	Reynolds-NY	.714	Garcia-Cle	46	Reynolds-NY	24	Shantz-Phi	5	Sain-NY	7
Garcia-Cle	22	Lemon-Cle	.667	Hooper-Phi	43	Wynn-Cle	19	Lemon-Cle	5		
Reynolds-NY	20	Garcia-Cle	.667			Garcia-Cle	19				

Innings Pitched		Fewest Hits/Game		Fewest BB/Game		Strikeouts		Strikeouts/Game		Ratio	
Lemon-Cle	309.2	Lemon-Cle	6.86	Shantz-Phi	2.03	Reynolds-NY	160	McDermott-Bos	6.50	Shantz-Phi	9.56
Garcia-Cle	292.1	Raschi-NY	7.02	Pillette-StL	2.41	Wynn-Cle	153	Reynolds-NY	5.89	Dobson-Chi	10.05
Wynn-Cle	285.2	Reynolds-NY	7.15	Marrero-Was	2.59	Shantz-Phi	152	Trucks-Det	5.89	Lemon-Cle	10.09
Shantz-Phi	279.2	Dobson-Chi	7.36	Houtteman-Det	2.65	Pierce-Chi	144	Gray-Det	5.54	Pierce-Chi	10.43
Pierce-Chi	255.1	Shantz-Phi	7.40	Garcia-Cle	2.68	Garcia-Cle	143	Grissom-Chi	5.26	Raschi-NY	10.94

Earned Run Average		Adjusted ERA		Opponents' Batting Avg.		Opponents' On Base Pct.		Starter Runs		Adjusted Starter Runs	
Reynolds-NY	2.06	Reynolds-NY	161	Lemon-Cle	.208	Shantz-Phi	.272	Reynolds-NY	43.8	Shantz-Phi	46.0
Garcia-Cle	2.37	Shantz-Phi	160	Raschi-NY	.216	Lemon-Cle	.279	Garcia-Cle	42.4	Reynolds-NY	34.2
Shantz-Phi	2.48	Dobson-Chi	145	Reynolds-NY	.218	Dobson-Chi	.280	Lemon-Cle	40.4	Garcia-Cle	31.6
Lemon-Cle	2.50	Pierce-Chi	142	Dobson-Chi	.222	Pierce-Chi	.289	Shantz-Phi	37.2	Pierce-Chi	30.5
Dobson-Chi	2.51	Garcia-Cle	141	Shantz-Phi	.225	Reynolds-NY	.300	Pierce-Chi	31.3	Lemon-Cle	29.1

Clutch Pitching Index		Relief Runs		Adjusted Relief Runs		Relief Ranking		Total Pitcher Index		Total Baseball Ranking	
Garcia-Cle	127	Dorish-Chi	12.2	Dorish-Chi	11.9	Dorish-Chi	17.4	Shantz-Phi	5.5	Shantz-Phi	5.5
Byrd-Phi	126	Kennedy-Chi	6.9	Kennedy-Chi	6.7	Kennedy-Chi	4.4	Lemon-Cle	4.6	Doby-Cle	5.1
Reynolds-NY	125	Consuegra-Was	5.1	Consuegra-Was	4.1	Consuegra-Was	3.6	Reynolds-NY	3.9	Mantle-NY	4.6
Porterfield-Was	120	Brissie-Cle	1.8	Littlefield-Det-SL	3.3	Littlefield-Det-SL	2.6	Garcia-Cle	3.6	Lemon-Cle	4.6
Hudson-Was-Bos	117	Littlefield-Det-SL	1.4	White-Det	.8	White-Det	1.1	Pierce-Chi	3.2	Fain-Phi	3.9

January 21 The Hall of Fame passes over Joe DiMaggio in his first year of eligibility and elects pitcher Dizzy Dean and outfielder Al Simmons to Cooperstown.

February 20 August A. Busch buys the Cardinals for $3.75 million and pledges not to move the team from St. Louis.

March 18 The Braves move to Milwaukee, the first franchise shift in baseball since 1903 when Baltimore moved to New York. The Braves had been in Boston for 77 years. Milwaukee assumes Pittsburgh's place in the Western Division for scheduling purposes.

April 9 August Busch buys Sportsman's Park for $800,000 from Browns owner Bill Veeck. Busch gives a five-year lease to the Browns, turning the tables in a manner of speaking, since the Cardinals had been tenants of the Browns since 1920. Busch initially renames Sportsman's Park Budweiser Park, but, in response to protests about the commercialization of his ballpark, Busch renames Budweiser Park Busch Stadium. The following season his company comes out with a new beer, Busch Bavarian Beer.

April 14 In a 3–2 victory, Braves outfielder Billy Bruton hits the first major league home run in Milwaukee's County Stadium, in the 10th inning off Gerry Staley of the Cards. This is the first ML game for the home crowd since 1901, when the Milwaukee Brewers were charter members of the AL.

April 29 Joe Adcock becomes the first major league player to homer into the center fielder bleacher seats in the Polo Grounds, over 475 feet away. Lou Brock and Hank Aaron will match it is as well in 1962. The Braves win the game 3-2 on a ninth-inning wild pitch by Hoyt Wilhelm.

May 25 Ralph Kiner becomes the 12th player to hit 300 home runs with a blast at Forbes Field against the Giants. He accomplishes the feat in less than eight seasons.

July 14 The NL wins its fourth All-Star Game in a row, 5–1 in Cincinnati's Crosley Field behind the stellar pitching of Robin Roberts and Warren Spahn. Cardinals outfielder Enos Slaughter gets two hits, scores twice, and robs Harvey Kuenn of an extra-base blow.

July 27 The veterans committee enshrines Chief Bender, Bobby Wallace, Harry Wright, executive Ed Barrow, and umpires Bill Klem and Tom Connolly into the Hall of Fame at Cooperstown.

August 23 Phil Paine, a former Boston Braves pitcher in military service with the U.S. Air Force in Japan, becomes the first ex-major league player to play in Japan, pitching in nine games for the Nishitetsu Lions.

September 6 Roy Campanella sets the major league mark for home runs by a catcher. His 38th tops the NL high of 37 hit by the Cubs' Gabby Hartnett in 1930. The next day, he sets the major league record for RBI by a catcher when he smacks a three-run home run in a 6-3 Dodgers' win over the Phils, surpassing Yogi Berra's 124 set in 1950.

September 20 Ernie Banks of the Cubs hits his first major league home run, against Gerry Staley, but the Cards win 11-6.

September 22 The Dodgers tie the record for the most wins in a home park, beating Pittsburgh 5-4. They go an incredible 60-17 at Ebbets Field, tying record of the St. Louis Cardinals in 1942. Only the 61 wins of the San Francisco Giants in 1962 in an 81-game home season will surpass this mark.

October 2 The World Series moves to Ebbets Field as Carl Erskine establishes a new Series strikeout record by fanning 14 Yanks, including Mickey Mantle and Joe Collins four times each. Roy Campanella breaks a 2-2 tie with a game-winning solo home run in the eighth for a 3-2 Brooklyn win

November 24 The Dodgers sign the relatively unknown Walter Alston to a one-year pact as their manager for 1954.

BROOKLYN

Pos	Player
M	C.Dressen
1B	G.Hodges
2B	J.Gilliam
SS	P.Reese
3B	B.Cox
LF	D.Thompson
CF	D.Snider
RF	C.Furillo
C	R.Campanella
O3	J.Robinson
3S	B.Morgan
O	G.Shuba
1	W.Belardi
C	R.Walker
O	D.Williams
O	B.Antonello
/O	C.Mauro
H	D.Howell
H	D.Teed
P	C.Erskine
P	R.Meyer
P	B.Loes
P	P.Roe
P	B.Milliken
RP	C.Labine
RP	B.Wade
RP	J.Hughes
P	J.Podres
P	J.Black
/P	R.Branca
/P	R.Moore
/P	G.Mickens
/P	E.Palica

CHICAGO

Pos	Player
M	P.Cavarretta
1B	D.Fondy
2B	E.Miksis
SS	R.Smalley
3B	R.Jackson
LF	R.Kiner
CF	F.Baumholtz
RF	H.Sauer
C	C.McCullough
O	J.Jeffcoat
23	B.Serena
C	J.Garagiola
S	T.Brown
O	C.Metkovich
O	P.Ward
C	T.Atwell
C	C.Sawatski
O	G.Hermanski
2	B.Ramazzotti
S	E.Banks
/O	B.Talbot
/2	G.Baker
H	P.Cavarretta
/O	B.Addis
/O	P.Schramka
P	W.Hacker
P	H.Minner
P	J.Klippstein
P	B.Rush
P	T.Lown
RP	D.Leonard
P	H.Pollet
P	B.Church
P	D.Simpson
P	J.Willis
P	S.Jones
P	B.Kelly
/P	B.Schultz
/P	F.Baczewski
/P	D.Elston
/P	B.Moisan

CINCINNATI

Pos	Player
M	R.Hornsby
1B	B.Mills
1B	T.Kluszewski
2B	R.Bridges
SS	R.McMillan
3B	B.Adams
LF	J.Greengrass
CF	G.Bell
RF	W.Marshall
C	A.Seminick
O	B.Borkowski
21	G.Hatton
C	H.Landrith
2	J.Temple
O	B.Marquis
O	W.Post
/C	F.Baldwin
/O	G.Lerchen
/C	H.Foiles
/O	J.Szekely
/C	E.Bailey
P	H.Perkowski
P	B.Podbielan
P	K.Raffensberger
P	J.Nuxhall
P	F.Baczewski
RP	H.Wehmeier
RP	C.King
P	F.Smith
P	H.Judson
/P	E.Nevel
/P	E.Erautt
/P	B.Martin
/P	E.Blake

MILWAUKEE

Pos	Player
M	C.Grimm
1B	J.Adcock
2B	J.Dittmer
SS	J.Logan
3B	E.Mathews
LF	S.Gordon
CF	B.Bruton
RF	A.Pafko
C	D.Crandall
C	J.Pendleton
32	W.Cooper
2	H.Hanebrink
C	E.St.Claire
/1	G.Crowe
O	B.Thorpe
2	S.Sisti
H	B.Klaus
/2	M.Roach
/C	P.Burris
P	W.Spahn
P	L.Burdette
P	J.Antonelli
P	M.Surkont
P	B.Buhl
RP	E.Johnson
RP	V.Bickford
P	D.Liddle
P	J.Wilson
P	D.Jolly
P	D.Cole
/P	J.Jay
/P	V.Jester

NEW YORK

Pos	Player
M	L.Durocher
1B	W.Lockman
2B	D.Williams
SS	A.Dark
3B	H.Thompson
LF	M.Irvin
CF	B.Thomson
RF	D.Mueller
C	W.Westrum
S3	D.Spencer
1	B.Hofman
O	D.Rhodes
1	T.Gilbert
C	R.Noble
C	S.Yvars
C	S.Calderone
/C	R.Katt
/O	B.Rigney
H	G.Wilson
P	R.Gomez
P	J.Hearn
P	L.Jansen
P	S.Maglie
P	D.Koslo
RP	H.Wilhelm
RP	A.Corwin
P	A.Worthington
P	M.Grissom
/P	F.Hiller
/P	M.Kennedy
/P	B.Connelly
/P	M.Lanier
/P	G.Spencer

PHILADELPHIA

Pos	Player
M	S.O'Neill
1B	E.Torgeson
2B	G.Hamner
SS	T.Kazanski
3B	W.Jones
LF	D.Ennis
CF	R.Ashburn
RF	J.Wyrostek
C	S.Burgess
2	C.Ryan
1	E.Waitkus
O	S.Lopata
	M.Clark
	T.Glaviano
	B.Nicholson
	J.Lohrke
	J.Mayo
/O	S.Palys
P	R.Roberts
P	C.Simmons
P	K.Drews
P	J.Konstanty
P	B.Miller
RP	S.Ridzik
RP	A.Hansen
P	T.Kipper
P	K.Peterson
	J.Lindell
/P	T.Qualters
/P	P.Stuffel

PITTSBURGH

Pos	Player
M	F.Haney
1B	P.Ward
2B	J.O'Brien
SS	E.O'Brien
3B	D.O'Connell
LF	H.Rice
CF	F.Thomas
RF	C.Abrams
C	M.Sandlock
S	D.Cole
1O	P.Smith
O	C.Bernier
23	E.Pellagrini
3	P.Castiglione
O	R.Kiner
C	T.Atwell
C	J.Vanowicz
C	J.Garagiola
O	G.Hermanski
O	F.Montemayor
S	D.Smith
/1	C.Metkovich
/O	B.Davis
/2	D.Hall
/C	E.FitzGerald
/C	N.Koback
/C	P.Naton
/C	J.Shepard
H	B.Addis
H	C.Koshorek
P	M.Dickson
P	J.Lindell
P	P.LaPalme
P	B.Friend
P	B.Hall
RP	R.Face
RP	J.Hetki
RP	R.Bowman
P	J.Waugh
P	P.Pettit
/P	C.Hogue
P	B.Schultz
/P	H.Pollet
/P	B.Macdonald
/P	W.Main

ST.LOUIS

Pos	Player
M	E.Stanky
1B	S.Bilko
2B	R.Schoendienst
SS	S.Hemus
3B	R.Jablonski
LF	S.Musial
CF	S.Repulski
RF	E.Slaughter
C	D.Rice
O2	P.Lowrey
O	H.Elliott
O	S.Yvars
3	P.Castiglione
1	D.Sisler
O	D.Schofield
C	F.Anderson
/C	D.Rand
C	E.Stanky
/O	G.Dunlap
	L.Fusselman
H	H.Rice
3	B.Johnson
H	V.Benson
H	V.Stallcup
/1	F.Marolewski
R	E.Phillips
P	H.Haddix
P	G.Staley
P	V.Mizell
P	J.Presko
P	S.Miller
RP	A.Brazle
RP	H.White
RP	C.Chambers
P	M.Clark
P	E.Erautt
/P	W.Schmidt
/P	J.Faszholz
/P	J.Collum
/P	J.Romonosky
/P	D.Bokelmann
/P	E.Yuhas

TEAM	G	W	L	PCT	GB	R	OR	AB	H	2B	3B	HR	BB	SO	AVG	OBP	SLG	PRO	PRO+	BR	/A	PF	CHI	RC	SB	CS	SBA	SBR
BRO	155	105	49	.682		955	689	5373	1529	274	59	208	655	686	.285	.366	.474	.840	121	188	167	102	101	963	90	47	66	-1
MIL	157	92	62	.597	13	738	589	5349	1422	227	52	156	439	637	.266	.325	.415	.740	104	-22	22	94	104	727	46	27	63	-2
STL	157	83	71	.539	22	768	713	5397	1474	281	56	140	574	617	.273	.347	.424	.771	107	53	54	100	95	806	18	22	45	-8
PHI	156	83	71	.539	22	716	666	5290	1400	228	62	115	530	597	.265	.335	.396	.731	97	-25	-21	99	101	727	42	21	67	0
NY	155	70	84	.455	35	768	747	5362	1452	195	45	176	499	608	.271	.336	.422	.758	101	20	6	102	101	771	31	21	60	-3
CIN	155	68	86	.442	37	714	788	5343	1396	190	34	166	485	701	.261	.325	.403	.728	94	-42	-47	101	103	711	25	20	56	-5
CHI	155	65	89	.422	40	633	835	5272	1372	204	57	137	514	746	.260	.328	.399	.727	93	-41	-56	102	92	697	49	21	70	2
PIT	154	50	104	.325	55	622	887	5253	1297	178	49	99	524	715	.247	.319	.356	.675	82	-130	-126	99	103	614	41	39	51	-11
TOT	622					5914		42639	11342	1777	414	1197	4220	5307	.266	.335	.411	.747							342	218	61	-28

TEAM	CG	SH	SV	IP	H	H/G	HR	BB	SO	RAT	ERA	ERA+	OAV	OOB	PR	/A	PF	CPI	FA	E	DP	FW	PW	BW	SBW	DIF
BRO	51	11	29	1380²	1337	8.7	169	509	817	12.1	4.10	104	.253	.320	29	25	99	97	.980	118	161	1.7	2.4	16.1	.2	7.6
MIL	72	14	15	1387	1282	8.3	107	539	738	12.0	3.30	119	.245	.318	153	96	92	106	.976	143	169	.4	9.2	2.1	.1	3.1
STL	51	11	36	1386²	1406	9.1	139	533	732	12.9	4.23	101	.262	.333	9	5	99	98	.977	138	161	.7	.5	5.2	-.4	.0
PHI	76	13	15	1369²	1410	9.3	138	410	637	12.1	3.80	111	.265	.320	74	62	98	104	.975	147	161	.0	6.0	-2.0	.3	1.6
NY	46	10	20	1365²	1403	9.2	146	610	647	13.4	4.25	101	.264	.343	5	6	100	103	.975	151	151	-.2	.6	.6	.0	-8.0
CIN	47	7	15	1365	1484	9.8	179	488	506	13.2	4.64	94	.279	.343	-53	-43	102	102	.978	129	176	1.1	-4.1	-4.5	-.1	-1.2
CHI	38	3	22	1359	1491	9.8	151	554	623	13.8	4.79	93	.276	.347	-76	-51	104	97	.967	193	141	-2.5	-4.9	-5.4	.5	.3
PIT	49	4	10	1358	1529	10.1	168	577	607	14.1	5.22	86	.285	.356	-141	-113	104	96	.973	163	139	-.9	-10.9	-12.1	-.7	-2.4
TOT	430	73	162	10971²		9.3				12.9	4.29		.266	.335					.975	1182	1259					

Runs		Hits		Doubles		Triples		Home Runs		Total Bases	
Snider-Bro	132	Ashburn-Phi	205	Musial-StL	53	Gilliam-Bro	17	Mathews-Mil	47	Snider-Bro	370
Musial-StL	127	Musial-StL	200	Dark-NY	41	Bruton-Mil	14	Snider-Bro	42	Mathews-Mil	363
Dark-NY	126	Snider-Bro	198	Snider-Bro	38	Hemus-StL	11	Campanella-Bro	41	Musial-StL	361
Gilliam-Bro	125	Dark-NY	194	Furillo-Bro	38	Fondy-Chi	11	Kluszewski-Cin	40	Kluszewski-Cin	325
		Schoendienst-StL	193	Bell-Cin	37			Kiner-Pit-Chi	35	Bell-Cin	320

Runs Batted In		Runs Produced		Bases On Balls		Batting Average		On Base Percentage		Slugging Average	
Campanella-Bro	142	Snider-Bro	216	Musial-StL	105	Furillo-Bro	.344	Musial-StL	.437	Snider-Bro	.627
Mathews-Mil	135	Musial-StL	210	Kiner-Pit-Chi	100	Schoendienst-StL	.342	Robinson-Bro	.425	Mathews-Mil	.627
Snider-Bro	126	Campanella-Bro	204	Gilliam-Bro	100	Musial-StL	.337	Snider-Bro	.419	Campanella-Bro	.611
Ennis-Phi	125	Mathews-Mil	198	Mathews-Mil	99	Snider-Bro	.336	Irvin-NY	.406	Musial-StL	.609
Hodges-Bro	122			Hemus-StL	86	Mueller-NY	.333	Mathews-Mil	.406	Furillo-Bro	.580

Production		Adjusted Production		Batter Runs		Adjusted Batter Runs		Clutch Hitting Index		Runs Created	
Snider-Bro	1.046	Mathews-Mil	175	Musial-StL	62.7	Mathews-Mil	63.8	Slaughter-StL	142	Musial-StL	166
Musial-StL	1.046	Musial-StL	169	Snider-Bro	59.3	Musial-StL	62.9	Jablonski-StL	128	Snider-Bro	161
Mathews-Mil	1.033	Snider-Bro	165	Mathews-Mil	54.9	Snider-Bro	56.2	Robinson-Bro	125	Mathews-Mil	157
Campanella-Bro	1.006	Campanella-Bro	154	Campanella-Bro	42.9	Campanella-Bro	40.4	Ennis-Phi	121	Campanella-Bro	128
Furillo-Bro	.973	Furillo-Bro	146	Kluszewski-Cin	35.0	Kluszewski-Cin	34.2	Campanella-Bro	119	Kluszewski-Cin	126

Total Average		Stolen Bases		Stolen Base Average		Stolen Base Runs		Fielding Runs		Total Player Rating	
Musial-StL	1.143	Bruton-Mil	26	Robinson-Bro	81.0	Reese-Bro	3.0	Ashburn-Phi	25.7	Schoendienst-StL	5.8
Snider-Bro	1.134	Reese-Bro	22	Reese-Bro	78.6	Robinson-Bro	2.7	Schoendienst-StL	25.3	Mathews-Mil	5.8
Mathews-Mil	1.119	Gilliam-Bro	21	Bruton-Mil	70.3	Torgeson-Phi	1.5	Logan-Mil	20.6	Campanella-Bro	4.7
Campanella-Bro	1.048	Robinson-Bro	17	Snider-Bro	69.6	Miksis-Chi	1.5	Crandall-Mil	14.8	Snider-Bro	4.6
Robinson-Bro	.988	Snider-Bro	16	Gilliam-Bro	60.0	Jeffcoat-Chi	1.5	Bell-Cin	13.7	Musial-StL	4.4

Wins		Win Percentage		Games		Complete Games		Shutouts		Saves	
Spahn-Mil	23	Erskine-Bro	.769	Wilhelm-NY	68	Roberts-Phi	33	Haddix-StL	6	Brazle-StL	18
Roberts-Phi	23	Spahn-Mil	.767	Brazle-StL	60	Spahn-Mil	24	Spahn-Mil	5	Wilhelm-NY	15
Haddix-StL	20	Meyer-Bro	.750	Hetki-Pit	54	Simmons-Phi	19	Roberts-Phi	5	Hughes-Bro	9
Erskine-Bro	20	Burdette-Mil	.750	Smith-Cin	50	Haddix-StL	19	Simmons-Phi	4	Leonard-Chi	8
Staley-StL	18	Haddix-StL	.690			Erskine-Bro	16	Erskine-Bro	4	Burdette-Mil	8

Innings Pitched		Fewest Hits/Game		Fewest BB/Game		Strikeouts		Strikeouts/Game		Ratio	
Roberts-Phi	346.2	Spahn-Mil	7.15	Roberts-Phi	1.58	Roberts-Phi	198	Mizell-StL	6.94	Spahn-Mil	9.55
Spahn-Mil	265.2	Gomez-NY	7.32	Raffensberger-Cin	1.71	Erskine-Bro	187	Erskine-Bro	6.82	Roberts-Phi	10.05
Haddix-StL	253.0	Mizell-StL	7.74	Minner-Chi	1.79	Mizell-StL	173	Antonelli-Mil	6.72	Haddix-StL	10.42
Erskine-Bro	246.2	Erskine-Bro	7.77	Staley-StL	2.11	Haddix-StL	163	Klippstein-Chi	6.07	Simmons-Phi	11.19
Simmons-Phi	238.0	Haddix-StL	7.83	Hacker-Chi	2.19	Spahn-Mil	148	Haddix-StL	5.80	Erskine-Bro	11.35

Earned Run Average		Adjusted ERA		Opponents' Batting Avg.		Opponents' On Base Pct.		Starter Runs		Adjusted Starter Runs	
Spahn-Mil	2.10	Spahn-Mil	187	Spahn-Mil	.217	Spahn-Mil	.270	Spahn-Mil	64.5	Roberts-Phi	56.1
Roberts-Phi	2.75	Roberts-Phi	153	Gomez-NY	.218	Roberts-Phi	.276	Roberts-Phi	59.1	Spahn-Mil	53.8
Haddix-StL	3.06	Haddix-StL	139	Mizell-StL	.227	Haddix-StL	.287	Haddix-StL	34.5	Haddix-StL	33.6
Antonelli-Mil	3.18	Simmons-Phi	131	Erskine-Bro	.230	Hacker-Chi	.299	Simmons-Phi	28.3	Simmons-Phi	26.3
Simmons-Phi	3.21	Gomez-NY	126	Haddix-StL	.232	Simmons-Phi	.302	Buhl-Mil	22.5	Gomez-NY	20.2

Clutch Pitching Index		Relief Runs		Adjusted Relief Runs		Relief Ranking		Total Pitcher Index		Total Baseball Ranking	
Raffensberger-Cin	115	Wilhelm-NY	20.1	Wilhelm-NY	20.1	Labine-Bro	27.9	Spahn-Mil	6.6	Spahn-Mil	6.6
Dickson-Pit	112	Labine-Bro	18.5	Labine-Bro	18.2	Wilhelm-NY	23.4	Roberts-Phi	6.1	Roberts-Phi	6.1
Drews-Phi	112	Johnson-Mil	14.6	White-StL	12.0	White-StL	16.3	Haddix-StL	4.7	Schoendienst-StL	5.8
Burdette-Mil	110	White-StL	12.3	Johnson-Mil	11.3	Johnson-Mil	8.8	Labine-Bro	2.7	Mathews-Mil	5.8
Roe-Bro	108	Hughes-Bro	7.8	Hughes-Bro	7.6	Hughes-Bro	7.3	Simmons-Phi	2.4	Haddix-StL	4.7

January 8 The Cleveland Indians bar night games with the Browns due to St. Louis owner Bill Veeck's refusal to share receipts of the telecasts.

February 13 The Athletics change the name of Shibe Park to Connie Mack Stadium, in honor of their longtime owner and manager.

February 19 Ted Williams safely crashlands his damaged Panther jet after flying a combat mission in Korea.

April 17 Mickey Mantle hits the longest home run in Griffith Stadium history, a 565-feet shot off Chuck Stobbs of the Washington Senators. The Yanks win 7-3.

May 6 Bobo Holloman of the St. Louis Browns pitches a no-hitter in his first major league start, only the third rookie to do so, in a 6-0 win over the A's. Within three months he will be out of the major leagues for good, the winner of just three games.

June 15 Duane Pillette of the Browns ends the Yankee win streak at 18 and the Browns team record 14-game losing streak with a 3–1 victory over New York in Yankee Stadium. Johnny Mize becomes the 93rd player in baseball history to get 2,000 hits when he singles in the Yankee run in the fifth.

June 18 Red Sox rookie outfielder Gene Stephens becomes the only AL player to get three hits in the same inning, as Boston scores 17 in the seventh inning in a 23-3 romp over Detroit. The Red Sox send 23 to the plate in the seventh, getting 14 hits and six walks before third baseman George Kell flies out to end it.

August 6 Ted Williams is back in a Red Sox uniform after military duty in Korea. He will finish with 13 home runs and a .407 mark.

September 14 The Yanks clinch their fifth straight pennant with an 8-5 win over the Indians. Second baseman Billy Martin has four RBI.

September 26 Billy Hunter becomes the last St. Louis Browns player to homer in a game. The Browns lose anyway, 6-3 to Chicago.

September 27 Washington's Mickey Vernon goes into the last game of the season still fighting for the batting title with Cleveland's Al Rosen. Near the end of the game Vernon is hitting .337 when word arrives that Rosen's game is over and Vernon is ahead by .0011 points. Instead of letting Vernon bat again, his teammates contrive to make an out to end the game.

September 27 The St. Louis Browns play both their last game in Sportsman's Park and the last game in the franchise's 52-year history, losing 2-1 to the Chicago White Sox in 10 innings for their 100th defeat of the season.

September 29 The AL adopts a constitutional amendment calling for expansion to 10 teams.

September 30 The Yanks defeat Brooklyn 9-5 in the first game of the World Series. Carl Erskine is ineffective, walking the first three batters, who score on a Hank Bauer triple. The Dodgers tie it up 5-5, but Clem Labine gets the loss in relief.

October 4 In Game 5, Mickey Mantle hits a grand slam off Russ Meyer, and the Yanks hold on to win 11-7.

October 5 The Yanks end the World Series in six as Billy Martin's 12th World Series hit, a record-breaking single to center in the bottom of the ninth, gives the Yankees their fifth championship in a row.

October 28 Red Barber resigns from the Dodger broadcast booth and takes a job with the rival New York Yankees.

November 17 The St. Louis Browns' name officially becomes the Baltimore Baseball Club Inc. The Baltimore franchise board officially changes its name to the "Orioles."

November 27 Indians third baseman Al Rosen is unanimously named the AL's MVP with a record 336 votes. In the NL, Dodger catcher Roy Campanella is named MVP.

BOSTON	CHICAGO	CLEVELAND	DETROIT	NEW YORK	PHILADELPHIA	ST.LOUIS	WASHINGTON
M L.Boudreau	M P.Richards	M A.Lopez	M F.Hutchinson	M C.Stengel	M J.Dykes	M M.Marion	M B.Harris
1B D.Gernert	1B F.Fain	1B B.Glynn	1B W.Dropo	1B J.Collins	1B E.Robinson	1B D.Kryhoski	1B M.Vernon
2B B.Goodman	2B N.Fox	2B B.Avila	2B J.Pesky	2B B.Martin	2B C.Michaels	2B B.Young	2B W.Terwilliger
SS M.Bolling	SS C.Carrasquel	SS G.Strickland	SS H.Kuenn	SS P.Rizzuto	SS J.DeMaestri	SS B.Hunter	SS P.Runnels
3B G.Kell	3B B.Elliott	3B A.Rosen	3B R.Boone	3B G.McDougald	3B L.Babe	3B J.Dyck	3B E.Yost
LF H.Evers	LF M.Minoso	LF D.Mitchell	LF B.Nieman	LF G.Woodling	LF G.Zernial	LF D.Kokos	LF C.Vollmer
CF T.Umphlett	CF J.Rivera	CF L.Doby	CF J.Delsing	CF M.Mantle	CF E.McGhee	CF J.Groth	CF J.Busby
RF J.Piersall	RF S.Mele	RF B.Kennedy	RF D.Lund	RF H.Bauer	RF D.Philley	RF V.Wertz	RF J.Jensen
C S.White	C S.Lollar	C J.Hegan	C M.Batts	C Y.Berra	C J.Astroth	C C.Courtney	C E.Fitz Gerald
O G.Stephens	1O B.Boyd	O H.Simpson	32 F.Hatfield	32 I.Noren	O P.Suder	O D.Lenhardt	C M.Grasso
32 F.Baker	C R.Wilson	O W.Westlake	O S.Souchock	1 D.Bollweg	1 R.Murray	1 R.Sievers	O G.Coan
2S T.Lepcio	O T.Wright	1 L.Easter	21 J.Priddy	O B.Renna	S E.Joost	C L.Moss	S J.Snyder
S J.Lipon	3 R.Krsnich	S A.Smith	C J.Bucha	S J.Mize	C C.Mauro	3 V.Stephens	Y.Davalillo
C D.Wilber	3 V.Stephens	S R.Boone	O P.Mullin	C C.Silvera	O E.Valo	3 B.Elliott	/O K.Thomas
O T.Williams	3S F.Marsh	C J.Ginsberg	2 O.Friend	O A.Carey	O A.Clark	O H.Edwards	2 M.Hoderlein
O A.Zarilla	O B.Stewart	C J.Tipton	O R.Sullivan	/1 T.Hamilton	32 K.Thomas	O N.Berry	/O K.Wood
32 B.Consolo	3 C.Ryan	2 O.Friend	C J.Ginsberg	O G.Triandos	/1 N.Watlington	/1 E.Mickelson	/O L.Peden
O K.Olson	C B.Sheely	2 H.Majeski	3 B.Hitchcock	2 J.Coleman		/1 J.Pisoni	/O C.Mauro
C G.Niarhos	/O B.Wilson	O J.Lemon	/2 A.Kaline	/3 R.Houk		/3 D.Lipon	/S G.Verble
/2 J.Merson	/1 A.Clark	H B.McCosky	/3 J.Baumgartner	/C B.Cerv		H D.Upright	/C F.Sacka
H D.DiMaggio	/2 N.Berry	/O F.Carswell	/O F.Carswell	/2 J.Brideweser		/3 M.Marion	/C B.Oldis
/S A.Richter	/S S.Dente	/C D.Aylward	/C B.Swift	R A.Schult		/S W.Miranda	H F.Campos
H C.Vollmer		R D.Weik	/2 R.Bertoia	/S F.Verdi		/1 F.Kellert	/2 T.Roig
			H G.Freese			/C B.Martin	/3 F.Baker
P M.Parnell	P B.Pierce	P B.Lemon	P B.Hoeft	P W.Ford	P H.Byrd	P D.Larsen	/O B.Barnes
P M.McDermott	P V.Trucks	P M.Garcia	P N.Garver	P J.Sain	P M.Fricano	P D.Pillette	P B.Porterfield
P H.Brown	P M.Fornieles	P E.Wynn	P T.Gray	P V.Raschi	P A.Kellner	P D.Littlefield	P W.Masterson
P S.Hudson	P S.Rogovin	P B.Feller	P S.Gromek	P E.Lopat	P C.Bishop	P H.Brecheen	P S.Shea
P W.Nixon	P S.Consuegra	P D.Hoskins	P R.Branca	P A.Reynolds	P B.Shantz	P B.Cain	P C.Stobbs
RP E.Kinder	RP H.Dorish	RP B.Hooper	RP D.Marlowe	RP B.Kuzava	P M.Martin	RP S.Paige	P C.Marrero
RP B.Flowers	RP G.Bearden	P A.Houtteman	RP R.Herbert	RP T.Gorman	RP F.Fanovich	RP M.Stuart	RP S.Dixon
RP I.Delock	P J.Dobson	/P B.Chakales	RP D.Madison	RP R.Scarborough	P C.Scheib	RP M.Blyzka	RP A.Sima
P B.Henry	P B.Keegan	P B.Wight	P A.Houtteman	P J.McDonald	P J.Coleman	P V.Trucks	RP J.Lane
P M.Grissom	P C.Johnson	P L.Brissie	P A.Aber	P B.Miller	RP B.Newsom	P L.Kretlow	P J.Schmitz
P H.Freeman	P L.Aloma	/P S.Gromek	P B.Miller	/P S.Kraly	/P B.Trice	P B.Holloman	P J.Moreno
P F.Sullivan	/P L.Kretlow	/P D.Tomanek	P H.Erickson	/P A.Schallock	P R.Monahan	P B.Turley	/P T.Byrne
P B.Kennedy	/P T.Byrne	/P A.Aber	P B.Wight	/P E.Blackwell	P D.Rozek	P M.Lanier	/P B.Stewart
P B.Werle	/P E.Harrist	/P T.Wilks	P H.Newhouser	/P J.Schmitz	P W.Kellner	P H.White	/P J.Pearce
/P K.Holcombe	/P H.Hudson		P R.Scarborough		P B.Harrington	/P B.Habenicht	/P D.Stone
			/P E.Harrist		P J.Mackinson		/P S.Consuegra
			/P D.Weik				
			/P M.Jordan				
			/P P.Foytack				
			/P F.Hutchinson				

TEAM	G	W	L	PCT	GB	R	OR	AB	H	2B	3B	HR	BB	SO	AVG	OBP	SLG	PRO	PRO+	BR	/A	PF	CHI	RC	SB	CS	SBA	SBR
NY	151	99	52	.656		801	547	5194	1420	226	52	139	656	644	.273	.359	.417	.776	120	113	141	97	100	809	34	44	44	-16
CLE	155	92	62	.597	8.5	770	627	5285	1426	201	29	160	609	683	.270	.349	.410	.759	114	77	98	97	100	780	33	29	53	-8
CHI	156	89	65	.578	11.5	716	592	5212	1345	226	53	74	601	530	.258	.341	.364	.705	93	-17	-37	103	106	666	73	55	57	-11
BOS	153	84	69	.549	16	656	632	5246	1385	255	37	101	496	601	.264	.332	.384	.716	94	-10	-45	105	98	683	33	45	42	-17
WAS	152	76	76	.500	23.5	687	614	5149	1354	230	53	69	596	604	.263	.343	.368	.711	100	-6	10	98	103	675	65	36	64	-2
DET	158	60	94	.390	40.5	695	923	5553	1479	259	44	108	506	603	.266	.331	.387	.718	100	-10	-2	99	99	716	30	35	46	-12
PHI	157	59	95	.383	41.5	632	799	5455	1398	205	38	116	498	602	.256	.321	.372	.693	89	-61	-85	104	100	658	41	24	63	-2
STL	154	54	100	.351	46.5	555	778	5264	1310	214	25	112	507	644	.249	.317	.363	.680	87	-83	-94	102	93	606	17	34	33	-15
TOT	618					5512		42358	11117	1816	331	879	4469	4911	.262	.336	.383	.720							326	302	52	-83

TEAM	CG	SH	SV	IP	H	H/G	HR	BB	SO	RAT	ERA	ERA+	OAV	OOB	PR	/A	PF	CPI	FA	E	DP	FW	PW	BW	SBW	DIF
NY	50	18	39	1358[1]	1286	8.5	94	500	604	12.1	3.20	115	.251	.321	120	74	92	110	.979	126	182	.3	7.4	14.1	-.6	2.2
CLE	81	11	15	1373	1311	8.6	92	519	586	12.2	3.64	103	.253	.325	53	16	94	99	.979	127	197	.4	1.6	9.8	.2	2.9
CHI	57	17	33	1403[2]	1299	8.3	113	583	714	12.2	3.41	118	.246	.324	91	95	101	105	.980	125	144	.6	9.5	-3.7	-.0	5.7
BOS	41	15	37	1373	1333	8.7	92	584	642	12.7	3.58	118	.254	.331	63	96	105	104	.975	148	173	-.9	9.6	-4.5	-.7	3.9
WAS	76	16	10	1344[2]	1313	8.8	112	478	515	12.2	3.66	106	.258	.324	50	35	98	103	.979	120	173	.7	3.5	1.0	.8	-6.0
DET	50	2	16	1415	1633	10.4	154	585	645	14.4	5.25	77	.291	.363	-198	-187	102	96	.978	135	149	.1	-18.7	-.2	-.2	2.0
PHI	51	7	11	1409	1475	9.4	121	594	566	13.6	4.67	92	.271	.349	-106	-60	107	93	.977	137	161	-.0	-6.0	-8.5	.8	-4.3
STL	28	10	24	1383[2]	1467	9.5	101	626	639	13.8	4.48	94	.273	.351	-74	-43	105	97	.974	152	165	-1.0	-4.3	-9.4	-.5	-7.8
TOT	434	96	185	11060[1]		9.0				12.9	3.99		.262	.336					.978	1070	1344					

Runs
Rosen-Cle 115
Yost-Was 107
Mantle-NY 105
Minoso-Chi 104
Vernon-Was 101

Hits
Kuenn-Det 209
Vernon-Was 205
Rosen-Cle 201
Philley-Phi 188
Busby-Was 183

Doubles
Vernon-Was 43
Kell-Bos 41
White-Bos 34
Kuenn-Det 33
Goodman-Bos 33

Triples
Rivera-Chi 16
Vernon-Was 11
Piersall-Bos 9
Philley-Phi 9

Home Runs
Rosen-Cle 43
Zernial-Phi 42
Doby-Cle 29
Berra-NY 27
Boone-Cle-Det 26

Total Bases
Rosen-Cle 367
Vernon-Was 315
Zernial-Phi 311
Philley-Phi 263
Berra-NY 263

Runs Batted In
Rosen-Cle 145
Vernon-Was 115
Boone-Cle-Det 114
Zernial-Phi 108
Berra-NY 108

Runs Produced
Rosen-Cle 217
Vernon-Was 201
Minoso-Chi 193
Boone-Cle-Det 182
Mantle-NY 176

Bases On Balls
Yost-Was 123
Fain-Chi 108
Doby-Cle 96
Gernert-Bos 88
Rosen-Cle 85

Batting Average
Vernon-Was .... .337
Rosen-Cle .... .336
Goodman-Bos .... .313
Minoso-Chi .... .313
Busby-Was .... .312

On Base Percentage
Woodling-NY ...... .429
Rosen-Cle .... .422
Minoso-Chi .... .410
Fain-Chi .... .405
Yost-Was .... .403

Slugging Average
Rosen-Cle .... .613
Zernial-Phi .... .559
Berra-NY .... .523
Boone-Cle-Det .... .519
Vernon-Was .... .518

Production
Rosen-Cle 1.034
Vernon-Was .... .921
Zernial-Phi .... .914
Boone-Cle-Det .... .909
Woodling-NY ...... .898

Adjusted Production
Rosen-Cle 181
Vernon-Was 151
Woodling-NY 147
Boone-Cle-Det 146
Mantle-NY 145

Batter Runs
Rosen-Cle 63.3
Vernon-Was 39.7
Minoso-Chi 30.6
Boone-Cle-Det 30.5
Zernial-Phi 30.4

Adjusted Batter Runs
Rosen-Cle 67.2
Vernon-Was 42.5
Boone-Cle-Det 32.0
Mantle-NY 30.4
Woodling-NY 30.1

Clutch Hitting Index
Rizzuto-NY 128
Dropo-Det 122
Fox-Chi 120
Vernon-Was 119
Robinson-Phi 118

Runs Created
Rosen-Cle 155
Vernon-Was 127
Zernial-Phi 113
Boone-Cle-Det 106
Minoso-Chi 106

Total Average
Rosen-Cle 1.078
Mantle-NY .... .943
Boone-Cle-Det .... .925
Zernial-Phi .... .917
Doby-Cle .... .912

Stolen Bases
Minoso-Chi 25
Rivera-Chi 22
Jensen-Was 18
Philley-Phi 13
Busby-Was 13

Stolen Base Average
Jensen-Was 69.2
Minoso-Chi 61.0
Rivera-Chi 59.5

Stolen Base Runs
Michaels-Phi 2.1
Coan-Was 2.1
Zernial-Phi 1.2
Souchock-Det 9
Philley-Phi 9

Fielding Runs
Busby-Was 18.9
Groth-StL 17.1
Piersall-Bos 16.1
Strickland-Cle 15.6
Hunter-StL 14.6

Total Player Rating
Rosen-Cle 6.2
Zernial-Phi 3.5
Berra-NY 3.4
Boone-Cle-Det 3.2
Vernon-Was 3.1

Wins
Porterfield-Was 22
Parnell-Bos 21
B.Lemon-Cle 21
Trucks-StL-Chi 20

Win Percentage
Lopat-NY .... .800
Ford-NY .... .750
Parnell-Bos .... .724
Porterfield-Was .... .688

Games
Kinder-Bos 69
Stuart-StL 60
Martin-Phi 58
Paige-StL 57
Dorish-Chi 55

Complete Games
Porterfield-Was 24
B.Lemon-Cle 23
Garcia-Cle 21
Pierce-Chi 19
Trucks-StL-Chi 17

Shutouts
Porterfield-Was 9
Pierce-Chi 7
Parnell-Bos 5
B.Lemon-Cle 5

Saves
Kinder-Bos 27
Dorish-Chi 18
Reynolds-NY 13
Paige-StL 11
Sain-NY 9

Innings Pitched
B.Lemon-Cle 286.2
Garcia-Cle 271.2
Pierce-Chi 271.1
Trucks-StL-Chi ... 264.1
Porterfield-Was ... 255.0

Fewest Hits/Game
Pierce-Chi 7.16
McDermott-Bos .. 7.37
Raschi-NY 7.46
Masterson-Was ... 7.85
Trucks-StL-Chi ... 7.97

Fewest BB/Game
Lopat-NY 1.61
Sain-NY 2.14
A.Kellner-Phi 2.28
Porterfield-Was ... 2.58
Hoeft-Det 2.64

Strikeouts
Pierce-Chi 186
Trucks-StL-Chi ... 149
Wynn-Cle 138
Parnell-Bos 136
Garcia-Cle 134

Strikeouts/Game
Pierce-Chi 6.17
Gray-Det 5.88
Masterson-Was ... 5.14
Parnell-Bos 5.08
Trucks-StL-Chi ... 5.07

Ratio
Raschi-NY 10.24
Lopat-NY 10.35
Pierce-Chi 10.65
Porterfield-Was ... 11.19
Sain-NY 11.29

Earned Run Average
Lopat-NY 2.42
Pierce-Chi 2.72
Trucks-StL-Chi ... 2.93
Sain-NY 3.00
Ford-NY 3.00

Adjusted ERA
Lopat-NY 152
Pierce-Chi 148
McDermott-Bos ... 140
Trucks-StL-Chi ... 139
Parnell-Bos 137

Opponents' Batting Avg.
Pierce-Chi .... .218
McDermott-Bos ... .224
Raschi-NY .... .224
Masterson-Was ... .232
Trucks-StL-Chi .... .238

Opponents' On Base Pct.
Raschi-NY .... .283
Lopat-NY .... .288
Pierce-Chi .... .292
Masterson-Was ... .304
Garcia-Cle .... .307

Starter Runs
Pierce-Chi 38.4
Trucks-StL-Chi ... 31.3
Lopat-NY 31.2
Parnell-Bos 25.0
Ford-NY 22.9

Adjusted Starter Runs
Pierce-Chi 39.3
Trucks-StL-Chi ... 33.9
Parnell-Bos 30.6
McDermott-Bos ... 27.4
Lopat-NY 25.1

Clutch Pitching Index
Ford-NY 127
Lopat-NY 123
Sain-NY 118
B.Lemon-Cle 113
Parnell-Bos 112

Relief Runs
Kinder-Bos 25.5
Dorish-Chi 9.7
Kuzava-NY 7.0
Bearden-Chi 6.9
Paige-StL 6.1

Adjusted Relief Runs
Kinder-Bos 28.0
Dorish-Chi 10.1
Paige-StL 8.7
Bearden-Chi 7.1
Kuzava-NY 3.9

Relief Ranking
Kinder-Bos 53.6
Dorish-Chi 12.8
Paige-StL 9.9
Bearden-Chi 6.5
Kuzava-NY 4.5

Total Pitcher Index
Kinder-Bos 5.9
McDermott-Bos ... 4.4
Trucks-StL-Chi ... 3.8
Pierce-Chi 3.5
Parnell-Bos 3.4

Total Baseball Ranking
Rosen-Cle 6.2
Kinder-Bos 5.9
McDermott-Bos ... 4.4
Trucks-StL-Chi ... 3.8
Zernial-Phi 3.5

March 13 Newly acquired Brave Bobby Thomson breaks his ankle sliding into third base in an exhibition game with the Pirates, thus opening the way for Henry Aaron to start in the outfield.

March 29 Phil Cavarretta gives Cubs owner Phil Wrigley an honest assessment of the team's chances, and is fired for his "defeatist attitude," the first manager to be given the gate during spring training.

April 11 To make room for promising rookie outfielder Wally Moon, the Cardinals trade long-time great Enos Slaughter to the Yankees. In what turns out to be a good deal for both teams, the Cardinals get center fielder Bill Virdon, pitcher Mel Wright, and outfielder Emil Tellinger in return. Virdon will become the NL Rookie of the Year in 1955, and Slaughter will help the Yankees to win 103 games.

April 13 Back in center field after two years in the Army, Willie Mays of the Giants hits a two-run shot that beats Brooklyn, 4–3.

April 23 At Sportsman's Park, Henry Aaron hits the first of his 755 major league home runs, off Vic Raschi of St. Louis. The Braves win in 14 innings 7-5.

May 2 Stan Musial hits five home runs in a doubleheader split with the Giants in St. Louis. In attendance is eight-year-old Nate Colbert, who will be the only other player in history to accomplish this feat.

May 24 In a unique Birdie Tebbetts shift against the Cards' Stan Musial, the Redlegs enlist a "fourth" outfielder in place of regular shortstop Roy McMillan. This causes a box score irregularity because left-handed outfielder Nino Escalero is officially listed as a left-handed shortstop. After all that, Art Fowler strikes out Musial as the Reds win 4–2.

June 12 Jim Wilson, 32, no-hits the Phillies, 2–0, before 28,218 in Milwaukee. Robin Roberts takes the loss, his first after nine straight wins over the Braves. It is Wilson's first start after pitching just 8⅓ innings of relief, giving up 7 runs. Ironically, the Braves asked waivers on Wilson two weeks earlier, with no takers.

July 31 Using a borrowed bat, Dodger killer Joe Adcock hits four home runs and a double for 18 total bases in the Braves' 15–7 victory at Ebbets Field. The 18 total bases is a major league mark and, combined with the seven total bases from the day before, gives him a two-day tally of 25, which ties the record of Ty Cobb.

August 29 A disappointed crowd of 45,922 at Milwaukee's County Stadium sees the Dodgers take two from the Braves, 12–4 and 11–4. In game one, the Dodgers break a tie with a record eight runs in the 11th. The Braves establish a new NL attendance mark of 1,841,666 on their way to a season total of 2,131,388.

September 10 Attempting to handle Hoyt Wilhelm's knuckleball against the Redlegs, catcher Ray Katt of the Giants sets a major league record with four passed balls in the eighth inning.

September 26 In his second start, rookie Brooklyn lefty Karl Spooner shuts out Pittsburgh 1-0 on a Gil Hodges home run in the eighth inning. He fans 12 for a total of 27 strikeouts in his first two major league games, establishing a new record. The home run by Hodges gives him 42 for the season, tying him with Duke Snider for the most by a Dodger.

September 29 In Game 1 of the World Series, Willie Mays of the Giants makes one of the greatest catches in history when he races back to deep center field in the Polo Grounds to make an over-the-head catch of Indian Vic Wertz's 462-foot drive in the eighth with the score tied at 2-2. In the 10th inning, Dusty Rhodes hits a pinch-hit, three-run, 260-foot home run off Bob Lemon to give the Giants a 5-2 victory.

October 2 In Game 4 the Giants sweep the AL team with the best record in history, as they score four runs in the fifth to take a 7-0 lead. The final is 7-4 as Don Liddle defeats Bob Lemon.

December 11 With the Athletics poised to move to Kansas City, the Phillies purchase Connie Mack Stadium.

	BROOKLYN		CHICAGO		CINCINNATI		MILWAUKEE		NEW YORK		PHILADELPHIA		PITTSBURGH		ST.LOUIS
M	W.Alston	M	S.Hack	M	B.Tebbetts	M	C.Grimm	M	L.Durocher	M	S.O'Neill	M	F.Haney	M	E.Stanky
1B	G.Hodges	1B	D.Fondy	1B	T.Kluszewski	1B	J.Adcock	1B	W.Lockman	M	T.Moore	1B	B.Skinner	1B	J.Cunningham
2B	J.Gilliam	2B	G.Baker	2B	J.Temple	2B	D.O'Connell	2B	D.Williams	1B	E.Torgeson	2B	C.Roberts	2B	R.Schoendienst
SS	P.Reese	SS	E.Banks	SS	R.McMillan	SS	J.Logan	SS	A.Dark	2B	G.Hamner	SS	G.Allie	SS	A.Grammas
3B	D.Hoak	3B	R.Jackson	3B	B.Adams	3B	E.Mathews	3B	H.Thompson	SS	B.Morgan	3B	D.Cole	3B	R.Jablonski
LF	J.Robinson	LF	R.Kiner	LF	J.Greengrass	LF	H.Aaron	LF	M.Irvin	3B	W.Jones	LF	D.Hall	LF	R.Repulski
CF	D.Snider	CF	B.Talbot	CF	G.Bell	CF	B.Bruton	CF	W.Mays	LF	D.Schell	CF	F.Thomas	CF	W.Moon
RF	C.Furillo	RF	H.Sauer	RF	W.Post	RF	A.Pafko	RF	D.Mueller	CF	R.Ashburn	RF	S.Gordon	RF	S.Musial
C	R.Campanella	C	J.Garagiola	C	A.Seminick	C	D.Crandall	C	W.Westrum	RF	D.Ennis	C	T.Atwell	C	B.Sarni
										C	S.Burgess				
O	S.Amoros	O	F.Baumholtz	3	C.Harmon	2	J.Dittmer	C	R.Katt			O	J.Lynch	S3	S.Hemus
32	B.Cox	C	W.Cooper	C	E.Bailey	O	J.Pendleton	O	D.Rhodes	C	S.Lopata	1O	P.Ward	1	T.Alston
C	R.Walker	C	E.Tappe	O	B.Borkowski	1O	C.Metkovich	12	B.Hofman	O1	J.Wyrostek	C	J.Shepard	C	D.Rice
O	W.Moryn	2	E.Miksis	O	L.Merriman	O	B.Thomson	32	B.Gardner	O	M.Clark	3	E.Pellagrini	O	J.Frazier
O	G.Shuba	1	S.Bilko	C	H.Landrith	C	C.White	/O	B.Taylor	S	T.Kazanski	O	H.Rice	O	P.Lowrey
O	D.Williams	O	C.McCullough	O	N.Escalera	/S	R.Smalley	C	E.St.Claire	/3	F.Baker	3	V.Janowicz	/O	S.Yvars
S	D.Zimmer	O	H.Rice	S2	R.Bridges	C	S.Calderone	/3	F.Castleman	/3	J.Command	O	C.Abrams	/O	T.Burgess
O	D.Thompson	3	V.Morgan	/O	J.Bolger	/1	M.Roach	/O	H.Evers	H	J.Lindell	/3	D.Smith	/1	S.Bilko
/C	T.Thompson	3	B.Serena	H	G.Hatton	/O	B.Queen	/C	J.Garagiola	/O	G.Niarhos	/O	G.Henley	S	D.Schofield
/1	C.Kress	C	J.Fanning	H	J.Lipon	R	S.Sisti	/O	E.Rodin	/O	S.Palys	/C	J.Mangan	/3	P.Castiglione
H	W.Belardi	O	L.Marquez	H	D.Murphy			/3	J.Amalfitano	H	S.Jok	/C	W.Cooper		
		/O	D.Robertson	H	C.Ryan			/2	R.Samford	/S	M.Micelotta	/C	N.Koback	P	H.Haddix
P	C.Erskine	H	B.Edwards			P	W.Spahn	H	H.Gentry			/O	L.Marquez	P	V.Raschi
P	R.Meyer	/S	C.Kitsos	P	A.Fowler	P	L.Burdette	H	B.Lennon	P	R.Roberts	/C	B.Hall	P	B.Lawrence
P	J.Podres			P	C.Valentine	P	G.Conley			P	C.Simmons	/O	S.Jethroe	P	G.Staley
P	B.Loes	P	B.Rush	P	J.Nuxhall	P	J.Wilson	P	J.Antonelli	P	M.Dickson			P	T.Poholsky
P	D.Newcombe	P	P.Minner	P	B.Podbielan	P	C.Nichols	P	R.Gomez	P	B.Miller	P	M.Surkont	RP	A.Brazle
RP	C.Labine	P	W.Hacker	P	F.Baczewski	RP	D.Jolly	P	S.Maglie	P	H.Wehmeier	P	B.Friend	RP	J.Presko
RP	J.Hughes	P	J.Klippstein	RP	H.Judson	RP	E.Johnson	P	J.Hearn	RP	S.Ridzik	P	V.Law	RP	C.Deal
RP	E.Palica	P	H.Pollet	RP	F.Smith	RP	R.Crone	P	D.Liddle	RP	J.Konstanty	P	D.Littlefield		
		RP	J.Davis	RP	J.Collum			RP	M.Grissom			P	B.Purkey	P	G.Jones
P	B.Milliken	RP	H.Jeffcoat			P	B.Buhl	RP	H.Wilhelm	P	R.Mrozinski	RP	J.Hetki	P	R.Lint
P	P.Roe	RP	B.Tremel	P	H.Perkowski	P	J.Jay	RP	W.McCall	P	B.Greenwood			P	R.Beard
P	B.Wade			P	K.Drews	P	D.Koslo			/P	K.Drews	P	J.Thies	P	S.Miller
P	P.Wojey	P	D.Cole	P	H.Wehmeier	P	P.Paine	P	L.Jansen	/P	P.Penson	P	P.LaPalme	P	B.Wade
/P	K.Spooner	P	J.Brosnan	/P	M.Savransky	/P	C.Gorin	P	A.Corwin	T.Kipper		P	G.O'Donnell	/P	M.Wright
/P	B.Darnell	P	J.Willis	/P	J.Lane			P	A.Worthington			P	L.Pepper	/P	C.Scheib
/P	T.Lasorda	P	T.Lown	/P	J.Pearce			/P	M.Picone			P	L.Yochim	/P	H.White
/P	J.Black	/P	M.Picone	/P	M.Picone			/P	A.Konikowski			/C	C.Hogue	/P	B.Greason
		/P	B.Zick	/P	K.Raffensberger			/P	G.Spencer			/P	J.Page	/P	M.Luna
		/P	B.Church	/P	G.Zuverink			/P	R.Monzant			/P	N.King		
		/P	A.Lary	/P	C.Ross			/P	P.Giel						
		/P	J.Pyecha												

TEAM	G	W	L	PCT	GB	R	OR	AB	H	2B	3B	HR	BB	SO	AVG	OBP	SLG	PRO	PRO+	BR	/A	PF	CHI	RC	SB	CS	SBA	SBR
NY	154	97	57	.630		732	**550**	5245	1386	194	42	**186**	522	561	.264	.335	.424	.759	102	17	13	101	102	747	30	23	57	-5
BRO	154	92	62	.597	5	778	740	5251	1418	246	56	**186**	**634**	625	.270	.353	**.444**	**.797**	110	**100**	**75**	103	96	**821**	46	39	54	-10
MIL	154	89	65	.578	8	670	556	5261	1395	217	41	139	471	619	.265	.330	.401	.731	103	-33	10	94	101	697	30	27	**64**	-2
PHI	154	75	79	.487	22	659	614	5184	1384	243	**58**	102	604	620	.267	.345	.395	.740	99	-2	-1	100	95	707	47	30	61	-7
CIN	154	74	80	.481	23	729	763	5234	1369	221	46	147	557	645	.262	.336	.406	.742	96	-8	-27	101	**105**	726	46	35	62	-4
STL	154	72	82	.468	25	**799**	790	5405	**1518**	**285**	**58**	119	582	586	.281	.354	.421	.775	107	65	59	101	102	807	**63**	46	58	-9
CHI	154	64	90	.416	33	700	766	5359	1412	229	45	159	478	693	.263	.327	.412	.739	97	-21	-28	101	103	717	46	31	60	-5
PIT	154	53	101	.344	44	557	845	5088	1260	181	57	76	566	737	.248	.326	.350	.676	83	-119	-111	99	98	596	21	13	62	-2
TOT	616					5624		42027	11142	1816	403	1114	4414	5086	.265	.338	.407	.745							337	240	58	-43

TEAM	CG	SH	SV	IP	H	H/G	HR	BB	SO	RAT	ERA	ERA+	OAV	OOB	PR	/A	PF	CPI	FA	E	DP	FW	PW	BW	SBW	DIF
NY	45	**19**	33	1390	**1258**	8.1	113	613	692	12.3	**3.09**	130	**.243**	.328	151	145	99	113	.975	154	172	-.5	**14.4**	1.3	.0	4.9
BRO	39	8	**36**	1393²	1399	9.0	164	533	**762**	12.6	4.31	95	.261	.330	-36	-35	100	93	.978	129	138	.8	-3.5	**7.4**	-.5	10.7
MIL	63	13	21	1394²	1296	8.4	106	553	698	12.1	3.19	117	.250	.326	137	83	92	110	**.981**	**116**	171	**1.5**	8.2	1.0	**.3**	.9
PHI	**78**	14	12	1365¹	1329	8.8	133	**450**	570	11.8	3.59	112	.256	**.318**	73	68	99	100	.975	145	133	-.0	6.7	-.0	-.2	-8.4
CIN	34	8	27	1367¹	1491	9.8	169	547	537	13.6	4.50	93	.282	.354	-65	-47	103	105	.977	137	**194**	.4	-4.7	-2.7	.1	3.8
STL	40	11	18	1390¹	1484	9.6	170	535	680	13.4	4.50	91	.275	.346	-66	-60	101	100	.976	146	178	-.0	-5.9	5.8	-.4	-4.4
CHI	41	6	19	1374¹	1375	9.0	131	619	622	13.2	4.51	93	.264	.345	-66	-46	103	92	.974	154	164	-.5	-4.6	-2.8	.0	-5.2
PIT	37	4	15	1346	1510	10.1	128	564	525	14.0	4.92	85	.287	.359	-127	-109	103	95	.971	173	136	-1.6	-10.8	-11.0	.3	-1.0
TOT	377	83	181	11021²		9.1				12.9	4.07		.265	.338					.976	1154	1286					

Runs
Snider-Bro ... 120
Musial-StL ... 120
Mays-NY ... 119
Ashburn-Phi ... 111
Gilliam-Bro ... 107

Hits
Mueller-NY ... 212
Snider-Bro ... 199
Musial-StL ... 195
Mays-NY ... 195
Moon-StL ... 193

Doubles
Musial-StL ... 41
Snider-Bro ... 39
Repulski-StL ... 39
Hamner-Phi ... 39

Triples
Mays-NY ... 13
Hamner-Phi ... 11
Snider-Bro ... 10

Home Runs
Kluszewski-Cin ... 49
Hodges-Bro ... 42
Sauer-Chi ... 41
Mays-NY ... 41

Total Bases
Snider-Bro ... 378
Mays-NY ... 377
Kluszewski-Cin ... 368
Musial-StL ... 359
Hodges-Bro ... 335

Runs Batted In
Kluszewski-Cin ... 141
Snider-Bro ... 130
Hodges-Bro ... 130
Musial-StL ... 126
Ennis-Phi ... 119

Runs Produced
Musial-StL ... 211
Snider-Bro ... 210
Kluszewski-Cin ... 196
Hodges-Bro ... 194

Bases On Balls
Ashburn-Phi ... 125
Mathews-Mil ... 113
Musial-StL ... 103
Thompson-NY ... 90
Reese-Bro ... 90

Batting Average
Mays-NY ... .345
Mueller-NY ... .342
Snider-Bro ... .341
Musial-StL ... .330
Kluszewski-Cin ... .326

On Base Percentage
Ashburn-Phi ... .442
Musial-StL ... .433
Mathews-Mil ... .428
Snider-Bro ... .427
Mays-NY ... .415

Slugging Average
Mays-NY ... .667
Snider-Bro ... .647
Kluszewski-Cin ... .642
Musial-StL ... .607
Mathews-Mil ... .603

Production
Mays-NY ... 1.083
Snider-Bro ... 1.074
Kluszewski-Cin ... 1.052
Musial-StL ... 1.040
Mathews-Mil ... 1.031

Adjusted Production
Mathews-Mil ... 177
Mays-NY ... 176
Snider-Bro ... 170
Musial-StL ... 166
Kluszewski-Cin ... 165

Batter Runs
Snider-Bro ... 64.6
Mays-NY ... 61.8
Musial-StL ... 60.7
Kluszewski-Cin ... 57.1
Mathews-Mil ... 48.6

Adjusted Batter Runs
Mays-NY ... 61.1
Snider-Bro ... 60.2
Musial-StL ... 59.6
Mathews-Mil ... 56.6
Kluszewski-Cin ... 53.4

Clutch Hitting Index
Ennis-Phi ... 132
Jablonski-StL ... 127
Post-Cin ... 126
Furillo-Bro ... 119
Bell-Cin ... 117

Runs Created
Snider-Bro ... 161
Mays-NY ... 155
Musial-StL ... 153
Kluszewski-Cin ... 151
Mathews-Mil ... 131

Total Average
Mathews-Mil ... 1.169
Mays-NY ... 1.158
Snider-Bro ... 1.156
Kluszewski-Cin ... 1.117
Musial-StL ... 1.087

Stolen Bases
Bruton-Mil ... 34
Temple-Cin ... 21
Fondy-Chi ... 20
Moon-StL ... 18
Ashburn-Phi ... 11

Stolen Base Average
Fondy-Chi ... 80.0
Temple-Cin ... 75.0
Bruton-Mil ... 72.3
Moon-StL ... 64.3

Stolen Base Runs
Fondy-Chi ... 3.0
Bruton-Mil ... 2.4
Temple-Cin ... 2.1
Torgeson-Phi ... 1.5

Fielding Runs
Schoendienst-StL ... 32.9
Grammas-StL ... 29.8
Ashburn-Phi ... 17.2
Mays-NY ... 15.5
Logan-Mil ... 14.4

Total Player Rating
Mays-NY ... 6.7
Mathews-Mil ... 5.2
Schoendienst-StL ... 4.8
Snider-Bro ... 4.6
Musial-StL ... 4.6

Wins
Roberts-Phi ... 23
Spahn-Mil ... 21
Antonelli-NY ... 21
Haddix-StL ... 18
Erskine-Bro ... 18

Win Percentage
Antonelli-NY ... .750
Lawrence-StL ... .714
Gomez-NY ... .654
Spahn-Mil ... .636
Roberts-Phi ... .605

Games
Hughes-Bro ... 60
Hetki-Pit ... 58
Brazle-StL ... 58
Wilhelm-NY ... 57
Grissom-NY ... 56

Complete Games
Roberts-Phi ... 29
Spahn-Mil ... 23
Simmons-Phi ... 21
Antonelli-NY ... 18

Shutouts
Antonelli-NY ... 6

Saves
Hughes-Bro ... 24
Smith-Cin ... 20
Grissom-NY ... 19
Jolly-Mil ... 10
Hetki-Pit ... 9

Innings Pitched
Roberts-Phi ... 336.2
Spahn-Mil ... 283.1
Erskine-Bro ... 260.1
Haddix-StL ... 259.2
Antonelli-NY ... 258.2

Fewest Hits/Game
Antonelli-NY ... 7.27
Roberts-Phi ... 7.73
Conley-Mil ... 7.92
Lawrence-StL ... 8.00
Wehmeier-Cin-Phi ... 8.02

Fewest BB/Game
Roberts-Phi ... 1.50
Minner-Chi ... 2.06
Hacker-Chi ... 2.10
Burdette-Mil ... 2.34
Meyer-Bro ... 2.45

Strikeouts
Roberts-Phi ... 185
Haddix-StL ... 184
Erskine-Bro ... 166
Antonelli-NY ... 152
Spahn-Mil ... 136

Strikeouts/Game
Haddix-StL ... 6.38
Erskine-Bro ... 5.74
Littlefield-Pit ... 5.34
Antonelli-NY ... 5.29
Conley-Mil ... 5.23

Ratio
Roberts-Phi ... 9.36
Antonelli-NY ... 10.72
Burdette-Mil ... 10.97
Spahn-Mil ... 11.09
Hacker-Chi ... 11.23

Earned Run Average
Antonelli-NY ... 2.30
Burdette-Mil ... 2.76
Simmons-Phi ... 2.81
Gomez-NY ... 2.88
Conley-Mil ... 2.96

Adjusted ERA
Antonelli-NY ... 176
Simmons-Phi ... 144
Gomez-NY ... 140
Roberts-Phi ... 136
Burdette-Mil ... 135

Opponents' Batting Avg.
Antonelli-NY ... .219
Roberts-Phi ... .231
Simmons-Phi ... .239
Littlefield-Pit ... .239
Wehmeier-Cin-Phi ... .239

Opponents' On Base Pct.
Roberts-Phi ... .267
Antonelli-NY ... .293
Spahn-Mil ... .302
Burdette-Mil ... .302
Hacker-Chi ... .304

Starter Runs
Antonelli-NY ... 51.0
Roberts-Phi ... 41.3
Simmons-Phi ... 35.5
Burdette-Mil ... 34.7
Gomez-NY ... 29.3

Adjusted Starter Runs
Antonelli-NY ... 50.0
Roberts-Phi ... 40.1
Simmons-Phi ... 34.6
Gomez-NY ... 28.4
Burdette-Mil ... 25.5

Clutch Pitching Index
Gomez-NY ... 130
Dickson-Phi ... 123
Fowler-Cin ... 116
Conley-Mil ... 116
Antonelli-NY ... 115

Relief Runs
Wilhelm-NY ... 24.4
Grissom-NY ... 23.4
Jolly-Mil ... 20.4
Johnson-Mil ... 13.9
Smith-Cin ... 12.7

Adjusted Relief Runs
Wilhelm-NY ... 23.9
Grissom-NY ... 22.9
Jolly-Mil ... 16.1
Smith-Cin ... 13.7
Johnson-Mil ... 10.1

Relief Ranking
Grissom-NY ... 36.6
Wilhelm-NY ... 34.3
Smith-Cin ... 27.5
Jolly-Mil ... 25.4
Hughes-Bro ... 15.6

Total Pitcher Index
Antonelli-NY ... 5.5
Grissom-NY ... 3.6
Roberts-Phi ... 3.6
Wilhelm-NY ... 3.4
Simmons-Phi ... 3.3

Total Baseball Ranking
Mays-NY ... 6.7
Antonelli-NY ... 5.5
Mathews-Mil ... 5.2
Schoendienst-StL ... 4.8
Snider-Bro ... 4.6

January 14 Joe DiMaggio marries Marilyn Monroe.

April 15 Clint Courtney of the Orioles hits the first home run in Memorial Stadium. Baltimore draws a record Opening Day crowd of 46,354 in a 3-1 win over the White Sox.

May 16 Ted Williams returns to action after breaking his collarbone and goes 8-for-9 with two home runs and seven RBI in a doubleheader against the Tigers.

July 13 In the All-Star Game, the AL breaks the NL's four-game winning streak with an 11–9 win. Larry Doby's pinch home run in the eighth, followed by Nellie Fox's two-run single, ends the highest scoring All-Star Game in history. The two teams combine for 31 hits, with the AL amassing 17. The Indians' Al Rosen has two home runs and drives in five runs.

July 30 Against Allie Reynolds, third baseman Bob Kennedy hits the first grand slam for the new Baltimore Orioles. The Orioles surpass the top season attendance the Browns had in their 52 years, as they draw 27,385 for the game, giving them 7,000 more than the 712,918 St. Louis drew in 1922.

August 12 Eddie Yost of the Senators draws his 100th walk for the fifth year in a row.

August 31 The Indians beat the Yanks, 6–1, to record their 26th win of the month, tying the 1931 A's.

September 12 A record crowd of 86,587 jams Cleveland's Memorial Stadium to see the Indians sweep a doubleheader from the Yanks, 4–1 and 3–2, behind Bob Lemon and Early Wynn.

September 18 The Indians clinch their third pennant in history and the first since 1948 with a 3–2 win over the Tigers.

September 25 Early Wynn two-hits the Tigers 11-1 for his league-leading 23rd win as the Indians notch their 111th victory, a new AL record eclipsing the 110 wins of the 1927 Yankees.

September 26 Art Ditmar of the Athletics defeats the Yanks 8-6 in the last game the franchise will play in Philadelphia before moving to Kansas City. Yogi Berra plays his only game at third base, and Mickey Mantle plays shortstop in Casey Stengel's "power line-up."

October 28 The major league owners vote down the sale of the Athletics to a Philadelphia syndicate. A week later, Arnold Johnson buys a controlling interest in the Athletics from the Mack family for $3.5 million and moves the team to Kansas City. Shortly thereafter, the Phillies purchase Connie Mack Stadium.

November 18 In an enormous two-part trade begun on November 14, the Yankees and Orioles exchange 17 players. Among those who change place is Don Larsen, who will pitch the only perfect game in World Series history for the Yankees in 1956.

BALTIMORE		BOSTON		CHICAGO		CLEVELAND		DETROIT		NEW YORK		PHILADELPHIA		WASHINGTON	
M	J.Dykes	M	L.Boudreau	M	P.Richards	M	A.Lopez	M	F.Hutchinson	M	C.Stengel	M	E.Joost	M	B.Harris
1B	E.Waitkus	1B	H.Agganis	M	M.Marion	1B	B.Glynn	1B	W.Dropo	1B	J.Collins	1B	L.Limmer	1B	M.Vernon
2B	B.Young	2B	T.Lepcio	1B	F.Fain	2B	B.Avila	2B	F.Bolling	2B	G.McDougald	2B	S.Jacobs	2B	W.Terwilliger
SS	B.Hunter	SS	M.Bolling	2B	N.Fox	SS	G.Strickland	SS	H.Kuenn	SS	P.Rizzuto	SS	J.DeMaestri	SS	P.Runnels
3B	V.Stephens	3B	G.Hatton	SS	C.Carrasquel	3B	A.Rosen	3B	R.Boone	3B	A.Carey	3B	J.Finigan	3B	E.Yost
LF	J.Fridley	LF	T.Williams	3B	C.Michaels	LF	A.Smith	LF	J.Delsing	LF	I.Noren	LF	G.Zernial	LF	R.Sievers
CF	C.Diering	CF	J.Jensen	LF	M.Minoso	CF	L.Doby	CF	B.Tuttle	CF	M.Mantle	CF	V.Power	CF	J.Busby
RF	C.Abrams	RF	J.Piersall	CF	J.Groth	RF	D.Philley	RF	A.Kaline	RF	H.Bauer	RF	B.Renna	RF	T.Umphlett
C	C.Courtney	C	S.White	RF	J.Rivera	C	J.Hegan	C	F.House	C	Y.Berra	C	J.Astroth	C	E.Fitz Gerald
O	G.Coan	21	B.Goodman	C	S.Lollar	1	V.Wertz	O	B.Nieman	2S	J.Coleman	1	D.Bollweg	O	T.Wright
3O	B.Kennedy	O	K.Olson	13	G.Kell	O	W.Westlake	1	W.Belardi	O	G.Woodling	O	E.Valo	2	J.Pesky
1	D.Kryhoski	S3	B.Consolo	C	M.Batts	3	R.Regalado	23	F.Hatfield	1	B.Skowron	O	B.Wilson	C	J.Tipton
O	S.Mele	1O	S.Mele	1	P.Cavarretta	S	S.Dente	C	R.Wilson	1	E.Robinson	23	P.Suder	S	J.Snyder
S2	J.Brideweser	O	C.Maxwell	C	C.Sawatski	23	H.Majeski	H	H.Evers	S	E.Slaughter	C	Bi.Shantz	O	J.Lemon
C	L.Moss	3	G.Kell	3	F.Marsh	O	D.Pope	O	D.Lund	C	W.Miranda	C	J.Robertson	O	C.Vollmer
O	V.Wertz	C	M.Owen	1	R.Jackson	C	H.Naragon	/O	S.Souchock	O	B.Cerv	O	J.Taylor	/S	M.Hoderlein
2	C.Garcia	O	D.Lenhardt	O	E.McGhee	/O	D.Mitchell	2	R.Bertoia	3	B.Brown	O	E.McGhee	/C	B.Oldis
C	R.Murray	C	D.Wilber	O	W.Marshall	H	L.Easter	/1	C.Kress	C	C.Silvera	/S	E.Joost	/O	C.Paula
O	J.Durham	/1	D.Gernert	O1	B.Boyd	/C	M.Grasso	/O	C.King	/C	L.Berberet	/S	J.Littrell	/2	R.Dietzel
/1	F.Kellert	/3	F.Baker	O	B.Wilson	/1	R.Nelson	/C	M.Batts	/1	F.Leja			/2	H.Killebrew
/O	D.Lenhardt	/O	H.Evers	3	G.Hatton	/C	J.Ginsberg	H	J.Pesky	/S	W.Held	P	A.Portocarrero	/3	J.Levan
/O	D.Kokos	H	G.Morton	/3	J.Kirrene	H	J.Dyck	/C	A.Lakeman	H	R.Houk	P	A.Kellner	/C	S.Korcheck
/S	N.Berry	P	F.Sullivan	/C	R.Wilson	/O	B.Kennedy	/S	G.Bullard	/C	G.Triandos	P	M.Fricano	P	B.Porterfield
P	B.Turley	P	W.Nixon	/O	B.Stewart	P	E.Wynn	/C	W.Streuli	P	W.Ford	P	B.Trice	P	M.McDermott
P	J.Coleman	P	T.Brewer	/3	S.Jok	P	M.Garcia	P	S.Gromek	P	B.Grim	P	J.Gray	P	J.Schmitz
P	D.Larsen	P	L.Kiely	R	B.Cain	P	B.Lemon	P	N.Garver	P	E.Lopat	RP	S.Dixon	P	C.Stobbs
P	D.Pillette	P	B.Henry	H	D.Nicholas	P	A.Houtteman	P	G.Zuverink	P	A.Reynolds	RP	M.Burtschy	P	D.Stone
P	L.Kretlow	RP	H.Brown	P	V.Trucks	P	B.Feller	P	B.Hoeft	P	T.Morgan	RP	A.Sima	RP	C.Pascual
RP	B.Chakales	RP	E.Kinder	P	B.Keegan	RP	D.Mossi	P	A.Aber	RP	J.Sain	P	C.Bishop	RP	G.Keriazakos
RP	M.Blyzka	RP	S.Hudson	P	B.Pierce	RP	R.Narleski	RP	D.Marlowe	P	H.Byrd	P	M.Martin	RP	B.Stewart
RP	H.Fox	P	M.Parnell	P	J.Harshman	RP	H.Newhouser	RP	R.Herbert	P	J.McDonald	P	A.Ditmar	P	S.Shea
P	M.Stuart	P	R.Kemmerer	P	S.Consuegra	P	B.Hooper	RP	B.Miller	/P	T.Byrne	/P	L.Wheat	P	C.Marrero
/P	B.Kuzava	P	T.Clevenger	RP	H.Dorish	P	D.Hoskins	P	T.Gray	P	B.Kuzava	/P	O.Van Brabant	P	S.Dixon
/P	B.O'Dell	P	T.Hurd	RP	M.Martin	/P	B.Chakales	P	R.Branca	P	T.Gorman	/P	B.Oster		
/P	D.Koslo	P	T.Herrin	P	D.Johnson	P	J.Santiago	/P	D.Weik	P	B.Wiesler	/P	D.Romberger		
/P	D.Littlefield	P	B.Werle	P	M.Fornieles	/P	D.Tomanek	/P	D.Donovan	P	J.Konstanty	/P	Bo.Shantz		
/P	V.Bickford	/P	J.Dobson	/P	D.Strahs			/P	F.Lary	P	M.Stuart	/P	B.Upton		
/P	J.Heard			/P	A.Sima					P	A.Schallock	/P	H.Raether		
/P	R.Duren			/P	T.Flanigan					P	R.Branca	/P	C.Scheib		
				/P	V.Valentinetti					P	B.Miller	/P	D.Rozek		

TEAM	G	W	L	PCT	GB	R	OR	AB	H	2B	3B	HR	BB	SO	AVG	OBP	SLG	PRO	PRO+	BR	/A	PF	CHI	RC	SB	CS	SBA	SBR
CLE	156	111	43	.721		746	**504**	5222	1368	188	39	**156**	637	668	.262	.345	.403	.748	109	76	64	102	102	739	30	33	48	-11
NY	155	103	51	.669	8	**805**	563	5226	1400	215	59	133	650	632	**.268**	**.351**	**.408**	**.759**	118	**101**	**128**	97	**106**	768	34	41	45	-14
CHI	155	94	60	.610	17	711	521	5168	1382	203	47	94	604	**536**	.267	.350	.379	.729	103	51	27	103	101	700	**98**	58	63	-5
BOS	156	69	85	.448	42	700	728	5399	**1436**	244	41	123	654	660	.266	.348	.395	.743	99	73	-9	111	93	749	51	30	63	-3
DET	155	68	86	.442	43	584	664	5233	1351	215	41	90	492	603	.258	.324	.367	.691	97	-37	-26	98	97	609	48	44	52	-12
WAS	155	66	88	.429	45	632	680	5249	1292	188	**69**	81	610	719	.246	.328	.355	.683	98	-44	-11	95	104	631	37	21	**64**	**-2**
BAL	154	54	100	.351	57	483	668	5206	1309	195	49	52	468	634	.251	.316	.338	.654	92	-104	-65	93	91	553	30	31	49	-10
PHI	156	51	103	.331	60	542	875	5206	1228	191	41	94	504	677	.236	.307	.342	.649	84	-117	-119	100	105	553	30	29	51	-8
TOT	621					5203		41909	10766	1639	386	823	4619	5129	.257	.334	.373	.707							358	287	56	-65

TEAM	CG	SH	SV	IP	H	H/G	HR	BB	SO	RAT	ERA	ERA+	OAV	OOB	PR	/A	PF	CPI	FA	E	DP	FW	PW	BW	SBW	DIF
CLE	**77**	12	36	1419¹	**1220**	7.7	89	486	678	10.9	2.78	132	.232	.299	148	141	99	100	.979	128	148	.7	14.6	6.6	-.3	12.4
NY	51	16	**37**	1379¹	1284	8.4	86	552	655	12.2	3.26	105	.251	.328	71	27	92	**107**	.979	126	**198**	.8	2.8	**13.2**	-.6	9.8
CHI	60	**23**	33	1383	1255	8.2	94	517	701	11.6	3.05	122	.244	.314	103	105	100	105	**.982**	108	149	1.8	10.8	2.8	.3	1.2
BOS	41	10	22	1412¹	1434	9.1	118	612	**707**	13.3	4.01	102	.265	.344	-46	15	110	101	.972	176	163	-2.0	1.5	-.9	.5	-7.2
DET	58	13	13	1383	1375	8.9	138	506	603	12.5	3.81	97	.261	.330	-13	-17	99	103	.978	129	131	.6	-1.8	-2.7	-.4	-4.8
WAS	69	10	7	1383¹	1396	9.1	79	573	562	13.0	3.84	93	.265	.340	-18	-43	96	99	.977	137	172	.2	-4.4	-1.1	.6	-6.2
BAL	58	6	8	1373¹	1279	8.4	**78**	688	668	13.0	3.88	92	.250	.341	-24	-45	96	94	.975	147	152	-.4	-4.6	-6.7	-.2	-11.0
PHI	49	3	13	1371¹	1523	10.0	141	685	555	14.7	5.18	75	.285	.370	-222	-194	105	95	.972	169	163	-1.6	-20.0	-12.3	.0	7.9
TOT	463	93	169	11105		8.7				12.6	3.72		.257	.334					.977	1120	1276					

Runs
Mantle-NY 129
Minoso-Chi 119
Avila-Cle 112
Fox-Chi 111
Carrasquel-Chi 106

Hits
Kuenn-Det 201
Fox-Chi 201
Avila-Cle 189
Busby-Was 187
Minoso-Chi 182

Doubles
Vernon-Was 33
Smith-Cle 29
Minoso-Chi 29

Triples
Minoso-Chi 18
Runnels-Was 15
Vernon-Was 14
Mantle-NY 12
Tuttle-Det 11

Home Runs
Doby-Cle 32
Williams-Bos 29
Mantle-NY 27
Jensen-Bos 25

Total Bases
Minoso-Chi 304
Vernon-Was 294
Mantle-NY 285
Berra-NY 285
Doby-Cle 279

Runs Batted In
Doby-Cle 126
Berra-NY 125
Jensen-Bos 117
Minoso-Chi 116

Runs Produced
Minoso-Chi 216
Mantle-NY 204
Berra-NY 191
Doby-Cle 188
Jensen-Bos 184

Bases On Balls
Williams-Bos 136
Yost-Was 131
Mantle-NY 102
Smith-Cle 88

Batting Average
Avila-Cle 341
Minoso-Chi 320
Noren-NY 319
Fox-Chi 319
Berra-NY 307

On Base Percentage
Williams-Bos 516
Minoso-Chi 416
Rosen-Cle 412
Mantle-NY 411
Yost-Was 406

Slugging Average
Minoso-Chi 535
Mantle-NY 525
Rosen-Cle 506
Vernon-Was 492
Berra-NY 488

Production
Williams-Bos 1.151
Minoso-Chi 951
Mantle-NY 936
Rosen-Cle 918
Avila-Cle 882

Adjusted Production
Williams-Bos 193
Mantle-NY 160
Minoso-Chi 154
Rosen-Cle 148
Noren-NY 140

Batter Runs
Williams-Bos 70.9
Minoso-Chi 47.3
Mantle-NY 42.8
Rosen-Cle 34.2
Avila-Cle 31.5

Adjusted Batter Runs
Williams-Bos 57.6
Mantle-NY 46.8
Minoso-Chi 43.2
Rosen-Cle 32.6
Avila-Cle 29.8

Clutch Hitting Index
Berra-NY 123
Minoso-Chi 122
Rosen-Cle 118
Sievers-Was 117
Doby-Cle 116

Runs Created
Williams-Bos 139
Mantle-NY 127
Minoso-Chi 125
Avila-Cle 109
Doby-Cle 108

Total Average
Williams-Bos 1.452
Mantle-NY 1.013
Minoso-Chi 969
Rosen-Cle 959
Doby-Cle 862

Stolen Bases
Jensen-Bos 22
Rivera-Chi 18
Minoso-Chi 18
Jacobs-Phi 17
Busby-Was 17

Stolen Base Average
Busby-Was 89.5
Jacobs-Phi 85.0
Jensen-Bos 75.9
Rivera-Chi 64.3
Fox-Chi 64.0

Stolen Base Runs
Busby-Was 3.9
Jacobs-Phi 3.3
Jensen-Bos 2.4
Cavarretta-Chi 1.2

Fielding Runs
Coleman-NY 17.9
Carey-NY 16.7
Lepcio-Bos 16.1
Bolling-Bos 15.3
Minoso-Chi 13.4

Total Player Rating
Williams-Bos 5.0
Minoso-Chi 5.0
Avila-Cle 4.7
Mantle-NY 4.1
Berra-NY 3.6

Wins
Wynn-Cle 23
Lemon-Cle 23
Grim-NY 20
Trucks-Chi 19
Garcia-Cle 19

Win Percentage
Consuegra-Chi 842
Grim-NY 769
Lemon-Cle 767
Garcia-Cle 704
Houtteman-Cle . . .682

Games
Dixon-Was-Phi 54
Martin-Phi-Chi 48
Pascual-Was 48
Kinder-Bos 48

Complete Games
Porterfield-Was . . . 21
Lemon-Cle 21
Wynn-Cle 20
Gromek-Det 17

Shutouts
Trucks-Chi 5
Garcia-Cle 5

Saves
Sain-NY 22
Kinder-Bos 15
Narleski-Cle 13

Innings Pitched
Wynn-Cle 270.2
Trucks-Chi 264.2
Garcia-Cle 258.2
Lemon-Cle 258.1
Gromek-Det 252.2

Fewest Hits/Game
Turley-Bal 6.48
Ford-NY 7.26
Wynn-Cle 7.48
Coleman-Bal 7.48
Reynolds-NY 7.61

Fewest BB/Game
Lopat-NY 1.75
Gromek-Det 2.03
Garver-Det 2.27
Garcia-Cle 2.47
Zuverink-Det 2.75

Strikeouts
Turley-Bal 185
Wynn-Cle 155
Trucks-Chi 152
Pierce-Chi 148
Harshman-Chi 134

Strikeouts/Game
Pierce-Chi 7.06
Harshman-Chi . . . 6.81
Turley-Bal 6.73
Hoeft-Det 5.86
Reynolds-NY 5.72

Ratio
Garcia-Cle 10.19
Wynn-Cle 10.24
Garver-Det 10.30
Gromek-Det 10.86
Trucks-Chi 10.88

Earned Run Average
Garcia-Cle 2.64
Lemon-Cle 2.72
Wynn-Cle 2.73
Gromek-Det 2.74
Trucks-Chi 2.79

Adjusted ERA
Garcia-Cle 139
Lemon-Cle 135
Wynn-Cle 135
Gromek-Det 135
Trucks-Chi 134

Opponents' Batting Avg.
Turley-Bal 203
Wynn-Cle 225
Ford-NY 227
Trucks-Chi 228
Garcia-Cle 229

Opponents' On Base Pct.
Garcia-Cle 284
Wynn-Cle 284
Garver-Det 287
Gromek-Det 297
Trucks-Chi 297

Starter Runs
Garcia-Cle 31.0
Wynn-Cle 30.0
Lemon-Cle 28.9
Gromek-Det 27.5
Trucks-Chi 27.5

Adjusted Starter Runs
Garcia-Cle 29.6
Wynn-Cle 28.5
Trucks-Chi 27.8
Lemon-Cle 27.5
Gromek-Det 26.7

Clutch Pitching Index
Keegan-Chi 126
Gromek-Det 116
Houtteman-Cle . . . 114
Lopat-NY 114
Harshman-Chi 114

Relief Runs
Mossi-Cle 18.5
Narleski-Cle 14.8
Dorish-Chi 12.1
Miller-Det 9.8
Sain-NY 4.9

Adjusted Relief Runs
Mossi-Cle 18.0
Narleski-Cle 14.3
Dorish-Chi 12.2
Miller-Det 9.6
Kinder-Bos 5.9

Relief Ranking
Mossi-Cle 15.2
Narleski-Cle 13.4
Dorish-Chi 11.6
Kinder-Bos 9.7
Sain-NY 4.9

Total Pitcher Index
Lemon-Cle 4.1
Gromek-Det 3.4
Wynn-Cle 3.3
Trucks-Chi 3.2
Garcia-Cle 2.9

Total Baseball Ranking
Williams-Bos 5.0
Minoso-Chi 5.0
Avila-Cle 4.7
Lemon-Cle 4.1
Mantle-NY 4.1

April 21 Brooklyn wins its 10th in a row, trouncing Robin Roberts of the Phils, 14–2. This sets a new major league record for consecutive wins to start a season, later topped by Atlanta and Oakland.

June 3 Stan Musial hits the 300th home run of his career, a three-run shot in the fifth-inning against Brooklyn's Johnny Podres. The Cards use a NL-record eight pitchers in a 12–5 loss.

June 8 The Dodgers option pitcher Tommy Lasorda to Montreal to make room on the roster for bonus baby Sandy Koufax, who has been on the injured list.

August 15 At Sportsman's Park in St. Louis, Braves pitcher Warren Spahn cracks a home run off Cardinals pitcher Mel Wright. It gives Spahn a home run in every National League park.

August 27 Dodgers bonus baby Sandy Koufax fans 14 Redlegs in a 7–0 win, as the two teams total 23 strikeouts.

September 5 Pitcher Don Newcombe wins his 20th game of the season 11-4 over the Phillies and hits his seventh homer of the season to set a new NL record for home runs by a pitcher.

September 8 Brooklyn clinches the pennant by beating the Braves 10-2 for their eighth straight win and break their own major league record for the earliest clinching, set in 1953.

September 19 Cubs slugger Ernie Banks hits his fifth grand slam of the season to set a new major league mark, but the Cubs lose 6-5 in 12 innings, to the Cardinals.

September 20 Giants slugger Willie Mays poles two home runs against the Pirates, giving him 50 for the year, making him only the seventh player in history to accomplish the feat.

September 25 Bobby Hofman of the Giants lines into a season-ending triple play against the Phillies in a 3–1 loss. The Giants win the opener, 5–2, as Willie Mays belts his 51st HR of the year.

October 2 Surprise Brooklyn starter rookie Roger Craig pitches six innings in World Series Game 1 for a 5–3 win. Two home runs by Duke Snider and one by Sandy Amoros in the first five innings prove too much for New York. Snider, who hit four home runs in the 1952 World Series, becomes the first player in history to do this more than once.

October 4 No more "wait till next year" as the Dodgers, behind the 2-0 pitching of Johnny Podres, brings the first World Series championship to Brooklyn in eight tries. Sixth-inning replacement Sandy Amoros races over to the wall in left field to one-hand an opposite-field bid for extra bases by Yogi Berra with the tying runs on. Amoros turns and fires to shortstop Pee Wee Reese who throws a bullet to Gil Hodges at first baseman for the double play on Yankee base runner Gil McDougald.

October 12 The Cardinals give manager Harry Walker his hat and replace him with Fred Hutchinson. With the departure of Walker, who pinch hit for the Cards during the season, the 1956 season will be the first one in NL history without a player-manager. The AL first went to all bench managers in 1930, then repeated in 1951.

October 25 Baseball great Branch Rickey steps down as GM of the Pirates and moves into an advisory role with the Pirates. Joe L. Brown, son of the actor, replaces him.

BROOKLYN

Pos	Player
M	W.Alston
1B	G.Hodges
2B	J.Gilliam
SS	P.Reese
3B	J.Robinson
LF	S.Amoros
CF	D.Snider
RF	C.Furillo
C	R.Campanella
3	D.Hoak
2S	D.Zimmer
C	R.Walker
1	F.Kellert
/O	G.Shuba
C	D.Howell
/O	B.Borkowski
/O	W.Moryn
H	B.Hamric
P	D.Newcombe
P	C.Erskine
P	J.Podres
P	B.Loes
P	K.Spooner
RP	C.Labine
RP	E.Roebuck
RP	D.Bessent
P	R.Craig
P	R.Meyer
P	J.Hughes
P	S.Koufax
/P	J.Black
/P	C.Templeton
/P	T.Lasorda

CHICAGO

Pos	Player
M	S.Hack
1B	D.Fondy
2B	G.Baker
SS	E.Banks
3B	R.Jackson
LF	H.Sauer
CF	E.Miksis
RF	J.King
C	H.Chiti
O	F.Baumholtz
O	B.Speake
O	J.Bolger
O	L.Merriman
C	W.Cooper
O	C.McCullough
O	T.Tappe
/O	G.Wade
/C	J.Fanning
/3	O.Friend
/3	V.Morgan
R	A.Lary
/C	E.Tappe
P	S.Jones
P	B.Rush
P	W.Hacker
P	P.Minner
P	J.Davis
RP	H.Jeffcoat
RP	H.Pollet
RP	D.Hillman
P	H.Perkowski
P	J.Andre
P	B.Tremel
P	D.Kaiser
P	H.Cohen
P	V.Amor
/P	B.Church
/P	B.Thorpe

CINCINNATI

Pos	Player
M	B.Tebbetts
1B	T.Kluszewski
2B	J.Temple
SS	R.McMillan
3B	R.Bridges
LF	S.Palys
CF	G.Bell
RF	W.Post
C	S.Burgess
3O	C.Harmon
3O	R.Jablonski
O	B.Thurman
3	B.Adams
3	M.Smith
C	H.Landrith
C	M.Batts
O	S.Mele
/1	B.Taylor
/C	B.Roselli
O	B.Borkowski
H	J.Brovia
/O	G.Gorbous
/C	A.Seminick
/O	B.Hazle
/O	A.Silvera
P	J.Nuxhall
P	A.Fowler
P	J.Klippstein
P	J.Collum
P	G.Staley
RP	R.Minarcin
RP	H.Freeman
P	J.Black
P	D.Gross
P	B.Podbielan
P	S.Ridzik
P	C.Valentine
/P	B.Hooper
/P	J.Lane
/P	M.Fisher
/P	J.Pearce
/P	F.Baczewski

MILWAUKEE

Pos	Player
M	C.Grimm
1B	G.Crowe
2B	D.O'Connell
SS	J.Logan
3B	E.Mathews
LF	B.Thomson
CF	B.Bruton
RF	H.Aaron
C	D.Crandall
O	C.Tanner
1	J.Adcock
O3	A.Pafko
2	J.Dittmer
O	D.Rice
C	D.White
/S	J.Pendleton
/1	B.Taylor
/C	B.Roselli
P	W.Spahn
P	L.Burdette
P	B.Buhl
P	G.Conley
P	C.Nichols
RP	E.Johnson
RP	D.Jolly
P	R.Crone
RP	H.Robinson
P	H.Paine
P	R.Vargas
P	J.Jay
/P	J.Edelman
P	C.Gorin
/P	D.Koslo

NEW YORK

Pos	Player
M	L.Durocher
1B	G.Harris
2B	W.Terwilliger
SS	A.Dark
3B	H.Thompson
LF	W.Lockman
CF	W.Mays
RF	D.Mueller
C	R.Katt
1C	B.Hofman
O	D.Rhodes
2	D.Williams
S3	B.Gardner
O	M.Irvin
O	S.Gordon
C	W.Westrum
/O	B.Taylor
/2	F.Castleman
/S	J.Amalfitano
/O	G.Coan
/C	M.Grasso
P	J.Antonelli
P	J.Hearn
P	R.Gomez
H	S.Maglie
P	D.Liddle
RP	H.Wilhelm
RP	W.McCall
RP	M.Grissom
P	R.Monzant
P	P.Giel
P	A.Corwin
/P	P.Burnside
/P	G.Spencer

PHILADELPHIA

Pos	Player
M	M.Smith
1B	M.Blaylock
2B	B.Morgan
SS	R.Smalley
3B	W.Jones
LF	D.Ennis
CF	R.Ashburn
RF	J.Greengrass
C	A.Seminick
2S	G.Hamner
C1	S.Lopata
O	G.Gorbous
1	E.Torgeson
1	E.Waitkus
O	P.Lowrey
O	S.Palys
/O	M.Clark
/C	S.Burgess
/S	T.Kazanski
/C	G.Niarhos
/3	F.Baker
H	J.Command
H	M.Micelotta
H	B.Bowman
H	D.Schell
H	J.Westlake
R	J.Easton
H	F.Van Dusen
P	R.Roberts
P	M.Dickson
P	H.Wehmeier
P	C.Simmons
RP	J.Meyer
RP	B.Miller
P	S.Rogovin
P	R.Negray
P	T.Kipper
P	R.Mrozinski
P	B.Kuzava
P	D.Cole
P	L.Lovenguth
/P	S.Ridzik
/P	J.Owens
/P	J.Spring
/P	B.Greenwood

PITTSBURGH

Pos	Player
M	F.Haney
1B	D.Long
2B	J.O'Brien
SS	D.Groat
3B	Gn.Freese
LF	J.Lynch
CF	F.Thomas
RF	R.Clemente
C	J.Shepard
32	D.Cole
O	E.O'Brien
O	T.Atwell
3	Gr.Freese
1	P.Ward
O	R.Mejias
O	T.Saffell
O	F.Montemayor
C	H.Peterson
/3	S.Gordon
/2	C.Roberts
/O	E.Smith
/C	N.Koback
/O	J.Powers
/S	D.Smith
P	V.Law
P	B.Friend
P	M.Surkont
P	R.Kline
P	D.Littlefield
P	R.Face
P	L.Donoso
P	D.Hall
P	B.Purkey
P	N.King
P	B.Wade
P	L.Pepper
P	R.Bowman
/P	A.Grunwald
/P	P.Martin
/P	F.Waters
/P	J.Thies
/P	R.Swanson
/P	B.Bell

ST.LOUIS

Pos	Player
M	E.Stanky
M	H.Walker
1B	S.Musial
2B	R.Schoendienst
SS	A.Grammas
3B	K.Boyer
LF	R.Repulski
CF	B.Virdon
RF	W.Moon
C	B.Sarni
32	S.Hemus
C	N.Burbrink
O	H.Elliott
O	P.Whisenant
S	B.Stephenson
O	J.Frazier
C	D.Rice
/2	D.Blasingame
/O	H.Walker
/C	D.Rand
/1	T.Alston
/S	D.Schofield
P	H.Haddix
P	L.Jackson
P	L.Arroyo
P	T.Poholsky
P	W.Schmidt
RP	B.Lawrence
RP	P.LaPalme
P	F.Wooldridge
P	G.Jones
P	F.Smith
P	M.Wright
P	B.Tiefenauer
P	B.Schultz
/P	B.Flowers
/P	H.Moford
/P	J.Mackinson
/P	L.McDaniel
/P	A.Gettel
/P	T.Jacobs
/P	V.Raschi

TEAM	G	W	L	PCT	GB	R	OR	AB	H	2B	3B	HR	BB	SO	AVG	OBP	SLG	PRO	PRO+	BR	/A	PF	CHI	RC	SB	CS	SBA	SBR
BRO	154	98	55	.641		857	650	5193	1406	230	44	201	674	718	.271	.359	.448	.807	116	142	118	103	100	834	79	56	59	-10
MIL	154	85	69	.552	13.5	743	668	5277	1377	219	55	182	504	735	.261	.329	.427	.756	109	27	63	95	102	733	42	27	61	-4
NY	154	80	74	.519	18.5	702	673	5288	1377	173	34	169	497	581	.260	.328	.402	.730	98	-15	-16	100	102	699	38	22	63	-2
PHI	154	77	77	.500	21.5	675	666	5092	1300	214	50	132	652	673	.255	.343	.395	.738	103	14	27	98	95	692	44	32	58	-6
CIN	154	75	79	.487	23.5	761	684	5270	1424	216	28	181	556	657	.270	.344	.425	.769	103	63	19	106	99	773	51	36	59	-6
CHI	154	72	81	.471	26	626	713	5214	1287	187	55	164	428	806	.247	.307	.398	.705	91	-75	-73	100	103	623	37	35	51	-10
STL	154	68	86	.442	30.5	654	757	5266	1375	228	36	143	458	597	.261	.324	.400	.724	96	-30	-29	100	99	662	64	59	52	-16
PIT	154	60	94	.390	38.5	560	767	5173	1262	210	60	91	471	652	.244	.310	.361	.671	84	-127	-119	99	100	567	22	22	50	-7
TOT	616					5578		41773	10808	1677	362	1263	4240	5419	.259	.330	.407	.737		377					289	57		-60

TEAM	CG	SH	SV	IP	H	H/G	HR	BB	SO	RAT	ERA	ERA+	OAV	OOB	PR	/A	PF	CPI	FA	E	DP	FW	PW	BW	SBW	DIF
BRO	46	11	37	1378	1296	8.5	168	483	773	11.7	3.68	110	.248	.314	54	58	101	100	.978	133	156	.5	5.8	11.7	-.2	3.8
MIL	61	5	12	1383	1339	8.7	138	591	654	12.7	3.85	98	.256	.333	29	-14	93	102	.975	152	155	-.6	-1.4	6.3	.4	3.4
NY	52	6	14	1386²	1347	8.7	155	560	721	12.7	3.77	107	.257	.334	41	39	100	107	.976	142	165	.0	3.9	-1.6	.5	.2
PHI	58	11	21	1356²	1291	8.6	161	477	657	11.9	3.93	101	.251	.318	17	6	98	96	.981	110	117	1.8	.6	2.7	.2	-5.2
CIN	38	12	22	1363	1373	9.1	161	443	576	12.1	3.95	107	.264	.324	13	43	105	102	.977	139	169	.2	4.3	1.9	.2	-8.5
CHI	47	10	23	1378¹	1306	8.5	153	601	686	12.6	4.17	98	.251	.332	-21	-13	101	95	.975	147	147	-.3	-1.3	-7.2	-.2	4.6
STL	42	10	15	1376²	1376	9.0	185	549	730	12.9	4.56	89	.262	.337	-80	-77	101	95	.975	146	152	-.2	-7.6	-2.9	-.8	2.6
PIT	41	5	16	1362	1480	9.8	142	536	622	13.5	4.39	94	.281	.350	-54	-42	102	104	.972	166	175	-1.4	-4.2	-11.8	.0	.3
TOT	385	70	160	10984¹		8.9				12.5	4.04		.259	.330					.976	1135	1236					

Runs
Snider-Bro 126
Mays-NY 123
Post-Cin 116
Kluszewski-Cin 116
Gilliam-Bro 110

Hits
Kluszewski-Cin 192
Aaron-Mil 189
Bell-Cin 188
Post-Cin 186

Doubles
Logan-Mil 37
Aaron-Mil 37
Snider-Bro 34
Post-Cin 33
Ashburn-Phi 32

Triples
Mays-NY 13
Long-Pit 13
Bruton-Mil 12
Clemente-Pit 11

Home Runs
Mays-NY 51
Kluszewski-Cin 47
Banks-Chi 44
Snider-Bro 42
Mathews-Mil 41

Total Bases
Mays-NY 382
Kluszewski-Cin 358
Banks-Chi 355
Post-Cin 345
Snider-Bro 338

Runs Batted In
Snider-Bro 136
Mays-NY 127
Ennis-Phi 120
Banks-Chi 117
Kluszewski-Cin 113

Runs Produced
Snider-Bro 220
Mays-NY 199
Post-Cin 185
Aaron-Mil 184
Kluszewski-Cin 182

Bases On Balls
Mathews-Mil 109
Ashburn-Phi 105
Snider-Bro 104
Thompson-NY 84

Batting Average
Ashburn-Phi 338
Mays-NY 319
Musial-StL 319
Campanella-Bro ...318
Aaron-Mil 314

On Base Percentage
Ashburn-Phi 449
Snider-Bro 421
Mathews-Mil 417
Musial-StL 411
Mays-NY 404

Slugging Average
Mays-NY 659
Snider-Bro 628
Mathews-Mil 601
Banks-Chi 596
Kluszewski-Cin ...585

Production
Mays-NY 1.063
Snider-Bro 1.050
Mathews-Mil ...1.018
Campanella-Bro ...985
Musial-StL 977

Adjusted Production
Mays-NY 176
Mathews-Mil 175
Snider-Bro 169
Musial-StL 156
Campanella-Bro ... 153

Batter Runs
Mays-NY 62.3
Snider-Bro 58.9
Mathews-Mil 50.0
Musial-StL 46.5
Kluszewski-Cin ... 44.9

Adjusted Batter Runs
Mays-NY 62.0
Mathews-Mil 56.3
Snider-Bro 55.2
Musial-StL 46.6
Ashburn-Phi 38.8

Clutch Hitting Index
Long-Pit 117
Jones-Phi 117
Mueller-NY 116
Ennis-Phi 116
Temple-Cin 115

Runs Created
Mays-NY 157
Snider-Bro 145
Kluszewski-Cin ... 136
Musial-StL 131
Mathews-Mil 131

Total Average
Mays-NY 1.180
Snider-Bro 1.147
Mathews-Mil ...1.124
Musial-StL 1.020
Campanella-Bro .1.000

Stolen Bases
Bruton-Mil 25
Mays-NY 24
Boyer-StL 22
Temple-Cin 19
Gilliam-Bro 15

Stolen Base Average
Mays-NY 85.7
Temple-Cin 82.6
Bruton-Mil 69.4
Boyer-StL 56.4

Stolen Base Runs
Mays-NY 4.8
Temple-Cin 3.3
Robinson-Bro 1.8
Blaylock-Phi 1.2

Fielding Runs
Mays-NY 19.8
McMillan-Cin 16.6
O'Connell-Mil ... 15.8
Groat-Pit 15.4
Bruton-Mil 14.7

Total Player Rating
Mays-NY 7.7
Banks-Chi 5.3
Mathews-Mil 4.9
Snider-Bro 4.7
Ashburn-Phi 4.0

Wins
Roberts-Phi 23
Newcombe-Bro 20
Spahn-Mil 17
Nuxhall-Cin 17

Win Percentage
Newcombe-Bro ...800
Roberts-Phi 622
Nuxhall-Cin 586
Spahn-Mil 548

Games
Labine-Bro 60
Wilhelm-NY 59
LaPalme-StL 56
Grissom-NY 55
Freeman-Cin 52

Complete Games
Roberts-Phi 26
Newcombe-Bro 17
Spahn-Mil 16

Shutouts
Nuxhall-Cin 5
Jones-Chi 4
Dickson-Phi 4

Saves
Meyer-Phi 16
Roebuck-Bro 12
Labine-Bro 11
Freeman-Cin 11
Grissom-NY 8

Innings Pitched
Roberts-Phi 305.0
Nuxhall-Cin 257.0
Spahn-Mil 245.2
Jones-Chi 241.2
Antonelli-NY 235.1

Fewest Hits/Game
Jones-Chi 6.52
Buhl-Mil 7.50
Rush-Chi 7.85
Antonelli-NY ... 7.88
Dickson-Phi 7.92

Fewest BB/Game
Newcombe-Bro ... 1.46
Roberts-Phi 1.56
Hacker-Chi 1.82
Friend-Pit 2.34
Spahn-Mil 2.38

Strikeouts
Jones-Chi 198
Roberts-Phi 160
Haddix-StL 150
Newcombe-Bro 143
Antonelli-NY 143

Strikeouts/Game
Jones-Chi 7.37
Haddix-StL 6.49
Podres-Bro 6.44
Conley-Mil 6.09
Newcombe-Bro 5.51

Ratio
Newcombe-Bro ...10.05
Roberts-Phi 10.24
Friend-Pit 10.42
Hacker-Chi 10.44
Rush-Chi 10.73

Earned Run Average
Friend-Pit 2.83
Newcombe-Bro ...3.20
Buhl-Mil 3.21
Spahn-Mil 3.26
Roberts-Phi 3.28

Adjusted ERA
Friend-Pit 145
Newcombe-Bro 127
Nuxhall-Cin 122
Roberts-Phi 121
Antonelli-NY 121

Opponents' Batting Avg.
Jones-Chi 206
Buhl-Mil 227
Rush-Chi 234
Antonelli-NY 234
Dickson-Phi 238

Opponents' On Base Pct.
Roberts-Phi 280
Newcombe-Bro ...280
Hacker-Chi 285
Friend-Pit 294
Rush-Chi 295

Starter Runs
Friend-Pit 26.9
Roberts-Phi 25.8
Newcombe-Bro ... 21.8
Spahn-Mil 21.2
Antonelli-NY 18.6

Adjusted Starter Runs
Friend-Pit 28.6
Roberts-Phi 23.5
Newcombe-Bro ... 22.5
Nuxhall-Cin 21.9
Schmidt-StL 18.5

Clutch Pitching Index
Minner-Chi 122
Spahn-Mil 114
Jackson-StL 113
Law-Pit 109
Friend-Pit 109

Relief Runs
Freeman-Cin 19.1
Miller-Phi 16.2
LaPalme-StL 13.1
Labine-Bro 12.8
Jeffcoat-Chi 12.2

Adjusted Relief Runs
Freeman-Cin 21.1
Miller-Phi 15.5
LaPalme-StL 13.4
Labine-Bro 13.1
Jeffcoat-Chi 12.7

Relief Ranking
Freeman-Cin 28.5
Miller-Phi 19.1
Jeffcoat-Chi 17.6
Labine-Bro 17.0
Bessent-Bro 13.3

Total Pitcher Index
Newcombe-Bro 4.2
Roberts-Phi 3.7
Friend-Pit 3.3
Freeman-Cin 3.1
Antonelli-NY 2.6

Total Baseball Ranking
Mays-NY 7.7
Banks-Chi 5.3
Mathews-Mil 4.9
Snider-Bro 4.7
Newcombe-Bro 4.2

April 12 After a big civic parade, the Athletics open their first season in Kansas City with a 6-2 win over the Tigers before 32,844.

April 14 Elston Howard becomes the first black to wear the Yankee uniform. He singles in his first at bat, against the Red Sox, as the Yanks win 8-4.

May 29 Larry Doby of the Indians hits the first major league home run over the outer wall in Kansas City, an estimated 500-foot clout. The Indians win 4-2.

June 24 Washington rookie infielder Harmon Killebrew hits his first home run in an 18-7 loss to the Detroit Tigers.

August 5 After playing 274 straight games at second base, Nellie Fox is given a day off by White Sox manager Marty Marion. Fox will come back the next day and play in 798 more consecutive games.

August 13 Larry Doby makes his first error in the outfield in 167 games, a new AL record.

September 7 Whitey Ford throws his second consecutive one-hitter, beating the A's 2-1. Jim Finigan hits a two-out single in the seventh for the Nats' only hit.

September 14 Herb Score of the Indians breaks Grover Cleveland Alexander's rookie record of 235 strikeouts. He finishes the season with 245.

September 17 Future Hall of Famer Brooks Robinson goes 2-4 in his first game as the O's top the Senators 3-1.

September 23 The Yanks clinch the pennant by beating the Red Sox 3-2.

September 25 Detroit outfielder Al Kaline becomes the youngest batting champ in history, as he takes the AL crown at age 20.

September 26 The Red Sox beat the Yankees, 8-1, as Ted Williams goes 1-for-2. Williams finishes the season at .356, well ahead of Kaline's .340, but does not have enough at bats to win the batting title. The same thing happened in 1954. Williams was walked 136 times in 1954 and 71 times (an AL-leading 17 were intentional) this year. A rule change will be made to recognize plate appearances, not times at bat.

September 28 The Yanks win the first game of the World Series, as Whitey Ford beats Don Newcombe 6-5. In a controversial play with Frank Kellert at bat, Jackie Robinson steals home in the eighth to bring the Dodgers to within a run of a tie. Films later disclose that Robinson is out by a whisker, but Yogi Berra actually balked on the play, receiving Whitey Ford's pitch before Kellert could swing at it.

BALTIMORE	BOSTON	CHICAGO	CLEVELAND	DETROIT	KANSAS CITY	NEW YORK	WASHINGTON
M P.Richards	M P.Higgins	M M.Marion	M A.Lopez	M B.Harris	M L.Boudreau	M C.Stengel	M C.Dressen
1B G.Triandos	1B N.Zauchin	1B W.Dropo	1B V.Wertz	1B E.Torgeson	1B V.Power	1B B.Skowron	1B M.Vernon
2B F.Marsh	2B B.Goodman	2B N.Fox	2B B.Avila	2B F.Hatfield	2B J.Finigan	2B G.McDougald	2B P.Runnels
SS W.Miranda	SS B.Klaus	SS C.Carrasquel	SS G.Strickland	SS H.Kuenn	SS J.DeMaestri	SS B.Hunter	SS J.Valdivielso
3B W.Causey	3B G.Hatton	3B G.Kell	3B A.Rosen	3B R.Boone	3B H.Lopez	3B A.Carey	3B E.Yost
LF D.Philley	LF T.Williams	LF M.Minoso	LF R.Kiner	LF J.Delsing	LF G.Zernial	LF I.Noren	LF R.Sievers
CF C.Diering	CF J.Piersall	CF J.Busby	CF L.Doby	CF B.Tuttle	CF H.Simpson	CF M.Mantle	CF T.Umphlett
RF C.Abrams	RF J.Jensen	RF J.Rivera	RF A.Smith	RF A.Kaline	RF E.Slaughter	RF H.Bauer	RF C.Paula
C H.Smith	C S.White	C S.Lollar	C J.Hegan	C F.House	C J.Astroth	C Y.Berra	C E.Fitz Gerald
O D.Pope	O B.Nieman	O B.Nieman	O G.Woodling	O B.Phillips	O B.Renna	O J.Collins	O E.Oravetz
O3 J.Dyck	3O F.Throneberry	3O B.Kennedy	C H.Naragon	2 H.Malmberg	O B.Wilson	1O E.Howard	C C.Courtney
32 B.Cox	3 T.Lepcio	1 J.Groth	1 F.Fain	C F.Fain	1 E.Valo	O E.Robinson	1 J.Busby
2 B.Young	S2 E.Joost	C R.Jackson	C H.Foiles	2 J.Phillips	2 Bi.Shantz	S P.Rizzuto	O J.Groth
O H.Evers	1 H.Agganis	C L.Moss	S3 S.Dente	S3 C.Maxwell	S2 Ct.Boyer	S2 J.Coleman	2 B.Kline
1 B.Hale	C P.Daley	S J.Brideweser	O D.Philley	3 R.Bertoia	O J.Littrell	O B.Cerv	3 J.Delis
O G.Woodling	O K.Olson	3 V.Stephens	3 D.Pope	/1 J.Porter	S J.Schypinski	2 B.Martin	2S J.Snyder
O G.Coan	S O.Friend	O W.Marshall	/1 J.Altobelli	/O C.King	1 D.Kryhoski	/2 B.Richardson	3 H.Killebrew
3 J.Pyburn	/O S.Mele	C C.Courtney	/O H.Evers	/O J.Small	/O T.Saffell	C C.Silvera	C B.Edwards
1 E.Waitkus	/1 D.Gernert	/3 B.Adams	/O D.Mitchell	/C W.Streuli	/2 S.Jacobs	H E.Slaughter	S T.Roig
O B.Kennedy	/S F.Malzone	/S B.Peterson	/C H.Majeski	/2 W.Belardi	/O B.Stewart	/S T.Carroll	C J.Schoonmaker
2 D.Leppert	/O B.Consolo	/O G.Coan	2 B.Young	/S R.Samford	/O D.Plarski	/C L.Berberet	C S.Korcheck
C L.Moss	/C H.Sullivan	/C R.Northey	/3 R.Regalado	H S.Souchock	/1 D.Bollweg	/O D.Tettelbach	/O J.Lemon
/3 H.Majeski	/S M.Bolling	O E.McGhee	/O W.Westlake	P F.Lary	/C J.Robertson	/1 J.Blanchard	H J.Levan
/O T.Nelson	/C J.Pagliaroni	/C E.Battey	S B.Harrell	/3 N.Garver	/3 H.Bevan	/1 F.Leja	/1 J.Becquer
C T.Gastall	/1	/1 P.Cavarretta	/O S.Locklin	P B.Hoeft	/C E.MacKenzie	/1 M.Throneberry	H T.Wright
/O W.Westlake	P F.Sullivan	/O S.Locklin	/O R.Colavito	P S.Gromek	P A.Ditmar	P W.Ford	/C B.Oldis
/3 B.Robinson	P W.Nixon	/O S.Esposito	/2 S.Pawloski	RP B.Birrer	P A.Kellner	P B.Turley	P D.Stone
/O A.Dagres	P T.Brewer	/3 S.Jok	/S K.Kuhn	RP A.Aber	P Bo.Shantz	P T.Byrne	P B.Porterfield
/3 K.Segrist	P G.Susce	/O E.White	H H.Simpson	RP P.Foytack	P A.Ceccarelli	P J.Kucks	P J.Schmitz
/3 V.Stephens	P I.Delock	H L.Merriman	RP E.Wynn	P D.Maas	RP A.Portocarrero	P D.Larsen	P M.McDermott
H C.Maxwell	RP L.Kiely	R L.Powell	RP H.Score	P J.Bunning	RP T.Gorman	RP J.Konstanty	P C.Stobbs
/O R.Marquis	RP T.Hurd	P B.Pierce	P B.Lemon	P L.Cristante	RP B.Harrington	RP T.Morgan	RP P.Ramos
P J.Wilson	RP E.Kinder	P D.Donovan	P M.Garcia	P G.Zuverink	P V.Raschi	RP T.Sturdivant	RP T.Abernathy
P E.Palica	P B.Henry	P J.Harshman	P A.Houtteman	P J.Coleman	P Cd.Boyer	P B.Grim	RP S.Shea
P R.Moore	P M.Parnell	P V.Trucks	RP R.Narleski	/P B.Miller	P R.Herbert	P E.Lopat	P C.Pascual
P B.Wight	/P F.Baumann	P C.Johnson	RP D.Mossi	/P D.Marlowe	P J.Sain	P B.Wiesler	P B.Chakales
RP A.Schallock	P D.Brodowski	RP S.Consuegra	P B.Feller	P B.Black	/P J.Gray	P R.Coleman	/P W.Clarke
RP D.Johnson	RP R.Kemmerer	RP D.Howell	/P J.Santiago	/P V.Fletcher	/P L.Sleater	/P J.Sain	/P B.Stewart
RP H.Dorish	P H.Brown	RP M.Martin	/P S.Maglie	/P B.Flowers	/P M.Kume	/P T.Gray	/P B.Currie
P G.Zuverink	/P H.Freeman	P H.Byrd	P B.Wight	/P B.Froats	P M.Fricano	/P A.Schallock	/P V.Gonzales
S S.Rogovin	/P B.Smith	P M.Fornieles	/P H.Aguirre	/P B.Schultz	P W.Craddock	/P G.Staley	/P D.Hyde
P H.Byrd	/P J.Trimble	P B.Keegan	/P B.Daley		/P G.Keriazakos		
P H.Brown		P H.Dorish	/P T.Gray		/P M.Burtschy		
P J.McDonald		/P B.Chakales	/P H.Newhouser		/P B.Trice		
P E.Lopat		/P A.Papai			/P C.Bishop		
P L.Kretlow		/P T.Gray			/P E.Blackwell		
/P D.Pillette					/P B.Spicer		
/P T.Gray					/P G.Cox		
P J.Coleman					/P S.Dixon		
/P B.Kuzava					/P O.Van Brabant		
/P D.Ferrarese					/P L.Wheat		
/P B.Alexander							
/P B.Miller							
/P C.Locke							
/P B.Harrison							

TEAM	G	W	L	PCT	GB	R	OR	AB	H	2B	3B	HR	BB	SO	AVG	OBP	SLG	PRO	PRO+	BR	/A	PF	CHI	RC	SB	CS	SBA	SBR
NY	154	96	58	.623		762	569	5161	1342	179	55	175	609	658	.260	.343	.418	.761	113	71	83	98	101	759	55	25	69	2
CLE	154	93	61	.604	3	698	601	5146	1325	195	31	148	723	715	.257	.353	.394	.747	104	60	32	104	93	741	28	24	54	-6
CHI	155	91	63	.591	5	725	557	5220	1401	204	36	116	567	595	.268	.347	.388	.735	101	31	11	103	101	712	69	45	61	-6
BOS	154	84	70	.545	12	755	652	5273	1392	241	39	137	707	733	.264	.354	.402	.756	101	77	7	109	97	773	43	17	72	3
DET	154	79	75	.513	17	775	658	5283	1407	211	38	130	641	583	.266	.348	.394	.742	108	46	63	98	104	736	41	22	65	-1
KC	155	63	91	.409	33	638	911	5335	1395	189	46	121	463	725	.261	.323	.382	.705	95	-40	-47	101	100	637	22	36	38	-15
BAL	156	57	97	.370	39	540	754	5257	1263	177	39	54	560	742	.240	.316	.320	.636	83	-159	-123	93	104	532	34	46	43	-17
WAS	154	53	101	.344	43	598	789	5142	1277	178	54	80	538	654	.248	.324	.351	.675	93	-86	-55	95	103	586	25	32	44	-12
TOT	618					5491		41817	10802	1574	338	961	4808	5405	.258	.339	.381	.720							317	247	56	-53

TEAM	CG	SH	SV	IP	H	H/G	HR	BB	SO	RAT	ERA	ERA+	OAV	OOB	PR	/A	PF	CPI	FA	E	DP	FW	PW	BW	SBW	DIF
NY	52	19	33	1372¹	1163	7.6	108	688	731	12.3	3.23	116	.232	.328	111	78	95	107	.978	128	180	.5	7.8	8.3	.9	1.5
CLE	45	15	36	1386¹	1285	8.3	111	558	877	12.1	3.39	118	.245	.320	88	92	101	101	.981	108	152	1.7	9.2	3.2	.0	1.9
CHI	55	20	23	1378	1301	8.5	111	497	720	11.9	3.37	117	.251	.319	90	89	100	103	.981	111	147	1.5	8.9	1.1	.0	2.4
BOS	44	9	34	1384¹	1333	8.7	128	582	674	12.7	3.72	115	.253	.331	37	88	108	102	.977	136	140	.0	8.8	.7	1.0	-3.5
DET	66	16	12	1380¹	1381	9.0	126	517	629	12.6	3.79	101	.261	.331	26	7	97	102	.976	139	159	-.2	.7	6.3	.6	-5.4
KC	29	9	22	1382	1486	9.7	175	707	572	14.6	5.35	78	.278	.367	-214	-181	105	94	.976	146	174	-.5	-18.1	-4.7	-.8	10.2
BAL	35	10	20	1388²	1403	9.1	103	625	595	13.4	4.21	91	.266	.348	-39	-61	96	99	.972	167	159	-1.7	-6.1	-12.3	-1.0	1.2
WAS	37	10	16	1354²	1450	9.6	99	634	607	14.2	4.62	83	.279	.362	-100	-119	97	98	.974	154	170	-1.0	-11.9	-5.5	-.5	-5.0
TOT	363	108	196	11026²		8.8				13.0	3.96		.258	.339					.977	1089	1281					

Runs		Hits		Doubles		Triples		Home Runs		Total Bases	
Smith-Cle	123	Kaline-Det	200	Kuenn-Det	38	Mantle-NY	11	Mantle-NY	37	Kaline-Det	321
Mantle-NY	121	Fox-Chi	198	Power-KC	34	Carey-NY	11	Zernial-KC	30	Mantle-NY	316
Kaline-Det	121	Power-KC	190	Goodman-Bos	31	Power-KC	10	Williams-Bos	28	Power-KC	301
Tuttle-Det	102	Kuenn-Det	190	White-Bos	30					Smith-Cle	287
Kuenn-Det	101	Smith-Cle	186	Finigan-KC	30					Jensen-Bos	275

Runs Batted In		Runs Produced		Bases On Balls		Batting Average		On Base Percentage		Slugging Average	
Jensen-Bos	116	Kaline-Det	196	Mantle-NY	113	Kaline-Det	.340	Mantle-NY	.433	Mantle-NY	.611
Boone-Det	116	Jensen-Bos	185	Goodman-Bos	99	Power-KC	.319	Kaline-Det	.425	Kaline-Det	.546
Berra-NY	108	Mantle-NY	183	Yost-Was	95	Kell-Chi	.312	Smith-Cle	.411	Zernial-KC	.508
Sievers-Was	106	Smith-Cle	178	Fain-Det-Cle	94	Fox-Chi	.311	Yost-Was	.410	Doby-Cle	.505
Kaline-Det	102	Tuttle-Det	166	Smith-Cle	93	Kuenn-Det	.306	Goodman-Bos	.397	Power-KC	.505

Production		Adjusted Production		Batter Runs		Adjusted Batter Runs		Clutch Hitting Index		Runs Created	
Mantle-NY	1.044	Mantle-NY	181	Williams-Bos	59.3	Mantle-NY	61.2	Kell-Chi	137	Mantle-NY	148
Kaline-Det	.971	Kaline-Det	163	Mantle-NY	59.0	Kaline-Det	53.2	Boone-Det	137	Kaline-Det	135
Smith-Cle	.884	Sievers-Was	136	Kaline-Det	50.2	Williams-Bos	50.1	Zauchin-Bos	114	Smith-Cle	128
Doby-Cle	.877	Vernon-Was	133	Smith-Cle	34.7	Smith-Cle	30.4	Jensen-Bos	111	Williams-Bos	118
Power-KC	.862	Smith-Cle	132	Valo-KC	24.8	Vernon-Was	25.2	Sievers-Was	111	Power-KC	103

Total Average		Stolen Bases		Stolen Base Average		Stolen Base Runs		Fielding Runs		Total Player Rating	
Mantle-NY	1.206	Rivera-Chi	25	Minoso-Chi	70.4	Torgeson-Det	2.7	Fox-Chi	26.9	Mantle-NY	6.3
Kaline-Det	.993	Minoso-Chi	19	Jensen-Bos	69.6	Busby-Was-Chi	1.8	McDougald-NY	19.4	Kaline-Det	5.0
Smith-Cle	.928	Jensen-Bos	16	Rivera-Chi	61.0	Mantle-NY	1.8	Miranda-Bal	19.0	Williams-Bos	4.4
Doby-Cle	.884	Busby-Was-Chi	12			Klaus-Bos	1.8	Lopez-KC	15.1	Fox-Chi	3.9
Jensen-Bos	.849	Smith-Cle	11					Tuttle-Det	14.9	McDougald-NY	3.5

Wins		Win Percentage		Games		Complete Games		Shutouts		Saves	
F.Sullivan-Bos	18	Byrne-NY	.762	Narleski-Cle	60	Ford-NY	18	Hoeft-Det	7	Narleski-Cle	19
Lemon-Cle	18	Ford-NY	.720	Mossi-Cle	57	Hoeft-Det	17	Wynn-Cle	6	Kinder-Bos	18
Ford-NY	18	Hoeft-Det	.696	Gorman-KC	57			Turley-NY	6	Gorman-KC	18
Wynn-Cle	17	Lemon-Cle	.643	Dorish-Chi-Bal	48			Pierce-Chi	6	Konstanty-NY	11
Turley-NY	17	Donovan-Chi	.625	Moore-Bal	46					Morgan-NY	10

Innings Pitched		Fewest Hits/Game		Fewest BB/Game		Strikeouts		Strikeouts/Game		Ratio	
F.Sullivan-Bos	260.0	Turley-NY	6.13	Gromek-Det	1.84	Score-Cle	245	Score-Cle	9.70	Pierce-Chi	10.02
Ford-NY	253.2	Score-Cle	6.26	Donovan-Chi	2.31	Turley-NY	210	Turley-NY	7.66	Ford-NY	10.71
Turley-NY	246.2	Ford-NY	6.67	Garcia-Cle	2.39	Pierce-Chi	157	Pierce-Chi	6.87	Hoeft-Det	10.96
Wilson-Bal	235.1	Pierce-Chi	7.09	Garver-Det	2.61	Ford-NY	137	Harshman-Chi	5.82	Wilson-Bal	11.13
Lary-Det	235.0	Harshman-Chi	7.23	Porterfield-Was	2.73	Hoeft-Det	133	Hoeft-Det	5.44	Wynn-Cle	11.35

Earned Run Average		Adjusted ERA		Opponents' Batting Avg.		Opponents' On Base Pct.		Starter Runs		Adjusted Starter Runs	
Pierce-Chi	1.97	Pierce-Chi	201	Turley-NY	.193	Pierce-Chi	.277	Pierce-Chi	45.5	Pierce-Chi	45.2
Ford-NY	2.63	F.Sullivan-Bos	148	Score-Cle	.194	Ford-NY	.297	Ford-NY	37.6	F.Sullivan-Bos	39.9
Wynn-Cle	2.82	Ford-NY	143	Ford-NY	.208	Hoeft-Det	.298	F.Sullivan-Bos	30.4	Ford-NY	31.5
Score-Cle	2.85	Wynn-Cle	142	Pierce-Chi	.213	Wilson-Bal	.300	Wynn-Cle	29.2	Wynn-Cle	29.9
F.Sullivan-Bos	2.91	Score-Cle	140	Harshman-Chi	.224	Wynn-Cle	.307	Score-Cle	28.1	Score-Cle	28.8

Clutch Pitching Index		Relief Runs		Adjusted Relief Runs		Relief Ranking		Total Pitcher Index		Total Baseball Ranking	
Pierce-Chi	119	Consuegra-Chi	18.6	Consuegra-Chi	18.4	Kinder-Bos	21.1	Pierce-Chi	5.3	Mantle-NY	6.3
Byrne-NY	119	Mossi-Cle	13.9	Kiely-Bos	14.9	Hurd-Bos	19.5	F.Sullivan-Bos	4.2	Pierce-Chi	5.3
F.Sullivan-Bos	116	Konstanty-NY	13.4	Mossi-Cle	14.2	Consuegra-Chi	16.7	Wynn-Cle	3.3	Kaline-Det	5.0
Lary-Det	115	Kiely-Bos	11.6	Konstanty-NY	11.6	Konstanty-NY	16.7	Ford-NY	3.1	Williams-Bos	4.4
Schmitz-Was	115	Dorish-Chi-Bal	10.4	Hurd-Bos	11.4	Mossi-Cle	14.5	Lary-Det	2.5	F.Sullivan-Bos	4.2

January 19 The City of Hoboken dedicates a plaque honoring the achievements of Alexander Cartwright in organizing early baseball at Elysian Field in the New Jersey city.

January 27 The New York Giants football team of the NFL switches its home games to Yankee Stadium, leading to speculation that the baseball team will soon vacate the Polo Grounds as well.

March 3 In an effort to keep the Giants in New York, Manhattan Borough President Hulan Jack makes plans for a new 110,000-seat stadium over the New York Central railroad tracks, on a 470,000-foot site stretching from 60th to 72nd streets on Manhattan's West Side. The $75 million estimated cost eventually dooms the project and will be a major factor in Horace Stoneham's decision to move to San Francisco.

April 28 Redlegs rookie left fielder Frank Robinson hits the first home run of his 586 lifetime blasts, off Cubs pitcher Paul Minner in Crosley Field. The Cubs lose the opener, 9–1. Cincinnati outfielder Wally Post hits four home runs in a doubleheader sweep for the Redlegs.

May 7 The future NL president, Bill White of the NY Giants, homers in his first time up in the major leagues. The Giants lose to St. Louis, 6–3.

May 19 Pirate slugger Dale Long hits a ninth-inning home run against the Cubs for the first of a string of eight home runs in eight games.

July 6 Ford Frick inaugurates the Cy Young Award, to honor the outstanding pitcher each year. The BBWAA will do the voting. Only one pitcher will be honored each year until 1967, when a pitcher in each league will be selected.

July 10 In the All-Star Game, Ken Boyer of the Cardinals makes three sparkling plays at third base and gets three hits as the NL defeats the AL, 7–3. Willie Mays, Mickey Mantle, Ted Williams, and Stan Musial all homer. Mays's pinch-hit two-run home run off Whitey Ford is his seventh straight hit against the Yankee lefty.

July 23 Joe Cronin and Hank Greenberg are officially inducted into the Hall of Fame at Cooperstown, NY.

July 25 Brooklyn's right fielder Carl Furillo is the first Dodger player to homer in Jersey City, as the Dodgers lose to the Reds 2-1 at Roosevelt Field.

September 11 Frank Robinson ties the NL record for home runs by a rookie with 38 in an 11-5 Redlegs win over New York.

September 30 Sandy Amoros and Duke Snider each hit two home runs against the Pirates, as the Dodgers win 8-6 to edge Milwaukee for the pennant on the last day of the season.

October 3 Sal Maglie and the Dodgers defeat the Yankees 6-3 in the first game of the World Series.

October 9 The Dodgers bounce back in Game 6. Clem Labine comes out of the bullpen to pitch a 1-0 victory in 10 innings. Enos Slaughter misjudges Jackie Robinson's line drive, and Jim Gilliam scores from second base.

November 21 Don Newcombe, who won the 1949 Rookie of the Year Award, wins the NL MVP and the first-ever Cy Young Award.

December 1 Cincinnati slugger Frank Robinson is unanimously voted the NL Rookie of the Year. White Sox shortstop Luis Aparicio is voted AL Rookie of the Year, beating out Oriole Tito Francona and Indian Rocky Colavito.

December 13 The Dodgers trade Jackie Robinson to the Giants for pitcher Dick Littlefield and $35,000. Robinson retires rather than accept the trade.

BROOKLYN		CHICAGO		CINCINNATI		MILWAUKEE		NEW YORK		PHILADELPHIA		PITTSBURGH		ST.LOUIS	
M	W.Alston	M	S.Hack	M	B.Tebbetts	M	C.Grimm	M	B.Rigney	M	M.Smith	M	B.Bragan	M	F.Hutchinson
1B	G.Hodges	1B	D.Fondy	1B	T.Kluszewski	M	F.Haney	1B	B.White	1B	M.Blaylock	1B	D.Long	1B	S.Musial
2B	J.Gilliam	2B	G.Baker	2B	J.Temple	1B	J.Adcock	2B	R.Schoendienst	2B	T.Kazanski	2B	B.Mazeroski	2B	D.Blasingame
SS	P.Reese	SS	E.Banks	SS	R.McMillan	2B	D.O'Connell	SS	D.Spencer	SS	G.Hamner	SS	D.Groat	SS	A.Dark
3B	R.Jackson	3B	D.Hoak	3B	R.Jablonski	SS	J.Logan	3B	F.Castleman	3B	W.Jones	3B	F.Thomas	3B	K.Boyer
LF	S.Amoros	LF	M.Irvin	LF	F.Robinson	3B	E.Mathews	LF	J.Brandt	LF	D.Ennis	LF	L.Walls	LF	R.Repulski
CF	D.Snider	CF	P.Whisenant	CF	G.Bell	LF	B.Thomson	CF	W.Mays	CF	R.Ashburn	CF	B.Virdon	CF	D.Del Greco
RF	C.Furillo	RF	W.Moryn	RF	W.Post	CF	B.Bruton	RF	D.Mueller	RF	E.Valo	RF	R.Clemente	RF	W.Moon
C	R.Campanella	C	H.Landrith	C	E.Bailey	RF	H.Aaron	C	B.Sarni	C	S.Lopata	C	J.Shepard	C	H.Smith
						C	D.Crandall								
32	J.Robinson	O	J.King	C	S.Burgess	O	D.Rhodes	O	J.Greengrass	O1	B.Skinner	O	W.Lockman		
C	R.Walker	3O	E.Miksis	1	G.Crowe	1	F.Torre	S	A.Dark	2	S.Hemus	C	H.Foiles	C	R.Katt
2	C.Neal	O	S.Drake	3S	A.Grammas	C	D.Rice	3O	H.Thompson	S	R.Smalley	32	G.Freese	2	R.Schoendienst
1	R.Nelson	C	H.Chiti	O	B.Thurman	O	W.Covington	O	W.Lockman	O	A.Seminick	2	J.O'Brien	C	H.Sauer
S	C.Fernandez	1	F.Kellert	S	S.Palys	2	J.Dittmer	S	E.Bressoud	F	F.Baumholtz	32	D.Cole	C	B.Sarni
O	G.Cimoli	S	J.Kindall	3	R.Bridges	O	A.Pafko	O	W.Westrum	O	G.Gorbous	C	D.Kravitz	23	B.Morgan
/O	D.Mitchell	/C	C.McCullough	/O	J.Frazier	/O	C.Tanner	C	R.Katt	/3	B.Morgan	2	C.Roberts	2	G.Hatton
/S	D.Zimmer	/3	E.Winceniak	/1	J.Dyck	S	F.Mantilla	/O	G.Wilson	/1	E.Bouchee	S	E.O'Brien	O	B.Virdon
/C	D.Howell	/O	G.Wade	/O	A.Schult	/C	T.Atwell	/C	B.Hofman	/C	J.Lonnett	2	S.Jacobs	C	W.Cooper
H	D.Williams	/C	J.Fanning	/C	B.Edwards	O	E.Hersh	O	B.Lennon	/O	B.Bowman	/3	P.Ward	1	R.Nelson
/O	D.Demeter	H	O.Friend	/O	C.Harmon	/S	J.Pendleton	1	G.Harris	H	W.Westlake	/O	J.Powers	O	C.Peete
H	B.Aspromonte	H	R.Myers	/O	B.Balcena	/C	B.Roselli	/O	M.Mangan		M.Burk	/O	B.DelGreco	J	J.Brandt
		/C	E.Tappe	H	M.Batts			/2	W.Terwilliger			/O	J.Lynch	/S	D.Schofield
P	D.Newcombe			H	C.Flood	P	W.Spahn	/3	O.Virgil	P	R.Roberts	/C	T.Atwell	/O	J.Frazier
P	R.Craig	P	B.Rush	P	J.Oldham	/O	L.Burdette	/O	B.Taylor	P	H.Haddix	/C	B.Hall	O	C.Harmon
P	S.Maglie	P	S.Jones	R	A.Silvera	P	B.Buhl	H	G.Coan	P	C.Simmons			/S	A.Grammas
P	C.Erskine	P	W.Hacker			P	R.Crone			P	S.Rogovin	P	B.Friend	H	S.Hemus
P	D.Drysdale	P	D.Kaiser	P	B.Lawrence	P	G.Conley	P	J.Antonelli	P	S.Miller	P	R.Kline	/1	J.Cunningham
RP	C.Labine	P	J.Brosnan	P	J.Klippstein	RP	B.Trowbridge	P	R.Gomez	RP	B.Miller	P	V.Law	/1	T.Alston
RP	E.Roebuck	RP	J.Davis	P	J.Nuxhall	RP	E.Johnson	RP	A.Worthington	P	J.Meyer	P	R.Munger		
RP	D.Bessent	RP	T.Lown	P	A.Fowler			P	J.Hearn	RP	R.Negray	RP	R.Face	P	V.Mizell
		RP	V.Valentinetti	P	H.Jeffcoat	P	T.Phillips	P	D.Littlefield			RP	N.King	P	T.Poholsky
P	D.Newcombe			RP	H.Freeman	P	J.Dolly	RP	S.Ridzik	P	B.Flowers	RP	F.Waters	P	M.Dickson
P	K.Lehman			RP	T.Acker	P	L.Sleater	RP	H.Wilhelm	P	J.Owens			P	H.Wehmeier
/P	C.Templeton	/P	M.Drabowsky	RP	J.Black	P	R.Murff	RP	M.Grissom	/P	M.Dickson	P	D.Hall	P	W.Schmidt
/P	J.Hughes	P	P.Minner							/P	D.Pillette	P	C.Naranjo	RP	L.McDaniel
/P	R.Branca	P	J.Hughes	P	D.Gross	/P	H.Robinson	P	J.Margoneri	/P	H.Wehmeier	P	L.Pepper	RP	L.Jackson
/P	B.Darnell	/P	D.Hillman	/P	L.Jansen	/P	P.Paine	P	W.McCall	P	J.Sanford	P	L.Arroyo	RP	J.Collum
/P	B.Loes	/P	J.Briggs	P	P.LaPalme			P	D.Liddle	P	A.LiPetri	P	H.Pollet		
		/P	G.Piktuzis	/P	P.Scantlebury			/P	M.Surkont	/P	T.Farrell	/P	D.Littlefield	P	B.Blaylock
		/P	B.Tremel	/P	F.Smith			/P	R.Monzant	/P	B.Ross	/P	J.McMahan	P	J.Konstanty
				/P	B.Kennedy			/P	M.McCormick			P	R.Swanson	P	E.Kinder
				/P	R.Meyer			/P	J.Constable			/P	B.Garber	/P	D.Liddle
								/P	R.Wright			/P	B.Purkey	/P	H.Haddix
												/P	L.Donoso	/P	B.Flowers
												/P	M.Surkont	P	G.Jones
														/P	D.Littlefield
														/P	S.Miller
														/P	M.Surkont
														/P	P.LaPalme

TEAM	G	W	L	PCT	GB	R	OR	AB	H	2B	3B	HR	BB	SO	AVG	OBP	SLG	PRO	PRO+	BR	/A	PF	CHI	RC	SB	CS	SBA	SBR
BRO	154	93	61	.604		720	601	5098	1315	212	36	179	**649**	738	.258	**.344**	.419	.763	103	81	24	108	97	728	65	37	64	-3
MIL	155	92	62	.597	1	709	**569**	5207	1350	212	54	177	486	714	.259	.325	.423	.748	**113**	38	**80**	94	101	714	29	20	59	-3
CIN	155	91	63	.591	2	775	658	5291	1406	201	32	**221**	528	760	.266	.338	**.441**	**.779**	107	**103**	54	106	100	**789**	45	22	67	0
STL	156	76	78	.494	17	678	698	5378	**1443**	**234**	49	124	503	622	**.268**	.335	.399	.734	103	-12	0	98	103	658	45	23	66	-9
PHI	154	71	83	.461	22	668	738	5204	1313	207	49	121	585	673	.252	.331	.381	.712	99	-85	-81	99	97	586	**67**	34	66	0
NY	154	67	87	.435	26	540	650	5190	1268	192	45	145	402	659	.244	.301	.382	.683	89	-70	-57	98	102	594	24	33	42	-13
PIT	157	66	88	.429	27	588	653	5221	1340	199	**57**	110	383	752	.257	.310	.380	.690	93	-79	-69	98	103	606	55	38	59	-6
CHI	157	60	94	.390	33	597	708	5260	1281	202	50	142	446	776	.244	.304	.382	.686	91	-79	-69	98	103	606	55	38	59	-6
TOT	621					5275		41849	10716	1659	372	1219	3982	5694	.256	.324	.401	.725							371	242	61	-34

TEAM	CG	SH	SV	IP	H	H/G	HR	BB	SO	RAT	ERA	ERA+	OAV	OOB	PR	/A	PF	CPI	FA	E	DP	FW	PW	BW	SBW	DIF
BRO	46	**12**	30	1368.2	1251	8.2	171	441	**772**	11.3	3.57	111	**.244**	.307	31	60	105	97	**.981**	111	149	1.4	6.1	2.5	.1	5.9
MIL	**64**	12	27	1393.1	1295	8.4	133	467	639	11.5	**3.11**	111	.247	.311	102	54	92	107	.979	130	159	.3	5.5	**8.2**	.1	.8
CIN	47	4	29	1389	1406	9.1	141	458	653	12.3	3.85	103	.265	.327	-12	20	106	101	**.981**	113	147	1.3	2.0	5.5	.4	4.6
STL	41	12	30	1388.2	1339	8.7	155	546	709	12.3	3.97	95	.257	.329	-30	-28	100	98	.978	134	172	.1	-2.9	2.6	-.5	-.3
PHI	57	4	15	1377.1	1407	9.2	172	**437**	750	12.2	4.20	89	.266	.325	-66	-73	99	95	.975	144	140	-.6	-7.5	.0	.4	1.6
NY	31	9	28	1378	1287	8.4	144	551	765	12.2	3.78	100	.250	.326	-1	1	100	98	.976	144	143	-.6	.1	-8.3	.4	-1.7
PIT	37	8	24	1376.1	1406	9.2	142	469	662	12.4	3.74	101	.267	.329	5	5	100	105	.973	162	140	-1.5	.5	-5.8	-.9	-3.3
CHI	37	6	17	1392	1325	8.6	161	613	744	12.7	3.96	95	.252	.334	-29	-29	100	100	.976	144	141	-.4	-3.0	-7.1	-.2	-6.4
TOT	360	67	200	11063.1		8.7				12.1	3.77		.256	.324					.977	1082	1191					

Runs
Robinson-Cin 122
Snider-Bro 112
Aaron-Mil 106
Mathews-Mil 103
Gilliam-Bro 102

Hits
Aaron-Mil 200
Ashburn-Phi 190
Virdon-StL-Pit 185
Musial-StL 184
Boyer-StL 182

Doubles
Aaron-Mil 34
Snider-Bro 33
Musial-StL 33
Lopata-Phi 33
Bell-Cin 31

Triples
Bruton-Mil 15
Aaron-Mil 14
Walls-Pit 11
Moon-StL 11
Virdon-StL-Pit 10

Home Runs
Snider-Bro 43
Robinson-Cin 38
Adcock-Mil 38
Mathews-Mil 37

Total Bases
Aaron-Mil 340
Snider-Bro 324
Mays-NY 322
Robinson-Cin 319
Musial-StL 310

Runs Batted In
Musial-StL 109
Adcock-Mil 103
Kluszewski-Cin 102
Snider-Bro 101
Boyer-StL 98

Runs Produced
Aaron-Mil 172
Snider-Bro 170
Musial-StL 169
Robinson-Cin 167
Boyer-StL 163

Bases On Balls
Snider-Bro 99
Gilliam-Bro 95
Jones-Phi 92
Mathews-Mil 91
Moon-StL 80

Batting Average
Aaron-Mil 328
Virdon-StL-Pit 319
Clemente-Pit 311
Musial-StL 310
Boyer-StL 306

On Base Percentage
Snider-Bro 402
Gilliam-Bro 400
Musial-StL 390
Moon-StL 390
Jones-Phi 387

Slugging Average
Snider-Bro 598
Adcock-Mil 597
Aaron-Mil 558
Robinson-Cin 558
Mays-NY 557

Production
Snider-Bro 1.000
Robinson-Cin 939
Adcock-Mil 936
Mays-NY 928
Aaron-Mil 927

Adjusted Production
Adcock-Mil 154
Aaron-Mil 154
Snider-Bro 152
Mays-NY 146
Mathews-Mil 146

Batter Runs
Snider-Bro 50.5
Robinson-Cin 39.1
Aaron-Mil 36.3
Musial-StL 36.3
Mays-NY 35.9

Adjusted Batter Runs
Aaron-Mil 43.1
Snider-Bro 41.1
Mays-NY 36.7
Musial-StL 36.3
Mathews-Mil 36.2

Clutch Hitting Index
McMillan-Cin 145
Thomson-Mil 123
Ennis-Phi 115
Jones-Phi 109
Long-Pit 109

Runs Created
Snider-Bro 128
Robinson-Cin 121
Musial-StL 119
Mays-NY 118
Aaron-Mil 115

Total Average
Snider-Bro 1.052
Mays-NY 972
Robinson-Cin 960
Mathews-Mil 946
Adcock-Mil 916

Stolen Bases
Mays-NY 40
Gilliam-Bro 21
White-NY 15
Temple-Cin 14
Reese-Bro 13

Stolen Base Average
Mays-NY 80.0
Gilliam-Bro 70.0

Stolen Base Runs
Mays-NY 6.0
Ashburn-Phi 2.4
Temple-Cin 1.8
Post-Cin 1.8
Mathews-Mil 1.8

Fielding Runs
McMillan-Cin 29.9
Ashburn-Phi 25.3
Blasingame-StL 21.9
Gilliam-Bro 17.7
Baker-Chi 17.2

Total Player Rating
Mays-NY 4.7
Aaron-Mil 4.4
McMillan-Cin 3.7
Gilliam-Bro 3.4
Musial-StL 3.3

Wins
Newcombe-Bro 27
Spahn-Mil 20
Antonelli-NY 20

Win Percentage
Newcombe-Bro 794
Buhl-Mil 692
Lawrence-Cin 655
Burdette-Mil 655
Spahn-Mil 645

Games
Face-Pit 68
Wilhelm-NY 64
Freeman-Cin 64
Labine-Bro 62
Lown-Chi 61

Complete Games
Roberts-Phi 22
Spahn-Mil 20
Friend-Pit 19
Newcombe-Bro 18
Burdette-Mil 16

Shutouts
Burdette-Mil 6
Newcombe-Bro 5
Antonelli-NY 5
Friend-Pit 4

Saves
Labine-Bro 19
Freeman-Cin 18
Lown-Chi 13
Jackson-StL 9
Bessent-Bro 9

Innings Pitched
Friend-Pit 314.1
Roberts-Phi 297.1
Spahn-Mil 281.1
Newcombe-Bro . . . 268.0
Kline-Pit 264.0

Fewest Hits/Game
Maglie-Bro 7.26
Newcombe-Bro 7.35
Jones-Chi 7.39
Mizell-StL 7.42
Craig-Bro 7.64

Fewest BB/Game
Roberts-Phi 1.21
Newcombe-Bro 1.54
Spahn-Mil 1.66
Fowler-Cin 1.77
Burdette-Mil 1.83

Strikeouts
Jones-Chi 176
Haddix-StL-Phi . . . 170
Friend-Pit 166
Roberts-Phi 157
Mizell-StL 153

Strikeouts/Game
Jones-Chi 8.40
Haddix-StL-Phi . . . 6.64
Mizell-StL 6.60
Nuxhall-Cin 5.38
Worthington-NY . . . 5.16

Ratio
Newcombe-Bro . . . 9.00
Spahn-Mil 9.73
Maglie-Bro 9.94
Burdette-Mil 10.15
Rush-Chi 10.18

Earned Run Average
Burdette-Mil 2.70
Spahn-Mil 2.78
Antonelli-NY 2.86
Maglie-Bro 2.87
Newcombe-Bro . . . 3.06

Adjusted ERA
Maglie-Bro 138
Antonelli-NY 132
Newcombe-Bro . . . 130
Burdette-Mil 128
Spahn-Mil 124

Opponents' Batting Avg.
Newcombe-Bro 221
Jones-Chi 221
Mizell-StL 222
Maglie-Bro 222
Craig-Bro 231

Opponents' On Base Pct.
Newcombe-Bro 257
Spahn-Mil 276
Maglie-Bro 281
Burdette-Mil 282
Rush-Chi 282

Starter Runs
Spahn-Mil 30.9
Burdette-Mil 30.4
Antonelli-NY 26.3
Newcombe-Bro . . . 21.3
Maglie-Bro 19.0

Adjusted Starter Runs
Newcombe-Bro . . . 27.1
Antonelli-NY 26.6
Maglie-Bro 23.2
Burdette-Mil 21.6
Spahn-Mil 21.2

Clutch Pitching Index
Conley-Mil 127
Klippstein-Cin . . . 111
Kline-Pit 110
Poholsky-StL 108
Jeffcoat-Cin 105

Relief Runs
Grissom-NY 19.8
Acker-Cin 13.1
Bessent-Bro 11.2
B.Miller-Phi 7.3
Labine-Bro 5.5

Adjusted Relief Runs
Grissom-NY 19.9
Acker-Cin 15.0
Bessent-Bro 13.0
Labine-Bro 8.0
Freeman-Cin 7.0

Relief Ranking
Freeman-Cin 13.7
Bessent-Bro 13.6
Labine-Bro 12.9
Acker-Cin 11.7
Grissom-NY 8.3

Total Pitcher Index
Newcombe-Bro . . . 4.3
Antonelli-NY 3.6
Spahn-Mil 2.9
Burdette-Mil 2.6
Dickson-Phi-StL . . 2.2

Total Baseball Ranking
Mays-NY 4.7
Aaron-Mil 4.4
Newcombe-Bro . . . 4.3
McMillan-Cin 3.7
Antonelli-NY 3.6

February 4 The AL says it will test the automatic intentional walk during spring training.

February 8 The legendary Connie Mack dies at age 93. He began his career with Washington in 1886 as a catcher. After managing the NL Pittsburgh club from 1894-96, he became a prominent figure in Ban Johnson's Western League and a founder of the AL and its Philadelphia franchise in 1901. In 50 years as the Athletics pilot he won nine pennants and five World Championships, but also finished last 17 times.

February 15 The Pirates and the Kansas City A's cancel an exhibition game in Birmingham, Alabama, because of a local ordinance barring black players from playing against white players.

April 24 AL umpire Frank Umont is the first to wear glasses in a regular season game, between Detroit and Kansas City. The former NFL tackle (New York Giants) still presents an intimidating appearance to most players and fans.

May 18 Mickey Mantle homers from both sides of the plate for the third time in his career, eclipsing the mark of Jim Russell. The visiting New Yorkers nip Chicago, 8–7, in 10 innings.

May 30 Mickey Mantle hits one of the most memorable home runs in his career, in the second game of a doubleheader with the Washington Senators. He tags a pitch from Pedro Ramos that comes within 18 inches of leaving Yankee Stadium, something never accomplished by any major leaguer. The ball was still climbing when it caromed off the upper-stand facade, about 396 feet from home plate. Estimates are that the ball could have traveled more than 600 feet. It is Mantle's 20th home run of the season; no one else has ever hit 20 home runs before June.

August 7 The Boston Red Sox fine Ted Williams $5,000 for spitting at Boston fans, as the Red Sox edge the Yanks in 11 innings on Williams's bases-loaded walk. The spitting started after the crowd of 36,350 started booing the Splendid Splinter for muffing Mickey Mantle's windblown fly in the 11th.

September 18 Mickey Mantle hits his 50th home run, off Chicago's Billy Pierce, as New York wins 3-2 to clinch another pennant. Mantle will win the Triple Crown with a .353 batting average, 52 home runs, and 130 RBI.

September 30 White Sox hurler Jim Derrington becomes the youngest pitcher since 1900 to start a game. He loses to Kansas City 7-6 at the age of 16 years and 10 months.

October 8 Series history is made by Don Larsen of the Yankees, who pitches a perfect game to defeat the Dodgers 2-0 in Game 5. He requires only 97 pitches.

October 10 In Game 7, the Yankees win their first World Series championship in three years as Johnny Kucks sets down the Bums 9-0. Yogi Berra hits a pair of two-run home runs and Bill Skowron hits a grand slam. Don Newcombe takes the loss, his fourth in Series competition.

December 18 Former Yankee shortstop Phil Rizzuto signs as a Yankee radio-TV announcer.

BALTIMORE	BOSTON	CHICAGO	CLEVELAND	DETROIT	KANSAS CITY	NEW YORK	WASHINGTON
M P.Richards	M P.Higgins	M M.Marion	M A.Lopez	M B.Harris	M L.Boudreau	M C.Stengel	M C.Dressen
1B B.Boyd	1B M.Vernon	1B W.Dropo	1B V.Wertz	1B E.Torgeson	1B V.Power	1B B.Skowron	1B P.Runnels
2B B.Gardner	2B B.Goodman	2B N.Fox	2B B.Avila	2B F.Bolling	2B J.Finigan	2B B.Martin	2B H.Plews
SS W.Miranda	SS B.Buddin	SS L.Aparicio	SS C.Carrasquel	SS H.Kuenn	SS J.DeMaestri	SS G.McDougald	SS J.Valdivielso
3B G.Kell	3B B.Klaus	3B F.Hatfield	3B A.Rosen	3B R.Boone	3B H.Lopez	3B A.Carey	3B E.Yost
LF B.Nieman	LF T.Williams	LF M.Minoso	LF A.Smith	LF C.Maxwell	LF L.Skizas	LF E.Howard	LF R.Sievers
CF D.Williams	CF J.Piersall	CF J.Rivera	CF J.Busby	CF B.Tuttle	CF J.Groth	CF M.Mantle	CF W.Herzog
RF T.Francona	RF J.Jensen	C S.Lollar	RF R.Colavito	RF A.Kaline	RF H.Simpson	RF H.Bauer	RF J.Lemon
C G.Triandos	C S.White	1O D.Philley	C J.Hegan	C F.House	C T.Thompson	C Y.Berra	C C.Courtney
C H.Smith	O1 D.Gernert	3S S.Esposito	O G.Woodling	O R.Wilson	O G.Zernial	O1 J.Collins	C L.Berberet
1 B.Hale	O G.Stephens	C L.Moss	2S G.Strickland	1 J.Phillips	2S A.Pilarcik	2S J.Coleman	C K.Olson
O J.Pyburn	23 T.Lepcio	O B.Phillips	1O P.Ward	O3 B.Kennedy	O E.Slaughter	O N.Siebern	C E.FitzGerald
O D.Philley	C P.Daley	3 G.Kell	C H.Naragon	S2 J.Brideweser	O J.Ginsberg	O B.Cerv	S J.Snyder
O H.Evers	O P.Philley	1 R.Jackson	O S.Mele	1 W.Belardi	1 E.Robinson	O E.Slaughter	S E.Oravetz
32 B.Adams	3 F.Malzone	O R.Northey	C E.Averill	O J.Small	C H.Smith	S B.Hunter	S L.Luttrell
O C.Diering	1 N.Zauchin	O J.Delsing	O D.Pope	2 R.Bertoia	2 C.Boyer	S J.Lumpe	2S T.Roig
3 W.Causey	O F.Throneberry	O B.Nieman	3 R.Regalado	S B.Hicks	O M.Baxes	S E.Robinson	3 H.Killebrew
O J.Frazier	/2 G.Mauch	/3 B.Consolo	O J.Caffie	2 J.Porter	2 S.Jacobs	S P.Rizzuto	O C.Paula
O T.Nelson	2 B.Consolo	S J.Brideweser	/O D.Mitchell	1 J.Delsing	1 R.Pless	O I.Noren	O D.Tettelbach
23 G.Hatton	H G.Hatton	/C E.Battey	S K.Kuhn	/2 F.Hatfield	O B.Renna	3 T.Carroll	H T.Wright
C T.Gastall	H M.Keough	/O C.Abrams	/O S.Locklin	/O C.King	/O J.Pisoni	/O G.Wilson	P C.Stobbs
3 B.Robinson	P T.Brewer	P B.Pierce	H H.Evers	/C C.Lau	/C J.Astroth	/C C.Silvera	P C.Pascual
/C J.Ginsberg	P F.Sullivan	P D.Donovan	/C H.Foiles	/C W.Streuli	/O E.Valo	/2 B.Richardson	P P.Ramos
/S F.Marsh	P W.Nixon	P J.Harshman	R B.Young	P F.Lary	/O D.Melton	H L.Skizas	P D.Stone
/O J.Dyck	P D.Sisler	P J.Wilson	P E.Wynn	P P.Foytack	P A.Ditmar	P W.Ford	P B.Wiesler
/O D.Pope	P M.Parnell	P B.Keegan	P B.Lemon	P B.Hoeft	P T.Gorman	RP J.Kucks	RP H.Griggs
P R.Moore	RP I.Delock	RP D.Howell	P H.Score	S P.Gromek	P W.Burnette	RP D.Larsen	RP B.Chakales
P C.Johnson	RP T.Hurd	P G.Staley	P M.Garcia	P V.Trucks	P L.Kretlow	RP T.Sturdivant	RP C.Grob
P B.Wight	P B.Porterfield	P P.LaPalme	RP D.Mossi	RP D.Maas	P T.Herriage	P B.Turley	P B.Stewart
P H.Brown	P G.Susce	P S.Consuegra	RP C.McLish	P A.Aber	RP J.Crimian	RP T.Byrne	P B.Byerly
P E.Palica	P L.Kiely	P E.Kinder	RP R.Narleski	P W.Masterson	RP B.Shantz	RP B.Grim	P T.Clevenger
RP D.Ferrarese	/P F.Baumann	P H.Pollet	P H.Aguirre	P J.Bunning	RP J.McMahan	RP T.Morgan	/P T.Abernathy
RP G.Zuverink	P H.Dorish	/P J.McDonald	P B.Feller	P B.Miller	P A.Kellner	P R.Coleman	/P E.Hernandez
RP B.Loes	/P R.Minarcin	P M.Martin	P B.Miller	/P N.Garver	P T.Lasorda	P M.McDermott	/P D.Brodowski
P M.Fornieles	/P J.Schmitz	/P M.Fornieles	/P B.Daley	/P D.Marlowe	P M.Burtschy	P R.Terry	
/P J.Wilson		/P C.Johnson	/P S.Maglie	/P B.Black	P B.Harrington	/P J.Konstanty	
P J.Schmitz		/P J.Derrington		/P J.Brady	/P G.Cox	/P S.Dixon	
P H.Dorish		/P H.Byrd		/P G.Host	/P J.Santiago	/P J.Coates	
/P F.Besana		/P J.Dahlke		/P H.Woodeshick	/P A.Ceccarelli	/P G.Staley	
/P C.Beamon		/P B.Fischer		/P P.Wojey	/P G.Brunet		
/P S.Consuegra		/P D.Marlowe			/P W.Craddock		
/P R.Moeller					/P A.Portocarrero		
/P B.O'Dell					/P C.Duser		
/P M.Held					/P B.Bradford		
/P B.Birrer					/P B.Spicer		
/P M.Martin							
/P B.Harrison							
/P G.Werley							
/P G.Sundin							

TEAM	G	W	L	PCT	GB	R	OR	AB	H	2B	3B	HR	BB	SO	AVG	OBP	SLG	PRO	PRO+	BR	/A	PF	CHI	RC	SB	CS	SBA	SBR
NY	154	97	57	.630		857	631	5312	1433	193	55	190	615	755	.270	.349	.434	.783	116	80	107	97	106	814	51	37	58	-7
CLE	155	88	66	.571	9	712	581	5148	1256	199	23	153	681	764	.244	.337	.381	.718	93	-35	-50	102	105	681	40	32	56	-7
CHI	154	85	69	.552	12	776	634	5286	1412	218	43	128	619	660	.267	.352	.397	.749	102	30	19	101	102	756	70	33	68	1
BOS	155	84	70	.545	13	780	751	5349	1473	261	45	139	727	687	.275	.365	.419	.784	101	100	-1	112	93	826	28	19	60	-3
DET	155	82	72	.532	15	789	699	5364	1494	209	50	150	644	618	.279	.359	.420	.779	111	84	82	100	97	816	43	26	62	-3
BAL	154	69	85	.448	28	571	705	5090	1242	198	34	91	563	725	.244	.322	.350	.672	90	-123	-80	92	101	572	39	42	48	-14
WAS	155	59	95	.383	38	652	924	5202	1302	198	62	112	690	877	.250	.343	.377	.720	96	-27	-26	100	94	681	37	34	52	-9
KC	154	52	102	.338	45	619	831	5256	1325	204	41	112	480	727	.252	.317	.370	.687	86	-108	-110	100	105	610	40	30	57	-6
TOT	618					5756		42007	10937	1680	353	1075	5019	5813	.260	.343	.394	.737							348	253	58	-47

TEAM	CG	SH	SV	IP	H	H/G	HR	BB	SO	RAT	ERA	ERA+	OAV	OOB	PR	/A	PF	CPI	FA	E	DP	FW	PW	BW	SBW	DIF
NY	50	10	35	1382	1285	8.4	114	652	732	12.9	3.63	107	.249	.337	82	37	93	105	.977	136	214	.6	3.6	10.5	-.1	5.4
CLE	67	17	24	1384	1233	8.0	116	564	845	11.9	3.32	127	.238	.316	129	136	101	100	.978	129	130	1.0	13.3	-4.9	-.1	1.7
CHI	65	11	13	1389	1351	8.8	118	524	722	12.3	3.73	110	.255	.325	67	58	99	99	.979	122	160	1.3	5.7	1.9	.7	-1.6
BOS	50	8	20	1398	1354	8.7	130	668	712	13.3	4.17	111	.254	.342	-1	71	111	96	.972	169	168	-1.2	7.0	-.0	.3	1.1
DET	62	10	15	1379	1389	9.1	140	655	788	13.6	4.06	101	.264	.351	15	9	99	108	.976	140	151	.4	.9	8.0	.3	-4.6
BAL	38	10	24	1360²	1362	9.0	99	547	715	12.8	4.20	93	.263	.337	-6	-42	94	93	.977	137	142	.5	-4.1	-7.8	-.8	4.2
WAS	36	1	18	1368²	1539	10.1	171	730	663	15.1	5.33	81	.287	.376	-179	-153	104	99	.972	171	173	-1.3	-15.0	-2.5	-.3	1.1
KC	30	3	18	1370¹	1424	9.4	187	679	636	14.1	4.86	89	.271	.359	-107	-81	104	101	.973	166	187	-1.1	-7.9	-10.8	.0	-5.2
TOT	398	70	167	11031²		8.9				13.2	4.16		.260	.343					.975	1170	1325					

Runs		Hits		Doubles		Triples		Home Runs		Total Bases	
Mantle-NY	132	Kuenn-Det	196	Piersall-Bos	40	Simpson-KC	11	Mantle-NY	52	Mantle-NY	376
Fox-Chi	109	Kaline-Det	194	Kuenn-Det	32	Minoso-Chi	11	Wertz-Cle	32	Kaline-Det	327
Minoso-Chi	106	Fox-Chi	192	Kaline-Det	32	Lemon-Was	11	Berra-NY	30	Jensen-Bos	287
		Mantle-NY	188			Jensen-Bos	11	Sievers-Was	29	Minoso-Chi	286
		Jensen-Bos	182					Maxwell-Det	28		

Runs Batted In		Runs Produced		Bases On Balls		Batting Average		On Base Percentage		Slugging Average	
Mantle-NY	130	Mantle-NY	210	Yost-Was	151	Mantle-NY	.353	Williams-Bos	.479	Mantle-NY	.705
Kaline-Det	128	Kaline-Det	197	Mantle-NY	112	Williams-Bos	.345	Mantle-NY	.467	Williams-Bos	.605
Wertz-Cle	106	Minoso-Chi	173	Williams-Bos	102	Kuenn-Det	.332	Nieman-Chi-Bal	.438	Maxwell-Det	.534
Simpson-KC	105	Kuenn-Det	172	Doby-Chi	102	Maxwell-Det	.326	Minoso-Chi	.430	Berra-NY	.534
Berra-NY	105	Berra-NY	168	Sievers-Was	100	Nieman-Chi-Bal	.320	Maxwell-Det	.420	Kaline-Det	.530

Production		Adjusted Production		Batter Runs		Adjusted Batter Runs		Clutch Hitting Index		Runs Created	
Mantle-NY	1.172	Mantle-NY	213	Mantle-NY	83.3	Mantle-NY	88.7	Kaline-Det	117	Mantle-NY	188
Williams-Bos	1.084	Williams-Bos	164	Williams-Bos	54.1	Minoso-Chi	41.5	Lollar-Chi	117	Minoso-Chi	130
Minoso-Chi	.954	Nieman-Chi-Bal	156	Minoso-Chi	43.2	Williams-Bos	40.9	Triandos-Bal	114	Kaline-Det	129
Maxwell-Det	.954	Maxwell-Det	150	Maxwell-Det	37.5	Nieman-Chi-Bal	38.8	Doby-Chi	113	Williams-Bos	121
Nieman-Chi-Bal	.934	Minoso-Chi	149	Kaline-Det	33.4	Maxwell-Det	37.3	Carey-NY	109	Maxwell-Det	118

Total Average		Stolen Bases		Stolen Base Average		Stolen Base Runs		Fielding Runs		Total Player Rating	
Mantle-NY	1.426	Aparicio-Chi	21	Aparicio-Chi	84.0	Aparicio-Chi	3.9	Piersall-Bos	17.6	Mantle-NY	8.7
Williams-Bos	1.255	Rivera-Chi	20	Avila-Cle	81.0	Avila-Cle	2.7	Kaline-Det	17.3	Kaline-Det	4.2
Minoso-Chi	1.031	Avila-Cle	17	Rivera-Chi	69.0	Mantle-NY	2.4	Hegan-Cle	15.6	Berra-NY	4.2
Maxwell-Det	1.015	Minoso-Chi	12					Buddin-Bos	13.9	Maxwell-Det	4.2
Nieman-Chi-Bal	.955							Maxwell-Det	13.1	Minoso-Chi	3.6

Wins		Win Percentage		Games		Complete Games		Shutouts		Saves	
Lary-Det	21	Ford-NY	.760	Zuverink-Bal	62	Pierce-Chi	21	Score-Cle	5	Zuverink-Bal	16
		Wynn-Cle	.690	Crimian-KC	54	Lemon-Cle	21			Mossi-Cle	11
		Score-Cle	.690	Gorman-KC	52	Lary-Det	20			Morgan-NY	11
		Pierce-Chi	.690	Mossi-Cle	48					Shantz-KC	9
		Brewer-Bos	.679	Delock-Bos	48					Delock-Bos	9

Innings Pitched		Fewest Hits/Game		Fewest BB/Game		Strikeouts		Strikeouts/Game		Ratio	
Lary-Det	294.0	Score-Cle	5.85	Stobbs-Was	2.03	Score-Cle	263	Score-Cle	9.49	Score-Cle	10.58
Wynn-Cle	277.2	Larsen-NY	6.66	Donovan-Chi	2.26	Pierce-Chi	192	Pascual-Was	7.73	Donovan-Chi	10.62
Pierce-Chi	276.1	Harshman-Chi	7.27	Kucks-NY	2.89	Foytack-Det	184	Foytack-Det	6.47	Wynn-Cle	10.66
Foytack-Det	256.0	Brewer-Bos	7.37	Wynn-Cle	2.95	Hoeft-Det	172	Pierce-Chi	6.25	Sturdivant-NY	10.80
Lemon-Cle	255.1	Foytack-Det	7.42	Sturdivant-NY	2.96	Lary-Det	165	Sturdivant-NY	6.25	Ford-NY	10.97

Earned Run Average		Adjusted ERA		Opponents' Batting Avg.		Opponents' On Base Pct.		Starter Runs		Adjusted Starter Runs	
Ford-NY	2.47	Score-Cle	166	Score-Cle	.186	Sturdivant-NY	.291	Score-Cle	45.2	Score-Cle	46.5
Score-Cle	2.53	Ford-NY	156	Larsen-NY	.204	Donovan-Chi	.292	Wynn-Cle	44.3	Wynn-Cle	45.7
Wynn-Cle	2.72	Wynn-Cle	154	Brewer-Bos	.220	Score-Cle	.292	Ford-NY	42.3	Ford-NY	35.0
Lemon-Cle	3.03	Lemon-Cle	139	Harshman-Chi	.221	Wynn-Cle	.294	Lary-Det	32.9	Lemon-Cle	33.3
Harshman-Chi	3.10	Sullivan-Bos	135	Sturdivant-NY	.224	Ford-NY	.303	Lemon-Cle	32.0	Sullivan-Bos	32.2

Clutch Pitching Index		Relief Runs		Adjusted Relief Runs		Relief Ranking		Total Pitcher Index		Total Baseball Ranking	
Lary-Det	117	Narleski-Cle	17.4	Narleski-Cle	17.7	Narleski-Cle	16.1	Lemon-Cle	5.2	Mantle-NY	8.7
Sullivan-Bos	116	Grim-NY	11.5	Grim-NY	9.1	Byerly-Was	9.6	Wynn-Cle	5.1	Lemon-Cle	5.2
Hoeft-Det	116	Byrne-NY	9.7	Byerly-Was	7.9	Delock-Bos	9.2	Score-Cle	4.8	Wynn-Cle	5.1
Ford-NY	114	Byerly-Was	6.9	Byrne-NY	6.1	Grim-NY	9.0	Ford-NY	4.5	Score-Cle	4.8
Stobbs-Was	114	Mossi-Cle	5.5	Mossi-Cle	6.0	Mossi-Cle	8.4	Brewer-Bos	4.1	Ford-NY	4.5

January 4 The Dodgers buy a 44-passenger twin-engine airplane for $775,000, which they will use to transport the club during the season. They are the first team to own their own plane.

April 18 New York Parks Commissioner Robert Moses proposes a 78-acre tract in Flushing Meadows as a site for a new NL stadium. The plan, submitted to Mayor Robert Wagner, includes a 50,000-seat stadium with a plastic dome, to be built by the Parks Department.

May 28 The NL approves the proposed moves of the Dodgers and the Giants to the West Coast, provided both clubs make their request before October 1 and move at the same time.

June 12 Cardinal Stan Musial plays in his 823rd game for a new NL consecutive-game streak, beating Gus Suhr's record.

June 28 By stuffing the ballot box, Cincinnati fans elect eight Redlegs as starters in the All-Star Game. Over protests from Reds fans, Commissioner Ford Frick names Stan Musial, Willie Mays, and Hank Aaron to replace Reds Gus Bell, George Crowe, and Wally Post in the starting lineup.

August 1 Gil Hodges hits his 13th career grand slam, the last in the history of the Brooklyn Dodgers, to establish a new NL record.

August 17 Richie Ashburn, known for his ability to foul pitches off, hits spectator Alice Roth twice in the same at bat. The first one breaks her nose, and the second one hits her while she is being removed from her seat on a stretcher. Ironically, she is the wife of Earl Roth, the sports editor of the Philadelphia *Bulletin*.

September 3 Warren Spahn of the Braves hurls his 41st shutout, the most by a NL lefthander, as he beats Chicago 8-0.

September 16 The Los Angeles City Council approves a 300-acre site in Chavez Ravine for a Dodger stadium if the club will finance a public recreation area.

September 21 Gail Harris is the last player to hit a home run as a New York Giant. New York beats the Pirates 9-5 in the second game of a doubleheader and Ruben Gomez gains the last New York Giants' victory.

September 22 Duke Snider's 39th and 40th home runs are the last that will be hit at Ebbets Field. The Duke of Flatbush ties Ralph Kiner's NL mark of hitting at least 40 home runs in five consecutive seasons. Phillie Robin Roberts, who has a penchant for throwing gopher balls, is the loser, 7-3.

September 23 The Milwaukee Braves clinch the pennant by beating the Cardinals 4-2 on Hank Aaron's 11th-inning home run.

September 24 In the last game at Ebbets Field, 6,702 fans watch Dodgers lefty Danny McDevitt prevail over the Pirates 2-0. Gil Hodges has the last RBI.

September 29 With 1895 manager Jack Doyle among the 11,606 looking on, the Giants lose their last game at the Polo Grounds 9-1. Pirate pitcher Bob Friend defeats Johnny Antonelli.

October 6 With the score tied at 5-5, Eddie Mathews of the Braves evens the World Series at two games with a two-run home run in the bottom of the 10th.

October 9 With Warren Spahn stricken by the flu, Lew Burdette, pitching with two days rest, achieves his third complete game and second shutout to beat New York 5-0. The Braves win their first World Series championship since the "Miracle Braves" of 1914 beat Connie Mack's Athletics.

November 28 Warren Spahn of the Braves wins the Cy Young Award as major league Pitcher of the Year almost unanimously. White Sox pitcher Dick Donovan receives one vote.

	BROOKLYN		CHICAGO		CINCINNATI		MILWAUKEE		NEW YORK		PHILADELPHIA		PITTSBURGH		ST. LOUIS
M	W.Alston	M	B.Scheffing	M	B.Tebbetts	M	F.Haney	M	B.Rigney	M	M.Smith	M	B.Bragan	M	F.Hutchinson
1B	G.Hodges	1B	D.Long	1B	G.Crowe	1B	F.Torre	1B	W.Lockman	1B	E.Bouchee	M	D.Murtaugh	1B	S.Musial
2B	J.Gilliam	2B	B.Morgan	2B	J.Temple	2B	R.Schoendienst	2B	D.O'Connell	2B	G.Hamner	1B	D.Fondy	2B	D.Blasingame
SS	C.Neal	SS	J.Littrell	SS	R.McMillan	SS	J.Logan	SS	D.Spencer	SS	C.Fernandez	2B	B.Mazeroski	SS	A.Dark
3B	P.Reese	3B	E.Banks	3B	D.Hoak	3B	E.Mathews	3B	R.Jablonski	3B	W.Jones	SS	D.Groat	3B	E.Kasko
LF	G.Cimoli	LF	L.Walls	LF	F.Robinson	LF	W.Covington	LF	H.Sauer	LF	H.Anderson	3B	G.Freese	LF	W.Moon
CF	D.Snider	CF	B.Speake	CF	G.Bell	CF	B.Bruton	CF	W.Mays	CF	R.Ashburn	LF	B.Skinner	CF	K.Boyer
RF	C.Furillo	RF	W.Moryn	RF	W.Post	RF	H.Aaron	RF	D.Mueller	RF	R.Repulski	CF	B.Virdon	RF	D.Ennis
C	R.Campanella	C	C.Neeman	C	E.Bailey	C	D.Crandall	C	V.Thomas	C	S.Lopata	RF	R.Clemente	C	H.Smith
												C	H.Foiles		
O	S.Amoros	O	J.Bolger	C	S.Burgess	O	A.Pafko	3O	O.Virgil	O	B.Bowman			1O	J.Cunningham
3S	D.Zimmer	O	C.Tanner	O	B.Thurman	1	J.Adcock	2	R.Schoendienst	32	T.Kazanski	3S	G.Baker	C	H.Landrith
C	R.Walker	3	B.Adams	1	T.Kluszewski	2	D.O'Connell	1	G.Harris	1	J.Lonnett	1O	F.Thomas	O	BG.Smith
O	E.Valo	23	J.Kindall	O	J.Lynch	S2	F.Mantilla	O	B.Thomson	2	S.Hemus	O	P.Smith	O	W.Cooper
3	R.Jackson	O	B.Will	O	J.Taylor	O	B.Thomson	O	D.Rhodes	O	C.Harmon	O	R.Mejias	S	D.Schofield
C	J.Roseboro	2	C.Wise	S2	A.Grammas	O	D.Rice	C	R.Katt	R	R.Smalley	C	D.Rand	O	E.Miksis
/O	B.Kennedy	C	J.Fanning	O	P.Whisenant	O	B.Hazle	S3	E.Bressoud	1	M.Blaylock	C	H.Peterson	/O	J.King
/C	J.Pignatano	/C	C.Silvera	/O	A.Schult	C	C.Sawatski	C	W.Westrum	H	R.Northey	/O	J.Pendleton	/O	I.Noren
/1	J.Gentile	1	D.Fondy	/C	D.Dotterer	1	N.Jones	S	A.Rodgers	/C	A.Seminick	C	D.Kravitz	/1	T.Alston
H	R.Miller	/S	E.Winceniak	/S	B.Henrich	O	C.Tanner	/3	F.Castleman	/O	D.Landrum	/O	J.Powers	/O	G.Green
		3	G.Baker	3	C.Flood	O	J.DeMerit	H	B.Taylor	H	F.Baumholtz	/1	D.Long	/O	D.Lassetter
P	D.Drysdale	O	B.DelGreco	/2	R.Bridges	/2	B.Malkmus	H	B.Hofman	/3	G.Gorbous	/O	L.Walls	/O	C.Harmon
P	D.Newcombe	/3	J.Goryl	/S	B.Durnbaugh	2	D.Cole			/2	B.Morgan	S	B.Pritchard		
P	J.Podres	O	F.Ernaga	H	D.Pavletich	/3	H.Hanebrink	P	R.Gomez			/S	K.Hamlin	P	L.Jackson
P	D.McDevitt	/O	E.Haas			/2	M.Roach	P	J.Antonelli					P	L.McDaniel
P	R.Craig	P	B.Lennon	P	B.Lawrence	/O	R.Shearer	P	C.Barclay	P	R.Roberts	P	B.Friend	P	S.Jones
RP	C.Labine	/C	G.Massa	P	H.Jeffcoat	/C	H.Taylor	P	S.Miller	P	J.Sanford	P	R.Kline	P	H.Wehmeier
RP	E.Roebuck	/1	E.Mickelson	P	J.Nuxhall			P	R.Crone	P	C.Simmons	P	B.Purkey	P	V.Mizell
		R	J.Woods	P	D.Gross			RP	A.Worthington	H	H.Haddix	P	V.Law	RP	W.Schmidt
P	S.Koufax			P	J.Klippstein	P	W.Spahn	RP	M.Grissom	P	D.Cardwell	RP	L.Arroyo	RP	L.Merritt
P	S.Maglie	P	M.Drabowsky	RP	T.Acker	P	L.Burdette	RP	R.Monzant	RP	T.Farrell	RP	R.Face	H.Wilhelm
P	C.Erskine	P	D.Drott	RP	A.Fowler	P	B.Buhl			RP	J.Hearn	RP	R.Swanson	
P	D.Bessent	P	B.Rush	RP	H.Freeman	P	G.Conley	RP	B.Miller					P	V.McDaniel
/P	R.Valdez	P	D.Elston			P	B.Trowbridge					P	B.Smith	P	M.Dickson
/P	B.Harris	P	D.Hillman	P	R.Sanchez	RP	T.Phillips	P	J.Margoneri			P	N.King	P	B.Muffett
/P	K.Lehman	RP	J.Brosnan	P	W.Hacker	RP	E.Johnson	P	P.Burnside	P	W.Hacker	P	W.Douglas	P	J.Davis
/P	J.Collum	RP	T.Lown	/P	V.Amor	RP	D.McMahon	P	J.Constable	P	S.Morehead	P	J.O'Brien	P	M.Martin
/P	F.Kipp	RP	D.Littlefield	/P	B.Podbielan			P	S.Ridzik	P	J.Meyer	/P	J.Trimble	/P	F.Barnes
/P	D.Elston			/P	B.Kennedy	P	J.Pizarro	P	G.Jones	/P	S.Rogovin	/P	E.O'Brien	/P	Bo.Smith
		P	T.Poholsky	/P	J.Hook	P	R.Crone	/P	J.Davis	/P	T.Qualters	/P	D.Hall	/P	T.Cheney
		P	D.Kaiser	/P	C.Rabe	P	D.Jolly	/P	M.Surkont			/P	L.Pepper	/P	L.Lovenguth
		P	B.Anderson	/P	D.Skaugstad	P	R.Murff	/P	S.Consuegra			/P	C.Churn	/P	B.Miller
		P	E.Singleton	/P	C.Osteen	P	P.Paine	/P	W.McCall			/P	B.Daniels	/P	B.Kuzava
		/P	V.Valentinetti			/P	J.Jay					/P	B.Kuzava		
		/P	J.Collum									/P	G.Witt		
		/P	E.Mayer												
		/P	J.Briggs												
		/P	G.Hobbie												

TEAM	G	W	L	PCT	GB	R	OR	AB	H	2B	3B	HR	BB	SO	AVG	OBP	SLG	PRO	PRO+	BR	/A	PF	CHI	RC	SB	CS	SBA	SBR
MIL	155	95	59	.617		772	613	5458	1469	221	62	199	461	729	.269	.329	.442	.771	121	82	138	93	101	787	35	16	69	1
STL	154	87	67	.565	8	737	666	5472	1497	235	43	132	493	672	.274	.336	.405	.741	103	36	22	102	102	731	58	44	57	-9
BRO	154	84	70	.545	11	690	591	5242	1325	188	38	147	550	848	.253	.328	.387	.715	89	-11	-75	110	104	664	60	34	64	-2
CIN	154	80	74	.519	15	747	781	5389	1452	251	33	187	546	752	.269	.341	.432	.773	106	97	42	107	95	794	51	36	59	-6
PHI	156	77	77	.500	18	623	656	5241	1311	213	44	117	534	758	.250	.325	.375	.700	97	-39	-19	97	99	635	57	26	69	2
NY	154	69	85	.448	26	643	701	5346	1349	171	54	157	447	669	.252	.313	.393	.706	95	-42	-40	100	103	646	64	38	63	-4
PIT	155	62	92	.403	33	586	696	5402	1447	231	60	92	374	733	.268	.318	.384	.702	97	-46	-27	97	93	649	46	35	57	-7
CHI	156	62	92	.403	33	628	722	5369	1312	223	31	147	461	989	.244	.307	.380	.687	91	-78	-68	98	105	623	28	25	53	-7
TOT	619					5426		42919	11162	1733	365	1178	3866	6150	.260	.325	.400	.724							399	254	61	-33

TEAM	CG	SH	SV	IP	H	H/G	HR	BB	SO	RAT	ERA	ERA+	OAV	OOB	PR	/A	PF	CPI	FA	E	DP	FW	PW	BW	SBW	DIF
MIL	60	9	24	1411	1347	8.6	124	570	693	12.3	3.47	101	.253	.327	64	4	90	107	.981	120	173	1.0	.4	14.0	.5	2.0
STL	46	11	29	1413¹	1385	8.8	140	506	778	12.2	3.78	105	.257	.324	16	29	102	100	.979	131	168	.4	2.9	2.2	-.5	5.0
BRO	44	18	29	1399	1285	8.3	144	456	891	11.4	3.35	124	.244	.307	82	127	107	101	.979	127	136	.6	12.9	-7.6	.2	.9
CIN	40	5	29	1395²	1486	9.6	179	429	707	12.7	4.62	89	.275	.334	-116	-79	106	95	.982	107	139	1.7	-8.0	4.3	-.2	5.3
PHI	54	9	23	1401²	1363	8.8	139	412	858	11.5	3.79	100	.254	.310	13	1	98	97	.976	136	117	.2	-.1	-1.9	.6	1.0
NY	35	9	20	1398²	1436	9.2	150	471	701	12.5	4.01	98	.267	.330	-20	-12	101	101	.974	161	180	-1.3	-1.2	-4.1		-1.4
PIT	47	9	15	1395	1463	9.4	158	421	663	12.3	3.88	98	.270	.325	0	-14	98	105	.972	170	143	-1.7	-1.4	-2.7	-.3	-8.8
CHI	30	5	26	1403¹	1397	9.0	144	601	859	13.0	4.13	94	.261	.339	-39	-40	100	100	.975	149	140	-.5	-4.1	-6.9	-.3	-3.2
TOT	356	75	195	11217²		9.0				12.2	3.88		.260	.325					.977	1101	1196					

Runs		Hits		Doubles		Triples		Home Runs		Total Bases	
Aaron-Mil	118	Schoendienst-NY-Mil	200	Hoak-Cin	39	Mays-NY	20	Aaron-Mil	44	Aaron-Mil	369
Banks-Chi	113	Aaron-Mil	198	Musial-StL	38	Virdon-Pit	11	Banks-Chi	43	Mays-NY	366
Mays-NY	112	Robinson-Cin	197	Bouchee-Phi	35	Mathews-Mil	9	Snider-Bro	40	Banks-Chi	344
Mathews-Mil	109	Mays-NY	195	Banks-Chi	34	Bruton-Mil	9	Mays-NY	35	Robinson-Cin	323
Blasingame-StL	108	Ashburn-Phi	186	Moryn-Chi	33			Mathews-Mil	32	Mathews-Mil	309

Runs Batted In		Runs Produced		Bases On Balls		Batting Average		On Base Percentage		Slugging Average	
Aaron-Mil	132	Aaron-Mil	206	Temple-Cin	94	Musial-StL	.351	Musial-StL	.428	Mays-NY	.626
Ennis-StL	105	Mays-NY	174	Ashburn-Phi	94	Mays-NY	.333	Mays-NY	.411	Musial-StL	.612
Musial-StL	102	Banks-Chi	172	Mathews-Mil	90	Robinson-Cin	.322	Bouchee-Phi	.396	Aaron-Mil	.600
Banks-Chi	102	Mathews-Mil	171	Bouchee-Phi	84	Aaron-Mil	.322	Ashburn-Phi	.392	Snider-Bro	.587
Hodges-Bro	98	Hodges-Bro	165	Snider-Bro	77	Groat-Pit	.315	Temple-Cin	.391	Banks-Chi	.579

Production		Adjusted Production		Batter Runs		Adjusted Batter Runs		Clutch Hitting Index		Runs Created	
Musial-StL	1.040	Mays-NY	174	Mays-NY	60.5	Mays-NY	61.0	McMillan-Cin	134	Mays-NY	145
Mays-NY	1.037	Musial-StL	172	Musial-StL	54.1	Aaron-Mil	57.5	Ennis-StL	131	Aaron-Mil	136
Aaron-Mil	.979	Aaron-Mil	170	Aaron-Mil	48.3	Musial-StL	51.8	Hamner-Phi	115	Musial-StL	129
Snider-Bro	.957	Mathews-Mil	157	Banks-Chi	38.6	Mathews-Mil	46.7	Post-Cin	112	Mathews-Mil	126
Banks-Chi	.942	Banks-Chi	150	Mathews-Mil	38.3	Banks-Chi	40.5	Hoak-Cin	112	Banks-Chi	123

Total Average		Stolen Bases		Stolen Base Average		Stolen Base Runs		Fielding Runs		Total Player Rating	
Musial-StL	1.103	Mays-NY	38	Temple-Cin	79.2	Temple-Cin	2.7	Ashburn-Phi	32.4	Mays-NY	6.3
Mays-NY	1.092	Gilliam-Bro	26	Fernandez-Phi	78.3	Fernandez-Phi	2.4	Blasingame-StL	25.8	Aaron-Mil	5.0
Aaron-Mil	.988	Blasingame-StL	21	Gilliam-Bro	72.2	Robinson-Cin	1.8	Logan-Mil	23.9	Mathews-Mil	4.8
Mathews-Mil	.973	Temple-Cin	19	Blasingame-StL	70.0	Gilliam-Bro	1.8	Robinson-Cin	18.7	Musial-StL	4.5
Snider-Bro	.962	Fernandez-Phi	18	Mays-NY	66.7			Campanella-Bro	16.0	Robinson-Cin	3.8

Wins		Win Percentage		Games		Complete Games		Shutouts		Saves	
Spahn-Mil	21	Buhl-Mil	.720	Lown-Chi	67	Spahn-Mil	18	Podres-Bro	6	Labine-Bro	17
Sanford-Phi	19	Sanford-Phi	.704	Face-Pit	59	Friend-Pit	17	Spahn-Mil	4	Grissom-NY	14
Buhl-Mil	18	Spahn-Mil	.656	Labine-Bro	58	Gomez-NY	16	Newcombe-Bro	4	Lown-Chi	12
Drysdale-Bro	17	Drysdale-Bro	.654	Worthington-NY	55	Sanford-Phi	15	Drysdale-Bro	4	Wilhelm-StL	11
Burdette-Mil	17	Burdette-Mil	.654	Grissom-NY	55						

Innings Pitched		Fewest Hits/Game		Fewest BB/Game		Strikeouts		Strikeouts/Game		Ratio	
Friend-Pit	277.0	Sanford-Phi	7.38	Newcombe-Bro	1.49	Sanford-Phi	188	Jones-StL	7.59	Podres-Bro	9.78
Spahn-Mil	271.0	Podres-Bro	7.71	Roberts-Phi	1.55	Drott-Chi	170	Haddix-Phi	7.17	Roberts-Phi	10.45
Burdette-Mil	256.2	Drott-Chi	7.86	Law-Pit	1.67	Drabowsky-Chi	170	Sanford-Phi	7.15	Newcombe-Bro	10.56
Lawrence-Cin	250.1	Buhl-Mil	7.93	Purkey-Pit	1.90	Jones-StL	154	Drott-Chi	6.68	Spahn-Mil	10.66
Roberts-Phi	249.2	Worthington-NY	7.99	Jeffcoat-Cin	2.00	Drysdale-Bro	148	Drabowsky-Chi	6.38	Law-Pit	10.74

Earned Run Average		Adjusted ERA		Opponents' Batting Avg.		Opponents' On Base Pct.		Starter Runs		Adjusted Starter Runs	
Podres-Bro	2.66	Podres-Bro	156	Sanford-Phi	.221	Podres-Bro	.274	Spahn-Mil	35.8	Drysdale-Bro	36.3
Drysdale-Bro	2.69	Drysdale-Bro	155	Podres-Bro	.230	Roberts-Phi	.284	Drysdale-Bro	29.2	Podres-Bro	32.7
Spahn-Mil	2.69	Law-Pit	132	Drott-Chi	.234	Newcombe-Bro	.290	Buhl-Mil	27.4	Spahn-Mil	24.3
Buhl-Mil	2.74	Spahn-Mil	130	Drysdale-Bro	.236	Law-Pit	.291	Podres-Bro	26.5	Sanford-Phi	19.0
Law-Pit	2.87	Buhl-Mil	128	Spahn-Mil	.237	Spahn-Mil	.293	Sanford-Phi	21.0	Buhl-Mil	18.2

Clutch Pitching Index		Relief Runs		Adjusted Relief Runs		Relief Ranking		Total Pitcher Index		Total Baseball Ranking	
Buhl-Mil	135	Farrell-Phi	13.9	Roebuck-Bro	15.6	Farrell-Phi	20.7	Drysdale-Bro	4.7	Mays-NY	6.3
Barclay-NY	117	Roebuck-Bro	12.5	Farrell-Phi	13.2	Roebuck-Bro	17.5	Podres-Bro	3.5	Aaron-Mil	5.0
Law-Pit	113	Grissom-NY	11.6	Grissom-NY	12.1	Grissom-NY	15.2	Spahn-Mil	3.0	Mathews-Mil	4.8
Spahn-Mil	109	Face-Pit	8.4	Labine-Bro	8.4	Labine-Bro	11.8	Roebuck-Bro	2.3	Drysdale-Bro	4.7
Antonelli-NY	108	Miller-Phi	8.0	Miller-Phi	7.5	Miller-Phi	9.5	Farrell-Phi	2.2	Musial-StL	4.5

February 25 The U.S. Supreme Court decides 6-3 that baseball is the only professional sport exempt from antitrust laws. The issue arises when pro football seeks similar protection from the laws.

March 19 In what is believed to be the largest offer for a player ever made to date, the Indians reject a million-dollar offer for lefty Herb Score from Red Sox GM Joe Cronin. Cleveland GM Hank Greenberg refuses, saying that the team is interested in building for the future, not in selling its best ballplayers. Six weeks later, Score's career is endangered when Gil McDougald's liner strikes his right eye.

May 7 Gil McDougald of the Yankees hits a wicked line-drive that strikes Cleveland's Herb Score in the right eye. Score is carried off the feld on a stretcher, with a broken nose and lacerations. Bob Lemon relieves and wins the game, 2–1. Score will return the following year, but his pitching will not be the same.

May 16 The Yankees celebrate Billy Martin's 29th birthday in a raucous fashion. An ensuing fight at Manhattan's Copacabana Club leads to $5,500 in fines and the eventual trade of Martin to Kansas City. Hank Bauer allegedly starts the fight by hitting a patron, although Bauer denies it. The Yanks fine Ford, Bauer, Berra, Mantle and Martin $1,000 each and Kucks $500.

May 22 The Red Sox tie an AL record by smashing four home runs in the sixth inning in an 11-0 win over Cleveland. Gene Mauch, Ted Williams, Dick Gernert, and Frank Malzone do the honors. Williams had set the record with Jimmie Foxx, Joe Cronin, and Jim Tabor in l940.

June 13 For the second time this year, the Red Sox' Ted Williams hits three home runs in a game, a 9–2 win over the Indians. Williams is the first to do this in the AL.

June 28 Ray Moore blanks Cleveland 6–0 as the Orioles pitching staff hurls its fourth consecutive shutout, for a new AL mark.

July 8 The owners decide to re-elect Commissioner Ford Frick to another seven-year term when his present contract is up in 1958.

July 9 At Sportsman's Park in St. Louis, the AL nips the NL, 6–5, in the 24th All-Star Game. Both teams score three in the ninth inning, but Minnie Minoso's running catch with the bases loaded chokes off the NL's last-half rally.

September 24 The Yankees clinch their 23rd pennant and eighth under Casey Stengel, as Kansas City tips the White Sox 6-5.

October 2 Whitey Ford wins 3-1 over Warren Spahn in Game 1 of the Series at Yankee Stadium.

October 8 The Yankees stay alive as Hank Bauer homers off the foul pole in left field to give the Yankees a 3-2 win behind the four-hit pitching of Bob Turley. The World Series is even at three apiece.

November 22 Mickey Mantle edges Ted Williams 233 to 209 votes to win the AL MVP. Williams, at 39 years of age, led the league in hitting with a .388 average, hit 38 home runs, and compiled a slugging average of .731. Red Sox owner Tom Yawkey brands the voting "incompetent and unqualified," noting that two Chicago writers listed Williams in the ninth and tenth places on their ballots.

	BALTIMORE		BOSTON		CHICAGO		CLEVELAND		DETROIT		KANSAS CITY		NEW YORK		WASHINGTON
M	P.Richards	M	P.Higgins	M	A.Lopez	M	K.Farrell	M	J.Tighe	M	L.Boudreau	M	C.Stengel	M	C.Dressen
1B	B.Boyd	1B	D.Gernert	1B	E.Torgeson	1B	V.Wertz	1B	R.Boone	1B	H.Craft	1B	B.Skowron	M	C.Lavagetto
2B	B.Gardner	2B	T.Lepcio	2B	N.Fox	2B	B.Avila	2B	F.Bolling	1B	V.Power	2B	B.Richardson	1B	P.Runnels
SS	W.Miranda	SS	B.Klaus	SS	L.Aparicio	SS	C.Carrasquel	SS	H.Kuenn	2B	B.Hunter	SS	G.McDougald	2B	H.Plews
3B	G.Kell	3B	F.Malzone	3B	B.Phillips	3B	A.Smith	3B	R.Bertoia	SS	J.DeMaestri	3B	A.Carey	SS	R.Bridges
LF	B.Nieman	LF	T.Williams	LF	M.Minoso	LF	G.Woodling	LF	C.Maxwell	3B	H.Lopez	LF	E.Howard	3B	E.Yost
CF	J.Busby	CF	J.Piersall	CF	L.Doby	CF	R.Maris	CF	B.Tuttle	LF	G.Zernial	CF	M.Mantle	LF	R.Sievers
RF	A.Pilarcik	RF	J.Jensen	RF	J.Landis	RF	R.Colavito	RF	A.Kaline	CF	W.Held	RF	H.Bauer	CF	B.Usher
C	G.Triandos	C	S.White	C	S.Lollar	C	J.Hegan	C	F.House	RF	L.Skizas	C	Y.Berra	RF	J.Lemon
										C	H.Smith			C	L.Berberet
O	T.Francona	O	G.Stephens	3S	S.Esposito	3S	L.Raines	C	R.Wilson			OS	T.Kubek		
3	B.Goodman	1	M.Vernon	O1	J.Rivera	O3	D.Williams	3	J.Finigan	O	B.Cerv	O	E.Slaughter	1	J.Becquer
C	J.Ginsberg	2	G.Mauch	1	W.Dropo	2S	G.Strickland	1O	D.Philley	23	B.Martin	O1	H.Simpson	2S	M.Bolling
O3	D.Williams	S2	B.Consolo	C	E.Battey	C	R.Nixon	OC	J.Porter	C	T.Thompson	23	J.Coleman	1O	A.Schult
O	J.Durham	C	P.Daley	C	L.Moss	C	H.Naragon	O	J.Groth	1O	H.Simpson	1O	J.Collins	C	C.Courtney
S	J.Brideweser	1	N.Zauchin	3	F.Hatfield	C	D.Brown	S2	R.Samford	1	I.Noren	23	B.Martin	O	F.Throneberry
3	B.Robinson	2	K.Aspromonte	O	T.Beard	O	J.Caffie	1	E.Torgeson	2	M.Graff	3	J.Lumpe	C	E.FitzGerald
/1	B.Hale	/O	M.Keough	O	D.Philley	1	J.Altobelli	O	B.Martyn	O	D.Johnson	S2	J.Snyder
O	C.Powis	H	B.Goodman	1	R.Jackson	O	J.Busby	/3	S.Boros	O	J.Pisoni	/O	Z.Bella	O	W.Herzog
O	J.Pyburn	H	M.Bolling	H	R.Northey	S	B.Harrell	O	B.Osborne	O	J.Groth	/O	B.DelGreco	O	N.Chrisley
O	L.Green	/C	H.Sullivan	H	B.Kennedy	2	K.Kuhn	/O	B.Taylor	/2	C.Boyer	H	W.Held	S	L.Luttrell
/O	T.Nelson	H	F.Throneberry	R	L.Powell	/1	E.Robinson	/3	J.Dittmer					/3	H.Killebrew
/S	B.Peterson					/1	P.Ward	/O	K.Olson	P	N.Garver	P	T.Sturdivant	O	J.Schoonmaker
/C	F.Zupo	P	F.Sullivan	P	B.Pierce	/O	B.Usher	/1	E.Robinson	P	T.Morgan	P	J.Kucks	/O	K.Olson
/2	W.Causey	P	T.Brewer	P	D.Donovan			/O	M.Clark	P	A.Kellner	P	B.Turley	/O	D.Tettelbach
H	E.Robinson	P	W.Nixon	P	J.Wilson	P	E.Wynn	P	J.Phillips	P	R.Terry	P	B.Shantz		
/C	T.Patton	P	M.Fornieles	P	J.Harshman	P	M.Garcia	/3	G.Thomas	P	J.Urban	P	D.Larsen	P	P.Ramos
H	E.Miksis	P	D.Sisler	P	B.Keegan	P	D.Mossi	/C	T.Yewcic	P	V.Trucks	RP	A.Ditmar	P	C.Stobbs
		RP	I.Delock	RP	G.Staley	P	R.Narleski			RP	W.Burnette	RP	T.Byrne	P	C.Pascual
P	C.Johnson			RP	D.Howell	P	C.McLish	P	J.Bunning	RP	M.McDermott	RP	B.Grim	P	R.Kemmerer
P	R.Moore	P	B.Porterfield			RP	B.Daley	P	F.Lary					RP	T.Clevenger
P	B.Loes	P	G.Susce	P	B.Fischer	RP	D.Tomanek	P	D.Maas	P	T.Gorman	P	W.Ford	P	D.Hyde
P	H.Brown	P	D.Stone	P	P.LaPalme	RP	S.Pitula	P	P.Foytack	P	A.Portocarrero	P	A.Cicotte	RP	B.Byerly
P	B.O'Dell	P	R.Minarcin	P	J.Derrington			P	B.Hoeft	P	R.Duren	/P	S.Maglie		
RP	G.Zuverink	P	B.Chakales	P	J.McDonald	P	B.Lemon	RP	L.Sleater	P	R.Coleman	/P	R.Terry	P	T.Abernathy
RP	K.Lehman	P	M.Wall	/P	B.Latman	/P	H.Score	RP	H.Byrd	P	G.Host			P	E.Hernandez
RP	A.Ceccarelli	/P	F.Baumann	/P	D.Rudolph	P	V.Valentinetti			P	G.Cox			/P	J.Heise
		/P	R.Meyer	/P	J.Hughes	P	H.Aguirre	P	D.Lee	/P	G.Brunet			/P	B.Chakales
P	B.Wight	/P	R.Kemmerer	/P	E.Kinder	/P	J.Gray	P	A.Aber	/P	H.Taylor			/P	B.Wiesler
P	M.Fornieles	/P	J.Spring	/P	S.McIlwain	/P	B.Alexander	P	S.Gromek	/P	A.Aber			/P	H.Griggs
P	J.Walker					/P	A.Houtteman	/P	J.Stump	/P	E.Blake			/P	J.Black
/P	D.Ferrarese					/P	H.Wilhelm	/P	J.Presko	/P	D.Hill			/P	D.Brodowski
/P	C.Beamon							/P	B.Shaw	/P	H.Raether			/P	R.Lumenti
/P	M.Pappas							/P	J.Crimian					/P	D.Minnick
/P	A.Houtteman							/P	J.Tsitouris					/P	G.Shifflett
/P	S.Consuegra							/P	C.Daniel					/P	D.Stone
/P	D.Trout							/P	P.Wojey						

TEAM	G	W	L	PCT	GB	R	OR	AB	H	2B	3B	HR	BB	SO	AVG	OBP	SLG	PRO	PRO+	BR	/A	PF	CHI	RC	SB	CS	SBA	SBR
NY	154	98	56	.636		723	534	5271	1412	200	54	145	562	709	.268	.341	.409	.750	113	76	88	98	99	729	49	38	56	-8
CHI	155	90	64	.584	8	707	566	5265	1369	208	41	106	633	745	.260	.347	.375	.722	103	40	36	101	100	708	109	51	68	2
BOS	154	82	72	.532	16	721	668	5267	1380	231	32	153	624	739	.262	.343	.405	.748	104	76	34	106	98	725	29	21	58	-4
DET	154	78	76	.506	20	614	614	5348	1376	224	37	116	504	643	.257	.324	.378	.702	96	-18	-35	103	96	644	36	47	43	-17
BAL	154	76	76	.500	21	597	588	5264	1326	191	39	87	504	699	.252	.321	.353	.674	96	-66	-30	94	101	600	57	35	62	-4
CLE	153	76	77	.497	21.5	682	722	5171	1304	199	26	140	591	786	.252	.332	.382	.714	102	10	17	99	103	661	40	47	46	-16
KC	154	59	94	.386	38.5	563	710	5170	1262	195	40	166	364	760	.244	.297	.394	.691	92	-60	-70	102	100	578	35	27	56	-6
WAS	154	55	99	.357	43	603	808	5231	1274	215	38	111	527	733	.244	.318	.363	.681	93	-56	-49	99	102	592	13	38	25	-19
TOT	616					5210		41987	10703	1663	307	1024	4309	5814	.255	.328	.382	.710							368	304	55	-72

TEAM	CG	SH	SV	IP	H	H/G	HR	BB	SO	RAT	ERA	ERA+	OAV	OOB	PR	/A	PF	CPI	FA	E	DP	FW	PW	BW	SBW	DIF
NY	41	13	42	1395¹	1198	7.7	110	580	810	11.7	3.00	120	.234	.317	122	91	95	109	.980	123	183	.2	9.4	9.1	.1	2.2
CHI	59	16	27	1401²	1305	8.4	124	470	665	11.6	3.35	112	.248	.313	69	61	99	102	.982	107	169	1.1	6.3	3.7	1.1	.7
BOS	55	9	23	1376²	1391	9.1	116	498	692	12.6	3.88	103	.264	.331	-14	17	105	100	.976	149	179	-1.2	1.8	3.5	.5	.4
DET	52	9	21	1417²	1330	8.4	147	505	756	11.9	3.56	108	.250	.320	37	47	102	104	.980	121	151	.3	4.9	-3.6	-.8	-.3
BAL	44	13	25	1408	1272	8.1	95	493	767	11.5	3.46	104	.243	.312	51	20	95	92	.981	112	159	.8	2.1	-3.1	.5	-.3
CLE	46	7	23	1380²	1381	9.0	130	618	807	13.3	4.06	92	.261	.343	-42	-53	98	101	.974	153	154	-1.4	-5.5	1.8	-.7	5.4
KC	26	6	19	1369²	1344	8.8	153	565	626	12.7	4.19	94	.260	.336	-61	-35	104	99	.979	125	162	.1	-3.6	-7.2	.3	-7.1
WAS	31	5	16	1377	1482	9.7	149	580	691	13.7	4.85	80	.278	.353	-162	-146	103	95	.979	128	159	-.0	-15.1	-5.1	-1.0	-.8
TOT	354	78	196	11126²		8.7				12.4	3.79		.255	.328					.979	1018	1316					

Runs		Hits		Doubles		Triples		Home Runs		Total Bases	
Mantle-NY	121	Fox-Chi	196	Minoso-Chi	36	Simpson-KC-NY	9	Sievers-Was	42	Sievers-Was	331
Fox-Chi	110	Malzone-Bos	185	Gardner-Bal	36	McDougald-NY	9	Williams-Bos	38	Mantle-NY	315
Piersall-Bos	103	Minoso-Chi	176	Malzone-Bos	31	Bauer-NY	9	Mantle-NY	34	Williams-Bos	307
Sievers-Was	99	Mantle-NY	173	Kuenn-Det	30	Fox-Chi	8	Wertz-Cle	28	Kaline-Det	276
		Kuenn-Det	173			Boyd-Bal	8	Zernial-KC	27	Malzone-Bos	271

Runs Batted In		Runs Produced		Bases On Balls		Batting Average		On Base Percentage		Slugging Average	
Sievers-Was	114	Minoso-Chi	187	Mantle-NY	146	Williams-Bos	.388	Williams-Bos	.528	Williams-Bos	.731
Wertz-Cle	105	Mantle-NY	181	Williams-Bos	119	Mantle-NY	.365	Mantle-NY	.515	Mantle-NY	.665
Minoso-Chi	103	Sievers-Was	171	Smith-Cle	79	Woodling-Cle	.321	Minoso-Chi	.413	Sievers-Was	.579
Malzone-Bos	103	Malzone-Bos	170	Minoso-Chi	79	Boyd-Bal	.318	Woodling-Cle	.412	Woodling-Cle	.521
Jensen-Bos	103	Fox-Chi	165	Wertz-Cle	78	Fox-Chi	.317	Fox-Chi	.404	Wertz-Cle	.485

Production		Adjusted Production		Batter Runs		Adjusted Batter Runs		Clutch Hitting Index		Runs Created	
Williams-Bos	1.259	Williams-Bos	227	Williams-Bos	89.9	Mantle-NY	91.4	Minoso-Chi	126	Mantle-NY	178
Mantle-NY	1.179	Mantle-NY	223	Mantle-NY	88.9	Williams-Bos	81.5	Doby-Chi	125	Williams-Bos	167
Sievers-Was	.968	Sievers-Was	163	Sievers-Was	47.3	Sievers-Was	48.7	Skowron-NY	123	Sievers-Was	131
Woodling-Cle	.933	Woodling-Cle	155	Woodling-Cle	33.0	Woodling-Cle	33.9	Malzone-Bos	117	Fox-Chi	109
Minoso-Chi	.867	Minoso-Chi	136	Minoso-Chi	32.7	Minoso-Chi	32.2	Jensen-Bos	114	Minoso-Chi	106

Total Average		Stolen Bases		Stolen Base Average		Stolen Base Runs		Fielding Runs		Total Player Rating	
Williams-Bos	1.599	Aparicio-Chi	28	Rivera-Chi	90.0	Rivera-Chi	4.2	Bridges-Was	29.3	Mantle-NY	8.6
Mantle-NY	1.534	Rivera-Chi	18	Mantle-NY	84.2	Aparicio-Chi	3.6	Fox-Chi	20.9	Williams-Bos	7.1
Sievers-Was	1.010	Minoso-Chi	18	Aparicio-Chi	77.8	Mantle-NY	3.0	Berra-NY	15.6	Fox-Chi	5.6
Woodling-Cle	.944	Mantle-NY	16	Minoso-Chi	54.5	Landis-Chi	1.8	Phillips-Chi	15.5	Sievers-Was	4.4
Maxwell-Det	.876					Martin-NY-KC	1.5	McDougald-NY	15.1	McDougald-NY	4.2

Wins		Win Percentage		Games		Complete Games		Shutouts		Saves	
Pierce-Chi	20	Sturdivant-NY	.727	Zuverink-Bal	56	Pierce-Chi	16	Wilson-Chi	5	Grim-NY	19
Bunning-Det	20	Donovan-Chi	.727	Hyde-Was	52	Donovan-Chi	16	Turley-NY	4	Narleski-Cle	16
Sturdivant-NY	16	Bunning-Det	.714	Clevenger-Was	52	Brewer-Bos	15	Pierce-Chi	4	Delock-Bos	11
Donovan-Chi	16	Wilson-Chi	.652	Delock-Bos	49					Zuverink-Bal	9
Brewer-Bos	16	Pierce-Chi	.625	Trucks-KC	48					Clevenger-Was	8

Innings Pitched		Fewest Hits/Game		Fewest BB/Game		Strikeouts		Strikeouts/Game		Ratio	
Bunning-Det	267.1	Turley-NY	6.12	F.Sullivan-Bos	1.80	Wynn-Cle	184	Turley-NY	7.76	F.Sullivan-Bos	9.76
Wynn-Cle	263.0	Bunning-Det	7.20	Donovan-Chi	1.84	Bunning-Det	182	Johnson-Bal	6.58	Bunning-Det	10.00
Pierce-Chi	257.0	Foytack-Det	7.43	Shantz-NY	2.08	Johnson-Bal	177	Wynn-Cle	6.30	Donovan-Chi	10.44
Johnson-Bal	242.0	Sturdivant-NY	7.59	Loes-Bal	2.14	Pierce-Chi	171	Bunning-Det	6.13	Johnson-Bal	10.45
F.Sullivan-Bos	240.2	F.Sullivan-Bos	7.70	Bunning-Det	2.42	Turley-NY	152	Pierce-Chi	5.99	Pierce-Chi	10.51

Earned Run Average		Adjusted ERA		Opponents' Batting Avg.		Opponents' On Base Pct.		Starter Runs		Adjusted Starter Runs	
Shantz-NY	2.45	Shantz-NY	147	Turley-NY	.194	F.Sullivan-Bos	.275	Bunning-Det	32.5	Bunning-Det	34.5
Sturdivant-NY	2.54	F.Sullivan-Bos	146	Bunning-Det	.218	Bunning-Det	.279	F.Sullivan-Bos	28.3	F.Sullivan-Bos	33.6
Bunning-Det	2.69	Bunning-Det	143	Foytack-Det	.226	Pierce-Chi	.287	Sturdivant-NY	27.9	Donovan-Chi	23.6
Turley-NY	2.71	Sturdivant-NY	141	F.Sullivan-Bos	.230	Johnson-Bal	.289	Shantz-NY	25.8	Sturdivant-NY	23.4
F.Sullivan-Bos	2.73	Donovan-Chi	135	Sturdivant-NY	.232	Donovan-Chi	.293	Donovan-Chi	24.9	Shantz-NY	22.0

Clutch Pitching Index		Relief Runs		Adjusted Relief Runs		Relief Ranking		Total Pitcher Index		Total Baseball Ranking	
Shantz-NY	131	Staley-Chi	20.2	Staley-Chi	19.6	Grim-NY	23.8	F.Sullivan-Bos	3.5	Mantle-NY	8.6
Sturdivant-NY	121	Zuverink-Bal	16.4	Zuverink-Bal	14.0	Zuverink-Bal	20.3	Bunning-Det	3.3	Williams-Bos	7.1
Narleski-Cle	112	Trucks-KC	9.8	Trucks-KC	12.0	Trucks-KC	16.5	Shantz-NY	3.1	Fox-Chi	5.6
Kemmerer-Bos-Was	110	Grim-NY	9.3	Byerly-Was	8.1	Staley-Chi	13.0	Grim-NY	2.6	Sievers-Was	4.4
Donovan-Chi	108	Lehman-Bal	7.6	Grim-NY	7.7	Byerly-Was	10.4	Donovan-Chi	2.5	McDougald-NY	4.2

January 29 Dodgers catcher Roy Campanella suffers a broken neck in an early morning auto accident on Long Island. His spinal column is nearly severed and his legs are permanently paralyzed.

April 7 The Dodgers erect a 42-foot screen in left field at the Los Angeles Coliseum to cut down on home runs, since it is only 250 feet down the line.

April 15 The San Francisco Giants defeat the Los Angeles Dodgers in the first major league game played at Seals Stadium, with Ruben Gomez pitching an 8–0 shutout. Giants shortstop Daryl Spencer hits the first home run. The Giants set an attendance record for Seals Stadium by drawing 23,192 fans.

April 18 Following a downtown parade in the morning, the Giants-Dodgers game in Los Angeles sets a NL single-game record with 78,682 fans in attendance, as the Dodgers prevail 6-5. Hank Sauer hits two home runs for the Giants, including the first at the Coliseum. After he scores what would have been the tying run in the ninth, Giant Jim Davenport is called out for failing to touch third.

May 13 With his pinch double in Wrigley Field off Moe Drabowsky, Stan Musial of the Cardinals becomes the eighth hitter in history to get 3,000 hits. The Cards win 5-3.

June 3 The "Dodger referendum" passes by a slim margin of 24,293 votes in Los Angeles. The proposition allows the city to sell 300 acres of Chavez Ravine to the Dodgers for their stadium. The NL president had stated that the Dodgers should vacate Los Angeles if the bill failed.

July 7 At the NL meeting, William Shea outlines plans for a $12 million stadium at Flushing Meadows, the eventual site of Shea Stadium.

August 20 Out of catchers, the Cubs put left-handed first baseman Dale Long behind the plate in the opener against the Pirates. He is the first lefty backstop since 1906. The Cubs lose 4-2, then win the nightcap 5-1 with Long back at first base.

September 13 The Braves' Warren Spahn becomes the first lefty to win 20 or more games nine times, as he beats St. Louis, 8–2. Eddie Plank and Lefty Grove each won 20 games eight times.

September 29 In a race that goes down to the last game, Philadelphia's Richie Ashburn wins the NL batting title with a 3-for-4 day that raises him to .350, three percentage points ahead of Mays, despite Willie's three hits in the Giants' 7–2 win over St. Louis.

October 1 In the World Series, the Braves pick up where they left off the previous year, defeating the Yankees behind Warren Spahn 4-3 in 10 innings.

October 5 Milwaukee goes up three games to one with a 3-0 shutout by Warren Spahn, who allows just two hits.

November 25 The BBWAA names Chicago Cubs slugger Ernie Banks the 1958 MVP. Willie Mays is the runner-up.

December 10 The University of Pittsburgh agrees to buy Forbes Field from the Pirates and lease it to them for five years, or until a new municipal stadium is built.

CHICAGO		CINCINNATI		LOS ANGELES		MILWAUKEE		PHILADELPHIA		PITTSBURGH		SAN FRANCISCO		ST.LOUIS	
M	B.Scheffing	M	B.Tebbetts	M	W.Alston	M	F.Haney	M	M.Smith	M	D.Murtaugh	M	B.Rigney	M	F.Hutchinson
1B	D.Long	M	J.Dykes	1B	G.Hodges	1B	F.Torre	M	E.Sawyer	1B	T.Kluszewski	1B	O.Cepeda	M	S.Hack
2B	T.Taylor	1B	G.Crowe	2B	C.Neal	2B	R.Schoendienst	1B	E.Bouchee	2B	B.Mazeroski	2B	D.O'Connell	1B	S.Musial
SS	E.Banks	2B	J.Temple	SS	D.Zimmer	SS	J.Logan	2B	S.Hemus	SS	D.Groat	SS	D.Spencer	2B	D.Blasingame
3B	A.Dark	SS	R.McMillan	LF	J.Gilliam	3B	E.Mathews	SS	C.Fernandez	3B	F.Thomas	3B	J.Davenport	3B	K.Boyer
LF	W.Moryn	3B	D.Hoak	CF	G.Cimoli	LF	A.Pafko	3B	W.Jones	LF	B.Skinner	LF	H.Sauer	LF	D.Ennis
CF	B.Thomson	LF	F.Robinson	RF	C.Furillo	CF	B.Bruton	LF	H.Anderson	CF	B.Virdon	CF	W.Mays	CF	C.Flood
RF	L.Walls	CF	G.Bell	C	J.Roseboro	RF	H.Aaron	CF	R.Ashburn	RF	R.Clemente	RF	W.Kirkland	RF	W.Moon
C	S.Taylor	RF	J.Lynch	O	D.Snider	C	D.Crandall	RF	W.Post	C	H.Foiles	C	B.Schmidt	C	H.Smith
32	J.Goryl	C	E.Bailey	O1	N.Larker	1O	J.Adcock	C	S.Lopata	1	D.Stuart	3	R.Jablonski	1O	J.Cunningham
C	C.Neeman	C	S.Burgess	S3	P.Reese	O	W.Covington	2S	T.Kazanski	O	R.Mejias	O	L.Wagner	OC	G.Green
O	J.Bolger	S3	A.Grammas	C	J.Pignatano	O2	F.Mantilla	O	R.Repulski	C	B.Hall	O	F.Alou	O	I.Noren
O	C.Tanner	O	B.Thurman	2	D.Demeter	2	M.Roach	C	D.Philley	C	D.Kravitz	C	V.Thomas	S2	G.Freese
1	B.Adams	O	P.Whisenant	1	S.Bilko	O	H.Hanebrink	1	B.Bowman	1	R.Stevens	2	E.Bressoud	C	H.Landrith
1O	J.Marshall	1	W.Dropo	1	E.Valo	C	D.Rice	C	C.Sawatski	O	J.Powers	O2	W.Lockman	S	D.Schofield
O	L.Jackson	1O	D.Fondy	S	B.Lillis	2	C.Wise	32	G.Hamner	3	G.Baker	S	B.Speake	S	BG.Smith
C	E.Tappe	O	V.Pinson	3	R.Jackson	O	B.Hazle	O	C.Essegian	/S	D.Schofield	S	A.Rodgers	/S	R.Amaro
/C	M.Thacker	1	S.Bilko	O	R.Fairly	/O	E.Haas	31	P.Herrera	/3	H.Bright	O	J.King	/S	A.Dark
/1	P.Smith	O3	E.Miksis	/1	J.Gentile	/C	C.Sawatski	2	B.Young	/3	G.Freese	O	J.Brandt	C	R.Katt
H	F.Ernaga	/C	D.Dotterer	/O	F.Howard	/S	J.Koppe	C	J.Hegan	/C	H.Peterson	O	D.Taussig	/S	L.Tate
/O	C.King	O	D.Morejon	/O	D.Miles	/O	H.Taylor	/C	J.Lonnett	H	J.Pendleton	/1	B.White	/O	E.Burton
/2	J.Kindall	/O	C.Coles	/3	E.Robinson	/O	J.DeMerit	/C	J.Coker	/1	P.Smith	/2	J.Finigan	/O	J.Taylor
H	F.Johnson	/O	J.Fridley	/O	B.Wilson	H	B.Roselli	/S	R.Smalley	H	J.O'Brien	O	N.Testa	/3	B.Valenzuela
/O	B.Will	/S	B.Henrich	P	D.Drysdale	P	W.Spahn	H	M.Burk	P	B.Friend	P	J.Antonelli	/S	J.O'Brien
H	G.Gabler	/2	F.Hatfield	P	J.Podres	P	L.Burdette	P	R.Roberts	P	R.Kline	P	R.Gomez	P	L.McDaniel
H	G.Massa	P	B.Purkey	P	S.Koufax	P	B.Rush	P	R.Semproch	P	V.Law	P	S.Miller	P	S.Jones
H	B.Morgan	P	H.Haddix	P	S.Williams	P	C.Willey	P	J.Sanford	P	C.Raydon	P	M.McCormick	P	L.Jackson
P	T.Phillips	P	B.Lawrence	P	C.Erskine	P	J.Pizarro	RP	D.Cardwell	P	G.Witt	P	R.Monzant	P	V.Mizell
P	G.Hobbie	P	J.Nuxhall	RP	C.Labine	RP	G.Conley	RP	T.Farrell	RP	B.Porterfield	RP	A.Worthington	P	J.Brosnan
P	D.Drott	P	D.Newcombe	RP	F.Kipp	RP	D.McMahon	RP	J.Meyer	RP	R.Face	RP	M.Grissom	P	B.Mabe
P	D.Hillman	RP	H.Jeffcoat	P	J.Klippstein	RP	B.Trowbridge	RP	J.Hearn	P	D.Gross	P	P.Giel	RP	B.Muffett
P	M.Drabowsky	RP	W.Schmidt	P	D.McDevitt	P	J.Jay	P	S.Morehead	P	R.Blackburn	P	G.Jones	RP	P.Paine
RP	D.Elston	P	T.Acker	P	E.Roebuck	P	B.Buhl	P	B.Miller	P	B.Smith	P	R.Crone	RP	B.Wight
RP	B.Henry	P	A.Kellner	P	B.Birrer	P	H.Robinson	/P	J.Gray	/P	B.Daniels	P	D.Johnson	P	L.McDaniel
P	J.Briggs	P	J.Klippstein	P	D.Newcombe	P	E.Johnson	/P	W.Hacker	/P	D.Williams	/P	C.Barclay	P	S.Maglie
P	B.Anderson	/P	C.Rabe	/P	R.Craig	/P	D.Littlefield	/P	J.Anderson	/P	E.O'Brien	/P	P.Burnside	P	C.Stobbs
/P	J.Brosnan	/P	O.Pena	/P	B.Giallombardo			/P	D.Erickson			/P	J.Constable	P	N.Chittum
P	M.Solis	P	T.Lown	P	D.Bessent			/P	B.Conley			/P	D.Zanni	P	M.Martin
P	D.Nichols	/P	H.Freeman	/P	R.Mauriello			/P	J.Owens			/P	J.Fitzgerald	/P	F.Barnes
P	G.Fodge	/P	J.O'Toole	/P	R.Negray			/P	H.Mason			/P	J.Shipley	/P	Bi.Smith
P	J.Buzhardt	/P	B.Wight	/P	L.Sherry			/P	A.LiPetri					P	P.Clark
P	E.Mayer	P	L.Hayden	/P	J.Collum			/P	T.Qualters					P	H.Wehmeier
/P	H.Freeman	/P	J.Hook											/P	V.McDaniel
/P	F.Rodriguez	/P	B.Kelly											/P	T.Flanigan
/P	E.Singleton	/P	T.Wieand												
/P	T.Lown														
/P	D.Ellsworth														

TEAM	G	W	L	PCT	GB	R	OR	AB	H	2B	3B	HR	BB	SO	AVG	OBP	SLG	PRO	PRO+	BR	/A	PF	CHI	RC	SB	CS	SBA	SBR
MIL	154	92	62	.597		675	**541**	5225	1388	221	21	167	478	646	**.266**	.331	.412	.743	111	14	**72**	92	98	705	26	8	**76**	3
PIT	154	84	70	.545	8	662	607	5247	1386	229	**68**	134	134	753	.264	.319	.410	.729	101	-21	-4	97	103	669	30	15	67	0
SF	154	80	74	.519	12	**727**	698	5318	1399	**250**	42	170	531	817	.263	.334	.422	.756	107	37	54	98	100	**747**	64	29	69	2
CIN	154	76	78	.494	16	695	621	5273	1359	242	40	123	572	765	.258	.333	.389	.722	92	-19	-54	105	104	690	61	38	62	-5
STL	154	72	82	.468	20	619	704	5255	1371	216	39	111	533	**637**	.261	.331	.380	.711	90	-38	-63	104	97	638	44	43	51	-13
CHI	154	72	82	.468	20	709	725	5289	1402	207	49	**182**	467	853	.265	.332	**.426**	**.758**	108	**39**	50	98	97	737	39	23	63	-2
LA	154	71	83	.461	21	668	761	5173	1297	166	50	172	495	850	.251	.319	.402	.721	93	-32	-52	103	**106**	650	**73**	47	61	-6
PHI	154	69	85	.448	23	664	762	5363	**1424**	238	56	124	**573**	871	**.266**	**.341**	.400	.741	103	20	30	99	93	729	51	33	61	-5
TOT	616					5419		42143	11026	1769	365	1183	4065	6192	.262	.330	.405	.735							388	236	62	-25

TEAM	CG	SH	SV	IP	H	H/G	HR	BB	SO	RAT	ERA	ERA+	OAV	OOB	PR	/A	PF	CPI	FA	E	DP	FW	PW	BW	SBW	DIF
MIL	**72**	**16**	17	1376	**1261**	8.2	125	426	773	**11.2**	**3.21**	110	**.244**	**.305**	113	47	89	99	.980	120	152	.8	4.7	**7.3**	**.6**	1.5
PIT	43	10	**41**	1367	1344	8.8	**123**	470	679	12.1	3.56	109	.261	.325	59	46	98	**105**	.978	133	173	.1	4.6	-.4	.3	2.3
SF	38	7	25	1389¹	1400	9.1	166	512	775	12.6	3.98	96	.263	.332	-4	-25	97	103	.975	152	156	-.9	-2.5	5.4	.5	.5
CIN	50	7	20	1385¹	1422	9.2	148	**419**	705	12.1	3.73	**111**	.267	.324	34	**64**	105	**105**	**.983**	**100**	148	**1.9**	**6.5**	-5.4	-.2	-3.7
STL	45	6	25	1381²	1398	9.1	158	567	822	13.1	4.12	100	.264	.340	-25	2	105	102	.974	153	163	-.9	.2	-6.4	-1.0	3.1
CHI	27	5	24	1361	1322	8.7	142	**419**	805	13.1	4.22	93	.254	.338	-40	-46	99	94	.975	150	161	-.8	-4.6	5.0	.1	-4.7
LA	30	7	31	1368¹	1399	9.2	173	606	**855**	13.4	4.47	92	.267	.347	-79	-57	104	100	.975	146	**198**	-.6	-5.7	-5.2	-.3	5.9
PHI	51	6	15	1397	1480	9.5	148	446	778	12.5	4.32	92	.272	.329	-58	-56	100	93	.978	129	136	.3	-5.6	3.0	-.2	-5.5
TOT	356	64	198	11025²		9.0				12.5	3.95		.262	.330					.977	1083	1287					

Runs
Mays-SF 121
Banks-Chi 119
Aaron-Mil 109
Boyer-StL 101
Ashburn-Phi 98

Hits
Ashburn-Phi 215
Mays-SF 208
Aaron-Mil 196
Banks-Chi 193
Cepeda-SF 188

Doubles
Cepeda-SF 38
Groat-Pit 36
Musial-StL 35
H.Anderson-Phi 34
Aaron-Mil 34

Triples
Ashburn-Phi 13
Virdon-Pit 11
Mays-SF 11
Banks-Chi 11

Home Runs
Banks-Chi 47
Thomas-Pit 35
Robinson-Cin 31
Mathews-Mil 31
Aaron-Mil 30

Total Bases
Banks-Chi 379
Mays-SF 350
Aaron-Mil 328
Cepeda-SF 309
Thomas-Pit 297

Runs Batted In
Banks-Chi 129
Thomas-Pit 109
H.Anderson-Phi 97
Mays-SF 96
Cepeda-SF 96

Runs Produced
Banks-Chi 201
Mays-SF 188
Aaron-Mil 174
Boyer-StL 168
Thomas-Pit 163

Bases On Balls
Ashburn-Phi 97
Temple-Cin 91
Mathews-Mil 85
Cunningham-StL 82

Batting Average
Ashburn-Phi .350
Mays-SF .347
Musial-StL .337
Aaron-Mil .326
Skinner-Pit .321

On Base Percentage
Ashburn-Phi .441
Musial-StL .426
Mays-SF .423
Temple-Cin .406
Skinner-Pit .390

Slugging Average
Banks-Chi .614
Mays-SF .583
Aaron-Mil .546
Thomas-Pit .528
Musial-StL .528

Production
Mays-SF 1.006
Banks-Chi .984
Musial-StL .953
Aaron-Mil .933
H.Anderson-Phi .900

Adjusted Production
Mays-SF 167
Banks-Chi 157
Aaron-Mil 157
Musial-StL 145
H.Anderson-Phi 137

Batter Runs
Mays-SF 55.3
Banks-Chi 45.7
Aaron-Mil 37.0
Musial-StL 36.7
Ashburn-Phi 36.5

Adjusted Batter Runs
Mays-SF 58.4
Banks-Chi 47.7
Aaron-Mil 46.9
Ashburn-Phi 38.2
Musial-StL 32.8

Clutch Hitting Index
H.Anderson-Phi 111
Fernandez-Phi 110
Long-Chi 103
Spencer-SF 103
Banks-Chi 103

Runs Created
Mays-SF 152
Banks-Chi 135
Ashburn-Phi 129
Aaron-Mil 121
Skinner-Pit 102

Total Average
Mays-SF 1.110
Banks-Chi .984
Musial-StL .970
Ashburn-Phi .929
Aaron-Mil .916

Stolen Bases
Mays-SF 31
Ashburn-Phi 30
T.Taylor-Chi 21
Blasingame-StL 20
Gilliam-LA 18

Stolen Base Average
Mays-SF 83.8
Blasingame-StL 80.0
T.Taylor-Chi 77.8
Ashburn-Phi 71.4
Gilliam-LA 62.1

Stolen Base Runs
Mays-SF 5.7
Zimmer-LA 3.0
Blasingame-StL 3.0
T.Taylor-Chi 2.7
Robinson-Cin 2.4

Fielding Runs
Zimmer-LA 32.6
Clemente-Pit 25.2
Boyer-StL 23.4
Ashburn-Phi 22.1
Flood-StL 19.3

Total Player Rating
Mays-SF 7.2
Banks-Chi 5.7
Ashburn-Phi 5.3
Aaron-Mil 4.1
Boyer-StL 4.0

Wins
Spahn-Mil 22
Friend-Pit 22
Burdette-Mil 20
Roberts-Phi 17
Purkey-Cin 17

Win Percentage
Spahn-Mil .667
Burdette-Mil .667
Friend-Pit .611
Purkey-Cin .607
Antonelli-SF .552

Games
Elston-Chi 69
Klippstein-Cin-LA 57
Face-Pit 57
Hobbie-Chi 55

Complete Games
Spahn-Mil 23
Roberts-Phi 21
Burdette-Mil 19
Purkey-Cin 17
Friend-Pit 16

Shutouts
Willey-Mil 4
Witt-Pit 3
Purkey-Cin 3
Jay-Mil 3
Burdette-Mil 3

Saves
Face-Pit 20
Labine-LA 14
Farrell-Phi 11

Innings Pitched
Spahn-Mil 290.0
Burdette-Mil 275.1
Friend-Pit 274.0
Roberts-Phi 269.2

Fewest Hits/Game
Jones-StL 7.34
Koufax-LA 7.49
Miller-SF 7.91
Spahn-Mil 7.98
Brosnan-Chi-StL 7.99

Fewest BB/Game
Burdette-Mil 1.63
Roberts-Phi 1.70
Law-Pit 1.73
Purkey-Cin 1.76
Newcombe-LA-Cin 1.93

Strikeouts
Jones-StL 225
Spahn-Mil 150
Podres-LA 143
Antonelli-SF 143
Friend-Pit 135

Strikeouts/Game
Jones-StL 8.10
Koufax-LA 7.43
Drott-Chi 6.83
Podres-LA 6.12
Miller-SF 5.88

Ratio
Spahn-Mil 10.40
Miller-SF 10.43
Roberts-Phi 10.78
Burdette-Mil 10.92
Purkey-Cin 11.23

Earned Run Average
Miller-SF 2.47
Jones-StL 2.88
Burdette-Mil 2.91
Spahn-Mil 3.07
Roberts-Phi 3.24

Adjusted ERA
Miller-SF 154
Jones-StL 143
Roberts-Phi 122
Brosnan-Chi-StL 121
Burdette-Mil 121

Opponents' Batting Avg.
Koufax-LA .220
Jones-StL .223
Miller-SF .233
Spahn-Mil .237
Antonelli-SF .239

Opponents' On Base Pct.
Miller-SF .286
Spahn-Mil .288
Roberts-Phi .294
Burdette-Mil .301
Purkey-Cin .306

Starter Runs
Burdette-Mil 31.9
Miller-SF 29.9
Jones-StL 29.8
Spahn-Mil 28.3
Witt-Pit 27.5

Adjusted Starter Runs
Jones-StL 34.7
Miller-SF 27.1
Witt-Pit 26.5
Roberts-Phi 21.6
Burdette-Mil 18.7

Clutch Pitching Index
Haddix-Cin 116
Newcombe-LA-Cin 115
Mizell-StL 114
Miller-SF 110
Podres-LA 109

Relief Runs
Elston-Chi 11.6
Face-Pit 9.9
Henry-Chi 9.7
Schmidt-Cin 8.4
Porterfield-Pit 6.5

Adjusted Relief Runs
Elston-Chi 11.2
Schmidt-Cin 9.9
Henry-Chi 9.4
Face-Pit 9.1
Farrell-Phi 6.4

Relief Ranking
Elston-Chi 20.3
Farrell-Phi 12.0
Face-Pit 11.7
Henry-Chi 10.9
Schmidt-Cin 10.3

Total Pitcher Index
Spahn-Mil 3.9
Burdette-Mil 3.1
Jones-StL 2.9
Roberts-Phi 2.5
Witt-Pit 2.5

Total Baseball Ranking
Mays-SF 7.2
Banks-Chi 5.7
Ashburn-Phi 5.3
Aaron-Mil 4.1
Boyer-StL 4.0

January 15 In a deal worth over a million dollars, the Yankees announce that they will televise 140 games in the 1958 season. Six days later, the Phillies agree to televise 78 games into the New York City area.

January 30 Commissioner Ford Frick announces that players and coaches, rather than the fans, will vote for the All-Star teams this year.

February 6 Ted Williams signs with the Red Sox for $135,000, making him the highest paid player in major league history.

March 11 Starting this season, AL batters will be required to wear batting helmets.

April 23 In an ongoing dispute, a Chicago Court orders Mrs. Dorothy Comiskey Rigney to distribute stock from her mother's estate, so she can not effectively bar her brother Charles A. Comiskey from sitting on the White Sox Board.

April 30 Ted Williams becomes the tenth major league player to get 1,000 extra-base hits.

June 2 Brooks Robinson, in a 2-1 Orioles loss to the Washington Senators, hits into the first of his record four triple plays.

July 8 The AL edges the NL, 4–3, in the All-Star Game played at Baltimore's Memorial Stadium. The Yankees' Gil McDougald singles to score Boston's Frank Malzone with the deciding run. Billy O'Dell of Baltimore pitches perfect ball for three innings and gets the save in the first All-Star Game played without an extra-base hit.

August 27 Owner Clark Griffith says that the Senators will probably accept a good offer from Minneapolis/St. Paul, if one is made. President Dwight D. Eisenhower says that the Senators should improve the team and stay in Washington, DC.

August 28 White Sox second baseman Nellie Fox sets a record for consecutive games without striking out (98).

September 14 The Yankees win their 24th pennant, and ninth under Casey

Stengel. This ties Casey for first with Connie Mack for the most AL pennants won.

September 20 Orioles pitcher Hoyt Wilhelm, in a rare start, pitches a 1–0 no-hitter, the first in O's history, against Don Larsen of the Yankees. The Orioles acquired Wilhelm in August for the $20,000 waiver price. The win, Wilhelm's first major league complete game, improves his record to 3-10. The winning margin is Gus Triandos's 30th home run.

October 8 The Yankees win the World Series on Moose Skowron's three-run homer off Lew Burdette in the eighth that puts the game on ice 6-2.

November 12 The Yankees' Bob Turley wins the Cy Young Award, gathering five votes to four for last year's winner, Warren Spahn.

November 26 The AL MVP is Boston slugger Jackie Jensen, winning over New York's Bob Turley and Cleveland's Rocky Colavito.

BALTIMORE		BOSTON		CHICAGO		CLEVELAND		DETROIT		KANSAS CITY		NEW YORK		WASHINGTON	
M	P.Richards	M	P.Higgins	M	A.Lopez	M	B.Bragan	M	J.Tighe	M	H.Craft	M	C.Stengel	M	C.Lavagetto
1B	B.Boyd	1B	D.Gernert	1B	E.Torgeson	M	J.Gordon	M	B.Norman	1B	V.Power	1B	B.Skowron	1B	N.Zauchin
2B	B.Gardner	2B	P.Runnels	2B	N.Fox	1B	M.Vernon	1B	G.Harris	2B	M.Baxes	2B	G.McDougald	2B	K.Aspromonte
SS	W.Miranda	SS	D.Buddin	SS	L.Aparicio	2B	B.Avila	2B	F.Bolling	SS	J.DeMaestri	SS	T.Kubek	SS	R.Bridges
3B	B.Robinson	3B	F.Malzone	3B	B.Goodman	SS	B.Hunter	SS	B.Martin	3B	H.Lopez	3B	A.Carey	3B	E.Yost
LF	G.Woodling	LF	T.Williams	LF	J.Rivera	3B	B.Harrell	3B	R.Bertoia	LF	B.Cerv	LF	N.Siebern	LF	R.Sievers
CF	J.Busby	CF	J.Piersall	CF	J.Landis	LF	M.Minoso	LF	C.Maxwell	CF	B.Tuttle	CF	M.Mantle	CF	A.Pearson
RF	A.Pilarcik	RF	J.Jensen	RF	A.Smith	CF	L.Doby	CF	H.Kuenn	RF	R.Maris	RF	H.Bauer	RF	J.Lemon
C	G.Triandos	C	S.White	C	S.Lollar	RF	R.Colavito	RF	A.Kaline	C	H.Chiti	C	Y.Berra	C	C.Courtney
						C	R.Nixon	C	R.Wilson						
S	F.Castleman	O	G.Stephens	3S	S.Esposito					O	B.Martyn	CO	E.Howard	O	N.Chrisley
O	B.Nieman	C	L.Berberet	3O	B.Phillips	2S	B.Moran	S	C.Veal	3C	H.Smith	3	J.Lumpe	23	H.Plews
O3	D.Williams	2	T.Lepcio	1	R.Boone	31	V.Power	3	O.Virgil	13	P.Ward	23	B.Richardson	S2	O.Alvarez
1	J.Marshall	O	M.Keough	C	E.Battey	O	G.Geiger	O	J.Groth	1O	H.Simpson	1	M.Throneberry	1	J.Becquer
C	J.Ginsberg	S	B.Klaus	O	D.Mueller	C	R.Maris	O	J.Hegan	C	F.House	O	E.Slaughter	O	E.FitzGerald
O	L.Green	2S	B.Consolo	1	R.Jackson	C	D.Brown	O	G.Zernial	3S	C.Carrasquel	O	H.Simpson	O	F.Throneberry
O	J.Taylor	C	P.Daley	O	T.Francona	S3	C.Carrasquel	1	R.Boone	O	W.Held	/C	D.Johnson	2	B.Malkmus
O	W.Tasby	O	B.Renna	O	J.Callison	31	P.Ward	O	T.Francona	O1	W.Herzog	O	B.DelGreco	O	S.Korcheck
/1	B.Hale	/2	K.Aspromonte	1	W.Dropo	OS	W.Held	C	C.Lau	S	B.Hunter	/2	F.Brickell	O	B.Allison
S	J.Adair			O	T.Beard	3	R.Jackson	O	B.Hazle	/1	K.Hadley			/3	H.Killebrew
S	R.Hansen	P	T.Brewer	/O	J.McAnany	C	J.Porter	/O	L.Skizas	/2	L.Klimchock	P	B.Turley	/2	J.Schaive
/O	C.Oertel	P	F.Sullivan	/O	N.Cash	3	E.Averill	S	M.Bolling	/O	D.Melton	P	W.Ford	/2	J.Snyder
/O	L.Burke	P	I.Delock	/C	J.Romano	O	C.Hardy	/O	B.Taylor	/O	J.Small	P	A.Ditmar	/C	L.Berberet
H	B.Hamric	P	D.Sisler	/C	C.Lindstrom	/1	V.Wertz	/C	T.Thompson	/2	M.Graff	P	B.Shantz	/O	W.Herzog
/S	E.Miksis	P	M.Fornieles	H	L.Moss	H	H.Naragon	/O	G.Alusik			P	J.Kucks		
/C	F.Zupo	RP	M.Wall			/2	L.Raines	2	S.Boros	P	R.Terry	P	R.Duren	P	P.Ramos
		RP	L.Kiely	P	D.Donovan	/O	R.Graber	H	B.Osborne	P	N.Garver	RP	Z.Monroe	P	R.Kemmerer
P	J.Harshman			P	B.Pierce	/3	F.Hatfield	/C	J.Feller	P	R.Herbert			P	C.Pascual
P	B.O'Dell	P	B.Smith	P	E.Wynn			/O	G.Thomas	P	J.Urban	P	D.Larsen	P	H.Griggs
P	A.Portocarrero	P	T.Bowsfield	P	J.Wilson	P	C.McLish			P	B.Grim	P	D.Maas	P	V.Valentinetti
P	M.Pappas	P	B.Monbouquette	P	R.Moore	P	M.Grant	P	F.Lary	RP	T.Gorman	P	T.Sturdivant	RP	T.Clevenger
P	C.Johnson	P	F.Baumann	RP	G.Staley	P	R.Narleski	RP	P.Foytack	RP	D.Tomanek	P	V.Trucks	RP	D.Hyde
RP	G.Zuverink	P	W.Nixon	RP	B.Shaw	P	G.Bell	P	J.Bunning	RP	B.Daley	/P	S.Maglie		
RP	K.Lehman	P	B.Byerly			P	D.Ferrarese	P	B.Hoeft			/P	M.Dickson	P	C.Stobbs
RP	C.Beamon	/P	A.Schroll	P	B.Latman	RP	D.Mossi	P	H.Moford	P	M.Dickson	P	B.Grim	P	J.Romonosky
		/P	D.Wilson	P	T.Qualters			RP	H.Aguirre	P	D.Maas	/P	J.James	P	A.Cicotte
P	B.Loes	/P	B.Porterfield	P	T.Lown	P	H.Wilhelm	RP	T.Morgan	P	W.Craddock			P	J.Constable
P	H.Brown	/P	J.Casale	P	B.Fischer	P	H.Woodeshick			/P	A.Kellner			P	B.Byerly
/P	H.Wilhelm	/P	G.Susce	P	B.Keegan	P	D.Tomanek	P	G.Susce	/P	B.Davis			/P	B.Fischer
/P	J.Walker			/P	D.Rudolph	P	H.Score	P	A.Cicotte	P	W.Burnette			/P	R.Lumenti
/P	L.Sleater			/P	S.McIlwain	P	B.Kelly	P	B.Fischer	P	V.Trucks			/P	B.Wiesler
/P	R.Moeller			/P	H.Trosky	P	B.Lemon	P	B.Shaw	P	H.Reed			/P	J.Spring
				/P	D.Howell	P	M.Martin	/P	H.Wehmeier	/P	G.Cox			/P	J.Albanese
				/P	J.McDonald	/P	D.Brodowski	/P	V.Valentinetti	/P	J.Tsitouris				
						/P	C.Churn	/P	J.Presko	/P	C.Duser				
						/P	J.Constable	/P	G.Spencer	/P	K.Johnson				
						/P	S.Ridzik	/P	L.Sleater						
						/P	M.Garcia	/P	D.Lee						
								/P	M.McDermott						

TEAM	G	W	L	PCT	GB	R	OR	AB	H	2B	3B	HR	BB	SO	AVG	OBP	SLG	PRO	PRO+	BR	/A	PF	CHI	RC	SB	CS	SBA	SBR
NY	155	92	62	.597		759	577	5294	1418	212	39	164	537	822	.268	.338	.416	.754	117	88	115	96	102	746	48	32	60	-5
CHI	155	82	72	.532	10	634	615	5249	1348	191	42	101	518	669	.257	.329	.367	.696	99	-13	0	98	99	647	101	33	75	11
BOS	155	79	75	.513	13	697	691	5218	1335	229	30	155	638	820	.256	.340	.400	.740	102	70	21	107	96	708	29	22	57	-5
CLE	153	77	76	.503	14.5	694	635	5201	1340	210	31	161	494	819	.258	.327	.403	.730	109	38	55	98	102	677	50	49	51	-14
DET	154	77	77	.500	15	659	606	5194	1384	229	41	109	463	678	.266	.329	.389	.718	96	20	-28	107	100	657	48	32	60	-5
BAL	154	74	79	.484	17.5	521	575	5111	1233	195	19	108	483	731	.241	.310	.350	.660	92	-85	-56	95	96	546	33	35	49	-11
KC	156	73	81	.474	19	642	713	5261	1297	196	50	138	542	747	.240	.309	.381	.690	93	-40	-51	102	106	601	22	36	38	-15
WAS	156	61	93	.396	31	553	747	5156	1240	161	38	121	477	751	.240	.309	.357	.666	91	-78	-67	98	99	555	22	41	35	-18
TOT	619					5159		41684	10595	1623	290	1057	4062	6037	.254	.324	.383	.707							353	280	56	-62

TEAM	CG	SH	SV	IP	H	H/G	HR	BB	SO	RAT	ERA	ERA+	OAV	OOB	PR	/A	PF	CPI	FA	E	DP	FW	PW	BW	SBW	DIF
NY	53	21	33	1379	1201	7.8	116	557	796	11.8	3.22	110	.235	.315	85	48	94	103	.978	128	182	-.1	5.0	11.9	.3	-2.0
CHI	55	15	25	1389²	1296	8.4	152	515	751	11.8	3.61	101	.250	.320	25	5	97	104	.981	114	160	.7	.5	.0	1.9	1.9
BOS	44	5	28	1380	1396	9.1	121	521	695	12.7	3.92	102	.264	.334	-23	13	106	101	.976	145	172	-1.1	1.3	2.2	.3	-.7
CLE	51	2	20	1373¹	1283	8.4	123	604	766	12.5	3.73	98	.249	.331	6	-12	97	101	.974	152	171	-1.5	-1.2	5.7	-.6	-1.8
DET	59	8	19	1357²	1294	8.6	133	437	797	11.8	3.59	112	.252	.316	26	67	107	101	.982	106	140	1.1	6.9	-2.9	.3	-5.4
BAL	55	15	28	1369²	1277	8.4	106	403	749	11.3	3.40	106	.249	.308	57	30	95	97	.980	114	159	.6	3.1	-5.8	-.3	-.1
KC	42	9	25	1398¹	1405	9.0	150	467	721	12.2	4.15	94	.262	.324	-59	-38	104	95	.979	125	166	.1	-3.9	-5.3	-.7	5.8
WAS	28	6	28	1376²	1443	9.4	156	558	762	13.3	4.53	84	.272	.344	-116	-110	101	98	.980	118	163	.5	-11.4	-6.9	-1.1	2.9
TOT	387	81	206	11024		8.6				12.2	3.77		.254	.324					.979	1002	1313					

Runs		Hits		Doubles		Triples		Home Runs		Total Bases	
Mantle-NY	127	Fox-Chi	187	Kuenn-Det	39	Power-KC-Cle	10	Mantle-NY	42	Mantle-NY	307
Runnels-Bos	103	Malzone-Bos	185	Power-KC-Cle	37	Tuttle-KC	9	Colavito-Cle	41	Cerv-KC	305
Power-KC-Cle	98	Power-KC-Cle	184	Kaline-Det	34	Lemon-Was	9	Sievers-Was	39	Colavito-Cle	303
Minoso-Cle	94	Runnels-Bos	183	Runnels-Bos	32	Aparicio-Chi	9	Cerv-KC	38	Sievers-Was	299
Cerv-KC	93	Kuenn-Det	179	Jensen-Bos	31	Harris-Det	8	Jensen-Bos	35	Jensen-Bos	293

Runs Batted In		Runs Produced		Bases On Balls		Batting Average		On Base Percentage		Slugging Average	
Jensen-Bos	122	Mantle-NY	182	Mantle-NY	129	Williams-Bos	.328	Williams-Bos	.462	Colavito-Cle	.620
Colavito-Cle	113	Jensen-Bos	170	Jensen-Bos	99	Runnels-Bos	.322	Mantle-NY	.445	Cerv-KC	.592
Sievers-Was	108	Power-KC-Cle	162	Williams-Bos	98	Kuenn-Det	.319	Runnels-Bos	.418	Mantle-NY	.592
Cerv-KC	104	Cerv-KC	159	Runnels-Bos	87	Kaline-Det	.313	Colavito-Cle	.407	Williams-Bos	.584
Mantle-NY	97			Colavito-Cle	84	Power-KC-Cle	.312	Jensen-Bos	.398	Sievers-Was	.544

Production		Adjusted Production		Batter Runs		Adjusted Batter Runs		Clutch Hitting Index		Runs Created	
Williams-Bos	1.046	Mantle-NY	189	Mantle-NY	64.2	Mantle-NY	69.2	Courtney-NY	131	Mantle-NY	147
Mantle-NY	1.036	Colavito-Cle	183	Williams-Bos	53.6	Colavito-Cle	55.7	Lollar-Chi	127	Colavito-Cle	122
Colavito-Cle	1.027	Williams-Bos	174	Colavito-Cle	52.8	Williams-Bos	46.3	F.Bolling-Det	117	Jensen-Bos	120
Cerv-KC	.964	Cerv-KC	158	Jensen-Bos	42.7	Cerv-KC	38.8	Harris-Det	116	Williams-Bos	112
Jensen-Bos	.933	Sievers-Was	148	Cerv-KC	40.7	Jensen-Bos	35.0	Skowron-NY	116	Runnels-Bos	107

Total Average		Stolen Bases		Stolen Base Average		Stolen Base Runs		Fielding Runs		Total Player Rating	
Mantle-NY	1.208	Aparicio-Chi	29	Rivera-Chi	87.5	Kaline-Det	5.1	Kaline-Det	23.0	Mantle-NY	6.5
Williams-Bos	1.163	Rivera-Chi	21	Mantle-NY	85.7	Rivera-Chi	4.5	Kubek-NY	20.0	Cerv-KC	5.1
Colavito-Cle	1.078	Landis-Chi	19	Aparicio-Chi	82.9	Mantle-NY	3.6	Cerv-KC	20.0	Colavito-Cle	5.0
Jensen-Bos	.980	Mantle-NY	18	Landis-Chi	73.1	Wilson-Det	3.0	Malzone-Bos	16.6	Runnels-Bos	3.8
Cerv-KC	.947	Minoso-Cle	14					Kuenn-Det	15.1	Kaline-Det	3.6

Wins		Win Percentage		Games		Complete Games		Shutouts		Saves	
Turley-NY	21	Turley-NY	.750	Clevenger-Was	55	Turley-NY	19	Ford-NY	7	Duren-NY	20
Pierce-Chi	17	McLish-Cle	.667	Tomanek-Cle-KC	54	Pierce-Chi	19	Turley-NY	6	Hyde-Was	18
McLish-Cle	16	Pierce-Chi	.607	Hyde-Was	53	Lary-Det	19	Wynn-Chi	4	Kiely-Bos	12
Lary-Det	16	Portocarrero-Bal	.577	Wall-Bos	52	Harshman-Bal	17	Ramos-Was	4	Wall-Bos	10
		Foytack-Det	.536					Donovan-Chi	4		

Innings Pitched		Fewest Hits/Game		Fewest BB/Game		Strikeouts		Strikeouts/Game		Ratio	
Lary-Det	260.1	Turley-NY	6.53	Donovan-Chi	1.92	Wynn-Chi	179	Pascual-Was	7.41	Ford-NY	9.81
Ramos-Was	259.1	Bell-Cle	6.97	O'Dell-Bal	2.07	Bunning-Det	177	Bunning-Det	7.25	Pierce-Chi	9.96
Donovan-Chi	248.0	Ford-NY	7.14	Sullivan-Bos	2.21	Turley-NY	168	Wynn-Chi	6.72	Portocarrero-Bal	10.25
Turley-NY	245.1	Pierce-Chi	7.49	Lary-Det	2.35	Harshman-Bal	161	Turley-NY	6.16	O'Dell-Bal	10.41
Pierce-Chi	245.0	Portocarrero-Bal	7.61	Pierce-Chi	2.42	Pascual-Was	146	Harshman-Bal	6.13	Harshman-Bal	10.74

Earned Run Average		Adjusted ERA		Opponents' Batting Avg.		Opponents' On Base Pct.		Starter Runs		Adjusted Starter Runs	
Ford-NY	2.01	Ford-NY	176	Turley-NY	.206	Ford-NY	.276	Ford-NY	42.9	Ford-NY	37.1
Pierce-Chi	2.68	Lary-Det	139	Bell-Cle	.213	Pierce-Chi	.280	Pierce-Chi	29.6	Lary-Det	32.8
Harshman-Bal	2.89	Pierce-Chi	136	Ford-NY	.217	Portocarrero-Bal	.286	Lary-Det	25.0	Pierce-Chi	26.0
Lary-Det	2.90	Harshman-Bal	124	Pierce-Chi	.227	O'Dell-Bal	.288	Harshman-Bal	23.0	Wilhelm-Cle-Bal	18.9
O'Dell-Bal	2.97	McLish-Cle	122	Grant-Cle	.228	Harshman-Bal	.294	Turley-NY	21.7	Harshman-Bal	18.4

Clutch Pitching Index		Relief Runs		Adjusted Relief Runs		Relief Ranking		Total Pitcher Index		Total Baseball Ranking	
McLish-Cle	120	Hyde-Was	23.1	Hyde-Was	23.7	Hyde-Was	36.2	Ford-NY	3.9	Mantle-NY	6.5
Ford-NY	117	Duren-NY	14.7	Duren-NY	12.7	Duren-NY	22.6	Hyde-Was	3.9	Cerv-KC	5.1
Pierce-Chi	114	Kiely-Bos	6.9	Kiely-Bos	9.1	Kiely-Bos	10.1	Lary-Det	3.6	Colavito-Cle	5.0
Lary-Det	113	Staley-Chi	5.7	Morgan-Det	6.1	Wall-Bos	7.5	Harshman-Bal	3.4	Ford-NY	3.9
Wilson-Chi	110	Morgan-Det	4.2	Wall-Bos	4.9	Morgan-Det	6.4	Pierce-Chi	2.8	Hyde-Was	3.9

February 1 Zack Wheat, Dodger favorite of the teens and twenties, is unanimously elected to the Hall of Fame by the 11-member veterans committee.

May 7 The Los Angeles Coliseum is jammed by 93,103 on "Roy Campanella Night" for an exhibition game between the Dodgers and the New York Yankees. This is the largest crowd to see a game featuring major leagues.

May 26 In a singular performance, Harvey Haddix of the Pirates pitches a perfect game against Milwaukee for 12 innings, only to lose in the 13th. Felix Mantilla opens the last inning by reaching base on an error. A sacrifice and an intentional walk to Hank Aaron bring up Joe Adcock, who hits one out of the park in right-center field for an apparent 3-0 victory. Aaron pulls a "Merkle," leaving the field, and Adcock passes him on the basepaths. Both are called out as Mantilla scores. Lew Burdette goes all the way for his eighth win, scattering 12 hits.

June 30 In Chicago, two balls are in play at the same time. On a wild pitch from Bob Anderson, Stan Musial draws a walk. As the pitch gets by catcher Sammy Taylor, Musial tries for second

base. In what can only be described as a reflex action, umpire Vic Delmore puts another ball in play by mistake. Taylor promptly throws the ball into center field. Third baseman Al Dark, who chased down the original ball, throws to shortstop Ernie Banks, who tags out a confused Musial. After a 10-minute conference, the umpires agree that Musial is out. Delmore will be fired because of the boner.

July 7 The NL defeats the AL, 5–4, in the All-Star Game at Forbes Field in Pittsburgh. Willie Mays knocks in Henry Aaron with the deciding run. Don Drysdale pitches perfect ball the first three innings.

July 30 In his major league debut, Willie McCovey goes 4-for-4 with two triples off Robin Roberts to lead the Giants to a 7-2 win over the Phils. McCovey was hitting .372 with 29 home runs at Phoenix when promoted.

August 18 Branch Rickey resigns as chairman of the Pirates to become president of the Continental League, which never plays a game.

August 31 Sandy Koufax breaks Dizzy Dean's NL mark and ties Bob Feller's

major league record of 18 strikeouts in a game against the Giants as 82,974 fans watch.

September 27 The Braves and Dodgers finish in a tie (86-68), with the Giants a close third (83-71).

September 29 The Dodgers win Game two of the playoff 6-5, and take the NL pennant. Los Angeles overcomes a 5-2, ninth-inning deficit to tie the game; they win it in the 12th when Gil Hodges scores from second on Felix Mantilla's off-balance heave past first on a difficult chance on Carl Furillo's grounder.

October 8 The Los Angeles Dodgers win 9-3 to take the Series in Chicago, again behind Larry Sherry, in relief of Johnny Podres. Each Dodger receives a record $11,231 winning share. The White Sox get a record $7,275 for losing.

November 4 "Mr. Cub" Ernie Banks wins his second MVP award in a row on the strength of his 45 home runs and 143 RBI. Eddie Mathews finishes second.

November 17 Giants slugger Willie McCovey is the NL Rookie of the Year. McCovey gets all 24 votes to make him the second Giant in a row to win the award unanimously.

	CHICAGO		CINCINNATI		LOS ANGELES		MILWAUKEE		PHILADELPHIA		PITTSBURGH		SAN FRANCISCO		ST.LOUIS
M	B.Scheffing	M	M.Smith	M	W.Alston	M	F.Haney	M	E.Sawyer	M	D.Murtaugh	M	B.Rigney	M	S.Hemus
1B	D.Long	M	F.Hutchinson	1B	G.Hodges	1B	J.Adcock	1B	E.Bouchee	1B	D.Stuart	1B	O.Cepeda	1B	S.Musial
2B	T.Taylor	1B	F.Robinson	2B	C.Neal	2B	F.Mantilla	2B	S.Anderson	2B	B.Mazeroski	2B	D.Spencer	2B	D.Blasingame
SS	E.Banks	2B	J.Temple	SS	D.Zimmer	SS	J.Logan	SS	J.Koppe	SS	D.Groat	SS	E.Bressoud	SS	A.Grammas
3B	A.Dark	SS	E.Kasko	3B	J.Gilliam	3B	E.Mathews	3B	G.Freese	3B	D.Hoak	3B	J.Davenport	3B	K.Boyer
LF	B.Thomson	3B	W.Jones	LF	W.Moon	LF	W.Covington	LF	H.Anderson	LF	B.Skinner	LF	J.Brandt	LF	G.Cimoli
CF	G.Altman	LF	J.Lynch	CF	D.Demeter	CF	B.Bruton	CF	R.Ashburn	CF	B.Virdon	CF	W.Mays	CF	C.Flood
RF	L.Walls	CF	V.Pinson	RF	D.Snider	RF	H.Aaron	RF	W.Post	RF	R.Clemente	RF	W.Kirkland	RF	J.Cunningham
C	S.Taylor	RF	G.Bell	C	J.Roseboro	C	D.Crandall	C	C.Sawatski	C	S.Burgess	C	H.Landrith	C	H.Smith
		C	E.Bailey												
1	J.Marshall	O	R.Fairly	1	F.Torre	O1	D.Philley	O	R.Mejias	O	F.Alou	O1	B.White
O	W.Moryn	3O	F.Thomas	1O	N.Larker	2	B.Avila	3	W.Jones	1	R.Nelson	S	A.Rodgers	O	G.Oliver
C3	E.Averill	S	R.McMillan	S	M.Wills	C	A.Pafko	C	V.Thomas	C	D.Kravitz	1	W.McCovey	1	G.Crowe
O	I.Noren	C	D.Dotterer	O	J.Pignatano	O	L.Maye	S	C.Fernandez	2	D.Schofield	C	B.Schmidt	S2	W.Shannon
1O	A.Schult	O3	J.Pendleton	O	R.Repulski	2	J.O'Brien	2	H.Hanebrink	O	T.Kluszewski	O	L.Wagner	3	R.Jablonski
C	C.Neeman	1	W.Lockman	O	C.Furillo	1	M.Vernon	C	J.Lonnett	C	H.Foiles	3	D.O'Connell	OC	G.Green
3	R.Jackson	O	P.Whisenant	3	D.Gray	2	C.Wise	O	B.Bowman	/O	H.Bright	H	D.Rhodes	O	BG.Smith
2	J.Goryl	/O	J.Powers	S	B.Lillis	O	S.Lopata	S	G.Hamner	/O	H.Simpson	3	J.Pagan	S	D.Gray
O	B.Williams	1	W.Dropo	O	C.Essegian	/2	M.Roach	O	S.Drake	C	J.Christopher	C	J.Hegan	S	L.Tate
H	L.Jackson	/3	C.Cook	3	J.Baxes	/C	D.Rice	C	J.Hegan	/S	K.Hamlin	/O	H.Sauer	/O	C.Essegian
/O	C.King	/O	B.Gilbert	/O	F.Howard	2	C.Cottier	/O	J.Bolger	/1	R.Stevens	H	B.Speake	C	J.Porter
/1	B.Adams	/O	D.Ennis	/O	S.Drake	/O	J.Pisoni	H	J.Easton	/C	H.Peterson	/C	R.McCardell	C	R.Katt
/3	D.Eaddy	H	B.Thurman	H	S.Amoros	/2	J.Morgan							T.McCarver
		/S	B.Henrich	H	N.Sherry	O	E.Slaughter	P	R.Roberts	P	V.Law	P	J.Antonelli	O	D.Carmel
P	B.Anderson	R	D.Pavletich	H	T.Davis	/1	R.Boone	P	J.Owens	P	B.Friend	P	S.Jones	/2	S.Hemus
P	G.Hobbie					/O	A.Spangler	P	G.Conley	P	H.Haddix	P	M.McCormick	/O	I.Noren
P	D.Hillman	P	D.Newcombe	P	D.Drysdale	P	J.DeMerit	P	D.Cardwell	P	R.Kline	P	J.Sanford	/O	C.King
P	M.Drabowsky	P	B.Purkey	P	J.Podres	/2	R.Schoendienst	P	R.Semproch	RP	B.Daniels	RP	S.Miller	/O	J.Durham
P	A.Ceccarelli	P	J.Nuxhall	P	S.Koufax			RP	J.Meyer	P	R.Face	P	A.Worthington	H	C.O'Rourke
RP	B.Henry	P	J.O'Toole	P	R.Craig	P	W.Spahn	RP	H.Robinson						
RP	D.Elston	RP	O.Pena	P	D.McDevitt	P	L.Burdette	RP	T.Phillips	P	G.Witt	P	G.Jones	P	L.Jackson
		RP	B.Lawrence	P	C.Labine	P	B.Buhl			P	R.Blackburn	P	E.Fisher	P	V.Mizell
P	J.Buzhardt	RP	W.Schmidt	RP	A.Fowler	P	J.Jay	P	R.Gomez	/P	B.Porterfield	P	J.Shipley	P	E.Broglio
P	E.Singleton					P	J.Pizarro	P	T.Farrell	P	F.Green	P	B.Byerly	P	G.Blaylock
/P	D.Drott	P	J.Brosnan	P	S.Williams	RP	D.McMahon	P	C.Short	P	D.Gross	/P	D.Zanni	RP	L.McDaniel
P	S.Morehead	P	J.Hook	P	L.Sherry			/P	J.Hearn	P	B.Smith	/P	B.Muffett	RP	M.Bridges
/P	B.Johnson	P	T.Acker	P	J.Klippstein	P	C.Willey	P	S.Morehead	/P	A.Jackson	/P	M.Renfroe		
/P	T.Phillips	P	B.Mabe	P	C.Churn	P	B.Rush	/P	C.Simmons	/P	D.Williams	/P	C.Barclay	P	B.Gibson
/P	E.Donnelly	P	H.Jeffcoat	P	G.Snyder	P	B.Trowbridge	/P	E.Keegan	/P	D.Hall			P	B.Miller
/P	J.Schaffernoth	P	L.Arroyo	P	C.Erskine	P	B.Giggie	/P	A.Schroll	/P	P.Giel			P	D.Ricketts
/P	B.Porterfield	/P	J.Bailey	/P	F.Kipp	/P	B.Hartman	/P	F.Rodriguez	/P	J.Umbricht			P	A.Kellner
/P	M.Martin	/P	C.Osteen	/P	B.Harris									P	J.Brosnan
/P	B.Smith	/P	D.Rudolph											P	D.Stone
		/P	M.Cuellar											P	B.Duliba
														P	H.Nunn
														P	H.Jeffcoat
														P	T.Cheney
														/P	J.Urban
														/P	B.Blaylock
														/P	Bi.Smith
														/P	P.Clark
														/P	T.Hughes
														/P	M.Grissom

TEAM	G	W	L	PCT	GB	R	OR	AB	H	2B	3B	HR	BB	SO	AVG	OBP	SLG	PRO	PRO+	BR	/A	PF	CHI	RC	SB	CS	SBA	SBR
LA	156	88	68	.564		705	670	5282	1360	196	46	148	591	891	.257	.335	.396	.731	94	17	-34	107	99	706	84	51	62	-5
MIL	157	86	70	.551	2	724	623	5388	1426	216	36	177	488	765	.265	.329	.417	.746	115	32	93	92	100	729	41	14	75	4
SF	154	83	71	.539	4	705	613	5281	1377	239	35	167	473	875	.261	.324	.414	.738	105	16	32	98	101	711	81	34	70	4
PIT	155	78	76	.506	9	651	680	5369	1414	230	42	112	442	715	.263	.322	.384	.706	95	-39	-33	99	101	653	32	26	55	-6
CIN	154	74	80	.481	13	764	738	5288	1448	258	34	161	499	763	.274	.340	.427	.767	108	76	54	103	101	764	65	28	70	3
CHI	155	74	80	.481	13	673	688	5296	1321	209	44	163	498	911	.249	.319	.398	.717	98	-23	-16	99	102	673	32	19	63	-2
STL	154	71	83	.461	16	641	725	5317	1432	244	49	118	485	747	.269	.333	.400	.733	96	14	-30	106	92	699	65	53	55	-12
PHI	155	64	90	.416	23	599	725	5109	1237	196	38	113	498	858	.242	.314	.362	.676	86	-92	-101	102	105	574	39	46	46	-16
TOT	620					5462		42330	11015	1788	324	1159	3974	6525	.260	.327	.400	.727		439					271		62	-31

TEAM	CG	SH	SV	IP	H	H/G	HR	BB	SO	RAT	ERA	ERA+	OAV	OOB	PR	/A	PF	CPI	FA	E	DP	FW	PW	BW	SBW	DIF
LA	43	14	26	1411²	1317	8.4	157	614	1077	12.6	3.79	111	.247	.331	24	68	107	103	.981	114	154	1.5	6.8	-3.4	-.1	5.2
MIL	69	18	18	1400²	1406	9.0	128	429	775	11.9	3.51	101	.260	.317	68	5	90	104	.979	127	138	.8	.5	9.4	.8	-3.4
SF	52	12	23	1376¹	1279	8.4	139	500	873	11.8	3.47	110	.246	.316	74	52	97	103	.974	152	118	-.8	5.2	3.2	.8	-2.5
PIT	48	7	17	1393¹	1432	9.2	134	418	730	12.1	3.90	99	.267	.323	-7	-5	98	100	.975	154	165	-.8	-.5	-3.3	-.2	5.9
CIN	44	7	26	1357¹	1460	9.7	162	456	690	12.9	4.31	94	.275	.337	-55	-39	103	102	.978	126	157	.7	-3.9	5.4	.7	-5.9
CHI	30	11	25	1391	1337	8.7	152	519	765	12.4	4.01	98	.254	.323	-10	-10	100	96	.977	140	142	-.0	-1.0	-1.6	.2	-.5
STL	36	8	21	1363	1427	9.4	137	564	846	13.3	4.34	98	.271	.344	-59	-15	107	100	.975	146	158	-.4	-1.5	-3.0	-.8	-.2
PHI	54	8	15	1354	1357	9.0	150	474	769	12.4	4.27	96	.261	.326	-49	-25	104	93	.973	154	132	-.8	-2.5	-10.2	-1.2	1.7
TOT	376	85	171	11047¹		9.0				12.4	3.95		.260	.327					.977	1113	1164					

Runs
Pinson-Cin 131
Mays-SF 125
Mathews-Mil 118
Aaron-Mil 116
Robinson-Cin 106

Hits
Aaron-Mil 223
Pinson-Cin 205
Cepeda-SF 192
Temple-Cin 186
Mathews-Mil 182

Doubles
Pinson-Cin 47
Aaron-Mil 46
Mays-SF 43
Cimoli-StL 40

Triples
Neal-LA 11
Moon-LA 11
White-StL 9
Pinson-Cin 9
Dark-Chi 9

Home Runs
Mathews-Mil 46
Banks-Chi 45
Aaron-Mil 39
Robinson-Cin 36
Mays-SF 34

Total Bases
Aaron-Mil 400
Mathews-Mil 352
Banks-Chi 351
Mays-SF 335
Pinson-Cin 330

Runs Batted In
Banks-Chi 143
Robinson-Cin 125
Aaron-Mil 123
Bell-Cin 115
Mathews-Mil 114

Runs Produced
Aaron-Mil 200
Robinson-Cin 195
Pinson-Cin 195
Mays-SF 195
Banks-Chi 195

Bases On Balls
Gilliam-LA 96
Cunningham-StL ... 88
Moon-LA 81
Mathews-Mil 80
Ashburn-Phi 79

Batting Average
Aaron-Mil .... .355
Cunningham-StL .. .345
Cepeda-SF .... .317
Pinson-Cin .... .316
Mays-SF .... .313

On Base Percentage
Cunningham-StL... .456
Aaron-Mil .... .406
Robinson-Cin ...... .397
Moon-LA .... .396
Mathews-Mil ...... .391

Slugging Average
Aaron-Mil .... .636
Banks-Chi .... .596
Mathews-Mil ...... .593
Robinson-Cin ...... .583
Mays-SF .... .583

Production
Aaron-Mil 1.042
Mathews-Mil ...... .984
Robinson-Cin ...... .980
Banks-Chi .... .975
Mays-SF .... .967

Adjusted Production
Aaron-Mil 188
Mathews-Mil 172
Mays-SF 157
Banks-Chi 156
Robinson-Cin 152

Batter Runs
Aaron-Mil 62.8
Mathews-Mil 48.4
Banks-Chi 44.4
Robinson-Cin 44.0
Mays-SF 42.6

Adjusted Batter Runs
Aaron-Mil 75.3
Mathews-Mil 59.4
Banks-Chi 45.8
Mays-SF 45.3
Robinson-Cin 40.7

Clutch Hitting Index
Bell-Cin 134
Post-Phi 128
Mazeroski-Pit 120
Bouchee-Phi 111
Cimoli-StL 111

Runs Created
Aaron-Mil 156
Mathews-Mil 143
Mays-SF 131
Banks-Chi 126
Pinson-Cin 124

Total Average
Aaron-Mil 1.089
Mathews-Mil 1.041
Mays-SF 1.037
Robinson-Cin 1.015
Cunningham-StL .. .978

Stolen Bases
Mays-SF 27
T.Taylor-Chi 23
Gilliam-LA 23
Cepeda-SF 23
Pinson-Cin 21

Stolen Base Average
Mays-SF 87.1
Pinson-Cin 77.8
Neal-LA 73.9
T.Taylor-Chi 71.9
Cepeda-SF 71.9

Stolen Base Runs
Mays-SF 5.7
Pinson-Cin 2.7
Temple-Cin 2.4
Aaron-Mil 2.4
Cimoli-StL 2.1

Fielding Runs
Virdon-Pit 23.5
Blasingame-StL .. 20.5
Neal-LA 20.0
Pinson-Cin 19.7
H.Anderson-Phi... 18.3

Total Player Rating
Aaron-Mil 6.6
Banks-Chi 6.2
Mathews-Mil 6.2
Mays-SF 5.0
Pinson-Cin 3.9

Wins
Spahn-Mil 21
S.Jones-SF 21
Burdette-Mil 21
Antonelli-SF 19

Win Percentage
Face-Pit .... .947
Law-Pit .... .667
Antonelli-SF .... .655
Buhl-Mil .... .625

Games
Henry-Chi 65
Elston-Chi 65
McDaniel-StL 62
McMahon-Mil 60
Miller-SF 59

Complete Games
Spahn-Mil 21
Law-Pit 20
Burdette-Mil 20
Roberts-Phi 19

Shutouts
Spahn-Mil 4
S.Jones-SF 4
Drysdale-LA 4
Craig-LA 4
Burdette-Mil 4
Buhl-Mil 4
Antonelli-SF 4

Saves
McMahon-Mil 15
McDaniel-StL 15
Elston-Chi 13
Henry-Chi 12

Innings Pitched
Spahn-Mil 292.0
Burdette-Mil 289.2
Antonelli-SF 282.0
S.Jones-SF 270.2
Drysdale-LA 270.2

Fewest Hits/Game
Haddix-Pit 7.58
S.Jones-SF 7.71
Hobbie-Chi 7.85
Drysdale-LA 7.88
Antonelli-SF 7.88

Fewest BB/Game
Newcombe-Cin ... 1.09
Burdette-Mil 1.18
Roberts-Phi 1.22
Purkey-Cin 1.78
Law-Pit 1.79

Strikeouts
Drysdale-LA 242
S.Jones-SF 209
Koufax-LA 173
Antonelli-SF 165
McCormick-SF 151

Strikeouts/Game
Drysdale-LA 8.05
S.Jones-SF 6.95
Podres-LA 6.69
Broglio-StL 6.60
McCormick-SF 6.02

Ratio
Haddix-Pit 9.63
Newcombe-Cin 10.05
Conley-Phi 10.15
Law-Pit 10.15
Antonelli-SF 10.40

Earned Run Average
S.Jones-SF 2.83
Miller-SF 2.84
Buhl-Mil 2.86
Spahn-Mil 2.96
Law-Pit 2.98

Adjusted ERA
Conley-Phi 137
S.Jones-SF 135
Miller-SF 134
Law-Pit 130
Jackson-StL 128

Opponents' Batting Avg.
S.Jones-SF .... .228
Haddix-Pit .... .228
Antonelli-SF .... .233
Drysdale-LA .... .233
Conley-Phi .... .235

Opponents' On Base Pct.
Haddix-Pit .... .273
Newcombe-Cin .... .280
Conley-Phi .... .281
Law-Pit .... .282
Antonelli-SF .... .286

Starter Runs
S.Jones-SF 33.7
Spahn-Mil 32.1
Craig-LA 32.0
Law-Pit 28.7
Antonelli-SF 26.7

Adjusted Starter Runs
Craig-LA 36.7
S.Jones-SF 29.6
Jackson-StL 26.6
Law-Pit 26.3
Drysdale-LA 23.1

Clutch Pitching Index
Miller-SF 134
Buhl-Mil 120
Spahn-Mil 105
Jackson-StL 104
S.Jones-SF 104

Relief Runs
Miller-SF 20.5
Henry-Chi 18.9
Face-Pit 12.9
McMahon-Mil 12.4
Elston-Chi 6.8

Adjusted Relief Runs
Henry-Chi 18.9
Miller-SF 18.0
Face-Pit 12.1
McMahon-Mil 8.7
Meyer-Phi 7.7

Relief Ranking
Henry-Chi 25.3
Face-Pit 25.1
Miller-SF 16.4
Elston-Chi 13.4
McDaniel-StL 12.5

Total Pitcher Index
Newcombe-Cin 3.5
S.Jones-SF 3.4
Craig-LA 3.2
Drysdale-LA 3.0
Spahn-Mil 2.8

Total Baseball Ranking
Aaron-Mil 6.6
Banks-Chi 6.2
Mathews-Mil 6.2
Mays-SF 5.0
Pinson-Cin 3.9

January 31 Joe Cronin, former Senators and Red Sox shortstop, becomes president of the AL.

March 10 Dorothy Comiskey Rigney, granddaughter of the Old Roman, sells her 54 percent ownership in the White Sox to Bill Veeck's syndicate for $2.7 million. Brother Chuck fails in his attempt to match or improve the bid. Comiskey control of the franchise ends after 60 years.

April 9 In the fifth inning against Washington, the Orioles become the first team in history to turn a triple play on Opening Day. Vice President Richard Nixon, a righthander, substitutes for President Dwight D. Eisenhower and watches the Senators win 9–2.

May 1 White Sox pitcher Early Wynn, 39, pitches a one-hitter for a 1–0 victory over Boston. He fans 14 and belts a home run in the eighth for the only run.

May 11 At Yankee Stadium, Yogi Berra's errorless streak of 148 games comes to an end when he blunders in a 7–6 loss to the Indians.

May 26 At Comiskey Park, a helicopter lands behind second base before a Sox-Indians game, and four midgets dressed as spacemen jump out. Capturing 5'9"

Nellie Fox and 5'10" Luis Aparicio, the spacemen, led by Eddie Gaedel, present the two with ray guns.

June 10 Rocky Colavito hits four consecutive home runs in Baltimore's Memorial Stadium to lead the Indians to an 11–8 win. Colavito joins Lou Gehrig and Bobby Lowe as the only major league players to hit four consecutive four-baggers.

July 12 NBC uses outfield TV cameras with 80-inch lenses to show the catchers' signals during a Yankee-Red Sox game. Commissioner Ford Frick requests that they halt their use.

July 21 Pumpsie Green pinch runs for the Red Sox, who become the last major league team to field a black player. The next day Green goes 0-for-3 against Early Wynn.

August 3 For the first time, there are two All-Star Games in the same year. With the managers picking the starting lineup, the AL wins this second contest 5–3, as five home runs are hit at the Los Angeles Coliseum.

September 22 The "Go-Go" White Sox clinch their first pennant in 40 years with a 4–2 win over the second-place Indians. Early Wynn gets the win, with Gerry

Staley saving the game in the ninth.

October 1 The Go-Go Sox change character at home and hammer the LA Dodgers 11-0 in the first game of the World Series, as Ted Kluszewski has two home runs and five RBI.

October 6 White Sox hurler Dick Donovan keeps the Series alive with a splendid 1-0 win over the Dodgers. Sherm Lollar's double play grounder scores the only run. The attendance mark falls for the second day in a row, as 92,706 fans jam the Coliseum.

November 12 The White Sox second baseman Nellie Fox wins the AL's MVP award. Teammates Luis Aparicio and Early Wynn finish second and third in the voting.

November 18 Outfielder Bob Allison of Washington is voted the AL Rookie of the Year. Cleveland's Jim Perry is a distant second.

December 11 The A's Arnold Johnson gives the New York Yankees an early Christmas present—Roger Maris. The Yankees acquire the slugger in a seven-player deal that sends pitcher Don Larsen, right fielder Hank Bauer, first baseman Marv Throneberry, and left fielder Norm Siebern to the Athletics.

	BALTIMORE		BOSTON		CHICAGO		CLEVELAND		DETROIT		KANSAS CITY		NEW YORK		WASHINGTON
M	P.Richards	M	P.Higgins	M	A.Lopez	M	J.Gordon	M	B.Norman	M	H.Craft	M	C.Stengel	M	C.Lavagetto
1B	B.Boyd	M	R.York	1B	E.Torgeson	1B	V.Power	M	J.Dykes	1B	K.Hadley	1B	B.Skowron	1B	R.Sievers
2B	B.Gardner	M	B.Jurges	2B	N.Fox	2B	B.Martin	1B	G.Harris	2B	W.Terwilliger	2B	B.Richardson	2B	R.Bertoia
SS	C.Carrasquel	1B	D.Gernert	SS	L.Aparicio	SS	W.Held	2B	F.Bolling	SS	J.DeMaestri	SS	T.Kubek	SS	B.Consolo
3B	B.Robinson	2B	P.Runnels	3B	B.Phillips	3B	G.Strickland	SS	R.Bridges	3B	D.Williams	3B	H.Lopez	3B	H.Killebrew
LF	G.Woodling	SS	D.Buddin	LF	A.Smith	LF	M.Minoso	3B	E.Yost	LF	B.Cerv	LF	N.Siebern	LF	J.Lemon
CF	W.Tasby	3B	F.Malzone	CF	J.Landis	CF	J.Piersall	LF	C.Maxwell	CF	B.Tuttle	CF	M.Mantle	CF	B.Allison
RF	A.Pilarcik	LF	G.Stephens	RF	J.Rivera	RF	R.Colavito	CF	A.Kaline	RF	R.Maris	RF	H.Bauer	RF	F.Throneberry
C	G.Triandos	CF	G.Geiger	C	S.Lollar	C	R.Nixon	RF	H.Kuenn	C	F.House	C	Y.Berra	C	H.Naragon
		RF	J.Jensen					C	L.Berberet						
S3	B.Klaus	C	S.White	3	B.Goodman	O1	T.Francona			2S	J.Lumpe	1C	E.Howard	1	J.Becquer
O	B.Nieman			O	J.McAnany	23	J.Baxes	C	R.Wilson	3C	H.Smith	2S	G.McDougald	S2	R.Samford
C	J.Ginsberg	O	M.Keough	C	J.Romano	C	D.Brown	S2	T.Lepcio	O	R.Snyder	1O	M.Throneberry	2S	K.Aspromonte
1	W.Dropo	1	V.Wertz	O	J.Callison	C	E.FitzGerald	C	B.Osborne	C	H.Chiti	S3	C.Boyer	O	L.Green
O	A.Pearson	O	T.Williams	1	N.Cash	1	R.Webster	1	G.Zernial	2	H.Lopez	3	A.Carey	C	C.Courtney
3	J.Finigan	2	P.Green	1	T.Kluszewski	S	G.Hamner	O	N.Chrisley	1	R.Boone	O	E.Slaughter	O	J.Porter
S3	W.Miranda	C	P.Daley	O	D.Ennis	O	C.Hardy	O	J.Groth	O	W.Herzog	C	J.Blanchard	2	A.Pearson
O	B.Shetrone	O	J.Busby	O	H.Simpson	O	C.Tanner	S	C.Veal	1	P.Ward	3	J.Lumpe	1	N.Zauchin
1	W.Lockman	2	B.Avila	3S	S.Esposito	3	G.Leek	O	L.Doby	O	Z.Bella	S	F.Brickell	C	E.FitzGerald
/1	B.Hale	S	J.Mahoney	C	E.Battey	C	H.Naragon	/3	S.Demeter	2	L.Klimchock	O	J.Pisoni	O	D.Dobbek
O	B.Avila	/O	B.Renna	O	L.Doby	O	E.Valo	/C	R.Shoop	S	R.Jablonski	/O	K.Hunt	2	J.Schaive
2	J.Adair	/O	J.Mallett	/1	R.Boone	/3	W.Jones	/C	C.Lau	/3	J.Morgan	/O	G.Windhorn	S	Z.Versalles
O	J.Taylor	/S	B.Consolo	/2	B.Moran	/2	B.Moran	H	O.Alvarez	/1	H.Simpson			C	S.Korcheck
O	L.Green	/2	H.Plews	/O	L.Skizas	/1	G.Coleman			/S	T.Carroll			/2	H.Plews
/O	F.Valentine	/C	D.Gile	/O	J.Hicks	H	D.Dillard	P	J.Bunning	R	B.Martyn	P	W.Ford	S	J.Valdivielso
/2	L.Burke	/2	T.Lepcio	/3	J.Martin	H	J.Bolger	P	P.Foytack			P	A.Ditmar	R	B.Malkmus
/S	R.Hansen	/C	H.Sullivan	H	D.Mueller	/3	R.Jackson	P	D.Mossi			P	B.Turley		
R	B.Saverine			/C	C.Carreon			P	F.Lary	P	B.Daley	P	D.Maas		
		P	T.Brewer			P	C.McLish	RP	R.Narleski	P	N.Garver	P	R.Terry	P	C.Pascual
P	H.Wilhelm	P	J.Casale	P	E.Wynn	P	G.Bell	RP	T.Morgan	P	R.Herbert	RP	J.Coates	P	R.Ramos
P	M.Pappas	P	F.Sullivan	P	B.Shaw	RP	M.Grant	RP	P.Burnside	P	J.Kucks	RP	B.Shantz	P	R.Kemmerer
P	B.O'Dell	P	B.Monbouquette	P	B.Pierce	P	H.Score			P	B.Grim	RP	R.Duren	P	B.Fischer
P	J.Walker	P	I.Delock	P	D.Donovan	P	J.Perry	P	D.Sisler	RP	R.Coleman			RP	T.Clevenger
P	H.Brown	RP	M.Fornieles	P	B.Latman	RP	M.Garcia	RP	J.Davie	RP	T.Sturdivant	P	D.Larsen	RP	H.Griggs
RP	B.Loes	RP	L.Kiely	RP	G.Staley			P	B.Schultz	RP	M.Dickson	P	E.Grba	P	C.Stobbs
RP	E.Johnson			RP	T.Lown							P	J.Bronstad		
		P	F.Baumann			P	B.Locke	/P	G.Susce	J.Tsitouris		P	G.Blaylock	/P	H.Woodeshick
P	A.Portocarrero	/P	T.Wills	P	R.Moore	P	D.Ferrarese	P	J.Harshman	/P	R.Terry	/P	T.Sturdivant	P	D.Hyde
P	J.Fisher	P	M.Wall	P	R.Arias	P	J.Harshman	/P	J.Stump	P	R.Meyer	/P	G.Gabler	/P	J.Romanosky
P	J.Harshman	P	A.Schroll	P	K.McBride	P	A.Cicotte	/P	B.Hoeft	P	H.Reed	/P	J.Kucks	/P	J.Kralick
P	B.Hoeft	P	N.Chittum	/P	J.Stanka	P	D.Brodowski	/P	H.Aguirre	P	D.Tomanek	/P	M.Freeman	/P	V.Valentinetti
/P	W.Stock	/P	J.Harshman	/P	C.Raymond	P	B.Smith	/P	J.Proctor	P	T.Gorman	/P	Z.Monroe	/P	J.Kaat
/P	G.Zuverink	/P	E.Wilson	/P	D.Rudolph	P	J.Briggs	/P	B.Bruce	P	A.Grunwald			/P	R.Lumenti
/P	G.Bamberger	/P	B.Hoeft	P	G.Peters	/P	B.Podbielan			P	K.Johnson			/P	T.McAvoy
/P	R.Coleman	/P	T.Bowsfield			/P	H.Robinson			P	M.Kutyna			/P	M.Wall
		/P	H.Moford			/P	J.Striker			/P	E.Killeen				
		/P	D.Sisler							/P	G.Brunet				
										/P	M.Freeman				

TEAM	G	W	L	PCT	GB	R	OR	AB	H	2B	3B	HR	BB	SO	AVG	OBP	SLG	PRO	PRO+	BR	/A	PF	CHI	RC	SB	CS	SBA	SBR
CHI	156	94	60	.610		669	588	5297	1325	220	46	97	580	634	.250	.330	.364	.694	97	-20	-11	99	100	653	113	53	68	2
CLE	154	89	65	.578	5	745	646	5288	1390	216	25	167	433	721	.263	.323	.408	.731	110	32	59	96	107	682	33	36	48	-12
NY	155	79	75	.513	15	687	647	5379	1397	224	40	153	457	828	.260	.321	.402	.723	107	17	41	97	98	695	45	22	67	0
DET	154	76	78	.494	18	713	732	5211	1346	196	30	160	580	737	.258	.338	.400	.738	102	57	17	105	97	720	34	17	67	0
BOS	154	75	79	.487	19	726	696	5225	1335	248	28	125	626	810	.256	.338	.385	.723	99	36	3	105	101	697	68	25	73	5
BAL	155	74	80	.481	20	551	621	5208	1240	182	23	109	536	690	.238	.312	.345	.657	88	-96	-83	98	96	563	36	24	60	-4
KC	154	66	88	.429	28	681	760	5264	1383	231	43	117	481	780	.263	.328	.390	.718	100	16	4	102	99	669	34	24	59	-4
WAS	154	63	91	.409	31	619	701	5092	1205	173	32	163	517	881	.237	.310	.379	.689	94	-43	-40	100	101	594	51	34	60	-5
TOT	618					5391		41964	10621	1690	267	1091	4210	6081	.253	.325	.384	.709							414	235	64	-17

TEAM	CG	SH	SV	IP	H	H/G	HR	BB	SO	RAT	ERA	ERA+	OAV	OOB	PR	/A	PF	CPI	FA	E	DP	FW	PW	BW	SBW	DIF
CHI	44	13	36	1425[1]	1297	8.2	129	525	761	11.7	3.29	114	.242	.313	91	74	97	106	.979	130	141	.6	7.5	-1.1	.4	9.6
CLE	58	7	23	1383[2]	1230	8.0	148	635	799	12.3	3.75	98	.239	.325	18	-10	95	101	.978	127	138	.7	-1.0	6.0	-1.0	7.3
NY	38	15	28	1399	1281	8.2	120	594	836	12.2	3.60	101	.244	.324	40	7	94	102	.978	131	160	.5	.7	4.2	.2	-3.6
DET	53	9	24	1360	1327	8.8	177	432	829	11.9	4.20	97	.254	.316	-52	-21	105	94	.978	124	131	.9	-2.1	1.7	.2	-1.7
BOS	38	9	25	1364	1386	9.1	135	589	724	13.2	4.17	97	.266	.343	-47	-17	105	104	.978	131	167	.5	-1.7	.3	.7	-1.8
BAL	45	15	30	1400[1]	1290	8.3	111	476	735	11.5	3.56	106	.246	.313	47	35	98	96	.976	146	163	-.4	3.5	-8.4	-.2	2.4
KC	44	8	21	1360[2]	1452	9.6	148	492	703	13.2	4.35	92	.274	.341	-74	-52	104	102	.973	160	156	-1.2	-5.3	.4	-.2	-4.7
WAS	46	10	21	1360	1358	9.0	123	467	694	12.3	4.01	98	.259	.324	-23	-14	101	96	.973	162	140	-1.4	-1.4	-4.0	-.3	-6.9
TOT	366	86	208	11053		8.6				12.3	3.86		.253	.325					.977	1111	1196					

Runs		Hits		Doubles		Triples		Home Runs		Total Bases	
Yost-Det	115	Kuenn-Det	198	Kuenn-Det	42	Allison-Was	9	Killebrew-Was	42	Colavito-Cle	301
Mantle-NY	104	Fox-Chi	191	Malzone-Bos	34	McDougald-NY	8	Colavito-Cle	42	Killebrew-Was	282
Power-Cle	102	Runnels-Bos	176	Fox-Chi	34			Lemon-Was	33	Kuenn-Det	281
Jensen-Bos	101	Power-Cle	172	Williams-KC	33			Maxwell-Det	31	Mantle-NY	278
Kuenn-Det	99	Minoso-Cle	172	Runnels-Bos	33			Mantle-NY	31	Allison-Was	275

Runs Batted In		Runs Produced		Bases On Balls		Batting Average		On Base Percentage		Slugging Average	
Jensen-Bos	112	Jensen-Bos	185	Yost-Det	135	Kuenn-Det	.353	Yost-Det	.437	Kaline-Det	.530
Colavito-Cle	111	Minoso-Cle	163	Runnels-Bos	95	Kaline-Det	.327	Runnels-Bos	.415	Killebrew-Was	.516
Killebrew-Was	105	Malzone-Bos	163	Mantle-NY	93	Runnels-Bos	.314	Kaline-Det	.414	Mantle-NY	.514
Lemon-Was	100	Kuenn-Det	161	Buddin-Bos	92	Fox-Chi	.306	Woodling-Bal	.405	Colavito-Cle	.512
Maxwell-Det	95	Killebrew-Was	161	Killebrew-Was	90	Minoso-Cle	.302	Kuenn-Det	.405	Lemon-Was	.510

Production		Adjusted Production		Batter Runs		Adjusted Batter Runs		Clutch Hitting Index		Runs Created	
Kaline-Det	.944	Mantle-NY	152	Kaline-Det	41.6	Francona-Cle	40.0	Strickland-Cle	125	Mantle-NY	117
Kuenn-Det	.906	Kaline-Det	149	Yost-Det	37.9	Mantle-NY	39.8	Fox-Chi	121	Kuenn-Det	117
Mantle-NY	.905	Kuenn-Det	140	Francona-Cle	36.6	Kaline-Det	35.8	Woodling-Bal	120	Yost-Det	115
Yost-Det	.873	Woodling-Bal	139	Kuenn-Det	36.2	Yost-Det	31.8	Jensen-Bos	115	Kaline-Det	114
Killebrew-Was	.873	Killebrew-Was	137	Mantle-NY	36.0	Kuenn-Det	30.6	Cerv-KC	115	Killebrew-Was	103

Total Average		Stolen Bases		Stolen Base Average		Stolen Base Runs		Fielding Runs		Total Player Rating	
Yost-Det	.992	Aparicio-Chi	56	Mantle-NY	87.5	Aparicio-Chi	9.0	Gardner-Bal	30.5	Mantle-NY	4.5
Mantle-NY	.985	Mantle-NY	21	Aparicio-Chi	81.2	Mantle-NY	4.5	Minoso-Cle	16.2	Kaline-Det	4.0
Kaline-Det	.983	Landis-Chi	20	Jensen-Bos	80.0	Jensen-Bos	3.0	Landis-Chi	15.8	Jensen-Bos	3.4
Kuenn-Det	.903	Jensen-Bos	20	Landis-Chi	69.0	Malzone-Bos	1.8	Jensen-Bos	15.1	Minoso-Cle	3.4
Jensen-Bos	.888	Allison-Was	13			Yost-Det	1.5	Colavito-Cle	11.6	Runnels-Bos	3.3

Wins		Win Percentage		Games		Complete Games		Shutouts		Saves	
Wynn-Chi	22	Shaw-Chi	.750	Staley-Chi	67	Pascual-Was	17	Pascual-Was	6	Lown-Chi	15
McLish-Cle	19	McLish-Cle	.704	Lown-Chi	60	Pappas-Bal	15	Wynn-Chi	5	Staley-Chi	14
Shaw-Chi	18	Wynn-Chi	.688	Clevenger-Was	50	Mossi-Det	15	Pappas-Bal	4	Loes-Bal	14
		Mossi-Det	.654	Shaw-Chi	47	Wynn-Chi	14			Duren-NY	14
						Bunning-Det	14			Fornieles-Bos	11

Innings Pitched		Fewest Hits/Game		Fewest BB/Game		Strikeouts		Strikeouts/Game		Ratio	
Wynn-Chi	255.2	Score-Cle	6.89	Brown-Bal	1.76	Bunning-Det	201	Score-Cle	8.23	Ditmar-NY	9.62
Bunning-Det	249.2	Ditmar-NY	6.95	Lary-Det	1.86	Pascual-Was	185	Bunning-Det	7.25	Pascual-Was	10.33
Foytack-Det	240.1	Wilhelm-Bal	7.09	Garver-KC	1.88	Wynn-Chi	179	Pascual-Was	6.98	Mossi-Det	10.34
Pascual-Was	238.2	Wynn-Chi	7.11	Mossi-Det	1.93	Score-Cle	147	Turley-NY	6.47	O'Dell-Bal	10.43
McLish-Cle	235.1	O'Dell-Bal	7.36	Ramos-Was	2.00	Wilhelm-Bal	139	Wynn-Chi	6.30	Brown-Bal	10.48

Earned Run Average		Adjusted ERA		Opponents' Batting Avg.		Opponents' On Base Pct.		Starter Runs		Adjusted Starter Runs	
Wilhelm-Bal	2.19	Wilhelm-Bal	173	Score-Cle	.210	Ditmar-NY	.270	Wilhelm-Bal	42.0	Wilhelm-Bal	40.0
Pascual-Was	2.64	Pascual-Was	148	Ditmar-NY	.211	Pascual-Was	.284	Pascual-Was	32.4	Pascual-Was	33.8
Shaw-Chi	2.69	Shaw-Chi	140	Wynn-Chi	.216	O'Dell-Bal	.286	Shaw-Chi	30.0	Shaw-Chi	27.3
Ditmar-NY	2.90	Walker-Bal	130	O'Dell-Bal	.220	Mossi-Det	.286	Ditmar-NY	21.7	Daley-KC	20.2
Walker-Bal	2.92	O'Dell-Bal	129	Wilhelm-Bal	.224	Brown-Bal	.290	Perry-Cle	20.6	O'Dell-Bal	18.8

Clutch Pitching Index		Relief Runs		Adjusted Relief Runs		Relief Ranking		Total Pitcher Index		Total Baseball Ranking	
Wilhelm-Bal	132	Staley-Chi	20.9	Staley-Chi	19.6	Staley-Chi	25.0	Pascual-Was	5.0	Pascual-Was	5.0
Daley-KC	122	Duren-NY	16.9	Duren-NY	15.0	Duren-NY	22.1	Wilhelm-Bal	3.7	Mantle-NY	4.5
Ford-NY	119	Shantz-NY	15.6	Shantz-NY	13.3	Shantz-NY	13.6	Daley-KC	3.1	Kaline-Det	4.0
Shaw-Chi	114	Coates-NY	11.0	Stobbs-Was	9.4	Lown-Chi	12.7	Perry-Cle	2.8	Wilhelm-Bal	3.7
McLish-Cle	114	Lown-Chi	10.0	Fornieles-Bos	9.0	Fornieles-Bos	10.6	Ford-NY	2.8	Jensen-Bos	3.4

January 21 Stan Musial asks for, and receives, a pay cut from $100,000 to $80,000 a year. Musial says he was overpaid in 1957 and 1958, and his salary should be cut, based on his performance in 1959.

February 4 For the second straight year, the BBWAA voters fail to elect a new Hall of Fame member. Edd Roush gets 146 votes, but 202 are necessary for election. Sam Rice (143) and Eppa Rixey (142) are next in line.

February 18 Walter O'Malley, owner of the Dodgers, completes the purchase of the Chavez Ravine area in Los Angeles by paying $494,000 for property valued at $92,000.

February 20 Branch Rickey meets with officials of the proposed Western Carolinas League about pooling talent for Continental League clubs.

April 17 Eddie Mathews hits his 300th homer, off Robin Roberts, plus a double and triple, as Milwaukee beats Philadelphia 8-4. Only Jimmie Foxx hit his 300th at a younger age.

May 4 When the Cubs pluck Lou Boudreau out of the broadcast booth to replace Charlie Grimm (6-11) as manager, Jolly Cholly takes Lou's chair behind the mike.

June 26 Hoping to speed up the election process, the Hall of Fame changes its voting procedures. The new rules allow the Special Veterans Committee to vote annually, rather than every other year, and to induct up to two players a year. The BBWAA is authorized to hold a runoff election of the top 30 vote getters if no one is elected in the first ballot.

July 18 The NL votes to expand to 10 clubs if the Continental League does not join Organized Baseball. The new NL clubs would invade CL territories.

July 19 In his major league debut, Giant Juan Marichal pitches no-hit ball until Clay Dalrymple pinch-hit singles with two out in the seventh. Marichal winds up with 12 strikeouts and a one-hit 2-0 win against the Phillies. Marichal is the first NL pitcher since 1900 to debut with a one-hitter.

August 18 Facing just 27 batters, Lew Burdette pitches a 1-0 no-hitter against the Phillies. Tony Gonzalez, the only Phil to reach base, is hit by a Burdette pitch in the fifth inning but is then erased on a double play.

September 15 Willie Mays ties the modern major league record with three triples in a game against the Phillies. His three-bagger off Turk Farrell gives the Giants an 8-6 win in 11 innings. Mays also strokes a double and single.

September 16 Warren Spahn, 39 years old, notches his 11th 20-win season with a no-hitter against the Phillies, winning 4-0.

September 25 For the first time since 1927, the Pirates are headed for the World Series. A gigantic torchlight victory parade in Pittsburgh's Golden Triangle at midnight celebrates the pennant.

October 14 In a 9-9 tie, Bill Mazeroski leads off the last of the ninth and hits what is the most dramatic home run in Series history, off Ralph Terry, to give Pittsburgh a 10-9 win and the World Championship.

October 16 The NL votes to admit Houston and New York to the league, the first structural change since 1900.

November 3 Pittsburgh's Vern Law is voted Cy Young Award winner. He outpolls Warren Spahn 8-4.

November 16 NL batting champion Dick Groat is named league MVP, outpolling Pirate teammate Don Hoak 276-162.

December 21 Cubs owner P. K. Wrigley says Chicago will have no manager but will use a college of coaches instead.

	CHICAGO		CINCINNATI		LOS ANGELES		MILWAUKEE		PHILADELPHIA		PITTSBURGH		SAN FRANCISCO		ST.LOUIS
M	C.Grimm	M	F.Hutchinson	M	W.Alston	M	C.Dressen	M	E.Sawyer	M	D.Murtaugh	M	B.Rigney	M	S.Hemus
M	L.Boudreau	1B	F.Robinson	1B	N.Larker	1B	J.Adcock	M	A.Cohen	1B	D.Stuart	1B	T.Sheehan	1B	B.White
1B	E.Bouchee	2B	B.Martin	2B	C.Neal	2B	C.Cottier	M	G.Mauch	2B	B.Mazeroski	1B	W.McCovey	2B	J.Javier
2B	J.Kindall	SS	R.McMillan	SS	M.Wills	SS	J.Logan	1B	P.Herrera	SS	D.Groat	2B	D.Blasingame	SS	D.Spencer
SS	E.Banks	3B	E.Kasko	3B	J.Gilliam	3B	E.Mathews	2B	T.Taylor	3B	D.Hoak	SS	E.Bressoud	3B	K.Boyer
3B	R.Santo	LF	W.Post	LF	W.Moon	LF	A.Spangler	SS	R.Amaro	LF	B.Skinner	3B	J.Davenport	LF	S.Musial
LF	R.Ashburn	CF	V.Pinson	CF	T.Davis	CF	B.Bruton	3B	A.Dark	CF	B.Virdon	LF	F.Alou	CF	C.Flood
CF	G.Altman	RF	G.Bell	RF	F.Howard	RF	H.Aaron	LF	B.Smith	RF	R.Clemente	CF	W.Mays	RF	J.Cunningham
RF	B.Will	C	E.Bailey	C	J.Roseboro	C	D.Crandall	CF	B.Del Greco	C	S.Burgess	RF	W.Kirkland	C	H.Smith
C	M.Thacker							RF	K.Walters			C	B.Schmidt		
		O	J.Lynch	13	G.Hodges	O	W.Covington	C	J.Coker	O	G.Cimoli			S2	A.Grammas
1O	F.Thomas	1	G.Coleman	O	D.Snider	2	R.Schoendienst			C	H.Smith	32	J.Amalfitano	O	W.Moryn
23	D.Zimmer	3	C.Cook	O	D.Demeter	2S	F.Mantilla	O	T.Curry	1	R.Nelson	O1	O.Cepeda	O	B.Nieman
C	S.Taylor	3	W.Jones	C	N.Sherry	O1	A.Dark	O	J.Callison	S2	D.Schofield	S3	A.Rodgers	C	C.Sawatski
O	W.Moryn	S	L.Cardenas	C	J.Pignatano	O2	M.Roach	O	T.Gonzalez	O	J.Christopher	C	H.Landrith	O	L.Wagner
C	E.Tappe	2	E.Chacon	O	W.Davis	O	L.Maye	3O	L.Walls	/3	G.Baker	1	J.Marshall	/1	G.Crowe
O	E.Averill	O	T.Gonzalez	O	C.Essegian	C	C.Lau	S	J.Koppe	C	B.Oldis	O	D.Philley	O	C.James
O	A.Heist	O	L.Walls	S3	B.Lillis	1	F.Torre	C	C.Neeman	1	M.Vernon	1	D.Long	O	D.Landrum
1	D.Gernert	C	D.Dotterer	3	C.Smith	/O	E.Haas	C	C.Dalrymple	/S	D.Barone	S	J.Pagan	O	J.Glenn
2	T.Taylor	1	H.Anderson	S	B.Aspromonte	/1	R.Boone	3S	T.Lepcio	/C	D.Kravitz	/C	N.Wilson	O	E.Burton
O	D.Murphy	C	J.Azcue	O	R.Fairly	/O	M.Krsnich	S2	B.Malkmus	H	H.Bright	/O	M.Alou	2	W.Shannon
O	L.Johnson	/C	F.House	H	I.Noren	/C	S.Lopata	O1	H.Anderson	/1	R.Stevens			/C	T.McCarver
C	D.Rice	/O	J.Gaines	/C	D.Camilli	/O	L.Gabrielson	O	W.Post	H	R.Mejias	P	M.McCormick	/C	C.Cannizzaro
O	B.Williams	/1	W.Lockman	/O	S.Amoros	H	J.Torre	3	J.Morgan			P	Sa.Jones	S	J.Gotay
C	J.Hegan	/1	R.Alvarez	/O	C.Furillo			1	E.Bouchee	P	B.Friend	P	J.Sanford	/2	D.Gray
/2	G.Hatton	H	P.Whisenant	/O	R.Repulski	P	L.Burdette	3	J.Woods	P	V.Law	P	B.O'Dell	/3	E.Olivares
/C	D.Bertell					P	W.Spahn	/O	D.Philley	P	H.Haddix	RP	J.Antonelli	/1	D.Carmel
/3	S.Drake	P	B.Purkey	P	D.Drysdale	P	B.Buhl	/S	B.Wine	P	V.Mizell	RP	S.Miller	/O	G.Kolb
/O	A.Schult	P	J.Hook	P	J.Podres	P	C.Willey			RP	R.Face			/O	D.Johnson
/C	C.Neeman	P	J.O'Toole	P	S.Williams	P	J.Jay	P	R.Roberts	RP	J.Gibbon	P	J.Marichal	/C	D.Rice
/1	I.Noren	P	C.McLish	P	S.Koufax	RP	D.McMahon	P	J.Buzhardt	RP	F.Green	P	G.Maranda	/2	B.Sadowski
/O	N.Mathews	RP	J.Nuxhall	P	R.Craig	RP	G.Brunet	P	G.Conley			P	B.Loes	/2	R.Bridges
/2	J.McKnight	RP	J.Brosnan	RP	L.Sherry	RP	R.Piche	P	J.Owens			P	Sh.Jones	O	D.Clemens
		RP	B.Henry	RP	E.Roebuck			P	D.Green	P	T.Cheney	P	B.Byerly		
P	G.Hobbie			RP	D.McDevitt			RP	C.Short	P	J.Umbricht	P	J.Shipley	P	L.Jackson
P	B.Anderson	P	D.Newcombe			P	J.Pizarro	RP	S.Daniels	P	B.Daniels	/P	E.Fisher	P	E.Broglio
P	D.Ellsworth	P	J.Maloney	P	E.Palmquist	/P	D.Nottebart	RP	T.Farrell	P	P.Giel	/P	D.Choate	P	R.Sadecki
P	D.Cardwell	P	C.Osteen	P	E.Rakow	/P	B.Rush	RP	R.Gomez	P	C.Labine	/P	R.Monzant	P	C.Simmons
RP	D.Elston	P	B.Grim	/P	C.Labine	/P	T.Fox			P	G.Witt			P	R.Kline
RP	S.Morehead	P	M.Bridges	/P	J.Golden	/P	K.MacKenzie	P	A.Mahaffey	/P	E.Francis			RP	L.McDaniel
RP	M.Freeman	/P	R.Sanchez	/P	P.Ortega	/P	B.Giggie	P	H.Robinson	/P	D.Olivo			
		/P	O.Pena					/P	D.Cardwell	/P	D.Gross			P	B.Gibson
P	D.Drott	/P	B.Lawrence					/P	J.Meyer					/P	V.Mizell
P	J.Schaffernoth	/P	T.Wieand					/P	T.Phillips					/P	B.Miller
P	M.Drabowsky	/P	D.Richards					/P	A.Neiger					P	B.Duliba
P	B.Johnson							/P	H.Mason					P	M.Bridges
/P	J.Brewer							/P	C.Simmons					P	B.Grim
/P	M.Wright													/P	E.Bauta
/P	A.Ceccarelli													/P	F.Barnes
/P	D.Burwell													/P	M.Nelson
/P	J.Goetz													/P	C.Browning
/P	A.Schroll														

TEAM	G	W	L	PCT	GB	R	OR	AB	H	2B	3B	HR	BB	SO	AVG	OBP	SLG	PRO	PRO+	BR	/A	PF	CHI	RC	SB	CS	SBA	SBR
PIT	155	95	59	.617	—	**734**	**593**	5406	**1493**	**236**	56	120	486	747	**.276**	**.338**	.407	**.745**	109	**72**	68	101	99	**737**	34	24	59	-4
MIL	154	88	66	.571	7	724	658	5263	1393	198	48	**170**	463	793	.265	.327	**.417**	.744	**118**	60	**114**	93	102	714	69	37	65	-2
STL	155	86	68	.558	9	639	616	5187	1317	213	48	138	501	792	.254	.323	.393	.716	94	13	-44	109	97	652	48	35	58	-7
LA	154	82	72	.532	13	662	**593**	5227	1333	216	38	126	529	837	.255	.327	.383	.710	94	6	-37	106	99	659	**95**	53	64	-3
SF	156	79	75	.513	16	671	631	5324	1357	220	**62**	130	467	846	.255	.319	.393	.712	106	1	41	94	102	663	86	45	**66**	-1
CIN	154	67	87	.435	28	640	692	5289	1324	230	40	140	512	858	.250	.320	.388	.708	98	-1	-12	102	97	661	73	37	**66**	0
CHI	156	60	94	.390	35	634	776	5311	1293	213	48	119	**531**	897	.243	.314	.369	.683	94	-48	-41	99	**103**	617	51	34	60	-5
PHI	154	59	95	.383	36	546	691	5169	1235	196	44	99	448	1054	.239	.304	.351	.655	85	-102	-103	100	102	546	45	48	48	-15
TOT	619					5250		42176	10745	1722	384	1042	3937	6824	.255	.322	.388	.710							501	313	62	-38

TEAM	CG	SH	SV	IP	H	H/G	HR	BB	SO	RAT	ERA	ERA+	OAV	OOB	PR	/A	PF	CPI	FA	E	DP	FW	PW	BW	SBW	DIF
PIT	47	11	33	1399²	1363	8.8	**105**	386	811	**11.3**	3.49	107	.257	**.309**	42	40	100	99	**.979**	**128**	163	.7	4.1	7.0	.0	6.1
MIL	**55**	13	28	1387¹	1327	8.6	130	518	807	12.2	3.76	91	.251	.322	0	-52	91	99	.976	141	137	-.0	-5.4	**11.7**	.3	4.4
STL	37	11	30	1371	1316	8.6	127	511	906	12.1	3.64	112	.253	.322	18	69	109	103	.976	141	152	.0	7.1	-4.5	-.2	6.6
LA	46	13	20	1398	**1218**	**7.8**	154	564	**1122**	11.7	**3.40**	117	**.234**	.312	**56**	89	106	103	**.979**	125	142	.9	9.2	-3.8	.2	-1.4
SF	**55**	**16**	26	1396	1288	8.3	107	512	897	11.8	3.44	101	.245	.315	50	6	93	99	.972	166	117	-1.3	.6	4.2	.4	-1.9
CIN	33	8	**35**	1390¹	1417	9.2	134	442	740	12.3	4.00	96	.267	.328	-37	-27	102	101	**.979**	125	155	.9	-2.8	-1.2	**.5**	-7.3
CHI	36	6	25	1402²	1393	8.9	152	565	805	12.8	4.35	87	.260	.335	-92	-89	100	96	.977	143	133	-.0	-9.2	-4.2	-.0	-3.6
PHI	45	6	16	1375¹	1423	9.3	133	439	736	12.3	4.01	97	.270	.328	-38	-20	103	101	.974	155	129	-.8	-2.1	-10.6	-1.1	-3.5
TOT	354	84	213	11120¹		8.7				12.1	3.76		.255	.322					.977	1124	1128					

Runs		Hits		Doubles		Triples		Home Runs		Total Bases	
Bruton-Mil	112	Mays-SF	190	Pinson-Cin	37	Bruton-Mil	13	Banks-Chi	41	Aaron-Mil	334
Mathews-Mil	108	Pinson-Cin	187	Cepeda-SF	36	Pinson-Cin	12	Aaron-Mil	40	Banks-Chi	331
Pinson-Cin	107	Groat-Pit	186	Skinner-Pit	33	Mays-SF	12	Mathews-Mil	39	Mays-SF	330
Mays-SF	107	Bruton-Mil	180	Robinson-Cin	33	Aaron-Mil	11	Boyer-StL	32	Boyer-StL	310
Aaron-Mil	102	Clemente-Pit	179	Banks-Chi	32			Robinson-Cin	31	Pinson-Cin	308

Runs Batted In		Runs Produced		Bases On Balls		Batting Average		On Base Percentage		Slugging Average	
Aaron-Mil	126	Mathews-Mil	193	Ashburn-Chi	116	Groat-Pit	.325	Ashburn-Chi	.416	Robinson-Cin	.595
Mathews-Mil	124	Aaron-Mil	188	Mathews-Mil	111	Larker-LA	.323	Robinson-Cin	.413	Aaron-Mil	.566
Banks-Chi	117	Mays-SF	181	Gilliam-LA	96	Mays-SF	.319	Mathews-Mil	.401	Boyer-StL	.562
Mays-SF	103	Banks-Chi	170	Robinson-Cin	82	Clemente-Pit	.314	Moon-LA	.387	Mays-SF	.555
Boyer-StL	97	Clemente-Pit	167	Spencer-StL	81	Boyer-StL	.304	Mays-SF	.386	Banks-Chi	.554

Production		Adjusted Production		Batter Runs		Adjusted Batter Runs		Clutch Hitting Index		Runs Created	
Robinson-Cin	1.007	Mathews-Mil	170	Robinson-Cin	47.8	Mathews-Mil	55.4	Larker-LA	149	Mathews-Mil	128
Mathews-Mil	.952	Robinson-Cin	169	Mathews-Mil	46.0	Mays-SF	50.7	Mathews-Mil	120	Mays-SF	124
Mays-SF	.941	Mays-SF	164	Mays-SF	43.5	Aaron-Mil	46.0	Bailey-Cin	120	Aaron-Mil	119
Boyer-StL	.934	Aaron-Mil	161	Boyer-StL	37.9	Robinson-Cin	46.0	Stuart-Pit	114	Banks-Chi	113
Aaron-Mil	.925	Banks-Chi	145	Aaron-Mil	37.4	Banks-Chi	35.6	Clemente-Pit	112	Robinson-Cin	113

Total Average		Stolen Bases		Stolen Base Average		Stolen Base Runs		Fielding Runs		Total Player Rating	
Robinson-Cin	1.069	Wills-LA	50	Javier-StL	82.6	Wills-LA	7.8	Mazeroski-Pit	25.4	Mays-SF	5.9
Mathews-Mil	1.029	Pinson-Cin	32	Wills-LA	80.6	Javier-StL	3.3	Wills-LA	20.5	Banks-Chi	5.8
Mays-SF	.953	T.Taylor-Chi-Phi	26	Ashburn-Chi	80.0	Blasingame-SF	3.0	Grammas-StL	19.8	Aaron-Mil	4.8
Aaron-Mil	.935	Mays-SF	25	Pinson-Cin	72.7	Pinson-Cin	2.4	Smith-StL	18.0	Robinson-Cin	4.5
Boyer-StL	.918	Bruton-Mil	22	Mays-SF	71.4	Ashburn-Chi	2.4	Mays-SF	13.7	Mathews-Mil	4.2

Wins		Win Percentage		Games		Complete Games		Shutouts		Saves	
Spahn-Mil	21	Broglio-StL	.700	Face-Pit	68	Spahn-Mil	18	Sanford-SF	6	McDaniel-StL	26
Broglio-StL	21	Law-Pit	.690	McDaniel-StL	65	Law-Pit	18	Drysdale-LA	5	Face-Pit	24
Law-Pit	20	Spahn-Mil	.677	Elston-Chi	60	Burdette-Mil	18			Henry-Cin	17
Burdette-Mil	19	Buhl-Mil	.640	Farrell-Phi	59	Hobbie-Chi	16			Brosnan-Cin	12
		Purkey-Cin	.607	Roebuck-LA	58	Friend-Pit	16				

Innings Pitched		Fewest Hits/Game		Fewest BB/Game		Strikeouts		Strikeouts/Game		Ratio	
Jackson-StL	282.0	Broglio-StL	6.84	Burdette-Mil	1.14	Drysdale-LA	246	Koufax-LA	10.13	Drysdale-LA	9.90
Friend-Pit	275.2	Koufax-LA	6.84	Roberts-Phi	1.29	Koufax-LA	197	Drysdale-LA	8.23	Friend-Pit	10.15
Burdette-Mil	275.2	Williams-LA	7.03	Law-Pit	1.33	S.Jones-SF	190	Williams-LA	7.60	Law-Pit	10.27
Law-Pit	271.2	Drysdale-LA	7.16	Friend-Pit	1.47	Broglio-StL	188	Broglio-StL	7.48	Burdette-Mil	10.35
Drysdale-LA	269.0	Buhl-Mil	7.62	Haddix-Pit	1.98	Friend-Pit	183	S.Jones-SF	7.31	Williams-LA	10.37

Earned Run Average		Adjusted ERA		Opponents' Batting Avg.		Opponents' On Base Pct.		Starter Runs		Adjusted Starter Runs	
McCormick-SF	2.70	Broglio-StL	149	Koufax-LA	.207	Drysdale-LA	.275	McCormick-SF	29.8	Broglio-StL	34.0
Broglio-StL	2.74	Drysdale-LA	140	Williams-LA	.210	Friend-Pit	.281	Drysdale-LA	27.5	Drysdale-LA	33.6
Drysdale-LA	2.84	Simmons-Phi-StL	134	Broglio-StL	.213	Williams-LA	.282	Broglio-StL	25.6	Friend-Pit	22.9
Williams-LA	3.00	Williams-LA	133	Drysdale-LA	.215	Law-Pit	.287	Friend-Pit	23.2	Williams-LA	22.4
Friend-Pit	3.00	Podres-LA	129	Buhl-Mil	.229	Burdette-Mil	.287	Law-Pit	20.6	Podres-LA	22.4

Clutch Pitching Index		Relief Runs		Adjusted Relief Runs		Relief Ranking		Total Pitcher Index		Total Baseball Ranking	
Simmons-Phi-StL	121	McDaniel-StL	21.6	McDaniel-StL	26.0	McDaniel-StL	45.2	McDaniel-StL	5.0	Mays-SF	5.9
Podres-LA	117	Brosnan-Cin	15.4	Brosnan-Cin	16.1	Farrell-Phi	22.2	Broglio-StL	4.8	Banks-Chi	5.8
O'Dell-SF	110	Roebuck-LA	12.8	Roebuck-LA	15.5	Face-Pit	20.3	Drysdale-LA	4.3	McDaniel-StL	5.0
Sadecki-StL	109	Farrell-Phi	12.2	Farrell-Phi	13.6	Brosnan-Cin	17.5	McCormick-SF	2.7	Aaron-Mil	4.8
Buhl-Mil	108	Face-Pit	10.9	Face-Pit	10.8	Roebuck-LA	15.5	Williams-LA	2.6	Broglio-StL	4.8

June 17 A two-run homer off Wynn Hawkins at Cleveland Municipal Stadium makes Ted Williams the fourth player in major league history to hit 500 homers. The Red Sox win 3-1.

July 27 William Shea, chairman of Mayor Robert Wagner's New York baseball committee, announces the formation of the Continental League. The five founding cities are New York, Houston, Toronto, Denver, and Minneapolis/St. Paul.

August 3 Frank Lane trades managers with Detroit's GM Bill DeWitt. The Indians' Joe Gordon (49-46) is dealt to the Tigers for Jimmy Dykes (44-52). For one game, until the pair can change places, Jo-Jo White pilots the Indians and Billy Hitchcock guides the Tigers.

September 2 In the first game of a doubleheader, Ted Williams homers off Don Lee of the Senators. Williams had homered against Lee's father, Thornton, 20 years earlier.

September 26 In his final major league plate appearance, against Baltimore's Jack Fisher, Ted Williams picks out a 1-1 pitch and drives it 450 feet into the right-center field seats behind the Boston bullpen. It is Williams's 521st and last homer, putting him third on the all-time list. Williams's homer gives the seventh-place Red Sox a 5-4 victory. Williams stays in the dugout, ignoring the crowd's cheers, but when he trots out to left field in the ninth, he is replaced immediately by Carroll Hardy. The Splendid Splinter retires as a standing crowd roars.

October 3 The Yankees head into the Series with a 15-game winning streak. New York's 193 homers are an AL record, three better than the 1956 Yanks.

October 5 In a portent of things to come, Bill Mazeroski's two-run fifth-inning homer off Jim Coates is the difference as Pittsburgh beats New York 6-4 in its first World Series win since 1925. Roy Face survives a two-run ninth-inning Elston Howard homer to preserve Vern Law's victory.

October 6 Mickey Mantle's two homers highlight New York's 16-3 victory at Forbes Field, evening the Series.

October 27 Trying to jump ahead of the NL, the AL admits Los Angeles and Washington to the league with plans to have the new clubs begin competition in 1961. Calvin Griffith is given permission to move the existing Washington Senators franchise to Minneapolis/St. Paul. League president Joe Cronin says the AL will play a 162-game schedule, with 18 games against each opponent.

November 2 Roger Maris nips Mickey Mantle for the AL's Most Valuable Player award, 225-222.

November 17 The new Washington franchise is awarded to Elwood Quesada, Washington native, head of the Federal Aviation Agency.

November 22 The AL proposes that both leagues expand to nine teams in 1961 and begin interleague play. It will delay entering the Los Angeles market if the NL agrees.

November 26 Twins is the appropriate new name chosen for the club transplanted from Washington to the Twin Cities of Minneapolis/St. Paul.

December 5 President Joe Cronin suggests that if the NL starts its new New York franchise in 1961, the AL will stay out of Los Angeles until 1962. The NL turned down the suggested compromise of November 22 because Houston will not be ready in 1961.

December 6 A group headed by movie star Gene Autry and former football star Bob Reynolds is awarded the new AL Los Angeles Angels. Fred Haney will be GM.

December 20 Charlie Finley buys 52 percent of the A's from the late Arnold Johnson's estate.

	BALTIMORE		BOSTON		CHICAGO		CLEVELAND		DETROIT		KANSAS CITY		NEW YORK		WASHINGTON
M	P.Richards	M	B.Jurges	M	A.Lopez	M	J.Gordon	M	J.Dykes	M	B.Elliott	M	C.Stengel	M	C.Lavagetto
1B	J.Gentile	M	D.Baker	1B	R.Sievers	M	J.White	M	B.Hitchcock	1B	M.Throneberry	1B	B.Skowron	1B	C.Becquer
2B	M.Breeding	M	P.Higgins	2B	N.Fox	M	J.Dykes	M	J.Gordon	2B	J.Lumpe	2B	B.Richardson	2B	B.Gardner
SS	R.Hansen	1B	V.Wertz	SS	L.Aparicio	1B	V.Power	1B	N.Cash	SS	K.Hamlin	SS	T.Kubek	SS	J.Valdivielso
3B	B.Robinson	2B	P.Runnels	3B	G.Freese	2B	K.Aspromonte	2B	F.Bolling	3B	A.Carey	3B	C.Boyer	3B	R.Bertoia
LF	G.Woodling	SS	D.Buddin	LF	M.Minoso	SS	W.Held	3B	C.Fernandez	LF	N.Siebern	LF	H.Lopez	LF	J.Lemon
CF	J.Brandt	3B	F.Malzone	CF	J.Landis	3B	B.Phillips	3B	E.Yost	CF	B.Tuttle	CF	M.Mantle	CF	L.Green
RF	G.Stephens	LF	T.Williams	RF	A.Smith	LF	T.Francona	LF	C.Maxwell	RF	R.Snyder	RF	R.Maris	RF	B.Allison
C	G.Triandos	CF	W.Tasby	C	S.Lollar	CF	J.Piersall	CF	A.Kaline	C	P.Daley	C	E.Howard	C	E.Battey
		RF	L.Clinton			RF	H.Kuenn	RF	R.Colavito						
O	A.Pilarcik	C	R.Nixon	1	T.Kluszewski	C	J.Romano	C	L.Berberet	O	H.Bauer	CO	Y.Berra	S2	B.Consolo
1	W.Dropo			3S	S.Esposito					31	D.Williams	32	G.McDougald	O	D.Dobbek
O	J.Busby	2S	P.Green	3	B.Goodman	23	J.Temple	O	N.Chrisley	O	W.Herzog	O	B.Cerv	13	H.Killebrew
C	C.Courtney	O	G.Geiger	C	J.Ginsberg	S	M.DeLaHoz	1	S.Bilko	C	H.Chiti	C	J.Blanchard	O	F.Throneberry
O	D.Nicholson	O	C.Hardy	1	E.Torgeson	O	M.Keough	C	R.Wilson	C	D.Kravitz	1	K.Hadley	O	P.Whisenant
O	W.Tasby	O	R.Repulski	O	J.Hicks	O	W.Bond	3	O.Virgil	S2	B.Johnson	O	B.Cerv	O	H.Naragon
1	B.Boyd	C	H.Sullivan	O	F.Robinson	C	R.Wilson	O	H.Chiti	O	B.Cerv	2S	J.DeMaestri	1	D.Mincher
O	A.Pearson	O	B.Thomson	C	D.Brown	C	R.Nixon	2S	C.Wise	O	J.Delsing	O	K.Hunt	/O	E.Valo
2S	R.Klaus	C	G.Stephens	/3	J.Martin	/1	B.Hale	O	S.Amoros	/O	L.Posada	O	J.Pisoni	S	Z.Versalles
/O	D.Philley	O	M.Keough	/C	C.Carreon	C	H.Foiles	S	C.Veal	/3	R.Jablonski	/C	J.Gonder	/2	J.Schaive
C	J.Ginsberg	C	E.Sadowski	O	J.Rivera	3	J.Morgan	/2	H.Foiles	C	C.Boak	/O	E.Valo	H	K.Aspromonte
/O	J.Powers	1	R.Boone	/C	E.Averill	S3	G.Strickland	1	D.Gernert	/3	J.McManus	/3	D.Johnson	H	J.Jacobs
/C	V.Thomas	C	J.Pagliaroni	/O	S.Johnson	/S	R.Bridges	/S	D.McAuliffe	/2	L.Klimchock	/3	A.Carey		
/O	R.Barker	C1	D.Gile	H	J.McAnany	/O	T.Cline	/O	J.Groth	/C	H.Foiles	/3	Bi.Shantz	P	P.Ramos
/O	B.Thomson	/1	R.Jackson			/O	C.Tanner	/3	R.Bridges	/2	W.Terwilliger			P	D.Lee
/2	J.Adair	2	M.Coughtry	P	E.Wynn	O	C.Hardy	/1	G.Harris			P	A.Ditmar	P	C.Pascual
/O	G.Green	/2	R.Webster	P	B.Pierce	/O	J.Powers	H	E.Lindbeck	P	R.Herbert	P	W.Ford	P	J.Kralick
/C	D.Rice	/O	J.Busby	P	B.Shaw	P	D.Dillard			P	B.Daley	P	B.Turley	RP	T.Clevenger
R	B.Shetrone			P	F.Baumann	/O	P.Whisenant	P	F.Lary	P	D.Hall	P	R.Terry	RP	C.Stobbs
		P	B.Monbouquette	P	R.Kemmerer	/3	S.Demeter	P	J.Bunning	N.Garver	P	J.Coates	RP	H.Woodeshick
P	C.Estrada	P	T.Brewer	P	G.Staley			P	D.Mossi	P	J.Kucks	RP	D.Maas		
P	M.Pappas	P	F.Sullivan	RP	D.Donovan	P	J.Perry	P	B.Bruce	RP	K.Johnson	RP	Bo.Shantz	P	B.Fischer
P	J.Fisher	P	I.Delock	RP	T.Lown	P	M.Grant	P	P.Burnside	RP	M.Kutyna	RP	G.Gabler	P	R.Moore
P	S.Barber	P	B.Muffett			P	G.Bell	RP	H.Aguirre					P	J.Kaat
P	H.Brown	RP	M.Fornieles	P	H.Score	P	B.Latman	RP	D.Sisler	P	D.Larsen	P	E.Grba	P	R.Hernandez
RP	G.Jones	RP	T.Sturdivant	P	R.Moore	P	D.Stigman	RP	B.Fischer	P	B.Trowbridge	P	B.Stafford	P	T.Morgan
		RP	T.Borland	P	M.Garcia	RP	J.Klippstein			P	J.Tsitouris	P	R.Duren	/P	R.Kemmerer
P	H.Wilhelm			/P	B.Rush	RP	D.Newcombe	P	P.Foytack	P	B.Davis	P	B.Short	/P	T.Sadowski
P	J.Walker	P	J.Casale	/P	K.McBride			P	P.Regan	L.Kiely	P	J.James	/P	D.Hyde
P	A.Portocarrero	P	E.Wilson	/P	A.Worthington	P	B.Locke	P	T.Morgan	P	B.Giggie	P	L.Arroyo	/P	T.Abernathy
P	W.Stock	P	D.Hillman	/P	D.Ferrarese	P	W.Hawkins	P	R.Semproch	/P	J.Briggs	/P	F.Kipp	/P	H.Maestri
P	B.Hoeft	P	T.Wills	/P	J.Striker	P	J.Harshman	P	C.Labine	P	G.Brunet	/P	H.Stowe		
/P	J.Anderson	/P	B.Bowsfield	/P	G.Peters	/P	T.Bowsfield	/P	G.Spencer	D.Wickersham				
/P	R.Coleman	/P	C.Nichols			P	J.Briggs			R.Blemker				
/P	B.Mabe	/P	A.Worthington			/P	F.Funk			H.Reed				
		/P	N.Chittum			/P	C.Mathias								
		/P	A.Earley			/P	C.Thomas								
		/P	T.Stallard			/P	M.Lee								
						/P	B.Tiefenauer								
						/P	B.Grim								

TEAM	G	W	L	PCT	GB	R	OR	AB	H	2B	3B	HR	BB	SO	AVG	OBP	SLG	PRO	PRO+	BR	/A	PF	CHI	RC	SB	CS	SBA	SBR
NY	155	97	57	.630		746	627	5290	1377	215	40	193	537	818	.260	.332	.426	.758	117	63	105	94	100	747	37	23	62	-3
BAL	154	89	65	.578	8	682	606	5170	1307	206	33	123	596	801	.253	.334	.377	.711	99	-8	1	99	103	659	37	24	61	-3
CHI	154	87	67	.565	10	741	617	5191	1402	242	38	112	567	648	.270	.348	.396	.744	108	57	64	99	101	726	122	48	72	8
CLE	154	76	78	.494	21	667	693	5296	1415	218	20	127	444	573	.267	.328	.388	.716	102	-11	10	97	101	673	58	25	70	2
WAS	154	73	81	.474	24	672	696	5248	1283	205	43	147	584	883	.244	.326	.384	.710	99	-18	-11	99	101	656	52	43	55	-10
DET	154	71	83	.461	26	633	644	5202	1243	188	34	150	636	728	.239	.326	.375	.701	93	-32	-50	103	97	651	66	32	67	1
BOS	154	65	89	.422	32	658	775	5215	1359	234	32	124	570	798	.261	.336	.389	.725	99	16	-8	104	95	674	34	28	55	-7
KC	155	58	96	.377	39	615	756	5226	1303	212	34	110	513	744	.249	.318	.366	.684	90	-68	-72	101	103	598	16	11	59	-2
TOT	617					5414		41838	10689	1720	274	1086	4447	5993	.255	.331	.388	.718							422	234	64	-14

TEAM	CG	SH	SV	IP	H	H/G	HR	BB	SO	RAT	ERA	ERA+	OAV	OOB	PR	/A	PF	CPI	FA	E	DP	FW	PW	BW	SBW	DIF
NY	38	16	42	1398	1225	7.9	123	609	712	12.0	3.52	102	.238	.322	55	10	93	98	.979	129	162	.2	1.0	10.6	-.1	8.3
BAL	48	11	22	1375²	1222	8.0	117	552	785	11.8	3.52	108	.241	.320	54	44	98	98	.982	108	172	1.4	4.5	.1	-.1	6.2
CHI	42	11	26	1381	1338	8.7	127	533	695	12.3	3.60	105	.258	.329	41	27	98	106	.982	109	175	1.4	2.7	6.5	1.0	-1.5
CLE	32	10	30	1382¹	1308	8.5	161	636	771	12.8	3.95	95	.252	.336	-12	-33	97	103	.978	128	165	.2	-3.3	1.0	.4	.8
WAS	34	10	35	1405¹	1392	8.9	130	538	775	12.6	3.77	103	.243	.260	16	18	100	103	.973	165	159	-2.1	1.8	-1.1	-.8	-1.7
DET	40	7	25	1405²	1336	8.6	141	474	824	11.9	3.64	109	.251	.317	37	50	102	99	.977	138	138	-.5	5.1	-5.1	.3	-5.8
BOS	34	6	23	1361	1440	9.5	127	580	767	13.6	4.62	87	.273	.349	-113	-88	104	94	.976	141	156	-.6	-8.9	-.8	-.5	-1.1
KC	44	4	14	1374	1428	9.4	160	525	664	13.1	4.38	91	.271	.342	-77	-60	103	100	.979	127	149	.3	-6.1	-7.3	-.0	-5.9
TOT	312	75	217	11083		8.7				12.5	3.87		.255	.331					.978	1045	1276					

Runs		Hits		Doubles		Triples		Home Runs		Total Bases	
Mantle-NY	119	Minoso-Chi	184	Francona-Cle	36	Fox-Chi	10	Mantle-NY	40	Mantle-NY	294
Maris-NY	98	Robinson-Bal	175	Skowron-NY	34	Robinson-Bal	9	Maris-NY	39	Maris-NY	290
Minoso-Chi	89	Fox-Chi	175	Minoso-Chi	32			Lemon-Was	38	Skowron-NY	284
Landis-Chi	89	Smith-Chi	169	Freese-Chi	32			Colavito-Det	35	Minoso-Chi	284
Sievers-Chi	87	Runnels-Bos	169					Killebrew-Was	31	Lemon-Was	268

Runs Batted In		Runs Produced		Bases On Balls		Batting Average		On Base Percentage		Slugging Average	
Maris-NY	112	Minoso-Chi	174	Yost-Det	125	Runnels-Bos	.320	Yost-Det	.416	Maris-NY	.581
Minoso-Chi	105	Mantle-NY	173	Mantle-NY	111	Smith-Chi	.315	Woodling-Bal	.403	Mantle-NY	.558
Wertz-Bos	103	Maris-NY	171	Allison-Was	92	Minoso-Chi	.311	Runnels-Bos	.403	Killebrew-Was	.534
Lemon-Was	100	Sievers-Chi	152	Woodling-Bal	84	Skowron-NY	.309	Mantle-NY	.402	Sievers-Chi	.534
Gentile-Bal	98	Robinson-Bal	148	Landis-Chi	80	Kuenn-Cle	.308	Sievers-Chi	.399	Skowron-NY	.528

Production		Adjusted Production		Batter Runs		Adjusted Batter Runs		Clutch Hitting Index		Runs Created	
Mantle-NY	.960	Mantle-NY	166	Mantle-NY	43.9	Mantle-NY	50.6	Wertz-Bos	149	Mantle-NY	125
Maris-NY	.955	Maris-NY	164	Williams-Bos	43.5	Maris-NY	42.3	Power-Cle	115	Maris-NY	111
Sievers-Chi	.933	Sievers-Chi	152	Maris-NY	36.5	Williams-Bos	40.4	Woodling-Bal	110	Minoso-Chi	104
Killebrew-Was	.911	Killebrew-Was	145	Sievers-Chi	32.1	Sievers-Chi	33.0	Fox-Chi	109	Lemon-Was	99
Skowron-NY	.884	Skowron-NY	144	Killebrew-Was	26.9	Skowron-NY	29.7	Minoso-Chi	109	Francona-Cle	96

Total Average		Stolen Bases		Stolen Base Average		Stolen Base Runs		Fielding Runs		Total Player Rating	
Mantle-NY	1.053	Aparicio-Chi	51	Aparicio-Chi	86.4	Aparicio-Chi	10.5	Aparicio-Chi	30.4	Mantle-NY	4.4
Maris-NY	.992	Landis-Chi	23	Kaline-Det	82.6	Landis-Chi	3.3	Boyer-NY	27.6	Maris-NY	3.8
Sievers-Chi	.960	Green-Was	21	Landis-Chi	79.3	Kaline-Det	3.3	Power-Cle	21.0	Aparicio-Chi	3.8
Killebrew-Was	.936	Kaline-Det	19	Piersall-Cle	78.3	Piersall-Cle	2.4	Tuttle-KC	17.1	Williams-Bos	3.3
Lemon-Was	.871	Piersall-Cle	18	Green-Was	72.4	Mantle-NY	2.4	Landis-Chi	12.9	Runnels-Bos	3.2

Wins		Win Percentage		Games		Complete Games		Shutouts		Saves	
Perry-Cle	18	Perry-Cle	.643	Fornieles-Bos	70	Lary-Det	15	Wynn-Chi	4	Klippstein-Cle	14
Estrada-Bal	18	Ditmar-NY	.625	Staley-Chi	64	Ramos-Was	14	Perry-Cle	4	Fornieles-Bos	14
B.Daley-KC	16	Estrada-Bal	.621	Clevenger-Was	53	Herbert-KC	14	Ford-NY	4	Moore-Chi-Was	13
		Pappas-Bal	.577	Moore-Chi-Was	51	Wynn-Chi	13			B.Shantz-NY	11
				Kutyna-KC	51	B.Daley-KC	13				

Innings Pitched		Fewest Hits/Game		Fewest BB/Game		Strikeouts		Strikeouts/Game		Ratio	
Lary-Det	274.1	Estrada-Bal	6.99	Brown-Bal	1.25	Bunning-Det	201	Bunning-Det	7.18	Brown-Bal	10.08
Ramos-Was	274.0	Turley-NY	7.17	Mossi-Det	1.82	Ramos-Was	160	Bell-Cle	6.34	Bunning-Det	10.43
Perry-Cle	261.1	Barber-Bal	7.33	Hall-KC	1.88	Wynn-Chi	158	Estrada-Bal	6.21	Baumann-Chi	10.83
Herbert-KC	252.2	Bunning-Det	7.75	Lary-Det	2.03	Lary-Det	149	Wynn-Chi	5.99	Mossi-Det	10.86
Bunning-Det	252.0	Ford-NY	7.85	Pierce-Chi	2.11	Estrada-Bal	144	Monbouquette-Bos	5.61	Ford-NY	10.93

Earned Run Average		Adjusted ERA		Opponents' Batting Avg.		Opponents' On Base Pct.		Starter Runs		Adjusted Starter Runs	
Baumann-Chi	2.67	Bunning-Det	142	Estrada-Bal	.218	Brown-Bal	.286	Bunning-Det	30.4	Bunning-Det	32.8
Bunning-Det	2.79	Baumann-Chi	141	Turley-NY	.222	Bunning-Det	.293	Baumann-Chi	24.7	Baumann-Chi	22.8
Brown-Bal	3.06	Brown-Bal	125	Barber-Bal	.226	Mossi-Det	.296	Ditmar-NY	18.0	Herbert-KC	19.7
Ditmar-NY	3.06	Herbert-KC	121	Ford-NY	.235	Ford-NY	.299	Ford-NY	16.9	Pascual-Was	14.5
Ford-NY	3.08	Barber-Bal	118	Bunning-Det	.236	Terry-NY	.300	Herbert-KC	16.7	Kralick-Was	14.2

Clutch Pitching Index		Relief Runs		Adjusted Relief Runs		Relief Ranking		Total Pitcher Index		Total Baseball Ranking	
Ditmar-NY	121	Staley-Chi	18.6	Staley-Chi	17.4	Staley-Chi	32.0	Staley-Chi	3.7	Mantle-NY	4.4
Perry-Cle	113	Fornieles-Bos	14.9	Fornieles-Bos	17.0	Fornieles-Bos	25.9	Fornieles-Bos	2.9	Maris-NY	3.8
Lee-Was	113	Sisler-Det	12.4	Sisler-Det	13.2	Sisler-Det	20.0	Bunning-Det	2.6	Aparicio-Chi	3.8
Baumann-Chi	113	Aguirre-Det	10.7	Aguirre-Det	11.6	Aguirre-Det	11.6	Herbert-KC	2.5	Staley-Chi	3.7
Herbert-KC	111	B.Shantz-NY	8.1	Stobbs-Was	7.5	Klippstein-Cle	11.2	Pascual-Was	2.2	Williams-Bos	3.3

January 31 Houston voters approve a bond to finance a luxury domed stadium, the final hurdle standing between the city and major league baseball.

February 9 Willie Mays signs for $85,000, currently the biggest contract in major league baseball.

March 14 George Weiss is lured from retirement to become president of the New York Mets.

March 24 The New York State Senate approves $55 million for a new baseball stadium at Flushing Meadows Park in Queens.

March 31 A Pacific Coast League proposal to use a designated batter for the pitcher is voted down 8-1 by the Professional Baseball Rules Committee. The committee also rules that every club must designate a manager within 30 minutes of game time, a move prompted by the Cubs' college of coaches.

April 23 Art Mahaffey fans a batter in each inning and 17 in all, a Phillies' record, while beating the Cubs 6-0. The Phils won the first game 1-0 behind Frank Sullivan.

April 28 Five days past his 40th birthday, Warren Spahn becomes the second-oldest major league pitcher (after Cy Young) to hurl a no-hitter, blanking San Francisco 1-0. Hank Aaron drives in the only run off loser Sam Jones. It is Spahn's 290th win and 52nd shutout.

April 30 Using Joey Amalfitano's bat, Willie Mays becomes the ninth player in major league history to enjoy a four-homer game. His eight RBI pace the Giants to a 14-4 win at Milwaukee's County Stadium.

May 3 Another brilliant Warren Spahn performance is spoiled when left fielder Mel Roach's misplay costs the Milwaukee ace a second no-hitter in a row. He settles for a two-hitter in topping the Dodgers 4-1.

June 23 With two home runs, Stan Musial passes Lou Gehrig on the all-time list for extra bases.

July 7 Pittsburgh puts Vern Law on the retired list, on doctor's orders, to rest his sore right arm.

July 11 Strong winds dominate the first All-Star Game of 1961. A capacity crowd sees pitcher Stu Miller blown off the mound in the ninth inning at Candlestick Park. A balk is called, and it enables the AL to forge a 3-3 tie before losing 5-4 in 10 innings.

August 3 A 19-0 rout of St. Louis by Pittsburgh matches the most lopsided shutout in the century. The first had been achieved by the Cubs against the Giants on June 7, 1906.

August 16 Cincinnati takes the NL lead for good with a shutout sweep 6-0 and 8-0 at Los Angeles before 72,140, a record crowd for a NL doubleheader. Jim O'Toole and Bob Purkey are the winning pitchers.

September 26 Cincinnati clinches its first NL pennant since 1940. Home runs by Frank Robinson and Jerry Lynch give the Reds a 6-3 win at Chicago.

September 27 Sandy Koufax fans seven Phils in the course of a 2-1 win to set a NL record for strikeouts in a season: 269. This surpasses Christy Mathewson's 267 in 1903, which was accomplished in 367 innings pitched, as opposed to Koufax's 255.

October 2 Casey Stengel agrees to come out of retirement to manage the NL expansion New York Mets next year.

October 10 An expansion draft to stock the new NL clubs takes place in Cincinnati. Houston selections include Bobby Shantz, Ken Johnson, Dick Farrell, and Bob Lillis. New York takes Roger Craig, Gil Hodges, Don Zimmer, and Gus Bell among others.

November 22 Right fielder Frank Robinson is the first Reds player in 21 years to win the NL MVP, taking 219 of 224 possible votes.

	CHICAGO		CINCINNATI		LOS ANGELES		MILWAUKEE		PHILADELPHIA		PITTSBURGH		SAN FRANCISCO		ST.LOUIS
M	V.Himsl	M	F.Hutchinson	M	W.Alston	M	C.Dressen	M	G.Mauch	M	D.Murtaugh	M	A.Dark	M	S.Hemus
M	H.Craft	1B	G.Coleman	1B	G.Hodges	1B	B.Tebbetts	1B	P.Herrera	1B	D.Stuart	1B	W.McCovey	M	J.Keane
M	V.Himsl	2B	D.Blasingame	2B	C.Neal	1B	J.Adcock	2B	T.Taylor	2B	B.Mazeroski	2B	J.Amalfitano	1B	B.White
M	E.Tappe	SS	E.Kasko	SS	M.Wills	2B	F.Bolling	SS	R.Amaro	SS	D.Groat	SS	J.Pagan	2B	J.Javier
M	H.Craft	3B	G.Freese	3B	J.Gilliam	SS	R.McMillan	3B	C.Smith	3B	D.Hoak	3B	J.Davenport	SS	A.Grammas
M	V.Himsl	LF	W.Post	LF	W.Moon	3B	E.Mathews	LF	J.Callison	LF	B.Skinner	LF	H.Kuenn	3B	K.Boyer
M	E.Tappe	CF	V.Pinson	CF	W.Davis	LF	F.Thomas	CF	T.Gonzalez	CF	B.Virdon	CF	W.Mays	LF	S.Musial
M	L.Klein	RF	F.Robinson	RF	T.Davis	CF	H.Aaron	RF	K.Walters	RF	R.Clemente	RF	F.Alou	CF	C.Flood
M	E.Tappe	C	J.Zimmerman	C	J.Roseboro	RF	L.Maye	C	C.Dalrymple	C	S.Burgess	C	E.Bailey	RF	C.James
1B	E.Bouchee					C	J.Torre							C	J.Schaffer
2B	D.Zimmer	O	G.Bell	O1	R.Fairly			2S	B.Malkmus	C	H.Smith	1O	O.Cepeda		
SS	E.Banks	O	J.Lynch	1	N.Larker	O	G.Cimoli	O1	D.Demeter	O	J.Christopher	2	C.Hiller	O1	J.Cunningham
3B	R.Santo	S	L.Cardenas	O	F.Howard	O	M.Jones	13	L.Walls	1	R.Nelson	O	M.Alou	O	D.Taussig
LF	B.Williams	C	J.Edwards	O	D.Snider	O	A.Spangler	O	B.Smith	3	D.Schofield	S	E.Bressoud	S2	B.Lillis
CF	A.Heist	2	E.Chacon	3	D.Spencer	S2	F.Mantilla	O	W.Covington	O	G.Cimoli	C	J.Orsino	O	C.Sawatski
RF	G.Altman	C	B.Schmidt	O	N.Sherry	C	C.Lau	O	B.DelGreco	O	W.Moryn	C	H.Landrith	O	C.Warwick
C	D.Bertell	1	D.Gernert	/3	B.Aspromonte	O	J.DeMerit	C	D.Johnson	C	D.Leppert	C	T.Haller	S	D.Spencer
		C	D.Johnson	O	G.Windhorn	C	S.White	3	B.Sadowski	/3	J.Logan	2S	E.Bowman	H	H.Smith
O	R.Ashburn	C	E.Bailey	O	D.Camilli	/1	B.Boyd	3	J.Woods	/O	D.Clendenon	/1	J.Marshall	2	R.Schoendienst
2S	J.Kindall	/2	J.Baumer	O	D.Demeter	/O	M.Roach	C	G.Coleman	/3	G.Baker	S	B.Farley	S	J.Buchek
C	S.Taylor	O	P.Whisenant	/3	C.Smith	/C	D.Crandall	/O	E.Valo	/C	B.Oldis	/C	B.Schmidt	/C	T.McCarver
1S	A.Rodgers	/3	W.Jones	O	C.Warwick	/O	H.Taylor	/O	T.Curry	/O	R.Mejias	H	D.Blasingame	O	D.Landrum
O	B.Will	/3	C.Cook	3	B.Lillis	/O	W.Covington	2	G.Williams					O	G.Oliver
/1	M.Roach	H	H.Anderson	/1	T.Harkness	/S	J.Logan	C	C.Neeman	P	B.Friend	P	M.McCormick	S	J.Gotay
C	M.Thacker	/O	J.Gaines			H	N.Chrisley	C	J.Coker	P	J.Gibbon	P	J.Sanford	/O	W.Moryn
C	C.Barragan			P	S.Koufax	H	B.Martin	C	A.Kenders	P	H.Haddix	P	J.Marichal	O	E.Olivares
/2	K.Hubbs			P	D.Drysdale	/C	P.Roof	/S	J.Koppe	P	E.Francis	P	S.Jones	/O	B.Nieman
/1	M.Morhardt	P	J.O'Toole	P	S.Williams					P	V.Mizell	P	B.Loes	/O	D.Clemens
/O	D.Murphy	P	J.Jay	P	J.Podres	P	L.Burdette	P	A.Mahaffey	RP	C.Labine	RP	B.O'Dell	H	G.Crowe
/O	L.Brock	P	B.Purkey	RP	R.Craig	P	W.Spahn	P	J.Buzhardt	RP	R.Face	RP	S.Miller	/C	C.Cannizzaro
/O	J.McAnany	P	K.Hunt	RP	L.Sherry	P	B.Buhl	P	F.Sullivan	RP	B.Shantz	RP	J.Duffalo		
/O	N.Mathews	RP	J.Maloney	RP	R.Perranoski	P	C.Willey	P	D.Ferrarese					P	R.Sadecki
/O	J.McAnany	RP	J.Brosnan			P	D.Nottebart	P	D.Green	P	T.Sturdivant	P	D.LeMay	P	L.Jackson
H	G.Freese	P	J.Hook	P	T.Farrell	RP	D.McMahon	RP	J.Baldschun	P	A.McBean	P	B.Bolin	P	B.Gibson
/O	S.Drake	RP	S.Jones	P	J.Golden			RP	K.Lehman	P	V.Law	P	E.Fisher	P	C.Simmons
				/P	P.Ortega	P	B.Hendley			/P	A.Jackson	/P	D.Zanni	P	E.Broglio
P	D.Cardwell	P	K.Johnson	/P	E.Palmquist	P	T.Cloninger	P	C.Short	P	F.Green			RP	L.McDaniel
P	G.Hobbie	P	B.Henry	/P	E.Roebuck	P	M.Drabowsky	P	R.Roberts	P	G.Witt			RP	A.Cicotte
P	D.Ellsworth	P	H.Nunn			P	R.Piche	P	J.Owens	/P	L.Foss			RP	B.Miller
P	J.Curtis	P	M.Bridges			P	C.Raymond	P	P.Brown	/P	J.Umbricht				
RP	B.Anderson	/P	C.Osteen			P	S.Morehead	/P	T.Farrell	/P	T.Cheney			P	C.Anderson
RP	D.Drott					/P	J.Antonelli	/P	J.Meyer					P	M.McDermott
RP	D.Elston					/P	K.MacKenzie							/P	R.Washburn
						/P	G.Brunet							P	E.Bauta
P	J.Brewer					/P	C.Olivo							/P	B.Tiefenauer
P	B.Schultz														
P	J.Schaffernoth														
P	M.Wright														
/P	D.Burwell														

TEAM	G	W	L	PCT	GB	R	OR	AB	H	2B	3B	HR	BB	SO	AVG	OBP	SLG	PRO	PRO+	BR	/A	PF	CHI	RC	SB	CS	SBA	SBR
CIN	154	93	61	.604		710	653	5243	1414	247	35	158	423	761	.270	.328	.421	.749	102	19	10	101	101	713	70	33	68	1
LA	154	89	65	.578	4	735	697	5189	1358	193	40	157	596	796	.262	.340	.405	.745	95	29	-35	109	100	722	86	45	66	-1
SF	155	85	69	.552	8	773	655	5233	1379	219	32	183	506	764	.264	.332	.423	.755	109	35	62	96	106	719	79	54	59	-9
MIL	155	83	71	.539	10	712	656	5288	1365	199	34	188	534	880	.258	.330	.415	.745	110	19	63	94	98	714	70	43	62	-5
STL	155	80	74	.519	13	703	668	5307	1436	236	51	103	494	745	.271	.336	.393	.729	90	-3	-72	110	100	702	46	28	62	-3
PIT	154	75	79	.487	18	694	675	5311	1428	232	57	112	428	721	.273	.330	.410	.740	101	8	6	100	99	694	26	30	46	-10
CHI	156	64	90	.416	29	689	800	5344	1364	238	51	176	539	1027	.255	.327	.418	.745	101	16	7	101	95	726	35	25	58	-5
PHI	155	47	107	.305	46	584	796	5213	1265	185	50	103	475	928	.243	.311	.357	.668	84	-123	-115	99	102	577	56	30	65	-1
TOT	619					5600		42128	11029	1749	350	1196	3995	6622	.262	.329	.405	.735							468	288	62	-32

TEAM	CG	SH	SV	IP	H	H/G	HR	BB	SO	RAT	ERA	ERA+	OAV	OOB	PR	/A	PF	CPI	FA	E	DP	FW	PW	BW	SBW	DIF
CIN	46	12	40	1370	1300	8.5	147	500	829	12.0	3.78	107	.250	.320	38	43	101	98	.977	134	124	.7	4.3	1.0	.5	9.6
LA	40	10	35	1378¹	1346	8.8	167	544	1105	12.7	4.04	107	.256	.331	-2	46	108	101	.975	144	162	.1	4.6	-3.5	.3	10.5
SF	39	9	30	1388	1306	8.5	152	502	924	11.9	3.77	101	.249	.318	40	6	95	98	.977	133	126	.8	.6	6.2	-.5	1.0
MIL	57	8	16	1391¹	1357	8.8	153	493	652	12.1	3.89	96	.258	.324	21	-24	93	101	.982	111	152	2.0	-2.4	6.3	-.0	.2
STL	49	10	24	1368²	1334	8.8	136	570	823	12.7	3.74	118	.256	.333	44	100	110	106	.972	166	165	-1.1	9.9	-7.1	.1	1.2
PIT	34	9	29	1362	1442	9.5	121	400	759	12.3	3.92	102	.274	.328	17	10	99	102	.975	150	187	-.2	1.0	.6	-.6	-2.8
CHI	34	6	25	1385	1492	9.7	165	465	755	12.9	4.48	93	.277	.338	-70	-47	104	99	.970	183	175	-2.0	-4.7	.7	-.0	-7.0
PHI	29	9	13	1383¹	1452	9.4	155	521	775	13.1	4.61	88	.273	.342	-88	-82	101	96	.976	146	179	.0	-8.1	-11.4	.3	-10.8
TOT	328	73	212	11026²		9.0				12.5	4.03		.262	.329					.976	1167	1270					

Runs
Mays-SF 129
Robinson-Cin 117
Aaron-Mil 115
Boyer-StL 109

Hits
Pinson-Cin 208
Clemente-Pit 201
Aaron-Mil 197
Boyer-StL 194
Cepeda-SF 182

Doubles
Aaron-Mil 39
Pinson-Cin 34
Santo-Chi 32
Robinson-Cin 32
Mays-SF 32

Triples
Altman-Chi 12
White-StL 11
Callison-Phi 11
Boyer-StL 11

Home Runs
Cepeda-SF 46
Mays-SF 40
Robinson-Cin 37
Stuart-Pit 35
Adcock-Mil 35

Total Bases
Aaron-Mil 358
Cepeda-SF 356
Mays-SF 334
Robinson-Cin 333
Clemente-Pit 320

Runs Batted In
Cepeda-SF 142
Robinson-Cin 124
Mays-SF 123
Aaron-Mil 120
Stuart-Pit 117

Runs Produced
Mays-SF 212
Robinson-Cin 204
Cepeda-SF 201
Aaron-Mil 201
Boyer-StL 180

Bases On Balls
Mathews-Mil 93
Moon-LA 89
Mays-SF 81
Gilliam-LA 79

Batting Average
Clemente-Pit .... .351
Pinson-Cin ...... .343
Boyer-StL .... .329
Moon-LA .... .328
Aaron-Mil .... .327

On Base Percentage
Moon-LA .... .438
Robinson-Cin .... .411
Mathews-Mil ..... .405
Boyer-StL .... .400
Mays-SF .... .395

Slugging Average
Robinson-Cin .... .611
Cepeda-SF .... .609
Aaron-Mil .... .594
Mays-SF .... .584
Stuart-Pit ...... .581

Production
Robinson-Cin 1.022
Aaron-Mil .... .979
Mays-SF .... .979
Cepeda-SF .... .972
Clemente-Pit .... .951

Adjusted Production
Aaron-Mil 165
Robinson-Cin 164
Mays-SF 162
Cepeda-SF 158
Mathews-Mil 156

Batter Runs
Robinson-Cin 52.4
Aaron-Mil 46.0
Mays-SF 45.8
Cepeda-SF 40.7
Mathews-Mil 40.4

Adjusted Batter Runs
Aaron-Mil 53.8
Robinson-Cin 50.8
Mays-SF 50.4
Mathews-Mil 47.8
Cepeda-SF 45.1

Clutch Hitting Index
Moon-LA 113
McMillan-Mil 110
Davenport-SF 110
Adcock-Mil 105
Cepeda-SF 105

Runs Created
Robinson-Cin 137
Aaron-Mil 132
Mays-SF 130
Mathews-Mil 128
Boyer-StL 126

Total Average
Robinson-Cin 1.119
Mays-SF 1.017
Moon-LA 1.003
Aaron-Mil .... .993
Mathews-Mil ..... .981

Stolen Bases
Wills-LA 35
Pinson-Cin 23
Robinson-Cin 22
Aaron-Mil 21
Mays-SF 18

Stolen Base Average
Robinson-Cin 88.0
Wills-LA 70.0
Aaron-Mil 70.0
Pinson-Cin 69.7
Mays-SF 66.7

Stolen Base Runs
Robinson-Cin 4.8
Maye-Mil 2.4
Williams-Chi 1.8
Wills-LA 1.5
Gonzalez-Phi 1.5

Fielding Runs
Mazeroski-Pit ... 30.5
Pinson-Cin 19.2
Malkmus-Phi 16.3
Clemente-Pit 14.4
Amaro-Phi 14.1

Total Player Rating
Aaron-Mil 5.6
Robinson-Cin 5.5
Mays-SF 5.0
Clemente-Pit 4.4
Mathews-Mil 4.2

Wins
Spahn-Mil 21
Jay-Cin 21
O'Toole-Cin 19

Win Percentage
Podres-LA .... .783
O'Toole-Cin ..... .679
Jay-Cin .... .677
Burdette-Mil .... .621
Spahn-Mil .... .618

Games
Baldschun-Phi ... 65
Miller-SF 63
Face-Pit 62
Elston-Chi 58
Anderson-Chi 57

Complete Games
Spahn-Mil 21
Koufax-LA 15
Jay-Cin 14
Burdette-Mil 14

Shutouts
Spahn-Mil 4
Jay-Cin 4

Saves
Miller-SF 17
Face-Pit 17
Henry-Cin 16
Brosnan-Cin 16
L.Sherry-LA 15

Innings Pitched
Burdette-Mil 272.1
Spahn-Mil 262.2
Cardwell-Chi 259.1
Koufax-LA 255.2
O'Toole-Cin 252.2

Fewest Hits/Game
Koufax-LA 7.46
Jay-Cin 7.90
Gibson-StL 7.92
Sadecki-StL 7.92
Spahn-Mil 8.09

Fewest BB/Game
Burdette-Mil 1.09
Friend-Pit 1.72
Purkey-Cin 1.86
Spahn-Mil 2.19
Ellsworth-Chi ... 2.31

Strikeouts
Koufax-LA 269
Williams-LA 205
Drysdale-LA 182
O'Toole-Cin 178
Gibson-StL 166

Strikeouts/Game
Koufax-LA 9.47
Williams-LA 7.84
Gibson-StL 7.07
Drysdale-LA 6.71
Gibbon-Pit 6.68

Ratio
Spahn-Mil 10.42
Burdette-Mil 10.94
Koufax-LA 10.95
Purkey-Cin 11.03
Jackson-StL 11.22

Earned Run Average
Spahn-Mil 3.02
O'Toole-Cin 3.10
Simmons-StL 3.13
McCormick-SF 3.20
Gibson-StL 3.24

Adjusted ERA
Simmons-StL 141
Gibson-StL 136
O'Toole-Cin 131
Spahn-Mil 124
Koufax-LA 123

Opponents' Batting Avg.
Koufax-LA .... .222
Jay-Cin .... .236
Sadecki-StL ..... .238
Gibson-StL ...... .239
O'Toole-Cin ..... .240

Opponents' On Base Pct.
Spahn-Mil .... .293
Koufax-LA .... .295
Burdette-Mil .... .296
Purkey-Cin ...... .297
Jackson-StL ..... .303

Starter Runs
Spahn-Mil 29.7
O'Toole-Cin 26.2
McCormick-SF 23.0
Simmons-StL 19.6
Gibson-StL 18.7

Adjusted Starter Runs
Simmons-StL 27.6
Gibson-StL 27.3
O'Toole-Cin 27.1
Koufax-LA 23.3
Spahn-Mil 21.2

Clutch Pitching Index
Simmons-StL 122
Ellsworth-Chi ... 121
Podres-LA 116
McCormick-SF 115
Gibson-StL 114

Relief Runs
Miller-SF 18.6
Perranoski-LA ... 14.1
McMahon-Mil 12.2
Henry-Cin 10.9
Schultz-Chi 9.9

Adjusted Relief Runs
Perranoski-LA ... 17.2
Miller-SF 15.6
Henry-Cin 11.1
Schultz-Chi 11.0
McMahon-Mil 9.2

Relief Ranking
Miller-SF 26.8
Perranoski-LA ... 22.8
Schultz-Chi 21.8
Brosnan-Cin 18.5
Henry-Cin 13.1

Total Pitcher Index
Spahn-Mil 3.9
Gibson-StL 3.3
Miller-SF 3.1
Simmons-StL 3.0
O'Toole-Cin 2.7

Total Baseball Ranking
Aaron-Mil 5.6
Robinson-Cin 5.5
Mays-SF 5.0
Clemente-Pit 4.4
Mathews-Mil 4.2

January 29 Billy Hamilton and Max Carey are voted into the Hall of Fame by the Special Veterans Committee.

May 9 Jim Gentile becomes the fourth player to hit grand slams in consecutive at bats (Tony Lazzeri in 1936, Jim Tabor in 1939, Rudy York in 1946 also hit two grand slams, but not in consecutive innings) when he homers off Pedro Ramos in the first and Paul Giel in the second. His eight RBI in consecutive innings set a record. Gentile also tacks on a SF to give him nine RBI in the 13-5 drubbing of the Twins.

May 12 Bill Monbouquette's 17 strikeouts for the Red Sox are a club record and the most yet by an AL pitcher in a night game. He beats Washington 2-1.

June 12 An ailing Bill Veeck sells his interest in the White Sox to Arthur Allyn. Allyn also buys Hank Greenberg's stock to acquire a controlling interest.

June 18 St. Louis Browns midget Eddie Gaedel dies of a heart attack following a mugging in Chicago. He was 36.

July 17 Following a year-long illness, Ty Cobb succumbs to cancer at age 74 at Emory University Hospital in Atlanta.

September 20 The Yankees' 155th game of 1961 (including a tie) is Roger Maris's last chance to beat the Babe, in compliance with Commissioner Ford Frick's statement that Maris must do it in the same number of games as Ruth. Maris's 59th homer of the year, off Jack Fisher, is short of the record, but helps NY beat Baltimore 4-2, clinching its 26th AL pennant.

September 22 Jim Gentile's fifth grand slam ties the ML single-season record in Baltimore's 8-6 win over Chicago. Each of Gentile's slams comes with Chuck Estrada pitching for the Orioles.

October 1 Maris's tortuous season long race against Babe Ruth ends in a dramatic at bat against Boston's Tracy Stallard. Maris's classic left-handed swing sends homer number 61 into the right field stands in "The House That Ruth Built." (Fan Sal Durante grabs the historic ball which he sells for $5,000.) New York's 1-0 win gives the Yanks 109 wins, one short of the club's 1927 record.

October 4 Whitey Ford's third straight World Series shutout, with home runs by Elston Howard and Bill Skowron, gives New York a 2-0 win in the opener against Cincinnati at Yankee Stadium.

October 9 Star reserves Johnny Blanchard and Hector Lopez spark a five-run first inning and 13-5 win for New York. Both hit home runs, and Lopez drives in five runs. Bud Daley's long relief effort wraps up the Series, as Ralph Houk becomes the third rookie pilot to guide a World Series winner.

October 31 A Federal judge rules that Birmingham, Alabama, laws against integrated playing fields are illegal, eliminating the last barrier against integration in the Southern Association.

November 8 Whitey Ford is voted the Cy Young Award over Warren Spahn.

November 15 Roger Maris is voted AL MVP with 202 votes to 198 for Mickey Mantle and 157 for Jim Gentile.

November 26 The Rules Committee votes 8-1 against legalizing the spitball. Only NL supervisor of umpires Cal Hubbard votes in favor.

BALTIMORE		BOSTON		CHICAGO		CLEVELAND		DETROIT	
M	P.Richards	M	P.Higgins	M	A.Lopez	M	J.Dykes	M	B.Scheffing
M	L.Harris	1B	P.Runnels	1B	R.Sievers	M	M.Harder	1B	N.Cash
1B	J.Gentile	2B	C.Schilling	2B	N.Fox	1B	V.Power	2B	J.Wood
2B	J.Adair	SS	D.Buddin	SS	L.Aparicio	2B	J.Temple	SS	C.Fernandez
SS	R.Hansen	3B	F.Malzone	3B	A.Smith	SS	W.Held	3B	S.Boros
3B	B.Robinson	LF	C.Yastrzemski	LF	M.Minoso	3B	B.Phillips	LF	R.Colavito
LF	R.Snyder	CF	G.Geiger	CF	J.Landis	LF	T.Francona	CF	B.Bruton
CF	J.Brandt	RF	J.Jensen	RF	F.Robinson	CF	J.Piersall	RF	A.Kaline
RF	W.Herzog	C	J.Pagliaroni	C	S.Lollar	RF	W.Kirkland	C	D.Brown
C	G.Triandos					C	J.Romano		
		1	V.Wertz	13	J.Martin			S3	D.McAuliffe
O1	D.Williams	O	C.Hardy	C	C.Carreon	P	M.Grant	C	M.Roarke
2	M.Breeding	C	R.Nixon			P	G.Bell		
O	E.Robinson	S	P.Green	P	J.Pizarro	P	J.Perry	P	F.Lary
				P	F.Baumann	P	B.Latman	P	J.Bunning
P	S.Barber	P	B.Monbouquette	P	B.Pierce	P	W.Hawkins	P	D.Mossi
P	C.Estrada	P	G.Conley	P	C.McLish	RP	B.Locke	P	P.Foytack
P	J.Fisher	P	D.Schwall	P	R.Herbert	RP	F.Funk	P	P.Regan
P	M.Pappas	P	I.Delock	RP	T.Lown	RP	B.Allen	RP	T.Fox
P	H.Brown	P	T.Stallard	RP	R.Kemmerer			RP	H.Aguirre
RP	H.Wilhelm	RP	M.Fornieles	RP	D.Larsen	P	D.Stigman		
RP	W.Stock	RP	B.Muffett					P	R.Kline
		RP	D.Hillman	P	E.Wynn				
P	B.Hoeft			P	B.Shaw				
P	D.Hall	P	G.Cisco	P	W.Hacker				
		P	C.Nichols						
		P	A.Earley						

KANSAS CITY		LOS ANGELES		MINNESOTA		NEW YORK		WASHINGTON	
M	J.Gordon	M	B.Rigney	M	C.Lavagetto	M	R.Houk	M	M.Vernon
M	H.Bauer	1B	S.Bilko	M	S.Mele	1B	B.Skowron	1B	D.Long
1B	N.Siebern	2B	K.Aspromonte	M	C.Lavagetto	2B	B.Richardson	2B	C.Cottier
2B	J.Lumpe	SS	J.Koppe	M	S.Mele	SS	T.Kubek	SS	C.Veal
SS	D.Howser	3B	E.Yost	1B	H.Killebrew	3B	C.Boyer	3B	D.O'Connell
3B	W.Causey	LF	L.Wagner	2B	B.Martin	LF	Y.Berra	LF	M.Keough
LF	L.Posada	CF	K.Hunt	SS	Z.Versalles	CF	M.Mantle	CF	W.Tasby
CF	B.Del Greco	RF	A.Pearson	3B	B.Tuttle	RF	R.Maris	RF	G.Woodling
RF	D.Johnson	C	E.Averill	LF	J.Lemon	C	E.Howard	C	G.Green
C	H.Sullivan			CF	L.Green				
		1	T.Kluszewski	RF	B.Allison	CO	J.Blanchard	O	J.King
C	J.Pignatano	O1	L.Thomas	C	E.Battey	O	H.Lopez	C	C.Hinton
		O3	G.Thomas					3S	B.Klaus
P	J.Archer	2S	R.Bridges	P	P.Ramos	P	W.Ford	S	B.Johnson
P	N.Bass			P	C.Pascual	P	B.Stafford	C	P.Daley
P	J.Walker	P	K.McBride	P	J.Kralick	P	R.Terry		
P	B.Shaw	P	E.Grba	P	J.Kaat	P	R.Sheldon	P	J.McClain
P	J.Nuxhall	P	T.Bowsfield	P	D.Lee	P	J.Coates	P	B.Daniels
RP	E.Rakow	P	R.Moeller	RP	B.Pleis	RP	L.Arroyo	P	D.Donovan
RP	B.Kunkel	P	R.Kline	RP	R.Moore			P	E.Hobaugh
RP	A.Ditmar	RP	J.Donohue			P	B.Daley	P	P.Burnside
		RP	R.Duren	P	A.Schroll	P	B.Turley	RP	M.Kutyna
P	R.Herbert	RP	T.Morgan			P	A.Ditmar	RP	J.Klippstein
P	B.Daley							RP	D.Sisler
P	L.Krausse	P	A.Fowler						
		P	J.James					P	G.Gabler
								P	T.Sturdivant

TEAM	G	W	L	PCT	GB	R	OR	AB	H	2B	3B	HR	BB	SO	AVG	OBP	SLG	PRO	PRO+	BR	/A	PF	CHI	RC	SB	CS	SBA	SBR
NY	163	109	53	.673		827	612	5559	1461	194	40	**240**	543	785	.263	.332	**.442**	**.774**	118	82	**125**	95	101	811	28	18	61	-2
DET	163	101	61	.623	8	**841**	671	5561	1481	215	**53**	180	673	867	**.266**	**.349**	.421	.770	109	96	72	103	99	**835**	98	36	73	**8**
BAL	163	95	67	.586	14	691	**588**	5481	1393	227	36	149	581	902	.254	.328	.390	.718	102	-16	9	97	97	699	39	30	57	-6
CHI	163	86	76	.531	23	765	726	5556	1475	216	46	138	550	**612**	.265	.338	.395	.733	104	17	29	98	101	754	**100**	40	71	6
CLE	161	78	83	.484	30.5	737	752	5609	**1493**	**257**	39	150	492	720	**.266**	.328	.406	.734	105	9	29	97	99	743	34	11	**76**	4
BOS	163	76	86	.469	33	729	792	5508	1401	251	37	112	647	847	.254	.336	.374	.710	94	-22	-39	102	101	704	56	36	61	-5
MIN	161	70	90	.438	38	707	778	5417	1353	215	40	167	597	840	.250	.328	.397	.725	95	-5	-45	106	98	698	47	43	52	-12
LA	162	70	91	.435	38.5	744	784	5424	1331	218	22	189	**681**	1068	.245	.333	.398	.731	91	12	-72	111	99	734	37	28	57	-6
WAS	161	61	100	.379	47.5	618	776	5366	1307	217	44	119	558	917	.244	.317	.367	.684	90	-83	-74	99	98	625	81	47	63	-4
KC	162	61	100	.379	47.5	683	863	5423	1342	216	47	90	580	772	.247	.323	.354	.677	85	-90	-101	102	**107**	642	58	22	73	4
TOT	811					7342		54904	14037	2226	404	1534	5902	8330	.256	.331	.395	.726							578	311	65	-13

TEAM	CG	SH	SV	IP	H	H/G	HR	BB	SO	RAT	ERA	ERA+	OAV	OOB	PR	/A	PF	CPI	FA	E	DP	FW	PW	BW	SBW	DIF
NY	47	14	**39**	1451	1288	8.0	137	542	866	11.5	3.46	107	.239	.312	91	42	92	99	**.980**	124	180	**1.6**	4.2	12.4	-.0	9.9
DET	**62**	12	30	1459¹	1404	8.7	170	**469**	836	11.7	3.55	116	.252	.313	78	90	102	**106**	.976	146	147	.3	8.9	7.1	**.9**	2.7
BAL	54	**21**	33	1471¹	**1226**	**7.5**	109	617	926	11.5	**3.22**	**120**	**.227**	**.310**	**132**	103	96	97	**.980**	128	173	1.4	**10.2**	.9	-.5	2.0
CHI	39	3	23	1448²	1491	9.3	158	498	814	12.4	4.06	97	.268	.329	-5	-23	97	102	**.980**	128	138	1.4	-2.3	2.9	.7	2.3
CLE	35	12	23	1443¹	1426	8.9	178	599	801	12.8	4.15	95	.258	.334	-20	-34	98	102	.977	139	142	.6	-3.4	2.9	.5	-3.2
BOS	35	6	30	1442²	1472	9.2	167	679	831	13.5	4.29	97	.266	.348	-43	-20	104	105	.977	144	170	.4	-2.0	-3.9	-.4	.8
MIN	49	14	23	1432¹	1415	8.9	163	570	914	12.8	4.28	99	.256	.331	-41	-6	95	95	.972	174	150	-1.4	-.6	-4.5	-1.1	-2.5
LA	25	5	34	1438	1391	8.7	180	713	**973**	13.4	4.31	105	.254	.343	-46	32	112	101	.969	192	154	-2.4	3.2	-7.1	-.5	-3.6
WAS	39	8	21	1425	1405	8.9	131	586	666	12.8	4.23	95	.260	.336	-33	-34	100	96	.975	156	171	-.4	-3.4	-7.3	-.3	-8.2
KC	32	5	23	1415	1519	9.7	141	629	703	14.0	4.74	88	.275	.355	-113	-89	104	97	.972	175	160	-1.4	-8.8	-10.0	.5	.2
TOT	417	100	289	14426²		8.8				12.6	4.02		.256	.331					.976	1506	1585					

Runs		Hits		Doubles		Triples		Home Runs		Total Bases	
Maris-NY	132	Cash-Det	193	Kaline-Det	41	Wood-Det	14	Maris-NY	61	Maris-NY	366
Mantle-NY	132	B.Robinson-Bal	192	B.Robinson-Bal	38	Lumpe-KC	9	Mantle-NY	54	Cash-Det	354
Colavito-Det	129	Kaline-Det	190	Kubek-NY	38	Keough-Was	9	Killebrew-Min	46	Mantle-NY	353
Cash-Det	119	Francona-Cle	178	Siebern-KC	36			Gentile-Bal	46	Colavito-Det	338
Kaline-Det	116	Richardson-NY	173	Power-Cle	34			Colavito-Det	45	Killebrew-Min	328

Runs Batted In		Runs Produced		Bases On Balls		Batting Average		On Base Percentage		Slugging Average	
Maris-NY	142	Colavito-Det	224	Mantle-NY	126	Cash-Det	.361	Cash-Det	.488	Mantle-NY	.687
Gentile-Bal	141	Maris-NY	213	Cash-Det	124	Kaline-Det	.324	Mantle-NY	.452	Cash-Det	.662
Colavito-Det	140	Cash-Det	210	Colavito-Det	113	Piersall-Cle	.322	Gentile-Bal	.428	Gentile-Bal	.646
Cash-Det	132	Mantle-NY	206	Killebrew-Min	107	Mantle-NY	.317	Pearson-LA	.422	Maris-NY	.620
Mantle-NY	128	Gentile-Bal	191	Allison-Min	103	Gentile-Bal	.302	Killebrew-Min	.409	Killebrew-Min	.606

Production		Adjusted Production		Batter Runs		Adjusted Batter Runs		Clutch Hitting Index		Runs Created	
Cash-Det	1.150	Mantle-NY	210	Cash-Det	86.1	Mantle-NY	84.4	Schilling-Bos	120	Cash-Det	178
Mantle-NY	1.138	Cash-Det	198	Mantle-NY	76.3	Cash-Det	81.5	Gentile-Bal	115	Mantle-NY	174
Gentile-Bal	1.074	Gentile-Bal	189	Gentile-Bal	59.1	Gentile-Bal	63.7	Malzone-Bos	115	Colavito-Det	141
Killebrew-Min	1.015	Maris-NY	170	Killebrew-Min	52.9	Maris-NY	56.5	Allison-Min	111	Gentile-Bal	138
Maris-NY	.997	Killebrew-Min	159	Colavito-Det	51.5	Colavito-Det	47.8	Siebern-KC	109	Maris-NY	138

Total Average		Stolen Bases		Stolen Base Average		Stolen Base Runs		Fielding Runs		Total Player Rating	
Mantle-NY	1.384	Aparicio-Chi	53	Hinton-Was	81.5	Aparicio-Chi	8.1	Boyer-NY	30.3	Mantle-NY	8.0
Cash-Det	1.358	Howser-KC	37	Howser-KC	80.4	Howser-KC	5.7	Landis-Chi	19.3	Cash-Det	7.1
Gentile-Bal	1.196	Wood-Det	30	Aparicio-Chi	80.3	Wood-Det	3.6	Power-Cle	18.1	Gentile-Bal	5.3
Killebrew-Min	1.098	Hinton-Was	22	Geiger-Bos	80.0	Kaline-Det	3.6	Cottier-Det-Was	16.9	Colavito-Det	4.7
Colavito-Det	1.051	Bruton-Det	22	Landis-Chi	79.2	Hinton-Was	3.6	Lumpe-KC	16.0	Howard-NY	4.2

Wins		Win Percentage		Games		Complete Games		Shutouts		Saves	
Ford-NY	25	Ford-NY	.862	Arroyo-NY	65	Lary-Det	22	Pascual-Min	8	Arroyo-NY	29
Lary-Det	23	Terry-NY	.842	Morgan-LA	59	Pascual-Min	15	Barber-Bal	8	Wilhelm-Bal	18
Barber-Bal	18	Arroyo-NY	.750	Lown-Chi	59	Barber-Bal	14	Pappas-Bal	4	Fornieles-Bos	15
Bunning-Det	17	Lary-Det	.719	Kunkel-KC	58			Lary-Det	4	Moore-Min	14
Terry-NY	16			Fornieles-Bos	57			Bunning-Det	4	Fox-Det	12

Innings Pitched		Fewest Hits/Game		Fewest BB/Game		Strikeouts		Strikeouts/Game		Ratio	
Ford-NY	283.0	Estrada-Bal	6.75	Mossi-Det	1.76	Pascual-Min	221	Pizarro-Chi	8.69	Donovan-Was	9.39
Lary-Det	275.1	Pappas-Bal	6.79	Brown-Bal	1.78	Ford-NY	209	Pascual-Min	7.88	Terry-NY	9.80
Bunning-Det	268.0	Barber-Bal	7.03	Donovan-Was	1.87	Bunning-Det	194	Estrada-Bal	6.79	Brown-Bal	10.10
Ramos-Min	264.1	Pascual-Min	7.31	Terry-NY	2.01	Pizarro-Chi	188	McBride-LA	6.70	Bunning-Det	10.48
Pascual-Min	252.1	Donovan-Was	7.36	McClain-Was	2.04	McBride-LA	180	Ford-NY	6.65	Lary-Det	10.59

Earned Run Average		Adjusted ERA		Opponents' Batting Avg.		Opponents' On Base Pct.		Starter Runs		Adjusted Starter Runs	
Donovan-Was	2.40	Donovan-Was	167	Estrada-Bal	.207	Donovan-Was	.269	Hoeft-Bal	30.7	Mossi-Det	30.5
Stafford-NY	2.68	Stafford-NY	139	Pappas-Bal	.208	Terry-NY	.277	Donovan-Was	30.4	Donovan-Was	30.3
Mossi-Det	2.96	Mossi-Det	139	Pascual-Min	.217	Bunning-Det	.285	Stafford-NY	29.2	Hoeft-Bal	28.0
Pappas-Bal	3.04	Archer-KC	131	Barber-Bal	.218	Brown-Bal	.286	Mossi-Det	28.5	Bunning-Det	27.1
Pizarro-Chi	3.05	Schwall-Bos	129	Donovan-Was	.224	Ford-NY	.292	Ford-NY	25.5	Lary-Det	26.5

Clutch Pitching Index		Relief Runs		Adjusted Relief Runs		Relief Ranking		Total Pitcher Index		Total Baseball Ranking	
Schwall-Bos	131	Arroyo-NY	24.2	Morgan-LA	21.9	Arroyo-NY	41.6	Arroyo-NY	4.3	Mantle-NY	8.0
Mossi-Det	119	Wilhelm-Bal	21.0	Arroyo-NY	20.2	Wilhelm-Bal	31.8	Lary-Det	3.7	Cash-Det	7.1
Shaw-Chi-KC	115	Morgan-LA	17.0	Wilhelm-Bal	18.9	Morgan-LA	26.9	Donovan-Was	3.7	Gentile-Bal	5.3
Monbouquette-Bos	115	Fox-Det	16.6	Fox-Det	17.1	Fox-Det	26.9	Wilhelm-Bal	3.2	Colavito-Det	4.7
McBride-LA	112	Lown-Chi	14.2	Lown-Chi	12.9	Lown-Chi	17.0	Fox-Det	2.8	Arroyo-NY	4.3

April 13 Just 12,447 Mets' fans welcome the return of NL baseball to New York. Sherman Jones drops a 4-3 decision to the Pirates at the Polo Grounds.

April 24 Sandy Koufax ties the modern major league record he shares with Bob Feller by fanning 18 Cubs in nine innings. The Dodgers win 10-2.

May 19 Stan Musial gets hit number 3,431, to break Honus Wagner's recognized NL record of 3,430 (since revised to 3,415), as St. Louis downs the Dodgers 8-1. Musial's ninth-inning single comes off Ron Perranoski.

June 30 With the aid of 13 strikeouts, Sandy Koufax no-hits Bob Miller and the Mets 5-0 in Los Angeles.

July 10 Roberto Clemente has three hits as the NL wins 3-1 in the first All-Star Game of 1962, at DC Stadium.

July 17 Sandy Koufax leaves after one inning of a 7-5 loss at Cincinnati. The 14-game winner has a circulatory problem in the index finger and palm of his pitching hand and will be sidelined until late September.

July 23 Bob Feller, Jackie Robinson, Bill McKechnie, and Edd Roush are inducted into the Baseball Hall of Fame.

July 25 Stan Musial becomes the NL's all-time leader in runs batted in with 1,862, driving in both of the Cardinal runs in a 5-2 loss to the Dodgers.

July 31 The NL rejects Commissioner Ford Frick's proposal for interleague play in 1963.

September 5 Ken Hubbs of the Cubs sets major league records at second base for consecutive games without an error (78) and consecutive chances accepted (418) without an error. His streak ends with a fourth-inning throwing error as Cincinnati beats Chicago 4-1.

September 18 Bob Aspromonte of the Colt .45s sets an NL record for third basemen with his 57th straight errorless game.

September 23 A 12-2 Dodger loss at St. Louis is enlivened by Maury Wills, who ties Ty Cobb's long-standing major league single-season record of 96 steals by swiping second base after singling in the third, and breaks it with a repeat performance in the seventh.

September 29 The Dodgers (101-59) send Don Drysdale against the Cardinals, but Ernie Broglio wins the pitching duel 2-0. The Dodgers lead by one game with one to play.

September 30 Willie Mays's 47th homer, an eighth-inning blast off Dick Farrell (10-20), gives the Giants a critical 2-1 win. They then stay in the clubhouse to hear results of the Dodger game. Gene Oliver's homer off Johnny Podres gives Curt Simmons and St. Louis a 1-0 win against the Dodgers and a three-game sweep at Chavez Ravine. The loss forces the fourth playoff in NL history.

October 3 A crowd of 45,693, giving the Dodgers a major league-record season attendance of 2,755,184, attends the deciding game of the NL season. In the seventh, Maury Wills collects his fourth single of the day, and his 103rd and 104th steals of the year. But the Giants score four in the ninth to win 6-4 and put themselves in the World Series.

November 23 Dodgers shortstop Maury Wills is named the NL's Most Valuable Player.

November 29 Major league officials and player representatives agree to return to a single All-Star Game in 1963. The players' pension fund will receive 95 percent of the one game's proceeds (not 60 percent of the two games).

CHICAGO		CINCINNATI		HOUSTON		LOS ANGELES		MILWAUKEE	
M	E.Tappe	M	F.Hutchinson	M	H.Craft	M	W.Alston	M	B.Tebbetts
M	L.Klein	1B	G.Coleman	1B	N.Larker	1B	R.Fairly	1B	J.Adcock
M	C.Metro	2B	D.Blasingame	2B	J.Amalfitano	2B	L.Burright	2B	F.Bolling
1B	E.Banks	SS	L.Cardenas	SS	B.Lillis	SS	M.Wills	SS	R.McMillan
2B	K.Hubbs	3B	E.Kasko	3B	B.Aspromonte	3B	J.Gilliam	3B	E.Mathews
SS	A.Rodgers	LF	W.Post	LF	A.Spangler	LF	T.Davis	LF	L.Maye
3B	R.Santo	CF	V.Pinson	CF	C.Warwick	CF	W.Davis	CF	H.Aaron
LF	B.Williams	RF	F.Robinson	RF	R.Mejias	RF	F.Howard	RF	M.Jones
CF	L.Brock	C	J.Edwards	C	H.Smith	C	J.Roseboro	C	D.Crandall
RF	G.Altman								
C	D.Bertell	O1	M.Keough	O	J.Pendleton	O1	W.Moon	1O	T.Aaron
		O	J.Lynch	C	M.Ranew			C	J.Torre
O	D.Landrum					P	D.Drysdale	O	G.Bell
		P	B.Purkey	P	T.Farrell	P	J.Podres	S2	A.Samuel
P	B.Buhl	P	J.Jay	P	K.Johnson	P	S.Williams	P	W.Spahn
P	D.Ellsworth	P	J.O'Toole	P	B.Bruce	P	S.Koufax	P	B.Shaw
P	D.Cardwell	P	J.Maloney	P	J.Golden	RP	E.Roebuck	P	B.Hendley
P	C.Koonce	RP	J.Klippstein	P	H.Woodeshick	RP	R.Perranoski	P	L.Burdette
P	G.Hobbie	RP	J.Brosnan	RP	B.Tiefenauer	RP	L.Sherry	P	T.Cloninger
RP	B.Anderson	RP	T.Wills	RP	D.McMahon			RP	J.Curtis
RP	B.Schultz			RP	R.Kemmerer	P	J.Moeller	RP	C.Willey
RP	D.Elston	P	M.Drabowsky			P	P.Richert	RP	D.Nottebart
		P	J.Nuxhall	P	D.Giusti	P	P.Ortega		
P	D.Gerard			P	J.Umbricht			P	D.Lemaster
				P	G.Brunet			P	R.Piche
				P	D.Stone				

NEW YORK		PHILADELPHIA		PITTSBURGH		SAN FRANCISCO		ST.LOUIS	
M	C.Stengel	M	G.Mauch	M	D.Murtaugh	M	A.Dark	M	J.Keane
1B	M.Throneberry	1B	R.Sievers	1B	D.Stuart	1B	O.Cepeda	1B	B.White
2B	C.Neal	2B	T.Taylor	2B	B.Mazeroski	2B	C.Hiller	2B	J.Javier
SS	E.Chacon	SS	B.Wine	SS	D.Groat	SS	J.Pagan	SS	J.Gotay
3B	F.Mantilla	3B	D.Demeter	3B	D.Hoak	3B	J.Davenport	3B	K.Boyer
LF	F.Thomas	LF	T.Savage	LF	B.Skinner	LF	H.Kuenn	LF	S.Musial
CF	J.Hickman	CF	T.Gonzalez	CF	B.Virdon	CF	W.Mays	CF	C.Flood
RF	R.Ashburn	RF	J.Callison	RF	R.Clemente	RF	F.Alou	RF	C.James
C	C.Cannizzaro	C	J.Dalrymple	C	S.Burgess	C	T.Haller	C	G.Oliver
O	J.Christopher	O	W.Covington	1O	D.Clendenon	C	E.Bailey	C	C.Sawatski
23	R.Kanehl	3S	B.Klaus			O1	W.McCovey		
		1	F.Torre	P	B.Friend			P	L.Jackson
P	R.Craig	S	R.Amaro	P	A.McBean	P	B.O'Dell	P	B.Gibson
P	A.Jackson			P	E.Francis	P	J.Sanford	P	E.Broglio
P	J.Hook	P	A.Mahaffey	P	H.Haddix	P	J.Marichal	P	R.Washburn
P	RL.Miller	P	J.Hamilton	P	V.Law	P	B.Pierce	P	C.Simmons
RP	C.Anderson	P	D.Bennett	RP	T.Sturdivant	P	M.McCormick	RP	L.McDaniel
RP	B.Moorhead	P	C.McLish	RP	R.Face	RP	S.Miller	RP	B.Shantz
RP	R.Daviault	P	C.Short	RP	D.Olivo	RP	B.Bolin	RP	D.Ferrarese
		RP	J.Baldschun			RP	D.Larsen		
P	RG.Miller	RP	P.Brown	P	J.Lamabe			P	R.Sadecki
P	K.MacKenzie	RP	B.Smith	P	J.Gibbon				
P	W.Hunter								
		P	D.Green						
		P	J.Owens						

TEAM	G	W	L	PCT	GB	R	OR	AB	H	2B	3B	HR	BB	SO	AVG	OBP	SLG	PRO	PRO+	BR	/A	PF	CHI	RC	SB	CS	SBA	SBR
SF	165	103	62	.624		878	690	5588	1552	235	32	204	523	822	.278	.344	.441	.785	119	123	138	98	102	838	73	50	59	-8
LA	165	102	63	.618	1	842	697	5628	1510	192	65	140	572	886	.268	.339	.400	.739	112	41	89	94	107	783	198	43	82	34
CIN	162	98	64	.605	3.5	802	685	5645	1523	252	40	167	498	903	.270	.333	.417	.750	104	54	29	103	102	779	66	39	63	-4
PIT	161	93	68	.578	8	706	626	5483	1468	240	65	108	432	836	.268	.323	.394	.717	99	-15	-16	100	102	682	50	39	56	-8
MIL	162	86	76	.531	15.5	730	665	5458	1376	204	38	181	581	975	.252	.328	.403	.731	105	16	36	97	99	720	57	27	68	1
STL	163	84	78	.519	17.5	774	664	5643	1528	221	31	137	515	846	.271	.337	.394	.731	94	22	-51	110	102	747	86	41	68	1
PHI	161	81	80	.503	20	705	759	5420	1410	199	39	142	531	923	.260	.332	.390	.722	103	4	26	97	98	705	79	42	65	-2
HOU	162	64	96	.400	36.5	592	717	5558	1370	170	47	105	493	806	.246	.312	.351	.663	91	-117	-72	93	97	605	42	30	58	-5
CHI	162	59	103	.364	42.5	632	827	5534	1398	196	56	126	504	1044	.253	.319	.377	.696	90	-53	-77	104	94	657	78	50	61	-7
NY	161	40	120	.250	60.5	617	948	5492	1318	166	40	139	616	991	.240	.320	.361	.681	88	-75	-86	102	94	640	59	48	55	-11
TOT	812					7278		55449	14453	2075	453	1449	5265	9032	.261	.329	.393	.722							788	409	66	-9

TEAM	CG	SH	SV	IP	H	H/G	HR	BB	SO	RAT	ERA	ERA+	OAV	OOB	PR	/A	PF	CPI	FA	E	DP	FW	PW	BW	SBW	DIF
SF	62	10	39	1461²	1399	8.6	148	503	886	11.9	3.79	100	.251	.316	24	0	96	95	.977	142	153	1.0	.0	13.8	-.7	6.5
LA	44	8	46	1488²	1386	8.4	115	588	1104	12.1	3.62	100	.245	.319	54	2	92	94	.970	193	144	-2.1	.2	8.9	3.5	9.0
CIN	51	13	35	1460²	1397	8.6	149	567	964	12.4	3.75	107	.254	.329	31	44	102	104	.977	145	144	.6	4.4	2.9	-.3	9.4
PIT	40	13	41	1432¹	1433	9.0	118	466	897	12.1	3.37	117	.262	.322	90	89	100	110	.976	152	177	.2	8.9	-1.6	-.7	5.8
MIL	59	10	24	1434²	1443	9.1	151	407	802	11.8	3.68	103	.262	.317	42	19	96	103	.980	124	154	1.9	1.9	3.6	.2	-2.6
STL	53	17	25	1463¹	1394	8.6	149	517	914	11.9	3.55	120	.252	.319	64	117	108	104	.979	132	170	1.5	11.7	-5.1	.2	-5.2
PHI	43	7	24	1426²	1469	9.3	155	574	863	13.2	4.28	90	.268	.343	-53	-65	98	102	.977	138	167	1.0	-6.5	2.6	-.1	3.5
HOU	34	9	19	1453²	1446	9.0	113	471	1047	12.1	3.83	98	.259	.321	19	-15	95	95	.973	173	149	-1.0	-1.5	-7.2	-.4	-5.9
CHI	29	4	26	1438¹	1509	9.4	159	601	783	13.5	4.54	91	.272	.348	-95	-62	105	99	.977	146	171	.6	-6.2	-7.7	-.6	-8.1
NY	43	4	10	1430	1577	9.9	192	571	772	13.8	5.04	83	.281	.352	-175	-137	106	96	.967	210	167	-3.3	-13.7	-8.6	-1.0	-13.4
TOT	458	95	289	14490		9.0				12.5	3.94		.261	.329					.975	1555	1596					

Runs		Hits		Doubles		Triples		Home Runs		Total Bases	
Robinson-Cin	134	T.Davis-LA	230	Robinson-Cin	51	Wills-LA	10	Mays-SF	49	Mays-SF	382
Wills-LA	130	Wills-LA	208	Mays-SF	36	Virdon-Pit	10	H.Aaron-Mil	45	Robinson-Cin	380
Mays-SF	130	Robinson-Cin	208	Groat-Pit	34	W.Davis-LA	10	Robinson-Cin	39	H.Aaron-Mil	366
H.Aaron-Mil	127	White-StL	199			Callison-Phi	10	Banks-Chi	37	T.Davis-LA	356
T.Davis-LA	120	Groat-Pit	199					Cepeda-SF	35	Cepeda-SF	324

Runs Batted In		Runs Produced		Bases On Balls		Batting Average		On Base Percentage		Slugging Average	
T.Davis-LA	153	T.Davis-LA	246	Mathews-Mil	101	T.Davis-LA	.346	Robinson-Cin	.424	Robinson-Cin	.624
Mays-SF	141	Robinson-Cin	231	Gilliam-LA	93	Robinson-Cin	.342	Musial-StL	.420	H.Aaron-Mil	.618
Robinson-Cin	136	Mays-SF	222	Ashburn-NY	81	Musial-StL	.330	Skinner-Pit	.397	Mays-SF	.615
H.Aaron-Mil	128	H.Aaron-Mil	210	Mays-SF	78	White-StL	.324	Altman-Chi	.394	Howard-LA	.560
Howard-LA	119					H.Aaron-Mil	.323	H.Aaron-Mil	.393	T.Davis-LA	.535

Production		Adjusted Production		Batter Runs		Adjusted Batter Runs		Clutch Hitting Index		Runs Created	
Robinson-Cin	1.048	Robinson-Cin	172	Robinson-Cin	66.6	Robinson-Cin	62.0	T.Davis-LA	125	Robinson-Cin	160
H.Aaron-Mil	1.012	H.Aaron-Mil	171	Mays-SF	54.1	H.Aaron-Mil	57.6	Howard-LA	122	Mays-SF	146
Mays-SF	1.001	Mays-SF	167	H.Aaron-Mil	54.0	Mays-SF	56.4	Musial-StL	112	H.Aaron-Mil	140
Musial-StL	.928	T.Davis-LA	151	T.Davis-LA	37.2	T.Davis-LA	44.7	Fairly-LA	112	T.Davis-LA	129
T.Davis-LA	.914	Howard-LA	149	Altman-Chi	31.5	Mathews-Mil	30.5	Santo-Chi	111	White-StL	114

Total Average		Stolen Bases		Stolen Base Average		Stolen Base Runs		Fielding Runs		Total Player Rating	
Robinson-Cin	1.125	Wills-LA	104	Mays-SF	90.0	Wills-LA	23.4	Mazeroski-Pit	41.1	Mays-SF	6.4
Mays-SF	1.060	W.Davis-LA	32	Wills-LA	88.9	W.Davis-LA	5.4	Callison-Phi	22.9	Robinson-Cin	6.0
H.Aaron-Mil	1.050	Pinson-Cin	26	W.Davis-LA	82.1	Mays-SF	4.2	Flood-StL	15.7	H.Aaron-Mil	5.5
Musial-StL	.957	Javier-StL	26	Clendenon-Pit	80.0	Pinson-Cin	3.0	Williams-Chi	15.5	Mazeroski-Pit	5.0
Skinner-Pit	.930	Taylor-Phi	20	Pinson-Cin	76.5			Kanehl-NY	14.5	Callison-Phi	3.9

Wins		Win Percentage		Games		Complete Games		Shutouts		Saves	
Drysdale-LA	25	Purkey-Cin	.821	Perranoski-LA	70	Spahn-Mil	22	Gibson-StL	5	Face-Pit	28
Sanford-SF	24	Sanford-SF	.774	Baldschun-Phi	67	O'Dell-SF	20	Friend-Pit	5	Perranoski-LA	20
Purkey-Cin	23	Drysdale-LA	.735	Roebuck-LA	64	Mahaffey-Phi	20			Miller-SF	19
Jay-Cin	21	Pierce-SF	.727	Face-Pit	63	Drysdale-LA	19			McDaniel-StL	14
		Shaw-Mil	.625	Olivo-Pit	62						

Innings Pitched		Fewest Hits/Game		Fewest BB/Game		Strikeouts		Strikeouts/Game		Ratio	
Drysdale-LA	314.1	Koufax-LA	6.54	Shaw-Mil	1.76	Drysdale-LA	232	Koufax-LA	10.55	Koufax-LA	9.42
Purkey-Cin	288.1	Gibson-StL	6.70	Friend-Pit	1.82	Koufax-LA	216	Johnson-Hou	8.13	Farrell-Hou	10.06
O'Dell-SF	280.2	Bennett-Phi	7.42	Spahn-Mil	1.84	Gibson-StL	208	Gibson-StL	8.01	Spahn-Mil	10.23
Mahaffey-Phi	274.0	Drysdale-LA	7.79	Pierce-SF	1.94	Farrell-Hou	203	Bennett-Phi	7.68	Pierce-SF	10.26
Jay-Cin	273.0	Broglio-StL	7.81	Purkey-Cin	2.00	O'Dell-SF	195	Farrell-Hou	7.56	Drysdale-LA	10.34

Earned Run Average		Adjusted ERA		Opponents' Batting Avg.		Opponents' On Base Pct.		Starter Runs		Adjusted Starter Runs	
Koufax-LA	2.54	Gibson-StL	150	Koufax-LA	.197	Koufax-LA	.261	Drysdale-LA	38.6	Purkey-Cin	38.9
Shaw-Mil	2.80	Purkey-Cin	143	Gibson-StL	.204	Farrell-Hou	.280	Purkey-Cin	36.3	Gibson-StL	36.8
Purkey-Cin	2.81	Koufax-LA	143	Bennett-Phi	.224	Drysdale-LA	.283	Koufax-LA	28.7	Broglio-StL	31.4
Drysdale-LA	2.83	Broglio-StL	142	Drysdale-LA	.230	Pierce-SF	.284	Shaw-Mil	28.5	Drysdale-LA	27.8
Gibson-StL	2.85	Shaw-Mil	136	Farrell-Hou	.233	Spahn-Mil	.287	Gibson-StL	28.3	Friend-Pit	25.4

Clutch Pitching Index		Relief Runs		Adjusted Relief Runs		Relief Ranking		Total Pitcher Index		Total Baseball Ranking	
Shaw-Mil	123	Face-Pit	20.8	Face-Pit	20.8	Face-Pit	45.2	Gibson-StL	5.0	Mays-SF	6.4
Friend-Pit	119	McMahon-Mil-Hou	19.9	Shantz-Hou-StL	18.9	McMahon-Mil-Hou	26.6	Face-Pit	4.5	Robinson-Cin	6.0
Broglio-StL	116	Shantz-Hou-StL	17.3	McMahon-Mil-Hou	18.1	Shantz-Hou-StL	23.9	Purkey-Cin	3.6	H.Aaron-Mil	5.5
McBean-Pit	114	Umbricht-Hou	14.3	Umbricht-Hou	12.8	Elston-Chi	23.9	Drysdale-LA	3.4	Gibson-StL	5.0
Koonce-Chi	111	Perranoski-LA	13.0	Elston-Chi	12.6	Baldschun-Phi	20.3	Spahn-Mil	3.1	Mazeroski-Pit	5.0

April 9 President John F. Kennedy throws out the first ball to open the baseball season at new District of Columbia Stadium. Despite rain, a record Washington crowd of 42,143 shows up to see Bennie Daniels stop Detroit with a five-hit, 4-1 win.

April 25 Harry Chiti is traded for himself. Cleveland sends catcher Harry Chiti to the Mets for a player to be named later, a deal completed June 15 when the Mets send Chiti back to Cleveland.

May 5 Angels rookie Bo Belinsky pitches a no-hitter against the Orioles, the organization from which the cocky lefty was drafted last year. Belinsky has 9 strikeouts and beats Steve Barber 2-0.

May 26 Al Kaline suffers a broken right collarbone while making a diving, game-saving catch to seal Detroit's 2-1 win against the Yankees. He will be out until June 23.

July 8 The Yankees complete a 3-game sweep in Minnesota, winning 7-5, 6-3, and 9-8 to regain first place. They will remain there the rest of the way.

July 26 Pitcher Gene Conley and infielder Pumpsie Green of the Red Sox mysteriously disappear after a game with the Yankees. They leave the team bus in traffic to use a restroom and fail to return. Conley decides he wants to fly to Israel, and goes to the airport, but is refused a ticket because he does not have a visa.

August 13 Bert Campaneris of Daytona Beach (Florida State League) pitches ambidextrously in a relief appearance.

August 26 The Twins Jack Kralick no-hits the A's and wins 1-0 on Lenny Green's sacrifice fly off Bill Fischer. A walk to George Alusik with one out in the ninth puts the only runner on.

September 12 Washington's Tom Cheney sets a major league mark with 21 strikeouts in a 16-inning game at Baltimore. Bud Zipfel's 16th-inning homer off Dick Hall gives the Senators a 2-1 win.

September 25 Whitey Ford beats Washington 8-3, as the Yankees clinch the AL pennant. Ralph Houk becomes the fifth manager to capture pennants in each of his first two seasons.

October 4 At Candlestick Park, in Game 1 of the World Series, Roger Maris stakes Whitey Ford to a two-run lead with a first-inning, two-run double. Only right fielder Felipe Alou's leaping effort keeps Maris's drive in the park. Whitey Ford's record consecutive-shutout-inning streak ends at 33⅔ innings when a surprise bunt by Jose Pagan brings Willie Mays home. Clete Boyer's seventh-inning homer gives the Yankees a 6-2 win, the last of a record 10 World Series victories for Ford.

October 16 New York scores the game's only run, as Tony Kubek grounds into a fifth-inning double play. In the ninth, with two outs and Matty Alou on first base, Willie Mays rips a double to right off Ralph Terry, but great fielding by Roger Maris keeps Alou from scoring. Willie McCovey then hits a screaming liner toward right, but second base Bobby Richardson gloves it, giving the Yankees a 1-0 win and a second straight World Series victory. Terry is named World Series MVP.

November 15 The White Sox release Early Wynn so that the 299-game winner will be free to deal with other clubs, and earn his 300th.

November 20 Mickey Mantle is named the AL Most Valuable Player for the third time.

	BALTIMORE		BOSTON		CHICAGO		CLEVELAND		DETROIT
M	B.Hitchcock	M	P.Higgins	M	A.Lopez	M	M.McGaha	M	B.Scheffing
1B	J.Gentile	1B	P.Runnels	1B	J.Cunningham	M	M.Harder	1B	N.Cash
2B	M.Breeding	2B	C.Schilling	2B	N.Fox	1B	T.Francona	2B	J.Wood
SS	J.Adair	SS	E.Bressoud	SS	L.Aparicio	2B	J.Kindall	SS	C.Fernandez
3B	B.Robinson	3B	F.Malzone	3B	A.Smith	SS	W.Held	3B	S.Boros
LF	B.Powell	LF	C.Yastrzemski	LF	F.Robinson	3B	B.Phillips	LF	R.Colavito
CF	J.Brandt	CF	G.Geiger	CF	J.Landis	LF	C.Essegian	CF	B.Bruton
RF	R.Snyder	RF	C.Hardy	RF	M.Hershberger	CF	T.Cline	RF	A.Kaline
C	G.Triandos	C	J.Pagliaroni	C	C.Carreon	RF	W.Kirkland	C	D.Brown
						C	J.Romano		
O	W.Herzog	O	L.Clinton	C	S.Lollar	O	A.Luplow	23	D.McAuliffe
O	D.Nicholson	C	B.Tillman	O	C.Maxwell			P	J.Bunning
2	J.Temple							P	H.Aguirre
		P	G.Conley	P	R.Herbert	P	D.Donovan	P	D.Mossi
P	C.Estrada	P	B.Monbouquette	P	J.Pizarro	P	P.Ramos	P	P.Regan
P	M.Pappas	P	E.Wilson	P	E.Fisher	P	J.Perry	P	P.Foytack
P	R.Roberts	P	D.Schwall	P	E.Wynn	P	B.Latman	RP	S.Jones
P	J.Fisher	RP	D.Radatz	P	J.Buzhardt	P	M.Grant	RP	R.Kline
P	S.Barber	RP	M.Fornieles	RP	D.Zanni	RP	G.Bell	RP	R.Nischwitz
RP	D.Hall	RP	A.Earley	RP	T.Lown	RP	F.Funk		
RP	B.Hoeft							P	F.Lary
RP	H.Wilhelm	P	I.Delock	P	F.Baumann	P	S.McDowell	P	T.Fox
		P	G.Cisco	P	J.Horlen				
P	H.Brown	P	H.Kolstad						
P	W.Stock	P	C.Nichols						

	KANSAS CITY		LOS ANGELES		MINNESOTA		NEW YORK		WASHINGTON
M	H.Bauer	M	B.Rigney	M	S.Mele	M	R.Houk	M	M.Vernon
1B	N.Siebern	1B	L.Thomas	1B	V.Power	1B	B.Skowron	1B	H.Bright
2B	J.Lumpe	2B	B.Moran	2B	B.Allen	2B	B.Richardson	2B	C.Cottier
SS	D.Howser	SS	J.Koppe	SS	Z.Versalles	SS	T.Tresh	SS	K.Hamlin
3B	E.Charles	3B	F.Torres	3B	R.Rollins	3B	C.Boyer	3B	B.Johnson
LF	M.Jimenez	LF	L.Wagner	LF	H.Killebrew	LF	H.Lopez	LF	C.Hinton
CF	B.Del Greco	CF	A.Pearson	CF	L.Green	CF	M.Mantle	CF	J.Piersall
RF	G.Cimoli	RF	G.Thomas	RF	B.Allison	RF	R.Maris	RF	J.King
C	H.Sullivan	C	B.Rodgers	C	E.Battey	C	E.Howard	C	K.Retzer
S3	W.Causey	P	D.Chance	O	B.Tuttle	OC	J.Blanchard	O	J.Hicks
O	J.Tartabull	P	B.Belinsky			CO	Y.Berra	C	B.Schmidt
C	J.Azcue	P	E.Grba	P	J.Kaat			32	D.O'Connell
O	G.Alusik	P	D.Lee	P	C.Pascual	P	R.Terry	O	D.Lock
		P	K.McBride	P	J.Kralick	P	W.Ford	3	J.Schaive
P	E.Rakow	RP	A.Fowler	P	D.Stigman	P	B.Stafford		
P	D.Pfister	RP	R.Duren	P	J.Bonikowski	P	J.Bouton	P	D.Stenhouse
P	J.Walker	RP	J.Spring	RP	L.Stange	P	R.Sheldon	P	D.Rudolph
P	B.Fischer			RP	G.Maranda	RP	J.Coates	P	T.Cheney
P	D.Segui	P	T.Bowsfield	RP	R.Moore	RP	B.Daley	P	B.Daniels
RP	J.Wyatt	P	B.Botz			RP	M.Bridges	P	C.Osteen
RP	D.McDevitt	P	T.Morgan	/P	D.Lee			RP	S.Hamilton
		P	D.Osinski			P	B.Turley	RP	M.Kutyna
P	D.Wickersham							RP	E.Hobaugh
P	O.Pena								
P	N.Bass							P	P.Burnside
								P	J.Hannan

TEAM	G	W	L	PCT	GB	R	OR	AB	H	2B	3B	HR	BB	SO	AVG	OBP	SLG	PRO	PRO+	BR	/A	PF	CHI	RC	SB	CS	SBA	SBR
NY	162	96	66	.593		817	680	5644	1509	240	29	199	584	842	.267	.339	.426	.765	116	87	113	97	99	816	42	29	59	-5
MIN	163	91	71	.562	5	798	713	5561	1445	215	39	185	649	823	.260	.340	.412	.752	104	67	38	104	100	789	33	20	62	-2
LA	162	86	76	.531	10	718	706	5499	1377	232	35	137	602	917	.250	.328	.380	.708	100	-23	-1	97	103	698	46	27	63	-2
DET	161	85	76	.528	10.5	758	692	5456	1352	191	36	209	651	894	.248	.332	.411	.743	102	41	14	104	100	757	69	21	77	8
CHI	162	85	77	.525	11	707	658	5514	1415	250	56	92	620	674	.257	.336	.372	.708	97	-13	-9	100	99	701	76	40	66	-1
CLE	162	80	82	.494	16	682	745	5484	1341	202	22	180	502	939	.245	.314	.388	.702	97	-46	-26	97	103	671	35	16	69	1
BAL	162	77	85	.475	19	652	680	5491	1363	225	34	156	516	931	.248	.316	.387	.703	101	-42	0	94	98	665	45	32	58	-6
BOS	160	76	84	.475	19	707	756	5530	1429	257	53	146	525	923	.258	.326	.403	.729	99	9	-14	103	98	716	39	33	54	-8
KC	162	72	90	.444	24	745	837	5576	1467	220	58	116	556	803	.263	.334	.386	.720	96	3	-31	105	102	738	76	21	78	10
WAS	162	60	101	.373	35.5	599	716	5484	1370	206	38	132	466	789	.250	.310	.373	.683	90	-82	-77	99	97	623	99	53	65	-2
TOT	809					7183		55239	14068	2238	400	1552	5671	8535	.255	.328	.394	.722							560	292	66	-7

TEAM	CG	SH	SV	IP	H	H/G	HR	BB	SO	RAT	ERA	ERA+	OAV	OOB	PR	/A	PF	CPI	FA	E	DP	FW	PW	BW	SBW	DIF
NY	33	10	42	1470[1]	1375	8.4	146	499	838	11.6	3.70	101	.247	.312	44	7	94	96	.979	131	151	.4	.7	11.4	-.4	3.0
MIN	53	11	27	1463[1]	1400	8.6	166	493	948	11.9	3.89	105	.253	.319	13	31	103	99	.980	129	173	.5	3.1	3.8	-.1	2.7
LA	23	15	47	1466	1412	8.7	118	616	858	12.8	3.70	104	.253	.332	45	27	97	104	.973	175	153	-2.2	2.7	-.1	-.1	4.7
DET	46	8	35	1443[2]	1452	9.1	169	503	873	12.4	3.81	107	.259	.323	26	42	103	105	.974	156	114	-1.1	4.2	1.4	.9	-.9
CHI	50	13	28	1451[2]	1380	8.6	123	537	821	12.0	3.73	105	.251	.320	38	28	98	97	.982	110	153	1.6	2.8	-.9	-.0	.6
CLE	45	12	31	1441	1410	8.8	174	594	780	12.7	4.14	94	.258	.334	-27	-43	98	102	.978	139	168	-.1	-4.3	-2.6	.2	5.9
BAL	32	8	33	1462[1]	1373	8.5	147	549	898	12.0	3.69	100	.249	.320	45	1	93	101	.980	122	152	.9	.1	-.0	-.5	-4.4
BOS	34	12	40	1437[2]	1416	8.9	159	632	923	13.1	4.22	91	.258	.339	-40	-14	104	101	.979	131	152	.3	-1.4	-1.4	-.7	-.7
KC	32	4	33	1434	1450	9.1	199	655	825	13.5	4.79	88	.263	.346	-131	-91	106	97	.979	132	131	.3	-9.1	-3.1	1.1	1.9
WAS	38	11	13	1445	1400	8.7	151	593	771	12.5	4.04	100	.256	.331	-12	-1	102	100	.978	139	160	-.1	-.1	-7.7	-.1	-12.4
TOT	386	104	329	14515		8.7				12.4	3.97		.255	.328					.978	1364	1507					

Runs		Hits		Doubles		Triples		Home Runs		Total Bases	
Pearson-LA	115	Richardson-NY	209	Robinson-Chi	45	Cimoli-KC	15	Killebrew-Min	48	Colavito-Det	309
Siebern-KC	114	Lumpe-KC	193	Yastrzemski-Bos	43	Robinson-Chi	10	Cash-Det	39	B.Robinson-Bal	308
Allison-Min	102	B.Robinson-Bal	192	Bressoud-Bos	40	Lumpe-KC	10	Wagner-LA	37	Wagner-LA	306
Yastrzemski-Bos	99	Yastrzemski-Bos	191	Richardson-NY	38	Clinton-Bos	10	Colavito-Det	37	Yastrzemski-Bos	303
Richardson-NY	99	Robinson-Chi	187							Killebrew-Min	301

Runs Batted In		Runs Produced		Bases On Balls		Batting Average		On Base Percentage		Slugging Average	
Killebrew-Min	126	Siebern-KC	206	Mantle-NY	122	Runnels-Bos	.326	Mantle-NY	.488	Mantle-NY	.605
Siebern-KC	117	Robinson-Chi	187	Siebern-KC	110	Mantle-NY	.321	Siebern-KC	.416	Killebrew-Min	.545
Colavito-Det	112	Rollins-Min	176	Killebrew-Min	106	Robinson-Chi	.312	Cunningham-Chi	.415	Colavito-Det	.514
Robinson-Chi	109	Allison-Min	175	Cash-Det	104	Hinton-Was	.310	Runnels-Bos	.411	Cash-Det	.513
Wagner-LA	107	Yastrzemski-Bos	174	Cunningham-Chi	101	Siebern-KC	.308	Robinson-Chi	.387	Allison-Min	.511

Production		Adjusted Production		Batter Runs		Adjusted Batter Runs		Clutch Hitting Index		Runs Created	
Mantle-NY	1.093	Mantle-NY	198	Mantle-NY	57.3	Mantle-NY	61.0	Siebern-KC	125	Siebern-KC	129
Killebrew-Min	.914	Siebern-KC	138	Siebern-KC	41.1	Siebern-KC	35.4	Robinson-Chi	124	Mantle-NY	126
Siebern-KC	.911	Killebrew-Min	137	Killebrew-Min	33.1	Killebrew-Min	29.1	Rollins-Min	121	Colavito-Det	117
Cash-Det	.897	Cash-Det	134	Colavito-Det	31.4	Kaline-Det	27.8	Howard-NY	115	Killebrew-Min	113
Colavito-Det	.889	Colavito-Det	132	Kaline-Det	30.7	Colavito-Det	27.5	L.Thomas-LA	111	Robinson-Chi	113

Total Average		Stolen Bases		Stolen Base Average		Stolen Base Runs		Fielding Runs		Total Player Rating	
Mantle-NY	1.385	Aparicio-Chi	31	Howser-KC	90.5	Wood-Det	5.4	Boyer-NY	36.2	Mantle-NY	5.0
Siebern-KC	.956	Hinton-Was	28	Wood-Det	88.9	Howser-KC	4.5	Versalles-Min	31.6	Boyer-NY	4.0
Cash-Det	.950	Wood-Det	24	Charles-KC	83.3	Charles-KC	3.6	Bressoud-Bos	24.5	Bressoud-Bos	3.8
Killebrew-Min	.945	Charles-KC	20	Tartabull-KC	79.2	Tartabull-KC	2.7	Kindall-Cle	20.7	Colavito-Det	3.6
Allison-Min	.901			Hinton-Was	73.7	Mantle-NY	2.7	Cottier-Was	20.5	Kaline-Det	3.4

Wins		Win Percentage		Games		Complete Games		Shutouts		Saves	
Terry-NY	23	Herbert-Chi	.690	Radatz-Bos	62	Pascual-Min	18	Pascual-Min	5	Radatz-Bos	24
Pascual-Min	20	Ford-NY	.680	Wyatt-KC	59	Kaat-Min	16	Kaat-Min	5	Bridges-NY	18
Herbert-Chi	20	Donovan-Cle	.667			Donovan-Cle	16	Donovan-Cle	5	Fox-Det	16
Donovan-Cle	20	Aguirre-Det	.667			Terry-NY	14	Monbouquette-Bos	4	Wilhelm-Bal	15
Bunning-Det	19	Terry-NY	.657					McBride-LA	4	Bell-Cle	12

Innings Pitched		Fewest Hits/Game		Fewest BB/Game		Strikeouts		Strikeouts/Game		Ratio	
Terry-NY	298.2	Aguirre-Det	6.75	Donovan-Cle	1.69	Pascual-Min	206	Pizarro-Chi	7.66	Terry-NY	9.55
Kaat-Min	269.0	Cheney-Was	6.96	Terry-NY	1.72	Bunning-Det	184	Cheney-Was	7.63	Aguirre-Det	9.67
Bunning-Det	258.0	Belinsky-LA	7.16	Mossi-Det	1.80	Terry-NY	176	Pascual-Min	7.20	Pascual-Min	10.37
Pascual-Min	257.2	Wilson-Bos	7.67	Roberts-Bal	1.93	Pizarro-Chi	173	Belinsky-LA	6.97	Roberts-Bal	10.40
Ford-NY	257.2	Stenhouse-Was	7.72	Pascual-Min	2.06	Kaat-Min	173	Estrada-Bal	6.65	Fisher-Chi	10.59

Earned Run Average		Adjusted ERA		Opponents' Batting Avg.		Opponents' On Base Pct.		Starter Runs		Adjusted Starter Runs	
Aguirre-Det	2.21	Aguirre-Det	184	Aguirre-Det	.205	Aguirre-Det	.269	Aguirre-Det	42.3	Aguirre-Det	44.7
Roberts-Bal	2.78	Roberts-Bal	133	Cheney-Was	.213	Terry-NY	.270	Ford-NY	30.7	Kaat-Min	28.1
Ford-NY	2.90	Chance-LA	130	Belinsky-LA	.216	Pascual-Min	.286	Terry-NY	25.8	Ford-NY	24.3
Chance-LA	2.96	Kaat-Min	130	Terry-NY	.231	Roberts-Bal	.289	Roberts-Bal	25.4	Pascual-Min	22.0
Fisher-Chi	3.10	Ford-NY	129	Wilson-Bos	.231	Fisher-Chi	.293	Kaat-Min	24.7	Monbouquette-Bos	21.0

Clutch Pitching Index		Relief Runs		Adjusted Relief Runs		Relief Ranking		Total Pitcher Index		Total Baseball Ranking	
Chance-LA	114	Radatz-Bos	24.0	Radatz-Bos	26.2	Radatz-Bos	39.5	Kaat-Min	4.2	Mantle-NY	5.0
Roberts-Bal	111	Hall-Bal	22.2	Hall-Bal	18.7	Wilhelm-Bal	36.5	Wilhelm-Bal	3.8	Kaat-Min	4.2
Ramos-Cle	110	Wilhelm-Bal	21.0	Wilhelm-Bal	18.2	Hall-Bal	19.1	Radatz-Bos	3.7	Boyer-NY	4.0
Ford-NY	110	Fox-Det	14.6	Fox-Det	15.2	Fox-Det	18.7	Aguirre-Det	3.7	Bressoud-Bos	3.8
Perry-Cle	109	Fowler-LA	10.0	Fowler-LA	9.0	Bridges-NY	10.0	Pascual-Min	3.4	Wilhelm-Bal	3.8

April 11 Warren Spahn's Opening Day, 6-1 victory over the Mets is the 328th of his career. He thus moves ahead of yesteryear's great Eddie Plank as the all-time winningest lefthander. Except for Duke Snider's home run, no Met gets past second base.

April 13 After 11 hitless at bats, Cincinnati second baseman Pete Rose records his first ML hit, a triple off Pittsburgh's Bob Friend.

May 8 A Stan Musial home run against the Dodgers gives him 1,357 extra-base hits, surpassing Babe Ruth's major league record. He will get 20 more and permanent possession of second place lifetime. The Cards lose 11-5.

June 9 The Colt .45s beat the Giants 3-0 in the major leagues' first Sunday night game. The exception is made because of Houston's oppressive daytime heat.

July 2 At 12:31 A.M. in San Francisco, Willie Mays's round-tripper off Warren Spahn in the bottom of the 16th gives Juan Marichal a 1-0 win, the NL's longest win ended by a home run.

July 9 Willie Mays is held to a single, but dominates a 5-3 NL win in the All-Star Game. He also walks, steals twice,

scores twice, bats in a pair, and makes a great catch. This All-Star Game also marks Stan Musial's 24th appearance, a record.

July 19 With one out and a man on in the 9th, Roy Sievers hits his 300th career home run to give the Phils a 2-1 win over the Mets. Roger Craig is the victim, his 13th straight loss.

August 9 Roger Craig's NL record-tying 18-game losing streak ends thanks to Jim Hickman's 9th-inning grand slam off Lindy McDaniel. New York beats the Cubs 7-3.

September 8 Braves pitcher Warren Spahn ties Christy Mathewson with his 13th 20-win season by notching a 3-2 victory in Philadelphia. At 42, Spahn becomes the oldest 20-game winner.

September 10 Stan Musial hits a home run in his first at bat as a grandfather, and Bob Gibson (17-8) blanks the Cubs 8–0.

September 15 The Alou brothers—Felipe, Matty, and Jesus—appear in the San Francisco outfield for one inning of a 13-5 win against the Pirates. This necessitates the "benching" of Willie Mays.

October 2 In the World Series opener, Sandy Koufax fans the first 5 batters he

faces en route to a World Series record 15. John Roseboro's three-run home run is the difference, as Los Angeles beats the Yankees 5-2 at New York.

October 5 Fans attending the first World Series game at Dodger Stadium see a pitching duel between Don Drysdale and Jim Bouton. A first-inning run is all Los Angeles needs to take a three games-to-none lead.

October 6 Sandy Koufax beats the Yanks again 2-1 for a shocking World Series sweep for the Dodgers. Whitey Ford gives up only two hits, both by Frank Howard, who crashes a long home run in the fifth to start the LA scoring. The Bronx Bombers bat just .171 and score only four runs, the second lowest total in World Series history.

October 24 Sandy Koufax is the unanimous winner of the Cy Young Award.

October 30 Sandy Koufax wins again, outpolling Pittsburgh's Dick Groat 237 to 190 for the NL MVP award.

November 26 Cincinnati second baseman Pete Rose is a landslide winner of NL Rookie of the Year honors, taking 17 of 20 votes.

	CHICAGO		CINCINNATI		HOUSTON		LOS ANGELES		MILWAUKEE
M	B.Kennedy	M	F.Hutchinson	M	H.Craft	M	W.Alston	M	B.Bragan
1B	E.Banks	1B	G.Coleman	1B	R.Staub	1B	R.Fairly	1B	G.Oliver
2B	K.Hubbs	2B	P.Rose	2B	E.Fazio	2B	J.Gilliam	2B	F.Bolling
SS	A.Rodgers	SS	L.Cardenas	SS	B.Lillis	SS	M.Wills	SS	R.McMillan
3B	R.Santo	3B	G.Freese	3B	B.Aspromonte	3B	K.McMullen	3B	E.Mathews
LF	B.Williams	LF	F.Robinson	LF	A.Spangler	LF	T.Davis	LF	L.Maye
CF	E.Burton	CF	V.Pinson	CF	H.Goss	CF	W.Davis	CF	M.Jones
RF	L.Brock	RF	T.Harper	RF	C.Warwick	RF	F.Howard	RF	H.Aaron
C	D.Bertell	C	J.Edwards	C	J.Bateman	C	J.Roseboro	C	J.Torre
O	D.Landrum	P	J.Maloney	12	P.Runnels	O	W.Moon	S3	D.Menke
		P	J.O'Toole	23	J.Temple	S2	D.Tracewski	C	D.Crandall
P	D.Ellsworth	P	J.Nuxhall	OS	J.Wynn	1	B.Skowron		
P	L.Jackson	P	J.Tsitouris					P	W.Spahn
P	B.Buhl	P	J.Jay	P	K.Johnson	P	D.Drysdale	P	D.Lemaster
P	G.Hobbie	RP	A.Worthington	P	T.Farrell	P	S.Koufax	P	B.Hendley
P	P.Toth	RP	B.Henry	P	D.Nottebart	P	J.Podres	P	B.Shaw
RP	L.McDaniel			P	B.Bruce	P	B.Miller	P	T.Cloninger
RP	D.Elston	P	B.Purkey	P	B.Brown	RP	R.Perranoski	RP	H.Fischer
RP	J.Brewer			RP	H.Woodeshick	RP	L.Sherry	RP	C.Raymond
				RP	D.McMahon			RP	R.Piche
P	C.Koonce			RP	J.Umbricht	P	P.Richert		
								P	B.Sadowski
				P	D.Drott			P	L.Burdette
				P	C.Zachary				

	NEW YORK		PHILADELPHIA		PITTSBURGH		SAN FRANCISCO		ST.LOUIS
M	C.Stengel	M	G.Mauch	M	D.Murtaugh	M	A.Dark	M	J.Keane
1B	T.Harkness	1B	R.Sievers	1B	D.Clendenon	1B	O.Cepeda	1B	B.White
2B	R.Hunt	2B	T.Taylor	2B	B.Mazeroski	2B	C.Hiller	2B	J.Javier
SS	A.Moran	SS	B.Wine	SS	D.Schofield	SS	J.Pagan	SS	D.Groat
3B	C.Neal	3B	D.Hoak	3B	B.Bailey	3B	J.Davenport	3B	K.Boyer
LF	F.Thomas	LF	T.Gonzalez	LF	W.Stargell	LF	W.McCovey	LF	C.James
CF	J.Hickman	CF	D.Demeter	CF	B.Virdon	CF	W.Mays	CF	C.Flood
RF	D.Snider	RF	J.Callison	RF	R.Clemente	RF	F.Alou	RF	G.Altman
C	C.Coleman	C	C.Dalrymple	C	J.Pagliaroni	C	E.Bailey	C	T.McCarver
O3	R.Kanehl	S3	R.Amaro	C	S.Burgess	C	T.Haller	O	S.Musial
O1	E.Kranepool	O	W.Covington	O	J.Lynch	O3	H.Kuenn		
								P	B.Gibson
P	R.Craig	P	C.McLish	P	B.Friend	P	J.Marichal	P	E.Broglio
P	A.Jackson	P	R.Culp	P	D.Cardwell	P	J.Sanford	P	C.Simmons
P	C.Willey	P	C.Short	P	D.Schwall	P	B.O'Dell	P	R.Sadecki
P	G.Cisco	P	A.Mahaffey	P	J.Gibbon	P	J.Fisher	P	L.Burdette
P	T.Stallard	P	D.Green	RP	A.McBean	RP	B.Bolin	RP	R.Taylor
RP	L.Bearnarth	RP	J.Baldschun	RP	T.Sisk	RP	B.Pierce	RP	B.Shantz
RP	K.MacKenzie	RP	J.Klippstein	RP	E.Francis	RP	G.Perry	RP	E.Bauta
RP	D.Rowe	RP	R.Duren						
				P	B.Veale	P	J.Duffalo	P	R.Washburn
P	J.Hook	P	D.Bennett	P	V.Law	P	D.Larsen		
P	G.Powell	P	J.Boozer	P	R.Face				
				P	H.Haddix				

TEAM	G	W	L	PCT	GB		R	OR	AB	H	2B	3B	HR	BB	SO		AVG	OBP	SLG	PRO	PRO+		BR	/A	PF	CHI	RC		SB	CS	SBA	SBR
LA	163	99	63	.611			640	**550**	5428	1361	178	34	110	453	**867**		.251	.311	.357	.668	106		-3	39	93	105	596		**124**	70	64	-5
STL	162	93	69	.574	6		**747**	628	5678	**1540**	**231**	**66**	128	458	915		**.271**	**.328**	.403	.731	107		**119**	50	109	99	**751**		77	42	**65**	**-2**
SF	162	88	74	.543	11		725	641	5579	1442	206	35	**197**	441	889		.258	.318	**.414**	**.732**	**118**		111	119	99	98	712		55	49	53	-13
PHI	162	87	75	.537	12		642	578	5524	1390	228	54	126	403	955		.252	.308	.381	.689	106		28	36	99	99	640		56	39	59	-7
CIN	162	86	76	.531	13		648	594	5416	1333	225	44	122	474	960		.246	.312	.371	.683	100		25	6	103	101	630		92	58	61	-7
MIL	163	84	78	.519	15		677	603	5518	1345	204	39	139	**525**	954		.244	.314	.370	.684	105		30	37	99	102	643		75	52	59	-9
CHI	162	82	80	.506	17		570	578	5404	1286	205	44	127	439	1049		.238	.300	.363	.663	92		-21	-53	105	97	573		68	60	53	-16
PIT	162	74	88	.457	25		567	595	5536	1385	181	49	108	454	940		.250	.310	.359	.669	98		-2	-6	101	92	603		57	41	58	-8
HOU	162	66	96	.407	33		464	640	5384	1184	170	39	62	456	938		.220	.284	.301	.585	80		-159	-132	94	103	461		39	30	57	-6
NY	162	51	111	.315	48		501	774	5336	1168	156	35	96	457	1078		.219	.286	.315	.601	79		-129	-137	102	**106**	477		41	52	44	-19
TOT	811						6181		54803	13434	1984	439	1215	4560	9545		.245	.307	.364	.671							684		493	58	-91

TEAM	CG	SH	SV	IP		H	H/G	HR	BB	SO	RAT		ERA	ERA+	OAV	OOB		PR	/A	PF	CPI		FA	E	DP		FW	PW	BW	SBW	DIF
LA	51	**24**	29	1469[2]		1329	8.1	111	402	**1095**	10.8		**2.85**	106	.239	**.294**		71	27	92	103		.975	159	129		-.0	2.9	4.2	.4	10.4
STL	49	17	32	1463		1329	8.2	124	463	978	11.3		3.32	107	.241	.305		-5	37	108	97		.976	147	136		.6	4.0	5.4	**.8**	1.2
SF	46	9	30	1469		1380	8.5	126	464	954	11.5		3.35	96	.246	.307		-9	-24	97	99		.975	156	113		.1	-2.6	**12.9**	-.4	-3.0
PHI	45	12	31	1457[1]		**1262**	**7.8**	113	553	1052	11.4		3.09	105	**.235**	.311		32	23	98	104		.978	142	147		.9	2.5	3.9	.2	-1.6
CIN	55	22	**36**	1439[2]		1307	8.2	117	425	1048	11.1		3.29	102	.242	.302		-1	8	102	96		.978	135	127		1.3	.9	.7	.2	1.9
MIL	**56**	18	25	1471[2]		1327	8.1	149	489	924	10.5		3.27	99	.241	.306		4	-8	98	103		**.980**	**129**	161		**1.8**	-.9	4.0	.0	-1.9
CHI	45	15	28	1457		1357	8.4	119	400	851	11.0		3.08	**114**	.249	.303		34	**70**	107	105		.976	155	172		.2	**7.6**	-5.8	-.8	-.3
PIT	34	16	33	1448		1350	8.4	99	457	900	11.5		3.10	107	.249	.313		31	33	100	**107**		.972	182	**195**		-1.4	3.6	-.7	.1	-8.6
HOU	36	16	20	1450[1]		1341	8.3	**95**	**378**	937	10.9		3.44	92	.245	.298		-24	-46	96	87		.974	162	100		-.3	-5.0	-14.3	.3	4.2
NY	42	5	12	1427[2]		1452	9.2	162	529	806	12.8		4.12	85	.263	.332		-132	-101	106	100		.967	210	151		-3.1	-11.0	-14.9	-1.1	.0
TOT	459	154	276	14553[1]			8.3				11.4		3.29		.245	.307							.975	1577	1431						

Runs		Hits		Doubles		Triples		Home Runs		Total Bases	
H.Aaron-Mil	121	Pinson-Cin	204	Groat-StL	43	Pinson-Cin	14	McCovey-SF	44	H.Aaron-Mil	370
Mays-SF	115	Groat-StL	201	Pinson-Cin	37	Gonzalez-Phi	12	H.Aaron-Mil	44	Mays-SF	347
Flood-StL	112	H.Aaron-Mil	201	Williams-Chi	36	Groat-StL	11	Mays-SF	38	Pinson-Cin	335
White-StL	106	White-StL	200	Gonzalez-Phi	36	Callison-Phi	11	Cepeda-SF	34	Cepeda-SF	326
McCovey-SF	103	Flood-StL	200	Callison-Phi	36	Brock-Chi	11	Howard-LA	28	White-StL	323

Runs Batted In		Runs Produced		Bases On Balls		Batting Average		On Base Percentage		Slugging Average	
H.Aaron-Mil	130	H.Aaron-Mil	207	Mathews-Mil	124	T.Davis-LA	.326	Mathews-Mil	.400	H.Aaron-Mil	.586
Boyer-StL	111	White-StL	188	Robinson-Cin	81	Clemente-Pit	.320	H.Aaron-Mil	.394	Mays-SF	.582
White-StL	109	Pinson-Cin	180	H.Aaron-Mil	78	Groat-StL	.319	Mays-SF	.384	McCovey-SF	.566
Pinson-Cin	106	Mays-SF	180	Boyer-StL	70	H.Aaron-Mil	.319	Robinson-Cin	.381	Cepeda-SF	.563
Mays-SF	103	Boyer-StL	173	Schofield-Pit	69	Cepeda-SF	.316	Groat-StL	.380	Pinson-Cin	.514

Production		Adjusted Production		Batter Runs		Adjusted Batter Runs		Clutch Hitting Index		Runs Created	
H.Aaron-Mil	.980	H.Aaron-Mil	180	H.Aaron-Mil	63.0	H.Aaron-Mil	64.5	Sievers-Phi	135	H.Aaron-Mil	149
Mays-SF	.966	Mays-SF	176	Mays-SF	55.8	Mays-SF	57.2	Fairly-LA	135	Mays-SF	131
Cepeda-SF	.930	Cepeda-SF	166	Cepeda-SF	45.4	Cepeda-SF	46.6	Robinson-Cin	126	White-StL	117
McCovey-SF	.916	McCovey-SF	161	McCovey-SF	41.1	McCovey-SF	42.2	Boyer-StL	120	Cepeda-SF	113
Pinson-Cin	.864	Mathews-Mil	147	Mathews-Mil	37.4	Mathews-Mil	38.6	Edwards-Cin	120	Pinson-Cin	113

Total Average		Stolen Bases		Stolen Base Average		Stolen Base Runs		Fielding Runs		Total Player Rating	
H.Aaron-Mil	1.063	Wills-LA	40	H.Aaron-Mil	86.1	H.Aaron-Mil	6.3	Mazeroski-Pit	56.7	Mays-SF	6.6
Mays-SF	.984	H.Aaron-Mil	31	Gilliam-LA	79.2	Pinson-Cin	3.3	Callison-Phi	22.7	H.Aaron-Mil	6.5
McCovey-SF	.911	Pinson-Cin	27	Pinson-Cin	77.1	Maye-Mil	3.0	Hubbs-Chi	20.1	Mazeroski-Pit	6.0
Cepeda-SF	.906	Robinson-Cin	26	Robinson-Cin	72.2	Harper-Cin	3.0	Flood-StL	19.5	Mathews-Mil	5.3
Mathews-Mil	.894	W.Davis-LA	25	Taylor-Phi	71.9	Gilliam-LA	2.7	Harkness-NY	16.4	Callison-Phi	4.8

Wins		Win Percentage		Games		Complete Games		Shutouts		Saves	
Marichal-SF	25	Perranoski-LA	.842	Perranoski-LA	69	Spahn-Mil	22	Koufax-LA	11	McDaniel-Chi	22
Koufax-LA	25	Koufax-LA	.833	Baldschun-Phi	65	Koufax-LA	20	Spahn-Mil	7	Perranoski-LA	21
Spahn-Mil	23	Spahn-Mil	.767	Bearnarth-NY	58	Ellsworth-Chi	19	Simmons-StL	6	Face-Pit	16
Maloney-Cin	23	Maloney-Cin	.767	Sisk-Pit	57	Marichal-SF	18	Maloney-Cin	6	Baldschun-Phi	16
Ellsworth-Chi	22	Marichal-SF	.758	McDaniel-Chi	57	Drysdale-LA	17			Henry-Cin	14

Innings Pitched		Fewest Hits/Game		Fewest BB/Game		Strikeouts		Strikeouts/Game		Ratio	
Marichal-SF	321.1	Koufax-LA	6.19	Friend-Pit	1.47	Koufax-LA	306	Maloney-Cin	9.53	Koufax-LA	7.96
Drysdale-LA	315.1	Culp-Phi	6.55	Farrell-Hou	1.56	Maloney-Cin	265	Koufax-LA	8.86	Farrell-Hou	8.81
Koufax-LA	311.0	Maloney-Cin	6.58	Nuxhall-Cin	1.62	Drysdale-LA	251	Culp-Phi	7.79	Marichal-SF	9.02
Ellsworth-Chi	290.2	Ellsworth-Chi	6.90	Drysdale-LA	1.63	Marichal-SF	248	Short-Phi	7.27	Ellsworth-Chi	9.29
Sanford-SF	284.1	Farrell-Hou	7.16	Koufax-LA	1.68	Gibson-StL	204	Lemaster-Mil	7.22	Friend-Pit	9.55

Earned Run Average		Adjusted ERA		Opponents' Batting Avg.		Opponents' On Base Pct.		Starter Runs		Adjusted Starter Runs	
Koufax-LA	1.88	Ellsworth-Chi	167	Koufax-LA	.189	Koufax-LA	.230	Koufax-LA	48.6	Ellsworth-Chi	45.3
Ellsworth-Chi	2.11	Koufax-LA	161	Maloney-Cin	.202	Marichal-SF	.256	Ellsworth-Chi	38.2	Koufax-LA	39.4
Friend-Pit	2.34	Simmons-StL	143	Culp-Phi	.206	Farrell-Hou	.256	Marichal-SF	31.4	Jackson-Chi	29.2
Marichal-SF	2.41	Friend-Pit	141	Ellsworth-Chi	.210	Ellsworth-Chi	.263	Friend-Pit	28.2	Friend-Pit	28.5
Simmons-StL	2.48	Jackson-Chi	137	Broglio-StL	.216	Friend-Pit	.269	Drysdale-LA	23.2	Marichal-SF	28.2

Clutch Pitching Index		Relief Runs		Adjusted Relief Runs		Relief Ranking		Total Pitcher Index		Total Baseball Ranking	
Schwall-Pit	118	Perranoski-LA	23.1	Veale-Pit	19.5	Perranoski-LA	32.7	Ellsworth-Chi	5.2	Mays-SF	6.6
Spahn-Mil	115	Veale-Pit	19.4	Perranoski-LA	19.3	Woodeshick-Hou	26.5	Jackson-Chi	4.1	H.Aaron-Mil	6.5
Short-Phi	111	Klippstein-Phi	16.9	Klippstein-Phi	16.9	Baldschun-Phi	20.6	Perranoski-LA	3.7	Mazeroski-Pit	6.0
Cardwell-Pit	110	Woodeshick-Hou	16.6	Woodeshick-Hou	14.9	Veale-Pit	17.5	Woodeshick-Hou	3.3	Mathews-Mil	5.3
Buhl-Chi	109	Baldschun-Phi	12.5	Baldschun-Phi	11.8	Klippstein-Phi	16.9	Spahn-Mil	3.2	Ellsworth-Chi	5.2

January 26 The Major League Rules Committee votes to expand the strike zone, restoring it to pre-1950 standards: from the top of the shoulders to the bottom of the knees.

January 27 The Hall of Fame Special Veterans Committee votes in Sam Rice, Eppa Rixey, Elmer Flick, and John Clarkson.

April 8 The Tigers claim young pitcher Denny McLain from the White Sox for the $25,000 waiver price.

June 23 A major league fielding record is set by Boston first baseman Dick Stuart as "Dr. Strangeglove" handles three first-inning grounders and tosses to pitcher Bob Heffner for putouts. Stuart's teammates and Fenway fans give him a standing ovation. Regardless, the Yankees beat the Sox, 8–0.

July 8 Reports of Charlie Finley's intention to move the Kansas City A's to Oakland surface during the All-Star break at Cleveland.

July 13 At Kansas City in the second game of a doubleheader, Cleveland's Early Wynn leaves with a lead after struggling through 5 innings. Four scoreless relief innings by Jerry Walker enable Wynn to score his 300th career victory 7-4.

August 21 Orioles shortstop Luis Aparicio becomes the first major league player since George Case in 1945 to reach 300 career steals.

September 6 Baseball historian Lee Allen says the Indians-Senators game is the 100,000th in major league history. Bennie Daniels celebrates by beating the Tribe 7-2.

September 13 Jim Bouton's 20th win, 2–0, at Minnesota, clinches the Yankees 28th pennant.

October 1 The season ends, and there are no full-schedule players in the AL for the first time since 1910. Brooks Robinson played in the most games, 161, missing only one. Ron Santo, Vada Pinson, and Bill White all play the full schedule in the NL.

October 12 In the first (and last) Hispanic American major league all-star game, the NL team beats the AL 5-2 at the Polo Grounds. The game features such names as Minnie Minoso, Tony Oliva, Roberto Clemente, Orlando Cepeda, Julian Javier, Felipe Alou, Luis Aparicio, and Zoilo Versalles. Vic Power receives a pregame award as the number-one Latin player. NL starter Juan Marichal strikes out 6 in 4 innings, though reliever Al McBean is the winner. Pinch hitter Manny Mota drives in 2 against loser Pedro Ramos.

October 24 Yogi Berra is appointed manager of the Yankees.

November 7 Catcher Elston Howard is named AL MVP. New York's Howard tops Detroit's Al Kaline 248 to 148.

December 2 The Major League Rules Committee bans oversized catcher's mitts, effective in 1965.

BALTIMORE		BOSTON		CHICAGO		CLEVELAND		DETROIT	
M	B.Hitchcock	M	J.Pesky	M	A.Lopez	M	B.Tebbetts	M	B.Scheffing
1B	J.Gentile	1B	D.Stuart	1B	T.McCraw	1B	F.Whitfield	M	C.Dressen
2B	J.Adair	2B	C.Schilling	2B	N.Fox	2B	W.Held	1B	N.Cash
SS	L.Aparicio	SS	E.Bressoud	SS	R.Hansen	SS	J.Kindall	2B	J.Wood
3B	B.Robinson	3B	F.Malzone	3B	P.Ward	3B	M.Alvis	SS	D.McAuliffe
LF	B.Powell	LF	C.Yastrzemski	LF	D.Nicholson	LF	T.Francona	3B	B.Phillips
CF	J.Brandt	CF	G.Geiger	CF	J.Landis	CF	V.Davalillo	LF	R.Colavito
RF	R.Snyder	RF	L.Clinton	RF	F.Robinson	RF	W.Kirkland	CF	B.Bruton
C	J.Orsino	C	B.Tillman	C	J.Martin	C	J.Azcue	RF	A.Kaline
								C	G.Triandos
O2	B.Saverine	O	R.Mejias	C	C.Carreon	1	J.Adcock		
O	A.Smith	C	R.Nixon	O	M.Hershberger	O	A.Luplow	C1	B.Freehan
2	B.Johnson			2S	A.Weis	C	J.Romano	32	D.Wert
		P	B.Monbouquette	1	J.Cunningham	S2	L.Brown		
P	S.Barber	P	E.Wilson					P	J.Bunning
P	R.Roberts	P	D.Morehead	P	G.Peters	P	M.Grant	P	H.Aguirre
P	M.Pappas	P	B.Heffner	P	R.Herbert	P	D.Donovan	P	P.Regan
P	M.McCormick	RP	J.Lamabe	P	J.Pizarro	P	J.Kralick	P	M.Lolich
P	D.McNally	RP	D.Radatz	P	J.Buzhardt	P	P.Ramos	P	D.Mossi
RP	S.Miller	RP	A.Earley	P	J.Horlen	P	B.Latman	RP	T.Fox
RP	D.Hall			RP	H.Wilhelm	RP	G.Bell	RP	B.Anderson
RP	W.Stock	P	W.Wood	RP	J.Brosnan	RP	J.Walker	RP	T.Sturdivant
		P	C.Nichols	RP	F.Baumann	RP	T.Abernathy		
								P	F.Lary
				P	E.Fisher	P	S.McDowell	P	B.Faul
				P	D.DeBusschere	P	B.Allen		
						P	E.Wynn		

KANSAS CITY		LOS ANGELES		MINNESOTA		NEW YORK		WASHINGTON	
M	E.Lopat	M	B.Rigney	M	S.Mele	M	R.Houk	M	M.Vernon
1B	N.Siebern	1B	L.Thomas	1B	V.Power	1B	J.Pepitone	M	E.Yost
2B	J.Lumpe	2B	B.Moran	2B	B.Allen	2B	B.Richardson	M	G.Hodges
SS	W.Causey	SS	J.Fregosi	SS	Z.Versalles	SS	T.Kubek	1B	B.Osborne
3B	E.Charles	3B	F.Torres	3B	R.Rollins	3B	C.Boyer	2B	C.Cottier
LF	B.Del Greco	LF	L.Wagner	LF	H.Killebrew	LF	H.Lopez	SS	E.Brinkman
CF	J.Tartabull	CF	A.Pearson	CF	J.Hall	CF	T.Tresh	3B	D.Zimmer
RF	G.Cimoli	RF	B.Perry	RF	B.Allison	RF	J.Reed	LF	C.Hinton
C	D.Edwards	C	B.Rodgers	C	E.Battey	C	E.Howard	CF	D.Lock
								RF	J.King
O	C.Essegian	1	C.Dees	O	L.Green	O	R.Maris	C	K.Retzer
1O	K.Harrelson			1	D.Mincher	O	J.Blanchard		
O	G.Alusik	P	K.McBride					O	M.Minoso
		P	D.Chance	P	C.Pascual	P	W.Ford	1	D.Phillips
P	D.Wickersham	P	D.Osinski	P	D.Stigman	P	R.Terry	2	D.Blasingame
P	O.Pena	P	D.Lee	P	J.Kaat	P	J.Bouton	C	D.Leppert
P	E.Rakow	RP	J.Navarro	P	J.Perry	P	A.Downing		
P	M.Drabowsky	RP	A.Fowler	P	L.Stange	P	S.Williams	P	C.Osteen
P	D.Segui	RP	P.Foytack	RP	B.Dailey	RP	H.Reniff	P	D.Rudolph
RP	T.Bowsfield			RP	B.Pleis	RP	S.Hamilton	P	B.Daniels
RP	B.Fischer	P	B.Turley	RP	G.Roggenburk			P	T.Cheney
RP	J.Wyatt	P	B.Belinsky			P	B.Stafford	P	J.Duckworth
		P	M.Nelson					RP	R.Kline
								RP	P.Burnside
P	T.Sturdivant							RP	E.Roebuck
								P	S.Ridzik
								P	D.Stenhouse
								P	J.Bronstad

TEAM	G	W	L	PCT	GB	R	OR	AB	H	2B	3B	HR	BB	SO	AVG	OBP	SLG	PRO	PRO+	BR	/A	PF	CHI	RC	SB	CS	SBA	SBR
NY	161	104	57	.646		714	547	5506	1387	197	35	188	434	**808**	.252	.310	.403	.713	106	27	33	99	**105**	686	42	26	62	-3
CHI	162	94	68	.580	10.5	683	**544**	5508	1379	208	**40**	114	571	896	.250	.325	.365	.690	101	4	15	98	101	675	64	28	70	2
MIN	161	91	70	.565	13	**767**	602	5531	**1408**	223	35	**225**	547	912	**.255**	.326	**.430**	**.756**	**115**	116	101	102	98	**777**	32	14	70	1
BAL	162	86	76	.531	18.5	644	621	5448	1359	207	32	146	469	940	.249	.312	.380	.692	102	-7	17	96	100	645	**97**	34	**74**	**9**
DET	162	79	83	.488	25.5	700	703	5500	1388	195	36	148	**592**	908	.252	**.329**	.382	.711	102	43	19	103	98	699	73	32	70	3
CLE	162	79	83	.488	25.5	635	702	5496	1314	214	29	169	460	1102	.239	.304	.381	.685	98	-26	-20	99	100	634	59	36	62	-4
BOS	161	76	85	.472	28	666	704	5575	1403	**247**	34	171	475	954	.252	.313	.400	.713	102	31	9	103	96	684	27	16	63	-2
KC	162	73	89	.451	31.5	615	704	5495	1356	225	38	95	529	829	.247	.316	.353	.669	88	-41	-76	106	99	616	47	26	64	-2
LA	161	70	91	.435	34	597	660	5506	1378	208	38	95	448	916	.250	.312	.354	.666	98	-53	-18	94	99	608	43	30	59	-5
WAS	162	56	106	.346	48.5	578	812	5446	1237	190	35	138	497	963	.227	.295	.351	.646	86	-95	-93	100	104	569	68	28	71	4
TOT	808					6599		55011	13609	2114	352	1489	5031	9228	.247	.314	.380	.694							552	270	67	4

TEAM	CG	SH	SV	IP	H	H/G	HR	BB	SO	RAT	ERA	ERA+	OAV	OOB	PR	/A	PF	CPI	FA	E	DP	FW	PW	BW	SBW	DIF
NY	**59**	19	31	1449	**1239**	7.7	115	476	965	10.8	3.07	114	**.232**	**.297**	89	71	97	98	.982	110	162	1.4	7.5	3.5	-.4	11.5
CHI	49	**21**	39	1469	1311	8.0	**100**	**440**	932	10.9	**2.97**	118	.239	.299	**107**	**87**	97	102	.979	131	163	.3	**9.1**	1.6	.2	1.9
MIN	58	13	30	1446¹	1322	8.2	162	459	941	11.3	3.28	111	.242	.303	56	59	100	**105**	.976	144	140	-.5	6.2	**10.6**	.0	-5.8
BAL	35	8	**43**	1452	1353	8.4	137	507	913	11.7	3.45	101	.248	.316	29	3	96	104	**.984**	**99**	157	**2.1**	.3	1.8	**.9**	-.0
DET	42	7	28	1456¹	1407	8.7	195	477	930	11.9	3.90	96	.253	.317	-44	-25	103	102	.982	113	124	1.3	-2.6	2.0	.3	-2.9
CLE	40	14	25	1449	1390	8.5	176	478	**1018**	11.6	3.79	95	.249	.311	-27	-28	100	98	.977	143	129	-.4	-2.9	-2.1	-.5	3.9
BOS	29	7	32	1449²	1367	8.5	152	539	1009	12.0	3.97	95	.248	.318	-55	-30	104	93	.978	135	119	-.0	-3.2	.9	-.2	-2.0
KC	35	11	29	1458	1417	8.7	156	540	887	12.4	3.92	100	.256	.327	-47	-3	108	101	.980	127	131	.5	-.3	-8.0	-.2	.0
LA	30	13	31	1455¹	1317	8.1	120	578	889	12.0	3.52	97	.242	.320	17	-16	94	100	.974	163	155	-1.6	-1.7	-1.9	-.6	-4.8
WAS	29	8	25	1447	1486	9.2	176	537	744	12.8	4.42	84	.266	.334	-126	-114	102	98	.971	182	**165**	-2.6	-12.0	-9.8	.4	-1.0
TOT	406	121	313	14551²		8.4				11.7	3.63		.247	.314					.978	1347	1445					

Runs		Hits		Doubles		Triples		Home Runs		Total Bases	
Allison-Min	99	Yastrzemski-Bos	183	Yastrzemski-Bos	40	Versalles-Min	13	Killebrew-Min	45	Stuart-Bos	319
Pearson-LA	92	Ward-Chi	177	Ward-Chi	34	Hinton-Was	12	Stuart-Bos	42	Ward-Chi	289
Yastrzemski-Bos	91	Pearson-LA	176	Torres-LA	32	Fregosi-LA	12	Allison-Min	35	Killebrew-Min	286
Tresh-NY	91	Kaline-Det	172	Causey-KC	32	Cimoli-KC	11	Hall-Min	33	Kaline-Det	283
Colavito-Det	91	Fregosi-LA	170	Alvis-Cle	32			Howard-NY	28	Allison-Min	281

Runs Batted In		Runs Produced		Bases On Balls		Batting Average		On Base Percentage		Slugging Average	
Stuart-Bos	118	Kaline-Det	163	Yastrzemski-Bos	95	Yastrzemski-Bos	.321	Yastrzemski-Bos	.419	Killebrew-Min	.555
Kaline-Det	101	Colavito-Det	160	Pearson-LA	92	Kaline-Det	.312	Pearson-LA	.403	Allison-Min	.533
Killebrew-Min	96	Stuart-Bos	157	Allison-Min	90	Rollins-Min	.307	Cash-Det	.388	Howard-NY	.528
Colavito-Det	91	Allison-Min	155	Cash-Det	89	Pearson-LA	.304	Allison-Min	.381	Stuart-Bos	.521
Allison-Min	91	Siebern-KC	147	Colavito-Det	84	Ward-Chi	.295	Kaline-Det	.378	Hall-Min	.521

Production		Adjusted Production		Batter Runs		Adjusted Batter Runs		Clutch Hitting Index		Runs Created	
Allison-Min	.914	Allison-Min	150	Yastrzemski-Bos	42.0	Yastrzemski-Bos	38.4	Hansen-Chi	127	Yastrzemski-Bos	118
Killebrew-Min	.908	Killebrew-Min	147	Allison-Min	38.6	Allison-Min	36.6	Torres-LA	115	Allison-Min	113
Yastrzemski-Bos	.894	Yastrzemski-Bos	145	Kaline-Det	34.3	Killebrew-Min	31.6	Siebern-KC	114	Kaline-Det	105
Kaline-Det	.891	Kaline-Det	142	Killebrew-Min	33.5	Kaline-Det	30.9	L.Thomas-LA	112	Ward-Chi	104
Howard-NY	.871	Howard-NY	141	Cash-Det	28.7	Pearson-LA	29.8	Phillips-Det	112	Pearson-LA	100

Total Average		Stolen Bases		Stolen Base Average		Stolen Base Runs		Fielding Runs		Total Player Rating	
Allison-Min	.967	Aparicio-Bal	40	Tartabull-KC	94.1	Aparicio-Bal	8.4	Hansen-Chi	27.0	Yastrzemski-Bos	4.4
Yastrzemski-Bos	.916	Hinton-Was	25	Aparicio-Bal	87.0	Tartabull-KC	4.2	Boyer-NY	22.3	Allison-Min	4.2
Killebrew-Min	.907	Wood-Det	18	Wood-Det	78.3	Weis-Chi	3.9	Moran-LA	15.2	Hansen-Chi	3.6
Tresh-NY	.879	Snyder-Bal	18	Snyder-Bal	78.3	Richardson-NY	3.9	Lock-Was	14.8	Battey-Min	3.1
Cash-Det	.876	Pearson-LA	17	Hinton-Was	73.5	Smith-Bal	2.7	Geiger-Bos	13.7	Pearson-LA	2.9

Wins		Win Percentage		Games		Complete Games		Shutouts		Saves	
Ford-NY	24	Ford-NY	.774	S.Miller-Bal	71	Terry-NY	18	Herbert-Chi	7	S.Miller-Bal	27
Pascual-Min	21	Bouton-NY	.750	Radatz-Bos	66	Pascual-Min	18	Bouton-NY	6	Radatz-Bos	25
Bouton-NY	21	Radatz-Bos	.714	Dailey-Min	66	Stigman-Min	15			Wyatt-KC	21
Monbouquette-Bos	20	Peters-Chi	.704	Lamabe-Bos	65	Herbert-Chi	14			Wilhelm-Chi	21
Barber-Bal	20	Pascual-Min	.700	Wyatt-KC	63	Aguirre-Det	14			Dailey-Min	21

Innings Pitched		Fewest Hits/Game		Fewest BB/Game		Strikeouts		Strikeouts/Game		Ratio	
Ford-NY	269.1	Downing-NY	5.84	Donovan-Cle	1.22	Pascual-Min	202	Downing-NY	8.76	Terry-NY	9.71
Terry-NY	268.0	Bouton-NY	6.89	Terry-NY	1.31	Bunning-Det	196	Ramos-Cle	8.24	Roberts-Bal	9.78
Monbouquette-Bos	266.2	Drabowsky-KC	6.97	Herbert-Chi	1.40	Stigman-Min	193	Pascual-Min	7.32	Ramos-Cle	9.80
Barber-Bal	258.2	Morehead-Bos	7.06	Monbouquette-Bos	1.42	Peters-Chi	189	Stigman-Min	7.21	Peters-Chi	9.93
Roberts-Bal	251.1	McBride-LA	7.10	Roberts-Bal	1.43	Ford-NY	189	Bunning-Det	7.10	Downing-NY	9.94

Earned Run Average		Adjusted ERA		Opponents' Batting Avg.		Opponents' On Base Pct.		Starter Runs		Adjusted Starter Runs	
Peters-Chi	2.33	Peters-Chi	150	Downing-NY	.184	Roberts-Bal	.272	Peters-Chi	35.0	Pascual-Min	32.6
Pizarro-Chi	2.39	Pascual-Min	148	Morehead-Bos	.211	Terry-NY	.273	Pascual-Min	32.2	Peters-Chi	31.7
Pascual-Min	2.46	Pizarro-Chi	147	Bouton-NY	.212	Ramos-Cle	.273	Bouton-NY	30.6	Bouton-NY	27.3
Bouton-NY	2.53	Bouton-NY	139	Drabowsky-KC	.214	Downing-NY	.277	Pizarro-Chi	29.6	Pizarro-Chi	26.6
Downing-NY	2.56	Stange-Min	139	Peters-Chi	.216	Peters-Chi	.278	Ford-NY	26.6	Ford-NY	23.2

Clutch Pitching Index		Relief Runs		Adjusted Relief Runs		Relief Ranking		Total Pitcher Index		Total Baseball Ranking	
Barber-Bal	126	Radatz-Bos	24.4	Radatz-Bos	26.7	Radatz-Bos	49.4	Radatz-Bos	5.0	Radatz-Bos	5.0
Osteen-Was	120	Dailey-Min	19.8	Dailey-Min	20.0	S.Miller-Bal	24.3	Pascual-Min	4.6	Pascual-Min	4.6
Stange-Min	120	S.Miller-Bal	17.3	S.Miller-Bal	15.4	Dailey-Min	23.6	Peters-Chi	4.5	Peters-Chi	4.5
Segui-KC	115	Wilhelm-Chi	15.0	Wilhelm-Chi	13.1	Wilhelm-Chi	15.8	S.Miller-Bal	3.0	Yastrzemski-Bos	4.4
Pascual-Min	115	Fowler-LA	12.0	Lamabe-Bos	10.7	Kline-Was	14.1	Dailey-Min	3.0	Allison-Min	4.2

February 2 The Hall of Fame Special Veterans Committee tabs Red Faber, Burleigh Grimes, Tim Keefe, Heinie Manush, John Montgomery Ward, and Miller Huggins for induction, the biggest veterans class ever.

February 15 Cubs second baseman Ken Hubbs, 22, dies when his private plane crashes near Provo, UT, while en route to Colton, CA. As a rookie in 1962, Hubbs had played in 78 consecutive games without making an error.

May 31 After Juan Marichal's 5-3, first-game win, SF holds a 6-1 lead in the second until New York rallies for 5 to tie in the seventh. Eventually, with two out in the 23rd, pinch hitter Del Crandall delivers a run-scoring double off Galen Cisco, and the Giants prevail 8-6 after 7 hours and 22 minutes—a record. Gaylord Perry pitches 10 scoreless innings to get the win. Thirty-two innings and an elapsed time of 9 hours and 50 minutes are doubleheader records, as are 47 strikeouts. NY's 22 K's in the second game are the most by one club in an overtime contest.

June 4 Sandy Koufax becomes the fourth pitcher to hurl three no-hitters by blanking the NL-leading Phillies 3-0 at Connie Mack Stadium. Koufax strikes out 12 and walks one.

June 21 On Father's Day at Shea Stadium, Jim Bunning pitches the first perfect game (excluding Don Larsen's 1956 World Series effort and Harvey Haddix's 1959 overtime loss) since Charlie Robertson's on April 30, 1922. He is also the first to win no-hitters in both leagues and drives in two runs as Philadelphia beats the Mets 6-0. Gus Triandos becomes the first catcher to catch a no-hitter in each league.

September 1 Southpaw relief pitcher Masanori Murakami becomes the first major league player from Japan. He debuts in a 4-1 SF loss at NY. His first 11 innings will be scoreless ones.

September 26 The Braves and Phillies set the ML record by using 43 players in a nine-inning game. The Braves' 25 match the high mark for NL clubs. Eight of the 25 are pitchers, tying the NL mark.

October 4 The Phils bomb the Reds 10-0 as both teams finish one game behind St. Louis. They then sit in the visitor's clubhouse and hope that Galen Cisco (6-18) can stop the Cards. The Mets take a 3-2 lead into the fifth, but St. Louis scores 3 runs to take the lead. The Mets score once more but the Cards complete their scoring with 3 in the eighth to win 11-5. Bob Gibson wins in relief. For St. Louis, it is their first pennant since 1946.

October 7 Ailing Whitey Ford struggles as St. Louis wins the World Series opener 9-4 at Busch Stadium. Ray Sadecki and Barney Schultz combine for the win.

October 15 St. Louis takes an early lead in the deciding World Series Game 7. Lou Brock's fifth-inning home run triggers a second three-run frame and a 6-0 lead for Bob Gibson. Brothers Ken and Clete Boyer become the only brothers to homer in the same Series game, and the Cards win 7-5 to become World Champs.

November 7 With their home attendance below 800,000 for the past two seasons, the NL orders the Braves to stay in Milwaukee in 1965, but permits a move to Atlanta in 1966.

November 24 Third baseman Ken Boyer of the Cardinals is voted NL MVP, with 243 votes to 187 for Philadelphia outfielder Johnny Callison.

CHICAGO		CINCINNATI		HOUSTON		LOS ANGELES		MILWAUKEE	
M	B.Kennedy	M	F.Hutchinson	M	H.Craft	M	W.Alston	M	B.Bragan
1B	E.Banks	M	D.Sisler	M	L.Harris	1B	R.Fairly	1B	G.Oliver
2B	J.Amalfitano	M	F.Hutchinson	1B	W.Bond	2B	N.Oliver	2B	F.Bolling
SS	A.Rodgers	M	D.Sisler	2B	N.Fox	SS	M.Wills	SS	D.Menke
3B	R.Santo	1B	D.Johnson	SS	E.Kasko	3B	J.Gilliam	3B	E.Mathews
LF	B.Williams	2B	P.Rose	3B	B.Aspromonte	LF	T.Davis	LF	R.Carty
CF	B.Cowan	SS	L.Cardenas	LF	A.Spangler	CF	W.Davis	CF	L.Maye
RF	L.Gabrielson	3B	S.Boros	CF	M.White	RF	F.Howard	RF	H.Aaron
C	D.Bertell	LF	T.Harper	RF	J.Gaines	C	J.Roseboro	C	J.Torre
		CF	V.Pinson	C	J.Grote				
2S	J.Stewart	RF	F.Robinson			O1	W.Parker	O1	F.Alou
O	L.Brock	C	J.Edwards	2S	B.Lillis	23	D.Tracewski	O	T.Cline
				1O	R.Staub	3O	D.Griffith	C	E.Bailey
P	L.Jackson	O	M.Keough	C	J.Bateman				
P	D.Ellsworth	32	C.Ruiz	O	J.Wynn	P	D.Drysdale	P	T.Cloninger
P	B.Buhl					P	S.Koufax	P	D.Lemaster
P	L.Burdette	P	J.O'Toole	P	K.Johnson	P	P.Ortega	P	W.Spahn
P	E.Broglio	P	J.Maloney	P	B.Bruce	P	J.Moeller	P	H.Fischer
RP	L.McDaniel	P	B.Purkey	P	T.Farrell	RP	B.Miller	P	B.Sadowski
RP	D.Elston	P	J.Jay	P	D.Nottebart	RP	R.Perranoski	RP	B.Tiefenauer
RP	S.Slaughter	P	J.Tsitouris	P	H.Brown	RP	J.Brewer	P	B.Hoeft
		RP	S.Ellis	RP	J.Owens			RP	C.Olivo
		RP	B.McCool	RP	C.Raymond	P	H.Reed		
		RP	B.Henry	RP	H.Woodeshick	P	L.Miller	P	W.Blasingame
		P	J.Nuxhall	P	D.Larsen				
				P	G.Jones				

NEW YORK		PHILADELPHIA		PITTSBURGH		SAN FRANCISCO		ST.LOUIS	
M	C.Stengel	M	G.Mauch	M	D.Murtaugh	M	A.Dark	M	J.Keane
1B	E.Kranepool	1B	J.Herrnstein	1B	D.Clendenon	1B	O.Cepeda	1B	B.White
2B	R.Hunt	2B	T.Taylor	2B	B.Mazeroski	2B	H.Lanier	2B	J.Javier
SS	R.McMillan	SS	B.Wine	SS	D.Schofield	SS	J.Pagan	SS	D.Groat
3B	C.Smith	3B	D.Allen	3B	B.Bailey	3B	J.Hart	3B	K.Boyer
LF	G.Altman	LF	W.Covington	LF	M.Mota	LF	H.Kuenn	LF	L.Brock
CF	J.Hickman	CF	T.Gonzalez	CF	B.Virdon	CF	W.Mays	CF	C.Flood
RF	J.Christopher	RF	J.Callison	RF	R.Clemente	RF	J.Alou	RF	M.Shannon
C	J.Gonder	C	C.Dalrymple	C	J.Pagliaroni	C	T.Haller	C	T.McCarver
2O	R.Kanehl	S1	R.Amaro	3	G.Freese	O	M.Alou	O	C.James
CO	H.Taylor	O2	C.Rojas	O	J.Lynch	S3	J.Davenport		
O	L.Elliot			O1	W.Stargell	O1	W.McCovey	P	B.Gibson
23	B.Klaus	P	J.Bunning	S	G.Alley	2	C.Hiller	P	C.Simmons
		P	C.Short					P	R.Sadecki
P	J.Fisher	P	De.Bennett	P	B.Veale	P	J.Marichal	P	R.Craig
P	T.Stallard	P	A.Mahaffey	P	B.Friend	P	G.Perry	RP	R.Taylor
P	A.Jackson	P	R.Culp	P	V.Law	P	B.Bolin	RP	M.Cuellar
P	G.Cisco	RP	J.Baldschun	P	J.Gibbon	P	B.Hendley	RP	B.Schultz
RP	B.Wakefield	RP	E.Roebuck	P	S.Blass	P	R.Herbel		
RP	L.Bearnarth	RP	R.Wise	RP	A.McBean	RP	B.Shaw	P	E.Broglio
				RP	R.Face	RP	B.O'Dell	P	R.Washburn
P	D.Ribant	P	Da.Bennett	RP	T.Butters	P	J.Duffalo		
P	F.Lary	P	J.Boozer						
				P	T.Sisk	P	J.Sanford		
				P	D.Schwall				

TEAM	G	W	L	PCT	GB	R	OR	AB	H	2B	3B	HR	BB	SO	AVG	OBP	SLG	PRO	PRO+	BR	/A	PF	CHI	RC	SB	CS	SBA	SBR
STL	162	93	69	.574		715	652	5625	**1531**	240	53	109	427	925	**.272**	.326	.392	.718	100	62	0	109	99	711	73	51	59	-9
PHI	162	92	70	.568	1	693	632	5493	1415	241	51	130	440	924	.258	.317	.391	.708	107	41	50	99	100	672	30	35	46	-12
CIN	163	92	70	.568	1	660	**566**	5561	1383	220	38	130	457	974	.249	.310	.372	.682	99	-10	-33	104	102	642	90	36	**71**	5
SF	162	90	72	.556	3	656	587	5535	1360	185	38	**165**	**505**	900	.246	.313	.382	.695	96	16	2	102	97	657	64	35	65	-2
MIL	162	88	74	.543	5	**803**	744	5591	1522	**274**	32	159	486	**825**	**.272**	**.335**	**.418**	**.753**	118	**132**	**127**	101	101	**764**	53	41	56	-9
PIT	162	80	82	.494	13	663	636	5566	1469	225	**54**	121	408	970	.264	.317	.389	.706	105	35	36	100	97	668	39	33	54	-8
LA	164	80	82	.494	13	614	572	5499	1375	180	39	79	438	893	.250	.308	.340	.648	96	-70	-28	93	105	581	**141**	60	70	**6**
CHI	162	76	86	.469	17	649	724	5545	1391	239	50	145	499	1041	.251	.316	.390	.706	101	37	9	104	94	679	70	49	59	-8
HOU	162	66	96	.407	27	495	628	5303	1214	162	41	70	381	872	.229	.287	.315	.602	81	-158	-132	94	**106**	469	40	48	45	-17
NY	163	53	109	.327	40	569	776	5566	1372	195	31	103	353	932	.246	.297	.348	.645	90	-84	-71	98	102	552	36	31	54	-8
TOT	812					6517		55284	14032	2161	427	1211	4394	9256	.254	.313	.374	.687							636	419	60	-61

TEAM	CG	SH	SV	IP	H	H/G	HR	BB	SO	RAT	ERA	ERA+	OAV	OOB	PR	/A	PF	CPI	FA	E	DP	FW	PW	BW	SBW	DIF
STL	47	10	38	1445¹	1405	8.7	133	410	877	11.5	3.43	111	.255	.310	17	60	108	104	.973	172	147	-.7	6.3	.0	-.3	6.7
PHI	37	17	**41**	1461	1402	8.6	129	440	1009	11.7	3.36	103	.252	.313	28	17	98	**106**	.975	157	150	.0	1.8	5.3	-.6	4.5
CIN	54	14	35	1467	1306	8.0	112	436	**1122**	10.9	3.07	**118**	.238	.298	75	**88**	102	100	**.979**	**130**	137	**1.6**	**9.3**	-3.5	1.2	2.4
SF	48	17	30	1476¹	1348	8.2	118	458	1023	11.4	3.19	112	.241	.306	57	61	101	102	.975	159	136	-.0	6.4	.2	.4	1.9
MIL	45	14	39	1434²	1411	8.9	160	452	906	11.8	4.12	86	.257	.316	-92	-95	100	94	.977	143	139	.8	-10.0	13.4	-.3	3.1
PIT	42	14	29	1443²	1429	8.9	92	476	951	12.1	3.52	100	.260	.322	2	-2	99	103	.972	177	**179**	-1.0	-.2	3.8	-.2	-3.4
LA	47	**19**	27	1483²	**1289**	**7.8**	88	458	1062	10.8	**2.95**	110	**.232**	**.294**	96	47	92	95	.973	170	126	-.5	5.0	-3.0	**1.3**	-3.8
CHI	**58**	11	19	1445	1510	9.4	144	423	737	12.1	4.08	91	.270	.323	-87	-59	105	98	.975	162	147	-.2	-6.2	1.0	-.2	.7
HOU	30	9	31	1428	1421	9.0	105	**353**	852	11.4	3.41	100	.260	.309	20	1	97	102	.976	149	124	.5	.1	-13.9	-1.2	-.5
NY	40	10	15	1438²	1511	9.5	130	466	717	12.7	4.25	84	.272	.334	-115	-108	101	98	.975	167	154	-.4	-11.4	-7.5	-.2	-8.5
TOT	448	135	304	14523¹		8.7				11.6	3.54		.254	.313					.975	1586	1439					

Runs		Hits		Doubles		Triples		Home Runs		Total Bases	
Allen-Phi	125	Flood-StL	211	Maye-Mil	44	Santo-Chi	13	Mays-SF	47	Allen-Phi	352
Mays-SF	121	Clemente-Pit	211	Clemente-Pit	40	Allen-Phi	13	Williams-Chi	33	Mays-SF	351
Brock-Chi-StL	111	Williams-Chi	201	Williams-Chi	39	Brock-Chi-StL	11	Hart-SF	31	Williams-Chi	343
Robinson-Cin	103	Allen-Phi	201	Robinson-Cin	38	Pinson-Cin	11	Cepeda-SF	31	Santo-Chi	334
Aaron-Mil	103	Brock-Chi-StL	200	Allen-Phi	38			Callison-Phi	31	Callison-Phi	322

Runs Batted In		Runs Produced		Bases On Balls		Batting Average		On Base Percentage		Slugging Average	
Boyer-StL	119	Boyer-StL	195	Santo-Chi	86	Clemente-Pit	.339	Santo-Chi	.401	Mays-SF	.607
Santo-Chi	114	Allen-Phi	187	Mathews-Mil	85	Carty-Mil	.330	Robinson-Cin	.399	Santo-Chi	.564
Mays-SF	111	Mays-SF	185	Mays-SF	82	Aaron-Mil	.328	Aaron-Mil	.394	Allen-Phi	.557
Torre-Mil	109	Santo-Chi	178	Robinson-Cin	79	Torre-Mil	.321	Carty-Mil	.391	Carty-Mil	.554
Callison-Phi	104	Torre-Mil	176	Boyer-StL	70	Allen-Phi	.318	Clemente-Pit	.391	Robinson-Cin	.548

Production		Adjusted Production		Batter Runs		Adjusted Batter Runs		Clutch Hitting Index		Runs Created	
Mays-SF	.992	Mays-SF	171	Mays-SF	56.5	Mays-SF	53.9	Fairly-LA	142	Mays-SF	136
Santo-Chi	.966	Allen-Phi	163	Santo-Chi	55.1	Allen-Phi	52.1	Boyer-StL	117	Santo-Chi	135
Robinson-Cin	.947	Santo-Chi	162	Allen-Phi	50.5	Santo-Chi	49.9	T.Davis-LA	116	Allen-Phi	135
Carty-Mil	.945	Carty-Mil	162	Robinson-Cin	49.5	Robinson-Cin	45.3	Torre-Mil	113	Robinson-Cin	127
Allen-Phi	.940	Robinson-Cin	158	Williams-Chi	42.5	Aaron-Mil	40.2	Javier-StL	111	Williams-Chi	125

Total Average		Stolen Bases		Stolen Base Average		Stolen Base Runs		Fielding Runs		Total Player Rating	
Mays-SF	1.059	Wills-LA	53	Harper-Cin	88.9	Wills-LA	5.7	Mazeroski-Pit	33.9	Santo-Chi	6.5
Robinson-Cin	1.012	Brock-Chi-StL	43	Aaron-Mil	84.6	Harper-Cin	5.4	W.Davis-LA	24.9	Mays-SF	6.5
Santo-Chi	.998	W.Davis-LA	42	Robinson-Cin	82.1	W.Davis-LA	4.8	Edwards-Cin	22.6	Allen-Phi	5.8
Allen-Phi	.944	Harper-Cin	24	Mays-SF	79.2	Aaron-Mil	4.2	Callison-Phi	19.4	Aaron-Mil	5.1
Carty-Mil	.920	Robinson-Cin	23	W.Davis-LA	76.4	Robinson-Cin	3.9	Rodgers-Chi	19.4	Robinson-Cin	4.6

Wins		Win Percentage		Games		Complete Games		Shutouts		Saves	
Jackson-Chi	24	Koufax-LA	.792	B.Miller-LA	74	Marichal-SF	22	Koufax-LA	7	Woodeshick-Hou	23
Marichal-SF	21	Marichal-SF	.724	Perranoski-LA	72	Drysdale-LA	21	Law-Pit	5	McBean-Pit	22
Sadecki-StL	20	O'Toole-Cin	.708	Baldschun-Phi	71	Jackson-Chi	19	Fischer-Mil	5	Baldschun-Phi	21
		Bunning-Phi	.704	Taylor-StL	63	Gibson-StL	17	Drysdale-LA	5	McDaniel-Chi	15
		Jackson-Chi	.686	McDaniel-Chi	63	Ellsworth-Chi	16	Bunning-Phi	5		

Innings Pitched		Fewest Hits/Game		Fewest BB/Game		Strikeouts		Strikeouts/Game		Ratio	
Drysdale-LA	321.1	Koufax-LA	6.22	Bunning-Phi	1.46	Veale-Pit	250	Koufax-LA	9.00	Koufax-LA	8.35
Jackson-Chi	297.2	Drysdale-LA	6.78	Bruce-Hou	1.47	Gibson-StL	245	Maloney-Cin	8.92	Drysdale-LA	8.96
Gibson-StL	287.1	Short-Phi	7.10	Law-Pit	1.50	Drysdale-LA	237	Veale-Pit	8.05	Short-Phi	9.34
Bunning-Phi	284.1	Veale-Pit	7.14	Marichal-SF	1.74	Koufax-LA	223	Gibson-StL	7.67	Bunning-Phi	9.75
Veale-Pit	279.2	Maloney-Cin	7.29	Jackson-Chi	1.75	Bunning-Phi	219	Lemaster-Mil	7.53	Jackson-Chi	9.80

Earned Run Average		Adjusted ERA		Opponents' Batting Avg.		Opponents' On Base Pct.		Starter Runs		Adjusted Starter Runs	
Koufax-LA	1.74	Koufax-LA	187	Koufax-LA	.191	Koufax-LA	.241	Drysdale-LA	48.2	Drysdale-LA	37.6
Drysdale-LA	2.18	Short-Phi	157	Drysdale-LA	.207	Drysdale-LA	.256	Koufax-LA	44.6	Koufax-LA	37.2
Short-Phi	2.20	Drysdale-LA	148	Veale-Pit	.217	Short-Phi	.268	Short-Phi	32.7	Marichal-SF	32.5
Marichal-SF	2.48	Marichal-SF	144	Short-Phi	.217	Jackson-Chi	.273	Marichal-SF	31.7	Short-Phi	31.0
Bunning-Phi	2.63	O'Toole-Cin	136	Bolin-SF	.220	Marichal-SF	.273	Bunning-Phi	28.7	Bunning-Phi	26.6

Clutch Pitching Index		Relief Runs		Adjusted Relief Runs		Relief Ranking		Total Pitcher Index		Total Baseball Ranking	
Craig-StL	122	McBean-Pit	16.2	McBean-Pit	16.0	McBean-Pit	26.5	Drysdale-LA	4.7	Santo-Chi	6.5
D.Bennett-Phi	119	B.Miller-LA	14.1	Ellis-Cin	14.1	Ellis-Cin	17.1	Koufax-LA	3.5	Mays-SF	6.5
Farrell-Hou	115	Ellis-Cin	13.1	McCool-Cin	11.9	McCool-Cin	15.2	Short-Phi	3.5	Allen-Phi	5.8
Tsitouris-Cin	115	Roebuck-Phi	11.4	Roebuck-Phi	10.8	Roebuck-Phi	13.8	Marichal-SF	3.4	Aaron-Mil	5.1
Hendley-SF	110	McCool-Cin	11.1	B.Miller-LA	9.5	Woodeshick-Hou	11.0	McBean-Pit	3.3	Drysdale-LA	4.7

January 15 Major League Baseball executives vote to hold a free-agent draft in New York City and also sign a new TV contract.

January 16 AL owners vote 9-1 against Charlie Finley's proposal to move the A's to Louisville. Finley is given an ultimatum to sign a lease in Kansas City or lose his franchise.

February 17 White Sox shortstop Luke Appling is voted into the Hall of Fame.

July 14 Oriole Bob Johnson's sixth straight hit as a pinch hitter sets an AL mark, but the Yankees win 4-3.

July 23 A's rookie Bert Campaneris sends Minnesota to defeat 4-3 with two homers in his major league debut. The 21-year-old Cuban joins Bob Nieman as the only player since 1900 with two home runs in his first major league game.

August 5 After weeks of negotiating, Ford Frick tells the league presidents and club owners he will not run for another term as commissioner.

August 12 Mickey Mantle homers from each side of the plate in the same game for the tenth and final time, a major league record, and New York beats Chicago 7-3 at Yankee Stadium.

August 14 Bo Belinsky is suspended by the Angels after attacking sportswriter Braven Dyer. Four days later Belinsky is assigned to Hawaii (Pacific Coast League), then suspended for the season when he refuses to report.

August 20 On the New York team bus following a 5–0 White Sox win, Phil Linz begins to play "Mary Had a Little Lamb" on his harmonica. Manager Yogi Berra orders Linz to stop, then slaps the instrument out of his hands when he continues playing. The incident is reported as indicating dissension on the club and Berra's lack of control, as well as the level of Linz's humor.

August 31 Ground is broken for Anaheim Stadium, future home of the Los Angeles (later California and Anaheim) Angels.

September 17 The Yankees whip the Angels, 6–2, to lock on to first place for good with a two-percentage-point lead over the idle White Sox and Orioles. Roger Maris and Mickey Mantle each have three hits. Mantle's include his 2,000th career hit and his 450th home run, his 31st of the year. The Yankees have won two in a row and will run their win streak to 11 games.

October 17 A World Series loss is enough reason for the Yankees to fire manager Yogi Berra (99-63).

November 18 Baltimore third baseman Brooks Robinson is voted AL MVP, outpolling Mickey Mantle 269 to 171.

December 4 Baseball approves a free-agent draft. At their winter meetings in Houston, the minor league and major league organizations establish a system, basically like that of professional football, which will take effect in January 1965 and be held every four months thereafter. Choices will be exercised by clubs in inverse order of their previous year's standing. Draftees must be included in their club's 40-man roster or be susceptible to claim at the waiver price the following season.

	BALTIMORE		BOSTON		CHICAGO		CLEVELAND		DETROIT
M	H.Bauer	M	J.Pesky	M	A.Lopez	M	G.Strickland	M	C.Dressen
1B	N.Siebern	M	.Herman	1B	T.McCraw	M	B.Tebbetts	1B	N.Cash
2B	J.Adair	1B	D.Stuart	2B	A.Weis	1B	B.Chance	2B	J.Lumpe
SS	L.Aparicio	2B	D.Jones	SS	R.Hansen	2B	L.Brown	SS	D.McAuliffe
3B	B.Robinson	SS	E.Bressoud	3B	P.Ward	SS	D.Howser	3B	D.Wert
LF	B.Powell	3B	F.Malzone	LF	F.Robinson	3B	M.Alvis	LF	G.Brown
CF	J.Brandt	LF	T.Conigliaro	CF	J.Landis	LF	L.Wagner	CF	G.Thomas
RF	S.Bowens	CF	C.Yastrzemski	RF	M.Hershberger	CF	V.Davalillo	RF	A.Kaline
C	D.Brown	RF	L.Thomas	C	J.Martin	RF	T.Francona	C	B.Freehan
		C	B.Tillman			C	J.Romano		
C	J.Orsino			23	D.Buford			O	B.Bruton
S1	B.Johnson	O2	F.Mantilla	O	D.Nicholson	2O	W.Held	O1	D.Demeter
				1	B.Skowron	1	F.Whitfield		
P	M.Pappas	P	B.Monbouquette			O2	C.Salmon	P	D.Wickersham
P	W.Bunker	P	E.Wilson	P	G.Peters	C	J.Azcue	P	M.Lolich
P	R.Roberts	P	J.Lamabe	P	J.Pizarro			P	H.Aguirre
P	D.McNally	P	D.Morehead	P	J.Horlen	P	J.Kralick	P	E.Rakow
P	S.Barber	RP	B.Heffner	P	J.Buzhardt	P	S.McDowell	P	P.Regan
RP	S.Miller	RP	D.Radatz	P	R.Herbert	P	D.Donovan	RP	F.Gladding
RP	H.Haddix	RP	B.Spanswick	RP	H.Wilhelm	P	S.Siebert	RP	L.Sherry
RP	D.Hall			RP	E.Fisher	P	P.Ramos	RP	T.Fox
		P	E.Connolly			RP	G.Bell		
P	C.Estrada	P	P.Charton	P	F.Talbot	RP	D.McMahon	P	D.McLain
P	D.Vineyard	P	A.Earley			RP	T.Abernathy	P	J.Sparma
						P	L.Tiant		
						P	T.John		
						P	L.Stange		
						P	M.Grant		

	KANSAS CITY		LOS ANGELES		MINNESOTA		NEW YORK		WASHINGTON
M	E.Lopat	M	B.Rigney	M	S.Mele	M	Y.Berra	M	G.Hodges
M	M.McGaha	1B	J.Adcock	1B	B.Allison	1B	J.Pepitone	1B	B.Skowron
1B	J.Gentile	2B	B.Knoop	2B	B.Allen	2B	B.Richardson	2B	D.Blasingame
2B	D.Green	SS	J.Fregosi	SS	Z.Versalles	SS	T.Kubek	SS	E.Brinkman
SS	W.Causey	3B	F.Torres	3B	R.Rollins	3B	C.Boyer	3B	J.Kennedy
3B	E.Charles	LF	W.Smith	LF	H.Killebrew	LF	T.Tresh	LF	C.Hinton
LF	J.Tartabull	CF	J.Piersall	CF	J.Hall	CF	M.Mantle	CF	D.Lock
CF	N.Mathews	RF	L.Clinton	RF	T.Oliva	RF	R.Maris	RF	J.King
RF	R.Colavito	C	B.Rodgers	C	E.Battey	C	E.Howard	C	M.Brumley
C	D.Edwards								
		O	A.Pearson	1	D.Mincher	S3	P.Linz	1	D.Phillips
O1	G.Alusik	31	T.Satriano			O	H.Lopez	O	F.Valentine
SO	B.Campaneris	O	B.Perry	P	C.Pascual			3	D.Zimmer
C	B.Bryan	13	V.Power	P	J.Kaat	P	J.Bouton		
O	M.Jimenez	O	E.Kirkpatrick	P	D.Stigman	P	W.Ford	P	C.Osteen
				P	M.Grant	P	A.Downing	P	B.Narum
P	O.Pena	P	D.Chance	RP	G.Arrigo	P	R.Terry	P	B.Daniels
P	D.Segui	P	F.Newman	RP	J.Perry	P	R.Sheldon	P	A.Koch
P	J.O'Donoghue	P	B.Latman			RP	P.Mikkelsen	RP	S.Ridzik
P	M.Drabowsky	P	B.Belinsky			RP	H.Reniff	RP	J.Hannan
RP	J.Wyatt	P	K.McBride	P	J.Roland	RP	B.Stafford	RP	R.Kline
RP	T.Bowsfield	RP	B.Lee	P	L.Stange				
RP	W.Stock	RP	D.Osinski	P	B.Pleis	P	M.Stottlemyre	P	D.Stenhouse
		RP	D.Lee			P	S.Williams	P	D.Rudolph
P	J.Santiago					P	S.Hamilton	P	J.Duckworth
		P	B.Duliba						
		P	A.Gatewood						

TEAM	G	W	L	PCT	GB	R	OR	AB	H	2B	3B	HR	BB	SO	AVG	OBP	SLG	PRO	PRO+	BR	/A	PF	CHI	RC	SB	CS	SBA	SBR
NY	164	99	63	.611		730	577	5705	**1442**	208	35	162	520	976	.253	.319	.387	.706	100	13	2	102	**105**	705	54	18	**75**	5
CHI	162	98	64	.605	1	642	**501**	5491	1356	184	40	106	**562**	**902**	.247	.323	.353	.676	98	-32	-15	97	101	643	75	39	66	-1
BAL	163	97	65	.599	2	679	567	5463	1357	229	20	162	537	1019	.248	.319	.387	.706	102	14	17	100	101	671	78	38	67	1
DET	163	85	77	.525	14	699	678	5513	1394	199	**57**	157	517	912	.253	.321	.395	.716	103	35	25	102	100	707	60	27	69	2
LA	162	82	80	.506	17	544	551	5362	1297	186	27	102	472	920	.242	.306	.344	.650	97	-89	-36	90	99	552	49	39	56	-9
MIN	163	79	83	.488	20	**737**	678	5610	1413	227	46	**221**	553	1019	.252	.324	**.427**	.751	113	98	93	101	95	**775**	46	22	68	1
CLE	164	79	83	.488	20	689	693	5603	1386	208	22	164	500	1063	.247	.315	.380	.695	100	-8	-3	99	104	666	**79**	51	61	-7
BOS	162	72	90	.444	27	688	793	5513	1425	**253**	29	186	504	917	**.258**	.324	.416	.740		76	40	105	94	725	18	16	53	-4
WAS	162	62	100	.383	37	578	733	5396	1246	199	28	125	514	1124	.231	.301	.348	.649	86	-95	-92	100	**105**	566	47	30	61	-4
KC	163	57	105	.352	42	621	836	5524	1321	216	29	166	548	1104	.239	.313	.379	.692	95	-14	-33	103	96	645	34	20	63	-2
TOT	814					6607		55180	13637	2109	333	1551	5227	9956	.247	.316	.382	.698							540	300	64	-18

TEAM	CG	SH	SV	IP	H	H/G	HR	BB	SO	RAT	ERA	ERA+	OAV	OOB	PR	/A	PF	CPI	FA	E	DP	FW	PW	BW	SBW	DIF
NY	46	18	**45**	1506²	1312	7.8	129	504	989	11.0	3.15	115	.234	.300	79	78	100	97	.983	109	158	1.1	8.2	.2	**.7**	7.8
CHI	44	20	**45**	1467²	**1216**	7.5	124	**401**	955	**10.1**	2.72	127	.226	.283	147	119	95	100	.981	122	164	.2	**12.5**	-1.6	.0	5.7
BAL	44	17	41	1458²	1292	8.0	129	456	939	11.0	3.16	113	.239	.302	76	67	99	100	**.985**	**95**	159	**1.9**	7.0	1.8	.3	5.0
DET	35	11	35	1453	1343	8.3	164	536	993	12.0	3.84	95	.244	.317	-35	-29	101	95	.982	111	137	1.0	-3.0	2.6	.4	3.1
LA	30	**28**	41	1450²	1273	7.9	**100**	530	965	11.5	2.91	113	.236	.310	115	60	91	**107**	.978	138	**168**	-.7	6.3	-3.8	-.8	-.0
MIN	**47**	4	29	1477²	1361	8.3	181	545	1099	11.8	3.58	100	.243	.314	8	1	99	102	.977	145	131	-1.1	.1	**9.8**	.3	-11.1
CLE	37	16	37	1487²	1443	8.7	154	565	**1162**	12.3	3.75	96	.255	.326	-21	-25	99	103	.981	118	149	.6	-2.6	-.3	-.5	.9
BOS	21	9	38	1422	1464	9.3	178	571	1094	13.1	4.50	86	.266	.339	-138	-102	106	97	.977	138	123	-.7	-10.7	4.2	-.2	-1.5
WAS	27	5	26	1435¹	1417	8.9	172	505	794	12.2	3.98	93	.259	.324	-57	-45	102	100	.979	127	145	-.0	-4.7	-9.7	-.2	-4.3
KC	18	6	27	1455²	1516	9.4	220	614	966	13.5	4.71	81	.269	.346	-175	-144	105	101	.975	158	152	-1.9	-15.1	-3.5	-.0	-3.5
TOT	349	134	364	14615		8.4				11.8	3.63		.247	.316					.980	1261	1486					

Runs		Hits		Doubles		Triples		Home Runs		Total Bases	
Oliva-Min	109	Oliva-Min	217	Oliva-Min	43	Versalles-Min	10	Killebrew-Min	49	Oliva-Min	374
Howser-Cle	101	B.Robinson-Bal	194	Bressoud-Bos	41	Rollins-Min	10	Powell-Bal	39	B.Robinson-Bal	319
Killebrew-Min	95	Richardson-NY	181	B.Robinson-Bal	35	Yastrzemski-Bos	9	Mantle-NY	35	Killebrew-Min	316
Wagner-Cle	94	Howard-NY	172	Versalles-Min	33	Oliva-Min	9	Colavito-KC	34	Colavito-KC	298
Versalles-Min	94	Versalles-Min	171			Fregosi-LA	9	Stuart-Bos	33	Stuart-Bos	296

Runs Batted In		Runs Produced		Bases On Balls		Batting Average		On Base Percentage		Slugging Average	
B.Robinson-Bal	118	B.Robinson-Bal	172	Siebern-Bal	106	Oliva-Min	.323	Mantle-NY	.426	Powell-Bal	.606
Stuart-Bos	114	Oliva-Min	171	Mantle-NY	99	B.Robinson-Bal	.317	Allison-Min	.406	Mantle-NY	.591
Mantle-NY	111	Mantle-NY	168	Killebrew-Min	93	Howard-NY	.313	Powell-Bal	.400	Oliva-Min	.557
Killebrew-Min	111	Wagner-Cle	163	Allison-Min	92	Mantle-NY	.303	Robinson-Chi	.388	Allison-Min	.553
Colavito-KC	102			Causey-KC	88	Robinson-Chi	.301	Kaline-Det	.385	Killebrew-Min	.548

Production		Adjusted Production		Batter Runs		Adjusted Batter Runs		Clutch Hitting Index		Runs Created	
Mantle-NY	1.017	Mantle-NY	177	Mantle-NY	53.0	Mantle-NY	51.2	Rodgers-LA	125	Oliva-Min	132
Powell-Bal	1.007	Powell-Bal	176	Allison-Min	45.0	Powell-Bal	44.5	Boyer-NY	118	Killebrew-Min	122
Allison-Min	.959	Allison-Min	163	Powell-Bal	44.1	Allison-Min	44.2	Pepitone-NY	118	Mantle-NY	121
Killebrew-Min	.927	Killebrew-Min	153	Killebrew-Min	43.1	Killebrew-Min	42.3	Mantle-NY	117	Allison-Min	119
Oliva-Min	.918	Oliva-Min	150	Oliva-Min	43.0	Oliva-Min	42.2	Cash-Det	116	B.Robinson-Bal	115

Total Average		Stolen Bases		Stolen Base Average		Stolen Base Runs		Fielding Runs		Total Player Rating	
Mantle-NY	1.122	Aparicio-Bal	57	Aparicio-Bal	77.0	Aparicio-Bal	6.9	Knoop-LA	37.2	Powell-Bal	4.4
Powell-Bal	1.081	Weis-Chi	22	Weis-Chi	75.9	Tresh-NY	3.9	Yastrzemski-Bos	27.7	Fregosi-LA	4.4
Allison-Min	1.058	Davalillo-Cle	21	Howser-Cle	74.1	Wagner-Cle	3.0	Boyer-NY	19.3	Hansen-Chi	4.3
Killebrew-Min	.956	Howser-Cle	20	Hinton-Was	73.9	Weis-Chi	2.4	Green-KC	16.5	Oliva-Min	4.1
Oliva-Min	.894	Hinton-Was	17	Davalillo-Cle	65.6	Allison-Min	2.4	Brandt-Bal	16.1	Yastrzemski-Bos	3.9

Wins		Win Percentage		Games		Complete Games		Shutouts		Saves	
Peters-Chi	20	Bunker-Bal	.792	Wyatt-KC	81	Chance-LA	15	Chance-LA	11	Radatz-Bos	29
Chance-LA	20	Ford-NY	.739	Radatz-Bos	79	Pascual-Min	14	Ford-NY	8	Wilhelm-Chi	27
Wickersham-Det	19	Peters-Chi	.714	Wilhelm-Chi	73	Pappas-Bal	13	Pappas-Bal	7	Miller-Bal	23
Pizarro-Chi	19	Pappas-Bal	.696	McMahon-Cle	70	Osteen-Was	13	Lolich-Det	6	Wyatt-KC	20
Bunker-Bal	19	Chance-LA	.690	Miller-Bal	66	Kaat-Min	13	Monbouquette-Bos	5	B.Lee-LA	19

Innings Pitched		Fewest Hits/Game		Fewest BB/Game		Strikeouts		Strikeouts/Game		Ratio	
Chance-LA	278.1	Horlen-Chi	6.07	Monbouquette-Bos	1.54	Downing-NY	217	McDowell-Cle	9.19	Horlen-Chi	8.59
Peters-Chi	273.2	Chance-LA	6.27	Pappas-Bal	1.72	Pascual-Min	213	Downing-NY	8.00	Chance-LA	9.12
Bouton-NY	271.1	Bunker-Bal	6.77	Newman-LA	1.85	Chance-LA	207	Pena-KC	7.55	Pizarro-Chi	9.45
Pascual-Min	267.1	Peters-Chi	7.14	Bouton-NY	1.99	Peters-Chi	205	Stigman-Min	7.53	Bunker-Bal	9.50
Osteen-Was	257.0	Pizarro-Chi	7.27	Pizarro-Chi	2.07	Lolich-Det	192	Morehead-Bos	7.51	Bouton-NY	9.72

Earned Run Average		Adjusted ERA		Opponents' Batting Avg.		Opponents' On Base Pct.		Starter Runs		Adjusted Starter Runs	
Chance-LA	1.65	Chance-LA	199	Horlen-Chi	.190	Horlen-Chi	.250	Chance-LA	61.1	Chance-LA	50.6
Horlen-Chi	1.88	Horlen-Chi	184	Chance-LA	.195	Chance-LA	.261	Horlen-Chi	40.9	Ford-NY	40.5
Ford-NY	2.13	Ford-NY	170	Bunker-Bal	.207	Pizarro-Chi	.267	Ford-NY	40.6	Horlen-Chi	36.9
Peters-Chi	2.50	Peters-Chi	138	Peters-Chi	.219	Bunker-Bal	.269	Peters-Chi	34.2	Peters-Chi	29.1
Pizarro-Chi	2.56	Pizarro-Chi	135	Pizarro-Chi	.219	Bouton-NY	.273	Pizarro-Chi	28.3	Pizarro-Chi	23.7

Clutch Pitching Index		Relief Runs		Adjusted Relief Runs		Relief Ranking		Total Pitcher Index		Total Baseball Ranking	
McDowell-Cle	123	B.Lee-LA	32.2	Radatz-Bos	27.3	Radatz-Bos	49.2	Radatz-Bos	5.1	Radatz-Bos	5.1
Roberts-Bal	121	Wilhelm-Chi	23.9	B.Lee-LA	27.0	Wilhelm-Chi	39.6	Chance-LA	4.7	Chance-LA	4.7
Kralick-Cle	118	Radatz-Bos	23.2	Wilhelm-Chi	21.4	Worthington-Min	31.2	Horlen-Chi	4.2	Powell-Bal	4.4
Grant-Cle-Min	112	Worthington-Min	18.1	Stock-Bal-KC	18.6	Kline-Was	27.7	Wilhelm-Chi	4.2	Fregosi-LA	4.4
Peters-Chi	111	Hall-Bal	17.3	Worthington-Min	17.8	B.Lee-LA	27.0	Ford-NY	4.2	Hansen-Chi	4.3

January 31 Pud Galvin is chosen for Hall of Fame induction by the Special Veterans Committee.

March 17 Jackie Robinson is signed as a member of the ABC-TV baseball broadcast team, the first black to receive a network position broadcasting baseball.

April 9 President Lyndon B. Johnson joins 47,878 fans for the opening of Harris County Domed Stadium (the Astrodome). The Astros win an exhibition with the Yankees 2-1 in 12 innings. Mickey Mantle hits the first home run in the new park.

June 8 Arizona star sophomore Rick Monday, selected by the Athletics, is the first player chosen in the initial major league free-agent draft of high school, college, and sandlot players. Picking second, the Mets take pitcher Les Rohr. The Mets finally take Nolan Ryan in the 10th round.

June 14 No-hit pitching and 18 strikeouts, tying the NL extra-inning record, net Cincinnati's Jim Maloney a 0-0 tie with the last-place Mets through 10 innings. Johnny Lewis's 11th-inning home run gives New York and reliever Larry Bearnarth a 1-0 win.

August 19 Jim Maloney's second no-hit effort of 1965 is another 0-0 duel through nine innings, until Reds shortstop Leo Cardenas homers off the left field foul pole in the 10th at Wrigley Field. Maloney allows a record 10 walks and fans 12 in his 1-0 win.

August 20 Eddie Mathews hits his 28th home run as the Braves win 4-3 at Pittsburgh. The duo of Mathews and Hank Aaron, in the period 1954-1965, becomes the top home run tandem in major league history, passing the Babe Ruth-Lou Gehrig total of 772 home runs.

August 29 Willie Mays sets a NL record for homers in one month with his 17th of August, 41st overall, as San Francisco beats the Mets 8-3.

August 30 Following his doctor's advice, Casey Stengel announces his retirement as manager of the Mets. He will head up Mets scouting in California. The 75-year-old Stengel has been in professional baseball since 1910.

September 9 A duel between Dodger Sandy Koufax and Bob Hendley of the Cubs is perfect until Dodger left fielder Lou Johnson walks in the fifth. Following a sacrifice, Johnson steals third and scores on catcher Chris Krug's wild throw. Johnson later gets the game's only hit, a seventh-inning single. Koufax's fourth no-hitter in four years is a perfect game.

October 3 The Cubs tie a major league record with their third triple play of the season—first baseman Ernie Banks to shortstop Don Kessinger—but Pittsburgh wins 6-3 at Forbes Field.

October 14 Working on two days' rest, Sandy Koufax pitches a three-hitter and blanks Minnesota 2-0, giving the Dodgers a second World Championship in three years. He is named World Series MVP.

November 3 Sandy Koufax is named Cy Young Award winner by a unanimous vote.

November 10 Willie Mays is named NL MVP, receiving 224 votes to 177 for Sandy Koufax.

CHICAGO		CINCINNATI		HOUSTON		LOS ANGELES		MILWAUKEE	
M	B.Kennedy	M	D.Sisler	M	L.Harris	M	W.Alston	M	B.Bragan
M	L.Klein	1B	T.Perez	1B	W.Bond	1B	W.Parker	1B	F.Alou
1B	E.Banks	2B	P.Rose	2B	J.Morgan	2B	J.Lefebvre	2B	F.Bolling
2B	G.Beckert	SS	L.Cardenas	SS	B.Lillis	SS	M.Wills	SS	W.Woodward
SS	D.Kessinger	3B	D.Johnson	3B	B.Aspromonte	3B	J.Kennedy	3B	E.Mathews
3B	R.Santo	LF	T.Harper	LF	L.Maye	LF	L.Johnson	LF	R.Carty
LF	D.Clemens	CF	V.Pinson	CF	J.Wynn	CF	W.Davis	CF	M.Jones
CF	D.Landrum	RF	F.Robinson	RF	R.Staub	RF	R.Fairly	RF	H.Aaron
RF	B.Williams	C	J.Edwards	C	R.Brand	C	J.Roseboro	C	J.Torre
C	V.Roznovsky								
		1	G.Coleman	O	J.Gaines	3O	J.Gilliam	C1	G.Oliver
OS	J.Stewart			1	J.Gentile			O	T.Cline
		P	S.Ellis	S	E.Kasko	P	S.Koufax		
P	L.Jackson	P	J.Maloney			P	D.Drysdale	P	T.Cloninger
P	D.Ellsworth	P	J.Jay	P	B.Bruce	P	C.Osteen	P	W.Blasingame
P	B.Buhl	P	J.Nuxhall	P	T.Farrell	P	J.Podres	P	K.Johnson
P	C.Koonce	P	J.Tsitouris	P	D.Nottebart	RP	R.Perranoski	P	D.Lemaster
RP	T.Abernathy	RP	B.McCool	P	L.Dierker	RP	B.Miller	P	B.Sadowski
RP	L.McDaniel	RP	T.Davidson	P	D.Giusti	RP	H.Reed	RP	B.O'Dell
RP	B.Humphreys	RP	R.Craig	RP	C.Raymond			RP	D.Osinski
				RP	J.Owens			RP	P.Niekro
P	B.Faul	P	J.O'Toole	RP	R.Taylor				
P	B.Hendley	P	G.Arrigo					P	H.Fischer
P	E.Broglio			P	R.Roberts				
P	B.Hoeft			P	M.Cuellar				
				/P	K.Johnson				

NEW YORK		PHILADELPHIA		PITTSBURGH		SAN FRANCISCO		ST.LOUIS	
M	C.Stengel	M	G.Mauch	M	H.Walker	M	H.Franks	M	R.Schoendienst
M	W.Westrum	1B	D.Stuart	1B	D.Clendenon	1B	W.McCovey	1B	B.White
1B	E.Kranepool	2B	T.Taylor	2B	B.Mazeroski	2B	H.Lanier	2B	J.Javier
2B	C.Hiller	SS	B.Wine	SS	G.Alley	SS	D.Schofield	SS	D.Groat
SS	R.McMillan	3B	D.Allen	3B	B.Bailey	3B	J.Hart	3B	K.Boyer
3B	C.Smith	LF	A.Johnson	LF	W.Stargell	LF	M.Alou	LF	L.Brock
LF	R.Swoboda	CF	T.Gonzalez	CF	B.Virdon	CF	W.Mays	CF	C.Flood
CF	J.Hickman	RF	J.Callison	RF	R.Clemente	RF	J.Alou	RF	M.Shannon
RF	J.Lewis	C	C.Dalrymple	C	J.Pagliaroni	C	T.Haller	C	T.McCarver
C	C.Cannizzaro								
		1S	R.Amaro	O	M.Mota	3S	J.Davenport	2O	P.Gagliano
O	J.Christopher	O	W.Covington			O	L.Gabrielson		
2S	B.Klaus	2O	C.Rojas	P	B.Veale			P	B.Gibson
		O	J.Briggs	P	D.Cardwell	P	J.Marichal	P	C.Simmons
P	J.Fisher			P	B.Friend	P	B.Shaw	P	T.Stallard
P	A.Jackson	P	C.Short	P	V.Law	P	G.Perry	P	R.Sadecki
P	W.Spahn	P	J.Bunning	P	J.Gibbon	P	R.Herbel	P	B.Purkey
P	G.Cisco	P	R.Culp	RP	A.McBean	P	B.Bolin	RP	N.Briles
RP	T.McGraw	P	R.Herbert	RP	T.Sisk	RP	F.Linzy	RP	H.Woodeshick
RP	T.Parsons	P	B.Belinsky	RP	D.Schwall	RP	M.Murakami	RP	D.Dennis
RP	G.Kroll	RP	G.Wagner						
		RP	J.Baldschun	P	W.Wood	P	J.Sanford	P	R.Washburn
P	L.Bearnarth	RP	E.Roebuck			P	W.Spahn		
P	F.Lary								
P	L.Miller	P	L.Burdette						
P	G.Richardson	P	A.Mahaffey						

TEAM	G	W	L	PCT	GB	R	OR	AB	H	2B	3B	HR	BB	SO	AVG	OBP	SLG	PRO	PRO+	BR	/A	PF	CHI	RC	SB	CS	SBA	SBR
LA	162	97	65	.599		608	521	5425	1329	193	32	78	492	891	.245	.314	.335	.649	96	-61	-22	93	103	593	172	77	69	5
SF	163	95	67	.586	2	682	593	5495	1384	169	43	159	476	844	.252	.315	.385	.700	101	24	6	103	101	649	47	27	64	-2
PIT	163	90	72	.556	7	675	580	5686	1506	217	57	111	419	1008	.265	.319	.382	.701	103	27	24	101	97	671	51	38	57	-8
CIN	162	89	73	.549	8	825	704	5658	1544	268	61	183	538	1003	.273	.341	.439	.780	118	188	129	107	95	842	82	46	67	1
MIL	162	86	76	.531	11	708	633	5542	1419	243	28	196	408	976	.256	.311	.416	.727	110	67	63	101	99	699	64	37	63	-3
PHI	162	85	76	.528	11.5	654	667	5528	1380	205	53	144	494	1091	.250	.315	.384	.699	105	24	36	98	96	665	46	32	59	-5
STL	162	80	81	.497	16.5	707	674	5579	1415	234	46	109	477	882	.254	.316	.371	.687	91	3	-59	109	107	659	150	52	66	-1
CHI	164	72	90	.444	25	635	723	5540	1316	202	33	134	532	948	.238	.309	.358	.667	92	-34	-49	102	101	613	65	47	58	-9
HOU	162	65	97	.401	32	569	711	5483	1299	188	42	97	502	877	.237	.306	.340	.646	96	-73	-33	93	98	574	90	37	71	5
NY	164	50	112	.309	47	495	752	5441	1202	203	27	107	392	1129	.221	.278	.327	.605	79	-164	-147	96	105	480	28	42	40	-17
TOT	813					6558		55377	13794	2122	422	1318	4730	9649	.249	.313	.374	.687							745	429	63	-34

TEAM	CG	SH	SV	IP	H	H/G	HR	BB	SO	RAT	ERA	ERA+	OAV	OOB	PR	/A	PF	CPI	FA	E	DP	FW	PW	BW	SBW	DIF
LA	58	23	34	1476	1223	7.5	127	425	1079	10.3	2.81	116	.224	.284	119	74	92	99	.979	134	135	.8	7.8	-2.3	.9	8.8
SF	42	17	42	1465¹	1325	8.1	137	408	1060	10.9	3.20	112	.238	.295	55	65	102	98	.976	148	124	.0	6.9	.6	.1	6.3
PIT	49	17	27	1479	1324	8.1	89	469	882	11.2	3.01	117	.241	.306	87	82	99	103	.977	152	189	-.1	8.7	2.5	-.5	-1.6
CIN	43	9	34	1457¹	1355	8.4	136	587	1113	12.3	3.88	96	.247	.325	-56	-22	106	96	.981	117	142	1.8	-2.3	13.6	.5	-5.6
MIL	43	4	38	1447²	1336	8.3	123	541	966	11.8	3.52	100	.246	.318	3	1	100	101	.978	140	145	.5	.1	6.7	.0	-2.3
PHI	50	18	21	1468²	1426	8.7	116	466	1071	12.0	3.53	98	.256	.320	2	-12	98	104	.975	157	153	-.5	-1.3	3.8	-.2	2.6
STL	40	11	35	1461¹	1414	8.7	166	467	916	11.8	3.77	102	.255	.317	-37	-12	109	102	.979	130	152	1.1	1.3	-6.2	-.3	3.2
CHI	33	9	35	1472	1470	9.0	154	481	855	12.1	3.78	98	.260	.321	-39	-15	104	104	.974	171	166	-1.2	-1.6	-5.2	-.6	-.5
HOU	29	7	26	1461	1459	9.0	123	388	931	11.6	3.84	87	.260	.312	-49	-79	95	94	.974	166	130	-1.0	-8.3	-3.5	.9	-4.1
NY	29	11	14	1454²	1462	9.0	147	498	776	12.4	4.06	87	.262	.328	-84	-86	100	99	.974	171	153	-1.2	-9.1	-15.5	-1.4	-3.8
TOT	416	126	306	14643		8.5				11.6	3.54		.249	.313					.977	1486	1489					

Runs		Hits		Doubles		Triples		Home Runs		Total Bases	
Harper-Cin	126	Rose-Cin	209	H.Aaron-Mil	40	Callison-Phi	16	Mays-SF	52	Mays-SF	360
Mays-SF	118	Pinson-Cin	204	Williams-Chi	39	Clendenon-Pit	14	McCovey-SF	39	Williams-Chi	356
Rose-Cin	117	Williams-Chi	203	Rose-Cin	35	Clemente-Pit	14	Williams-Chi	34	Pinson-Cin	324
Williams-Chi	115	Clemente-Pit	194	Brock-StL	35	Allen-Phi	14	Santo-Chi	33	H.Aaron-Mil	319
		Flood-StL	191	Pinson-Cin	34	Morgan-Hou	12	Robinson-Cin	33	Johnson-Cin	317

Runs Batted In		Runs Produced		Bases On Balls		Batting Average		On Base Percentage		Slugging Average	
Johnson-Cin	130	Johnson-Cin	190	Morgan-Hou	97	Clemente-Pit	.329	Mays-SF	.399	Mays-SF	.645
Robinson-Cin	113	Williams-Chi	189	Santo-Chi	88	H.Aaron-Mil	.318	Robinson-Cin	.388	H.Aaron-Mil	.560
Mays-SF	112	Robinson-Cin	189	McCovey-SF	88	Mays-SF	.317	H.Aaron-Mil	.384	Williams-Chi	.552
Williams-Chi	108	Rose-Cin	187	Wynn-Hou	84	Williams-Chi	.315	McCovey-SF	.383	Robinson-Cin	.540
Stargell-Pit	107	Mays-SF	178	Harper-Cin	78	Rose-Cin	.312	Rose-Cin	.383	McCovey-SF	.539

Production		Adjusted Production		Batter Runs		Adjusted Batter Runs		Clutch Hitting Index		Runs Created	
Mays-SF	1.044	Mays-SF	184	Mays-SF	64.7	Mays-SF	61.2	Stargell-Pit	120	Mays-SF	143
H.Aaron-Mil	.943	H.Aaron-Mil	161	Williams-Chi	49.3	Williams-Chi	46.4	Johnson-Cin	118	Williams-Chi	132
Williams-Chi	.932	Williams-Chi	155	H.Aaron-Mil	45.9	H.Aaron-Mil	45.4	Boyer-StL	118	H.Aaron-Mil	122
Robinson-Cin	.928	McCovey-SF	152	Robinson-Cin	45.9	McCovey-SF	38.9	Stuart-Phi	118	Santo-Chi	121
McCovey-SF	.922	Robinson-Cin	148	McCovey-SF	41.8	Allen-Phi	38.4	Flood-StL	118	Robinson-Cin	120

Total Average		Stolen Bases		Stolen Base Average		Stolen Base Runs		Fielding Runs		Total Player Rating	
Mays-SF	1.114	Wills-LA	94	Wynn-Hou	91.5	Wynn-Hou	10.5	Alley-Pit	29.5	Mays-SF	7.3
H.Aaron-Mil	.980	Brock-StL	63	H.Aaron-Mil	85.7	Wills-LA	9.6	Mazeroski-Pit	25.6	Wynn-Hou	6.1
McCovey-SF	.945	Wynn-Hou	43	Harper-Cin	85.4	Harper-Cin	6.9	Wine-Phi	21.7	H.Aaron-Mil	5.5
Robinson-Cin	.938	Harper-Cin	35	Wills-LA	75.2	H.Aaron-Mil	4.8	Wills-LA	21.2	Santo-Chi	5.4
Williams-Chi	.935	W.Davis-LA	25	W.Davis-LA	73.5	Allen-Phi	3.3	Wynn-Hou	20.1	Williams-Chi	4.3

Wins		Win Percentage		Games		Complete Games		Shutouts		Saves	
Koufax-LA	26	Koufax-LA	.765	Abernathy-Chi	84	Koufax-LA	27	Marichal-SF	10	Abernathy-Chi	31
Cloninger-Mil	24	Maloney-Cin	.690	Woodesh'k-Hou-StL	78	Marichal-SF	24	Koufax-LA	8	McCool-Cin	21
Drysdale-LA	23	Ellis-Cin	.688	McDaniel-Chi	71	Gibson-StL	20	Veale-Pit	7	Linzy-SF	21
Marichal-SF	22	Cloninger-Mil	.686	Baldschun-Phi	65	Drysdale-LA	20	Drysdale-LA	7		
Ellis-Cin	22	Bunning-Phi	.679			Cloninger-Mil	16	Bunning-Phi	7		

Innings Pitched		Fewest Hits/Game		Fewest BB/Game		Strikeouts		Strikeouts/Game		Ratio	
Koufax-LA	335.2	Koufax-LA	5.79	Marichal-SF	1.40	Koufax-LA	382	Koufax-LA	10.24	Koufax-LA	7.83
Drysdale-LA	308.1	Maloney-Cin	6.66	Law-Pit	1.45	Veale-Pit	276	Veale-Pit	9.34	Marichal-SF	8.35
Gibson-StL	299.0	Marichal-SF	6.83	Bruce-Hou	1.49	Gibson-StL	270	Maloney-Cin	8.60	Law-Pit	9.11
Short-Phi	297.1	Bolin-SF	6.90	Farrell-Hou	1.51	Bunning-Phi	268	Bunning-Phi	8.29	Bunning-Phi	10.11
Marichal-SF	295.1	Gibson-StL	7.31	Johnson-Hou-Mil	1.87	Maloney-Cin	244	Gibson-StL	8.13	Drysdale-LA	10.16

Earned Run Average		Adjusted ERA		Opponents' Batting Avg.		Opponents' On Base Pct.		Starter Runs		Adjusted Starter Runs	
Koufax-LA	2.04	Marichal-SF	169	Koufax-LA	.179	Koufax-LA	.228	Koufax-LA	56.0	Marichal-SF	48.1
Marichal-SF	2.13	Law-Pit	163	Marichal-SF	.205	Marichal-SF	.240	Marichal-SF	46.1	Koufax-LA	45.7
Law-Pit	2.15	Koufax-LA	160	Maloney-Cin	.206	Law-Pit	.264	Law-Pit	33.5	Maloney-Cin	34.3
Maloney-Cin	2.54	Maloney-Cin	148	Bolin-SF	.214	Drysdale-LA	.280	Bunning-Phi	30.4	Law-Pit	32.8
Bunning-Phi	2.60	Shaw-SF	136	Gibson-StL	.222	Shaw-SF	.280	Maloney-Cin	28.4	Bunning-Phi	27.8

Clutch Pitching Index		Relief Runs		Adjusted Relief Runs		Relief Ranking		Total Pitcher Index		Total Baseball Ranking	
Law-Pit	115	Linzy-SF	19.1	Linzy-SF	19.7	Linzy-SF	37.4	Marichal-SF	6.0	Mays-SF	7.3
Koonce-Chi	112	O'Dell-Mil	16.8	Abernathy-Chi	16.8	O'Dell-Mil	27.4	Koufax-LA	5.0	Wynn-Hou	6.1
Culp-Phi	108	McBean-Pit	15.8	O'Dell-Mil	16.6	Woodesh'k-Hou-StL	23.5	Linzy-SF	4.9	Marichal-SF	6.0
Spahn-NY-SF	107	Perranoski-LA	15.2	McDaniel-Chi	15.7	McBean-Pit	20.2	Law-Pit	4.6	H.Aaron-Mil	5.5
Buhl-Chi	107	Abernathy-Chi	14.6	McBean-Pit	15.5	Abernathy-Chi	19.7	Maloney-Cin	4.6	Santo-Chi	5.4

June 15 Tigers pitcher Denny McLain makes a first-inning relief appearance and fans the first seven batters he faces, setting a major league record. He has 14 strikeouts in 6⅔ innings as Detroit rallies to beat Boston 6–5. Bill Freehan posts a record-tying 19 putouts at catcher.

July 9 Senators left fielder Frank Howard ties a major league record with seven strikeouts in Washington's twin bill split with the Red Sox.

July 20 Mel Stottlemyre of the Yankees becomes the first pitcher to hit an inside-the-park grand slam since Deacon Phillippe did it for the Pirates in 1910. Stottlemyre's bases-loaded drive assures him a 6-3 victory over the Red Sox.

August 18 In a 3–2 Orioles' win over the Red Sox, Brooks Robinson hits into his third triple play against Boston, tying the record of George Sisler in 1921, '22, and '26.

September 3 Preparing a move to Anaheim, the Angels change their name from Los Angeles to California.

September 8 Bert Campaneris plays all nine positions against the Angels in a promotion to boost attendance at Kansas City. He leaves the game in the ninth after a collision with Angels catcher Ed Kirkpatrick. The Angels win it in the 13th inning 5-3.

September 16 An eventful day in Boston includes the firing of general manager Mike Higgins and a no-hitter by Dave Morehead. Boston beats Cleveland, 2–0. Morehead lost a no-hitter against Cleveland in 1963 on Fred Whitfield's bad-hop single in the eighth inning.

September 18 On Mickey Mantle Day at Yankee Stadium, 50,180 fans see Mantle play his 2,000th game.

September 25 Another Kansas City publicity stunt makes the great Satchel Paige baseball's oldest performer. At 59, Paige hurls the first three innings, garners one strikeout, and allows just one hit, to Carl Yastrzemski, in Paige's first major league appearance since 1953. The Red Sox jump on reliever Don Mossi for a 5-2 win.

September 26 Minnesota gains its first AL pennant by defeating Washington, 2–1. Jim Kaat (17-11) wins the clincher.

October 3 Knuckleballer Eddie Fisher of the White Sox sets an AL record with his 82nd appearance, one more than John Wyatt in 1964.

October 6 Minnesota's six-run third inning routs Dodger Don Drysdale and sparks an 8-2 Twins win in the first game of the World Series. Jim Grant gets the win.

October 13 Twins pitcher Jim "Mudcat" Grant does it all himself. He smacks a three-run home run and pitches a 5–1 win at Minnesota to knot the World Series with the Dodgers.

November 17 Retired Air Force Lieutenant-General William Eckert is unanimously elected commissioner of baseball. Ford Frick leaves office after 14 years.

November 18 Zoilo Versalles is named AL MVP. The Minnesota shortstop gets 275 votes to 174 for outfield teammate Tony Oliva.

November 22 Baltimore outfielder Curt Blefary edges Angels pitcher Marcelino Lopez for AL Rookie of the Year honors.

	BALTIMORE		BOSTON		CALIFORNIA		CHICAGO		CLEVELAND
M	H.Bauer	M	B.Herman	M	B.Rigney	M	A.Lopez	M	B.Tebbetts
1B	B.Powell	1B	L.Thomas	1B	V.Power	1B	B.Skowron	1B	F.Whitfield
2B	J.Adair	2B	F.Mantilla	2B	B.Knoop	2B	D.Buford	2B	P.Gonzalez
SS	L.Aparicio	SS	R.Petrocelli	SS	J.Fregosi	SS	R.Hansen	SS	L.Brown
3B	B.Robinson	3B	F.Malzone	3B	P.Schaal	3B	P.Ward	3B	M.Alvis
LF	C.Blefary	LF	C.Yastrzemski	LF	W.Smith	LF	D.Cater	LF	L.Wagner
CF	P.Blair	CF	L.Green	CF	J.Cardenal	CF	K.Berry	CF	V.Davalillo
RF	R.Snyder	RF	T.Conigliaro	RF	A.Pearson	RF	F.Robinson	RF	R.Colavito
C	D.Brown	C	B.Tillman	C	B.Rodgers	C	J.Martin	C	J.Azcue
1	N.Siebern	S	E.Bressoud	1	J.Adcock	1O	T.McCraw	O1	C.Hinton
1S	B.Johnson	3	D.Jones	O	L.Clinton	C	J.Romano	S2	D.Howser
O	J.Brandt	O	J.Gosger			2	A.Weis		
C	J.Orsino			P	F.Newman			P	S.McDowell
O	S.Bowens	P	E.Wilson	P	D.Chance	P	J.Horlen	P	L.Tiant
		P	B.Monbouquette	P	M.Lopez	P	J.Buzhardt	P	S.Siebert
P	M.Pappas	P	D.Morehead	P	G.Brunet	P	T.John	P	R.Terry
P	S.Barber	P	J.Lonborg	P	R.May	P	G.Peters	P	L.Stange
P	D.McNally	P	D.Bennett	RP	B.Lee	P	B.Howard	RP	G.Bell
P	W.Bunker	RP	D.Radatz	RP	A.Gatewood	RP	E.Fisher	RP	J.Kralick
P	R.Roberts	RP	A.Earley			RP	H.Wilhelm	RP	D.McMahon
RP	S.Miller	RP	J.Ritchie			RP	B.Locker		
RP	D.Hall							P	F.Weaver
RP	D.Larsen	P	B.Duliba			P	J.Pizarro	P	S.Hargan
		P	J.Stephenson						
P	J.Miller								
P	J.Palmer								

	DETROIT		KANSAS CITY		MINNESOTA		NEW YORK		WASHINGTON
M	B.Swift	M	M.McGaha	M	S.Mele	M	J.Keane	M	G.Hodges
M	C.Dressen	M	H.Sullivan	1B	D.Mincher	1B	J.Pepitone	1B	D.Nen
1B	N.Cash	1B	K.Harrelson	2B	J.Kindall	2B	B.Richardson	2B	D.Blasingame
2B	J.Lumpe	2B	D.Green	SS	Z.Versalles	SS	T.Kubek	SS	E.Brinkman
SS	D.McAuliffe	SS	B.Campaneris	3B	R.Rollins	3B	C.Boyer	3B	K.McMullen
3B	D.Wert	3B	E.Charles	LF	B.Allison	LF	M.Mantle	LF	F.Howard
LF	W.Horton	LF	T.Reynolds	CF	J.Hall	CF	T.Tresh	CF	D.Lock
CF	D.Demeter	CF	J.Landis	RF	T.Oliva	RF	H.Lopez	RF	W.Held
RF	A.Kaline	RF	M.Hershberger	C	E.Battey	C	E.Howard	C	M.Brumley
C	B.Freehan	C	B.Bryan						
				13	H.Killebrew	1	R.Barker	2S	K.Hamlin
O	G.Brown	S2	W.Causey	O	S.Valdespino	S	P.Linz	O	J.King
O	J.Northrup	O	J.Tartabull			O	R.Repoz	O	W.Kirkland
		C	R.Lachemann	P	M.Grant			C3	D.Zimmer
P	M.Lolich			P	J.Kaat	P	M.Stottlemyre	1	J.Cunningham
P	D.McLain	P	F.Talbot	P	J.Perry	P	W.Ford		
P	H.Aguirre	P	R.Sheldon	P	C.Pascual	P	A.Downing	P	P.Richert
P	D.Wickersham	P	J.O'Donoghue	P	D.Boswell	P	J.Bouton	P	P.Ortega
P	J.Sparma	P	D.Segui	RP	A.Worthington	P	B.Stafford	P	B.Narum
RP	L.Sherry	P	C.Hunter	RP	J.Klippstein	RP	P.Ramos	P	M.McCormick
RP	T.Fox	RP	W.Stock	RP	D.Stigman	RP	H.Reniff	P	B.Daniels
RP	F.Gladding	RP	J.Wyatt			RP	P.Mikkelsen	RP	S.Ridzik
		RP	J.Dickson	P	J.Merritt			RP	R.Kline
P	O.Pena			P	M.Nelson	P	J.Cullen	RP	F.Kreutzer
P	P.Regan	P	D.Mossi	P	B.Pleis	P	S.Hamilton		
		P	J.Aker					P	H.Koplitz
								P	J.Duckworth
								P	M.Bridges

TEAM	G	W	L	PCT	GB	R	OR	AB	H	2B	3B	HR	BB	SO	AVG	OBP	SLG	PRO	PRO+	BR	/A	PF	CHI	RC	SB	CS	SBA	SBR
MIN	162	102	60	.630		774	600	5488	1396	257	42	150	554	969	.254	.327	.399	.726	107	84	52	104	106	730	92	33	74	8
CHI	162	95	67	.586	7	647	555	5509	1354	200	38	125	533	916	.246	.317	.364	.681	106	1	41	94	99	636	50	33	60	-5
BAL	162	94	68	.580	8	641	578	5450	1299	227	38	125	529	907	.238	.309	.363	.672	95	-21	-33	102	103	607	67	31	68	2
DET	162	89	73	.549	13	680	602	5368	1278	190	27	162	554	952	.238	.314	.374	.688	101	10	3	101	106	628	57	41	58	-8
CLE	162	87	75	.537	15	663	613	5469	1367	198	21	156	506	857	.250	.317	.379	.696	103	26	21	101	99	667	109	46	70	5
NY	162	77	85	.475	25	611	604	5470	1286	196	31	149	489	951	.235	.300	.364	.664	95	-42	-38	99	103	593	35	20	64	-2
CAL	162	75	87	.463	27	527	569	5354	1279	200	36	92	443	973	.239	.300	.341	.641	90	-81	-69	98	97	549	107	59	64	-3
WAS	162	70	92	.432	32	591	721	5374	1227	179	33	136	570	1125	.228	.306	.350	.656	94	-47	-38	99	101	586	30	19	61	-1
BOS	162	62	100	.383	40	669	791	5487	1378	244	40	165	607	964	.251	.329	.400	.729	107	95	51	106	90	715	47	24	66	0
KC	162	59	103	.364	43	585	755	5393	1294	186	59	110	521	1020	.240	.311	.358	.669	97	-25	-16	99	96	604	110	51	68	2
TOT	810					6388		54362	13158	2077	365	1370	5306	9634	.242	.313	.369	.682							704	357	66	-3

TEAM	CG	SH	SV	IP	H	H/G	HR	BB	SO	RAT	ERA	ERA+	OAV	OOB	PR	/A	PF	CPI	FA	E	DP	FW	PW	BW	SBW	DIF
MIN	32	12	45	1457¹	1278	7.9	166	503	934	11.2	3.14	113	.235	.303	52	68	103	107	.973	172	158	-2.3	7.3	5.5	.9	9.6
CHI	21	14	53	1481²	1261	7.7	122	460	946	10.6	2.99	107	.231	.294	76	33	92	98	.980	127	156	.6	3.5	4.4	-.5	6.0
BAL	32	15	41	1477²	1268	7.7	120	510	939	11.0	2.98	116	.233	.302	78	80	100	104	.980	126	152	.6	8.5	-3.5	.2	7.1
DET	45	14	31	1455	1283	7.9	137	509	1069	11.4	3.35	104	.237	.308	17	20	101	99	.981	116	126	1.3	2.1	.3	-.8	5.1
CLE	41	13	31	1458¹	1254	7.7	129	500	1156	11.0	3.30	106	.232	.300	26	30	101	94	.981	114	127	1.4	3.2	2.2	.6	-1.4
NY	41	11	31	1459²	1337	8.2	126	511	1001	11.6	3.28	104	.245	.313	29	20	98	104	.978	137	166	-.0	2.1	-4.1	-.2	-1.8
CAL	39	14	33	1441²	1259	7.9	91	563	847	11.5	3.17	107	.237	.313	46	37	98	100	.981	123	149	.8	3.9	-7.4	-.3	-3.1
WAS	21	8	40	1435²	1376	8.6	160	633	867	12.8	3.93	88	.254	.336	-75	-73	101	105	.977	143	148	-.4	-7.8	-4.1	-.2	1.5
BOS	33	9	25	1439¹	1443	9.0	158	543	993	12.6	4.24	88	.260	.329	-125	-82	108	95	.974	162	129	-1.6	-8.7	5.4	.0	-14.1
KC	18	7	32	1433	1399	8.8	161	574	882	12.6	4.24	82	.256	.331	-124	-119	101	96	.977	139	142	-.2	-12.7	-1.7	.2	-7.6
TOT	323	117	372	14539¹		8.1				11.6	3.46		.242	.313					.978	1359	1453					

Runs		Hits		Doubles		Triples		Home Runs		Total Bases	
Versalles-Min	126	Oliva-Min	185	Yastrzemski-Bos	45	Versalles-Min	12	Conigliaro-Bos	32	Versalles-Min	308
Oliva-Min	107	Versalles-Min	182	Versalles-Min	45	Campaneris-KC	12	Cash-Det	30	Tresh-NY	287
Tresh-NY	94	Colavito-Cle	170	Oliva-Min	40	Aparicio-Bal	10	Horton-Det	29	Oliva-Min	283
Buford-Chi	93	Tresh-NY	168	Tresh-NY	29	W.Smith-Cal	9	Wagner-Cle	28	Colavito-Cle	277
Colavito-Cle	92	Fregosi-Cal	167	Richardson-NY	28					Conigliaro-Bos	267

Runs Batted In		Runs Produced		Bases On Balls		Batting Average		On Base Percentage		Slugging Average	
Colavito-Cle	108	Oliva-Min	189	Colavito-Cle	93	Oliva-Min	.321	Yastrzemski-Bos	.398	Yastrzemski-Bos	.536
Horton-Det	104	Versalles-Min	184	Blefary-Bal	88	Yastrzemski-Bos	.312	Colavito-Cle	.387	Conigliaro-Bos	.512
Oliva-Min	98	Colavito-Cle	174	Mantilla-Bos	79	Davalillo-Cle	.301	Oliva-Min	.384	Cash-Det	.512
Mantilla-Bos	92	Hall-Min	147	Cash-Det	77	Robinson-Bal	.297	Blefary-Bal	.382	Wagner-Cle	.495
Whitfield-Cle	90	Horton-Det	144	Robinson-Chi	76	Wagner-Cle	.294	Mantilla-Bos	.377	Oliva-Min	.491

Production		Adjusted Production		Batter Runs		Adjusted Batter Runs		Clutch Hitting Index		Runs Created	
Yastrzemski-Bos	.935	Yastrzemski-Bos	154	Yastrzemski-Bos	41.6	Yastrzemski-Bos	35.6	Mantilla-Bos	126	Colavito-Cle	110
Cash-Det	.886	Cash-Det	147	Oliva-Min	35.3	Colavito-Cle	33.7	Horton-Det	120	Oliva-Min	109
Oliva-Min	.876	Wagner-Cle	143	Colavito-Cle	34.6	Oliva-Min	30.8	Powell-Bal	116	Yastrzemski-Bos	102
Wagner-Cle	.866	Oliva-Min	141	Cash-Det	31.0	Cash-Det	30.1	Allison-Min	116	Versalles-Min	102
Colavito-Cle	.855	Colavito-Cle	140	Wagner-Cle	29.6	Wagner-Cle	28.8	Adair-Bal	115	Tresh-NY	101

Total Average		Stolen Bases		Stolen Base Average		Stolen Base Runs		Fielding Runs		Total Player Rating	
Yastrzemski-Bos	.931	Campaneris-KC	51	Hinton-Cle	85.0	Versalles-Min	5.1	Boyer-NY	25.9	Yastrzemski-Bos	3.6
Cash-Det	.894	Cardenal-Cal	37	Versalles-Min	84.4	Campaneris-KC	3.9	Hansen-Chi	16.7	Weis-Chi	3.4
Wagner-Cle	.882	Versalles-Min	27	Howser-Cal	81.0	Davalillo-Cle	3.6	Davalillo-Cle	14.7	Buford-Chi	3.3
Blefary-Bal	.876	Davalillo-Cle	26	Davalillo-Cle	78.8	Aparicio-Bal	3.6	Conigliaro-Bos	13.5	Oliva-Min	3.3
Oliva-Min	.863	Aparicio-Bal	26	Aparicio-Bal	78.8	Hinton-Cle	3.3	Knoop-Cal	12.8	Colavito-Cle	3.1

Wins		Win Percentage		Games		Complete Games		Shutouts		Saves	
Grant-Min	21	Grant-Min	.750	Fisher-Chi	82	Stottlemyre-NY	18	Grant-Min	6	Kline-Was	29
Stottlemyre-NY	20	McLain-Det	.727	Kline-Was	74	McDowell-Cle	14	Stottlemyre-NY	4	S.Miller-Bal	24
Kaat-Min	18	Stottlemyre-NY	.690	B.Lee-Cal	69	Grant-Min	14	McLain-Det	4	Fisher-Chi	24
McDowell-Cle	17	Fisher-Chi	.682	Dickson-KC	68	McLain-Det	13	Horlen-Chi	4	B.Lee-Cal	23
		Siebert-Cle	.667	S.Miller-Bal	67			Chance-Cal	4	Radatz-Bos	22

Innings Pitched		Fewest Hits/Game		Fewest BB/Game		Strikeouts		Strikeouts/Game		Ratio	
Stottlemyre-NY	291.0	McDowell-Cle	5.87	Terry-Cle	1.25	McDowell-Cle	325	McDowell-Cle	10.71	Fisher-Chi	8.87
McDowell-Cle	273.0	Fisher-Chi	6.42	Monbouquette-Bos	1.57	Lolich-Det	226	Siebert-Cle	9.11	Siebert-Cle	9.06
Grant-Min	270.1	Siebert-Cle	6.63	Horlen-Chi	1.60	McLain-Det	192	Lolich-Det	8.35	Terry-Cle	9.67
Kaat-Min	264.1	Richert-Was	6.77	Ford-NY	1.84	Siebert-Cle	191	McLain-Det	7.84	McLain-Det	9.72
Newman-Cal	260.2	Brunet-Cal	6.81	Grant-Min	2.03	Downing-NY	179	Morehead-Bos	7.61	Newman-Cal	10.01

Earned Run Average		Adjusted ERA		Opponents' Batting Avg.		Opponents' On Base Pct.		Starter Runs		Adjusted Starter Runs	
McDowell-Cle	2.18	McDowell-Cle	160	McDowell-Cle	.185	Siebert-Cle	.262	McDowell-Cle	38.9	McDowell-Cle	39.5
Fisher-Chi	2.40	Siebert-Cle	143	Fisher-Chi	.205	Fisher-Chi	.262	Stottlemyre-NY	26.8	Stottlemyre-NY	25.0
Siebert-Cle	2.43	Perry-Min	135	Siebert-Cle	.206	Terry-Cle	.269	Siebert-Cle	21.5	Siebert-Cle	21.9
Brunet-Cal	2.56	Richert-Was	134	Brunet-Cal	.209	McLain-Det	.273	Pappas-Bal	21.1	Kaat-Min	21.4
Richert-Was	2.60	Pappas-Bal	133	Richert-Was	.210	Pappas-Bal	.281	McLain-Det	20.7	Pappas-Bal	21.3

Clutch Pitching Index		Relief Runs		Adjusted Relief Runs		Relief Ranking		Total Pitcher Index		Total Baseball Ranking	
Kaat-Min	123	Wilhelm-Chi	26.3	Wilhelm-Chi	22.1	S.Miller-Bal	41.5	S.Miller-Bal	4.7	S.Miller-Bal	4.7
Perry-Min	117	B.Lee-Cal	22.5	B.Lee-Cal	21.6	B.Lee-Cal	31.1	McDowell-Cle	4.1	McDowell-Cle	4.1
Peters-Chi	113	S.Miller-Bal	20.9	S.Miller-Bal	21.0	Worthington-Min	30.8	Worthington-Min	3.6	Worthington-Min	3.6
Richert-Was	110	Fisher-Chi	19.5	Fisher-Chi	14.6	Wilhelm-Chi	25.3	Kaat-Min	3.5	Yastrzemski-Bos	3.6
Pappas-Bal	110	Hamilton-NY	13.4	Hamilton-NY	13.1	Fisher-Chi	21.7	B.Lee-Cal	3.4	Kaat-Min	3.5

March 8 The Hall of Fame Special Veterans Committee waives election rules and inducts Casey Stengel, recently retired manager of the Mets.

March 30 Sandy Koufax and Don Drysdale end their 32-day holdout, signing for $130,000 and $105,000 respectively.

April 3 Tom Seaver, University of Southern California pitcher, signs with the Mets for a reported $50,000 bonus. A selection of the Braves in the January free-agent draft, Seaver was signed by Atlanta's Richmond farm club a month later, after USC had begun its baseball schedule. The violation netted Richmond a $500 fine and forbade Atlanta from signing Seaver for three years. However, Seaver was also declared ineligible at the college level, so an unprecedented special draft is held. Three clubs willing to match Richmond's $40,000 contract—the Indians, Phillies, and Mets—participate. New York's name is drawn from a hat as the winner.

April 12 The Braves lose their first game in Atlanta 3-2 to Pittsburgh in 13 innings, with 50,761 fans on hand.

April 24 Atlanta's 5–2 win at Atlanta-Fulton County Stadium in the first game of a doubleheader is an NL-record 18th straight home win against the Mets. "Home" for 17 of those wins, though, was actually Milwaukee.

May 4 Willie Mays hits a NL record 512th home run—topping another Giant, Mel Ott—and the Giants beat the Dodgers 6-1.

May 12 The Cardinals open new Busch Memorial Stadium with a 12-inning, 4-3 win over the Braves.

June 7 The New York Mets, picking first in the June free-agent draft, pass up Arizona State outfielder Reggie Jackson to select catcher Steve Chilcott. Chilcott will retire after six years in the minors and will be the first number-one pick to never play in the major leagues. The A's take Jackson with the second pick.

July 3 Pitcher Tony Cloninger hits two grand slams and drives in nine runs, as the Braves rout the Giants at Candlestick Park 17-3. Cloninger is the only NL player to hit two in a game, and his nine RBI are a major league record for pitchers.

July 12 St. Louis hosts a hot midsummer All-Star classic. Maury Wills's 10th-inning single scores Tim McCarver, as the NL wins 2-1 in 105-degree heat. Brooks Robinson's three hits at the plate and eight chances in the field earn him the game MVP.

August 16 Willie Mays hits his 534th home run, matching Jimmie Foxx's record for righthanded batters, as Gaylord Perry beats the Cardinals 3-1.

September 29 Sandy Koufax pitches a four-hitter, beats the Cards 2-1, and becomes the first major league pitcher to achieve a third 300-strikeout season since Amos Rusie in 1890-92.

November 1 Sandy Koufax becomes the first three-time winner of the Cy Young Award. He is a unanimous winner for the second-straight year. This is the last year that only one award is given for pitchers in both of the major leagues.

November 12 The Dodgers complete an 18-game tour of Japan with a 9-8-1 record, the most losses ever for a major league club touring the Far East.

November 16 Pirate outfielder Roberto Clemente is named MVP in the NL. He edges Koufax by 10 votes.

November 18 Sandy Koufax announces his retirement, due to increasing pain in his arthritic left elbow.

November 25 Cincinnati's Tommy Helms is voted NL Rookie of the Year.

ATLANTA		CHICAGO		CINCINNATI		HOUSTON		LOS ANGELES	
M	B.Bragan	M	L.Durocher	M	D.Heffner	M	G.Hatton	M	W.Alston
M	B.Hitchcock	1B	E.Banks	M	D.Bristol	1B	C.Harrison	1B	W.Parker
1B	F.Alou	2B	G.Beckert	1B	T.Perez	2B	J.Morgan	2B	J.Lefebvre
2B	W.Woodward	SS	D.Kessinger	2B	P.Rose	SS	S.Jackson	SS	M.Wills
SS	D.Menke	3B	R.Santo	SS	L.Cardenas	3B	B.Aspromonte	3B	J.Kennedy
3B	E.Mathews	LF	B.Browne	3B	T.Helms	LF	L.Maye	LF	L.Johnson
LF	R.Carty	CF	A.Phillips	LF	D.Johnson	CF	J.Wynn	CF	W.Davis
CF	M.Jones	RF	B.Williams	CF	V.Pinson	RF	R.Staub	RF	R.Fairly
RF	H.Aaron	C	R.Hundley	RF	T.Harper	C	J.Bateman	C	J.Roseboro
C	J.Torre			C	J.Edwards				
		O1	J.Boccabella			O	D.Nicholson	O	T.Davis
2	F.Bolling			C1	D.Pavletich			3	J.Gilliam
		P	D.Ellsworth	O	A.Shamsky	P	M.Cuellar		
P	T.Cloninger	P	K.Holtzman	1	G.Coleman	P	D.Giusti	P	S.Koufax
P	K.Johnson	P	F.Jenkins			P	L.Dierker	P	D.Drysdale
P	D.Lemaster	P	B.Hands	P	J.Maloney	P	T.Farrell	P	C.Osteen
RP	C.Carroll	RP	C.Koonce	P	S.Ellis	P	B.Bruce	P	D.Sutton
RP	C.Olivo	RP	B.Hendley	P	M.Pappas	RP	C.Raymond	RP	P.Regan
RP	T.Abernathy			P	J.O'Toole	RP	R.Taylor	RP	B.Miller
		P	C.Simmons	P	J.Nuxhall	RP	J.Owens	RP	R.Perranoski
P	D.Kelley	P	E.Broglio	RP	D.Nottebart				
P	W.Blasingame	P	B.Faul	RP	B.McCool	P	B.Latman	P	J.Moeller
P	P.Jarvis			RP	T.Davidson	P	R.Roberts		
P	P.Niekro					P	C.Zachary		
				P	J.Jay				
				P	J.Baldschun				

NEW YORK		PHILADELPHIA		PITTSBURGH		SAN FRANCISCO		ST.LOUIS	
M	W.Westrum	M	G.Mauch	M	H.Walker	M	H.Franks	M	R.Schoendienst
1B	E.Kranepool	1B	B.White	1B	D.Clendenon	1B	W.McCovey	1B	O.Cepeda
2B	R.Hunt	2B	C.Rojas	2B	B.Mazeroski	2B	H.Lanier	2B	J.Javier
SS	E.Bressoud	SS	D.Groat	SS	G.Alley	SS	T.Fuentes	SS	D.Maxvill
3B	K.Boyer	3B	D.Allen	3B	B.Bailey	3B	J.Hart	3B	C.Smith
LF	R.Swoboda	LF	T.Gonzalez	LF	W.Stargell	LF	J.Alou	LF	L.Brock
CF	C.Jones	CF	J.Briggs	CF	M.Alou	CF	W.Mays	CF	C.Flood
RF	A.Luplow	RF	J.Callison	RF	R.Clemente	RF	O.Brown	RF	M.Shannon
C	J.Grote	C	C.Dalrymple	C	J.Pagliaroni	C	T.Haller	C	T.McCarver
23	C.Hiller	23	T.Taylor	O	M.Mota	S3	J.Davenport	2S	J.Buchek
S	R.McMillan	C	B.Uecker	3S	J.Pagan	O	L.Gabrielson	3	P.Gagliano
P	J.Fisher	P	J.Bunning	P	B.Veale	P	J.Marichal	P	B.Gibson
P	D.Ribant	P	C.Short	P	W.Fryman	P	G.Perry	P	A.Jackson
P	B.Shaw	P	L.Jackson	P	V.Law	P	B.Bolin	P	R.Washburn
P	R.Gardner	P	B.Buhl	P	S.Blass	P	R.Herbel	P	N.Briles
RP	J.Hamilton	P	R.Culp	P	T.Sisk	P	R.Sadecki	P	L.Jaster
RP	D.Selma	RP	D.Knowles	RP	P.Mikkelsen	RP	L.McDaniel	RP	J.Hoerner
RP	B.Hepler	RP	R.Herbert	RP	A.McBean	RP	F.Linzy	RP	H.Woodeshick
				RP	B.O'Dell	RP	B.Priddy	RP	D.Dennis
P	B.Friend	P	R.Wise						
P	T.McGraw			P	D.Cardwell	P	J.Gibbon	/P	S.Carlton
P	L.Bearnarth			P	R.Face			P	T.Stallard

TEAM	G	W	L	PCT	GB	R	OR	AB	H	2B	3B	HR	BB	SO	AVG	OBP	SLG	PRO	PRO+	BR	/A	PF	CHI	RC	SB	CS	SBA	SBR
LA	162	95	67	.586		606	**490**	5471	1399	201	27	108	430	**830**	.256	.316	.362	.678	103	-37	12	92	98	615	94	64	59	-10
SF	161	93	68	.578	1.5	675	626	5539	1373	195	31	181	414	860	.248	.304	.392	.696	96	-14	-33	103	105	633	29	30	49	-9
PIT	162	92	70	.568	3	759	641	5676	**1586**	238	66	158	405	1011	**.279**	**.331**	**.428**	**.759**	116	117	116	100	96	779	64	60	52	-17
PHI	162	87	75	.537	8	696	640	5607	1448	224	49	117	510	969	.258	.323	.378	.701	101	12	11	100	101	683	56	42	57	-8
ATL	163	85	77	.525	10	**782**	683	5617	1476	220	32	**207**	**512**	913	.263	.324	.424	.753	113	106	94	102	100	775	59	47	56	-11
STL	162	83	79	.512	12	571	577	5480	1377	196	61	108	345	977	.251	.300	.368	.668	91	-66	-69	101	99	592	**144**	61	**70**	**7**
CIN	160	76	84	.475	18	692	702	5521	1434	232	33	149	394	877	.260	.311	.395	.706	94	7	-51	109	105	658	70	50	58	-9
HOU	163	72	90	.444	23	612	695	5511	1405	203	35	112	491	885	.255	.320	.365	.685	104	-19	25	93	94	640	90	47	66	-1
NY	161	66	95	.410	28.5	587	761	5371	1286	187	35	98	446	992	.239	.303	.342	.645	87	-99	-87	98	**108**	546	55	46	54	-11
CHI	162	59	103	.364	36	644	809	5592	1418	203	43	140	457	998	.254	.315	.380	.695	98	-6	-14	101	97	665	76	47	62	-5
TOT	809					6624		55385	14202	2099	412	1378	4404	9312	.256	.315	.384	.699							737	494	60	-75

TEAM	CG	SH	SV	IP	H	H/G	HR	BB	SO	RAT	ERA	ERA+	OAV	OOB	PR	/A	PF	CPI	FA	E	DP	FW	PW	BW	SBW	DIF
LA	**52**	**20**	35	1458	**1287**	7.9	84	356	1084	10.3	**2.62**	126	**.237**	.288	159	109	91	102	.979	133	128	.9	**11.4**	-1.3	-.3	.7
SF	**52**	14	27	1476²	1370	8.3	140	359	973	10.7	3.24	113	.244	.294	61	71	102	96	.974	168	131	-1.2	7.4	-3.5	-.2	9.8
PIT	35	12	**43**	1463¹	1445	8.9	125	463	898	12.0	3.52	101	.261	.322	13	8	99	105	.978	141	215	.4	.8	**12.2**	-1.0	-1.4
PHI	**52**	15	23	1459²	1439	8.9	137	412	928	11.8	3.57	101	.258	.316	6	4	100	102	**.982**	113	147	**2.0**	.4	1.2	-.0	2.5
ATL	37	10	36	1469¹	1430	8.8	129	485	884	11.9	3.68	99	.257	.319	-12	-7	101	98	.976	154	139	-.3	-.7	9.9	-.4	-4.5
STL	47	19	32	1459²	1345	8.3	130	448	892	11.3	3.11	115	.246	.307	80	77	100	**107**	.977	145	166	.2	8.1	-7.2	**1.5**	-.6
CIN	28	10	30	1436	1408	8.8	153	490	1043	12.2	4.08	96	.258	.324	-76	-28	108	94	.980	122	133	1.4	-2.9	-5.3	-.2	3.0
HOU	34	13	26	1443²	1468	9.2	130	391	929	11.8	3.76	91	.262	.314	-24	-54	95	96	.972	174	126	-1.4	-5.7	2.6	.7	-5.3
NY	37	9	22	1427	1497	9.4	166	521	773	12.9	4.17	87	.272	.339	-89	-85	101	104	.975	159	171	-.6	-8.9	-9.1	-.4	-8.7
CHI	28	6	24	1458	1513	9.3	184	479	908	12.5	4.33	85	.268	.328	-118	-106	102	97	.974	166	132	-1.0	-11.1	-1.5	.3	-8.7
TOT	402	128	303	14551¹		8.8				11.7	3.61		.256	.315					.977	1475	1488					

Runs		Hits		Doubles		Triples		Home Runs		Total Bases	
Alou-Atl	122	Alou-Atl	218	Callison-Phi	40	McCarver-StL	13	Aaron-Atl	44	Alou-Atl	355
Aaron-Atl	117	Rose-Cin	205	Rose-Cin	38	Brock-StL	12	Allen-Phi	40	Clemente-Pit	342
Allen-Phi	112	Clemente-Pit	202	Pinson-Cin	35	Clemente-Pit	11	Mays-SF	37	Allen-Phi	331
Clemente-Pit	105	Beckert-Chi	188	Alou-Atl	32			Torre-Atl	36	Aaron-Atl	325
Williams-Chi	100							McCovey-SF	36	Mays-SF	307

Runs Batted In		Runs Produced		Bases On Balls		Batting Average		On Base Percentage		Slugging Average	
Aaron-Atl	127	Aaron-Atl	200	Santo-Chi	95	Alou-Pit	.342	Santo-Chi	.417	Allen-Phi	.632
Clemente-Pit	119	Clemente-Pit	195	Morgan-Hou	89	Morgan-Hou	.327	Morgan-Hou	.412	McCovey-SF	.586
Allen-Phi	110	Allen-Phi	182	McCovey-SF	76	Carty-Atl	.326	Allen-Phi	.398	Stargell-Pit	.581
White-Phi	103	White-Phi	166	Aaron-Atl	76	Allen-Phi	.317	Carty-Atl	.396	Torre-Atl	.560
Mays-SF	103			Menke-Atl	71	Clemente-Pit	.317	McCovey-SF	.394	Mays-SF	.556

Production		Adjusted Production		Batter Runs		Adjusted Batter Runs		Clutch Hitting Index		Runs Created	
Allen-Phi	1.030	Allen-Phi	181	Allen-Phi	56.8	Allen-Phi	56.7	White-Phi	125	Allen-Phi	131
McCovey-SF	.979	Stargell-Pit	164	Santo-Chi	51.2	Santo-Chi	49.7	Beckert-Chi	117	Santo-Chi	127
Stargell-Pit	.965	McCovey-SF	163	McCovey-SF	46.9	McCovey-SF	43.8	Clemente-Pit	117	Alou-Atl	123
Santo-Chi	.955	Santo-Chi	161	Torre-Atl	43.0	Torre-Atl	41.4	Woodward-Atl	117	McCovey-SF	119
Torre-Atl	.945	Torre-Atl	157	Stargell-Pit	41.1	Stargell-Pit	41.0	Staub-Hou	116	Clemente-Pit	119

Total Average		Stolen Bases		Stolen Base Average		Stolen Base Runs		Fielding Runs		Total Player Rating	
Allen-Phi	1.088	Brock-StL	74	Aaron-Atl	87.5	Brock-StL	11.4	Mazeroski-Pit	40.8	Santo-Chi	7.5
McCovey-SF	1.039	Jackson-Hou	49	Brock-StL	80.4	Jackson-Hou	6.3	Santo-Chi	28.8	Clemente-Pit	4.6
Santo-Chi	.988	Wills-LA	38	Jackson-Hou	77.8	Aaron-Atl	4.5	Lanier-SF	28.2	Allen-Phi	4.5
Stargell-Pit	.980	Phillips-Phi-Chi	32	Harper-Cin	74.4	Harper-Cin	2.7	Maxvill-StL	23.8	Mazeroski-Pit	4.5
Mays-SF	.941	Harper-Cin	29	White-Phi	72.7			Clemente-Pit	15.4	Aaron-Atl	4.3

Wins		Win Percentage		Games		Complete Games		Shutouts		Saves	
Koufax-LA	27	Marichal-SF	.806	Carroll-Atl	73	Koufax-LA	27	L.Jackson-Chi-Phi	5	Regan-LA	21
Marichal-SF	25	Koufax-LA	.750	Mikkelsen-Pit	71	Marichal-SF	25	Maloney-Cin	5	McCool-Cin	18
Perry-SF	21	Perry-SF	.724	Knowles-Phi	69	Gibson-StL	20	Koufax-LA	5	Face-Pit	18
Gibson-StL	21	Short-Phi	.667	Regan-LA	65	Short-Phi	19	Jaster-StL	5	Raymond-Hou	16
Short-Phi	20	Maloney-Cin	.667	McDaniel-SF	64	Bunning-Phi	16	Gibson-StL	5	Linzy-SF	16
								Bunning-Phi	5		

Innings Pitched		Fewest Hits/Game		Fewest BB/Game		Strikeouts		Strikeouts/Game		Ratio	
Koufax-LA	323.0	Marichal-SF	6.68	Marichal-SF	1.05	Koufax-LA	317	Koufax-LA	8.83	Marichal-SF	7.88
Bunning-Phi	314.0	Koufax-LA	6.72	Law-Pit	1.22	Bunning-Phi	252	Maloney-Cin	8.65	Koufax-LA	8.86
Marichal-SF	307.1	Gibson-StL	6.74	Perry-SF	1.41	Veale-Pit	229	Sutton-LA	8.34	Gibson-StL	9.41
Gibson-StL	280.1	Maloney-Cin	6.97	Drysdale-LA	1.48	Gibson-StL	225	Veale-Pit	7.68	Bunning-Phi	9.57
Drysdale-LA	273.2	Bolin-SF	6.98	Bunning-Phi	1.58	Marichal-SF	222	Jenkins-Phi-Chi	7.32	Cuellar-Hou	9.70

Earned Run Average		Adjusted ERA		Opponents' Batting Avg.		Opponents' On Base Pct.		Starter Runs		Adjusted Starter Runs	
Koufax-LA	1.73	Koufax-LA	191	Marichal-SF	.202	Marichal-SF	.230	Koufax-LA	67.4	Koufax-LA	56.3
Cuellar-Hou	2.22	Marichal-SF	165	Koufax-LA	.205	Koufax-LA	.253	Marichal-SF	47.2	Marichal-SF	49.2
Marichal-SF	2.23	Cuellar-Hou	154	Gibson-StL	.207	Gibson-StL	.267	Bunning-Phi	41.8	Bunning-Phi	41.4
Bunning-Phi	2.41	Bunning-Phi	149	Bolin-SF	.211	Bunning-Phi	.270	Gibson-StL	36.3	Gibson-StL	35.8
Gibson-StL	2.44	Gibson-StL	147	Maloney-Cin	.214	Cuellar-Hou	.274	Cuellar-Hou	35.1	Cuellar-Hou	30.5

Clutch Pitching Index		Relief Runs		Adjusted Relief Runs		Relief Ranking		Total Pitcher Index		Total Baseball Ranking	
Jackson-StL	117	Regan-LA	25.8	Regan-LA	21.7	Regan-LA	33.9	Marichal-SF	5.8	Santo-Chi	7.5
L.Jackson-Chi-Phi	110	Carroll-Atl	19.8	Carroll-Atl	20.4	McCool-Cin	29.2	Koufax-LA	5.4	Marichal-SF	5.8
Ellsworth-Chi	108	Hoerner-StL	17.5	Hoerner-StL	17.3	Carroll-Atl	22.5	Gibson-StL	4.4	Koufax-LA	5.4
Johnson-Atl	108	McCool-Cin	13.2	McCool-Cin	16.7	Hoerner-StL	19.0	Jackson-StL	4.2	Clemente-Pit	4.6
Osteen-LA	107	Woodeshick-StL	13.2	McDaniel-SF	13.6	McDaniel-SF	16.6	Bunning-Phi	4.1	Allen-Phi	4.5

January 20 The BBWAA voters elect Ted Williams to the Hall of Fame. Williams receives 282 of a possible 302 votes.

March 5 Player representatives elect Marvin Miller, assistant to the president of the United Steelworkers, as executive director of the Major Leagues Players' Association.

April 11 A crowd of 44,468, including Vice President Hubert Humphrey, attends a historic opener at Washington. Emmett Ashford becomes the ML's first black umpire in Cleveland's 5-2 win against the Senators.

April 19 In the first regular season game at Anaheim Stadium, California drops a 3-1 decision to the White Sox before 31,660 fans. Rick Reichardt hits the Angels' first regular-season home run in the new facility.

April 28 Cleveland ties the Brooklyn Dodgers' record with its 10th straight win since Opening Day. Wilfred "Sonny" Siebert defeats the Angels, 2–1. Cleveland will finally lose tomorrow, 4-1, to Gary Peters and the White Sox.

May 8 Orioles right fielder Frank Robinson hits the first ball ever hit completely out of Baltimore's Memorial Stadium, a 451-foot shot, ending Luis Tiant's scoreless-innings streak at 27. Baltimore wins 8-3 and ties Cleveland for first place.

June 9 Minnesota rocks Kansas City with the first five-home run inning in AL history. Rich Rollins, Zoilo Versalles, Tony Oliva, Don Mincher, and Harmon Killebrew connect in the seventh inning to give the Twins a 9-4 victory.

June 10 Sonny Siebert pitches a no-hitter against the Senators. Leon Wagner homers off loser Phil Ortega, as first-place Cleveland wins 2-0.

September 17 Cleveland pitchers set an AL record by fanning 19 batters in the first nine innings of a 10-inning 6-2 win at Detroit.

September 22 The Orioles beat the A's 6–1 to clinch their first AL pennant. Frank Robinson, who drives in two runs in the clincher, will end the year as the Triple Crown winner, the first to achieve the feat since Mickey Mantle in 1956. He

clinches with a batting average of .316, 49 home runs, and 122 RBI.

October 5 With first-inning homers by Frank Robinson and Brooks Robinson and 11 strikeouts from relief pitcher Moe Drabowsky, the Orioles win Game 1 of the World Series 5-2.

October 9 Dave McNally wraps up Baltimore's brilliant pitching display, and a World Championship, with a four-hit, 1-0 win. Frank Robinson's home run off Don Drysdale gives Baltimore a surprising sweep of the defending champion Dodgers. The 33 consecutive scoreless innings pitched by Baltimore are a World Series record.

November 8 Frank Robinson of the Orioles is the unanimous choice as AL MVP. He is the first player to win the award in both leagues.

November 23 Chicago outfielder Tommie Agee is voted AL Rookie of the Year, gathering 16 of the 18 votes. Kansas City pitcher Jim Nash gets the other two. Agee had been brought up briefly the past four seasons before finding a permanent spot this year.

BALTIMORE		BOSTON		CALIFORNIA		CHICAGO		CLEVELAND	
M	H.Bauer	M	B.Herman	M	B.Rigney	M	E.Stanky	M	B.Tebbetts
1B	B.Powell	M	P.Runnels	1B	N.Siebern	1B	T.McCraw	M	G.Strickland
2B	D.Johnson	1B	G.Scott	2B	B.Knoop	2B	A.Weis	1B	F.Whitfield
SS	L.Aparicio	2B	G.Smith	SS	J.Fregosi	SS	L.Elia	2B	P.Gonzalez
3B	B.Robinson	SS	R.Petrocelli	3B	P.Schaal	3B	D.Buford	SS	L.Brown
LF	C.Blefary	3B	J.Foy	LF	R.Reichardt	LF	K.Berry	3B	M.Alvis
CF	P.Blair	LF	C.Yastrzemski	CF	J.Cardenal	CF	T.Agee	LF	L.Wagner
RF	F.Robinson	CF	D.Demeter	RF	E.Kirkpatrick	RF	F.Robinson	CF	V.Davalillo
C	A.Etchebarren	RF	T.Conigliaro	C	B.Rodgers	C	J.Romano	RF	R.Colavito
		C	M.Ryan					C	J.Azcue
O	R.Snyder			C1	T.Satriano	S2	J.Adair		
O	S.Bowens	2	D.Jones	O	J.Johnstone	1	B.Skowron	O	C.Hinton
		C	B.Tillman	1	J.Adcock	O3	P.Ward	S2	C.Salmon
P	D.McNally								
P	J.Palmer	P	J.Lonborg	P	D.Chance	P	T.John	P	G.Bell
P	E.Watt	P	J.Santiago	P	G.Brunet	P	J.Horlen	P	S.Siebert
P	W.Bunker	P	B.Brandon	P	M.Lopez	P	G.Peters	P	S.McDowell
P	S.Barber	P	L.Stange	P	F.Newman	P	J.Buzhardt	P	S.Hargan
RP	M.Drabowsky	P	E.Wilson	RP	J.Sanford	P	B.Howard	P	L.Tiant
RP	S.Miller	RP	D.Stigman	RP	B.Lee	RP	B.Locker	RP	J.Kralick
RP	E.Fisher	RP	D.McMahon	RP	M.Rojas	RP	D.Higgins	RP	D.Radatz
		RP	J.Wyatt			RP	J.Pizarro	RP	B.Allen
P	J.Miller			P	C.Wright				
P	G.Brabender	P	R.Sheldon	P	L.Burdette	P	J.Lamabe	P	J.O'Donoghue
P	D.Hall	P	D.Bennett	P	J.McGlothlin	P	H.Wilhelm	P	T.Kelley
P	F.Bertaina	P	D.Osinski						
		P	J.Stephenson						

DETROIT		KANSAS CITY		MINNESOTA		NEW YORK		WASHINGTON	
M	C.Dressen	M	A.Dark	M	S.Mele	M	J.Keane	M	G.Hodges
M	B.Swift	1B	K.Harrelson	1B	D.Mincher	M	R.Houk	1B	D.Nen
M	F.Skaff	2B	D.Green	2B	B.Allen	1B	J.Pepitone	2B	B.Saverine
1B	N.Cash	SS	B.Campaneris	SS	Z.Versalles	2B	B.Richardson	SS	E.Brinkman
2B	J.Lumpe	3B	E.Charles	3B	H.Killebrew	SS	H.Clarke	3B	K.McMullen
SS	D.McAuliffe	LF	L.Stahl	LF	J.Hall	3B	C.Boyer	LF	F.Howard
3B	D.Wert	CF	J.Nossek	CF	T.Uhlaender	LF	T.Tresh	CF	D.Lock
LF	W.Horton	RF	M.Hershberger	RF	T.Oliva	CF	M.Mantle	RF	F.Valentine
CF	A.Kaline	C	P.Roof	C	E.Battey	RF	R.Maris	P.Casanova
RF	J.Northrup					C	E.Howard	
C	B.Freehan	13	D.Cater	2S	C.Tovar			O	J.King
		O1	R.Repoz	3	R.Rollins	O	R.White	O	W.Kirkland
2	J.Wood	O	J.Gosger					1	K.Harrelson
O	M.Stanley			P	J.Kaat	P	M.Stottlemyre	2	D.Blasingame
S	R.Oyler	P	L.Krausse	P	M.Grant	P	F.Peterson		
		P	C.Hunter	P	J.Perry	P	A.Downing	P	P.Richert
P	D.McLain	P	J.Nash	P	D.Boswell	P	F.Talbot	P	M.McCormick
P	M.Lolich	P	P.Lindblad	P	J.Merritt	P	J.Bouton	P	P.Ortega
P	E.Wilson	RP	J.Aker	RP	A.Worthington	RP	H.Reniff	P	J.Hannan
P	D.Wickersham	RP	K.Sanders	RP	P.Cimino	RP	P.Ramos	RP	C.Cox
P	J.Podres			RP	D.Siebler	RP	S.Hamilton	RP	B.Humphreys
RP	O.Pena	P	B.Odom					RP	R.Kline
RP	L.Sherry	P	C.Dobson	P	C.Pascual	P	D.Womack		
RP	F.Gladding	P	R.Sheldon			P	W.Ford	P	D.Lines
		P	F.Talbot					P	D.Segui
P	H.Aguirre	P	R.Terry					P	B.Moore
P	B.Monbouquette								
P	J.Sparma								

TEAM	G	W	L	PCT	GB	R	OR	AB	H	2B	3B	HR	BB	SO	AVG	OBP	SLG	PRO	PRO+	BR	/A	PF	CHI	RC	SB	CS	SBA	SBR
BAL	160	97	63	.606		755	601	5529	1426	243	35	175	514	926	.258	.325	.409	.734	119	114	126	98	100	727	55	43	56	-9
MIN	162	89	73	.549	9	663	581	5390	1341	219	33	144	513	844	.249	.319	.382	.701	101	49	6	106	98	643	67	42	61	-5
DET	162	88	74	.543	10	719	698	5507	1383	224	45	179	551	987	.251	.323	.406	.729	112	102	85	102	96	714	41	34	55	-8
CHI	163	83	79	.512	15	574	517	5348	1235	193	40	87	476	872	.231	.299	.331	.630	93	-83	-47	93	106	539	153	78	66	-1
CLE	162	81	81	.500	17	574	586	5474	1300	156	25	155	450	914	.237	.299	.360	.659	95	-38	-38	100	97	579	53	41	56	-9
CAL	162	80	82	.494	18	604	643	5360	1244	179	54	122	525	1062	.232	.305	.354	.659	98	-29	-13	97	101	582	80	54	60	-8
KC	160	74	86	.463	23	564	648	5328	1259	212	56	70	421	982	.236	.295	.337	.632	90	-84	-67	97	107	535	132	50	73	10
WAS	159	71	88	.447	25.5	557	659	5318	1245	185	40	126	450	1069	.234	.296	.355	.651	94	-50	-44	99	99	548	53	37	59	-6
BOS	162	72	90	.444	26	655	731	5498	1318	228	44	145	542	1020	.240	.312	.376	.688	93	24	-44	110	98	640	35	24	59	-4
NY	160	70	89	.440	26.5	611	612	5330	1254	182	36	162	485	817	.235	.302	.374	.676	104	-5	18	96	100	598	49	29	63	-3
TOT	806					6276		54082	13005	2021	408	1365	4927	9493	.240	.308	.369	.676							718	432	62	-44

TEAM	CG	SH	SV	IP	H	H/G	HR	BB	SO	RAT	ERA	ERA+	OAV	OOB	PR	/A	PF	CPI	FA	E	DP	FW	PW	BW	SBW	DIF
BAL	23	13	51	1466¹	1267	7.8	127	514	1070	11.1	3.32	100	.233	.303	19	2	97	97	.981	115	142	1.3	.2	13.5	-.5	2.4
MIN	52	11	28	1438²	1246	7.8	139	392	1015	10.4	3.13	115	.232	.287	48	74	105	97	.977	139	118	.0	8.0	.6	-.0	-.6
DET	36	11	38	1454¹	1356	8.4	185	520	1026	11.9	3.85	94	.247	.317	-67	-60	101	102	.980	120	142	1.1	-6.4	9.1	-.4	3.6
CHI	38	22	34	1475¹	1229	7.5	101	403	896	10.2	2.68	118	.226	.283	123	80	92	100	.976	159	149	-1.1	8.6	-5.1	.4	-.8
CLE	49	15	28	1467¹	1260	7.7	129	489	1111	10.9	3.23	107	.232	.299	34	35	100	98	.978	138	132	.0	3.8	-4.1	-.5	.7
CAL	31	12	40	1467¹	1364	8.4	136	511	836	11.8	3.56	94	.251	.320	-21	-33	98	105	.979	136	186	.2	-3.5	-1.4	-.4	4.1
KC	19	11	47	1435	1281	8.0	106	630	854	12.2	3.56	96	.241	.326	-19	-25	99	101	.977	139	154	-.0	-2.7	-7.2	1.5	2.4
WAS	25	6	35	1419	1282	8.1	154	448	866	11.1	3.70	93	.242	.304	-42	-39	101	95	.977	142	139	-.3	-4.4	-4.7	-.2	.9
BOS	32	10	31	1463²	1402	8.6	164	577	977	12.4	3.92	97	.253	.327	-78	-18	111	103	.975	155	153	-.9	-1.9	-4.7	.0	-1.5
NY	29	7	32	1415²	1318	8.4	124	443	842	11.3	3.41	97	.248	.308	3	-14	97	102	.977	142	142	-.3	-1.5	1.9	.1	-9.8
TOT	334	118	364	14492²		8.1				11.3	3.44		.240	.308					.978	1385	1457					

Runs
F.Robinson-Bal . . . 122
Oliva-Min 99
Cash-Det 98
Agee-Chi 98

Hits
Oliva-Min 191
F.Robinson-Bal 182
Aparicio-Bal 182
Agee-Chi 172
Cash-Det 168

Doubles
Yastrzemski-Bos . . . 39
B.Robinson-Bal 35
F.Robinson-Bal 34
Oliva-Min 32
Fregosi-Cal 32

Triples
Knoop-Cal 11
Campaneris-KC 10
Brinkman-Was 9

Home Runs
F.Robinson-Bal 49
Killebrew-Min 39
Powell-Bal 34
Cash-Det 32
Pepitone-NY 31

Total Bases
F.Robinson-Bal 367
Oliva-Min 312
Killebrew-Min 306
Cash-Det 288
Agee-Chi 281

Runs Batted In
F.Robinson-Bal . . . 122
Killebrew-Min . . . 110
Powell-Bal 109
B.Robinson-Bal . . . 100
Horton-Det 100

Runs Produced
F.Robinson-Bal 195
B.Robinson-Bal 168
Agee-Chi 162
Oliva-Min 161
Killebrew-Min 160

Bases On Balls
Killebrew-Min 103
Foy-Bos 91
F.Robinson-Bal 87
Tresh-NY 86
Yastrzemski-Bos . . . 84

Batting Average
F.Robinson-Bal 316
Oliva-Min 307
Kaline-Det 288
Powell-Bal 287
Killebrew-Min 281

On Base Percentage
F.Robinson-Bal 415
Kaline-Det 396
Killebrew-Min 393
McAuliffe-Det 375
Powell-Bal 374

Slugging Average
F.Robinson-Bal 637
Killebrew-Min 538
Kaline-Det 534
Powell-Bal 532
McAuliffe-Det 509

Production
F.Robinson-Bal . . .1.052
Killebrew-Min 931
Kaline-Det 931
Powell-Bal 905
McAuliffe-Det 884

Adjusted Production
F.Robinson-Bal . . . 200
Kaline-Det 161
Powell-Bal 159
Killebrew-Min 155
McAuliffe-Det 148

Batter Runs
F.Robinson-Bal . . . 73.6
Killebrew-Min 49.9
Kaline-Det 42.1
Powell-Bal 36.3
Oliva-Min 33.2

Adjusted Batter Runs
F.Robinson-Bal . . .75.9
Killebrew-Min 42.4
Kaline-Det 39.8
Powell-Bal 37.8
Mantle-NY 31.4

Clutch Hitting Index
Powell-Bal 119
Horton-Det 119
Green-KC 116
Hershberger-KC . . . 115
D.Johnson-Bal 113

Runs Created
F.Robinson-Bal . . . 146
Killebrew-Min 122
Oliva-Min 106
Kaline-Det 105
Cash-Det 101

Total Average
F.Robinson-Bal . . .1.104
Kaline-Det 969
Killebrew-Min 967
Powell-Bal 898
McAuliffe-Det 877

Stolen Bases
Campaneris-KC 52
Buford-Chi 51
Agee-Chi 44
Aparicio-Bal 25
Cardenal-Cal 24

Stolen Base Average
Campaneris-KC . . . 83.9
Tartabull-KC-Bos . . 82.6
Tovar-Min 72.7
Agee-Chi 71.0
Buford-Chi 69.9

Stolen Base Runs
Campaneris-KC 9.6
Tartabull-KC-Bos . . 3.3
Salmon-Cle 2.4
Agee-Chi 2.4

Fielding Runs
Weis-Chi 36.9
Tresh-NY 27.7
Boyer-NY 19.9
Yastrzemski-Bos . . 16.6
Knoop-Cal 16.5

Total Player Rating
F.Robinson-Bal . . . 6.7
Tresh-NY 4.1
Fregosi-Cal 3.9
Kaline-Det 3.9
Oliva-Min 3.5

Wins
Kaat-Min 25
McLain-Det 20
Wilson-Bos-Det 18
Siebert-Cle 16
Palmer-Bal 15

Win Percentage
Siebert-Cle 667
Kaat-Min 658
Wilson-Bos-Det 621
Palmer-Bal 600
McLain-Det 588

Games
Fisher-Chi-Bal 67
Cox-Was 66
Aker-KC 66
Worthington-Min . . . 65
Kline-Was 63

Complete Games
Kaat-Min 19
McLain-Det 14
Wilson-Bos-Det 13
Bell-Cle 12

Shutouts
Tiant-Cle 5
McDowell-Cle 5
John-Chi 5

Saves
Aker-KC 32
Kline-Was 23
Sherry-Det 20
Fisher-Chi-Bal 19
S.Miller-Bal 18

Innings Pitched
Kaat-Min 304.2
McLain-Det 264.1
Wilson-Bos-Det . . 264.0
Chance-Cal 259.2
Bell-Cle 254.1

Fewest Hits/Game
McDowell-Cle . . . 6.02
Boswell-Min 6.38
Peters-Chi 6.86
McLain-Det 6.98
Chance-Cal 7.14

Fewest BB/Game
Kaat-Min 1.62
Peterson-NY 1.67
Grant-Min 1.77
Peters-Chi 1.98
Hargan-Cle 2.11

Strikeouts
McDowell-Cle 225
Kaat-Min 205
Wilson-Bos-Det . . . 200
Richert-Was 195
Bell-Cle 194

Strikeouts/Game
McDowell-Cle . . . 10.42
Boswell-Min 9.19
Lolich-Det 7.64
Richert-Was 7.14
Bell-Cle 6.87

Ratio
Peters-Chi 8.97
Kaat-Min 9.72
Richert-Was 9.74
Siebert-Cle 9.75
Ortega-Was 9.85

Earned Run Average
Peters-Chi 1.98
Horlen-Chi 2.43
Hargan-Cle 2.48
Perry-Min 2.54
John-Chi 2.62

Adjusted ERA
Peters-Chi 160
Perry-Min 142
Hargan-Cle 138
Kaat-Min 131
Horlen-Chi 130

Opponents' Batting Avg.
McDowell-Cle 188
Boswell-Min 197
Peters-Chi 212
McLain-Det 214
Richert-Was 215

Opponents' On Base Pct.
Peters-Chi 261
Richert-Was 271
Kaat-Min 271
Ortega-Was 276
Siebert-Cle 278

Starter Runs
Peters-Chi 33.1
Horlen-Chi 23.5
Kaat-Min 23.3
Hargan-Cle 20.3
John-Chi 20.1

Adjusted Starter Runs
Kaat-Min 28.8
Peters-Chi 27.1
Perry-Min 21.7
Hargan-Cle 20.4
Nash-KC 18.9

Clutch Pitching Index
McNally-Bal 118
Horlen-Chi 114
Brunet-Cal 114
Perry-Min 113
Hargan-Cle 110

Relief Runs
Aker-KC 18.1
Wilhelm-Chi 16.0
S.Miller-Bal 12.1
Fisher-Chi-Bal 10.8
Lines-Was 10.7

Adjusted Relief Runs
Aker-KC 17.7
Wilhelm-Chi 13.7
Worthington-Min . . 11.5
S.Miller-Bal 11.1
Lines-Was 10.9

Relief Ranking
Aker-KC 26.8
McMahon-Cle-Bos . 20.5
S.Miller-Bal 18.4
Kline-Was 16.1
Worthington-Min . . .14.2

Total Pitcher Index
Kaat-Min 4.1
Peters-Chi 3.9
Wilson-Bos-Det . . . 3.3
Aker-KC 3.2
Perry-Min 2.4

Total Baseball Ranking
F.Robinson-Bal . . . 6.7
Tresh-NY 4.1
Kaat-Min 4.1
Fregosi-Cal 3.9
Peters-Chi 3.9

January 29 Branch Rickey and Lloyd Waner are elected to the Baseball Hall of Fame by a unanimous vote of the Special Veterans Committee.

February 16 Red Ruffing is selected for the Hall of Fame through a special runoff election, since nobody received the required 75 percent vote in January.

May 10 In the eighth inning against Jim Bunning of the Phillies, Hank Aaron drives a ball to deep center field and scores ahead of the relay. It will be the only inside-the-park home run among his 755.

June 4 Curt Flood's record string of 568 straight chances without an error ends when he drops a fly ball during a 4-3 win over the Cubs at St. Louis. The Cardinals center fielder had played a NL-record 227 straight games without an error beginning September 3, 1965.

July 12 Reds third baseman Tony Perez ends the longest All-Star Game (15 innings, three hours and 41 minutes) with a home run off Catfish Hunter. Homers by NL third baseman Richie Allen and AL third baseman Brooks Robinson account for the other runs in a 2-1 NL triumph.

July 14 Eddie Mathews becomes the seventh member of the 500-home run club, connecting off loser Juan Marichal as the Astros beat the Giants 8-6.

October 1 Pittsburgh right fielder Roberto Clemente ends his season with a flourish, winning his fourth batting title with a .357 average by going 2-for-5 with a triple and his 23rd home run, as the Pirates wallop the Astros 10-3.

October 4 Cardinals left fielder Lou Brock has four hits, two stolen bases, and scores twice, as St. Louis edges Boston 2-1 to open the World Series at Fenway Park. Bob Gibson has 10 strikeouts and outduels Jose Santiago, whose home run is Boston's only score.

October 8 Bob Gibson is overpowering again in a five-hit 6-0 win in Game 4.

Roger Maris and Tim McCarver each drive in two runs for St. Louis.

October 9 Roger Maris homers for the Cardinals in the ninth, but Jim Lonborg's 3-1 win sends the World Series back to Boston.

October 12 The Cardinals earn their second World Championship of the decade with a 7-2 victory. Bob Gibson notches his third World Series win with a three-hitter, 10 strikeouts, and a fifth-inning home run. Lou Brock steals three bases for a record seven thefts in a seven-game World Series.

October 31 San Francisco's Mike McCormick is the NL Cy Young Award winner, as pitchers are honored in each league for the first time.

November 7 Orlando Cepeda of the Cards is the first unanimous selection as NL MVP.

November 20 Mets pitcher Tom Seaver (16-12) is named NL Rookie of the Year.

ATLANTA		CHICAGO		CINCINNATI		HOUSTON		LOS ANGELES	
M	B.Hitchcock	M	L.Durocher	M	D.Bristol	M	G.Hatton	M	W.Alston
M	K.Silvestri	1B	E.Banks	1B	L.May	1B	E.Mathews	1B	W.Parker
1B	F.Alou	2B	G.Beckert	2B	T.Helms	2B	J.Morgan	2B	R.Hunt
2B	W.Woodward	SS	D.Kessinger	SS	L.Cardenas	SS	S.Jackson	SS	G.Michael
SS	D.Menke	3B	R.Santo	3B	T.Perez	3B	B.Aspromonte	3B	J.Lefebvre
3B	C.Boyer	LF	B.Williams	LF	P.Rose	LF	R.Davis	LF	L.Johnson
LF	R.Carty	CF	A.Phillips	CF	V.Pinson	CF	J.Wynn	CF	W.Davis
CF	M.Jones	RF	T.Savage	RF	T.Harper	RF	R.Staub	RF	R.Fairly
RF	H.Aaron	C	R.Hundley	C	J.Edwards	C	J.Bateman	C	J.Roseboro
C	J.Torre								
		P	F.Jenkins	13	D.Johnson	2S	J.Gotay	3O	B.Bailey
1	T.Francona	P	R.Nye	23	C.Ruiz	C	R.Brand	O	A.Ferrara
		P	J.Niekro	C	D.Pavletich			O	L.Gabrielson
P	D.Lemaster	P	R.Culp			P	M.Cuellar	2S	N.Oliver
P	K.Johnson	P	B.Hands	P	G.Nolan	P	D.Giusti	S	D.Schofield
P	P.Niekro	RP	C.Hartenstein	P	M.Pappas	P	D.Wilson		
P	P.Jarvis	RP	B.Stoneman	P	M.Queen	P	B.Belinsky	P	C.Osteen
RP	D.Kelley	RP	C.Koonce	P	J.Maloney	P	L.Dierker	P	D.Drysdale
RP	C.Carroll			P	S.Ellis	RP	B.Latman	P	D.Sutton
RP	J.Ritchie	P	K.Holtzman	RP	T.Abernathy	RP	C.Sembera	P	B.Singer
		P	C.Simmons	RP	D.Nottebart	RP	D.Eilers	P	J.Brewer
P	T.Cloninger			RP	G.Arrigo			RP	R.Perranoski
P	R.Hernandez					P	W.Blasingame	RP	P.Regan
				P	B.McCool	P	D.Schneider	RP	B.Miller
				P	B.Lee	P	B.Von Hoff		

NEW YORK		PHILADELPHIA		PITTSBURGH		SAN FRANCISCO		ST.LOUIS	
M	W.Westrum	M	G.Mauch	M	H.Walker	M	H.Franks	M	R.Schoendienst
M	S.Parker	1B	B.White	M	D.Murtaugh	1B	W.McCovey	1B	O.Cepeda
1B	E.Kranepool	2B	C.Rojas	1B	D.Clendenon	2B	T.Fuentes	2B	J.Javier
2B	J.Buchek	SS	B.Wine	2B	B.Mazeroski	SS	H.Lanier	SS	D.Maxvill
SS	B.Harrelson	3B	D.Allen	SS	G.Alley	3B	J.Hart	3B	M.Shannon
3B	E.Charles	LF	T.Gonzalez	3B	M.Wills	LF	J.Alou	LF	L.Brock
LF	T.Davis	CF	J.Briggs	LF	W.Stargell	CF	W.Mays	CF	C.Flood
CF	C.Jones	RF	J.Callison	CF	M.Alou	RF	O.Brown	RF	R.Maris
RF	R.Swoboda	C	C.Dalrymple	RF	R.Clemente	C	T.Haller	C	T.McCarver
C	J.Grote			C	J.May				
		O	D.Lock			3S	J.Davenport	O1	B.Tolan
O	T.Reynolds	SO	G.Sutherland	O	M.Mota	23	P.Gagliano		
21	B.Johnson	13	T.Taylor	3O	J.Pagan	P	G.Perry	P	D.Hughes
		C	G.Oliver			P	M.McCormick	P	S.Carlton
P	T.Seaver			P	T.Sisk	P	J.Marichal	P	R.Washburn
P	J.Fisher	P	J.Bunning	P	B.Veale	P	R.Sadecki	P	B.Gibson
P	D.Cardwell	P	L.Jackson	P	D.Ribant	P	R.Herbel	P	N.Briles
P	B.Shaw	P	C.Short	P	S.Blass	RP	F.Linzy	RP	A.Jackson
RP	D.Selma	P	R.Wise	P	W.Fryman	P	J.Gibbon	RP	R.Willis
RP	R.Taylor	P	D.Ellsworth	RP	A.McBean	RP	L.McDaniel	RP	J.Hoerner
RP	D.Shaw	RP	T.Farrell	RP	J.Pizarro				
		RP	D.Hall	RP	R.Face	P	B.Bolin	P	L.Jaster
P	D.Frisella	RP	G.Jackson						
P	B.Hendley			P	V.Law				
P	B.Denehy	P	J.Boozer	P	B.O'Dell				
				P	P.Mikkelsen				

TEAM	G	W	L	PCT	GB	R	OR	AB	H	2B	3B	HR	BB	SO	AVG	OBP	SLG	PRO	PRO+	BR	/A	PF	CHI	RC	SB	CS	SBA	SBR
STL	161	101	60	.627		695	557	5566	1462	225	40	115	443	919	.263	.322	.379	.701	109	52	61	99	103	676	102	54	65	-2
SF	162	91	71	.562	10.5	652	551	5524	1354	201	39	140	520	978	.245	.315	.372	.687	104	24	33	99	100	641	22	30	42	-11
CHI	162	87	74	.540	14	702	624	5463	1373	211	49	128	509	912	.251	.319	.378	.697	101	44	13	105	105	654	63	50	56	-11
CIN	162	87	75	.537	14.5	604	563	5519	1366	251	54	109	372	969	.248	.299	.372	.671	88	-20	-88	111	102	592	92	63	59	-10
PHI	162	82	80	.506	19.5	612	581	5401	1306	221	47	103	545	1033	.242	.314	.357	.671	98	-1	-7	101	99	604	79	62	56	-14
PIT	163	81	81	.500	20.5	679	693	5724	1585	193	62	91	387	914	.277	.327	.380	.707	108	63	60	101	97	693	79	37	68	2
ATL	162	77	85	.475	24.5	631	640	5450	1307	191	29	158	512	947	.240	.309	.372	.681	102	10	19	99	100	615	55	45	55	-11
LA	162	73	89	.451	28.5	519	595	5456	1285	203	38	82	485	881	.236	.303	.332	.635	97	-74	-30	92	95	541	56	47	54	-11
HOU	162	69	93	.426	32.5	626	742	5506	1372	259	46	93	537	934	.249	.319	.364	.683	107	20	42	97	97	640	88	38	70	4
NY	162	61	101	.377	40.5	498	672	5417	1288	178	23	83	362	981	.238	.290	.325	.615	83	-118	-110	98	103	500	58	44	57	-9
TOT	810					6218		55026	13698	2133	427	1102	4672	9468	.249	.312	.363	.675							694	470	60	-74

TEAM	CG	SH	SV	IP	H	H/G	HR	BB	SO	RAT	ERA	ERA+	OAV	OOB	PR	/A	PF	CPI	FA	E	DP	FW	PW	BW	SBW	DIF
STL	44	17	45	1465	1313	8.1	97	431	956	10.9	3.05	108	.239	.299	54	39	97	98	.978	140	127	.0	4.2	6.6	.6	9.1
SF	64	17	25	1474¹	1283	7.8	113	453	990	10.8	2.92	113	.234	.296	75	61	97	101	.979	134	149	.4	6.6	3.6	-.4	-.2
CHI	47	7	28	1457	1352	8.4	142	463	888	11.4	3.48	102	.246	.308	-17	10	105	99	.981	121	143	1.1	1.1	1.4	-.4	3.3
CIN	34	18	39	1468	1328	8.1	101	498	1065	11.5	3.05	123	.241	.309	54	115	111	104	.980	121	124	1.1	12.5	-9.5	-.3	2.2
PHI	46	17	23	1453²	1372	8.5	86	403	967	11.2	3.10	110	.250	.306	44	50	101	102	.978	137	174	.2	5.4	-.8	-.7	-3.2
PIT	35	5	35	1458¹	1439	8.9	108	561	820	12.5	3.74	90	.261	.332	-59	-61	100	103	.978	141	186	.0	-6.6	6.5	1.0	-.9
ATL	35	5	32	1454	1377	8.5	118	449	862	11.6	3.47	96	.251	.313	-16	-24	98	100	.978	138	148	.2	-2.6	2.1	-.4	-3.2
LA	41	17	24	1473	1421	8.7	93	393	967	11.3	3.21	96	.254	.308	27	-19	92	102	.975	160	144	-1.1	-2.1	-3.2	-.4	-1.2
HOU	35	8	21	1445²	1444	9.0	120	485	1060	12.3	4.03	82	.260	.324	-105	-115	98	93	.974	159	120	-1.0	-12.5	4.5	1.2	-4.3
NY	36	10	19	1433²	1369	8.6	124	536	893	12.1	3.73	91	.253	.323	-56	-54	100	99	.975	157	147	-.9	-5.8	-11.9	-.2	-1.1
TOT	417	121	291	14582²		8.5				11.6	3.38		.249	.312					.978	1408	1462					

Runs		Hits		Doubles		Triples		Home Runs		Total Bases	
Brock-StL	113	Clemente-Pit	209	Staub-Hou	44	Pinson-Cin	13	Aaron-Atl	39	Aaron-Atl	344
Aaron-Atl	113	Brock-StL	206	Cepeda-StL	37	Williams-Chi	12	Wynn-Hou	37	Brock-StL	325
Santo-Chi	107	Pinson-Cin	187	Aaron-Atl	37	Brock-StL	12	Santo-Chi	31	Clemente-Pit	324
Clemente-Pit	103	Wills-Pit	186			Morgan-Hou	11	McCovey-SF	31	Williams-Chi	305
Wynn-Hou	102	Alou-Pit	186					Hart-SF	29	Santo-Chi	300

Runs Batted In		Runs Produced		Bases On Balls		Batting Average		On Base Percentage		Slugging Average	
Cepeda-StL	111	Clemente-Pit	190	Santo-Chi	96	Clemente-Pit	.357	Allen-Phi	.404	Aaron-Atl	.573
Clemente-Pit	110	Aaron-Atl	183	Morgan-Hou	81	Gonzalez-Phi	.339	Cepeda-StL	.403	Allen-Phi	.566
Aaron-Atl	109	Cepeda-StL	177	Phillips-Chi	80	Alou-Pit	.338	Staub-Hou	.402	Clemente-Pit	.554
Wynn-Hou	107	Santo-Chi	174	Hart-SF	77	Flood-StL	.335	Clemente-Pit	.402	McCovey-SF	.535
Perez-Cin	102	Wynn-Hou	172	Allen-Phi	75	Staub-Hou	.333	Santo-Chi	.401	Cepeda-StL	.524

Production		Adjusted Production		Batter Runs		Adjusted Batter Runs		Clutch Hitting Index		Runs Created	
Allen-Phi	.970	Allen-Phi	173	Clemente-Pit	52.1	Aaron-Atl	51.8	Shannon-StL	141	Clemente-Pit	126
Clemente-Pit	.956	Clemente-Pit	170	Aaron-Atl	50.1	Clemente-Pit	51.6	Lanier-SF	125	Aaron-Atl	126
Aaron-Atl	.946	Aaron-Atl	169	Santo-Chi	47.9	Cepeda-StL	48.8	Maxvill-StL	120	Santo-Chi	120
Cepeda-StL	.927	Cepeda-StL	166	Cepeda-StL	47.3	Allen-Phi	45.1	Fairly-LA	118	Cepeda-StL	118
McCovey-SF	.916	McCovey-SF	162	Allen-Phi	46.1	Santo-Chi	42.5	Boyer-Atl	117	Hart-SF	111

Total Average		Stolen Bases		Stolen Base Average		Stolen Base Runs		Fielding Runs		Total Player Rating	
Allen-Phi	1.054	Brock-StL	52	Morgan-Hou	85.3	Morgan-Hou	5.7	Santo-Chi	30.6	Santo-Chi	7.3
Aaron-Atl	.965	Wills-Pit	29	Wynn-Hou	80.0	Brock-StL	4.8	Lanier-SF	28.9	Aaron-Atl	6.1
Clemente-Pit	.959	Morgan-Hou	29	Allen-Phi	80.0	Pinson-Cin	3.0	Wine-Phi	28.9	Clemente-Pit	5.8
Cepeda-StL	.950	Pinson-Cin	26	Davis-LA	76.9	Allen-Phi	3.0	Fuentes-SF	24.5	Cepeda-StL	4.4
McCovey-SF	.941	Phillips-Chi	24	Pinson-Cin	76.5	Wills-Pit	2.7	Mazeroski-Pit	16.7	Allen-Phi	4.4

Wins		Win Percentage		Games		Complete Games		Shutouts		Saves	
McCormick-SF	22	Hughes-StL	.727	Perranoski-LA	70	Jenkins-Chi	20	Bunning-Phi	6	Abernathy-Cin	28
Jenkins-Chi	20	McCormick-SF	.688	Abernathy-Cin	70	Seaver-NY	18	Osteen-LA	5	Linzy-SF	17
Osteen-LA	17	Veale-Pit	.667	Willis-StL	65	Perry-SF	18	Nolan-Cin	5	Face-Pit	17
Bunning-Phi	17	Jenkins-Chi	.606	Face-Pit	61	Marichal-SF	18	McCormick-SF	5	Perranoski-LA	16
		Jarvis-Atl	.600					L.Jackson-Phi	4	Hoerner-StL	15

Innings Pitched		Fewest Hits/Game		Fewest BB/Game		Strikeouts		Strikeouts/Game		Ratio	
Bunning-Phi	302.1	Hughes-StL	6.64	Pappas-Cin	1.57	Bunning-Phi	253	Nolan-Cin	8.18	Hughes-StL	8.78
Perry-SF	293.0	Wilson-Hou	6.90	Osteen-LA	1.62	Jenkins-Chi	236	Veale-Pit	7.94	Bunning-Phi	9.73
Jenkins-Chi	289.1	Perry-SF	7.10	Johnson-Atl	1.63	Perry-SF	230	Carlton-StL	7.83	Queen-Cin	9.80
Osteen-LA	288.1	Queen-Cin	7.13	Niekro-Chi	1.70	Nolan-Cin	206	Wilson-Hou	7.78	Perry-SF	9.80
Drysdale-LA	282.0	Niekro-Atl	7.13	L.Jackson-Phi	1.86	Cuellar-Hou	203	Gibson-StL	7.55	Niekro-Atl	9.83

Earned Run Average		Adjusted ERA		Opponents' Batting Avg.		Opponents' On Base Pct.		Starter Runs		Adjusted Starter Runs	
Niekro-Atl	1.87	Niekro-Atl	178	Hughes-StL	.203	Hughes-StL	.252	Bunning-Phi	36.4	Bunning-Phi	37.5
Bunning-Phi	2.29	Bunning-Phi	149	Wilson-Hou	.209	Bunning-Phi	.273	Niekro-Atl	34.6	Niekro-Atl	33.4
Short-Phi	2.39	Nolan-Cin	145	Perry-SF	.214	Queen-Cin	.273	Perry-SF	24.9	Nolan-Cin	29.5
Nolan-Cin	2.58	Short-Phi	142	Queen-Cin	.215	Perry-SF	.274	Short-Phi	21.8	Jenkins-Chi	24.0
Perry-SF	2.61	Queen-Cin	136	Bunning-Phi	.217	Jenkins-Chi	.277	Nolan-Cin	20.0	Short-Phi	22.5

Clutch Pitching Index		Relief Runs		Adjusted Relief Runs		Relief Ranking		Total Pitcher Index		Total Baseball Ranking	
Ellis-Cin	123	Abernathy-Cin	24.9	Abernathy-Cin	29.3	Abernathy-Cin	39.7	Abernathy-Cin	4.5	Santo-Chi	7.3
Niekro-Atl	121	Linzy-SF	19.9	Linzy-SF	19.0	Linzy-SF	32.5	Bunning-Phi	4.1	Aaron-Atl	6.1
Seaver-NY	114	Nottebart-Cin	12.8	Nottebart-Cin	16.1	Hall-Phi	24.2	Linzy-SF	3.9	Clemente-Pit	5.8
Marichal-SF	114	McBean-Pit	12.1	Farrell-Hou-Phi	12.1	Farrell-Hou-Phi	20.0	Niekro-Atl	3.8	Abernathy-Cin	4.5
Short-Phi	114	Farrell-Hou-Phi	11.9	McBean-Pit	12.0	Face-Pit	15.3	Jenkins-Chi	3.1	Cepeda-StL	4.4

March 3 The White Sox are given permission to use a semi-designated hitter in training camp. With home club permission, clubs will be allowed to use a designated pinch hitter twice in the same game.

April 14 Red Sox rookie Billy Rohr debuts at Yankee Stadium. He startles everyone by taking a no-hitter to the ninth inning, but Elston Howard lines a 3-2 pitch for a single to right-center with 2 outs. Carl Yastrzemski had kept the no-hitter alive with a spectacular grab of a Tom Tresh drive to deep left field to open the ninth. The Red Sox go on to win 3-0. Rohr will pitch only one more game for Boston before returning to the minors.

May 14 Mickey Mantle becomes the sixth member of the 500-home run club in New York's 6-5 win against Baltimore. Mantle connects batting left-handed off Stu Miller.

June 7 The last-place Yankees have the first pick in the free-agent draft and use it to take Ron Blomberg.

July 25 Race riots in Detroit force postponement of a Tigers-Orioles game. The games scheduled for the 26th and 27th are shifted to Baltimore.

August 6 Against Chicago, Brooks Robinson of the Orioles hits into the fourth triple play of his career for a major league mark.

August 18 A baseball tragedy occurs when Tony Conigliaro of the Red Sox is beaned by the Angels Jack Hamilton. Hit on the left cheekbone, just below the eye socket, Conigliaro will miss the rest of 1967 and all of 1968. He was hitting .267 with 20 homers and 67 RBI in 95 games.

August 26 Dean Chance pitches a 2-1 no-hitter, and the Twins sweep Cleveland to take the AL lead. The victory gives Chance a 17-9 record and lowers his ERA to 2.42.

October 1 Boston clinches the AL pennant with a 5-3 win over Minnesota, Jim Lonborg besting Dean Chance. Carl Yastrzemski goes 4-for-4 and has 10 hits in his final 13 at bats to win the Triple Crown (.326, 44, 121). Detroit, which could tie for the lead with a sweep, beats California in the opener 6-4. They then drop the second game 8-5 despite sending eight pitchers to the mound. The four teams combined for a 6-12 record over the final week, while Boston wins the pennant with a .568 winning percentage, the lowest in league history.

October 11 A World Series record three home runs in one inning—consecutively, by Yaz, Reggie Smith, and Rico Petrocelli—power Boston to an 8-4 win that evens the Series at three games each.

November 3 Boston's Jim Lonborg is named American League Cy Young Award winner.

November 15 Boston's Carl Yastrzemski is the overwhelming selection as AL MVP.

November 22 Minnesota second baseman Rod Carew (.292) is the runaway choice for AL Rookie of the Year.

	BALTIMORE		BOSTON		CALIFORNIA		CHICAGO		CLEVELAND
M	H.Bauer	M	D.Williams	M	B.Rigney	M	E.Stanky	M	J.Adcock
1B	B.Powell	1B	G.Scott	1B	D.Mincher	1B	T.McCraw	1B	T.Horton
2B	D.Johnson	2B	M.Andrews	2B	B.Knoop	2B	W.Causey	2B	P.Gonzalez
SS	L.Aparicio	SS	R.Petrocelli	SS	J.Fregosi	SS	R.Hansen	SS	L.Brown
3B	B.Robinson	3B	J.Foy	3B	P.Schaal	3B	D.Buford	3B	M.Alvis
LF	C.Blefary	LF	C.Yastrzemski	LF	R.Reichardt	LF	P.Ward	LF	L.Wagner
CF	P.Blair	CF	R.Smith	CF	J.Cardenal	CF	T.Agee	CF	V.Davalillo
RF	F.Robinson	RF	T.Conigliaro	RF	J.Hall	RF	K.Berry	RF	C.Hinton
C	A.Etchebarren	C	M.Ryan	C	B.Rodgers	C	J.Martin	C	J.Azcue
O	R.Snyder	O	J.Tartabull	O	J.Johnstone	O	W.Williams	O	L.Maye
		3S	J.Adair	O	B.Morton			1	F.Whitfield
P	T.Phoebus			3C	T.Satriano	P	G.Peters	C	D.Sims
P	P.Richert	P	J.Lonborg			P	J.Horlen	2	V.Fuller
P	B.Dillman	P	L.Stange	P	G.Brunet	P	T.John	O1	C.Salmon
P	D.McNally	P	G.Bell	P	J.McGlothlin	P	B.Howard		
P	J.Hardin	P	B.Brandon	P	R.Clark	RP	B.Locker	P	S.McDowell
RP	E.Watt	RP	J.Santiago	P	J.Hamilton	RP	W.Wood	P	S.Hargan
RP	M.Drabowsky	RP	J.Wyatt	RP	M.Rojas	RP	D.McMahon	P	L.Tiant
RP	E.Fisher	RP	D.Osinski	RP	B.Kelso			P	S.Siebert
				RP	P.Cimino	P	J.Buzhardt	P	J.O'Donoghue
P	G.Brabender	P	D.Bennett			P	H.Wilhelm	RP	O.Pena
P	W.Bunker					P	J.O'Toole	RP	G.Culver
P	S.Miller			P	C.Wright			RP	S.Bailey
P	S.Barber			P	J.Coates				
								P	S.Williams
								/P	G.Bell
								P	B.Allen

	DETROIT		KANSAS CITY		MINNESOTA		NEW YORK		WASHINGTON
M	M.Smith	M	A.Dark	M	S.Mele	M	R.Houk	M	G.Hodges
1B	N.Cash	M	L.Appling	M	C.Ermer	1B	M.Mantle	1B	M.Epstein
2B	D.McAuliffe	1B	R.Webster	1B	H.Killebrew	2B	H.Clarke	2B	B.Allen
SS	R.Oyler	2B	J.Donaldson	2B	R.Carew	SS	R.Amaro	SS	E.Brinkman
3B	D.Wert	SS	B.Campaneris	SS	Z.Versalles	3B	C.Smith	3B	K.McMullen
LF	J.Northrup	3B	D.Green	3B	R.Rollins	LF	T.Tresh	LF	F.Howard
CF	M.Stanley	LF	J.Gosger	LF	B.Allison	CF	J.Pepitone	CF	F.Valentine
RF	A.Kaline	CF	R.Monday	CF	T.Uhlaender	RF	S.Whitaker	RF	C.Peterson
C	B.Freehan	RF	M.Hershberger	RF	T.Oliva	C	J.Gibbs	C	P.Casanova
		C	P.Roof	C	J.Zimmerman				
O	W.Horton					O	B.Robinson	O	H.Allen
		3O	D.Cater	O3	C.Tovar	O3	R.White	S2	T.Cullen
P	E.Wilson							1	D.Nen
P	D.McLain	P	C.Hunter	P	D.Chance	P	M.Stottlemyre	2S	B.Saverine
P	J.Sparma	P	J.Nash	P	J.Kaat	P	A.Downing	O	E.Stroud
P	M.Lolich	P	C.Dobson	P	J.Merritt	P	F.Peterson		
RP	D.Wickersham	P	L.Krausse	P	D.Boswell	P	F.Talbot	P	P.Ortega
RP	F.Gladding	P	B.Odom	P	J.Perry	P	B.Monbouquette	P	C.Pascual
RP	J.Hiller	RP	P.Lindblad	RP	A.Worthington	RP	T.Tillotson	P	B.Moore
		RP	T.Pierce	RP	R.Kline	RP	D.Womack	P	J.Coleman
P	J.Podres	RP	J.Aker			RP	J.Verbanic	P	F.Bertaina
P	M.Marshall			P	M.Grant			RP	D.Knowles
		P	D.Segui			P	S.Barber	RP	B.Priddy
						P	S.Hamilton	RP	B.Humphreys
								P	D.Lines
								P	C.Cox
								P	D.Baldwin
								P	P.Richert
								/P	D.Bosman

TEAM	G	W	L	PCT	GB	R	OR	AB	H	2B	3B	HR	BB	SO	AVG	OBP	SLG	PRO	PRO+	BR	/A	PF	CHI	RC	SB	CS	SBA	SBR
BOS	162	92	70	.568		**722**	614	5471	**1394**	216	39	**158**	522	1020	**.255**	.323	**.395**	**.718**	109	118	60	108	100	**694**	68	59	54	-15
MIN	164	91	71	.562	1	671	590	5458	1309	**216**	48	131	512	976	.240	.310	.369	.679	99	44	-8	108	104	625	55	37	60	-6
DET	163	91	71	.562	1	683	587	5410	1315	192	36	152	**626**	994	.243	**.327**	.376	**.703**	111	100	**81**	103	96	681	37	21	64	-2
CHI	162	89	73	.549	3	531	**491**	5383	1209	181	34	89	480	**849**	.225	.293	.320	.613	90	-80	-61	96	104	504	124	82	60	-12
CAL	161	84	77	.522	7.5	567	587	5307	1265	170	37	114	453	1021	.238	.302	.349	.651	102	-12	10	96	99	553	40	36	53	-10
WAS	161	76	85	.472	15.5	550	637	5441	1211	168	25	115	472	1037	.223	.289	.326	.615	92	-81	-61	96	**107**	512	53	37	59	-6
BAL	161	76	85	.472	15.5	654	592	5456	1312	215	44	138	531	1002	.240	.313	.372	.685	110	54	59	99	99	639	54	37	59	-6
CLE	162	75	87	.463	17	559	613	5461	1282	213	35	131	413	984	.235	.295	.359	.654	98	-15	-20	101	96	563	53	65	45	-23
NY	163	72	90	.444	20	522	621	5443	1225	166	17	100	532	1043	.225	.298	.317	.615	91	-74	-54	96	98	522	63	37	63	-3
KC	161	62	99	.385	29.5	533	660	5349	1244	212	**50**	69	452	1019	.233	.297	.330	.627	94	-54	-37	97	100	539	**132**	59	**69**	4
TOT	810					5992		54179	12766	1949	365	1197	4993	9945	.236	.305	.351	.656							679	470	59	-78

TEAM	CG	SH	SV	IP	H	H/G	HR	BB	SO	RAT	ERA	ERA+	OAV	OOB	PR	/A	PF	CPI	FA	E	DP	FW	PW	BW	SBW	DIF
BOS	41	9	44	1459[1]	1307	8.1	142	477	1010	11.3	3.36	104	.239	.306	-21	20	108	101	.977	142	142	-.6	2.2	6.6	-.8	3.6
MIN	**58**	18	24	1461	1336	8.2	115	**396**	1089	10.9	3.14	110	.243	.298	15	53	107	101	.978	132	123	.1	5.9	-.9	.2	4.7
DET	46	17	40	1443[2]	1230	7.7	151	472	1038	10.8	3.32	98	.230	.297	-14	-9	101	97	.978	132	126	.0	-1.0	**8.9**	.6	1.3
CHI	36	**24**	39	1490[1]	**1197**	**7.2**	**87**	465	927	**10.4**	**2.45**	**127**	**.219**	**.288**	**129**	**108**	96	**106**	.979	138	149	-.3	**11.9**	-6.7	-.5	3.6
CAL	19	14	**46**	1430[1]	1246	7.8	118	525	892	11.4	3.19	98	.237	.311	6	-8	97	105	**.982**	**111**	135	**1.3**	-.9	1.1	-.2	2.2
WAS	24	14	39	1473[1]	1334	8.1	113	495	878	11.4	3.38	93	.242	.309	-25	-36	98	98	.978	144	**167**	-.8	-4.0	-6.7	-.2	6.8
BAL	29	17	36	1457[1]	1218	7.5	116	566	1034	11.2	3.32	95	.228	.305	-15	-27	98	95	.980	124	144	.5	-3.0	6.5	.2	-3.5
CLE	49	14	27	1477[2]	1258	7.7	120	559	**1189**	11.3	3.25	101	.231	.307	-3	3	101	99	.981	116	138	1.0	.3	-2.2	-1.7	-3.5
NY	37	16	27	1480[2]	1375	8.4	110	480	898	11.5	3.24	97	.249	.313	-2	-19	97	**106**	.976	154	144	-1.3	-2.1	-6.0	.5	-.2
KC	26	10	34	1428	1265	8.0	125	558	990	11.7	3.68	87	.238	.315	-71	-79	99	94	.978	132	120	-.0	-8.7	-4.1	**1.3**	-7.0
TOT	365	153	356	14601[2]		7.9				11.2	3.23		.236	.305					.979	1325	1388					

Runs
Yastrzemski-Bos . 112
Killebrew-Min 105
Tovar-Min 98
Kaline-Det 94
McAuliffe-Det 92

Hits
Yastrzemski-Bos . . . 189
Tovar-Min 173
Scott-Bos 171
Fregosi-Cal 171
B.Robinson-Bal 164

Doubles
Oliva-Min 34
Tovar-Min 32
Yastrzemski-Bos . . . 31
D.Johnson-Bal 30
Campaneris-KC 29

Triples
Blair-Bal 12
Buford-Chi 9

Home Runs
Yastrzemski-Bos . . . 44
Killebrew-Min 44
Howard-Was 36
F.Robinson-Bal 30

Total Bases
Yastrzemski-Bos . . 360
Killebrew-Min 305
F.Robinson-Bal . . . 276
B.Robinson-Bal . . . 265
Howard-Was 265

Runs Batted In
Yastrzemski-Bos . 121
Killebrew-Min 113
F.Robinson-Bal 94
Howard-Was 89
Oliva-Min 83

Runs Produced
Yastrzemski-Bos . . 189
Killebrew-Min 174
F.Robinson-Bal . . . 147
Kaline-Det 147
B.Robinson-Bal . . . 143

Bases On Balls
Killebrew-Min 131
Mantle-NY 107
McAuliffe-Det 105
Yastrzemski-Bos . . . 91
Kaline-Det 83

Batting Average
Yastrzemski-Bos . .326
F.Robinson-Bal . .311
Kaline-Det 308
Scott-Bos 303
Blair-Bal 293

On Base Percentage
Yastrzemski-Bos . .421
Kaline-Det 415
Killebrew-Min 413
F.Robinson-Bal . .408
Mantle-NY 394

Slugging Average
Yastrzemski-Bos . .622
F.Robinson-Bal . .576
Killebrew-Min 558
Kaline-Det 541
Howard-Was 511

Production
Yastrzemski-Bos . 1.043
F.Robinson-Bal . . .984
Killebrew-Min 970
Kaline-Det 957
Mincher-Cal 855

Adjusted Production
Yastrzemski-Bos . . 189
F.Robinson-Bal . . . 189
Kaline-Det 176
Killebrew-Min 170
Mincher-Cal 156

Batter Runs
Yastrzemski-Bos . 76.4
Killebrew-Min 62.3
F.Robinson-Bal . . 53.3
Kaline-Det 48.4
Scott-Bos 33.8

Adjusted Batter Runs
Yastrzemski-Bos . .65.3
F.Robinson-Bal . .54.2
Killebrew-Min . . . 52.2
Kaline-Det 45.7
Mincher-Cal 34.6

Clutch Hitting Index
Hershberger-KC . . .124
D.Johnson-Bal 113
Hansen-Chi 111
Northrup-Det 109
Versalles-Min 108

Runs Created
Yastrzemski-Bos . . 155
Killebrew-Min 131
F.Robinson-Bal . . . 113
Kaline-Det 104
Scott-Bos 97

Total Average
Yastrzemski-Bos . 1.134
Killebrew-Min 1.058
F.Robinson-Bal . . 1.029
Kaline-Det 1.009
Mantle-NY 874

Stolen Bases
Campaneris-KC 55
Buford-Chi 34
Agee-Chi 28
McCraw-Chi 24
Clarke-NY 21

Stolen Base Average
Valentine-Was 85.0
Clarke-NY 84.0
Aparicio-Chi 78.3
Campaneris-KC . . . 77.5
Agee-Chi 73.7

Stolen Base Runs
Campaneris-KC 6.9
Clarke-NY 3.9
Valentine-Was 3.3

Fielding Runs
B.Robinson-Bal . . . 30.8
Blair-Bal 20.9
Smith-Bos 16.5
Monday-KC 15.2
Clarke-NY 15.2

Total Player Rating
Yastrzemski-Bos . . 7.3
Kaline-Det 5.2
B.Robinson-Bal . . . 5.0
F.Robinson-Bal . . . 4.8
Blair-Bal 4.1

Wins
Wilson-Det 22
Lonborg-Bos 22
Chance-Min 20
Horlen-Chi 19
McLain-Det 17

Win Percentage
Horlen-Chi 731
Lonborg-Bos 710
Wilson-Det 667
Sparma-Det 640
Peters-Chi 593

Games
Locker-Chi 77
Rojas-Cal 72
Kelso-Cal 69
Womack-NY 65
McMahon-Bos-Chi . 63

Complete Games
Chance-Min 18
Lonborg-Bos 15
Hargan-Cle 15

Shutouts
McGlothlin-Cal 6
Lolich-Det 6
John-Chi 6
Horlen-Chi 6
Hargan-Cle 6

Saves
Rojas-Cal 27
Wyatt-Bos 20
Locker-Chi 20
Womack-NY 18
Worthington-Min . . . 16

Innings Pitched
Chance-Min 283.2
Lonborg-Bos 273.1
Wilson-Det 264.0
Kaat-Min 263.1
Peters-Chi 260.0

Fewest Hits/Game
Peters-Chi 6.47
Boswell-Min 6.55
Horlen-Chi 6.56
Siebert-Cle 6.60
Downing-NY 7.05

Fewest BB/Game
Merritt-Min 1.19
Kaat-Min 1.44
Stange-Bos 1.59
Horlen-Chi 2.02
Peterson-NY 2.13

Strikeouts
Lonborg-Bos 246
McDowell-Cle 236
Chance-Min 220
Tiant-Cle 219
Peters-Chi 215

Strikeouts/Game
Tiant-Cle 9.22
McDowell-Cle 8.99
Boswell-Min 8.25
Lonborg-Bos 8.10
Phoebus-Bal 7.75

Ratio
Horlen-Chi 8.72
Merritt-Min 9.21
Siebert-Cle 9.52
John-Chi 9.84
Peters-Chi 10.00

Earned Run Average
Horlen-Chi 2.06
Peters-Chi 2.28
Siebert-Cle 2.38
John-Chi 2.47
Merritt-Min 2.53

Adjusted ERA
Horlen-Chi 151
Siebert-Cle 137
Merritt-Min 137
Peters-Chi 136
Chance-Min 127

Opponents' Batting Avg.
Peters-Chi 199
Boswell-Min 202
Siebert-Cle 202
Horlen-Chi 203
Downing-NY 217

Opponents' On Base Pct.
Horlen-Chi 253
Merritt-Min 262
Siebert-Cle 268
John-Chi 277
Peters-Chi 277

Starter Runs
Horlen-Chi 33.6
Peters-Chi 27.3
Merritt-Min 17.7
Siebert-Cle 17.5
Chance-Min 15.8

Adjusted Starter Runs
Horlen-Chi 30.0
Peters-Chi 23.7
Merritt-Min 23.5
Chance-Min 23.0
Siebert-Cle 18.3

Clutch Pitching Index
Clark-Cal 121
Stottlemyre-NY . . . 117
Kaat-Min 108
Tiant-Cle 107
Stange-Bos 105

Relief Runs
Wilhelm-Chi 18.9
Drabowsky-Bal . . . 17.2
Locker-Chi 15.7
McMahon-Bos-Chi . 15.2
Baldwin-Was 11.6

Adjusted Relief Runs
Wilhelm-Chi 17.7
Drabowsky-Bal . . . 16.4
McMahon-Bos-Chi . 14.5
Locker-Chi 14.0
Baldwin-Was 11.1

Relief Ranking
Wilhelm-Chi 24.6
Drabowsky-Bal . . . 22.8
Wyatt-Bos 19.0
Rojas-Cal 17.0
Locker-Chi 16.7

Total Pitcher Index
Peters-Chi 3.7
Horlen-Chi 3.5
Drabowsky-Bal 2.9
Wilhelm-Chi 2.6
Chance-Min 2.4

Total Baseball Ranking
Yastrzemski-Bos . . 7.3
Kaline-Det 5.2
B.Robinson-Bal . . . 5.0
F.Robinson-Bal . . . 4.8
Blair-Bal 4.1

January 23 Joe Medwick is voted into the Baseball Hall of Fame.

January 28 Goose Goslin and Kiki Cuyler are admitted to the Hall of Fame by unanimous vote of the Special Veterans Committee.

April 15 Three records are smashed when the Astros score an unearned run in the 24th inning to squeeze by the Mets 1-0. It is the longest NL game played to completion, in terms of innings, the longest ML night game, and the first 23 innings are the longest ML scoreless game. The game ties the AL's longest complete game: A's 4, Red Sox 1, in 24 frames, on September 1, 1906.

June 8 Don Drysdale works four scoreless innings against Philadelphia before finally allowing a run, after 58⅔ shutout innings, on Howie Bedell's sacrifice fly. Drysdale breaks the ML record of 56 consecutive scoreless innings set by Walter Johnson in 1913.

July 1 A first inning wild pitch breaks Bob Gibson's streak of 47⅔ innings of scoreless pitching as the Cards beat the Dodgers in Los Angeles 8-1.

July 9 Appropriately, pitching dominates the All-Star Game. Willie Mays tallies an unearned run in the first inning against AL starter Luis Tiant to complete the scoring for the day—the first All-Star Game to end 1-0. Don Drysdale, Juan Marichal, Steve Carlton, Tom Seaver, Ron Reed, and Jerry Koosman hold the AL to three hits.

July 14 Houston's Don Wilson fans 18 batters, tying the ML record set by Bob Feller. He also ties the ML record with 8 strikeouts in a row. For all his efforts, Wilson is not the winner.

September 17 Gaylord Perry hurls a no-hitter at Candlestick, as the Giants edge the Cards and Bob Gibson 1-0. Perry evens his record at 14-14.

September 18 Sixteen hours after Perry's feat, Ray Washburn of the Cards makes major league history by hurling a second consecutive no-hitter in one park. Run-scoring hits by Mike Shannon and Curt Flood down the Giants 2-0.

September 27 A 1-0 win and 11 strikeouts against the Astros enable Cardinal Bob Gibson to lower his ERA to 1.12, a new NL season mark. His phenomenal campaign includes 28 complete games, 268 strikeouts, and 13 shutouts.

October 2 For the first time, two soon-to-be-named MVPs oppose each other. St. Louis Bob Gibson records a World Series-record 17 strikeouts and a 4-0 win over Denny McLain. Detroit manager Mayo Smith moves Gold Glove center fielder Mickey Stanley to shortstop, improving his offense by opening a spot for Al Kaline.

October 14 In the NL expansion draft, the Expos choose 30 players, including Maury Wills, Jim Grant, Donn Clendenon, and Manny Mota. San Diego's 30 selections include Dave Giusti, Nate Colbert, Zoilo Versalles, Al McBean, and Clarence Gaston.

November 13 Bob Gibson edges Pete Rose to win the NL MVP award.

November 22 Reds catcher Johnny Bench is named NL Rookie of the Year, getting 10½ votes to edge out NY's Jerry Koosman who had 9½.

ATLANTA	CHICAGO	CINCINNATI	HOUSTON	LOS ANGELES
M L.Harris	M L.Durocher	M D.Bristol	M G.Hatton	M W.Alston
1B D.Johnson	1B E.Banks	1B L.May	M H.Walker	1B W.Parker
2B F.Millan	2B G.Beckert	2B T.Helms	1B R.Staub	2B P.Popovich
SS S.Jackson	SS D.Kessinger	SS L.Cardenas	2B D.Menke	SS Z.Versalles
3B C.Boyer	3B R.Santo	3B T.Perez	SS H.Torres	3B B.Bailey
LF M.Lum	LF B.Williams	LF A.Johnson	3B D.Rader	LF L.Gabrielson
CF F.Alou	CF A.Phillips	CF V.Pinson	LF J.Wynn	CF W.Davis
RF H.Aaron	RF J.Hickman	RF P.Rose	CF R.Davis	RF R.Fairly
C J.Torre	C R.Hundley	C J.Bench	RF N.Miller	C T.Haller
			C J.Bateman	
O1 T.Francona	O L.Johnson	O M.Jones		O J.Fairey
S3 M.Martinez			3O B.Aspromonte	23 J.Lefebvre
O1 T.Aaron	P F.Jenkins	P G.Culver	O L.Thomas	31 K.Boyer
C B.Tillman	P B.Hands	P J.Maloney		
	P K.Holtzman	P G.Arrigo	P D.Giusti	P B.Singer
P P.Niekro	P J.Niekro	P G.Nolan	P L.Dierker	P C.Osteen
P P.Jarvis	P R.Nye	RP T.Abernathy	P D.Lemaster	P D.Drysdale
P R.Reed	RP P.Regan	RP C.Carroll	P D.Wilson	P D.Sutton
P K.Johnson	RP J.Lamabe	RP B.Lee	P M.Cuellar	P M.Kekich
P M.Pappas			RP J.Buzhardt	RP M.Grant
RP C.Upshaw		P T.Cloninger	RP J.Ray	RP J.Brewer
RP J.Britton		P M.Pappas	RP T.Dukes	RP J.Billingham
RP C.Raymond		P J.Ritchie		
		P B.Kelso		P J.Purdin
		P B.McCool		
P D.Kelley				
P G.Stone				

NEW YORK	PHILADELPHIA	PITTSBURGH	SAN FRANCISCO	ST.LOUIS
M G.Hodges	M G.Mauch	M L.Shepard	M H.Franks	M R.Schoendienst
1B E.Kranepool	M G.Myatt	1B D.Clendenon	1B W.McCovey	1B O.Cepeda
2B P.Linz	M B.Skinner	2B B.Mazeroski	2B R.Hunt	2B J.Javier
SS B.Harrelson	1B B.White	SS G.Alley	SS H.Lanier	SS D.Maxvill
3B E.Charles	2B C.Rojas	3B M.Wills	3B J.Davenport	3B M.Shannon
LF C.Jones	SS R.Pena	LF W.Stargell	LF J.Alou	LF L.Brock
CF T.Agee	3B T.Taylor	CF M.Alou	CF W.Mays	CF C.Flood
RF R.Swoboda	LF D.Allen	RF R.Clemente	RF B.Bonds	RF R.Maris
C J.Grote	CF T.Gonzalez	C J.May	C D.Dietz	C T.McCarver
	RF J.Callison			
O1 A.Shamsky	C M.Ryan	O M.Mota	O1 T.Cline	O B.Tolan
2 K.Boswell		S F.Patek	3O J.Hart	C J.Edwards
S2 A.Weis	O1 J.Briggs		C1 J.Hiatt	
C1 J.Martin	O D.Lock	P B.Veale		
	C C.Dalrymple	P S.Blass	P J.Marichal	P B.Gibson
P T.Seaver		P A.McBean	P G.Perry	P N.Briles
P J.Koosman	P C.Short	P B.Moose	P R.Sadecki	P S.Carlton
P D.Cardwell	P L.Jackson	P J.Bunning	P M.McCormick	P R.Washburn
P D.Selma	P W.Fryman	RP R.Kline	P B.Bolin	P L.Jaster
P N.Ryan	P R.Wise	RP T.Sisk	RP F.Linzy	RP R.Willis
RP C.Koonce	P J.James	RP L.Walker		RP D.Hughes
RP R.Taylor	RP T.Farrell			RP M.Nelson
RP D.Frisella	RP G.Wagner			
	RP J.Boozer	P D.Ellis		
		P R.Face		
P A.Jackson				
P J.McAndrew	P J.Johnson			
	P G.Jackson			

TEAM	G	W	L	PCT	GB	R	OR	AB	H	2B	3B	HR	BB	SO	AVG	OBP	SLG	PRO	PRO+	BR	/A	PF	CHI	RC	SB	CS	SBA	SBR
STL	162	97	65	.599		583	472	5561	1383	227	**48**	73	378	897	.249	.300	.346	.646	102	2	9	99	104	581	110	45	**71**	**6**
SF	163	88	74	.543	9	599	529	5441	1301	162	33	108	**508**	904	.239	.310	.341	.651	103	20	21	100	103	577	50	37	57	-7
CHI	163	84	78	.519	13	612	611	5458	1319	203	43	**130**	415	854	.242	.300	.366	.666	100	36	-4	107	104	593	41	30	58	-6
CIN	163	83	79	.512	14	**690**	673	5767	**1573**	281	36	106	379	938	**.273**	**.322**	**.389**	**.711**	114	130	85	106	98	**688**	59	55	52	-15
ATL	163	81	81	.500	16	514	549	5552	1399	179	31	80	414	**782**	.252	.308	.339	.647	101	9	7	100	90	564	83	44	65	-2
PIT	163	80	82	.494	17	583	532	5569	1404	180	44	80	422	953	.252	.309	.343	.652	105	19	28	99	100	580	**130**	59	69	4
PHI	162	76	86	.469	21	543	615	5372	1253	178	30	100	462	1003	.233	.297	.333	.630	96	-24	-24	100	104	527	58	51	53	-13
LA	162	76	86	.469	21	470	509	5354	1234	202	36	67	439	980	.230	.291	.319	.610	97	-61	-25	92	97	501	57	43	57	-9
NY	163	73	89	.451	24	473	499	5503	1252	178	30	81	379	1203	.228	.283	.315	.598	86	-91	-93	101	102	486	72	45	62	-5
HOU	162	72	90	.444	25	510	588	5336	1233	205	28	66	479	988	.231	.300	.317	.617	94	-41	-31	98	100	505	44	51	46	-17
TOT	813					5577		54913	13351	1995	359	891	4275	9502	.243	.302	.341	.643							704	460	60	-65

TEAM	CG	SH	SV	IP	H	H/G	HR	BB	SO	RAT	ERA	ERA+	OAV	OOB	PR	/A	PF	CPI	FA	E	DP	FW	PW	BW	SBW	DIF
STL	63	**30**	32	1479¹	1282	7.8	82	375	971	10.3	**2.49**	116	.234	.286	**82**	67	97	105	.978	140	135	-.0	**7.7**	1.0	**1.4**	5.9
SF	**77**	20	16	1469	1302	8.0	86	**344**	942	**10.2**	2.71	109	.236	**.283**	45	38	99	96	.975	162	125	-1.3	4.4	2.4	-.0	1.6
CHI	46	12	32	1453²	1399	8.7	138	392	894	11.3	3.41	93	.254	.306	-69	-40	106	100	**.981**	119	149	**1.2**	-4.6	-.5	.0	6.8
CIN	24	16	**38**	1490¹	1399	8.4	114	573	963	12.2	3.56	89	.250	.324	-96	-66	106	100	.978	144	144	-.2	-7.6	**9.8**	-1.0	1.0
ATL	44	16	29	1474²	1326	8.1	87	362	871	10.5	2.92	103	.241	.292	11	13	100	96	.980	125	139	.9	1.5	.8	.5	-3.7
PIT	42	19	30	1487	1322	8.0	73	485	897	11.2	2.74	101	.240	.306	40	31	98	**107**	.979	139	162	.0	3.6	3.2	1.2	-9.0
PHI	42	12	27	1448¹	1416	8.8	91	421	935	11.7	3.36	89	.257	.315	-61	-57	101	100	.980	127	**163**	.7	-6.5	-2.8	-.7	4.3
LA	38	23	31	1448²	1293	8.0	**65**	414	994	10.8	2.69	103	.241	.300	48	12	93	104	.977	144	144	-.3	1.4	-2.9	-.3	-2.9
NY	45	25	32	1483¹	**1250**	**7.6**	87	430	1014	10.5	2.72	111	**.230**	.292	43	49	101	98	.979	133	142	.4	5.6	-10.7	.2	-3.5
HOU	50	12	23	1446²	1362	8.5	68	479	**1021**	11.7	3.26	91	.249	.313	-44	-49	99	96	.975	156	129	-1.0	-5.6	-3.6	-1.2	2.4
TOT	471	185	290	14681		8.2				11.0	2.99		.243	.302					.978	1389	1432					

Runs		Hits		Doubles		Triples		Home Runs		Total Bases	
Beckert-Chi	98	Rose-Cin	210	Brock-StL	46	Brock-StL	14	McCovey-SF	36	Williams-Chi	321
Rose-Cin	94	Alou-Atl	210	Rose-Cin	42	Clemente-Pit	12	Allen-Phi	33	H.Aaron-Atl	302
Perez-Cin	93	Beckert-Chi	189	Bench-Cin	40	Davis-LA	10	Banks-Chi	32	Rose-Cin	294
Brock-StL	92	A.Johnson-Cin	188	Staub-Hou	37	Allen-Phi	9	Williams-Chi	30	Alou-Atl	290
Williams-Chi	91	Flood-StL	186	Alou-Atl	37	Williams-Chi	8	H.Aaron-Atl	29	McCovey-SF	285

Runs Batted In		Runs Produced		Bases On Balls		Batting Average		On Base Percentage		Slugging Average	
McCovey-SF	105	Perez-Cin	167	Santo-Chi	96	Rose-Cin	.335	Rose-Cin	.394	McCovey-SF	.545
Williams-Chi	98	Williams-Chi	159	Wynn-Hou	90	Alou-Pit	.332	McCovey-SF	.383	Allen-Phi	.520
Santo-Chi	98	Santo-Chi	158	Hunt-SF	78	Alou-Atl	.317	Wynn-Hou	.378	Williams-Chi	.500
Perez-Cin	92	McCovey-SF	150	Allen-Phi	74	A.Johnson-Cin	.312	Mays-SF	.376	H.Aaron-Atl	.498
Allen-Phi	90	Allen-Phi	144	Staub-Hou	73	Flood-StL	.301	Staub-Hou	.376	Mays-SF	.488

Production		Adjusted Production		Batter Runs		Adjusted Batter Runs		Clutch Hitting Index		Runs Created	
McCovey-SF	.928	McCovey-SF	176	McCovey-SF	48.8	McCovey-SF	48.9	Hundley-Chi	134	Rose-Cin	113
Allen-Phi	.876	Allen-Phi	160	Rose-Cin	44.5	Wynn-Hou	40.4	Staub-Hou	123	McCovey-SF	110
Mays-SF	.864	Mays-SF	158	H.Aaron-Atl	39.0	H.Aaron-Atl	38.7	Clendenon-Pit	122	Williams-Chi	107
Rose-Cin	.863	Wynn-Hou	158	Wynn-Hou	38.4	Allen-Phi	38.0	Santo-Chi	117	H.Aaron-Atl	104
H.Aaron-Atl	.855	H.Aaron-Atl	154	Allen-Phi	38.0	Rose-Cin	37.8	Swoboda-NY	117	Alou-Atl	103

Total Average		Stolen Bases		Stolen Base Average		Stolen Base Runs		Fielding Runs		Total Player Rating	
McCovey-SF	.953	Brock-StL	62	H.Aaron-Atl	84.8	Brock-StL	11.4	Mazeroski-Pit	25.7	H.Aaron-Atl	5.5
Allen-Phi	.869	Wills-Pit	52	Brock-StL	83.8	H.Aaron-Atl	5.4	Alley-Pit	25.6	McCovey-SF	4.6
Mays-SF	.853	Davis-LA	36	Taylor-Phi	81.5	Davis-LA	4.8	Kessinger-Chi	17.9	Wynn-Hou	4.5
H.Aaron-Atl	.852	H.Aaron-Atl	28	Davis-LA	78.3	Taylor-Phi	3.6	Flood-StL	17.5	Santo-Chi	4.0
Wynn-Hou	.826	Jones-NY	23			Wills-Pit	3.0	Santo-Chi	17.3	Clemente-Pit	3.9

Wins		Win Percentage		Games		Complete Games		Shutouts		Saves	
Marichal-SF	26	Blass-Pit	.750	Abernathy-Cin	78	Marichal-SF	30	Gibson-StL	13	Regan-LA-Chi	25
Gibson-StL	22	Marichal-SF	.743	Regan-LA-Chi	73	Gibson-StL	28	Drysdale-LA	8	Carroll-Atl-Cin	17
Jenkins-Chi	20	Gibson-StL	.710	Carroll-Atl-Cin	68	Jenkins-Chi	20	Koosman-NY	7	Hoerner-StL	17
		Briles-StL	.633	Taylor-NY	58	Perry-SF	19	Blass-Pit	7	Brewer-LA	14
				Linzy-SF	57	Koosman-NY	17				

Innings Pitched		Fewest Hits/Game		Fewest BB/Game		Strikeouts		Strikeouts/Game		Ratio	
Marichal-SF	326.0	Gibson-StL	5.85	Hands-Chi	1.25	Gibson-StL	268	Singer-LA	7.97	Gibson-StL	7.89
Jenkins-Chi	308.0	Bolin-SF	6.52	Marichal-SF	1.27	Jenkins-Chi	260	Gibson-StL	7.92	Jarvis-Atl	8.93
Gibson-StL	304.2	Veale-Pit	6.86	Seaver-NY	1.56	Singer-LA	227	Maloney-Cin	7.87	Bolin-SF	9.07
Perry-SF	291.0	Jarvis-Atl	7.10	Pappas-Cin-Atl	1.57	Marichal-SF	218	Jenkins-Chi	7.60	Seaver-NY	9.08
Seaver-NY	277.2	Moose-Pit	7.14	Niekro-Atl	1.58	Sadecki-SF	206	Wilson-Hou	7.55	Hands-Chi	9.15

Earned Run Average		Adjusted ERA		Opponents' Batting Avg.		Opponents' On Base Pct.		Starter Runs		Adjusted Starter Runs	
Gibson-StL	1.12	Gibson-StL	258	Gibson-StL	.184	Gibson-StL	.233	Gibson-StL	63.1	Gibson-StL	60.0
Bolin-SF	1.99	Bolin-SF	148	Bolin-SF	.200	Jarvis-Atl	.255	Koosman-NY	26.5	Koosman-NY	27.5
Veale-Pit	2.05	Koosman-NY	145	Veale-Pit	.211	Bolin-SF	.258	Veale-Pit	25.4	Seaver-NY	25.2
Koosman-NY	2.08	Veale-Pit	142	Jarvis-Atl	.214	Seaver-NY	.262	Seaver-NY	24.1	Veale-Pit	23.8
Blass-Pit	2.12	Blass-Pit	138	Moose-Pit	.218	Hands-Chi	.264	Drysdale-LA	22.3	Blass-Pit	19.6

Clutch Pitching Index		Relief Runs		Adjusted Relief Runs		Relief Ranking		Total Pitcher Index		Total Baseball Ranking	
Blass-Pit	125	Kline-Pit	16.4	Kline-Pit	15.6	Kline-Pit	23.4	Gibson-StL	7.3	Gibson-StL	7.3
Briles-StL	124	Regan-LA-Chi	10.7	Regan-LA-Chi	13.0	Regan-LA-Chi	20.1	Seaver-NY	3.1	H.Aaron-Atl	5.5
Koosman-NY	123	Linzy-SF	9.4	Abernathy-Cin	10.3	Linzy-SF	17.0	Koosman-NY	3.0	McCovey-SF	4.6
Lemaster-Hou	122	Grant-LA	9.4	Linzy-SF	9.0	Abernathy-Cin	13.9	Marichal-SF	2.7	Wynn-Hou	4.5
Drysdale-LA	117	Abernathy-Cin	7.7	Carroll-Atl-Cin	7.2	Upshaw-Atl	9.6	Kline-Pit	2.4	Santo-Chi	4.0

March 21 Royals is chosen as the name of the new Kansas City AL franchise.

March 31 The name for Seattle's AL club is the Pilots.

May 9 Oakland's Jim "Catfish" Hunter pitches a perfect game against the Twins, winning 3-0. The 22-year-old right-hander hurls the first AL regular season perfecto in 46 years. He strikes out 11 and drives in all three A's runs.

May 15 The first AL game played in Milwaukee since 1901 is a 4-2 California win against Chicago before 23,403 fans. This is the first of nine games the White Sox will play in Milwaukee in 1968.

May 18 Frank Howard ties the AL record with a home run in his sixth consecutive game to lead Washington to an 8-4 win over Detroit. For Detroit, Al Kaline belts a pinch home run off Steve Jones. For Kaline, it is his 307th home run, surpassing Hank Greenberg's 306 in a Tiger uniform.

July 3 Luis Tiant registers 19 strikeouts in 10 innings, as Cleveland beats Minnesota 1-0.

July 24 Hoyt Wilhelm's 907th game breaks Cy Young's record for major league pitching appearances, but he loses a 2-1 decision to Oakland.

September 14 Denny McLain becomes the first 30-game winner since Dizzy Dean in 1934, as the Tigers beat the A's 5-4. Denny gives up six hits and strikes out 10.

September 17 Detroit clinches the AL pennant with a 2-1 win over the Yankees.

September 19 Denny McLain's 31st win is overshadowed by Mickey Mantle's 535th home run. McLain says he purposely fed a belt-high fastball to the aging slugger. The home run gives Mantle undisputed hold of third place on the all-time home run list.

September 22 Cesar Tovar becomes the second player to play every position in a game. Minnesota's all-purpose star leads the Twins to a 2-1 win over the Oakland A's. Bert Campaneris of the Kansas City A's was the first to pull off this stunt in 1965.

September 29 Carl Yastrzemski maintains a .3005 BA, to win his second straight batting crown with the lowest championship average ever. Yaz is the AL's only .300 hitter: Oakland's Danny Cater is second with .290.

September 29 White Sox relief pitcher Wilbur Wood ends his season with a 7-6 win at California and a major league record 88 appearances.

October 9 Denny McLain returns to form, scattering nine singles, as Detroit evens the World Series with a 10-run third inning and 13-1 win at St. Louis.

October 10 Mickey Lolich bests Bob Gibson and brings Detroit its first World Series championship since 1945. The hefty lefty hurls a five-hitter, giving Detroit a 4-1 win.

October 15 Roger Nelson is the initial choice of the Royals in the AL expansion draft. Don Mincher is the Pilots' first choice. Other Seattle selections include Tommy Harper, Tommy Davis, Gary Bell, and Lou Piniella. Kansas City chooses Wally Bunker, Moe Drabowsky, Hoyt Wilhelm, and Joe Foy.

November 1 Denny McLain is the unanimous AL winner of the Cy Young Award.

November 5 Denny McLain is the unanimous choice as AL MVP.

November 19 Yankees pitcher Stan Bahnsen, who was 17-12, is named AL Rookie of the Year.

BALTIMORE

M	H.Bauer
M	E.Weaver
1B	B.Powell
2B	D.Johnson
SS	M.Belanger
3B	B.Robinson
LF	C.Blefary
CF	P.Blair
RF	F.Robinson
C	A.Etchebarren
O2	D.Buford
O	C.Motton
P	D.McNally
P	J.Hardin
P	T.Phoebus
P	D.Leonhard
P	G.Brabender
RP	E.Watt
RP	P.Richert
RP	M.Drabowsky
P	W.Bunker
P	R.Nelson

BOSTON

M	D.Williams
1B	G.Scott
2B	M.Andrews
SS	R.Petrocelli
3B	J.Foy
LF	C.Yastrzemski
CF	R.Smith
RF	K.Harrelson
C	R.Gibson
12	D.Jones
S2	J.Adair
C	E.Howard
P	R.Culp
P	G.Bell
P	D.Ellsworth
P	J.Santiago
P	J.Lonborg
RP	L.Stange
RP	S.Lyle
RP	B.Landis
P	J.Pizarro
P	G.Waslewski
P	J.Stephenson
P	D.Morehead

CALIFORNIA

M	B.Rigney
1B	D.Mincher
2B	B.Knoop
SS	J.Fregosi
3B	A.Rodriguez
LF	R.Reichardt
CF	V.Davalillo
RF	R.Repoz
C	B.Rodgers
1O	C.Hinton
C2	T.Satriano
3	P.Schaal
P	G.Brunet
P	J.McGlothlin
P	S.Ellis
P	C.Wright
P	T.Murphy
RP	M.Pattin
RP	A.Messersmith
RP	T.Burgmeier
P	R.Clark
P	M.Rojas

CHICAGO

M	E.Stanky
M	L.Moss
M	A.Lopez
M	L.Moss
M	A.Lopez
1B	T.McCraw
2B	S.Alomar
SS	L.Aparicio
3B	P.Ward
LF	T.Davis
CF	K.Berry
RF	B.Bradford
C	D.Josephson
P	J.Horlen
P	J.Fisher
P	T.John
P	G.Peters
P	C.Carlos
RP	W.Wood
RP	H.Wilhelm
RP	B.Locker
P	B.Priddy

CLEVELAND

M	A.Dark
1B	T.Horton
2B	V.Fuller
SS	L.Brown
3B	M.Alvis
LF	L.Maye
CF	J.Cardenal
RF	T.Harper
C	J.Azcue
23	C.Salmon
C1	D.Sims
O	R.Snyder
O	L.Johnson
P	S.McDowell
P	L.Tiant
P	S.Siebert
P	S.Williams
P	S.Hargan
RP	E.Fisher
RP	M.Paul
RP	V.Romo

DETROIT

M	M.Smith
1B	N.Cash
2B	D.McAuliffe
SS	R.Oyler
3B	D.Wert
LF	W.Horton
CF	M.Stanley
RF	J.Northrup
C	B.Freehan
O1	A.Kaline
S2	T.Matchick
S3	D.Tracewski
P	D.McLain
P	E.Wilson
P	M.Lolich
P	J.Sparma
P	J.Hiller
RP	P.Dobson
RP	D.Patterson

MINNESOTA

M	C.Ermer
1B	R.Reese
2B	R.Carew
SS	J.Hernandez
3B	C.Tovar
LF	B.Allison
CF	T.Uhlaender
RF	T.Oliva
C	J.Roseboro
3S	R.Clark
13	H.Killebrew
23	R.Rollins
3	
P	D.Chance
P	J.Merritt
P	J.Kaat
P	D.Boswell
P	J.Perry
RP	R.Perranoski
RP	A.Worthington
RP	B.Miller
P	J.Roland

NEW YORK

M	R.Houk
1B	M.Mantle
2B	H.Clarke
SS	T.Tresh
3B	B.Cox
LF	R.White
CF	B.Robinson
RF	A.Kosco
C	J.Gibbs
O1	J.Pepitone
P	M.Stottlemyre
P	S.Bahnsen
P	F.Peterson
P	S.Barber
P	F.Talbot
RP	J.Verbanic
RP	D.Womack
RP	L.McDaniel
P	B.Monbouquette
P	A.Downing
P	S.Hamilton

OAKLAND

M	B.Kennedy
1B	D.Cater
2B	J.Donaldson
SS	B.Campaneris
3B	S.Bando
LF	M.Hershberger
CF	R.Monday
RF	R.Jackson
C	D.Duncan
2	D.Green
P	C.Hunter
P	B.Odom
P	J.Nash
P	C.Dobson
P	L.Krausse
RP	D.Segui
RP	J.Aker
RP	E.Sprague
P	P.Lindblad

WASHINGTON

M	J.Lemon
1B	M.Epstein
2B	B.Allen
SS	R.Hansen
3B	K.McMullen
LF	F.Howard
CF	D.Unser
RF	E.Stroud
C	P.Casanova
O	C.Peterson
P	J.Coleman
P	C.Pascual
P	J.Hannan
P	D.Bosman
P	F.Bertaina
RP	D.Higgins
RP	B.Humphreys
P	B.Moore
P	P.Ortega

TEAM	G	W	L	PCT	GB	R	OR	AB	H	2B	3B	HR	BB	SO	AVG	OBP	SLG	PRO	PRO+	BR	/A	PF	CHI	RC	SB	CS	SBA	SBR
DET	164	103	59	.636		**671**	492	5490	1292	190	39	**185**	521	964	.235	.309	**.385**	**.694**	114	**102**	82	103	100	646	26	32	45	-11
BAL	162	91	71	.562	12	579	497	5275	1187	**215**	28	133	570	1019	.225	.306	.352	.658	106	41	40	100	97	585	78	32	**71**	4
CLE	162	86	75	.534	16.5	516	504	5416	1266	210	36	75	427	858	.234	.294	.327	.621	96	-34	-26	99	100	525	115	61	65	-2
BOS	162	86	76	.531	17	614	611	5303	1253	207	17	125	582	974	**.236**	.316	.318	**.668**	102	62	21	107	99	590	76	62	55	-14
NY	164	83	79	.512	20	536	531	5310	1137	154	34	109	566	958	.214	.293	.318	.611	95	-46	-30	97	**106**	507	90	50	64	-3
OAK	163	82	80	.506	21	569	544	5406	**1300**	192	40	94	472	1022	**.240**	.306	.343	.649	108	19	47	95	99	580	**147**	61	**71**	**8**
MIN	162	79	83	.488	24	562	546	5373	1274	207	**41**	105	445	966	.237	.301	.350	.651	99	20	-8	105	99	564	98	54	64	-3
CAL	162	67	95	.414	36	498	615	5331	1209	170	33	83	447	1080	.227	.293	.318	.611	90	-51	-33	96	100	498	62	50	55	-11
CHI	162	67	95	.414	36	463	527	5405	1233	169	33	71	397	**840**	.228	.286	.311	.597	86	-82	-87	101	99	480	90	50	64	-3
WAS	161	65	96	.404	37.5	524	665	5400	1208	160	37	124	454	960	.224	.289	.336	.625	99	-31	-14	97	101	518	29	19	60	-3
TOT	812					5532		53709	12359	1874	338	1104	4881	9641	.230	.299	.339	.639							811	471	63	-39

TEAM	CG	SH	SV	IP	H	H/G	HR	BB	SO	RAT	ERA	ERA+	OAV	OOB	PR	/A	PF	CPI	FA	E	DP	FW	PW	BW	SBW	DIF
DET	**59**	19	29	1489²	1180	7.1	129	486	1115	10.3	2.71	111	.217	**.285**	44	**49**	101	100	**.983**	105	133	2.0	5.6	9.4	-.8	5.8
BAL	53	16	31	1451¹	1111	6.9	101	502	1044	10.3	2.66	110	.212	.287	51	43	98	96	.981	120	131	1.0	4.9	4.6	.9	-1.5
CLE	48	**23**	32	1464¹	**1087**	**6.7**	98	540	**1157**	10.3	2.66	111	**.206**	.286	53	49	99	93	.979	127	130	.6	**5.6**	-3.0	.2	2.0
BOS	55	17	31	1447	1303	8.1	115	523	972	11.7	3.33	95	.241	.313	-57	-28	106	100	.979	128	147	.6	-3.2	2.4	-1.2	6.4
NY	45	14	27	1467¹	1308	8.0	99	424	831	10.8	2.79	104	.240	.298	31	18	97	100	.979	139	142	.0	2.1	-3.4	.1	3.3
OAK	45	18	29	1455²	1220	7.5	124	505	997	10.9	2.94	96	.227	.297	6	-20	95	101	.977	145	136	-.4	-2.3	5.4	**1.4**	-3.1
MIN	46	14	29	1433¹	1224	7.7	**92**	**414**	996	10.5	2.89	107	.229	.290	13	31	104	94	.977	170	117	-2.0	3.6	-.9	.1	-2.8
CAL	29	11	31	1437	1234	7.7	131	519	869	11.2	3.43	85	.233	.306	-72	-83	98	94	.977	140	**156**	-.2	-9.5	-3.8	-.8	.3
CHI	20	11	**40**	1468	1290	7.9	97	451	834	11.1	2.75	110	.236	.303	38	46	102	**110**	.977	151	152	-.8	5.3	-10.0	.1	-8.6
WAS	26	11	28	1439²	1402	8.8	118	517	826	12.3	3.64	80	.258	.327	-106	-116	98	104	.976	148	144	-.7	-13.3	-1.6	.1	.0
TOT	426	154	307	14553¹		7.6				10.9	2.98		.230	.299					.978	1373	1388					

Runs		Hits		Doubles		Triples		Home Runs		Total Bases	
McAuliffe-Det	95	Campaneris-Oak	177	Smith-Bos	37	Fregosi-Cal	13	F.Howard-Was	44	F.Howard-Was	330
Yastrzemski-Bos	90	Tovar-Min	167	B.Robinson-Bal	36	McCraw-Chi	12	Horton-Det	36	Horton-Det	278
White-NY	89	F.Howard-Was	164	Yastrzemski-Bos	32	Stroud-Was	10	Harrelson-Bos	35	Harrelson-Bos	277
Tovar-Min	89	Aparicio-Chi	164	Tovar-Min	31	McAuliffe-Det	10	Jackson-Oak	29	Yastrzemski-Bos	267
Stanley-Det	88	Yastrzemski-Bos	162			Campaneris-Oak	9			Northrup-Det	259

Runs Batted In		Runs Produced		Bases On Balls		Batting Average		On Base Percentage		Slugging Average	
Harrelson-Bos	109	Harrelson-Bos	153	Yastrzemski-Bos	119	Yastrzemski-Bos	.301	Yastrzemski-Bos	.429	F.Howard-Was	.552
F.Howard-Was	106	Northrup-Det	145	Mantle-NY	106	Cater-Oak	.290	F.Robinson-Bal	.391	Horton-Det	.543
Northrup-Det	90	Yastrzemski-Bos	141	Foy-Bos	84	Oliva-Min	.289	Mantle-NY	.387	Harrelson-Bos	.518
Powell-Bal	85	F.Howard-Was	141	McAuliffe-Det	82	Horton-Det	.285	Monday-Oak	.373	Yastrzemski-Bos	.495
Horton-Det	85	Stanley-Det	137	Andrews-Bos	81	Uhlaender-Min	.283	Andrews-Bos	.369	Oliva-Min	.477

Production		Adjusted Production		Batter Runs		Adjusted Batter Runs		Clutch Hitting Index		Runs Created	
Yastrzemski-Bos	.924	F.Howard-Was	172	Yastrzemski-Bos	57.5	Yastrzemski-Bos	49.9	Foy-Bos	118	Yastrzemski-Bos	121
Horton-Det	.900	Yastrzemski-Bos	168	F.Howard-Was	45.1	F.Howard-Was	48.5	Cater-Oak	116	F.Howard-Was	110
F.Howard-Was	.892	Horton-Det	165	Horton-Det	41.1	Horton-Det	38.3	Powell-Bal	113	Horton-Det	95
Harrelson-Bos	.877	Harrelson-Bos	153	Harrelson-Bos	40.2	Harrelson-Bos	34.0	Tresh-NY	111	Harrelson-Bos	94
Oliva-Min	.837	F.Robinson-Bal	153	Freehan-Det	32.7	Freehan-Det	30.0	Harrelson-Bos	111	Freehan-Det	94

Total Average		Stolen Bases		Stolen Base Average		Stolen Base Runs		Fielding Runs		Total Player Rating	
Yastrzemski-Bos	1.000	Campaneris-Oak	62	McCraw-Chi	80.0	Campaneris-Oak	5.4	Clarke-NY	29.5	Yastrzemski-Bos	6.6
F.Howard-Was	.872	Cardenal-Cle	40	Nelson-Cle	76.7	McCraw-Chi	3.0	Aparicio-Chi	24.7	Freehan-Det	4.8
Horton-Det	.867	Tovar-Min	35	Foy-Bos	76.5	Foy-Bos	3.0	Unser-Was	18.8	F.Howard-Was	4.6
F.Robinson-Bal	.865	Buford-Bal	33	Clarke-NY	74.1	Tovar-Min	2.7	Yastrzemski-Bos	17.3	Campaneris-Oak	3.8
Harrelson-Bos	.835	Foy-Bos	26	Campaneris-Oak	73.8	Nelson-Cle	2.7	B.Robinson-Bal	16.6	Aparicio-Chi	3.7

Wins		Win Percentage		Games		Complete Games		Shutouts		Saves	
McLain-Det	31	McLain-Det	.838	Wood-Chi	88	McLain-Det	28	Tiant-Cle	9	Worthington-Min	18
McNally-Bal	22	Culp-Bos	.727	Wilhelm-Chi	72	Tiant-Cle	19			Wood-Chi	16
Tiant-Cle	21	Tiant-Cle	.700	Locker-Chi	70	Stottlemyre-NY	19			Higgins-Was	13
Stottlemyre-NY	21	Ellsworth-Bos	.696	Perranoski-Min	66	McNally-Bal	18				
Hardin-Bal	18	McNally-Bal	.688			Hardin-Bal	16				

Innings Pitched		Fewest Hits/Game		Fewest BB/Game		Strikeouts		Strikeouts/Game		Ratio	
McLain-Det	336.0	Tiant-Cle	5.30	Peterson-NY	1.23	McDowell-Cle	283	McDowell-Cle	9.47	McNally-Bal	7.91
Chance-Min	292.0	McNally-Bal	5.77	McLain-Det	1.69	McLain-Det	280	Tiant-Cle	9.20	Tiant-Cle	7.98
Stottlemyre-NY	278.2	McDowell-Cle	6.06	Ellsworth-Bos	1.70	Tiant-Cle	264	Lolich-Det	8.06	McLain-Det	8.30
McNally-Bal	273.0	Siebert-Cle	6.33	Kaat-Min	1.73	Chance-Min	234	Culp-Bos	7.90	Chance-Min	9.15
McDowell-Cle	269.0	McLain-Det	6.46	McNally-Bal	1.81	McNally-Bal	202	McLain-Det	7.50	Peterson-NY	9.32

Earned Run Average		Adjusted ERA		Opponents' Batting Avg.		Opponents' On Base Pct.		Starter Runs		Adjusted Starter Runs	
Tiant-Cle	1.60	Tiant-Cle	185	Tiant-Cle	.168	Tiant-Cle	.233	Tiant-Cle	39.5	McLain-Det	39.3
McDowell-Cle	1.81	McDowell-Cle	164	McNally-Bal	.182	McNally-Bal	.234	McLain-Det	38.2	Tiant-Cle	38.9
McNally-Bal	1.95	McLain-Det	154	McDowell-Cle	.189	McLain-Det	.243	McDowell-Cle	35.0	McDowell-Cle	34.4
McLain-Det	1.96	John-Chi	153	Siebert-Cle	.198	Chance-Min	.261	McNally-Bal	31.4	McNally-Bal	29.7
John-Chi	1.98	McNally-Bal	150	McLain-Det	.200	Nash-Oak	.270	Bahnsen-NY	27.5	Bahnsen-NY	25.2

Clutch Pitching Index		Relief Runs		Adjusted Relief Runs		Relief Ranking		Total Pitcher Index		Total Baseball Ranking	
Horlen-Chi	133	Wood-Chi	19.6	Wood-Chi	20.5	Wood-Chi	33.6	McLain-Det	4.9	Yastrzemski-Bos	6.6
John-Chi	119	Wilhelm-Chi	13.0	Wilhelm-Chi	13.5	Romo-Cle	14.7	Tiant-Cle	4.2	McLain-Det	4.9
Fisher-Chi	116	Romo-Cle	12.6	Romo-Cle	12.4	Wilhelm-Chi	14.3	McDowell-Cle	4.0	Freehan-Det	4.8
McDowell-Cle	113	McMahon-Chi-Det	9.0	McMahon-Chi-Det	9.4	Drabowsky-Bal	9.9	McNally-Bal	3.9	F.Howard-Was	4.6
Bahnsen-NY	111	Drabowsky-Bal	7.3	Locker-Chi	7.4	Locker-Chi	8.5	Wood-Chi	3.9	Tiant-Cle	4.2

January 21 Stan Musial and Roy Campanella are voted into the Hall of Fame by BBWAA members.

February 2 Stan Coveleski and Waite Hoyt are voted into the Hall of Fame by the Veterans Committee.

February 4 Attorney Bowie Kuhn is a compromise choice for commissioner and is elected on a temporary basis.

June 29 On Billy Williams Day in Chicago, the Cubs outfielder passes Stan Musial's NL record for consecutive games played (896).

July 9 With one out in the ninth, Chicago's Jimmy Qualls bloops a single to left-center field, the only blemish on Tom Seaver's 4-0 near-perfect win before a record crowd (59,083) at Shea Stadium.

July 23 Willie McCovey hits two homers as the NL beats the AL 9-3 for its seventh straight All-Star Game win. Mel Stottlemyre starts for the AL when Denny McLain is late arriving from a dental appointment.

August 11 Don Drysdale retires because of damage to his right shoulder. Drysdale is the last Brooklyn Dodger active with the Los Angeles Dodgers.

August 13 Commissioner Bowie Kuhn is elected for a seven-year term.

September 13 Bobby Bonds becomes the fourth 30-homer, 30-steal player in major league history. His 32nd steal, on August 13, erased Willie Mays's SF record of 31.

September 15 Steve Carlton of the Cardinals fans a major league-record 19 batters and still loses. Ron Swoboda hits a pair of two-run home runs, and New York beats St. Louis 4-3.

September 22 Willie Mays joins Babe Ruth in the 600-homer club, while batting for rookie George Foster. Bobby Bonds sets a major league record with his 176th strikeout, as SF beats SD 4-2.

October 6 New York rallies twice and wins the first NLCS. Tommie Agee, Ken Boswell, and Wayne Garrett hit homers in a 7-4 win.

October 15 A memorable World Series game pits Tom Seaver against Mike Cuellar. Right fielder Ron Swoboda's dive at Brooks Robinson's sinking liner

with runners at first base and third in the ninth results in a brilliant catch, even though Frank Robinson tags and scores the tying run. In the 10th pinch-hitter J. C. Martin, running illegally inside the first base line, is hit on the wrist by pitcher Pete Richert's errant throw, enabling pinch-runner Rod Gaspar to score from second as the Mets win 2-1.

October 16 In Game 5 Cleon Jones, awarded first base when shoe polish on the ball proves he was hit by a pitch, scores on Donn Clendenon's home run. Al Weis's home run an inning later ties the game. Ron Swoboda's double and two Baltimore errors in the eighth give New York a 5-3 win and the Series. Jerry Koosman completes the Mets achievement with a five-hitter.

October 29 Tom Seaver is voted the NL Cy Young Award.

November 20 SF's Willie McCovey edges Tom Seaver as NL MVP.

November 28 Second baseman Ted Sizemore becomes the seventh Dodger to win NL Rookie honors.

	ATLANTA		CHICAGO		CINCINNATI		HOUSTON		LOS ANGELES		MONTREAL
M	L.Harris	M	L.Durocher	M	D.Bristol	M	H.Walker	M	W.Alston	M	G.Mauch
1B	O.Cepeda	1B	E.Banks	1B	L.May	1B	C.Blefary	1B	W.Parker	1B	B.Bailey
2B	F.Millan	2B	G.Beckert	2B	T.Helms	2B	J.Morgan	2B	T.Sizemore	2B	G.Sutherland
SS	S.Jackson	SS	D.Kessinger	SS	W.Woodward	SS	D.Menke	SS	M.Wills	SS	B.Wine
3B	C.Boyer	3B	R.Santo	3B	T.Perez	3B	D.Rader	3B	B.Sudakis	3B	C.Laboy
LF	T.Gonzalez	LF	B.Williams	LF	A.Johnson	LF	J.Alou	LF	W.Crawford	LF	M.Jones
CF	F.Alou	CF	D.Young	CF	B.Tolan	CF	J.Wynn	CF	W.Davis	CF	A.Phillips
RF	H.Aaron	RF	J.Hickman	RF	P.Rose	RF	N.Miller	RF	A.Kosco	RF	R.Staub
C	B.Didier	C	R.Hundley	C	J.Bench	C	J.Edwards	C	T.Haller	C	R.Brand
O	R.Carty	O1	W.Smith	O2	J.Stewart	P	L.Dierker	O	B.Russell	O1	T.Cline
O	M.Lum	O	A.Spangler	S	D.Chaney	P	D.Lemaster	O	M.Mota	1O	R.Fairly
S	G.Garrido					P	D.Wilson	32	J.Lefebvre	C	J.Bateman
		P	F.Jenkins	P	J.Merritt	P	T.Griffin				
P	P.Niekro	P	B.Hands	P	T.Cloninger	RP	J.Ray	P	C.Osteen	P	B.Stoneman
P	R.Reed	P	K.Holtzman	P	J.Maloney	RP	J.Billingham	P	B.Singer	P	J.Robertson
P	P.Jarvis	P	D.Selma	P	J.Fisher	RP	F.Gladding	P	D.Sutton	P	M.Wegener
P	G.Stone	RP	P.Regan	P	G.Nolan			P	A.Foster	P	G.Waslewski
P	M.Pappas	RP	T.Abernathy	RC	C.Carroll	P	W.Blasingame	RP	J.Brewer	P	H.Reed
RP	C.Upshaw	RP	R.Nye	RP	W.Granger	P	D.Womack	RP	P.Mikkelsen	RP	D.McGinn
RP	G.Neibauer			RP	P.Ramos			RP	J.Moeller	RP	D.Shaw
RP	C.Raymond									RP	R.Face
				P	G.Culver			P	D.Drysdale		
P	J.Britton			P	G.Arrigo			/P	J.Bunning	P	S.Renko
										P	L.Jaster
										P	M.Grant

	NEW YORK		PHILADELPHIA		PITTSBURGH		SAN DIEGO		SAN FRANCISCO		ST.LOUIS
M	G.Hodges	M	B.Skinner	M	L.Shepard	M	P.Gomez	M	C.King	M	R.Schoendienst
1B	E.Kranepool	M	G.Myatt	1B	A.Oliver	1B	N.Colbert	1B	W.McCovey	1B	J.Torre
2B	K.Boswell	1B	D.Allen	2B	B.Mazeroski	2B	J.Arcia	2B	R.Hunt	2B	J.Javier
SS	B.Harrelson	2B	C.Rojas	SS	F.Patek	SS	T.Dean	SS	H.Lanier	SS	D.Maxvill
3B	W.Garrett	SS	D.Money	3B	R.Hebner	3B	E.Spiezio	3B	J.Davenport	3B	M.Shannon
LF	C.Jones	3B	T.Taylor	LF	W.Stargell	LF	A.Ferrara	LF	K.Henderson	LF	L.Brock
CF	T.Agee	LF	J.Briggs	CF	M.Alou	CF	C.Gaston	CF	W.Mays	CF	C.Flood
RF	R.Swoboda	CF	L.Hisle	RF	R.Clemente	RF	O.Brown	RF	B.Bonds	RF	V.Pinson
C	J.Grote	RF	J.Callison	C	M.Sanguillen	C	C.Cannizzaro	C	D.Dietz	C	T.McCarver
		C	M.Ryan								
O	R.Gaspar					O	I.Murrell	1O	B.Burda	P	B.Gibson
O	A.Shamsky	O3	D.Johnson	3O	J.Pagan	S2	R.Pena	O	D.Marshall	P	S.Carlton
S2	A.Weis	31	R.Joseph	O1	C.Taylor	2	J.Sipin	23	D.Mason	P	N.Briles
32	B.Pfeil	O	R.Stone	2S	G.Alley	32	V.Kelly	O	J.Hart	P	R.Washburn
1	D.Clendenon	S2	T.Harmon							P	C.Taylor
				P	B.Veale	P	C.Kirby	P	G.Perry	RP	M.Grant
P	T.Seaver	P	G.Jackson	P	D.Ellis	P	J.Niekro	P	J.Marichal	RP	J.Hoerner
P	J.Koosman	P	W.Fryman	P	S.Blass	P	A.Santorini	P	M.McCormick		
P	G.Gentry	P	R.Wise	P	B.Moose	P	D.Kelley	P	B.Bolin	P	M.Torrez
P	D.Cardwell	P	J.Johnson	P	J.Bunning	RP	T.Sisk	P	R.Sadecki	P	D.Giusti
P	J.McAndrew	P	B.Champion	RP	C.Hartenstein	RP	G.Ross	RP	F.Linzy		
RP	T.McGraw	RP	J.Boozer	RP	B.Dal Canton	RP	F.Reberger	RP	R.Herbel		
RP	C.Koonce	RP	T.Farrell	RP	J.Gibbon						
RP	R.Taylor	RP	A.Raffo			P	J.Baldschun	P	R.Bryant		
				P	L.Walker	P	J.Podres				
P	N.Ryan	P	L.Palmer			P	B.McCool				
P	J.DiLauro	P	B.Wilson								

TEAM	G	W	L	PCT	GB	R	OR	AB	H	2B	3B	HR	BB	SO	AVG	OBP	SLG	PRO	PRO+	BR	/A	PF	CHI	RC	SB	CS	SBA	SBR
EAST
NY	162	100	62	.617		632	541	5427	1311	184	41	109	527	1089	.242	.313	.351	.664	91	-52	-65	102	**105**	601	66	43	61	-6
CHI	163	92	70	.568	8	720	611	5530	1400	215	40	142	559	928	.253	.326	.384	.710	94	37	-53	113	102	693	30	32	48	-10
PIT	162	88	74	.543	12	725	652	5626	1557	220	**52**	119	454	944	**.277**	.336	.398	.734	115	84	**100**	98	97	742	74	34	**69**	**2**
STL	162	87	75	.537	13	595	**540**	5536	1403	**228**	44	90	503	876	.253	.318	.359	.677	96	-25	-27	100	94	632	87	49	64	-3
PHI	162	63	99	.389	37	645	745	5408	1304	227	35	137	549	1130	.241	.314	.372	.686	102	-12	5	97	101	629	73	49	60	-8
MON	162	52	110	.321	48	582	791	5419	1300	202	33	125	529	962	.240	.312	.359	.671	94	-40	-42	100	100	596	52	52	50	-16
WEST
ATL	162	93	69	.574		691	631	5460	1411	195	22	141	485	**665**	.258	.323	.380	.703	104	20	18	100	103	655	59	48	55	-11
SF	162	90	72	.556	3	713	636	5474	1389	217	28	136	711	1054	.254	.326	.361	.697	104	32	45	98	100	690	71	32	**69**	**2**
CIN	163	89	73	.549	4	**798**	768	5634	**1558**	224	42	**171**	474	1042	**.277**	**.338**	**.422**	**.760**	114	**133**	92	105	99	**791**	79	56	59	-10
LA	162	85	77	.525	8	645	561	5532	1405	185	**52**	97	484	823	.254	.316	.359	.675	103	-31	13	93	103	626	80	51	61	-7
HOU	162	81	81	.500	12	676	668	5348	1284	208	40	104	699	972	.240	.332	.352	.684	101	7	20	98	101	649	**101**	58	64	-5
SD	162	52	110	.321	41	468	746	5357	1203	180	42	99	423	1143	.225	.286	.329	.615	81	-153	-134	96	98	491	45	44	51	-13
TOT	973					7890		65751	16461	2455	471	1470	6397	11628	.250	.321	.369	.690							817	548	60	-84

TEAM	CG	SH	SV	IP	H	H/G	HR	BB	SO	RAT	ERA	ERA+	OAV	OOB	PR	/A	PF	CPI	FA	E	DP	FW	PW	BW	SBW	DIF
EAST
NY	51	**28**	35	1468¹	1217	7.5	119	517	1012	**10.8**	2.99	122	**.227**	.298	99	109	102	99	.980	122	146	1.4	11.4	-6.8	.1	12.9
CHI	58	22	27	1454¹	1366	8.5	118	475	1017	11.6	3.34	120	.248	.311	41	**110**	112	101	.979	136	149	.6	**11.5**	-5.6	-.3	4.7
PIT	39	9	33	1445²	1348	8.4	**96**	553	1124	12.1	3.61	97	.248	.322	-3	-20	97	95	.975	155	169	-.5	-2.1	**10.5**	**.9**	-1.9
STL	63	12	26	1460¹	1289	7.9	99	511	1004	11.3	**2.94**	121	.237	.307	**106**	102	99	**105**	.978	138	144	.5	10.7	-2.8	.4	-2.8
PHI	47	14	21	1434	1494	9.4	134	570	921	13.2	4.14	86	.270	.342	-88	-96	99	102	.978	137	157	.5	-10.1	.5	-.1	-8.9
MON	26	8	21	1426	1429	9.0	145	702	973	13.8	4.33	85	.258	.353	-117	-104	102	102	.971	184	179	-2.1	-10.9	-4.4	-.9	-10.6
WEST
ATL	38	7	42	1445	1334	8.3	144	438	893	11.2	3.53	102	.245	.304	11	13	100	95	**.981**	**115**	114	**1.8**	1.4	1.9	-.4	7.4
SF	**71**	15	17	1473²	1381	8.4	120	461	906	11.5	3.26	108	.248	.309	55	40	97	102	.974	169	155	-1.3	4.2	4.7	**.9**	.4
CIN	23	11	**44**	1465	1478	9.1	149	611	818	13.0	4.11	92	.262	.340	-84	-57	105	104	.974	167	158	-1.1	-6.0	9.7	-.3	5.8
LA	47	20	31	1457	1324	8.2	122	**420**	975	11.0	3.08	108	.242	.301	83	39	93	102	.980	126	130	1.2	4.1	1.4	.0	-2.6
HOU	52	11	34	1435²	1347	8.4	111	547	**1221**	12.1	3.60	98	.247	.319	-1	-9	99	96	.975	153	136	-.4	-.9	2.1	.2	-1.0
SD	16	9	25	1422¹	1454	9.2	113	592	764	13.2	4.24	83	.267	.343	-102	-111	98	97	.975	156	140	-.5	-11.7	-14.1	-.6	-2.1
TOT	531	166	356	17387¹		8.5				12.1	3.59		.250	.321					.977	1758	1777					

Runs		Hits		Doubles		Triples		Home Runs		Total Bases	
Rose-Cin	120	Alou-Pit	231	Alou-Pit	41	Clemente-Pit	12	McCovey-SF	45	H.Aaron-Atl	332
Bonds-SF	120	Rose-Cin	218	Kessinger-Chi	38	Rose-Cin	11	H.Aaron-Atl	44	Perez-Cin	331
Wynn-Hou	113	Brock-StL	195	Williams-Chi	33	Williams-Chi	10	May-Cin	38	McCovey-SF	322
Kessinger-Chi	109	Tolan-Cin	194	Rose-Cin	33	Tolan-Cin	10	Perez-Cin	37	Rose-Cin	321
Alou-Pit	105	Williams-Chi	188	Brock-StL	33	Brock-StL	10	Wynn-Hou	33	May-Cin	321

Runs Batted In		Runs Produced		Bases On Balls		Batting Average		On Base Percentage		Slugging Average	
McCovey-SF	126	Santo-Chi	191	Wynn-Hou	148	Rose-Cin	.348	McCovey-SF	.458	McCovey-SF	.656
Santo-Chi	123	Perez-Cin	188	McCovey-SF	121	Clemente-Pit	.345	Wynn-Hou	.440	H.Aaron-Atl	.607
Perez-Cin	122	Rose-Cin	186	Staub-Mon	110	Jones-NY	.340	Rose-Cin	.432	Allen-Phi	.573
May-Cin	110	McCovey-SF	182	Morgan-Hou	110	Alou-Pit	.331	Staub-Mon	.427	Stargell-Pit	.556
Banks-Chi	106	Bonds-SF	178	Santo-Chi	96	McCovey-SF	.320	Jones-NY	.424	Clemente-Pit	.544

Production		Adjusted Production		Batter Runs		Adjusted Batter Runs		Clutch Hitting Index		Runs Created	
McCovey-SF	1.114	McCovey-SF	212	McCovey-SF	76.1	McCovey-SF	78.7	Menke-Hou	134	McCovey-SF	151
H.Aaron-Atl	1.005	H.Aaron-Atl	177	H.Aaron-Atl	56.3	H.Aaron-Atl	55.9	Rader-Hou	132	Rose-Cin	138
Clemente-Pit	.958	Clemente-Pit	170	Rose-Cin	56.0	Wynn-Hou	53.4	Banks-Chi	132	Staub-Mon	128
Staub-Mon	.953	Wynn-Hou	168	Staub-Mon	52.6	Staub-Mon	52.2	Santo-Chi	122	H.Aaron-Atl	128
Allen-Phi	.952	Allen-Phi	168	Wynn-Hou	51.0	Rose-Cin	49.3	D.Johnson-Phi	121	Wynn-Hou	126

Total Average		Stolen Bases		Stolen Base Average		Stolen Base Runs		Fielding Runs		Total Player Rating	
McCovey-SF	1.296	Brock-StL	53	Bonds-SF	91.8	Bonds-SF	11.1	Lanier-SF	28.6	McCovey-SF	6.3
Wynn-Hou	1.118	Morgan-Hou	49	Brock-StL	79.1	Brock-StL	7.5	Kessinger-Chi	24.6	Wynn-Hou	6.0
H.Aaron-Atl	1.032	Bonds-SF	45	Morgan-Hou	77.8	Morgan-Hou	6.3	Maxvill-StL	21.1	H.Aaron-Atl	5.2
Staub-Mon	1.018	Wills-Mon-LA	40	Wynn-Hou	76.7	Wynn-Hou	2.7	Grote-NY	19.3	Staub-Mon	5.0
Allen-Phi	.988	Tolan-Cin	26	Alou-Pit	73.3	Millan-Atl	2.4	Money-Phi	17.3	Clemente-Pit	4.9

Wins		Win Percentage		Games		Complete Games		Shutouts		Saves	
Seaver-NY	25	Seaver-NY	.781	Granger-Cin	90	Gibson-StL	28	Marichal-SF	8	Gladding-Hou	29
Niekro-Atl	23	Marichal-SF	.656	McGinn-Mon	74	Marichal-SF	27	Osteen-LA	7	Upshaw-Atl	27
Marichal-SF	21	Merritt-Cin	.654	Regan-Chi	71	Perry-SF	26	Jenkins-Chi	7	Granger-Cin	27
Jenkins-Chi	21	Koosman-NY	.654	Carroll-Cin	71	Jenkins-Chi	23	Koosman-NY	6	Brewer-LA	20
		Reed-Atl	.643	Reberger-SD	67	Niekro-Atl	21	Holtzman-Chi	6	Regan-Chi	17

Innings Pitched		Fewest Hits/Game		Fewest BB/Game		Strikeouts		Strikeouts/Game		Ratio	
Perry-SF	325.1	Seaver-NY	6.65	Marichal-SF	1.62	Jenkins-Chi	273	Griffin-Hou	9.56	Marichal-SF	9.13
Osteen-LA	321.0	Maloney-Cin	6.80	Niekro-Atl	1.80	Gibson-StL	269	Wilson-Hou	9.40	Dierker-Hou	9.23
Singer-LA	315.2	Singer-LA	6.96	Jenkins-Chi	2.05	Singer-LA	247	Moose-Pit	8.74	Singer-LA	9.35
Gibson-StL	314.0	Koosman-NY	6.98	Niekro-Chi-SD	2.07	Wilson-Hou	235	Selma-SD-Chi	8.54	Niekro-Atl	9.40
Jenkins-Chi	311.1	Carlton-StL	7.05	Osteen-LA	2.07	Perry-SF	233	Veale-Pit	8.49	Seaver-NY	9.58

Earned Run Average		Adjusted ERA		Opponents' Batting Avg.		Opponents' On Base Pct.		Starter Runs		Adjusted Starter Runs	
Marichal-SF	2.10	Marichal-SF	166	Seaver-NY	.207	Dierker-Hou	.262	Marichal-SF	49.6	Hands-Chi	51.1
Carlton-StL	2.17	Seaver-NY	166	Maloney-Cin	.208	Marichal-SF	.263	Gibson-StL	49.3	Gibson-StL	48.6
Gibson-StL	2.18	Carlton-StL	165	Singer-LA	.210	Singer-LA	.263	Singer-LA	44.0	Marichal-SF	46.5
Seaver-NY	2.21	Gibson-StL	164	Dierker-Hou	.214	Niekro-Atl	.264	Dierker-Hou	42.9	Seaver-NY	44.0
Koosman-NY	2.28	Hands-Chi	162	Carlton-StL	.216	Seaver-NY	.273	Seaver-NY	42.1	Dierker-Hou	41.1

Clutch Pitching Index		Relief Runs		Adjusted Relief Runs		Relief Ranking		Total Pitcher Index		Total Baseball Ranking	
Carlton-StL	122	McGraw-NY	15.1	McGraw-NY	15.7	McGraw-NY	21.2	Gibson-StL	6.0	McCovey-SF	6.3
Perry-SF	117	Granger-Cin	12.8	Granger-Cin	15.5	Granger-Cin	20.9	Seaver-NY	5.6	Gibson-StL	6.0
Veale-Pit	114	Brewer-LA	10.3	DiLauro-NY	8.8	Taylor-NY	14.0	Hands-Chi	5.5	Wynn-Hou	6.0
Robertson-Mon	113	Gibbon-SF-Pit	9.5	Gibbon-SF-Pit	8.7	Brewer-LA	14.0	Marichal-SF	5.4	Seaver-NY	5.6
Hands-Chi	111	DiLauro-NY	8.4	Upshaw-Atl	8.2	Gibbon-SF-Pit	13.9	Carlton-StL	4.9	Hands-Chi	5.5

March 1 Mickey Mantle retires.

April 7 At RFK Stadium, 45,000 fans, including President Richard Nixon, look on as Ted Williams makes his managerial debut for the Senators. The Yanks spoil it, winning 8-4.

April 8 Expansion teams Kansas City Royals, Montreal Expos, San Diego Padres, and Seattle Pilots make things look easy by winning their first regular season games.

April 8 After a long recovery following a 1967 beaning, Tony Conigliaro starts his first game for Boston. His dramatic two-run tenth-inning home run gives the Red Sox a brief lead, and his 12th-inning run wins it.

April 27 Harmon Killebrew hits his 400th home run, and the Twins take first place in the AL West by beating Chicago 4-3.

June 7 The Washington Senators name Jeff Burroughs the number one pick in the June free-agent draft. The Astros choose J. R. Richard as the second pick.

July 16 Rod Carew steals home for the seventh time, as the AL West leading Twins sweep the White Sox. Carew ties Pete Reiser's record for steals of home in a season.

July 21 A gala All-Star Game banquet in Washington is one of baseball's great events. An all-time team and all-time living team is announced. Babe Ruth is selected Greatest All-Time Player, and Joe DiMaggio Greatest Living Player.

July 22 For the first time, the All-Star Game is postponed due to rain.

August 13 Baltimore's Jim Palmer leaves no doubt about his comeback with an 8-0 no-hitter against Oakland. Reggie Jackson, leading the AL with 42 home runs, walks three times, as the A's drop two games behind the Twins in the West. Palmer, now 11-2, pushes the O's lead to a comfortable 14½ games.

September 29 Rico Petrocelli blasts his 40th home run, a season record for shortstops, as Boston wins 8-5 over Washington. Petrocelli is hitting .301 with only 14 errors in the field.

October 2 The Pilots play what will be their last game in Seattle in a 3-1 loss to Oakland. A crowd of 5,473 fans show up to pay their respects.

October 4 The first League Championship Series begin in Atlanta and Baltimore. New York survives homers by Hank Aaron and Tony Gonzalez off Tom Seaver and scores five runs off Phil Niekro in the eighth to coast 9-5. Paul Blair's 12th-inning squeeze bunt gives the Orioles a 4-3 win over Minnesota.

October 6 Baltimore wins the first ALCS as Paul Blair delivers five hits and Don Buford has four in an 11-2 win at Minnesota.

October 11 Don Buford's leadoff home run starts a 4-1 Baltimore win over New York to open the World Series. Mike Cuellar bests Tom Seaver.

November 6 Denny McLain and Mike Cuellar finish dead even in AL Cy Young Award voting.

November 12 Minnesota's Harmon Killebrew is voted AL MVP honors.

November 25 Kansas City's Lou Piniella is voted AL Rookie of the Year.

BALTIMORE		BOSTON		CALIFORNIA		CHICAGO		CLEVELAND		DETROIT	
M	E.Weaver	M	D.Williams	M	B.Rigney	M	A.Lopez	M	A.Dark	M	M.Smith
1B	B.Powell	M	E.Popowski	M	L.Phillips	1B	G.Hopkins	1B	T.Horton	1B	N.Cash
2B	D.Johnson	1B	D.Jones	1B	J.Spencer	2B	B.Knoop	2B	V.Fuller	2B	D.McAuliffe
SS	M.Belanger	2B	M.Andrews	2B	S.Alomar	SS	L.Aparicio	SS	L.Brown	SS	T.Tresh
3B	B.Robinson	SS	R.Petrocelli	SS	J.Fregosi	3B	B.Melton	3B	M.Alvis	3B	D.Wert
LF	D.Buford	3B	G.Scott	3B	A.Rodriguez	LF	C.May	LF	R.Snyder	LF	W.Horton
CF	P.Blair	LF	C.Yastrzemski	LF	R.Reichardt	CF	K.Berry	CF	J.Cardenal	CF	J.Northrup
RF	F.Robinson	CF	R.Smith	CF	J.Johnstone	RF	W.Williams	RF	K.Harrelson	RF	A.Kaline
C	E.Hendricks	RF	T.Conigliaro	RF	B.Voss	C	E.Herrmann	C	D.Sims	C	B.Freehan
C	A.Etchebarren	C	R.Gibson	C	J.Azcue						
								O	R.Scheinblum	OS	M.Stanley
		O	J.Lahoud	O1	R.Repoz	13	P.Ward	32	L.Klimchock	23	T.Matchick
P	M.Cuellar	3S	S.O'Brien			O	B.Bradford	23	Z.Versalles		
P	D.McNally	2S	D.Schofield	P	A.Messersmith	1O	T.McCraw	S	E.Leon	P	D.McLain
P	T.Phoebus			P	T.Murphy					P	M.Lolich
P	J.Palmer	P	R.Culp	P	J.McGlothlin	P	J.Horlen	P	S.McDowell	P	E.Wilson
P	J.Hardin	P	M.Nagy	P	R.May	P	T.John	P	L.Tiant	P	M.Kilkenny
RP	D.Leonhard	P	S.Siebert	P	G.Brunet	P	G.Peters	P	S.Hargan	RP	P.Dobson
RP	E.Watt	P	J.Lonborg	RP	E.Fisher	P	B.Wynne	P	D.Ellsworth	RP	J.Hiller
RP	M.Lopez	P	L.Stange	RP	K.Tatum	RP	W.Wood	RP	S.Williams	RP	T.Timmerman
		RP	V.Romo	RP	H.Wilhelm	RP	D.Osinski	RP	M.Paul		
P	D.Hall	RP	S.Lyle	P	C.Wright	RP	C.Carlos	RP	J.Pizarro	P	J.Sparma
P	P.Richert	RP	B.Landis								
						P	P.Edmondson	P	R.Law		
		P	R.Jarvis			P	J.Nyman				
		P	B.Lee								

KANSAS CITY		MINNESOTA		NEW YORK		OAKLAND		SEATTLE		WASHINGTON	
M	J.Gordon	M	B.Martin	M	R.Houk	M	H.Bauer	M	J.Schultz	M	T.Williams
1B	M.Fiore	1B	R.Reese	1B	J.Pepitone	M	J.McNamara	1B	D.Mincher	1B	M.Epstein
2B	J.Adair	2B	R.Carew	2B	H.Clarke	1B	D.Cater	2B	J.Donaldson	2B	B.Allen
SS	J.Hernandez	SS	L.Cardenas	SS	G.Michael	2B	D.Green	SS	R.Oyler	SS	E.Brinkman
3B	J.Foy	3B	H.Killebrew	3B	J.Kenney	SS	B.Campaneris	3B	T.Harper	3B	K.McMullen
LF	L.Piniella	LF	T.Uhlaender	LF	R.White	3B	S.Bando	LF	T.Davis	LF	F.Howard
CF	B.Oliver	CF	C.Tovar	CF	R.Woods	LF	T.Reynolds	CF	W.Comer	CF	D.Unser
RF	P.Kelly	RF	T.Oliva	RF	B.Murcer	CF	R.Monday	RF	S.Hovley	RF	H.Allen
C	E.Rodriguez	C	J.Roseboro	C	J.Gibbs	RF	R.Jackson	C	J.McNertney	C	P.Casanova
						C	P.Roof				
O	E.Kirkpatrick	32	F.Quilici	CO	F.Fernandez			O1	M.Hegan	O	B.Alyea
1	C.Harrison	O3	G.Nettles	O	B.Robinson	S2	T.Kubiak	32	G.Gil	2	T.Cullen
C	B.Martinez			O	J.Hall	O	J.Tartabull			O	E.Stroud
3	P.Schaal	P	J.Perry					P	G.Brabender	O	L.Maye
		P	D.Boswell	P	M.Stottlemyre	P	C.Hunter	P	M.Pattin		
P	W.Bunker	P	J.Kaat	P	F.Peterson	P	C.Dobson	P	F.Talbot	P	J.Coleman
P	D.Drago	P	T.Hall	P	S.Bahnsen	P	B.Odom	RP	D.Segui	P	D.Bosman
P	B.Butler	RP	R.Perranoski	P	B.Burbach	P	L.Krausse	RP	J.Gelnar	P	C.Cox
P	R.Nelson	RP	B.Miller	P	A.Downing	P	J.Nash	RP	J.Bouton	P	J.Hannan
P	J.Rooker	RP	D.Woodson	RP	L.McDaniel	RP	R.Fingers			P	B.Moore
RP	M.Drabowsky			RP	J.Aker	RP	J.Roland	P	M.Marshall	RP	J.Shellenback
RP	T.Burgmeier	P	D.Chance	RP	S.Hamilton	RP	P.Lindblad	P	S.Barber	RP	D.Higgins
RP	D.Wickersham	P	A.Worthington					P	B.Locker	RP	D.Knowles
				P	M.Kekich	P	G.Lauzerique	P	J.O'Donoghue		
P	M.Hedlund							P	G.Brunet	P	B.Humphreys
								P	G.Bell	P	D.Baldwin
										P	C.Pascual

TEAM	G	W	L	PCT	GB	R	OR	AB	H	2B	3B	HR	BB	SO	AVG	OBP	SLG	PRO	PRO+	BR	/A	PF	CHI	RC	SB	CS	SBA	SBR
EAST																												
BAL	162	109	53	.673		779	**517**	5518	1465	234	29	175	634	806	.265	**.346**	.414	**.760**	118	**135**	**128**	101	96	791	82	45	65	-2
DET	162	90	72	.556	19	701	601	5441	1316	188	29	182	578	922	.242	.318	.387	.705	99	17	-12	104	104	674	35	28	56	-6
BOS	162	87	75	.537	22	743	736	5494	1381	234	37	**197**	658	923	.251	.335	**.415**	.750	110	110	69	105	96	761	41	47	47	-16
WAS	162	86	76	.531	23	694	644	5447	1365	171	40	148	630	900	.251	.332	.378	.710	111	38	75	95	99	675	52	40	57	-8
NY	162	80	81	.497	28.5	562	587	5308	1247	210	44	94	565	840	.235	.310	.344	.654	92	-74	-53	96	99	572	119	74	62	-9
CLE	161	62	99	.385	46.5	573	717	5365	1272	173	24	119	535	906	.237	.309	.345	.654	86	-77	-96	103	101	568	85	37	70	3
WEST																												
MIN	162	97	65	.599		**790**	618	5677	**1520**	**246**	32	163	599	906	**.268**	.342	.408	.750	114	118	101	102	98	**794**	115	70	62	-8
OAK	162	88	74	.543	9	740	678	5614	1400	210	28	148	617	953	.249	.330	.376	.706	109	32	63	96	103	712	100	39	72	7
CAL	163	71	91	.438	28	528	652	5316	1221	151	29	88	516	929	.230	.302	.319	.621	84	-137	-112	95	**105**	518	54	39	58	-7
KC	163	69	93	.426	28	586	688	5462	1311	179	32	98	522	901	.240	.311	.338	.649	87	-84	-87	101	102	577	129	70	65	-3
CHI	162	68	94	.420	29	625	723	5450	1346	210	27	112	552	844	.247	.322	.357	.679	92	-25	-56	105	98	638	54	22	71	3
SEA	163	64	98	.395	33	639	799	5444	1276	179	27	125	626	1015	.234	.317	.346	.663	94	-53	-43	98	104	622	**167**	59	**74**	15
TOT	973					7960		65536	16120	2385	378	1649	7032	10845	.246	.323	.369	.693							1033	570	64	-32

TEAM	CG	SH	SV	IP	H	H/G	HR	BB	SO	RAT	ERA	ERA+	OAV	OOB	PR	/A	PF	CPI	FA	E	DP	FW	PW	BW	SBW	DIF
EAST																										
BAL	50	20	36	1473²	**1194**	7.3	117	498	897	10.5	2.83	126	.223	.291	130	121	98	97	**.984**	101	145	2.2	12.7	13.4	.0	-.4
DET	55	20	28	1455¹	1250	7.7	128	586	1032	11.6	3.31	113	.232	.312	50	67	103	98	.979	130	130	.5	7.0	-1.3	-.3	3.0
BOS	30	7	41	1466²	1423	8.7	155	685	935	11.3	3.92	97	.256	.343	-49	-19	105	106	.975	157	**178**	-1.0	-2.0	7.2	-1.4	3.2
WAS	28	10	41	1447¹	1310	8.1	135	656	835	12.4	3.49	99	.244	.330	22	-4	96	**107**	.978	140	159	-.0	-.4	7.9	-.6	-1.8
NY	53	13	20	1440²	1258	7.9	118	522	801	11.2	3.23	108	.236	.306	63	40	96	97	.979	131	158	.5	4.2	-5.6	-.7	1.0
CLE	35	7	22	1437	1330	8.3	134	681	1000	12.9	3.94	96	.248	.338	-51	-27	104	99	.976	145	153	-.4	-2.8	-10.1	.6	-5.8
WEST																										
MIN	41	8	**43**	1497²	1388	8.3	119	524	906	11.7	3.24	113	.246	.315	64	69	101	104	.977	150	177	-.6	7.2	10.6	-.6	-.7
OAK	42	14	36	1480²	1356	8.2	163	586	887	12.0	3.71	93	.245	.322	-15	-45	95	100	.979	136	162	.2	-4.7	6.6	1.0	3.9
CAL	25	9	39	1438¹	1294	8.1	126	517	885	11.7	3.54	98	.242	.315	13	-9	96	96	.978	136	164	.2	-.9	-11.7	-.5	2.9
KC	42	10	25	1464²	1357	8.3	136	560	894	11.9	3.72	94	.246	.319	-15	-5	102	95	.975	157	114	-1.0	-.5	-9.1	-.0	-1.4
CHI	29	10	25	1437²	1470	9.2	146	564	810	12.9	4.21	92	.267	.339	-93	-56	107	99	.981	122	163	-1.0	-5.9	-5.9	-.6	-2.8
SEA	21	6	33	1463²	1490	9.2	172	653	963	13.5	4.35	84	.264	.345	-118	-116	100	101	.974	167	149	-1.5	-12.2	-4.5	1.9	-.6
TOT	451	134	389	17503¹		8.3				12.1	3.62		.246	.323					.978	1672	1852					

Runs
Jackson-Oak 123
F.Robinson-Bal ... 111
Howard-Was 111
Killebrew-Min 106
Bando-Oak 106

Hits
Oliva-Min 197
Clarke-NY 183
Blair-Bal 178
Howard-Was 175
Horton-Cle 174

Doubles
Oliva-Min 39
Jackson-Oak 36
Johnson-Bal 34
Petrocelli-Bos 32
Blair-Bal 32

Triples
Unser-Was 8
Smith-Bos 7
Clarke-NY 7

Home Runs
Killebrew-Min 49
Howard-Was 48
Jackson-Oak 47
Yastrzemski-Bos .. 40
Petrocelli-Bos 40

Total Bases
Howard-Was 340
Jackson-Oak 334
Killebrew-Min 324
Oliva-Min 316
Petrocelli-Bos 315

Runs Batted In
Killebrew-Min 140
Powell-Bal 121
Jackson-Oak 118
Bando-Oak 113

Runs Produced
Killebrew-Min 197
Jackson-Oak 194
Bando-Oak 188
F.Robinson-Bal ... 179

Bases On Balls
Killebrew-Min 145
Jackson-Oak 114
Bando-Oak 111
Howard-Was 102
Yastrzemski-Bos .. 101

Batting Average
Carew-Min .... .332
Smith-Bos .... .309
Oliva-Min .... .309
F.Robinson-Bal ... .308
Powell-Bal .... .304

On Base Percentage
Killebrew-Min ..... .430
F.Robinson-Bal ... .417
Jackson-Oak ...... .410
Petrocelli-Bos .... .407
Howard-Was ...... .403

Slugging Average
Jackson-Oak ...... .608
Petrocelli-Bos .... .589
Killebrew-Min .... .584
Howard-Was ...... .574
Powell-Bal .... .559

Production
Jackson-Oak 1.019
Killebrew-Min 1.014
Petrocelli-Bos .... .996
Howard-Was ...... .978
F.Robinson-Bal ... .957

Adjusted Production
Jackson-Oak 190
Howard-Was 180
Killebrew-Min 177
Petrocelli-Bos 167
F.Robinson-Bal ... 164

Batter Runs
Killebrew-Min 65.6
Jackson-Oak 62.0
Howard-Was 56.8
Petrocelli-Bos 54.8
F.Robinson-Bal ... 49.9

Adjusted Batter Runs
Jackson-Oak 67.9
Howard-Was 63.8
Killebrew-Min 62.6
F.Robinson-Bal ... 48.8
Petrocelli-Bos 48.4

Clutch Hitting Index
White-NY 128
Cater-Oak 120
Bando-Oak 118
Foy-KC 116
T.Conigliaro-Bos ... 113

Runs Created
Killebrew-Min 146
Jackson-Oak 144
Howard-Was 132
Petrocelli-Bos 129
F.Robinson-Bal ... 126

Total Average
Killebrew-Min 1.143
Jackson-Oak 1.139
Petrocelli-Bos 1.048
F.Robinson-Bal ... 1.026
Howard-Was 1.004

Stolen Bases
Harper-Sea 73
Campaneris-Oak ... 62
Tovar-Min 45
Kelly-KC 40
Foy-KC 37

Stolen Base Average
Campaneris-Oak .. 88.6
Alomar-Chi-Cal ... 87.0
Cardenal-Cle 85.7
Aparicio-Chi 85.7
Davis-Sea 82.6

Stolen Base Runs
Campaneris-Oak .. 13.8
Harper-Sea 11.1
Cardenal-Cle 7.2
Tovar-Min 6.3
Aparicio-Chi 4.8

Fielding Runs
Cardenas-Min 33.5
Aparicio-Chi 29.3
Blair-Bal 24.8
Knoop-Cal-Chi 24.5
Quilici-Min 24.2

Total Player Rating
Petrocelli-Bos 6.9
Jackson-Oak 6.6
Cardenas-Min 5.6
Aparicio-Chi 5.1
F.Robinson-Bal 4.2

Wins
McLain-Det 24
Cuellar-Bal 23

Win Percentage
Palmer-Bal .... .800
Perry-Min .... .769
McNally-Bal ...... .741
McLain-Det .... .727
Odom-Oak .... .714

Games
Wood-Chi 76
Perranoski-Min ... 75
Lyle-Bos 71
Locker-Chi-Sea ... 68
Segui-Sea 66

Complete Games
Stottlemyre-NY 24
McLain-Det 23
McDowell-Cle 18
Cuellar-Bal 18
Peterson-NY 16

Shutouts
McLain-Det 9
Palmer-Bal 6
Cuellar-Bal 5

Saves
Perranoski-Min 31
K.Tatum-Cal 22
Lyle-Bos 17
Watt-Bal 16
Higgins-Was 16

Innings Pitched
McLain-Det 325.0
Stottlemyre-NY ... 303.0
Cuellar-Bal 290.2
McDowell-Cle 285.0
Lolich-Det 280.2

Fewest Hits/Game
Messersmith-Cal . 6.08
Palmer-Bal 6.51
Cuellar-Bal 6.60
Lolich-Det 6.86
Odom-Oak 6.96

Fewest BB/Game
Peterson-NY 1.42
Bosman-Was 1.82
McLain-Det 1.86
Perry-Min 2.27
Cuellar-Bal 2.45

Strikeouts
McDowell-Cle 279
Lolich-Det 271
Messersmith-Cal .. 211
Boswell-Min 190

Strikeouts/Game
McDowell-Cle 8.81
Lolich-Det 8.69
Messersmith-Cal .. 7.60
Butler-KC 7.25
Williams-Cle 7.01

Ratio
Peterson-NY 9.07
Cuellar-Bal 9.07
Bosman-Was 9.19
Palmer-Bal 9.75
Messersmith-Cal .. 9.86

Earned Run Average
Bosman-Was 2.19
Palmer-Bal 2.34
Cuellar-Bal 2.38
Messersmith-Cal .. 2.52
Peterson-NY 2.55

Adjusted ERA
Bosman-Was 158
Palmer-Bal 153
Cuellar-Bal 150
Messersmith-Cal .. 138
Peterson-NY 136

Opponents' Batting Avg.
Messersmith-Cal .. .190
Palmer-Bal .... .200
Cuellar-Bal ...... .204
Lolich-Det .... .210
McDowell-Cle ..... .213

Opponents' On Base Pct.
Cuellar-Bal .... .261
Bosman-Was ..... .262
Peterson-NY ..... .263
Palmer-Bal .... .272
Messersmith-Cal .. .276

Starter Runs
Cuellar-Bal 40.0
Peterson-NY 32.5
Bosman-Was 30.7
Messersmith-Cal .. 30.6
McLain-Det 29.8

Adjusted Starter Runs
Cuellar-Bal 38.1
McLain-Det 33.7
Peterson-NY 28.1
Bosman-Was 27.3
Messersmith-Cal .. 26.8

Clutch Pitching Index
Cox-Was 128
Nagy-Bos 119
Tiant-Cle 118
John-Chi 114
Wilson-Det 112

Relief Runs
K.Tatum-Cal 21.7
Perranoski-Min ... 20.2
Watt-Bal 15.6
Roland-Oak 13.7
Knowles-Was 12.9

Adjusted Relief Runs
Perranoski-Min ... 20.6
K.Tatum-Cal 20.4
Watt-Bal 15.1
Lyle-Bos 14.4
Hall-Bal 12.0

Relief Ranking
Perranoski-Min ... 41.3
K.Tatum-Cal 30.9
Watt-Bal 21.1
Wood-Chi 21.0
Lyle-Bos 19.2

Total Pitcher Index
Perranoski-Min 4.4
Cuellar-Bal 4.1
Stottlemyre-NY ... 3.8
K.Tatum-Cal 3.8
Peterson-NY 3.7

Total Baseball Ranking
Petrocelli-Bos 6.9
Jackson-Oak 6.6
Cardenas-Min 5.6
Aparicio-Chi 5.1
Perranoski-Min 4.4

January 16 Curt Flood, Cardinals Gold Glove outfielder, files a civil lawsuit challenging Major League Baseball's reserve clause, a suit that will have historic implications. Flood refused to report to the Phillies after he was traded by the Cardinals three months ago, contending the baseball rule violates Federal anti-trust laws.

April 22 Tom Seaver strikes out 19 Padres, including the last 10 in succession—both major league records—in winning 2-1 for the Mets. To date, only Steve Carlton has struck out as many in a game in this century, and no one has ever struck out 10 in a row.

May 10 While losing 6-5 to St. Louis, the Braves Hoyt Wilhelm becomes the first pitcher ever to appear in 1,000 games.

May 12 Ernie Banks becomes the eighth member of the 500 homer club, connecting off Pat Jarvis during a 4-3 Cub win over the Braves.

May 17 During a 7-6 Atlanta loss to Cincinnati in the second game of a doubleheader, Hank Aaron collects his 3,000th career hit. The ninth man to amass 3,000 hits, Aaron is the first to also have 500 homers.

May 30 All-Star voting is returned to the fans, as computerized punch-card ballots appear in stores and ballparks coast to coast. Since 1958 the All-Star squads had been selected by managers, coaches, and players.

July 14 The NL wins its eighth straight All-Star Game, a thrilling 12-inning 5-4 victory in Cincinnati. Pete Rose crashes into Cleveland catcher Ray Fosse to score the winning run.

July 18 During a 10-1 win over Montreal, the Giants' Willie Mays singles off Mike Wegener. It is career hit number 3,000 for Mays.

August 11 Jim Bunning notches his 100th NL victory, a 6-5 Phillies win over the Astros. Bunning is the first pitcher since Cy Young to win 100 games in each league.

August 12 Curt Flood loses his $4.1 million antitrust suit against baseball, as Federal Judge Irving Ben Cooper upholds the legality of the sport's reserve clause. Cooper does recommend changes in the reserve system, to be achieved through negotiation between players and owners. Less than six years

later, this recommendation would become a reality.

September 3 After an NL record 1,117 consecutive games, Billy Williams asks to sit one out.

October 1 The Angels' Alex Johnson grounds out and then hits two singles in the final game of the season to edge Boston's Carl Yastrzemski for the AL batting title, .3290 to .3286. Johnson leaves the game after his second hit.

October 4 Major league umpires return after a one-day walkout in quest of higher wages. Minor league umps had been pressed into service for the opening LCS games the day before. There had been rumors of a strike for several days as negotiations between the umpires and Major League Baseball had reached an impasse.

November 3 Bob Gibson wins the NL Cy Young Award by a 118-51 margin over Giant Gaylord Perry. Gibson posted a 23-7 record for the Cardinals.

November 18 Johnny Bench wins the NL MVP Award with 326 points, 108 more than the Cubs' Billy Williams. Bench had 45 homers, 148 RBI, and a .293 average for the Reds.

ATLANTA		CHICAGO		CINCINNATI		HOUSTON		LOS ANGELES		MONTREAL	
M	L.Harris	M	L.Durocher	M	S.Anderson	M	H.Walker	M	W.Alston	M	G.Mauch
1B	O.Cepeda	1B	E.Banks	1B	L.May	1B	B.Watson	1B	W.Parker	1B	R.Fairly
2B	F.Millan	2B	G.Beckert	2B	T.Helms	2B	J.Morgan	2B	T.Sizemore	2B	G.Sutherland
SS	S.Jackson	SS	D.Kessinger	SS	D.Concepcion	SS	D.Menke	SS	M.Wills	SS	B.Wine
3B	C.Boyer	3B	R.Santo	3B	T.Perez	3B	D.Rader	3B	B.Grabarkewitz	3B	C.Laboy
LF	R.Carty	LF	B.Williams	LF	B.Carbo	LF	J.Wynn	LF	M.Mota	LF	M.Jones
CF	T.Gonzalez	CF	J.Hickman	CF	B.Tolan	CF	C.Cedeno	CF	W.Davis	CF	A.Phillips
RF	H.Aaron	RF	J.Callison	RF	P.Rose	RF	J.Alou	RF	W.Crawford	RF	R.Staub
C	B.Tillman	C	R.Hundley	C	J.Bench	C	J.Edwards	C	T.Haller	C	J.Bateman
S2	G.Garrido	O	C.James	O2	J.Stewart	1O	J.Pepitone	23	J.Lefebvre	3O	B.Bailey
O	M.Lum	O1	J.Pepitone	S3	W.Woodward	O	N.Miller	O	B.Russell	2	M.Staehle
C	H.King					O	T.Davis	C3	B.Sudakis	O1	J.Gosger
								O	A.Kosco	O	J.Fairey
P	P.Jarvis	P	F.Jenkins	P	G.Nolan	P	L.Dierker				
P	P.Niekro	P	K.Holtzman	P	J.Merritt	P	J.Billingham	P	D.Sutton	P	C.Morton
P	J.Nash	P	B.Hands	P	J.McGlothlin	P	J.Wilson	P	C.Osteen	P	S.Renko
P	G.Stone	P	M.Pappas	P	W.Simpson	P	D.Lemaster	P	A.Foster	P	B.Stoneman
P	R.Reed	P	J.Decker	P	T.Cloninger	P	T.Griffin	P	J.Moeller	P	M.Wegener
RP	H.Wilhelm	RP	P.Regan	RP	C.Carroll	RP	J.Ray	P	S.Vance	RP	D.McGinn
RP	B.Priddy	RP	J.Colborn	RP	W.Granger	RP	R.Cook	RP	J.Brewer	RP	H.Reed
				RP	D.Gullett	RP	J.Bouton	RP	F.Norman	RP	C.Raymond
P	M.McQueen							RP	P.Mikkelsen		
				P	R.Washburn	P	W.Blasingame			P	J.Strohmayer
						P	F.Gladding	P	B.Singer	P	M.Marshall
								P	R.Lamb		
								P	J.Pena		

NEW YORK		PHILADELPHIA		PITTSBURGH		SAN DIEGO		SAN FRANCISCO		ST.LOUIS	
M	G.Hodges	M	F.Lucchesi	M	D.Murtaugh	M	P.Gomez	M	C.King	M	R.Schoendienst
1B	D.Clendenon	1B	D.Johnson	1B	B.Robertson	1B	N.Colbert	M	C.Fox	1B	J.Hague
2B	K.Boswell	2B	D.Doyle	2B	B.Mazeroski	2B	D.Campbell	1B	W.McCovey	2B	J.Javier
SS	B.Harrelson	SS	L.Bowa	SS	G.Alley	SS	J.Arcia	2B	R.Hunt	SS	D.Maxvill
3B	J.Foy	3B	D.Money	3B	R.Hebner	3B	E.Spiezio	SS	H.Lanier	3B	J.Torre
LF	C.Jones	LF	J.Briggs	LF	W.Stargell	LF	A.Ferrara	3B	A.Gallagher	LF	L.Brock
CF	T.Agee	CF	L.Hisle	CF	M.Alou	CF	C.Gaston	LF	K.Henderson	CF	J.Cardenal
RF	R.Swoboda	RF	R.Stone	RF	R.Clemente	RF	O.Brown	CF	W.Mays	RF	L.Lee
C	J.Grote	C	M.Ryan	C	M.Sanguillen	C	C.Cannizzaro	RF	B.Bonds	C	T.Simmons
								C	D.Dietz		
32	W.Garrett	O	B.Browne	O1	A.Oliver	O	I.Murrell			13	D.Allen
O1	A.Shamsky	23	T.Taylor	S	F.Patek	S3	S.Huntz	2S	T.Fuentes	O	V.Davalillo
		O	O.Gamble	3	J.Pagan			3O	J.Hart	O1	Ca.Taylor
				2	D.Cash						
P	T.Seaver					P	P.Dobson				
P	J.Koosman	P	R.Wise	P	B.Veale	P	C.Kirby	P	G.Perry	P	B.Gibson
P	G.Gentry	P	J.Bunning	P	D.Ellis	P	D.Coombs	P	J.Marichal	P	S.Carlton
P	J.McAndrew	P	C.Short	P	S.Blass	P	D.Roberts	P	R.Robertson	P	M.Torrez
P	R.Sadecki	P	G.Jackson	P	B.Moose	P	M.Corkins	P	F.Reberger	P	J.Reuss
RP	T.McGraw	P	B.Lersch	P	L.Walker	RP	R.Herbel	RP	R.Bryant	P	N.Briles
RP	R.Taylor	RP	D.Selma	RP	D.Giusti	RP	T.Dukes	RP	D.McMahon	RP	Ch.Taylor
RP	D.Frisella	RP	L.Palmer	RP	B.Dal Canton	RP	G.Ross	RP	Je.Johnson	RP	F.Linzy
		RP	B.Wilson							RP	S.Campisi
P	N.Ryan					P	A.Santorini	P	S.Pitlock	P	G.Culver
		P	W.Fryman	P	J.Nelson	P	E.Wilson	P	M.McCormick		
		P	J.Hoerner			P	R.Willis	P	Ja.Johnson		

TEAM	G	W	L	PCT	GB	R	OR	AB	H	2B	3B	HR	BB	SO	AVG	OBP	SLG	PRO	PRO+	BR	/A	PF	CHI	RC	SB	CS	SBA	SBR
EAST																												
PIT	162	89	73	.549		729	664	5637	**1522**	235	**70**	130	444	871	**.270**	.328	.406	.734	105	12	28	98	99	740	66	34	66	-1
CHI	162	84	78	.519	5	806	679	5491	1424	228	44	179	607	844	.259	.335	.415	.750	95	49	-44	112	**104**	773	39	16	71	2
NY	162	83	79	.512	6	695	**630**	5443	1358	211	42	120	684	1062	.249	.336	.370	.706	96	-23	-24	100	98	689	118	54	69	3
STL	162	76	86	.469	13	744	747	5689	1497	218	51	113	569	961	.263	.333	.379	.712	95	-20	-35	102	103	719	117	47	71	7
PHI	161	73	88	.453	15.5	594	730	5456	1299	224	58	101	519	1066	.238	.307	.356	.663	85	-125	-109	97	101	582	72	64	53	-17
MON	162	73	89	.451	16	687	807	5411	1284	211	35	136	659	972	.237	.324	.365	.689	91	-62	-61	100	103	658	65	45	59	-8
WEST																												
CIN	162	102	60	.630		775	681	5540	1498	253	45	**191**	547	984	.270	.339	**.436**	**.775**	113	94	92	100	94	814	115	52	69	3
LA	161	87	74	.540	14.5	749	664	5606	1515	233	67	87	541	841	**.270**	.337	.382	.719	104	-4	28	96	102	730	**138**	57	71	7
SF	162	86	76	.531	16	**831**	826	5578	1460	**257**	35	165	**729**	1005	.262	**.353**	.409	.762	112	92	**102**	99	98	**821**	83	27	**75**	9
HOU	162	79	83	.488	23	744	763	5574	1446	250	47	129	598	911	.259	.334	.391	.725	104	5	36	99	100	728	114	41	74	**10**
ATL	162	76	86	.469	26	736	772	5546	1495	215	24	160	522	**736**	**.270**	.337	.404	.741	99	32	-13	106	97	742	58	34	63	-3
SD	162	63	99	.389	39	681	788	5494	1353	208	36	172	500	1164	.246	.314	.391	.705	98	-49	-22	96	102	669	60	45	57	-9
TOT	971					8771		66465	17151	2743	554	1683	6919	11417	.258	.332	.392	.724							1045	516	67	4

TEAM	CG	SH	SV	IP	H	H/G	HR	BB	SO	RAT	ERA	ERA+	OAV	OOB	PR	/A	PF	CPI	FA	E	DP	FW	PW	BW	SBW	DIF
EAST																										
PIT	36	13	43	1453²	1386	8.6	106	625	990	12.7	3.70	106	.255	.336	56	33	96	**106**	.979	137	**195**	.3	3.3	2.8	-.1	1.8
CHI	**59**	9	25	1435	1402	8.8	143	**475**	1000	11.9	3.76	120	.256	.318	46	**118**	111	101	.978	137	146	.3	**11.8**	-4.4	.2	-4.8
NY	47	10	32	1459²	**1260**	**7.8**	135	575	1064	11.5	3.45	117	**.233**	**.310**	97	93	99	98	.979	124	136	1.0	9.3	-2.4	.3	-6.2
STL	51	11	20	1475²	1483	9.0	102	632	960	13.0	4.06	101	.263	.340	-2	10	102	100	.977	150	159	-.4	1.0	-3.5	.7	-2.8
PHI	24	8	36	1461	1483	9.1	132	538	1047	12.7	4.17	96	.265	.333	-20	-29	99	98	**.981**	**114**	134	**1.5**	-2.9	-10.9	-1.7	6.5
MON	29	10	32	1438²	1434	9.0	162	716	914	13.8	4.50	91	.261	.351	-73	-63	102	101	.977	141	193	.0	-6.3	-6.1	-.8	5.1
WEST																										
CIN	32	15	**60**	1444²	1370	8.5	118	592	843	12.4	3.69	109	.251	.327	57	55	100	102	.976	151	173	-.5	5.5	9.2	.3	6.6
LA	37	**17**	42	1458²	1394	8.6	164	496	880	11.9	3.82	100	.250	.316	37	2	95	99	.978	135	135	.4	.2	2.8	.7	2.5
SF	50	7	30	1457²	1514	9.3	156	604	931	13.3	4.50	88	.267	.341	-74	-86	98	99	.973	170	153	-1.5	-8.6	**10.2**	.9	4.1
HOU	36	6	35	1456	1491	9.2	131	577	942	13.0	4.23	92	.265	.338	-30	-58	96	99	.978	140	144	.1	-5.8	3.6	**1.0**	-.9
ATL	45	9	24	1430²	1451	9.1	185	478	960	12.3	4.33	99	.261	.322	-45	-6	106	96	.977	141	118	.0	-.6	-1.3	-.3	-2.9
SD	24	9	32	1440¹	1483	9.3	149	611	886	13.3	4.36	91	.267	.344	-50	-61	98	102	.975	158	159	-.9	-6.1	-2.2	-.9	-7.9
TOT	470	124	411	17411²		8.9				12.6	4.05		.258	.332					.977	1698	1845					

Runs		Hits		Doubles		Triples		Home Runs		Total Bases	
Williams-Chi	137	Williams-Chi	205	Parker-LA	47	Davis-LA	16	Bench-Cin	45	Williams-Chi	373
Bonds-SF	134	Rose-Cin	205	McCovey-SF	39	Kessinger-Chi	14	Williams-Chi	42	Bench-Cin	355
Rose-Cin	120	Torre-StL	203	Rose-Cin	37	Clemente-Pit	10	Perez-Cin	40	Perez-Cin	346
Brock-StL	114	Brock-StL	202	Dietz-SF	36	Bonds-SF	10	McCovey-SF	39	Bonds-SF	334
Tolan-Cin	112	Alou-Pit	201	Bonds-SF	36					Gaston-SD	317

Runs Batted In		Runs Produced		Bases On Balls		Batting Average		On Base Percentage		Slugging Average	
Bench-Cin	148	Williams-Chi	224	McCovey-SF	137	Carty-Atl	.366	Carty-Atl	.456	McCovey-SF	.612
Williams-Chi	129	Bench-Cin	200	Staub-Mon	112	Torre-StL	.325	McCovey-SF	.446	Perez-Cin	.589
Perez-Cin	129	Perez-Cin	196	Dietz-SF	109	Sanguillen-Pit	.325	Dietz-SF	.430	Bench-Cin	.587
McCovey-SF	126	Bonds-SF	186	Wynn-Hou	106	Williams-Chi	.322	Hickman-Chi	.421	Williams-Chi	.586
H.Aaron-Atl	118			Morgan-Hou	102	Parker-LA	.319	Perez-Cin	.405	Carty-Atl	.584

Production		Adjusted Production		Batter Runs		Adjusted Batter Runs		Clutch Hitting Index		Runs Created	
McCovey-SF	1.058	McCovey-SF	183	McCovey-SF	62.0	McCovey-SF	63.6	Parker-LA	126	Williams-Chi	147
Carty-Atl	1.040	Carty-Atl	167	Carty-Atl	54.4	Perez-Cin	51.7	Dietz-SF	122	McCovey-SF	140
Hickman-Chi	1.003	Perez-Cin	162	Perez-Cin	52.1	Carty-Atl	47.5	Wine-Mon	118	Perez-Cin	140
Perez-Cin	.994	Dietz-SF	154	Williams-Chi	51.1	Dietz-SF	42.2	Santo-Chi	117	Bonds-SF	134
Williams-Chi	.979	Hickman-Chi	148	Hickman-Chi	49.5	Carbo-Cin	40.2	Davis-LA	115	Hickman-Chi	129

Total Average		Stolen Bases		Stolen Base Average		Stolen Base Runs		Fielding Runs		Total Player Rating	
McCovey-SF	1.214	Tolan-Cin	57	Henderson-SF	87.0	Bonds-SF	8.4	Maxvill-StL	37.5	McCovey-SF	6.2
Carty-Atl	1.102	Brock-StL	51	Harrelson-NY	85.2	Brock-StL	6.3	Alley-Pit	33.7	Bench-Cin	4.5
Hickman-Chi	1.080	Bonds-SF	48	Wynn-Hou	82.8	Tolan-Cin	5.1	Mazeroski-Pit	23.9	Perez-Cin	4.3
Perez-Cin	1.045	Morgan-Hou	42	Bonds-SF	82.8	Morgan-Hou	4.8	Rader-Hou	23.8	Wynn-Hou	4.2
Williams-Chi	1.018	Davis-LA	38	Cedeno-Hou	81.0	Harrelson-NY	4.5	Wine-Mon	19.7	Carty-Atl	4.2

Wins		Win Percentage		Games		Complete Games		Shutouts		Saves	
Perry-SF	23	Gibson-StL	.767	Herbel-SD-NY	76	Jenkins-Chi	24	Perry-SF	5	Granger-Cin	35
Gibson-StL	23	Nolan-Cin	.720	Selma-Phi	73	Perry-SF	23	Sutton-LA	4	Giusti-Pit	26
Jenkins-Chi	22	Walker-Pit	.714	Linzy-SF-StL	67	Gibson-StL	23	Osteen-LA	4	Brewer-LA	24
Merritt-Cin	20	Perry-SF	.639	Granger-Cin	67	Seaver-NY	19	Morton-Mon	4	Raymond-Mon	23
		Merritt-Cin	.625	Giusti-Pit	66	Dierker-Hou	17	Ellis-Pit	4	Selma-Phi	22

Innings Pitched		Fewest Hits/Game		Fewest BB/Game		Strikeouts		Strikeouts/Game		Ratio	
Perry-SF	328.2	Simpson-Cin	6.39	Jenkins-Chi	1.73	Seaver-NY	283	Seaver-NY	8.76	Jenkins-Chi	9.55
Jenkins-Chi	313.0	Seaver-NY	7.12	Marichal-SF	1.78	Jenkins-Chi	274	Gibson-StL	8.39	Seaver-NY	9.82
Gibson-StL	294.0	Walker-Pit	7.12	Osteen-LA	1.81	Gibson-StL	274	Veale-Pit	7.93	McAndrew-NY	10.06
Seaver-NY	290.2	Gentry-NY	7.41	McAndrew-NY	1.86	Perry-SF	214	Jenkins-Chi	7.88	Perry-SF	10.52
Holtzman-Chi	287.2	Jenkins-Chi	7.62	Merritt-Cin	2.04	Holtzman-Chi	202	Stoneman-Mon	7.63	Gibson-StL	10.84

Earned Run Average		Adjusted ERA		Opponents' Batting Avg.		Opponents' On Base Pct.		Starter Runs		Adjusted Starter Runs	
Seaver-NY	2.82	Seaver-NY	143	Simpson-Cin	.198	Jenkins-Chi	.265	Seaver-NY	39.7	Seaver-NY	38.9
Simpson-Cin	3.02	Simpson-Cin	134	Seaver-NY	.214	Seaver-NY	.273	Perry-SF	30.7	Jenkins-Chi	38.5
Walker-Pit	3.04	Pappas-Atl-Chi	133	Walker-Pit	.219	McAndrew-NY	.281	Gibson-StL	30.2	Holtzman-Chi	35.8
Gibson-StL	3.12	Holtzman-Chi	133	Jenkins-Chi	.224	Perry-SF	.290	Jenkins-Chi	22.7	Gibson-StL	32.4
Koosman-NY	3.14	Jenkins-Chi	133	Gentry-NY	.224	Gibson-StL	.296	Nolan-Cin	21.7	Perry-SF	28.1

Clutch Pitching Index		Relief Runs		Adjusted Relief Runs		Relief Ranking		Total Pitcher Index		Total Baseball Ranking	
Ellis-Pit	119	Selma-Phi	19.4	Selma-Phi	18.5	Selma-Phi	27.6	Seaver-NY	4.5	McCovey-SF	6.2
Morton-Mon	118	Carroll-Cin	16.9	Carroll-Cin	16.8	Granger-Cin	26.5	Gibson-StL	4.2	Seaver-NY	4.5
Coombs-SD	113	Gullett-Cin	13.9	C.Taylor-StL	13.8	Carroll-Cin	24.3	Carroll-Cin	4.0	Bench-Cin	4.5
Pappas-Atl-Chi	109	Granger-Cin	13.1	Gullett-Cin	13.8	Hoerner-Phi	21.5	Holtzman-Chi	3.4	Perez-Cin	4.3
Dobson-SD	108	C.Taylor-StL	12.9	Granger-Cin	12.9	McMahon-SF	18.8	Selma-Phi	3.0	Gibson-StL	4.2

January 20 Lou Boudreau achieves the Hall of Fame, receiving 232 votes in the BBWAA election. Ralph Kiner finishes with 167, 58 votes short.

February 1 The Hall of Fame Special Committee on Veterans selects Ford Frick, Earle Combs, and Jesse Haines for enshrinement.

April 1 The Milwaukee Brewers Baseball Club, headed by Bud Selig, purchases the Seattle Pilots for $10,800,000. Brewers tickets go on sale tomorrow.

April 7 Major League Baseball returns to Wisconsin as the Brewers play their first game in Milwaukee, losing to California 12-0 before a crowd of 37,237.

April 13 Oakland uses gold-colored bases during the club's home opener. The Rules Committee subsequently bans this innovation.

June 21 Detroit's Cesar Gutierrez goes 7-for-7 to tie a record set in 1892, in a 12-inning 9-8 win over Cleveland. Mickey Stanley's homer wins it for the Tigers. Gutierrez will collect just seven hits in all of 1971, and 128 hits for his career.

July 1 The return of Denny McLain following his suspension is witnessed by a gathering of 53,863 fans and 71 writers. He is knocked out of the box in the sixth inning, but the Tigers rally to beat the Yankees in the eleventh 6-5.

July 2 Detroit's Joe Niekro no-hits the Yankees until Horace Clarke singles in the ninth inning. The Tigers win 5-0. This is the third time in the month that Clarke has broken up a no-hitter, having spoiled bids by KC's Jim Rooker (June 4) and Boston's Sonny Siebert (June 19).

June 3 In pregame ceremonies, California's Clyde Wright is inducted into the National Association of Intercollegiate Athletics (NAIA) Hall of Fame for his pitching while at Carson-Newman College. He then hurls a no-hitter against Oakland, winning 4-0.

September 21 The A's Vida Blue no-hits the Twins 6-0, becoming the youngest pitcher to perform the feat since Paul Dean, 36 years ago to the day. The only base runner is Harmon Killebrew, who walks in the fourth. An Oakland crowd of only 4,284 watches Blue's second major league start.

October 10 Baltimore overcomes a 3-0 deficit to beat the Reds 4-3 in the World Series opener at Riverfront Stadium as Boog Powell, Ellie Hendricks, and Brooks Robinson contribute homers.

October 15 For the third time the Orioles overcome a 3-0 deficit to bury the Reds 9-3 and win the World Championship four games to one. Brooks Robinson, the "human vacuum cleaner," easily wins the Series MVP award.

November 6 The Twins Jim Perry wins the AL Cy Young Award in a close race. Perry, who won 24 games during the season, receives 55 points to edge out Dave McNally (47), Sam McDowell (45), and Mike Cuellar (44).

November 11 Boog Powell, who batted .297 with 35 homers and 114 RBI for Baltimore, is named AL MVP.

November 25 Yankee catcher Thurman Munson receives 23 of 24 votes in being named AL Rookie of the Year.

	BALTIMORE		BOSTON		CALIFORNIA		CHICAGO		CLEVELAND		DETROIT
M	E.Weaver	M	E.Kasko	M	L.Phillips	M	D.Gutteridge	M	A.Dark	M	M.Smith
1B	B.Powell	1B	C.Yastrzemski	1B	J.Spencer	M	B.Adair	1B	T.Horton	1B	N.Cash
2B	D.Johnson	2B	M.Andrews	2B	S.Alomar	M	C.Tanner	2B	E.Leon	2B	D.McAuliffe
SS	M.Belanger	SS	R.Petrocelli	SS	J.Fregosi	1B	G.Hopkins	SS	J.Heidemann	SS	C.Gutierrez
3B	B.Robinson	3B	G.Scott	3B	K.McMullen	2B	B.Knoop	3B	G.Nettles	3B	D.Wert
LF	D.Buford	LF	B.Conigliaro	LF	A.Johnson	SS	L.Aparicio	LF	R.Foster	LF	W.Horton
CF	P.Blair	CF	R.Smith	CF	J.Johnstone	3B	B.Melton	CF	T.Uhlaender	CF	M.Stanley
RF	F.Robinson	RF	T.Conigliaro	RF	R.Repoz	LF	C.May	RF	V.Pinson	RF	J.Northrup
C	E.Hendricks	C	J.Moses	C	J.Azcue	CF	K.Berry	C	R.Fosse	C	B.Freehan
						RF	W.Williams				
O	M.Rettenmund	P	R.Culp	C	T.Egan	C	E.Herrmann	1O	C.Hinton	O1	A.Kaline
C	A.Etchebarren	P	S.Siebert					CO	D.Sims	3O	E.Maddox
		P	G.Peters	P	C.Wright	1O	T.McCraw				
P	J.Palmer	P	K.Brett	P	T.Murphy	32	S.O'Brien	P	S.McDowell	P	M.Lolich
P	M.Cuellar	P	M.Nagy	P	R.May	C	D.Josephson	P	R.Hand	P	J.Niekro
P	D.McNally	P	V.Romo	P	A.Messersmith			P	D.Chance	P	L.Cain
P	J.Hardin	RP	S.Lyle	RP	E.Fisher	P	T.John	P	S.Hargan	P	M.Kilkenny
P	T.Phoebus			RP	K.Tatum	P	J.Janeski	RP	D.Higgins	P	E.Wilson
RP	M.Lopez	P	C.Koonce	RP	G.Garrett	P	J.Horlen	RP	M.Paul	RP	J.Hiller
RP	D.Hall					RP	W.Wood	RP	P.Hennigan	RP	T.Timmermann
RP	E.Watt			P	T.Bradley	RP	J.Crider			RP	D.Patterson
				P	M.Queen	RP	D.Murphy	P	S.Dunning		
P	P.Richert			P	D.LaRoche			P	B.Moore	P	D.McLain
						P	B.Johnson	P	R.Austin	P	F.Scherman
						P	B.Moore	P	F.Lasher		
						P	B.Miller				
						P	F.Weaver				

	KANSAS CITY		MILWAUKEE		MINNESOTA		NEW YORK		OAKLAND		WASHINGTON
M	C.Metro	M	D.Bristol	M	B.Rigney	M	R.Houk	M	J.McNamara	M	T.Williams
M	B.Lemon	1B	M.Hegan	1B	R.Reese	1B	D.Cater	1B	D.Mincher	1B	M.Epstein
1B	B.Oliver	2B	T.Kubiak	2B	D.Thompson	2B	H.Clarke	2B	D.Green	2B	T.Cullen
2B	C.Rojas	SS	R.Pena	SS	L.Cardenas	SS	G.Michael	SS	B.Campaneris	SS	E.Brinkman
SS	J.Hernandez	3B	T.Harper	3B	H.Killebrew	3B	J.Kenney	3B	S.Bando	3B	A.Rodriguez
3B	P.Schaal	LF	D.Walton	LF	J.Holt	LF	R.White	LF	F.Alou	LF	F.Howard
LF	L.Piniella	CF	D.May	CF	C.Tovar	CF	B.Murcer	CF	R.Monday	CF	E.Stroud
CF	A.Otis	RF	R.Snyder	RF	T.Oliva	RF	C.Blefary	RF	R.Jackson	RF	D.Unser
RF	P.Kelly	C	P.Roof	C	G.Mitterwald	C	T.Munson	C	F.Fernandez	C	P.Casanova
C	E.Kirkpatrick										
		C1	J.McNertney	23	F.Quilici	1	J.Ellis	1O	J.Rudi	23	B.Allen
S2	R.Severson	O	T.Savage	O	B.Alyea	O	R.Woods	C	D.Duncan	O	R.Reichardt
C	E.Rodriguez	O	B.Burda					O	T.Davis	O	L.Maye
				P	J.Perry	P	M.Stottlemyre				
P	D.Drago	P	M.Pattin	P	J.Kaat	P	F.Peterson	P	C.Dobson	P	D.Bosman
P	B.Johnson	P	L.Krausse	P	B.Blyleven	P	S.Bahnsen	P	C.Hunter	P	J.Coleman
P	J.Rooker	P	S.Lockwood	P	B.Zepp	P	S.Kline	P	D.Segui	P	C.Cox
P	B.Butler	P	B.Bolin	RP	T.Hall	P	M.Kekich	P	B.Odom	P	J.Hannan
P	D.Morehead	P	G.Brabender	RP	S.Williams	RP	L.McDaniel	P	R.Fingers	P	G.Brunet
RP	A.Fitzmorris	RP	K.Sanders	RP	R.Perranoski	RP	R.Klimkowski	RP	M.Grant	RP	D.Knowles
RP	T.Burgmeier	RP	J.Gelnar			RP	J.Aker	RP	P.Lindblad	RP	J.Grzenda
RP	T.Abernathy			P	L.Tiant			RP	M.Lachemann	RP	H.Pina
		P	A.Downing	P	D.Boswell	P	J.Cumberland				
P	W.Bunker	P	J.Morris			P	G.Waslewski	P	B.Locker	P	J.Shellenback
P	K.Wright									P	J.Brown
										P	D.Such

TEAM	G	W	L	PCT	GB	R	OR	AB	H	2B	3B	HR	BB	SO	AVG	OBP	SLG	PRO	PRO+	BR	/A	PF	CHI	RC	SB	CS	SBA	SBR
EAST																												
BAL	162	108	54	.667		**792**	**574**	5545	1424	213	25	179	717	952	.257	**.346**	.401	.747	112	101	**92**	101	99	**795**	84	39	68	2
NY	163	93	69	.574	15	680	612	5492	1381	208	**41**	111	588	**808**	.251	.327	.365	.692	102	-18	16	95	103	662	105	61	63	-5
BOS	162	87	75	.537	21	786	722	5535	**1450**	252	28	**203**	594	855	**.262**	.338	**.428**	**.766**	109	**119**	63	107	98	786	50	48	51	-14
DET	162	79	83	.488	29	666	731	5377	1282	207	38	148	656	825	.238	.325	.374	.699	98	-4	-9	101	99	658	29	30	49	-9
CLE	162	76	86	.469	32	649	675	5463	1358	197	23	183	503	909	.249	.316	.394	.710	96	3	-30	105	97	670	25	36	41	-14
WAS	162	70	92	.432	38	626	689	5460	1302	184	28	138	635	989	.238	.323	.358	.681	92	-36	-5	95	97	638	72	42	63	-4
WEST																												
MIN	162	98	64	.605		744	605	5483	1438	230	**41**	153	501	905	**.262**	.329	.403	.732	107	50	40	101	103	709	57	52	52	-14
OAK	162	89	73	.549	9	678	593	5376	1338	208	24	171	584	977	.249	.327	.392	.719	108	28	53	96	98	689	**131**	68	66	-2
CAL	162	86	76	.531	12	631	630	5532	1391	197	40	114	447	922	.251	.311	.363	.674	95	-64	-43	97	104	622	69	27	**72**	5
MIL	163	65	97	.401	33	613	751	5395	1305	202	24	126	592	985	.242	.321	.358	.679	92	-42	-46	101	97	618	91	73	55	-17
KC	162	65	97	.401	33	611	705	5503	1341	202	**41**	97	514	958	.244	.311	.348	.659	88	-88	-87	100	**105**	593	97	53	65	-3
CHI	162	56	106	.346	42	633	822	5514	1394	192	20	123	477	872	.253	.317	.362	.679	90	-50	-74	104	102	627	53	33	62	-4
TOT	973					8109		65675	16404	2492	373	1746	6808	10957	.250	.324	.379	.703							863	562	61	-78

TEAM	CG	SH	SV	IP	H	H/G	HR	BB	SO	RAT	ERA	ERA+	OAV	OOB	PR	/A	PF	CPI	FA	E	DP	FW	PW	BW	SBW	DIF
EAST																										
BAL	60	12	31	1478²	1317	8.0	139	469	941	11.0	3.15	116	.240	**.302**	93	82	98	102	.981	117	148	**1.1**	8.5	9.5	.9	7.0
NY	36	6	49	1471²	1386	8.5	**130**	**451**	777	11.4	3.24	108	.249	.308	77	45	95	**103**	.980	130	146	.4	4.7	1.7	.2	5.1
BOS	38	8	44	1446¹	1391	8.7	156	594	1003	12.6	3.87	102	.251	.329	-25	14	107	100	.974	156	131	-1.2	1.5	6.5	-.8	-.0
DET	33	9	39	1447¹	1443	9.0	153	623	1045	13.1	4.09	91	.260	.338	-61	-59	100	100	.978	133	142	.2	-6.1	-.9	-.3	5.2
CLE	34	8	35	1451¹	1333	8.3	163	689	**1076**	13.4	3.91	101	.247	.337	-31	8	107	**103**	.979	133	168	.2	.8	-3.1	-.8	-2.1
WAS	20	11	40	1457²	1375	8.5	139	611	823	12.4	3.80	94	.252	.330	-13	-39	96	100	**.982**	**116**	173	**1.1**	-4.0	-.5	.3	-7.8
WEST																										
MIN	26	12	**58**	1448¹	1329	8.3	**130**	486	940	11.5	3.23	115	.244	.310	78	79	100	**103**	.980	123	130	.7	8.2	4.1	-.8	4.7
OAK	33	**15**	40	1442²	**1253**	**7.8**	134	542	858	11.4	3.30	107	**.234**	.308	66	38	95	98	.977	141	152	-.3	3.9	5.5	.5	-1.6
CAL	21	10	49	1462¹	1280	7.9	154	559	922	11.6	3.48	104	.237	.313	37	21	97	99	.980	127	169	.5	2.2	-4.5	**1.2**	5.6
MIL	31	2	27	1446¹	1397	8.7	146	587	895	12.6	4.21	90	.255	.332	-79	-67	102	93	.978	136	142	.0	-6.8	-4.8	-1.1	-3.2
KC	30	11	25	1463²	1346	8.3	138	641	915	12.4	3.78	99	.247	.331	-11	-7	101	99	.976	152	162	-.9	-.7	-9.0	.4	-5.7
CHI	20	6	30	1430¹	1554	9.8	164	556	762	13.6	4.54	86	.280	.350	-132	-103	105	101	.975	165	**187**	-1.7	-10.7	-7.7	-.4	-5.2
TOT	382	110	467	17447		8.5				12.2	3.71		.250	.324					.978	1629	1850					

Runs	Hits	Doubles	Triples	Home Runs	Total Bases
Yastrzemski-Bos .. 125	Oliva-Min......204	Tovar-Min 36	Tovar-Min 13	Howard-Was 44	Yastrzemski-Bos ... 335
Tovar-Min 120	Johnson-Cal ... 202	Otis-KC 36	Stanley-Det 11	Killebrew-Min ... 41	Oliva-Min 323
White-NY 109	Tovar-Min ... 195	Oliva-Min 36	Otis-KC 9	Yastrzemski-Bos ... 40	Harper-Mil 315
Smith-Bos...... 109	Yastrzemski-Bos... 186	Harper-Mil 35		T.Conigliaro-Bos ... 36	Howard-Was 309
Harper-Mil 104	White-NY 180	Cardenas-Min 34		Powell-Bal 35	Powell-Bal 289

Runs Batted In	Runs Produced	Bases On Balls	Batting Average	On Base Percentage	Slugging Average
Howard-Was ... 126	Yastrzemski-Bos... 187	Howard-Was ... 132	Johnson-Cal 329	Yastrzemski-Bos ...453	Yastrzemski-Bos ...592
T.Conigliaro-Bos .. 116	White-NY 181	Yastrzemski-Bos ... 128	Yastrzemski-Bos ...329	Howard-Was ...420	Powell-Bal ...549
Powell-Bal ... 114	Oliva-Min ... 180	Killebrew-Min ... 128	Oliva-Min ...325	Powell-Bal ...417	Killebrew-Min ...546
Killebrew-Min 113	Howard-Was ... 172	Bando-Oak ... 118	Aparicio-Chi 313	Killebrew-Min ...416	Howard-Was ...546
Oliva-Min 107	T.Conigliaro-Bos ... 169	Buford-Bal 109	F.Robinson-Bal ...306	Buford-Bal ...409	Harper-Mil ...522

Production	Adjusted Production	Batter Runs	Adjusted Batter Runs	Clutch Hitting Index	Runs Created
Yastrzemski-Bos .1.045	Yastrzemski-Bos ... 174	Yastrzemski-Bos ... 71.7	Yastrzemski-Bos ...61.7	Piniella-KC 128	Yastrzemski-Bos ... 157
Powell-Bal 967	Howard-Was ... 173	Howard-Was ... 54.1	Howard-Was 60.5	Cater-NY 117	Howard-Was ... 130
Howard-Was 966	Powell-Bal ... 163	Killebrew-Min ... 49.5	Powell-Bal 47.9	McMullen-Was-Cal 116	Powell-Bal 123
Killebrew-Min 962	Killebrew-Min ... 161	Powell-Bal ... 49.2	Killebrew-Min ...47.8	Howard-Was ... 116	Harper-Mil 122
F.Robinson-Bal ...922	F.Robinson-Bal 151	Harper-Mil 37.5	White-NY 38.2	Belanger-Bal 115	Killebrew-Min 116

Total Average	Stolen Bases	Stolen Base Average	Stolen Base Runs	Fielding Runs	Total Player Rating
Yastrzemski-Bos .1.170	Campaneris-Oak .. 42	Otis-KC 94.3	Otis-KC 8.7	Knoop-Cal 35.1	Yastrzemski-Bos ... 5.2
Powell-Bal 1.034	Harper-Mil 38	Johnson-Cal 89.5	Campaneris-Oak .. 6.6	Brinkman-Was ... 31.1	Aparicio-Chi 4.6
Howard-Was ...1.026	Alomar-Cal 35	Campaneris-Oak .. 80.8	Stroud-Was 3.9	Nettles-Cle 27.8	Oliva-Min 4.3
Killebrew-Min 1.000	Kelly-KC 34	Stroud-Was 78.4	Johnson-Cal 3.9	Cullen-Was 26.5	Fregosi-Cal 4.2
F.Robinson-Bal ...944	Otis-KC 33	Kenney-NY 76.9	Alomar-Cal 3.3	Mitterwald-Min ... 24.3	Howard-Was 4.2

Wins	Win Percentage	Games	Complete Games	Shutouts	Saves
Perry-Min 24	Cuellar-Bal .... .750	Wood-Chi 77	Cuellar-Bal 21	Palmer-Bal 5	Perranoski-Min 34
McNally-Bal 24	McNally-Bal 727	Grant-Oak 72	McDowell-Cle 19	Dobson-Oak 5	McDaniel-NY ... 29
Cuellar-Bal 24	Perry-Min 667	Knowles-Was....... 71	Palmer-Bal 17	Peters-Bos 4	Timmermann-Det ... 27
Wright-Cal 22	Palmer-Bal 667	Williams-Min 68	McNally-Bal 16	Perry-Min 4	Knowles-Was ... 27
	Siebert-Bos 652		Culp-Bos 15	Cuellar-Bal 4	Grant-Oak 24

Innings Pitched	Fewest Hits/Game	Fewest BB/Game	Strikeouts	Strikeouts/Game	Ratio
Palmer-Bal 305.0	Messersmith-Cal . 6.66	Peterson-NY 1.38	McDowell-Cle ... 304	McDowell-Cle ... 8.97	Peterson-NY 10.03
McDowell-Cle ...305.0	McDowell-Cle ... 6.96	Perry-Min 1.84	Lolich-Det ... 230	Johnson-KC ... 8.66	Cuellar-Bal 10.37
Cuellar-Bal ...297.2	Segui-Oak 7.22	Cox-Was 2.06	Johnson-KC ... 206	Cain-Det 7.77	Perry-Min 10.46
McNally-Bal ...296.0	Johnson-KC 7.49	Cuellar-Bal 2.09	Palmer-Bal ... 199	Lolich-Det 7.59	Blyleven-Min 10.54
Perry-Min 278.2	Culp-Bos 7.56	Horlen-Chi 2.14	Culp-Bos 197	Messersmith-Cal . 7.49	Messersmith-Cal .10.54

Earned Run Average	Adjusted ERA	Opponents' Batting Avg.	Opponents' On Base Pct.	Starter Runs	Adjusted Starter Runs
Segui-Oak........2.56	Segui-Oak 139	Messersmith-Cal ...205	Peterson-NY 280	Palmer-Bal 33.9	McDowell-Cle 35.2
Palmer-Bal 2.71	McDowell-Cle ... 136	McDowell-Cle 213	Cuellar-Bal 286	McDowell-Cle ... 26.9	Palmer-Bal 31.6
Wright-Cal 2.83	Palmer-Bal 134	Segui-Oak 222	Perry-Min 287	Wright-Cal 25.6	Culp-Bos 25.6
Peterson-NY 2.90	Culp-Bos 130	Culp-Bos 224	Blyleven-Min......289	Peterson-NY 23.4	Wright-Cal 22.7
McDowell-Cle 2.92	Wright-Cal 128	Johnson-KC 228	Messersmith-Cal ..290	Perry-Min 21.0	Perry-Min 21.2

Clutch Pitching Index	Relief Runs	Adjusted Relief Runs	Relief Ranking	Total Pitcher Index	Total Baseball Ranking
Stottlemyre-NY ...113	Grant-Oak 25.9	Grant-Oak 23.5	Knowles-Was 32.8	Knowles-Was ... 3.5	Yastrzemski-Bos ... 5.2
Kaat-Min 112	Knowles-Was ... 22.2	Williams-Min ... 21.9	McDaniel-NY ...30.0	Perry-Min 3.3	Aparicio-Chi 4.6
Bahnsen-NY 109	Williams-Min ... 21.8	Sanders-Mil ... 20.9	Wood-Chi 28.6	McDaniel-NY ... 3.3	Oliva-Min 4.3
Segui-Oak 108	McDaniel-NY ... 21.1	Hall-Min 20.2	Perranoski-Min ...28.5	Wood-Chi........ 3.2	Fregosi-Cal 4.2
Wright-Cal 107	Sanders-Mil ... 20.1	Knowles-Was 20.1	Williams-Min 24.5	McDowell-Cle ... 3.0	Howard-Was 4.2

January 21 The BBWAA fails to elect anyone in the annual Hall of Fame election. With 270 votes required, the nearest finishers are Yogi Berra (242) and Early Wynn (240).

January 31 The Hall of Fame Special Veterans Committee selects seven men for enshrinement: former players Jake Beckley, Joe Kelley, Harry Hooper, Rube Marquard, Chick Hafey, Dave Bancroft, and executive George Weiss.

February 9 Satchel Paige is nominated for the Hall of Fame. The Hall's new Special Committee on the Negro Leagues will formally select Paige for induction on June 10.

April 10 The Phillies debut in new $49.5 million Veterans Stadium, beating Montreal 4-1. Don Money connects for the park's first homer.

April 27 Hank Aaron becomes the third member of the 600-home run club, but one of the other two members—the Giants' Willie Mays—hits a 10th-inning single to beat Aaron's Braves.

May 28 The Braves' Clete Boyer, involved in a dispute with owner Paul Richards and manager Lum Harris over alleged silly rules and mismanagement, gets his release and retires. Boyer had hit safely in the last nine games of his ca-

reer, including five home runs and 14 RBI.

May 30 Willie Mays hits his 638th career home run for the Giants, adding his NL record 1,950th run scored in the process. Stan Musial had been the record holder with 1,949 runs.

June 3 Cub southpaw Ken Holtzman tosses the second no-hitter of his career, victimizing the Reds 1-0. Holtzman scores the only run, in the third inning.

June 6 Willie Mays strokes a 12th-inning home run off Joe Hoerner of the Phillies in the second game of a doubleheader. It is his 22nd—and last—career extra-inning belt, a major league record.

June 23 Phillie Rick Wise no-hits the Reds 4-0 and hits two home runs to drive in all the runs in the game.

August 14 Before 30,678 Pittsburgh fans, Cardinals ace Bob Gibson, 35, hurls the first no-hitter of his career, an 11-0 shellacking of the Pirates. The Cards make it easy for Gibson by scoring five runs in the top of the first inning.

September 5 Astros pitcher J. R. Richard makes his major league debut, striking out 15 Giants in a 5-3 win.

September 29 In the sixth inning of the Expos' 6–5 win over the Cubs, Ron Hunt

is hit by a Milt Pappas pitch. It is the 50th HBP for Hunt in 1971, setting a major league record.

October 6 The Pirates outslug the Giants 9-5 to win the LCS 3 games to 1, as Richie Hebner's bat takes Pittsburgh into the World Series. Hebner has three hits and three RBI, including a homer.

October 14 Nelson Briles hurls a two-hit shutout and Robertson slugs his sixth postseason homer as the Pirates win the fifth game 4-0 and take a 3-2 Series advantage. Roberto Clemente hits safely in his 12th straight Series game.

October 17 Steve Blass hurls a four-hitter and Clemente homers as the Pirates win Game 7 of the World Series 2-1, becoming World Champions for the first time since 1960.

November 10 Joe Torre, who hit 24 homers for the Cardinals and led the NL in RBI (137) and batting (.363), wins the MVP Award.

November 24 Earl Williams, who belted 33 home runs and knocked in 87 runs for the Braves, wins the NL Rookie of the Year honors. Williams gets 18 of 24 votes, with the others going to Willie Montanez of the Phillies.

December 1 The Cubs release Ernie Banks and sign him as a coach.

ATLANTA		CHICAGO		CINCINNATI		HOUSTON		LOS ANGELES		MONTREAL	
M	L.Harris	M	L.Durocher	M	S.Anderson	M	H.Walker	M	W.Alston	M	G.Mauch
1B	H.Aaron	1B	J.Pepitone	1B	L.May	1B	D.Menke	1B	W.Parker	1B	R.Fairly
2B	F.Millan	2B	G.Beckert	2B	T.Helms	2B	J.Morgan	2B	J.Lefebvre	2B	R.Hunt
SS	M.Perez	SS	D.Kessinger	SS	D.Concepcion	SS	R.Metzger	SS	M.Wills	SS	B.Wine
3B	D.Evans	3B	R.Santo	3B	T.Perez	3B	D.Rader	3B	S.Garvey	3B	B.Bailey
LF	R.Garr	LF	B.Williams	LF	H.McRae	LF	J.Alou	LF	D.Allen	LF	J.Fairey
CF	S.Jackson	CF	B.Davis	CF	G.Foster	CF	C.Cedeno	CF	W.Davis	CF	B.Day
RF	M.Lum	RF	J.Callison	RF	P.Rose	RF	J.Wynn	RF	B.Buckner	RF	R.Staub
C	E.Williams	C	C.Cannizzaro	C	J.Bench	C	J.Edwards	C	D.Sims	C	J.Bateman
1	O.Cepeda	O1	J.Hickman	O	B.Carbo	O1	B.Watson	O	W.Crawford	2S	G.Sutherland
		23	P.Popovich	S3	W.Woodward			S3	B.Valentine		
								O	M.Mota		
P	P.Niekro					P	D.Wilson	2O	B.Russell	P	B.Stoneman
P	R.Reed	P	F.Jenkins	P	G.Nolan	P	J.Billingham	C	T.Haller	P	S.Renko
P	G.Stone	P	M.Pappas	P	D.Gullett	P	K.Forsch			P	C.Morton
P	P.Jarvis	P	B.Hands	P	J.McGlothlin	P	L.Dierker	P	D.Sutton	P	E.McAnally
P	T.Kelley	P	K.Holtzman	P	R.Grimsley	P	W.Blasingame	P	A.Downing	P	J.Strohmayer
RP	C.Upshaw	P	J.Pizarro	P	W.Simpson	RP	J.Ray	P	C.Osteen	RP	M.Marshall
RP	S.Barber	RP	P.Regan	RP	W.Granger	RP	G.Culver	P	B.Singer	RP	D.McGinn
RP	B.Priddy	RP	B.Bonham	RP	C.Carroll	RP	D.Lemaster	RP	J.Brewer	RP	H.Reed
				RP	J.Gibbon			RP	P.Mikkelsen		
P	J.Nash					P	F.Gladding	RP	J.Moeller	P	C.Raymond
P	M.McQueen	P	J.Merritt								
P	R.Herbel	P	T.Cloninger					P	D.Alexander		

NEW YORK		PHILADELPHIA		PITTSBURGH		SAN DIEGO		SAN FRANCISCO		ST.LOUIS	
M	G.Hodges	M	F.Lucchesi	M	D.Murtaugh	M	P.Gomez	M	C.Fox	M	R.Schoendienst
1B	E.Kranepool	1B	D.Johnson	1B	B.Robertson	1B	N.Colbert	1B	W.McCovey	1B	J.Hague
2B	K.Boswell	2B	D.Doyle	2B	D.Cash	2B	D.Mason	2B	T.Fuentes	2B	T.Sizemore
SS	B.Harrelson	SS	L.Bowa	SS	G.Alley	SS	E.Hernandez	SS	C.Speier	SS	D.Maxvill
3B	B.Aspromonte	3B	J.Vukovich	3B	R.Hebner	3B	E.Spiezio	3B	A.Gallagher	3B	J.Torre
LF	C.Jones	LF	O.Gamble	LF	W.Stargell	LF	L.Stahl	LF	K.Henderson	LF	L.Brock
CF	T.Agee	CF	W.Montanez	CF	A.Oliver	CF	C.Gaston	CF	W.Mays	CF	M.Alou
RF	K.Singleton	RF	R.Freed	RF	R.Clemente	RF	O.Brown	RF	B.Bonds	RF	J.Cardenal
C	J.Grote	C	T.McCarver	C	M.Sanguillen	C	B.Barton	C	D.Dietz	C	T.Simmons
23	T.Foli	3O	D.Money	O	G.Clines	23	D.Campbell	32	H.Lanier	O	J.Cruz
O	D.Hahn	2	T.Harmon	O1	V.Davalillo	O	I.Murrell			2	J.Javier
O	D.Marshall			S	J.Hernandez	O	L.Lee	P	G.Perry		
1	D.Clendenon	P	R.Wise					P	J.Marichal	P	S.Carlton
3	W.Garrett	P	B.Lersch	P	S.Blass	P	D.Roberts	P	J.Cumberland	P	B.Gibson
		P	C.Short	P	D.Ellis	P	C.Kirby	P	R.Bryant	P	R.Cleveland
P	T.Seaver	P	K.Reynolds	P	B.Johnson	P	S.Arlin	P	S.Stone	P	J.Reuss
P	G.Gentry	P	W.Fryman	P	L.Walker	P	T.Phoebus	RP	J.Johnson	RP	C.Taylor
P	J.Koosman	RP	B.Champion	P	B.Moose	P	F.Norman	RP	D.McMahon	RP	M.Drabowsky
P	R.Sadecki	RP	B.Brandon	RP	D.Giusti	RP	A.Severinsen	RP	R.Robertson	RP	F.Linzy
P	N.Ryan	RP	J.Hoerner	RP	M.Grant	RP	B.Miller				
RP	T.McGraw					RP	D.Kelley	P	D.Carrithers	P	C.Zachary
RP	D.Frisella	P	J.Bunning	1971	N.Briles					P	D.Shaw
RP	C.Williams	P	B.Wilson	P	B.Kison	P	D.Coombs			P	A.Santorini
P	J.McAndrew										
P	R.Taylor										

TEAM	G	W	L	PCT	GB	R	OR	AB	H	2B	3B	HR	BB	SO	AVG	OBP	SLG	PRO	PRO+	BR	/A	PF	CHI	RC	SB	CS	SBA	SBR
EAST																												
PIT	162	97	65	.599		788	599	5674	**1555**	223	**61**	**154**	469	919	.274	.333	**.416**	**.749**	119	121	125	100	103	776	65	31	68	1
STL	163	90	72	.556	7	739	699	5610	1542	225	54	95	543	757	**.275**	**.342**	.385	.727	108	91	62	104	100	736	**124**	53	70	5
NY	162	83	79	.512	14	588	**550**	5477	1365	203	29	98	547	958	.249	.321	.351	.672	98	-20	-11	99	95	614	89	43	67	1
CHI	162	83	79	.512	14	637	648	5438	1401	202	34	128	527	772	.258	.327	.378	.705	99	41	-56	115	95	663	44	32	58	-6
MON	162	71	90	.441	25.5	622	729	5335	1312	197	29	88	543	800	.246	.325	.343	.668	96	-20	-22	100	102	598	51	43	54	-11
PHI	162	67	95	.414	30	558	688	5538	1289	209	35	123	499	1031	.233	.300	.350	.650	90	-74	-73	100	99	586	63	39	62	-5
WEST																												
SF	162	90	72	.556		706	644	5461	1348	224	36	140	**654**	1042	.247	.331	.385	.709	109	57	68	98	101	699	101	36	**74**	**9**
LA	162	89	73	.549	1	663	587	5523	1469	213	38	95	489	755	.266	.328	.370	.698	111	28	68	94	100	661	76	40	66	-1
ATL	162	82	80	.506	8	643	699	5575	1434	192	30	153	434	**747**	.257	.314	.385	.699	98	18	-23	106	98	658	57	46	55	-11
HOU	162	79	83	.488	11	585	567	5492	1319	**230**	52	71	478	888	.240	.304	.340	.644	90	-81	-67	97	**107**	573	101	51	66	0
CIN	162	79	83	.488	11	586	581	5414	1306	203	28	138	438	907	.241	.301	.366	.667	96	-45	-33	98	103	586	59	33	64	-6
SD	161	61	100	.379	28.5	486	610	5366	1250	184	31	96	438	966	.233	.294	.332	.626	89	-117	-84	93	98	513	70	45	61	-6
TOT	972					7601		65903	16590	2505	457	1379	6059	10542	.252	.318	.366	.685					900	492	65	-25		

TEAM	CG	SH	SV	IP	H	H/G	HR	BB	SO	RAT	ERA	ERA+	OAV	OOB	PR	/A	PF	CPI	FA	E	DP	FW	PW	BW	SBW	DIF
EAST																										
PIT	43	15	**48**	1461	1426	8.8	108	470	813	11.9	3.31	102	.257	.318	26	12	98	105	.979	133	164	.0	1.3	**13.4**	.3	.9
STL	56	14	22	1467	1482	9.1	104	576	911	12.9	3.85	93	.263	.336	-63	-41	104	99	.978	142	155	-.4	-4.4	6.6	.8	6.4
NY	42	13	22	1466¹	**1227**	**7.5**	100	529	**1157**	11.0	**2.99**	114	**.227**	**.300**	78	68	98	94	.981	114	135	1.2	**7.3**	-1.2	.3	-5.6
CHI	75	17	13	1444	1458	9.1	132	411	900	11.8	3.61	109	.262	.316	-23	52	114	101	.980	126	150	.5	5.6	-6.0	-.4	2.4
MON	49	8	25	1434¹	1418	8.9	133	658	829	13.2	4.12	86	.260	.344	-104	-94	102	100	.976	150	164	-.9	-10.1	-2.4	-1.0	4.8
PHI	31	10	25	1470²	1396	8.5	132	525	838	12.0	3.71	95	.254	.323	-41	-31	102	98	.981	122	158	.7	-3.3	-7.8	-.3	-3.3
WEST																										
SF	45	14	30	1454²	1324	8.2	128	471	831	11.3	3.32	102	.242	.306	24	13	98	97	.972	179	153	-2.6	1.4	7.3	**1.2**	1.7
LA	48	**18**	33	1449²	1363	8.5	110	**399**	853	11.1	3.23	100	.250	.304	37	-1	93	98	.979	131	159	.2	-.1	7.3	.1	.5
ATL	40	11	31	1474²	1529	9.3	152	485	823	12.5	3.75	99	.269	.330	-46	-6	107	108	.977	146	180	-.7	-.6	-2.5	-1.0	5.7
HOU	43	10	25	1471¹	1318	8.1	**75**	475	914	11.3	3.13	107	.241	.309	55	38	97	95	.983	106	152	1.6	4.1	-7.2	.2	-.8
CIN	27	11	38	1444	1298	8.1	112	501	750	11.4	3.35	102	.243	.311	18	0	97	97	**.984**	103	174	**1.8**	.3	-3.5	.0	-.3
SD	47	10	17	1438	1351	8.5	93	559	923	12.1	3.22	102	.249	.323	39	12	95	106	.974	161	144	-1.6	1.3	-9.0	-.4	-9.8
TOT	546	151	329	17475²		8.5				11.9	3.47		.252	.318					.979	1613	1888					

Runs		Hits		Doubles		Triples		Home Runs		Total Bases	
Brock-StL	126	Torre-StL	230	Cedeno-Hou	40	Morgan-Hou	11	Stargell-Pit	48	Torre-StL	352
Bonds-SF	110	Garr-Atl	219	Brock-StL	37	Metzger-Hou	11	H.Aaron-Atl	47	H.Aaron-Atl	331
Stargell-Pit	104	Brock-StL	200	Torre-StL	34	Davis-LA	10	May-Cin	39	Stargell-Pit	321
Garr-Atl	101	Davis-LA	198	Staub-Mon	34	Gaston-SD	9	Johnson-Phi	34	Bonds-SF	317
Torre-StL	97			Davis-LA	33					Williams-Chi	300

Runs Batted In		Runs Produced		Bases On Balls		Batting Average		On Base Percentage		Slugging Average	
Torre-StL	137	Torre-StL	210	Mays-SF	112	Torre-StL	.363	Mays-SF	.429	H.Aaron-Atl	.669
Stargell-Pit	125	Stargell-Pit	181	Dietz-SF	97	Garr-Atl	.343	Torre-StL	.424	Stargell-Pit	.628
H.Aaron-Atl	118	Brock-StL	180	Bailey-Mon	97	Beckert-Chi	.342	H.Aaron-Atl	.414	Torre-StL	.555
Bonds-SF	102	Bonds-SF	179	Allen-LA	93	Clemente-Pit	.341	Hunt-Mon	.403	May-Cin	.532
Montanez-Phi	99	Staub-Mon	172	Morgan-Hou	88	H.Aaron-Atl	.327	Stargell-Pit	.401	Bonds-SF	.512

Production		Adjusted Production		Batter Runs		Adjusted Batter Runs		Clutch Hitting Index		Runs Created	
H.Aaron-Atl	1.082	H.Aaron-Atl	190	H.Aaron-Atl	65.2	Stargell-Pit	59.3	Fairly-Mon	129	Torre-StL	145
Stargell-Pit	1.029	Stargell-Pit	188	Torre-StL	62.5	H.Aaron-Atl	57.7	Sanguillen-Pit	125	H.Aaron-Atl	137
Torre-StL	.979	Torre-StL	169	Stargell-Pit	58.7	Torre-StL	57.3	Bailey-Mon	123	Stargell-Pit	131
Mays-SF	.911	Mays-SF	160	Williams-Chi	39.4	Allen-LA	41.1	Watson-Hou	121	Bonds-SF	115
Williams-Chi	.889	Allen-LA	154	Staub-Mon	38.5	Mays-SF	39.1	Simmons-StL	120	Brock-StL	114

Total Average		Stolen Bases		Stolen Base Average		Stolen Base Runs		Fielding Runs		Total Player Rating	
H.Aaron-Atl	1.178	Brock-StL	64	Mays-SF	88.5	Brock-StL	7.8	Maxvill-StL	29.2	Stargell-Pit	5.8
Stargell-Pit	1.117	Morgan-Hou	40	Henderson-SF	85.7	Morgan-Hou	7.2	Garr-Atl	16.2	H.Aaron-Atl	4.2
Mays-SF	1.067	Garr-Atl	30	Morgan-Hou	83.3	Mays-SF	5.1	Robertson-Pit	15.2	Torre-StL	4.1
Torre-StL	.998			Agee-NY	82.4	Agee-NY	4.8	Helms-Cin	14.4	Staub-Mon	3.6
Bonds-SF	.876			Hernandez-SD	80.8	Harrelson-NY	4.2	Barton-SD	14.0	Mays-SF	3.6

Wins		Win Percentage		Games		Complete Games		Shutouts		Saves	
Jenkins-Chi	24	Gullett-Cin	.727	Granger-Cin	70	Jenkins-Chi	30	Pappas-Chi	5	Giusti-Pit	30
Seaver-NY	20	Downing-LA	.690	J.Johnson-SF	67	Seaver-NY	21	Gibson-StL	5	Marshall-Mon	23
Downing-LA	20	Carlton-StL	.690	Marshall-Mon	66	Stoneman-Mon	20	Downing-LA	5	Brewer-LA	22
Carlton-StL	20	Ellis-Pit	.679	McMahon-SF	61	Gibson-StL	20	Blass-Pit	5	J.Johnson-SF	18
Ellis-Pit	19	Seaver-NY	.667	Carroll-Cin	61					Upshaw-Atl	17

Innings Pitched		Fewest Hits/Game		Fewest BB/Game		Strikeouts		Strikeouts/Game		Ratio	
Jenkins-Chi	325.0	Wilson-Hou	6.55	Jenkins-Chi	1.02	Seaver-NY	289	Seaver-NY	9.08	Seaver-NY	8.64
Stoneman-Mon	294.2	Seaver-NY	6.60	Marichal-SF	1.81	Jenkins-Chi	263	Kirby-SD	7.78	Wilson-Hou	9.44
Seaver-NY	286.1	Kirby-SD	7.17	Stone-Atl	1.82	Stoneman-Mon	251	Stoneman-Mon	7.67	Jenkins-Chi	9.58
Perry-SF	280.0	Gentry-NY	7.39	Hands-Chi	1.86	Kirby-SD	231	Jenkins-Chi	7.28	Marichal-SF	9.77
Marichal-SF	279.0	Stoneman-Mon	7.42	Sutton-LA	1.87	Sutton-LA	194	Gentry-NY	6.86	Sutton-LA	9.87

Earned Run Average		Adjusted ERA		Opponents' Batting Avg.		Opponents' On Base Pct.		Starter Runs		Adjusted Starter Runs	
Seaver-NY	1.76	Seaver-NY	194	Wilson-Hou	.202	Seaver-NY	.253	Seaver-NY	54.3	Seaver-NY	52.4
Roberts-SD	2.10	Roberts-SD	157	Seaver-NY	.206	Wilson-Hou	.268	Roberts-SD	40.9	Jenkins-Chi	42.1
Wilson-Hou	2.45	Jenkins-Chi	142	Kirby-SD	.216	Jenkins-Chi	.271	Wilson-Hou	30.2	Roberts-SD	35.8
Forsch-Hou	2.53	Wilson-Hou	137	Cumberland-SF	.223	Marichal-SF	.274	Sutton-LA	27.2	Wilson-Hou	27.2
Sutton-LA	2.54	Forsch-Hou	133	Gentry-NY	.224	Nolan-Cin	.275	Jenkins-Chi	25.2	Niekro-Atl	21.8

Clutch Pitching Index		Relief Runs		Adjusted Relief Runs		Relief Ranking		Total Pitcher Index		Total Baseball Ranking	
Roberts-SD	120	McGraw-NY	21.7	McGraw-NY	21.0	McGraw-NY	29.0	Seaver-NY	6.5	Seaver-NY	6.5
Downing-LA	115	Miller-Chi-SD-Pit	18.9	Miller-Chi-SD-Pit	18.9	Miller-Chi-SD-Pit	26.7	Jenkins-Chi	6.4	Jenkins-Chi	6.4
Short-Phi	115	Frisella-NY	14.9	Frisella-NY	14.3	Frisella-NY	22.7	Roberts-SD	4.6	Stargell-Pit	5.8
Johnson-Pit	112	Ray-Hou	14.6	Ray-Hou	13.5	Brewer-LA	22.3	Wise-Phi	3.4	Roberts-SD	4.6
Wise-Phi	112	Brewer-LA	14.3	Hoerner-Phi	12.6	Ray-Hou	18.4	McGraw-NY	3.4	H.Aaron-Atl	4.2

January 11 Tigers pitcher John Hiller, age 27, suffers a heart attack. He will miss the season before making a remarkable comeback.

April 27 Curt Flood jumps the Senators after 13 games and departs for Denmark, ending his playing career. He will continue his antitrust suit which will eventually reach the Supreme Court.

June 21 Indians slugger Ken Harrelson announces his retirement from baseball to join the pro golf tour.

June 26 Last year's AL batting king Alex Johnson is suspended by the Angels following a series of incidents (including five benchings and 29 fines) resulting from his failure to hustle.

July 13 In an All-Star Game featuring homers by Johnny Bench, Hank Aaron, Roberto Clemente, Reggie Jackson, Frank Robinson, and Harmon Killebrew, the AL triumphs at Detroit 6-4. It is the only AL All-Star win between 1962 and 1983. Jackson's homer goes 520 feet.

August 10 Harmon Killebrew becomes the tenth player to amass 500 homers, and adds his 501st, but the Orioles beat the Twins 5-4.

August 10 Sixteen baseball researchers at Cooperstown form the Society for American Baseball Research (SABR), with founder L. Robert Davids as president.

September 26 Jim Palmer becomes the fourth member of the Orioles pitching staff to notch his 20th victory. Only one other team in major league history—the 1920 White Sox—boasted four 20-game winners.

September 28 Arbitrator Lewis Gill rules that Alex Johnson was "emotionally incapacitated" during events leading to his June suspension, and that he should be treated the same as a physically disabled player. Johnson wins nearly $30,000 in back salary from the Angels.

September 28 Baltimore achieves 108 wins for the season with doubleheader victories at Boston 10-2 and 5-4. The Orioles become only the third team to win 100 games in three straight seasons.

September 30 The Senators, in their final game in Washington, hold a 7-5 lead over the Yankees with two outs in the ninth. Fans then swarm onto the field, causing the game to be forfeited.

October 5 The Orioles overcome two Reggie Jackson home runs to complete a sweep of Oakland in the LCS with a 5-3 victory.

October 9 The Orioles win Game 1 of the World Series over the Pirates 5-3 behind Dave McNally's three-hitter and Merv Rettenmund's three-run homer.

October 11 Brooks Robinson ties a Series record by reaching base five straight times on three hits and two walks as Baltimore rolls over Pittsburgh 11-3 to take a 2-0 Series advantage.

October 26 Vida Blue wins the AL Cy Young Award. Blue was 24-8 for the A's, posting 301 strikeouts, eight shutouts, and a 1.82 ERA. Ferguson Jenkins won the Cy Young Award in the NL.

November 10 Vida Blue adds the AL MVP to his list of awards.

December 10 The Angels trade shortstop Jim Fregosi to the Mets for four players, including outfielder Leroy Stanton and pitcher Nolan Ryan. This will rank as probably the Angels' best trade.

BALTIMORE

Pos	Player
M	E.Weaver
1B	B.Powell
2B	D.Johnson
SS	M.Belanger
3B	B.Robinson
LF	D.Buford
CF	P.Blair
RF	M.Rettenmund
C	E.Hendricks
O1	F.Robinson
C	A.Etchebarren
P	M.Cuellar
P	J.Palmer
P	P.Dobson
P	D.McNally
RP	G.Jackson
P	D.Leonhard

BOSTON

Pos	Player
M	E.Kasko
1B	G.Scott
2B	D.Griffin
SS	L.Aparicio
3B	R.Petrocelli
LF	C.Yastrzemski
CF	B.Conigliaro
RF	R.Smith
C	D.Josephson
O	J.Lahoud
2S	J.Kennedy
C	B.Montgomery
P	R.Culp
P	S.Siebert
P	G.Peters
P	J.Lonborg
RP	B.Lee
RP	B.Bolin
RP	K.Brett
P	L.Tiant
P	R.Moret
P	K.Tatum
P	S.Lyle

CALIFORNIA

Pos	Player
M	L.Phillips
1B	J.Spencer
2B	S.Alomar
SS	J.Fregosi
3B	K.McMullen
LF	T.Gonzalez
CF	K.Berry
RF	R.Repoz
C	J.Stephenson
O	M.Rivers
O	T.Conigliaro
S	S.O'Brien
O	A.Johnson
P	C.Wright
P	A.Messersmith
P	T.Murphy
P	R.May
RP	E.Fisher
RP	L.Allen
RP	D.LaRoche
P	M.Queen

CHICAGO

Pos	Player
M	C.Tanner
1B	C.May
2B	M.Andrews
SS	L.Alvarado
3B	B.Melton
LF	R.Reichardt
CF	J.Johnstone
RF	W.Williams
C	E.Herrmann
2O	R.McKinney
SO	L.Richard
C	T.Egan
O	P.Kelly
P	W.Wood
P	T.Bradley
P	T.John
P	B.Johnson
P	J.Horlen
RP	S.Kealey
RP	V.Romo
RP	T.Forster

CLEVELAND

Pos	Player
M	A.Dark
M	J.Lipon
1B	C.Chambliss
2B	E.Leon
SS	J.Heidemann
3B	G.Nettles
LF	T.Uhlaender
CF	V.Pinson
RF	R.Foster
C	R.Fosse
P	S.McDowell
P	S.Dunning
P	A.Foster
P	R.Lamb
P	S.Hargan
RP	V.Colbert
RP	P.Hennigan
RP	E.Farmer
P	M.Paul
P	R.Hand
P	S.Mingori

DETROIT

Pos	Player
M	B.Martin
1B	N.Cash
2B	D.McAuliffe
SS	E.Brinkman
3B	A.Rodriguez
LF	W.Horton
CF	M.Stanley
RF	A.Kaline
C	B.Freehan
O1	J.Northrup
P	M.Lolich
P	J.Coleman
P	L.Cain
P	J.Niekro
RP	F.Scherman
RP	D.Chance
RP	M.Kilkenny
P	T.Timmerman

KANSAS CITY

Pos	Player
M	B.Lemon
1B	G.Hopkins
2B	C.Rojas
SS	F.Patek
3B	P.Schaal
LF	L.Piniella
CF	A.Otis
RF	J.Keough
C	J.May
OC	E.Kirkpatrick
1O	B.Oliver
P	D.Drago
P	M.Hedlund
P	P.Splittorff
P	B.Dal Canton
P	A.Fitzmorris
RP	J.York
RP	T.Burgmeier
RP	T.Abernathy
P	K.Wright
P	J.Rooker

MILWAUKEE

Pos	Player
M	D.Bristol
1B	J.Briggs
2B	R.Theobald
SS	R.Auerbach
3B	T.Matchick
LF	T.Harper
CF	D.May
RF	B.Voss
C	E.Rodriguez
O1	A.Kosco
13	R.Pena
2S	T.Kubiak
P	M.Pattin
P	B.Parsons
P	S.Lockwood
P	L.Krausse
P	J.Slaton
RP	K.Sanders
RP	J.Morris
RP	M.Lopez

MINNESOTA

Pos	Player
M	B.Rigney
1B	R.Reese
2B	R.Carew
SS	L.Cardenas
3B	S.Braun
LF	C.Tovar
CF	J.Holt
RF	T.Oliva
C	G.Mitterwald
13	H.Killebrew
P	B.Blyleven
P	J.Perry
P	J.Kaat
RP	R.Corbin
RP	T.Hall
RP	S.Williams
P	S.Luebber

NEW YORK

Pos	Player
M	R.Houk
1B	D.Cater
2B	H.Clarke
SS	G.Michael
3B	J.Kenney
LF	R.White
CF	B.Murcer
RF	F.Alou
C	T.Munson
1	J.Ellis
C	J.Gibbs
P	F.Peterson
P	M.Stottlemyre
P	S.Bahnsen
P	S.Kline
P	M.Kekich
RP	L.McDaniel
RP	J.Aker

OAKLAND

Pos	Player
M	D.Williams
1B	M.Epstein
2B	D.Green
SS	B.Campaneris
3B	S.Bando
LF	J.Rudi
CF	R.Monday
RF	R.Jackson
C	D.Duncan
O	A.Mangual
1O	T.Davis
P	V.Blue
P	C.Hunter
P	C.Dobson
P	D.Segui
P	B.Odom
RP	R.Fingers
RP	B.Locker
RP	D.Knowles

WASHINGTON

Pos	Player
M	T.Williams
1B	D.Mincher
2B	T.Cullen
SS	T.Harrah
3B	D.Nelson
LF	F.Howard
CF	E.Maddox
RF	D.Unser
C	P.Casanova
23	B.Allen
CO	D.Billings
O1	T.McCraw
2	L.Randle
P	D.Bosman
P	D.McLain
P	P.Broberg
P	B.Gogolewski
P	J.Shellenback
RP	C.Cox
RP	P.Lindblad
RP	D.Riddleberger
P	J.Grzenda
P	M.Thompson
P	J.Janeski
P	H.Pina

TEAM	G	W	L	PCT	GB	R	OR	AB	H	2B	3B	HR	BB	SO	AVG	OBP	SLG	PRO	PRO+	BR	/A	PF	CHI	RC	SB	CS	SBA	SBR
EAST																												
BAL	158	101	57	.639		**742**	530	5303	1382	207	25	158	**672**	844	**.261**	.349	.398	**.747**	120	133	140	99	97	750	66	38	63	-3
DET	162	91	71	.562	12	701	645	5502	1399	214	38	**179**	540	854	.254	.327	**.405**	.732	110	88	60	104	97	715	35	43	45	-15
BOS	162	85	77	.525	18	691	667	5401	1360	**246**	28	161	552	871	.252	.325	.397	.722	104	68	19	107	100	686	51	34	60	-5
NY	162	82	80	.506	21	648	641	5413	1377	195	**43**	97	581	**717**	.254	.331	.360	.691	109	22	62	94	99	643	75	55	58	-11
WAS	159	63	96	.396	38.5	537	660	5290	1219	189	30	86	575	956	.230	.309	.324	.635	91	-86	-56	94	102	538	68	45	60	-7
CLE	162	60	102	.370	43	543	747	5467	1303	200	20	109	467	868	.238	.302	.342	.644	81	-83	-133	99	101	558	57	37	61	-5
WEST																												
OAK	161	101	60	.627		691	544	5494	1383	195	25	160	542	1018	.252	.323	.384	.707	109	42	56	98	102	681	80	53	60	-8
KC	161	85	76	.528	16	603	566	5295	1323	225	40	80	490	819	.250	.316	.353	.669	97	-28	-23	99	104	594	**130**	46	**74**	**11**
CHI	162	79	83	.488	22.5	617	597	5382	1346	185	30	138	562	870	.250	.327	.373	.700	102	33	13	103	94	661	83	65	56	-14
CAL	162	76	86	.469	25.5	511	576	5495	1271	213	18	96	441	827	.231	.292	.329	.621	88	-131	-96	93	**104**	518	72	34	68	1
MIN	160	74	86	.463	26.5	654	649	5414	**1406**	197	31	116	512	846	.260	.326	.372	.698	101	28	8	103	101	641	66	44	60	-7
MIL	161	69	92	.429	32	534	609	5185	1188	200	23	104	543	924	.229	.306	.329	.635	87	-88	-82	99	103	534	82	53	61	-7
TOT	966					7472		64641	15957	2426	351	1484	6477	10414	.247	.320	.364	.684							865	547	61	-69

TEAM	CG	SH	SV	IP	H	H/G	HR	BB	SO	RAT	ERA	ERA+	OAV	OOB	PR	/A	PF	CPI	FA	E	DP	FW	PW	BW	SBW	DIF
EAST																										
BAL	71	15	22	1415¹	1257	8.0	125	**416**	793	10.8	**2.99**	112	.239	**.297**	74	57	97	101	.981	112	148	.7	6.1	**15.1**	.3	-.2
DET	53	11	32	1468¹	1355	8.3	126	609	**1000**	12.3	3.63	99	.247	.327	-28	-7	104	99	**.983**	106	156	**1.2**	-.8	6.5	-1.0	4.1
BOS	44	11	35	1443	1424	8.9	136	535	871	12.5	3.80	97	.259	.329	-55	-18	107	100	.981	116	149	.6	-1.9	2.0	.0	3.2
NY	67	15	12	1452	1382	8.6	126	423	707	11.3	3.43	94	.252	.308	4	-33	93	97	.981	125	159	.1	-3.5	6.7	-.6	-1.7
WAS	30	10	26	1418²	1376	8.7	132	554	762	12.5	3.70	89	.258	.333	-37	-62	96	100	.977	141	170	-1.0	-6.7	-6.0	-.1	-2.7
CLE	21	7	32	1440	1352	8.4	154	770	937	13.6	4.28	89	.252	.351	-130	-72	111	99	.981	116	159	.6	-7.7	-14.3	.0	.3
WEST																										
OAK	57	18	36	1469¹	**1229**	**7.5**	131	501	999	10.8	3.05	109	**.228**	.298	67	46	96	97	.981	117	157	.5	4.9	6.0	-.2	9.2
KC	34	15	**44**	1420¹	1301	8.2	**84**	496	775	11.6	3.25	106	.247	.316	33	28	99	98	.979	132	**178**	-.4	3.0	-2.5	**1.8**	2.5
CHI	46	19	32	1450¹	1348	8.4	100	468	976	11.4	3.12	**115**	.247	.309	55	**75**	104	101	.975	160	128	-1.9	**8.1**	1.4	-.9	-8.6
CAL	39	11	32	1481	1246	7.6	101	607	904	11.5	3.10	104	.230	.312	60	23	94	98	.980	131	159	-.2	2.5	-10.3	.7	2.4
MIN	43	9	25	1416²	1384	8.8	139	529	895	12.4	3.81	93	.257	.328	-55	-41	103	100	.980	118	134	.4	-4.4	.9	-.1	-2.7
MIL	32	**23**	32	1416¹	1303	8.3	130	569	795	12.1	3.38	103	.247	.324	13	14	100	**106**	.977	138	152	-.7	1.5	-8.8	-.1	-3.3
TOT	537	164	360	17291¹		8.3				11.9	3.46		.247	.320					.980	1512	1849					

Runs
Buford-Bal	99
Tovar-Min	94
Murcer-NY	94
Carew-Min	88
Jackson-Oak	87

Hits
Tovar-Min	204
Alomar-Cal	179
Carew-Min	177
Smith-Bos	175
Murcer-NY	175

Doubles
Smith-Bos	33
Schaal-KC	31
Rodriguez-Det	30
Oliva-Min	30

Triples
Patek-KC	11
Carew-Min	10
Blair-Bal	8

Home Runs
Melton-Chi	33
Jackson-Oak	32
Cash-Det	32
Smith-Bos	30

Total Bases
Smith-Bos	302
Jackson-Oak	288
Murcer-NY	287
Melton-Chi	267
Oliva-Min	266

Runs Batted In
Killebrew-Min	119
F.Robinson-Bal	99
Smith-Bos	96
Murcer-NY	94
Bando-Oak	94

Runs Produced
Murcer-NY	163
F.Robinson-Bal	153
Killebrew-Min	152
White-NY	151
Smith-Bos	151

Bases On Balls
Killebrew-Min	114
Yastrzemski-Bos	106
Schaal-KC	103
Petrocelli-Bos	91
Murcer-NY	91

Batting Average
Oliva-Min	.337
Murcer-NY	.331
Rettenmund-Bal	.318
Tovar-Min	.311
Carew-Min	.307

On Base Percentage
Murcer-NY	.429
Rettenmund-Bal	.424
Kaline-Det	.421
Buford-Bal	.415
White-NY	.399

Slugging Average
Oliva-Min	.546
Murcer-NY	.543
Cash-Det	.531
F.Robinson-Bal	.510
Jackson-Oak	.508

Production
Murcer-NY	.972
Oliva-Min	.918
Cash-Det	.905
F.Robinson-Bal	.900
Buford-Bal	.891

Adjusted Production
Murcer-NY	185
White-NY	155
F.Robinson-Bal	154
Buford-Bal	153
Oliva-Min	152

Batter Runs
Murcer-NY	53.7
Rettenmund-Bal	34.8
Buford-Bal	34.5
White-NY	33.7
Oliva-Min	33.6

Adjusted Batter Runs
Murcer-NY	61.1
White-NY	39.8
Rettenmund-Bal	35.7
Buford-Bal	35.3
F.Robinson-Bal	33.8

Clutch Hitting Index
Killebrew-Min	140
Powell-Bal	137
Alou-Oak-NY	123
F.Robinson-Bal	121
May-Chi	120

Runs Created
Murcer-NY	126
Smith-Bos	106
Jackson-Oak	103
White-NY	103
Rettenmund-Bal	99

Total Average
Murcer-NY	1.035
Buford-Bal	.970
Cash-Det	.933
F.Robinson-Bal	.905
Rettenmund-Bal	.904

Stolen Bases
Otis-KC	52
Patek-KC	49
Alomar-Cal	39
Campaneris-Oak	34

Stolen Base Average
Harper-Mil	89.3
Otis-KC	86.7
Campaneris-Oak	82.9
Pinson-Cle	80.6
Alomar-Cal	79.6

Stolen Base Runs
Otis-KC	10.8
Patek-KC	6.3
Campaneris-Oak	6.0
Harper-Mil	5.7
Alomar-Cal	5.7

Fielding Runs
Nettles-Cle	42.3
Melton-Chi	27.0
Alomar-Cal	21.4
Cullen-Was	20.5
Otis-KC	19.8

Total Player Rating
Murcer-NY	5.5
Nettles-Cle	5.3
Melton-Chi	5.1
White-NY	4.5
Otis-KC	4.2

Wins
Lolich-Det	25
Blue-Oak	24
Wood-Chi	22
McNally-Bal	21
Hunter-Oak	21

Win Percentage
McNally-Bal	.808
Dobson-Oak	.750
Blue-Oak	.750
Dobson-Bal	.714

Games
Sanders-Mil	83
Scherman-Det	69
Burgmeier-KC	67
Abernathy-KC	63

Complete Games
Lolich-Det	29
Blue-Oak	24
Wood-Chi	22
Cuellar-Bal	21
Palmer-Bal	20

Shutouts
Blue-Oak	8
Wood-Chi	7
Stottlemyre-NY	7
Bradley-Chi	6

Saves
Sanders-Mil	31
Abernathy-KC	23
Scherman-Det	20
Fingers-Oak	17
Burgmeier-KC	17

Innings Pitched
Lolich-Det	376.0
Wood-Chi	334.0
Blue-Oak	312.0
Cuellar-Bal	292.1
Coleman-Det	286.0

Fewest Hits/Game
Blue-Oak	6.03
McDowell-Cle	6.71
May-Cal	6.91
Messersmith-Cal	7.29
Wright-Cal	7.32

Fewest BB/Game
Peterson-NY	1.38
Kline-NY	1.50
Kaat-Min	1.62
Wood-Chi	1.67
Drago-KC	1.72

Strikeouts
Lolich-Det	308
Blue-Oak	301
Coleman-Det	236
Blyleven-Min	224
Wood-Chi	210

Strikeouts/Game
Blue-Oak	8.68
McDowell-Cle	8.05
Johnson-Chi	7.74
Coleman-Det	7.43
Lolich-Det	7.37

Ratio
Blue-Oak	8.68
Wood-Chi	9.19
Kline-NY	9.84
Dobson-Bal	9.98
McNally-Bal	10.07

Earned Run Average
Blue-Oak	1.82
Wood-Chi	1.91
Palmer-Bal	2.68
Hedlund-KC	2.71
Blyleven-Min	2.81

Adjusted ERA
Wood-Chi	188
Blue-Oak	183
Siebert-Bos	127
Hedlund-KC	126
Blyleven-Min	126

Opponents' Batting Avg.
Blue-Oak	.189
McDowell-Cle	.207
May-Cal	.213
Messersmith-Cal	.218
Palmer-Bal	.221

Opponents' On Base Pct.
Blue-Oak	.252
Wood-Chi	.264
Kline-NY	.276
Dobson-Bal	.279
Hunter-Oak	.282

Starter Runs
Wood-Chi	57.5
Blue-Oak	57.0
Palmer-Bal	24.5
Lolich-Det	22.6
Blyleven-Min	20.0

Adjusted Starter Runs
Wood-Chi	62.2
Blue-Oak	52.6
Lolich-Det	28.0
Blyleven-Min	22.8
Palmer-Bal	21.0

Clutch Pitching Index
Drago-KC	119
Krausse-Mil	118
Johnson-Chi	117
Bosman-Was	112
Wood-Chi	112

Relief Runs
Sanders-Mil	23.4
Burgmeier-KC	17.0
Mingori-Cle	12.8
Queen-Cal	12.3
Grzenda-Was	12.0

Adjusted Relief Runs
Sanders-Mil	23.5
Burgmeier-KC	16.7
Mingori-Cle	15.1
Scherman-Det	11.1
Lee-Bos	10.9

Relief Ranking
Sanders-Mil	41.6
Burgmeier-KC	34.4
Scherman-Det	19.4
Abernathy-KC	13.8
Grzenda-Was	11.4

Total Pitcher Index
Wood-Chi	6.6
Blue-Oak	4.9
Sanders-Mil	4.7
Burgmeier-KC	4.4
Siebert-Bos	3.5

Total Baseball Ranking
Wood-Chi	6.6
Murcer-NY	5.5
Nettles-Cle	5.3
Melton-Chi	5.1
Blue-Oak	4.9

January 13 Former umpire, now housewife Bernice Gera wins her suit against baseball, initiated on March 15, 1971. Mrs. Gera is slated to umpire in the New York-Pennsylvania League starting in June.

April 2 Mets manager Gil Hodges dies of a heart attack at West Palm Beach, Florida, two days shy of his 48th birthday. Yogi Berra is named manager.

April 6 For the first time in history, the major league season fails to open due to a general player strike. The strike, announced April 1, will erase 86 games from major league schedules.

April 13 The end of the baseball strike is announced, with an abbreviated schedule to start two days later.

April 16 In Chicago, 22-year-old rookie Burt Hooton of the Cubs no-hits the Phillies 4-0. It is Hooton's fourth major league game over two seasons and he has allowed just 8 hits in 30 innings. Throwing his knuckle curve, Hooton walks 7 and fans 7.

May 11 The Giants trade future Hall of Famer Willie Mays to the Mets for minor league pitcher Charlie Williams and cash.

June 18 By a 5-3 vote, the U.S. Supreme Court confirms lower court rulings in the Curt Flood case, upholding baseball's exemption from antitrust laws and the legitimacy of its reserve clause. Its decision is narrowly construed, however, and leaves the way open for legislation or collective bargaining to undercut the reserve system. By the year's end, owners will agree to salary arbitration.

August 1 Nate Colbert ties one major league record with five home runs, and sets another with 13 RBI, as the Padres take a doubleheader from the Braves, 9–0 and 11–7.

August 29 During a 3-0 win over St. Louis, San Francisco's Jim Barr retires the first 20 batters to face him. Six days earlier, Barr had gotten out the last 21 men to face him. This gives Barr a major league record of 41 consecutive batsmen retired.

September 2 Milt Pappas of the Cubs hurls a no-hit game in beating the Padres 8-0. Pappas has a perfect game until pinch hitter Larry Stahl walks with two outs in the ninth inning. Pappas and catcher Randy Hundley both said of the pitches to Stahl, "They were so close I don't know how Stahl could take them, but they were balls."

September 30 During a 5-0 win over the Mets, the Pirates' Roberto Clemente doubles off Jon Matlack in the fourth inning for his 3,000th—and final—career hit in regular-season play.

October 2 Bill Stoneman of Montreal pitches his second no-hitter, beating the Mets 7-0.

October 11 The Pirates lead the Reds 3-2 in the bottom of the ninth inning of the final game of the NLCS. Johnny Bench homers to tie the game, and two singles and a Bob Moose wild pitch later, the Reds are NL champs.

October 24 Hall of Famer Jackie Robinson dies of heart disease at age 53.

November 2 Steve Carlton caps off a remarkable season with a unanimous NL Cy Young Award.

November 22 Johnny Bench wins the NL MVP.

December 10 The major leagues adopt the save as an official statistic.

December 31 A plane carrying Roberto Clemente to Nicaragua on a mercy mission for earthquake victims crashes into the Atlantic Ocean. Clemente, who batted .317 in 18 seasons with the Pirates, is presumed dead at age 38.

ATLANTA		CHICAGO		CINCINNATI		HOUSTON		LOS ANGELES		MONTREAL	
M	L.Harris	M	L.Durocher	M	S.Anderson	M	H.Walker	M	W.Alston	M	G.Mauch
M	E.Mathews	M	W.Lockman	1B	T.Perez	M	S.Parker	1B	W.Parker	1B	M.Jorgensen
1B	H.Aaron	1B	J.Hickman	2B	J.Morgan	M	L.Durocher	2B	L.Lacy	2B	R.Hunt
2B	F.Millan	2B	G.Beckert	SS	D.Concepcion	1B	L.May	SS	B.Russell	SS	T.Foli
SS	M.Perez	SS	D.Kessinger	3B	D.Menke	2B	T.Helms	3B	S.Garvey	3B	B.Bailey
3B	D.Evans	3B	R.Santo	LF	P.Rose	SS	R.Metzger	LF	M.Mota	LF	K.Singleton
LF	R.Carty	LF	B.Williams	CF	B.Tolan	3B	D.Rader	CF	W.Davis	CF	B.Day
CF	D.Baker	CF	R.Monday	RF	C.Geronimo	LF	B.Watson	RF	F.Robinson	RF	C.Mashore
RF	R.Garr	RF	J.Cardenal	C	J.Bench	CF	C.Cedeno	C	C.Cannizzaro	C	J.Boccabella
C	E.Williams	C	R.Hundley			RF	J.Wynn				
				P	J.Billingham	C	J.Edwards	O1	B.Buckner	O1	R.Fairly
O	M.Lum	31	C.Fanzone	P	R.Grimsley	O	W.Crawford	O	R.Woods	
		1	J.Pepitone	P	G.Nolan	P	D.Wilson	23	B.Valentine	CO	T.McCarver
P	P.Niekro			P	J.McGlothlin	P	L.Dierker			C	T.Humphrey
P	R.Reed	P	F.Jenkins	P	D.Gullett	P	D.Roberts	P	D.Sutton	
P	R.Schueler	P	B.Hooton	RP	T.Hall	P	J.Reuss	P	C.Osteen	P	B.Stoneman
P	T.Kelley	P	M.Pappas	RP	C.Carroll	P	K.Forsch	P	A.Downing	P	M.Torrez
P	G.Stone	P	B.Hands			RP	G.Culver	P	T.John	P	C.Morton
RP	P.Jarvis	P	R.Reuschel	P	W.Simpson	RP	T.Griffin	P	B.Singer	P	E.McAnally
RP	C.Upshaw	RP	T.Phoebus	P	E.Sprague	RP	J.Ray	RP	J.Brewer	P	B.Moore
		RP	J.Aker					RP	P.Mikkelsen	RP	M.Marshall
P	J.Hardin	RP	D.McGinn					RP	P.Richert	RP	J.Strohmayer
P	M.McQueen									RP	T.Walker
P	D.McLain	P	J.Pizarro								
		P	B.Bonham							P	S.Renko

NEW YORK		PHILADELPHIA		PITTSBURGH		SAN DIEGO		SAN FRANCISCO		ST.LOUIS	
M	Y.Berra	M	F.Lucchesi	M	B.Virdon	M	P.Gomez	M	C.Fox	M	R.Schoendienst
1B	E.Kranepool	M	P.Owens	1B	W.Stargell	M	D.Zimmer	1B	W.McCovey	1B	M.Alou
2B	K.Boswell	1B	T.Hutton	2B	D.Cash	1B	N.Colbert	2B	T.Fuentes	2B	T.Sizemore
SS	B.Harrelson	2B	D.Doyle	SS	G.Alley	2B	D.Thomas	SS	C.Speier	SS	D.Maxvill
3B	J.Fregosi	SS	L.Bowa	3B	R.Hebner	SS	E.Hernandez	3B	A.Gallagher	3B	J.Torre
LF	J.Milner	3B	D.Money	LF	V.Davalillo	3B	D.Roberts	LF	K.Henderson	LF	L.Brock
CF	T.Agee	LF	G.Luzinski	CF	A.Oliver	LF	L.Lee	CF	G.Maddox	CF	J.Cruz
RF	R.Staub	CF	W.Montanez	RF	R.Clemente	CF	J.Jeter	RF	B.Bonds	RF	L.Melendez
C	D.Dyer	RF	B.Robinson	C	M.Sanguillen	RF	C.Gaston	C	D.Rader	C	T.Simmons
		C	J.Bateman			C	F.Kendall				
32	W.Garrett			O	G.Clines			31	D.Kingman	O	B.Carbo
2S	T.Martinez	1	D.Johnson	1O	B.Robertson	O	J.Morales			S2	E.Crosby
O1	C.Jones	2S	T.Harmon	2O	R.Stennett	O	L.Stahl	P	R.Bryant	
C	J.Grote					23	G.Jestadt	P	J.Barr	P	B.Gibson
		P	S.Carlton	P	S.Blass			P	J.Marichal	P	R.Wise
P	T.Seaver	P	K.Reynolds	P	B.Moose	P	S.Arlin	P	S.McDowell	P	R.Cleveland
P	J.Matlack	P	B.Champion	P	N.Briles	P	C.Kirby	P	S.Stone	P	A.Santorini
P	G.Gentry	P	W.Fryman	P	D.Ellis	P	F.Norman	RP	J.Johnson	P	S.Spinks
P	J.Koosman	RP	W.Twitchell	P	B.Kison	P	M.Caldwell	RP	R.Moffitt	RP	D.Segui
P	J.McAndrew	RP	B.Brandon	RP	D.Giusti	P	B.Greif	RP	D.McMahon	
RP	T.McGraw	RP	B.Lersch	RP	R.Hernandez	RP	M.Corkins			
RP	R.Sadecki			RP	B.Miller	RP	G.Ross	P	F.Reberger	
RP	D.Frisella	P	D.Selma			RP	E.Acosta	P	D.Carrithers	
				P	B.Johnson			P	J.Willoughby	
P	B.Capra			P	L.Walker					

TEAM	G	W	L	PCT	GB	R	OR	AB	H	2B	3B	HR	BB	SO	AVG	OBP	SLG	PRO	PRO+	BR	/A	PF	CHI	RC	SB	CS	SBA	SBR
EAST																												
PIT	155	96	59	.619		691	512	5490	1505	251	47	110	404	871	.274	.327	.397	.724	114	74	89	98	100	701	49	30	62	-3
CHI	156	85	70	.548	11	685	567	5247	1346	206	40	133	566	815	.257	.332	.387	.719	100	74	2	111	100	670	69	47	59	-8
NY	156	83	73	.532	13.5	528	578	5135	1154	175	31	105	589	990	.225	.309	.332	.641	91	-68	-54	97	99	530	41	41	50	-12
STL	156	75	81	.481	21.5	568	600	5326	1383	214	42	70	437	793	.260	.319	.355	.674	99	-14	-6	99	96	591	104	48	68	2
MON	156	70	86	.449	26.5	513	609	5156	1205	156	22	91	474	828	.234	.304	.325	.629	84	-92	-101	102	102	513	68	66	51	-19
PHI	156	59	97	.378	37.5	503	635	5248	1240	200	36	98	487	930	.236	.304	.344	.648	88	-65	-78	103	94	545	42	50	46	-17
WEST																												
CIN	154	95	59	.617		707	557	5241	1317	214	44	124	606	914	.251	.333	.380	.713	116	67	107	94	104	676	140	63	69	4
HOU	153	84	69	.549	10.5	708	636	5267	1359	233	38	134	524	907	.258	.329	.393	.722	114	75	89	98	103	686	111	56	66	0
LA	155	85	70	.548	10.5	584	527	5270	1349	178	39	98	480	786	.256	.321	.360	.681	102	1	16	98	96	610	82	39	68	1
ATL	155	70	84	.455	25	628	730	5278	1363	186	17	144	532	770	.258	.330	.382	.712	100	60	-1	109	94	661	47	35	57	-7
SF	155	69	86	.445	26.5	662	649	5245	1281	211	36	150	480	964	.244	.311	.384	.695	102	17	8	101	107	630	123	45	73	10
SD	153	58	95	.379	36.5	488	665	5213	1181	168	38	102	407	976	.227	.284	.332	.616	87	-130	-98	93	106	489	78	46	63	-4
TOT	930					7265		63116	15683	2392	430	1359	5985	10544	.248	.317	.365	.682							954	566	63	-53

TEAM	CG	SH	SV	IP	H	H/G	HR	BB	SO	RAT	ERA	ERA+	OAV	OOB	PR	/A	PF	CPI	FA	E	DP	FW	PW	BW	SBW	DIF
EAST																										
PIT	39	15	48	1414¹	1282	8.2	90	433	838	11.1	2.81	118	.243	.304	102	81	96	108	.978	136	171	-.0	8.7	9.6	.2	.1
CHI	54	19	32	1398²	1329	8.6	112	421	824	11.5	3.22	118	.251	.311	37	92	110	105	.979	132	148	.2	9.9	.2	-.4	-2.4
NY	32	12	41	1414²	1263	8.0	118	486	1059	11.3	3.26	103	.240	.308	30	15	97	99	.980	116	122	1.1	1.6	-5.8	-.8	8.9
STL	64	13	13	1399²	1290	8.3	87	531	912	11.8	3.42	99	.247	.319	5	-3	99	97	.977	141	146	-.3	.0	-.6	-.7	-2.4
MON	39	11	23	1401¹	1281	8.2	103	579	888	12.1	3.59	99	.245	.323	-21	-6	103	97	.978	134	141	.0	-.6	-10.9	-1.6	5.0
PHI	43	13	15	1400	1318	8.5	117	536	927	12.1	3.66	98	.251	.324	-33	-11	104	99	.981	116	142	1.1	-1.2	-8.4	-1.3	-9.2
WEST																										
CIN	25	15	60	1412²	1313	8.4	129	435	806	11.3	3.21	100	.247	.307	38	0	93	104	.982	110	143	1.3	.0	11.5	.9	4.3
HOU	38	14	31	1385¹	1340	8.7	114	498	971	12.2	3.77	89	.256	.325	-48	-62	97	98	.980	116	151	.9	-6.7	9.6	.5	3.2
LA	50	23	29	1403	1196	7.7	83	429	856	10.6	2.78	120	.230	.292	104	85	97	96	.974	162	145	-1.5	9.1	1.7	.6	-2.5
ATL	40	4	27	1377	1412	9.2	155	512	732	12.7	4.27	89	.266	.333	-126	-74	110	97	.974	156	180	-1.1	-8.0	-.1	-.3	2.5
SF	44	8	23	1386¹	1309	8.5	130	507	771	12.0	3.69	94	.250	.320	-37	-32	101	99	.974	156	121	-1.1	-3.4	-7.5	1.6	-6.3
SD	39	17	19	1403²	1350	8.7	121	618	960	12.9	3.78	98	.255	.337	-50	-76	95	103	.976	144	146	-.6	-8.2	-10.5	.0	.7
TOT	507	164	361	16796²		8.4				11.8	3.45		.248	.317					.978	1619	1706					

Runs		Hits		Doubles		Triples		Home Runs		Total Bases	
Morgan-Cin	122	Rose-Cin	198	Montanez-Phi	39	Bowa-Phi	13	Bench-Cin	40	Williams-Chi	348
Bonds-SF	118	Brock-StL	193	Cedeno-Hou	39	Rose-Cin	11	Colbert-SD	38	Cedeno-Hou	300
Wynn-Hou	117	Williams-Chi	191	Simmons-StL	36	Sanguillen-Pit	8	Williams-Chi	37	Bench-Cin	291
Rose-Cin	107	Simmons-StL	180	Williams-Chi	34	Cedeno-Hou	8	Aaron-Atl	34	May-Hou	290
Cedeno-Hou	103	Garr-Atl	180			Brock-StL	8	Stargell-Pit	33	Colbert-SD	286

Runs Batted In		Runs Produced		Bases On Balls		Batting Average		On Base Percentage		Slugging Average	
Bench-Cin	125	Wynn-Hou	183	Morgan-Cin	115	Williams-Chi	.333	Morgan-Cin	.419	Williams-Chi	.606
Williams-Chi	122	Williams-Chi	180	Wynn-Hou	103	Garr-Atl	.325	Williams-Chi	.403	Stargell-Pit	.558
Stargell-Pit	112	Morgan-Cin	179	Bench-Cin	100	Baker-Atl	.321	Santo-Chi	.397	Bench-Cin	.541
Colbert-SD	111	Bonds-SF	172	Aaron-Atl	92	Cedeno-Hou	.320	Aaron-Atl	.391	Cedeno-Hou	.537
May-Hou	98	Bench-Cin	172	Evans-Atl	90	Watson-Hou	.312	Wynn-Hou	.391	Aaron-Atl	.514

Production		Adjusted Production		Batter Runs		Adjusted Batter Runs		Clutch Hitting Index		Runs Created	
Williams-Chi	1.010	Bench-Cin	171	Williams-Chi	61.1	Bench-Cin	50.6	Parker-LA	140	Williams-Chi	137
Stargell-Pit	.935	Stargell-Pit	166	Bench-Cin	44.0	Williams-Chi	48.2	Tolan-Cin	131	Morgan-Cin	117
Bench-Cin	.927	Williams-Chi	166	Cedeno-Hou	42.9	Cedeno-Hou	45.2	Helms-Hou	120	Cedeno-Hou	115
Cedeno-Hou	.924	Cedeno-Hou	163	Stargell-Pit	39.6	Morgan-Cin	43.5	Sanguillen-Pit	119	Bench-Cin	110
Aaron-Atl	.906	Hebner-Pit	155	Morgan-Cin	37.2	Stargell-Pit	41.7	Oliver-Pit	117	Rose-Cin	109

Total Average		Stolen Bases		Stolen Base Average		Stolen Base Runs		Fielding Runs		Total Player Rating	
Williams-Chi	1.050	Brock-StL	63	Hernandez-SD	88.9	Bonds-SF	9.6	Helms-Hou	26.5	Cedeno-Hou	5.6
Morgan-Cin	.973	Morgan-Cin	58	Bonds-SF	88.0	Brock-StL	8.1	Money-Phi	20.3	Morgan-Cin	5.5
Cedeno-Hou	.959	Cedeno-Hou	55	Davis-LA	87.0	Morgan-Cin	7.2	Rader-Hou	18.0	Bench-Cin	5.1
Stargell-Pit	.958	Bonds-SF	44	Brock-StL	77.8	Hernandez-SD	5.4	Rose-Cin	16.1	Rose-Cin	4.3
Aaron-Atl	.945	Tolan-Cin	42	Morgan-Cin	77.3	Davis-LA	4.2	Russell-LA	15.0	Williams-Chi	4.1

Wins		Win Percentage		Games		Complete Games		Shutouts		Saves	
Carlton-Phi	27	Nolan-Cin	.750	Marshall-Mon	65	Carlton-Phi	30	Sutton-LA	9	Carroll-Cin	37
Seaver-NY	21	Carlton-Phi	.730	Carroll-Cin	65	Jenkins-Chi	23	Carlton-Phi	8	McGraw-NY	27
Osteen-LA	20	Pappas-Chi	.708	Borbon-Cin	62	Gibson-StL	23	Norman-SD	6	Giusti-Pit	22
Jenkins-Chi	20	Blass-Pit	.704	Ross-SD	60	Wise-StL	20	Jenkins-Chi	5	Marshall-Mon	18
		Ellis-Pit	.682			Sutton-LA	18	Dierker-Hou	5		

Innings Pitched		Fewest Hits/Game		Fewest BB/Game		Strikeouts		Strikeouts/Game		Ratio	
Carlton-Phi	346.1	Sutton-LA	6.14	Pappas-Chi	1.34	Carlton-Phi	310	Seaver-NY	8.55	Sutton-LA	8.35
Jenkins-Chi	289.1	Carlton-Phi	6.68	Nolan-Cin	1.53	Seaver-NY	249	Reuss-NY	8.16	Carlton-Phi	8.97
Niekro-Atl	282.1	Gibson-StL	7.32	Niekro-Atl	1.69	Gibson-StL	208	Koosman-NY	8.12	Nolan-Cin	9.10
Gibson-StL	278.0	Seaver-NY	7.39	Ellis-Pit	1.82	Sutton-LA	207	Carlton-Phi	8.06	McAndrew-NY	9.86
Sutton-LA	272.2	Bryant-SF	7.40	Moose-Pit	1.87	Jenkins-Chi	184	Norman-SD	7.10	Niekro-Atl	9.95

Earned Run Average		Adjusted ERA		Opponents' Batting Avg.		Opponents' On Base Pct.		Starter Runs		Adjusted Starter Runs	
Carlton-Phi	1.97	Carlton-Phi	182	Sutton-LA	.189	Sutton-LA	.240	Carlton-Phi	56.9	Carlton-Phi	62.2
Nolan-Cin	1.99	Nolan-Cin	161	Carlton-Phi	.206	Carlton-Phi	.259	Sutton-LA	41.6	Sutton-LA	38.0
Sutton-LA	2.08	Sutton-LA	160	Gibson-StL	.224	Nolan-Cin	.262	Gibson-StL	30.7	Gibson-StL	29.1
Matlack-NY	2.32	Matlack-NY	145	Seaver-NY	.224	Niekro-Atl	.275	Matlack-NY	30.6	Matlack-NY	28.1
Gibson-StL	2.46	Gibson-StL	138	Bryant-SF	.224	McAndrew-NY	.278	Nolan-Cin	28.5	Hooton-Chi	24.4

Clutch Pitching Index		Relief Runs		Adjusted Relief Runs		Relief Ranking		Total Pitcher Index		Total Baseball Ranking	
Blass-Pit	131	Marshall-Mon	21.5	Marshall-Mon	22.8	Marshall-Mon	46.8	Carlton-Phi	7.4	Carlton-Phi	7.4
Nolan-Cin	115	McGraw-NY	20.7	McGraw-NY	18.0	Brewer-LA	39.8	Marshall-Mon	5.3	Cedeno-Hou	5.6
Hooton-Chi	115	Brewer-LA	19.1	Brewer-LA	18.0	McGraw-NY	34.5	Brewer-LA	4.5	Morgan-Cin	5.5
Matlack-NY	115	R.Hernandez-Pit	13.9	R.Hernandez-Pit	12.8	Giusti-Pit	23.0	Gibson-StL	4.2	Marshall-Mon	5.3
Downing-LA	115	Carroll-Cin	12.8	Giusti-Pit	11.6	Carroll-Cin	18.5	Sutton-LA	3.9	Bench-Cin	5.1

January 19 The BBWAA elects Sandy Koufax (344 votes), Yogi Berra (339), and Early Wynn (301) to the Hall of Fame. Koufax makes it in his first try and, at 36, is the youngest honoree in history.

February 2 The Special Veterans Committee selects Lefty Gomez, Ross Youngs, and William Harridge for the Hall of Fame.

February 8 Commissioner Bowie Kuhn announces the Hall of Fame selection of Josh Gibson and Buck Leonard by the Special Committee on the Negro Leagues.

May 13 The Brewers score in the top of the 22nd to win 4-3, then lose to the Twins 4-3 in 15 innings. The two games take nine hours and 23 minutes to complete and sets an AL record for consecutive innings played in two days.

July 14 In a ML first, the plate umpire and the catcher in a game are brothers. Bill Haller is the ump and Tom Haller is the Tigers catcher during a game with the Royals. Kansas City wins 1-0.

August 5 During a 4-3 win over Cleveland, Detroit shortstop Ed Brinkman commits an error, thus ending his major

league-record streak of 72 games and 331 total chances without a miscue.

August 23 Chicago's Dick Allen becomes the fourth major league player (Jimmie Foxx, Hank Greenberg, and Alex Johnson are the others) to hit a ball into the center field bleachers in Comiskey Park when he connects off New York's Lindy McDaniel.

October 2 After a pinch RBI single, White Sox reliever Terry Forster steals second. Forster, later described by David Letterman as "a fat tub of goo," is the last AL pitcher to steal a base.

October 3 Roric Harrison homers as Baltimore beats Cleveland 4-3 in the second game of a doubleheader. With the DH rule on the horizon, it will be the last homer hit by an AL pitcher.

October 4 Ted Williams manages his final game as the Rangers lose to the Royals 4-0. Williams will be replaced by Whitey Herzog.

October 12 Oakland takes the AL flag with a 2-1 win in the fifth game of the LCS. The A's Reggie Jackson steals home, but pulls a hamstring in the process, sidelining him for the Series.

October 14 Catcher Gene Tenace be-

comes the first player ever to homer in each of his first two World Series at bats, leading the A's to a 3-2 opening-game win over the Reds.

October 18 With runners at second base and third base and a 3-2 count, the A's fake an intentional walk and strike out Johnny Bench looking.

October 22 The A's win their first World Championship in 42 years with a 3-2 victory in Game 7.

October 31 Gaylord Perry wins the AL Cy Young award by a 64-58 margin over Chicago's Wilbur Wood. Perry won 24 games for the fifth-place Indians.

November 15 The White Sox' Dick Allen wins the AL MVP Award by an overwhelming margin.

November 21 Boston's Carlton Fisk is the unanimous choice for AL Rookie of the Year, the first time this has happened. Jon Matlack of the Mets is named NL Rookie of the Year.

December 10 The AL votes unanimously to adopt the designated-hitter rule for a three-year experiment. In the December 1975 meeting the AL will vote to permanently adopt the DH. The NL declines to go along with the AL.

BALTIMORE		BOSTON		CALIFORNIA		CHICAGO		CLEVELAND		DETROIT	
M	E.Weaver	M	E.Kasko	M	D.Rice	M	C.Tanner	M	K.Aspromonte	M	B.Martin
1B	B.Powell	1B	D.Cater	1B	B.Oliver	1B	D.Allen	1B	C.Chambliss	1B	N.Cash
2B	D.Johnson	2B	D.Griffin	2B	S.Alomar	2B	M.Andrews	2B	J.Brohamer	2B	D.McAuliffe
SS	M.Belanger	SS	L.Aparicio	SS	L.Cardenas	SS	R.Morales	SS	F.Duffy	SS	E.Brinkman
3B	B.Robinson	3B	R.Petrocelli	3B	K.McMullen	3B	E.Spiezio	3B	G.Nettles	3B	A.Rodriguez
LF	D.Buford	LF	C.Yastrzemski	LF	V.Pinson	LF	C.May	LF	A.Johnson	LF	W.Horton
CF	P.Blair	CF	T.Harper	CF	K.Berry	CF	J.Johnstone	CF	D.Unser	CF	M.Stanley
RF	M.Rettenmund	RF	R.Smith	RF	L.Stanton	RF	P.Kelly	RF	B.Bell	RF	J.Northrup
C	J.Oates	C	C.Fisk	C	A.Kusnyer	C	E.Herrmann	C	R.Fosse	C	B.Freehan
O	D.Baylor	O	B.Oglivie	1O	J.Spencer	S2	L.Alvarado	O1	T.McCraw	O	G.Brown
O1	T.Crowley	2S	J.Kennedy			O	R.Reichardt	2S	E.Leon	O1	A.Kaline
S2	B.Grich			P	N.Ryan	O	W.Williams			2	T.Taylor
		P	M.Pattin	P	C.Wright	3	B.Melton	P	G.Perry		
P	J.Palmer	P	S.Siebert	P	R.May			P	D.Tidrow	P	M.Lolich
P	P.Dobson	P	L.Tiant	P	A.Messersmith	P	W.Wood	P	M.Wilcox	P	J.Coleman
P	M.Cuellar	P	J.Curtis	P	R.Clark	P	T.Bradley	P	R.Lamb	P	T.Timmermann
P	D.McNally	P	L.McGlothen	RP	L.Allen	P	S.Bahnsen	P	S.Dunning	P	W.Fryman
P	D.Alexander	RP	G.Peters	RP	E.Fisher	P	D.Lemonds	RP	P.Hennigan	RP	C.Seelbach
RP	R.Harrison	RP	B.Lee	RP	S.Barber	P	T.Forster	RP	E.Farmer	RP	F.Scherman
		RP	L.Krausse			RP	R.Gossage	RP	M.Kilkenny	RP	J.Niekro
						RP	S.Kealey				
		P	R.Culp					P	V.Colbert	P	B.Slayback
						P	V.Romo	P	S.Mingori		
								P	D.Riddleberger		

KANSAS CITY		MILWAUKEE		MINNESOTA		NEW YORK		OAKLAND		TEXAS	
M	B.Lemon	M	D.Bristol	M	B.Rigney	M	R.Houk	M	D.Williams	M	T.Williams
1B	J.Mayberry	M	R.McMillan	M	F.Quilici	1B	R.Blomberg	1B	M.Epstein	1B	F.Howard
2B	C.Rojas	M	D.Crandall	1B	H.Killebrew	2B	H.Clarke	2B	T.Cullen	2B	L.Randle
SS	F.Patek	1B	G.Scott	2B	R.Carew	SS	G.Michael	SS	B.Campaneris	SS	T.Harrah
3B	P.Schaal	2B	R.Theobald	SS	D.Thompson	3B	C.Sanchez	3B	S.Bando	3B	D.Nelson
LF	L.Piniella	SS	R.Auerbach	3B	E.Soderholm	LF	R.White	LF	J.Rudi	LF	L.Biittner
CF	A.Otis	3B	M.Ferraro	LF	S.Brye	CF	B.Murcer	CF	R.Jackson	CF	J.Lovitto
RF	R.Scheinblum	LF	J.Briggs	CF	B.Darwin	RF	J.Callison	RF	A.Mangual	RF	T.Ford
C	E.Kirkpatrick	CF	D.May	RF	C.Tovar	C	T.Munson	C	D.Duncan	C	D.Billings
		RF	J.Lahoud	C	P.Roof						
O	S.Hovley	C	E.Rodriguez			1O	F.Alou	1	M.Hegan	O	E.Maddox
				32	S.Braun	32	B.Allen	C	G.Tenace		
P	D.Drago	23	B.Heise	O	J.Nettles					P	P.Broberg
P	P.Splittorff			1O	R.Reese	P	M.Stottlemyre	P	C.Hunter	P	D.Bosman
P	R.Nelson	P	J.Lonborg			P	F.Peterson	P	K.Holtzman	P	R.Hand
P	B.Dal Canton	P	B.Parsons	P	B.Blyleven	P	S.Kline	P	B.Odom	P	M.Paul
P	M.Hedlund	P	S.Lockwood	P	D.Woodson	P	M.Kekich	P	V.Blue	P	B.Gogolewski
RP	A.Fitzmorris	P	J.Colborn	P	J.Perry	P	R.Gardner	P	D.Hamilton	RP	P.Lindblad
RP	T.Abernathy	P	K.Brett	P	R.Corbin	RP	S.Lyle	RP	R.Fingers	RP	J.Panther
RP	T.Burgmeier	RP	K.Sanders	P	J.Kaat	RP	L.McDaniel	RP	J.Horlen	RP	H.Pina
		RP	E.Stephenson	RP	D.LaRoche	RP	F.Beene	RP	B.Locker		
P	J.Rooker	RP	F.Linzy	RP	W.Granger					P	D.Stanhouse
P	T.Murphy							P	D.Knowles	P	C.Cox
/P	M.Montgomery	P	G.Ryerson	P	D.Goltz					P	J.Shellenback
		P	J.Bell								

TEAM	G	W	L	PCT	GB	R	OR	AB	H	2B	3B	HR	BB	SO	AVG	OBP	SLG	PRO	PRO+	BR	/A	PF	CHI	RC	SB	CS	SBA	SBR
EAST																												
DET	156	86	70	.551		558	514	5099	1206	179	32	122	483	793	.237	.306	.356	.662	100	18	0	103	101	549	17	21	45	-8
BOS	155	85	70	.548	0.5	**640**	620	5208	1289	**229**	**34**	124	522	858	.248	.320	**.376**	**.696**	108	83	49	106	102	**634**	66	30	**69**	**2**
BAL	154	80	74	.519	5	519	**430**	5028	1153	193	29	100	507	935	.229	.304	.339	.643	96	-12	-25	103	100	523	78	41	66	-1
NY	155	79	76	.510	6.5	557	527	5168	1288	201	24	103	491	**689**	.249	.318	.357	.675	111	45	65	97	95	588	71	42	63	-4
CLE	156	72	84	.462	14	472	519	5207	1220	187	18	91	420	762	.234	.295	.330	.625	89	-54	-70	103	98	495	49	53	48	-17
MIL	156	65	91	.417	21	493	595	5124	1204	167	22	88	472	868	.235	.303	.328	.631	96	-35	-26	98	99	495	64	57	53	-15
WEST																												
OAK	155	93	62	.600		604	457	5200	1248	195	29	**134**	463	886	.240	.308	.366	.674	113	37	67	95	104	584	87	48	64	-3
CHI	154	87	67	.565	5.5	566	538	5083	1208	170	28	108	511	991	.238	.311	.346	.657	100	14	3	102	103	550	100	52	66	-1
MIN	154	77	77	.500	15.5	537	535	5234	1277	182	31	93	478	905	.244	.311	.344	.655	96	9	-18	105	97	554	53	41	56	-9
KC	154	76	78	.494	16.5	580	545	5167	**1317**	220	26	78	**534**	711	**.255**	**.329**	.353	.682	111	65	**68**	100	95	601	85	44	66	-1
CAL	155	75	80	.484	18	454	533	5165	1249	171	26	78	503	850	.242	.294	.330	.624	98	-55	-28	94	97	487	57	37	61	-5
TEX	154	54	100	.351	38.5	461	628	5029	1092	166	17	56	503	926	.217	.292	.290	.582	83	-115	-97	96	**111**	438	**126**	73	63	-6
TOT	929					6441		61712	14751	2260	316	1175	5742	10174	.239	.308	.343	.651							853	539	61	-68

TEAM	CG	SH	SV	IP	H	H/G	HR	BB	SO	RAT	ERA	ERA+	OAV	OOB	PR	/A	PF	CPI	FA	E	DP	FW	PW	BW	SBW	DIF
EAST																										
DET	46	11	33	1388¹	1212	7.9	101	465	952	11.2	2.96	106	.236	.306	15	28	103	102	**.984**	96	137	**1.9**	3.2	.0	-.3	3.2
BOS	48	20	25	1382²	1309	8.5	101	512	918	12.1	3.47	93	.251	.323	-63	-39	105	100	.978	130	141	-.0	-4.4	5.6	**.9**	5.6
BAL	**62**	20	21	1371²	1116	7.3	**85**	**395**	788	10.0	**2.53**	121	.224	**.283**	81	**82**	100	97	.983	100	150	1.6	**9.3**	-2.8	.5	-5.6
NY	35	19	39	1373¹	1306	8.6	87	419	625	11.5	3.05	97	.252	.312	2	-15	96	105	.978	134	**179**	-.3	-1.7	7.4	.2	-4.1
CLE	47	13	24	1410	1232	7.9	123	534	846	11.5	2.92	110	.237	.313	23	47	105	**112**	.981	116	157	.8	-5.3	-8.0	-1.3	-2.9
MIL	37	14	32	1391²	1289	8.3	116	486	740	11.7	3.45	94	.247	.315	-61	-65	99	97	.977	139	145	-.5	-7.4	-3.0	-1.1	-1.0
WEST																										
OAK	42	**23**	**43**	1417²	1170	7.4	96	418	862	10.2	2.58	110	.226	.286	76	42	93	99	.979	130	146	-.0	4.8	7.6	.3	2.9
CHI	36	14	42	1385¹	1269	8.2	94	431	936	11.2	3.12	100	.245	.307	-9	1	102	99	.977	135	136	-.4	.1	.3	.5	9.4
MIN	37	17	34	1399¹	1188	7.6	105	444	838	10.7	2.84	113	.230	.296	35	58	105	99	.974	159	133	-1.8	6.6	-2.0	-.4	-2.4
KC	44	16	29	1381¹	1293	8.4	**85**	405	801	11.3	3.24	94	.251	.309	-27	-32	99	97	.981	116	164	.7	-3.6	**7.7**	.5	-6.3
CAL	57	18	16	1377²	**1109**	7.2	90	620	**1000**	11.5	3.06	95	**.222**	.312	0	-23	95	96	.981	114	135	-.2	-2.6	-3.2	.0	2.4
TEX	11	8	34	1374²	1258	8.2	92	613	868	12.6	3.53	85	.246	.332	-71	-79	94	99	.972	166	147	-2.2	-9.0	-11.0	-.0	.8
TOT	502	193	372	16653²		8.0				11.3	3.06		.239	.308					.979	1535	1770					

Runs		Hits		Doubles		Triples		Home Runs		Total Bases	
Murcer-NY	102	Rudi-Oak	181	Piniella-KC	33	Rudi-Oak	9	D.Allen-Chi	37	Murcer-NY	314
Rudi-Oak	94	Piniella-KC	179	Rudi-Oak	32	Fisk-Bos	9	Murcer-NY	33	D.Allen-Chi	305
Harper-Bos	92	Murcer-NY	171	Murcer-NY	30	Blair-Bal	8	Killebrew-Min	26	Rudi-Oak	288
D.Allen-Chi	90	Carew-Min	170	White-NY	29	Murcer-NY	7	Epstein-Oak	26	Mayberry-KC	255
Tovar-Min	86	May-Chi	161	Harper-Bos	29	Kelly-Chi	7			Piniella-KC	253

Runs Batted In		Runs Produced		Bases On Balls		Batting Average		On Base Percentage		Slugging Average	
D.Allen-Chi	113	D.Allen-Chi	166	White-NY	99	Carew-Min	.318	D.Allen-Chi	.422	D.Allen-Chi	.603
Mayberry-KC	100	Murcer-NY	165	D.Allen-Chi	99	Piniella-KC	.312	May-Chi	.408	Fisk-Bos	.538
Murcer-NY	96	Rudi-Oak	150	Killebrew-Min	94	D.Allen-Chi	.308	Mayberry-KC	.396	Murcer-NY	.537
Scott-Mil	88	Mayberry-KC	140	May-Chi	79	May-Chi	.308	White-NY	.385	Mayberry-KC	.507
Powell-Bal	81					Rudi-Oak	.305	Scheinblum-KC	.385	Epstein-Oak	.490

Production		Adjusted Production		Batter Runs		Adjusted Batter Runs		Clutch Hitting Index		Runs Created	
D.Allen-Chi	1.025	D.Allen-Chi	199	D.Allen-Chi	66.1	D.Allen-Chi	63.6	Billings-Tex	138	D.Allen-Chi	131
Fisk-Bos	.909	Murcer-NY	171	Murcer-NY	44.9	Murcer-NY	48.6	Rojas-KC	123	Murcer-NY	114
Mayberry-KC	.903	Mayberry-KC	168	Mayberry-KC	43.0	Mayberry-KC	43.5	Scheinblum-KC	123	Mayberry-KC	101
Murcer-NY	.900	Epstein-Oak	166	Fisk-Bos	37.1	Epstein-Oak	37.6	Petrocelli-Bos	122	May-Chi	96
Epstein-Oak	.868	Fisk-Bos	159	May-Chi	36.7	Rudi-Oak	35.8	Bando-Oak	121	Rudi-Oak	95

Total Average		Stolen Bases		Stolen Base Average		Stolen Base Runs		Fielding Runs		Total Player Rating	
D.Allen-Chi	1.121	Campaneris-Oak	52	Baylor-Bal	92.3	Campaneris-Oak	7.2	Patek-KC	29.5	Murcer-NY	5.5
Mayberry-KC	.910	Nelson-Tex	51	Patek-KC	82.5	Baylor-Bal	6.0	Rodriguez-Det	24.0	D.Allen-Chi	5.4
Fisk-Bos	.908	Patek-KC	33	Scott-Mil	80.0	Patek-KC	5.7	Michael-NY	23.7	Fisk-Bos	4.4
Murcer-NY	.888	Kelly-Chi	32	Campaneris-Oak	78.8	Nelson-Tex	5.1	Belanger-Bal	20.8	Patek-KC	3.8
Epstein-Oak	.885	Otis-KC	28	Harper-Bos	78.1	Kelly-Chi	4.2	May-Mil	14.9	White-NY	3.4

Wins		Win Percentage		Games		Complete Games		Shutouts		Saves	
Wood-Chi	24	Hunter-Oak	.750	Lindblad-Tex	66	Perry-Cle	29	Ryan-Cal	9	Lyle-NY	35
Perry-Cle	24	Tiant-Bos	.714	Fingers-Oak	65	Lolich-Det	23	Wood-Chi	8	Forster-Chi	29
Lolich-Det	22	Odom-Oak	.714	Granger-Min	63	Wood-Chi	20	Stottlemyre-NY	7	Fingers-Oak	21
		Palmer-Bal	.677			Ryan-Cal	20			Granger-Min	19
		Kline-NY	.640			Palmer-Bal	18			Sanders-Mil	17

Innings Pitched		Fewest Hits/Game		Fewest BB/Game		Strikeouts		Strikeouts/Game		Ratio	
Wood-Chi	376.2	Ryan-Cal	5.26	Peterson-NY	1.58	Ryan-Cal	329	Ryan-Cal	10.43	Nelson-KC	7.89
Perry-Cle	342.2	Hunter-Oak	6.09	Nelson-KC	1.61	Lolich-Det	250	Messersmith-Cal	7.53	Hunter-Oak	8.32
Lolich-Det	327.1	Nelson-KC	6.23	Kline-NY	1.68	Perry-Cle	234	May-Cal	7.41	Perry-Cle	9.11
Hunter-Oak	295.1	Tiant-Bos	6.44	Holtzman-Oak	1.76	Blyleven-Min	228	Bradley-Chi	7.23	Palmer-Bal	9.51
Blyleven-Min	287.1	Messersmith-Cal	6.63	Wood-Chi	1.77	Coleman-Det	222	Blyleven-Min	7.14	Wood-Chi	9.70

Earned Run Average		Adjusted ERA		Opponents' Batting Avg.		Opponents' On Base Pct.		Starter Runs		Adjusted Starter Runs	
Tiant-Bos	1.91	Tiant-Bos	168	Ryan-Cal	.171	Nelson-KC	.236	Perry-Cle	43.5	Perry-Cle	49.5
Perry-Cle	1.92	Perry-Cle	168	Hunter-Oak	.189	Hunter-Oak	.242	Hunter-Oak	33.4	Palmer-Bal	30.7
Hunter-Oak	2.04	Palmer-Bal	149	Nelson-KC	.196	Perry-Cle	.261	Palmer-Bal	30.3	Hunter-Oak	26.3
Palmer-Bal	2.07	Nelson-KC	146	Tiant-Bos	.202	Palmer-Bal	.269	Ryan-Cal	24.6	Tiant-Bos	25.9
Nelson-KC	2.08	Hunter-Oak	139	Perry-Cle	.205	Tiant-Bos	.277	Wood-Chi	23.1	Wood-Chi	25.8

Clutch Pitching Index		Relief Runs		Adjusted Relief Runs		Relief Ranking		Total Pitcher Index		Total Baseball Ranking	
Paul-Tex	128	Lyle-NY	13.6	Lyle-NY	12.3	Lyle-NY	23.3	Perry-Cle	7.0	Perry-Cle	7.0
Odom-Oak	124	Knowles-Oak	12.3	Bell-Mil	10.8	Forster-Chi	16.0	Palmer-Bal	4.2	Murcer-NY	5.5
Wilcox-Cle	119	Bell-Mil	11.0	Knowles-Oak	10.7	Knowles-Oak	12.9	Wood-Chi	3.1	D.Allen-Chi	5.4
Lonborg-Mil	112	Forster-Chi	9.0	Forster-Chi	9.7	Abernathy-KC	11.0	Tiant-Bos	3.0	Fisk-Bos	4.4
Lolich-Det	111	Abernathy-KC	8.8	Abernathy-KC	8.6	Fingers-Oak	8.5	Lyle-NY	2.7	Palmer-Bal	4.2

January 24 Warren Spahn is elected to the Hall of Fame in his first try, receiving 316 of 380 votes.

January 28 The Hall of Fame Special Veterans Committee selects players Mickey Welch and George Kelly, plus umpire Billy Evans, for enshrinement.

February 1 Commissioner Bowie Kuhn announces the selection of Monte Irvin for the Hall of Fame by the Special Committee on the Negro Leagues.

February 25 A new three-year Basic Agreement is reached between players and owners, and spring training is slated to start March 1. Among the provisions of the agreement are a $15,000 minimum salary, salary arbitration, and the "10 and 5" trade rule, which permits a player with 10 years in the major league, the last 5 of which are with his current team, to veto any trade involving him.

March 20 In a special election held by the BBWAA, the late Roberto Clemente receives 393 of 424 votes to earn entry in the Hall of Fame. The Hall's Board of Directors had earlier waived the five-year-wait rule for Clemente. His number 21 will be retired in Pittsburgh 17 days later.

May 8 For the second time in his career, Pirate Willie Stargell poles one out of Dodger Stadium. His blast off Andy Messersmith hits the right field pavilion roof 470 feet away. His first such homer, a 506-foot shot, came off Alan Foster on August 5, 1969. No other player has hit one out of the stadium.

June 20 Bobby Bonds leads off with a homer, but the Giants lose 7-5 to the Reds. It is Bonds's 22nd leadoff homer, breaking Lou Brock's NL record.

June 23 Phillies pitcher Ken Brett beats the Expos, 7–2, and hits a home run for a major league-record fourth consecutive game. He hit home runs on June 9, 13, and 18: he will total 10 for his career.

July 21 Hank Aaron hits a Ken Brett fastball for a two-run home run during the Braves' 8–4 loss to the Phillies. It is the 700th career homer for Aaron, only the second player to reach that milestone.

August 6 Roberto Clemente and Warren Spahn head the list of new inductees at Cooperstown. Clemente is the first Latin-born player to achieve membership at Cooperstown.

August 17 Willie Mays hits the 660th—and last—home run of his major league career off Don Gullett of Cincinnati.

October 10 Tom Seaver hurls the Mets into the Series with a 7-2 victory over the Reds. New York has 13 hits in the contest.

October 14 The Mets win Game 2, 10-7, scoring four runs in an eleventh inning, featuring the last major league hit by Willie Mays and two errors by Oakland second base Mike Andrews. Andrews is subsequently put on the "disabled list" by Finley,

October 31 Tom Seaver wins the NL Cy Young Award, the first time the honor has gone to a player with fewer than 20 wins. Seaver was 19-10 and led the league in ERA (2.08) and strikeouts (251).

November 21 Pete Rose wins the NL MVP in a controversial vote, edging out Willie Stargell. Rose led the league with 230 hits and won his third batting crown with a .338 mark. Stargell led with 44 homers, 119 RBI, and a .646 slugging average while batting .299.

November 27 Gary Matthews receives 11 of 24 nominations for the NL Rookie of the Year Award. The Giants outfielder batted .300 in 145 games.

ATLANTA		CHICAGO		CINCINNATI		HOUSTON		LOS ANGELES		MONTREAL	
M	E.Mathews	M	W.Lockman	M	S.Anderson	M	L.Durocher	M	W.Alston	M	G.Mauch
1B	M.Lum	1B	J.Hickman	1B	T.Perez	1B	L.May	1B	B.Buckner	1B	M.Jorgensen
2B	D.Johnson	2B	G.Beckert	2B	J.Morgan	2B	T.Helms	2B	D.Lopes	2B	R.Hunt
SS	M.Perez	SS	D.Kessinger	SS	D.Concepcion	SS	R.Metzger	SS	B.Russell	SS	T.Foli
3B	D.Evans	3B	R.Santo	3B	D.Menke	3B	D.Rader	3B	R.Cey	3B	B.Bailey
LF	H.Aaron	LF	B.Williams	LF	P.Rose	LF	B.Watson	LF	M.Mota	LF	R.Fairly
CF	D.Baker	CF	R.Monday	CF	C.Geronimo	CF	C.Cedeno	CF	W.Davis	CF	R.Woods
RF	R.Garr	RF	J.Cardenal	RF	B.Tolan	RF	J.Wynn	RF	W.Crawford	RF	K.Singleton
C	J.Oates	C	R.Hundley	C	J.Bench	C	S.Jutze	C	J.Ferguson	C	J.Boccabella
OS	S.Jackson	O	G.Hiser	S2	D.Chaney	C	J.Edwards	1O	S.Garvey	1	H.Breeden
C	P.Casanova	2	P.Popovich	31	D.Driessen	O	T.Agee			O	B.Day
								P	D.Sutton	S2	P.Frias
P	C.Morton	P	F.Jenkins	P	J.Billingham	P	J.Reuss	P	A.Messersmith		
P	P.Niekro	P	B.Hooton	P	R.Grimsley	P	D.Roberts	P	C.Osteen	P	S.Renko
P	R.Schueler	P	R.Reuschel	P	D.Gullett	P	D.Wilson	P	T.John	P	M.Torrez
P	R.Harrison	P	M.Pappas	P	F.Norman	P	K.Forsch	P	A.Downing	P	B.Moore
P	R.Reed	P	B.Bonham	RP	P.Borbon	P	T.Griffin	RP	C.Hough	P	E.McAnally
RP	T.House	RP	B.Locker	RP	T.Hall	RP	J.Crawford	RP	J.Brewer	P	S.Rogers
		RP	R.Burris	RP	C.Carroll	RP	J.Ray	RP	D.Rau	RP	M.Marshall
P	G.Gentry	RP	J.Aker			RP	J.York			RP	T.Walker
P	P.Dobson							P	P.Richert		
		P	L.Gura	P	J.McGlothlin	P	J.Richard			P	B.Stoneman
		P	D.LaRoche	P	R.Nelson						

NEW YORK		PHILADELPHIA		PITTSBURGH		SAN DIEGO		SAN FRANCISCO		ST.LOUIS	
M	Y.Berra	M	D.Ozark	M	B.Virdon	M	D.Zimmer	M	C.Fox	M	R.Schoendienst
1B	J.Milner	1B	W.Montanez	M	D.Murtaugh	1B	N.Colbert	1B	W.McCovey	1B	J.Torre
2B	F.Millan	2B	D.Doyle	1B	B.Robertson	2B	R.Morales	2B	T.Fuentes	2B	T.Sizemore
SS	B.Harrelson	SS	L.Bowa	2B	D.Cash	SS	D.Thomas	SS	C.Speier	SS	M.Tyson
3B	W.Garrett	3B	M.Schmidt	SS	D.Maxvill	3B	D.Roberts	3B	E.Goodson	3B	K.Reitz
LF	C.Jones	LF	G.Luzinski	3B	R.Hebner	LF	L.Lee	LF	G.Matthews	LF	L.Brock
CF	D.Hahn	CF	D.Unser	LF	W.Stargell	CF	J.Grubb	CF	G.Maddox	CF	L.Melendez
RF	R.Staub	RF	B.Robinson	CF	A.Oliver	RF	C.Gaston	RF	B.Bonds	RF	J.Cruz
C	J.Grote	C	B.Boone	RF	R.Zisk	C	F.Kendall	C	D.Rader	C	T.Simmons
				C	M.Sanguillen						
1O	E.Kranepool	1	T.Hutton			O	J.Morales	31	D.Kingman	O	B.Carbo
SO	T.Martinez	3O	C.Tovar	O	G.Clines	S	E.Hernandez	1O	G.Thomasson	1C	T.McCarver
O1	W.Mays			C	M.May	32	D.Hilton				
		P	S.Carlton	2S	R.Stennett	O1	I.Murrell	P	R.Bryant	P	R.Wise
P	T.Seaver	P	W.Twitchell					P	J.Barr	P	R.Cleveland
P	J.Koosman	P	K.Brett	P	N.Briles	P	B.Greif	P	T.Bradley	P	A.Foster
P	J.Matlack	P	J.Lonborg	P	B.Moose	P	C.Kirby	P	J.Marichal	P	B.Gibson
P	G.Stone	P	D.Ruthven	P	D.Ellis	P	S.Arlin	P	J.Willoughby	RP	D.Segui
P	R.Sadecki	RP	B.Lersch	P	J.Rooker	P	R.Troedson	RP	E.Sosa	RP	R.Folkers
RP	T.McGraw	RP	M.Scarce	P	L.Walker	P	R.Jones	RP	R.Moffitt	P	O.Pena
RP	H.Parker	RP	B.Brandon	RP	D.Giusti	RP	M.Caldwell	RP	D.Carrithers		
				RP	B.Johnson	RP	M.Corkins			P	T.Murphy
P	J.McAndrew			RP	R.Hernandez	RP	V.Romo			P	A.Hrabosky
				P	S.Blass	P	G.Ross				
						P	F.Norman				

TEAM	G	W	L	PCT	GB	R	OR	AB	H	2B	3B	HR	BB	SO	AVG	OBP	SLG	PRO	PRO+	BR	/A	PF	CHI	RC	SB	CS	SBA	SBR
EAST																												
NY	161	82	79	.509		608	588	5457	1345	198	24	85	540	805	.246	.317	.338	.655	89	-81	-72	98	104	583	27	22	55	-5
STL	162	81	81	.500	1.5	643	603	5478	1418	240	35	75	531	796	.259	.328	.357	.685	96	-24	-22	100	100	635	100	46	68	2
PIT	162	80	82	.494	2.5	704	693	5608	1465	**257**	44	154	432	842	.261	.317	.405	.722	109	30	48	97	101	697	23	30	43	-11
MON	162	79	83	.488	3.5	668	702	5369	1345	190	23	125	**695**	777	.251	**.341**	.364	.705	98	30	5	104	94	672	77	68	53	-18
CHI	161	77	84	.478	5	614	655	5363	1322	201	21	117	575	855	.247	.322	.357	.679	98	-35	-81	107	99	605	65	58	53	-15
PHI	162	71	91	.438	11.5	642	717	5546	1381	218	29	134	476	979	.249	.312	.371	.683	93	-40	-56	103	102	641	51	47	52	-13
WEST																												
CIN	162	99	63	.611		741	621	5505	1398	232	34	137	639	947	.254	.335	.383	.718	**111**	43	81	95	102	724	**148**	55	73	11
LA	162	95	66	.590	3.5	675	**565**	5604	1473	219	29	110	497	795	.263	.326	.371	.697	104	-5	25	96	100	676	109	50	69	3
SF	162	88	74	.543	11	739	702	5537	1452	212	**52**	161	590	913	.262	.337	.407	.744	108	87	56	104	96	765	112	52	68	2
HOU	162	82	80	.506	17	681	672	5532	1391	216	35	134	469	962	.251	.314	.376	.690	97	-28	-26	100	**107**	639	92	48	66	-1
ATL	162	76	85	.472	22.5	**799**	748	5631	**1497**	219	34	**206**	608	870	**.266**	**.341**	.447	**.768**	**111**	**134**	73	108	97	**826**	84	40	68	5
SD	162	60	102	.370	39	548	770	5457	1330	198	26	112	401	966	.244	.298	.351	.649	92	-110	-67	92	102	566	88	36	71	5
TOT	971					8062		66087	16817	2600	386	1550	6453	10507	.254	.324	.376	.700							976	552	64	-38

TEAM	CG	SH	SV	IP	H	H/G	HR	BB	SO	RAT	ERA	ERA+	OAV	OOB	PR	/A	PF	CPI	FA	E	DP	FW	PW	BW	SBW	DIF
EAST																										
NY	47	15	40	1465	1345	8.3	127	490	**1027**	11.4	3.26	111	.245	.309	65	58	99	101	.980	126	140	1.1	6.0	-7.5	-.2	2.0
STL	42	14	36	1460²	1366	8.4	**105**	486	867	11.6	3.25	112	.248	.312	66	63	100	100	.975	159	149	-.7	6.6	-2.3	.5	-4.1
PIT	26	11	**44**	1450²	1426	8.8	110	564	839	12.6	3.73	94	.258	.331	-12	-35	96	100	.976	151	156	-.3	-3.6	5.0	-.8	-1.3
MON	26	6	38	1451²	1356	8.4	128	681	866	12.8	3.71	103	.250	.337	-9	16	104	103	.974	163	156	-.9	1.7	.5	-1.5	-1.7
CHI	27	13	40	1437²	1471	9.2	128	**438**	885	12.1	3.66	108	.267	.325	1	46	108	104	.975	157	155	-.7	4.8	-8.4	-1.2	2.0
PHI	**49**	11	22	1447¹	1435	8.9	131	632	919	13.1	3.99	95	.263	.343	-53	-31	104	103	.979	134	**179**	.7	-3.2	-5.8	-1.0	-.6
WEST																										
CIN	39	**17**	43	1473	1389	8.5	135	518	801	11.8	3.40	100	.252	.319	42	0	93	105	**.982**	115	162	**1.8**	.0	8.4	1.5	6.3
LA	45	15	38	1491	**1270**	**7.7**	129	461	961	**10.6**	**3.00**	**115**	**.231**	.294	109	72	94	97	.981	125	166	1.2	**7.5**	2.6	.6	2.5
SF	33	8	**44**	1452¹	1442	8.9	145	485	787	12.1	3.79	101	.257	.320	-21	4	104	97	.974	163	138	-.9	.4	5.8	.5	1.2
HOU	45	14	26	1460²	1389	8.6	111	575	907	12.3	3.75	97	.252	.325	-14	-19	99	95	.981	116	140	1.7	-2.0	-2.7	.2	3.7
ATL	34	9	35	1462	1467	9.0	144	575	803	12.7	4.25	93	.263	.335	-95	-51	107	95	.974	166	142	-1.1	-5.3	7.6	.4	-6.1
SD	34	10	23	1430	1461	9.2	157	548	845	12.8	4.16	83	.267	.336	-79	-110	95	100	.973	170	152	-1.3	-11.5	-7.0	.9	-2.1
TOT	447	143	429	17482		8.7				12.2	3.66		.254	.324					.977	1745	1835					

Runs
Bonds-SF 131
Morgan-Cin 116
Rose-Cin 115
Evans-Atl 114
Brock-StL 110

Hits
Rose-Cin 230
Garr-Atl 200
Brock-StL 193
Simmons-StL 192
Oliver-Pit 191

Doubles
Stargell-Pit 43
Oliver-Pit 38
Staub-NY 36
Simmons-StL 36
Rose-Cin 36

Triples
Metzger-Hou 14
Matthews-SF 10
Maddox-SF 10
Davis-LA 9

Home Runs
Stargell-Pit 44
Johnson-Atl 43
Evans-Atl 41
Aaron-Atl 40
Bonds-SF 39

Total Bases
Bonds-SF 341
Stargell-Pit 337
Evans-Atl 331
Johnson-Atl 305
Oliver-Pit 303

Runs Batted In
Stargell-Pit 119
May-Hou 105
Evans-Atl 104
Bench-Cin 104
Singleton-Mon 103

Runs Produced
Bonds-SF 188
Stargell-Pit 181
Singleton-Mon 180
Baker-Atl 179
Evans-Atl 177

Bases On Balls
Evans-Atl 124
Cedeno-Hou 123
Morgan-Cin 111
McCovey-SF 105
Monday-Chi 92

Batting Average
Rose-Cin .... .338
Cedeno-Hou .... .320
Maddox-SF .... .319
Perez-Cin .... .314
Watson-Hou .... .312

On Base Percentage
Singleton-Mon .... .429
Fairly-Mon .... .422
Morgan-Cin .... .408
Evans-Atl .... .407
Watson-Hou .... .405

Slugging Average
Stargell-Pit ..... .646
Evans-Atl .... .556
Johnson-Atl ...... .546
Cedeno-Hou .... .537
Bonds-SF .... .530

Production
Stargell-Pit 1.041
Evans-Atl .... .964
Perez-Cin .... .923
Johnson-Atl ...... .917
Cedeno-Hou .... .914

Adjusted Production
Stargell-Pit 189
Perez-Cin 162
Morgan-Cin 157
Evans-Atl 153
Cedeno-Hou 151

Batter Runs
Stargell-Pit 57.8
Evans-Atl 54.8
Aaron-Atl 45.5
Singleton-Mon 44.8
Morgan-Cin 41.6

Adjusted Batter Runs
Stargell-Pit 61.0
Morgan-Cin 47.8
Perez-Cin 47.2
Evans-Atl 45.0
Singleton-Mon 40.6

Clutch Hitting Index
Cey-LA 126
Sizemore-StL 123
Bench-Cin 121
Speier-SF 119
Tolan-Cin 116

Runs Created
Evans-Atl 143
Stargell-Pit 136
Bonds-SF 130
Morgan-Cin 128
Rose-Cin 119

Total Average
Stargell-Pit 1.129
Evans-Atl 1.048
Morgan-Cin 1.034
Cedeno-Hou .... .949
Johnson-Atl ...... .947

Stolen Bases
Brock-StL 70
Morgan-Cin 67
Cedeno-Hou 56
Bonds-SF 43
Lopes-LA 36

Stolen Base Average
Baker-Atl 88.9
Morgan-Cin 81.7
Concepcion-Cin ... 81.5
Cedeno-Hou 78.9
Brock-StL 77.8

Stolen Base Runs
Morgan-Cin 11.1
Brock-StL 9.0
Cedeno-Hou 7.8
Baker-Atl 5.4
Garr-Atl 3.9

Fielding Runs
Schmidt-Phi 21.2
Kessinger-Chi 17.0
Unser-Phi 16.7
Rose-Cin 16.7
Cey-LA 16.2

Total Player Rating
Stargell-Pit 6.3
Morgan-Cin 6.1
Cedeno-Hou 5.3
Evans-Atl 5.2
Rose-Cin 4.6

Wins
Bryant-SF 24
Seaver-NY 19
Billingham-Cin ... 19
Sutton-LA 18
Gullett-Cin 18

Win Percentage
John-LA .... .696
Gullett-Cin ...... .692
Bryant-SF .... .667
Seaver-NY .... .655
Billingham-Cin ... .655

Games
Marshall-Mon 92
Borbon-Cin 80
Sosa-SF 71
Giusti-Pit 67
Segui-StL 65

Complete Games
Seaver-NY 18
Carlton-Phi 18
Billingham-Cin ... 16

Shutouts
Billingham-Cin 7
Roberts-Hou 6
Wise-StL 5
Twitchell-Phi 5

Saves
Marshall-Mon 31
McGraw-NY 25
Giusti-Pit 20
Brewer-LA 20

Innings Pitched
Carlton-Phi 293.1
Billingham-Cin ... 293.1
Seaver-NY 290.0
Reuss-Hou 279.1
Jenkins-Chi 271.0

Fewest Hits/Game
Seaver-NY 6.80
Sutton-LA 6.88
Twitchell-Phi 6.93
Wilson-Hou 7.03
Messersmith-LA ... 7.07

Fewest BB/Game
Marichal-SF 1.61
Jenkins-Chi 1.89
Barr-SF 1.91
Sutton-LA 1.97
Seaver-NY 1.99

Strikeouts
Seaver-NY 251
Carlton-Phi 223
Matlack-NY 205
Sutton-LA 200

Strikeouts/Game
Seaver-NY 7.79
Moore-Mon 7.71
Matlack-NY 7.62
Sutton-LA 7.02
Carlton-Phi 6.84

Ratio
Seaver-NY 8.91
Sutton-LA 9.02
Messersmith-LA ... 10.06
Gibson-StL 10.11
Rooker-Pit 10.41

Earned Run Average
Seaver-NY 2.08
Sutton-LA 2.42
Twitchell-Phi 2.50
Marshall-Mon 2.66
Messersmith-LA ... 2.70

Adjusted ERA
Seaver-NY 174
Twitchell-Phi 152
Marshall-Mon 143
Sutton-LA 142
Renko-Mon 136

Opponents' Batting Avg.
Seaver-NY .... .206
Sutton-LA .... .209
Wilson-Hou .... .213
Messersmith-LA ... .214
Renko-Mon .... .218

Opponents' On Base Pct.
Seaver-NY .... .254
Sutton-LA .... .258
Messersmith-LA ... .279
Gibson-StL .... .284
Briles-Pit .... .288

Starter Runs
Seaver-NY 51.0
Sutton-LA 35.3
Rogers-Mon 31.5
Twitchell-Phi 28.8
Messersmith-LA ... 26.6

Adjusted Starter Runs
Seaver-NY 49.5
Rogers-Mon 33.8
Twitchell-Phi 32.2
Sutton-LA 28.9
Renko-Mon 27.8

Clutch Pitching Index
Marshall-Mon 134
Roberts-Hou 122
Twitchell-Phi 121
Grimsley-Cin 116
Moose-Pit 113

Relief Runs
Borbon-Cin 20.2
Marshall-Mon 19.8
Giusti-Pit 14.1
Moffitt-SF 13.8
Locker-Chi 13.3

Adjusted Relief Runs
Marshall-Mon 22.9
Borbon-Cin 16.8
Locker-Chi 16.6
Moffitt-SF 15.6
Giusti-Pit 12.6

Relief Ranking
Marshall-Mon 36.8
Locker-Chi 28.2
Borbon-Cin 22.7
Giusti-Pit 17.8
Scarce-Phi 16.1

Total Pitcher Index
Seaver-NY 5.4
Marshall-Mon 4.4
Rogers-Mon 4.1
Renko-Mon 3.6
Locker-Chi 3.1

Total Baseball Ranking
Stargell-Pit 6.3
Morgan-Cin 6.1
Seaver-NY 5.4
Cedeno-Hou 5.3
Evans-Atl 5.2

January 3 A group of investors, headed by shipbuilder George Steinbrenner, purchases the New York Yankees from CBS for $10 million.

April 6 Yankee Ron Blomberg, facing Boston's Luis Tiant, becomes the first official DH in the major league. Blomberg walks with the bases loaded and winds up 1-for-3 in the 15-5 loss to the Red Sox.

April 27 In 50-degree Detroit weather, Royals rookie Steve Busby no-hits the Tigers 3-0. It is the first Royals no-hitter, and Busby is the first no-hit game pitcher not to bat.

May 15 California's Nolan Ryan strikes out 12 and hurls his first career no-hitter in beating Kansas City 3-0.

June 7 The Rangers make Texas high school pitcher David Clyde the number-one pick in the free-agent draft. He will make his major league debut later this month. Dave Winfield, the number-four pick, will go straight to the major leagues. Winfield was also taken in the NBA and NFL drafts. John Stearns is taken second by the Phillies, and the Brewers, picking third, take Robin Yount.

June 27 David Clyde, 18 and fresh out of Houston's Westchester High School, makes his eagerly awaited debut with the Rangers, before 35,698, the largest Rangers' crowd of the year. Clyde goes five innings and is the winner 4-3.

July 15 Before 41,411 in Detroit, Angel Nolan Ryan hurls his second no-hitter of the season in taming the Tigers 6-0. Ryan fans 17 batters.

July 20 Chicago's Wilbur Wood starts and loses both games of a doubleheader with the Yankees 12-2 and 7-0.

July 30 The Rangers Jim Bibby no-hits first-place Oakland 6-0. Bibby, who came to Texas in a June 6 trade with the Cardinals, strikes out 13 batters.

August 1 Thurman Munson and Carlton Fisk brawl at Fenway. With a 2-2 score in the top of the ninth, Munson, attempting to score from third on a missed bunt, crashes into Fisk and they both come up swinging. Boston wins 3-2 in the bottom of the inning.

September 19 The Angels down the Rangers 6-2 and 9-4 at Arlington Stadium. Frank Robinson homers in the 32nd different park of his major league career—a record.

September 27 Nolan Ryan fans 16 in 11 innings, beating the Twins 5-4. The final strikeout victim, Rich Reese, is 383 of the season for Ryan, enabling him to surpass the major league record set by Sandy Koufax in 1965.

October 21 Oakland wins the World Championship for the second straight year as Campaneris and MVP Jackson homer in the 5-2, seventh-game victory.

November 14 Reggie Jackson wins the AL MVP Award unanimously. The Oakland star led the league in runs (99), homers (32), RBI (117), and slugging (.531). Jim Palmer is named the AL Cy Young winner.

BALTIMORE		BOSTON		CALIFORNIA		CHICAGO		CLEVELAND		DETROIT	
M	E.Weaver	M	E.Kasko	M	B.Winkles	M	C.Tanner	M	K.Aspromonte	M	B.Martin
1B	B.Powell	M	E.Popowski	1B	M.Epstein	1B	T.Muser	1B	C.Chambliss	M	J.Schultz
2B	B.Grich	1B	C.Yastrzemski	2B	S.Alomar	2B	J.Orta	2B	J.Brohamer	1B	N.Cash
SS	M.Belanger	2B	D.Griffin	SS	R.Meoli	SS	E.Leon	SS	F.Duffy	2B	D.McAuliffe
3B	B.Robinson	SS	L.Aparicio	3B	A.Gallagher	3B	B.Melton	3B	B.Bell	SS	E.Brinkman
LF	D.Baylor	3B	R.Petrocelli	LF	V.Pinson	LF	C.May	LF	C.Spikes	3B	A.Rodriguez
CF	P.Blair	LF	T.Harper	CF	K.Berry	CF	J.Jeter	CF	G.Hendrick	LF	W.Horton
RF	R.Coggins	CF	R.Miller	RF	L.Stanton	RF	P.Kelly	RF	R.Torres	CF	M.Stanley
C	E.Williams	RF	D.Evans	C	J.Torborg	C	E.Herrmann	C	D.Duncan	RF	J.Northrup
DH	T.Davis	C	C.Fisk	DH	F.Robinson	DH	K.Henderson	DH	O.Gamble	C	B.Freehan
		DH	O.Cepeda							DH	G.Brown
O	A.Bumbry			O1	T.McCraw	1	D.Allen	CD	J.Ellis		
O	M.Rettenmund	O	R.Smith	3O	B.Oliver	O1	J.Hairston	O2	J.Lowenstein	O1	A.Kaline
		S2	M.Guerrero	O	R.Scheinblum	2S	L.Alvarado	OD	W.Williams	2	T.Taylor
P	J.Palmer									C	D.Sims
P	M.Cuellar	P	B.Lee	P	N.Ryan	P	W.Wood	P	G.Perry	D	F.Howard
P	D.McNally	P	L.Tiant	P	B.Singer	P	S.Bahnsen	P	D.Tidrow		
P	D.Alexander	P	J.Curtis	P	C.Wright	P	S.Stone	P	M.Wilcox	P	M.Lolich
P	J.Jefferson	P	M.Pattin	P	R.May	P	T.Forster	P	T.Timmermann	P	J.Coleman
RP	B.Reynolds	P	R.Moret	RP	S.Barber	P	E.Fisher	P	B.Strom	P	J.Perry
RP	G.Jackson	RP	B.Bolin	RP	D.Sells	RP	C.Acosta	RP	T.Hilgendorf	P	W.Fryman
RP	E.Watt					RP	R.Gossage	RP	R.Lamb	RP	J.Hiller
		P	D.Pole	P	R.Hand			RP	J.Johnson	RP	F.Scherman
		P	R.Culp	P	D.Lange	P	B.Johnson			RP	L.LaGrow
								P	D.Bosman		
								P	M.Kekich	P	M.Strahler

KANSAS CITY		MILWAUKEE		MINNESOTA		NEW YORK		OAKLAND		TEXAS	
M	J.McKeon	M	D.Crandall	M	F.Quilici	M	R.Houk	M	D.Williams	M	W.Herzog
1B	J.Mayberry	1B	G.Scott	1B	J.Lis	1B	F.Alou	1B	G.Tenace	M	D.Wilber
2B	C.Rojas	2B	P.Garcia	2B	R.Carew	2B	H.Clarke	2B	D.Green	M	B.Martin
SS	F.Patek	SS	T.Johnson	SS	D.Thompson	SS	G.Michael	SS	B.Campaneris	1B	J.Spencer
3B	P.Schaal	3B	D.Money	3B	S.Braun	3B	G.Nettles	3B	S.Bando	2B	D.Nelson
LF	L.Piniella	LF	J.Briggs	LF	J.Holt	LF	R.White	LF	J.Rudi	SS	J.Mason
CF	A.Otis	CF	D.May	CF	L.Hisle	CF	B.Murcer	CF	B.North	3B	T.Harrah
RF	E.Kirkpatrick	RF	B.Coluccio	RF	B.Darwin	RF	M.Alou	RF	R.Jackson	LF	R.Carty
C	F.Healy	C	D.Porter	C	G.Mitterwald	C	T.Munson	C	R.Fosse	CF	V.Harris
DH	H.McRae	DH	O.Brown	DH	T.Oliva	DH	J.Hart	DH	D.Johnson	RF	J.Burroughs
										C	K.Suarez
32	K.Bevacqua	CD	El.Rodriguez	S3	J.Terrell	D1	R.Blomberg	2S	T.Kubiak	DH	A.Johnson
OD	S.Hovley	DO	J.Lahoud	O	S.Brye						
				1	H.Killebrew					O	E.Maddox
P	P.Splittorff	P	J.Colborn			P	M.Stottlemyre	P	K.Holtzman	C	D.Billings
P	S.Busby	P	J.Slaton	P	B.Blyleven	P	D.Medich	P	V.Blue	O1	L.Biittner
P	D.Drago	P	J.Bell	P	J.Kaat	P	F.Peterson	P	C.Hunter	31	B.Sudakis
P	G.Garber	P	S.Lockwood	P	J.Decker	P	L.McDaniel	P	B.Odom		
P	B.Dal Canton	P	B.Champion	P	B.Hands	P	P.Dobson	RP	R.Fingers	P	J.Bibby
RP	D.Bird	RP	Ed.Rodriguez	P	D.Woodson	RP	S.Lyle	RP	D.Knowles	P	J.Merritt
RP	S.Mingori	RP	C.Short	RP	R.Corbin			RP	H.Pina	P	S.Siebert
		RP	F.Linzy	RP	E.Bane	P	S.McDowell			P	P.Broberg
P	A.Fitzmorris			RP	B.Campbell	P	F.Beene	P	P.Lindblad	RP	B.Gogolewski
P	K.Wright	P	B.Parsons			P	S.Kline	P	D.Hamilton	RP	M.Paul
P	W.Simpson			P	D.Goltz					RP	J.Brown
				P	D.Fife						
										P	S.Dunning
										P	D.Clyde
										P	D.Stanhouse
										P	C.Hudson
										P	S.Foucault

TEAM	G	W	L	PCT	GB	R	OR	AB	H	2B	3B	HR	BB	SO	AVG	OBP	SLG	PRO	PRO+	BR	/A	PF	CHI	RC	SB	CS	SBA	SBR
EAST																												
BAL	162	97	65	.599		754	561	5537	1474	229	48	119	648	752	.266	.348	.389	.737	108	61	67	99	98	765	146	64	70	5
BOS	162	89	73	.549	8	738	647	5513	1472	235	30	147	581	799	.267	.340	.401	.741	102	58	14	106	98	751	114	45	72	7
DET	162	85	77	.525	12	642	674	5508	1400	213	32	157	509	722	.254	.322	.390	.712	94	-9	-54	107	95	674	28	30	48	-10
NY	162	80	82	.494	17	641	610	5492	1435	212	17	131	489	680	.261	.324	.378	.702	101	-25	-2	97	98	655	47	43	52	-12
MIL	162	74	88	.457	23	708	731	5526	1399	229	40	145	563	977	.253	.327	.388	.715	103	2	17	98	101	702	110	66	63	-7
CLE	162	71	91	.438	26	680	826	5592	1429	205	29	158	471	793	.256	.317	.387	.704	95	-27	-38	102	103	666	60	68	47	-23
WEST																												
OAK	162	94	68	.580		758	615	5507	1431	216	28	147	595	919	.260	.336	.389	.725	110	28	66	95	104	730	128	57	69	4
KC	162	88	74	.543	6	755	752	5508	1440	239	40	114	644	696	.261	.342	.381	.723	96	31	-25	108	103	720	105	69	60	-10
MIN	162	81	81	.500	13	738	692	5625	1521	240	44	120	598	954	.270	.344	.393	.737	103	56	26	104	97	756	87	46	65	-2
CAL	162	79	83	.488	15	629	657	5505	1395	183	29	93	509	816	.253	.320	.348	.668	95	-84	-38	92	104	609	59	47	56	-11
CHI	162	77	85	.475	17	652	705	5475	1400	228	38	111	537	952	.256	.326	.372	.698	93	-28	-50	103	99	647	83	73	53	-19
TEX	162	57	105	.352	37	619	844	5488	1397	195	29	110	503	791	.255	.320	.361	.681	95	-63	-37	96	100	629	91	53	63	-5
TOT	972					8314		66276	17193	2624	404	1552	6647	9851	.259	.331	.381	.712							1058	661	62	-79

TEAM	CG	SH	SV	IP	H	H/G	HR	BB	SO	RAT	ERA	ERA+	OAV	OOB	PR	/A	PF	CPI	FA	E	DP	FW	PW	BW	SBW	DIF
EAST																										
BAL	67	14	26	1461²	1297	8.0	124	475	715	11.0	3.07	122	.240	.303	122	108	98	102	.981	119	184	1.3	11.0	6.9	1.2	-4.4
BOS	67	10	33	1440¹	1417	8.9	158	499	808	12.2	3.65	110	.259	.325	27	59	105	106	.979	127	162	.8	6.0	1.4	1.4	-1.7
DET	39	11	46	1447²	1468	9.1	154	493	911	12.4	3.90	105	.265	.328	-13	30	107	101	.982	112	144	1.7	3.1	-5.5	-.3	5.1
NY	47	16	39	1427²	1379	8.7	109	457	708	11.7	3.34	110	.254	.315	75	51	96	102	.976	156	172	-.8	5.2	-.2	-.6	-4.7
MIL	50	11	28	1454	1476	9.1	119	623	671	13.2	3.98	94	.265	.342	-27	-36	99	101	.977	145	167	-.2	-3.7	1.7	-.0	-4.8
CLE	55	9	21	1464²	1532	9.4	172	602	883	13.4	4.58	85	.271	.345	-125	-108	103	96	.978	139	174	.2	-11.0	-3.9	-1.7	6.5
WEST																										
OAK	46	16	41	1457¹	1311	8.1	143	494	797	11.3	3.29	108	.241	.308	86	42	93	100	.978	137	170	.3	4.3	6.8	1.1	.6
KC	40	7	41	1449¹	1521	9.4	114	617	790	13.5	4.19	98	.273	.349	-60	-13	108	100	.974	167	192	-1.4	-1.3	-2.6	-.3	12.7
MIN	48	18	34	1451²	1443	8.9	115	519	879	12.4	3.77	105	.259	.327	7	30	104	97	.978	139	147	.2	3.1	2.7	.5	-6.4
CAL	72	13	19	1456¹	1351	8.3	104	614	1010	12.4	3.53	100	.246	.326	46	3	93	99	.975	156	153	-.8	-.3	-3.9	-.5	2.8
CHI	48	15	35	1456	1484	9.2	110	574	848	13.0	3.86	102	.266	.338	-8	15	104	101	.977	144	165	-.1	1.5	-5.1	-1.3	1.0
TEX	35	10	27	1430	1514	9.5	130	680	831	14.1	4.64	80	.273	.357	-131	-146	98	96	.974	161	164	-1.1	-14.9	-3.8	.2	-4.4
TOT	614	150	390	17396²		8.9				12.5	3.82		.259	.331					.977	1702	1994					

Runs		Hits		Doubles		Triples		Home Runs		Total Bases	
Jackson-Oak	99	Carew-Min	203	Garcia-Min	32	Carew-Min	11	Jackson-Oak	32	Scott-Mil	295
Scott-Mil	98	May-Mil	189	Bando-Oak	32	Bumbry-Bal	11	Robinson-Cal	30	May-Mil	295
North-Oak	98	Murcer-NY	187	Scott-Mil	30	Orta-Chi	10	Burroughs-Tex	30	Bando-Oak	295
Carew-Min	98	Scott-Mil	185	Chambliss-Cle	30	Coggins-Bal	9	Bando-Oak	29	Murcer-NY	286
Bando-Oak	97	Johnson-Tex	179	Carew-Min	30	Coluccio-Mil	8			Jackson-Oak	286

Runs Batted In		Runs Produced		Bases On Balls		Batting Average		On Base Percentage		Slugging Average	
Jackson-Oak	117	Jackson-Oak	184	Mayberry-KC	122	Carew-Min	.350	Mayberry-KC	.420	Jackson-Oak	.531
Scott-Mil	107	Scott-Mil	181	Grich-Bal	107	Scott-Mil	.306	Carew-Min	.415	Bando-Oak	.498
Mayberry-KC	100	Bando-Oak	166	Yastrzemski-Bos	105	Davis-Bal	.306	Yastrzemski-Bos	.411	Robinson-Cal	.489
Bando-Oak	98	May-Mil	164	Tenace-Oak	101	Murcer-NY	.304	Tenace-Oak	.391	Scott-Mil	.488
Robinson-Cal	97	Mayberry-KC	161	Briggs-Mil	87	May-Mil	.303	Jackson-Oak	.387	Munson-NY	.487

Production		Adjusted Production		Batter Runs		Adjusted Batter Runs		Clutch Hitting Index		Runs Created	
Jackson-Oak	.918	Jackson-Oak	165	Mayberry-KC	41.0	Jackson-Oak	46.4	Davis-Bal	134	Bando-Oak	113
Mayberry-KC	.898	Robinson-Cal	153	Jackson-Oak	40.5	Bando-Oak	41.5	Robinson-Bal	124	Carew-Min	113
Carew-Min	.885	Bando-Oak	153	Carew-Min	38.9	Robinson-Cal	38.1	Piniella-KC	123	Mayberry-KC	113
Bando-Oak	.876	Scott-Mil	144	Yastrzemski-Bos	36.8	Carew-Min	34.5	Johnson-Oak	122	Jackson-Oak	112
Yastrzemski-Bos	.874	Carew-Min	143	Bando-Oak	35.5	Scott-Mil	33.9	May-Chi	119	Scott-Mil	106

Total Average		Stolen Bases		Stolen Base Average		Stolen Base Runs		Fielding Runs		Total Player Rating	
Mayberry-KC	.995	Harper-Bos	54	Rojas-KC	81.8	Harper-Bos	7.8	Patek-KC	35.3	Carew-Min	5.3
Jackson-Oak	.953	North-Oak	53	Money-Mil	81.5	Campaneris-Oak	4.2	Nettles-NY	26.0	Grich-Bal	4.7
Carew-Min	.885	Nelson-Tex	43	Harper-Bos	79.4	Baylor-Bal	4.2	Bell-Cle	24.3	Jackson-Oak	4.6
Yastrzemski-Bos	.879	Carew-Min	41	Baylor-Bal	78.0	North-Oak	3.9	North-Oak	23.6	Munson-NY	3.8
Bando-Oak	.876	Patek-KC	36	Campaneris	77.3	Money-Mil	3.6	Grich-Bal	21.0	Robinson-Cal	3.8

Wins		Win Percentage		Games		Complete Games		Shutouts		Saves	
Wood-Chi	24	Hunter-Oak	.808	Hiller-Det	65	Perry-Cle	29	Blyleven-Min	9	Hiller-Det	38
Coleman-Det	23	Palmer-Bal	.710	Fingers-Oak	62	Ryan-Cal	26	Perry-Cle	7	Lyle-NY	27
Palmer-Bal	22	Blue-Oak	.690	Bird-KC	54	Blyleven-Min	25	Palmer-Bal	6	Fingers-Oak	22
		Splittorff-KC	.645	Knowles-Oak	52	Tiant-Bos	23			Bird-KC	20
		Colborn-Mil	.625			Colborn-Mil	22			Acosta-Chi	18

Innings Pitched		Fewest Hits/Game		Fewest BB/Game		Strikeouts		Strikeouts/Game		Ratio	
Wood-Chi	359.1	Bibby-Tex	6.04	Kaat-Min-Chi	1.73	Ryan-Cal	383	Ryan-Cal	10.57	Tiant-Bos	9.99
Perry-Cle	344.0	Ryan-Cal	6.57	Blyleven-Min	1.86	Blyleven-Min	258	Bibby-Tex	7.74	Hunter-Oak	10.25
Ryan-Cal	326.0	Palmer-Bal	6.83	Holtzman-Oak	2.00	Singer-Cal	241	Blyleven-Min	7.14	Blyleven-Min	10.30
Blyleven-Min	325.0	Tiant-Bos	7.18	Wood-Chi	2.28	Perry-Cle	238	Stone-Chi	7.04	Palmer-Bal	10.36
Singer-Cal	315.2	Blue-Oak	7.30	Lolich-Det	2.30	Lolich-Det	214	Singer-Cal	6.87	Holtzman-Oak	10.44

Earned Run Average		Adjusted ERA		Opponents' Batting Avg.		Opponents' On Base Pct.		Starter Runs		Adjusted Starter Runs	
Palmer-Bal	2.40	Blyleven-Min	157	Bibby-Tex	.192	Tiant-Bos	.281	Blyleven-Min	46.8	Blyleven-Min	51.9
Blyleven-Min	2.52	Palmer-Bal	156	Ryan-Cal	.203	Hunter-Oak	.284	Palmer-Bal	46.6	Palmer-Bal	43.9
Lee-Bos	2.75	Lee-Bos	146	Palmer-Bal	.211	Blyleven-Min	.287	Ryan-Cal	34.2	Lee-Bos	40.1
Ryan-Cal	2.87	Medich-NY	124	Tiant-Bos	.219	Holtzman-Oak	.287	Lee-Bos	33.7	Ryan-Cal	24.4
Medich-NY	2.95	Ryan-Cal	123	Blue-Oak	.224	Palmer-Bal	.289	Holtzman-Oak	28.1	Perry-Cle	20.8

Clutch Pitching Index		Relief Runs		Adjusted Relief Runs		Relief Ranking		Total Pitcher Index		Total Baseball Ranking	
Lee-Bos	119	Hiller-Det	33.1	Hiller-Det	36.9	Hiller-Det	64.9	Hiller-Det	6.7	Hiller-Det	6.7
Forster-Chi	116	Fingers-Oak	26.7	Fingers-Oak	26.7	Acosta-Chi	35.4	Blyleven-Min	5.7	Blyleven-Min	5.7
Curtis-Bos	113	Reynolds-Bal	23.1	Reynolds-Bal	22.0	Fingers-Oak	33.3	Palmer-Bal	4.5	Carew-Min	5.3
Drago-KC	112	Acosta-Chi	17.1	Acosta-Chi	18.6	Reynolds-Bal	25.4	Lee-Bos	4.0	Grich-Bal	4.7
Bahnsen-Chi	112	Jackson-Bal	17.1	Jackson-Bal	16.3	Lyle-NY	23.8	Acosta-Chi	3.6	Jackson-Oak	4.6

January 25 Ray Kroc, fast-food entrepreneur (McDonald's), buys the Padres for $12 million.

April 4 In his first swing of the season, Hank Aaron hits a three-run home run off Jack Billingham, but the Braves lose to the Reds 7–6. It is home run 714 for Aaron to tie him with Babe Ruth as the top slugger of all time.

April 8 In the fourth inning, of the Braves home opener against the Dodgers, Henry Aaron parks an Al Downing pitch in the left-center field stands for career homer 715, breaking Ruth's once unapproachable record.

May 27 The Pirates' Ken Brett no-hits the Padres until the ninth inning, settling for a two-hit 6-0 shutout.

June 10 During a 12-0 win over the Astros, Phillie third baseman Mike Schmidt hits a ball off the public address speaker hanging from the Astrodome roof, 117 feet up and 300 feet from the plate. Schmidt must settle for a titanic single.

July 3 Pitching in his major league record 13th consecutive game for the Dodgers, Mike Marshall saves Tommy John's 4–1 win over the Reds in the first game of a doubleheader.

July 17 Cardinals pitching great Bob Gibson fans the Reds' Cesar Geronimo to become the second hurler to strike out 3,000 batters. Geronimo will become Nolan Ryan's 3,000th K victim six years later.

July 23 The NL triumphs in the All-Star Game at Pittsburgh, winning 7-2. Write-in choice Dodger first baseman Steve Garvey is the game's MVP.

August 12 Nolan Ryan strikes out 19 as the Angels top the Red Sox 4-2.

September 3 John Montefusco makes his major league debut, homers in his first official time at bat, and pitches nine innings of relief for the Giants to earn a 9–5 victory over the Dodgers.

September 10 The Cardinals lose to the Phillies 8-2, but Lou Brock breaks Maury Wills's major league record by stealing his 104th and 105th bases of the season. It also gives him 740 career stolen bases, breaking Max Carey's National League record of 738.

October 2 During a 13–0 win over Reds, Hank Aaron homers off Rawly Eastwick. It is Aaron's 733rd career clout and comes in his last NL at bat.

October 9 Los Angeles advances to the World Series with a 12-1 win over the Bucs as Don Sutton wins his second LCS game and eleventh in a row.

November 2 The Braves trade Hank Aaron to the Brewers for outfielder Dave May and a minor league pitcher to be named later. Aaron will finish his major league career in Milwaukee, where he started it in 1954.

November 6 The Dodgers' Mike Marshall becomes the first relief pitcher to win the Cy Young Award, setting major league records with 106 appearances and 208 innings in relief.

November 13 The Dodgers' Steve Garvey wins the NL MVP Award.

November 27 Cardinals outfielder Bake McBride wins the NL Rookie of the Year Award.

ATLANTA		CHICAGO		CINCINNATI		HOUSTON		LOS ANGELES		MONTREAL	
M	E.Mathews	M	W.Lockman	M	S.Anderson	M	P.Gomez	M	W.Alston	M	G.Mauch
M	C.King	M	J.Marshall	1B	T.Perez	1B	L.May	1B	S.Garvey	1B	M.Jorgensen
1B	D.Johnson	1B	A.Thornton	2B	J.Morgan	2B	T.Helms	2B	D.Lopes	2B	J.Cox
2B	M.Perez	2B	V.Harris	SS	D.Concepcion	SS	R.Metzger	SS	B.Russell	SS	T.Foli
SS	C.Robinson	SS	D.Kessinger	3B	D.Driessen	3B	D.Rader	3B	R.Cey	3B	R.Hunt
3B	D.Evans	3B	B.Madlock	LF	P.Rose	LF	B.Watson	LF	B.Buckner	LF	B.Bailey
LF	H.Aaron	LF	J.Morales	CF	C.Geronimo	CF	C.Cedeno	CF	J.Wynn	CF	W.Davis
CF	D.Baker	CF	R.Monday	RF	G.Foster	RF	G.Gross	RF	W.Crawford	RF	K.Singleton
RF	R.Garr	RF	J.Cardenal	C	J.Bench	C	M.May	C	S.Yeager	C	B.Foote
C	J.Oates	C	S.Swisher								
				32	D.Chaney	O	B.Gallagher	CO	J.Ferguson	1O	R.Fairly
O	R.Office	1O	B.Williams	O	K.Griffey	2	L.Milbourne			2S	L.Lintz
1O	M.Lum	C	G.Mitterwald	O	M.Rettenmund			P	A.Messersmith		
C	V.Correll					P	L.Dierker	P	D.Sutton	P	S.Rogers
		P	B.Bonham	P	D.Gullett	P	T.Griffin	P	D.Rau	P	S.Renko
P	P.Niekro	P	R.Reuschel	P	C.Kirby	P	D.Wilson	P	T.John	P	M.Torrez
P	C.Morton	P	B.Hooton	P	J.Billingham	P	D.Roberts	P	A.Downing	P	D.Blair
P	B.Capra	P	S.Stone	P	F.Norman	P	C.Osteen	RP	M.Marshall	P	E.McAnally
P	R.Reed	RP	K.Frailing	RP	P.Borbon	RP	K.Forsch	RP	C.Hough	RP	C.Taylor
P	R.Harrison	RP	D.LaRoche	RP	C.Carroll	RP	M.Cosgrove			RP	T.Walker
RP	T.House	RP	J.Todd	RP	T.Hall	RP	F.Scherman	P	G.Zahn	RP	J.Montague
RP	M.Leon										
RP	L.Krausse	P	O.Zamora	P	R.Nelson	P	J.Richard			P	D.Murray
		P	R.Burris	P	T.Carroll					P	D.Carrithers
		P	T.Dettore							P	D.DeMola

NEW YORK		PHILADELPHIA		PITTSBURGH		SAN DIEGO		SAN FRANCISCO		ST.LOUIS	
M	Y.Berra	M	D.Ozark	M	D.Murtaugh	M	J.McNamara	M	C.Fox	M	R.Schoendienst
1B	J.Milner	1B	W.Montanez	1B	B.Robertson	1B	W.McCovey	M	W.Westrum	1B	J.Torre
2B	F.Millan	2B	D.Cash	2B	R.Stennett	2B	D.Thomas	1B	D.Kingman	2B	T.Sizemore
SS	B.Harrelson	SS	L.Bowa	SS	F.Taveras	SS	E.Hernandez	2B	T.Fuentes	SS	M.Tyson
3B	W.Garrett	3B	M.Schmidt	3B	R.Hebner	3B	D.Roberts	SS	C.Speier	3B	K.Reitz
LF	C.Jones	LF	G.Luzinski	LF	W.Stargell	LF	D.Winfield	3B	S.Ontiveros	LF	L.Brock
CF	D.Hahn	CF	D.Unser	CF	A.Oliver	CF	J.Grubb	LF	G.Matthews	CF	B.McBride
RF	R.Staub	RF	M.Anderson	RF	R.Zisk	RF	B.Tolan	CF	G.Maddox	RF	R.Smith
C	J.Grote	C	B.Boone	C	M.Sanguillen	C	F.Kendall	RF	B.Bonds	C	T.Simmons
								C	D.Rader		
S3	T.Martinez	O	B.Robinson	O	G.Clines	1O	N.Colbert			O	J.Cruz
O	D.Schneck	1O	T.Hutton	1O	E.Kirkpatrick	O	C.Gaston	1	E.Goodson		
23	K.Boswell	O	J.Johnstone	O	D.Parker	32	D.Hilton	32	M.Phillips	P	J.Gibson
O1	E.Kranepool							O1	G.Thomasson	P	L.McGlothen
		P	S.Carlton	P	J.Rooker	P	B.Greif			P	J.Curtis
P	J.Matlack	P	J.Lonborg	P	J.Reuss	P	D.Freisleben	P	J.Barr	P	A.Foster
P	J.Koosman	P	D.Ruthven	P	K.Brett	P	R.Jones	P	J.D'Acquisto	P	S.Siebert
P	T.Seaver	P	R.Schueler	P	D.Ellis	P	D.Spillner	P	M.Caldwell	RP	R.Folkers
P	H.Parker	P	W.Twitchell	P	B.Kison	RP	L.Hardy	P	T.Bradley	RP	A.Hrabosky
P	R.Sadecki	RP	M.Scarce	RP	D.Giusti	RP	V.Romo	P	R.Bryant	RP	M.Garman
RP	B.Apodaca	RP	G.Garber	RP	R.Hernandez	RP	D.Tomlin	RP	R.Moffitt		
RP	T.McGraw			RP	J.Morlan			RP	E.Sosa	P	B.Forsch
RP	B.Miller					P	L.Palmer	P	C.Williams		
				P	L.Demery	P	S.Arlin				
P	G.Stone					P	M.Corkins	P	E.Halicki		

TEAM	G	W	L	PCT	GB	R	OR	AB	H	2B	3B	HR	BB	SO	AVG	OBP	SLG	PRO	PRO+	BR	/A	PF	CHI	RC	SB	CS	SBA	SBR
EAST																												
PIT	162	88	74	.543		751	657	5702	**1560**	238	46	114	514	828	**.274**	.338	.391	.729	114	66	94	96	100	745	55	31	64	-2
STL	161	86	75	.534	1.5	677	643	5620	1492	216	46	83	531	752	.265	.334	.365	.699	102	9	15	99	98	687	**172**	62	74	**14**
PHI	162	80	82	.494	8	676	701	5494	1434	233	**50**	95	469	822	.261	.322	.373	.695	96	-7	-34	104	**104**	658	115	58	66	0
MON	161	79	82	.491	8.5	662	657	5343	1355	201	29	86	652	812	.254	.338	.350	.688	93	2	-35	106	99	657	124	49	72	8
NY	162	71	91	.438	17	572	646	5468	1286	183	22	96	590	**735**	.235	.314	.329	.643	86	-99	-89	98	100	571	43	23	65	-1
CHI	162	66	96	.407	22	669	826	5574	1397	221	42	110	621	857	.251	.329	.365	.694	96	-1	-29	104	98	668	78	73	52	-20
WEST																												
LA	162	102	60	.630		798	**561**	5557	1511	231	34	**139**	597	820	.272	**.346**	**.401**	**.747**	120	103	135	96	102	774	149	75	67	0
CIN	163	98	64	.605	4	776	631	5535	1437	**271**	35	135	**693**	940	.260	.345	.394	.739	115	95	107	99	99	**776**	146	49	**75**	**14**
ATL	163	88	74	.543	14	661	563	5533	1375	202	37	120	571	772	.249	.321	.363	.684	93	-23	-51	104	101	649	72	44	62	-5
HOU	162	81	81	.500	21	653	632	5489	1441	222	41	110	471	864	.263	.324	.378	.702	107	6	35	96	98	663	108	65	62	-7
SF	162	72	90	.444	30	634	723	5482	1380	228	38	93	548	869	.252	.323	.358	.681	92	-28	-58	105	100	642	107	51	68	2
SD	162	60	102	.370	42	541	830	5415	1239	196	27	99	564	900	.229	.304	.330	.634	87	-122	-99	96	101	555	85	45	65	-2
TOT	972					8070		66212	16907	2642	447	1280	6828	9971	.255	.328	.367	.695							1254	625	67	1

TEAM	CG	SH	SV	IP	H	H/G	HR	BB	SO	RAT	ERA	ERA+	OAV	OOB	PR	/A	PF	CPI	FA	E	DP	FW	PW	BW	SBW	DIF
EAST																										
PIT	**51**	9	17	1466	1428	8.8	93	543	721	12.3	3.49	99	.256	.326	21	-7	95	100	.975	162	154	-.5	-.7	9.8	-.2	-1.4
STL	37	13	20	1473¹	1399	8.5	97	616	794	12.5	3.48	103	.254	.331	22	15	99	**104**	.977	147	**192**	.4	1.6	1.6	**1.4**	.6
PHI	46	4	19	1447¹	1394	8.7	111	682	892	13.1	3.91	97	.257	.343	-47	-22	104	101	.976	148	168	.4	-2.3	-3.5	-.0	4.5
MON	35	8	**27**	1429	1340	8.4	99	544	822	12.0	3.60	107	.249	.321	3	38	106	94	.976	153	157	.0	-4.0	-3.6	.8	-2.6
NY	46	15	14	1470¹	1433	8.8	99	504	908	12.0	3.42	104	.257	.322	33	24	99	102	.975	158	150	-.2	2.5	-9.3	-.1	-2.9
CHI	23	6	26	1466¹	1593	9.8	122	576	895	13.6	4.28	89	.277	.347	-108	-76	105	100	.969	199	141	-2.6	-7.9	-3.0	-2.1	.7
WEST																										
LA	33	19	23	1465¹	1272	7.8	112	**464**	943	10.8	2.97	114	**.233**	.296	105	70	94	96	.975	157	122	-.2	7.3	**14.1**	-.0	-.2
CIN	34	11	**27**	1466¹	1364	8.4	126	536	875	11.8	3.41	102	.247	.316	33	12	96	100	.979	134	151	1.2	1.2	11.1	**1.4**	1.9
ATL	46	**21**	22	1474¹	1343	8.2	97	488	772	11.3	3.05	**124**	.244	.309	93	**119**	104	102	.979	132	161	1.3	**12.4**	-5.3	-.5	-.9
HOU	36	18	18	1450²	1396	8.7	**84**	601	738	12.6	3.46	100	.255	.333	25	0	105	104	**.982**	113	161	**2.4**	.0	3.6	-.7	-5.3
SF	27	11	25	1439	1409	8.8	116	559	756	12.5	3.78	101	.257	.328	-26	3	105	97	.972	175	153	-1.2	-.3	-6.0	.2	-2.2
SD	25	7	19	1445²	1536	9.6	124	715	855	14.3	4.58	78	.275	.362	-155	-165	98	99	.973	170	126	-.9	-17.2	-10.3	-.2	7.6
TOT	439	142	257	17493²		8.7				12.4	3.62		.255	.328					.976	1848	1836					

Runs
Rose-Cin	110
Schmidt-Phi	108
Bench-Cin	108
Morgan-Cin	107
Brock-StL	105

Hits
Garr-Atl	214
Cash-Phi	206
Garvey-LA	200
Oliver-Pit	198
Stennett-Pit	196

Doubles
Rose-Cin	45
Oliver-Pit	38
Bench-Cin	38
Stargell-Pit	37

Triples
Garr-Atl	17
Oliver-Pit	12
Cash-Phi	11
Metzger-Hou	10
Bowa-Phi	10

Home Runs
Schmidt-Phi	36
Bench-Cin	33
Wynn-LA	32
Perez-Cin	28
Cedeno-Hou	26

Total Bases
Bench-Cin	315
Schmidt-Phi	310
Garr-Atl	305
Garvey-LA	301
Oliver-Pit	293

Runs Batted In
Bench-Cin	129
Schmidt-Phi	116
Garvey-LA	111
Wynn-LA	108
Simmons-StL	103

Runs Produced
Bench-Cin	204
Schmidt-Phi	188
Garvey-LA	185
Wynn-LA	180
Cedeno-Hou	171

Bases On Balls
Evans-Atl	126
Morgan-Cin	120
Wynn-LA	108
Schmidt-Phi	106
Rose-Cin	106

Batting Average
Garr-Atl	.353
Oliver-Pit	.321
Gross-Hou	.314
Buckner-LA	.314
Madlock-Chi	.313

On Base Percentage
Morgan-Cin	.430
Stargell-Pit	.409
Bailey-Mon	.400
Schmidt-Phi	.398
Smith-StL	.394

Slugging Average
Schmidt-Phi	.546
Stargell-Pit	.537
Smith-StL	.528
Bench-Cin	.507
Garr-Atl	.503

Production
Stargell-Pit	.947
Schmidt-Phi	.944
Morgan-Cin	.924
Smith-StL	.922
Wynn-LA	.891

Adjusted Production
Stargell-Pit	169
Morgan-Cin	160
Smith-StL	158
Schmidt-Phi	156
Wynn-LA	154

Batter Runs
Schmidt-Phi	48.3
Morgan-Cin	45.2
Stargell-Pit	44.4
Smith-StL	38.5
Wynn-LA	36.4

Adjusted Batter Runs
Stargell-Pit	48.5
Morgan-Cin	46.9
Schmidt-Phi	43.4
Wynn-LA	40.8
Smith-StL	39.4

Clutch Hitting Index
Sizemore-StL	128
Singleton-Mon	123
Montanez-Phi	121
Cey-LA	120
Zisk-Pit	119

Runs Created
Schmidt-Phi	130
Morgan-Cin	125
Stargell-Pit	115
Bench-Cin	114
Garr-Atl	113

Total Average
Morgan-Cin	1.108
Schmidt-Phi	1.017
Stargell-Pit	.997
Smith-StL	.920
Wynn-LA	.915

Stolen Bases
Brock-StL	118
Lopes-LA	59
Morgan-Cin	58
Cedeno-Hou	57
Lintz-Mon	50

Stolen Base Average
Lintz-Mon	87.7
Concepcion-Cin	87.2
Morgan-Cin	82.9
Bonds-SF	78.8
Hernandez-SD	78.7

Stolen Base Runs
Brock-StL	15.6
Lintz-Mon	10.8
Morgan-Cin	10.2
Concepcion-Cin	8.7

Fielding Runs
Cash-Phi	29.1
Schmidt-Phi	26.3
Cedeno-Hou	20.9
Foli-Mon	19.4
Rose-Cin	17.6

Total Player Rating
Schmidt-Phi	6.9
Morgan-Cin	5.2
Stargell-Pit	4.5
Wynn-LA	4.3
Concepcion-Cin	4.3

Wins
P.Niekro-Atl	20
Messersmith-LA	20
Sutton-LA	19
Billingham-Cin	19

Win Percentage
Messersmith-LA	.769
Sutton-LA	.679
Capra-Atl	.667
Torrez-Mon	.652
Billingham-Cin	.633

Games
Marshall-LA	106
Hardy-SD	76
Borbon-Cin	73
Forsch-Hou	70
Sosa-SF	68

Complete Games
P.Niekro-Atl	18
Carlton-Phi	17
Lonborg-Phi	16
Rooker-Pit	15

Shutouts
Matlack-NY	7
P.Niekro-Atl	6

Saves
Marshall-LA	21
Moffitt-SF	15
Borbon-Cin	14
Giusti-Pit	12

Innings Pitched
P.Niekro-Atl	302.1
Messersmith-LA	292.1
Carlton-Phi	291.0
Lonborg-Phi	283.0
Sutton-LA	276.0

Fewest Hits/Game
Capra-Atl	6.76
Messersmith-LA	6.99
P.Niekro-Atl	7.41
Gullett-Cin	7.44
Wilson-Hou	7.48

Fewest BB/Game
Barr-SF	1.76
Reed-Atl	1.98
Ellis-Pit	2.09
Lonborg-Phi	2.23
Marshall-LA	2.42

Strikeouts
Carlton-Phi	240
Messersmith-LA	221
Seaver-NY	201
P.Niekro-Atl	195
Matlack-NY	195

Strikeouts/Game
Seaver-NY	7.67
Carlton-Phi	7.42
Bonham-Chi	7.08
D'Acquisto-SF	6.99
Norman-Cin	6.81

Ratio
Messersmith-LA	9.97
P.Niekro-Atl	10.21
Barr-SF	10.21
Matlack-NY	10.24
Reed-Atl	10.35

Earned Run Average
Capra-Atl	2.28
P.Niekro-Atl	2.38
Matlack-NY	2.41
Marshall-LA	2.42
Messersmith-LA	2.59

Adjusted ERA
Capra-Atl	166
P.Niekro-Atl	159
Matlack-NY	148
Marshall-LA	141
Barr-SF	139

Opponents' Batting Avg.
Capra-Atl	.208
Messersmith-LA	.212
Gullett-Cin	.222
P.Niekro-Atl	.225
Matlack-NY	.226

Opponents' On Base Pct.
Messersmith-LA	.278
Matlack-NY	.285
P.Niekro-Atl	.286
Reed-Atl	.286
Capra-Atl	.287

Starter Runs
P.Niekro-Atl	41.5
Matlack-NY	35.6
Messersmith-LA	33.5
Capra-Atl	32.2
Rooker-Pit	24.6

Adjusted Starter Runs
P.Niekro-Atl	46.9
Capra-Atl	36.1
Matlack-NY	34.0
Barr-SF	28.1
Messersmith-LA	26.4

Clutch Pitching Index
Caldwell-SF	117
Morton-Atl	117
Marshall-LA	116
Schueler-Phi	113
McGlothen-StL	112

Relief Runs
Marshall-LA	27.7
Murray-Mon	20.0
House-Atl	19.3
Taylor-Mon	17.3
C.Carroll-Cin	16.5

Adjusted Relief Runs
Marshall-LA	22.7
Murray-Mon	21.7
House-Atl	21.1
Taylor-Mon	19.9
C.Carroll-Cin	15.0

Relief Ranking
Marshall-LA	31.6
C.Carroll-Cin	24.8
House-Atl	19.9
Taylor-Mon	17.9
Leon-Atl	13.4

Total Pitcher Index
P.Niekro-Atl	5.2
Capra-Atl	3.7
Marshall-LA	3.5
Messersmith-LA	3.4
Rooker-Pit	3.2

Total Baseball Ranking
Schmidt-Phi	6.9
P.Niekro-Atl	5.2
Morgan-Cin	5.2
Stargell-Pit	4.5
Wynn-LA	4.3

January 1 Lee MacPhail takes over as AL president, succeeding Joe Cronin, who retires.

January 16 The BBWAA elects former Yankee teammates Mickey Mantle and Whitey Ford to the Hall of Fame. Mantle becomes only the seventh player to make it in his first try.

January 28 The Hall of Fame Special Veterans Committee selects Sam Thompson, Jim Bottomley, and umpire Jocko Conlan.

February 11 Forty-eight major league players invoke the new arbitration procedure established to settle contract differences. The first is pitcher Dick Woodson (seeking a contract for $29,000) and his team, the Twins (offering $23,000), who present their respective cases to Detroit lawyer and labor arbitrator Harry H. Platt, who must decide on one of the monetary amounts presented. Woodson wins.

February 13 Speedster James "Cool Papa" Bell is named for Hall of Fame honors by the Special Committee on the Negro Leagues.

July 19 Cleveland's Dick Bosman no-hits Oakland 4-0. He has no one but himself to blame for not picking up a rare perfect game. His throwing error in the fourth puts the only A's runner on base.

September 24 Al Kaline doubles off Dave McNally for his 3,000th career hit, as the Tigers beat the Orioles 5-4.

October 3 Frank Robinson becomes the first black manager in the major leagues, as the Indians name him to replace Ken Aspromonte for the 1975 season.

October 9 The A's get just one hit, but draw 11 walks in beating the Orioles 2-1 to take the pennant in four games.

October 12 Oakland slugging star Reggie Jackson connects for a homer off Andy Messersmith to start the scoring, and pitcher Ken Holtzman scores the second run in the fifth on a suicide squeeze. The A's win the World Series opener 3-2 as the Dodgers strand 12 base runners.

October 13 Hall of Fame outfielder Sam Rice dies at Rossmor, Maryland, at age 84, leaving a letter—opened at Cooperstown—confirming his controversial catch in the 1925 World Series.

October 17 Vida Blue and Don Sutton are tied 2-2 going into the bottom of the sixth when Mike Marshall relieves and retires the side. In the seventh, a shower of debris halts the game for 15 minutes. When play is resumed, Joe Rudi hits Marshall's first pitch for a homer to give the A's a third 3-2 win, clinching a third straight World Championship for the team.

October 30 Catfish Hunter is named the AL Cy Young Award winner. He led the league with 25 wins and a 2.49 ERA.

November 20 Jeff Burroughs, the Texas outfielder who batted .301 with 25 homers and a league-leading 118 RBI, wins the AL MVP Award.

November 26 Catfish Hunter meets with Charlie Finley in the American Arbitration Association office in New York City for a hearing to determine the validity of Hunter's breach-of-contract claim. Hunter contends that Finley failed to pay $50,000, half of Hunter's salary, to a life insurance fund. The case will go to arbitration. On December 13 Hunter wins his claim against Finley and is declared a free agent by arbitrator Peter Seitz.

December 31 The Yankees sign Hunter to a 5-year contract worth a reported $3.75 million. This is triple the salary of any other major league player.

	BALTIMORE		BOSTON		CALIFORNIA		CHICAGO		CLEVELAND		DETROIT
M	E.Weaver	M	D.Johnson	M	B.Winkles	M	C.Tanner	M	K.Aspromonte	M	R.Houk
1B	B.Powell	1B	C.Yastrzemski	M	W.Herzog	1B	D.Allen	1B	J.Ellis	1B	B.Freehan
2B	B.Grich	2B	D.Griffin	M	D.Williams	2B	J.Orta	2B	J.Brohamer	2B	G.Sutherland
SS	M.Belanger	SS	M.Guerrero	1B	J.Doherty	SS	B.Dent	SS	F.Duffy	SS	E.Brinkman
3B	B.Robinson	3B	R.Petrocelli	2B	D.Doyle	3B	B.Melton	3B	B.Bell	3B	A.Rodriguez
LF	D.Baylor	LF	B.Carbo	SS	D.Chalk	LF	C.May	LF	J.Lowenstein	LF	W.Horton
CF	P.Blair	CF	J.Beniquez	3B	P.Schaal	CF	K.Henderson	CF	G.Hendrick	CF	M.Stanley
RF	R.Coggins	RF	D.Evans	LF	J.Lahoud	RF	B.Sharp	RF	C.Spikes	RF	J.Northrup
C	E.Williams	C	B.Montgomery	CF	M.Rivers	C	E.Herrmann	C	D.Duncan	C	J.Moses
DH	T.Davis	DH	T.Harper	RF	L.Stanton	DH	P.Kelly	DH	O.Gamble	DH	A.Kaline
				C	E.Rodriguez						
O	A.Bumbry	S2	R.Burleson	DH	F.Robinson	CO	B.Downing	O	R.Torres	O	R.LeFlore
		O	R.Miller			1D	T.Muser	O	L.Lee	O1	B.Oglivie
P	R.Grimsley	1D	C.Cooper	13	B.Oliver	D2	R.Santo				
P	M.Cuellar	23	D.McAuliffe	OS	B.Valentine			P	G.Perry	P	M.Lolich
P	D.McNally					P	W.Wood	P	J.Perry	P	J.Coleman
P	J.Palmer	P	L.Tiant	P	N.Ryan	P	J.Kaat	P	F.Peterson	P	L.LaGrow
P	D.Alexander	P	B.Lee	P	F.Tanana	P	S.Bahnsen	P	D.Bosman	P	W.Fryman
RP	B.Reynolds	P	R.Cleveland	P	A.Hassler	P	B.Johnson	RP	T.Buskey	RP	J.Hiller
RP	G.Jackson	P	D.Drago	P	D.Lange	RP	T.Forster	RP	F.Beene	RP	J.Ray
RP	J.Jefferson	P	R.Moret	P	B.Singer	RP	S.Pitlock	RP	M.Wilcox		
		RP	D.Segui	RP	S.Lockwood	RP	R.Gossage			P	L.Walker
P	W.Garland							P	B.Johnson	P	D.Lemanczyk
P	D.Hood	P	J.Marichal	P	E.Figueroa			P	S.Kline	P	B.Slayback
				P	B.Stoneman						

	KANSAS CITY		MILWAUKEE		MINNESOTA		NEW YORK		OAKLAND		TEXAS
M	J.McKeon	M	D.Crandall	M	F.Quilici	M	B.Virdon	M	A.Dark	M	B.Martin
1B	J.Mayberry	1B	G.Scott	1B	C.Kusick	1B	C.Chambliss	1B	G.Tenace	1B	M.Hargrove
2B	C.Rojas	2B	P.Garcia	2B	R.Carew	2B	S.Alomar	2B	D.Green	2B	D.Nelson
SS	F.Patek	SS	R.Yount	SS	D.Thompson	SS	J.Mason	SS	B.Campaneris	SS	T.Harrah
3B	G.Brett	3B	D.Money	3B	E.Soderholm	3B	G.Nettles	3B	S.Bando	3B	L.Randle
LF	J.Wohlford	LF	J.Briggs	LF	L.Hisle	LF	L.Piniella	LF	J.Rudi	LF	C.Tovar
CF	A.Otis	CF	B.Coluccio	CF	S.Brye	CF	E.Maddox	CF	B.North	CF	J.Lovitto
RF	V.Pinson	RF	D.May	RF	B.Darwin	RF	B.Murcer	RF	R.Jackson	RF	J.Burroughs
C	F.Healy	C	D.Porter	C	G.Borgmann	C	T.Munson	C	L.Haney	C	J.Sundberg
DH	H.McRae	DH	B.Mitchell	DH	T.Oliva	DH	R.Blomberg	DH	J.Alou	DH	J.Spencer
O	A.Cowens	OD	K.Berry	O3	S.Braun	OD	R.White	2S	T.Kubiak	OD	A.Johnson
2S	F.White	S2	T.Johnson	D1	H.Killebrew	D1	B.Sudakis	OD	A.Mangual	DO	T.Grieve
1D	T.Solaita	C	C.Moore	S2	J.Terrell			DO	C.Washington	13	J.Fregosi
						P	P.Dobson	C	R.Fosse		
P	S.Busby	P	J.Slaton	P	B.Blyleven	P	D.Medich			P	F.Jenkins
P	P.Splittorff	P	C.Wright	P	J.Decker	P	D.Tidrow	P	C.Hunter	P	J.Bibby
P	A.Fitzmorris	P	J.Colborn	P	D.Goltz	P	R.May	P	V.Blue	P	J.Brown
P	B.Dal Canton	P	K.Kobel	P	V.Albury	P	M.Stottlemyre	P	K.Holtzman	P	S.Hargan
P	M.Pattin	P	B.Champion	P	B.Hands	RP	S.Lyle	P	D.Hamilton	P	D.Clyde
RP	L.McDaniel	RP	T.Murphy	RP	B.Campbell	RP	C.Upshaw	P	G.Abbott	RP	S.Foucault
RP	D.Bird	RP	E.Rodriguez	RP	T.Burgmeier	RP	M.Wallace	RP	R.Fingers		
RP	S.Mingori	RP	B.Travers					RP	P.Lindblad		
				P	R.Corbin	/P	L.Gura	RP	B.Odom		
P	N.Briles	P	E.Sprague	P	B.Butler						
								P	D.Knowles		

TEAM	G	W	L	PCT	GB	R	OR	AB	H	2B	3B	HR	BB	SO	AVG	OBP	SLG	PRO	PRO+	BR	/A	PF	CHI	RC	SB	CS	SBA	SBR
EAST																												
BAL	162	91	71	.562		659	612	5535	1418	226	27	116	509	770	.256	.325	.370	.695	103	-2	19	97	98	671	145	58	**71**	9
NY	162	89	73	.549	2	671	623	5524	1451	220	30	101	515	**690**	.263	.328	.368	.696	102	1	12	98	100	666	53	35	60	-5
BOS	162	84	78	.519	7	**696**	661	5499	1449	**236**	31	109	**569**	811	.264	.336	.377	.713	98	39	-11	107	98	699	104	58	64	-4
CLE	162	77	85	.475	14	662	694	5474	1395	201	19	131	432	756	.255	.312	.370	.682	97	-36	-30	99	**108**	610	79	68	54	-17
MIL	162	76	86	.469	15	647	660	5472	1335	228	**49**	120	500	909	.244	.310	.369	.679	96	-41	-37	99	105	622	106	75	59	-13
DET	162	72	90	.444	19	620	768	5568	1375	200	35	131	436	784	.247	.304	.366	.670	89	-64	-85	104	104	607	67	38	64	-3
WEST																												
OAK	162	90	72	.556		689	**551**	5331	1315	205	37	132	568	876	.247	.324	.373	.697	107	1	44	94	105	648	**164**	93	64	-7
TEX	161	84	76	.525	5	690	698	5449	1482	198	39	99	508	710	**.272**	**.338**	.377	.715	**108**	42	**60**	98	98	677	113	80	59	-14
MIN	163	82	80	.506	8	673	669	5632	**1530**	190	37	111	520	791	**.272**	**.338**	.378	.716	103	44	21	103	93	**707**	74	45	62	-5
CHI	163	80	80	.500	9	684	721	5577	1492	225	23	**135**	519	858	.268	.333	**.389**	**.722**	104	49	32	102	95	701	64	53	55	-13
KC	162	77	85	.475	13	667	662	5582	1448	232	42	89	550	768	.259	.329	.364	.693	94	-2	-40	106	99	668	146	76	66	-2
CAL	163	68	94	.420	22	618	657	5401	1372	203	31	95	509	801	.254	.323	.356	.679	101	-30	6	94	99	615	119	79	60	-12
TOT	973					7976		66044	17062	2564	400	1369	6135	9524	.258	.325	.371	.697							1234	758	62	-85

TEAM	CG	SH	SV	IP	H	H/G	HR	BB	SO	RAT	ERA	ERA+	OAV	OOB	PR	/A	PF	CPI	FA	E	DP	FW	PW	BW	SBW	DIF
EAST																										
BAL	57	**16**	25	1474	1393	8.5	101	480	701	11.6	3.27	105	.253	.316	56	29	95	102	**.980**	128	174	1.0	3.0	2.0	**1.7**	2.3
NY	53	13	24	1455¹	1402	8.7	104	528	829	12.1	3.31	106	.256	.325	50	35	97	**107**	.977	142	158	.2	3.7	1.3	.2	2.7
BOS	**71**	12	18	1455¹	1462	9.0	126	463	751	12.1	3.72	103	.262	.322	-16	20	106	99	.977	145	156	.0	2.1	-1.2	.3	1.7
CLE	45	9	27	1448²	1419	8.8	138	479	650	12.0	3.80	95	.260	.323	-30	-31	100	98	.977	146	157	-.0	-3.2	-3.1	-1.0	3.4
MIL	43	11	24	1457²	1476	9.1	126	493	621	12.3	3.76	96	.266	.329	-23	-23	100	102	**.980**	127	168	1.1	-2.4	-3.9	-.6	.8
DET	54	7	15	1455²	1443	8.9	148	621	869	13.0	4.16	91	.262	.341	-88	-58	105	99	.975	158	155	-.7	-6.1	-8.9	.4	6.2
WEST																										
OAK	49	12	28	1439²	**1322**	8.3	**90**	430	755	**11.1**	2.95	112	.246	.305	107	59	92	103	.977	141	154	.3	**6.2**	4.6	.0	-2.0
TEX	62	**16**	12	1433²	1423	8.9	126	449	871	12.0	3.82	93	.260	.321	-33	-41	99	95	.974	163	164	-1.1	-4.3	**6.3**	-.7	3.8
MIN	43	11	**29**	1455¹	1436	8.9	115	513	934	12.3	3.64	102	.260	.327	-4	13	103	101	.976	151	164	-.3	1.4	2.2	.2	-2.5
CHI	55	11	**29**	1465²	1470	9.0	103	548	826	12.7	3.94	95	.263	.334	-52	-34	103	96	.977	147	**188**	-.0	-3.6	3.3	-.6	.9
KC	54	13	17	1471²	1477	9.0	91	482	731	12.2	3.51	109	.263	.325	17	50	106	101	.976	152	166	-.4	5.2	-4.2	.5	-5.2
CAL	64	13	12	1439	1339	8.4	101	649	**986**	12.7	3.52	98	.248	.334	15	-14	95	102	.976	147	150	-.0	-1.5	.6	-.5	-11.6
TOT	650	144	260	17448²		8.8				12.2	3.62		.258	.325					.977	1747	1954					

Runs
Yastrzemski-Bos . . . 93
Grich-Bal 92
Jackson-Oak 90
Otis-KC 87
Carew-Min 86

Hits
Carew-Min 218
Davis-Bal 181
Money-Mil 178
K.Henderson-Chi . . 176
Rudi-Oak 174

Doubles
Rudi-Oak 39
Scott-Mil 36
McRae-KC 36
K.Henderson-Chi . . 35
Burroughs-Tex 33

Triples
Rivers-Cal 11
Otis-KC 9

Home Runs
D.Allen-Chi 32
Jackson-Oak 29
Tenace-Oak 26
Darwin-Min 25
Burroughs-Tex 25

Total Bases
Rudi-Oak 287
K.Henderson-Chi . . 281
Burroughs-Tex 279
Carew-Min 267

Runs Batted In
Burroughs-Tex . . . 118
Bando-Oak 103
Rudi-Oak 99
K.Henderson-Chi . . 95
Darwin-Min 94

Runs Produced
Burroughs-Tex . . . 177
Bando-Oak 165
Yastrzemski-Bos . . 157
Grich-Bal 155
Jackson-Oak 154

Bases On Balls
Tenace-Oak 110
Yastrzemski-Bos . . 104
Burroughs-Tex 91
Grich-Bal 90

Batting Average
Carew-Min 364
Orta-Chi 316
McRae-KC 310
Piniella-NY 305
Maddox-NY 303

On Base Percentage
Carew-Min 435
Yastrzemski-Bos . . .421
Burroughs-Tex 405
Maddox-NY 397
Jackson-Oak 396

Slugging Average
D.Allen-Chi 563
Jackson-Oak 514
Burroughs-Tex 504
Rudi-Oak 484
McRae-KC 475

Production
D.Allen-Chi 942
Jackson-Oak 910
Burroughs-Tex 908
Carew-Min 880
Yastrzemski-Bos . . .866

Adjusted Production
Jackson-Oak 171
Burroughs-Tex 164
D.Allen-Chi 164
Carew-Min 149
Robinson-Cal-Cle . . 143

Batter Runs
Burroughs-Tex 45.3
Carew-Min 44.7
Jackson-Oak 41.0
D.Allen-Chi 39.3
Yastrzemski-Bos . . 38.1

Adjusted Batter Runs
Burroughs-Tex 48.2
Jackson-Oak 48.1
Carew-Min 40.9
D.Allen-Chi 37.0
Grich-Bal 31.3

Clutch Hitting Index
Murcer-NY 134
Bando-Oak 132
Burroughs-Tex 131
Petrocelli-Bos 119
Evans-Bos 115

Runs Created
Carew-Min 118
Burroughs-Tex 113
Jackson-Oak 109
Yastrzemski-Bos . . 102
K.Henderson-Chi . . 100

Total Average
Jackson-Oak 992
D.Allen-Chi 953
Burroughs-Tex 919
Yastrzemski-Bos . . .900
Carew-Min 879

Stolen Bases
North-Oak 54
Carew-Min 38
Lowenstein-Cle . . . 36
Campaneris-Oak . . 34
Patek-KC 33

Stolen Base Average
Jackson-Oak 83.3
Coggins-Bal 81.3
Pinson-KC 80.8
Otis-KC 78.3
Money-Mil 76.0

Stolen Base Runs
Jackson-Oak 4.5
Coggins-Bal 4.2
Pinson-KC 3.3
Miller-Bos 2.7
Blair-Bal 2.7

Fielding Runs
Terrell-Min 23.3
Rodriguez-Det 21.6
Robinson-Bal 20.5
North-Oak 18.4
Doyle-Cal 16.4

Total Player Rating
Carew-Min 6.0
Jackson-Oak 5.6
Grich-Bal 4.8
Burroughs-Tex 3.3
Robinson-Bal 3.2

Wins
Jenkins-Tex 25
Hunter-Oak 25

Win Percentage
Cuellar-Bal 688
Jenkins-Tex 676
Hunter-Oak 676
Tiant-Bos 629

Games
Fingers-Oak 76
Murphy-Mil 70
Foucault-Tex 69
Lyle-NY 66
Campbell-Min 63

Complete Games
Jenkins-Tex 29
G.Perry-Cle 28
Lolich-Det 27
Ryan-Cal 26
Tiant-Bos 25

Shutouts
Tiant-Bos 7
Jenkins-Tex 6
Hunter-Oak 6
Cuellar-Bal 5
Bibby-Tex 5

Saves
Forster-Chi 24
Murphy-Mil 20
Campbell-Min 19
Buskey-NY-Cle 18
Fingers-Oak 18

Innings Pitched
Ryan-Cal 332.2
Jenkins-Tex 328.1
G.Perry-Cle 322.1
Wood-Chi 320.1
Hunter-Oak 318.1

Fewest Hits/Game
Ryan-Cal 5.98
G.Perry-Cle 6.42
DalCanton-KC 6.93
Hassler-Cal 7.33
Hunter-Oak 7.58

Fewest BB/Game
Jenkins-Tex 1.23
Hunter-Oak 1.30
Holtzman-Oak 1.80
Kaat-Chi 2.04
Wright-Mil 2.09

Strikeouts
Ryan-Cal 367
Blyleven-Min 249
Jenkins-Tex 225
G.Perry-Cle 216
Lolich-Det 202

Strikeouts/Game
Ryan-Cal 9.93
Blyleven-Min 7.98
Jenkins-Tex 6.17
Busby-KC 6.10
G.Perry-Cle 6.03

Ratio
Hunter-Oak 8.99
Jenkins-Tex 9.29
G.Perry-Cle 9.35
Grimsley-Bal 10.53
Blyleven-Min 10.57

Earned Run Average
Hunter-Oak 2.49
G.Perry-Cle 2.51
Hassler-Cal 2.61
Blyleven-Min 2.66
Fitzmorris-KC 2.79

Adjusted ERA
G.Perry-Cle 144
Blyleven-Min 140
Fitzmorris-KC 137
Hunter-Oak 133
Hassler-Cal 132

Opponents' Batting Avg.
Ryan-Cal 190
G.Perry-Cle 204
DalCanton-KC 211
Hassler-Cal 225
Hunter-Oak 229

Opponents' On Base Pct.
Hunter-Oak 260
Jenkins-Tex 264
G.Perry-Cle 272
Blyleven-Min 292
Tiant-Bos 293

Starter Runs
Hunter-Oak 39.9
G.Perry-Cle 39.6
Blyleven-Min 29.9
Jenkins-Tex 29.0
Ryan-Cal 26.7

Adjusted Starter Runs
G.Perry-Cle 39.4
Blyleven-Min 33.3
Tiant-Bos 31.9
Hunter-Oak 29.3
Jenkins-Tex 27.0

Clutch Pitching Index
Goltz-Min 124
Hassler-Cal 121
Lee-Bos 119
Fitzmorris-KC 116
Tanana-Cal 113

Relief Runs
Lyle-NY 24.8
Murphy-Mil 23.4
Foucault-Tex 22.0
Lindblad-Oak 17.5
Hiller-Det 16.3

Adjusted Relief Runs
Lyle-NY 23.6
Murphy-Mil 23.4
Foucault-Tex 21.1
Hiller-Det 19.4
Campbell-Min 14.8

Relief Ranking
Murphy-Mil 42.9
Hiller-Det 39.8
Lyle-NY 29.4
Foucault-Tex 26.4
Campbell-Min 21.9

Total Pitcher Index
Murphy-Mil 4.9
G.Perry-Cle 4.4
Blyleven-Min 4.0
Hiller-Det 3.9
Lyle-NY 3.0

Total Baseball Ranking
Carew-Min 6.0
Jackson-Oak 5.6
Murphy-Mil 4.9
Grich-Bal 4.8
G.Perry-Cle 4.4

January 23 Ralph Kiner earns Hall of Fame membership by a single vote.

February 3 Billy Herman, Earl Averill, and Bucky Harris are selected for the Hall of Fame by the Special Veterans Committee.

February 10 The Special Committee on the Negro Leagues picks William "Judy" Johnson for the Hall of Fame.

May 4 The Giants beat the Astros 8-6 in the first game of a doubleheader at Candlestick. In the second inning, Houston's Bob Watson scores what is calculated as Major League Baseball's one-millionth run of all time (the Philadelphia Nationals' Wes Fisler scored the first run on April 22, 1876).

August 9 Davey Lopes steals his 32nd consecutive base for the Dodgers without being caught in a 2-0 win over the Mets. This breaks the major league record set by Max Carey in 1922.

August 21 Pitching brothers Rick and Paul Reuschel combine to hurl the Cubs to a 7-0 victory over the Dodgers—the first time brothers have collaborated on a shutout.

September 1 Mets ace Tom Seaver shuts out the Pirates 3-0 and reaches 200 strikeouts for a major league record eighth straight season.

September 7 The Reds clinch the NL West flag with an 8-4 win over the Giants. It is the earliest clinching date in league history.

September 16 Rennie Stennett ties Wilbert Robinson's major league record, set June 10, 1892, by going 7-for-7 in a nine-inning game.

October 7 Pittsburgh's John Candelaria strikes out 14 Reds, but is knocked out of the box by Pete Rose's eighth-inning homer. The Reds complete their sweep of the NLCS with a 5-3 win.

October 14 In a game featuring six homers, three by each team, the Reds prevail 6-5 in the tenth inning. The game is marred by a controversial play involving Cincinnati's Ed Armbrister and Boston's Carlton Fisk. Armbrister lays down a sacrifice bunt in the tenth and seemingly hesitates breaking out of the batter's box; Fisk's subsequent throwing error leads to the Reds' winning run. The Sox claim interference, to no avail.

October 22 The Sox take a 3-0 lead but the Reds rally to tie it in the seventh. Jim Willoughby is relieved by Jim Burton and Joe Morgan's single wins the deciding game 4-3. Rose is named the World Series MVP.

November 12 The Mets' Tom Seaver wins his third Cy Young Award. He led the NL with 22 wins, notched 243 strikeouts, and had a 2.38 ERA.

November 19 By the most overwhelming margin ever, the Reds' Joe Morgan is named NL MVP. Morgan batted .327, with 67 stolen bases, and a league-leading 132 walks.

ATLANTA		CHICAGO		CINCINNATI		HOUSTON		LOS ANGELES		MONTREAL	
M	C.King	M	J.Marshall	M	S.Anderson	M	P.Gomez	M	W.Alston	M	G.Mauch
M	C.Ryan	1B	A.Thornton	1B	T.Perez	M	B.Virdon	1B	S.Garvey	1B	M.Jorgensen
1B	E.Williams	2B	M.Trillo	2B	J.Morgan	1B	B.Watson	2B	D.Lopes	2B	P.Mackanin
2B	M.Perez	SS	D.Kessinger	SS	D.Concepcion	2B	R.Andrews	SS	B.Russell	SS	T.Foli
SS	L.Blanks	3B	B.Madlock	3B	P.Rose	SS	R.Metzger	3B	R.Cey	3B	L.Parrish
3B	D.Evans	LF	J.Cardenal	LF	G.Foster	3B	D.Rader	LF	B.Buckner	LF	L.Biittner
LF	R.Garr	CF	R.Monday	CF	C.Geronimo	LF	W.Howard	CF	J.Wynn	CF	P.Mangual
CF	R.Office	RF	J.Morales	RF	K.Griffey	CF	C.Cedeno	RF	W.Crawford	RF	G.Carter
RF	D.Baker	C	S.Swisher	C	J.Bench	RF	G.Gross	C	S.Yeager	C	B.Foote
C	V.Correll					C	M.May				
		1O	P.LaCock	1O	D.Driessen			2O	L.Lacy	O	B.Bailey
1O	M.Lum	C1	G.Mitterwald			O1	E.Cabell	O	J.Hale		
O	D.May			P	G.Nolan	O	J.Cruz	CO	J.Ferguson	P	S.Rogers
23	R.Gilbreath	P	R.Burris	P	J.Billingham	1C	C.Johnson			P	S.Renko
		P	R.Reuschel	P	F.Norman			P	A.Messersmith	P	D.Warthen
P	C.Morton	P	B.Bonham	P	D.Gullett	P	L.Dierker	P	D.Rau	P	D.Blair
P	P.Niekro	P	S.Stone	P	P.Darcy	P	J.Richard	P	D.Sutton	P	W.Fryman
RP	M.Leon	RP	D.Knowles	RP	P.Borbon	P	D.Roberts	P	B.Hooton	RP	D.Murray
RP	T.House	RP	T.Dettore	RP	C.Carroll	P	D.Konieczny	P	R.Rhoden	RP	D.DeMola
RP	M.Beard	RP	O.Zamora	RP	W.McEnaney	P	K.Forsch	RP	M.Marshall	RP	F.Scherman
						RP	J.Niekro	RP	C.Hough		
P	B.Capra	P	G.Zahn	P	C.Kirby	RP	J.Crawford			P	D.Carrithers
P	R.Reed	P	K.Frailing	P	R.Eastwick	RP	W.Granger	P	A.Downing	P	D.McNally
P	J.Easterly									P	C.Taylor
P	B.DalCanton					P	T.Griffin				
P	R.Sadecki					P	M.Cosgrove				
P	E.Sosa										
P	B.Odom										
P	R.Harrison										
P	M.Thompson										

NEW YORK		PHILADELPHIA		PITTSBURGH		SAN DIEGO		SAN FRANCISCO		ST.LOUIS	
M	Y.Berra	M	D.Ozark	M	D.Murtaugh	M	J.McNamara	M	W.Westrum	M	R.Schoendienst
M	R.McMillan	1B	D.Allen	1B	W.Stargell	1B	W.McCovey	1B	W.Montanez	1B	R.Smith
1B	E.Kranepool	2B	D.Cash	2B	R.Stennett	2B	T.Fuentes	2B	D.Thomas	2B	T.Sizemore
2B	F.Millan	SS	L.Bowa	SS	F.Taveras	SS	E.Hernandez	SS	C.Speier	SS	M.Tyson
SS	M.Phillips	3B	M.Schmidt	3B	R.Hebner	3B	T.Kubiak	3B	S.Ontiveros	3B	K.Reitz
3B	W.Garrett	LF	G.Luzinski	LF	R.Zisk	LF	B.Tolan	LF	G.Matthews	LF	L.Brock
LF	D.Kingman	CF	G.Maddox	CF	A.Oliver	CF	J.Grubb	CF	V.Joshua	CF	B.McBride
CF	D.Unser	RF	M.Anderson	RF	D.Parker	RF	D.Winfield	RF	B.Murcer	RF	W.Davis
RF	R.Staub	C	B.Boone	C	M.Sanguillen	C	F.Kendall	C	D.Rader	C	T.Simmons
C	J.Grote										
		1O	T.Hutton	O	B.Robinson	13	M.Ivie	32	B.Miller	1O	R.Fairly
31	J.Torre	O	J.Johnstone			O	G.Locklear	O1	G.Thomasson	O	L.Melendez
O1	J.Milner	C	J.Oates	P	J.Reuss	S3	H.Torres				
O	G.Clines			P	J.Rooker			P	J.Montefusco	P	L.McGlothen
		P	S.Carlton	P	B.Kison	P	R.Jones	P	J.Barr	P	B.Forsch
P	T.Seaver	P	T.Underwood	P	D.Ellis	P	J.McIntosh	P	P.Falcone	P	R.Reed
P	J.Koosman	P	L.Christenson	P	J.Candelaria	P	D.Freisleben	P	M.Caldwell	P	J.Curtis
P	J.Matlack	P	J.Lonborg	RP	L.Demery	P	D.Spillner	P	E.Halicki	P	J.Denny
P	R.Tate	P	W.Twitchell	RP	D.Giusti	P	R.Folkers	RP	C.Williams	RP	A.Hrabosky
P	H.Webb	RP	G.Garber	RP	B.Moose	RP	D.Frisella	RP	G.Lavelle	RP	M.Garman
RP	R.Baldwin	RP	T.McGraw			RP	D.Tomlin	RP	R.Moffitt		
RP	B.Apodaca	RP	T.Hilgendorf	P	K.Brett	RP	B.Greif			P	B.Gibson
RP	T.Hall			P	R.Hernandez			P	D.Heaverlo	P	E.Rasmussen
		P	R.Schueler	P	K.Tekulve	P	B.Strom				
P	G.Stone					P	J.Johnson				

TEAM	G	W	L	PCT	GB	R	OR	AB	H	2B	3B	HR	BB	SO	AVG	OBP	SLG	PRO	PRO+	BR	/A	PF	CHI	RC	SB	CS	SBA	SBR
EAST																												
PIT	161	92	69	.571		712	565	5489	1444	255	47	**138**	468	832	.263	.325	**.402**	.727	109	44	50	99	102	709	49	28	64	-2
PHI	162	86	76	.531	6.5	735	694	5592	1506	**283**	42	125	610	960	.269	.344	**.402**	.746	109	98	67	104	94	785	126	57	69	4
NY	162	82	80	.506	10.5	646	625	5587	1430	217	34	101	501	805	.256	.321	.361	.682	100	-36	-7	95	102	639	32	26	55	-6
STL	163	82	80	.506	10.5	662	689	5597	**1527**	239	46	81	444	**649**	**.273**	.329	.375	.704	99	7	-17	104	99	683	116	49	70	5
MON	162	75	87	.463	17.5	601	690	5518	1346	216	31	98	579	954	.244	.319	.348	.667	87	-63	-89	104	99	623	108	58	65	-2
CHI	162	75	87	.463	17.5	712	827	5470	1419	229	41	95	650	802	.259	.341	.368	.709	99	33	2	104	100	702	67	55	55	-13
WEST																												
CIN	162	108	54	.667		**840**	586	5581	1515	278	37	124	**691**	916	.271	**.355**	.401	**.756**	114	**128**	**113**	102	103	**829**	168	36	82	29
LA	162	88	74	.543	20	648	**534**	5453	1346	231	31	118	611	825	.248	.328	.365	.693	103	-10	-18	96	98	667	138	52	73	10
SF	161	80	81	.497	27.5	659	671	5447	1412	235	45	84	604	775	.259	.336	.365	.701	97	11	-17	104	98	673	99	47	68	2
SD	162	71	91	.438	37	552	683	5429	1324	215	22	78	506	754	.244	.313	.335	.648	92	-100	-66	94	99	571	85	50	63	-5
ATL	161	67	94	.416	40.5	583	739	5424	1323	179	28	107	543	759	.244	.315	.346	.661	86	-75	-96	104	101	587	55	38	59	-6
HOU	162	64	97	.398	43.5	664	711	5515	1401	218	**54**	84	523	762	.254	.322	.359	.681	102	-36	9	93	**106**	643	133	62	68	3
TOT	971					8014		66102	17002	2781	458	1233	6730	9793	.257	.329	.369	.698							1176	558	68	18

TEAM	CG	SH	SV	IP	H	H/G	HR	BB	SO	RAT	ERA	ERA+	OAV	OOB	PR	/A	PF	CPI	FA	E	DP	FW	PW	BW	SBW	DIF
EAST																										
PIT	43	14	31	1437¹	1302	8.2	**79**	551	768	11.7	3.01	**118**	.243	.315	98	**85**	98	103	.976	151	147	.2	**8.9**	5.2	-.4	-2.4
PHI	33	11	30	1455	1353	8.4	111	546	897	11.9	3.82	98	.249	.320	-33	-15	103	89	.976	152	156	.2	-1.6	7.0	.3	-.9
NY	40	14	31	1466	1344	8.3	99	580	**989**	12.0	3.39	102	.246	.321	38	10	95	98	.976	151	144	.3	1.0	-.7	-.8	1.2
STL	33	13	36	1454²	1452	9.0	98	571	824	12.7	3.57	105	.260	.331	8	30	104	102	.973	171	140	-.8	3.1	-1.8	.4	.0
MON	30	12	25	1480	1448	8.8	102	665	831	13.1	3.72	103	.259	.341	-17	17	106	103	.973	180	**179**	-1.3	1.8	-9.3	-.4	3.2
CHI	27	8	33	1444¹	1587	9.9	130	551	850	13.6	4.49	88	.281	.349	-140	-105	106	98	.972	179	152	-1.3	-11.0	.2	-1.5	7.6
WEST																										
CIN	22	8	**50**	1459	1422	8.8	112	487	663	10.9	3.37	107	.257	.321	41	36	99	105	**.984**	102	173	**3.0**	3.8	**11.8**	**2.9**	5.6
LA	51	18	21	1469²	1215	7.4	104	**448**	894	10.4	2.92	116	**.225**	.287	114	78	94	88	.979	127	106	1.6	8.1	1.9	.9	-5.5
SF	37	9	24	1432²	1406	8.8	92	612	856	12.9	3.74	102	.259	.339	-19	10	105	101	.976	146	164	.5	1.0	-1.8	.0	-.3
SD	40	12	20	1463¹	1494	9.2	99	521	713	12.5	3.48	100	.266	.331	23	-1	96	**107**	.971	188	163	-1.8	-.1	-6.9	-.7	-.5
ATL	32	4	24	1430	1543	9.7	101	519	669	13.3	3.91	96	.278	.344	-47	-23	104	105	.972	175	147	-1.1	-2.4	-10.0	-.8	.8
HOU	39	6	25	1458¹	1436	8.9	106	679	839	13.3	4.04	83	.262	.347	-67	-108	93	99	.979	137	166	1.1	-11.3	.9	.2	-7.4
TOT	427	129	350	17450¹		8.8				12.4	3.62		.257	.329					.976	1859	1837					

Runs		Hits		Doubles		Triples		Home Runs		Total Bases	
Rose-Cin	112	Cash-Phi	213	Rose-Cin	47	Garr-Atl	11	Schmidt-Phi	38	Luzinski-Phi	322
Cash-Phi	111	Rose-Cin	210	Cash-Phi	40	Parker-Pit	10	Kingman-NY	36	Garvey-LA	314
Lopes-LA	108	Garvey-LA	210	Oliver-Pit	39	Kessinger-Chi	10	Luzinski-Phi	34	Parker-Pit	302
Morgan-Cin	107	Simmons-StL	193	Bench-Cin	39	Joshua-SF	10	Bench-Cin	28	Schmidt-Phi	294
Thomas-SF	99	Millan-NY	191	Garvey-LA	38	Gross-Hou	10			Rose-Cin	286

Runs Batted In		Runs Produced		Bases On Balls		Batting Average		On Base Percentage		Slugging Average	
Luzinski-Phi	120	Morgan-Cin	184	Morgan-Cin	132	Madlock-Chi	.354	Morgan-Cin	.471	Parker-Pit	.541
Bench-Cin	110	Staub-NY	179	Wynn-LA	110	Simmons-StL	.332	Wynn-LA	.407	Luzinski-Phi	.540
Perez-Cin	109	Rose-Cin	179	Evans-Atl	105	Sanguillen-Pit	.328	Rose-Cin	.407	Schmidt-Phi	.523
Staub-NY	105	Luzinski-Phi	171	Schmidt-Phi	101	Morgan-Cin	.327	Madlock-Chi	.406	Bench-Cin	.519
		Bench-Cin	165			Watson-Hou	.324	Murcer-SF	.404	Foster-Cin	.518

Production		Adjusted Production		Batter Runs		Adjusted Batter Runs		Clutch Hitting Index		Runs Created	
Morgan-Cin	.979	Morgan-Cin	168	Morgan-Cin	57.1	Morgan-Cin	54.9	Perez-Cin	133	Morgan-Cin	145
Luzinski-Phi	.939	Luzinski-Phi	152	Luzinski-Phi	47.5	Luzinski-Phi	42.6	Morales-Chi	133	Luzinski-Phi	128
Parker-Pit	.899	Watson-Hou	152	Simmons-StL	35.7	Parker-Pit	32.5	Trillo-Chi	132	Rose-Cin	120
Stargell-Pit	.894	Parker-Pit	148	Thornton-Chi	35.4	Simmons-StL	32.1	Montanez-Phi-SF	127	Schmidt-Phi	113
Schmidt-Phi	.890	Stargell-Pit	147	Schmidt-Phi	33.7	Thornton-Chi	31.7	Murcer-SF	123	Simmons-StL	108

Total Average		Stolen Bases		Stolen Base Average		Stolen Base Runs		Fielding Runs		Total Player Rating	
Morgan-Cin	1.279	Lopes-LA	77	Morgan-Cin	87.0	Lopes-LA	15.9	Schmidt-Phi	24.0	Morgan-Cin	7.1
Luzinski-Phi	.956	Morgan-Cin	67	Lopes-LA	86.5	Morgan-Cin	14.1	Evans-Atl	23.4	Schmidt-Phi	5.7
Schmidt-Phi	.943	Brock-StL	56	Maddox-SF-Phi	86.2	Brock-StL	7.2	Maddox-SF-Phi	21.0	Bench-Cin	3.9
Bench-Cin	.901	Cedeno-Hou	50	Winfield-SD	85.2	Concepcion-Cin	6.3	Mackanin-Mon	18.2	Parker-Pit	3.7
Stargell-Pit	.895	Cardenal-Chi	34	Concepcion-Cin	84.6	Maddox-SF-Phi	5.1	Trillo-Chi	16.0	Evans-Atl	3.5

Wins		Win Percentage		Games		Complete Games		Shutouts		Saves	
Seaver-NY	22	Gullett-Cin	.789	Garber-Phi	71	Messersmith-LA	19	Messersmith-LA	7	Hrabosky-StL	22
Jones-SD	20	Seaver-NY	.710	McEnaney-Cin	70	Jones-SD	18	Reuss-Pit	6	Eastwick-Cin	22
Messersmith-LA	19	Hooton-Chi-LA	.667	Tomlin-SD	67	Seaver-NY	15	Jones-SD	6	Giusti-Pit	17
Hooton-Chi-LA	18	Murray-Mon	.652	Borbon-Cin	67	Reuss-Pit	15	Seaver-NY	5	McEnaney-Cin	15
Reuss-Pit	18			Garman-StL	66					Knowles-Chi	15

Innings Pitched		Fewest Hits/Game		Fewest BB/Game		Strikeouts		Strikeouts/Game		Ratio	
Messersmith-LA	321.2	Messersmith-LA	6.83	Nolan-Cin	1.24	Seaver-NY	243	Montefusco-SF	7.94	Jones-SD	9.41
Jones-SD	285.0	Seaver-NY	6.97	Montefusco-SF	1.77	Montefusco-SF	215	Richard-Hou	7.80	Sutton-LA	9.45
Seaver-NY	280.1	Warthen-Mon	6.98	Reed-Atl-StL	1.91	Messersmith-LA	213	Seaver-NY	7.80	Messersmith-LA	9.65
Morton-Atl	277.2	Sutton-LA	7.15	Rau-LA	2.13	Carlton-Phi	192	Warthen-Mon	6.87	Hooton-Chi-LA	9.89
Niekro-Atl	275.2	Hooton-Chi-LA	7.29	Barr-SF	2.14	Richard-Hou	176	Carlton-Phi	6.77	Nolan-Cin	9.91

Earned Run Average		Adjusted ERA		Opponents' Batting Avg.		Opponents' On Base Pct.		Starter Runs		Adjusted Starter Runs	
Jones-SD	2.24	Jones-SD	155	Messersmith-LA	.213	Sutton-LA	.264	Messersmith-LA	47.4	Messersmith-LA	39.5
Messersmith-LA	2.29	Messersmith-LA	148	Sutton-LA	.213	Jones-SD	.271	Jones-SD	43.7	Jones-SD	39.0
Seaver-NY	2.38	Seaver-NY	145	Seaver-NY	.214	Hooton-Chi-LA	.276	Seaver-NY	38.8	Seaver-NY	33.5
Reuss-Pit	2.54	Reuss-Pit	139	Warthen-Mon	.217	Messersmith-LA	.276	Reuss-Pit	28.5	Reuss-Pit	26.4
Forsch-StL	2.86	Montefusco-SF	132	Hooton-Chi-LA	.219	Nolan-Cin	.278	Sutton-LA	21.3	Montefusco-SF	24.8

Clutch Pitching Index		Relief Runs		Adjusted Relief Runs		Relief Ranking		Total Pitcher Index		Total Baseball Ranking	
Reuss-Pit	122	Hrabosky-StL	21.2	Hrabosky-StL	22.6	Hrabosky-StL	44.9	Jones-SD	4.9	Morgan-Cin	7.1
Niekro-Atl	122	Apodaca-NY	20.1	Apodaca-NY	20.1	Apodaca-NY	20.1	Hrabosky-StL	4.8	Schmidt-Phi	5.7
Blair-Mon	114	Hilgendorf-Phi	15.9	Hilgendorf-Phi	17.1	Garman-StL	18.4	Seaver-NY	4.3	Jones-SD	4.9
Koosman-NY	113	McEnaney-Cin	11.6	Garman-StL	12.0	Hilgendorf-Phi	15.9	Messersmith-LA	4.1	Hrabosky-StL	4.8
Barr-SF	110	Garman-StL	10.8	McEnaney-Cin	11.3	McGraw-Phi	13.9	Reuss-Pit	3.7	Seaver-NY	4.3

April 8 Frank Robinson, making his debut as the Indians player-manager, homers in his first at bat (as a DH) during a 5-3 win over the Yankees. It is Robby's eighth Opening Day homer, setting a major league record.

April 11 In Milwaukee, 48,160 fans brave 37 degree weather to welcome home Hank Aaron. Hank drives in a run as the Brewers whip the Indians 6-2.

June 6 Nolan Ryan's bid for a second no-hitter in a row is foiled by Hank Aaron's single in the sixth inning. Ryan gives up one other hit in overpowering the Brewers 6-0.

September 28 In a major league first, four pitchers share in a no-hitter, as the A's shut down the Angels 5-0. Vida Blue, Glenn Abbott, Paul Lindblad, and Rollie Fingers are the unique quartet.

October 7 The Red Sox match Cincinnati with a 5-3 win and three-game sweep over Oakland.

October 11 Boston's Luis Tiant shuts down the Big Red Machine and scores the first run as the Red Sox win the opening game of the World Series 6-0.

October 21 Fred Lynn's three-run first-inning homer is matched by teammate Bernie Carbo's pinch homer in the eighth to tie the game at 6-all. The Sox then fill the bases with no outs in the ninth but fail to bring in a run. But Boston evens the Series again with a 7-6 victory, won by Carlton Fisk's dramatic 12th-inning home run.

November 4 The Orioles Jim Palmer wins his second Cy Young Award, after pacing the AL in wins (23), shutouts (10), and ERA (2.09).

November 10 The Royals release slugger Harmon Killebrew, ending a 22-year career marked by 573 homers, good for fifth on the all-time list.

December 23 Arbitrator Peter Seitz announces a landmark decision in favor of the Players' Association, making pitchers Andy Messersmith and Dave McNally free agents. Seitz is immediately fired by John Gaherin, chairman of the owners' Player Relations Committee. McNally, who retired June 8, will not return to the major leagues, finishing with a 184-119 career record.

November 26 Fred Lynn, already named Rookie of the Year, becomes the first novice to win MVP honors, taking the AL award. Lynn batted .331 with 21 homers, 105 RBI, and league-leading figures in runs (103), doubles (47), and slugging (.566).

BALTIMORE

Pos	Player
M	E.Weaver
1B	L.May
2B	B.Grich
SS	M.Belanger
3B	B.Robinson
LF	D.Baylor
CF	P.Blair
RF	K.Singleton
C	D.Duncan
DH	T.Davis
DO	A.Bumbry
C	E.Hendricks
P	J.Palmer
P	M.Torrez
P	M.Cuellar
P	R.Grimsley
P	D.Alexander
RP	G.Jackson
P	W.Garland
P	P.Mitchell

BOSTON

Pos	Player
M	D.Johnson
1B	C.Yastrzemski
2B	D.Griffin
SS	R.Burleson
3B	R.Petrocelli
LF	B.Carbo
CF	F.Lynn
RF	D.Evans
C	C.Fisk
DH	J.Rice
D1	C.Cooper
2	D.Doyle
OD	J.Beniquez
P	L.Tiant
P	B.Lee
P	B.Wise
P	R.Cleveland
P	R.Moret
RP	D.Drago
RP	D.Segui
RP	J.Burton
P	D.Pole

CALIFORNIA

Pos	Player
M	D.Williams
1B	B.Bochte
2B	J.Remy
SS	M.Miley
3B	D.Chalk
LF	M.Nettles
CF	M.Rivers
RF	L.Stanton
C	E.Rodriguez
DH	T.Harper
OD	D.Collins
P	F.Tanana
P	E.Figueroa
P	N.Ryan
P	B.Singer
P	A.Hassler
RP	D.Kirkwood
RP	M.Scott
P	D.Lange

CHICAGO

Pos	Player
M	C.Tanner
1B	C.May
2B	J.Orta
SS	B.Dent
3B	B.Melton
LF	N.Nyman
CF	K.Henderson
RF	P.Kelly
C	B.Downing
DH	D.Johnson
23	B.Stein
O	J.Hairston
P	J.Kaat
P	W.Wood
P	C.Osteen
P	J.Jefferson
RP	R.Gossage
RP	D.Hamilton
RP	O.Osborn
P	S.Bahnsen
P	B.Gogolewski

CLEVELAND

Pos	Player
M	F.Robinson
1B	B.Powell
2B	D.Kuiper
SS	F.Duffy
3B	B.Bell
LF	O.Gamble
CF	R.Manning
RF	G.Hendrick
C	A.Ashby
DH	R.Carty
O	C.Spikes
C	J.Ellis
OD	J.Lowenstein
2	J.Brohamer
P	D.Eckersley
P	F.Peterson
P	D.Hood
P	R.Harrison
P	G.Perry
RP	D.LaRoche
RP	T.Buskey
RP	J.Brown
P	J.Bibby
P	E.Raich
P	J.Kern
P	R.Waits

DETROIT

Pos	Player
M	R.Houk
1B	J.Pierce
2B	G.Sutherland
SS	T.Veryzer
3B	A.Rodriguez
LF	B.Oglivie
CF	R.LeFlore
RF	L.Roberts
C	B.Freehan
DH	W.Horton
O1	D.Meyer
P	M.Lolich
P	J.Coleman
P	V.Ruhle
P	L.LaGrow
P	R.Bare
RP	J.Hiller
P	T.Walker
P	D.Lemanczyk
P	F.Arroyo

KANSAS CITY

Pos	Player
M	J.McKeon
M	W.Herzog
1B	J.Mayberry
2B	C.Rojas
SS	F.Patek
3B	G.Brett
LF	H.McRae
CF	A.Otis
RF	A.Cowens
C	B.Martinez
DH	H.Killebrew
O	V.Pinson
2S	F.White
O	J.Wohlford
D1	T.Solaita
P	S.Busby
P	A.Fitzmorris
P	D.Leonard
P	M.Pattin
P	P.Splittorff
RP	D.Bird
RP	L.McDaniel
RP	S.Mingori
P	N.Briles

MILWAUKEE

Pos	Player
M	D.Crandall
M	H.Kuenn
1B	G.Scott
2B	P.Garcia
SS	R.Yount
3B	D.Money
LF	B.Sharp
CF	G.Thomas
RF	S.Lezcano
C	D.Porter
DH	H.Aaron
32	K.Bevacqua
CO	C.Moore
OD	B.Mitchell
O1	M.Hegan
P	P.Broberg
P	J.Slaton
P	J.Colborn
P	B.Travers
P	T.Hausman
RP	E.Rodriguez
RP	T.Murphy
P	B.Champion
P	B.Castro
P	E.Sprague

MINNESOTA

Pos	Player
M	F.Quilici
1B	C.Kusick
2B	R.Carew
SS	D.Thompson
3B	E.Soderholm
LF	S.Braun
CF	D.Ford
RF	L.Bostock
C	G.Borgmann
DH	T.Oliva
S2	J.Terrell
1O	J.Briggs
OD	L.Hisle
O	S.Brye
P	B.Blyleven
P	J.Hughes
P	D.Goltz
P	V.Albury
RP	B.Campbell
RP	T.Burgmeier
P	R.Corbin
P	B.Butler

NEW YORK

Pos	Player
M	B.Virdon
M	B.Martin
1B	C.Chambliss
2B	S.Alomar
SS	J.Mason
3B	G.Nettles
LF	R.White
CF	E.Maddox
RF	B.Bonds
C	T.Munson
DH	E.Herrmann
S2	F.Stanley
P	C.Hunter
P	D.Medich
P	R.May
P	P.Dobson
P	L.Gura
RP	S.Lyle
RP	D.Tidrow

OAKLAND

Pos	Player
M	A.Dark
1B	J.Rudi
2B	P.Garner
SS	B.Campaneris
3B	S.Bando
LF	C.Washington
CF	B.North
RF	R.Jackson
C	G.Tenace
DH	B.Williams
1	J.Holt
P	V.Blue
P	K.Holtzman
P	D.Bosman
P	G.Abbott
P	S.Bahnsen
RP	R.Fingers
RP	J.Todd
RP	P.Lindblad
P	J.Perry
P	S.Siebert

TEXAS

Pos	Player
M	B.Martin
M	F.Lucchesi
1B	J.Spencer
2B	L.Randle
SS	T.Harrah
3B	R.Howell
LF	M.Hargrove
CF	D.Moates
RF	J.Burroughs
C	J.Sundberg
DH	C.Tovar
OD	T.Grieve
S2	R.Smalley
P	F.Jenkins
P	S.Hargan
P	G.Perry
P	B.Hands
RP	J.Umbarger
RP	S.Foucault
RP	S.Thomas
P	C.Wright
P	J.Brown
P	J.Bibby
P	S.Perzanowski

TEAM	G	W	L	PCT	GB	R	OR	AB	H	2B	3B	HR	BB	SO	AVG	OBP	SLG	PRO	PRO+	BR	/A	PF	CHI	RC	SB	CS	SBA	SBR
EAST																												
BOS	160	95	65	.594		796	709	5448	1500	284	44	134	565	741	.275	.347	.417	.764	106	108	41	109	99	776	66	58	53	-15
BAL	159	90	69	.566	4.5	682	553	5474	1382	224	33	124	580	834	.252	.328	.373	.701	105	-14	30	94	100	680	104	55	65	-2
NY	160	83	77	.519	12	681	588	5415	1430	230	39	110	486	710	.264	.328	.382	.710	102	-3	8	98	101	665	102	59	63	-5
CLE	159	79	80	.497	15.5	688	703	5404	1409	201	25	153	525	667	.261	.329	.392	.721	103	17	18	100	99	672	106	89	54	-22
MIL	162	68	94	.420	28	675	792	5378	1343	242	34	146	553	922	.250	.323	.389	.712	100	-2	-5	101	99	663	65	64	50	-19
DET	159	57	102	.358	37.5	570	786	5366	1338	171	39	125	383	872	.249	.303	.366	.669	84	-94	-119	104	101	573	63	57	53	-15
WEST																												
OAK	162	98	64	.605		758	606	5415	1376	220	33	151	609	846	.254	.335	.391	.726	107	34	51	98	104	725	183	82	69	6
KC	162	91	71	.562	7	710	649	5491	1431	263	58	118	591	675	.261	.336	.394	.730	103	40	21	103	96	736	155	75	67	2
TEX	162	79	83	.488	19	714	733	5599	1431	208	17	134	613	863	.256	.332	.371	.703	99	-10	-4	99	102	693	102	62	62	-7
MIN	159	76	83	.478	20.5	724	736	5514	1497	215	28	121	563	746	.271	.343	.386	.729	105	46	36	101	97	732	81	48	63	-5
CHI	161	75	86	.466	22.5	655	703	5490	1400	209	38	94	611	800	.255	.334	.358	.692	95	-24	-33	101	97	659	101	54	65	-2
CAL	161	72	89	.447	25.5	628	723	5377	1324	195	41	55	593	811	.246	.324	.328	.652	91	-99	-58	93	106	596	220	108	67	1
TOT	963					8281		65371	16861	2662	429	1465	6672	9487	.258	.330	.379	.709							1348	811	62	-82

TEAM	CG	SH	SV	IP	H	H/G	HR	BB	SO	RAT	ERA	ERA+	OAV	OOB	PR	/A	PF	CPI	FA	E	DP	FW	PW	BW	SBW	DIF
EAST																										
BOS	62	11	31	1436²	1463	9.2	145	490	720	12.4	3.98	102	.265	.327	-33	14	108	99	.977	139	142	.9	1.4	4.2	-.8	9.3
BAL	70	19	21	1451	1285	8.0	110	500	717	11.1	3.17	111	.242	.308	98	55	93	100	.983	107	175	2.6	5.6	3.1	.5	-1.3
NY	70	11	20	1424	1325	8.4	104	502	809	11.7	3.29	112	.249	.317	78	62	97	103	.978	135	148	1.1	6.3	.8	.2	-5.4
CLE	37	6	33	1435¹	1395	8.7	136	599	800	12.7	3.84	98	.258	.335	-10	-10	100	103	.978	134	156	1.1	-1.0	1.8	-1.5	-.9
MIL	36	10	34	1431²	1496	9.4	133	624	643	13.3	4.34	88	.271	.351	-89	-81	101	100	.971	180	162	-1.4	-8.3	-4.5	-1.2	-1.6
DET	52	10	17	1396	1496	9.6	137	533	787	13.3	4.27	94	.275	.343	-77	-40	106	100	.972	173	141	-1.1	-4.1	-12.2		-4.3
WEST																										
OAK	36	10	44	1448	1267	7.9	102	523	784	11.4	3.27	111	.236	.308	82	58	96	94	.977	143	140	.7	5.9	5.2	1.3	3.8
KC	52	11	25	1456²	1422	8.8	108	498	815	12.0	3.47	111	.258	.322	50	62	102	102	.976	155	151	.0	6.3	2.1	.9	.6
TEX	60	16	17	1465²	1456	8.9	123	518	792	12.4	3.86	97	.261	.329	-14	-17	99	98	.971	191	173	-2.0	-1.7	-.4	-.0	2.1
MIN	57	7	22	1423	1381	8.7	137	617	846	12.9	4.05	94	.257	.337	-43	-35	101	98	.973	170	147	-.9	-3.6	3.7	.2	-2.8
CHI	34	7	39	1452¹	1489	9.2	107	655	799	13.5	3.93	99	.268	.349	-24	-9	103	105	.978	140	155	.9	-.9	-3.4	.5	-2.6
CAL	59	19	16	1453¹	1386	8.6	123	613	975	12.6	3.89	91	.253	.333	-18	-55	94	97	.971	184	164	-1.6	-5.6	-5.9	.8	3.9
TOT	625	137	319	17273²		8.8				12.5	3.78		.258	.330					.975	1851	1854					

Runs		Hits		Doubles		Triples		Home Runs		Total Bases	
Lynn-Bos	103	Brett-KC	195	Lynn-Bos	47	Rivers-Cal	13	Scott-Mil	36	Scott-Mil	318
Mayberry-KC	95	Carew-Min	192	Jackson-Oak	39	Brett-KC	13	Jackson-Oak	36	Mayberry-KC	303
Bonds-NY	93	Munson-NY	190	McRae-KC	38	Orta-Chi	10	Mayberry-KC	34	Jackson-Oak	303
Rice-Bos	92	C.Washington-Oak	182	Mayberry-KC	38	Cowens-KC	8	Bonds-NY	32	Lynn-Bos	299
				Chambliss-NY	38					Brett-KC	289

Runs Batted In		Runs Produced		Bases On Balls		Batting Average		On Base Percentage		Slugging Average	
Scott-Mil	109	Lynn-Bos	187	Mayberry-KC	119	Carew-Min	.359	Carew-Min	.428	Lynn-Bos	.566
Mayberry-KC	106	Munson-NY	173	Singleton-Bal	118	Lynn-Bos	.331	Mayberry-KC	.419	Mayberry-KC	.547
Lynn-Bos	105	Rice-Bos	172	Grich-Bal	107	Munson-NY	.318	Singleton-Bal	.418	Powell-Cle	.524
Jackson-Oak	104	Mayberry-KC	167	Tenace-Oak	106	Rice-Bos	.309	Harrah-Tex	.406	Scott-Mil	.515
		Brett-KC	162	Harrah-Tex	98	C.Washington-Oak	.308	Lynn-Bos	.405	Bonds-NY	.512

Production		Adjusted Production		Batter Runs		Adjusted Batter Runs		Clutch Hitting Index		Runs Created	
Lynn-Bos	.971	Mayberry-KC	167	Mayberry-KC	56.0	Mayberry-KC	52.6	Stanton-Cal	135	Mayberry-KC	135
Mayberry-KC	.966	Carew-Min	159	Lynn-Bos	49.4	Singleton-Bal	49.2	Robinson-Bal	130	Lynn-Bos	120
Carew-Min	.926	Lynn-Bos	158	Carew-Min	44.4	Carew-Min	42.9	Munson-NY	122	Singleton-Bal	118
Powell-Cle	.906	Singleton-Bal	156	Singleton-Bal	41.3	Lynn-Bos	39.7	Duffy-Cle	116	Carew-Min	118
Bonds-NY	.891	Powell-Cle	154	Bonds-NY	35.4	Bonds-NY	37.2	Bando-Oak	115	Harrah-Tex	105

Total Average		Stolen Bases		Stolen Base Average		Stolen Base Runs		Fielding Runs		Total Player Rating	
Mayberry-KC	1.059	Rivers-Cal	70	Hisle-Min	85.0	Rivers-Cal	12.6	Belanger-Bal	28.0	Harrah-Tex	6.2
Lynn-Bos	1.000	C.Washington-Oak	40	Bumbry-Bal	84.2	Patek-KC	5.4	Dent-Chi	27.2	Grich-Bal	5.8
Carew-Min	.986	Otis-KC	39	Rivers-Cal	83.3	Otis-KC	5.1	Grich-Bal	24.0	Carew-Min	5.7
Tenace-Oak	.919	Carew-Min	35	Alomar-NY	82.4	Carew-Min	5.1	Rodriguez-Det	20.7	Lynn-Bos	4.7
Harrah-Tex	.914	Remy-Cal	34	Patek-KC	82.1	Alomar-NY	4.8	North-Oak	19.6	Mayberry-KC	4.6

Wins		Win Percentage		Games		Complete Games		Shutouts		Saves	
Palmer-Bal	23	Torrez-Bal	.690	Fingers-Oak	75	Hunter-NY	30	Palmer-Bal	10	Gossage-Chi	26
Hunter-NY	23	Leonard-KC	.682	Lindblad-Oak	68	G.Perry-Cle-Tex	25	Hunter-NY	7	Fingers-Oak	24
Blue-Oak	22	Palmer-Bal	.676	Gossage-Chi	62	Palmer-Bal	25			Murphy-Mil	20
Torrez-Bal	20	Blue-Oak	.667	LaRoche-Cle	61	Jenkins-Tex	22			LaRoche-Cle	17
Kaat-Chi	20	Lee-Bos	.654	Foucault-Tex	59	Blyleven-Min	20			Drago-Bos	15

Innings Pitched		Fewest Hits/Game		Fewest BB/Game		Strikeouts		Strikeouts/Game		Ratio	
Hunter-NY	328.0	Hunter-NY	6.80	Jenkins-Tex	1.87	Tanana-Cal	269	Tanana-Cal	9.41	Hunter-NY	9.22
Palmer-Bal	323.0	Ryan-Cal	6.91	G.Perry-Cle-Tex	2.06	G.Perry-Cle-Tex	233	Ryan-Cal	8.45	Palmer-Bal	9.33
G.Perry-Cle-Tex	305.2	Palmer-Bal	7.05	Grimsley-Bal	2.15	Blyleven-Min	233	Blyleven-Min	7.61	Blyleven-Min	10.02
Kaat-Chi	303.2	Eckersley-Cle	7.09	Palmer-Bal	2.23	Palmer-Bal	193	Eckersley-Cle	7.33	Tanana-Cal	10.18
Wood-Chi	291.1	Blyleven-Min	7.15	Hunter-NY	2.28	Blue-Oak	189	G.Perry-Cle-Tex	6.86	G.Perry-Cle-Tex	10.33

Earned Run Average		Adjusted ERA		Opponents' Batting Avg.		Opponents' On Base Pct.		Starter Runs		Adjusted Starter Runs	
Palmer-Bal	2.09	Palmer-Bal	168	Hunter-NY	.208	Hunter-NY	.263	Palmer-Bal	60.6	Palmer-Bal	51.0
Hunter-NY	2.58	Eckersley-Cle	145	Ryan-Cal	.213	Palmer-Bal	.267	Hunter-NY	43.7	Hunter-NY	40.1
Eckersley-Cle	2.60	Hunter-NY	143	Eckersley-Cle	.215	Blyleven-Min	.283	Tanana-Cal	33.0	Tanana-Cal	26.4
Tanana-Cal	2.62	Tanana-Cal	135	Palmer-Bal	.216	G.Perry-Cle-Tex	.284	Eckersley-Cle	24.4	Kaat-Chi	25.7
Figueroa-Cal	2.91	Blyleven-Min	127	Blyleven-Min	.219	Tanana-Cal	.288	Blyleven-Min	23.7	Blyleven-Min	25.1

Clutch Pitching Index		Relief Runs		Adjusted Relief Runs		Relief Ranking		Total Pitcher Index		Total Baseball Ranking	
Kaat-Chi	119	Gossage-Chi	30.5	Gossage-Chi	32.0	Gossage-Chi	47.7	Palmer-Bal	6.1	Harrah-Tex	6.2
Eckersley-Cle	116	Todd-Oak	20.2	Todd-Oak	18.2	LaRoche-Cle	19.5	Gossage-Chi	5.2	Palmer-Bal	6.1
Torrez-Bal	111	LaRoche-Cle	14.6	LaRoche-Cle	14.6	Todd-Oak	18.8	Hunter-NY	3.9	Grich-Bal	5.8
Osteen-Chi	110	Lindblad-Oak	14.4	Hiller-Det	14.5	Hiller-Det	15.7	Tanana-Cal	3.3	Carew-Min	5.7
Hargan-Tex	108	Hiller-Det	12.7	Lindblad-Oak	12.3	Fingers-Oak	14.1	Busby-KC	2.6	Gossage-Chi	5.2

January 14 Ted Turner completes the purchase of 100 percent of the Atlanta Braves.

April 25 Cubs outfielder Rick Monday snatches an American flag from two fans who are about to set it on fire in the outfield during a game at Dodger Stadium. The Dodgers win 5-4 in 10 innings. The next day, the Illinois legislature unanimously approves May 4 as Rick Monday Day.

May 29 The only homer Joe Niekro hits in his 22-year career comes at the expense of brother Phil.

June 15 The scheduled game at the Astrodome is canceled when heavy rains make it difficult for the visiting team and umpires to get through flooded streets to the stadium.

June 22 Randy Jones pitches the Padres to a 4-2 win over the Giants, and ties Christy Mathewson's 63-year-old NL record by going 68 innings without a base on balls. He receives a standing ovation from the home crowd after striking out Darrell Evans to end the seventh. His streak ends when he walks Marc Hill leading off the eighth. It is Jones's 13th win of the year.

September 29 The Dodgers' Walter Alston, after 23 years and 2,040 victories, steps down as manager. Third base coach Tommy Lasorda is promoted to the post.

October 3 The Cubs' Bill Madlock wrests the NL crown from the Reds' Ken Griffey by collecting four singles in an 11-1 win over the Braves. The hits raise Madlock from .333 to .339, one point ahead of the idle Griffey, who belatedly joins the Reds' 8-2 win over the Expos and goes 0-for-2, dipping his average to .336.

October 12 The Reds score seven times in the final three innings to secure a 7-6 win and complete a sweep of the LCS. Johnny Bench and George Foster hit successive homers to start the rally.

October 16 Don Gullett and Pedro Borbon combine on a five-hitter, as the Reds win Game 1 of the World Series 5-1 over the Yankees. Three hits by Perez, the first World Series designated hitter, and a Joe Morgan homer supply the offense.

October 21 The Reds take a 3-0 lead against Ed Figueroa, but the Yankees close it to 3-2. A four-run splurge in the ninth, topped by Johnny Bench's second homer of the game, ices Cincinnati's 7-2 win and a four-game sweep of the Yankees. World Series MVP Johnny Bench has two homers and five RBI, and demolishes the Yankees with .533 hitting. The Reds become the first team ever to go through an entire LCS and World Series without a defeat.

November 2 Padre Randy Jones beats out Met Jerry Koosman for the NL Cy Young Award. Jones led the league with 315 innings, and posted a 22-14 record for the fifth-place Padres.

November 24 The Reds' Joe Morgan outpoints teammate George Foster to win his second straight NL MVP Award. Morgan led with a .576 slugging average, and hit .320, scored 113 runs, knocked in 111, and stole 60 bases. Thurman Munson, who hit .302 with 17 homers and 105 RBI, was named the AL MVP a week earlier.

	ATLANTA		CHICAGO		CINCINNATI		HOUSTON		LOS ANGELES		MONTREAL
M	D.Bristol	M	J.Marshall	M	S.Anderson	M	B.Virdon	M	W.Alston	M	K.Kuehl
1B	W.Montanez	1B	P.LaCock	1B	T.Perez	1B	B.Watson	M	T.Lasorda	M	C.Fox
2B	R.Gilbreath	2B	M.Trillo	2B	J.Morgan	2B	R.Andrews	1B	S.Garvey	1B	M.Jorgensen
SS	D.Chaney	SS	M.Kelleher	SS	D.Concepcion	SS	R.Metzger	2B	D.Lopes	2B	P.Mackanin
3B	J.Royster	3B	B.Madlock	3B	P.Rose	3B	E.Cabell	SS	B.Russell	SS	T.Foli
LF	J.Wynn	LF	J.Cardenal	LF	G.Foster	LF	J.Cruz	3B	R.Cey	3B	L.Parrish
CF	R.Office	CF	R.Monday	CF	C.Geronimo	CF	C.Cedeno	LF	B.Buckner	LF	D.Unser
RF	K.Henderson	RF	J.Morales	RF	K.Griffey	RF	G.Gross	CF	D.Baker	CF	J.White
C	V.Correll	C	S.Swisher	C	J.Bench	C	E.Herrmann	RF	R.Smith	RF	E.Valentine
								C	S.Yeager	C	B.Foote
O	D.May	C1	G.Mitterwald	1O	D.Driessen	CO	C.Johnson				
O1	T.Paciorek	O	J.Wallis	23	D.Flynn	O	L.Roberts	2	T.Sizemore	1C	J.Morales
		S	D.Rosello							CO	G.Carter
P	P.Niekro			P	G.Nolan	P	J.Richard	P	D.Sutton	O	P.Mangual
P	D.Ruthven	P	R.Reuschel	P	P.Zachry	P	L.Dierker	P	D.Rau		
P	A.Messersmith	P	R.Burris	P	F.Norman	P	J.Andujar	P	B.Hooton	P	S.Rogers
P	C.Morton	P	B.Bonham	P	J.Billingham	P	J.Niekro	P	T.John	P	W.Fryman
P	F.LaCorte	P	S.Renko	P	S.Alcala	RP	K.Forsch	P	R.Rhoden	P	D.Stanhouse
RP	R.Moret	RP	P.Reuschel	RP	P.Borbon	RP	G.Pentz	RP	C.Hough	RP	D.Carrithers
RP	A.Devine	RP	B.Sutter	RP	R.Eastwick	RP	G.Rondon	RP	M.Marshall	RP	D.Murray
RP	B.Dal Canton	RP	J.Coleman	RP	W.McEnaney			RP	S.Wall	RP	S.Dunning
						P	D.Larson			RP	C.Lang
P	P.Torrealba	P	M.Garman	P	D.Gullett	P	M.Cosgrove				
		P	S.Stone			P	B.McLaughlin			P	D.Warthen
		P	D.Knowles			P	J.Sambito			P	C.Kirby
		P	O.Zamora							P	J.Kerrigan

	NEW YORK		PHILADELPHIA		PITTSBURGH		SAN DIEGO		SAN FRANCISCO		ST.LOUIS
M	J.Frazier	M	D.Ozark	M	D.Murtaugh	M	J.McNamara	M	B.Rigney	M	R.Schoendienst
1B	E.Kranepool	1B	D.Allen	1B	W.Stargell	1B	M.Ivie	1B	D.Evans	1B	K.Hernandez
2B	F.Millan	2B	D.Cash	2B	R.Stennett	2B	T.Fuentes	2B	M.Perez	2B	M.Tyson
SS	B.Harrelson	SS	L.Bowa	SS	F.Taveras	SS	E.Hernandez	SS	C.Speier	SS	D.Kessinger
3B	R.Staiger	3B	M.Schmidt	3B	R.Hebner	3B	D.Rader	3B	K.Reitz	3B	H.Cruz
LF	J.Milner	LF	G.Luzinski	LF	R.Zisk	LF	J.Grubb	LF	G.Matthews	LF	L.Brock
CF	D.Unser	CF	G.Maddox	CF	A.Oliver	CF	W.Davis	CF	L.Herndon	CF	J.Mumphrey
RF	D.Kingman	RF	J.Johnstone	RF	D.Parker	RF	D.Winfield	RF	B.Murcer	RF	W.Crawford
C	J.Grote	C	B.Boone	C	M.Sanguillen	C	F.Kendall	C	D.Rader	C	T.Simmons
1	J.Torre	O	J.Martin	O3	B.Robinson	O	J.Turner	O1	G.Thomasson	2O	V.Harris
O	B.Boisclair	1O	B.Tolan			S	H.Torres	2	D.Thomas	O	B.McBride
S2	M.Phillips	O	O.Brown			32	T.Kubiak	1	W.Montanez	S	G.Templeton
32	W.Garrett			P	J.Candelaria	1	W.McCovey				
		P	S.Carlton	P	J.Reuss			P	J.Montefusco	P	P.Falcone
P	T.Seaver	P	J.Kaat	P	J.Rooker			P	J.Barr	P	J.Denny
P	J.Matlack	P	J.Lonborg	P	B.Kison	P	R.Jones	P	E.Halicki	P	L.McGlothen
P	J.Koosman	P	L.Christenson	P	D.Medich	P	B.Strom	P	R.Dressler	P	B.Forsch
P	M.Lolich	P	T.Underwood	RP	K.Tekulve	P	D.Freisleben	P	J.D'Acquisto	P	E.Rasmussen
P	C.Swan	RP	R.Reed	RP	B.Moose	P	D.Spillner	RP	G.Lavelle	RP	A.Hrabosky
RP	S.Lockwood	RP	T.McGraw	RP	D.Giusti	RP	B.Metzger	RP	M.Caldwell	RP	M.Wallace
RP	B.Apodaca	RP	G.Garber			RP	D.Tomlin	RP	R.Moffitt	RP	B.Greif
		P	W.Twitchell	P	L.Demery	RP	R.Folkers	P	C.Williams	P	J.Curtis
		P	R.Schueler			P	A.Foster	P	D.Heaverlo		
						P	R.Sawyer				
						P	T.Griffin				

TEAM	G	W	L	PCT	GB	R	OR	AB	H	2B	3B	HR	BB	SO	AVG	OBP	SLG	PRO	PRO+	BR	/A	PF	CHI	RC	SB	CS	SBA	SBR
EAST																												
PHI	162	101	61	.623		770	557	5528	1505	259	45	110	542	793	.272	.342	.395	.737	112	106	83	103	101	746	127	70	64	-4
PIT	162	92	70	.568	9	708	630	5604	1499	249	56	110	433	807	.267	.323	.391	.714	107	50	44	101	102	700	130	45	74	12
NY	162	86	76	.531	15	615	**538**	5415	1334	198	34	102	561	797	.246	.320	.352	.672	103	-19	17	94	99	608	66	58	53	-15
CHI	162	75	87	.463	26	611	728	5519	1386	216	24	105	490	834	.251	.316	.356	.672	89	-27	-83	109	99	605	74	74	50	-22
STL	162	72	90	.444	29	629	671	5516	1432	243	57	63	512	860	.260	.325	.359	.684	99	1	-5	101	97	644	123	55	69	4
MON	162	55	107	.340	46	531	734	5428	1275	224	32	94	433	841	.235	.293	.340	.633	82	-109	-131	104	102	539	86	44	66	-1
WEST																												
CIN	162	102	60	.630		**857**	633	5702	1599	271	63	141	681	902	**.280**	.360	.424	.784	126	214	193	102	95	907	210	57	79	29
LA	162	92	70	.568	10	608	543	5472	1371	200	34	91	486	744	.251	.315	.349	.664	96	-39	-28	98	101	604	144	55	72	10
HOU	162	80	82	.494	22	625	657	5464	1401	195	50	66	530	719	.256	.325	.347	.672	107	-20	36	91	101	622	150	57	72	11
SF	162	74	88	.457	28	595	686	5452	1340	211	37	85	518	778	.246	.314	.345	.659	90	-48	-66	103	100	591	88	55	62	-7
SD	162	73	89	.451	29	570	662	5369	1327	216	37	64	488	716	.247	.313	.337	.650	98	-65	-19	92	100	570	92	46	67	0
ATL	162	70	92	.432	32	620	700	5345	1309	170	30	66	589	811	.245	.322	.334	.656	87	-44	-82	106	**104**	579	74	61	55	-14
TOT	972					7739		65814	16778	2652	499	1113	6263	9602	.255	.323	.361	.684							1364	677	67	3

TEAM	CG	SH	SV	IP	H	H/G	HR	BB	SO	RAT	ERA	ERA+	OAV	OOB	PR	/A	PF	CPI	FA	E	DP	FW	PW	BW	SBW	DIF
EAST																										
PHI	34	9	44	1459	1377	8.5	98	**397**	918	11.1	3.08	115	.250	.303	69	**76**	101	102	.981	115	148	1.7	**8.1**	8.8	-.5	1.8
PIT	45	12	35	1466¹	1402	8.6	95	460	762	11.5	3.36	104	.253	.313	22	20	100	99	.975	163	142	-1.0	2.1	4.7	1.2	4.0
NY	**53**	18	25	1449	**1248**	**7.8**	97	419	**1025**	10.5	**2.94**	112	**.233**	**.292**	91	57	94	95	.979	131	116	.8	6.1	1.8	-1.6	-2.1
CHI	27	12	33	1471¹	1511	9.2	123	490	850	12.4	3.93	98	.268	.332	-71	-12	110	100	.978	140	145	.3	-1.3	-8.8	-2.4	6.2
STL	35	15	26	1453²	1416	8.8	91	581	731	12.5	3.60	98	.260	.332	-16	-11	101	103	.973	174	163	-1.7	-1.2	-.5	-.4	-6.0
MON	26	10	21	1440	1442	9.0	89	659	783	13.4	3.99	93	.266	.350	-79	-44	106	102	.976	155	**179**	-.6	-4.7	-13.9	-.1	-6.7
WEST																										
CIN	33	12	**45**	1471	1436	8.8	100	491	790	11.9	3.51	100	.258	.321	-1	0	100	101	**.984**	**102**	157	**2.5**	.0	20.5	3.1	-5.0
LA	47	17	28	1470²	1330	8.1	97	479	747	11.2	3.02	112	.243	.307	79	60	97	**104**	.980	128	154	1.0	6.4	-3.0	1.0	5.6
HOU	42	17	29	1444¹	1349	8.4	82	662	780	12.7	3.56	90	.250	.335	-9	-59	91	101	.978	140	155	.3	-6.3	3.8	1.1	.0
SF	27	**18**	31	1461²	1464	9.0	**68**	518	746	12.3	3.53	103	.263	.328	-4	16	104	100	.971	186	153	-2.4	1.7	-7.0	-.8	1.4
SD	47	11	18	1432¹	1368	8.6	87	543	652	12.1	3.65	90	.253	.323	-24	-61	93	95	.978	141	148	.2	-6.5	-2.0	-.0	.3
ATL	33	13	27	1438	1435	9.0	86	564	818	12.8	3.86	98	.261	.335	-58	-12	108	97	.973	167	151	-1.3	-1.3	-8.7	-1.5	1.8
TOT	449	164	362	17457¹		8.6				12.0	3.50		.255	.323					.977	1742	1811					

Runs
Rose-Cin 130
Morgan-Cin 113
Schmidt-Phi 112
Griffey-Cin 111
Monday-Chi 107

Hits
Rose-Cin 215
Montanez-SF-Atl . . 206
Garvey-LA 200
Buckner-LA 193

Doubles
Rose-Cin 42
Johnstone-Phi 38
Maddox-Phi 37
Garvey-LA 37

Triples
Cash-Phi 12
Geronimo-Cin 11
Parker-Pit 10
W.Davis-SD 10

Home Runs
Schmidt-Phi 38
Kingman-NY 37
Monday-Chi 32
Foster-Cin 29
Morgan-Cin 27

Total Bases
Schmidt-Phi 306
Rose-Cin 299
Foster-Cin 298
Garvey-LA 284

Runs Batted In
Foster-Cin 121
Morgan-Cin 111
Schmidt-Phi 107
Watson-Hou 102
Luzinski-Phi 95

Runs Produced
Morgan-Cin 197
Rose-Cin 183
Schmidt-Phi 181
Griffey-Cin 179
Foster-Cin 178

Bases On Balls
Wynn-Atl 127
Morgan-Cin 114
Schmidt-Phi 100
Cey-LA 89
Rose-Cin 86

Batting Average
Madlock-Chi 339
Griffey-Cin 336
Maddox-Phi 330
Rose-Cin 323
Morgan-Cin 320

On Base Percentage
Morgan-Cin 453
Madlock-Chi 415
Rose-Cin 406
Griffey-Cin 403
Cey-LA 389

Slugging Average
Morgan-Cin 576
Foster-Cin 530
Schmidt-Phi 524
Monday-Chi 507
Kingman-NY 506

Production
Morgan-Cin 1.029
Madlock-Chi 915
Schmidt-Phi 904
Foster-Cin 899
Rose-Cin 855

Adjusted Production
Morgan-Cin 186
Watson-Hou 151
Schmidt-Phi 150
Foster-Cin 149
Madlock-Chi 146

Batter Runs
Morgan-Cin 61.4
Schmidt-Phi 42.7
Madlock-Chi 40.6
Rose-Cin 39.6
Foster-Cin 36.7

Adjusted Batter Runs
Morgan-Cin 58.4
Schmidt-Phi 39.2
Watson-Hou 38.3
Rose-Cin 36.8
Foster-Cin 34.3

Clutch Hitting Index
Cruz-StL 119
Brock-StL 117
Milner-NY 117
Bench-Cin 116
Reitz-SF 116

Runs Created
Morgan-Cin 144
Rose-Cin 123
Schmidt-Phi 121
Foster-Cin 111
Griffey-Cin 109

Total Average
Morgan-Cin 1.319
Schmidt-Phi 944
Foster-Cin 911
Madlock-Chi 882
Griffey-Cin 876

Stolen Bases
Lopes-LA 63
Morgan-Cin 60
Taveras-Pit 58
Cedeno-Hou 58
Brock-StL 56

Stolen Base Average
Morgan-Cin 87.0
Lopes-LA 86.3
Foster-Cin 85.0
Taveras-Pit 84.1
Geronimo-Cin . . . 81.5

Stolen Base Runs
Lopes-LA 12.9
Morgan-Cin 12.6
Taveras-Pit 10.8
Cedeno-Hou 8.4
Cabell-Hou 5.7

Fielding Runs
Schmidt-Phi 24.7
Maddox-Phi 24.3
Trillo-Chi 18.3
Stennett-Pit 17.4
Royster-Atl 16.6

Total Player Rating
Schmidt-Phi 6.4
Morgan-Cin 5.8
Maddox-Phi 4.5
Cedeno-Hou 4.4
Concepcion-Cin . . . 4.1

Wins
Jones-SD 22
Sutton-LA 21
Koosman-NY 21
Richard-Hou 20
Carlton-Phi 20

Win Percentage
Carlton-Phi 741
Candelaria-Pit 696
Sutton-LA 677
Koosman-NY 677
Rooker-Pit 652

Games
Murray-Mon 81
Metzger-SD 77
Hough-LA 77
Eastwick-Cin 71
Borbon-Cin 69

Complete Games
Jones-SD 25
Koosman-NY 17
Matlack-NY 16
Sutton-LA 15
Richard-Hou 14

Shutouts
Montefusco-SF 6
Matlack-NY 6
Seaver-NY 5
Jones-SD 5

Saves
Eastwick-Cin 26
Lockwood-NY 19
Forsch-Hou 19
Hough-LA 18
Metzger-SD 16

Innings Pitched
Jones-SD 315.1
Richard-Hou 291.0
Seaver-NY 271.0
Niekro-Atl 270.2
Sutton-LA 267.2

Fewest Hits/Game
Richard-Hou 6.84
Seaver-NY 7.01
Candelaria-Pit . . . 7.08
Messersmith-Atl . . 7.21
Falcone-StL 7.34

Fewest BB/Game
Nolan-Cin 1.02
Kaat-Phi 1.27
Jones-SD 1.43
Matlack-NY 1.96
Lonborg-Phi 2.03

Strikeouts
Seaver-NY 235
Richard-Hou 214
Koosman-NY 200
Carlton-Phi 195
Niekro-Atl 173

Strikeouts/Game
Seaver-NY 7.80
Koosman-NY 7.28
Carlton-Phi 6.95
Richard-Hou 6.62
Zachry-Cin 6.31

Ratio
Jones-SD 9.36
Candelaria-Pit . . . 9.61
Seaver-NY 9.70
Nolan-Cin 9.78
Koosman-NY 9.90

Earned Run Average
Denny-StL 2.52
Rau-LA 2.57
Seaver-NY 2.59
Koosman-NY 2.69
Zachry-Cin 2.74

Adjusted ERA
Denny-StL 140
Rau-LA 132
Zachry-Cin 128
Montefusco-SF . . . 128
Seaver-NY 127

Opponents' Batting Avg.
Richard-Hou 212
Seaver-NY 213
Candelaria-Pit 216
Messersmith-Atl . . .219
Falcone-StL 222

Opponents' On Base Pct.
Jones-SD 267
Candelaria-Pit 273
Seaver-NY 273
Nolan-Cin 276
Koosman-NY 279

Starter Runs
Seaver-NY 27.4
Jones-SD 26.7
Richard-Hou 24.2
Rau-LA 23.9
Denny-StL 22.5

Adjusted Starter Runs
Denny-StL 23.3
Montefusco-SF . . . 22.1
Seaver-NY 21.2
Rau-LA 20.8
Burris-Chi 20.8

Clutch Pitching Index
Rau-LA 139
Denny-StL 129
Burris-Chi 118
Christenson-Phi . . . 112
Fryman-Mon 112

Relief Runs
Hough-LA 20.5
Eastwick-Cin 16.9
Reed-Phi 14.8
Moffitt-SF 14.1
Forsch-Hou 13.8

Adjusted Relief Runs
Hough-LA 18.6
Eastwick-Cin 16.9
Moffitt-SF 15.5
Reed-Phi 15.4
Twitchell-Phi 12.3

Relief Ranking
Eastwick-Cin 31.8
Hough-LA 28.8
Moffitt-SF 21.0
Reed-Phi 20.1
Lavelle-SF 17.8

Total Pitcher Index
Hough-LA 3.3
Eastwick-Cin 3.1
Barr-SF 2.8
Denny-StL 2.7
Rau-LA 2.6

Total Baseball Ranking
Schmidt-Phi 6.4
Morgan-Cin 5.8
Maddox-Phi 4.5
Cedeno-Hou 4.4
Concepcion-Cin . . . 4.1

January 22 Pitchers Robin Roberts and Bob Lemon are voted into the Hall of Fame.

February 2 The Special Veterans Committee selects old-time players Roger Connor and Fred Lindstrom, and umpire Cal Hubbard, for Cooperstown. Hubbard becomes the first man elected to both the Pro Football and Baseball Halls of Fame.

February 9 Oscar Charleston is selected for the Hall of Fame by the Special Committee on the Negro Leagues.

April 15 Newly remodeled Yankee Stadium is jammed with 52,613 fans for Opening Day ceremonies. The 1923 Yankee team is honored, and Bob Shawkey, winner of the 1923 Stadium opener, throws out the first ball.

May 13 The Royals beat the White Sox 13-2 as George Brett sets a major league record by collecting three hits for the sixth consecutive game, breaking Rod Carew's record.

July 20 Hank Aaron hits the 755th, and last, homer of his career, connecting off Dick Drago of the California Angels.

July 28 Blue Moon Odom and Francisco Barrios combine on a no-hitter as the White Sox top the A's 2-1. Odom walks nine in five innings and is lifted after throwing a ball in the sixth. For Odom (2-0), this is his last major league victory.

September 11 Minnie Minoso comes to bat for the White Sox after a 12-year hiatus. He goes hitless in his three at bats against Frank Tanana, but his appearance makes him one of a handful of major league players to play in four decades. His at bat in 1980 will match him with Nick Altrock as a five-decade player.

October 3 George Brett edges Royals teammate Hal McRae for the AL batting title, .333 to .332, when his blooper drops in front of Twins outfielder Steve Brye and skips over his head for an inside-the-park homer.

October 14 In the final LCS game, the Yankees take the early lead only to see the Royals even it up on Brett's 3-run homer in the eighth. Chris Chambliss then connects on a dramatic ninth-inning homer off relief ace Mark Littell to win the game 7-6 and the pennant for the Yankees. By the time Chambliss reaches second base, he is surrounded by screaming fans who escort him around the bases. After he reaches the dugout he returns with a police escort to make sure he touches third base and home.

November 4 The first mass market free-agent re-entry draft is held at New York's Plaza Hotel. Among those available are Reggie Jackson, Joe Rudi, Don Gullett, Gene Tenace, Rollie Fingers, Don Baylor, Bobby Grich, and Willie McCovey.

November 5 New AL franchises in Seattle and Toronto fill up their rosters by selecting 30 players apiece from unprotected players on other AL rosters. Outfielder Ruppert Jones (Seattle) and infielder-outfielder Bob Bailor (Toronto) are the first choices.

November 5 Baltimore's Jim Palmer easily outpoints Detroit's sensational rookie Mark Fidrych to win the AL Cy Young Award.

BALTIMORE

Pos	Player
M	E.Weaver
1B	T.Muser
2B	B.Grich
SS	M.Belanger
3B	D.DeCinces
LF	K.Singleton
CF	P.Blair
RF	R.Jackson
C	D.Duncan
DH	L.May
OD	A.Bumbry
DO	A.Mora
3	B.Robinson
P	J.Palmer
P	W.Garland
P	R.May
P	R.Grimsley
P	M.Cuellar
RP	D.Miller
P	K.Holtzman
P	M.Flanagan
P	D.Alexander

BOSTON

Pos	Player
M	D.Johnson
M	D.Zimmer
1B	C.Yastrzemski
2B	D.Doyle
SS	R.Burleson
3B	B.Hobson
LF	J.Rice
CF	F.Lynn
RF	D.Evans
C	C.Fisk
DH	C.Cooper
O	R.Miller
3	R.Petrocelli
P	L.Tiant
P	R.Wise
P	F.Jenkins
P	R.Cleveland
P	D.Pole
RP	J.Willoughby
RP	T.Murphy
P	R.Jones
P	B.Lee

CALIFORNIA

Pos	Player
M	D.Williams
M	N.Sherry
1B	B.Bochte
2B	J.Remy
SS	D.Chalk
3B	R.Jackson
LF	L.Stanton
CF	R.Torres
RF	B.Bonds
C	A.Etchebarren
DH	T.Davis
OD	D.Collins
D1	B.Melton
2S	M.Guerrero
1O	D.Briggs
1	T.Solaita
P	F.Tanana
P	N.Ryan
P	G.Ross
P	P.Hartzell
P	D.Kirkwood
RP	D.Drago
P	S.Monge

CHICAGO

Pos	Player
M	P.Richards
1B	J.Spencer
2B	J.Brohamer
SS	B.Dent
3B	K.Bell
LF	J.Orta
CF	C.Lemon
RF	R.Garr
C	B.Downing
DH	P.Kelly
23	B.Stein
D1	L.Johnson
P	R.Gossage
P	B.Johnson
P	K.Brett
P	F.Barrios
P	T.Forster
RP	D.Hamilton
RP	C.Carroll
P	P.Vuckovich
P	J.Jefferson
/P	W.Wood
P	C.Knapp
/P	K.Kravec

CLEVELAND

Pos	Player
M	F.Robinson
1B	B.Powell
2B	D.Kuiper
SS	F.Duffy
3B	B.Bell
LF	G.Hendrick
CF	R.Manning
RF	C.Spikes
C	A.Ashby
DH	R.Carty
S2	L.Blanks
C	R.Fosse
OD	J.Lowenstein
P	P.Dobson
P	D.Eckersley
P	J.Brown
P	J.Bibby
P	R.Waits
RP	J.Kern
RP	S.Thomas
RP	D.LaRoche
P	T.Buskey
P	D.Hood

DETROIT

Pos	Player
M	R.Houk
1B	J.Thompson
2B	P.Garcia
SS	T.Veryzer
3B	A.Rodriguez
LF	A.Johnson
CF	R.LeFlore
RF	R.Staub
C	B.Kimm
DH	W.Horton
O1	D.Meyer
O	B.Oglivie
C	B.Freehan
2S	C.Scrivener
O1	M.Stanley
P	D.Roberts
P	M.Fidrych
P	V.Ruhle
P	R.Bare
P	J.Crawford
RP	J.Hiller
RP	S.Grilli
P	B.Laxton
P	D.Lemanczyk
P	J.Coleman

KANSAS CITY

Pos	Player
M	W.Herzog
1B	J.Mayberry
2B	F.White
SS	F.Patek
3B	G.Brett
LF	T.Poquette
CF	A.Otis
RF	A.Cowens
C	B.Martinez
DH	H.McRae
O	J.Wohlford
C	B.Stinson
P	D.Leonard
P	A.Fitzmorris
P	D.Bird
P	P.Splittorff
P	M.Pattin
RP	M.Littell
RP	S.Mingori
P	A.Hassler
P	S.Busby
P	L.Gura

MILWAUKEE

Pos	Player
M	A.Grammas
1B	G.Scott
2B	T.Johnson
SS	R.Yount
3B	D.Money
LF	S.Lezcano
CF	V.Joshua
RF	G.Thomas
C	D.Porter
DH	H.Aaron
CO	M.Moore
DO	M.Hegan
P	J.Slaton
P	B.Travers
P	J.Colborn
P	J.Augustine
P	E.Rodriguez
RP	B.Castro
RP	D.Frisella
P	P.Broberg

MINNESOTA

Pos	Player
M	G.Mauch
1B	R.Carew
2B	B.Randall
SS	R.Smalley
3B	M.Cubbage
LF	L.Hisle
CF	L.Bostock
RF	D.Ford
C	B.Wynegar
DH	C.Kusick
DO	S.Braun
O	S.Brye
P	D.Goltz
P	J.Hughes
P	B.Singer
P	S.Luebber
P	P.Redfern
RP	B.Campbell
RP	T.Burgmeier
RP	V.Albury
P	B.Blyleven
P	E.Bane
P	J.Decker

NEW YORK

Pos	Player
M	B.Martin
1B	C.Chambliss
2B	W.Randolph
SS	F.Stanley
3B	G.Nettles
LF	R.White
CF	M.Rivers
RF	O.Gamble
C	T.Munson
DH	C.May
OD	L.Piniella
S	J.Mason
P	C.Hunter
P	E.Figueroa
P	D.Ellis
P	K.Holtzman
P	D.Alexander
RP	S.Lyle
RP	D.Tidrow
RP	G.Jackson
P	R.May

OAKLAND

Pos	Player
M	C.Tanner
1B	G.Tenace
2B	P.Garner
SS	B.Campaneris
3B	S.Bando
LF	J.Rudi
CF	B.North
RF	C.Washington
C	L.Haney
DH	B.Williams
O1	D.Baylor
31	K.McMullen
P	V.Blue
P	M.Torrez
P	S.Bahnsen
P	P.Mitchell
P	D.Bosman
RP	R.Fingers
P	P.Lindblad
P	J.Todd
P	M.Norris
P	G.Abbott

TEXAS

Pos	Player
M	F.Lucchesi
1B	M.Hargrove
2B	L.Randle
SS	T.Harrah
3B	R.Howell
LF	G.Clines
CF	J.Beniquez
RF	J.Burroughs
C	J.Sundberg
DH	T.Grieve
P	G.Perry
P	N.Briles
P	B.Blyleven
P	J.Umbarger
P	S.Hargan
RP	S.Foucault
RP	M.Bacsik
RP	J.Terpko
P	T.Boggs
P	S.Barr
P	B.Singer

TEAM	G	W	L	PCT	GB	R	OR	AB	H	2B	3B	HR	BB	SO	AVG	OBP	SLG	PRO	PRO+	BR	/A	PF	CHI	RC	SB	CS	SBA	SBR
EAST																												
NY	159	97	62	.610		730	**575**	5555	1496	231	36	120	470	**616**	.269	.330	.389	.719	111	64	**71**	99	103	723	163	65	71	10
BAL	162	88	74	.543	10.5	619	598	5457	1326	213	28	119	519	883	.243	.311	.358	.669	102	-33	5	94	102	612	150	61	71	8
BOS	162	83	79	.512	15.5	716	660	5511	1448	257	53	**134**	500	832	.263	.327	**.402**	**.729**	101	**80**	-8	112	98	709	95	70	58	-14
CLE	159	81	78	.509	16	615	615	5412	1423	189	38	85	479	631	.263	.324	.359	.683	101	-2	5	99	97	611	75	69	52	-19
DET	161	74	87	.460	24	609	709	5441	1401	207	38	101	450	730	.257	.318	.365	.683	96	-7	-31	104	97	611	107	59	64	-3
MIL	161	66	95	.410	32	570	655	5396	1326	170	38	88	511	909	.246	.314	.340	.654	93	-57	-46	98	98	575	62	61	50	-18
WEST																												
KC	162	90	72	.556		713	611	5540	1490	259	**57**	65	484	650	.269	.331	.371	.702	104	37	32	101	103	687	218	106	67	2
OAK	161	87	74	.540	2.5	686	598	5353	1319	208	33	113	**592**	818	.246	.327	.361	.688	105	13	40	96	**105**	663	**341**	123	**73**	**29**
MIN	162	85	77	.525	5	**743**	704	5574	**1526**	222	51	81	550	714	**.274**	**.343**	.375	.718	108	78	63	102	100	**727**	146	75	66	-1
TEX	162	76	86	.469	14	616	652	5555	1390	213	26	80	568	809	.250	.323	.341	.664	93	-32	-45	102	98	616	87	45	66	-1
CAL	162	76	86	.469	14	550	631	5385	1265	210	23	63	534	812	.235	.309	.318	.627	90	-105	-72	94	102	531	126	80	61	-10
CHI	161	64	97	.398	25.5	586	745	5532	1410	209	46	73	471	739	.255	.317	.349	.666	94	-36	-40	101	96	622	120	53	69	4
TOT	967					7753		65711	16820	2588	467	1122	6128	9143	.256	.323	.361	.684							1690	867	66	-13

TEAM	CG	SH	SV	IP	H	H/G	HR	BB	SO	RAT	ERA	ERA+	OAV	OOB	PR	/A	PF	CPI	FA	E	DP	FW	PW	BW	SBW	DIF
EAST																										
NY	62	15	37	1455	**1300**	8.0	97	448	674	**10.9**	3.19	107	**.241**	**.301**	53	36	97	95	.980	126	141	.9	3.8	**7.5**	1.2	4.1
BAL	59	16	23	1468[2]	1396	8.6	**80**	489	678	11.7	3.32	99	.255	.318	33	-7	93	101	**.982**	**118**	157	**1.5**	-.7	.5	1.0	4.8
BOS	49	13	27	1458	1495	9.2	109	**409**	673	12.0	3.52	**111**	.267	.320	-1	**62**	111	104	.978	141	148	.2	**6.6**	-.8	-1.4	-2.5
CLE	30	**17**	**46**	1432	1361	8.6	**80**	533	928	12.1	3.47	101	.255	.326	8	3	99	101	.980	121	159	1.2	.3	.5	-1.9	1.4
DET	55	12	20	1431[1]	1426	9.0	101	550	738	12.6	3.87	96	.263	.334	-56	-25	105	99	.974	168	161	-1.4	-2.7	-3.3	-.2	1.1
MIL	45	10	27	1435[1]	1406	8.8	99	567	677	12.6	3.64	96	.260	.334	-20	-24	99	104	.975	152	160	-.5	-2.5	-4.9	-1.8	-4.8
WEST																										
KC	41	12	35	1472[1]	1356	8.3	83	493	735	11.5	3.21	109	.247	.312	51	48	100	99	.978	139	147	.3	5.1	3.4	.3	-.1
OAK	39	15	29	1459[1]	1412	8.7	96	415	711	11.5	3.26	103	.255	.310	42	16	95	101	.977	144	130	-.0	1.7	4.2	**3.2**	-2.6
MIN	29	11	23	1459	1421	8.8	89	610	762	12.8	3.69	97	.259	.337	-29	-20	102	102	.973	172	**182**	-1.6	-2.1	6.7	.0	1.0
TEX	63	15	15	1472	1464	9.0	106	461	735	12.9	3.45	104	.262	.322	10	21	102	**105**	.976	156	142	-.7	2.2	-4.8	.0	-1.8
CAL	**64**	15	17	1477[1]	1323	8.1	95	553	**992**	11.7	3.36	99	**.241**	.315	26	-5	95	96	.977	150	139	-.3	-.5	-7.6	-.9	4.5
CHI	54	10	22	1448	1460	9.1	87	600	802	13.0	4.25	84	.266	.342	-118	-111	101	92	.979	130	155	.7	-11.8	-4.2	-.4	-1.8
TOT	590	161	321	17468[1]		8.7				12.0	3.52		.256	.323					.977	1717	1821					

Runs		Hits		Doubles		Triples		Home Runs		Total Bases	
White-NY	104	Brett-KC	215	Otis-KC	40	Brett-KC	14	Nettles-NY	32	Brett-KC	298
Carew-Min	97	Carew-Min	200	McRae-KC	34	Garner-Oak	12	R.Jackson-Bal	27	Chambliss-NY	283
Rivers-NY	95	Chambliss-NY	188	Evans-Bos	34	Carew-Min	12	Bando-Oak	27	Rice-Bos	280
Brett-KC	94	Munson-NY	186	Carty-Cle	34	Poquette-KC	10			Carew-Min	280
		Rivers-NY	184	Brett-KC	34	Bostock-Min	9			Nettles-NY	277

Runs Batted In		Runs Produced		Bases On Balls		Batting Average		On Base Percentage		Slugging Average	
L.May-Bal	109	Carew-Min	178	Hargrove-Tex	97	Brett-KC	.333	McRae-KC	.412	R.Jackson-Bal	.502
Munson-NY	105	Munson-NY	167	Harrah-Tex	91	McRae-KC	.332	Hargrove-Tex	.401	Rice-Bos	.482
Yastrzemski-Bos	102	Hisle-Min	163	Grich-Bal	86	Carew-Min	.331	Carew-Min	.398	Nettles-NY	.475
		Otis-KC	161	White-NY	83	Bostock-Min	.323	Staub-Det	.392	Lynn-Bos	.467
				Staub-Det	83	LeFlore-Det	.316	Carty-Cle	.384	Carew-Min	.463

Production		Adjusted Production		Batter Runs		Adjusted Batter Runs		Clutch Hitting Index		Runs Created	
McRae-KC	.873	R.Jackson-Bal	158	Carew-Min	40.0	McRae-KC	38.1	Mayberry-KC	137	Brett-KC	114
Carew-Min	.861	McRae-KC	154	McRae-KC	38.8	Brett-KC	37.7	Rudi-Oak	131	Carew-Min	111
R.Jackson-Bal	.855	Tenace-Oak	150	Brett-KC	36.2	Brett-KC	35.4	L.May-Bal	127	McRae-KC	101
Brett-KC	.843	Carew-Min	149	Staub-Det	33.2	R.Jackson-Bal	34.3	Yastrzemski-Bos	124	Staub-Det	99
Lynn-Bos	.842	Brett-KC	145	Carty-Cle	29.8	Carty-Cle	30.8	Hisle-Min	124	White-NY	98

Total Average		Stolen Bases		Stolen Base Average		Stolen Base Runs		Fielding Runs		Total Player Rating	
McRae-KC	.862	North-Oak	75	Rivers-NY	86.0	Campaneris-Oak	9.0	White-KC	21.1	Nettles-NY	4.1
R.Jackson-Bal	.857	LeFlore-Det	58	Campaneris-Oak	81.8	Rivers-NY	8.7	Kuiper-Cle	20.0	Brett-KC	4.0
Tenace-Oak	.855	Campaneris-Oak	54	Baylor-Oak	81.3	Baylor-Oak	8.4	Beniquez-Tex	19.5	Grich-Bal	3.9
Carew-Min	.854	Baylor-Oak	52	Bumbry-Bal	80.8	Bumbry-Bal	6.6	Brohamer-Chi	18.0	R.Jackson-Bal	3.7
Brett-KC	.797	Patek-KC	51	R.Jackson-Bal	80.0	Patek-KC	6.3	Nettles-NY	17.2	Belanger-Bal	3.6

Wins		Win Percentage		Games		Complete Games		Shutouts		Saves	
Palmer-Bal	22	Campbell-Min	.773	Campbell-Min	78	Fidrych-Det	24	Ryan-Cal	7	Lyle-NY	23
Tiant-Bos	21	Garland-Bal	.741	Fingers-Oak	70	Tanana-Cal	23	Blyleven-Min-Tex	6	LaRoche-Cle	21
Garland-Bal	20	Ellis-NY	.680	Lindblad-Oak	65	Palmer-Bal	23	Palmer-Bal	6	Fingers-Oak	20
		Fidrych-Det	.679	Lyle-NY	64			Blue-Oak	6	Campbell-Min	20
				LaRoche-Cle	61					Littell-KC	16

Innings Pitched		Fewest Hits/Game		Fewest BB/Game		Strikeouts		Strikeouts/Game		Ratio	
Palmer-Bal	315.0	Ryan-Cal	6.11	Bird-KC	1.41	Ryan-Cal	327	Ryan-Cal	10.35	Tanana-Cal	9.18
Hunter-NY	298.2	Tanana-Cal	6.62	Jenkins-Bos	1.85	Tanana-Cal	261	Eckersley-Cle	9.03	Fidrych-Det	9.81
Blue-Oak	298.1	Eckersley-Cle	7.00	Perry-Tex	1.87	Blyleven-Min-Tex	219	Tanana-Cal	8.15	Palmer-Bal	9.91
Blyleven-Min-Tex	297.2	Palmer-Bal	7.29	Blue-Oak	1.90	Eckersley-Cle	200	Blyleven-Min-Tex	6.62	Blue-Oak	10.02
Slaton-Mil	292.2	Brett-NY-Chi	7.67	Fidrych-Det	1.91	Hunter-NY	173	Campbell-Min	6.17	Perry-Tex	10.21

Earned Run Average		Adjusted ERA		Opponents' Batting Avg.		Opponents' On Base Pct.		Starter Runs		Adjusted Starter Runs	
Fidrych-Det	2.34	Fidrych-Det	159	Ryan-Cal	.195	Tanana-Cal	.261	Blue-Oak	38.6	Fidrych-Det	38.1
Blue-Oak	2.35	Blue-Oak	142	Tanana-Cal	.203	Fidrych-Det	.279	Palmer-Bal	35.1	Blue-Oak	33.1
Tanana-Cal	2.43	Tanana-Cal	137	Eckersley-Cle	.214	Blue-Oak	.280	Tanana-Cal	34.7	Tanana-Cal	28.5
Torrez-Oak	2.50	Torrez-Oak	134	Palmer-Bal	.224	Palmer-Bal	.282	Fidrych-Det	32.8	Palmer-Bal	26.5
Palmer-Bal	2.51	Palmer-Bal	130	Brett-NY-Chi	.233	Bird-KC	.283	Torrez-Oak	30.1	Tiant-Bos	26.2

Clutch Pitching Index		Relief Runs		Adjusted Relief Runs		Relief Ranking		Total Pitcher Index		Total Baseball Ranking	
Hartzell-Cal	124	Littell-KC	16.7	Hiller-Det	17.9	Hiller-Det	30.9	Fidrych-Det	5.0	Fidrych-Det	5.0
Travers-Mil	120	Fingers-Oak	15.6	Littell-KC	16.4	Fingers-Oak	25.5	Palmer-Bal	3.6	Nettles-NY	4.1
Umbarger-Tex	118	Hiller-Det	15.3	Kern-Cle	14.6	Lyle-NY	24.0	Hiller-Det	3.3	Brett-KC	4.0
Garland-Bal	116	Kern-Cle	15.0	Thomas-Cle	14.0	Kern-Cle	23.2	Tanana-Cal	3.2	Grich-Bal	3.9
Torrez-Oak	115	Lyle-NY	14.5	Burgmeier-Min	13.8	Littell-KC	22.8	Blue-Oak	3.1	R.Jackson-Bal	3.7

January 2 Commissioner Kuhn suspends Braves owner Ted Turner for one year as a result of tampering charges in the Gary Matthews free-agency signing, but the Braves are permitted to keep the outfielder.

January 19 The BBWAA elects Ernie Banks to the Hall of Fame in his first year of eligibility.

January 31 The Special Veterans Committee selects Joe Sewell, Amos Rusie, and Al Lopez for the Hall of Fame.

February 3 The Hall of Fame's Special Committee on the Negro Leagues picks Martin Dihigo and John Lloyd for induction. The committee then dissolves, its functions being taken over by the Veterans Committee.

May 11 With the Braves mired in a 16-game losing streak, owner Ted Turner takes over as field manager. After the Braves lose again 2-1, Turner is relieved of his new job by NL president Chub Feeney. A league rule prohibits a manager from owning part of his club.

June 15 The Mets trade ace pitcher Tom Seaver to the Reds. In return they get pitcher Pat Zachry, infielder Doug Flynn, and minor leaguers Steve Henderson and Dan Norman. The Mets also trade slugger Dave Kingman to the Padres for utility player Bobby Valentine and a minor league pitcher.

July 19 At Yankee Stadium, the NL scores four times in the opening inning off Jim Palmer, en route to a 7-5 All-Star Game victory. Don Sutton, hurling three scoreless innings, is named MVP.

August 29 The Cardinals' Lou Brock steals second base in a 4-3 loss to the Padres. It is career steal 893 for Brock, breaking Ty Cobb's modern record.

September 3 Sadaharu Oh hits the 756th homer of his career to surpass Hank Aaron's total and make him the most prolific homer hitter in professional baseball history.

October 2 Dusty Baker homers in his final at bat of the season. It is Baker's 30th homer of the year, enabling him to join teammates Steve Garvey (33), Reggie Smith (32), and Ron Cey (30) in making the Dodgers the first team ever to boast four 30-homer hitters in one season.

October 7 Down 5-3 with two outs in the ninth inning, the Dodgers catch lightning in a bottle. Pinch hitter Vic Davalillo beats out a two-strike drag bunt, and pinch hitter Manny Mota follows with a long double. Los Angeles pulls out a 6-5 victory over the Phillies to win the NLCS.

November 2 The Phillies' Steve Carlton outpoints LA's Tommy John to win his second Cy Young Award. Carlton led the NL with 23 wins, losing 10, and posting a 2.64 ERA.

November 9 The Reds' George Foster wins the NL MVP Award.

November 22 Montreal's Andre Dawson wins the NL Rookie of the Year Award by one vote over New York's Steve Henderson.

	ATLANTA		CHICAGO		CINCINNATI		HOUSTON		LOS ANGELES		MONTREAL
M	D.Bristol	M	H.Franks	M	S.Anderson	M	B.Virdon	M	T.Lasorda	M	D.Williams
M	T.Turner	1B	B.Buckner	1B	D.Driessen	1B	B.Watson	1B	S.Garvey	1B	T.Perez
M	V.Benson	2B	M.Trillo	2B	J.Morgan	2B	A.Howe	2B	D.Lopes	2B	D.Cash
M	D.Bristol	SS	I.DeJesus	SS	D.Concepcion	SS	R.Metzger	SS	B.Russell	SS	C.Speier
1B	W.Montanez	3B	S.Ontiveros	3B	P.Rose	3B	E.Cabell	3B	R.Cey	3B	L.Parrish
2B	R.Gilbreath	LF	J.Cardenal	LF	G.Foster	LF	T.Puhl	LF	D.Baker	LF	W.Cromartie
SS	P.Rockett	CF	J.Morales	CF	C.Geronimo	CF	C.Cedeno	CF	R.Monday	CF	A.Dawson
3B	J.Moore	RF	B.Murcer	RF	K.Griffey	RF	J.Cruz	RF	R.Smith	RF	E.Valentine
LF	G.Matthews	C	G.Mitterwald	C	J.Bench	C	J.Ferguson	C	S.Yeager	C	G.Carter
CF	R.Office										
RF	J.Burroughs	1O	L.Biittner	P	F.Norman	S2	J.Gonzalez	P	D.Sutton	O1	D.Unser
C	B.Pocoroba	O	G.Gross	P	T.Seaver			P	B.Hooton		
		O	G.Clines	P	J.Billingham	P	J.Richard	P	T.John	P	S.Rogers
O3	B.Bonnell	C	S.Swisher	P	P.Moskau	P	M.Lemongello	P	R.Rhoden	P	J.Brown
3S	J.Royster			P	D.Capilla	P	J.Niekro	P	D.Rau	P	D.Stanhouse
S2	D.Chaney	P	R.Reuschel	RP	P.Borbon	P	J.Andujar	RP	C.Hough	P	W.Twitchell
		P	R.Burris	RP	D.Murray	P	F.Bannister	RP	E.Sosa	P	S.Bahnsen
P	P.Niekro	P	B.Bonham			RP	J.Sambito	RP	M.Garman	RP	J.Kerrigan
P	D.Ruthven	P	M.Krukow	P	W.Fryman	RP	G.Pentz			RP	W.McEnaney
P	B.Capra	RP	W.Hernandez	P	P.Zachry	RP	K.Forsch			RP	B.Atkinson
P	A.Messersmith	RP	B.Sutter	P	M.Soto						
RP	D.Campbell	RP	P.Reuschel			P	D.Larson			P	S.Alcala
RP	M.Leon					P	B.McLaughlin				
RP	R.Camp	P	D.Roberts								
		P	S.Renko								
P	E.Solomon										
P	D.Collins										
P	P.Hanna										
P	J.Easterly										

	NEW YORK		PHILADELPHIA		PITTSBURGH		SAN DIEGO		SAN FRANCISCO		ST.LOUIS
M	J.Frazier	M	D.Ozark	M	C.Tanner	M	J.McNamara	M	J.Altobelli	M	V.Rapp
M	J.Torre	1B	R.Hebner	1B	B.Robinson	M	B.Skinner	1B	W.McCovey	1B	K.Hernandez
1B	J.Milner	2B	T.Sizemore	2B	R.Stennett	M	A.Dark	2B	R.Andrews	2B	M.Tyson
2B	F.Millan	SS	L.Bowa	SS	F.Taveras	1B	M.Ivie	SS	T.Foli	SS	G.Templeton
SS	B.Harrelson	3B	M.Schmidt	3B	P.Garner	2B	M.Champion	3B	B.Madlock	3B	K.Reitz
3B	L.Randle	LF	G.Luzinski	LF	A.Oliver	SS	B.Almon	LF	G.Thomasson	LF	L.Brock
LF	S.Henderson	CF	G.Maddox	CF	O.Moreno	3B	T.Ashford	CF	D.Thomas	CF	J.Mumphrey
CF	L.Mazzilli	RF	J.Johnstone	RF	D.Parker	LF	G.Richards	RF	J.Clark	RF	H.Cruz
RF	M.Vail	C	B.Boone	C	D.Dyer	CF	G.Hendrick	C	M.Hill	C	T.Simmons
C	J.Stearns					RF	D.Winfield				
		1	T.Hutton	C	E.Ott	C	G.Tenace	O1	D.Evans	O	T.Scott
O1	E.Kranepool	O	J.Martin					O	T.Whitfield		
O	B.Boisclair	O	B.McBride	P	J.Candelaria	O	M.Rettenmund			P	E.Rasmussen
S2	D.Flynn			P	J.Reuss	O	J.Turner	P	E.Halicki	P	B.Forsch
O1	D.Kingman	P	S.Carlton	P	J.Rooker			P	J.Barr	P	J.Denny
		P	L.Christenson	P	B.Kison	P	B.Shirley	P	B.Knepper	P	J.Urrea
P	J.Koosman	P	R.Lerch	P	O.Jones	P	B.Owchinko	P	J.Montefusco	P	P.Falcone
P	N.Espinosa	P	J.Kaat	RP	R.Gossage	P	T.Griffin	RP	C.Williams	RP	B.Metzger
P	J.Matlack	P	J.Lonborg	RP	K.Tekulve	P	R.Jones	RP	G.Lavelle	RP	C.Carroll
P	C.Swan	RP	R.Reed	RP	G.Jackson	RP	D.Freisleben	RP	D.Heaverlo	RP	A.Hrabosky
P	P.Zachry	RP	G.Garber			RP	R.Fingers				
RP	S.Lockwood	P	T.McGraw	P	L.Demery	RP	D.Spillner	P	R.Moffitt	P	T.Underwood
RP	B.Myrick			P	T.Forster	RP	R.Sawyer	P	L.McGlothen	P	B.Schultz
RP	B.Apodaca	P	W.Brusstar					P	J.Curtis	P	R.Eastwick
						P	D.Tomlin				
P	T.Seaver					P	D.Wehrmeister				
P	J.Todd										
P	R.Baldwin										

TEAM	G	W	L	PCT	GB	R	OR	AB	H	2B	3B	HR	BB	SO	AVG	OBP	SLG	PRO	PRO+	BR	/A	PF	CHI	RC	SB	CS	SBA	SBR
EAST																												
PHI	162	101	61	.623		847	668	5546	1548	266	56	186	573	806	.279	.351	.448	.799	114	143	105	104	98	865	135	68	67	0
PIT	162	96	66	.593	5	734	665	5662	1550	278	57	133	474	878	.274	.334	.413	.747	102	37	17	103	98	776	260	120	68	6
STL	162	83	79	.512	18	737	688	5527	1490	252	56	96	489	823	.270	.332	.388	.720	100	-13	-1	98	107	690	134	112	54	-27
CHI	162	81	81	.500	20	692	739	5604	1489	271	37	111	534	796	.266	.333	.387	.720	88	-11	-90	111	98	709	64	45	59	-8
MON	162	75	87	.463	26	665	736	5675	1474	294	50	138	478	877	.260	.320	.402	.722	101	-20	0	97	95	715	88	50	64	-4
NY	162	64	98	.395	37	587	663	5410	1319	227	30	88	529	887	.244	.315	.346	.661	87	-125	-99	95	103	577	98	81	55	-19
WEST																												
LA	162	98	64	.605		769	582	5589	1484	223	28	191	563	896	.266	.338	.418	.756	109	58	62	100	98	794	114	62	65	-3
CIN	162	88	74	.543	10	802	725	5524	1513	269	42	181	600	911	.274	.348	.436	.784	113	115	100	102	97	847	170	64	73	13
HOU	162	81	81	.500	17	680	650	5530	1405	263	60	114	515	839	.254	.322	.385	.707	104	-41	18	91	102	697	187	72	72	13
SF	162	75	87	.463	23	673	711	5497	1392	227	41	134	568	842	.253	.326	.383	.709	95	-35	-32	100	100	683	90	59	60	-8
SD	162	69	93	.426	29	692	834	5602	1397	245	49	120	602	1057	.249	.325	.375	.700	104	-49	21	90	102	700	133	57	70	6
ATL	162	61	101	.377	37	678	895	5534	1404	218	20	139	537	876	.254	.322	.376	.698	82	-58	-136	112	104	660	82	53	61	-7
TOT	972					8556		66700	17465	3033	526	1631	6487	10488	.262	.330	.396	.727							1555	843	65	-39

TEAM	CG	SH	SV	IP	H	H/G	HR	BB	SO	RAT	ERA	ERA+	OAV	OOB	PR	/A	PF	CPI	FA	E	DP	FW	PW	BW	SBW	DIF
EAST																										
PHI	31	7	47	1455²	1451	9.0	134	482	856	12.1	3.71	108	.263	.325	32	47	102	103	.981	120	168	1.3	4.8	10.6	.3	3.0
PIT	25	15	39	1481²	1406	8.5	149	485	890	11.6	3.61	110	.252	.314	50	62	102	99	.977	145	137	-.0	6.3	1.7	.9	6.1
STL	26	10	31	1446	1420	8.8	139	532	768	12.3	3.81	101	.260	.329	16	6	98	102	.978	139	174	.3	.6	-.1	-2.4	3.6
CHI	16	10	44	1468	1500	9.2	128	489	942	12.3	4.01	100	.266	.327	-16	61	112	96	.977	153	147	-.5	6.2	-9.1	-.5	3.9
MON	31	11	33	1481	1426	8.7	135	579	856	12.3	4.01	95	.255	.327	-17	-34	97	94	.980	129	128	.8	-3.4	.0	-.0	-3.3
NY	27	12	28	1433²	1378	8.7	118	490	911	11.9	3.77	99	.254	.319	22	-6	96	94	.978	134	132	.5	-.6	-10.0	-1.6	-5.3
WEST																										
LA	34	13	39	1475¹	1393	8.5	119	438	930	11.3	3.22	119	.251	.309	113	99	98	104	.981	124	160	1.1	10.0	6.3	.0	-.4
CIN	33	12	32	1437¹	1469	9.2	156	544	868	12.8	4.21	93	.267	.337	-49	-46	101	100	.984	95	154	2.7	-4.7	10.1	1.6	-2.8
HOU	37	11	28	1465²	1384	8.5	110	545	871	12.0	3.54	101	.251	.321	61	5	91	99	.978	142	136	.0	.5	1.8	1.6	-4.1
SF	27	10	33	1459	1501	9.3	114	529	854	12.7	3.75	104	.267	.333	26	26	100	104	.972	179	136	-2.0	2.6	-3.2	-.5	-2.9
SD	6	5	44	1466¹	1556	9.6	160	673	827	13.8	4.43	80	.276	.355	-85	-146	91	105	.971	189	142	-2.5	-14.8	2.1	.9	2.2
ATL	28	5	31	1445¹	1581	9.8	169	701	915	14.5	4.85	92	.279	.363	-151	-65	114	101	.972	175	127	-1.7	-6.6	-13.8	-.4	2.5
TOT	321	121	429	17515		9.0				12.5	3.91		.262	.330					.977	1724	1741					

Runs		Hits		Doubles		Triples		Home Runs		Total Bases	
Foster-Cin	124	Parker-Pit	215	Parker-Pit	44	Templeton-StL	18	Foster-Cin	52	Foster-Cin	388
Griffey-Cin	117	Rose-Cin	204	Cash-Mon	42	Schmidt-Phi	11	Burroughs-Atl	41	Parker-Pit	338
Schmidt-Phi	114	Templeton-StL	200	Hernandez-StL	41	Richards-SD	11	Luzinski-Phi	39	Luzinski-Phi	329
Morgan-Cin	113	Foster-Cin	197	Cromartie-Mon	41	Almon-SD	11	Schmidt-Phi	38	Garvey-LA	322
Parker-Pit	107	Garvey-LA	192					Garvey-LA	33	Schmidt-Phi	312

Runs Batted In		Runs Produced		Bases On Balls		Batting Average		On Base Percentage		Slugging Average	
Foster-Cin	149	Foster-Cin	221	Tenace-SD	125	Parker-Pit	.338	Smith-LA	.432	Foster-Cin	.631
Luzinski-Phi	130	Luzinski-Phi	190	Morgan-Cin	117	Templeton-StL	.322	Morgan-Cin	.420	Luzinski-Phi	.594
Garvey-LA	115	Schmidt-Phi	177	Smith-LA	104	Foster-Cin	.320	Tenace-SD	.417	Smith-LA	.576
Burroughs-Atl	114	Parker-Pit	174	Schmidt-Phi	104	Griffey-Cin	.318	Simmons-StL	.410	Schmidt-Phi	.574
		Garvey-LA	173	Cey-LA	93	Simmons-StL	.318	Parker-Pit	.399	Bench-Cin	.540

Production		Adjusted Production		Batter Runs		Adjusted Batter Runs		Clutch Hitting Index		Runs Created	
Foster-Cin	1.017	Smith-LA	168	Foster-Cin	56.0	Foster-Cin	53.6	Watson-Hou	121	Foster-Cin	144
Smith-LA	1.008	Foster-Cin	165	Smith-LA	50.3	Smith-LA	50.9	Cey-LA	116	Luzinski-Phi	132
Luzinski-Phi	.993	Luzinski-Phi	155	Luzinski-Phi	48.6	Luzinski-Phi	43.3	Bench-Cin	114	Parker-Pit	130
Schmidt-Phi	.972	Schmidt-Phi	151	Schmidt-Phi	45.8	Schmidt-Phi	40.5	Robinson-Pit	114	Schmidt-Phi	129
Parker-Pit	.929	Hendrick-SD	148	Parker-Pit	42.0	Parker-Pit	38.7	Evans-SF	114	Smith-LA	129

Total Average		Stolen Bases		Stolen Base Average		Stolen Base Runs		Fielding Runs		Total Player Rating	
Smith-LA	1.121	Taveras-Pit	70	Bowa-Phi	91.4	Taveras-Pit	10.2	DeJesus-Chi	35.8	Schmidt-Phi	6.7
Morgan-Cin	1.054	Cedeno-Hou	61	McBride-StL-Phi	83.7	Cedeno-Hou	9.9	Parker-Pit	32.5	Foster-Cin	6.1
Schmidt-Phi	1.046	Richards-SD	56	Morgan-Cin	83.1	Richards-SD	9.6	Trillo-Chi	30.1	Parker-Pit	5.8
Luzinski-Phi	1.043	Moreno-Pit	53	Richards-SD	82.4	Morgan-Cin	8.7	Schmidt-Phi	28.8	Hendrick-SD	3.8
Foster-Cin	1.039	Morgan-Cin	49	Cedeno-Hou	81.3	Bowa-Phi	7.8	Tyson-StL	22.0	Smith-LA	3.7

Wins		Win Percentage		Games		Complete Games		Shutouts		Saves	
Carlton-Phi	23	Candelaria-Pit	.800	Fingers-SD	78	Niekro-Atl	20	Seaver-NY-Cin	7	Fingers-SD	35
Seaver-NY-Cin	21	Seaver-NY-Cin	.778	Tomlin-SD	76	Seaver-NY-Cin	19	Rogers-Mon	4	Sutter-Chi	31
		Christenson-Phi	.760	Spillner-SD	76	Rogers-Mon	17	R.Reuschel-Chi	4	Gossage-Pit	26
		John-LA	.741	Metzger-SD-StL	75	Carlton-Phi	17			Hough-LA	22
		Forsch-StL	.741			Richard-Hou	13				

Innings Pitched		Fewest Hits/Game		Fewest BB/Game		Strikeouts		Strikeouts/Game		Ratio	
Niekro-Atl	330.1	Seaver-NY-Cin	6.85	Candelaria-Pit	1.95	Niekro-Atl	262	Koosman-NY	7.62	Seaver-NY-Cin	9.13
Rogers-Mon	301.2	Richard-Hou	7.15	John-LA	2.04	Richard-Hou	214	Richard-Hou	7.21	Candelaria-Pit	9.72
Carlton-Phi	283.0	Carlton-Phi	7.28	Rau-LA	2.08	Rogers-Mon	206	Niekro-Atl	7.14	Hooton-LA	9.95
Richard-Hou	267.0	Hooton-LA	7.41	Barr-SF	2.15	Carlton-Phi	198	Seaver-NY-Cin	6.75	Carlton-Phi	10.24
Seaver-NY-Cin	261.1	Candelaria-Pit	7.69	Lemongello-Hou	2.18	Seaver-NY-Cin	196	Matlack-NY	6.55	Sutton-LA	10.45

Earned Run Average		Adjusted ERA		Opponents' Batting Avg.		Opponents' On Base Pct.		Starter Runs		Adjusted Starter Runs	
Candelaria-Pit	2.34	Candelaria-Pit	170	Seaver-NY-Cin	.209	Seaver-NY-Cin	.260	Candelaria-Pit	40.2	R.Reuschel-Chi	44.8
Seaver-NY-Cin	2.58	R.Reuschel-Chi	157	Richard-Hou	.218	Candelaria-Pit	.276	Carlton-Phi	39.9	Carlton-Phi	42.7
Hooton-LA	2.62	Carlton-Phi	151	Carlton-Phi	.223	Hooton-LA	.281	Seaver-NY-Cin	38.5	Candelaria-Pit	42.1
Carlton-Phi	2.64	Seaver-NY-Cin	149	Hooton-LA	.225	Carlton-Phi	.287	Hooton-LA	32.0	Seaver-NY-Cin	37.0
John-LA	2.78	Hooton-LA	146	Koosman-NY	.232	Sutton-LA	.291	R.Reuschel-Chi	31.4	Hooton-LA	29.9

Clutch Pitching Index		Relief Runs		Adjusted Relief Runs		Relief Ranking		Total Pitcher Index		Total Baseball Ranking	
Candelaria-Pit	126	Gossage-Pit	33.8	Sutter-Chi	36.3	Gossage-Pit	61.1	Gossage-Pit	6.4	Schmidt-Phi	6.7
John-LA	120	Sutter-Chi	30.6	Gossage-Pit	34.9	Sutter-Chi	51.8	Carlton-Phi	6.0	Gossage-Pit	6.4
Rooker-Pit	118	Lavelle-SF	24.4	Lavelle-SF	24.4	Lavelle-SF	34.4	R.Reuschel-Chi	5.8	Foster-Cin	6.1
Lemongello-Hou	116	Garber-Phi	17.9	Garber-Phi	18.9	Garber-Phi	30.2	Sutter-Chi	5.6	Carlton-Phi	6.0
Rau-LA	114	Reed-Phi	16.0	Reed-Phi	17.2	W.Hernandez-Chi	21.6	Candelaria-Pit	4.7	R.Reuschel-Chi	5.8

January 4 Mary Shane is hired by the Chicago White Sox as the first woman TV play-by-play announcer.

March 21 Mark Fidrych, the 1976 Rookie of the Year, rips the cartilage in his left knee and will undergo surgery ten days later. The injury will effectively end the fabled career of the Bird.

March 28 The Rangers' Lenny Randle, angry for having been benched during spring training, attacks 50-year-old manager Frank Lucchesi, sending him to the hospital with a shattered cheekbone. Lucchesi helped precipitate the incident by calling the good-natured Randle "a punk." Randle's days in Texas are numbered.

April 6 The Seattle Mariners make their debut, losing to Frank Tanana and the Angels 7-0.

April 7 Al Woods hits a pinch home run in his first major league at bat and the Toronto Blue Jays make a successful debut in a 9-5 win over the White Sox at Exhibition Stadium.

May 14 Jim Colborn hurls a no-hit game as Kansas City beats Texas, 6-0.

May 30 Twenty-two-year-old Dennis Eckersley fires a no-hitter as the Indians top the Angels 1-0.

June 7 The White Sox select Harold Baines with the number one pick in the draft. Bill Veeck had first seen Baines play Little League ball and had followed his career.

June 8 Nolan Ryan notches his fourth career 19-strikeout game, hurling the first 10 innings of a game against Toronto.

July 4 The Red Sox wallop a major league-record eight home runs, including seven solo shots, in beating Toronto, 9-6, at Fenway. Four home runs come in the eighth inning.

July 24 Seattle's John Montague pitches $6\tfrac{1}{3}$ innings of perfect relief against California, giving him 33 consecutive batsmen retired over two games to tie the AL record.

September 9 In the second game of a doubleheader in Boston, Tiger rookies Lou Whitaker and Allan Trammell debut together. They will hold down the second base and shortstop jobs in Detroit for a record 19 years.

September 16 Seattle beats Kansas City 4-1 to end the Royals' winning streak at 16 games—the longest in the majors in 24 years.

September 18 Boston's Ted Cox goes 4-for-4 in his first major league game, a 10-4 win over the Orioles to spoil Brooks Robinson Night in Baltimore. Cox will get two more hits the following day against the Yankees, setting a major league record for consecutive hits at the start of a career.

October 9 For the second year in succession, the Yanks score in the ninth inning of the fifth game to beat the Royals in the LCS. Mickey Rivers gets the game-winning hit.

October 11 The Yankees win the opening game of the World Series 4-3 in 12 innings as Willie Randolph doubles and scores the winning run on a single by Paul Blair.

October 18 Reggie Jackson becomes "Mr. October." Three homers in three swings lead the Yankees to an 8-4, Series-clinching victory.

BALTIMORE	BOSTON	CALIFORNIA	CHICAGO	CLEVELAND	DETROIT	KANSAS CITY
M E.Weaver	M D.Zimmer	M N.Sherry	M B.Lemon	M F.Robinson	M R.Houk	M W.Herzog
1B L.May	1B G.Scott	1B D.Garcia	1B J.Spencer	M J.Torborg	1B J.Thompson	1B J.Mayberry
2B B.Smith	2B D.Doyle	1B T.Solaita	2B J.Orta	1B A.Thornton	2B T.Fuentes	2B F.White
SS M.Belanger	SS R.Burleson	2B J.Remy	SS A.Bannister	2B D.Kuiper	SS T.Veryzer	SS F.Patek
3B D.DeCinces	3B B.Hobson	SS R.Mulliniks	3B E.Soderholm	SS F.Duffy	3B A.Rodriguez	3B G.Brett
LF P.Kelly	LF C.Yastrzemski	3B D.Chalk	LF R.Garr	3B B.Bell	LF S.Kemp	LF T.Poquette
CF A.Bumbry	CF F.Lynn	LF J.Rudi	CF C.Lemon	LF B.Bochte	CF R.LeFlore	CF A.Otis
RF K.Singleton	RF R.Miller	CF G.Flores	RF R.Zisk	CF J.Norris	RF B.Oglivie	RF A.Cowens
C R.Dempsey	C C.Fisk	RF B.Bonds	C J.Essian	RF P.Dade	C M.May	C D.Porter
DH E.Murray	DH J.Rice	C T.Humphrey	DH O.Gamble	C F.Kendall	DH R.Staub	DH H.McRae
1O T.Muser	O D.Evans	DH D.Baylor	D1 L.Johnson	DH R.Carty	3 P.Mankowski	O J.Zdeb
2 R.Dauer	O B.Carbo	13 R.Jackson		S3 L.Blanks	O M.Stanley	1D P.LaCock
O A.Mora	SD M.Guerrero	O T.Bosley	P F.Barrios	O R.Manning	P D.Rozema	P D.Leonard
C D.Skaggs	P F.Jenkins	P N.Ryan	P S.Stone	C R.Fosse	P F.Arroyo	P J.Colborn
P J.Palmer	P R.Cleveland	P F.Tanana	P K.Kravec	O R.Pruitt	P B.Sykes	P P.Splittorff
P R.May	P L.Tiant	P P.Hartzell	P C.Knapp	P W.Garland	P D.Roberts	P A.Hassler
P M.Flanagan	P B.Stanley	P K.Brett	P W.Wood	P D.Eckersley	P J.Crawford	P M.Pattin
P R.Grimsley	P R.Wise	P W.Simpson	RP L.LaGrow	P J.Bibby	RP J.Hiller	RP D.Bird
P D.Martinez	RP B.Campbell	RP D.Miller	RP D.Hamilton	P R.Waits	RP S.Foucault	RP L.Gura
RP T.Martinez	RP J.Willoughby	RP D.LaRoche	P B.Johnson	P A.Fitzmorris	RP S.Grilli	RP M.Littell
P S.McGregor	P B.Lee	RP M.Barlow	P K.Brett	RP D.Hood	P M.Wilcox	P S.Mingori
	P M.Paxton	P G.Ross	/P S.Renko	RP J.Kern	P M.Fidrych	
	P D.Aase			P P.Dobson	P V.Ruhle	

MILWAUKEE	MINNESOTA	NEW YORK	OAKLAND	SEATTLE	TEXAS	TORONTO
M A.Grammas	M G.Mauch	M B.Martin	M J.McKeon	M D.Johnson	M F.Lucchesi	M R.Hartsfield
1B C.Cooper	1B R.Carew	1B C.Chambliss	M B.Winkles	1B D.Meyer	M E.Stanky	1B D.Ault
2B D.Money	2B B.Randall	2B W.Randolph	1B D.Allen	2B J.Baez	C R.Ryan	2B S.Staggs
SS R.Yount	SS R.Smalley	SS B.Dent	2B M.Perez	SS C.Reynolds	M B.Hunter	SS H.Torres
3B S.Bando	3B M.Cubbage	3B G.Nettles	SS R.Picciolo	3B B.Stein	1B M.Hargrove	3B R.Howell
LF J.Wohlford	LF L.Hisle	LF R.White	3B W.Gross	LF S.Braun	2B B.Wills	LF A.Woods
CF V.Joshua	CF L.Bostock	CF M.Rivers	LF M.Page	CF Ru.Jones	SS B.Campaneris	CF B.Bailor
RF S.Lezcano	RF D.Ford	RF R.Jackson	CF T.Armas	RF L.Stanton	3B T.Harrah	RF O.Velez
C C.Moore	C B.Wynegar	C T.Munson	RF J.Tyrone	C B.Stinson	LF C.Washington	C A.Ashby
DH J.Quirk	DH C.Kusick	DH C.May	C J.Newman	DH J.Bernhardt	CF J.Beniquez	DH R.Fairly
O S.Brye	DO R.Chiles	OD L.Piniella	DH M.Sanguillen	OD D.Collins	RF D.May	OD S.Ewing
	DO G.Adams		2S R.Scott	O C.Lopez	C J.Sundberg	3D D.Rader
	32 J.Terrell		DC E.Williams	2S L.Milbourne	DH W.Horton	23 D.McKay
P J.Slaton		P E.Figueroa	1O M.Jorgensen		O K.Henderson	O J.Scott
P J.Augustine	P D.Goltz	P M.Torrez		P G.Abbott	OD T.Grieve	O G.Woods
P M.Haas	P P.Thormodsgard	P R.Guidry	P V.Blue	P J.Montague		
P E.Rodriguez	P G.Zahn	P D.Gullett	P R.Langford	P D.Pole	P G.Perry	P D.Lemanczyk
P L.Sorensen	RP P.Redfern	P D.Tidrow	P D.Medich	RP E.Romo	P D.Alexander	P J.Garvin
RP S.Hinds	RP T.Johnson	RP S.Lyle	RP J.Coleman	RP D.Segui	P B.Blyleven	P J.Jefferson
RP B.McClure	RP R.Schueler	RP K.Clay	RP B.Lacey	RP M.Kekich	P D.Ellis	RP P.Vuckovich
RP B.Castro	RP T.Burgmeier	P C.Hunter	RP P.Torrealba	P T.House	P N.Briles	RP M.Willis
P B.Travers	P D.Johnson	P K.Holtzman	P D.Bair	P G.Wheelock	P A.Devine	RP J.Johnson
P M.Caldwell			P M.Norris	P B.Laxton	RP P.Lindblad	P J.Byrd
P G.Beare			P D.Giusti	P D.Pagan	RP G.Knowles	P J.Clancy
				P S.Thomas	P R.Moret	P B.Singer
						P T.Murphy

TEAM	G	W	L	PCT	GB	R	OR	AB	H	2B	3B	HR	BB	SO	AVG	OBP	SLG	PRO	PRO+	BR	/A	PF	CHI	RC	SB	CS	SBA	SBR
EAST																												
NY	162	100	62	.617		831	**651**	5605	1576	267	47	184	533	681	.281	.347	.444	.791	115	104	**113**	99	98	853	93	57	62	-6
BAL	161	97	64	.602	2.5	719	653	5494	1433	231	25	148	560	945	.261	.332	.393	.725	103	-23	21	94	102	711	90	51	64	-4
BOS	161	97	64	.602	2.5	859	712	5510	1551	258	56	**213**	528	905	.281	.349	**.465**	**.814**	107	**144**	43	112	98	**875**	66	47	58	-8
DET	162	74	88	.457	26	714	751	5604	1480	228	45	166	452	764	.264	.321	.410	.731	93	-25	-62	105	101	717	60	46	57	-10
CLE	161	71	90	.441	28.5	676	739	5491	1476	221	46	100	531	688	.269	.337	.380	.717	98	-31	-9	97	96	682	87	87	50	-26
MIL	162	67	95	.414	33	639	765	5517	1425	255	46	125	443	862	.258	.316	.389	.705	91	-73	-72	100	99	660	85	67	56	-15
TOR	161	54	107	.335	45.5	605	822	5418	1367	230	41	100	499	819	.252	.318	.365	.683	85	-106	-115	101	99	610	65	55	54	-14
WEST																												
KC	162	102	60	.630		822	**651**	5594	1549	**299**	**77**	146	522	687	.277	.343	.436	.779	110	82	75	101	100	835	170	87	**66**	**-1**
TEX	162	94	68	.580	8	767	657	5541	1497	265	39	135	**596**	904	.270	.345	.405	.750	103	34	26	101	98	780	154	85	64	-5
CHI	162	90	72	.556	12	844	771	5633	1568	254	52	192	559	**666**	.278	.347	.444	.791	110	107	109	100	99	858	42	44	49	-14
MIN	161	84	77	.522	17.5	**867**	776	5639	**1588**	273	60	123	563	754	**.282**	**.351**	.417	.768	110	71	83	99	105	827	105	65	62	-8
CAL	162	74	88	.457	28	675	695	5410	1380	233	40	131	542	880	.255	.327	.386	.713	97	-47	-20	96	100	681	159	89	64	-6
SEA	162	64	98	.395	38	624	855	5460	1398	218	33	133	426	769	.256	.314	.381	.695	89	-91	-85	99	100	643	110	67	62	-2
OAK	161	63	98	.391	38.5	605	749	5358	1284	176	37	117	516	910	.240	.311	.352	.663	81	-145	-137	99	**107**	589	176	89	**66**	**-1**
TOT	1131					10247		77274	20572	3408	644	2013	7270	11234	.266	.333	.405	.738							1462	936	61	-123

TEAM	CG	SH	SV	IP	H	H/G	HR	BB	SO	RAT	ERA	ERA+	OAV	OOB	PR	/A	PF	CPI	FA	E	DP	FW	PW	BW	SBW	DIF
EAST																										
NY	52	16	34	1449^{1}	1395	8.7	139	486	758	11.8	3.61	109	.254	.318	73	54	97	101	.979	132	151	.6	5.4	**11.2**	.3	1.5
BAL	**65**	11	23	1451	1414	8.8	124	494	737	12.0	3.74	101	.260	.325	51	8	93	101	**.983**	**106**	189	**2.0**	.8	2.1	.5	11.1
BOS	40	13	40	1428	1555	9.8	158	**378**	758	12.3	4.11	109	.278	.327	-8	60	111	102	.978	133	162	.5	6.0	4.3	.0	5.7
DET	44	3	23	1457	1526	9.4	162	470	784	12.5	4.13	104	.271	.329	-11	26	106	100	.979	142	153	.0	2.6	-6.2	-.1	-3.3
CLE	45	8	30	1452^{1}	1441	8.9	136	550	876	12.5	4.10	96	.261	.331	-6	-25	97	96	.979	130	145	.7	-2.5	-.9	-.7	-5.1
MIL	38	6	25	1431	1461	9.2	136	566	719	13.0	4.32	94	.268	.341	-42	-40	100	99	.978	139	165	.2	-4.0	-7.2	-.6	-2.5
TOR	40	3	20	1428^{1}	1538	9.7	152	623	771	13.7	4.57	92	.278	.354	-81	-59	103	101	.974	164	133	-1.2	-5.9	-11.4	-.5	-7.4
WEST																										
KC	41	15	**42**	1460^{2}	**1377**	8.5	110	499	850	11.8	**3.52**	115	.251	.318	88	84	99	98	.978	137	145	.3	**8.3**	7.5	**.8**	4.1
TEX	49	**17**	31	1472^{1}	1412	8.6	134	471	864	**11.7**	3.56	114	.255	**.317**	81	**84**	101	101	.982	117	156	1.5	**8.3**	2.6	.4	.2
CHI	34	3	40	1444^{2}	1557	9.7	136	516	842	13.2	4.25	96	.277	.342	-31	-27	101	101	.974	159	125	-.9	-2.7	10.8	-.5	2.3
MIN	35	4	15	1442	1546	9.6	151	507	737	13.0	4.36	91	.278	.342	-48	-60	98	101	.979	143	184	-.0	-6.0	8.2	.0	1.2
CAL	53	13	26	1437^{2}	1383	8.7	136	572	**965**	12.5	3.72	105	.256	.333	54	31	96	**105**	.976	147	137	-.2	3.1	-2.0	.3	-8.1
SEA	18	1	31	1433	1508	9.5	194	578	785	13.5	4.83	85	.272	.347	-123	-114	101	96	.976	147	162	-.2	-11.3	-8.4	.2	2.8
OAK	32	4	26	1436^{1}	1459	9.4	145	560	788	12.8	4.04	100	.256	.336	3	-3	99	102	.970	190	136	-2.7	-.3	-13.6	.8	-1.6
TOT	586	117	416	20224		9.2				12.6	4.06		.266	.333					.977	1986	2143					

Runs
Carew-Min 128
Fisk-Bos 106
Brett-KC 105

Hits
Carew-Min 239
LeFlore-Det 212
Rice-Bos 206
Bostock-Min 199
Burleson-Bos 194

Doubles
McRae-KC 54
Jackson-NY 39
Lemon-Chi 38
Carew-Min 38

Triples
Carew-Min 16
Rice-Bos 15
Cowens-KC 14
Brett-KC 13
Bostock-Min 12

Home Runs
Rice-Bos 39
Nettles-NY 37
Bonds-Cal 37
Scott-Bos 33
Jackson-NY 32

Total Bases
Rice-Bos 382
Carew-Min 351
McRae-KC 330
Cowens-KC 318
LeFlore-Det 310

Runs Batted In
Hisle-Min 119
Bonds-Cal 115
Rice-Bos 114
Hobson-Bos 112
Cowens-KC 112

Runs Produced
Carew-Min 214
Cowens-KC 187
Hisle-Min 186
Fisk-Bos 182
Bonds-Cal 181

Bases On Balls
Harrah-Tex 109
Singleton-Bal 107
Hargrove-Tex 103
Gross-Oak 86
Mayberry-KC 83

Batting Average
Carew-Min .... .388
Bostock-Min ...... .336
Singleton-Bal .... .328
Rivers-NY .... .326
LeFlore-Det ...... .325

On Base Percentage
Carew-Min .... .452
Singleton-Bal .... .442
Hargrove-Tex ..... .424
Fisk-Bos .... .408
Page-Oak .... .407

Slugging Average
Rice-Bos .... .593
Carew-Min .... .570
Jackson-NY .... .550
Hisle-Min .... .533
Brett-KC .... .532

Production
Carew-Min 1.022
Rice-Bos .... .972
Singleton-Bal .... .949
Fisk-Bos .... .929
Page-Oak .... .928

Adjusted Production
Carew-Min 179
Singleton-Bal 168
Page-Oak 153
Jackson-NY 151
Thornton-Cle .....

Batter Runs
Carew-Min 67.0
Rice-Bos 51.4
Singleton-Bal 48.5
Fisk-Bos 39.9
Hargrove-Tex 37.8

Adjusted Batter Runs
Carew-Min 69.3
Singleton-Bal 56.5
Page-Oak 39.0
Bostock-Min 37.6
Jackson-NY 36.8

Clutch Hitting Index
Wynegar-Min 130
Doyle-Bos 128
Sundberg-Tex 128
Carty-Cle 123
Staub-Det 116

Runs Created
Carew-Min 160
Rice-Bos 136
Singleton-Bal 124
McRae-KC 119
Page-Oak 117

Total Average
Carew-Min 1.093
Page-Oak 1.064
Singleton-Bal ... 1.011
Jackson-NY .... .997
Harrah-Tex .... .964

Stolen Bases
Patek-KC 53
Page-Oak 42
Remy-Cal 41
Bonds-Cal 41
LeFlore-Det 39

Stolen Base Average
Page-Oak 89.4
Jackson-NY 85.0
Harrah-Tex 84.4
White-KC 82.1
Patek-KC 80.3

Stolen Base Runs
Page-Oak 9.6
Patek-KC 8.1
Harrah-Tex 5.1
White-KC 3.9

Fielding Runs
Lemon-Chi 34.9
Sundberg-Tex 22.9
R.Jones-Sea 22.0
Belanger-Bal 20.7
Smalley-Min 18.7

Total Player Rating
Carew-Min 6.3
Singleton-Bal 4.9
Page-Oak 4.9
Brett-KC 4.4
Lemon-Chi 4.0

Wins
Palmer-Bal 20
Leonard-KC 20
Goltz-Min 20
Ryan-Cal 19

Win Percentage
Splittorff-KC .... .727
T.Johnson-Min .... .696
Guidry-NY .... .696
Rozema-Det .... .682

Games
Lyle-NY 72
T.Johnson-Min 71
Campbell-Bos 69
McClure-Mil 68
LaGrow-Chi 66

Complete Games
Ryan-Cal 22
Palmer-Bal 22
Leonard-KC 21
Garland-Cle 21
Tanana-Cal 20

Shutouts
Tanana-Cal 7
Leonard-KC 5
Guidry-NY 5
Blyleven-Tex 5

Saves
Campbell-Bos 31
Lyle-NY 26
LaGrow-Chi 25
Kern-Cle 18
LaRoche-Cle-Cal .. 17

Innings Pitched
Palmer-Bal 319.0
Goltz-Min 303.0
Ryan-Cal 299.0
Leonard-KC 292.2
Garland-Cle 282.2

Fewest Hits/Game
Ryan-Cal 5.96
Blyleven-Tex 6.94
Palmer-Bal 7.42
Guidry-NY 7.43
Tanana-Cal 7.50

Fewest BB/Game
Rozema-Det 1.40
Jenkins-Bos 1.68
Hartzell-Cal 1.81
Eckersley-Cle 1.96
Cleveland-Bos 2.03

Strikeouts
Ryan-Cal 341
Leonard-KC 244
Tanana-Cal 205
Palmer-Bal 193
Eckersley-Cle 191

Strikeouts/Game
Ryan-Cal 10.26
Tanana-Cal 7.65
Guidry-NY 7.52
Leonard-KC 7.50
Blyleven-Tex 6.98

Ratio
Blyleven-Tex 9.86
Eckersley-Cle ... 10.01
Guidry-NY 10.21
Tanana-Cal 10.22
Leonard-KC 10.24

Earned Run Average
Tanana-Cal 2.54
Blyleven-Tex 2.72
Ryan-Cal 2.77
Guidry-NY 2.82
Palmer-Bal 2.91

Adjusted ERA
Tanana-Cal 154
Blyleven-Tex 150
Ryan-Cal 141
Guidry-NY 140
Rozema-Det 139

Opponents' Batting Avg.
Ryan-Cal .... .193
Blyleven-Tex ..... .214
Guidry-NY .... .224
Tanana-Cal .... .227
Leonard-KC .... .227

Opponents' On Base Pct.
Eckersley-Cle .... .278
Blyleven-Tex ..... .279
Guidry-NY .... .284
Leonard-KC .... .285
Tanana-Cal .... .286

Starter Runs
Ryan-Cal 42.8
Palmer-Bal 40.8
Tanana-Cal 40.8
Blyleven-Tex 34.8
Leonard-KC 33.0

Adjusted Starter Runs
Ryan-Cal 38.0
Tanana-Cal 36.9
Blyleven-Tex 35.3
Leonard-KC 32.2
Palmer-Bal 31.3

Clutch Pitching Index
Slaton-Mil 118
Rozema-Det 116
Grimsley-Bal 110
Splittorff-KC 108
Tanana-Cal 106

Relief Runs
Lyle-NY 28.8
Torrealba-Oak 18.6
LaGrow-Chi 17.5
Campbell-Bos 17.1
Coleman-Oak 15.6

Adjusted Relief Runs
Lyle-NY 27.0
Campbell-Bos 18.5
Torrealba-Oak 18.1
LaGrow-Chi 17.8
Romo-Sea 16.2

Relief Ranking
Campbell-Bos 45.6
Lyle-NY 43.4
Romo-Sea 28.1
LaGrow-Chi 26.3
T.Johnson-Min 22.8

Total Pitcher Index
Lyle-NY 4.4
Ryan-Cal 4.2
Campbell-Bos 3.9
Blyleven-Tex 3.8
Tanana-Cal 3.7

Total Baseball Ranking
Carew-Min 6.3
Singleton-Bal 4.9
Page-Oak 4.9
Brett-KC 4.4
Lyle-NY 4.4

January 25 The Padres trade pitcher Dave Tomlin and an estimated $125,000 in cash to the Rangers for aging pitcher Gaylord Perry. Perry will win the NL Cy Young Award with San Diego in 1978.

January 30 Commissioner Bowie Kuhn voids the Vida Blue deal between the A's and the Reds, suggesting a restructuring of the trade in which the A's and Reds would send Blue to Cincinnati for outfielder Dave Revering and $1.75 million cash.

March 21 The Padres fire manager Alvin Dark, replacing him with pitching coach Roger Craig. Dark becomes the only manager besides the Cubs' Phil Cavarretta in 1954 to be fired during spring training.

April 23 Reds second baseman Joe Morgan commits an error during a 2-1 win over the Giants, ending his major league record streak of 91 consecutive errorless games since July 6, 1977.

May 5 Pete Rose singles off Montreal's Steve Rogers for career hit 3,000. The Expos beat the Reds 4-3.

June 3 The Phils' Davey Johnson breaks up a 1-1, ninth-inning tie with Los Angeles by hitting his second pinch grand slam of the year. His first came on April 30 when he broke up a fifth-inning tie in San Diego. Johnson is the first major league player to accomplish this feat, but Mike Ivie will duplicate it this month.

June 16 In the 12th major league season of a career speckled with near-misses, Cincinnati's Tom Seaver finally hurls a no-hitter, beating the Cardinals 4-0.

July 11 At San Diego, the NL wins another All-Star Game 7-3. Steve Garvey singles and triples to earn the game's MVP trophy. Vida Blue starts for the NL, the first pitcher to start for both leagues. Blue also started in 1971 and 1975 for the AL.

July 31 Pete Rose singles off Phil Niekro to extend his hitting streak to 44 games, as the Reds edge the Braves 3-2. Rose ties Willie Keeler's 81-year-old NL record.

September 14 Jim Bouton, 38, earns a 4-1 win for the Braves over the Giants. It is Bouton's first major league victory since 1970, and the last of his career.

September 30 The Phillies overcome a first inning grand slam by Willie Stargell to beat the Pirates 10-8 and clinch the NL East title.

October 7 The Dodgers win the NLCS 4-3 as Bill Russell's tenth-inning single scores Ron Cey.

October 7 Veteran Roy White leads the Yanks to victory, snapping a 1-1 tie with a homer in the sixth inning. New York gains its third straight championship series over Kansas City.

October 10 Davey Lopes collects 2 homers and 5 RBI to lead the Dodgers to an 11-5 victory over the Yankees in Game 1 of the World Series.

October 25 Gaylord Perry of the Padres becomes the first pitcher to win the Cy Young Award in both leagues. Perry copped the NL honors with a 21-6 record and a 2.72 ERA.

November 15 The Pirates' Dave Parker wins the NL MVP Award, 320-194 over the Dodgers' Steve Garvey.

ATLANTA		CHICAGO		CINCINNATI		HOUSTON		LOS ANGELES		MONTREAL	
M	B.Cox	M	H.Franks	M	S.Anderson	M	B.Virdon	M	T.Lasorda	M	D.Williams
1B	D.Murphy	1B	B.Buckner	1B	D.Driessen	1B	B.Watson	1B	S.Garvey	1B	T.Perez
2B	J.Royster	2B	M.Trillo	2B	J.Morgan	2B	A.Howe	2B	D.Lopes	2B	D.Cash
SS	D.Chaney	SS	I.DeJesus	SS	D.Concepcion	SS	J.Sexton	SS	B.Russell	SS	C.Speier
3B	B.Horner	3B	S.Ontiveros	3B	P.Rose	3B	E.Cabell	3B	R.Cey	3B	L.Parrish
LF	J.Burroughs	LF	D.Kingman	LF	G.Foster	LF	D.Walling	LF	D.Baker	LF	W.Cromartie
CF	R.Office	CF	G.Gross	CF	C.Geronimo	CF	T.Puhl	CF	B.North	CF	A.Dawson
RF	G.Matthews	RF	B.Murcer	RF	K.Griffey	RF	J.Cruz	RF	R.Smith	RF	E.Valentine
C	B.Pocoroba	C	D.Rader	C	J.Bench	C	J.Pujols	C	S.Yeager	C	G.Carter
1	B.Beall	1O	L.Biittner	O	D.Collins	1O	D.Bergman	O2	L.Lacy	1O	D.Unser
O3	B.Bonnell	O	G.Clines			2S	J.Gonzalez	O	R.Monday		
32	R.Gilbreath	3O	R.Scott			S	R.Landestoy			P	R.Grimsley
C	J.Nolan			P	T.Seaver			P	D.Sutton	P	S.Rogers
				P	F.Norman					P	D.Schatzeder
		P	R.Reuschel	P	T.Hume	P	J.Richard	P	B.Hooton	P	R.May
P	P.Niekro	P	D.Lamp	P	P.Moskau	P	M.Lemongello	P	T.John	P	W.Twitchell
P	P.Hanna	P	R.Burris	P	B.Bonham	P	J.Niekro	P	D.Rau	RP	S.Bahnsen
P	M.Mahler	P	D.Roberts	RP	M.Sarmiento	P	T.Dixon	P	R.Rhoden	RP	D.Knowles
P	L.McWilliams	P	M.Krukow	P	D.Bair	P	J.Andujar	RP	C.Hough	RP	M.Garman
RP	E.Solomon	RP	D.Moore	RP	P.Borbon	RP	K.Forsch	RP	T.Forster		
RP	G.Garber	RP	B.Sutter			RP	J.Sambito	RP	L.Rautzhan		
RP	J.Easterly	RP	L.McGlothen	P	M.LaCoss					P	H.Dues
				P	D.Tomlin	P	F.Bannister	P	B.Welch	P	W.Fryman
P	D.Ruthven	P	W.Hernandez			P	V.Ruhle			P	S.Sanderson
P	R.Camp	P	W.Fryman								
P	D.Campbell	P	K.Holtzman								
P	A.Devine										
P	C.Skok										
P	T.Boggs										

NEW YORK		PHILADELPHIA		PITTSBURGH		SAN DIEGO		SAN FRANCISCO		ST.LOUIS	
M	J.Torre	M	D.Ozark	M	C.Tanner	M	R.Craig	M	J.Altobelli	M	V.Rapp
1B	W.Montanez	1B	R.Hebner	1B	W.Stargell	1B	G.Tenace	1B	W.McCovey	M	J.Krol
2B	D.Flynn	2B	T.Sizemore	2B	R.Stennett	2B	F.Gonzalez	2B	B.Madlock	M	K.Boyer
SS	T.Foli	SS	L.Bowa	SS	F.Taveras	SS	O.Smith	SS	J.LeMaster	1B	K.Hernandez
3B	L.Randle	3B	M.Schmidt	3B	P.Garner	3B	B.Almon	3B	D.Evans	2B	M.Tyson
LF	S.Henderson	LF	G.Luzinski	LF	B.Robinson	LF	G.Richards	LF	T.Whitfield	SS	G.Templeton
CF	L.Mazzilli	CF	G.Maddox	CF	O.Moreno	CF	D.Winfield	CF	L.Herndon	3B	K.Reitz
RF	E.Maddox	RF	B.McBride	RF	D.Parker	RF	O.Gamble	RF	J.Clark	LF	L.Brock
C	J.Stearns	C	B.Boone	C	E.Ott	C	R.Sweet	C	M.Hill	CF	G.Hendrick
										RF	J.Morales
O	B.Boisclair	O	J.Martin	O1	J.Milner	O2	D.Thomas	1O	M.Ivie	C	T.Simmons
O2	J.Youngblood	1O	J.Cardenal	1C	M.Sanguillen	O	J.Turner	S	R.Metzger		
						1	B.Perkins			O	J.Mumphrey
P	J.Koosman	P	S.Carlton	P	B.Blyleven	P	G.Perry	P	B.Knepper	O	T.Scott
P	C.Swan	P	L.Christenson	P	D.Robinson	P	R.Jones	P	V.Blue		
P	N.Espinosa	P	R.Lerch	P	J.Candelaria	P	B.Owchinko	P	J.Montefusco	P	B.Forsch
P	P.Zachry	P	D.Ruthven	P	J.Rooker	P	B.Shirley	P	E.Halicki	P	J.Denny
P	M.Bruhert	P	J.Kaat	P	J.Bibby	P	E.Rasmussen	P	J.Barr	P	P.Vuckovich
RP	S.Lockwood	RP	R.Reed	RP	K.Tekulve	RP	R.Fingers	RP	G.Lavelle	P	S.Martinez
RP	D.Murray	RP	T.McGraw	RP	G.Jackson	RP	J.D'Acquisto	RP	R.Moffitt	P	J.Urrea
RP	D.Bernard	RP	W.Brusstar	RP	E.Whitson	RP	M.Lee	RP	J.Curtis	RP	M.Littell
										RP	B.Schultz
P	K.Kobel	P	J.Lonborg	P	B.Kison					RP	A.Lopez
P	T.Hausman			P	J.Reuss						
										P	P.Falcone
										P	E.Rasmussen
										P	T.Bruno

TEAM	G	W	L	PCT	GB	R	OR	AB	H	2B	3B	HR	BB	SO	AVG	OBP	SLG	PRO	PRO+	BR	/A	PF	CHI	RC	SB	CS	SBA	SBR
EAST																												
PHI	162	90	72	.556		708	586	5448	1404	248	32	133	552	866	.258	.331	.388	.719	106	49	43	101	101	715	152	58	72	11
PIT	161	88	73	.547	1.5	684	637	5406	1390	239	54	115	480	874	.257	.323	.385	.708	100	21	-9	105	104	676	**213**	90	70	10
CHI	162	79	83	.488	11	664	724	5532	**1461**	224	48	72	562	746	.264	.334	.361	.695	90	11	-70	112	99	673	110	58	65	-2
MON	162	76	86	.469	14	633	611	5530	1404	269	31	121	396	881	.254	.308	.379	.687	98	-27	-20	99	103	629	80	42	66	-1
STL	162	69	93	.426	21	600	657	5415	1351	263	44	79	420	713	.249	.306	.358	.664	92	-66	-58	99	**106**	583	97	42	70	4
NY	162	66	96	.407	24	607	690	5433	1332	227	47	86	549	829	.245	.317	.352	.669	96	-47	-25	96	101	600	100	77	56	-16
WEST																												
LA	162	95	67	.586		727	573	5437	1435	251	27	**149**	610	818	.264	.340	**.402**	**.742**	114	98	101	100	96	763	137	52	72	10
CIN	161	92	69	.571	2.5	710	688	5392	1378	**270**	32	136	**636**	899	.256	.337	.393	.730	110	75	75	100	97	730	137	58	70	6
SF	162	89	73	.549	6	613	594	5364	1331	240	41	117	554	814	.248	.320	.374	.694	104	-1	24	96	95	647	87	54	62	-6
SD	162	84	78	.519	11	591	598	5360	1349	208	42	75	536	848	.252	.323	.348	.671	102	-37	-10	92	98	624	152	70	68	4
HOU	162	74	88	.457	21	605	634	5408	1408	231	45	70	434	743	.258	.315	.355	.670	101	-49	-5	93	103	608	178	59	**75**	18
ATL	162	69	93	.426	26	600	750	5381	1313	191	39	123	550	874	.244	.317	.363	.680	86	-28	-97	111	98	608	90	65	58	-12
TOT	971					7742		65156	16556	2861	482	1276	6279	9905	.254	.323	.372	.694							1533	725	68	25

TEAM	CG	SH	SV	IP	H	H/G	HR	BB	SO	RAT	ERA	ERA+	OAV	OOB	PR	/A	PF	CPI	FA	E	DP	FW	PW	BW	SBW	DIF
EAST																										
PHI	38	9	29	1436¹	1343	8.4	118	**393**	813	11.0	3.33	107	.251	**.305**	39	37	100	99	**.983**	104	156	2.0	3.9	4.5	.9	-2.4
PIT	30	13	44	1444²	1366	8.5	103	499	880	11.8	3.41	108	.249	.315	26	46	104	98	.973	167	133	-1.4	4.9	-1.0	.8	4.2
CHI	24	7	38	1455¹	1475	9.1	125	539	768	12.7	4.05	99	.265	.333	-77	-4	113	98	.978	144	154	-.2	-.4	-7.4	-.4	6.4
MON	42	13	32	1446	1332	8.3	117	572	740	12.0	3.42	103	.249	.325	24	16	99	106	.979	134	150	.4	1.7	-2.1	-.3	-4.6
STL	32	13	22	1437²	**1300**	8.1	94	600	859	12.1	3.58	98	**.245**	.326	-1	-11	98	97	.978	136	155	.3	-1.2	-6.1	-.2	-5.2
NY	21	7	26	1455¹	1447	8.9	114	531	775	12.4	3.87	90	.265	.334	-48	-62	98	101	.979	132	160	.5	-6.6	-2.6	-1.9	-4.4
WEST																										
LA	46	16	38	1440¹	1362	8.5	107	440	800	11.4	**3.12**	112	.250	.309	73	62	98	106	.978	140	138	.0	6.6	10.7	.8	-4.1
CIN	16	10	46	1448¹	1437	8.9	122	567	908	12.6	3.81	93	.261	.332	-38	-42	99	102	.978	134	120	.3	-4.4	7.9	.4	7.3
SF	42	**17**	29	1455	1377	8.5	84	453	840	11.5	3.30	104	.252	.311	44	23	96	98	.977	146	118	-.3	2.4	2.5	-.9	4.1
SD	21	10	**55**	1433²	1385	8.7	**74**	483	744	11.8	3.28	101	.257	.320	47	8	93	104	.975	160	**171**	-1.0	.8	1.1	.2	1.9
HOU	48	17	32	1440¹	1328	8.3	86	578	**930**	12.1	3.63	91	.247	.323	-9	-52	93	94	.978	133	109	.4	-5.5	-.5	**1.7**	-3.1
ATL	29	12	32	1440¹	1404	8.8	132	624	848	12.9	4.08	99	.257	.337	-81	-5	113	98	.975	153	126	-.6	-.5	-10.3	-1.5	.9
TOT	389	144	414	17333¹		8.6				12.0	3.57		.254	.323					.978	1683	1690					

Runs
DeJesus-Chi 104
Rose-Cin 103
Parker-Pit 102
Foster-Cin 97
Moreno-Pit 95

Hits
Garvey-LA 202
Rose-Cin 198
Cabell-Hou 195
Parker-Pit 194
Bowa-Phi 192

Doubles
Rose-Cin 51
Clark-SF 46
Simmons-StL 40
Parrish-Mon 39
Perez-Mon 38

Triples
Templeton-StL 13
Richards-SD 12
Parker-Pit 12

Home Runs
Foster-Cin 40
Luzinski-Phi 35
Parker-Pit 30
Smith-LA 29

Total Bases
Parker-Pit 340
Foster-Cin 330
Garvey-LA 319
Clark-SF 318
Winfield-SD 293

Runs Batted In
Foster-Cin 120
Parker-Pit 117
Garvey-LA 113
Luzinski-Phi 101
Clark-SF 98

Runs Produced
Parker-Pit 189
Garvey-LA 181
Foster-Cin 177
Clark-SF 163
Winfield-SD 161

Bases On Balls
Burroughs-Atl 117
Evans-SF 105
Tenace-SD 101
Luzinski-Phi 100
Cey-LA 96

Batting Average
Parker-Pit 334
Garvey-LA 316
Cruz-Hou 315
Madlock-SF 309
Winfield-SD 308

On Base Percentage
Burroughs-Atl 436
Parker-Pit 395
Tenace-SD 394
Smith-LA 392
Luzinski-Phi 390

Slugging Average
Parker-Pit 585
Smith-LA 559
Foster-Cin 546
Clark-SF 537
Burroughs-Atl 529

Production
Parker-Pit 981
Burroughs-Atl 965
Smith-LA 951
Luzinski-Phi 916
Foster-Cin 909

Adjusted Production
Smith-LA 164
Parker-Pit 163
Clark-SF 155
Winfield-SD 153
Luzinski-Phi 152

Batter Runs
Parker-Pit 52.9
Burroughs-Atl 50.1
Luzinski-Phi 40.9
Foster-Cin 39.2
Smith-LA 37.8

Adjusted Batter Runs
Parker-Pit 47.6
Clark-SF 40.0
Luzinski-Phi 39.9
Foster-Cin 39.2
Winfield-SD 38.6

Clutch Hitting Index
Morgan-Cin 134
Reitz-StL 126
Montanez-NY 119
Watson-Hou 118
B.Robinson-Pit 117

Runs Created
Parker-Pit 134
Burroughs-Atl 116
Foster-Cin 115
Luzinski-Phi 114
Clark-SF 109

Total Average
Burroughs-Atl 1.042
Parker-Pit 1.025
Smith-LA 1.009
Luzinski-Phi 957
Foster-Cin 893

Stolen Bases
Moreno-Pit 71
Taveras-Pit 46
Lopes-LA 45
DeJesus-Chi 41
Smith-SD 40

Stolen Base Average
Cedeno-Hou 92.0
Lopes-LA 91.8
McBride-Phi 90.3
Sexton-Hou 88.9
Bowa-Phi 84.4

Stolen Base Runs
Lopes-LA 11.1
Moreno-Pit 8.1
McBride-Phi 6.6

Fielding Runs
Trillo-Chi 28.9
Smith-SD 25.6
Cromartie-Mon 24.7
Templeton-StL 22.9
Dawson-Mon 21.1

Total Player Rating
Parker-Pit 5.3
Clark-SF 4.7
Foster-Cin 4.0
Lopes-LA 4.0
Templeton-StL 3.8

Wins
Perry-SD 21
Grimsley-Mon 20
Niekro-Atl 19
Hooton-LA 19

Win Percentage
Perry-SD 778
Hooton-LA 655
Grimsley-Mon 645
Blue-SF 643
John-LA 630

Games
Tekulve-Pit 91
Littell-StL 72
Moore-Chi 71
Moffitt-SF 70
Bair-Cin 70

Complete Games
Niekro-Atl 22
Grimsley-Mon 19
Richard-Hou 16
Knepper-SF 16

Shutouts
Knepper-SF 6
Niekro-Atl 4
Halicki-SF 4
Blyleven-Pit 4
Blue-SF 4

Saves
Fingers-SD 37
Tekulve-Pit 31
Bair-Cin 28
Sutter-Chi 27
Garber-Phi-Atl 25

Innings Pitched
Niekro-Atl 334.1
Richard-Hou 275.1
Grimsley-Mon 263.0
Perry-SD 260.2
Knepper-SF 260.0

Fewest Hits/Game
Richard-Hou 6.28
Swan-NY 7.12
Hooton-LA 7.47
Halicki-SF 7.51
Knepper-SF 7.55

Fewest BB/Game
Christensen-Phi . . . 1.86
Barr-SF 1.93
R.Reuschel-Chi 2.00
Halicki-SF 2.04
Sutton-LA 2.04

Strikeouts
Richard-Hou 303
Niekro-Atl 248
Seaver-Cin 226
Blyleven-Pit 182
Montefusco-SF 177

Strikeouts/Game
Richard-Hou 9.90
Seaver-Cin 7.83
Vuckovich-StL 6.76
Blyleven-Pit 6.72
Niekro-Atl 6.68

Ratio
Swan-NY 9.72
Hooton-LA 9.80
Halicki-SF 9.86
Christenson-Phi 10.14
Rogers-Mon 10.36

Earned Run Average
Swan-NY 2.43
Rogers-Mon 2.47
Vuckovich-StL 2.54
Knepper-SF 2.63
Hooton-LA 2.71

Adjusted ERA
Swan-NY 143
Rogers-Mon 143
Niekro-Atl 140
Vuckovich-StL 138
Knepper-SF 131

Opponents' Batting Avg.
Richard-Hou 196
Swan-NY 219
Halicki-SF 221
Hooton-LA 226
Seaver-Cin 227

Opponents' On Base Pct.
Halicki-SF 271
Swan-NY 277
Hooton-LA 277
Christenson-Phi 284
D.Robinson-Pit 286

Starter Runs
Knepper-SF 27.3
Rogers-Mon 27.0
Swan-NY 26.4
Niekro-Atl 25.8
Perry-SD 24.5

Adjusted Starter Runs
Niekro-Atl 43.3
Rogers-Mon 25.7
Swan-NY 24.3
Knepper-SF 23.6
Vuckovich-StL 21.4

Clutch Pitching Index
Rau-LA 134
Vuckovich-StL 124
Carlton-Phi 121
Jones-SD 114
Rogers-Mon 113

Relief Runs
Tekulve-Pit 18.6
Garber-Phi-Atl 18.5
Bair-Cin 17.9
Reed-Phi 16.2
D'Acquisto-SD 14.9

Adjusted Relief Runs
Garber-Phi-Atl 22.5
Tekulve-Pit 20.5
Bair-Cin 17.5
Reed-Phi 16.1
D'Acquisto-SD 12.4

Relief Ranking
Bair-Cin 30.8
Tekulve-Pit 30.4
Garber-Phi-Atl 29.2
Fingers-SD 22.4
Forster-LA 22.4

Total Pitcher Index
Niekro-Atl 5.7
Tekulve-Pit 3.5
Carlton-Phi 3.3
Bair-Cin 3.2
Garber-Phi-Atl 3.2

Total Baseball Ranking
Niekro-Atl 5.7
Parker-Pit 5.3
Clark-SF 4.7
Foster-Cin 4.0
Lopes-LA 4.0

January 19 The BBWAA elects Eddie Mathews to the Hall of Fame. The former third baseman is named on 301 of 379 ballots.

January 30 Pitcher Addie Joss and former executive Larry MacPhail are voted into the Hall of Fame by the Special Veterans Committee.

April 9 The Brewers complete a stunning season-opening, three-game sweep of the Orioles by scores of 11–3, 16–3, and 13–5. Sixto Lezcano, Gorman Thomas, and Cecil Cooper provided the Brewers with a grand slam in each game to set a major league mark.

June 17 Ron Guidry strikes out 18 batters in a 4-hit 4-0 shutout of the Angels, setting an AL record for lefthanders. The victory raises the Yankee southpaw's record to 11-0.

June 30 Larry Doby becomes the second black major league manager, replacing Bob Lemon as skipper of the White Sox. Chicago has a 34-40 record at the time, and will go 37-50 the rest of the way.

September 7 The Yankees, four games behind the Red Sox in the AL East, arrive in Boston for a crucial four-game series. The Yanks begin the "Boston Massacre" with a 15–3 route. Willie Randolph drives in five of the runs.

September 24 Ron Guidry gains his third 2-hit shutout of the month 4-0 over the Indians. It is Guidry's ninth shutout of the year, a Yankee record, and just one short of the AL record for southpaws set by Boston lefty Babe Ruth in 1916. The Red Sox stay one game in back of New York by topping Toronto 7-6.

September 26 New York District Court Judge Constance Baker Motley rules that women sportswriters cannot be banned from locker rooms in the state.

October 2 The Yankees and Red Sox, tied for first at the end of the regular season, play a dramatic one-game playoff at Fenway for the AL East title. New York prevails 5-4 behind Bucky Dent's three-run homer off Mike Torrez and

Guidry's 25th win against just three losses. Guidry's .893 percentage is a major league record for a 20-game winner.

October 13 Spectacular defense at third base by Graig Nettles highlights the Yankees' first World Series win 5-1. Ron Guidry gets the victory.

October 17 The Yanks win their fourth straight game 7-2 to clinch their second consecutive World Series over the Dodgers as Brian Doyle and Series MVP Bucky Dent have three hits apiece.

November 1 Guidry is the unanimous choice for the AL Cy Young Award. The southpaw led the league in wins, percentage, shutouts (9), and ERA (1.74).

November 7 Boston's Jim Rice outpoints New York's Ron Guidry, 353-291, to win the AL MVP Award. Rice led the league in hits (213), triples (15), homers (46), RBI (139), and slugging (.600), and became the first AL player to accumulate 400 total bases in a season since Joe DiMaggio in 1937.

	BALTIMORE		BOSTON		CALIFORNIA		CHICAGO		CLEVELAND		DETROIT		KANSAS CITY
M	E.Weaver	M	D.Zimmer	M	D.Garcia	M	B.Lemon	M	J.Torborg	M	R.Houk	M	W.Herzog
1B	E.Murray	1B	G.Scott	M	J.Fregosi	M	L.Doby	1B	A.Thornton	1B	J.Thompson	1B	P.LaCock
2B	R.Dauer	2B	J.Remy	1B	R.Fairly	1B	M.Squires	2B	D.Kuiper	2B	L.Whitaker	2B	F.White
SS	M.Belanger	SS	R.Burleson	2B	B.Grich	2B	J.Orta	SS	T.Veryzer	SS	A.Trammell	SS	F.Patek
3B	D.DeCinces	3B	B.Hobson	SS	D.Chalk	SS	D.Kessinger	3B	B.Bell	3B	A.Rodriguez	3B	G.Brett
LF	P.Kelly	LF	C.Yastrzemski	3B	C.Lansford	3B	E.Soderholm	LF	J.Grubb	LF	S.Kemp	LF	W.Wilson
CF	L.Harlow	CF	F.Lynn	LF	J.Rudi	LF	R.Garr	CF	R.Manning	CF	R.LeFlore	CF	A.Otis
RF	K.Singleton	RF	D.Evans	CF	R.Miller	CF	C.Lemon	RF	P.Dade	RF	T.Corcoran	RF	A.Cowens
C	R.Dempsey	C	C.Fisk	RF	L.Bostock	RF	C.Washington	C	G.Alexander	C	M.May	C	D.Porter
DH	L.May	DH	J.Rice	C	B.Downing	C	B.Nahorodny	DH	B.Carbo	DH	R.Staub	DH	H.McRae
				DH	D.Baylor	DH	La.Johnson						
O	C.Lopez	3D	J.Brohamer					OD	J.Norris	C	L.Parrish	O1	C.Hurdle
2	B.Smith			13	R.Jackson	OD	B.Molinaro	O3	T.Cox	3	P.Mankowski	O	T.Poquette
O	A.Mora	P	D.Eckersley	O	K.Landreaux	2S	G.Pryor	P	R.Waits			P	D.Leonard
		P	M.Torrez			O	T.Bosley	P	R.Wise	P	J.Slaton	P	P.Splittorff
P	J.Palmer	P	L.Tiant	P	F.Tanana	OD	W.Nordhagen	P	M.Paxton	P	M.Wilcox	P	L.Gura
P	M.Flanagan	P	B.Lee	P	N.Ryan			P	D.Hood	P	D.Rozema	P	R.Gale
P	D.Martinez	P	J.Wright	P	C.Knapp	P	S.Stone	P	D.Clyde	P	J.Billingham	RP	D.Bird
P	S.McGregor	RP	B.Stanley	P	D.Aase	P	K.Kravec	P	J.Kern	P	K.Young	RP	M.Pattin
RP	D.Stanhouse	RP	D.Drago	P	K.Brett	P	F.Barrios	RP	S.Monge	RP	J.Hiller	RP	A.Hrabosky
RP	J.Kerrigan	RP	T.Burgmeier	P	R.Hartzell	P	W.Wood	RP	D.Spillner				
RP	T.Martinez			RP	D.LaRoche	RP	J.Willoughby			P	J.Morris		
		P	A.Ripley	RP	D.Miller	RP	L.LaGrow			P	B.Sykes	P	S.Mingori
P	N.Briles	P	B.Campbell			RP	R.Schueler	P	P.Reuschel	P	S.Baker	P	A.Hassler
		P	D.Frost	P	R.Hinton								
		P	T.Griffin	P	M.Proly								
				/P	R.Wortham								
				P	P.Torrealba								
				P	J.Kucek								

	MILWAUKEE		MINNESOTA		NEW YORK		OAKLAND		SEATTLE		TEXAS		TORONTO
M	G.Bamberger	M	G.Mauch	M	B.Martin	M	B.Winkles	M	D.Johnson	M	B.Hunter	M	R.Hartsfield
1B	C.Cooper	1B	R.Carew	M	D.Howser	M	J.McKeon	1B	D.Meyer	M	P.Corrales	1B	J.Mayberry
2B	P.Molitor	2B	B.Randall	M	B.Lemon	1B	D.Revering	2B	J.Cruz	1B	M.Hargrove	2B	D.McKay
SS	R.Yount	SS	R.Smalley	1B	C.Chambliss	2B	M.Edwards	SS	C.Reynolds	2B	B.Wills	SS	L.Gomez
3B	S.Bando	3B	M.Cubbage	2B	W.Randolph	SS	M.Guerrero	3B	B.Stein	SS	B.Campaneris	3B	R.Howell
LF	B.Oglivie	LF	W.Norwood	SS	B.Dent	3B	W.Gross	LF	B.Bochte	3B	T.Harrah	LF	O.Velez
CF	G.Thomas	CF	D.Ford	3B	G.Nettles	LF	M.Page	CF	Ru.Jones	LF	A.Oliver	CF	R.Bosetti
RF	S.Lezcano	RF	H.Powell	LF	L.Piniella	CF	M.Dilone	RF	L.Roberts	RF	J.Beniquez	RF	B.Bailor
C	C.Moore	C	B.Wynegar	CF	M.Rivers	RF	T.Armas	C	B.Stinson	RF	B.Bonds	C	R.Cerone
DH	L.Hisle	DH	G.Adams	RF	R.Jackson	C	J.Essian	DH	L.Stanton	C	J.Sundberg	DH	R.Carty
				C	T.Munson	DH	G.Alexander			DH	R.Zisk		
12	D.Money	D	J.Morales	DH	C.Johnson			O	J.Hale			C	A.Ashby
C	B.Martinez	O	B.Rivera			32	T.Duncan	OD	T.Paciorek	3D	K.Bevacqua	OD	W.Upshaw
DO	D.Davis	3	L.Wolfe	OD	R.White	C1	J.Newman	3S	L.Milbourne			O	A.Woods
						O	J.Wallis			P	J.Matlack		
P	M.Caldwell	P	R.Erickson	P	R.Guidry	O	G.Burke	P	P.Mitchell	P	F.Jenkins	P	J.Jefferson
P	L.Sorensen	P	G.Zahn	P	E.Figueroa			P	G.Abbott	P	D.Alexander	P	T.Underwood
P	J.Augustine	P	D.Goltz	P	D.Tidrow	P	M.Keough	P	R.Honeycutt	P	D.Medich	P	J.Clancy
P	B.Travers	P	G.Serum	P	J.Beattie	P	J.Johnson	P	T.House	P	D.Ellis	P	J.Garvin
P	A.Replogle	RP	M.Marshall	P	C.Hunter	P	R.Langford	P	J.Colborn	RP	R.Cleveland	P	B.Moore
RP	R.Stein			RP	R.Gossage	P	P.Broberg	RP	S.Rawley	RP	L.Barker	P	M.Willis
RP	B.McClure	P	D.Jackson	RP	S.Lyle	P	S.Renko	RP	J.Todd			RP	T.Murphy
DO	B.Castro	P	P.Thormodsgard	RP	K.Clay	RP	D.Heaverlo	RP	E.Romo	P	S.Comer	RP	J.Coleman
		P	S.Perzanowski			RP	B.Lacey			P	J.Umbarger		
P	E.Rodriguez			RP	E.Sosa	P	B.McLaughlin					P	D.Lemanczyk
						P	D.Pole					P	D.Kirkwood
				P	A.Wirth	P	M.Parrott						

TEAM	G	W	L	PCT	GB	R	OR	AB	H	2B	3B	HR	BB	SO	AVG	OBP	SLG	PRO	PRO+	BR	/A	PF	CHI	RC	SB	CS	SBA	SBR
EAST																												
NY	163	100	63	.613		735	**582**	5583	1489	228	38	125	505	695	.267	.332	.388	.720	105	14	31	98	**105**	720	98	42	70	4
BOS	163	99	64	.607	1	796	657	5587	1493	270	46	172	582	835	.267	.339	.424	.763	102	96	12	111	100	793	74	51	59	-8
MIL	162	93	69	.574	6.5	804	650	5536	**1530**	265	38	**173**	520	805	**.276**	**.342**	**.432**	**.774**	116	**114**	**112**	100	100	**822**	95	53	64	-3
BAL	161	90	71	.559	9	659	633	5422	1397	248	19	154	552	864	.258	.329	.396	.725	110	18	61	94	95	691	75	61	55	-14
DET	162	86	76	.531	13.5	714	653	5601	1520	218	34	129	563	695	.271	.341	.392	.733	103	45	24	103	96	748	90	38	70	4
CLE	159	69	90	.434	29	639	694	5365	1400	223	45	106	488	698	.261	.326	.379	.705	99	-19	-11	99	99	649	64	63	50	-19
TOR	161	59	102	.366	40	590	775	5430	1358	217	39	98	448	645	.250	.310	.359	.669	86	-93	-105	102	103	587	28	52	35	-23
WEST																												
KC	162	92	70	.568		743	634	5474	1469	**305**	**59**	98	498	644	.268	.333	.399	.732	102	34	15	103	104	739	**216**	**84**	**72**	**14**
TEX	162	87	75	.537	5	692	632	5347	1353	216	36	132	**624**	779	.253	.335	.381	.716	101	11	10	100	100	696	196	91	68	4
CAL	162	87	75	.537	5	691	666	5472	1417	226	28	108	539	682	.259	.333	.370	.703	101	-14	12	96	103	669	86	69	55	-16
MIN	162	73	89	.451	19	666	678	5522	1472	259	47	82	604	684	.267	**.342**	.375	.717	99	21	7	102	92	715	99	56	64	-4
CHI	161	71	90	.441	20.5	634	731	5393	1423	221	41	106	409	**625**	.264	.320	.379	.699	95	-35	-41	101	102	635	83	68	55	-16
OAK	162	69	93	.426	23	532	690	5321	1304	200	31	100	433	800	.245	.305	.351	.656	89	-117	-89	95	99	552	144	117	55	-27
SEA	160	56	104	.350	35	614	834	5358	1327	229	37	97	522	702	.248	.317	.359	.676	91	-73	-69	99	103	620	123	47	**72**	9
TOT	1131					9509		76411	19952	3325	538	1680	7287	10153	.261	.329	.385	.714							1471	892	62	-94

TEAM	CG	SH	SV	IP	H	H/G	HR	BB	SO	RAT	ERA	ERA+	OAV	OOB	PR	/A	PF	CPI	FA	E	DP	FW	PW	BW	SBW	DIF
EAST																										
NY	39	16	**36**	1460²	1321	**8.1**	111	478	817	**11.3**	3.18	114	**.243**	**.308**	95	72	96	99	**.982**	113	134	1.5	7.4	3.2	1.1	5.2
BOS	57	15	26	1472²	1530	9.4	137	464	706	12.4	3.54	116	.270	.329	37	**94**	109	111	.977	146	171	-.3	**9.7**	1.2	-.1	7.1
MIL	62	**19**	24	1436	1442	9.0	109	**398**	577	11.8	3.65	103	.262	.316	17	17	100	95	.977	150	144	-.6	1.8	**11.5**	.4	-1.0
BAL	**65**	16	33	1429	1340	8.4	107	509	754	11.7	3.56	98	.251	.318	32	-11	93	95	**.982**	110	166	**1.6**	-1.1	6.3	-.8	3.5
DET	60	12	21	1455²	1441	8.9	135	503	684	12.2	3.64	106	.263	.329	20	36	103	106	.981	118	**177**	1.2	3.7	2.5	1.1	-3.5
CLE	36	6	28	1407¹	1397	8.9	**100**	568	739	12.7	3.97	94	.261	.335	-33	-37	99	95	.980	123	142	.8	-3.8	-1.1	-1.3	-5.1
TOR	35	5	23	1429¹	1529	9.6	149	614	758	13.6	4.54	86	.279	.353	-123	-98	104	100	.979	131	163	.4	-10.1	-10.8	-1.7	.7
WEST																										
KC	53	14	33	1439	1350	8.4	108	478	657	11.6	3.44	111	.251	.316	52	61	102	98	.976	150	153	-.6	6.3	1.5	**2.1**	1.7
TEX	54	12	25	1456¹	1431	8.8	108	421	776	11.6	3.36	112	.259	.315	66	63	100	102	.976	153	140	-.8	6.5	1.0	1.1	-1.8
CAL	44	13	33	1455²	1382	8.5	125	599	**892**	12.4	3.65	99	.253	.330	19	-6	96	102	.978	136	136	.2	-.6	1.2	-1.0	6.2
MIN	48	9	26	1459²	1468	9.1	102	520	703	12.5	3.69	103	.266	.333	11	20	102	102	.977	146	171	-.4	2.1	.7	.3	-10.7
CHI	38	9	33	1409¹	1380	8.8	128	586	710	12.8	4.21	90	.259	.337	-71	-65	101	94	.977	139	130	-.0	-6.7	-4.2	-1.0	2.4
OAK	26	12	14	1433¹	1401	8.8	106	582	750	12.6	3.62	100	.259	.333	22	3	97	103	.971	179	145	-2.3	.3	-9.2	-2.1	1.2
SEA	28	4	20	1419¹	1540	9.8	155	567	630	13.6	4.67	81	.280	.352	-144	-136	101	98	.978	141	174	-.2	-14.0	-7.1	1.6	-4.3
TOT	645	161	390	20163¹		8.9				12.4	3.76		.261	.329					.978	1935	2146					

Runs		**Hits**		**Doubles**		**Triples**		**Home Runs**		**Total Bases**	
LeFlore-Det	126	Rice-Bos	213	Brett-KC	45	Rice-Bos	15	Rice-Bos	46	Rice-Bos	406
Rice-Bos	121	LeFlore-Det	198	McRae-KC	39	Ford-Min	10	Hisle-Mil	34	Murray-Bal	293
Baylor-Cal	103	Carew-Min	188	Fisk-Bos	39	Carew-Min	10	Baylor-Cal	34	Staub-Det	279
Thornton-Cle	97	Munson-NY	183	DeCinces-Bal	37	Yount-Mil	9	Thornton-Cle	33	Baylor-Cal	279
Hisle-Mil	96	Staub-Det	175	Ford-Min	36	Garr-Chi	9	Thomas-Mil	32	Thompson-Det	278

Runs Batted In		**Runs Produced**		**Bases On Balls**		**Batting Average**		**On Base Percentage**		**Slugging Average**	
Rice-Bos	139	Rice-Bos	214	Hargrove-Tex	107	Carew-Min	.333	Carew-Min	.415	Rice-Bos	.600
Staub-Det	121	Hisle-Mil	177	Singleton-Bal	98	Oliver-Tex	.324	Singleton-Bal	.410	Hisle-Mil	.533
Hisle-Mil	115	LeFlore-Det	176	Kemp-Det	97	Rice-Bos	.315	Hargrove-Tex	.391	DeCinces-Bal	.526
Thornton-Cle	105	Staub-Det	172	Thornton-Cle	93	Piniella-NY	.314	Otis-KC	.387	Otis-KC	.525
		Thornton-Cle	169	Smalley-Min	85	Oglivie-Mil	.303	Randolph-NY	.385	Thornton-Cle	.516

Production		**Adjusted Production**		**Batter Runs**		**Adjusted Batter Runs**		**Clutch Hitting Index**		**Runs Created**	
Rice-Bos	.973	Singleton-Bal	154	Rice-Bos	58.7	Rice-Bos	44.1	Staub-Det	136	Rice-Bos	147
Otis-KC	.911	Rice-Bos	153	Hisle-Mil	36.3	Singleton-Bal	40.4	L.Johnson-Chi	127	LeFlore-Det	105
Hisle-Mil	.909	Hisle-Mil	153	Thornton-Cle	35.6	Thornton-Cle	36.8	Whitaker-Det	119	Carew-Min	105
Thornton-Cle	.898	Thornton-Cle	152	Otis-KC	35.2	Hisle-Mil	36.8	Chambliss-NY	117	Thompson-Det	104
Roberts-Sea	.881	DeCinces-Bal	152	Singleton-Bal	34.0	Murray-Bal	33.7	Cowens-KC	116	Murray-Bal	104

Total Average		**Stolen Bases**		**Stolen Base Average**		**Stolen Base Runs**		**Fielding Runs**		**Total Player Rating**	
Rice-Bos	.973	LeFlore-Det	68	Cruz-Sea	85.5	Cruz-Sea	11.7	Belanger-Bal	33.8	Smalley-Min	5.3
Otis-KC	.972	Cruz-Sea	59	Campaneris-Tex	84.6	LeFlore-Det	10.8	Bell-Cle	28.3	Rice-Bos	4.8
Hisle-Mil	.907	Wills-Tex	52	Lowenstein-Tex	84.2	Wills-Tex	7.2	Bosetti-Tor	25.1	Yount-Mil	4.5
Singleton-Bal	.900	Dilone-Oak	50	Randolph-NY	83.7	Wilson-KC	6.6	Yount-Mil	21.9	Otis-KC	4.2
Thornton-Cle	.897	Wilson-KC	46	Rivers-NY	83.3	Randolph-NY	6.6	Wills-Tex	21.3	DeCinces-Bal	4.0

Wins		**Win Percentage**		**Games**		**Complete Games**		**Shutouts**		**Saves**	
Guidry-NY	25	Guidry-NY	.893	Lacey-Oak	74	Caldwell-Mil	23	Guidry-NY	9	Gossage-NY	27
Caldwell-Mil	22	Stanley-Bos	.882	Heaverlo-Oak	69	Leonard-KC	20	Palmer-Bal	6	LaRoche-Cal	25
Palmer-Bal	21	Gura-KC	.800	Sosa-Oak	68	Palmer-Bal	19	Caldwell-Mil	6	Stanhouse-Bal	24
Leonard-KC	21	Eckersley-Bos	.714	Gossage-NY	63	Matlack-Tex	18	Tiant-Bos	5	Marshall-Min	21
		Caldwell-Mil	.710							Hrabosky-KC	20

Innings Pitched		**Fewest Hits/Game**		**Fewest BB/Game**		**Strikeouts**		**Strikeouts/Game**		**Ratio**	
Palmer-Bal	296.0	Guidry-NY	6.15	Jenkins-Tex	1.48	Ryan-Cal	260	Ryan-Cal	9.97	Guidry-NY	8.55
Leonard-KC	294.2	Ryan-Cal	7.02	Sorensen-Mil	1.60	Guidry-NY	248	Guidry-NY	8.16	Caldwell-Mil	9.79
Caldwell-Mil	293.1	Gura-KC	7.43	Caldwell-Mil	1.66	Leonard-KC	183	Kravec-Chi	6.83	Jenkins-Tex	9.83
Flanagan-Bal	281.1	Palmer-Bal	7.48	Matlack-Tex	1.70	Flanagan-Bal	167	Underwood-Tor	6.33	Gura-KC	10.03
Sorensen-Mil	280.2	Tiant-Bos	7.84	Rozema-Det	1.76	Eckersley-Bos	162	Knapp-Cal	6.02	Matlack-Tex	10.23

Earned Run Average		**Adjusted ERA**		**Opponents' Batting Avg.**		**Opponents' On Base Pct.**		**Starter Runs**		**Adjusted Starter Runs**	
Guidry-NY	1.74	Guidry-NY	208	Guidry-NY	.193	Guidry-NY	.250	Guidry-NY	61.4	Guidry-NY	57.1
Matlack-Tex	2.27	Matlack-Tex	165	Ryan-Cal	.220	Caldwell-Mil	.274	Caldwell-Mil	45.7	Caldwell-Mil	45.5
Caldwell-Mil	2.36	Caldwell-Mil	159	Palmer-Bal	.227	Jenkins-Tex	.279	Matlack-Tex	44.9	Matlack-Tex	44.3
Palmer-Bal	2.46	Goltz-Min	153	Gura-KC	.229	Matlack-Tex	.284	Palmer-Bal	42.8	Palmer-Bal	34.0
Goltz-Min	2.49	Palmer-Bal	142	Tiant-Bos	.234	Gura-KC	.286	Goltz-Min	31.1	Eckersley-Bos	33.6

Clutch Pitching Index		**Relief Runs**		**Adjusted Relief Runs**		**Relief Ranking**		**Total Pitcher Index**		**Total Baseball Ranking**	
Lee-Bos	130	Gossage-NY	26.2	Gossage-NY	24.0	Gossage-NY	44.7	Guidry-NY	6.2	Guidry-NY	6.2
Zahn-Min	129	Stanley-Bos	18.2	Stanley-Bos	23.7	Marshall-Min	37.2	Caldwell-Mil	5.0	Smalley-Min	5.3
Goltz-Min	125	Hiller-Det	14.6	Hiller-Det	15.7	Stanley-Bos	29.4	Matlack-Tex	4.7	Caldwell-Mil	5.0
Gale-KC	115	Marshall-Min	14.4	Marshall-Min	15.0	Hiller-Det	25.6	Gossage-NY	4.7	Rice-Bos	4.8
Eckersley-Bos	115	Sosa-Oak	13.6	Sosa-Oak	12.1	LaRoche-Cal	19.9	Palmer-Bal	4.3	Matlack-Tex	4.7

January 23 Willie Mays receives 409 of 432 votes in the BBWAA election to earn enshrinement in the Hall of Fame.

March 7 The Special Veterans Committee selects Warren Giles and slugger Hack Wilson for the Hall of Fame.

April 7 In the earliest no-hitter in major league history, the Astros' Ken Forsch shuts downs the Braves 6-0, making him and his brother Bob the first brothers to pitch no-hit games.

May 17 The wind is really blowing out at Wrigley as the Cubs and the Phillies combine for a major-league-record-tying 11 homers during a wild 10-inning slugfest won 23-22 by the Phils. Dave Kingman has 3 homers and 6 RBI for the Cubs. Teammate Bill Buckner has a grand slam and 7 RBI. Mike Schmidt's 2 homers include the game-winner in the 10th.

August 13 Lou Brock collects his 3,000th career hit, a single off Dennis Lamp, as the Cardinals top the Cubs 3-2.

September 23 St. Louis legend Lou Brock steals the 938th—and final—base of his career in a 7-4 win against the New York Mets. He tops nineteenth century speedster Billy Hamilton by one.

September 24 Pete Rose singles in the Phillies 7-2 loss to the Cardinals, giving him 200 hits in a season for the tenth time. He breaks the major league record of nine formerly held by Ty Cobb.

September 26 Atlanta's Phil Niekro notches his 20th win of the season by beating his brother Joe, the NL's only other 20-game winner, in a 9-4 victory. The Niekro brothers are the second pair (the other was Jim and Gaylord Perry) to win 20 games in the same year.

September 28 Switch-hitting Cardinal shortstop Garry Templeton collects three hits against the Mets and becomes the first player to get 100 hits from each side of the plate. During the last nine games, he bats righthanded exclusively.

October 5 The Pirates complete a sweep of the LCS, beating the Reds 7-1. Willie Stargell hits another homer and is named series MVP.

October 17 In Game 7, Stargell's third World Series homer propels Pittsburgh to its third straight win 4-1, and the World Championship. Pops is named Series MVP.

October 31 Mike Flanagan, who posted a 23-9 record for the Orioles, is named the winner of the AL Cy Young Award by a comfortable margin over the Yankees' Tommy John.

November 7 Reliever Bruce Sutter, who had a 2.23 ERA and saved 37 of the Cubs' 80 victories, wins the NL Cy Young Award by a 72-66 margin over the Astros' Joe Niekro.

November 13 For the first time in history, two players share the MVP Award. The co-winners are Willie Stargell, the Pirates' spiritual leader, who batted .281 with 32 homers, and the Cardinals Keith Hernandez, who led the NL in runs (116), doubles (48), and batting (.344).

November 14 California's Don Baylor, who led the AL in runs and RBI, is named the league's MVP.

	ATLANTA		CHICAGO		CINCINNATI		HOUSTON		LOS ANGELES		MONTREAL
M	B.Cox	M	H.Franks	M	J.McNamara	M	B.Virdon	M	T.Lasorda	M	D.Williams
1B	D.Murphy	M	J.Amalfitano	1B	D.Driessen	1B	C.Cedeno	1B	S.Garvey	1B	T.Perez
2B	G.Hubbard	1B	B.Buckner	2B	J.Morgan	2B	R.Landestoy	2B	D.Lopes	2B	R.Scott
SS	P.Frias	2B	T.Sizemore	SS	D.Concepcion	SS	C.Reynolds	SS	B.Russell	SS	C.Speier
3B	B.Horner	SS	I.DeJesus	3B	R.Knight	3B	E.Cabell	3B	R.Cey	3B	L.Parrish
LF	J.Burroughs	3B	S.Ontiveros	LF	G.Foster	LF	J.Cruz	LF	D.Baker	LF	W.Cromartie
CF	R.Office	LF	D.Kingman	CF	C.Geronimo	CF	T.Puhl	CF	D.Thomas	CF	A.Dawson
RF	G.Matthews	CF	J.Martin	RF	K.Griffey	RF	J.Leonard	RF	G.Thomasson	RF	E.Valentine
C	B.Benedict	RF	S.Thompson	C	J.Bench	C	A.Ashby	C	S.Yeager	C	G.Carter
		C	B.Foote								
1	M.Lum			O1	D.Collins	23	A.Howe	CO	J.Ferguson	P	S.Rogers
O	B.Bonnell	O1	L.Biittner	2	J.Kennedy			O	R.Smith	P	B.Lee
32	J.Royster					P	J.Richard			P	S.Sanderson
C	J.Nolan	P	R.Reuschel	P	T.Seaver	P	J.Niekro	P	R.Sutcliffe	P	D.Schatzeder
		P	L.McGlothen	P	M.LaCoss	P	J.Andujar	P	D.Sutton	P	R.Grimsley
P	P.Niekro	P	D.Lamp	P	F.Norman	P	K.Forsch	P	B.Hooton	RP	E.Sosa
P	E.Solomon	P	M.Krukow	P	B.Bonham	P	R.Williams	P	J.Reuss	RP	R.May
P	R.Matula	P	K.Holtzman	P	P.Moskau	RP	J.Sambito	P	C.Hough	RP	S.Bahnsen
P	T.Brizzolara	RP	D.Tidrow	RP	T.Hume	RP	R.Niemann	RP	D.Patterson		
P	M.Mahler	RP	B.Sutter	RP	D.Bair					P	D.Palmer
RP	G.Garber	RP	W.Hernandez	RP	D.Tomlin	P	V.Ruhle	P	B.Welch	P	W.Fryman
RP	J.McLaughlin							P	A.Messersmith		
RP	A.Devine	P	B.Caudill	P	F.Pastore			P	D.Rau		
		P	D.Moore								
P	L.McWilliams										
P	C.Skok										
P	B.McLaughlin										

	NEW YORK		PHILADELPHIA		PITTSBURGH		SAN DIEGO		SAN FRANCISCO		ST.LOUIS
M	J.Torre	M	D.Ozark	M	C.Tanner	M	R.Craig	M	J.Altobelli	M	K.Boyer
1B	W.Montanez	M	D.Green	1B	W.Stargell	1B	G.Tenace	M	D.Bristol	1B	K.Hernandez
2B	D.Flynn	1B	P.Rose	2B	R.Stennett	2B	F.Gonzalez	1B	M.Ivie	2B	K.Oberkfell
SS	F.Taveras	2B	M.Trillo	SS	T.Foli	SS	O.Smith	2B	J.Strain	SS	G.Templeton
3B	R.Hebner	SS	L.Bowa	3B	B.Madlock	3B	P.Dade	SS	J.LeMaster	3B	K.Reitz
LF	S.Henderson	3B	M.Schmidt	LF	B.Robinson	LF	J.Turner	3B	D.Evans	LF	L.Brock
CF	L.Mazzilli	LF	G.Luzinski	CF	O.Moreno	CF	G.Richards	LF	L.Herndon	CF	T.Scott
RF	J.Youngblood	CF	G.Maddox	RF	D.Parker	RF	D.Winfield	CF	B.North	RF	G.Hendrick
C	J.Stearns	RF	B.McBride	C	E.Ott	C	B.Fahey	RF	J.Clark	C	T.Simmons
		C	B.Boone					C	D.Littlejohn		
O3	E.Maddox			23	P.Garner	2S	B.Almon			O	J.Mumphrey
C3	A.Trevino	O	G.Gross	O1	J.Milner	32	K.Bevacqua	1	W.McCovey		
						1O	D.Briggs	O	T.Whitfield		
P	C.Swan	P	S.Carlton	P	B.Blyleven	O1	J.Johnstone	S2	R.Metzger	P	P.Vuckovich
P	P.Falcone	P	R.Lerch	P	J.Candelaria			2	B.Madlock	P	B.Forsch
P	K.Kobel	P	N.Espinosa	P	B.Kison	P	R.Jones			P	S.Martinez
RP	N.Allen	P	D.Ruthven	P	D.Robinson	P	G.Perry	P	V.Blue	P	J.Denny
RP	D.Murray	P	L.Christenson	P	J.Bibby	P	B.Shirley	P	B.Knepper	P	J.Fulgham
RP	A.Hassler	RP	R.Reed	RP	K.Tekulve	P	E.Rasmussen	P	J.Montefusco	RP	M.Littell
		RP	T.McGraw	RP	E.Romo	P	B.Owchinko	P	E.Halicki	RP	R.Thomas
P	D.Ellis	RP	R.Eastwick	RP	G.Jackson	RP	J.D'Acquisto	P	J.Curtis	RP	W.McEnaney
P	T.Hausman					RP	R.Fingers	RP	G.Lavelle		
P	W.Twitchell	P	D.Noles	P	J.Rooker	RP	S.Mura	RP	T.Griffin	P	B.Sykes
P	E.Glynn	P	K.Saucier	P	E.Whitson			RP	G.Minton		
P	M.Scott	P	D.Bird			P	M.Lee				
								P	P.Nastu		
								P	E.Whitson		

TEAM	G	W	L	PCT	GB	R	OR	AB	H	2B	3B	HR	BB	SO	AVG	OBP	SLG	PRO	PRO+	BR	/A	PF	CHI	RC	SB	CS	SBA	SBR
EAST																												
PIT	163	98	64	.605		775	643	5661	1541	264	52	148	483	855	.272	.333	.416	.749	105	68	32	105	101	781	180	66	73	14
MON	160	95	65	.594	2	701	581	5465	1445	273	42	143	432	890	.264	.321	.408	.729	105	23	29	99	102	701	121	56	68	3
STL	163	86	76	.531	12	731	693	5734	1594	279	63	100	460	838	.278	.335	.401	.736	106	46	40	101	98	757	116	69	63	-7
PHI	163	84	78	.519	14	683	718	5463	1453	250	53	119	602	764	.266	.343	.396	.739	106	63	39	103	91	743	128	76	63	-7
CHI	162	80	82	.494	18	706	707	5550	1494	250	43	135	478	762	.269	.331	.403	.734	97	40	-28	110	98	726	73	52	58	-9
NY	163	63	99	.389	35	593	706	5591	1399	255	41	74	498	817	.250	.315	.350	.665	90	-90	-68	96	99	615	135	79	63	-7
WEST																												
CIN	161	90	71	.559		731	644	5477	1445	266	31	132	614	902	.264	.340	.396	.736	106	55	51	101	99	741	99	47	68	2
HOU	162	89	73	.549	1.5	583	582	5394	1382	224	52	49	461	745	.256	.317	.344	.661	91	-93	-60	94	102	591	190	95	67	0
LA	162	79	83	.488	11.5	739	717	5490	1443	220	24	183	556	834	.263	.333	.412	.745	111	62	73	99	99	743	106	46	70	4
SF	162	71	91	.438	19.5	672	751	5395	1328	192	36	125	580	925	.246	.322	.365	.687	100	-46	-3	93	106	644	140	73	66	-2
SD	161	68	93	.422	22	603	681	5436	1316	193	53	93	534	770	.242	.313	.348	.661	91	-97	-62	94	103	600	100	58	63	-5
ATL	160	66	94	.413	23.5	669	763	5422	1389	220	28	126	490	818	.256	.320	.377	.697	89	-31	-78	107	105	654	98	50	66	-1
TOT	971					8186		66088	17229	2886	518	1427	6188	9920	.261	.327	.385	.712							1486	767	66	-14

TEAM	CG	SH	SV	IP	H	H/G	HR	BB	SO	RAT	ERA	ERA+	OAV	OOB	PR	/A	PF	CPI	FA	E	DP	FW	PW	BW	SBW	DIF
EAST																										
PIT	24	7	52	1493^1	1424	8.6	125	504	904	11.8	3.41	114	.254	.318	53	77	104	103	.979	134	163	.4	7.9	3.3	1.6	3.8
MON	33	18	39	1447^1	1379	8.6	116	450	813	11.5	3.14	117	.253	.312	95	84	98	107	.979	131	123	.4	8.7	3.0	.4	2.5
STL	38	10	25	1486^2	1449	8.8	127	501	788	11.9	3.72	101	.258	.321	1	6	101	97	.980	132	166	.5	.6	4.1	-.6	.3
PHI	33	14	29	1441^1	1455	9.1	135	477	787	12.2	4.16	94	.266	.328	-69	-54	103	94	.983	106	148	2.1	-5.6	4.0	-.6	3.1
CHI	20	11	44	1446^2	1500	9.3	127	521	933	12.8	3.88	106	.270	.338	-24	37	110	105	.975	159	163	-1.1	3.8	-2.9	-.9	.0
NY	16	10	36	1482^2	1486	9.0	120	607	819	12.9	3.84	95	.266	.341	-18	-34	98	105	.978	140	168	.0	-3.5	-7.0	-.6	-6.9
WEST																										
CIN	27	10	40	1440^1	1415	8.8	103	485	773	12.0	3.58	104	.260	.322	24	24	100	99	.980	124	152	.9	2.5	5.3	.3	.5
HOU	55	19	31	1447^2	1278	7.9	90	504	854	11.2	3.20	110	.237	.306	86	51	94	93	.978	138	146	.1	5.3	-6.2	.1	8.7
LA	30	6	34	1444	1425	8.9	101	555	811	12.5	3.83	95	.260	.331	-15	-31	97	97	.981	118	123	1.3	-3.2	7.5	.5	-8.2
SF	25	6	34	1436	1484	9.3	143	577	841	13.1	4.16	94	.269	.341	-69	-107	94	101	.974	163	138	-1.4	-11.0	-.3	-.0	2.8
SD	29	7	25	1453	1438	8.9	108	513	779	12.2	3.69	96	.263	.328	6	-27	95	101	.978	141	154	-.1	-2.8	-6.4	-.4	-2.8
ATL	32	3	34	1407^2	1496	9.6	132	494	779	13.0	4.18	97	.272	.337	-70	-21	109	99	.970	183	139	-2.7	-2.2	-8.0	.0	-1.1
TOT	362	121	423	17426^2		8.9				12.3	3.73		.261	.327					.978	1669	1783					

Runs
Hernandez-StL 116
Moreno-Pit 110
Schmidt-Phi 109
Parker-Pit 109
Lopes-LA 109

Hits
Templeton-StL 211
Hernandez-StL 210
Rose-Phi 208
Garvey-LA 204
Moreno-Pit 196

Doubles
Hernandez-StL 48
Cromartie-Mon 46
Parker-Pit 45
Reitz-StL 41
Rose-Phi 40

Triples
Templeton-StL 19
Moreno-Pit 12
McBride-Phi 12
Dawson-Mon 12

Home Runs
Kingman-Chi 48
Schmidt-Phi 45
Winfield-SD 34
Horner-Atl 33
Stargell-Pit 32

Total Bases
Winfield-SD 333
Parker-Pit 327
Kingman-Chi 326
Garvey-LA 322
Matthews-Atl 317

Runs Batted In
Winfield-SD 118
Kingman-Chi 115
Schmidt-Phi 114
Garvey-LA 110
Hernandez-StL 105

Runs Produced
Hernandez-StL 210
Winfield-SD 181
Schmidt-Phi 178
Parker-Pit 178
Garvey-LA 174

Bases On Balls
Schmidt-Phi 120
Tenace-SD 105
Lopes-LA 97
North-SF 96
Rose-Phi 95

Batting Average
Hernandez-StL ...... .344
Rose-Phi ...... .331
Knight-Cin ...... .318
Garvey-LA ...... .315
Horner-Atl ...... .314

On Base Percentage
Hernandez-StL ...... .421
Rose-Phi ...... .421
Tenace-SD ...... .407
Mazzilli-NY ...... .397
Winfield-SD ...... .396

Slugging Average
Kingman-Chi ...... .613
Schmidt-Phi ...... .564
Foster-Cin ...... .561
Winfield-SD ...... .558
Horner-Atl ...... .552

Production
Kingman-Chi ...... .960
Schmidt-Phi ...... .955
Winfield-SD ...... .954
Foster-Cin ...... .950
Hernandez-StL ...... .934

Adjusted Production
Winfield-SD 167
Foster-Cin 155
Schmidt-Phi 153
Hernandez-StL 152
Parrish-Mon 146

Batter Runs
Winfield-SD 47.4
Hernandez-StL 47.1
Schmidt-Phi 44.9
Parker-Pit 39.3
Kingman-Chi 37.8

Adjusted Batter Runs
Winfield-SD 55.0
Hernandez-StL 46.1
Schmidt-Phi 41.1
Parker-Pit 33.8
Foster-Cin 33.1

Clutch Hitting Index
Foli-NY-Pit 140
Hebner-NY 137
Flynn-NY 124
Luzinski-Phi 122
Concepcion-Cin 114

Runs Created
Hernandez-StL 135
Winfield-SD 132
Parker-Pit 131
Schmidt-Phi 123
Matthews-Atl 118

Total Average
Schmidt-Phi 1.024
Winfield-SD ...... .988
Kingman-Chi ...... .972
Hernandez-StL ...... .961
Foster-Cin ...... .959

Stolen Bases
Moreno-Pit 77
North-SF 58
Taveras-Pit-NY 44
Lopes-LA 44
Scott-Mon 39

Stolen Base Average
Lopes-LA 91.7
Parker-Pit 83.3
Morgan-Cin 82.4
Royster-Atl 81.4
Smith-SD 80.0

Stolen Base Runs
Lopes-LA 10.8
Moreno-Pit 10.5
Royster-Atl 5.7
Morgan-Cin 4.8

Fielding Runs
Maddox-Phi 26.9
Moreno-Pit 22.8
Evans-SF 22.4
Smith-SD 21.0
Cromartie-Mon 20.4

Total Player Rating
Winfield-SD 5.9
Schmidt-Phi 5.8
Hernandez-StL 5.6
Templeton-StL 4.7
Parker-Pit 4.0

Wins
Niekro-Atl 21
Niekro-Hou 21
Richard-Hou 18
Reuschel-Chi 18
Carlton-Phi 18

Win Percentage
Seaver-Cin ...... .727
Niekro-Hou ...... .656
Martinez-StL ...... .652
Sutcliffe-LA ...... .630
Carlton-Phi ...... .621

Games
Tekulve-Pit 94
Romo-Pit 84
Jackson-Pit 72
Lavelle-SF 70
Garber-Atl 68

Complete Games
Niekro-Atl 23
Richard-Hou 19
Rogers-Mon 13
Carlton-Phi 13
Hooton-LA 12

Shutouts
Seaver-Cin 5
Rogers-Mon 5
Niekro-Hou 5
Richard-Hou 4
Carlton-Phi 4

Saves
Sutter-Chi 37
Tekulve-Pit 31
Garber-Atl 25
Sambito-Hou 22
Lavelle-SF 20

Innings Pitched
Niekro-Atl 342.0
Richard-Hou 292.1
Niekro-Hou 263.2
Jones-SD 263.0
Swan-NY 251.1

Fewest Hits/Game
Richard-Hou 6.77
Carlton-Phi 7.24
Niekro-Hou 7.54
Schatzeder-Mon 7.56
Andujar-Hou 7.79

Fewest BB/Game
Forsch-Hou 1.77
Candelaria-Pit 1.78
Hume-Cin 1.82
Lee-Mon 1.86
Swan-NY 2.04

Strikeouts
Richard-Hou 313
Carlton-Phi 213
Niekro-Atl 208
Blyleven-Pit 172
McGlothen-Chi 147

Strikeouts/Game
Richard-Hou 9.64
Carlton-Phi 7.64
Sanderson-Mon 7.39
Blyleven-Pit 6.52
Krukow-Chi 6.50

Ratio
Forsch-Hou 9.62
Richard-Hou 9.88
Seaver-Cin 10.38
Sutton-LA 10.47
Carlton-Phi 10.61

Earned Run Average
Richard-Hou 2.71
Hume-Cin 2.76
Schatzeder-Mon 2.83
Hooton-LA 2.97
Niekro-Hou 3.00

Adjusted ERA
Hume-Cin 135
Richard-Hou 130
Schatzeder-Mon 129
Hooton-LA 122
Rogers-Mon 122

Opponents' Batting Avg.
Richard-Hou ...... .209
Carlton-Phi ...... .219
Schatzeder-Mon ...... .225
Niekro-Hou ...... .228
Andujar-Hou ...... .233

Opponents' On Base Pct.
Forsch-Hou ...... .275
Richard-Hou ...... .278
Seaver-Cin ...... .291
Sutton-LA ...... .291
Carlton-Phi ...... .292

Starter Runs
Richard-Hou 33.2
Niekro-Hou 21.3
Rogers-Mon 20.1
Fulgham-StL 19.5
Hooton-LA 17.9

Adjusted Starter Runs
Richard-Hou 26.0
Niekro-Atl 24.8
Fulgham-StL 20.0
Rogers-Mon 18.2
Bibby-Pit 16.3

Clutch Pitching Index
Hume-Cin 117
Lamp-Chi 114
Lee-Mon 113
Kobel-NY 112
Blyleven-Pit 112

Relief Runs
Sambito-Hou 19.9
Sosa-Mon 19.1
Hume-Cin 17.6
Minton-SF 17.0
Sutter-Chi 17.0

Adjusted Relief Runs
Sutter-Chi 21.3
Sosa-Mon 18.4
Sambito-Hou 17.6
Hume-Cin 17.6
Tekulve-Pit 16.9

Relief Ranking
Sutter-Chi 38.8
Sambito-Hou 34.8
Sosa-Mon 32.7
Tekulve-Pit 28.4
Littell-StL 25.2

Total Pitcher Index
Sutter-Chi 4.3
Sambito-Hou 4.1
Niekro-Atl 3.4
Sosa-Mon 3.3
Tekulve-Pit 3.1

Total Baseball Ranking
Winfield-SD 5.9
Schmidt-Phi 5.8
Hernandez-StL 5.6
Templeton-StL 4.7
Sutter-Chi 4.3

February 3 The Twins trade seven-time batting champion Rod Carew to the Angels for outfielder Ken Landreaux, third baseman Dave Engle, and two pitchers.

April 5 Baltimore manager Earl Weaver wins his 1,000th game as a skipper.

May 31 Pat Underwood makes his major league debut for Detroit, pitching 8⅓ innings in shutting out Toronto 1-0. The losing pitcher is Pat's brother, Tom.

June 8 The Mariners make Al Chambers the number-one pick in the free-agent draft. Kansas City picks football players on the fourth (Dan Marino) and the 17th (John Elway) rounds.

June 12 The Tigers fire manager Les Moss, hiring Sparky Anderson.

June 24 Rickey Henderson makes his major league debut for Oakland in a 5-1 loss to Texas in the first game of a doubleheader. Henderson has a single and double and steals the first base of his major league career.

July 13 California's Nolan Ryan and Boston's Steve Renko each lose no-hitters in the ninth inning, and each settle for one-hit victories, 6–1 over New York and 2–0 over Oakland, respectively.

August 2 Thurman Munson, 32, perishes at Canton, Ohio, in a crash of the plane he was piloting. A crowd of 51,151 will attend the memorial tribute at Yankee Stadium the following day.

September 5 Matt Keough of the A's beats the Brewers, 6–1, for his first victory after 14 straight losses. He ended 1978 with four defeats and barely avoided tying the AL record of 19 consecutive losses.

September 12 Boston's Carl Yastrzemski singles off New York's Jim Beattie for his 3,000th career hit. The Sox win 9-2 and Yaz becomes the first AL player to collect both 3,000 hits and 400 homers.

September 15 Boston's Bob Watson hits for the cycle in a 10–2 win over the Orioles. Watson becomes the first player to accomplish the feat in the AL and NL.

September 16 Willie Wilson hits his fifth inside-the-park homer this season in a 6–3 loss to Seattle at Kansas City. It is the most inside jobs hit in a season since Kiki Cuyler hit eight for the Pirates in 1925.

October 6 Scott McGregor's 8-0 shutout of the Angels gives the Orioles the AL pennant. Pat Kelly notches three RBI with a homer and a single.

October 10 The Orioles score five times in the first inning of the World Series, hanging on to defeat the Pirates 5-4 in Game 1. Dave Parker has four hits for the losers.

October 13 Baltimore scores six runs in the eighth inning en route to a 9-6 win, taking a three-games-to-one advantage.

October 31 Mike Flanagan, who posted a 23-9 record for the Orioles, is named the winner of the AL Cy Young Award by a comfortable margin over the Yankees' Tommy John.

November 14 California's Don Baylor, who led the AL in runs and RBI, is named the league's MVP.

	BALTIMORE		BOSTON		CALIFORNIA		CHICAGO		CLEVELAND		DETROIT		KANSAS CITY
M	E.Weaver	M	D.Zimmer	M	J.Fregosi	M	D.Kessinger	M	J.Torborg	M	L.Moss	M	W.Herzog
1B	E.Murray	1B	B.Watson	1B	R.Carew	M	T.LaRussa	M	D.Garcia	M	D.Tracewski	1B	P.LaCock
2B	R.Dauer	2B	J.Remy	2B	B.Grich	1B	M.Squires	1B	A.Thornton	M	S.Anderson	2B	F.White
SS	K.Garcia	SS	R.Burleson	SS	B.Campaneris	2B	A.Bannister	2B	D.Kuiper	1B	J.Thompson	SS	F.Patek
3B	D.DeCinces	3B	B.Hobson	3B	C.Lansford	SS	G.Pryor	SS	T.Veryzer	2B	L.Whitaker	3B	G.Brett
LF	G.Roenicke	LF	J.Rice	LF	J.Rudi	3B	K.Bell	3B	T.Harrah	SS	A.Trammell	LF	W.Wilson
CF	A.Bumbry	CF	F.Lynn	CF	R.Miller	LF	R.Torres	LF	J.Norris	3B	A.Rodriguez	CF	A.Otis
RF	K.Singleton	RF	D.Evans	RF	D.Ford	CF	C.Lemon	CF	R.Manning	LF	S.Kemp	RF	A.Cowens
C	R.Dempsey	C	G.Allenson	C	B.Downing	RF	C.Washington	RF	B.Bonds	CF	R.LeFlore	C	D.Porter
DH	L.May	DH	C.Yastrzemski	DH	D.Baylor	C	M.May	C	G.Alexander	RF	J.Morales	DH	H.McRae
						DH	J.Orta	DH	C.Johnson	C	L.Parrish		
S	M.Belanger	DC	C.Fisk	1D	W.Aikens					DH	R.Staub	S2	U.Washington
O	J.Lowenstein			S3	J.Anderson	OD	R.Garr	O1	M.Hargrove				
		P	M.Torrez			1D	L.Johnson	C	R.Hassey	OD	C.Summers	P	P.Splittorff
P	D.Martinez	P	D.Eckersley	P	D.Frost	23	J.Morrison			1C	J.Wockenfuss	P	D.Leonard
P	M.Flanagan	P	B.Stanley	P	N.Ryan	3	E.Soderholm	P	R.Wise	O	L.Jones	P	L.Gura
P	S.Stone	P	S.Renko	P	J.Barr	OD	J.Moore	P	R.Waits			P	R.Gale
P	S.McGregor	P	C.Rainey	P	D.Aase			P	M.Paxton	P	J.Morris	RP	E.Rodriguez
P	J.Palmer	RP	D.Drago	P	C.Knapp	P	K.Kravec	P	D.Spillner	P	M.Wilcox	RP	A.Hrabosky
RP	T.Martinez	RP	T.Burgmeier	RP	M.Clear	P	R.Wortham	P	L.Barker	P	J.Billingham		
RP	D.Stanhouse	RP	B.Campbell	RP	D.LaRoche	P	R.Baumgarten	RP	S.Monge	P	P.Underwood	P	S.Busby
RP	T.Stoddard			RP	M.Barlow	P	S.Trout	RP	V.Cruz	P	D.Petry	P	M.Pattin
		P	A.Ripley			RP	R.Scarbery			RP	A.Lopez	P	C.Chamberlain
P	S.Stewart	P	J.Finch	P	F.Tanana	RP	M.Proly	P	W.Garland	RP	J.Hiller		
						RP	E.Farmer	P	E.Wilkins	RP	D.Tobik		
						P	F.Barrios			P	D.Rozema		
						P	F.Howard			P	S.Baker		

	MILWAUKEE		MINNESOTA		NEW YORK		OAKLAND		SEATTLE		TEXAS		TORONTO
M	G.Bamberger	M	G.Mauch	M	B.Lemon	M	J.Marshall	M	D.Johnson	M	P.Corrales	M	R.Hartsfield
1B	C.Cooper	1B	R.Jackson	M	B.Martin	1B	D.Revering	1B	B.Bochte	1B	P.Putnam	1B	J.Mayberry
2B	P.Molitor	2B	R.Wilfong	1B	C.Chambliss	2B	M.Edwards	2B	J.Cruz	2B	B.Wills	2B	D.Ainge
SS	R.Yount	SS	R.Smalley	2B	W.Randolph	SS	R.Picciolo	SS	M.Mendoza	SS	N.Norman	SS	A.Griffin
3B	S.Bando	3B	J.Castino	SS	B.Dent	3B	W.Gross	3B	D.Meyer	3B	B.Bell	3B	R.Howell
LF	B.Oglivie	LF	B.Rivera	3B	G.Nettles	LF	R.Henderson	LF	L.Roberts	LF	B.Sample	LF	A.Woods
CF	G.Thomas	CF	K.Landreaux	LF	L.Piniella	CF	D.Murphy	CF	R.Jones	CF	A.Oliver	CF	R.Bosetti
RF	S.Lezcano	RF	H.Powell	CF	B.Murcer	RF	L.Murray	RF	J.Simpson	RF	R.Zisk	RF	B.Bailor
C	C.Moore	C	B.Wynegar	RF	R.Jackson	C	J.Newman	C	L.Cox	C	J.Sundberg	C	R.Cerone
DH	D.Davis	DH	J.Morales	C	T.Munson	DH	M.Page	DH	W.Horton	DH	J.Ellis	DH	R.Carty
				DH	J.Spencer								
D3	D.Money	DO	G.Adams	C3	J.Essian	S2	L.Milbourne	O	J.Grubb	O	O.Velez
32	J.Gantner	OD	W.Norwood	O	M.Rivers	O	T.Armas	O1	T.Paciorek	O	M.Rivers	
		3D	M.Cubbage	DO	R.White	OC	M.Heath	32	B.Stein			P	T.Underwood
P	L.Sorensen	O	D.Edwards			2S	D.Chalk	C	B.Stinson	P	F.Jenkins	P	P.Huffman
P	M.Caldwell			P	T.John					P	S.Comer	P	D.Lemanczyk
P	J.Slaton	P	J.Koosman	P	R.Guidry	P	R.Langford	P	M.Parrott	P	D.Medich	P	B.Moore
P	B.Travers	P	D.Goltz	P	L.Tiant	P	S.McCatty	P	R.Honeycutt	P	D.Alexander	P	D.Stieb
P	M.Haas	P	G.Zahn	P	C.Hunter	P	M.Keough	P	F.Bannister	RP	J.Kern	RP	D.Freisleben
RP	J.Augustine	P	P.Hartzell	P	E.Figueroa	P	M.Norris	P	O.Jones	RP	S.Lyle	RP	T.Buskey
RP	R.Cleveland	P	R.Erickson	P	R.Davis	P	C.Minetto	P	G.Abbott	P	D.Rajsich		
RP	B.McClure	RP	M.Marshall	RP	K.Clay	RP	D.Heaverlo	RP	B.McLaughlin			P	J.Jefferson
		RP	P.Redfern	RP	D.Hood	RP	D.Hamilton	RP	J.Montague	P	J.Matlack	P	M.Lemongello
P	P.Mitchell	RP	D.Jackson			RP	J.Todd	RP	S.Rawley	P	J.Johnson	P	J.Clancy
P	B.Galasso			P	J.Beattie					P	D.Darwin	/P	B.Edge
		P	M.Bacsik	P	R.Gossage	P	B.Kingman	P	R.Dressler				
		P	G.Serum	P	J.Kaat	P	J.Johnson						
						P	M.Morgan						

TEAM	G	W	L	PCT	GB	R	OR	AB	H	2B	3B	HR	BB	SO	AVG	OBP	SLG	PRO	PRO+	BR	/A	PF	CHI	RC	SB	CS	SBA	SBR
EAST																												
BAL	159	102	57	.642		757	**582**	5371	1401	258	24	181	608	847	.261	.339	.419	.758	107	25	54	96	98	758	99	49	67	0
MIL	161	95	66	.590	8	807	722	5536	1552	291	41	185	549	745	.280	.347	.448	.795	113	95	95	100	94	**850**	100	53	65	-2
BOS	160	91	69	.569	11.5	841	711	5538	1567	**310**	34	**194**	512	708	**.283**	.347	**.456**	**.803**	109	**108**	61	106	97	848	60	43	58	-8
NY	160	89	71	.556	13.5	734	672	5421	1443	226	40	150	509	590	.266	.331	.406	.737	100	-21	-5	98	102	708	65	46	59	-9
DET	161	85	76	.528	18	770	738	5375	1446	221	35	164	575	814	.269	.342	.415	.757	100	24	0	103	101	754	176	86	67	1
CLE	161	81	80	.503	22	760	805	5376	1388	206	29	138	**657**	786	.258	.344	.384	.728	96	-21	-24	100	103	720	143	90	61	-11
TOR	162	53	109	.327	50.5	613	862	5423	1362	253	34	95	448	663	.251	.313	.363	.676	81	-142	-149	101	104	602	75	56	57	-11
WEST																												
CAL	162	88	74	.543		**866**	768	5550	1563	242	43	164	589	843	.282	**.354**	.429	.783	**114**	83	**112**	97	101	842	100	53	65	-2
KC	162	85	77	.525	3	851	816	5653	**1596**	286	**79**	116	528	879	.282	.347	.422	.769	104	51	35	102	103	836	**207**	76	**73**	17
TEX	162	83	79	.512	5	750	698	5562	1549	252	26	140	461	607	.278	.337	.409	.746	101	-1	-8	99	99	750	79	51	61	-7
MIN	162	82	80	.506	6	764	725	5544	1544	256	46	112	526	693	.278	.344	.402	.746	96	7	-22	104	99	770	66	45	59	-7
CHI	160	73	87	.456	14	730	748	5463	1505	290	33	127	454	668	.275	.335	.410	.745	100	-4	-4	100	99	726	97	62	61	-8
SEA	162	67	95	.414	21	711	820	5544	1490	250	52	132	515	725	.269	.334	.404	.738	96	-17	-30	102	96	733	126	52	71	7
OAK	162	54	108	.333	34	573	860	5348	1276	188	32	108	482	751	.239	.304	.346	.650	79	-189	-160	95	**106**	552	104	69	60	-10
TOT	1128					10527		76704	20682	3529	548	2006	7413	10115	.270	.337	.408	.746							1497	831	64	-50

TEAM	CG	SH	SV	IP	H	H/G	HR	BB	SO	RAT	ERA	ERA+	OAV	OOB	PR	/A	PF	CPI	FA	E	DP	FW	PW	BW	SBW	DIF
EAST																										
BAL	52	**12**	30	1434¹	**1279**	8.0	133	467	786	**11.0**	3.26	123	**.241**	.304	152	119	95	100	.980	125	161	.8	**11.6**	5.3	.3	4.5
MIL	**61**	12	23	1439²	1563	9.8	162	**381**	580	12.3	4.03	103	.279	.327	29	21	99	105	.980	127	153	.7	2.0	9.3	.1	2.3
BOS	47	11	29	1431¹	1487	9.4	123	463	731	12.5	4.03	110	.270	.330	29	61	105	100	.977	142	166	-.2	6.0	6.0	-.4	-.3
NY	43	10	37	1432¹	1446	9.1	123	455	731	12.0	3.83	106	.268	.326	61	38	97	102	**.981**	122	183	1.0	3.7	-.5	-.4	5.2
DET	25	5	37	1423¹	1429	9.0	167	547	802	12.8	4.27	101	.265	.338	-9	8	103	101	**.981**	120	184	1.1	.8	.0	.4	2.1
CLE	28	7	32	1431²	1502	9.4	138	570	781	13.2	4.57	93	.272	.343	-56	-50	101	94	.978	134	149	.3	-4.9	-2.3	-.7	8.1
TOR	44	7	11	1417	1537	9.8	165	594	613	13.8	4.82	90	.281	.356	-95	-75	103	100	.975	159	187	-1.0	-7.3	-14.5	-.7	-4.4
WEST																										
CAL	46	9	33	1436	1463	9.2	131	573	**820**	13.0	4.34	94	.267	.340	-19	-42	97	96	.978	135	172	.3	-4.1	**10.9**	.1	-.3
KC	42	7	22	1448¹	1477	9.2	165	536	640	12.7	4.45	96	.267	.335	-38	-30	101	95	.977	146	160	-.3	-2.9	3.4	**2.0**	1.8
TEX	26	10	**42**	1437	1371	8.6	135	532	773	12.1	3.86	107	.253	.323	56	45	98	97	.979	130	151	.6	4.4	.8	-.3	-3.5
MIN	31	6	33	1444¹	1590	9.9	128	452	721	12.8	4.13	106	.285	.340	14	40	104	**106**	.979	134	**203**	.4	3.9	-2.1	-.3	-.8
CHI	28	9	37	1409	1365	8.7	**114**	618	675	12.9	4.10	104	.256	.338	18	23	101	96	.972	173	142	-1.9	2.2	-.4	-.4	-6.5
SEA	37	7	26	1438	1567	9.8	151	571	736	13.6	4.58	95	.281	.351	-57	-34	103	103	.978	141	170	.0	-3.3	-2.9	1.0	-8.8
OAK	41	4	20	1429¹	1606	10.1	147	654	726	14.5	4.75	85	.288	.367	-84	-112	96	105	.972	174	137	-1.9	-10.9	-15.6	-.6	2.0
TOT	551	116	417	20051²		9.3				12.8	4.22		.270	.337					.978	1962	2318					

Runs
Baylor-Cal 120
Brett-KC 119
Rice-Bos 117
Lynn-Bos 116
Lansford-Cal 114

Hits
Brett-KC 212
Rice-Bos 201
Bell-Tex 200
Molitor-Mil 188
Lansford-Cal 188

Doubles
Lemon-Chi 44
Cooper-Mil 44
Lynn-Bos 42
Brett-KC 42
Bell-Tex 42

Triples
Brett-KC 20
Molitor-Mil 16
Wilson-KC 13
Randolph-NY 13

Home Runs
Thomas-Mil 45
Rice-Bos 39
Lynn-Bos 39
Baylor-Cal 36
Singleton-Bal 35

Total Bases
Rice-Bos 369
Brett-KC 363
Lynn-Bos 338
Baylor-Cal 333
Singleton-Bal 304

Runs Batted In
Baylor-Cal 139
Rice-Bos 130
Thomas-Mil 123
Lynn-Bos 122
Porter-KC 112

Runs Produced
Baylor-Cal 223
Rice-Bos 208
Brett-KC 203
Lynn-Bos 199
Porter-KC 193

Bases On Balls
Porter-KC 121
Singleton-Bal 109
Thomas-Mil 98
Randolph-NY 95
Thornton-Cle 90

Batting Average
Lynn-Bos .... .333
Brett-KC .... .329
Downing-Cal .... .326
Rice-Bos .... .325
Oliver-Tex .... .323

On Base Percentage
Porter-KC .... .429
Lynn-Bos .... .426
Downing-Cal .... .420
Lezcano-Mil .... .420
Singleton-Bal ...... .409

Slugging Average
Lynn-Bos .... .637
Rice-Bos .... .596
Lezcano-Mil .... .573
Brett-KC .... .563
Jackson-NY .... .544

Production
Lynn-Bos 1.063
Lezcano-Mil .... .992
Rice-Bos .... .981
Kemp-Det .... .946
Singleton-Bal ...... .942

Adjusted Production
Lynn-Bos 173
Lezcano-Mil 165
Singleton-Bal 158
Rice-Bos 152
Jackson-NY 151

Batter Runs
Lynn-Bos 62.1
Rice-Bos 50.2
Lezcano-Mil 44.6
Singleton-Bal 44.4
Brett-KC 42.8

Adjusted Batter Runs
Lynn-Bos 54.7
Singleton-Bal 49.2
Lezcano-Mil 44.6
Rice-Bos 42.9
Baylor-Cal 40.8

Clutch Hitting Index
Porter-KC 123
Baylor-Cal 121
Sundberg-Tex 120
Cerone-Tor 117
Dauer-Bal 114

Runs Created
Lynn-Bos 147
Rice-Bos 138
Brett-KC 134
Singleton-Bal 127
Baylor-Cal 126

Total Average
Lynn-Bos 1.162
Lezcano-Mil 1.051
Rice-Bos .... .993
Singleton-Bal ...... .993
Porter-KC .... .982

Stolen Bases
Wilson-KC 83
LeFlore-Det 78
Cruz-Sea 49
Bumbry-Bal 37
Wills-Tex 35

Stolen Base Average
Wilson-KC 87.4
Otis-KC 85.7
LeFlore-Det 84.8
Cruz-Sea 84.5
Lowenstein-Bal 80.0

Stolen Base Runs
Wilson-KC 17.7
LeFlore-Det 15.0
Cruz-Sea 9.3
Otis-KC 6.0
Manning-Cle 4.2

Fielding Runs
Smalley-Min 33.1
Dent-NY 32.0
Mendoza-Sea 27.5
Burleson-Bos 21.7
Wilfong-Min 20.7

Total Player Rating
Smalley-Min 5.6
Lynn-Bos 5.2
Brett-KC 4.9
Grich-Cal 4.2
Lezcano-Mil 4.0

Wins
Flanagan-Bal 23
John-NY 21
Koosman-Min 20
Guidry-NY 18

Win Percentage
Caldwell-Mil .... .727
Flanagan-Bal .... .719
Morris-Det .... .708
John-NY .... .700
Guidry-NY .... .692

Games
Marshall-Min 90
Monge-Cle 76
Kern-Tex 71
Lyle-Tex 67
Heaverlo-Oak 62

Complete Games
D.Martinez-Bal 18
Ryan-Cal 17
John-NY 17
Eckersley-Bos 17

Shutouts
Ryan-Cal 5
Leonard-KC 5
Flanagan-Bal 5
Stanley-Bos 4
Caldwell-Mil 4

Saves
Marshall-Min 32
Kern-Tex 29
Stanhouse-Bal 21
Lopez-Det 21
Monge-Cle 19

Innings Pitched
D.Martinez-Bal 292.1
John-NY 276.1
Flanagan-Bal 265.2
Koosman-Min 263.2
Jenkins-Tex 259.0

Fewest Hits/Game
Ryan-Cal 6.83
Kravec-Chi 7.49
Guidry-NY 7.73
Morris-Det 8.15
Baumgarten-Chi 8.26

Fewest BB/Game
McGregor-Bal 1.19
Caldwell-Mil 1.49
Sorensen-Mil 1.61
Stanley-Bos 1.83
John-NY 2.12

Strikeouts
Ryan-Cal 223
Guidry-NY 201
Flanagan-Bal 190
Jenkins-Tex 164
Koosman-Min 157

Strikeouts/Game
Ryan-Cal 9.01
Guidry-NY 7.65
Flanagan-Bal 6.44
Jenkins-Tex 5.70
Bannister-Sea 5.68

Ratio
McGregor-Bal 9.79
Guidry-NY 10.43
Flanagan-Bal 10.77
Leonard-KC 10.83
Eckersley-Bos 10.91

Earned Run Average
Guidry-NY 2.78
John-NY 2.96
Eckersley-Bos 2.99
Flanagan-Bal 3.08
Morris-Det 3.28

Adjusted ERA
Eckersley-Bos 148
Guidry-NY 146
John-NY 137
Morris-Det 132
Flanagan-Bal 130

Opponents' Batting Avg.
Ryan-Cal .... .212
Kravec-Chi .... .233
Guidry-NY .... .236
Baumgarten-Chi ..... .243
Morris-Det .... .244

Opponents' On Base Pct.
McGregor-Bal .... .275
Guidry-NY .... .294
Flanagan-Bal .... .297
Eckersley-Bos ...... .298
Leonard-KC .... .299

Starter Runs
John-NY 38.4
Guidry-NY 37.7
Eckersley-Bos 33.5
Flanagan-Bal 33.4
Koosman-Min 24.5

Adjusted Starter Runs
Eckersley-Bos 39.0
John-NY 34.0
Guidry-NY 33.9
Koosman-Min 29.3
Flanagan-Bal 27.4

Clutch Pitching Index
Eckersley-Bos 115
Keough-Oak 114
McCatty-Oak 114
Travers-Mil 113
Koosman-Min 112

Relief Runs
Kern-Tex 42.0
Monge-Cle 26.4
Lopez-Det 25.5
Marshall-Min 24.8
Stoddard-Bal 16.2

Adjusted Relief Runs
Kern-Tex 40.9
Marshall-Min 27.4
Lopez-Det 27.0
Monge-Cle 26.9
Burgmeier-Bos 16.5

Relief Ranking
Kern-Tex 65.0
Marshall-Min 57.1
Monge-Cle 49.5
Lopez-Det 38.8
Drago-Bos 26.6

Total Pitcher Index
Kern-Tex 6.7
Marshall-Min 5.7
Monge-Cle 5.0
Eckersley-Bos 4.0
John-NY 3.8

Total Baseball Ranking
Kern-Tex 6.7
Marshall-Min 5.7
Smalley-Min 5.6
Lynn-Bos 5.2
Monge-Cle 5.0

January 28 Henry Aaron refuses an award from Commissioner Bowie Kuhn honoring him for hitting his 715th home run. Aaron charges that baseball's treatment of retired black ballplayers falls far short of what is needed.

July 30 Attempting to throw for the first time since being hospitalized for tests last week, J. R. Richard suffers a stroke and is rushed to Houston's Methodist Hospital for emergency surgery to remove a life-threatening blood clot in his neck. He will never pitch in the major leagues again.

September 10 Expos 21-year-old pitcher Bill Gullickson strikes out 18 Cubs in a 4-2 win at Olympic Stadium, setting a major league record for rookies and falling one short of the all-time record for strikeouts in a nine-inning game.

October 5 Capping an improbable comeback, the Dodgers beat the Astros for the third day in a row to force a one-game playoff for the NL West title. Los Angeles trailed Houston by three games with three games left in the season, and won all three by a single run.

October 6 The Astros finally win, whipping the Dodgers 7-1 in a one-game playoff at Dodger Stadium. Art Howe drives in four runs with a home run and two singles and Joe Niekro wins his 20th game of the season to put Houston in the postseason for the first time.

October 11 In one of the most exciting and controversial games in playoff history, the Phillies tie the NLCS at two games apiece with a 10-inning 5-3 win over the Astros. In the fourth inning, Houston is deprived of an apparent triple play when the umpires rule that pitcher Vern Ruhle had trapped Garry Maddox's soft line drive. In the sixth, Houston loses a run when Gary Woods leaves the base early on Luis Pujols' would-be sacrifice fly.

October 12 The Phillies capture their first NL pennant since 1950 with a 10-inning 8-7 win over the Astros in the fifth and final game of the NLCS.

October 21 The Phillies win the first world championship in their 98-year history by beating the Royals 4-1 in Game 6 of the World Series. Philadelphia's Mike Schmidt is named MVP, hitting .381 with two home runs and seven RBI, while KC's Willie Wilson is the goat, striking out a record 12 times.

November 4 Steve Carlton joins Sandy Koufax, Tom Seaver, and Jim Palmer as the only pitchers to win three Cy Young Awards, garnering 23 of 24 first-place votes to take NL honors. Carlton was 24-9 with a 2.34 ERA and led the NL with 286 strikeouts.

November 4 Sadaharu Oh, professional baseball's all-time home run king with 868 in 22 seasons in Japan, retires at the age of 40.

November 26 Mike Schmidt is a unanimous choice as NL MVP. The slugging third baseman hit .286 with career highs of 48 home runs and 121 RBI.

ATLANTA		CHICAGO		CINCINNATI		HOUSTON		LOS ANGELES		MONTREAL	
M	B.Cox	M	P.Gomez	M	J.McNamara	M	B.Virdon	M	T.Lasorda	M	D.Williams
1B	C.Chambliss	M	J.Amalfitano	1B	D.Driessen	1B	A.Howe	1B	S.Garvey	1B	W.Cromartie
2B	G.Hubbard	1B	B.Buckner	2B	J.Kennedy	2B	J.Morgan	2B	D.Lopes	2B	R.Scott
SS	L.Gomez	2B	M.Tyson	SS	D.Concepcion	SS	C.Reynolds	SS	B.Russell	SS	C.Speier
3B	B.Horner	SS	I.DeJesus	3B	R.Knight	3B	E.Cabell	3B	R.Cey	3B	L.Parrish
LF	J.Burroughs	3B	L.Randle	LF	G.Foster	LF	J.Cruz	LF	D.Baker	LF	R.LeFlore
CF	D.Murphy	LF	D.Kingman	CF	D.Collins	CF	C.Cedeno	CF	R.Law	CF	A.Dawson
RF	G.Matthews	CF	J.Martin	RF	K.Griffey	RF	T.Puhl	RF	R.Smith	RF	R.Office
C	B.Benedict	RF	M.Vail	C	J.Bench	C	A.Ashby	C	S.Yeager	C	G.Carter
		C	T.Blackwell								
23	J.Royster			O	C.Geronimo	2S	R.Landestoy	O	J.Johnstone	O	J.White
S3	L.Blanks	1O	L.Biittner	2S	R.Oester	1O	D.Walling	OS	D.Thomas	O	E.Valentine
O	B.Asselstine	32	S.Dillard			C	L.Pujols				
		O	J.Figueroa	P	M.Soto	O1	J.Leonard	P	J.Reuss	P	S.Rogers
P	P.Niekro	23	M.Kelleher	P	F.Pastore			P	B.Welch	P	S.Sanderson
P	D.Alexander	O1	S.Thompson	P	C.Leibrandt	P	J.Niekro	P	D.Sutton	P	B.Gullickson
P	T.Boggs	C	B.Foote	P	M.LaCoss	P	N.Ryan	P	B.Hooton	P	D.Palmer
P	R.Matula			P	T.Seaver	P	K.Forsch	P	D.Goltz	P	B.Lee
P	L.McWilliams	P	R.Reuschel	RP	T.Hume	P	V.Ruhle	RP	R.Sutcliffe	RP	F.Norman
RP	R.Camp	P	M.Krukow	RP	D.Bair	P	J.Andujar	RP	B.Castillo	RP	E.Sosa
RP	G.Garber	P	D.Lamp			RP	D.Smith	RP	S.Howe	RP	S.Bahnsen
RP	P.Hanna	P	L.McGlothen	P	P.Moskau	RP	J.Sambito				
		RP	B.Caudill	P	J.Price	RP	F.LaCorte			P	C.Lea
P	A.Hrabosky	RP	D.Tidrow					P	J.Beckwith	P	W.Fryman
P	L.Bradford	RP	W.Hernandez			P	J.Richard				
		P	B.Sutter								
		P	D.Capilla								

NEW YORK		PHILADELPHIA		PITTSBURGH		SAN DIEGO		SAN FRANCISCO		ST.LOUIS	
M	J.Torre	M	D.Green	M	C.Tanner	M	J.Coleman	M	D.Bristol	M	K.Boyer
1B	L.Mazzilli	1B	P.Rose	1B	J.Milner	1B	W.Montanez	1B	M.Ivie	M	J.Krol
2B	D.Flynn	2B	M.Trillo	2B	P.Garner	2B	D.Cash	2B	R.Stennett	M	W.Herzog
SS	F.Taveras	SS	L.Bowa	SS	T.Foli	SS	O.Smith	SS	J.LeMaster	M	R.Schoendienst
3B	E.Maddox	3B	M.Schmidt	3B	B.Madlock	3B	A.Rodriguez	3B	D.Evans	1B	K.Hernandez
LF	S.Henderson	LF	G.Luzinski	LF	M.Easler	LF	G.Richards	LF	L.Herndon	2B	K.Oberkfell
CF	J.Youngblood	CF	G.Maddox	CF	O.Moreno	CF	J.Mumphrey	CF	B.North	SS	G.Templeton
RF	C.Washington	RF	B.McBride	RF	D.Parker	RF	D.Winfield	RF	J.Clark	3B	K.Reitz
C	A.Trevino	C	B.Boone	C	E.Ott	C	G.Tenace	C	M.May	LF	B.Bonds
										CF	T.Scott
1O	M.Jorgensen	O	G.Gross	O	L.Lacy	23	T.Flannery	O	T.Whitfield	RF	K.Hendrick
C1	J.Stearns	O	L.Smith	1O	B.Robinson	C	B.Fahey			C	T.Simmons
				3S	D.Berra			P	V.Blue		
P	R.Burris	P	S.Carlton	1	W.Stargell	P	J.Curtis	P	B.Knepper	O	D.Iorg
P	P.Zachry	P	D.Ruthven			P	S.Mura	P	E.Whitson	O	L.Durham
P	M.Bomback	P	B.Walk	P	J.Bibby	P	R.Wise	P	A.Ripley	CO	T.Kennedy
P	P.Falcone	P	R.Lerch	P	J.Candelaria	P	R.Jones	P	J.Montefusco	2S	T.Herr
P	C.Swan	RP	T.McGraw	P	B.Blyleven	RP	B.Shirley	RP	T.Griffin		
RP	T.Hausman	RP	R.Reed	P	D.Robinson	RP	E.Rasmussen	RP	G.Lavelle	P	P.Vuckovich
RP	J.Reardon	RP	D.Noles	P	E.Romo	RP	R.Fingers	RP	G.Minton	P	B.Forsch
RP	N.Allen			RP	K.Tekulve					P	B.Sykes
		P	N.Espinosa	RP	G.Jackson	P	J.Eichelberger	P	A.Holland	P	S.Martinez
P	J.Pacella	P	L.Christenson			P	D.Kinney	P	A.Hargesheimer	RP	J.Kaat
P	R.Jackson	P	K.Saucier	P	E.Solomon	P	J.D'Acquisto			RP	D.Hood
P	E.Glynn									RP	J.Littlefield
										P	J.Fulgham
										P	J.Urrea
										P	J.Otten
										P	R.Thomas

TEAM	G	W	L	PCT	GB	R	OR	AB	H	2B	3B	HR	BB	SO	AVG	OBP	SLG	PRO	PRO+	BR	/A	PF	CHI	RC	SB	CS	SBA	SBR
EAST																												
PHI	162	91	71	.562		728	639	5625	1517	272	54	117	472	**708**	.270	.330	**.400**	.730	103	61	21	106	100	**736**	140	62	69	5
MON	162	90	72	.556	1	694	629	5465	1407	250	61	114	547	865	.257	.327	.388	.715	105	36	35	100	101	709	237	82	74	22
PIT	162	83	79	.512	8	666	646	5517	1469	249	38	116	452	760	.266	.325	.388	.713	102	27	17	102	98	686	209	102	67	2
STL	162	74	88	.457	17	**738**	710	5608	**1541**	**300**	49	101	451	781	**.275**	**.331**	**.400**	**.731**	106	**63**	41	102	102	724	117	54	68	3
NY	162	67	95	.414	24	611	702	5478	1407	218	41	61	501	840	.257	.322	.345	.667	95	-52	-35	97	102	601	158	99	61	-12
CHI	162	64	98	.395	27	614	728	5619	1411	251	35	107	471	912	.251	.311	.365	.676	88	-47	-93	107	100	627	93	64	59	-11
WEST																												
HOU	163	93	70	.571		637	**589**	5566	1455	231	**67**	75	540	755	.261	.328	.367	.695	**109**	2	**55**	92	96	688	194	74	72	14
LA	163	92	71	.564	1	663	591	5568	1462	209	24	**148**	492	846	.263	.325	.388	.713	106	29	42	98	96	699	123	72	63	-6
CIN	163	89	73	.549	3.5	707	670	5516	1445	256	45	113	537	852	.262	.330	.386	.716	105	39	39	100	101	716	156	43	**78**	21
ATL	161	81	80	.503	11	630	660	5402	1352	226	22	144	434	899	.250	.308	.380	.688	94	-27	-47	103	**104**	616	73	52	58	-9
SF	161	75	86	.466	17	573	634	5368	1310	199	44	80	509	840	.244	.311	.342	.653	90	-82	-69	98	102	571	100	58	63	-5
SD	163	73	89	.451	19.5	591	654	5540	1410	195	43	67	**563**	791	.255	.326	.342	.668	98	-48	-12	94	96	641	**239**	73	77	**28**
TOT	973					7852		66272	17186	2856	523	1243	5969	9849	.259	.323	.374	.697							1839	835	69	51

TEAM	CG	SH	SV	IP	H	H/G	HR	BB	SO	RAT	ERA	ERA+	OAV	OOB	PR	/A	PF	CPI	FA	E	DP	FW	PW	BW	SBW	DIF
EAST																										
PHI	25	8	40	1480	1419	8.6	87	530	889	12.0	3.43	110	.255	.322	28	**59**	105	100	.979	136	136	.2	**6.2**	2.2	.0	1.2
MON	33	15	36	1456²	1447	8.9	100	460	823	11.9	3.48	102	.261	.320	20	14	99	102	.977	144	126	-.2	1.5	3.7	1.9	2.1
PIT	25	8	**43**	1458¹	1422	8.8	110	**451**	832	11.7	3.58	102	.259	.318	4	10	101	99	.978	137	154	.2	1.1	1.8	-.2	-.8
STL	**34**	9	27	1447	1454	9.0	90	495	664	12.3	3.93	94	.265	.329	-53	-39	103	94	.981	122	**174**	1.0	-4.1	4.3	-.1	-8.1
NY	17	9	33	1451¹	1473	9.1	140	510	886	12.4	3.85	94	.267	.331	-40	-48	99	104	.975	154	132	-.7	-5.1	-3.7	-1.7	-2.8
CHI	13	6	35	1479	1525	9.3	109	589	923	13.0	3.89	101	.272	.344	-47	4	107	**106**	.974	174	149	-1.7	.4	-9.8	-1.6	-4.2
WEST																										
HOU	31	18	41	1482²	1367	**8.3**	69	466	**929**	11.3	**3.10**	106	**.246**	**.307**	82	31	91	96	.978	140	145	.0	3.3	**5.8**	1.0	1.3
LA	24	**19**	42	1472²	**1358**	**8.3**	105	480	835	**11.3**	3.25	108	.247	.309	58	41	97	100	.981	123	149	1.0	4.3	4.4	-1.1	1.8
CIN	30	12	37	1459¹	1404	8.7	113	506	833	11.9	3.85	93	.255	.319	-40	-44	99	92	**.983**	106	144	**1.9**	-4.6	4.1	1.8	4.9
ATL	29	9	37	1428	1397	8.8	131	454	696	11.8	3.77	99	.258	.318	-27	-4	104	97	.975	162	156	-1.2	-.4	-5.0	-1.4	8.4
SF	27	10	35	1448¹	1446	9.0	92	492	811	12.2	3.46	94	.261	.325	24	13	98	104	.975	159	124	-1.0	1.4	-7.3	-1.0	2.4
SD	19	9	39	1466¹	1474	9.0	97	536	728	12.4	3.65	94	.267	.333	-8	-36	95	105	.980	132	157	.5	-3.8	-1.3	**2.5**	-5.9
TOT	307	132	445	17529²		8.8				12.0	3.60		.259	.323					.978	1689	1746					

Runs		Hits		Doubles		Triples		Home Runs		Total Bases	
Hernandez-StL	111	Garvey-LA	200	Rose-Phi	42	Scott-Mon	13	Schmidt-Phi	48	Schmidt-Phi	342
Schmidt-Phi	104	Richards-SD	193	Dawson-Mon	41	Moreno-Pit	13	Horner-Atl	35	Garvey-LA	307
Murphy-Atl	98	Hernandez-StL	191	Buckner-Chi	41	LeFlore-Mon	11	Murphy-Atl	33	Hernandez-StL	294
Dawson-Mon	96	Buckner-Chi	187	Knight-Cin	39	Herndon-SF	11	Carter-Mon	29	Baker-LA	291
				Hernandez-StL	39			Baker-LA	29	Murphy-Atl	290

Runs Batted In		Runs Produced		Bases On Balls		Batting Average		On Base Percentage		Slugging Average	
Schmidt-Phi	121	Hernandez-StL	194	Morgan-Hou	93	Buckner-Chi	.324	Hernandez-StL	.410	Schmidt-Phi	.624
Hendrick-StL	109	Schmidt-Phi	177	Driessen-Cin	93	Hernandez-StL	.321	Cedeno-Hou	.390	Clark-SF	.517
Garvey-LA	106	Dawson-Mon	166	Tenace-SD	92	Templeton-StL	.319	Clark-SF	.390	Murphy-Atl	.510
Carter-Mon	101	Simmons-StL	161	Schmidt-Phi	89	McBride-Phi	.309	Schmidt-Phi	.388	Simmons-StL	.505
Hernandez-StL	99	Griffey-Cin	161	Hernandez-StL	86	Cedeno-Hou	.309	Driessen-Cin	.382	Baker-LA	.503

Production		Adjusted Production		Batter Runs		Adjusted Batter Runs		Clutch Hitting Index		Runs Created	
Schmidt-Phi	1.012	Schmidt-Phi	169	Schmidt-Phi	56.5	Schmidt-Phi	49.7	Montanez-SD-Mon	124	Schmidt-Phi	137
Clark-SF	.907	Clark-SF	155	Hernandez-StL	43.3	Hernandez-StL	39.7	Rose-Phi	117	Hernandez-StL	122
Hernandez-StL	.904	Cedeno-Hou	150	Easler-Pit	37.2	Easler-Pit	35.9	Youngblood-NY	117	Dawson-Mon	105
Simmons-StL	.885	Hernandez-StL	147	Clark-SF	31.1	Cedeno-Hou	33.6	Simmons-StL	117	Murphy-Atl	101
Murphy-Atl	.859	Simmons-StL	140	Simmons-StL	29.6	Clark-SF	33.1	Concepcion-Cin	116	Griffey-Cin	99

Total Average		Stolen Bases		Stolen Base Average		Stolen Base Runs		Fielding Runs		Total Player Rating	
Schmidt-Phi	1.095	LeFlore-Mon	97	Griffey-Cin	95.8	LeFlore-Mon	17.7	Smith-SD	40.8	Schmidt-Phi	7.3
Hernandez-StL	.915	Moreno-Pit	96	Mumphrey-SD	91.2	Mumphrey-SD	12.6	Templeton-StL	27.6	Dawson-Mon	4.8
Clark-SF	.906	Collins-Cin	79	LeFlore-Mon	83.6	Scott-Mon	11.1	Moreno-Pit	27.4	Templeton-StL	4.7
Cedeno-Hou	.890	Scott-Mon	63	Maddox-Phi	83.3	Collins-Cin	11.1	Schmidt-Phi	23.2	Smith-SD	4.7
Simmons-StL	.872	Richards-SD	61	Scott-Mon	82.9	Moreno-Pit	9.0	Dawson-Mon	20.1	Cedeno-Hou	4.3

Wins		Win Percentage		Games		Complete Games		Shutouts		Saves	
Carlton-Phi	24	Bibby-Pit	.760	Tidrow-Pit	84	Rogers-Mon	14	Reuss-LA	6	Sutter-Chi	28
Niekro-Hou	20	Reuss-LA	.750	Tekulve-Pit	78	Carlton-Phi	13	Rogers-Mon	4	Hume-Cin	25
Bibby-Pit	19	Carlton-Phi	.727	Hume-Cin	78	Niekro-Atl	11	Richard-Hou	4	Fingers-SD	23
Reuss-LA	18	Ruthven-Phi	.630	Camp-Atl	77	Niekro-Hou	11			Camp-Atl	22
Ruthven-Phi	17	Niekro-Hou	.625	Romo-Pit	74					Allen-NY	22

Innings Pitched		Fewest Hits/Game		Fewest BB/Game		Strikeouts		Strikeouts/Game		Ratio	
Carlton-Phi	304.0	Soto-Cin	5.96	Forsch-StL	1.38	Carlton-Phi	286	Soto-Cin	8.61	Sutter-Chi	8.99
Rogers-Mon	281.0	Sutton-LA	6.91	Reuss-LA	1.57	Ryan-Hou	200	Carlton-Phi	8.47	Reuss-LA	9.14
Niekro-Atl	275.0	Carlton-Phi	7.19	Forsch-Hou	1.66	Soto-Cin	182	Ryan-Hou	7.70	Pastore-Cin	9.89
Reuschel-Chi	257.0	Seaver-Cin	7.50	Candelaria-Pit	1.93	Niekro-Atl	176	Blyleven-Pit	6.98	Carlton-Phi	9.92
Niekro-Hou	256.0	Reuss-LA	7.57	Sutton-LA	1.99	Blyleven-Pit	168	Welch-LA	5.94	Soto-Cin	10.02

Earned Run Average		Adjusted ERA		Opponents' Batting Avg.		Opponents' On Base Pct.		Starter Runs		Adjusted Starter Runs	
Sutton-LA	2.20	Carlton-Phi	162	Soto-Cin	.187	Sutton-LA	.258	Carlton-Phi	42.6	Carlton-Phi	49.0
Carlton-Phi	2.34	Sutton-LA	159	Sutton-LA	.211	Reuss-LA	.261	Sutton-LA	33.0	Sutton-LA	30.5
Reuss-LA	2.51	Reuss-LA	139	Carlton-Phi	.218	Pastore-Cin	.277	Reuss-LA	27.8	Reuss-LA	25.1
Blue-SF	2.97	Rogers-Mon	120	Seaver-Cin	.225	Carlton-Phi	.278	Ruhle-Hou	21.8	Rogers-Mon	18.3
Rogers-Mon	2.98	Blue-SF	119	Reuss-LA	.227	Soto-Cin	.279	Richard-Hou	21.5	Richard-Hou	17.5

Clutch Pitching Index		Relief Runs		Adjusted Relief Runs		Relief Ranking		Total Pitcher Index		Total Baseball Ranking	
Reuschel-Chi	119	McGraw-Phi	21.9	Caudill-Chi	24.5	McGraw-Phi	32.6	Carlton-Phi	5.3	Schmidt-Phi	7.3
Bomback-NY	116	Camp-Atl	20.3	McGraw-Phi	23.9	Camp-Atl	28.4	McGraw-Phi	3.6	Carlton-Phi	5.3
Zachry-NY	114	Caudill-Chi	20.1	Camp-Atl	22.0	Hume-Cin	25.6	Camp-Atl	3.4	Dawson-Mon	4.8
Ruthven-Phi	112	Smith-Hou	19.1	Holland-SF	16.4	Sutter-Chi	25.5	Hume-Cin	3.1	Templeton-StL	4.7
Sanderson-Mon	111	Holland-SF	16.9	Smith-Hou	15.5	Fryman-Mon	20.1	Sutter-Chi	2.7	Smith-SD	4.7

January 9 Al Kaline and Duke Snider are elected to the Hall of Fame by the BBWAA. Kaline is the tenth player to be elected in his first year of eligibility, while Snider is making his eleventh appearance on the ballot.

February 12 The AL's offer to buy out the remaining eight years of the Oakland A's lease at the Oakland Coliseum expires, effectively blocking the sale of the club from Charlie Finley to oil man Marvin Davis. Davis had planned to move the club to Denver, but the Oakland Coliseum Board, backed by the city council, refuses the American League's $4 million offer.

March 8 While waiting for the team bus outside his hotel during the Cleveland Indians three-game exhibition series against the Mexico City Reds, rookie outfielder Joe Charboneau is stabbed by a crazed fan wielding a ball-point pen. The pen penetrates one inch and strikes a rib, sidelining Charboneau for four days,

but he will recover to win the AL Rookie of the Year award.

March 12 Slugger Chuck Klein and former Red Sox owner Tom Yawkey are elected to the Hall of Fame by the Special Veterans Committee. Yawkey is the first club owner selected who never served as a player, manager, or general manager.

May 3 Rangers pitcher Ferguson Jenkins defeats the Orioles 3-2 to become only the fourth pitcher to win 100 games in each league. He won 149 games for the Phillies and Cubs before joining the AL in 1974.

August 23 A's owner Charlie Finley sells the club for $12.7 million to the Haas family of San Francisco, owners of the Levi Strauss clothing empire, keeping the team in Oakland.

October 4 The Yankees clinch their fourth AL East title in five seasons, beating Detroit 5-2 in the first game of a doubleheader. Reggie Jackson hits his 41st home run of the season and will

share the AL home run crown with Milwaukee's Ben Oglivie.

October 10 George Brett puts Kansas City into its first World Series with a three-run home run off Yankees reliever Rich Gossage in the seventh inning. The Royals win 4-2 win for a three-game sweep of the ALCS.

November 12 Baltimore's Steve Stone, who led the AL in wins with a 25-7 record, edges Oakland's Mike Norris for the AL Cy Young Award.

November 18 Despite having missed 45 games with injuries, George Brett is named AL MVP. The 27-year-old third baseman's .390 average was the highest in the major league since Ted Williams's .406 in 1941, and he added 24 home runs and 118 RBI to lead Kansas City to its first AL pennant.

December 15 Outfielder Dave Winfield becomes the highest-paid player in baseball when he signs a 10-year, $15 million contract with the New York Yankees.

BALTIMORE		BOSTON		CALIFORNIA		CHICAGO		CLEVELAND		DETROIT		KANSAS CITY	
M	E.Weaver	M	D.Zimmer	M	J.Fregosi	M	T.LaRussa	M	D.Garcia	M	S.Anderson	M	J.Frey
1B	E.Murray	M	J.Pesky	1B	R.Carew	1B	M.Squires	1B	M.Hargrove	1B	R.Hebner	1B	W.Aikens
2B	R.Dauer	1B	T.Perez	2B	B.Grich	2B	J.Morrison	2B	J.Brohamer	2B	L.Whitaker	2B	F.White
SS	M.Belanger	2B	D.Stapleton	SS	F.Patek	SS	T.Cruz	SS	T.Veryzer	SS	A.Trammell	SS	U.Washington
3B	D.DeCinces	SS	R.Burleson	3B	C.Lansford	3B	K.Bell	3B	T.Harrah	3B	T.Brookens	3B	G.Brett
LF	G.Roenicke	3B	G.Hoffman	LF	J.Rudi	LF	W.Nordhagen	LF	M.Dilone	LF	S.Kemp	LF	W.Wilson
CF	A.Bumbry	LF	J.Rice	CF	R.Miller	CF	C.Lemon	CF	R.Manning	CF	R.Peters	CF	A.Otis
RF	K.Singleton	CF	F.Lynn	RF	L.Harlow	RF	H.Baines	RF	J.Orta	RF	A.Cowens	RF	C.Hurdle
C	R.Dempsey	RF	D.Evans	C	T.Donohue	C	B.Kimm	C	R.Hassey	C	L.Parrish	C	D.Porter
DH	T.Crowley	C	C.Fisk	DH	J.Thompson	DH	L.Johnson	DH	J.Charboneau	DH	C.Summers	DH	H.McRae
		DH	C.Yastrzemski										
S2	K.Garcia			OD	D.Baylor	OD	B.Molinaro	S2	J.Dybzinski	1D	J.Wockenfuss	1O	P.LaCock
O	J.Lowenstein	3D	B.Hobson	S2	D.Thon	S3	G.Pryor	2O	A.Bannister			CO	J.Wathan
C	D.Graham	OD	J.Dwyer	O	B.Clark			C	B.Diaz	P	J.Morris		
D	L.May	2	J.Remy	OD	D.Ford	P	B.Burns			P	M.Wilcox	P	L.Gura
OD	P.Kelly			S	B.Campaneris	P	S.Trout	P	L.Barker	P	D.Schatzeder	P	D.Leonard
						P	R.Dotson	P	R.Waits	P	D.Petry	P	P.Splittorff
P	S.McGregor	P	M.Torrez	P	F.Tanana	P	R.Baumgarten	P	D.Spillner	P	D.Rozema	P	R.Gale
P	S.Stone	P	D.Eckersley	P	D.Aase	P	L.Hoyt	P	W.Garland	RP	A.Lopez	P	R.Martin
P	M.Flanagan	P	B.Stanley	P	A.Martinez	RP	M.Proly	P	B.Owchinko	RP	P.Underwood	RP	D.Quisenberry
P	J.Palmer	P	S.Renko	P	C.Knapp	RP	E.Farmer	RP	S.Monge			RP	M.Pattin
P	S.Stewart	P	D.Drago	RP	D.LaRoche	RP	R.Wortham	RP	M.Stanton	P	R.Weaver		
RP	T.Stoddard	RP	T.Burgmeier	RP	M.Clear			RP	V.Cruz	P	D.Tobik		
RP	T.Martinez	P	J.Tudor	RP	A.Hassler	P	K.Kravec			P	B.Robbins		
RP	D.Ford	P	C.Rainey					P	J.Denny				
				P	D.Frost			P	R.Grimsley				
P	D.Martinez			P	J.Montague								
				P	B.Kison								
				P	J.Barr								
				P	D.Lemanczyk								

MILWAUKEE		MINNESOTA		NEW YORK		OAKLAND		SEATTLE		TEXAS		TORONTO	
M	B.Rodgers	M	G.Mauch	M	D.Howser	M	B.Martin	M	D.Johnson	M	P.Corrales	M	B.Mattick
M	G.Bamberger	M	J.Goryl	1B	B.Watson	1B	D.Revering	M	M.Wills	1B	P.Putnam	1B	J.Mayberry
M	B.Rodgers	1B	R.Jackson	2B	W.Randolph	2B	D.McKay	1B	B.Bochte	2B	B.Wills	2B	D.Garcia
1B	C.Cooper	2B	R.Wilfong	SS	B.Dent	SS	M.Guerrero	2B	J.Cruz	SS	P.Frias	SS	A.Griffin
2B	P.Molitor	SS	R.Smalley	3B	G.Nettles	3B	W.Gross	SS	M.Mendoza	3B	B.Bell	3B	R.Howell
SS	R.Yount	3B	J.Castino	LF	L.Piniella	LF	R.Henderson	3B	T.Cox	LF	A.Oliver	LF	B.Bailor
3B	J.Gantner	LF	B.Sofield	CF	B.Brown	CF	D.Murphy	LF	D.Meyer	CF	M.Rivers	CF	B.Bonnell
LF	B.Oglivie	CF	K.Landreaux	RF	R.Jackson	RF	T.Armas	CF	J.Simpson	RF	J.Norris	RF	L.Moseby
CF	G.Thomas	RF	H.Powell	C	R.Cerone	C	J.Essian	RF	L.Roberts	C	J.Sundberg	C	E.Whitt
RF	S.Lezcano	C	B.Wynegar	DH	E.Soderholm	DH	M.Page	C	L.Cox	DH	R.Zisk	DH	O.Velez
C	C.Moore	DH	J.Morales					DH	W.Horton				
DH	D.Davis			OD	B.Murcer	1C	J.Newman			O	J.Grubb	OD	A.Woods
		DO	G.Adams	1D	J.Spencer	CD	M.Heath	S3	J.Anderson	3S	D.Roberts	23	G.Iorg
31	D.Money	13	M.Cubbage	O	R.Jones	S2	R.Picciolo	2S	L.Milbourne	D1	R.Staub	C	B.Davis
3D	S.Bando	2S	P.Mackanin					O1	T.Paciorek	O	B.Sample		
C	B.Martinez	O	D.Edwards	P	T.John	P	R.Langford	O	R.Craig			P	J.Clancy
				P	R.Guidry	P	M.Norris	O	J.Beniquez			P	D.Stieb
P	M.Haas	P	J.Koosman	P	T.Underwood	P	M.Keough			P	J.Matlack	P	P.Mirabella
P	M.Caldwell	P	G.Zahn	P	R.May	P	S.McCatty	P	F.Bannister	P	D.Medich	P	J.Jefferson
P	L.Sorensen	P	R.Erickson	P	L.Tiant	P	B.Kingman	P	G.Abbott	P	F.Jenkins	RP	J.McLaughlin
P	B.Travers	P	D.Jackson	RP	R.Davis	RP	B.Lacey	P	R.Honeycutt	RP	D.Darwin	RP	J.Garvin
P	R.Cleveland	P	P.Redfern	RP	R.Gossage			P	J.Beattie	RP	S.Lyle	RP	J.Kucek
RP	B.McClure	RP	D.Corbett	RP	D.Bird			P	R.Dressler	RP	J.Kern		
RP	B.Castro	RP	J.Verhoeven					RP	S.Rawley			P	J.Todd
RP	J.Augustine			P	E.Figueroa			RP	B.McLaughlin	P	C.Hough	P	T.Buskey
		P	F.Arroyo	P	M.Griffin			RP	D.Roberts			P	B.Moore
P	P.Mitchell	P	A.Williams	P	G.Perry							P	L.Leal
												P	M.Barlow
						P	M.Parrott						
						P	D.Heaverlo						

TEAM	G	W	L	PCT	GB	R	OR	AB	H	2B	3B	HR	BB	SO	AVG	OBP	SLG	PRO	PRO+	BR	/A	PF	CHI	RC	SB	CS	SBA	SBR
EAST																												
NY	162	103	59	.636		820	662	5553	1484	239	34	189	643	739	.267	.346	.425	.771	112	79	93	98	100	820	86	36	70	4
BAL	162	100	62	.617	3	805	**640**	5585	1523	258	29	156	587	766	.273	.344	.413	.757	107	52	60	99	102	788	111	38	74	11
MIL	162	86	76	.531	17	811	682	5653	1555	**298**	36	**203**	455	745	.275	.332	**.448**	**.780**	116	78	**104**	97	100	**834**	131	56	70	6
BOS	160	83	77	.519	19	757	767	5603	1588	297	36	162	475	720	.283	.343	.436	.779	107	**86**	45	105	93	810	79	48	62	-5
DET	163	84	78	.519	19	**830**	757	5648	1543	232	53	143	**645**	844	.273	.351	.409	.760	106	66	47	102	101	804	75	68	52	-18
CLE	160	79	81	.494	23	738	807	5470	1517	221	40	89	617	625	.277	**.355**	.381	.736	102	26	23	100	97	739	118	58	67	1
TOR	162	67	95	.414	36	624	762	5571	1398	249	53	126	448	813	.251	.310	.383	.693	85	-92	-121	105	99	640	67	72	48	-23
WEST																												
KC	162	97	65	.599		809	694	5714	**1633**	266	**59**	115	508	709	**.286**	.348	.413	.761	107	62	56	101	100	826	**185**	43	**81**	**30**
OAK	162	83	79	.512	14	686	642	5495	1424	212	35	137	506	824	.259	.324	.385	.709	100	-51	-4	93	102	680	175	82	68	3
MIN	161	77	84	.478	19.5	670	724	5530	1468	252	46	99	436	703	.265	.322	.381	.703	86	-65	-113	107	103	655	62	46	57	-9
TEX	163	76	85	.472	20.5	756	752	5690	1616	263	27	124	480	**589**	.284	.342	.405	.747	107	30	53	97	98	768	91	49	65	-2
CHI	162	70	90	.438	26	587	722	5444	1408	255	38	91	399	670	.259	.314	.370	.684	87	-104	-101	100	98	608	68	54	56	-12
CAL	160	65	95	.406	31	698	797	5443	1441	236	32	106	539	889	.265	.335	.378	.713	97	-33	-16	98	102	681	91	63	59	-11
SEA	163	59	103	.364	38	610	793	5489	1359	211	35	104	483	727	.248	.311	.356	.667	81	-136	-141	101	**105**	598	116	62	65	-2
TOT	1132					10201		77888	20958	3489	553	1844	7221	10363	.269	.334	.399	.733							1455	775	65	-29

TEAM	CG	SH	SV	IP	H	H/G	HR	BB	SO	RAT	ERA	ERA+	OAV	OOB	PR	/A	PF	CPI	FA	E	DP	FW	PW	BW	SBW	DIF
EAST																										
NY	29	**15**	**50**	1464[1]	1433	8.8	**102**	463	845	11.8	3.58	109	.259	.319	73	55	97	98	.978	138	160	.0	5.5	9.3	.6	6.6
BAL	42	10	41	1460	1438	8.9	134	507	789	12.1	3.64	109	.261	.325	63	50	98	104	**.985**	**95**	178	**2.4**	5.0	6.0	1.3	4.3
MIL	48	14	30	1450	1530	9.5	137	**420**	575	12.3	3.71	104	.273	.326	53	26	96	**107**	.977	147	189	-.5	2.6	**10.4**	.8	-8.3
BOS	30	8	43	1441[1]	1557	9.7	129	481	696	12.9	4.38	96	.279	.340	-55	-26	105	97	.977	149	**206**	-.7	-2.6	4.5	-.3	2.1
DET	40	9	30	1467[1]	1505	9.2	152	558	741	12.8	4.25	97	.267	.336	-35	-23	102	98	.979	133	165	.3	-2.3	4.7	-1.6	1.9
CLE	35	8	32	1428	1519	9.6	137	552	843	13.3	4.68	87	.275	.344	-103	-97	101	92	.983	165	143	1.8	-9.7	2.3	-.3	-1.8
TOR	39	9	23	1466	1523	9.3	135	635	705	13.4	4.19	103	.274	.351	-26	17	107	105	.979	133	206	.3	1.7	-12.1	-2.1	-1.8
WEST																										
KC	37	10	42	1459[1]	1496	9.2	129	465	614	12.2	3.83	106	.267	.325	33	36	100	100	.978	141	150	-.2	3.6	5.6	**3.2**	3.8
OAK	94	9	13	1471[2]	**1347**	**8.2**	142	521	769	**11.6**	**3.46**	109	**.244**	**.312**	94	50	93	99	.979	130	115	.5	5.0	-.4	.5	-3.5
MIN	35	9	30	1451	1502	9.3	120	468	744	12.4	3.93	**111**	.272	.331	16	**68**	108	100	.977	148	192	-.6	**6.8**	-11.3	-.7	2.3
TEX	35	6	25	1451[2]	1561	9.7	119	519	**890**	13.1	4.02	97	.277	.342	2	-21	97	104	.977	147	169	-.5	-2.1	5.3	-.0	-7.2
CHI	32	12	42	1435[1]	1434	9.0	108	563	724	12.8	3.92	103	.263	.337	18	17	100	99	.973	171	162	-1.9	1.7	-10.1	-1.0	1.2
CAL	22	6	30	1428[1]	1548	9.8	141	529	725	13.3	4.52	93	.278	.345	-77	-94	97	97	.978	134	144	.1	-9.4	-1.6	-.9	-3.3
SEA	31	7	26	1457[1]	1565	9.7	159	540	703	13.2	4.38	94	.278	.344	-56	-40	102	101	.977	149	189	-.6	-4.0	-14.1	.5	-3.4
TOT	549	132	457	20331[2]		9.3				12.7	4.03		.269	.334					.978	1920	2368					

Runs		Hits		Doubles		Triples		Home Runs		Total Bases	
Wilson-KC	133	Wilson-KC	230	Yount-Mil	49	Wilson-KC	15	Oglivie-Mil	41	Cooper-Mil	335
Yount-Mil	121	Cooper-Mil	219	Oliver-Tex	43	Griffin-Tor	15	Jackson-NY	41	Oglivie-Mil	333
Bumbry-Bal	118	Rivers-Tex	210	Morrison-Chi	40	Washington-KC	11	Thomas-Mil	38	Murray-Bal	322
Henderson-Oak	111	Oliver-Tex	209	McRae-KC	39	Landreaux-Min	11	Armas-Oak	35	Yount-Mil	317
Trammell-Det	107	Bumbry-Bal	205	Evans-Bos	37	Yount-Mil	10	Murray-Bal	32	Oliver-Tex	315

Runs Batted In		Runs Produced		Bases On Balls		Batting Average		On Base Percentage		Slugging Average	
Cooper-Mil	122	Oliver-Tex	194	Randolph-NY	119	G.Brett-KC	.390	G.Brett-KC	.461	G.Brett-KC	.664
Oglivie-Mil	118	Cooper-Mil	193	Cooper-Mil	117	Cooper-Mil	.352	Randolph-NY	.429	Jackson-NY	.597
G.Brett-KC	118	Yount-Mil	185	Hargrove-Cle	111	Dilone-Cle	.341	Henderson-Oak	.422	Oglivie-Mil	.563
Oliver-Tex	117	Murray-Bal	184	Murphy-Oak	102	Rivers-Tex	.333	Hargrove-Cle	.421	Cooper-Mil	.539
Murray-Bal	116	G.Brett-KC	181	Harrah-Cle	98	Carew-Cal	.331	Thompson-Det-Cal	.402	Yount-Mil	.519

Production		Adjusted Production		Batter Runs		Adjusted Batter Runs		Clutch Hitting Index		Runs Created	
G.Brett-KC	1.124	G.Brett-KC	202	G.Brett-KC	64.8	G.Brett-KC	63.8	Manning-Cle	125	G.Brett-KC	135
Jackson-NY	.996	Jackson-NY	172	Jackson-NY	49.1	Jackson-NY	51.1	Thompson-Det-Cal	125	Cooper-Mil	126
Cooper-Mil	.931	Cooper-Mil	157	Cooper-Mil	42.9	Cooper-Mil	46.9	Hargrove-Cle	122	Jackson-NY	125
Oglivie-Mil	.930	Oglivie-Mil	156	Oglivie-Mil	39.2	Oglivie-Mil	43.0	Whitaker-Det	122	Oglivie-Mil	121
Singleton-Bal	.885	Singleton-Bal	143	Singleton-Bal	35.4	Henderson-Oak	36.6	Aikens-KC	122	Henderson-Oak	120

Total Average		Stolen Bases		Stolen Base Average		Stolen Base Runs		Fielding Runs		Total Player Rating	
G.Brett-KC	1.258	Henderson-Oak	100	Otis-KC	94.1	Wilson-KC	17.7	Castino-Min	27.8	Henderson-Oak	6.6
Jackson-NY	1.060	Wilson-KC	79	Harrah-Cle	89.5	Henderson-Oak	14.4	Burleson-Bos	25.5	G.Brett-KC	6.4
Henderson-Oak	.973	Dilone-Cle	61	Kelly-Bal	88.9	Cruz-Sea	9.3	DeCinces-Bal	24.5	Oglivie-Mil	5.4
Randolph-NY	.952	Cruz-Sea	45	Wilson-KC	88.8	Dilone-Cle	7.5	Murphy-Oak	23.9	Bell-Tex	4.7
Oglivie-Mil	.925	Bumbry-Bal	44	Cruz-Sea	86.5	Bumbry-Bal	6.6	Henderson-Oak	23.3	Cooper-Mil	4.3

Wins		Win Percentage		Games		Complete Games		Shutouts		Saves	
Stone-Bal	25	Stone-Bal	.781	Quisenberry-KC	75	Langford-Oak	28	John-NY	6	Quisenberry-KC	33
Norris-Oak	22	May-NY	.750	Corbett-Min	73	Norris-Oak	24	Zahn-Min	5	Gossage-NY	33
John-NY	22	McGregor-Bal	.714	Monge-Cle	67	Keough-Oak	20	Stieb-Tor	4	Farmer-Chi	30
McGregor-Bal	20	Norris-Oak	.710	Lopez-Det	67	John-NY	16	McGregor-Bal	4	Stoddard-Bal	26
Leonard-KC	20	John-NY	.710			Gura-KC	16	Gura-KC	4	Burgmeier-Bos	24

Innings Pitched		Fewest Hits/Game		Fewest BB/Game		Strikeouts		Strikeouts/Game		Ratio	
Langford-Oak	290.0	Norris-Oak	6.81	Matlack-Tex	1.84	Barker-Cle	187	Barker-Cle	6.83	May-NY	9.39
Norris-Oak	284.1	May-NY	7.39	Splittorff-KC	1.90	Norris-Oak	180	May-NY	6.83	Norris-Oak	9.62
Gura-KC	283.1	John-NY	7.79	John-NY	1.90	Guidry-NY	166	Guidry-NY	6.80	Langford-Oak	10.58
Leonard-KC	280.1	Underwood-NY	7.84	Tanana-Cal	1.99	Leonard-KC	155	Bannister-Sea	6.41	Burns-Chi	10.59
John-NY	265.1	Keough-Oak	7.85	Langford-Oak	1.99	Bannister-Sea	155	Perry-Tex-NY	5.91	Eckersley-Bos	10.65

Earned Run Average		Adjusted ERA		Opponents' Batting Avg.		Opponents' On Base Pct.		Starter Runs		Adjusted Starter Runs	
May-NY	2.46	May-NY	159	Norris-Oak	.209	May-NY	.268	Norris-Oak	47.4	Norris-Oak	39.0
Norris-Oak	2.53	Norris-Oak	149	May-NY	.224	Norris-Oak	.272	Gura-KC	34.0	Gura-KC	34.5
Burns-Chi	2.84	Burns-Chi	142	Clancy-Tor	.233	Eckersley-Bos	.291	Burns-Chi	31.7	Burns-Chi	31.5
Keough-Oak	2.92	Gura-KC	137	Keough-Oak	.236	Burns-Chi	.295	Keough-Oak	31.0	May-NY	28.4
Gura-KC	2.95	Erickson-Min	134	Underwood-NY	.237	Bannister-Sea	.296	May-NY	30.6	Clancy-Tor	27.8

Clutch Pitching Index		Relief Runs		Adjusted Relief Runs		Relief Ranking		Total Pitcher Index		Total Baseball Ranking	
Sorensen-Mil	126	Corbett-Min	31.1	Corbett-Min	36.0	Corbett-Min	46.8	Norris-Oak	4.7	Henderson-Oak	6.6
Stanley-Bos	117	Burgmeier-Bos	22.4	Burgmeier-Bos	33.1	Burgmeier-Bos	33.1	Corbett-Min	4.5	G.Brett-KC	6.4
Keough-Oak	113	Gossage-NY	19.4	Garvin-Tor	18.5	Gossage-NY	26.6	Burgmeier-Bos	3.7	Oglivie-Mil	5.4
Trout-Chi	113	Darwin-Tex	17.1	Gossage-NY	18.1	Quisenberry-KC	26.2	Burns-Chi	3.5	Norris-Oak	4.7
Perry-Tex-NY	112	Garvin-Tor	16.0	Proly-Chi	15.6	Garvin-Tor	26.1	Gura-KC	3.3	Bell-Tex	4.7

January 15 In his first year of eligibility, former Cardinals pitcher Bob Gibson is elected to the Hall of Fame.

March 11 Johnny Mize and Andrew "Rube" Foster are elected to the Hall of Fame by the Veterans Committee.

April 9 Pressed into service on Opening Day when scheduled starter Jerry Reuss pulls a calf muscle, Dodgers pitcher Fernando Valenzuela shuts out the Astros, 2–0, on five hits in his first major league start.

April 18 The Reds' Tom Seaver strikes out Keith Hernandez in the fourth inning of a 10-4 loss to the Cardinals, becoming the fifth pitcher in major league history with 3,000 career strikeouts.

April 27 "Fernandomania" hits fever pitch at Dodger Stadium as a sellout crowd watches the 20-year-old rookie pitch his fourth shutout in five starts, 5-0 versus the Giants. Valenzuela is 5-0 with a 0.20 ERA and is batting .438.

April 29 Philadelphia's Steve Carlton strikes out the side (Tim Raines, Jerry Manuel, and Tim Wallach) in the first inning of a 6–2 win over the Expos to become the first lefthander in major league history (and sixth pitcher overall) to record 3,000 career strikeouts.

May 31 Playing before their 10th consecutive home sellout, the Dodgers pound the Reds, 16–4, and raise their season attendance to 1,026,725 in 22 dates. It is the earliest any team has cracked the million attendance barrier.

June 5 Houston's Nolan Ryan passes Early Wynn as baseball's all-time walk leader, walking two batters in a 3–0 win over the Mets to raise his total to 1,777. Ryan also fans 10 batters while pitching a five-hitter.

June 10 Phillies first baseman Pete Rose singles off Nolan Ryan in the first inning to tie Stan Musial as the NL's all-time hit leader with 3,630.

September 17 Fernando Valenzuela sets the NL rookie record with his eighth shutout of the season, a 2-0 three-hitter versus the Braves.

September 26 Nolan Ryan no-hits the Dodgers 5-0 to become the only major league pitcher to toss five career no-hitters. Ryan had shared the record of four with Dodger great Sandy Koufax, but had not pitched a no-hitter since June 1, 1975. The 34-year-old Ryan strikes out 11 and retires the last 19 batters in a row.

October 3 In Cincinnati, Bob Horner homers twice and scores the winning run on Ron Oester's eighth-inning throwing error to give the Braves a 4-3 win over the Reds and give the Astros the second-half title in the NL West. Cincinnati, which lost the first-half title to the Dodgers by one-half game, will finish with the best overall record (66-42) in the major leagues, but will not make the playoffs.

October 11 After being down two games to none, LA shuts out Houston 4-0 behind Jerry Reuss to take the playoff.

October 19 In Game 5 of the NLCS, Rick Monday hits a solo home run with two out in the top of the ninth against Montreal to give Los Angeles a 2-1 victory and a trip to the World Series.

October 28 Pedro Guerrero drives in five runs and the Dodgers beat the Yankees 9-2 to win the World Series in six. In a remarkable postseason, the Dodgers came from behind to win three series (down 2-0 to Houston and 2-0 to Montreal in the best-of-5 series). Guerrero, Ron Cey, and Steve Yeager are named co-MVPs.

November 11 Fernando Valenzuela becomes the first rookie ever to win a Cy Young Award, edging the Reds' Tom Seaver 70-67 for NL honors. He was the first rookie since Herb Score in 1955 to lead his league in strikeouts, with 180.

November 18 Phillies third baseman Mike Schmidt wins his second consecutive NL MVP Award, joining Ernie Banks and Joe Morgan as the only NL players to win the award back-to-back. Schmidt hit .316 with 31 home runs and 91 RBI in the abbreviated season and also led the league in runs and walks.

ATLANTA		CHICAGO		CINCINNATI		HOUSTON		LOS ANGELES		MONTREAL	
M	B.Cox	M	J.Amalfitano	M	J.McNamara	M	B.Virdon	M	T.Lasorda	M	D.Williams
1B	C.Chambliss	1B	B.Buckner	1B	D.Driessen	1B	C.Cedeno	1B	S.Garvey	M	J.Fanning
2B	G.Hubbard	2B	M.Tyson	2B	R.Oester	2B	J.Pittman	2B	D.Lopes	1B	W.Cromartie
SS	R.Ramirez	SS	I.DeJesus	SS	D.Concepcion	SS	C.Reynolds	SS	B.Russell	2B	R.Scott
3B	B.Horner	3B	K.Reitz	3B	R.Knight	3B	A.Howe	3B	R.Cey	SS	C.Speier
LF	R.Linares	LF	S.Henderson	LF	G.Foster	LF	J.Cruz	LF	D.Baker	3B	L.Parrish
CF	D.Murphy	CF	J.Morales	CF	K.Griffey	CF	T.Scott	CF	K.Landreaux	LF	T.Raines
RF	C.Washington	RF	L.Durham	RF	D.Collins	RF	T.Puhl	RF	P.Guerrero	CF	A.Dawson
C	B.Benedict	C	J.Davis	C	J.Nolan	C	A.Ashby	C	M.Scioscia	RF	J.White
										C	G.Carter
32	J.Royster	P	M.Krukow	P	M.Soto	P	J.Niekro	2S	D.Thomas		
P		P	R.Martz	P	T.Seaver	P	D.Sutton			O1	T.Wallach
P	G.Perry	P	R.Reuschel	P	F.Pastore	P	B.Knepper	P	F.Valenzuela		
P	T.Boggs	P	K.Kravec	P	B.Berenyi	P	N.Ryan	P	J.Reuss	P	S.Rogers
P	P.Niekro	P	D.Bird	P	M.LaCoss	P	V.Ruhle	P	B.Hooton	P	B.Gullickson
P	R.Mahler	RP	D.Tidrow	RP	T.Hume	RP	D.Smith	P	B.Welch	P	S.Sanderson
RP	J.Montefusco	RP	B.Caudill	RP	P.Moskau	RP	J.Sambito	RP	D.Goltz	P	R.Burris
RP	R.Camp	RP	L.Smith	RP	J.Price	RP	F.LaCorte	RP	S.Howe	RP	B.Lee
RP	G.Garber							RP	B.Castillo	RP	S.Bahnsen
		P	L.McGlothen							RP	W.Fryman
		P	M.Griffin								
		P	D.Capilla							P	C.Lea

NEW YORK		PHILADELPHIA		PITTSBURGH		SAN DIEGO		SAN FRANCISCO		ST.LOUIS	
M	J.Torre	M	D.Green	M	C.Tanner	M	F.Howard	M	F.Robinson	M	W.Herzog
1B	D.Kingman	1B	P.Rose	1B	J.Thompson	1B	B.Perkins	1B	E.Cabell	1B	K.Hernandez
2B	D.Flynn	2B	M.Trillo	2B	P.Garner	2B	J.Bonilla	2B	J.Morgan	2B	T.Herr
SS	F.Taveras	SS	L.Bowa	SS	T.Foli	SS	O.Smith	SS	J.LeMaster	SS	G.Templeton
3B	H.Brooks	3B	M.Schmidt	3B	B.Madlock	3B	L.Salazar	3B	D.Evans	3B	K.Oberkfell
LF	L.Mazzilli	LF	G.Matthews	LF	M.Easler	LF	G.Richards	LF	L.Herndon	LF	D.Iorg
CF	M.Wilson	CF	G.Maddox	CF	O.Moreno	CF	R.Jones	CF	J.Martin	CF	G.Hendrick
RF	E.Valentine	RF	B.McBride	RF	D.Parker	RF	J.Lefebvre	RF	J.Clark	RF	S.Lezcano
C	J.Stearns	C	B.Boone	C	T.Pena	C	T.Kennedy	C	M.May	C	D.Porter
3	M.Cubbage	O	G.Gross	3S	D.Berra	1	R.Bass	P	D.Alexander	P	L.Sorensen
1O	M.Jorgensen			O	L.Lacy			P	T.Griffin	P	B.Forsch
1	R.Staub	P	S.Carlton			P	J.Eichelberger	P	V.Blue	P	J.Martin
		P	D.Ruthven	P	R.Rhoden	P	S.Mura	P	E.Whitson	P	S.Martinez
P	P.Zachry	P	L.Christenson	P	E.Solomon	P	C.Welsh	P	A.Ripley	RP	B.Sutter
P	M.Scott	P	N.Espinosa	P	J.Bibby	P	R.Wise	RP	A.Holland	RP	B.Shirley
P	E.Lynch	RP	S.Lyle	P	P.Perez	P	T.Lollar	RP	G.Minton	RP	J.Kaat
P	G.Harris	RP	M.Proly	RP	R.Scurry	RP	G.Lucas	RP	F.Breining		
RP	P.Falcone	RP	R.Reed	RP	K.Tekulve	RP	J.Curtis			P	J.Andujar
RP	N.Allen			RP	E.Romo	RP	J.Littlefield	P	G.Lavelle		
RP	D.Miller	P	D.Noles								
		/P	M.Bystrom	/P	L.Tiant	P	D.Boone				
P	R.Jones			P	D.Boone						

TEAM	G	W	L	PCT	GB	R	OR	AB	H	2B	3B	HR	BB	SO	AVG	OBP	SLG	PRO	PRO+	BR	/A	PF	CHI	RC	SB	CS	SBA	SBR
EAST Split Season: First-half Winner PHI (34-21); Second-half Winner MON (30-23)																												
STL	103	59	43	.578		464	417	3537	936	158	45	50	379	495	.265	.339	.377	.716	106	43	31	103	102	454	88	45	66	-1
MON	108	60	48	.556	2	443	394	3591	883	146	28	81	368	498	.246	.319	.370	.689	100	3	-2	101	105	435	138	40	78	17
PHI	107	59	48	.551	2.5	491	472	3665	1002	165	25	69	372	432	.273	.344	.389	.733	109	66	45	104	100	495	103	46	69	3
PIT	103	46	56	.451	13	407	425	3576	920	176	30	55	278	494	.257	.314	.369	.683	96	-9	-21	103	102	417	122	52	70	5
NY	105	41	62	.398	18.5	348	432	3493	868	136	35	57	304	603	.248	.311	.356	.667	96	-26	-20	98	93	387	103	42	71	6
CHI	106	38	65	.369	21.5	370	483	3546	838	138	29	57	342	611	.236	.306	.340	.646	84	-52	-68	104	104	368	72	41	64	-3
WEST Split Season: First-half Winner LA (36-21); Second-half Winner HOU (33-20)																												
CIN	108	66	42	.611		464	440	3637	972	190	24	64	375	553	.267	.339	.385	.724	109	53	45	102	97	469	58	37	61	-5
LA	110	63	47	.573	4	450	356	3751	984	133	20	82	331	550	.262	.325	.374	.699	108	16	32	96	101	450	73	46	61	-6
HOU	110	61	49	.555	6	394	331	3693	948	160	35	45	340	488	.257	.321	.356	.677	103	-12	0	95	95	425	81	43	65	-2
SF	111	56	55	.505	11.5	427	414	3766	941	161	26	63	386	543	.250	.322	.357	.679	100	-8	0	99	99	431	89	50	64	-3
ATL	107	50	56	.472	15	395	416	3642	886	148	22	64	321	540	.243	.308	.349	.657	90	-41	-51	103	105	391	98	39	72	6
SD	110	41	69	.373	26	382	455	3757	963	170	35	32	311	525	.256	.316	.346	.662	90	-33	-4	93	96	400	83	62	57	-12
TOT	644					5035		43654	11141	1881	354	719	4107	6332	.255	.322	.364	.686						1108	543	67	7	

TEAM	CG	SH	SV	IP	H	H/G	HR	BB	SO	RAT	ERA	ERA+	OAV	OOB	PR	/A	PF	CPI	FA	E	DP	FW	PW	BW	SBW	DIF
STL	11	5	33	943	902	8.6	52	290	388	11.5	3.63	98	.255	.314	-14	-7	102	91	.981	82	108	.6	-.8	3.3	-.2	5.0
MON	20	12	23	975	902	8.3	58	268	520	11.0	3.30	106	.247	.302	21	21	100	92	.980	81	88	.9	2.3	-.2	1.8	1.3
PHI	19	5	23	960[1]	967	9.1	72	347	580	12.4	4.05	90	.267	.333	-60	-45	104	97	.980	86	90	.6	-4.8	4.8	.3	4.6
PIT	11	5	29	942	953	9.1	60	346	492	12.6	3.56	101	.266	.333	-8	3	103	107	.979	86	106	.4	.3	-2.3	.5	-4.0
NY	7	3	24	926[1]	906	8.8	74	336	490	12.2	3.55	98	.259	.326	-6	-7	100	105	.968	130	89	-1.6	-.8	-2.1	.6	-6.5
CHI	6	2	20	956[2]	983	9.2	59	388	532	13.1	4.01	92	.270	.344	-55	-33	106	101	.974	113	103	-.8	-3.5	-7.3	-.4	-1.5
CIN	25	14	20	965[2]	863	8.0	67	393	593	11.8	3.73	95	.241	.318	-26	-19	102	90	.981	80	99	1.0	-2.0	4.8	-.6	8.8
LA	26	19	24	997	904	8.2	54	302	603	11.0	3.01	110	.245	.304	54	35	95	100	.980	87	101	.7	3.8	3.4	-.7	.8
HOU	23	19	25	990	842	7.7	40	300	610	10.5	2.66	124	.231	.291	91	69	94	96	.980	87	81	.7	7.4	1.0	-.3	-2.8
SF	8	9	33	1009[1]	970	8.6	57	393	561	12.4	3.28	105	.256	.330	23	17	98	109	.977	102	102	.0	1.8	.0	-.4	-1.0
ATL	11	4	24	968	936	8.7	62	330	471	11.9	3.45	104	.257	.321	4	14	103	93	.976	102	93	-.2	1.5	-5.5	.6	.6
SD	9	6	23	1002	1013	9.1	64	414	492	13.0	3.72	88	.268	.343	-25	-51	93	108	.977	102	117	-.0	-5.5	-.4	-1.3	-6.7
TOT	176	103	301	11635[1]		8.6				11.9	3.49		.255	.322					.978	1138	1177					

Runs		Hits		Doubles		Triples		Home Runs		Total Bases	
Schmidt-Phi	78	Rose-Phi	140	Buckner-Chi	35	Richards-SD	12	Schmidt-Phi	31	Schmidt-Phi	228
Rose-Phi	73	Buckner-Chi	131	Jones-SD	34	Reynolds-Hou	12	Dawson-Mon	24	Dawson-Mon	218
Dawson-Mon	71	Concepcion-Cin	129	Concepcion-Cin	28	Herr-StL	9	Kingman-NY	22	Foster-Cin	215
Hendrick-StL	67	Baker-LA	128	Hernandez-StL	27			Foster-Cin	22	Buckner-Chi	202
		Griffey-Cin	123	Chambliss-Atl	25			Hendrick-StL	18	Hendrick-StL	191

Runs Batted In		Runs Produced		Bases On Balls		Batting Average		On Base Percentage		Slugging Average	
Schmidt-Phi	91	Schmidt-Phi	138	Schmidt-Phi	73	Madlock-Pit	.341	Schmidt-Phi	.439	Schmidt-Phi	.644
Foster-Cin	90	Foster-Cin	132	Morgan-SF	66	Rose-Phi	.325	Madlock-Pit	.418	Dawson-Mon	.553
Buckner-Chi	75	Matthews-Phi	120	Hernandez-StL	61	Baker-LA	.320	Hernandez-StL	.405	Foster-Cin	.519
Carter-Mon	68	Concepcion-Cin	119	Thompson-Pit	59	Schmidt-Phi	.316	Matthews-Phi	.404	Madlock-Pit	.495
		Garvey-LA	117	Matthews-Phi	59	Buckner-Chi	.311	Raines-Mon	.394	Hendrick-StL	.485

Production		Adjusted Production		Batter Runs		Adjusted Batter Runs		Clutch Hitting Index		Runs Created	
Schmidt-Phi	1.083	Schmidt-Phi	195	Schmidt-Phi	50.1	Schmidt-Phi	46.0	Concepcion-Cin	141	Schmidt-Phi	102
Dawson-Mon	.923	Dawson-Mon	157	Dawson-Mon	28.8	Dawson-Mon	28.0	Herr-StL	127	Dawson-Mon	83
Madlock-Pit	.912	Madlock-Pit	153	Foster-Cin	27.7	Foster-Cin	26.5	Matthews-Phi	126	Foster-Cin	81
Foster-Cin	.895	Foster-Cin	150	Hernandez-StL	24.6	Hernandez-StL	22.8	Foster-Cin	126	Hernandez-StL	73
Hernandez-StL	.868	Cey-LA	145	Matthews-Phi	22.0	Madlock-Pit	20.4	Maddox-Phi	122	Matthews-Phi	71

Total Average		Stolen Bases		Stolen Base Average		Stolen Base Runs		Fielding Runs		Total Player Rating	
Schmidt-Phi	1.227	Raines-Mon	71	Lopes-LA	90.9	Raines-Mon	14.7	Smith-SD	25.9	Schmidt-Phi	7.0
Raines-Mon	1.034	Moreno-Pit	39	Lacy-Pit	88.9	Lacy-Pit	5.4	Schmidt-Phi	22.5	Dawson-Mon	5.0
Dawson-Mon	.989	Scott-Mon	30	Dawson-Mon	86.7	Dawson-Mon	5.4	Dawson-Mon	17.8	Foster-Cin	3.4
Madlock-Pit	.959			Raines-Mon	86.6	Scott-Mon	4.8	Flynn-NY	12.2	Raines-Mon	3.1
Matthews-Phi	.908			Puhl-Hou	84.6	Lopes-LA	4.8	Clark-SF	11.9	Hernandez-StL	2.5

Wins		Win Percentage		Games		Complete Games		Shutouts		Saves	
Seaver-Cin	14	Seaver-Cin	.875	Lucas-SD	57	Valenzuela-LA	11	Valenzuela-LA	8	Sutter-StL	25
Valenzuela-LA	13	Carlton-Phi	.765	Minton-SF	55	Soto-Cin	10	Knepper-Hou	5	Minton-SF	21
Carlton-Phi	13	Ryan-Hou	.688	Tidrow-Chi	51	Carlton-Phi	10	Hooton-LA	4	Allen-NY	18
		Valenzuela-LA	.650	Hume-Cin	51	Reuss-LA	8			Camp-Atl	17
		Hooton-LA	.647	Sambito-Hou	49	Rogers-Mon	7				

Innings Pitched		Fewest Hits/Game		Fewest BB/Game		Strikeouts		Strikeouts/Game		Ratio	
Valenzuela-LA	192.1	Ryan-Hou	5.98	Perry-Atl	1.43	Valenzuela-LA	180	Carlton-Phi	8.48	Sutton-Hou	9.19
Carlton-Phi	190.0	Seaver-Cin	6.49	Reuss-LA	1.59	Carlton-Phi	179	Ryan-Hou	8.46	Valenzuela-LA	9.45
Soto-Cin	175.0	Valenzuela-LA	6.55	Sutton-Hou	1.64	Soto-Cin	151	Valenzuela-LA	8.42	Knepper-Hou	9.77
Seaver-Cin	166.1	Berenyi-Cin	6.93	Sorensen-StL	1.67	Ryan-Hou	140	Soto-Cin	7.77	Reuss-LA	9.96
Niekro-Hou	166.0	Blue-SF	7.00	Solomon-Pit	1.91	Gullickson-Mon	115	Berenyi-Cin	7.57	Hooton-LA	10.05

Earned Run Average		Adjusted ERA		Opponents' Batting Avg.		Opponents' On Base Pct.		Starter Runs		Adjusted Starter Runs	
Ryan-Hou	1.69	Ryan-Hou	195	Ryan-Hou	.188	Sutton-Hou	.268	Ryan-Hou	29.8	Ryan-Hou	26.5
Knepper-Hou	2.18	Knepper-Hou	151	Valenzuela-LA	.205	Valenzuela-LA	.271	Knepper-Hou	22.8	Carlton-Phi	25.6
Hooton-LA	2.28	Carlton-Phi	150	Seaver-Cin	.205	Knepper-Hou	.280	Carlton-Phi	22.7	Knepper-Hou	19.4
Reuss-LA	2.30	Hooton-LA	146	Berenyi-Cin	.211	Sanderson-Mon	.281	Valenzuela-LA	21.6	Seaver-Cin	18.7
Carlton-Phi	2.42	Reuss-LA	144	Blue-SF	.217	Ryan-Hou	.281	Reuss-LA	20.2	Valenzuela-LA	17.9

Clutch Pitching Index		Relief Runs		Adjusted Relief Runs		Relief Ranking		Total Pitcher Index		Total Baseball Ranking	
Mahler-Atl	124	Lucas-SD	14.9	Camp-Atl	15.2	Camp-Atl	29.3	Ryan-Hou	3.3	Schmidt-Phi	7.0
Solomon-Pit	124	Camp-Atl	14.5	Lucas-SD	12.6	Lucas-SD	21.7	Camp-Atl	3.1	Dawson-Mon	5.0
Alexander-SF	122	Holland-SF	12.0	Holland-SF	11.4	Sambito-Hou	18.2	Valenzuela-LA	2.5	Foster-Cin	3.4
Blue-SF	112	Sambito-Hou	11.7	Sambito-Hou	10.3	Fryman-Mon	15.7	Lucas-SD	2.3	Ryan-Hou	3.3
Zachry-NY	111	Reardon-NY-Mon	10.3	Reardon-NY-Mon	10.3	Holland-SF	14.0	Carlton-Phi	2.2	Camp-Atl	3.1

February 12 Arbitrator Raymond Goetz declares Red Sox catcher Carlton Fisk a free agent on the grounds that the club mailed his contract two days after the December 20 deadline.

April 10 In his first game for Chicago, Carlton Fisk belts a three-run home run in the eighth inning to lead Chicago to a 5-3 win over his former Red Sox teammates at Fenway Park.

April 18 The International League Pawtucket Red Sox and Rochester Red Wings play 32 innings before suspending play at 4:07 a.m. on April 19, tied 2-2. The game resumes on June 23.

May 15 The Indians' Len Barker pitches a perfect game, 3-0 over the Blue Jays before just 7,290 fans on a rainy night in Cleveland.

May 25 Carl Yastrzemski plays in his 3,000th major league game, scoring the winning run in Boston's 8-7 triumph over Cleveland. Yaz joins Ty Cobb, Stan Musial, and Hank Aaron as the only major leaguers to appear in 3,000 games.

June 12 At 12:30 A.M., the longest labor action to that point in American sports history begins. By the time the season resumes on August 10, 706 games (38 percent of the major league schedule) will have been canceled.

June 23 Dave Koza scores Marty Barrett with a bases-loaded single in the bottom of the 33rd inning, giving Pawtucket a 3-2 win over Rochester and ending the longest game in professional baseball history. The game had been suspended April 19 after 32 innings and 8 hours, 7 minutes of play, but the continuation took only 18 minutes to complete. Bob Ojeda pitches one inning to earn the win. Future major league stars Wade Boggs and Cal Ripken go a combined 6-for-25.

August 6 As a result of the nearly two-month interruption in play because of the strike the ML owners elect to split the season in half, with the first-place teams from each half in each division (or a wild card team if the same club wins both halves) meeting in a best-of-five divisional playoff series. The last time the majors played a split season was 1892. The A's, Yankees, Phillies, and Dodgers suddenly find themselves guaranteed playoff spots as first-half champions.

October 3 The Brewers (since 1970) and Expos (1969) clinch their first-ever post-season appearances. Milwaukee beats Detroit 2-1 to wrap up the second-half title in the AL East, while Montreal edges New York 5-4 to win the NL East's second playoff spot.

October 5 Kansas City shuts out Cleveland 9-0 in the first game of a scheduled doubleheader to clinch the second-half title in the AL West. The second game is canceled as irrelevant.

October 9 The A's sweep Kansas City by winning 4-1.

October 11 Yankee bats are too much for the Brewers. Three home runs, including the second of the series by Jackson, and 13 hits provide a 7-3 win and a trip to the ALCS.

October 15 The Yankees wrap up their third AL pennant with a 4-0 win over the A's, completing a 3-game sweep of the ALCS.

October 20 In a World Series rematch of the 1978 teams, the Yankees take Game 1 over the Dodgers 5-3.

November 3 Brewers reliever Rollie Fingers (28 saves, 1.04 ERA) wins the AL Cy Young Award, collecting 22 of 28 possible first-place votes.

November 25 Rollie Fingers becomes the first relief pitcher ever to win the AL MVP Award, edging Oakland's Rickey Henderson 319-308.

	BALTIMORE		BOSTON		CALIFORNIA		CHICAGO		CLEVELAND		DETROIT		KANSAS CITY
M	E.Weaver	M	R.Houk	M	J.Fregosi	M	T.LaRussa	M	D.Garcia	M	S.Anderson	M	J.Frey
1B	E.Murray	1B	T.Perez	M	G.Mauch	1B	M.Squires	1B	M.Hargrove	1B	R.Hebner	M	D.Howser
2B	R.Dauer	2B	J.Remy	1B	R.Carew	2B	T.Bernazard	2B	D.Kuiper	2B	L.Whitaker	1B	W.Aikens
SS	M.Belanger	SS	G.Hoffman	2B	B.Grich	SS	B.Almon	SS	T.Veryzer	SS	A.Trammell	2B	F.White
3B	D.DeCinces	3B	C.Lansford	SS	B.Burleson	3B	J.Morrison	3B	T.Harrah	3B	T.Brookens	SS	U.Washington
LF	J.Lowenstein	LF	J.Rice	3B	B.Hobson	LF	R.LeFlore	LF	M.Dilone	LF	S.Kemp	3B	G.Brett
CF	A.Bumbry	CF	R.Miller	LF	B.Downing	CF	C.Lemon	CF	R.Manning	CF	A.Cowens	LF	W.Wilson
RF	G.Roenicke	RF	D.Evans	CF	F.Lynn	RF	H.Baines	RF	J.Orta	RF	K.Gibson	CF	A.Otis
C	R.Dempsey	C	R.Gedman	RF	D.Ford	C	C.Fisk	C	R.Hassey	C	L.Parrish	RF	C.Geronimo
DH	T.Crowley	DH	C.Yastrzemski	C	E.Ott	DH	G.Luzinski	DH	A.Thornton	DH	J.Wockenfuss	C	J.Wathan
				DH	D.Baylor							DH	H.McRae
O	J.Dwyer	S3	D.Stapleton			O	R.Kuntz	O2	A.Bannister	O	L.Jones		
OD	K.Singleton			P	G.Zahn	O	W.Nordhagen			OD	R.Peters	P	D.Leonard
		P	D.Eckersley	P	K.Forsch			P	B.Blyleven			P	L.Gura
P	D.Martinez	P	F.Tanana	P	M.Witt	P	B.Burns	P	L.Barker	P	J.Morris	P	R.Gale
P	S.McGregor	P	M.Torrez	P	S.Renko	P	R.Dotson	P	J.Denny	P	M.Wilcox	P	P.Splittorff
P	J.Palmer	P	J.Tudor	RP	J.Jefferson	P	D.Lamp	P	R.Waits	P	D.Petry	P	M.Jones
P	M.Flanagan	P	B.Ojeda	RP	A.Hassler	P	S.Trout	P	D.Spillner	P	D.Rozema	RP	D.Quisenberry
P	S.Stewart	RP	B.Stanley	RP	D.Aase	P	R.Baumgarten	RP	S.Monge	P	D.Schatzeder	RP	R.Martin
RP	T.Martinez	RP	M.Clear			RP	L.Hoyt	RP	M.Stanton	RP	A.Lopez	RP	K.Brett
RP	D.Ford	RP	T.Burgmeier			RP	E.Farmer			RP	D.Tobik		
RP	T.Stoddard					RP	K.Hickey	P	W.Garland	RP	K.Saucier	P	J.Wright
		P	S.Crawford										
P	S.Stone												

	MILWAUKEE		MINNESOTA		NEW YORK		OAKLAND		SEATTLE		TEXAS		TORONTO
M	B.Rodgers	M	J.Goryl	M	G.Michael	M	B.Martin	M	M.Wills	M	D.Zimmer	M	B.Mattick
1B	C.Cooper	M	B.Gardner	M	B.Lemon	1B	J.Spencer	M	R.Lachemann	1B	P.Putnam	1B	J.Mayberry
2B	J.Gantner	1B	D.Goodwin	1B	B.Watson	2B	S.Babitt	1B	B.Bochte	2B	B.Wills	3B	D.Garcia
SS	R.Yount	2B	R.Wilfong	2B	W.Randolph	SS	R.Picciolo	2B	J.Cruz	SS	M.Mendoza	SS	A.Griffin
3B	D.Money	SS	R.Smalley	SS	B.Dent	3B	W.Gross	SS	J.Anderson	3B	B.Bell	3B	D.Ainge
LF	B.Oglivie	3B	J.Castino	3B	G.Nettles	LF	R.Henderson	3B	L.Randle	LF	B.Sample	LF	A.Woods
CF	G.Thomas	LF	G.Ward	CF	D.Winfield	CF	D.Murphy	LF	T.Paciorek	CF	M.Rivers	CF	L.Moseby
RF	M.Brouhard	CF	M.Hatcher	RF	J.Mumphrey	RF	T.Armas	CF	J.Simpson	RF	L.Roberts	RF	B.Bonnell
C	T.Simmons	RF	D.Engle	C	R.Jackson	C	M.Heath	RF	J.Burroughs	C	J.Sundberg	C	E.Whitt
DH	L.Hisle	C	S.Butera	DH	R.Cerone	DH	C.Johnson	C	J.Narron	DH	A.Oliver	DH	O.Velez
		DH	G.Adams	DH	B.Murcer			DH	R.Zisk				
3D	R.Howell					32	D.McKay			O	J.Grubb	23	G.Iorg
OD	P.Molitor	2S	P.Mackanin	OD	O.Gamble	C1	J.Newman	1D	G.Gray				
		O	H.Powell			3O	D.Meyer			P	D.Darwin	P	D.Stieb
P	P.Vuckovich			P	R.May	P	R.Langford	P	G.Abbott	P	D.Medich	P	L.Leal
P	M.Caldwell	P	A.Williams	P	T.John	P	S.McCatty	P	F.Bannister	P	R.Honeycutt	P	J.Clancy
P	M.Haas	P	M.Redfern	P	R.Guidry	P	M.Norris	P	K.Clay	P	F.Jenkins	P	J.Todd
P	J.Slaton	P	F.Arroyo	P	D.Righetti	P	M.Keough	P	B.Clark	P	J.Matlack	P	M.Bomback
P	R.Lerch	P	J.Koosman	RP	R.Reuschel	RP	B.Kingman	P	M.Parrott	RP	S.Comer	RP	R.Jackson
RP	R.Fingers	RP	R.Erickson	RP	R.Davis	P	J.Jones	RP	S.Rawley	RP	D.Schmidt	RP	J.McLaughlin
RP	R.Cleveland	RP	D.Corbett	RP	D.LaRoche	RP	B.Owchinko	RP	L.Andersen			RP	J.Garvin
RP	J.Easterly	RP	D.Cooper	RP	R.Gossage			RP	D.Drago	P	C.Hough		
		RP	J.Verhoeven			P	T.Underwood						
P	J.Augustine			P	D.Bird							J.Berenguer	
		P	B.Havens					P	J.Gleaton				
								P	J.Beattie				

TEAM	G	W	L	PCT	GB	R	OR	AB	H	2B	3B	HR	BB	SO	AVG	OBP	SLG	PRO	PRO+	BR	/A	PF	CHI	RC	SB	CS	SBA	SBR
EAST Split Season: First-half Winner NY (34-22); Second-half Winner MIL (31-22)																												
MIL	109	62	47	.569		493	459	3743	961	173	20	96	300	461	.257	.317	.391	.708	109	9	33	95	108	451	39	36	52	-10
BAL	105	59	46	.562	1	429	437	3516	883	165	11	88	**404**	454	.251	.331	.379	.710	104	22	23	100	95	431	41	34	55	-8
NY	107	59	48	.551	2	421	**343**	3529	889	148	22	100	391	434	.252	.328	.391	.719	108	29	35	99	92	445	47	30	61	-4
DET	109	60	49	.550	2	427	404	3600	922	148	29	65	**404**	500	.256	.334	.368	.702	98	14	-2	104	94	442	61	37	62	-4
BOS	108	59	49	.546	2.5	**519**	481	3820	**1052**	168	17	90	378	520	.275	.343	.399	.742	107	65	33	106	99	**514**	32	31	51	-9
CLE	103	52	51	.505	7	431	442	3507	922	150	21	39	343	379	.263	.331	.351	.682	98	-11	-5	99	104	414	119	37	76	14
TOR	106	37	69	.349	23.5	329	466	3521	797	137	23	61	284	556	.226	.288	.330	.618	73	-103	-124	106	105	326	66	57	54	-14
WEST Split Season: First-half Winner OAK (37-23); Second-half Winner KC (30-23)																												
OAK	109	64	45	.587		458	403	3677	910	119	26	**104**	342	647	.247	.314	.379	.693	104	-8	13	95	106	438	98	47	68	1
TEX	105	57	48	.543	5	452	389	3581	968	**178**	15	49	295	396	.270	.329	.369	.698	107	5	28	95	105	425	46	41	53	-11
CHI	106	54	52	.509	8.5	476	423	3615	982	135	27	76	322	518	.272	.338	.387	.725	**110**	41	**51**	98	100	471	86	44	66	-1
KC	103	50	53	.485	11	397	405	3560	952	169	29	61	301	419	.267	.327	.383	.710	105	17	21	99	90	437	100	53	65	-2
CAL	110	51	59	.464	13.5	476	453	3688	944	134	16	97	393	571	.256	.332	.380	.712	105	26	26	100	100	463	44	33	57	-7
SEA	110	44	65	.404	20	426	521	3780	950	148	13	89	329	553	.251	.316	.368	.684	93	-19	-36	104	98	441	100	50	67	0
MIN	110	41	68	.376	23	378	486	3676	884	147	**36**	47	275	497	.240	.295	.338	.633	77	-87	-111	107	109	355	34	27	56	-6
TOT	750					6112		50813	13016	2119	305	1062	4761	6905	.256	.323	.373	.696							913	557	62	-60

TEAM	CG	SH	SV	IP	H	H/G	HR	BB	SO	RAT	ERA	ERA+	OAV	OOB	PR	/A	PF	CPI	FA	E	DP	FW	PW	BW	SBW	DIF
MIL	11	4	**35**	986	994	9.1	72	352	448	12.4	3.91	88	.266	.331	-27	-53	94	99	.982	79	**135**	.3	-5.6	3.5	-.6	9.9
BAL	25	10	23	940	923	8.8	83	347	489	12.3	3.70	98	.260	.328	-4	-7	99	**104**	.983	68	114	.8	-.7	2.4	-.4	4.4
NY	16	**13**	30	948	**827**	7.9	**64**	287	**606**	10.7	**2.90**	**123**	**.235**	**.295**	80	71	99	98	.982	72	100	.7	**7.5**	3.7	.0	-6.3
DET	33	**13**	22	969¹	840	**7.8**	83	373	476	11.5	3.53	107	.236	.313	14	26	103	94	**.984**	67	109	**1.0**	2.7	-.2	.0	1.9
BOS	19	4	24	987¹	983	9.0	90	354	536	12.4	3.81	102	.262	.330	-17	7	106	103	.979	91	108	-.4	.7	3.5	-.5	1.7
CLE	33	10	13	931	989	9.6	67	311	569	12.7	3.88	94	.274	.333	-23	-26	99	102	.978	87	91	-.4	-2.7	-.5	**1.9**	2.2
TOR	20	4	18	953¹	908	8.6	72	377	451	12.5	3.81	103	.252	.329	-17	13	108	97	.975	105	102	-1.3	1.4	-13.0	-1.0	-2.0
WEST																										
OAK	**60**	11	10	993	883	8.0	80	370	505	11.6	3.30	105	.240	.314	40	20	95	101	.980	81	74	.2	2.1	1.4	.6	5.3
TEX	23	**13**	18	940¹	851	8.1	67	322	488	11.4	3.40	105	.243	.310	27	7	95	95	**.984**	69	102	.7	.7	2.9	-.7	.8
CHI	20	8	23	940²	891	8.5	73	336	529	12.0	3.47	103	.252	.321	19	11	98	102	.979	87	113	-.3	1.2	**5.4**	.3	-5.6
KC	24	8	24	922¹	909	8.9	75	**273**	404	11.7	3.56	101	.260	.317	10	5	99	101	.982	72	94	.5	.2	2.2	-.2	-4.9
CAL	27	8	19	971¹	958	8.9	81	323	426	12.1	3.70	94	.261	.324	-4	-5	100	102	.977	101	120	-.9	-.5	2.7	-.3	-5.0
SEA	10	5	23	997¹	1039	9.4	76	360	478	12.8	4.23	91	.271	.336	-64	-42	105	95	.979	91	122	-.3	-4.4	-3.8	-.3	-2.5
MIN	13	6	22	979²	1021	9.4	79	376	500	13.0	3.98	99	.272	.341	-35	-3	108	**104**	.978	96	103	-.6	-.3	-11.6	-.2	-.8
TOT	334	117	304	13459²		8.7				12.1	3.66		.256	.323					.980	1166	1487					

Runs		Hits		Doubles		Triples		Home Runs		Total Bases	
Henderson-Oak	89	Henderson-Oak	135	Cooper-Mil	35	Castino-Min	9	Murray-Bal	22	Evans-Bos	215
Evans-Bos	84	Lansford-Bos	134	Oliver-Tex	29	Wilson-KC	7	Grich-Cal	22	Armas-Oak	211
Cooper-Mil	70	Wilson-KC	133	Paciorek-Sea	28	Henderson-Oak	7	Evans-Bos	22	Paciorek-Sea	206
Harrah-Cle	64	Cooper-Mil	133	Dauer-Bal	27	G.Brett-KC	7	Armas-Oak	22	Cooper-Mil	206
Rivers-Tex	62	Paciorek-Sea	132	G.Brett-KC	27	Baines-Chi	7			Murray-Bal	202

Runs Batted In		Runs Produced		Bases On Balls		Batting Average		On Base Percentage		Slugging Average	
Murray-Bal	78	Evans-Bos	133	Evans-Bos	85	Lansford-Bos	.336	Hargrove-Cle	.432	Grich-Cal	.543
Armas-Oak	76	Henderson-Oak	118	Murphy-Oak	73	Paciorek-Sea	.326	Evans-Bos	.418	Murray-Bal	.534
Oglivie-Mil	72	Cooper-Mil	118	Kemp-Det	70	Cooper-Mil	.320	Henderson-Oak	.411	Evans-Bos	.522
Evans-Bos	71	Murray-Bal	113	Henderson-Oak	64	Henderson-Oak	.319	Kemp-Det	.393	Paciorek-Sea	.509
Winfield-NY	68	Oglivie-Mil	111	Aikens-KC	62	Hargrove-Cle	.317	Lansford-Bos	.391	Cooper-Mil	.495

Production		Adjusted Production		Batter Runs		Adjusted Batter Runs		Clutch Hitting Index		Runs Created	
Evans-Bos	.940	Grich-Cal	164	Evans-Bos	39.8	Evans-Bos	34.2	Yastrzemski-Bos	139	Evans-Bos	95
Grich-Cal	.924	Evans-Bos	160	Paciorek-Sea	28.4	Henderson-Oak	30.8	Wills-Tex	132	Henderson-Oak	81
Murray-Bal	.897	Murray-Bal	156	Grich-Cal	28.3	Grich-Cal	28.3	Hargrove-Cle	129	Paciorek-Sea	76
Paciorek-Sea	.894	Lemon-Chi	155	Henderson-Oak	26.9	Cooper-Mil	27.3	Oglivie-Mil	128	Grich-Cal	73
Lemon-Chi	.879	Cooper-Mil	154	Murray-Bal	25.9	Murray-Bal	26.0	Murphy-Oak	125	Murray-Bal	70

Total Average		Stolen Bases		Stolen Base Average		Stolen Base Runs		Fielding Runs		Total Player Rating	
Evans-Bos	1.007	Henderson-Oak	56	Manning-Cle	89.3	Cruz-Sea	8.1	Bell-Tex	30.0	Henderson-Oak	5.2
Grich-Cal	.917	Cruz-Sea	43	Bannister-Cle	89.3	Manning-Cle	5.7	Yount-Mil	27.5	Bell-Tex	4.6
Henderson-Oak	.899	LeFlore-Chi	36	Cruz-Sea	84.3	Wilson-KC	5.4	Wilson-KC	22.1	Yount-Mil	4.5
Murray-Bal	.864	Wilson-KC	34	Wilson-KC	81.0	LeFlore-Chi	4.2	Burleson-Cal	21.0	Grich-Cal	4.5
Paciorek-Sea	.846	Dilone-Cle	29	Gibson-Det	77.3			Henderson-Oak	20.1	Evans-Bos	4.5

Wins		Win Percentage		Games		Complete Games		Shutouts		Saves	
Vuckovich-Mil	14	Vuckovich-Mil	.778	Corbett-Min	54	Langford-Oak	18	Medich-Tex	4	Fingers-Mil	28
Morris-Det	14	D.Martinez-Bal	.737	Fingers-Mil	47	McCatty-Oak	16	McCatty-Oak	4	Gossage-NY	20
McCatty-Oak	14	McGregor-Bal	.722	Rawley-Sea	46	Morris-Det	15	Forsch-Cal	4	Quisenberry-KC	18
D.Martinez-Bal	14	Guidry-NY	.688	Easterly-Mil	44	Norris-Oak	12	Dotson-Chi	4	Corbett-Min	17
						Gura-KC	12			Saucier-Det	13

Innings Pitched		Fewest Hits/Game		Fewest BB/Game		Strikeouts		Strikeouts/Game		Ratio	
Leonard-KC	201.2	McCatty-Oak	6.79	Honeycutt-Tex	1.20	Barker-Cle	127	Barker-Cle	7.41	Guidry-NY	9.00
Morris-Det	198.0	Morris-Det	6.95	Forsch-Cal	1.59	Burns-Chi	108	Guidry-NY	7.37	Gura-KC	9.30
Langford-Oak	195.1	Guidry-NY	7.09	Gura-KC	1.83	Leonard-KC	107	Bannister-Sea	6.30	Honeycutt-Tex	9.66
McCatty-Oak	185.2	Darwin-Tex	7.09	Leonard-KC	1.83	Blyleven-Cle	107	Burns-Chi	6.20	McCatty-Oak	9.84
Stieb-Tor	183.2	Stewart-Bal	7.13	Guidry-NY	1.84	Guidry-NY	104	Blyleven-Cle	6.04	Forsch-Cal	10.24

Earned Run Average		Adjusted ERA		Opponents' Batting Avg.		Opponents' On Base Pct.		Starter Runs		Adjusted Starter Runs	
McCatty-Oak	2.33	Stewart-Bal	156	McCatty-Oak	.211	Guidry-NY	.257	Guidry-NY	27.5	McCatty-Oak	23.8
Stewart-Bal	2.32	McCatty-Oak	149	Guidry-NY	.214	Gura-KC	.269	Righetti-NY	18.8	Righetti-NY	17.8
Lamp-Chi	2.41	Lamp-Chi	148	Darwin-Tex	.218	Honeycutt-Tex	.272	Gura-KC	18.0	Gura-KC	17.1
John-NY	2.63	John-NY	136	Morris-Det	.218	McCatty-Oak	.279	Burns-Chi	17.7	Lamp-Chi	16.5
Burns-Chi	2.64	Burns-Chi	135	Lamp-Chi	.222	Forsch-Cal	.289	Lamp-Chi	17.6	Burns-Chi	16.3

Clutch Pitching Index		Relief Runs		Adjusted Relief Runs		Relief Ranking		Total Pitcher Index		Total Baseball Ranking	
Stewart-Bal	145	Fingers-Mil	22.7	Fingers-Mil	20.7	Fingers-Mil	37.9	Fingers-Mil	4.2	Henderson-Oak	5.2
John-NY	129	Gossage-NY	15.0	Gossage-NY	14.5	Gossage-NY	27.8	Gossage-NY	3.1	Bell-Tex	4.6
Burns-Chi	121	Quisenberry-KC	13.3	Corbett-Min	13.4	Saucier-Det	19.5	McCatty-Oak	2.8	Yount-Mil	4.5
Denny-Cle	119	Saucier-Det	10.9	Quisenberry-KC	13.0	Quisenberry-KC	17.7	Quisenberry-KC	2.2	Grich-Cal	4.5
McGregor-Bal	116	Corbett-Min	10.6	Saucier-Det	11.5	Corbett-Min	16.8	Saucier-Det	2.0	Evans-Bos	4.5

January 13 Hank Aaron and Frank Robinson become the 12th and 13th players elected to the Hall of Fame by the BBWAA in their first year of eligibility. Aaron falls nine votes shy of becoming the first-ever unanimous selection, and his 97.8 election percentage is second only to Ty Cobb's 98.2 percent in the inaugural 1936 election.

February 8 The Dodgers break up the longest-playing infield unit in ML history by trading veteran second baseman Davey Lopes to the A's for minor-leaguer Lance Hudson. Lopes, first baseman Steve Garvey, third baseman Ron Cey, and shortstop Bill Russell had been LA's starting infield since 1974.

March 10 Travis Jackson and Happy Chandler are elected to the Hall of Fame by the Special Veterans Committee. Jackson hit .291 in 15 seasons as the Giants shortstop in the 1920s and 30s, while Chandler was baseball's second commissioner and oversaw—and encouraged—the dismantling of the color barrier in 1947.

April 20 By defeating Cincinnati 4-2 for its twelfth victory in a row, Atlanta breaks the modern ML record for con-secutive wins at the start of a season. Steve Bedrosian pitches 4⅓ innings of relief to earn his first ML win.

June 7 The Cubs select shortstop Shawon Dunston, who batted .790 this season for Brooklyn's Thomas Jefferson HS, with the first pick in the annual June free-agent draft. Dwight Gooden is taken fifth, by the Mets, and the Yankees select high school shortstop Bo Jackson in the second round, but he opts for Auburn instead.

June 20 Phillies Pete Rose plays in his 3,000th major league game (a 3-1 loss to the Pirates), joining Ty Cobb, Stan Musial, Hank Aaron, and Carl Yastrzemski as the only players to reach that plateau.

August 4 Outfielder Joel Youngblood becomes the first major league player ever to play for two different teams in two different cities on the same day, and collects a hit in each game. After going 1-for-2 off Fergie Jenkins in an afternoon game at Wrigley Field, Youngblood is traded from the Mets to the Expos and flies to Philadelphia in time to enter the game that night in the sixth inning, going 1-for-1 off Steve Carlton.

September 6 Veteran first baseman Willie Stargell, whose number is retired, is saluted by 38,000 fans on his day at Pittsburgh's Three Rivers Stadium. The 41-year-old slugger delivers a pinch single in the Pirates' 6-1 win over the Mets.

October 10 St. Louis wins its first pennant since 1968 by defeating the Braves 6-2 to complete a 3-game sweep of the NLCS. Catcher Darrell Porter, who hit .556, is named series MVP.

October 20 St. Louis rallies for three runs in the sixth inning, and Bruce Sutter saves Game 7, registering a 6-3 win to give the Cards the World Championship.

October 26 Steve Carlton wins the NL Cy Young Award for the fourth time. The Phils 37-year-old lefthander, who led the NL in wins (23), innings (295⅔), strikeouts (286), and shutouts (6), was a previous winner in 1972, 1977, and 1980. He joins Walter Johnson and Willie Mays as the only players to be voted MVP or Cy Young winner 10 or more years apart.

November 17 Dale Murphy wins the NL MVP Award, becoming the first Brave to be so honored since Hank Aaron in 1957.

ATLANTA		CHICAGO		CINCINNATI		HOUSTON		LOS ANGELES		MONTREAL	
M	J.Torre	M	L.Elia	M	J.McNamara	M	B.Virdon	M	T.Lasorda	M	J.Fanning
1B	C.Chambliss	1B	B.Buckner	1B	D.Driessen	1B	R.Knight	1B	S.Garvey	1B	A.Oliver
2B	G.Hubbard	2B	B.Wills	2B	R.Oester	2B	P.Garner	2B	S.Sax	2B	D.Flynn
SS	R.Ramirez	SS	L.Bowa	SS	D.Concepcion	SS	D.Thon	SS	B.Russell	SS	C.Speier
3B	B.Horner	3B	R.Sandberg	3B	J.Bench	3B	A.Howe	3B	R.Cey	3B	T.Wallach
LF	R.Linares	LF	K.Moreland	LF	E.Milner	LF	J.Cruz	LF	D.Baker	LF	T.Raines
CF	D.Murphy	CF	G.Woods	CF	C.Cedeno	CF	T.Scott	CF	K.Landreaux	CF	A.Dawson
RF	C.Washington	RF	L.Durham	RF	P.Householder	RF	T.Puhl	RF	P.Guerrero	RF	W.Cromartie
C	B.Benedict	C	J.Davis	C	A.Trevino	C	A.Ashby	C	M.Scioscia	C	G.Carter
3O	J.Royster	O	J.Johnstone					O	R.Monday	P	S.Rogers
O	B.Butler	2S	J.Kennedy	O1	L.Biittner	P	J.Niekro	O	R.Roenicke	P	B.Gullickson
		O	S.Henderson	O	D.Walker	P	N.Ryan			P	S.Sanderson
P	P.Niekro					P	D.Sutton	P	F.Valenzuela	P	C.Lea
P	R.Mahler	P	F.Jenkins	P	M.Soto	P	B.Knepper	P	J.Reuss	P	R.Burris
P	R.Camp	P	D.Bird	P	B.Berenyi	P	V.Ruhle	P	B.Welch	RP	J.Reardon
P	B.Walk	P	D.Noles	P	F.Pastore	RP	M.LaCoss	P	D.Stewart	RP	B.Smith
RP	S.Bedrosian	P	R.Martz	P	B.Shirley	RP	F.LaCorte	P	B.Hooton	RP	W.Fryman
RP	G.Garber	P	A.Ripley	P	T.Seaver	RP	D.Smith	RP	S.Howe		
		RP	L.Smith	RP	G.Harris			RP	T.Forster	P	D.Palmer
P	P.Perez	RP	D.Tidrow	RP	J.Kern			RP	T.Niedenfuer		
P	K.Dayley	RP	B.Campbell	RP	J.Price						
P	J.Cowley										
		P	M.Proly	P	C.Leibrandt						
		P	W.Hernandez	P	T.Hume						

NEW YORK		PHILADELPHIA		PITTSBURGH		SAN DIEGO		SAN FRANCISCO		ST.LOUIS	
M	G.Bamberger	M	P.Corrales	M	C.Tanner	M	D.Williams	M	F.Robinson	M	W.Herzog
1B	D.Kingman	1B	P.Rose	1B	J.Thompson	1B	B.Perkins	1B	R.Smith	1B	K.Hernandez
2B	W.Backman	2B	M.Trillo	2B	J.Ray	2B	T.Flannery	2B	J.Morgan	2B	T.Herr
SS	R.Gardenhire	SS	I.DeJesus	SS	D.Berra	SS	G.Templeton	SS	J.LeMaster	SS	O.Smith
3B	H.Brooks	3B	M.Schmidt	3B	B.Madlock	3B	L.Salazar	3B	D.Evans	3B	K.Oberkfell
LF	G.Foster	LF	G.Matthews	LF	M.Easler	LF	G.Richards	LF	J.Leonard	LF	L.Smith
CF	M.Wilson	CF	G.Maddox	CF	O.Moreno	CF	R.Jones	CF	C.Davis	CF	W.McGee
RF	E.Valentine	RF	G.Vukovich	RF	L.Lacy	RF	S.Lezcano	RF	J.Clark	RF	G.Hendrick
C	J.Stearns	C	B.Diaz	C	T.Pena	C	T.Kennedy	C	M.May	C	D.Porter
S2	B.Bailor	O	G.Gross	O	D.Parker	3O	J.Lefebvre	1	D.Bergman	O1	D.Iorg
1O	M.Jorgensen	O	B.Dernier			O	A.Wiggins	2	D.Kuiper	23	M.Ramsey
O1	R.Staub			P	R.Rhoden			O	J.Wohlford		
C	R.Hodges	P	S.Carlton	P	D.Robinson	P	T.Lollar	3	T.O'Malley	P	J.Andujar
O	J.Youngblood	P	L.Christenson	P	J.Candelaria	P	J.Montefusco			P	B.Forsch
		P	M.Krukow	P	M.Sarmiento	P	J.Eichelberger	P	B.Laskey	P	S.Mura
P	C.Puleo	P	D.Ruthven	RP	L.McWilliams	P	E.Show	P	A.Hammaker	P	D.LaPoint
P	P.Falcone	RP	R.Reed	RP	K.Tekulve	P	C.Welsh	P	R.Gale	P	J.Stuper
P	C.Swan	RP	E.Farmer	RP	R.Scurry	RP	L.DeLeon	P	R.Martin	RP	B.Sutter
P	M.Scott	RP	S.Monge	RP	E.Romo	RP	G.Lucas	RP	F.Breining	RP	D.Bair
P	E.Lynch					RP	F.Chiffer	RP	A.Holland	RP	J.Kaat
RP	J.Orosco	P	M.Bystrom					RP	J.Barr		
RP	N.Allen					P	J.Curtis			P	J.Martin
						P	D.Dravecky	G.Minton		P	J.Lahti
P	P.Zachry					P	A.Hawkins	P	G.Lavelle		
P	R.Jones							P	A.Fowlkes		
/P	R.Ownbey										

TEAM	G	W	L	PCT	GB	R	OR	AB	H	2B	3B	HR	BB	SO	AVG	OBP	SLG	PRO	PRO+	BR	/A	PF	CHI	RC	SB	CS	SBA	SBR
EAST																												
STL	162	92	70	.568		685	**609**	5455	1439	239	**52**	67	569	805	.264	**.337**	.364	.701	101	24	17	101	99	682	**200**	91	69	5
PHI	162	89	73	.549	3	664	654	5454	1417	245	25	112	506	831	.260	.325	.376	.701	100	14	-1	102	99	654	128	76	63	-7
MON	162	86	76	.531	6	697	616	5557	1454	270	38	133	503	816	.262	.327	.396	.723	106	52	38	102	97	725	156	56	**74**	**13**
PIT	162	84	78	.519	8	724	696	5614	**1535**	**272**	40	134	447	862	**.273**	.330	**.408**	**.738**	109	**80**	58	103	97	**745**	161	75	68	3
CHI	162	73	89	.451	19	676	709	5531	1436	239	46	102	460	869	.260	.319	.375	.694	90	-4	-22	103	103	662	132	70	65	-2
NY	162	65	97	.401	27	609	723	5510	1361	227	26	97	456	1005	.247	.307	.350	.657	90	-75	-71	99	105	595	137	58	70	6
WEST																												
ATL	162	89	73	.549		**739**	702	5507	1411	215	22	**146**	554	869	.256	.327	.383	.710	100	33	4	104	105	697	151	77	66	-1
LA	162	88	74	.543	1	691	612	5642	1487	222	32	138	528	804	.264	.330	.388	.718	**110**	47	**65**	98	95	735	151	56	73	12
SF	162	87	75	.537	2	673	687	5499	1393	213	30	133	**607**	915	.253	.329	.376	.705	103	27	28	100	97	685	130	56	70	5
SD	162	81	81	.500	8	675	658	5575	1435	217	**52**	81	429	877	.257	.313	.359	.672	99	-49	-17	95	**110**	626	165	77	68	3
HOU	162	77	85	.475	12	569	620	5440	1342	236	48	74	435	830	.247	.305	.349	.654	95	-84	-42	92	102	578	140	61	70	5
CIN	162	61	101	.377	28	545	661	5479	1375	228	34	82	470	817	.251	.313	.350	.663	89	-63	-75	102	92	588	131	69	66	-2
TOT	972					7947		66263	17085	2823	445	1299	5964	10300	.258	.322	.373	.695							1782	822	68	41

TEAM	CG	SH	SV	IP	H	H/G	HR	BB	SO	RAT	ERA	ERA+	OAV	OOB	PR	/A	PF	CPI	FA	E	DP	FW	PW	BW	SBW	DIF
EAST																										
STL	25	10	47	1465¹	1420	8.7	94	502	689	11.9	3.37	107	.258	.322	37	40	101	105	**.981**	124	169	.9	4.2	1.8	.2	3.9
PHI	**38**	13	33	1456¹	1395	8.6	86	472	**1002**	11.7	3.61	102	.255	.317	-1	9	102	93	**.981**	121	138	**1.1**	.9	-.1	-1.1	7.1
MON	34	10	43	1460²	1371	8.4	110	**448**	936	11.3	3.31	**110**	.250	.309	46	**53**	101	99	.980	122	117	**1.1**	5.6	4.0	**1.0**	-6.6
PIT	19	7	39	1466²	1434	8.8	118	521	933	12.2	3.81	97	.257	.324	-34	-17	103	96	.977	145	133	-.3	-1.8	6.1	-.0	-1.0
CHI	9	7	43	1447¹	1510	9.4	125	452	764	12.4	3.92	96	.272	.330	-51	-30	104	102	.979	132	110	.5	-3.2	-2.3	-.6	-2.4
NY	15	5	37	1447¹	1508	9.4	119	582	759	13.1	3.88	94	.273	.344	-45	-40	101	**109**	.972	175	134	-2.0	-4.2	-7.5	.3	-2.6
WEST																										
ATL	15	11	**51**	1463	1484	9.1	126	502	813	12.4	3.82	98	.267	.331	-36	-15	104	103	.979	137	**186**	.2	-1.6	.4	-.5	9.4
LA	37	**16**	28	1488¹	1356	**8.2**	81	468	932	**11.2**	**3.26**	106	**.244**	**.305**	56	34	96	92	.979	139	131	.0	3.6	**6.8**	.9	-4.4
SF	18	4	45	1465¹	1507	9.3	109	466	810	12.3	3.64	99	.270	.329	-6	-7	100	106	.973	173	125	-1.9	-.7	2.9	.2	5.5
SD	20	11	41	1476	1348	**8.2**	139	502	765	11.4	3.52	97	**.244**	.310	13	-16	95	96	.976	152	142	-.7	-1.7	-1.8	-.0	4.2
HOU	37	**16**	31	1446²	**1338**	8.3	87	479	899	11.5	3.42	97	.247	.312	30	-16	92	94	.978	136	154	.3	-1.7	-4.4	.2	1.7
CIN	22	7	31	1460¹	1414	8.7	105	570	998	12.4	3.66	101	.258	.330	-10	6	103	102	.980	128	158	.7	.6	-7.9	-.6	-12.9
TOT	289	117	469	17543¹		8.8				12.0	3.60		.258	.322					.978	1684	1697					

Runs		Hits		Doubles		Triples		Home Runs		Total Bases	
L.Smith-StL	120	Oliver-Mon	204	Oliver-Mon	43	Thon-Hou	10	Kingman-NY	37	Oliver-Mon	317
Murphy-Atl	113	Buckner-Chi	201	Kennedy-SD	42	Wilson-NY	9	Murphy-Atl	36	Guerrero-LA	308
Schmidt-Phi	108	Dawson-Mon	183	Dawson-Mon	37	Puhl-Hou	9	Schmidt-Phi	35	Murphy-Atl	303
Dawson-Mon	107	L.Smith-StL	182	Knight-Hou	36	Moreno-Pit	9	Horner-Atl	32	Dawson-Mon	303
Sandberg-Chi	103	Ray-Pit	182					Guerrero-LA	32	Buckner-Chi	290

Runs Batted In		Runs Produced		Bases On Balls		Batting Average		On Base Percentage		Slugging Average	
Oliver-Mon	109	Murphy-Atl	186	Schmidt-Phi	107	Oliver-Mon	.331	Schmidt-Phi	.407	Schmidt-Phi	.547
Murphy-Atl	109	Buckner-Chi	183	Thompson-Pit	101	Madlock-Pit	.319	Hernandez-StL	.404	Guerrero-LA	.536
Buckner-Chi	105	L.Smith-StL	181	Hernandez-StL	100	Durham-Chi	.312	Morgan-SF	.402	Durham-Chi	.521
Hendrick-StL	104	Oliver-Mon	177	Murphy-Atl	93	L.Smith-StL	.307	Thompson-Pit	.397	Oliver-Mon	.514
Clark-SF	103	Madlock-Pit	168	Clark-SF	90	Buckner-Chi	.306	Oliver-Mon	.394	Thompson-Pit	.511

Production		Adjusted Production		Batter Runs		Adjusted Batter Runs		Clutch Hitting Index		Runs Created	
Schmidt-Phi	.954	Schmidt-Phi	161	Schmidt-Phi	47.2	Schmidt-Phi	44.7	Hernandez-StL	129	Oliver-Mon	125
Guerrero-LA	.915	Guerrero-LA	157	Oliver-Mon	42.7	Guerrero-LA	43.1	Hendrick-StL	128	Guerrero-LA	120
Durham-Chi	.910	Oliver-Mon	149	Thompson-Pit	40.7	Oliver-Mon	40.5	DeJesus-Phi	123	Murphy-Atl	118
Oliver-Mon	.908	Lezcano-SD	149	Guerrero-LA	40.3	Thompson-Pit	37.4	Buckner-Chi	123	Schmidt-Phi	118
Thompson-Pit	.908	Durham-Chi	148	Murphy-Atl	37.8	Durham-Chi	35.0	Lezcano-SD	115	Thompson-Pit	117

Total Average		Stolen Bases		Stolen Base Average		Stolen Base Runs		Fielding Runs		Total Player Rating	
Schmidt-Phi	1.026	Raines-Mon	78	Bailor-NY	87.0	Raines-Mon	13.8	O.Smith-StL	33.1	Schmidt-Phi	6.1
Guerrero-LA	.959	L.Smith-StL	68	Morgan-SF	85.7	Wilson-NY	7.8	Dawson-Mon	20.8	Carter-Mon	5.4
Thompson-Pit	.951	Moreno-Pit	60	Wiggins-SD	84.6	Wiggins-SD	6.3	Hubbard-Atl	19.9	Dawson-Mon	4.7
Morgan-SF	.923	Wilson-NY	58	Matthews-Phi	84.0	Thon-Hou	6.3	Schmidt-Phi	18.8	Guerrero-LA	4.6
Durham-Chi	.917	S.Sax-LA	49	O.Smith-StL	83.3	Dawson-Mon	5.7	Davis-SF	17.9	Lezcano-SD	4.6

Wins		Win Percentage		Games		Complete Games		Shutouts		Saves	
Carlton-Phi	23	Niekro-Atl	.810	Tekulve-Pit	85	Carlton-Phi	19	Carlton-Phi	6	Sutter-StL	36
Valenzuela-LA	19	Rogers-Mon	.704	Minton-SF	78	Valenzuela-LA	18	Niekro-Hou	5	Minton-SF	30
Rogers-Mon	19	Carlton-Phi	.676	Scurry-Pit	76	Niekro-Hou	16	Andujar-StL	5	Garber-Atl	30
Reuss-LA	18	Lollar-SD	.640	Reardon-Mon	75	Rogers-Mon	14			Reardon-Mon	26
		Forsch-StL	.625	Hernandez-Chi	75	Soto-Cin	13			Tekulve-Pit	20

Innings Pitched		Fewest Hits/Game		Fewest BB/Game		Strikeouts		Strikeouts/Game		Ratio	
Carlton-Phi	295.2	Ryan-Hou	7.05	Bird-Chi	1.41	Carlton-Phi	286	Soto-Cin	9.57	Soto-Cin	9.68
Valenzuela-LA	285.0	Soto-Cin	7.06	Hammaker-SF	1.44	Soto-Cin	274	Ryan-Hou	8.81	Niekro-Hou	9.77
Rogers-Mon	277.0	Lea-Mon	7.35	Andujar-StL	1.69	Ryan-Hou	245	Carlton-Phi	8.71	Andujar-StL	9.96
Niekro-Hou	270.0	Lollar-SD	7.43	Reuss-LA	1.77	Valenzuela-LA	199	Candelaria-Pit	6.85	Sutton-Hou	9.97
Andujar-StL	265.2	Niekro-Hou	7.47	Candelaria-Pit	1.91	Rogers-Mon	179	Welch-LA	6.72	Reuss-LA	10.04

Earned Run Average		Adjusted ERA		Opponents' Batting Avg.		Opponents' On Base Pct.		Starter Runs		Adjusted Starter Runs	
Rogers-Mon	2.40	Rogers-Mon	151	Ryan-Hou	.213	Soto-Cin	.273	Rogers-Mon	36.8	Rogers-Mon	38.0
Niekro-Hou	2.47	Andujar-StL	146	Soto-Cin	.215	Reuss-LA	.278	Niekro-Hou	34.0	Andujar-StL	33.8
Andujar-StL	2.47	Niekro-Hou	134	Lea-Mon	.222	Sutton-Hou	.279	Andujar-StL	33.3	Soto-Cin	25.9
Soto-Cin	2.79	Soto-Cin	132	Lollar-SD	.224	Niekro-Hou	.279	Soto-Cin	23.1	Niekro-Hou	25.5
Valenzuela-LA	2.87	Candelaria-Pit	126	Niekro-Hou	.229	Andujar-StL	.282	Valenzuela-LA	23.0	Valenzuela-LA	18.8

Clutch Pitching Index		Relief Runs		Adjusted Relief Runs		Relief Ranking		Total Pitcher Index		Total Baseball Ranking	
Camp-Atl	124	Minton-SF	24.2	Minton-SF	24.1	Minton-SF	35.7	Minton-SF	3.9	Schmidt-Phi	6.1
Jenkins-Chi	121	Scurry-Pit	21.5	Scurry-Pit	22.7	Garber-Atl	33.7	Garber-Atl	3.9	Carter-Mon	5.4
Krukow-Phi	120	Reardon-Mon	18.6	Bedrosian-Atl	20.1	Reardon-Mon	25.8	Rogers-Mon	3.7	Dawson-Mon	4.7
Gale-SF	114	Bedrosian-Atl	18.1	Reardon-Mon	19.1	DeLeon-SD	23.9	Andujar-StL	3.2	Guerrero-LA	4.6
Mura-StL	110	DeLeon-SD	17.8	Garber-Atl	18.5	Scurry-Pit	23.4	Soto-Cin	2.7	Lezcano-SD	4.6

January 22 Free-agent outfielder Reggie Jackson ends his tumultuous five seasons as a Yankee by signing a reported four-year contract with the California Angels for nearly $1 million per year.

May 6 Gaylord Perry becomes the 15th pitcher to win 300 career games, beating the Yankees 7-3 at the Kingdome.

July 8 Billy Martin records his 1,000th career win as a manager as the A's beat the Yankees 6–3.

July 19 In the first annual Cracker Jack Old-Timers Classic at Washington's Robert F. Kennedy Stadium, 75-year-old Luke Appling hits a 250-foot homer off Warren Spahn to help the AL to a 7-2 win over the NL.

August 2 Oakland's Rickey Henderson steals his 100th base of the season in a 6–5 win over Seattle, tying the AL record he set in 1981.

August 21 Milwaukee's Rollie Fingers records his 300th career save in a 3–2 win at Seattle, becoming the first player to reach that milestone.

August 23 Seattle pitcher Gaylord Perry is ejected in the seventh inning of a 4-3 loss to the Red Sox for doctoring the baseball. It is the first time in his 20 major league seasons that the self-proclaimed spitball king has been bounced for that offense.

August 24 Kansas City's John Wathan steals his 31st base of the season in a 5-3 win over the Rangers, breaking the single-season record for catchers set by Ray Schalk in 1916. Wathan will finish the season with a career-high 36 stolen bases.

August 27 Rickey Henderson steals four bases in Oakland's 5-4 loss to Milwaukee to raise his total to 122 and break Lou Brock's single-season record of 118.

October 2 The Angels clinch the AL West title with a 6-4 win over the Rangers.

October 3 Robin Yount smacks two home runs and a triple as Milwaukee whips Baltimore 10-2 to win the AL East championship. Don Sutton, 4-1 since being acquired by the Brewers in late August, is the winning pitcher.

October 10 In Game 5 of the ALCS, the Brewers complete their comeback from a 2-0 deficit by edging the Angels 4-3 to earn their first-ever trip to the World Series. Angels outfielder Fred Lynn bats .611 for the series and is named MVP in a losing cause.

October 12 Paul Molitor goes 5-for-6 to become the first player ever to collect 5 hits in a World Series game, and teammate Robin Yount goes 4-for-6 as the Brewers rout the Cardinals 10-0 in Game 1.

October 17 Robin Yount records his second four-hit game of the Series to lead the Brewers to a 6-4 win in Game 5 and give Milwaukee a 3-2 lead overall. Yount is the first player ever to have two four-hit games in one World Series.

November 3 Pete Vuckovich becomes the Brewers' second consecutive AL Cy Young Award winner, edging Jim Palmer. Vuckovich was 18-6 with a 3.34 ERA for the AL champions, and has the highest winning percentage in the majors for the past two seasons.

November 9 Robin Yount, who hit .331 for Milwaukee and led the league in hits (210), doubles (46), and slugging percentage (.578), is a unanimous choice as AL MVP.

	BALTIMORE		BOSTON		CALIFORNIA		CHICAGO		CLEVELAND		DETROIT		KANSAS CITY
M	E.Weaver	M	R.Houk	M	G.Mauch	M	T.LaRussa	M	D.Garcia	M	S.Anderson	M	D.Howser
1B	E.Murray	1B	D.Stapleton	1B	R.Carew	1B	M.Squires	1B	M.Hargrove	1B	E.Cabell	1B	W.Aikens
2B	R.Dauer	2B	J.Remy	2B	B.Grich	2B	T.Bernazard	2B	J.Perconte	2B	L.Whitaker	2B	F.White
SS	L.Sakata	SS	G.Hoffman	SS	T.Foli	SS	B.Almon	SS	M.Fischlin	SS	A.Trammell	SS	U.Washington
3B	C.Ripken	3B	C.Lansford	3B	D.DeCinces	3B	A.Rodriguez	3B	T.Harrah	3B	T.Brookens	3B	G.Brett
LF	G.Roenicke	LF	J.Rice	LF	B.Downing	LF	S.Kemp	LF	M.Dilone	LF	L.Herndon	LF	W.Wilson
CF	A.Bumbry	CF	R.Miller	CF	F.Lynn	CF	R.Law	CF	R.Manning	CF	G.Wilson	CF	A.Otis
RF	D.Ford	RF	D.Evans	RF	Re.Jackson	RF	H.Baines	RF	V.Hayes	RF	C.Lemon	RF	J.Martin
C	R.Dempsey	C	G.Allenson	C	B.Boone	C	C.Fisk	C	R.Hassey	C	L.Parrish	C	J.Wathan
DH	K.Singleton	DH	C.Yastrzemski	DH	D.Baylor	DH	G.Luzinski	DH	A.Thornton	DH	M.Ivie	DH	H.McRae
O	J.Lowenstein	13	W.Boggs	O	J.Beniquez	S3	V.Law	O2	A.Bannister	O	K.Gibson	S2	O.Concepcion
C	J.Nolan	C	R.Gedman	O	B.Clark	1	T.Paciorek	2S	L.Milbourne	1O	R.Leach		
		O	R.Nichols			O	R.LeFlore	S	J.Dybzinski	DO	J.Turner		
P	D.Martinez			P	G.Zahn							P	L.Gura
P	M.Flanagan	P	D.Eckersley	P	K.Forsch	P	L.Hoyt	P	L.Barker	P	J.Morris	P	V.Blue
P	J.Palmer	P	J.Tudor	P	M.Witt	P	R.Dotson	P	R.Sutcliffe	P	D.Petry	P	P.Splittorff
P	S.McGregor	P	M.Torrez	P	S.Renko	P	D.Lamp	P	L.Sorensen	P	M.Wilcox	P	D.Leonard
P	S.Stewart	P	B.Stanley	P	B.Kison	P	J.Koosman	P	J.Denny	P	J.Ujdur	RP	D.Quisenberry
RP	T.Martinez	P	C.Rainey	RP	L.Sanchez	P	B.Burns	P	R.Waits	P	P.Underwood	RP	M.Armstrong
RP	T.Grimsley	RP	M.Clear	P	A.Hassler	RP	S.Barojas	RP	D.Spillner	RP	D.Tobik	RP	D.Hood
RP	T.Stoddard	RP	T.Burgmeier	RP	D.Corbett	RP	K.Hickey	RP	E.Whitson	RP	D.Rucker		
		RP	L.Aponte			RP	C.Escarrega	RP	E.Glynn	RP	E.Sosa	P	B.Black
P	S.Davis			P	D.Goltz							P	D.Frost
		P	B.Hurst	P	D.Aase	P	S.Trout	P	T.Brennan	P	L.Pashnick	P	B.Castro
		P	B.Ojeda					P	B.Anderson				

	MILWAUKEE		MINNESOTA		NEW YORK		OAKLAND		SEATTLE		TEXAS		TORONTO
M	B.Rodgers	M	B.Gardner	M	B.Lemon	M	B.Martin	M	R.Lachemann	M	D.Zimmer	M	B.Cox
M	H.Kuenn	1B	K.Hrbek	M	G.Michael	1B	D.Meyer	1B	G.Gray	M	D.Johnson	1B	W.Upshaw
1B	C.Cooper	2B	J.Castino	M	C.King	2B	D.Lopes	2B	J.Cruz	1B	D.Hostetler	2B	D.Garcia
2B	J.Gantner	SS	R.Washington	1B	J.Mayberry	SS	F.Stanley	SS	T.Cruz	2B	M.Richardt	SS	A.Griffin
SS	R.Yount	3B	G.Gaetti	2B	W.Randolph	3B	W.Gross	3B	M.Castillo	SS	M.Wagner	3B	R.Mulliniks
3B	P.Molitor	LF	G.Ward	SS	R.Smalley	LF	R.Henderson	LF	B.Bochte	3B	B.Bell	LF	B.Bonnell
LF	B.Oglivie	CF	B.Mitchell	3B	G.Nettles	CF	D.Murphy	CF	D.Henderson	LF	B.Sample	CF	L.Moseby
CF	G.Thomas	RF	T.Brunansky	LF	D.Winfield	RF	T.Armas	RF	A.Cowens	CF	G.Wright	RF	J.Barfield
RF	C.Moore	C	T.Laudner	CF	J.Mumphrey	C	M.Heath	C	R.Sweet	RF	L.Parrish	C	E.Whitt
C	T.Simmons	DH	R.Johnson	C	K.Griffey	DH	C.Johnson	DH	R.Zisk	C	J.Sundberg	DH	D.Revering
DH	R.Howell			C	R.Cerone					DH	L.Johnson		
		OD	M.Hatcher	DH	O.Gamble	DO	J.Burroughs	O	J.Simpson			32	G.Iorg
D3	D.Money	S	L.Faedo			C	J.Newman	O	B.Brown	OD	J.Grubb	OD	H.Powell
				O1	D.Collins	23	D.McKay	1	J.Maler	2S	D.Flynn	C	B.Martinez
P	M.Caldwell	P	B.Castillo	DO	L.Piniella							OD	A.Woods
P	P.Vuckovich	P	B.Havens			P	R.Langford	P	F.Bannister	P	C.Hough		
P	M.Haas	P	A.Williams	P	R.Guidry	P	M.Keough	P	G.Perry	P	F.Tanana	P	D.Stieb
P	B.McClure	P	F.Viola	P	T.John	P	M.Norris	P	J.Beattie	P	R.Honeycutt	P	J.Clancy
P	J.Slaton	P	J.O'Connor	P	D.Righetti	P	S.McCatty	P	M.Moore	P	J.Matlack	P	L.Leal
RP	R.Fingers	RP	T.Felton	P	S.Rawley	P	B.Kingman	P	G.Nelson	P	D.Medich	P	J.Gott
RP	D.Bernard	RP	R.Davis	P	M.Morgan	RP	T.Underwood	RP	B.Caudill	RP	S.Comer	RP	D.Murray
		RP	J.Pacella	RP	G.Frazier	RP	B.Owchinko	RP	L.Andersen	RP	D.Darwin	RP	R.Jackson
P	R.Lerch			RP	R.May	RP	D.Beard	RP	E.Vande Berg	RP	P.Mirabella	RP	J.McLaughlin
P	D.Medich	P	P.Redfern	RP	R.Gossage								
P	J.Augustine	P	P.Boris					P	B.Clark	P	D.Schmidt	P	M.Bomback
/P	D.Sutton			P	R.Erickson	P	M.Stanton	/P	B.Stoddard	P	J.Butcher	P	J.Garvin
				P	D.Alexander								
				P	D.LaRoche								

TEAM	G	W	L	PCT	GB	R	OR	AB	H	2B	3B	HR	BB	SO	AVG	OBP	SLG	PRO	PRO+	BR	/A	PF	CHI	RC	SB	CS	SBA	SBR
EAST																												
MIL	163	95	67	.586		**891**	717	5733	1599	277	41	**216**	484	714	.279	.337	**.455**	**.792**	123	**109**	**162**	94	105	**865**	84	52	62	-6
BAL	163	94	68	.580	1	774	687	5557	1478	259	27	179	634	796	.266	.344	.419	.763	108	67	70	100	96	795	49	38	56	-8
BOS	162	89	73	.549	6	753	713	5596	1536	271	31	136	547	736	.274	.342	.407	.749	99	39	-6	106	98	755	42	39	52	-11
DET	162	83	79	.512	12	729	685	5590	1489	237	40	177	470	807	.266	.326	.418	.744	103	15	12	100	99	752	93	66	58	-12
NY	162	79	83	.488	16	709	716	5526	1417	225	37	161	590	719	.256	.331	.398	.729	101	-5	7	98	98	716	69	45	61	-6
TOR	162	78	84	.481	17	651	701	5526	1447	262	45	106	415	749	.262	.317	.383	.700	83	-70	-129	109	102	655	118	81	59	-13
CLE	162	78	84	.481	17	683	748	5559	1458	225	32	109	**651**	625	.262	.343	.373	.716	97	-13	-9	100	94	723	151	68	69	5
WEST																												
CAL	162	93	69	.574		814	**670**	5532	1518	268	26	186	613	760	.274	**.350**	.433	.783	114	108	108	100	96	834	55	53	51	-15
KC	162	90	72	.556	3	784	717	5629	**1603**	295	58	132	442	758	**.285**	.340	.428	.768	109	67	66	100	99	802	133	48	**73**	11
CHI	162	87	75	.537	6	786	710	5575	1523	266	52	136	533	866	.273	.340	.413	.753	106	43	43	100	102	784	136	58	70	6
SEA	162	76	86	.469	17	651	712	5626	1431	259	33	130	456	806	.254	.313	.381	.694	87	-84	-102	103	102	657	131	82	62	-10
OAK	162	68	94	.420	25	691	819	5448	1286	211	27	149	582	948	.236	.312	.367	.679	90	-106	-79	96	**113**	644	**232**	87	**73**	**17**
TEX	162	64	98	.395	29	590	749	5445	1354	204	26	115	447	750	.249	.309	.359	.668	87	-128	-100	95	103	593	63	45	58	-8
MIN	162	60	102	.370	33	657	819	5544	1427	234	44	148	474	887	.257	.319	.396	.715	93	-43	-61	103	98	676	38	33	54	-8
TOT	1135					10163		77886	20566	3493	519	2080	7338	10921	.264	.330	.402	.733							1394	795	64	-59

TEAM	CG	SH	SV	IP	H	H/G	HR	BB	SO	RAT	ERA	ERA+	OAV	OOB	PR	/A	PF	CPI	FA	E	DP	FW	PW	BW	SBW	DIF
EAST																										
MIL	34	6	47	1467[1]	1514	9.3	152	511	717	12.5	3.98	95	.270	.333	15	-32	93	106	.980	125	**185**	.1	-3.2	**16.2**	-.2	1.1
BAL	38	8	34	1462[1]	1436	8.8	147	488	719	**12.0**	3.99	101	.257	**.320**	14	7	99	95	**.984**	**101**	140	**1.4**	.7	7.0	-.4	4.3
BOS	23	11	33	1453	1557	9.6	155	478	816	12.8	4.03	107	.276	.336	7	44	106	**108**	.981	121	172	.3	4.4	-.6	-.7	4.6
DET	**45**	5	27	1451	**1371**	**8.5**	172	554	740	12.1	**3.80**	107	**.251**	.323	**44**	42	100	104	.981	117	165	.5	4.2	1.2	-.8	-3.1
NY	24	8	39	1459	1471	9.1	113	491	939	12.1	3.99	100	.264	.326	13	-1	98	95	.979	128	158	-.0	-.1	.7	-.2	-2.3
TOR	41	**13**	25	1443[2]	1428	8.9	147	493	776	12.1	3.95	**113**	.257	.321	20	**85**	110	97	.978	136	146	-.5	**8.5**	-12.9	-.9	2.8
CLE	31	9	30	1468[1]	1433	8.8	122	589	882	12.5	4.11	99	.257	.330	-5	-5	100	94	.980	123	129	.2	-.5	-.9	.9	-2.7
WEST																										
CAL	40	10	27	1464	1436	8.8	124	482	728	**12.0**	3.82	106	.259	.322	42	38	100	98	.983	108	171	1.0	3.8	10.8	-1.1	-2.5
KC	16	12	45	1431	1443	9.1	163	471	650	12.2	4.08	100	.262	.323	-1	0	100	98	.979	127	140	-.0	.0	6.6	1.5	.9
CHI	30	10	41	1439	1502	9.4	**99**	**460**	753	12.4	3.87	104	.270	.329	33	27	99	100	.976	154	173	-1.5	2.7	4.3	1.0	-.5
SEA	23	11	39	1476[1]	1431	8.7	173	547	**1002**	12.2	3.88	109	.256	.325	32	60	104	104	.978	139	158	-.7	6.0	-10.2	-.6	.5
OAK	42	6	22	1456	1506	9.3	177	648	697	13.5	4.54	86	.268	.346	-76	-103	96	100	.974	160	140	-1.8	-10.3	-7.9	2.1	4.9
TEX	32	5	24	1431	1554	9.8	128	483	690	13.1	4.28	90	.281	.342	-33	-66	95	102	.981	121	169	.3	-6.6	-10.0	-.4	-.3
MIN	26	7	30	1433	1484	9.3	208	643	812	13.4	4.72	90	.269	.347	-103	-77	104	101	.982	108	162	1.0	-7.7	-6.1	-.4	-7.8
TOT	445	121	463	20335		9.1				12.5	4.07		.264	.330					.980	1768	2208					

Runs		Hits		Doubles		Triples		Home Runs		Total Bases	
Molitor-Mil	136	Yount-Mil	210	Yount-Mil	46	Wilson-KC	15	Thomas-Mil	39	Yount-Mil	367
Yount-Mil	129	Cooper-Mil	205	McRae-KC	46	Herndon-Det	13	R.Jackson-Cal	39	Cooper-Mil	345
Evans-Bos	122	Molitor-Mil	201	White-KC	45	Yount-Mil	12	Winfield-NY	37	McRae-KC	332
Henderson-Oak	119	Wilson-KC	194	DeCinces-Cal	42	Mumphrey-NY	10	Oglivie-Mil	34	Evans-Bos	325
Downing-Cal	109	McRae-KC	189	Cowens-Sea	39					DeCinces-Cal	315

Runs Batted In		Runs Produced		Bases On Balls		Batting Average		On Base Percentage		Slugging Average	
McRae-KC	133	Yount-Mil	214	Henderson-Oak	116	Wilson-KC	.332	Evans-Bos	.403	Yount-Mil	.578
Cooper-Mil	121	McRae-KC	197	Evans-Bos	112	Yount-Mil	.331	Harrah-Cle	.400	Winfield-NY	.560
Thornton-Cle	116	Cooper-Mil	193	Thornton-Cle	109	Carew-Cal	.319	Henderson-Oak	.399	Murray-Bal	.549
Yount-Mil	114	Molitor-Mil	188	Hargrove-Cle	101	Murray-Bal	.316	Carew-Cal	.399	DeCinces-Cal	.548
Thomas-Mil	112	Evans-Bos	188	Murphy-Oak	94	Cooper-Mil	.313	Murray-Bal	.395	McRae-KC	.542

Production		Adjusted Production		Batter Runs		Adjusted Batter Runs		Clutch Hitting Index		Runs Created	
Yount-Mil	.962	Yount-Mil	170	Yount-Mil	50.3	Yount-Mil	58.7	Otis-Cal	137	Yount-Mil	136
Murray-Bal	.944	Murray-Bal	157	Evans-Bos	48.5	Murray-Bal	42.9	Foli-Cal	137	Evans-Bos	134
Evans-Bos	.937	DeCinces-Cal	149	Murray-Bal	42.5	Evans-Bos	40.9	Hayes-Cle	128	Harrah-Cle	123
DeCinces-Cal	.922	R.Jackson-Cal	147	DeCinces-Cal	38.1	Harrah-Cle	38.6	Boone-Cal	124	McRae-KC	123
McRae-KC	.912	McRae-KC	146	Harrah-Cle	38.0	DeCinces-Cal	38.1	Murphy-Oak	122	Cooper-Mil	118

Total Average		Stolen Bases		Stolen Base Average		Stolen Base Runs		Fielding Runs		Total Player Rating	
Evans-Bos	.976	Henderson-Oak	130	Sexton-Oak	100.0	Henderson-Oak	13.8	Bell-Tex	34.4	Yount-Mil	7.0
Yount-Mil	.969	Garcia-Tor	54	Fisk-Chi	89.5	Molitor-Mil	6.9	Bernazard-Chi	24.6	DeCinces-Cal	5.3
Murray-Bal	.957	J.Cruz-Sea	46	Dilone-Cle	86.8	Dilone-Cle	6.9	Murphy-Oak	21.8	Bell-Tex	5.1
Henderson-Oak	.934	Molitor-Mil	41	Harrah-Cle	85.0	J.Cruz-Sea	6.0	DeCinces-Cal	20.6	Evans-Bos	4.2
Harrah-Cle	.931	Wilson-KC	37	Brown-Sea	82.4	Wathan-KC	5.4	Almon-Chi	20.0	Henderson-Oak	4.0

Wins		Win Percentage		Games		Complete Games		Shutouts		Saves	
Hoyt-Chi	19	Vuckovich-Mil	.750	VandeBerg-Sea	78	Stieb-Tor	19	Stieb-Tor	5	Quisenberry-KC	35
Zahn-Cal	18	Palmer-Bal	.750	T.Martinez-Bal	76	Morris-Det	17	Zahn-Cal	4	Gossage-NY	30
Vuckovich-Mil	18	Zahn-Cal	.692	Quisenberry-KC	72	Langford-Oak	15	Forsch-Cal	4	Fingers-Mil	29
Gura-KC	18	Petry-Det	.625	Caudill-Sea	70	Hoyt-Chi	14			Caudill-Sea	26
		Gura-KC	.600	Spillner-Cle	65					Davis-Min	22

Innings Pitched		Fewest Hits/Game		Fewest BB/Game		Strikeouts		Strikeouts/Game		Ratio	
Stieb-Tor	288.1	Sutcliffe-Cle	7.25	John-NY-Cal	1.58	Bannister-Sea	209	Righetti-NY	8.02	Palmer-Bal	10.39
Clancy-Tor	266.2	Ujdur-Det	7.58	Eckersley-Bos	1.73	Barker-Cle	187	Bannister-Sea	7.62	Eckersley-Bos	10.95
Morris-Det	266.1	Righetti-NY	7.62	Hoyt-Chi	1.80	Righetti-NY	163	Beattie-Sea	7.31	Stieb-Tor	10.96
Caldwell-Mil	258.0	Palmer-Bal	7.73	Haas-Mil	1.82	Guidry-NY	162	Barker-Cle	6.88	Barker-Cle	11.11
D.Martinez-Bal	252.0	Barker-Cle	7.76	Langford-Oak	1.86	Tudor-Bos	146	Tudor-Bos	6.72	Bannister-Sea	11.11

Earned Run Average		Adjusted ERA		Opponents' Batting Avg.		Opponents' On Base Pct.		Starter Runs		Adjusted Starter Runs	
Sutcliffe-Cle	2.96	Stanley-Bos	139	Sutcliffe-Cle	.226	Palmer-Bal	.287	Sutcliffe-Cle	26.8	Stieb-Tor	39.4
Stanley-Bos	3.10	Stieb-Tor	138	Righetti-NY	.229	Eckersley-Bos	.297	Stieb-Tor	26.5	Sutcliffe-Cle	26.9
Palmer-Bal	3.13	Sutcliffe-Cle	138	Ujdur-Det	.230	Stieb-Tor	.299	Palmer-Bal	23.7	Petry-Det	23.0
Petry-Det	3.22	Palmer-Bal	129	Palmer-Bal	.231	Barker-Cle	.301	Petry-Det	23.3	Palmer-Bal	22.7
Stieb-Tor	3.25	Beattie-Sea	127	Barker-Cle	.232	Clancy-Tor	.302	Vuckovich-Mil	18.2	Clancy-Tor	22.6

Clutch Pitching Index		Relief Runs		Adjusted Relief Runs		Relief Ranking		Total Pitcher Index		Total Baseball Ranking	
Vuckovich-Mil	131	Spillner-Cle	23.5	Spillner-Cle	23.6	Caudill-Sea	51.7	Caudill-Sea	5.1	Yount-Mil	7.0
Tudor-Bos	121	Quisenberry-KC	22.9	Quisenberry-KC	23.0	Spillner-Cle	43.0	Quisenberry-KC	4.4	DeCinces-Cal	5.3
Dotson-Chi	118	Burgmeier-Bos	20.3	Burgmeier-Bos	23.0	Quisenberry-KC	37.2	Stieb-Tor	4.2	Caudill-Sea	5.1
Wilcox-Det	113	Gossage-NY	19.1	Stanley-Bos	22.5	Clear-Bos	34.5	Spillner-Cle	4.2	Bell-Tex	5.1
Stanley-Bos	110	Caudill-Sea	18.3	Caudill-Sea	20.1	Gossage-NY	28.7	Clear-Bos	3.5	Quisenberry-KC	4.5

January 12 Brooks Robinson and Juan Marichal are elected to the Hall of Fame by the BBWAA. Robinson becomes the 14th player elected in his first year of eligibility.

March 3 Steve Carlton agrees to a four-year, $4.15 million contract with the Phillies that will make him the highest-paid pitcher in baseball history.

March 10 Walter Alston, who managed the Dodgers to four World Championships, and George Kell, who hit .306 over 15 major league seasons, are elected to the Hall of Fame by the Special Veterans Committee.

April 27 In a 4-2 win over the Expos, Nolan Ryan strikes out Brad Mills to move a strikeout ahead of Walter Johnson and become baseball's all-time leader at 3,509.

July 29 Steve Garvey's consecutive-game streak ends at 1,207 when he dislocates his left thumb in a home-plate collision with Braves pitcher Pascual Perez. The injury keeps him from playing the second game of the doubleheader.

August 24 First baseman Pete Rose does not play in the Phillies 5-3 loss to the Giants, ending his consecutive games played streak at 745. Manager Paul Owens had planned to use Rose as a pinch hitter in the 10th inning, but Joel Youngblood ends the game with a two-run home run off Steve Carlton in the bottom of the ninth.

August 25 The Louisville Redbirds (American Association) become the first minor league team to draw one million fans in a season.

August 28 Greg Luzinski becomes the first player to park three home runs onto the roof at Comiskey Park, connecting off Boston's Oil Can Boyd. Jimmie Foxx and Ted Williams each accomplished the feat twice.

September 17 A record regular-season crowd of 53,790 packs Cincinnati's Riverfront Stadium on Johnny Bench Night, and he responds with a two-run home run and a single.

September 28 Whipping the Cubs 13-6 for their 12th win in their last 13 games, the Phillies clinch the NL East championship. Bo Diaz goes 5-for-5 with a pair of home runs and Joe Morgan has his third four-hit game of the month.

September 30 The Dodgers beat the Giants 4-3 and the Padres beat the Braves 3-2, giving Los Angeles the NL West title.

October 4 In the NLCS opener, Mike Schmidt's first-inning homer and Al Holland's clutch relieving to get out of an eighth-inning bases-loaded jam are enough for Philadelphia to top LA 1-0.

October 5 Five-hit pitching by LaMarr Hoyt is the margin in the 2-1 White Sox victory over the Orioles in Game 1 of the ALCS.

October 11 In the World Series opener, homers account for all the scoring as the Phillies top Baltimore 2-1.

November 2 John Denny wins the NL Cy Young Award, collecting 20 of 24 first-place votes to defeat runner-up Mario Soto. Denny was 19-6 with a 2.37 ERA for the NL champion Phillies.

November 8 Atlanta's Dale Murphy wins his second consecutive NL MVP Award, joining Ernie Banks, Joe Morgan, and Mike Schmidt, who also accomplished that feat.

ATLANTA		CHICAGO		CINCINNATI		HOUSTON		LOS ANGELES		MONTREAL	
M	J.Torre	M	L.Elia	M	R.Nixon	M	B.Lillis	M	T.Lasorda	M	B.Virdon
1B	C.Chambliss	M	C.Fox	1B	D.Driessen	1B	R.Knight	1B	G.Brock	1B	A.Oliver
2B	G.Hubbard	1B	B.Buckner	2B	R.Oester	2B	B.Doran	2B	S.Sax	2B	D.Flynn
SS	R.Ramirez	2B	R.Sandberg	SS	D.Concepcion	SS	D.Thon	SS	B.Russell	SS	C.Speier
3B	B.Horner	SS	L.Bowa	3B	N.Esasky	3B	P.Garner	3B	P.Guerrero	3B	T.Wallach
LF	B.Butler	3B	R.Cey	LF	G.Redus	LF	J.Cruz	LF	D.Baker	LF	T.Raines
CF	D.Murphy	LF	L.Durham	CF	E.Milner	CF	O.Moreno	CF	K.Landreaux	CF	A.Dawson
RF	C.Washington	CF	M.Hall	RF	P.Householder	RF	T.Puhl	RF	M.Marshall	RF	W.Cromartie
C	B.Benedict	RF	K.Moreland	C	D.Bilardello	C	A.Ashby	C	S.Yeager	C	G.Carter
		C	J.Davis								
32	J.Royster			31	J.Bench	13	D.Walling	OS	D.Thomas	O1	T.Francona
O	T.Harper	P	C.Rainey	O1	C.Cedeno					S2	B.Little
		P	S.Trout	O	D.Walker	P	J.Niekro	P	F.Valenzuela		
P	C.McMurtry	P	F.Jenkins			P	B.Knepper	P	J.Reuss	P	S.Rogers
P	P.Perez	P	D.Ruthven	P	M.Soto	P	N.Ryan	P	B.Welch	P	B.Gullickson
P	P.Niekro	P	D.Noles	P	B.Berenyi	P	M.Scott	P	A.Pena	P	C.Lea
P	R.Camp	RP	B.Campbell	P	F.Pastore	P	M.LaCoss	P	B.Hooton	P	B.Smith
P	P.Falcone	RP	L.Smith	P	C.Puleo	RP	V.Ruhle	RP	T.Niedenfuer	P	R.Burris
RP	S.Bedrosian	RP	C.Lefferts	P	J.Price	RP	B.Dawley	RP	D.Stewart	RP	J.Reardon
RP	T.Forster			RP	T.Power	RP	D.Smith	RP	J.Beckwith	RP	D.Schatzeder
RP	D.Moore	P	M.Proly	RP	B.Scherrer					RP	B.James
		P	W.Brusstar	RP	R.Gale	P	M.Madden	P	S.Howe		
P	K.Dayley					P	F.DiPino	P	P.Zachry	P	S.Sanderson
P	G.Garber			P	B.Hayes	P	F.LaCorte				
				P	J.Russell						
				P	T.Hume						

NEW YORK		PHILADELPHIA		PITTSBURGH		SAN DIEGO		SAN FRANCISCO		ST.LOUIS	
M	G.Bamberger	M	P.Corrales	M	C.Tanner	M	D.Williams	M	F.Robinson	M	W.Herzog
M	F.Howard	M	P.Owens	1B	J.Thompson	1B	S.Garvey	1B	D.Evans	1B	G.Hendrick
1B	K.Hernandez	1B	P.Rose	2B	J.Ray	2B	J.Bonilla	2B	B.Wellman	2B	T.Herr
2B	B.Giles	2B	J.Morgan	SS	D.Berra	SS	G.Templeton	SS	J.LeMaster	SS	O.Smith
SS	J.Oquendo	SS	I.DeJesus	3B	B.Madlock	3B	L.Salazar	3B	T.O'Malley	3B	K.Oberkfell
3B	H.Brooks	3B	M.Schmidt	LF	M.Easler	LF	A.Wiggins	LF	J.Leonard	LF	L.Smith
LF	G.Foster	LF	G.Matthews	CF	M.Wynne	CF	R.Jones	CF	C.Davis	CF	W.McGee
CF	M.Wilson	CF	G.Maddox	RF	D.Parker	RF	S.Lezcano	RF	J.Clark	RF	D.Green
RF	D.Strawberry	RF	V.Hayes	C	T.Pena	C	T.Kennedy	C	B.Brenly	C	D.Porter
C	R.Hodges	C	B.Diaz								
				O	L.Lacy	O	T.Gwynn	23	J.Youngblood	2S	M.Ramsey
S2	B.Bailor	O	G.Gross	O	L.Mazzilli	O	G.Richards	O	M.Venable	O3	A.Van Slyke
O1	D.Heep	O	J.Lefebvre			O	B.Brown			1	K.Hernandez
1	D.Kingman	O	B.Dernier	P	R.Rhoden	32	T.Flannery	P	F.Breining		
1O	R.Staub	1	T.Perez	P	L.McWilliams			P	M.Krukow	P	J.Andujar
				P	J.Candelaria	P	E.Show	P	A.Hammaker	P	J.Stuper
P	T.Seaver	P	S.Carlton	P	L.Tunnell	P	D.Dravecky	P	B.Laskey	P	D.LaPoint
P	M.Torrez	P	J.Denny	P	J.DeLeon	P	T.Lollar	P	A.McGaffigan	P	B.Forsch
P	E.Lynch	P	C.Hudson	RP	C.Guante	P	E.Whitson	RP	G.Minton	P	N.Allen
P	W.Terrell	P	M.Bystrom	RP	K.Tekulve	RP	A.Hawkins	RP	R.Martin	RP	B.Sutter
P	C.Swan	RP	R.Reed	RP	M.Sarmiento	RP	L.DeLeon	P	J.Barr	RP	J.Lahti
RP	J.Orosco	RP	W.Hernandez			RP	G.Lucas			RP	D.Von Ohlen
RP	D.Sisk	RP	A.Holland	P	J.Bibby	RP	E.Sosa	P	M.Davis		
RP	S.Holman			P	R.Scurry			P	G.Lavelle	P	D.Cox
		P	K.Gross			P	M.Thurmond			P	J.Martin
		P	T.McGraw			P	J.Montefusco				
P	C.Diaz					P	S.Monge				
P	N.Allen										

TEAM	G	W	L	PCT	GB	R	OR	AB	H	2B	3B	HR	BB	SO	AVG	OBP	SLG	PRO	PRO+	BR	/A	PF	CHI	RC	SB	CS	SBA	SBR
EAST																												
PHI	163	90	72	.556		696	635	5426	1352	209	45	125	**640**	906	.249	.331	.373	.704	102	17	25	99	101	676	143	75	66	-2
PIT	162	84	78	.519	6	659	648	5531	1460	238	29	121	497	873	.264	.327	.383	.710	100	17	0	103	96	682	124	77	62	-9
MON	163	82	80	.506	8	677	646	5611	1482	**297**	41	102	509	733	.264	.329	.386	.715	105	30	34	99	95	716	138	44	**76**	**15**
STL	162	79	83	.488	11	679	710	5550	**1496**	262	**63**	83	543	879	.261	.337	.384	.721	**106**	47	**47**	100	94	725	**207**	89	70	9
CHI	162	71	91	.438	19	701	719	5512	1436	272	42	140	470	868	.261	.322	**.401**	.723	101	35	2	105	100	707	84	40	68	1
NY	162	68	94	.420	22	575	680	5444	1314	172	26	112	436	1031	.241	.301	.344	.645	85	-112	-107	99	107	562	141	64	69	4
WEST																												
LA	163	91	71	.562		654	**609**	5440	1358	197	34	**146**	541	925	.250	.320	.379	.699	100	-6	-2	99	100	663	166	76	69	4
ATL	162	88	74	.543	3	**746**	640	5472	1489	218	45	130	582	847	**.272**	**.344**	.400	**.744**	104	**91**	35	107	98	**744**	146	88	62	-9
HOU	162	85	77	.525	6	643	646	5502	1412	239	60	97	517	869	.257	.323	.375	.698	**106**	-7	34	94	97	673	164	95	63	-8
SD	163	81	81	.500	10	653	653	5527	1384	207	34	93	482	822	.250	.313	.351	.664	93	-74	-53	97	**110**	609	179	67	73	14
SF	162	79	83	.488	12	687	697	5369	1324	206	30	142	619	990	.247	.328	.375	.703	104	11	33	97	102	662	140	78	64	-5
CIN	162	74	88	.457	17	623	710	5333	1274	236	35	107	588	1006	.239	.317	.356	.673	89	-49	-70	104	103	606	154	77	67	0
TOT	974					7993		65717	16781	2753	484	1398	6424	10749	.255	.324	.376	.700							1786	870	67	14

TEAM	CG	SH	SV	IP	H	H/G	HR	BB	SO	RAT	ERA	ERA+	OAV	OOB	PR	/A	PF	CPI	FA	E	DP	FW	PW	BW	SBW	DIF
EAST																										
PHI	20	10	41	1461²	1429	8.8	111	464	**1092**	11.8	3.34	107	.256	.316	47	37	98	103	.976	152	117	-.7	3.9	2.6	-.3	3.6
PIT	25	14	41	1462¹	1378	8.5	109	563	1061	12.1	3.55	104	.252	.323	12	25	102	99	**.982**	115	165	1.4	2.6	.0	-1.1	.0
MON	**38**	**15**	34	1471	1406	8.6	120	479	899	11.7	3.58	100	.254	.317	8	1	99	98	.981	116	130	1.4	.1	3.6	**1.4**	-5.5
STL	22	10	27	1460²	1479	9.1	115	525	709	12.5	3.79	96	.256	.332	-26	-28	100	102	.976	152	173	-.8	-2.9	**4.9**	-.0	-4.0
CHI	9	10	42	1428²	1496	9.4	117	498	807	12.7	4.08	93	.274	.337	-71	-45	105	100	**.982**	115	164	1.4	-4.7	.2	-.0	-6.9
NY	18	7	33	1451	1384	8.6	97	615	717	12.5	3.68	99	.256	.334	-8	-8	100	100	.976	151	171	-.7	-.8	-11.2	.3	-.6
WEST																										
LA	27	12	40	1464	1336	8.2	97	495	1000	**11.4**	**3.10**	116	.244	**.309**	85	79	99	101	.974	168	132	-1.7	**8.3**	-.2	.3	3.3
ATL	18	4	**48**	1440²	1412	8.8	132	540	895	12.3	3.67	106	.260	.329	-7	33	107	**105**	.978	137	**176**	.1	3.4	3.7	-1.1	.8
HOU	22	14	**48**	1466¹	**1276**	**7.8**	**94**	570	904	11.5	3.45	99	**.236**	.312	29	-8	94	90	.977	147	165	-.5	-.8	3.6	-1.0	2.7
SD	23	5	44	1467²	1389	8.5	144	528	850	11.9	3.62	96	.253	.322	1	-22	96	102	.979	129	135	.6	-2.3	-5.5	1.3	5.8
SF	20	9	47	1445²	1431	8.9	127	520	881	12.6	3.70	96	.259	.326	-11	-27	97	101	.973	171	109	-1.9	-2.8	3.4	-.6	-.0
CIN	34	5	29	1441¹	1365	8.5	135	627	934	12.6	3.98	95	.253	.333	-57	-29	105	97	.981	**114**	121	**1.5**	-3.0	-7.3	-.1	2.0
TOT	276	115	474	17461		8.6				12.1	3.63		.255	.324					.978	1667	1758					

Runs		Hits		Doubles		Triples		Home Runs		Total Bases	
Raines-Mon	133	Dawson-Mon	189	Ray-Pit	38	Butler-Atl	13	Schmidt-Phi	40	Dawson-Mon	341
Murphy-Atl	131	Cruz-Hou	189	Oliver-Mon	38	Moreno-Hou	11	Murphy-Atl	36	Murphy-Atl	318
Schmidt-Phi	104	Ramirez-Atl	185	Buckner-Chi	38	Green-StL	10	Guerrero-LA	32	Guerrero-LA	310
Dawson-Mon	104	Oliver-Mon	184	Carter-Mon	37	Dawson-Mon	10	Dawson-Mon	32	Thon-Hou	283
		Raines-Mon	183					Evans-SF	30	Schmidt-Phi	280

Runs Batted In		Runs Produced		Bases On Balls		Batting Average		On Base Percentage		Slugging Average	
Murphy-Atl	121	Murphy-Atl	216	Schmidt-Phi	128	Madlock-Pit	.323	Schmidt-Phi	.402	Murphy-Atl	.540
Dawson-Mon	113	Raines-Mon	193	Thompson-Pit	99	L.Smith-StL	.321	Hernandez-StL-NY	.398	Dawson-Mon	.539
Schmidt-Phi	109	Dawson-Mon	185	Raines-Mon	97	Cruz-Hou	.318	Murphy-Atl	.396	Guerrero-LA	.531
Guerrero-LA	103	Schmidt-Phi	173	Murphy-Atl	90	Hendrick-StL	.318	Raines-Mon	.395	Schmidt-Phi	.524
Kennedy-SD	98	Cruz-Hou	163	Morgan-Phi	89	Knight-Hou	.304	Madlock-Pit	.389	Evans-SF	.516

Production		Adjusted Production		Batter Runs		Adjusted Batter Runs		Clutch Hitting Index		Runs Created	
Murphy-Atl	.936	Schmidt-Phi	156	Murphy-Atl	46.2	Schmidt-Phi	44.6	Kennedy-SD	122	Murphy-Atl	131
Schmidt-Phi	.926	Evans-SF	151	Schmidt-Phi	43.2	Guerrero-LA	38.4	Rose-Phi	121	Raines-Mon	120
Guerrero-LA	.908	Guerrero-LA	150	Guerrero-LA	37.8	Murphy-Atl	37.5	Garner-Hou	115	Guerrero-LA	118
Evans-SF	.896	Murphy-Atl	146	Evans-SF	33.0	Evans-SF	36.2	Hendrick-StL	115	Schmidt-Phi	117
Dawson-Mon	.886	Cruz-Hou	143	Dawson-Mon	32.4	Cruz-Hou	34.5	McGee-StL	112	Dawson-Mon	113

Total Average		Stolen Bases		Stolen Base Average		Stolen Base Runs		Fielding Runs		Total Player Rating	
Murphy-Atl	1.014	Raines-Mon	90	Morgan-Phi	90.0	Raines-Mon	18.6	Sandberg-Chi	41.1	Schmidt-Phi	6.4
Schmidt-Phi	.986	Wiggins-SD	66	Murphy-Atl	88.2	Wiggins-SD	12.0	Schmidt-Phi	23.3	Thon-Hou	5.9
Raines-Mon	.959	S.Sax-LA	56	Raines-Mon	86.5	McGee-StL	6.9	Hubbard-Atl	21.6	Raines-Mon	5.8
Guerrero-LA	.935	Wilson-NY	54	Bailor-NY	85.7	Wilson-NY	6.6	Buckner-Chi	21.0	Guerrero-LA	4.6
Evans-SF	.908	L.Smith-StL	43	Wiggins-SD	83.5	Murphy-Atl	6.6	Thon-Hou	20.8	Murphy-Atl	4.6

Wins		Win Percentage		Games		Complete Games		Shutouts		Saves	
Denny-Phi	19	Denny-Phi	.760	Campbell-Chi	82	Soto-Cin	18	Rogers-Mon	5	Smith-Chi	29
Soto-Cin	17	Perez-Atl	.652	Tekulve-Pit	76	Rogers-Mon	13	Valenzuela-LA	4	Holland-Phi	25
Rogers-Mon	17	McWilliams-Pit	.652	Hernandez-Chi-Phi	74	Gullickson-Mon	10	McWilliams-Pit	4	Minton-SF	22
Gullickson-Mon	17	Candelaria-Pit	.652	Scherrer-Cin	73			Lea-Mon	4	Sutter-StL	21
Lea-Mon	16	McMurtry-Atl	.625	Minton-SF	73					Reardon-Mon	21

Innings Pitched		Fewest Hits/Game		Fewest BB/Game		Strikeouts		Strikeouts/Game		Ratio	
Carlton-Phi	283.2	Ryan-Hou	6.14	Hammaker-SF	1.67	Carlton-Phi	275	Carlton-Phi	8.73	Hammaker-SF	9.50
Soto-Cin	273.2	Soto-Cin	6.81	Ruthven-Chi-Phi	1.87	Soto-Cin	242	Ryan-Hou	8.39	Soto-Cin	10.10
Rogers-Mon	273.0	Welch-LA	7.24	Denny-Phi	1.97	McWilliams-Pit	199	Soto-Cin	7.96	Pena-LA	10.37
Niekro-Hou	263.2	Hammaker-SF	7.68	Reuss-LA	2.01	Valenzuela-LA	189	McWilliams-Pit	7.53	Welch-LA	10.54
Valenzuela-LA	257.0	Pena-LA	7.73	Candelaria-Pit	2.05	Ryan-Hou	183	Berenyi-Cin	7.29	Denny-Phi	10.61

Earned Run Average		Adjusted ERA		Opponents' Batting Avg.		Opponents' On Base Pct.		Starter Runs		Adjusted Starter Runs	
Hammaker-SF	2.25	Hammaker-SF	157	Ryan-Hou	.195	Hammaker-SF	.267	Denny-Phi	33.8	Soto-Cin	33.7
Denny-Phi	2.37	Denny-Phi	150	Soto-Cin	.208	Soto-Cin	.280	Soto-Cin	28.3	Denny-Phi	32.1
Welch-LA	2.65	Soto-Cin	141	Welch-LA	.222	Pena-LA	.285	Hammaker-SF	26.4	Hammaker-SF	24.6
Soto-Cin	2.70	Welch-LA	136	Hammaker-SF	.228	Welch-LA	.294	Welch-LA	22.2	Welch-LA	21.4
Pena-LA	2.75	Pena-LA	131	Pena-LA	.229	Denny-Phi	.294	Smith-Mon	19.6	McMurtry-Atl	19.8

Clutch Pitching Index		Relief Runs		Adjusted Relief Runs		Relief Ranking		Total Pitcher Index		Total Baseball Ranking	
Rhoden-Pit	119	Orosco-NY	26.3	Orosco-NY	26.3	Orosco-NY	50.6	Orosco-NY	5.8	Schmidt-Phi	6.4
Niekro-Atl	117	Smith-Chi	22.6	Smith-Chi	24.5	Smith-Chi	42.6	Smith-Chi	4.6	Thon-Hou	5.9
Reuss-LA	116	Tekulve-Pit	21.9	Tekulve-Pit	22.7	Tekulve-Pit	32.4	Howe-LA	3.6	Raines-Mon	5.8
Denny-Phi	115	Niedenfuer-LA	18.1	Niedenfuer-LA	17.8	Howe-LA	31.6	Denny-Phi	3.5	Orosco-NY	5.8
Knepper-Hou	111	Howe-LA	16.7	Howe-LA	16.4	Niedenfuer-LA	22.4	Tekulve-Pit	3.5	Guerrero-LA	4.6

July 6 In the 50th anniversary All-Star Game at Chicago's Comiskey Park, the AL routs the NL 13-3 for its first win since 1971. The AL breaks the game open with 7 runs in the fourth inning, highlighted by Fred Lynn's grand slam—the first ever in All-Star competition.

July 24 In the memorable "Pine Tar Game" at Yankee Stadium, George Brett hits an apparent two-run home run off Rich Gossage to give the Royals a 5-4 lead with two outs in the ninth inning, only to have it taken away when Yankees manager Billy Martin points out that the pine tar on Brett's bat handle exceeds the 17 inches allowed in the rules. As a result, Brett is called out for illegally batting the ball, giving New York a 4-3 victory. The Royals immediately protest, and AL President Lee MacPhail overrules his umpires for the first time, saying that while the rules should certainly be rewritten and clarified, the home run will stand and the game will be resumed from that point on August 18.

August 18 In the continuation of the "Pine Tar Game," Hal McRae strikes out and Dan Quisenberry retires the Yankees in order in the bottom of the ninth to preserve the Royals' 5-4 victory. The conclusion took just 12 minutes (and 16 pitches) and, as the only game scheduled at the Stadium, was witnessed by a crowd of just 1,245.

October 8 The Phillies and Orioles each win Game 4 of their respective LCS to advance to the World Series. Philadelphia gets home runs from Gary Matthews and Sixto Lezcano in a 7-2 victory, while Baltimore's Tito Landrum hits a solo home run in the top of the tenth inning to break a scoreless tie, sparking the Orioles to a 3-0 win.

October 10 John E. Fetzer sells the Tigers to Michigan businessman Tom Monaghan, the founder and president of Domino's Pizza.

October 16 Eddie Murray slams a pair of home runs and Scott McGregor pitches a five-hitter as the Orioles beat the Phillies 5-0 and win the World Series 4-1. Baltimore catcher Rick Dempsey, who hit .385 with four doubles and a home run, is the Series MVP.

October 25 White Sox pitcher LaMarr Hoyt, who led the AL with 24 wins but whose 3.66 ERA was not among the league's 15 best, wins the AL Cy Young Award, beating out the Royals' Dan Quisenberry and the Tigers' Jack Morris.

November 15 Cal Ripken is named MVP of the AL, edging Orioles teammate Eddie Murray. Ripken hit .318 and led the league in hits (211) and runs (111) while playing every inning of every game, and is the first player ever to win the Rookie of the Year and MVP Awards in consecutive seasons.

November 17 Kansas City Royals teammates Willie Wilson, Willie Aikens, and Jerry Martin, who, along with former teammate Vida Blue, had pleaded guilty to attempting to purchase cocaine, are each sentenced to 3 months in prison.

December 8 Dr. Bobby Brown, who played third base for the Yankees before embarking on a successful medical career, is elected president of the AL by the club owners.

BALTIMORE

Pos	Player
M	J.Altobelli
1B	E.Murray
2B	R.Dauer
SS	C.Ripken
3B	T.Cruz
LF	J.Lowenstein
CF	J.Shelby
RF	D.Ford
C	R.Dempsey
DH	K.Singleton
OD	J.Dwyer
OD	A.Bumbry
O	G.Roenicke
3	L.Hernandez
P	S.McGregor
P	S.Davis
P	M.Boddicker
P	D.Martinez
P	M.Flanagan
RP	S.Stewart
RP	T.Martinez
RP	T.Stoddard
P	J.Palmer
P	A.Ramirez

BOSTON

Pos	Player
M	R.Houk
1B	D.Stapleton
2B	J.Remy
SS	G.Hoffman
3B	W.Boggs
LF	J.Rice
CF	T.Armas
RF	D.Evans
C	G.Allenson
DH	C.Yastrzemski
O	R.Miller
OD	R.Nichols
C	R.Gedman
P	J.Tudor
P	B.Hurst
P	D.Eckersley
P	B.Ojeda
P	M.Brown
RP	B.Stanley
RP	M.Clear
RP	L.Aponte
P	O.Boyd
P	D.Bird
P	J.Johnson

CALIFORNIA

Pos	Player
M	J.McNamara
1B	R.Carew
2B	B.Grich
SS	T.Foli
3B	D.DeCinces
LF	B.Downing
CF	F.Lynn
RF	E.Valentine
C	B.Boone
DH	Re.Jackson
31	Ro.Jackson
1D	D.Sconiers
O	J.Beniquez
O	B.Clark
P	T.John
P	K.Forsch
P	G.Zahn
P	M.Witt
P	B.Kison
RP	L.Sanchez
RP	J.Curtis
P	D.Goltz
P	R.Steirer
P	B.McLaughlin

CHICAGO

Pos	Player
M	T.LaRussa
1B	M.Squires
2B	J.Cruz
SS	J.Dybzinski
3B	V.Law
LF	R.Kittle
CF	R.Law
RF	H.Baines
C	C.Fisk
DH	G.Luzinski
S2	S.Fletcher
O	J.Hairston
1O	T.Paciorek
1D	G.Walker
2	T.Bernazard
P	L.Hoyt
P	R.Dotson
P	F.Bannister
P	B.Burns
P	J.Koosman
RP	D.Lamp
RP	D.Tidrow
RP	S.Barojas

CLEVELAND

Pos	Player
M	M.Ferraro
M	P.Corrales
1B	M.Hargrove
2B	M.Trillo
SS	J.Franco
3B	T.Harrah
LF	A.Bannister
CF	G.Thomas
RF	G.Vukovich
C	R.Hassey
DH	A.Thornton
O3	P.Tabler
OD	M.McBride
2S	M.Fischlin
P	R.Sutcliffe
P	L.Sorensen
P	B.Blyleven
P	L.Barker
P	N.Heaton
RP	D.Spillner
RP	B.Anderson
RP	J.Easterly
P	J.Eichelberger

DETROIT

Pos	Player
M	S.Anderson
1B	E.Cabell
2B	L.Whitaker
SS	A.Trammell
3B	T.Brookens
LF	L.Herndon
CF	C.Lemon
RF	G.Wilson
C	L.Parrish
DH	K.Gibson
1O	R.Leach
DC	J.Wockenfuss
P	J.Morris
P	D.Petry
P	M.Wilcox
P	J.Berenguer
P	D.Rozema
RP	A.Lopez
RP	H.Bailey
RP	D.Bair

KANSAS CITY

Pos	Player
M	D.Howser
1B	W.Aikens
2B	F.White
SS	U.Washington
3B	G.Brett
LF	W.Wilson
CF	A.Otis
RF	P.Sheridan
C	J.Wathan
DH	H.McRae
C	D.Slaught
32	O.Concepcion
O	L.Roberts
P	L.Gura
P	B.Black
P	P.Splittorff
P	S.Renko
RP	D.Quisenberry
RP	M.Armstrong
P	K.Creel
P	V.Blue
P	G.Perry
P	D.Leonard
P	E.Rasmussen

MILWAUKEE

Pos	Player
M	H.Kuenn
1B	C.Cooper
2B	J.Gantner
SS	R.Yount
3B	P.Molitor
LF	B.Oglivie
CF	R.Manning
RF	C.Moore
C	N.Yost
DH	T.Simmons
P	M.Caldwell
P	D.Sutton
P	M.Haas
P	B.McClure
P	C.Porter
RP	J.Slaton
RP	T.Tellmann
RP	J.Augustine
P	B.Gibson
P	T.Candiotti

MINNESOTA

Pos	Player
M	B.Gardner
1B	K.Hrbek
2B	J.Castino
SS	R.Washington
3B	G.Gaetti
LF	G.Ward
CF	D.Brown
RF	T.Brunansky
C	D.Engle
DH	R.Bush
OD	M.Hatcher
P	F.Viola
P	K.Schrom
P	A.Williams
P	B.Castillo
RP	R.Lysander
RP	R.Davis
RP	L.Whitehouse
P	P.Filson
P	J.O'Connor
P	B.Havens
P	M.Walters

NEW YORK

Pos	Player
M	B.Martin
1B	K.Griffey
2B	W.Randolph
SS	R.Smalley
3B	G.Nettles
LF	D.Winfield
CF	J.Mumphrey
RF	S.Kemp
C	B.Wynegar
DH	D.Baylor
S2	A.Robertson
O1	D.Mattingly
C	R.Cerone
P	R.Guidry
P	S.Rawley
P	D.Righetti
P	B.Shirley
RP	R.Fontenot
RP	G.Frazier
RP	D.Murray
RP	R.Gossage
P	J.Howell
P	M.Keough

OAKLAND

Pos	Player
M	S.Boros
1B	W.Gross
2B	D.Lopes
SS	T.Phillips
3B	C.Lansford
LF	R.Henderson
CF	D.Murphy
RF	M.Davis
C	B.Kearney
DH	J.Burroughs
S3	B.Almon
O1	G.Hancock
CO	M.Heath
P	C.Codiroli
P	S.McCatty
P	T.Conroy
P	B.Krueger
RP	T.Underwood
RP	T.Burgmeier
RP	K.Atherton
P	M.Norris
P	G.Heimueller
P	M.Warren
P	D.Beard
P	S.Baker

SEATTLE

Pos	Player
M	R.Lachemann
M	D.Crandall
1B	P.Putnam
2B	T.Bernazard
SS	S.Owen
3B	J.Allen
LF	S.Henderson
CF	D.Henderson
RF	R.Nelson
C	R.Sweet
DH	R.Zisk
OD	A.Cowens
S	T.Cruz
31	M.Castillo
P	M.Young
P	J.Beattie
P	B.Stoddard
P	B.Clark
P	M.Moore
RP	R.Thomas
RP	B.Caudill
RP	M.Stanton
P	G.Perry
P	G.Abbott
P	E.Vande Berg

TEXAS

Pos	Player
M	D.Rader
1B	P.O'Brien
2B	W.Tolleson
SS	B.Dent
3B	B.Bell
LF	R.Sample
CF	G.Wright
RF	L.Parrish
C	J.Sundberg
DH	D.Hostetler
DO	M.Rivers
21	B.Stein
P	C.Hough
P	M.Smithson
P	D.Darwin
P	R.Honeycutt
P	F.Tanana
RP	J.Matlack
RP	O.Jones
P	J.Butcher
/P	D.Stewart

TORONTO

Pos	Player
M	B.Cox
1B	W.Upshaw
2B	D.Garcia
SS	A.Griffin
3B	R.Mulliniks
LF	B.Bonnell
CF	L.Moseby
RF	J.Barfield
C	E.Whitt
DH	C.Johnson
O	D.Collins
32	G.Iorg
DO	J.Orta
C	B.Martinez
P	D.Stieb
P	J.Clancy
P	L.Leal
P	J.Gott
P	D.Alexander
RP	J.Acker
RP	R.Jackson
RP	J.McLaughlin
P	R.Moffitt
P	D.Geisel

TEAM	G	W	L	PCT	GB	R	OR	AB	H	2B	3B	HR	BB	SO	AVG	OBP	SLG	PRO	PRO+	BR	/A	PF	CHI	RC	SB	CS	SBA	SBR
EAST																												
BAL	162	98	64	.605		799	652	5546	1492	283	27	168	601	800	.269	**.343**	.421	.764	111	70	85	98	99	794	61	33	65	-2
DET	162	92	70	.568	6	789	679	5592	1530	283	53	156	508	831	.274	.338	.427	.765	112	67	88	97	99	799	93	53	64	-4
NY	162	91	71	.562	7	770	703	5631	1535	269	40	153	533	686	.273	.339	.416	.755	110	52	81	96	98	783	84	42	67	0
TOR	162	89	73	.549	9	795	726	5581	1546	268	58	167	510	810	**.277**	.341	**.436**	**.777**	106	**89**	39	106	97	**818**	131	72	65	-4
MIL	162	87	75	.537	11	764	708	5620	**1556**	281	57	132	475	665	**.277**	.336	.418	.754	**115**	44	**103**	92	98	774	101	49	67	1
BOS	162	78	84	.481	20	724	775	5590	1512	**287**	32	142	536	758	.270	.337	.409	.746	97	35	-20	107	94	749	30	26	54	-7
CLE	162	70	92	.432	28	704	785	5476	1451	249	31	86	**605**	691	.265	.341	.369	.710	92	-23	-50	104	100	687	109	71	61	-10
WEST																												
CHI	162	99	63	.611		**800**	650	5484	1439	270	42	157	527	888	.262	.332	.413	.745	100	26	-2	104	**107**	762	165	50	77	20
KC	163	79	83	.488	20	696	767	5598	1515	273	54	109	397	722	.271	.322	.397	.719	99	-31	-32	100	102	711	182	47	**79**	**26**
TEX	163	77	85	.475	22	639	**609**	5610	1429	242	33	106	442	767	.255	.312	.366	.678	88	-108	-96	98	104	633	119	60	66	0
OAK	162	74	88	.457	25	708	782	5640	1447	237	28	121	524	872	.262	.330	.381	.711	101	-34	-7	94	100	694	**235**	98	71	12
CAL	162	70	92	.432	29	722	779	5640	1467	241	22	154	509	835	.260	.325	.393	.718	98	-29	-23	99	102	702	41	39	51	-11
MIN	162	70	92	.432	29	709	822	5601	1463	280	41	141	467	802	.261	.321	.401	.722	94	-29	-48	104	101	701	44	29	60	-4
SEA	162	60	102	.370	39	558	740	5336	1280	247	31	111	460	840	.240	.330	.360	.663	79	-135	-156	101	100	574	144	80	64	-5
TOT	1135					10177		77821	20662	3710	549	1903	7094	10967	.266	.330	.401	.731							1539	749	67	12

TEAM	CG	SH	SV	IP	H	H/G	HR	BB	SO	RAT	ERA	ERA+	OAV	OOB	PR	/A	PF	CPI	FA	E	DP	FW	PW	BW	SBW	DIF
EAST																										
BAL	36	**15**	38	1452¹	1451	9.0	130	452	774	11.9	3.63	109	.261	.318	70	53	97	104	.981	121	159	.5	5.3	8.5	-.3	3.0
DET	42	9	28	1451	**1318**	**8.2**	170	522	875	11.6	3.80	103	**.242**	.312	42	17	96	96	.980	125	142	.3	1.7	8.8	-.5	.7
NY	**47**	12	32	1456²	1449	9.0	116	455	892	11.9	3.86	101	.260	.318	33	6	96	95	.978	139	157	-.5	.6	8.1	-.0	1.9
TOR	43	8	32	1445¹	1434	8.9	145	517	835	12.4	4.12	104	.259	.327	-10	29	106	97	.981	115	148	.9	2.9	3.9	-.5	.8
MIL	35	10	43	1454	1513	9.4	133	491	689	12.6	4.02	93	.270	.332	6	-46	92	103	**.982**	113	162	**1.0**	-4.6	**10.3**	-.1	-.7
BOS	29	7	42	1446¹	1572	9.8	158	493	767	13.0	4.34	100	.279	.340	-44	2	107	104	.979	130	168	.0	.2	-2.0	-.8	-.5
CLE	34	8	25	1441²	1531	9.6	120	529	794	13.1	4.43	96	.275	.342	-60	-32	104	97	.980	122	174	.5	-3.2	-5.0	-1.1	-2.2
WEST																										
CHI	35	12	48	1445¹	1355	8.4	128	**447**	877	**11.4**	3.67	114	.248	**.309**	63	83	103	94	.981	120	158	.6	8.3	-.2	1.9	7.4
KC	19	8	**49**	1437²	1535	9.6	133	471	593	12.7	4.25	96	.274	.339	-30	-28	100	99	.974	165	178	-1.9	-2.8	-3.2	**2.5**	3.4
TEX	43	11	32	1466²	1392	8.5	**97**	471	826	11.7	**3.31**	121	.252	.315	**122**	113	99	104	**.982**	113	151	**1.0**	11.3	-9.6	-.0	-6.6
OAK	22	12	33	1454¹	1462	9.0	135	626	719	13.1	4.34	89	.263	.340	-46	-79	95	97	.974	157	**190**	-1.5	-7.9	.7	1.1	.5
CAL	39	7	23	1474	1636	10.0	130	496	668	13.2	4.31	93	.284	.344	-41	-49	99	104	.977	154	190	-1.3	-4.9	-2.3	-1.2	-1.3
MIN	20	5	39	1437¹	1559	9.8	163	580	748	13.6	4.66	91	.280	.351	-96	-67	105	102	.980	121	170	.5	-6.7	-4.8	-.5	-.4
SEA	25	9	39	1418¹	1455	9.2	145	544	**910**	12.9	4.12	100	.268	.339	-9	22	105	**105**	.978	136	159	-.3	2.2	-15.6	-.6	-6.7
TOT	469	133	503	20281		9.2				12.5	4.06		.266	.330					.979	1831	2273					

Runs		Hits		Doubles		Triples		Home Runs		Total Bases	
Ripken-Bal	121	Ripken-Bal	211	Ripken-Bal	47	Yount-Mil	10	Rice-Bos	39	Rice-Bos	344
Murray-Bal	115	Boggs-Bos	210	Boggs-Bos	44	Herndon-Det	9	Armas-Bos	36	Ripken-Bal	343
Cooper-Mil	106	Whitaker-Det	206	Yount-Mil	42	Griffin-Tor	9	Kittle-Chi	35	Cooper-Mil	336
Henderson-Oak	105	Cooper-Mil	203	Parrish-Det	42	Gibson-Det	9	Murray-Bal	33	Murray-Bal	313
Moseby-Tor	104	Rice-Bos	191							Winfield-NY	307

Runs Batted In		Runs Produced		Bases On Balls		Batting Average		On Base Percentage		Slugging Average	
Rice-Bos	126	Cooper-Mil	202	Henderson-Oak	103	Boggs-Bos	.361	Boggs-Bos	.449	Brett-KC	.563
Cooper-Mil	126	Ripken-Bal	196	Singleton-Bal	99	Carew-Cal	.339	Henderson-Oak	.415	Rice-Bos	.550
Winfield-NY	116	Murray-Bal	193	Boggs-Bos	92	Whitaker-Det	.320	Carew-Cal	.411	Murray-Bal	.538
Parrish-Det	114	Winfield-NY	183	Thornton-Cle	87	Trammell-Det	.319	Murray-Bal	.398	Fisk-Chi	.518
Murray-Bal	111	Rice-Bos	177	Murray-Bal	86	Ripken-Bal	.318	Singleton-Bal	.395	Ripken-Bal	.517

Production		Adjusted Production		Batter Runs		Adjusted Batter Runs		Clutch Hitting Index		Runs Created	
Brett-KC	.949	Murray-Bal	158	Boggs-Bos	50.6	Murray-Bal	47.3	Simmons-Mil	124	Boggs-Bos	130
Murray-Bal	.936	Brett-KC	157	Murray-Bal	44.9	Yount-Mil	43.6	Franco-Cle	122	Murray-Bal	127
Boggs-Bos	.935	Yount-Mil	155	Rice-Bos	38.7	Boggs-Bos	41.4	Murphy-Oak	116	Ripken-Bal	120
Rice-Bos	.914	Boggs-Bos	147	Ripken-Bal	37.1	Ripken-Bal	39.4	Cooper-Mil	116	Yount-Mil	115
Upshaw-Tor	.891	Ripken-Bal	145	Brett-KC	36.3	Brett-KC	36.1	Singleton-Bal	113	Whitaker-Det	114

Total Average		Stolen Bases		Stolen Base Average		Stolen Base Runs		Fielding Runs		Total Player Rating	
Henderson-Oak	1.048	Henderson-Oak	108	Wilson-KC	88.1	Henderson-Oak	21.0	Ward-Min	25.9	Ripken-Bal	6.7
Murray-Bal	.971	R.Law-Chi	77	R.Law-Chi	86.5	R.Law-Chi	15.9	T.Cruz-Sea-Bal	25.4	Henderson-Oak	5.7
Boggs-Bos	.964	Wilson-KC	59	Washington-KC	85.1	Wilson-KC	12.9	Dempsey-Bal	20.6	Yount-Mil	5.2
Brett-KC	.964	J.Cruz-Sea-Chi	57	Henderson-Oak	85.0	J.Cruz-Sea-Chi	9.9	Fletcher-Chi	18.2	Boggs-Bos	4.5
Yount-Mil	.897	Sample-Tex	44			Sample-Tex	8.4	Brunansky-Min	17.8	Grich-Cal	4.5

Wins		Win Percentage		Games		Complete Games		Shutouts		Saves	
Hoyt-Chi	24	Dotson-Chi	.759	Quisenberry-KC	69	Guidry-NY	21	Boddicker-Bal	5	Quisenberry-KC	45
Dotson-Chi	22	McGregor-Bal	.720	VandeBerg-Sea	68	Morris-Det	20	Stieb-Tor	4	Stanley-Bos	33
Guidry-NY	21	Hoyt-Chi	.706	Davis-Min	66	Stieb-Tor	14	Burns-Chi	4	Davis-Min	30
Morris-Det	20	Guidry-NY	.700	T.Martinez-Bal	65	Rawley-NY	13			Caudill-Sea	26
Petry-Det	19	Boddicker-Bal	.667	Stanley-Bos	64	McGregor-Bal	12			Ladd-Mil	25

Innings Pitched		Fewest Hits/Game		Fewest BB/Game		Strikeouts		Strikeouts/Game		Ratio	
Morris-Det	293.2	Boddicker-Bal	7.09	Hoyt-Chi	1.07	Morris-Det	232	Bannister-Chi	7.99	Hoyt-Chi	9.25
Stieb-Tor	278.0	Stieb-Tor	7.22	McGregor-Bal	1.56	Bannister-Chi	193	Morris-Det	7.11	Boddicker-Bal	9.70
Petry-Det	266.1	Conroy-Oak	7.82	John-Cal	1.88	Stieb-Tor	187	Righetti-NY	7.01	Morris-Det	10.51
Hoyt-Chi	260.2	Hough-Tex	7.82	Honeycutt-Tex	1.91	Righetti-NY	169	Conroy-Oak	6.21	Guidry-NY	10.57
McGregor-Bal	260.0	Dotson-Chi	7.84	Eckersley-Bos	1.99	Sutcliffe-Cle	160	Gott-Tor	6.16	Stieb-Tor	10.68

Earned Run Average		Adjusted ERA		Opponents' Batting Avg.		Opponents' On Base Pct.		Starter Runs		Adjusted Starter Runs	
Honeycutt-Tex	2.42	Honeycutt-Tex	165	Boddicker-Bal	.216	Hoyt-Chi	.262	Honeycutt-Tex	31.8	Stieb-Tor	38.8
Boddicker-Bal	2.77	Boddicker-Bal	143	Stieb-Tor	.219	Boddicker-Bal	.274	Stieb-Tor	31.4	Honeycutt-Tex	30.7
Stieb-Tor	3.04	Stieb-Tor	141	Conroy-Oak	.232	Morris-Det	.289	Boddicker-Bal	25.8	Dotson-Chi	25.6
Hough-Tex	3.18	Young-Sea	130	Bannister-Chi	.233	Guidry-NY	.291	McGregor-Bal	25.3	Boddicker-Bal	23.6
McGregor-Bal	3.18	Dotson-Chi	130	Morris-Det	.233	Stieb-Tor	.293	Hough-Tex	24.7	Hough-Tex	23.1

Clutch Pitching Index		Relief Runs		Adjusted Relief Runs		Relief Ranking		Total Pitcher Index		Total Baseball Ranking	
Honeycutt-Tex	139	Quisenberry-KC	32.7	Quisenberry-KC	32.9	Quisenberry-KC	38.7	Honeycutt-Tex	4.3	Ripken-Bal	6.7
Zahn-Cal	118	T.Martinez-Bal	19.6	Stanley-Bos	24.2	Stanley-Bos	38.2	Quisenberry-KC	4.2	Henderson-Oak	5.7
Hurst-Bos	113	Stanley-Bos	19.6	T.Martinez-Bal	18.4	Gossage-NY	37.3	Stieb-Tor	3.9	Yount-Mil	5.2
Dotson-Chi	113	Gossage-NY	17.4	Barojas-Chi	16.6	T.Martinez-Bal	26.8	Stanley-Bos	3.7	Boggs-Bos	4.5
McGregor-Bal	113	Lopez-Det	16.0	Gossage-NY	15.8	Lopez-Det	23.1	Gossage-NY	3.7	Grich-Cal	4.5

January 10 Luis Aparicio, Harmon Killebrew, and Don Drysdale are elected to the Hall of Fame by the BBWAA.

March 4 Shortstop Pee Wee Reese and catcher Rick Ferrell are elected to the Hall of Fame by the Special Veterans Committee. Reese hit .269 in 16 seasons with the Dodgers while Ferrell batted .281 with 28 home runs in 18 seasons for the Browns, Red Sox, and Senators.

June 24 Oakland's Joe Morgan hits his 265th career home run as a second baseman, breaking Rogers Hornsby's major league record for that position.

July 10 On the 50th anniversary of Carl Hubbell's legendary five consecutive strikeouts in the 1934 All-Star Game, NL pitchers Fernando Valenzuela and Dwight Gooden combine to fan six in a row for a new All-Star record in the NL's 3-1 triumph. After Valenzuela whiffs Dave Winfield, Reggie Jackson, and George Brett in the fourth inning, Gooden, the youngest All-Star ever at age 19, fans Lance Parrish, Chet Lemon, and Alvin Davis in the fifth.

August 12 In one of the ugliest brawl-filled games in ML history, the Braves beat the Padres 5-3 in Atlanta. Atlanta's Pascual Perez hits Alan Wiggins in the back with the first pitch of the game. Padres pitchers retaliate by throwing at Perez all four times he comes to the plate. All in all, the game features two bench-clearing brawls, the second of which includes several fans, and 19 ejections, including both managers and both replacement managers. Padres manager Dick Williams will be suspended for 10 days and fined $10,000, while Braves manager Joe Torre and five players will each receive three-game suspensions.

August 16 After a nearly six-year absence, Pete Rose is reunited with his hometown Reds in a trade for infielder Tom Lawless, and Cincinnati immediately names him player-manager, replacing Vern Rapp.

September 12 Dwight Gooden strikes out 16 Pirates in a 2-0 victory to break Herb Score's major league rookie strikeout record of 245.

September 20 The Padres clinch their first NL West title with a 5-4 win over the Giants. The key blow is winning pitcher Tim Lollar's three-run home run, his third home run of the season.

September 24 Rick Sutcliffe pitches a two-hitter in a 4-1 win over Pittsburgh to clinch the NL East title for the Cubs, who will be making their first postseason appearance since 1945.

October 2 The Cubs clobber the Padres 13-0 to take a 1-0 lead in the NL series. The ALCS opens with a convincing 8-1 Tiger trouncing of KC.

October 7 San Diego rallies for four runs in the seventh inning to beat Chicago 6-3 and earn its first trip to the World Series.

October 23 Rick Sutcliffe, who was 16-1 for the Cubs after arriving from Cleveland two days before the June 15 trading deadline, is a unanimous choice as NL Cy Young Award winner.

November 13 Ryne Sandberg wins the NL MVP Award, becoming the first Cub to do so since Ernie Banks in 1959.

ATLANTA	CHICAGO	CINCINNATI	HOUSTON	LOS ANGELES	MONTREAL
M J.Torre	M J.Frey	M V.Rapp	M B.Lillis	M T.Lasorda	M B.Virdon
1B C.Chambliss	1B L.Durham	M P.Rose	1B E.Cabell	1B G.Brock	M J.Fanning
2B G.Hubbard	2B R.Sandberg	1B D.Driessen	2B B.Doran	2B S.Sax	1B T.Francona
SS R.Ramirez	SS L.Bowa	2B R.Oester	SS C.Reynolds	SS D.Anderson	2B D.Flynn
3B R.Johnson	3B R.Cey	SS D.Concepcion	3B P.Garner	3B G.Rivera	SS A.Salazar
LF B.Komminsk	LF G.Matthews	3B N.Esasky	LF J.Cruz	LF M.Marshall	3B T.Wallach
CF D.Murphy	CF B.Dernier	LF G.Redus	CF J.Mumphrey	CF K.Landreaux	LF J.Wohlford
RF C.Washington	RF K.Moreland	CF E.Milner	RF T.Puhl	RF C.Maldonado	CF T.Raines
C B.Benedict	C J.Davis	RF D.Parker	C M.Bailey	C M.Scioscia	RF A.Dawson
		C B.Gulden			C G.Carter
1O G.Perry	O H.Cotto		O K.Bass	3O P.Guerrero	SO D.Thomas
C A.Trevino		O1 C.Cedeno	31 R.Knight	SO B.Russell	1O P.Rose
23 J.Royster	P S.Trout	S2 T.Foley	31 D.Walling	O R.Reynolds	2 B.Little
	P D.Eckersley	3 W.Krenchicki		1O F.Stubbs	
P R.Mahler	P R.Sutcliffe		P J.Niekro	P F.Valenzuela	P B.Gullickson
P P.Perez	P S.Sanderson	P M.Soto	P B.Knepper	P A.Pena	P C.Lea
P C.McMurtry	P D.Ruthven	P J.Russell	P N.Ryan	P O.Hershiser	P B.Smith
P R.Camp	RP L.Smith	P J.Price	P M.Scott	P R.Honeycutt	P S.Rogers
P L.Barker	RP T.Stoddard	P J.Tibbs	P M.LaCoss	P B.Welch	P D.Schatzeder
RP G.Garber	RP R.Bordi	P F.Pastore	RP B.Dawley	RP B.Hooton	RP B.James
RP S.Bedrosian	P R.Reuschel	RP T.Hume	RP V.Ruhle	RP P.Zachry	RP J.Reardon
RP J.Dedmon	P C.Rainey	RP T.Power	RP D.Smith	RP K.Howell	RP G.Lucas
	P W.Brusstar	RP B.Owchinko			
P P.Falcone	P G.Frazier	P J.Franco	P F.DiPino	P J.Reuss	P D.Palmer
P D.Moore	P D.Noles	P B.Scherrer	P J.Solano		
		P B.Berenyi			

NEW YORK	PHILADELPHIA	PITTSBURGH	SAN DIEGO	SAN FRANCISCO	ST.LOUIS
M D.Johnson	M P.Owens	M C.Tanner	M D.Williams	M F.Robinson	M W.Herzog
1B K.Hernandez	1B L.Matuszek	1B J.Thompson	1B S.Garvey	1B S.Thompson	1B D.Green
2B W.Backman	2B J.Samuel	2B J.Ray	2B A.Wiggins	2B M.Trillo	2B T.Herr
SS J.Oquendo	SS I.DeJesus	SS D.Berra	SS G.Templeton	SS J.LeMaster	SS O.Smith
3B H.Brooks	3B M.Schmidt	3B B.Madlock	3B G.Nettles	3B J.Youngblood	3B T.Pendleton
LF G.Foster	LF G.Wilson	LF L.Lacy	LF C.Martinez	LF J.Leonard	LF L.Smith
CF M.Wilson	CF V.Hayes	CF M.Wynne	CF K.McReynolds	CF D.Gladden	CF W.McGee
RF D.Strawberry	RF S.Lezcano	RF D.Frobel	RF T.Gwynn	RF C.Davis	RF G.Hendrick
C M.Fitzgerald	C O.Virgil	C T.Pena	C T.Kennedy		C D.Porter
				C B.Brenly	
O1 D.Heep	1O T.Corcoran	O L.Mazzilli	3O L.Salazar	O D.Baker	O T.Landrum
S2 R.Gardenhire	O1 G.Gross	32 J.Morrison		1 A.Oliver	O3 A.Van Slyke
	O G.Maddox		P E.Show	2S B.Wellman	
P D.Gooden	P S.Carlton	P R.Rhoden	P T.Lollar	O J.Clark	P J.Andujar
P W.Terrell	P J.Koosman	P L.McWilliams	P E.Whitson		P D.LaPoint
P R.Darling	P C.Hudson	P J.Tudor	P M.Thurmond	P B.Laskey	P D.Cox
P E.Lynch	P J.Denny	P J.DeLeon	P D.Dravecky	P M.Krukow	P R.Horton
P B.Berenyi	P S.Rawley	P J.Candelaria	RP C.Lefferts	P M.Davis	P K.Kepshire
RP J.Orosco	RP K.Gross	RP D.Robinson	RP R.Gossage	P J.Robinson	RP B.Sutter
RP B.Gaff	RP A.Holland	RP K.Tekulve	RP G.Booker	RP G.Minton	RP N.Allen
RP D.Sisk	RP L.Andersen	RP L.Tunnell		RP F.Williams	RP J.Lahti
			P A.Hawkins	RP G.Lavelle	
P S.Fernandez	P B.Campbell				P D.Rucker
P T.Gorman	P M.Bystrom			P R.Lerch	P J.Stuper
P T.Leary				P M.Grant	P B.Forsch
				P B.Lacey	

TEAM	G	W	L	PCT	GB	R	OR	AB	H	2B	3B	HR	BB	SO	AVG	OBP	SLG	PRO	PRO+	BR	/A	PF	CHI	RC	SB	CS	SBA	SBR
EAST																												
CHI	161	96	65	.596		**762**	658	5437	1415	240	47	136	**567**	967	.260	.333	.397	.730	102	78	12	109	104	729	154	66	70	7
NY	162	90	72	.556	6.5	652	676	5438	1400	235	25	107	500	1001	.257	.322	.369	.691	102	1	11	99	100	645	149	54	73	12
STL	162	84	78	.519	12.5	652	645	5433	1369	225	44	75	516	924	.252	.319	.351	.670	97	-35	-19	97	**106**	623	**220**	71	76	**23**
PHI	162	81	81	.500	15.5	720	690	5614	1494	**248**	51	147	555	1084	**.266**	**.335**	**.407**	**.742**	112	102	90	102	93	766	186	60	76	20
MON	161	78	83	.484	18	593	585	5439	1367	242	36	96	470	**782**	.251	.314	.362	.676	101	-32	-4	96	96	630	131	38	**78**	17
PIT	162	75	87	.463	21.5	615	**567**	5537	1412	237	33	98	438	841	.255	.312	.363	.675	95	-37	-37	100	99	611	96	62	61	-8
WEST																												
SD	162	92	70	.568		686	634	5504	1425	207	42	109	472	810	.259	.320	.371	.691	100	-1	0	100	105	645	152	68	69	5
HOU	162	80	82	.494	12	693	630	5548	1465	222	**67**	79	494	837	.264	.326	.371	.697	110	14	63	93	100	679	105	61	63	-5
ATL	162	80	82	.494	12	632	649	5422	1338	234	27	111	555	896	.247	.319	.361	.680	90	-18	-64	107	99	623	140	85	62	-9
LA	162	79	83	.488	13	580	600	5399	1316	213	23	102	488	829	.244	.308	.348	.656	91	-68	-62	99	100	573	109	69	61	-9
CIN	162	70	92	.432	22	627	747	5498	1342	238	30	106	566	978	.244	.316	.356	.672	91	-34	-62	105	100	635	160	63	72	10
SF	162	66	96	.407	26	682	807	5650	**1499**	229	26	112	528	980	.265	.330	.375	.705	108	31	54	97	97	686	126	76	62	-8
TOT	971					7894		65919	16842	2770	451	1278	6149	10929	.255	.321	.369	.691							1728	773	69	55

TEAM	CG	SH	SV	IP	H	H/G	HR	BB	SO	RAT	ERA	ERA+	OAV	OOB	PR	/A	PF	CPI	FA	E	DP	FW	PW	BW	SBW	DIF
EAST																										
CHI	19	8	50	1434	1458	9.2	99	**442**	879	12.1	3.75	104	.267	.324	-26	25	109	99	.981	121	137	1.1	2.6	1.3	.3	10.3
NY	12	15	50	1442[1]	1371	8.6	104	573	1028	12.3	3.60	98	.252	.326	-2	-10	99	101	.979	129	154	.7	-1.1	1.2	.8	7.4
STL	19	12	**51**	1449	1427	8.9	94	494	808	12.1	3.58	97	.262	.326	1	-18	97	103	**.982**	118	184	**1.3**	-1.9	-2.0	**1.9**	3.6
PHI	11	6	35	1458[1]	1416	8.7	101	448	904	11.6	3.62	100	.253	**.310**	-5	2	101	92	.975	161	112	-1.2	.2	**9.5**	1.6	-10.1
MON	19	10	44	1431	1333	8.4	114	474	861	11.3	3.31	103	.249	.312	45	18	95	103	.978	132	147	.4	1.9	-.4	1.3	-5.7
PIT	27	13	34	1470	1344	**8.2**	102	502	995	**11.4**	**3.11**	116	.246	.310	78	80	100	**105**	.980	128	142	.7	**8.4**	-3.9	-1.3	-9.9
WEST																										
SD	13	**17**	44	1460[1]	**1327**	**8.2**	122	563	812	11.8	3.48	102	**.244**	.317	17	14	99	99	.978	138	144	.1	1.5	.0	.0	9.3
HOU	24	13	29	1449[1]	1350	8.4	91	502	950	11.6	3.32	96	.248	.314	44	0	93	99	.979	133	160	.4	.0	6.6	-1.0	-7.1
ATL	17	7	49	1447	1401	8.7	122	525	859	12.1	3.57	108	.257	.324	3	46	107	**105**	.978	139	153	.0	4.8	-6.7	-1.4	2.2
LA	**39**	16	27	1460[2]	1381	8.5	**76**	499	**1033**	11.7	3.17	111	.250	.314	68	59	98	102	.975	163	146	-1.3	6.2	-6.5	-1.4	1.1
CIN	25	6	25	1461[1]	1445	8.9	128	578	946	12.6	4.19	91	.259	.330	-92	-62	105	94	.977	139	116	.0	-6.5	-6.5	.6	1.4
SF	9	7	38	1461	1589	9.8	125	549	854	13.4	4.39	80	.278	.345	-131	-143	98	99	.973	173	134	-1.9	-15.0	5.7	-1.3	-2.4
TOT	234	130	480	17424[2]		8.7				12.0	3.59		.255	.321					.978	1674	1729					

Runs		Hits		Doubles		Triples		Home Runs		Total Bases	
Sandberg-Chi	114	Gwynn-SD	213	Ray-Pit	38	Sandberg-Chi	19	Schmidt-Phi	36	Murphy-Atl	332
Wiggins-SD	106	Sandberg-Chi	200	Raines-Mon	38	Samuel-Phi	19	Murphy-Atl	36	Sandberg-Chi	331
Raines-Mon	106	Raines-Mon	192	Sandberg-Chi	36	Cruz-Hou	13	Carter-Mon	27	Samuel-Phi	310
Samuel-Phi	105	Samuel-Phi	191	Samuel-Phi	36			Strawberry-NY	26	Carter-Mon	290
Matthews-Chi	101	Cruz-Hou	187					Cey-Chi	25	Schmidt-Phi	283

Runs Batted In		Runs Produced		Bases On Balls		Batting Average		On Base Percentage		Slugging Average	
Schmidt-Phi	106	Sandberg-Chi	179	Matthews-Chi	103	Gwynn-SD	.351	Matthews-Chi	.417	Murphy-Atl	.547
Carter-Mon	106	Cruz-Hou	179	Hernandez-NY	97	Lacy-Pit	.321	Hernandez-NY	.415	Schmidt-Phi	.536
Murphy-Atl	100	Matthews-Chi	169	Schmidt-Phi	92	C.Davis-SF	.315	Gwynn-SD	.411	Sandberg-Chi	.520
Strawberry-NY	97	Schmidt-Phi	163	Thompson-Pit	87	Sandberg-Chi	.314	Raines-Mon	.395	C.Davis-SF	.507
Cey-Chi	97	Hernandez-NY	162	Raines-Mon	87	Ray-Pit	.312	Schmidt-Phi	.388	Durham-Chi	.505

Production		Adjusted Production		Batter Runs		Adjusted Batter Runs		Clutch Hitting Index		Runs Created	
Schmidt-Phi	.924	Schmidt-Phi	155	Murphy-Atl	43.8	Schmidt-Phi	39.5	Mumphrey-Hou	132	Sandberg-Chi	126
Murphy-Atl	.920	C.Davis-SF	149	Schmidt-Phi	41.2	Cruz-Hou	38.4	Davis-SF	125	Raines-Mon	124
Sandberg-Chi	.889	Cruz-Hou	148	Sandberg-Chi	37.9	Hernandez-NY	37.0	Garvey-SD	125	Murphy-Atl	123
Durham-Chi	.877	Murphy-Atl	145	Hernandez-NY	35.5	Murphy-Atl	35.5	Cey-Chi	120	Cruz-Hou	111
C.Davis-SF	.876	Hernandez-NY	145	Gwynn-SD	33.9	Raines-Mon	35.4	Concepcion-Cin	118	Carter-Mon	108

Total Average		Stolen Bases		Stolen Base Average		Stolen Base Runs		Fielding Runs		Total Player Rating	
Raines-Mon	.953	Raines-Mon	75	Dilone-Mon	93.1	Raines-Mon	16.5	O.Smith-StL	26.2	Sandberg-Chi	6.4
Murphy-Atl	.942	Samuel-Phi	72	Raines-Mon	88.2	Samuel-Phi	12.6	Sandberg-Chi	23.3	Raines-Mon	5.8
Schmidt-Phi	.933	Wiggins-SD	70	Cedeno-Cin	86.4	Wilson-NY	8.4	Garner-Hou	23.1	Cruz-Hou	4.9
Sandberg-Chi	.913	L.Smith-StL	50	VanSlyke-StL	84.8	Wiggins-SD	8.4	Martinez-SD	20.6	Schmidt-Phi	4.8
Matthews-Chi	.888			Stone-Phi	84.4	Redus-Cin	7.8	Hubbard-Atl	19.6	Hernandez-NY	4.6

Wins		Win Percentage		Games		Complete Games		Shutouts		Saves	
Andujar-StL	20	Sutcliffe-Chi	.941	Power-Cin	78	Soto-Cin	13	Pena-LA	4	Sutter-StL	45
Soto-Cin	18	Soto-Cin	.720	Lavelle-SF	77	Valenzuela-LA	12	Hershiser-LA	4	Smith-Chi	33
Gooden-NY	17	Gooden-NY	.654	Minton-SF	74	Andujar-StL	12	Andujar-StL	4	Orosco-NY	31
Sutcliffe-Chi	16	Show-SD	.625	Tekulve-Pit	72	Knepper-Hou	11			Holland-Phi	29
Niekro-Hou	16			Sutter-StL	71	Mahler-Atl	9			Gossage-SD	25

Innings Pitched		Fewest Hits/Game		Fewest BB/Game		Strikeouts		Strikeouts/Game		Ratio	
Andujar-StL	261.1	Gooden-NY	6.65	Gullickson-Mon	1.47	Gooden-NY	276	Gooden-NY	11.39	Gooden-NY	9.74
Valenzuela-LA	261.0	Soto-Cin	6.86	Candelaria-Pit	1.65	Valenzuela-LA	240	Ryan-Hou	9.65	Hershiser-LA	10.15
Niekro-Hou	248.1	DeLeon-Pit	6.88	Whitson-SD	2.00	Ryan-Hou	197	Valenzuela-LA	8.28	Andujar-StL	10.16
Rhoden-Pit	238.1	Ryan-Hou	7.01	Pena-LA	2.08	Soto-Cin	185	Berenyi-Cin-NY	7.27	Soto-Cin	10.35
Soto-Cin	237.1	Andujar-StL	7.51	Knepper-Hou	2.12	Carlton-Phi	163	DeLeon-Pit	7.16	Candelaria-Pit	10.39

Earned Run Average		Adjusted ERA		Opponents' Batting Avg.		Opponents' On Base Pct.		Starter Runs		Adjusted Starter Runs	
Pena-LA	2.48	Pena-LA	142	Gooden-NY	.202	Gooden-NY	.270	Pena-LA	24.5	Rhoden-Pit	23.3
Gooden-NY	2.60	Gooden-NY	136	Soto-Cin	.209	Hershiser-LA	.279	Gooden-NY	23.9	Pena-LA	23.2
Hershiser-LA	2.66	Hershiser-LA	133	Ryan-Hou	.211	Soto-Cin	.286	Rhoden-Pit	23.0	Gooden-NY	22.6
Rhoden-Pit	2.72	Rhoden-Pit	132	DeLeon-Pit	.214	Andujar-StL	.286	Hershiser-LA	19.6	Sutcliffe-Chi	20.3
Candelaria-Pit	2.72	Candelaria-Pit	132	Hershiser-LA	.225	Ryan-Hou	.288	Denny-Phi	19.5	Denny-Phi	20.3

Clutch Pitching Index		Relief Runs		Adjusted Relief Runs		Relief Ranking		Total Pitcher Index		Total Baseball Ranking	
McWilliams-Pit	130	Sutter-StL	27.9	Sutter-StL	26.3	Sutter-StL	40.7	Sutter-StL	4.4	Sandberg-Chi	6.4
Terrell-NY	124	Dawley-Hou	18.1	Lefferts-SD	16.9	Bedrosian-Atl	25.6	Rhoden-Pit	3.5	Raines-Mon	5.8
Candelaria-Pit	122	Lefferts-SD	17.1	Dawley-Hou	15.1	Dawley-Hou	22.3	Gooden-NY	2.9	Cruz-Hou	4.9
Honeycutt-LA	117	Sisk-NY	13.0	Bedrosian-Atl	13.8	Orosco-NY	21.1	Sutcliffe-Chi	2.8	Schmidt-Phi	4.8
Trout-Chi	117	Andersen-Phi	12.1	Andersen-Phi	12.6	Power-Cin	17.5	Mahler-Atl	2.6	Hernandez-NY	4.6

May 9 The longest—and slowest—game in AL history ends in the 25th inning when Harold Baines homers off Chuck Porter to give the White Sox a 7-6 victory over the Brewers. The game falls one inning shy of the major league record, but takes by far the most time to play: 8 hours and 6 minutes. The contest was suspended yesterday after 17 innings with the score tied 3-3, and each team scores three more runs in the 21st. Tom Seaver pitches the final inning to earn the win, then wins the regularly scheduled game as well 5-4.

September 17 Reggie Jackson hits his 500th career home run in the seventh inning off Bud Black, but the Royals beat California 10-1 to move into first place in the AL West. Jackson is the thirteenth player in major league history to hit 500 home runs.

September 18 The Tigers clinch the AL East championship with a 3-0 win over the Brewers as starter Randy O'Neal records his first major league win. Detroit becomes the fourth team this century to be in first place every day of the season, joining the 1923 Giants, the 1927 Yankees, and the 1955 Dodgers.

September 28 Kansas City clinches the AL West title with a 6-5 win over Oakland.

September 30 On the final day of the regular season, California's Mike Witt fans 10 and needs just 97 pitches to complete a perfect game, 1-0 over Texas.

September 30 In the dramatic race for the AL batting title, Don Mattingly goes 4-for-5 in the Yankees season-ending 4-2 win over the Tigers to edge teammate Dave Winfield .343 to .340.

October 5 In Game 3, Milt Wilcox and Willie Hernandez combine on a 1-0 three-hitter to give the Tigers a three-game sweep of the Royals in the ALCS.

October 9 The Tigers win the World Series opener as Jack Morris pitches a complete-game 3-2 victory. Larry Herndon's two-run home run in the fifth is the margin.

October 14 Series MVP Kirk Gibson blasts two upper-deck home runs at Tiger Stadium in Game 5, including a three-run shot off Rich Gossage in the eighth inning, to lead Detroit to an 8-4 win and its first World Championship since 1968.

October 16 Gene Mauch, who resigned as the Angels' manager after the 1982 season, is hired again.

October 30 Tigers reliever Willie Hernandez wins the AL Cy Young Award, edging fellow reliever Dan Quisenberry of the Royals.

November 6 Willie Hernandez wins the AL MVP Award, joining Rollie Fingers as the only relief pitcher to be named MVP and Cy Young Award winner in the same season.

	BALTIMORE		BOSTON		CALIFORNIA		CHICAGO		CLEVELAND		DETROIT		KANSAS CITY
M	J.Altobelli	M	R.Houk	M	J.McNamara	M	T.LaRussa	M	P.Corrales	M	S.Anderson	M	D.Howser
1B	E.Murray	1B	B.Buckner	1B	R.Carew	1B	G.Walker	1B	M.Hargrove	1B	D.Bergman	1B	S.Balboni
2B	R.Dauer	2B	M.Barrett	2B	R.Wilfong	2B	J.Cruz	2B	T.Bernazard	2B	L.Whitaker	2B	F.White
SS	C.Ripken	SS	J.Gutierrez	SS	D.Schofield	SS	S.Fletcher	SS	J.Franco	SS	A.Trammell	SS	O.Concepcion
3B	W.Gross	3B	W.Boggs	3B	D.DeCinces	3B	V.Law	3B	B.Jacoby	3B	H.Johnson	3B	G.Pryor
LF	G.Roenicke	LF	J.Rice	LF	B.Downing	LF	R.Kittle	LF	M.Hall	LF	L.Herndon	LF	D.Motley
CF	J.Shelby	CF	T.Armas	CF	G.Pettis	CF	R.Law	CF	B.Butler	CF	C.Lemon	CF	W.Wilson
RF	M.Young	RF	D.Evans	RF	F.Lynn	RF	H.Baines	RF	G.Vukovich	RF	K.Gibson	RF	P.Sheridan
C	R.Dempsey	C	R.Gedman	C	B.Boone	C	C.Fisk	C	J.Willard	C	L.Parrish	C	D.Slaught
DH	K.Singleton	DH	M.Easler	DH	Re.Jackson	DH	G.Luzinski	DH	A.Thornton	DH	D.Evans	DH	H.McRae
O	A.Bumbry	P	B.Hurst	O	J.Beniquez	OD	J.Hairston	1O	P.Tabler	3S	T.Brookens	3	G.Brett
OD	J.Lowenstein	P	B.Ojeda	21	B.Grich	1O	T.Paciorek	O	J.Carter	13	B.Garbey	DO	J.Orta
C3	F.Rayford	P	O.Boyd			13	M.Squires	C	C.Bando	O	R.Jones	C1	J.Wathan
		P	A.Nipper	P	M.Witt			O	C.Castillo			1O	D.Iorg
P	M.Boddicker	P	R.Clemens	P	R.Romanick	P	R.Dotson			P	J.Morris		
P	M.Flanagan	RP	B.Stanley	P	G.Zahn	P	T.Seaver	P	B.Blyleven	P	D.Petry	P	B.Black
P	S.Davis	RP	M.Clear	P	T.John	P	L.Hoyt	P	N.Heaton	P	M.Wilcox	P	M.Gubicza
P	S.McGregor	RP	J.Johnson	P	J.Slaton	P	F.Bannister	P	S.Comer	P	J.Berenguer	P	L.Gura
P	D.Martinez			RP	D.Corbett	P	B.Burns	P	S.Farr	P	D.Rozema	P	B.Saberhagen
RP	S.Stewart	P	M.Brown	RP	L.Sanchez	RP	R.Reed	RP	E.Camacho	RP	W.Hernandez	P	C.Leibrandt
RP	T.Martinez	/P	D.Eckersley	RP	C.Kaufman	RP	J.Agosto	RP	T.Waddell	RP	A.Lopez	RP	D.Quisenberry
RP	T.Underwood	P	S.Crawford			RP	D.Spillner	RP	M.Jeffcoat	RP	D.Bair	RP	J.Beckwith
				P	B.Kison							RP	M.Huisman
P	B.Swaggerty					P	G.Nelson	P	R.Sutcliffe				
								P	D.Schulze			P	M.Jones
								P	R.Smith			P	D.Jackson
								P	J.Easterly				
								P	D.Spillner				
								P	L.Aponte				

	MILWAUKEE		MINNESOTA		NEW YORK		OAKLAND		SEATTLE		TEXAS		TORONTO
M	R.Lachemann	M	B.Gardner	M	Y.Berra	M	S.Boros	M	D.Crandall	M	D.Rader	M	B.Cox
1B	C.Cooper	1B	K.Hrbek	1B	D.Mattingly	M	J.Moore	M	C.Cottier	1B	P.O'Brien	1B	W.Upshaw
2B	J.Gantner	2B	T.Teufel	2B	W.Randolph	1B	B.Bochte	1B	A.Davis	2B	W.Tolleson	2B	D.Garcia
SS	R.Yount	SS	H.Jimenez	SS	B.Meacham	2B	J.Morgan	2B	J.Perconte	SS	C.Wilkerson	SS	A.Griffin
3B	E.Romero	3B	G.Gaetti	3B	T.Harrah	SS	T.Phillips	SS	S.Owen	3B	B.Bell	3B	R.Mulliniks
LF	B.Oglivie	LF	M.Hatcher	LF	K.Griffey	3B	C.Lansford	3B	J.Presley	LF	B.Sample	LF	D.Collins
CF	R.Manning	CF	K.Puckett	CF	O.Moreno	LF	R.Henderson	LF	P.Bradley	CF	G.Wright	CF	L.Moseby
RF	D.James	RF	T.Brunansky	RF	D.Winfield	CF	D.Murphy	CF	D.Henderson	RF	G.Ward	RF	G.Bell
C	J.Sundberg	C	D.Engle	C	B.Wynegar	RF	M.Davis	RF	A.Cowens	C	D.Scott	C	E.Whitt
DH	T.Simmons	DH	R.Bush	DH	D.Baylor	C	M.Heath	C	B.Kearney	DH	L.Parrish	DH	C.Johnson
						DH	D.Kingman	DH	K.Phelps				
C	B.Schroeder	C	T.Laudner	OD	S.Kemp					DO	M.Rivers	O	J.Barfield
		OD	D.Brown	3S	R.Smalley	O1	B.Almon	O3	B.Bonnell	C	N.Yost	3	G.Iorg
				3	M.Pagliarulo	O2	D.Lopes	OD	S.Henderson			C	B.Martinez
P	D.Sutton							32	L.Milbourne	P	C.Hough	D	W.Aikens
P	M.Haas	P	F.Viola							P	F.Tanana	S3	T.Fernandez
P	J.Cocanower	P	M.Smithson	P	P.Niekro	P	R.Burris	P	M.Langston	P	D.Darwin		
P	B.McClure	P	J.Butcher	P	R.Guidry	P	L.Sorensen	P	M.Moore	P	D.Stewart	P	D.Stieb
P	M.Caldwell	P	K.Schrom	P	R.Fontenot	P	S.McCatty	P	J.Beattie	P	M.Mason	P	D.Alexander
RP	P.Ladd	P	E.Hodge	P	D.Rasmussen	P	B.Krueger	P	M.Young	RP	D.Schmidt	P	L.Leal
RP	T.Tellmann	RP	P.Filson	RP	B.Shirley	P	C.Young	RP	E.Vande Berg	RP	O.Jones	P	J.Clancy
RP	R.Waits	RP	R.Davis	RP	J.Howell	RP	K.Atherton	RP	B.Stoddard			P	J.Gott
		RP	R.Lysander	RP	D.Righetti	RP	B.Caudill	RP	D.Beard	P	D.Noles	RP	R.Jackson
						RP	T.Conroy					RP	D.Lamp
P	C.Porter			P	J.Cowley							RP	J.Acker
P	B.Gibson	P	A.Williams	P	J.Rijo	P	M.Warren	P	S.Barojas				
				P	J.Montefusco	P	C.Codiroli	P	P.Mirabella			P	J.Key
				P	M.Armstrong			P	E.Nunez				
								P	M.Stanton				
								P	R.Thomas				

TEAM	G	W	L	PCT	GB	R	OR	AB	H	2B	3B	HR	BB	SO	AVG	OBP	SLG	PRO	PRO+	BR	/A	PF	CHI	RC	SB	CS	SBA	SBR
EAST																												
DET	162	104	58	.642		**829**	**643**	5644	1529	254	46	**187**	602	941	.271	**.345**	.432	.777	**114**	103	**109**	99	99	**843**	106	68	61	-9
TOR	163	89	73	.549	15	750	696	5687	1555	275	**68**	143	460	816	.273	.333	.421	.754	103	52	24	104	96	808	**193**	67	**74**	**18**
NY	162	87	75	.537	17	758	679	5661	1560	275	32	130	534	673	.276	.342	.404	.746	110	47	78	96	97	773	62	38	62	-4
BOS	162	86	76	.531	18	810	764	5648	**1598**	259	45	181	500	842	**.283**	.343	**.441**	**.784**	110	**113**	75	105	97	832	38	25	60	-4
BAL	162	85	77	.525	19	681	667	5456	1374	234	23	160	**620**	884	.252	.331	.391	.722	101	-4	12	98	96	705	51	36	59	-6
CLE	163	75	87	.463	29	761	766	5643	1498	222	39	123	600	815	.265	.339	.384	.723	98	4	-9	102	103	732	126	77	62	-8
MIL	161	67	94	.416	36.5	641	734	5511	1446	232	36	96	432	673	.262	.319	.370	.689	94	-75	-50	96	103	621	52	57	48	-19
WEST																												
KC	162	84	78	.519		673	686	5543	1487	269	52	117	400	832	.268	.320	.399	.719	97	-23	-28	101	99	685	106	64	62	-7
CAL	162	81	81	.500	3	696	697	5470	1363	211	30	150	556	928	.249	.322	.381	.703	95	-46	-41	99	**105**	663	80	51	61	-7
MIN	162	81	81	.500	3	673	675	5562	1473	259	33	114	437	735	.265	.321	.385	.706	90	-45	-75	100	102	669	39	30	57	-6
OAK	162	77	85	.475	7	738	796	5457	1415	257	29	158	568	871	.259	.332	.404	.736	109	18	67	93	101	736	145	64	69	5
SEA	162	74	88	.457	10	682	774	5546	1429	244	34	129	519	871	.258	.326	.384	.710	97	-32	-23	99	100	700	116	62	65	-2
CHI	162	74	88	.457	10	679	736	5513	1360	225	38	172	523	883	.247	.316	.395	.711	91	-37	-67	105	101	690	109	49	69	3
TEX	161	69	92	.429	14.5	656	714	5569	1452	227	29	120	420	807	.261	.315	.377	.692	88	-75	-95	103	104	643	81	50	62	-6
TOT	1134					10027		77910	20539	3443	534	1980	7171	11571	.264	.329	.398	.727							1304	738	64	-52

TEAM	CG	SH	SV	IP	H	H/G	HR	BB	SO	RAT	ERA	ERA+	OAV	OOB	PR	/A	PF	CPI	FA	E	DP	FW	PW	BW	SBW	DIF
EAST																										
DET	19	8	51	1464	**1358**	8.3	130	489	914	**11.5**	3.49	112	.246	.311	81	**70**	98	98	.979	127	162	.3	7.0	11.0	-.5	5.2
TOR	34	10	33	1464	1433	8.8	140	528	875	12.3	3.86	106	.257	.325	21	38	103	99	.980	123	166	.6	3.8	2.4	**2.2**	-1.0
NY	15	12	43	1465¹	1485	9.1	**120**	518	**992**	12.4	3.78	100	.264	.328	35	2	95	102	.977	142	**177**	-.5	.2	7.8	-.0	-1.5
BOS	40	12	32	1442	1524	9.5	141	517	927	12.9	4.18	100	.270	.334	-29	-2	104	99	.977	143	128	-.6	-.2	7.5	-.0	-1.7
BAL	**48**	**13**	32	1439¹	1393	8.7	137	512	714	12.1	3.71	104	.256	.323	44	25	97	102	**.981**	123	166	.5	2.5	1.2	-.2	-.0
CLE	21	7	35	1467²	1523	9.3	141	545	803	12.8	4.26	96	.269	.336	-43	-27	102	98	.977	146	163	-.7	-2.7	-.9	-.4	-1.2
MIL	13	7	41	1433	1532	9.6	137	480	785	12.8	4.06	95	.274	.334	-10	-33	96	103	.978	136	156	-.3	-3.3	-5.0	-1.5	-3.4
WEST																										
KC	18	9	50	1444	1426	8.9	136	**433**	724	11.8	3.92	103	.258	.315	11	17	101	93	.979	131	157	.0	1.7	-2.8	-.3	4.4
CAL	36	12	26	1458	1526	9.4	143	474	754	12.5	3.96	100	.271	.331	6	2	99	**104**	.980	128	170	.2	-.4	-2.1	-.3	4.0
MIN	32	9	38	1437²	1429	8.9	159	463	713	12.1	3.85	109	.261	.321	23	56	105	101	.980	120	134	.7	5.6	-7.2	-.2	1.5
OAK	15	6	44	1430	1554	9.8	155	592	695	13.7	4.48	84	.278	.351	-78	-117	94	100	.975	146	159	-.8	-11.8	6.7	.9	.9
SEA	26	4	35	1442	1497	9.3	138	619	972	13.5	4.31	94	.270	.348	-50	-51	100	102	.979	128	143	.2	-5.1	-2.3	.2	.0
CHI	43	9	32	1454¹	1416	8.8	155	483	840	12.0	4.13	101	.256	.320	-23	4	104	93	**.981**	122	160	.6	.4	-6.7	.7	-1.9
TEX	38	6	21	1438²	1443	9.0	148	518	863	12.5	3.91	106	.261	.327	13	38	104	101	.977	138	138	-.4	3.8	-9.6	-.2	-5.2
TOT	398	124	513	20280		9.1				12.5	3.99		.264	.329					.979	1853	2179					

Runs		Hits		Doubles		Triples		Home Runs		Total Bases	
Evans-Bos	121	Mattingly-NY	207	Mattingly-NY	44	Moseby-Tor	15	Armas-Bos	43	Armas-Bos	339
Henderson-Oak	113	Boggs-Bos	203	Parrish-Tex	42	Collins-Tor	15	Kingman-Oak	35	Evans-Bos	335
Boggs-Bos	109	Ripken-Bal	195	Bell-Tor	39	Gibson-Det	10	Thornton-Cle	33	Ripken-Bal	327
Butler-Cle	108	Winfield-NY	193	Ripken-Bal	37	Baines-Chi	10	Parrish-Det	33	Mattingly-NY	324
Armas-Bos	107			Evans-Bos	37			Murphy-Oak	33	Easler-Bos	310

Runs Batted In		Runs Produced		Bases On Balls		Batting Average		On Base Percentage		Slugging Average	
Armas-Bos	123	Evans-Bos	193	Murray-Bal	107	Mattingly-NY	.343	Murray-Bal	.415	Baines-Chi	.541
Rice-Bos	122	Rice-Bos	192	Davis-Sea	97	Winfield-NY	.340	Boggs-Bos	.409	Mattingly-NY	.537
Kingman-Oak	118	Winfield-NY	187	Evans-Bos	96	Boggs-Bos	.325	Henderson-Oak	.401	Evans-Bos	.532
Davis-Sea	116	Armas-Bos	187	Thornton-Cle	91	Bell-Tex	.315	Winfield-NY	.397	Armas-Bos	.531
				Boggs-Bos	89	Trammell-Det	.314	Davis-Sea	.395	Hrbek-Min	.522

Production		Adjusted Production		Batter Runs		Adjusted Batter Runs		Clutch Hitting Index		Runs Created	
Evans-Bos	.924	Mattingly-NY	159	Murray-Bal	46.8	Murray-Bal	49.7	Franco-Cle	132	Evans-Bos	132
Mattingly-NY	.923	Murray-Bal	157	Evans-Bos	46.6	Mattingly-NY	46.0	Davis-Sea	127	Murray-Bal	130
Murray-Bal	.923	Winfield-NY	156	Mattingly-NY	41.3	Winfield-NY	42.8	Rice-Bos	124	Ripken-Bal	122
Winfield-NY	.912	Henderson-Oak	147	Winfield-NY	38.4	Evans-Bos	40.6	Simmons-Mil	121	Mattingly-NY	120
Hrbek-Min	.909	Davis-Sea	147	Davis-Sea	37.5	Ripken-Bal	39.3	Tabler-Cle	116	Easler-Bos	118

Total Average		Stolen Bases		Stolen Base Average		Stolen Base Runs		Fielding Runs		Total Player Rating	
Murray-Bal	.993	Henderson-Oak	66	Wilson-KC	90.4	Wilson-KC	11.1	Ripken-Bal	38.8	Ripken-Bal	9.1
Henderson-Oak	.971	Collins-Tor	60	Tolleson-Tex	84.6	Collins-Tor	9.6	Puckett-Min	30.1	Yount-Mil	5.0
Evans-Bos	.942	Butler-Cle	52	Perconte-Sea	82.9	Henderson-Oak	9.0	Cruz-Chi	22.1	Murray-Bal	4.9
Davis-Sea	.928	Pettis-Cal	48	Moseby-Tor	81.3	Garcia-Tor	6.6	Boggs-Bos	21.0	Mattingly-NY	4.9
Gibson-Det	.926	Wilson-KC	47	Collins-Tor	81.1	Moseby-Tor	6.3	Murphy-Oak	21.0	Henderson-Oak	4.7

Wins		Win Percentage		Games		Complete Games		Shutouts		Saves	
Boddicker-Bal	20	Alexander-Tor	.739	Hernandez-Det	80	Hough-Tex	17	Zahn-Cal	5	Quisenberry-KC	44
Morris-Det	19	Blyleven-Cle	.731	Quisenberry-KC	72	Boddicker-Bal	16	Ojeda-Bos	5	Caudill-Oak	36
Blyleven-Cle	19	Petry-Det	.692	Lopez-Det	71	Dotson-Chi	14			Hernandez-Det	32
Viola-Min	18	Wilcox-Det	.680	Camacho-Cle	69	Blyleven-Cle	12			Righetti-NY	31
Petry-Det	18			Caudill-Oak	68	Beattie-Sea	12			Davis-Min	29

Innings Pitched		Fewest Hits/Game		Fewest BB/Game		Strikeouts		Strikeouts/Game		Ratio	
Stieb-Tor	267.0	Stieb-Tor	7.25	Hoyt-Chi	1.64	Langston-Sea	204	Langston-Sea	8.16	Black-KC	10.30
Hough-Tex	266.0	Blyleven-Cle	7.49	Smithson-Min	1.93	Stieb-Tor	198	Witt-Cal	7.15	Alexander-Tor	10.32
Alexander-Tor	261.2	Boddicker-Bal	7.51	Guidry-NY	2.02	Witt-Cal	196	Moore-Sea	6.71	Mason-Tex	10.35
Boddicker-Bal	261.1	Langston-Sea	7.52	Alexander-Tor	2.03	Blyleven-Cle	170	Stieb-Tor	6.67	Blyleven-Cle	10.43
Viola-Min	257.2	Mason-Tex	7.76	Haas-Mil	2.04	Hough-Tex	164	Berenguer-Det	6.31	Boddicker-Bal	10.47

Earned Run Average		Adjusted ERA		Opponents' Batting Avg.		Opponents' On Base Pct.		Starter Runs		Adjusted Starter Runs	
Boddicker-Bal	2.79	Stieb-Tor	145	Stieb-Tor	.221	Black-KC	.283	Boddicker-Bal	34.9	Stieb-Tor	37.5
Stieb-Tor	2.83	Blyleven-Cle	143	Blyleven-Cle	.224	Blyleven-Cle	.287	Stieb-Tor	34.4	Blyleven-Cle	33.3
Blyleven-Cle	2.87	Boddicker-Bal	139	Boddicker-Bal	.228	Alexander-Tor	.287	Blyleven-Cle	30.7	Boddicker-Bal	31.4
Niekro-NY	3.09	Alexander-Tor	131	Langston-Sea	.230	Mason-Tex	.288	Alexander-Tor	25.0	Viola-Min	28.3
Zahn-Cal	3.12	Viola-Min	131	Berenguer-Det	.232	Seaver-Chi	.290	Black-KC	25.0	Alexander-Tor	28.1

Clutch Pitching Index		Relief Runs		Adjusted Relief Runs		Relief Ranking		Total Pitcher Index		Total Baseball Ranking	
Niekro-NY	125	Hernandez-Det	32.2	Hernandez-Det	31.1	Hernandez-Det	38.1	Boddicker-Bal	4.2	Ripken-Bal	9.1
Fontenot-NY	119	Quisenberry-KC	19.4	Quisenberry-KC	19.9	Camacho-Cle	31.6	Hernandez-Det	3.9	Yount-Mil	5.0
Cocanower-Mil	114	Righetti-NY	17.7	Camacho-Cle	18.4	Righetti-NY	26.0	Blyleven-Cle	3.4	Murray-Bal	4.9
Hurst-Bos	113	Corbett-Cal	17.7	Corbett-Cal	17.5	Quisenberry-KC	25.9	Stieb-Tor	3.3	Mattingly-NY	4.9
Burris-Oak	112	Camacho-Cle	17.3	Righetti-NY	15.6	Caudill-Oak	24.8	Camacho-Cle	3.2	Henderson-Oak	4.7

July 2 Houston's Joe Niekro wins his 200th career game 3-2 over the Padres. Joe and Phil Niekro join Jim and Gaylord Perry as the only pitching brothers to win at least 200 games each in the majors.

July 4 In a marathon game that borders on the surreal, the Mets endure two rain delays and 6:10 of playing time to beat the Braves 16-13 in 19 innings on Fireworks Night in Atlanta. The Mets had taken a 10-8 lead in the top of the thirteenth inning, only to watch the Braves tie it up. The Mets score again in the 18th, but relief hurler Rick Camp (a .060 hitter who was batting because Atlanta had no more position players) ties the score with his first major league home run on a two-out two-strike pitch in the bottom of the inning. No pitcher ever homered that late in a game before. Finally the Mets erupt for five runs in the 19th off Camp, and Atlanta can respond only with two. The game ends at 3:55 AM on July 5, the latest finish in major league history. At 4:01 A.M. the postgame fireworks display begins, causing

folks to think the city is under attack.

August 20 Dwight Gooden fans 16 batters on the way to his thirteenth consecutive victory, 5-0 over the Giants, raising his season strikeout total to 208. Gooden (19-3) joins Herb Score as the only pitchers this century to strike out 200 batters in each of their first two seasons.

September 11 Pete Rose becomes baseball's all-time hit leader, singling to left center off Eric Show in the first inning of the Reds' 2-0 win over San Diego. His 4,192nd career hit breaks Ty Cobb's record before 47,237 fans at Cincinnati's Riverfront Stadium. In 1981, it was discovered that Cobb had once been credited twice for the same two-hit game, actually giving him 4,189, but commissioner Bowie Kuhn declined to change Cobb's stats.

October 2 The Dodgers clinch the NL West title with a 9-3 win over the Braves. Orel Hershiser raises his record to 19-3 with his eleventh consecutive victory.

October 5 The Cardinals, Royals, and Blue Jays all clinch their division cham-

pionships. John Tudor pitches a four-hitter as St. Louis beats the Cubs 7-1. It is Tudor's 20th win in 21 decisions. Willie Wilson singles home the winning run as Kansas City beats Oakland 5-4 in 10 innings, and Doyle Alexander pitches a five-hitter, as Toronto beats second-place New York 5-1 to wrap up its first AL East crown.

October 19 St. Louis wins the opener of the "I-70 Series" behind ace John Tudor 3-1.

November 18 Willie McGee wins the NL MVP Award, capping a season in which he led the league in batting average (.353) and hits (216) and also stole 56 bases for St. Louis.

November 18 Dwight Gooden (NL) and Bret Saberhagen (AL) win the Cy Young Award in their respective leagues.

November 27 Vince Coleman, who stole 110 bases for the Cardinals, joins Frank Robinson, Orlando Cepeda, and Willie McCovey as the only unanimous winners of the NL Rookie of the Year Award.

ATLANTA		CHICAGO		CINCINNATI		HOUSTON		LOS ANGELES		MONTREAL	
M	E.Haas	M	J.Frey	M	P.Rose	M	B.Lillis	M	T.Lasorda	M	B.Rodgers
M	B.Wine	1B	L.Durham	1B	P.Rose	1B	G.Davis	1B	G.Brock	1B	D.Driessen
1B	B.Horner	2B	R.Sandberg	2B	R.Oester	2B	B.Doran	2B	S.Sax	2B	V.Law
2B	G.Hubbard	SS	S.Dunston	SS	D.Concepcion	SS	C.Reynolds	SS	M.Duncan	SS	H.Brooks
SS	R.Ramirez	3B	R.Cey	3B	B.Bell	3B	P.Garner	3B	D.Anderson	3B	T.Wallach
3B	K.Oberkfell	LF	G.Matthews	LF	G.Redus	LF	J.Cruz	LF	C.Maldonado	LF	T.Raines
LF	T.Harper	CF	B.Dernier	CF	E.Milner	CF	K.Bass	CF	K.Landreaux	CF	H.Winningham
CF	D.Murphy	RF	K.Moreland	RF	D.Parker	RF	J.Mumphrey	RF	M.Marshall	RF	A.Dawson
RF	C.Washington	C	J.Davis	C	D.Van Gorder	C	M.Bailey	C	M.Scioscia	C	M.Fitzgerald
C	R.Cerone										
		O	T.Bosley	3O	N.Esasky	31	D.Walling	O3	P.Guerrero	1O	T.Francona
1	C.Chambliss	O	D.Lopes	O1	C.Cedeno	S	D.Thon	O	R.Reynolds	O	M.Webster
O	B.Komminsk	S3	C.Speier								
1	G.Perry			P	T.Browning	P	B.Knepper	P	F.Valenzuela	P	B.Smith
C	B.Benedict	P	D.Eckersley	P	M.Soto	P	N.Ryan	P	O.Hershiser	P	B.Gullickson
		P	R.Fontenot	P	J.Tibbs	P	M.Scott	P	J.Reuss	P	J.Hesketh
P	R.Mahler	P	S.Trout	P	R.Robinson	P	J.Niekro	P	B.Welch	P	D.Palmer
P	S.Bedrosian	P	R.Sutcliffe	P	J.Stuper	RP	B.Dawley	P	R.Honeycutt	P	D.Schatzeder
P	Z.Smith	P	S.Sanderson	RP	J.Franco	RP	D.Smith	RP	T.Niedenfuer	RP	T.Burke
RP	R.Camp	RP	L.Smith	RP	T.Power	RP	F.DiPino	RP	K.Howell	RP	J.Reardon
RP	G.Garber	RP	L.Sorensen	RP	T.Hume			RP	C.Diaz	RP	R.St.Claire
RP	B.Sutter	RP	G.Frazier			P	R.Mathis				
				P	A.McGaffigan	P	J.Calhoun	P	B.Castillo	P	F.Youmans
P	P.Perez	P	D.Ruthven	P	J.Price	P	J.Heathcock			P	G.Lucas
P	J.Dedmon	P	W.Brusstar	P	F.Pastore					P	B.Roberge
P	J.Johnson	P	J.Baller								
P	L.Barker	P	S.Engel								
P	S.Shields										
P	T.Forster										

NEW YORK		PHILADELPHIA		PITTSBURGH		SAN DIEGO		SAN FRANCISCO		ST.LOUIS	
M	D.Johnson	M	J.Felske	M	C.Tanner	M	D.Williams	M	J.Davenport	M	W.Herzog
1B	K.Hernandez	1B	M.Schmidt	1B	J.Thompson	1B	S.Garvey	M	R.Craig	1B	J.Clark
2B	W.Backman	2B	J.Samuel	2B	J.Ray	2B	T.Flannery	1B	D.Green	2B	T.Herr
SS	R.Santana	SS	S.Jeltz	SS	S.Khalifa	SS	G.Templeton	2B	M.Trillo	SS	O.Smith
3B	H.Johnson	3B	R.Schu	3B	B.Madlock	3B	G.Nettles	SS	J.Uribe	3B	T.Pendleton
LF	G.Foster	LF	V.Hayes	LF	J.Orsulak	LF	C.Martinez	3B	C.Brown	LF	V.Coleman
CF	M.Wilson	CF	G.Maddox	CF	M.Wynne	CF	K.McReynolds	LF	J.Leonard	CF	W.McGee
RF	D.Strawberry	RF	G.Wilson	RF	G.Hendrick	RF	T.Gwynn	CF	D.Gladden	RF	A.Van Slyke
C	G.Carter	C	O.Virgil	C	T.Pena	C	T.Kennedy	RF	C.Davis	C	T.Nieto
								C	B.Brenly		
O	D.Heep	1	T.Corcoran	SO	B.Almon	23	J.Royster			C	D.Porter
3	R.Knight	O	J.Stone	32	J.Morrison			O	J.Youngblood		
O	L.Dykstra	O1	J.Russell	O	S.Kemp	P	E.Show			P	J.Tudor
				O	M.Brown	P	A.Hawkins	P	D.LaPoint	P	J.Andujar
P	D.Gooden	P	J.Denny			P	D.Dravecky	P	M.Krukow	P	D.Cox
P	R.Darling	P	K.Gross	P	R.Rhoden	P	L.Hoyt	P	A.Hammaker	P	K.Kepshire
P	E.Lynch	P	S.Rawley	P	R.Reuschel	P	M.Thurmond	P	J.Gott	P	B.Forsch
P	S.Fernandez	P	C.Hudson	P	J.DeLeon	RP	C.Lefferts	P	V.Blue	RP	R.Horton
P	R.Aguilera	P	J.Koosman	P	L.Tunnell	RP	R.Gossage	RP	M.Davis	RP	J.Lahti
RP	R.McDowell	RP	D.Carman	P	L.McWilliams	RP	T.Stoddard	RP	S.Garrelts	RP	K.Dayley
RP	J.Orosco	RP	D.Rucker	RP	C.Guante			RP	G.Minton		
RP	D.Sisk	RP	L.Andersen	RP	D.Robinson					P	B.Campbell
				RP	J.Winn			P	B.Laskey		
P	T.Leach	P	S.Carlton					P	F.Williams		
P	T.Gorman	P	K.Tekulve	P	A.Holland						
				/P	B.Walk						
				P	J.Candelaria						

TEAM	G	W	L	PCT	GB	R	OR	AB	H	2B	3B	HR	BB	SO	AVG	OBP	SLG	PRO	PRO+	BR	/A	PF	CHI	RC	SB	CS	SBA	SBR
EAST																												
STL	162	101	61	.623		**747**	572	5467	1446	245	**59**	87	586	853	**.264**	**.338**	.379	**.717**	108	52	58	99	**105**	733	**314**	96	77	**37**
NY	162	98	64	.605	3	695	**568**	5549	1425	239	35	134	546	872	.257	.326	.385	.711	108	31	49	98	99	691	117	53	69	3
MON	161	84	77	.522	16.5	633	636	5429	1342	242	49	118	492	880	.247	.313	.375	.688	104	-19	17	94	101	633	169	77	69	5
CHI	162	77	84	.478	23.5	686	729	5492	1397	239	28	**150**	562	937	.254	.326	**.390**	.716	95	40	-37	111	98	710	182	49	**79**	25
PHI	162	75	87	.463	26	667	673	5477	1343	238	47	141	527	1095	.245	.314	.383	.697	97	0	-18	103	102	657	122	51	71	6
PIT	161	57	104	.354	43.5	568	708	5436	1340	251	28	80	514	842	.247	.313	.347	.660	91	-64	-58	99	97	587	110	60	65	-3
WEST																												
LA	162	95	67	.586		682	579	5502	1434	226	28	129	539	846	.261	.330	.382	.712	108	38	**59**	97	97	704	136	58	70	6
CIN	162	89	72	.553	5.5	677	666	5431	1385	249	34	114	576	856	.255	.329	.376	.705	98	26	-8	105	99	672	159	70	69	6
SD	162	83	79	.512	12	650	622	5507	1405	241	28	109	513	**809**	.255	.321	.368	.689	101	-9	-1	99	100	645	60	39	61	-5
HOU	162	83	79	.512	12	706	691	5582	**1457**	**261**	42	121	477	873	.261	.322	.388	.710	107	25	45	97	103	684	96	56	63	-5
ATL	162	66	96	.407	29	632	781	5526	1359	213	28	126	553	849	.246	.317	.363	.680	91	-28	-66	106	99	622	72	52	58	-10
SF	162	62	100	.383	33	556	674	5420	1263	217	31	115	488	962	.233	.301	.348	.649	91	-93	-66	95	100	564	99	55	64	-3
TOT	971					7899		65818	16596	2861	437	1424	6373	10674	.252	.321	.374	.695							1636	716	70	61

TEAM	CG	SH	SV	IP	H	H/G	HR	BB	SO	RAT	ERA	ERA+	OAV	OOB	PR	/A	PF	CPI	FA	E	DP	FW	PW	BW	SBW	DIF
EAST																										
STL	**37**	20	44	1464	1343	8.3	**98**	453	798	11.2	3.10	114	.246	.307	79	70	98	102	**.983**	**108**	166	**1.7**	7.4	6.1	**3.4**	1.5
NY	32	19	37	1488	1306	**7.9**	111	515	**1039**	11.1	3.11	111	.237	.304	80	57	96	99	.982	115	138	1.3	6.0	5.2	-.2	4.8
MON	13	13	**53**	1457	1346	8.3	99	509	870	11.6	3.55	96	.247	.313	7	-25	94	93	.981	121	152	.8	-2.6	1.8	-.0	3.5
CHI	20	8	42	1442[1]	1492	9.3	156	519	820	12.7	4.16	96	.271	.336	-91	-27	111	103	.979	134	150	.1	-2.8	-3.9	2.1	1.0
PHI	24	9	30	1447	1424	8.9	115	596	899	12.7	3.68	100	.259	.334	-15	0	103	105	.978	139	142	-.2	-1.0	-1.9	.0	-4.0
PIT	15	6	29	1445[1]	1406	8.8	107	584	962	12.6	3.97	90	.255	.330	-61	-64	100	94	.979	133	127	.1	-6.7	-6.1	-.9	-9.9
WEST																										
LA	**37**	**21**	36	1465	**1280**	**7.9**	102	462	979	**10.8**	**2.96**	**117**	**.234**	**.296**	102	84	97	98	.974	166	131	-1.8	**8.8**	**6.2**	.0	.7
CIN	24	11	45	1451[1]	1347	8.4	131	535	910	11.8	3.71	102	.248	.317	-19	12	105	96	.980	122	142	.8	1.3	-.8	.0	7.1
SD	26	19	44	1451[1]	1399	8.7	127	**443**	727	11.6	3.40	104	.257	.316	30	21	98	**106**	.980	124	158	.7	2.2	.1	-1.1	.0
HOU	17	9	42	1458	1393	8.6	119	543	909	12.1	3.66	95	.254	.324	-11	-32	96	100	.976	152	159	-1.0	-3.4	4.7	-1.1	2.7
ATL	9	9	29	1457[1]	1512	9.3	134	642	776	13.5	4.19	92	.271	.349	-98	-56	107	104	.976	159	**197**	-1.4	-5.9	-6.9	-1.6	.8
SF	13	5	24	1448	1348	8.4	125	572	985	12.1	3.61	95	.247	.321	-3	-28	96	99	.976	148	134	-.7	-2.9	-6.9	-.9	-7.5
TOT	267	149	455	17474[2]		8.5				12.0	3.59		.252	.321					.979	1621	1796					

Runs		**Hits**		**Doubles**		**Triples**		**Home Runs**		**Total Bases**	
Murphy-Atl	118	McGee-StL	216	Parker-Cin	42	McGee-StL	18	Murphy-Atl	37	Parker-Cin	350
Raines-Mon	115	Parker-Cin	198	Wilson-Phi	39	Samuel-Phi	13	Parker-Cin	34	Murphy-Atl	332
McGee-StL	114	Gwynn-SD	197	Herr-StL	38	Raines-Mon	13	Schmidt-Phi	33	McGee-StL	308
Sandberg-Chi	113	Sandberg-Chi	186	Wallach-Mon	36	Garner-Hou	10	Guerrero-LA	33	Sandberg-Chi	307
Coleman-StL	107	Murphy-Atl	185			Coleman-StL	10	Carter-NY	32	Schmidt-Phi	292

Runs Batted In		**Runs Produced**		**Bases On Balls**		**Batting Average**		**On Base Percentage**		**Slugging Average**	
Parker-Cin	125	Herr-StL	199	Murphy-Atl	90	McGee-StL	.353	Guerrero-LA	.425	Guerrero-LA	.577
Murphy-Atl	111	Murphy-Atl	192	Schmidt-Phi	87	Guerrero-LA	.320	Scioscia-LA	.409	Parker-Cin	.551
Herr-StL	110	McGee-StL	186	Martinez-SD	87	Raines-Mon	.320	Raines-Mon	.407	Murphy-Atl	.539
Moreland-Chi	106	Parker-Cin	179	Rose-Cin	86	Gwynn-SD	.317	Rose-Cin	.398	Schmidt-Phi	.532
Wilson-Phi	102	Sandberg-Chi	170	Law-Mon	86	Parker-Cin	.312	Clark-StL	.397	Marshall-LA	.515

Production		**Adjusted Production**		**Batter Runs**		**Adjusted Batter Runs**		**Clutch Hitting Index**		**Runs Created**	
Guerrero-LA	1.002	Guerrero-LA	183	Guerrero-LA	52.8	Guerrero-LA	56.3	Herr-StL	161	Murphy-Atl	131
Murphy-Atl	.929	Raines-Mon	155	Murphy-Atl	47.6	Raines-Mon	43.9	Pendleton-StL	139	Raines-Mon	124
Parker-Cin	.918	Clark-StL	151	Parker-Cin	42.5	Murphy-Atl	40.4	Moreland-Chi	128	McGee-StL	123
Schmidt-Phi	.911	McGee-StL	148	Schmidt-Phi	38.5	McGee-StL	37.6	Wilson-Phi	128	Guerrero-LA	121
Clark-StL	.899	Murphy-Atl	148	Raines-Mon	37.5	Parker-Cin	36.8	Brooks-Mon	125	Sandberg-Chi	117

Total Average		**Stolen Bases**		**Stolen Base Average**		**Stolen Base Runs**		**Fielding Runs**		**Total Player Rating**	
Guerrero-LA	1.086	Coleman-StL	110	Lopes-Chi	92.2	Coleman-StL	18.0	Hubbard-Atl	61.8	Raines-Mon	6.6
Raines-Mon	1.022	Raines-Mon	70	Herr-StL	91.2	Raines-Mon	15.6	Wallach-Mon	36.7	Guerrero-LA	6.3
Murphy-Atl	.960	McGee-StL	56	Raines-Mon	88.6	Lopes-Chi	11.7	McReynolds-SD	23.1	McGee-StL	5.4
Schmidt-Phi	.927	Sandberg-Chi	54	VanSlyke-StL	85.0	Sandberg-Chi	9.6	Pendleton-StL	22.7	Hubbard-Atl	5.4
McGee-StL	.920	Samuel-Phi	53	Davis-Cin	84.2	Herr-StL	7.5	Wilson-Phi	20.4	Sandberg-Chi	4.6

Wins		**Win Percentage**		**Games**		**Complete Games**		**Shutouts**		**Saves**	
Gooden-NY	24	Hershiser-LA	.864	Burke-Mon	78	Gooden-NY	16	Tudor-StL	10	Reardon-Mon	41
Tudor-StL	21	Gooden-NY	.857	M.Davis-SF	77	Valenzuela-LA	14	Gooden-NY	8	Smith-Chi	33
Andujar-StL	21	Smith-Mon	.783	Garrelts-SF	74	Tudor-StL	14	Valenzuela-LA	5	Smith-Hou	27
Browning-Cin	20	Darling-NY	.727	Carman-Phi	71	Cox-StL	10	Hershiser-LA	5	Power-Cin	27
Hershiser-LA	19	Tudor-StL	.724	Minton-SF	68	Andujar-StL	10			Gossage-SD	26

Innings Pitched		**Fewest Hits/Game**		**Fewest BB/Game**		**Strikeouts**		**Strikeouts/Game**		**Ratio**	
Gooden-NY	276.2	Fernandez-NY	5.71	Hoyt-SD	.86	Gooden-NY	268	Fernandez-NY	9.51	Tudor-StL	8.61
Tudor-StL	275.0	Gooden-NY	6.44	Eckersley-Chi	1.01	Soto-Cin	214	Gooden-NY	8.72	Gooden-NY	8.75
Valenzuela-LA	272.1	Hershiser-LA	6.72	Lynch-NY	1.27	Ryan-Hou	209	DeLeon-Pit	8.24	Eckersley-Chi	8.88
Andujar-StL	269.2	Tudor-StL	6.84	Tudor-StL	1.60	Valenzuela-LA	208	Ryan-Hou	8.11	Hershiser-LA	9.50
Mahler-Atl	266.2	Soto-Cin	6.87	Smith-Mon	1.66	Fernandez-NY	180	Soto-Cin	7.50	Smith-Mon	9.51

Earned Run Average		**Adjusted ERA**		**Opponents' Batting Avg.**		**Opponents' On Base Pct.**		**Starter Runs**		**Adjusted Starter Runs**	
Gooden-NY	1.53	Gooden-NY	226	Fernandez-NY	.181	Tudor-StL	.249	Gooden-NY	63.4	Gooden-NY	59.2
Tudor-StL	1.93	Tudor-StL	183	Gooden-NY	.201	Gooden-NY	.254	Tudor-StL	50.7	Tudor-StL	48.9
Hershiser-LA	2.03	Hershiser-LA	171	Hershiser-LA	.206	Eckersley-Chi	.255	Hershiser-LA	41.6	Hershiser-LA	38.5
Reuschel-Pit	2.27	Reuschel-Pit	157	Tudor-StL	.209	Hershiser-LA	.268	Valenzuela-LA	34.6	Valenzuela-LA	31.2
Welch-LA	2.31	Welch-LA	150	Soto-Cin	.211	Smith-Mon	.269	Reuschel-Pit	28.4	Reuschel-Pit	28.1

Clutch Pitching Index		**Relief Runs**		**Adjusted Relief Runs**		**Relief Ranking**		**Total Pitcher Index**		**Total Baseball Ranking**	
Darling-NY	120	Burke-Mon	16.0	Franco-Cin	17.6	Franco-Cin	28.1	Gooden-NY	7.3	Gooden-NY	7.3
Hawkins-SD	119	Gossage-SD	15.5	Carman-Phi	15.3	Smith-Hou	23.6	Tudor-StL	5.5	Raines-Mon	6.6
Show-SD	119	Franco-Cin	15.5	Gossage-SD	15.2	Gossage-SD	23.2	Hershiser-LA	4.2	Guerrero-LA	6.3
Reuss-LA	115	Garrelts-SF	15.2	Garrelts-SF	13.3	Carman-Phi	23.1	Reuschel-Pit	4.0	Tudor-StL	5.5
Gooden-NY	115	Carman-Phi	14.4	Burke-Mon	13.3	Power-Cin	21.4	Valenzuela-LA	3.6	McGee-StL	5.4

January 7 Lou Brock and Hoyt Wilhelm are elected to the Hall of Fame.

March 6 Enos Slaughter and Arky Vaughan are elected to the Hall of Fame by the Special Veterans Committee.

June 3 The Brewers select University of North Carolina catcher B. J. Surhoff with the first pick in what will prove to be an extremely fruitful free-agent draft. Fellow Olympians Will Clark (Mississippi State), Bobby Witt (University of Oklahoma), and Barry Larkin (University of Michigan) are drafted second, third, and fourth by the Giants, Rangers, and Reds, respectively.

October 6 Phil Niekro finally wins his 300th career game 8-0 over the Blue Jays on the final day of the regular season. At 46, he is the oldest hurler ever to pitch a complete-game shutout.

October 16 Baseball gets its first intrastate World Series since 1974, as the Royals and Cardinals win their respective playoff series. Kansas City beats Toronto 6-2 in Game 7 to cap a comeback from a deficit of three games to one. In Los Angeles, Jack Clark drills a three-run home run off Tom Niedenfuer with two outs in the top of the ninth and first base open to give the Cardinals a 7-5 victory and a 4-2 series win.

October 22 Bret Saberhagen gives Kansas City its first World Series win with a 6-1 win.

October 26 Aided by a blown call, a bungled pop-up, and a passed ball, Kansas City scores two runs in the bottom of the ninth to beat St. Louis 2-1 and even the World Series at three games apiece. The Cardinals are three outs away from a championship when Jorge Orta reaches base on a disputed infield single. The next batter, Steve Balboni, lofts a foul pop that Jack Clark lets fall untouched, then singles. After Darrell Porter's passed ball puts runners on second and third, and Hal McRae is intentionally walked to load the bases, pinch hitter Dane Iorg singles home two runs to end the game.

October 27 The Royals rout the Cardinals 11-0 in Game 7 to become only the sixth team to rally from a three games to one deficit and win the World Series. Series MVP Bret Saberhagen pitches the shutout while Cardinals ace John Tudor allows five runs in 2⅓ innings, and fellow 20-game winner Joaquin Andujar is ejected for arguing balls and strikes during Kansas City's six-run fifth inning. The Cardinals finish the World Series with a .185 team batting average, lowest ever for a seven-game Series.

October 27 Billy Martin is fired by the Yankees for an unprecedented fourth time and is replaced by former Yankees outfielder Lou Piniella, who had been the team's hitting instructor since retiring as a player in 1984.

November 20 Don Mattingly easily wins the AL MVP Award, becoming the first player from a non-championship team to do so since 1978.

BALTIMORE		BOSTON		CALIFORNIA		CHICAGO		CLEVELAND		DETROIT		KANSAS CITY	
M	J.Altobelli	M	J.McNamara	M	G.Mauch	M	T.LaRussa	M	P.Corrales	M	S.Anderson	M	D.Howser
M	C.Ripken	1B	B.Buckner	1B	R.Carew	1B	G.Walker	1B	P.Tabler	1B	D.Evans	1B	S.Balboni
M	E.Weaver	2B	M.Barrett	2B	B.Grich	2B	J.Cruz	2B	T.Bernazard	2B	L.Whitaker	2B	F.White
1B	E.Murray	SS	J.Gutierrez	SS	D.Schofield	SS	O.Guillen	SS	J.Franco	SS	A.Trammell	SS	O.Concepcion
2B	A.Wiggins	3B	W.Boggs	3B	D.DeCinces	3B	T.Hulett	3B	B.Jacoby	3B	D.Brookens	3B	G.Brett
SS	C.Ripken	LF	J.Rice	LF	B.Downing	LF	R.Law	LF	J.Carter	LF	L.Herndon	LF	L.Smith
3B	F.Rayford	CF	S.Lyons	CF	G.Pettis	CF	D.Boston	CF	B.Butler	CF	C.Lemon	CF	W.Wilson
LF	M.Young	RF	D.Evans	RF	R.Jones	RF	H.Baines	RF	G.Vukovich	RF	K.Gibson	RF	D.Motley
CF	F.Lynn	C	R.Gedman	C	B.Boone	C	C.Fisk	C	J.Willard	C	L.Parrish	C	J.Sundberg
RF	L.Lacy	DH	M.Easler	DH	R.Jackson	DH	R.Kittle	DH	A.Thornton	DH	J.Grubb	DH	H.McRae
C	R.Dempsey												
DH	L.Sheets	OD	T.Armas	O1	J.Beniquez	3S	S.Fletcher	1	M.Hargrove	OD	N.Simmons	O	L.Jones
		S	G.Hoffman	2	R.Wilfong	O3	L.Salazar	1O	O.Nixon	1O	B.Garbey	D	J.Orta
O	J.Dwyer											O	P.Sheridan
3D	W.Gross	P	O.Boyd	P	M.Witt	P	T.Seaver	P	N.Heaton	P	J.Morris		
OD	G.Roenicke	P	B.Hurst	P	R.Romanick	P	B.Burns	P	B.Blyleven	P	D.Petry	P	C.Leibrandt
23	R.Dauer	P	A.Nipper	P	K.McCaskill	P	F.Bannister	RP	V.Ruhle	P	W.Terrell	P	B.Saberhagen
O	J.Shelby	P	B.Ojeda	P	J.Slaton	P	G.Nelson	RP	T.Waddell	P	F.Tanana	P	D.Jackson
		RP	S.Crawford	RP	D.Moore	RP	B.James	RP	J.Easterly	RP	W.Hernandez	P	B.Black
P	S.McGregor	RP	B.Stanley	RP	S.Cliburn	RP	D.Spillner			RP	A.Lopez	P	M.Gubicza
P	M.Boddicker	RP	M.Clear	RP	P.Clements	RP	J.Agosto	P	D.Schulze	RP	B.Scherrer	RP	D.Quisenberry
P	D.Martinez							P	R.Thompson			RP	J.Beckwith
P	S.Davis	P	R.Clemens	P	U.Lugo	P	T.Lollar	P	J.Reed	P	J.Berenguer	RP	M.Jones
P	K.Dixon	P	B.Kison	P	J.Candelaria	P	J.Davis	P	C.Wardle	P	R.O'Neal		
RP	S.Stewart	P	M.Trujillo	P	L.Sanchez	/P	R.Dotson	P	R.Romero				
RP	N.Snell	P	T.Lollar					P	B.Clark				
RP	D.Aase							P	K.Creel				
								P	R.Smith				
P	M.Flanagan												
P	T.Martinez												

MILWAUKEE		MINNESOTA		NEW YORK		OAKLAND		SEATTLE		TEXAS		TORONTO	
M	G.Bamberger	M	B.Gardner	M	Y.Berra	M	J.Moore	M	C.Cottier	M	D.Rader	M	B.Cox
1B	C.Cooper	M	R.Miller	M	B.Martin	1B	B.Bochte	1B	A.Davis	M	B.Valentine	1B	W.Upshaw
2B	J.Gantner	1B	K.Hrbek	1B	D.Mattingly	2B	D.Hill	2B	J.Perconte	1B	P.O'Brien	2B	D.Garcia
SS	E.Riles	2B	T.Teufel	2B	W.Randolph	SS	A.Griffin	SS	S.Owen	2B	T.Harrah	SS	T.Fernandez
3B	P.Molitor	SS	G.Gagne	SS	B.Meacham	3B	C.Lansford	3B	J.Presley	SS	C.Wilkerson	3B	R.Mulliniks
LF	B.Oglivie	3B	G.Gaetti	3B	M.Pagliarulo	LF	D.Collins	LF	P.Bradley	3B	B.Bell	LF	G.Bell
CF	R.Yount	LF	M.Hatcher	LF	K.Griffey	CF	D.Murphy	CF	D.Henderson	LF	G.Ward	CF	L.Moseby
RF	P.Householder	CF	K.Puckett	CF	R.Henderson	RF	M.Davis	RF	A.Cowens	CF	O.McDowell	RF	J.Barfield
C	C.Moore	RF	T.Brunansky	RF	D.Winfield	C	M.Heath	RF	B.Kearney	RF	G.Wright	C	E.Whitt
DH	T.Simmons	C	M.Salas	C	B.Wynegar	DH	D.Kingman	DH	G.Thomas	C	D.Slaught	DH	J.Burroughs
		DH	R.Smalley	DH	D.Baylor					DH	C.Johnson		
S2	E.Romero					1O	D.Baker	O	I.Calderon			32	G.Iorg
O	R.Manning	OD	R.Bush	C	R.Hassey	C	M.Tettleton			S2	W.Tolleson		
								P	M.Moore	OD	L.Parrish	P	D.Stieb
P	D.Darwin	P	M.Smithson	P	R.Guidry	P	C.Codiroli	P	M.Young	3	S.Buechele	P	D.Alexander
P	T.Higuera	P	F.Viola	P	P.Niekro	P	D.Sutton	P	M.Langston			P	J.Key
P	R.Burris	P	J.Butcher	P	J.Cowley	P	B.Krueger	P	F.Wills	P	C.Hough	P	J.Clancy
P	M.Haas	P	K.Schrom	P	E.Whitson	P	T.Birtsas	P	B.Swift	P	M.Mason	P	D.Lamp
P	J.Cocanower	P	B.Blyleven	P	D.Rasmussen	RP	K.Atherton	RP	R.Thomas	P	B.Hooton	RP	J.Acker
RP	B.Gibson	RP	P.Filson	RP	B.Shirley	RP	J.Howell	RP	E.Nunez	P	D.Noles	RP	G.Lavelle
RP	B.McClure	RP	R.Davis	RP	D.Righetti	RP	S.McCatty	RP	E.Vande Berg	P	G.Harris		
RP	R.Fingers	RP	F.Eufemia	RP	B.Fisher					RP	D.Rozema	P	B.Caudill
						P	S.Ontiveros	P	J.Beattie	RP	D.Schmidt	P	L.Leal
P	P.Vuckovich	P	R.Lysander	P	R.Bordi	P	J.Rijo	P	S.Barojas			P	R.Musselman
						P	R.Langford			P	D.Stewart		
										P	F.Tanana		
										P	C.Welsh		
										P	J.Russell		

TEAM	G	W	L	PCT	GB	R	OR	AB	H	2B	3B	HR	BB	SO	AVG	OBP	SLG	PRO	PRO+	BR	/A	PF	CHI	RC	SB	CS	SBA	SBR
EAST																												
TOR	161	99	62	.615		759	**588**	5508	1482	281	**53**	158	503	807	.269	.334	.425	.759	103	43	24	103	98	767	144	77	65	-3
NY	161	97	64	.602	2	**839**	660	5458	1458	272	31	176	620	771	.267	.347	.425	.772	**113**	82	**102**	98	102	821	**155**	53	**75**	**15**
DET	161	84	77	.522	15	729	688	5575	1413	254	45	202	526	926	.253	.321	.424	.745	112	8	13	99	97	765	75	41	65	-2
BAL	161	83	78	.516	16	818	764	5517	1451	234	22	**214**	604	908	.263	.338	**.430**	.768	112	64	86	97	102	794	69	43	62	-5
BOS	163	81	81	.500	18.5	800	720	5720	**1615**	**292**	31	162	562	816	**.282**	**.350**	.429	**.779**	108	**96**	61	104	93	**844**	66	27	71	4
MIL	161	71	90	.441	28	690	802	5568	1467	250	44	101	462	**746**	.263	.322	.379	.701	91	-68	-65	100	103	666	69	34	67	0
CLE	162	60	102	.370	39.5	729	861	5527	1465	254	31	116	492	817	.265	.327	.385	.712	95	-44	-39	99	106	681	132	72	65	-4
WEST																												
KC	162	91	71	.562		687	639	5500	1384	261	49	154	473	840	.252	.315	.401	.716	94	-47	-49	100	101	687	128	48	73	10
CAL	162	90	72	.556	1	732	703	5442	1364	215	31	153	**648**	902	.251	.335	.386	.721	97	-17	-13	100	100	711	106	51	68	1
CHI	163	85	77	.525	6	736	720	5470	1386	247	37	146	471	843	.253	.318	.392	.710	90	-55	-81	104	**110**	674	108	56	66	-1
MIN	162	77	85	.475	14	705	782	5509	1453	282	41	141	502	779	.264	.329	.407	.736	95	-1	-43	106	97	729	68	44	61	-6
OAK	162	77	85	.475	14	757	787	5581	1475	230	34	155	508	861	.264	.327	.401	.728	106	-15	39	93	104	725	117	58	67	0
SEA	162	74	88	.457	17	719	818	5521	1410	277	38	171	564	942	.255	.328	.412	.740	100	7	3	101	96	739	94	35	73	7
TEX	161	62	99	.385	28.5	617	785	5361	1359	213	41	129	530	819	.253	.324	.381	.705	91	-54	-63	101	93	652	130	76	63	-7
TOT	1132					10317		77257	20182	3562	528	2178	7465	11777	.261	.330	.406	.735							1461	715	67	9

TEAM	CG	SH	SV	IP	H	H/G	HR	BB	SO	RAT	ERA	ERA+	OAV	OOB	PR	/A	PF	CPI	FA	E	DP	FW	PW	BW	SBW	DIF
EAST																										
TOR	18	9	47	1448	**1312**	8.2	147	484	823	**11.3**	**3.31**	127	.243	**.308**	135	145	102	107	.980	125	164	.2	**14.3**	2.4	-.4	1.9
NY	25	9	**49**	1440¹	1373	8.6	157	518	907	11.3	3.69	109	.251	.318	74	50	97	104	.979	126	172	.2	4.9	**10.1**	**1.4**	-.1
DET	31	**11**	40	1456	1313	**8.1**	141	556	943	11.7	3.78	108	**.240**	.316	59	47	98	94	.977	129	143	-.8	-5.4	1.3	-.3	-1.4
BAL	32	6	33	1427¹	1480	9.3	160	568	793	13.1	4.38	102	.270	.341	-36	-55	97	102	.979	129	168	-.0	-5.4	8.5	-.6	-.0
BOS	35	8	29	1461¹	1487	9.2	130	540	913	12.7	4.06	106	.265	.333	14	37	103	101	.977	145	161	-.8	3.7	6.0	.3	-9.2
MIL	34	5	37	1437	1510	9.5	175	499	777	12.8	4.39	95	.271	.334	-39	-36	100	101	.977	142	153	-.7	-3.6	-6.4	-.0	1.3
CLE	24	7	28	1421	1556	9.9	170	547	702	13.6	4.91	84	.281	.350	-121	-123	100	98	.977	141	161	-.6	-12.2	-3.9	-.5	-3.9
WEST																										
KC	27	**11**	41	1461	1433	8.8	**103**	463	846	11.9	3.49	119	.257	.317	107	109	100	103	.980	127	160	.1	10.8	-4.8	.9	3.0
CAL	22	8	41	1457¹	1453	9.0	171	514	767	12.3	3.91	106	.263	.328	38	32	99	**108**	**.982**	102	**202**	.0	3.2	-1.3	-.0	6.1
CHI	20	8	39	1451²	1411	8.7	161	569	**1023**	12.5	4.07	106	.256	.330	13	40	104	101	**.982**	111	152	**1.1**	4.0	-8.0	-.2	7.1
MIN	**41**	7	34	1426¹	1468	9.3	164	**462**	767	12.4	4.48	98	.268	.329	-53	-11	106	95	.980	120	139	.5	-1.1	-4.3	-.7	1.5
OAK	10	6	41	1453	1451	9.0	172	607	785	12.9	4.41	87	.259	.334	-84	-89	93	97	.977	140	137	-.6	-8.8	3.9	-.0	1.6
SEA	23	8	30	1432	1456	9.2	154	637	868	13.4	4.68	90	.264	.346	-65	-74	102	96	.980	122	156	.4	-7.3	.3	.6	-1.0
TEX	18	5	33	1411²	1479	9.4	173	501	863	12.9	4.56	93	.269	.334	-65	-52	102	97	.980	120	145	.5	-5.1	-6.2	-.8	-6.9
TOT	360	108	522	20184		9.0				12.5	4.15		.261	.330					.979	1803	2222					

Runs
Henderson-NY ... 146
Ripken-Bal ... 116
Murray-Bal ... 111
Evans-Bos ... 110
Brett-KC ... 108

Hits
Boggs-Bos ... 240
Mattingly-NY ... 211
Buckner-Bos ... 201
Puckett-Min ... 199
Baines-Chi ... 198

Doubles
Mattingly-NY ... 48
Buckner-Bos ... 46
Boggs-Bos ... 42
Cooper-Mil ... 39

Triples
Wilson-KC ... 21
Butler-Cle ... 14
Puckett-Min ... 13
Fernandez-Tor ... 10

Home Runs
Evans-Det ... 40
Fisk-Chi ... 37
Balboni-KC ... 36
Mattingly-NY ... 35
G.Thomas-Sea ... 32

Total Bases
Mattingly-NY ... 370
Brett-KC ... 322
Bradley-Sea ... 319
Boggs-Bos ... 312
Murray-Bal ... 305

Runs Batted In
Mattingly-NY ... 145
Murray-Bal ... 124
Winfield-NY ... 114
Baines-Chi ... 113
Brett-KC ... 112

Runs Produced
Mattingly-NY ... 217
Murray-Bal ... 204
Ripken-Bal ... 200
Henderson-NY ... 194
Winfield-NY ... 193

Bases On Balls
Evans-Bos ... 114
Harrah-Tex ... 113
Brett-KC ... 103
Henderson-NY ... 99
Boggs-Bos ... 96

Batting Average
Boggs-Bos ... .368
Brett-KC ... .335
Mattingly-NY ... .324
Henderson-NY ... .314
Butler-Cle ... .311

On Base Percentage
Boggs-Bos ... .452
Brett-KC ... .442
Harrah-Tex ... .437
Henderson-NY ... .422
Murray-Bal ... .387

Slugging Average
Brett-KC ... .585
Mattingly-NY ... .567
Barfield-Tor ... .536
Murray-Bal ... .523
Evans-Det ... .519

Production
Brett-KC ... 1.028
Mattingly-NY ... .946
Henderson-NY ... .938
Boggs-Bos ... .929
Murray-Bal ... .910

Adjusted Production
Brett-KC ... 178
Henderson-NY ... 159
Mattingly-NY ... 159
Murray-Bal ... 150
Boggs-Bos ... 149

Batter Runs
Brett-KC ... 63.4
Boggs-Bos ... 54.8
Mattingly-NY ... 47.5
Henderson-NY ... 45.5
Murray-Bal ... 38.4

Adjusted Batter Runs
Brett-KC ... 63.0
Mattingly-NY ... 50.8
Boggs-Bos ... 48.9
Henderson-NY ... 48.5
Murray-Bal ... 41.6

Clutch Hitting Index
Franco-Cle ... 137
Meacham-NY ... 137
Mattingly-NY ... 132
Boone-Cal ... 130
Thornton-Cle ... 125

Runs Created
Brett-KC ... 146
Boggs-Bos ... 143
Henderson-NY ... 138
Mattingly-NY ... 136
Murray-Bal ... 122

Total Average
Henderson-NY ... 1.155
Brett-KC ... 1.150
Gibson-Det ... .953
Boggs-Bos ... .952
Murray-Bal ... .938

Stolen Bases
Henderson-NY ... 80
Pettis-Cal ... 56
Butler-Cle ... 47
Wilson-KC ... 43
Smith-KC ... 40

Stolen Base Average
Percone-Sea ... 93.9
Henderson-NY ... 88.9
Gibson-Det ... 88.2
Pettis-Cal ... 86.2
Smith-KC ... 85.1

Stolen Base Runs
Henderson-NY ... 18.0
Pettis-Cal ... 11.4
Percone-Sea ... 8.1
Smith-KC ... 7.8
Gibson-Det ... 6.6

Fielding Runs
Owen-Sea ... 30.3
Buckner-Bos ... 25.4
Barfield-Tor ... 21.9
Butler-Cle ... 21.8
Puckett-Min ... 21.2

Total Player Rating
Henderson-NY ... 7.4
Brett-KC ... 7.2
Boggs-Bos ... 5.3
Barfield-Tor ... 4.8
Murray-Bal ... 4.4

Wins
Guidry-NY ... 22
Saberhagen-KC ... 20
Viola-Min ... 18
Burns-Chi ... 18

Win Percentage
Guidry-NY ... .786
Saberhagen-KC ... .769
Leibrandt-KC ... .654
Higuera-Mil ... .652

Games
Quisenberry-KC ... 84
VandeBerg-Sea ... 76
Righetti-NY ... 74
Hernandez-Det ... 74
Nunez-Sea ... 70

Complete Games
Blyleven-Cle-Min ... 24
Moore-Sea ... 14
Hough-Tex ... 14
Morris-Det ... 13
Boyd-Bos ... 13

Shutouts
Blyleven-Cle-Min ... 5
Morris-Det ... 4
Burns-Chi ... 4

Saves
Quisenberry-KC ... 37
James-Chi ... 32
Moore-Cal ... 31
Hernandez-Det ... 31

Innings Pitched
Blyleven-Cle-Min ... 293.2
Boyd-Bos ... 272.1
Stieb-Tor ... 265.0
Alexander-Tor ... 260.2
Guidry-NY ... 259.0

Fewest Hits/Game
Stieb-Tor ... 7.00
Hough-Tex ... 7.12
Petry-Det ... 7.16
Morris-Det ... 7.42
Higuera-Mil ... 7.88

Fewest BB/Game
Haas-Mil ... 1.39
Saberhagen-KC ... 1.45
Guidry-NY ... 1.46
Butcher-Min ... 1.86
Key-Tor ... 2.12

Strikeouts
Blyleven-Cle-Min ... 206
Bannister-Chi ... 198
Morris-Det ... 191
Hurst-Bos ... 189
Witt-Cal ... 180

Strikeouts/Game
Bannister-Chi ... 8.46
Hurst-Bos ... 7.42
Burns-Chi ... 6.82
Morris-Det ... 6.69
Tanana-Tex-Det ... 6.66

Ratio
Saberhagen-KC ... 9.56
Guidry-NY ... 9.90
Key-Tor ... 10.16
Petry-Det ... 10.33
Hough-Tex ... 10.35

Earned Run Average
Stieb-Tor ... 2.48
Leibrandt-KC ... 2.69
Saberhagen-KC ... 2.87
Key-Tor ... 3.00
Blyleven-Cle-Min ... 3.16

Adjusted ERA
Stieb-Tor ... 170
Leibrandt-KC ... 155
Saberhagen-KC ... 145
Key-Tor ... 140
Seaver-Chi ... 136

Opponents' Batting Avg.
Stieb-Tor ... .213
Hough-Tex ... .215
Petry-Det ... .217
Morris-Det ... .225
Higuera-Mil ... .235

Opponents' On Base Pct.
Saberhagen-KC ... .273
Guidry-NY ... .279
Key-Tor ... .284
Hough-Tex ... .285
Petry-Det ... .285

Starter Runs
Stieb-Tor ... 49.1
Leibrandt-KC ... 38.5
Saberhagen-KC ... 33.4
Blyleven-Cle-Min ... 32.3
Key-Tor ... 27.0

Adjusted Starter Runs
Stieb-Tor ... 50.9
Leibrandt-KC ... 38.8
Blyleven-Cle-Min ... 35.4
Saberhagen-KC ... 33.8
Seaver-Chi ... 30.5

Clutch Pitching Index
Leibrandt-KC ... 121
Romanick-Cal ... 117
Boddicker-Bal ... 115
Alexander-Tor ... 114
Stieb-Tor ... 112

Relief Runs
Moore-Cal ... 25.5
Quisenberry-KC ... 25.4
James-Chi ... 24.7
Cliburn-Cal ... 22.6
Harris-Tex ... 21.1

Adjusted Relief Runs
James-Chi ... 26.8
Quisenberry-KC ... 25.4
Moore-Cal ... 25.0
Cliburn-Cal ... 22.2
Harris-Tex ... 22.1

Relief Ranking
Moore-Cal ... 49.7
James-Chi ... 48.0
Quisenberry-KC ... 44.7
Hernandez-Det ... 33.9
Righetti-NY ... 31.0

Total Pitcher Index
Stieb-Tor ... 5.5
Moore-Cal ... 5.1
James-Chi ... 4.8
Quisenberry-KC ... 4.6
Leibrandt-KC ... 4.5

Total Baseball Ranking
Henderson-NY ... 7.4
Brett-KC ... 7.2
Stieb-Tor ... 5.5
Boggs-Bos ... 5.3
Moore-Cal ... 5.1

January 8 Willie McCovey is the only player elected this year to the Hall of Fame by the BBWAA.

March 10 Ernie Lombardi, the NL MVP in 1938, and Bobby Doerr, a nine-time AL All-Star, are elected to the Hall of Fame by the Special Veterans Committee.

June 7 The Pirates take University of Arkansas's Jeff King as the first choice in the June draft. Gregg Swindell is the next pick and will be in the majors after just three starts in the minors.

June 10 The NL announces that Yale University president A. Bartlett Giamatti will be its next president, after Chub Feeney's retirement in December.

July 6 Bob Horner becomes the 11th player to hit four home runs in a game, but it isn't enough as the Braves fall to the Expos 11-8.

September 17 The Mets clinch the NL East Championship with a 4-2 win over the Cubs at Shea Stadium as Dwight Gooden tosses a six-hitter. The Mets will win 108 games this season, most in the NL since the 1975 Reds.

September 25 Houston's Mike Scott pitches a 2-0 no-hitter against the Giants at the Astrodome, clinching the NL West title for the Astros. It's the first time a pennant has ever been decided by a no-hitter, and the third consecutive game in which Astros pitchers have allowed two hits or less.

October 2 Mike Scott strikes out eight Giants in a 2-1 Astros victory to run his season total to 306, joining Sandy Koufax and J. R. Richard as the only NL pitchers to fan 300 batters in one season. Scott loses his bid for a second consecutive no-hitter when Will Clark doubles in the seventh inning.

October 15 In the longest game in postseason history, the Mets beat the Astros 7-6 in 16 innings to earn their first trip to the World Series since 1973. New York scores three runs in the top of the ninth to force extra innings. The Mets score three more runs in the top of the 16th and Houston answers with two of its own before Jesse Orosco fans Kevin Bass to end the game.

October 25 Trailing 5-3 with two out and no one on base in the bottom of the 10th inning, New York rallies to win Game 6 of the World Series 6-5 and force a deciding seventh game. After Gary Carter, Kevin Mitchell, and Ray Knight single, Bob Stanley uncorks a wild pitch that permits the tying run to score, and a hobbled Bill Buckner lets Mookie Wilson's slow bouncer skip through his legs, allowing Knight to score the winning run.

October 27 The Mets win Game 7 of the World Series 8-5 at Shea Stadium. Third baseman Ray Knight, whose home run triggers a three-run rally in the seventh inning, is named MVP.

November 11 Houston's Mike Scott (18-10) beats Fernando Valenzuela (21-11) for the NL Cy Young Award.

November 19 Phillies third baseman Mike Schmidt wins the NL MVP Award, joining Stan Musial and Roy Campanella as the only three-time winners. Schmidt led the NL with 37 home runs and 119 RBI.

ATLANTA		CHICAGO		CINCINNATI		HOUSTON		LOS ANGELES		MONTREAL	
M	C.Tanner	M	J.Frey	M	P.Rose	M	H.Lanier	M	T.Lasorda	M	B.Rodgers
1B	B.Horner	M	J.Vukovich	1B	N.Esasky	1B	G.Davis	1B	G.Brock	1B	A.Galarraga
2B	G.Hubbard	M	G.Michael	2B	R.Oester	2B	B.Doran	2B	S.Sax	2B	V.Law
SS	A.Thomas	1B	L.Durham	SS	K.Stillwell	SS	D.Thon	SS	M.Duncan	SS	H.Brooks
3B	K.Oberkfell	2B	R.Sandberg	3B	B.Bell	3B	D.Walling	3B	B.Madlock	3B	T.Wallach
LF	T.Harper	SS	S.Dunston	LF	E.Davis	LF	J.Cruz	LF	F.Stubbs	LF	T.Raines
CF	D.Murphy	3B	R.Cey	CF	E.Milner	CF	B.Hatcher	CF	R.Williams	CF	M.Webster
RF	O.Moreno	LF	G.Matthews	RF	D.Parker	RF	K.Bass	RF	M.Marshall	RF	A.Dawson
C	O.Virgil	CF	B.Dernier	C	B.Diaz	C	A.Ashby	C	M.Scioscia	C	D.Bilardello
		RF	K.Moreland								
1	C.Chambliss	C	J.Davis	O	M.Venable	3	P.Garner	1O	E.Cabell	13	W.Krenchicki
S3	R.Ramirez			S1	D.Concepcion	S	C.Reynolds	O	K.Landreaux	C	M.Fitzgerald
O	K.Griffey	O	J.Mumphrey	1	P.Rose			OS	B.Russell	S2	T.Foley
O	B.Sample			1	T.Perez	P	M.Scott	3S	D.Anderson		
		P	D.Eckersley			P	B.Knepper	C	A.Trevino	P	F.Youmans
P	R.Mahler	P	R.Sutcliffe	P	B.Gullickson	P	N.Ryan			P	J.Tibbs
P	D.Palmer	P	S.Sanderson	P	T.Browning	P	J.Deshaies	P	F.Valenzuela	P	B.Smith
P	Z.Smith	P	S.Trout	P	J.Denny	RP	C.Kerfeld	P	B.Welch	P	D.Martinez
P	D.Alexander	P	E.Lynch	P	C.Welsh	RP	A.Lopez	P	O.Hershiser	RP	A.McGaffigan
RP	J.Dedmon	RP	L.Smith	P	M.Soto	RP	L.Andersen	P	R.Honeycutt	RP	T.Burke
RP	C.McMurtry	RP	G.Hoffman	RP	T.Power			RP	K.Howell	RP	J.Reardon
RP	G.Garber	RP	D.Gumpert	RP	R.Robinson	P	D.Smith	RP	T.Niedenfuer		
				RP	J.Franco	P	D.Darwin	RP	E.Vande Berg	P	B.Sebra
P	J.Acker	P	J.Moyer							P	J.Hesketh
P	J.Johnson	P	R.Fontenot	P	S.Terry			P	J.Reuss	P	B.McClure
P	P.Assenmacher	P	J.Baller	P	C.Willis			P	A.Pena	P	D.Schatzeder
		P	G.Frazier	P	R.Murphy			P	D.Powell		

NEW YORK		PHILADELPHIA		PITTSBURGH		SAN DIEGO		SAN FRANCISCO		ST.LOUIS	
M	D.Johnson	M	J.Felske	M	J.Leyland	M	S.Boros	M	R.Craig	M	W.Herzog
1B	K.Hernandez	1B	V.Hayes	1B	S.Bream	1B	S.Garvey	1B	W.Clark	1B	J.Clark
2B	W.Backman	2B	J.Samuel	2B	J.Ray	2B	T.Flannery	2B	R.Thompson	2B	T.Herr
SS	R.Santana	SS	S.Jeltz	SS	R.Belliard	SS	G.Templeton	SS	J.Uribe	SS	O.Smith
3B	R.Knight	3B	M.Schmidt	3B	J.Morrison	3B	G.Nettles	3B	C.Brown	3B	T.Pendleton
LF	M.Wilson	LF	G.Redus	LF	R.Reynolds	LF	K.McReynolds	LF	C.Maldonado	LF	V.Coleman
CF	L.Dykstra	CF	M.Thompson	CF	B.Bonds	CF	M.Wynne	CF	D.Gladden	CF	W.McGee
RF	D.Strawberry	RF	G.Wilson	RF	J.Orsulak	RF	T.Gwynn	RF	C.Davis	RF	A.Van Slyke
C	G.Carter	C	J.Russell	C	T.Pena	C	T.Kennedy	C	B.Brenly	C	M.LaValliere
OS	K.Mitchell	O	R.Roenicke	O3	B.Almon	O	J.Kruk	O	J.Youngblood	O	C.Ford
2	T.Teufel	O	J.Stone	O1	M.Diaz	O1	C.Martinez	C	J.Leonard	O	T.Landrum
O	G.Foster	3	R.Schu	O	M.Brown	2	B.Roberts	C	B.Melvin		
3S	H.Johnson					3S	J.Royster	1O	M.Aldrete	P	B.Forsch
		P	K.Gross	P	R.Rhoden					P	D.Cox
P	D.Gooden	P	S.Rawley	P	R.Reuschel	P	A.Hawkins	P	M.Krukow	P	J.Tudor
P	R.Darling	P	B.Ruffin	P	M.Bielecki	P	D.Dravecky	P	M.LaCoss	P	G.Mathews
P	B.Ojeda	P	C.Hudson	P	B.Walk	P	L.Hoyt	P	S.Garrelts	P	T.Conroy
P	S.Fernandez	RP	D.Carman	P	B.Kipper	P	E.Show	P	V.Blue	RP	T.Worrell
P	R.Aguilera	RP	K.Tekulve	RP	L.McWilliams	RP	L.McCullers	RP	J.Robinson	RP	R.Horton
RP	R.McDowell	RP	T.Hume	RP	J.Winn	RP	C.Lefferts	RP	M.Davis	RP	P.Perry
RP	J.Orosco			RP	C.Guante	RP	G.Walter	P	J.Berenguer		
RP	D.Sisk	P	S.Bedrosian							P	R.Burris
		P	S.Carlton	P	D.Robinson	P	E.Whitson	P	K.Downs		
P	R.Anderson	P	M.Maddux	P	P.Clements	P	M.Thurmond	P	G.Minton		
						P	R.Gossage	P	R.Mason		
						P	D.LaPoint	P	T.Mulholland		
								P	F.Williams		

TEAM	G	W	L	PCT	GB	R	OR	AB	H	2B	3B	HR	BB	SO	AVG	OBP	SLG	PRO	PRO+	BR	/A	PF	CHI	RC	SB	CS	SBA	SBR
EAST																												
NY	162	108	54	.667		783	578	5558	1462	261	31	148	631	968	.263	.341	.401	.742	114	84	107	97	101	773	118	48	71	7
PHI	161	86	75	.534	21.5	739	713	5483	1386	266	39	154	589	1154	.253	.330	.400	.730	103	50	24	104	101	739	153	59	72	11
STL	161	79	82	.491	28.5	601	611	5378	1270	216	48	58	568	905	.236	.311	.327	.638	83	-119	-114	99	109	584	262	78	77	32
MON	161	78	83	.484	29.5	637	688	5508	1401	255	50	110	537	1016	.254	.324	.379	.703	101	-1	-5	99	94	676	193	95	67	1
CHI	160	70	90	.438	37	680	781	5499	1409	258	27	155	508	966	.256	.321	.398	.719	96	21	-33	108	94	697	132	62	68	2
PIT	162	64	98	.395	44	663	700	5456	1366	273	33	111	569	929	.250	.323	.374	.697	96	-12	-27	102	100	654	152	84	64	-5
WEST																												
HOU	162	96	66	.593		654	569	5441	1388	244	32	125	538	916	.255	.325	.381	.706	104	3	22	97	98	668	163	75	68	4
CIN	162	86	76	.531	10	732	717	5536	1404	237	35	144	586	920	.254	.327	.387	.714	99	21	-9	104	104	712	177	53	77	21
SF	162	83	79	.512	13	698	618	5501	1394	269	25	114	456	1087	.253	.325	.375	.699	104	-9	24	95	104	674	148	93	61	-11
SD	162	74	88	.457	22	656	723	5515	1442	239	25	136	484	917	.261	.323	.388	.711	104	9	23	98	97	671	96	68	59	-12
LA	162	73	89	.451	23	638	679	5471	1373	232	14	130	478	966	.251	.315	.370	.685	102	-42	2	93	102	639	155	67	70	6
ATL	161	72	89	.447	23.5	615	719	5384	1348	241	24	138	538	904	.250	.321	.381	.702	94	-5	-42	106	93	646	93	76	55	-18
TOT	969					8096		65730	16643	2991	387	1523	6560	11648	.253	.324	.380	.704						1842	858	68	38	

TEAM	CG	SH	SV	IP	H	H/G	HR	BB	SO	RAT	ERA	ERA+	OAV	OOB	PR	/A	PF	CPI	FA	E	DP	FW	PW	BW	SBW	DIF
EAST																										
NY	27	11	46	1484	1304	7.9	103	509	1083	11.2	3.11	114	.236	.304	100	70	95	98	.978	138	145	.1	7.3	11.1	.4	8.1
PHI	22	11	39	1451²	1473	9.1	130	553	874	12.7	3.85	100	.265	.334	-22	0	104	105	.978	137	157	.1	.0	2.5	.8	2.1
STL	17	4	46	1466¹	1364	8.4	135	485	761	11.5	3.37	108	.250	.314	56	44	98	106	.981	123	178	.9	4.6	-11.8	3.0	1.9
MON	15	9	50	1466¹	1350	8.3	119	566	1051	12.0	3.78	98	.246	.320	-11	-15	99	93	.979	133	132	.3	-1.6	.5	-.2	-1.6
CHI	11	6	42	1445	1546	9.6	143	557	962	13.2	4.49	90	.279	.346	-124	-72	109	94	.980	124	147	.8	-7.5	-3.4	-.1	.2
PIT	17	9	30	1450²	1397	8.7	138	570	924	12.4	3.90	98	.255	.329	-30	-11	103	100	.978	143	134	-.2	-1.1	-2.8	-.8	-12.0
WEST																										
HOU	18	19	51	1456¹	1203	7.4	116	523	1160	10.8	3.15	114	.225	.297	92	73	97	93	.979	130	108	.6	7.6	2.3	.0	4.5
CIN	14	8	45	1468	1465	9.0	136	524	924	12.3	3.91	99	.264	.329	-32	-7	104	101	.978	140	160	.0	-.7	-.9	1.9	4.8
SF	18	10	35	1460¹	1264	7.8	121	591	992	11.6	3.33	106	.236	.316	62	30	95	101	.977	143	149	-.2	3.1	2.5	-1.5	-2.0
SD	13	7	32	1443¹	1406	8.8	150	607	934	12.7	3.99	92	.258	.335	-44	-54	98	102	.978	137	135	.2	-5.6	2.4	-1.6	-2.4
LA	35	14	25	1454¹	1428	8.8	115	499	1051	12.1	3.76	92	.256	.320	-7	-51	93	96	.971	181	118	-2.2	-5.3	.2	.3	-1.0
ATL	17	5	39	1424²	1443	9.1	117	576	932	12.9	3.97	100	.266	.340	-41	0	107	103	.978	141	181	-.1	.0	-4.4	-2.2	-1.8
TOT	224	113	480	17471		8.6				12.1	3.72		.253	.324					.978	1670	1744					

Runs
Hayes-Phi	107
Gwynn-SD	107
Schmidt-Phi	97
Davis-Cin	97

Hits
Gwynn-SD	211
Sax-LA	210
Raines-Mon	194
Hayes-Phi	186
Bass-Hou	184

Doubles
Hayes-Phi	46
Sax-LA	43
Dunston-Chi	37
Bream-Pit	37
Samuel-Phi	36

Triples
Webster-Mon	13
Samuel-Phi	12
Raines-Mon	10
Coleman-StL	8

Home Runs
Schmidt-Phi	37
Parker-Cin	31
Davis-Hou	31
Murphy-Atl	29

Total Bases
Parker-Cin	304
Schmidt-Phi	302
Gwynn-SD	300
Murphy-Atl	293
Hayes-Phi	293

Runs Batted In
Schmidt-Phi	119
Parker-Cin	116
Carter-NY	105
Davis-Hou	101
Hayes-Phi	98

Runs Produced
Hayes-Phi	186
Schmidt-Phi	179
Parker-Cin	174
Hernandez-NY	164
Carter-NY	162

Bases On Balls
Hernandez-NY	94
Schmidt-Phi	89
C.Davis-SF	84
Oberkfell-Atl	83
Doran-Hou	81

Batting Average
Raines-Mon	.334
Sax-LA	.332
Gwynn-SD	.329
Bass-Hou	.311
Hernandez-NY	.310

On Base Percentage
Raines-Mon	.415
Hernandez-NY	.414
Schmidt-Phi	.395
Sax-LA	.391
Gwynn-SD	.382

Slugging Average
Schmidt-Phi	.547
Strawberry-NY	.507
McReynolds-SD	.504
Davis-Hou	.493
Bass-Hou	.486

Production
Schmidt-Phi	.942
Raines-Mon	.891
Strawberry-NY	.871
McReynolds-SD	.867
Hayes-Phi	.861

Adjusted Production
Schmidt-Phi	152
Raines-Mon	146
Strawberry-NY	142
Hernandez-NY	141
McReynolds-SD	140

Batter Runs
Schmidt-Phi	44.0
Raines-Mon	38.0
Hernandez-NY	32.2
Hayes-Phi	30.3
Gwynn-SD	28.4

Adjusted Batter Runs
Schmidt-Phi	40.0
Raines-Mon	39.0
Hernandez-NY	35.3
Sax-LA	33.4
Gwynn-SD	30.6

Clutch Hitting Index
Carter-NY	132
Pendleton-StL	123
Cruz-NY	121
Uribe-SF	121
Jeltz-Phi	120

Runs Created
Raines-Mon	130
Schmidt-Phi	122
Gwynn-SD	113
Hayes-Phi	111
Sax-LA	110

Total Average
Raines-Mon	1.040
Schmidt-Phi	.988
Strawberry-NY	.910
Hernandez-NY	.873
McReynolds-SD	.848

Stolen Bases
Coleman-StL	107
Davis-Cin	80
Raines-Mon	70
Duncan-LA	48

Stolen Base Average
Dernier-Chi	93.1
Raines-Mon	88.6
Coleman-StL	88.4
Davis-Cin	87.9
Leonard-SF	84.2

Stolen Base Runs
Coleman-StL	23.7
Davis-Cin	17.4
Raines-Mon	15.6
Dernier-Chi	6.9

Fielding Runs
Hubbard-Atl	41.0
Pendleton-StL	24.2
Bream-Pit	22.8
Wilson-Pit	20.6
Dunston-Chi	20.3

Total Player Rating
Raines-Mon	6.2
Gwynn-SD	5.2
Hernandez-NY	4.4
Sax-LA	3.7
Hubbard-Atl	3.5

Wins
Valenzuela-LA	21
Krukow-SF	20
Scott-Hou	18
Ojeda-NY	18

Win Percentage
Ojeda-NY	.783
Gooden-NY	.739
Fernandez-NY	.727
Darling-NY	.714
Krukow-SF	.690

Games
Lefferts-SD	83
McDowell-NY	75
Worrell-StL	74
Franco-Cin	74
Tekulve-Phi	73

Complete Games
Valenzuela-LA	20
Rhoden-Pit	12
Gooden-NY	12
Krukow-SF	10

Shutouts
Scott-Hou	5
Knepper-Hou	5
Welch-LA	3
Valenzuela-LA	3

Saves
Worrell-StL	36
Reardon-Mon	35
Smith-Hou	33
Smith-Chi	31

Innings Pitched
Scott-Hou	275.1
Valenzuela-LA	269.1
Knepper-Hou	258.0
Rhoden-Pit	253.2
Gooden-NY	250.0

Fewest Hits/Game
Scott-Hou	5.95
Youmans-Mon	5.96
Ryan-Hou	6.02
Fernandez-NY	7.09
Gooden-NY	7.09

Fewest BB/Game
Eckersley-Chi	1.93
Sanderson-Chi	1.96
Krukow-SF	2.02
Welch-LA	2.10
Ojeda-NY	2.15

Strikeouts
Scott-Hou	306
Valenzuela-LA	242
Youmans-Mon	202
Gooden-NY	200
Fernandez-NY	200

Strikeouts/Game
Scott-Hou	10.00
Ryan-Hou	9.81
Fernandez-NY	8.81
Youmans-Mon	8.30
Valenzuela-LA	8.09

Ratio
Scott-Hou	8.37
Krukow-SF	9.66
Ojeda-NY	9.90
Gooden-NY	10.12
Rhoden-Pit	10.25

Earned Run Average
Scott-Hou	2.22
Ojeda-NY	2.57
Darling-NY	2.81
Rhoden-Pit	2.84
Gooden-NY	2.84

Adjusted ERA
Scott-Hou	162
Ojeda-NY	138
Rhoden-Pit	135
Darling-NY	126
Cox-StL	125

Opponents' Batting Avg.
Scott-Hou	.186
Ryan-Hou	.188
Youmans-Mon	.188
Gooden-NY	.215
Fernandez-NY	.216

Opponents' On Base Pct.
Scott-Hou	.244
Krukow-SF	.271
Ojeda-NY	.279
Gooden-NY	.280
Ryan-Hou	.285

Starter Runs
Scott-Hou	45.7
Ojeda-NY	27.7
Rhoden-Pit	24.7
Gooden-NY	24.2
Darling-NY	23.9

Adjusted Starter Runs
Scott-Hou	42.1
Rhoden-Pit	28.0
Ojeda-NY	23.3
Ruffin-Phi	22.6
Gooden-NY	19.2

Clutch Pitching Index
Dravecky-SD	115
Darling-NY	113
Garrelts-SF	110
Tudor-StL	109
Gullickson-Cin	109

Relief Runs
Worrell-StL	18.8
McGaffigan-Mon	16.9
Horton-StL	16.4
Tekulve-Phi	14.4
McCullers-SD	14.2

Adjusted Relief Runs
Worrell-StL	17.9
McGaffigan-Mon	16.5
Tekulve-Phi	16.1
Horton-StL	15.6
McCullers-SD	13.2

Relief Ranking
Worrell-StL	40.8
Smith-Chi	23.1
Tekulve-Phi	22.1
Orosco-NY	21.9
Garber-Atl	21.3

Total Pitcher Index
Scott-Hou	4.3
Worrell-StL	4.2
Rhoden-Pit	4.0
Smith-Chi	2.4
Garber-Atl	2.4

Total Baseball Ranking
Raines-Mon	6.2
Gwynn-SD	5.2
Hernandez-NY	4.4
Scott-Hou	4.3
Worrell-StL	4.1

March 27 Baseball's Rules Committee votes to change the DH rule for the World Series, allowing a DH to be used in all games played in the AL club's home park. Since 1976, the DH had been used in all games in alternating years.

April 29 Twenty-three-year-old Red Sox pitcher Roger Clemens strikes out 20 batters in a 3-1 win over Seattle, breaking the ML record of 19 shared by Nolan Ryan, Steve Carlton, and Tom Seaver. Clemens doesn't walk a batter, allows just three hits, and ties the AL record with eight consecutive strikeouts in the middle innings.

June 18 California's Don Sutton becomes the 19th pitcher in major league history to win 300 games, beating the Rangers 3-1 on a three-hitter.

June 21 Bo Jackson, Heisman Trophy winner in 1985 and the first pick (by Tampa Bay) in the NFL draft, stuns observers nationwide by signing with the Kansas City Royals instead.

October 4 On the next-to-last day of the season, Dave Righetti saves both ends of the Yankees' doubleheader sweep of the Red Sox to give him a record 46 saves. Bruce Sutter and Dan Quisenberry had shared the record with 45.

October 12 One loss away from elimination and trailing 5-2 entering the ninth, the Red Sox stage one of the most improbable comebacks in postseason history, winning 7-6 over the Angels in 11 innings. After Don Baylor's ninth-inning home run reduces the deficit to 5-4, reserve outfielder Dave Henderson slugs a two-out, two-run home run off Donnie Moore to give Boston a 6-5 lead. California ties the score with a run in the bottom of the ninth but Henderson, who had appeared to be the goat when he dropped Bobby Grich's long fly ball over the fence for a home run in the seventh inning, delivers a sacrifice fly in the eleventh for the winning run.

October 15 Boston routs California 8-1 in the seventh game of the ALCS and advances to the World Series. The game caps yet another heartbreaking failure for Angels skipper Gene Mauch, who in Game 5 was one strike away from reaching his first World Series in 25 seasons as a major league manager.

October 18 Boston wins Game 1 of the World Series 1-0 when Tim Teufel botches Rich Gedman's routine grounder in the seventh inning, allowing Jim Rice to score the game's only run. Bruce Hurst and Calvin Schiraldi combine on a four-hitter for the Red Sox.

November 12 Roger Clemens wins the AL Cy Young Award unanimously, joining Denny McLain (1968) as the only pitchers to do so.

November 18 Roger Clemens becomes the first starting pitcher to win the AL MVP Award since Vida Blue in 1971.

	BALTIMORE		BOSTON		CALIFORNIA		CHICAGO		CLEVELAND		DETROIT		KANSAS CITY
M	E.Weaver	M	J.McNamara	M	G.Mauch	M	T.LaRussa	M	P.Corrales	M	S.Anderson	M	D.Howser
1B	E.Murray	1B	B.Buckner	1B	W.Joyner	M	D.Rader	1B	P.Tabler	1B	D.Evans	M	M.Ferraro
2B	J.Bonilla	2B	M.Barrett	2B	R.Wilfong	M	J.Fregosi	2B	T.Bernazard	2B	L.Whitaker	1B	S.Balboni
SS	C.Ripken	SS	E.Romero	SS	D.Schofield	1B	G.Walker	SS	J.Franco	SS	A.Trammell	2B	F.White
3B	F.Rayford	3B	W.Boggs	3B	D.DeCinces	2B	J.Cruz	3B	B.Jacoby	3B	D.Coles	SS	A.Salazar
LF	J.Shelby	LF	J.Rice	LF	B.Downing	SS	O.Guillen	LF	M.Hall	LF	D.Collins	3B	G.Brett
CF	F.Lynn	CF	T.Armas	CF	G.Pettis	3B	T.Hulett	CF	B.Butler	CF	C.Lemon	LF	L.Smith
RF	L.Lacy	RF	D.Evans	RF	R.Jones	LF	R.Nichols	RF	J.Carter	RF	K.Gibson	CF	W.Wilson
C	R.Dempsey	C	R.Gedman	C	B.Boone	CF	J.Cangelosi	C	A.Allanson	C	L.Parrish	RF	R.Law
DH	L.Sheets	DH	D.Baylor	DH	R.Jackson	RF	H.Baines	DH	A.Thornton	DH	J.Grubb	C	J.Sundberg
						C	C.Fisk					DH	J.Orta
O3	J.Beniquez	P	R.Clemens	21	B.Grich	DH	R.Kittle	O	O.Nixon	32	T.Brookens		
OD	M.Young	P	O.Boyd	O	G.Hendrick			OS	C.Snyder	OD	L.Herndon	S2	B.Biancalana
2	A.Wiggins	P	B.Hurst	DS	R.Burleson	D1	J.Hairston	C	C.Bando	O	P.Sheridan	D	H.McRae
1D	J.Traber	P	A.Nipper			3S	W.Tolleson	OD	C.Castillo			C3	J.Quirk
		P	T.Seaver	P	M.Witt	O1	B.Bonilla			P	J.Morris	O	D.Motley
P	M.Boddicker	RP	B.Stanley	P	K.McCaskill			P	T.Candiotti	P	W.Terrell	O	M.Kingery
P	S.McGregor	RP	S.Stewart	P	D.Sutton	P	R.Dotson	P	P.Niekro	P	F.Tanana		
P	K.Dixon	RP	S.Crawford	P	R.Romanick	P	F.Bannister	P	K.Schrom	P	E.King	P	C.Leibrandt
P	M.Flanagan			RP	D.Corbett	P	J.Cowley	RP	S.Bailes	P	R.O'Neal	P	D.Leonard
P	S.Davis	P	J.Sellers	RP	D.Moore	P	N.Allen	RP	R.Yett	RP	W.Hernandez	P	D.Jackson
RP	R.Bordi	P	M.Brown			P	J.Davis	RP	B.Oelkers	RP	B.Campbell	P	M.Gubicza
RP	D.Aase	P	C.Schiraldi	P	J.Candelaria	RP	G.Nelson			RP	M.Thurmond	P	B.Saberhagen
RP	N.Snell			P	J.Slaton	RP	B.Dawley	P	D.Schulze			RP	B.Black
						RP	D.Schmidt	P	N.Heaton	P	D.Petry	RP	S.Farr
P	B.Havens							/P	G.Swindell	P	D.LaPoint	RP	D.Quisenberry
						P	J.DeLeon	P	E.Camacho				
						P	T.Seaver	P	D.Noles			P	S.Bankhead
						P	S.Carlton	P	J.Butcher				
						P	B.James						

	MILWAUKEE		MINNESOTA		NEW YORK		OAKLAND		SEATTLE		TEXAS		TORONTO
M	G.Bamberger	M	R.Miller	M	L.Piniella	M	J.Moore	M	C.Cottier	M	B.Valentine	M	J.Williams
M	T.Trebelhorn	M	T.Kelly	1B	D.Mattingly	M	J.Newman	M	M.Martinez	1B	P.O'Brien	1B	W.Upshaw
1B	B.Robidoux	1B	K.Hrbek	2B	W.Randolph	M	T.LaRussa	D	D.Williams	2B	T.Harrah	2B	D.Garcia
2B	J.Gantner	2B	S.Lombardozzi	SS	W.Tolleson	1B	B.Bochte	1B	A.Davis	SS	S.Fletcher	SS	T.Fernandez
SS	E.Riles	SS	G.Gagne	3B	M.Pagliarulo	2B	T.Phillips	2B	H.Reynolds	3B	S.Buechele	3B	R.Mulliniks
3B	P.Molitor	3B	G.Gaetti	LF	D.Pasqua	SS	A.Griffin	SS	S.Owen	LF	R.Sierra	LF	G.Bell
LF	R.Manning	LF	R.Bush	CF	R.Henderson	3B	C.Lansford	3B	J.Presley	CF	O.McDowell	CF	L.Moseby
CF	R.Yount	CF	K.Puckett	RF	D.Winfield	LF	J.Canseco	LF	P.Bradley	RF	P.Incaviglia	RF	J.Barfield
RF	R.Deer	RF	T.Brunansky	C	B.Wynegar	CF	D.Murphy	CF	J.Moses	C	D.Slaught	C	E.Whitt
C	C.Moore	C	M.Salas	DH	M.Easler	RF	M.Davis	RF	D.Tartabull	DH	L.Parrish	DH	C.Johnson
DH	C.Cooper	DH	R.Smalley			C	M.Tettleton	C	B.Kearney				
				P	D.Rasmussen	DH	D.Kingman	DH	G.Thomas	O	G.Ward	32	G.Iorg
OD	B.Oglivie	OD	M.Hatcher	P	R.Guidry					2S	C.Wilkerson	DO	R.Leach
32	D.Sveum			P	D.Drabek	23	D.Hill	OD	D.Henderson	O1	T.Paciorek		
C1	B.Schroeder	P	B.Blyleven	P	B.Tewksbury	OD	D.Baker	1D	K.Phelps			P	J.Key
C	R.Cerone	P	F.Viola	P	J.Niekro					P	C.Hough	P	J.Clancy
O	G.Braggs	P	M.Smithson	RP	D.Righetti	P	C.Young	P	M.Moore	P	E.Correa	P	D.Stieb
		P	N.Heaton	RP	B.Shirley	P	J.Rijo	P	M.Langston	P	J.Guzman	P	J.Cerutti
P	T.Higuera	P	M.Portugal	RP	B.Fisher	P	J.Andujar	P	M.Morgan	P	B.Witt	P	D.Alexander
P	B.Wegman	RP	K.Atherton			P	D.Stewart	P	B.Swift	P	M.Mason	RP	M.Eichhorn
P	T.Leary	RP	F.Pastore	P	T.John	P	E.Plunk	RP	M.Young	RP	G.Harris	RP	T.Henke
P	J.Nieves			P	S.Nielsen	RP	B.Mooneyham	RP	M.Huismann	RP	M.Williams	RP	D.Lamp
P	D.Darwin					RP	S.Ontiveros	RP	L.Guetterman	RP	J.Russell		
RP	D.Plesac	P	A.Anderson			RP	J.Howell					P	J.Johnson
RP	M.Clear	P	J.Butcher					P	P.Ladd	P	D.Mohorcic	P	J.Acker
RP	B.Clutterbuck					P	C.Codiroli	P	M.Wilcox	P	M.Mahler		
						P	M.Haas						
						P	R.Langford						

TEAM	G	W	L	PCT	GB	R	OR	AB	H	2B	3B	HR	BB	SO	AVG	OBP	SLG	PRO	PRO+	BR	/A	PF	CHI	RC	SB	CS	SBA	SBR
EAST																												
BOS	161	95	66	.590		794	696	5498	1488	320	21	144	595	707	.271	.349	.415	.764	107	59	57	100	98	792	41	34	55	-8
NY	162	90	72	.556	5.5	797	738	5570	1512	275	23	188	645	911	.271	.350	.430	.780	112	89	99	99	94	843	139	48	74	13
DET	162	87	75	.537	8.5	798	714	5512	1447	234	30	198	613	885	.263	.341	.424	.765	107	52	55	100	99	814	138	58	70	7
TOR	163	86	76	.531	9.5	809	733	5716	1540	285	35	181	496	848	.269	.331	.427	.758	102	29	10	102	103	796	110	59	65	-2
CLE	163	84	78	.519	11.5	831	841	5702	1620	270	45	157	456	944	.284	.340	.430	.770	110	57	72	98	102	822	141	54	72	10
MIL	161	77	84	.478	18	667	734	5461	1393	255	38	127	530	986	.255	.324	.385	.709	89	-59	-80	103	98	682	100	50	67	0
BAL	162	73	89	.451	22.5	708	760	5524	1425	223	13	169	563	862	.258	.330	.395	.725	97	-28	-17	99	99	708	64	34	65	-1
WEST																												
CAL	162	92	70	.568		786	684	5433	1387	236	36	167	671	860	.255	.341	.404	.745	103	22	31	99	101	765	109	42	72	8
TEX	162	87	75	.537	5	771	743	5529	1479	248	43	184	511	1088	.267	.333	.428	.761	103	37	18	102	99	761	103	85	55	-20
KC	162	76	86	.469	16	654	673	5561	1403	264	45	137	474	919	.252	.315	.390	.705	88	-77	-90	102	99	683	97	46	68	2
OAK	162	76	86	.469	16	731	760	5435	1370	213	25	163	553	983	.252	.325	.390	.715	101	-48	3	93	106	700	139	61	70	5
CHI	162	72	90	.444	20	644	699	5406	1335	197	34	121	487	940	.247	.313	.363	.676	81	-125	-144	103	107	614	115	54	68	2
MIN	162	71	91	.438	21	741	839	5531	1446	257	39	196	501	977	.261	.327	.428	.755	100	21	2	103	97	756	81	61	57	-12
SEA	162	67	95	.414	25	718	835	5498	1392	243	41	158	572	1148	.253	.327	.399	.726	95	-28	-33	101	100	706	93	76	55	-18
TOT	1134					10449		77376	20237	3520	468	2290	7667	13058	.262	.332	.408	.740							1470	762	66	-16

TEAM	CG	SH	SV	IP	H	H/G	HR	BB	SO	RAT	ERA	ERA+	OAV	OOB	PR	/A	PF	CPI	FA	E	DP	FW	PW	BW	SBW	DIF
EAST																										
BOS	36	6	41	1429²	1469	9.2	167	474	1033	12.4	3.93	106	.266	.327	38	36	100	106	.979	129	146	-.2	3.5	5.6	-.7	6.2
NY	13	8	58	1443¹	1461	9.1	175	492	878	12.3	4.11	99	.263	.325	11	-3	98	100	.979	127	153	.0	-.3	9.7	1.4	-1.8
DET	33	12	38	1443²	1374	8.6	183	571	880	12.3	4.02	102	.251	.325	25	16	99	100	.982	108	163	1.1	1.6	5.4	.8	-2.9
TOR	16	12	44	1476	1467	8.9	164	487	1002	12.2	4.08	103	.261	.325	16	23	101	99	.984	100	150	1.7	2.3	1.0	-.0	.2
CLE	31	7	34	1447²	1548	9.6	167	605	744	13.7	4.58	91	.273	.349	-64	-70	99	101	.975	157	148	-1.7	-6.9	7.1	1.1	3.4
MIL	29	12	32	1431²	1478	9.3	158	494	952	12.6	4.01	108	.267	.330	26	50	104	104	.976	146	146	-1.2	4.9	-7.9	.1	.5
BAL	17	6	39	1436²	1451	9.1	177	535	954	12.6	4.30	96	.263	.330	-20	-27	99	98	.978	135	163	-.5	-2.7	-1.7	.0	-3.2
WEST																										
CAL	29	12	40	1456	1356	8.4	153	478	955	11.5	3.84	107	.248	.311	54	44	98	94	.983	107	156	1.2	4.3	3.0	.9	1.5
TEX	15	8	41	1450¹	1356	8.4	145	736	1059	13.2	4.11	105	.249	.342	11	31	103	100	.980	122	160	.3	3.0	1.8	-1.9	2.7
KC	24	13	31	1440²	1413	8.8	121	499	888	12.1	3.82	111	.258	.322	56	68	102	98	.980	123	153	.2	6.7	-8.8		-3.4
OAK	22	8	37	1433	1334	8.4	166	667	937	12.8	4.31	90	.247	.333	-21	-70	93	94	.978	135	120	-.5	-6.9	.3	.6	1.4
CHI	18	8	38	1442¹	1361	8.5	143	561	937	12.2	3.93	110	.251	.325	39	61	103	97	.981	117	142	.6	6.0	-14.2	-.9	-1.8
MIN	39	6	24	1432²	1579	9.9	200	503	937	13.4	4.77	90	.281	.345	-94	-74	103	101	.980	118	168	.5	-7.3	.2	-1.1	-2.4
SEA	33	5	27	1439²	1590	9.9	171	585	944	13.9	4.65	91	.283	.355	-76	-65	102	105	.975	156	191	-1.7	-6.4	-3.2	-1.7	-1.0
TOT	355	123	524	20203¹		9.0				12.7	4.18		.262	.332					.979	1780	2159					

Runs
Henderson-NY 130
Puckett-Min 119
Mattingly-NY 117
Carter-Cle 108

Hits
Mattingly-NY 238
Puckett-Min 223
Fernandez-Tor 213
Boggs-Bos 207

Doubles
Mattingly-NY 53
Boggs-Bos 47
Rice-Bos 39
Buckner-Bos 39
Barrett-Bos 39

Triples
Butler-Cle 14
Sierra-Tex 10
Fernandez-Tor 9
Carter-Cle 9

Home Runs
Barfield-Tor 40
Kingman-Oak 35
Gaetti-Min 34
Deer-Mil 33
Canseco-Oak 33

Total Bases
Mattingly-NY 388
Puckett-Min 365
Carter-Cle 341
Bell-Tor 341
Barfield-Tor 329

Runs Batted In
Carter-Cle 121
Canseco-Oak 117
Mattingly-NY 113
Rice-Bos 110

Runs Produced
Carter-Cle 200
Mattingly-NY 199
Rice-Bos 188
Puckett-Min 184
Bell-Tor 178

Bases On Balls
Boggs-Bos 105
Evans-Bos 97
Randolph-NY 94
Jackson-Cal 92
Evans-Det 91

Batting Average
Boggs-Bos .... .357
Mattingly-NY .... .352
Puckett-Min .... .328
Tabler-Cle .... .326
Rice-Bos .... .324

On Base Percentage
Boggs-Bos .... .455
P.Bradley-Sea .... .406
Brett-KC .... .404
Murray-Bal .... .400
Mattingly-NY .... .399

Slugging Average
Mattingly-NY .... .573
Barfield-Tor .... .559
Puckett-Min .... .537
Bell-Tor .... .532
Gaetti-Min .... .518

Production
Mattingly-NY .... .973
Boggs-Bos .... .942
Barfield-Tor .... .929
Puckett-Min .... .903
Brett-KC .... .885

Adjusted Production
Mattingly-NY 163
Boggs-Bos 156
Barfield-Tor 145
Puckett-Min 138
Rice-Bos 137

Batter Runs
Mattingly-NY 55.6
Boggs-Bos 51.6
Barfield-Tor 39.0
Puckett-Min 37.1
Rice-Bos 32.6

Adjusted Batter Runs
Mattingly-NY 57.3
Boggs-Bos 51.1
Barfield-Tor 36.1
Puckett-Min 34.1
Rice-Bos 32.3

Clutch Hitting Index
Phillips-Oak 135
Buckner-Bos 127
Cooper-Mil 126
Canseco-Oak 125
Downing-Cal 122

Runs Created
Mattingly-NY 150
Boggs-Bos 133
Puckett-Min 127
Barfield-Tor 122
Carter-Cle 116

Total Average
Boggs-Bos .... .987
Mattingly-NY .... .969
Gibson-Det .... .950
Barfield-Tor .... .931
Henderson-NY .... .931

Stolen Bases
Henderson-NY 87
Pettis-Cal 50
Cangelosi-Chi 50
Wilson-KC 34
Gibson-Det 34

Stolen Base Average
Felder-Mil 88.9
Davis-Oak 87.1
Gibson-Det 85.0
Henderson-NY 82.9

Stolen Base Runs
Henderson-NY 15.3
Pettis-Cal 7.2
Gibson-Det 6.6
Davis-Oak 5.7
Wilson-KC 5.4

Fielding Runs
Owen-Sea-Bos 31.9
Reynolds-Sea 29.0
Barfield-Tor 20.9
Pettis-Cal 20.7
Buckner-Bos 20.1

Total Player Rating
Barfield-Tor 4.8
Ripken-Bal 4.4
Boggs-Bos 4.3
Rice-Bos 4.2
Henderson-NY 4.2

Wins
Clemens-Bos 24
Morris-Det 21
Higuera-Mil 20
Witt-Cal 18
Rasmussen-NY 18

Win Percentage
Clemens-Bos .... .857
Rasmussen-NY .... .750
Morris-Det .... .724
Higuera-Mil .... .645
Witt-Cal .... .643

Games
Williams-Tex 80
Righetti-NY 74
Harris-Tex 73
Eichhorn-Tor 69

Complete Games
Candiotti-Cle 17
Blyleven-Min 16
Morris-Det 15
Higuera-Mil 15
Witt-Cal 14

Shutouts
Morris-Det 6
Hurst-Bos 4
Higuera-Mil 4

Saves
Righetti-NY 46
Aase-Bal 34
Henke-Tor 27
Hernandez-Det 24
Moore-Cal 21

Innings Pitched
Blyleven-Min 271.2
Witt-Cal 269.0
Morris-Det 267.0
Moore-Sea 266.0
Clemens-Bos 254.0

Fewest Hits/Game
Clemens-Bos 6.34
Rasmussen-NY 7.13
Witt-Cal 7.29
Hough-Tex 7.35
Cowley-Chi 7.37

Fewest BB/Game
Guidry-NY 1.78
Boyd-Bos 1.89
Blyleven-Min 1.92
Wegman-Mil 1.95
Sutton-Cal 2.13

Strikeouts
Langston-Sea 245
Clemens-Bos 238
Morris-Det 223
Blyleven-Min 215
Witt-Cal 208

Strikeouts/Game
Langston-Sea 9.21
Hurst-Bos 8.62
Clemens-Bos 8.43
Correa-Tex 8.41
Rijo-Oak 8.18

Ratio
Clemens-Bos 8.86
Witt-Cal 9.84
Morris-Det 10.48
Rasmussen-NY 10.51
Sutton-Cal 10.61

Earned Run Average
Clemens-Bos 2.48
Higuera-Mil 2.79
Witt-Cal 2.84
Hurst-Bos 2.99
D.Jackson-KC 3.20

Adjusted ERA
Clemens-Bos 168
Higuera-Mil 155
Witt-Cal 144
Hurst-Bos 139
D.Jackson-KC 133

Opponents' Batting Avg.
Clemens-Bos .... .195
Rasmussen-NY .... .217
Witt-Cal .... .221
Hough-Tex .... .221
Correa-Tex .... .223

Opponents' On Base Pct.
Clemens-Bos .... .253
Witt-Cal .... .277
Morris-Det .... .287
Sutton-Cal .... .288
Rasmussen-NY .... .290

Starter Runs
Clemens-Bos 47.8
Witt-Cal 39.8
Higuera-Mil 38.2
Morris-Det 26.9
Hurst-Bos 22.9

Adjusted Starter Runs
Clemens-Bos 47.5
Higuera-Mil 42.4
Witt-Cal 37.8
Morris-Det 25.3
Hurst-Bos 22.6

Clutch Pitching Index
Hurst-Bos 123
D.Jackson-KC 121
Higuera-Mil 119
Stieb-Tor 119
Niekro-Cle 117

Relief Runs
Eichhorn-Tor 42.8
Righetti-NY 20.5
Harris-Tex 16.7
Clear-Mil 16.2
Mohorcic-Tex 14.7

Adjusted Relief Runs
Eichhorn-Tor 43.6
Righetti-NY 19.4
Harris-Tex 18.2
Clear-Mil 17.4
Mohorcic-Tex 15.8

Relief Ranking
Eichhorn-Tor 55.3
Righetti-NY 42.6
Harris-Tex 32.8
Clear-Mil 28.6
Plesac-Mil 27.2

Total Pitcher Index
Eichhorn-Tor 5.7
Clemens-Bos 4.9
Higuera-Mil 4.8
Righetti-NY 4.3
Witt-Cal 4.0

Total Baseball Ranking
Eichhorn-Tor 5.7
Clemens-Bos 4.9
Higuera-Mil 4.8
Barfield-Tor 4.8
Ripken-Bal 4.4

April 8 Faced with a storm of criticism, the Dodgers fire VP Al Campanis for racially insensitive remarks he made on the April 6 telecast of ABC-TV's *Nightline* news show.

April 19 Cardinals ace John Tudor suffers a broken leg when Mets catcher Barry Lyons crashes into him in the St. Louis dugout while chasing a foul pop. Tudor, who was not pitching, will be sidelined until August.

June 22 Tom Seaver abandons his comeback attempt with the injury-riddled Mets and retires with a career W-L record of 311-205, an ERA of 2.86, 3,640 K's (third behind Nolan Ryan and Steve Carlton), and 61 shutouts.

July 14 Tim Raines caps a 3-for-3 performance in the All-Star Game with a two-run triple in the top of the thirteenth inning, giving the NL a 2-0 victory.

July 14 The BBWAA votes to rename the Rookie of the Year Award in honor of Jackie Robinson, who broke baseball's color barrier on the way to winning the first Rookie of the Year Award in 1947.

August 10 Phillies pitcher Kevin Gross becomes the second pitcher in eight days to be ejected for scuffing the baseball when umpires discover sandpaper in his glove during the fifth inning of a 4-2 win over the Cubs. Like Joe Niekro, Gross will be suspended for 10 games.

September 1 Williamsport (Eastern League) Bills catcher Dave Bresnahan introduces a new wrinkle to baseball—the hidden potato. With a Reading runner, Rick Rudblad, on third, Bresnahan returns from a time out with a shaved potato hidden in his mitt. On the next pitch he throws the potato wildly on a pickoff attempt. When the runner trots home, Bresnahan tags him out with the real ball. The umpire, unamused, rules the runner safe, gives the catcher an error, and fines him $50. He is released the following day. That same night, their last game of the season, the Bills admit any fan for a $1 and a potato. On each potato, Bresnahan autographs, "This spud's for you."

September 21 Darryl Strawberry joins Howard Johnson as the first teammates ever to achieve 30 homers and 30 steals in the same season.

September 28 The Giants and Twins win their divisions, ending 16- and 17-year droughts, respectively. SF clinches its first NL West title since 1971 with a 5-4 win at San Diego, while Minnesota clinches its first AL West title since 1970 with a 5-3 win at Texas.

October 14 Danny Cox pitches the Cardinals' second consecutive shutout 6-0 over the Giants in Game 7 of the NLCS, to send St. Louis to the World Series for the third time in the 1980s. Giants outfielder Jeffrey Leonard (.417, 4 home runs) is named series MVP.

November 10 In the closest vote in the award's history, Steve Bedrosian edges Rick Sutcliffe 57-55 to win the NL Cy Young Award. Bedrosian is the third reliever to win the award in the NL.

November 18 Cubs outfielder Andre Dawson becomes the first player from a last-place club to win an MVP Award.

	ATLANTA		CHICAGO		CINCINNATI		HOUSTON		LOS ANGELES		MONTREAL
M	C.Tanner	M	G.Michael	M	P.Rose	M	H.Lanier	M	T.Lasorda	M	B.Rodgers
1B	G.Perry	1B	F.Lucchesi	1B	N.Esasky	1B	G.Davis	1B	F.Stubbs	1B	A.Galarraga
2B	G.Hubbard	1B	L.Durham	2B	R.Oester	2B	B.Doran	2B	S.Sax	2B	V.Law
SS	A.Thomas	2B	R.Sandberg	SS	B.Larkin	SS	C.Reynolds	SS	M.Duncan	SS	H.Brooks
3B	K.Oberkfell	SS	S.Dunston	3B	B.Bell	3B	D.Walling	3B	M.Hatcher	3B	T.Wallach
LF	K.Griffey	3B	K.Moreland	LF	T.Jones	LF	J.Cruz	LF	P.Guerrero	LF	T.Raines
CF	D.James	LF	J.Mumphrey	CF	E.Davis	CF	B.Hatcher	CF	J.Shelby	CF	H.Winningham
RF	D.Murphy	CF	D.Martinez	RF	D.Parker	RF	K.Bass	RF	M.Marshall	RF	M.Webster
C	O.Virgil	RF	A.Dawson	C	B.Diaz	C	A.Ashby	C	M.Scioscia	C	M.Fitzgerald
		C	J.Davis								
3	G.Nettles			21	D.Concepcion	O	G.Young	S3	D.Anderson	2O	C.Candaele
O	A.Hall	O	B.Dayett	O	K.Daniels	3	K.Caminiti	O	K.Landreaux	S2	T.Foley
		13	M.Trillo	1	T.Francona					C	J.Reed
P	Z.Smith	O1	R.Palmeiro	S2	K.Stillwell	M.Scott		P	O.Hershiser		
P	R.Mahler					P	N.Ryan	P	B.Welch	N.Heaton
P	D.Palmer	P	R.Sutcliffe	P	T.Power	P	D.Darwin	P	F.Valenzuela	P	B.Sebra
P	C.Puleo	P	J.Moyer	P	T.Browning	P	B.Knepper	P	R.Honeycutt	P	B.Smith
P	D.Alexander	P	G.Maddux	P	B.Gullickson	P	J.Deshaies	RP	T.Leary	P	D.Martinez
RP	J.Acker	P	S.Sanderson	P	G.Hoffman	RP	L.Andersen	RP	A.Pena	P	F.Youmans
RP	J.Dedmon	P	L.Lancaster	P	R.Robinson	RP	D.Smith	RP	B.Holton	RP	A.McGaffigan
RP	G.Garber	RP	E.Lynch	RP	F.Williams	RP	D.Meads			RP	T.Burke
		RP	L.Smith	RP	R.Murphy			P	S.Hillegas	RP	R.St.Claire
P	R.O'Neal	RP	F.DiPino	RP	J.Franco			P	K.Howell		
P	P.Assenmacher							P	M.Young	P	J.Tibbs
/P	T.Glavine	P	S.Trout	P	B.Landrum					P	P.Perez
		P	D.Noles							P	J.Parrett
										P	B.McClure

	NEW YORK		PHILADELPHIA		PITTSBURGH		SAN DIEGO		SAN FRANCISCO		ST.LOUIS
M	D.Johnson	M	J.Felske	M	J.Leyland	M	L.Bowa	M	R.Craig	M	W.Herzog
1B	K.Hernandez	M	L.Elia	1B	S.Bream	1B	J.Kruk	1B	W.Clark	1B	J.Clark
2B	T.Teufel	1B	V.Hayes	2B	J.Ray	2B	T.Flannery	2B	R.Thompson	2B	T.Herr
SS	R.Santana	2B	J.Samuel	SS	A.Pedrique	SS	G.Templeton	SS	J.Uribe	SS	O.Smith
3B	H.Johnson	SS	S.Jeltz	3B	B.Bonilla	3B	R.Ready	3B	K.Mitchell	3B	T.Pendleton
LF	K.McReynolds	3B	M.Schmidt	LF	B.Bonds	LF	S.Jefferson	LF	J.Leonard	LF	V.Coleman
CF	L.Dykstra	LF	C.James	CF	A.Van Slyke	CF	S.Mack	CF	C.Davis	CF	W.McGee
RF	D.Strawberry	CF	M.Thompson	RF	R.Reynolds	RF	T.Gwynn	RF	C.Maldonado	RF	C.Ford
C	G.Carter	RF	G.Wilson	C	M.LaValliere	C	B.Santiago	C	B.Brenly	C	T.Pena
		C	L.Parrish								
O	M.Wilson			O	J.Cangelosi	O1	C.Martinez	O1	M.Aldrete	O	J.Morris
2	W.Backman	O1	G.Gross	O1	M.Diaz	O	M.Wynne	O	E.Milner	O2	J.Oquendo
		S	L.Aguayo	3S	J.Morrison	2	J.Cora	23	C.Speier	O1	J.Lindeman
P	R.Darling			S	R.Belliard			C	B.Melvin		
P	D.Gooden	P	S.Rawley			P	E.Whitson	S3	M.Williams	P	D.Cox
P	S.Fernandez	P	D.Carman	P	B.Fisher	P	E.Show			P	G.Mathews
P	R.Aguilera	P	B.Ruffin	P	R.Reuschel	P	J.Jones	P	K.Downs	P	B.Forsch
P	J.Mitchell	P	K.Gross	P	D.Drabek	P	A.Hawkins	P	M.LaCoss	P	J.Magrane
RP	T.Leach	RP	M.Jackson	P	M.Dunne	P	M.Grant	P	A.Hammaker	P	J.Tudor
RP	R.McDowell	RP	K.Tekulve	P	B.Walk	RP	L.McCullers	P	M.Krukow	RP	R.Horton
RP	D.Sisk	RP	S.Bedrosian	RP	J.Smiley	RP	D.Dravecky	P	D.Dravecky	RP	B.Dawley
				RP	D.Robinson	RP	G.Booker	RP	S.Garrelts	RP	T.Worrell
P	D.Cone	P	T.Hume					RP	J.Robinson		
P	J.Orosco	P	W.Ritchie	P	B.Kipper	P	E.Nolte	P	J.Gott	P	L.Tunnell
P	R.Myers			P	D.Taylor	P	S.Davis			P	P.Perry
						P	M.Davis	P	M.Davis	P	K.Dayley
						P	R.Gossage	P	M.Grant		
						P	C.Lefferts	/P	R.Reuschel		

TEAM	G	W	L	PCT	GB	R	OR	AB	H	2B	3B	HR	BB	SO	AVG	OBP	SLG	PRO	PRO+	BR	/A	PF	CHI	RC	SB	CS	SBA	SBR
EAST																												
STL	162	95	67	.586		798	693	5500	1449	252	49	94	644	933	.263	.343	.378	.721	95	-9	-23	102	**109**	740	**248**	72	78	**31**
NY	162	92	70	.568	3	**823**	698	5601	**1499**	287	34	192	592	1012	.268	.341	**.434**	**.775**	117	81	124	95	100	848	159	49	76	18
MON	162	91	71	.562	4	741	720	5527	1467	**310**	39	120	501	918	.265	.330	.401	.731	96	-6	-28	103	103	734	166	74	69	5
PIT	162	80	82	.494	15	723	744	5536	1464	282	45	131	535	914	.264	.332	.403	.735	99	3	-1	101	98	741	140	58	71	7
PHI	162	80	82	.494	15	702	749	5475	1390	248	**51**	169	587	1109	.264	.329	.410	.739	98	8	-16	103	95	730	111	49	69	4
CHI	161	76	85	.472	18.5	720	801	5583	1475	244	33	**209**	504	1064	.264	.327	.432	.759	102	40	10	104	94	785	109	48	69	4
WEST																												
SF	162	90	72	.556		783	**669**	5608	1458	274	32	205	511	1094	.260	.326	.430	.756	110	33	70	95	102	768	126	97	57	-20
CIN	162	84	78	.519	6	783	752	5560	1478	262	29	192	514	928	.266	.331	.427	.758	102	42	8	104	102	786	169	46	**79**	23
HOU	162	76	86	.469	14	648	678	5485	1386	238	28	122	526	936	.253	.321	.373	.694	94	-78	-54	96	100	669	162	46	78	21
LA	162	73	89	.451	17	635	675	5517	1389	236	23	125	445	923	.252	.311	.371	.682	88	-108	-92	97	104	627	128	59	68	3
ATL	161	69	92	.429	20.5	747	829	5428	1401	284	24	152	641	**834**	.258	.341	.403	.744	98	28	-9	105	98	747	135	68	67	0
SD	162	65	97	.401	25	668	763	5456	1419	209	48	113	577	992	.260	.334	.378	.712	99	-34	-97	96	96	693	198	91	69	5
TOT	971					8771		66276	17275	3126	435	1824	6577	11657	.261	.331	.404	.734							1851	757	71	101

TEAM	CG	SH	SV	IP	H	H/G	HR	BB	SO	RAT	ERA	ERA+	OAV	OOB	PR	/A	PF	CPI	FA	E	DP	FW	PW	BW	SBW	DIF
EAST																										
STL	10	7	48	1466	1484	9.1	**129**	533	873	12.5	3.91	106	.265	.332	28	40	102	103	**.982**	116	172	.9	4.0	-2.3	**2.2**	9.2
NY	16	7	**51**	1454	1407	8.7	135	510	1032	12.1	3.84	98	.254	.321	38	-11	93	97	.978	137	137	-.3	-1.1	**12.3**	1.0	-.9
MON	16	8	50	1450[1]	1428	8.9	145	**446**	1012	**11.8**	3.92	**107**	.257	**.315**	26	**46**	103	95	.976	147	122	-.9	**4.6**	-2.8	-.3	9.4
PIT	25	**13**	39	1445	1377	8.6	164	562	914	12.2	4.20	98	.253	.326	-19	-14	101	95	.980	123	147	.5	-1.4	-.0	-.1	.2
PHI	13	7	48	1448[1]	1453	9.0	167	587	877	12.9	4.18	101	.263	.338	-16	9	104	103	.980	121	137	.6	.9	-1.6	-.4	-.5
CHI	11	5	48	1434[2]	1524	9.6	159	628	1024	13.7	4.55	94	.275	.352	-76	-44	105	103	.979	130	154	.0	-4.4	1.0	-.4	-.7
WEST																										
SF	19	10	38	1471	1407	8.6	146	547	1038	12.1	**3.68**	105	.255	.325	66	27	94	106	.980	129	183	.1	2.7	7.0	-2.8	2.0
CIN	7	6	44	1452[1]	1486	9.2	170	485	919	12.4	4.24	100	.267	.328	-27	0	104	99	.979	130	137	.0	.0	.8	1.5	.7
HOU	13	**13**	33	1441[1]	**1363**	**8.5**	141	525	**1137**	12.0	3.84	102	**.250**	.319	38	12	96	96	.981	116	113	.9	1.2	-5.4	1.3	-2.9
LA	**29**	8	32	1455	1415	8.8	130	565	1097	12.4	3.72	**107**	.255	.327	59	40	97	103	.975	155	144	-1.3	4.0	-9.2	-.5	-.9
ATL	16	4	32	1427[2]	1529	9.6	163	587	837	13.6	4.63	94	.276	.350	-87	-45	107	101	**.982**	116	170	.8	-4.5	-.9	-.8	-6.1
SD	14	10	33	1433[1]	1402	8.8	175	602	897	12.8	4.27	93	.256	.334	-30	-50	97	98	.976	147	135	-.9	-5.0	-.9	-.3	-8.9
TOT	189	98	496	17379		8.9				12.5	4.08		.261	.331					.979	1567	1751					

Runs
Raines-Mon 123
Coleman-StL 121
Davis-Cin 120
Gwynn-SD 119
Murphy-Atl 115

Hits
Gwynn-SD 218
Guerrero-LA 184
Smith-StL 182
Coleman-StL 180

Doubles
Wallach-Mon 42
Smith-StL 40
Galarraga-Mon 40

Triples
Samuel-Phi 15
Gwynn-SD 13
VanSlyke-Pit 11
McGee-StL 11
Coleman-StL 10

Home Runs
Dawson-Chi 49
Murphy-Atl 44
Strawberry-NY 39
Davis-Cin 37
Johnson-NY 36

Total Bases
Dawson-Chi 353
Samuel-Phi 329
Murphy-Atl 328
Strawberry-NY 310
Clark-SF 307

Runs Batted In
Dawson-Chi 137
Wallach-Mon 123
Schmidt-Phi 113
Clark-StL 106

Runs Produced
Wallach-Mon 186
Samuel-Phi 185
Davis-Cin 183
Smith-StL 179
Dawson-Chi 178

Bases On Balls
Clark-StL 136
Hayes-Phi 121
Murphy-Atl 115
Strawberry-NY 97
Raines-Mon 90

Batting Average
Gwynn-SD ...... .370
Guerrero-LA ...... .338
Raines-Mon ...... .330
Kruk-SD ...... .313
James-Atl ...... .312

On Base Percentage
Clark-StL ...... .461
Gwynn-SD ...... .450
Raines-Mon ...... .431
Guerrero-LA ...... .421
Murphy-Atl ...... .420

Slugging Average
Clark-StL ...... .597
Davis-Cin ...... .593
Strawberry-NY ...... .583
Clark-SF ...... .580
Murphy-Atl ...... .580

Production
Clark-StL 1.058
Murphy-Atl 1.000
Davis-Cin ...... .994
Strawberry-NY ...... .984
Gwynn-SD ...... .961

Adjusted Production
Clark-StL 174
Strawberry-NY 165
Gwynn-SD 160
Guerrero-LA 156
Clark-SF 155

Batter Runs
Clark-StL 54.3
Murphy-Atl 53.3
Gwynn-SD 49.6
Strawberry-NY 44.7
Raines-Mon 43.2

Adjusted Batter Runs
Gwynn-SD 54.3
Clark-StL 52.0
Strawberry-NY 51.1
Murphy-Atl 46.8
Guerrero-LA 45.7

Clutch Hitting Index
Herr-StL 172
Pendleton-StL 131
Smith-StL 130
McGee-StL 126
Diaz-Cin 124

Runs Created
Murphy-Atl 143
Gwynn-SD 143
Strawberry-NY 132
Raines-Mon 132
Clark-StL 127

Total Average
Clark-StL 1.258
Davis-Cin 1.182
Raines-Mon 1.133
Murphy-Atl 1.106
Strawberry-NY 1.103

Stolen Bases
Coleman-StL 109
Gwynn-SD 56
Hatcher-Hou 53
Raines-Mon 50
Davis-Cin 50

Stolen Base Average
Sandberg-Chi 91.3
Raines-Mon 90.9
Davis-Cin 89.3
Hatcher-Hou 85.5
Coleman-StL 83.2

Stolen Base Runs
Coleman-StL 19.5
Raines-Mon 12.0
Davis-Cin 11.4
Hatcher-Hou 10.5
Gwynn-SD 9.6

Fielding Runs
Hubbard-Atl 28.2
Davis-Cin 28.1
Bonds-Pit 19.7
Smith-StL 19.3
Hernandez-NY 17.7

Total Player Rating
Davis-Cin 6.9
Gwynn-SD 6.6
Raines-Mon 6.1
Murphy-Atl 5.4
Strawberry-NY 5.0

Wins
Sutcliffe-Chi 18
Rawley-Phi 17
Scott-Hou 16
Hershiser-LA 16

Win Percentage
Gooden-NY ...... .682
Sutcliffe-Chi ...... .643
Welch-LA ...... .625
Rawley-Phi ...... .607
Z.Smith-Atl ...... .600

Games
Tekulve-Phi 90
Murphy-Cin 87
Williams-Cin 85
J.Robinson-SF-Pit 81
McCullers-SD 78

Complete Games
Reuschel-Pit-SF 12
Valenzuela-LA 12
Hershiser-LA 10
Z.Smith-Atl 9
Scott-Hou 8

Shutouts
Reuschel-Pit-SF 4
Welch-LA 4

Saves
Bedrosian-Phi 40
Smith-Chi 36
Worrell-StL 33
Franco-Cin 32
McDowell-NY 25

Innings Pitched
Hershiser-LA 264.2
Welch-LA 251.2
Valenzuela-LA 251.0
Scott-Hou 247.2
Z.Smith-Atl 242.0

Fewest Hits/Game
Ryan-Hou 6.55
Scott-Hou 7.23
Welch-LA 7.30
Dunne-Pit 7.88
Darling-NY 7.93

Fewest BB/Game
Reuschel-Pit-SF 1.67
Heaton-Min 1.72
Gullickson-Cin 2.13
Forsch-StL 2.26
Drabek-Pit 2.35

Strikeouts
Ryan-Hou 270
Scott-Hou 233
Welch-LA 196
Valenzuela-LA 190
Hershiser-LA 190

Strikeouts/Game
Ryan-Hou 11.48
Scott-Hou 8.47
Sebra-Mon 7.92
Gooden-NY 7.41
Darling-NY 7.24

Ratio
Reuschel-Pit-SF 10.19
Scott-Hou 10.25
Ryan-Hou 10.42
Welch-LA 10.51
Drabek-Pit 10.77

Earned Run Average
Ryan-Hou 2.76
Dunne-Pit 3.03
Hershiser-LA 3.06
Reuschel-Pit-SF 3.09
Gooden-NY 3.21

Adjusted ERA
Ryan-Hou 142
Dunne-Pit 136
Reuschel-Pit-SF 131
Hershiser-LA 130
Welch-LA 123

Opponents' Batting Avg.
Ryan-Hou ...... .199
Scott-Hou ...... .217
Welch-LA ...... .221
Darling-NY ...... .233
Dunne-Pit ...... .240

Opponents' On Base Pct.
Scott-Hou ...... .282
Ryan-Hou ...... .284
Reuschel-Pit-SF ...... .284
Welch-LA ...... .291
Drabek-Pit ...... .296

Starter Runs
Ryan-Hou 30.9
Hershiser-LA 30.0
Reuschel-Pit-SF 24.9
Welch-LA 24.1
Scott-Hou 23.3

Adjusted Starter Runs
Ryan-Hou 27.1
Hershiser-LA 26.6
Reuschel-Pit-SF 24.1
Welch-LA 20.9
Dunne-Pit 19.6

Clutch Pitching Index
LaCoss-SF 124
Cox-StL 120
Dravecky-SD-SF 113
Ruffin-Phi 112
Grant-SF-SD 111

Relief Runs
Burke-Mon 29.3
McGaffigan-Mon 24.2
Williams-Cin 20.9
J.Robinson-SF-Pit 16.9
Smith-Hou 16.2

Adjusted Relief Runs
Burke-Mon 30.5
McGaffigan-Mon 24.2
Williams-Cin 22.8
Worrell-StL 15.7
Franco-Cin 15.7

Relief Ranking
Franco-Cin 33.1
Burke-Mon 31.7
Worrell-StL 30.5
Smith-Chi 24.3
Bedrosian-Phi 22.3

Total Pitcher Index
Hershiser-LA 3.6
Franco-Cin 3.3
Burke-Mon 3.2
Worrell-StL 3.1
Reuschel-Pit-SF 2.5

Total Baseball Ranking
Davis-Cin 6.9
Gwynn-SD 6.6
Raines-Mon 6.1
Murphy-Atl 5.4
Strawberry-NY 5.0

January 14 Catfish Hunter and Billy Williams are elected to the Hall of Fame by the BBWAA.

March 3 Ray Dandridge, a legendary third baseman from the Negro Leagues, is the only player elected to the Hall of Fame by the Special Veterans Committee.

June 2 The Mariners select Ken Griffey, Jr., the son of Braves outfielder Ken Griffey, with the first pick overall in the free-agent draft.

July 18 Don Mattingly hits a home run in his eighth consecutive game, tying the major league record set by Dale Long in 1956. His streak will end tomorrow when the Rangers romp 20-3.

August 26 Paul Molitor goes 0-for-4 in Milwaukee's 1-0, 10-inning win over the Indians, ending his hitting streak at 39 consecutive games, the longest in the AL since Joe DiMaggio's 56-game streak.

August 30 Kirby Puckett goes 6-for-6 with two home runs, tying the AL record for hits in a nine-inning game. Combined with yesterday's 4-for-5, two-home run performance, Puckett has a major

league-record-tying 10 hits in two games.

September 14 In an 18-3 rout of the Orioles, the Blue Jays erupt for a major league-record 10 home runs. Ernie Whitt leads the parade with three round trippers, Rance Mulliniks and George Bell hit two, and Lloyd Moseby, Rob Ducey, and Fred McGriff each add one.

September 29 Don Mattingly hits his major league-record sixth grand slam of the season off Boston's Bruce Hurst in a 6-0 Yankees victory, eclipsing the mark shared by Ernie Banks (1955) and Jim Gentile (1961).

October 4 On the last day of the regular season, Detroit beats second-place Toronto 1-0 at Tiger Stadium to win the AL East title. The Tigers were one game behind the Blue Jays entering their three-game season-ending showdown, and won each game by a single run (4-3, 3-2, and 1-0). Frank Tanana outduels Jimmy Key in the finale, and Larry Herndon's second-inning home run provides the game's only run.

October 12 Minnesota beats Detroit 9-5

in game 5 of the ALCS to wrap up its first AL championship since 1965. Third baseman Gary Gaetti is named MVP.

October 17 In the first indoor World Series game ever (at Minnesota's Metrodome), Dan Gladden's grand slam caps a 7-run fourth inning and leads the Twins to a 10-1 win over St. Louis in Game 1.

October 25 Series MVP Frank Viola and reliever Jeff Reardon hold the Cardinals to six hits as the Twins capture game seven 4-2 to win their first World Championship in Minnesota.

November 11 Roger Clemens becomes the first pitcher since Jim Palmer in 1975-76 to win consecutive Cy Young Awards, collecting 21 of 28 first-place votes to easily beat runner-up Jimmy Key.

November 17 George Bell becomes the first Blue Jay ever to win the AL MVP Award, edging Detroit's Alan Trammell 332-311. Bell hit .308 last season with 47 home runs and a league-leading 134 RBI.

	BALTIMORE		BOSTON		CALIFORNIA		CHICAGO		CLEVELAND		DETROIT		KANSAS CITY
M	C.Ripken	M	J.McNamara	M	G.Mauch	M	J.Fregosi	M	P.Corrales	M	S.Anderson	M	B.Gardner
1B	E.Murray	1B	D.Evans	1B	W.Joyner	1B	G.Walker	M	D.Edwards	1B	D.Evans	M	J.Wathan
2B	B.Ripken	2B	M.Barrett	2B	M.McLemore	2B	F.Manrique	1B	J.Carter	2B	L.Whitaker	1B	G.Brett
SS	C.Ripken	SS	S.Owen	SS	D.Schofield	SS	O.Guillen	2B	T.Bernazard	SS	A.Trammell	2B	F.White
3B	R.Knight	3B	W.Boggs	3B	D.DeCinces	3B	T.Hulett	SS	J.Franco	3B	T.Brookens	SS	A.Salazar
LF	K.Gerhart	LF	J.Rice	LF	J.Howell	LF	G.Redus	3B	B.Jacoby	LF	K.Gibson	3B	K.Seitzer
CF	F.Lynn	CF	E.Burks	CF	G.Pettis	CF	K.Williams	LF	M.Hall	CF	C.Lemon	LF	B.Jackson
RF	L.Sheets	RF	M.Greenwell	RF	D.White	RF	I.Calderon	RF	B.Butler	RF	P.Sheridan	CF	W.Wilson
C	T.Kennedy	C	M.Sullivan	C	B.Boone	C	C.Fisk	RF	C.Snyder	C	M.Nokes	RF	D.Tartabull
DH	M.Young	DH	D.Baylor	DH	B.Downing	DH	H.Baines	C	C.Bando	DH	B.Madlock	C	J.Quirk
								DH	P.Tabler			DH	S.Balboni
D2	A.Wiggins	1	B.Buckner	P	M.Witt	O	D.Boston			CO	M.Heath		
O	L.Lacy	2S	E.Romero	P	D.Sutton	23	D.Hill	2	T.Hinzo	OD	L.Herndon	P	B.Saberhagen
DO	J.Dwyer	O	T.Benzinger	W	W.Fraser			DO	C.Castillo			P	M.Gubicza
2	R.Burleson			P	J.Lazorko	P	F.Bannister			P	J.Morris	P	C.Leibrandt
		P	R.Clemens	P	J.Candelaria	P	R.Dotson	P	T.Candiotti	P	W.Terrell	P	D.Jackson
P	M.Boddicker	P	B.Hurst	P	D.Buice	P	J.DeLeon	P	K.Schrom	P	F.Tanana	P	B.Black
P	E.Bell	P	A.Nipper	RP	C.Finley	P	B.Long	P	P.Niekro	P	D.Petry	RP	S.Farr
P	D.Schmidt	P	B.Stanley	RP	G.Minton	RP	J.Winn	P	S.Bailes	P	J.Robinson	RP	J.Gleaton
P	J.Habyan	P	J.Sellers			P	B.Thigpen	P	S.Carlton	RP	E.King	RP	D.Quisenberry
P	K.Dixon	RP	W.Gardner	P	J.Reuss	RP	R.Searage	RP	R.Yett	RP	M.Henneman		
RP	M.Williamson	RP	C.Schiraldi	P	K.McCaskill			RP	D.Jones	RP	M.Thurmond		
RP	T.Arnold	RP	S.Crawford	P	G.Lucas	P	D.LaPoint	RP	E.Vande Berg				
RP	T.Niedenfuer					P	S.Nielsen			P	D.Alexander		
		P	T.Bolton			P	J.Davis	P	G.Swindell				
P	M.Flanagan					P	B.James	P	D.Akerfelds				
P	S.McGregor					P	N.Allen	P	J.Farrell				
P	M.Griffin												
P	J.Ballard												

	MILWAUKEE		MINNESOTA		NEW YORK		OAKLAND		SEATTLE		TEXAS		TORONTO
M	T.Trebelhorn	M	T.Kelly	M	L.Piniella	M	T.LaRussa	M	D.Williams	M	B.Valentine	M	J.Williams
1B	G.Brock	1B	K.Hrbek	1B	D.Mattingly	1B	M.McGwire	1B	A.Davis	1B	P.O'Brien	1B	W.Upshaw
2B	J.Castillo	2B	S.Lombardozzi	2B	W.Randolph	2B	T.Phillips	2B	H.Reynolds	2B	J.Browne	2B	G.Iorg
SS	D.Sveum	SS	G.Gagne	SS	W.Tolleson	SS	A.Griffin	SS	R.Quinones	SS	S.Fletcher	SS	T.Fernandez
3B	E.Riles	3B	G.Gaetti	3B	M.Pagliarulo	3B	C.Lansford	3B	J.Presley	3B	S.Buechele	3B	K.Gruber
LF	R.Deer	LF	D.Gladden	LF	G.Ward	LF	J.Canseco	LF	P.Bradley	LF	P.Incaviglia	LF	G.Bell
CF	R.Yount	CF	K.Puckett	CF	C.Washington	CF	L.Polonia	CF	J.Moses	CF	O.McDowell	CF	L.Moseby
RF	G.Braggs	RF	T.Brunansky	RF	D.Winfield	RF	M.Davis	RF	M.Kingery	RF	R.Sierra	RF	J.Barfield
C	B.Surhoff	C	T.Laudner	C	R.Cerone	C	T.Steinbach	C	S.Bradley	C	D.Slaught	C	E.Whitt
DH	C.Cooper	DH	R.Smalley	DH	R.Kittle	DH	R.Jackson	DH	K.Phelps	DH	L.Parrish	DH	F.McGriff
O	M.Felder	O	R.Bush	OD	D.Pasqua	O	D.Murphy	O	M.Brantley	O	B.Brower	OD	R.Leach
O	M.Manning	O	M.Davidson	OD	R.Henderson	2	T.Bernazard	CD	D.Valle	C3	G.Petralli	3D	R.Mulliniks
D3	P.Molitor	S2	A.Newman	S2	B.Meacham					C1	M.Stanley		
23	J.Gantner	D1	G.Larkin					P	M.Langston			P	J.Key
C	B.Schroeder			P	T.John	P	D.Stewart	P	M.Moore	P	C.Hough	P	J.Clancy
		P	B.Blyleven	P	R.Rhoden	P	C.Young	P	M.Morgan	P	J.Guzman	P	D.Stieb
P	T.Higuera	P	F.Viola	P	C.Hudson	P	S.Ontiveros	P	S.Bankhead	P	B.Witt	P	J.Cerutti
P	B.Wegman	P	L.Straker	P	D.Rasmussen	P	G.Nelson	P	L.Guetterman	P	M.Williams	RP	M.Eichhorn
P	J.Nieves	P	M.Smithson	P	R.Guidry	RP	D.Eckersley	RP	J.Reed	RP	D.Mohorcic	RP	J.Nunez
P	C.Bosio	P	J.Niekro	RP	D.Righetti	RP	E.Plunk	RP	B.Wilkinson	RP	J.Russell	RP	T.Henke
RP	C.Crim	RP	J.Berenguer	RP	T.Stoddard			RP	M.Trujillo				
RP	D.Plesac	RP	G.Frazier	RP	P.Clements	P	J.Rijo					P	J.Musselman
RP	M.Clear	RP	J.Reardon	/P	J.Niekro	P	J.Andujar			P	P.Kilgus	P	J.Johnson
						P	D.Lamp			P	E.Correa		
P	M.Knudson	P	K.Atherton			P	D.Leiper			P	M.Loynd		
P	J.Aldrich												

TEAM	G	W	L	PCT	GB	R	OR	AB	H	2B	3B	HR	BB	SO	AVG	OBP	SLG	PRO	PRO+	BR	/A	PF	CHI	RC	SB	CS	SBA	SBR
EAST																												
DET	162	98	64	.605		896	735	5649	1535	274	32	225	653	913	.272	.352	.451	.803	116	91	131	96	98	910	106	50	68	2
TOR	162	96	66	.593	2	845	655	5635	1514	277	38	215	555	970	.269	.338	.446	.784	103	42	26	102	100	841	126	50	72	8
MIL	162	91	71	.562	7	862	817	5625	1552	272	46	163	598	1040	.276	.349	.428	.777	102	40	17	103	101	852	176	74	70	8
NY	162	89	73	.549	9	788	758	5511	1445	239	16	196	604	949	.262	.338	.418	.756	100	-6	3	99	100	773	105	43	71	6
BOS	162	78	84	.481	20	842	825	5586	1554	273	26	174	606	825	.278	.355	.424	.785	104	61	38	103	97	855	77	45	63	-4
BAL	162	67	95	.414	31	729	880	5576	1437	219	20	211	524	939	.258	.324	.418	.742	98	-47	-27	97	99	736	69	45	61	-6
CLE	162	61	101	.377	37	742	957	5606	1476	267	30	187	489	977	.263	.326	.422	.748	95	-35	-40	101	98	772	140	54	72	10
WEST																												
MIN	162	85	77	.525		786	806	5441	1422	258	35	196	523	898	.261	.330	.430	.760	96	-8	-35	104	103	757	113	65	63	-5
KC	162	83	79	.512	2	715	691	5499	1443	239	40	168	590	1034	.262	.330	.412	.742	93	-40	-58	102	97	747	125	43	74	12
OAK	162	81	81	.500	4	806	789	5511	1432	263	33	199	593	1056	.260	.336	.428	.764	108	4	58	93	101	796	140	63	69	4
SEA	162	78	84	.481	7	760	801	5508	1499	282	48	161	500	863	.272	.337	.428	.765	96	9	-31	105	96	788	174	73	70	8
CHI	162	77	85	.475	8	748	746	5538	1427	283	36	173	487	971	.258	.321	.415	.736	91	-57	-74	102	103	737	138	52	73	10
TEX	162	75	87	.463	10	823	849	5564	1478	264	35	194	567	1081	.266	.336	.430	.766	101	9	8	100	102	798	120	71	63	-7
CAL	162	75	87	.463	10	770	803	5570	1406	257	26	172	590	926	.252	.328	.401	.729	95	-65	-39	97	105	744	125	44	74	11
TOT	1134					11112		77819	20620	3667	461	2634	7812	13442	.265	.336	.425	.761						1734	772	69	57	

TEAM	CG	SH	SV	IP	H	H/G	HR	BB	SO	RAT	ERA	ERA+	OAV	OOB	PR	/A	PF	CPI	FA	E	DP	FW	PW	BW	SBW	DIF
EAST																										
DET	33	10	31	1456	1430	8.8	180	563	976	12.5	4.02	105	.256	.328	70	32	95	103	.980	122	147	.1	3.1	12.5	-.2	1.6
TOR	18	8	43	1454	1323	8.2	158	567	1064	11.8	3.74	120	.244	.318	115	121	101	100	.982	111	148	.8	11.5	2.5	.4	-.2
MIL	28	6	45	1464	1548	9.5	169	529	1039	12.9	4.62	99	.271	.336	-27	-8	103	96	.976	145	155	-1.3	-.8	1.6	.4	10.1
NY	19	10	47	1446[1]	1475	9.2	179	542	900	12.8	4.36	101	.266	.334	16	5	98	101	.983	102	155	1.3	.5	.3	.2	5.7
BOS	47	13	16	1436	1584	9.9	190	517	1034	13.4	4.77	95	.282	.346	-50	-37	102	102	.982	110	158	.8	-3.5	3.6	-.8	-3.2
BAL	17	6	30	1439[2]	1555	9.7	226	547	870	13.3	5.01	88	.276	.343	-88	-97	99	98	.982	111	174	.8	-9.2	-2.6	-1.0	-2.0
CLE	24	8	25	1422[2]	1566	9.9	219	606	849	14.1	5.28	86	.278	.354	-131	-120	102	97	.975	153	128	-1.8	-11.4	-3.8	.6	-3.5
WEST																										
MIN	16	4	39	1427[1]	1465	9.2	210	564	990	13.1	4.63	100	.266	.339	-27	-2	104	100	.984	98	147	1.6	-.2	-3.3	-.9	6.8
KC	44	11	26	1424	1424	9.0	128	548	923	12.7	3.86	118	.261	.333	95	111	102	105	.979	131	151	-.5	10.6	-5.5	.8	-3.4
OAK	18	6	40	1445[2]	1442	9.0	176	531	1042	12.5	4.32	96	.258	.327	22	-31	93	96	.977	142	122	-1.1	-3.0	.5	.0	-1.4
SEA	39	10	33	1430[2]	1503	9.5	199	497	919	12.8	4.49	105	.272	.335	-5	37	106	102	.980	122	150	.3	3.5	-3.0		-4.0
CHI	29	12	37	1447[2]	1436	8.9	189	537	792	12.5	4.30	107	.259	.329	26	46	103	99	.981	116	174	.5	4.4	-7.1	.6	-2.4
TEX	20	3	27	1444[1]	1388	8.6	199	760	1103	13.7	4.63	97	.253	.350	-28	-25	100	100	.976	151	148	-1.7	-2.4	.8	-1.1	-1.6
CAL	20	7	36	1457[1]	1481	9.1	212	504	941	12.5	4.38	98	.264	.329	13	-13	97	101	.981	117	162	.4	-1.2	-3.7	.7	-2.1
TOT	372	114	475	20195[2]		9.2				12.9	4.46		.265	.336					.980	1731	2119					

Runs		Hits		Doubles		Triples		Home Runs		Total Bases	
Molitor-Mil	114	Seitzer-KC	207	Molitor-Mil	41	Wilson-KC	15	McGwire-Oak	49	Bell-Tor	369
Bell-Tor	111	Puckett-Min	207	Boggs-Bos	40	Polonia-Oak	10	Bell-Tor	47	McGwire-Oak	344
Whitaker-Det	110	Trammell-Det	205			P.Bradley-Sea	10			Puckett-Min	333
Downing-Cal	110	Boggs-Bos	200			Yount-Mil	9			Trammell-Det	329
		Yount-Mil	198							Boggs-Bos	324

Runs Batted In		Runs Produced		Bases On Balls		Batting Average		On Base Percentage		Slugging Average	
Bell-Tor	134	Evans-Bos	198	Evans-Bos	106	Boggs-Bos	.363	Boggs-Bos	.467	McGwire-Oak	.618
Evans-Bos	123	Bell-Tor	198	Downing-Cal	106	Molitor-Mil	.353	Molitor-Mil	.438	Bell-Tor	.605
McGwire-Oak	118	Trammell-Det	186	Boggs-Bos	105	Trammell-Det	.343	Evans-Bos	.422	Boggs-Bos	.588
Joyner-Cal	117	Joyner-Cal	183	Evans-Det	100	Puckett-Min	.332	Randolph-NY	.415	Evans-Bos	.569
Mattingly-NY	115	Yount-Mil	181	Butler-Cle	91	Mattingly-NY	.327	Trammell-Det	.406	Molitor-Mil	.566

Production		Adjusted Production		Batter Runs		Adjusted Batter Runs		Clutch Hitting Index		Runs Created	
Boggs-Bos	1.055	Boggs-Bos	173	Boggs-Bos	66.6	Boggs-Bos	62.7	Randolph-NY	141	Boggs-Bos	154
Molitor-Mil	1.004	McGwire-Oak	168	Evans-Bos	49.6	McGwire-Oak	53.0	Griffin-Oak	127	Trammell-Det	137
McGwire-Oak	.992	Molitor-Mil	159	Molitor-Mil	44.8	Trammell-Det	49.5	Owen-Bos	118	Evans-Bos	134
Evans-Bos	.991	Trammell-Det	157	McGwire-Oak	44.2	Evans-Bos	46.1	Tabler-Cle	117	McGwire-Oak	131
Bell-Tor	.962	Evans-Bos	155	Trammell-Det	43.7	Molitor-Mil	41.8	Ward-NY	117	Molitor-Mil	125

Total Average		Stolen Bases		Stolen Base Average		Stolen Base Runs		Fielding Runs		Total Player Rating	
Molitor-Mil	1.171	Reynolds-Sea	60	McDowell-Tex	92.3	Wilson-KC	11.1	Barrett-Bos	32.3	Boggs-Bos	5.8
Boggs-Bos	1.169	Wilson-KC	59	Trammell-Det	91.3	Redus-Chi	9.0	Salazar-KC	21.8	Trammell-Det	5.4
Evans-Bos	1.059	Redus-Chi	52	Schofield-Cal	86.4	Moseby-Tor	7.5	Manrique-Chi	18.9	Molitor-Mil	3.5
McGwire-Oak	1.042	Molitor-Mil	45	Moseby-Tor	84.8	Molitor-Mil	7.5	Reynolds-Sea	18.8	Henderson-NY	3.5
Trammell-Det	1.015	Henderson-NY	41	Wilson-KC	84.3	Henderson-NY	7.5	Gagne-Min	16.9	McGwire-Oak	3.3

Wins		Win Percentage		Games		Complete Games		Shutouts		Saves	
Stewart-Oak	20	Clemens-Bos	.690	Eichhorn-Tor	89	Clemens-Bos	18	Clemens-Bos	7	Henke-Tor	34
Clemens-Bos	20	Key-Tor	.680	Williams-Tex	85	Saberhagen-KC	15	Saberhagen-KC	4	Righetti-NY	31
Langston-Sea	19	Saberhagen-KC	.643	Mohorcic-Tex	74	Hurst-Bos	15			Reardon-Min	31
		Higuera-Mil	.643	Henke-Tor	72	Langston-Sea	14			Plesac-Mil	23
				Musselman-Tor	68	Higuera-Mil	14			Buice-Cal	17

Innings Pitched		Fewest Hits/Game		Fewest BB/Game		Strikeouts		Strikeouts/Game		Ratio	
Hough-Tex	285.1	Key-Tor	7.24	Long-Chi	1.49	Langston-Sea	262	Langston-Sea	8.67	Key-Tor	9.59
Clemens-Bos	281.2	Hough-Tex	7.51	Saberhagen-KC	1.86	Clemens-Bos	256	Higuera-Mil	8.25	Bannister-Chi	10.43
Langston-Sea	272.0	Morris-Det	7.68	Sutton-Cal	1.93	Higuera-Mil	240	Clemens-Bos	8.18	Saberhagen-KC	10.68
Blyleven-Min	267.0	Stewart-Oak	7.71	Bannister-Chi	1.93	Hough-Tex	223	Bosio-Mil	7.94	Young-Oak	10.68
Morris-Det	266.0	DeLeon-Chi	7.73	Young-Oak	1.95	Morris-Det	208	Nieves-Mil	7.50	Viola-Min	10.80

Earned Run Average		Adjusted ERA		Opponents' Batting Avg.		Opponents' On Base Pct.		Starter Runs		Adjusted Starter Runs	
Key-Tor	2.76	Key-Tor	163	Key-Tor	.221	Key-Tor	.273	Key-Tor	49.2	Key-Tor	50.3
Viola-Min	2.90	Viola-Min	159	Hough-Tex	.223	Bannister-Chi	.286	Clemens-Bos	46.5	Clemens-Bos	49.0
Clemens-Bos	2.97	Clemens-Bos	153	Morris-Det	.228	Viola-Min	.294	Viola-Min	43.6	Viola-Min	48.1
Saberhagen-KC	3.36	Saberhagen-KC	135	Stewart-Oak	.229	Morris-Det	.294	Morris-Det	31.7	Saberhagen-KC	34.0
Morris-Det	3.38	Leibrandt-KC	134	DeLeon-Chi	.230	Young-Oak	.295	Saberhagen-KC	31.2	Leibrandt-KC	30.6

Clutch Pitching Index		Relief Runs		Adjusted Relief Runs		Relief Ranking		Total Pitcher Index		Total Baseball Ranking	
Viola-Min	115	Henke-Tor	20.5	Henke-Tor	20.9	Plesac-Mil	32.4	Viola-Min	4.6	Boggs-Bos	5.8
Rhoden-NY	112	Eckersley-Oak	18.3	Eichhorn-Tor	18.7	Thigpen-Chi	29.3	Key-Tor	4.4	Trammell-Det	5.4
Terrell-Det	110	Eichhorn-Tor	18.2	Thigpen-Chi	18.3	Henke-Tor	28.3	Clemens-Bos	4.4	Viola-Min	4.6
Blyleven-Min	109	Thigpen-Chi	17.1	Plesac-Mil	17.3	Mohorcic-Tex	25.0	Leibrandt-KC	3.5	Key-Tor	4.4
Gubicza-KC	107	Plesac-Mil	16.3	Mohorcic-Tex	16.4	Eichhorn-Tor	22.4	Saberhagen-KC	3.4	Clemens-Bos	4.4

February 23 A committee of Chicago aldermen vote 7-2 to allow the Cubs to install lights and play up to 18 night games a year at Wrigley Field. The Cubs had feared losing the 1990 All-Star Game, as well as future playoff and World Series games, if lights were not installed.

May 14 Infielder Jose Oquendo becomes the first non-pitcher in 20 years to get a major league decision in the Cardinals' 7-5, 19-inning loss to the Braves. St. Louis had used seven pitchers when Oquendo is brought in to pitch the 16th inning. He shuts out the Braves for three innings before surrendering the game-winning runs.

August 9 The Cubs and Mets play the first official night game at Wrigley Field, a 6-4 Chicago victory.

September 8 NL president Bart Giamatti is unanimously elected baseball's seventh commissioner, and will succeed Peter Ueberroth next season.

September 26 The Dodgers beat the Padres 3-2 to clinch the NL West title and earn a playoff date with the Mets, who won 10 of their 11 meetings this season.

September 28 In his last start of the regular season, Orel Hershiser pitches 10 shutout innings to extend his consecutive-scoreless-inning streak to 59, breaking Dodger Don Drysdale's major league record by one. San Diego's Andy Hawkins also pitches 10 shutout innings and the Padres eventually win 2-1 on Mark Parent's home run in the bottom of the 16th.

October 8 Dodgers ace reliever Jay Howell is ejected in the eighth inning of Game 3 of the NLCS for having pine tar on his glove, and the Mets go on to score five times in the inning on the way to an 8-4 win. Howell will be suspended for three days by the NL.

October 12 Series MVP Orel Hershiser shuts out New York on five hits to win Game 7 of the NLCS 6-0 and put the Dodgers into the World Series for the first time since 1981.

October 15 In one of the most improbable finishes in World Series history, pinch hitter Kirk Gibson hits a two-run home run off Dennis Eckersley with two out in the bottom of the ninth inning to give the Dodgers a 5-4 win in Game 1. The injured Gibson was not expected to play in the NLCS, and will not play again in the Series.

October 20 Series MVP Orel Hershiser ends his dream season with a 5-2 four-hitter over the A's in Game 5 of the World Series, which gives the Dodgers their first World Championship since 1981. Los Angeles is the only team to win more than one World Series in the 1980s.

November 10 Orel Hershiser (23-8) is a unanimous choice as NL Cy Young Award winner.

November 15 Dodgers outfielder Kirk Gibson wins the NL MVP Award, edging Mets Darryl Strawberry and Kevin McReynolds. Gibson hit .290 with 25 home runs and just 76 RBI.

	ATLANTA		CHICAGO		CINCINNATI		HOUSTON		LOS ANGELES		MONTREAL
M	C.Tanner	M	D.Zimmer	M	P.Rose	M	H.Lanier	M	T.Lasorda	M	B.Rodgers
M	R.Nixon	1B	M.Grace	M	T.Helms	1B	G.Davis	1B	F.Stubbs	1B	A.Galarraga
1B	G.Perry	2B	R.Sandberg	M	P.Rose	2B	B.Doran	2B	S.Sax	2B	T.Foley
2B	R.Gant	SS	S.Dunston	1B	N.Esasky	SS	R.Ramirez	SS	A.Griffin	SS	L.Rivera
SS	A.Thomas	3B	V.Law	2B	J.Treadway	3B	B.Bell	3B	J.Hamilton	3B	T.Wallach
3B	K.Oberkfell	LF	R.Palmeiro	SS	B.Larkin	LF	B.Hatcher	LF	K.Gibson	LF	T.Raines
LF	D.James	CF	D.Jackson	3B	C.Sabo	CF	G.Young	CF	J.Shelby	CF	O.Nixon
CF	A.Hall	RF	A.Dawson	LF	K.Daniels	RF	K.Bass	RF	M.Marshall	RF	H.Brooks
RF	D.Murphy	C	D.Berryhill	CF	E.Davis	C	A.Trevino	C	M.Scioscia	C	N.Santovenia
C	O.Virgil			RF	P.O'Neill						
		O	M.Webster	C	B.Diaz	O	T.Puhl	S3	D.Anderson	O	M.Webster
C	B.Benedict	O	D.Martinez	O	D.Collins	C	A.Ashby	O	M.Davis	2S	R.Hudler
		C	J.Davis					31	P.Guerrero		
P	R.Mahler					P	N.Ryan			P	De.Martinez
P	P.Smith	P	G.Maddux	P	D.Jackson	P	M.Scott	P	O.Hershiser	P	B.Smith
P	T.Glavine	P	R.Sutcliffe	P	T.Browning	P	J.Deshaies	P	T.Leary	P	P.Perez
P	Z.Smith	P	J.Moyer	P	J.Rijo	P	D.Darwin	P	T.Belcher	P	J.Dopson
RP	C.Puleo	P	C.Schiraldi	RP	J.Franco	P	B.Knepper	P	F.Valenzuela	P	B.Holman
RP	J.Alvarez	P	J.Pico	RP	R.Murphy	RP	J.Agosto	RP	A.Pena	RP	J.Parrett
RP	P.Assenmacher	RP	F.DiPino	RP	T.Birtsas	RP	L.Andersen	RP	B.Holton	RP	A.McGaffigan
		RP	L.Lancaster			RP	D.Smith	RP	T.Crews	RP	T.Burke
P	K.Coffman			P	M.Soto						
P	J.Smoltz	P	A.Nipper	P	R.Robinson	P	J.Andujar	P	D.Sutton	P	D.Martinez
P	G.Jimenez			P	J.Armstrong			P	J.Howell	P	N.Heaton
				P	F.Williams			P	S.Hillegas	P	F.Youmans
				P	N.Charlton			P	J.Orosco	P	J.Hesketh
				P	R.Dibble			/P	J.Tudor		
				P	D.Rasmussen						

	NEW YORK		PHILADELPHIA		PITTSBURGH		SAN DIEGO		SAN FRANCISCO		ST.LOUIS
M	D.Johnson	M	L.Elia	M	J.Leyland	M	L.Bowa	M	R.Craig	M	W.Herzog
1B	K.Hernandez	M	J.Vukovich	1B	S.Bream	M	J.McKeon	1B	W.Clark	1B	B.Horner
2B	W.Backman	1B	V.Hayes	2B	J.Lind	1B	K.Moreland	2B	R.Thompson	2B	L.Alicea
SS	K.Elster	2B	J.Samuel	SS	R.Belliard	2B	R.Alomar	SS	J.Uribe	SS	O.Smith
3B	H.Johnson	SS	S.Jeltz	3B	B.Bonilla	SS	G.Templeton	3B	K.Mitchell	3B	T.Pendleton
LF	K.McReynolds	3B	M.Schmidt	LF	B.Bonds	3B	C.Brown	LF	M.Aldrete	LF	V.Coleman
CF	L.Dykstra	LF	P.Bradley	CF	A.Van Slyke	LF	C.Martinez	CF	B.Butler	CF	W.McGee
RF	D.Strawberry	CF	M.Thompson	RF	R.Reynolds	CF	M.Wynne	RF	C.Maldonado	RF	T.Brunansky
C	G.Carter	RF	C.James	C	M.LaValliere	RF	T.Gwynn	C	B.Melvin	C	T.Pena
		C	L.Parrish			C	B.Santiago				
13	D.Magadan			O	D.Coles			C	B.Brenly	23	J.Oquendo
O	M.Wilson	O1	G.Gross			1O	J.Kruk				
2	T.Teufel	1	R.Jordan	P	D.Drabek	32	R.Ready	P	R.Reuschel	P	J.DeLeon
				P	B.Walk	S	D.Thon	P	D.Robinson	P	J.Magrane
P	D.Gooden	P	K.Gross	P	J.Smiley			P	K.Downs	P	J.Tudor
P	R.Darling	P	D.Carman	P	M.Dunne	P	E.Show	P	A.Hammaker	P	L.McWilliams
P	D.Cone	P	S.Rawley	P	B.Fisher	P	A.Hawkins	P	M.Krukow	P	B.Forsch
P	B.Ojeda	P	D.Palmer	RP	J.Robinson	P	E.Whitson	RP	S.Garrelts	RP	S.Terry
P	S.Fernandez	RP	B.Ruffin	RP	J.Gott	P	J.Jones	RP	C.Lefferts	RP	T.Worrell
RP	T.Leach	RP	G.Harris	RP	B.Kipper	P	D.Rasmussen	P	J.Price	RP	K.Dayley
RP	R.McDowell	RP	K.Tekulve			RP	L.McCullers			
RP	R.Myers			P	B.Jones	RP	M.Grant	P	M.LaCoss	P	D.Cox
		P	M.Maddux	/P	D.LaPoint	RP	M.Davis			P	G.Mathews
		P	S.Bedrosian							P	R.O'Neal
		P	M.Freeman			P	G.Booker			P	J.Costello
						P	D.Leiper			

TEAM	G	W	L	PCT	GB	R	OR	AB	H	2B	3B	HR	BB	SO	AVG	OBP	SLG	PRO	PRO+	BR	/A	PF	CHI	RC	SB	CS	SBA	SBR
EAST																												
NY	160	100	60	.625		**703**	**532**	5408	1387	251	24	**152**	544	842	.256	**.328**	**.396**	**.724**	120	**95**	**131**	95	97	**717**	140	51	73	11
PIT	160	85	75	.531	15	651	616	5379	1327	240	45	110	**553**	947	.247	.321	.369	.690	105	33	42	99	99	648	119	60	66	0
MON	163	81	81	.500	20	628	592	5573	1400	260	**48**	107	454	1053	.251	.311	.373	.684	98	12	-18	105	97	636	189	89	68	3
CHI	163	77	85	.475	24	660	694	5675	**1481**	**262**	46	113	403	910	**.261**	.312	.383	.695	100	31	1	105	99	673	120	46	72	8
STL	162	76	86	.469	25	578	633	5518	1373	207	33	71	484	**827**	.249	.312	.337	.649	92	-47	-53	101	99	601	**234**	64	**79**	**32**
PHI	162	65	96	.404	35.5	597	734	5403	1294	246	31	106	489	981	.239	.308	.355	.663	94	-22	-35	102	100	599	112	49	70	4
WEST																												
LA	162	94	67	.584		628	544	5431	1346	217	25	99	437	947	.248	.308	.352	.660	99	-32	-14	97	**107**	590	131	46	74	12
CIN	161	87	74	.540	7	641	596	5426	1334	246	25	122	479	922	.246	.311	.368	.679	97	6	-19	104	102	639	207	56	**79**	29
SD	161	83	78	.516	11	594	583	5366	1325	205	35	94	494	892	.247	.313	.351	.664	99	-19	-8	98	99	594	123	50	71	7
SF	162	83	79	.512	11.5	670	626	5450	1353	227	44	113	550	1023	.248	.321	.368	.689	109	32	61	96	101	650	121	78	61	-11
HOU	162	82	80	.506	12.5	617	631	5494	1338	239	31	96	474	840	.244	.308	.351	.659	99	-32	-9	96	103	620	198	71	74	17
ATL	160	54	106	.338	39.5	555	741	5440	1319	228	28	96	432	848	.242	.301	.348	.649	94	-56	-84	105	99	549	95	69	58	-13
TOT	969					7522		65563	16277	2828	415	1279	5793	11032	.248	.313	.363	.675							1789	729	71	99

TEAM	CG	SH	SV	IP	H	H/G	HR	BB	SO	RAT	ERA	ERA+	OAV	OOB	PR	/A	PF	CPI	FA	E	DP	FW	PW	BW	SBW	DIF
EAST																										
NY	31	22	46	1439	**1253**	7.8	**78**	404	**1100**	10.6	2.91	111	.235	.293	86	50	93	97	**.981**	115	127	.9	5.4	**14.1**	.3	-.7
PIT	12	11	46	1440²	1349	8.4	108	469	790	11.6	3.47	98	.250	.314	-3	-10	99	101	.980	125	128	.3	-1.1	4.5	-.9	2.1
MON	18	12	43	1482²	1310	8.0	122	476	923	11.1	3.08	**117**	.238	.303	60	**84**	104	**105**	.978	142	145	-.5	**9.1**	-1.9	-.6	-6.0
CHI	30	10	29	1464¹	1494	9.2	115	490	897	12.4	3.84	94	.265	.327	-64	-38	105	102	.980	125	128	.5	-4.1	.1	-.0	-.4
STL	17	14	42	1470²	1387	8.5	91	486	881	11.6	3.47	100	.252	.314	-4	1	101	99	**.981**	121	131	.6	.1	-5.7	**2.6**	-2.6
PHI	16	6	36	1433	1447	9.1	118	628	859	13.3	4.14	86	.265	.344	-110	-92	103	102	.976	145	139	-.7	-9.9	-3.8	-.5	-.6
WEST																										
LA	**32**	**24**	**49**	1463¹	1291	7.9	84	473	1029	11.0	2.96	112	.237	.301	78	59	97	102	.977	142	126	-.5	6.4	-1.5	.4	8.8
CIN	24	13	43	1455	1271	7.9	121	504	934	11.1	3.35	107	.237	.306	16	38	104	98	.980	125	131	.4	4.1	-2.0	2.2	1.9
SD	30	9	39	1449	1332	8.3	112	439	885	11.1	3.28	104	.247	.306	27	19	99	102	**.981**	120	**147**	.6	2.0	-.9	-.1	.8
SF	25	13	42	1462¹	1323	8.1	99	422	875	10.9	3.39	96	.242	.300	10	-20	95	93	.978	129	145	.2	-2.2	6.6	-2.1	-.9
HOU	21	15	40	1474²	1339	8.2	123	478	1049	11.3	3.41	97	.242	.307	7	-14	96	99	.978	138	124	-.3	-1.5	-1.0	.9	2.9
ATL	14	4	25	1446	1481	9.2	108	524	810	12.7	4.09	90	.268	.336	-103	-67	107	100	.976	151	138	-1.1	-7.2	-9.1	-2.3	-6.3
TOT	270	153	480	17480²		8.4				11.6	3.45		.248	.313					.979	1578	1609					

Runs		Hits		Doubles		Triples		Home Runs		Total Bases	
Butler-SF	109	Galarraga-Mon	184	Galarraga-Mon	42	VanSlyke-Pit	15	Strawberry-NY	39	Galarraga-Mon	329
Gibson-LA	106	Dawson-Chi	179	Palmeiro-Chi	41	Coleman-StL	10	Davis-Hou	30	Dawson-Chi	298
Clark-SF	102	Palmeiro-Chi	178	Sabo-Cin	40	Young-Hou	9	Galarraga-Mon	29	VanSlyke-Pit	297
VanSlyke-Pit	101	Sax-LA	175	Bream-Pit	37	Samuel-Phi	9	Clark-SF	29	Strawberry-NY	296
Strawberry-NY	101	Larkin-Cin	174			Butler-SF	9	McReynolds-NY	27	Clark-SF	292

Runs Batted In		Runs Produced		Bases On Balls		Batting Average		On Base Percentage		Slugging Average	
Clark-SF	109	Clark-SF	182	Clark-SF	100	Gwynn-SD	.313	Daniels-Cin	.400	Strawberry-NY	.545
Strawberry-NY	101	VanSlyke-Pit	176	Butler-SF	97	Palmeiro-Chi	.307	Butler-SF	.395	Galarraga-Mon	.540
VanSlyke-Pit	100	Strawberry-NY	163	Daniels-Cin	87	Dawson-Chi	.303	Clark-SF	.392	Clark-SF	.508
Bonilla-Pit	100	Bonilla-Pit	163	Johnson-NY	86	Galarraga-Mon	.302	Gibson-LA	.381	VanSlyke-Pit	.506
		Galarraga-Mon	162			Perry-Atl	.300	Gwynn-SD	.374	Dawson-Chi	.504

Production		Adjusted Production		Batter Runs		Adjusted Batter Runs		Clutch Hitting Index		Runs Created	
Strawberry-NY	.916	Strawberry-NY	168	Clark-SF	44.3	Clark-SF	49.3	Moreland-SD	131	Clark-SF	120
Clark-SF	.900	Clark-SF	163	Strawberry-NY	42.0	Strawberry-NY	47.4	Gwynn-SD	118	Galarraga-Mon	114
Galarraga-Mon	.894	Gibson-LA	151	Galarraga-Mon	39.2	Gibson-LA	36.9	Maldonado-SF	114	Strawberry-NY	111
Gibson-LA	.864	Bonds-Pit	147	Gibson-LA	33.8	Galarraga-Mon	34.3	Bream-Pit	114	Gibson-LA	107
Daniels-Cin	.863	Galarraga-Mon	147	Daniels-Cin	33.2	Bonilla-Pit	33.6	Davis-Cin	113	VanSlyke-Pit	107

Total Average		Stolen Bases		Stolen Base Average		Stolen Base Runs		Fielding Runs		Total Player Rating	
Strawberry-NY	.957	Coleman-StL	81	McReynolds-NY	100.0	Smith-StL	11.7	Smith-StL	22.9	Strawberry-NY	5.2
Clark-SF	.955	Young-Hou	65	Davis-Cin	92.1	McGee-StL	8.7	Bream-Pit	20.9	VanSlyke-Pit	5.1
Gibson-LA	.929	Smith-StL	57	Gibson-LA	88.6	Davis-Cin	8.7	Sabo-Cin	18.8	Smith-StL	5.1
Davis-Cin	.927	Sabo-Cin	46	McGee-StL	87.2	Coleman-StL	8.1	Murphy-Atl	17.5	Gibson-LA	5.0
Daniels-Cin	.924	Nixon-Mon	46	Smith-StL	86.4	Larkin-Cin	7.8	VanSlyke-Pit	16.7	Larkin-Cin	4.5

Wins		Win Percentage		Games		Complete Games		Shutouts		Saves	
Jackson-Cin	23	Cone-NY	.870	Murphy-Cin	76	Jackson-Cin	15	Hershiser-LA	8	Franco-Cin	39
Hershiser-LA	23	Browning-Cin	.783	Robinson-Pit	75	Hershiser-LA	15	Leary-LA	6	Gott-Pit	34
Cone-NY	20	Jackson-Cin	.742	Agosto-Hou	75	Show-SD	13	Jackson-Cin	6	Worrell-StL	32
Reuschel-SF	19	Hershiser-LA	.742	Tekulve-Phi	70	Sutcliffe-Chi	12	Scott-Hou	5	Davis-SD	28
		Maddux-Chi	.692	Franco-Cin	70	Gooden-NY	10	Ojeda-NY	5	Bedrosian-Phi	28

Innings Pitched		Fewest Hits/Game		Fewest BB/Game		Strikeouts		Strikeouts/Game		Ratio	
Hershiser-LA	267.0	Fernandez-NY	6.11	B.Smith-Mon	1.45	Ryan-Hou	228	Ryan-Hou	9.33	Perez-Mon	8.81
Jackson-Cin	260.2	Perez-Mon	6.37	Mahler-Atl	1.52	Cone-NY	213	Fernandez-NY	9.10	Scott-Hou	9.18
Browning-Cin	250.2	Rijo-Cin	6.67	Reuschel-SF	1.54	DeLeon-StL	208	Rijo-Cin	8.89	Ojeda-NY	9.22
Mahler-Atl	249.0	Scott-Hou	6.67	Ojeda-NY	1.56	Scott-Hou	190	DeLeon-StL	8.31	Hershiser-LA	9.61
Maddux-Chi	249.0	Cone-NY	6.93	Tudor-StL-LA	1.87	Fernandez-NY	189	Cone-NY	8.29	Jackson-Cin	9.63

Earned Run Average		Adjusted ERA		Opponents' Batting Avg.		Opponents' On Base Pct.		Starter Runs		Adjusted Starter Runs	
Magrane-StL	2.18	Magrane-StL	160	Fernandez-NY	.191	Perez-Mon	.253	Hershiser-LA	35.3	Hershiser-LA	31.8
Cone-NY	2.22	Rijo-Cin	150	Perez-Mon	.196	Scott-Hou	.261	Cone-NY	31.6	Cone-NY	25.8
Hershiser-LA	2.26	Tudor-StL-LA	148	Scott-Hou	.204	Ojeda-NY	.264	Tudor-StL-LA	24.7	Jackson-Cin	24.7
Tudor-StL-LA	2.32	Hershiser-LA	147	Rijo-Cin	.209	Hershiser-LA	.271	Magrane-StL	23.3	Tudor-StL-LA	24.5
Rijo-Cin	2.39	Perez-Mon	147	Cone-NY	.213	Fernandez-NY	.274	Perez-Mon	21.0	Perez-Mon	24.1

Clutch Pitching Index		Relief Runs		Adjusted Relief Runs		Relief Ranking		Total Pitcher Index		Total Baseball Ranking	
Tudor-StL-LA	135	Franco-Cin	17.9	Franco-Cin	19.2	Franco-Cin	39.9	Franco-Cin	4.5	Strawberry-NY	5.2
Rawley-Phi	122	Holton-LA	16.4	Holton-LA	15.3	Davis-SD	28.5	Hershiser-LA	4.5	VanSlyke-Pit	5.1
Moyer-Chi	118	Pena-LA	16.1	Davis-SD	15.1	Myers-NY	22.8	Davis-SD	3.6	Smith-StL	5.1
Robinson-SF	113	Davis-SD	15.7	Pena-LA	14.9	Pena-LA	21.9	Jackson-Cin	3.2	Gibson-LA	5.0
D.Martinez-Mon	112	Myers-NY	13.0	Harris-Phi	14.3	Holton-LA	16.6	D.Martinez-Mon	3.0	Franco-Cin	4.5

January 12 Former Pirates slugger Willie Stargell is the only player elected this year to the Hall of Fame by the BBWAA, and becomes the 17th player to be elected in his first year of eligibility. Jim Bunning falls four votes shy of the 321 needed for election in his 13th year on the ballot.

April 28 The Orioles set an AL record with their 21st consecutive loss, 4-2 to the Twins, breaking the record shared by the 1906 Red Sox and the 1916 and 1943 A's.

May 9 Oakland beats Detroit 3-1 to extend its club-record winning streak to 14 consecutive games, the longest in the majors since 1977.

June 11 DH Rick Rhoden for the Yankees hits a sacrifice fly in New York's 8-6 win over Baltimore. He's the first pitcher to start a game as a DH since the rule was adopted in 1973.

June 25 Cal Ripken, Jr. plays in his 1,000th consecutive game, a 10-3 loss to Boston. Ripken's streak is the sixth longest in major league history.

June 30 Alarmed by threats by the White Sox to move to St. Petersburg, Florida, Illinois lawmakers grant state subsidies for a new stadium to replace venerable but decaying Comiskey Park.

July 3 While pinch running for Don Baylor in a 9-8, 16-inning win over Toronto, Oakland's Gene Nelson steals a base to become the first AL pitcher to steal a base since John "Blue Moon" Odom in 1973.

July 12 After being maligned by the press as an unworthy All-Star starter, A's catcher Terry Steinbach hits a solo home run and a sacrifice fly to lead the AL to a 2-1 victory at Riverfront Stadium and is named the game's MVP.

August 14 Detroit pounds the Red Sox 18-6 at Fenway Park to end Boston's AL-record home winning streak at 24 games, two shy of the major league record held by the 1916 Giants. Roger Clemens gives up eight runs in 1⅓ innings.

September 23 Oakland's Jose Canseco becomes the founder of baseball's 40-home run, 40-stolen base club by stealing two bases in a 9-8, 14-inning win over Milwaukee. He also hits his 41st home run.

September 30 The Red Sox lose to Cleveland 3-2 but clinch the AL East title anyway when second-place Milwaukee loses to Oakland 7-1.

September 30 Dave Stieb is one out away from a no-hitter for the second consecutive game, but falls short again when Jim Traber bloops a single over the head of first baseman Fred McGriff. Stieb finishes with his second straight one-hitter, 4-0 over the Orioles.

October 9 Oakland beats Boston 4-1 to complete a four-game sweep of the ALCS. Dennis Eckersley saves all four games and is named series MVP.

November 16 Jose Canseco becomes the first unanimous AL MVP since Reggie Jackson in 1973.

	BALTIMORE		BOSTON		CALIFORNIA		CHICAGO		CLEVELAND		DETROIT		KANSAS CITY
M	C.Ripken	M	J.McNamara	M	C.Rojas	M	J.Fregosi	M	D.Edwards	M	S.Anderson	M	J.Wathan
M	F.Robinson	M	J.Morgan	M	M.Stubing	1B	G.Walker	1B	W.Upshaw	1B	R.Knight	1B	G.Brett
1B	J.Traber	1B	T.Benzinger	1B	W.Joyner	2B	F.Manrique	2B	J.Franco	2B	L.Whitaker	2B	F.White
2B	B.Ripken	2B	M.Barrett	2B	J.Ray	SS	O.Guillen	SS	J.Bell	SS	A.Trammell	SS	K.Stillwell
SS	C.Ripken	SS	J.Reed	SS	D.Schofield	3B	S.Lyons	3B	B.Jacoby	3B	T.Brookens	3B	K.Seitzer
3B	R.Gonzales	3B	W.Boggs	3B	J.Howell	LF	D.Boston	LF	M.Hall	LF	P.Sheridan	LF	B.Jackson
LF	P.Stanicek	LF	M.Greenwell	LF	T.Armas	CF	D.Gallagher	CF	J.Carter	CF	G.Pettis	CF	W.Wilson
CF	F.Lynn	CF	E.Burks	CF	D.White	RF	D.Pasqua	RF	C.Snyder	RF	C.Lemon	RF	D.Tartabull
RF	J.Orsulak	RF	D.Evans	RF	C.Davis	C	C.Fisk	C	A.Allanson	C	M.Nokes	C	J.Quirk
C	M.Tettleton	C	R.Gedman	C	B.Boone	DH	H.Baines	DH	R.Kittle	DH	D.Evans	DH	B.Buckner
DH	E.Murray	DH	J.Rice	DH	B.Downing								
						O	I.Calderon	S	R.Washington	1D	D.Bergman	DO	P.Tabler
OD	L.Sheets	C	R.Cerone	2	M.McLemore	O	G.Redus	D	T.Francona	OS	L.Salazar	C	M.Macfarlane
O	K.Gerhart	S	S.Owen			23	D.Hill			C	M.Heath	OD	J.Eisenreich
3	R.Schu					O3	K.Williams	P	G.Swindell				
C	T.Kennedy	P	R.Clemens	P	M.Witt			P	T.Candiotti	P	J.Morris	P	M.Gubicza
		P	B.Hurst	P	W.Fraser	P	M.Perez	P	J.Farrell	P	D.Alexander	P	B.Saberhagen
P	J.Bautista	P	W.Gardner	P	C.Finley	P	J.Reuss	P	S.Bailes	P	W.Terrell	P	C.Leibrandt
P	J.Tibbs	P	O.Boyd	P	K.McCaskill	P	B.Long	P	R.Yett	P	F.Tanana	P	F.Bannister
P	J.Ballard	P	M.Smithson	P	D.Petry	RP	D.LaPoint	RP	D.Jones	P	J.Robinson	RP	S.Farr
P	M.Boddicker	RP	B.Stanley	RP	S.Cliburn	P	J.McDowell	RP	D.Gordon	RP	P.Gibson	RP	J.Montgomery
P	D.Schmidt	RP	L.Smith	RP	G.Minton	RP	R.Horton	RP	B.Havens	RP	M.Henneman		
RP	D.Sisk	RP	D.Lamp	RP	B.Harvey	RP	B.Thigpen			RP	W.Hernandez	P	T.Power
RP	M.Thurmond					RP	Jn.Davis	P	R.Nichols				
RP	T.Niedenfuer	P	M.Boddicker	P	T.Clark			P	B.Black	P	E.King		
		P	J.Sellers			P	J.Bittiger						
P	M.Williamson												
P	O.Peraza												
P	M.Morgan												

	MILWAUKEE		MINNESOTA		NEW YORK		OAKLAND		SEATTLE		TEXAS		TORONTO
M	T.Trebelhorn	M	T.Kelly	M	B.Martin	M	T.LaRussa	M	D.Williams	M	B.Valentine	M	J.Williams
1B	G.Brock	1B	K.Hrbek	M	L.Piniella	1B	M.McGwire	M	J.Snyder	1B	P.O'Brien	1B	F.McGriff
2B	J.Gantner	2B	S.Lombardozzi	1B	D.Mattingly	2B	G.Hubbard	1B	A.Davis	2B	C.Wilkerson	2B	M.Lee
SS	D.Sveum	SS	G.Gagne	2B	W.Randolph	SS	W.Weiss	2B	H.Reynolds	SS	S.Fletcher	SS	T.Fernandez
3B	P.Molitor	3B	G.Gaetti	SS	R.Santana	3B	C.Lansford	SS	R.Quinones	3B	S.Buechele	3B	K.Gruber
LF	J.Leonard	LF	D.Gladden	3B	M.Pagliarulo	LF	S.Javier	3B	J.Presley	LF	C.Espy	LF	G.Bell
CF	R.Yount	CF	K.Puckett	LF	R.Henderson	CF	D.Henderson	LF	M.Brantley	CF	O.McDowell	CF	L.Moseby
RF	R.Deer	RF	R.Bush	CF	C.Washington	RF	J.Canseco	CF	H.Cotto	RF	R.Sierra	RF	J.Barfield
C	B.Surhoff	C	T.Laudner	RF	D.Winfield	C	R.Hassey	RF	G.Wilson	C	G.Petralli	C	E.Whitt
DH	J.Meyer	DH	G.Larkin	C	D.Slaught	DH	D.Baylor	C	S.Bradley	DH	L.Parrish	DH	R.Mulliniks
				DH	J.Clark			DH	K.Phelps				
OD	G.Braggs	O	M.Davidson			2S	M.Gallego			OD	P.Incaviglia	2D	N.Liriano
		O	J.Moses	C	J.Skinner	DO	D.Parker	D1	S.Balboni	CD	M.Stanley		
P	T.Higuera	3S	A.Newman	O1	G.Ward	C	T.Steinbach	C	D.Valle	2	J.Browne	P	M.Flanagan
P	B.Wegman	2	T.Herr			O	L.Polonia			OD	B.Brower	P	D.Stieb
P	C.Bosio			P	R.Rhoden	3O	T.Phillips	P	M.Langston			P	J.Clancy
P	D.August	P	F.Viola	P	T.John			P	M.Moore	P	C.Hough	P	J.Key
P	M.Birkbeck	P	B.Blyleven	P	R.Dotson	P	D.Stewart	P	B.Swift	P	J.Guzman	P	T.Stottlemyre
RP	C.Crim	P	A.Anderson	P	J.Candelaria	P	B.Welch	P	S.Bankhead	P	P.Kilgus	RP	J.Cerutti
RP	O.Jones	P	C.Lea	P	C.Hudson	P	S.Davis	P	M.Campbell	P	J.Russell	RP	D.Ward
RP	P.Mirabella	P	F.Toliver	RP	N.Allen	P	C.Young	RP	M.Jackson	P	B.Witt	RP	T.Henke
		RP	J.Berenguer	RP	D.Righetti	P	T.Burns	P	J.Reed	RP	M.Williams		
P	J.Nieves	RP	K.Atherton	RP	S.Shields	RP	G.Nelson	RP	M.Schooler	RP	C.McMurtry	P	J.Musselman
P	T.Filer	RP	J.Reardon			RP	R.Honeycutt			RP	D.Mohorcic	P	M.Eichhorn
P	D.Plesac			P	C.Guante	RP	E.Plunk	P	S.Trout			P	D.Wells
		P	L.Straker	P	A.Leiter					P	R.Hayward		
		P	M.Portugal	P	R.Guidry	P	D.Eckersley						
				P	T.Stoddard	P	G.Cadaret						
						P	S.Ontiveros						

TEAM	G	W	L	PCT	GB	R	OR	AB	H	2B	3B	HR	BB	SO	AVG	OBP	SLG	PRO	PRO+	BR	/A	PF	CHI	RC	SB	CS	SBA	SBR
EAST																												
BOS	162	89	73	.549		**813**	689	5545	**1569**	**310**	39	124	**623**	728	**.283**	**.360**	.420	**.780**	113	**140**	**104**	104	94	**842**	65	36	64	-2
DET	162	88	74	.543	1	703	658	5433	1358	213	28	143	588	841	.250	.326	.378	.704	100	-20	6	96	103	673	87	42	67	1
TOR	162	87	75	.537	2	763	680	5557	1491	271	**47**	158	521	935	.268	.334	.419	.753	109	68	65	100	98	771	107	36	75	11
MIL	162	87	75	.537	2	682	**616**	5488	1409	258	26	113	439	911	.257	.316	.375	.691	92	-56	-61	101	**107**	648	**159**	55	74	15
NY	161	85	76	.528	3.5	772	748	5592	1469	272	12	148	588	935	.263	.336	.395	.731	105	33	39	99	102	754	146	39	**79**	**20**
CLE	162	78	84	.481	11	666	731	5505	1435	235	28	134	416	866	.261	.317	.387	.704	94	-35	-52	103	101	667	97	50	66	-1
BAL	161	54	107	.335	34.5	550	789	5358	1275	199	20	137	504	869	.238	.307	.359	.666	88	-101	-85	97	94	581	69	44	61	-6
WEST																												
OAK	162	104	58	.642		800	620	5602	1474	251	22	156	580	926	.263	.339	.399	.738	110	50	77	97	103	763	129	54	70	6
MIN	162	91	71	.562	13	759	672	5510	1508	294	31	151	528	832	.274	.343	**.421**	**.764**	110	94	71	103	95	785	107	63	63	-6
KC	161	84	77	.522	19.5	704	648	5469	1419	275	40	121	486	944	.259	.324	.391	.715	98	-9	-15	101	102	696	137	54	72	9
CAL	162	75	87	.463	29	714	771	5582	1458	258	31	124	469	819	.261	.324	.385	.709	101	-18	1	97	103	690	86	52	62	-5
CHI	161	71	90	.441	32.5	631	757	5449	1327	224	35	132	446	908	.244	.305	.370	.675	88	-52	-90	100	105	609	98	46	68	2
TEX	161	70	91	.435	33.5	637	735	5479	1378	227	39	112	542	1022	.252	.323	.368	.691	91	-47	-63	102	97	661	130	57	70	5
SEA	161	68	93	.422	35.5	664	744	5436	1397	271	27	148	461	787	.257	.319	.398	.717	95	-7	-37	104	97	673	95	61	61	-8
TOT	1131					9858		77005	19967	3558	425	1901	7191	12323	.259	.327	.391	.718							1512	689	69	40

TEAM	CG	SH	SV	IP	H	H/G	HR	BB	SO	RAT	ERA	ERA+	OAV	OOB	PR	/A	PF	CPI	FA	E	DP	FW	PW	BW	SBW	DIF
EAST																										
BOS	26	14	37	1426¹	1415	8.9	143	493	**1085**	12.3	3.97	104	.259	.324	-1	23	104	99	.984	93	123	1.6	2.3	**10.5**	-.5	-5.9
DET	34	8	36	1445²	1361	8.5	150	497	890	11.8	3.71	103	.248	.314	41	17	96	99	.982	109	129	.6	1.7	.6	-.2	4.2
TOR	16	**17**	47	1449	1404	8.7	143	528	904	12.4	3.80	104	.256	.328	27	22	99	**105**	.982	110	170	.6	2.2	6.6	.8	-4.2
MIL	30	8	51	1449¹	1355	8.4	125	437	832	**11.2**	3.45	**115**	.248	**.306**	84	**85**	100	99	.981	120	146	-.0	**8.6**	-6.2	1.2	2.4
NY	16	5	43	1456	1512	9.3	157	487	861	12.7	4.26	92	.267	.331	-48	-52	99	99	.978	134	161	-.9	-5.3	3.9	**1.7**	5.0
CLE	35	10	46	1434	1501	9.4	120	442	812	12.4	4.16	99	.270	.328	-31	-8	104	97	.980	124	131	-.3	-.8	-5.3	-.4	3.7
BAL	20	7	26	1416	1506	9.6	153	523	709	13.1	4.54	86	.274	.342	-90	-100	98	97	.980	119	172	-1.0	-10.1	-8.6	-.9	-6.9
WEST																										
OAK	22	9	**64**	1489¹	1376	8.3	116	553	983	11.8	**3.44**	110	.247	.318	**87**	56	95	104	.983	105	151	.9	5.7	7.8	.3	8.4
MIN	18	9	52	1431²	1457	9.2	146	453	897	12.3	3.93	104	.266	.327	6	22	103	104	**.986**	84	155	**2.1**	2.2	7.2	-.9	-.6
KC	29	12	32	1428¹	1415	9.0	**102**	465	886	12.1	3.65	109	.258	.320	49	52	101	100	.980	124	147	-.3	5.3	-1.5	.6	-.6
CAL	26	9	33	1455²	1503	9.3	135	568	817	13.1	4.32	89	.270	.342	-57	-74	97	101	.979	135	175	-.9	-7.5	.1	-.8	3.1
CHI	11	9	43	1439	1467	9.2	138	533	754	12.7	4.12	96	.266	.332	-25	-24	100	101	.976	154	177	-1.0	-2.4	-9.1	-.0	4.2
TEX	**41**	11	31	1438²	**1310**	**8.2**	129	654	912	12.6	4.05	101	**.244**	.332	-13	5	103	95	.979	131	145	-.7	.5	-6.4	.2	-4.1
SEA	28	11	28	1428	1385	8.7	144	558	981	12.5	4.15	100	.256	.330	-30	1	105	97	.980	123	168	-.2	.1	-3.7	-1.1	-7.5
TOT	352	139	569	20187		8.9				12.4	3.97		.259	.327					.981	1665	2150					

Runs
Boggs-Bos 128
Canseco-Oak 120
Henderson-NY 118
Molitor-Mil 115
Puckett-Min 109

Hits
Puckett-Min 234
Boggs-Bos 214
Greenwell-Bos 192
Yount-Mil 190
Molitor-Mil 190

Doubles
Boggs-Bos 45
Ray-Cal 42
Puckett-Min 42
Brett-KC 42
Fernandez-Tor 41

Triples
Yount-Mil 11
Wilson-KC 11
Reynolds-Sea 11
Greenwell-Bos 8

Home Runs
Canseco-Oak 42
McGriff-Tor 34
McGwire-Oak 32
Murray-Bal 28
Gaetti-Min 28

Total Bases
Puckett-Min 358
Canseco-Oak 347
Greenwell-Bos 313
Brett-KC 300
Carter-Cle 297

Runs Batted In
Canseco-Oak 124
Puckett-Min 121
Greenwell-Bos 119
Evans-Bos 111
Winfield-NY 107

Runs Produced
Puckett-Min 206
Canseco-Oak 202
Evans-Bos 186
Greenwell-Bos 183
Boggs-Bos 181

Bases On Balls
Boggs-Bos 125
Clark-NY 113
C.Ripken-Bal 102
Davis-Sea 95
Greenwell-Bos 87

Batting Average
Boggs-Bos .... .366
Puckett-Min ..... .356
Greenwell-Bos ... .325
Winfield-NY ..... .322
Molitor-Mil ..... .312

On Base Percentage
Boggs-Bos .... .480
Greenwell-Bos ... .420
Davis-Sea .... .416
Winfield-NY ..... .398
Henderson-NY .... .397

Slugging Average
Canseco-Oak ..... .569
McGriff-Tor ..... .552
Gaetti-Min ...... .551
Puckett-Min ..... .545
Greenwell-Bos ... .531

Production
Boggs-Bos .... .970
Canseco-Oak ..... .963
Greenwell-Bos ... .950
McGriff-Tor ..... .930
Winfield-NY ..... .928

Adjusted Production
Canseco-Oak 172
Boggs-Bos 165
Winfield-NY 159
Greenwell-Bos ... 158
McGriff-Tor 156

Batter Runs
Boggs-Bos 65.8
Canseco-Oak 54.1
Greenwell-Bos ... 53.4
Puckett-Min 45.5
Winfield-NY 43.4

Adjusted Batter Runs
Boggs-Bos 59.7
Canseco-Oak 58.9
Greenwell-Bos ... 47.9
Winfield-NY 44.4
Puckett-Min 42.0

Clutch Hitting Index
Barrett-Bos 135
Hall-Cle 123
Larkin-Min 121
Evans-Bos 120
Clark-NY 118

Runs Created
Boggs-Bos 140
Canseco-Oak 136
Greenwell-Bos ... 134
Puckett-Min 126
Brett-KC 119

Total Average
Boggs-Bos 1.043
Canseco-Oak 1.011
Greenwell-Bos .. 1.000
McGriff-Tor ..... .958
Henderson-NY .... .955

Stolen Bases
Henderson-NY 93
Pettis-Det 44
Molitor-Mil 41
Canseco-Oak 40

Stolen Base Average
Javier-Oak 95.2
Redus-Chi 92.9
Cotto-Sea 90.0
Henderson-NY 87.7
Yount-Mil 84.6

Stolen Base Runs
Henderson-NY 20.1
Pettis-Det 7.2
Redus-Chi 6.6

Fielding Runs
Guillen-Chi 42.6
Gruber-Tor 25.1
Schofield-Cal ... 23.2
Puckett-Min 19.5
Gladden-Min 16.3

Total Player Rating
Canseco-Oak 6.4
Puckett-Min 5.4
Boggs-Bos 5.3
Greenwell-Bos 4.9
Henderson-NY 4.7

Wins
Viola-Min 24
Stewart-Oak 21
Gubicza-KC 20

Win Percentage
Viola-Min .... .774
Hurst-Bos .... .750
Gubicza-KC ...... .714
Davis-Oak .... .696
Stieb-Tor .... .667

Games
Crim-Mil 70
Thigpen-Chi 68
Williams-Tex 67
Henneman-Det 65

Complete Games
Stewart-Oak 14
Clemens-Bos 14
Witt-Tex 13
Witt-Cal 12
Swindell-Cle 12

Shutouts
Clemens-Bos 8
Swindell-Cle 4
Stieb-Tor 4
Gubicza-KC 4

Saves
Eckersley-Oak 45
Reardon-Min 42
Jones-Cle 37
Thigpen-Chi 34
Plesac-Mil 30

Innings Pitched
Stewart-Oak 275.2
Gubicza-KC 269.2
Clemens-Bos 264.0
Langston-Sea 261.1
Saberhagen-KC ... 260.2

Fewest Hits/Game
Robinson-Det 6.33
Higuera-Mil 6.65
Stieb-Tor 6.82
Witt-Tex 6.92
Hough-Tex 7.21

Fewest BB/Game
Anderson-Min 1.65
Swindell-Cle 1.67
Alexander-Det ... 1.81
Bosio-Mil 1.88
Viola-Min 1.90

Strikeouts
Clemens-Bos 291
Langston-Sea 235
Viola-Min 193
Stewart-Oak 192
Higuera-Mil 192

Strikeouts/Game
Clemens-Bos 9.92
Langston-Sea 8.09
Witt-Tex 7.64
Higuera-Mil 7.60
Moore-Sea 7.16

Ratio
Higuera-Mil 9.22
Clemens-Bos 9.72
Robinson-Det ... 10.26
Moore-Sea 10.31
Viola-Min 10.33

Earned Run Average
Anderson-Min 2.45
Higuera-Mil 2.45
Viola-Min 2.64
Gubicza-KC 2.70
Clemens-Bos 2.93

Adjusted ERA
Anderson-Min 166
Higuera-Mil 162
Viola-Min 154
Gubicza-KC 147
Clemens-Bos 140

Opponents' Batting Avg.
Robinson-Det .... .197
Higuera-Mil ..... .207
Stieb-Tor .... .210
Witt-Tex .... .216
Clemens-Bos ..... .220

Opponents' On Base Pct.
Higuera-Mil ..... .265
Clemens-Bos ..... .270
Robinson-Det .... .284
Moore-Sea .... .287
Swindell-Cle .... .287

Starter Runs
Higuera-Mil 38.2
Gubicza-KC 37.8
Viola-Min 37.5
Anderson-Min 34.1
Clemens-Bos 30.3

Adjusted Starter Runs
Viola-Min 40.4
Higuera-Mil 38.5
Gubicza-KC 38.4
Anderson-Min 36.5
Clemens-Bos 34.6

Clutch Pitching Index
Anderson-Min 138
Davis-Oak 121
Candiotti-Cle ... 116
Leibrandt-KC 116
Viola-Min 115

Relief Runs
Henneman-Det 21.2
Jones-Cle 15.7
Harvey-Cal 15.5
Mirabella-Mil ... 15.4
Jackson-Sea 14.8

Adjusted Relief Runs
Henneman-Det 19.7
Jones-Cle 17.1
Jackson-Sea 16.9
Mirabella-Mil ... 15.5
Harvey-Cal 14.6

Relief Ranking
Henneman-Det 37.6
Harvey-Cal 26.6
Jones-Cle 26.5
Reardon-Min 23.0
Eckersley-Oak ... 21.3

Total Pitcher Index
Viola-Min 4.6
Anderson-Min 4.5
Higuera-Mil 4.3
Gubicza-KC 4.2
Henneman-Det 3.9

Total Baseball Ranking
Canseco-Oak 6.4
Puckett-Min 5.4
Boggs-Bos 5.3
Greenwell-Bos 4.9
Henderson-NY 4.7

January 9 Johnny Bench and Carl Yastrzemski are elected to the Hall of Fame by the BBWAA in their first year of eligibility. Bench was named on 96.4 percent of the ballots, the third-highest figure in history behind Ty Cobb and Hank Aaron.

January 29 The game-winning RBI is dropped as an official statistic after nine years of use. The Mets Keith Hernandez is the all-time leader with 129.

February 2 Bill White, a six-time All-Star and longtime Yankees broadcaster, is elected president of the NL. He becomes the highest-ranking black official in American professional sports.

February 16 Orel Hershiser becomes the first player to sign a contract that calls for a $3 million salary by inking a 3-year, $7.9 million contract with LA that will pay him $3,166,667 in 1991.

February 28 Red Schoendienst and Al Barlick, a major league umpire for over 29 seasons, are elected to the Hall of Fame by the Special Veterans Committee.

April 6 In his first start of the season, Orel Hershiser gives up a run in the first inning of a 4-3 loss to the Reds to end his major league-record consecutive-scoreless-inning streak at 59.

May 29 Phillies third baseman Mike Schmidt, 39, retires. He is seventh on the all-time home run list with 548.

May 31 The Senior Professional Baseball Association announces that it will begin its inaugural season on November 1 with eight teams of players age 35 and over.

June 3 Houston beats Los Angeles 5-4 in 22 innings in a game that takes 7:14 to complete. Third baseman Jeff Hamilton becomes the losing pitcher and pitcher Fernando Valenzuela finishes the game at first base.

July 5 Barry Bonds homers in Pittsburgh's 6-4 loss to SF, giving Barry and father Bobby the father-and-son home run record with 408. The Bells (Gus and Buddy) and the Berras (Yogi and Dale) had shared the record at 407.

August 24 After weeks of legal wrangling, Commissioner Bart Giamatti permanently bans Pete Rose from baseball for his alleged gambling on major league games. Although the five-page document signed by both parties includes no formal findings, Giamatti says that he considers Rose's acceptance of the ban to be a no-contest plea to the charges.

August 28 Frank Viola and the Mets outduel Orel Hershiser and LA, 1-0 in the first-ever regular-season matchup of defending Cy Young winners.

September 13 Fay Vincent is elected baseball's eighth commissioner, succeeding the late Bart Giamatti, whom he served as deputy commissioner.

October 4 Will Clark goes 4-for-4 with two home runs, including the first NLCS grand slam since 1977, to lead the Giants to an 11-3 win over the Cubs in Game 1 of the NL playoffs.

October 9 The Giants win their first NL pennant since 1962 by defeating the Cubs 3-2 in Game 5 of the NLCS. Will Clark bats .650 in the series with 8 RBI to win MVP honors.

November 14 Padres reliever Mark Davis wins the NL Cy Young Award. He saved 44 games with a 1.85 ERA.

November 21 Giants Kevin Mitchell, who led the big leagues with 47 home runs and 125 RBI, wins the NL MVP Award.

ATLANTA	CHICAGO	CINCINNATI	HOUSTON	LOS ANGELES	MONTREAL
M R.Nixon	M D.Zimmer	M P.Rose	M A.Howe	M T.Lasorda	M B.Rodgers
1B G.Perry	1B M.Grace	M T.Helms	1B G.Davis	1B E.Murray	1B A.Galarraga
2B J.Treadway	2B R.Sandberg	1B T.Benzinger	2B B.Doran	2B W.Randolph	2B T.Foley
SS A.Thomas	SS S.Dunston	2B R.Oester	SS R.Ramirez	SS A.Griffin	SS S.Owen
3B J.Blauser	3B V.Law	SS B.Larkin	3B K.Caminiti	3B J.Hamilton	3B T.Wallach
LF L.Smith	LF D.Smith	3B C.Sabo	LF B.Hatcher	LF K.Gibson	LF T.Raines
CF O.McDowell	CF J.Walton	LF R.Roomes	CF G.Young	CF J.Shelby	CF Da.Martinez
RF D.Murphy	RF A.Dawson	CF E.Davis	RF T.Puhl	RF M.Marshall	RF H.Brooks
C J.Davis	C D.Berryhill	RF P.O'Neill	C C.Biggio	C M.Scioscia	C N.Santovenia
		C J.Reed			
13 D.Evans	O M.Webster		2S C.Reynolds	O J.Gonzalez	C M.Fitzgerald
O1 T.Gregg	O1 L.McClendon	O K.Griffey	O K.Bass	O3 M.Hatcher	O O.Nixon
3O R.Gant		23 L.Quinones			2 D.Garcia
	P G.Maddux	O H.Winningham	P M.Scott	P O.Hershiser	
P J.Smoltz	P R.Sutcliffe		P J.Deshaies	P T.Belcher	P De.Martinez
P T.Glavine	P M.Bielecki	P T.Browning	P J.Clancy	P F.Valenzuela	P B.Smith
P D.Lilliquist	P S.Sanderson	P R.Mahler	P B.Knepper	P M.Morgan	P K.Gross
P P.Smith	P P.Kilgus	P D.Jackson	P M.Portugal	P T.Leary	P P.Perez
P M.Clary	RP J.Pico	P J.Rijo	RP D.Darwin	RP J.Howell	P M.Langston
RP J.Acker	RP S.Wilson	P S.Scudder	RP B.Forsch	RP A.Pena	RP T.Burke
RP J.Boever	RP M.Williams	RP R.Dibble	RP L.Andersen	RP T.Crews	RP A.McGaffigan
RP M.Eichhorn		RP N.Charlton			RP Z.Smith
	P C.Schiraldi	RP J.Franco	P R.Rhoden	P J.Wetteland	
P Z.Smith	P L.Lancaster		P J.Agosto	P R.Martinez	
P P.Assenmacher		P T.Leary	P D.Smith		
P J.Alvarez		P R.Robinson	P D.Schatzeder		
		P T.Birtsas			
		P K.Tekulve			

NEW YORK	PHILADELPHIA	PITTSBURGH	SAN DIEGO	SAN FRANCISCO	ST.LOUIS
M D.Johnson	M N.Leyva	M J.Leyland	M J.McKeon	M R.Craig	M W.Herzog
1B D.Magadan	1B R.Jordan	1B G.Redus	1B Ja.Clark	1B W.Clark	1B P.Guerrero
2B G.Jefferies	2B T.Herr	2B J.Lind	2B R.Alomar	2B R.Thompson	2B J.Oquendo
SS K.Elster	SS D.Thon	SS J.Bell	SS G.Templeton	SS J.Uribe	SS O.Smith
3B H.Johnson	3B C.Hayes	3B B.Bonilla	3B L.Salazar	3B E.Riles	3B T.Pendleton
LF K.McReynolds	LF J.Kruk	LF B.Bonds	LF C.James	LF K.Mitchell	LF V.Coleman
CF J.Samuel	CF L.Dykstra	CF A.Van Slyke	CF M.Wynne	CF B.Butler	CF M.Thompson
RF D.Strawberry	RF V.Hayes	RF R.Reynolds	RF T.Gwynn	RF C.Maldonado	RF T.Brunansky
C B.Lyons	C D.Daulton	C J.Ortiz	C B.Santiago	C T.Kennedy	C T.Pena
O M.Wilson	O C.Ford	O J.Cangelosi	O1 C.Martinez	3S M.Williams	P J.DeLeon
21 T.Teufel	S3 S.Jeltz	O1 G.Wilson	O3 B.Roberts	C K.Manwaring	P J.Magrane
1 K.Hernandez	O B.Dernier	S R.Quinones			P K.Hill
		13 J.King			P S.Terry
P D.Cone	P K.Howell	P D.Drabek	P B.Hurst	P R.Reuschel	RP F.DiPino
P S.Fernandez	P D.Carman	P J.Smiley	P E.Whitson	P D.Robinson	RP D.Quisenberry
P R.Darling	P B.Ruffin	P B.Walk	P D.Rasmussen	P S.Garrelts	RP K.Dayley
P B.Ojeda	P L.McWilliams	P N.Heaton	P W.Terrell	P M.LaCoss	
P D.Gooden	P D.Cook	P R.Kramer	P E.Show	RP C.Lefferts	P T.Power
RP R.Myers	RP J.Parrett	RP J.Robinson	RP G.Harris	RP J.Brantley	P C.Carpenter
RP R.Aguilera	RP G.Harris	RP B.Kipper	RP M.Grant	RP A.Hammaker	P J.Costello
RP D.Aase	RP T.Frohwirth	RP B.Landrum	RP M.Davis		P T.Worrell
				P K.Downs	
P F.Viola	P T.Mulholland	P D.Bair	P A.Benes	P B.Knepper	
	P R.McDowell	P R.Reed		P S.Bedrosian	

TEAM	G	W	L	PCT	GB	R	OR	AB	H	2B	3B	HR	BB	SO	AVG	OBP	SLG	PRO	PRO+	BR	/A	PF	CHI	RC	SB	CS	SBA	SBR
EAST																												
CHI	162	93	69	.574		**702**	623	5513	**1438**	235	45	124	472	921	**.261**	.322	.387	**.709**	101	54	3	107	101	685	136	57	70	7
NY	162	87	75	.537	6	683	595	5489	1351	**280**	21	**147**	504	934	.246	.313	.385	.698	110	30	62	95	102	676	158	53	**75**	**16**
STL	164	86	76	.531	7	632	608	5492	1418	263	47	73	507	848	.258	**.323**	.363	.686	99	16	-5	103	97	652	155	54	74	14
MON	162	81	81	.500	12	632	630	5482	1353	267	30	100	**572**	958	.247	.322	.361	.683	100	13	4	101	96	645	**160**	70	70	6
PIT	164	74	88	.457	19	637	680	5539	1334	263	**53**	95	563	914	.241	.314	.359	.673	102	-13	9	97	100	629	155	69	69	5
PHI	163	67	95	.414	26	629	735	5447	1324	215	36	123	558	926	.243	.316	.364	.680	100	1	1	100	99	634	106	50	68	2
WEST																												
SF	162	92	70	.568		699	600	5469	1365	241	52	141	508	1071	.250	.318	**.390**	.708	**111**	50	**69**	97	102	683	87	54	62	-6
SD	162	89	73	.549	3	642	626	5422	1360	215	32	120	552	1013	.251	.321	.369	.690	103	22	21	100	98	644	136	67	67	1
HOU	162	86	76	.531	6	647	669	5516	1316	239	28	97	530	860	.239	.308	.345	.653	95	-50	-29	97	**109**	606	144	62	70	6
LA	160	77	83	.481	14	554	**536**	5465	1313	241	17	89	507	885	.240	.308	.339	.647	93	-61	-51	98	96	576	81	54	60	-8
CIN	162	75	87	.463	17	632	691	5520	1363	242	35	118	493	1028	.247	.312	.370	.682	97	1	-21	103	99	639	128	71	64	-4
ATL	161	63	97	.394	28	584	680	5463	1281	201	22	128	485	996	.234	.300	.350	.650	89	-64	-79	103	103	575	83	54	61	-8
TOT	973					7673		65817	16215	2903	411	1365	6251	11354	.246	.315	.365	.680							1529	715	68	30

TEAM	CG	SH	SV	IP	H	H/G	HR	BB	SO	RAT	ERA	ERA+	OAV	OOB	PR	/A	PF	CPI	FA	E	DP	FW	PW	BW	SBW	DIF
EAST																										
CHI	18	10	**55**	1460¹	1369	8.4	106	532	918	11.9	3.43	110	.250	.319	11	54	108	104	.980	124	130	.6	5.8	.3	.5	4.8
NY	24	12	38	1454¹	**1260**	**7.8**	115	532	**1108**	11.3	3.29	99	**.231**	**.303**	33	-5	93	95	.976	144	110	-.6	-.5	6.6	**1.4**	-1.0
STL	18	18	43	1461	1330	8.2	**84**	482	844	11.3	3.36	108	.243	.308	21	43	104	95	**.982**	112	134	**1.4**	4.6	-.5	1.2	-1.7
MON	20	13	35	1468¹	1344	8.2	120	1059	11.6	3.48	102	.245	.314	3	9	101	101	.979	136	126	-.1	1.0	.4	.4	-1.7
PIT	20	9	40	1487²	1394	8.4	121	539	827	11.9	3.64	92	.248	.317	-24	-47	96	98	.975	160	130	-1.4	-5.0	1.0	.3	-1.8
PHI	10	10	33	1433¹	1408	8.8	127	613	899	12.9	4.04	88	.259	.337	-87	-80	101	101	.979	133	136	.1	-8.6	.1	-.0	-5.6
WEST																										
SF	12	16	47	1457	1320	8.2	120	471	802	11.2	3.30	102	.243	.307	31	11	97	102	**.982**	114	135	1.2	1.2	**7.4**	-.9	2.2
SD	21	11	52	1457¹	1359	8.4	133	481	933	11.5	3.38	103	.249	.312	19	19	100	106	.976	154	147	-1.1	2.0	2.2	-.2	5.0
HOU	19	12	38	1479¹	1379	8.4	105	551	965	11.9	3.64	93	.243	.318	-25	-42	97	96	.977	142	121	-.4	-4.5	-3.1	-.4	12.7
LA	**25**	**19**	36	1463¹	1278	**7.9**	95	504	1052	**11.1**	**2.95**	**116**	**.237**	.306	**89**	**76**	98	**107**	.981	118	**153**	.8	**8.1**	-5.5	-1.1	-5.4
CIN	16	9	37	1464¹	1404	8.6	125	559	981	11.5	3.73	96	.253	.326	-38	-21	103	102	.980	121	108	.8	-2.2	-2.2	-.7	-1.6
ATL	15	8	33	1447²	1370	8.5	114	**468**	966	11.5	3.70	99	.250	.311	-33	-8	104	94	.976	152	124	-1.1	-.9	-8.4	-1.1	-5.5
TOT	218	147	487	17534		8.3				11.7	3.49		.246	.315					.978	1610	1554					

Runs
Sandberg-Chi 104
Johnson-NY 104
Clark-SF 104
Mitchell-SF 100
Butler-SF 100

Hits
Gwynn-SD 203
Clark-SF 196
R.Alomar-SD 184
Guerrero-StL 177
Sandberg-Chi 176

Doubles
Wallach-Mon 42
Guerrero-StL 42
Johnson-NY 41
Clark-SF 38
Bonilla-Pit 37

Triples
Thompson-SF 11
Bonilla-Pit 10
VanSlyke-Pit 9
Coleman-StL 9
Clark-SF 9

Home Runs
Mitchell-SF 47
Johnson-NY 36
Davis-Hou 34
Davis-Cin 34
Sandberg-Chi 30

Total Bases
Mitchell-SF 345
Clark-SF 321
Johnson-NY 319
Bonilla-Pit 302
Sandberg-Chi 301

Runs Batted In
Mitchell-SF 125
Guerrero-StL 117
Clark-SF 111
Johnson-NY 101
Davis-Cin 101

Runs Produced
Clark-SF 192
Mitchell-SF 178
Johnson-NY 169
Guerrero-StL 160
Bonilla-Pit 158

Bases On Balls
J.Clark-SD 132
V.Hayes-Phi 101
Raines-Mon 93
Bonds-Pit 93

Batting Average
Gwynn-SD 336
Clark-SF 333
L.Smith-Atl 315
Grace-Chi 314
Guerrero-StL 311

On Base Percentage
L.Smith-Atl 420
J.Clark-SD 413
Clark-SF 412
Grace-Chi 407
Guerrero-StL 398

Slugging Average
Mitchell-SF 635
Johnson-NY 559
Clark-SF 546
Davis-Cin 541
L.Smith-Atl 533

Production
Mitchell-SF 1.027
Clark-SF 958
L.Smith-Atl 953
Johnson-NY 932
Davis-Cin 916

Adjusted Production
Mitchell-SF 194
Clark-SF 177
Johnson-NY 171
L.Smith-Atl 166
Davis-Cin 154

Batter Runs
Mitchell-SF 62.1
Clark-SF 55.6
L.Smith-Atl 47.0
Johnson-NY 45.7
Guerrero-StL 38.3

Adjusted Batter Runs
Mitchell-SF 65.8
Clark-SF 59.2
Johnson-NY 51.3
L.Smith-Atl 44.2
Bonilla-Pit 36.1

Clutch Hitting Index
Guerrero-StL 132
Hatcher-Hou-Pit . . . 121
J.Clark-SD 120
Doran-Hou 117
Murphy-Atl 115

Runs Created
Clark-SF 136
Mitchell-SF 136
Johnson-NY 127
L.Smith-Atl 113
Guerrero-StL 109

Total Average
Mitchell-SF 1.099
Johnson-NY 1.026
L.Smith-Atl 1.023
Clark-SF 1.010
J.Clark-SD 969

Stolen Bases
Coleman-StL 65
Samuel-Phi-NY 42
R.Alomar-SD 42
Raines-Mon 41
Johnson-NY 41

Stolen Base Average
Doran-Hou 88.0
Biggio-Hou 87.5
Coleman-StL 86.7
D.Martinez-Mon . . . 85.2
Johnson-NY 83.7

Stolen Base Runs
Coleman-StL 13.5
Johnson-NY 7.5
Raines-Mon 6.9
Samuel-Phi-NY 5.4
Doran-Hou 4.8

Fielding Runs
Pendleton-StL 30.2
Young-Hou 26.3
Oquendo-StL 20.4
Foley-Mon 19.8
Bonds-Pit 19.7

Total Player Rating
Mitchell-SF 7.0
L.Smith-Atl 5.2
Clark-SF 5.0
Bonds-Pit 4.2
Bonilla-Pit 4.2

Wins
Scott-Hou 20
Maddux-Chi 19
Magrane-StL 18
Bielecki-Chi 18
Reuschel-SF 17

Win Percentage
Bielecki-Chi 720
D.Martinez-Mon 696
Reuschel-SF 680
Scott-Hou 667
Magrane-StL 667

Games
Williams-Chi 76
Dibble-Cin 74
Parrett-Phi 72
Dayley-StL 71
Agosto-Hou 71

Complete Games
Hurst-SD 10
Belcher-LA 10
Scott-Hou 9
Magrane-StL 9
Browning-Cin 9

Shutouts
Belcher-LA 8
Drabek-Pit 5
Langston-Mon 4
Hershiser-LA 4
Glavine-Atl 4

Saves
Davis-SD 44
Williams-Chi 36
Franco-Cin 32
Howell-LA 28
Burke-Mon 28

Innings Pitched
Hershiser-LA 256.2
Browning-Cin 249.2
Hurst-SD 244.2
DeLeon-StL 244.2
Drabek-Pit 244.1

Fewest Hits/Game
DeLeon-StL 6.36
Fernandez-NY 6.44
Howell-Phi 6.84
Smoltz-Atl 6.92
Garrelts-SF 6.94

Fewest BB/Game
Robinson-StL 1.69
Lilliquist-Atl 1.85
D.Martinez-Mon . . . 1.90
Whitson-SD 1.90
Glavine-Atl 1.94

Strikeouts
DeLeon-StL 201
Belcher-LA 200
Fernandez-NY 198
Cone-NY 190
Hurst-SD 179

Strikeouts/Game
Langston-Mon 8.92
Fernandez-NY 8.12
Belcher-LA 7.83
Cone-NY 7.78
DeLeon-StL 7.39

Ratio
Garrelts-SF 9.08
DeLeon-StL 9.53
Scott-Hou 9.63
Fernandez-NY 9.77
B.Smith-Mon 9.81

Earned Run Average
Garrelts-SF 2.28
Hershiser-LA 2.31
Langston-Mon 2.39
Whitson-SD 2.66
Hurst-SD 2.69

Adjusted ERA
Garrelts-SF 148
Hershiser-LA 148
Langston-Mon 147
Whitson-SD 132
Hurst-SD 130

Opponents' Batting Avg.
DeLeon-StL 197
Fernandez-NY 198
Smoltz-Atl 212
Garrelts-SF 212
Scott-Hou 212

Opponents' On Base Pct.
Garrelts-SF 260
Scott-Hou 268
DeLeon-StL 269
Fernandez-NY 272
Smiley-Pit 276

Starter Runs
Hershiser-LA 33.7
Garrelts-SF 26.1
Hurst-SD 22.0
Langston-Mon 21.6
Whitson-SD 21.2

Adjusted Starter Runs
Hershiser-LA 31.4
Garrelts-SF 23.4
Langston-Mon 22.3
Hurst-SD 22.0
Maddux-Chi 21.5

Clutch Pitching Index
Langston-Mon 135
Hershiser-LA 124
Lilliquist-Atl 117
Maddux-Chi 115
Drabek-Pit 113

Relief Runs
Andersen-Hou 19.0
Lancaster-Chi 17.2
Davis-SD 17.0
Howell-LA 16.9
Landrum-Pit 16.5

Adjusted Relief Runs
Lancaster-Chi 19.3
Andersen-Hou 18.0
Davis-SD 17.0
Dibble-Cin 16.6
Howell-LA 16.2

Relief Ranking
Davis-SD 26.0
Howell-LA 24.9
McDowell-NY-Phi . . 24.6
Dibble-Cin 23.2
Lancaster-Chi 18.2

Total Pitcher Index
Hershiser-LA 4.6
Maddux-Chi 3.4
McDowell-NY-Phi . . 3.1
Langston-Mon 2.7
Howell-LA 2.7

Total Baseball Ranking
Mitchell-SF 7.0
L.Smith-Atl 5.2
Clark-SF 5.0
Hershiser-LA 4.6
Bonds-Pit 4.2

April 10 Dave Stieb pitches a one-hitter against the Yankees, giving him three one-hitters in his last four starts (dating back to last September). Jamie Quirk's fifth-inning single is the only hit off Stieb in the 8-0 Blue Jays' victory.

July 2 Brewers outfielder Robin Yount, 33, collects his 2,500th hit in a 10-2 win over the Yankees.

July 11 Bo Jackson and Wade Boggs lead off the bottom of the first inning with back-to-back home runs off Rick Reuschel to spark the AL to a 5-3 win in the All-Star Game at Anaheim Stadium. Jackson earns MVP honors

August 4 Hard-luck pitcher Dave Stieb loses a perfect game when New York's Roberto Kelly doubles with two out in the ninth inning, and Stieb finishes with a 2-1 two-hitter. It's the third time that Stieb has lost a no-hitter with two out in the ninth.

September 27 The two San Francisco Bay teams clinch their divisions. Oak-land wins the AL West by beating Texas 5-0, while San Francisco loses 1-0 to the Dodgers but is assured of the NL West crown when the second-place Padres lose to the Reds 2-1 in 13 innings.

October 1 Minnesota's Kirby Puckett and San Diego's Tony Gwynn each win batting titles on the final day of the regular season. Puckett goes 2-for-5 to edge Carney Lansford .339 to .336, while Gwynn goes 3-for-4 to beat Will Clark .336 to .333.

October 8 Oakland beats Toronto 4-3 to win the ALCS 4-1 and advance to the World Series for the second straight year. Rickey Henderson, who hit .400 with eight stolen bases, is named series MVP.

October 14 Dave Stewart shuts out the Giants 5-0 on five hits in Game 1 of the World Series. He is the first pitcher to start consecutive World Series openers since the Reds' Don Gullett in 1975 and '76.

October 17 Game 3 of the World Series is postponed when an earthquake strikes the San Francisco Bay area a half hour before game time, causing minor damage to Candlestick Park and major damage to the surrounding area.

October 28 The A's take an 8-0 lead and beat the Giants 9-6 to complete a sweep of the World Series, the first since 1976. Oakland's Dave Stewart, who won two games, is named MVP.

November 15 Twenty-five-year-old Bret Saberhagen becomes the fourth pitcher ever to win the AL Cy Young Award twice, getting 27 of a possible 28 first-place votes for his 23-6, 2.16 ERA season.

November 20 Brewers center fielder Robin Yount edges the Rangers' Ruben Sierra to win his second AL MVP Award. Yount, who won as a shortstop in 1982, hit .318 last season with 21 home runs and 103 RBI.

BALTIMORE		BOSTON		CALIFORNIA		CHICAGO		CLEVELAND		DETROIT		KANSAS CITY	
M	F.Robinson	M	J.Morgan	M	D.Rader	M	J.Torborg	M	D.Edwards	M	S.Anderson	M	J.Wathan
1B	R.Milligan	1B	N.Esasky	1B	W.Joyner	1B	G.Walker	M	J.Hart	1B	D.Bergman	1B	G.Brett
2B	B.Ripken	2B	M.Barrett	2B	J.Ray	2B	S.Lyons	1B	P.O'Brien	2B	L.Whitaker	2B	F.White
SS	C.Ripken	SS	L.Rivera	SS	D.Schofield	SS	O.Guillen	2B	J.Browne	SS	A.Trammell	SS	K.Stillwell
3B	C.Worthington	3B	W.Boggs	3B	J.Howell	3B	C.Martinez	SS	F.Fermin	3B	R.Schu	3B	K.Seitzer
LF	P.Bradley	LF	M.Greenwell	LF	C.Davis	LF	D.Boston	3B	B.Jacoby	LF	F.Lynn	LF	B.Jackson
CF	M.Devereaux	CF	E.Burks	CF	D.White	CF	D.Gallagher	LF	J.Carter	CF	G.Pettis	CF	W.Wilson
RF	J.Orsulak	RF	K.Romine	RF	C.Washington	RF	I.Calderon	CF	B.Komminsk	RF	C.Lemon	RF	J.Eisenreich
C	M.Tettleton	C	R.Cerone	C	L.Parrish	C	C.Fisk	RF	C.Snyder	C	M.Heath	C	B.Boone
DH	L.Sheets	DH	D.Evans	DH	B.Downing	DH	H.Baines	C	A.Allanson	DH	K.Moreland	DH	D.Tartabull
								DH	D.Clark				
C	B.Melvin	O1	D.Heep	S	K.Anderson	O	D.Pasqua			O1	G.Ward	OD	P.Tabler
O	B.Anderson	S2	J.Reed	O	T.Armas	2	S.Fletcher	OD	D.James	CD	M.Nokes	2S	B.Wellman
1	J.Traber	C	R.Gedman			3	E.Williams	O	O.McDowell	O	K.Williams		
O	S.Finley	D	J.Rice					OD	A.Belle	S2	M.Brumley	P	B.Saberhagen
						P	B.Blyleven					P	M.Gubicza
P	B.Milacki	P	R.Clemens	P	M.Witt	P	M.Perez	P	B.Black	P	F.Tanana	P	T.Gordon
P	J.Ballard	P	M.Boddicker	P	K.McCaskill	P	E.King	P	J.Farrell	P	D.Alexander	P	C.Leibrandt
P	D.Schmidt	P	J.Dopson	P	C.Finley	P	S.Rosenberg	P	T.Candiotti	P	J.Morris	P	L.Aquino
P	P.Harnisch	P	M.Smithson	P	J.Abbott	P	G.Hibbard	P	G.Swindell	RP	P.Gibson	RP	J.Montgomery
RP	B.Holton	RP	D.Lamp	RP	W.Fraser	P	J.Reuss	P	S.Bailes	RP	M.Henneman	RP	T.Leach
RP	M.Williamson	RP	R.Murphy	RP	G.Minton	RP	S.Hillegas	RP	D.Jones	RP	F.Williams	RP	S.Farr
RP	M.Thurmond	RP	B.Stanley	RP	B.Harvey	RP	D.Pall	RP	J.Orosco				
						RP	B.Thigpen			P	J.Robinson	P	F.Bannister
P	D.Johnson	P	W.Gardner	P	B.McClure			P	R.Yett	P	K.Ritz	P	S.Crawford
P	G.Olson	P	L.Smith	P	D.Petry	P	R.Dotson	P	R.Nichols	P	C.Hudson		
P	J.Bautista	P	J.Price			P	B.Long			P	E.Nunez		
P	J.Tibbs	P	O.Boyd			P	T.McCarthy						
		P	E.Hetzel			P	K.Patterson						

MILWAUKEE		MINNESOTA		NEW YORK		OAKLAND		SEATTLE		TEXAS		TORONTO	
M	T.Trebelhorn	M	T.Kelly	M	D.Green	M	T.LaRussa	M	J.Lefebvre	M	B.Valentine	M	J.Williams
1B	G.Brock	1B	K.Hrbek	M	B.Dent	1B	M.McGwire	1B	A.Davis	1B	R.Palmeiro	M	C.Gaston
2B	J.Gantner	2B	A.Newman	1B	D.Mattingly	2B	T.Phillips	2B	H.Reynolds	2B	J.Franco	1B	F.McGriff
SS	B.Spiers	SS	G.Gagne	2B	S.Sax	SS	M.Gallego	SS	O.Vizquel	SS	S.Fletcher	2B	N.Liriano
3B	P.Molitor	3B	G.Gaetti	SS	A.Espinoza	3B	C.Lansford	3B	J.Presley	3B	S.Buechele	SS	T.Fernandez
LF	G.Braggs	LF	D.Gladden	3B	M.Pagliarulo	LF	R.Henderson	LF	G.Briley	LF	P.Incaviglia	3B	K.Gruber
CF	R.Yount	CF	K.Puckett	LF	M.Hall	CF	D.Henderson	CF	K.Griffey	CF	C.Espy	LF	G.Bell
RF	R.Deer	RF	R.Bush	CF	R.Kelly	RF	S.Javier	RF	D.Coles	RF	R.Sierra	CF	L.Moseby
C	B.Surhoff	C	B.Harper	RF	J.Barfield	C	T.Steinbach	C	D.Valle	C	C.Kreuter	RF	J.Felix
DH	J.Meyer	DH	J.Dwyer	C	D.Slaught	DH	D.Parker	DH	J.Leonard	DH	H.Baines	C	E.Whitt
				DH	S.Balboni							DH	R.Mulliniks
OD	M.Felder	1D	G.Larkin			C	R.Hassey	C	S.Bradley	SO	J.Kunkel		
S3	G.Sheffield	CD	T.Laudner	O	R.Henderson	S	W.Weiss	O	H.Cotto	DO	R.Leach	2S	M.Lee
1D	T.Francona	O	J.Moses	O	L.Polonia	O	J.Canseco	O	J.Buhner			CD	P.Borders
		2	W.Backman	C	B.Geren	O	L.Polonia					O	M.Wilson
P	C.Bosio	OD	C.Castillo					P	S.Bankhead	P	N.Ryan		
P	D.August			A.Hawkins		P	D.Stewart	P	B.Holman	P	B.Witt		
P	T.Higuera	P	A.Anderson	P	C.Parker	P	M.Moore	P	R.Johnson	P	K.Brown	P	J.Key
P	M.Knudson	P	F.Viola	P	D.LaPoint	P	B.Welch	P	B.Swift	P	C.Hough	P	D.Stieb
P	J.Navarro	P	R.Smith	P	C.Cary	P	S.Davis	P	E.Hanson	P	M.Jeffcoat	P	J.Cerutti
RP	C.Crim	P	S.Rawley	RP	L.Guetterman	P	C.Young	P	J.Reed	RP	K.Rogers	P	M.Flanagan
RP	B.Krueger	RP	J.Berenguer	RP	L.McCullers	RP	T.Burns	RP	M.Jackson	RP	J.Russell	RP	T.Stottlemyre
RP	D.Plesac	RP	J.Reardon	RP	E.Plunk	RP	G.Nelson	RP	M.Schooler	RP	C.Guante	RP	D.Ward
		RP	G.Wayne			RP	R.Honeycutt					RP	T.Henke
P	T.Filer			P	G.Cadaret			P	M.Dunne	P	J.Moyer	RP	D.Wells
P	B.Clutterbuck	P	R.Aguilera	P	W.Terrell	P	D.Eckersley	P	M.Langston	P	D.Hall		
P	T.Fossas	P	M.Dyer	P	D.Righetti			P	C.Zavaras	P	G.Mielke	P	F.Wills
P	B.Wegman	P	M.Guthrie	P	T.John								
		P	F.Oliveras	P	D.Mohorcic								
				P	R.Dotson								

TEAM	G	W	L	PCT	GB	R	OR	AB	H	2B	3B	HR	BB	SO	AVG	OBP	SLG	PRO	PRO+	BR	/A	PF	CHI	RC	SB	CS	SBA	SBR
EAST																												
TOR	162	89	73	.549		731	651	5581	1449	265	40	142	521	923	.260	.326	.398	.724	105	18	32	98	102	724	144	58	71	8
BAL	162	87	75	.537	2	708	686	5440	1369	238	33	129	593	957	.252	.329	.379	.708	102	-6	15	97	102	678	118	55	68	2
BOS	162	83	79	.512	6	**774**	735	5666	**1571**	**326**	30	108	**643**	755	**.277**	**.355**	**.403**	**.758**	106	**106**	**55**	106	93	**802**	56	35	62	-4
MIL	162	81	81	.500	8	707	679	5473	1415	235	32	126	455	791	.259	.321	.382	.703	98	-22	-15	99	**106**	677	**165**	62	73	12
NY	161	74	87	.460	14.5	698	792	5458	1470	229	23	130	502	831	.269	.334	.391	.725	98	26	35	99	98	709	137	60	70	5
CLE	162	73	89	.451	16	604	654	5463	1340	221	26	127	499	934	.245	.312	.365	.677	89	-72	-82	102	98	622	74	51	59	-8
DET	162	59	103	.364	30	617	816	5432	1315	198	24	116	585	899	.242	.320	.351	.671	91	-74	-60	98	100	616	103	50	67	1
WEST																												
OAK	162	99	63	.611		712	**576**	5416	1414	220	25	127	562	855	.261	.334	.381	.715	105	12	37	96	101	687	157	55	74	14
KC	162	92	70	.568	7	690	635	5475	1428	227	41	101	554	897	.261	.332	.373	.705	98	-9	-6	100	101	682	154	51	**75**	**16**
CAL	162	91	71	.562	8	669	578	5545	1422	208	37	**145**	429	1011	.256	.313	.386	.699	98	-38	-26	98	103	663	89	40	69	3
TEX	162	83	79	.512	16	695	714	5458	1433	260	**46**	122	503	989	.263	.329	.394	.723	101	18	7	102	98	694	101	49	67	1
MIN	162	80	82	.494	19	740	738	5581	1542	278	35	117	478	**743**	.276	.338	.402	.740	101	53	3	107	98	751	111	53	68	2
SEA	162	73	89	.451	26	694	728	5512	1417	237	29	134	489	838	.257	.323	.384	.707	95	-16	-38	103	103	679	81	55	60	-9
CHI	161	69	92	.429	29.5	693	750	5504	1493	262	36	94	464	873	.271	.331	.383	.714	103	4	21	98	100	696	97	52	65	-2
TOT	1133					9732		77004	20078	3404	457	1718	7277	12296	.261	.328	.384	.712							1587	726	69	41

TEAM	CG	SH	SV	IP	H	H/G	HR	BB	SO	RAT	ERA	ERA+	OAV	OOB	PR	/A	PF	CPI	FA	E	DP	FW	PW	BW	SBW	DIF
EAST																										
TOR	12	12	38	1467	1408	8.6	99	478	849	11.8	3.58	105	.255	.320	49	31	97	99	.980	127	164	-.1	3.2	3.3	.5	1.2
BAL	16	7	44	1448¹	1518	9.4	134	486	676	12.6	4.00	95	.272	.333	-19	-33	98	104	**.986**	87	163	**2.3**	-3.4	1.5	-.0	5.6
BOS	14	9	42	1460¹	1448	8.9	131	548	1054	12.5	4.01	102	.261	.331	-20	15	106	99	.980	127	162	-.1	1.5	**5.6**	-.7	-4.3
MIL	16	8	45	1432¹	1463	9.2	129	457	812	12.2	3.80	101	.265	.324	14	7	99	102	.975	155	164	-1.8	.7	-1.5	.9	1.7
NY	15	9	44	1414²	1550	9.9	150	521	787	13.4	4.50	86	.281	.347	-98	-100	100	102	.980	122	**183**	.1	-10.2	3.6	.2	-.2
CLE	23	13	38	1453	1423	8.8	107	**452**	844	11.8	3.65	109	.257	.315	38	50	102	96	.981	118	126	.4	5.1	-8.3	-1.1	-4.1
DET	24	4	26	1427¹	1514	9.5	150	652	831	13.9	4.53	84	.274	.355	-103	-114	98	103	.979	130	153	-.3	-11.6	-6.1	-.2	-3.8
WEST																										
OAK	17	**20**	**57**	1448¹	1287	**8.0**	103	510	930	**11.3**	**3.09**	**119**	**.238**	**.307**	**128**	**95**	95	103	.979	129	159	-.2	**9.7**	3.8	1.1	3.7
KC	27	13	38	1451²	1415	8.8	**86**	455	978	11.7	3.55	109	.257	.316	54	49	99	97	.982	114	139	.7	5.0	-.6	**1.3**	4.6
CAL	**32**	20	38	1454¹	1384	8.6	113	465	897	11.6	3.28	116	.253	.315	97	86	98	**107**	.985	96	173	1.7	8.8	-2.6	.0	2.1
TEX	26	7	44	1434¹	**1279**	8.0	119	654	**1112**	12.4	3.91	101	.239	.327	-4	9	102	92	.978	136	137	-.6	.9	.7	-.2	1.2
MIN	19	8	38	1429¹	1495	9.4	139	500	851	12.8	4.28	97	.264	.334	-63	-23	107	97	.982	107	141	1.1	-2.3	.3	-.0	.0
SEA	15	10	44	1438	1422	8.9	114	560	897	12.7	4.00	101	.259	.333	-19	4	104	98	.977	143	168	-1.1	.4	-3.9	-1.2	-2.3
CHI	9	5	46	1422	1472	9.3	144	539	778	12.9	4.23	90	.269	.338	-54	-67	98	101	.975	151	176	-1.6	-6.8	2.1	-.5	-4.7
TOT	265	145	582	20181		9.0				12.4	3.88		.261	.328					.980	1742	2208					

Runs		Hits		Doubles		Triples		Home Runs		Total Bases	
R.Henderson-NY-Oak	113	Puckett-Min	215	Boggs-Bos	51	Sierra-Tex	14	McGriff-Tor	36	Sierra-Tex	344
Boggs-Bos	113	Sax-NY	205	Puckett-Min	45	White-Cal	13	Carter-Cle	35	Yount-Mil	314
Yount-Mil	101	Boggs-Bos	205	Reed-Bos	42	Bradley-Bal	10	McGwire-Oak	33	Carter-Cle	303
Sierra-Tex	101	Yount-Mil	195	Bell-Tor	41			Jackson-KC	32	Mattingly-NY	301
McGriff-Tor	98			Yount-Mil	38			Esasky-Bos	30	Puckett-Min	295

Runs Batted In		Runs Produced		Bases On Balls		Batting Average		On Base Percentage		Slugging Average	
Sierra-Tex	119	Sierra-Tex	191	R.Henderson-NY-Oak	126	Puckett-Min	.339	Boggs-Bos	.434	Sierra-Tex	.543
Mattingly-NY	113	Yount-Mil	183	McGriff-Tor	119	Lansford-Oak	.336	Davis-Sea	.428	McGriff-Tor	.525
Esasky-Bos	108	Bell-Tor	174	Boggs-Bos	107	Boggs-Bos	.330	R.Henderson-NY-Oak	.413	Yount-Mil	.511
Jackson-KC	105	Mattingly-NY	169	Seitzer-KC	102	Yount-Mil	.318	McGriff-Tor	.402	Esasky-Bos	.500
Carter-Cle	105	Greenwell-Bos	168	Davis-Sea	101	Franco-Tex	.316	Evans-Bos	.402	Davis-Sea	.496

Production		Adjusted Production		Batter Runs		Adjusted Batter Runs		Clutch Hitting Index		Runs Created	
McGriff-Tor	.927	McGriff-Tor	162	McGriff-Tor	46.8	McGriff-Tor	49.1	Evans-Bos	122	Yount-Mil	125
Davis-Sea	.924	Boggs-Bos	155	Boggs-Bos	46.6	Yount-Mil	42.3	Brett-KC	121	Boggs-Bos	122
Yount-Mil	.898	Yount-Mil	152	Davis-Sea	44.2	Davis-Sea	40.7	Mattingly-NY	119	Sierra-Tex	122
Sierra-Tex	.895	Sierra-Tex	146	Yount-Mil	41.2	Boggs-Bos	38.7	Ray-Cal	118	McGriff-Tor	121
Boggs-Bos	.883	Baines-Chi-Tex	144	Sierra-Tex	37.4	Sierra-Tex	35.6	Greenwell-Bos	113	R.Henderson-NY-Oak	110

Total Average		Stolen Bases		Stolen Base Average		Stolen Base Runs		Fielding Runs		Total Player Rating	
McGriff-Tor	.986	R.Henderson-NY-Oak	77	Thurman-KC	100.0	R.Henderson-NY-Oak	14.7	Reynolds-Sea	27.0	R.Henderson-NY-Oak	5.2
R.Henderson-NY-Oak	.983	Espy-Tex	45	Franco-Tex	87.5	Thurman-KC	4.8	Howell-Cal	22.5	Yount-Mil	4.6
Davis-Sea	.975	White-Cal	44	Yount-Mil	86.4	Felder-Mil	4.8	Gruber-Tor	19.2	Sierra-Tex	3.9
Yount-Mil	.926	Sax-NY	43	Finley-Bal	85.0	Franco-Tex	4.5	Snyder-Cle	18.6	Puckett-Min	3.9
Boggs-Bos	.882	Pettis-Det	43	R.Henderson-NY-Oak	84.6			Puckett-Min	18.4	McGriff-Tor	3.5

Wins		Win Percentage		Games		Complete Games		Shutouts		Saves	
Saberhagen-KC	23	Saberhagen-KC	.793	Crim-Mil	76	Saberhagen-KC	12	Blyleven-Cal	5	Russell-Tex	38
Stewart-Oak	21	Blyleven-Cal	.773	Murphy-Bos	74	Morris-Det	10	Saberhagen-KC	4	Thigpen-Chi	34
Moore-Oak	19	Davis-Oak	.731	Rogers-Tex	73	Finley-Cal	9	McCaskill-Cal	4	Schooler-Sea	33
Davis-Oak	19	Stewart-Oak	.700	Russell-Tex	71					Plesac-Mil	33
Ballard-Bal	18	Ballard-Bal	.692	Guetterman-NY	70					Eckersley-Oak	33

Innings Pitched		Fewest Hits/Game		Fewest BB/Game		Strikeouts		Strikeouts/Game		Ratio	
Saberhagen-KC	262.1	Ryan-Tex	6.09	Key-Tor	1.13	Ryan-Tex	301	Ryan-Tex	11.32	Saberhagen-KC	8.71
Stewart-Oak	257.2	Gordon-KC	6.74	Saberhagen-KC	1.48	Clemens-Bos	230	Gordon-KC	8.45	Ryan-Tex	10.12
Gubicza-KC	255.0	Stieb-Tor	7.14	Blyleven-Cal	1.64	Saberhagen-KC	193	Clemens-Bos	8.17	Blyleven-Cal	10.34
Clemens-Bos	253.1	Saberhagen-KC	7.17	Bosio-Mil	1.84	Gubicza-KC	173	Witt-Tex	7.69	Moore-Oak	10.35
Milacki-Bal	243.0	Moore-Oak	7.19	Witt-Cal	1.96	Bosio-Mil	173	Viola-Min	7.07	Key-Tor	10.67

Earned Run Average		Adjusted ERA		Opponents' Batting Avg.		Opponents' On Base Pct.		Starter Runs		Adjusted Starter Runs	
Saberhagen-KC	2.16	Saberhagen-KC	178	Ryan-Tex	.187	Saberhagen-KC	.252	Saberhagen-KC	50.2	Saberhagen-KC	49.2
Finley-Cal	2.57	Finley-Cal	148	Gordon-KC	.210	Ryan-Tex	.276	Moore-Oak	34.3	Blyleven-Cal	29.1
Moore-Oak	2.61	Moore-Oak	141	Saberhagen-KC	.217	Moore-Oak	.288	Blyleven-Cal	31.0	Moore-Oak	28.8
Blyleven-Cal	2.73	Blyleven-Cal	140	Stieb-Tor	.219	Blyleven-Cal	.289	Finley-Cal	29.1	Finley-Cal	27.6
McCaskill-Cal	2.93	Clemens-Bos	131	Moore-Oak	.219	Bosio-Mil	.291	Bosio-Mil	24.2	Clemens-Bos	27.4

Clutch Pitching Index		Relief Runs		Adjusted Relief Runs		Relief Ranking		Total Pitcher Index		Total Baseball Ranking	
Cerutti-Tor	130	Montgomery-KC	25.7	Montgomery-KC	25.3	Jones-Cle	37.6	Saberhagen-KC	5.5	Saberhagen-KC	5.5
Ballard-Bal	123	Olson-Bal	20.7	Lamp-Bos	22.2	Russell-Tex	34.5	Moore-Oak	4.0	R.Henderson-NY-Oak	5.2
Finley-Cal	123	Lamp-Bos	19.5	Olson-Bal	19.8	Montgomery-KC	33.5	Jones-Cle	4.0	Yount-Mil	4.6
McCaskill-Cal	116	Henke-Tor	19.4	Henke-Tor	18.3	Henke-Tor	27.5	Russell-Tex	3.8	Moore-Oak	4.0
Davis-Oak	113	Burns-Oak	17.6	Orosco-Cle	16.3	Olson-Bal	25.7	Montgomery-KC	3.5	Jones-Cle	4.0

February 4 The St. Petersburg Pelicans get home runs from Lamar Johnson and Steve Kemp and rout the West Palm Beach Tropics 12-4 to win the first-ever championship of the Senior Professional Baseball Association.

April 20 Less than a year after being banished from baseball for his illegal gambling activities, all-time hit king Pete Rose pleads guilty to two felony counts of filing false income tax returns. On July 19, he will be sentenced to five months in prison and fined $50,000.

April 29 The Cubs' Greg Maddux sets a record for ML pitchers with seven putouts in a 4-0 win over the Dodgers.

May 18 In a 7-0 loss to the Astros, Cubs second baseman Ryne Sandberg finally commits an error. This ends his major league-record errorless streaks at 123 games and 584 chances.

May 22 Andre Dawson sets a major league record when he is intentionally walked five times during a 2-1 Cubs win over the Reds. Cincinnati issues seven intentional passes altogether to tie a record set by Houston in 1984.

June 4 The Braves select Florida high school shortstop Chipper Jones with the first pick in the annual free-agent draft.

June 14 The NL announces plans to expand from 12 to 14 teams for the 1993 season. The price of admission is $95 million.

August 28 Ryne Sandberg homers in the Cubs' 5–2 win over the Astros to become the first second baseman ever to post back-to-back 30-home run seasons.

September 29 The Reds clinch the NL West title during a rain delay of their 3-1 loss to the second-place Dodgers when the second-place Dodgers lose 4-3 to San Francisco. The Reds, never out of first place, are the first NL team ever to lead from wire to wire in a 162-game schedule.

September 30 Pittsburgh beats St. Louis 2-0 behind Doug Drabek's three-hitter to clinch its first NL East title since 1979.

October 12 Danny Jackson, Norm Charlton, and Randy Myers combine on a one-hitter, as Cincinnati beats the Pirates 2-1 to win the NLCS in six games.

October 16 In Game 1 of the World Series, the Reds rout the A's 7-0, ending Oakland's 10-game postseason winning streak.

October 20 The talk of an Oakland dynasty is proven premature, as Cincinnati beats Oakland 2-1 to complete one of the most stunning sweeps in World Series history. Series MVP Jose Rijo (2-0, 0.59 ERA) retires the last 20 batters he faces to give the Reds their first World Championship since 1976.

November 14 Doug Drabek (22-6) wins the NL Cy Young Award, collecting 23 of a possible 24 first-place votes.

November 19 Pittsburgh's Barry Bonds wins the NL MVP Award, easily outdistancing teammate and runner-up Bobby Bonilla. Bonds hit .301 with 23 home runs, 114 RBI, and 52 stolen bases.

December 5 In a major trade, the Blue Jays send first baseman Fred McGriff and veteran shortstop Tony Fernandez to San Diego for second baseman Roberto Alomar and outfielder Joe Carter.

ATLANTA		CHICAGO		CINCINNATI		HOUSTON		LOS ANGELES		MONTREAL	
M	R.Nixon	M	D.Zimmer	M	L.Piniella	M	A.Howe	M	T.Lasorda	M	B.Rodgers
M	B.Cox	1B	M.Grace	1B	T.Benzinger	1B	G.Davis	1B	E.Murray	1B	A.Galarraga
1B	D.Justice	2B	R.Sandberg	2B	M.Duncan	2B	B.Doran	2B	J.Samuel	2B	D.DeShields
2B	J.Treadway	SS	S.Dunston	SS	B.Larkin	SS	R.Ramirez	SS	A.Griffin	SS	S.Owen
SS	J.Blauser	3B	L.Salazar	3B	C.Sabo	3B	K.Caminiti	3B	M.Sharperson	3B	T.Wallach
3B	J.Presley	LF	D.Dascenzo	LF	B.Hatcher	LF	F.Stubbs	LF	K.Daniels	LF	T.Raines
LF	L.Smith	CF	J.Walton	CF	E.Davis	CF	E.Yelding	CF	S.Javier	CF	Da.Martinez
CF	R.Gant	RF	A.Dawson	RF	P.O'Neill	RF	G.Wilson	RF	H.Brooks	RF	L.Walker
RF	D.Murphy	C	J.Girardi	C	J.Oliver	C	C.Biggio	C	M.Scioscia	C	M.Fitzgerald
C	G.Olson										
		3S	D.Ramos	1	H.Morris	O2	C.Candaele	O	J.Gonzalez	O	M.Grissom
1O	T.Gregg	O	D.Smith	O	G.Braggs	O	E.Anthony	O	C.Gwynn	O	O.Nixon
32	M.Lemke							32	L.Harris		
O	O.McDowell	P	G.Maddux	P	T.Browning	P	J.Deshaies	O	K.Gibson	P	De.Martinez
S	A.Thomas	P	M.Harkey	P	J.Rijo	P	M.Scott			P	O.Boyd
		P	M.Bielecki	P	J.Armstrong	P	M.Portugal	P	R.Martinez	P	K.Gross
P	J.Smoltz	P	S.Wilson	P	R.Mahler	P	B.Gullickson	P	M.Morgan	P	M.Gardner
P	T.Glavine	P	S.Boskie	P	D.Jackson	P	D.Darwin	P	F.Valenzuela	P	Z.Smith
P	C.Leibrandt	RP	L.Lancaster	RP	N.Charlton	RP	J.Agosto	P	T.Belcher	RP	B.Sampen
P	M.Clary	RP	P.Assenmacher	RP	R.Dibble	RP	J.Clancy	RP	T.Crews	RP	T.Burke
P	S.Avery	RP	J.Pico	RP	R.Myers	RP	L.Andersen	RP	M.Hartley	RP	D.Hall
RP	T.Castillo							RP	J.Howell		
RP	R.Luecken	P	M.Williams	P	T.Layana	P	D.Schatzeder			P	C.Nabholz
RP	M.Grant	P	J.Nunez	P	S.Scudder	P	X.Hernandez	P	J.Neidlinger	P	S.Frey
		P	B.Long	P	T.Birtsas	P	D.Smith	P	J.Gott	P	D.Mohorcic
P	P.Smith										
P	D.Lilliquist										

NEW YORK		PHILADELPHIA		PITTSBURGH		SAN DIEGO		SAN FRANCISCO		ST.LOUIS	
M	D.Johnson	M	N.Leyva	M	J.Leyland	M	J.McKeon	M	R.Craig	M	W.Herzog
M	B.Harrelson	1B	R.Jordan	1B	S.Bream	M	G.Riddoch	M	W.Clark	M	R.Schoendienst
1B	D.Magadan	2B	T.Herr	2B	J.Lind	1B	Ja.Clark	2B	R.Thompson	M	J.Torre
2B	G.Jefferies	SS	D.Thon	SS	J.Bell	2B	R.Alomar	SS	J.Uribe	1B	P.Guerrero
SS	K.Elster	3B	C.Hayes	3B	J.King	SS	G.Templeton	3B	M.Williams	2B	J.Oquendo
3B	H.Johnson	LF	J.Kruk	LF	B.Bonds	3B	M.Pagliarulo	LF	K.Mitchell	SS	O.Smith
LF	K.McReynolds	CF	L.Dykstra	CF	A.Van Slyke	LF	B.Roberts	CF	B.Butler	3B	T.Pendleton
CF	D.Boston	RF	V.Hayes	RF	B.Bonilla	CF	J.Carter	RF	M.Kingery	LF	V.Coleman
RF	D.Strawberry	C	D.Daulton	C	M.LaValliere	RF	T.Gwynn	C	T.Kennedy	CF	W.McGee
C	M.Sasser					C	B.Santiago			RF	M.Thompson
		O2	R.Ready	32	W.Backman			C	G.Carter	C	T.Zeile
O2	K.Miller	O	D.Murphy	C	D.Slaught	1	P.Stephenson	O	K.Bass		
				1	G.Redus			O2	G.Litton	1O	D.Collins
				O	R.Reynolds					C	T.Pagnozzi
P	F.Viola	P	P.Combs			P	E.Whitson	P	J.Burkett	O2	R.Hudler
P	D.Gooden	P	T.Mulholland			P	B.Hurst	P	S.Garrelts		
P	D.Cone	P	B.Ruffin	P	D.Drabek	P	A.Benes	P	D.Robinson	P	J.Magrane
P	S.Fernandez	P	D.Cook	P	J.Smiley	P	D.Rasmussen	P	T.Wilson	P	J.DeLeon
P	R.Darling	P	J.DeJesus	P	N.Heaton	RP	G.Harris	RP	J.Brantley	P	J.Tudor
RP	A.Pena	RP	D.Akerfelds	P	B.Walk	RP	E.Show	RP	S.Bedrosian	P	B.Tewksbury
RP	J.Franco	RP	D.Carman	RP	B.Patterson	RP	C.Schiraldi	RP	A.Hammaker	P	B.Smith
RP	W.Whitehurst	RP	R.McDowell	RP	B.Landrum					RP	F.DiPino
				RP	B.Kipper	P	C.Lefferts			RP	K.Dayley
P	B.Ojeda	P	K.Howell			P	D.Lilliquist	P	R.Reuschel	RP	S.Terry
		P	J.Parrett					P	M.LaCoss		
		P	J.Grimsley	P	W.Terrell			P	K.Downs	P	K.Hill
				P	R.Tomlin			P	M.Thurmond	P	L.Smith
				P	Z.Smith			P	F.Oliveras	P	T.Niedenfuer
				P	S.Belinda					P	G.Mathews
				P	R.Reed						
				P	T.Power						

TEAM	G	W	L	PCT	GB	R	OR	AB	H	2B	3B	HR	BB	SO	AVG	OBP	SLG	PRO	PRO+	BR	/A	PF	CHI	RC	SB	CS	SBA	SBR
EAST																												
PIT	162	95	67	.586		733	619	5388	1395	288	42	138	582	914	.259	.334	.405	.739	113	64	92	96	99	738	137	52	72	10
NY	162	91	71	.562	4	775	613	5504	1410	278	21	172	536	851	.256	.326	.408	.734	107	48	50	100	106	748	110	33	77	13
MON	162	85	77	.525	10	662	598	5453	1363	227	43	114	576	1024	.250	.325	.370	.695	101	-18	7	96	99	672	235	99	70	11
PHI	162	77	85	.475	18	646	729	5535	1410	237	27	103	582	915	.255	.329	.363	.692	96	-19	-17	96	99	675	151	36	76	11
CHI	162	77	85	.475	18	690	774	5600	1474	240	36	136	406	869	.263	.316	.392	.708	93	-7	-56	107	103	695	108	35	76	15
STL	162	70	92	.432	25	599	698	5462	1398	255	41	73	517	844	.256	.323	.358	.681	93	-46	-49	100	95	650	221	74	75	22
WEST																												
CIN	162	91	71	.562		693	597	5525	1466	284	40	125	466	913	.265	.327	.399	.726	101	35	5	104	97	726	166	66	72	10
LA	162	86	76	.531	5	728	685	5491	1436	222	27	129	538	952	.262	.331	.382	.713	105	17	37	97	104	699	141	65	68	3
SF	162	85	77	.525	6	719	710	5573	1459	221	35	152	509	973	.262	.325	.396	.721	108	24	50	96	101	724	109	56	66	-1
SD	162	75	87	.463	16	673	673	5554	1429	243	35	123	509	902	.257	.323	.380	.703	98	-8	-13	101	99	682	138	59	70	6
HOU	162	75	87	.463	16	573	656	5371	1301	209	32	94	548	997	.242	.315	.345	.660	90	-83	-66	97	97	596	179	83	68	4
ATL	162	65	97	.401	26	682	821	5504	1376	263	26	162	473	1010	.250	.312	.396	.708	95	-8	-47	106	103	675	92	55	63	-5
TOT	972						8173	65968	16917	2967	405	1521	6221	11164	.256	.324	.383	.707							1787	727	71	100

TEAM	CG	SH	SV	IP	H	H/G	HR	BB	SO	RAT	ERA	ERA+	OAV	OOB	PR	/A	PF	CPI	FA	E	DP	FW	PW	BW	SBW	DIF
EAST																										
PIT	18	8	43	1447	1367	8.5	135	413	848	11.3	3.40	106	.251	.307	63	35	95	103	.979	134	125	-.4	3.6	9.5	.2	1.2
NY	18	14	41	1440	1339	8.4	119	444	1217	11.3	3.42	109	.246	.306	59	51	99	97	.978	132	107	-.3	5.3	5.2	.5	-.6
MON	18	11	50	1473¹	1349	8.2	127	510	991	11.6	3.37	108	.245	.313	70	46	96	103	.982	110	134	.9	4.7	.7	.3	-2.7
PHI	18	7	35	1449	1381	8.6	124	651	840	12.8	4.07	94	.253	.336	-45	-40	101	97	.981	117	150	.5	-4.1	-1.8	.3	1.1
CHI	13	7	42	1442²	1510	9.4	121	572	877	13.2	4.34	94	.271	.342	-87	-42	108	98	.980	124	136	.1	-4.3	-5.8	.7	5.3
STL	8	13	39	1443¹	1432	8.9	98	475	833	12.1	3.87	98	.261	.324	-13	-9	101	95	.979	130	114	-.2	-.9	-5.1	1.4	-6.2
WEST																										
CIN	14	12	50	1456¹	1338	8.3	124	543	1029	11.8	3.39	116	.246	.318	64	89	104	105	.983	102	126	1.4	9.2	.5	.2	-1.3
LA	29	12	29	1442	1364	8.5	137	478	1021	11.7	3.72	98	.249	.313	11	-10	97	96	.979	130	123	-.2	-1.0	3.8	-.5	3.0
SF	14	6	45	1446¹	1477	9.2	131	553	788	12.8	4.08	89	.267	.335	-46	-70	96	101	.983	107	148	1.1	-7.2	5.2	-1.0	5.9
SD	21	12	35	1461²	1437	8.8	147	507	928	12.1	3.68	104	.258	.322	19	24	101	106	.977	141	141	-.8	2.5	-1.3	-.2	-6.0
HOU	12	6	37	1450	1396	9.2	130	496	854	12.0	3.61	106	.255	.321	30	17	98	104	.978	131	124	-.3	1.8	-6.8	-.4	-.2
ATL	17	8	30	1429²	1527	9.6	128	579	938	13.4	4.58	88	.275	.346	-125	-86	106	97	.974	158	133	-1.8	-8.9	-4.8	-1.4	.9
TOT	200	116	476	17381¹		8.8				12.2	3.79		.256	.324					.980	1516	1561					

Runs		Hits		Doubles		Triples		Home Runs		Total Bases	
Sandberg-Chi	116	Dykstra-Phi	192	Jefferies-NY	40	Duncan-Cin	11	Sandberg-Chi	40	Sandberg-Chi	344
Bonilla-Pit	112	Butler-SF	192	Bonilla-Pit	39	Gwynn-SD	10	Strawberry-NY	37	Bonilla-Pit	324
Butler-SF	108	Sandberg-Chi	188	Sabo-Cin	38	L.Smith-Atl	9	Mitchell-SF	35	Gant-Atl	310
Gant-Atl	107	Wallach-Mon	185	Wallach-Mon	37	Coleman-StL	9	Williams-SF	33	Williams-SF	301
Dykstra-Phi	106	Larkin-Cin	185	Johnson-NY	37	Butler-SF	9	Bonds-Pit	33	Wallach-Mon	295

Runs Batted In		Runs Produced		Bases On Balls		Batting Average		On Base Percentage		Slugging Average	
Williams-SF	122	Bonilla-Pit	200	J.Clark-SD	104	McGee-StL	.335	Magadan-NY	.425	Bonds-Pit	.565
Bonilla-Pit	120	Bonds-Pit	185	Bonds-Pit	93	Murray-LA	.330	Dykstra-Phi	.420	Sandberg-Chi	.559
Carter-SD	115	Williams-SF	176	Butler-SF	90	Magadan-NY	.328	Murray-LA	.417	Mitchell-SF	.544
Bonds-Pit	114	Sandberg-Chi	176	Dykstra-Phi	89	Dykstra-Phi	.325	Bonds-Pit	.410	Gant-Atl	.539
Strawberry-NY	108	Carter-SD	170	V.Hayes-Phi	87	Dawson-Chi	.310	Butler-SF	.401	Justice-Atl	.535

Production		Adjusted Production		Batter Runs		Adjusted Batter Runs		Clutch Hitting Index		Runs Created	
Bonds-Pit	.974	Bonds-Pit	172	Bonds-Pit	48.1	Bonds-Pit	52.6	Carter-SD	130	Bonds-Pit	128
Murray-LA	.936	Murray-LA	160	Murray-LA	44.7	Murray-LA	48.0	Magadan-NY	123	Sandberg-Chi	124
Daniels-LA	.923	Daniels-LA	156	Sandberg-Chi	37.9	J.Clark-SD	35.9	Kruk-Phi	121	Dykstra-Phi	121
Sandberg-Chi	.918	Mitchell-SF	151	J.Clark-SD	36.5	Mitchell-SF	35.0	Guerrero-StL	119	Murray-LA	118
Justice-Atl	.909	Magadan-NY	143	Dykstra-Phi	34.3	Daniels-LA	34.9	V.Hayes-Phi	119	Gant-Atl	109

Total Average		Stolen Bases		Stolen Base Average		Stolen Base Runs		Fielding Runs		Total Player Rating	
Bonds-Pit	1.115	Coleman-StL	77	Gibson-LA	92.9	Coleman-StL	12.9	Thompson-SF	27.7	Bonds-Pit	7.2
Daniels-LA	.945	Yelding-Hou	64	Grissom-Mon	91.7	Bonds-Pit	7.8	Grace-Chi	26.7	Dykstra-Phi	5.8
Murray-LA	.945	Bonds-Pit	52	Dawson-Chi	88.9	Nixon-Mon	7.2	C.Hayes-Phi	23.6	Sandberg-Chi	4.3
Justice-Atl	.941	Butler-SF	51	Davis-Cin	87.5	Dykstra-Phi	6.9	Dykstra-Phi	20.1	Larkin-Cin	4.3
Dykstra-Phi	.941	Nixon-Mon	50	Dykstra-Phi	86.8			Larkin-Cin	19.9	Murray-LA	4.1

Wins		Win Percentage		Games		Complete Games		Shutouts		Saves	
Drabek-Pit	22	Drabek-Pit	.786	Agosto-Hou	82	Martinez-LA	12	Morgan-LA	4	Franco-NY	33
Viola-NY	20	Martinez-LA	.769	Assenmacher-Chi	74	Hurst-SD	9	Hurst-SD	4	Myers-Cin	31
Martinez-LA	20	Gooden-NY	.731	Harris-SD	73	Drabek-Pit	9			L.Smith-StL	27
Gooden-NY	19	Viola-NY	.625	McDowell-Phi	72	Maddux-Chi	8			Smith-Hou	23
		Browning-Cin	.625	Akerfelds-Phi	71					Lefferts-SD	23

Innings Pitched		Fewest Hits/Game		Fewest BB/Game		Strikeouts		Strikeouts/Game		Ratio	
Viola-NY	249.2	Fernandez-NY	6.52	Darwin-Hou	1.72	Cone-NY	233	Cone-NY	9.91	Darwin-Hou	9.46
Maddux-Chi	237.0	Rijo-Cin	6.90	Whitson-SD	1.85	Martinez-LA	223	Fernandez-NY	9.08	Drabek-Pit	9.69
Martinez-LA	234.1	Martinez-LA	7.34	Leibrandt-Atl	1.94	Gooden-NY	223	Gooden-NY	8.63	D.Martinez-Mon	9.80
Gooden-NY	232.2	Drabek-Pit	7.39	D.Martinez-Mon	1.95	Viola-NY	182	Martinez-LA	8.56	Martinez-LA	10.06
		Darwin-Hou	7.52	Browning-Cin	2.06	Fernandez-NY	181	DeLeon-StL	8.08	Fernandez-NY	10.14

Earned Run Average		Adjusted ERA		Opponents' Batting Avg.		Opponents' On Base Pct.		Starter Runs		Adjusted Starter Runs	
Darwin-Hou	2.21	Darwin-Hou	168	Fernandez-NY	.200	Darwin-Hou	.267	Viola-NY	31.2	Whitson-SD	31.1
Smith-Mon-Pit	2.55	Whitson-SD	147	Rijo-Cin	.212	Drabek-Pit	.275	Whitson-SD	30.3	Viola-NY	29.8
Whitson-SD	2.60	Rijo-Cin	146	Martinez-LA	.220	D.Martinez-Mon	.275	Smith-Mon-Pit	29.7	Rijo-Cin	27.3
Viola-NY	2.67	Smith-Mon-Pit	143	Drabek-Pit	.225	Martinez-LA	.279	Darwin-Hou	28.5	Darwin-Hou	27.1
Rijo-Cin	2.70	Viola-NY	140	Darwin-Hou	.225	Fernandez-NY	.280	Drabek-Pit	26.4	Smith-Mon-Pit	26.0

Clutch Pitching Index		Relief Runs		Adjusted Relief Runs		Relief Ranking		Total Pitcher Index		Total Baseball Ranking	
Gullickson-Hou	121	Dibble-Cin	22.3	Dibble-Cin	23.9	Myers-Cin	30.5	Viola-NY	3.6	Bonds-Pit	7.2
Smith-Mon-Pit	118	Brantley-SF	21.5	Charlton-Cin	20.6	Dibble-Cin	29.1	Whitson-SD	3.4	Dykstra-Phi	5.8
Whitson-SD	115	Harris-SD	19.4	Brantley-SF	20.1	Harris-SD	27.1	Drabek-Pit	3.4	Sandberg-Chi	4.3
Rasmussen-SD	114	Charlton-Cin	18.0	Harris-SD	19.8	Charlton-Cin	25.7	Myers-Cin	3.3	Larkin-Cin	4.3
Darwin-Hou	107	Myers-Cin	16.5	Myers-Cin	18.0	Brantley-SF	24.8	Rijo-Cin	3.1	Murray-LA	4.1

January 9 Jim Palmer, a three-time AL Cy Young Award winner, and Joe Morgan, a two-time NL MVP, are elected to the Hall of Fame in their first years of eligibility.

June 11 Ageless Nolan Ryan pitches his unprecedented sixth career no-hitter, striking out 14 batters in a 5-0 win over the A's.

June 29 Oakland's Dave Stewart and the Dodgers' Fernando Valenzuela both throw no-hitters. Stewart blanks the Blue Jays 5-0, and a few hours later Valenzuela beats the Cardinals 6-0.

July 17 The Twins pull a major league first—two triple plays in the same game. Both are started on grounders to third baseman Gary Gaetti.

August 31 Ken Griffeys—Jr. in center and Sr. in left—become the first father-and-son combination in major league history to play as teammates, and they each go 1-for-4 in Seattle's 5-2 win over the Royals. The Mariners had signed the elder Griffey after he was waived by the Reds last week.

September 2 In the year of no-hitters, Dave Stieb pitches the ninth and final one of the season, blanking Cleveland 3-0. It is the first no-hitter in Blue Jays' history, and the first for Stieb after numerous close calls.

September 25 The Oakland A's clinch their third straight AL West title by beating Kansas City 5-0.

September 30 The White Sox beat Seattle 2-1 in the last game played at historic Comiskey Park, which is to be torn down after 80 seasons of major league ball. Chicago will play next season at the new Comiskey Park located across the street.

October 3 Boston beats Chicago 3-1 on the final day of the season to wrap up its third AL East title in five seasons.

October 3 George Brett pinch hits a single in Kansas City's finale to end the season at .329 and win the AL batting crown, his third in three decades. Willie McGee's .335 wins the NL batting title despite having been traded out of the league in August.

October 10 After Red Sox starter Roger Clemens is ejected in the second inning for cursing at home plate umpire Terry Cooney, Oakland beats Boston 3-1 to complete a four-game sweep of the ALCS and earn its third straight trip to the World Series.

November 13 Oakland's Bob Welch wins the AL Cy Young Award. His 27 wins were the most in the majors since Steve Carlton in 1972.

November 20 Oakland's Rickey Henderson edges Detroit's Cecil Fielder for the AL MVP Award. Henderson hit .325 with 28 home runs and a major league-best 65 stolen bases.

December 6 At Leland's auction house in New York City, Shoeless Joe Jackson's signature is sold for $23,100, the most money ever paid for a baseball signature. Jackson, who could not read or write, copied the signature from one written out by his wife. The signature, which was resold within hours, was cut from an unknown document.

	BALTIMORE		BOSTON		CALIFORNIA		CHICAGO		CLEVELAND		DETROIT		KANSAS CITY
M	F.Robinson	M	J.Morgan	M	D.Rader	M	J.Torborg	M	J.McNamara	M	S.Anderson	M	J.Wathan
1B	R.Milligan	1B	C.Quintana	1B	W.Joyner	1B	C.Martinez	1B	B.Jacoby	1B	C.Fielder	1B	G.Brett
2B	B.Ripken	2B	Jo.Reed	2B	J.Ray	2B	S.Fletcher	2B	J.Browne	2B	L.Whitaker	2B	F.White
SS	C.Ripken	SS	L.Rivera	SS	D.Schofield	SS	O.Guillen	SS	F.Fermin	SS	A.Trammell	SS	K.Stillwell
3B	C.Worthington	3B	W.Boggs	3B	J.Howell	3B	R.Ventura	3B	C.Baerga	3B	T.Phillips	3B	K.Seitzer
LF	P.Bradley	LF	M.Greenwell	LF	D.Bichette	LF	I.Calderon	LF	C.Maldonado	LF	G.Ward	LF	W.Wilson
CF	M.Devereaux	CF	E.Burks	CF	D.White	CF	L.Johnson	CF	M.Webster	CF	L.Moseby	CF	B.Jackson
RF	S.Finley	RF	T.Brunansky	RF	D.Winfield	RF	S.Sosa	RF	C.Snyder	RF	C.Lemon	RF	J.Eisenreich
C	M.Tettleton	C	T.Pena	C	L.Parrish	C	C.Fisk	C	S.Alomar	C	M.Heath	C	M.Macfarlane
DH	S.Horn	DH	D.Evans	DH	B.Downing	DH	D.Pasqua	DH	C.James	DH	D.Bergman	DH	G.Perry
O	J.Orsulak	2S	J.Reed	DO	C.Davis	D1	R.Kittle	1O	D.James	OD	L.Sheets	OD	D.Tartabull
CD	B.Melvin			2S	D.Hill			O	A.Cole	3S	T.Fryman	2S	B.Pecota
OD	B.Anderson	OD	L.Polonia			P	G.Hibbard			O	J.Shelby		
		1	L.Stevens			P	J.McDowell	P	G.Swindell			P	T.Gordon
P	P.Harnisch	P	G.Harris			P	M.Perez	P	T.Candiotti	P	J.Morris	P	K.Appier
P	D.Johnson	P	D.Kiecker	P	C.Finley	P	E.King	P	B.Black	P	F.Tanana	P	B.Saberhagen
P	B.Milacki	P	T.Bolton	RP	M.Langston	RP	W.Edwards	P	S.Valdez	P	D.Petry	P	S.Davis
P	J.Ballard	RP	D.Lamp	P	J.Abbott	RP	B.Thigpen	P	J.Farrell	P	J.Robinson	RP	S.Farr
P	B.McDonald	RP	W.Gardner	P	K.McCaskill	RP	D.Pall	RP	S.Olin	RP	P.Gibson	RP	J.Montgomery
RP	M.Williamson	RP	R.Murphy	P	B.Blyleven			RP	D.Jones	RP	M.Henneman	RP	S.Crawford
RP	G.Olson			RP	M.Eichhorn	P	A.Fernandez	RP	J.Orosco	RP	J.Gleaton		
RP	J.Price	P	J.Gray	RP	W.Fraser	P	A.Peterson					P	M.Gubicza
		P	J.Reardon	RP	M.Fetters	P	B.Jones	P	M.Walker	P	E.Nunez	P	A.McGaffigan
P	J.Mitchell					P	K.Patterson			P	S.Searcy	P	M.Davis
P	B.Holton			P	B.Harvey	P	S.Radinsky			P	W.Terrell	P	L.Aquino
P	J.Tibbs									P	B.DuBois		
										P	C.Parker		

	MILWAUKEE		MINNESOTA		NEW YORK		OAKLAND		SEATTLE		TEXAS		TORONTO
M	T.Trebelhorn	M	T.Kelly	M	B.Dent	M	T.LaRussa	M	J.Lefebvre	M	B.Valentine	M	C.Gaston
1B	G.Brock	1B	K.Hrbek	1B	D.Mattingly	1B	M.McGwire	1B	P.O'Brien	1B	R.Palmeiro	1B	F.McGriff
2B	J.Gantner	2B	A.Newman	2B	S.Sax	2B	W.Randolph	2B	H.Reynolds	2B	J.Franco	2B	M.Lee
SS	B.Spiers	SS	G.Gagne	SS	W.Weiss	SS	O.Vizquel	SS	J.Huson	SS	T.Fernandez	
3B	G.Sheffield	3B	G.Gaetti	SS	A.Espinoza	3B	C.Lansford	3B	E.Martinez	3B	S.Buechele	3B	K.Gruber
LF	M.Felder	LF	D.Gladden	3B	R.Velarde	LF	R.Henderson	LF	G.Briley	LF	P.Incaviglia	LF	G.Bell
CF	R.Yount	CF	K.Puckett	LF	O.Azocar	CF	D.Henderson	CF	K.Griffey	CF	G.Pettis	CF	M.Wilson
RF	R.Deer	RF	S.Mack	CF	R.Kelly	RF	F.Jose	RF	H.Cotto	RF	R.Sierra	RF	J.Felix
C	B.Surhoff	C	B.Harper	RF	J.Barfield	C	T.Steinbach	C	D.Valle	C	G.Petralli	C	P.Borders
DH	D.Parker	DH	G.Larkin	C	B.Geren	DH	J.Canseco	DH	A.Davis	DH	H.Baines	DH	J.Olerud
				DH	S.Balboni								
21	P.Molitor	OD	J.Moses			2S	M.Gallego	C	S.Bradley	O1	J.Daugherty	OD	G.Hill
O	G.Vaughn	2	F.Manrique	DO	M.Hall	CD	R.Hassey	OD	J.Leonard	S3	J.Kunkel	C	G.Myers
S2	E.Diaz			3O	J.Leyritz					CD	M.Stanley		
				1D	K.Maas								
P	T.Higuera	P	K.Tapani	CD	M.Nokes	P	D.Stewart	P	E.Hanson	P	B.Witt	P	D.Stieb
P	M.Knudson	P	R.Smith			P	B.Welch	P	M.Young	P	C.Hough	P	T.Stottlemyre
P	J.Navarro	P	D.West	P	T.Leary	P	S.Sanderson	P	R.Johnson	P	N.Ryan	P	D.Wells
P	R.Robinson	P	M.Guthrie	P	D.LaPoint	P	M.Moore	P	B.Holman	P	K.Brown	P	J.Key
P	C.Bosio	RP	J.Berenguer	P	A.Hawkins	P	C.Young	RP	B.Swift	P	J.Moyer	P	J.Cerutti
RP	T.Edens	RP	T.Drummond	RP	C.Cary	RP	T.Burns	RP	M.Jackson	RP	M.Jeffcoat	RP	D.Ward
RP	C.Crim	RP	T.Leach	P	M.Witt	RP	G.Nelson	RP	M.Schooler	RP	K.Rogers	RP	F.Wills
RP	D.Plesac			RP	G.Cadaret	RP	D.Eckersley			RP	B.Arnsberg	P	J.Acker
		P	S.Erickson	RP	L.Guetterman	P	R.Honeycutt	P	K.Comstock				
P	B.Krueger	RP	R.Aguilera	RP	J.Robinson							P	T.Henke
P	P.Mirabella	P	J.Candelaria									P	W.Blair
				P	E.Plunk								
				P	D.Righetti								
				P	J.Jones								

TEAM	G	W	L	PCT	GB	R	OR	AB	H	2B	3B	HR	BB	SO	AVG	OBP	SLG	PRO	PRO+	BR	/A	PF	CHI	RC	SB	CS	SBA	SBR
EAST																												
BOS	162	88	74	.543		699	664	5516	**1502**	298	31	106	598	795	.272	.346	.395	.741	102	57	22	105	92	733	53	52	50	-15
TOR	162	86	76	.531	2	**767**	661	5589	1479	263	**50**	167	526	970	.265	.331	**.419**	**.750**	106	56	42	102	101	**769**	111	52	68	2
DET	162	79	83	.488	9	750	754	5479	1418	241	32	**172**	634	952	.259	.339	.409	.748	101	**62**	57	101	98	754	82	57	59	-10
CLE	162	77	85	.475	11	732	737	5485	1465	266	41	110	458	836	.267	.327	.391	.718	101	-5	-2	100	107	694	107	52	67	1
BAL	161	76	85	.472	11.5	669	698	5410	1328	234	22	132	**660**	962	.245	.332	.370	.702	99	-21	1	97	98	676	94	52	64	-3
MIL	162	74	88	.457	14	732	760	5503	1408	247	36	128	519	821	.256	.324	.384	.708	98	-24	-19	99	**109**	692	**164**	72	69	6
NY	162	67	95	.414	21	603	749	5483	1322	208	19	147	427	1027	.241	.302	.366	.668	86	-109	-111	100	105	605	119	45	**73**	9
WEST																												
OAK	162	103	59	.636		733	**570**	5433	1379	209	22	164	651	992	.254	.339	.391	.730	**108**	31	**61**	96	100	739	141	54	72	**10**
CHI	162	94	68	.580	9	682	633	5402	1393	251	44	106	478	903	.258	.322	.379	.701	97	-35	-21	98	105	651	140	90	61	-12
TEX	162	83	79	.512	20	676	696	5469	1416	257	27	110	575	1054	.259	.333	.376	.709	98	-11	-12	100	98	688	115	48	71	6
CAL	162	80	82	.494	23	690	706	5570	1448	237	27	147	566	1000	.260	.331	.391	.722	103	10	24	98	96	691	69	43	62	-5
SEA	162	77	85	.475	26	640	680	5474	1465	251	26	107	596	749	.259	.336	.373	.709	97	-7	-15	101	92	691	105	51	67	1
KC	161	75	86	.466	27.5	707	709	5488	1465	**316**	44	100	498	879	.267	.331	.395	.726	104	14	25	98	101	706	107	62	63	-5
MIN	162	74	88	.457		666	729	5499	1458	281	39	100	445	749	.265	.326	.385	.711	92	-17	-61	107	99	673	96	53	64	-3
TOT	1133					9746		76800	19900	3559	460	1796	7631	12689	.259	.330	.388	.718							1503	783	66	-19

TEAM	CG	SH	SV	IP	H	H/G	HR	BB	SO	RAT	ERA	ERA+	OAV	OOB	PR	/A	PF	CPI	FA	E	DP	FW	PW	BW	SBW	DIF
EAST																										
BOS	15	13	44	1442	1439	9.0	**92**	519	997	12.5	3.72	110	.261	.329	30	57	104	100	.980	123	154	-.2	5.8	2.2	-1.4	.6
TOR	6	9	48	1454	1434	8.9	143	**445**	892	11.9	3.84	103	.260	.319	11	17	101	99	**.986**	86	144	**2.0**	1.7	4.3	.3	-3.4
DET	15	12	45	1430	1401	8.8	154	661	856	13.3	4.39	90	.259	.345	-76	-68	101	98	.979	131	178	-.7	-6.9	5.8	-.9	.7
CLE	12	10	47	1427[1]	1491	9.4	163	518	860	12.9	4.26	92	.270	.337	-57	-55	100	102	.981	117	146	.2	-5.6	-.2	.2	1.4
BAL	10	5	43	1435[1]	1445	9.1	161	537	776	12.5	4.04	94	.264	.332	-21	-39	97	103	.985	93	151	1.6	-4.0	.1	-.2	-2.0
MIL	23	13	42	1445	1558	9.7	121	469	771	12.9	4.08	95	.275	.335	-28	-34	99	101	.976	149	152	-1.8	-3.5	-1.9	.7	-.6
NY	15	6	41	1444[2]	1430	8.9	144	618	909	12.9	4.21	94	.261	.339	-49	-39	102	99	.980	126	164	-.4	-4.0	-11.3	1.1	.6
WEST																										
OAK	18	**16**	64	1456	**1287**	8.0	123	494	831	**11.2**	3.18	117	.238	.305	118	87	95	101	**.986**	87	152	2.0	8.9	6.2	1.2	3.8
CHI	17	10	**68**	1449[1]	1313	8.2	106	548	914	11.8	3.61	106	.244	.318	48	34	98	95	.980	124	169	-.3	3.5	-2.1	-1.1	13.0
TEX	**25**	9	36	1444[2]	1343	8.4	113	623	997	12.5	3.83	102	.248	.330	12	14	100	97	.979	133	161	-.8	1.4	-1.2	.7	1.9
CAL	21	13	42	1454	1482	9.2	106	544	944	12.8	3.79	101	.267	.337	18	3	98	**105**	.978	142	**186**	-1.4	.3	2.4	-.4	-2.0
SEA	21	7	41	1443[1]	1319	8.2	120	606	**1064**	12.3	3.69	107	.243	.324	34	42	101	97	.979	130	152	-.6	4.3	-1.5	.2	-6.4
KC	18	8	33	1420[2]	1449	9.2	116	560	1006	13.0	3.93	97	.264	.337	-5	-16	98	102	.980	122	161	-.2	-1.6	2.5	-.4	-5.9
MIN	13	13	43	1435[2]	1509	9.5	134	489	872	12.7	4.12	101	.273	.335	-35	-4	106	101	.983	101	161	1.1	.4	-6.2	-.2	-2.2
TOT	229	144	637	20182[1]		8.9				12.5	3.91		.259	.330					.981	1664	2231					

Runs
R.Henderson-Oak . 119
Fielder-Det . 104
Reynolds-Sea . 100
Yount-Mil . 98
Phillips-Det . 97

Hits
Palmeiro-Tex . 191
Boggs-Bos . 187
Kelly-NY . 183
Greenwell-Bos . 181

Doubles
J.Reed-Bos . 45
Brett-KC . 45
Calderon-Chi . 44
Boggs-Bos . 44
Harper-Min . 42

Triples
Fernandez-Tor . 17
Sosa-Chi . 10
Polonia-NY-Cal . 9
Liriano-Tor-Min . 9
Johnson-Chi . 9

Home Runs
Fielder-Det . 51
McGwire-Oak . 39
J.Canseco-Oak . 37
McGriff-Tor . 35
Gruber-Tor . 31

Total Bases
Fielder-Det . 339
Gruber-Tor . 303
McGriff-Tor . 295
K.Griffey-Sea . 287
Burks-Bos . 286

Runs Batted In
Fielder-Det . 132
Gruber-Tor . 118
McGwire-Oak . 108
J.Canseco-Oak . 101
Sierra-Tex . 96

Runs Produced
Fielder-Det . 185
Gruber-Tor . 179
Yount-Mil . 158
Burks-Bos . 157
McGwire-Oak . 156

Bases On Balls
McGwire-Oak . 110
Tettleton-Bal . 106
Phillips-Det . 99
R.Henderson-Oak . 97
McGriff-Tor . 94

Batting Average
Brett-KC . 329
R.Henderson-Oak . 325
Palmeiro-Tex . 319
Trammell-Det . 304
Boggs-Bos . 302

On Base Percentage
R.Henderson-Oak . 441
McGriff-Tor . 403
E.Martinez-Sea . 399
Davis-Sea . 393
Brett-KC . 392

Slugging Average
Fielder-Det . 592
R.Henderson-Oak . 577
J.Canseco-Oak . 543
McGriff-Tor . 530
Brett-KC . 515

Production
R.Henderson-Oak . 1.017
Fielder-Det . 972
McGriff-Tor . 932
J.Canseco-Oak . 917
Brett-KC . 906

Adjusted Production
R.Henderson-Oak . 190
Fielder-Det . 167
J.Canseco-Oak . 160
McGriff-Tor . 156
Brett-KC . 154

Batter Runs
R.Henderson-Oak . 57.5
Fielder-Det . 51.3
McGriff-Tor . 45.5
Brett-KC . 37.0
J.Canseco-Oak . 34.3

Adjusted Batter Runs
R.Henderson-Oak . 62.7
Fielder-Det . 50.4
McGriff-Tor . 43.4
Brett-KC . 38.7
J.Canseco-Oak . 38.4

Clutch Hitting Index
Leonard-Sea . 138
Guillen-Chi . 122
Fletcher-Chi . 121
Gaetti-Min . 118
Gruber-Tor . 117

Runs Created
R.Henderson-Oak . 137
Fielder-Det . 129
McGriff-Tor . 124
Brett-KC . 106
K.Griffey-Sea . 103

Total Average
R.Henderson-Oak . 1.241
Fielder-Det . 1.007
McGriff-Tor . 983
J.Canseco-Oak . 943
McGwire-Oak . 903

Stolen Bases
R.Henderson-Oak . 65
Sax-NY . 43
Kelly-NY . 42
Cole-Cle . 40
Pettis-Tex . 38

Stolen Base Average
Cotto-Sea . 87.5
R.Henderson-Oak . 86.7
Molitor-Mil . 85.7
Gantner-Mil . 85.7
Wilson-Tor . 85.2

Stolen Base Runs
R.Henderson-Oak . 13.5
Sax-NY . 7.5
Cole-Cle . 6.6
Wilson-Tor . 4.5
Cotto-Sea . 4.5

Fielding Runs
Espinoza-NY . 21.1
Reynolds-Sea . 15.1
Quintana-Bos . 14.5
Gaetti-Min . 13.8
Gallego-Oak . 13.7

Total Player Rating
R.Henderson-Oak . 8.2
Fielder-Det . 4.2
McGriff-Tor . 4.1
J.Canseco-Oak . 4.0
Fisk-Chi . 3.5

Wins
Welch-Oak . 27
Stewart-Oak . 22
Clemens-Bos . 21

Win Percentage
Welch-Oak . .818
Clemens-Bos . .778
Stieb-Tor . .750
Boddicker-Bos . .680

Games
Thigpen-Chi . 77
Ward-Tor . 73
Montgomery-KC . 73
Rogers-Tex . 69
Henneman-Det . 69

Complete Games
Stewart-Oak . 11
Morris-Det . 11

Shutouts
Stewart-Oak . 4
Clemens-Bos . 4
Perez-Chi . 3
Morris-Det . 3
Appier-KC . 3

Saves
Thigpen-Chi . 57
Eckersley-Oak . 48
Jones-Cle . 43
Olson-Bal . 37
Righetti-NY . 36

Innings Pitched
Stewart-Oak . 267.0
Morris-Det . 249.2
Welch-Oak . 238.0
Hanson-Sea . 236.0
Finley-Cal . 236.0

Fewest Hits/Game
Ryan-Tex . 6.04
Johnson-Sea . 7.13
Clemens-Bos . 7.61
Stewart-Oak . 7.62
Stieb-Tor . 7.72

Fewest BB/Game
Anderson-Min . 1.86
Swindell-Cle . 1.97
Clemens-Bos . 2.13
Knudson-Mil . 2.14
Wells-Tor . 2.14

Strikeouts
Ryan-Tex . 232
Witt-Tex . 221
Hanson-Sea . 211
Clemens-Bos . 209
Langston-Cal . 195

Strikeouts/Game
Ryan-Tex . 10.24
Witt-Tex . 8.96
Clemens-Bos . 8.24
Gordon-KC . 8.06
Hanson-Sea . 8.05

Ratio
Ryan-Tex . 9.62
Clemens-Bos . 10.01
Wells-Tor . 10.10
Hanson-Sea . 10.49
Stewart-Oak . 10.58

Earned Run Average
Clemens-Bos . 1.93
Finley-Cal . 2.40
Stewart-Oak . 2.56
Appier-KC . 2.76
Stieb-Tor . 2.93

Adjusted ERA
Clemens-Bos . 211
Finley-Cal . 159
Stewart-Oak . 145
Appier-KC . 139
Stieb-Tor . 134

Opponents' Batting Avg.
Ryan-Tex . .188
Johnson-Sea . .216
Clemens-Bos . .228
Stieb-Tor . .230
Stewart-Oak . .231

Opponents' On Base Pct.
Ryan-Tex . .269
Clemens-Bos . .280
Wells-Tor . .283
Hanson-Sea . .289
Black-Cle-Tor . .293

Starter Runs
Clemens-Bos . 50.1
Stewart-Oak . 39.9
Finley-Cal . 39.4
Welch-Oak . 23.6
Appier-KC . 23.6

Adjusted Starter Runs
Clemens-Bos . 54.3
Finley-Cal . 37.1
Stewart-Oak . 34.2
Stieb-Tor . 23.4
Appier-KC . 22.0

Clutch Pitching Index
Finley-Cal . 136
Appier-KC . 121
Clemens-Bos . 118
Welch-Oak . 117
Johnson-Bal . 113

Relief Runs
Farr-KC . 27.1
Eckersley-Oak . 26.8
Swift-Sea . 21.5
Thigpen-Chi . 20.5
Nelson-Oak . 19.4

Adjusted Relief Runs
Farr-KC . 26.1
Eckersley-Oak . 25.3
Swift-Sea . 22.3
Thigpen-Chi . 19.6
Nelson-Oak . 17.8

Relief Ranking
Eckersley-Oak . 45.1
Thigpen-Chi . 40.1
Farr-KC . 37.3
Olson-Bal . 24.1
Jones-Cle . 23.9

Total Pitcher Index
Clemens-Bos . 6.7
Eckersley-Oak . 4.7
Thigpen-Chi . 4.4
Finley-Cal . 4.1
Stewart-Oak . 4.1

Total Baseball Ranking
R.Henderson-Oak . 8.2
Clemens-Bos . 6.7
Eckersley-Oak . 4.7
Thigpen-Chi . 4.4
Fielder-Det . 4.2

January 8 For the first time since 1984, three players are elected to the Hall of Fame: two 300-game winners, Gaylord Perry and Ferguson Jenkins, and a 3,000-hit player, Rod Carew. Ironically, none of the three players ever appeared in a World Series.

February 26 Bill Veeck, the colorful owner of the Browns, Indians and White Sox (twice), and Yankee great "Poosh 'Em Up Tony" Lazzeri are elected to the Hall of Fame by the Veterans Committee.

March 22 At Sotheby's in New York, a 1909-10 tobacco card in mint condition of Honus Wagner sells for $451,000 to hockey star Wayne Gretzky and LA Kings owner Bruce McNall.

April 21 In the greatest extra-inning comeback in major league history, Pittsburgh scores six in the bottom of the 11th inning to erase a five-run Cub lead built in the top of the inning on Andre Dawson's grand slam. The Pirates had rallied earlier from a 7-2 deficit to tie the game

in the ninth.

May 7 Darryl Strawberry homers twice in his first game back at Shea Stadium since signing with the Dodgers as a free agent, but he grounds out with the tying run on third as the Mets hold on for a 6-5 win.

May 23 Philadelphia's Tommy Greene tosses the season's second no-hitter, a 2-0 win over Montreal.

July 28 Dennis Martinez pitches the 13th perfect game in baseball history, a 2-0 win at Los Angeles. Ron Hassey, who caught Len Barker's perfecto in Cleveland in 1981, is behind the plate for Martinez.

August 13 Atlanta, now 22-10 since the All-Star break, goes 11 games over .500 for the first time since 1984 as Tom Glavine wins again; this time a 9-2 triumph over the Giants.

August 25 Doug Dascenzo commits his first career error after 242 games, an NL

record, in the Cubs' 12-9 loss to the Padres.

September 13 A 55-ton block collapses in Montreal's Olympic Stadium. The Expos, already in last place, will have to play the rest of their home games on the road.

October 5 After eleven lead changes or ties in the closing weeks of the NL West race, the Braves finally clinch the division on the second-to-last day of the season.

October 17 The Braves take the well-below capacity crowd at Three Rivers Stadium out of the game quickly on Brian Hunter's two-run home run in the first inning. It's all John Smoltz needs as he tosses a 4-0 shutout to bring the first pennant to Atlanta.

October 22 It takes 12 innings, but the first World Series game ever in Atlanta goes to the Braves. Mark Lemke singles in David Justice for the 5-4 win.

	ATLANTA		CHICAGO		CINCINNATI		HOUSTON		LOS ANGELES		MONTREAL
M	B.Cox	M	D.Zimmer	M	L.Piniella	M	A.Howe	M	T.Lasorda	M	B.Rodgers
1B	B.Hunter	M	J.Altobelli	1B	H.Morris	1B	J.Bagwell	1B	E.Murray	M	T.Runnells
2B	M.Lemke	M	J.Essian	2B	B.Doran	2B	C.Candaele	2B	J.Samuel	1B	A.Galarraga
SS	R.Belliard	1B	M.Grace	SS	B.Larkin	SS	E.Yelding	SS	A.Griffin	2B	D.DeShields
3B	T.Pendleton	2B	R.Sandberg	3B	C.Sabo	3B	K.Caminiti	3B	L.Harris	SS	S.Owen
LF	O.Nixon	SS	S.Dunston	LF	B.Hatcher	LF	L.Gonzalez	LF	K.Daniels	3B	T.Wallach
CF	R.Gant	3B	L.Salazar	CF	E.Davis	CF	G.Young	CF	B.Butler	LF	I.Calderon
RF	D.Justice	LF	G.Bell	RF	P.O'Neill	RF	S.Finley	RF	D.Strawberry	CF	M.Grissom
C	G.Olson	CF	J.Walton	C	J.Oliver	C	C.Biggio	C	M.Scioscia	RF	Da.Martinez
		RF	A.Dawson							C	G.Reyes
S2	J.Blauser	C	R.Wilkins	2S	M.Duncan	S2	R.Ramirez	C1	G.Carter		
O	L.Smith			23	L.Quinones	S	A.Cedeno	O	S.Javier	O1	L.Walker
2	J.Treadway	O	D.Dascenzo	O	H.Winningham			3S	M.Sharperson		
1	S.Bream	3O	C.Walker	C	J.Reed	P	P.Harnisch			P	De.Martinez
				O	G.Braggs	P	M.Portugal	P	M.Morgan	P	M.Gardner
P	T.Glavine	P	G.Maddux			P	J.Deshaies	P	R.Martinez	P	B.Barnes
P	J.Smoltz	P	M.Bielecki	P	T.Browning	P	D.Kile	P	T.Belcher	P	C.Nabholz
P	C.Leibrandt	P	S.Boskie	P	J.Rijo	P	J.Jones	P	B.Ojeda	P	O.Boyd
P	S.Avery	P	F.Castillo	P	J.Armstrong	RP	A.Osuna	P	O.Hershiser	RP	B.Sampen
RP	M.Stanton	P	R.Sutcliffe	P	S.Scudder	RP	J.Corsi	RP	K.Gross	RP	B.Jones
RP	K.Mercker	RP	L.Lancaster	P	C.Hammond	RP	C.Schilling	RP	J.Gott	RP	S.Ruskin
RP	J.Berenguer	RP	B.Scanlan	RP	R.Myers			RP	T.Crews		
		RP	P.Assenmacher	RP	N.Charlton	P	R.Bowen			P	C.Haney
				RP	T.Power	P	D.Henry	P	M.Hartley	P	J.Fassero
		P	C.McElroy			P	X.Hernandez	P	J.Howell		
		P	D.Jackson	P	K.Gross	P	J.Clancy				
		P	H.Slocumb	P	R.Dibble						

	NEW YORK		PHILADELPHIA		PITTSBURGH		SAN DIEGO		SAN FRANCISCO		ST.LOUIS
M	B.Harrelson	M	N.Leyva	M	J.Leyland	M	G.Riddoch	M	R.Craig	M	J.Torre
M	M.Cubbage	M	J.Fregosi	1B	O.Merced	1B	F.McGriff	1B	W.Clark	1B	P.Guerrero
1B	D.Magadan	1B	J.Kruk	2B	J.Lind	2B	B.Roberts	2B	R.Thompson	2B	J.Oquendo
2B	G.Jefferies	2B	M.Morandini	SS	J.Bell	SS	T.Fernandez	SS	J.Uribe	SS	O.Smith
SS	K.Elster	SS	D.Thon	3B	B.Bonilla	3B	J.Howell	3B	M.Williams	3B	T.Zeile
3B	H.Johnson	3B	C.Hayes	LF	B.Bonds	LF	J.Clark	LF	M.Felder	LF	M.Thompson
LF	K.McReynolds	LF	W.Chamberlain	CF	A.Van Slyke	CF	D.Jackson	CF	W.McGee	CF	R.Lankford
CF	D.Boston	CF	V.Hayes	RF	G.Varsho	RF	T.Gwynn	RF	K.Bass	RF	F.Jose
RF	H.Brooks	RF	D.Murphy	C	M.LaValliere	C	B.Santiago	C	S.Decker	C	T.Pagnozzi
C	R.Cerone	C	D.Daulton								
				1O	G.Redus	O	T.Howard	S1	D.Anderson	O1	R.Hudler
O	M.Carreon	1	R.Jordan	C	D.Slaught	23	T.Teufel	O	K.Mitchell	2	G.Pena
2O	K.Miller	O	L.Dykstra					O	D.Lewis	1	G.Perry
O	V.Coleman	2	R.Ready	P	D.Drabek	P	A.Benes			O	B.Gilkey
CO	M.Sasser			P	Z.Smith	P	B.Hurst	P	B.Black		
S1	G.Templeton	P	T.Mulholland	P	J.Smiley	P	D.Rasmussen	P	J.Burkett	P	B.Smith
		P	T.Greene	P	R.Tomlin	P	G.Harris	P	T.Wilson	P	B.Tewksbury
P	D.Cone	P	J.DeJesus	P	B.Walk	RP	M.Maddux	P	D.Robinson	P	K.Hill
P	F.Viola	P	B.Ruffin	RP	V.Palacios	RP	R.Rodriguez	RP	K.Downs	P	O.Olivares
P	D.Gooden	P	D.Cox	RP	S.Belinda	RP	C.Lefferts	RP	J.Brantley	P	J.DeLeon
P	W.Whitehurst	RP	J.Boever	RP	B.Landrum			RP	F.Oliveras	RP	J.Agosto
P	R.Darling	RP	M.Williams			P	J.Melendez			RP	S.Terry
RP	P.Schourek	RP	R.McDowell	P	N.Heaton	P	E.Whitson	P	D.Righetti	RP	L.Smith
RP	J.Innis			P	B.Patterson	P	A.Peterson	P	P.McClellan		
RP	A.Pena	P	P.Combs	P	B.Kipper	P	R.Bones	P	R.Beck	P	R.Cormier
		P	J.Grimsley					P	B.Hickerson	P	C.Carpenter
P	D.Simons	P	D.Akerfelds								
P	T.Burke	P	W.Ritchie								
P	J.Franco										

TEAM	G	W	L	PCT	GB	R	OR	AB	H	2B	3B	HR	BB	SO	AVG	OBP	SLG	PRO	PRO+	BR	/A	PF	CHI	RC	SB	CS	SBA	SBR
EAST																												
PIT	162	98	64	.605		**768**	632	5449	**1433**	259	50	126	**620**	901	.263	.342	.398	**.740**	116	104	117	98	98	762	124	46	73	**10**
STL	162	84	78	.519	14	651	648	5362	1366	239	**53**	68	532	857	.255	.324	.357	.681	96	-13	-17	101	102	628	202	110	65	-5
PHI	162	78	84	.481	20	629	680	5521	1332	248	33	111	490	1026	.241	.306	.358	.664	93	-60	-53	99	**104**	609	92	30	**75**	**10**
CHI	160	77	83	.481	20	695	734	5522	1395	232	26	159	442	879	.253	.312	.390	.702	97	11	-21	105	103	675	123	64	66	-2
NY	161	77	84	.478	20.5	640	646	5359	1305	250	24	117	578	**789**	.244	.320	.365	.685	99	-9	-4	99	99	641	153	70	69	4
MON	161	71	90	.441	26.5	579	655	5412	1329	236	42	95	484	1056	.246	.311	.357	.668	94	-47	-38	99	95	607	**221**	100	69	6
WEST																												
ATL	162	94	68	.580		749	644	5456	1407	255	30	141	563	906	.258	.331	.393	.724	103	65	22	106	102	719	165	76	68	4
LA	162	93	69	.574	1	665	**565**	5408	1366	191	29	108	583	957	.253	.328	.359	.687	101	1	16	98	100	650	126	68	65	-3
SD	162	84	78	.519	10	636	646	5408	1321	204	36	121	501	1069	.244	.312	.362	.674	92	-35	-54	103	102	605	101	64	61	-8
SF	162	75	87	.463	19	649	697	5463	1345	215	48	141	471	973	.246	.311	.381	.692	103	-9	-12	97	100	647	95	57	63	-6
CIN	162	74	88	.457	20	689	691	5501	1419	250	37	**164**	488	1006	.258	.322	**.403**	.725	105	57	30	104	96	721	124	56	69	4
HOU	162	65	97	.401	29	605	717	5504	1345	240	43	79	502	1027	.244	.312	.347	.659	97	-64	-29	94	101	606	125	68	65	-3
TOT	970					7955		65365	16363	2819	441	1430	6254	11446	.250	.319	.373	.692							1651	809	67	10

TEAM	CG	SH	SV	IP	H	H/G	HR	BB	SO	RAT	ERA	ERA+	OAV	OOB	PR	/A	PF	CPI	FA	E	DP	FW	PW	BW	SBW	DIF
EAST																										
PIT	18	11	51	1456²	1411	8.7	117	**401**	919	11.4	3.44	104	.256	.309	39	21	97	103	.981	120	134	.4	2.2	12.2	1.0	1.3
STL	9	5	51	1435¹	1367	8.6	114	454	822	11.7	3.69	101	.255	.318	0	5	101	100	**.982**	107	133	1.1	.5	-1.8	-.6	3.8
PHI	16	11	35	1463	1346	8.3	111	670	988	12.7	3.86	95	.246	.332	-29	-32	100	99	.981	119	111	.4	-3.3	-5.5	1.0	4.5
CHI	12	4	40	1456²	1415	8.7	117	542	927	12.3	4.03	96	.257	.327	-57	-24	105	96	**.982**	113	120	.7	-2.5	-2.2	-.3	1.3
NY	12	11	39	1437¹	1403	8.8	108	410	1028	11.5	3.56	102	.257	.311	20	13	99	100	.977	143	112	-1.0	1.4	-.4	.3	-3.7
MON	12	**14**	39	1440¹	**1304**	**8.1**	111	584	909	12.0	3.64	99	.244	.322	7	-4	98	100	.979	133	128	-.4	-.4	-4.0	.5	-5.2
WEST																										
ATL	18	7	48	1452²	**1304**	8.1	118	481	969	**11.2**	3.49	111	**.240**	**.305**	32	64	106	95	.978	138	122	-.7	6.7	2.3	.3	4.4
LA	15	**14**	40	1458	1312	**8.1**	96	500	1028	11.4	**3.06**	**117**	.241	.308	**101**	**86**	98	**107**	.980	123	126	.2	**9.0**	1.7	-.4	1.6
SD	14	11	47	1452²	1385	8.6	139	457	921	11.5	3.57	106	.252	.311	18	36	103	102	**.982**	113	130	.8	3.8	-5.6	-.9	5.0
SF	10	10	45	1442	1397	8.7	143	544	905	12.3	4.03	89	.257	.329	-56	-72	97	100	**.982**	109	**151**	1.0	-7.5	1.3	-.7	.0
CIN	7	11	43	1440	1372	8.6	127	560	997	12.3	3.83	99	.253	.326	-24	-5	103	101	.979	155	131	.0	-.5	3.1	.3	-10.0
HOU	7	13	36	1453	1347	8.3	129	651	560	12.6	4.00	88	.247	.330	-51	-80	95	97	.974	161	129	-2.0	-8.4	-3.0	-.4	-2.2
TOT	150	122	514	17387²		8.5				11.9	3.68		.250	.319					.980	1504	1527					

Runs		Hits		Doubles		Triples		Home Runs		Total Bases	
Butler-LA	112	Pendleton-Atl	187	Bonilla-Pit	44	Lankford-StL	15	Johnson-NY	38	Pendleton-Atl	303
Johnson-NY	108	Butler-LA	182	Jose-StL	40	Gwynn-SD	11	Williams-SF	34	Clark-SF	303
Sandberg-Chi	104	Sabo-Cin	175	Zeile-StL	36	Finley-Hou	10	Gant-Atl	32	Johnson-NY	302
Bonilla-Pit	102	Bonilla-Pit	174	O'Neill-Cin	36	Grissom-Mon	9	McGriff-SD	31	Williams-SF	294
Gant-Atl	101	Jose-StL	173			Gonzalez-Hou	9	Dawson-Chi	31	Sabo-Cin	294

Runs Batted In		Runs Produced		Bases On Balls		Batting Average		On Base Percentage		Slugging Average	
Johnson-NY	117	Johnson-NY	187	Butler-LA	108	Pendleton-Atl	.319	Bonds-Pit	.419	Clark-SF	.536
Clark-SF	116	Bonds-Pit	186	Bonds-Pit	107	Morris-Cin	.318	Butler-LA	.402	Johnson-NY	.535
Bonds-Pit	116	Bonilla-Pit	184	McGriff-SD	105	Gwynn-SD	.317	McGriff-SD	.400	Pendleton-Atl	.517
McGriff-SD	106	Sandberg-Chi	178	DeShields-Mon	95	McGee-SF	.312	Bonilla-Pit	.398	Bonds-Pit	.514
Gant-Atl	105	Gant-Atl	174	Bonilla-Pit	90	Jose-StL	.305	Bagwell-Hou	.391	Larkin-Cin	.506

Production		Adjusted Production		Batter Runs		Adjusted Batter Runs		Clutch Hitting Index		Runs Created	
Bonds-Pit	.932	Bonds-Pit	163	Bonds-Pit	45.5	Bonds-Pit	47.3	Pagnozzi-StL	129	Bonds-Pit	118
Clark-SF	.897	Clark-SF	154	Bonilla-Pit	39.5	Bonilla-Pit	41.3	Bonds-Pit	127	Sandberg-Chi	114
McGriff-SD	.894	Bonilla-Pit	151	McGriff-SD	38.4	Clark-SF	38.1	Murray-LA	118	Bonilla-Pit	114
Bonilla-Pit	.890	Johnson-NY	147	Sandberg-Chi	34.8	McGriff-SD	35.2	Magadan-NY	117	Clark-SF	110
Larkin-Cin	.886	McGriff-SD	146	Clark-SF	34.7	Johnson-NY	33.5	Daniels-LA	116	Pendleton-Atl	107

Total Average		Stolen Bases		Stolen Base Average		Stolen Base Runs		Fielding Runs		Total Player Rating	
Bonds-Pit	1.055	Grissom-Mon	76	Dykstra-Phi	85.7	Grissom-Mon	12.6	Pendleton-Atl	27.9	Bonds-Pit	6.4
McGriff-SD	.937	Nixon-Atl	72	Redus-Pit	85.0	Nixon-Atl	9.0	Belliard-Atl	26.1	Pendleton-Atl	5.9
Larkin-Cin	.923	DeShields-Mon	56	Landrum-Chi	84.4	O.Smith-StL	5.1	Lind-Pit	22.6	Larkin-Cin	5.8
Johnson-NY	.902	Lankford-StL	44	Jefferies-NY	83.9	Landrum-Chi	5.1	Grissom-Mon	20.4	Sandberg-Chi	4.7
Sandberg-Chi	.896	Bonds-Pit	43	Grissom-Mon	81.7	Bonds-Pit	5.1	Grace-Chi	20.0	Bonilla-Pit	4.1

Wins		Win Percentage		Games		Complete Games		Shutouts		Saves	
Smiley-Pit	20	Smiley-Pit	.714	Jones-Mon	77	D.Martinez-Mon	9	D.Martinez-Mon	5	L.Smith-StL	47
Glavine-Atl	20	Rijo-Cin	.714	Assenmacher-Chi	75	Glavine-Atl	9	Martinez-LA	4	Dibble-Cin	31
Avery-Atl	18	Avery-Atl	.692	Stanton-Atl	74	Mulholland-Phi	8	Smith-Pit	3	Williams-Phi	30
Martinez-LA	17	Hurst-SD	.652	Burke-Mon-NY	72	Maddux-Chi	7	Mulholland-Phi	3	Franco-NY	30
		Glavine-Atl	.645	Agosto-StL	72			Black-SF	3	Righetti-SF	24

Innings Pitched		Fewest Hits/Game		Fewest BB/Game		Strikeouts		Strikeouts/Game		Ratio	
Maddux-Chi	263.0	Harnisch-Hou	7.02	Smith-Pit	1.14	Cone-NY	241	Cone-NY	9.32	Rijo-Cin	9.82
Glavine-Atl	246.2	Tewksbury-StL	7.27	Tewksbury-StL	1.79	Maddux-Chi	198	Rijo-Cin	7.58	Glavine-Atl	9.92
Morgan-LA	236.1	DeJesus-Phi	7.28	Mulholland-Phi	1.90	Glavine-Atl	192	Harnisch-Hou	7.14	Morgan-LA	9.94
Drabek-Pit	234.2	Hill-StL	7.30	Smiley-Pit	1.91	Rijo-Cin	172	Gooden-NY	7.11	D.Martinez-Mon	10.26
Cone-NY	232.2	Glavine-Atl	7.33	B.Smith-StL	2.04	Harnisch-Hou	172	Glavine-Atl	7.01	Benes-SD	10.37

Earned Run Average		Adjusted ERA		Opponents' Batting Avg.		Opponents' On Base Pct.		Starter Runs		Adjusted Starter Runs	
D.Martinez-Mon	2.39	Glavine-Atl	152	Harnisch-Hou	.212	Rijo-Cin	.274	D.Martinez-Mon	31.9	Glavine-Atl	36.5
Rijo-Cin	2.51	Rijo-Cin	151	Rijo-Cin	.219	Glavine-Atl	.279	Glavine-Atl	31.0	D.Martinez-Mon	30.2
Glavine-Atl	2.55	D.Martinez-Mon	151	Glavine-Atl	.222	Morgan-LA	.279	Rijo-Cin	26.6	Rijo-Cin	29.3
Belcher-LA	2.62	DeLeon-StL	137	Hill-StL	.224	D.Martinez-Mon	.283	Belcher-LA	24.7	Harris-SD	23.1
Harnisch-Hou	2.70	Belcher-LA	137	DeJesus-Phi	.224	Benes-SD	.286	Morgan-LA	23.7	Belcher-LA	22.6

Clutch Pitching Index		Relief Runs		Adjusted Relief Runs		Relief Ranking		Total Pitcher Index		Total Baseball Ranking	
DeLeon-StL	131	McElroy-Chi	19.5	McElroy-Chi	21.7	Williams-Phi	30.0	Glavine-Atl	5.5	Bonds-Pit	6.4
Drabek-Pit	127	Maddux-SD	13.4	Maddux-SD	14.6	L.Smith-StL	24.6	D.Martinez-Mon	3.9	Pendleton-Atl	5.9
Tewksbury-StL	121	Williams-Phi	13.2	Williams-Phi	13.0	McElroy-Chi	16.5	Williams-Phi	3.1	Larkin-Cin	5.8
Ojeda-LA	121	Brantley-SF	13.0	Brantley-SF	11.9	Pena-NY-Atl	15.3	Rijo-Cin	3.0	Glavine-Atl	5.5
Belcher-LA	118	Pena-NY-Atl	11.7	Pena-NY-Atl	11.8	McDowell-Phi-LA	14.0	L.Smith-StL	2.5	Sandberg-Chi	4.7

March 11 Jim Palmer, who is in the Orioles camp as a non-roster player, has a shaky outing against the Red Sox, giving up five hits and two runs in two innings. Palmer, who retired in 1984, will retire again tomorrow, citing a hamstring injury.

April 18 New Comiskey Park opens with fanfare and a rout. The Tigers are the stars of the day as Detroit mauls the White Sox 16-0.

May 1 Rickey Henderson steals third base in the fourth inning for his 939th career theft to break Lou Brock's all-time stolen base record. The A's knock off the Yankees 7-4.

May 1 The 44-year-old flame-thrower Nolan Ryan strikes out 16 Blue Jays en route to his seventh career no-hitter, a 3-0 win.

May 15 The Red Sox and White Sox play the slowest nine-inning game in major league history (four hours, 11 minutes), but Boston rallies from a 5-0 deficit for a 9-6 win.

June 6 Albert Belle is shipped to the minors for not running out a ground ball in Cleveland's 2-1 loss to the White Sox.

July 9 At Toronto's SkyDome, the AL wins the All-Star Game 4-2 on Cal Ripken's three-run home run off Montreal's Dennis Martinez. The Baltimore shortstop earns MVP honors.

August 11 Wilson Alvarez hurls a no-hitter in his first big league start as the White Sox stop Baltimore 7-0.

October 12 The Blue Jays chase Twins starter Kevin Tapani for the second time in the ALCS, but Minnesota's bullpen and bats lead to six unanswered runs at the SkyDome as the Twins win their third pennant, four games to one.

October 26 Kirby Puckett prevents two Atlanta runs with a leaping catch in the third inning and then he lofts a sacrifice fly in the fifth to give the Twins the lead. The Braves tie it in the seventh, but Puckett turns out the lights in the 10th with a home run to force Game 7.

October 27 In a Game 7 that rivals any in World Series history, the Braves and Twins go through the first nine innings without scoring. Lonnie Smith is decoyed into pausing at second base to keep him from scoring the winner for Atlanta in the eighth. Series MVP Jack Morris makes the Braves pay for that hesitation. Gene Larkin's single over a drawn-in outfield in the 10th is the difference in the first extra-inning Game 7 in 67 years.

BALTIMORE		BOSTON		CALIFORNIA		CHICAGO		CLEVELAND		DETROIT		KANSAS CITY	
M	F.Robinson	M	J.Morgan	M	D.Rader	M	J.Torborg	M	J.McNamara	M	S.Anderson	M	J.Wathan
M	J.Oates	1B	C.Quintana	M	B.Rodgers	1B	D.Pasqua	M	M.Hargrove	1B	D.Bergman	M	B.Schaefer
1B	R.Milligan	2B	J.Reed	1B	W.Joyner	2B	S.Fletcher	1B	B.Jacoby	2B	L.Whitaker	M	H.McRae
2B	B.Ripken	SS	L.Rivera	2B	L.Sojo	SS	O.Guillen	2B	M.Lewis	SS	A.Trammell	1B	T.Benzinger
SS	C.Ripken	3B	W.Boggs	SS	D.Schofield	3B	R.Ventura	SS	F.Fermin	3B	T.Fryman	2B	T.Shumpert
3B	L.Gomez	LF	M.Greenwell	3B	G.Gaetti	LF	T.Raines	3B	C.Baerga	LF	L.Moseby	SS	K.Stillwell
LF	B.Anderson	CF	E.Burks	LF	L.Polonia	CF	L.Johnson	LF	A.Belle	CF	M.Cuyler	3B	B.Pecota
CF	M.Devereaux	RF	T.Brunansky	CF	D.Gallagher	RF	S.Sosa	CF	A.Cole	RF	R.Deer	LF	J.Eisenreich
RF	J.Orsulak	C	T.Pena	RF	D.Winfield	C	C.Fisk	RF	M.Whiten	C	M.Tettleton	CF	B.McRae
C	C.Hoiles	DH	J.Clark	C	L.Parrish	DH	F.Thomas	C	J.Skinner	DH	C.Fielder	RF	D.Tartabull
DH	S.Horn			DH	D.Parker			DH	C.James			C	B.Mayne
		1D	M.Vaughn			2	J.Cora			OD	P.Incaviglia	DH	G.Brett
2S	J.Bell	O2	S.Lyons	O	J.Felix	32	C.Grebeck	2O	J.Browne	O3	T.Phillips		
OD	D.Evans			2S	D.Hill			D1	C.Martinez			OD	K.Gibson
C	B.Melvin	P	R.Clemens			P	J.McDowell			P	B.Gullickson	C	M.Macfarlane
O	C.Martinez	P	G.Harris	P	M.Langston	P	C.Hough	P	G.Swindell	P	W.Terrell	S2	D.Howard
1O	D.Segui	P	J.Hesketh	P	J.Abbott	P	G.Hibbard	P	C.Nagy	P	F.Tanana	3	K.Seitzer
32	T.Hulett	P	M.Gardiner	P	C.Finley	P	A.Fernandez	P	E.King	P	M.Leiter		
		P	T.Bolton	P	K.McCaskill	RP	M.Perez	P	R.Nichols	RP	P.Gibson	P	K.Appier
P	B.Milacki	RP	D.Lamp	RP	M.Eichhorn	RP	S.Radinsky	P	T.Candiotti	RP	J.Cerutti	P	B.Saberhagen
P	B.McDonald	RP	J.Gray	RP	B.Harvey	RP	D.Pall	RP	S.Hillegas	RP	M.Henneman	P	M.Boddicker
P	J.Mesa	RP	J.Reardon	RP	J.Robinson			RP	J.Shaw			P	T.Gordon
P	J.Ballard					P	R.Garcia	RP	D.Jones	P	J.Gleaton	P	L.Aquino
P	J.Robinson	P	M.Young	P	J.Grahe	P	B.Thigpen			P	D.Gakeler	RP	S.Davis
RP	M.Flanagan	P	K.Morton	P	S.Lewis	P	K.Patterson	P	D.Otto	P	S.Aldred	P	J.Montgomery
RP	T.Frohwirth	P	D.Darwin	P	S.Bailes	P	W.Alvarez	P	S.Olin	P	D.Petry	RP	M.Davis
RP	M.Williamson	P	T.Fossas										
												P	M.Gubicza
P	M.Mussina											P	M.Magnante
P	D.Johnson												
P	R.Smith												
P	G.Olson												
P	P.Kilgus												

MILWAUKEE		MINNESOTA		NEW YORK		OAKLAND		SEATTLE		TEXAS		TORONTO	
M	T.Trebelhorn	M	T.Kelly	M	S.Merrill	M	T.LaRussa	M	J.Lefebvre	M	B.Valentine	M	C.Gaston
1B	F.Stubbs	1B	K.Hrbek	1B	D.Mattingly	1B	M.McGwire	1B	P.O'Brien	1B	R.Palmeiro	M	G.Tenace
2B	W.Randolph	2B	C.Knoblauch	2B	S.Sax	2B	M.Gallego	2B	H.Reynolds	2B	J.Franco	M	C.Gaston
SS	B.Spiers	SS	G.Gagne	SS	A.Espinoza	SS	M.Bordick	SS	O.Vizquel	SS	J.Huson	1B	J.Olerud
3B	J.Gantner	3B	M.Pagliarulo	3B	P.Kelly	3B	E.Riles	3B	E.Martinez	3B	S.Buechele	2B	R.Alomar
LF	G.Vaughn	LF	D.Gladden	LF	R.Kelly	LF	R.Henderson	LF	G.Briley	LF	J.Gonzalez	SS	M.Lee
CF	R.Yount	CF	K.Puckett	CF	B.Williams	CF	D.Henderson	CF	K.Griffey	CF	G.Pettis	3B	K.Gruber
RF	D.Bichette	RF	S.Mack	RF	M.Hall	RF	J.Canseco	RF	J.Buhner	RF	R.Sierra	LF	C.Maldonado
C	B.Surhoff	C	B.Harper	C	M.Nokes	C	T.Steinbach	C	D.Valle	C	I.Rodriguez	CF	D.White
DH	P.Molitor	DH	C.Davis	DH	K.Maas	DH	H.Baines	DH	A.Davis	DH	B.Downing	RF	J.Carter
												C	G.Myers
O	D.Hamilton	O1	G.Larkin	OD	H.Meulens	O	W.Wilson	P	R.Johnson	OD	K.Reimer	DH	R.Mulliniks
S3	D.Sveum	3S	S.Leius	O	J.Barfield	C	J.Quirk	P	B.Holman	3O	D.Palmer		
		S2	A.Newman					P	R.DeLucia			C	P.Borders
P	J.Navarro			P	S.Sanderson	P	D.Stewart	P	B.Krueger	P	K.Brown	OD	M.Wilson
P	C.Bosio	P	J.Morris	P	J.Johnson	P	B.Welch	P	E.Hanson	P	N.Ryan		
P	B.Wegman	P	K.Tapani	P	T.Leary	P	M.Moore	RP	B.Swift	RP	J.Guzman	P	T.Stottlemyre
P	D.August	P	S.Erickson	P	W.Taylor	RP	J.Slusarski	RP	M.Jackson	RP	K.Rogers	P	J.Key
RP	D.Plesac	P	A.Anderson	RP	G.Cadaret	RP	D.Eckersley	RP	R.Swan	RP	G.Alexander	P	D.Wells
RP	C.Crim	RP	M.Guthrie	RP	E.Plunk	RP	C.Young			RP	J.Barfield	P	J.Guzman
RP	J.Machado	RP	C.Willis	P	J.Habyan	P	J.Klink	P	S.Bankhead			RP	T.Candiotti
		RP	S.Bedrosian							P	B.Witt	RP	M.Timlin
P	D.Holmes			P	L.Guetterman	P	A.Hawkins			P	M.Jeffcoat	RP	D.Ward
P	M.Lee	P	D.West	P	P.Perez	P	R.Darling			Je.Russell		RP	J.Acker
P	K.Brown	P	R.Aguilera	P	D.Eiland	P	S.Chitren			P	W.Rosenthal		
		P	T.Leach	P	S.Farr	P	E.Show			P	O.Boyd	/P	D.Stieb
				/P	S.Kamieniecki					P	B.Bohanon	P	R.MacDonald
				P	C.Cary					P	T.Mathews	P	T.Henke

TEAM	G	W	L	PCT	GB	R	OR	AB	H	2B	3B	HR	BB	SO	AVG	OBP	SLG	PRO	PRO+	BR	/A	PF	CHI	RC	SB	CS	SBA	SBR
EAST																												
TOR	162	91	71	.562		684	622	5489	1412	295	45	133	499	1043	.257	.326	.400	.726	96	-7	-33	104	96	724	148	53	74	13
DET	162	84	78	.519	7	817	794	5547	1372	259	26	209	699	1185	.247	.335	.416	.751	105	50	39	101	103	800	109	47	70	5
BOS	162	84	78	.519	7	731	712	5530	1486	305	25	126	593	820	.269	.340	.396	.736	106	42	4	105	95	756	59	39	60	-6
MIL	162	83	79	.512	8	799	744	5611	1523	247	53	116	556	802	.271	.340	.396	.736	106	24	43	98	105	745	106	68	61	-9
NY	162	71	91	.438	20	674	777	5541	1418	249	19	147	473	861	.256	.319	.387	.706	94	-47	-48	100	101	683	109	36	75	11
BAL	162	67	95	.414	24	686	796	5604	1421	256	29	170	528	974	.254	.321	.401	.722	102	-17	12	96	96	707	50	33	60	-5
CLE	162	57	105	.352	34	576	759	5470	1390	236	26	79	449	888	.254	.316	.350	.666	83	-118	-122	101	98	591	84	58	59	-10
WEST																												
MIN	162	95	67	.586		776	652	5556	1557	270	42	140	526	747	.280	.347	.420	.767	106	45	105	96	108	787	107	68	61	-9
CHI	162	87	75	.537	8	758	681	5594	1464	226	39	139	610	896	.262	.338	.391	.729	103	12	30	98	101	741	134	74	64	-4
TEX	162	85	77	.525	10	829	814	5703	1539	288	31	177	596	1039	.270	.343	.424	.767	113	85	100	98	99	831	102	50	51	1
OAK	162	84	78	.519	11	760	776	5410	1342	246	19	159	642	981	.248	.333	.389	.722	105	-2	39	94	106	711	151	64	70	7
SEA	162	83	79	.512	12	702	664	5494	1400	268	29	126	588	811	.255	.331	.383	.714	97	-21	-22	100	99	698	97	44	69	3
KC	162	82	80	.506	13	727	722	5584	1475	290	41	117	523	969	.264	.331	.394	.725	100	-4	-7	100	101	720	119	68	64	-5
CAL	162	81	81	.500	14	653	649	5470	1396	245	29	115	448	928	.255	.316	.374	.690	90	-78	-77	100	104	640	94	56	63	-5
TOT	1134					10172		77603	20195	3680	453	1953	7730	12944	.260	.331	.395	.726		1469	758				66			-14

TEAM	CG	SH	SV	IP	H	H/G	HR	BB	SO	RAT	ERA	ERA+	OAV	OOB	PR	/A	PF	CPI	FA	E	DP	FW	PW	BW	SBW	DIF
EAST																										
TOR	10	16	60	1462²	1301	8.0	121	523	971	11.5	3.50	120	.238	.309	96	114	103	96	.980	127	115	-.6	11.4	-3.3	1.4	1.1
DET	18	8	38	1450¹	1570	9.7	148	593	739	13.6	4.51	92	.280	.352	-66	-57	101	105	.983	104	171	.7	-5.7	3.9	.6	3.5
BOS	15	13	45	1439²	1405	8.8	147	530	999	12.3	4.01	107	.257	.326	13	46	105	100	.981	116	165	.0	4.6	.4	-.5	-1.5
MIL	23	11	41	1463²	1498	9.2	147	527	859	12.7	4.14	96	.266	.334	-8	-28	97	102	.981	118	176	-.0	-2.8	4.3	-.8	1.4
NY	3	11	37	1444	1510	9.4	152	506	936	12.8	4.42	94	.271	.336	-52	-45	101	99	.979	133	181	-.9	-4.5	-4.8	1.2	-1.0
BAL	8	8	42	1457²	1534	9.5	147	504	868	12.8	4.59	86	.273	.335	-80	-103	97	95	.985	91	172	1.4	-10.3	1.2	-.4	-5.9
CLE	22	8	33	1441¹	1551	9.7	110	441	862	12.7	4.23	98	.276	.333	-22	-31	101	98	.976	149	163	-1.8	-1.3	-12.2	-.9	-7.8
WEST																										
MIN	21	12	53	1449¹	1402	8.7	139	488	876	11.9	3.69	115	.255	.319	64	92	104	104	.985	95	161	1.2	9.2	4.5	-.8	-.0
CHI	28	8	40	1478	1302	7.9	154	601	923	11.8	3.79	105	.235	.318	50	30	97	98	.982	116	151	.0	3.0	3.0	-.3	.3
TEX	9	10	41	1479	1486	9.0	151	662	1022	13.3	4.47	90	.262	.344	-61	-72	98	98	.979	134	138	-1.0	-7.2	10.0	.2	2.0
OAK	14	10	49	1444¹	1425	8.9	155	655	892	13.3	4.57	84	.260	.345	-77	-119	94	97	.982	107	150	.5	-11.9	3.9	.8	9.7
SEA	10	13	48	1464¹	1387	8.5	136	628	1003	12.7	3.79	109	.253	.335	50	54	101	107	.983	110	187	.3	5.4	-2.2	-.4	-1.9
KC	17	12	41	1466	1473	9.0	105	529	1004	12.6	3.92	101	.261	.329	28	32	101	99	.980	125	141	-.5	3.2	-.7	-.4	-.6
CAL	18	10	50	1441²	1351	8.4	141	543	990	12.1	3.69	111	.250	.323	65	66	100	105	.984	102	156	.8	6.6	-7.7	-.4	.7
TOT	216	150	618	20382		8.9				12.6	4.09		.260	.331					.981	1627	2214					

Runs
Molitor-Mil . . . 133
Palmeiro-Tex 115
Canseco-Oak 115
White-Tor 110
Sierra-Tex 110

Hits
Molitor-Mil 216
C.Ripken-Bal 210
Sierra-Tex 203
Palmeiro-Tex 203
Franco-Tex 201

Doubles
Palmeiro-Tex . . . 49
C.Ripken-Bal . . . 46
Sierra-Tex 44

Triples
Molitor-Mil . . . 13
Johnson-Chi 13
Alomar-Tor 11
White-Tor 10
Devereaux-Bal . . . 10

Home Runs
Fielder-Det 44
Canseco-Oak 44
C.Ripken-Bal . . . 34
Carter-Tor 33
Thomas-Chi 32

Total Bases
C.Ripken-Bal 368
Palmeiro-Tex 336
Sierra-Tex 332
Molitor-Mil 325
Carter-Tor 321

Runs Batted In
Fielder-Det 133
Canseco-Oak . . . 122
Sierra-Tex 116
C.Ripken-Bal 114
Thomas-Chi 109

Runs Produced
Sierra-Tex 201
Canseco-Oak 193
Molitor-Mil 191
Fielder-Det 191
Thomas-Chi 181

Bases On Balls
Thomas-Chi 138
Tettleton-Det 101
R.Henderson-Oak . . 98
Clark-Bos 96
Davis-Min 95

Batting Average
Franco-Tex 341
Boggs-Bos 332
Randolph-Mil 327
K.Griffey-Sea 327
Molitor-Mil 325

On Base Percentage
Thomas-Chi 454
Randolph-Mil 427
Boggs-Bos 425
Franco-Tex 409
E.Martinez-Sea 407

Slugging Average
Tartabull-KC 593
C.Ripken-Bal 566
Canseco-Oak 556
Thomas-Chi 553
Palmeiro-Tex 532

Production
Thomas-Chi . . . 1.007
Tartabull-KC 993
C.Ripken-Bal 945
K.Griffey-Sea 932
Palmeiro-Tex 925

Adjusted Production
Thomas-Chi 181
Tartabull-KC 170
C.Ripken-Bal . . . 164
Canseco-Oak . . . 159
Palmeiro-Tex 156

Batter Runs
Thomas-Chi 65.9
C.Ripken-Bal 48.5
Tartabull-KC 46.4
Palmeiro-Tex 45.6
K.Griffey-Sea 42.3

Adjusted Batter Runs
Thomas-Chi 69.4
C.Ripken-Bal . . . 53.9
Palmeiro-Tex . . . 47.9
Tartabull-KC . . . 45.9
Canseco-Oak . . . 44.7

Clutch Hitting Index
Davis-Sea 135
Surhoff-Mil 125
Yount-Mil 124
Randolph-Mil 122
Hrbek-Min 119

Runs Created
Thomas-Chi 145
C.Ripken-Bal 134
Molitor-Mil 132
Palmeiro-Tex . . . 129
K.Griffey-Sea . . . 118

Total Average
Thomas-Chi . . . 1.109
Tartabull-KC . . . 1.044
K.Griffey-Sea 969
Canseco-Oak 962
Whitaker-Det 942

Stolen Bases
R.Henderson-Oak . . 58
Alomar-Tor 53
Raines-Chi 51
Polonia-Cal 48
Cuyler-Det 41

Stolen Base Average
Cotto-Sea 84.2
Knoblauch-Min . . . 83.3
Alomar-Tor 82.8
Gibson-KC 81.8
Canseco-Oak . . . 81.3

Stolen Base Runs
Alomar-Tor 9.3
R.Henderson-Oak . . 6.6
Raines-Chi 6.3
Cuyler-Det 6.3
Franco-Tex 5.4

Fielding Runs
Gaetti-Cal 24.6
Vizquel-Sea 23.5
Espinoza-NY 20.3
Buechele-Tex 19.9
Sojo-Cal 19.5

Total Player Rating
C.Ripken-Bal 8.3
Thomas-Chi 5.5
K.Griffey-Sea . . . 4.9
Canseco-Oak . . . 4.2
R.Henderson-Oak . . 4.1

Wins
Gullickson-Det . . . 20
Erickson-Min 20
Langston-Cal 19

Win Percentage
Erickson-Min 714
Langston-Cal 704
Gullickson-Det 690
Wegman-Mil 682
Moore-Oak 680

Games
D.Ward-Tor 81
Olson-Bal 72
Jackson-Sea 72
Swift-Sea 71

Complete Games
McDowell-Chi . . . 15
Clemens-Bos . . . 13
Navarro-Mil 10
Morris-Min 10
Terrell-Det 8

Shutouts
Clemens-Bos 4
McDowell-Chi . . . 3
Holman-Sea 3
Erickson-Min 3
Appier-KC 3

Saves
Harvey-Cal 46
Eckersley-Oak . . . 43
Aguilera-Min . . . 42
Reardon-Bos . . . 40
Montgomery-KC . . . 33

Innings Pitched
Clemens-Bos . . . 271.1
McDowell-Chi . . . 253.2
Morris-Min 246.2
Langston-Cal . . . 246.1
Tapani-Min 244.0

Fewest Hits/Game
Ryan-Tex 5.31
Johnson-Sea . . . 6.75
Langston-Cal . . . 6.94
Clemens-Bos . . . 7.26
McDowell-Chi . . . 7.52

Fewest BB/Game
Swindell-Cle 1.17
Sanderson-NY . . . 1.25
Tapani-Min 1.48
Gullickson-Det . . . 1.75
Wegman-Mil 1.86

Strikeouts
Clemens-Bos 241
Johnson-Sea . . . 228
Ryan-Tex 203
McDowell-Chi . . . 191
Langston-Cal . . . 183

Strikeouts/Game
Ryan-Tex 10.56
Johnson-Sea . . . 10.19
Clemens-Bos . . . 7.99
Hanson-Sea . . . 7.37
Appier-KC 6.85

Ratio
Ryan-Tex 9.31
Clemens-Bos . . . 9.59
Tapani-Min 9.85
Sanderson-NY . . . 10.04
Saberhagen-KC . . . 10.04

Earned Run Average
Clemens-Bos 2.62
Candiotti-Cle-Tor . 2.65
Wegman-Mil 2.84
J.Abbott-Cal 2.89
Ryan-Tex 2.91

Adjusted ERA
Clemens-Bos 164
Candiotti-Cle-Tor . 158
Tapani-Min 143
J.Abbott-Cal . . . 142
Wegman-Mil 140

Opponents' Batting Avg.
Ryan-Tex 172
Johnson-Sea 213
Langston-Cal 215
Clemens-Bos 221
Candiotti-Cle-Tor . .228

Opponents' On Base Pct.
Ryan-Tex 267
Clemens-Bos 272
Tapani-Min 278
Sanderson-NY 281
Saberhagen-KC 281

Starter Runs
Clemens-Bos 44.4
Candiotti-Cle-Tor . 38.3
J.Abbott-Cal . . . 32.5
Langston-Cal . . . 30.1
Tapani-Min 30.0

Adjusted Starter Runs
Clemens-Bos 50.6
Candiotti-Cle-Tor . 40.6
Tapani-Min 34.7
J.Abbott-Cal . . . 32.8
Langston-Cal . . . 30.3

Clutch Pitching Index
Krueger-Sea 130
Holman-Sea 117
Terrell-Det 117
Guzman-Tex 116
Tanana-Det 115

Relief Runs
Frohwirth-Bal 23.8
Harvey-Cal 21.8
Swift-Sea 21.1
Eichhorn-Cal . . . 19.2
Flanagan-Bal . . . 18.7

Adjusted Relief Runs
Frohwirth-Bal 22.3
Harvey-Cal 21.9
Swift-Sea 21.3
Eichhorn-Cal . . . 19.2
Habyan-NY 18.4

Relief Ranking
Harvey-Cal 36.1
Aguilera-Min . . . 32.0
Farr-NY 27.8
D.Ward-Tor 24.8
Radinsky-Chi . . . 22.4

Total Pitcher Index
Clemens-Bos 4.8
Candiotti-Cle-Tor . 4.3
J.Abbott-Cal . . . 4.1
Harvey-Cal 3.7
Key-Tor 3.5

Total Baseball Ranking
C.Ripken-Bal 8.3
Thomas-Chi 5.5
K.Griffey-Sea . . . 4.9
Clemens-Bos . . . 4.8
Candiotti-Cle-Tor . 4.3

January 7 Tom Seaver, one of the greatest starting pitchers of all-time, and Rollie Fingers, who helped revolutionize the role of the reliever, are elected to the Hall of Fame.

March 17 Hal Newhouser, a two-time MVP pitcher with the Tigers, and umpire Bill McGowan are elected to the Hall of Fame by the Veterans Committee.

May 17 Gary Carter, back with the Expos, joins Bob Boone and Carlton Fisk in the exclusive 2,000-games caught club.

June 4 San Jose voters tell the Giants they don't want them by rejecting a plan to build a new stadium in their town. Then the Astros add insult to injury by swatting the ball every which way in a 12-6 drubbing at Candlestick Park in front of just 8,850.

June 6 Eddie Murray of the Mets becomes the all-time leader in RBI by a switch hitter. He passes Mickey Mantle with RBI No. 1,510.

July 27 Houston starts its club-record 26-game road trip with a grand slam by Eric Anthony. The Astros are sent away so the Republican National Convention can take over the Astrodome.

August 7 The Giants announce that the team has been sold to Tampa Bay investors for a reported $110 million and will move to St. Petersburg for the 1993 season. The move will be blocked by other owners in November.

August 26 In the first matchup of NL knuckleballers in ten years, Pittsburgh's Tim Wakefield outduels Tom Candiotti of the Dodgers. The last time knuckleballs floated to batters on both teams came when Phil and Joe Niekro squared off in 1982.

August 27 The Mets, who are rapidly falling through the NL East standings, trade David Cone to Toronto, the AL East front-runner, for Jeff Kent and Ryan Thompson. Cone comes within one strikeout of becoming the first pitcher in almost 50 years to lead to lead the NL in strikeouts for three straight years; one strikeout by Atlanta's John Smoltz on the final day of the season denies him that honor.

August 29 Atlanta's Charlie Leibrandt records his 1,000th strikeout and decides to save the ball. He rolls the ball towards the dugout for safekeeping, but neglects to call time out so Ricky Jordan takes second base on the error.

September 4 Eddie Murray ties Al Simmons for most consecutive years (16) with at least 75 RBI.

September 19 Barry Bonds joins his father, Bobby, as well as Willie Mays, Howard Johnson, and Ron Gant as the only player to have two 30-home run, 30-steal seasons.

October 14 The usually sure-handed Jose Lind bobbles a grounder in the ninth that helps set the stage for Atlanta's three-run rally in Game 7 against Pittsburgh. Little-used pinch-hitter Francisco Cabrera singles in the tying and winning runs to give the Braves the pennant.

October 17 Tom Glavine goes the distance to give the Braves a 3-1 win over the Blue Jays in Game 1 of the World Series.

	ATLANTA		CHICAGO		CINCINNATI		HOUSTON		LOS ANGELES		MONTREAL
M	B.Cox	M	J.Lefebvre	M	L.Piniella	M	A.Howe	M	T.Lasorda	M	T.Runnells
1B	S.Bream	1B	M.Grace	1B	H.Morris	1B	J.Bagwell	1B	E.Karros	M	F.Alou
2B	M.Lemke	2B	R.Sandberg	2B	B.Doran	2B	C.Biggio	2B	L.Harris	1B	T.Wallach
SS	R.Belliard	SS	R.Sanchez	SS	B.Larkin	SS	A.Cedeno	SS	J.Offerman	2B	D.DeShields
3B	T.Pendleton	3B	S.Buechele	3B	C.Sabo	3B	K.Caminiti	3B	D.Hansen	SS	S.Owen
LF	R.Gant	LF	D.May	LF	R.Sanders	LF	L.Gonzalez	LF	E.Davis	3B	B.Barberie
CF	O.Nixon	CF	D.Dascenzo	CF	D.Martinez	CF	S.Finley	CF	B.Butler	LF	M.Alou
RF	D.Justice	RF	A.Dawson	RF	P.O'Neill	RF	E.Anthony	RF	M.Webster	CF	M.Grissom
C	G.Olson	C	J.Girardi	C	J.Oliver	C	E.Taubensee	C	M.Scioscia	RF	L.Walker
										C	G.Carter
C	D.Berryhill	3O	L.Salazar	O2	B.Roberts	S3	C.Candaele	O1	T.Benzinger		
S2	J.Blauser	S3	J.Vizcaino	O	G.Braggs	O	P.Incaviglia	23	M.Sharperson	O	J.Vander Wal
1	B.Hunter	O	S.Sosa			C	S.Servais			13	A.Cianfrocco
O	D.Sanders	C	R.Wilkins	P	T.Belcher			P	O.Hershiser	C	D.Fletcher
		O	Dw.Smith	P	G.Swindell	P	P.Harnisch	P	Ke.Gross		
P	J.Smoltz			P	J.Rijo	P	B.Henry	P	T.Candiotti	P	D.Martinez
P	S.Avery	P	G.Maddux	P	C.Hammond	P	J.Jones	P	B.Ojeda	P	K.Hill
P	T.Glavine	P	M.Morgan	RP	D.Henry	P	D.Kile	P	R.Martinez	P	C.Nabholz
P	C.Leibrandt	P	F.Castillo	RP	N.Charlton	P	M.Portugal	RP	J.Gott	P	M.Gardner
RP	K.Mercker	P	D.Jackson	RP	S.Bankhead	RP	D.Jones	RP	R.McDowell	P	B.Barnes
RP	M.Stanton	RP	B.Scanlan			RP	X.Hernandez	RP	T.Crews	RP	M.Rojas
RP	M.Freeman	RP	J.Bullinger	P	T.Browning	RP	J.Boever			RP	J.Fassero
		RP	C.McElroy	P	R.Dibble			P	P.Astacio	RP	J.Wetteland
P	M.Bielecki			P	S.Ruskin	P	B.Williams	P	S.Wilson		
P	P.Smith	P	S.Boskie	P	S.Foster	P	W.Blair			P	B.Sampen
		P	J.Robinson			P	A.Osuna				
		P	P.Assenmacher			P	R.Murphy				

	NEW YORK		PHILADELPHIA		PITTSBURGH		SAN DIEGO		SAN FRANCISCO		ST.LOUIS
M	J.Torborg	M	J.Fregosi	M	J.Leyland	M	G.Riddoch	M	R.Craig	M	J.Torre
1B	E.Murray	1B	J.Kruk	1B	O.Merced	M	J.Riggleman	1B	W.Clark	1B	A.Galarraga
2B	W.Randolph	2B	M.Morandini	2B	J.Lind	1B	F.McGriff	2B	R.Thompson	2B	L.Alicea
SS	D.Schofield	SS	J.Bell	SS	J.Bell	2B	K.Stillwell	SS	R.Clayton	SS	O.Smith
3B	D.Magadan	3B	D.Hollins	3B	S.Buechele	SS	T.Fernandez	3B	M.Williams	3B	T.Zeile
LF	D.Boston	LF	M.Duncan	LF	B.Bonds	3B	G.Sheffield	LF	M.Felder	LF	B.Gilkey
CF	H.Johnson	CF	L.Dykstra	CF	A.Van Slyke	LF	J.Clark	CF	D.Lewis	CF	R.Lankford
RF	B.Bonilla	RF	R.Amaro	RF	C.Espy	CF	D.Jackson	RF	W.McGee	RF	F.Jose
C	T.Hundley	C	D.Daulton	C	M.LaValliere	RF	T.Gwynn	C	K.Manwaring	C	T.Pagnozzi
						C	B.Santiago				
O	D.Gallagher	O	S.Javier	31	J.King			O	C.James	O	M.Thompson
3S	B.Pecota	1O	R.Jordan	O	G.Varsho	O	O.Azocar	O1	C.Snyder	2	G.Pena
32	C.Walker	O	W.Chamberlain	C	D.Slaught	23	T.Teufel	O	K.Bass		
O	V.Coleman			O	A.Cole					P	B.Tewksbury
		P	T.Mulholland			P	A.Benes	P	J.Burkett	P	O.Olivares
P	S.Fernandez	P	C.Schilling	P	D.Drabek	P	B.Hurst	P	B.Black	P	R.Cormier
P	D.Gooden	P	K.Abbott	P	R.Tomlin	P	C.Lefferts	P	B.Swift	P	D.Osborne
P	D.Cone	P	B.Rivera	P	Z.Smith	P	Gr.Harris	P	T.Wilson	P	M.Clark
P	P.Schourek	RP	Mt.Williams	P	B.Walk	P	F.Seminara	RP	J.Brantley	RP	M.Perez
P	B.Saberhagen	RP	C.Brantley	RP	R.Mason	RP	R.Rodriguez	RP	B.Beck	RP	C.Carpenter
RP	A.Young	RP	M.Hartley	RP	D.Neagle	RP	J.Melendez	RP	B.Hickerson	RP	L.Smith
RP	W.Whitehurst			RP	S.Belinda	RP	R.Myers				
RP	J.Innis	P	T.Greene					P	M.Jackson	P	J.DeLeon
		P	B.Jones	P	T.Wakefield	P	J.Deshaies	P	D.Righetti	P	T.Worrell
P	P.Gibson	P	G.Mathews	P	D.Jackson	P	M.Maddux	P	D.Burba	P	B.McClure
P	E.Hillman			P	B.Patterson			P	K.Downs		
				P	V.Palacios						

TEAM	G	W	L	PCT	GB	R	OR	AB	H	2B	3B	HR	BB	SO	AVG	OBP	SLG	PRO	PRO+	BR	/A	PF	CHI	RC	SB	CS	SBA	SBR
EAST																												
PIT	162	96	66	.593		**693**	595	5527	1409	272	54	106	569	872	.255	.327	.381	.708	107	48	56	99	101	699	110	53	67	1
MON	162	87	75	.537	9	648	581	5477	1381	263	37	102	463	976	.252	.315	.370	.685	101	-4	2	99	104	651	196	63	76	**21**
STL	162	83	79	.512	13	631	604	5594	**1464**	262	44	94	495	996	**.262**	.325	.375	.700	107	30	51	97	94	680	**208**	118	64	-8
CHI	162	78	84	.481	18	593	624	5590	1420	221	41	104	417	**816**	.254	.309	.364	.673	94	-31	-46	103	99	617	77	51	60	-8
NY	162	72	90	.444	24	599	653	5340	1254	259	17	93	**572**	956	.235	.312	.342	.654	92	-54	-46	98	106	583	129	52	71	8
PHI	162	70	92	.432	26	686	717	5500	1392	255	36	118	509	1059	.253	.322	.377	.699	104	27	29	100	104	684	127	31	**80**	20
WEST																												
ATL	162	98	64	.605		682	**569**	5480	1391	223	48	**138**	493	924	.254	.318	**.388**	.706	99	34	-6	106	103	686	126	60	68	2
CIN	162	90	72	.556	8	660	609	5460	1418	**281**	44	99	563	888	.260	**.331**	.382	**.713**	105	58	39	103	96	689	125	65	66	-2
SD	162	82	80	.506	16	617	636	5476	1396	255	30	135	453	864	.255	.315	.386	.701	102	22	11	102	96	648	69	52	57	-11
HOU	162	81	81	.500	17	608	668	5480	1350	255	38	96	505	1025	.246	.316	.359	.675	102	-20	7	96	100	616	139	54	72	9
SF	162	72	90	.444	26	574	647	5456	1330	220	36	105	435	1067	.244	.304	.355	.659	97	-57	-26	94	102	584	112	64	64	-5
LA	162	63	99	.389	35	548	636	5368	1333	201	34	72	503	899	.248	.316	.339	.655	93	-54	-45	98	97	579	142	78	65	-4
TOT	972					7539		65748	16538	2967	459	1262	5978	11342	.252	.318	.368	.686							1560	741	68	23

TEAM	CG	SH	SV	IP	H	H/G	HR	BB	SO	RAT	ERA	ERA+	OAV	OOB	PR	/A	PF	CPI	FA	E	DP	FW	PW	BW	SBW	DIF
EAST																										
PIT	20	20	43	1479²	1410	8.6	101	455	844	11.5	3.35	103	.254	.314	25	14	98	103	.984	101	144	.9	1.5	**6.0**	-.1	6.7
MON	11	14	49	1468	**1296**	**7.9**	92	525	1014	11.5	3.25	107	**.238**	.310	41	35	99	97	.980	124	113	-.4	3.8	.2	**2.1**	.4
STL	10	9	47	1480	1405	8.5	118	**400**	842	**11.2**	3.38	105	.250	.305	20	1	97	99	**.985**	94	146	**1.3**	.1	5.5	-1.1	-3.8
CHI	16	11	37	1469	1337	8.2	107	575	901	12.0	3.39	106	.246	.323	18	34	103	104	.982	114	142	.2	3.7	-5.0	-1.1	-.8
NY	17	13	34	1446²	1404	8.7	98	481	1025	12.0	3.66	95	.256	.321	-25	-30	99	99	.981	116	134	.0	-3.2	-5.0	.7	-1.5
PHI	**27**	7	34	1428	1387	8.7	113	549	851	12.4	4.11	85	.257	.328	-96	-98	100	92	.978	131	128	-.8	-10.6	3.1	1.9	-4.7
WEST																										
ATL	26	**24**	41	1460	1321	8.1	89	489	948	11.3	**3.14**	116	.242	.307	58	**83**	104	99	.982	109	121	.4	**8.9**	-.6	.0	8.3
CIN	9	11	**55**	1449²	1362	8.5	109	470	**1060**	11.5	3.46	104	.251	.314	6	21	103	100	.984	96	128	1.2	2.3	4.2	-.4	1.8
SD	9	11	46	1461¹	1444	8.9	111	439	971	11.7	3.56	100	.261	.318	-9	3	102	102	.982	115	127	.0	.3	1.2	-1.4	.8
HOU	5	12	45	1459¹	1386	8.5	114	539	978	12.1	3.72	90	.252	.323	-35	-58	96	96	.981	114	125	.2	-6.2	.8	.8	4.6
SF	9	12	30	1461	1385	8.5	128	502	927	11.8	3.61	91	.253	.320	-17	-50	94	102	.982	113	**174**	.2	-5.4	-2.8	-.7	-.3
LA	18	13	29	1438	1401	8.8	**82**	553	981	12.4	3.41	101	.257	.328	15	5	98	**106**	.972	174	136	-3.2	.5	-4.8	-.6	-9.8
TOT	177	157	490	17500²		8.5				11.8	3.50		.252	.318					.981	1401	1618					

Runs
Bonds-Pit 109
Hollins-Phi 104
VanSlyke-Pit 103
Sandberg-Chi 100
Grissom-Mon 99

Hits
VanSlyke-Pit 199
Pendleton-Atl 199
Sandberg-Chi 186
Grace-Chi 185
Sheffield-SD 184

Doubles
VanSlyke-Pit 45
Lankford-StL 40
Duncan-Phi 40
Clark-SF 40

Triples
Sanders-Atl 14
Finley-Hou 13
VanSlyke-Pit 12
Butler-LA 11
Alicea-StL 11

Home Runs
McGriff-SD 35
Bonds-Pit 34
Sheffield-SD 33
Hollins-Phi 27
Daulton-Phi 27

Total Bases
Sheffield-SD 323
Sandberg-Chi 312
VanSlyke-Pit 310
Pendleton-Atl 303

Runs Batted In
Daulton-Phi 109
Pendleton-Atl 105
McGriff-SD 104
Bonds-Pit 103
Sheffield-SD 100

Runs Produced
Pendleton-Atl 182
VanSlyke-Pit 178
Bonds-Pit 178
Hollins-Phi 170
Bagwell-Hou 165

Bases On Balls
Bonds-Pit 127
McGriff-SD 96
Butler-LA 95
Biggio-Hou 94
Kruk-Phi 92

Batting Average
Sheffield-SD 330
VanSlyke-Pit 324
Kruk-Phi 323
Roberts-Cin 323
Gwynn-SD 317

On Base Percentage
Bonds-Pit 461
Kruk-Phi 428
Butler-LA 413
McGriff-SD 396
Roberts-Cin 396

Slugging Average
Bonds-Pit 624
Sheffield-SD 580
McGriff-SD 556
Daulton-Phi 524
Sandberg-Chi 510

Production
Bonds-Pit 1.085
Sheffield-SD 969
McGriff-SD 952
Daulton-Phi 912
VanSlyke-Pit 891

Adjusted Production
Bonds-Pit 207
Sheffield-SD 168
McGriff-SD 164
Daulton-Phi 157
Clark-SF 153

Batter Runs
Bonds-Pit 71.8
Sheffield-SD 50.1
McGriff-SD 48.1
VanSlyke-Pit 40.2
Kruk-Phi 38.6

Adjusted Batter Runs
Bonds-Pit 73.3
Sheffield-SD 48.2
McGriff-SD 46.2
VanSlyke-Pit 41.4
Kruk-Phi 38.9

Clutch Hitting Index
Murray-NY 126
Daulton-Phi 124
Lind-Pit 120
Karros-LA 115
Larkin-Cin 114

Runs Created
Bonds-Pit 148
VanSlyke-Pit 122
Sheffield-SD 118
Sandberg-Chi 117
McGriff-SD 116

Total Average
Bonds-Pit 1.335
Daulton-Phi 994
McGriff-SD 987
Sheffield-SD 945
Kruk-Phi 900

Stolen Bases
Grissom-Mon 78
DeShields-Mon 46
Roberts-Cin 44
Finley-Hou 44
O.Smith-StL 43

Stolen Base Average
Davis-LA 95.0
Alou-Mon 88.9
Duncan-Phi 88.5

Stolen Base Runs
Grissom-Mon 15.6
Finley-Hou 7.8
O.Smith-StL 7.5
Bonds-Pit 6.9
Dykstra-Phi 6.0

Fielding Runs
Belliard-Atl 26.6
Jackson-SD 24.2
Thompson-SF 20.3
Wallach-Mon 18.2
Harris-LA 16.6

Total Player Rating
Bonds-Pit 9.2
Sheffield-SD 5.8
Sandberg-Chi 5.7
VanSlyke-Pit 5.4
Larkin-Cin 4.7

Wins
Maddux-Chi 20
Glavine-Atl 20

Win Percentage
Tewksbury-StL 762
Glavine-Atl 714
Leibrandt-Atl 682
Morgan-Chi 667
Maddux-Chi 645

Games
Boever-Hou 81
D.Jones-Hou 80
Perez-StL 77
Hernandez-Hou 77
Innis-NY 76

Complete Games
Mulholland-Phi 12
Schilling-Phi 10
Drabek-Pit 10
Smoltz-Atl 9
Maddux-Chi 9

Shutouts
Glavine-Atl 5
Cone-NY 5

Saves
L.Smith-StL 43
Myers-SD 38
Wetteland-Mon 37
D.Jones-Hou 36
M.Williams-Phi 29

Innings Pitched
Maddux-Chi 268.0
Drabek-Pit 256.2
Smoltz-Atl 246.2
Morgan-Chi 240.0
Avery-Atl 233.2

Fewest Hits/Game
Schilling-Phi 6.56
Maddux-Chi 6.75
Fernandez-NY 6.79
Martinez-Mon 6.84
Cone-NY 7.41

Fewest BB/Game
Tewksbury-StL 77
Cormier-StL 1.60
Swindell-Cin 1.73
Mulholland-Phi 1.81
Tomlin-Pit 1.81

Strikeouts
Smoltz-Atl 215
Cone-NY 214
Maddux-Chi 199
Fernandez-NY 193
Drabek-Pit 177

Strikeouts/Game
Cone-NY 9.79
Fernandez-NY 8.09
Smoltz-Atl 7.84
Rijo-Cin 7.29
Harnisch-Hou 7.14

Ratio
Schilling-Phi 8.95
Tewksbury-StL 9.27
Maddux-Chi 9.57
Martinez-Mon 9.58
Drabek-Pit 9.75

Earned Run Average
Swift-SF 2.08
Tewksbury-StL 2.16
Maddux-Chi 2.18
Schilling-Phi 2.35
Martinez-Mon 2.47

Adjusted ERA
Maddux-Chi 165
Swift-SF 159
Tewksbury-StL 157
Schilling-Phi 149
Morgan-Chi 141

Opponents' Batting Avg.
Schilling-Phi 201
Maddux-Chi 210
Fernandez-NY 210
Martinez-Mon 211
Cone-NY 223

Opponents' On Base Pct.
Schilling-Phi 256
Tewksbury-StL 267
Martinez-Mon 273
Maddux-Chi 273
Drabek-Pit 277

Starter Runs
Maddux-Chi 39.3
Tewksbury-StL 34.7
Schilling-Phi 29.1
Swift-SF 26.1
Martinez-Mon 26.1

Adjusted Starter Runs
Maddux-Chi 42.2
Tewksbury-StL 31.7
Schilling-Phi 28.7
Morgan-Chi 28.0
Martinez-Mon 25.1

Clutch Pitching Index
Swift-SF 131
Tewksbury-StL 120
Swindell-Cin 119
Morgan-Chi 115
Ojeda-LA 113

Relief Runs
Rojas-Mon 23.2
D.Jones-Hou 20.5
Beck-SF 17.8
Hernandez-Hou 17.2
Perez-StL 17.2

Adjusted Relief Runs
Rojas-Mon 22.7
D.Jones-Hou 18.7
Perez-StL 16.0
Beck-SF 15.8
Hernandez-Hou 15.4

Relief Ranking
D.Jones-Hou 39.4
Rojas-Mon 20.3
Perez-StL 18.6
Beck-SF 14.5
Hernandez-Hou 14.2

Total Pitcher Index
Maddux-Chi 6.2
D.Jones-Hou 4.2
Martinez-Mon 3.5
Glavine-Atl 3.3
Rijo-Cin 3.2

Total Baseball Ranking
Bonds-Pit 9.2
Maddux-Chi 6.2
Sheffield-SD 5.8
Sandberg-Chi 5.7
VanSlyke-Pit 5.4

June 15 Jeff Reardon of the Red Sox breaks Rollie Fingers's all-time save record with No. 342 in a 1-0 win over the Yankees.

July 14 The AL wins its fifth straight All-Star Game and does it in convincing fashion. The AL scores the first 10 runs en route to a 13-6 romp. Ken Griffey Jr. goes 3-for-3 with a home run and, like his dad 12 years before, he earned MVP honors.

July 26 The Ryan express keeps on rolling. Nolan Ryan strikes out his 100th batter of the season for a major-league record 23rd consecutive year. He also gets a 6-2 win over the Orioles—thanks to the longest home run yet at Camden Yards, a 450-foot shot to center off the bat of Juan Gonzalez—to pass Phil Niekro as No. 12 on the all-time win list with 319.

August 19 The Boones become the first three-generation family of major leaguers when Bret Boone debuts for the Mariners. His father, Bob, played for 19 years, and grandfather, Ray, logged 13 seasons in the majors.

August 23 Dennis Eckersley becomes the first pitcher to record 40 saves in four different seasons.

September 9 Robin Yount becomes the 17th player in major league history to collect 3,000 hits when the Brewers outfielder connects against the Indians before an adoring crowd at County Stadium.

September 24 Toronto's Dave Winfield becomes the oldest player in major league history to reach the 100-RBI plateau. The 40-year-old does the trick in his 2,700th career game.

September 30 George Brett collects his 3,000th career hit with his fourth hit of the game against the Angels. Moments after the milestone, Brett is picked off by pitcher Tim Fortugno.

October 2 Carlos Baerga becomes the first second baseman in AL history to hit .300 with 200 hits, 20 home runs, and 100 RBI.

October 11 Dennis Eckersley, who saved 51 games for Oakland during the season, surrenders a two-run home run to Roberto Alomar that sends Game 4 into extra innings. The Blue Jays go on to win, 7-6, in 11 innings and take a three games-to-one edge in the ALCS.

October 14 Joe Carter and Candy Maldonado hit homers and Juan Guzman cruises on the mound in the 9-2 clincher for the Blue Jays in Game 6 of the ALCS.

October 18 Ed Sprague's two-run home run in the ninth inning off Jeff Reardon evens the World Series at one game apiece.

October 20 The first World Series game ever played in Canada, fittingly, belongs to the Blue Jays. Despite a blown call on what should have been a Toronto triple play, Joe Carter and Kelly Gruber hit home runs to give the Blue Jays the Series lead.

October 24 The Braves rally to tie the game in the ninth inning of Game 6, but Dave Winfield's double in the 11th is the key blow as the Blue Jays hold on for Canada's first world championship.

BALTIMORE	BOSTON	CALIFORNIA	CHICAGO	CLEVELAND	DETROIT	KANSAS CITY
M J.Oates	M B.Hobson	M B.Rodgers	M G.Lamont	M M.Hargrove	M S.Anderson	M H.McRae
1B R.Milligan	1B M.Vaughn	M J.Wathan	1B F.Thomas	1B P.Sorrento	1B D.Bergman	1B W.Joyner
2B B.Ripken	2B J.Reed	M B.Rodgers	2B S.Sax	2B C.Baerga	2B L.Whitaker	2B K.Miller
SS C.Ripken	SS L.Rivera	1B L.Stevens	SS C.Grebeck	SS M.Lewis	SS T.Fryman	SS D.Howard
3B L.Gomez	3B W.Boggs	2B L.Sojo	3B R.Ventura	3B B.Jacoby	3B S.Livingstone	3B G.Jefferies
LF B.Anderson	LF B.Hatcher	SS G.DiSarcina	LF T.Raines	LF T.Howard	LF D.Gladden	LF K.McReynolds
CF M.Devereaux	CF B.Zupcic	3B G.Gaetti	CF L.Johnson	CF K.Lofton	CF M.Cuyler	CF B.McRae
RF J.Orsulak	RF T.Brunansky	LF L.Polonia	RF S.Abner	RF M.Whiten	RF R.Deer	RF J.Eisenreich
C C.Hoiles	C T.Pena	CF J.Felix	C R.Karkovice	C S.Alomar	C M.Tettleton	C M.Macfarlane
DH G.Davis	DH J.Clark	RF C.Curtis	DH G.Bell	DH A.Belle	DH C.Fielder	DH G.Brett
2D M.McLemore	13 S.Cooper	C M.Fitzgerald	O D.Pasqua	OD G.Hill	OD M.Carreon	S2 C.Wilkerson
1O D.Segui	O H.Winningham	DH H.Brooks	P J.McDowell	C J.Ortiz	O2 T.Phillips	C B.Mayne
P M.Mussina	OD P.Plantier	32 R.Gonzales	P K.McCaskill	13 C.Martinez	P B.Gullickson	O G.Thurman
P R.Sutcliffe	O E.Burks	O V.Hayes	P A.Fernandez	S3 F.Fermin	P F.Tanana	P K.Appier
P B.McDonald	P R.Clemens	P M.Langston	P C.Hough	P C.Nagy	P W.Terrell	P H.Pichardo
P B.Milacki	P F.Viola	P J.Abbott	P G.Hibbard	P J.Armstrong	P M.Leiter	P M.Gubicza
RP T.Frohwirth	P D.Darwin	P C.Finley	RP W.Alvarez	P D.Cook	RP J.Doherty	P R.Reed
RP A.Mills	P J.Hesketh	P J.Valera	RP T.Leach	P S.Scudder	RP L.Lancaster	RP T.Gordon
RP S.Davis	P J.Dopson	P B.Blyleven	RP D.Pall	P R.Nichols	RP M.Henneman	RP R.Meacham
P A.Rhodes	RP G.Harris	RP J.Grahe	P R.Hernandez	RP T.Power	P K.Ritz	RP M.Magnante
P J.Mesa	RP M.Young	RP C.Crim	P S.Radinsky	RP S.Olin	P E.King	M.Boddicker
P G.Olson	RP P.Quantrill	RP M.Eichhorn	P B.Thigpen	RP E.Plunk	P K.Knudsen	J.Montgomery
	P M.Gardiner			P J.Mesa	P S.Aldred	L.Aquino
				P D.Otto	P D.Haas	S.Shifflett
				P D.Lilliquist	P J.Kiely	

MILWAUKEE	MINNESOTA	NEW YORK	OAKLAND	SEATTLE	TEXAS	TORONTO
M P.Garner	M T.Kelly	M B.Showalter	M T.LaRussa	M B.Plummer	M B.Valentine	M C.Gaston
1B F.Stubbs	1B K.Hrbek	1B D.Mattingly	1B M.McGwire	1B P.O'Brien	M T.Harrah	1B J.Olerud
2B S.Fletcher	2B C.Knoblauch	2B P.Kelly	2B M.Bordick	2B H.Reynolds	1B R.Palmeiro	2B R.Alomar
SS P.Listach	SS G.Gagne	SS A.Stankiewicz	SS W.Weiss	SS O.Vizquel	2B A.Newman	SS M.Lee
3B K.Seitzer	3B S.Leius	3B C.Hayes	3B C.Lansford	3B E.Martinez	SS D.Thon	3B K.Gruber
LF G.Vaughn	LF S.Mack	LF M.Hall	LF R.Henderson	LF H.Cotto	3B D.Palmer	LF C.Maldonado
CF R.Yount	CF K.Puckett	CF R.Kelly	CF W.Wilson	CF K.Griffey	LF K.Reimer	CF D.White
RF D.Hamilton	RF P.Munoz	RF D.Tartabull	RF J.Canseco	RF J.Buhner	CF J.Gonzalez	RF J.Carter
C B.Surhoff	C B.Harper	C M.Nokes	C T.Steinbach	C D.Valle	RF R.Sierra	C P.Borders
DH P.Molitor	DH C.Davis	DH K.Maas	DH H.Baines	DH T.Martinez	C I.Rodriguez	DH D.Winfield
O D.Bichette	OD R.Bush	S3 R.Velarde	2O L.Blankenship	OD K.Mitchell	DH B.Downing	P J.Morris
23 J.Gantner	1O G.Larkin	O B.Williams	3O J.Browne	OD G.Briley	S2 J.Huson	P J.Key
P B.Wegman	P J.Smiley	P M.Perez	P M.Moore	P D.Fleming	P K.Brown	P J.Guzman
P J.Navarro	P K.Tapani	P S.Sanderson	P R.Darling	P R.Johnson	P J.Guzman	P T.Stottlemyre
P C.Bosio	P S.Erickson	P S.Kamieniecki	P D.Stewart	P E.Hanson	P B.Witt	P D.Stieb
P R.Bones	P B.Krueger	P T.Leary	P B.Welch	P R.Swan	P N.Ryan	RP D.Wells
P C.Eldred	RP C.Willis	RP G.Cadaret	RP J.Parrett	RP R.DeLucia	RP T.Burns	RP D.Ward
RP D.Plesac	RP T.Edens	RP R.Monteleone	RP D.Eckersley	RP J.Nelson	RP K.Rogers	RP T.Henke
RP D.Henry	RP M.Guthrie	RP J.Habyan	RP K.Campbell	P B.Fisher	RP Je.Russell	/P D.Cone
RP M.Fetters	P W.Banks	P S.Hillegas	P K.Downs	P M.Grant	P R.Pavlik	/P P.Hentgen
P J.Austin	P P.Mahomes	/P S.Militello	P J.Slusarski	P C.Jones		
P B.Ruffin	/P R.Aguilera	P J.Johnson	P G.Nelson	P D.Powell		
		P S.Farr		P M.Schooler		
		/P B.Wickman				

TEAM	G	W	L	PCT	GB	R	OR	AB	H	2B	3B	HR	BB	SO	AVG	OBP	SLG	PRO	PRO+	BR	/A	PF	CHI	RC	SB	CS	SBA	SBR
EAST																												
TOR	162	96	66	.593		780	682	5536	1458	265	40	163	561	933	.263	.336	.414	**.750**	104	63	29	105	102	779	129	39	**77**	15
MIL	162	92	70	.568	4	740	**604**	5504	1477	272	35	82	511	779	.268	.334	.375	.709	100	-10	4	98	108	700	**256**	115	69	8
BAL	162	89	73	.549	7	705	656	5485	1423	243	36	148	647	827	.259	.343	.398	.741	104	56	37	103	92	754	89	48	65	-2
NY	162	76	86	.469	20	733	746	5593	1462	281	18	163	536	903	.261	.331	.406	.737	106	33	39	99	99	742	78	37	68	1
CLE	162	76	86	.469	20	674	746	5620	1495	227	24	127	448	885	.266	.325	.383	.708	100	-22	-10	98	99	686	144	67	68	3
DET	162	75	87	.463	21	**791**	794	5515	1411	256	16	**182**	675	1055	.256	.340	.407	.747	107	63	59	101	102	769	66	45	59	-7
BOS	162	73	89	.451	23	599	669	5461	1343	259	21	84	591	865	.246	.323	.347	.670	83	-84	-125	107	98	617	44	48	48	-16
WEST																												
OAK	162	96	66	.593		745	672	5387	1389	219	24	142	**707**	831	.258	**.349**	.386	.735	**112**	54	**95**	95	98	748	143	59	71	8
MIN	162	90	72	.556	6	747	653	5582	**1544**	275	27	104	527	834	**.277**	.345	.391	.736	103	46	22	103	99	742	123	74	62	-8
CHI	162	86	76	.531	10	738	690	5498	1434	269	36	110	622	784	.261	.339	.383	.722	103	19	28	99	102	728	160	57	74	14
TEX	162	77	85	.475	19	682	753	5537	1387	266	23	159	550	1036	.250	.324	.393	.717	104	-5	20	96	98	708	81	44	65	-2
KC	162	72	90	.444	24	610	667	5501	1411	**284**	**42**	75	439	**741**	.256	.317	.364	.681	88	-73	-90	103	99	629	131	71	65	-3
CAL	162	72	90	.444	24	579	671	5364	1306	202	20	88	416	882	.243	.303	.338	.641	79	-152	-155	101	**112**	529	160	101	61	-13
SEA	162	64	98	.395	32	679	799	5564	1406	278	24	149	474	841	.263	.326	.402	.728	102	13	9	101	96	708	100	55	65	-3
TOT	1134					9802		77147	20006	3596	386	1776	7704	12196	.259	.331	.385	.716							1704	860	66	-5

TEAM	CG	SH	SV	IP	H	H/G	HR	BB	SO	RAT	ERA	ERA+	OAV	OOB	PR	/A	PF	CPI	FA	E	DP	FW	PW	BW	SBW	DIF
EAST																										
TOR	18	14	49	1440²	1346	8.4	124	541	954	12.1	3.91	104	.248	.321	5	27	104	93	.985	93	109	1.4	2.7	3.0	**1.6**	6.3
MIL	19	14	39	1457	**1344**	**8.3**	127	**435**	793	**11.3**	3.43	112	**.246**	.307	82	65	97	98	**.986**	89	146	**1.6**	6.6	.4	.8	1.5
BAL	20	**16**	48	1464	1419	8.7	124	518	846	12.1	3.79	106	.256	.324	25	38	102	99	.985	93	168	1.4	3.9	3.8	-.2	-.9
NY	20	9	44	1452²	1453	9.0	129	612	851	13.0	4.21	93	.263	.341	-43	-47	99	99	.982	114	165	.2	-4.8	4.0	.1	-4.6
CLE	13	4	46	1470	1507	9.2	159	566	890	12.9	4.11	95	.268	.339	-28	-33	99	106	.978	141	**176**	-1.3	-3.4	-1.0	.3	.3
DET	10	4	36	1435²	1534	9.6	155	564	693	13.3	4.60	86	.277	.346	-105	-103	100	99	.981	116	164	.1	-10.5	6.0	-.7	-1.0
BOS	22	13	39	1448²	1403	8.7	107	535	943	12.3	3.58	117	.255	.326	57	**101**	107	103	.978	139	170	-1.2	**10.3**	-12.7	-1.6	-2.8
WEST																										
OAK	8	9	**58**	1447	1396	8.7	129	601	843	12.7	3.73	100	.256	.335	34	3	95	**107**	.979	125	158	-.4	.3	**9.7**	.8	4.5
MIN	16	13	50	1453	1391	8.6	121	479	923	11.8	3.70	109	.254	.318	38	56	103	98	.985	95	155	1.3	5.7	2.2	-.8	.5
CHI	21	5	52	1461²	1400	8.6	123	550	801	12.3	3.82	101	.252	.326	19	6	98	98	.979	129	134	-.6	.6	2.9	1.5	.7
TEX	19	3	42	1460¹	1471	9.1	113	598	**1034**	13.0	4.09	93	.264	.341	-24	-47	96	100	.975	154	153	-2.0	-4.8	2.0	-.2	.9
KC	9	12	44	1447¹	1426	8.9	**106**	512	834	12.3	3.81	106	.259	.327	21	39	103	98	.980	122	164	-.2	4.0	-9.2	-.3	-3.3
CAL	**26**	13	42	1446	1449	9.0	130	532	888	12.6	3.84	104	.264	.333	16	23	101	106	.979	134	172	-.9	2.3	-15.8	-1.3	6.6
SEA	21	9	30	1445	1467	9.1	129	661	894	13.6	4.55	87	.266	.351	-97	-92	101	96	.982	112	170	.3	-9.4	-.9	-.3	-8.6
TOT	242	141	619	20329		8.9				12.5	3.94		.259	.331					.981	1656	2204					

Runs		Hits		Doubles		Triples		Home Runs		Total Bases	
Phillips-Det	114	Puckett-Min	210	Thomas-Chi	46	Johnson-Chi	12	Gonzalez-Tex	43	Puckett-Min	313
Thomas-Chi	108	Baerga-Cle	205	E.Martinez-Sea	46	Devereaux-Bal	11	McGwire-Oak	42	Carter-Tor	310
Alomar-Tor	105	Molitor-Mil	195	Yount-Mil	40	Anderson-Bal	10	Fielder-Det	35	Gonzalez-Tex	309
Puckett-Min	104	Mack-Min	189	Mattingly-NY	40	Raines-Chi	9	Carter-Tor	34	Thomas-Chi	307
Knoblauch-Min	104	Thomas-Chi	185	Griffey-Sea	39			Belle-Cle	34	Devereaux-Bal	303

Runs Batted In		Runs Produced		Bases On Balls		Batting Average		On Base Percentage		Slugging Average	
Fielder-Det	124	Thomas-Chi	199	Thomas-Chi	122	E.Martinez-Sea	.343	McGwire-Oak	.446	McGwire-Oak	.585
Carter-Tor	119	Puckett-Min	195	Tettleton-Det	122	Puckett-Min	.329	Tartabull-NY	.410	E.Martinez-Sea	.544
Thomas-Chi	115	Carter-Tor	182	Phillips-Det	114	Thomas-Chi	.323	E.Martinez-Sea	.408	Thomas-Chi	.536
Belle-Cle	112	Baerga-Cle	177	Milligan-Bal	106	Molitor-Mil	.320	Alomar-Tor	.406	Griffey-Sea	.535
Bell-Chi	112	Winfield-Tor	174	Tartabull-NY	103	Mack-Min	.315	Molitor-Mil	.396	Gonzalez-Tex	.529

Production		Adjusted Production		Batter Runs		Adjusted Batter Runs		Clutch Hitting Index		Runs Created	
Thomas-Chi	.981	McGwire-Oak	180	Thomas-Chi	62.4	Thomas-Chi	64.3	Surhoff-Mil	136	Thomas-Chi	142
McGwire-Oak	.976	Thomas-Chi	176	E.Martinez-Sea	44.9	McGwire-Oak	50.3	Lansford-Oak	134	Anderson-Bal	118
E.Martinez-Sea	.951	E.Martinez-Sea	164	McGwire-Oak	44.4	E.Martinez-Sea	44.4	Devereaux-Bal	120	E.Martinez-Sea	116
Tartabull-NY	.900	Tartabull-NY	152	Griffey-Sea	34.2	Molitor-Mil	35.7	Felix-Cal	120	Molitor-Mil	116
Griffey-Sea	.898	Griffey-Sea	148	Mack-Min	33.8	R.Henderson-Oak	35.6	Ventura-Chi	119	Mack-Min	114

Total Average		Stolen Bases		Stolen Base Average		Stolen Base Runs		Fielding Runs		Total Player Rating	
Thomas-Chi	1.066	Lofton-Cle	66	Cotto-Sea	92.0	Lofton-Cle	12.6	Reed-Bos	23.8	R.Henderson-Oak	4.7
McGwire-Oak	1.040	Listach-Mil	54	White-Tor	90.2	Raines-Chi	9.9	Ventura-Chi	23.7	Ventura-Chi	4.6
Tartabull-NY	.972	Anderson-Bal	53	Raines-Chi	88.2	Alomar-Tor	9.3	Gagne-Min	20.9	E.Martinez-Sea	4.6
E.Martinez-Sea	.970	Polonia-Cal	51	R.Kelly-NY	84.8	White-Tor	8.7	Lofton-Cle	16.7	Thomas-Chi	4.3
Alomar-Tor	.915	Alomar-Tor	49	Lofton-Cle	84.6	R.Henderson-Oak	7.8	White-Tor	15.1	Anderson-Bal	4.2

Wins		Win Percentage		Games		Complete Games		Shutouts		Saves	
Morris-Tor	21	Mussina-Bal	.783	Rogers-Tex	81	McDowell-Chi	13	Clemens-Bos	5	Eckersley-Oak	51
Brown-Tex	21	Morris-Tor	.778	D.Ward-Tor	79	Clemens-Bos	11	Mussina-Bal	4	Aguilera-Min	41
McDowell-Chi	20	Guzman-Tor	.762	Olin-Chi	72	Brown-Tex	11	Fleming-Sea	4	Montgomery-KC	39
Mussina-Bal	18	Bosio-Mil	.727	Lilliquist-Cle	71	Perez-NY	10			Olson-Bal	36
Clemens-Bos	18	McDowell-Chi	.667	Harris-Bos	70	Nagy-Cle	10			Henke-Tor	34

Innings Pitched		Fewest Hits/Game		Fewest BB/Game		Strikeouts		Strikeouts/Game		Ratio	
Brown-Tex	265.2	Johnson-Sea	6.59	Bosio-Mil	1.71	Johnson-Sea	241	Johnson-Sea	10.31	Mussina-Bal	9.78
Wegman-Mil	261.2	Guzman-Tor	6.73	Mussina-Bal	1.79	Perez-NY	218	Guzman-Tor	8.22	Clemens-Bos	10.00
McDowell-Chi	260.2	Appier-KC	7.21	Wegman-Mil	1.89	Clemens-Bos	208	Perez-NY	7.92	Appier-KC	10.24
Nagy-Cle	252.0	Clemens-Bos	7.41	Tapani-Min	1.96	Guzman-Tex	179	Clemens-Bos	7.59	Smiley-Min	10.31
Perez-NY	247.2	Smiley-Min	7.66	Gullickson-Det	2.03	McDowell-Chi	178	Guzman-Tex	7.19	Guzman-Tor	10.36

Earned Run Average		Adjusted ERA		Opponents' Batting Avg.		Opponents' On Base Pct.		Starter Runs		Adjusted Starter Runs	
Clemens-Bos	2.41	Clemens-Bos	175	Johnson-Sea	.206	Mussina-Bal	.279	Clemens-Bos	42.0	Clemens-Bos	49.4
Appier-KC	2.46	Appier-KC	165	Guzman-Tor	.207	Clemens-Bos	.280	Mussina-Bal	37.5	Mussina-Bal	39.7
Mussina-Bal	2.54	Mussina-Bal	158	Appier-KC	.217	Appier-KC	.282	Appier-KC	34.2	Appier-KC	36.8
Guzman-Tor	2.64	Guzman-Tor	155	Clemens-Bos	.224	Guzman-Tor	.287	Perez-NY	29.4	Guzman-Tor	28.9
Abbott-Cal	2.77	Abbott-Cal	144	Smiley-Min	.231	Smiley-Min	.288	Abbott-Cal	27.4	Perez-NY	28.8

Clutch Pitching Index		Relief Runs		Adjusted Relief Runs		Relief Ranking		Total Pitcher Index		Total Baseball Ranking	
Abbott-Cal	132	D.Ward-Tor	22.4	D.Ward-Tor	24.0	Eckersley-Oak	31.7	Clemens-Bos	5.8	Clemens-Bos	5.8
Finley-Cal	124	Hernandez-Chi	18.1	Harris-Bos	20.4	Olin-Chi	28.6	Appier-KC	3.8	R.Henderson-Oak	4.7
Erickson-Min	113	Eckersley-Oak	18.0	Frohwirth-Bal	18.4	D.Ward-Tor	28.1	Mussina-Bal	3.5	Ventura-Chi	4.6
Perez-NY	110	Frohwirth-Bal	17.4	Hernandez-Chi	17.5	Hernandez-Chi	27.0	Eckersley-Oak	3.5	E.Martinez-Sea	4.6
Moore-Oak	108	Harris-Bos	17.1	Montgomery-KC	17.2	J.Russell-Tex-Oak	27.0	Perez-NY	3.2	Thomas-Chi	4.3

April 5 The first new NL teams since 1969 both play their first games. The Rockies are 3-0 losers to the Mets at Shea Stadium. The Marlins are 6-3 winners over LA at Joe Robbie Stadium.

April 27 Pittsburgh knuckleballer Tim Wakefield throws 171 pitches in a 10-inning 6-2 win over the Braves. The last pitcher to throw that many pitches was Fernando Valenzuela in 1987.

May 27 Dale Murphy calls it a career. Just two home runs shy of 400, the former two-time NL MVP announces his retirement as a member of the Rockies.

July 7 Tom Browning decides that he has seen the view from the dugout often enough, so he leaves Wrigley Field and watches the Reds beat the Cubs, 4-3, from the roof of a three-story building across Sheffield Avenue. He is fined $500 for leaving the dugout—not to mention the ballpark—during a game.

July 16 San Francisco outfielder Darren Lewis plays in his 267th consecutive errorless game to snap the record set by Don Demeter with Philadelphia and Detroit from 1962 to 1965.

July 28 Anthony Young's major league record 27-game losing streak finally ends. The Mets come from behind for a 4-3 win against the Marlins after Young's error allows Florida to take the lead.

September 7 Mark Whiten, who never hit more than 15 at any professional level, hits four homers and drives in 12 runs in the second game of a doubleheader for the Cardinals. His misplay of a fly ball leads to the winning runs in a 14-13 loss to the Reds in the first game, but he more than makes up for it in the nightcap. He hits a grand slam his first time up, adds three-run shots in the sixth and seventh innings and caps his prodigious night with a two-run shot in the ninth.

September 8 Houston's Darryl Kile throws the third no-hitter of the season in a 7-1 victory over the Mets. Kile fans nine and walks one in the first no-hitter by an Astro since Mike Scott's gem that clinched the 1986 NL West title.

September 9 Baseball joins the other major sports and expands the postseason as well as its divisions. The measure passes by a 27-1 vote.

October 3 The Giants need to beat the Dodgers on the final day of the season to force a one-game playoff with the Braves for the NL West title, but the Dodgers have other plans. LA rips San Francisco 12-1 to end the Giants' postseason dreams. At 103-59, San Francisco becomes the first team since the 1954 New York Yankees to win that many games and not play in the postseason.

October 13 The Phillies end the Braves' two-year reign as NL champions with a 6-3 win in Game 6 of the NLCS as Tommy Greene outpitches Greg Maddux. Curt Schilling wins the NLCS MVP even though he didn't win a game.

ATLANTA	CHICAGO	CINCINNATI	COLORADO	FLORIDA	HOUSTON	LOS ANGELES
M B.Cox	M J.Lefebvre	M T.Perez	M D.Baylor	M R.Lachemann	M A.Howe	M T.Lasorda
1B S.Bream	1B M.Grace	M D.Johnson	1B A.Galarraga	1B O.Destrade	1B J.Bagwell	1B E.Karros
2B M.Lemke	2B R.Sandberg	1B H.Morris	2B E.Young	2B B.Barberie	2B C.Biggio	2B J.Reed
SS J.Blauser	SS R.Sanchez	2B J.Samuel	SS V.Castilla	SS W.Weiss	SS A.Cedeno	SS J.Offerman
3B T.Pendleton	3B S.Buechele	SS B.Larkin	3B C.Hayes	3B G.Sheffield	3B K.Caminiti	3B T.Wallach
LF R.Gant	LF D.May	3B C.Sabo	LF J.Clark	LF J.Conine	LF L.Gonzalez	LF E.Davis
CF O.Nixon	CF D.Smith	LF K.Mitchell	CF A.Cole	CF C.Carr	CF S.Finley	CF B.Butler
RF D.Justice	RF S.Sosa	CF J.Brumfield	RF D.Bichette	RF D.Whitmore	RF E.Anthony	RF C.Snyder
C D.Berryhill	C R.Wilkins	RF R.Sanders	C J.Girardi	C B.Santiago	C E.Taubensee	C M.Piazza
		C J.Oliver				
O D.Sanders	S3 J.Vizcaino		O D.Boston	O G.Briley	O K.Bass	23 L.Harris
C G.Olson	O W.Wilson	S2 J.Branson	2 R.Mejia	23 R.Renteria	C S.Servais	
1 F.McGriff		O R.Kelly	C D.Sheaffer	23 A.Arias		P O.Hershiser
	P M.Morgan	2O B.Roberts	S2 F.Benavides	3 D.Magadan	P D.Drabek	P T.Candiotti
P G.Maddux	P G.Hibbard	1 R.Milligan	O C.Jones	O J.Felix	P P.Harnisch	P R.Martinez
P J.Smoltz	P J.Guzman				P M.Portugal	P Ke.Gross
P T.Glavine	P M.Harkey	P J.Rijo	P A.Reynoso	P C.Hough	P G.Swindell	P P.Astacio
P S.Avery	P F.Castillo	P T.Pugh	P W.Blair	P J.Armstrong	P D.Kile	RP P.Martinez
RP G.McMichael	RP J.Bautista	P T.Belcher	RP B.Ruffin	P C.Hammond	RP X.Hernandez	RP J.Gott
RP K.Mercker	RP B.Scanlan	P T.Browning	RP S.Reed	P R.Bowen	RP D.Jones	RP R.McDowell
RP J.Howell	RP R.Myers	P J.Smiley	RP J.Parrett	RP L.Aquino	RP B.Williams	
		RP B.Ayala		RP R.Lewis		P R.Trlicek
P P.Smith		RP J.Reardon	P D.Nied	RP B.Harvey		
P M.Stanton	P S.Boskie	RP J.Spradlin	P B.Henry			
P S.Bedrosian	P D.Plesac	P J.Roper	P K.Bottenfield	P P.Rapp		
		P L.Luebbers	P G.Harris	P M.Turner		
			P D.Holmes			
			P G.Wayne			
			P C.Leskanic			
			P A.Ashby			

MONTREAL	NEW YORK	PHILADELPHIA	PITTSBURGH	SAN DIEGO	SAN FRANCISCO	ST.LOUIS
M F.Alou	M J.Torborg	M J.Fregosi	M J.Leyland	M J.Riggleman	M D.Baker	M J.Torre
1B G.Colbrunn	M D.Green	1B J.Kruk	1B K.Young	1B F.McGriff	1B W.Clark	1B G.Jefferies
2B D.DeShields	1B E.Murray	2B M.Morandini	2B C.Garcia	2B J.Gardner	2B R.Thompson	2B L.Alicea
SS W.Cordero	2B J.Kent	SS K.Stocker	SS J.Bell	SS R.Gutierrez	SS R.Clayton	SS O.Smith
3B S.Berry	SS T.Bogar	3B D.Hollins	3B J.King	3B G.Sheffield	3B M.Williams	3B T.Zeile
LF M.Alou	3B H.Johnson	LF M.Thompson	LF A.Martin	LF P.Plantier	LF B.Bonds	LF B.Gilkey
CF M.Grissom	LF V.Coleman	CF L.Dykstra	CF A.Van Slyke	CF D.Bell	CF D.Lewis	CF R.Lankford
RF L.Walker	CF D.Orsulak	RF J.Eisenreich	RF O.Merced	RF T.Gwynn	RF W.McGee	RF M.Whiten
C D.Fletcher	RF B.Bonilla	C D.Daulton	C D.Slaught	C K.Higgins	C K.Manwaring	C T.Pagnozzi
	C T.Hundley					
O L.Frazier	O D.Gallagher	2S M.Duncan	O D.Clark	O1 P.Clark	O D.Martinez	O1 R.Brewer
3S M.Lansing	S2 J.McKnight	O P.Incaviglia		S3 C.Shipley		2 G.Pena
1O J.Vander Wal	23 C.Walker	O W.Chamberlain		31 A.Cianfrocco		CO E.Pappas
13 F.Bolick	O R.Thompson			2 T.Teufel		O B.Jordan
	O J.Burnitz					
P D.Martinez		P C.Schilling	P S.Cooke	P A.Benes	P B.Swift	P B.Tewksbury
P K.Hill		P D.Jackson	P B.Walk	P Gr.Harris	P J.Burkett	P R.Arocha
P C.Nabholz	P D.Gooden	P T.Mulholland	P P.Wagner	P D.Brocail	P T.Wilson	P D.Osborne
RP J.Fassero	P F.Tanana	RP B.Rivera	P T.Wakefield	P W.Whitehurst	RP B.Hickerson	P R.Cormier
RP B.Barnes	P E.Hillman	P T.Greene	P R.Tomlin	P T.Worrell	RP J.Brantley	RP J.Magrane
RP J.Shaw	RP B.Saberhagen	RP Mt.Williams	RP B.Minor	RP K.Taylor	RP D.Burba	RP O.Olivares
	P P.Schourek	RP L.Andersen	RP D.Neagle	RP Ge.Harris		RP M.Perez
P M.Rojas	RP A.Young		RP D.Otto	RP T.Hoffman	P B.Black	RP R.Murphy
P K.Rueter	RP J.Innis	P Mi.Williams	P Z.Smith		P K.Rogers	
P J.Wetteland	RP M.Maddux	P R.Mason	P J.Ballard	P A.Ashby	P R.Beck	P A.Watson
P K.Bottenfield			P J.Johnston	/P S.Sanders	P M.Jackson	P T.Urbani
P G.Heredia	P S.Fernandez			P R.Mason		P L.Lancaster
	P D.Telgheder					P L.Smith
	/P B.Jones					

TEAM	G	W	L	PCT	GB	R	OR	AB	H	2B	3B	HR	BB	SO	AVG	OBP	SLG	PRO	PRO+	BR	/A	PF	CHI	RC	SB	CS	SBA	SBR
EAST																												
PHI	162	97	65	.599		**877**	740	5685	**1555**	297	51	156	665	1049	.274	**.354**	.426	**.780**	116	117	**130**	99	99	**880**	91	32	74	8
MON	163	94	68	.580	3	732	682	5493	1410	270	36	122	542	860	.257	.329	.386	.715	92	-25	-55	104	104	727	**228**	56	**80**	35
STL	162	87	75	.537	10	758	744	5551	1508	262	34	118	588	882	.272	.344	.395	.739	105	32	48	98	99	759	153	72	68	3
CHI	163	84	78	.519	13	738	739	5627	1521	259	32	161	446	923	.270	.328	.414	.742	105	18	31	98	99	748	100	43	70	4
PIT	162	75	87	.463	22	707	806	5549	1482	267	50	110	536	972	.267	.338	.393	.731	101	10	12	100	95	734	92	55	63	-5
FLA	162	64	98	.395	33	581	724	5475	1356	197	31	94	498	1054	.248	.316	.346	.662	79	-124	-157	106	98	604	117	56	68	2
NY	162	59	103	.364	38	672	744	5448	1350	228	37	158	448	879	.248	.308	.390	.698	92	-72	-64	99	**105**	646	79	50	61	-6
WEST																												
ATL	162	104	58	.642		767	**559**	5515	1444	239	29	**169**	560	946	.262	.334	.408	.742	103	26	19	101	101	754	125	48	72	9
SF	162	103	59	.636	1	808	636	5557	1534	269	33	168	516	930	**.276**	.343	**.427**	.770	115	82	107	97	99	803	120	65	65	-3
HOU	162	85	77	.525	19	716	630	5464	1459	288	37	138	487	911	.267	.333	.409	.742	107	24	51	96	96	733	103	60	63	-5
LA	162	81	81	.500	23	675	662	5588	1458	234	28	130	492	937	.261	.324	.383	.707	100	-45	-5	94	98	696	126	61	67	1
CIN	162	73	89	.451	31	722	785	5517	1457	261	28	137	485	1025	.264	.327	.396	.723	98	-13	-14	100	102	720	142	59	71	7
COL	162	67	95	.414	37	758	967	5517	1507	278	**59**	142	388	944	.273	.346	.422	.748	90	28	-93	116	102	731	146	90	62	-10
SD	162	61	101	.377	43	679	772	5503	1386	239	28	153	443	1046	.252	.314	.389	.703	91	-58	-69	102	103	672	92	41	69	3
TOT	1135					10190		77489	20427	3588	513	1956	7104	13358	.264	.330	.399	.729							1714	788	69	41

TEAM	CG	SH	SV	IP	H	H/G	HR	BB	SO	RAT	ERA	ERA+	OAV	OOB	PR	/A	PF	CPI	FA	E	DP	FW	PW	BW	SBW	DIF
EAST																										
PHI	**24**	11	46	1472²	1419	8.7	129	573	**1117**	12.4	3.95	100	.251	.324	14	1	98	94	.977	141	123	-.4	.0	**13.0**	.5	2.8
MON	8	7	**61**	1456²	1369	8.5	119	521	934	12.0	3.55	118	.249	.319	80	101	103	101	.975	159	144	-1.4	10.1	-5.5	**3.2**	6.6
STL	5	7	54	1453	1553	9.6	152	**383**	775	12.3	4.09	97	.276	.327	-8	-20	98	102	.975	159	157	-1.4	-2.0	4.8	.0	4.6
CHI	8	5	56	1449²	1514	9.4	153	470	905	12.6	4.18	95	.273	.335	-22	-31	99	103	.982	115	162	1.1	-3.1	3.1	.1	1.8
PIT	12	5	34	1445²	1557	9.7	153	485	832	13.0	4.77	85	.280	.342	-117	-116	100	95	.983	105	161	1.7	-11.6	1.2	-.8	3.5
FLA	4	5	48	1440¹	1437	9.0	135	598	945	12.9	4.13	105	.261	.337	-14	30	107	100	.980	125	130	.5	3.0	-15.7	-.0	-4.8
NY	16	8	22	1438	1483	9.3	139	434	867	12.3	4.05	99	.263	.328	-2	-6	99	100	.975	156	143	-1.3	-.6	-6.4	-.9	-12.9
WEST																										
ATL	18	**16**	46	1455	**1297**	8.0	101	480	1036	11.1	3.14	128	.240	.305	146	142	99	101	.983	108	146	1.5	**14.2**	1.9	.6	4.8
SF	4	9	50	1456²	1385	8.6	168	442	982	11.6	3.61	108	.253	.315	69	47	97	105	**.984**	101	169	1.9	4.7	10.7	-.6	5.3
HOU	18	14	42	1441¹	1363	8.5	117	476	1056	11.7	3.49	111	.251	.316	88	61	96	101	.979	126	141	.5	6.1	5.1	-.8	-6.8
LA	17	9	36	1472²	1406	8.6	103	567	1043	12.3	3.50	109	.254	.327	88	51	94	**105**	.979	133	141	.0	5.1	-.5	-.2	-4.5
CIN	11	8	37	1434	1510	9.5	158	508	996	12.9	4.51	89	.272	.338	-74	-77	100	97	.980	121	133	.8	-7.7	-1.4	.4	-.0
COL	9	0	35	1431¹	1664	10.5	181	609	913	14.6	5.41	88	.294	.367	-218	-102	118	98	.973	167	149	-1.9	-10.2	-9.3	-1.3	8.7
SD	8	6	32	1437²	1470	9.2	148	558	957	12.6	4.23	98	.266	.337	-30	-15	102	100	.974	160	129	-1.5	-1.5	-6.9	.0	-10.1
TOT	162	110	599	20284²		9.1				12.5	4.04		.264	.330					.978	1876	2028					

Runs
Dykstra-Phi 143
Bonds-SF 129
Gant-Atl 113
McGriff-SD-Atl 111
Blauser-Atl 110

Hits
Dykstra-Phi 194
Grace-Chi 193
Grissom-Mon 188
Bell-Pit 187
Jefferies-StL 186

Doubles
Hayes-Col 45
Dykstra-Phi 44
Bichette-Col 43
Gwynn-SD 41
Biggio-Hou 41

Triples
Finley-Hou 13
Butler-LA 10
Morandini-Phi 9
Bell-Pit 9

Home Runs
Bonds-SF 46
Justice-Atl 40
Williams-SF 38
McGriff-SD-Atl 37
Gant-Atl 36

Total Bases
Bonds-SF 365
Williams-SF 325
Gant-Atl 309
Piazza-LA 307
Dykstra-Phi 307

Runs Batted In
Bonds-SF 123
Justice-Atl 120
Gant-Atl 117
Piazza-LA 112
Williams-SF 110

Runs Produced
Bonds-SF 206
Gant-Atl 194
Dykstra-Phi 190
Grissom-Mon 180
Hollins-Phi 179

Bases On Balls
Dykstra-Phi 129
Bonds-SF 126
Daulton-Phi 117
Kruk-Phi 111
Butler-LA 86

Batting Average
Galarraga-Col ..... .370
Gwynn-SD ..... .358
Jefferies-StL ..... .342
Bonds-SF ..... .336
Grace-Chi ..... .325

On Base Percentage
Bonds-SF ..... .463
Kruk-Phi ..... .433
Dykstra-Phi ..... .423
Merced-Pit ..... .415
Jefferies-StL ..... .411

Slugging Average
Bonds-SF ..... .677
Galarraga-Col ..... .602
Williams-SF ..... .561
Piazza-LA ..... .561
McGriff-SD-Atl ..... .549

Production
Bonds-SF 1.140
Galarraga-Col 1.010
Piazza-LA ..... .935
McGriff-SD-Atl ..... .927
Bagwell-Hou ..... .909

Adjusted Production
Bonds-SF 207
Piazza-LA 155
Bagwell-Hou 146
Kruk-Phi 145
Dykstra-Phi 144

Batter Runs
Bonds-SF 82.0
Dykstra-Phi 43.3
Galarraga-Col 42.3
Kruk-Phi 38.1
McGriff-SD-Atl 34.8

Adjusted Batter Runs
Bonds-SF 87.0
Dykstra-Phi 45.3
Piazza-LA 40.5
Kruk-Phi 39.9
Bagwell-Hou 35.4

Clutch Hitting Index
Zeile-StL 128
King-Pit 127
May-Chi 126
Oliver-Cin 125
Daulton-Phi 122

Runs Created
Bonds-SF 172
Dykstra-Phi 142
Kruk-Phi 117
McGriff-SD-Atl 115
Jefferies-StL 113

Total Average
Bonds-SF 1.339
Galarraga-Col 1.006
Dykstra-Phi 1.000
Kruk-Phi ..... .974
Daulton-Phi ..... .971

Stolen Bases
Carr-Fla 58
Grissom-Mon 53
Nixon-Atl 47
Lewis-SF 46
Jefferies-StL 46

Stolen Base Average
Frazier-Mon 89.5
Davis-LA 86.8
Grissom-Mon 84.1
Bell-SD 83.9
Jefferies-StL 83.6

Stolen Base Runs
Grissom-Mon 9.9
Jefferies-StL 8.4
DeShields-Mon 6.9
Davis-LA 6.9
Nixon-Atl 6.3

Fielding Runs
Bell-Pit 25.7
King-Pit 20.5
Gonzalez-Hou 20.2
Reed-LA 19.4
O.Smith-StL 18.2

Total Player Rating
Bonds-SF 8.8
Dykstra-Phi 6.1
Bell-Pit 5.7
Piazza-LA 5.1
Wilkins-Chi 4.2

Wins
Glavine-Atl 22
Burkett-SF 22
Swift-SF 21
Maddux-Atl 20

Win Percentage
Portugal-Hou ..... .818
Greene-Phi ..... .800
Glavine-Atl ..... .786
Burkett-SF ..... .759
Avery-Atl ..... .750

Games
Jackson-SF 81
West-Phi 76
Beck-SF 76
McMichael-Atl 74

Complete Games
Maddux-Atl 8

Shutouts
Harnisch-Hou 4
R.Martinez-LA 3

Saves
Myers-Chi 53
Beck-SF 48
Harvey-Fla 45

Innings Pitched
Maddux-Atl 267.0
Rijo-Cin 257.1
Smoltz-Atl 243.2
Glavine-Atl 239.1
Drabek-Hou 237.2

Fewest Hits/Game
Harnisch-Hou 7.07
Swift-SF 7.54
Rijo-Cin 7.62
Smoltz-Atl 7.68
Maddux-Atl 7.69

Fewest BB/Game
Tewksbury-StL ..... .84
Arocha-StL 1.48
Burkett-SF 1.55
Avery-Atl 1.73
Maddux-Atl 1.75

Strikeouts
Rijo-Cin 227
Smoltz-Atl 208
Maddux-Atl 197
Schilling-Phi 186
Harnisch-Hou 185

Strikeouts/Game
Rijo-Cin 7.94
Smoltz-Atl 7.68
Guzman-Chi 7.68
Harnisch-Hou 7.65
Greene-Phi 7.52

Ratio
Maddux-Atl 9.64
Rijo-Cin 9.86
Swift-SF 9.90
Mulholland-Phi 10.37
Avery-Atl 10.44

Earned Run Average
Maddux-Atl 2.36
Rijo-Cin 2.48
Portugal-Hou 2.77
Swift-SF 2.82
Avery-Atl 2.94

Adjusted ERA
Maddux-Atl 170
Rijo-Cin 162
Portugal-Hou 140
Swift-SF 138
Avery-Atl 136

Opponents' Batting Avg.
Harnisch-Hou ..... .214
Swift-SF ..... .226
Rijo-Cin ..... .230
Smoltz-Atl ..... .230
Maddux-Atl ..... .232

Opponents' On Base Pct.
Maddux-Atl ..... .274
Swift-SF ..... .278
Rijo-Cin ..... .278
Mulholland-Phi ..... .283
Harnisch-Hou ..... .290

Starter Runs
Maddux-Atl 49.8
Rijo-Cin 44.5
Swift-SF 31.4
Portugal-Hou 29.4
Avery-Atl 27.2

Adjusted Starter Runs
Maddux-Atl 49.0
Rijo-Cin 44.0
Swift-SF 28.0
Avery-Atl 26.5
Portugal-Hou 25.4

Clutch Pitching Index
Portugal-Hou 120
Glavine-Atl 116
R.Martinez-LA 116
Reynoso-Col 113
Avery-Atl 110

Relief Runs
Fassero-Mon 29.2
Wetteland-Mon 26.5
McMichael-Atl 20.1
Harvey-Fla 18.0
P.Martinez-LA 17.0

Adjusted Relief Runs
Fassero-Mon 31.3
Wetteland-Mon 26.5
Harvey-Fla 20.1
McMichael-Atl 19.9
Beck-SF 15.4

Relief Ranking
Wetteland-Mon 56.4
Harvey-Fla 38.1
Fassero-Mon 32.4
Gott-LA 25.0
Beck-SF 22.9

Total Pitcher Index
Maddux-Atl 6.1
Wetteland-Mon 5.7
Rijo-Cin 4.8
Swift-SF 4.2
Harvey-Fla 3.9

Total Baseball Ranking
Bonds-SF 8.8
Dykstra-Phi 6.1
Maddux-Atl 6.1
Wetteland-Mon 5.7
Bell-Pit 5.7

January 5 Reggie Jackson is the lone player elected to the Hall of Fame. Jackson, whose .262 lifetime batting average is the lowest of any outfielder in the Hall, receives 93.6 percent of the vote. His 563 career home runs certainly didn't hurt in his first year of eligibility.

March 22 Cleveland pitcher Steve Olin is killed instantly and new teammate Tim Crews dies several hours later as a result of a boating accident at Little Lake Nellie in Clermont, Florida. Bob Ojeda is seriously injured as well, but he will survive and make a comeback.

May 29 Jose Canseco, who three days earlier had a ball bounce off his head for a home run, pitches an inning in a blowout in Boston. Besides the Rangers' 15-1 loss, Canseco winds up having to undergo season-ending elbow surgery from his ill-advised outing.

June 28 Carlton Fisk is released by the White Sox after 12 years with the team. The 45-year-old caught more games and hit more homers than any catcher.

July 12 Kirby Puckett homers and doubles to earn MVP honors in the AL's 9-3 All-Star victory at Baltimore's Camden Yards.

July 28 Ken Griffey Jr. hits home runs in eight consecutive games to tie the major league record. Six travel more than 400 feet and one is a grand slam. Dale Long (1956) and Don Mattingly (1987) are the only others to go deep in eight straight games.

September 4 Jim Abbott becomes the eighth Yankee pitcher to throw a no-hitter with a 4-0 triumph over the Indians. Abbott, who was born without a right hand, throws 118 pitches and does not allow a runner past first base—despite five walks.

September 16 Minnesota's Dave Winfield becomes the 19th member of the 3,000-hit club with a single off Oakland's Dennis Eckersley. Only Cap Anson, who was 46 when he became the charter member of the 3,000-hit club,

reached the milestone at an older age than the 41-year-old Winfield.

October 12 Dave Stewart captures the pennant and the ALCS MVP with a 6-3 win over the White Sox in Game 6. Paul Molitor triples home two runs and Devon White's ninth-inning home run sparks a three-run rally in the clincher.

October 20 The Blue Jays hammer Mitch Williams and the Phillies relief corps for six runs in the eighth inning to overcome a four-run deficit. Reliever Duane Ward retires all four batters he faces in Toronto's 15-14 win. The 4-hour, 14-minute marathon is the longest and highest scoring game in World Series history.

October 23 In one of the most dramatic endings in World Series history, Joe Carter hits a three-run ninth-inning home run off Mitch Williams for an 8-6 win and Toronto's second straight world championship. Paul Molitor, who hit .500 in 24 at bats, is MVP.

BALTIMORE		BOSTON		CALIFORNIA		CHICAGO		CLEVELAND		DETROIT		KANSAS CITY	
M	J.Oates	M	B.Hobson	M	B.Rodgers	M	G.Lamont	M	M.Hargrove	M	S.Anderson	M	H.McRae
1B	D.Segui	1B	M.Vaughn	1B	J.Snow	1B	F.Thomas	1B	P.Sorrento	1B	C.Fielder	1B	W.Joyner
2B	H.Reynolds	2B	S.Fletcher	2B	T.Lovullo	2B	J.Cora	2B	C.Baerga	2B	L.Whitaker	2B	J.Lind
SS	C.Ripken	SS	J.Valentin	SS	G.DiSarcina	SS	O.Guillen	SS	F.Fermin	SS	A.Trammell	SS	G.Gagne
3B	T.Hulett	3B	S.Cooper	3B	R.Gonzales	3B	R.Ventura	3B	A.Espinoza	3B	T.Fryman	3B	G.Gaetti
LF	B.Anderson	LF	M.Greenwell	LF	L.Polonia	LF	T.Raines	LF	A.Belle	LF	T.Phillips	LF	K.McReynolds
CF	M.Devereaux	CF	B.Hatcher	CF	C.Curtis	CF	L.Johnson	CF	K.Lofton	CF	M.Cuyler	CF	B.McRae
RF	M.McLemore	RF	B.Zupcic	RF	T.Salmon	RF	E.Burks	RF	W.Kirby	RF	R.Deer	RF	F.Jose
C	C.Hoiles	C	T.Pena	C	G.Myers	C	R.Karkovice	C	J.Ortiz	C	C.Kreuter	C	M.Macfarlane
DH	H.Baines	DH	A.Dawson	DH	C.Davis	DH	G.Bell	DH	R.Jefferson	DH	K.Gibson	DH	G.Brett
3	L.Gomez	1O	C.Quintana	O1	S.Javier	OD	B.Jackson	32	J.Treadway	3D	S.Livingstone	O	C.Gwynn
		OD	I.Calderon	23	D.Easley			31	C.Martinez	1C	M.Tettleton	3	P.Hiatt
P	B.McDonald					P	J.McDowell	C	S.Alomar	O	D.Gladden	C	B.Mayne
P	F.Valenzuela	P	D.Darwin	P	M.Langston	P	A.Fernandez						
P	M.Mussina	P	R.Clemens	P	C.Finley	P	W.Alvarez	P	J.Mesa	P	M.Moore	P	D.Cone
P	R.Sutcliffe	P	F.Viola	P	S.Sanderson	P	J.Bere	P	T.Kramer	P	D.Wells	P	K.Appier
P	J.Moyer	P	J.Dopson	RP	K.Patterson	P	K.McCaskill	P	M.Clark	P	J.Doherty	P	H.Pichardo
RP	A.Mills	P	A.Sele	RP	J.Grahe	RP	R.Hernandez	P	J.Hernandez	P	B.Gullickson	P	T.Gordon
RP	T.Frohwirth	RP	P.Quantrill	RP	J.Valera	RP	D.Pall	RP	E.Plunk	P	M.Leiter	P	C.Haney
RP	M.Williamson	RP	G.Harris			RP	S.Radinsky	RP	D.Lilliquist	RP	T.Bolton	RP	M.Gubicza
		RP	S.Bankhead	P	J.Farrell					RP	B.Krueger	RP	J.Montgomery
P	A.Rhodes			P	P.Leftwich	P	T.Belcher	P	J.Mutis	RP	M.Henneman		
P	J.Poole	P	J.Hesketh	P	R.Springer	P	J.Schwarz	P	M.Young			P	M.Gardner
		P	K.Ryan	P	H.Hathaway			P	M.Bielecki	P	R.MacDonald		
				P	G.Nelson			P	B.Wertz				
								P	C.Young				
								P	J.DiPoto				
								P	D.Cook				
								/P	A.Lopez				

MILWAUKEE		MINNESOTA		NEW YORK		OAKLAND		SEATTLE		TEXAS		TORONTO	
M	P.Garner	M	T.Kelly	M	B.Showalter	M	T.LaRussa	M	L.Piniella	M	K.Kennedy	M	C.Gaston
1B	J.Jaha	1B	K.Hrbek	1B	D.Mattingly	1B	M.Aldrete	1B	T.Martinez	1B	R.Palmeiro	1B	J.Olerud
2B	B.Spiers	2B	C.Knoblauch	2B	P.Kelly	2B	B.Gates	2B	R.Amaral	2B	D.Strange	2B	R.Alomar
SS	P.Listach	SS	P.Meares	SS	S.Owen	SS	M.Bordick	SS	O.Vizquel	SS	M.Lee	SS	T.Fernandez
3B	B.Surhoff	3B	M.Pagliarulo	3B	W.Boggs	3B	C.Paquette	3B	M.Blowers	3B	D.Palmer	3B	E.Sprague
LF	G.Vaughn	LF	P.Munoz	LF	D.James	LF	R.Henderson	LF	M.Felder	LF	J.Gonzalez	LF	T.Ward
CF	R.Yount	CF	S.Mack	CF	B.Williams	CF	D.Henderson	CF	K.Griffey	CF	D.Hulse	CF	D.White
RF	D.Hamilton	RF	K.Puckett	RF	P.O'Neill	RF	R.Sierra	RF	J.Buhner	RF	J.Canseco	RF	J.Carter
C	D.Nilsson	C	B.Harper	C	M.Stanley	C	T.Steinbach	C	D.Valle	C	I.Rodriguez	C	P.Borders
DH	K.Reimer	DH	D.Winfield	DH	D.Tartabull	DH	T.Neel	DH	P.O'Brien	DH	J.Franco	DH	P.Molitor
2S	J.Bell	O1	D.McCarty	S2	M.Gallego	O3	J.Browne	2	B.Boone	O	G.Redus	O	J.Guzman
S3	D.Thon	S3	J.Reboulet	1O	J.Leyritz	31	K.Seitzer	13	D.Magadan	S3	M.Diaz	P	P.Hentgen
O	T.Brunansky			OS	R.Velarde	O2	L.Blankenship					P	T.Stottlemyre
		P	K.Tapani	CD	M.Nokes	C	S.Hemond	P	R.Johnson	P	K.Brown	P	D.Stewart
P	C.Eldred	P	S.Erickson			O1	S.Brosius	P	E.Hanson	P	K.Rogers	P	J.Morris
P	J.Navarro	P	W.Banks	P	J.Key			P	T.Leary	P	R.Pavlik	RP	D.Cox
P	R.Bones	P	J.Deshaies	P	J.Abbott	P	B.Witt	P	D.Fleming	P	C.Leibrandt	RP	M.Eichhorn
P	B.Wegman	RP	M.Trombley	P	M.Perez	P	R.Darling	P	C.Bosio	RP	B.Bohanon	RP	D.Ward
P	A.Miranda	RP	M.Hartley	P	S.Kamieniecki	P	B.Welch	RP	J.Nelson	RP	C.Lefferts		
RP	G.Lloyd	RP	R.Aguilera	P	B.Wickman	RP	K.Downs	RP	D.Henry	RP	T.Henke	P	A.Leiter
RP	M.Fetters			RP	R.Monteleone	RP	J.Boever	RP	D.Powell			P	M.Timlin
RP	J.Orosco	P	E.Guardado	RP	S.Howe	RP	E.Nunez					P	T.Castillo
		P	G.Tsamis							P	M.Whiteside		
P	R.Novoa	P	C.Willis			P	T.Van Poppel			P	N.Ryan		
P	D.Henry	P	L.Casian			P	D.Eckersley			P	T.Burns		
P	M.Boddicker					P	M.Mohler			P	B.Patterson		
						P	S.Davis						
						P	S.Hillegas						

TEAM	G	W	L	PCT	GB	R	OR	AB	H	2B	3B	HR	BB	SO	AVG	OBP	SLG	PRO	PRO+	BR	/A	PF	CHI	RC	SB	CS	SBA	SBR
EAST																												
TOR	162	95	67	.586		847	742	5579	1556	317	42	159	588	861	**.279**	.353	.436	.789	110	85	81	101	99	867	**170**	49	**78**	**22**
NY	162	88	74	.543	7	821	761	5615	**1568**	294	24	178	629	910	**.279**	.356	.435	.791	**115**	93	122	97	95	861	39	35	53	-9
BAL	162	85	77	.525	10	786	745	5508	1470	287	24	157	655	930	.267	.349	.413	.762	100	36	3	104	98	796	73	54	57	-11
DET	162	85	77	.525	10	**899**	837	5620	1546	282	38	178	**765**	1122	.275	**.365**	.434	**.799**	**115**	**120**	**126**	99	98	**916**	104	63	62	-7
BOS	162	80	82	.494	15	686	698	5496	1451	**319**	29	114	508	871	.264	.333	.395	.728	89	-41	-85	106	96	713	73	38	66	-1
CLE	162	76	86	.469	19	790	813	5619	1547	264	31	141	488	843	.275	.339	.409	.748	100	-5	-2	100	104	776	159	55	74	15
MIL	162	69	93	.426	26	733	792	5525	1426	240	25	125	555	932	.258	.330	.378	.708	91	-77	-67	99	108	686	138	63	60	-14
WEST																												
CHI	162	94	68	.580		776	664	5483	1454	228	**44**	162	604	834	.265	.342	.411	.753	103	11	28	98	100	773	106	57	65	-2
TEX	162	86	76	.531	8	835	751	5510	1472	284	39	**181**	483	984	.267	.332	.431	.763	107	16	46	96	**109**	777	113	67	63	-6
KC	162	84	78	.519	10	675	694	5522	1455	294	35	125	428	936	.263	.322	.397	.719	87	-67	-107	106	100	692	100	75	57	-15
SEA	162	82	80	.506	12	734	731	5494	1429	272	24	161	624	901	.260	.342	.406	.748	99	3	-8	101	95	758	91	68	57	-14
CAL	162	71	91	.438	23	684	770	5391	1399	259	24	114	564	930	.260	.334	.380	.714	88	-63	-85	103	101	679	169	100	63	-9
MIN	162	71	91	.438	23	693	830	5601	1480	261	27	121	493	850	.264	.329	.385	.714	91	-70	-72	100	101	692	83	59	58	-11
OAK	162	68	94	.420	26	715	846	5543	1408	260	21	158	622	1048	.254	.333	.394	.727	101	-42	1	94	99	735	131	59	69	4
TOT	1134					10674		77506	20661	3861	427	2074	8006	12952	.267	.340	.408	.748							1549	872	64	-59

TEAM	CG	SH	SV	IP	H	H/G	HR	BB	SO	RAT	ERA	ERA+	OAV	OOB	PR	/A	PF	CPI	FA	E	DP	FW	PW	BW	SBW	DIF
EAST																										
TOR	11	11	**50**	1441¹	1441	9.0	134	620	1023	13.1	4.21	103	.261	.339	18	17	100	99	.982	107	144	.5	1.7	7.9	**2.5**	1.5
NY	11	**13**	38	1438¹	1467	9.2	170	552	899	12.8	4.35	95	.266	.336	-5	-31	96	100	.983	105	166	.6	-3.0	11.9	-.5	-2.0
BAL	21	10	42	1442²	1427	8.9	153	579	900	12.8	4.31	104	.261	.336	2	26	104	98	.984	100	171	.9	2.5	.3	-.7	1.0
DET	11	7	36	1436²	1547	9.7	188	542	828	13.4	4.65	92	.276	.345	-52	-58	99	102	.979	132	148	-1.0	-5.6	**12.3**	-.3	-1.3
BOS	9	11	44	1452¹	**1379**	**8.5**	127	552	997	**12.3**	3.77	**122**	**.252**	.325	88	**136**	107	100	.980	122	155	-.4	**13.2**	-8.3	.3	-5.9
CLE	7	8	45	1445²	1591	9.9	182	591	888	13.8	4.58	95	.281	.353	-41	-40	100	**107**	.976	148	**174**	-1.9	-3.9	-.2	1.9	-.8
MIL	**26**	6	29	1447	1511	9.4	153	522	810	13.0	4.45	95	.271	.340	-21	-33	98	99	.979	131	148	-.9	-3.2	-6.5	-1.0	-.4
WEST																										
CHI	16	11	48	1454	1398	8.7	125	566	974	12.4	**3.70**	113	.255	.330	**100**	77	97	105	.982	112	153	.2	7.5	2.7	.2	2.4
TEX	20	6	45	1438¹	1476	9.2	144	562	957	13.0	4.28	97	.267	.339	6	-21	96	100	.979	132	145	-1.0	-2.0	4.5	-.2	3.8
KC	16	6	48	1445¹	**1379**	8.6	**105**	571	985	12.4	4.04	113	.254	.329	45	86	106	93	**.985**	**90**	173	**1.5**	8.4	-10.4	-1.1	5.1
SEA	22	10	41	1453²	1421	8.8	135	605	**1083**	13.0	4.20	105	.259	.340	20	33	102	99	.980	120	161	-.3	2.5	-.8	-1.0	-1.9
CAL	**26**	6	41	1430¹	1482	9.3	153	550	843	13.1	4.34	104	.270	.342	-3	26	104	100	.980	100	161	-.3	2.5	-8.3	-.5	-3.5
MIN	5	3	44	1444¹	1591	9.9	148	**514**	901	13.4	4.71	92	.283	.348	-63	-57	101	99	.984	100	160	.9	-5.5	-7.0	-.7	2.4
OAK	8	2	42	1452¹	1551	9.6	157	680	864	14.1	4.90	83	.276	.359	-94	-134	94	98	.982	111	161	.2	-13.0	.0	.8	-1.1
TOT	209	110	593	20222¹		9.2				13.0	4.32		.267	.340					.981	1607	2209					

Runs
Palmeiro-Tex 124
Molitor-Tor 121
White-Tor 116
Lofton-Cle 116
Henderson-Oak-Tor 114

Hits
Molitor-Tor 211
Olerud-Tor 200
Baerga-Cle 200
Alomar-Tor 192
Lofton-Cle 185

Doubles
Olerud-Tor 54
White-Tor 42
Valentin-Bos 40
Palmeiro-Tex 40
Puckett-Min 39

Triples
Johnson-Chi 14
Cora-Chi 13
Hulse-Tex 10
McRae-KC 9
Fernandez-Tor 9

Home Runs
Gonzalez-Tex 46
Griffey-Sea 45
Thomas-Chi 41
Belle-Cle 38
Palmeiro-Tex 37

Total Bases
Griffey-Sea 359
Gonzalez-Tex 339
Thomas-Chi 333
Palmeiro-Tex 331
Olerud-Tor 330

Runs Batted In
Belle-Cle 129
Thomas-Chi 128
Carter-Tor 121
Gonzalez-Tex 118
Fielder-Det 117

Runs Produced
Molitor-Tor 210
Baerga-Cle 198
Thomas-Chi 193
Palmeiro-Tex 192
Olerud-Tor 192

Bases On Balls
Phillips-Det 132
Henderson-Oak-Tor 120
Olerud-Tor 114
Thomas-Chi 112
Tettleton-Det 109

Batting Average
Olerud-Tor ..... .363
Molitor-Tor ..... .332
Alomar-Tor ..... .326
Lofton-Cle ..... .325
Baerga-Cle ..... .321

On Base Percentage
Olerud-Tor ..... .478
Phillips-Det ..... .446
Henderson-Oak-Tor .... .435
Thomas-Chi ..... .434
Hoiles-Bal ..... .419

Slugging Average
Gonzalez-Tex ..... .632
Griffey-Sea ..... .617
Thomas-Chi ..... .607
Olerud-Tor ..... .599
Hoiles-Bal ..... .585

Production
Olerud-Tor 1.077
Thomas-Chi 1.041
Griffey-Sea 1.029
Hoiles-Bal 1.003
Gonzalez-Tex 1.001

Adjusted Production
Olerud-Tor 186
Thomas-Chi 180
Gonzalez-Tex 170
Griffey-Sea 170
Hoiles-Bal 160

Batter Runs
Olerud-Tor 74.4
Thomas-Chi 62.3
Griffey-Sea 60.1
Gonzalez-Tex 44.4
Molitor-Tor 41.0

Adjusted Batter Runs
Olerud-Tor 73.6
Thomas-Chi 65.5
Griffey-Sea 58.1
Gonzalez-Tex 49.0
Palmeiro-Tex 42.9

Clutch Hitting Index
McLemore-Bal 122
Surhoff-Mil 120
Baerga-Cle 119
Davis-Cal 117
Kirby-Cle 115

Runs Created
Olerud-Tor 161
Thomas-Chi 149
Griffey-Sea 147
Molitor-Tor 136
Palmeiro-Tex 128

Total Average
Olerud-Tor 1.230
Thomas-Chi 1.160
Henderson-Oak-Tor 1.106
Griffey-Sea 1.104
Hoiles-Bal 1.077

Stolen Bases
Lofton-Cle 70
Polonia-Cal 55
Alomar-Tor 55
Henderson-Oak-Tor 53
Curtis-Cal 48

Stolen Base Average
White-Tor 89.5
Palmeiro-Tex 88.0
Henderson-Oak-Tor 86.9
Molitor-Tor 84.6
Fletcher-Bos 84.2

Stolen Base Runs
Lofton-Cle 12.6
Henderson-Oak-Tor 11.1
White-Tor 7.8
Alomar-Tor 7.5
Johnson-Chi 6.3

Fielding Runs
Vizquel-Sea 23.1
Pena-Bos 21.6
Joyner-KC 20.4
Boggs-NY 19.7
Belle-Cle 19.1

Total Player Rating
Olerud-Tor 5.8
Henderson-Oak-Tor 5.3
Griffey-Sea 5.3
Belle-Cle 5.2
Gonzalez-Tex 4.9

Wins
McDowell-Chi 22
Johnson-Sea 19
Hentgen-Tor 19

Win Percentage
Key-NY ..... .750
Johnson-Sea ..... .704
Appier-KC ..... .692
McDowell-Chi ..... .688
Hentgen-Tor ..... .679

Games
Harris-Bos 80
Radinsky-Chi 73
D.Ward-Tor 71
Nelson-Sea 71
Fossas-Bos 71

Complete Games
Finley-Cal 13
Brown-Tex 12
McDowell-Chi 10
Johnson-Sea 10
Eldred-Mil 8

Shutouts
McDowell-Chi 4
Moore-Det 3
Johnson-Sea 3
Brown-Tex 3

Saves
D.Ward-Tor 45
Montgomery-KC 45
Henke-Tex 40
Hernandez-Chi 38
Eckersley-Oak 36

Innings Pitched
Eldred-Mil 258.0
McDowell-Chi 256.2
Langston-Cal 256.1
Johnson-Sea 255.1
Cone-KC 254.0

Fewest Hits/Game
Johnson-Sea 6.52
Appier-KC 6.90
Cone-KC 7.26
Alvarez-Chi 7.28
McDonald-Bal 7.56

Fewest BB/Game
Key-NY 1.64
Darwin-Bos 1.92
Wells-Det 2.02
Tapani-Min 2.27
Doherty-Det 2.34

Strikeouts
Johnson-Sea 308
Langston-Cal 196
Guzman-Tor 194
Cone-KC 191
Finley-Cal 187

Strikeouts/Game
Johnson-Sea 10.86
Perez-NY 8.17
Guzman-Tor 7.90
Clemens-Bos 7.51
Banks-Min 7.25

Ratio
Darwin-Bos 9.73
Appier-KC 9.99
Key-NY 10.00
Johnson-Sea 10.57
Fernandez-Chi 10.70

Earned Run Average
Appier-KC 2.56
Alvarez-Chi 2.95
Key-NY 3.00
Fernandez-Chi 3.13
Viola-Bos 3.14

Adjusted ERA
Appier-KC 179
Viola-Bos 147
Finley-Cal 143
Alvarez-Chi 142
Darwin-Bos 142

Opponents' Batting Avg.
Johnson-Sea ..... .203
Appier-KC ..... .212
Cone-KC ..... .223
McDonald-Bal ..... .228
Bosio-Sea ..... .229

Opponents' On Base Pct.
Darwin-Bos ..... .274
Appier-KC ..... .280
Key-NY ..... .282
Johnson-Sea ..... .292
Fernandez-Chi ..... .296

Starter Runs
Appier-KC 46.6
Key-NY 34.6
Fernandez-Chi 32.7
Finley-Cal 32.7
Langston-Cal 32.1

Adjusted Starter Runs
Appier-KC 53.4
Finley-Cal 37.8
Langston-Cal 37.3
Cone-KC 35.3
Darwin-Bos 34.6

Clutch Pitching Index
Alvarez-Chi 129
Viola-Bos 123
Pavlik-Tex 119
Banks-Min 118
Finley-Cal 115

Relief Runs
Montgomery-KC 19.9
Hernandez-Chi 17.8
D.Ward-Tor 17.4
Lilliquist-Cle 14.7
Henneman-Det 13.4

Adjusted Relief Runs
Montgomery-KC 22.4
D.Ward-Tor 17.4
Hernandez-Chi 16.5
Lilliquist-Cle 14.8
Mills-Bal 13.9

Relief Ranking
Montgomery-KC 47.7
D.Ward-Tor 29.7
Hernandez-Chi 27.0
Henke-Tex 21.9
Henneman-Det 20.8

Total Pitcher Index
Appier-KC 4.8
Montgomery-KC 4.3
Langston-Cal 3.9
Finley-Cal 3.7
Darwin-Bos 3.4

Total Baseball Ranking
Olerud-Tor 5.8
Henderson-Oak-Tor 5.3
Griffey-Sea 5.3
Belle-Cle 5.2
Gonzalez-Tex 4.9

January 12 Steve Carlton, winner of 329 games and four Cy Young Awards, is elected to the Baseball Hall of Fame.

February 25 The Hall of Fame Veterans Committee taps Leo Durocher, who hit .247 over a 17-year career, but had a .540 winning percentage in 24 years as a manager, and Yankee great Phil Rizzuto, who had waited in vain for years for enshrinement.

April 4 Cubs outfielder Karl "Tuffy" Rhodes, who hit three home runs in all of 1993, hits three home runs off Mets starter Dwight Gooden on Opening Day at Wrigley Field. New York holds on for the 12-8 win.

April 8 Braves lefthander Kent Mercker no-hits the Dodgers, 6-0, in his first career complete game.

April 8 Chan Ho Park of the Dodgers becomes the first Korean-born player to appear in an ML game.

April 10* The Texas League witnesses two no-hitters on a single evening.

April 15* Beloit (Midwest League) southpaw Kelly Wunsch fans five Springfield Sultan batters in a single inning. Two batters reach first when third strikes get past the Beloit catcher.

May 14 St. Louis shortstop Ozzie Smith homers in back-to-back games, the first time this has happened in his 16-year ML career.

June 13 Ryne Sandberg of the Cubs, considered by many as one of the best second basemen in NL history, abruptly announces his retirement. He is hitting just .238.

June 22 Mets reliever John Franco earns his 253rd career save to break Dave Righetti's record for most saves by a lefthander.

June 24 Jeff Bagwell of the Astros becomes the 28th player to hit two home runs in one inning when he connects twice in the sixth inning against the Dodgers. Bagwell adds another homer in the eighth.

June 30 Giants center fielder Darren Lewis commits his first major league error to break his record of 392 flawless games in the outfield.

July 14 Cardinals shortstop Ozzie Smith breaks Luis Aparicio's record for assists by a shortstop with his 8,017th in an 8-1 loss to Colorado.

July 31 Matt Williams hits his 40th home run of the season to set a NL record for most homers by the end of July. Williams reaches 40 homers sooner than any player since Reggie Jackson in 1969.

August 5 Fred McGriff becomes the seventh player to hit 30 or more home runs for seven consecutive seasons.

August 12 Major league players go on strike to produce the eighth work stoppage since 1972.

September 14 Major League Baseball cancels the World Series. It makes the first season without a World Series in 90 years.

	ATLANTA		CHICAGO		CINCINNATI		COLORADO		FLORIDA		HOUSTON		LOS ANGELES
M	B.Cox	M	T.Trebelhorn	M	D.Johnson	M	D.Baylor	M	R.Lachemann	M	T.Collins	M	T.Lasorda
1B	F.McGriff	1B	M.Grace	1B	H.Morris	1B	A.Galarraga	1B	G.Colbrunn	1B	J.Bagwell	1B	E.Karros
2B	M.Lemke	2B	R.Sandberg	2B	B.Boone	2B	N.Liriano	2B	B.Barberie	2B	C.Biggio	2B	D.DeShields
SS	J.Blauser	SS	S.Dunston	SS	B.Larkin	SS	W.Weiss	SS	K.Abbott	SS	A.Cedeno	SS	J.Offerman
3B	T.Pendleton	3B	S.Buechele	3B	T.Fernandez	3B	C.Hayes	3B	J.Browne	3B	K.Caminiti	3B	T.Wallach
LF	R.Klesko	LF	D.May	LF	K.Mitchell	LF	H.Johnson	LF	J.Conine	LF	L.Gonzalez	LF	H.Rodriguez
CF	R.Kelly	CF	G.Hill	CF	D.Sanders	CF	M.Kingery	CF	C.Carr	CF	S.Finley	CF	B.Butler
RF	D.Justice	RF	S.Sosa	RF	R.Sanders	RF	D.Bichette	RF	G.Sheffield	RF	J.Mouton	RF	R.Mondesi
C	J.Lopez	C	R.Wilkins	C	B.Dorsett	C	J.Girardi	C	B.Santiago	C	S.Servais	C	M.Piazza
O	T.Tarasco	O	K.Rhodes	1	J.Rijo	1	J.Vander Wal	O	M.Carrillo	O	K.Bass	O	C.Snyder
O	D.Gallagher	2S	R.Sanchez	O	J.Smiley	O	E.Young	31	D.Magadan			O	M.Webster
					E.Hanson					P	D.Drabek		
P	G.Maddux	P	S.Trachsel	P	J.Roper	P	G.Harris	P	D.Weathers	P	G.Swindell	P	R.Martinez
P	T.Glavine	P	W.Banks	P	P.Schourek	P	D.Nied	P	P.Rapp	P	D.Kile	P	K.Gross
P	S.Avery	P	A.Young	RP	J.Ruffin	P	M.Freeman	P	C.Hough	P	S.Reynolds	P	T.Candiotti
P	J.Smoltz	P	J.Bullinger	RP	J.Brantley	P	M.Harkey	P	M.Gardner	P	P.Harnisch	P	P.Astacio
P	K.Mercker	P	M.Morgan	RP	C.McElroy	P	K.Ritz	P	C.Hammond	RP	T.Jones	P	O.Hershiser
RP	G.McMichael	RP	J.Bautista			RP	W.Blair	RP	R.Nen	RP	T.Edens	RP	T.Worrell
RP	M.Wohlers	RP	C.Crim	P	H.Carrasco	RP	S.Reed	RP	R.Lewis	RP	D.Veres	RP	R.McDowell
RP	M.Stanton	RP	D.Plesac			RP	B.Ruffin	RP	L.Aquino			RP	J.Gott
										P	B.Williams		
		P	K.Foster			P	L.Painter						
						/P	A.Reynoso						

	MONTREAL		NEW YORK		PHILADELPHIA		PITTSBURGH		SAN DIEGO		SAN FRANCISCO		ST.LOUIS
M	F.Alou	M	D.Green	M	J.Fregosi	M	J.Leyland	M	J.Riggleman	M	D.Baker	M	J.Torre
1B	C.Floyd	1B	D.Segui	1B	J.Kruk	1B	B.Hunter	1B	E.Williams	1B	T.Benzinger	1B	G.Jefferies
2B	M.Lansing	2B	J.Kent	2B	M.Morandini	2B	C.Garcia	2B	B.Roberts	2B	J.Patterson	2B	G.Pena
SS	W.Cordero	SS	J.Vizcaino	SS	K.Stocker	SS	J.Bell	SS	R.Gutierrez	SS	R.Clayton	SS	O.Smith
3B	S.Berry	3B	B.Bonilla	3B	D.Hollins	3B	J.King	3B	C.Shipley	3B	M.Williams	3B	T.Zeile
LF	M.Alou	LF	J.Cangelosi	LF	M.Thompson	LF	A.Martin	LF	P.Plantier	LF	B.Bonds	LF	B.Gilkey
CF	M.Grissom	CF	R.Thompson	CF	L.Dykstra	CF	A.Van Slyke	CF	D.Bell	CF	D.Lewis	CF	R.Lankford
RF	L.Walker	RF	J.Orsulak	RF	J.Eisenreich	RF	O.Merced	RF	T.Gwynn	RF	D.Martinez	RF	M.Whiten
C	D.Fletcher	C	T.Hundley	C	D.Daulton	C	D.Slaught	C	B.Ausmus	C	K.Manwaring	C	T.Pagnozzi
O	L.Frazier	23	F.Vina	23	M.Duncan	O	D.Clark	O1	B.Bean	P	J.Burkett	2	L.Alicea
				O	P.Incaviglia			S2	L.Lopez	P	M.Portugal		
P	K.Hill	P	B.Saberhagen	1	R.Jordan	P	Z.Smith			P	B.Swift	P	B.Tewksbury
P	P.Martinez	P	B.Jones	3S	K.Batiste	P	D.Neagle	P	A.Benes	P	B.Hickerson	P	V.Palacios
P	J.Fassero	P	P.Smith			P	S.Cooke	P	A.Ashby	P	Van Landingham	P	A.Watson
P	B.Henry	P	M.Gozzo	P	D.Jackson	P	P.Wagner	P	S.Sanders	RP	D.Burba	P	T.Urbani
P	K.Rueter	RP	R.Mason	P	B.Munoz	P	J.Lieber	P	J.Hamilton	RP	R.Beck	P	O.Olivares
RP	M.Rojas	RP	D.Linton	P	D.West	RP	R.White	RP	P.Martinez	RP	R.Monteleone	RP	R.Arocha
RP	G.Heredia	RP	J.Franco	P	S.Boskie	RP	M.Dewey	RP	T.Hoffman			RP	B.Eversgerd
RP	J.Shaw			P	C.Schilling	RP	R.Manzanillo	RP	T.Mauser	P	S.Torres	RP	R.Rodriguez
		P	M.Remlinger	RP	H.Slocumb					P	B.Black		
/P	J.Jacome			RP	D.Jones			P	W.Whitehurst				
P	J.Wetteland											P	R.Sutcliffe
P	T.Scott												
				P	M.Williams								

TEAM	G	W	L	PCT	GB	R	OR	AB	H	2B	3B	HR	BB	SO	AVG	OBP	SLG	PRO	PRO+	BR	/A	PF	CHI	RC	SB	CS	SBA	SBR
EAST																												
MON	114	74	40	.649		585	454	4000	1111	246	30	108	379	669	.278	.346	.435	.781	107	47	42	101	99	615	**137**	36	**79**	20
ATL	114	68	46	.596	6	542	**448**	3861	1031	198	18	**137**	377	**668**	.267	.336	.434	.770	103	25	14	102	99	548	48	31	61	-4
NY	113	55	58	.487	18.5	506	526	3869	966	164	21	117	336	807	.250	.334	.394	.712	91	-57	-52	99	109	484	25	26	49	-8
PHI	115	54	61	.470	20.5	521	497	3927	1028	208	28	80	396	711	.262	.334	.390	.724	92	-31	-43	102	104	515	67	24	74	6
FLA	115	51	64	.443	23.5	468	576	3926	1043	180	24	94	349	746	.266	.332	.396	.728	92	-29	-43	103	94	519	65	26	71	4
CENTRAL																												
CIN	115	66	48	.579		**609**	490	3999	**1142**	211	36	124	388	738	**.286**	**.353**	**.449**	**.802**	115	**78**	85	99	98	**633**	119	51	70	5
HOU	115	66	49	.574	0.5	602	503	3955	1099	**252**	25	120	394	718	.278	.350	.445	.795	**118**	66	**98**	95	99	624	124	44	74	11
STL	115	53	61	.465	13	535	621	3902	1026	213	27	108	**434**	686	.263	.342	.414	.756	104	14	25	98	98	555	76	46	62	-5
PIT	114	53	61	.465	13	466	580	3864	1001	198	23	80	349	725	.259	.324	.384	.708	88	-57	-63	101	102	478	53	25	68	1
CHI	113	49	64	.434	16.5	500	549	3918	1015	189	26	109	364	750	.259	.326	.404	.730	96	-29	-22	99	101	507	69	53	57	-11
WEST																												
LA	114	58	56	.509		532	509	3904	1055	160	29	115	366	687	.270	.336	.414	.750	107	1	36	93	101	538	74	37	67	0
SF	115	55	60	.478	3.5	504	500	3869	963	159	32	123	364	719	.249	.320	.402	.722	97	-44	-21	95	105	504	114	40	74	10
COL	117	53	64	.453	6.5	573	638	4006	1098	206	**39**	125	378	761	.274	.340	.439	.779	92	40	-54	116	99	584	91	53	63	-5
SD	117	47	70	.402	12.5	479	531	4068	1117	200	19	92	319	762	.275	.332	.401	.733	99	-24	-8	97	93	526	79	37	68	2
TOT	803					7422		55068	14695	2784	377	1532	5193	10147	.267	.335	.415	.750							1141	529	68	25

TEAM	CG	SH	SV	IP	H	H/G	HR	BB	SO	RAT	ERA	ERA+	OAV	OOB	PR	/A	PF	CPI	FA	E	DP	FW	PW	BW	SBW	DIF
EAST																										
MON	4	8	46	1036²	970	8.4	100	288	805	11.3	3.56	119	.247	**.305**	75	76	100	95	.979	94	90	-.5	7.5	4.1	**1.8**	4.1
ATL	**16**	8	26	1026¹	**929**	8.1	76	378	865	11.7	3.57	119	.242	.314	73	77	101	93	.982	81	85	.3	**7.6**	1.4	-.6	2.3
NY	7	3	35	1023	1069	9.4	117	332	640	12.5	4.13	101	.271	.331	9	4	99	103	.980	89	112	-.2	.4	-5.1	-1.0	4.4
PHI	7	6	30	1024¹	1028	9.0	98	377	699	12.6	3.85	111	.261	.330	41	50	102	103	.978	94	96	-.4	4.9	-4.2	.4	-4.2
FLA	5	7	30	1015	1069	9.5	120	428	649	13.6	4.50	97	.274	.352	-32	-15	104	104	.978	95	111	-.5	-1.5	-4.2	.2	-.5
CENTRAL																										
CIN	6	6	27	1038¹	1037	9.2	117	339	799	12.2	3.78	109	.262	.324	50	41	98	**106**	.983	73	91	.8	4.0	8.4	.3	-4.5
HOU	9	6	29	1029²	1043	9.1	102	367	739	12.6	3.97	100	.265	.333	28	-2	94	104	.983	76	110	.6	-.2	**9.6**	.9	-2.5
STL	7	7	29	1018	1154	10.2	134	355	632	13.7	5.14	81	.289	.353	-105	-111	99	97	.982	80	119	.4	-10.9	2.5	-.7	4.7
PIT	8	2	24	1005²	1094	9.8	117	370	650	13.5	4.64	93	.281	.350	-47	-36	103	102	.982	90	110	-.3	-3.5	-6.2	-.0	6.1
CHI	5	5	27	1023²	1054	9.3	120	392	717	12.9	4.47	93	.268	.338	-29	-36	99	97	.982	81	110	.2	-3.5	-2.2	-1.3	-.8
WEST																										
LA	14	5	20	1014	1041	9.2	90	354	732	12.5	4.17	94	.267	.333	4	-28	93	97	.980	88	104	-.1	-2.8	3.5	-.2	.5
SF	2	4	33	1025¹	1014	8.9	122	372	655	12.5	3.99	100	.262	.333	26	2	95	106	**.985**	68	113	**1.1**	.2	-2.1	.8	-2.5
COL	4	5	28	1031	1185	10.3	120	448	703	14.7	5.15	96	.292	.369	-108	-21	118	101	.981	84	117	.2	-2.1	-5.3	-.7	2.3
SD	8	6	27	1045²	1008	8.7	99	393	862	12.3	4.08	101	.252	.323	15	3	98	91	.975	111	82	-1.3	.3	-.8	.0	-9.7
TOT	102	78	411	14356²		9.2				12.8	4.21		.267	.335					.980	1205	1471					

Runs
Bagwell-Hou ... 104
Grissom-Mon ... 96
Lankford-StL ... 89
Bonds-SF ... 89
Biggio-Hou ... 88

Hits
Gwynn-SD ... 165
Bichette-Col ... 147
Bagwell-Hou ... 147
Morris-Cin ... 146
Conine-Fla ... 144

Doubles
Walker-Mon ... 44
Biggio-Hou ... 44
Gwynn-SD ... 35
Bell-Pit ... 35
Bichette-Col ... 33

Triples
Lewis-SF ... 9
Butler-LA ... 8
R.Sanders-Cin ... 8
Mondesi-LA ... 8
Kingery-Col ... 8

Home Runs
Williams-SF ... 43
Bagwell-Hou ... 39
Bonds-SF ... 37
McGriff-Atl ... 34
Galarraga-Col ... 31

Total Bases
Bagwell-Hou ... 300
Williams-SF ... 270
Bichette-Col ... 265
McGriff-Atl ... 264
Bonds-SF ... 253

Runs Batted In
Bagwell-Hou ... 116
Williams-SF ... 96
Bichette-Col ... 95
McGriff-Atl ... 94
Piazza-LA ... 92

Runs Produced
Bagwell-Hou ... 181
Walker-Mon ... 143
Bichette-Col ... 142
McGriff-Atl ... 141
Biggio-Hou ... 138

Bases On Balls
Bonds-SF ... 74
Justice-Atl ... 69
Dykstra-Phi ... 68
Butler-LA ... 68
Bagwell-Hou ... 65

Batting Average
Gwynn-SD ... .394
Bagwell-Hou ... .368
Alou-Mon ... .339
Morris-Cin ... .335
Mitchell-Cin ... .326

On Base Percentage
Bagwell-Hou ... .461
Gwynn-SD ... .458
Mitchell-Cin ... .438
Bonds-SF ... .429
Justice-Atl ... .428

Slugging Average
Bagwell-Hou ... .750
Mitchell-Cin ... .681
Bonds-SF ... .647
McGriff-Atl ... .623
Williams-SF ... .607

Production
Bagwell-Hou ... 1.211
Mitchell-Cin ... 1.119
Bonds-SF ... 1.076
Gwynn-SD ... 1.026
McGriff-Atl ... 1.014

Adjusted Production
Bagwell-Hou ... 220
Mitchell-Cin ... 188
Bonds-SF ... 184
Gwynn-SD ... 171
McGriff-Atl ... 156

Batter Runs
Bagwell-Hou ... 64.7
Bonds-SF ... 44.9
Gwynn-SD ... 42.2
Mitchell-Cin ... 40.3
McGriff-Atl ... 35.6

Adjusted Batter Runs
Bagwell-Hou ... 71.2
Bonds-SF ... 49.9
Gwynn-SD ... 45.2
Mitchell-Cin ... 41.3
McGriff-Atl ... 33.7

Clutch Hitting Index
Gonzalez-Hou ... 132
Blauser-Atl ... 121
Piazza-LA ... 120
Morris-Cin ... 116
Sheffield-Fla ... 116

Runs Created
Bagwell-Hou ... 137
Bonds-SF ... 115
Gwynn-SD ... 104
McGriff-Atl ... 103
Biggio-Hou ... 98

Total Average
Bagwell-Hou ... 1.413
Bonds-SF ... 1.256
Mitchell-Cin ... 1.244
Gwynn-SD ... 1.069
McGriff-Atl ... 1.063

Stolen Bases
Biggio-Hou ... 39
D.Sanders-Atl-Cin ... 38
Grissom-Mon ... 36
Carr-Fla ... 32
Lewis-SF ... 30

Stolen Base Average
Larkin-Cin ... 92.9
Biggio-Hou ... 90.7
Clayton-SF ... 88.5
Grissom-Mon ... 85.7
Cordero-Mon ... 84.2

Stolen Base Runs
Biggio-Hou ... 9.3
Grissom-Mon ... 7.2
Larkin-Cin ... 6.6
Clayton-SF ... 5.1
Carr-Fla ... 4.8

Fielding Runs
Sanchez-Chi ... 28.5
Bell-Pit ... 19.3
Bagwell-Hou ... 17.1
Grissom-Mon ... 16.3
Karros-LA ... 16.0

Total Player Rating
Bagwell-Hou ... 7.6
Bonds-SF ... 5.6
Gwynn-SD ... 4.5
Mitchell-Cin ... 4.2
Biggio-Hou ... 3.6

Wins
Maddux-Atl ... 16
Hill-Mon ... 16
Saberhagen-NY ... 14
Jackson-Phi ... 14
Glavine-Atl ... 13

Win Percentage
Saberhagen-NY ... .778
Hill-Mon ... .762
Maddux-Atl ... .727
Jackson-Phi ... .700
Martinez-Mon ... .688

Games
Reed-Col ... 61
Rojas-Mon ... 58
Bautista-Chi ... 58
Munoz-Col ... 57
Burba-SF ... 57

Complete Games
Maddux-Atl ... 10
Drabek-Hou ... 6
Candiotti-LA ... 5

Shutouts
Martinez-LA ... 3
Maddux-Atl ... 3
Drabek-Hou ... 2
Benes-SD ... 2

Saves
Franco-NY ... 30
Beck-SF ... 28
Jones-Phi ... 27
Wetteland-Mon ... 25

Innings Pitched
Maddux-Atl ... 202.0
Jackson-Phi ... 179.1
Saberhagen-NY ... 177.1
Rijo-Cin ... 172.1
Benes-SD ... 172.1

Fewest Hits/Game
Maddux-Atl ... 6.68
Martinez-Mon ... 7.15
Drabek-Hou ... 7.21
Avery-Atl ... 7.54
Fassero-Mon ... 7.72

Fewest BB/Game
Saberhagen-NY ... .66
Tewksbury-StL ... 1.27
Maddux-Atl ... 1.38
Reynolds-Hou ... 1.52
Swindell-Hou ... 1.58

Strikeouts
Benes-SD ... 189
Rijo-Cin ... 171
Maddux-Atl ... 156
Saberhagen-NY ... 143
Martinez-Mon ... 142

Strikeouts/Game
Benes-SD ... 9.87
Rijo-Cin ... 8.93
Martinez-Mon ... 8.83
Neagle-Pit ... 8.01
Reynolds-Hou ... 7.98

Ratio
Maddux-Atl ... 8.33
Saberhagen-NY ... 9.44
Drabek-Hou ... 9.78
Fassero-Mon ... 10.38
Ashby-SD ... 10.46

Earned Run Average
Maddux-Atl ... 1.56
Saberhagen-NY ... 2.74
Drabek-Hou ... 2.84
Fassero-Mon ... 2.99
Reynolds-Hou ... 3.05

Adjusted ERA
Maddux-Atl ... 272
Saberhagen-NY ... 152
Fassero-Mon ... 141
Drabek-Hou ... 139
Rijo-Cin ... 134

Opponents' Batting Avg.
Maddux-Atl ... .207
Martinez-Mon ... .220
Drabek-Hou ... .220
Avery-Atl ... .227
Fassero-Mon ... .229

Opponents' On Base Pct.
Maddux-Atl ... .245
Saberhagen-NY ... .273
Drabek-Hou ... .277
Fassero-Mon ... .286
Ashby-SD ... .286

Starter Runs
Maddux-Atl ... 59.5
Saberhagen-NY ... 29.0
Drabek-Hou ... 25.0
Rijo-Cin ... 21.6
Henry-Mon ... 21.2

Adjusted Starter Runs
Maddux-Atl ... 60.2
Saberhagen-NY ... 28.2
Freeman-Col ... 27.2
Henry-Mon ... 21.3
Jackson-Phi ... 20.4

Clutch Pitching Index
Rijo-Cin ... 125
Rapp-Fla ... 121
Smith-Pit ... 118
Burkett-SF ... 118
Trachsel-Chi ... 116

Relief Runs
Jackson-SF ... 12.8
Brantley-Cin ... 12.6
Carrasco-Chi ... 12.4
Jones-Phi ... 12.3
Jones-Hou ... 12.0

Adjusted Relief Runs
Jones-Phi ... 12.7
Brantley-Cin ... 12.0
Carrasco-Chi ... 11.9
Jackson-SF ... 11.8
McElroy-Cin ... 11.5

Relief Ranking
Brantley-Cin ... 24.6
Jones-Phi ... 23.9
Carrasco-Chi ... 23.1
Wetteland-Mon ... 20.7
Nen-Fla ... 18.3

Total Pitcher Index
Maddux-Atl ... 7.3
Saberhagen-NY ... 3.1
Freeman-Col ... 2.8
Drabek-Hou ... 2.7
Brantley-Cin ... 2.5

Total Baseball Ranking
Bagwell-Hou ... 7.6
Maddux-Atl ... 7.3
Bonds-SF ... 5.6
Gwynn-SD ... 4.5
Mitchell-Cin ... 4.2

March 27 The all-women Colorado Silver Bullets drops their first exhibition game 10-2 to the Chet Lemon All-Stars. Bullets pitcher Lisa Martinez fans Lemon, a 16-year major league veteran.

April 9 Basketball legend Michael Jordan makes his professional baseball debut with an 0-for-3 day for Birmingham. Chattanooga beats the White Sox minor league team 10-3.

April 21 Indians first baseman Eddie Murray hits home runs from both sides of the plate in a game for the 11th time in his career to break Mickey Mantle's record.

April 27 Twins righthander Scott Erickson no-hits the Brewers 6-0 for Minnesota's first no-hitter since 1967.

April 30 Blue Jays outfielder Joe Carter finishes April with 31 RBI to set a ML record for the month. Colorado's Andres Galarraga sets the NL mark with 30.

May 14 Gary Gaetti participates in his seventh career triple play. He starts the play when he spears Geronimo Berroa's grounder, steps on third and goes around the horn to end an Oakland rally.

June 8 Gene Budig, chancellor of University of Kansas, replaces Dr. Bobby Brown as AL president.

June 13 Don Mattingly of the Yankees plays in his 1,469th game at first base to move past Wally Pipp into second place in Yankee history. Only Hall of Famer Lou Gehrig played in more (2,137).

June 19 The Tigers tie a major league record by hitting a home run in their 25th consecutive game when Mickey Tettleton goes deep against the Blue Jays.

June 22 Seattle's Ken Griffey Jr. breaks Babe Ruth's record for most home runs hit by the end of June when he connects for his 31st in a 12-3 win over the Angels.

July 1 The Orioles and the California Angels combine to hit 11 home runs to tie a major league record in Baltimore's 14-7 victory at Camden Yards.

July 9 Red Sox shortstop John Valentin records the 10th unassisted triple play in major league history.

July 18 Blue Jays outfielder Joe Carter reaches the 20-home run mark for the ninth consecutive year.

July 27 Tigers manager Sparky Anderson moves into fourth place on the all-time list for managerial wins with his 2,126th in a 3-1 win over the Mariners. Anderson passes Joe McCarthy with the win.

July 28 Kenny Rogers of the Rangers throws the 14th perfect game in major league history—and the first by a left-hander in AL history—with a 4-0 win over the Angels.

August 1 Cal Ripken Jr. plays in his 2,000th consecutive game.

August 11 In what would be the last game of the 1994 season, Ken Griffey hits a grand slam—his 40th home run in 111 games—in an 8-1 win over Oakland.

	BALTIMORE		BOSTON		CALIFORNIA		CHICAGO		CLEVELAND		DETROIT		KANSAS CITY
M	J.Oates	M	B.Hobson	M	B.Rodgers	M	G.Lamont	M	M.Hargrove	M	S.Anderson	M	H.McRae
1B	R.Palmeiro	1B	M.Vaughn	M	B.Knoop	1B	F.Thomas	1B	P.Sorrento	1B	C.Fielder	1B	W.Joyner
2B	M.McLemore	2B	S.Fletcher	M	M.Lachemann	2B	J.Cora	2B	C.Baerga	2B	L.Whitaker	2B	J.Lind
SS	C.Ripken	SS	J.Valentin	1B	J.Snow	SS	O.Guillen	SS	O.Vizquel	SS	A.Trammell	SS	G.Gagne
3B	L.Gomez	3B	S.Cooper	2B	H.Reynolds	3B	R.Ventura	3B	J.Thome	3B	T.Fryman	3B	G.Gaetti
LF	B.Anderson	LF	M.Greenwell	SS	G.DiSarcina	LF	T.Raines	LF	A.Belle	LF	T.Phillips	LF	V.Coleman
CF	M.Devereaux	CF	O.Nixon	3B	S.Owen	CF	L.Johnson	CF	K.Lofton	CF	M.Cuyler	CF	B.McRae
RF	J.Hammonds	RF	T.Brunansky	LF	J.Edmonds	RF	D.Jackson	RF	M.Ramirez	RF	J.Felix	RF	F.Jose
C	C.Hoiles	C	D.Berryhill	CF	C.Curtis	C	R.Karkovice	C	S.Alomar	C	C.Kreuter	C	M.Macfarlane
DH	H.Baines	DH	A.Dawson	RF	T.Salmon	DH	J.Franco	DH	E.Murray	DH	K.Gibson	DH	B.Hamelin
				C	C.Turner								
3O	C.Sabo	23	T.Naehring	DH	C.Davis	P	J.McDowell	3S	A.Espinoza	S2	C.Gomez	P	D.Cone
						P	A.Fernandez	O	W.Kirby	C1	M.Tettleton	P	T.Gordon
P	M.Mussina	P	R.Clemens	32	D.Easley	P	W.Alvarez					P	K.Appier
P	B.McDonald	P	A.Sele	O	B.Jackson	P	J.Bere	P	D.Martinez	P	T.Belcher	P	M.Gubicza
P	J.Moyer	P	J.Hesketh			P	S.Sanderson	P	C.Nagy	P	M.Moore	RP	H.Pichardo
P	S.Fernandez	P	D.Darwin	P	C.Finley	RP	J.DeLeon	P	J.Morris	P	B.Gullickson	RP	R.Meacham
RP	M.Eichhorn	RP	K.Ryan	P	M.Langston	RP	K.McCaskill	P	M.Clark	P	D.Wells	RP	S.Belinda
RP	M.Williamson	RP	G.Harris	P	P.Leftwich	RP	R.Hernandez	P	J.Grimsley	P	J.Doherty		
RP	A.Mills	RP	C.Howard	P	B.Anderson			RP	J.Mesa	RP	J.Boever	P	B.Milacki
				P	J.Magrane			RP	E.Plunk	RP	M.Gardiner		
P	M.Oquist			RP	M.Leiter					RP	S.Davis		
P	A.Rhodes			RP	J.Dopson								
				RP	R.Springer								

	MILWAUKEE		MINNESOTA		NEW YORK		OAKLAND		SEATTLE		TEXAS		TORONTO
M	P.Garner	M	T.Kelly	M	B.Showalter	M	T.LaRussa	M	L.Piniella	M	K.Kennedy	M	C.Gaston
1B	J.Jaha	1B	K.Hrbek	1B	D.Mattingly	1B	T.Neel	1B	T.Martinez	1B	W.Clark	1B	J.Olerud
2B	J.Reed	2B	C.Knoblauch	2B	P.Kelly	2B	B.Gates	2B	R.Amaral	2B	J.Frye	2B	R.Alomar
SS	J.Valentin	SS	P.Meares	SS	M.Gallego	SS	M.Bordick	SS	F.Fermin	SS	M.Lee	SS	D.Schofield
3B	K.Seitzer	3B	S.Leius	3B	W.Boggs	3B	S.Brosius	3B	E.Martinez	3B	D.Palmer	3B	E.Sprague
LF	G.Vaughn	LF	S.Mack	LF	L.Polonia	LF	R.Henderson	LF	E.Anthony	LF	J.Gonzalez	LF	M.Huff
CF	T.Ward	CF	A.Cole	CF	B.Williams	CF	S.Javier	CF	K.Griffey	CF	D.Hulse	CF	D.White
RF	M.Mieske	RF	K.Puckett	RF	P.O'Neill	RF	R.Sierra	RF	J.Buhner	RF	R.Greer	RF	J.Carter
C	D.Nilsson	C	M.Walbeck	C	M.Stanley	C	T.Steinbach	C	D.Wilson	C	I.Rodriguez	C	P.Borders
DH	B.Harper	DH	D.Winfield	DH	D.Tartabull	DH	G.Berroa	DH	R.Jefferson	DH	J.Canseco	DH	P.Molitor
O	A.Diaz	OD	P.Munoz	CD	J.Leyritz	O1	M.Aldrete	31	M.Blowers	23	D.Strange	P	P.Hentgen
3S	B.Spiers	S2	J.Reboulet	S3	R.Velarde	C2	S.Hemond	2S	L.Sojo			P	J.Guzman
P	C.Eldred	P	K.Tapani	P	J.Key	P	R.Darling	P	R.Johnson	P	K.Brown	P	T.Stottlemyre
P	R.Bones	P	S.Erickson	P	J.Abbott	P	B.Witt	P	C.Bosio	P	K.Rogers	P	D.Stewart
P	B.Wegman	P	J.Deshaies	P	M.Perez	P	T.Van Poppel	P	D.Fleming	P	H.Fajardo	P	A.Leiter
P	B.Scanlan	P	P.Mahomes	P	T.Mulholland	P	S.Ontiveros	RP	G.Hibbard	RP	M.Whiteside	RP	T.Castillo
P	J.Navarro	P	C.Pulido	P	S.Kamieniecki	RP	C.Reyes	RP	B.Ayala	RP	C.Carpenter	RP	W.Williams
RP	M.Ignasiak	RP	C.Willis	RP	B.Wickman	RP	B.Welch	RP	B.Risley	RP	D.Oliver	RP	M.Timlin
RP	G.Lloyd	RP	M.Guthrie	RP	S.Hitchcock	RP	J.Briscoe	RP	T.Davis				
RP	M.Fetters	RP	M.Trombley	RP	S.Howe					P	J.Dettmer		
								P	J.Cummings	/P	R.Helling		
P	T.Higuera							P	R.Salkeld	P	R.Pavlik		

TEAM	G	W	L	PCT	GB	R	OR	AB	H	2B	3B	HR	BB	SO	AVG	OBP	SLG	PRO	PRO+	BR	/A	PF	CHI	RC	SB	CS	SBA	SBR
EAST																												
NY	113	70	43	.619		670	534	3986	1155	238	16	139	530	660	.290	.377	.462	.839	120	97	124	96	94	692	55	40	58	-8
BAL	112	63	49	.563	6.5	589	497	3856	1047	185	20	139	438	655	.272	.352	.438	.790	97	13	-17	105	99	606	69	13	84	13
TOR	115	55	60	.478	16	566	579	3962	1064	210	30	115	387	691	.269	.339	.424	.763	95	-30	-32	100	100	570	79	26	75	8
BOS	115	54	61	.470	17	552	621	3940	1038	222	19	120	404	723	.263	.337	.421	.758	90	-39	-65	100	100	558	81	38	68	2
DET	115	53	62	.461	18	652	671	3955	1048	216	25	161	404	520	.265	.355	.454	.809	107	42	39	100	100	646	46	33	58	-6
CENTRAL																												
CHI	113	67	46	.593		633	498	3942	1133	175	39	121	497	568	.287	.370	.444	.814	111	58	71	98	95	660	77	27	74	7
CLE	113	66	47	.584	1	679	562	4022	1165	240	20	167	382	629	.290	.354	.484	.838	113	73	72	100	101	686	131	48	73	11
KC	115	64	51	.557	4	574	532	3911	1051	211	38	100	376	698	.269	.338	.419	.757	90	-38	-60	104	105	558	140	62	69	5
MIN	113	53	60	.469	14	594	688	3952	1092	239	23	103	359	635	.276	.343	.427	.770	90	-20	-20	100	105	578	94	30	76	10
MIL	115	53	62	.461	15	547	586	3978	1045	238	21	99	417	680	.263	.338	.408	.746	87	-53	-78	105	100	549	59	37	61	-5
WEST																												
TEX	114	52	62	.456		618	697	3983	1114	198	27	124	437	730	.280	.356	.436	.792	103	20	22	100	98	622	82	35	70	4
OAK	114	51	63	.447	1	549	589	3885	1009	178	13	113	417	686	.260	.334	.399	.733	96	-68	-25	92	106	527	91	39	70	4
SEA	112	49	63	.438	2	569	616	3883	1045	211	18	153	372	652	.269	.337	.451	.788	99	-1	-12	102	98	585	48	21	70	2
CAL	115	47	68	.409	5.5	543	660	3943	1042	178	16	120	402	715	.264	.336	.409	.745	90	-54	-62	101	101	536	65	54	55	-13
TOT	797					8330		55198	15048	2939	325	1774	5938	9619	.273	.348	.434	.782		1117	503						69	33

TEAM	CG	SH	SV	IP	H	H/G	HR	BB	SO	RAT	ERA	ERA+	OAV	OOB	PR	/A	PF	CPI	FA	E	DP	FW	PW	BW	SBW	DIF
EAST																										
NY	8	2	31	1019²	1045	9.2	120	398	656	12.9	4.34	105	.267	.337	52	26	95	103	.982	80	122	.1	2.4	11.5	-1.0	.4
BAL	13	4	37	997²	1005	9.1	131	351	666	12.5	4.31	116	.263	.330	54	77	104	102	.986	57	103	1.5	7.1	-1.6	1.0	-1.0
TOR	13	4	26	1025	1053	9.2	127	482	832	13.8	4.70	103	.266	.351	12	14	100	102	.981	81	105	.2	1.3	-3.0	.5	-1.5
BOS	6	3	30	1029¹	1104	9.7	120	450	729	13.9	4.93	102	.276	.354	-15	11	105	99	.981	81	124	.2	1.0	-6.0	-.0	1.3
DET	15	1	20	1018	1139	10.1	148	449	560	14.3	5.38	90	.282	.358	-66	-61	101	98	.981	82	90	.1	-5.6	3.6	-.8	-1.8
CENTRAL																										
CHI	13	9	20	1011¹	964	8.6	115	377	754	12.1	3.96	118	.250	.320	94	79	97	100	.981	79	91	.2	7.3	6.6	.4	-4.0
CLE	17	5	21	1018²	1097	9.7	94	404	666	13.6	4.36	108	.275	.348	49	40	98	105	.980	90	119	-.4	3.7	6.7	.8	-1.2
KC	5	6	38	1031²	1018	8.9	95	392	717	12.6	4.23	118	.260	.332	65	88	104	97	.982	80	102	.2	8.1	-5.5	.2	3.4
MIN	6	4	29	1005	1197	10.7	153	388	602	14.5	5.68	86	.299	.365	-98	-91	101	100	.982	75	99	.4	-8.4	-1.8	.7	5.6
MIL	11	3	23	1036	1071	9.3	127	421	577	13.2	4.62	109	.269	.343	20	47	105	101	.981	85	130	-.0	4.3	-7.2	-.7	-.9
WEST																										
TEX	10	4	26	1023	1176	10.3	157	394	683	14.1	5.45	88	.287	.355	-75	-72	100	98	.976	106	106	-1.4	-6.7	2.0	.1	.8
OAK	12	9	23	1003¹	979	8.8	128	510	732	13.7	4.80	92	.257	.350	0	-42	92	98	.979	88	105	-.3	-3.9	-2.3	.1	.3
SEA	13	7	21	984	1051	9.6	109	486	763	14.3	4.99	98	.274	.360	-21	-12	102	99	.977	95	102	-.8	-1.1	-1.1	-.0	-4.0
CAL	11	4	21	1027	1149	10.1	150	436	682	14.3	5.42	90	.287	.363	-70	-61	102	100	.983	76	110	.5	-5.6	-5.7	-1.4	1.8
TOT	153	65	366	14229²		9.5				13.5	4.80		.273	.348					.981	1155	1508					

Runs
Thomas-Chi	106
Lofton-Cle	105
Griffey-Sea	94
Phillips-Det	91
Belle-Cle	90

Hits
Lofton-Cle	160
Molitor-Tor	155
Belle-Cle	147
Thomas-Chi	141

Doubles
Knoblauch-Min	45
Belle-Cle	35
Thomas-Chi	34
Fryman-Det	34

Triples
L.Johnson-Chi	14
Coleman-KC	12
Lofton-Cle	9
Diaz-Mil	7

Home Runs
Griffey-Sea	40
Thomas-Chi	38
Belle-Cle	36
Canseco-Tex	31
Fielder-Det	28

Total Bases
Belle-Cle	294
Griffey-Sea	292
Thomas-Chi	291
Lofton-Cle	246
Palmeiro-Bal	240

Runs Batted In
Puckett-Min	112
Carter-Tor	103
Thomas-Chi	101
Belle-Cle	101
Franco-Chi	98

Runs Produced
Puckett-Min	171
Thomas-Chi	169
Belle-Cle	155
Lofton-Cle	150
Franco-Chi	150

Bases On Balls
Thomas-Chi	109
Tettleton-Det	97
Phillips-Det	95
O'Neill-NY	72
Henderson-Oak	72

Batting Average
O'Neill-NY	.359
Belle-Cle	.357
Thomas-Chi	.353
Lofton-Cle	.349
Boggs-NY	.342

On Base Percentage
Thomas-Chi	.494
O'Neill-NY	.464
Belle-Cle	.442
Boggs-NY	.437
Clark-Tex	.436

Slugging Average
Thomas-Chi	.729
Belle-Cle	.714
Griffey-Sea	.674
O'Neill-NY	.603
Hamelin-KC	.599

Production
Thomas-Chi	1.223
Belle-Cle	1.156
Griffey-Sea	1.078
O'Neill-NY	1.067
Hamelin-KC	.992

Adjusted Production
Thomas-Chi	214
Belle-Cle	191
O'Neill-NY	179
Griffey-Sea	168
Davis-Cal	147

Batter Runs
Thomas-Chi	71.3
Belle-Cle	56.3
Griffey-Sea	44.7
O'Neill-NY	42.8
Vaughn-Bos	30.7

Adjusted Batter Runs
Thomas-Chi	74.0
Belle-Cle	56.0
O'Neill-NY	46.8
Griffey-Sea	42.6
Lofton-Cle	30.5

Clutch Hitting Index
Puckett-Min	143
Clark-Tex	122
Sorrento-Cle	120
Franco-Chi	120
Fryman-Det	118

Runs Created
Thomas-Chi	145
Belle-Cle	131
Griffey-Sea	117
Lofton-Cle	111
Molitor-Tor	101

Total Average
Thomas-Chi	1.453
Belle-Cle	1.304
Griffey-Sea	1.174
O'Neill-NY	1.152
Lofton-Cle	1.101

Stolen Bases
Lofton-Cle	60
Coleman-KC	50
Nixon-Bos	42
Knoblauch-Min	35
Anderson-Bal	31

Stolen Base Average
Molitor-Tor	100.0
Anderson-Bal	96.9
Hulse-Tex	90.0
Coleman-KC	86.2
Shumpert-KC	85.7

Stolen Base Runs
Lofton-Cle	10.8
Coleman-KC	10.2
Anderson-Bal	8.7
Knoblauch-Min	6.9
Nixon-Bos	6.6

Fielding Runs
Valentin-Mil	28.1
Espinoza-Cle	24.4
Gallego-NY	19.6
Fielder-Det	15.7
Curtis-Cal	14.6

Total Player Rating
Belle-Cle	5.0
Thomas-Chi	5.0
Griffey-Sea	4.2
Lofton-Cle	4.2
O'Neill-NY	4.1

Wins
Key-NY	17
Mussina-Bal	16
Cone-KC	16
McDonald-Bal	14

Win Percentage
Bere-Chi	.857
Key-NY	.810
Clark-Cle	.786
Mussina-Bal	.762
Cone-KC	.762

Games
Wickman-NY	53
Mesa-Cle	51
Guthrie-Min	50
Brewer-KC	50
Willis-Min	49

Complete Games
Johnson-Sea	9
Martinez-Cle	7
Finley-Cal	7

Shutouts
Johnson-Sea	4

Saves
L.Smith-Bal	33
Montgomery-KC	27
Aguilera-Min	23
Eckersley-Oak	19
Ayala-Sea	18

Innings Pitched
Finley-Cal	183.1
McDowell-Chi	181.0
Eldred-Mil	179.0
Martinez-Cle	176.2
Mussina-Bal	176.1

Fewest Hits/Game
Clemens-Bos	6.54
Cone-KC	6.82
Johnson-Sea	6.91
Ontiveros-Oak	7.26
Bere-Chi	7.56

Fewest BB/Game
Gubicza-KC	1.80
Gullickson-Det	1.95
Wegman-Mil	2.02
Ontiveros-Oak	2.03
McDowell-Chi	2.09

Strikeouts
Johnson-Sea	204
Clemens-Bos	168
Finley-Cal	148
Hentgen-Tor	147
Appier-KC	145

Strikeouts/Game
Johnson-Sea	10.67
Clemens-Bos	8.86
Appier-KC	8.42
Langston-Cal	8.22
Bere-Chi	8.07

Ratio
Ontiveros-Oak	9.75
Cone-KC	10.01
Clemens-Bos	10.49
Mussina-Bal	10.51
Johnson-Sea	10.99

Earned Run Average
Ontiveros-Oak	2.65
Clemens-Bos	2.85
Cone-KC	2.94
Mussina-Bal	3.06
Johnson-Sea	3.19

Adjusted ERA
Clemens-Bos	177
Cone-KC	170
Ontiveros-Oak	167
Mussina-Bal	163
Johnson-Sea	153

Opponents' Batting Avg.
Clemens-Bos	.203
Cone-KC	.209
Johnson-Sea	.216
Ontiveros-Oak	.217
Bere-Chi	.229

Opponents' On Base Pct.
Ontiveros-Oak	.272
Cone-KC	.279
Clemens-Bos	.291
Mussina-Bal	.294
Martinez-Cle	.301

Starter Runs
Clemens-Bos	37.0
Cone-KC	35.5
Mussina-Bal	34.0
Johnson-Sea	30.7
Key-NY	28.6

Adjusted Starter Runs
Clemens-Bos	41.4
Cone-KC	39.4
Mussina-Bal	38.1
Johnson-Sea	32.4
Bones-Mil	30.4

Clutch Pitching Index
Kamieniecki-NY	124
Key-NY	122
Clark-Cle	117
Mahomes-Min	115
Stottlemyre-Tor	114

Relief Runs
Eichhorn-Bal	20.9
Plunk-Cle	17.9
Castillo-Tor	17.3
Howe-NY	13.3
Wickman-NY	13.3

Adjusted Relief Runs
Eichhorn-Bal	22.5
Castillo-Tor	17.4
Plunk-Cle	17.2
Ryan-Bos	13.8
Ayala-Sea	12.8

Relief Ranking
Eichhorn-Bal	32.0
Ayala-Sea	22.1
Risley-Sea	21.7
Fetters-Mil	21.6
Plunk-Cle	21.1

Total Pitcher Index
Cone-KC	4.4
Mussina-Bal	3.9
Johnson-Sea	3.3
Eichhorn-Bal	3.2
Key-NY	3.2

Total Baseball Ranking
Belle-Cle	5.0
Thomas-Chi	5.0
Cone-KC	4.4
Griffey-Sea	4.2
Lofton-Cle	4.2

January 8 Mike Schmidt, who hit 548 home runs and won two MVP Awards in 18 years with the Phillies, is elected to the Baseball Hall of Fame.

March 7 The Veterans Committee makes four selections for the Hall of Fame: Phillies great Richie Ashburn; William Hulbert, the NL's first president; Vic Willis, an eight-time 20-game winner in a 13-year major league career starting in 1898; and Negro League pitcher Leon Day.

March 31 The longest strike in sports history ends—in a courtroom. A U.S. District court order forbids owners from implementing new financial working conditions in the wake of the negotiations impasse. The court decides that conditions will revert to the old rules from the previous season. Because of the timing of the court order, 18 games will have to be trimmed from the major league schedule.

July 11 The NL is held without a hit by Randy Johnson, Kevin Appier, and Dennis Martinez for an All-Star record 5⅔ innings, but rallies for single runs in the sixth, seventh and eighth innings to pull out a 3-2 win at the Ballpark at Arlington. Jeff Conine homers against Steve Ontiveros in his only at bat for the game-winner to earn MVP honors.

August 18 Cardinals reliever Tom Henke earns his 300th career save in a 4-3 win over the Braves.

September 19 Andres Galarraga homers in a 15-4 loss to the Padres, but the home run makes the Rockies the second team to have four players hit 30 or more homers (the 1977 Dodgers were the other). Galarraga joins Dante Bichette, Larry Walker, and Vinny Castilla with 30 home runs for Colorado.

September 19 Padres third baseman Ken Caminiti drives in eight runs and homers from both sides of the plate for the third time in four games. Caminiti is the first player to perform this trick so many times in four days or fewer.

September 21 Rockies pinch hitter John Vander Wal sets a major league record with his 26th pinch-hit of the season. The record-setting hit is a home run in a 5-3 loss to the Giants.

October 1 The Rockies are the first team to make the postseason before their eighth year in existence and are the NL's first wild card winner following a 10-9 win over the Giants. The Rockies' .535 percentage (77-67 record) is the best ever for a third-year team.

October 6 The Reds hit three home runs and cruise to a 10-1 win over the Dodgers for a sweep of the Division Series.

October 7 The Braves wrap up the Division Series with a 10-4 win over the Rockies. Marquis Grissom hit .524 for Atlanta in the four-game win.

October 14 Mike Devereaux hits a three-run home run to seal Atlanta's 6-0 win for a four-game sweep of the Reds in the NLCS. Devereaux, who also had the game-winning single in the 11th inning of Game 1, earns MVP honors.

October 28 David Justice hears the boos from the home crowd after he questions Atlanta fans' loyalty—and he turns them to cheers with a sixth inning home run in Game 6. Series MVP Tom Glavine receives most of the cheers, however, with a one-hitter over eight innings. Mark Wohlers makes Justice's home run stand up in the ninth as the Braves win 1-0 for the first championship in Atlanta history.

ATLANTA
Pos	Player
M	B.Cox
1B	F.McGriff
2B	M.Lemke
SS	J.Blauser
3B	C.Jones
LF	R.Klesko
CF	M.Grissom
RF	D.Justice
C	J.Lopez
O	M.Kelly
O	D.Smith
P	G.Maddux
P	T.Glavine
P	J.Smoltz
P	S.Avery
P	K.Mercker
RP	G.McMichael
RP	B.Clontz
RP	M.Wohlers

CHICAGO
Pos	Player
M	J.Riggleman
1B	M.Grace
2B	R.Sanchez
SS	S.Dunston
3B	T.Zeile
LF	L.Gonzalez
CF	B.McRae
RF	S.Sosa
C	S.Servais
O	S.Bullett
S2	J.Hernandez
P	J.Navarro
P	F.Castillo
P	K.Foster
P	S.Trachsel
P	J.Bullinger
RP	M.Perez
RP	T.Wendell
RP	R.Myers

CINCINNATI
Pos	Player
M	D.Johnson
1B	H.Morris
2B	B.Boone
SS	B.Larkin
3B	J.Branson
LF	R.Gant
CF	J.Walton
RF	R.Sanders
C	B.Santiago
31	L.Harris
1O	T.Howard
2O	E.Taubensee
C	
P	P.Schourek
P	J.Smiley
P	T.Pugh
P	X.Hernandez
RP	H.Carrasco
RP	J.Brantley
P	K.Jarvis
P	M.Portugal
P	D.Wells
P	J.Rijo
P	D.Burba

COLORADO
Pos	Player
M	D.Baylor
1B	A.Galarraga
2B	J.Bates
SS	W.Weiss
3B	V.Castilla
LF	D.Bichette
CF	M.Kingery
RF	L.Walker
C	J.Girardi
O	E.Burks
1O	J.Vander Wal
2O	E.Young
P	K.Ritz
P	B.Swift
P	M.Freeman
P	A.Reynoso
RP	C.Leskanic
RP	S.Reed
RP	R.Bailey
P	B.Rekar
P	D.Holmes
P	J.Acevedo
P	J.Grahe
P	M.Thompson

FLORIDA
Pos	Player
M	R.Lachemann
1B	G.Colbrunn
2B	Q.Veras
SS	K.Abbott
3B	T.Pendleton
LF	J.Conine
CF	C.Carr
RF	G.Sheffield
C	C.Johnson
S3	A.Arias
O	A.Dawson
P	J.Burkett
P	P.Rapp
P	C.Hammond
P	B.Witt
P	D.Weathers
RP	M.Gardner
RP	T.Mathews
RP	R.Nen
/P	W.Banks

HOUSTON
Pos	Player
M	T.Collins
1B	J.Bagwell
2B	C.Biggio
SS	O.Miller
3B	D.Magadan
LF	J.Mouton
CF	B.Hunter
RF	D.Bell
C	T.Eusebio
O	J.Cangelosi
3S	C.Shipley
O	M.Thompson
O	L.Gonzalez
O	D.May
P	S.Reynolds
P	D.Drabek
P	G.Swindell
P	M.Hampton
P	D.Kile
RP	D.Veres
RP	T.Jones
RP	D.Brocail
P	J.Dougherty

LOS ANGELES
Pos	Player
M	T.Lasorda
1B	E.Karros
2B	D.DeShields
SS	J.Offerman
3B	T.Wallach
LF	B.Ashley
CF	R.Kelly
RF	R.Mondesi
C	M.Piazza
S2	C.Fonville
3	D.Hansen
P	R.Martinez
P	I.Valdes
P	H.Nomo
P	T.Candiotti
RP	P.Astacio
RP	T.Worrell
RP	A.Osuna
P	K.Tapani

MONTREAL
Pos	Player
M	F.Alou
1B	D.Segui
2B	M.Lansing
SS	W.Cordero
3B	S.Berry
LF	M.Alou
CF	R.White
RF	T.Tarasco
C	D.Fletcher
S3	M.Grudzielanek
31	S.Andrews
P	P.Martinez
P	J.Fassero
P	C.Perez
P	B.Henry
RP	G.Heredia
RP	M.Rojas
RP	T.Scott
P	J.Shaw

NEW YORK
Pos	Player
M	D.Green
1B	R.Brogna
2B	J.Kent
SS	J.Vizcaino
3B	E.Alfonzo
LF	J.Orsulak
CF	B.Butler
RF	T.Everett
C	T.Hundley
3O	B.Bonilla
O	R.Thompson
P	B.Jones
P	D.Mlicki
P	B.Pulsipher
P	B.Saberhagen
P	P.Harnisch
RP	J.DiPoto
RP	D.Henry
RP	J.Franco
P	J.Isringhausen
P	R.Cornelius

PHILADELPHIA
Pos	Player
M	J.Fregosi
1B	D.Hollins
2B	M.Morandini
SS	K.Stocker
3B	C.Hayes
LF	J.Eisenreich
CF	L.Dykstra
RF	M.Whiten
C	D.Daulton
1O	G.Jefferies
O	A.Van Slyke
P	P.Quantrill
P	T.Green
P	M.Mimbs
P	C.Schilling
RP	W.Williams
RP	R.Bottalico
P	T.Borland
P	S.Fernandez
P	H.Slocumb
P	J.Juden

PITTSBURGH
Pos	Player
M	J.Leyland
1B	M.Johnson
2B	C.Garcia
SS	J.Bell
3B	J.King
LF	A.Martin
CF	J.Brumfield
RF	O.Merced
C	M.Parent
2	N.Liriano
P	D.Neagle
P	E.Loaiza
P	P.Wagner
P	J.Ericks
RP	M.Dyer
RP	J.McCurry
RP	D.Plesac
P	S.Parris
P	J.Lieber
P	D.Miceli
P	J.Christiansen
P	R.White

SAN DIEGO
Pos	Player
M	B.Bochy
1B	E.Williams
2B	J.Reed
SS	A.Cedeno
3B	K.Caminiti
LF	M.Nieves
CF	S.Finley
RF	T.Gwynn
C	B.Ausmus
13	S.Livingstone
1	R.Petagine
O2	B.Roberts
C	B.Johnson
P	J.Hamilton
P	A.Ashby
P	A.Benes
P	G.Dishman
P	F.Valenzuela
RP	W.Blair
RP	B.Williams
RP	B.Florie
P	S.Sanders
P	T.Hoffman

SAN FRANCISCO
Pos	Player
M	D.Baker
1B	M.Carreon
2B	R.Thompson
SS	R.Clayton
3B	M.Williams
LF	B.Bonds
CF	D.Lewis
RF	G.Hill
C	K.Manwaring
2	J.Patterson
1	J.Phillips
32	S.Scarsone
O	D.Sanders
P	M.Leiter
P	T.Mulholland
P	Van Landingham
RP	M.Portugal
RP	J.Bautista
RP	R.Beck
RP	C.Hook
P	T.Wilson
P	J.Brewington
P	S.Valdez

ST.LOUIS
Pos	Player
M	J.Torre
M	M.Jorgensen
1B	J.Mabry
2B	J.Oquendo
SS	T.Cromer
3B	S.Cooper
LF	B.Gilkey
CF	R.Lankford
RF	B.Jordan
C	D.Sheaffer
C	T.Pagnozzi
P	M.Petkovsek
P	A.Watson
P	D.Osborne
P	K.Hill
P	M.Morgan
RP	R.DeLucia
RP	J.Parrett
RP	T.Henke
P	D.Jackson
P	T.Urbani
P	R.Arocha

TEAM	G	W	L	PCT	GB	R	OR	AB	H	2B	3B	HR	BB	SO	AVG	OBP	SLG	PRO	PRO+	BR	/A	PF	CHI	RC	SB	CS	SBA	SBR
EAST																												
ATL	144	90	54	.625		645	540	4814	1202	210	27	168	520	933	.250	.328	.409	.737	96	-10	-31	103	100	647	73	43	63	-4
NY	144	69	75	.479	21	657	618	4958	1323	218	34	125	446	994	.267	.333	.400	.733	101	-15	6	97	100	657	58	39	60	-6
PHI	144	69	75	.479	21	615	658	4950	1296	263	30	94	497	884	.262	.338	.384	.719	94	-33	-37	101	96	648	72	25	74	7
FLA	143	67	76	.469	22.5	673	673	4886	1278	214	29	144	517	916	.262	.338	.406	.744	101	9	7	100	99	681	131	53	71	8
MON	144	66	78	.458	24	621	638	4905	1268	265	24	118	400	901	.259	.322	.394	.716	90	-49	-70	104	103	619	120	49	71	7
CENTRAL																												
CIN	144	85	59	.590		747	623	4903	1326	277	35	161	519	946	.270	.345	.440	.785	112	77	81	100	100	757	190	68	74	16
HOU	144	76	68	.528	9	747	674	5097	1403	260	22	109	566	992	.275	.356	.399	.755	113	43	95	93	100	745	176	60	75	17
CHI	144	73	71	.507	12	693	671	4963	1315	267	39	158	440	920	.265	.329	.430	.759	106	23	36	98	101	698	105	37	74	9
STL	143	62	81	.434	22.5	563	658	4779	1182	238	24	107	436	920	.247	.316	.374	.690	86	-89	-87	100	102	669	79	46	63	-4
PIT	144	58	86	.403	27	629	736	4937	1281	245	27	125	456	972	.259	.325	.396	.721	93	-39	-50	102	101	634	84	55	60	-8
WEST																												
LA	144	78	66	.542		634	609	4942	1303	191	31	140	468	1023	.264	.331	.400	.731	106	-18	39	91	98	662	127	45	74	11
COL	144	77	67	.535	1	785	783	4994	1406	259	43	200	484	943	.282	.352	.471	.823	94	141	-85	129	96	815	125	59	68	2
SD	144	70	74	.486	8	668	672	4950	1345	231	20	116	447	872	.272	.336	.397	.733	102	-11	12	97	103	657	124	46	73	10
SF	144	67	77	.465	11	652	776	4971	1256	229	33	152	472	1060	.253	.325	.404	.729	100	-28	-8	97	101	663	138	45	75	14
TOT	1007					9329		69049	18184	3367	418	1917	6668	13309	.263	.334	.408	.741							1602	671	70	78

TEAM	CG	SH	SV	IP	H	H/G	HR	BB	SO	RAT	ERA	ERA+	OAV	OOB	PR	/A	PF	CPI	FA	E	DP	FW	PW	BW	SBW	DIF
EAST																										
ATL	18	11	34	1291²	1184	8.2	107	436	1087	11.5	3.44	124	.244	.311	106	118	102	99	.982	100	113	.6	11.6	-3.0	-.9	9.7
NY	9	9	36	1291	1296	9.0	133	401	901	12.1	3.88	104	.262	.322	44	24	97	101	.979	115	125	-.3	2.4	.6	-1.1	-4.6
PHI	8	8	41	1290¹	1241	8.7	134	538	980	12.8	4.21	100	.254	.335	-4	3	101	97	.982	97	139	.8	.3	-3.6	.1	-.6
FLA	12	7	29	1286	1299	9.1	139	562	994	13.3	4.27	99	.262	.345	-13	-8	101	103	.979	115	143	-.3	-.8	.7	.2	-4.3
MON	7	9	42	1283²	1286	9.0	128	416	950	12.3	4.11	104	.262	.327	10	26	103	97	.980	109	119	.1	2.6	-6.9	.1	-1.9
CENTRAL																										
CIN	8	10	38	1289¹	1270	8.9	131	424	903	12.0	4.03	102	.260	.323	21	12	99	97	.986	79	140	1.9	1.2	8.0	1.0	.9
HOU	6	8	32	1320¹	1357	9.2	118	460	1056	12.7	4.06	95	.266	.333	17	-29	93	100	.979	121	120	-.6	-2.9	9.3	1.1	-3.0
CHI	6	12	45	1301	1313	9.1	162	518	926	12.9	4.13	99	.262	.335	7	-4	98	105	.979	115	115	-.3	-.4	3.5	.3	-2.2
STL	4	6	38	1265²	1290	9.2	135	445	842	12.6	4.09	102	.268	.335	13	14	100	104	.980	113	156	-.2	1.4	-8.6	-.9	-1.2
PIT	11	7	29	1275¹	1407	9.9	130	477	871	13.7	4.70	92	.283	.353	-74	-56	103	101	.978	122	138	-.7	-5.5	-4.9	-1.3	-1.6
WEST																										
LA	16	11	37	1295	1188	8.3	125	462	1060	11.7	3.66	104	.243	.313	76	20	91	96	.976	130	120	-1.2	2.0	3.8	.5	.8
COL	1	1	43	1288¹	1443	10.1	160	512	891	13.9	4.97	106	.286	.357	-113	60	129	101	.981	107	146	.2	5.9	-8.4	-.4	7.6
SD	6	10	35	1284²	1242	8.7	142	512	1047	12.6	4.13	97	.255	.332	7	-15	96	99	.980	108	130	.2	-1.5	1.2	.4	-2.3
SF	12	5	34	1293²	1368	9.5	173	505	801	13.4	4.86	84	.275	.348	-98	-112	98	98	.980	108	142	.2	-11.0	-.8	.8	5.8
TOT	124	114	513	18056		9.1				12.7	4.18		.263	.334					.980	1539	1846					

Runs		Hits		Doubles		Triples		Home Runs		Total Bases	
Biggio-Hou	123	Gwynn-SD	197	Grace-Chi	51	Butler-NY-LA	9	Bichette-Col	40	Bichette-Col	359
Bonds-SF	109	Bichette-Col	197	McRae-Chi	38	Young-SD	9	Walker-Col	36	Walker-Col	300
Finley-SD	104	Grace-Chi	180	Bichette-Col	38	D.Sanders-Cin-SF	8	Sosa-Chi	36	Castilla-Col	297
Bichette-Col	102			R.Sanders-Cin	36	Gonzalez-Hou-Chi	8	Bonds-SF	33	Karros-LA	295
Larkin-Cin	98					Finley-SD	8			Bonds-SF	292

Runs Batted In		Runs Produced		Bases On Balls		Batting Average		On Base Percentage		Slugging Average	
Bichette-Col	128	Bichette-Col	190	Bonds-SF	120	Gwynn-SD	.368	Bonds-SF	.434	Bichette-Col	.620
Sosa-Chi	119	Bonds-SF	180	Weiss-Col	98	Piazza-LA	.346	Biggio-Hou	.411	Walker-Col	.607
Galarraga-Col	106	Biggio-Hou	178	Veras-Fla	80	Bichette-Col	.340	Gwynn-SD	.408	Piazza-LA	.606
Karros-LA	105	Grace-Chi	173	Biggio-Hou	80	Bell-Hou	.334	Weiss-Col	.404	R.Sanders-Cin	.579
Conine-Fla	105	Sosa-Chi	172	Bagwell-Hou	79	Grace-Chi	.326	Bagwell-Hou	.403	Bonds-SF	.577

Production		Adjusted Production		Batter Runs		Adjusted Batter Runs		Clutch Hitting Index		Runs Created	
Bonds-SF	1.011	Piazza-LA	177	Bonds-SF	51.4	Bonds-SF	55.4	Bell-Hou	138	Bonds-SF	134
Piazza-LA	1.007	Bonds-SF	169	Bichette-Col	42.1	Piazza-LA	45.7	Hayes-Phi	128	Bichette-Col	121
Walker-Col	.991	R.Sanders-Cin	155	Walker-Col	39.0	R.Sanders-Cin	39.2	King-Pit	121	Biggio-Hou	121
Bichette-Col	.989	Karros-LA	149	R.Sanders-Cin	38.6	Biggio-Hou	39.0	Bagwell-Hou	121	R.Sanders-Cin	115
R.Sanders-Cin	.980	Gant-Cin	146	Piazza-LA	37.0	Karros-LA	36.9	Conine-Fla	116	Grace-Chi	115

Total Average		Stolen Bases		Stolen Base Average		Stolen Base Runs		Fielding Runs		Total Player Rating	
Bonds-SF	1.156	Veras-Fla	56	Larkin-Cin	91.1	Larkin-Cin	12.3	Branson-Cin	21.5	Bonds-SF	6.7
R.Sanders-Cin	1.067	Larkin-Cin	51	Roberts-SD	90.9	Sosa-Chi	6.0	Reed-SD	18.0	Biggio-Hou	4.8
Walker-Col	1.047	DeShields-LA	39	Tarasco-Mon	88.9	Mondesi-LA	5.7	Bagwell-Hou	18.0	Piazza-LA	4.4
Piazza-LA	1.034	R.Sanders-Cin	36	Mondesi-LA	87.1	Lansing-Mon	5.7	Bonds-SF	15.0	R.Sanders-Cin	4.3
Larkin-Cin	1.014	Finley-SD	36	Lansing-Mon	87.1	Tarasco-Mon	5.4	C.Garcia-Pit	14.4	Caminiti-SD	3.8

Wins		Win Percentage		Games		Complete Games		Shutouts		Saves	
Maddux-Atl	19	Maddux-Atl	.905	Leskanic-Col	76	Maddux-Atl	10	Nomo-LA	3	Myers-Chi	38
Schourek-Cin	18	Schourek-Cin	.720	Veres-Hou	72	Leiter-SF	7	Maddux-Atl	3	Henke-StL	36
Martinez-LA	17	Martinez-LA	.708	Reed-Col	71	Valdes-LA	6			Beck-SF	33
Glavine-Atl	16	Glavine-Atl	.696	Perez-Fla	69	Neagle-Pit	5			Worrell-LA	32
										Slocumb-Phi	32

Innings Pitched		Fewest Hits/Game		Fewest BB/Game		Strikeouts		Strikeouts/Game		Ratio	
Neagle-Pit	209.2	Nomo-LA	5.83	Maddux-Atl	.99	Nomo-LA	236	Nomo-LA	11.10	Maddux-Atl	7.47
Maddux-Atl	209.2	Maddux-Atl	6.31	Reynolds-Hou	1.76	Smoltz-Atl	193	Smoltz-Atl	9.02	Nomo-LA	9.74
Martinez-LA	206.1	Martinez-Mon	7.30	Neagle-Pit	1.93	Maddux-Atl	181	Reynolds-Hou	8.32	Schourek-Cin	9.98
Hamilton-SD	204.1	Schourek-Cin	7.47	Saberhagen-NY-Col	1.94	Reynolds-Hou	175	Martinez-Mon	8.04	Valdes-LA	10.02
Navarro-Chi	200.1	Valdes-LA	7.65	Smiley-Cin	1.99	Martinez-Mon	174	Foster-Chi	7.84	Martinez-Mon	10.86

Earned Run Average		Adjusted ERA		Opponents' Batting Avg.		Opponents' On Base Pct.		Starter Runs		Adjusted Starter Runs	
Maddux-Atl	1.63	Maddux-Atl	261	Nomo-LA	.182	Maddux-Atl	.225	Maddux-Atl	59.4	Maddux-Atl	61.3
Nomo-LA	2.54	Nomo-LA	149	Maddux-Atl	.197	Nomo-LA	.271	Nomo-LA	34.9	Nomo-LA	26.6
Ashby-SD	2.94	Glavine-Atl	138	Martinez-Mon	.227	Valdes-LA	.279	Ashby-SD	26.5	Glavine-Atl	26.1
Valdes-LA	3.05	Ashby-SD	137	Valdes-LA	.228	Schourek-Cin	.283	Hamilton-SD	24.9	Smoltz-Atl	23.3
Glavine-Atl	3.08	Smoltz-Atl	134	Schourek-Cin	.228	Reynolds-Hou	.300	Valdes-LA	24.8	Ashby-SD	23.3

Clutch Pitching Index		Relief Runs		Adjusted Relief Runs		Relief Ranking		Total Pitcher Index		Total Baseball Ranking	
Ashby-SD	127	Veres-Hou	22.0	Reed-Col	30.3	Wohlers-Atl	32.4	Maddux-Atl	6.8	Maddux-Atl	6.8
Neagle-Pit	113	Reed-Col	19.0	Leskanic-Col	21.7	Reed-Col	24.6	Glavine-Atl	3.5	Bonds-SF	6.7
Rapp-Fla	111	Bottalico-Phi	16.7	Veres-Hou	18.4	Slocumb-Phi	23.0	Wohlers-Atl	3.2	Biggio-Hou	4.4
Swindell-Hou	111	Wohlers-Atl	15.0	Bottalico-Phi	17.2	Franco-NY	22.0	Ritz-Col	2.9	Piazza-LA	4.4
Castillo-Chi	110	Worrell-LA	15.0	Holmes-Col	15.9	Leskanic-Col	21.8	Reed-Col	2.6	R.Sanders-Cin	4.3

May 3 David Bell makes his major league debut at third base for the Indians in a 14-7 victory over the Tigers. His appearance makes the Bells—with his father Buddy and his grandfather Gus—the second three-generation family in major league history (the Boones are the other). Gus Bell dies four days later.

May 28 The White Sox and Tigers combine for a major league record 12 home runs at Tiger Stadium. The Tigers hit seven home runs, but still lose the 14-12 slugfest.

June 30 Eddie Murray collects his 3,000th career hit against Minnesota's Mike Trombley in a 4-1 Cleveland win at the Metrodome. The Indians slugger is the 20th player to reach the milestone and the third in franchise history.

August 30 Tigers teammates Lou Whitaker and Alan Trammell play in their 1,914th game together in a 10-7 loss to the White Sox.

September 6 Cal Ripken, Jr. breaks Lou Gehrig's record for consecutive games played before a home town crowd at Camden Yards. After the Angels are retired in the top of the fifth inning, the game becomes official, and fans go wild. Although Ripken comes out repeatedly to tip his cap to the crowd, fans persist with their cheering. Finally, teammates Rafael Palmeiro and Bobby Bonilla gently push him out of the dugout, and Ripken takes a lap around the park, shaking hands and giving high fives to fans, ball girls, ushers and every member of the Angels. The ovation lasts for more than 22 minutes. Ripken homers, and the Orioles ultimately win 4-2.

September 8 Cleveland ends a 41-year postseason drought by clinching the AL Central with a 3-2 win over the Orioles.

September 30 Indians outfielder Albert Belle hits his 50th home run of the season in a 5-2 win over Royals to become the first player ever to have 50 home runs and 50 doubles in the same season.

October 2 The Mariners defeat the Angels 9-1 in a one-game playoff for the AL West title. The win sends the Mariners to the postseason for the first time in their 19-year history.

October 6 The Indians sweep the Division Series with an 8-2 victory over the Red Sox at Fenway Park.

October 8 Edgar Martinez drives home the tying and winning runs with a double to left field to rally the Mariners to a 6-5 win in the bottom of the 11th inning to win the Division Series. Martinez bats .571 with 10 RBI against the Yankees in the five-game series. Ken Griffey Jr., who beat the relay throw home to score the winning run, has five home runs in the series.

October 17 The Indians win their third straight game to win the AL pennant for the first time in 41 years. Dennis Martinez allows just four hits in seven innings as the Indians are 4-0 winners over Seattle. Orel Hershiser, who won both his starts and had a 1.29 ERA in the ALCS, earns MVP honors.

October 24 Eddie Murray singles home pinch-runner Alvaro Espinoza in the bottom of the 11th inning to give the Indians their first win in a World Series in 47 years. The Tribe's 7-6 win fittingly occurs in the first-ever Series game at Jacobs Field.

	BALTIMORE		BOSTON		CALIFORNIA		CHICAGO		CLEVELAND		DETROIT		KANSAS CITY
M	P.Regan	M	K.Kennedy	M	M.Lachemann	M	G.Lamont	M	M.Hargrove	M	S.Anderson	M	B.Boone
1B	R.Palmeiro	1B	M.Vaughn	1B	J.Snow	M	T.Bevington	1B	P.Sorrento	1B	C.Fielder	1B	W.Joyner
2B	M.Alexander	2B	L.Alicea	2B	D.Easley	1B	D.Martinez	2B	C.Baerga	2B	L.Whitaker	2B	K.Lockhart
SS	C.Ripken	SS	J.Valentin	SS	G.DiSarcina	2B	R.Durham	SS	O.Vizquel	SS	C.Gomez	SS	G.Gagne
3B	J.Manto	3B	T.Naehring	3B	T.Phillips	SS	O.Guillen	3B	J.Thome	3B	T.Fryman	3B	G.Gaetti
LF	B.Anderson	LF	M.Greenwell	LF	G.Anderson	3B	R.Ventura	LF	A.Belle	LF	B.Higginson	LF	V.Coleman
CF	C.Goodwin	CF	L.Tinsley	CF	J.Edmonds	LF	T.Raines	CF	K.Lofton	CF	C.Curtis	CF	T.Goodwin
RF	K.Bass	RF	T.O'Leary	RF	T.Salmon	CF	L.Johnson	RF	M.Ramirez	RF	D.Bautista	RF	J.Nunnally
C	C.Hoiles	C	M.Macfarlane	C	J.Fabregas	RF	M.Devereaux	C	T.Pena	C	J.Flaherty	C	B.Mayne
DH	H.Baines	DH	J.Canseco	DH	C.Davis	C	R.Karkovice	DH	E.Murray	DH	K.Gibson	DH	B.Hamelin
						DH	F.Thomas						
2	B.Barberie	O	W.McGee	CD	G.Myers			O	W.Kirby	S	A.Trammell	2S	D.Howard
O3	B.Bonilla	2O	R.Hudler			P	A.Fernandez	C	S.Alomar				
		P	T.Wakefield	3S	S.Owen	P	W.Alvarez			P	F.Lira	P	M.Gubicza
P	M.Mussina	P	E.Hanson			P	J.Bere	P	D.Martinez	P	S.Bergman	P	K.Appier
P	K.Brown	P	R.Clemens	P	C.Finley	P	J.Abbott	P	C.Nagy	P	M.Moore	P	T.Gordon
P	J.Moyer	P	Z.Smith	P	M.Langston	P	B.Keyser	P	O.Hershiser	P	D.Wells	RP	J.Montgomery
P	S.Erickson	RP	R.Cormier	P	S.Boskie	RP	K.McCaskill	P	M.Clark	RP	J.Doherty	RP	H.Pichardo
RP	M.Oquist	RP	M.Maddux	P	B.Anderson	P	J.DeLeon	P	C.Ogea	RP	B.Bohanon	RP	R.Meacham
RP	J.Orosco	RP	S.Belinda	RP	T.Percival	RP	R.Hernandez	RP	J.Tavarez	RP	J.Boever		
RP	A.Benitez			RP	M.James			RP	E.Plunk			P	J.Jacome
		P	V.Eshelman	RP	B.Patterson			RP	J.Mesa	P	J.Lima	P	C.Haney
P	B.McDonald									P	M.Christopher		
P	R.Krivda			J.Abbott		P	K.Hill	P	B.Maxcy		
P	A.Rhodes			P	M.Bielecki		P	J.Poole				
				P	M.Harkey								
				P	R.Springer								
				P	M.Butcher								

	MILWAUKEE		MINNESOTA		NEW YORK		OAKLAND		SEATTLE		TEXAS		TORONTO
M	P.Garner	M	T.Kelly	M	B.Showalter	M	T.LaRussa	M	L.Piniella	M	J.Oates	M	C.Gaston
1B	J.Jaha	1B	S.Stahoviak	1B	D.Mattingly	1B	M.McGwire	1B	T.Martinez	1B	W.Clark	1B	J.Olerud
2B	F.Vina	2B	C.Knoblauch	2B	P.Kelly	2B	B.Gates	2B	J.Cora	2B	J.Frye	2B	R.Alomar
SS	J.Valentin	SS	P.Meares	SS	T.Fernandez	SS	M.Bordick	SS	L.Sojo	SS	B.Gil	SS	A.Gonzalez
3B	J.Cirillo	3B	S.Leius	3B	W.Boggs	3B	C.Paquette	3B	M.Blowers	3B	M.Pagliarulo	3B	E.Sprague
LF	D.Hulse	LF	M.Cordova	LF	G.Williams	LF	R.Henderson	LF	R.Amaral	LF	M.McLemore	LF	J.Carter
CF	D.Hamilton	CF	R.Becker	CF	B.Williams	CF	S.Javier	CF	A.Diaz	CF	O.Nixon	CF	D.White
RF	M.Mieske	RF	K.Puckett	RF	P.O'Neill	RF	R.Sierra	RF	J.Buhner	RF	R.Greer	RF	S.Green
C	J.Oliver	C	M.Walbeck	C	M.Stanley	C	T.Steinbach	C	D.Wilson	C	I.Rodriguez	C	L.Parrish
DH	G.Vaughn	DH	P.Munoz	DH	R.Sierra	DH	G.Berroa	DH	E.Martinez	DH	J.Gonzalez	DH	P.Molitor
2S	P.Listach	S3	J.Reboulet	2S	R.Velarde	3O	S.Brosius	O	K.Griffey	OD	M.Tettleton	P	P.Hentgen
31	K.Seitzer			C1	J.Leyritz			S2	F.Fermin			P	A.Leiter
O1	B.Surhoff	P	B.Radke	O	L.Polonia	P	T.Stottlemyre			P	K.Rogers	P	J.Guzman
OD	D.Nilsson	P	K.Tapani	OD	D.James	P	T.Van Poppel	P	R.Johnson	P	R.Pavlik	P	D.Cone
		P	M.Trombley			P	S.Ontiveros	P	T.Belcher	P	K.Gross	RP	T.Castillo
P	S.Sparks	P	F.Rodriguez	J.McDowell	P	R.Darling	P	C.Bosio	P	B.Tewksbury	RP	W.Williams
P	R.Bones	P	S.Erickson	A.Pettitte	RP	C.Reyes	RP	J.Nelson	RP	R.McDowell	RP	D.Cox
P	S.Karl	RP	P.Mahomes	RP	S.Hitchcock	RP	M.Acre	RP	B.Wells	RP	M.Whiteside		
P	B.Givens	RP	E.Guardado	P	D.Cone	RP	D.Eckersley	RP	B.Ayala	RP	D.Oliver	P	P.Menhart
RP	A.Miranda	RP	D.Stevens	S.Kamieniecki							E.Hurtado
RP	B.Wegman			RP	B.Wickman	P	D.Stewart	P	S.Torres	P	B.Witt	P	D.Darwin
RP	M.Kiefer	P	J.Parra	P	J.Wetteland	P	M.Harkey	P	A.Benes				
		P	R.Robertson	RP	S.Howe	P	A.Prieto	P	B.Risley				
P	S.Roberson					P	D.Johns						
P	B.Scanlan			M.Perez								
				M.Rivera								

TEAM	G	W	L	PCT	GB	R	OR	AB	H	2B	3B	HR	BB	SO	AVG	OBP	SLG	PRO	PRO+	BR	/A	PF	CHI	RC	SB	CS	SBA	SBR
EAST																												
BOS	144	86	58	.597		791	698	4997	1399	286	31	175	560	923	.280	.360	.455	.815	106	76	49	103	97	818	99	44	69	3
NY	145	79	65	.549	7	749	688	4947	1365	280	34	122	625	851	.276	.362	.420	.782	104	28	36	99	98	755	50	30	63	-3
BAL	144	71	73	.493	15	704	640	4837	1267	229	27	173	574	803	.262	.345	.428	.773	99	-3	-14	102	99	716	92	45	67	1
DET	144	60	84	.417	26	654	844	4865	1204	228	29	159	551	987	.247	.329	.404	.733	90	-78	-74	99	102	649	73	36	67	0
TOR	144	56	88	.389	30	642	777	5036	1309	275	27	140	492	906	.260	.331	.409	.740	92	-69	-64	99	97	687	75	16	82	13
CENTRAL																												
CLE	144	100	44	.694		840	607	5028	1461	279	23	207	542	766	.291	.364	.479	.843	115	122	110	101	98	868	132	53	71	8
KC	144	70	74	.486	30	629	691	4903	1275	240	35	119	475	849	.260	.331	.396	.727	87	-88	-96	101	100	647	120	53	69	4
CHI	145	68	76	.472	32	755	758	5060	1417	252	37	146	576	767	.280	.357	.431	.788	109	33	69	95	97	793	110	39	74	10
MIL	144	65	79	.451	35	740	747	5000	1329	249	42	128	502	840	.266	.338	.409	.747	88	-50	-88	106	109	702	105	40	72	8
MIN	144	56	88	.389	44	703	889	5005	1398	270	34	120	471	916	.279	.348	.419	.767	98	-11	-12	100	99	710	105	57	65	-3
WEST																												
SEA	145	79	66	.545		796	708	4996	1377	276	20	182	549	871	.276	.352	.448	.800	105	45	38	101	102	794	110	41	73	8
CAL	145	78	67	.538	1	801	697	5019	1390	252	25	186	564	889	.277	.354	.448	.802	108	51	59	99	102	795	58	39	60	-6
TEX	144	74	70	.514	4.5	691	720	4913	1304	247	24	138	526	877	.265	.340	.410	.750	92	-43	-59	102	102	688	90	47	66	-1
OAK	144	67	77	.465	11.5	730	761	4916	1296	228	18	169	565	911	.264	.345	.420	.765	104	-15	24	95	102	725	112	46	71	6
TOT	1010					10225		69522	18791	3591	406	2164	7572	12116	.270	.347	.427	.774		1331	586				69	48		

TEAM	CG	SH	SV	IP	H	H/G	HR	BB	SO	RAT	ERA	ERA+	OAV	OOB	PR	/A	PF	CPI	FA	E	DP	FW	PW	BW	SBW	DIF
EAST																										
BOS	7	9	39	1292²	1338	9.3	127	476	888	12.9	4.39	111	.268	.337	46	68	103	98	.978	120	151	-1.2	6.4	4.6	-.0	4.3
NY	18	5	35	1284²	1286	9.0	159	535	908	13.0	4.56	101	.261	.337	22	8	98	97	.986	74	121	1.4	.8	3.4	-.6	2.1
BAL	19	10	29	1267	1165	8.3	149	523	930	12.3	4.31	110	.245	.325	56	62	101	93	.986	72	141	1.4	5.8	-1.3	-.2	-6.7
DET	5	3	38	1275	1509	10.7	170	536	729	14.8	5.49	87	.296	.368	-110	-104	101	100	.981	106	143	-.4	-9.8	-6.9	-.3	5.5
TOR	16	8	22	1292²	1336	9.3	145	654	894	14.2	4.88	96	.267	.358	-24	-25	100	99	.982	97	131	.0	-2.3	-6.0	.9	-8.6
CENTRAL																										
CLE	10	10	50	1301	1261	8.7	135	445	926	12.1	3.83	122	.255	.322	127	125	100	103	.982	101	142	-.2	11.7	10.3	.4	5.7
KC	11	10	37	1284²	1323	9.2	142	503	763	13.0	4.49	107	.268	.340	32	43	102	100	.984	90	168	.4	4.0	-9.0	.0	2.5
CHI	12	4	36	1284²	1374	9.6	164	617	892	14.2	4.85	92	.275	.359	-20	-57	95	104	.980	108	131	-.5	-5.3	6.5	.6	-5.2
MIL	7	4	31	1286	1391	9.7	146	603	699	14.3	4.82	103	.280	.364	-16	23	106	106	.981	105	186	-.4	2.2	-8.3	.4	-.9
MIN	7	2	27	1272²	1450	10.3	210	533	790	14.3	5.76	38	.287	.359	-149	-141	100	95	.981	100	141	-.1	-13.2	-1.1	-.6	-.9
WEST																										
SEA	9	8	39	1289¹	1343	9.4	149	591	1068	13.8	4.50	105	.265	.350	31	35	101	105	.980	104	108	-.3	3.3	3.6	.4	-.5
CAL	8	9	42	1284¹	1310	9.2	163	486	901	12.9	4.52	104	.265	.336	28	25	100	99	.982	95	120	.2	2.3	5.5	-.9	-1.7
TEX	14	4	34	1285	1385	9.7	152	514	838	13.6	4.66	104	.278	.349	8	24	102	102	.982	98	156	.0	2.3	-5.5	-.4	5.7
OAK	8	4	34	1273	1320	9.3	153	556	890	13.6	4.93	91	.269	.350	-31	-66	95	96	.981	102	151	-.2	-6.2	2.3	.2	-1.1
TOT	151	90	493	17976		9.4				13.5	4.71		.270	.347					.982	1372	1990					

Runs		Hits		Doubles		Triples		Home Runs		Total Bases	
E.Martinez-Sea	121	Johnson-Chi	186	E.Martinez-Sea	52	Lofton-Cle	13	Belle-Cle	50	Belle-Cle	377
Belle-Cle	121	E.Martinez-Sea	182	Belle-Cle	52	Johnson-Chi	12	F.Thomas-Chi	40	Palmeiro-Bal	323
Edmonds-Cal	120	Knoblauch-Min	179	Puckett-Min	39	Anderson-Bal	10	Buhner-Sea	40	E.Martinez-Sea	321
Phillips-Cal	119	Salmon-Cal	177	Valentin-Bos	37	B.Williams-NY	9			Salmon-Cal	319
Salmon-Cal	111	Baerga-Cle	175	T.Martinez-Sea	35	Knoblauch-Min	8			Vaughn-Bos	316

Runs Batted In		Runs Produced		Bases On Balls		Batting Average		On Base Percentage		Slugging Average	
Vaughn-Bos	126	E.Martinez-Sea	205	F.Thomas-Chi	136	E.Martinez-Sea	.356	E.Martinez-Sea	.482	Belle-Cle	.690
Belle-Cle	126	Belle-Cle	197	E.Martinez-Sea	116	Knoblauch-Min	.333	F.Thomas-Chi	.463	E.Martinez-Sea	.628
Buhner-Sea	121	Edmonds-Cal	194	Phillips-Cal	113	Salmon-Cal	.330	Thome-Cle	.440	F.Thomas-Chi	.606
E.Martinez-Sea	113	Vaughn-Bos	185	Tettleton-Tex	107	Boggs-NY	.324	Davis-Cal	.437	Salmon-Cal	.594
		Valentin-Bos	183	Thome-Cle	97	Murray-Cle	.323	Salmon-Cal	.432	Palmeiro-Bal	.583

Production		Adjusted Production		Batter Runs		Adjusted Batter Runs		Clutch Hitting Index		Runs Created	
E.Martinez-Sea	1.110	E.Martinez-Sea	184	E.Martinez-Sea	71.5	E.Martinez-Sea	70.1	Blowers-Sea	127	E.Martinez-Sea	161
Belle-Cle	1.094	F.Thomas-Chi	184	F.Thomas-Chi	61.9	F.Thomas-Chi	68.8	Stanley-NY	121	F.Thomas-Chi	144
F.Thomas-Chi	1.069	Belle-Cle	175	Belle-Cle	60.6	Belle-Cle	58.7	Clark-Tex	120	Belle-Cle	144
Salmon-Cal	1.026	Salmon-Cal	165	Salmon-Cal	52.7	Salmon-Cal	54.0	Joyner-KC	118	Salmon-Cal	142
Thome-Cle	.998	Thome-Cle	155	McGwire-Oak	45.0	McGwire-Oak	50.7	Snow-Cal	113	Palmeiro-Bal	123

Total Average		Stolen Bases		Stolen Base Average		Stolen Base Runs		Fielding Runs		Total Player Rating	
E.Martinez-Sea	1.300	Lofton-Cle	54	Amaral-Sea	91.3	Johnson-Chi	8.4	Fryman-Det	26.6	Salmon-Cal	5.9
F.Thomas-Chi	1.238	Nixon-Tex	50	Alomar-Tor	90.9	Javier-Oak	7.8	Valentin-Mil	19.7	Belle-Cle	5.8
Belle-Cle	1.150	Goodwin-KC	50	Javier-Oak	87.8	Lofton-Cle	7.2	Edmonds-Cal	19.4	E.Martinez-Sea	5.3
Salmon-Cal	1.112	Knoblauch-Min	46	Johnson-Chi	87.0	Alomar-Tor	7.2	Cordova-Min	18.7	Valentin-Bos	4.7
Thome-Cle	1.106	Coleman-KC-Sea	42	Goodwin-Bal	84.6	Amaral-Sea	5.1	Gil-Tex	16.2	F.Thomas-Chi	4.0

Wins		Win Percentage		Games		Complete Games		Shutouts		Saves	
Mussina-Bal	19	Johnson-Sea	.900	Orosco-Bal	65	McDowell-NY	8	Mussina-Bal	4	Mesa-Cle	46
Cone-Tor-NY	18	Hanson-Bos	.750	McDowell-Tex	64	Erickson-Min-Bal	7	Johnson-Sea	3	Smith-Cal	37
Johnson-Sea	18	Nagy-Cle	.727	Wickman-NY	63	Mussina-Bal	7			Aguilera-Min-Bos	32
Rogers-Tex	17	Hershiser-Cle	.727	Belinda-Bos	63					Hernandez-Chi	32
		Rogers-Tex	.708	Ayala-Sea	63						

Innings Pitched		Fewest Hits/Game		Fewest BB/Game		Strikeouts		Strikeouts/Game		Ratio	
Cone-Tor-NY	229.1	Johnson-Sea	6.68	Mussina-Bal	2.03	Johnson-Sea	294	Johnson-Sea	12.35	Johnson-Sea	9.66
Mussina-Bal	221.2	Appier-KC	7.29	Martinez-Cle	2.21	Stottlemyre-Oak	205	Stottlemyre-Oak	8.80	Mussina-Bal	9.66
McDowell-NY	217.2	Wakefield-Bos	7.51	Radke-Min	2.34	Finley-Cal	195	Finley-Cal	8.65	Wakefield-Bos	11.06
Johnson-Sea	214.1	Mussina-Bal	7.59	K.Brown-Bal	2.51	Cone-Tor-NY	191	Appier-KC	8.27	K.Brown-Bal	11.07
Gubicza-KC	213.1	Cone-Tor-NY	7.65	Gubicza-KC	2.62	Appier-KC	185	Leiter-Tor	7.52	Hershiser-Cle	11.13

Earned Run Average		Adjusted ERA		Opponents' Batting Avg.		Opponents' On Base Pct.		Starter Runs		Adjusted Starter Runs	
Johnson-Sea	2.48	Johnson-Sea	191	Johnson-Sea	.201	Johnson-Sea	.267	Johnson-Sea	53.2	Johnson-Sea	53.8
Wakefield-Bos	2.95	Wakefield-Bos	165	Appier-KC	.221	Mussina-Bal	.271	Wakefield-Bos	38.3	Wakefield-Bos	41.7
Martinez-Cle	3.08	Martinez-Cle	152	Mussina-Bal	.226	Wakefield-Bos	.302	Mussina-Bal	35.1	Mussina-Bal	36.0
Mussina-Bal	3.29	Mussina-Bal	144	Wakefield-Bos	.227	K.Brown-Bal	.303	Martinez-Cle	33.9	Rogers-Tex	33.5
Rogers-Tex	3.38	Rogers-Tex	143	Cone-Tor-NY	.228	Appier-KC	.304	Rogers-Tex	30.9	Martinez-Cle	33.5

Clutch Pitching Index		Relief Runs		Adjusted Relief Runs		Relief Ranking		Total Pitcher Index		Total Baseball Ranking	
Bosio-Sea	117	Mesa-Cle	25.5	Mesa-Cle	25.4	Mesa-Cle	44.3	Johnson-Sea	4.6	Salmon-Cal	5.9
Wakefield-Bos	115	Percival-Cal	22.7	Percival-Cal	22.6	Aguilera-Min-Bos	27.9	Wakefield-Bos	4.5	Belle-Cle	5.8
Gubicza-KC	113	Nelson-Sea	22.5	Nelson-Sea	22.4	Tavarez-Cle	27.1	Mesa-Cle	4.3	E.Martinez-Sea	5.3
Martinez-Cle	113	Tavarez-Cle	21.5	Tavarez-Cle	21.3	Nelson-Sea	26.7	Mussina-Bal	3.9	Valentin-Bos	4.7
Rogers-Tex	112	Plunk-Cle	14.5	Plunk-Cle	14.4	Wetteland-NY	20.7	Rogers-Tex	3.6	Johnson-Sea	4.6

March 5 Earl Weaver and Jim Bunning are elected into the Hall of Fame by the Veterans Committee. Also chosen are turn-of-the-century manager Ned Hanlon and Negro League pitcher Bill Foster.

April 27 Barry Bonds homers twice to reach the 300-home run mark. Bonds joins his father Bobby, godfather Willie Mays, and Andre Dawson as the only players with 300 homers and 300 steals.

July 29 Tom Lasorda calls it quits after 20 seasons as Dodger manager following a heart attack and an angioplasty in June.

August 16 The Padres and Mets play the first regular season ML game ever played in Mexico. The Padres take a big lead, but the Mets close the gap with seven runs in the ninth inning in a 15-10 Padres triumph. The series is moved from San Diego because of a perceived conflict with the G.O.P. National Convention.

September 14 Todd Hundley's opposite-field home run ties the game between the Mets and Braves and breaks Roy Campanella's record for homers by a catcher with 41.

September 17 Hideo Nomo pitches a no-hitter at hitter-friendly Coors Field against the NL's best hitting team. The Dodger righthander walks four Rockies and fans eight in his 110-pitch 9-0 win.

October 5 Chipper Jones starts an Atlanta rally in the first inning and caps another rally with a home run in the fourth. The Braves make it stand up in a 5-2 win over the Dodgers for a sweep of the Division Series.

October 17 With the NLCS tied at three games each, the Braves explode in the first and keep on exploding. Tom Glavine pitches seven shutout innings and adds a three-run triple as Atlanta cruises to the pennant with a 15-0 rout.

October 20 The Braves make a strong case for back-to-back world championships. John Smoltz pitches 5⅔ hitless innings and rookie Andruw Jones becomes the youngest player to homer in World Series history—in fact he does it twice—as the Braves blast the Yankees 12-1 in the opener.

November 6 Todd Hollandsworth continues a Dodger tradition. The outfielder is the fifth consecutive Dodger to win the NL Rookie of the Year prize.

November 11 John Smoltz, who won a ML-high 24 games for the Braves, wins the NL Cy Young Award in a runaway. Smoltz, the NL leader in strikeouts (276), innings (253⅔), and winning percentage (.750), receives 26 of 28 first-place votes. Kevin Brown of the Marlins, NL ERA leader (1.89), receives the other two first-place votes.

November 13 Padres third baseman Ken Caminiti is the fourth unanimous winner of the NL MVP. The slick-fielding Caminiti set team records for home runs (40), RBI (130), and slugging (.621), while leading the Padres to the NL West title for the first time in 12 years.

	ATLANTA		CHICAGO		CINCINNATI		COLORADO		FLORIDA		HOUSTON		LOS ANGELES
M	B.Cox	M	J.Riggleman	M	R.Knight	M	D.Baylor	M	R.Lachemann	M	T.Collins	M	T.Lasorda
1B	F.McGriff	1B	M.Grace	1B	H.Morris	1B	A.Galarraga	M	C.Rojas	1B	J.Bagwell	M	B.Russell
2B	M.Lemke	2B	R.Sandberg	2B	B.Boone	2B	E.Young	M	J.Boles	2B	C.Biggio	1B	E.Karros
SS	J.Blauser	SS	R.Sanchez	SS	B.Larkin	SS	W.Weiss	1B	G.Colbrunn	SS	O.Miller	2B	D.DeShields
3B	C.Jones	3B	W.Greene	3B	W.Greene	3B	V.Castilla	2B	Q.Veras	3B	S.Berry	SS	G.Gagne
LF	R.Klesko	LF	L.Gonzalez	LF	T.Howard	LF	E.Burks	SS	E.Renteria	LF	J.Mouton	3B	M.Blowers
CF	M.Grissom	CF	B.McRae	CF	E.Davis	CF	Q.McCracken	3B	T.Pendleton	CF	B.Hunter	LF	T.Hollandsworth
RF	J.Dye	RF	S.Sosa	RF	R.Sanders	RF	D.Bichette	LF	J.Conine	RF	D.Bell	CF	R.Cedeno
C	J.Lopez	C	S.Servais	C	J.Oliver	C	J.Reed	CF	D.White	C	R.Wilkins	RF	R.Mondesi
								RF	G.Sheffield			C	M.Piazza
O	D.Smith	O	S.Bullett	3S	J.Branson	O1	J.Vander Wal	C	C.Johnson	O	J.Cangelosi		
		S3	J.Hernandez	O3	L.Harris	O	L.Walker			O	D.May	O2	C.Fonville
P	J.Smoltz			C	E.Taubensee			S3	K.Abbott	3	B.Spiers	P	H.Nomo
P	G.Maddux	O	E.Owens			P	K.Ritz	3S	A.Arias	S	R.Gutierrez	P	I.Valdes
P	T.Glavine	P	J.Navarro			P	Ma.Thompson	O	J.Orsulak			P	P.Astacio
P	S.Avery	P	S.Trachsel	P	J.Smiley	P	A.Reynoso	O	J.Tavarez	P	S.Reynolds	P	R.Martinez
RP	G.McMichael	P	F.Castillo	P	D.Burba	RP	M.Freeman			P	D.Kile	P	T.Candiotti
RP	B.Clontz	P	J.Bullinger	P	M.Portugal	RP	D.Holmes	P	K.Brown	P	D.Drabek	RP	C.Park
RP	M.Wohlers	P	A.Telemaco	RP	K.Jarvis	RP	S.Reed	P	A.Leiter	P	M.Hampton	RP	A.Osuna
		RP	T.Adams	P	R.Salkeld	P	C.Leskanic	P	P.Rapp	P	D.Wall	RP	M.Guthrie
P	M.Bielecki	RP	T.Wendell	RP	J.Shaw			P	J.Burkett	RP	X.Hernandez		
P	T.Wade	RP	R.Myers	RP	H.Carrasco	P	J.Wright	RP	R.Nen	RP	T.Jones	P	T.Worrell
P	J.Schmidt			RP	J.Brantley	P	R.Bailey	RP	C.Hammond	RP	D.Brocail	P	S.Radinsky
		P	K.Foster			P	B.Ruffin	RP	D.Weathers				
		P	K.Bottenfield			P	B.Rekar			P	B.Wagner		
		P	B.Patterson			P	P.Schourek	P	J.Powell				
						P	J.Ruffin	P	M.Hutton				
						P	L.Painter	P	T.Mathews				

	MONTREAL		NEW YORK		PHILADELPHIA		PITTSBURGH		SAN DIEGO		SAN FRANCISCO		ST.LOUIS
M	F.Alou	M	D.Green	M	J.Fregosi	M	J.Leyland	M	B.Bochy	M	D.Baker	M	T.LaRussa
1B	D.Segui	M	B.Valentine	1B	G.Jefferies	1B	M.Johnson	1B	W.Joyner	1B	M.Carreon	1B	J.Mabry
2B	M.Lansing	1B	B.Huskey	2B	M.Morandini	2B	C.Garcia	2B	J.Reed	2B	S.Scarsone	2B	L.Alicea
SS	M.Grudzielanek	2B	J.Vizcaino	SS	K.Stocker	SS	J.Bell	SS	C.Gomez	SS	R.Aurilia	SS	R.Clayton
3B	S.Andrews	SS	R.Ordonez	3B	T.Zeile	3B	C.Hayes	3B	K.Caminiti	3B	M.Williams	3B	G.Gaetti
LF	H.Rodriguez	3B	J.Kent	LF	P.Incaviglia	LF	A.Martin	LF	R.Henderson	LF	B.Bonds	LF	R.Gant
CF	F.Santangelo	LF	B.Gilkey	CF	F.Otero	CF	M.Kingery	CF	S.Finley	CF	M.Benard	CF	R.Lankford
RF	M.Alou	CF	L.Johnson	RF	J.Eisenreich	RF	O.Merced	RF	T.Gwynn	RF	G.Hill	RF	B.Jordan
C	D.Fletcher	RF	A.Ochoa	C	B.Santiago	C	J.Kendall	C	J.Flaherty	C	T.Lampkin	C	T.Pagnozzi
		C	T.Hundley										
O	C.Floyd			P	C.Schilling	12	J.King	13	S.Livingstone	S	S.Dunston	O	W.McGee
O	R.White	23	E.Alfonzo	P	M.Williams	2	N.Liriano	C	B.Johnson	O	S.Javier	O1	M.Sweeney
		O	C.Everett	P	T.Mulholland	O	J.Allensworth			2	R.Thompson	S	O.Smith
P	J.Fassero			P	M.Mimbs	O	D.Clark	P	J.Hamilton	3	B.Mueller		
P	P.Martinez	P	M.Clark	RP	R.Springer			P	B.Tewksbury			P	An.Benes
P	R.Cormier	P	B.Jones	RP	T.Borland	P	D.Neagle	P	F.Valenzuela	P	A.Watson	P	T.Stottlemyre
P	U.Urbina	P	P.Harnisch	RP	K.Ryan	P	D.Darwin	P	A.Ashby	P	Van Landingham	P	D.Osborne
RP	O.Daal	P	J.Isringhausen			RP	J.Lieber	P	S.Sanders	P	M.Gardner	P	Al.Benes
RP	B.Manuel	P	P.Wilson	P	M.Grace	RP	F.Cordova	RP	T.Worrell	P	O.Fernandez	P	M.Morgan
RP	M.Rojas	RP	D.Mlicki	P	R.Hunter	RP	D.Miceli	RP	S.Bergman	P	M.Leiter	RP	M.Petkovsek
		RP	J.DiPoto	P	R.Bottalico			RP	T.Hoffman	RP	M.Dewey	RP	T.Mathews
P	K.Rueter	RP	D.Henry	P	S.Fernandez	P	Z.Smith			RP	J.Bautista	RP	D.Eckersley
P	D.Veres					P	P.Wagner	W.Blair		RP	R.DeLucia		
P	M.Dyer	P	R.Person			P	M.Wilkins	D.Bochtler				P	C.Bailey
P	M.Leiter	P	J.Franco			P	D.Plesac			P	S.Estes		
P	J.Paniagua					P	C.Peters			P	R.Beck		
						P	M.Ruebel						
						P	E.Loaiza						

TEAM	G	W	L	PCT	GB	R	OR	AB	H	2B	3B	HR	BB	SO	AVG	OBP	SLG	PRO	PRO+	BR	/A	PF	CHI	RC	SB	CS	SBA	SBR
EAST																												
ATL	162	96	66	.593		773	648	5614	1514	264	28	197	530	1032	.270	.336	.432	.768	101	49	4	106	95	798	83	43	66	-1
MON	162	88	74	.543	8	741	668	5505	1441	297	27	148	492	1077	.262	.329	.406	.735	96	-14	-32	103	101	739	108	34	**76**	12
FLA	162	80	82	.494	16	688	703	5498	1413	240	30	150	445	1122	.257	.327	.412	.739	106	-29	0	96	95	713	99	46	68	2
NY	162	71	91	.438	25	746	779	5618	1515	267	**47**	147	445	1069	.270	.327	.412	.739	106	-10	41	93	100	748	97	48	67	0
PHI	162	67	95	.414	29	650	790	5499	1405	249	39	132	536	1092	.256	.327	.387	.714	91	-52	-70	103	93	704	117	41	74	11
CENTRAL																												
STL	162	88	74	.543		759	706	5502	1468	281	31	142	495	1089	.267	.332	.407	.739	100	-5	-7	100	102	743	149	58	72	10
HOU	162	82	80	.506	6	753	792	5508	1445	297	29	129	554	1057	.262	.339	.397	.736	109	-1	68	91	99	758	180	63	74	16
CIN	162	81	81	.500	7	778	773	5455	1398	259	36	191	604	1134	.256	.334	.422	.756	105	29	35	99	99	780	171	63	73	14
CHI	162	76	86	.469	12	772	771	5531	1388	267	19	175	523	1090	.251	.322	.401	.723	94	-39	-48	101	**108**	713	108	50	68	2
PIT	162	73	89	.451	15	776	833	5665	1509	**319**	33	138	510	989	.266	.331	.407	.738	96	-6	-29	103	102	771	126	49	72	8
WEST																												
SD	162	91	71	.562		771	682	5655	1499	285	24	147	601	1015	.265	.341	.402	.743	106	13	53	95	97	772	109	55	66	0
LA	162	90	72	.556	1	703	652	5538	1396	215	33	150	516	1190	.252	.318	.384	.702	98	-80	-25	92	105	684	124	40	**76**	13
COL	162	83	79	.512	8	**961**	964	5590	**1607**	297	37	**221**	527	1108	**.287**	**.357**	**.472**	**.829**	96	**178**	-82	129	102	**951**	**201**	66	75	**21**
SF	162	68	94	.420	23	752	862	5533	1400	245	21	153	**615**	1189	.253	.333	.388	.721	99	-32	-1	96	102	730	113	53	68	2
TOT	1134					10623		77711	20398	3782	434	2220	7501	15253	.262	.333	.408	.741							1785	709	72	110

TEAM	CG	SH	SV	IP	H	H/G	HR	BB	SO	RAT	ERA	ERA+	OAV	OOB	PR	/A	PF	CPI	FA	E	DP	FW	PW	BW	SBW	DIF
EAST																									
ATL	**14**	9	46	1469	1372	**8.4**	120	**451**	**1245**	**11.3**	3.52	125	**.247**	**.306**	113	**143**	104	96	.980	130	143	-.1	**14.0**	.4	-.9	1.7
MON	11	7	43	1441¹	**1353**	**8.4**	152	482	1206	11.8	3.78	114	**.247**	.315	70	85	102	98	.980	126	121	.0	8.3	-3.1	.4	1.3
FLA	8	**13**	41	1443	1386	8.6	**113**	598	1050	12.7	3.95	102	.256	.336	42	15	96	100	.982	111	**187**	1.0	1.5	.0	-.6	-2.9
NY	10	10	41	1440	1517	9.5	159	532	999	13.1	4.22	93	.272	.340	-1	-47	93	105	.974	159	163	-1.9	-4.6	4.0	-.8	-6.7
PHI	12	6	42	1423¹	1463	9.3	160	510	1044	12.7	4.48	97	.267	.333	-42	-18	104	96	.981	116	145	.7	-1.8	-6.8	.3	-6.4
CENTRAL																									
STL	13	11	43	1452¹	1380	8.6	173	539	1050	12.7	3.97	107	.251	.322	39	42	101	100	.980	125	139	.2	4.1	-.7	.2	3.2
HOU	13	4	35	1447	1541	9.6	154	539	1163	13.4	4.37	88	.274	.345	-24	-87	91	104	.978	138	130	-.6	-8.5	**6.6**	.8	2.7
CIN	6	8	**52**	1443	1447	9.0	167	591	1089	13.0	4.32	96	.263	.339	-16	-26	99	101	.980	121	145	.4	-2.5	3.4	.6	-1.9
CHI	10	10	34	1456¹	1447	8.9	184	546	1027	12.7	4.36	98	.260	.332	-23	-16	101	99	**.983**	104	147	1.4	-1.6	-4.7	-.6	.4
PIT	5	7	37	1453¹	1602	9.9	183	479	1044	13.2	4.61	95	.281	.342	-63	-37	104	102	.980	128	144	-.0	-3.6	-2.8	.0	-1.5
WEST																									
SD	5	11	47	1489	1395	**8.4**	138	506	1194	11.8	3.72	107	.248	.315	81	44	95	97	.981	118	136	.6	4.3	5.2	-.8	.7
LA	6	9	50	1466¹	1378	8.5	125	534	1213	12.0	**3.46**	111	.250	.320	**123**	63	91	106	.980	125	143	.2	6.2	-2.4	.5	4.6
COL	5	4	34	1422²	1597	10.1	198	624	932	14.5	5.59	97	.285	.364	-218	-25	129	95	.976	149	167	-1.3	-2.4	-8.0	**1.3**	12.5
SF	9	8	35	1442¹	1520	9.5	194	570	997	13.5	4.71	87	.273	.348	-80	-100	97	102	.978	136	165	-.5	-9.8	-.0	-.6	-2.0
TOT	127	117	580	20289		9.0				12.7	4.21		.262	.333					.979	1786	2075					

Runs		Hits		Doubles		Triples		Home Runs		Total Bases	
Burks-Col	142	Johnson-NY	227	Bagwell-Hou	48	Johnson-NY	21	Galarraga-Col	47	Burks-Col	392
Finley-SD	126	Burks-Col	211	Finley-SD	45	Howard-Cin	10	Sheffield-Fla	42	Galarraga-Col	376
Bonds-SF	122	Grissom-Atl	207	Burks-Col	45	Grissom-Atl	10	Bonds-SF	42	Finley-SD	348
Galarraga-Col	119	Grudzielanek-Mon	201	Gilkey-NY	44	Finley-SD	9	Hundley-NY	41	Castilla-Col	345
Sheffield-Fla	118	Bichette-Col	198	Rodriguez-Mon	42					Caminiti-SD	339

Runs Batted In		Runs Produced		Bases On Balls		Batting Average		On Base Percentage		Slugging Average	
Galarraga-Col	150	Burks-Col	230	Bonds-SF	151	Gwynn-SD	.353	Sheffield-Fla	.469	Burks-Col	.639
Bichette-Col	141	Bichette-Col	224	Sheffield-Fla	142	Burks-Col	.344	Bonds-SF	.465	Sheffield-Fla	.624
Caminiti-SD	130	Galarraga-Col	222	Bagwell-Hou	135	Piazza-LA	.336	Bagwell-Hou	.454	Caminiti-SD	.621
Bonds-SF	129	Bonds-SF	209	Henderson-SD	125	Johnson-NY	.333	Piazza-LA	.423	Bonds-SF	.615
Burks-Col	128	Bagwell-Hou	200	Larkin-Cin	96	Grace-Chi	.331	Larkin-Cin	.415	Galarraga-Col	.601

Production		Adjusted Production		Batter Runs		Adjusted Batter Runs		Clutch Hitting Index		Runs Created	
Sheffield-Fla	1.094	Sheffield-Fla	193	Sheffield-Fla	72.3	Sheffield-Fla	78.6	Jordan-StL	128	Bonds-SF	162
Bonds-SF	1.080	Bonds-SF	190	Bonds-SF	69.2	Bagwell-Hou	77.6	Bell-Hou	128	Sheffield-Fla	159
Burks-Col	1.048	Bagwell-Hou	185	Bagwell-Hou	63.3	Bonds-SF	75.7	Pendleton-Fla-Atl	121	Burks-Col	158
Caminiti-SD	1.035	Caminiti-SD	177	Burks-Col	61.6	Caminiti-SD	60.9	Joyner-SD	121	Bagwell-Hou	156
Bagwell-Hou	1.025	Piazza-LA	171	Caminiti-SD	54.2	Piazza-LA	57.6	Reed-SD	121	Caminiti-SD	138

Total Average		Stolen Bases		Stolen Base Average		Stolen Base Runs		Fielding Runs		Total Player Rating	
Bonds-SF	1.338	Young-Col	53	Bell-Hou	90.6	Johnson-NY	7.8	Young-Col	27.8	Bonds-SF	8.5
Sheffield-Fla	1.268	Johnson-NY	50	Walker-Col	90.0	DeShields-LA	7.8	Castilla-Col	27.6	Caminiti-SD	7.0
Bagwell-Hou	1.175	DeShields-LA	48	Renteria-Fla	88.9	Bonds-SF	7.8	Gilkey-NY	24.1	Bagwell-Hou	6.8
Burks-Col	1.136	Bonds-SF	40	Owens-Cin	88.9	Bell-Hou	6.9	Andrews-Mon	21.0	Gilkey-NY	6.6
Caminiti-SD	1.101	Martin-Pit	38	Bonds-SF	85.1	Lankford-StL	6.3	Lopez-Atl	18.3	Sheffield-Fla	6.2

Wins		Win Percentage		Games		Complete Games		Shutouts		Saves	
Smoltz-Atl	24	Smoltz-Atl	.750	Clontz-Atl	81	Schilling-Phi	8	Brown-Fla	3	Worrell-LA	44
A.Benes-StL	18	Martinez-LA	.714	Patterson-Chi	79	Smoltz-Atl	6			Brantley-Cin	44
Ritz-Col	17	Valdes-LA	.682	Shaw-Cin	78					Hoffman-SD	42
Brown-Fla	17	A.Benes-StL	.643	Dewey-SF	78					Wohlers-Atl	39
		Neagle-Pit-Atl	.640	Wohlers-Atl	77					Rojas-Mon	36

Innings Pitched		Fewest Hits/Game		Fewest BB/Game		Strikeouts		Strikeouts/Game		Ratio	
Smoltz-Atl	253.2	Leiter-Fla	6.39	Maddux-Atl	1.03	Smoltz-Atl	276	Smoltz-Atl	9.79	Smoltz-Atl	9.08
Maddux-Atl	245.0	Smoltz-Atl	7.06	Brown-Fla	1.27	Nomo-LA	234	Nomo-LA	9.22	Brown-Fla	9.12
Reynolds-Hou	239.0	Nomo-LA	7.09	Darwin-Pit-Hou	1.48	Martinez-Mon	222	Martinez-Mon	9.22	Maddux-Atl	9.40
Navarro-Chi	236.2	Brown-Fla	7.22	Reynolds-Hou	1.66	Fassero-Mon	222	Kile-Hou	9.00	Schilling-Phi	9.92
Glavine-Atl	235.1	Schilling-Phi	7.31	Tewksbury-SD	1.87	Kile-Hou	219	Schilling-Phi	8.93	Reynolds-Hou	10.51

Earned Run Average		Adjusted ERA		Opponents' Batting Avg.		Opponents' On Base Pct.		Starter Runs		Adjusted Starter Runs	
Brown-Fla	1.89	Brown-Fla	214	Leiter-Fla	.202	Smoltz-Atl	.261	Brown-Fla	60.1	Brown-Fla	55.7
Maddux-Atl	2.72	Maddux-Atl	162	Smoltz-Atl	.216	Brown-Fla	.263	Maddux-Atl	40.7	Maddux-Atl	45.8
Leiter-Fla	2.93	Smoltz-Atl	149	Nomo-LA	.218	Maddux-Atl	.265	Smoltz-Atl	35.8	Smoltz-Atl	41.0
Smoltz-Atl	2.94	Glavine-Atl	147	Brown-Fla	.220	Schilling-Phi	.280	Glavine-Atl	32.2	Glavine-Atl	37.0
Glavine-Atl	2.98	Trachsel-Chi	141	Schilling-Phi	.223	Reynolds-Hou	.290	Leiter-Fla	30.8	Trachsel-Chi	28.0

Clutch Pitching Index		Relief Runs		Adjusted Relief Runs		Relief Ranking		Total Pitcher Index		Total Baseball Ranking	
Trachsel-Chi	119	Nen-Fla	20.9	Nen-Fla	19.3	Hoffman-SD	38.6	Brown-Fla	7.2	Bonds-SF	8.5
Martinez-LA	119	Shaw-Cin	20.0	Shaw-Cin	19.3	Nen-Fla	26.9	Maddux-Atl	5.6	Brown-Fla	7.2
Valenzuela-SD	118	Hoffman-SD	19.2	Ryan-Phi	19.1	J.Franco-NY	24.5	Smoltz-Atl	5.4	Caminiti-SD	7.0
Drabek-Hou	114	Ryan-Phi	17.7	Hoffman-SD	17.0	Shaw-Cin	24.5	Glavine-Atl	4.8	Bagwell-Hou	6.8
Astacio-LA	113	Guthrie-LA	16.2	Bielecki-Atl	14.8	Ruffin-Col	23.8	Hoffman-SD	3.8	Gilkey-NY	6.6

March 31 The first Opening Day in history in March takes place in Seattle.

May 14 Dwight Gooden, who sat out part of the previous two seasons for drug-related suspensions, no-hits the Mariners. Gooden walks six and fans five in the 10th no-hitter in Yankees history.

May 21 Ken Griffey Jr. hits his 200th career home run at age 26. Only seven other players did it faster, and six are in the Hall of Fame.

July 12 Kirby Puckett, a career .318 hitter in 12 seasons, announces his retirement because of a damaged retina.

July 15 After 2,216 consecutive games at shortstop, Cal Ripken moves to third base, the first time that Ripken hasn't started at shortstop since 1982.

September 6 Eddie Murray's 500th career home run ties the game between the Orioles and Tigers in the seventh, but Detroit wins 5-4 in 12 innings. Murray joins an exclusive circle of Hank Aaron and Willie Mays as the only players with 500 home runs and 3,000 hits.

September 16 Paul Molitor of the Twins becomes the 21st player to reach 3,000 hits—and the first to reach the milestone with a triple.

September 18 Roger Clemens ties his own ML record with 20 strikeouts against the Tigers. The Red Sox fireballer allows five singles and walks none.

September 27 Baltimore's Roberto Alomar spits at home plate umpire John Hirschbeck during an argument and is given a five-game suspension, but he appeals and is allowed to play the next night; he hits a home run that clinches the wild card spot for the Orioles.

October 9 The Yankees win the ALCS opener when a 12-year-old fan sticks his glove out and turns a fly ball into a home run to tie the game. Bernie Williams homers in the bottom of the 11th to give New York a 5-4 win over the Orioles.

October 23 The Braves jump to a 6-0 lead, but the Yanks mount their biggest World Series comeback with a three-run home run by Jim Leyritz that ties the game in the eighth. After Bernie Williams is intentionally walked with runners on first and second in the 10th, Steve Avery walks Wade Boggs to bring in the deciding run.

October 26 A three-run third inning is all the Yankees need. Series MVP John Wetteland pitches out of trouble in the ninth as the Yankees win the World Series for the first time since 1978.

November 5 Yankees shortstop Derek Jeter is the unanimous choice as AL Rookie of the Year. He is the eighth Yankee to win the award and the fifth unanimous choice in AL history.

November 12 Toronto's Pat Hentgen edges Andy Pettitte of the Yankees for the Cy Young Award. Hentgen (20-10) outpoints Pettitte (21-8) by a narrow margin of 110-104. Yankees middle reliever Mariano Rivera finishes third in the voting.

BALTIMORE		BOSTON		CALIFORNIA		CHICAGO		CLEVELAND		DETROIT		KANSAS CITY	
M	D.Johnson	M	K.Kennedy	M	M.Lachemann	M	T.Bevington	M	M.Hargrove	M	B.Bell	M	B.Boone
1B	R.Palmeiro	1B	M.Vaughn	M	J.McNamara	1B	F.Thomas	1B	J.Franco	1B	T.Clark	1B	J.Offerman
2B	R.Alomar	2B	J.Frye	1B	J.Snow	2B	R.Durham	2B	C.Baerga	2B	M.Lewis	2B	K.Lockhart
SS	C.Ripken	SS	J.Valentin	2B	R.Velarde	SS	O.Guillen	SS	O.Vizquel	SS	A.Cedeno	SS	D.Howard
3B	B.Surhoff	3B	T.Naehring	SS	G.DiSarcina	3B	R.Ventura	3B	J.Thome	3B	T.Fryman	3B	J.Randa
LF	M.Devereaux	LF	M.Greenwell	3B	G.Arias	LF	T.Phillips	LF	A.Belle	LF	B.Higginson	LF	T.Goodwin
CF	B.Anderson	CF	L.Tinsley	LF	G.Anderson	CF	D.Lewis	CF	K.Lofton	CF	C.Curtis	CF	J.Damon
RF	B.Bonilla	RF	T.O'Leary	CF	J.Edmonds	RF	D.Tartabull	RF	M.Ramirez	RF	M.Nieves	RF	M.Tucker
C	C.Hoiles	C	M.Stanley	RF	T.Salmon	C	R.Karkovice	C	S.Alomar	C	B.Ausmus	C	M.Macfarlane
DH	E.Murray	DH	J.Canseco	C	J.Fabregas	DH	H.Baines	DH	E.Murray	DH	E.Williams	DH	J.Vitiello
				DH	C.Davis								
O	J.Hammonds	DO	R.Jefferson			O1	D.Martinez	P	C.Nagy	O	K.Bartee	3O	C.Paquette
		C	B.Haselman	2O	R.Hudler	OD	L.Mouton	P	O.Hershiser	1D	C.Fielder	2D	B.Roberts
P	M.Mussina	O	D.Bragg	O	D.Erstad			P	J.McDowell	OD	C.Pride	D1	B.Hamelin
P	D.Wells			C	D.Slaught	P	A.Fernandez	P	C.Ogea				
P	S.Erickson	P	R.Clemens			P	K.Tapani	P	D.Martinez	P	F.Lira	P	T.Belcher
P	R.Coppinger	P	T.Gordon	P	C.Finley	P	W.Alvarez	RP	J.Tavarez	P	O.Olivares	P	C.Haney
RP	R.Myers	P	T.Wakefield	P	S.Boskie	P	J.Baldwin	RP	E.Plunk	P	B.Williams	P	K.Appier
RP	R.McDowell	P	A.Sele	P	J.Abbott	RP	R.Hernandez	RP	J.Mesa	RP	R.Lewis	P	M.Gubicza
RP	J.Orosco	RP	V.Eshelman	P	J.Grimsley	RP	B.Simas			RP	J.Lima	P	J.Rosado
		RP	H.Slocumb	P	M.Langston	RP	B.Keyser	P	A.Lopez	RP	M.Myers	RP	H.Pichardo
P	J.Haynes	RP	M.Maddux	RP	M.James			P	P.Shuey			RP	J.Montgomery
P	R.Krivda			RP	T.Percival	P	M.Karchner	P	B.Anderson			RP	J.Valera
P	K.Mercker	P	J.Moyer			P	J.Magrane			P	G.Gohr		
P	A.Mills	P	M.Stanton	P	D.Springer	P	K.McCaskill			P	G.Keagle	P	D.Linton
P	A.Rhodes									P	A.Sager	P	M.Magnante
										P	J.Thompson		

MILWAUKEE		MINNESOTA		NEW YORK		OAKLAND		SEATTLE		TEXAS		TORONTO	
M	P.Garner	M	T.Kelly	M	J.Torre	M	A.Howe	M	L.Piniella	M	J.Oates	M	C.Gaston
1B	K.Seitzer	1B	S.Stahoviak	1B	T.Martinez	1B	M.McGwire	1B	P.Sorrento	1B	W.Clark	1B	J.Olerud
2B	F.Vina	2B	C.Knoblauch	2B	M.Duncan	2B	R.Bournigal	2B	J.Cora	2B	M.McLemore	2B	T.Perez
SS	J.Valentin	SS	P.Meares	SS	D.Jeter	SS	M.Bordick	SS	A.Rodriguez	SS	K.Elster	SS	A.Gonzalez
3B	J.Cirillo	3B	D.Hollins	3B	W.Boggs	3B	S.Brosius	3B	R.Davis	3B	D.Palmer	3B	E.Sprague
LF	G.Vaughn	LF	M.Cordova	LF	G.Williams	LF	P.Plantier	LF	R.Amaral	LF	R.Greer	LF	J.Carter
CF	P.Listach	CF	R.Becker	CF	B.Williams	CF	E.Young	CF	K.Griffey	CF	D.Hamilton	CF	O.Nixon
RF	M.Mieske	RF	R.Kelly	RF	P.O'Neill	RF	J.Herrera	RF	J.Buhner	RF	J.Gonzalez	RF	S.Green
C	M.Matheny	C	G.Myers	C	J.Girardi	C	T.Steinbach	C	D.Wilson	C	I.Rodriguez	C	C.O'Brien
DH	J.Jaha	DH	P.Molitor	DH	R.Sierra	DH	G.Berroa	DH	E.Martinez	DH	M.Tettleton	DH	C.Delgado
C	J.Levis	S3	J.Reboulet	23	A.Fox	1O	J.Giambi	32	L.Sojo	O	W.Newson	O	J.Brumfield
OD	D.Nilsson	O	M.Lawton	C3	J.Leyritz	2	B.Gates					2	D.Cedeno
		1O	R.Coomer	OD	D.Strawberry	23	T.Batista	P	S.Hitchcock	P	K.Hill	C	A.Martinez
		C	M.Walbeck	O	T.Raines			P	B.Wolcott	P	R.Pavlik	O	R.Perez
P	B.McDonald			D	C.Fielder	P	D.Wengert	P	B.Wells	P	B.Witt		
P	S.Karl	P	B.Radke			P	D.Johns	RP	R.Carmona	P	D.Oliver	P	P.Hentgen
P	R.Bones	P	F.Rodriguez	P	A.Pettitte	P	J.Wasdin	RP	N.Charlton	P	K.Gross	P	E.Hanson
RP	A.Miranda	P	R.Robertson	P	K.Rogers	P	A.Prieto	RP	M.Jackson	RP	G.Heredia	P	J.Guzman
RP	R.Garcia	P	S.Aldred	P	D.Gooden	RP	C.Reyes			RP	D.Cook	RP	P.Quantrill
RP	M.Fetters	P	R.Aguilera	P	J.Key	RP	M.Mohler	P	M.Wagner	RP	J.Russell	RP	T.Castillo
		RP	G.Hansell	P	M.Rivera	RP	B.Groom	P	J.Moyer			RP	T.Crabtree
P	S.Sparks	RP	E.Guardado	RP	B.Wickman			P	T.Mulholland			RP	M.Timlin
P	J.D'Amico	RP	J.Parra	RP	J.Nelson	P	S.Wojciechowski	P	B.Ayala	J.Burkett		
P	C.Eldred					P	D.Telgheder	P	C.Bosio				
P	T.Van Egmond					P	W.Adams	P	R.Johnson			P	M.Janzen
P	G.Lloyd	P	M.Trombley	P	D.Cone	P	J.Corsi					P	H.Flener
		P	D.Stevens	P	J.Wetteland	P	T.Van Poppel					P	W.Williams
		P	D.Naulty	P	R.Mendoza	P	B.Taylor						
						P	B.Chouinard						

TEAM	G	W	L	PCT	GB	R	OR	AB	H	2B	3B	HR	BB	SO	AVG	OBP	SLG	PRO	PRO+	BR	/A	PF	CHI	RC	SB	CS	SBA	SBR
EAST																												
NY	162	92	70	.568		871	787	5628	1621	293	28	162	632	909	.288	.364	.436	.800	99	16	0	102	98	890	96	46	68	1
BAL	163	88	74	.543	4	949	903	5689	1557	299	29	**257**	645	915	.274	.354	.472	.826	108	50	63	99	102	948	76	40	66	-1
BOS	162	85	77	.525	7	928	921	5756	1631	308	31	209	642	1020	.283	.362	.457	.819	102	47	15	103	99	948	91	44	67	1
TOR	162	74	88	.457	18	766	809	5599	1451	302	35	177	529	1105	.259	.333	.420	.753	89	-101	-104	100	101	794	116	38	75	12
DET	162	53	109	.327	39	783	1103	5530	1413	257	21	204	546	1268	.256	.326	.420	.746	88	-121	-115	99	**108**	746	87	50	64	-4
CENTRAL																												
CLE	161	99	62	.615		952	**769**	5681	**1665**	335	23	218	671	**844**	**.293**	**.372**	.475	.847	112	109	110	100	96	1003	160	50	**76**	18
CHI	162	85	77	.525	14.5	898	794	5644	1586	284	33	195	**701**	927	.281	.364	.447	.811	109	35	86	95	98	926	105	41	72	7
MIL	162	80	82	.494	19.5	894	899	5662	1578	304	40	178	624	986	.279	.356	.441	.797	95	0	-47	105	102	899	101	48	68	2
MIN	162	78	84	.481	21.5	877	900	5673	1633	332	**47**	118	576	958	.288	.360	.425	.785	95	-15	-30	102	103	860	143	53	73	11
KC	161	75	86	.466	24	746	786	5542	1477	286	38	123	529	943	.267	.335	.398	.733	86	-132	-113	97	104	750	**195**	85	70	8
WEST																												
TEX	163	90	72	.556		928	799	5702	1622	323	32	221	660	1041	.284	.362	.469	.831	101	67	3	107	98	975	83	26	**76**	9
SEA	161	85	76	.528	4.5	**993**	895	5668	1625	**343**	19	245	670	1052	.287	.366	.488	**.854**	**114**	**117**	**122**	100	99	**1024**	90	39	70	4
OAK	162	78	84	.481	12	861	900	5630	1492	283	21	243	640	1114	.265	.346	.452	.798	103	-8	27	96	100	880	58	35	62	-4
CAL	161	70	91	.435	19.5	762	943	5686	1571	256	24	192	527	974	.276	.341	.431	.772	95	-62	-44	98	96	814	53	39	58	-8
TOT	1133					12208		79090	21922	4205	421	2742	8592	14056	.277	.353	.445	.798							1454	634	70	56

TEAM	CG	SH	SV	IP	H	H/G	HR	BB	SO	RAT	ERA	ERA+	OAV	OOB	PR	/A	PF	CPI	FA	E	DP	FW	PW	BW	SBW	DIF
EAST																										
NY	6	**9**	**52**	1440	**1469**	9.2	143	610	1139	13.3	4.65	109	**.265**	.343	55	64	101	94	.985	91	146	1.2	5.8	.0	-.3	4.2
BAL	13	1	44	1468²	1604	9.8	209	597	1047	13.7	5.14	95	.280	.352	-25	-40	103	98	.984	97	173	.9	-3.6	5.7	-.5	4.4
BOS	17	5	37	1458	1606	9.9	185	722	**1165**	14.7	4.98	103	.279	.364	1	26	103	103	.978	135	152	-1.2	2.4	1.4	-.3	1.8
TOR	**19**	7	35	1445²	1476	9.2	187	610	1033	14.2	4.57	111	.266	.343	68	77	101	101	.982	110	187	.2	7.0	-9.5	.7	-5.4
DET	10	4	22	1432²	1699	10.7	241	784	957	16.1	6.38	79	.296	.389	-221	-209	101	97	.978	137	157	-1.4	-19.0	-10.5	-.7	3.6
CENTRAL																										
CLE	13	**9**	46	1452¹	1530	9.5	173	484	1033	**12.7**	**4.34**	113	.271	**.333**	105	89	98	102	.980	124	156	-.7	8.1	10.0	**1.3**	-.2
CHI	7	4	43	1461	1529	9.4	174	616	1039	13.4	4.52	104	.270	.345	77	29	94	102	.982	109	145	.2	2.6	7.8	.3	-7.0
MIL	6	4	42	1447¹	1570	9.8	213	635	846	14.1	5.14	102	.278	.357	-23	20	105	101	.978	134	180	-1.2	1.8	-4.3	-.2	2.8
MIN	13	5	31	1439²	1561	9.8	233	581	959	13.6	5.28	97	.277	.348	-46	-23	103	96	.984	94	142	1.1	-2.1	-2.7	.6	.1
KC	17	8	35	1450	1563	9.7	176	**460**	926	12.9	4.55	107	.277	.338	71	54	98	101	.982	111	184	.0	4.9	-10.3	.4	-.6
WEST																										
TEX	**19**	6	43	1449¹	1569	9.7	168	582	976	13.6	4.65	**114**	.278	.350	55	**106**	106	103	**.986**	87	150	**1.5**	9.7	.3	.5	-2.9
SEA	4	4	34	1431²	1562	9.8	216	605	1000	14.0	5.21	95	.287	.356	-35	-45	99	99	.981	110	155	.1	-4.1	**11.1**	.0	-2.6
OAK	7	5	34	1456¹	1638	10.1	205	644	884	14.3	5.20	92	.287	.365	-33	-63	96	**104**	.984	103	195	.6	-5.7	2.5	-.7	.5
CAL	12	8	38	1439	1546	9.7	219	662	1052	14.3	5.30	92	.275	.360	-49	-65	98	99	.979	128	156	-.9	-5.9	-4.0	-1.1	1.4
TOT	163	79	536	20271²		9.7				13.9	4.99		.277	.353					.982	1570	2278					

Runs
Rodriguez-Sea 141
Knoblauch-Min 140
Lofton-Cle........ 132
Alomar-Bal 132
Griffey-Sea 125

Hits
Molitor-Sea 225
Rodriguez-Sea 215
Lofton-Cle....... 210
Vaughn-Bos 207
Knoblauch-Min 197

Doubles
Rodriguez-Sea 54
E.Martinez-Sea 52
Rodriguez-Tex 47
Cordova-Min 46
Cirillo-Mil 46

Triples
Knoblauch-Min 14
Vina-Mil 10

Home Runs
McGwire-Oak 52
Anderson-Bal 50
Griffey-Sea 49
Belle-Cle 48
Gonzalez-Tex 47

Total Bases
Rodriguez-Sea 379
Belle-Cle 375
Vaughn-Bos 370
Anderson-Bal 369
Gonzalez-Tex 348

Runs Batted In
Belle-Cle 148
Gonzalez-Tex 144
Vaughn-Bos 143
Palmeiro-Bal 142
Griffey-Sea 140

Runs Produced
Rodriguez-Sea 228
Belle-Cle 224
Vaughn-Bos 217
Griffey-Sea 216
Palmeiro-Bal 213

Bases On Balls
Phillips-Chi 125
Thome-Cle 123
E.Martinez-Sea 123
McGwire-Oak 116
F.Thomas-Chi 109

Batting Average
Rodriguez-Sea 358
F.Thomas-Chi 349
Molitor-Min 341
Knoblauch-Min 341
Greer-Tex 332

On Base Percentage
McGwire-Oak 468
E.Martinez-Sea 467
F.Thomas-Chi 465
Knoblauch-Min 452
Thome-Cle 451

Slugging Average
McGwire-Oak 730
Gonzalez-Tex 643
Anderson-Bal 637
Rodriguez-Sea 631
Griffey-Sea 628

Production
McGwire-Oak 1.199
F.Thomas-Chi 1.091
Thome-Cle 1.063
E.Martinez-Sea 1.062
Rodriguez-Sea 1.049

Adjusted Production
McGwire-Oak 205
F.Thomas-Chi 182
E.Martinez-Sea 167
Thome-Cle 165
Rodriguez-Sea 161

Batter Runs
McGwire-Oak..... 67.3
F.Thomas-Chi 63.3
E.Martinez-Sea 57.1
Thome-Cle 55.6
Rodriguez-Sea 54.6

Adjusted Batter Runs
McGwire-Oak 73.0
F.Thomas-Chi 71.8
E.Martinez-Sea 57.8
Thome-Cle 55.7
Rodriguez-Sea 55.3

Clutch Hitting Index
Molitor-Min 129
Cordova-Min 120
Elster-Tex 117
Tartabull-Chi 117
O'Leary-Bos 116

Runs Created
Vaughn-Bos 158
Rodriguez-Sea 157
Belle-Cle 156
Anderson-Bal 150
F.Thomas-Chi 150

Total Average
McGwire-Oak 1.420
E.Martinez-Sea 1.209
Thome-Cle 1.207
F.Thomas-Chi 1.203
Griffey-Sea 1.139

Stolen Bases
Lofton-Cle 75
Goodwin-KC 66
Nixon-Tor 54
Knoblauch-Min 45
Vizquel-Cle 35

Stolen Base Average
Griffey-Sea 94.1
Durham-Chi 88.2
Listach-Mil 83.3
Damon-KC 83.3
Frye-Bos 81.8

Stolen Base Runs
Lofton-Cle 12.3
Nixon-Tor 8.4
Goodwin-KC 6.6
Durham-Chi 6.6

Fielding Runs
Becker-Min 23.9
Gonzalez-Tor 23.0
McLemore-Tex 20.1
Howard-KC 18.8
Fryman-Det 16.7

Total Player Rating
Rodriguez-Sea 5.4
Griffey-Sea 5.4
Alomar-Bal 5.4
Belle-Cle 5.3
McGwire-Oak 5.1

Wins
Pettitte-NY 21
Hentgen-Tor 20
Mussina-Bal 19
Nagy-Cle 17

Win Percentage
Nagy-Cle .... .773
Pettitte-NY .... .724
Hentgen-Tor .... .667
Pavlik-Tex .... .652
Mussina-Bal .... .633

Games
Myers-Det 83
Guardado-Min 83
Stanton-Bos-Tex 81
Slocumb-Bos 75

Complete Games
Hentgen-Tor 10
Pavlik-Tex 7
Hill-Tex 7

Shutouts
Robertson-Min 3
Hill-Tex 3
Hentgen-Tor 3
Lira-Det 2
Clemens-Bos 2

Saves
Wetteland-NY 43
Mesa-Cle 39
Hernandez-Chi 38
Percival-Cal 36
Fetters-Mil 32

Innings Pitched
Hentgen-Tor 265.2
Fernandez-Chi 258.0
Hill-Tex 250.2
Mussina-Bal 243.1
Clemens-Bos 242.2

Fewest Hits/Game
Guzman-Tor 7.58
Clemens-Bos 8.01
Hentgen-Tor 8.06
Appier-KC 8.18
Fernandez-Chi 8.65

Fewest BB/Game
Haney-KC 2.01
Wells-Bal 2.05
Radke-Min 2.21
Nagy-Cle 2.47
Fernandez-Chi 2.51

Strikeouts
Clemens-Bos 257
Finley-Cal 215
Appier-KC 207
Mussina-Bal 204
Fernandez-Chi 200

Strikeouts/Game
Clemens-Bos 9.53
Appier-KC 8.82
Finley-Cal 8.13
Guzman-Tor 7.91
Mussina-Bal 7.55

Ratio
Guzman-Tor 10.45
Radke-Min 11.33
Nagy-Cle 11.39
Fernandez-Chi 11.41
Hentgen-Tor 11.42

Earned Run Average
Guzman-Tor 2.93
Hentgen-Tor 3.22
Nagy-Cle 3.41
Fernandez-Chi 3.45
Appier-KC 3.62

Adjusted ERA
Guzman-Tor 173
Hentgen-Tor 157
Hill-Tex 146
Nagy-Cle 144
Clemens-Bos 141

Opponents' Batting Avg.
Guzman-Tor .... .228
Clemens-Bos .... .237
Hentgen-Tor .... .241
Appier-KC .... .245
Fernandez-Chi .... .253

Opponents' On Base Pct.
Guzman-Tor .... .290
Radke-Min .... .304
Nagy-Cle .... .307
Fernandez-Chi .... .309
Hentgen-Tor .... .310

Starter Runs
Hentgen-Tor 52.3
Fernandez-Chi 44.1
Guzman-Tor 43.1
Nagy-Cle 39.1
Hill-Tex 38.0

Adjusted Starter Runs
Hentgen-Tor 54.1
Hill-Tex 46.9
Guzman-Tor 44.3
Clemens-Bos 40.6
Nagy-Cle 36.6

Clutch Pitching Index
Belcher-KC 116
Fernandez-Chi 113
Hill-Tex 112
Pettitte-NY 111
Boskie-Cal 110

Relief Runs
M.Rivera-NY 34.7
Hernandez-Chi 28.9
Plunk-Cle 22.1
Percival-Cal 22.0
James-Cal 20.9

Adjusted Relief Runs
M.Rivera-NY 35.4
Hernandez-Chi 26.2
Percival-Cal 21.2
Plunk-Cle 21.2
James-Cal 20.0

Relief Ranking
Hernandez-Chi 52.9
M.Rivera-NY 35.7
Slocumb-Bos 35.0
Wetteland-NY 31.3
Percival-Cal 24.8

Total Pitcher Index
Hentgen-Tor 5.3
Hernandez-Chi 4.9
Hill-Tex 3.9
Guzman-Tor 3.9
Fernandez-Chi 3.5

Total Baseball Ranking
Rodriguez-Sea 5.4
Griffey-Sea 5.4
Alomar-Bal 5.4
Hentgen-Tor 5.3
Belle-Cle 5.3

The All-Time Leaders: Introduction

This section is divided into two parts: lifetime leaders and single-season leaders. Both groups command our attention and convey the pleasures of the game, which lie as much in contemplation of the past as in experiencing the present: Henry Aaron, 755; Babe Ruth, 714; Willie Mays, 660—this is no mere aggregation of names and numbers, as in a telephone directory . . . it comprises the romance and lore of the home run, and of baseball itself. Jack Chesbro, 41, 1904; Bob Gibson, 1.12, 1968; Nolan Ryan, 383, 1973 . . . you can fill in the blanks that tell the story of pitching's most glorious seasons.

What follows are the all-time great achievements in 219 categories, both the traditional statistics and the new. For most of these we will give not the top 10 or 20 but the top 100, because some categories would otherwise be dominated by players of a certain era (for example, slugging average by batters of the 1920s and 1930s, earned run average by pitchers of 1900–1919). And for many stats we will offer a second kind of ranking, broken down into six distinct eras of baseball, with the top 10 or 15 leaders in each. For example, breaking down single-season home runs this way would produce lists topped by these men:

    1876–1892: Ned Williamson, 27, 1884
    1893–1919: Babe Ruth, 29, 1919
    1920–1941: Babe Ruth, 60, 1927
    1942–1960: Ralph Kiner, 54, 1949
    1961–1976: Roger Maris, 61, 1961
    1977–1996: George Foster, 52, 1977;
        Mark McGwire, 1996

And for single-season Adjusted ERA (normalized to league average and adjusted for home-park factor), we get:

    1876–1892: Tim Keefe, 294
        (adjusted from actual 0.80), 1880
    1893–1919: Dutch Leonard, 280
        (adjusted from actual 0.96), 1914
    1920–1941: Lefty Grove, 218
        (adjusted from actual 2.06), 1931
    1942–1960: Billy Pierce, 201
        (adjusted from actual 1.97), 1955
    1961–1976: Bob Gibson, 258
        (adjusted from actual 1.12), 1968
    1977–1996: Greg Maddux, 266
        (adjusted from actual 1.56), 1994

This is quite a different lineup from the traditional list of ERA leaders (which relegates pre-1900 pitching to the shadows), where of the 15 top spots, 14 are accorded to pitchers active from 1905 to 1918. Is there a baseball fan alive who thinks that all the great pitchers were created in that 14-year span and that the mold was then broken?

We also present certain categories in a per game fashion that illuminates some hidden great performers. While it is not surprising to find such names as Babe Ruth, Lou Gehrig, and Jimmie Foxx among the top ten all-time at runs batted in per game, few fans would expect to find Cap Anson listed seventh, or to find that the best of the best was nineteenth-century slugger Sam Thompson.

But we go one step further and rank several batting categories by position, thus recognizing and illustrating the greater demands for fielding skill at such positions as shortstop, catcher, and second base, and the comparatively plentiful supply of batting talent in the outfield and at first base. Having Mark McGwire hit 52 home runs for you is great, but he cannot play anywhere but first base; a team of nine McGwires (or ten, in the AL) would finish dead last. For example, here is the list of the top ten lifetime batting averages:

    Ty Cobb, .366
    Rogers Hornsby, .358
    Joe Jackson, .356
    Ed Delahanty, .346
    Tris Speaker, .345
    Ted Williams, .344
    Billy Hamilton, .344
    Dan Brouthers, .342
    Babe Ruth, .342
    Harry Heilmann, .342

This would be a formidable team indeed, but it would not win, for it includes a first baseman, a second baseman, and eight outfielders. Here, as food for thought, is a list of the top ten lifetime leading averages among catchers, that indispensable class of men. ("You gotta have a catcher," Casey Stengel explained, "because if you don't, the ball rolls all the way to the backstop.")

    Mickey Cochrane, .320
    Bill Dickey, .313
    Spud Davis, .308
    Ernie Lombardi, .306
    Gabby Hartnett, .297
    Manny Sanguillen, .296
    Smoky Burgess, .295
    Thurman Munson, .292
    Hank Severeid, .289
    Jack Clements, .286

This team would not win, either. But the point is that

the section that follows will, if perused carefully, make you think differently about the game and its statistics. And that's a large part of what *Total Baseball* is about.

For example, the batting average itself is a flawed measure, as we have discussed in "The History of Major League Baseball Statistics" and "Sabermetrics." While batting average is not as good as, say, Production (on base plus slugging), it is not worthless, either. And when we report batting average in a form which relates it to the league average at the time, it becomes far more useful as an evaluative tool.

Remember that list above of the top ten lifetime batting averages? Here are the top ten batting averages *as compared to* the league batting averages in the years in which the men played (individual batting average divided by league batting average, expressed in three digits, so that a man who batted at exactly his league average over the course of his career would have a mark of 100):

> Ty Cobb, 134.7
> Joe Jackson, 133.1
> Pete Browning, 131.6
> Ted Williams, 128.1
> Dan Brouthers, 127.8
> Tony Gwynn, 127.7
> Nap Lajoie, 127.3
> Wade Boggs, 127.1
> Rod Carew, 127.0
> Rogers Hornsby, 126.2

Says something, doesn't it? But enough expostulation and fulmination. Let's set some ground rules, define some terms that may still be unfamiliar after you've browsed through the Player and Pitcher registers, and get on with the show.

To be eligible for a lifetime pitching category that is stated as an average, a man must have pitched 1,500 or more innings, or 750 or more innings if he is a relief pitcher, in the major leagues; for a counting statistic, he must simply have attained the necessary quantity to crack the list. For a single-season category expressed as an average, he must have pitched one inning per league scheduled game or have attained the necessary quantity (wins, strikeouts, saves) to head a counted list.

To be eligible for a lifetime batting category that is stated as an average, a man must have played in 1,000 or more games; for counting stats such as strikeouts, a Rob Deer earned his place on the list before he played his 1,000th game. For Pitcher Batting Average, the criterion is 1,500 innings pitched or 100 hits. And to reach the single-season batting lists, a man must have 3.1 plate appearances per scheduled game.

We provide tables of the top fielding performances, too, sorted by position as you would expect (and, in this edition, including only games played at the position, rather than combining data from secondary positions under the dominant position). As we establish a 1,000-game minimum for inclusion in all but a few batting and baserunning categories, we likewise establish for these positional rankings a minimum of 1,000 games played at the position.

For the three principal categories—Total Player Rating, Total Pitcher Index, and Total Baseball Ranking—we have introduced several variations. For example, TPR and

TBR are shown 500 deep for lifetime leaders—sorted first by highest value; then alphabetically so that the reader may find a particular player without scanning 500 names; and last by the above-named eras, the top 25 in each. Total Pitcher Index is also sorted this way, but because far fewer pitchers than position players meet the longevity criteria, the lifetime groupings go 300 and 200 deep rather than 500 and 300.

Ties are calculated to as many decimal places as needed to break them, but averages are shown to only three places. When two or more players are tied in an averaged category with a narrow base of data, such as a season's won-lost percentage, the reader can presume a numerical dead heat (and obviously this goes for counting stats, too—one man's 39 doubles are as good as another's). But where there is a tie for batting average, earned run average, or any of the sabermetric measures, the reader may assume that the man listed above the other(s) has the minutely higher average.

Here are the few stats carried in this section that are not carried in the Annual Record or Registers, with definitions where the terms are not self-explanatory (see Glossary for formulas):

Batting, Baserunning, Fielding

Runs (Scored) Per Game   Broken down by era

Home Run Percentage   Home runs per 100 at bats

Bases on Balls Percentage   Walks (most) per 100 appearances (at bats plus walks)

At-Bats Per Strikeout   Broken down by era

Relative Batting Average   Normalized to league average

Isolated Power   Slugging average minus batting average

Extra Base Hits

Pinch Hits

Pinch Hit Batting Average

Pinch Hit Home Runs

Strikeout Percentage

Total Player Rating Per 150 Games   Highlighting the achievements of modern players and those with comparatively short careers (though at least 1,000 games)

Total Chances Per Game   Broken down by position

Chances Accepted Per Game   Broken down by position

Putouts   Broken down by position

Putouts Per Game   Broken down by position

Assists   Broken down by position

Assists Per Game   Broken down by position

Double Plays   Broken down by position

Pitching

Wins Above Team   How many wins a pitcher garnered beyond those expected of an average pitcher for that team;

the formula is weighted so that a pitcher on a good team has a chance to compete with pitchers on poor teams who otherwise would benefit from the larger potential spread between their team's won-lost percentage and their own; see Glossary for more information.

Wins Above League   A pitcher's won-lost record restated by adding his Pitching Wins above the league average to the record that a league-average pitcher would have had with the same number of decisions (for example, Tom Seaver goes 20–10 with 7 Pitching Wins; applying the 7 wins to a 15–15 mark in the same 30 decisions results in a WAL of 22–8).

Percentage of Team Wins

Relief Games

Pitchers' Batting Runs

Pitchers' Fielding Runs

Relief Wins   This statistic, like the relief stats below, includes only games in relief.

Relief Losses

Relief Innings Pitched

Relief Points   Relief wins plus saves minus losses

Games

1	Pete Rose	3562
2	Carl Yastrzemski	3308
3	Hank Aaron	3298
4	Ty Cobb	3035
5	Stan Musial	3026
6	Willie Mays	2992
7	Dave Winfield	2973
8	Eddie Murray	2971
9	Rusty Staub	2951
10	Brooks Robinson	2896
11	Robin Yount	2856
12	Al Kaline	2834
13	Eddie Collins	2826
14	Reggie Jackson	2820
15	Frank Robinson	2808
16	Honus Wagner	2792
17	Tris Speaker	2789
18	Tony Perez	2777
19	Mel Ott	2730
20	George Brett	2707
21	Graig Nettles	2700
22	Darrell Evans	2687
23	Rabbit Maranville	2670
24	Joe Morgan	2649
25	Andre Dawson	2627
26	Lou Brock	2616
27	Dwight Evans	2606
28	Luis Aparicio	2599
29	Willie McCovey	2588
30	Ozzie Smith	2573
31	Paul Waner	2549
32	Ernie Banks	2528
33	Bill Buckner	2517
	Sam Crawford	2517
35	Babe Ruth	2503
36	Carlton Fisk	2499
37	Dave Concepcion	2488
	Billy Williams	2488
39	Nap Lajoie	2480
40	Max Carey	2476
41	Rod Carew	2469
	Vada Pinson	2469
43	Dave Parker	2466
44	Ted Simmons	2456
45	Bill Dahlen	2443
46	Ron Fairly	2442
47	Harmon Killebrew	2435
48	Roberto Clemente	2433
49	Willie Davis	2429
50	Luke Appling	2422
	Paul Molitor	2422
52	Zack Wheat	2410
53	Mickey Vernon	2409
54	Buddy Bell	2405
55	Sam Rice	2404
	Mike Schmidt	2404
57	Mickey Mantle	2401
58	Eddie Mathews	2391
59	Lou Whitaker	2390
60	Jake Beckley	2386
61	Bobby Wallace	2383
62	Cal Ripken	2381
63	Enos Slaughter	2380
64	George Davis	2368
	Al Oliver	2368
66	Nellie Fox	2367
67	Willie Stargell	2360
68	Jose Cruz	2353
69	Brian Downing	2344
70	Rickey Henderson	2340
71	Steve Garvey	2332
72	Bert Campaneris	2328
73	Harold Baines	2326
74	Frank White	2324
75	Charlie Gehringer	2323
76	Jimmie Foxx	2317
77	Frankie Frisch	2311
78	Harry Hooper	2309
79	Gary Carter	2296
80	Alan Trammell	2293
81	Don Baylor	2292
	Ted Williams	2292
83	Goose Goslin	2287
84	Jimmy Dykes	2282
85	Cap Anson	2276
86	Lave Cross	2275
87	Bob Boone	2264
88	Chris Speier	2260
89	Rogers Hornsby	2259
90	Larry Bowa	2247
91	Ron Santo	2243
92	Fred Clarke	2242
93	Doc Cramer	2239
94	Red Schoendienst	2216
95	Al Simmons	2215
96	Tim Wallach	2212
97	Joe Torre	2209
98	Willie Randolph	2202
99	Tommy Corcoran	2200
100	Tony Taylor	2195

At Bats

1	Pete Rose	14053
2	Hank Aaron	12364
3	Carl Yastrzemski	11988
4	Ty Cobb	11434
5	Eddie Murray	11169
6	Robin Yount	11008
7	Dave Winfield	11003
8	Stan Musial	10972
9	Willie Mays	10881
10	Brooks Robinson	10654
11	Honus Wagner	10430
12	George Brett	10349
13	Lou Brock	10332
14	Luis Aparicio	10230
15	Tris Speaker	10195
16	Al Kaline	10116
17	Rabbit Maranville	10078
18	Frank Robinson	10006
19	Eddie Collins	9949
20	Andre Dawson	9927
21	Reggie Jackson	9864
22	Paul Molitor	9795
23	Tony Perez	9778
24	Rusty Staub	9720
25	Vada Pinson	9645
26	Nap Lajoie	9589
27	Sam Crawford	9570
28	Jake Beckley	9526
29	Paul Waner	9459
30	Mel Ott	9456
31	Roberto Clemente	9454
32	Ernie Banks	9421
33	Bill Buckner	9397
34	Ozzie Smith	9396
35	Max Carey	9363
36	Dave Parker	9358
37	Billy Williams	9350
38	Rod Carew	9315
39	Joe Morgan	9277
40	Sam Rice	9269
41	Nellie Fox	9232
42	Cal Ripken	9217
43	Willie Davis	9174
44	Doc Cramer	9140
45	Frankie Frisch	9112
46	Zack Wheat	9106
47	Cap Anson	9101
48	Lave Cross	9072
49	Al Oliver	9049
50	Bill Dahlen	9031
	George Davis	9031
52	Dwight Evans	8996
53	Buddy Bell	8995
54	Graig Nettles	8986
55	Darrell Evans	8973
56	Charlie Gehringer	8860
57	Luke Appling	8856
58	Steve Garvey	8835
59	Tommy Corcoran	8804
60	Harry Hooper	8785
61	Al Simmons	8759
62	Carlton Fisk	8756
63	Mickey Vernon	8731
64	Dave Concepcion	8723
65	Bert Campaneris	8684
66	Ted Simmons	8680
67	Goose Goslin	8656
68	Bobby Wallace	8618
69	Willie Keeler	8591
70	Lou Whitaker	8570
71	Fred Clarke	8568
72	Eddie Mathews	8537
73	Rickey Henderson	8528
74	Red Schoendienst	8479
75	Jesse Burkett	8421
76	Larry Bowa	8418
77	Babe Ruth	8399
78	Harold Baines	8366
79	Richie Ashburn	8365
80	Mike Schmidt	8352
81	Bid McPhee	8291
82	Alan Trammell	8288
83	George Sisler	8267
84	Jim Rice	8225
85	Don Baylor	8198
86	Willie McCovey	8197
87	Rogers Hornsby	8173
88	Jimmy Ryan	8164
89	Harmon Killebrew	8147
90	Ron Santo	8143
91	Jimmie Foxx	8134
92	Mickey Mantle	8102
93	Wade Boggs	8100
94	Tim Wallach	8099
95	Pee Wee Reese	8058
96	Jimmy Dykes	8046
97	George Van Haltren	8021
98	Willie Randolph	8018
99	Lou Gehrig	8001
100	Joe Kuhel	7984

Runs

1	Ty Cobb	2246
2	Hank Aaron	2174
	Babe Ruth	2174
4	Pete Rose	2165
5	Willie Mays	2062
6	Stan Musial	1949
7	Lou Gehrig	1888
8	Tris Speaker	1882
9	Mel Ott	1859
10	Rickey Henderson	1829
	Frank Robinson	1829
12	Eddie Collins	1821
13	Carl Yastrzemski	1816
14	Ted Williams	1798
15	Charlie Gehringer	1774
16	Jimmie Foxx	1751
17	Honus Wagner	1736
18	Jesse Burkett	1720
19	Cap Anson	1719
	Willie Keeler	1719
21	Billy Hamilton	1690
22	Bid McPhee	1678
23	Mickey Mantle	1677
24	Dave Winfield	1669
25	Joe Morgan	1650
26	Paul Molitor	1644
27	Jimmy Ryan	1642
28	George Van Haltren	1639
29	Robin Yount	1632
30	Paul Waner	1627
31	Al Kaline	1622
32	Roger Connor	1620
33	Fred Clarke	1619
34	Eddie Murray	1614
35	Lou Brock	1610
36	Jake Beckley	1600
37	Ed Delahanty	1599
38	Bill Dahlen	1589
39	George Brett	1583
40	Rogers Hornsby	1579
41	Hugh Duffy	1552
42	Reggie Jackson	1551
43	Max Carey	1545
44	George Davis	1539
45	Frankie Frisch	1532
46	Dan Brouthers	1523
47	Tom Brown	1521
48	Sam Rice	1514
49	Eddie Mathews	1509
50	Al Simmons	1507
51	Mike Schmidt	1506
52	Nap Lajoie	1504
53	Harry Stovey	1492
54	Goose Goslin	1483
55	Arlie Latham	1478
56	Dwight Evans	1470
57	Herman Long	1455
58	Jim O'Rourke	1446
59	Harry Hooper	1429
60	Dummy Hoy	1426
61	Rod Carew	1424
62	Joe Kelley	1421
63	Tim Raines	1419
64	Roberto Clemente	1416
65	Billy Williams	1410
66	John Ward	1408
67	Mike Griffin	1405
68	Sam Crawford	1391
69	Joe DiMaggio	1390
70	Lou Whitaker	1386
71	Andre Dawson	1373
72	Wade Boggs	1367
73	Vada Pinson	1366
	Cal Ripken	1366
75	Doc Cramer	1357
	King Kelly	1357
77	Tommy Leach	1355
78	Darrell Evans	1344
79	Pee Wee Reese	1338
80	Luis Aparicio	1335
81	Lave Cross	1333
82	George Gore	1327
83	Richie Ashburn	1322
84	Luke Appling	1319
85	Patsy Donovan	1318
86	Mike Tiernan	1313
87	Brett Butler	1307
88	Ernie Banks	1305
	Kiki Cuyler	1305
90	Jimmy Sheckard	1296
91	Harry Heilmann	1291
92	Zack Wheat	1289
93	Heinie Manush	1287
94	George Sisler	1284
95	Harmon Killebrew	1283
96	Donie Bush	1280
97	Nellie Fox	1279
98	Fred Tenney	1278
99	Carlton Fisk	1276
100	2 players tied	1272

Runs per Game (by era)

1876-1892

1	George Gore	1.01
2	Harry Stovey	1.00
3	King Kelly	.93
4	Dan Brouthers	.91
5	Arlie Latham	.91
6	Sam Thompson	.89
7	Buck Ewing	.86
8	Tom Brown	.85
9	Hardy Richardson	.84
10	Tommy McCarthy	.84
11	Tip O'Neill	.83
12	Denny Lyons	.83
13	Curt Welch	.83
14	Jim O'Rourke	.82
15	Roger Connor	.81

1893-1919

1	Billy Hamilton	1.06
2	John McGraw	.93
3	Mike Griffin	.93
4	Hugh Duffy	.89
5	Mike Tiernan	.89
6	Ed Delahanty	.87
7	Cupid Childs	.83
8	Jesse Burkett	.83
9	George Van Haltren	.83
10	Jimmy Ryan	.82
11	Willie Keeler	.81
12	Dummy Hoy	.79
13	Herman Long	.78
14	Hughie Jennings	.77
15	Joe Kelley	.77

1920-1941

1	Lou Gehrig	.87
2	Babe Ruth	.87
3	Earle Combs	.82
4	Red Rolfe	.80
5	Charlie Gehringer	.76
6	Jimmie Foxx	.76
7	Hank Greenberg	.75
8	Earl Averill	.73
9	Max Bishop	.72
10	Lu Blue	.71
11	Mickey Cochrane	.70
12	Rogers Hornsby	.70
13	Kiki Cuyler	.69
14	Mel Ott	.68
15	Al Simmons	.68

1942-1960

1	Joe DiMaggio	.80
2	Ted Williams	.78
3	Dom DiMaggio	.75
4	Tommy Henrich	.70
5	Mickey Mantle	.70
6	Jackie Robinson	.69
7	Johnny Pesky	.68
8	Ralph Kiner	.66
9	Eddie Stanky	.64
10	Stan Musial	.64
11	George Case	.64
12	Eddie Mathews	.63
13	Larry Doby	.63
14	Charlie Keller	.62
15	Minnie Minoso	.62

1961-1976

1	Willie Mays	.69
2	Bobby Bonds	.68
3	Hank Aaron	.66
4	Frank Robinson	.65
5	Dick Allen	.63
6	Joe Morgan	.62
7	Lou Brock	.62
8	Pete Rose	.61
9	Roberto Clemente	.58
10	Rod Carew	.58
11	Jim Wynn	.58
12	Al Kaline	.57
13	Billy Williams	.57
14	Reggie Smith	.57
15	Roger Maris	.56

1977-1996

1	Rickey Henderson	.78
2	Barry Bonds	.71
3	Paul Molitor	.68
4	Tim Raines	.67
5	Ron LeFlore	.67
6	Ken Griffey Jr.	.66
7	Jose Canseco	.64
8	Wade Boggs	.64
9	Roberto Alomar	.64
10	Lenny Dykstra	.63
11	Mike Schmidt	.63
12	Ellis Burks	.63
13	Barry Larkin	.62
14	Ryne Sandberg	.62
15	Vince Coleman	.62

Hits

1	Pete Rose	4256
2	Ty Cobb	4189
3	Hank Aaron	3771
4	Stan Musial	3630
5	Tris Speaker	3514
6	Carl Yastrzemski	3419
7	Honus Wagner	3415
8	Eddie Collins	3315
9	Willie Mays	3283
10	Nap Lajoie	3242
11	Eddie Murray	3218
12	George Brett	3154
13	Paul Waner	3152
14	Robin Yount	3142
15	Dave Winfield	3110
16	Rod Carew	3053
17	Lou Brock	3023
18	Paul Molitor	3014
19	Al Kaline	3007
20	Roberto Clemente	3000
21	Cap Anson	2995
22	Sam Rice	2987
23	Sam Crawford	2961
24	Frank Robinson	2943
25	Willie Keeler	2932
26	Jake Beckley	2930
	Rogers Hornsby	2930
28	Al Simmons	2927
29	Zack Wheat	2884
30	Frankie Frisch	2880
31	Mel Ott	2876
32	Babe Ruth	2873
33	Jesse Burkett	2850
34	Brooks Robinson	2848
35	Charlie Gehringer	2839
36	George Sisler	2812
37	Andre Dawson	2774
38	Vada Pinson	2757
39	Luke Appling	2749
40	Al Oliver	2743
41	Goose Goslin	2735
42	Tony Perez	2732
43	Lou Gehrig	2721
44	Rusty Staub	2716
45	Bill Buckner	2715
46	Dave Parker	2712
47	Billy Williams	2711
48	Doc Cramer	2705
49	Wade Boggs	2697
50	Luis Aparicio	2677
51	Fred Clarke	2672
52	Max Carey	2665
53	Nellie Fox	2663
54	George Davis	2660
	Harry Heilmann	2660
56	Ted Williams	2654
57	Jimmie Foxx	2646
58	Lave Cross	2645
59	Rabbit Maranville	2605
60	Steve Garvey	2599
61	Ed Delahanty	2596
62	Reggie Jackson	2584
63	Ernie Banks	2583
64	Richie Ashburn	2574
65	Willie Davis	2561
66	Tony Gwynn	2560
67	Cal Ripken	2549
68	George Van Haltren	2532
69	Heinie Manush	2524
70	Joe Morgan	2517
71	Buddy Bell	2514
72	Jimmy Ryan	2502
73	Mickey Vernon	2495
74	Ted Simmons	2472
75	Joe Medwick	2471
76	Roger Connor	2467
77	Harry Hooper	2466
78	Ozzie Smith	2460
79	Lloyd Waner	2459
80	Bill Dahlen	2457
81	Jim Rice	2452
82	Rickey Henderson	2450
83	Red Schoendienst	2449
84	Dwight Evans	2446
85	Harold Baines	2425
86	Pie Traynor	2416
87	Mickey Mantle	2415
88	Stuffy McInnis	2405
89	Enos Slaughter	2383
90	Edd Roush	2376
91	Lou Whitaker	2369
92	Alan Trammell	2365
93	Carlton Fisk	2356
94	Joe Judge	2352
	Tim Raines	2352
96	Orlando Cepeda	2351
97	Billy Herman	2345
98	Joe Torre	2342
99	Dave Concepcion	2326
	Jake Daubert	2326

Doubles

1	Tris Speaker	792
2	Pete Rose	746
3	Stan Musial	725
4	Ty Cobb	724
5	George Brett	665
6	Nap Lajoie	657
7	Carl Yastrzemski	646
8	Honus Wagner	640
9	Hank Aaron	624
10	Paul Waner	605
11	Robin Yount	583
12	Charlie Gehringer	574
13	Eddie Murray	553
14	Paul Molitor	544
15	Harry Heilmann	542
16	Rogers Hornsby	541
17	Joe Medwick	540
	Dave Winfield	540
19	Al Simmons	539
20	Lou Gehrig	534
21	Al Oliver	529
22	Cap Anson	528
	Frank Robinson	528
24	Dave Parker	526
25	Ted Williams	525
26	Willie Mays	523
27	Ed Delahanty	522
28	Wade Boggs	518
29	Joe Cronin	515
30	Babe Ruth	506
31	Tony Perez	505
32	Andre Dawson	503
33	Goose Goslin	500
34	Rusty Staub	499
35	Bill Buckner	498
	Al Kaline	498
	Sam Rice	498
38	Heinie Manush	491
39	Mickey Vernon	490
40	Mel Ott	488
41	Cal Ripken	487
42	Lou Brock	486
	Billy Herman	486
44	Vada Pinson	485
45	Hal McRae	484
46	Dwight Evans	483
	Ted Simmons	483
48	Brooks Robinson	482
49	Zack Wheat	476
50	Jake Beckley	473
51	Frankie Frisch	466
52	Jim Bottomley	465
53	Reggie Jackson	463
54	Dan Brouthers	460
55	Sam Crawford	458
	Jimmie Foxx	458
57	Jimmy Dykes	453
58	George Davis	451
	Jimmy Ryan	451
60	Joe Morgan	449
61	Rod Carew	445
62	George Burns	444
63	Dick Bartell	442
	Don Mattingly	442
65	Roger Connor	441
66	Luke Appling	440
	Roberto Clemente	440
	Steve Garvey	440
69	Eddie Collins	438
70	Cesar Cedeno	436
	Joe Sewell	436
72	Wally Moses	435
73	Billy Williams	434
74	Joe Judge	433
75	Tim Wallach	432
76	Red Schoendienst	427
77	Keith Hernandez	426
78	Buddy Bell	425
	Sherry Magee	425
	George Sisler	425
81	Willie Stargell	423
82	Carlton Fisk	421
83	Lou Whitaker	420
84	Max Carey	419
85	Orlando Cepeda	417
86	Harold Baines	416
87	Cecil Cooper	415
88	Jim O'Rourke	414
	Kirby Puckett	414
90	Bill Dahlen	413
	Enos Slaughter	413
92	Rickey Henderson	412
	Joe Kuhel	412
	Alan Trammell	412
95	Lave Cross	411
	Tony Gwynn	411
97	Mike Schmidt	408
98	Ernie Banks	407
	Ben Chapman	407
	Frank White	407

Triples

1	Sam Crawford	309
2	Ty Cobb	295
3	Honus Wagner	252
4	Jake Beckley	243
5	Roger Connor	233
6	Tris Speaker	222
7	Fred Clarke	220
8	Dan Brouthers	205
9	Joe Kelley	194
10	Paul Waner	191
11	Bid McPhee	188
12	Eddie Collins	187
13	Ed Delahanty	185
14	Sam Rice	184
15	Jesse Burkett	182
	Edd Roush	182
17	Ed Konetchy	181
18	Buck Ewing	178
19	Rabbit Maranville	177
	Stan Musial	177
21	Harry Stovey	174
22	Goose Goslin	173
23	Tommy Leach	172
	Zack Wheat	172
25	Rogers Hornsby	169
26	Joe Jackson	168
27	Roberto Clemente	166
	Sherry Magee	166
29	Jake Daubert	165
30	Elmer Flick	164
	George Sisler	164
	Pie Traynor	164
33	Bill Dahlen	163
	George Davis	163
	Lou Gehrig	163
	Nap Lajoie	163
37	Mike Tiernan	162
38	George Van Haltren	161
39	Harry Hooper	160
	Heinie Manush	160
	Sam Thompson	160
42	Max Carey	159
	Joe Judge	159
44	Ed McKean	158
45	Kiki Cuyler	157
	Jimmy Ryan	157
47	Tommy Corcoran	155
48	Earle Combs	154
49	Jim Bottomley	151
	Harry Heilmann	151
51	Kip Selbach	149
	Al Simmons	149
53	Wally Pipp	148
	Enos Slaughter	148
55	Bobby Veach	147
	Willie Wilson	147
57	Charlie Gehringer	146
58	Harry Davis	145
	Willie Keeler	145
60	Bobby Wallace	143
61	Lou Brock	141
62	Willie Mays	140
63	John Reilly	139
64	Tom Brown	138
	Willie Davis	138
	Frankie Frisch	138
	Jimmy Williams	138
68	George Brett	137
69	Babe Ruth	136
	Jimmy Sheckard	136
	Elmer Smith	136
72	Lave Cross	135
	Pete Rose	135
74	Shano Collins	133
75	Jim O'Rourke	132
	George Wood	132
77	Joe DiMaggio	131
	Buck Freeman	131
79	Buddy Myer	130
80	Oyster Burns	129
	Larry Gardner	129
82	Earl Averill	128
	Brett Butler	128
	Arky Vaughan	128
85	Vada Pinson	127
86	Hardy Richardson	126
	Robin Yount	126
88	Jimmie Foxx	125
89	John Anderson	124
	Cap Anson	124
	Hal Chase	124
	Frank Schulte	124
93	Larry Doyle	123
	Duke Farrell	123
95	Dummy Hoy	121
96	Mickey Vernon	120
97	Hugh Duffy	119
	Fred Pfeffer	119
99	3 players tied	118

Triples (by era)

1876-1892

1	Roger Connor	233
2	Dan Brouthers	205
3	Bid McPhee	188
4	Buck Ewing	178
5	Harry Stovey	174
6	Sam Thompson	160
7	John Reilly	139
8	Tom Brown	138
9	Jim O'Rourke	132
	George Wood	132
11	Oyster Burns	129
12	Hardy Richardson	126
13	Cap Anson	124
14	Fred Pfeffer	119
15	Bill Kuehne	115

1893-1919

1	Sam Crawford	309
2	Ty Cobb	295
3	Honus Wagner	252
4	Jake Beckley	243
5	Tris Speaker	222
6	Fred Clarke	220
7	Joe Kelley	194
8	Eddie Collins	187
9	Ed Delahanty	185
10	Jesse Burkett	182
11	Ed Konetchy	181
12	Tommy Leach	172
	Zack Wheat	172
14	Joe Jackson	168
15	Sherry Magee	166

1920-1941

1	Paul Waner	191
2	Sam Rice	184
3	Edd Roush	182
4	Rabbit Maranville	177
5	Goose Goslin	173
6	Rogers Hornsby	169
7	George Sisler	164
	Pie Traynor	164
9	Lou Gehrig	163
10	Heinie Manush	160
11	Max Carey	159
	Joe Judge	159
13	Kiki Cuyler	157
14	Earle Combs	154
15	2 players tied	151

1942-1960

1	Stan Musial	177
2	Enos Slaughter	148
3	Joe DiMaggio	131
4	Mickey Vernon	120
5	Nellie Fox	112
6	Wally Moses	110
7	Richie Ashburn	109
8	Bill Bruton	102
	Jeff Heath	102
10	Phil Cavarretta	99
11	Dixie Walker	96
12	Bob Elliott	94
13	Bobby Doerr	89
14	Duke Snider	85
15	2 players tied	83

1961-1976

1	Roberto Clemente	166
2	Lou Brock	141
3	Willie Mays	140
4	Willie Davis	138
5	Pete Rose	135
6	Vada Pinson	127
7	Rod Carew	112
8	Hank Aaron	98
9	Joe Morgan	96
10	Luis Aparicio	92
11	Ernie Banks	90
12	Johnny Callison	89
13	Billy Williams	88
14	Bert Campaneris	86
	Tony Taylor	86

1977-1996

1	Willie Wilson	147
2	George Brett	137
3	Brett Butler	128
4	Robin Yount	126
5	Tim Raines	109
6	Garry Templeton	106
7	Paul Molitor	105
8	Larry Bowa	99
	Lance Johnson	99
10	Andre Dawson	98
	Juan Samuel	98
12	Jose Cruz	94
13	Andy Van Slyke	91
14	3 players tied	89

Home Runs

1	Hank Aaron	755
2	Babe Ruth	714
3	Willie Mays	660
4	Frank Robinson	586
5	Harmon Killebrew	573
6	Reggie Jackson	563
7	Mike Schmidt	548
8	Mickey Mantle	536
9	Jimmie Foxx	534
10	Willie McCovey	521
	Ted Williams	521
12	Ernie Banks	512
	Eddie Mathews	512
14	Mel Ott	511
15	Eddie Murray	501
16	Lou Gehrig	493
17	Stan Musial	475
	Willie Stargell	475
19	Dave Winfield	465
20	Carl Yastrzemski	452
21	Dave Kingman	442
22	Andre Dawson	438
23	Billy Williams	426
24	Darrell Evans	414
25	Duke Snider	407
26	Al Kaline	399
27	Dale Murphy	398
28	Graig Nettles	390
29	Johnny Bench	389
30	Dwight Evans	385
31	Frank Howard	382
	Jim Rice	382
33	Orlando Cepeda	379
	Tony Perez	379
35	Norm Cash	377
36	Carlton Fisk	376
37	Rocky Colavito	374
38	Gil Hodges	370
39	Ralph Kiner	369
40	Joe DiMaggio	361
41	Johnny Mize	359
42	Yogi Berra	358
43	Joe Carter	357
44	Lee May	354
45	Cal Ripken	353
46	Dick Allen	351
47	George Foster	348
48	Ron Santo	342
49	Jack Clark	340
50	Dave Parker	339
	Boog Powell	339
52	Don Baylor	338
53	Joe Adcock	336
54	Barry Bonds	334
55	Bobby Bonds	332
56	Hank Greenberg	331
57	Mark McGwire	329
58	Jose Canseco	328
59	Willie Horton	325
60	Gary Carter	324
	Lance Parrish	324
62	Harold Baines	323
63	Roy Sievers	318
64	George Brett	317
	Fred McGriff	317
66	Ron Cey	316
67	Gary Gaetti	315
68	Reggie Smith	314
69	Darryl Strawberry	308
70	Greg Luzinski	307
	Al Simmons	307
72	Fred Lynn	306
73	Rogers Hornsby	301
74	Chuck Klein	300
75	Chili Davis	298
76	Kent Hrbek	293
77	Rusty Staub	292
78	Jim Wynn	291
79	Cecil Fielder	289
80	Del Ennis	288
	Bob Johnson	288
	Hank Sauer	288
83	Frank Thomas	286
84	Ken Boyer	282
85	Ted Kluszewski	279
86	Rudy York	277
87	Brian Downing	275
	Roger Maris	275
89	Steve Garvey	272
90	Tom Brunansky	271
	George Scott	271
92	Ryne Sandberg	270
93	Joe Morgan	268
	Brooks Robinson	268
	Gorman Thomas	268
96	George Hendrick	267
97	Vic Wertz	266
98	George Bell	265
99	Bobby Thomson	264
100	Danny Tartabull	262

Home Runs (by era)

1876-1892

1	Roger Connor	138
2	Sam Thompson	127
3	Harry Stovey	122
4	Dan Brouthers	106
5	Cap Anson	97
6	Fred Pfeffer	94
7	Jack Clements	77
8	Jerry Denny	74
9	Buck Ewing	71
10	Hardy Richardson	70
11	King Kelly	69
	John Reilly	69
13	George Wood	68
14	Oyster Burns	65
	Bug Holliday	65

1893-1919

1	Zack Wheat	132
2	Gavvy Cravath	119
3	Jimmy Ryan	118
	Tilly Walker	118
5	Ty Cobb	117
	Tris Speaker	117
7	Hugh Duffy	106
	Mike Tiernan	106
9	Ed Delahanty	101
	Honus Wagner	101
11	Sam Crawford	97
12	Frank Baker	96
13	Frank Schulte	92
14	Herman Long	91
15	Jake Beckley	86

1920-1941

1	Babe Ruth	714
2	Jimmie Foxx	534
3	Mel Ott	511
4	Lou Gehrig	493
5	Hank Greenberg	331
6	Al Simmons	307
7	Rogers Hornsby	301
8	Chuck Klein	300
9	Bob Johnson	288
10	Cy Williams	251
11	Goose Goslin	248
12	Hack Wilson	244
13	Wally Berger	242
14	Dolph Camilli	239
15	Earl Averill	238

1942-1960

1	Mickey Mantle	536
2	Ted Williams	521
3	Eddie Mathews	512
4	Stan Musial	475
5	Duke Snider	407
6	Gil Hodges	370
7	Ralph Kiner	369
8	Joe DiMaggio	361
9	Johnny Mize	359
10	Yogi Berra	358
11	Joe Adcock	336
12	Roy Sievers	318
13	Del Ennis	288
	Hank Sauer	288
15	Frank Thomas	286

1961-1976

1	Hank Aaron	755
2	Willie Mays	660
3	Frank Robinson	586
4	Harmon Killebrew	573
5	Willie McCovey	521
6	Ernie Banks	512
7	Willie Stargell	475
8	Carl Yastrzemski	452
9	Billy Williams	426
10	Al Kaline	399
11	Johnny Bench	389
12	Frank Howard	382
13	Orlando Cepeda	379
	Tony Perez	379
15	Norm Cash	377

1977-1996

1	Reggie Jackson	563
2	Mike Schmidt	548
3	Eddie Murray	501
4	Dave Winfield	465
5	Dave Kingman	442
6	Andre Dawson	438
7	Darrell Evans	414
8	Dale Murphy	398
9	Graig Nettles	390
10	Dwight Evans	385
11	Jim Rice	382
12	Carlton Fisk	376
13	Joe Carter	357
14	Cal Ripken	353
15	George Foster	348

Home Run Percentage

1	Babe Ruth	8.50
2	Mark McGwire	8.06
3	Ralph Kiner	7.09
4	Harmon Killebrew	7.03
5	Ted Williams	6.76
6	Dave Kingman	6.62
7	Mickey Mantle	6.62
8	Cecil Fielder	6.60
9	Jimmie Foxx	6.57
10	Mike Schmidt	6.56
11	Jose Canseco	6.47
12	Hank Greenberg	6.37
13	Willie McCovey	6.36
14	Fred McGriff	6.18
15	Lou Gehrig	6.16
16	Hank Aaron	6.11
17	Darryl Strawberry	6.11
18	Willie Mays	6.07
19	Barry Bonds	6.03
20	Hank Sauer	6.01
21	Eddie Mathews	6.00
22	Jay Buhner	5.99
23	Willie Stargell	5.99
24	Ken Griffey Jr.	5.97
25	Matt Williams	5.97
26	Rob Deer	5.93
27	Frank Howard	5.89
28	Frank Robinson	5.86
29	Kevin Mitchell	5.78
30	Bob Horner	5.77
31	Roy Campanella	5.76
32	Rocky Colavito	5.75
33	Gus Zernial	5.74
34	Gorman Thomas	5.73
35	Reggie Jackson	5.71
36	Dick Stuart	5.70
37	Duke Snider	5.68
38	Norm Cash	5.62
39	Eric Davis	5.62
40	Johnny Mize	5.57
41	Dick Allen	5.54
42	Ernie Banks	5.43
43	Mel Ott	5.40
44	Roger Maris	5.39
45	Joe DiMaggio	5.29
46	Gil Hodges	5.26
47	Wally Post	5.24
48	Danny Tartabull	5.24
49	Mickey Tettleton	5.20
50	Al Rosen	5.15
51	Hack Wilson	5.13
52	Ron Gant	5.12
53	Glenn Davis	5.11
54	Bob Allison	5.09
55	Joe Adcock	5.09
56	Johnny Bench	5.08
57	Boog Powell	5.07
58	Jesse Barfield	5.06
59	Nate Colbert	5.06
60	Dale Murphy	5.00
61	Charlie Keller	4.99
62	Roy Sievers	4.98
63	Cliff Johnson	4.97
64	Don Mincher	4.97
65	Jack Clark	4.97
66	Pete Incaviglia	4.96
67	George Foster	4.96
68	Tony Armas	4.86
69	Joe Carter	4.81
70	Andy Thornton	4.78
71	Orlando Cepeda	4.78
72	Leon Wagner	4.77
73	Jim Lemon	4.76
74	Yogi Berra	4.74
75	Don Demeter	4.73
76	Kent Hrbek	4.73
77	Larry Doby	4.73
78	Greg Luzinski	4.72
79	Bobby Bonds	4.71
80	Ted Kluszewski	4.71
81	Rudy York	4.70
82	Wally Berger	4.69
83	John Mayberry	4.68
84	Lee May	4.65
85	Jim Rice	4.64
86	Chuck Klein	4.63
87	Howard Johnson	4.62
88	Darrell Evans	4.61
89	Lance Parrish	4.58
90	Gene Tenace	4.58
91	Charlie Maxwell	4.56
92	Billy Williams	4.56
93	Frank Thomas	4.55
94	Andres Galarraga	4.51
95	Jim Ray Hart	4.49
96	Eddie Murray	4.49
97	Gary Roenicke	4.47
98	Dolph Camilli	4.46
99	Reggie Smith	4.46
100	Woodie Held	4.45

Home Run Pctg. (by era)

1876-1892

1	Sam Thompson	2.12
2	Harry Stovey	1.99
3	Jack Clements	1.80
4	Roger Connor	1.77
5	Dan Brouthers	1.58
6	Jerry Denny	1.50
7	John Reilly	1.47
8	Denny Lyons	1.44
9	Charlie Bennett	1.44
10	Fred Pfeffer	1.43
11	Ned Williamson	1.41
12	Oyster Burns	1.40
13	Buck Ewing	1.32
14	George Wood	1.27
15	Hardy Richardson	1.24

1893-1919

1	Gavvy Cravath	3.01
2	Tilly Walker	2.33
3	Buck Freeman	1.95
4	Mike Tiernan	1.79
5	Fred Luderus	1.73
6	Frank Baker	1.60
7	Hugh Duffy	1.51
8	Charlie Hickman	1.48
9	Zack Wheat	1.45
10	Jimmy Ryan	1.45
11	Frank Schulte	1.41
12	Casey Stengel	1.40
13	Ed Delahanty	1.35
14	Mike Donlin	1.32
15	Chief Wilson	1.28

1920-1941

1	Babe Ruth	8.50
2	Jimmie Foxx	6.57
3	Hank Greenberg	6.37
4	Lou Gehrig	6.16
5	Mel Ott	5.40
6	Hack Wilson	5.13
7	Wally Berger	4.69
8	Chuck Klein	4.63
9	Dolph Camilli	4.46
10	Hal Trosky	4.42
11	Bob Johnson	4.16
12	Ken Williams	4.03
13	Earl Averill	3.75
14	Cy Williams	3.70
15	Rogers Hornsby	3.68

1942-1960

1	Ralph Kiner	7.09
2	Ted Williams	6.76
3	Mickey Mantle	6.62
4	Hank Sauer	6.01
5	Eddie Mathews	6.00
6	Roy Campanella	5.76
7	Gus Zernial	5.74
8	Duke Snider	5.68
9	Johnny Mize	5.57
10	Joe DiMaggio	5.29
11	Gil Hodges	5.26
12	Wally Post	5.24
13	Al Rosen	5.15
14	Joe Adcock	5.09
15	Charlie Keller	4.99

1961-1976

1	Harmon Killebrew	7.03
2	Willie McCovey	6.36
3	Hank Aaron	6.11
4	Willie Mays	6.07
5	Willie Stargell	5.99
6	Frank Howard	5.89
7	Frank Robinson	5.86
8	Rocky Colavito	5.75
9	Dick Stuart	5.70
10	Norm Cash	5.62
11	Dick Allen	5.54
12	Ernie Banks	5.43
13	Roger Maris	5.39
14	Bob Allison	5.09
15	Johnny Bench	5.08

1977-1996

1	Mark McGwire	8.06
2	Dave Kingman	6.62
3	Cecil Fielder	6.60
4	Mike Schmidt	6.56
5	Jose Canseco	6.47
6	Fred McGriff	6.18
7	Darryl Strawberry	6.11
8	Barry Bonds	6.03
9	Jay Buhner	5.99
10	Ken Griffey Jr.	5.97
11	Matt Williams	5.97
12	Rob Deer	5.93
13	Kevin Mitchell	5.78
14	Bob Horner	5.77
15	Gorman Thomas	5.73

Total Bases

1	Hank Aaron	6856
2	Stan Musial	6134
3	Willie Mays	6066
4	Ty Cobb	5854
5	Babe Ruth	5793
6	Pete Rose	5752
7	Carl Yastrzemski	5539
8	Frank Robinson	5373
9	Eddie Murray	5344
10	Dave Winfield	5221
11	Tris Speaker	5101
12	Lou Gehrig	5060
13	George Brett	5044
14	Mel Ott	5041
15	Jimmie Foxx	4956
16	Ted Williams	4884
17	Honus Wagner	4862
18	Al Kaline	4852
19	Reggie Jackson	4834
20	Andre Dawson	4787
21	Robin Yount	4730
22	Rogers Hornsby	4712
23	Ernie Banks	4706
24	Al Simmons	4685
25	Billy Williams	4599
26	Tony Perez	4532
27	Mickey Mantle	4511
28	Roberto Clemente	4492
29	Paul Waner	4478
30	Nap Lajoie	4474
31	Paul Molitor	4428
32	Dave Parker	4405
33	Mike Schmidt	4404
34	Eddie Mathews	4349
35	Sam Crawford	4328
36	Goose Goslin	4325
37	Brooks Robinson	4270
38	Eddie Collins	4268
39	Vada Pinson	4264
40	Charlie Gehringer	4257
41	Lou Brock	4238
42	Dwight Evans	4230
43	Willie McCovey	4219
44	Willie Stargell	4190
45	Rusty Staub	4185
46	Cal Ripken	4181
47	Jake Beckley	4147
48	Harmon Killebrew	4143
49	Jim Rice	4129
50	Zack Wheat	4100
51	Al Oliver	4083
52	Cap Anson	4062
53	Harry Heilmann	4053
54	Carlton Fisk	3999
55	Rod Carew	3998
56	Joe Morgan	3962
57	Orlando Cepeda	3959
58	Sam Rice	3955
59	Joe DiMaggio	3948
60	Steve Garvey	3941
61	Frankie Frisch	3937
62	Harold Baines	3906
63	George Sisler	3871
64	Darrell Evans	3866
65	Duke Snider	3865
66	Joe Medwick	3852
67	Bill Buckner	3833
68	Ted Simmons	3793
69	Ed Delahanty	3791
70	Roger Connor	3788
71	Graig Nettles	3779
	Ron Santo	3779
73	Willie Davis	3778
74	Jesse Burkett	3759
75	Mickey Vernon	3741
76	Jim Bottomley	3737
77	Dale Murphy	3733
78	Rickey Henderson	3712
79	Fred Clarke	3674
80	Heinie Manush	3665
81	George Davis	3656
82	Buddy Bell	3654
83	Lou Whitaker	3651
84	Johnny Bench	3644
85	Yogi Berra	3643
86	Wade Boggs	3640
87	Johnny Mize	3621
	Jimmy Ryan	3621
89	Max Carey	3612
90	Ryne Sandberg	3607
91	Enos Slaughter	3599
92	Don Baylor	3571
93	Willie Keeler	3562
94	Joe Torre	3560
95	Joe Cronin	3546
96	Luke Appling	3528
97	Chuck Klein	3522
98	Luis Aparicio	3504
99	Bob Johnson	3501
100	Gary Carter	3497

Runs Batted In

1	Hank Aaron	2297
2	Babe Ruth	2213
3	Lou Gehrig	1995
4	Stan Musial	1951
5	Ty Cobb	1937
6	Jimmie Foxx	1922
7	Willie Mays	1903
8	Eddie Murray	1899
9	Cap Anson	1879
10	Mel Ott	1860
11	Carl Yastrzemski	1844
12	Ted Williams	1839
13	Dave Winfield	1833
14	Al Simmons	1827
15	Frank Robinson	1812
16	Honus Wagner	1732
17	Reggie Jackson	1702
18	Tony Perez	1652
19	Ernie Banks	1636
20	Goose Goslin	1609
21	Nap Lajoie	1599
22	George Brett	1595
	Mike Schmidt	1595
24	Andre Dawson	1591
25	Rogers Hornsby	1584
	Harmon Killebrew	1584
27	Al Kaline	1583
28	Jake Beckley	1575
29	Willie McCovey	1555
30	Willie Stargell	1540
31	Harry Heilmann	1539
32	Joe DiMaggio	1537
33	Tris Speaker	1529
34	Sam Crawford	1525
35	Mickey Mantle	1509
36	Dave Parker	1493
37	Billy Williams	1475
38	Rusty Staub	1466
39	Ed Delahanty	1464
40	Eddie Mathews	1453
41	Jim Rice	1451
42	George Davis	1437
43	Yogi Berra	1430
44	Charlie Gehringer	1427
45	Joe Cronin	1424
46	Jim Bottomley	1422
47	Robin Yount	1406
48	Ted Simmons	1389
49	Dwight Evans	1384
50	Joe Medwick	1383
51	Johnny Bench	1376
52	Lave Cross	1371
53	Cal Ripken	1369
54	Orlando Cepeda	1365
55	Brooks Robinson	1357
56	Harold Baines	1356
57	Darrell Evans	1354
58	Johnny Mize	1337
59	Duke Snider	1333
60	Ron Santo	1331
61	Carlton Fisk	1330
62	Al Oliver	1326
63	Roger Connor	1322
64	Graig Nettles	1314
	Pete Rose	1314
66	Mickey Vernon	1311
67	Paul Waner	1309
68	Steve Garvey	1308
69	Roberto Clemente	1305
70	Enos Slaughter	1304
71	Hugh Duffy	1302
72	Eddie Collins	1300
73	Sam Thompson	1299
74	Dan Brouthers	1296
75	Del Ennis	1284
76	Bob Johnson	1283
77	Joe Carter	1280
78	Don Baylor	1276
	Hank Greenberg	1276
80	Gil Hodges	1274
81	Pie Traynor	1273
82	Dale Murphy	1266
83	Zack Wheat	1248
84	Bobby Doerr	1247
85	Frankie Frisch	1244
	Lee May	1244
87	George Foster	1239
88	Bill Dahlen	1233
89	Gary Carter	1225
90	Dave Kingman	1210
91	Bill Dickey	1209
92	Bill Buckner	1208
93	Chuck Klein	1201
94	Chili Davis	1195
	Bob Elliott	1195
96	Joe Kelley	1194
97	Tony Lazzeri	1191
98	Boog Powell	1187
99	Joe Torre	1185
100	Heinie Manush	1183

Runs Batted In (by era)

1876-1892

1	Cap Anson	1879
2	Roger Connor	1322
3	Sam Thompson	1299
4	Dan Brouthers	1296
5	Bid McPhee	1067
6	Fred Pfeffer	1019
7	Jim O'Rourke	1010
8	Billy Nash	977
9	King Kelly	950
10	Harry Stovey	908
11	Charlie Comiskey	883
	Buck Ewing	883
13	John Ward	867
14	Henry Larkin	836
15	Lou Bierbauer	835

1893-1919

1	Ty Cobb	1937
2	Honus Wagner	1732
3	Nap Lajoie	1599
4	Jake Beckley	1575
5	Tris Speaker	1529
6	Sam Crawford	1525
7	Ed Delahanty	1464
8	George Davis	1437
9	Lave Cross	1371
10	Hugh Duffy	1302
11	Eddie Collins	1300
12	Zack Wheat	1248
13	Bill Dahlen	1233
14	Joe Kelley	1194
15	Sherry Magee	1176

1920-1941

1	Babe Ruth	2213
2	Lou Gehrig	1995
3	Jimmie Foxx	1922
4	Mel Ott	1860
5	Al Simmons	1827
6	Goose Goslin	1609
7	Rogers Hornsby	1584
8	Harry Heilmann	1539
9	Charlie Gehringer	1427
10	Joe Cronin	1424
11	Jim Bottomley	1422
12	Joe Medwick	1383
13	Paul Waner	1309
14	Bob Johnson	1283
15	Hank Greenberg	1276

1942-1960

1	Stan Musial	1951
2	Ted Williams	1839
3	Joe DiMaggio	1537
4	Mickey Mantle	1509
5	Eddie Mathews	1453
6	Yogi Berra	1430
7	Johnny Mize	1337
8	Duke Snider	1333
9	Mickey Vernon	1311
10	Enos Slaughter	1304
11	Del Ennis	1284
12	Gil Hodges	1274
13	Bobby Doerr	1247
14	Bob Elliott	1195
15	Vic Wertz	1178

1961-1976

1	Hank Aaron	2297
2	Willie Mays	1903
3	Carl Yastrzemski	1844
4	Frank Robinson	1812
5	Tony Perez	1652
6	Ernie Banks	1636
7	Harmon Killebrew	1584
8	Al Kaline	1583
9	Willie McCovey	1555
10	Willie Stargell	1540
11	Billy Williams	1475
12	Rusty Staub	1466
13	Johnny Bench	1376
14	Orlando Cepeda	1365
15	Brooks Robinson	1357

1977-1996

1	Eddie Murray	1899
2	Dave Winfield	1833
3	Reggie Jackson	1702
4	George Brett	1595
	Mike Schmidt	1595
6	Andre Dawson	1591
7	Dave Parker	1493
8	Jim Rice	1451
9	Robin Yount	1406
10	Ted Simmons	1389
11	Dwight Evans	1384
12	Cal Ripken	1369
13	Harold Baines	1356
14	Darrell Evans	1354
15	Carlton Fisk	1330

Runs Batted In per Game

1	Sam Thompson	.92
2	Lou Gehrig	.92
3	Hank Greenberg	.92
4	Joe DiMaggio	.89
5	Babe Ruth	.88
6	Jimmie Foxx	.83
7	Cap Anson	.83
8	Al Simmons	.82
9	Ted Williams	.80
10	Ed Delahanty	.80
11	Hack Wilson	.79
12	Dan Brouthers	.77
13	Jose Canseco	.77
14	Bob Meusel	.76
15	Hal Trosky	.75
16	Hugh Duffy	.75
17	Rudy York	.72
18	Tip O'Neill	.72
19	Harry Heilmann	.72
20	Jim Bottomley	.71
21	Johnny Mize	.71
22	Henry Larkin	.71
23	Roy Campanella	.70
24	Goose Goslin	.70
25	Mark McGwire	.70
26	Rogers Hornsby	.70
27	Oyster Burns	.70
28	Cecil Fielder	.70
29	Earl Averill	.70
30	Joe Medwick	.70
31	Hank Aaron	.70
32	Jim Rice	.69
33	Ralph Kiner	.69
34	Bob Johnson	.69
35	Al Rosen	.69
36	Ken Griffey Jr.	.69
37	Chuck Klein	.69
38	Tony Lazzeri	.68
39	Vern Stephens	.68
40	Mel Ott	.68
41	Ed McKean	.68
42	Bill Dickey	.68
43	Del Ennis	.67
44	Yogi Berra	.67
45	Denny Lyons	.67
46	Bob Horner	.67
47	Joe Carter	.67
48	Buck Ewing	.67
49	Joe Cronin	.67
50	Jay Buhner	.67
51	Bobby Doerr	.67
52	Dick Stuart	.67
53	Wally Berger	.67
54	Mike Schmidt	.66
55	Roger Connor	.66
56	Jake Beckley	.66
57	Dave Foutz	.66
58	Danny Tartabull	.66
59	Pie Traynor	.66
60	Hughie Jennings	.65
61	Matt Williams	.65
62	Ken Williams	.65
63	King Kelly	.65
64	Willie Stargell	.65
65	Harmon Killebrew	.65
66	Charlie Keller	.65
67	Chick Hafey	.65
68	John Reilly	.65
69	Ernie Banks	.65
70	Darryl Strawberry	.65
71	Glenn Wright	.65
72	Jackie Jensen	.65
73	Frank Robinson	.65
74	Nap Lajoie	.64
75	Stan Musial	.64
76	Joe Kelley	.64
77	Orlando Cepeda	.64
78	Babe Herman	.64
79	Ruben Sierra	.64
80	Jeff Heath	.64
81	Bobby Veach	.64
82	Dick Allen	.64
83	Eddie Murray	.64
84	Ty Cobb	.64
85	Johnny Bench	.64
86	Dolph Camilli	.64
87	Willie Mays	.64
88	Irish Meusel	.64
89	Charlie Comiskey	.64
90	Buck Freeman	.63
91	Larry Doby	.63
92	Vic Wertz	.63
93	Kevin Mitchell	.63
94	George Bell	.63
95	Will Clark	.63
96	Billy Nash	.63
97	Patsy Tebeau	.63
98	Rocky Colavito	.63
99	George Kelly	.63
100	Gus Zernial	.63

Walks

1	Babe Ruth	2056
2	Ted Williams	2019
3	Joe Morgan	1865
4	Carl Yastrzemski	1845
5	Mickey Mantle	1733
6	Mel Ott	1708
7	Rickey Henderson	1675
8	Eddie Yost	1614
9	Darrell Evans	1605
10	Stan Musial	1599
11	Pete Rose	1566
12	Harmon Killebrew	1559
13	Lou Gehrig	1508
14	Mike Schmidt	1507
15	Eddie Collins	1499
16	Willie Mays	1464
17	Jimmie Foxx	1452
18	Eddie Mathews	1444
19	Frank Robinson	1420
20	Hank Aaron	1402
21	Dwight Evans	1391
22	Tris Speaker	1381
23	Reggie Jackson	1375
24	Willie McCovey	1345
25	Eddie Murray	1318
26	Luke Appling	1302
27	Wade Boggs	1280
28	Al Kaline	1277
29	Ken Singleton	1263
30	Jack Clark	1262
31	Rusty Staub	1255
32	Ty Cobb	1249
33	Willie Randolph	1243
34	Jim Wynn	1224
35	Dave Winfield	1216
36	Pee Wee Reese	1210
37	Richie Ashburn	1198
38	Brian Downing	1197
	Lou Whitaker	1197
40	Billy Hamilton	1187
41	Charlie Gehringer	1186
42	Tim Raines	1168
43	Donie Bush	1158
44	Max Bishop	1153
	Toby Harrah	1153
46	Harry Hooper	1136
47	Jimmy Sheckard	1135
48	Ron Santo	1108
49	Tony Phillips	1099
50	George Brett	1096
51	Lu Blue	1092
	Stan Hack	1092
53	Paul Waner	1091
54	Graig Nettles	1088
55	Brett Butler	1087
	Bobby Grich	1087
57	Barry Bonds	1082
58	Bob Johnson	1075
59	Ozzie Smith	1072
60	Harlond Clift	1070
	Keith Hernandez	1070
62	Bill Dahlen	1064
63	Joe Cronin	1059
64	Ron Fairly	1052
65	Billy Williams	1045
66	Norm Cash	1043
	Eddie Joost	1043
68	Roy Thomas	1042
69	Max Carey	1040
70	Rogers Hornsby	1038
71	Jim Gilliam	1036
72	Sal Bando	1031
73	Jesse Burkett	1029
74	Chili Davis	1022
75	Rod Carew	1018
	Enos Slaughter	1018
77	Ron Cey	1012
78	Ralph Kiner	1011
79	Dummy Hoy	1004
	Paul Molitor	1004
81	Miller Huggins	1003
82	Roger Connor	1002
83	Boog Powell	1001
84	Eddie Stanky	996
85	Cupid Childs	991
86	Dale Murphy	986
87	Gene Tenace	984
88	Bid McPhee	981
89	Joe Kuhel	980
	Earl Torgeson	980
91	Augie Galan	979
92	Duke Snider	971
93	Bob Elliott	967
94	Robin Yount	966
95	Mike Hargrove	965
	Joe Judge	965
	Buddy Myer	965
98	Honus Wagner	963
99	Cal Ripken	960
100	Jimmy Dykes	958

Walk Percentage

1	Ted Williams	20.76
2	Max Bishop	20.42
3	Babe Ruth	19.67
4	Eddie Stanky	18.80
5	Ferris Fain	18.70
6	Gene Tenace	18.31
7	Roy Cullenbine	18.03
8	Eddie Yost	18.01
9	Mickey Mantle	17.62
10	John McGraw	17.56
11	Charlie Keller	17.14
12	Mickey Tettleton	16.89
13	Joe Morgan	16.74
14	Earl Torgeson	16.47
15	Bernie Carbo	16.45
16	Roy Thomas	16.44
17	Rickey Henderson	16.42
18	Barry Bonds	16.35
19	Ralph Kiner	16.26
20	Mark McGwire	16.20
21	Harmon Killebrew	16.06
22	Billy Hamilton	15.92
23	Lou Gehrig	15.86
24	Elmer Valo	15.78
25	Joe Ferguson	15.77
26	Harlond Clift	15.74
27	Eddie Joost	15.69
28	Lu Blue	15.61
29	Jack Clark	15.56
30	Jim Wynn	15.54
31	Mel Ott	15.30
32	Miller Huggins	15.29
33	Mike Schmidt	15.29
34	Darrell Evans	15.17
35	Jimmie Foxx	15.15
36	Joe Cunningham	15.12
37	Dolph Camilli	15.03
38	Cupid Childs	14.99
39	Ken Singleton	14.94
40	Elbie Fletcher	14.85
41	Merv Rettenmund	14.83
42	Mike Hargrove	14.78
43	Dave Magadan	14.75
44	Topsy Hartsel	14.72
45	Dwayne Murphy	14.66
46	Darren Daulton	14.60
47	Wayne Garrett	14.59
48	Tony Phillips	14.58
49	Jason Thompson	14.52
50	Eddie Mathews	14.47
51	John Kruk	14.28
52	Mickey Cochrane	14.22
53	Andy Thornton	14.20
54	Augie Galan	14.16
55	Gene Woodling	14.15
56	Willie McCovey	14.10
57	Hank Greenberg	14.09
58	Darrell Porter	14.04
59	Larry Doby	14.01
60	John Mayberry	13.92
61	Alvin Davis	13.91
62	Johnny Briggs	13.87
63	Billy North	13.85
64	Donie Bush	13.84
65	Wally Schang	13.79
66	Roger Bresnahan	13.74
67	Paul Radford	13.69
68	Steve Braun	13.69
69	Fred McGriff	13.67
70	Wade Boggs	13.65
71	Norm Siebern	13.64
72	Bob Allison	13.64
73	Bobby Grich	13.63
74	Al Rosen	13.61
75	Toby Harrah	13.48
76	Lee Mazzilli	13.47
77	Norm Cash	13.46
78	Mike Jorgensen	13.46
79	Bob Johnson	13.45
80	Willie Randolph	13.42
81	Tommy Henrich	13.40
82	Dwight Evans	13.39
83	Rick Ferrell	13.38
84	Wayne Gross	13.36
85	Carl Yastrzemski	13.34
86	Grady Hatton	13.31
87	Lyn Lary	13.28
88	Danny Tartabull	13.25
89	Brian Downing	13.23
90	Ed Bailey	13.21
91	Jackie Robinson	13.17
92	Jack Graney	13.14
93	Eddie Collins	13.09
94	Rick Monday	13.09
95	Don Mincher	13.08
96	Pee Wee Reese	13.06
97	Jeff Burroughs	13.05
98	Stan Hack	13.05
99	Gary Roenicke	13.04
100	Boog Powell	13.03

Strikeouts

1	Reggie Jackson	2597
2	Willie Stargell	1936
3	Mike Schmidt	1883
4	Tony Perez	1867
5	Dave Kingman	1816
6	Bobby Bonds	1757
7	Dale Murphy	1748
8	Lou Brock	1730
9	Mickey Mantle	1710
10	Harmon Killebrew	1699
11	Dwight Evans	1697
12	Dave Winfield	1686
13	Lee May	1570
14	Dick Allen	1556
15	Willie McCovey	1550
16	Dave Parker	1537
17	Frank Robinson	1532
18	Lance Parrish	1527
19	Willie Mays	1526
20	Rick Monday	1513
21	Andre Dawson	1509
22	Greg Luzinski	1495
23	Eddie Murray	1490
24	Eddie Mathews	1487
25	Chili Davis	1484
26	Frank Howard	1460
27	Jack Clark	1441
28	Jim Wynn	1427
29	Jim Rice	1423
30	George Foster	1419
31	George Scott	1418
32	Darrell Evans	1410
33	Rob Deer	1409
34	Juan Samuel	1401
35	Gary Gaetti	1398
36	Carl Yastrzemski	1393
37	Carlton Fisk	1386
38	Hank Aaron	1383
39	Larry Parrish	1359
40	Danny Tartabull	1358
41	Robin Yount	1350
42	Jose Canseco	1349
43	Ron Santo	1343
44	Gorman Thomas	1339
45	Babe Ruth	1330
46	Andres Galarraga	1328
47	Deron Johnson	1318
48	Willie Horton	1313
49	Jimmie Foxx	1311
50	Tim Wallach	1307
51	Mickey Tettleton	1295
52	Kirk Gibson	1285
53	Johnny Bench	1278
	Bobby Grich	1278
55	Claudell Washington	1266
56	Ken Singleton	1246
57	Tony Phillips	1237
	Duke Snider	1237
	Darryl Strawberry	1237
60	Ernie Banks	1236
61	Ron Cey	1235
62	Jesse Barfield	1234
63	Roberto Clemente	1230
64	Boog Powell	1226
65	Harold Baines	1225
66	Joe Carter	1221
	Pete Incaviglia	1221
68	Graig Nettles	1209
69	Tony Armas	1201
70	Vada Pinson	1196
71	Rickey Henderson	1191
72	Tom Brunansky	1187
73	Dave Concepcion	1186
74	Orlando Cepeda	1169
75	Ryne Sandberg	1166
76	Devon White	1146
77	Willie Wilson	1144
78	Pete Rose	1143
79	Bert Campaneris	1142
80	Donn Clendenon	1140
81	Gil Hodges	1137
82	Jeff Burroughs	1135
	Leo Cardenas	1135
	Fred McGriff	1135
	Lloyd Moseby	1135
86	Paul Molitor	1130
87	Brian Downing	1127
88	Bob Bailey	1126
89	Gary Matthews	1125
90	Cecil Fielder	1118
91	Fred Lynn	1116
92	Dave Henderson	1105
93	Lou Whitaker	1099
94	Jim Fregosi	1097
95	Eric Davis	1096
96	Joe Torre	1094
97	Garry Templeton	1092
98	Norm Cash	1091
99	Tony Taylor	1083
100	Tommy Harper	1080

At Bats per Strikeout

1	Joe Sewell	62.6
2	Lloyd Waner	44.9
3	Nellie Fox	42.7
4	Tommy Holmes	40.9
5	Andy High	33.8
6	Sam Rice	33.7
7	Frankie Frisch	33.5
8	Dale Mitchell	33.5
9	Johnny Cooney	31.5
10	Frank McCormick	30.3
11	Don Mueller	29.9
12	Billy Southworth	29.5
13	Rip Radcliff	28.9
14	Edd Roush	28.3
15	Pie Traynor	27.2
16	Doc Cramer	26.5
17	Carson Bigbee	26.0
18	Hank Severeid	25.5
19	George Sisler	25.3
20	Paul Waner	25.2
21	Sparky Adams	24.9
22	Lou Finney	24.9
23	Deacon White	24.8
24	Jack Rowe	24.8
25	Irish Meusel	24.6
26	Ezra Sutton	24.6
27	Red Schoendienst	24.5
28	Vic Power	24.5
29	Arky Vaughan	24.0
30	Felix Millan	23.9
31	Mickey Cochrane	23.8
32	Charlie Gehringer	23.8
33	John Ward	23.5
34	George Kell	23.4
35	George Cutshaw	23.2
36	Jack Tobin	23.1
37	Taffy Wright	23.1
38	Hughie Critz	23.1
39	Mark Koenig	22.5
40	Ernie Lombardi	22.3
41	Heinie Manush	22.2
42	Bobby Richardson	22.2
43	Jo-Jo Moore	22.0
44	Earl Sheely	21.8
45	Bill Dickey	21.8
46	Johnny Pesky	21.8
47	Rick Ferrell	21.8
48	Glenn Beckert	21.4
49	Dick Siebert	21.2
50	Tony Gwynn	21.0
51	Eddie Waitkus	20.9
52	Max Flack	20.8
53	Bill Buckner	20.7
54	Dixie Walker	20.7
55	Everett Scott	20.7
56	Earle Combs	20.7
57	Paul Hines	20.6
58	Freddy Lindstrom	20.3
59	Mickey Owen	20.2
60	Joe Vosmik	20.1
61	Lou Boudreau	19.5
62	Milt Stock	19.5
63	Willard Marshall	19.3
64	Debs Garms	19.3
65	Charlie Grimm	19.3
66	Harry Rice	19.3
67	Skeeter Newsome	19.2
68	Curt Walker	19.1
69	Peanuts Lowrey	19.1
70	Charlie Jamieson	19.0
71	Muddy Ruel	19.0
72	Tommy Griffith	18.9
73	Tommy Thevenow	18.8
74	Joe Stripp	18.6
75	Joe DiMaggio	18.5
76	Bob Fothergill	18.5
77	Bing Miller	18.3
78	Riggs Stephenson	18.3
79	Yogi Berra	18.2
80	Billy Herman	18.0
81	Lee Magee	18.0
82	Dave Cash	18.0
83	Elmer Valo	17.7
84	Heinie Groh	17.6
85	Luke Sewell	17.5
86	Rich Dauer	17.5
87	Buddy Lewis	17.4
88	Billy Goodman	17.2
89	Jim Gilliam	17.1
90	Harvey Kuenn	17.1
91	Gus Mancuso	17.1
92	Jimmie Wilson	17.1
93	Billy Cox	17.0
94	Ken Williams	16.9
95	George Case	16.9
96	Cecil Travis	16.9
97	Luke Appling	16.8
98	Jackie Hayes	16.8
99	Brian Harper	16.8
100	Jackie Robinson	16.8

Batting Average

1	Ty Cobb	.366
2	Rogers Hornsby	.358
3	Joe Jackson	.356
4	Ed Delahanty	.346
5	Tris Speaker	.345
6	Ted Williams	.344
7	Billy Hamilton	.344
8	Dan Brouthers	.342
9	Babe Ruth	.342
10	Harry Heilmann	.342
11	Pete Browning	.341
12	Willie Keeler	.341
13	Bill Terry	.341
14	George Sisler	.340
15	Lou Gehrig	.340
16	Jesse Burkett	.338
17	Nap Lajoie	.338
18	Tony Gwynn	.337
19	Riggs Stephenson	.336
20	Al Simmons	.334
21	John McGraw	.334
22	Paul Waner	.333
23	Eddie Collins	.333
24	Wade Boggs	.333
25	Mike Donlin	.333
26	Stan Musial	.331
27	Sam Thompson	.331
28	Heinie Manush	.330
29	Cap Anson	.329
30	Rod Carew	.328
31	Honus Wagner	.327
32	Tip O'Neill	.326
33	Bob Fothergill	.325
34	Jimmie Foxx	.325
35	Earle Combs	.325
36	Joe DiMaggio	.325
37	Babe Herman	.324
38	Hugh Duffy	.324
39	Joe Medwick	.324
40	Edd Roush	.323
41	Sam Rice	.322
42	Ross Youngs	.322
43	Kiki Cuyler	.321
44	Charlie Gehringer	.320
45	Chuck Klein	.320
46	Pie Traynor	.320
47	Mickey Cochrane	.320
48	Ken Williams	.319
49	Kirby Puckett	.318
50	Earl Averill	.318
51	Arky Vaughan	.318
52	Roberto Clemente	.317
53	Chick Hafey	.317
54	Joe Kelley	.317
55	Zack Wheat	.317
56	Roger Connor	.317
57	Lloyd Waner	.316
58	Frankie Frisch	.316
59	Goose Goslin	.316
60	George Van Haltren	.316
61	Bibb Falk	.314
62	Cecil Travis	.314
63	Hank Greenberg	.313
64	Jack Fournier	.313
65	Elmer Flick	.313
66	Bill Dickey	.313
67	Dale Mitchell	.312
68	Johnny Mize	.312
69	Joe Sewell	.312
70	Fred Clarke	.312
71	Barney McCosky	.312
72	Hughie Jennings	.311
73	Freddy Lindstrom	.311
74	Bing Miller	.311
75	Jackie Robinson	.311
76	Baby Doll Jacobson	.311
77	Taffy Wright	.311
78	Rip Radcliff	.311
79	Ginger Beaumont	.311
80	Mike Tiernan	.311
81	Denny Lyons	.310
82	Elmer Smith	.310
83	Luke Appling	.310
84	Irish Meusel	.310
85	Bobby Veach	.310
86	Jim O'Rourke	.310
87	Jim Bottomley	.310
88	John Stone	.310
89	Sam Crawford	.309
90	Bob Meusel	.309
91	Mark Grace	.309
92	Jack Tobin	.309
93	Spud Davis	.308
94	Richie Ashburn	.308
95	Paul Molitor	.308
96	King Kelly	.308
97	Jake Beckley	.308
98	Stuffy McInnis	.307
99	Don Mattingly	.307
100	Joe Vosmik	.307

Batting Average (by era)

1876-1892

1	Dan Brouthers	.342
2	Pete Browning	.341
3	Sam Thompson	.331
4	Cap Anson	.329
5	Tip O'Neill	.326
6	Roger Connor	.317
7	Denny Lyons	.310
8	Jim O'Rourke	.310
9	King Kelly	.308
10	Deacon White	.303
11	Buck Ewing	.303
12	Henry Larkin	.303
13	George Gore	.301
14	Paul Hines	.301
15	Oyster Burns	.300

1893-1919

1	Ty Cobb	.366
2	Joe Jackson	.356
3	Ed Delahanty	.346
4	Tris Speaker	.345
5	Billy Hamilton	.344
6	Willie Keeler	.341
7	Jesse Burkett	.338
8	Nap Lajoie	.338
9	John McGraw	.334
10	Eddie Collins	.333
11	Mike Donlin	.333
12	Honus Wagner	.327
13	Hugh Duffy	.324
14	Joe Kelley	.317
15	Zack Wheat	.317

1920-1941

1	Rogers Hornsby	.358
2	Babe Ruth	.342
3	Harry Heilmann	.342
4	Bill Terry	.341
5	George Sisler	.340
6	Lou Gehrig	.340
7	Riggs Stephenson	.336
8	Al Simmons	.334
9	Paul Waner	.333
10	Heinie Manush	.330
11	Bob Fothergill	.325
12	Jimmie Foxx	.325
13	Earle Combs	.325
14	Babe Herman	.324
15	Joe Medwick	.324

1942-1960

1	Ted Williams	.344
2	Stan Musial	.331
3	Joe DiMaggio	.325
4	Dale Mitchell	.312
5	Johnny Mize	.312
6	Barney McCosky	.312
7	Jackie Robinson	.311
8	Taffy Wright	.311
9	Richie Ashburn	.308
10	Johnny Pesky	.307
11	George Kell	.306
12	Dixie Walker	.306
13	Harvey Kuenn	.303
14	Tommy Holmes	.302
15	Enos Slaughter	.300

1961-1976

1	Rod Carew	.328
2	Roberto Clemente	.317
3	Matty Alou	.307
4	Ralph Garr	.306
5	Hank Aaron	.305
6	Tony Oliva	.304
7	Manny Mota	.304
8	Pete Rose	.303
9	Willie Mays	.302
10	Rico Carty	.299
11	Joe Torre	.297
12	Al Kaline	.297
13	Orlando Cepeda	.297
14	Manny Sanguillen	.296
15	Bob Watson	.295

1977-1996

1	Tony Gwynn	.337
2	Wade Boggs	.333
3	Kirby Puckett	.318
4	Mark Grace	.309
5	Paul Molitor	.308
6	Don Mattingly	.307
7	George Brett	.305
8	Bill Madlock	.305
9	Al Oliver	.303
10	Mike Greenwell	.303
11	Julio Franco	.303
12	Ken Griffey Jr.	.302
13	Roberto Alomar	.302
14	Will Clark	.300
15	John Kruk	.300

Batting Average (by position)

First Base

1	Dan Brouthers	.342
2	Bill Terry	.341
3	George Sisler	.340
4	Lou Gehrig	.340
5	Cap Anson	.329
6	Rod Carew	.328
7	Jimmie Foxx	.325
8	Roger Connor	.317
9	Hank Greenberg	.313
10	Jack Fournier	.313

Second Base

1	Rogers Hornsby	.358
2	Nap Lajoie	.338
3	Eddie Collins	.333
4	Charlie Gehringer	.320
5	Frankie Frisch	.316
6	Cupid Childs	.306
7	Billy Herman	.304
8	Buddy Myer	.303
9	Roberto Alomar	.302
10	Del Pratt	.292

Shortstop

1	Honus Wagner	.327
2	Arky Vaughan	.318
3	Joe Sewell	.312
4	Luke Appling	.310
5	Ed McKean	.302
6	Joe Cronin	.301
7	Barry Larkin	.298
8	Lou Boudreau	.295
9	George Davis	.295
10	Glenn Wright	.294

Third Base

1	Wade Boggs	.333
2	Pie Traynor	.320
3	Denny Lyons	.310
4	Frank Baker	.307
5	George Kell	.306
6	George Brett	.305
7	Bill Madlock	.305
8	Stan Hack	.301
9	Kevin Seitzer	.296
10	Pinky Whitney	.295

Outfield

1	Ty Cobb	.366
2	Joe Jackson	.356
3	Ed Delahanty	.346
4	Tris Speaker	.345
5	Ted Williams	.344
6	Billy Hamilton	.344
7	Babe Ruth	.342
8	Harry Heilmann	.342
9	Willie Keeler	.341
10	Jesse Burkett	.338
11	Tony Gwynn	.337
12	Al Simmons	.334
13	Paul Waner	.333
14	Stan Musial	.331
15	Sam Thompson	.331
16	Heinie Manush	.330
17	Tip O'Neill	.326
18	Earle Combs	.325
19	Joe DiMaggio	.325
20	Babe Herman	.324

Catcher

1	Mickey Cochrane	.320
2	Bill Dickey	.313
3	Spud Davis	.308
4	Ernie Lombardi	.306
5	Gabby Hartnett	.297
6	Manny Sanguillen	.296
7	Smoky Burgess	.295
8	Thurman Munson	.292
9	Hank Severeid	.289
10	Jack Clements	.286

Relative Batting Average

1	Ty Cobb	134.8
2	Joe Jackson	133.1
3	Pete Browning	131.6
4	Ted Williams	128.1
5	Tony Gwynn	127.9
6	Dan Brouthers	127.8
7	Nap Lajoie	127.4
8	Rod Carew	127.0
9	Rogers Hornsby	126.2
10	Wade Boggs	126.1
11	Tris Speaker	125.4
12	Tip O'Neill	125.3
13	Willie Keeler	124.6
14	Stan Musial	123.9
15	Mike Donlin	123.6
16	Honus Wagner	123.1
17	Billy Hamilton	122.7
18	Cap Anson	122.7
19	Ed Delahanty	122.6
20	Eddie Collins	121.8
21	Jesse Burkett	121.7
22	Sam Thompson	121.1
23	Kirby Puckett	121.0
24	Roberto Clemente	120.7
25	Tony Oliva	120.4
26	Harry Heilmann	119.4
27	Babe Ruth	119.2
28	George Sisler	118.9
29	Sam Crawford	118.9
30	King Kelly	118.2
31	Jim O'Rourke	118.1
32	Matty Alou	117.9
33	Joe Medwick	117.8
34	Paul Waner	117.8
35	Elmer Flick	117.4
36	Roger Connor	117.4
37	Bill Terry	117.3
38	Lou Gehrig	117.2
39	Joe DiMaggio	117.1
40	Mark Grace	117.1
41	Ginger Beaumont	117.0
42	Don Mattingly	116.9
43	Ralph Garr	116.7
44	Manny Mota	116.4
45	George Brett	116.3
46	Dale Mitchell	116.3
47	Paul Molitor	116.3
48	John McGraw	116.2
49	Henry Larkin	116.2
50	Deacon White	116.1
51	Hank Aaron	116.0
52	Paul Hines	115.8
53	George Gore	115.7
54	Jackie Robinson	115.7
55	Pete Rose	115.6
56	Al Simmons	115.4
57	Frank Baker	115.4
58	Al Kaline	115.4
59	Bill Madlock	115.2
60	Arky Vaughan	115.1
61	Al Oliver	115.1
62	Riggs Stephenson	115.0
63	Mickey Mantle	115.0
64	Johnny Mize	115.0
65	Zack Wheat	114.9
66	Hugh Duffy	114.8
67	George Kell	114.8
68	Barney McCosky	114.7
69	Julio Franco	114.7
70	Richie Ashburn	114.6
71	Mike Greenwell	114.6
72	Hardy Richardson	114.6
73	Pedro Guerrero	114.5
74	Johnny Pesky	114.5
75	Harvey Kuenn	114.5
76	Rico Carty	114.4
77	Willie Mays	114.3
78	John Kruk	114.2
79	Roberto Alomar	114.2
80	Fred Clarke	114.0
81	Heinie Manush	114.0
82	Cy Seymour	113.9
83	Ken Griffey Jr.	113.9
84	Jimmie Foxx	113.8
85	Joe Torre	113.8
86	Will Clark	113.8
87	Edd Roush	113.8
88	Denny Lyons	113.6
89	Cecil Cooper	113.5
90	Jim Rice	113.5
91	Frank Robinson	113.4
92	Tommy Davis	113.4
93	Taffy Wright	113.4
94	Minnie Minoso	113.1
95	Willie McGee	113.0
96	Jimmy Wolf	113.0
97	Tommy Holmes	113.0
98	Joe Kelley	112.9
99	Orlando Cepeda	112.9
100	Barry Larkin	112.9

On Base Percentage

1	Ted Williams	.483
2	Babe Ruth	.474
3	John McGraw	.466
4	Billy Hamilton	.455
5	Lou Gehrig	.447
6	Rogers Hornsby	.434
7	Ty Cobb	.433
8	Jimmie Foxx	.428
	Tris Speaker	.428
10	Wade Boggs	.425
	Ferris Fain	.425
12	Eddie Collins	.424
13	Max Bishop	.423
	Dan Brouthers	.423
	Joe Jackson	.423
	Mickey Mantle	.423
17	Mickey Cochrane	.419
18	Stan Musial	.418
19	Cupid Childs	.416
20	Jesse Burkett	.415
21	Mel Ott	.414
22	Roy Thomas	.413
23	Hank Greenberg	.412
24	Ed Delahanty	.411
25	Harry Heilmann	.410
	Charlie Keller	.410
	Jackie Robinson	.410
	Eddie Stanky	.410
29	Rickey Henderson	.409
30	Roy Cullenbine	.408
31	Barry Bonds	.407
	Denny Lyons	.407
	Riggs Stephenson	.407
34	Joe Cunningham	.406
	Arky Vaughan	.406
36	Charlie Gehringer	.404
	Paul Waner	.404
38	Pete Browning	.403
39	Lu Blue	.402
	Joe Kelley	.402
41	Mike Hargrove	.400
	John Kruk	.400
43	Luke Appling	.399
	Elmer Valo	.399
	Ross Youngs	.399
46	Joe DiMaggio	.398
	Ralph Kiner	.398
	Elmer Smith	.398
49	Richie Ashburn	.397
	Earle Combs	.397
	Roger Connor	.397
	Johnny Mize	.397
53	Cap Anson	.395
	Earl Averill	.395
	Rod Carew	.395
	Dave Magadan	.395
	Joe Morgan	.395
	Hack Wilson	.395
	Eddie Yost	.395
60	Frank Chance	.394
	Stan Hack	.394
	Johnny Pesky	.394
63	Bob Johnson	.393
	Wally Schang	.393
	Bill Terry	.393
	Ken Williams	.393
67	Jack Fournier	.392
	George Grantham	.392
	Tony Gwynn	.392
	Tip O'Neill	.392
	Frank Robinson	.392
	Mike Tiernan	.392
73	Minnie Minoso	.391
	Joe Sewell	.391
	Ken Singleton	.391
	Gene Tenace	.391
	Honus Wagner	.391
78	Harlond Clift	.390
	Joe Cronin	.390
	Augie Galan	.390
	Hughie Jennings	.390
82	Bernie Carbo	.389
	Elmer Flick	.389
	Buddy Myer	.389
85	Dolph Camilli	.388
	Mike Griffin	.388
	Keith Hernandez	.388
	Willie Keeler	.388
	Tim Raines	.388
	Gene Woodling	.388
91	Larry Doby	.387
	Goose Goslin	.387
	Willie Mays	.387
	Earl Torgeson	.387
95	9 players tied	.386

Slugging Average

1	Babe Ruth	.690
2	Ted Williams	.634
3	Lou Gehrig	.632
4	Jimmie Foxx	.609
5	Hank Greenberg	.605
6	Joe DiMaggio	.579
7	Rogers Hornsby	.577
8	Johnny Mize	.562
9	Stan Musial	.559
10	Willie Mays	.557
11	Mickey Mantle	.557
12	Hank Aaron	.555
13	Ken Griffey Jr.	.549
14	Ralph Kiner	.548
15	Barry Bonds	.548
16	Hack Wilson	.545
17	Mark McGwire	.544
18	Chuck Klein	.543
19	Duke Snider	.540
20	Frank Robinson	.537
21	Al Simmons	.535
22	Dick Allen	.534
23	Earl Averill	.534
24	Mel Ott	.533
25	Babe Herman	.532
26	Ken Williams	.530
27	Fred McGriff	.530
28	Willie Stargell	.529
29	Kevin Mitchell	.528
30	Mike Schmidt	.527
31	Chick Hafey	.526
32	Hal Trosky	.522
33	Wally Berger	.522
34	Jose Canseco	.521
35	Harry Heilmann	.520
36	Dan Brouthers	.519
37	Charlie Keller	.518
38	Joe Jackson	.517
39	Willie McCovey	.515
40	Ty Cobb	.512
41	Eddie Mathews	.509
42	Jeff Heath	.509
43	Harmon Killebrew	.509
44	Bob Johnson	.506
45	Bill Terry	.506
46	Ed Delahanty	.505
47	Sam Thompson	.505
48	Joe Medwick	.505
49	Darryl Strawberry	.504
50	Jim Rice	.502
51	Tris Speaker	.500
52	Jim Bottomley	.500
53	Goose Goslin	.500
54	Roy Campanella	.500
55	Ernie Banks	.500
56	Orlando Cepeda	.499
57	Bob Horner	.499
58	Frank Howard	.499
59	Matt Williams	.498
60	Ted Kluszewski	.498
61	Rafael Palmeiro	.498
62	Jay Buhner	.497
63	Bob Meusel	.497
64	Danny Tartabull	.497
65	Hank Sauer	.496
66	Cecil Fielder	.495
67	Al Rosen	.495
68	Will Clark	.492
69	Billy Williams	.492
70	Ripper Collins	.492
71	Dolph Camilli	.492
72	Ellis Burks	.491
73	Tommy Henrich	.491
74	Larry Doby	.490
75	Reggie Jackson	.490
76	Dick Stuart	.489
77	Reggie Smith	.489
78	Gabby Hartnett	.489
79	Rocky Colavito	.489
80	Norm Cash	.488
81	George Brett	.487
82	Bobby Bonilla	.487
83	Gil Hodges	.487
84	Bill Dickey	.486
85	Roger Connor	.486
86	Andres Galarraga	.486
87	Gus Zernial	.486
88	Joe Adcock	.485
89	Wally Post	.485
90	Fred Lynn	.484
91	Jack Fournier	.483
92	Rudy York	.483
93	Andre Dawson	.482
94	Yogi Berra	.482
95	Eric Davis	.481
96	Kent Hrbek	.481
97	Charlie Gehringer	.480
98	Pedro Guerrero	.480
99	George Foster	.480
100	Al Kaline	.480

Production

1	Babe Ruth	1.163
2	Ted Williams	1.116
3	Lou Gehrig	1.080
4	Jimmie Foxx	1.038
5	Hank Greenberg	1.017
6	Rogers Hornsby	1.010
7	Mickey Mantle	.979
8	Joe DiMaggio	.977
	Stan Musial	.977
10	Johnny Mize	.959
11	Barry Bonds	.955
12	Mel Ott	.947
13	Ralph Kiner	.946
14	Ty Cobb	.945
15	Willie Mays	.944
16	Dan Brouthers	.942
17	Joe Jackson	.940
	Hack Wilson	.940
19	Ken Griffey Jr.	.933
20	Hank Aaron	.932
21	Harry Heilmann	.930
22	Frank Robinson	.929
23	Earl Averill	.928
	Charlie Keller	.928
	Mark McGwire	.928
	Tris Speaker	.928
27	Ken Williams	.924
28	Chuck Klein	.922
29	Duke Snider	.921
30	Ed Delahanty	.917
31	Fred McGriff	.916
32	Babe Herman	.915
	Al Simmons	.915
34	Dick Allen	.914
35	Mike Schmidt	.912
36	Bob Johnson	.899
	Bill Terry	.899
38	Chick Hafey	.898
39	Mickey Cochrane	.897
40	Kevin Mitchell	.895
41	Willie McCovey	.892
	Willie Stargell	.892
	Hal Trosky	.892
44	Eddie Mathews	.888
	Sam Thompson	.888
46	Goose Goslin	.887
	Billy Hamilton	.887
	Harmon Killebrew	.887
49	Charlie Gehringer	.884
50	Roger Connor	.883
	Jackie Robinson	.883
52	Al Rosen	.882
53	Wally Berger	.881
54	Dolph Camilli	.880
	Riggs Stephenson	.880
56	Jose Canseco	.879
	Jeff Heath	.879
58	Paul Waner	.878
59	Larry Doby	.877
60	Will Clark	.876
	John McGraw	.876
62	Wade Boggs	.875
	Jack Fournier	.875
64	Tommy Henrich	.873
65	Jim Bottomley	.869
	Pete Browning	.869
	Rafael Palmeiro	.869
68	Bill Dickey	.868
	Danny Tartabull	.868
70	Joe Medwick	.867
71	Norm Cash	.865
72	Darryl Strawberry	.863
73	Jesse Burkett	.862
74	George Brett	.861
	Roy Campanella	.861
76	Kiki Cuyler	.860
77	Earle Combs	.859
	Al Kaline	.859
	Reggie Smith	.859
	Arky Vaughan	.859
81	Jack Clark	.858
	Gavvy Cravath	.858
	Gabby Hartnett	.858
	Jim Rice	.858
85	Joe Cronin	.857
	Honus Wagner	.857
87	Heinie Manush	.856
	Billy Williams	.856
89	Jay Buhner	.855
90	Mike Donlin	.854
	George Grantham	.854
	Pedro Guerrero	.854
	Mike Tiernan	.854
94	Eddie Collins	.853
	Frank Howard	.853
	Joe Kelley	.853
97	5 players tied	.852

Adjusted Production

1	Babe Ruth	209
2	Ted Williams	186
3	Lou Gehrig	182
4	Rogers Hornsby	176
5	Mickey Mantle	173
6	Dan Brouthers	170
7	Joe Jackson	169
8	Ty Cobb	167
9	Pete Browning	164
10	Barry Bonds	162
11	Jimmie Foxx	161
12	Hank Greenberg	157
	Willie Mays	157
	Mark McGwire	157
	Johnny Mize	157
	Stan Musial	157
17	Hank Aaron	156
	Dick Allen	156
	Joe DiMaggio	156
	Tris Speaker	156
21	Mel Ott	155
22	Roger Connor	154
	Frank Robinson	154
24	Ed Delahanty	152
	Charlie Keller	152
26	Nap Lajoie	150
	Honus Wagner	150
28	Gavvy Cravath	149
	Elmer Flick	149
30	Harry Heilmann	148
	Ralph Kiner	148
	Willie McCovey	148
33	Ken Griffey Jr.	147
	Kevin Mitchell	147
	Mike Schmidt	147
	Willie Stargell	147
37	Sam Thompson	146
38	Eddie Mathews	145
	Hack Wilson	145
40	Fred McGriff	144
41	Sam Crawford	143
	Jack Fournier	143
	Frank Howard	143
44	Eddie Collins	142
	Mike Donlin	142
	Harmon Killebrew	142
	Harry Stovey	142
48	Babe Herman	141
	Henry Larkin	141
50	Wally Berger	140
	Jesse Burkett	140
	Will Clark	140
	Jeff Heath	140
	Reggie Jackson	140
	Tip O'Neill	140
	Darryl Strawberry	140
57	Jose Canseco	139
	Billy Hamilton	139
	Bob Johnson	139
	Denny Lyons	139
61	Cap Anson	138
	Norm Cash	138
	Jack Clark	138
	Pedro Guerrero	138
	Al Rosen	138
	Duke Snider	138
	Mike Tiernan	138
68	Larry Doby	137
	Rickey Henderson	137
	Sherry Magee	137
	Gene Tenace	137
	Bill Terry	137
73	Frank Baker	136
	King Kelly	136
	Reggie Smith	136
	Arky Vaughan	136
	Ken Williams	136
78	George Brett	135
	Oyster Burns	135
	Frank Chance	135
	Chuck Klein	135
	John McGraw	135
83	Wade Boggs	134
	Dolph Camilli	134
	George Gore	134
	Al Kaline	134
	John Kruk	134
	Boog Powell	134
89	Orlando Cepeda	133
	Chick Hafey	133
	Charlie Hickman	133
	Paul Hines	133
	Joe Medwick	133
	Joe Morgan	133
	Bill Nicholson	133
	Jim O'Rourke	133
	Rafael Palmeiro	133
	Danny Tartabull	133
	Paul Waner	133
100	11 players tied	132

Batting Runs

Rank	Player	Runs
1	Babe Ruth	1322
2	Ted Williams	1166
3	Ty Cobb	1031
4	Stan Musial	983
5	Lou Gehrig	917
6	Hank Aaron	878
7	Rogers Hornsby	844
8	Tris Speaker	843
9	Willie Mays	827
10	Jimmie Foxx	803
	Mickey Mantle	803
12	Frank Robinson	773
13	Mel Ott	767
14	Honus Wagner	664
15	Dan Brouthers	636
16	Carl Yastrzemski	617
17	Eddie Collins	608
18	Mike Schmidt	592
19	Nap Lajoie	556
20	Cap Anson	548
	Roger Connor	548
22	Harmon Killebrew	532
23	Ed Delahanty	525
24	Willie McCovey	524
25	Johnny Mize	520
26	Harry Heilmann	517
27	Al Kaline	513
28	George Brett	511
29	Joe DiMaggio	507
30	Jesse Burkett	504
31	Sam Crawford	493
32	Wade Boggs	492
33	Paul Waner	491
34	Willie Stargell	483
35	Eddie Mathews	480
36	Barry Bonds	475
37	Billy Hamilton	471
38	Dick Allen	470
39	Hank Greenberg	468
40	Reggie Jackson	466
41	Billy Williams	463
42	Joe Jackson	452
43	Rickey Henderson	441
	Duke Snider	441
45	Joe Morgan	438
46	Rod Carew	431
	Eddie Murray	431
48	Dwight Evans	418
49	Pete Rose	416
50	Frank Thomas	409
51	Al Simmons	399
52	Ralph Kiner	391
53	Norm Cash	390
54	Dave Winfield	382
55	Reggie Smith	379
56	Fred Clarke	376
	Charlie Gehringer	376
	Joe Kelley	376
59	Chuck Klein	375
60	Jack Clark	367
	Jim Rice	367
62	Bob Johnson	366
63	Arky Vaughan	361
64	Sam Thompson	360
65	Pete Browning	356
66	Roberto Clemente	354
	Joe Medwick	354
68	Harry Stovey	347
69	Ron Santo	345
70	Elmer Flick	342
	Fred McGriff	342
72	Goose Goslin	341
	Willie Keeler	341
74	Orlando Cepeda	337
75	Earl Averill	334
	Paul Molitor	334
	Zack Wheat	334
78	Ken Singleton	332
79	Sherry Magee	331
80	Tony Gwynn	326
81	Frank Howard	324
82	Dolph Camilli	319
83	Rusty Staub	318
	Bill Terry	318
85	King Kelly	313
86	Keith Hernandez	310
87	Fred Lynn	309
88	Enos Slaughter	306
89	Boog Powell	305
	Hack Wilson	305
91	Babe Herman	304
92	Tim Raines	300
93	Minnie Minoso	299
94	Joe Torre	298
95	Rocky Colavito	297
96	Jim O'Rourke	293
97	Tony Perez	292
98	4 players tied	291

Adjusted Batting Runs

Rank	Player	Runs
1	Babe Ruth	1382
2	Ted Williams	1024
3	Lou Gehrig	1005
4	Ty Cobb	1004
5	Hank Aaron	914
6	Stan Musial	899
7	Rogers Hornsby	874
8	Mickey Mantle	863
9	Willie Mays	844
10	Tris Speaker	793
11	Mel Ott	776
12	Jimmie Foxx	746
13	Frank Robinson	744
14	Honus Wagner	631
15	Eddie Collins	622
16	Dan Brouthers	609
17	Eddie Mathews	559
18	Nap Lajoie	558
19	Roger Connor	549
20	Ed Delahanty	543
	Mike Schmidt	543
22	Willie McCovey	540
23	Harry Heilmann	532
24	Joe DiMaggio	529
25	Reggie Jackson	519
26	Rickey Henderson	514
27	Barry Bonds	506
28	Johnny Mize	490
29	George Brett	488
	Willie Stargell	488
31	Harmon Killebrew	482
32	Joe Morgan	478
33	Jesse Burkett	474
	Carl Yastrzemski	474
35	Eddie Murray	472
36	Dick Allen	469
37	Al Kaline	468
38	Sam Crawford	464
	Paul Waner	464
40	Wade Boggs	440
	Dave Winfield	440
42	Frank Thomas	437
43	Joe Jackson	433
44	Hank Greenberg	422
45	Cap Anson	417
46	Billy Hamilton	414
47	Rod Carew	411
48	Duke Snider	388
49	Bob Johnson	387
50	Pete Browning	384
51	Jack Clark	377
52	Billy Williams	371
53	Fred Clarke	366
	Pete Rose	366
55	Roberto Clemente	363
	Ralph Kiner	363
57	Al Simmons	361
58	Ken Singleton	359
59	Frank Howard	357
60	Norm Cash	355
61	Elmer Flick	353
62	Arky Vaughan	352
63	Paul Molitor	351
64	Goose Goslin	347
65	Sam Thompson	344
66	Tony Gwynn	342
	Reggie Smith	342
68	Orlando Cepeda	338
	Bill Terry	338
70	Mark McGwire	336
71	Zack Wheat	335
72	Rusty Staub	334
73	Charlie Gehringer	332
74	Dwight Evans	331
75	Sherry Magee	324
	Fred McGriff	324
77	Babe Herman	323
78	Joe Kelley	321
79	Keith Hernandez	320
80	Will Clark	315
	Tim Raines	315
82	Mike Tiernan	314
83	Hack Wilson	311
84	Joe Medwick	310
	Boog Powell	310
86	Jack Fournier	308
87	Jake Beckley	299
	Joe Torre	299
89	Chuck Klein	298
90	Minnie Minoso	297
91	Earl Averill	296
92	Harry Stovey	294
93	Charlie Keller	293
94	Jim Wynn	289
95	Rocky Colavito	287
96	Willie Keeler	286
	Jim O'Rourke	286
98	Larry Doby	285
99	Jeff Bagwell	279
100	Pedro Guerrero	277

Batting Wins

Rank	Player	Wins
1	Babe Ruth	127.5
2	Ted Williams	115.9
3	Ty Cobb	106.3
4	Stan Musial	99.7
5	Hank Aaron	91.1
6	Tris Speaker	86.1
7	Willie Mays	85.5
8	Lou Gehrig	85.3
9	Rogers Hornsby	84.9
10	Mickey Mantle	82.9
11	Frank Robinson	80.7
12	Mel Ott	76.2
13	Jimmie Foxx	75.3
14	Honus Wagner	68.5
15	Carl Yastrzemski	64.3
16	Eddie Collins	62.4
17	Mike Schmidt	61.8
18	Nap Lajoie	57.0
19	Harmon Killebrew	55.8
20	Dan Brouthers	55.6
21	Willie McCovey	54.9
22	Al Kaline	53.4
23	Sam Crawford	52.5
24	Johnny Mize	52.2
25	George Brett	51.4
26	Willie Stargell	51.0
27	Harry Heilmann	50.8
28	Dick Allen	50.0
29	Eddie Mathews	49.2
30	Barry Bonds	48.6
31	Joe DiMaggio	48.6
32	Billy Williams	48.6
33	Paul Waner	48.6
34	Cap Anson	48.5
35	Wade Boggs	48.4
36	Reggie Jackson	47.9
37	Roger Connor	47.9
38	Joe Jackson	47.4
39	Ed Delahanty	46.3
40	Jesse Burkett	46.2
41	Joe Morgan	45.9
42	Rod Carew	44.7
43	Hank Greenberg	44.5
44	Duke Snider	44.4
45	Pete Rose	43.9
46	Rickey Henderson	43.8
47	Eddie Murray	43.0
48	Dwight Evans	42.2
49	Norm Cash	41.1
50	Billy Hamilton	41.1
51	Reggie Smith	40.3
52	Frank Thomas	39.5
53	Ralph Kiner	39.1
54	Dave Winfield	38.6
55	Jack Clark	38.0
56	Al Simmons	37.4
57	Jim Rice	36.9
58	Roberto Clemente	36.8
59	Chuck Klein	36.7
60	Fred Clarke	36.7
61	Arky Vaughan	36.4
62	Ron Santo	36.3
63	Sherry Magee	35.8
64	Joe Medwick	35.8
65	Bob Johnson	35.2
66	Charlie Gehringer	35.1
67	Orlando Cepeda	35.1
68	Elmer Flick	34.8
69	Joe Kelley	34.6
70	Fred McGriff	34.5
71	Frank Howard	34.4
72	Zack Wheat	34.4
73	Ken Singleton	34.0
74	Tony Gwynn	33.6
75	Rusty Staub	33.3
76	Willie Keeler	33.0
77	Paul Molitor	32.9
78	Boog Powell	32.4
79	Keith Hernandez	32.4
80	Dolph Camilli	32.2
81	Goose Goslin	31.9
82	Joe Torre	31.4
83	Sam Thompson	31.2
84	Fred Lynn	31.1
85	Pete Browning	31.0
86	Enos Slaughter	30.9
87	Earl Averill	30.8
88	Rocky Colavito	30.8
89	Bill Terry	30.8
90	Tony Perez	30.6
91	Tim Raines	30.6
92	Harry Stovey	30.6
93	Minnie Minoso	30.3
94	Greg Luzinski	30.1
95	Ernie Banks	29.8
96	Gavvy Cravath	29.7
97	Hack Wilson	29.5
98	Babe Herman	29.5
99	Will Clark	29.4
100	Tony Oliva	28.9

Adjusted Batting Wins

Rank	Player	Wins
1	Babe Ruth	133.3
2	Ty Cobb	103.6
3	Ted Williams	101.7
4	Hank Aaron	94.8
5	Lou Gehrig	93.5
6	Stan Musial	91.1
7	Mickey Mantle	89.1
8	Rogers Hornsby	87.9
9	Willie Mays	87.3
10	Tris Speaker	81.0
11	Frank Robinson	77.7
12	Mel Ott	77.1
13	Jimmie Foxx	69.9
14	Honus Wagner	65.1
15	Eddie Collins	63.8
16	Eddie Mathews	57.3
17	Nap Lajoie	57.2
18	Mike Schmidt	56.7
19	Willie McCovey	56.6
20	Reggie Jackson	53.4
21	Dan Brouthers	53.2
22	Harry Heilmann	52.2
23	Barry Bonds	51.8
24	Willie Stargell	51.5
25	Rickey Henderson	51.0
26	Joe DiMaggio	50.8
27	Harmon Killebrew	50.6
28	Joe Morgan	50.1
29	Dick Allen	49.8
30	Carl Yastrzemski	49.4
31	Sam Crawford	49.4
32	Johnny Mize	49.2
33	George Brett	49.1
34	Al Kaline	48.7
35	Roger Connor	48.0
36	Ed Delahanty	47.9
37	Eddie Murray	47.1
38	Paul Waner	45.9
39	Joe Jackson	45.4
40	Dave Winfield	44.5
41	Jesse Burkett	43.5
42	Wade Boggs	43.3
43	Rod Carew	42.7
44	Frank Thomas	42.2
45	Hank Greenberg	40.1
46	Duke Snider	39.1
47	Jack Clark	39.1
48	Billy Williams	39.0
49	Pete Rose	38.6
50	Frank Howard	37.9
51	Roberto Clemente	37.8
52	Norm Cash	37.5
53	Bob Johnson	37.2
54	Cap Anson	36.9
55	Ken Singleton	36.7
56	Reggie Smith	36.4
57	Ralph Kiner	36.3
58	Billy Hamilton	36.1
59	Elmer Flick	35.9
60	Fred Clarke	35.7
61	Arky Vaughan	35.5
62	Tony Gwynn	35.3
63	Orlando Cepeda	35.2
64	Sherry Magee	35.1
65	Rusty Staub	35.0
66	Paul Molitor	34.6
67	Zack Wheat	34.5
68	Al Simmons	33.8
69	Pete Browning	33.4
70	Keith Hernandez	33.4
71	Dwight Evans	33.4
72	Mark McGwire	33.0
73	Boog Powell	32.9
74	Bill Terry	32.7
75	Fred McGriff	32.7
76	Goose Goslin	32.5
77	Tim Raines	32.1
78	Will Clark	31.9
79	Joe Torre	31.5
80	Joe Medwick	31.4
81	Babe Herman	31.3
82	Jack Fournier	31.1
83	Charlie Gehringer	31.0
84	Jim Wynn	30.6
85	Minnie Minoso	30.1
86	Hack Wilson	30.1
87	Sam Thompson	29.8
88	Rocky Colavito	29.8
89	Joe Kelley	29.5
90	Chuck Klein	29.2
91	Charlie Keller	29.2
92	Pedro Guerrero	29.0
93	Bobby Bonds	28.6
94	Larry Doby	28.4
95	Tony Perez	28.3
96	Jeff Bagwell	28.3
97	Darryl Strawberry	27.9
98	Brian Downing	27.8
99	Ron Santo	27.7
100	Jim Rice	27.6

Runs Created

1	Babe Ruth	2847
2	Ty Cobb	2810
3	Stan Musial	2625
4	Hank Aaron	2550
5	Ted Williams	2538
6	Willie Mays	2372
7	Tris Speaker	2325
8	Lou Gehrig	2321
9	Mel Ott	2235
	Honus Wagner	2235
11	Pete Rose	2220
12	Jimmie Foxx	2191
13	Carl Yastrzemski	2147
14	Frank Robinson	2126
15	Rogers Hornsby	2074
16	Mickey Mantle	2069
17	Eddie Collins	2062
18	Eddie Murray	1926
19	Nap Lajoie	1907
20	George Brett	1878
21	Paul Waner	1853
22	Al Kaline	1846
23	Ed Delahanty	1832
24	Dave Winfield	1813
25	Jesse Burkett	1804
	Joe Morgan	1804
27	Charlie Gehringer	1787
28	Al Simmons	1777
29	Reggie Jackson	1772
30	Rickey Henderson	1764
31	Mike Schmidt	1757
32	Cap Anson	1756
33	Eddie Mathews	1738
34	Paul Molitor	1724
35	Sam Crawford	1716
36	Goose Goslin	1707
37	Billy Hamilton	1706
38	Harry Heilmann	1698
39	Willie Keeler	1688
40	Jake Beckley	1685
41	Fred Clarke	1677
42	Billy Williams	1671
43	Robin Yount	1655
44	Roger Connor	1648
45	Willie McCovey	1638
46	George Davis	1634
47	Dan Brouthers	1624
48	Dwight Evans	1611
49	Harmon Killebrew	1609
50	Joe DiMaggio	1606
51	Wade Boggs	1595
	Rod Carew	1595
53	George Van Haltren	1566
54	Jimmy Ryan	1562
55	Roberto Clemente	1557
56	Zack Wheat	1540
57	Joe Kelley	1535
58	Rusty Staub	1534
59	Willie Stargell	1531
60	Tony Perez	1523
61	Andre Dawson	1519
62	Ernie Banks	1513
63	Lou Brock	1512
64	Bill Dahlen	1508
	Hugh Duffy	1508
66	Johnny Mize	1502
67	Sam Rice	1501
68	Darrell Evans	1499
69	George Sisler	1498
70	Luke Appling	1493
71	Duke Snider	1487
72	Tim Raines	1485
73	Max Carey	1472
74	Frankie Frisch	1464
75	Dave Parker	1452
76	Enos Slaughter	1432
77	Joe Cronin	1426
78	Bob Johnson	1418
79	Cal Ripken	1417
80	Lou Whitaker	1396
81	Vada Pinson	1394
82	Heinie Manush	1389
83	Mickey Vernon	1387
84	Richie Ashburn	1386
85	Jim Bottomley	1384
86	Jim Rice	1382
87	Ron Santo	1379
88	Chuck Klein	1378
89	Carlton Fisk	1375
90	Joe Medwick	1372
91	Earl Averill	1358
	Harold Baines	1358
	Brooks Robinson	1358
94	Harry Hooper	1349
95	Al Oliver	1348
96	Bid McPhee	1345
97	Orlando Cepeda	1338
98	Kiki Cuyler	1336
99	Hank Greenberg	1331
100	Sherry Magee	1328

Total Average

1	Babe Ruth	1.399
2	Ted Williams	1.320
3	Lou Gehrig	1.229
4	Billy Hamilton	1.191
5	John McGraw	1.153
6	Jimmie Foxx	1.143
7	Hank Greenberg	1.105
	Rogers Hornsby	1.105
9	Mickey Mantle	1.091
10	Barry Bonds	1.069
11	Ty Cobb	1.066
12	Dan Brouthers	1.061
13	Mel Ott	1.036
14	Ed Delahanty	1.035
15	Stan Musial	1.028
16	Joe DiMaggio	1.012
17	Tris Speaker	1.011
18	Joe Jackson	1.008
19	Ralph Kiner	1.006
20	Johnny Mize	1.005
	Hack Wilson	1.005
22	Charlie Keller	1.000
23	Willie Mays	.982
24	Rickey Henderson	.981
25	Mark McGwire	.973
26	Mike Tiernan	.970
27	Harry Heilmann	.963
28	Joe Kelley	.961
	Frank Robinson	.961
30	Ken Griffey Jr.	.959
31	Earl Averill	.957
32	Denny Lyons	.955
33	Mike Schmidt	.954
34	Roger Connor	.952
35	Mickey Cochrane	.947
	Honus Wagner	.947
37	Pete Browning	.946
38	Chuck Klein	.944
39	Jesse Burkett	.943
	Ken Williams	.943
41	Eddie Collins	.942
	Babe Herman	.942
43	Hank Aaron	.940
44	Jackie Robinson	.939
	Sam Thompson	.939
46	Fred McGriff	.936
47	Duke Snider	.933
48	Dick Allen	.930
	Hugh Duffy	.930
50	Dolph Camilli	.928
51	Harry Stovey	.924
52	Frank Chance	.920
	Bob Johnson	.920
54	Eddie Mathews	.916
55	Elmer Flick	.915
56	Mike Donlin	.914
57	Willie McCovey	.912
58	Elmer Smith	.911
59	Charlie Gehringer	.910
	Harmon Killebrew	.910
	Joe Morgan	.910
62	Eric Davis	.908
	Chick Hafey	.908
64	Gavvy Cravath	.905
	Mike Griffin	.905
	Al Simmons	.905
67	Kiki Cuyler	.901
	Goose Goslin	.901
69	Cupid Childs	.900
70	Riggs Stephenson	.899
	Bill Terry	.899
72	Tip O'Neill	.897
	Tim Raines	.897
74	Arky Vaughan	.894
75	Larry Doby	.893
	Tommy Henrich	.893
77	Willie Stargell	.889
	Hal Trosky	.889
79	Paul Waner	.888
80	Darryl Strawberry	.887
81	Jack Fournier	.884
82	Fred Clarke	.883
	Hughie Jennings	.883
84	George Grantham	.882
85	Roy Cullenbine	.881
	Kevin Mitchell	.881
	George Van Haltren	.881
88	Jose Canseco	.877
89	Will Clark	.876
90	Norm Cash	.875
	Al Rosen	.875
92	Wade Boggs	.874
93	Oyster Burns	.873
94	Wally Berger	.870
	Jimmy Ryan	.870
96	Jeff Heath	.869
97	Cap Anson	.867
	Jack Glasscock	.867
99	Danny Tartabull	.866
100	Dummy Hoy	.865

Runs Produced

1	Ty Cobb	4066
2	Hank Aaron	3716
3	Babe Ruth	3673
4	Cap Anson	3501
5	Stan Musial	3425
6	Lou Gehrig	3390
7	Honus Wagner	3367
8	Pete Rose	3319
9	Willie Mays	3305
10	Tris Speaker	3294
11	Mel Ott	3208
	Carl Yastrzemski	3208
13	Jimmie Foxx	3139
14	Ted Williams	3116
15	Jake Beckley	3089
16	Eddie Collins	3074
17	Frank Robinson	3055
18	Dave Winfield	3037
19	Al Simmons	3027
20	Nap Lajoie	3020
21	Charlie Gehringer	3017
22	Eddie Murray	3012
23	Ed Delahanty	2962
24	George Davis	2903
25	Rogers Hornsby	2862
26	George Brett	2861
27	Goose Goslin	2844
28	Paul Waner	2823
29	Sam Crawford	2819
30	Al Kaline	2806
31	Roger Connor	2804
32	Robin Yount	2787
33	Hugh Duffy	2748
34	Bill Dahlen	2738
35	Dan Brouthers	2713
36	Bid McPhee	2692
37	Reggie Jackson	2690
38	Frankie Frisch	2671
39	Lave Cross	2657
40	Mickey Mantle	2650
41	Harry Heilmann	2647
42	Jimmy Ryan	2617
43	Jesse Burkett	2597
44	George Van Haltren	2584
45	Paul Molitor	2573
46	Fred Clarke	2567
47	Joe DiMaggio	2566
48	Sam Rice	2558
49	Mike Schmidt	2553
50	Joe Kelley	2550
51	Tony Perez	2545
52	Andre Dawson	2526
53	Joe Morgan	2515
54	Willie Keeler	2496
55	Joe Cronin	2487
56	Roberto Clemente	2481
57	Rickey Henderson	2472
58	Dwight Evans	2469
59	Billy Williams	2459
60	Eddie Mathews	2450
61	Ernie Banks	2429
62	Sam Thompson	2428
63	Dave Parker	2426
64	Herman Long	2419
65	Jim O'Rourke	2406
66	Zack Wheat	2405
67	Pie Traynor	2398
68	Luke Appling	2390
69	Billy Hamilton	2386
70	Cal Ripken	2382
	Enos Slaughter	2382
72	Jim Bottomley	2380
73	Joe Medwick	2376
74	Rusty Staub	2363
75	Lou Brock	2361
76	Heinie Manush	2360
77	George Sisler	2357
78	Rod Carew	2347
79	Mickey Vernon	2335
80	Brooks Robinson	2321
81	Jim Rice	2318
82	Al Oliver	2296
83	Harmon Killebrew	2294
84	Tommy Corcoran	2285
	Ed McKean	2285
86	Darrell Evans	2284
87	Vada Pinson	2280
88	Harry Stovey	2278
89	Max Carey	2275
90	Willie McCovey	2263
91	Willie Stargell	2260
92	John Ward	2249
93	Yogi Berra	2247
94	Kiki Cuyler	2242
95	King Kelly	2238
96	Bob Johnson	2234
97	Carlton Fisk	2230
98	Lou Whitaker	2226
99	Ted Simmons	2215
100	Sherry Magee	2205

Clutch Hitting Index

1	Cap Anson	132
2	Earl Sheely	127
3	Tommy Thevenow	126
4	Bobby Veach	124
5	Pat Tabler	120
	Pie Traynor	120
7	Sam Mertes	119
8	Hughie Jennings	118
	Duffy Lewis	118
	Jack Rowe	118
	Luke Sewell	118
12	Rube Bressler	117
	Tommy Davis	117
	Bob Fothergill	117
	Chick Gandil	117
	King Kelly	117
	Cookie Lavagetto	117
	Muddy Ruel	117
	Ray Schalk	117
	Billy Sullivan	117
21	John Anderson	116
	Frank Bowerman	116
	Sherry Magee	116
	Elmer Smith	116
	Red Smith	116
26	Kitty Bransfield	115
	Lou Criger	115
	Ron Fairly	115
	Sam Mele	115
	Lee Tannehill	115
	Pinky Whitney	115
	Possum Whitted	115
33	Roy Campanella	114
	Sam Crawford	114
	George Cutshaw	114
	Art Devlin	114
	Jack Doyle	114
	Ferris Fain	114
	Carl Furillo	114
	Red Murray	114
	B.J. Surhoff	114
	Denny Walling	114
	Deacon White	114
	Jimmie Wilson	114
	Heinie Zimmerman	114
46	Darren Daulton	113
	Bob Elliott	113
	Larry Gardner	113
	Frank LaPorte	113
	Stuffy McInnis	113
	Enos Slaughter	113
	Frank Snyder	113
	Vic Wertz	113
	Taffy Wright	113
55	Alan Ashby	112
	Frank Baker	112
	Larry Biittner	112
	Smoky Burgess	112
	Frank Chance	112
	Johnny Edwards	112
	Kid Elberfeld	112
	Art Fletcher	112
	Sherm Lollar	112
	Frank McCormick	112
	Ed McKean	112
	Keith Moreland	112
	Manny Mota	112
	Jack O'Connor	112
	Mickey Owen	112
	Terry Pendleton	112
	Fred Pfeffer	112
	Boog Powell	112
	Cy Seymour	112
	Ted Simmons	112
	Sam Thompson	112
	Mike Tresh	112
77	Bob Boone	111
	Sid Bream	111
	Steve Brodie	111
	Gavvy Cravath	111
	Joe Cronin	111
	Lave Cross	111
	Hugh Duffy	111
	Hank Gowdy	111
	Ron Hassey	111
	Jim Kaat	111
	Willie Kamm	111
	Ed Kirkpatrick	111
	Steve O'Neill	111
	Del Pratt	111
	Wilbert Robinson	111
	Rusty Staub	111
	Harry Steinfeldt	111
	Riggs Stephenson	111
	Patsy Tebeau	111
	Joe Tinker	111
	Robin Ventura	111
	Jimmy Williams	111
	Glenn Wright	111
100	22 players tied	110

Isolated Power

1	Babe Ruth	.348
2	Lou Gehrig	.292
3	Hank Greenberg	.292
4	Ted Williams	.289
5	Mark McGwire	.286
6	Jimmie Foxx	.284
7	Ralph Kiner	.269
8	Mike Schmidt	.260
9	Barry Bonds	.260
10	Mickey Mantle	.259
11	Willie Mays	.256
12	Joe DiMaggio	.254
13	Harmon Killebrew	.252
14	Johnny Mize	.250
15	Hank Aaron	.250
16	Jose Canseco	.249
17	Willie Stargell	.247
18	Ken Griffey Jr.	.247
19	Willie McCovey	.245
20	Darryl Strawberry	.245
21	Fred McGriff	.244
22	Duke Snider	.244
23	Frank Robinson	.243
24	Dave Kingman	.242
25	Dick Allen	.242
26	Kevin Mitchell	.240
27	Cecil Fielder	.239
28	Eddie Mathews	.238
29	Jay Buhner	.238
30	Hack Wilson	.238
31	Matt Williams	.234
32	Charlie Keller	.231
33	Hank Sauer	.230
34	Mel Ott	.229
35	Stan Musial	.228
36	Reggie Jackson	.228
37	Dick Stuart	.225
38	Ernie Banks	.225
39	Frank Howard	.225
40	Danny Tartabull	.224
41	Roy Campanella	.224
42	Chuck Klein	.223
43	Gorman Thomas	.223
44	Rob Deer	.223
45	Rocky Colavito	.223
46	Bob Horner	.222
47	Wally Berger	.221
48	Gus Zernial	.221
49	Wally Post	.220
50	Eric Davis	.219
51	Hal Trosky	.219
52	Rogers Hornsby	.218
53	Ron Gant	.218
54	Norm Cash	.217
55	Bob Allison	.217
56	Roger Maris	.216
57	Earl Averill	.216
58	Jeff Heath	.216
59	Dolph Camilli	.215
60	Gil Hodges	.214
61	Ken Williams	.211
62	Jesse Barfield	.210
63	Al Rosen	.210
64	Bob Johnson	.210
65	Tommy Henrich	.209
66	Chick Hafey	.209
67	Jack Clark	.209
68	Joe Carter	.208
69	Johnny Bench	.208
70	Roy Sievers	.208
71	Rudy York	.208
72	Glenn Davis	.208
73	Joe Adcock	.208
74	Mickey Tettleton	.208
75	Nate Colbert	.207
76	Babe Herman	.207
77	Larry Doby	.207
78	Pete Incaviglia	.206
79	George Foster	.206
80	Jim Rice	.204
81	Dale Murphy	.204
82	Bobby Bonilla	.203
83	Bobby Bonds	.203
84	Orlando Cepeda	.203
85	Andre Dawson	.203
86	Billy Williams	.202
87	Greg Luzinski	.202
88	Cliff Johnson	.202
89	Reggie Smith	.202
90	Ellis Burks	.202
91	Fred Lynn	.201
92	Andres Galarraga	.201
93	Al Simmons	.201
94	Don Mincher	.201
95	Tony Armas	.200
96	Ted Kluszewski	.200
97	Rafael Palmeiro	.199
98	Leon Durham	.199
99	Dwight Evans	.198
100	Jim Lemon	.198

Extra Base Hits

1	Hank Aaron	1477
2	Stan Musial	1377
3	Babe Ruth	1356
4	Willie Mays	1323
5	Lou Gehrig	1190
6	Frank Robinson	1186
7	Carl Yastrzemski	1157
8	Ty Cobb	1136
9	Tris Speaker	1131
10	George Brett	1119
11	Jimmie Foxx	1117
	Ted Williams	1117
13	Dave Winfield	1093
14	Eddie Murray	1089
15	Reggie Jackson	1075
16	Mel Ott	1071
17	Pete Rose	1041
18	Andre Dawson	1039
19	Mike Schmidt	1015
20	Rogers Hornsby	1011
21	Ernie Banks	1009
22	Al Simmons	995
23	Honus Wagner	993
24	Al Kaline	972
25	Tony Perez	963
26	Robin Yount	960
27	Willie Stargell	953
28	Mickey Mantle	952
29	Billy Williams	948
30	Dwight Evans	941
31	Dave Parker	940
32	Eddie Mathews	938
33	Goose Goslin	921
34	Willie McCovey	920
35	Paul Waner	909
36	Charlie Gehringer	904
37	Nap Lajoie	903
38	Harmon Killebrew	887
39	Cal Ripken	883
40	Joe DiMaggio	881
41	Harry Heilmann	876
42	Paul Molitor	869
43	Vada Pinson	868
44	Sam Crawford	864
45	Joe Medwick	858
46	Duke Snider	850
47	Roberto Clemente	846
48	Carlton Fisk	844
49	Rusty Staub	838
50	Jim Bottomley	835
51	Jim Rice	834
52	Al Oliver	825
53	Orlando Cepeda	823
54	Brooks Robinson	818
55	Joe Morgan	813
56	Roger Connor	812
57	Johnny Mize	809
58	Ed Delahanty	808
59	Joe Cronin	803
60	Jake Beckley	802
61	Johnny Bench	794
62	Harold Baines	787
	Dale Murphy	787
64	Joe Carter	785
65	Mickey Vernon	782
66	Hank Greenberg	781
67	Zack Wheat	780
68	Darrell Evans	779
	Bob Johnson	779
70	Ted Simmons	778
71	Lou Brock	776
72	Ron Santo	774
73	Chuck Klein	772
74	Dan Brouthers	771
75	Earl Averill	767
76	Heinie Manush	761
77	Steve Garvey	755
78	Dick Allen	750
79	Cap Anson	749
80	Graig Nettles	746
81	Hal McRae	741
82	Fred Lynn	737
83	Reggie Smith	734
84	Don Baylor	732
85	Enos Slaughter	730
86	Lou Whitaker	729
87	Yogi Berra	728
	Tim Wallach	728
89	Gary Gaetti	727
90	Gary Carter	726
	Jimmy Ryan	726
92	Lee May	725
93	Ryne Sandberg	723
94	Bill Buckner	721
95	Barry Bonds	718
96	Sam Rice	716
97	Willie Davis	715
	Del Ennis	715
	Rickey Henderson	715
100	Gil Hodges	713

Pinch Hits

1	Manny Mota	150
2	Smoky Burgess	145
3	Greg Gross	143
4	Jose Morales	123
5	Jerry Lynch	116
6	Red Lucas	114
7	Steve Braun	113
8	Terry Crowley	108
	Denny Walling	108
10	Gates Brown	107
11	Mike Lum	103
12	Jim Dwyer	102
13	Rusty Staub	100
14	Larry Biittner	95
	Vic Davalillo	95
	Gerald Perry	95
17	Jerry Hairston	94
18	Dave Philley	93
	Joel Youngblood	93
20	Jay Johnstone	92
21	Ed Kranepool	90
	Elmer Valo	90
23	Dwight Smith	87
24	Dave Collins	85
25	Jesus Alou	82
	Thad Bosley	82
	Kurt Bevacqua	82
	Tim McCarver	82

Pinch Hit Average
(150 at-bats minimum)

1	Tommy Davis	.320
2	Frenchy Bordagaray	.312
3	Frankie Baumholtz	.307
4	Sid Bream	.306
5	Mark Carreon	.306
6	Chip Hale	.304
7	Red Schoendienst	.303
8	Bob Fothergill	.300
9	Dave Philley	.299
10	Manny Mota	.297
11	Ted Easterly	.296
12	Harvey Hendrick	.295
13	Larry Herndon	.294
14	Rance Mulliniks	.292
15	Terry Puhl	.289
16	Manny Sanguillen	.288
17	Ricky Jordan	.287
18	Smoky Burgess	.286
19	Rick Miller	.286
20	Johnny Mize	.283
21	John Vander Wal	.282
22	Ken Griffey Sr.	.282
23	Dave Hansen	.281
	Bubba Morton	.281
25	Steve Braun	.281

Pinch Hit Home Runs

1	Cliff Johnson	20
2	Jerry Lynch	18
3	Gates Brown	16
	Smoky Burgess	16
	Willie McCovey	16
6	George Crowe	14
7	Joe Adcock	12
	Bob Cerv	12
	Jose Morales	12
	Graig Nettles	12
11	Jeff Burroughs	11
	Jay Johnstone	11
	Candy Maldonado	11
	Fred Whitfield	11
	Cy Williams	11
16	Mark Carreon	10
	Jim Dwyer	10
	Mike Lum	10
	Ken McMullen	10
	Don Mincher	10
	Wally Post	10
	Champ Summers	10
	Jerry Turner	10
	Gus Zernial	10

Total Player Rating / 150g

1	Babe Ruth	6.45
2	Barry Bonds	6.13
3	Nap Lajoie	5.70
4	Ted Williams	5.61
5	Rogers Hornsby	5.39
6	Rickey Henderson	4.97
7	Mike Schmidt	4.89
8	Mickey Mantle	4.75
9	Tris Speaker	4.65
10	Willie Mays	4.62
11	Lou Gehrig	4.55
12	Ty Cobb	4.50
13	Honus Wagner	4.36
14	Barry Larkin	4.25
15	Joe Jackson	4.22
16	Hank Aaron	4.08
17	Joe DiMaggio	4.05
18	Ken Griffey Jr.	3.95
19	Lou Boudreau	3.76
20	Tim Raines	3.71
21	Eddie Collins	3.70
22	Dan Brouthers	3.69
23	Frank Robinson	3.69
24	Pete Browning	3.65
25	Ed Delahanty	3.62
26	Jimmie Foxx	3.50
27	Stan Musial	3.49
28	Jackie Robinson	3.45
29	Mel Ott	3.45
30	Buck Ewing	3.37
31	Tony Gwynn	3.33
32	Bobby Grich	3.29
33	Eddie Mathews	3.24
34	Arky Vaughan	3.24
35	George Davis	3.23
36	Hank Greenberg	3.23
37	Frank Baker	3.22
38	Roger Connor	3.21
39	Joe Morgan	3.19
40	Mickey Cochrane	3.18
41	Bill Dahlen	3.16
42	Wade Boggs	3.15
43	Bobby Doerr	3.14
44	Jack Glasscock	3.12
45	Cupid Childs	3.09
46	Hardy Richardson	3.08
47	Hughie Jennings	3.06
48	Sam Thompson	3.04
49	Dick Allen	3.03
50	Gabby Hartnett	3.02
51	Charlie Keller	3.01
52	Lenny Dykstra	2.99
53	Bill Dickey	2.97
54	Ralph Kiner	2.94
55	Elmer Flick	2.91
56	Johnny Mize	2.88
57	Charlie Gehringer	2.87
58	Bob Johnson	2.87
59	Ryne Sandberg	2.82
60	Bid McPhee	2.82
61	Kevin Mitchell	2.81
62	Joe Cronin	2.78
63	Dave Bancroft	2.76
64	Darryl Strawberry	2.76
65	Jose Canseco	2.75
66	Joe Sewell	2.72
67	Charlie Bennett	2.71
68	Joe Gordon	2.70
69	Eric Davis	2.69
70	Roy Campanella	2.67
71	Denny Lyons	2.65
72	Roberto Clemente	2.64
73	Reggie Smith	2.64
74	Ron Santo	2.64
75	Cal Ripken	2.60
76	Jim Wynn	2.59
77	Yogi Berra	2.56
78	King Kelly	2.55
79	Frankie Frisch	2.53
80	Art Fletcher	2.52
81	Luke Appling	2.52
82	Bill Mazeroski	2.52
83	Ozzie Smith	2.51
84	Billy Hamilton	2.49
85	Billy Herman	2.47
86	Keith Hernandez	2.47
87	Wally Berger	2.47
88	Kirby Puckett	2.45
89	Mark McGwire	2.43
90	Heinie Groh	2.42
91	Matt Williams	2.41
92	Bobby Bonds	2.39
93	Frank Chance	2.39
94	Al Kaline	2.36
95	Art Devlin	2.35
96	Jack Fournier	2.34
97	Jack Clark	2.34
98	Roy Thomas	2.33
99	Gavvy Cravath	2.32
100	Bobby Wallace	2.32

Stolen Bases

1	Rickey Henderson	1186
2	Lou Brock	938
3	Billy Hamilton	912
4	Ty Cobb	892
5	Tim Raines	787
6	Vince Coleman	752
7	Eddie Collins	744
8	Arlie Latham	739
9	Max Carey	738
10	Honus Wagner	722
11	Joe Morgan	689
12	Willie Wilson	668
13	Tom Brown	657
14	Bert Campaneris	649
15	George Davis	616
16	Dummy Hoy	594
17	Maury Wills	586
18	George Van Haltren	583
19	Ozzie Smith	580
20	Hugh Duffy	574
21	Bid McPhee	568
22	Davey Lopes	557
23	Cesar Cedeno	550
24	Bill Dahlen	547
25	Brett Butler	543
26	John Ward	540
27	Herman Long	534
28	Patsy Donovan	518
29	Jack Doyle	516
30	Harry Stovey	509
31	Luis Aparicio	506
	Fred Clarke	506
33	Otis Nixon	498
34	Willie Keeler	495
	Clyde Milan	495
36	Omar Moreno	487
37	Paul Molitor	484
38	Mike Griffin	473
39	Tommy McCarthy	468
40	Jimmy Sheckard	465
41	Bobby Bonds	461
42	Ed Delahanty	455
	Ron LeFlore	455
44	Curt Welch	453
45	Steve Sax	444
46	Joe Kelley	443
47	Sherry Magee	441
48	John McGraw	436
49	Tris Speaker	432
50	Bob Bescher	428
	Mike Tiernan	428
52	Charlie Comiskey	419
	Frankie Frisch	419
54	Jimmy Ryan	418
55	Tommy Harper	408
56	Donie Bush	404
57	Frank Chance	401
58	Bill Lange	399
59	Willie Davis	398
60	Sam Mertes	396
61	Dave Collins	395
	Billy North	395
63	Jesse Burkett	389
64	Tommy Corcoran	387
65	Tom Daly	385
	Freddie Patek	385
67	George Burns	383
	Hugh Nicol	383
69	Fred Pfeffer	382
70	Walt Wilmot	381
71	Barry Bonds	380
	Nap Lajoie	380
73	Juan Samuel	378
74	Harry Hooper	375
	George Sisler	375
76	Jack Glasscock	372
77	Lonnie Smith	370
78	King Kelly	368
79	Sam Crawford	366
	Tommy Dowd	366
81	Hal Chase	363
82	Tommy Leach	361
83	Hughie Jennings	359
	Fielder Jones	359
85	Buck Ewing	354
	Gary Pettis	354
87	Rod Carew	353
88	Tommy Tucker	352
89	Sam Rice	351
90	George Case	349
91	Paul Radford	346
92	Julio Cruz	343
93	Amos Otis	341
94	John Anderson	338
	Willie Mays	338
96	Ryne Sandberg	337
97	Joe Tinker	336
98	Kip Selbach	334
99	Elmer Flick	330
	Willie McGee	330

Stolen Base Average

1	Eric Davis	85.9
2	Tim Raines	85.2
3	Barry Larkin	84.4
4	Stan Javier	84.1
5	Henry Cotto	83.3
6	Willie Wilson	83.3
7	Davey Lopes	83.0
8	Marquis Grissom	82.6
9	Kenny Lofton	82.2
10	Julio Cruz	81.5
11	Joe Morgan	81.0
12	Vince Coleman	80.9
13	Rickey Henderson	80.9
14	Andy Van Slyke	80.6
15	Mickey Mantle	80.1
16	Lenny Dykstra	79.8
17	Ozzie Smith	79.7
18	Enzo Hernandez	79.6
19	Gary Redus	79.5
20	Paul Molitor	79.5
21	Roberto Alomar	79.2
22	Devon White	79.2
23	R. J. Reynolds	79.0
24	Luis Aparicio	78.8
25	Amos Otis	78.6
26	Kirk Gibson	78.5
27	Gregg Jefferies	77.9
28	Tommy Harper	77.9
29	Rudy Law	77.8
30	Mike Felder	77.8
31	Joe Carter	77.7
32	Bob Dernier	77.6
33	Barry Bonds	77.6
34	Miguel Dilone	77.4
35	Brady Anderson	77.3
36	Gary Pettis	77.3
37	Lance Johnson	77.0
38	Mookie Wilson	76.9
39	Larry Walker	76.7
40	Hank Aaron	76.7
41	Willie Mays	76.6
42	Ryne Sandberg	76.6
43	Bert Campaneris	76.5
44	Milt Thompson	76.4
45	Ron LeFlore	76.2
46	George Case	76.2
47	Chuck Knoblauch	76.2
48	Oddibe McDowell	76.1
49	Otis Nixon	75.7
50	Mariano Duncan	75.7

Stolen Base Runs

1	Rickey Henderson	188
2	Tim Raines	154
3	Willie Wilson	120
4	Vince Coleman	119
5	Joe Morgan	110
6	Davey Lopes	99
7	Lou Brock	97
8	Ozzie Smith	85
9	Bert Campaneris	75
10	Luis Aparicio	70
	Paul Molitor	70
12	Eric Davis	66
13	Cesar Cedeno	58
14	Julio Cruz	56
	Marquis Grissom	56
	Kenny Lofton	56
17	Tommy Harper	53
	Otis Nixon	53
19	Barry Larkin	52
20	Ron LeFlore	51
	Maury Wills	51
22	Barry Bonds	48
23	Amos Otis	47
	Gary Redus	47
25	Roberto Alomar	45
26	Gary Pettis	44
27	Lenny Dykstra	42
28	Willie Davis	41
29	Willie Mays	40
30	George Case	39
	Ryne Sandberg	39
	Devon White	39
	Mookie Wilson	39
34	Kirk Gibson	38
	Andy Van Slyke	38
36	Bobby Bonds	37
	Omar Moreno	37
	Freddie Patek	37
39	Dave Collins	35
40	Lance Johnson	34
	Juan Samuel	34
42	Miguel Dilone	33
43	Larry Bowa	32
	Stan Javier	32
45	Dave Concepcion	31
	Willie McGee	31
47	Andre Dawson	29
	Delino DeShields	29
	Rudy Law	29
	Lloyd Moseby	29

Stolen Base Wins

1	Rickey Henderson	18.7
2	Tim Raines	15.7
3	Vince Coleman	12.1
4	Willie Wilson	12.0
5	Joe Morgan	11.5
6	Davey Lopes	10.2
7	Lou Brock	10.2
8	Ozzie Smith	8.8
9	Bert Campaneris	7.9
10	Luis Aparicio	7.3
11	Paul Molitor	6.9
12	Eric Davis	6.8
13	Cesar Cedeno	6.1
14	Marquis Grissom	5.7
15	Tommy Harper	5.6
16	Julio Cruz	5.6
17	Kenny Lofton	5.4
18	Maury Wills	5.3
19	Barry Larkin	5.3
20	Otis Nixon	5.3
21	Ron LeFlore	5.2
22	Barry Bonds	4.9
23	Amos Otis	4.9
24	Gary Redus	4.8
25	Roberto Alomar	4.5
26	Gary Pettis	4.4
27	Lenny Dykstra	4.3
28	Willie Davis	4.3
29	Willie Mays	4.1
30	Mookie Wilson	4.1
31	Ryne Sandberg	4.0
32	Andy Van Slyke	3.9
33	George Case	3.9
34	Freddie Patek	3.8
35	Devon White	3.8
36	Omar Moreno	3.8
37	Bobby Bonds	3.8
38	Kirk Gibson	3.8
39	Dave Collins	3.6
40	Juan Samuel	3.5
41	Miguel Dilone	3.4
42	Larry Bowa	3.3
43	Lance Johnson	3.3
44	Dave Concepcion	3.2
45	Willie McGee	3.2
46	Stan Javier	3.2
47	Andre Dawson	3.0
48	Delino DeShields	2.9
49	Bob Dernier	2.9
50	Rudy Law	2.9

Games

First Base
1	Eddie Murray	2413
2	Jake Beckley	2377
3	Mickey Vernon	2237
4	Lou Gehrig	2137
5	Charlie Grimm	2131
6	Joe Judge	2084
7	Ed Konetchy	2073
8	Steve Garvey	2059
9	Cap Anson	2058
10	Joe Kuhel	2057

Second Base
1	Eddie Collins	2650
2	Joe Morgan	2527
3	Lou Whitaker	2308
4	Nellie Fox	2295
5	Charlie Gehringer	2206
6	Willie Randolph	2152
7	Frank White	2150
8	Bid McPhee	2126
9	Bill Mazeroski	2094
10	Nap Lajoie	2035

Shortstop
1	Luis Aparicio	2581
2	Ozzie Smith	2511
3	Cal Ripken	2299
4	Larry Bowa	2222
5	Luke Appling	2218
6	Dave Concepcion	2178
7	Rabbit Maranville	2153
8	Alan Trammell	2139
9	Bill Dahlen	2132
10	Bert Campaneris	2097

Third Base
1	Brooks Robinson	2870
2	Graig Nettles	2412
3	Mike Schmidt	2212
4	Buddy Bell	2183
5	Eddie Mathews	2181
6	Ron Santo	2130
7	Tim Wallach	2054
8	Eddie Yost	2008
9	Ron Cey	1989
10	Wade Boggs	1987

Outfield
1	Ty Cobb	2935
2	Willie Mays	2842
3	Hank Aaron	2760
4	Tris Speaker	2698
5	Lou Brock	2507
6	Al Kaline	2488
7	Dave Winfield	2469
8	Max Carey	2421
9	Vada Pinson	2403
10	Roberto Clemente	2370
11	Zack Wheat	2337
12	Willie Davis	2323
	Andre Dawson	2323
14	Mel Ott	2313
15	Sam Crawford	2299
16	Paul Waner	2288
17	Harry Hooper	2284
18	Sam Rice	2270
19	Babe Ruth	2241
20	Goose Goslin	2188

Catcher
1	Carlton Fisk	2229
2	Bob Boone	2225
3	Gary Carter	2056
4	Jim Sundberg	1927
5	Al Lopez	1918
6	Tony Pena	1912
7	Lance Parrish	1818
8	Rick Ferrell	1806
9	Gabby Hartnett	1793
10	Ted Simmons	1771

Pitcher
1	Hoyt Wilhelm	1070
2	Kent Tekulve	1050
3	Rich Gossage	1002
4	Lee Smith	997
5	Lindy McDaniel	987
6	Dennis Eckersley	964
7	Rollie Fingers	944
8	Gene Garber	931
9	Cy Young	906
10	Sparky Lyle	899

Fielding Average

First Base
1	Steve Garvey	.996
2	Don Mattingly	.996
3	Wes Parker	.996
4	Dan Driessen	.995
5	Jim Spencer	.995
6	Frank McCormick	.995
7	Mark Grace	.995
8	Rafael Palmeiro	.995
9	Wally Joyner	.994
10	Keith Hernandez	.994
11	Kent Hrbek	.994
12	Vic Power	.994

Second Base
1	Ryne Sandberg	.990
2	Tom Herr	.989
3	Jose Lind	.988
4	Jody Reed	.988
5	Jim Gantner	.985
6	Frank White	.984
7	Bobby Grich	.984
8	Jerry Lumpe	.984
9	Lou Whitaker	.984
10	Cookie Rojas	.984

Shortstop
1	Larry Bowa	.980
2	Tony Fernandez	.980
3	Omar Vizquel	.980
4	Cal Ripken	.979
5	Ozzie Smith	.978
6	Spike Owen	.977
7	Alan Trammell	.977
8	Mark Belanger	.977
9	Bucky Dent	.976
10	Dick Schofield	.976

Third Base
1	Brooks Robinson	.971
2	Ken Reitz	.970
3	George Kell	.969
4	Steve Buechele	.968
5	Don Money	.968
6	Don Wert	.968
7	Willie Kamm	.967
8	Heinie Groh	.967
9	Carney Lansford	.966
10	Clete Boyer	.965

Outfield
1	Terry Puhl	.993
2	Brett Butler	.992
3	Pete Rose	.991
4	Amos Otis	.991
5	Joe Rudi	.991
6	Mickey Stanley	.991
7	Paul O'Neill	.991
8	Robin Yount	.990
9	Jim Piersall	.990
10	Jim Landis	.989
11	Ken Berry	.989
12	Otis Nixon	.989
13	Tommy Holmes	.989
14	Kirby Puckett	.989
15	Gene Woodling	.989
16	Cesar Geronimo	.988
17	Fred Lynn	.988
18	Mike Devereaux	.988
19	Paul Blair	.988
20	Tim Raines	.988

Catcher
1	Bill Freehan	.993
2	Elston Howard	.993
3	Jim Sundberg	.993
4	Sherm Lollar	.992
5	Johnny Edwards	.992
6	Tom Haller	.992
7	Lance Parrish	.991
8	Jerry Grote	.991
9	Ernie Whitt	.991
10	Gary Carter	.991

Pitcher
1	Don Mossi	.990
2	Gary Nolan	.990
3	Rick Rhoden	.989
4	Lon Warneke	.988
5	Jim Wilson	.988
6	Woodie Fryman	.988
7	Larry Gura	.986
8	Pete Alexander	.985
9	Alvin Crowder	.984
10	Bill Monbouquette	.984

Total Chances per Game

First Base
1	Tom Jones	11.38
2	George Stovall	11.30
3	George Kelly	11.09
4	Candy LaChance	11.05
5	Wally Pipp	11.05
6	Ed Konetchy	11.04
7	George Burns	10.92
8	Bill Terry	10.91
9	Cap Anson	10.86
10	Walter Holke	10.83
11	Bill Phillips	10.83
12	Fred Tenney	10.83

Second Base
1	Fred Pfeffer	6.95
2	Bid McPhee	6.70
3	Cub Stricker	6.59
4	Lou Bierbauer	6.50
5	Cupid Childs	6.32
6	Ski Melillo	6.16
7	Hughie Critz	6.07
8	Frankie Frisch	6.05
9	Bobby Lowe	6.01
10	Bucky Harris	6.00
11	Nap Lajoie	6.00

Shortstop
1	Herman Long	6.38
2	Dave Bancroft	6.33
3	Bill Dahlen	6.26
4	George Davis	6.22
5	Rabbit Maranville	6.10
6	Bobby Wallace	6.10
7	Tommy Corcoran	6.09
8	Monte Cross	6.06
9	Bones Ely	6.06
10	Honus Wagner	5.99

Third Base
1	Jerry Denny	4.21
2	Billy Shindle	4.15
3	Billy Nash	4.07
4	Arlie Latham	4.04
5	Denny Lyons	3.98
6	Jimmy Collins	3.89
7	Hick Carpenter	3.81
8	Jimmy Austin	3.74
9	Lave Cross	3.73
10	Frank Baker	3.64

Outfield
1	Taylor Douthit	3.16
2	Richie Ashburn	3.04
3	Dom DiMaggio	2.99
4	Mike Kreevich	2.95
5	Dwayne Murphy	2.92
6	Sam Chapman	2.91
7	Sam West	2.88
8	Max Carey	2.87
9	Fred Schulte	2.84
10	Lloyd Waner	2.81
11	Vince DiMaggio	2.80
12	Joe DiMaggio	2.78
13	Tris Speaker	2.77
14	Devon White	2.77
15	Billy North	2.76
16	Terry Moore	2.75
17	Garry Maddox	2.74
18	Jimmy McAleer	2.73
19	Wally Berger	2.71
20	Gary Pettis	2.71
21	Kirby Puckett	2.71

Catcher
1	Johnny Edwards	6.98
2	Johnny Roseboro	6.83
3	Bill Freehan	6.79
4	Mike Scioscia	6.59
5	Jerry Grote	6.53
6	Tim McCarver	6.41
7	Gary Carter	6.38
8	Tony Pena	6.37
9	Tom Haller	6.33
10	Bill Killefer	6.27

Pitcher
1	Nick Altrock	3.70
2	Harry Howell	3.61
3	Addie Joss	3.59
4	Ed Walsh	3.49
5	Nixey Callahan	3.47
6	Willie Sudhoff	3.33
7	George Mullin	3.20
8	Barney Pelty	3.17
9	Chick Fraser	3.12
10	Red Donahue	2.95
11	Ed Willett	2.95

Chances Accepted per Game

First Base
1	Tom Jones	11.21
2	George Stovall	11.14
3	George Kelly	11.00
4	Wally Pipp	10.96
5	Ed Konetchy	10.93
6	Candy LaChance	10.87
7	Bill Terry	10.82
8	George Burns	10.77
9	Walter Holke	10.75
10	Fred Tenney	10.65

Second Base
1	Fred Pfeffer	6.39
2	Bid McPhee	6.33
3	Lou Bierbauer	6.07
4	Ski Melillo	6.00
5	Cub Stricker	5.97
6	Hughie Critz	5.91
7	Frankie Frisch	5.89
8	Cupid Childs	5.88
9	Bucky Harris	5.79
10	Nap Lajoie	5.78

Shortstop
1	Dave Bancroft	5.98
2	George Davis	5.85
3	Rabbit Maranville	5.81
4	Bill Dahlen	5.80
5	Herman Long	5.78
6	Bobby Wallace	5.73
7	Travis Jackson	5.67
8	Dick Bartell	5.64
9	Tommy Corcoran	5.63
10	Honus Wagner	5.63

Third Base
1	Jerry Denny	3.72
2	Billy Shindle	3.70
3	Billy Nash	3.65
4	Jimmy Collins	3.61
5	Arlie Latham	3.52
6	Denny Lyons	3.51
7	Lave Cross	3.50
8	Jimmy Austin	3.49
9	Frank Baker	3.43
10	Bill Bradley	3.38

Outfield
1	Taylor Douthit	3.07
2	Richie Ashburn	2.98
3	Dom DiMaggio	2.92
4	Mike Kreevich	2.89
5	Dwayne Murphy	2.88
6	Sam Chapman	2.83
7	Sam West	2.83
8	Max Carey	2.77
9	Fred Schulte	2.77
10	Lloyd Waner	2.76
11	Vince DiMaggio	2.75
12	Devon White	2.73
13	Joe DiMaggio	2.72
14	Terry Moore	2.71
15	Billy North	2.71
16	Garry Maddox	2.70
17	Tris Speaker	2.69
18	Kirby Puckett	2.68
19	Robin Yount	2.68
20	Gary Pettis	2.67

Catcher
1	Johnny Edwards	6.92
2	Johnny Roseboro	6.76
3	Bill Freehan	6.75
4	Mike Scioscia	6.51
5	Jerry Grote	6.47
6	Tim McCarver	6.35
7	Gary Carter	6.32
8	Tony Pena	6.31
9	Tom Haller	6.28
10	Earl Battey	6.15

Pitcher
1	Nick Altrock	3.57
2	Addie Joss	3.47
3	Harry Howell	3.46
4	Ed Walsh	3.36
5	Nixey Callahan	3.25
6	Willie Sudhoff	3.13
7	George Mullin	3.03
8	Barney Pelty	2.97
9	Chick Fraser	2.90
10	Red Donahue	2.81
11	Christy Mathewson	2.81
12	Doc White	2.81

Putouts

First Base
1	Jake Beckley	23709
2	Ed Konetchy	21361
3	Eddie Murray	21255
4	Cap Anson	20794
5	Charlie Grimm	20711
6	Stuffy McInnis	19962
7	Mickey Vernon	19808
8	Jake Daubert	19634
9	Lou Gehrig	19510
10	Joe Kuhel	19386

Second Base
1	Bid McPhee	6545
2	Eddie Collins	6526
3	Nellie Fox	6090
4	Joe Morgan	5742
5	Nap Lajoie	5496
6	Charlie Gehringer	5369
7	Bill Mazeroski	4974
8	Bobby Doerr	4928
9	Willie Randolph	4859
10	Billy Herman	4780

Shortstop
1	Rabbit Maranville	5139
2	Bill Dahlen	4850
3	Dave Bancroft	4623
4	Honus Wagner	4576
5	Tommy Corcoran	4550
6	Luis Aparicio	4548
7	Luke Appling	4398
8	Ozzie Smith	4249
9	Herman Long	4225
10	Bobby Wallace	4142

Third Base
1	Brooks Robinson	2697
2	Jimmy Collins	2372
3	Eddie Yost	2356
4	Lave Cross	2306
5	Pie Traynor	2289
6	Billy Nash	2219
7	Frank Baker	2154
8	Willie Kamm	2151
9	Eddie Mathews	2049
10	Willie Jones	2045

Outfield
1	Willie Mays	7095
2	Tris Speaker	6788
3	Max Carey	6363
4	Ty Cobb	6361
5	Richie Ashburn	6089
6	Hank Aaron	5539
7	Willie Davis	5449
8	Doc Cramer	5412
9	Rickey Henderson	5310
10	Andre Dawson	5158
11	Brett Butler	5133
12	Vada Pinson	5097
13	Willie Wilson	5060
14	Al Kaline	5035
15	Zack Wheat	4996
16	Chet Lemon	4993
17	Al Simmons	4988
18	Dave Winfield	4975
19	Amos Otis	4936
20	Paul Waner	4872

Catcher
1	Gary Carter	11785
2	Carlton Fisk	11369
3	Bob Boone	11260
4	Tony Pena	11021
5	Bill Freehan	9941
6	Jim Sundberg	9767
7	Lance Parrish	9647
8	Johnny Roseboro	9291
9	Johnny Bench	9249
10	Johnny Edwards	8925

Pitcher
1	Jack Morris	387
2	Phil Niekro	386
3	Fergie Jenkins	363
4	Gaylord Perry	349
5	Don Sutton	334
6	Tony Mullane	328
	Rick Reuschel	328
	Tom Seaver	328
9	Pud Galvin	324
10	Robin Roberts	316

Putouts per Game

First Base
1	Tom Jones	10.53
2	Candy LaChance	10.48
3	George Stovall	10.45
4	George Kelly	10.37
5	Wally Pipp	10.33
6	Ed Konetchy	10.31
7	Bill Phillips	10.22
8	Walter Holke	10.20
9	Charlie Comiskey	10.15
10	John Reilly	10.12
11	Bill Terry	10.12

Second Base
1	Bid McPhee	3.08
2	Fred Pfeffer	3.07
3	Cub Stricker	3.02
4	Lou Bierbauer	2.74
5	Jerry Priddy	2.74
6	Bucky Harris	2.73
7	Nap Lajoie	2.71
8	Bobby Doerr	2.67
9	Cupid Childs	2.66
10	Nellie Fox	2.66

Shortstop
1	Dave Bancroft	2.47
2	Honus Wagner	2.43
3	Rabbit Maranville	2.39
4	Monte Cross	2.38
5	George Davis	2.36
6	Herman Long	2.36
7	Dick Bartell	2.31
8	Bill Dahlen	2.28
9	Ivy Olson	2.27
10	Bobby Wallace	2.27

Third Base
1	Jerry Denny	1.61
2	Denny Lyons	1.55
3	Billy Nash	1.52
4	Jimmy Austin	1.43
5	Billy Shindle	1.43
6	Jimmy Collins	1.41
7	Frank Baker	1.40
8	Hick Carpenter	1.37
9	Lave Cross	1.34
10	Hans Lobert	1.30

Outfield
1	Taylor Douthit	3.01
2	Richie Ashburn	2.90
3	Dom DiMaggio	2.82
4	Dwayne Murphy	2.82
5	Mike Kreevich	2.81
6	Sam Chapman	2.74
7	Sam West	2.74
8	Fred Schulte	2.70
9	Lloyd Waner	2.68
10	Devon White	2.67
11	Billy North	2.65
12	Garry Maddox	2.64
13	Max Carey	2.63
14	Joe DiMaggio	2.63
15	Vince DiMaggio	2.63
16	Terry Moore	2.63
17	Robin Yount	2.63
18	Gary Pettis	2.62
19	Lance Johnson	2.61
20	Chet Lemon	2.60

Catcher
1	Johnny Edwards	6.42
2	Johnny Roseboro	6.30
3	Bill Freehan	6.29
4	Jerry Grote	6.00
5	Mike Scioscia	5.98
6	Tim McCarver	5.92
7	Tom Haller	5.85
8	Tony Pena	5.77
9	Gary Carter	5.74
10	Earl Battey	5.69

Pitcher
1	Greg Maddux	0.90
2	Kevin Brown	0.84
3	Dave Foutz	0.78
4	Nick Altrock	0.77
5	Chick Fraser	0.73
6	Mike Boddicker	0.72
7	Carl Morton	0.72
8	Doug Drabek	0.71
9	Jack Morris	0.71
10	Dan Petry	0.69

Assists

First Base
1	Eddie Murray	1865
2	Keith Hernandez	1682
3	George Sisler	1529
4	Mickey Vernon	1448
5	Fred Tenney	1363
6	Bill Buckner	1351
	Chris Chambliss	1351
8	Norm Cash	1317
9	Jake Beckley	1315
10	Joe Judge	1301

Second Base
1	Eddie Collins	7630
2	Charlie Gehringer	7068
3	Joe Morgan	6967
4	Bid McPhee	6905
5	Bill Mazeroski	6685
6	Lou Whitaker	6653
7	Nellie Fox	6373
8	Willie Randolph	6336
9	Nap Lajoie	6262
10	Frank White	6250

Shortstop
1	Ozzie Smith	8375
2	Luis Aparicio	8016
3	Bill Dahlen	7500
4	Rabbit Maranville	7354
5	Luke Appling	7218
6	Tommy Corcoran	7106
7	Cal Ripken	6978
8	Larry Bowa	6857
9	Dave Concepcion	6594
10	Dave Bancroft	6561

Third Base
1	Brooks Robinson	6205
2	Graig Nettles	5279
3	Mike Schmidt	5045
4	Buddy Bell	4925
5	Ron Santo	4581
6	Eddie Mathews	4322
7	Aurelio Rodriguez	4150
8	Ron Cey	4018
9	Tim Wallach	3992
10	Gary Gaetti	3927

Outfield
1	Tris Speaker	449
2	Ty Cobb	392
3	Jimmy Ryan	375
4	Tom Brown	348
	George Van Haltren	348
6	Harry Hooper	344
7	Max Carey	339
8	Jimmy Sheckard	307
9	Clyde Milan	294
10	Orator Shaffer	289
11	King Kelly	285
12	Sam Thompson	283
13	Sam Rice	278
14	Dummy Hoy	273
15	Jesse Burkett	270
16	Sam Crawford	268
	Tommy McCarthy	268
18	Roberto Clemente	266
19	Patsy Donovan	264
20	Willie Keeler	258

Catcher
1	Deacon McGuire	1859
2	Ray Schalk	1811
3	Steve O'Neill	1698
4	Red Dooin	1590
5	Chief Zimmer	1580
6	Johnny Kling	1552
7	Ivey Wingo	1487
8	Wilbert Robinson	1454
9	Bill Bergen	1444
10	Wally Schang	1420

Pitcher
1	Cy Young	2014
2	Christy Mathewson	1503
3	Pete Alexander	1419
4	Pud Galvin	1382
5	Walter Johnson	1351
6	Burleigh Grimes	1252
7	George Mullin	1244
8	Jack Quinn	1240
9	Ed Walsh	1208
10	Eppa Rixey	1195

Assists per Game

First Base
1	Bill Buckner	0.87
2	Mark Grace	0.87
3	Ferris Fain	0.84
4	Keith Hernandez	0.84
5	Vic Power	0.83
6	Wally Joyner	0.82
7	Eddie Murray	0.78
8	Pete O'Brien	0.78
9	George Sisler	0.78
10	Rudy York	0.77

Second Base
1	Hughie Critz	3.54
2	Frankie Frisch	3.42
3	Ski Melillo	3.38
4	Lou Bierbauer	3.34
5	Glenn Hubbard	3.34
6	Fred Pfeffer	3.33
7	Rogers Hornsby	3.31
8	Bid McPhee	3.25
9	Ryne Sandberg	3.25
10	Tony Cuccinello	3.23

Shortstop
1	Germany Smith	3.70
2	Art Fletcher	3.55
3	Bill Dahlen	3.52
4	Dave Bancroft	3.51
5	Bones Ely	3.50
6	Travis Jackson	3.50
7	George Davis	3.49
8	Jack Glasscock	3.46
9	Bobby Wallace	3.46
10	Tommy Corcoran	3.43
11	Herman Long	3.43

Third Base
1	Mike Schmidt	2.29
2	Billy Shindle	2.27
3	Buddy Bell	2.26
4	Arlie Latham	2.26
5	Clete Boyer	2.24
6	Terry Pendleton	2.21
7	Jimmy Collins	2.20
8	Graig Nettles	2.19
9	George Brett	2.18
10	Darrell Evans	2.17
11	Brooks Robinson	2.17

Outfield
1	Tommy McCarthy	0.23
2	Pop Corkhill	0.22
3	Jimmy Wolf	0.22
4	Sam Thompson	0.21
5	Tom Brown	0.20
6	Jimmy Ryan	0.20
7	George Van Haltren	0.20
8	Curt Welch	0.20
9	Ed Delahanty	0.19
10	George Gore	0.19
11	Paul Hines	0.18
12	Gavvy Cravath	0.17
13	Mike Griffin	0.17
14	Ned Hanlon	0.17
15	Joe Hornung	0.17
16	Mike Mitchell	0.17
17	Tris Speaker	0.17
18	Tilly Walker	0.17
19	George Wood	0.17
20	Ross Youngs	0.17

Catcher
1	Duke Farrell	1.42
2	Red Dooin	1.34
3	Johnny Kling	1.33
4	Bill Killefer	1.32
5	Oscar Stanage	1.29
6	Chief Zimmer	1.28
7	John Warner	1.27
8	Ivey Wingo	1.21
9	Billy Sullivan	1.18
10	George Gibson	1.17

Pitcher
1	Addie Joss	2.96
2	Harry Howell	2.84
3	Ed Walsh	2.81
4	Nick Altrock	2.80
5	Willie Sudhoff	2.75
6	Nixey Callahan	2.60
7	George Mullin	2.56
8	Ed Willett	2.54
9	Barney Pelty	2.48
10	Red Donahue	2.47

Double Plays

First Base
1	Mickey Vernon	2044
2	Eddie Murray	2033
3	Joe Kuhel	1769
4	Charlie Grimm	1733
5	Chris Chambliss	1687
6	Keith Hernandez	1654
7	Gil Hodges	1614
8	Lou Gehrig	1575
9	Jim Bottomley	1562
10	Jimmie Foxx	1528

Second Base
1	Bill Mazeroski	1706
2	Nellie Fox	1619
3	Willie Randolph	1547
4	Lou Whitaker	1527
5	Bobby Doerr	1507
6	Joe Morgan	1505
7	Charlie Gehringer	1444
8	Frank White	1382
9	Red Schoendienst	1368
10	Bobby Grich	1302

Shortstop
1	Ozzie Smith	1590
2	Cal Ripken	1565
3	Luis Aparicio	1553
4	Luke Appling	1424
5	Alan Trammell	1307
6	Roy McMillan	1304
7	Dave Concepcion	1290
8	Larry Bowa	1265
9	Pee Wee Reese	1246
10	Dick Groat	1237

Third Base
1	Brooks Robinson	618
2	Graig Nettles	470
3	Mike Schmidt	450
4	Buddy Bell	430
5	Gary Gaetti	411
6	Aurelio Rodriguez	408
7	Ron Santo	395
8	Wade Boggs	382
9	Eddie Mathews	369
10	Ken Boyer	355

Outfield
1	Tris Speaker	139
2	Ty Cobb	107
3	Max Carey	86
4	Tom Brown	85
5	Harry Hooper	81
6	Jimmy Sheckard	80
7	Mike Griffin	75
8	Dummy Hoy	72
9	Jimmy Ryan	71
10	Fielder Jones	70
11	Patsy Donovan	69
12	Sam Rice	67
13	George Van Haltren	64
14	Jesse Burkett	62
15	Sam Thompson	61
16	Willie Keeler	60
	Willie Mays	60
	Tommy McCarthy	60
	Mel Ott	60
20	Sam Crawford	59

Catcher
1	Ray Schalk	226
2	Steve O'Neill	193
3	Yogi Berra	175
4	Gabby Hartnett	163
5	Bob Boone	154
6	Tony Pena	153
	Jimmie Wilson	153
8	Gary Carter	149
	Wally Schang	149
10	Carlton Fisk	147

Pitcher
1	Phil Niekro	83
2	Warren Spahn	82
3	Freddie Fitzsimmons	79
4	Bob Lemon	78
5	Bucky Walters	76
6	Burleigh Grimes	74
7	Walter Johnson	72
8	Tommy John	69
9	Jim Kaat	65
10	Dizzy Trout	63

Fielding Runs

1	Nap Lajoie	367
2	Bill Mazeroski	362
3	Bill Dahlen	348
4	Bid McPhee	313
5	Fred Pfeffer	266
6	Mike Schmidt	265
7	George Davis	249
8	Tris Speaker	248
9	Ozzie Smith	243
10	Jack Glasscock	240
11	Clete Boyer	233
12	Glenn Hubbard	229
13	Richie Ashburn	227
14	Bobby Wallace	211
15	Joe Tinker	208
16	Dave Bancroft	198
	Max Carey	198
18	Buddy Bell	191
19	Terry Pendleton	187
20	Aurelio Rodriguez	183
21	Bobby Doerr	181
22	Willie Mays	180
23	Dick Bartell	178
	Mickey Doolan	178
25	Roberto Clemente	175
26	Joe Gerhardt	173
27	George McBride	169
28	Mark Belanger	167
29	Darrell Evans	165
	Lee Tannehill	165
31	Art Fletcher	162
	Rickey Henderson	162
33	Dal Maxvill	160
34	Germany Smith	157
35	Danny Richardson	156
36	Rabbit Maranville	155
37	Ski Melillo	151
	Brooks Robinson	151
39	Lou Bierbauer	150
	Hughie Jennings	150
	Bobby Knoop	150
42	Frankie Frisch	149
	Jim Hegan	149
	Carl Yastrzemski	149
45	Keith Hernandez	148
	Pop Snyder	148
47	Lave Cross	146
48	Garry Maddox	142
49	Billy Jurges	140
50	Barry Bonds	138
	Ron Santo	138
52	Jimmy Collins	137
	Willie Davis	137
	Fred Dunlap	137
	Kirby Puckett	137
	Bobby Wine	137
57	Lou Boudreau	134
58	John Ward	133
59	Rafael Belliard	132
	Hal Lanier	132
	Graig Nettles	132
62	Bill Killefer	131
63	Lou Criger	130
64	Manny Trillo	129
65	Mick Kelleher	128
66	Bill Buckner	127
67	Gene Alley	125
68	Fred Tenney	124
69	Andre Dawson	123
	Vic Power	123
71	Al Weis	121
72	Tony Gwynn	120
73	Bill Bergen	119
74	Ryne Sandberg	118
75	Chet Lemon	116
	Harold Reynolds	116
77	Everett Scott	115
78	Jesse Barfield	114
	Curt Flood	114
	Tommy Leach	114
	Tony Pena	114
82	Johnny Callison	113
	Hank DeBerry	113
	Hardy Richardson	113
85	Hughie Critz	111
	Jose Cruz	111
	Hobe Ferris	111
88	Brett Butler	110
	Jim Wynn	110
90	Jerry Denny	109
91	Devon White	108
92	Joe Sewell	107
	Curt Welch	107
94	Tommy Corcoran	106
95	Johnny Logan	105
	Tim Raines	105
97	Alvaro Espinoza	104
98	5 players tied	103

Fielding Runs (by position)

First Base
1	Keith Hernandez	150
2	Fred Tenney	129
3	Vic Power	124
4	Bill Buckner	121
5	George Sisler	89
6	Sid Bream	76
	Darrell Evans	76
8	Mark Grace	74
9	Wally Joyner	67
	Bill Terry	67

Second Base
1	Nap Lajoie	369
2	Bill Mazeroski	363
3	Bid McPhee	314
4	Fred Pfeffer	257
5	Glenn Hubbard	229
6	Bobby Doerr	180
7	Joe Gerhardt	160
8	Lou Bierbauer	153
9	Bobby Knoop	150
10	Ski Melillo	148

Shortstop
1	Bill Dahlen	302
2	Jack Glasscock	243
3	Ozzie Smith	242
4	Joe Tinker	210
5	Dave Bancroft	200
6	George Davis	187
7	Rabbit Maranville	174
8	George McBride	172
9	Mickey Doolan	168
10	Mark Belanger	164

Third Base
1	Mike Schmidt	265
2	Clete Boyer	201
3	Buddy Bell	199
4	Terry Pendleton	188
5	Aurelio Rodriguez	184
6	Brooks Robinson	152
7	Jimmy Collins	136
	Graig Nettles	136
9	Ron Santo	135
10	Lave Cross	133

Outfield
1	Tris Speaker	248
2	Richie Ashburn	227
3	Max Carey	202
4	Willie Mays	184
5	Roberto Clemente	173
6	Rickey Henderson	162
7	Carl Yastrzemski	143
8	Garry Maddox	142
9	Kirby Puckett	139
10	Barry Bonds	138
11	Willie Davis	137
12	Andre Dawson	124
13	Tony Gwynn	119
	Chet Lemon	119
15	Jim Wynn	118
16	Curt Flood	116
17	Johnny Callison	114
18	Jesse Barfield	112
19	Jose Cruz	111
20	Jim Fogarty	110

Catcher
1	Pop Snyder	151
2	Jim Hegan	149
3	Lou Criger	133
4	Bill Killefer	131
5	Bill Bergen	119
6	Tony Pena	113
7	Chief Zimmer	103
8	Ossee Schreckengost	98
	Jim Sundberg	98
10	Johnny Edwards	97

Pitcher
1	Ed Walsh	84
2	Carl Mays	74
3	Christy Mathewson	69
4	Freddie Fitzsimmons	61
5	Bob Lemon	59
6	Burleigh Grimes	58
7	Tommy John	56
	Greg Maddux	56
9	Harry Gumbert	51
10	Harry Howell	50

Fielding Wins

1	Bill Mazeroski	37.7
2	Nap Lajoie	37.7
3	Bill Dahlen	33.1
4	Mike Schmidt	27.7
5	Bid McPhee	27.2
6	Tris Speaker	25.3
7	Ozzie Smith	25.3
8	Clete Boyer	24.2
9	Glenn Hubbard	23.8
10	George Davis	23.4
11	Fred Pfeffer	23.2
12	Richie Ashburn	22.7
13	Joe Tinker	21.9
14	Bobby Wallace	21.3
15	Jack Glasscock	21.3
16	Max Carey	20.3
17	Dave Bancroft	20.2
18	Buddy Bell	19.6
19	Terry Pendleton	19.2
20	Aurelio Rodriguez	19.1
21	Mickey Doolan	19.0
22	Willie Mays	18.6
23	Roberto Clemente	18.2
24	George McBride	18.2
25	Lee Tannehill	17.9
26	Bobby Doerr	17.8
27	Dick Bartell	17.5
28	Mark Belanger	17.5
29	Art Fletcher	17.3
30	Darrell Evans	17.0
31	Dal Maxvill	16.9
32	Bobby Knoop	16.2
33	Rickey Henderson	16.1
34	Brooks Robinson	15.9
35	Rabbit Maranville	15.7
36	Carl Yastrzemski	15.5
37	Joe Gerhardt	15.5
38	Keith Hernandez	15.5
39	Jim Hegan	14.9
40	Garry Maddox	14.9
41	Frankie Frisch	14.6
42	Ron Santo	14.5
43	Bobby Wine	14.4
44	Willie Davis	14.4
45	Bill Killefer	14.2
46	Billy Jurges	14.2
47	Barry Bonds	14.1
48	Ski Melillo	14.1
49	Hal Lanier	14.1
50	Graig Nettles	13.7
51	Rafael Belliard	13.6
52	Danny Richardson	13.6
53	Kirby Puckett	13.5
54	Germany Smith	13.5
55	Lou Boudreau	13.5
56	Manny Trillo	13.5
57	Lave Cross	13.4
58	Mick Kelleher	13.4
59	Gene Alley	13.3
60	Jimmy Collins	13.2
61	Pop Snyder	13.2
62	Hughie Jennings	13.2
63	Lou Criger	13.2
64	Bill Buckner	13.1
65	Al Weis	12.9
66	Andre Dawson	12.7
67	Lou Bierbauer	12.7
68	Bill Bergen	12.6
69	Vic Power	12.6
70	Fred Dunlap	12.4
71	Tony Gwynn	12.4
72	Fred Tenney	12.3
73	Ryne Sandberg	12.3
74	Curt Flood	11.9
75	Tommy Leach	11.9
76	Johnny Callison	11.9
77	Hobe Ferris	11.8
78	John Ward	11.7
79	Everett Scott	11.7
80	Tony Pena	11.7
81	Chet Lemon	11.6
82	Jim Wynn	11.6
83	Jose Cruz	11.6
84	Harold Reynolds	11.5
85	Jesse Barfield	11.4
86	Brett Butler	11.2
87	Hank DeBerry	10.9
88	Hughie Critz	10.7
89	Al Weis	10.7
90	Tim Raines	10.7
91	Omar Moreno	10.7
92	Devon White	10.6
93	Lenny Dykstra	10.6
94	Johnny Logan	10.6
95	Hank Aaron	10.5
96	Honus Wagner	10.4
97	Eddie Miller	10.4
98	Dwayne Murphy	10.2
99	Alvaro Espinoza	10.2
100	Johnny Edwards	10.2

Total Player Rating

1	Babe Ruth	107.7
2	Nap Lajoie	94.2
3	Willie Mays	92.2
4	Ty Cobb	91.0
5	Hank Aaron	89.8
6	Tris Speaker	86.5
7	Ted Williams	85.7
8	Honus Wagner	81.2
9	Rogers Hornsby	81.1
10	Mike Schmidt	78.4
11	Rickey Henderson	77.5
12	Mickey Mantle	76.1
13	Stan Musial	70.5
14	Eddie Collins	69.8
15	Frank Robinson	69.0
16	Lou Gehrig	65.7
17	Barry Bonds	64.7
18	Mel Ott	62.7
19	Joe Morgan	56.3
20	Jimmie Foxx	54.0
21	Tim Raines	52.3
22	Eddie Mathews	51.6
23	Bill Dahlen	51.4
24	George Davis	51.0
25	Joe DiMaggio	46.9
26	Carl Yastrzemski	45.5
27	Wade Boggs	44.6
	Al Kaline	44.6
29	Charlie Gehringer	44.4
30	Ed Delahanty	44.3
31	Bobby Grich	44.0
32	Tony Gwynn	43.2
33	Robin Yount	43.1
34	Ozzie Smith	43.0
35	Roberto Clemente	42.9
36	Reggie Jackson	42.8
37	Roger Connor	42.7
38	Lou Boudreau	41.3
	Cal Ripken	41.3
40	Dan Brouthers	41.2
41	Luke Appling	40.7
42	Gabby Hartnett	40.1
	Bid McPhee	40.1
44	Ron Santo	39.5
45	Joe Cronin	39.4
46	Arky Vaughan	39.2
47	George Brett	39.0
	Bobby Doerr	39.0
	Frankie Frisch	39.0
50	Dave Winfield	38.5
51	Ryne Sandberg	38.2
52	Barry Larkin	37.6
53	Joe Jackson	37.5
54	Bobby Wallace	36.9
55	Willie McCovey	36.5
56	Bill Mazeroski	36.3
57	Yogi Berra	36.2
	Johnny Mize	36.2
59	Jack Glasscock	36.1
	Paul Waner	36.1
61	Bob Johnson	35.6
62	Bill Dickey	35.4
63	Dick Allen	35.3
	Paul Molitor	35.3
65	Dave Bancroft	35.2
66	Eddie Murray	35.0
	Reggie Smith	35.0
68	Darrell Evans	34.6
69	Joe Sewell	34.5
70	Keith Hernandez	34.4
71	Frank Baker	33.8
72	Jim Wynn	33.2
73	Willie Stargell	32.8
74	Harry Heilmann	32.3
75	Jackie Robinson	31.8
76	Rod Carew	31.7
	Billy Herman	31.7
78	Mickey Cochrane	31.4
79	Jack Clark	31.1
	Billy Williams	31.1
81	Cap Anson	30.8
82	Sam Crawford	30.4
	Dwight Evans	30.4
84	Richie Ashburn	30.2
85	Cupid Childs	30.0
	Hank Greenberg	30.0
87	Andre Dawson	29.9
88	Gary Carter	29.6
89	Bobby Bonds	29.5
	Buck Ewing	29.5
91	Frank Thomas	29.3
92	Kirby Puckett	29.1
93	Ralph Kiner	28.9
94	Pete Browning	28.8
	Jose Cruz	28.8
	Elmer Flick	28.8
97	Fred Clarke	28.7
98	Jesse Burkett	28.5
	Sam Thompson	28.5
100	Cesar Cedeno	28.3

Total Player Rating

101	Joe Gordon	28.2
102	Dick Bartell	27.9
103	Ken Griffey Jr.	27.8
104	Rusty Staub	27.6
105	Norm Cash	27.5
106	Fred Dunlap	27.4
107	Hardy Richardson	27.3
108	Stan Hack	27.2
109	Joe Medwick	27.1
	Jim Rice	27.1
111	Heinie Groh	27.0
112	Darryl Strawberry	26.6
113	Sherry Magee	26.5
114	Billy Hamilton	26.4
	Harmon Killebrew	26.4
116	Hughie Jennings	26.2
117	Jeff Bagwell	26.1
118	Goose Goslin	26.0
	Minnie Minoso	26.0
120	Ernie Banks	25.9
121	Art Fletcher	25.8
122	Al Simmons	25.6
123	Lenny Dykstra	25.5
124	Rocky Colavito	25.2
125	Lou Whitaker	25.0
126	Tony Oliva	24.9
	Bill Terry	24.9
128	King Kelly	24.7
129	Jose Canseco	24.6
130	Johnny Bench	24.3
	Zack Wheat	24.3
132	Carlton Fisk	24.0
	Travis Jackson	24.0
134	Jack Fournier	23.9
135	Charlie Keller	23.5
136	Albert Belle	23.3
137	Jimmy Collins	23.1
	Willie Randolph	23.1
	Joe Tinker	23.1
140	Dave Parker	23.0
141	Jake Beckley	22.9
	Buddy Bell	22.9
143	Brett Butler	22.8
	Roy Thomas	22.8
145	Harland Clift	22.7
	George Sisler	22.7
147	Max Carey	22.6
148	George Foster	22.3
	Ed Konetchy	22.3
	Chet Lemon	22.3
	Fred Lynn	22.3
	Duke Snider	22.3
153	Wally Berger	22.2
154	Eric Davis	22.0
155	Ron Cey	21.9
156	Alan Trammell	21.8
157	Fred Pfeffer	21.7
158	Roy Campanella	21.6
	Kevin Mitchell	21.6
160	Harry Stovey	21.5
161	Chuck Klein	21.4
162	Frank Howard	21.3
	Graig Nettles	21.3
164	Larry Doby	21.2
165	Roy White	21.1
166	Ken Singleton	20.9
	Fred Tenney	20.9
168	Charley Jones	20.7
	Pie Traynor	20.7
170	Art Devlin	20.6
	Jim Fregosi	20.6
172	Frank Chance	20.5
	Mike Griffin	20.5
174	Del Pratt	20.4
175	Andy Van Slyke	20.3
176	Glenn Hubbard	20.2
	Joe Kelley	20.2
178	Pete Rose	20.0
179	Denny Lyons	19.8
	Mark McGwire	19.8
	Brooks Robinson	19.8
182	Roger Bresnahan	19.7
183	Vern Stephens	19.6
	Joe Torre	19.6
185	Jimmy Sheckard	19.5
186	Will Clark	19.4
187	Dale Murphy	19.3
	Amos Otis	19.3
189	Roberto Alomar	19.2
	Charlie Bennett	19.2
	Edgar Martinez	19.2
192	Fred McGriff	19.1
193	Bill Nicholson	19.0
	Rafael Palmeiro	19.0
195	Gavvy Cravath	18.9
	Bill Joyce	18.9
197	Bob Elliott	18.8
198	Bobby Bonilla	18.6
	Ken Boyer	18.6
	Brian Downing	18.6

Total Player Rating

201	Eddie Stanky	18.4
202	Roy Cullenbine	18.1
	Miller Huggins	18.1
	Wally Schang	18.1
205	Gene Alley	18.0
	Matt Williams	18.0
207	Craig Biggio	17.9
	Rico Carty	17.9
209	Ferris Fain	17.8
210	Earl Averill	17.6
211	Tommy Leach	17.4
212	Babe Herman	17.3
	Johnny Logan	17.3
	Ernie Lombardi	17.3
	Ken Williams	17.3
216	Paul Hines	17.2
217	Tony Lazzeri	16.9
218	Harold Baines	16.8
	Gil McDougald	16.8
	Ted Simmons	16.8
221	Orlando Cepeda	16.7
	Pedro Guerrero	16.7
	Mike Piazza	16.7
224	Jesse Barfield	16.4
	Jeff Heath	16.4
	Dwayne Murphy	16.4
227	Enos Slaughter	16.3
228	George Gore	16.1
	Jim O'Rourke	16.1
230	Kirk Gibson	16.0
	John McGraw	16.0
	Jimmy Williams	16.0
233	Kiki Cuyler	15.8
	Phil Rizzuto	15.8
	Chief Zimmer	15.8
236	Mike Hargrove	15.7
237	Davey Johnson	15.6
	Jocko Milligan	15.6
	Danny Tartabull	15.6
	Hack Wilson	15.6
241	Ray Chapman	15.4
	Tony Fernandez	15.4
243	Chili Davis	15.3
	Gene Tenace	15.3
245	Thurman Munson	15.2
246	Sid Gordon	15.1
247	Mark Belanger	15.0
	Bobby Knoop	15.0
249	Jay Bell	14.9
	Henry Larkin	14.9
	Boog Powell	14.9
252	Benny Kauff	14.8
	Mike Scioscia	14.8
	Bobby Veach	14.8
255	Sixto Lezcano	14.7
	Paul O'Neill	14.7
257	Lave Cross	14.6
	Duke Farrell	14.6
	Augie Galan	14.6
	Greg Luzinski	14.6
	Pee Wee Reese	14.6
262	Tommy Henrich	14.5
	Kevin McReynolds	14.5
264	Bob Allison	14.3
265	Ron Hansen	14.2
	Kenny Lofton	14.2
267	Johnny Callison	14.1
268	Ben Chapman	14.0
269	Larry Walker	13.9
270	Roy Smalley	13.8
271	Gil Hodges	13.7
272	Willie Kamm	13.6
	Kip Selbach	13.6
274	Fred Carroll	13.5
	Tommy Holmes	13.5
	Tim Salmon	13.5
	George Stone	13.5
	Richie Zisk	13.5
279	David Justice	13.4
	Chief Meyers	13.4
	Al Oliver	13.4
282	Jimmy Ryan	13.3
283	Bill Freehan	13.2
	Dave Orr	13.2
	Roger Peckinpaugh	13.2
286	Doug DeCinces	13.1
	Mark Grace	13.1
	Edd Roush	13.1
	John Titus	13.1
290	Johnny Evers	12.9
	Bobby Murcer	12.9
	Mike Tiernan	12.9
293	Kal Daniels	12.8
	Red Smith	12.8
	Riggs Stephenson	12.8
296	Lou Brock	12.7
	Jack Clements	12.7
	Roy Sievers	12.7
299	Clete Boyer	12.6
	Dolph Camilli	12.6

Total Player Rating

	Kid Elberfeld	12.6
	Bernard Gilkey	12.6
	Chick Hafey	12.6
	Harry Hooper	12.6
	Deacon McGuire	12.6
	Billy Nash	12.6
307	Rabbit Maranville	12.5
308	Luis Aparicio	12.4
	Ken Griffey Sr.	12.4
	Johnny Pesky	12.4
	Al Rosen	12.4
	Gary Sheffield	12.4
313	Lance Parrish	12.1
	Darrell Porter	12.1
	Bob Watson	12.1
316	Gary Matthews	12.0
317	Nellie Fox	11.9
	Julio Franco	11.9
	Lonny Frey	11.9
	Ossee Schreckengost	11.9
	Robby Thompson	11.9
322	Rick Burleson	11.8
	Jake Daubert	11.8
	Ray Lankford	11.8
325	Lou Criger	11.7
	Jim Gentile	11.7
	Roger Maris	11.7
	Jerry Priddy	11.7
	Andy Thornton	11.7
	Robin Ventura	11.7
331	Earle Combs	11.6
	Ken Keltner	11.6
	Hal McRae	11.6
	Lefty O'Doul	11.6
	Stan Spence	11.6
336	Johnny Kling	11.5
	Lonnie Smith	11.5
338	Dan McGann	11.4
	Orator Shaffer	11.4
340	Buck Herzog	11.3
	Andy Seminick	11.3
	Ed Swartwood	11.3
343	Toby Harrah	11.2
	Don Mattingly	11.2
	Danny Murphy	11.2
	Tony Phillips	11.2
347	Ron Gant	11.1
	Tom Haller	11.1
	George Van Haltren	11.1
350	Freddy Lindstrom	11.0
	Terry Pendleton	11.0
	Hank Sauer	11.0
	John Valentin	11.0
354	Don Baylor	10.9
	Harry Davis	10.9
	Monte Irvin	10.9
	Ben Oglivie	10.9
358	Earl Battey	10.8
	Tony Cuccinello	10.8
	Willie Davis	10.8
	Dom DiMaggio	10.8
	Joe Harris	10.8
	Jackie Jensen	10.8
	John Kruk	10.8
	Ross Youngs	10.8
366	Tom Daly	10.7
	Mike Greenwell	10.7
368	Jay Buhner	10.6
	Mike Donlin	10.6
	Red Schoendienst	10.6
	Dixie Walker	10.6
	Curt Welch	10.6
	Deacon White	10.6
374	Ken Caminiti	10.5
	Billy Jurges	10.5
	Ed McFarland	10.5
	Maury Wills	10.5
378	Willie Keeler	10.4
	Tip O'Neill	10.4
	Cy Seymour	10.4
381	Whitey Kurowski	10.3
	Rico Petrocelli	10.3
383	Carlos Baerga	10.2
	Bill Melton	10.2
	Buddy Myer	10.2
	Cecil Travis	10.2
	Jimmy Wolf	10.2
	Rudy York	10.2
389	Jack Crooks	10.1
	Rick Ferrell	10.1
391	Larry Hisle	10.0
	Reggie Sanders	10.0
	Ned Williamson	10.0
394	Jerry Denny	9.9
	Charlie Hickman	9.9
	Tony Perez	9.9
397	Doug Rader	9.8
398	Luis Gonzalez	9.7
	Marquis Grissom	9.7
	Johnny Romano	9.7

Total Player Rating

401	Oscar Gamble	9.5
	Wally Joyner	9.5
	Elmer Smith	9.5
	Heinie Zimmerman	9.5
405	John Farrell	9.4
	Vic Wertz	9.4
407	Oyster Burns	9.3
	Walker Cooper	9.3
	Kent Hrbek	9.3
	Bump Wills	9.3
411	Don Buford	9.2
	Dave Concepcion	9.2
	Jimmy Dykes	9.2
	Hank Gowdy	9.2
	Sherm Lollar	9.2
	Wes Westrum	9.2
417	Bill Lange	9.1
	Sam Rice	9.1
419	Claude Ritchey	9.0
420	Bill Bradley	8.9
	Del Ennis	8.9
	Pinky May	8.9
423	Juan Gonzalez	8.8
	Garry Maddox	8.8
	Marty McManus	8.8
	Vada Pinson	8.8
	Gene Woodling	8.8
428	Dal Maxvill	8.7
	Bernie Williams	8.7
430	Bob Nieman	8.6
431	Bernie Carbo	8.5
	Happy Felsch	8.5
	Fred Luderus	8.5
	Rick Monday	8.5
435	Sal Bando	8.4
	Ellis Burks	8.4
	Bert Campaneris	8.4
	Eddie Joost	8.4
	Willie McGee	8.4
440	Steve Kemp	8.3
441	Del Crandall	8.2
	George Selkirk	8.2
	Snuffy Stirnweiss	8.2
444	Hank DeBerry	8.1
	Topsy Hartsel	8.1
	Pinky Whitney	8.1
447	Mike Mitchell	7.9
	Jody Reed	7.9
	Jim Sundberg	7.9
	Bill Sweeney	7.9
	Al Weis	7.9
	Ernie Whitt	7.9
453	Bob Allen	7.8
	Jimmy Barrett	7.8
	Johnny Bassler	7.8
	Frank Fennelly	7.8
	Travis Fryman	7.8
	John Ward	7.8
	Devon White	7.8
460	Solly Hemus	7.7
	Billy Werber	7.7
462	Cecil Cooper	7.6
	Elbie Fletcher	7.6
464	Dusty Baker	7.5
	Johnny Mostil	7.5
	Pop Snyder	7.5
	Mickey Tettleton	7.5
468	Donie Bush	7.4
	Cecil Fielder	7.4
	Phil Garner	7.4
	Cliff Johnson	7.4
	Harry Steinfeldt	7.4
473	Joe Adcock	7.3
	Johnny Bates	7.3
	Phil Bradley	7.3
	Ken McMullen	7.3
	Jim McTamany	7.3
	Danny Richardson	7.3
479	Matty McIntyre	7.2
	Socks Seybold	7.2
	Lee Tannehill	7.2
482	Julio Cruz	7.1
	Dick Dietz	7.1
	Ival Goodman	7.1
	Raul Mondesi	7.1
	Perry Werden	7.1
	Cy Williams	7.1
488	Dave Brain	7.0
	Spud Davis	7.0
	Joe Gerhardt	7.0
	Elston Howard	7.0
	Mick Kelleher	7.0
	Buddy Lewis	7.0
	Charlie Maxwell	7.0
	Bake McBride	7.0
	Johnny Ray	7.0
	Pete Reiser	7.0
	Jim Thome	7.0
499	3 players tied	6.9

Total Player Rating (alpha.)

Hank Aaron	89.8
Joe Adcock	7.3
Dick Allen	35.3
Bob Allen	7.8
Gene Alley	18.0
Bob Allison	14.3
Roberto Alomar	19.2
Cap Anson	30.8
Luis Aparicio	12.4
Luke Appling	40.7
Richie Ashburn	30.2
Earl Averill	17.6
Carlos Baerga	10.2
Jeff Bagwell	26.1
Harold Baines	16.8
Frank Baker	33.8
Dusty Baker	7.5
Dave Bancroft	35.2
Sal Bando	8.4
Ernie Banks	25.9
Jesse Barfield	16.4
Jimmy Barrett	7.8
Dick Bartell	27.9
Johnny Bassler	7.8
Johnny Bates	7.3
Earl Battey	10.8
Don Baylor	10.9
Jake Beckley	22.9
Mark Belanger	15.0
Buddy Bell	22.9
Jay Bell	14.9
Albert Belle	23.3
Johnny Bench	24.3
Charlie Bennett	19.2
Wally Berger	22.2
Yogi Berra	36.2
Craig Biggio	17.9
Wade Boggs	44.6
Barry Bonds	64.7
Bobby Bonds	29.5
Bobby Bonilla	18.6
Lou Boudreau	41.3
Clete Boyer	12.6
Ken Boyer	18.6
Phil Bradley	7.3
Bill Bradley	8.9
Dave Brain	7.0
Roger Bresnahan	19.7
George Brett	39.0
Lou Brock	12.7
Dan Brouthers	41.2
Pete Browning	28.8
Don Buford	9.2
Jay Buhner	10.6
Jesse Burkett	28.5
Ellis Burks	8.4
Rick Burleson	11.8
Oyster Burns	9.3
Donie Bush	7.4
Brett Butler	22.8
Johnny Callison	14.1
Dolph Camilli	12.6
Ken Caminiti	10.5
Roy Campanella	21.6
Bert Campaneris	8.4
Jose Canseco	24.6
Bernie Carbo	8.5
Rod Carew	31.7
Max Carey	22.6
Fred Carroll	13.5
Gary Carter	29.6
Rico Carty	17.9
Norm Cash	27.5
Cesar Cedeno	28.3
Orlando Cepeda	16.7
Ron Cey	21.9
Frank Chance	20.5
Ray Chapman	15.4
Ben Chapman	14.0
Cupid Childs	30.0
Jack Clark	31.1
Will Clark	19.4
Fred Clarke	28.7
Roberto Clemente	42.9
Jack Clements	12.7
Harlond Clift	22.7
Ty Cobb	91.0
Mickey Cochrane	31.4
Rocky Colavito	25.2
Eddie Collins	69.8
Jimmy Collins	23.1
Earle Combs	11.6
Dave Concepcion	9.2
Roger Connor	42.7
Cecil Cooper	7.6
Walker Cooper	9.3
Del Crandall	8.2
Gavvy Cravath	18.9
Sam Crawford	30.4
Lou Criger	11.7

Total Player Rating (alpha.)

Joe Cronin	39.4
Jack Crooks	10.1
Lave Cross	14.6
Jose Cruz	28.8
Julio Cruz	7.1
Tony Cuccinello	10.8
Roy Cullenbine	18.1
Kiki Cuyler	15.8
Bill Dahlen	51.4
Tom Daly	10.7
Kal Daniels	12.8
Jake Daubert	11.8
Chili Davis	15.3
Eric Davis	22.0
George Davis	51.0
Harry Davis	10.9
Spud Davis	7.0
Willie Davis	10.8
Andre Dawson	29.9
Hank DeBerry	8.1
Doug DeCinces	13.1
Ed Delahanty	44.3
Jerry Denny	9.9
Art Devlin	20.6
Bill Dickey	35.4
Dick Dietz	7.1
Dom DiMaggio	10.8
Joe DiMaggio	46.9
Larry Doby	21.2
Bobby Doerr	39.0
Mike Donlin	10.6
Brian Downing	18.6
Fred Dunlap	27.4
Jimmy Dykes	9.2
Lenny Dykstra	25.5
Kid Elberfeld	12.6
Bob Elliott	18.8
Del Ennis	8.9
Darrell Evans	34.6
Dwight Evans	30.4
Johnny Evers	12.9
Buck Ewing	29.5
Ferris Fain	17.8
Duke Farrell	14.6
John Farrell	9.4
Happy Felsch	8.5
Frank Fennelly	7.8
Tony Fernandez	15.4
Rick Ferrell	10.1
Cecil Fielder	7.4
Carlton Fisk	24.0
Art Fletcher	25.8
Elbie Fletcher	7.6
Elmer Flick	28.8
George Foster	22.3
Jack Fournier	23.9
Nellie Fox	11.9
Jimmie Foxx	54.0
Julio Franco	11.9
Bill Freehan	13.2
Jim Fregosi	20.6
Lonny Frey	11.9
Frankie Frisch	39.0
Travis Fryman	7.8
Augie Galan	14.6
Oscar Gamble	9.5
Ron Gant	11.1
Phil Garner	7.4
Lou Gehrig	65.7
Charlie Gehringer	44.4
Jim Gentile	11.7
Joe Gerhardt	7.0
Kirk Gibson	16.0
Bernard Gilkey	12.6
Jack Glasscock	36.1
Juan Gonzalez	8.8
Luis Gonzalez	9.7
Ival Goodman	7.1
Joe Gordon	28.2
Sid Gordon	15.1
George Gore	16.1
Goose Goslin	26.0
Hank Gowdy	9.2
Mark Grace	13.1
Hank Greenberg	30.0
Mike Greenwell	10.7
Bobby Grich	44.0
Ken Griffey Jr.	27.8
Ken Griffey Sr.	12.4
Mike Griffin	20.5
Marquis Grissom	9.7
Heinie Groh	27.0
Pedro Guerrero	16.7
Tony Gwynn	43.2
Stan Hack	27.2
Chick Hafey	12.6
Tom Haller	11.1
Billy Hamilton	26.4
Ron Hansen	14.2
Mike Hargrove	15.7

Total Player Rating (alpha.)

Toby Harrah	11.2
Joe Harris	10.8
Gabby Hartnett	40.1
Topsy Hartsel	8.1
Jeff Heath	16.4
Harry Heilmann	32.3
Solly Hemus	7.7
Rickey Henderson	77.5
Tommy Henrich	14.5
Babe Herman	17.3
Billy Herman	31.7
Keith Hernandez	34.4
Buck Herzog	11.3
Charlie Hickman	9.9
Paul Hines	17.2
Larry Hisle	10.0
Gil Hodges	13.7
Tommy Holmes	13.5
Harry Hooper	12.6
Rogers Hornsby	81.1
Elston Howard	7.0
Frank Howard	21.3
Kent Hrbek	9.3
Glenn Hubbard	20.2
Miller Huggins	18.1
Monte Irvin	10.9
Joe Jackson	37.5
Reggie Jackson	42.8
Travis Jackson	24.0
Hughie Jennings	26.2
Jackie Jensen	10.8
Cliff Johnson	7.4
Davey Johnson	15.6
Bob Johnson	35.6
Charley Jones	20.7
Eddie Joost	8.4
Bill Joyce	18.9
Wally Joyner	9.5
Billy Jurges	10.5
David Justice	13.4
Al Kaline	44.6
Willie Kamm	13.6
Benny Kauff	14.8
Willie Keeler	10.4
Mick Kelleher	7.0
Charlie Keller	23.5
Joe Kelley	20.2
King Kelly	24.7
Ken Keltner	11.6
Steve Kemp	8.3
Harmon Killebrew	26.4
Ralph Kiner	28.9
Chuck Klein	21.4
Johnny Kling	11.5
Bobby Knoop	15.0
Ed Konetchy	22.3
John Kruk	10.8
Whitey Kurowski	10.3
Nap Lajoie	94.2
Bill Lange	9.1
Ray Lankford	11.8
Barry Larkin	37.6
Henry Larkin	14.9
Tony Lazzeri	16.9
Tommy Leach	17.4
Chet Lemon	22.3
Buddy Lewis	7.0
Sixto Lezcano	14.7
Freddy Lindstrom	11.0
Kenny Lofton	14.2
Johnny Logan	17.3
Sherm Lollar	9.2
Ernie Lombardi	17.3
Fred Luderus	8.5
Greg Luzinski	14.6
Fred Lynn	22.3
Denny Lyons	19.8
Garry Maddox	8.8
Sherry Magee	26.5
Mickey Mantle	76.1
Rabbit Maranville	12.5
Roger Maris	11.7
Edgar Martinez	19.2
Eddie Mathews	51.6
Gary Matthews	12.0
Don Mattingly	11.2
Dal Maxvill	8.7
Charlie Maxwell	7.0
Pinky May	8.9
Willie Mays	92.2
Bill Mazeroski	36.3
Bake McBride	7.0
Willie McCovey	36.5
Gil McDougald	16.8
Ed McFarland	10.5
Dan McGann	11.4
Willie McGee	8.4
John McGraw	16.0
Fred McGriff	19.1
Deacon McGuire	12.6

Total Player Rating (alpha.)

Mark McGwire	19.8
Matty McIntyre	7.2
Marty McManus	8.8
Ken McMullen	7.3
Bid McPhee	40.1
Hal McRae	11.6
Kevin McReynolds	14.5
Jim McTamany	7.3
Joe Medwick	27.1
Bill Melton	10.2
Chief Meyers	13.4
Jocko Milligan	15.6
Minnie Minoso	26.0
Kevin Mitchell	21.6
Mike Mitchell	7.9
Johnny Mize	36.2
Paul Molitor	35.3
Rick Monday	8.5
Raul Mondesi	7.1
Joe Morgan	56.3
Johnny Mostil	7.5
Thurman Munson	15.2
Bobby Murcer	12.9
Dale Murphy	19.3
Danny Murphy	11.2
Dwayne Murphy	16.4
Eddie Murray	35.0
Stan Musial	70.5
Buddy Myer	10.2
Billy Nash	12.6
Graig Nettles	21.3
Bill Nicholson	19.0
Bob Nieman	8.6
Lefty O'Doul	11.6
Ben Oglivie	10.9
Tony Oliva	24.9
Al Oliver	13.4
Tip O'Neill	10.4
Paul O'Neill	14.7
Jim O'Rourke	16.1
Dave Orr	13.2
Amos Otis	19.3
Mel Ott	62.7
Rafael Palmeiro	19.0
Dave Parker	23.0
Lance Parrish	12.1
Roger Peckinpaugh	13.2
Terry Pendleton	11.0
Tony Perez	9.9
Johnny Pesky	12.4
Rico Petrocelli	10.3
Fred Pfeffer	21.7
Tony Phillips	11.2
Mike Piazza	16.7
Vada Pinson	8.8
Darrell Porter	12.1
Boog Powell	14.9
Del Pratt	20.4
Jerry Priddy	11.7
Kirby Puckett	29.1
Doug Rader	9.8
Tim Raines	52.3
Willie Randolph	23.1
Johnny Ray	7.0
Jody Reed	7.9
Pee Wee Reese	14.6
Pete Reiser	7.0
Sam Rice	9.1
Jim Rice	27.1
Hardy Richardson	27.3
Danny Richardson	7.3
Cal Ripken	41.3
Claude Ritchey	9.0
Phil Rizzuto	15.8
Brooks Robinson	19.8
Frank Robinson	69.0
Jackie Robinson	31.8
Johnny Romano	9.7
Pete Rose	20.0
Al Rosen	12.4
Edd Roush	13.1
Babe Ruth	107.7
Jimmy Ryan	13.3
Tim Salmon	13.5
Ryne Sandberg	38.2
Reggie Sanders	10.0
Ron Santo	39.5
Hank Sauer	11.0
Wally Schang	18.1
Mike Schmidt	78.4
Red Schoendienst	10.6
Ossee Schreckengost	11.9
Mike Scioscia	14.8
Kip Selbach	13.6
George Selkirk	8.2
Andy Seminick	11.3
Joe Sewell	34.5
Socks Seybold	7.2
Cy Seymour	10.4
Orator Shaffer	11.4

Total Player Rating (alpha.)

Jimmy Sheckard	19.5
Gary Sheffield	12.4
Roy Sievers	12.7
Al Simmons	25.6
Ted Simmons	16.8
Ken Singleton	20.9
George Sisler	22.7
Enos Slaughter	16.3
Roy Smalley	13.8
Reggie Smith	35.0
Elmer Smith	9.5
Red Smith	12.8
Lonnie Smith	11.5
Ozzie Smith	43.0
Duke Snider	22.3
Pop Snyder	7.5
Tris Speaker	86.5
Stan Spence	11.6
Eddie Stanky	18.4
Willie Stargell	32.8
Rusty Staub	27.6
Harry Steinfeldt	7.4
Vern Stephens	19.6
Riggs Stephenson	12.8
Snuffy Stirnweiss	8.2
George Stone	13.5
Harry Stovey	21.5
Darryl Strawberry	26.6
Jim Sundberg	7.9
Ed Swartwood	11.3
Bill Sweeney	7.9
Lee Tannehill	7.2
Danny Tartabull	15.6
Gene Tenace	15.3
Fred Tenney	20.9
Bill Terry	24.9
Mickey Tettleton	7.5
Frank Thomas	29.3
Roy Thomas	22.8
Jim Thome	7.0
Robby Thompson	11.9
Sam Thompson	28.5
Andy Thornton	11.7
Mike Tiernan	12.9
Joe Tinker	23.1
John Titus	13.1
Joe Torre	19.6
Alan Trammell	21.8
Cecil Travis	10.2
Pie Traynor	20.7
John Valentin	11.0
George Van Haltren	11.1
Andy Van Slyke	20.3
Arky Vaughan	39.2
Bobby Veach	14.8
Robin Ventura	11.7
Honus Wagner	81.2
Dixie Walker	10.6
Larry Walker	13.9
Bobby Wallace	36.9
Paul Waner	36.1
John Ward	7.8
Bob Watson	12.1
Al Weis	7.9
Curt Welch	10.6
Billy Werber	7.7
Perry Werden	7.1
Vic Wertz	9.4
Wes Westrum	9.2
Zack Wheat	24.3
Lou Whitaker	25.0
Devon White	7.8
Deacon White	10.6
Roy White	21.1
Pinky Whitney	8.1
Ernie Whitt	7.9
Bernie Williams	8.7
Billy Williams	31.1
Cy Williams	7.1
Jimmy Williams	16.0
Ken Williams	17.3
Matt Williams	18.0
Ted Williams	85.7
Ned Williamson	10.0
Bump Wills	9.3
Maury Wills	10.5
Hack Wilson	15.6
Dave Winfield	38.5
Jimmy Wolf	10.2
Gene Woodling	8.8
Jim Wynn	33.2
Carl Yastrzemski	45.5
Rudy York	10.2
Ross Youngs	10.8
Robin Yount	43.1
Chief Zimmer	15.8
Heinie Zimmerman	9.5
Richie Zisk	13.5

Total Player Rating (by era)

1876-1892

1	Roger Connor	42.7
2	Dan Brouthers	41.2
3	Bid McPhee	40.1
4	Jack Glasscock	36.1
5	Cap Anson	30.8
6	Buck Ewing	29.5
7	Pete Browning	28.8
8	Sam Thompson	28.5
9	Fred Dunlap	27.4
10	Hardy Richardson	27.3
11	King Kelly	24.7
12	Fred Pfeffer	21.7
13	Harry Stovey	21.5
14	Charley Jones	20.7
15	Denny Lyons	19.8
16	Charlie Bennett	19.2
17	Paul Hines	17.2
18	George Gore	16.1
19	Jim O'Rourke	16.1
20	Jocko Milligan	15.6
21	Henry Larkin	14.9
22	Fred Carroll	13.5
23	Dave Orr	13.2
24	Jack Clements	12.7
25	Billy Nash	12.6

1893-1919

1	Nap Lajoie	94.2
2	Ty Cobb	91.0
3	Tris Speaker	86.5
4	Honus Wagner	81.2
5	Eddie Collins	69.8
6	Bill Dahlen	51.4
7	George Davis	51.0
8	Ed Delahanty	44.3
9	Joe Jackson	37.5
10	Bobby Wallace	36.9
11	Frank Baker	33.8
12	Sam Crawford	30.4
13	Cupid Childs	30.0
14	Elmer Flick	28.8
15	Fred Clarke	28.7
16	Jesse Burkett	28.5
17	Heinie Groh	27.0
18	Sherry Magee	26.5
19	Billy Hamilton	26.4
20	Hughie Jennings	26.2
21	Art Fletcher	25.8
22	Zack Wheat	24.3
23	Jimmy Collins	23.1
	Joe Tinker	23.1
25	Jake Beckley	22.9

1920-1941

1	Babe Ruth	107.7
2	Rogers Hornsby	81.1
3	Lou Gehrig	65.7
4	Mel Ott	62.7
5	Jimmie Foxx	54.0
6	Charlie Gehringer	44.4
7	Luke Appling	40.7
8	Gabby Hartnett	40.1
9	Joe Cronin	39.4
10	Arky Vaughan	39.2
11	Frankie Frisch	37.7
12	Paul Waner	36.1
13	Bob Johnson	35.6
14	Bill Dickey	35.4
15	Dave Bancroft	35.2
16	Joe Sewell	34.5
17	Harry Heilmann	32.3
18	Billy Herman	31.7
19	Mickey Cochrane	31.4
20	Hank Greenberg	30.0
21	Dick Bartell	27.9
22	Stan Hack	27.2
23	Joe Medwick	27.1
24	Goose Goslin	26.0
25	Al Simmons	25.6

Total Player Rating (by era)

1942-1960

1	Ted Williams	85.7
2	Mickey Mantle	76.1
3	Stan Musial	70.5
4	Eddie Mathews	51.6
5	Joe DiMaggio	46.9
6	Lou Boudreau	41.3
7	Bobby Doerr	39.0
8	Yogi Berra	36.2
	Johnny Mize	36.2
10	Jackie Robinson	31.8
11	Richie Ashburn	30.2
12	Ralph Kiner	28.9
13	Joe Gordon	28.2
14	Minnie Minoso	26.0
15	Charlie Keller	23.5
16	Duke Snider	22.3
17	Roy Campanella	21.6
18	Larry Doby	21.2
19	Vern Stephens	19.6
20	Bill Nicholson	19.0
21	Bob Elliott	18.8
22	Eddie Stanky	18.4
23	Roy Cullenbine	18.1
24	Ferris Fain	17.8
25	Johnny Logan	17.3

1961-1976

1	Willie Mays	92.2
2	Hank Aaron	89.8
3	Frank Robinson	69.0
4	Joe Morgan	56.3
5	Carl Yastrzemski	45.5
6	Al Kaline	44.6
7	Roberto Clemente	42.9
8	Ron Santo	39.5
9	Willie McCovey	36.5
10	Bill Mazeroski	36.3
11	Dick Allen	35.3
12	Reggie Smith	35.0
13	Jim Wynn	33.2
14	Willie Stargell	32.8
15	Rod Carew	31.7
16	Billy Williams	31.1
17	Bobby Bonds	29.5
18	Rusty Staub	27.6
19	Norm Cash	27.5
20	Harmon Killebrew	26.4
21	Ernie Banks	25.9
22	Rocky Colavito	25.2
23	Tony Oliva	24.9
24	Johnny Bench	24.3
25	Frank Howard	21.3

1977-1996

1	Mike Schmidt	78.4
2	Rickey Henderson	77.5
3	Barry Bonds	64.7
4	Tim Raines	52.3
5	Wade Boggs	44.6
6	Bobby Grich	44.0
7	Tony Gwynn	43.2
8	Robin Yount	43.1
9	Ozzie Smith	43.0
10	Reggie Jackson	42.8
11	Cal Ripken	41.3
12	George Brett	39.0
13	Dave Winfield	38.5
14	Ryne Sandberg	38.2
15	Barry Larkin	37.6
16	Paul Molitor	35.3
17	Eddie Murray	35.0
18	Darrell Evans	34.6
19	Keith Hernandez	34.4
20	Jack Clark	31.1
21	Dwight Evans	30.4
22	Andre Dawson	29.9
23	Gary Carter	29.6
24	Frank Thomas	29.3
25	Kirby Puckett	29.1

Wins

#	Player	
1	Cy Young	511
2	Walter Johnson	417
3	Pete Alexander	373
	Christy Mathewson	373
5	Warren Spahn	363
6	Kid Nichols	361
7	Pud Galvin	360
8	Tim Keefe	342
9	Steve Carlton	329
10	John Clarkson	328
11	Eddie Plank	326
12	Nolan Ryan	324
	Don Sutton	324
14	Phil Niekro	318
15	Gaylord Perry	314
16	Tom Seaver	311
17	Charley Radbourn	309
18	Mickey Welch	307
19	Lefty Grove	300
	Early Wynn	300
21	Tommy John	288
22	Bert Blyleven	287
23	Robin Roberts	286
24	Fergie Jenkins	284
	Tony Mullane	284
26	Jim Kaat	283
27	Red Ruffing	273
28	Burleigh Grimes	270
29	Jim Palmer	268
30	Bob Feller	266
	Eppa Rixey	266
32	Jim McCormick	265
33	Gus Weyhing	264
34	Ted Lyons	260
35	Red Faber	254
	Jack Morris	254
37	Carl Hubbell	253
38	Bob Gibson	251
39	Vic Willis	249
40	Jack Quinn	247
41	Joe McGinnity	246
	Amos Rusie	246
43	Jack Powell	245
44	Juan Marichal	243
45	Herb Pennock	241
46	Dennis Martinez	240
	Frank Tanana	240
48	Mordecai Brown	239
49	Clark Griffith	237
	Waite Hoyt	237
51	Whitey Ford	236
52	Charlie Buffinton	233
53	Sam Jones	229
	Luis Tiant	229
	Will White	229
56	George Mullin	228
57	Jim Bunning	224
	Catfish Hunter	224
59	Paul Derringer	223
	Mel Harder	223
61	Hooks Dauss	222
	Jerry Koosman	222
63	Joe Niekro	221
64	Jerry Reuss	220
65	Bob Caruthers	218
	Earl Whitehill	218
67	Freddie Fitzsimmons	217
	Mickey Lolich	217
69	Wilbur Cooper	216
	Charlie Hough	216
71	Stan Coveleski	215
	Jim Perry	215
73	Rick Reuschel	214
74	Chief Bender	212
75	Bobo Newsom	211
	Billy Pierce	211
	Bob Welch	211
78	Jesse Haines	210
79	Vida Blue	209
	Don Drysdale	209
	Milt Pappas	209
82	Eddie Cicotte	208
	Carl Mays	208
84	Bob Lemon	207
	Hal Newhouser	207
86	Al Orth	204
87	Lew Burdette	203
	Silver King	203
	Jack Stivetts	203
90	Rube Marquard	201
	Charlie Root	201
92	George Uhle	200
93	Jack Chesbro	198
	Bucky Walters	198
95	Larry French	197
	Bob Friend	197
	Jesse Tannehill	197
	Adonis Terry	197
	Dazzy Vance	197
100	2 players tied	196

Losses

#	Player	
1	Cy Young	316
2	Pud Galvin	308
3	Nolan Ryan	292
4	Walter Johnson	279
5	Phil Niekro	274
6	Gaylord Perry	265
7	Don Sutton	256
8	Jack Powell	254
9	Eppa Rixey	251
10	Bert Blyleven	250
11	Robin Roberts	245
	Warren Spahn	245
13	Steve Carlton	244
	Early Wynn	244
15	Jim Kaat	237
16	Frank Tanana	236
17	Gus Weyhing	232
18	Tommy John	231
19	Bob Friend	230
	Ted Lyons	230
21	Fergie Jenkins	226
22	Tim Keefe	225
	Red Ruffing	225
24	Bobo Newsom	222
25	Tony Mullane	220
26	Jack Quinn	218
27	Sam Jones	217
28	Charlie Hough	216
29	Jim McCormick	214
30	Red Faber	213
31	Paul Derringer	212
	Chick Fraser	212
	Burleigh Grimes	212
34	Mickey Welch	210
35	Jerry Koosman	209
36	Pete Alexander	208
	Kid Nichols	208
38	Tom Seaver	205
	Vic Willis	205
40	Joe Niekro	204
	Jim Whitney	204
42	George Mullin	196
	Adonis Terry	196
44	Claude Osteen	195
	Charley Radbourn	195
46	Eddie Plank	194
47	Mickey Lolich	191
	Rick Reuschel	191
	Jerry Reuss	191
	Tom Zachary	191
51	Al Orth	189
52	Christy Mathewson	188
53	Mel Harder	186
	Jack Morris	186
55	Earl Whitehill	185
56	Jim Bunning	184
57	Joe Bush	183
	Larry Jackson	183
	Curt Simmons	183
60	Hooks Dauss	182
	Waite Hoyt	182
	Dennis Martinez	182
63	Murry Dickson	181
	Dutch Leonard	181
	Rick Wise	181
66	Lee Meadows	180
67	Pink Hawley	179
	Dolf Luque	179
69	John Clarkson	178
	Wilbur Cooper	178
71	Bill Dinneen	177
	Rube Marquard	177
73	Mike Moore	175
	Red Donahue	175
	Tom Hughes	175
76	Doyle Alexander	174
	Bob Gibson	174
	Jim Perry	174
	Amos Rusie	174
80	Luis Tiant	172
81	Larry French	171
82	Ted Breitenstein	170
	Camilo Pascual	170
84	Billy Pierce	167
85	Red Ames	167
	Jim Clancy	167
	Bert Cunningham	167
	Red Ehret	167
89	Don Drysdale	166
	Howard Ehmke	166
	Catfish Hunter	166
	George Uhle	166
	Will White	166
94	Mark Baldwin	165
	Dennis Eckersley	165
	Bump Hadley	165
	Si Johnson	165
98	Milt Gaston	164
	Win Mercer	164
	Milt Pappas	164

Winning Percentage

#	Player	
1	Dave Foutz	.690
2	Whitey Ford	.690
3	Bob Caruthers	.688
4	Lefty Grove	.680
5	Vic Raschi	.667
6	Larry Corcoran	.665
7	Christy Mathewson	.665
8	Sam Leever	.660
9	Sal Maglie	.657
10	Sandy Koufax	.655
11	Johnny Allen	.654
12	Ron Guidry	.651
13	Lefty Gomez	.649
14	John Clarkson	.648
15	Mordecai Brown	.648
16	Dwight Gooden	.646
17	Dizzy Dean	.644
18	Pete Alexander	.642
19	Jim Palmer	.638
20	Kid Nichols	.634
21	Deacon Phillippe	.634
22	Joe McGinnity	.634
23	Roger Clemens	.634
24	Ed Reulbach	.632
25	Juan Marichal	.631
26	Mort Cooper	.631
27	Allie Reynolds	.630
28	David Cone	.630
29	Jesse Tannehill	.627
30	Ray Kremer	.627
31	Firpo Marberry	.627
32	Eddie Plank	.627
33	Tommy Bond	.627
34	Chief Bender	.625
35	Don Newcombe	.623
36	Nig Cuppy	.623
37	Carl Mays	.623
38	Addie Joss	.623
39	Fred Goldsmith	.622
40	Doc Crandall	.622
41	Carl Hubbell	.622
42	Bob Feller	.621
43	Mel Parnell	.621
44	Randy Johnson	.619
	John Tudor	.619
46	Clark Griffith	.619
47	Bob Lemon	.618
48	Cy Young	.618
49	John Ward	.617
50	Urban Shocker	.615
51	Jeff Tesreau	.615
52	Jim Maloney	.615
53	Lon Warneke	.613
54	Greg Maddux	.613
55	Charley Radbourn	.613
56	Jimmy Key	.612
57	Gary Nolan	.611
58	Schoolboy Rowe	.610
59	Carl Erskine	.610
60	Ed Walsh	.607
61	Charlie Ferguson	.607
62	Dave McNally	.607
63	Jack McDowell	.607
64	Hooks Wiltse	.607
65	Jack Stivetts	.606
66	Art Nehf	.605
67	Charlie Buffinton	.605
68	Orval Overall	.603
69	Tim Keefe	.603
70	Tom Seaver	.603
71	Stan Coveleski	.602
72	Preacher Roe	.602
73	Tom Glavine	.602
74	Wes Ferrell	.601
75	J.R. Richard	.601
76	Jack Chesbro	.600
77	Walter Johnson	.599
78	Herb Pennock	.598
79	Freddie Fitzsimmons	.598
80	Ed Lopat	.597
81	Warren Spahn	.597
82	Rip Sewell	.596
83	Mike Garcia	.594
84	Mickey Welch	.594
85	Pat Malone	.593
86	Alvin Crowder	.592
87	John Candelaria	.592
88	Harry Brecheen	.591
89	Bob Welch	.591
90	Jim Bagby	.591
91	Bob Gibson	.591
92	Dutch Ruether	.591
93	Denny McLain	.590
94	Eddie Rommel	.590
95	Jack Coombs	.590
96	Tiny Bonham	.589
97	Mike Cuellar	.587
98	Bill Bernhard	.586
99	Amos Rusie	.586
100	Jeff Pfeffer	.585

Games

#	Player	
1	Hoyt Wilhelm	1070
2	Kent Tekulve	1050
3	Rich Gossage	1002
4	Lee Smith	997
5	Lindy McDaniel	987
6	Dennis Eckersley	964
7	Rollie Fingers	944
8	Gene Garber	931
9	Cy Young	906
10	Sparky Lyle	899
11	Jim Kaat	898
12	Jesse Orosco	885
13	Jeff Reardon	880
14	Don McMahon	874
15	Phil Niekro	864
16	Charlie Hough	858
17	Roy Face	848
18	Tug McGraw	824
19	Nolan Ryan	807
20	Walter Johnson	802
21	Rick Honeycutt	795
22	Gaylord Perry	777
23	Don Sutton	774
24	Darold Knowles	765
25	Tommy John	760
26	Jack Quinn	756
27	Ron Reed	751
28	Warren Spahn	750
29	Tom Burgmeier	745
	Gary Lavelle	745
31	Willie Hernandez	744
32	Steve Carlton	741
33	Ron Perranoski	737
34	Ron Kline	736
35	Steve Bedrosian	732
36	Clay Carroll	731
37	Mike Marshall	723
	Roger McDowell	723
39	Dave Righetti	718
40	John Franco	712
41	Johnny Klippstein	711
42	Greg Minton	710
43	Stu Miller	704
44	Greg Harris	703
45	Joe Niekro	702
46	Bill Campbell	700
47	Larry Andersen	699
48	Bob McClure	698
49	Pud Galvin	697
50	Pete Alexander	696
	Craig Lefferts	696
52	Bob Miller	694
53	Bert Blyleven	692
	Grant Jackson	692
	Eppa Rixey	692
56	Early Wynn	691
57	Eddie Fisher	690
58	Paul Assenmacher	685
59	Ted Abernathy	681
60	Robin Roberts	676
61	Waite Hoyt	674
	Dan Quisenberry	674
63	Red Faber	669
64	Dave Giusti	668
65	Fergie Jenkins	664
66	Bruce Sutter	661
67	Tom Seaver	656
68	Paul Lindblad	655
69	Danny Darwin	652
70	Wilbur Wood	651
71	Sam Jones	647
	Dave LaRoche	647
73	Tom Henke	642
74	Dutch Leonard	640
	Gerry Staley	640
76	Dennis Lamp	639
	Diego Segui	639
78	Frank Tanana	638
79	Bob Stanley	637
80	Christy Mathewson	635
81	Charlie Root	632
82	Dennis Martinez	630
	Jim Perry	630
84	Jerry Reuss	628
85	Lew Burdette	626
86	Murry Dickson	625
	Woodie Fryman	625
88	Red Ruffing	624
89	Mike Jackson	623
	Eddie Plank	623
91	Kid Nichols	620
	Dick Tidrow	620
93	Herb Pennock	617
94	Burleigh Grimes	616
	Lefty Grove	616
96	Terry Forster	614
97	Jerry Koosman	612
	Mitch Williams	612
99	Dave Smith	609
100	Dan Plesac	607

Games Started

1	Cy Young	815
2	Nolan Ryan	773
3	Don Sutton	756
4	Phil Niekro	716
5	Steve Carlton	709
6	Tommy John	700
7	Gaylord Perry	690
8	Bert Blyleven	685
9	Pud Galvin	681
10	Walter Johnson	666
11	Warren Spahn	665
12	Tom Seaver	647
13	Jim Kaat	625
14	Frank Tanana	616
15	Early Wynn	612
16	Robin Roberts	609
17	Pete Alexander	600
18	Fergie Jenkins	594
	Tim Keefe	594
20	Kid Nichols	561
21	Eppa Rixey	553
22	Christy Mathewson	551
23	Mickey Welch	549
24	Dennis Martinez	548
25	Jerry Reuss	547
26	Red Ruffing	536
27	Eddie Plank	529
	Rick Reuschel	529
29	Jerry Koosman	527
	Jack Morris	527
31	Jim Palmer	521
32	Jim Bunning	519
33	John Clarkson	518
34	Jack Powell	516
35	Tony Mullane	504
36	Charley Radbourn	503
	Gus Weyhing	503
38	Joe Niekro	500
39	Bob Friend	497
	Burleigh Grimes	497
41	Mickey Lolich	496
42	Claude Osteen	488
43	Sam Jones	487
44	Jim McCormick	485
45	Bob Feller	484
	Ted Lyons	484
	Luis Tiant	484
48	Red Faber	483
	Bobo Newsom	483
50	Bob Gibson	482
51	Catfish Hunter	476
52	Vida Blue	473
	Earl Whitehill	473
54	Vic Willis	471
55	Don Drysdale	465
	Milt Pappas	465
57	Doyle Alexander	464
58	Bob Welch	462
59	Curt Simmons	461
60	Mike Torrez	458
61	Lefty Grove	457
	Juan Marichal	457
63	Rick Wise	455
64	Jim Perry	447
65	Paul Derringer	445
66	Jack Quinn	443
67	Charlie Hough	440
	Mike Moore	440
69	Whitey Ford	438
70	Mel Harder	433
71	Billy Pierce	432
72	Carl Hubbell	431
73	Larry Jackson	429
74	George Mullin	428
75	Amos Rusie	427
76	Freddie Fitzsimmons	426
77	Waite Hoyt	423
78	Bob Forsch	422
79	Frank Viola	420
80	Herb Pennock	419
81	Bob Knepper	413
82	Ken Holtzman	410
83	Dave Stieb	409
84	Tom Zachary	408
85	Wilbur Cooper	407
	Scott Sanderson	407
87	Lee Meadows	406
	Adonis Terry	406
	Fernando Valenzuela	406
90	Rube Marquard	405
91	Mike Flanagan	404
	Camilo Pascual	404
93	Will White	401
94	Mark Langston	398
	Bucky Walters	398
96	Charlie Buffinton	396
	Dave McNally	396
	Jim Whitney	396
99	Al Orth	394
100	Steve Rogers	393

Games Started (by era)

1876-1892

1	Pud Galvin	681
2	Tim Keefe	594
3	Mickey Welch	549
4	John Clarkson	518
5	Tony Mullane	504
6	Charley Radbourn	503
	Gus Weyhing	503
8	Jim McCormick	485
9	Adonis Terry	406
10	Will White	401
11	Charlie Buffinton	396
	Jim Whitney	396
13	Silver King	371
14	Bill Hutchison	346
15	Jack Stivetts	333

1893-1919

1	Cy Young	815
2	Walter Johnson	666
3	Pete Alexander	600
4	Kid Nichols	561
5	Christy Mathewson	551
6	Eddie Plank	529
7	Jack Powell	516
8	Vic Willis	471
9	George Mullin	428
10	Amos Rusie	427
11	Rube Marquard	405
12	Al Orth	394
13	Hooks Dauss	388
	Chick Fraser	388
15	Joe McGinnity	381

1920-1941

1	Eppa Rixey	553
2	Red Ruffing	536
3	Burleigh Grimes	497
4	Sam Jones	487
5	Ted Lyons	484
6	Red Faber	483
	Bobo Newsom	483
8	Earl Whitehill	473
9	Lefty Grove	457
10	Paul Derringer	445
11	Jack Quinn	443
12	Mel Harder	433
13	Carl Hubbell	431
14	Freddie Fitzsimmons	426
15	Waite Hoyt	423

1942-1960

1	Warren Spahn	665
2	Early Wynn	612
3	Robin Roberts	609
4	Bob Friend	497
5	Bob Feller	484
6	Curt Simmons	461
7	Whitey Ford	438
8	Billy Pierce	432
9	Dutch Leonard	375
10	Hal Newhouser	374
11	Lew Burdette	373
12	Bob Buhl	369
13	Vern Law	364
14	Bob Lemon	350

1961-1976

1	Don Sutton	756
2	Phil Niekro	716
3	Steve Carlton	709
4	Tommy John	700
5	Gaylord Perry	690
6	Tom Seaver	647
7	Jim Kaat	625
8	Fergie Jenkins	594
9	Jerry Koosman	527
10	Jim Palmer	521
11	Jim Bunning	519
12	Mickey Lolich	496
13	Claude Osteen	488
14	Luis Tiant	484
15	Bob Gibson	482

1977-1996

1	Nolan Ryan	773
2	Bert Blyleven	685
3	Frank Tanana	616
4	Dennis Martinez	548
5	Jerry Reuss	547
6	Rick Reuschel	529
7	Jack Morris	527
8	Joe Niekro	500
9	Vida Blue	473
10	Doyle Alexander	464
11	Bob Welch	462
12	Charlie Hough	440
	Mike Moore	440
14	Bob Forsch	422
15	Frank Viola	420

Complete Games

1	Cy Young	749
2	Pud Galvin	639
3	Tim Keefe	554
4	Walter Johnson	531
	Kid Nichols	531
6	Mickey Welch	525
7	Charley Radbourn	489
8	John Clarkson	485
9	Tony Mullane	468
10	Jim McCormick	466
11	Gus Weyhing	448
12	Pete Alexander	437
13	Christy Mathewson	434
14	Jack Powell	422
15	Eddie Plank	410
16	Will White	394
17	Amos Rusie	393
18	Vic Willis	388
19	Warren Spahn	382
20	Jim Whitney	377
21	Adonis Terry	367
22	Ted Lyons	356
23	George Mullin	353
24	Charlie Buffinton	351
25	Chick Fraser	342
26	Clark Griffith	337
27	Red Ruffing	335
28	Silver King	328
29	Al Orth	324
30	Bill Hutchison	321
31	Burleigh Grimes	314
	Joe McGinnity	314
33	Red Donahue	312
	Guy Hecker	312
35	Bill Dinneen	306
36	Robin Roberts	305
37	Gaylord Perry	303
38	Ted Breitenstein	300
39	Bob Caruthers	298
	Lefty Grove	298
41	Pink Hawley	297
	Ed Morris	297
43	Mark Baldwin	295
44	Tommy Bond	294
45	Brickyard Kennedy	293
46	Eppa Rixey	290
	Early Wynn	290
48	Bill Donovan	289
	Bobby Mathews	289
50	Bert Cunningham	286
51	Wilbur Cooper	279
	Bob Feller	279
	Sadie McMahon	279
54	Jack Stivetts	278
	Jack Taylor	278
56	Charlie Getzien	277
57	Red Faber	273
58	Mordecai Brown	271
	Frank Dwyer	271
60	Jouett Meekin	270
61	Fergie Jenkins	267
62	Elton Chamberlain	264
	Matt Kilroy	264
64	Jesse Tannehill	263
65	Doc White	262
66	Rube Waddell	261
67	Jack Chesbro	260
	Red Ehret	260
	Carl Hubbell	260
70	Larry Corcoran	256
71	Chief Bender	255
	Bob Gibson	255
73	Steve Carlton	254
74	Frank Killen	253
	Win Mercer	253
76	Paul Derringer	251
77	Sam Jones	250
	Ed Walsh	250
79	Eddie Cicotte	249
	Stump Wiedman	249
81	Herb Pennock	247
82	Bobo Newsom	246
83	George Bradley	245
	Hooks Dauss	245
	Phil Niekro	245
86	Harry Howell	244
	Juan Marichal	244
	John Ward	244
89	Jack Quinn	243
90	Bert Blyleven	242
	Deacon Phillippe	242
	Bucky Walters	242
93	Sam Leever	241
94	Kid Gleason	240
95	Addie Joss	234
96	George Uhle	232
97	Carl Mays	231
	Tom Seaver	231
	Harry Staley	231
100	Earl Moore	230

Complete Games (by era)

1876-1892

1	Pud Galvin	639
2	Tim Keefe	554
3	Mickey Welch	525
4	Charley Radbourn	489
5	John Clarkson	485
6	Tony Mullane	468
7	Jim McCormick	466
8	Gus Weyhing	448
9	Will White	394
10	Jim Whitney	377
11	Adonis Terry	367
12	Charlie Buffinton	351
13	Silver King	328
14	Bill Hutchison	321
15	Guy Hecker	312

1893-1919

1	Cy Young	749
2	Walter Johnson	531
	Kid Nichols	531
4	Pete Alexander	437
5	Christy Mathewson	434
6	Jack Powell	422
7	Eddie Plank	410
8	Amos Rusie	393
9	Vic Willis	388
10	George Mullin	353
11	Chick Fraser	342
12	Clark Griffith	337
13	Al Orth	324
14	Joe McGinnity	314
15	Red Donahue	312

1920-1941

1	Ted Lyons	356
2	Red Ruffing	335
3	Burleigh Grimes	314
4	Lefty Grove	298
5	Eppa Rixey	290
6	Wilbur Cooper	279
7	Red Faber	273
8	Carl Hubbell	260
9	Paul Derringer	251
10	Sam Jones	250
11	Herb Pennock	247
12	Bobo Newsom	246
13	Jack Quinn	243
14	Bucky Walters	242
15	George Uhle	232

1942-1960

1	Warren Spahn	382
2	Robin Roberts	305
3	Early Wynn	290
4	Bob Feller	279
5	Hal Newhouser	212
6	Billy Pierce	193
7	Dutch Leonard	192
8	Bob Lemon	188
9	Ed Lopat	164
10	Bob Friend	163
	Curt Simmons	163
12	Lew Burdette	158
	Dizzy Trout	158
14	Whitey Ford	156
	Jim Tobin	156

1961-1976

1	Gaylord Perry	303
2	Fergie Jenkins	267
3	Bob Gibson	255
4	Steve Carlton	254
5	Phil Niekro	245
6	Juan Marichal	244
7	Tom Seaver	231
8	Jim Palmer	211
9	Mickey Lolich	195
10	Luis Tiant	187
11	Catfish Hunter	181
12	Jim Kaat	180
13	Don Sutton	178
14	Mike Cuellar	172
15	Don Drysdale	167

1977-1996

1	Bert Blyleven	242
2	Nolan Ryan	222
3	Jack Morris	175
4	Vida Blue	143
	Frank Tanana	143
6	Steve Rogers	129
7	Jerry Reuss	127
8	Dennis Martinez	121
9	Fernando Valenzuela	112
10	Charlie Hough	107
	Joe Niekro	107
12	Dennis Leonard	103
	Dave Stieb	103
14	Rick Reuschel	102
15	Mike Flanagan	101

Shutouts

1	Walter Johnson	110
2	Pete Alexander	90
3	Christy Mathewson	79
4	Cy Young	76
5	Eddie Plank	69
6	Warren Spahn	63
7	Nolan Ryan	61
	Tom Seaver	61
9	Bert Blyleven	60
10	Don Sutton	58
11	Pud Galvin	57
	Ed Walsh	57
13	Bob Gibson	56
14	Mordecai Brown	55
	Steve Carlton	55
16	Jim Palmer	53
	Gaylord Perry	53
18	Juan Marichal	52
19	Rube Waddell	50
	Vic Willis	50
21	Don Drysdale	49
	Fergie Jenkins	49
	Luis Tiant	49
	Early Wynn	49
25	Kid Nichols	48
26	Tommy John	46
	Jack Powell	46
28	Whitey Ford	45
	Addie Joss	45
	Phil Niekro	45
	Robin Roberts	45
	Red Ruffing	45
	Doc White	45
34	Babe Adams	44
	Bob Feller	44
36	Milt Pappas	43
37	Catfish Hunter	42
	Bucky Walters	42
39	Mickey Lolich	41
	Hippo Vaughn	41
	Mickey Welch	41
42	Chief Bender	40
	Jim Bunning	40
	Larry French	40
	Sandy Koufax	40
	Claude Osteen	40
	Ed Reulbach	40
	Mel Stottlemyre	40
49	Tim Keefe	39
	Sam Leever	39
	Jerry Reuss	39
52	Roger Clemens	38
	Stan Coveleski	38
	Billy Pierce	38
	Nap Rucker	38
56	Vida Blue	37
	John Clarkson	37
	Larry Jackson	37
	Eppa Rixey	37
	Steve Rogers	37
61	Mike Cuellar	36
	Bob Friend	36
	Carl Hubbell	36
	Sam Jones	36
	Camilo Pascual	36
	Allie Reynolds	36
	Curt Simmons	36
	Will White	36
69	Tommy Bond	35
	Joe Bush	35
	Jack Chesbro	35
	Eddie Cicotte	35
	Jack Coombs	35
	Wilbur Cooper	35
	Bill Donovan	35
	Burleigh Grimes	35
	Lefty Grove	35
	George Mullin	35
	Herb Pennock	35
	Charley Radbourn	35
81	Bill Doak	34
	Earl Moore	34
	Frank Tanana	34
	Jesse Tannehill	34
85	Tommy Bridges	33
	Lew Burdette	33
	Dean Chance	33
	Mort Cooper	33
	Jerry Koosman	33
	Lefty Leifield	33
	Dutch Leonard	33
	Jim McCormick	33
	Dave McNally	33
	Hal Newhouser	33
	Bob Shawkey	33
	Virgil Trucks	33
97	Paul Derringer	32
	Joe McGinnity	32
	Jim Perry	32
100	7 players tied	31

Saves

1	Lee Smith	473
2	Jeff Reardon	367
3	Dennis Eckersley	353
4	Rollie Fingers	341
5	John Franco	323
6	Tom Henke	311
7	Rich Gossage	310
8	Bruce Sutter	300
9	Randy Myers	274
10	Dave Righetti	252
11	Dan Quisenberry	244
12	Doug Jones	242
	Jeff Montgomery	242
14	Sparky Lyle	238
15	Hoyt Wilhelm	227
16	Todd Worrell	221
17	Gene Garber	218
18	Dave Smith	216
19	Rick Aguilera	211
20	Bobby Thigpen	201
21	Roy Face	193
	Mike Henneman	193
23	Mitch Williams	192
24	Mike Marshall	188
25	Jeff Russell	186
26	Steve Bedrosian	184
	Kent Tekulve	184
28	Tug McGraw	180
	John Wetteland	180
30	Ron Perranoski	179
31	Bryan Harvey	177
32	Lindy McDaniel	172
	Gregg Olson	172
34	Rod Beck	162
35	Roger McDowell	159
36	Jay Howell	155
37	Stu Miller	154
38	Don McMahon	153
39	Greg Minton	150
40	Ted Abernathy	148
	Dan Plesac	148
42	Willie Hernandez	147
43	Dave Giusti	145
44	Clay Carroll	143
	Darold Knowles	143
46	Gary Lavelle	136
47	Roberto Hernandez	134
48	Jesse Orosco	133
49	Jim Brewer	132
	Steve Farr	132
	Bob Stanley	132
52	Ron Davis	130
53	Jeff Brantley	129
54	Terry Forster	127
55	Bill Campbell	126
	Dave LaRoche	126
57	John Hiller	125
58	Jack Aker	123
59	Dick Radatz	122
60	Duane Ward	121
61	Tippy Martinez	115
62	Frank Linzy	111
63	Al Worthington	110
64	Fred Gladding	109
	Mel Rojas	109
66	Wayne Granger	108
	Ron Kline	108
68	Johnny Murphy	107
69	Bill Caudill	106
70	Ron Reed	103
	John Wyatt	103
72	Tom Burgmeier	102
	Tim Burke	102
	Ellis Kinder	102
75	Craig Lefferts	101
	Firpo Marberry	101
77	Joe Hoerner	99
78	Trevor Hoffman	98
	Mike Schooler	98
80	Al Hrabosky	97
	Tom Niedenfuer	97
82	Mark Davis	96
	Clem Labine	96
	Randy Moffitt	96
85	Bob Locker	95
86	Aurelio Lopez	93
87	Tom Hume	92
	Phil Regan	92
89	Jim Gott	91
	Steve Howe	91
91	Bill Henry	90
92	Rob Dibble	89
	Donnie Moore	89
94	Jim Kern	88
95	Jose Mesa	87
96	Ken Sanders	86
	Cecil Upshaw	86
98	Joe Sambito	84
99	4 players tied	83

Innings Pitched

1	Cy Young	7356.0
2	Pud Galvin	5941.1
3	Walter Johnson	5914.1
4	Phil Niekro	5404.1
5	Nolan Ryan	5386.0
6	Gaylord Perry	5350.1
7	Don Sutton	5282.1
8	Warren Spahn	5243.2
9	Steve Carlton	5217.1
10	Pete Alexander	5190.0
11	Kid Nichols	5056.1
12	Tim Keefe	5047.2
13	Bert Blyleven	4970.0
14	Mickey Welch	4802.0
15	Tom Seaver	4782.2
16	Christy Mathewson	4780.2
17	Tommy John	4710.1
18	Robin Roberts	4688.2
19	Early Wynn	4564.0
20	John Clarkson	4536.1
21	Charley Radbourn	4535.1
22	Tony Mullane	4531.1
23	Jim Kaat	4530.1
24	Fergie Jenkins	4500.2
25	Eddie Plank	4495.2
26	Eppa Rixey	4494.2
27	Jack Powell	4389.0
28	Red Ruffing	4344.0
29	Gus Weyhing	4324.1
30	Jim McCormick	4275.2
31	Frank Tanana	4188.1
32	Burleigh Grimes	4179.2
33	Ted Lyons	4161.0
34	Red Faber	4086.2
35	Vic Willis	3996.0
36	Jim Palmer	3948.0
37	Lefty Grove	3940.2
38	Jack Quinn	3920.1
39	Bob Gibson	3884.1
40	Sam Jones	3883.0
41	Dennis Martinez	3859.2
42	Jerry Koosman	3839.1
43	Bob Feller	3827.0
44	Jack Morris	3824.0
45	Charlie Hough	3801.1
46	Amos Rusie	3778.2
47	Waite Hoyt	3762.1
48	Jim Bunning	3760.1
49	Bobo Newsom	3759.1
50	George Mullin	3686.2
51	Jerry Reuss	3669.2
52	Paul Derringer	3645.0
53	Mickey Lolich	3638.1
54	Bob Friend	3611.0
55	Carl Hubbell	3590.1
56	Joe Niekro	3584.0
57	Herb Pennock	3571.2
58	Earl Whitehill	3564.2
59	Rick Reuschel	3548.1
60	Will White	3542.2
61	Adonis Terry	3514.0
62	Juan Marichal	3507.1
63	Jim Whitney	3496.1
64	Luis Tiant	3486.1
65	Wilbur Cooper	3480.0
66	Claude Osteen	3460.1
67	Catfish Hunter	3449.1
68	Joe McGinnity	3441.1
69	Don Drysdale	3432.0
70	Mel Harder	3426.1
71	Charlie Buffinton	3404.0
72	Hooks Dauss	3390.2
73	Clark Griffith	3385.2
74	Doyle Alexander	3367.2
75	Chick Fraser	3356.0
76	Al Orth	3354.2
77	Curt Simmons	3348.1
78	Vida Blue	3343.1
79	Rube Marquard	3306.2
	Billy Pierce	3306.2
81	Jim Perry	3285.2
82	Larry Jackson	3262.2
83	Freddie Fitzsimmons	3223.2
84	Eddie Cicotte	3223.0
85	Dolf Luque	3220.1
86	Dutch Leonard	3218.1
87	Jesse Haines	3208.2
88	Red Ames	3198.0
89	Charlie Root	3197.1
90	Dennis Eckersley	3193.0
91	Milt Pappas	3186.0
92	Silver King	3181.2
93	Mordecai Brown	3172.1
94	Whitey Ford	3170.1
95	Lee Meadows	3160.2
96	Larry French	3152.0
97	Rick Wise	3127.0
98	Tom Zachary	3126.1
99	George Uhle	3119.2
100	Bucky Walters	3104.2

Innings Pitched (by era)

1876-1892

1	Pud Galvin	5941.1
2	Tim Keefe	5047.2
3	Mickey Welch	4802.0
4	John Clarkson	4536.1
5	Charley Radbourn	4535.1
6	Tony Mullane	4531.1
7	Gus Weyhing	4324.1
8	Jim McCormick	4275.2
9	Will White	3542.2
10	Adonis Terry	3514.0
11	Jim Whitney	3496.1
12	Charlie Buffinton	3404.0
13	Silver King	3181.2
14	Bill Hutchison	3078.0
15	Guy Hecker	2924.0

1893-1919

1	Cy Young	7356.0
2	Walter Johnson	5914.1
3	Pete Alexander	5190.0
4	Kid Nichols	5056.1
5	Christy Mathewson	4780.2
6	Eddie Plank	4495.2
7	Jack Powell	4389.0
8	Vic Willis	3996.0
9	Amos Rusie	3778.2
10	George Mullin	3686.2
11	Joe McGinnity	3441.1
12	Hooks Dauss	3390.2
13	Clark Griffith	3385.2
14	Chick Fraser	3356.0
15	Al Orth	3354.2

1920-1941

1	Eppa Rixey	4494.2
2	Red Ruffing	4344.0
3	Burleigh Grimes	4179.2
4	Ted Lyons	4161.0
5	Red Faber	4086.2
6	Lefty Grove	3940.2
7	Jack Quinn	3920.1
8	Sam Jones	3883.0
9	Waite Hoyt	3762.1
10	Bobo Newsom	3759.1
11	Paul Derringer	3645.0
12	Carl Hubbell	3590.1
13	Herb Pennock	3571.2
14	Earl Whitehill	3564.2
15	Wilbur Cooper	3480.0

1942-1960

1	Warren Spahn	5243.2
2	Robin Roberts	4688.2
3	Early Wynn	4564.0
4	Bob Feller	3827.0
5	Bob Friend	3611.0
6	Curt Simmons	3348.1
7	Billy Pierce	3306.2
8	Dutch Leonard	3218.1
9	Whitey Ford	3170.1
10	Lew Burdette	3067.1
11	Murry Dickson	3052.1
12	Hal Newhouser	2993.0
13	Bob Lemon	2850.0
14	Dizzy Trout	2725.2
15	Virgil Trucks	2682.1

1961-1976

1	Phil Niekro	5404.1
2	Gaylord Perry	5350.1
3	Don Sutton	5282.1
4	Steve Carlton	5217.1
5	Tom Seaver	4782.2
6	Tommy John	4710.1
7	Jim Kaat	4530.1
8	Fergie Jenkins	4500.2
9	Jim Palmer	3948.0
10	Bob Gibson	3884.1
11	Jerry Koosman	3839.1
12	Jim Bunning	3760.1
13	Mickey Lolich	3638.1
14	Juan Marichal	3507.1
15	Luis Tiant	3486.1

1977-1996

1	Nolan Ryan	5386.0
2	Bert Blyleven	4970.0
3	Frank Tanana	4188.1
4	Dennis Martinez	3859.2
5	Jack Morris	3824.0
6	Charlie Hough	3801.1
7	Jerry Reuss	3669.2
8	Joe Niekro	3584.0
9	Rick Reuschel	3548.1
10	Doyle Alexander	3367.2
11	Vida Blue	3343.1
12	Dennis Eckersley	3193.0
13	Bob Welch	3092.0
14	Dave Stieb	2845.0
15	Fernando Valenzuela	2841.0

Hits per Game

1	Nolan Ryan	6.56
2	Sandy Koufax	6.79
3	Sid Fernandez	6.85
4	J.R. Richard	6.88
5	Andy Messersmith	6.94
6	Randy Johnson	6.94
7	Hoyt Wilhelm	7.01
8	Sam McDowell	7.03
9	Ed Walsh	7.12
10	Bob Turley	7.18
11	Orval Overall	7.22
12	Jeff Tesreau	7.24
13	Ed Reulbach	7.24
14	Mario Soto	7.26
15	Addie Joss	7.30
16	Jose DeLeon	7.38
17	Jim Maloney	7.39
18	David Cone	7.40
19	Rich Gossage	7.45
20	Tom Seaver	7.47
21	Walter Johnson	7.48
22	Rube Waddell	7.48
23	Bob Gibson	7.60
24	Don Wilson	7.61
25	Jim Palmer	7.63
26	Roger Clemens	7.65
27	Larry Cheney	7.68
28	Mordecai Brown	7.68
29	Sam Jones	7.68
30	Bob Feller	7.69
31	Johnny Vander Meer	7.69
32	John Smoltz	7.71
33	Catfish Hunter	7.72
34	Al Downing	7.72
35	Jim Scott	7.73
36	Charlie Hough	7.77
37	Bobby Bolin	7.79
38	Stan Williams	7.79
39	Rollie Fingers	7.80
40	Dean Chance	7.81
41	Frank Smith	7.82
42	Tug McGraw	7.83
43	Barney Pelty	7.84
44	Whitey Ford	7.85
45	Denny McLain	7.85
46	Bob Veale	7.87
47	Chief Bender	7.89
48	George McQuillan	7.89
49	Jack Coombs	7.89
50	Tim Keefe	7.90
51	Moe Drabowsky	7.90
52	Vida Blue	7.91
53	Nap Rucker	7.92
54	Allie Reynolds	7.92
55	Eddie Plank	7.92
56	Luis Tiant	7.94
57	Christy Mathewson	7.94
58	Rudy May	7.94
59	Dwight Gooden	7.95
60	Ray Culp	7.95
61	Dave Stieb	7.95
62	Bill Donovan	7.99
63	Howie Camnitz	7.99
64	Don Sutton	7.99
65	Juan Pizarro	7.99
66	Greg Maddux	8.00
67	Gary Bell	8.01
68	Earl Moore	8.02
69	Sonny Siebert	8.03
70	Lefty Tyler	8.03
71	Hal Newhouser	8.04
72	Claude Hendrix	8.06
73	Steve Carlton	8.06
74	Hooks Wiltse	8.06
75	Mark Langston	8.07
76	Amos Rusie	8.07
77	Jose Rijo	8.07
78	Willie Mitchell	8.07
79	Larry Corcoran	8.08
80	Bill Singer	8.08
81	Bob Lemon	8.08
82	Mike Scott	8.08
83	Stu Miller	8.09
84	Don Drysdale	8.09
85	Gary Nolan	8.09
86	Eddie Cicotte	8.09
87	Juan Marichal	8.09
88	Doc White	8.10
89	Virgil Trucks	8.11
90	Hippo Vaughn	8.11
91	Blue Moon Odom	8.12
92	Kirby Higbe	8.13
93	Jim Shaw	8.13
94	Mike Cuellar	8.13
95	Billy Pierce	8.14
96	Mort Cooper	8.15
97	Red Ames	8.15
98	Vic Willis	8.16
99	Harry Brecheen	8.17
100	Earl Wilson	8.17

Home Runs Allowed

1	Robin Roberts	505
2	Fergie Jenkins	484
3	Phil Niekro	482
4	Don Sutton	472
5	Frank Tanana	448
6	Warren Spahn	434
7	Bert Blyleven	430
8	Steve Carlton	414
9	Gaylord Perry	399
10	Jim Kaat	395
11	Jack Morris	389
12	Charlie Hough	383
13	Tom Seaver	380
14	Catfish Hunter	374
15	Jim Bunning	372
16	Dennis Martinez	356
17	Mickey Lolich	347
18	Luis Tiant	346
19	Early Wynn	338
20	Dennis Eckersley	332
21	Doyle Alexander	324
22	Nolan Ryan	321
23	Juan Marichal	320
24	Pedro Ramos	315
25	Jim Perry	308
26	Jim Palmer	303
27	Murry Dickson	302
	Tommy John	302
29	Milt Pappas	298
30	Scott Sanderson	297
31	Frank Viola	294
32	Mudcat Grant	292
33	Floyd Bannister	291
	Mike Moore	291
35	Jerry Koosman	290
36	Lew Burdette	289
37	Bob Friend	286
38	Billy Pierce	284
39	Mark Langston	283
40	Bill Gullickson	282
41	Don Drysdale	280
42	Jim Slaton	277
43	Joe Niekro	276
44	Danny Darwin	272
45	Vern Law	268
46	Bob Welch	267
47	Dave Stewart	264
48	Vida Blue	263
49	Rick Wise	261
50	Larry Jackson	259
51	Bruce Hurst	258
52	Bob Gibson	257
53	Camilo Pascual	256
54	Mike McCormick	255
	Curt Simmons	255
56	Red Ruffing	254
57	Don Newcombe	252
58	Mike Flanagan	251
59	Ken Holtzman	249
	Claude Osteen	249
61	Steve Renko	248
62	John Candelaria	245
	Jerry Reuss	245
64	Jim Clancy	244
65	Denny McLain	242
	Johnny Podres	242
67	Harvey Haddix	240
	Ray Sadecki	240
69	Ron Darling	239
70	Bob Buhl	238
71	Tom Browning	236
	Rick Sutcliffe	236
	Earl Wilson	236
74	Scott McGregor	235
75	Joe Coleman	234
76	Jim Lonborg	233
77	Dave McNally	230
78	Whitey Ford	228
	Bob Knepper	228
80	Carl Hubbell	227
81	Kevin Gross	226
	Ron Guidry	226
83	Don Cardwell	225
	Jimmy Key	225
85	Bob Feller	224
86	Stan Bahnsen	223
	Ted Lyons	223
	Mike Torrez	223
89	Mike Cuellar	222
90	Ray Burris	221
	Rick Reuschel	221
92	Dave Stieb	219
93	Mike Caldwell	218
	Ron Kline	218
	Dan Petry	218
96	Bud Black	217
97	Bob Forsch	216
	Ralph Terry	216
99	Fernando Valenzuela	214
100	Ned Garver	213

Home Runs Allowed (by era)

1876-1892

1	John Clarkson	161
2	Jack Stivetts	131
3	Pud Galvin	122
4	Gus Weyhing	120
5	Charley Radbourn	117
6	Mickey Welch	106
7	Bill Hutchison	104
8	Tony Mullane	98
9	Charlie Getzien	95
10	Harry Staley	92
11	Charlie Buffinton	87
12	Jim McCormick	84
13	Mark Baldwin	82
14	Jim Whitney	79
15	Adonis Terry	76

1893-1919

1	Pete Alexander	164
2	Kid Nichols	156
3	Cy Young	138
4	Jack Powell	110
5	Frank Dwyer	109
6	Rube Marquard	107
7	Walter Johnson	97
8	Brickyard Kennedy	93
9	Christy Mathewson	91
10	Hooks Dauss	87
11	Ad Gumbert	81
12	Kid Carsey	80
13	Ted Breitenstein	79
14	Bill Dinneen	78
15	Clark Griffith	76

1920-1941

1	Red Ruffing	254
2	Carl Hubbell	227
3	Ted Lyons	223
4	Bobo Newsom	206
5	Earl Whitehill	192
6	Charlie Root	187
7	Freddie Fitzsimmons	186
8	Tommy Bridges	181
9	Lon Warneke	175
10	George Blaeholder	173
	Syl Johnson	173
12	Bump Hadley	167
13	Jesse Haines	165
14	Larry French	164
15	Rube Walberg	163

1942-1960

1	Robin Roberts	505
2	Warren Spahn	434
3	Early Wynn	338
4	Pedro Ramos	315
5	Murry Dickson	302
6	Lew Burdette	289
7	Bob Friend	286
8	Billy Pierce	284
9	Vern Law	268
10	Curt Simmons	255
11	Don Newcombe	252
12	Johnny Podres	242
13	Harvey Haddix	240
14	Bob Buhl	238
15	Whitey Ford	228

1961-1976

1	Fergie Jenkins	484
2	Phil Niekro	482
3	Don Sutton	472
4	Steve Carlton	414
5	Gaylord Perry	399
6	Jim Kaat	395
7	Tom Seaver	380
8	Catfish Hunter	374
9	Jim Bunning	372
10	Mickey Lolich	347
11	Luis Tiant	346
12	Juan Marichal	320
13	Jim Perry	308
14	Jim Palmer	303
15	Tommy John	302

1977-1996

1	Frank Tanana	448
2	Bert Blyleven	430
3	Jack Morris	389
4	Charlie Hough	383
5	Dennis Martinez	356
6	Dennis Eckersley	332
7	Doyle Alexander	324
8	Nolan Ryan	321
9	Scott Sanderson	297
10	Frank Viola	294
11	Floyd Bannister	291
	Mike Moore	291
13	Mark Langston	283
14	Bill Gullickson	282
15	Jim Slaton	277

Walks

1	Nolan Ryan	2795
2	Steve Carlton	1833
3	Phil Niekro	1809
4	Early Wynn	1775
5	Bob Feller	1764
6	Bobo Newsom	1732
7	Amos Rusie	1707
8	Charlie Hough	1665
9	Gus Weyhing	1566
10	Red Ruffing	1541
11	Bump Hadley	1442
12	Warren Spahn	1434
13	Earl Whitehill	1431
14	Tony Mullane	1408
15	Sam Jones	1396
16	Jack Morris	1390
	Tom Seaver	1390
18	Gaylord Perry	1379
19	Mike Torrez	1371
20	Walter Johnson	1363
21	Don Sutton	1343
22	Bob Gibson	1336
23	Chick Fraser	1332
24	Bert Blyleven	1322
25	Sam McDowell	1312
26	Jim Palmer	1311
27	Mark Baldwin	1307
28	Adonis Terry	1298
29	Mickey Welch	1297
30	Burleigh Grimes	1295
31	Kid Nichols	1268
32	Joe Bush	1263
33	Joe Niekro	1262
34	Allie Reynolds	1261
35	Tommy John	1259
36	Frank Tanana	1255
37	Bob Lemon	1251
38	Hal Newhouser	1249
39	George Mullin	1238
40	Tim Keefe	1236
41	Cy Young	1217
42	Red Faber	1213
43	Vic Willis	1212
44	Ted Breitenstein	1203
45	Brickyard Kennedy	1201
46	Jerry Koosman	1198
47	Tommy Bridges	1192
48	John Clarkson	1191
49	Mark Langston	1190
50	Lefty Grove	1187
51	Vida Blue	1185
52	Billy Pierce	1178
53	Mike Moore	1156
54	Jack Stivetts	1155
55	Bill Hutchison	1132
	Johnny Vander Meer	1132
57	Jerry Reuss	1127
58	Ted Lyons	1121
	Bucky Walters	1121
	Bobby Witt	1121
61	Mel Harder	1118
62	Dennis Martinez	1117
63	Earl Moore	1108
64	Bob Buhl	1105
	Fernando Valenzuela	1105
66	Luis Tiant	1104
67	Mickey Lolich	1099
68	Lefty Gomez	1095
69	Virgil Trucks	1088
70	Whitey Ford	1086
71	Jim Kaat	1083
72	Eppa Rixey	1082
73	Rick Sutcliffe	1081
74	Eddie Plank	1072
75	Camilo Pascual	1069
76	Bob Turley	1068
77	Hooks Dauss	1067
78	Elton Chamberlain	1065
79	Bert Cunningham	1064
80	Curt Simmons	1063
81	Bill Donovan	1059
82	Murry Dickson	1058
	Jouett Meekin	1058
84	Vern Kennedy	1049
85	Dizzy Trout	1046
86	Howard Ehmke	1042
87	Wes Ferrell	1040
88	Tommy Byrne	1037
89	Red Ames	1034
	Dave Stewart	1034
	Bob Welch	1034
92	Rube Walberg	1031
93	Jack Powell	1021
94	Bob Shawkey	1018
95	Dave Stieb	1017
96	Steve Renko	1010
97	Jim Slaton	1004
98	Joe Coleman	1003
	Waite Hoyt	1003
100	Jim Bunning	1000

Fewest Walks per Game

1876-1892
1	Tommy Bond	0.58
2	George Bradley	0.67
3	Terry Larkin	0.71
4	John Ward	0.92
5	Fred Goldsmith	0.96
6	Jim Whitney	1.06
7	Bobby Mathews	1.11
8	Pud Galvin	1.13
9	Will White	1.26
10	Jack Lynch	1.38
11	Guy Hecker	1.51
12	Lee Richmond	1.53
13	Jim McCormick	1.58
14	Jumbo McGinnis	1.65
15	Ed Morris	1.67

1893-1919
1	Deacon Phillippe	1.25
2	Babe Adams	1.29
3	Addie Joss	1.41
4	Cy Young	1.49
5	Jesse Tannehill	1.56
6	Christy Mathewson	1.59
7	Nick Altrock	1.62
8	Pete Alexander	1.65
9	Noodles Hahn	1.69
10	Dick Rudolph	1.77
11	Al Orth	1.77
12	Slim Sallee	1.83
13	Bill Bernhard	1.83
14	Ed Siever	1.86
15	Ed Walsh	1.87

1920-1941
1	Red Lucas	1.61
2	Pete Donohue	1.80
3	Jesse Barnes	1.80
4	Carl Hubbell	1.82
5	Curt Davis	1.85
6	Paul Derringer	1.88
7	Bill Swift	1.93
8	Sherry Smith	1.93
9	Watty Clark	1.97
10	Jack Quinn	1.97
11	Syl Johnson	2.03
12	Dizzy Dean	2.07
13	Art Nehf	2.13
14	Sloppy Thurston	2.15
15	Eppa Rixey	2.17

1942-1960
1	Tiny Bonham	1.67
2	Robin Roberts	1.73
3	Lew Burdette	1.84
4	Ken Raffensberger	1.88
5	Vern Law	2.01
6	Don Newcombe	2.05
7	Dutch Leonard	2.06
8	Hal Brown	2.08
9	Larry Jansen	2.09
10	Bob Purkey	2.17
11	Dick Donovan	2.21
12	Bob Friend	2.23
13	Don Mossi	2.24
14	Preacher Roe	2.37
15	Ed Lopat	2.40

1961-1976
1	Fritz Peterson	1.73
2	Juan Marichal	1.82
3	Fergie Jenkins	1.99
4	Jim Barr	2.04
5	Bill Monbouquette	2.12
6	Ken Johnson	2.14
7	Jim Kaat	2.15
8	Ralph Terry	2.17
9	Gary Nolan	2.22
10	Don Drysdale	2.24
11	Bill Hands	2.27
12	Larry Jackson	2.27
13	Don Sutton	2.29
14	Ron Reed	2.30
15	Rick Wise	2.31

1977-1996
1	Bret Saberhagen	1.70
2	Greg Swindell	1.96
3	Dennis Eckersley	2.04
4	Lary Sorensen	2.08
5	John Candelaria	2.11
6	Bryn Smith	2.17
7	Scott McGregor	2.18
8	Bill Gullickson	2.19
9	Scott Sanderson	2.20
10	Jimmy Key	2.20
11	Mike Caldwell	2.23
12	Greg Maddux	2.24
13	Terry Mulholland	2.24
14	John Smiley	2.34
15	Randy Jones	2.34

Strikeouts

1	Nolan Ryan	5714
2	Steve Carlton	4136
3	Bert Blyleven	3701
4	Tom Seaver	3640
5	Don Sutton	3574
6	Gaylord Perry	3534
7	Walter Johnson	3509
8	Phil Niekro	3342
9	Fergie Jenkins	3192
10	Bob Gibson	3117
11	Jim Bunning	2855
12	Mickey Lolich	2832
13	Cy Young	2803
14	Frank Tanana	2773
15	Roger Clemens	2590
16	Warren Spahn	2583
17	Bob Feller	2581
18	Tim Keefe	2560
19	Jerry Koosman	2556
20	Christy Mathewson	2502
21	Don Drysdale	2486
22	Jack Morris	2478
23	Jim Kaat	2461
24	Sam McDowell	2453
25	Luis Tiant	2416
26	Sandy Koufax	2396
27	Charlie Hough	2362
28	Robin Roberts	2357
29	Mark Langston	2335
30	Dennis Eckersley	2334
	Early Wynn	2334
32	Rube Waddell	2316
33	Juan Marichal	2303
34	Lefty Grove	2266
35	Eddie Plank	2246
36	Tommy John	2245
37	Jim Palmer	2212
38	Pete Alexander	2198
39	Vida Blue	2175
40	Camilo Pascual	2167
41	Bobo Newsom	2082
42	Dennis Martinez	2070
43	Dazzy Vance	2045
44	Rick Reuschel	2015
45	Fernando Valenzuela	2013
46	Catfish Hunter	2012
47	Dwight Gooden	2001
48	Billy Pierce	1999
49	Red Ruffing	1987
50	John Clarkson	1978
51	Bob Welch	1969
52	Whitey Ford	1956
53	Amos Rusie	1950
54	Jerry Reuss	1907
55	Kid Nichols	1873
56	Mickey Welch	1850
57	Frank Viola	1844
58	Charley Radbourn	1830
59	David Cone	1812
60	Tony Mullane	1803
61	Pud Galvin	1799
62	Hal Newhouser	1796
63	Ron Guidry	1778
64	Danny Darwin	1769
65	Rudy May	1760
66	Joe Niekro	1747
67	Dave Stewart	1741
68	Sid Fernandez	1740
69	Ed Walsh	1736
70	Bob Friend	1734
71	Joe Coleman	1728
	Milt Pappas	1728
73	Floyd Bannister	1723
74	Chief Bender	1711
75	Larry Jackson	1709
	Randy Johnson	1709
77	Kevin Gross	1707
78	Jim McCormick	1704
79	Bob Veale	1703
80	Red Ames	1702
81	Charlie Buffinton	1700
82	Curt Simmons	1697
83	Bruce Hurst	1689
84	Orel Hershiser	1679
	Rick Sutcliffe	1679
86	Carl Hubbell	1677
87	Tommy Bridges	1674
88	John Candelaria	1673
89	Mike Moore	1667
90	Gus Weyhing	1665
91	Vic Willis	1651
92	Rick Wise	1647
93	Greg Maddux	1643
94	Dave Stieb	1642
95	Al Downing	1639
96	Mike Cuellar	1632
97	Chris Short	1629
98	Andy Messersmith	1625
99	Jack Powell	1621
	Steve Rogers	1621

Strikeouts per Game

1	Randy Johnson	10.11
2	Nolan Ryan	9.55
3	Sandy Koufax	9.28
4	Sam McDowell	8.86
5	Sid Fernandez	8.41
6	Roger Clemens	8.40
7	J.R. Richard	8.37
8	David Cone	8.18
9	Bob Veale	7.96
10	Jose Rijo	7.84
11	Jim Maloney	7.81
12	Dwight Gooden	7.70
13	Bobby Witt	7.65
14	John Smoltz	7.62
15	Mark Langston	7.58
16	Jose DeLeon	7.56
17	Mario Soto	7.54
18	Sam Jones	7.54
19	Rich Gossage	7.47
20	Andy Benes	7.31
21	Bob Gibson	7.22
22	Steve Carlton	7.13
23	Rube Waddell	7.04
24	Mickey Lolich	7.01
25	Chuck Finley	6.87
26	Rollie Fingers	6.87
27	Tom Seaver	6.85
28	Jim Bunning	6.83
29	Juan Pizarro	6.73
30	Bobby Bolin	6.71
31	Bert Blyleven	6.70
32	Ron Guidry	6.69
33	Ray Culp	6.69
34	Stan Williams	6.66
35	Camilo Pascual	6.65
36	Bob Turley	6.65
37	Don Wilson	6.60
38	Tug McGraw	6.59
39	Dennis Eckersley	6.58
40	Denny Lemaster	6.57
41	Andy Messersmith	6.56
42	Don Drysdale	6.52
43	Al Downing	6.50
44	Floyd Bannister	6.49
45	Toad Ramsey	6.49
46	Diego Segui	6.46
47	Dean Chance	6.43
48	Hoyt Wilhelm	6.43
49	Mike Scott	6.39
50	Fergie Jenkins	6.38
51	Fernando Valenzuela	6.38
52	Moe Drabowsky	6.37
53	Earl Wilson	6.37
54	Harvey Haddix	6.34
55	Sonny Siebert	6.32
56	Chris Short	6.31
57	Bruce Hurst	6.29
58	Bill Singer	6.27
59	Greg Maddux	6.25
60	Jack McDowell	6.24
61	Kevin Gross	6.24
62	Luis Tiant	6.24
63	Turk Farrell	6.21
64	Dazzy Vance	6.20
65	Stu Miller	6.18
66	Clay Kirby	6.17
67	Gary Bell	6.15
68	Gary Peters	6.14
69	Greg Swindell	6.12
70	Denny McLain	6.12
71	Bret Saberhagen	6.10
72	Don Sutton	6.09
73	Todd Stottlemyre	6.07
74	Mike Krukow	6.07
75	Bob Feller	6.07
76	Ron Darling	6.06
77	Joe Coleman	6.05
78	Fred Norman	6.05
79	Rudy May	6.04
80	Jerry Koosman	5.99
81	John Smiley	5.97
82	Orel Hershiser	5.97
83	John Candelaria	5.96
84	Frank Tanana	5.96
85	Dave Stewart	5.96
86	Gaylord Perry	5.94
87	Tim Belcher	5.94
88	Woodie Fryman	5.92
89	Juan Marichal	5.91
90	Steve Barber	5.89
91	John Montefusco	5.89
92	Danny Darwin	5.87
93	Mike Witt	5.86
94	Vida Blue	5.85
95	Tom Candiotti	5.85
96	Frank Viola	5.85
97	Jack Morris	5.83
98	Joey Jay	5.81
99	Ray Sadecki	5.81
100	Doug Drabek	5.80

Ratio

1	Addie Joss	8.9
2	Ed Walsh	9.2
3	John Ward	9.4
4	Christy Mathewson	9.6
5	Tommy Bond	9.8
	Mordecai Brown	9.8
7	George Bradley	9.9
	Walter Johnson	9.9
9	Babe Adams	10.0
	Larry Corcoran	10.0
	Sandy Koufax	10.0
	Juan Marichal	10.0
13	Charlie Ferguson	10.1
	Terry Larkin	10.1
	Deacon Phillippe	10.1
16	Pete Alexander	10.2
	Jim McCormick	10.2
	Ed Morris	10.2
	Tom Seaver	10.2
	Will White	10.2
21	Chief Bender	10.3
	Catfish Hunter	10.3
	Tim Keefe	10.3
	Rube Waddell	10.3
25	Nick Altrock	10.4
	Tiny Bonham	10.4
	Fred Goldsmith	10.4
	Noodles Hahn	10.4
	Fergie Jenkins	10.4
	George McQuillan	10.4
	Gary Nolan	10.4
	Charley Radbourn	10.4
	Bret Saberhagen	10.4
	Don Sutton	10.4
	Doc White	10.4
	Jim Whitney	10.4
	Hoyt Wilhelm	10.4
	Hooks Wiltse	10.4
	Cy Young	10.4
40	Eddie Cicotte	10.5
	Sid Fernandez	10.5
	Greg Maddux	10.5
	Andy Messersmith	10.5
	Eddie Plank	10.5
	Dick Rudolph	10.5
	Jeff Tesreau	10.5
47	Dennis Eckersley	10.6
	Rollie Fingers	10.6
	Carl Hubbell	10.6
	Sam Leever	10.6
	Denny McLain	10.6
	Robin Roberts	10.6
53	Bob Caruthers	10.7
	Jack Chesbro	10.7
	Roger Clemens	10.7
	Don Drysdale	10.7
	Ron Guidry	10.7
	Guy Hecker	10.7
	Jumbo McGinnis	10.7
	Orval Overall	10.7
	Jim Palmer	10.7
	Ed Reulbach	10.7
	Slim Sallee	10.7
	Frank Smith	10.7
	George Winter	10.7
66	John Candelaria	10.8
	Mike Cuellar	10.8
	Bob Ewing	10.8
	Pud Galvin	10.8
	Barney Pelty	10.8
	Gaylord Perry	10.8
	Nap Rucker	10.8
	Dupee Shaw	10.8
	Mario Soto	10.8
	Warren Spahn	10.8
	Ralph Terry	10.8
77	Harry Brecheen	10.9
	Phil Douglas	10.9
	Eddie Fisher	10.9
	Dave Foutz	10.9
	Bob Gibson	10.9
	Claude Hendrix	10.9
	Fritz Peterson	10.9
	Jim Scott	10.9
	Jack Taylor	10.9
	Luis Tiant	10.9
	Fred Toney	10.9
	John Tudor	10.9
	Carl Weilman	10.9
90	13 players tied	11.0

Earned Run Average

Rank	Player	ERA
1	Ed Walsh	1.82
2	Addie Joss	1.89
3	Mordecai Brown	2.06
4	John Ward	2.10
5	Christy Mathewson	2.13
6	Rube Waddell	2.16
7	Walter Johnson	2.17
8	Orval Overall	2.23
9	Tommy Bond	2.25
10	Ed Reulbach	2.28
	Will White	2.28
12	Jim Scott	2.30
13	Eddie Plank	2.35
14	Larry Corcoran	2.36
15	Eddie Cicotte	2.38
	Ed Killian	2.38
	George McQuillan	2.38
18	Doc White	2.39
19	Nap Rucker	2.42
20	Terry Larkin	2.43
	Jim McCormick	2.43
	Jeff Tesreau	2.43
23	Chief Bender	2.46
24	Sam Leever	2.47
	Lefty Leifield	2.47
	Hooks Wiltse	2.47
27	Bob Ewing	2.49
	Hippo Vaughn	2.49
29	George Bradley	2.50
30	Hoyt Wilhelm	2.52
31	Noodles Hahn	2.55
32	Pete Alexander	2.56
	Slim Sallee	2.56
34	Deacon Phillippe	2.59
	Frank Smith	2.59
36	Ed Siever	2.60
37	Bob Rhoads	2.61
38	Tim Keefe	2.62
39	Red Ames	2.63
	Barney Pelty	2.63
	Vic Willis	2.63
	Cy Young	2.63
43	Claude Hendrix	2.65
44	Joe McGinnity	2.66
	Dick Rudolph	2.66
	Jack Taylor	2.66
47	Nick Altrock	2.67
	Charlie Ferguson	2.67
	Charley Radbourn	2.67
	Carl Weilman	2.67
51	Jack Chesbro	2.68
	Cy Falkenberg	2.68
53	Bill Donovan	2.69
	Fred Toney	2.69
55	Larry Cheney	2.70
56	Mickey Welch	2.71
57	Fred Goldsmith	2.73
58	Harry Howell	2.74
59	Howie Camnitz	2.75
	Whitey Ford	2.75
	Dummy Taylor	2.75
62	Babe Adams	2.76
	Sandy Koufax	2.76
	Dutch Leonard	2.76
65	Jeff Pfeffer	2.77
66	Jack Coombs	2.78
	Earl Moore	2.78
68	Tully Sparks	2.79
	Jesse Tannehill	2.79
70	Phil Douglas	2.80
71	John Clarkson	2.81
72	Ray Fisher	2.82
	Ed Morris	2.82
	George Mullin	2.82
75	Bob Caruthers	2.83
76	Dave Foutz	2.84
77	Greg Maddux	2.86
	Andy Messersmith	2.86
	Jim Palmer	2.86
	Tom Seaver	2.86
81	Pud Galvin	2.87
	George Winter	2.87
83	Willie Mitchell	2.88
84	Wilbur Cooper	2.89
	Stan Coveleski	2.89
	Juan Marichal	2.89
87	Rollie Fingers	2.90
88	Bob Gibson	2.91
89	Harry Brecheen	2.92
	Dean Chance	2.92
	Doc Crandall	2.92
	Carl Mays	2.92
93	Dave Davenport	2.93
	Guy Hecker	2.93
95	Don Drysdale	2.95
	Jumbo McGinnis	2.95
	Kid Nichols	2.95
	Lefty Tyler	2.95
99	Charlie Buffinton	2.96
100	4 players tied	2.97

Earned Run Average (by era)

1876-1892

Rank	Player	ERA
1	John Ward	2.10
2	Tommy Bond	2.25
3	Will White	2.28
4	Larry Corcoran	2.36
5	Terry Larkin	2.43
	Jim McCormick	2.43
7	George Bradley	2.50
8	Tim Keefe	2.62
9	Charlie Ferguson	2.67
	Charley Radbourn	2.67
11	Mickey Welch	2.71
12	Fred Goldsmith	2.73
13	John Clarkson	2.81
14	Ed Morris	2.82
15	Bob Caruthers	2.83

1893-1919

Rank	Player	ERA
1	Ed Walsh	1.82
2	Addie Joss	1.89
3	Mordecai Brown	2.06
4	Christy Mathewson	2.13
5	Rube Waddell	2.16
6	Walter Johnson	2.17
7	Orval Overall	2.23
8	Ed Reulbach	2.28
9	Jim Scott	2.30
10	Eddie Plank	2.35
11	Eddie Cicotte	2.38
	Ed Killian	2.38
	George McQuillan	2.38
14	Doc White	2.39
15	Nap Rucker	2.42

1920-1941

Rank	Player	ERA
1	Wilbur Cooper	2.89
	Stan Coveleski	2.89
3	Carl Mays	2.92
4	Carl Hubbell	2.98
5	Dizzy Dean	3.02
6	Lefty Grove	3.06
7	Bob Shawkey	3.09
8	Red Faber	3.15
	Eppa Rixey	3.15
10	Urban Shocker	3.17
11	Lon Warneke	3.18
12	Art Nehf	3.20
13	Jesse Barnes	3.22
14	George Mogridge	3.23
15	2 players tied	3.24

1942-1960

Rank	Player	ERA
1	Hoyt Wilhelm	2.52
2	Whitey Ford	2.75
3	Harry Brecheen	2.92
4	Mort Cooper	2.97
5	Max Lanier	3.01
6	Tiny Bonham	3.06
	Hal Newhouser	3.06
8	Warren Spahn	3.09
9	Sal Maglie	3.15
10	Ed Lopat	3.21
11	Bob Lemon	3.23
	Dizzy Trout	3.23
13	Stu Miller	3.24
14	Bob Feller	3.25
	Dutch Leonard	3.25

1961-1976

Rank	Player	ERA
1	Sandy Koufax	2.76
2	Andy Messersmith	2.86
	Jim Palmer	2.86
	Tom Seaver	2.86
5	Juan Marichal	2.89
6	Rollie Fingers	2.90
7	Bob Gibson	2.91
8	Dean Chance	2.92
9	Don Drysdale	2.95
10	Mel Stottlemyre	2.97
11	Bob Veale	3.07
12	Gary Nolan	3.08
13	Joe Horlen	3.11
	Gaylord Perry	3.11
15	2 players tied	3.14

1977-1996

Rank	Player	ERA
1	Greg Maddux	2.86
2	Rich Gossage	3.01
3	Roger Clemens	3.06
4	John Tudor	3.12
5	J.R. Richard	3.15
6	David Cone	3.16
	Orel Hershiser	3.16
	Jose Rijo	3.16
9	Steve Rogers	3.17
10	Nolan Ryan	3.19
11	Dwight Gooden	3.24
12	Bret Saberhagen	3.26
13	Vida Blue	3.27
14	Ron Guidry	3.29
15	Bert Blyleven	3.31

Adjusted Earned Run Average

Rank	Player	Adj.
1	Lefty Grove	148
2	Walter Johnson	147
3	Hoyt Wilhelm	146
4	Ed Walsh	145
5	Roger Clemens	144
6	Addie Joss	142
7	Greg Maddux	139
	Kid Nichols	139
9	Cy Young	138
10	Mordecai Brown	137
11	Christy Mathewson	136
12	Pete Alexander	135
	Rube Waddell	135
14	John Clarkson	134
15	Harry Brecheen	133
	Whitey Ford	133
	Noodles Hahn	133
18	Sandy Koufax	131
19	Dizzy Dean	130
	Carl Hubbell	130
	Hal Newhouser	130
	Amos Rusie	130
23	Stan Coveleski	128
24	Nig Cuppy	127
	Bob Gibson	127
	Sal Maglie	127
	Tom Seaver	127
28	Tommy Bridges	126
	Bret Saberhagen	126
30	David Cone	125
	Lefty Gomez	125
	Rich Gossage	125
	Tim Keefe	125
	Max Lanier	125
	Jim Palmer	125
	Mel Parnell	125
	Dazzy Vance	125
38	Dave Foutz	124
	Urban Shocker	124
	Dizzy Trout	124
41	Bob Caruthers	123
	Eddie Cicotte	123
	Mort Cooper	123
	Sam Leever	123
	Orval Overall	123
	John Tudor	123
47	Larry Corcoran	122
	Bob Feller	122
	Charlie Ferguson	122
	Randy Johnson	122
	Jimmy Key	122
	Silver King	122
	Juan Marichal	122
	Eddie Plank	122
	Ed Reulbach	122
	Jose Rijo	122
	Eddie Rommel	122
	Dave Stieb	122
59	Don Drysdale	121
	Clark Griffith	121
	Andy Messersmith	121
	Jack Stivetts	121
63	Tiny Bonham	120
	Joe McGinnity	120
	Deacon Phillippe	120
	Charley Radbourn	120
	Jim Scott	120
	Hippo Vaughn	120
	Will White	120
70	Dean Chance	119
	Red Faber	119
	Rollie Fingers	119
	Ron Guidry	119
	Orel Hershiser	119
	Thornton Lee	119
	Bob Lemon	119
	Dutch Leonard	119
	Carl Mays	119
	Billy Pierce	119
	Nap Rucker	119
	Bobby Shantz	119
	Lon Warneke	119
83	Babe Adams	118
	Kevin Brown	118
	Ted Lyons	118
	Sadie McMahon	118
	Tony Mullane	118
	Warren Spahn	118
	John Ward	118
	Vic Willis	118
91	Bert Blyleven	117
	Wes Ferrell	117
	Chuck Finley	117
	Mike Garcia	117
	Dolf Luque	117
	Jim McCormick	117
	Gaylord Perry	117
	Toad Ramsey	117
	Bob Stanley	117
	Virgil Trucks	117

Adjusted ERA (by era)

1876-1892

Rank	Player	Adj.
1	John Clarkson	134
2	Tim Keefe	125
3	Dave Foutz	124
4	Bob Caruthers	123
5	Larry Corcoran	122
	Charlie Ferguson	122
	Silver King	122
8	Jack Stivetts	121
9	Charley Radbourn	120
	Will White	120
11	Sadie McMahon	118
	Tony Mullane	118
	John Ward	118
14	Jim McCormick	117
	Toad Ramsey	117

1893-1919

Rank	Player	Adj.
1	Walter Johnson	147
2	Ed Walsh	145
3	Addie Joss	142
4	Kid Nichols	139
5	Cy Young	138
6	Mordecai Brown	137
7	Christy Mathewson	136
8	Pete Alexander	135
	Rube Waddell	135
10	Noodles Hahn	133
11	Amos Rusie	130
12	Nig Cuppy	127
13	Eddie Cicotte	123
	Sam Leever	123
	Orval Overall	123

1920-1941

Rank	Player	Adj.
1	Lefty Grove	148
2	Dizzy Dean	130
	Carl Hubbell	130
4	Stan Coveleski	128
5	Tommy Bridges	126
6	Lefty Gomez	125
	Dazzy Vance	125
8	Urban Shocker	124
9	Eddie Rommel	122
10	Red Faber	119
	Thornton Lee	119
	Carl Mays	119
	Lon Warneke	119
14	Ted Lyons	118
15	2 players tied	117

1942-1960

Rank	Player	Adj.
1	Hoyt Wilhelm	146
2	Harry Brecheen	133
	Whitey Ford	133
4	Hal Newhouser	130
5	Sal Maglie	127
6	Max Lanier	125
	Mel Parnell	125
8	Dizzy Trout	124
9	Mort Cooper	123
10	Bob Feller	122
11	Tiny Bonham	120
12	Bob Lemon	119
	Dutch Leonard	119
	Billy Pierce	119
	Bobby Shantz	119

1961-1976

Rank	Player	Adj.
1	Sandy Koufax	131
2	Bob Gibson	127
	Tom Seaver	127
4	Jim Palmer	125
5	Juan Marichal	122
6	Don Drysdale	121
	Andy Messersmith	121
8	Dean Chance	119
	Rollie Fingers	119
10	Gaylord Perry	117
11	Tug McGraw	116
	Gary Nolan	116
13	4 players tied	115

1977-1996

Rank	Player	Adj.
1	Roger Clemens	144
2	Greg Maddux	139
3	Bret Saberhagen	126
4	David Cone	125
	Rich Gossage	125
6	John Tudor	123
7	Randy Johnson	122
	Jimmy Key	122
	Jose Rijo	122
	Dave Stieb	122
11	Ron Guidry	119
	Orel Hershiser	119
13	Kevin Brown	118
14	3 players tied	117

Pitching Runs

```
  1  Cy Young . . . . . . . . . .  753
  2  Walter Johnson . . . . . .   706
  3  Lefty Grove . . . . . . . .   595
  4  Kid Nichols . . . . . . . .   531
  5  Pete Alexander . . . . . .   484
  6  Warren Spahn . . . . . .     470
  7  Christy Mathewson . . . . . 420
  8  Tom Seaver . . . . . . . .   419
  9  Amos Rusie . . . . . . . .   418
 10  Tim Keefe . . . . . . . . .  404
 11  Carl Hubbell . . . . . . .   394
 12  Whitey Ford . . . . . . . .  386
 13  Bob Feller . . . . . . . . . 385
 14  Jim Palmer . . . . . . . .   374
 15  John Clarkson . . . . . .    371
 16  Roger Clemens . . . . . .    366
 17  Lefty Gomez . . . . . . .    322
 18  Ted Lyons . . . . . . . . .  313
 19  Gaylord Perry . . . . . .    311
 20  Ed Walsh . . . . . . . . .   310
     Hoyt Wilhelm . . . . . . .   310
 22  Nolan Ryan . . . . . . . .   309
 23  Charley Radbourn . . . . .   302
 24  Red Faber . . . . . . . . .  294
 25  Bob Gibson . . . . . . . .   290
 26  Dazzy Vance . . . . . . .    281
 27  Mordecai Brown . . . . . .   279
 28  Red Ruffing . . . . . . . .  272
 29  Bert Blyleven . . . . . . .  271
 30  Dutch Leonard . . . . . .    267
 31  Don Drysdale . . . . . . .   266
 32  Robin Roberts . . . . . . .  264
 33  Juan Marichal . . . . . . .  262
 34  Stan Coveleski . . . . . .   259
     Don Sutton . . . . . . . .   259
 36  Greg Maddux . . . . . . .    257
     Hal Newhouser . . . . . .    257
     Eddie Plank . . . . . . . .  257
 39  Tommy Bridges . . . . . .    256
 40  Bob Lemon . . . . . . . .    251
     Eppa Rixey . . . . . . . .   251
 42  Billy Pierce . . . . . . . . 250
 43  Dolf Luque . . . . . . . .   245
     Tony Mullane . . . . . . .   245
 45  Sandy Koufax . . . . . . .   243
 46  Rube Waddell . . . . . . .   240
 47  Steve Carlton . . . . . . .  236
 48  Clark Griffith . . . . . . . 233
 49  Carl Mays . . . . . . . . .  217
 50  Addie Joss . . . . . . . . . 216
     Mickey Welch . . . . . . .   216
 52  Bob Caruthers . . . . . . .  214
     Tommy John . . . . . . . .   214
 54  Waite Hoyt . . . . . . . .   210
     Urban Shocker . . . . . .    210
 56  Orel Hershiser . . . . . .   205
 57  Silver King . . . . . . . .  204
 58  Jim McCormick . . . . . .    202
 59  Ron Guidry . . . . . . . .   201
     Bret Saberhagen . . . . .    201
 61  Eddie Cicotte . . . . . . .  200
     Nig Cuppy . . . . . . . . .  200
 63  Dave Stieb . . . . . . . .   199
 64  Will White . . . . . . . . . 198
 65  Harry Brecheen . . . . . .   194
 66  Jimmy Key . . . . . . . .    192
     Phil Niekro . . . . . . . .  192
 68  Mel Harder . . . . . . . .   190
 69  Lon Warneke . . . . . . .    188
 70  Dizzy Dean . . . . . . . .   187
 71  David Cone . . . . . . . .   186
     Ed Lopat . . . . . . . . .   186
     Joe McGinnity . . . . . . .  186
 74  Jim Bunning . . . . . . . .  179
     Ed Morris . . . . . . . . .  179
     Eddie Rommel . . . . . . .   179
 77  Larry French . . . . . . .   178
 78  Dizzy Trout . . . . . . . .  177
 79  Spud Chandler . . . . . .    176
 80  Sam Leever . . . . . . . .   175
 81  Kevin Appier . . . . . . .   174
     Freddie Fitzsimmons . . . .  174
     Mike Garcia . . . . . . . .  174
 84  Sadie McMahon . . . . . .    172
     Andy Messersmith . . . . .   172
     Vic Willis . . . . . . . . . 172
 87  Early Wynn . . . . . . . .   170
 88  Thornton Lee . . . . . . .   169
 89  Wilbur Cooper . . . . . .    168
 90  Dennis Eckersley . . . . .   163
 91  Charlie Buffinton . . . . .  162
 92  Babe Adams . . . . . . . .   161
     Noodles Hahn . . . . . . .   161
 94  Pud Galvin . . . . . . . .   160
 95  Ed Reulbach . . . . . . . .  159
 96  Rich Gossage . . . . . . .   158
 97  Fergie Jenkins . . . . . .   157
 98  Sal Maglie . . . . . . . .   156
     Firpo Marberry . . . . . . . 156
100  2 players tied . . . . . . . 153
```

Adjusted Pitching Runs

```
  1  Cy Young . . . . . . . . . .  819
  2  Walter Johnson . . . . . .    668
  3  Kid Nichols . . . . . . . .   653
  4  Lefty Grove . . . . . . . .   643
  5  Pete Alexander . . . . . .    522
  6  John Clarkson . . . . . .     480
  7  Roger Clemens . . . . . .     418
  8  Tom Seaver . . . . . . . .    411
  9  Christy Mathewson . . . . .   403
 10  Amos Rusie . . . . . . . .    384
 11  Tim Keefe . . . . . . . . .   375
 12  Carl Hubbell . . . . . . .    355
 13  Bob Gibson . . . . . . . .    335
 14  Warren Spahn . . . . . .      330
 15  Bert Blyleven . . . . . . .   317
 16  Whitey Ford . . . . . . . .   315
     Jim Palmer . . . . . . . .    315
 18  Hal Newhouser . . . . . .     305
     Gaylord Perry . . . . . .     305
 20  Ted Lyons . . . . . . . . .   302
 21  Bob Feller . . . . . . . . .  301
 22  Phil Niekro . . . . . . . .   299
 23  Greg Maddux . . . . . . .     297
 24  Tommy Bridges . . . . . .     291
 25  Hoyt Wilhelm . . . . . . .    288
 26  Steve Carlton . . . . . . .   277
 27  Stan Coveleski . . . . . .    276
 28  Red Faber . . . . . . . . .   274
 29  Tony Mullane . . . . . . .    270
     Ed Walsh . . . . . . . . .    270
 31  Mordecai Brown . . . . . .    267
     Charley Radbourn . . . . .    267
 33  Clark Griffith . . . . . . .  266
     Dazzy Vance . . . . . . .     266
 35  Fergie Jenkins . . . . . .    254
     Eddie Plank . . . . . . . .   254
 37  Silver King . . . . . . . .   251
 38  Eppa Rixey . . . . . . . .    248
 39  Juan Marichal . . . . . . .   247
     Jack Stivetts . . . . . . .   247
     Rube Waddell . . . . . . .    247
 42  Dave Stieb . . . . . . . .    240
 43  Nig Cuppy . . . . . . . . .   239
 44  Robin Roberts . . . . . . .   236
 45  Dizzy Trout . . . . . . . .   232
 46  Don Drysdale . . . . . . .    230
 47  Lefty Gomez . . . . . . .     229
     Billy Pierce . . . . . . . .  229
 49  Urban Shocker . . . . . .     226
 50  Dutch Leonard . . . . . .     224
 51  Sandy Koufax . . . . . . .    221
 52  Nolan Ryan . . . . . . . .    218
 53  Eddie Rommel . . . . . . .    217
 54  Bret Saberhagen . . . . .     208
     Vic Willis . . . . . . . . .  208
 56  Joe McGinnity . . . . . .     207
 57  Bob Caruthers . . . . . . .   206
     Addie Joss . . . . . . . . .  206
 59  Harry Brecheen . . . . . .    205
 60  Dizzy Dean . . . . . . . .    201
     Dennis Eckersley . . . . .    201
     Jim McCormick . . . . . .     201
 63  Dolf Luque . . . . . . . .    200
 64  Mickey Welch . . . . . . .    196
 65  Wes Ferrell . . . . . . . .   195
 66  Eddie Cicotte . . . . . . .   194
 67  Bob Lemon . . . . . . . .     193
 68  Jim Bunning . . . . . . . .   192
     Jimmy Key . . . . . . . .     192
 70  Carl Mays . . . . . . . . .   189
 71  Lon Warneke . . . . . . .     188
 72  Noodles Hahn . . . . . . .    187
 73  Kevin Appier . . . . . . .    186
 74  Rick Reuschel . . . . . . .   183
 75  Mel Harder . . . . . . . .    182
     Sadie McMahon . . . . . .     182
     Jack Quinn . . . . . . . .    182
 78  Wilbur Cooper . . . . . .     180
 79  Tommy John . . . . . . . .    179
     Will White . . . . . . . . .  179
 81  Frank Dwyer . . . . . . .     178
 82  David Cone . . . . . . . .    177
 83  Red Ruffing . . . . . . . .   174
 84  Waite Hoyt . . . . . . . .    173
     Luis Tiant . . . . . . . . .  173
 86  Thornton Lee . . . . . . .    172
 87  Larry French . . . . . . .    171
 88  Mel Parnell . . . . . . . .   170
 89  Orel Hershiser . . . . . .    169
     Sam Leever . . . . . . . .    169
 91  Bucky Walters . . . . . .     168
 92  Ron Guidry . . . . . . . .    167
     Virgil Trucks . . . . . . .   167
 94  Pud Galvin . . . . . . . .    162
 95  Babe Adams . . . . . . . .    161
     Charlie Buffinton . . . . .   161
 97  Sal Maglie . . . . . . . .    160
 98  Larry Jackson . . . . . . .   155
 99  Rich Gossage . . . . . . .    154
     Steve Rogers . . . . . . .    154
```

Pitching Wins

```
  1  Walter Johnson . . . . . . .  73.2
  2  Cy Young . . . . . . . . . .  70.8
  3  Lefty Grove . . . . . . . .   55.5
  4  Pete Alexander . . . . . .    49.7
  5  Warren Spahn . . . . . .      47.4
  6  Kid Nichols . . . . . . . .   47.1
  7  Christy Mathewson . . . . .   44.2
  8  Tom Seaver . . . . . . . .    43.8
  9  Whitey Ford . . . . . . . .   39.3
 10  Jim Palmer . . . . . . . .    38.8
 11  Carl Hubbell . . . . . . .    38.8
 12  Bob Feller . . . . . . . . .  37.5
 13  Tim Keefe . . . . . . . . .   36.3
 14  Amos Rusie . . . . . . . .    35.9
 15  Roger Clemens . . . . . .     35.9
 16  Ed Walsh . . . . . . . . .    33.4
 17  John Clarkson . . . . . .     33.1
 18  Gaylord Perry . . . . . .     32.6
 19  Nolan Ryan . . . . . . . .    32.1
 20  Hoyt Wilhelm . . . . . . .    31.9
 21  Bob Gibson . . . . . . . .    30.5
 22  Lefty Gomez . . . . . . .     29.9
 23  Mordecai Brown . . . . . .    29.7
 24  Ted Lyons . . . . . . . . .   29.4
 25  Red Faber . . . . . . . . .   28.9
 26  Bert Blyleven . . . . . . .   27.8
 27  Don Drysdale . . . . . . .    27.7
 28  Juan Marichal . . . . . . .   27.6
 29  Eddie Plank . . . . . . . .   27.2
 30  Dazzy Vance . . . . . . .     27.0
 31  Don Sutton . . . . . . . .    26.9
 32  Charley Radbourn . . . . .    26.9
 33  Robin Roberts . . . . . . .   26.6
 34  Dutch Leonard . . . . . .     26.4
 35  Greg Maddux . . . . . . .     26.4
 36  Hal Newhouser . . . . . .     26.0
 37  Stan Coveleski . . . . . .    25.9
 38  Red Ruffing . . . . . . . .   25.6
 39  Rube Waddell . . . . . . .    25.2
 40  Eppa Rixey . . . . . . . .    25.2
 41  Sandy Koufax . . . . . . .    25.1
 42  Billy Pierce . . . . . . . .  25.1
 43  Bob Lemon . . . . . . . .     25.0
 44  Steve Carlton . . . . . . .   24.7
 45  Tommy Bridges . . . . . .     24.1
 46  Dolf Luque . . . . . . . .    23.9
 47  Addie Joss . . . . . . . . .  23.4
 48  Tommy John . . . . . . . .    22.1
 49  Carl Mays . . . . . . . . .   22.0
 50  Tony Mullane . . . . . . .    21.5
 51  Eddie Cicotte . . . . . . .   21.4
 52  Orel Hershiser . . . . . .    20.9
 53  Clark Griffith . . . . . . .  20.8
 54  Urban Shocker . . . . . .     20.5
 55  Waite Hoyt . . . . . . . .    20.2
 56  Ron Guidry . . . . . . . .    20.1
 57  Bret Saberhagen . . . . .     20.0
 58  Phil Niekro . . . . . . . .   20.0
 59  Dave Stieb . . . . . . . .    19.9
 60  Mickey Welch . . . . . . .    19.7
 61  Harry Brecheen . . . . . .    19.6
 62  Lon Warneke . . . . . . .     18.9
 63  Jimmy Key . . . . . . . .     18.8
 64  Bob Caruthers . . . . . . .   18.8
 65  David Cone . . . . . . . .    18.8
 66  Ed Lopat . . . . . . . . .    18.8
 67  Jim Bunning . . . . . . . .   18.6
 68  Joe McGinnity . . . . . .     18.6
 69  Dizzy Dean . . . . . . . .    18.6
 70  Jim McCormick . . . . . .     18.4
 71  Will White . . . . . . . . .  18.2
 72  Andy Messersmith . . . . .    18.2
 73  Mel Harder . . . . . . . .    18.1
 74  Dizzy Trout . . . . . . . .   17.9
 75  Sam Leever . . . . . . . .    17.8
 76  Vic Willis . . . . . . . . .  17.6
 77  Spud Chandler . . . . . .     17.6
 78  Silver King . . . . . . . .   17.6
 79  Larry French . . . . . . .    17.6
 80  Wilbur Cooper . . . . . .     17.5
 81  Mike Garcia . . . . . . . .   17.4
 82  Early Wynn . . . . . . . .    17.2
 83  Ed Reulbach . . . . . . . .   17.1
 84  Freddie Fitzsimmons . . . .   17.1
 85  Nig Cuppy . . . . . . . . .   17.0
 86  Eddie Rommel . . . . . . .    17.0
 87  Kevin Appier . . . . . . .    16.9
 88  Babe Adams . . . . . . . .    16.7
 89  Dennis Eckersley . . . . .    16.5
 90  Fergie Jenkins . . . . . .    16.4
 91  Thornton Lee . . . . . . .    16.3
 92  Rich Gossage . . . . . . .    16.2
 93  Ed Morris . . . . . . . . .   16.0
 94  Vida Blue . . . . . . . . .   15.9
 95  Noodles Hahn . . . . . . .    15.8
 96  Joe Wood . . . . . . . . .    15.7
 97  Sal Maglie . . . . . . . .    15.6
 98  Bucky Walters . . . . . .     15.4
 99  Deacon Phillippe . . . . .    15.4
100  Steve Rogers . . . . . . .    15.3
```

Adjusted Pitching Wins

```
  1  Cy Young . . . . . . . . . .  77.0
  2  Walter Johnson . . . . . .    69.2
  3  Lefty Grove . . . . . . . .   59.9
  4  Kid Nichols . . . . . . . .   57.9
  5  Pete Alexander . . . . . .    53.6
  6  Tom Seaver . . . . . . . .    43.0
  7  John Clarkson . . . . . .     42.8
  8  Christy Mathewson . . . . .   42.4
  9  Roger Clemens . . . . . .     41.0
 10  Bob Gibson . . . . . . . .    35.2
 11  Carl Hubbell . . . . . . .    35.0
 12  Tim Keefe . . . . . . . . .   33.7
 13  Warren Spahn . . . . . .      33.3
 14  Amos Rusie . . . . . . . .    33.0
 15  Jim Palmer . . . . . . . .    32.7
 16  Bert Blyleven . . . . . . .   32.6
 17  Whitey Ford . . . . . . . .   32.1
 18  Gaylord Perry . . . . . .     32.0
 19  Phil Niekro . . . . . . . .   31.2
 20  Hal Newhouser . . . . . .     30.9
 21  Greg Maddux . . . . . . .     30.5
 22  Hoyt Wilhelm . . . . . . .    29.6
 23  Bob Feller . . . . . . . . .  29.3
 24  Ed Walsh . . . . . . . . .    29.1
 25  Steve Carlton . . . . . . .   29.0
 26  Mordecai Brown . . . . . .    28.4
 27  Ted Lyons . . . . . . . . .   28.4
 28  Stan Coveleski . . . . . .    27.6
 29  Tommy Bridges . . . . . .     27.4
 30  Red Faber . . . . . . . . .   27.0
 31  Eddie Plank . . . . . . . .   26.9
 32  Fergie Jenkins . . . . . .    26.5
 33  Juan Marichal . . . . . . .   26.0
 34  Rube Waddell . . . . . . .    26.0
 35  Dazzy Vance . . . . . . .     25.6
 36  Eppa Rixey . . . . . . . .    24.9
 37  Dave Stieb . . . . . . . .    24.0
 38  Don Drysdale . . . . . . .    24.0
 39  Robin Roberts . . . . . . .   23.8
 40  Clark Griffith . . . . . . .  23.8
 41  Charley Radbourn . . . . .    23.7
 42  Tony Mullane . . . . . . .    23.7
 43  Dizzy Trout . . . . . . . .   23.5
 44  Billy Pierce . . . . . . . .  23.0
 45  Sandy Koufax . . . . . . .    22.9
 46  Nolan Ryan . . . . . . . .    22.6
 47  Addie Joss . . . . . . . . .  22.3
 48  Dutch Leonard . . . . . .     22.1
 49  Urban Shocker . . . . . .     22.1
 50  Silver King . . . . . . . .   21.6
 51  Vic Willis . . . . . . . . .  21.3
 52  Lefty Gomez . . . . . . .     21.3
 53  Jack Stivetts . . . . . . .   20.9
 54  Bret Saberhagen . . . . .     20.7
 55  Harry Brecheen . . . . . .    20.7
 56  Eddie Cicotte . . . . . . .   20.7
 57  Joe McGinnity . . . . . .     20.7
 58  Eddie Rommel . . . . . . .    20.6
 59  Nig Cuppy . . . . . . . . .   20.4
 60  Dennis Eckersley . . . . .    20.3
 61  Dizzy Dean . . . . . . . .    20.0
 62  Jim Bunning . . . . . . . .   19.9
 63  Dolf Luque . . . . . . . .    19.5
 64  Bob Lemon . . . . . . . .     19.2
 65  Rick Reuschel . . . . . . .   19.1
 66  Carl Mays . . . . . . . . .   19.1
 67  Lon Warneke . . . . . . .     18.9
 68  Jimmy Key . . . . . . . .     18.8
 69  Wilbur Cooper . . . . . .     18.7
 70  Tommy John . . . . . . . .    18.5
 71  Jim McCormick . . . . . .     18.4
 72  Noodles Hahn . . . . . . .    18.3
 73  Luis Tiant . . . . . . . . .  18.2
 74  Jack Quinn . . . . . . . .    18.1
 75  Bob Caruthers . . . . . . .   18.1
 76  Kevin Appier . . . . . . .    18.0
 77  Wes Ferrell . . . . . . . .   18.0
 78  David Cone . . . . . . . .    17.9
 79  Mickey Welch . . . . . . .    17.9
 80  Mel Harder . . . . . . . .    17.3
 81  Orel Hershiser . . . . . .    17.2
 82  Sam Leever . . . . . . . .    17.2
 83  Bucky Walters . . . . . .     17.1
 84  Virgil Trucks . . . . . . .   16.9
 85  Larry French . . . . . . .    16.9
 86  Mel Parnell . . . . . . . .   16.8
 87  Babe Adams . . . . . . . .    16.7
 88  Ron Guidry . . . . . . . .    16.7
 89  Waite Hoyt . . . . . . . .    16.6
 90  Thornton Lee . . . . . . .    16.5
 91  Hippo Vaughn . . . . . . .    16.5
 92  Will White . . . . . . . . .  16.5
 93  Red Ruffing . . . . . . . .   16.4
 94  Larry Jackson . . . . . . .   16.1
 95  Steve Rogers . . . . . . .    16.1
 96  Sal Maglie . . . . . . . .    15.8
 97  Rich Gossage . . . . . . .    15.8
 98  Ed Reulbach . . . . . . . .   15.7
 99  Joe Wood . . . . . . . . .    15.6
100  Sadie McMahon . . . . . .     15.5
```

Opponents' Batting Average

1. Nolan Ryan .204
2. Sandy Koufax .205
3. Sid Fernandez .209
4. Andy Messersmith .212
   J.R. Richard .212
6. Randy Johnson .213
7. Sam McDowell .215
8. Hoyt Wilhelm .216
9. Ed Walsh .218
10. Mario Soto .220
    Bob Turley .220
12. David Cone .223
    Addie Joss .223
    Orval Overall .223
    Jeff Tesreau .223
16. Jose DeLeon .224
    Jim Maloney .224
    Ed Reulbach .224
19. Larry Corcoran .226
    Tim Keefe .226
    Tom Seaver .226
22. Walter Johnson .227
23. Bob Gibson .228
    Rich Gossage .228
    Rube Waddell .228
    Don Wilson .228
27. Roger Clemens .229
28. Sam Jones .230
    Jim Palmer .230
30. Bobby Bolin .231
    Bob Feller .231
    Catfish Hunter .231
    John Smoltz .231
34. Al Downing .232
    Johnny Vander Meer .232
    Stan Williams .232
37. Mordecai Brown .233
    Charlie Ferguson .233
    Charlie Hough .233
40. Dean Chance .234
    Larry Cheney .234
    Denny McLain .234
    Toad Ramsey .234
    Amos Rusie .234
45. Ray Culp .235
    Rollie Fingers .235
    Whitey Ford .235
    Dave Foutz .235
    Ed Morris .235
    John Ward .235
51. Moe Drabowsky .236
    Christy Mathewson .236
    Tony Mullane .236
    Don Sutton .236
    Luis Tiant .236
    Bob Veale .236
57. Vida Blue .237
    Dwight Gooden .237
    Juan Marichal .237
    Tug McGraw .237
    Juan Pizarro .237
    Frank Smith .237
63. Greg Maddux .238
    Rudy May .238
    Allie Reynolds .238
    Jim Scott .238
    Sonny Siebert .238
68. Gary Bell .239
    Chief Bender .239
    Bill Donovan .239
    Don Drysdale .239
    Hal Newhouser .239
    Gary Nolan .239
    Barney Pelty .239
    Eddie Plank .239
    Dupee Shaw .239
    Dave Stieb .239
    Will White .239
79. Steve Carlton .240
    Bob Caruthers .240
    John Clarkson .240
    Mort Cooper .240
    Billy Pierce .240
    Jose Rijo .240
    Mike Scott .240
    Bill Singer .240
    Virgil Trucks .240
88. Jack Coombs .241
    Kirby Higbe .241
    Mark Langston .241
    Bob Lemon .241
    George McQuillan .241
    Earl Moore .241
    Charley Radbourn .241
    Hooks Wiltse .241
96. 9 players tied .242

Opponents' On Base Pctg.

1. John Ward .254
2. Addie Joss .260
3. George Bradley .262
4. Terry Larkin .263
5. Larry Corcoran .264
   Ed Walsh .264
7. Tommy Bond .267
8. Will White .268
9. Charlie Ferguson .270
10. Christy Mathewson .273
    Ed Morris .273
12. Jim McCormick .274
13. Fred Goldsmith .275
    Tim Keefe .275
    Jim Whitney .275
16. Sandy Koufax .276
17. Mordecai Brown .278
    Juan Marichal .278
    Charley Radbourn .278
20. Walter Johnson .279
    Dupee Shaw .279
22. Guy Hecker .281
    Jumbo McGinnis .281
24. Deacon Phillippe .283
25. Babe Adams .284
    Pud Galvin .284
27. Bob Caruthers .285
    Bobby Mathews .285
    Tom Seaver .285
30. Dave Foutz .286
31. Catfish Hunter .287
    Gary Nolan .287
    Don Sutton .287
    Cy Young .287
35. Pete Alexander .288
    Sid Fernandez .288
    Rube Waddell .288
38. Tiny Bonham .289
    Henry Boyle .289
    Noodles Hahn .289
    Fergie Jenkins .289
    Jack Lynch .289
    Andy Messersmith .289
    Bret Saberhagen .289
45. Hoyt Wilhelm .290
    Hooks Wiltse .290
47. Nick Altrock .291
    Chief Bender .291
    John Clarkson .291
    Dennis Eckersley .291
    Carl Hubbell .291
    Greg Maddux .291
53. Charlie Buffinton .292
    Denny McLain .292
    Mickey Welch .292
    Doc White .292
57. Roger Clemens .293
    Sam Leever .293
    Eddie Plank .293
    Robin Roberts .293
61. Don Drysdale .294
    Ron Guidry .294
    George McQuillan .294
64. Rollie Fingers .295
    Toad Ramsey .295
    Jeff Tesreau .295
67. Jim Palmer .296
    Mario Soto .296
    Ralph Terry .296
70. Jack Chesbro .297
    Eddie Cicotte .297
    Gaylord Perry .297
    Frank Smith .297
    Warren Spahn .297
    George Winter .297
76. Harry Brecheen .298
    John Candelaria .298
    Dizzy Dean .298
    Tony Mullane .298
    Orval Overall .298
    Lee Richmond .298
    Dick Rudolph .298
    Jack Taylor .298
    Luis Tiant .298
85. Jim Bunning .299
    Mike Cuellar .299
    Eddie Fisher .299
    Bob Gibson .299
    Don Mossi .299
    Don Newcombe .299
    Ed Reulbach .299
    Slim Sallee .299
93. David Cone .300
    Mort Cooper .300
    Dwight Gooden .300
    Joe Horlen .300
    Kid Nichols .300
    Fritz Peterson .300
    Mike Scott .300
    John Smoltz .300

Wins Above Team

1. Cy Young 99.7
2. Walter Johnson 90.0
3. Pete Alexander 81.6
4. Christy Mathewson 64.9
5. Lefty Grove 62.9
6. Tom Seaver 58.9
7. Jim McCormick 56.3
8. Pud Galvin 53.7
9. Charley Radbourn 50.3
10. Warren Spahn 45.8
11. Clark Griffith 45.6
12. Whitey Ford 44.4
13. Will White 43.5
14. Roger Clemens 40.8
15. Juan Marichal 38.7
16. Bob Feller 36.8
    Amos Rusie 36.8
    Mickey Welch 36.8
19. Ted Lyons 36.2
    Phil Niekro 36.2
21. Tony Mullane 35.8
    Eddie Plank 35.8
23. Jesse Tannehill 35.2
24. Charlie Buffinton 35.0
25. Wes Ferrell 34.8
26. Carl Hubbell 34.6
27. Dwight Gooden 34.4
    Kid Nichols 34.4
29. Steve Carlton 33.5
30. Dazzy Vance 33.5
31. Jim Devlin 32.5
32. Joe McGinnity 32.4
33. Guy Hecker 31.5
    Ed Walsh 31.5
35. Bob Gibson 31.0
36. Ed Morris 30.8
    Eddie Rommel 30.8
38. Sandy Koufax 30.6
39. Bob Caruthers 30.4
40. Jim Palmer 30.2
    Urban Shocker 30.2
42. Robin Roberts 30.0
43. Sadie McMahon 29.5
44. Fergie Jenkins 29.3
45. Ron Guidry 29.1
46. Mordecai Brown 29.0
47. Addie Joss 28.7
48. Dizzy Dean 27.6
49. Bobby Mathews 26.7
50. Schoolboy Rowe 26.5
51. David Cone 26.3
52. Randy Johnson 25.7
    Mark Langston 25.7
    Sam Leever 25.7
55. Rip Sewell 25.4
56. Greg Maddux 25.3
57. Mike Mussina 25.2
58. Frank Killen 25.1
59. Jack Chesbro 24.8
60. Nap Rucker 24.7
61. Red Lucas 24.5
    Herb Pennock 24.5
63. Russ Ford 24.3
64. John Candelaria 23.9
65. Charlie Ferguson 23.6
66. Red Faber 23.5
67. Johnny Allen 23.4
    Chief Bender 23.4
69. John Clarkson 23.2
    Orel Hershiser 23.2
71. Gaylord Perry 23.1
    Rick Reuschel 23.1
73. Joe Wood 23.0
74. Noodles Hahn 22.9
    Firpo Marberry 22.9
76. Sal Maglie 22.7
77. Gus Weyhing 22.6
78. Tim Keefe 22.5
79. Tommy John 22.2
    Bret Saberhagen 22.2
81. Carl Mays 21.9
    Bob Welch 21.9
83. Burleigh Grimes 21.3
    Claude Passeau 21.3
    Hippo Vaughn 21.3
86. Spud Chandler 21.2
87. Dutch Leonard 21.1
    J.R. Richard 21.1
89. John Tudor 21.0
    George Uhle 21.0
    Bucky Walters 21.0
92. Jim Maloney 20.9
93. Slim Sallee 20.6
94. Vida Blue 20.4
    Hal Newhouser 20.4
96. Bert Blyleven 20.3
    Freddie Fitzsimmons 20.3
98. Babe Adams 20.2
    Allie Reynolds 20.2
100. 2 players tied 20.1

Wins Above League

1. Cy Young 413.5
2. Walter Johnson 348.0
3. Pud Galvin 334.0
4. Nolan Ryan 308.0
5. Warren Spahn 304.0
6. Phil Niekro 296.0
7. Pete Alexander 290.5
8. Don Sutton 290.0
9. Gaylord Perry 289.5
10. Steve Carlton 286.5
11. Kid Nichols 284.5
12. Tim Keefe 283.5
13. Christy Mathewson 280.5
14. Early Wynn 272.0
15. Bert Blyleven 268.5
16. Robin Roberts 265.5
17. Jim Kaat 260.0
    Eddie Plank 260.0
19. Tommy John 259.5
20. Eppa Rixey 258.5
    Mickey Welch 258.5
22. Tom Seaver 258.0
23. Fergie Jenkins 255.0
24. John Clarkson 253.0
25. Tony Mullane 252.0
    Charley Radbourn 252.0
27. Jack Powell 249.5
28. Red Ruffing 249.0
29. Gus Weyhing 248.0
30. Ted Lyons 245.0
31. Burleigh Grimes 241.0
32. Jim McCormick 239.5
33. Frank Tanana 238.0
34. Red Faber 233.5
35. Jack Quinn 232.5
36. Vic Willis 227.0
37. Sam Jones 223.0
38. Lefty Grove 220.5
39. Jack Morris 220.0
40. Paul Derringer 217.5
41. Bobo Newsom 216.5
42. Charlie Hough 216.0
43. Jerry Koosman 215.5
44. Bob Feller 214.0
45. Bob Friend 213.5
46. Bob Gibson 212.5
    Joe Niekro 212.5
48. George Mullin 212.0
49. Dennis Martinez 211.0
50. Jim Palmer 210.0
    Amos Rusie 210.0
52. Waite Hoyt 209.5
53. Jerry Reuss 205.5
54. Mel Harder 204.5
55. Jim Bunning 204.0
    Mickey Lolich 204.0
57. Carl Hubbell 203.5
58. Rick Reuschel 202.5
59. Hooks Dauss 202.0
60. Herb Pennock 201.5
    Earl Whitehill 201.5
62. Luis Tiant 200.5
63. Will White 197.5
    Jim Whitney 197.5
65. Wilbur Cooper 197.0
66. Al Orth 196.5
    Adonis Terry 196.5
68. Claude Osteen 195.5
69. Catfish Hunter 195.0
70. Jim Perry 194.5
71. Joe McGinnity 194.0
72. Chick Fraser 193.5
73. Charlie Buffinton 192.5
    Juan Marichal 192.5
75. Clark Griffith 191.5
76. Billy Pierce 190.0
77. Joe Bush 189.0
    Rube Marquard 189.0
79. Larry Jackson 188.5
    Tom Zachary 188.5
81. Curt Simmons 188.0
82. Don Drysdale 187.5
83. Dolf Luque 186.5
    Milt Pappas 186.5
85. Dutch Leonard 186.0
86. Vida Blue 185.0
87. Mordecai Brown 184.5
    Rick Wise 184.5
89. Doyle Alexander 184.0
    Larry French 184.0
    Jesse Haines 184.0
    Lee Meadows 184.0
93. George Uhle 183.0
94. Freddie Fitzsimmons 181.5
95. Charlie Root 180.5
96. Bucky Walters 179.0
97. 5 players tied 178.5

Relief Games

1	Kent Tekulve	1050
2	Hoyt Wilhelm	1018
3	Lee Smith	991
4	Rich Gossage	965
5	Gene Garber	922
6	Lindy McDaniel	913
7	Rollie Fingers	907
8	Sparky Lyle	899
9	Jesse Orosco	881
10	Jeff Reardon	880
11	Don McMahon	872
12	Roy Face	821
13	Tug McGraw	785
14	Darold Knowles	757
15	Tom Burgmeier	742
	Gary Lavelle	742
17	Ron Perranoski	736
18	Willie Hernandez	733
19	Roger McDowell	721
20	John Franco	712
21	Clay Carroll	703
	Greg Minton	703
23	Mike Marshall	699
24	Larry Andersen	698
25	Bill Campbell	691
26	Steve Bedrosian	686
27	Paul Assenmacher	684
28	Dan Quisenberry	674
29	Bruce Sutter	661
30	Craig Lefferts	651
31	Ted Abernathy	647
32	Tom Henke	642
33	Dave LaRoche	632
34	Dave Righetti	629
35	Eddie Fisher	627
36	Bob McClure	625
37	Paul Lindblad	623
38	Mike Jackson	616
39	Stu Miller	611
40	Grant Jackson	609
	Mitch Williams	609
42	Dave Smith	608
43	Greg Harris	605
44	Elias Sosa	598
45	Rob Murphy	597
46	Bob Miller	595
47	Randy Myers	593
	Dan Plesac	593
49	Pedro Borbon	589
50	Doug Bair	579

Relief Wins

1	Hoyt Wilhelm	124
2	Lindy McDaniel	119
3	Rich Gossage	115
4	Rollie Fingers	107
5	Sparky Lyle	99
6	Roy Face	96
7	Gene Garber	94
	Kent Tekulve	94
9	Mike Marshall	92
10	Don McMahon	90
11	Tug McGraw	89
12	Clay Carroll	88
13	Bob Stanley	85
14	Bill Campbell	80
	Gary Lavelle	80
16	Tom Burgmeier	79
	Stu Miller	79
	Ron Perranoski	79
19	Jesse Orosco	74
20	Johnny Murphy	73
	Jeff Reardon	73
22	John Franco	72
	John Hiller	72
24	Mark Clear	71
	Dick Hall	71
	Lee Smith	71
27	Willie Hernandez	70
	Roger McDowell	70
29	Pedro Borbon	69
30	Bruce Sutter	68
31	Steve Bedrosian	65
32	Al Hrabosky	64
33	Darold Knowles	63
	Clem Labine	63
	Dave LaRoche	63
36	Jim Brewer	62
	Turk Farrell	62
	Eddie Fisher	62
	Grant Jackson	62
	Paul Lindblad	62
	Frank Linzy	62
42	Joe Heving	60
43	Johnny Klippstein	59
	Elias Sosa	59
45	Aurelio Lopez	58
	Phil Regan	58
47	Ted Abernathy	57
	Mike Henneman	57
	Bob Locker	57
	Greg Minton	57

Relief Losses

1	Gene Garber	108
2	Hoyt Wilhelm	103
3	Rollie Fingers	101
4	Mike Marshall	98
5	Kent Tekulve	90
6	Lindy McDaniel	88
7	Lee Smith	86
8	Rich Gossage	85
9	Roy Face	82
10	Jeff Reardon	77
11	Sparky Lyle	76
12	Gary Lavelle	75
13	Ron Perranoski	74
14	Darold Knowles	71
	Bruce Sutter	71
16	Roger McDowell	69
	Tug McGraw	69
18	Stu Miller	67
	Jesse Orosco	67
20	Clay Carroll	66
	Don McMahon	66
22	Bill Campbell	65
23	Greg Minton	62
24	Steve Bedrosian	61
	Bob Stanley	61
26	Doug Jones	59
27	John Hiller	58
28	John Franco	57
	Frank Linzy	57
30	Willie Hernandez	55
	Mitch Williams	55
32	Craig Lefferts	54
33	Tom Burgmeier	53
	Ron Davis	53
	Greg Harris	53
	Dave Smith	53
37	Jim Kern	52
	Randy Moffitt	52
	Dave Righetti	52
40	Turk Farrell	51
	Eddie Fisher	51
	Dave LaRoche	51
	Claude Raymond	51
44	Mark Davis	50
	Dale Murray	50
	Al Worthington	50
47	Jim Brewer	49
	Elias Sosa	49
49	Ted Abernathy	48
	Mark Clear	48

Relief Innings Pitched

1	Hoyt Wilhelm	1871.0
2	Lindy McDaniel	1694.0
3	Rich Gossage	1558.1
4	Rollie Fingers	1501.0
5	Gene Garber	1454.1
6	Kent Tekulve	1437.0
7	Sparky Lyle	1391.0
8	Tug McGraw	1302.0
9	Don McMahon	1297.0
10	Mike Marshall	1260.0
11	Tom Burgmeier	1250.1
12	Lee Smith	1232.1
13	Roy Face	1213.0
14	Clay Carroll	1206.1
15	Eddie Fisher	1186.0
16	Bill Campbell	1178.0
17	Ron Perranoski	1172.1
18	Bob Stanley	1157.0
19	Jeff Reardon	1133.0
20	Stu Miller	1096.1
21	Greg Minton	1088.0
22	Gary Lavelle	1079.1
23	Jesse Orosco	1060.1
24	Darold Knowles	1053.0
25	Paul Lindblad	1044.0
	Dan Quisenberry	1044.0
27	Bruce Sutter	1043.0
28	Johnny Klippstein	1042.1
29	Roger McDowell	1041.1
30	Pedro Borbon	1017.0
31	Willie Hernandez	995.0
32	Bob Miller	994.1
33	Larry Andersen	992.1
34	Dave LaRoche	976.0
35	Ted Abernathy	970.0
36	John Hiller	964.1
37	Steve Bedrosian	931.0
38	Greg Harris	923.0
39	Elias Sosa	905.0
40	Dale Murray	902.0
41	Doug Bair	890.0
42	Terry Forster	888.0
43	Craig Lefferts	883.1
44	Bob Locker	879.0
45	John Franco	876.0
	Dennis Lamp	876.0
47	Ron Reed	875.0
48	Jim Brewer	861.0
49	Aurelio Lopez	860.0
50	Dick Tidrow	859.1

Relief Points

1	Lee Smith	1002
2	Jeff Reardon	803
3	Rollie Fingers	795
4	Rich Gossage	765
5	Dennis Eckersley	757
6	John Franco	733
7	Bruce Sutter	665
8	Tom Henke	662
9	Hoyt Wilhelm	599
10	Sparky Lyle	598
11	Dan Quisenberry	554
12	Dave Righetti	544
13	Jeff Montgomery	530
14	Doug Jones	519
15	Gene Garber	516
16	Randy Myers	507
17	Roy Face	496
18	Lindy McDaniel	494
19	Todd Worrell	492
20	Dave Smith	485
21	Tug McGraw	469
22	Kent Tekulve	466
23	Mike Marshall	462
24	Mike Henneman	458
25	Rick Aguilera	443
26	Ron Perranoski	442
27	Steve Bedrosian	437
28	Bobby Thigpen	428
29	Don McMahon	420
30	Mitch Williams	419
31	Jeff Russell	406
32	Stu Miller	399
33	Clay Carroll	396
34	Roger McDowell	389
35	John Wetteland	388
36	Willie Hernandez	379
37	Bob Stanley	373
38	Jay Howell	369
39	Gregg Olson	366
40	Dave Giusti	363
	Bryan Harvey	363
42	Ted Abernathy	362
43	Gary Lavelle	357
44	Greg Minton	352
45	Bill Campbell	347
	Jesse Orosco	347
47	Darold Knowles	341
48	Jim Brewer	339
49	John Hiller	336
50	Dan Plesac	330

Relief Ranking

1	Hoyt Wilhelm	355
2	Rich Gossage	316
3	Lee Smith	246
4	John Franco	242
5	Dan Quisenberry	219
6	Tom Henke	215
7	Kent Tekulve	207
8	Rollie Fingers	204
9	Mike Marshall	196
10	John Hiller	189
11	Sparky Lyle	186
12	Bruce Sutter	184
13	Jeff Montgomery	183
14	Dennis Eckersley	172
15	Ellis Kinder	166
16	Bob Stanley	163
17	Tug McGraw	161
	Jesse Orosco	161
19	Lindy McDaniel	158
20	John Wetteland	152
21	Ron Perranoski	150
22	Gary Lavelle	146
23	Roy Face	143
24	Stu Miller	141
25	Rick Aguilera	140
26	Mark Eichhorn	137
27	Gene Garber	136
28	Doug Jones	134
29	Dave Righetti	131
30	Jeff Reardon	130
31	Todd Worrell	127
32	Mike Henneman	125
33	Clay Carroll	123
34	Jeff Russell	122
35	Bryan Harvey	119
	Willie Hernandez	119
37	Lefty Grove	117
	Dave Smith	117
39	Roberto Hernandez	113
40	Tom Burgmeier	111
41	Frank Linzy	110
	Dick Radatz	110
43	Gregg Olson	108
44	Jim Brewer	107
	Johnny Murphy	107
46	Jay Howell	106
47	Ted Abernathy	103
	Dan Plesac	103
49	Steve Farr	102
50	4 players tied	100

Relievers' Runs

1	Hoyt Wilhelm	261
2	Rich Gossage	185
3	Rollie Fingers	156
4	Dan Quisenberry	144
5	Tom Henke	129
6	Kent Tekulve	128
7	Lee Smith	123
8	Mark Eichhorn	122
9	Sparky Lyle	121
10	Dennis Eckersley	120
11	John Franco	117
	Jesse Orosco	117
13	Tug McGraw	110
14	Jeff Montgomery	109
15	Clay Carroll	100
	Mike Marshall	100
	Ron Perranoski	100
18	John Hiller	99
	Gary Lavelle	99
	Don McMahon	99
21	Stu Miller	96
22	Lindy McDaniel	94
23	Bob Stanley	93
24	Eric Plunk	91
	Bruce Sutter	91
26	Dave Smith	89
27	Greg Minton	88
28	Johnny Murphy	85
29	Ellis Kinder	82
30	Mike Henneman	80
	Jeff Reardon	80
	John Wetteland	80
33	Tom Burgmeier	78
34	Greg Harris	76
35	Steve Farr	75
	Jay Howell	75
	Doug Jones	75
	Jeff Russell	75
39	Willie Hernandez	74
	Mike Jackson	74
41	Jim Brewer	73
42	Tim Burke	72
43	Terry Forster	71
	Roger McDowell	71
45	Larry Andersen	70
	Bob Miller	70
47	Rick Aguilera	69
	Firpo Marberry	69
49	Jeff Brantley	68
	Bryan Harvey	68

Adjusted Relievers' Runs

1	Hoyt Wilhelm	243
2	Rich Gossage	178
3	Dan Quisenberry	147
4	Lee Smith	144
5	Kent Tekulve	142
6	Tom Henke	130
7	Mark Eichhorn	125
8	John Franco	123
9	Bob Stanley	121
10	Rollie Fingers	120
11	Sparky Lyle	119
12	Bruce Sutter	117
13	John Hiller	115
14	Tug McGraw	113
	Jeff Montgomery	113
16	Jesse Orosco	112
17	Lindy McDaniel	108
18	Mike Marshall	103
19	Dennis Eckersley	102
20	Ellis Kinder	99
21	Clay Carroll	97
22	Gary Lavelle	96
23	Gene Garber	93
24	Greg Harris	91
25	Tom Burgmeier	86
26	Don McMahon	85
	Eric Plunk	85
28	Willie Hernandez	84
	Ron Perranoski	84
	Jeff Reardon	84
31	Stu Miller	82
32	Jeff Russell	80
33	John Wetteland	79
34	Terry Forster	78
	Mike Henneman	78
36	Steve Farr	76
	Mike Jackson	76
	Doug Jones	76
39	Greg Minton	75
40	Ron Reed	74
41	Dave Smith	73
42	Rick Aguilera	72
43	Larry Andersen	70
	Tim Burke	70
45	Bryan Harvey	68
46	Lefty Grove	67
47	Ted Abernathy	66
	Johnny Murphy	66
49	Grant Jackson	64
	Gerry Staley	64

Clutch Pitching Index

1	Bob Rhoads	117
2	Ed Killian	116
	Ed Siever	116
4	Win Mercer	115
5	Ron Kline	113
	Bill Lee	113
	Will White	113
8	Al Benton	112
	Chuck Finley	112
	Ed Lopat	112
	Bob Stanley	112
	Tom Zachary	112
13	Frank Dwyer	111
	Whitey Ford	111
	Preacher Roe	111
16	Max Lanier	110
	Bob Miller	110
	Gerry Staley	110
	Bill Wight	110
20	Steve Blass	109
	Bob Buhl	109
	Max Butcher	109
	Dan Casey	109
	Lefty Leifield	109
	Sal Maglie	109
	Mel Parnell	109
	Bob Shaw	109
	Geoff Zahn	109
29	Jim Abbott	108
	Steve Barber	108
	Sheriff Blake	108
	Nixey Callahan	108
	Lefty Grove	108
	Carl Morton	108
	George Mullin	108
	Dizzy Trout	108
	Bob Veale	108
38	Mark Baldwin	107
	Nelson Briles	107
	Lloyd Brown	107
	Nig Cuppy	107
	Larry French	107
	Clark Griffith	107
	Claude Osteen	107
	Eddie Rommel	107
	Dutch Ruether	107
	Eddie Smith	107
	Dummy Taylor	107
	Steve Trout	107
	Mickey Welch	107
51	Jim Bagby	106
	Roger Craig	106
	Red Donahue	106
	Red Faber	106
	Dave Foutz	106
	Mel Harder	106
	Joe Haynes	106
	Guy Hecker	106
	Tommy John	106
	Jim McCormick	106
	Cal McLish	106
	Jeff Pfeffer	106
	Togie Pittinger	106
	Howie Pollet	106
	Nap Rucker	106
	Jim Scott	106
	Sherry Smith	106
	Sloppy Thurston	106
	John Tudor	106
	Rube Waddell	106
	Bucky Walters	106
72	30 players tied	105

Pitcher Batting Runs

1	Red Ruffing	143
2	Bob Caruthers	111
3	Wes Ferrell	100
4	Walter Johnson	99
5	Red Lucas	98
6	George Uhle	92
7	Guy Hecker	90
	Bob Lemon	90
9	Jim Whitney	89
10	Warren Spahn	88
11	George Mullin	87
12	Don Newcombe	79
13	Babe Ruth	78
14	Schoolboy Rowe	76
15	Early Wynn	72
16	Bob Gibson	65
	Jack Stivetts	65
18	Carl Mays	64
19	Al Orth	63
20	Don Drysdale	60
21	Christy Mathewson	59
22	Gary Peters	57
	Bucky Walters	57
	Earl Wilson	57
25	Jesse Tannehill	55
26	Doc Crandall	54
	Jim Tobin	54
28	Burleigh Grimes	52
	Ad Gumbert	52
30	Claude Hendrix	50
	Tony Mullane	50
32	Joe Bush	49
	Steve Carlton	49
	Charlie Ferguson	49
35	Bob Forsch	48
	Scott Stratton	48
37	Don Larsen	46
38	Dave Foutz	45
	Vern Law	45
	Rick Rhoden	45
	Dutch Ruether	45
	Adonis Terry	45
43	Frank Killen	44
	Jack Scott	44
45	Tommy Byrne	41
	Jim Kaat	41
	Don Robinson	41
48	Charley Radbourn	40
	Johnny Sain	40
50	Wilbur Cooper	39
	Fred Hutchinson	39
52	Claude Osteen	38
	Sloppy Thurston	38
54	Dolf Luque	37
	Doc White	37
56	Jack Coombs	36
	Mickey McDermott	36
58	Ken Brett	35
	Clark Griffith	35
	Harvey Haddix	35
	Win Mercer	35
	Frank Smith	35
	Jack Taylor	35
64	Orel Hershiser	34
	Art Nehf	34
	Robin Roberts	34
	Rick Wise	34
68	Chief Bender	33
	Catfish Hunter	33
	Ben Sanders	33
71	Hooks Dauss	32
	Ted Lyons	32
	Al Maul	32
	Fernando Valenzuela	32
75	Ray Caldwell	31
	Dizzy Trout	31
	John Ward	31
	Joe Wood	31
79	Ed Brandt	30
	Lew Burdette	30
	Lefty Tyler	30
82	Dwight Gooden	29
	Jack Harshman	29
	Ed Lopat	29
	Jouett Meekin	29
	Camilo Pascual	29
	Juan Pizarro	29
88	Joe Nuxhall	28
	Tom Seaver	28
	Urban Shocker	28
91	Charlie Buffinton	27
	Whitey Ford	27
	Brickyard Kennedy	27
	Frank Kitson	27
	Bill Sherdel	27
	Lon Warneke	27
97	Jim Maloney	26
	Clarence Mitchell	26
	Blue Moon Odom	26
100	8 players tied	25

Pitcher Fielding Runs

1	Ed Walsh	83
2	Carl Mays	74
3	Christy Mathewson	68
4	Freddie Fitzsimmons	60
	Bob Lemon	60
6	Burleigh Grimes	58
7	Greg Maddux	56
8	Tommy John	55
9	Harry Howell	51
10	Harry Gumbert	50
11	John Clarkson	46
12	Bill Doak	43
13	Willis Hudlin	42
	Dennis Martinez	42
	Eddie Rommel	42
16	Jack Quinn	40
17	Pud Galvin	39
	Rick Reuschel	39
	Bobby Shantz	39
20	Hooks Dauss	38
	Dizzy Trout	38
22	Jack Russell	36
	Mel Stottlemyre	36
24	Charlie Buffinton	35
	Johnny Schmitz	35
	Willie Sudhoff	35
27	Nick Altrock	34
	Fernando Valenzuela	34
29	Tony Mullane	33
30	Red Ames	32
	Murry Dickson	32
	Howard Ehmke	32
	Randy Jones	32
34	Pete Alexander	31
	Russ Christopher	31
	Curt Davis	31
	John Denny	31
38	Tommy Bond	30
	Orel Hershiser	30
	Addie Joss	30
	Hal Schumacher	30
42	Chick Fraser	29
	Gerry Staley	29
	Dave Stieb	29
45	Mike Boddicker	28
	Ben Cantwell	28
	Sid Hudson	28
	Matt Kilroy	28
	George Mullin	28
	Phil Niekro	28
	Ed Willett	28
52	Ted Abernathy	27
	Tom Burgmeier	27
	Spud Chandler	27
	Amos Rusie	27
	Bucky Walters	27
	Vic Willis	27
58	Nixey Callahan	26
	Whitey Ford	26
	Frank Smith	26
	Sherry Smith	26
62	Kevin Brown	25
	Don Drysdale	25
	Guy Hecker	25
	Larry Jackson	25
	Charlie Leibrandt	25
	Dan Quisenberry	25
	Doc White	25
69	Mike Caldwell	24
	Frank Corridon	24
	Ned Garvin	24
	Dutch Leonard	24
	John Ward	24
74	Jean Dubuc	23
	Lindy McDaniel	23
	Roger McDowell	23
	Cy Seymour	23
78	Tom Brewer	22
	Bill Hart	22
	Joe Horlen	22
	Carl Hubbell	22
	Jim McCormick	22
	Stu Miller	22
	Mike Moore	22
	Hal Newhouser	22
	Frank Owen	22
	Dan Petry	22
	Ed Reulbach	22
	Bob Stanley	22
	Kent Tekulve	22
91	Elden Auker	21
	Joe Bush	21
	Benny Frey	21
	Mark Gubicza	21
	Sadie McMahon	21
	Gaylord Perry	21
	Bob Purkey	21
	Jack Taylor	21
	Lefty Tyler	21
100	13 players tied	20

Pitcher Batting Average

1	Jack Stivetts	.297
2	George Uhle	.289
3	Charlie Ferguson	.288
4	Win Mercer	.286
5	Doc Crandall	.285
6	Bob Caruthers	.282
	Guy Hecker	.282
8	Red Lucas	.281
9	Wes Ferrell	.280
10	Dave Foutz	.276
11	Jack Scott	.275
	John Ward	.275
13	Scott Stratton	.274
14	Nixey Callahan	.273
	Ad Gumbert	.273
	Al Orth	.273
17	Don Newcombe	.271
18	Sloppy Thurston	.270
19	Red Ruffing	.269
20	Carl Mays	.268
21	Schoolboy Rowe	.263
22	George Mullin	.262
23	Kid Gleason	.261
	Brickyard Kennedy	.261
	Jim Whitney	.261
26	Dutch Ruether	.258
	Joe Shaute	.258
28	Lee Richmond	.257
29	Jesse Tannehill	.256
30	Joe Bush	.253
31	Clarence Mitchell	.252
	Jack Taylor	.252
33	Adonis Terry	.249
34	Ray Caldwell	.248
	Burleigh Grimes	.248
36	Amos Rusie	.247
37	Pete Donohue	.246
38	Charlie Buffinton	.245
	Johnny Sain	.245
40	Vern Kennedy	.244
41	Jouett Meekin	.243
	Tony Mullane	.243
	Elam Vangilder	.243
	Bucky Walters	.243
45	Don Larsen	.242
	Bob Smith	.242
47	Duke Esper	.241
	Pink Hawley	.241
	Claude Hendrix	.241
	Frank Killen	.241
51	Frank Kitson	.240
52	Wilbur Cooper	.239
53	Ed Crane	.238
	Rick Rhoden	.238
55	Tommy Bond	.236
	Ed Brandt	.236
	Jim McCormick	.236
58	Jack Coombs	.235
	Walter Johnson	.235
	Terry Larkin	.235
	Charley Radbourn	.235
62	Fritz Ostermueller	.234
63	Nig Cuppy	.233
	Clark Griffith	.233
	Ted Lyons	.233
	Sherry Smith	.233
67	Bob Lemon	.232
68	Ben Cantwell	.231
	Murry Dickson	.231
	Don Robinson	.231
71	George Earnshaw	.230
	Jim Tobin	.230
73	Vic Aldridge	.229
	Frank Dwyer	.229
75	George Bradley	.228
	Nels Potter	.228
77	George Haddock	.227
	Dolf Luque	.227
	Bill Swift	.227
80	Jim Bagby	.226
	Catfish Hunter	.226
	Kid Nichols	.226
	Ed Stein	.226
	Tom Zachary	.226
85	Dizzy Dean	.225
86	Frank Foreman	.224
	Fred Goldsmith	.224
	Mickey Welch	.224
89	Hal Carlson	.223
	Larry Corcoran	.223
	George Hemming	.223
	Bill Sherdel	.223
	Jack Taylor	.223
	Lon Warneke	.223
95	Matt Kilroy	.222
	Gary Peters	.222
97	Van Mungo	.221
98	Sid Hudson	.220
99	3 players tied	.219

Total Pitcher Index

#	Player	
1	Walter Johnson	90.5
2	Cy Young	79.8
3	Pete Alexander	64.9
4	Christy Mathewson	62.7
5	Lefty Grove	61.2
6	Kid Nichols	60.9
7	John Clarkson	48.7
8	Tom Seaver	48.2
9	Warren Spahn	47.0
10	Bob Gibson	44.0
11	Ed Walsh	43.3
12	Roger Clemens	40.9
13	Hal Newhouser	40.8
14	Hoyt Wilhelm	39.7
15	Carl Hubbell	39.2
16	Greg Maddux	39.1
	Amos Rusie	39.1
18	Bob Lemon	37.4
19	Whitey Ford	37.2
	Tim Keefe	37.2
21	Ted Lyons	36.7
22	Carl Mays	36.2
23	Jim Palmer	35.5
24	Phil Niekro	35.4
25	Mordecai Brown	34.8
26	Dizzy Trout	34.5
27	Gaylord Perry	34.4
28	Don Drysdale	34.0
29	Steve Carlton	33.2
30	Tony Mullane	32.6
31	Wes Ferrell	32.3
32	Fergie Jenkins	30.9
33	Bert Blyleven	30.8
34	Clark Griffith	29.7
35	Rich Gossage	29.5
36	Bob Caruthers	29.4
37	Juan Marichal	28.9
38	Tommy Bridges	28.7
	Charley Radbourn	28.7
40	Bucky Walters	28.6
41	Bob Feller	28.5
42	Jack Stivetts	28.2
43	Stan Coveleski	27.5
44	Dave Stieb	27.2
45	Red Faber	27.0
	Eddie Plank	27.0
	Dazzy Vance	27.0
48	Red Ruffing	26.9
49	Dennis Eckersley	26.5
50	John Franco	26.4
51	Dolf Luque	26.3
52	Eddie Rommel	26.0
53	Eppa Rixey	25.9
	Urban Shocker	25.9
55	Dutch Leonard	25.8
56	Rick Reuschel	25.5
57	Harry Brecheen	25.4
	Orel Hershiser	25.4
	Addie Joss	25.4
60	Eddie Cicotte	25.2
61	Tommy John	25.0
62	Robin Roberts	24.9
63	Dan Quisenberry	24.8
64	Rube Waddell	24.6
65	Joe Wood	24.2
66	Burleigh Grimes	24.0
67	Guy Hecker	23.9
68	Jack Quinn	23.6
	Kent Tekulve	23.6
70	Bret Saberhagen	23.5
	Lee Smith	23.5
72	Billy Pierce	23.3
73	Freddie Fitzsimmons	23.1
74	Silver King	22.9
75	Lon Warneke	22.7
76	Nig Cuppy	22.4
77	Dizzy Dean	22.2
78	Curt Davis	22.1
79	Vic Willis	22.0
80	Rollie Fingers	21.7
81	Jesse Tannehill	21.3
82	Tom Henke	21.2
	Jim McCormick	21.2
84	Bobby Shantz	21.1
85	Mike Marshall	20.9
86	Nolan Ryan	20.8
87	Spud Chandler	20.6
	John Hiller	20.6
	Jimmy Key	20.6
90	Charlie Buffinton	20.3
91	Mel Harder	20.0
	Sparky Lyle	20.0
93	Bruce Sutter	19.8
94	Wilbur Cooper	19.7
	Murry Dickson	19.7
96	Dave Foutz	19.6
97	Joe McGinnity	19.5
98	Doc White	19.1
99	Jim Kaat	19.0
100	Don Newcombe	18.9

Total Pitcher Index

#	Player	
101	David Cone	18.8
	Larry Jackson	18.8
103	Sandy Koufax	18.5
	Red Lucas	18.5
	Wilbur Wood	18.5
106	Ron Guidry	18.2
107	Ed Lopat	18.1
	Mel Parnell	18.1
109	Lefty Gomez	17.9
	Hippo Vaughn	17.9
111	Ed Reulbach	17.7
112	Tom Glavine	17.6
113	Jeff Montgomery	17.5
	Jose Rijo	17.5
115	Ned Garver	17.4
	Schoolboy Rowe	17.4
117	Bob Stanley	17.3
	Mel Stottlemyre	17.3
119	Larry French	17.2
120	Andy Messersmith	17.1
	Jesse Orosco	17.1
	Babe Ruth	17.1
	Luis Tiant	17.1
124	Kevin Appier	16.9
	Dwight Gooden	16.9
	Noodles Hahn	16.9
	Thornton Lee	16.9
128	Stu Miller	16.7
	Jack Taylor	16.7
130	Early Wynn	16.6
131	Claude Passeau	16.5
132	Harry Howell	16.4
133	Max Lanier	16.3
	Hal Schumacher	16.3
135	Gene Garber	16.1
136	Dennis Martinez	16.0
137	Sadie McMahon	15.9
	Virgil Trucks	15.9
139	Kevin Brown	15.8
140	Johnny Antonelli	15.7
	Deacon Phillippe	15.7
	Dave Righetti	15.7
143	Ron Perranoski	15.5
144	Ellis Kinder	15.4
145	Steve Rogers	15.3
146	John Tudor	15.2
147	Babe Adams	15.0
	Doug Jones	15.0
	Sam Leever	15.0
150	John Candelaria	14.9
	Frank Dwyer	14.9
	Charlie Hough	14.9
153	Bob Shawkey	14.8
	Mickey Welch	14.8
155	Jim Whitney	14.7
156	Gary Lavelle	14.6
	Frank Linzy	14.6
	Lindy McDaniel	14.6
159	Mike Garcia	14.5
	George Mullin	14.5
161	Mark Eichhorn	14.4
	Chuck Finley	14.4
	Claude Hendrix	14.4
	Waite Hoyt	14.4
	Tug McGraw	14.4
166	Mark Langston	14.2
167	Rick Aguilera	14.1
	Fred Hutchinson	14.1
	John Ward	14.1
170	Larry Corcoran	14.0
	Frank Viola	14.0
172	Frank Lary	13.9
173	Chief Bender	13.8
	Charlie Ferguson	13.8
	Nap Rucker	13.8
176	Sal Maglie	13.7
	Howie Pollet	13.7
178	Jim Bunning	13.6
	Don Sutton	13.6
180	Bill Hutchison	13.5
	George Uhle	13.5
182	Clay Carroll	13.4
	Jim Maloney	13.4
184	Frank Tanana	13.3
185	Jim Devlin	13.2
	Roy Face	13.2
	Claude Osteen	13.2
188	Jerry Koosman	13.1
	Firpo Marberry	13.1
190	Jim Tobin	13.0
191	Mort Cooper	12.9
	Pud Galvin	12.9
	Frank Killen	12.9
194	Tom Burgmeier	12.8
	Van Mungo	12.8
	John Smoltz	12.8
197	Todd Worrell	12.7
198	Tom Candiotti	12.6
	Mike Mussina	12.6
	Curt Simmons	12.6

Total Pitcher Index

#	Player	
201	John Wetteland	12.5
202	Milt Pappas	12.4
203	Mike Henneman	12.3
	Sherry Smith	12.3
205	Will White	12.2
206	Willie Hernandez	12.1
	Jon Matlack	12.1
208	Steve Farr	12.0
	Bryan Harvey	12.0
210	Ewell Blackwell	11.9
	Greg Minton	11.9
212	Jake Weimer	11.8
213	Ted Breitenstein	11.7
214	Harvey Haddix	11.6
	Orval Overall	11.6
216	Lefty Leifield	11.5
	Gregg Olson	11.5
218	Johnny Sain	11.4
	Fernando Valenzuela	11.4
220	Al Brazle	11.3
	Jack Chesbro	11.3
	Terry Forster	11.3
	Randy Johnson	11.3
224	Bob Rush	11.2
	Dave Smith	11.2
226	Gary Peters	11.1
227	Jim Kern	11.0
228	Russ Ford	10.9
	Camilo Pascual	10.9
230	Nixey Callahan	10.8
	Dean Chance	10.8
	Roberto Hernandez	10.8
233	Mike Boddicker	10.7
234	Jack McDowell	10.6
	Dick Radatz	10.6
	Charlie Root	10.6
237	Doug Drabek	10.5
238	Mark Gubicza	10.4
	Tex Hughson	10.4
	Matt Kilroy	10.4
	Charlie Leibrandt	10.4
	Roger McDowell	10.4
	Jeff Russell	10.4
	Sonny Siebert	10.4
245	Randy Myers	10.3
	Jeff Reardon	10.3
	Ben Sanders	10.3
	Al Worthington	10.3
	Tom Zachary	10.3
250	Vida Blue	10.2
	Jim Brewer	10.2
	Danny Darwin	10.2
	Win Mercer	10.2
	Johnny Murphy	10.2
255	Bob Ewing	10.1
	Don McMahon	10.1
	Jeff Pfeffer	10.1
	Rip Sewell	10.1
	Frank Sullivan	10.1
	Hooks Wiltse	10.1
261	Elton Chamberlain	10.0
	Joe Dobson	10.0
	Sam McDowell	10.0
	Fritz Ostermueller	10.0
265	Hooks Dauss	9.9
	Jay Howell	9.9
267	Clint Brown	9.8
	Jeff Fassero	9.8
269	Tim Burke	9.7
	Bob Locker	9.7
	Art Nehf	9.7
	Jim Perry	9.7
273	Mickey McDermott	9.6
	Al Orth	9.6
275	Ned Garvin	9.5
	Steve Howe	9.5
	Monte Pearson	9.5
278	Slim Sallee	9.4
	Gerry Staley	9.4
280	Teddy Higuera	9.3
	Jim Scott	9.3
282	Larry Jansen	9.2
	Tippy Martinez	9.2
	Ed Morris	9.2
285	Howard Ehmke	9.1
	Greg Harris	9.1
287	Pink Hawley	9.0
	Dan Plesac	9.0
289	Johnny Allen	8.9
	Mark Baldwin	8.9
	Al Benton	8.9
	Bob Welch	8.9
293	Harry Coveleski	8.8
	Darold Knowles	8.8
	Ray Kremer	8.8
	Johnny Rigney	8.8
	Bill Swift	8.8
298	Red Ames	8.7
	Al McBean	8.7
	Jeff Tesreau	8.7

Total Pitcher Index (alpha.)

Player	
Babe Adams	15.0
Rick Aguilera	14.1
Pete Alexander	64.9
Johnny Allen	8.9
Red Ames	8.7
Johnny Antonelli	15.7
Kevin Appier	16.9
Mark Baldwin	8.9
Chief Bender	13.8
Al Benton	8.9
Ewell Blackwell	11.9
Vida Blue	10.2
Bert Blyleven	30.8
Mike Boddicker	10.7
Al Brazle	11.3
Harry Brecheen	25.4
Ted Breitenstein	11.7
Jim Brewer	10.2
Tommy Bridges	28.7
Clint Brown	9.8
Kevin Brown	15.8
Mordecai Brown	34.8
Charlie Buffinton	20.3
Jim Bunning	13.6
Tom Burgmeier	12.8
Tim Burke	9.7
Nixey Callahan	10.8
John Candelaria	14.9
Tom Candiotti	12.6
Steve Carlton	33.2
Clay Carroll	13.4
Bob Caruthers	29.4
Elton Chamberlain	10.0
Dean Chance	10.8
Spud Chandler	20.6
Jack Chesbro	11.3
Eddie Cicotte	25.2
John Clarkson	48.7
Roger Clemens	40.9
David Cone	18.8
Wilbur Cooper	19.7
Mort Cooper	12.9
Larry Corcoran	14.0
Harry Coveleski	8.8
Stan Coveleski	27.5
Nig Cuppy	22.4
Danny Darwin	10.2
Hooks Dauss	9.9
Curt Davis	22.1
Dizzy Dean	22.2
Jim Devlin	13.2
Murry Dickson	19.7
Joe Dobson	10.0
Doug Drabek	10.5
Don Drysdale	34.0
Frank Dwyer	14.9
Dennis Eckersley	26.5
Howard Ehmke	9.1
Mark Eichhorn	14.4
Bob Ewing	10.1
Red Faber	27.0
Roy Face	13.2
Steve Farr	12.0
Jeff Fassero	9.8
Bob Feller	28.5
Charlie Ferguson	13.8
Wes Ferrell	32.3
Rollie Fingers	21.7
Chuck Finley	14.4
Freddie Fitzsimmons	23.1
Whitey Ford	37.2
Russ Ford	10.9
Terry Forster	11.3
Dave Foutz	19.6
John Franco	26.4
Larry French	17.2
Pud Galvin	12.9
Gene Garber	16.1
Mike Garcia	14.5
Ned Garver	17.4
Ned Garvin	9.5
Bob Gibson	44.0
Tom Glavine	17.6
Lefty Gomez	17.9
Dwight Gooden	16.9
Rich Gossage	29.5
Clark Griffith	29.7
Burleigh Grimes	24.0
Lefty Grove	61.2
Mark Gubicza	10.4
Ron Guidry	18.2
Harvey Haddix	11.6
Noodles Hahn	16.9
Mel Harder	20.0
Greg Harris	9.1
Bryan Harvey	12.0
Pink Hawley	9.0
Guy Hecker	23.9
Claude Hendrix	14.4
Tom Henke	21.2

Total Pitcher Index (alpha.)

Mike Henneman	12.3
Willie Hernandez	12.1
Roberto Hernandez	10.8
Orel Hershiser	25.4
Teddy Higuera	9.3
John Hiller	20.6
Charlie Hough	14.9
Steve Howe	9.5
Harry Howell	16.4
Jay Howell	9.9
Waite Hoyt	14.4
Carl Hubbell	39.2
Tex Hughson	10.4
Fred Hutchinson	14.1
Bill Hutchison	13.5
Larry Jackson	18.8
Larry Jansen	9.2
Fergie Jenkins	30.9
Tommy John	25.0
Randy Johnson	11.3
Walter Johnson	90.5
Doug Jones	15.0
Addie Joss	25.4
Jim Kaat	19.0
Tim Keefe	37.2
Jim Kern	11.0
Jimmy Key	20.6
Frank Killen	12.9
Matt Kilroy	10.4
Ellis Kinder	15.4
Silver King	22.9
Darold Knowles	8.8
Jerry Koosman	13.1
Sandy Koufax	18.5
Ray Kremer	8.8
Mark Langston	14.2
Max Lanier	16.3
Frank Lary	13.9
Gary Lavelle	14.6
Thornton Lee	16.9
Sam Leever	15.0
Charlie Leibrandt	10.4
Lefty Leifield	11.5
Bob Lemon	37.4
Dutch Leonard	25.8
Frank Linzy	14.6
Bob Locker	9.7
Ed Lopat	18.1
Red Lucas	18.5
Dolf Luque	26.3
Sparky Lyle	20.0
Ted Lyons	36.7
Greg Maddux	39.1
Sal Maglie	13.7
Jim Maloney	13.4
Firpo Marberry	13.1
Juan Marichal	28.9
Mike Marshall	20.9
Tippy Martinez	9.2
Dennis Martinez	16.0
Christy Mathewson	62.7
Jon Matlack	12.1
Carl Mays	36.2
Jim McCormick	21.2
Lindy McDaniel	14.6
Mickey McDermott	9.6
Jack McDowell	10.6
Roger McDowell	10.4
Sam McDowell	10.0
Joe McGinnity	19.5
Tug McGraw	14.4
Don McMahon	10.1
Sadie McMahon	15.9
Win Mercer	10.2
Andy Messersmith	17.1
Stu Miller	16.7
Greg Minton	11.9
Jeff Montgomery	17.5
Ed Morris	9.2
Tony Mullane	32.6
George Mullin	14.5
Van Mungo	12.8
Johnny Murphy	10.2
Mike Mussina	12.6
Randy Myers	10.3
Al McBean	8.7
Art Nehf	9.7
Don Newcombe	18.9
Hal Newhouser	40.8
Kid Nichols	60.9
Phil Niekro	35.4
Gregg Olson	11.5
Jesse Orosco	17.1
Al Orth	9.6
Claude Osteen	13.2
Fritz Ostermueller	10.0
Orval Overall	11.6
Jim Palmer	35.5
Milt Pappas	12.4
Mel Parnell	18.1

Total Pitcher Index (alpha.)

Camilo Pascual	10.9
Claude Passeau	16.5
Monte Pearson	9.5
Ron Perranoski	15.5
Gaylord Perry	34.4
Jim Perry	9.7
Gary Peters	11.1
Jeff Pfeffer	10.1
Deacon Phillippe	15.7
Billy Pierce	23.3
Eddie Plank	27.0
Dan Plesac	9.0
Howie Pollet	13.7
Jack Quinn	23.6
Dan Quisenberry	24.8
Dick Radatz	10.6
Charley Radbourn	28.7
Jeff Reardon	10.3
Ed Reulbach	17.7
Rick Reuschel	25.5
Dave Righetti	15.7
Johnny Rigney	8.8
Jose Rijo	17.5
Eppa Rixey	25.9
Robin Roberts	24.9
Steve Rogers	15.3
Eddie Rommel	26.0
Charlie Root	10.6
Schoolboy Rowe	17.4
Nap Rucker	13.8
Red Ruffing	26.9
Bob Rush	11.2
Amos Rusie	39.1
Jeff Russell	10.4
Babe Ruth	17.1
Nolan Ryan	20.8
Bret Saberhagen	23.5
Johnny Sain	11.4
Slim Sallee	9.4
Ben Sanders	10.3
Hal Schumacher	16.3
Jim Scott	9.3
Tom Seaver	48.2
Rip Sewell	10.1
Bobby Shantz	21.1
Bob Shawkey	14.8
Urban Shocker	25.9
Sonny Siebert	10.4
Curt Simmons	12.6
Dave Smith	11.2
Lee Smith	23.5
Sherry Smith	12.3
John Smoltz	12.8
Warren Spahn	47.0
Gerry Staley	9.4
Bob Stanley	17.3
Dave Stieb	27.2
Jack Stivetts	28.2
Mel Stottlemyre	17.3
Frank Sullivan	10.1
Bruce Sutter	19.8
Don Sutton	13.6
Bill Swift	8.8
Frank Tanana	13.3
Jesse Tannehill	21.3
Jack Taylor	16.7
Kent Tekulve	23.6
Jeff Tesreau	8.7
Luis Tiant	17.1
Jim Tobin	13.0
Dizzy Trout	34.5
Virgil Trucks	15.9
John Tudor	15.2
George Uhle	13.5
Fernando Valenzuela	11.4
Dazzy Vance	27.0
Hippo Vaughn	17.9
Frank Viola	14.0
Rube Waddell	24.6
Ed Walsh	43.3
Bucky Walters	28.6
John Ward	14.1
Lon Warneke	22.7
Jake Weimer	11.8
Mickey Welch	14.8
Bob Welch	8.9
John Wetteland	12.5
Doc White	19.1
Will White	12.2
Jim Whitney	14.7
Hoyt Wilhelm	39.7
Vic Willis	22.0
Hooks Wiltse	10.1
Joe Wood	24.2
Wilbur Wood	18.5
Todd Worrell	12.7
Al Worthington	10.3
Early Wynn	16.6
Cy Young	79.8
Tom Zachary	10.3

Total Pitcher Index (by era)

1876-1892

1	John Clarkson	48.7
2	Tim Keefe	37.2
3	Tony Mullane	32.6
4	Bob Caruthers	29.4
5	Charley Radbourn	28.7
6	Jack Stivetts	28.2
7	Guy Hecker	23.9
8	Silver King	22.9
9	Jim McCormick	21.2
10	Charlie Buffinton	20.3
11	Dave Foutz	19.6
12	Sadie McMahon	15.9
13	Mickey Welch	14.8
14	Jim Whitney	14.7
15	John Ward	14.1
16	Larry Corcoran	14.0
17	Charlie Ferguson	13.8
18	Bill Hutchison	13.5
19	Jim Devlin	13.2
20	Pud Galvin	12.9
21	Will White	12.2
22	Matt Kilroy	10.4
23	Ben Sanders	10.3
24	Elton Chamberlain	10.0
25	Ed Morris	9.2

1893-1919

1	Walter Johnson	90.5
2	Cy Young	79.8
3	Pete Alexander	64.9
4	Christy Mathewson	62.7
5	Kid Nichols	60.9
6	Ed Walsh	43.3
7	Amos Rusie	39.1
8	Mordecai Brown	34.8
9	Clark Griffith	29.7
10	Eddie Plank	27.0
11	Addie Joss	25.4
12	Eddie Cicotte	25.2
13	Rube Waddell	24.6
14	Joe Wood	24.2
15	Nig Cuppy	22.4
16	Vic Willis	22.0
17	Jesse Tannehill	21.3
18	Joe McGinnity	19.5
19	Doc White	19.1
20	Hippo Vaughn	17.9
21	Ed Reulbach	17.7
22	Babe Ruth	17.1
23	Noodles Hahn	16.9
24	Jack Taylor	16.7
25	Harry Howell	16.4

1920-1941

1	Lefty Grove	61.2
2	Carl Hubbell	39.2
3	Ted Lyons	36.7
4	Carl Mays	36.2
5	Wes Ferrell	32.3
6	Tommy Bridges	28.7
7	Bucky Walters	28.6
8	Stan Coveleski	27.5
9	Red Faber	27.0
	Dazzy Vance	27.0
11	Red Ruffing	26.9
12	Dolf Luque	26.3
13	Eddie Rommel	26.0
14	Eppa Rixey	25.9
	Urban Shocker	25.9
16	Burleigh Grimes	24.0
17	Jack Quinn	23.6
18	Freddie Fitzsimmons	23.1
19	Lon Warneke	22.7
20	Dizzy Dean	22.2
21	Curt Davis	22.1
22	Mel Harder	20.0
23	Wilbur Cooper	19.7
24	Red Lucas	18.5
25	Lefty Gomez	17.9

Total Pitcher Index (by era)

1942-1960

1	Warren Spahn	47.0
2	Hal Newhouser	40.8
3	Hoyt Wilhelm	39.7
4	Bob Lemon	37.4
5	Whitey Ford	37.2
6	Dizzy Trout	34.5
7	Bob Feller	28.5
8	Dutch Leonard	25.8
9	Harry Brecheen	25.4
10	Robin Roberts	24.9
11	Billy Pierce	23.3
12	Bobby Shantz	21.1
13	Spud Chandler	20.6
14	Murry Dickson	19.7
15	Don Newcombe	18.9
16	Ed Lopat	18.1
	Mel Parnell	18.1
18	Ned Garver	17.4
19	Stu Miller	16.7
20	Early Wynn	16.6
21	Max Lanier	16.3
22	Virgil Trucks	15.9
23	Johnny Antonelli	15.7
24	Ellis Kinder	15.4
25	Mike Garcia	14.5

1961-1976

1	Tom Seaver	48.2
2	Bob Gibson	44.0
3	Jim Palmer	35.5
4	Phil Niekro	35.4
5	Gaylord Perry	34.4
6	Don Drysdale	34.0
7	Steve Carlton	33.2
8	Fergie Jenkins	30.9
9	Juan Marichal	28.9
10	Tommy John	25.0
11	Rollie Fingers	21.7
12	Mike Marshall	20.9
13	John Hiller	20.6
14	Sparky Lyle	20.0
15	Jim Kaat	19.0
16	Larry Jackson	18.8
17	Sandy Koufax	18.5
	Wilbur Wood	18.5
19	Mel Stottlemyre	17.3
20	Andy Messersmith	17.1
	Luis Tiant	17.1
22	Ron Perranoski	15.5
23	Frank Linzy	14.6
	Lindy McDaniel	14.6
25	Tug McGraw	14.4

1977-1996

1	Roger Clemens	40.9
2	Greg Maddux	39.1
3	Bert Blyleven	30.8
4	Rich Gossage	29.5
5	Dave Stieb	27.2
6	Dennis Eckersley	26.5
7	John Franco	26.4
8	Rick Reuschel	25.5
9	Orel Hershiser	25.4
10	Dan Quisenberry	24.8
11	Kent Tekulve	23.6
12	Bret Saberhagen	23.5
	Lee Smith	23.5
14	Tom Henke	21.2
15	Nolan Ryan	20.8
16	Jimmy Key	20.6
17	Bruce Sutter	19.8
18	David Cone	18.8
19	Ron Guidry	18.2
20	Tom Glavine	17.6
21	Jeff Montgomery	17.5
	Jose Rijo	17.5
23	Bob Stanley	17.3
24	Jesse Orosco	17.1
25	2 players tied	16.9

Total Baseball Ranking

Rank	Player	Score
1	Babe Ruth	124.8
2	Nap Lajoie	94.2
3	Willie Mays	92.2
4	Ty Cobb	91.1
5	Walter Johnson	90.1
6	Hank Aaron	89.8
7	Tris Speaker	86.5
8	Ted Williams	85.7
9	Honus Wagner	81.2
10	Rogers Hornsby	81.1
11	Cy Young	79.8
12	Mike Schmidt	78.4
13	Rickey Henderson	77.5
14	Mickey Mantle	76.1
15	Stan Musial	70.5
16	Eddie Collins	69.8
17	Frank Robinson	69.0
18	Lou Gehrig	65.7
19	Pete Alexander	64.9
20	Barry Bonds	64.7
21	Christy Mathewson	62.7
	Mel Ott	62.7
23	Lefty Grove	61.2
24	Kid Nichols	60.9
25	Joe Morgan	56.3
26	Jimmie Foxx	54.3
27	Tim Raines	52.3
28	Eddie Mathews	51.6
29	Bill Dahlen	51.4
30	George Davis	49.9
31	John Clarkson	48.7
32	Tom Seaver	48.2
33	Warren Spahn	47.0
34	Joe DiMaggio	46.9
35	Carl Yastrzemski	45.5
36	Wade Boggs	44.6
	Al Kaline	44.6
38	Charlie Gehringer	44.4
39	Ed Delahanty	44.3
40	Bob Gibson	44.0
	Bobby Grich	44.0
42	Ed Walsh	43.3
43	Tony Gwynn	43.2
44	Robin Yount	43.1
45	Ozzie Smith	43.0
46	Roberto Clemente	42.9
47	Reggie Jackson	42.8
48	Roger Connor	42.7
49	Lou Boudreau	41.3
	Cal Ripken	41.3
51	Roger Clemens	40.9
52	Hal Newhouser	40.8
53	Luke Appling	40.7
	Dan Brouthers	40.7
	Bobby Wallace	40.7
56	Gabby Hartnett	40.1
	Bid McPhee	40.1
58	Hoyt Wilhelm	39.7
59	Ron Santo	39.5
60	Joe Cronin	39.4
61	Carl Hubbell	39.2
	Arky Vaughan	39.2
63	Greg Maddux	39.1
	Amos Rusie	39.1
65	George Brett	39.0
	Bobby Doerr	39.0
	Frankie Frisch	39.0
68	Dave Winfield	38.5
69	Ryne Sandberg	38.2
70	Barry Larkin	37.6
71	Joe Jackson	37.5
72	Whitey Ford	37.2
	Tim Keefe	37.2
74	Bob Lemon	36.9
75	Ted Lyons	36.7
76	Willie McCovey	36.5
77	Bill Mazeroski	36.3
78	Carl Mays	36.2
	Yogi Berra	36.2
	Jack Glasscock	36.2
	Johnny Mize	36.2
82	Paul Waner	36.1
83	Bob Johnson	35.6
84	Jim Palmer	35.5
85	Phil Niekro	35.4
	Bill Dickey	35.4
87	Dick Allen	35.3
	Paul Molitor	35.3
89	Dave Bancroft	35.2
90	Eddie Murray	35.0
	Reggie Smith	35.0
92	Mordecai Brown	34.8
93	Darrell Evans	34.6
94	Dizzy Trout	34.5
	Joe Sewell	34.5
96	Gaylord Perry	34.4
	Keith Hernandez	34.4
98	Don Drysdale	34.0
99	Frank Baker	33.8
100	Steve Carlton	33.2

Total Baseball Ranking

Rank	Player	Score
	Jim Wynn	33.2
102	Willie Stargell	32.8
103	Wes Ferrell	32.4
104	Harry Heilmann	32.3
105	Jackie Robinson	31.8
106	Rod Carew	31.7
	Billy Herman	31.7
108	Bob Caruthers	31.5
109	Mickey Cochrane	31.4
110	Tony Mullane	31.1
	Jack Clark	31.1
	Billy Williams	31.1
113	Fergie Jenkins	30.9
114	Bert Blyleven	30.8
115	Sam Crawford	30.4
	Dwight Evans	30.4
117	Richie Ashburn	30.2
118	Cap Anson	30.0
	Cupid Childs	30.0
	Hank Greenberg	30.0
121	Andre Dawson	29.9
122	Gary Carter	29.6
	Buck Ewing	29.6
124	Rich Gossage	29.5
	Bobby Bonds	29.5
126	Frank Thomas	29.3
127	Kirby Puckett	29.1
128	Clark Griffith	29.0
129	Juan Marichal	28.9
	Ralph Kiner	28.9
131	Jose Cruz	28.8
	Elmer Flick	28.8
133	Tommy Bridges	28.7
	Fred Clarke	28.7
135	Bob Feller	28.5
	Sam Thompson	28.5
137	Cesar Cedeno	28.3
138	Joe Gordon	28.2
139	Dick Bartell	27.9
140	Ken Griffey Jr.	27.8
141	Rusty Staub	27.6
142	Stan Coveleski	27.5
	Norm Cash	27.5
144	Dave Stieb	27.2
	Fred Dunlap	27.2
	Stan Hack	27.2
147	Joe Medwick	27.1
	Jim Rice	27.1
149	Red Faber	27.0
	Eddie Plank	27.0
	Dazzy Vance	27.0
	Heinie Groh	27.0
	Hardy Richardson	27.0
154	Pete Browning	26.9
155	Red Ruffing	26.8
156	Darryl Strawberry	26.6
157	Dennis Eckersley	26.5
	Sherry Magee	26.5
159	John Franco	26.4
	Bucky Walters	26.4
	Jesse Burkett	26.4
	Billy Hamilton	26.4
	Harmon Killebrew	26.4
164	Dolf Luque	26.3
	Jack Stivetts	26.3
166	Charley Radbourn	26.2
	Hughie Jennings	26.2
168	Jeff Bagwell	26.1
169	Eddie Rommel	26.0
	Goose Goslin	26.0
	Minnie Minoso	26.0
172	Eppa Rixey	25.9
	Urban Shocker	25.9
	Ernie Banks	25.9
175	Dutch Leonard	25.8
	Art Fletcher	25.8
177	Rocky Colavito	25.6
	Al Simmons	25.6
179	Rick Reuschel	25.5
	Lenny Dykstra	25.5
181	Harry Brecheen	25.4
	Orel Hershiser	25.4
	Addie Joss	25.4
184	Eddie Cicotte	25.2
185	Tommy John	25.0
	Lou Whitaker	25.0
187	Robin Roberts	24.9
	Tony Oliva	24.9
	Bill Terry	24.9
190	Dan Quisenberry	24.8
191	Rube Waddell	24.6
	Jose Canseco	24.6
193	King Kelly	24.4
194	Johnny Bench	24.3
	Zack Wheat	24.3
196	Burleigh Grimes	24.0
	Carlton Fisk	24.0
	Travis Jackson	24.0
	George Sisler	24.0
200	Jack Fournier	23.9

Total Baseball Ranking

Rank	Player	Score
201	Jack Quinn	23.6
	Kent Tekulve	23.6
203	Bret Saberhagen	23.5
	Lee Smith	23.5
	Charlie Keller	23.5
206	Billy Pierce	23.3
	Albert Belle	23.3
208	Freddie Fitzsimmons	23.1
	Jimmy Collins	23.1
	Willie Randolph	23.1
	Joe Tinker	23.1
212	Dave Parker	23.0
213	Silver King	22.9
	Buddy Bell	22.9
215	Joe Wood	22.8
	Brett Butler	22.8
	Roy Thomas	22.8
218	Lon Warneke	22.7
	Jake Beckley	22.7
	Harlond Clift	22.7
221	Max Carey	22.6
222	Nig Cuppy	22.4
223	George Foster	22.3
	Ed Konetchy	22.3
	Chet Lemon	22.3
	Fred Lynn	22.3
	Duke Snider	22.3
228	Dizzy Dean	22.2
	Wally Berger	22.2
230	Curt Davis	22.1
231	Vic Willis	22.0
	Eric Davis	22.0
233	Ron Cey	21.9
	Fred Pfeffer	21.9
	John Ward	21.9
236	Alan Trammell	21.8
237	Rollie Fingers	21.7
238	Roy Campanella	21.6
	Kevin Mitchell	21.6
240	Harry Stovey	21.5
241	Chuck Klein	21.4
242	Guy Hecker	21.3
	Frank Howard	21.3
	Graig Nettles	21.3
245	Tom Henke	21.2
	Jim McCormick	21.2
	Larry Doby	21.2
248	Bobby Shantz	21.1
	Roy White	21.1
250	Mike Marshall	20.9
	Ken Singleton	20.9
	Fred Tenney	20.9
253	Nolan Ryan	20.8
254	Charley Jones	20.7
	Pie Traynor	20.7
256	Spud Chandler	20.6
	John Hiller	20.6
	Jimmy Key	20.6
	Art Devlin	20.6
	Jim Fregosi	20.6
261	Frank Chance	20.5
	Mike Griffin	20.5
263	Del Pratt	20.4
264	Andy Van Slyke	20.3
265	Jesse Tannehill	20.2
	Glenn Hubbard	20.2
	Joe Kelley	20.2
268	Mel Harder	20.0
	Sparky Lyle	20.0
	Pete Rose	20.0
271	Bruce Sutter	19.8
	Roger Bresnahan	19.8
	Denny Lyons	19.8
	Mark McGwire	19.8
	Brooks Robinson	19.8
276	Wilbur Cooper	19.7
	Murry Dickson	19.7
278	Vern Stephens	19.6
	Joe Torre	19.6
280	Joe McGinnity	19.5
	Jimmy Sheckard	19.5
282	Will Clark	19.4
283	Dale Murphy	19.3
	Amos Otis	19.3
285	Roberto Alomar	19.2
	Charlie Bennett	19.2
	Edgar Martinez	19.2
288	Fred McGriff	19.1
289	Jim Kaat	19.0
	Bill Nicholson	19.0
	Rafael Palmeiro	19.0
292	Don Newcombe	18.9
	Gavvy Cravath	18.9
	Bill Joyce	18.9
295	David Cone	18.8
	Larry Jackson	18.8
	Bob Elliott	18.8
298	Bobby Bonilla	18.6
	Ken Boyer	18.6
	Brian Downing	18.6

Total Baseball Ranking

Rank	Player	Score
301	Sandy Koufax	18.5
	Wilbur Wood	18.5
303	Eddie Stanky	18.4
304	Ron Guidry	18.2
305	Ed Lopat	18.1
	Mel Parnell	18.1
	Roy Cullenbine	18.1
	Miller Huggins	18.1
	Wally Schang	18.1
310	Gene Alley	18.0
	Matt Williams	18.0
312	Lefty Gomez	17.9
	Hippo Vaughn	17.9
	Craig Biggio	17.9
	Rico Carty	17.9
316	Red Lucas	17.8
	Ferris Fain	17.8
318	Ed Reulbach	17.7
	Doc White	17.7
320	Tom Glavine	17.6
	Earl Averill	17.6
322	Jeff Montgomery	17.5
	Jose Rijo	17.5
324	Ned Garver	17.4
	Schoolboy Rowe	17.4
	Tommy Leach	17.4
327	Bob Stanley	17.3
	Mel Stottlemyre	17.3
	Babe Herman	17.3
	Johnny Logan	17.3
	Ernie Lombardi	17.3
	Ken Williams	17.3
333	Larry French	17.2
	Paul Hines	17.2
335	Andy Messersmith	17.1
	Jesse Orosco	17.1
	Luis Tiant	17.1
338	Kevin Appier	16.9
	Dwight Gooden	16.9
	Noodles Hahn	16.9
	Thornton Lee	16.9
	Tony Lazzeri	16.9
343	Harold Baines	16.8
	Gil McDougald	16.8
	Ted Simmons	16.8
346	Stu Miller	16.7
	Jack Taylor	16.7
	Orlando Cepeda	16.7
	Pedro Guerrero	16.7
	Mike Piazza	16.7
351	Early Wynn	16.6
352	Claude Passeau	16.5
353	Jesse Barfield	16.4
	Jeff Heath	16.4
	Dwayne Murphy	16.4
356	Max Lanier	16.3
	Hal Schumacher	16.3
	Enos Slaughter	16.3
359	Cy Seymour	16.2
360	Gene Garber	16.1
	George Gore	16.1
	Jim O'Rourke	16.1
363	Dennis Martinez	16.0
	Kirk Gibson	16.0
	John McGraw	16.0
	Jimmy Williams	16.0
367	Sadie McMahon	15.9
	Virgil Trucks	15.9
369	Kevin Brown	15.8
	Kiki Cuyler	15.8
	Phil Rizzuto	15.8
	Chief Zimmer	15.8
373	Johnny Antonelli	15.7
	Deacon Phillippe	15.7
	Dave Righetti	15.7
	Mike Hargrove	15.7
377	Davey Johnson	15.6
	Jocko Milligan	15.6
	Danny Tartabull	15.6
	Hack Wilson	15.6
381	Ron Perranoski	15.5
382	Ellis Kinder	15.4
	Ray Chapman	15.4
	Tony Fernandez	15.4
385	Steve Rogers	15.3
	Chili Davis	15.3
	Gene Tenace	15.3
388	John Tudor	15.2
	Thurman Munson	15.2
	Elmer Smith	15.2
391	Sid Gordon	15.1
392	Babe Adams	15.0
	Doug Jones	15.0
	Sam Leever	15.0
	Mark Belanger	15.0
	Bobby Knoop	15.0
397	Charlie Buffinton	14.9
	John Candelaria	14.9
	Frank Dwyer	14.9

Total Baseball Ranking		Total Baseball Rank (alpha.)		Total Baseball Rank (alpha.)		Total Baseball Rank (alpha.)	
	Charlie Hough	14.9	Hank Aaron	89.8	Kiki Cuyler	15.8	Keith Hernandez	34.4
	Jay Bell	14.9	Babe Adams	15.0	Bill Dahlen	51.4	Orel Hershiser	25.4
	Henry Larkin	14.9	Rick Aguilera	14.1	Kal Daniels	12.8	John Hiller	20.6
	Boog Powell	14.9	Pete Alexander	64.9	Curt Davis	22.1	Paul Hines	17.2
404	Bob Shawkey	14.8	Dick Allen	35.3	Chili Davis	15.3	Gil Hodges	13.7
	Mickey Welch	14.8	Gene Alley	18.0	Eric Davis	22.0	Tommy Holmes	13.5
	Benny Kauff	14.8	Bob Allison	14.3	George Davis	49.9	Rogers Hornsby	81.1
	Mike Scioscia	14.8	Roberto Alomar	19.2	Andre Dawson	29.9	Charlie Hough	14.9
408	Sixto Lezcano	14.7	Cap Anson	30.0	Dizzy Dean	22.2	Frank Howard	21.3
	Paul O'Neill	14.7	Johnny Antonelli	15.7	Doug DeCinces	13.1	Harry Howell	13.9
	Bobby Veach	14.7	Kevin Appier	16.9	Ed Delahanty	44.3	Waite Hoyt	14.4
411	Gary Lavelle	14.6	Luke Appling	40.7	Jim Devlin	13.2	Glenn Hubbard	20.2
	Frank Linzy	14.6	Richie Ashburn	30.2	Art Devlin	20.6	Carl Hubbell	39.2
	Lindy McDaniel	14.6	Earl Averill	17.6	Bill Dickey	35.4	Miller Huggins	18.1
	Lave Cross	14.6	Jeff Bagwell	26.1	Murry Dickson	19.7	Fred Hutchinson	14.0
	Duke Farrell	14.6	Harold Baines	16.8	Joe DiMaggio	46.9	Bill Hutchison	13.5
	Augie Galan	14.6	Frank Baker	33.8	Larry Doby	21.2	Larry Jackson	18.8
	Greg Luzinski	14.6	Dave Bancroft	35.2	Bobby Doerr	39.0	Joe Jackson	37.5
	Pee Wee Reese	14.6	Ernie Banks	25.9	Brian Downing	18.6	Reggie Jackson	42.8
419	Mike Garcia	14.5	Jesse Barfield	16.4	Don Drysdale	34.0	Travis Jackson	24.0
	Tommy Henrich	14.5	Dick Bartell	27.9	Fred Dunlap	27.2	Fergie Jenkins	30.9
	Kevin McReynolds	14.5	Jake Beckley	22.7	Frank Dwyer	14.9	Hughie Jennings	26.2
422	Mark Eichhorn	14.4	Mark Belanger	15.0	Lenny Dykstra	25.5	Tommy John	25.0
	Chuck Finley	14.4	Buddy Bell	22.9	Dennis Eckersley	26.5	Walter Johnson	90.1
	Claude Hendrix	14.4	Jay Bell	14.9	Mark Eichhorn	14.4	Davey Johnson	15.6
	Waite Hoyt	14.4	Albert Belle	23.3	Bob Elliott	18.8	Bob Johnson	35.6
	Tug McGraw	14.4	Johnny Bench	24.3	Darrell Evans	34.6	Doug Jones	15.0
427	Bob Allison	14.3	Chief Bender	13.8	Dwight Evans	30.4	Charley Jones	20.7
428	Mark Langston	14.2	Charlie Bennett	19.2	Johnny Evers	12.9	Addie Joss	25.4
	Ron Hansen	14.2	Wally Berger	22.2	Buck Ewing	29.6	Bill Joyce	18.9
	Kenny Lofton	14.2	Yogi Berra	36.2	Red Faber	27.0	David Justice	13.4
431	Rick Aguilera	14.1	Craig Biggio	17.9	Roy Face	13.2	Jim Kaat	19.0
	Johnny Callison	14.1	Bert Blyleven	30.8	Ferris Fain	17.8	Al Kaline	44.6
433	Fred Hutchinson	14.0	Wade Boggs	44.6	Duke Farrell	14.6	Willie Kamm	13.6
	George Mullin	14.0	Barry Bonds	64.7	Bob Feller	28.5	Benny Kauff	14.8
	Frank Viola	14.0	Bobby Bonds	29.5	Charlie Ferguson	13.8	Tim Keefe	37.2
436	Harry Howell	13.9	Bobby Bonilla	18.6	Tony Fernandez	15.4	Charlie Keller	23.5
	Frank Lary	13.9	Lou Boudreau	41.3	Wes Ferrell	32.4	Joe Kelley	20.2
	Jimmy Ryan	13.9	Ken Boyer	18.6	Rollie Fingers	21.7	King Kelly	24.4
	Larry Walker	13.9	Harry Brecheen	25.4	Chuck Finley	14.4	Jimmy Key	20.6
440	Chief Bender	13.8	Roger Bresnahan	19.8	Carlton Fisk	24.0	Harmon Killebrew	26.4
	Charlie Ferguson	13.8	George Brett	39.0	Freddie Fitzsimmons	23.1	Frank Killen	12.9
	Nap Rucker	13.8	Tommy Bridges	28.7	Art Fletcher	25.8	Ellis Kinder	15.4
	Roy Smalley	13.8	Lou Brock	12.7	Elmer Flick	28.8	Ralph Kiner	28.9
444	Sal Maglie	13.7	Dan Brouthers	40.7	Whitey Ford	37.2	Silver King	22.9
	Howie Pollet	13.7	Kevin Brown	15.8	George Foster	22.3	Chuck Klein	21.4
	Gil Hodges	13.7	Mordecai Brown	34.8	Jack Fournier	23.9	Bobby Knoop	15.0
447	Jim Bunning	13.6	Pete Browning	26.9	Dave Foutz	12.7	Ed Konetchy	22.3
	Don Sutton	13.6	Charlie Buffinton	14.9	Jimmie Foxx	54.3	Jerry Koosman	13.1
	Ben Chapman	13.6	Jim Bunning	13.6	John Franco	26.4	Sandy Koufax	18.5
	Willie Kamm	13.6	Tom Burgmeier	12.8	Bill Freehan	13.2	Nap Lajoie	94.2
	Kip Selbach	13.6	Jesse Burkett	26.4	Jim Fregosi	20.6	Mark Langston	14.2
452	Bill Hutchison	13.5	Brett Butler	22.8	Larry French	17.2	Max Lanier	16.3
	George Uhle	13.5	Johnny Callison	14.1	Frankie Frisch	39.0	Barry Larkin	37.6
	Fred Carroll	13.5	Roy Campanella	21.6	Augie Galan	14.6	Henry Larkin	14.9
	Tommy Holmes	13.5	John Candelaria	14.9	Pud Galvin	12.9	Frank Lary	13.9
	Tim Salmon	13.5	Jose Canseco	24.6	Gene Garber	16.1	Gary Lavelle	14.6
	George Stone	13.5	Rod Carew	31.7	Mike Garcia	14.5	Tony Lazzeri	16.9
	George Van Haltren	13.5	Max Carey	22.6	Ned Garver	17.4	Tommy Leach	17.4
	Richie Zisk	13.5	Steve Carlton	33.2	Lou Gehrig	65.7	Thornton Lee	16.9
460	Clay Carroll	13.4	Clay Carroll	13.4	Charlie Gehringer	44.4	Sam Leever	15.0
	Jim Maloney	13.4	Fred Carroll	13.5	Bob Gibson	44.0	Bob Lemon	36.9
	David Justice	13.4	Gary Carter	29.6	Kirk Gibson	16.0	Chet Lemon	22.3
	Chief Meyers	13.4	Rico Carty	17.9	Jack Glasscock	36.2	Dutch Leonard	25.8
	Al Oliver	13.4	Bob Caruthers	31.5	Tom Glavine	17.6	Sixto Lezcano	14.7
465	Frank Tanana	13.3	Norm Cash	27.5	Lefty Gomez	17.9	Frank Linzy	14.6
466	Jim Devlin	13.2	Cesar Cedeno	28.3	Dwight Gooden	16.9	Kenny Lofton	14.2
	Roy Face	13.2	Orlando Cepeda	16.7	Joe Gordon	28.2	Johnny Logan	17.3
	Claude Osteen	13.2	Ron Cey	21.9	Sid Gordon	15.1	Ernie Lombardi	17.3
	Bill Freehan	13.2	Frank Chance	20.5	George Gore	16.1	Ed Lopat	18.1
	Dave Orr	13.2	Spud Chandler	20.6	Goose Goslin	26.0	Red Lucas	17.8
	Roger Peckinpaugh	13.2	Ray Chapman	15.4	Rich Gossage	29.5	Dolf Luque	26.3
472	Jerry Koosman	13.1	Ben Chapman	13.6	Mark Grace	13.1	Greg Luzinski	14.6
	Firpo Marberry	13.1	Cupid Childs	30.0	Hank Greenberg	30.0	Sparky Lyle	20.0
	Doug DeCinces	13.1	Eddie Cicotte	25.2	Bobby Grich	44.0	Fred Lynn	22.3
	Mark Grace	13.1	Jack Clark	31.1	Ken Griffey Jr.	27.8	Ted Lyons	36.7
	Edd Roush	13.1	Will Clark	19.4	Mike Griffin	20.5	Denny Lyons	19.8
	John Titus	13.1	Fred Clarke	28.7	Clark Griffith	29.0	Greg Maddux	39.1
478	Jim Tobin	13.0	John Clarkson	48.7	Burleigh Grimes	24.0	Sherry Magee	26.5
479	Mort Cooper	12.9	Roger Clemens	40.9	Heinie Groh	27.0	Sal Maglie	13.7
	Pud Galvin	12.9	Roberto Clemente	42.9	Lefty Grove	61.2	Jim Maloney	13.4
	Frank Killen	12.9	Jack Clements	12.7	Pedro Guerrero	16.7	Mickey Mantle	76.1
	Jim Whitney	12.9	Harlond Clift	22.7	Ron Guidry	18.2	Firpo Marberry	13.1
	Johnny Evers	12.9	Ty Cobb	91.1	Tony Gwynn	43.2	Juan Marichal	28.9
	Bobby Murcer	12.9	Mickey Cochrane	31.4	Stan Hack	27.2	Mike Marshall	20.9
485	Tom Burgmeier	12.8	Rocky Colavito	25.6	Noodles Hahn	16.9	Dennis Martinez	16.0
	Van Mungo	12.8	Eddie Collins	69.8	Billy Hamilton	26.4	Edgar Martinez	19.2
	John Smoltz	12.8	Jimmy Collins	23.1	Ron Hansen	14.2	Eddie Mathews	51.6
	Kal Daniels	12.8	David Cone	18.8	Mel Harder	20.0	Christy Mathewson	62.7
	Red Smith	12.8	Roger Connor	42.7	Mike Hargrove	15.7	Carl Mays	36.2
	Riggs Stephenson	12.8	Wilbur Cooper	19.7	Gabby Hartnett	40.1	Willie Mays	92.2
491	Dave Foutz	12.7	Mort Cooper	12.9	Jeff Heath	16.4	Bill Mazeroski	36.3
	Todd Worrell	12.7	Stan Coveleski	27.5	Guy Hecker	21.3	Jim McCormick	21.2
	Lou Brock	12.7	Gavvy Cravath	18.9	Harry Heilmann	32.3	Willie McCovey	36.5
	Jack Clements	12.7	Sam Crawford	30.4	Rickey Henderson	77.5	Lindy McDaniel	14.6
	Roy Sievers	12.7	Joe Cronin	39.4	Claude Hendrix	14.4	Gil McDougald	16.8
496	11 players tied	12.6	Lave Cross	14.6	Tom Henke	21.2	Joe McGinnity	19.5
			Jose Cruz	28.8	Tommy Henrich	14.5	Tug McGraw	14.4
			Roy Cullenbine	18.1	Babe Herman	17.3	John McGraw	16.0
			Nig Cuppy	22.4	Billy Herman	31.7	Fred McGriff	19.1

Total Baseball Rank (alpha.)

Player	Rank
Mark McGwire	19.8
Sadie McMahon	15.9
Bid McPhee	40.1
Kevin McReynolds	14.5
Joe Medwick	27.1
Andy Messersmith	17.1
Chief Meyers	13.4
Stu Miller	16.7
Jocko Milligan	15.6
Minnie Minoso	26.0
Kevin Mitchell	21.6
Johnny Mize	36.2
Paul Molitor	35.3
Jeff Montgomery	17.5
Joe Morgan	56.3
Tony Mullane	31.1
George Mullin	14.0
Van Mungo	12.8
Thurman Munson	15.2
Bobby Murcer	12.9
Dale Murphy	19.3
Dwayne Murphy	16.4
Eddie Murray	35.0
Stan Musial	70.5
Graig Nettles	21.3
Don Newcombe	18.9
Hal Newhouser	40.8
Kid Nichols	60.9
Bill Nicholson	19.0
Phil Niekro	35.4
Paul O'Neill	14.7
Jim O'Rourke	16.1
Tony Oliva	24.9
Al Oliver	13.4
Jesse Orosco	17.1
Dave Orr	13.2
Claude Osteen	13.2
Amos Otis	19.3
Mel Ott	62.7
Rafael Palmeiro	19.0
Jim Palmer	35.5
Dave Parker	23.0
Mel Parnell	18.1
Claude Passeau	16.5
Roger Peckinpaugh	13.2
Ron Perranoski	15.5
Gaylord Perry	34.4
Fred Pfeffer	21.9
Deacon Phillippe	15.7
Mike Piazza	16.7
Billy Pierce	23.3
Eddie Plank	27.0
Howie Pollet	13.7
Boog Powell	14.9
Del Pratt	20.4
Kirby Puckett	29.1
Jack Quinn	23.6
Dan Quisenberry	24.8
Charley Radbourn	26.2
Tim Raines	52.3
Willie Randolph	23.1
Ed Reulbach	17.7
Rick Reuschel	25.5
Jim Rice	27.1
Hardy Richardson	27.0
Dave Righetti	15.7
Jose Rijo	17.5
Cal Ripken	41.3
Eppa Rixey	25.9
Phil Rizzuto	15.8
Robin Roberts	24.9
Brooks Robinson	19.8
Frank Robinson	69.0
Jackie Robinson	31.8
Steve Rogers	15.3
Eddie Rommel	26.0
Pete Rose	20.0
Edd Roush	13.1
Schoolboy Rowe	17.4
Nap Rucker	13.8
Red Ruffing	26.8
Amos Rusie	39.1
Babe Ruth	124.8
Nolan Ryan	20.8
Jimmy Ryan	13.9
Bret Saberhagen	23.5
Tim Salmon	13.5
Ryne Sandberg	38.2
Ron Santo	39.5
Wally Schang	18.1
Mike Schmidt	78.4
Hal Schumacher	16.3
Mike Scioscia	14.8
Tom Seaver	48.2
Kip Selbach	13.6
Joe Sewell	34.5
Cy Seymour	16.2
Bobby Shantz	21.1
Bob Shawkey	14.8

Total Baseball Rank (alpha.)

Player	Rank
Jimmy Sheckard	19.5
Urban Shocker	25.9
Roy Sievers	12.7
Al Simmons	25.6
Ted Simmons	16.8
Ken Singleton	20.9
George Sisler	24.0
Enos Slaughter	16.3
Roy Smalley	13.8
Lee Smith	23.5
Reggie Smith	35.0
Elmer Smith	15.2
Red Smith	12.8
Ozzie Smith	43.0
John Smoltz	12.8
Duke Snider	22.3
Warren Spahn	47.0
Tris Speaker	86.5
Eddie Stanky	18.4
Bob Stanley	17.3
Willie Stargell	32.8
Rusty Staub	27.6
Vern Stephens	19.6
Riggs Stephenson	12.8
Dave Stieb	27.2
Jack Stivetts	26.3
George Stone	13.5
Mel Stottlemyre	17.3
Harry Stovey	21.5
Darryl Strawberry	26.6
Bruce Sutter	19.8
Don Sutton	13.6
Frank Tanana	13.3
Jesse Tannehill	20.2
Danny Tartabull	15.6
Jack Taylor	16.7
Kent Tekulve	23.6
Gene Tenace	15.3
Fred Tenney	20.9
Bill Terry	24.9
Frank Thomas	29.3
Roy Thomas	22.8
Sam Thompson	28.5
Luis Tiant	17.1
Joe Tinker	23.1
John Titus	13.1
Jim Tobin	13.0
Joe Torre	19.6
Alan Trammell	21.8
Pie Traynor	20.7
Dizzy Trout	34.5
Virgil Trucks	15.9
John Tudor	15.2
George Uhle	13.5
Dazzy Vance	27.0
George Van Haltren	13.5
Andy Van Slyke	20.3
Arky Vaughan	39.2
Hippo Vaughn	17.9
Bobby Veach	14.7
Frank Viola	14.0
Rube Waddell	24.6
Honus Wagner	81.2
Larry Walker	13.9
Bobby Wallace	40.7
Ed Walsh	43.3
Bucky Walters	26.4
Paul Waner	36.1
John Ward	21.9
Lon Warneke	22.7
Pee Wee Reese	14.6
Mickey Welch	14.8
Zack Wheat	24.3
Lou Whitaker	25.0
Doc White	17.7
Roy White	21.1
Jim Whitney	12.9
Hoyt Wilhelm	39.7
Billy Williams	31.1
Jimmy Williams	16.0
Ken Williams	17.3
Matt Williams	18.0
Ted Williams	85.7
Vic Willis	22.0
Hack Wilson	15.6
Dave Winfield	38.5
Joe Wood	22.8
Wilbur Wood	18.5
Todd Worrell	12.7
Early Wynn	16.6
Jim Wynn	33.2
Carl Yastrzemski	45.5
Cy Young	79.8
Robin Yount	43.1
Chief Zimmer	15.8
Richie Zisk	13.5

Total Baseball Rank (by era)

1876-1892

	Player	Rank
1	John Clarkson	48.7
2	Roger Connor	42.7
3	Dan Brouthers	40.7
4	Bid McPhee	40.1
5	Tim Keefe	37.2
6	Jack Glasscock	36.2
7	Bob Caruthers	31.5
8	Tony Mullane	31.1
9	Cap Anson	30.0
10	Buck Ewing	29.6
11	Sam Thompson	28.5
12	Fred Dunlap	27.2
13	Hardy Richardson	27.0
14	Pete Browning	26.9
15	Jack Stivetts	26.3
16	Charley Radbourn	26.2
17	King Kelly	24.4
18	Silver King	22.9
19	Fred Pfeffer	21.9
	John Ward	21.9
21	Harry Stovey	21.5
22	Guy Hecker	21.3
23	Jim McCormick	21.2
24	Charley Jones	20.7
25	Denny Lyons	19.8

1893-1919

	Player	Rank
1	Nap Lajoie	94.2
2	Ty Cobb	91.1
3	Walter Johnson	90.1
4	Tris Speaker	86.5
5	Honus Wagner	81.2
6	Cy Young	79.8
7	Eddie Collins	69.8
8	Pete Alexander	64.9
9	Christy Mathewson	62.7
10	Kid Nichols	60.9
11	Bill Dahlen	51.4
12	George Davis	49.9
13	Ed Delahanty	44.3
14	Ed Walsh	43.3
15	Bobby Wallace	40.7
16	Amos Rusie	39.1
17	Joe Jackson	37.5
18	Mordecai Brown	34.8
19	Frank Baker	33.8
20	Sam Crawford	30.4
21	Cupid Childs	30.0
22	Clark Griffith	29.0
23	Elmer Flick	28.8
24	Fred Clarke	28.7
25	2 players tied	27.0

1920-1941

	Player	Rank
1	Babe Ruth	124.8
2	Rogers Hornsby	81.1
3	Lou Gehrig	65.7
4	Mel Ott	62.7
5	Lefty Grove	61.2
6	Jimmie Foxx	54.3
7	Charlie Gehringer	44.4
8	Luke Appling	40.7
9	Gabby Hartnett	40.1
10	Joe Cronin	39.4
11	Carl Hubbell	39.2
	Arky Vaughan	39.2
13	Frankie Frisch	39.0
14	Ted Lyons	36.7
15	Carl Mays	36.2
16	Paul Waner	36.1
17	Bob Johnson	35.6
18	Bill Dickey	35.4
19	Dave Bancroft	35.2
20	Joe Sewell	34.5
21	Wes Ferrell	32.4
22	Harry Heilmann	32.3
23	Billy Herman	31.7
24	Mickey Cochrane	31.4
25	Hank Greenberg	30.0

Total Baseball Rank (by era)

1942-1960

	Player	Rank
1	Ted Williams	85.7
2	Mickey Mantle	76.1
3	Stan Musial	70.5
4	Eddie Mathews	51.6
5	Warren Spahn	47.0
6	Joe DiMaggio	46.9
7	Lou Boudreau	41.3
8	Hal Newhouser	40.8
9	Hoyt Wilhelm	39.7
10	Bobby Doerr	39.0
11	Whitey Ford	37.2
12	Bob Lemon	36.9
13	Yogi Berra	36.2
	Johnny Mize	36.2
15	Dizzy Trout	34.5
16	Jackie Robinson	31.8
17	Richie Ashburn	30.2
18	Ralph Kiner	28.9
19	Bob Feller	28.5
20	Joe Gordon	28.2
21	Minnie Minoso	26.0
22	Dutch Leonard	25.8
23	Harry Brecheen	25.4
24	Robin Roberts	24.9
25	Charlie Keller	23.5

1961-1976

	Player	Rank
1	Willie Mays	92.2
2	Hank Aaron	89.8
3	Frank Robinson	69.0
4	Joe Morgan	56.3
5	Tom Seaver	48.2
6	Carl Yastrzemski	45.5
7	Al Kaline	44.6
8	Bob Gibson	44.0
9	Roberto Clemente	42.9
10	Ron Santo	39.5
11	Willie McCovey	36.5
12	Bill Mazeroski	36.3
13	Jim Palmer	35.5
14	Phil Niekro	35.4
15	Dick Allen	35.3
16	Reggie Smith	35.0
17	Gaylord Perry	34.4
18	Don Drysdale	34.0
19	Steve Carlton	33.2
	Jim Wynn	33.2
21	Willie Stargell	32.8
22	Rod Carew	31.7
23	Billy Williams	31.1
24	Fergie Jenkins	30.9
25	Bobby Bonds	29.5

1977-1996

	Player	Rank
1	Mike Schmidt	78.4
2	Rickey Henderson	77.5
3	Barry Bonds	64.7
4	Tim Raines	52.3
5	Wade Boggs	44.6
6	Bobby Grich	44.0
7	Tony Gwynn	43.2
8	Robin Yount	43.1
9	Ozzie Smith	43.0
10	Reggie Jackson	42.8
11	Cal Ripken	41.3
12	Roger Clemens	40.9
13	Greg Maddux	39.1
14	George Brett	39.0
15	Dave Winfield	38.5
16	Ryne Sandberg	38.2
17	Barry Larkin	37.6
18	Paul Molitor	35.3
19	Eddie Murray	35.0
20	Darrell Evans	34.6
21	Keith Hernandez	34.4
22	Jack Clark	31.1
23	Bert Blyleven	30.8
24	Dwight Evans	30.4
25	Andre Dawson	29.9

At Bats

1	Willie Wilson, 1980	705
2	Juan Samuel, 1984	701
3	Dave Cash, 1975	699
4	Matty Alou, 1969	698
5	Woody Jensen, 1936	696
6	Maury Wills, 1962	695
	Omar Moreno, 1979	695
8	Bobby Richardson, 1962	692
9	Kirby Puckett, 1985	691
10	Lou Brock, 1967	689
	Sandy Alomar, 1971	689
12	Dave Cash, 1974	687
	Tony Fernandez, 1986	687
14	Horace Clarke, 1970	686
15	Lance Johnson, 1996	682
16	Lloyd Waner, 1931	681
	Jo-Jo Moore, 1935	681
18	Pete Rose, 1973	680
	Frank Taveras, 1979	680
	Kirby Puckett, 1986	680
21	Harvey Kuenn, 1953	679
	Curt Flood, 1964	679
	Bobby Richardson, 1964	679
24	Dick Groat, 1962	678
25	Matty Alou, 1970	677
	Jim Rice, 1978	677
	Don Mattingly, 1986	677
28	Felix Millan, 1975	676
	Omar Moreno, 1980	676
30	Rennie Stennett, 1974	673
	Bill Buckner, 1985	673
32	Rabbit Maranville, 1922	672
	Tony Oliva, 1964	672
	Sandy Alomar, 1970	672
	Garry Templeton, 1979	672
36	Jack Tobin, 1921	671
	Marquis Grissom, 1996	671
38	Al Simmons, 1932	670
	Pete Rose, 1965	670
	Buddy Bell, 1979	670
41	Vada Pinson, 1965	669
	Larry Bowa, 1974	669
43	Buddy Lewis, 1937	668
	Brooks Robinson, 1961	668
	Ralph Garr, 1973	668
46	Carl Furillo, 1951	667
47	Billy Herman, 1935	666
	Zoilo Versalles, 1965	666
	Felipe Alou, 1966	666
	Dave Cash, 1976	666
	Ron LeFlore, 1978	666
	Paul Molitor, 1982	666
53	Tommy Davis, 1962	665
	Pete Rose, 1976	665
	Paul Molitor, 1991	665
56	Taylor Douthit, 1930	664
	Bobby Richardson, 1965	664
	Don Kessinger, 1969	664
	Lou Brock, 1970	664
60	Jake Wood, 1961	663
	Bill Virdon, 1962	663
	Bobby Bonds, 1970	663
	Rick Burleson, 1977	663
	Cal Ripken, 1983	663
	Juan Samuel, 1985	663
	Joe Carter, 1986	663
67	Lloyd Waner, 1929	662
	Hughie Critz, 1930	662
	Richie Ashburn, 1949	662
	Granny Hamner, 1949	662
	Bobby Richardson, 1961	662
	Curt Flood, 1963	662
	Felipe Alou, 1968	662
	Pete Rose, 1975	662
	Kenny Lofton, 1996	662
76	Doc Cramer, 1933	661
	Doc Cramer, 1940	661
	Ken Hubbs, 1962	661
	Cecil Cooper, 1983	661
	Ruben Sierra, 1991	661
81	Tom Brown, 1892	660
	Doc Cramer, 1941	660
	Lou Brock, 1968	660
	Enos Cabell, 1978	660
	Paul Molitor, 1996	660
86	Lloyd Waner, 1928	659
	Hughie Critz, 1932	659
	Red Schoendienst, 1947	659
	Billy Moran, 1962	659
	Zoilo Versalles, 1964	659
	Luis Aparicio, 1966	659
	Steve Garvey, 1975	659
	Warren Cromartie, 1979	659
	Travis Fryman, 1992	659
95	Heinie Manush, 1933	658
	Doc Cramer, 1938	658
	Bill White, 1963	658
	Dave Cash, 1978	658
	Steve Garvey, 1980	658
	Julio Franco, 1984	658

Runs

1	Billy Hamilton, 1894	192
2	Tom Brown, 1891	177
	Babe Ruth, 1921	177
4	Tip O'Neill, 1887	167
	Lou Gehrig, 1936	167
6	Billy Hamilton, 1895	166
7	Willie Keeler, 1894	165
	Joe Kelley, 1894	165
9	Arlie Latham, 1887	163
	Babe Ruth, 1928	163
	Lou Gehrig, 1931	163
12	Willie Keeler, 1895	162
13	Hugh Duffy, 1890	161
14	Fred Dunlap, 1884	160
	Hugh Duffy, 1894	160
	Jesse Burkett, 1896	160
17	Hughie Jennings, 1895	159
18	Bobby Lowe, 1894	158
	Babe Ruth, 1920	158
	Babe Ruth, 1927	158
	Chuck Klein, 1930	158
22	John McGraw, 1894	156
	Rogers Hornsby, 1929	156
24	King Kelly, 1886	155
	Kiki Cuyler, 1930	155
26	Dan Brouthers, 1887	153
	Jesse Burkett, 1895	153
	Willie Keeler, 1896	153
29	Arlie Latham, 1886	152
	Mike Griffin, 1889	152
	Harry Stovey, 1889	152
	Billy Hamilton, 1896	152
	Billy Hamilton, 1897	152
	Lefty O'Doul, 1929	152
	Woody English, 1930	152
	Al Simmons, 1930	152
	Chuck Klein, 1932	152
38	Babe Ruth, 1923	151
	Jimmie Foxx, 1932	151
	Joe DiMaggio, 1937	151
41	George Gore, 1886	150
	Babe Ruth, 1930	150
	Ted Williams, 1949	150
44	Herman Long, 1893	149
	Bill Dahlen, 1894	149
	Ed Delahanty, 1895	149
	Lou Gehrig, 1927	149
	Babe Ruth, 1931	149
49	Hub Collins, 1890	148
	Jake Stenzel, 1894	148
	Joe Kelley, 1895	148
	Joe Kelley, 1896	148
53	Mike Tiernan, 1889	147
	Hugh Duffy, 1893	147
	Ed Delahanty, 1894	147
	Ty Cobb, 1911	147
57	Darby O'Brien, 1889	146
	Tom Brown, 1890	146
	Hack Wilson, 1930	146
	Rickey Henderson, 1985	146
61	Jesse Burkett, 1893	145
	Cupid Childs, 1893	145
	Ed Delahanty, 1893	145
	Patsy Donovan, 1894	145
	Willie Keeler, 1897	145
	Nap Lajoie, 1901	145
	Harland Clift, 1936	145
68	Hugh Duffy, 1889	144
	Billy Hamilton, 1889	144
	Ty Cobb, 1915	144
	Kiki Cuyler, 1925	144
	Charlie Gehringer, 1930	144
	Al Simmons, 1932	144
	Charlie Gehringer, 1936	144
	Hank Greenberg, 1938	144
76	Cupid Childs, 1894	143
	John McGraw, 1898	143
	Babe Ruth, 1924	143
	Babe Herman, 1930	143
	Lou Gehrig, 1930	143
	Earle Combs, 1932	143
	Red Rolfe, 1937	143
	Lenny Dykstra, 1993	143
84	Mike Griffin, 1887	142
	Harry Stovey, 1890	142
	Jesse Burkett, 1901	142
	Paul Waner, 1928	142
	Ted Williams, 1946	142
	Ellis Burks, 1996	142
90	Billy Hamilton, 1891	141
	Rogers Hornsby, 1922	141
	Ted Williams, 1942	141
	Alex Rodriguez, 1996	141
94	9 players tied	140

Runs per Game (by era)

1876-1892

1	Ross Barnes, 1876	1.91
2	Fred Dunlap, 1884	1.58
3	George Gore, 1890	1.42
4	Tip O'Neill, 1887	1.35
5	King Kelly, 1886	1.31
6	Tom Brown, 1891	1.29
7	George Gore, 1886	1.27
8	Dan Brouthers, 1887	1.24
9	Orator Shaffer, 1884	1.23
10	Mike Tiernan, 1889	1.20
11	Harry Stovey, 1890	1.20
12	Arlie Latham, 1887	1.20
13	Harry Stovey, 1884	1.19
14	George Gore, 1882	1.18
15	George Gore, 1881	1.18

1893-1919

1	Billy Hamilton, 1894	1.49
2	Billy Hamilton, 1895	1.35
3	Billy Hamilton, 1893	1.34
4	Herman Long, 1894	1.31
5	Ed Delahanty, 1894	1.29
6	Ed Delahanty, 1895	1.28
7	Hugh Duffy, 1894	1.28
8	Willie Keeler, 1894	1.28
	Joe Kelley, 1894	1.28
10	John McGraw, 1894	1.26
11	Willie Keeler, 1895	1.24
12	Bill Dahlen, 1894	1.23
13	Jimmy Ryan, 1894	1.22
14	Willie Keeler, 1896	1.21
15	Hughie Jennings, 1895	1.21

1920-1941

1	Babe Ruth, 1921	1.16
2	Babe Ruth, 1920	1.11
3	Al Simmons, 1930	1.10
4	Lou Gehrig, 1936	1.08
5	Babe Ruth, 1928	1.06
6	Lou Gehrig, 1931	1.05
7	Jimmie Foxx, 1939	1.05
8	Babe Ruth, 1927	1.05
9	Babe Ruth, 1930	1.03
10	Babe Ruth, 1931	1.03
11	Chuck Klein, 1930	1.01
12	Rogers Hornsby, 1929	1.00
	Joe DiMaggio, 1937	1.00
14	Kiki Cuyler, 1930	.99
15	Babe Ruth, 1923	.99

1942-1960

1	Ted Williams, 1949	.97
2	Ted Williams, 1946	.95
3	Tommy Henrich, 1948	.95
4	Ted Williams, 1942	.94
5	Dom DiMaggio, 1950	.93
6	Ted Williams, 1948	.91
7	Johnny Mize, 1947	.89
8	Eddie Joost, 1949	.89
9	Mickey Mantle, 1954	.88
10	Johnny Pesky, 1950	.88
11	Mickey Mantle, 1956	.88
12	Stan Musial, 1948	.87
13	Goody Rosen, 1945	.87
	Dom DiMaggio, 1949	.87
15	Johnny Pesky, 1948	.87

1961-1976

1	Mickey Mantle, 1961	.86
2	Bobby Bonds, 1970	.85
3	Billy Williams, 1970	.85
4	Willie Mays, 1961	.84
5	Frank Robinson, 1962	.83
6	Roger Maris, 1961	.82
7	Joe Morgan, 1972	.82
8	Bobby Bonds, 1973	.82
9	Hank Aaron, 1962	.81
10	Don Buford, 1971	.81
11	Reggie Jackson, 1969	.81
12	Jim Wynn, 1972	.81
13	Lou Brock, 1971	.80
14	Willie Mays, 1962	.80
	Pete Rose, 1976	.80

1977-1996

1	Rickey Henderson, 1985	1.02
2	Paul Molitor, 1987	.97
3	Alex Rodriguez, 1996	.97
4	Jeff Bagwell, 1994	.95
5	Frank Thomas, 1994	.94
6	Kenny Lofton, 1994	.94
7	Eric Davis, 1987	.93
8	Chuck Knoblauch, 1996	.92
9	Ellis Burks, 1996	.91
10	Ken Griffey Jr., 1996	.89
11	Lenny Dykstra, 1993	.89
12	Tim Raines, 1987	.88
13	Rickey Henderson, 1990	.88
14	Marquis Grissom, 1994	.87
15	Craig Biggio, 1995	.87

Hits

1	George Sisler, 1920	257
2	Lefty O'Doul, 1929	254
	Bill Terry, 1930	254
4	Al Simmons, 1925	253
5	Rogers Hornsby, 1922	250
	Chuck Klein, 1930	250
7	Ty Cobb, 1911	248
8	George Sisler, 1922	246
9	Heinie Manush, 1928	241
	Babe Herman, 1930	241
11	Jesse Burkett, 1896	240
	Wade Boggs, 1985	240
13	Willie Keeler, 1897	239
	Rod Carew, 1977	239
15	Ed Delahanty, 1899	238
	Don Mattingly, 1986	238
17	Hugh Duffy, 1894	237
	Harry Heilmann, 1921	237
	Paul Waner, 1927	237
	Joe Medwick, 1937	237
21	Jack Tobin, 1921	236
22	Rogers Hornsby, 1921	235
23	Lloyd Waner, 1929	234
	Kirby Puckett, 1988	234
25	Joe Jackson, 1911	233
26	Nap Lajoie, 1901	232
	Earl Averill, 1936	232
28	Earle Combs, 1927	231
	Freddy Lindstrom, 1928	231
	Freddy Lindstrom, 1930	231
	Matty Alou, 1969	231
32	Stan Musial, 1948	230
	Tommy Davis, 1962	230
	Joe Torre, 1971	230
	Pete Rose, 1973	230
	Willie Wilson, 1980	230
37	Rogers Hornsby, 1929	229
38	Kiki Cuyler, 1930	228
	Stan Musial, 1946	228
40	Nap Lajoie, 1910	227
	Rogers Hornsby, 1924	227
	Jim Bottomley, 1925	227
	Sam Rice, 1925	227
	Billy Herman, 1935	227
	Charlie Gehringer, 1936	227
	Lance Johnson, 1996	227
47	Jesse Burkett, 1901	226
	Joe Jackson, 1912	226
	Ty Cobb, 1912	226
	Bill Terry, 1929	226
	Chuck Klein, 1932	226
52	Tip O'Neill, 1887	225
	Jesse Burkett, 1895	225
	Ty Cobb, 1917	225
	Harry Heilmann, 1925	225
	Johnny Hodapp, 1930	225
	Bill Terry, 1932	225
	Paul Molitor, 1996	225
59	Eddie Collins, 1920	224
	George Sisler, 1925	224
	Joe Medwick, 1935	224
	Tommy Holmes, 1945	224
63	Frankie Frisch, 1923	223
	Lloyd Waner, 1927	223
	Paul Waner, 1928	223
	Chuck Klein, 1933	223
	Joe Medwick, 1936	223
	Hank Aaron, 1959	223
	Kirby Puckett, 1986	223
70	Sam Thompson, 1893	222
	Tris Speaker, 1912	222
	Charlie Jamieson, 1923	222
73	Jesse Burkett, 1899	221
	Zack Wheat, 1925	221
	Lloyd Waner, 1928	221
	Heinie Manush, 1933	221
	Richie Ashburn, 1951	221
78	Pete Browning, 1887	220
	Billy Hamilton, 1894	220
	Kiki Cuyler, 1925	220
	Lou Gehrig, 1930	220
	Stan Musial, 1943	220
83	Ed Delahanty, 1893	219
	Willie Keeler, 1894	219
	Jimmy Williams, 1899	219
	Cy Seymour, 1905	219
	Chuck Klein, 1929	219
	Lefty O'Doul, 1932	219
	Paul Waner, 1937	219
	Ralph Garr, 1971	219
	Cecil Cooper, 1980	219
92	12 players tied	218

Doubles

1	Earl Webb, 1931	67
2	George Burns, 1926	64
	Joe Medwick, 1936	64
4	Hank Greenberg, 1934	63
5	Paul Waner, 1932	62
6	Charlie Gehringer, 1936	60
7	Tris Speaker, 1923	59
	Chuck Klein, 1930	59
9	Billy Herman, 1935	57
	Billy Herman, 1936	57
11	Joe Medwick, 1937	56
	George Kell, 1950	56
13	Ed Delahanty, 1899	55
	Gee Walker, 1936	55
15	Hal McRae, 1977	54
	John Olerud, 1993	54
	Alex Rodriguez, 1996	54
18	Tris Speaker, 1912	53
	Al Simmons, 1926	53
	Paul Waner, 1936	53
	Stan Musial, 1953	53
	Don Mattingly, 1986	53
23	Tip O'Neill, 1887	52
	Tris Speaker, 1921	52
	Tris Speaker, 1926	52
	Lou Gehrig, 1927	52
	Johnny Frederick, 1929	52
	Enos Slaughter, 1939	52
	Albert Belle, 1995	52
	Edgar Martinez, 1995	52
	Edgar Martinez, 1996	52
32	Hugh Duffy, 1894	51
	Nap Lajoie, 1910	51
	Baby Doll Jacobson, 1926	51
	George Burns, 1927	51
	Johnny Hodapp, 1930	51
	Beau Bell, 1937	51
	Joe Cronin, 1938	51
	Stan Musial, 1944	51
	Mickey Vernon, 1946	51
	Frank Robinson, 1962	51
	Pete Rose, 1978	51
	Wade Boggs, 1989	51
	Mark Grace, 1995	51
45	Tris Speaker, 1920	50
	Harry Heilmann, 1927	50
	Paul Waner, 1928	50
	Kiki Cuyler, 1930	50
	Chuck Klein, 1932	50
	Charlie Gehringer, 1934	50
	Odell Hale, 1936	50
	Ben Chapman, 1936	50
	Hank Greenberg, 1940	50
	Stan Musial, 1946	50
	Stan Spence, 1946	50
56	Ned Williamson, 1883	49
	Ed Delahanty, 1895	49
	Nap Lajoie, 1904	49
	George Sisler, 1920	49
	Heinie Manush, 1930	49
	Riggs Stephenson, 1932	49
	Hank Greenberg, 1937	49
	Robin Yount, 1980	49
	Rafael Palmeiro, 1991	49
65	Joe Kelley, 1894	48
	Nap Lajoie, 1901	48
	Nap Lajoie, 1906	48
	Tris Speaker, 1922	48
	Joe Sewell, 1927	48
	Babe Herman, 1930	48
	Dick Bartell, 1932	48
	Earl Averill, 1934	48
	Wally Moses, 1937	48
	Joe Medwick, 1939	48
	Stan Musial, 1943	48
	Keith Hernandez, 1979	48
	Don Mattingly, 1985	48
	Jeff Bagwell, 1996	48
79	25 players tied	47

Triples

1	Chief Wilson, 1912	36
2	Dave Orr, 1886	31
	Heinie Reitz, 1894	31
4	Perry Werden, 1893	29
5	Harry Davis, 1897	28
6	George Davis, 1893	27
	Sam Thompson, 1894	27
	Jimmy Williams, 1899	27
9	John Reilly, 1890	26
	George Treadway, 1894	26
	Joe Jackson, 1912	26
	Sam Crawford, 1914	26
	Kiki Cuyler, 1925	26
14	Roger Connor, 1894	25
	Buck Freeman, 1899	25
	Sam Crawford, 1903	25
	Larry Doyle, 1911	25
	Tom Long, 1915	25
19	Ed McKean, 1893	24
	Ty Cobb, 1911	24
	Ty Cobb, 1917	24
22	Harry Stovey, 1884	23
	Sam Thompson, 1887	23
	Elmer Smith, 1893	23
	Dan Brouthers, 1894	23
	Nap Lajoie, 1897	23
	Ty Cobb, 1912	23
	Sam Crawford, 1913	23
	Earle Combs, 1927	23
	Adam Comorosky, 1930	23
	Dale Mitchell, 1949	23
32	Roger Connor, 1887	22
	Bid McPhee, 1890	22
	Jake Beckley, 1890	22
	Joe Visner, 1890	22
	Willie Keeler, 1894	22
	Kip Selbach, 1895	22
	John Anderson, 1898	22
	Honus Wagner, 1900	22
	Tommy Leach, 1902	22
	Sam Crawford, 1902	22
	Bill Bradley, 1903	22
	Elmer Flick, 1906	22
	Mike Mitchell, 1911	22
	Birdie Cree, 1911	22
	Tris Speaker, 1913	22
	Hy Myers, 1920	22
	Jake Daubert, 1922	22
	Paul Waner, 1926	22
	Earle Combs, 1930	22
	Snuffy Stirnweiss, 1945	22
52	Dave Orr, 1885	21
	Mike Tiernan, 1890	21
	Billy Shindle, 1890	21
	Tom Brown, 1891	21
	Ed Delahanty, 1892	21
	Sam Thompson, 1895	21
	Mike Tiernan, 1895	21
	Tom McCreery, 1896	21
	George Van Haltren, 1896	21
	Bobby Wallace, 1897	21
	Jimmy Williams, 1901	21
	Bill Keister, 1901	21
	Jimmy Williams, 1902	21
	Cy Seymour, 1905	21
	Frank Schulte, 1911	21
	Frank Baker, 1912	21
	Sam Crawford, 1912	21
	Vic Saier, 1913	21
	Joe Jackson, 1916	21
	Edd Roush, 1924	21
	Earle Combs, 1928	21
	Willie Wilson, 1985	21
	Lance Johnson, 1996	21
75	36 players tied	20

Triples (by era)

1876-1892

1	Dave Orr, 1886	31
2	John Reilly, 1890	26
3	Harry Stovey, 1884	23
	Sam Thompson, 1887	23
5	Roger Connor, 1887	22
	Bid McPhee, 1890	22
	Jake Beckley, 1890	22
	Joe Visner, 1890	22
9	Dave Orr, 1885	21
	Mike Tiernan, 1890	21
	Billy Shindle, 1890	21
	Tom Brown, 1891	21
	Ed Delahanty, 1892	21
14	10 players tied	20

1893-1919

1	Chief Wilson, 1912	36
2	Heinie Reitz, 1894	31
3	Perry Werden, 1893	29
4	Harry Davis, 1897	28
5	George Davis, 1893	27
	Sam Thompson, 1894	27
	Jimmy Williams, 1899	27
8	George Treadway, 1894	26
	Joe Jackson, 1912	26
	Sam Crawford, 1914	26
11	Roger Connor, 1894	25
	Buck Freeman, 1899	25
	Sam Crawford, 1903	25
	Larry Doyle, 1911	25
	Tom Long, 1915	25

1920-1941

1	Kiki Cuyler, 1925	26
2	Earle Combs, 1927	23
	Adam Comorosky, 1930	23
4	Hy Myers, 1920	22
	Jake Daubert, 1922	22
	Paul Waner, 1926	22
	Earle Combs, 1930	22
8	Edd Roush, 1924	21
	Earle Combs, 1928	21
10	12 players tied	20

1942-1960

1	Dale Mitchell, 1949	23
2	Snuffy Stirnweiss, 1945	22
3	Stan Musial, 1943	20
	Stan Musial, 1946	20
	Willie Mays, 1957	20
6	Johnny Barrett, 1944	19
7	Stan Musial, 1948	18
	Minnie Minoso, 1954	18
9	Enos Slaughter, 1942	17
	Jim Gilliam, 1953	17
11	6 players tied	16

1961-1976

1	Ralph Garr, 1974	17
2	Johnny Callison, 1965	16
	Willie Davis, 1970	16
4	Gino Cimoli, 1962	15
5	Jake Wood, 1961	14
	Vada Pinson, 1963	14
	Dick Allen, 1965	14
	Roberto Clemente, 1965	14
	Donn Clendenon, 1965	14
	Lou Brock, 1968	14
	Don Kessinger, 1970	14
	Roger Metzger, 1973	14
	George Brett, 1976	14
14	10 players tied	13

1977-1996

1	Willie Wilson, 1985	21
	Lance Johnson, 1996	21
3	George Brett, 1979	20
4	Garry Templeton, 1979	19
	Juan Samuel, 1984	19
	Ryne Sandberg, 1984	19
7	Garry Templeton, 1977	18
	Willie McGee, 1985	18
9	Tony Fernandez, 1990	17
10	Rod Carew, 1977	16
	Paul Molitor, 1979	16
12	11 players tied	15

Home Runs

1	Roger Maris, 1961	61
2	Babe Ruth, 1927	60
3	Babe Ruth, 1921	59
4	Jimmie Foxx, 1932	58
	Hank Greenberg, 1938	58
6	Hack Wilson, 1930	56
7	Babe Ruth, 1920	54
	Babe Ruth, 1928	54
	Ralph Kiner, 1949	54
	Mickey Mantle, 1961	54
11	Mickey Mantle, 1956	52
	Willie Mays, 1965	52
	George Foster, 1977	52
	Mark McGwire, 1996	52
15	Ralph Kiner, 1947	51
	Johnny Mize, 1947	51
	Willie Mays, 1955	51
	Cecil Fielder, 1990	51
19	Jimmie Foxx, 1938	50
	Albert Belle, 1995	50
	Brady Anderson, 1996	50
22	Babe Ruth, 1930	49
	Lou Gehrig, 1934	49
	Lou Gehrig, 1936	49
	Ted Kluszewski, 1954	49
	Willie Mays, 1962	49
	Harmon Killebrew, 1964	49
	Frank Robinson, 1966	49
	Harmon Killebrew, 1969	49
	Andre Dawson, 1987	49
	Mark McGwire, 1987	49
	Ken Griffey, Jr., 1996	49
33	Jimmie Foxx, 1933	48
	Harmon Killebrew, 1962	48
	Frank Howard, 1969	48
	Willie Stargell, 1971	48
	Dave Kingman, 1979	48
	Mike Schmidt, 1980	48
	Albert Belle, 1996	48
40	Babe Ruth, 1926	47
	Lou Gehrig, 1927	47
	Ralph Kiner, 1950	47
	Eddie Mathews, 1953	47
	Ted Kluszewski, 1955	47
	Ernie Banks, 1958	47
	Willie Mays, 1964	47
	Reggie Jackson, 1969	47
	Hank Aaron, 1971	47
	George Bell, 1987	47
	Kevin Mitchell, 1989	47
	Andres Galarraga, 1996	47
	Juan Gonzalez, 1996	47
53	Babe Ruth, 1924	46
	Babe Ruth, 1929	46
	Babe Ruth, 1931	46
	Lou Gehrig, 1931	46
	Joe DiMaggio, 1937	46
	Eddie Mathews, 1959	46
	Orlando Cepeda, 1961	46
	Jim Gentile, 1961	46
	Harmon Killebrew, 1961	46
	Jim Rice, 1978	46
	Barry Bonds, 1993	46
	Juan Gonzalez, 1993	46
65	Ernie Banks, 1959	45
	Rocky Colavito, 1961	45
	Hank Aaron, 1962	45
	Harmon Killebrew, 1963	45
	Willie McCovey, 1969	45
	Johnny Bench, 1970	45
	Mike Schmidt, 1979	45
	Gorman Thomas, 1979	45
	Ken Griffey Jr., 1993	45
74	Jimmie Foxx, 1934	44
	Hank Greenberg, 1946	44
	Ernie Banks, 1955	44
	Hank Aaron, 1957	44
	Hank Aaron, 1963	44
	Willie McCovey, 1963	44
	Hank Aaron, 1966	44
	Harmon Killebrew, 1967	44
	Carl Yastrzemski, 1967	44
	Frank Howard, 1968	44
	Hank Aaron, 1969	44
	Frank Howard, 1970	44
	Willie Stargell, 1973	44
	Dale Murphy, 1987	44
	Jose Canseco, 1991	44
	Cecil Fielder, 1991	44
	Jay Buhner, 1996	44
	Mo Vaughn, 1996	44
92	10 players tied	43

Home Runs (by era)

1876-1892

1	Ned Williamson, 1884	27
2	Fred Pfeffer, 1884	25
3	Abner Dalrymple, 1884	22
4	Cap Anson, 1884	21
5	Sam Thompson, 1889	20
6	Billy O'Brien, 1887	19
	Bug Holliday, 1889	19
	Harry Stovey, 1889	19
9	Jerry Denny, 1889	18
10	Roger Connor, 1887	17
	Jimmy Ryan, 1889	17
12	5 players tied	16

1893-1919

1	Babe Ruth, 1919	29
2	Buck Freeman, 1899	25
3	Gavvy Cravath, 1915	24
4	Frank Schulte, 1911	21
5	Ed Delahanty, 1893	19
	Gavvy Cravath, 1913	19
	Gavvy Cravath, 1914	19
8	Hugh Duffy, 1894	18
	Sam Thompson, 1895	18
	Fred Luderus, 1913	18
	Vic Saier, 1914	18
12	5 players tied	17

1920-1941

1	Babe Ruth, 1927	60
2	Babe Ruth, 1921	59
3	Jimmie Foxx, 1932	58
	Hank Greenberg, 1938	58
5	Hack Wilson, 1930	56
6	Babe Ruth, 1920	54
	Babe Ruth, 1928	54
8	Jimmie Foxx, 1938	50
9	Babe Ruth, 1930	49
	Lou Gehrig, 1934	49
	Lou Gehrig, 1936	49
12	Jimmie Foxx, 1933	48
13	Babe Ruth, 1926	47
	Lou Gehrig, 1927	47
15	5 players tied	46

1942-1960

1	Ralph Kiner, 1949	54
2	Mickey Mantle, 1956	52
3	Ralph Kiner, 1947	51
	Johnny Mize, 1947	51
	Willie Mays, 1955	51
6	Ted Kluszewski, 1954	49
7	Ralph Kiner, 1950	47
	Eddie Mathews, 1953	47
	Ted Kluszewski, 1955	47
	Ernie Banks, 1958	47
11	Eddie Mathews, 1959	46
12	Ernie Banks, 1959	45
13	Hank Greenberg, 1946	44
	Ernie Banks, 1955	44
	Hank Aaron, 1957	44

1961-1976

1	Roger Maris, 1961	61
2	Mickey Mantle, 1961	54
3	Willie Mays, 1965	52
4	Willie Mays, 1962	49
	Harmon Killebrew, 1964	49
	Frank Robinson, 1966	49
	Harmon Killebrew, 1969	49
8	Harmon Killebrew, 1962	48
	Frank Howard, 1969	48
	Willie Stargell, 1971	48
11	Willie Mays, 1964	47
	Reggie Jackson, 1969	47
	Hank Aaron, 1971	47
14	3 players tied	46

1977-1996

1	George Foster, 1977	52
	Mark McGwire, 1996	52
3	Cecil Fielder, 1990	51
4	Albert Belle, 1995	50
	Brady Anderson, 1996	50
6	Andre Dawson, 1987	49
	Mark McGwire, 1987	49
	Ken Griffey Jr., 1996	49
9	Dave Kingman, 1979	48
	Mike Schmidt, 1980	48
	Albert Belle, 1996	48
12	George Bell, 1987	47
	Kevin Mitchell, 1989	47
	Andres Galarraga, 1996	47
	Juan Gonzalez, 1996	47

Home Run Percentage

1	Mark McGwire, 1996	12.29
2	Babe Ruth, 1920	11.79
3	Babe Ruth, 1927	11.11
4	Babe Ruth, 1921	10.93
5	Mickey Mantle, 1961	10.51
6	Hank Greenberg, 1938	10.43
7	Roger Maris, 1961	10.34
8	Babe Ruth, 1928	10.07
9	Jimmie Foxx, 1932	9.91
10	Ralph Kiner, 1949	9.84
11	Mickey Mantle, 1956	9.76
12	Jeff Bagwell, 1994	9.75
13	Kevin Mitchell, 1994	9.68
14	Matt Williams, 1994	9.66
15	Hack Wilson, 1930	9.57
16	Frank Thomas, 1994	9.52
17	Babe Ruth, 1926	9.49
	Hank Aaron, 1971	9.49
19	Jim Gentile, 1961	9.47
20	Barry Bonds, 1994	9.46
21	Babe Ruth, 1930	9.46
22	Willie Stargell, 1971	9.39
23	Willie Mays, 1965	9.32
24	Ken Griffey, Jr. 1994	9.24
25	Babe Ruth, 1929	9.22
26	Boog Powell, 1964	9.20
27	Willie McCovey, 1969	9.16
28	Albert Belle, 1995	9.16
29	Ted Williams, 1957	9.05
30	Ralph Kiner, 1947	9.03
31	Dave Kingman, 1979	9.02
32	Mark McGwire, 1992	8.99
33	Ken Griffey Jr., 1996	8.99
34	Babe Ruth, 1932	8.97
35	Cecil Fielder, 1990	8.90
36	Jimmie Foxx, 1938	8.85
37	Harmon Killebrew, 1969	8.83
38	Mark McGwire, 1987	8.80
39	Willie Mays, 1955	8.79
40	Mike Schmidt, 1980	8.76
41	Mike Schmidt, 1981	8.76
42	Harmon Killebrew, 1963	8.74
	Albert Belle, 1994	8.74
44	Johnny Mize, 1947	8.70
45	Babe Ruth, 1924	8.70
	Harmon Killebrew, 1962	8.70
47	Juan Gonzalez, 1996	8.69
48	Kevin Mitchell, 1989	8.66
49	Brady Anderson, 1996	8.64
50	Babe Ruth, 1922	8.62
51	Babe Ruth, 1931	8.61
52	Ralph Kiner, 1950	8.59
53	Juan Gonzalez, 1993	8.58
54	Reggie Jackson, 1969	8.56
55	Ted Kluszewski, 1954	8.55
56	Barry Bonds, 1993	8.53
57	Jay Buhner, 1995	8.51
58	Frank Robinson, 1966	8.51
59	Harmon Killebrew, 1961	8.50
60	Harmon Killebrew, 1964	8.49
61	Lou Gehrig, 1934	8.46
	Lou Gehrig, 1936	8.46
63	George Foster, 1977	8.46
64	Willie Stargell, 1973	8.43
65	Hank Greenberg, 1946	8.41
66	Eddie Mathews, 1954	8.40
67	Gary Sheffield, 1996	8.39
68	Rocky Colavito, 1958	8.38
69	Jimmie Foxx, 1933	8.38
70	Joe Adcock, 1956	8.37
71	Jack Clark, 1987	8.35
72	Mike Schmidt, 1979	8.32
73	Eddie Mathews, 1955	8.22
74	Jimmie Foxx, 1934	8.16
75	Willie Mays, 1964	8.13
76	Barry Bonds, 1996	8.12
77	Eddie Mathews, 1953	8.12
78	Ted Williams, 1941	8.11
79	Frank Thomas, 1995	8.11
80	Frank Howard, 1969	8.11
81	Mickey Mantle, 1958	8.09
	Gary Sheffield, 1996	8.09
83	Gorman Thomas, 1979	8.08
84	Lou Gehrig, 1927	8.05
85	Harmon Killebrew, 1967	8.04
	Hank Aaron, 1969	8.04
87	Sammy Sosa, 1996	8.03
88	Fred McGriff, 1994	8.02
89	Reggie Jackson, 1980	7.98
90	Albert Belle, 1996	7.97
91	Mickey Mantle, 1962	7.96
92	Greg Vaughn, 1996	7.95
93	Duke Snider, 1956	7.93
94	Darrell Evans, 1985	7.92
95	Ralph Kiner, 1951	7.91
96	Roy Campanella, 1953	7.90
97	Willie Mays, 1962	7.89
	Andre Dawson, 1987	7.89
99	Hank Sauer, 1954	7.88
100	Willie McCovey, 1970	7.88

Home Run Pctg.(by era)

1876-1892

1	Ned Williamson, 1884	6.47
2	Fred Pfeffer, 1884	5.35
3	Cap Anson, 1884	4.42
4	Abner Dalrymple, 1884	4.22
5	Billy O'Brien, 1887	4.19
6	Sam Thompson, 1889	3.75
7	Roger Connor, 1887	3.61
8	Dan Brouthers, 1884	3.52
9	Harry Stovey, 1889	3.42
10	Bug Holliday, 1889	3.37
11	Fred Pfeffer, 1887	3.34
12	Harry Stovey, 1883	3.33
13	Charlie Duffee, 1889	3.14
14	Jerry Denny, 1889	3.11
15	Dan Brouthers, 1881	2.96

1893-1919

1	Babe Ruth, 1919	6.71
2	Bill Joyce, 1894	4.79
3	Gavvy Cravath, 1915	4.60
4	Jack Clements, 1893	4.52
5	Buck Freeman, 1899	4.25
6	Gavvy Cravath, 1914	3.81
7	Jim Canavan, 1894	3.65
8	Frank Schulte, 1911	3.64
9	Gavvy Cravath, 1913	3.62
10	Bill Joyce, 1895	3.59
11	Sherry Magee, 1911	3.37
12	Vic Saier, 1914	3.35
13	Sam Thompson, 1895	3.35
14	Hugh Duffy, 1894	3.34
15	Ed Delahanty, 1893	3.19

1920-1941

1	Babe Ruth, 1920	11.79
2	Babe Ruth, 1927	11.11
3	Babe Ruth, 1921	10.93
4	Hank Greenberg, 1938	10.43
5	Babe Ruth, 1928	10.07
6	Jimmie Foxx, 1932	9.91
7	Hack Wilson, 1930	9.57
8	Babe Ruth, 1926	9.49
9	Babe Ruth, 1930	9.46
10	Babe Ruth, 1929	9.22
11	Babe Ruth, 1932	8.97
12	Jimmie Foxx, 1938	8.85
13	Babe Ruth, 1924	8.70
14	Babe Ruth, 1922	8.62
15	Babe Ruth, 1931	8.61

1942-1960

1	Ralph Kiner, 1949	9.84
2	Mickey Mantle, 1956	9.76
3	Ted Williams, 1957	9.05
4	Ralph Kiner, 1947	9.03
5	Willie Mays, 1955	8.79
6	Johnny Mize, 1947	8.70
7	Ralph Kiner, 1950	8.59
8	Ted Kluszewski, 1954	8.55
9	Hank Greenberg, 1946	8.41
10	Eddie Mathews, 1954	8.40
11	Rocky Colavito, 1958	8.38
12	Joe Adcock, 1956	8.37
13	Eddie Mathews, 1955	8.22
14	Eddie Mathews, 1953	8.12
15	Mickey Mantle, 1958	8.09

1961-1976

1	Mickey Mantle, 1961	10.51
2	Roger Maris, 1961	10.34
3	Hank Aaron, 1971	9.49
4	Jim Gentile, 1961	9.47
5	Willie Stargell, 1971	9.39
6	Willie Mays, 1965	9.32
7	Boog Powell, 1964	9.20
8	Willie McCovey, 1969	9.16
9	Harmon Killebrew, 1969	8.83
10	Harmon Killebrew, 1963	8.74
11	Harmon Killebrew, 1962	8.70
12	Reggie Jackson, 1969	8.56
13	Frank Robinson, 1966	8.51
14	Harmon Killebrew, 1961	8.50
15	Harmon Killebrew, 1964	8.49

1977-1996

1	Mark McGwire, 1996	12.29
2	Jeff Bagwell, 1994	9.75
3	Kevin Mitchell, 1994	9.68
4	Matt Williams, 1994	9.66
5	Frank Thomas, 1994	9.52
6	Barry Bonds, 1994	9.46
7	Ken Griffey Jr., 1994	9.24
8	Albert Belle, 1995	9.16
9	Dave Kingman, 1979	9.02
10	Mark McGwire, 1992	8.99
11	Ken Griffey Jr., 1996	8.99
12	Cecil Fielder, 1990	8.90
13	Mark McGwire, 1987	8.80
14	Mike Schmidt, 1980	8.76
15	Mike Schmidt, 1981	8.76

Total Bases

1	Babe Ruth, 1921	457
2	Rogers Hornsby, 1922	450
3	Lou Gehrig, 1927	447
4	Chuck Klein, 1930	445
5	Jimmie Foxx, 1932	438
6	Stan Musial, 1948	429
7	Hack Wilson, 1930	423
8	Chuck Klein, 1932	420
9	Lou Gehrig, 1930	419
10	Joe DiMaggio, 1937	418
11	Babe Ruth, 1927	417
12	Babe Herman, 1930	416
13	Lou Gehrig, 1931	410
14	Rogers Hornsby, 1929	409
	Lou Gehrig, 1934	409
16	Joe Medwick, 1937	406
	Jim Rice, 1978	406
18	Chuck Klein, 1929	405
	Hal Trosky, 1936	405
20	Jimmie Foxx, 1933	403
	Lou Gehrig, 1936	403
22	Hank Aaron, 1959	400
23	George Sisler, 1920	399
	Babe Ruth, 1923	399
25	Jimmie Foxx, 1938	398
26	Lefty O'Doul, 1929	397
	Hank Greenberg, 1937	397
28	Al Simmons, 1925	392
	Bill Terry, 1930	392
	Al Simmons, 1930	392
	Ellis Burks, 1996	392
32	Babe Ruth, 1924	391
33	Hank Greenberg, 1935	389
34	Babe Ruth, 1920	388
	George Foster, 1977	388
	Don Mattingly, 1986	388
37	Earl Averill, 1936	385
38	Hank Greenberg, 1940	384
39	Stan Musial, 1949	382
	Willie Mays, 1955	382
	Willie Mays, 1962	382
	Jim Rice, 1977	382
43	Rogers Hornsby, 1925	381
44	Babe Ruth, 1928	380
	Hank Greenberg, 1938	380
	Frank Robinson, 1962	380
47	Babe Ruth, 1930	379
	Ernie Banks, 1958	379
	Alex Rodriguez, 1996	379
50	Rogers Hornsby, 1921	378
	Duke Snider, 1954	378
52	Willie Mays, 1954	377
	Albert Belle, 1995	377
54	Mickey Mantle, 1956	376
	Andres Galarraga, 1996	376
56	Albert Belle, 1996	375
57	Hugh Duffy, 1894	374
	Babe Ruth, 1931	374
	Hal Trosky, 1934	374
	Tony Oliva, 1964	374
61	Rogers Hornsby, 1924	373
	Al Simmons, 1929	373
	Bill Terry, 1932	373
	Billy Williams, 1970	373
65	Lou Gehrig, 1932	370
	Duke Snider, 1953	370
	Hank Aaron, 1963	370
	Don Mattingly, 1985	370
	Mo Vaughn, 1996	370
70	Kiki Cuyler, 1925	369
	Ripper Collins, 1934	369
	Jimmie Foxx, 1936	369
	Hank Aaron, 1957	369
	Jim Rice, 1979	369
	George Bell, 1987	369
	Brady Anderson, 1996	369
77	Johnny Mize, 1940	368
	Ted Williams, 1949	368
	Ted Kluszewski, 1954	368
	Cal Ripken, 1991	368
81	Ty Cobb, 1911	367
	Ken Williams, 1922	367
	Heinie Manush, 1928	367
	Al Simmons, 1932	367
	Joe Medwick, 1936	367
	Joe DiMaggio, 1936	367
	Tommy Holmes, 1945	367
	Al Rosen, 1953	367
	Frank Robinson, 1966	367
	Robin Yount, 1982	367
91	Lou Gehrig, 1937	366
	Stan Musial, 1946	366
	Willie Mays, 1957	366
	Roger Maris, 1961	366
	Hank Aaron, 1962	366
96	6 players tied	365

Runs Batted In

1	Hack Wilson, 1930	190
2	Lou Gehrig, 1931	184
3	Hank Greenberg, 1937	183
4	Lou Gehrig, 1927	175
	Jimmie Foxx, 1938	175
6	Lou Gehrig, 1930	174
7	Babe Ruth, 1921	171
8	Chuck Klein, 1930	170
	Hank Greenberg, 1935	170
10	Jimmie Foxx, 1932	169
11	Joe DiMaggio, 1937	167
12	Sam Thompson, 1887	166
13	Sam Thompson, 1895	165
	Al Simmons, 1930	165
	Lou Gehrig, 1934	165
16	Babe Ruth, 1927	164
17	Babe Ruth, 1931	163
	Jimmie Foxx, 1933	163
19	Hal Trosky, 1936	162
20	Hack Wilson, 1929	159
	Lou Gehrig, 1937	159
	Ted Williams, 1949	159
	Vern Stephens, 1949	159
24	Al Simmons, 1929	157
25	Jimmie Foxx, 1930	156
26	Ken Williams, 1922	155
	Joe DiMaggio, 1948	155
28	Babe Ruth, 1929	154
	Joe Medwick, 1937	154
30	Babe Ruth, 1930	153
	Tommy Davis, 1962	153
32	Rogers Hornsby, 1922	152
	Lou Gehrig, 1936	152
34	Mel Ott, 1929	151
	Lou Gehrig, 1932	151
	Al Simmons, 1932	151
37	Hank Greenberg, 1940	150
	Andres Galarraga, 1996	150
39	Rogers Hornsby, 1929	149
	George Foster, 1977	149
41	Johnny Bench, 1970	148
	Albert Belle, 1996	148
43	Cap Anson, 1886	147
44	Hardy Richardson, 1890	146
	Ed Delahanty, 1893	146
	Babe Ruth, 1926	146
	Hank Greenberg, 1938	146
48	Hugh Duffy, 1894	145
	Chuck Klein, 1929	145
	Ted Williams, 1939	145
	Al Rosen, 1953	145
	Don Mattingly, 1985	145
53	Walt Dropo, 1950	144
	Vern Stephens, 1950	144
	Juan Gonzalez, 1996	144
56	Rogers Hornsby, 1925	143
	Earl Averill, 1931	143
	Don Hurst, 1932	143
	Jimmie Foxx, 1936	143
	Ernie Banks, 1959	143
	Mo Vaughn, 1996	143
62	Lou Gehrig, 1928	142
	Babe Ruth, 1928	142
	Hal Trosky, 1934	142
	Roy Campanella, 1953	142
	Orlando Cepeda, 1961	142
	Roger Maris, 1961	142
	Rafael Palmeiro, 1996	142
69	Sam Thompson, 1894	141
	Ted Kluszewski, 1954	141
	Jim Gentile, 1961	141
	Willie Mays, 1962	141
	Dante Bichette, 1996	141
74	Joe DiMaggio, 1938	140
	Rocky Colavito, 1961	140
	Harmon Killebrew, 1969	140
	Ken Griffey Jr., 1996	140
78	Harry Heilmann, 1921	139
	Lou Gehrig, 1933	139
	Hank Greenberg, 1934	139
	Jim Rice, 1978	139
	Don Baylor, 1979	139
83	Bob Meusel, 1925	138
	Goose Goslin, 1930	138
	Joe Medwick, 1936	138
	Zeke Bonura, 1936	138
	Johnny Mize, 1947	138
	Jay Buhner, 1996	138
89	Ed Delahanty, 1899	137
	Babe Ruth, 1920	137
	Jim Bottomley, 1929	137
	Dale Alexander, 1929	137
	Chuck Klein, 1932	137
	Babe Ruth, 1932	137
	Johnny Mize, 1940	137
	Ted Williams, 1942	137
	Vern Stephens, 1948	137
	Joe Torre, 1971	137
	Andre Dawson, 1987	137
100	6 players tied	136

Runs Batted In per Game

1	Sam Thompson, 1894	1.42
2	Sam Thompson, 1895	1.39
3	Sam Thompson, 1887	1.31
4	Hack Wilson, 1930	1.23
5	Al Simmons, 1930	1.20
6	Hank Greenberg, 1937	1.19
7	Lou Gehrig, 1931	1.19
8	Cap Anson, 1886	1.18
9	Jimmie Foxx, 1938	1.17
10	Hugh Duffy, 1894	1.16
11	Dave Orr, 1890	1.16
12	Ed Delahanty, 1894	1.15
13	Babe Ruth, 1929	1.14
14	Lou Gehrig, 1930	1.13
15	Lou Gehrig, 1927	1.13
16	Babe Ruth, 1921	1.13
17	Babe Ruth, 1931	1.12
18	Hardy Richardson, 1890	1.12
19	Hank Greenberg, 1935	1.12
20	Ed Delahanty, 1893	1.11
21	Joe DiMaggio, 1937	1.11
22	Al Simmons, 1929	1.10
23	Jimmie Foxx, 1932	1.10
24	Jimmie Foxx, 1933	1.09
25	Chuck Klein, 1930	1.09
26	Babe Ruth, 1927	1.09
27	Oyster Burns, 1890	1.08
28	Juan Gonzalez, 1996	1.07
29	Hal Trosky, 1936	1.07
30	Lou Gehrig, 1934	1.07
31	Ed McKean, 1893	1.06
32	Hack Wilson, 1929	1.06
33	Dave Foutz, 1887	1.06
	Walt Dropo, 1950	1.06
35	Babe Ruth, 1930	1.06
36	Jeff Bagwell, 1994	1.05
37	Buck Ewing, 1893	1.05
38	Lave Cross, 1894	1.05
39	Joe DiMaggio, 1939	1.05
40	George Davis, 1897	1.05
41	Dan Brouthers, 1894	1.04
42	Kirby Puckett, 1994	1.04
43	Rogers Hornsby, 1925	1.04
44	Jim O'Rourke, 1890	1.04
45	Babe Ruth, 1932	1.03
46	Ted Williams, 1949	1.03
	Vern Stephens, 1949	1.03
48	Ed Delahanty, 1896	1.02
49	Steve Brodie, 1895	1.02
	Joe Kelley, 1895	1.02
51	Jimmie Foxx, 1930	1.02
52	Dave Orr, 1884	1.02
53	Hank Greenberg, 1940	1.01
54	Ken Williams, 1922	1.01
	Joe DiMaggio, 1948	1.01
56	Lou Gehrig, 1937	1.01
57	Cap Anson, 1882	1.01
58	George Decker, 1894	1.01
59	George Brett, 1980	1.01
60	Joe DiMaggio, 1940	1.01
61	Mel Ott, 1929	1.01
62	Nap Lajoie, 1897	1.00
	Al Simmons, 1931	1.00
	Ken Griffey Jr., 1996	1.00
65	Roger Connor, 1889	.99
66	Tommy McCarthy, 1894	.99
67	Tip O'Neill, 1887	.99
68	Jake Beckley, 1890	.99
69	Dan Brouthers, 1883	.99
70	Joe Medwick, 1937	.99
71	Rogers Hornsby, 1922	.99
72	Roy Campanella, 1953	.99
73	Jimmy Collins, 1897	.99
74	Ed McKean, 1894	.98
75	Bug Holliday, 1894	.98
76	Lou Gehrig, 1936	.98
77	Al Simmons, 1932	.98
78	Walt Wilmot, 1894	.98
79	Cap Anson, 1881	.98
80	Chuck Klein, 1929	.97
	Ted Williams, 1939	.97
82	Heinie Reitz, 1894	.97
83	Lou Gehrig, 1932	.97
84	Vern Stephens, 1950	.97
85	Joe DiMaggio, 1938	.97
86	Babe Ruth, 1920	.96
87	Cap Anson, 1885	.96
88	Hugh Duffy, 1897	.96
89	Sam Thompson, 1893	.96
90	Billy Nash, 1893	.96
91	Babe Ruth, 1926	.96
92	Jay Buhner, 1996	.96
93	Harry Heilmann, 1929	.96
94	Tommy McCarthy, 1893	.96
95	Rogers Hornsby, 1929	.96
96	Hughie Jennings, 1895	.95
	Nap Lajoie, 1901	.95
98	Don Hurst, 1932	.95
99	Albert Belle, 1994	.95
100	Jim Gentile, 1961	.95

Walks

1	Babe Ruth, 1923	170
2	Ted Williams, 1947	162
	Ted Williams, 1949	162
4	Ted Williams, 1946	156
5	Eddie Yost, 1956	151
	Barry Bonds, 1996	151
7	Eddie Joost, 1949	149
8	Babe Ruth, 1920	148
	Eddie Stanky, 1945	148
	Jim Wynn, 1969	148
11	Jimmy Sheckard, 1911	147
12	Mickey Mantle, 1957	146
13	Ted Williams, 1941	145
	Ted Williams, 1942	145
	Harmon Killebrew, 1969	145
16	Babe Ruth, 1921	144
	Babe Ruth, 1926	144
	Eddie Stanky, 1950	144
	Ted Williams, 1951	144
20	Babe Ruth, 1924	142
	Gary Sheffield, 1996	142
22	Eddie Yost, 1950	141
23	Babe Ruth, 1927	138
	Frank Thomas, 1991	138
25	Eddie Stanky, 1946	137
	Roy Cullenbine, 1947	137
	Ralph Kiner, 1951	137
	Willie McCovey, 1970	137
29	Jack Crooks, 1892	136
	Babe Ruth, 1930	136
	Ferris Fain, 1949	136
	Ted Williams, 1954	136
	Jack Clark, 1987	136
	Frank Thomas, 1995	136
35	Babe Ruth, 1928	135
	Eddie Yost, 1959	135
	Jeff Bagwell, 1996	135
38	Ferris Fain, 1950	133
39	Lou Gehrig, 1935	132
	Frank Howard, 1970	132
	Joe Morgan, 1975	132
	Jack Clark, 1989	132
	Tony Phillips, 1993	132
44	Bob Elliott, 1948	131
	Eddie Yost, 1954	131
	Harmon Killebrew, 1967	131
47	Babe Ruth, 1932	130
	Lou Gehrig, 1936	130
49	Eddie Yost, 1952	129
	Mickey Mantle, 1958	129
	Lenny Dykstra, 1993	129
52	Max Bishop, 1929	128
	Max Bishop, 1930	128
	Babe Ruth, 1931	128
	Harmon Killebrew, 1970	128
	Carl Yastrzemski, 1970	128
	Mike Schmidt, 1983	128
58	Lu Blue, 1931	127
	Lou Gehrig, 1937	127
	Eddie Stanky, 1951	127
	Jim Wynn, 1976	127
	Barry Bonds, 1992	127
63	Billy Hamilton, 1894	126
	Lu Blue, 1929	126
	Ted Williams, 1948	126
	Eddie Yost, 1951	126
	Mickey Mantle, 1961	126
	Darrell Evans, 1974	126
	Rickey Henderson, 1989	126
	Barry Bonds, 1993	126
71	Richie Ashburn, 1954	125
	Eddie Yost, 1960	125
	Gene Tenace, 1977	125
	Wade Boggs, 1988	125
	Rickey Henderson, 1996	125
	Tony Phillips, 1996	125
77	John McGraw, 1899	124
	Norm Cash, 1961	124
	Eddie Mathews, 1963	124
	Darrell Evans, 1973	124
81	Bill Joyce, 1890	123
	Eddie Yost, 1953	123
	Ken Singleton, 1973	123
	Edgar Martinez, 1996	123
	Jim Thome, 1996	123
86	Jimmy Sheckard, 1912	122
	Lou Gehrig, 1929	122
	Luke Appling, 1935	122
	Ralph Kiner, 1950	122
	Eddie Joost, 1952	122
	Mickey Mantle, 1962	122
	John Mayberry, 1973	122
	Mickey Tettleton, 1992	122
	Frank Thomas, 1992	122
95	7 players tied	121

Strikeouts

1	Bobby Bonds, 1970	189
2	Bobby Bonds, 1969	187
3	Rob Deer, 1987	186
4	Pete Incaviglia, 1986	185
5	Cecil Fielder, 1990	182
6	Mike Schmidt, 1975	180
7	Rob Deer, 1986	179
8	Dave Nicholson, 1963	175
	Gorman Thomas, 1979	175
	Jose Canseco, 1986	175
	Rob Deer, 1991	175
12	Jim Presley, 1986	172
	Bo Jackson, 1989	172
14	Reggie Jackson, 1968	171
15	Gorman Thomas, 1980	170
16	Andres Galarraga, 1990	169
	Rob Deer, 1993	169
18	Juan Samuel, 1984	168
	Pete Incaviglia, 1987	168
20	Gary Alexander, 1978	166
	Steve Balboni, 1985	166
	Cory Snyder, 1987	166
23	Donn Clendenon, 1968	163
24	Butch Hobson, 1977	162
	Juan Samuel, 1987	162
26	Dick Allen, 1968	161
	Reggie Jackson, 1971	161
28	Mickey Tettleton, 1990	160
	Henry Rodriguez, 1996	160
30	Jay Buhner, 1996	159
31	Bo Jackson, 1987	158
	Andres Galarraga, 1989	158
	Rob Deer, 1989	158
	Jose Canseco, 1990	158
	Melvin Nieves, 1996	158
36	Danny Tartabull, 1986	157
	Jose Canseco, 1987	157
	Jim Presley, 1987	157
	Andres Galarraga, 1996	157
40	Tommie Agee, 1970	156
	Dave Kingman, 1982	156
	Reggie Jackson, 1982	156
	Tony Armas, 1984	156
	Danny Tartabull, 1993	156
45	Frank Howard, 1967	155
	Jeff Burroughs, 1975	155
47	Willie Stargell, 1971	154
	Larry Parrish, 1987	154
	Dean Palmer, 1992	154
	Dean Palmer, 1993	154
	Mo Vaughn, 1996	154
52	Dave Kingman, 1975	153
	Andres Galarraga, 1988	153
	Rob Deer, 1988	153
	Pete Incaviglia, 1988	153
56	George Scott, 1966	152
	Larry Hisle, 1969	152
	Jose Canseco, 1991	152
59	Don Lock, 1963	151
	Greg Luzinski, 1975	151
	Juan Samuel, 1988	151
	Delino DeShields, 1991	151
	Cecil Fielder, 1991	151
	Cecil Fielder, 1992	151
65	Dick Allen, 1965	150
	Nate Colbert, 1970	150
	Ron Kittle, 1983	150
	Jesse Barfield, 1989	150
	Jesse Barfield, 1990	150
	Sammy Sosa, 1990	150
	Mo Vaughn, 1995	150
72	Billy Grabarkewitz, 1970	149
	Mike Schmidt, 1976	149
	Fred McGriff, 1988	149
	Travis Fryman, 1991	149
76	Bobby Bonds, 1973	148
	Mike Schmidt, 1983	148
	Gorman Thomas, 1983	148
	Roberto Kelly, 1990	148
80	Rob Deer, 1990	147
	Ray Lankford, 1992	147
	Cory Snyder, 1993	147
	Benji Gil, 1995	147
84	Deron Johnson, 1971	146
	Nate Colbert, 1973	146
	Steve Balboni, 1986	146
	Jesse Barfield, 1986	146
	Bo Jackson, 1988	146
	Pete Incaviglia, 1990	146
	Jay Buhner, 1992	146
	Andres Galarraga, 1995	146
	Todd Hundley, 1996	146
	Ed Sprague, 1996	146
94	Lee May, 1972	145
	Bobby Darwin, 1972	145
	Dale Murphy, 1978	145
	Jack Clark, 1989	145
	Dean Palmer, 1996	145
	Jose Valentin, 1996	145
100	5 players tied	144

At Bats per Strikeout

1876-1892
1	Mike McGeary, 1876	276.0
2	Cap Anson, 1878	261.0
3	John Peters, 1876	158.0
4	John Clapp, 1876	149.0
5	Joe Start, 1877	135.5
6	Joe Start, 1876	132.0
7	Levi Meyerle, 1876	128.0
8	Jim Holdsworth, 1876	120.5
9	Lon Knight, 1876	120.0
10	Ezra Sutton, 1876	118.0
11	Bobby Mathews, 1876	109.0
12	Paul Hines, 1876	101.7
13	Deacon White, 1876	101.0
14	Al Spalding, 1876	97.3
15	Davy Force, 1876	95.7

1893-1919
1	Jack Doyle, 1894	140.7
2	John Ward, 1893	117.6
3	Willie Keeler, 1894	98.3
4	Joe Quinn, 1895	90.5
5	John Ward, 1894	90.0
6	Joe Quinn, 1893	78.1
7	Lave Cross, 1894	75.6
8	Steve Brodie, 1894	71.6
9	Jack Glasscock, 1893	69.7
10	Lave Cross, 1895	66.9
11	Ed McKean, 1896	63.4
12	Dummy Hoy, 1893	62.7
13	Patsy Donovan, 1893	62.4
14	Farmer Vaughn, 1896	61.9
15	Willie Keeler, 1896	60.4

1920-1941
1	Joe Sewell, 1932	167.7
2	Joe Sewell, 1925	152.0
3	Joe Sewell, 1929	144.5
4	Joe Sewell, 1933	131.0
5	Charlie Hollocher, 1922	118.4
6	Stuffy McInnis, 1922	107.4
7	Stuffy McInnis, 1924	96.8
8	Joe Sewell, 1926	96.3
9	Joe Sewell, 1927	81.3
10	Pie Traynor, 1929	77.1
11	Sam Rice, 1929	68.4
12	Tris Speaker, 1927	65.4
13	Joe Sewell, 1928	65.3
14	Sam Rice, 1925	64.9
15	Stuffy McInnis, 1921	64.9

1942-1960
1	Tommy Holmes, 1945	70.7
2	Emil Verban, 1947	67.5
3	Lou Boudreau, 1948	62.2
4	Dale Mitchell, 1949	58.2
5	Tommy Holmes, 1944	57.4
6	Dale Mitchell, 1952	56.8
7	Nellie Fox, 1958	56.6
8	Tommy Holmes, 1942	55.8
9	Jimmy Brown, 1942	55.1
10	Nellie Fox, 1951	54.9
11	Lou Boudreau, 1947	53.8
12	Nellie Fox, 1954	52.6
13	Harvey Kuenn, 1954	50.5
14	Don Mueller, 1955	50.4
15	Yogi Berra, 1950	49.8

1961-1976
1	Nellie Fox, 1962	51.8
2	Dave Cash, 1976	51.2
3	Nellie Fox, 1961	50.5
4	Matty Alou, 1970	37.6
5	Felix Millan, 1974	37.0
6	Vic Power, 1961	35.2
7	Nellie Fox, 1964	34.0
8	Glenn Beckert, 1968	32.2
9	Nellie Fox, 1963	31.7
10	Felix Millan, 1973	29.0
11	Bobby Richardson, 1962	28.8
12	Bobby Richardson, 1961	28.8
13	Bobby Richardson, 1963	28.6
14	Felix Millan, 1976	27.9
15	Glenn Beckert, 1972	27.9

1977-1996
1	Tim Foli, 1979	38.0
2	Tony Gwynn, 1995	35.7
3	Felix Fermin, 1993	34.3
4	Tony Gwynn, 1992	32.5
5	Bill Buckner, 1980	32.1
6	Tim Foli, 1981	31.6
7	Ozzie Smith, 1993	30.3
8	Bob Bailor, 1978	29.6
9	Rich Dauer, 1980	29.3
10	Tony Gwynn, 1991	27.9
11	Tony Gwynn, 1984	26.3
12	Bill Buckner, 1981	26.3
13	Tony Gwynn, 1993	25.7
14	Bill Buckner, 1982	25.3
15	Bill Buckner, 1986	25.2

Strikeout Percentage

1876-1892
1	Frank Meinke, 1884	26.10
2	Pud Galvin, 1883	24.53
3	Sam Wise, 1884	24.41
4	Pud Galvin, 1879	21.13
5	Charlie Bastian, 1885	21.08
6	Will White, 1878	20.81
7	Silver Flint, 1883	20.78
8	John Morrill, 1884	19.86
9	John Morrill, 1885	19.80
10	Charlie Bastian, 1886	19.57
11	Jim Lillie, 1886	19.23
12	Will White, 1879	19.05
13	John Morrill, 1886	18.84
14	Sam Wise, 1883	18.23
15	Bill Crowley, 1884	18.18

1893-1919
1	Gus Williams, 1914	24.05
2	Grover Gilmore, 1914	20.38
3	Gavvy Cravath, 1916	19.87
4	Ed McDonald, 1912	19.83
5	Art Wilson, 1914	18.18
6	Gavvy Cravath, 1912	17.66
7	Cozy Dolan, 1914	17.58
8	Max Carey, 1911	17.56
9	Danny Moeller, 1913	17.49
10	Doug Baird, 1915	17.19
11	Al Boucher, 1914	17.05
12	Wally Pipp, 1915	16.91
13	Joe Agler, 1914	16.85
14	Ray Powell, 1919	16.81
15	Cy Williams, 1917	16.67

1920-1941
1	Vince DiMaggio, 1938	24.81
2	Vince DiMaggio, 1937	22.52
3	Chet Ross, 1940	22.32
4	Dolph Camilli, 1941	21.74
5	Joe Orengo, 1940	21.69
6	Jimmie Foxx, 1941	21.15
7	Boze Berger, 1935	21.04
8	Jimmie Foxx, 1936	20.34
9	Dolph Camilli, 1938	19.84
10	Babe Ruth, 1922	19.70
11	Babe Ruth, 1933	19.61
12	Jimmy Dykes, 1922	19.56
13	Hank Greenberg, 1939	19.00
14	Vince DiMaggio, 1941	18.94
15	Dolph Camilli, 1939	18.94

1942-1960
1	Pancho Herrera, 1960	26.56
2	Jim Lemon, 1956	25.65
3	Dick Stuart, 1960	24.43
4	Frank Howard, 1960	24.11
5	Harmon Killebrew, 1960	23.98
6	Jim Lemon, 1958	23.95
7	Mickey Mantle, 1960	23.72
8	Larry Doby, 1953	23.59
9	Pat Seerey, 1945	23.43
10	Mickey Mantle, 1959	23.29
11	Mickey Mantle, 1958	23.12
12	Wally Post, 1956	23.01
13	Woodie Held, 1959	22.48
14	Gil Hodges, 1959	22.28
15	Norm Zauchin, 1955	22.01

1961-1976
1	Dave Nicholson, 1963	38.98
2	Dick Allen, 1969	32.88
3	Mike Schmidt, 1975	32.03
4	Reggie Jackson, 1970	31.69
5	Larry Hisle, 1969	31.54
6	Reggie Jackson, 1968	30.92
7	Dick Allen, 1968	30.90
8	Dave Kingman, 1975	30.48
9	Willie Stargell, 1971	30.14
10	Bobby Bonds, 1969	30.06
11	Frank Howard, 1967	29.87
12	Rick Monday, 1968	29.67
13	Dave Kingman, 1972	29.66
14	Willie Mays, 1971	29.50
15	Jim Wynn, 1969	28.69

1977-1996
1	Rob Deer, 1987	39.24
2	Rob Deer, 1991	39.06
3	Rob Deer, 1986	38.41
4	Rob Deer, 1993	36.27
5	Mickey Tettleton, 1990	36.04
6	Benji Gil, 1995	35.42
7	Pete Incaviglia, 1986	34.26
8	Rob Deer, 1989	33.91
9	Rob Deer, 1990	33.41
10	Bo Jackson, 1989	33.40
11	Gary Alexander, 1978	33.33
12	Jack Clark, 1987	33.17
13	Pete Incaviglia, 1987	33.01
14	Jose Canseco, 1990	32.85
15	Jack Clark, 1989	31.87

Batting Average

1	Hugh Duffy, 1894	.440
2	Tip O'Neill, 1887	.435
3	Ross Barnes, 1876	.429
4	Nap Lajoie, 1901	.426
5	Willie Keeler, 1897	.424
6	Rogers Hornsby, 1924	.424
7	George Sisler, 1922	.420
8	Ty Cobb, 1911	.420
9	Fred Dunlap, 1884	.412
10	Ed Delahanty, 1899	.410
11	Jesse Burkett, 1896	.410
12	Jesse Burkett, 1895	.409
13	Ty Cobb, 1912	.409
14	Joe Jackson, 1911	.408
15	Sam Thompson, 1894	.407
16	George Sisler, 1920	.407
17	Ed Delahanty, 1894	.407
18	Ted Williams, 1941	.406
19	Billy Hamilton, 1894	.404
20	Ed Delahanty, 1895	.404
21	Rogers Hornsby, 1925	.403
22	Harry Heilmann, 1923	.403
23	Pete Browning, 1887	.402
24	Rogers Hornsby, 1922	.401
25	Bill Terry, 1930	.401
26	Hughie Jennings, 1896	.401
27	Ty Cobb, 1922	.401
28	Cap Anson, 1881	.399
29	Lefty O'Doul, 1929	.398
30	Harry Heilmann, 1927	.398
31	Rogers Hornsby, 1921	.397
32	Ed Delahanty, 1896	.397
33	Jesse Burkett, 1899	.396
34	Joe Jackson, 1912	.395
35	Tony Gwynn, 1994	.394
36	Harry Heilmann, 1921	.394
37	Babe Ruth, 1923	.393
38	Harry Heilmann, 1925	.393
39	Babe Herman, 1930	.393
40	Joe Kelley, 1894	.393
41	Sam Thompson, 1895	.392
42	John McGraw, 1899	.391
43	Ty Cobb, 1913	.390
44	Fred Clarke, 1897	.390
45	Al Simmons, 1931	.390
46	George Brett, 1980	.390
47	Tris Speaker, 1925	.389
48	Bill Lange, 1895	.389
49	Billy Hamilton, 1895	.389
50	Ty Cobb, 1921	.389
51	Ted Williams, 1957	.388
52	King Kelly, 1886	.388
53	Rod Carew, 1977	.388
54	Luke Appling, 1936	.388
55	Tris Speaker, 1920	.388
56	Al Simmons, 1925	.387
57	Deacon White, 1877	.387
58	Rogers Hornsby, 1928	.387
59	Tris Speaker, 1916	.386
60	Willie Keeler, 1896	.386
61	Chuck Klein, 1930	.386
62	Lave Cross, 1894	.386
	Hughie Jennings, 1895	.386
64	Willie Keeler, 1898	.385
65	Arky Vaughan, 1935	.385
66	Rogers Hornsby, 1923	.384
67	Ty Cobb, 1919	.384
68	Nap Lajoie, 1910	.384
69	Ty Cobb, 1910	.383
70	Jesse Burkett, 1897	.383
71	Tris Speaker, 1912	.383
72	Ty Cobb, 1917	.383
73	Lefty O'Doul, 1930	.383
74	Joe Jackson, 1920	.382
75	Ty Cobb, 1918	.382
76	Honus Wagner, 1900	.381
77	Babe Herman, 1929	.381
78	Joe DiMaggio, 1939	.381
79	Al Simmons, 1930	.381
80	Paul Waner, 1927	.380
81	Rogers Hornsby, 1929	.380
82	Billy Hamilton, 1893	.380
83	Tris Speaker, 1923	.380
84	Goose Goslin, 1928	.379
85	Freddy Lindstrom, 1930	.379
86	Willie Keeler, 1899	.379
87	Lou Gehrig, 1930	.379
88	John Cassidy, 1877	.378
89	Pete Browning, 1882	.378
90	Ty Cobb, 1925	.378
91	Babe Ruth, 1924	.378
92	Sam Crawford, 1911	.378
93	Tris Speaker, 1922	.378
94	Earl Averill, 1936	.378
95	Babe Ruth, 1921	.378
96	Heinie Manush, 1928	.378
97	Heinie Manush, 1926	.378
98	Ed Delahanty, 1897	.377
99	Willie Keeler, 1895	.377
100	Ty Cobb, 1909	.377

Batting Average (by era)

1876-1892
1	Tip O'Neill, 1887	.435
2	Ross Barnes, 1876	.429
3	Fred Dunlap, 1884	.412
4	Pete Browning, 1887	.402
5	Cap Anson, 1881	.399
6	King Kelly, 1886	.388
7	Deacon White, 1877	.387
8	John Cassidy, 1877	.378
9	Pete Browning, 1882	.378
10	Dan Brouthers, 1883	.374
11	Pete Browning, 1890	.373
12	Dan Brouthers, 1889	.373
13	Sam Thompson, 1887	.372
14	Tommy Tucker, 1889	.372
15	Roger Connor, 1885	.371

1893-1919
1	Hugh Duffy, 1894	.440
2	Nap Lajoie, 1901	.426
3	Willie Keeler, 1897	.424
4	Ty Cobb, 1911	.420
5	Ed Delahanty, 1899	.410
6	Jesse Burkett, 1896	.410
7	Jesse Burkett, 1895	.409
8	Ty Cobb, 1912	.409
9	Joe Jackson, 1911	.408
10	Sam Thompson, 1894	.407
11	Ed Delahanty, 1894	.407
12	Billy Hamilton, 1894	.404
13	Ed Delahanty, 1895	.404
14	Hughie Jennings, 1896	.401
15	Ed Delahanty, 1896	.397

1920-1941
1	Rogers Hornsby, 1924	.424
2	George Sisler, 1922	.420
3	George Sisler, 1920	.407
4	Ted Williams, 1941	.406
5	Rogers Hornsby, 1925	.403
6	Harry Heilmann, 1923	.403
7	Rogers Hornsby, 1922	.401
8	Bill Terry, 1930	.401
9	Ty Cobb, 1922	.401
10	Lefty O'Doul, 1929	.398
11	Harry Heilmann, 1927	.398
12	Rogers Hornsby, 1921	.397
13	Harry Heilmann, 1921	.394
14	Babe Ruth, 1923	.393
15	Harry Heilmann, 1925	.393

1942-1960
1	Ted Williams, 1957	.388
2	Stan Musial, 1948	.376
3	Ted Williams, 1948	.369
4	Stan Musial, 1946	.365
5	Mickey Mantle, 1957	.365
6	Harry Walker, 1947	.363
7	Dixie Walker, 1944	.357
8	Stan Musial, 1943	.357
9	Ted Williams, 1942	.356
10	Phil Cavarretta, 1945	.355
11	Lou Boudreau, 1948	.355
12	Stan Musial, 1951	.355
13	Hank Aaron, 1959	.355
14	Billy Goodman, 1950	.354
15	Harvey Kuenn, 1959	.353

1961-1976
1	Rico Carty, 1970	.366
2	Rod Carew, 1974	.364
3	Joe Torre, 1971	.363
4	Norm Cash, 1961	.361
5	Rod Carew, 1975	.359
6	Roberto Clemente, 1967	.357
7	Bill Madlock, 1975	.354
8	Ralph Garr, 1974	.353
9	Roberto Clemente, 1961	.351
10	Rod Carew, 1973	.350
11	Pete Rose, 1969	.348
12	Tommy Davis, 1962	.346
13	Roberto Clemente, 1969	.345
14	Ralph Garr, 1971	.343
15	Vada Pinson, 1961	.343

1977-1996
1	Tony Gwynn, 1994	.394
2	George Brett, 1980	.390
3	Rod Carew, 1977	.388
4	Andres Galarraga, 1993	.370
5	Tony Gwynn, 1987	.370
6	Tony Gwynn, 1995	.368
7	Wade Boggs, 1985	.368
8	Jeff Bagwell, 1994	.368
9	Wade Boggs, 1988	.366
10	Wade Boggs, 1987	.363
	John Olerud, 1993	.363
12	Wade Boggs, 1983	.361
13	Paul O'Neill, 1994	.359
14	Tony Gwynn, 1993	.358
15	Alex Rodriguez, 1996	.358

Batting Average (by position)

First Base
1 George Sisler, 1922 ..... .420
2 George Sisler, 1920 ..... .407
3 Bill Terry, 1930 .... .401
4 Cap Anson, 1881 ...... .399
5 Rod Carew, 1977 ...... .388
6 Lou Gehrig, 1930 ...... .379
7 Dan Brouthers, 1883 .... .374
8 Lou Gehrig, 1928 ...... .374
9 Lou Gehrig, 1927 ...... .373
10 Dan Brouthers, 1889 .... .373

Second Base
1 Ross Barnes, 1876 ...... .429
2 Nap Lajoie, 1901 ...... .426
3 Rogers Hornsby, 1924 ... .424
4 Fred Dunlap, 1884 ..... .412
5 Rogers Hornsby, 1925 ... .403
6 Rogers Hornsby, 1922 ... .401
7 Rogers Hornsby, 1921 ... .397
8 Rogers Hornsby, 1928 ... .387
9 Nap Lajoie, 1910 ...... .384
10 Rogers Hornsby, 1929 ... .380

Shortstop
1 Hughie Jennings, 1896 ... .401
2 Luke Appling, 1936 ..... .388
3 Hughie Jennings, 1895 ... .386
4 Arky Vaughan, 1935 .... .385
5 Honus Wagner, 1905 ... .363
6 Alex Rodriguez, 1996 ... .358
7 Hughie Jennings, 1897 ... .355
8 Honus Wagner, 1903 ... .355
9 Honus Wagner, 1908 ... .354
10 Honus Wagner, 1907 ... .350

Third Base
1 John McGraw, 1899 ..... .391
2 George Brett, 1980 ..... .390
3 Lave Cross, 1894 ...... .386
4 Freddy Lindstrom, 1930 .. .379
5 Heinie Zimmerman, 1912 . .372
6 John McGraw, 1895 .... .369
7 Wade Boggs, 1985 ..... .368
8 Denny Lyons, 1887 ..... .367
9 Wade Boggs, 1988 ..... .366
10 Pie Traynor, 1930 ...... .366

Outfield
1 Hugh Duffy, 1894 ...... .440
2 Tip O'Neill, 1887 ...... .435
3 Willie Keeler, 1897 ..... .424
4 Ty Cobb, 1911 .... .420
5 Ty Cobb, 1912 .... .410
6 Ed Delahanty, 1899 .... .410
7 Jesse Burkett, 1896 .... .410
8 Jesse Burkett, 1895 .... .409
9 Joe Jackson, 1911 ..... .408
10 Sam Thompson, 1894 ... .407
11 Ed Delahanty, 1894 .... .407
12 Ted Williams, 1941 ..... .406
13 Billy Hamilton, 1894 .... .404
14 Ed Delahanty, 1895 .... .404
15 Harry Heilmann, 1923 ... .403
16 Pete Browning, 1887 .... .402
17 Ty Cobb, 1922 .... .401
18 Lefty O'Doul, 1929 ..... .399
19 Harry Heilmann, 1927 ... .398
20 Ed Delahanty, 1896 .... .397

Catcher
1 Cal McVey, 1877 ...... .368
2 Mickey Cochrane, 1930 .. .357
3 Wilbert Robinson, 1894 .. .353
4 Spud Davis, 1933 ...... .349
5 Mickey Cochrane, 1931 .. .349
6 Mike Piazza, 1995 ..... .346
7 Ernie Lombardi, 1938 ... .342
8 Gabby Hartnett, 1930 ... .339
9 Mickey Cochrane, 1927 .. .338
10 Mike Piazza, 1996 ..... .336

Relative Batting Average

1 Ross Barnes, 1876 ..... 1.608
2 Tip O'Neill, 1887 ...... 1.564
3 Nap Lajoie, 1910 ...... 1.537
4 Ty Cobb, 1910 .... 1.534
5 Pete Browning, 1882 .... 1.526
6 Cap Anson, 1881 ...... 1.512
7 King Kelly, 1886 ...... 1.508
8 Roger Connor, 1885 .... 1.506
9 Tris Speaker, 1916 ..... 1.506
10 Ty Cobb, 1917 .... 1.501
11 Ty Cobb, 1912 .... 1.501
12 Nap Lajoie, 1901 ...... 1.501
13 Nap Lajoie, 1904 ...... 1.499
14 Ty Cobb, 1911 .... 1.493
15 Ty Cobb, 1909 .... 1.493
16 Ted Williams, 1957 ..... 1.476
17 Ty Cobb, 1913 .... 1.475
18 Ted Williams, 1941 ..... 1.472
19 Ty Cobb, 1918 .... 1.469
20 George Gore, 1880 ..... 1.462
21 Rogers Hornsby, 1924 .. 1.461
22 Rod Carew, 1977 ...... 1.458
23 Dan Brouthers, 1885 ... 1.455
24 Joe Jackson, 1911 ..... 1.452
25 Joe Jackson, 1912 ..... 1.451
26 Dan Brouthers, 1882 ... 1.449
27 Dave Orr, 1884 .... 1.448
28 George Brett, 1980 .... 1.448
29 Ty Cobb, 1915 .... 1.448
30 Pete Browning, 1887 .... 1.446
31 Ty Cobb, 1916 .... 1.445
32 Cap Anson, 1886 ...... 1.442
33 Pete Browning, 1885 ... 1.439
34 Dan Brouthers, 1886 ... 1.439
35 Tony Gwynn, 1994 ..... 1.436
36 Honus Wagner, 1908 ... 1.434
37 George Sisler, 1922 .... 1.433
38 Cap Anson, 1882 ...... 1.428
39 Cy Seymour, 1905 ..... 1.425
40 Willie Keeler, 1897 ..... 1.422
41 Ed Delahanty, 1899 .... 1.414
42 Wade Boggs, 1988 ..... 1.413
43 King Kelly, 1884 ...... 1.411
44 Joe Jackson, 1913 ..... 1.411
45 Rod Carew, 1974 ...... 1.408
46 Wade Boggs, 1985 ..... 1.407
47 Tris Speaker, 1912 ..... 1.406
48 Deacon White, 1877 .... 1.405
49 Dan Brouthers, 1883 ... 1.402
50 Jimmy Wolf, 1890 ...... 1.401
51 George Stone, 1906 .... 1.400
52 Stan Musial, 1948 ..... 1.400
53 Cap Anson, 1888 ...... 1.399
54 George Sisler, 1920 .... 1.398
55 Joe Torre, 1971 .... 1.397
56 Hugh Duffy, 1894 ...... 1.394
57 Stan Musial, 1946 ..... 1.393
58 Ed Swartwood, 1883 ... 1.392
59 Ty Cobb, 1919 .... 1.392
60 Rod Carew, 1975 ...... 1.391
61 Tommy Tucker, 1889 ... 1.391
62 Nap Lajoie, 1906 ...... 1.390
63 John Reilly, 1884 ...... 1.389
64 Harry Heilmann, 1923 ... 1.389
65 Mickey Mantle, 1957 ... 1.388
66 Willie Keeler, 1898 .... 1.387
67 Honus Wagner, 1907 ... 1.387
68 Roberto Clemente, 1967 . 1.385
69 George Sisler, 1917 .... 1.383
70 Jim O'Rourke, 1884 .... 1.383
71 Pete Browning, 1886 .... 1.382
72 Tris Speaker, 1917 ..... 1.380
73 Ezra Sutton, 1884 ..... 1.380
74 Ty Cobb, 1907 .... 1.379
75 Hick Carpenter, 1882 ... 1.379
76 Roger Connor, 1886 .... 1.378
77 Jesse Burkett, 1896 .... 1.378
78 Paul Hines, 1879 ...... 1.377
79 Tony Gwynn, 1987 ..... 1.375
80 Pete Browning, 1884 .... 1.374
81 Tris Speaker, 1913 ..... 1.374
82 Kirby Puckett, 1988 .... 1.374
83 John Cassidy, 1877 .... 1.373
84 Eddie Collins, 1909 .... 1.373
85 Honus Wagner, 1905 ... 1.372
86 Dave Orr, 1886 .... 1.372
87 Rico Carty, 1970 ...... 1.372
88 George Hall, 1876 ..... 1.372
89 Tip O'Neill, 1888 ...... 1.370
90 Wade Boggs, 1987 ..... 1.370
91 Ty Cobb, 1922 .... 1.370
92 Dan Brouthers, 1889 ... 1.370
93 Cap Anson, 1880 ...... 1.368
94 Norm Cash, 1961 ...... 1.368
95 Jesse Burkett, 1899 .... 1.367
96 Andres Galarraga, 1993 . 1.366
97 Jesse Burkett, 1901 .... 1.365
98 Hardy Richardson, 1886 . 1.365
99 Willie Keeler, 1904 .... 1.365
100 Wade Boggs, 1986 ..... 1.365

On Base Percentage

1 Ted Williams, 1941 ..... .551
2 John McGraw, 1899 .... .547
3 Babe Ruth, 1923 ...... .545
4 Babe Ruth, 1920 ...... .530
5 Ted Williams, 1957 .... .528
6 Billy Hamilton, 1894 ... .523
7 Ted Williams, 1954 .... .516
8 Babe Ruth, 1926 ...... .516
9 Mickey Mantle, 1957 ... .515
10 Babe Ruth, 1924 ...... .513
11 Babe Ruth, 1921 ...... .512
12 Rogers Hornsby, 1924 .. .507
13 John McGraw, 1900 .... .505
14 Joe Kelley, 1894 ...... .502
15 Hugh Duffy, 1894 ..... .502
16 Ed Delahanty, 1895 .... .500
17 Ted Williams, 1942 .... .499
18 Ted Williams, 1947 .... .499
19 Rogers Hornsby, 1928 .. .498
20 Ted Williams, 1946 .... .497
21 Ted Williams, 1948 .... .497
22 Bill Joyce, 1894 ...... .496
23 Babe Ruth, 1931 ...... .495
24 Frank Thomas, 1994 ... .494
25 Babe Ruth, 1930 ...... .493
26 Arky Vaughan, 1935 ... .491
27 Ted Williams, 1949 .... .490
28 Billy Hamilton, 1895 ... .490
29 Billy Hamilton, 1893 ... .490
30 Tip O'Neill, 1887 ...... .490
31 Rogers Hornsby, 1925 .. .489
   Babe Ruth, 1932 ...... .489
33 Norm Cash, 1961 ...... .488
34 Mickey Mantle, 1962 ... .488
35 Babe Ruth, 1927 ...... .487
36 Ty Cobb, 1915 .... .486
37 Jesse Burkett, 1895 .... .486
38 Tris Speaker, 1920 .... .483
39 King Kelly, 1886 ...... .483
40 Edgar Martinez, 1995 ... .482
41 Harry Heilmann, 1923 ... .481
42 Wade Boggs, 1988 ..... .480
43 Billy Hamilton, 1898 ... .480
44 Tris Speaker, 1925 .... .479
   Ted Williams, 1956 .... .479
46 Ed Delahanty, 1894 .... .478
47 John Olerud, 1993 ..... .478
48 Lou Gehrig, 1936 ...... .478
49 Billy Hamilton, 1896 ... .477
50 Cupid Childs, 1894 .... .475
51 John McGraw, 1898 .... .475
52 Harry Heilmann, 1927 ... .475
53 Tris Speaker, 1922 .... .474
54 Lou Gehrig, 1927 ...... .474
55 Luke Appling, 1936 .... .474
56 Lou Gehrig, 1930 ...... .473
57 Lou Gehrig, 1937 ...... .473
58 Hughie Jennings, 1896 .. .472
59 Ed Delahanty, 1896 .... .472
60 John McGraw, 1897 .... .471
61 Joe Morgan, 1975 ..... .471
62 Dan Brouthers, 1891 ... .471
63 Tris Speaker, 1916 .... .470
64 Bill Joyce, 1896 ...... .470
65 Joe Kelley, 1896 ...... .469
66 Tris Speaker, 1923 .... .469
   Gary Sheffield, 1996 ... .469
68 Jimmie Foxx, 1932 ..... .469
69 Jesse Burkett, 1897 .... .468
70 Ty Cobb, 1925 .... .468
71 Mark McGwire, 1996 ... .468
72 Joe Jackson, 1911 ..... .468
73 Lou Gehrig, 1928 ...... .467
74 Ty Cobb, 1913 .... .467
75 George Sisler, 1922 .... .467
76 Mike Griffin, 1894 ..... .467
77 Cupid Childs, 1896 .... .467
78 Mickey Mantle, 1956 ... .467
79 Edgar Martinez, 1996 ... .467
80 Wade Boggs, 1987 ..... .467
81 Ty Cobb, 1911 .... .467
82 Dan Brouthers, 1890 ... .466
83 Lou Gehrig, 1935 ...... .466
84 Lou Gehrig, 1934 ...... .465
85 Lefty O'Doul, 1929 .... .465
86 Frank Thomas, 1996 ... .465
87 Barry Bonds, 1996 ..... .465
88 Jimmie Foxx, 1939 ..... .464
89 Tris Speaker, 1912 .... .464
90 Ed Delahanty, 1899 .... .464
91 Pete Browning, 1887 ... .464
92 Ted Williams, 1951 .... .464
93 Willie Keeler, 1897 .... .464
94 Paul O'Neill, 1994 ..... .464
95 Bob Caruthers, 1887 ... .463
96 Barry Bonds, 1993 ..... .463
97 Cupid Childs, 1893 .... .463
98 Jimmie Foxx, 1929 ..... .463
99 Hughie Jennings, 1897 .. .463
100 Nap Lajoie, 1901 ...... .463

Slugging Average

1 Babe Ruth, 1920 ...... .847
2 Babe Ruth, 1921 ...... .846
3 Babe Ruth, 1927 ...... .772
4 Lou Gehrig, 1927 ...... .765
5 Babe Ruth, 1923 ...... .764
6 Rogers Hornsby, 1925 .. .756
7 Jeff Bagwell, 1994 ..... .750
8 Jimmie Foxx, 1932 ..... .749
9 Babe Ruth, 1924 ...... .739
10 Babe Ruth, 1926 ...... .737
11 Ted Williams, 1941 ..... .735
12 Babe Ruth, 1930 ...... .732
13 Ted Williams, 1957 ..... .731
14 Mark McGwire, 1996 .... .730
15 Frank Thomas, 1994 .... .729
16 Hack Wilson, 1930 ..... .723
17 Rogers Hornsby, 1922 .. .722
18 Lou Gehrig, 1930 ...... .721
19 Albert Belle, 1994 ..... .714
20 Babe Ruth, 1928 ...... .709
21 Al Simmons, 1930 ..... .708
22 Lou Gehrig, 1934 ...... .706
23 Mickey Mantle, 1956 .... .705
24 Jimmie Foxx, 1938 ..... .704
25 Jimmie Foxx, 1933 ..... .703
26 Stan Musial, 1948 ..... .702
27 Babe Ruth, 1931 ...... .700
28 Babe Ruth, 1929 ...... .697
29 Lou Gehrig, 1936 ...... .696
30 Rogers Hornsby, 1924 .. .696
31 Hugh Duffy, 1894 ..... .694
32 Jimmie Foxx, 1939 ..... .694
33 Tip O'Neill, 1887 ...... .691
34 Albert Belle, 1995 ..... .690
35 Mickey Mantle, 1961 .... .687
36 Chuck Klein, 1930 ..... .687
37 Sam Thompson, 1894 ... .686
38 Hank Greenberg, 1938 .. .683
39 Kevin Mitchell, 1994 ... .681
40 Rogers Hornsby, 1929 .. .679
41 Babe Herman, 1930 .... .678
42 Barry Bonds, 1993 ..... .677
43 Ken Griffey Jr., 1994 ... .674
44 Joe DiMaggio, 1937 .... .673
45 Babe Ruth, 1922 ...... .672
46 Joe DiMaggio, 1939 .... .671
47 Hank Greenberg, 1940 .. .670
48 Hank Aaron, 1971 ..... .669
49 Hank Greenberg, 1937 .. .668
50 Ted Williams, 1946 ..... .667
51 Willie Mays, 1954 ..... .667
52 Mickey Mantle, 1957 ... .665
53 George Brett, 1980 .... .664
54 Lou Gehrig, 1931 ...... .662
55 Norm Cash, 1961 ...... .662
56 Babe Ruth, 1932 ...... .661
57 Willie Mays, 1955 ..... .659
58 Ralph Kiner, 1949 ..... .658
59 Chuck Klein, 1929 ..... .657
60 Babe Ruth, 1919 ...... .657
61 Willie McCovey, 1969 ... .656
62 Sam Thompson, 1895 ... .654
63 Jimmie Foxx, 1934 ..... .653
64 Chick Hafey, 1930 ..... .652
65 Ted Williams, 1949 .... .650
66 Bill Joyce, 1894 ...... .648
67 Lou Gehrig, 1928 ...... .648
68 Ted Williams, 1942 .... .648
69 Duke Snider, 1954 ..... .647
70 Barry Bonds, 1994 ..... .647
71 Chuck Klein, 1932 ..... .646
72 Jim Gentile, 1961 ..... .646
73 Willie Stargell, 1973 ... .646
74 Willie Mays, 1965 ..... .645
75 Mike Schmidt, 1981 .... .644
76 Hal Trosky, 1936 ...... .644
77 Nap Lajoie, 1901 ...... .643
78 Joe DiMaggio, 1941 .... .643
   Juan Gonzalez, 1996 ... .643
80 Lou Gehrig, 1937 ...... .643
81 Ted Kluszewski, 1954 ... .642
82 Al Simmons, 1929 ..... .642
83 Joe Medwick, 1937 ..... .641
84 Al Simmons, 1931 ..... .641
85 Ellis Burks, 1996 ...... .639
86 Ralph Kiner, 1947 ..... .639
87 Rogers Hornsby, 1921 .. .639
88 Brady Anderson, 1996 .. .637
89 Frank Robinson, 1966 .. .637
90 Jimmie Foxx, 1930 ..... .637
91 Fred Lynn, 1979 .... .637
92 Hank Aaron, 1959 ..... .636
93 Johnny Mize, 1940 ..... .636
94 Jimmie Foxx, 1935 ..... .636
95 Kevin Mitchell, 1989 ... .635
96 Mel Ott, 1929 .... .635
97 Ted Williams, 1954 .... .635
98 Ted Williams, 1947 .... .634
99 Chick Hafey, 1929 ..... .632
100 Juan Gonzalez, 1993 ... .632

Production

1	Babe Ruth, 1920	1.378
2	Babe Ruth, 1921	1.358
3	Babe Ruth, 1923	1.309
4	Ted Williams, 1941	1.286
5	Babe Ruth, 1927	1.259
6	Ted Williams, 1957	1.259
7	Babe Ruth, 1926	1.253
8	Babe Ruth, 1924	1.252
9	Rogers Hornsby, 1925	1.245
10	Lou Gehrig, 1927	1.240
11	Babe Ruth, 1930	1.225
12	Frank Thomas, 1994	1.223
13	Jimmie Foxx, 1932	1.218
14	Jeff Bagwell, 1994	1.211
15	Rogers Hornsby, 1924	1.203
16	Mark McGwire, 1996	1.199
17	Hugh Duffy, 1894	1.196
18	Babe Ruth, 1931	1.195
19	Lou Gehrig, 1930	1.194
20	Rogers Hornsby, 1922	1.181
21	Tip O'Neill, 1887	1.180
22	Mickey Mantle, 1957	1.179
23	Hack Wilson, 1930	1.177
24	Lou Gehrig, 1936	1.174
25	Mickey Mantle, 1956	1.172
26	Lou Gehrig, 1934	1.172
27	Babe Ruth, 1928	1.170
28	Jimmie Foxx, 1938	1.166
29	Ted Williams, 1946	1.164
30	Jimmie Foxx, 1939	1.158
31	Albert Belle, 1994	1.156
32	Jimmie Foxx, 1933	1.153
33	Stan Musial, 1948	1.152
34	Ted Williams, 1954	1.151
35	Babe Ruth, 1932	1.150
36	Norm Cash, 1961	1.150
37	Ted Williams, 1942	1.147
38	Sam Thompson, 1894	1.145
39	Bill Joyce, 1894	1.143
40	Ted Williams, 1949	1.141
41	Barry Bonds, 1993	1.140
42	Rogers Hornsby, 1929	1.139
43	Mickey Mantle, 1961	1.138
44	Ted Williams, 1947	1.133
45	Babe Herman, 1930	1.132
46	Al Simmons, 1930	1.130
47	Rogers Hornsby, 1928	1.130
48	Babe Ruth, 1929	1.128
49	George Brett, 1980	1.124
50	Chuck Klein, 1930	1.123
51	Hank Greenberg, 1938	1.122
52	Joe DiMaggio, 1939	1.119
53	Kevin Mitchell, 1994	1.119
54	Ed Delahanty, 1895	1.117
55	Lou Gehrig, 1937	1.116
56	Lou Gehrig, 1928	1.115
57	Babe Ruth, 1919	1.114
58	Willie McCovey, 1969	1.114
59	Harry Heilmann, 1923	1.113
60	Ted Williams, 1948	1.112
61	Edgar Martinez, 1995	1.110
62	Lou Gehrig, 1931	1.108
63	Nap Lajoie, 1901	1.106
64	Babe Ruth, 1922	1.106
65	Hank Greenberg, 1937	1.105
66	Joe Kelley, 1894	1.104
67	Hank Greenberg, 1940	1.103
68	Ed Delahanty, 1896	1.103
69	Jimmie Foxx, 1934	1.102
70	Arky Vaughan, 1935	1.098
71	Rogers Hornsby, 1921	1.097
72	Jimmie Foxx, 1935	1.096
73	Gary Sheffield, 1996	1.094
74	Albert Belle, 1995	1.094
75	Mickey Mantle, 1962	1.093
76	Frank Thomas, 1996	1.091
77	Harry Heilmann, 1927	1.091
78	Ralph Kiner, 1949	1.089
79	Jimmie Foxx, 1929	1.088
80	Ty Cobb, 1911	1.088
81	Lefty O'Doul, 1929	1.087
82	Rogers Hornsby, 1923	1.086
83	Al Simmons, 1931	1.085
84	Barry Bonds, 1992	1.085
85	Joe DiMaggio, 1937	1.085
86	Sam Thompson, 1895	1.085
87	Ted Williams, 1956	1.084
88	Mel Ott, 1929	1.084
89	Joe DiMaggio, 1941	1.083
90	Willie Mays, 1954	1.083
91	Mike Schmidt, 1981	1.083
92	Hank Aaron, 1971	1.082
93	George Sisler, 1920	1.082
94	Barry Bonds, 1996	1.080
95	Tris Speaker, 1922	1.080
96	Ralph Kiner, 1951	1.079
97	Tris Speaker, 1923	1.079
98	Ken Griffey Jr., 1994	1.078
99	John Olerud, 1993	1.077
100	Barry Bonds, 1994	1.076

Adjusted Production

1	Babe Ruth, 1920	252
2	Babe Ruth, 1923	238
3	Babe Ruth, 1921	236
4	Ted Williams, 1941	232
5	Babe Ruth, 1927	229
6	Pete Browning, 1882	229
7	Babe Ruth, 1926	228
8	Ted Williams, 1957	227
9	Lou Gehrig, 1927	224
10	Babe Ruth, 1919	224
11	Babe Ruth, 1931	223
12	Mickey Mantle, 1957	223
13	Rogers Hornsby, 1924	223
14	Ross Barnes, 1876	222
15	Babe Ruth, 1924	221
16	Jeff Bagwell, 1994	220
17	Babe Ruth, 1930	216
18	Frank Thomas, 1994	214
19	Ted Williams, 1942	214
20	Lou Gehrig, 1934	213
21	Mickey Mantle, 1956	213
22	Willie McCovey, 1969	212
23	Ted Williams, 1946	211
24	Mickey Mantle, 1961	210
25	Babe Ruth, 1928	210
26	Rogers Hornsby, 1922	210
27	Ty Cobb, 1917	210
28	George Hall, 1876	208
29	Rogers Hornsby, 1925	208
30	Lou Gehrig, 1930	207
31	Barry Bonds, 1993	207
32	Barry Bonds, 1992	207
33	Babe Ruth, 1932	206
34	Nap Lajoie, 1904	205
35	Tip O'Neill, 1887	205
36	Honus Wagner, 1908	205
37	Mark McGwire, 1996	205
38	Rogers Hornsby, 1928	204
39	Dan Brouthers, 1886	204
40	Ty Cobb, 1912	203
41	Jimmie Foxx, 1932	203
42	Roger Connor, 1885	203
43	George Brett, 1980	203
44	Ty Cobb, 1910	202
45	Frank Robinson, 1966	200
46	Jimmie Foxx, 1933	199
47	Ted Williams, 1947	199
48	Lou Gehrig, 1931	199
49	Dan Brouthers, 1885	199
50	Babe Ruth, 1929	199
51	Dick Allen, 1972	199
52	Norm Cash, 1961	198
53	Mickey Mantle, 1962	198
54	Dan Brouthers, 1882	198
55	Nap Lajoie, 1910	198
56	Dave Orr, 1885	197
57	Ed Swartwood, 1882	197
58	Lou Gehrig, 1928	197
59	Stan Musial, 1948	196
60	Ty Cobb, 1918	196
61	Ty Cobb, 1913	196
62	Nap Lajoie, 1901	196
63	Orator Shaffer, 1878	196
64	Mike Schmidt, 1981	195
65	George Stone, 1906	195
66	Harry Heilmann, 1923	195
67	Dave Orr, 1884	195
68	Kevin Mitchell, 1989	194
69	Lou Gehrig, 1936	193
70	Gary Sheffield, 1996	193
71	Ed Delahanty, 1899	193
72	Ty Cobb, 1911	193
73	Ted Williams, 1954	193
74	Joe Jackson, 1911	192
75	Ed Delahanty, 1896	192
76	Rogers Hornsby, 1921	191
77	Albert Belle, 1994	191
78	Ty Cobb, 1909	190
79	Joe Jackson, 1913	190
80	Rickey Henderson, 1990	190
81	Pete Browning, 1885	190
82	Hank Aaron, 1971	190
83	Reggie Jackson, 1969	190
84	Deacon White, 1877	190
85	Joe Jackson, 1912	190
86	Barry Bonds, 1996	190
87	Rogers Hornsby, 1920	190
88	Cap Anson, 1881	189
89	Jim Gentile, 1961	189
90	Cupid Childs, 1890	189
91	Carl Yastrzemski, 1967	189
92	Mickey Mantle, 1958	189
93	Frank Robinson, 1967	189
94	Willie Stargell, 1973	189
95	Willie Stargell, 1971	189
96	King Kelly, 1879	188
97	Jimmie Foxx, 1934	188
98	Hank Aaron, 1959	188
99	Kevin Mitchell, 1994	188
100	Roger Connor, 1882	188

Batting Runs

1	Babe Ruth, 1921	119
2	Babe Ruth, 1923	119
3	Babe Ruth, 1920	113
4	Ted Williams, 1941	102
5	Lou Gehrig, 1927	101
6	Babe Ruth, 1924	101
7	Babe Ruth, 1927	101
8	Babe Ruth, 1926	97
9	Jimmie Foxx, 1932	97
10	Ted Williams, 1946	94
11	Rogers Hornsby, 1924	94
12	Ted Williams, 1942	93
13	Babe Ruth, 1931	92
14	Ted Williams, 1947	91
15	Stan Musial, 1948	90
16	Rogers Hornsby, 1922	90
17	Ted Williams, 1957	90
18	Babe Ruth, 1930	90
19	Mickey Mantle, 1957	89
20	Ted Williams, 1949	89
21	Lou Gehrig, 1930	88
22	Rogers Hornsby, 1925	87
23	Tip O'Neill, 1887	86
24	Norm Cash, 1961	86
25	Lou Gehrig, 1934	86
26	Babe Ruth, 1928	84
27	Mickey Mantle, 1956	83
28	Jimmie Foxx, 1933	83
29	Lou Gehrig, 1936	82
30	Barry Bonds, 1993	82
31	Lou Gehrig, 1931	80
32	Ty Cobb, 1911	78
33	Jimmie Foxx, 1938	78
34	Carl Yastrzemski, 1967	76
35	Mickey Mantle, 1961	76
36	Willie McCovey, 1969	76
37	Lou Gehrig, 1928	76
38	Ted Williams, 1948	76
39	Hugh Duffy, 1894	76
40	Hack Wilson, 1930	75
41	Rogers Hornsby, 1921	74
42	Ty Cobb, 1917	74
43	John Olerud, 1993	74
44	Rogers Hornsby, 1929	74
45	Nap Lajoie, 1901	74
46	Frank Robinson, 1966	74
47	Lou Gehrig, 1932	73
48	George Sisler, 1920	73
49	Tris Speaker, 1912	73
50	Rogers Hornsby, 1928	72
51	Stan Musial, 1949	72
52	Gary Sheffield, 1996	72
53	Arky Vaughan, 1935	72
54	Barry Bonds, 1992	72
55	Joe Jackson, 1911	72
56	Carl Yastrzemski, 1970	72
57	Ty Cobb, 1915	72
58	Edgar Martinez, 1995	71
59	Frank Thomas, 1994	71
60	Babe Ruth, 1932	71
61	Ted Williams, 1954	71
62	Tris Speaker, 1923	71
63	Stan Musial, 1946	71
64	Ralph Kiner, 1951	71
65	Harry Heilmann, 1923	71
66	Joe Jackson, 1912	70
67	Stan Musial, 1951	70
68	Ralph Kiner, 1949	70
69	Barry Bonds, 1996	69
70	Chuck Klein, 1933	69
71	Joe Medwick, 1937	69
72	Hank Greenberg, 1940	69
73	Johnny Mize, 1939	69
74	Babe Herman, 1930	69
75	Lou Gehrig, 1932	69
76	Lefty O'Doul, 1929	69
77	Nap Lajoie, 1910	68
78	Chuck Klein, 1932	68
79	Ty Cobb, 1910	68
80	Ed Delahanty, 1899	68
81	Chuck Klein, 1930	67
82	Mark McGwire, 1996	67
83	Jimmie Foxx, 1935	67
84	Hank Greenberg, 1937	67
85	Ty Cobb, 1912	67
86	Rod Carew, 1977	67
87	Frank Robinson, 1962	67
88	Wade Boggs, 1987	67
89	Babe Ruth, 1919	67
90	Jimmie Foxx, 1934	66
91	Ed Delahanty, 1895	66
92	Jimmie Foxx, 1939	66
93	Dick Allen, 1972	66
94	Hank Greenberg, 1938	66
95	Dan Brouthers, 1886	66
96	Frank Thomas, 1991	66
97	Wade Boggs, 1988	66
98	Ty Cobb, 1909	66
99	Harmon Killebrew, 1969	66
100	Joe Jackson, 1913	66

Adjusted Batting Runs

1	Babe Ruth, 1923	116
2	Babe Ruth, 1921	115
3	Lou Gehrig, 1927	107
4	Babe Ruth, 1920	107
5	Babe Ruth, 1927	106
6	Babe Ruth, 1931	102
7	Babe Ruth, 1924	101
8	Babe Ruth, 1926	100
9	Rogers Hornsby, 1922	99
10	Lou Gehrig, 1934	98
11	Babe Ruth, 1930	98
12	Ted Williams, 1941	98
13	Rogers Hornsby, 1924	97
14	Lou Gehrig, 1930	97
15	Mickey Mantle, 1957	91
16	Jimmie Foxx, 1932	90
17	Lou Gehrig, 1931	90
18	Babe Ruth, 1928	89
19	Lou Gehrig, 1936	89
20	Mickey Mantle, 1956	89
21	Barry Bonds, 1993	87
22	Ted Williams, 1942	87
23	Ted Williams, 1946	85
24	Mickey Mantle, 1961	84
25	Rogers Hornsby, 1925	83
26	Norm Cash, 1961	82
27	Ted Williams, 1957	82
28	Lou Gehrig, 1928	81
29	Jimmie Foxx, 1933	81
30	Stan Musial, 1948	81
31	Rogers Hornsby, 1928	80
32	Ted Williams, 1947	79
33	Babe Ruth, 1932	79
34	Willie McCovey, 1969	79
35	Gary Sheffield, 1996	79
36	Rogers Hornsby, 1921	78
37	Jeff Bagwell, 1996	78
38	Lou Gehrig, 1932	77
39	Ted Williams, 1949	77
40	Frank Robinson, 1966	76
41	Barry Bonds, 1996	76
42	Hank Aaron, 1959	75
43	Ty Cobb, 1917	75
44	Hack Wilson, 1930	74
45	Babe Ruth, 1919	74
46	Frank Thomas, 1994	74
47	Rogers Hornsby, 1929	74
48	Harry Heilmann, 1923	74
49	John Olerud, 1993	74
50	Ed Delahanty, 1899	73
51	Barry Bonds, 1992	73
52	Mark McGwire, 1996	73
53	Lou Gehrig, 1937	72
54	Jimmie Foxx, 1934	72
55	Frank Thomas, 1996	72
56	Ty Cobb, 1912	72
57	Babe Ruth, 1929	71
58	Jeff Bagwell, 1994	71
59	Tris Speaker, 1923	71
60	Babe Herman, 1930	71
61	Ty Cobb, 1911	71
62	Jimmie Foxx, 1938	70
63	Joe Jackson, 1911	70
64	Edgar Martinez, 1995	70
65	Lou Gehrig, 1935	70
66	Frank Thomas, 1991	69
67	Rod Carew, 1977	69
68	Mickey Mantle, 1958	69
69	Stan Musial, 1951	69
70	Frank Thomas, 1995	69
71	Lou Gehrig, 1933	68
72	George Sisler, 1920	68
73	Jimmie Foxx, 1935	68
74	Ted Williams, 1948	68
75	Reggie Jackson, 1969	68
76	Tip O'Neill, 1887	68
77	Rogers Hornsby, 1920	68
78	Nap Lajoie, 1901	68
79	Arky Vaughan, 1935	67
80	Al Rosen, 1953	67
81	Ed Delahanty, 1896	67
82	Ralph Kiner, 1951	67
83	Nap Lajoie, 1910	66
84	Joe DiMaggio, 1941	66
85	Ralph Kiner, 1949	66
86	Joe Medwick, 1937	66
87	Jesse Burkett, 1901	66
88	Kevin Mitchell, 1989	66
89	Ed Delahanty, 1895	66
90	Joe Jackson, 1912	66
91	Frank Thomas, 1993	66
92	Stan Musial, 1949	66
93	Carl Yastrzemski, 1967	65
94	Honus Wagner, 1908	65
95	Tris Speaker, 1912	65
96	Stan Musial, 1946	65
97	Billy Hamilton, 1894	65
98	Hank Aaron, 1963	64
99	Ty Cobb, 1915	64
100	Frank Thomas, 1992	64

Batting Wins

1	Babe Ruth, 1923	11.5
2	Babe Ruth, 1921	11.1
3	Babe Ruth, 1920	11.0
4	Ted Williams, 1941	9.9
5	Ted Williams, 1946	9.9
6	Lou Gehrig, 1927	9.6
7	Babe Ruth, 1927	9.6
8	Babe Ruth, 1924	9.5
9	Ted Williams, 1942	9.5
10	Ted Williams, 1947	9.4
11	Babe Ruth, 1926	9.4
12	Rogers Hornsby, 1924	9.3
13	Ted Williams, 1957	9.3
14	Mickey Mantle, 1957	9.2
15	Stan Musial, 1948	9.0
16	Jimmie Foxx, 1932	8.9
17	Ted Williams, 1949	8.6
18	Norm Cash, 1961	8.5
19	Babe Ruth, 1931	8.5
20	Rogers Hornsby, 1922	8.5
21	Carl Yastrzemski, 1967	8.4
22	Ty Cobb, 1917	8.3
23	Barry Bonds, 1993	8.2
24	Rogers Hornsby, 1925	8.2
25	Mickey Mantle, 1956	8.2
26	Babe Ruth, 1928	8.1
27	Babe Ruth, 1930	8.1
28	Lou Gehrig, 1930	8.0
29	Willie McCovey, 1969	8.0
30	Lou Gehrig, 1934	8.0
31	Frank Robinson, 1966	7.9
32	Jimmie Foxx, 1933	7.8
33	Barry Bonds, 1992	7.7
34	Ty Cobb, 1911	7.7
35	Ty Cobb, 1915	7.6
36	Nap Lajoie, 1910	7.6
37	Mickey Mantle, 1961	7.6
38	Honus Wagner, 1908	7.5
39	Ty Cobb, 1910	7.5
40	Stan Musial, 1946	7.5
41	Dick Allen, 1972	7.5
42	Carl Yastrzemski, 1970	7.4
43	Lou Gehrig, 1931	7.4
44	Rogers Hornsby, 1921	7.3
45	Lou Gehrig, 1928	7.3
46	Ted Williams, 1948	7.3
47	Ted Williams, 1954	7.3
48	Chuck Klein, 1933	7.3
49	Tris Speaker, 1912	7.3
50	Lou Gehrig, 1936	7.3
51	John Olerud, 1993	7.2
52	Ty Cobb, 1909	7.2
53	Stan Musial, 1949	7.2
54	Tris Speaker, 1916	7.1
55	Ralph Kiner, 1951	7.1
56	George Sisler, 1920	7.1
57	Rogers Hornsby, 1928	7.1
58	Gary Sheffield, 1996	7.1
59	Jimmie Foxx, 1938	7.1
60	Joe Jackson, 1911	7.1
61	Joe Jackson, 1912	7.0
62	Stan Musial, 1951	7.0
63	Tip O'Neill, 1887	7.0
64	Hank Aaron, 1971	7.0
65	Stan Musial, 1943	7.0
66	Arky Vaughan, 1935	7.0
67	Nap Lajoie, 1904	7.0
68	Joe Jackson, 1913	7.0
69	Babe Ruth, 1919	7.0
70	Ralph Kiner, 1949	6.9
71	Harmon Killebrew, 1967	6.9
72	Harmon Killebrew, 1969	6.9
73	Johnny Mize, 1939	6.9
74	Tris Speaker, 1923	6.9
75	Willie Mays, 1965	6.8
76	Harry Heilmann, 1923	6.8
77	Hank Aaron, 1963	6.8
78	Joe Medwick, 1937	6.8
79	Barry Bonds, 1996	6.8
80	Chuck Klein, 1932	6.7
81	Rogers Hornsby, 1929	6.7
82	Lou Gehrig, 1937	6.7
83	Cy Seymour, 1905	6.7
84	Ty Cobb, 1912	6.7
85	Rogers Hornsby, 1920	6.7
86	Edgar Martinez, 1995	6.7
87	Joe Torre, 1971	6.7
88	Nap Lajoie, 1901	6.7
89	Hack Wilson, 1930	6.7
90	Rod Carew, 1977	6.7
91	Wade Boggs, 1988	6.7
92	Frank Robinson, 1962	6.6
93	Kevin Mitchell, 1989	6.6
94	Mickey Mantle, 1958	6.6
95	Carl Yastrzemski, 1968	6.6
96	Frank Thomas, 1991	6.6
97	Frank Thomas, 1994	6.6
98	Babe Ruth, 1932	6.6
99	Billy Williams, 1972	6.6
100	Joe Morgan, 1976	6.5

Adjusted Batting Wins

1	Babe Ruth, 1923	11.2
2	Babe Ruth, 1921	10.7
3	Babe Ruth, 1920	10.3
4	Lou Gehrig, 1927	10.1
5	Babe Ruth, 1927	10.1
6	Babe Ruth, 1926	9.7
7	Rogers Hornsby, 1924	9.6
8	Babe Ruth, 1924	9.5
9	Ted Williams, 1941	9.5
10	Babe Ruth, 1931	9.5
11	Mickey Mantle, 1957	9.4
12	Rogers Hornsby, 1922	9.3
13	Lou Gehrig, 1934	9.1
14	Ted Williams, 1946	8.9
15	Ted Williams, 1942	8.9
16	Babe Ruth, 1930	8.9
17	Lou Gehrig, 1930	8.8
18	Barry Bonds, 1993	8.7
19	Mickey Mantle, 1956	8.7
20	Babe Ruth, 1928	8.6
21	Ted Williams, 1957	8.4
22	Lou Gehrig, 1931	8.4
23	Mickey Mantle, 1961	8.4
24	Ty Cobb, 1917	8.3
25	Jimmie Foxx, 1932	8.3
26	Willie McCovey, 1969	8.3
27	Ted Williams, 1947	8.2
28	Frank Robinson, 1966	8.2
29	Norm Cash, 1961	8.1
30	Stan Musial, 1948	8.1
31	Barry Bonds, 1992	7.9
32	Rogers Hornsby, 1928	7.8
33	Lou Gehrig, 1928	7.8
34	Lou Gehrig, 1936	7.8
35	Rogers Hornsby, 1925	7.8
36	Babe Ruth, 1919	7.7
37	Gary Sheffield, 1996	7.7
38	Rogers Hornsby, 1921	7.7
39	Jimmie Foxx, 1933	7.7
40	Jeff Bagwell, 1996	7.6
41	Hank Aaron, 1959	7.6
42	Honus Wagner, 1908	7.5
43	Ted Williams, 1949	7.5
44	Barry Bonds, 1996	7.4
45	Nap Lajoie, 1910	7.4
46	Babe Ruth, 1932	7.3
47	Rogers Hornsby, 1920	7.2
48	Dick Allen, 1972	7.2
49	Carl Yastrzemski, 1967	7.2
50	Ty Cobb, 1912	7.2
51	John Olerud, 1993	7.2
52	Mickey Mantle, 1958	7.2
53	Lou Gehrig, 1932	7.1
54	Harry Heilmann, 1923	7.1
55	Reggie Jackson, 1969	7.1
56	Nap Lajoie, 1904	7.1
57	Kevin Mitchell, 1989	7.0
58	Jeff Bagwell, 1994	7.0
59	Hank Aaron, 1963	7.0
60	Frank Thomas, 1991	7.0
61	George Stone, 1906	6.9
62	Ty Cobb, 1911	6.9
63	Stan Musial, 1951	6.9
64	Joe Jackson, 1911	6.9
65	Tris Speaker, 1923	6.9
66	Stan Musial, 1946	6.9
67	Rod Carew, 1977	6.9
68	Frank Thomas, 1994	6.8
69	Ty Cobb, 1915	6.8
70	Al Rosen, 1953	6.7
71	Babe Ruth, 1929	6.7
72	Rogers Hornsby, 1929	6.7
73	Jimmie Foxx, 1934	6.7
74	Frank Howard, 1969	6.7
75	Ralph Kiner, 1951	6.7
76	Mark McGwire, 1996	6.7
77	Ed Delahanty, 1899	6.7
78	Lou Gehrig, 1937	6.6
79	George Sisler, 1920	6.6
80	Ty Cobb, 1910	6.6
81	Ted Williams, 1948	6.6
82	Joe Jackson, 1912	6.6
83	Bobby Murcer, 1971	6.6
84	Ty Cobb, 1909	6.6
85	Joe Jackson, 1913	6.6
86	Edgar Martinez, 1995	6.6
87	Harmon Killebrew, 1969	6.6
88	Lou Gehrig, 1935	6.6
89	Ralph Kiner, 1949	6.6
90	Hack Wilson, 1930	6.5
91	Frank Thomas, 1992	6.5
92	Frank Thomas, 1996	6.5
93	Arky Vaughan, 1935	6.5
94	Joe Medwick, 1937	6.5
95	Tris Speaker, 1912	6.5
96	Lou Gehrig, 1933	6.5
97	Stan Musial, 1949	6.5
98	Willie Mays, 1965	6.5
99	Jesse Burkett, 1901	6.5
100	Frank Thomas, 1995	6.4

Runs Created

1	Babe Ruth, 1921	238
2	Babe Ruth, 1923	223
3	Hugh Duffy, 1894	217
4	Lou Gehrig, 1927	212
5	Babe Ruth, 1920	211
6	Babe Ruth, 1927	208
7	Jimmie Foxx, 1932	207
8	Billy Hamilton, 1894	207
9	Ty Cobb, 1911	207
10	Babe Ruth, 1924	205
11	Ted Williams, 1941	202
12	Rogers Hornsby, 1922	200
13	Lou Gehrig, 1936	199
14	Babe Ruth, 1926	196
15	Lou Gehrig, 1930	195
16	Lou Gehrig, 1934	195
17	Tip O'Neill, 1887	194
18	Ted Williams, 1949	193
19	Babe Ruth, 1931	192
20	Babe Ruth, 1930	191
21	Pete Browning, 1887	191
22	Stan Musial, 1948	191
23	Hack Wilson, 1930	189
24	Jimmie Foxx, 1938	189
25	Ted Williams, 1946	188
26	Mickey Mantle, 1956	188
27	Rogers Hornsby, 1925	187
28	Ted Williams, 1947	186
29	Rogers Hornsby, 1924	186
30	Chuck Klein, 1930	186
31	Lou Gehrig, 1931	185
32	Ted Williams, 1942	185
33	Jimmie Foxx, 1933	184
34	Rogers Hornsby, 1929	183
35	Babe Herman, 1930	183
36	Joe Kelley, 1894	182
37	Babe Ruth, 1928	182
38	Lou Gehrig, 1937	181
39	Lefty O'Doul, 1929	180
40	Nap Lajoie, 1901	179
41	Mickey Mantle, 1957	178
42	Billy Hamilton, 1895	178
43	Joe Kelley, 1896	178
44	Norm Cash, 1961	178
45	Hank Greenberg, 1937	178
46	Ed Delahanty, 1895	176
47	George Sisler, 1920	176
48	Willie Keeler, 1897	176
49	Ed Delahanty, 1899	175
50	Benny Kauff, 1914	175
51	Tris Speaker, 1912	175
52	Joe Jackson, 1911	175
53	Mickey Mantle, 1961	174
54	Stan Musial, 1949	173
55	Joe DiMaggio, 1937	173
56	Ty Cobb, 1912	173
57	Barry Bonds, 1993	172
58	Hank Greenberg, 1938	172
59	Ted Williams, 1948	172
60	Chuck Klein, 1932	171
61	Hank Greenberg, 1940	171
62	Ed Delahanty, 1896	170
63	Joe Medwick, 1937	170
64	Bill Terry, 1930	170
65	Stan Musial, 1951	169
66	Lou Gehrig, 1928	169
67	Rogers Hornsby, 1921	169
68	Earl Averill, 1936	168
69	Jimmie Foxx, 1936	168
70	Lou Gehrig, 1932	168
71	Sam Thompson, 1895	167
72	Ted Williams, 1957	167
73	Ed Delahanty, 1893	167
74	Jesse Burkett, 1896	166
75	Stan Musial, 1953	166
76	Joe Jackson, 1912	166
77	Tris Speaker, 1923	166
78	Jimmie Foxx, 1934	165
79	Ralph Kiner, 1951	165
80	Jake Stenzel, 1894	165
81	Jesse Burkett, 1895	165
82	Ty Cobb, 1917	164
83	Stan Musial, 1946	164
84	Ralph Kiner, 1949	163
85	Arky Vaughan, 1935	163
86	Jimmie Foxx, 1935	163
87	Al Simmons, 1930	163
88	Johnny Mize, 1939	162
89	Chuck Klein, 1933	162
90	Barry Bonds, 1996	162
91	George Sisler, 1922	162
92	Joe DiMaggio, 1941	162
93	Duke Snider, 1954	161
94	Hank Greenberg, 1935	161
95	Duke Snider, 1953	161
96	John Olerud, 1993	161
97	Edgar Martinez, 1995	161
98	Bill Lange, 1895	160
99	Rod Carew, 1977	160
100	Denny Lyons, 1887	160

Total Average

1	Babe Ruth, 1920	1.797
2	Babe Ruth, 1921	1.745
3	Ted Williams, 1941	1.688
4	Babe Ruth, 1923	1.683
5	Hugh Duffy, 1894	1.619
6	Babe Ruth, 1926	1.606
7	Billy Hamilton, 1894	1.605
8	John McGraw, 1899	1.601
9	Ted Williams, 1957	1.599
10	Babe Ruth, 1927	1.571
11	Babe Ruth, 1924	1.558
12	Rogers Hornsby, 1925	1.539
13	Mickey Mantle, 1957	1.534
14	Bill Joyce, 1894	1.528
15	Ed Delahanty, 1895	1.517
16	Tip O'Neill, 1887	1.514
17	Babe Ruth, 1930	1.509
18	Joe Kelley, 1894	1.503
19	Lou Gehrig, 1927	1.500
20	Babe Ruth, 1931	1.487
21	Ty Cobb, 1911	1.464
22	Frank Thomas, 1994	1.453
23	Ted Williams, 1954	1.452
24	Jimmie Foxx, 1932	1.451
25	Billy Hamilton, 1895	1.443
26	Babe Ruth, 1932	1.432
27	Ted Williams, 1946	1.431
28	Joe Kelley, 1896	1.430
29	Lou Gehrig, 1936	1.426
30	Mickey Mantle, 1956	1.426
31	Rogers Hornsby, 1924	1.424
32	Pete Browning, 1887	1.422
33	Mark McGwire, 1996	1.420
34	Jeff Bagwell, 1994	1.413
35	Hack Wilson, 1930	1.411
36	Rogers Hornsby, 1928	1.409
37	Sam Thompson, 1894	1.409
38	Ed Delahanty, 1896	1.405
39	Babe Ruth, 1928	1.405
40	Lou Gehrig, 1934	1.401
41	Ted Williams, 1942	1.394
42	Jimmie Foxx, 1938	1.392
43	Ted Williams, 1947	1.391
44	Lou Gehrig, 1930	1.389
45	Billy Hamilton, 1893	1.386
46	Mickey Mantle, 1962	1.385
47	Mickey Mantle, 1961	1.384
48	Bill Lange, 1895	1.373
49	Bob Caruthers, 1887	1.368
50	King Kelly, 1886	1.366
51	Babe Ruth, 1919	1.358
52	Norm Cash, 1961	1.358
53	Rogers Hornsby, 1922	1.353
54	Babe Herman, 1930	1.351
55	Jimmie Foxx, 1933	1.348
56	Ted Williams, 1948	1.347
57	Ted Williams, 1949	1.347
58	Lou Gehrig, 1937	1.339
59	Barry Bonds, 1993	1.339
60	Rogers Hornsby, 1929	1.338
61	Barry Bonds, 1996	1.338
62	Barry Bonds, 1992	1.335
63	Nap Lajoie, 1901	1.327
64	Ty Cobb, 1912	1.321
65	Ty Cobb, 1910	1.321
66	Jake Stenzel, 1894	1.320
67	Joe Morgan, 1976	1.319
68	Arky Vaughan, 1935	1.317
69	Billy Hamilton, 1896	1.316
70	Ty Cobb, 1913	1.310
71	Jimmie Foxx, 1934	1.310
72	Tris Speaker, 1912	1.310
73	Joe Jackson, 1911	1.308
74	Bill Joyce, 1896	1.306
75	Hank Greenberg, 1938	1.306
76	Albert Belle, 1994	1.304
77	Jimmie Foxx, 1939	1.304
78	Edgar Martinez, 1995	1.300
79	Stan Musial, 1948	1.298
80	Willie McCovey, 1969	1.296
81	Ed Delahanty, 1894	1.290
82	Joe Kelley, 1895	1.289
83	Jimmie Foxx, 1935	1.288
84	Babe Ruth, 1929	1.288
85	Harry Heilmann, 1923	1.288
86	Mel Ott, 1929	1.287
87	Joe Morgan, 1975	1.279
88	Benny Kauff, 1914	1.278
89	Hank Greenberg, 1937	1.277
90	Chuck Klein, 1930	1.274
91	Al Simmons, 1930	1.272
92	Tris Speaker, 1922	1.272
93	Fred Clarke, 1897	1.272
94	Billy Hamilton, 1891	1.270
95	Sam Thompson, 1895	1.269
96	Gary Sheffield, 1996	1.268
97	Lou Gehrig, 1931	1.267
98	Harry Heilmann, 1927	1.265
99	Jesse Burkett, 1895	1.265
100	Hughie Jennings, 1896	1.263

Runs Produced

1	Lou Gehrig, 1931	301
2	Babe Ruth, 1921	289
3	Chuck Klein, 1930	288
4	Hugh Duffy, 1894	287
5	Al Simmons, 1930	281
6	Hughie Jennings, 1895	280
	Hack Wilson, 1930	280
	Hank Greenberg, 1937	280
9	Sam Thompson, 1895	278
10	Lou Gehrig, 1927	277
11	Tip O'Neill, 1887	276
	Kiki Cuyler, 1930	276
	Lou Gehrig, 1930	276
14	Billy Hamilton, 1894	275
15	Ed Delahanty, 1894	274
16	Sam Thompson, 1887	273
17	Ed Delahanty, 1893	272
	Joe Kelley, 1895	272
	Joe DiMaggio, 1937	272
20	Joe Kelley, 1894	270
	Lou Gehrig, 1936	270
22	Ty Cobb, 1911	266
	Rogers Hornsby, 1929	266
	Babe Ruth, 1931	266
	Ted Williams, 1949	266
26	Jimmie Foxx, 1938	264
27	Ed Delahanty, 1899	263
28	Babe Ruth, 1927	262
	Jimmie Foxx, 1932	262
30	Al Simmons, 1932	260
	Lou Gehrig, 1937	260
32	Hardy Richardson, 1890	259
	Hugh Duffy, 1893	259
	Walt Wilmot, 1894	259
35	Dan Brouthers, 1894	256
	Bobby Lowe, 1894	256
	Jake Stenzel, 1894	256
	Nap Lajoie, 1901	256
39	Hack Wilson, 1929	255
	Lou Gehrig, 1932	255
	Hank Greenberg, 1935	255
42	Cap Anson, 1886	254
	Willie Keeler, 1894	254
	Lou Gehrig, 1928	254
	Babe Ruth, 1930	254
46	Harry Stovey, 1889	252
47	Pete Browning, 1887	251
	Rogers Hornsby, 1922	251
	Babe Ruth, 1928	251
	Earl Averill, 1931	251
	Chuck Klein, 1932	251
52	Charlie Gehringer, 1934	250
53	Hugh Duffy, 1897	248
54	John McGraw, 1894	247
	Mel Ott, 1929	247
56	Hughie Jennings, 1896	246
	Tris Speaker, 1923	246
	Jimmie Foxx, 1930	246
	Zeke Bonura, 1936	246
	Tommy Davis, 1962	246
61	Sam Thompson, 1893	245
	Bill Terry, 1930	245
	Lou Gehrig, 1933	245
	Charlie Gehringer, 1936	245
	Ted Williams, 1939	245
66	Arlie Latham, 1887	244
	Tom Brown, 1891	244
	Steve Brodie, 1894	244
	Ed Delahanty, 1895	244
	Ed Delahanty, 1896	244
	Ken Williams, 1922	244
	Lou Gehrig, 1934	244
	Hal Trosky, 1936	244
74	Dan Brouthers, 1887	242
	Ed McKean, 1895	242
	Lefty O'Doul, 1929	242
	Ted Williams, 1942	242
78	Lave Cross, 1894	241
	Bill Dahlen, 1894	241
	Babe Ruth, 1920	241
	Babe Ruth, 1923	241
82	Dan Brouthers, 1892	240
	Joe Kelley, 1896	240
	Ty Cobb, 1915	240
	George Sisler, 1920	240
	Joe Cronin, 1930	240
	Jimmie Foxx, 1933	240
88	Hughie Jennings, 1894	239
	Vern Stephens, 1950	239
90	Charlie Comiskey, 1887	238
	George Davis, 1897	238
	Babe Ruth, 1926	238
	Babe Herman, 1930	238
	Hank Greenberg, 1940	238
95	Rogers Hornsby, 1925	237
	Al Simmons, 1929	237
	Joe DiMaggio, 1938	237
98	8 players tied	236

Clutch Hitting Index

1	Cap Anson, 1880	178
2	Tom Herr, 1987	172
3	Ed Abbaticchio, 1907	166
4	Bill McClellan, 1878	165
	Ed McKean, 1892	165
6	Lon Knight, 1881	164
7	Jack Barry, 1913	163
8	George Stovall, 1911	163
9	John Sullivan, 1943	162
10	Tom Herr, 1985	161
11	Fred Hartman, 1902	160
12	Cookie Lavagetto, 1941	160
13	Cap Anson, 1886	158
14	Sherry Magee, 1918	158
15	John Gochnauer, 1903	155
16	Tommy Davis, 1969	155
17	Maurice Van Robays, 1940	154
18	George Davis, 1906	154
19	Art Devlin, 1904	154
20	Frank LaPorte, 1910	154
21	Jack Rowe, 1888	153
22	Pete Hotaling, 1888	153
23	John Ward, 1886	153
24	Sam Crawford, 1910	153
25	Johnny Berardino, 1941	152
26	Jackie Hayes, 1937	152
27	Rebel Oakes, 1915	152
28	Bill Harbidge, 1878	151
	Pop Corkhill, 1886	151
	Frank LaPorte, 1914	151
31	Possum Whitted, 1920	151
32	Heinie Reitz, 1896	151
33	Earl Sheely, 1931	151
34	Joe Gerhardt, 1879	150
	Oyster Burns, 1890	150
	Socks Seybold, 1907	150
37	Cy Seymour, 1908	150
38	Tom Burns, 1888	150
39	Joe Battin, 1876	150
40	Norm Larker, 1960	149
41	Earl Sheely, 1924	149
42	Chick Galloway, 1925	149
43	Sam Thompson, 1887	149
44	Vic Wertz, 1960	149
45	Jack Crooks, 1890	149
46	Hugh Duffy, 1896	148
47	Cap Anson, 1893	148
48	Roger Connor, 1884	148
49	Farmer Vaughn, 1893	148
	Bill Brubaker, 1936	148
51	Pie Traynor, 1928	147
52	Reddy Mack, 1889	147
	Larry Kopf, 1920	147
54	Pete Hotaling, 1880	147
55	Fred Pfeffer, 1882	147
56	Doc Gessler, 1911	147
57	Stuffy McInnis, 1914	147
58	Heinie Zimmerman, 1917	146
59	Bill Dahlen, 1904	146
60	Bill Holbert, 1882	146
61	Deacon White, 1885	146
62	Ned Williamson, 1885	146
	Clyde Barnhart, 1925	146
64	Jimmy Brown, 1942	146
65	Nap Lajoie, 1912	145
66	Cap Anson, 1881	145
	Cap Anson, 1890	145
68	Cap Anson, 1885	145
69	Dave Foutz, 1889	145
70	Mike Mowrey, 1916	145
71	Roy McMillan, 1956	145
72	Joe Kelley, 1898	145
73	Larry Gardner, 1920	144
74	Lave Cross, 1903	144
75	Jose Cardenal, 1971	144
76	Ty Cobb, 1907	143
77	Cap Anson, 1882	143
	Ed Delahanty, 1900	143
79	Hal Chase, 1909	143
80	Cal McVey, 1879	143
	Jim O'Rourke, 1887	143
	Ferris Fain, 1949	143
83	Kirby Puckett, 1994	143
84	John Ward, 1881	143
	Maurice Van Robays, 1941	143
	Joe Medwick, 1942	143
87	Eddie Collins, 1919	143
	Bobby Veach, 1922	143
89	Bill Hague, 1878	142
	Ron Fairly, 1964	142
91	Hick Carpenter, 1886	142
	Ross Youngs, 1921	142
93	Bob Ferguson, 1877	142
94	Monte Cross, 1900	142
	Milt Stock, 1921	142
	Enos Slaughter, 1953	142
97	Deacon White, 1876	142
98	Fred Pfeffer, 1892	142
99	Cupid Childs, 1895	141
100	2 players tied	141

Isolated Power

1	Babe Ruth, 1920	.472
2	Babe Ruth, 1921	.469
3	Mark McGwire, 1996	.418
4	Babe Ruth, 1927	.417
5	Lou Gehrig, 1927	.392
6	Babe Ruth, 1928	.386
7	Jimmie Foxx, 1932	.385
8	Jeff Bagwell, 1994	.382
9	Frank Thomas, 1994	.376
10	Albert Belle, 1995	.374
11	Babe Ruth, 1930	.373
12	Babe Ruth, 1923	.372
13	Mickey Mantle, 1961	.370
14	Hank Greenberg, 1938	.369
15	Hack Wilson, 1930	.368
16	Babe Ruth, 1926	.366
17	Babe Ruth, 1924	.361
18	Babe Ruth, 1922	.357
19	Albert Belle, 1994	.357
20	Jimmie Foxx, 1938	.356
21	Kevin Mitchell, 1994	.355
22	Rogers Hornsby, 1925	.353
23	Mickey Mantle, 1956	.353
24	Babe Ruth, 1929	.353
25	Ken Griffey Jr., 1994	.351
26	Roger Maris, 1961	.351
27	Ralph Kiner, 1949	.348
28	Jimmie Foxx, 1933	.347
29	Willie Stargell, 1973	.347
30	Kevin Mitchell, 1989	.344
31	Lou Gehrig, 1934	.344
32	Jim Gentile, 1961	.344
33	Ted Williams, 1957	.343
34	Lou Gehrig, 1930	.343
35	Lou Gehrig, 1936	.342
36	Hank Aaron, 1971	.341
37	Barry Bonds, 1993	.341
38	Brady Anderson, 1996	.340
39	Willie Mays, 1955	.340
40	Matt Williams, 1994	.339
41	Mike Schmidt, 1980	.338
42	Willie McCovey, 1969	.336
43	Babe Ruth, 1919	.336
44	Barry Bonds, 1994	.335
45	Jimmie Foxx, 1939	.334
46	Reggie Jackson, 1969	.333
47	Willie Stargell, 1971	.333
48	Hank Greenberg, 1937	.332
49	Hank Greenberg, 1940	.330
50	Juan Gonzalez, 1996	.329
51	Ted Williams, 1941	.329
52	Mark McGwire, 1987	.329
53	Willie Mays, 1965	.328
54	Babe Ruth, 1931	.328
55	Mike Schmidt, 1981	.328
56	Hank Greenberg, 1946	.327
57	Joe DiMaggio, 1937	.327
58	Al Simmons, 1930	.327
59	Stan Musial, 1948	.326
60	Ralph Kiner, 1947	.326
61	Dave Kingman, 1979	.325
62	Ted Williams, 1946	.325
63	Ken Griffey Jr., 1996	.325
64	Eddie Mathews, 1953	.325
65	Willie McCovey, 1970	.323
66	Juan Gonzalez, 1993	.323
67	Willie Mays, 1954	.322
68	Lou Gehrig, 1931	.321
69	Johnny Mize, 1940	.321
70	Frank Robinson, 1966	.321
71	Rogers Hornsby, 1922	.321
72	Duke Snider, 1955	.320
73	Babe Ruth, 1932	.319
74	Jimmie Foxx, 1934	.319
75	Ralph Kiner, 1951	.318
76	Ralph Kiner, 1950	.318
77	Harmon Killebrew, 1961	.318
78	Bob Hamelin, 1994	.317
79	Rocky Colavito, 1958	.317
80	Mark McGwire, 1992	.317
81	Chick Hafey, 1930	.316
82	Boog Powell, 1964	.316
83	Ted Kluszewski, 1954	.316
84	Dick Allen, 1966	.315
85	Cecil Fielder, 1990	.314
86	Eddie Mathews, 1954	.313
87	Duke Snider, 1957	.313
88	Barry Bonds, 1992	.313
89	Eddie Mathews, 1955	.313
90	Albert Belle, 1996	.312
91	Johnny Mize, 1947	.312
92	Willie Mays, 1964	.311
93	Willie Mays, 1962	.311
94	George Foster, 1977	.311
95	Mike Schmidt, 1979	.311
96	Jack Clark, 1987	.310
97	Gary Sheffield, 1996	.310
98	Hank Greenberg, 1939	.310
99	Harmon Killebrew, 1969	.308
100	Ken Griffey Jr., 1993	.308

Extra Base Hits

1	Babe Ruth, 1921	119
2	Lou Gehrig, 1927	117
3	Chuck Klein, 1930	107
4	Chuck Klein, 1932	103
	Hank Greenberg, 1937	103
	Stan Musial, 1948	103
	Albert Belle, 1995	103
8	Rogers Hornsby, 1922	102
9	Lou Gehrig, 1930	100
	Jimmie Foxx, 1932	100
11	Babe Ruth, 1920	99
	Babe Ruth, 1923	99
	Hank Greenberg, 1940	99
14	Hank Greenberg, 1935	98
15	Babe Ruth, 1927	97
	Hack Wilson, 1930	97
	Joe Medwick, 1937	97
18	Hank Greenberg, 1934	96
	Hal Trosky, 1936	96
	Joe DiMaggio, 1937	96
21	Lou Gehrig, 1934	95
	Joe Medwick, 1936	95
23	Rogers Hornsby, 1929	94
	Chuck Klein, 1929	94
	Babe Herman, 1930	94
	Jimmie Foxx, 1933	94
27	Jim Bottomley, 1928	93
	Al Simmons, 1930	93
	Lou Gehrig, 1936	93
	Ellis Burks, 1996	93
31	Babe Ruth, 1924	92
	Lou Gehrig, 1931	92
	Jimmie Foxx, 1938	92
	Stan Musial, 1953	92
	Hank Aaron, 1959	92
	Frank Robinson, 1962	92
	Brady Anderson, 1996	92
38	Babe Ruth, 1928	91
	Alex Rodriguez, 1996	91
40	Rogers Hornsby, 1925	90
	Stan Musial, 1949	90
	Willie Mays, 1962	90
	Willie Stargell, 1973	90
44	Hal Trosky, 1934	89
	Duke Snider, 1954	89
	Andres Galarraga, 1996	89
	Albert Belle, 1996	89
48	Joe DiMaggio, 1936	88
	Barry Bonds, 1993	88
50	Tris Speaker, 1923	87
	Kiki Cuyler, 1925	87
	Lou Gehrig, 1928	87
	Ripper Collins, 1934	87
	Charlie Gehringer, 1936	87
	Johnny Mize, 1940	87
	Willie Mays, 1954	87
	Robin Yount, 1982	87
	Kevin Mitchell, 1989	87
59	George Sisler, 1920	86
	Babe Ruth, 1930	86
	Wally Moses, 1937	86
	Johnny Mize, 1939	86
	Ted Williams, 1939	86
	Stan Musial, 1946	86
	Eddie Mathews, 1953	86
	Reggie Jackson, 1969	86
	Hal McRae, 1977	86
	Jim Rice, 1978	86
	Don Mattingly, 1985	86
	Don Mattingly, 1986	86
	Ken Griffey Jr., 1993	86
72	Tip O'Neill, 1887	85
	Hugh Duffy, 1894	85
	Chick Hafey, 1929	85
	Goose Goslin, 1930	85
	Lou Gehrig, 1932	85
	Lou Gehrig, 1933	85
	Earl Averill, 1934	85
	Hank Greenberg, 1938	85
	Rudy York, 1940	85
	Ted Williams, 1949	85
	Stan Musial, 1954	85
	Frank Robinson, 1966	85
	George Foster, 1977	85
	George Brett, 1979	85
	Cal Ripken, 1991	85
87	Sam Thompson, 1895	84
	Ken Williams, 1922	84
	Al Simmons, 1929	84
	Ed Morgan, 1930	84
	Earl Webb, 1931	84
	Joe DiMaggio, 1941	84
	Duke Snider, 1953	84
	Tony Oliva, 1964	84
	Johnny Bench, 1970	84
	Jim Rice, 1979	84
	Steve Finley, 1996	84
98	11 players tied	83

Pinch Hits

1	John Vander Wal, 1995	28
2	Jose Morales, 1976	25
3	Dave Philley, 1961	24
	Vic Davalillo, 1970	24
	Rusty Staub, 1983	24
	Gerald Perry, 1993	24
7	Sam Leslie, 1932	22
	Peanuts Lowrey, 1953	21
	Red Schoendienst, 1962	22
	Wallace Johnson, 1988	22
11	Doc Miller, 1913	21
	Smoky Burgess, 1966	21
	Merv Rettenmund, 1977	21
14	Ed Coleman, 1936	20
	Frenchy Bordagaray, 1938	20
	Joe Frazier, 1954	20
	Smoky Burgess, 1965	20
	Ken Boswell, 1976	20
	Jerry Turner, 1978	20
	Thad Bosley, 1985	20
	Chris Chambliss, 1986	20
22	Many players tied	19

Pinch Hit Average
(30 at-bats minimum)

1	Ed Kranepool, 1974	.486
2	Smead Jolley, 1931	.467
3	Frenchy Bordagaray, 1938	.465
4	Rick Miller, 1983	.457
5	Jose Pagan, 1969	.452
6	Elmer Valo, 1955	.452
	Mark Johnson, 1996	.452
8	Gates Brown, 1968	.450
9	Ted Easterly, 1912	.433
	Milt Thompson, 1985	.433
	Randy Bush, 1986	.433
12	Joe Cronin, 1943	.429
	Don Dillard, 1961	.429
14	Candy Maldonado, 1986	.425
15	Richie Ashburn, 1962	.419
	Dick Williams, 1962	.419
17	Merritt Ranew, 1963	.415
	Carl Taylor, 1969	.415
19	Kurt Bevacqua, 1983	.412
20	Jerry Turner, 1978	.408
21	Bob Bowman, 1958	.406
	Chico Walker, 1991	.406
	Sid Bream, 1994	.406
24	Frankie Baumholtz, 1955	.405
25	7 players tied	.400

Pinch Hit Home Runs

1	Johnny Frederick, 1932	6
2	Joe Cronin, 1943	5
	Butch Nieman, 1945	5
	Gene Freese, 1959	5
	Jerry Lynch, 1961	5
	Cliff Johnson, 1974	5
	Lee Lacy, 1978	5
	Jerry Turner, 1978	5
	Billy Ashley, 1996	5
10	Ernie Lombardi, 1946	4
	Del Wilber, 1953	4
	Bill Taylor, 1955	4
	Bob Thurman, 1957	4
	Rip Repulski, 1958	4
	George Crowe, 1959	4
	George Crowe, 1960	4
	Johnny Blanchard, 1961	4
	Carl Sawatski, 1961	4
	Jerry Lynch, 1963	4
	Don Mincher, 1964	4
	Hal Breeden, 1973	4
	Mike Ivie, 1978	4
	Del Unser, 1979	4
	Jeff Burroughs, 1982	4
	Danny Heep, 1983	4
	Candy Maldonado, 1986	4
	Mark Carreon, 1989	4
	Tommy Gregg, 1990	4
	Ernest Riles, 1990	4
	Howard Johnson, 1994	4
	John Vander Wal, 1995	4
	Jack Howell, 1996	4
	Mark Johnson, 1996	4

Total Player Rating / 150g

1	Babe Ruth, 1923	10.46
2	Jeff Bagwell, 1994	10.36
3	Mike Schmidt, 1981	10.29
4	Fred Dunlap, 1884	10.25
5	Pete Browning, 1882	10.22
6	Nap Lajoie, 1901	10.19
7	Nap Lajoie, 1903	10.08
8	Barry Bonds, 1992	9.86
9	Babe Ruth, 1921	9.28
10	Babe Ruth, 1927	9.14
11	Babe Ruth, 1920	9.08
12	Rickey Henderson, 1990	9.04
13	Mickey Mantle, 1957	8.96
14	Rogers Hornsby, 1924	8.92
15	Mickey Mantle, 1956	8.70
16	Cal Ripken, 1984	8.43
17	Ross Barnes, 1876	8.41
18	Ty Cobb, 1917	8.39
19	Babe Ruth, 1924	8.33
20	Barry Bonds, 1993	8.30
21	Nap Lajoie, 1906	8.29
	Babe Ruth, 1926	8.29
23	Ted Williams, 1941	8.29
24	Rogers Hornsby, 1922	8.28
25	George Brett, 1980	8.21
26	Fred Pfeffer, 1884	8.17
27	Rogers Hornsby, 1920	8.15
28	Ted Williams, 1942	8.10
29	Barry Bonds, 1996	8.07
30	Ted Williams, 1957	8.07
31	Eric Davis, 1987	8.02
32	Nap Lajoie, 1910	8.02
33	Cupid Childs, 1890	7.98
34	Rogers Hornsby, 1917	7.97
35	Ted Williams, 1946	7.90
36	Mickey Mantle, 1961	7.84
37	Lou Gehrig, 1927	7.84
38	Lou Boudreau, 1944	7.80
39	Tris Speaker, 1913	7.77
40	Rickey Henderson, 1985	7.76
41	Hughie Jennings, 1896	7.73
42	Nap Lajoie, 1904	7.71
43	Honus Wagner, 1906	7.71
44	Cal Ripken, 1991	7.69
45	Willie Mays, 1955	7.60
46	King Kelly, 1879	7.60
	George Sisler, 1920	7.60
	Lou Gehrig, 1934	7.60
49	Babe Ruth, 1930	7.55
	Babe Ruth, 1931	7.55
51	Tris Speaker, 1912	7.55
52	Cupid Childs, 1896	7.50
	Barry Bonds, 1994	7.50
54	Nap Lajoie, 1908	7.45
55	Honus Wagner, 1905	7.45
56	Nap Lajoie, 1900	7.35
57	Nap Lajoie, 1907	7.34
58	Honus Wagner, 1903	7.33
59	Jack Glasscock, 1882	7.32
60	Ed Delahanty, 1896	7.32
61	Mike Schmidt, 1980	7.30
62	Ty Cobb, 1911	7.29
	Joe Morgan, 1975	7.29
64	Andre Dawson, 1981	7.28
65	Babe Ruth, 1919	7.27
66	Ron Santo, 1966	7.26
67	Rickey Henderson, 1981	7.22
68	Tris Speaker, 1914	7.22
69	Ken Caminiti, 1996	7.19
70	Ty Cobb, 1910	7.18
71	Ed Delahanty, 1893	7.16
72	Frankie Frisch, 1927	7.16
73	Barry Bonds, 1990	7.15
74	Dick Bartell, 1937	7.15
75	Joe DiMaggio, 1939	7.13
76	Buddy Bell, 1981	7.11
77	Charley Jones, 1877	7.11
	Snuffy Stirnweiss, 1945	7.11
	Willie Mays, 1958	7.11
80	Albert Belle, 1994	7.08
81	Barry Larkin, 1991	7.07
82	Robin Yount, 1981	7.03
83	Barry Bonds, 1995	6.98
84	Willie Mays, 1965	6.97
85	George Sisler, 1922	6.97
86	Harlond Clift, 1937	6.97
	George Brett, 1985	6.97
88	Honus Wagner, 1908	6.95
89	Bobby Wallace, 1901	6.94
90	Joe Jackson, 1911	6.94
91	Hughie Jennings, 1897	6.92
	Rogers Hornsby, 1929	6.92
	Ted Williams, 1947	6.92
94	Rogers Hornsby, 1921	6.92
	Snuffy Stirnweiss, 1944	6.92
96	Joe DiMaggio, 1941	6.91
97	Orator Shaffer, 1878	6.90
98	Pedro Guerrero, 1985	6.90
99	Bob Ferguson, 1878	6.89
100	Hughie Jennings, 1895	6.87

Stolen Bases

1	Hugh Nicol, 1887	138
2	Rickey Henderson, 1982	130
3	Arlie Latham, 1887	129
4	Lou Brock, 1974	118
5	Charlie Comiskey, 1887	117
6	John Ward, 1887	111
	Billy Hamilton, 1889	111
	Billy Hamilton, 1891	111
9	Vince Coleman, 1985	110
10	Arlie Latham, 1888	109
	Vince Coleman, 1987	109
12	Rickey Henderson, 1983	108
13	Vince Coleman, 1986	107
14	Tom Brown, 1891	106
15	Maury Wills, 1962	104
16	Pete Browning, 1887	103
	Hugh Nicol, 1888	103
18	Jim Fogarty, 1887	102
	Billy Hamilton, 1890	102
20	Rickey Henderson, 1980	100
21	Jim Fogarty, 1889	99
22	Billy Hamilton, 1894	98
23	Harry Stovey, 1890	97
	Billy Hamilton, 1895	97
	Ron LeFlore, 1980	97
26	Ty Cobb, 1915	96
	Omar Moreno, 1980	96
28	Bid McPhee, 1887	95
	Curt Welch, 1888	95
30	Mike Griffin, 1887	94
	Maury Wills, 1965	94
32	Tommy McCarthy, 1888	93
	Rickey Henderson, 1988	93
34	Darby O'Brien, 1889	91
35	Tim Raines, 1983	90
36	Curt Welch, 1887	89
	Herman Long, 1889	89
38	Tom Poorman, 1887	88
	Blondie Purcell, 1887	88
	John Ward, 1892	88
	Clyde Milan, 1912	88
42	Harry Stovey, 1888	87
	Arlie Latham, 1891	87
	Joe Kelley, 1896	87
	Rickey Henderson, 1986	87
46	Cub Stricker, 1887	86
47	Tommy Tucker, 1887	85
	Hub Collins, 1890	85
	Hugh Duffy, 1891	85
50	King Kelly, 1887	84
	Chippy McGarr, 1887	84
	Billy Sunday, 1890	84
	Bill Lange, 1896	84
54	Tommy McCarthy, 1890	83
	Billy Hamilton, 1896	83
	Ty Cobb, 1911	83
	Willie Wilson, 1979	83
58	Dummy Hoy, 1888	82
	John Reilly, 1888	82
60	Eddie Collins, 1910	81
	Bob Bescher, 1911	81
	Vince Coleman, 1988	81
63	Emmett Seery, 1888	80
	Hugh Nicol, 1889	80
	Rickey Henderson, 1985	80
	Eric Davis, 1986	80
67	Tom Brown, 1890	79
	Dave Collins, 1980	79
	Willie Wilson, 1980	79
70	Hugh Duffy, 1890	78
	Tom Brown, 1892	78
	John McGraw, 1894	78
	Ron LeFlore, 1979	78
	Tim Raines, 1982	78
	Marquis Grissom, 1992	78
76	Ted Scheffler, 1890	77
	Jimmy Sheckard, 1899	77
	Davey Lopes, 1975	77
	Omar Moreno, 1979	77
	Rudy Law, 1983	77
	Rickey Henderson, 1989	77
	Vince Coleman, 1990	77
83	Ed McKean, 1887	76
	Walt Wilmot, 1890	76
	Dusty Miller, 1896	76
	Ty Cobb, 1909	76
	Marquis Grissom, 1991	76
88	Yank Robinson, 1887	75
	George Van Haltren, 1891	75
	Clyde Milan, 1913	75
	Benny Kauff, 1914	75
	Billy North, 1976	75
	Tim Raines, 1984	75
	Kenny Lofton, 1996	75
95	Frank Fennelly, 1887	74
	Harry Stovey, 1887	74
	Walt Wilmot, 1894	74
	Fritz Maisel, 1914	74
	Lou Brock, 1966	74
100	7 players tied	73

Stolen Base Average

1	Kevin McReynolds, 1988	100.0
	Paul Molitor, 1994	100.0
3	Brady Anderson, 1994	96.9
4	Max Carey, 1922	96.2
5	Ken Griffey Jr., 1980	95.8
6	Stan Javier, 1988	95.2
7	Amos Otis, 1970	94.3
8	Jack Perconte, 1985	93.9
9	Miguel Dilone, 1984	93.1
	Bob Dernier, 1986	93.1
11	Kirk Gibson, 1990	92.9
	Barry Larkin, 1994	92.9
13	Don Baylor, 1972	92.3
	Oddibe McDowell, 1987	92.3
15	Davey Lopes, 1985	92.2
16	Eric Davis, 1988	92.1
17	Henry Cotto, 1992	92.0
18	Bobby Bonds, 1969	91.8
	Davey Lopes, 1978	91.8
20	Davey Lopes, 1979	91.7
	Marquis Grissom, 1990	91.7
22	Jim Wynn, 1965	91.5
23	Larry Bowa, 1977	91.4
24	Ryne Sandberg, 1987	91.3
	Alan Trammell, 1987	91.3
	Rich Amaral, 1995	91.3
27	Jerry Mumphrey, 1980	91.2
28	Tom Herr, 1985	91.2
29	Barry Larkin, 1995	91.1
30	Jack Smith, 1925	90.9
	Davey Lopes, 1981	90.9
	Tim Raines, 1987	90.9
	Bip Roberts, 1995	90.9
	Roberto Alomar, 1995	90.9
35	Craig Biggio, 1994	90.7
36	Derek Bell, 1996	90.6
37	Willie Wilson, 1984	90.4
38	Bake McBride, 1978	90.3
39	Devon White, 1992	90.2
40	Henry Cotto, 1988	90.0
41	Devon White, 1993	89.5
42	Mitchell Page, 1977	89.4
43	Tommy Harper, 1971	89.3
	Rick Manning, 1981	89.3
	Eric Davis, 1987	89.3
46	8 players tied	88.9

Stolen Base Runs

1	Vince Coleman, 1986 . . .	24
2	Maury Wills, 1962	23
3	Rickey Henderson, 1983 .	21
4	Rickey Henderson, 1988 .	20
5	Vince Coleman, 1987 . . .	20
6	Tim Raines, 1983	19
7	Vince Coleman, 1985 . . .	18
	Rickey Henderson, 1985 .	18
9	Willie Wilson, 1979	18
	Ron LeFlore, 1980	18
	Willie Wilson, 1980	18
12	Eric Davis, 1986	17
13	Tim Raines, 1984	17
14	Davey Lopes, 1975	16
	Rudy Law, 1983	16
16	Lou Brock, 1974	16
	Tim Raines, 1985	16
	Tim Raines, 1986	16
	Marquis Grissom, 1992 . .	16
20	Rickey Henderson, 1986 .	15
21	Ron LeFlore, 1979	15
22	Tim Raines, 1981	15
	Rickey Henderson, 1989 .	15
24	Rickey Henderson, 1980 .	14
25	Max Carey, 1922	14
	Joe Morgan, 1975	14
27	Bert Campaneris, 1969 . .	14
	Tim Raines, 1982	14
	Rickey Henderson, 1982 .	14
30	Vince Coleman, 1989 . . .	14
	Rickey Henderson, 1990 .	14
32	Davey Lopes, 1976	13
	Willie Wilson, 1983	13
	Vince Coleman, 1990 . . .	13
35	Mickey Rivers, 1975	13
	Joe Morgan, 1976	13
	Jerry Mumphrey, 1980 . .	13
	Juan Samuel, 1984	13
	Marquis Grissom, 1991 . .	13
	Kenny Lofton, 1992	13
	Kenny Lofton, 1993	13
42	Barry Larkin, 1995	12
	Kenny Lofton, 1996	12
44	Fritz Maisel, 1914	12
	Alan Wiggins, 1983	12
	Tim Raines, 1987	12
47	Julio Cruz, 1978	12
	Davey Lopes, 1985	12
	Ozzie Smith, 1988	12
50	4 players tied	11

Stolen Base Wins

1	Vince Coleman, 1986	2.5
2	Maury Wills, 1962	2.3
3	Rickey Henderson, 1983 .	2.1
4	Rickey Henderson, 1988 .	2.0
5	Tim Raines, 1983	1.9
6	Vince Coleman, 1987 . . .	1.9
7	Vince Coleman, 1985 . . .	1.9
8	Ron LeFlore, 1980	1.9
9	Eric Davis, 1986	1.8
10	Rickey Henderson, 1985 .	1.8
11	Willie Wilson, 1980	1.8
12	Tim Raines, 1984	1.7
13	Willie Wilson, 1979	1.7
14	Marquis Grissom, 1992 . .	1.7
15	Davey Lopes, 1975	1.7
16	Tim Raines, 1985	1.6
17	Lou Brock, 1974	1.6
18	Tim Raines, 1986	1.6
19	Rudy Law, 1983	1.6
20	Tim Raines, 1981	1.6
21	Rickey Henderson, 1986 .	1.5
22	Rickey Henderson, 1989 .	1.5
23	Joe Morgan, 1975	1.5
24	Ron LeFlore, 1979	1.5
25	Tim Raines, 1982	1.4
26	Bert Campaneris, 1969 . .	1.4
27	Vince Coleman, 1989 . . .	1.4
28	Rickey Henderson, 1980 .	1.4
29	Rickey Henderson, 1982 .	1.4
30	Rickey Henderson, 1990 .	1.4
31	Davey Lopes, 1976	1.4
32	Joe Morgan, 1976	1.3
33	Jerry Mumphrey, 1980 . .	1.3
34	Max Carey, 1922	1.3
35	Vince Coleman, 1990 . . .	1.3
36	Fritz Maisel, 1914	1.3
37	Juan Samuel, 1984	1.3
38	Marquis Grissom, 1991 . .	1.3
39	Lou Brock, 1968	1.3
40	Willie Wilson, 1983	1.3
41	Mickey Rivers, 1975	1.3
42	Kenny Lofton, 1992	1.3
43	Ozzie Smith, 1988	1.3
44	Alan Wiggins, 1983	1.3
45	Davey Lopes, 1985	1.2
46	Kenny Lofton, 1993	1.2
47	Barry Larkin, 1995	1.2
48	Julio Cruz, 1978	1.2
49	Lou Brock, 1966	1.2
50	Tim Raines, 1987	1.2

Fielding Average

First Base

1	Steve Garvey, 1984	1.000
2	Stuffy McInnis, 1921	.999
3	Frank McCormick, 1946 . .	.999
4	Steve Garvey, 1981	.999
5	Jim Spencer, 1973	.999
6	Wes Parker, 1968	.999
7	Eddie Murray, 1981	.999
8	Hal Morris, 1992	.999
9	Jim Spencer, 1976	.998
10	Jim Spencer, 1981	.998

Second Base

1	Bobby Grich, 1985	.997
2	Jose Oquendo, 1990	.996
3	Ryne Sandberg, 1991 . . .	.995
4	Jody Reed, 1994	.995
5	Rob Wilfong, 1980	.995
6	Bobby Grich, 1973	.995
7	Frank White, 1988	.994
8	Mark Lemke, 1994	.994
9	Jose Oquendo, 1989	.994
10	Bret Boone, 1995	.994

Shortstop

1	Cal Ripken, 1990	.996
2	Tony Fernandez, 1989 . . .	.992
3	Larry Bowa, 1979	.991
4	Ed Brinkman, 1972	.990
5	Cal Ripken, 1989	.990
6	Spike Owen, 1990	.989
7	Omar Vizquel, 1992	.989
8	Cal Ripken, 1995	.989
9	Tony Fernandez, 1990 . . .	.989
10	Dick Schofield, 1992	.988

Third Base

1	Tony Fernandez, 1994 . . .	.991
2	Don Money, 1974	.989
3	Hank Majeski, 1947	.988
4	Aurelio Rodriguez, 1978 .	.987
5	Willie Kamm, 1933	.984
6	Steve Buechele, 1991 . . .	.983
7	George Kell, 1946	.983
8	Heinie Groh, 1924	.983
9	Carney Lansford, 1979 . .	.983
10	Gary Gaetti, 1994	.982

Outfield

1	Danny Litwhiler, 1942 . . .	1.000
	Willard Marshall, 1951 . . .	1.000
	Tony Gonzalez, 1962 . . .	1.000
	Don Demeter, 1963	1.000
	Rocky Colavito, 1965 . . .	1.000
	Curt Flood, 1966	1.000
	Johnny Callison, 1968 . . .	1.000
	Mickey Stanley, 1968 . . .	1.000
	Ken Harrelson, 1968	1.000
	Ken Berry, 1969	1.000
	Mickey Stanley, 1970 . . .	1.000
	Roy White, 1971	1.000
	Al Kaline, 1971	1.000
	Ken Berry, 1972	1.000
	Carl Yastrzemski, 1977 . .	1.000
	Terry Puhl, 1979	1.000
	Gary Roenicke, 1980 . . .	1.000
	Ken Landreaux, 1981 . . .	1.000
	Terry Puhl, 1981	1.000
	Ken Singleton, 1981	1.000
	Brian Downing, 1982	1.000
	John Lowenstein, 1982 . .	1.000
	Brian Downing, 1984	1.000
	Brett Butler, 1991	1.000
	Darryl Hamilton, 1992 . . .	1.000
	Brett Butler, 1993	1.000
	Darren Lewis, 1993	1.000
	Tim Raines, 1993	1.000
	Lance Johnson, 1994 . . .	1.000
	Milt Thompson, 1994 . . .	1.000
	Jim Eisenreich 1995	1.000
	Stan Javier, 1995	1.000
	Darryl Hamilton, 1996 . . .	1.000
	Paul O'Neill, 1996	1.000

Catcher

1	Spud Davis, 1939	1.000
	Buddy Rosar, 1946	1.000
	Lou Berberet, 1957	1.000
	Pete Daley, 1957	1.000
	Yogi Berra, 1958	1.000
	Rick Cerone, 1988	1.000
7	Tom Pagnozzi, 1992	.999
8	Joe Azcue, 1967	.999
9	Wes Westrum, 1950	.999
10	Terry Steinbach, 1994 . . .	.998

Pitcher (92 chances accepted)

1	Kid Nichols, 1896	1.000
	Frank Owen, 1904	1.000
	Mordecai Brown, 1908 . . .	1.000
	Pete Alexander, 1913 . . .	1.000
	Walter Johnson, 1913 . . .	1.000
	Eppa Rixey, 1917	1.000
	Walter Johnson, 1917 . . .	1.000
	Hal Schumacher, 1935 . . .	1.000
	Larry Jackson, 1964	1.000
	Randy Jones, 1976	1.000
	Greg Maddux, 1990	1.000

Total Chances per Game

First Base

1	Joe Gerhardt, 1876	13.28
2	Jiggs Donahue, 1907 . . .	12.73
3	Oscar Walker, 1879	12.60
4	Joe Start, 1878	12.54
5	Tim Murnane, 1878	12.52
6	Joe Start, 1879	12.49
7	Jake Goodman, 1878 . . .	12.45
8	Herman Dehlman, 1876 . .	12.36
9	Phil Todt, 1926	12.36
10	Joe Start, 1877	12.35

Second Base

1	Thorny Hawkes, 1879 . . .	8.44
2	Chick Fulmer, 1879	8.34
3	Jack Burdock, 1878	8.30
4	Ed Somerville, 1876	8.28
5	Joe Gerhardt, 1877	8.12
6	Fred Pfeffer, 1884	8.08
7	Jack Burdock, 1879	7.88
8	Joe Quest, 1878	7.81
9	Pop Smith, 1885	7.74
10	Joe Quest, 1879	7.73

Shortstop

1	Herman Long, 1889	7.27
2	Hughie Jennings, 1895 . .	7.16
3	Dave Bancroft, 1918	7.14
4	Phil Tomney, 1889	7.12
5	George Davis, 1899	7.08
6	Hughie Jennings, 1896 . .	7.07
7	Hughie Jennings, 1897 . .	7.03
8	Bobby Wallace, 1901 . . .	6.97
9	Monte Cross, 1897	6.97
10	Bill Dahlen, 1895	6.93

Third Base

1	Al Nichols, 1876	5.81
2	Bob Ferguson, 1877	5.61
3	Jumbo Davis, 1888	5.13
5	Cap Anson, 1876	5.03
6	George Bradley, 1880 . . .	4.93
7	Billy Shindle, 1892	4.93
8	Jack Gleason, 1882	4.90
9	Bill Bradley, 1900	4.87
10	Will Foley, 1877	4.79

Outfield

1	Fred Treacey, 1876	4.39
2	Redleg Snyder, 1876 . . .	3.84
3	Charley Jones, 1877	3.77
4	Taylor Douthit, 1928	3.68
5	Mike Mansell, 1879	3.64
6	Richie Ashburn, 1951 . . .	3.64
7	Chet Lemon, 1977	3.60
8	Thurman Tucker, 1944 . . .	3.58
9	Kirby Puckett, 1984	3.57
10	Irv Noren, 1951	3.53
11	Richie Ashburn, 1949 . . .	3.49
12	Carden Gillenwater, 1945 .	3.46
13	Taylor Douthit, 1926	3.43
14	Sam West, 1935	3.41
15	Richie Ashburn, 1956 . . .	3.40
16	Dom DiMaggio, 1948 . . .	3.39
17	Richie Ashburn, 1957 . . .	3.38
18	Lloyd Waner, 1932	3.37
19	Lloyd Waner, 1931	3.37
20	Richie Ashburn, 1958 . . .	3.36

Catcher

1	Bill Holbert, 1883	10.63
2	Sam Trott, 1884	10.35
3	Bill Holbert, 1884	9.51
4	Jocko Milligan, 1884	9.40
5	Mert Hackett, 1884	9.35
6	Barney Gilligan, 1884 . . .	9.30
7	Mike Hines, 1883	9.27
8	George Baker, 1884	8.99
9	Jocko Milligan, 1885	8.82
10	Lew Brown, 1877	8.65

Pitcher

1	Harry Howell, 1905	5.42
2	Harry Howell, 1904	5.12
3	Will White, 1882	4.76
4	Ed Walsh, 1907	4.75
5	George Mullin, 1904	4.53
6	Tony Mullane, 1882	4.38
7	Red Donahue, 1902	4.37
8	Harry Howell, 1906	4.34
9	Jack Katoll, 1902	4.31
10	Nick Altrock, 1904	4.26
	Nick Altrock, 1905	4.26

Chances Accepted per Game

First Base
1 Jiggs Donahue, 1907 . . . 12.65
2 Joe Gerhardt, 1876 . . . . 12.54
3 Phil Todt, 1926 . . . . . . 12.21
4 Joe Start, 1879 . . . . . . 12.15
5 George Burns, 1914 . . . . 12.10
6 Stuffy McInnis, 1918 . . . 12.10
7 George Stovall, 1908 . . . 12.08
8 George Kelly, 1920 . . . . 12.01
9 Joe Start, 1878 . . . . 12.00
10 Oscar Walker, 1879 . . . . 11.92

Second Base
1 Jack Burdock, 1878 . . . . 7.62
2 Thorny Hawkes, 1879 . . . 7.56
3 Chick Fulmer, 1879 . . . . 7.55
4 Fred Pfeffer, 1884 . . . . . 7.29
5 Joe Gerhardt, 1877 . . . . 7.21
6 Ed Somerville, 1876 . . . . 7.20
7 Jack Burdock, 1879 . . . . 7.18
8 Joe Quest, 1879 . . . . . . 7.16
9 Pop Smith, 1885 . . . . . . 7.13
10 Bid McPhee, 1886 . . . . . 7.09

Shortstop
1 Hughie Jennings, 1895 . . 6.73
2 George Davis, 1899 . . . . 6.69
3 Dave Bancroft, 1918 . . . . 6.62
4 Hughie Jennings, 1896 . . 6.56
5 Hughie Jennings, 1897 . . 6.55
6 Rabbit Maranville, 1919 . . 6.48
7 Bobby Wallace, 1901 . . . 6.48
8 Monte Cross, 1897 . . . . 6.41
9 Dave Bancroft, 1920 . . . . 6.40
10 George Davis, 1900 . . . . 6.39

Third Base
1 Bob Ferguson, 1877 . . . . 4.71
2 Al Nichols, 1876 . . . . . . 4.53
3 Billy Shindle, 1892 . . . . . 4.34
4 Jumbo Davis, 1888 . . . . 4.33
5 Billy Alvord, 1891 . . . . . 4.31
6 Bill Bradley, 1900 . . . . . 4.29
7 Cap Anson, 1876 . . . . . 4.27
8 George Bradley, 1880 . . . 4.23
9 Joe Battin, 1883 . . . . . . 4.17
10 Bill Hague, 1878 . . . . . . 4.16

Outfield
1 Fred Treacey, 1876 . . . . 3.70
2 Taylor Douthit, 1928 . . . . 3.62
3 Richie Ashburn, 1951 . . . 3.59
4 Thurman Tucker, 1944 . . . 3.55
5 Kirby Puckett, 1984 . . . . 3.55
6 Chet Lemon, 1977 . . . . . 3.52
7 Irv Noren, 1951 . . . . . . 3.45
8 Richie Ashburn, 1949 . . . 3.42
9 Carden Gillenwater, 1945 . 3.39
10 Sam West, 1935 . . . . . . 3.38
11 Richie Ashburn, 1956 . . . 3.34
12 Richie Ashburn, 1957 . . . 3.33
13 Dom DiMaggio, 1948 . . . 3.33
14 Lloyd Waner, 1932 . . . . 3.32
15 Jim Busby, 1953 . . . . . . 3.31
16 Richie Ashburn, 1958 . . . 3.31
17 Jim Busby, 1952 . . . . . . 3.31
18 Richie Ashburn, 1953 . . . 3.29
19 Lloyd Waner, 1931 . . . . 3.29
20 Dwayne Murphy, 1980 . . . 3.29

Catcher
1 Bill Holbert, 1883 . . . . . 9.78
2 Sam Trott, 1884 . . . . . . 9.63
3 Jocko Milligan, 1884 . . . . 8.83
4 Bill Holbert, 1884 . . . . . 8.75
5 Mert Hackett, 1884 . . . . 8.68
6 Barney Gilligan, 1884 . . . 8.63
7 Duffy Dyer, 1972 . . . . . 8.25
8 Jocko Milligan, 1885 . . . . 8.25
9 Mike Hines, 1883 . . . . . 8.22
10 George Baker, 1884 . . . . 8.06

Pitcher
1 Harry Howell, 1905 . . . . 5.24
2 Harry Howell, 1904 . . . . 4.97
3 Ed Walsh, 1907 . . . . . . 4.68
4 Will White, 1882 . . . . . . 4.56
5 George Mullin, 1904 . . . . 4.24
6 Nick Altrock, 1905 . . . . . 4.21
7 Tony Mullane, 1882 . . . . 4.20
8 Willie Sudhoff, 1904 . . . . 4.19
9 Red Donahue, 1902 . . . . 4.14
10 Nick Altrock, 1904 . . . . . 4.13

Putouts

First Base
1 Jiggs Donahue, 1907 . . . 1846
2 George Kelly, 1920 1759
3 Phil Todt, 1926 1755
4 Wally Pipp, 1926 1710
5 Jiggs Donahue, 1906 . . . 1697
6 Candy LaChance, 1904 . . 1691
7 Tom Jones, 1907 1687
8 Ernie Banks, 1965 1682
9 Wally Pipp, 1922 1667
10 Lou Gehrig, 1927 1662

Second Base
1 Bid McPhee, 1886 529
2 Bobby Grich, 1974 484
3 Bucky Harris, 1922 483
4 Nellie Fox, 1956 478
5 Lou Bierbauer, 1889 472
6 Billy Herman, 1933 466
7 Bill Wambsganss, 1924 . . 463
8 Cub Stricker, 1887 461
9 Buddy Myer, 1935 460
10 Bill Sweeney, 1912 459

Shortstop
1 Hughie Jennings, 1895 . . 425
  Donie Bush, 1914 425
3 Joe Cassidy, 1905 408
4 Rabbit Maranville, 1914 . . 407
5 Dave Bancroft, 1922 405
  Eddie Miller, 1940 405
7 Monte Cross, 1898 404
8 Dave Bancroft, 1921 396
9 Mickey Doolan, 1906 . . . 395
10 Buck Weaver, 1913 392

Third Base
1 Denny Lyons, 1887 255
2 Jimmy Williams, 1899 . . . 251
  Jimmy Collins, 1900 251
4 Jimmy Collins, 1898 243
  Willie Kamm, 1928 243
6 Willie Kamm, 1927 236
7 Frank Baker, 1913 233
8 Bill Coughlin, 1901 232
9 Ernie Courtney, 1905 . . . 229
10 Jimmy Austin, 1911 228

Outfield
1 Taylor Douthit, 1928 547
2 Richie Ashburn, 1951 . . . 538
3 Richie Ashburn, 1949 . . . 514
4 Chet Lemon, 1977 512
5 Dwayne Murphy, 1980 . . . 507
6 Dom DiMaggio, 1948 . . . 503
  Richie Ashburn, 1956 . . . 503
8 Richie Ashburn, 1957 . . . 502
9 Richie Ashburn, 1953 . . . 496
10 Richie Ashburn, 1958 . . . 495
11 Jim Busby, 1954 491
12 Omar Moreno, 1979 490
13 Baby Doll Jacobson, 1924 488
  Bobby Thomson, 1949 . . 488
  Al Bumbry, 1980 488
16 Lloyd Waner, 1931 484
17 Richie Ashburn, 1954 . . . 483
18 Jim Busby, 1953 482
  Willie Wilson, 1980 482
20 Omar Moreno, 1980 479

Catcher
1 Johnny Edwards, 1969 . . 1135
2 Mike Piazza, 1996 1056
3 Johnny Edwards, 1963 . . 1008
4 Javy Lopez, 1996 994
5 Darren Daulton, 1993 . . . 981
6 Randy Hundley, 1969 . . . 978
7 Tony Pena, 1983 976
8 Bill Freehan, 1968 971
9 Gary Carter, 1985 956
10 Gary Carter, 1982 954

Pitcher
1 Dave Foutz, 1886 57
2 Tony Mullane, 1882 54
3 George Bradley, 1876 . . . 50
  Guy Hecker, 1884 50
5 Mike Boddicker, 1984 . . . 49
6 Larry Corcoran, 1884 . . . 47
7 Al Spalding, 1876 45
  Ted Breitenstein, 1895 . . . 45
9 Jim Devlin, 1876 44
  Dave Foutz, 1887 44
  Bill Hutchison, 1890 44

Putouts per Game

First Base
1 Joe Gerhardt, 1876 . . . . . 12.30
2 Joe Start, 1879 . . . . 11.98
3 Joe Start, 1878 . . . . 11.79
4 Jiggs Donahue, 1907 . . . 11.76
5 Joe Start, 1877 . . . . 11.73
6 Herman Dehlman, 1876 . . 11.72
7 Joe Start, 1880 . . . . 11.63
8 Jake Goodman, 1878 . . . 11.55
9 George Burns, 1914 . . . . 11.53
10 Oscar Walker, 1879 . . . . 11.50

Second Base
1 Jack Burdock, 1878 . . . . 4.08
2 Jack Burdock, 1880 . . . . 3.81
3 Bid McPhee, 1886 . . . . . 3.78
4 Bid McPhee, 1884 . . . . . 3.71
5 Joe Quest, 1878 . . . . . . 3.68
6 Cub Stricker, 1887 . . . . . 3.66
7 Lou Bierbauer, 1889 . . . . 3.63
8 Jack Burdock, 1879 . . . . 3.61
9 Chick Fulmer, 1879 . . . . 3.59
10 Bob Ferguson, 1880 . . . . 3.59

Shortstop
1 Hughie Jennings, 1895 . . 3.24
2 Dave Bancroft, 1918 . . . . 2.97
3 Hughie Jennings, 1896 . . 2.90
4 Hughie Jennings, 1897 . . 2.89
5 George Davis, 1898 . . . . 2.88
6 George Davis, 1899 . . . . 2.88
7 Rabbit Maranville, 1919 . . 2.76
8 Honus Wagner, 1913 . . . 2.75
9 Kid Elberfeld, 1901 . . . . . 2.74
10 Buck Weaver, 1914 . . . . 2.74

Third Base
1 Al Nichols, 1876 . . . . . . 2.16
2 Cap Anson, 1876 . . . . . 2.05
3 Hick Carpenter, 1880 . . . 2.03
4 Bob Ferguson, 1877 . . . . 1.95
5 Denny Lyons, 1887 . . . . 1.86
6 Patsy Tebeau, 1890 . . . . 1.85
7 Cap Anson, 1877 . . . . . 1.85
8 Joe Battin, 1876 . . . . . . 1.83
9 Jerry Denny, 1883 . . . . . 1.82
10 Frank Hankinson, 1881 . . 1.80

Outfield
1 Taylor Douthit, 1928 . . . . 3.55
2 Fred Treacey, 1876 . . . . 3.54
3 Richie Ashburn, 1951 . . . 3.49
4 Thurman Tucker, 1944 . . . 3.45
5 Chet Lemon, 1977 . . . . . 3.44
6 Kirby Puckett, 1984 . . . . 3.42
7 Richie Ashburn, 1949 . . . 3.34
8 Irv Noren, 1951 . . . . . . 3.33
9 Sam West, 1935 . . . . . . 3.33
10 Jim Busby, 1952 . . . . . . 3.28
11 Richie Ashburn, 1956 . . . 3.27
12 Richie Ashburn, 1958 . . . 3.26
13 Lloyd Waner, 1932 . . . . 3.25
14 Dom DiMaggio, 1948 . . . 3.25
15 Carden Gillenwater, 1945 . 3.22
16 Richie Ashburn, 1957 . . . 3.22
17 Jim Busby, 1953 . . . . . . 3.21
18 Baby Doll Jacobson, 1924 3.21
19 Dwayne Murphy, 1980 . . . 3.21
20 Taylor Douthit, 1926 . . . . 3.19

Catcher
1 Sam Trott, 1884 . . . . . . 8.18
2 Bill Holbert, 1883 . . . . . 7.75
3 Duffy Dyer, 1972 . . . . . 7.58
4 Dan Wilson, 1995 . . . . . 7.52
5 Johnny Edwards, 1969 . . 7.52
6 Barney Gilligan, 1884 . . . 7.47
7 Javy Lopez, 1994 . . . . . 7.45
8 Johnny Romano, 1964 . . . 7.44
9 Johnny Edwards, 1964 . . 7.42
10 Joe Azcue, 1967 . . . . . . 7.40

Pitcher
1 Kevin Brown, 1995 . . . . . 1.54
2 Mike Boddicker, 1984 . . . 1.44
3 Oil Can Boyd, 1985 . . . . 1.20
4 Nick Altrock, 1904 . . . . . 1.13
5 Greg Maddux, 1990 . . . . 1.11
6 Dave Foutz, 1887 . . . . . 1.10
7 Dwight Gooden, 1986 . . . 1.09
8 Dan Petry, 1984 . . . . . . 1.09
9 Greg Maddux, 1993 . . . . 1.08
10 Nat Hudson, 1888 . . . . . 1.08
  Al Nipper, 1986 . . . . . . 1.08

Assists

First Base
1 Bill Buckner, 1985 184
2 Mark Grace, 1990 180
3 Mark Grace, 1991 167
4 Sid Bream, 1986 166
5 Bill Buckner, 1983 161
6 Bill Buckner, 1982 159
7 Bill Buckner, 1986 157
8 Mickey Vernon, 1949 . . . 155
9 Fred Tenney, 1905 152
  Eddie Murray, 1985 152

Second Base
1 Frankie Frisch, 1927 641
2 Hughie Critz, 1926 588
3 Rogers Hornsby, 1927 . . . 582
4 Ski Melillo, 1930 572
5 Ryne Sandberg, 1983 . . . 571
6 Rabbit Maranville, 1924 . . 568
7 Frank Parkinson, 1922 . . . 562
8 Tony Cuccinello, 1936 . . . 559
9 Johnny Hodapp, 1930 . . . 557
10 Lou Bierbauer, 1892 555

Shortstop
1 Ozzie Smith, 1980 621
2 Glenn Wright, 1924 601
3 Dave Bancroft, 1920 598
4 Tommy Thevenow, 1926 . 597
5 Ivan DeJesus, 1977 595
6 Cal Ripken, 1984 583
7 Whitey Wietelmann, 1943 581
8 Dave Bancroft, 1922 579
9 Rabbit Maranville, 1914 . . 574
10 Don Kessinger, 1968 . . . 573

Third Base
1 Graig Nettles, 1971 412
2 Graig Nettles, 1973 410
  Brooks Robinson, 1974 . . 410
4 Harlond Clift, 1937 405
  Brooks Robinson, 1967 . . 405
6 Mike Schmidt, 1974 404
7 Doug DeCinces, 1982 . . . 399
8 Clete Boyer, 1962 396
  Mike Schmidt, 1977 396
  Buddy Bell, 1982 396

Outfield
1 Orator Shaffer, 1879 50
2 Hugh Nicol, 1884 48
3 Hardy Richardson, 1881 . . 45
4 Tommy McCarthy, 1888 . . 44
  Chuck Klein, 1930 44
6 Charlie Duffee, 1889 43
  Jimmy Bannon, 1894 . . . 43
8 Jim Fogarty, 1889 42
9 Orator Shaffer, 1883 41
  Jim Lillie, 1884 41
11 Jim Fogarty, 1887 39
  Tom Brown, 1893 39
  Mike Mitchell, 1907 39
14 King Kelly, 1883 38
  Harry Stovey, 1889 38
  Tommy McCarthy, 1889 . . 38
17 Jack Manning, 1883 37
  Tom Brown, 1892 37
19 Lon Knight, 1884 36
  Jimmy Ryan, 1889 36
  Jack McGeachy, 1889 . . . 36
  Jimmy Sheckard, 1903 . . 36

Catcher
1 Bill Rariden, 1915 238
2 Bill Rariden, 1914 215
3 Pat Moran, 1903 214
4 Oscar Stanage, 1911 . . . 212
  Art Wilson, 1914 212
6 Gabby Street, 1909 210
7 Frank Snyder, 1915 204
8 George Gibson, 1910 . . . 203
9 Bill Bergen, 1909 202
  Claude Berry, 1914 202

Pitcher
1 Ed Walsh, 1907 227
2 Will White, 1882 223
3 Ed Walsh, 1908 190
4 Harry Howell, 1905 178
5 Tony Mullane, 1882 177
6 John Clarkson, 1885 174
7 John Clarkson, 1889 172
8 Jack Chesbro, 1904 166
9 George Mullin, 1904 163
10 Ed Walsh, 1911 160

Assists per Game

First Base
1 Mark Grace, 1990 . . . . . . 1.18
2 Bill Buckner, 1986 . . . . . 1.14
3 Bill Buckner, 1985 . . . . . 1.14
4 Jeff Bagwell, 1995 . . . . . 1.13
5 Bill Buckner, 1983 . . . . . 1.12
6 Jeff Bagwell, 1994 . . . . . 1.10
7 Sid Bream, 1986 . . . . . . 1.08
8 Eric Karros, 1994 . . . . . 1.08
9 Cecil Fielder, 1994 . . . . . 1.06
10 Ferris Fain, 1951 . . . . . . 1.05

Second Base
1 Joe Gerhardt, 1877 . . . . . 4.28
2 Frankie Frisch, 1927 . . . . 4.19
3 Thorny Hawkes, 1879 . . . . 4.13
4 Hughie Critz, 1933 . . . . . 4.07
5 Frank Parkinson, 1922 . . 4.04
6 Joe Quest, 1879 . . . . . . 3.99
7 Chick Fulmer, 1879 . . . . . 3.96
8 Ed Somerville, 1876 . . . . 3.92
9 Ski Melillo, 1930 . . . . . . 3.86
10 Glenn Hubbard, 1985 . . . 3.85

Shortstop
1 Germany Smith, 1885 . . . 4.21
2 Arthur Irwin, 1880 . . . . . 4.13
3 Art Fletcher, 1919 . . . . . 4.10
4 Bill Dahlen, 1895 . . . . . . 4.09
5 Phil Tomney, 1889 . . . . . 4.05
6 Bobby Wallace, 1901 . . . . 4.04
7 Jack Glasscock, 1887 . . . . 4.04
8 Germany Smith, 1892 . . . . 4.04
9 Henry Easterday, 1888 . . . 3.99
10 Dave Bancroft, 1920 . . . . 3.99

Third Base
1 Jumbo Davis, 1888 . . . . . 2.96
2 Buddy Bell, 1981 . . . . . . 2.93
3 George Bradley, 1880 . . . . 2.89
4 Bill Hague, 1878 . . . . . . 2.85
5 Billy Shindle, 1892 . . . . . 2.85
6 Bob Ferguson, 1877 . . . . 2.77
7 Ned Williamson, 1879 . . . 2.76
8 Arlie Latham, 1884 . . . . . 2.75
9 Bill Bradley, 1900 . . . . . . 2.75
10 Arlie Latham, 1891 . . . . . 2.74

Outfield
1 Orator Shaffer, 1879 . . . . 0.69
2 Hardy Richardson, 1881 . 0.57
3 Hugh Nicol, 1884 . . . . . . 0.55
4 King Kelly, 1878 . . . . . . 0.51
5 John Cassidy, 1878 . . . . . 0.50
   King Kelly, 1880 . . . . . . 0.50
7 King Kelly, 1883 . . . . . . 0.46
8 Jake Evans, 1882 . . . . . . 0.46
9 Orator Shaffer, 1878 . . . . 0.44
10 Dick Higham, 1878 . . . . . 0.44
11 Orator Shaffer, 1883 . . . . 0.43
12 King Kelly, 1881 . . . . . . 0.43
13 Orator Shaffer, 1880 . . . . 0.42
14 Jake Evans, 1879 . . . . . . 0.42
15 Jack Manning, 1883 . . . . 0.38
16 Jake Evans, 1881 . . . . . . 0.37
17 Jimmy Wolf, 1883 . . . . . 0.37
18 Hugh Nicol, 1883 . . . . . . 0.37
19 Jim Lillie, 1884 . . . . 0.36
20 Buttercup Dickerson, 1883 . 0.36

Catcher
1 Bill Holbert, 1884 . . . . . . 2.41
2 Tom Daly, 1887 . . . . 2.31
3 Bill Holbert, 1882 . . . . . . 2.14
4 Pop Snyder, 1884 . . . . . . 2.08
5 Bill Holbert, 1883 . . . . . . 2.03
6 Buck Ewing, 1881 . . . . . . 2.02
7 Pat Moran, 1903 . . . . . . 2.00
8 Charlie Reipschlager, 1885 . 1.98
9 Connie Mack, 1888 . . . . . 1.92
10 King Kelly, 1888 . . . . . . 1.92

Pitcher
1 Harry Howell, 1905 . . . . . 4.68
2 Harry Howell, 1904 . . . . . 4.21
3 Will White, 1882 . . . . . . 4.13
4 Ed Walsh, 1907 . . . . 4.05
5 Willie Sudhoff, 1904 . . . . 3.85
6 Red Donahue, 1902 . . . . . 3.71
7 George Mullin, 1904 . . . . 3.62
8 Frank Owen, 1904 . . . . . 3.51
9 Carl Mays, 1918 . . . . . . 3.49
10 Jack Katoll, 1902 . . . . . . 3.44

Double Plays

First Base
1 Ferris Fain, 1949 194
2 Ferris Fain, 1950 192
3 Donn Clendenon, 1966 . . 182
4 Ron Jackson, 1979 175
5 Gil Hodges, 1951 171
6 Mickey Vernon, 1949 168
7 Ted Kluszewski, 1954 166
8 Rudy York, 1944 163
9 Donn Clendenon, 1965 . . 161
   Rod Carew, 1977 161

Second Base
1 Bill Mazeroski, 1966 161
2 Jerry Priddy, 1950 150
3 Bill Mazeroski, 1961 144
   Nellie Fox, 1957 141
   Dave Cash, 1974 141
6 Buddy Myer, 1935 138
   Bill Mazeroski, 1962 138
   Carlos Baerga, 1992 138
9 Jerry Coleman, 1950 137
   Jackie Robinson, 1951 . . 137
   Red Schoendienst, 1954 . . 137

Shortstop
1 Rick Burleson, 1980 147
2 Roy Smalley, 1979 144
3 Bobby Wine, 1970 137
4 Lou Boudreau, 1944 134
5 Spike Owen, 1986 133
6 Rafael Ramirez, 1982 130
7 Roy McMillan, 1954 129
8 Hod Ford, 1928 128
   Vern Stephens, 1949 128
   Gene Alley, 1966 128

Third Base
1 Graig Nettles, 1971 54
2 Harlond Clift, 1937 50
3 Johnny Pesky, 1949 48
   Paul Molitor, 1982 48
5 Sammy Hale, 1927 46
   Clete Boyer, 1965 46
   Gary Gaetti, 1983 46
8 Eddie Yost, 1950 45
   Frank Malzone, 1961 45
   Darrell Evans, 1974 45

Outfield
1 Happy Felsch, 1919 15
2 Jimmy Sheckard, 1899 . . . 14
3 Tom Brown, 1893 13
4 Tom Brown, 1886 12
   Tommy McCarthy, 1888 . . 12
   Jimmy Bannon, 1894 12
   Mike Griffin, 1895 12
   Danny Green, 1899 12
   Cy Seymour, 1905 12
   Ginger Beaumont, 1907 . . 12
   Ty Cobb, 1907 12
   Tris Speaker, 1909 12
   Jimmy Sheckard, 1911 . . . 12
   Tris Speaker, 1914 12
   Mel Ott, 1929 12
16 Sam Thompson, 1886 . . . 11
   Tommy McCarthy, 1889 . . 11
   Billy Sunday, 1890 11
   Sam Thompson, 1896 . . . 11
   Bill Lange, 1899 11
   Fielder Jones, 1902 11
   Jimmy Sebring, 1903 11
   Ben Koehler, 1905 11
   Burt Shotton, 1913 11
   Chief Wilson, 1914 11

Catcher
1 Steve O'Neill, 1916 36
2 Frankie Hayes, 1945 29
3 Ray Schalk, 1920 25
   Yogi Berra, 1951 25
5 Jack Lapp, 1915 23
   Muddy Ruel, 1924 23
   Tom Haller, 1968 23
8 Steve O'Neill, 1914 22
   Bob O'Farrell, 1922 22
10 Gabby Hartnett, 1927 . . . 21
   Wes Westrum, 1950 21

Pitcher
1 Bob Lemon, 1953 15
2 Eddie Rommel, 1924 12
   Curt Davis, 1934 12
   Randy Jones, 1976 12
5 Scott Perry, 1919 11
   Tom Rogers, 1919 11
   Art Nehf, 1920 11
   Burleigh Grimes, 1925 . . . 11
   Gene Bearden, 1948 11
10 10 players tied 10

Fielding Runs

1 Glenn Hubbard, 1985 . . . 61.8
2 Danny Richardson, 1892 . 57.6
3 Bill Mazeroski, 1963 . . . . 56.7
4 Rabbit Maranville, 1914 . . 51.8
5 Freddie Maguire, 1928 . . . 50.5
6 Nap Lajoie, 1908 . . . . . . 49.4
7 Danny Richardson, 1891 . 49.1
8 Frankie Frisch, 1927 . . . . 48.6
9 Hughie Critz, 1933 . . . . . 46.5
10 George Davis, 1899 . . . . 46.3
11 Nap Lajoie, 1907 . . . . . . 45.9
12 Fred Pfeffer, 1884 . . . . . 45.5
13 Dick Bartell, 1936 . . . . . 44.8
14 Ozzie Guillen, 1988 . . . . 42.6
15 Dave Shean, 1910 . . . . . 42.5
   Lee Tannehill, 1911 . . . . 42.5
17 Cupid Childs, 1896 . . . . . 42.4
18 Graig Nettles, 1971 . . . . 42.3
19 Joe Gerhardt, 1890 . . . . . 41.5
20 Bid McPhee, 1889 . . . . . 41.1
   Bill Mazeroski, 1962 . . . . 41.1
   Ryne Sandberg, 1983 . . . 41.1
23 Harlond Clift, 1937 . . . . . 41.0
   Glenn Hubbard, 1986 . . . 41.0
25 Bill Mazeroski, 1966 . . . . 40.8
   Ozzie Smith, 1980 . . . . . 40.8
27 Nap Lajoie, 1903 . . . . . . 40.1
28 Germany Smith, 1885 . . . 39.9
29 Arlie Latham, 1884 . . . . . 39.5
30 Lee Tannehill, 1906 . . . . 39.3
31 John Kerins, 1886 . . . . . 39.0
   Dave Bancroft, 1920 . . . . 39.0
33 Bobby Wallace, 1899 . . . . 38.8
   Cal Ripken, 1984 . . . . . . 38.8
35 Bob Allen, 1890 . . . . . . 38.6
36 Fred Pfeffer, 1888 . . . . . 38.3
37 Everett Scott, 1921 . . . . . 38.1
38 Bill Dahlen, 1908 . . . . . . 37.5
   Dick Bartell, 1937 . . . . . 37.5
   Dal Maxvill, 1970 . . . . . . 37.5
41 Bobby Knoop, 1964 . . . . 37.2
42 Al Weis, 1966 . . . . 36.9
43 Billy Shindle, 1888 . . . . . 36.8
44 Tim Wallach, 1985 . . . . . 36.7
45 Lou Bierbauer, 1889 . . . . 36.6
46 Miller Huggins, 1905 . . . . 36.2
   Clete Boyer, 1962 . . . . . 36.2
48 Tommy Leach, 1904 . . . . 35.8
   Ivan DeJesus, 1977 . . . . . 35.8
50 Hughie Jennings, 1895 . . 35.7
51 Bill Dahlen, 1895 . . . . . . 35.6
   Harry Steinfeldt, 1900 . . . 35.6
53 Jack Glasscock, 1889 . . . . 35.5
   Billy Shindle, 1892 . . . . . 35.5
55 Freddie Patek, 1973 . . . . 35.3
56 Bobby Knoop, 1970 . . . . 35.1
57 Jack Glasscock, 1887 . . . . 35.0
58 Chet Lemon, 1977 . . . . . 34.9
59 Jimmy Bloodworth, 1941 . 34.7
60 George Davis, 1898 . . . . 34.6
61 Bill Holbert, 1883 . . . . . 34.4
   Buddy Bell, 1982 . . . . . . 34.4
63 Hughie Jennings, 1896 . . 34.2
   Doc Lavan, 1916 . . . . . . 34.2
65 Art Fletcher, 1915 . . . . . 34.1
66 Bid McPhee, 1893 . . . . . 34.0
   Shorty Fuller, 1895 . . . . . 34.0
68 Joe Cassidy, 1905 . . . . . 33.9
   Bill Mazeroski, 1964 . . . . 33.9
70 Mark Belanger, 1978 . . . . 33.8
71 Eddie Collins, 1910 . . . . 33.7
   Gene Alley, 1970 . . . . . . 33.7
73 Buck Weaver, 1913 . . . . . 33.6
74 Lave Cross, 1895 . . . . . . 33.5
   John Farrell, 1902 . . . . . 33.5
   Donie Bush, 1914 . . . . . 33.5
   Leo Cardenas, 1969 . . . . 33.5
78 Pop Smith, 1885 . . . . . . 33.2
79 Hughie Jennings, 1894 . . 33.1
   Ski Melillo, 1931 . . . . . . 33.1
   Roy Smalley, 1979 . . . . . 33.1
   Ozzie Smith, 1982 . . . . . 33.1
83 Mickey Doolan, 1915 . . . . 33.0
84 Tom Daly, 1887 . . . . . . 32.9
   Red Schoendienst, 1952 . . 32.9
   Red Schoendienst, 1954 . . 32.9
87 Lave Cross, 1899 . . . . . . 32.7
88 Don Zimmer, 1958 . . . . . 32.6
89 Dave Parker, 1977 . . . . . 32.5
90 Richie Ashburn, 1957 . . . 32.4
91 Richie Ashburn, 1951 . . . 32.3
   Marty Barrett, 1987 . . . . 32.3
93 Herman Long, 1889 . . . . 32.2
94 Germany Smith, 1887 . . . 32.0
   George McBride, 1908 . . . 32.0
   Wally Gerber, 1928 . . . . . 32.0
   Bucky Dent, 1979 . . . . . 32.0
98 Spike Owen, 1986 . . . . . 31.9
99 Heinie Wagner, 1908 . . . . 31.8
   Pep Young, 1938 . . . . . . 31.8

Fielding Runs

First Base
1 Mark Grace, 1990 27
2 Bill Buckner, 1985 25
3 Chick Gandil, 1914 24
4 Sid Bream, 1986 24
5 Fred Tenney, 1905 22
6 Bill Buckner, 1983 22
7 Vic Power, 1960 21
8 Sid Bream, 1988 21
9 Jake Beckley, 1892 21
10 Jiggs Donahue, 1907 21

Second Base
1 Glenn Hubbard, 1985 . . . 62
2 Bill Mazeroski, 1963 57
3 Freddie Maguire, 1928 . . . 50
4 Frankie Frisch, 1927 49
5 Nap Lajoie, 1908 48
6 Hughie Critz, 1933 46
7 Fred Pfeffer, 1884 46
8 Danny Richardson, 1891 . 44
9 Nap Lajoie, 1907 44
10 Dave Shean, 1910 42

Shortstop
1 Rabbit Maranville, 1914 . . 52
2 George Davis, 1899 46
3 Dick Bartell, 1936 45
4 Ozzie Guillen, 1988 43
5 Ozzie Smith, 1980 41
6 Germany Smith, 1885 . . . 40
7 Dave Bancroft, 1920 39
8 Cal Ripken, 1984 39
9 Bob Allen, 1890 39
10 Everett Scott, 1921 38

Third Base
1 Graig Nettles, 1971 42
2 Harlond Clift, 1937 41
3 Arlie Latham, 1884 40
4 Billy Shindle, 1892 38
5 Billy Shindle, 1888 37
6 Tim Wallach, 1985 37
7 Clete Boyer, 1962 36
8 Tommy Leach, 1904 36
9 Lee Tannehill, 1906 35
10 Buddy Bell, 1982 35

Outfield
1 Chet Lemon, 1977 35
2 Dave Parker, 1977 33
3 Richie Ashburn, 1957 . . . 32
4 Richie Ashburn, 1951 . . . 32
5 Jim Fogarty, 1887 32
6 Kirby Puckett, 1984 30
7 Tommy McCarthy, 1888 . . 30
8 Max Carey, 1916 30
9 Eric Davis, 1987 28
10 Tris Speaker, 1914 28
11 Omar Moreno, 1980 27
12 Tom Brown, 1893 27
13 Garry Maddox, 1979 27
14 Carl Yastrzemski, 1964 . . . 27
15 Gerald Young, 1989 26
16 Ed Delahanty, 1893 26
17 Gary Ward, 1983 26
18 Richie Ashburn, 1953 . . . 26
19 Mike Griffin, 1891 26
20 Richie Ashburn, 1956 . . . 25

Catcher
1 John Kerins, 1886 37
2 Bill Holbert, 1883 36
3 Tom Daly, 1887 32
4 Duke Farrell, 1894 30
5 John Kerins, 1887 27
6 Pop Snyder, 1884 26
7 Wilbert Robinson, 1888 . . 26
8 Connie Mack, 1892 25
9 Pop Snyder, 1879 25
10 George Mitterwald, 1970 . . 24

Pitcher
1 Ed Walsh, 1907 22
2 Harry Howell, 1905 18
3 Ed Walsh, 1911 15
4 Ed Walsh, 1908 14
5 Will White, 1882 13
6 John Clarkson, 1889 11
7 Sadie McMahon, 1890 . . . 11
8 Tony Mullane, 1882 11
9 Carl Mays, 1926 10
10 Frank Smith, 1909 10

Fielding Wins

1	Glenn Hubbard, 1985	6.5
2	Bill Mazeroski, 1963	6.2
3	Nap Lajoie, 1908	5.6
4	Rabbit Maranville, 1914	5.6
5	Danny Richardson, 1892	5.3
6	Nap Lajoie, 1907	5.1
7	Freddie Maguire, 1928	4.9
8	Hughie Critz, 1933	4.9
9	Frankie Frisch, 1927	4.8
10	Graig Nettles, 1971	4.6
11	Dave Shean, 1910	4.5
12	Danny Richardson, 1891	4.4
13	Dick Bartell, 1936	4.4
14	Bill Dahlen, 1908	4.3
15	Lee Tannehill, 1906	4.3
16	Ozzie Smith, 1980	4.3
17	Ozzie Guillen, 1988	4.3
18	Ryne Sandberg, 1983	4.3
19	Bill Mazeroski, 1966	4.3
20	Glenn Hubbard, 1986	4.3
21	George Davis, 1899	4.2
22	Dave Bancroft, 1920	4.2
23	Lee Tannehill, 1911	4.2
24	Nap Lajoie, 1903	4.2
25	Bill Mazeroski, 1962	4.1
26	Fred Pfeffer, 1884	4.1
27	Al Weis, 1966	4.0
28	Bobby Knoop, 1964	3.9
29	Cal Ripken, 1984	3.9
30	Tim Wallach, 1985	3.9
31	Doc Lavan, 1916	3.8
32	Art Fletcher, 1915	3.8
33	Tommy Leach, 1904	3.8
34	Harland Clift, 1937	3.8
35	Fred Pfeffer, 1888	3.8
36	Miller Huggins, 1905	3.8
37	Eddie Collins, 1910	3.7
38	Dal Maxvill, 1970	3.7
39	Joe Cassidy, 1905	3.7
40	Dick Bartell, 1937	3.7
41	Donie Bush, 1914	3.7
42	Joe Gerhardt, 1890	3.6
43	George McBride, 1908	3.6
44	Bobby Knoop, 1970	3.6
45	Clete Boyer, 1962	3.6
46	Ivan DeJesus, 1977	3.6
47	Heinie Wagner, 1908	3.6
48	Freddie Patek, 1973	3.6
49	Arlie Latham, 1884	3.6
50	Cupid Childs, 1896	3.6
51	Germany Smith, 1885	3.6
52	Bill Mazeroski, 1964	3.6
53	Buck Weaver, 1913	3.6
54	Everett Scott, 1921	3.6
55	Mickey Doolan, 1915	3.6
56	John Farrell, 1902	3.5
57	Joe Tinker, 1908	3.5
58	Bobby Wallace, 1899	3.5
59	Leo Cardenas, 1969	3.5
60	Mark Belanger, 1978	3.5
61	Ozzie Smith, 1982	3.5
62	Bid McPhee, 1889	3.5
63	Chet Lemon, 1977	3.5
64	Buddy Bell, 1982	3.4
65	Buck Herzog, 1915	3.4
66	Bob Allen, 1890	3.4
67	John Kerins, 1886	3.4
68	Max Carey, 1916	3.4
69	Red Schoendienst, 1952	3.4
70	Brooks Robinson, 1967	3.4
71	Billy Shindle, 1888	3.4
72	Nap Lajoie, 1906	3.4
73	Horace Clarke, 1968	3.4
74	Nap Lajoie, 1916	3.4
75	Jimmy Bloodworth, 1941	3.4
76	Gene Alley, 1970	3.4
77	Freddie Patek, 1972	3.4
78	Ron Santo, 1967	3.3
79	Johnny Evers, 1904	3.3
80	Buck Herzog, 1914	3.3
81	Richie Ashburn, 1957	3.3
82	Dave Parker, 1977	3.3
83	Don Zimmer, 1958	3.3
84	Billy Shindle, 1892	3.3
85	Red Schoendienst, 1954	3.3
86	Harry Steinfeldt, 1900	3.3
87	Bruno Betzel, 1916	3.2
88	Richie Ashburn, 1951	3.2
89	George Davis, 1898	3.2
90	Roy Smalley, 1979	3.2
91	Terry Pendleton, 1989	3.2
92	Ed Brinkman, 1970	3.2
93	Pep Young, 1938	3.2
94	Rabbit Maranville, 1919	3.2
95	Zoilo Versalles, 1962	3.2
96	Dave Bancroft, 1917	3.2
97	Buddy Bell, 1981	3.1
98	Johnny Evers, 1907	3.1
99	Spike Owen, 1986	3.1
100	Billy Jurges, 1932	3.1

Total Player Rating

1	Babe Ruth, 1923	10.6
2	Babe Ruth, 1921	9.4
3	Babe Ruth, 1927	9.2
	Barry Bonds, 1992	9.2
5	Cal Ripken, 1984	9.1
6	Nap Lajoie, 1901	8.9
7	Barry Bonds, 1993	8.8
8	Mickey Mantle, 1956	8.7
9	Babe Ruth, 1920	8.6
	Mickey Mantle, 1957	8.6
11	Nap Lajoie, 1910	8.5
	Ty Cobb, 1917	8.5
	Rogers Hornsby, 1922	8.5
	Rogers Hornsby, 1924	8.5
	Babe Ruth, 1924	8.5
	Barry Bonds, 1996	8.5
17	Nap Lajoie, 1903	8.4
	Nap Lajoie, 1906	8.4
	Babe Ruth, 1926	8.4
20	Cal Ripken, 1991	8.3
21	Rickey Henderson, 1990	8.2
22	Rogers Hornsby, 1920	8.1
	Lou Gehrig, 1927	8.1
	Ted Williams, 1942	8.1
25	Mickey Mantle, 1961	8.0
26	Ted Williams, 1941	7.9
	Ted Williams, 1946	7.9
28	Nap Lajoie, 1908	7.8
	George Sisler, 1920	7.8
	Lou Gehrig, 1934	7.8
	Lou Boudreau, 1944	7.8
32	Tris Speaker, 1912	7.7
	Rogers Hornsby, 1917	7.7
	Willie Mays, 1955	7.7
35	Tris Speaker, 1914	7.6
	Jeff Bagwell, 1994	7.6
37	Ron Santo, 1966	7.5
38	Rickey Henderson, 1985	7.4
39	Honus Wagner, 1905	7.3
	Honus Wagner, 1906	7.3
	Tris Speaker, 1913	7.3
	Frankie Frisch, 1927	7.3
	Babe Ruth, 1930	7.3
	Babe Ruth, 1931	7.3
	Willie Mays, 1965	7.3
	Ron Santo, 1967	7.3
	Carl Yastrzemski, 1967	7.3
	Mike Schmidt, 1980	7.3
49	Nap Lajoie, 1904	7.2
	Rogers Hornsby, 1929	7.2
	Harland Clift, 1937	7.2
	Snuffy Stirnweiss, 1945	7.2
	Ted Williams, 1947	7.2
	Willie Mays, 1958	7.2
	George Brett, 1985	7.2
	Barry Bonds, 1990	7.2
57	Ty Cobb, 1911	7.1
	Rogers Hornsby, 1921	7.1
	Snuffy Stirnweiss, 1944	7.1
	Ted Williams, 1957	7.1
	Norm Cash, 1961	7.1
	Joe Morgan, 1975	7.1
63	Honus Wagner, 1908	7.0
	Eddie Collins, 1910	7.0
	Babe Ruth, 1928	7.0
	Mike Schmidt, 1981	7.0
	Robin Yount, 1982	7.0
	Kevin Mitchell, 1989	7.0
	Ken Caminiti, 1996	7.0
70	Fred Dunlap, 1884	6.9
	Joe Jackson, 1912	6.9
	Rogers Hornsby, 1927	6.9
	Lou Gehrig, 1930	6.9
	Lou Boudreau, 1948	6.9
	Rico Petrocelli, 1969	6.9
	Mike Schmidt, 1974	6.9
	Eric Davis, 1987	6.9
78	Joe Jackson, 1911	6.8
	Jackie Robinson, 1951	6.8
	Jeff Bagwell, 1996	6.8
81	Cupid Childs, 1890	6.7
	Hughie Jennings, 1896	6.7
	Nap Lajoie, 1907	6.7
	Ty Cobb, 1910	6.7
	Joe Cronin, 1930	6.7
	Jimmie Foxx, 1933	6.7
	Lou Boudreau, 1943	6.7
	Ted Williams, 1949	6.7
	Willie Mays, 1954	6.7
	Frank Robinson, 1966	6.7
	Mike Schmidt, 1977	6.7
	Cal Ripken, 1983	6.7
	Barry Bonds, 1995	6.7
94	11 players tied	6.6

Total Player Rating (alpha.)

Jeff Bagwell, 1994	7.6
Jeff Bagwell, 1996	6.8
Barry Bonds, 1990	7.2
Barry Bonds, 1992	9.2
Barry Bonds, 1993	8.8
Barry Bonds, 1995	6.7
Barry Bonds, 1996	8.5
Lou Boudreau, 1943	6.7
Lou Boudreau, 1944	7.8
Lou Boudreau, 1948	6.9
George Brett, 1985	7.2
Ken Caminiti, 1996	7.0
Norm Cash, 1961	7.1
Cupid Childs, 1890	6.7
Harlond Clift, 1937	7.2
Ty Cobb, 1910	6.7
Ty Cobb, 1911	7.1
Ty Cobb, 1917	8.5
Eddie Collins, 1910	7.0
Joe Cronin, 1930	6.7
Eric Davis, 1987	6.9
Fred Dunlap, 1884	6.9
Jimmie Foxx, 1933	6.7
Frankie Frisch, 1927	7.3
Lou Gehrig, 1927	8.1
Lou Gehrig, 1930	6.9
Lou Gehrig, 1934	7.8
Rickey Henderson, 1985	7.4
Rickey Henderson, 1990	8.2
Rogers Hornsby, 1917	7.7
Rogers Hornsby, 1920	8.1
Rogers Hornsby, 1921	7.1
Rogers Hornsby, 1922	8.5
Rogers Hornsby, 1924	8.5
Rogers Hornsby, 1927	6.9
Rogers Hornsby, 1929	7.2
Joe Jackson, 1911	6.8
Joe Jackson, 1912	6.9
Hughie Jennings, 1896	6.7
Nap Lajoie, 1901	8.9
Nap Lajoie, 1903	8.4
Nap Lajoie, 1904	7.2
Nap Lajoie, 1906	8.4
Nap Lajoie, 1907	6.7
Nap Lajoie, 1908	7.8
Nap Lajoie, 1910	8.5
Mickey Mantle, 1956	8.7
Mickey Mantle, 1957	8.6
Mickey Mantle, 1961	8.0
Willie Mays, 1954	6.7
Willie Mays, 1955	7.7
Willie Mays, 1958	7.2
Willie Mays, 1965	7.3
Kevin Mitchell, 1989	7.0
Joe Morgan, 1975	7.1
Rico Petrocelli, 1969	6.9
Cal Ripken, 1983	6.7
Cal Ripken, 1984	9.1
Cal Ripken, 1991	8.3
Jackie Robinson, 1951	6.8
Frank Robinson, 1966	6.7
Babe Ruth, 1920	8.6
Babe Ruth, 1921	9.4
Babe Ruth, 1923	10.6
Babe Ruth, 1924	8.5
Babe Ruth, 1926	8.4
Babe Ruth, 1927	9.2
Babe Ruth, 1928	7.0
Babe Ruth, 1930	7.3
Babe Ruth, 1931	7.3
Ron Santo, 1966	7.5
Ron Santo, 1967	7.3
Mike Schmidt, 1974	6.9
Mike Schmidt, 1977	6.7
Mike Schmidt, 1980	7.3
Mike Schmidt, 1981	7.0
George Sisler, 1920	7.8
Tris Speaker, 1912	7.7
Tris Speaker, 1913	7.3
Tris Speaker, 1914	7.6
Snuffy Stirnweiss, 1944	7.1
Snuffy Stirnweiss, 1945	7.2
Honus Wagner, 1905	7.3
Honus Wagner, 1906	7.3
Honus Wagner, 1908	7.0
Ted Williams, 1941	7.9
Ted Williams, 1942	8.1
Ted Williams, 1946	7.9
Ted Williams, 1947	7.2
Ted Williams, 1949	6.7
Ted Williams, 1957	7.1
Carl Yastrzemski, 1967	7.3
Robin Yount, 1982	7.0

Total Player Rating (by era)

1876-1892

1	Fred Dunlap, 1884	6.9
2	Cupid Childs, 1890	6.7
3	Fred Pfeffer, 1884	6.1
	Dan Brouthers, 1892	6.1
5	Jack Glasscock, 1889	5.9
6	Billy Nash, 1888	4.9
	Harry Stovey, 1889	4.9
	Jack Glasscock, 1890	4.9
9	Hardy Richardson, 1886	4.8
	Denny Lyons, 1890	4.8
11	Pete Browning, 1882	4.7
	Ned Williamson, 1884	4.7
	Tip O'Neill, 1887	4.7
14	3 players tied	4.6

1893-1919

1	Nap Lajoie, 1901	8.9
2	Nap Lajoie, 1910	8.5
	Ty Cobb, 1917	8.5
4	Nap Lajoie, 1903	8.4
	Nap Lajoie, 1906	8.4
6	Nap Lajoie, 1908	7.8
7	Tris Speaker, 1912	7.7
	Rogers Hornsby, 1917	7.7
9	Tris Speaker, 1914	7.6
10	Honus Wagner, 1905	7.3
	Honus Wagner, 1906	7.3
	Tris Speaker, 1913	7.3
13	Nap Lajoie, 1904	7.2
14	Ty Cobb, 1911	7.1
15	2 players tied	7.0

1920-1941

1	Babe Ruth, 1923	10.6
2	Babe Ruth, 1921	9.4
3	Babe Ruth, 1927	9.2
4	Babe Ruth, 1920	8.6
5	Rogers Hornsby, 1922	8.5
	Rogers Hornsby, 1924	8.5
	Babe Ruth, 1924	8.5
8	Babe Ruth, 1926	8.4
9	Rogers Hornsby, 1920	8.1
	Lou Gehrig, 1927	8.1
11	Ted Williams, 1941	7.9
12	George Sisler, 1920	7.8
	Lou Gehrig, 1934	7.8
14	3 players tied	7.3

1942-1960

1	Mickey Mantle, 1956	8.7
2	Mickey Mantle, 1957	8.6
3	Ted Williams, 1942	8.1
4	Ted Williams, 1946	7.9
5	Lou Boudreau, 1944	7.8
6	Willie Mays, 1955	7.7
7	Snuffy Stirnweiss, 1945	7.2
	Ted Williams, 1947	7.2
	Willie Mays, 1958	7.2
10	Snuffy Stirnweiss, 1944	7.1
	Ted Williams, 1957	7.1
12	Lou Boudreau, 1948	6.9
13	Jackie Robinson, 1951	6.8
14	3 players tied	6.7

1961-1976

1	Mickey Mantle, 1961	8.0
2	Ron Santo, 1966	7.5
3	Willie Mays, 1965	7.3
	Ron Santo, 1967	7.3
	Carl Yastrzemski, 1967	7.3
6	Norm Cash, 1961	7.1
	Joe Morgan, 1975	7.1
8	Rico Petrocelli, 1969	6.9
	Mike Schmidt, 1974	6.9
10	Frank Robinson, 1966	6.7
11	Willie Mays, 1963	6.6
	Carl Yastrzemski, 1968	6.6
	Reggie Jackson, 1969	6.6
14	3 players tied	6.5

1977-1996

1	Barry Bonds, 1992	9.2
2	Cal Ripken, 1984	9.1
3	Barry Bonds, 1993	8.8
4	Barry Bonds, 1996	8.5
5	Cal Ripken, 1991	8.3
6	Rickey Henderson, 1990	8.2
7	Jeff Bagwell, 1994	7.6
8	Rickey Henderson, 1985	7.4
9	Mike Schmidt, 1980	7.3
10	George Brett, 1985	7.2
	Barry Bonds, 1990	7.2
12	Mike Schmidt, 1981	7.0
	Robin Yount, 1982	7.0
	Kevin Mitchell, 1989	7.0
	Ken Caminiti, 1996	7.0

Wins

1	Charley Radbourn, 1884	59
2	John Clarkson, 1885	53
3	Guy Hecker, 1884	52
4	John Clarkson, 1889	49
5	Charley Radbourn, 1883	48
	Charlie Buffinton, 1884	48
7	Al Spalding, 1876	47
	John Ward, 1879	47
9	Pud Galvin, 1883	46
	Pud Galvin, 1884	46
	Matt Kilroy, 1887	46
12	George Bradley, 1876	45
	Jim McCormick, 1880	45
	Silver King, 1888	45
15	Mickey Welch, 1885	44
	Bill Hutchison, 1891	44
17	Billy Taylor, 1884	43
	Tommy Bond, 1879	43
	Will White, 1879	43
	Larry Corcoran, 1880	43
	Will White, 1883	43
22	Lady Baldwin, 1886	42
	Tim Keefe, 1886	42
	Bill Hutchison, 1890	42
25	Charlie Sweeney, 1884	41
	Tim Keefe, 1883	41
	Dave Foutz, 1886	41
	Ed Morris, 1886	41
	Jack Chesbro, 1904	41
30	Jim McCormick, 1884	40
	Tommy Bond, 1877	40
	Tommy Bond, 1878	40
	Will White, 1882	40
	Bill Sweeney, 1884	40
	Bob Caruthers, 1885	40
	Bob Caruthers, 1889	40
	Ed Walsh, 1908	40
38	John Ward, 1880	39
	Mickey Welch, 1884	39
	Ed Morris, 1885	39
41	Toad Ramsey, 1886	38
	John Clarkson, 1887	38
	Kid Gleason, 1890	38
44	Pud Galvin, 1879	37
	Jim Whitney, 1883	37
	Tim Keefe, 1884	37
	Jack Lynch, 1884	37
	Toad Ramsey, 1887	37
	Christy Mathewson, 1908	37
50	Jim McCormick, 1882	36
	Tony Mullane, 1884	36
	John Clarkson, 1886	36
	Sadie McMahon, 1890	36
	Bill Hutchison, 1892	36
	Cy Young, 1892	36
	Frank Killen, 1893	36
	Amos Rusie, 1894	36
	Walter Johnson, 1913	36
59	Jim Devlin, 1877	35
	Tony Mullane, 1883	35
	Larry Corcoran, 1884	35
	Tim Keefe, 1887	35
	Tim Keefe, 1888	35
	Ed Seward, 1888	35
	Silver King, 1889	35
	Sadie McMahon, 1891	35
	Kid Nichols, 1892	35
	Jack Stivetts, 1892	35
	Cy Young, 1895	35
	Joe McGinnity, 1904	35
71	Mickey Welch, 1880	34
	Larry Corcoran, 1883	34
	Ed Morris, 1884	34
	Will White, 1884	34
	Elmer Smith, 1887	34
	Scott Stratton, 1890	34
	George Haddock, 1891	34
	Kid Nichols, 1893	34
	Cy Young, 1893	34
	Joe Wood, 1912	34
81	Charley Radbourn, 1882	33
	Dave Foutz, 1885	33
	Henry Porter, 1885	33
	Mickey Welch, 1886	33
	Tony Mullane, 1886	33
	John Clarkson, 1888	33
	Mark Baldwin, 1890	33
	John Clarkson, 1891	33
	Amos Rusie, 1891	33
	Jack Stivetts, 1891	33
	Amos Rusie, 1893	33
	Jouett Meekin, 1894	33
	Cy Young, 1901	33
	Christy Mathewson, 1904	33
	Walter Johnson, 1912	33
	Pete Alexander, 1916	33
97	10 players tied	32

Wins (by era)

1876-1892

1	Charley Radbourn, 1884	59
2	John Clarkson, 1885	53
3	Guy Hecker, 1884	52
4	John Clarkson, 1889	49
5	Charley Radbourn, 1883	48
	Charlie Buffinton, 1884	48
7	Al Spalding, 1876	47
	John Ward, 1879	47
9	Pud Galvin, 1883	46
	Pud Galvin, 1884	46
	Matt Kilroy, 1887	46
12	George Bradley, 1876	45
	Jim McCormick, 1880	45
	Silver King, 1888	45
15	2 players tied	44

1893-1919

1	Jack Chesbro, 1904	41
2	Ed Walsh, 1908	40
3	Christy Mathewson, 1908	37
4	Frank Killen, 1893	36
	Amos Rusie, 1894	36
	Walter Johnson, 1913	36
7	Cy Young, 1895	35
	Joe McGinnity, 1904	35
9	Kid Nichols, 1893	34
	Cy Young, 1893	34
	Joe Wood, 1912	34
12	6 players tied	33

1920-1941

1	Jim Bagby, 1920	31
	Lefty Grove, 1931	31
3	Dizzy Dean, 1934	30
4	Dazzy Vance, 1924	28
	Lefty Grove, 1930	28
	Dizzy Dean, 1935	28
7	Pete Alexander, 1920	27
	Carl Mays, 1921	27
	Urban Shocker, 1921	27
	Eddie Rommel, 1922	27
	Dolf Luque, 1923	27
	George Uhle, 1926	27
	Bucky Walters, 1939	27
	Bob Feller, 1940	27
15	7 players tied	26

1942-1960

1	Hal Newhouser, 1944	29
2	Robin Roberts, 1952	28
3	Dizzy Trout, 1944	27
	Don Newcombe, 1956	27
5	Hal Newhouser, 1946	26
	Bob Feller, 1946	26
7	Hal Newhouser, 1945	25
	Dave Ferriss, 1946	25
	Mel Parnell, 1949	25
10	Johnny Sain, 1948	24
	Bobby Shantz, 1952	24
12	13 players tied	23

1961-1976

1	Denny McLain, 1968	31
2	Sandy Koufax, 1966	27
	Steve Carlton, 1972	27
4	Sandy Koufax, 1965	26
	Juan Marichal, 1968	26
6	Whitey Ford, 1961	25
	Don Drysdale, 1962	25
	Sandy Koufax, 1963	25
	Juan Marichal, 1963	25
	Juan Marichal, 1966	25
	Jim Kaat, 1966	25
	Tom Seaver, 1969	25
	Mickey Lolich, 1971	25
	Catfish Hunter, 1974	25
	Fergie Jenkins, 1974	25

1977-1996

1	Bob Welch, 1990	27
2	Ron Guidry, 1978	25
	Steve Stone, 1980	25
4	Steve Carlton, 1980	24
	La Marr Hoyt, 1983	24
	Dwight Gooden, 1985	24
	Roger Clemens, 1986	24
	Frank Viola, 1988	24
	John Smoltz, 1996	24
10	Steve Carlton, 1977	23
	Mike Flanagan, 1979	23
	Steve Carlton, 1982	23
	Orel Hershiser, 1988	23
	Danny Jackson, 1988	23
	Bret Saberhagen, 1989	23

Losses

1	John Coleman, 1883	48
2	Will White, 1880	42
3	Larry McKeon, 1884	41
4	George Bradley, 1879	40
	Jim McCormick, 1879	40
6	Henry Porter, 1888	37
	Kid Carsey, 1891	37
	George Cobb, 1892	37
9	Stump Wiedman, 1886	36
	Bill Hutchison, 1892	36
11	Jim Devlin, 1876	35
	Pud Galvin, 1880	35
	Fleury Sullivan, 1884	35
	Adonis Terry, 1884	35
	Hardie Henderson, 1885	35
	Red Donahue, 1897	35
17	Bobby Mathews, 1876	34
	Bob Barr, 1884	34
	Matt Kilroy, 1886	34
	Al Mays, 1887	34
	Mark Baldwin, 1889	34
	Amos Rusie, 1890	34
23	Hardie Henderson, 1883	33
	Dupee Shaw, 1884	33
	Harry McCormick, 1879	33
	Jim Whitney, 1881	33
	Lee Richmond, 1882	33
	Frank Mountain, 1883	33
	Jersey Bakely, 1888	33
30	Lee Richmond, 1880	32
	John Harkins, 1884	32
	Jim Whitney, 1885	32
	Jim Whitney, 1886	32
34	Sam Weaver, 1878	31
	Will White, 1879	31
	Charley Radbourn, 1886	31
	Dupee Shaw, 1886	31
	Billy Crowell, 1887	31
	Amos Rusie, 1892	31
40	Mickey Welch, 1880	30
	Jim McCormick, 1881	30
	Jim McCormick, 1882	30
	Jersey Bakely, 1884	30
	Jack Lynch, 1886	30
	Phenomenal Smith, 1887	30
	Toad Ramsey, 1888	30
	John Ewing, 1889	30
	Ed Beatin, 1890	30
	Ted Breitenstein, 1895	30
	Jim Hughey, 1899	30
51	Tommy Bond, 1880	29
	Pud Galvin, 1883	29
	John Healy, 1887	29
	Hank O'Day, 1888	29
	Bert Cunningham, 1888	29
	Red Ehret, 1889	29
	Silver King, 1891	29
	Bill Hart, 1896	29
	Jack Taylor, 1898	29
	Vic Willis, 1905	29
61	Jim McCormick, 1880	28
	Doc Landis, 1882	28
	Hank O'Day, 1884	28
	Hugh Daily, 1884	28
	Gus Weyhing, 1887	28
	Mark Baldwin, 1891	28
	Duke Esper, 1893	28
	Bill Hill, 1896	28
69	Pud Galvin, 1879	27
	Tim Keefe, 1881	27
	Tim Keefe, 1883	27
	Charlie Buffinton, 1885	27
	Al Mays, 1886	27
	Tony Mullane, 1886	27
	Toad Ramsey, 1886	27
	Toad Ramsey, 1887	27
	Park Swartzel, 1889	27
	Phil Knell, 1891	27
	Mark Baldwin, 1892	27
	Pink Hawley, 1894	27
	Chick Fraser, 1896	27
	Bill Hart, 1897	27
	Willie Sudhoff, 1898	27
	Bill Carrick, 1899	27
	Dummy Taylor, 1901	27
	George Bell, 1910	27
	Paul Derringer, 1933	27
88	21 players tied	26

Winning Percentage

1	Roy Face, 1959	.947
2	Greg Maddux, 1995	.905
3	Randy Johnson, 1995	.900
4	Ron Guidry, 1978	.893
5	Freddie Fitzsimmons, 1940	.889
6	Lefty Grove, 1931	.886
7	Preacher Roe, 1951	.880
8	Fred Goldsmith, 1880	.875
9	Joe Wood, 1912	.872
10	David Cone, 1988	.870
11	Orel Hershiser, 1985	.864
12	Bill Donovan, 1907	.862
	Whitey Ford, 1961	.862
14	Dwight Gooden, 1985	.857
	Roger Clemens, 1986	.857
16	Chief Bender, 1914	.850
17	Lefty Grove, 1930	.848
18	Tom Hughes, 1916	.842
	Emil Yde, 1924	.842
	Schoolboy Rowe, 1940	.842
	Sandy Consuegra, 1954	.842
	Ralph Terry, 1961	.842
	Ron Perranoski, 1963	.842
24	Lefty Gomez, 1934	.839
25	Bill Hoffer, 1895	.838
	Denny McLain, 1968	.838
27	Walter Johnson, 1913	.837
28	King Cole, 1910	.833
	Spud Chandler, 1943	.833
	Sandy Koufax, 1963	.833
31	Charley Radbourn, 1884	.831
32	Ed Reulbach, 1906	.826
	Elmer Riddle, 1941	.826
34	Jim Hughes, 1899	.824
	Jack Chesbro, 1902	.824
	Dazzy Vance, 1924	.824
37	Chief Bender, 1910	.821
	Bob Purkey, 1962	.821
39	Sal Maglie, 1950	.818
	Bob Welch, 1990	.818
	Mark Portugal, 1993	.818
42	Joe McGinnity, 1904	.814
43	Mordecai Brown, 1906	.813
	Russ Ford, 1910	.813
	Eddie Plank, 1912	.813
	Carl Hubbell, 1936	.813
47	Dizzy Dean, 1934	.811
48	Ed Reulbach, 1907	.810
	Doc Crandall, 1910	.810
	Johnny Allen, 1932	.810
	Ted Wilks, 1944	.810
	Phil Niekro, 1982	.810
	Jimmy Key, 1994	.810
54	Alvin Crowder, 1928	.808
	Bobo Newsom, 1940	.808
	Tiny Bonham, 1942	.808
	Larry Jansen, 1947	.808
	Dave McNally, 1971	.808
	Catfish Hunter, 1973	.808
60	Christy Mathewson, 1909	.806
	Howie Camnitz, 1909	.806
	Dave Ferriss, 1946	.806
	Juan Marichal, 1966	.806
64	Eddie Cicotte, 1919	.806
65	Mickey Welch, 1885	.800
	Ed Doheny, 1902	.800
	Sam Leever, 1905	.800
	Bert Humphries, 1913	.800
	Stan Coveleski, 1925	.800
	Firpo Marberry, 1931	.800
	Robin Roberts, 1952	.800
	Ed Lopat, 1953	.800
	Don Newcombe, 1955	.800
	Jim Palmer, 1969	.800
	John Candelaria, 1977	.800
	Larry Gura, 1978	.800
	Tommy Greene, 1993	.800
78	Al Spalding, 1876	.797
79	Don Newcombe, 1956	.794
80	Jocko Flynn, 1886	.793
	Ellis Kinder, 1949	.793
	Sal Maglie, 1951	.793
	Bret Saberhagen, 1989	.793
84	Dutch Leonard, 1914	.792
	Sandy Koufax, 1964	.792
	Wally Bunker, 1964	.792
87	Fred Klobedanz, 1897	.788
	Bill James, 1914	.788
	Joe Bush, 1922	.788
90	Jouett Meekin, 1894	.786
	Lon Warneke, 1932	.786
	Tex Hughson, 1942	.786
	Ron Guidry, 1985	.786
	Doug Drabek, 1990	.786
	Tom Glavine, 1993	.786
96	Bob Caruthers, 1889	.784
97	George Mullin, 1909	.784
98	9 players tied	.783

Winning Percentage (by era)

1876-1892
1	Fred Goldsmith, 1880	.875
2	Charley Radbourn, 1884	.831
3	Mickey Welch, 1885	.800
4	Al Spalding, 1876	.797
5	Jocko Flynn, 1886	.793
6	Bob Caruthers, 1889	.784
7	Jack Manning, 1876	.783
8	Will White, 1882	.769
	Charlie Ferguson, 1886	.769
	John Clarkson, 1885	.768
11	Lady Baldwin, 1886	.764
12	Bob Caruthers, 1887	.763
	Charlie Buffinton, 1891	.763
14	George Haddock, 1891	.756
15	Bob Caruthers, 1885	.755

1893-1919
1	Joe Wood, 1912	.872
2	Bill Donovan, 1907	.862
3	Chief Bender, 1914	.850
4	Tom Hughes, 1916	.842
5	Bill Hoffer, 1895	.838
6	Walter Johnson, 1913	.837
7	King Cole, 1910	.833
8	Ed Reulbach, 1906	.826
9	Jim Hughes, 1899	.824
	Jack Chesbro, 1902	.824
11	Chief Bender, 1910	.821
12	Joe McGinnity, 1904	.814
13	Mordecai Brown, 1906	.813
	Russ Ford, 1910	.813
	Eddie Plank, 1912	.813

1920-1941
1	Freddie Fitzsimmons, 1940	.889
2	Lefty Grove, 1931	.886
3	Lefty Grove, 1930	.848
4	Emil Yde, 1924	.842
	Schoolboy Rowe, 1940	.842
6	Lefty Gomez, 1934	.839
7	Elmer Riddle, 1941	.826
8	Dazzy Vance, 1924	.824
9	Carl Hubbell, 1936	.813
10	Dizzy Dean, 1934	.811
11	Johnny Allen, 1932	.810
12	Alvin Crowder, 1928	.808
	Bobo Newsom, 1940	.808
14	Stan Coveleski, 1925	.800
	Firpo Marberry, 1931	.800

1942-1960
1	Roy Face, 1959	.947
2	Preacher Roe, 1951	.880
3	Sandy Consuegra, 1954	.842
4	Spud Chandler, 1943	.833
5	Sal Maglie, 1950	.818
6	Ted Wilks, 1944	.810
7	Tiny Bonham, 1942	.808
	Larry Jansen, 1947	.808
9	Dave Ferriss, 1946	.806
10	Robin Roberts, 1952	.800
	Ed Lopat, 1953	.800
	Don Newcombe, 1955	.800
13	Don Newcombe, 1956	.794
14	Ellis Kinder, 1949	.793
	Sal Maglie, 1951	.793

1961-1976
1	Whitey Ford, 1961	.862
2	Ralph Terry, 1961	.842
	Ron Perranoski, 1963	.842
4	Denny McLain, 1968	.838
5	Sandy Koufax, 1963	.833
6	Bob Purkey, 1962	.821
7	Dave McNally, 1971	.808
	Catfish Hunter, 1973	.808
9	Juan Marichal, 1966	.806
10	Jim Palmer, 1969	.800
11	Sandy Koufax, 1964	.792
	Wally Bunker, 1964	.792
13	Johnny Podres, 1961	.783
14	Tom Seaver, 1969	.781
15	2 players tied	.774

1977-1996
1	Greg Maddux, 1995	.905
2	Randy Johnson, 1995	.900
3	Ron Guidry, 1978	.893
4	David Cone, 1988	.870
5	Orel Hershiser, 1985	.864
6	Dwight Gooden, 1985	.857
	Roger Clemens, 1986	.857
8	Bob Welch, 1990	.818
	Mark Portugal, 1993	.818
10	Phil Niekro, 1982	.810
	Jimmy Key, 1994	.810
12	John Candelaria, 1977	.800
	Larry Gura, 1978	.800
	Tommy Greene, 1993	.800
15	Bret Saberhagen, 1989	.793

Games

1	Mike Marshall, 1974	106
2	Kent Tekulve, 1979	94
3	Mike Marshall, 1973	92
4	Kent Tekulve, 1978	91
5	Wayne Granger, 1969	90
	Mike Marshall, 1979	90
	Kent Tekulve, 1987	90
8	Mark Eichhorn, 1987	89
9	Wilbur Wood, 1968	88
10	Rob Murphy, 1987	87
11	Kent Tekulve, 1982	85
	Frank Williams, 1987	85
	Mitch Williams, 1987	85
14	Ted Abernathy, 1965	84
	Enrique Romo, 1979	84
	Dick Tidrow, 1980	84
	Dan Quisenberry, 1985	84
18	Ken Sanders, 1971	83
	Craig Lefferts, 1986	83
	Eddie Guardado, 1996	83
	Mike Myers, 1996	83
22	Eddie Fisher, 1965	82
	Bill Campbell, 1983	82
	Juan Agosto, 1990	82
25	John Wyatt, 1964	81
	Dale Murray, 1976	81
	Jeff Robinson, 1987	81
	Duane Ward, 1991	81
	Joe Boever, 1992	81
	Kenny Rogers, 1992	81
	Mike Jackson, 1993	81
	Brad Clontz, 1996	81
	Mike Stanton, 1996	81
34	Mudcat Grant, 1970	80
	Pedro Borbon, 1973	80
	Willie Hernandez, 1984	80
	Mitch Williams, 1986	80
	Doug Jones, 1992	80
	Greg Harris, 1993	80
40	Dick Radatz, 1964	79
	Duane Ward, 1992	79
	Bob Patterson, 1996	79
43	Hal Woodeshick, 1965	78
	Ted Abernathy, 1968	78
	Bill Campbell, 1976	78
	Rollie Fingers, 1977	78
	Tom Hume, 1980	78
	Kent Tekulve, 1980	78
	Greg Minton, 1982	78
	Ed Vande Berg, 1982	78
	Ted Power, 1984	78
	Tim Burke, 1985	78
	Lance McCullers, 1987	78
	Mark Dewey, 1996	78
	Jeff Shaw, 1996	78
56	Dick Tidrow, 1979	77
	Bob Locker, 1967	77
	Wilbur Wood, 1970	77
	Charlie Hough, 1976	77
	Butch Metzger, 1976	77
	Rick Camp, 1980	77
	Gary Lavelle, 1984	77
	Mark Davis, 1985	77
	Craig Lefferts, 1987	77
	Bobby Thigpen, 1990	77
	Barry Jones, 1991	77
	Xavier Hernandez, 1992	77
	Mike Perez, 1992	77
	Mark Wohlers, 1996	77
70	Will White, 1879	76
	Pud Galvin, 1883	76
	Charley Radbourn, 1883	76
	Wilbur Wood, 1969	76
	Ron Herbel, 1970	76
	Larry Hardy, 1974	76
	Rollie Fingers, 1974	76
	Dan Spillner, 1977	76
	Dave Tomlin, 1977	76
	Sid Monge, 1979	76
	Rod Scurry, 1982	76
	Tippy Martinez, 1982	76
	Kent Tekulve, 1983	76
	Ed Vande Berg, 1985	76
	Rob Murphy, 1988	76
	Mitch Williams, 1989	76
	Chuck Crim, 1989	76
	Jeff Innis, 1992	76
	Rod Beck, 1993	76
	David West, 1993	76
	Curt Leskanic, 1995	76
91	16 players tied	75

Games (by era)

1876-1892
1	Will White, 1879	76
	Pud Galvin, 1883	76
	Charley Radbourn, 1883	76
4	Charley Radbourn, 1884	75
	Guy Hecker, 1884	75
	Bill Hutchison, 1892	75
7	Jim McCormick, 1880	74
	Lee Richmond, 1880	74
9	John Clarkson, 1889	73
10	Pud Galvin, 1884	72
11	Bill Hutchison, 1890	71
12	John Ward, 1879	70
	John Ward, 1880	70
	John Clarkson, 1885	70
15	Matt Kilroy, 1887	69

1893-1919
1	Ed Walsh, 1908	66
2	Ed Walsh, 1912	62
3	Dave Davenport, 1916	59
4	Amos Rusie, 1893	56
	Ted Breitenstein, 1894	56
	Pink Hawley, 1895	56
	Ed Walsh, 1907	56
	Christy Mathewson, 1908	56
	Ed Walsh, 1911	56
	Reb Russell, 1916	56
11	Frank Killen, 1893	55
	Joe McGinnity, 1903	55
	Jack Chesbro, 1904	55
	Dave Davenport, 1915	55
15	3 players tied	54

1920-1941
1	Firpo Marberry, 1926	64
2	Clint Brown, 1939	61
3	Garland Braxton, 1927	58
	Russ Van Atta, 1935	58
5	Eddie Rommel, 1923	56
	Firpo Marberry, 1927	56
	Hugh Mulcahy, 1937	56
8	Firpo Marberry, 1925	55
	Bump Hadley, 1931	55
	Jim Walkup, 1935	55
11	George Uhle, 1923	54
	Firpo Marberry, 1932	54
	Jack Russell, 1934	54
	Chubby Dean, 1939	54
	Clyde Shoun, 1940	54

1942-1960
1	Jim Konstanty, 1950	74
2	Hoyt Wilhelm, 1952	71
3	Ace Adams, 1943	70
	Mike Fornieles, 1960	70
5	Ellis Kinder, 1953	69
	Don Elston, 1958	69
7	Hoyt Wilhelm, 1953	68
	Roy Face, 1956	68
	Roy Face, 1960	68
10	Andy Karl, 1945	67
	Turk Lown, 1957	67
	Gerry Staley, 1959	67
13	6 players tied	65

1961-1976
1	Mike Marshall, 1974	106
2	Mike Marshall, 1973	92
3	Wayne Granger, 1969	90
4	Wilbur Wood, 1968	88
5	Ted Abernathy, 1965	84
6	Ken Sanders, 1971	83
7	Eddie Fisher, 1965	82
8	John Wyatt, 1964	81
	Dale Murray, 1976	81
10	Mudcat Grant, 1970	80
	Pedro Borbon, 1973	80
12	Dick Radatz, 1964	79
13	Hal Woodeshick, 1965	78
	Ted Abernathy, 1968	78
	Bill Campbell, 1976	78

1977-1996
1	Kent Tekulve, 1979	94
2	Kent Tekulve, 1978	91
3	Mike Marshall, 1979	90
	Kent Tekulve, 1987	90
5	Mark Eichhorn, 1987	89
6	Rob Murphy, 1987	87
7	Kent Tekulve, 1982	85
	Frank Williams, 1987	85
	Mitch Williams, 1987	85
10	Enrique Romo, 1979	84
	Dick Tidrow, 1980	84
	Dan Quisenberry, 1985	84
13	Craig Lefferts, 1986	83
	Eddie Guardado, 1996	83
	Mike Myers, 1996	83

Games Started

1	Will White, 1879	75
	Pud Galvin, 1883	75
3	Jim McCormick, 1880	74
4	Charley Radbourn, 1884	73
	Guy Hecker, 1884	73
6	Pud Galvin, 1884	72
	John Clarkson, 1889	72
8	John Clarkson, 1885	70
	Bill Hutchison, 1892	70
10	Matt Kilroy, 1887	69
11	Jim Devlin, 1876	68
	Charley Radbourn, 1883	68
	Tim Keefe, 1883	68
	Matt Kilroy, 1886	68
15	John Ward, 1880	67
	Jim McCormick, 1882	67
	Charlie Buffinton, 1884	67
	Toad Ramsey, 1886	67
19	Dupee Shaw, 1884	66
	Pud Galvin, 1879	66
	Lee Richmond, 1880	66
	Bill Hutchison, 1890	66
23	Jim McCormick, 1884	65
	Mickey Welch, 1884	65
	Tony Mullane, 1884	65
	Silver King, 1888	65
27	George Bradley, 1876	64
	Tommy Bond, 1879	64
	Mickey Welch, 1880	64
	Will White, 1883	64
	Tim Keefe, 1886	64
	Toad Ramsey, 1887	64
33	Jim Whitney, 1881	63
	Ed Morris, 1885	63
	Ed Morris, 1885	63
36	Will White, 1880	62
	Amos Rusie, 1890	62
	Amos Rusie, 1892	62
39	Jim Devlin, 1877	61
	John Coleman, 1883	61
	Hardie Henderson, 1885	61
	Jersey Bakely, 1888	61
43	Al Spalding, 1876	60
	Jim McCormick, 1879	60
	John Ward, 1879	60
	Larry Corcoran, 1880	60
	Larry McKeon, 1884	60
	Bill Sweeney, 1884	60
49	Billy Taylor, 1884	59
	Tommy Bond, 1878	59
	Frank Mountain, 1883	59
	Larry Corcoran, 1884	59
	Mickey Welch, 1886	59
	John Clarkson, 1887	59
	Mark Baldwin, 1889	59
56	Tommy Bond, 1877	58
	Terry Larkin, 1879	58
	Jim McCormick, 1881	58
	Tim Keefe, 1884	58
	Hugh Daily, 1884	58
	Charley Radbourn, 1886	58
	Bill Hutchison, 1891	58
	Sadie McMahon, 1891	58
64	Tommy Bond, 1880	57
	Dave Foutz, 1886	57
	Ed Seward, 1888	57
	Sadie McMahon, 1890	57
	Amos Rusie, 1891	57
69	Charlie Sweeney, 1884	56
	Bobby Mathews, 1876	56
	Terry Larkin, 1877	56
	Terry Larkin, 1878	56
	Jim Whitney, 1883	56
	Lady Baldwin, 1886	56
	Tony Mullane, 1886	56
	Tim Keefe, 1887	56
	Matt Kilroy, 1889	56
	Mark Baldwin, 1890	56
	Silver King, 1890	56
	Jack Stivetts, 1891	56
81	George Derby, 1881	55
	Tony Mullane, 1882	55
	Adonis Terry, 1884	55
	Mickey Welch, 1885	55
	John Clarkson, 1886	55
	Phenomenal Smith, 1887	55
	Gus Weyhing, 1887	55
	Ed Morris, 1888	55
	Kid Gleason, 1890	55
90	George Bradley, 1879	54
	Harry McCormick, 1879	54
	Pud Galvin, 1880	54
	Will White, 1882	54
	Henry Porter, 1885	54
	John Clarkson, 1888	54
	Henry Porter, 1888	54
	Ed Beatin, 1890	54
	Bob Barr, 1890	54
99	9 players tied	53

Games Started (by era)

1876-1892

1	Will White, 1879	75
	Pud Galvin, 1883	75
3	Jim McCormick, 1880	74
4	Charley Radbourn, 1884	73
	Guy Hecker, 1884	73
6	Pud Galvin, 1884	72
	John Clarkson, 1889	72
8	John Clarkson, 1885	70
	Bill Hutchison, 1892	70
10	Matt Kilroy, 1887	69
11	Jim Devlin, 1876	68
	Charley Radbourn, 1883	68
	Tim Keefe, 1883	68
	Matt Kilroy, 1886	68
15	4 players tied	67

1893-1919

1	Amos Rusie, 1893	52
2	Jack Chesbro, 1904	51
3	Ted Breitenstein, 1894	50
	Amos Rusie, 1894	50
	Ted Breitenstein, 1895	50
	Pink Hawley, 1895	50
	Frank Killen, 1896	50
8	Ed Walsh, 1908	49
9	Frank Killen, 1893	48
	Jouett Meekin, 1894	48
	Joe McGinnity, 1903	48
12	Cy Young, 1894	47
	Amos Rusie, 1895	47
	Jack Taylor, 1898	47
15	8 players tied	46

1920-1941

1	George Uhle, 1923	44
2	Pete Alexander, 1920	40
	Stan Coveleski, 1921	40
	George Uhle, 1922	40
	George Caster, 1938	40
	Bobo Newsom, 1938	40
	Bob Feller, 1941	40
8	Red Faber, 1920	39
	Red Faber, 1921	39
	Hooks Dauss, 1923	39
	Howard Ehmke, 1923	39
	George Earnshaw, 1930	39
	Alvin Crowder, 1932	39
	Kirby Higbe, 1941	39
15	24 players tied	38

1942-1960

1	Bob Feller, 1946	42
	Bob Friend, 1956	42
3	Bill Voiselle, 1944	41
	Robin Roberts, 1953	41
5	Dizzy Trout, 1944	40
6	Johnny Sain, 1948	39
	Robin Roberts, 1950	39
	Warren Spahn, 1950	39
	Vern Bickford, 1950	39
	Robin Roberts, 1951	39
	Ron Kline, 1956	39
	Lew Burdette, 1959	39
13	10 players tied	38

1961-1976

1	Wilbur Wood, 1972	49
2	Wilbur Wood, 1973	48
3	Mickey Lolich, 1971	45
4	Wilbur Wood, 1975	43
5	Don Drysdale, 1963	42
	Jack Sanford, 1963	42
	Don Drysdale, 1965	42
	Jim Kaat, 1965	42
	Fergie Jenkins, 1969	42
	Wilbur Wood, 1971	42
	Stan Bahnsen, 1973	42
	Mickey Lolich, 1973	42
	Wilbur Wood, 1974	42
14	22 players tied	41

1977-1996

1	Phil Niekro, 1979	44
2	Phil Niekro, 1977	43
3	Phil Niekro, 1978	42
4	Steve Rogers, 1977	40
	Mike Flanagan, 1978	40
	Dennis Leonard, 1978	40
	Jim Clancy, 1982	40
	Charlie Hough, 1987	40
9	9 players tied	39

Complete Games

1	Will White, 1879	75
2	Charley Radbourn, 1884	73
3	Jim McCormick, 1880	72
	Pud Galvin, 1883	72
	Guy Hecker, 1884	72
6	Pud Galvin, 1884	71
7	Tim Keefe, 1883	68
	John Clarkson, 1885	68
	John Clarkson, 1889	68
10	Bill Hutchison, 1892	67
11	Jim Devlin, 1876	66
	Charley Radbourn, 1883	66
	Matt Kilroy, 1886	66
	Toad Ramsey, 1886	66
	Matt Kilroy, 1887	66
16	Pud Galvin, 1879	65
	Jim McCormick, 1882	65
	Bill Hutchison, 1890	65
19	Mickey Welch, 1880	64
	Will White, 1883	64
	Tony Mullane, 1884	64
	Silver King, 1888	64
23	Jim McCormick, 1884	63
	George Bradley, 1876	63
	Charlie Buffinton, 1884	63
	Ed Morris, 1885	63
	Ed Morris, 1886	63
28	Mickey Welch, 1884	62
	Tim Keefe, 1886	62
30	Jim Devlin, 1877	61
	Toad Ramsey, 1887	61
32	Dupee Shaw, 1884	60
	Jersey Bakely, 1888	60
34	Billy Taylor, 1884	59
	Tommy Bond, 1879	59
	Jim McCormick, 1879	59
	John Ward, 1880	59
	John Coleman, 1883	59
	Larry McKeon, 1884	59
	Hardie Henderson, 1885	59
	Amos Rusie, 1892	59
42	Tommy Bond, 1877	58
	John Ward, 1879	58
	Will White, 1880	58
	Bill Sweeney, 1884	58
46	Tommy Bond, 1878	57
	Terry Larkin, 1879	57
	Larry Corcoran, 1880	57
	Lee Richmond, 1880	57
	Jim McCormick, 1881	57
	Jim Whitney, 1881	57
	Frank Mountain, 1883	57
	Larry Corcoran, 1884	57
	Charley Radbourn, 1886	57
	Ed Seward, 1888	57
56	Terry Larkin, 1878	56
	Tim Keefe, 1884	56
	Hugh Daily, 1884	56
	Mickey Welch, 1886	56
	John Clarkson, 1887	56
	Amos Rusie, 1890	56
	Bill Hutchison, 1891	56
63	Bobby Mathews, 1876	55
	Terry Larkin, 1877	55
	George Derby, 1881	55
	Mickey Welch, 1885	55
	Lady Baldwin, 1886	55
	Dave Foutz, 1886	55
	Tony Mullane, 1886	55
	Matt Kilroy, 1889	55
	Sadie McMahon, 1890	55
72	Jim Whitney, 1883	54
	Adonis Terry, 1884	54
	Tim Keefe, 1887	54
	Phenomenal Smith, 1887	54
	Ed Morris, 1888	54
	Mark Baldwin, 1889	54
	Kid Gleason, 1890	54
79	Charlie Sweeney, 1884	53
	Al Spalding, 1876	53
	George Bradley, 1879	53
	Jack Lynch, 1884	53
	Bob Caruthers, 1885	53
	Henry Porter, 1885	53
	Gus Weyhing, 1887	53
	John Clarkson, 1888	53
	Henry Porter, 1888	53
	Ed Beatin, 1890	53
	Mark Baldwin, 1890	53
	Sadie McMahon, 1891	53
91	Will White, 1878	52
	Will White, 1882	52
	Will White, 1884	52
	Ed Seward, 1887	52
	Bob Barr, 1890	52
	Amos Rusie, 1891	52
97	7 players tied	51

Complete Games (by era)

1876-1892

1	Will White, 1879	75
2	Charley Radbourn, 1884	73
3	Jim McCormick, 1880	72
	Pud Galvin, 1883	72
	Guy Hecker, 1884	72
6	Pud Galvin, 1884	71
7	Tim Keefe, 1883	68
	John Clarkson, 1885	68
	John Clarkson, 1889	68
10	Bill Hutchison, 1892	67
11	Jim Devlin, 1876	66
	Charley Radbourn, 1883	66
	Matt Kilroy, 1886	66
	Toad Ramsey, 1886	66
	Matt Kilroy, 1887	66

1893-1919

1	Amos Rusie, 1893	50
2	Jack Chesbro, 1904	48
3	Ted Breitenstein, 1894	46
	Ted Breitenstein, 1895	46
5	Amos Rusie, 1894	45
	Vic Willis, 1902	45
7	Cy Young, 1894	44
	Pink Hawley, 1895	44
	Frank Killen, 1896	44
	Joe McGinnity, 1903	44
11	Kid Nichols, 1893	43
12	7 players tied	42

1920-1941

1	Pete Alexander, 1920	33
	Burleigh Grimes, 1923	33
3	Red Faber, 1921	32
	George Uhle, 1926	32
5	Red Faber, 1922	31
	Wes Ferrell, 1935	31
	Bobo Newsom, 1938	31
	Bucky Walters, 1939	31
	Bob Feller, 1940	31
10	8 players tied	30

1942-1960

1	Bob Feller, 1946	36
2	Dizzy Trout, 1944	33
	Robin Roberts, 1953	33
4	Robin Roberts, 1952	30
5	Hal Newhouser, 1945	29
	Hal Newhouser, 1946	29
	Robin Roberts, 1954	29
8	Jim Tobin, 1942	28
	Jim Tobin, 1944	28
	Johnny Sain, 1948	28
	Bob Lemon, 1952	28
12	Bucky Walters, 1944	27
	Mel Parnell, 1949	27
	Vern Bickford, 1950	27
	Bobby Shantz, 1952	27

1961-1976

1	Juan Marichal, 1968	30
	Fergie Jenkins, 1971	30
	Steve Carlton, 1972	30
	Catfish Hunter, 1975	30
5	Mickey Lolich, 1971	29
	Gaylord Perry, 1972	29
	Gaylord Perry, 1973	29
	Fergie Jenkins, 1974	29
9	Bob Gibson, 1968	28
	Denny McLain, 1968	28
	Bob Gibson, 1969	28
	Gaylord Perry, 1974	28
13	4 players tied	27

1977-1996

1	Rick Langford, 1980	28
2	Mike Norris, 1980	24
	Bert Blyleven, 1985	24
4	Mike Caldwell, 1978	23
	Phil Niekro, 1979	23
6	Jim Palmer, 1977	22
	Nolan Ryan, 1977	22
	Phil Niekro, 1978	22
9	Wayne Garland, 1977	21
	Dennis Leonard, 1977	21
	Ron Guidry, 1983	21
12	6 players tied	20

Shutouts

1	George Bradley, 1876	16
	Pete Alexander, 1916	16
3	Jack Coombs, 1910	13
	Bob Gibson, 1968	13
5	Pud Galvin, 1884	12
	Ed Morris, 1886	12
	Pete Alexander, 1915	12
8	Tommy Bond, 1879	11
	Charley Radbourn, 1884	11
	Dave Foutz, 1886	11
	Christy Mathewson, 1908	11
	Ed Walsh, 1908	11
	Walter Johnson, 1913	11
	Sandy Koufax, 1963	11
	Dean Chance, 1964	11
16	Jim McCormick, 1884	10
	John Clarkson, 1885	10
	Cy Young, 1904	10
	Ed Walsh, 1906	10
	Joe Wood, 1912	10
	Dave Davenport, 1915	10
	Carl Hubbell, 1933	10
	Mort Cooper, 1942	10
	Bob Feller, 1946	10
	Bob Lemon, 1948	10
	Juan Marichal, 1965	10
	Jim Palmer, 1975	10
	John Tudor, 1985	10
29	Tommy Bond, 1878	9
	George Derby, 1881	9
	Cy Young, 1892	9
	Joe McGinnity, 1904	9
	Mordecai Brown, 1906	9
	Addie Joss, 1906	9
	Mordecai Brown, 1908	9
	Addie Joss, 1908	9
	Orval Overall, 1909	9
	Pete Alexander, 1913	9
	Walter Johnson, 1914	9
	Cy Falkenberg, 1914	9
	Babe Ruth, 1916	9
	Stan Coveleski, 1917	9
	Pete Alexander, 1919	9
	Bill Lee, 1938	9
	Bob Porterfield, 1953	9
	Luis Tiant, 1968	9
	Denny McLain, 1969	9
	Don Sutton, 1972	9
	Nolan Ryan, 1972	9
	Bert Blyleven, 1973	9
	Ron Guidry, 1978	9
52	Al Spalding, 1876	8
	John Ward, 1880	8
	Will White, 1882	8
	Charlie Buffinton, 1884	8
	Tim Keefe, 1888	8
	Ben Sanders, 1888	8
	John Clarkson, 1889	8
	Christy Mathewson, 1902	8
	Jack Chesbro, 1902	8
	Rube Waddell, 1904	8
	Christy Mathewson, 1905	8
	Ed Killian, 1905	8
	Lefty Leifield, 1906	8
	Rube Waddell, 1906	8
	Orval Overall, 1907	8
	Christy Mathewson, 1907	8
	Eddie Plank, 1907	8
	Mordecai Brown, 1909	8
	Christy Mathewson, 1909	8
	Ed Walsh, 1909	8
	Russ Ford, 1910	8
	Walter Johnson, 1910	8
	Reb Russell, 1913	8
	Jeff Tesreau, 1914	8
	Al Mamaux, 1915	8
	Jeff Tesreau, 1915	8
	Joe Bush, 1916	8
	Pete Alexander, 1917	8
	Jim Bagby, 1917	8
	Walter Johnson, 1917	8
	Hippo Vaughn, 1918	8
	Walter Johnson, 1918	8
	Carl Mays, 1918	8
	Babe Adams, 1920	8
	Hal Newhouser, 1945	8
	Steve Barber, 1961	8
	Camilo Pascual, 1961	8
	Whitey Ford, 1964	8
	Sandy Koufax, 1965	8
	Don Drysdale, 1968	8
	Juan Marichal, 1969	8
	Vida Blue, 1971	8
	Steve Carlton, 1972	8
	Wilbur Wood, 1972	8
	Fernando Valenzuela, 1981	8
	Dwight Gooden, 1985	8
	Orel Hershiser, 1988	8
	Roger Clemens, 1988	8
	Tim Belcher, 1989	8

Saves

1	Bobby Thigpen, 1990	57
2	Randy Myers, 1993	53
3	Dennis Eckersley, 1992	51
4	Dennis Eckersley, 1990	48
	Rod Beck, 1993	48
6	Lee Smith, 1991	47
7	Lee Smith, 1993	46
	Dave Righetti, 1986	46
	Bryan Harvey, 1991	46
	Jose Mesa, 1995	46
11	Dan Quisenberry, 1983	45
	Bruce Sutter, 1984	45
	Dennis Eckersley, 1988	45
	Bryan Harvey, 1993	45
	Jeff Montgomery, 1993	45
	Duane Ward, 1993	45
17	Dan Quisenberry, 1984	44
	Mark Davis, 1989	44
	Jeff Brantley, 1996	44
	Todd Worrell, 1996	44
21	Doug Jones, 1990	43
	Dennis Eckersley, 1991	43
	Lee Smith, 1992	43
	John Wetteland, 1993	43
	Mitch Williams, 1993	43
	John Wetteland, 1996	43
27	Jeff Reardon, 1988	42
	Rick Aguilera, 1991	42
	Trevor Hoffman, 1996	42
30	Jeff Reardon, 1985	41
	Rick Aguilera, 1992	41
32	Steve Bedrosian, 1987	40
	Jeff Reardon, 1991	40
	Tom Henke, 1993	40
35	John Franco, 1988	39
	Jeff Montgomery, 1992	39
	Mark Wohlers, 1996	39
	Jose Mesa, 1996	39
39	John Hiller, 1973	38
	Jeff Russell, 1989	38
	Randy Myers, 1992	38
	Roberto Hernandez, 1993	38
	Randy Myers, 1995	38
	Roberto Hernandez, 1996	38
45	Clay Carroll, 1972	37
	Rollie Fingers, 1978	37
	Bruce Sutter, 1979	37
	Dan Quisenberry, 1985	37
	Doug Jones, 1988	37
	Gregg Olson, 1990	37
	John Wetteland, 1992	37
	Lee Smith, 1995	37
53	Bruce Sutter, 1982	36
	Bill Caudill, 1984	36
	Todd Worrell, 1986	36
	Lee Smith, 1987	36
	Mitch Williams, 1989	36
	Dave Righetti, 1990	36
	Doug Jones, 1992	36
	Gregg Olson, 1992	36
	Dennis Eckersley, 1993	36
	Tom Henke, 1995	36
	Mel Rojas, 1996	36
	Troy Percival, 1996	36
65	Wayne Granger, 1970	35
	Sparky Lyle, 1972	35
	Rollie Fingers, 1977	35
	Dan Quisenberry, 1982	35
	Jeff Reardon, 1986	35
	Rod Beck, 1996	35
	Robb Nen, 1996	35
72	Ron Perranoski, 1970	34
	Don Aase, 1986	34
	Tom Henke, 1987	34
	Jim Gott, 1988	34
	Bobby Thigpen, 1988	34
	Bobby Thigpen, 1989	34
	Tom Henke, 1992	34
	Rick Aguilera, 1993	34
	Ricky Bottalico, 1996	34
81	Rich Gossage, 1980	33
	Dan Quisenberry, 1980	33
	Bob Stanley, 1983	33
	Lee Smith, 1984	33
	Lee Smith, 1985	33
	Dave Smith, 1986	33
	Todd Worrell, 1987	33
	Dennis Eckersley, 1989	33
	Dan Plesac, 1989	33
	Mike Schooler, 1989	33
	John Franco, 1990	33
	Jeff Montgomery, 1991	33
	Jeff Russell, 1993	33
	Lee Smith, 1994	33
	Rod Beck, 1995	33
96	16 players tied	32

Innings Pitched

1	Will White, 1879	680.0
2	Charley Radbourn, 1884	678.2
3	Guy Hecker, 1884	670.2
4	Jim McCormick, 1880	657.2
5	Pud Galvin, 1883	656.1
6	Pud Galvin, 1884	636.1
7	Charley Radbourn, 1883	632.1
8	John Clarkson, 1885	623.0
9	Jim Devlin, 1876	622.0
	Bill Hutchison, 1892	622.0
11	John Clarkson, 1889	620.0
12	Tim Keefe, 1883	619.0
13	Bill Hutchison, 1890	603.0
14	Jim McCormick, 1882	595.2
15	John Ward, 1880	595.0
16	Pud Galvin, 1879	593.0
17	Lee Richmond, 1880	590.2
18	Matt Kilroy, 1887	589.1
19	Toad Ramsey, 1886	588.2
20	John Ward, 1879	587.0
	Charlie Buffinton, 1884	587.0
22	Silver King, 1888	585.2
23	Matt Kilroy, 1886	583.0
24	Ed Morris, 1885	581.0
25	Will White, 1883	577.0
26	Mickey Welch, 1880	574.0
27	George Bradley, 1876	573.0
28	Jim McCormick, 1884	569.0
29	Tony Mullane, 1884	567.0
30	Toad Ramsey, 1887	561.0
	Bill Hutchison, 1891	561.0
32	Jim Devlin, 1877	559.0
33	Mickey Welch, 1884	557.1
34	Tommy Bond, 1879	555.1
	Ed Morris, 1886	555.1
36	Jim Whitney, 1881	552.1
37	Amos Rusie, 1890	548.2
38	Jim McCormick, 1879	546.1
39	Dupee Shaw, 1884	543.1
40	Amos Rusie, 1892	541.0
41	Hardie Henderson, 1885	539.1
42	John Coleman, 1883	538.1
43	Bill Sweeney, 1884	538.0
44	Larry Corcoran, 1880	536.1
45	Tim Keefe, 1886	535.0
46	Tommy Bond, 1878	532.2
	Jersey Bakely, 1888	532.2
48	Tony Mullane, 1886	529.2
49	Al Spalding, 1876	528.2
50	Jim McCormick, 1881	526.0
51	Billy Taylor, 1884	523.0
	John Clarkson, 1887	523.0
53	Tommy Bond, 1877	521.0
54	Ed Seward, 1888	518.2
55	Will White, 1880	517.1
56	Larry Corcoran, 1884	516.2
57	Bobby Mathews, 1876	516.0
58	Jim Whitney, 1883	514.0
59	Mark Baldwin, 1889	513.2
60	Terry Larkin, 1879	513.1
61	Jim McKeon, 1884	512.0
62	Charley Radbourn, 1886	509.1
63	Sadie McMahon, 1890	509.0
64	Terry Larkin, 1878	506.0
	Kid Gleason, 1890	506.0
66	Dave Foutz, 1886	504.0
67	Frank Mountain, 1883	503.0
	Sadie McMahon, 1891	503.0
69	Terry Larkin, 1877	501.0
70	Hugh Daily, 1884	500.2
71	Amos Rusie, 1891	500.1
72	Mickey Welch, 1886	500.0
73	Jack Lynch, 1884	496.0
74	George Derby, 1881	494.2
75	Bob Barr, 1890	493.1
76	Tommy Bond, 1880	493.0
77	Charlie Sweeney, 1884	492.0
	Mickey Welch, 1885	492.0
	Mark Baldwin, 1890	492.0
80	Phenomenal Smith, 1887	491.1
81	George Bradley, 1879	487.0
	Lady Baldwin, 1886	487.0
83	John Clarkson, 1888	483.1
84	Tim Keefe, 1884	483.0
85	Bob Caruthers, 1885	482.1
86	Amos Rusie, 1893	482.0
87	Henry Porter, 1885	481.2
88	Matt Kilroy, 1889	480.2
89	Will White, 1882	480.0
	Guy Hecker, 1885	480.0
	Ed Morris, 1888	480.0
92	Tim Keefe, 1887	476.2
93	Adonis Terry, 1884	476.0
94	Ed Beatin, 1890	474.1
95	Pud Galvin, 1881	474.0
	Charley Radbourn, 1882	474.0
	Henry Porter, 1888	474.0
98	Larry Corcoran, 1883	473.2
99	Ed Seward, 1887	470.2
100	Gus Weyhing, 1892	469.2

Innings Pitched (by era)

1876-1892

1	Will White, 1879	680.0
2	Charley Radbourn, 1884	678.2
3	Guy Hecker, 1884	670.2
4	Jim McCormick, 1880	657.2
5	Pud Galvin, 1883	656.1
6	Pud Galvin, 1884	636.1
7	Charley Radbourn, 1883	632.1
8	John Clarkson, 1885	623.0
9	Jim Devlin, 1876	622.0
	Bill Hutchison, 1892	622.0
11	John Clarkson, 1889	620.0
12	Tim Keefe, 1883	619.0
13	Bill Hutchison, 1890	603.0
14	Jim McCormick, 1882	595.2
15	John Ward, 1880	595.0

1893-1919

1	Amos Rusie, 1893	482.0
2	Ed Walsh, 1908	464.0
3	Jack Chesbro, 1904	454.2
4	Ted Breitenstein, 1894	447.1
5	Pink Hawley, 1895	444.1
6	Amos Rusie, 1894	444.0
7	Joe McGinnity, 1903	434.0
8	Frank Killen, 1896	432.1
9	Ted Breitenstein, 1895	429.2
10	Kid Nichols, 1893	425.0
11	Cy Young, 1893	422.2
12	Ed Walsh, 1907	422.1
13	Frank Killen, 1893	415.0
14	Cy Young, 1896	414.1
15	Vic Willis, 1902	410.0

1920-1941

1	Pete Alexander, 1920	363.1
2	George Uhle, 1923	357.2
3	Red Faber, 1922	352.0
4	Urban Shocker, 1922	348.0
5	Bob Feller, 1941	343.0
6	Jim Bagby, 1920	339.2
7	Carl Mays, 1921	336.2
8	Red Faber, 1921	330.2
	Burleigh Grimes, 1928	330.2
10	Bobo Newsom, 1938	329.2
11	Wilbur Cooper, 1920	327.0
	Wilbur Cooper, 1921	327.0
	Burleigh Grimes, 1923	327.0
	Alvin Crowder, 1932	327.0
15	Urban Shocker, 1921	326.2

1942-1960

1	Bob Feller, 1946	371.1
2	Dizzy Trout, 1944	352.1
3	Robin Roberts, 1953	346.2
4	Robin Roberts, 1954	336.2
5	Robin Roberts, 1952	330.0
6	Robin Roberts, 1951	315.0
7	Johnny Sain, 1948	314.2
8	Bob Friend, 1956	314.1
9	Hal Newhouser, 1945	313.1
10	Bill Voiselle, 1944	312.2
11	Hal Newhouser, 1944	312.1
12	Vern Bickford, 1950	311.2
13	Warren Spahn, 1951	310.2
14	Bob Lemon, 1952	309.2
15	Robin Roberts, 1955	305.0

1961-1976

1	Wilbur Wood, 1972	376.2
2	Mickey Lolich, 1971	376.0
3	Wilbur Wood, 1973	359.1
4	Steve Carlton, 1972	346.1
5	Gaylord Perry, 1973	344.0
6	Gaylord Perry, 1972	342.2
7	Denny McLain, 1968	336.0
8	Sandy Koufax, 1965	335.2
9	Wilbur Wood, 1971	334.0
10	Nolan Ryan, 1974	332.2
11	Gaylord Perry, 1970	328.2
12	Fergie Jenkins, 1974	328.1
13	Catfish Hunter, 1975	328.0
14	Mickey Lolich, 1972	327.1
15	2 players tied	326.0

1977-1996

1	Phil Niekro, 1979	342.0
2	Phil Niekro, 1978	334.1
3	Phil Niekro, 1977	330.1
4	Jim Palmer, 1977	319.0
5	Steve Carlton, 1980	304.0
6	Dave Goltz, 1977	303.0
7	Steve Rogers, 1977	301.2
8	Nolan Ryan, 1977	299.0
9	Jim Palmer, 1978	296.0
10	Steve Carlton, 1982	295.2
11	Dennis Leonard, 1978	294.2
12	Jack Morris, 1983	293.2
	Bert Blyleven, 1985	293.2
14	Mike Caldwell, 1978	293.1
15	Dennis Leonard, 1977	292.2

Hits per Game

1	Nolan Ryan, 1972	5.26
2	Luis Tiant, 1968	5.30
3	Nolan Ryan, 1991	5.31
4	Ed Reulbach, 1906	5.33
5	Dutch Leonard, 1914	5.57
6	Carl Lundgren, 1907	5.65
7	Sid Fernandez, 1985	5.71
8	Tommy Byrne, 1949	5.74
9	Dave McNally, 1968	5.77
10	Sandy Koufax, 1965	5.79
11	Russ Ford, 1910	5.83
12	Tim Keefe, 1880	5.83
13	Hideo Nomo, 1995	5.83
14	Al Downing, 1963	5.84
15	Herb Score, 1956	5.85
16	Bob Gibson, 1968	5.85
17	Sam McDowell, 1965	5.87
18	Ed Walsh, 1910	5.89
19	Mike Scott, 1986	5.95
20	Mario Soto, 1980	5.96
21	Floyd Youmans, 1986	5.96
22	Nolan Ryan, 1977	5.96
23	Nolan Ryan, 1974	5.98
24	Nolan Ryan, 1981	5.98
25	Nolan Ryan, 1986	6.02
26	Sam McDowell, 1966	6.02
27	Vida Blue, 1971	6.03
28	Walter Johnson, 1913	6.03
29	Nolan Ryan, 1990	6.04
30	Pete Alexander, 1915	6.05
31	Sam McDowell, 1968	6.06
32	Joe Horlen, 1964	6.07
33	Andy Messersmith, 1969	6.08
34	Nolan Ryan, 1989	6.09
35	Stan Coveleski, 1917	6.09
36	Catfish Hunter, 1972	6.09
37	Nolan Ryan, 1976	6.11
38	Sid Fernandez, 1988	6.11
39	Bob Turley, 1957	6.12
40	Bob Turley, 1955	6.13
41	Don Sutton, 1972	6.14
42	Nolan Ryan, 1983	6.14
43	Ron Guidry, 1978	6.15
44	Mordecai Brown, 1908	6.17
45	Sandy Koufax, 1963	6.19
46	Jack Pfiester, 1906	6.21
47	Sandy Koufax, 1964	6.22
48	Roger Nelson, 1972	6.23
49	Herb Score, 1955	6.26
50	Cy Morgan, 1909	6.26
51	Dean Chance, 1964	6.27
52	Christy Mathewson, 1909	6.28
	J.R. Richard, 1978	6.28
54	Art Fromme, 1909	6.28
55	Greg Maddux, 1995	6.31
56	Walter Johnson, 1912	6.32
57	Jack Coombs, 1910	6.32
58	Rube Waddell, 1905	6.33
59	Vean Gregg, 1911	6.33
60	Jeff Robinson, 1988	6.33
61	Larry Cheney, 1916	6.33
62	Sonny Siebert, 1968	6.33
63	Allie Reynolds, 1943	6.34
64	Roger Clemens, 1986	6.34
65	Willie Mitchell, 1913	6.35
66	Jose DeLeon, 1989	6.36
67	Pascual Perez, 1988	6.37
68	Walter Johnson, 1910	6.37
69	Dave Boswell, 1966	6.38
70	Harry Krause, 1909	6.38
71	Dutch Leonard, 1915	6.38
72	Eddie Cicotte, 1917	6.39
73	Wayne Simpson, 1970	6.39
74	Al Leiter, 1996	6.39
75	Babe Ruth, 1916	6.40
76	Spec Shea, 1947	6.40
77	Jim Bibby, 1973	6.42
78	Ed Reulbach, 1905	6.42
79	Gaylord Perry, 1974	6.42
80	Eddie Fisher, 1965	6.42
81	Addie Joss, 1908	6.42
82	Mordecai Brown, 1906	6.43
83	Luis Tiant, 1972	6.44
84	Frank Smith, 1908	6.44
85	Dwight Gooden, 1985	6.44
86	Orval Overall, 1909	6.44
87	Sid Fernandez, 1989	6.44
88	Denny McLain, 1968	6.46
89	Mordecai Brown, 1909	6.46
90	Ray Caldwell, 1914	6.46
91	Fred Toney, 1915	6.47
92	Gary Peters, 1967	6.47
93	Bob Turley, 1954	6.48
94	Ed Walsh, 1909	6.49
95	Guy Hecker, 1882	6.49
96	Frank Smith, 1910	6.49
97	Tom Seaver, 1981	6.49
98	Al Mamaux, 1915	6.51
99	Claude Hendrix, 1914	6.51
	Jim Palmer, 1969	6.51

Hits per Game (by era)

1876-1892

1	Tim Keefe, 1880	5.83
2	Guy Hecker, 1882	6.49
3	Tim Keefe, 1888	6.57
4	Charlie Sweeney, 1884	6.59
5	Adonis Terry, 1888	6.69
6	Silver King, 1888	6.72
7	Frank Knauss, 1890	6.73
8	Ed Seward, 1888	6.73
9	Tim Keefe, 1885	6.75
10	Tony Mullane, 1892	6.77
11	Larry Corcoran, 1880	6.78
12	Mickey Welch, 1885	6.80
13	Cannonball Titcomb, 1888	6.81
14	Amos Rusie, 1892	6.82
15	Toad Ramsey, 1886	6.83

1893-1919

1	Ed Reulbach, 1906	5.33
2	Dutch Leonard, 1914	5.57
3	Carl Lundgren, 1907	5.65
4	Russ Ford, 1910	5.83
5	Ed Walsh, 1910	5.89
6	Walter Johnson, 1913	6.03
7	Pete Alexander, 1915	6.05
8	Stan Coveleski, 1917	6.09
9	Mordecai Brown, 1908	6.17
10	Jack Pfiester, 1906	6.21
11	Cy Morgan, 1909	6.26
12	Christy Mathewson, 1909	6.28
13	Art Fromme, 1909	6.28
14	Walter Johnson, 1912	6.32
15	Jack Coombs, 1910	6.32

1920-1941

1	Johnny Vander Meer, 1941	6.84
2	Bob Feller, 1940	6.88
3	Bob Feller, 1939	6.89
4	Hal Schumacher, 1933	6.92
5	Dazzy Vance, 1924	6.95
6	Whit Wyatt, 1941	6.96
7	Bucky Walters, 1939	7.05
8	Johnny Vander Meer, 1938	7.07
9	Bucky Walters, 1940	7.11
10	Lefty Gomez, 1934	7.13
11	Ernie White, 1941	7.24
12	Dazzy Vance, 1928	7.26
13	Bump Hadley, 1931	7.26
14	Dolf Luque, 1920	7.28
15	Bob Feller, 1938	7.29

1942-1960

1	Tommy Byrne, 1949	5.74
2	Herb Score, 1956	5.85
3	Bob Turley, 1957	6.12
4	Bob Turley, 1955	6.13
5	Herb Score, 1955	6.26
6	Allie Reynolds, 1943	6.34
7	Spec Shea, 1947	6.40
8	Bob Turley, 1954	6.48
9	Sam Jones, 1955	6.52
10	Bob Turley, 1958	6.53
11	Hal Newhouser, 1946	6.61
12	Johnny Niggeling, 1943	6.66
13	Don Larsen, 1956	6.66
14	Whitey Ford, 1955	6.67
15	Mort Cooper, 1942	6.69

1961-1976

1	Nolan Ryan, 1972	5.26
2	Luis Tiant, 1968	5.30
3	Dave McNally, 1968	5.77
4	Sandy Koufax, 1965	5.79
5	Al Downing, 1963	5.84
6	Bob Gibson, 1968	5.85
7	Sam McDowell, 1965	5.87
8	Nolan Ryan, 1974	5.98
9	Sam McDowell, 1966	6.02
10	Vida Blue, 1971	6.03
11	Sam McDowell, 1968	6.06
12	Joe Horlen, 1964	6.07
13	Andy Messersmith, 1969	6.08
14	Catfish Hunter, 1972	6.09
15	Nolan Ryan, 1976	6.11

1977-1996

1	Nolan Ryan, 1991	5.31
2	Sid Fernandez, 1985	5.71
3	Hideo Nomo, 1995	5.83
4	Mike Scott, 1986	5.95
5	Mario Soto, 1980	5.96
6	Floyd Youmans, 1986	5.96
7	Nolan Ryan, 1977	5.96
8	Nolan Ryan, 1981	5.98
9	Nolan Ryan, 1986	6.02
10	Nolan Ryan, 1990	6.04
11	Nolan Ryan, 1989	6.09
12	Sid Fernandez, 1988	6.11
13	Nolan Ryan, 1983	6.14
14	Ron Guidry, 1978	6.15
15	J.R. Richard, 1978	6.28

Home Runs Allowed

1	Bert Blyleven, 1986	50
2	Robin Roberts, 1956	46
	Bert Blyleven, 1987	46
4	Pedro Ramos, 1957	43
5	Denny McLain, 1966	42
6	Robin Roberts, 1955	41
	Phil Niekro, 1979	41
8	Bill Gullickson, 1987	40
	Robin Roberts, 1957	40
	Ralph Terry, 1962	40
	Orlando Pena, 1964	40
	Phil Niekro, 1970	40
	Fergie Jenkins, 1979	40
	Jack Morris, 1986	40
	Shawn Boskie, 1996	40
	Brad Radke, 1996	40
17	Murry Dickson, 1948	39
	Pedro Ramos, 1961	39
	Jim Perry, 1971	39
	Catfish Hunter, 1973	39
	Jack Morris, 1987	39
22	Warren Hacker, 1955	38
	Pedro Ramos, 1958	38
	Lew Burdette, 1959	38
	Jim Bunning, 1963	38
	Don Sutton, 1970	38
	Mickey Lolich, 1974	38
	Matt Keough, 1982	38
	Floyd Bannister, 1987	38
	Don Sutton, 1987	38
	Curt Young, 1987	38
	Tim Wakefield, 1996	38
33	Jim Bunning, 1959	37
	Earl Wilson, 1964	37
	Luis Tiant, 1969	37
	Fergie Jenkins, 1975	37
	Jack Morris, 1982	37
	Dan Petry, 1983	37
	Frank Viola, 1986	37
	Mark Leiter, 1996	37
41	Dennis Rasmussen, 1987	36
	Larry Jansen, 1949	36
	Art Mahaffey, 1962	36
	Pete Richert, 1966	36
	Mickey Lolich, 1971	36
	Ed Whitson, 1987	36
	Charlie Hough, 1987	36
	Tom Browning, 1988	36
49	Larry Corcoran, 1884	35
	Warren Hacker, 1953	35
	Robin Roberts, 1954	35
	Don Newcombe, 1955	35
	Jim Perry, 1960	35
	Roger Craig, 1962	35
	Robin Roberts, 1963	35
	Sammy Ellis, 1966	35
	Denny McLain, 1967	35
	Fergie Jenkins, 1973	35
	Mickey Lolich, 1973	35
	Mike Caldwell, 1983	35
	Mike Smithson, 1984	35
	Scott McGregor, 1986	35
	Scott Bankhead, 1987	35
	Bruce Hurst, 1987	35
	Bill Gullickson, 1992	35
	Mike Moore, 1993	35
67	Preacher Roe, 1950	34
	Johnny Sain, 1950	34
	Ken Raffensberger, 1950	34
	Robin Roberts, 1959	34
	Paul Foytack, 1959	34
	Juan Marichal, 1962	34
	Dick Ellsworth, 1964	34
	Bill Monbouquette, 1964	34
	Bob Gibson, 1965	34
	Mudcat Grant, 1965	34
	Earl Wilson, 1967	34
	Catfish Hunter, 1969	34
	Mike Cuellar, 1970	34
	Gaylord Perry, 1973	34
	Rick Wise, 1975	34
	Frank Viola, 1983	34
	Danny Darwin, 1985	34
	Scott McGregor, 1985	34
	Ken Schrom, 1986	34
	Don Carman, 1987	34
	Mike Witt, 1987	34
	Alex Fernandez, 1996	34
	Kevin Tapani, 1996	34
90	17 players tied	33

Home Runs Allowed (by era)

1876-1892

1	Larry Corcoran, 1884	35
2	Charlie Getzien, 1889	27
3	Bill Hutchison, 1891	26
4	Charlie Getzien, 1887	24
	John Healy, 1887	24
6	Pud Galvin, 1884	23
	Mark Baldwin, 1887	23
	Lev Shreve, 1888	23
9	Billy Serad, 1884	21
	John Clarkson, 1885	21
	Park Swartzel, 1889	21
	George Cobb, 1892	21
13	8 players tied	20

1893-1919

1	Frank Dwyer, 1894	27
	Jack Stivetts, 1894	27
3	Kid Nichols, 1894	23
4	Harry Staley, 1893	22
	Kid Carsey, 1894	22
6	Ted Breitenstein, 1894	21
7	Jack Stivetts, 1896	20
8	Tom Parrott, 1894	19
	Cy Young, 1894	19
10	Kid Gleason, 1893	18
	Al Orth, 1902	18
12	5 players tied	17

1920-1941

1	Lon Warneke, 1937	32
2	Phil Collins, 1934	30
	Bobo Newsom, 1938	30
4	Ray Kremer, 1930	29
	Lynn Nelson, 1938	29
6	George Earnshaw, 1932	28
	George Earnshaw, 1934	28
8	Roy Mahaffey, 1932	27
	Carl Hubbell, 1935	27
	Luke Hamlin, 1939	27
	Lynn Nelson, 1939	27
	Johnny Marcum, 1939	27
13	Freddie Fitzsimmons, 1930	26
	Gordon Rhodes, 1936	26
	Nels Potter, 1939	26

1942-1960

1	Robin Roberts, 1956	46
2	Pedro Ramos, 1957	43
3	Robin Roberts, 1955	41
4	Robin Roberts, 1957	40
5	Murry Dickson, 1948	39
6	Warren Hacker, 1955	38
	Pedro Ramos, 1958	38
	Lew Burdette, 1959	38
9	Jim Bunning, 1959	37
10	Larry Jansen, 1949	36
11	Warren Hacker, 1953	35
	Robin Roberts, 1954	35
	Don Newcombe, 1955	35
	Jim Perry, 1960	35
15	5 players tied	34

1961-1976

1	Denny McLain, 1966	42
2	Ralph Terry, 1962	40
	Orlando Pena, 1964	40
	Phil Niekro, 1970	40
5	Pedro Ramos, 1961	39
	Jim Perry, 1971	39
	Catfish Hunter, 1973	39
8	Jim Bunning, 1963	38
	Don Sutton, 1970	38
	Mickey Lolich, 1974	38
11	Earl Wilson, 1964	37
	Luis Tiant, 1969	37
	Fergie Jenkins, 1975	37
14	3 players tied	36

1977-1996

1	Bert Blyleven, 1986	50
2	Bert Blyleven, 1987	46
3	Phil Niekro, 1979	41
4	Bill Gullickson, 1987	40
	Fergie Jenkins, 1979	40
	Jack Morris, 1986	40
	Shawn Boskie, 1996	40
	Brad Radke, 1996	40
9	Jack Morris, 1987	39
10	Matt Keough, 1982	38
	Floyd Bannister, 1987	38
	Don Sutton, 1987	38
	Curt Young, 1987	38
	Tim Wakefield, 1996	38

Walks

1	Amos Rusie, 1890	289
2	Mark Baldwin, 1889	274
3	Amos Rusie, 1892	270
4	Amos Rusie, 1891	262
5	Mark Baldwin, 1890	249
6	Jack Stivetts, 1891	232
7	Mark Baldwin, 1891	227
8	Phil Knell, 1891	226
9	Bob Barr, 1890	219
10	Amos Rusie, 1893	218
11	Cy Seymour, 1898	213
12	Gus Weyhing, 1889	212
13	Ed Crane, 1890	208
	Bob Feller, 1938	208
15	Toad Ramsey, 1886	207
16	Elton Chamberlain, 1891	206
17	Mike Morrison, 1887	205
18	Henry Gruber, 1890	204
	Nolan Ryan, 1977	204
20	Ed Crane, 1891	203
	John Clarkson, 1889	203
22	Nolan Ryan, 1974	202
23	Bert Cunningham, 1890	201
24	Amos Rusie, 1894	200
25	Bill Hutchison, 1890	199
26	Mark Baldwin, 1892	194
	Bob Feller, 1941	194
28	Bobo Newsom, 1938	192
29	Ted Breitenstein, 1894	191
30	Bill Hutchison, 1892	190
31	Ed Crane, 1892	189
	Tony Mullane, 1893	189
33	Tony Mullane, 1891	187
	Kid Gleason, 1893	187
35	Ed Beatin, 1890	186
36	Sam Jones, 1955	185
37	Tom Vickery, 1890	184
38	Nolan Ryan, 1976	183
39	Matt Kilroy, 1886	182
	Frank Killen, 1892	182
41	Willie McGill, 1893	181
	Bob Harmon, 1911	181
	Bob Turley, 1954	181
44	Jack Stivetts, 1890	179
	Gus Weyhing, 1890	179
	Tommy Byrne, 1949	179
47	Bill Hutchison, 1891	178
	Ted Breitenstein, 1895	178
49	Bob Turley, 1955	177
50	Phenomenal Smith, 1887	176
	George Hemming, 1893	176
52	Silver King, 1892	171
	Jack Stivetts, 1892	171
	Jouett Meekin, 1894	171
	Bump Hadley, 1932	171
56	Elton Chamberlain, 1892	170
	Ed Stein, 1894	170
	Cy Seymour, 1899	170
59	Willie McGill, 1891	168
	Gus Weyhing, 1892	168
	Brickyard Kennedy, 1893	168
	Elmer Myers, 1916	168
63	Toad Ramsey, 1887	167
	Gus Weyhing, 1887	167
	Darby O'Brien, 1889	167
	Kid Gleason, 1890	167
	Bill Daley, 1890	167
	Bobo Newsom, 1937	167
69	Tony Mullane, 1886	166
	Sadie McMahon, 1890	166
	Phil Knell, 1890	166
	Chick Fraser, 1896	166
73	Elton Chamberlain, 1889	165
	Dan Casey, 1890	165
	Kid Gleason, 1891	165
	Weldon Wyckoff, 1915	165
77	Cy Seymour, 1897	164
	Earl Moore, 1911	164
	Phil Niekro, 1977	164
80	Mickey Welch, 1886	163
	Silver King, 1890	163
	George Haddock, 1892	163
83	Johnny Vander Meer, 1943	162
	Nolan Ryan, 1973	162
85	Hank O'Day, 1890	161
	John Sowders, 1890	161
	Kid Carsey, 1891	161
	Gus Weyhing, 1891	161
89	Tommy Byrne, 1950	160
90	George Hemming, 1894	159
	Amos Rusie, 1895	159
	Marty O'Toole, 1912	159
93	Joe Coleman, 1974	158
94	Matt Kilroy, 1887	157
	Bert Cunningham, 1888	157
	Pink Hawley, 1896	157
	Grover Lowdermilk, 1915	157
	Nolan Ryan, 1972	157
99	5 players tied	156

Fewest Walks/Game (by era)

1876-1892

1	George Zettlein, 1876	0.23
2	Cherokee Fisher, 1876	0.24
3	George Bradley, 1880	0.28
4	Tommy Bond, 1876	0.29
5	Tommy Bond, 1879	0.39
6	Bobby Mathews, 1876	0.42
7	Guy Hecker, 1882	0.43
8	Dale Williams, 1876	0.43
9	Al Spalding, 1876	0.44
10	Pud Galvin, 1879	0.47
11	George Bradley, 1879	0.48
12	Sam Weaver, 1878	0.49
13	Terry Larkin, 1879	0.53
14	Jim Devlin, 1876	0.54
15	Denny Driscoll, 1882	0.54

1893-1919

1	Christy Mathewson, 1913	0.62
2	Christy Mathewson, 1914	0.66
3	Cy Young, 1904	0.69
4	Cy Young, 1906	0.78
5	Babe Adams, 1919	0.79
6	Slim Sallee, 1919	0.79
7	Slim Sallee, 1918	0.82
8	Addie Joss, 1908	0.83
9	Cy Young, 1905	0.84
10	Deacon Phillippe, 1902	0.86
11	Cy Young, 1901	0.90
12	Deacon Phillippe, 1903	0.90
13	Christy Mathewson, 1908	0.97
14	Christy Mathewson, 1915	0.97
15	Jesse Tannehill, 1902	0.97

1920-1941

1	Babe Adams, 1920	0.62
2	Red Lucas, 1933	0.74
3	Babe Adams, 1922	0.79
4	Pete Alexander, 1923	0.89
5	Babe Adams, 1921	1.01
6	Paul Derringer, 1939	1.05
7	Carl Hubbell, 1934	1.06
8	Bill Swift, 1932	1.09
9	Pete Alexander, 1925	1.11
10	Herb Pennock, 1930	1.15
11	Red Lucas, 1932	1.17
12	Pete Alexander, 1921	1.18
13	Watty Clark, 1935	1.22
14	Pete Donohue, 1926	1.23
15	Pete Alexander, 1922	1.25

1942-1960

1	Tiny Bonham, 1942	0.96
2	Don Newcombe, 1959	1.09
3	Tiny Bonham, 1945	1.10
4	Lew Burdette, 1960	1.14
5	Lew Burdette, 1959	1.18
6	Robin Roberts, 1956	1.21
7	Robin Roberts, 1959	1.22
8	Robin Roberts, 1952	1.23
9	Hal Brown, 1960	1.25
10	Ray Prim, 1945	1.25
11	Robin Roberts, 1960	1.29
12	Fred Hutchinson, 1951	1.29
13	Ted Lyons, 1942	1.30
14	Schoolboy Rowe, 1943	1.31
15	Vern Law, 1960	1.33

1961-1976

1	Gary Nolan, 1976	1.02
2	Fergie Jenkins, 1971	1.02
3	Juan Marichal, 1966	1.05
4	Lew Burdette, 1961	1.09
5	Jim Merritt, 1967	1.19
6	Vern Law, 1966	1.22
7	Dick Donovan, 1963	1.22
8	Fritz Peterson, 1968	1.23
9	Fergie Jenkins, 1974	1.23
10	Gary Nolan, 1975	1.24
11	Ralph Terry, 1965	1.25
12	Bill Hands, 1968	1.25
13	Jim Kaat, 1976	1.27
14	Juan Marichal, 1968	1.27
15	Catfish Hunter, 1974	1.30

1977-1996

1	Bret Saberhagen, 1994	0.66
2	Bob Tewksbury, 1992	0.77
3	Bob Tewksbury, 1993	0.84
4	La Marr Hoyt, 1985	0.86
5	Greg Maddux, 1995	0.99
6	Dennis Eckersley, 1985	1.01
7	Greg Maddux, 1996	1.03
8	La Marr Hoyt, 1983	1.07
9	Jimmy Key, 1989	1.13
10	Zane Smith, 1991	1.14
11	Greg Swindell, 1991	1.17
12	Scott McGregor, 1979	1.19
13	Rick Honeycutt, 1981	1.20
14	Scott Sanderson, 1991	1.25
15	Bob Tewksbury, 1994	1.27

Strikeouts

1	Matt Kilroy, 1886	513
2	Toad Ramsey, 1886	499
3	Hugh Daily, 1884	483
4	Dupee Shaw, 1884	451
5	Charley Radbourn, 1884	441
6	Charlie Buffinton, 1884	417
7	Guy Hecker, 1884	385
8	Nolan Ryan, 1973	383
9	Sandy Koufax, 1965	382
10	Bill Sweeney, 1884	374
11	Pud Galvin, 1884	369
12	Mark Baldwin, 1889	368
13	Nolan Ryan, 1974	367
14	Tim Keefe, 1883	359
15	Toad Ramsey, 1887	355
16	Rube Waddell, 1904	349
17	Bob Feller, 1946	348
18	Hardie Henderson, 1884	346
19	Jim Whitney, 1883	345
	Mickey Welch, 1884	345
21	Jim McCormick, 1884	343
22	Amos Rusie, 1890	341
	Nolan Ryan, 1977	341
24	Charlie Sweeney, 1884	337
	Amos Rusie, 1891	337
26	Tim Keefe, 1888	335
27	Tim Keefe, 1884	334
28	Nolan Ryan, 1972	329
29	Nolan Ryan, 1976	327
30	Ed Morris, 1886	326
31	Tony Mullane, 1884	325
	Sam McDowell, 1965	325
33	Lady Baldwin, 1886	323
34	Sandy Koufax, 1966	317
35	Charley Radbourn, 1883	315
36	John Clarkson, 1886	313
	Walter Johnson, 1910	313
	J.R. Richard, 1979	313
39	Bill Hutchison, 1892	312
40	Steve Carlton, 1972	310
41	Larry McKeon, 1884	308
	John Clarkson, 1885	308
	Mickey Lolich, 1971	308
	Randy Johnson, 1993	308
45	Sandy Koufax, 1963	306
	Mike Scott, 1986	306
47	Amos Rusie, 1892	304
	Sam McDowell, 1970	304
49	Walter Johnson, 1912	303
	J.R. Richard, 1978	303
51	Ed Morris, 1884	302
	Rube Waddell, 1903	302
53	Vida Blue, 1971	301
	Nolan Ryan, 1989	301
55	Ed Morris, 1885	298
56	Tim Keefe, 1886	297
57	Randy Johnson, 1995	294
58	Jack Lynch, 1884	292
59	Sadie McMahon, 1890	291
	Roger Clemens, 1988	291
61	Bill Hutchison, 1890	289
	Jack Stivetts, 1890	289
	Tom Seaver, 1971	289
64	Rube Waddell, 1905	287
65	Bobby Mathews, 1884	286
	Bobby Mathews, 1885	286
	Steve Carlton, 1980	286
	Steve Carlton, 1982	286
69	Billy Taylor, 1884	284
	John Clarkson, 1889	284
71	Dave Foutz, 1886	283
	Sam McDowell, 1968	283
	Tom Seaver, 1970	283
74	Denny McLain, 1968	280
75	Pud Galvin, 1883	279
	Sam McDowell, 1969	279
77	Bob Veale, 1965	276
	Dwight Gooden, 1984	276
	John Smoltz, 1996	276
80	Hal Newhouser, 1946	275
	Steve Carlton, 1983	275
82	Bob Gibson, 1970	274
	Fergie Jenkins, 1970	274
	Mario Soto, 1982	274
85	Fergie Jenkins, 1969	273
86	Larry Corcoran, 1884	272
	Mickey Welch, 1886	272
	Ed Seward, 1888	272
89	Mickey Lolich, 1969	271
90	Jim Whitney, 1884	270
	Bob Gibson, 1965	270
	Nolan Ryan, 1987	270
93	Ed Walsh, 1908	269
	Sandy Koufax, 1961	269
	Bob Gibson, 1969	269
	Frank Tanana, 1975	269
97	5 players tied	268

Strikeouts (by era)

1876-1892

1	Matt Kilroy, 1886	513
2	Toad Ramsey, 1886	499
3	Hugh Daily, 1884	483
4	Dupee Shaw, 1884	451
5	Charley Radbourn, 1884	441
6	Charlie Buffinton, 1884	417
7	Guy Hecker, 1884	385
8	Bill Sweeney, 1884	374
9	Pud Galvin, 1884	369
10	Mark Baldwin, 1889	368
11	Tim Keefe, 1883	359
12	Toad Ramsey, 1887	355
13	Hardie Henderson, 1884	346
14	Jim Whitney, 1883	345
	Mickey Welch, 1884	345

1893-1919

1	Rube Waddell, 1904	349
2	Walter Johnson, 1910	313
3	Walter Johnson, 1912	303
4	Rube Waddell, 1903	302
5	Rube Waddell, 1905	287
6	Ed Walsh, 1908	269
7	Christy Mathewson, 1903	267
8	Christy Mathewson, 1908	259
9	Ed Walsh, 1910	258
	Joe Wood, 1912	258
11	Ed Walsh, 1911	255
12	Ed Walsh, 1912	254
13	Walter Johnson, 1913	243
14	Pete Alexander, 1915	241

1920-1941

1	Dazzy Vance, 1924	262
2	Bob Feller, 1940	261
3	Bob Feller, 1941	260
4	Bob Feller, 1939	246
5	Bob Feller, 1938	240
6	Van Mungo, 1936	238
7	Bobo Newsom, 1938	226
8	Dazzy Vance, 1925	221
9	Lefty Grove, 1930	209
10	Johnny Vander Meer, 1941	202
11	Dazzy Vance, 1928	200
12	Dizzy Dean, 1933	199
13	Dazzy Vance, 1923	197
14	Dizzy Dean, 1934	195
	Dizzy Dean, 1936	195

1942-1960

1	Bob Feller, 1946	348
2	Hal Newhouser, 1946	275
3	Herb Score, 1956	263
4	Don Drysdale, 1960	246
5	Herb Score, 1955	245
6	Don Drysdale, 1959	242
7	Sam Jones, 1958	225
8	Hal Newhouser, 1945	212
9	Bob Turley, 1955	210
10	Sam Jones, 1959	209
11	Jim Bunning, 1959	201
	Jim Bunning, 1960	201
13	Robin Roberts, 1953	198
	Sam Jones, 1955	198
15	Sandy Koufax, 1960	197

1961-1976

1	Nolan Ryan, 1973	383
2	Sandy Koufax, 1965	382
3	Nolan Ryan, 1974	367
4	Nolan Ryan, 1972	329
5	Nolan Ryan, 1976	327
6	Sam McDowell, 1965	325
7	Sandy Koufax, 1966	317
8	Steve Carlton, 1972	310
9	Mickey Lolich, 1971	308
10	Sandy Koufax, 1963	306
11	Sam McDowell, 1970	304
12	Vida Blue, 1971	301
13	Tom Seaver, 1971	289
14	Sam McDowell, 1968	283
	Tom Seaver, 1970	283

1977-1996

1	Nolan Ryan, 1977	341
2	J.R. Richard, 1979	313
3	Randy Johnson, 1993	308
4	Mike Scott, 1986	306
5	J.R. Richard, 1978	303
6	Nolan Ryan, 1989	301
7	Randy Johnson, 1995	294
8	Roger Clemens, 1988	291
9	Steve Carlton, 1980	286
	Steve Carlton, 1982	286
11	Dwight Gooden, 1984	276
	John Smoltz, 1996	276
13	Steve Carlton, 1983	275
14	Mario Soto, 1982	274
15	Nolan Ryan, 1987	270

Strikeouts per Game

1	Randy Johnson, 1995	12.35
2	Nolan Ryan, 1987	11.48
3	Dwight Gooden, 1984	11.39
4	Nolan Ryan, 1989	11.32
5	Hideo Nomo, 1995	11.10
6	Randy Johnson, 1993	10.86
7	Sam McDowell, 1965	10.71
8	Randy Johnson, 1994	10.67
9	Nolan Ryan, 1973	10.57
10	Nolan Ryan, 1991	10.56
11	Sandy Koufax, 1962	10.55
12	Nolan Ryan, 1972	10.43
13	Sam McDowell, 1966	10.42
14	Nolan Ryan, 1976	10.35
15	Randy Johnson, 1992	10.31
16	Nolan Ryan, 1977	10.26
17	Sandy Koufax, 1965	10.24
18	Nolan Ryan, 1990	10.24
19	Randy Johnson, 1991	10.19
20	Sandy Koufax, 1960	10.13
21	Mike Scott, 1986	10.00
22	Nolan Ryan, 1978	9.97
23	Nolan Ryan, 1974	9.93
24	Roger Clemens, 1988	9.92
25	David Cone, 1990	9.91
26	J.R. Richard, 1978	9.90
27	Andy Benes, 1994	9.87
28	Nolan Ryan, 1986	9.81
29	John Smoltz, 1996	9.79
30	Herb Score, 1955	9.70
31	Nolan Ryan, 1984	9.65
32	J.R. Richard, 1979	9.64
33	Mario Soto, 1982	9.57
34	Tom Griffin, 1969	9.56
35	Roger Clemens, 1996	9.53
36	Jim Maloney, 1963	9.53
37	Sid Fernandez, 1985	9.51
38	Herb Score, 1956	9.49
39	Sandy Koufax, 1961	9.47
40	Sam McDowell, 1968	9.47
41	David Cone, 1992	9.41
42	Frank Tanana, 1975	9.41
43	Don Wilson, 1969	9.40
44	Bob Veale, 1965	9.34
45	Nolan Ryan, 1988	9.33
46	David Cone, 1991	9.32
47	Luis Tiant, 1967	9.22
48	Hideo Nomo, 1996	9.22
49	Pedro Martinez, 1996	9.22
50	Mark Langston, 1986	9.21
51	Luis Tiant, 1968	9.20
52	Dave Boswell, 1966	9.19
53	Sam McDowell, 1964	9.19
54	Sonny Siebert, 1965	9.11
55	Sid Fernandez, 1988	9.10
56	Tom Seaver, 1971	9.08
57	Sid Fernandez, 1990	9.08
58	Dennis Eckersley, 1976	9.03
59	John Smoltz, 1995	9.02
60	Nolan Ryan, 1979	9.01
61	Sandy Koufax, 1964	9.00
	Darryl Kile, 1996	9.00
63	Sam McDowell, 1967	8.99
64	Sam McDowell, 1970	8.97
65	Bobby Witt, 1990	8.96
66	Curt Schilling, 1996	8.93
67	Jose Rijo, 1994	8.93
68	Jim Maloney, 1964	8.92
69	Jose Rijo, 1988	8.89
70	Roger Clemens, 1994	8.86
71	Sandy Koufax, 1963	8.86
72	Pedro Martinez, 1994	8.83
73	Sandy Koufax, 1966	8.83
74	Kevin Appier, 1996	8.82
75	Sam McDowell, 1969	8.81
76	Sid Fernandez, 1986	8.81
77	Nolan Ryan, 1982	8.81
78	Todd Stottlemyre, 1995	8.80
79	Tom Seaver, 1970	8.76
80	Al Downing, 1963	8.76
81	Bob Moose, 1969	8.74
82	Steve Carlton, 1983	8.73
83	Dwight Gooden, 1985	8.72
84	Steve Carlton, 1982	8.71
85	Juan Pizarro, 1961	8.69
86	Mickey Lolich, 1969	8.69
87	Vida Blue, 1971	8.68
88	Hugh Daily, 1884	8.68
89	Mark Langston, 1987	8.67
90	Bob Johnson, 1970	8.66
91	Jim Maloney, 1966	8.65
92	Chuck Finley, 1995	8.65
93	Dwight Gooden, 1990	8.63
94	Jeff Fassero, 1996	8.62
95	Bruce Hurst, 1986	8.62
96	Mario Soto, 1980	8.61
97	Jim Maloney, 1965	8.60
98	Ramon Martinez, 1990	8.56
99	Tom Seaver, 1972	8.55
100	Dick Selma, 1969	8.54

Strikeouts per Game (by era)

1876-1892
1	Hugh Daily, 1884	8.68
2	Matt Kilroy, 1886	7.92
3	Charlie Gagus, 1884	7.92
4	John Clarkson, 1884	7.78
5	Toad Ramsey, 1886	7.63
6	Dupee Shaw, 1884	7.47
7	Jim Whitney, 1884	7.23
8	Mike Dorgan, 1884	7.17
9	James Burke, 1884	7.13
10	Hardie Henderson, 1884	7.09
11	Tim Keefe, 1888	6.94
12	Bob Black, 1884	6.80
13	Lady Baldwin, 1885	6.78
14	Jack Stivetts, 1889	6.71
15	Toad Ramsey, 1890	6.63

1893-1919
1	Rube Waddell, 1903	8.39
2	Rube Waddell, 1904	8.20
3	Rube Waddell, 1905	7.86
4	Rube Marquard, 1911	7.68
5	Walter Johnson, 1910	7.61
6	Joe Wood, 1911	7.54
7	Walter Johnson, 1912	7.39
8	Rube Waddell, 1907	7.33
9	Rube Waddell, 1908	7.31
10	Dutch Leonard, 1914	7.05
11	Red Ames, 1906	6.90
12	Rube Waddell, 1902	6.84
13	Red Ames, 1905	6.78
14	Joe Wood, 1912	6.75
15	Orval Overall, 1908	6.68

1920-1941
1	Johnny Vander Meer, 1941	8.03
2	Bob Feller, 1938	7.78
3	Dazzy Vance, 1924	7.65
4	Dazzy Vance, 1925	7.50
5	Bob Feller, 1939	7.46
6	Dazzy Vance, 1926	7.46
7	Bob Feller, 1940	7.33
8	Van Mungo, 1936	6.87
9	Bob Feller, 1941	6.82
10	Van Mungo, 1937	6.82
11	Lefty Grove, 1926	6.77
12	Bill Hallahan, 1930	6.71
13	George Earnshaw, 1928	6.65
14	Red Ruffing, 1932	6.60
15	Lefty Grove, 1930	6.46

1942-1960
1	Sandy Koufax, 1960	10.13
2	Herb Score, 1955	9.70
3	Herb Score, 1956	9.49
4	Hal Newhouser, 1946	8.46
5	Bob Feller, 1946	8.43
6	Sam Jones, 1956	8.40
7	Herb Score, 1959	8.23
8	Don Drysdale, 1960	8.23
9	Sam Jones, 1958	8.10
10	Don Drysdale, 1959	8.05
11	Bob Turley, 1957	7.76
12	Camilo Pascual, 1956	7.73
13	Bob Turley, 1955	7.66
14	Stan Williams, 1960	7.60
15	Sam Jones, 1957	7.59

1961-1976
1	Sam McDowell, 1965	10.71
2	Nolan Ryan, 1973	10.57
3	Sandy Koufax, 1962	10.55
4	Nolan Ryan, 1972	10.43
5	Sam McDowell, 1966	10.42
6	Nolan Ryan, 1976	10.35
7	Sandy Koufax, 1965	10.24
8	Nolan Ryan, 1974	9.93
9	Tom Griffin, 1969	9.56
10	Jim Maloney, 1963	9.53
11	Sandy Koufax, 1961	9.47
12	Sam McDowell, 1968	9.47
13	Frank Tanana, 1975	9.41
14	Don Wilson, 1969	9.40
15	Bob Veale, 1965	9.34

1977-1996
1	Randy Johnson, 1995	12.35
2	Nolan Ryan, 1987	11.48
3	Dwight Gooden, 1984	11.39
4	Nolan Ryan, 1989	11.32
5	Hideo Nomo, 1995	11.10
6	Randy Johnson, 1993	10.86
7	Randy Johnson, 1994	10.67
8	Nolan Ryan, 1991	10.56
9	Randy Johnson, 1992	10.31
10	Nolan Ryan, 1977	10.26
11	Nolan Ryan, 1990	10.24
12	Randy Johnson, 1991	10.19
13	Mike Scott, 1986	10.00
14	Nolan Ryan, 1978	9.97
15	Roger Clemens, 1988	9.92

Ratio

1	Guy Hecker, 1882	6.92
2	Tim Keefe, 1880	7.20
3	Walter Johnson, 1913	7.26
4	Addie Joss, 1908	7.31
5	Charlie Sweeney, 1884	7.35
6	Christy Mathewson, 1909	7.45
7	Greg Maddux, 1995	7.47
8	Ed Walsh, 1910	7.47
9	George Bradley, 1880	7.53
10	Christy Mathewson, 1908	7.60
11	Henry Boyle, 1884	7.68
12	Mordecai Brown, 1908	7.72
13	Denny Driscoll, 1882	7.79
14	Pete Alexander, 1915	7.82
15	Sandy Koufax, 1965	7.83
16	Juan Marichal, 1966	7.88
17	Bob Gibson, 1968	7.89
18	Roger Nelson, 1972	7.89
19	Dave McNally, 1968	7.91
20	Ed Walsh, 1908	7.91
21	Sandy Koufax, 1963	7.96
22	Luis Tiant, 1968	7.98
23	George Bradley, 1876	7.98
24	Jim Whitney, 1884	8.01
25	Guy Hecker, 1884	8.02
26	Cy Young, 1905	8.03
27	Mordecai Brown, 1909	8.04
28	Cy Young, 1908	8.07
29	Tommy Bond, 1876	8.12
30	Babe Adams, 1919	8.17
31	Russ Ford, 1910	8.17
32	John Ward, 1880	8.26
33	Lady Baldwin, 1885	8.28
34	Eddie Cicotte, 1917	8.28
35	Dutch Leonard, 1914	8.29
36	Charley Radbourn, 1884	8.30
37	Denny McLain, 1968	8.30
38	Catfish Hunter, 1972	8.32
39	Doc White, 1906	8.33
40	Greg Maddux, 1994	8.33
41	Silver King, 1888	8.34
42	Pete Alexander, 1919	8.35
43	Juan Marichal, 1965	8.35
44	Don Sutton, 1972	8.35
45	Sandy Koufax, 1964	8.35
46	Ed Morris, 1884	8.36
47	Mike Scott, 1986	8.37
48	Christy Mathewson, 1905	8.42
49	Larry Corcoran, 1880	8.44
50	Addie Joss, 1908	8.49
51	Reb Russell, 1916	8.51
52	Cy Young, 1904	8.53
53	Mordecai Brown, 1906	8.53
54	Walter Johnson, 1910	8.54
55	Ron Guidry, 1978	8.55
56	Claude Hendrix, 1914	8.55
57	Walter Johnson, 1912	8.56
58	Warren Hacker, 1952	8.56
59	Jack Lynch, 1884	8.56
60	Jack Chesbro, 1904	8.57
61	John Clarkson, 1885	8.58
62	Joe Horlen, 1964	8.59
63	Ed Walsh, 1909	8.60
64	Perry Werden, 1884	8.60
65	Chief Bender, 1910	8.60
66	John Tudor, 1985	8.61
67	Bill Burns, 1908	8.62
68	Addie Joss, 1909	8.64
69	Tom Seaver, 1971	8.64
70	Russ Ford, 1914	8.66
71	Tim Keefe, 1883	8.67
72	Bill Bernhard, 1902	8.68
73	Tim Keefe, 1888	8.68
74	Vida Blue, 1971	8.68
75	Tim Keefe, 1884	8.68
76	Charlie Buffinton, 1888	8.70
77	Lady Baldwin, 1886	8.70
78	Larry Corcoran, 1882	8.70
79	Frank Smith, 1908	8.71
80	Tony Mullane, 1883	8.71
81	Bret Saberhagen, 1989	8.71
82	Christy Mathewson, 1907	8.71
83	Joe Horlen, 1967	8.72
84	Jim Devlin, 1876	8.73
85	Frank Smith, 1909	8.73
86	Mordecai Brown, 1907	8.73
87	Charlie Getzien, 1884	8.74
88	Dwight Gooden, 1985	8.75
89	Fred Anderson, 1917	8.78
90	Charlie Ferguson, 1886	8.78
91	Dick Hughes, 1967	8.78
92	Ray Caldwell, 1914	8.79
93	Walter Johnson, 1918	8.81
94	Turk Farrell, 1963	8.81
95	Pascual Perez, 1988	8.81
96	Charley Radbourn, 1883	8.81
97	Addie Joss, 1903	8.82
98	Dick Rudolph, 1916	8.86
99	Chief Bender, 1909	8.86
100	Fred Goldsmith, 1880	8.86

Earned Run Average

1	Tim Keefe, 1880	0.86
2	Dutch Leonard, 1914	0.96
3	Mordecai Brown, 1906	1.04
4	Bob Gibson, 1968	1.12
5	Christy Mathewson, 1909	1.14
6	Walter Johnson, 1913	1.14
7	Jack Pfiester, 1907	1.15
8	Addie Joss, 1908	1.16
9	Carl Lundgren, 1907	1.17
10	Denny Driscoll, 1882	1.21
11	Pete Alexander, 1915	1.22
12	George Bradley, 1876	1.23
13	Cy Young, 1908	1.26
14	Ed Walsh, 1910	1.27
15	Walter Johnson, 1918	1.27
16	Christy Mathewson, 1905	1.28
17	Guy Hecker, 1882	1.30
18	Jack Coombs, 1910	1.30
19	Mordecai Brown, 1909	1.31
20	Jack Taylor, 1902	1.33
21	Walter Johnson, 1910	1.36
22	George Bradley, 1880	1.38
23	Charley Radbourn, 1884	1.38
24	Walter Johnson, 1912	1.39
25	Mordecai Brown, 1907	1.39
26	Harry Krause, 1909	1.39
27	Ed Walsh, 1909	1.41
28	Ed Walsh, 1908	1.42
29	Ed Reulbach, 1905	1.42
30	Orval Overall, 1909	1.42
31	Christy Mathewson, 1908	1.43
32	Fred Anderson, 1917	1.44
33	Mordecai Brown, 1908	1.47
34	Rube Waddell, 1905	1.48
35	Joe Wood, 1915	1.49
36	Walter Johnson, 1919	1.49
37	Jack Pfiester, 1906	1.51
38	John Ward, 1878	1.51
39	Harry McCormick, 1882	1.52
40	Doc White, 1906	1.52
41	George McQuillan, 1908	1.53
42	Dwight Gooden, 1985	1.53
43	Eddie Cicotte, 1917	1.53
44	Will White, 1882	1.54
45	Cy Morgan, 1910	1.55
46	Pete Alexander, 1916	1.55
47	Walter Johnson, 1915	1.55
48	Howie Camnitz, 1908	1.56
49	Greg Maddux, 1994	1.56
50	Jim Devlin, 1876	1.56
51	Tim Keefe, 1885	1.58
52	Fred Toney, 1915	1.58
53	Eddie Cicotte, 1913	1.58
54	Rube Marquard, 1916	1.58
55	Chief Bender, 1910	1.58
56	Barney Pelty, 1906	1.59
57	Addie Joss, 1904	1.59
58	Ed Walsh, 1907	1.60
59	Luis Tiant, 1968	1.60
60	Joe McGinnity, 1904	1.61
61	Ray Collins, 1910	1.62
62	Rube Waddell, 1904	1.62
63	Howie Camnitz, 1909	1.62
64	Cy Young, 1901	1.62
65	Greg Maddux, 1995	1.63
66	Spud Chandler, 1943	1.64
67	Ernie Shore, 1915	1.64
68	Silver King, 1888	1.64
69	Ed Summers, 1908	1.64
70	Dean Chance, 1964	1.65
71	Walter Johnson, 1908	1.65
72	Ed Reulbach, 1906	1.65
73	Russ Ford, 1910	1.65
74	Chief Bender, 1909	1.66
75	Sam Leever, 1907	1.66
76	Carl Hubbell, 1933	1.66
77	Mickey Welch, 1885	1.66
78	Candy Cummings, 1876	1.67
79	Tommy Bond, 1876	1.68
80	Orval Overall, 1907	1.68
81	Ed Reulbach, 1907	1.69
82	Claude Hendrix, 1914	1.69
83	Nolan Ryan, 1981	1.69
84	Jim McCormick, 1878	1.69
85	Joe Wood, 1910	1.69
86	Rube Foster, 1914	1.70
87	Charlie Sweeney, 1884	1.70
	Bill Burns, 1908	1.70
89	Addie Joss, 1909	1.71
90	Ed Killian, 1909	1.71
91	Walter Johnson, 1914	1.72
92	Ned Garvin, 1904	1.72
93	Doc White, 1909	1.72
94	Bill Doak, 1914	1.72
95	Addie Joss, 1906	1.72
	Pete Alexander, 1919	1.72
97	Sandy Koufax, 1966	1.73
98	Bob Ewing, 1907	1.73
99	Vic Willis, 1906	1.73
100	Sandy Koufax, 1964	1.74

Earned Run Average (by era)

1876-1892
1	Tim Keefe, 1880	0.86
2	Denny Driscoll, 1882	1.21
3	George Bradley, 1876	1.23
4	Guy Hecker, 1882	1.30
5	George Bradley, 1880	1.38
6	Charley Radbourn, 1884	1.38
7	John Ward, 1878	1.51
8	Harry McCormick, 1882	1.52
9	Will White, 1882	1.54
10	Jim Devlin, 1876	1.56
11	Tim Keefe, 1885	1.58
12	Silver King, 1888	1.64
13	Mickey Welch, 1885	1.66
14	Candy Cummings, 1876	1.67
15	Tommy Bond, 1876	1.68

1893-1919
1	Dutch Leonard, 1914	0.96
2	Mordecai Brown, 1906	1.04
3	Christy Mathewson, 1909	1.14
4	Walter Johnson, 1913	1.14
5	Jack Pfiester, 1907	1.15
6	Addie Joss, 1908	1.16
7	Carl Lundgren, 1907	1.17
8	Pete Alexander, 1915	1.22
9	Cy Young, 1908	1.26
10	Ed Walsh, 1910	1.27
11	Walter Johnson, 1918	1.27
12	Christy Mathewson, 1905	1.28
13	Jack Coombs, 1910	1.30
14	Mordecai Brown, 1909	1.31
15	Jack Taylor, 1902	1.33

1920-1941
1	Carl Hubbell, 1933	1.66
2	Pete Alexander, 1920	1.91
3	Dolf Luque, 1923	1.93
4	Lon Warneke, 1933	2.00
5	Lefty Grove, 1931	2.06
6	Dazzy Vance, 1928	2.09
7	Babe Adams, 1920	2.16
8	Hal Schumacher, 1933	2.16
9	Dazzy Vance, 1924	2.16
10	Burleigh Grimes, 1920	2.22
11	Elmer Riddle, 1941	2.24
12	Bill Walker, 1931	2.26
13	Wilcy Moore, 1927	2.28
14	Bucky Walters, 1939	2.29
15	Carl Hubbell, 1934	2.30

1942-1960
1	Spud Chandler, 1943	1.64
2	Mort Cooper, 1942	1.78
3	Hal Newhouser, 1945	1.81
4	Max Lanier, 1943	1.90
5	Hal Newhouser, 1946	1.94
6	Billy Pierce, 1955	1.97
7	Whitey Ford, 1958	2.01
8	Al Benton, 1945	2.02
9	Allie Reynolds, 1952	2.06
10	Ted Lyons, 1942	2.10
11	Howie Pollet, 1946	2.10
12	Spud Chandler, 1946	2.10
13	Warren Spahn, 1953	2.10
14	Dizzy Trout, 1944	2.12
15	Roger Wolff, 1945	2.12

1961-1976
1	Bob Gibson, 1968	1.12
2	Luis Tiant, 1968	1.60
3	Dean Chance, 1964	1.65
4	Sandy Koufax, 1966	1.73
5	Sandy Koufax, 1964	1.74
6	Tom Seaver, 1971	1.76
7	Sam McDowell, 1968	1.81
8	Vida Blue, 1971	1.82
9	Phil Niekro, 1967	1.87
10	Joe Horlen, 1964	1.88
11	Sandy Koufax, 1963	1.88
12	Luis Tiant, 1972	1.91
13	Wilbur Wood, 1971	1.91
14	Gaylord Perry, 1972	1.92
15	Dave McNally, 1968	1.95

1977-1996
1	Dwight Gooden, 1985	1.53
2	Greg Maddux, 1994	1.56
3	Greg Maddux, 1995	1.63
4	Nolan Ryan, 1981	1.69
5	Ron Guidry, 1978	1.74
6	Kevin Brown, 1996	1.89
7	John Tudor, 1985	1.93
8	Roger Clemens, 1990	1.93
9	Orel Hershiser, 1985	2.03
10	Bill Swift, 1992	2.08
11	Bret Saberhagen, 1989	2.16
12	Bob Tewksbury, 1992	2.16
13	Joe Magrane, 1988	2.18
14	Greg Maddux, 1992	2.18
15	Bob Knepper, 1981	2.18

Adjusted Earned Run Average

1 Tim Keefe, 1880 294
2 Dutch Leonard, 1914 . . . 280
3 Greg Maddux, 1994 272
4 Greg Maddux, 1995 261
5 Walter Johnson, 1913 . . . 258
6 Bob Gibson, 1968 258
7 Mordecai Brown, 1906 . . 254
8 Walter Johnson, 1912 . . . 240
9 Christy Mathewson, 1905 . 230
10 Dwight Gooden, 1985 . . . 226
11 Pete Alexander, 1915 . . . 225
12 Christy Mathewson, 1909 . 223
13 Lefty Grove, 1931 218
14 Cy Young, 1901 217
15 Jack Pfiester, 1907 216
16 Denny Driscoll, 1882 216
17 Walter Johnson, 1919 . . . 216
18 Walter Johnson, 1918 . . . 215
19 Kevin Brown, 1996 214
20 Carl Lundgren, 1907 213
21 Roger Clemens, 1990 . . . 211
22 Ed Reulbach, 1905 210
23 Ron Guidry, 1978 208
24 Addie Joss, 1908 206
25 Charley Radbourn, 1884 . 205
26 Jack Taylor, 1902 203
27 Billy Pierce, 1955 201
28 Dolf Luque, 1923 200
29 Dean Chance, 1964 199
30 Silver King, 1888 198
31 Spud Chandler, 1943 . . . 197
32 Al Maul, 1895 196
33 Nolan Ryan, 1981 195
34 Cy Young, 1908 195
35 Hal Newhouser, 1945 . . . 194
36 Tom Seaver, 1971 194
37 Mordecai Brown, 1909 . . 193
38 Carl Hubbell, 1933 193
39 Mort Cooper, 1942 193
40 Walter Johnson, 1915 . . . 191
41 Monty Stratton, 1937 . . . 191
42 Randy Johnson, 1995 . . . 191
43 Guy Hecker, 1882 191
44 Lefty Gomez, 1937 191
45 Sandy Koufax, 1966 191
46 Ed Siever, 1902 191
47 Clark Griffith, 1898 191
48 Dazzy Vance, 1928 191
49 Lefty Grove, 1936 189
50 Vean Gregg, 1911 189
51 Ed Walsh, 1910 189
52 Amos Rusie, 1894 189
53 Hal Newhouser, 1946 . . . 189
54 Dazzy Vance, 1930 188
55 Billy Rhines, 1896 188
56 Wilbur Wood, 1971 188
57 Jack Stivetts, 1889 188
58 Joe Wood, 1915 187
59 Warren Spahn, 1953 187
60 Sandy Koufax, 1964 187
61 Lefty Grove, 1939 186
62 Eddie Cicotte, 1913 185
63 Luis Tiant, 1968 185
64 Lefty Grove, 1930 184
65 Hank Aguirre, 1962 184
66 Joe Horlen, 1964 184
67 Henry Boyle, 1886 184
68 Vida Blue, 1971 183
69 John Tudor, 1985 183
70 Walter Johnson, 1910 . . . 183
71 Harry Brecheen, 1948 . . . 183
72 Jack Coombs, 1910 182
73 Billy Rhines, 1890 182
74 Steve Carlton, 1972 182
75 Fred Toney, 1915 182
76 Johnny Allen, 1937 181
77 Rube Waddell, 1905 180
78 Mordecai Brown, 1907 . . 179
79 Orval Overall, 1909 179
80 Rube Waddell, 1902 179
81 Kevin Appier, 1993 179
82 Joe Wood, 1912 178
83 Bret Saberhagen, 1989 . . 178
84 Phil Niekro, 1967 178
85 Max Lanier, 1943 177
86 Roger Clemens, 1994 . . . 177
87 Fred Anderson, 1917 177
88 Cy Young, 1892 176
89 Johnny Antonelli, 1954 . . 176
90 Whitey Ford, 1958 176
91 Lefty Grove, 1935 176
92 Jack Pfiester, 1906 175
93 Eddie Cicotte, 1919 175
94 Roger Clemens, 1992 . . . 175
95 Mel Harder, 1934 174
96 Lefty Gomez, 1934 174
97 Harry McCormick, 1882 . . 174
98 Al Benton, 1945 174
99 George Bradley, 1876 . . . 174
100 Tom Seaver, 1973 174

Adjusted ERA (by era)

1876-1892

1 Tim Keefe, 1880 294
2 Denny Driscoll, 1882 216
3 Charley Radbourn, 1884 . 205
4 Silver King, 1888 198
5 Guy Hecker, 1882 191
6 Jack Stivetts, 1889 188
7 Henry Boyle, 1886 184
8 Billy Rhines, 1890 182
9 Cy Young, 1892 176
10 Harry McCormick, 1882 . . 174
11 George Bradley, 1876 . . . 174
12 Jim Devlin, 1876 174
13 Will White, 1882 172
14 Guy Hecker, 1884 172
15 Jim McCormick, 1883 . . . 171

1893-1919

1 Dutch Leonard, 1914 . . . 280
2 Walter Johnson, 1913 . . . 258
3 Mordecai Brown, 1906 . . 254
4 Walter Johnson, 1912 . . . 240
5 Christy Mathewson, 1905 . 230
6 Pete Alexander, 1915 . . . 225
7 Christy Mathewson, 1909 . 223
8 Cy Young, 1901 217
9 Jack Pfiester, 1907 216
10 Walter Johnson, 1919 . . . 216
11 Walter Johnson, 1918 . . . 215
12 Carl Lundgren, 1907 213
13 Ed Reulbach, 1905 210
14 Addie Joss, 1908 206
15 Jack Taylor, 1902 203

1920-1941

1 Lefty Grove, 1931 218
2 Dolf Luque, 1923 200
3 Carl Hubbell, 1933 193
4 Monty Stratton, 1937 . . . 191
5 Lefty Gomez, 1937 191
6 Dazzy Vance, 1928 191
7 Lefty Gomez, 1936 189
8 Dazzy Vance, 1930 188
9 Lefty Grove, 1939 186
10 Lefty Grove, 1930 184
11 Johnny Allen, 1937 181
12 Lefty Grove, 1935 176
13 Mel Harder, 1934 174
14 Lefty Gomez, 1934 174
15 Dazzy Vance, 1924 173

1942-1960

1 Billy Pierce, 1955 201
2 Spud Chandler, 1943 . . . 197
3 Hal Newhouser, 1945 . . . 194
4 Mort Cooper, 1942 193
5 Hal Newhouser, 1946 . . . 189
6 Warren Spahn, 1953 187
7 Harry Brecheen, 1948 . . . 183
8 Max Lanier, 1943 177
9 Johnny Antonelli, 1954 . . 176
10 Whitey Ford, 1958 176
11 Al Benton, 1945 174
12 Hoyt Wilhelm, 1959 173
13 Ted Lyons, 1942 172

1961-1976

1 Bob Gibson, 1968 258
2 Dean Chance, 1964 199
3 Tom Seaver, 1971 194
4 Sandy Koufax, 1966 191
5 Wilbur Wood, 1971 188
6 Sandy Koufax, 1964 187
7 Luis Tiant, 1968 185
8 Hank Aguirre, 1962 184
9 Joe Horlen, 1964 184
10 Vida Blue, 1971 183
11 Steve Carlton, 1972 182
12 Phil Niekro, 1967 178
13 Tom Seaver, 1973 174
14 Whitey Ford, 1964 170
15 Juan Marichal, 1965 169

1977-1996

1 Greg Maddux, 1994 272
2 Greg Maddux, 1995 261
3 Dwight Gooden, 1985 . . . 226
4 Kevin Brown, 1996 214
5 Roger Clemens, 1990 . . . 211
6 Ron Guidry, 1978 208
7 Nolan Ryan, 1981 195
8 Randy Johnson, 1995 . . . 191
9 John Tudor, 1985 183
10 Kevin Appier, 1993 179
11 Bret Saberhagen, 1989 . . 178
12 Roger Clemens, 1994 . . . 177
13 Roger Clemens, 1992 . . . 175
14 Juan Guzman, 1996 173
15 Orel Hershiser, 1985 . . . 171

Pitching Runs

1 Amos Rusie, 1894 . . . . . 125.7
2 Charley Radbourn, 1884 . 120.9
3 Guy Hecker, 1884 . . . . . . 108.0
4 Silver King, 1888 . . . . . . 92.3
5 John Clarkson, 1889 . . . . 88.7
6 Cy Young, 1901 . . . . 84.2
7 Matt Kilroy, 1887 . . . . . . 80.4
8 Pink Hawley, 1895 . . . . . 79.1
9 Walter Johnson, 1912 . . . 79.1
10 Silver King, 1890 . . . . . . 78.9
11 Will White, 1883 . . . . 77.7
12 Amos Rusie, 1893 . . . . . . 76.9
13 Charley Radbourn, 1883 . 76.5
14 Dave Foutz, 1886 . . . . . . 75.2
15 Lefty Grove, 1931 . . . . . . 74.5
16 Dolf Luque, 1923 . . . . . . 74.2
17 Jouett Meekin, 1894 . . . . 73.9
18 Scott Stratton, 1890 . . . . 72.3
19 Billy Rhines, 1890 . . . . . . 72.2
20 Lefty Gomez, 1937 . . . . . 70.9
21 Pud Galvin, 1884 . . . . . . 69.8
22 Walter Johnson, 1913 . . . 68.8
23 George Bradley, 1876 . . . 68.8
24 Cy Young, 1892 . . . . 68.5
25 Kid Nichols, 1897 . . . . . . 68.4
26 Lefty Grove, 1930 . . . . . . 68.4
27 Dazzy Vance, 1930 . . . . . 67.9
28 Lefty Gomez, 1934 . . . . . 67.7
29 Elmer Smith, 1887 . . . . . 67.6
30 Sandy Koufax, 1966 . . . . 67.5
31 John Clarkson, 1885 . . . . 67.1
32 Red Faber, 1921 . . . . 66.4
33 Toad Ramsey, 1886 . . . . 65.7
34 Christy Mathewson, 1905 . 65.0
35 Warren Spahn, 1953 . . . . 64.5
36 Pete Alexander, 1915 . . . 64.1
37 Kid Nichols, 1898 . . . . . . 63.5
38 Amos Rusie, 1897 . . . . . . 63.5
39 Kid Nichols, 1896 . . . . . . 63.5
40 Ted Breitenstein, 1893 . . 63.4
41 Dwight Gooden, 1985 . . . 63.4
42 Kid Nichols, 1890 . . . . . . 63.2
43 Mickey Welch, 1885 . . . . 63.1
44 Bob Gibson, 1968 . . . . . 63.1
45 Bob Caruthers, 1885 . . . . 63.1
46 Bob Feller, 1940 . . . . 63.0
47 Lefty Grove, 1936 . . . . . . 62.8
48 Cy Young, 1894 . . . . 62.7
49 Clark Griffith, 1898 . . . . . 62.6
50 Cy Young, 1895 . . . . 62.5
51 Ed Morris, 1886 . . . . 61.9
52 Amos Rusie, 1890 . . . . . . 61.6
53 Ron Guidry, 1978 . . . . . . 61.4
54 Carl Hubbell, 1934 . . . . . 61.3
55 Will White, 1882 . . . . 61.3
56 Cy Young, 1893 . . . . 61.1
57 Dean Chance, 1964 . . . . 61.1
58 Tim Keefe, 1883 . . . . 61.1
59 Cy Young, 1902 . . . . 60.8
60 Jim Palmer, 1975 . . . . . . 60.6
61 Ed Seward, 1888 . . . . . . 60.5
62 Kevin Brown, 1996 . . . . . 60.1
63 Greg Maddux, 1994 . . . . 59.5
64 Thornton Lee, 1941 . . . . 59.4
65 Greg Maddux, 1995 . . . . 59.4
66 Dazzy Vance, 1928 . . . . . 59.3
67 Robin Roberts, 1953 . . . . 59.1
68 Charlie Ferguson, 1886 . . 58.6
69 Dazzy Vance, 1924 . . . . . 58.5
70 Bob Feller, 1939 . . . . 58.3
71 Bill Hutchison, 1890 . . . . 58.2
72 Lady Baldwin, 1886 . . . . . 58.2
73 Bucky Walters, 1939 . . . . 57.8
74 Kid Nichols, 1895 . . . . . . 57.8
75 Carl Hubbell, 1936 . . . . . 57.8
76 John Clarkson, 1887 . . . . 57.7
77 Ed Morris, 1885 . . . . 57.7
78 Jesse Duryea, 1889 . . . . 57.5
79 Carl Hubbell, 1933 . . . . . 57.5
80 Wilbur Wood, 1971 . . . . . 57.4
81 Guy Hecker, 1885 . . . . . . 57.2
82 Tony Mullane, 1883 . . . . 57.0
83 Vida Blue, 1971 . . . . 57.0
84 Steve Carlton, 1972 . . . . 56.9
85 Walter Johnson, 1919 . . . 56.1
86 Sandy Koufax, 1965 . . . . 56.0
87 Win Mercer, 1894 . . . . . . 55.7
88 Warren Spahn, 1947 . . . . 55.7
89 Tim Keefe, 1885 . . . . 55.3
90 Bill Hoffer, 1895 . . . . 54.9
91 Walter Johnson, 1918 . . . 54.6
92 Bob Feller, 1946 . . . . 54.5
93 Charlie Buffinton, 1884 . . 54.5
94 Kid Nichols, 1893 . . . . . . 54.3
95 Tom Seaver, 1971 . . . . . . 54.3
96 Hal Newhouser, 1945 . . . 54.2
97 Joe Wood, 1912 . . . . 53.9
98 Toad Ramsey, 1887 . . . . 53.7
99 Charlie Sweeney, 1884 . . 53.7
100 Mel Harder, 1934 . . . . . . 53.6

Adjusted Pitching Runs

1 Amos Rusie, 1894 . . . . . 121.7
2 Charley Radbourn, 1884 . 108.9
3 Silver King, 1888 . . . . . . 105.2
4 John Clarkson, 1889 . . . . 98.9
5 Guy Hecker, 1884 . . . . . . 95.9
6 Silver King, 1890 . . . . . . 84.5
7 John Clarkson, 1885 . . . . 82.2
8 Pud Galvin, 1884 . . . . . . 81.9
9 John Clarkson, 1887 . . . . 81.8
10 Walter Johnson, 1912 . . . 79.8
11 Jim Devlin, 1876 . . . . 79.7
12 Cy Young, 1901 . . . . 78.6
13 Lefty Grove, 1931 . . . . . . 78.2
14 Toad Ramsey, 1886 . . . . 78.1
15 Amos Rusie, 1893 . . . . . . 76.4
16 Kid Nichols, 1897 . . . . . . 74.9
17 Dave Foutz, 1886 . . . . . . 74.6
18 Will White, 1883 . . . . 74.1
19 Cy Young, 1892 . . . . 73.7
20 Charley Radbourn, 1883 . 72.7
21 Kid Nichols, 1890 . . . . . . 71.8
22 Billy Rhines, 1890 . . . . . . 71.7
23 Cy Young, 1893 . . . . 71.4
24 Scott Stratton, 1890 . . . . 71.4
25 Kid Nichols, 1895 . . . . . . 71.3
26 Cy Young, 1895 . . . . 70.9
27 Kid Nichols, 1896 . . . . . . 70.9
28 Lefty Grove, 1936 . . . . . . 70.6
29 Jouett Meekin, 1894 . . . . 70.3
30 Elmer Smith, 1887 . . . . . 69.9
31 Walter Johnson, 1913 . . . 69.6
32 Dolf Luque, 1923 . . . . . . 69.3
33 Lefty Grove, 1930 . . . . . . 69.1
34 Cy Young, 1894 . . . . 69.0
35 Matt Kilroy, 1887 . . . . . . 67.4
36 Kid Nichols, 1898 . . . . . . 67.3
37 Kid Nichols, 1893 . . . . . . 67.1
38 Tony Mullane, 1883 . . . . 66.3
39 Dazzy Vance, 1930 . . . . . 66.2
40 Ted Breitenstein, 1893 . . 66.2
41 Pink Hawley, 1895 . . . . . 66.2
42 Jack Stivetts, 1891 . . . . . 65.7
43 Lefty Gomez, 1937 . . . . . 65.5
44 Jim Devlin, 1877 . . . . 65.5
45 Red Faber, 1921 . . . . 64.6
46 Bob Caruthers, 1885 . . . . 64.3
47 Bill Hutchison, 1890 . . . . 64.2
48 John Clarkson, 1886 . . . . 64.0
49 Tim Keefe, 1883 . . . . 63.8
50 Pete Alexander, 1915 . . . 63.7
51 Vic Willis, 1899 . . . . 63.4
52 Christy Mathewson, 1905 . 62.3
53 Wilbur Wood, 1971 . . . . . 62.2
54 Steve Carlton, 1972 . . . . 62.2
55 Lefty Grove, 1935 . . . . . . 61.9
56 Clark Griffith, 1898 . . . . . 61.6
57 Greg Maddux, 1995 . . . . 61.3
58 Cy Young, 1902 . . . . 60.8
59 Greg Maddux, 1994 . . . . 60.2
60 Jesse Duryea, 1889 . . . . 60.1
61 Bob Gibson, 1968 . . . . . 60.0
62 Cy Young, 1896 . . . . 59.9
63 Kid Nichols, 1891 . . . . . . 59.8
64 Toad Ramsey, 1887 . . . . 59.7
65 Dan Casey, 1887 . . . . . . 59.5
66 Hal Newhouser, 1945 . . . 59.4
67 Dwight Gooden, 1985 . . . 59.2
68 Elton Chamberlain, 1889 . 59.0
69 Dazzy Vance, 1928 . . . . . 58.8
70 Will White, 1882 . . . . 58.8
71 Matt Kilroy, 1889 . . . . . . 58.7
72 Lady Baldwin, 1886 . . . . . 58.3
73 Charlie Ferguson, 1886 . . 58.1
74 Ed Morris, 1886 . . . . 58.0
75 Amos Rusie, 1897 . . . . . . 57.9
76 George Bradley, 1876 . . . 57.8
77 Thornton Lee, 1941 . . . . 57.7
78 Kid Gleason, 1890 . . . . . . 57.5
79 Amos Rusie, 1890 . . . . . . 57.5
80 Cy Young, 1899 . . . . 57.4
81 Ron Guidry, 1978 . . . . . . 57.1
82 Bob Feller, 1940 . . . . 57.1
83 Joe Wood, 1912 . . . . 57.0
84 Nig Cuppy, 1895 . . . . 56.7
85 Dizzy Trout, 1944 . . . . . . 56.6
86 Bobo Newsom, 1940 . . . . 56.5
87 Nig Cuppy, 1896 . . . . 56.5
88 Sandy Koufax, 1966 . . . . 56.3
89 Ed Seward, 1888 . . . . . . 56.2
90 Robin Roberts, 1953 . . . . 56.1
91 Tony Mullane, 1884 . . . . 56.1
92 Guy Hecker, 1885 . . . . . . 56.0
93 Hal Newhouser, 1946 . . . 55.8
94 Ed Morris, 1885 . . . . 55.8
95 Kevin Brown, 1996 . . . . . 55.7
96 Walter Johnson, 1919 . . . 55.5
97 Silver King, 1889 . . . . . . 55.1
98 Mel Harder, 1934 . . . . . . 55.0
99 Mickey Welch, 1885 . . . . 54.8
100 Bucky Walters, 1939 . . . . 54.8

Pitching Wins

1	Charley Radbourn, 1884	10.8
2	Guy Hecker, 1884	9.9
3	Amos Rusie, 1894	9.6
4	Silver King, 1888	8.5
5	Walter Johnson, 1912	7.9
6	John Clarkson, 1889	7.7
7	Cy Young, 1901	7.6
8	Walter Johnson, 1913	7.3
9	Bob Gibson, 1968	7.2
10	Dolf Luque, 1923	7.1
11	Pete Alexander, 1915	7.1
12	Sandy Koufax, 1966	7.1
13	Lefty Grove, 1931	6.9
14	Will White, 1883	6.8
15	Christy Mathewson, 1905	6.7
16	Charley Radbourn, 1883	6.7
17	Dwight Gooden, 1985	6.7
18	Dave Foutz, 1886	6.6
19	Lefty Gomez, 1937	6.5
20	Matt Kilroy, 1887	6.5
21	Dean Chance, 1964	6.4
22	Billy Rhines, 1890	6.4
23	Pink Hawley, 1895	6.4
24	Scott Stratton, 1890	6.4
25	Cy Young, 1892	6.3
26	Ron Guidry, 1978	6.3
27	John Clarkson, 1885	6.3
28	Amos Rusie, 1893	6.3
29	Lefty Gomez, 1934	6.3
30	Silver King, 1890	6.3
31	Pud Galvin, 1884	6.2
32	Warren Spahn, 1953	6.2
33	Red Faber, 1921	6.2
34	Jim Palmer, 1975	6.2
35	Lefty Grove, 1930	6.2
36	Wilbur Wood, 1971	6.2
37	Vida Blue, 1971	6.1
38	Steve Carlton, 1972	6.1
39	Walter Johnson, 1918	6.1
40	Carl Hubbell, 1933	6.1
41	George Bradley, 1876	6.1
42	Dazzy Vance, 1930	6.0
43	Carl Hubbell, 1934	6.0
44	Bob Feller, 1940	5.9
45	Kid Nichols, 1898	5.9
46	Mickey Welch, 1885	5.9
47	Sandy Koufax, 1965	5.9
48	Kevin Brown, 1996	5.9
49	Walter Johnson, 1919	5.9
50	Kid Nichols, 1897	5.9
51	Greg Maddux, 1994	5.9
52	Clark Griffith, 1898	5.8
53	Greg Maddux, 1995	5.8
54	Tom Seaver, 1971	5.8
55	Dazzy Vance, 1924	5.8
56	Hal Newhouser, 1945	5.8
57	Dazzy Vance, 1928	5.8
58	Bucky Walters, 1939	5.8
59	Cy Young, 1902	5.8
60	Toad Ramsey, 1886	5.8
61	Thornton Lee, 1941	5.8
62	Ed Walsh, 1908	5.7
63	Bob Feller, 1946	5.7
64	Ed Walsh, 1910	5.7
65	Robin Roberts, 1953	5.7
66	Bob Caruthers, 1885	5.7
67	Jouett Meekin, 1894	5.7
68	Carl Hubbell, 1936	5.6
69	Will White, 1882	5.6
70	Kid Nichols, 1890	5.6
71	Ed Seward, 1888	5.6
72	Lefty Grove, 1936	5.5
73	Jack Taylor, 1902	5.5
74	Walter Johnson, 1915	5.5
75	Warren Spahn, 1947	5.5
76	Amos Rusie, 1890	5.5
77	Elmer Smith, 1887	5.5
78	Mordecai Brown, 1906	5.5
79	Amos Rusie, 1897	5.4
80	Ed Morris, 1886	5.4
81	Mordecai Brown, 1909	5.4
82	Joe McGinnity, 1904	5.4
83	Dizzy Trout, 1944	5.4
84	Joe Wood, 1912	5.4
85	Kid Nichols, 1896	5.4
86	Tim Keefe, 1883	5.4
87	Bob Feller, 1939	5.4
88	Hal Newhouser, 1946	5.3
89	John Tudor, 1985	5.3
90	Ed Reulbach, 1905	5.3
91	Tom Seaver, 1973	5.3
92	Jack Coombs, 1910	5.3
93	Pete Alexander, 1920	5.3
94	Charlie Ferguson, 1886	5.3
95	Pete Alexander, 1916	5.3
96	Walter Johnson, 1910	5.3
97	Sandy Koufax, 1963	5.3
98	Lady Baldwin, 1886	5.3
99	Tim Keefe, 1888	5.2
100	Juan Marichal, 1969	5.2

Adjusted Pitching Wins

1	Charley Radbourn, 1884	9.7
2	Silver King, 1888	9.7
3	Amos Rusie, 1894	9.3
4	Guy Hecker, 1884	8.8
5	John Clarkson, 1889	8.6
6	Walter Johnson, 1912	8.0
7	John Clarkson, 1885	7.7
8	Walter Johnson, 1913	7.4
9	Pud Galvin, 1884	7.3
10	Lefty Grove, 1931	7.3
11	Cy Young, 1901	7.1
12	Pete Alexander, 1915	7.1
13	Jim Devlin, 1876	7.0
14	John Clarkson, 1887	6.9
15	Bob Gibson, 1968	6.9
16	Toad Ramsey, 1886	6.8
17	Cy Young, 1892	6.8
18	Silver King, 1890	6.7
19	Wilbur Wood, 1971	6.7
20	Steve Carlton, 1972	6.7
21	Dolf Luque, 1923	6.7
22	Dave Foutz, 1886	6.5
23	Will White, 1883	6.5
24	Christy Mathewson, 1905	6.5
25	Kid Nichols, 1897	6.4
26	Kid Nichols, 1890	6.4
27	Billy Rhines, 1890	6.4
28	Hal Newhouser, 1945	6.4
29	Charley Radbourn, 1883	6.3
30	Kid Nichols, 1898	6.3
31	Scott Stratton, 1890	6.3
32	Amos Rusie, 1893	6.3
33	Lefty Grove, 1930	6.3
34	Lefty Gomez, 1934	6.2
35	Dwight Gooden, 1985	6.2
36	Red Faber, 1921	6.0
37	Greg Maddux, 1995	6.0
38	Kid Nichols, 1896	6.0
39	Lefty Gomez, 1937	6.0
40	Dizzy Trout, 1944	6.0
41	Greg Maddux, 1994	5.9
42	Sandy Koufax, 1966	5.9
43	Walter Johnson, 1918	5.9
44	Ron Guidry, 1978	5.9
45	Cy Young, 1893	5.9
46	Hal Newhouser, 1946	5.8
47	Dazzy Vance, 1930	5.8
48	Jim Devlin, 1877	5.8
49	Tony Mullane, 1883	5.8
50	Walter Johnson, 1919	5.8
51	Lefty Grove, 1935	5.8
52	John Clarkson, 1886	5.8
53	Bob Caruthers, 1885	5.8
54	Kid Nichols, 1895	5.8
55	Cy Young, 1902	5.8
56	Clark Griffith, 1898	5.8
57	Dazzy Vance, 1928	5.7
58	Vic Willis, 1899	5.7
59	Cy Young, 1895	5.7
60	Joe Wood, 1912	5.7
61	Bill Hutchison, 1890	5.7
62	Elmer Smith, 1887	5.7
63	Jack Stivetts, 1891	5.7
64	Vida Blue, 1971	5.7
65	Walter Johnson, 1915	5.6
66	Gaylord Perry, 1972	5.6
67	Carl Hubbell, 1933	5.6
68	Tom Seaver, 1971	5.6
69	Tim Keefe, 1883	5.6
70	Pete Alexander, 1920	5.6
71	Thornton Lee, 1941	5.6
72	Roger Clemens, 1990	5.5
73	Kid Nichols, 1893	5.5
74	Bucky Walters, 1939	5.5
75	Mordecai Brown, 1906	5.5
76	Mort Cooper, 1942	5.5
77	Matt Kilroy, 1887	5.5
78	Pete Alexander, 1916	5.4
79	Kevin Brown, 1996	5.4
80	Ted Breitenstein, 1893	5.4
81	Robin Roberts, 1953	5.4
82	Will White, 1882	5.4
83	Dazzy Vance, 1924	5.4
84	Bob Feller, 1940	5.4
85	Jouett Meekin, 1894	5.4
86	Bill Hands, 1969	5.4
87	Pink Hawley, 1895	5.4
88	Joe McGinnity, 1904	5.3
89	Kid Nichols, 1891	5.3
90	Bobo Newsom, 1940	5.3
91	Dean Chance, 1964	5.3
92	Carl Hubbell, 1934	5.3
93	Bert Blyleven, 1973	5.3
94	Dizzy Dean, 1934	5.3
95	Cy Young, 1894	5.3
96	Ed Walsh, 1908	5.3
97	Lady Baldwin, 1886	5.3
98	Curt Davis, 1934	5.3
99	Ed Reulbach, 1905	5.3
100	Charlie Ferguson, 1886	5.3

Opponents' Batting Average

1	Luis Tiant, 1968	.168
2	Nolan Ryan, 1972	.171
3	Nolan Ryan, 1991	.172
4	Ed Reulbach, 1906	.175
5	Tim Keefe, 1880	.178
6	Sandy Koufax, 1965	.179
7	Dutch Leonard, 1914	.180
8	Sid Fernandez, 1985	.181
9	Hideo Nomo, 1995	.182
10	Dave McNally, 1968	.182
11	Tommy Byrne, 1949	.183
12	Al Downing, 1963	.184
13	Bob Gibson, 1968	.184
14	Sam McDowell, 1965	.185
15	Carl Lundgren, 1907	.185
16	Herb Score, 1956	.186
17	Mike Scott, 1986	.186
18	Nolan Ryan, 1989	.187
19	Ed Walsh, 1910	.187
20	Mario Soto, 1980	.187
21	Walter Johnson, 1913	.187
22	Nolan Ryan, 1981	.188
23	Russ Ford, 1910	.188
24	Nolan Ryan, 1986	.188
25	Nolan Ryan, 1990	.188
26	Floyd Youmans, 1986	.188
27	Sam McDowell, 1966	.188
28	Guy Hecker, 1882	.188
29	Sandy Koufax, 1963	.189
30	Sam McDowell, 1968	.189
31	Don Sutton, 1972	.189
32	Catfish Hunter, 1972	.189
33	Vida Blue, 1971	.189
34	Nolan Ryan, 1974	.190
35	Andy Messersmith, 1969	.190
36	Joe Horlen, 1964	.190
37	Sid Fernandez, 1988	.191
38	Pete Alexander, 1915	.191
39	Sandy Koufax, 1964	.191
40	Bob Turley, 1955	.193
41	Nolan Ryan, 1977	.193
42	Fred Beebe, 1908	.193
43	Charlie Sweeney, 1884	.193
44	Ron Guidry, 1978	.193
45	Stan Coveleski, 1917	.194
46	Bob Turley, 1957	.194
47	Herb Score, 1955	.194
48	Jack Pfiester, 1906	.194
49	Mordecai Brown, 1908	.195
50	Nolan Ryan, 1976	.195
51	Nolan Ryan, 1983	.195
52	Dean Chance, 1964	.195
53	Roger Clemens, 1986	.195
54	Tim Keefe, 1888	.196
55	Walter Johnson, 1912	.196
56	Roger Nelson, 1972	.196
57	J.R. Richard, 1978	.196
58	Pascual Perez, 1988	.196
59	Greg Maddux, 1995	.197
60	Jeff Robinson, 1988	.197
61	Lady Baldwin, 1885	.197
62	Jose DeLeon, 1989	.197
63	Dave Boswell, 1966	.197
64	Sandy Koufax, 1962	.197
65	Addie Joss, 1908	.197
66	Sonny Siebert, 1968	.198
67	Sid Fernandez, 1989	.198
68	Toad Ramsey, 1886	.198
69	Larry Cheney, 1916	.198
70	Wayne Simpson, 1970	.198
71	Orval Overall, 1909	.198
72	Gary Peters, 1967	.199
73	Larry Corcoran, 1880	.199
74	Willie Mitchell, 1913	.199
75	Adonis Terry, 1888	.199
76	Nolan Ryan, 1987	.199
77	Mordecai Brown, 1904	.199
78	Christy Mathewson, 1909	.200
79	Rube Waddell, 1905	.200
80	Denny McLain, 1968	.200
81	Larry Corcoran, 1882	.200
82	Silver King, 1888	.200
	Bobby Bolin, 1968	.200
	Jim Palmer, 1969	.200
	Sid Fernandez, 1990	.200
86	Christy Mathewson, 1908	.200
87	Spec Shea, 1947	.200
88	Ed Seward, 1888	.200
89	Tony Mullane, 1892	.201
90	Art Fromme, 1909	.201
91	Babe Ruth, 1916	.201
92	Randy Johnson, 1995	.201
93	Dwight Gooden, 1985	.201
94	Cannonball Titcomb, 1888	.201
95	Curt Schilling, 1992	.201
96	Hal Newhouser, 1946	.201
97	Ed Reulbach, 1905	.201
98	Jack Coombs, 1910	.201
99	Dwight Gooden, 1984	.202
100	Jim Maloney, 1963	.202

Opponents' On Base Pctg.

1	Guy Hecker, 1882	.199
2	Charlie Sweeney, 1884	.211
3	Tim Keefe, 1880	.212
4	Henry Boyle, 1884	.215
5	George Bradley, 1880	.217
6	Walter Johnson, 1913	.217
7	Denny Driscoll, 1882	.218
8	Addie Joss, 1908	.218
9	Jim Whitney, 1884	.223
10	George Bradley, 1876	.224
11	Greg Maddux, 1995	.225
12	Christy Mathewson, 1908	.225
13	Guy Hecker, 1884	.226
14	Ed Walsh, 1910	.226
15	Tommy Bond, 1876	.227
16	Lady Baldwin, 1885	.228
17	Sandy Koufax, 1965	.228
18	Christy Mathewson, 1909	.228
19	Sandy Koufax, 1963	.230
20	Juan Marichal, 1966	.230
21	John Ward, 1880	.232
22	Mordecai Brown, 1908	.232
23	Ed Walsh, 1908	.232
24	Luis Tiant, 1968	.233
25	Bob Gibson, 1968	.233
26	Pete Alexander, 1915	.234
27	Dave McNally, 1968	.234
28	Larry Corcoran, 1882	.234
29	Charley Radbourn, 1884	.234
30	Ed Morris, 1884	.234
31	Perry Werden, 1884	.235
32	Jim Devlin, 1876	.235
33	Jack Lynch, 1884	.236
34	Larry Corcoran, 1880	.236
35	Roger Nelson, 1972	.236
36	Charlie Getzien, 1884	.237
37	Tim Keefe, 1883	.237
38	Silver King, 1888	.237
39	Tony Mullane, 1883	.238
40	John Clarkson, 1885	.239
41	Tim Keefe, 1884	.239
42	Mordecai Brown, 1909	.239
43	Fred Corey, 1880	.239
44	Juan Marichal, 1965	.240
45	Cy Young, 1908	.240
46	Don Sutton, 1972	.240
47	Cy Young, 1905	.241
48	Babe Adams, 1919	.241
49	Sandy Koufax, 1964	.241
50	Catfish Hunter, 1972	.242
51	Pete Conway, 1888	.243
52	Harry McCormick, 1882	.243
53	Denny McLain, 1968	.243
54	Tim Keefe, 1888	.243
55	Lady Baldwin, 1886	.243
56	Mike Scott, 1986	.244
57	Charley Radbourn, 1883	.244
58	Will White, 1883	.244
59	Charlie Ferguson, 1886	.244
60	Charlie Buffinton, 1888	.244
61	Will White, 1882	.244
62	Charlie Buffinton, 1884	.244
63	Russ Ford, 1910	.245
64	Pete Alexander, 1919	.245
65	Christy Mathewson, 1905	.245
66	Greg Maddux, 1994	.245
67	Dutch Leonard, 1914	.246
68	Bobby Mathews, 1882	.246
69	Pud Galvin, 1884	.246
70	Charley Radbourn, 1882	.246
71	Sam Weaver, 1878	.247
72	Charlie Gagus, 1884	.247
73	Christy Mathewson, 1907	.247
74	Warren Hacker, 1952	.247
75	Jim McCormick, 1880	.247
76	Ed Morris, 1885	.247
77	Fred Goldsmith, 1880	.247
78	Dupee Shaw, 1884	.247
79	Eddie Cicotte, 1917	.248
80	Walter Johnson, 1912	.248
81	Doc White, 1906	.249
82	John Clarkson, 1884	.249
83	Jumbo McGinnis, 1883	.249
84	John Tudor, 1985	.249
85	Henry Gruber, 1888	.249
86	Hugh Daily, 1884	.250
87	Ron Guidry, 1978	.250
88	Joe Horlen, 1964	.250
89	Terry Larkin, 1879	.250
90	John Ward, 1879	.250
91	John Ward, 1878	.251
92	Billy Taylor, 1884	.251
93	Candy Cummings, 1876	.251
94	Jim Whitney, 1883	.251
95	Cy Young, 1904	.251
96	Claude Hendrix, 1914	.251
97	Dick Burns, 1884	.252
98	Vida Blue, 1971	.252
99	Jack Chesbro, 1904	.252
100	Mordecai Brown, 1906	.252

Wins Above Team

#	Player, Year	
1	George Bradley, 1876	22.5
2	Will White, 1879	21.5
3	Charley Radbourn, 1884	20.1
4	Jim McCormick, 1880	19.4
5	Guy Hecker, 1884	18.0
6	Pud Galvin, 1883	17.6
7	Jim Devlin, 1877	17.5
8	Charley Radbourn, 1883	15.7
9	Matt Kilroy, 1887	15.4
10	Pud Galvin, 1884	15.1
11	Jim Devlin, 1876	15.0
12	Charlie Buffinton, 1884	14.9
13	Walter Johnson, 1913	14.7
14	Jim McCormick, 1884	14.6
15	Jack Chesbro, 1904	14.0
16	Tony Mullane, 1884	13.9
17	Sadie McMahon, 1890	13.4
18	Will White, 1882	13.1
19	Ed Morris, 1885	12.9
20	Joe Wood, 1912	12.8
21	Bill Sweeney, 1884	12.7
	Ed Walsh, 1908	12.7
23	John Clarkson, 1889	12.1
24	Tommy Bond, 1879	12.0
25	Lefty Grove, 1931	11.8
26	Steve Carlton, 1972	11.7
27	Cy Young, 1901	11.6
28	Bill Hutchison, 1891	11.4
	Denny McLain, 1968	11.4
30	Terry Larkin, 1878	11.2
	Mickey Welch, 1884	11.2
	Bob Caruthers, 1889	11.2
33	Henry Porter, 1885	11.0
	Bill Hoffer, 1895	11.0
	Christy Mathewson, 1908	11.0
36	Cy Young, 1902	10.9
37	Cy Young, 1895	10.7
38	Dazzy Vance, 1924	10.6
	Robin Roberts, 1952	10.6
	Ron Guidry, 1978	10.6
41	Bobby Mathews, 1876	10.5
	Dizzy Dean, 1934	10.5
43	Toad Ramsey, 1886	10.2
	Cy Young, 1892	10.2
	Joe McGinnity, 1904	10.2
	Eddie Rommel, 1922	10.2
47	Lefty Grove, 1930	10.1
48	Ed Morris, 1886	10.0
	Bill Donovan, 1907	10.0
50	Frank Mountain, 1883	9.9
	Eddie Cicotte, 1919	9.9
	Lefty Gomez, 1934	9.9
53	Kid Gleason, 1890	9.8
	Pete Alexander, 1915	9.8
	Hal Newhouser, 1944	9.8
56	Bobby Mathews, 1885	9.7
	Russ Ford, 1910	9.7
	Roger Clemens, 1986	9.7
59	Charlie Ferguson, 1886	9.6
	Pete Conway, 1888	9.6
	Eddie Plank, 1912	9.6
62	Pete Alexander, 1916	9.5
	Carl Hubbell, 1936	9.5
	Dwight Gooden, 1985	9.5
65	Jouett Meekin, 1894	9.4
	Walter Johnson, 1912	9.4
	Claude Hendrix, 1914	9.4
68	Joe McGinnity, 1900	9.3
	Sandy Koufax, 1963	9.3
70	Bert Cunningham, 1898	9.2
	Walter Johnson, 1911	9.2
	Bobby Shantz, 1952	9.2
	Don Newcombe, 1956	9.2
	Juan Marichal, 1966	9.2
	Bob Gibson, 1970	9.2
	Bob Welch, 1990	9.2
77	Tim Keefe, 1888	9.1
	Whitey Ford, 1961	9.1
79	Jim McCormick, 1882	9.0
	Cy Young, 1893	9.0
	Preacher Roe, 1951	9.0
82	Frank Killen, 1892	8.9
	Red Faber, 1921	8.9
84	Tim Keefe, 1883	8.8
	Tim Keefe, 1887	8.8
	Christy Mathewson, 1909	8.8
	Dolf Luque, 1923	8.8
88	Lee Richmond, 1881	8.7
	Frank Killen, 1893	8.7
	Jim Hughes, 1899	8.7
	Juan Marichal, 1963	8.7
	Juan Marichal, 1968	8.7
93	Jim McCormick, 1883	8.6
	Lefty Grove, 1933	8.6
	Bob Feller, 1946	8.6
	Roy Face, 1959	8.6
97	7 players tied	8.5

Wins Above League

#	Player, Year	
1	Charley Radbourn, 1884	45.2
2	Guy Hecker, 1884	44.8
3	Charley Radbourn, 1883	42.8
4	Silver King, 1888	42.7
5	John Clarkson, 1889	42.6
6	John Clarkson, 1885	42.2
7	Pud Galvin, 1884	41.3
8	Pud Galvin, 1883	40.4
9	Jim McCormick, 1880	40.1
10	Tim Keefe, 1883	39.6
11	Bill Hutchison, 1892	39.6
12	Jim Devlin, 1876	39.5
13	Will White, 1879	39.4
14	Toad Ramsey, 1886	39.3
15	Bill Hutchison, 1890	39.2
16	Will White, 1883	39.0
17	Matt Kilroy, 1887	38.0
18	George Bradley, 1876	37.1
19	Toad Ramsey, 1887	36.8
20	Amos Rusie, 1890	36.6
21	Ed Morris, 1885	36.5
22	John Clarkson, 1887	36.4
23	Charlie Buffinton, 1884	36.3
24	Tony Mullane, 1884	36.1
25	Jim Devlin, 1877	35.8
26	Jim McCormick, 1884	35.6
27	Ed Morris, 1886	35.6
28	Jim McCormick, 1882	35.6
29	Dave Foutz, 1886	35.0
30	Lee Richmond, 1880	34.9
31	Tim Keefe, 1886	34.5
32	John Ward, 1880	34.5
33	Bill Hutchison, 1891	34.4
34	John Ward, 1879	34.3
35	Pud Galvin, 1879	34.0
36	Sadie McMahon, 1891	34.0
37	Tommy Bond, 1879	34.0
38	Amos Rusie, 1894	33.8
39	Amos Rusie, 1892	33.6
40	Billy Taylor, 1884	33.5
41	Jim Whitney, 1883	33.3
42	Amos Rusie, 1893	33.3
43	Jack Stivetts, 1891	33.2
44	Dupee Shaw, 1884	33.1
45	Al Spalding, 1876	33.1
46	Jim Whitney, 1881	33.0
47	Mark Baldwin, 1890	32.8
48	Ed Walsh, 1908	32.8
49	Lady Baldwin, 1886	32.8
50	Larry Corcoran, 1884	32.7
51	Silver King, 1890	32.7
52	Mickey Welch, 1885	32.7
53	Mickey Welch, 1884	32.6
54	Kid Gleason, 1890	32.6
55	Charlie Sweeney, 1884	32.3
56	John Clarkson, 1886	32.3
57	Bob Caruthers, 1885	32.3
58	Ed Seward, 1888	32.2
59	Tommy Bond, 1877	32.1
60	Matt Kilroy, 1889	32.0
61	Will White, 1880	31.9
62	Mickey Welch, 1880	31.9
63	Pink Hawley, 1895	31.9
64	Matt Kilroy, 1886	31.8
65	Guy Hecker, 1885	31.5
66	Jack Chesbro, 1904	31.5
67	Sadie McMahon, 1890	31.5
68	Will White, 1882	31.4
69	Tim Keefe, 1884	31.2
70	Larry Corcoran, 1880	31.2
71	George Derby, 1881	31.2
72	Tommy Bond, 1878	31.2
73	Elmer Smith, 1887	31.2
74	Bill Sweeney, 1884	31.0
75	Cy Young, 1893	30.9
76	Tony Mullane, 1883	30.8
77	Cy Young, 1892	30.8
78	Jesse Duryea, 1889	30.6
79	Mark Baldwin, 1889	30.6
80	Walter Johnson, 1912	30.5
81	Jim McCormick, 1879	30.4
82	Hardie Henderson, 1885	30.4
83	Scott Stratton, 1890	30.3
84	Larry Corcoran, 1883	30.2
85	Silver King, 1889	30.2
86	Charley Radbourn, 1886	30.0
87	Charley Radbourn, 1882	30.0
88	John Clarkson, 1891	29.9
89	Tim Keefe, 1887	29.9
90	Phil Knell, 1891	29.9
91	Tony Mullane, 1882	29.8
92	Joe McGinnity, 1903	29.8
93	Amos Rusie, 1891	29.7
94	Jersey Bakely, 1888	29.6
95	Kid Nichols, 1893	29.5
96	Henry Porter, 1885	29.5
97	Kid Nichols, 1890	29.4
98	Gus Weyhing, 1892	29.3
99	Tony Mullane, 1886	29.1
100	Gus Weyhing, 1889	29.0

Relief Games

#	Player, Year	
1	Mike Marshall, 1974	106
2	Kent Tekulve, 1979	94
3	Mike Marshall, 1973	92
4	Kent Tekulve, 1978	91
5	Wayne Granger, 1969	90
	Kent Tekulve, 1987	90
7	Mike Marshall, 1979	89
	Mark Eichhorn, 1987	89
9	Rob Murphy, 1987	87
10	Wilbur Wood, 1968	86
11	Kent Tekulve, 1982	85
	Frank Williams, 1987	85
13	Ted Abernathy, 1965	84
	Enrique Romo, 1979	84
	Dick Tidrow, 1980	84
	Dan Quisenberry, 1985	84
	Mitch Williams, 1987	84
18	Ken Sanders, 1971	83
	Craig Lefferts, 1986	83
	Eddie Guardado, 1996	83
	Mike Myers, 1996	83
22	Eddie Fisher, 1965	82
	Bill Campbell, 1983	82
	Juan Agosto, 1990	82
25	John Wyatt, 1964	81
	Dale Murray, 1976	81
	Jeff Robinson, 1987	81
	Duane Ward, 1991	81
	Joe Boever, 1992	81
	Kenny Rogers, 1992	81
	Mike Jackson, 1993	81
	Brad Clontz, 1996	81
	Mike Stanton, 1996	81
34	Mudcat Grant, 1970	80
	Pedro Borbon, 1973	80
	Willie Hernandez, 1984	80
	Mitch Williams, 1986	80
	Doug Jones, 1992	80
	Greg Harris, 1993	80
40	Dick Radatz, 1964	79
	Duane Ward, 1992	79
	Bob Patterson, 1996	79
43	13 players tied	78

Relief Wins

#	Player, Year	
1	Roy Face, 1959	18
2	John Hiller, 1974	17
	Bill Campbell, 1976	17
4	Jim Konstanty, 1950	16
	Ron Perranoski, 1963	16
	Dick Radatz, 1964	16
	Tom Johnson, 1977	16
8	Mace Brown, 1938	15
	Hoyt Wilhelm, 1952	15
	Luis Arroyo, 1961	15
	Dick Radatz, 1963	15
	Eddie Fisher, 1965	15
	Mike Marshall, 1974	15
	Dale Murray, 1975	15
15	Joe Page, 1947	14
	Joe Black, 1952	14
	Hersh Freeman, 1956	14
	Stu Miller, 1961	14
	Stu Miller, 1965	14
	Phil Regan, 1966	14
	Frank Linzy, 1969	14
	Mike Marshall, 1972	14
	Mike Marshall, 1973	14
	Ron Davis, 1979	14
	Mark Clear, 1982	14
	Jim Slaton, 1983	14
	Roger McDowell, 1986	14
	Mark Eichhorn, 1986	14
29	Dick Tidrow, 1979	13
	Earl Caldwell, 1946	13
	Joe Page, 1949	13
	Clyde King, 1951	13
	Lindy McDaniel, 1959	13
	Larry Sherry, 1960	13
	Gerry Staley, 1960	13
	Lindy McDaniel, 1963	13
	Al Hrabosky, 1975	13
	Rollie Fingers, 1976	13
	Bill Campbell, 1977	13
	Sparky Lyle, 1977	13
	Gary Lavelle, 1978	13
	Bob Stanley, 1978	13
	Ron Reed, 1979	13
	Jim Kern, 1979	13
	Aurelio Lopez, 1980	13
	Jesse Orosco, 1983	13
	Rich Gossage, 1983	13
48	30 players tied	12

Relief Losses

1	Gene Garber, 1979	16
2	Darold Knowles, 1970	14
	John Hiller, 1974	14
	Mike Marshall, 1975	14
	Mike Marshall, 1979	14
6	Wilbur Wood, 1970	13
	Rollie Fingers, 1978	13
	Skip Lockwood, 1978	13
9	Roy Face, 1956	12
	Roy Face, 1961	12
	Ken Sanders, 1971	12
	Mike Marshall, 1974	12
	Gene Garber, 1975	12
	Jim Willoughby, 1976	12
	Charlie Hough, 1977	12
	Mike Marshall, 1978	12
	Kent Tekulve, 1980	12
	Ken Howell, 1986	12
	Roger Mason, 1993	12
20	Nels Potter, 1949	11
	Frank Funk, 1961	11
	Dick Radatz, 1965	11
	Frank Linzy, 1966	11
	Wilbur Wood, 1968	11
	Wilbur Wood, 1969	11
	Mike Marshall, 1973	11
	Rollie Fingers, 1976	11
	Rich Gossage, 1978	11
	Dave Heaverlo, 1979	11
	Mark Clear, 1980	11
	Greg Minton, 1983	11
	Ron Davis, 1984	11
	Mark Davis, 1985	11
	Joe Boever, 1989	11
35	45 players tied	10

Relief Innings Pitched

1	Mike Marshall, 1974	208.1
2	Mike Marshall, 1973	179.0
3	Bob Stanley, 1982	168.1
4	Bill Campbell, 1976	167.2
5	Andy Karl, 1945	166.2
6	Eddie Fisher, 1965	165.1
7	Hoyt Wilhelm, 1952	159.1
8	Dick Radatz, 1964	157.0
	Mark Eichhorn, 1986	157.0
10	Jim Konstanty, 1950	152.0
11	John Hiller, 1974	150.0
12	Tom Johnson, 1977	146.2
13	Garland Braxton, 1927	146.0
14	Bob Stanley, 1983	145.1
15	Hoyt Wilhelm, 1953	145.0
	Wilbur Wood, 1968	145.0
17	Allan Russell, 1923	144.2
	Wayne Granger, 1969	144.2
19	Steve Foucault, 1974	144.1
20	Hoyt Wilhelm, 1965	144.0
21	Jim Kern, 1979	143.0
22	Charlie Hough, 1976	142.2
23	Rich Gossage, 1975	141.2
24	Mike Marshall, 1979	140.2
25	Sammy Stewart, 1983	140.1
	Willie Hernandez, 1984	140.1
27	Bill Campbell, 1977	140.0
28	Jack Lamabe, 1963	139.2
29	Pedro Borbon, 1974	139.0
	Dan Quisenberry, 1983	139.0
31	Lindy McDaniel, 1973	138.1
32	Aurelio Lopez, 1984	137.2
33	Clay Carroll, 1966	137.1
34	Sparky Lyle, 1977	137.0
	Tom Hume, 1980	137.0
36	Dan Quisenberry, 1982	136.2
37	Ted Abernathy, 1965	136.1
	Ken Sanders, 1971	136.1
	Doug Corbett, 1980	136.1
40	Mudcat Grant, 1970	135.1
	Joe Page, 1949	135.1
42	Bruce Sutter, 1982	135.0
	Kent Tekulve, 1978	135.0
44	Ted Abernathy, 1968	134.2
	Phil Regan, 1968	134.2
	Rollie Fingers, 1976	134.2
47	Bill Henry, 1959	134.1
	Dick Selma, 1970	134.1
	Rich Gossage, 1978	134.1
	Kent Tekulve, 1979	134.1

Relief Points

1	Bobby Thigpen, 1990	116
2	Dennis Eckersley, 1992	115
3	Randy Myers, 1993	106
4	Lee Smith, 1991	103
5	Dennis Eckersley, 1990	102
6	Rod Beck, 1993	101
	John Wetteland, 1993	101
8	Dave Righetti, 1986	100
9	Jeff Montgomery, 1993	99
10	Jose Mesa, 1995	98
11	Dan Quisenberry, 1983	97
	Dan Quisenberry, 1984	97
	Trevor Hoffman, 1996	97
14	Dennis Eckersley, 1988	96
15	Bruce Sutter, 1984	93
	Mark Davis, 1989	93
17	Lee Smith, 1993	92
	Dennis Eckersley, 1991	92
	Bryan Harvey, 1991	92
20	John Hiller, 1973	91
	Doug Jones, 1990	91
	Duane Ward, 1993	91
23	Todd Worrell, 1996	90
24	Jeff Brantley, 1996	88
25	Steve Bedrosian, 1987	87
	Rick Aguilera, 1991	87
	Bryan Harvey, 1993	87
	John Wetteland, 1996	87
29	Doug Jones, 1992	86
30	Lee Smith, 1992	85
	Mitch Williams, 1993	85
	Tom Henke, 1993	85
33	John Franco, 1988	84
	Jeff Reardon, 1988	84
	Jeff Russell, 1989	84
36	Luis Arroyo, 1961	83
	Sparky Lyle, 1972	83
	Dan Quisenberry, 1980	83
	Bill Caudill, 1984	83
	Roberto Hernandez, 1996	83
41	Clay Carroll, 1972	82
	Bruce Sutter, 1982	82
	Mel Rojas, 1996	82
44	Dick Radatz, 1964	81
	Dan Quisenberry, 1982	81
	Dan Quisenberry, 1985	81
	Gregg Olson, 1990	81
48	Bruce Sutter, 1979	80
	Todd Worrell, 1986	80
	Rick Aguilera, 1992	80

Relief Ranking

1	Jim Kern, 1979	65.0
2	John Hiller, 1973	64.9
3	Rich Gossage, 1977	61.1
4	Lindy McDaniel, 1960	57.5
5	John Wetteland, 1993	56.4
6	Mike Marshall, 1979	56.2
7	Mark Eichhorn, 1986	55.3
8	Ellis Kinder, 1953	53.6
9	Roberto Hernandez, 1996	53.0
10	Bruce Sutter, 1977	51.8
11	Bill Caudill, 1982	51.7
12	Jesse Orosco, 1983	50.6
13	Donnie Moore, 1985	49.7
14	Sid Monge, 1979	49.5
15	Dick Radatz, 1963	49.4
16	Dick Radatz, 1964	49.2
17	Bob James, 1985	48.0
18	Rich Gossage, 1975	47.7
19	Jeff Montgomery, 1993	47.7
20	Mike Marshall, 1972	46.8
21	Doug Corbett, 1980	46.8
22	Bill Campbell, 1977	45.5
23	Roy Face, 1962	45.2
24	Dennis Eckersley, 1990	45.1
25	Al Hrabosky, 1975	44.9
26	Dan Quisenberry, 1985	44.7
27	Rich Gossage, 1978	44.7
28	Jose Mesa, 1995	44.3
29	Sparky Lyle, 1977	43.4
30	Dan Spillner, 1982	43.0
31	Tom Murphy, 1974	42.9
32	Lee Smith, 1983	42.6
33	Dave Righetti, 1986	42.6
34	Ken Sanders, 1971	41.6
35	Luis Arroyo, 1961	41.6
36	Stu Miller, 1965	41.5
37	Ron Perranoski, 1969	41.3
38	Todd Worrell, 1986	40.8
39	Bruce Sutter, 1984	40.7
40	Joe Page, 1949	40.3
41	Bobby Thigpen, 1990	40.1
42	John Franco, 1988	39.9
43	Jim Brewer, 1972	39.8
44	John Hiller, 1974	39.8
45	Ted Abernathy, 1967	39.7
46	Hoyt Wilhelm, 1964	39.6
47	Dick Radatz, 1962	39.5
48	Jim Konstanty, 1950	39.4
49	Doug Jones, 1992	39.4
50	Aurelio Lopez, 1979	38.8

Relievers' Runs

1	Mark Eichhorn, 1986	42.8
2	Jim Kern, 1979	42.0
3	Mariano Rivera, 1996	34.7
4	Rich Gossage, 1977	33.8
5	John Hiller, 1973	33.1
6	Dan Quisenberry, 1983	32.7
7	Willie Hernandez, 1984	32.2
8	Doug Corbett, 1980	31.1
9	Bruce Sutter, 1977	30.6
10	Rich Gossage, 1975	30.5
11	Tim Burke, 1987	29.3
12	Roberto Hernandez, 1996	29.0
13	Sparky Lyle, 1977	28.8
14	Lindy McDaniel, 1960	28.6
15	Bob Lee, 1964	28.4
16	Mudcat Grant, 1970	28.3
17	Garland Braxton, 1927	28.2
18	Bruce Sutter, 1984	27.9
19	Mike Marshall, 1974	27.7
20	Dennis Eckersley, 1990	26.8
21	Sid Monge, 1979	26.4
22	Jesse Orosco, 1983	26.3
23	Hoyt Wilhelm, 1965	26.3
24	Rich Gossage, 1978	26.2
25	Phil Regan, 1966	25.8
26	Jeff Montgomery, 1989	25.7
27	Jose Mesa, 1995	25.5
28	Ellis Kinder, 1953	25.5
29	Aurelio Lopez, 1979	25.5
30	Donnie Moore, 1985	25.5
31	Dan Quisenberry, 1985	25.4
32	John Wetteland, 1993	25.3
33	Ellis Kinder, 1951	25.1
34	Jim Konstanty, 1950	25.0
35	Ted Abernathy, 1967	24.9
36	Mike Marshall, 1979	24.9
37	Sparky Lyle, 1974	24.8
38	Bob James, 1985	24.7
39	Rollie Fingers, 1973	24.5
40	Gary Lavelle, 1977	24.4
41	Dick Radatz, 1963	24.4
42	Hoyt Wilhelm, 1954	24.4
43	Joe Black, 1952	24.2
44	Greg Minton, 1982	24.2
45	Luis Arroyo, 1961	24.2
46	Joe Page, 1949	24.1
47	Dick Radatz, 1962	24.0
48	Hoyt Wilhelm, 1964	23.9
49	Todd Frohwirth, 1991	23.8
50	Dan Spillner, 1982	23.5

Adjusted Relievers' Runs

1	Mark Eichhorn, 1986	43.6
2	Jim Kern, 1979	40.9
3	John Hiller, 1973	36.9
4	Bruce Sutter, 1977	36.3
5	Doug Corbett, 1980	36.0
6	Mariano Rivera, 1996	35.4
7	Rich Gossage, 1977	34.9
8	Dan Quisenberry, 1983	32.9
9	Lindy McDaniel, 1960	32.5
10	Rich Gossage, 1975	32.0
11	Willie Hernandez, 1984	31.1
12	Tim Burke, 1987	30.5
13	Steve Reed, 1995	30.3
14	Ellis Kinder, 1951	29.3
15	Ted Abernathy, 1967	29.3
16	Ellis Kinder, 1953	28.0
17	Mike Marshall, 1979	27.4
18	Dick Radatz, 1964	27.3
19	Aurelio Lopez, 1979	27.0
20	Sparky Lyle, 1977	27.0
21	Sid Monge, 1979	26.9
22	Bob James, 1985	26.8
23	Dick Radatz, 1963	26.7
24	John Wetteland, 1993	26.5
25	Jesse Orosco, 1983	26.3
26	Bruce Sutter, 1984	26.3
27	Dick Radatz, 1962	26.2
28	Roberto Hernandez, 1996	26.2
29	Mudcat Grant, 1970	25.6
30	Dan Quisenberry, 1985	25.6
31	Jose Mesa, 1995	25.4
32	Jeff Montgomery, 1989	25.3
33	Dennis Eckersley, 1990	25.3
34	Donnie Moore, 1985	25.0
35	Lee Smith, 1983	24.5
36	Gary Lavelle, 1977	24.4
37	Tom Burgmeier, 1980	24.4
38	Bob Lee, 1964	24.3
39	Bob Stanley, 1983	24.2
40	Andy McGaffigan, 1987	24.2
41	Greg Minton, 1982	24.1
42	Rich Gossage, 1978	24.0
43	Duane Ward, 1992	24.0
44	Rob Dibble, 1990	23.9
45	Hoyt Wilhelm, 1954	23.9
46	Tug McGraw, 1980	23.9
47	Bill Campbell, 1977	23.8
48	Dick Hyde, 1958	23.7
49	Sparky Lyle, 1974	23.6
50	Dan Spillner, 1982	23.6

Percent of Team Wins (by era)

1876-1892

1	Will White, 1879	100.0
	Bobby Mathews, 1876	100.0
	Jim Devlin, 1877	100.0
	Jim Devlin, 1876	100.0
	George Bradley, 1876	100.0
6	Tommy Bond, 1878	97.6
7	Terry Larkin, 1878	96.7
8	Jim McCormick, 1880	95.7
9	Tommy Bond, 1877	95.2
10	Terry Larkin, 1877	93.5
11	Al Spalding, 1876	90.4
	Jim Galvin, 1883	88.5
13	Will White, 1880	85.7
	Jim McCormick, 1882	85.7
15	Mickey Welch, 1880	82.9

1893-1919

1	Ted Breitenstein, 1895	48.7
2	Amos Rusie, 1893	48.5
3	Ted Breitenstein, 1894	48.2
4	Cy Young, 1893	46.6
5	Ed Walsh, 1908	45.5
	Frank Killen, 1896	45.5
7	Ted Breitenstein, 1896	45.0
8	Jack Chesbro, 1904	44.6
9	Frank Killen, 1893	44.4
10	Pink Hawley, 1895	43.7
11	Win Mercer, 1896	43.1
12	Noodles Hahn, 1901	42.3
13	Cy Young, 1901	41.8
14	Cy Young, 1895	41.6
15	Cy Young, 1902	41.6

1920-1941

1	Eddie Rommel, 1922	41.5
2	Red Faber, 1921	40.3
3	Buck Newsom, 1938	36.4
4	Jimmy Ring, 1923	36.0
	Pete Alexander, 1920	36.0
6	Ted Lyons, 1930	35.5
7	Curt Davis, 1934	33.9
8	Urban Shocker, 1921	33.3
	Bob Feller, 1941	33.3
	Ed Morris, 1928	33.3
11	Howard Ehmke, 1923	32.8
12	Dazzy Vance, 1925	32.4
	Paul Derringer, 1935	32.4
14	Wes Ferrell, 1935	32.1
15	George Uhle, 1923	31.7

1942-1960

1	Ned Garver, 1951	38.5
2	Bob Feller, 1946	38.2
3	Murry Dickson, 1952	33.3
4	Robin Roberts, 1952	32.2
5	Bill Voiselle, 1944	31.3
6	Murry Dickson, 1951	31.3
7	Phil Marchildon, 1942	30.9
8	Dizzy Trout, 1944	30.7
9	Robin Roberts, 1954	30.7
10	Bobby Shantz, 1952	30.4
11	Ewell Blackwell, 1947	30.1
12	Robin Roberts, 1955	29.9
13	Johnny Antonelli, 1956	29.9
14	Dave Ferriss, 1945	29.6
15	2 players tied	29.0

1961-1976

1	Steve Carlton, 1972	45.8
2	Gaylord Perry, 1972	33.3
3	Nolan Ryan, 1974	32.4
4	Larry Jackson, 1964	31.6
5	Wilbur Wood, 1973	31.2
6	Bob Gibson, 1970	30.3
7	Randy Jones, 1976	30.1
8	Denny McLain, 1968	30.1
9	Fergie Jenkins, 1974	29.8
10	Juan Marichal, 1968	29.5
11	Sam McDowell, 1969	29.0
12	Fergie Jenkins, 1971	28.9
13	Steve Busby, 1974	28.6
14	Sandy Koufax, 1966	28.4
15	Juan Marichal, 1963	28.4

1977-1996

1	Phil Niekro, 1979	31.8
2	Dave Stieb, 1981	29.7
3	Fernando Valenzuela, 1986	28.8
4	Phil Niekro, 1978	27.5
5	Kevin Brown, 1992	27.3
6	Pat Hentgen, 1996	27.0
7	Mike Mussina, 1995	26.8
8	Randy Johnson, 1994	26.5
9	Mike Norris, 1980	26.5
10	Danny Jackson, 1988	26.4
11	Steve Carlton, 1980	26.4
	Frank Viola, 1988	26.4
13	Ross Grimsley, 1978	26.3
14	Phil Niekro, 1977	26.2
15	Bob Welch, 1990	26.2

Clutch Pitching Index

1	Doc White, 1904	152.8
2	Mordecai Brown, 1903	152.7
3	Ned Garvin, 1904	152.6
4	Jim McCormick, 1878	152.3
5	Max Lanier, 1943	150.8
6	Pete Schneider, 1917	145.4
7	Sammy Stewart, 1981	144.8
8	Ed Killian, 1907	144.4
9	Carl Lundgren, 1902	144.0
10	Bill Burns, 1909	142.4
11	Cy Morgan, 1910	142.2
12	Ed Summers, 1908	142.1
13	Andy Coakley, 1905	141.7
	Fred Olmstead, 1910	141.7
15	Ben Tincup, 1914	141.6
16	Dick Rudolph, 1919	141.2
17	Sherry Smith, 1919	141.1
18	Fred Blanding, 1913	140.8
19	Charlie Hodnett, 1884	140.3
20	Ed Poole, 1902	139.7
21	Ed Willett, 1908	139.6
22	Bert Humphries, 1915	139.5
23	Doug Rau, 1976	139.2
24	Sloppy Thurston, 1923	139.0
25	Vic Willis, 1906	138.7
	Al Benton, 1945	138.7
	Al Brazle, 1947	138.7
28	Dummy Taylor, 1902	138.2
29	Allan Anderson, 1988	137.8
30	Mark Baldwin, 1888	137.4
31	Al Maul, 1895	137.0
32	Bob Rhoads, 1908	136.8
33	Mike Sullivan, 1892	136.3
34	Spud Chandler, 1942	136.2
	Chuck Finley, 1990	136.2
36	Red Faber, 1917	135.9
37	Mal Eason, 1902	135.8
	King Cole, 1910	135.8
39	Clark Griffith, 1898	135.4
40	Bob Buhl, 1957	134.8
	John Tudor, 1988	134.8
42	Doug Rau, 1978	134.5
43	Stu Miller, 1959	134.4
44	Ken Chase, 1940	134.2
	Dutch Leonard, 1948	134.2
46	Andy Coakley, 1908	134.1
47	Win Mercer, 1894	133.9
	Ed Siever, 1904	133.9
	Joe McGinnity, 1908	133.9
50	Mike Marshall, 1973	133.7
51	Ned Garvin, 1902	133.4
52	Joe Horlen, 1968	133.1
53	Eddie Plank, 1911	132.9
	Art Nehf, 1928	132.9
55	Charlie Chech, 1905	132.7
56	Andy Coakley, 1907	132.6
57	Gene Bearden, 1948	132.3
	Hoyt Wilhelm, 1959	132.3
59	Stan Baumgartner, 1924	132.1
60	Ed Killian, 1909	131.9
	Bump Hadley, 1939	131.9
62	Lew Brockett, 1909	131.8
63	Jim Abbott, 1992	131.7
64	Win Mercer, 1897	131.6
65	Jose DeLeon, 1991	131.5
66	Steve Blass, 1972	131.3
67	Chick Fraser, 1900	131.2
68	Don Schwall, 1961	131.1
69	Mike O'Neill, 1904	131.0
70	Ted Lyons, 1942	130.9
	Bobby Shantz, 1957	130.9
72	Tony Mullane, 1890	130.7
73	Rick Honeycutt, 1983	130.6
	Lon Warneke, 1933	130.6
	Pete Vuckovich, 1982	130.6
	Bill Swift, 1992	130.6
77	Bill Lee, 1978	130.5
78	Bill Bernhard, 1904	130.4
79	Hal McKain, 1929	130.3
	Bill Krueger, 1991	130.3
81	Larry Pape, 1911	130.2
	Hi Bithorn, 1942	130.2
	John Cerutti, 1989	130.2
84	Vean Gregg, 1913	130.0
85	Brickyard Kennedy, 1899	129.9
	Rollie Naylor, 1920	129.9
87	Earl Moore, 1911	129.6
	Ruben Gomez, 1954	129.6
	Larry McWilliams, 1984	129.6
90	Pud Galvin, 1886	129.5
	Wilson Alvarez, 1993	129.5
92	Lefty Weinert, 1922	129.4
93	Harry Moran, 1915	129.3
	Ned Garver, 1948	129.3
95	Tom Hughes, 1912	129.2
	Clarence Mitchell, 1929	129.2
	Atley Donald, 1944	129.2
	Joe Hatten, 1946	129.2
99	Bill Walker, 1929	129.1
	John Denny, 1976	129.1

Pitcher Batting Runs

1. Guy Hecker, 1884 . . . . 26.2
2. Bob Caruthers, 1886 . . . . 24.5
3. Jim Whitney, 1882 . . . . . . 22.3
4. Wes Ferrell, 1935 . . . . 21.5
5. Don Drysdale, 1965 . . . . 20.2
6. Don Newcombe, 1955 . . 20.1
7. Guy Hecker, 1886 . . . . . . 19.4
8. Jim Whitney, 1883 . . . . . . 18.1
9. Wes Ferrell, 1931 . . . . 17.8
10. Charlie Ferguson, 1885 . . 16.8
11. Tony Mullane, 1884 . . . . . 16.7
12. Schoolboy Rowe, 1943 . . 16.7
13. Bob Caruthers, 1887 . . . . 16.7
14. George Uhle, 1923 . . . . . . 16.4
15. Babe Ruth, 1917 . . . . 16.3
16. Scott Stratton, 1890 . . . . 16.1
17. Warren Spahn, 1958 . . . . 16.0
18. Walter Johnson, 1925 . . . 15.9
19. Bob Caruthers, 1889 . . . . 15.8
20. Red Ruffing, 1930 . . . . . . 15.6
21. Bob Lemon, 1950 . . . . . . 15.6
22. Don Newcombe, 1959 . . . 15.1
23. Jack Stivetts, 1892 . . . . . 15.1
24. Jack Stivetts, 1890 . . . . . 14.9
25. Jack Bentley, 1923 . . . . . 14.8
26. John Ward, 1879 . . . . 14.7
27. Bob Lemon, 1949 . . . . . . 14.7
28. Red Lucas, 1930 . . . . 14.7
29. Claude Hendrix, 1912 . . . 14.6
30. Babe Ruth, 1915 . . . . 14.5
31. Dave Foutz, 1887 . . . . . . 14.3
32. Charlie Ferguson, 1887 . . 14.2
33. Jim Tobin, 1942 . . . . 14.0
34. Frank Killen, 1893 . . . . . . 13.9
35. Red Ruffing, 1936 . . . . . . 13.8
36. Pete Conway, 1888 . . . . . 13.8
37. Red Lucas, 1932 . . . . 13.7
38. Robin Roberts, 1955 . . . . 13.6
39. Terry Larkin, 1878 . . . . . . 13.6
40. Elam Vangilder, 1922 . . . . 13.4
41. Babe Ruth, 1916 . . . . 13.1
42. Scott Stratton, 1888 . . . . 13.1
43. Joe Bush, 1924 . . . . 13.0
44. Adonis Terry, 1890 . . . . . 13.0
45. Jack Coombs, 1911 . . . . . 12.9
46. Pink Hawley, 1895 . . . . . . 12.9
47. Clark Griffith, 1901 . . . . . 12.8
48. Bucky Walters, 1939 . . . . 12.7
49. Bob Lemon, 1948 . . . . . . 12.6
50. Red Lucas, 1933 . . . . 12.5
51. Schoolboy Rowe, 1935 . . 12.5
52. Red Ruffing, 1932 . . . . . . 12.5
53. Doc Crandall, 1915 . . . . . 12.4
54. Cy Young, 1903 . . . . 12.3
55. Curt Davis, 1939 . . . . 12.3
56. Red Ruffing, 1935 . . . . . . 12.2
57. Bob Gibson, 1970 . . . . . . 12.2
58. Red Ruffing, 1928 . . . . . . 12.2
59. Ad Gumbert, 1891 . . . . . . 12.1
60. Catfish Hunter, 1971 . . . . 12.1
61. Wes Ferrell, 1936 . . . . . . 11.9
62. Dizzy Trout, 1944 . . . . . . 11.9
63. Joe Bowman, 1939 . . . . . 11.8
64. Charley Radbourn, 1883 . . 11.8
65. Billy Taylor, 1884 . . . . 11.8
66. Fergie Jenkins, 1971 . . . . 11.7
67. Johnny Sain, 1947 . . . . . . 11.7
68. Dutch Ruether, 1921 . . . . 11.6
69. Erv Brame, 1929 . . . . 11.5
70. Babe Ruth, 1918 . . . . 11.5
71. Jouett Meekin, 1896 . . . . 11.5
72. Jack Stivetts, 1896 . . . . . 11.5
73. George Mullin, 1904 . . . . 11.3
74. Adonis Terry, 1889 . . . . . 11.3
75. Charlie Ferguson, 1886 . . 11.2
76. Schoolboy Rowe, 1934 . . 11.2
77. George Van Haltren, 1888 . . 11.1
78. Tim Keefe, 1884 . . . . 11.1
79. Carl Mays, 1921 . . . . 11.0
80. Guy Hecker, 1887 . . . . . . 11.0
81. Jim Whitney, 1881 . . . . . . 11.0
82. Mickey Welch, 1880 . . . . 10.9
83. Red Lucas, 1931 . . . . 10.9
84. Dave Ferriss, 1945 . . . . . 10.9
85. Ad Gumbert, 1889 . . . . . . 10.8
86. Bob Caruthers, 1891 . . . . 10.8
87. Charlie Buffinton, 1884 . . 10.8
88. Red Ruffing, 1941 . . . . . . 10.8
89. Erv Brame, 1930 . . . . 10.8
90. Jack Stivetts, 1894 . . . . . 10.7
91. Red Lucas, 1929 . . . . 10.7
92. Jim Whitney, 1887 . . . . . . 10.7
93. Tom Parrott, 1895 . . . . . . 10.7
94. Fred Hutchinson, 1947 . . 10.7
95. Joe Wood, 1912 . . . . 10.6
96. Frank Foreman, 1891 . . . . 10.6
97. Burleigh Grimes, 1928 . . . 10.6
98. Burleigh Grimes, 1920 . . . 10.5
99. Blue Moon Odom, 1969 . . 10.5
100. Matt Kilroy, 1889 . . . . 10.4

Pitcher Fielding Runs

1. Ed Walsh, 1907 . . . . 21.7
2. Harry Howell, 1905 . . . . . 17.8
3. Ed Walsh, 1911 . . . . 14.8
4. Ed Walsh, 1908 . . . . 13.6
5. Will White, 1882 . . . . 12.9
6. John Clarkson, 1889 . . . . 11.3
7. Tony Mullane, 1882 . . . . . 10.7
    Sadie McMahon, 1890 . . . 10.7
9. Carl Mays, 1926 . . . . 10.1
10. Frank Smith, 1909 . . . . . . 10.0
11. Tommy Bond, 1880 . . . . . 9.8
    Greg Maddux, 1996 . . . . . 9.8
13. Mike Morrison, 1887 . . . . 9.7
    Ed Walsh, 1910 . . . . 9.7
15. Christy Mathewson, 1908 . . 9.6
16. Tony Mullane, 1884 . . . . . 9.5
    Matt Kilroy, 1887 . . . . 9.5
    Charlie Buffinton, 1888 . . 9.5
19. Harry Howell, 1904 . . . . . 9.4
20. Ed Scott, 1900 . . . . 9.1
    Elmer Stricklett, 1906 . . . 9.1
    Carl Mays, 1916 . . . . 9.1
    Carl Mays, 1918 . . . . 9.1
    Curt Davis, 1934 . . . . 9.1
25. John Clarkson, 1887 . . . . 9.0
    Elmer Stricklett, 1905 . . . 9.0
27. Hooks Dauss, 1915 . . . . . 8.9
28. Addie Joss, 1907 . . . . 8.7
29. Gene Packard, 1914 . . . . . 8.6
30. Park Swartzel, 1889 . . . . . 8.5
    Bucky Walters, 1936 . . . . 8.5
32. Jack Taylor, 1898 . . . . 8.4
    Hooks Dauss, 1920 . . . . . 8.4
    Wilcy Moore, 1927 . . . . . . 8.4
    Bob Lemon, 1948 . . . . . . 8.4
36. Cy Seymour, 1898 . . . . . . 8.3
    Harry Howell, 1907 . . . . . 8.3
    Randy Jones, 1976 . . . . . 8.3
39. Burleigh Grimes, 1925 . . . 8.2
40. Matt Kilroy, 1889 . . . . 8.1
    George Mullin, 1904 . . . . 8.1
    Carl Mays, 1924 . . . . 8.1
    Eddie Rommel, 1924 . . . . 8.1
44. Fred Newman, 1965 . . . . . 8.0
45. Cy Young, 1895 . . . . 7.9
    Cy Young, 1896 . . . . 7.9
    Nick Altrock, 1905 . . . . . . 7.9
    Bob Lemon, 1953 . . . . . . 7.9
    Mel Stottlemyre, 1969 . . . 7.9
50. John Clarkson, 1885 . . . . 7.8
    Pud Galvin, 1887 . . . . 7.8
    Carl Mays, 1917 . . . . 7.8
    Freddie Fitzsimmons, 1931 . . 7.8
    Harry Gumbert, 1938 . . . . 7.8
    John Denny, 1978 . . . . . . 7.8
56. Amos Rusie, 1894 . . . . . . 7.7
    Joe Wood, 1912 . . . . 7.7
    Mel Harder, 1933 . . . . . . 7.7
    Harry Gumbert, 1937 . . . . 7.7
    Russ Christopher, 1943 . . 7.7
61. Larry McKeon, 1884 . . . . 7.6
    Cy Seymour, 1897 . . . . . . 7.6
    Ed Walsh, 1906 . . . . 7.6
64. Willie Sudhoff, 1898 . . . . 7.5
    Christy Mathewson, 1901 . . 7.5
    Ned Garvin, 1903 . . . . . . 7.5
    Harry Howell, 1906 . . . . . 7.5
    Jean Dubuc, 1913 . . . . . . 7.5
    Greg Maddux, 1990 . . . . . 7.5
70. Christy Mathewson, 1911 . . 7.4
    Carl Hubbell, 1933 . . . . . 7.4
72. Tommy Bond, 1879 . . . . . 7.3
    Charlie Buffinton, 1887 . . 7.3
    Bob Caruthers, 1887 . . . . 7.3
    Bill Doak, 1915 . . . . 7.3
76. Pud Galvin, 1881 . . . . 7.2
    Eddie Cicotte, 1913 . . . . . 7.2
    Russ Christopher, 1945 . . 7.2
79. Pud Galvin, 1884 . . . . 7.1
    George Mullin, 1905 . . . . 7.1
    Ed Walsh, 1912 . . . . 7.1
    Harry Coveleski, 1914 . . . 7.1
83. Doc White, 1908 . . . . 7.0
    Red Ames, 1909 . . . . 7.0
    Hal Schumacher, 1935 . . . 7.0
86. Guy Hecker, 1884 . . . . . . 6.9
    Dave Foutz, 1885 . . . . . . 6.9
    Red Donahue, 1902 . . . . . 6.9
    Elmer Stricklett, 1907 . . . 6.9
    Lefty Tyler, 1913 . . . . 6.9
    Gene Krapp, 1915 . . . . . . 6.9
    Larry Jackson, 1964 . . . . . 6.9
93. 9 players tied 6.8

Total Pitcher Index

1. Guy Hecker, 1884 . . . . . . 12.6
2. Silver King, 1888 . . . . 11.4
3. Walter Johnson, 1912 . . . 11.2
4. Amos Rusie, 1894 . . . . . . 11.0
5. Walter Johnson, 1913 . . . 10.9
6. John Clarkson, 1889 . . . . 10.1
7. Charley Radbourn, 1884 . . 9.8
8. Christy Mathewson, 1905 . . 9.6
9. Dizzy Trout, 1944 . . . . . . 9.1
10. John Clarkson, 1885 . . . . 8.9
    Scott Stratton, 1890 . . . . 8.9
12. Lefty Grove, 1931 . . . . . . 8.7
13. Joe Wood, 1912 . . . . 8.6
    Pete Alexander, 1915 . . . . 8.6
15. Bucky Walters, 1939 . . . . 8.5
16. Charley Radbourn, 1883 . . 8.4
17. John Clarkson, 1887 . . . . 8.3
    Cy Young, 1901 . . . . 8.3
19. Dave Foutz, 1886 . . . . . . 8.1
    Ed Walsh, 1908 . . . . 8.1
21. Curt Davis, 1934 . . . . 7.8
    Hal Newhouser, 1945 . . . . 7.8
23. Tony Mullane, 1884 . . . . . 7.7
    Jack Stivetts, 1891 . . . . . 7.7
    Walter Johnson, 1915 . . . 7.7
26. Walter Johnson, 1918 . . . 7.6
27. Carl Hubbell, 1933 . . . . . 7.5
28. Pink Hawley, 1895 . . . . . . 7.4
    Dolf Luque, 1923 . . . . . . 7.4
    Steve Carlton, 1972 . . . . . 7.4
31. Jim Devlin, 1876 . . . . 7.3
    Will White, 1882 . . . . 7.3
    Matt Kilroy, 1887 . . . . 7.3
    Kid Nichols, 1897 . . . . . . 7.3
    Christy Mathewson, 1908 . . 7.3
    Walter Johnson, 1914 . . . 7.3
    Pete Alexander, 1916 . . . . 7.3
    Lefty Grove, 1930 . . . . . . 7.3
    Bob Gibson, 1968 . . . . . . 7.3
    Dwight Gooden, 1985 . . . 7.3
    Greg Maddux, 1994 . . . . . 7.3
42. Amos Rusie, 1893 . . . . . . 7.2
    Walter Johnson, 1919 . . . 7.2
    Wes Ferrell, 1935 . . . . . . 7.2
    Kevin Brown, 1996 . . . . . 7.2
46. Silver King, 1890 . . . . 7.1
    Ed Walsh, 1910 . . . . 7.1
    Pete Alexander, 1920 . . . . 7.1
    Hal Newhouser, 1946 . . . . 7.1
50. Cy Young, 1895 . . . . 7.0
    Christy Mathewson, 1909 . . 7.0
    Red Faber, 1921 . . . . 7.0
    Dazzy Vance, 1928 . . . . . 7.0
    Lefty Grove, 1936 . . . . . . 7.0
    Gaylord Perry, 1972 . . . . 7.0
56. Matt Kilroy, 1889 . . . . 6.9
    Amos Rusie, 1890 . . . . . . 6.9
    Kid Nichols, 1898 . . . . . . 6.9
    Jack Chesbro, 1904 . . . . . 6.9
60. Pud Galvin, 1884 . . . . 6.8
    Bob Caruthers, 1886 . . . . 6.8
    Mordecai Brown, 1906 . . 6.8
    Bob Lemon, 1948 . . . . . . 6.8
    Greg Maddux, 1995 . . . . . 6.8
65. Jesse Duryea, 1889 . . . . . 6.7
    Kid Nichols, 1890 . . . . . . 6.7
    Christy Mathewson, 1911 . . 6.7
    John Hiller, 1973 . . . . 6.7
    Jim Kern, 1979 . . . . 6.7
    Roger Clemens, 1990 . . . 6.7
71. Tim Keefe, 1883 . . . . 6.6
    Will White, 1883 . . . . 6.6
    Bob Caruthers, 1885 . . . . 6.6
    Guy Hecker, 1885 . . . . . . 6.6
    Cy Young, 1892 . . . . 6.6
    Kid Nichols, 1896 . . . . . . 6.6
    Ed Walsh, 1912 . . . . 6.6
    Dazzy Vance, 1930 . . . . . 6.6
    Thornton Lee, 1941 . . . . . 6.6
    Warren Spahn, 1953 . . . . 6.6
    Wilbur Wood, 1971 . . . . . 6.6
82. John Clarkson, 1886 . . . . 6.5
    Charlie Ferguson, 1886 . . 6.5
    Toad Ramsey, 1886 . . . . . 6.5
    Billy Rhines, 1890 . . . . . . 6.5
    Joe Wood, 1911 . . . . 6.5
    Lefty Gomez, 1937 . . . . . 6.5
    Hal Newhouser, 1944 . . . . 6.5
    Tom Seaver, 1971 . . . . . . 6.5
90. Cy Young, 1893 . . . . 6.4
    Cy Young, 1896 . . . . 6.4
    Ed Walsh, 1907 . . . . 6.4
    Walter Johnson, 1911 . . . 6.4
    Dizzy Dean, 1934 . . . . . . 6.4
    Mel Harder, 1934 . . . . . . 6.4
    Lefty Grove, 1935 . . . . . . 6.4
    Fergie Jenkins, 1971 . . . . 6.4
    Rich Gossage, 1977 . . . . 6.4
99. Charlie Sweeney, 1884 . . 6.3
    Jack Taylor, 1902 . . . . . . 6.3

Total Pitcher Index (alpha.)

Pete Alexander, 1915 . . . . 8.6
Pete Alexander, 1916 . . . . 7.3
Pete Alexander, 1920 . . . . 7.1
Mordecai Brown, 1906 . . . 6.8
Kevin Brown, 1996 . . . . . . 7.2
Steve Carlton, 1972 . . . . . 7.4
Bob Caruthers, 1885 . . . . 6.6
Bob Caruthers, 1886 . . . . 6.8
Jack Chesbro, 1904 . . . . . 6.9
John Clarkson, 1885 . . . . 8.9
John Clarkson, 1886 . . . . 6.5
John Clarkson, 1887 . . . . 8.3
John Clarkson, 1889 . . . . 10.1
Roger Clemens, 1990 . . . . 6.7
Curt Davis, 1934 . . . . 7.8
Dizzy Dean, 1934 . . . . . . 6.4
Jim Devlin, 1876 . . . . 7.3
Jesse Duryea, 1889 . . . . . 6.7
Red Faber, 1921 . . . . 7.0
Charlie Ferguson, 1886 . . 6.5
Wes Ferrell, 1935 . . . . . . 7.2
Dave Foutz, 1886 . . . . . . 8.1
Pud Galvin, 1884 . . . . 6.8
Bob Gibson, 1968 . . . . . . 7.3
Lefty Gomez, 1937 . . . . . 6.5
Dwight Gooden, 1985 . . . 7.3
Rich Gossage, 1977 . . . . 6.4
Lefty Grove, 1930 . . . . . . 7.3
Lefty Grove, 1931 . . . . . . 8.7
Lefty Grove, 1935 . . . . . . 6.4
Lefty Grove, 1936 . . . . . . 7.0
Mel Harder, 1934 . . . . . . 6.4
Pink Hawley, 1895 . . . . . . 7.4
Guy Hecker, 1884 . . . . . . 12.6
Guy Hecker, 1885 . . . . . . 6.6
John Hiller, 1973 . . . . 6.7
Carl Hubbell, 1933 . . . . . 7.5
Fergie Jenkins, 1971 . . . . 6.4
Walter Johnson, 1911 . . . 6.4
Walter Johnson, 1912 . . . 11.2
Walter Johnson, 1913 . . . 10.9
Walter Johnson, 1914 . . . 7.3
Walter Johnson, 1915 . . . 7.7
Walter Johnson, 1918 . . . 7.6
Walter Johnson, 1919 . . . 7.2
Tim Keefe, 1883 . . . . 6.6
Jim Kern, 1979 . . . . 6.7
Matt Kilroy, 1887 . . . . 7.3
Matt Kilroy, 1889 . . . . 6.9
Silver King, 1888 . . . . 11.4
Silver King, 1890 . . . . 7.1
Thornton Lee, 1941 . . . . . 6.6
Bob Lemon, 1948 . . . . . . 6.8
Dolf Luque, 1923 . . . . . . 7.4
Greg Maddux, 1994 . . . . . 7.3
Greg Maddux, 1995 . . . . . 6.8
Christy Mathewson, 1905 . . 9.6
Christy Mathewson, 1908 . . 7.3
Christy Mathewson, 1909 . . 7.0
Christy Mathewson, 1911 . . 6.7
Tony Mullane, 1884 . . . . . 7.7
Hal Newhouser, 1944 . . . . 6.5
Hal Newhouser, 1945 . . . . 7.8
Hal Newhouser, 1946 . . . . 7.1
Kid Nichols, 1890 . . . . . . 6.7
Kid Nichols, 1896 . . . . . . 6.6
Kid Nichols, 1897 . . . . . . 7.3
Kid Nichols, 1898 . . . . . . 6.9
Gaylord Perry, 1972 . . . . 7.0
Charley Radbourn, 1883 . . 8.4
Charley Radbourn, 1884 . . 9.8
Toad Ramsey, 1886 . . . . . 6.5
Billy Rhines, 1890 . . . . . . 6.5
Amos Rusie, 1890 . . . . . . 6.9
Amos Rusie, 1893 . . . . . . 7.2
Amos Rusie, 1894 . . . . . . 11.0
Tom Seaver, 1971 . . . . . . 6.5
Warren Spahn, 1953 . . . . 6.6
Jack Stivetts, 1891 . . . . . 7.7
Scott Stratton, 1890 . . . . 8.9
Charlie Sweeney, 1884 . . 6.3
Jack Taylor, 1902 . . . . . . 6.3
Dizzy Trout, 1944 . . . . . . 9.1
Dazzy Vance, 1928 . . . . . 7.0
Dazzy Vance, 1930 . . . . . 6.6
Ed Walsh, 1907 . . . . 6.4
Ed Walsh, 1908 . . . . 8.1
Ed Walsh, 1910 . . . . 7.1
Ed Walsh, 1912 . . . . 6.6
Bucky Walters, 1939 . . . . 8.5
Will White, 1882 . . . . 7.3
Will White, 1883 . . . . 6.6
Joe Wood, 1911 . . . . 6.5
Joe Wood, 1912 . . . . 8.6
Wilbur Wood, 1971 . . . . . 6.6
Cy Young, 1892 . . . . 6.6
Cy Young, 1893 . . . . 6.4
Cy Young, 1895 . . . . 7.0
Cy Young, 1896 . . . . 6.4
Cy Young, 1901 . . . . 8.3

Total Pitcher Index (by era)

1876-1892

1	Guy Hecker, 1884	12.6
2	Silver King, 1888	11.4
3	John Clarkson, 1889	10.1
4	Charley Radbourn, 1884	9.8
5	John Clarkson, 1885	8.9
	Scott Stratton, 1890	8.9
7	Charley Radbourn, 1883	8.4
8	John Clarkson, 1887	8.3
9	Dave Foutz, 1886	8.1
10	Tony Mullane, 1884	7.7
	Jack Stivetts, 1891	7.7
12	Jim Devlin, 1876	7.3
	Will White, 1882	7.3
	Matt Kilroy, 1887	7.3
15	Silver King, 1890	7.1

1893-1919

1	Walter Johnson, 1912	11.2
2	Amos Rusie, 1894	11.0
3	Walter Johnson, 1913	10.9
4	Christy Mathewson, 1905	9.6
5	Joe Wood, 1912	8.6
	Pete Alexander, 1915	8.6
7	Cy Young, 1901	8.3
8	Ed Walsh, 1908	8.1
9	Walter Johnson, 1915	7.7
10	Walter Johnson, 1918	7.6
11	Pink Hawley, 1895	7.4
12	Kid Nichols, 1897	7.3
	Christy Mathewson, 1908	7.3
	Walter Johnson, 1914	7.3
	Pete Alexander, 1916	7.3

1920-1941

1	Lefty Grove, 1931	8.7
2	Bucky Walters, 1939	8.5
3	Curt Davis, 1934	7.8
4	Carl Hubbell, 1933	7.5
5	Dolf Luque, 1923	7.4
6	Lefty Grove, 1930	7.3
7	Wes Ferrell, 1935	7.2
8	Pete Alexander, 1920	7.1
9	Red Faber, 1921	7.0
	Dazzy Vance, 1928	7.0
	Lefty Grove, 1936	7.0
12	Dazzy Vance, 1930	6.6
	Thornton Lee, 1941	6.6
14	Lefty Gomez, 1937	6.5
15	3 players tied	6.4

1942-1960

1	Dizzy Trout, 1944	9.1
2	Hal Newhouser, 1945	7.8
3	Hal Newhouser, 1946	7.1
4	Bob Lemon, 1948	6.8
5	Warren Spahn, 1953	6.6
6	Hal Newhouser, 1944	6.5
7	Robin Roberts, 1953	6.1
8	Johnny Sain, 1946	5.9
	Ellis Kinder, 1953	5.9
10	Spud Chandler, 1943	5.7
	Bob Lemon, 1949	5.7
	Ned Garver, 1950	5.7
13	5 players tied	5.5

1961-1976

1	Steve Carlton, 1972	7.4
2	Bob Gibson, 1968	7.3
3	Gaylord Perry, 1972	7.0
4	John Hiller, 1973	6.7
5	Wilbur Wood, 1971	6.6
6	Tom Seaver, 1971	6.5
7	Fergie Jenkins, 1971	6.4
8	Jim Palmer, 1975	6.1
9	Juan Marichal, 1965	6.0
	Bob Gibson, 1969	6.0
11	Juan Marichal, 1966	5.8
12	Bert Blyleven, 1973	5.7
13	Tom Seaver, 1969	5.6
14	Bill Hands, 1969	5.5
15	3 players tied	5.4

1977-1996

1	Dwight Gooden, 1985	7.3
	Greg Maddux, 1994	7.3
3	Kevin Brown, 1996	7.2
4	Greg Maddux, 1995	6.8
5	Jim Kern, 1979	6.7
	Roger Clemens, 1990	6.7
7	Rich Gossage, 1977	6.4
8	Ron Guidry, 1978	6.2
	Greg Maddux, 1992	6.2
10	Greg Maddux, 1993	6.1
11	Steve Carlton, 1977	6.0
12	Rick Reuschel, 1977	5.8
	Jesse Orosco, 1983	5.8
	Roger Clemens, 1992	5.8
15	4 players tied	5.7

Total Baseball Ranking

1	Guy Hecker, 1884	12.6
2	Silver King, 1888	11.4
3	Walter Johnson, 1912	11.2
4	Amos Rusie, 1894	11.0
5	Walter Johnson, 1913	10.9
6	Babe Ruth, 1923	10.6
7	John Clarkson, 1889	10.1
8	Charley Radbourn, 1884	9.8
9	Christy Mathewson, 1905	9.6
10	Babe Ruth, 1921	9.4
11	Babe Ruth, 1927	9.2
	Barry Bonds, 1992	9.2
13	Dizzy Trout, 1944	9.1
	Cal Ripken, 1984	9.1
15	John Clarkson, 1885	8.9
	Scott Stratton, 1890	8.9
	Nap Lajoie, 1901	8.9
18	Barry Bonds, 1993	8.8
19	Lefty Grove, 1931	8.7
	Mickey Mantle, 1956	8.7
21	Joe Wood, 1912	8.6
	Pete Alexander, 1915	8.6
	Babe Ruth, 1920	8.6
	Mickey Mantle, 1957	8.6
25	Bucky Walters, 1939	8.5
	Nap Lajoie, 1910	8.5
	Ty Cobb, 1917	8.5
	Rogers Hornsby, 1922	8.5
	Rogers Hornsby, 1924	8.5
	Babe Ruth, 1924	8.5
	Barry Bonds, 1996	8.5
32	Charley Radbourn, 1883	8.4
	Nap Lajoie, 1903	8.4
	Nap Lajoie, 1906	8.4
	Babe Ruth, 1926	8.4
36	John Clarkson, 1887	8.3
	Cy Young, 1901	8.3
	Cal Ripken, 1991	8.3
39	Rickey Henderson, 1990	8.2
40	Dave Foutz, 1886	8.1
	Ed Walsh, 1908	8.1
	Rogers Hornsby, 1920	8.1
	Lou Gehrig, 1927	8.1
	Ted Williams, 1942	8.1
45	Mickey Mantle, 1961	8.0
46	Ted Williams, 1941	7.9
	Ted Williams, 1946	7.9
48	Curt Davis, 1934	7.8
	Hal Newhouser, 1945	7.8
	Nap Lajoie, 1908	7.8
	George Sisler, 1920	7.8
	Lou Gehrig, 1934	7.8
	Lou Boudreau, 1944	7.8
54	Tony Mullane, 1884	7.7
	Jack Stivetts, 1891	7.7
	Walter Johnson, 1915	7.7
	Tris Speaker, 1912	7.7
	Rogers Hornsby, 1917	7.7
	Willie Mays, 1955	7.7
60	Walter Johnson, 1918	7.6
	Tris Speaker, 1914	7.6
	Jeff Bagwell, 1994	7.6
63	Carl Hubbell, 1933	7.5
	Ron Santo, 1966	7.5
65	Pink Hawley, 1895	7.4
	Dolf Luque, 1923	7.4
	Steve Carlton, 1972	7.4
	Rickey Henderson, 1985	7.4
69	Jim Devlin, 1876	7.3
	Will White, 1882	7.3
	Matt Kilroy, 1887	7.3
	Kid Nichols, 1897	7.3
	Christy Mathewson, 1908	7.3
	Walter Johnson, 1914	7.3
	Pete Alexander, 1916	7.3
	Lefty Grove, 1930	7.3
	Bob Gibson, 1968	7.3
	Dwight Gooden, 1985	7.3
	Greg Maddux, 1994	7.3
	Honus Wagner, 1905	7.3
	Honus Wagner, 1906	7.3
	Tris Speaker, 1913	7.3
	Frankie Frisch, 1927	7.3
	Babe Ruth, 1930	7.3
	Babe Ruth, 1931	7.3
	Willie Mays, 1965	7.3
	Ron Santo, 1967	7.3
	Carl Yastrzemski, 1967	7.3
	Mike Schmidt, 1980	7.3
90	12 players tied	7.2

Total Baseball Rank (alpha.)

Pete Alexander, 1915	8.6
Pete Alexander, 1916	7.3
Jeff Bagwell, 1994	7.6
Barry Bonds, 1992	9.2
Barry Bonds, 1993	8.8
Barry Bonds, 1996	8.5
Lou Boudreau, 1944	7.8
Steve Carlton, 1972	7.4
John Clarkson, 1885	8.9
John Clarkson, 1887	8.3
John Clarkson, 1889	10.1
Ty Cobb, 1917	8.5
Curt Davis, 1934	7.8
Jim Devlin, 1876	7.3
Dave Foutz, 1886	8.1
Frankie Frisch, 1927	7.3
Lou Gehrig, 1927	8.1
Lou Gehrig, 1934	7.8
Bob Gibson, 1968	7.3
Dwight Gooden, 1985	7.3
Lefty Grove, 1930	7.3
Lefty Grove, 1931	8.7
Pink Hawley, 1895	7.4
Guy Hecker, 1884	12.6
Rickey Henderson, 1985	7.4
Rickey Henderson, 1990	8.2
Rogers Hornsby, 1917	7.7
Rogers Hornsby, 1920	8.1
Rogers Hornsby, 1922	8.5
Rogers Hornsby, 1924	8.5
Carl Hubbell, 1933	7.5
Walter Johnson, 1912	11.2
Walter Johnson, 1913	10.9
Walter Johnson, 1914	7.3
Walter Johnson, 1915	7.7
Walter Johnson, 1918	7.6
Matt Kilroy, 1887	7.3
Silver King, 1888	11.4
Nap Lajoie, 1901	8.9
Nap Lajoie, 1903	8.4
Nap Lajoie, 1906	8.4
Nap Lajoie, 1908	7.8
Nap Lajoie, 1910	8.5
Dolf Luque, 1923	7.4
Greg Maddux, 1994	7.3
Mickey Mantle, 1956	8.7
Mickey Mantle, 1957	8.6
Mickey Mantle, 1961	8.0
Christy Mathewson, 1905	9.6
Christy Mathewson, 1908	7.3
Willie Mays, 1955	7.7
Willie Mays, 1965	7.3
Tony Mullane, 1884	7.7
Hal Newhouser, 1945	7.8
Kid Nichols, 1897	7.3
Charley Radbourn, 1883	8.4
Charley Radbourn, 1884	9.8
Cal Ripken, 1984	9.1
Cal Ripken, 1991	8.3
Amos Rusie, 1894	11.0
Babe Ruth, 1920	8.6
Babe Ruth, 1921	9.4
Babe Ruth, 1923	10.6
Babe Ruth, 1924	8.5
Babe Ruth, 1926	8.4
Babe Ruth, 1927	9.2
Babe Ruth, 1930	7.3
Babe Ruth, 1931	7.3
Ron Santo, 1966	7.5
Ron Santo, 1967	7.3
Mike Schmidt, 1980	7.3
George Sisler, 1920	7.8
Tris Speaker, 1912	7.7
Tris Speaker, 1913	7.3
Tris Speaker, 1914	7.6
Jack Stivetts, 1891	7.7
Scott Stratton, 1890	8.9
Dizzy Trout, 1944	9.1
Honus Wagner, 1905	7.3
Honus Wagner, 1906	7.3
Ed Walsh, 1908	8.1
Bucky Walters, 1939	8.5
Will White, 1882	7.3
Ted Williams, 1941	7.9
Ted Williams, 1942	8.1
Ted Williams, 1946	7.9
Joe Wood, 1912	8.6
Carl Yastrzemski, 1967	7.3
Cy Young, 1901	8.3

Total Baseball Rank (by era)

1876-1892

1	Guy Hecker, 1884	12.6
2	Silver King, 1888	11.4
3	John Clarkson, 1889	10.1
4	Charley Radbourn, 1884	9.8
5	John Clarkson, 1885	8.9
	Scott Stratton, 1890	8.9
7	Charley Radbourn, 1883	8.4
8	John Clarkson, 1887	8.3
9	Dave Foutz, 1886	8.1
10	Tony Mullane, 1884	7.7
	Jack Stivetts, 1891	7.7
12	Jim Devlin, 1876	7.3
	Will White, 1882	7.3
	Matt Kilroy, 1887	7.3
15	Silver King, 1890	7.1

1893-1919

1	Walter Johnson, 1912	11.2
2	Amos Rusie, 1894	11.0
3	Walter Johnson, 1913	10.9
4	Christy Mathewson, 1905	9.6
5	Nap Lajoie, 1901	8.9
6	Joe Wood, 1912	8.6
	Pete Alexander, 1915	8.6
8	Nap Lajoie, 1910	8.5
	Ty Cobb, 1917	8.5
10	Nap Lajoie, 1903	8.4
	Nap Lajoie, 1906	8.4
12	Cy Young, 1901	8.3
13	Ed Walsh, 1908	8.1
14	Nap Lajoie, 1908	7.8
15	3 players tied	7.7

1920-1941

1	Babe Ruth, 1923	10.6
2	Babe Ruth, 1921	9.4
3	Babe Ruth, 1927	9.2
4	Lefty Grove, 1931	8.7
5	Babe Ruth, 1920	8.6
6	Bucky Walters, 1939	8.5
	Rogers Hornsby, 1922	8.5
	Rogers Hornsby, 1924	8.5
	Babe Ruth, 1924	8.5
10	Babe Ruth, 1926	8.4
11	Rogers Hornsby, 1920	8.1
	Lou Gehrig, 1927	8.1
13	Ted Williams, 1941	7.9
14	3 players tied	7.8

1942-1960

1	Dizzy Trout, 1944	9.1
2	Mickey Mantle, 1956	8.7
3	Mickey Mantle, 1957	8.6
4	Ted Williams, 1942	8.1
5	Ted Williams, 1946	7.9
6	Hal Newhouser, 1945	7.8
	Lou Boudreau, 1944	7.8
8	Willie Mays, 1955	7.7
9	Snuffy Stirnweiss, 1945	7.2
	Ted Williams, 1947	7.2
	Willie Mays, 1958	7.2
12	Hal Newhouser, 1946	7.1
	Snuffy Stirnweiss, 1944	7.1
	Ted Williams, 1957	7.1
15	Lou Boudreau, 1948	6.9

1961-1976

1	Mickey Mantle, 1961	8.0
2	Ron Santo, 1966	7.5
3	Steve Carlton, 1972	7.4
4	Bob Gibson, 1968	7.3
	Willie Mays, 1965	7.3
	Ron Santo, 1967	7.3
	Carl Yastrzemski, 1967	7.3
8	Norm Cash, 1961	7.1
	Joe Morgan, 1975	7.1
10	Gaylord Perry, 1972	7.0
11	Rico Petrocelli, 1969	6.9
	Mike Schmidt, 1974	6.9
13	John Hiller, 1973	6.7
	Frank Robinson, 1966	6.7
15	4 players tied	6.6

1977-1996

1	Barry Bonds, 1992	9.2
2	Cal Ripken, 1984	9.1
3	Barry Bonds, 1993	8.8
4	Barry Bonds, 1996	8.5
5	Cal Ripken, 1991	8.3
6	Rickey Henderson, 1990	8.2
7	Jeff Bagwell, 1994	7.6
8	Rickey Henderson, 1985	7.4
9	Dwight Gooden, 1985	7.3
	Greg Maddux, 1994	7.3
	Mike Schmidt, 1980	7.3
12	Kevin Brown, 1996	7.2
	George Brett, 1985	7.2
	Barry Bonds, 1990	7.2
15	4 players tied	7.0

Manager Roster

This section details the managerial record of every man who ever held the reins of a major league club from 1871 through 1996. For many years, the assignment of wins and losses was thought a relatively simple task—almost as simple as identifying the managers themselves. In recent years, however, Richard Topp and Robert Tiemann wondered how it was that "managers" who never set foot on the field to lead their charges or even accompanied their clubs on road trips could be regarded as managers at all, at least in the commonly understood sense of field manager rather than business manager. Topp and Tiemann wondered how John McGraw, for example, could be credited as manager of the New York Giants for all of 1924 when a knee injury kept him from the bench for seven weeks: Somebody else must have run the team, they figured, so why not credit that man as interim manager?

That there were record-keeping errors in the 1870s or even the early 1900s may strike the average fan as unsurprising, but the incorrect assignment of decisions to helmsmen has been characteristic of every decade, up to and including the 1990s. Tiemann and Topp undertook a complete review of managerial records dating back to the National Association and found that the records published in previous baseball encyclopedias were wrong—so wrong that they had to be refigured from scratch. Here are the criteria they established for their groundbreaking study:

1. *Definition* A manager is the person designated by the club ownership to run the club on the field.

2. *Absences* When the regular manager is unable to be with the team for 30 or more days, the assistant in charge during his absence should be credited with the team's record from the time the absence begins until the regular manager returns to active duty.

3. *Interim manager* When a manager is removed, either by resignation or by being fired, and his designated replacement is not present to replace him, the assistant temporarily in charge of the team shall be credited with the team's record during the interim.

4. *Head coaches* From 1961 through 1964, the Chicago Cubs had a "panel of coaches" rather than a single manager. One of these coaches was designated *head coach* for a period of time; and that coach is credited with the team's record during his term as head coach.

5. *Captains* During the early years of professional baseball, the man who had the title of "manager" often served merely as the club's business manager, while the captain (a player) was responsible for the team on the field. Some captains were also managers. Each ambiguous situation is judged according to its particular circumstances, but in general the captain, rather than the manager, is credited with the team's record if the manager did not travel with the team or did not have previous baseball experience.

6. *Suspended games* If a game was suspended when one man was managing the team and was completed on a later date when another man was managing, the second manager is credited if the game was suspended before five innings were completed. If the game was suspended after five or more innings were played, then:

   (a) credit the first manager with a win if the team was leading at the point of suspension and maintained the lead to win the game; or

   (b) credit the first manager with a loss if the team was losing at the point of suspension and remained behind to lose the game; or

   (c) credit the second manager with a win (or tie) if the team was losing at the point of suspension but came back to tie the score or win the game; or

   (d) credit the second manager with a loss if the team was winning at the point of suspension but then lost the lead and/or game; or

   (e) credit the second manager with the win or loss if the score was tied at the point of suspension.

7. *Protested games* If a protest was granted and the game was ordered resumed from the point of protest, then the same rules used for suspended games apply. If a protested game of at least five innings' duration was ordered replayed in its entirety, then no win or loss is credited, but both managers are credited with a no-decision game.

8. *Forfeited games* All forfeited games are counted as games managed, even if the game did not start or if it did not go five innings.

9. *Split seasons* In 1892 the National League played a split season, the winners meeting for the championship. In 1981, because of a players' strike, the National and American Leagues played split seasons. The managers' totals will have entries for each half-season.

10. *Replacement clubs* In the American Association (1882–1891), there were three instances in which one club dropped out and was replaced by another club. In 1884 Richmond replaced Washington; in 1890 Baltimore replaced Brooklyn; and in 1891 Milwaukee replaced Cincinnati. In each case, the new club inherited the old club's record. Therefore, the manager of the new club is credited with starting in the position (standing) in which the old club finished.

In the Union Association (1884), when a new club

replaced an old one, the new club started with a 0–0 record rather than inheriting the old club's record, except in the case of the Chicago franchise, which moved to Pittsburgh. Therefore, all such Union Association managers are credited with a finish as if their teams had begun their season at the beginning of the league season. The finish for each manager is his club's standing in the eight-team league when (a) he left the job, (b) his club dropped out of the league, or (c) his club finished the season. The clubs that dropped out were Altoona (replaced by Kansas City); Philadelphia (replaced by Wilmington); Wilmington (replaced by St. Paul); and Pittsburgh (replaced by Milwaukee).

In a typical entry in the Manager Roster (a hypothetical entry has been created below), the column marked STANDING will, in cases where a team has had only one manager throughout the year, show the team's final standing (in the example below, see the entry for 1972). In the case of a manager who began the season but was replaced midway, however, the figure on the left of the column shows the team's standing when he departed and the figure on the right shows the team's final standing (in the example below, see the entry for 1976). In the case of a manager who finished the season but did not begin it, the team's standing when he took over is shown on the left and the final standing on the right (see the entry for 1978). In the case of a manager who began when the season was already under way but who failed to finish, the figure on the left of the column shows the team's standing when he took over; the middle figure shows the team's standing when he departed; and a third figure shows the team's final standing (see the entry for 1977). The figure in the next column represents the number of wins predicted by the team's runs scored and runs allowed, with about ten extra runs being required for each win beyond .500. Last, the number of wins in the A-E column, which may be a positive figure or a negative figure, reflects the extent to which a manager may have stretched (or hindered) his available talent. The bottom line of a manager's entry provides his career totals, beginning at the left with the number of years, full or partial, in which he managed a major league club. The symbols shown in the sample entry are explained after the example.

Whenever a manager served two or more teams in the same year, the totals for each club are shown separately (see the entry above for 1973). The split seasons of 1892 and 1981 are indicated with separate records for each half. A figure to the right of the year indicates first half or second half (see entry above for 1981).

TM/L	Team and League
G	Games managed (including ties)
W	Wins
L	Losses
PCT	Percentage of games won
M/Y	Manager/Year (The latter figure indicates how many managers the team employed that year, while the former indicates the chronological position of the manager whose entry it is; "2/5," for example, would mean that this manager was the second of the team's five managers during that year.)
W-EXP	Expected Wins Calculated for the team based on its actual runs scored and allowed, not its predicted runs scored and runs allowed. A team that allows exactly as many runs as it scores is predicted to play .500 ball. The equation for expected wins is:

$$\frac{(\text{Runs Scored} - \text{Runs Allowed})}{\text{Runs Per Win}} + \frac{(\text{Wins} + \text{Losses})}{2}$$

A-E	Actual Wins Minus Expected Wins (A measure of the extent to which a team outperformed or underperformed its talent; for a single season or two a high figure may be attributable to chance, but over time one must credit good managing.)
E	Eastern Division
W	Western Division
*	Indicates playing manager; for vital statistics, consult the player or pitcher register
▲	Tied for first place, involved in league or division playoff
●	Tied for position in standings
♦	League Championship Series win
★	World Series win
■	Wild Card
○	Lost Divisional Playoffs

The team and league abbreviations used in this section can be found on the last page of the book.

YEAR	TM/L	G	W	L	PCT	STANDING			M/Y	W-EXP	A-E
Blow, Josiah H. "Joe"											
1969	Det-A*	134	71	63	.530	3 E	3 E		1/2	66.8	4.2
1971	Tex-A*	23	9	14	.391	6 W	6 W		3/3	12.0	-3.0
1972	Tex-A	161	84	76	.525	2 W				79.1	4.9
1973	Tex-A	95	44	51	.463	4 W	3 W		1/2	44.2	-0.2
1973	NY-A	56	30	26	.535	3 E	3 E		2/2	28.7	1.3
1974	NY-A	159	97	62	.610	★♦1 E				82.8	14.2
1975	NY-A	162	100	62	.617	♦1 E				90.0	10.0
1976	NY-A	94	52	42	.553	▲♦3 E	1 E		1/3	53.8	-1.8
1977	Bos-A	95	55	40	.579	4 E	4 E	2 E	2/3	50.4	4.6
1978	Oak-A	152	83	69	.546	●5 W	2 W		2/2	75.2	7.8
1979	Oak-A	60	37	23	.617	1 W	2 W		1/2	33.0	4.0
1980	Oak-A	49	27	22	.551	2 W	3 W		2/2	27.4	-0.4
1981(1)	Oak-A	62	24	38	.387	6 W				32.4	-7.6
1981(2)	Oak-A	100	44	56	.440	5 W				57.0	-13.0
1982	NY-A	162	91	71	.562	3 E				81.5	10.5
1983	NY-A	145	91	54	.628	6 E	2 E		2/2	84.0	7.0
1996	Atl-N	10	3	7	.300	■○♦6 E	2 E		1/2	6.0	-3.0
	15	1719	942	776	.548						39.5

Adair, Marion Danne "Bill"

YEAR	TM/L	G	W	L	PCT	STANDING			M/Y	W-EXP	A-E
1970	Chi-A	10	4	6	.400	6 W	6 W	6 W	2/3	3.8	0.2

Adcock, Joseph Wilbur "Joe"

YEAR	TM/L	G	W	L	PCT	STANDING			M/Y	W-EXP	A-E
1967	Cle-A	162	75	87	.463	8				75.0	0.0

Addy, Robert Edward "Bob"

YEAR	TM/L	G	W	L	PCT	STANDING			M/Y	W-EXP	A-E
1875	Phi-n*	7	3	4	.429	4	5		2/2	4.3	-1.3
1877	Cin-N*	24	5	19	.208	6	6	6	2/3	5.3	-0.3
	2	31	8	23	.258						-1.6

Allen, Robert Gilman "Bob"

YEAR	TM/L	G	W	L	PCT	STANDING			M/Y	W-EXP	A-E
1890	Phi-N*	35	25	10	.714	3	2	3	4/5	20.2	4.8
1900	Cin-N*	144	62	77	.446	7				65.5	-3.5
	2	179	87	87	.500						1.3

Allison, Andrew K. "Andy"

YEAR	TM/L	G	W	L	PCT	STANDING			M/Y	W-EXP	A-E
1872	Eck-n*	11	0	11	.000	10	9		1/3	-1.2	1.2

Allison, Douglas L. "Doug"

YEAR	TM/L	G	W	L	PCT	STANDING			M/Y	W-EXP	A-E
1873	Res-n*	23	2	21	.087	8				-3.0	5.0

Alou, Felipe Rojas

YEAR	TM/L	G	W	L	PCT	STANDING			M/Y	W-EXP	A-E
1992	Mon-N	125	70	55	.560	4 E	2 E		2/2	68.1	1.9
1993	Mon-N	163	94	68	.580	2 E				86.1	7.9
1994	Mon-N	114	74	40	.649	1 E				70.0	4.0
1995	Mon-N	144	66	78	.458	5 E				70.3	-4.3
1996	Mon-N	162	88	74	.543	2 E				88.4	-0.4
	5	708	392	315	.554						9.1

Alston, Walter Emmons

YEAR	TM/L	G	W	L	PCT	STANDING			M/Y	W-EXP	A-E
1954	Bro-N	154	92	62	.597	2				80.6	11.4
1955	Bro-N	154	98	55	.641	★1				96.4	1.6
1956	Bro-N	154	93	61	.604	1				89.2	3.8
1957	Bro-N	154	84	70	.545	3				87.3	-3.3
1958	LA-N	154	71	83	.461	7				67.8	3.2
1959	LA-N	156	88	68	.564	▲★1				81.5	6.5
1960	LA-N	154	82	72	.532	4				84.3	-2.3
1961	LA-N	154	89	65	.578	2				80.7	8.3
1962	LA-N	165	102	63	.618	▲2				96.7	5.3
1963	LA-N	163	99	63	.611	★1				91.0	8.0
1964	LA-N	164	80	82	.494	●6				85.7	-5.7
1965	LA-N	162	97	65	.599	★1				90.9	6.1
1966	LA-N	162	95	67	.586	1				94.4	0.6
1967	LA-N	162	73	89	.451	8				72.3	0.7
1968	LA-N	162	76	86	.469	●7				76.2	-0.2
1969	LA-N	162	85	77	.525	4 W				90.2	-5.2
1970	LA-N	161	87	74	.540	2 W				87.0	-0.0
1971	LA-N	162	89	73	.549	2 W				89.2	-0.2
1972	LA-N	155	85	70	.548	3 W				83.9	1.1
1973	LA-N	162	95	66	.590	2 W				92.4	2.6
1974	LA-N	162	102	60	.630	♦1 W				105.6	-3.6
1975	LA-N	162	88	74	.543	2 W				93.7	-5.7
1976	LA-N	158	90	68	.570	2 W	2 W		1/2	86.1	3.9
	23	3658	2040	1613	.558						36.8

Altobelli, Joseph "Joe"

YEAR	TM/L	G	W	L	PCT	STANDING			M/Y	W-EXP	A-E
1977	SF-N	162	75	87	.463	4 W				77.1	-2.1
1978	SF-N	162	89	73	.549	3 W				83.1	5.9
1979	SF-N	140	61	79	.436	4 W	4 W		1/2	63.1	-2.1
1983	Bal-A	162	98	64	.605	★1 E				95.7	2.3
1984	Bal-A	162	85	77	.525	5 E				82.5	2.5
1985	Bal-A	55	29	26	.527	4 E	4 E		1/3	29.3	-0.3
1991	Chi-N	1	0	1	.000	4 E	5 E	4 E	2/3	0.5	-0.5
	7	844	437	407	.518						5.8

Amalfitano, John Joseph "Joey"

YEAR	TM/L	G	W	L	PCT	STANDING			M/Y	W-EXP	A-E
1979	Chi-N	7	2	5	.286	5 E	5 E		2/2	3.5	-1.5
1980	Chi-N	72	26	46	.361	6 E	6 E		2/2	30.7	-4.7
1981(1)	Chi-N	54	15	37	.288	6 E					
(2)	Chi-N	52	23	28	.451	5 E				39.5	-1.5
	3	185	66	116	.363						-7.8

Anderson, George Lee "Sparky"

YEAR	TM/L	G	W	L	PCT	STANDING			M/Y	W-EXP	A-E
1970	Cin-N	162	102	60	.630	♦1 W				90.4	11.6
1971	Cin-N	162	79	83	.488	●4 W				81.6	-2.6
1972	Cin-N	154	95	59	.617	♦1 W				92.7	2.3
1973	Cin-N	162	99	63	.611	1 W				93.4	5.6
1974	Cin-N	163	98	64	.605	2 W				95.8	2.2
1975	Cin-N	162	108	54	.667	★1 W				106.7	1.3
1976	Cin-N	162	102	60	.630	★1 W				103.2	-1.2
1977	Cin-N	162	88	74	.543	2 W				88.5	-0.5
1978	Cin-N	161	92	69	.571	2 W				82.7	9.3
1979	Det-A	106	56	50	.528	5 E	5 E		3/3	55.1	0.9
1980	Det-A	163	84	78	.519	5 E				88.0	-4.0
1981(1)	Det-A	57	31	26	.544	4 E					
(2)	Det-A	52	29	23	.558	●2 E				57.0	3.0
1982	Det-A	162	83	79	.512	4 E				85.5	-2.5
1983	Det-A	162	92	70	.568	2 E				92.0	0.0
1984	Det-A	162	104	58	.642	★1 E				99.5	4.5
1985	Det-A	161	84	77	.522	3 E				84.6	-0.6
1986	Det-A	162	87	75	.537	3 E				89.2	-2.2
1987	Det-A	162	98	64	.605	1 E				96.2	1.8
1988	Det-A	162	88	74	.543	2 E				85.7	2.3
1989	Det-A	162	59	103	.364	7 E				60.9	-1.9
1990	Det-A	162	79	83	.488	3 E				80.6	-1.6
1991	Det-A	162	84	78	.519	●2 E				83.2	0.8
1992	Det-A	162	75	87	.463	6 E				80.7	-5.7
1993	Det-A	162	85	77	.525	●3 E				86.7	-1.7
1994	Det-A	115	53	62	.461	5 E				55.8	-2.8
1995	Det-A	144	60	84	.417	4 E				54.3	5.7
	26	4030	2194	1834	.545						23.9

Anson, Adrian Constantine "Cap"

YEAR	TM/L	G	W	L	PCT	STANDING			M/Y	W-EXP	A-E
1875	Ath-n*	8	4	2	.667	2	2		2/2	4.9	-0.9
1879	Chi-N*	64	41	21	.661	2	4		1/2	32.9	8.1
1880	Chi-N*	86	67	17	.798	1				63.0	4.0
1881	Chi-N*	84	56	28	.667	1				57.4	-1.4
1882	Chi-N*	84	55	29	.655	1				64.3	-9.3
1883	Chi-N*	98	59	39	.602	2				60.8	-1.8
1884	Chi-N*	113	62	50	.554	●4				71.5	-9.5
1885	Chi-N*	113	87	25	.777	1				88.1	-1.1
1886	Chi-N*	126	90	34	.726	1				92.5	-2.5
1887	Chi-N*	127	71	50	.587	3				68.9	2.1
1888	Chi-N*	136	77	58	.570	2				74.5	2.5
1889	Chi-N*	136	67	65	.508	3				70.5	-3.5
1890	Chi-N*	139	84	53	.613	2				82.5	1.5
1891	Chi-N*	137	82	53	.607	2				76.6	5.4
1892(1)	Chi-N*	71	31	39	.443	8				63.2	6.8
(2)	Chi-N*	76	39	37	.513	7				59.8	-3.8
1893	Chi-N*	128	56	71	.441	9				64.1	-7.1
1894	Chi-N*	137	57	75	.432	8				64.1	-7.1
1895	Chi-N*	133	72	58	.554	4				66.0	6.0
1896	Chi-N*	132	71	57	.555	5				65.4	5.6
1897	Chi-N*	138	59	73	.447	9				60.7	-1.7
1898	NY-N	22	9	13	.409	6	7	7	2/3	11.5	-2.5
	21	2288	1296	947	.578						-3.2

Appling, Lucius Benjamin "Luke"

YEAR	TM/L	G	W	L	PCT	STANDING			M/Y	W-EXP	A-E
1967	KC-A	40	10	30	.250	10	10		2/2	16.5	-6.5

Armour, William Clark "Bill"

YEAR	TM/L	G	W	L	PCT	STANDING			M/Y	W-EXP	A-E
1902	Cle-A	137	69	67	.507	5				69.8	-0.8
1903	Cle-A	140	77	63	.550	3				76.1	0.9
1904	Cle-A	154	86	65	.570	4				93.8	-7.8
1905	Det-A	154	79	74	.516	3				66.5	12.5
1906	Det-A	151	71	78	.477	6				65.6	5.4
	5	736	382	347	.524						10.3

Aspromonte, Kenneth Joseph "Ken"

YEAR	TM/L	G	W	L	PCT	STANDING			M/Y	W-EXP	A-E
1972	Cle-A	156	72	84	.462	5 E				72.4	-0.4
1973	Cle-A	162	71	91	.438	6 E				66.6	4.4
1974	Cle-A	162	77	85	.475	4 E				77.7	-0.7
	3	480	220	260	.458						3.3

Austin, James Philip "Jimmy"

YEAR	TM/L	G	W	L	PCT	STANDING			M/Y	W-EXP	A-E
1913	StL-A*	8	2	6	.250	7	7	8	2/3	3.3	-1.3
1918	StL-A*	16	7	9	.438	6	6	5	2/3	7.7	-0.7
1923	StL-A*	51	22	29	.431	3	5		2/2	24.4	-2.4
	3	75	31	44	.413						-4.5

Baker, Delmer David "Del"

YEAR	TM/L	G	W	L	PCT	STANDING			M/Y	W-EXP	A-E
1933	Det-A	2	2	0	1.000	5	5		2/2	1.0	1.0
1936	Det-A	34	18	16	.529	3	4	2	2/3	18.0	0.0
1937	Det-A	54	34	20	.630	3	3	2	2/5	29.9	4.1
	Det-A	10	7	3	.700	2	2	2	4/5	5.5	1.5
1938	Det-A	57	37	19	.661	5	4		2/2	30.2	6.8
1939	Det-A	155	81	73	.526	5				85.1	-4.1
1940	Det-A	155	90	64	.584	●1				92.9	-2.9
1941	Det-A	155	75	79	.487	●4				71.4	3.6
1942	Det-A	156	73	81	.474	5				77.2	-4.2
1960	Bos-A	7	2	5	.286	8	8	7	2/3	3.0	-1.0
	9	785	419	360	.538						4.7

Baker, Johnnie B "Dusty"

YEAR	TM/L	G	W	L	PCT	STANDING			M/Y	W-EXP	A-E
1993	SF-N	162	103	59	.636	2 W				98.3	4.7
1994	SF-N	115	55	60	.478	2 W				57.9	-2.9
1995	SF-N	144	67	77	.465	4 W				60.2	6.8
1996	SF-N	162	68	94	.420	4 W				70.5	-2.5
	4	583	293	290	.503						6.1

Bamberger, George Irvin

YEAR	TM/L	G	W	L	PCT	STANDING			M/Y	W-EXP	A-E
1978	Mil-A	162	93	69	.574	3 E				96.4	-3.4
1979	Mil-A	161	95	66	.590	2 E				88.8	6.2
1980	Mil-A	92	47	45	.511	2 E	4 E	3 E	2/3	53.2	-6.2
1982	NY-N	162	65	97	.401	6 E				69.1	-4.1
1983	NY-N	46	16	30	.348	6 E	6 E		1/2	19.8	-3.8
1985	Mil-A	161	71	90	.441	6 E				69.5	1.5
1986	Mil-A	152	71	81	.467	6 E	6 E		1/2	69.6	1.4
	7	936	458	478	.489						-8.3

Bancroft, David James "Dave"

YEAR	TM/L	G	W	L	PCT	STANDING			M/Y	W-EXP	A-E
1924	Bos-N*	154	53	100	.346	8				47.8	5.2
1925	Bos-N*	153	70	83	.458	5				67.5	2.5
1926	Bos-N*	153	66	86	.434	7				66.4	-0.4
1927	Bos-N*	155	60	94	.390	7				65.1	-5.1
	4	615	249	363	.407						2.2

Bancroft, Frank Carter

YEAR	TM/L	G	W	L	PCT	STANDING			M/Y	W-EXP	A-E
1880	Wor-N	85	40	43	.482	5				45.7	-5.7
1881	Det-N	84	41	43	.488	4				42.9	-1.9
1882	Det-N	86	42	41	.506	6				34.0	8.0
1883	Cle-N	100	55	42	.567	4				51.8	3.2
1884	Pro-N	114	84	28	.750	1				83.3	0.7
1885	Pro-N	110	53	57	.482	4				46.0	7.0
1887	Phi-a	55	26	29	.473	6	5		1/2	27.6	-1.6

YEAR	TM/L	G	W	L	PCT	STANDING			M/Y	W-EXP	A-E
1889	Ind-N	68	25	43	.368	7	7		1/2	30.8	-5.8
1902	Cin-N	16	9	7	.563	6	6	4	2/3	8.8	0.2
	9	718	375	333	.530						4.1

Barkley, Samuel E. "Sam"

YEAR	TM/L	G	W	L	PCT	STANDING			M/Y	W-EXP	A-E
1888	KC-a*	58	21	36	.368	8	8	8	2/3	16.2	4.8

Barnie, William Harrison "Billy"

YEAR	TM/L	G	W	L	PCT	STANDING			M/Y	W-EXP	A-E
1883	Bal-a*	96	28	68	.292	8				25.1	2.9
1884	Bal-a	109	63	43	.594	6				64.1	-1.1
1885	Bal-a	110	41	68	.376	8				41.7	-0.7
1886	Bal-a	139	48	83	.366	8				42.4	5.6
1887	Bal-a	141	77	58	.570	3				77.0	0.0
1888	Bal-a	139	57	80	.416	5				56.8	0.2
1889	Bal-a	139	70	65	.519	5				67.1	2.9
1890	Bal-a	38	15	19	.441	8				16.0	-1.0
1891	Bal-a	139	71	64	.526	3				72.0	-1.0
1892(1)	Was-N	2	0	2	.000	●11	7		1/2	0.8	-0.8
1893	Lou-N	126	50	75	.400	11				47.6	2.4
1894	Lou-N	131	36	94	.277	12				39.3	-3.3
1897	Bro-N	136	61	71	.462	●6				62.3	-1.3
1898	Bro-N	35	15	20	.429	9	10		1/3	13.5	1.5
	14	1480	632	810	.438						6.1

Barrow, Edward Grant "Ed"

YEAR	TM/L	G	W	L	PCT	STANDING			M/Y	W-EXP	A-E
1903	Det-A	137	65	71	.478	5				71.0	-6.0
1904	Det-A	84	32	46	.410	7	7		1/2	31.9	0.1
1918	Bos-A	126	75	51	.595	★1				73.8	1.2
1919	Bos-A	138	66	71	.482	6				69.8	-3.8
1920	Bos-A	154	72	81	.471	5				71.6	0.4
	5	639	310	320	.492						-8.1

Barry, John Joseph "Jack"

YEAR	TM/L	G	W	L	PCT	STANDING			M/Y	W-EXP	A-E
1917	Bos-A*	157	90	62	.592	2				88.0	2.0

Battin, Joseph V. "Joe"

YEAR	TM/L	G	W	L	PCT	STANDING			M/Y	W-EXP	A-E
1883	Pit-a*	13	2	11	.154	7	7		3/3	4.2	-2.2
1884	Pit-a*	13	6	7	.462	11	10	10	3/5	2.9	3.1
	Pit-U*	6	1	5	.167	5	5		1/2	2.7	-1.7
	2	32	9	23	.281						-0.9

Bauer, Henry Albert "Hank"

YEAR	TM/L	G	W	L	PCT	STANDING			M/Y	W-EXP	A-E
1961	KC-A*	102	35	67	.343	8	●9		2/2	39.9	-4.9
1962	KC-A	162	72	90	.444	9				72.2	-0.2
1964	Bal-A	163	97	65	.599	3				93.2	3.8
1965	Bal-A	162	94	68	.580	3				87.9	6.1
1966	Bal-A	160	97	63	.606	★1				95.9	1.1
1967	Bal-A	161	76	85	.472	●6				87.2	-11.2
1968	Bal-A	80	43	37	.538	3	2		1/2	44.7	-1.7
1969	Oak-A	149	80	69	.537	2 W	2 W		1/2	80.3	-0.3
	8	1139	594	544	.522						-7.2

Baylor, Donald Edward "Don"

YEAR	TM/L	G	W	L	PCT	STANDING			M/Y	W-EXP	A-E
1993	Col-N	162	67	95	.414	6 W				61.8	5.2
1994	Col-N	117	53	64	.453	3 W				52.4	0.6
1995	Col-N	144	77	67	.535	○■2 W				72.2	4.8
1996	Col-N	162	82	79	.509	3 W				80.7	2.3
	4	585	279	305	.478						12.9

Bell, David Gus "Buddy"

YEAR	TM/L	G	W	L	PCT	STANDING			M/Y	W-EXP	A-E
1996	Det-A	162	53	109	.327	5 E				52.9	0.1

Benson, Vernon Adair "Vern"

YEAR	TM/L	G	W	L	PCT	STANDING			M/Y	W-EXP	A-E
1977	Atl-N	1	1	0	1.000	6 W	6 W	6 W	3/4	0.4	0.6

Berra, Lawrence Peter "Yogi"

YEAR	TM/L	G	W	L	PCT	STANDING			M/Y	W-EXP	A-E
1964	NY-A	164	99	63	.611	1				97.3	1.7
1972	NY-N	156	83	73	.532	3 E				72.4	10.6
1973	NY-N	161	82	79	.509	♦1 E				82.7	-0.7
1974	NY-N	162	71	91	.438	5 E				72.9	-1.9
1975	NY-N	109	56	53	.514	3 E	●3 E		1/2	56.0	-0.0
1984	NY-A	162	87	75	.537	3 E				89.0	-2.0
1985	NY-A	16	6	10	.375	7 E	2 E		1/2	9.7	-3.7
	7	930	484	444	.522						4.0

Bevington, Terry Paul

YEAR	TM/L	G	W	L	PCT	STANDING			M/Y	W-EXP	A-E
1995	Chi-A	113	57	56	.504	4 C	3 C		2/2	56.3	0.7
1996	Chi-A	162	85	77	.525	2 C				90.7	-5.7
	2	275	142	133	.516						-4.9

Bezdek, Hugo Frank

YEAR	TM/L	G	W	L	PCT	STANDING			M/Y	W-EXP	A-E
1917	Pit-N	91	30	59	.337	8	8		3/3	35.8	-5.8
1918	Pit-N	126	65	60	.520	4				68.6	-3.6
1919	Pit-N	139	71	68	.511	4				70.2	0.8
	3	356	166	187	.470						-8.6

Bickerson

YEAR	TM/L	G	W	L	PCT	STANDING			M/Y	W-EXP	A-E
1884	Was-a	1	0	1	.000	12	12		2/2	0.2	-0.2

Birmingham, Joseph Leo "Joe"

YEAR	TM/L	G	W	L	PCT	STANDING			M/Y	W-EXP	A-E
1912	Cle-A*	28	21	7	.750	6	5		2/2	13.9	7.1
1913	Cle-A*	155	86	66	.566	3				86.6	-0.6
1914	Cle-A*	157	51	102	.333	8				58.3	-7.3
1915	Cle-A	28	12	16	.429	6	7		1/2	11.4	0.6
	4	368	170	191	.471						-0.2

Bissonette, Adelphia Louis "Del"

YEAR	TM/L	G	W	L	PCT	STANDING			M/Y	W-EXP	A-E
1945	Bos-N	60	25	34	.424	7	6		2/2	29.2	-4.2

Blackburne, Russell Aubrey "Lena"

YEAR	TM/L	G	W	L	PCT	STANDING			M/Y	W-EXP	A-E
1928	Chi-A*	80	40	40	.500	6	5		2/2	36.4	3.6
1929	Chi-A*	152	59	93	.388	7				59.8	-0.8

YEAR	TM/L	G	W	L	PCT	STANDING			M/Y	W-EXP	A-E
	2	232	99	133	.427						2.8

Blades, Francis Raymond "Ray"

YEAR	TM/L	G	W	L	PCT	STANDING			M/Y	W-EXP	A-E
1939	StL-N	155	92	61	.601	2				91.0	1.0
1940	StL-N	39	14	24	.368	6	3		1/3	20.2	-6.2
1948	Bro-N	1	1	0	1.000	5	5	3	2/3	0.5	0.5
	3	195	107	85	.557						-4.7

Blair, Walter Allen "Walter"

YEAR	TM/L	G	W	L	PCT	STANDING			M/Y	W-EXP	A-E
1915	Buf-F*	2	1	1	.500	8	8	6	2/3	0.9	0.1

Bluege, Oswald Louis "Ossie"

YEAR	TM/L	G	W	L	PCT	STANDING			M/Y	W-EXP	A-E
1943	Was-A	153	84	69	.549	2				83.9	0.1
1944	Was-A	154	64	90	.416	8				69.4	-5.4
1945	Was-A	156	87	67	.565	2				83.5	3.5
1946	Was-A	155	76	78	.494	4				66.9	9.1
1947	Was-A	154	64	90	.416	7				57.5	6.5
	5	772	375	394	.488						13.7

Bochy, Bruce Douglas

YEAR	TM/L	G	W	L	PCT	STANDING			M/Y	W-EXP	A-E
1995	SD-N	144	70	74	.486	3 W				71.6	-1.6
1996	SD-N	162	91	71	.562	○1 W				89.9	1.1
	2	306	161	145	.526						-0.5

Boles, John

YEAR	TM/L	G	W	L	PCT	STANDING			M/Y	W-EXP	A-E
1996	Fla-N	75	40	35	.533	4 E	3 E		3/3	36.8	3.2

Bond, Thomas Henry "Tommy"

YEAR	TM/L	G	W	L	PCT	STANDING			M/Y	W-EXP	A-E
1882	Wor-N*	6	2	4	.333	8	8	8	2/3	1.3	0.7

Boone, Robert Raymond "Bob"

YEAR	TM/L	G	W	L	PCT	STANDING			M/Y	W-EXP	A-E
1995	KC-A	144	70	74	.486	2 C				65.9	4.1
1996	KC-A	161	75	86	.466	5 C				76.6	-1.6
	2	305	145	160	.475						2.5

Boros, Stephen "Steve"

YEAR	TM/L	G	W	L	PCT	STANDING			M/Y	W-EXP	A-E
1983	Oak-A	162	74	88	.457	4 W				73.7	0.3
1984	Oak-A	44	20	24	.455	5 W	4 W		1/2	20.5	-0.5
1986	SD-N	162	74	88	.457	4 W				74.1	-0.1
	3	368	168	200	.457						-0.3

Bottomley, James Leroy "Jim"

YEAR	TM/L	G	W	L	PCT	STANDING			M/Y	W-EXP	A-E
1937	StL-A*	78	21	56	.273	7	8		2/2	24.7	-3.7

Boudreau, Louis "Lou"

YEAR	TM/L	G	W	L	PCT	STANDING			M/Y	W-EXP	A-E
1942	Cle-A*	156	75	79	.487	4				69.7	5.3
1943	Cle-A*	153	82	71	.536	3				79.0	3.0
1944	Cle-A*	155	72	82	.468	●5				73.5	-1.5
1945	Cle-A*	147	73	72	.503	5				73.5	-0.5
1946	Cle-A*	156	68	86	.442	6				66.0	2.0
1947	Cle-A*	157	80	74	.519	4				87.4	-7.4
1948	Cle-A*	156	97	58	.626	▲★1				104.7	-7.7
1949	Cle-A*	154	89	65	.578	3				87.6	1.4
1950	Cle-A*	155	92	62	.597	4				91.9	0.1
1952	Bos-A*	154	76	78	.494	6				78.0	-2.0
1953	Bos-A	153	84	69	.549	4				79.0	5.0
1954	Bos-A	156	69	85	.448	4				74.2	-5.2
1955	KC-A	154	63	91	.409	6				51.1	11.9
1956	KC-A	154	52	102	.338	8				56.3	-4.3
1957	KC-A	104	36	67	.350	7	7		1/2	41.2	-5.2
1960	Chi-N	139	54	83	.394	7			2/2	55.9	-1.9
	16	2404	1162	1224	.487						-6.9

Bowa, Lawrence Robert "Larry"

YEAR	TM/L	G	W	L	PCT	STANDING			M/Y	W-EXP	A-E
1987	SD-N	162	65	97	.401	6 W				71.4	-6.4
1988	SD-N	46	16	30	.348	5 W	3 W		1/2	23.3	-7.3
	2	208	81	127	.389						-13.8

Bowerman, Frank Eugene "Frank"

YEAR	TM/L	G	W	L	PCT	STANDING			M/Y	W-EXP	A-E
1909	Bos-N*	76	22	54	.289	8	8		1/2	24.2	-2.2

Boyd, William J. "Bill"

YEAR	TM/L	G	W	L	PCT	STANDING			M/Y	W-EXP	A-E
1875	Atl-n*	2	0	2	.000	12	12		2/2	-0.2	0.2

Boyer, Kenton Lloyd "Ken"

YEAR	TM/L	G	W	L	PCT	STANDING			M/Y	W-EXP	A-E
1978	StL-N	143	62	81	.434	6 E	5 E		3/3	66.1	-4.1
1979	StL-N	163	86	76	.531	3 E				84.9	1.1
1980	StL-N	51	18	33	.353	6 E	4 E		1/4	26.4	-8.4
	3	357	166	190	.466						-11.3

Bradley, William Joseph "Bill"

YEAR	TM/L	G	W	L	PCT	STANDING			M/Y	W-EXP	A-E
1905	Cle-A*	41	20	21	.488	●1	2	5	2/3	19.9	0.1
1914	Bro-F*	157	77	77	.500	5				75.5	1.5
	2	198	97	98	.497						1.6

Bragan, Robert Randall "Bobby"

YEAR	TM/L	G	W	L	PCT	STANDING			M/Y	W-EXP	A-E
1956	Pit-N	157	66	88	.429	7				70.1	-4.1
1957	Pit-N	104	36	67	.350	7	●7		1/2	43.8	-7.8
1958	Cle-A	67	31	36	.463	6	4		1/2	36.1	-5.1
1963	Mil-N	163	84	78	.519	6				88.9	-4.9
1964	Mil-N	162	88	74	.543	5				86.7	1.3
1965	Mil-N	162	86	76	.531	5				88.8	-2.8
1966	Atl-N	112	52	59	.468	7			1/2	62.3	-10.3
	7	927	443	478	.481						-33.8

Bresnahan, Roger Philip

YEAR	TM/L	G	W	L	PCT	STANDING			M/Y	W-EXP	A-E
1909	StL-N*	154	54	98	.355	7				60.8	-6.8
1910	StL-N*	153	63	90	.412	7				68.5	-5.5
1911	StL-N*	158	75	74	.503	5				67.1	7.9
1912	StL-N*	153	63	90	.412	6				60.1	2.9
1915	Chi-N*	157	73	80	.477	4				71.1	1.9
	5	775	328	432	.432						0.5

Bristol, James David "Dave"

YEAR	TM/L	G	W	L	PCT	STANDING			M/Y	W-EXP	A-E
1966	Cin-N	77	39	38	.506	8	7		2/2	38.0	1.0
1967	Cin-N	162	87	75	.537	4				85.6	1.4
1968	Cin-N	163	83	79	.512	4				82.8	0.2
1969	Cin-N	163	89	73	.549	3 W				83.9	5.1
1970	Mil-A	163	65	97	.401	●4 W				66.7	-1.7
1971	Mil-A	161	69	92	.429	6 W				72.1	-3.1
1972	Mil-A	30	10	20	.333	6 E	6 E		1/3	12.8	-2.8
1976	Atl-N	162	70	92	.432	6 W				72.6	-2.6
1977	Atl-N	29	8	21	.276	6 W	6 W		1/4	10.8	-2.8
	Atl-N	131	52	79	.397	6 W	6 W		4/4	48.6	3.4
1979	SF-N	22	10	12	.455	4 W	4 W		2/2	9.9	0.1
1980	SF-N	161	75	86	.466	5 W				73.8	1.2
11		1424	657	764	.462						-0.5

Brown, Freeman

YEAR	TM/L	G	W	L	PCT	STANDING			M/Y	W-EXP	A-E
1882	Wor-N	41	9	32	.220	8	8		1/3	9.1	-0.1

Brown, Mordecai Peter Centennial "Three Finger"

YEAR	TM/L	G	W	L	PCT	STANDING			M/Y	W-EXP	A-E
1914	StL-F*	114	50	63	.442	7	8		1/2	46.1	3.9

Brown, Thomas T. "Tom"

YEAR	TM/L	G	W	L	PCT	STANDING			M/Y	W-EXP	A-E
1897	Was-N*	99	52	46	.531	11	●6		2/2	48.2	3.8
1898	Was-N*	38	12	26	.316	11	11		1/4	13.6	-1.6
2		137	64	72	.471						2.2

Brucker, Earle Francis Sr

YEAR	TM/L	G	W	L	PCT	STANDING			M/Y	W-EXP	A-E
1952	Cin-N	5	3	2	.600	7	7	6	2/3	2.4	0.6

Buckenberger, Albert C. "Al"

YEAR	TM/L	G	W	L	PCT	STANDING			M/Y	W-EXP	A-E
1889	Col-a	140	60	78	.435	6				56.5	3.5
1890	Col-a	80	39	41	.488	5	2		1/3	51.9	-12.9
1892(1)	Pit-N	29	15	14	.517	7	6		1/2		
(2)		66	38	27	.585	10	4		2/2	47.3	5.7
1893	Pit-N	131	81	48	.628	2				81.3	-0.3
1894	Pit-N	110	53	55	.491	7	7		1/2	52.9	0.1
1895	StL-N	50	16	34	.320	11	11		1/4	16.0	-0.0
1902	Bos-N	142	73	64	.533	3				74.6	-1.6
1903	Bos-N	140	58	80	.420	6				57.0	1.0
1904	Bos-N	155	55	98	.359	7				49.1	5.9
9		1043	488	539	.475						1.3

Buffinton, Charles G. "Charlie"

YEAR	TM/L	G	W	L	PCT	STANDING			M/Y	W-EXP	A-E
1890	Phi-P*	116	61	54	.530	5	5		2/2	63.6	-2.6

Burdock, John Joseph "Jack"

YEAR	TM/L	G	W	L	PCT	STANDING			M/Y	W-EXP	A-E
1883	Bos-N*	54	30	24	.556	4	1		1/2	37.4	-7.4

Burke, James Timothy "Jimmy"

YEAR	TM/L	G	W	L	PCT	STANDING			M/Y	W-EXP	A-E
1905	StL-N*	90	34	56	.378	7	6	6		32.8	1.2
1918	StL-A	61	29	31	.483	6	5		3/3	28.8	0.2
1919	StL-A	140	67	72	.482	5				65.9	1.1
1920	StL-A	154	76	77	.497	4				79.4	-3.4
4		445	206	236	.466						-0.9

Burnham, George Walter "Watch"

YEAR	TM/L	G	W	L	PCT	STANDING			M/Y	W-EXP	A-E
1887	Ind-N	28	6	22	.214	8	8		1/3	7.7	-1.7

Burns, Thomas Everett "Tom"

YEAR	TM/L	G	W	L	PCT	STANDING			M/Y	W-EXP	A-E
1892(1)	Pit-N*	47	22	25	.468	7	6		2/2		
(2)	Pit-N*	13	5	7	.417	10	4		1/2	29.7	-2.7
1898	Chi-N	152	85	65	.567	4				89.2	-4.2
1899	Chi-N	152	75	73	.507	8				78.6	-3.6
3		364	187	170	.524						-10.5

Burwell, William Edwin "Bill"

YEAR	TM/L	G	W	L	PCT	STANDING			M/Y	W-EXP	A-E
1947	Pit-N	1	1	0	1.000	8	●7		2/2	0.5	0.5

Bush, Owen Joseph "Donie"

YEAR	TM/L	G	W	L	PCT	STANDING			M/Y	W-EXP	A-E
1923	Was-A*	155	75	78	.490	4				73.9	1.1
1927	Pit-N	156	94	60	.610	1				92.4	1.6
1928	Pit-N	152	85	67	.559	4				88.5	-3.5
1929	Pit-N	119	67	51	.568	2	2		1/2	67.7	-0.7
1930	Chi-A	154	62	92	.403	7				62.6	-0.6
1931	Chi-A	156	56	97	.366	8				54.8	1.2
1933	Cin-N	153	58	94	.382	8				59.8	-1.8
7		1045	497	539	.480						-2.7

Butler, Ormond Hook

YEAR	TM/L	G	W	L	PCT	STANDING			M/Y	W-EXP	A-E
1883	Pit-a	53	17	36	.321	6	6		2/3	17.3	-0.3

Byrne, Charles H. "Charlie"

YEAR	TM/L	G	W	L	PCT	STANDING			M/Y	W-EXP	A-E
1885	Bro-a	75	38	37	.507	7	●5		2/2	36.0	2.0
1886	Bro-a	141	76	61	.555	3				68.5	7.5
1887	Bro-a	138	60	74	.448	6				65.8	-5.8
3		354	174	172	.503						3.7

Callahan, James Joseph "Jim"

YEAR	TM/L	G	W	L	PCT	STANDING			M/Y	W-EXP	A-E
1903	Chi-A*	138	60	77	.438	7				58.3	1.7
1904	Chi-A*	42	23	18	.561	4	3		1/2	24.1	-1.1
1912	Chi-A*	158	78	76	.506	4				76.1	1.9
1913	Chi-A*	153	78	74	.513	5				74.8	3.2
1914	Chi-A	157	70	84	.455	●6				68.5	1.5
1916	Pit-N	157	65	89	.422	6				65.3	-0.3
1917	Pit-N	61	20	40	.333	8	8		1/3	24.1	-4.1
7		866	394	458	.462						2.8

Campau, Charles Columbus "Count"

YEAR	TM/L	G	W	L	PCT	STANDING			M/Y	W-EXP	A-E
1890	StL-a*	42	27	14	.659	5	2	3	4/6	24.1	2.9

Cantillon, Joseph D. "Joe"

YEAR	TM/L	G	W	L	PCT	STANDING			M/Y	W-EXP	A-E
1907	Was-A	154	49	102	.325	8				55.6	-6.6
1908	Was-A	155	67	85	.441	7				69.0	-2.0
1909	Was-A	156	42	110	.276	8				43.9	-1.9
3		465	158	297	.347						-10.4

Carey, Max George

YEAR	TM/L	G	W	L	PCT	STANDING			M/Y	W-EXP	A-E
1932	Bro-N	154	81	73	.526	3				77.5	3.5
1933	Bro-N	157	65	88	.425	6				68.4	-3.4
2		311	146	161	.476						0.1

Carey, Thomas John "Tom"

YEAR	TM/L	G	W	L	PCT	STANDING			M/Y	W-EXP	A-E
1873	Bal-n*	24	14	9	.609	3	3		2/2	16.9	-2.9
1874	Mut-n*	25	13	12	.520	3	2		1/2	16.4	-3.4
2		49	27	21	.563						-6.3

Carrigan, William Francis "Bill"

YEAR	TM/L	G	W	L	PCT	STANDING			M/Y	W-EXP	A-E
1913	Bos-A*	70	40	30	.571	5	4		2/2	36.0	4.0
1914	Bos-A*	159	91	62	.595	2				85.5	5.5
1915	Bos-A*	155	101	50	.669	★1				94.1	6.9
1916	Bos-A*	156	91	63	.591	★1				85.2	5.8
1927	Bos-A	154	51	103	.331	8				51.7	-0.7
1928	Bos-A	154	57	96	.373	8				58.2	-1.2
1929	Bos-A	155	58	96	.377	8				57.3	0.7
7		1003	489	500	.494						21.0

Caruthers, Robert Lee "Bob"

YEAR	TM/L	G	W	L	PCT	STANDING			M/Y	W-EXP	A-E
1892(2)	StL-N*	50	16	32	.333	12	11		3/3	17.5	-1.5

Cavarretta, Philip Joseph "Phil"

YEAR	TM/L	G	W	L	PCT	STANDING			M/Y	W-EXP	A-E
1951	Chi-N*	74	27	47	.365	7	8		2/2	30.4	-3.4
1952	Chi-N*	155	77	77	.500	5				76.7	0.3
1953	Chi-N*	155	65	89	.422	7				57.3	7.7
3		384	169	213	.442						4.6

Caylor, Oliver Perry "O.P."

YEAR	TM/L	G	W	L	PCT	STANDING			M/Y	W-EXP	A-E
1885	Cin-a	112	63	49	.563	2				62.1	0.9
1886	Cin-a	141	65	73	.471	5				70.5	-5.5
1887	NY-a	100	35	60	.368	7	7		3/3	27.6	7.4
3		353	163	182	.472						2.7

Chance, Frank Leroy

YEAR	TM/L	G	W	L	PCT	STANDING			M/Y	W-EXP	A-E
1905	Chi-N*	90	55	33	.625	4	3		2/2	58.5	-3.5
1906	Chi-N*	155	116	36	.763	1				112.7	3.3
1907	Chi-N*	155	107	45	.704	★1				98.1	8.9
1908	Chi-N*	158	99	55	.643	★1				95.7	3.3
1909	Chi-N*	155	104	49	.680	2				105.1	-1.1
1910	Chi-N*	154	104	50	.675	1				99.8	4.2
1911	Chi-N*	158	92	62	.597	2				92.3	-0.3
1912	Chi-N*	153	91	59	.607	3				83.6	7.4
1913	NY-A*	153	57	94	.377	7				60.6	-3.6
1914	NY-A*	137	60	74	.448	7	●6		1/2	65.7	-5.7
1923	Bos-A	154	61	91	.401	8				53.6	7.4
11		1622	946	648	.593						20.3

Chapman, John Curtis "Jack"

YEAR	TM/L	G	W	L	PCT	STANDING			M/Y	W-EXP	A-E
1876	Lou-N*	69	30	36	.455	5				26.6	3.4
1877	Lou-N	61	35	25	.583	2				34.8	0.2
1878	Mil-N	61	15	45	.250	6				18.0	-3.0
1882	Wor-N	37	7	30	.189	8	8		3/3	8.2	-1.2
1883	Det-N	101	40	58	.408	7				37.9	2.1
1884	Det-N	114	28	84	.250	8				28.9	-0.9
1885	Buf-N	88	31	57	.352	7	7		2/2	25.3	5.7
1889	Lou-a	7	1	6	.143	8	8		4/4	1.5	-0.5
1890	Lou-a	136	88	44	.667	1				87.5	0.5
1891	Lou-a	141	55	84	.396	7				53.7	1.3
1892(1)	Lou-N	54	21	33	.389	10	11		1/2	21.6	-0.6
11		869	351	502	.411						7.0

Chapman, William Benjamin "Ben"

YEAR	TM/L	G	W	L	PCT	STANDING			M/Y	W-EXP	A-E
1945	Phi-N*	85	28	57	.329	8	8		2/2	25.2	2.8
1946	Phi-N*	155	69	85	.448	5				61.8	7.2
1947	Phi-N	155	62	92	.403	●7				66.8	-4.8
1948	Phi-N	79	37	42	.468	7	6		1/3	32.2	4.8
4		474	196	276	.415						10.1

Chase, Harold Homer "Hal"

YEAR	TM/L	G	W	L	PCT	STANDING			M/Y	W-EXP	A-E
1910	NY-A*	14	10	4	.714	3	2		2/2	7.7	2.3
1911	NY-A*	153	76	76	.500	6				72.0	4.0
2		167	86	80	.518						6.3

Clapp, John Edgar

YEAR	TM/L	G	W	L	PCT	STANDING			M/Y	W-EXP	A-E
1872	Man-n*	24	5	19	.208	8				4.1	0.9
1878	Ind-N*	63	24	36	.400	5				26.7	-2.7
1879	Buf-N*	79	46	32	.590	3				41.8	4.2
1880	Cin-N*	82	21	59	.262	8				22.6	-1.6
1881	Cle-N*	74	32	41	.438	6	7		2/2	34.6	-2.6
1883	NY-N*	98	46	50	.479	6				43.8	2.2
6		420	174	237	.423						0.3

Clarke, Fred Clifford

YEAR	TM/L	G	W	L	PCT	STANDING			M/Y	W-EXP	A-E
1897	Lou-N*	92	35	54	.393	9	11		2/2	32.9	2.1
1898	Lou-N*	154	70	81	.464	9				65.6	4.4
1899	Lou-N*	156	75	77	.493	9				80.9	-5.9
1900	Pit-N*	140	79	60	.568	2				81.2	-2.2
1901	Pit-N*	140	90	49	.647	1				93.2	-3.2
1902	Pit-N*	142	103	36	.741	1				103.9	-0.9
1903	Pit-N*	141	91	49	.650	1				87.1	3.9
1904	Pit-N*	156	87	66	.569	4				85.2	1.8
1905	Pit-N*	155	96	57	.627	2				89.3	6.7

YEAR	TM/L	G	W	L	PCT	STANDING			M/Y	W-EXP	A-E
1906	Pit-N*	154	93	60	.608	3				93.7	-0.7
1907	Pit-N*	157	91	63	.591	2				90.8	0.2
1908	Pit-N*	155	98	56	.636	●2				90.3	7.7
1909	Pit-N*	154	110	42	.724	★1				103.7	6.3
1910	Pit-N*	154	86	67	.562	3				84.9	1.1
1911	Pit-N*	156	85	69	.552	3				96.4	-11.4
1912	Pit-N	153	93	58	.616	2				94.5	-1.5
1913	Pit-N*	155	78	71	.523	4				83.8	-5.8
1914	Pit-N*	158	69	85	.448	7				72.7	-3.7
1915	Pit-N*	157	73	81	.474	5				81.2	-8.2
19		2829	1602	1181	.576						-9.3

Clements, John J. "Jack"

YEAR	TM/L	G	W	L	PCT	STANDING			M/Y	W-EXP	A-E
1890	Phi-N*	19	13	6	.684	1	2	3	2/5	11.0	2.0

Cobb, Tyrus Raymond "Ty"

YEAR	TM/L	G	W	L	PCT	STANDING			M/Y	W-EXP	A-E
1921	Det-A*	154	71	82	.464	6				79.3	-8.3
1922	Det-A*	155	79	75	.513	3				80.4	-1.4
1923	Det-A*	155	83	71	.539	2				85.5	-2.5
1924	Det-A*	156	86	68	.558	3				81.9	4.1
1925	Det-A*	156	81	73	.526	4				83.7	-2.7
1926	Det-A*	157	79	75	.513	6				73.5	5.5
6		933	479	444	.519						-5.3

Cochrane, Gordon Stanley "Mickey"

YEAR	TM/L	G	W	L	PCT	STANDING			M/Y	W-EXP	A-E
1934	Det-A*	154	101	53	.656	1				99.8	1.2
1935	Det-A*	152	93	58	.616	★1				99.1	-6.1
1936	Det-A*	53	29	24	.547	3	2		1/3	28.0	1.0
	Det-A*	67	36	31	.537	4	2		3/3	35.4	0.6
1937	Det-A*	29	16	13	.552	3	2		1/5	16.1	-0.1
	Det-A*	47	26	20	.565	3	2	2	3/5	25.5	0.5
1938	Det-A*	98	47	51	.480	5	4		1/2	52.9	-5.9
5		600	348	250	.582						-8.8

Cohen, Andrew Howard "Andy"

YEAR	TM/L	G	W	L	PCT	STANDING			M/Y	W-EXP	A-E
1960	Phi-N	1	1	0	1.000	●6	●4	8	2/3	0.4	0.6

Coleman, Gerald Francis "Jerry"

YEAR	TM/L	G	W	L	PCT	STANDING			M/Y	W-EXP	A-E
1980	SD-N	163	73	89	.451	6 W				74.2	-1.2

Coleman, Robert Hunter "Bob"

YEAR	TM/L	G	W	L	PCT	STANDING			M/Y	W-EXP	A-E
1943	Bos-N	46	21	25	.457	6	6		1/2	18.0	3.0
1944	Bos-N	155	65	89	.422	6				68.5	-3.5
1945	Bos-N	94	42	51	.452	7	6		1/2	46.1	-4.1
3		295	128	165	.437						-4.6

Collins, Edward Trowbridge Sr. "Eddie"

YEAR	TM/L	G	W	L	PCT	STANDING			M/Y	W-EXP	A-E
1924	Chi-A*	27	14	13	.519	6			3/4	12.4	1.6
1925	Chi-A*	154	79	75	.513	5				80.8	-1.8
1926	Chi-A*	155	81	72	.529	5				83.0	-2.0
3		336	174	160	.521						-2.3

Collins, James Joseph "Jimmy"

YEAR	TM/L	G	W	L	PCT	STANDING			M/Y	W-EXP	A-E
1901	Bos-A*	138	79	57	.581	2				82.4	-3.4
1902	Bos-A*	138	77	60	.562	3				74.8	2.2
1903	Bos-A*	141	91	47	.659	★1				89.9	1.1
1904	Bos-A*	157	95	59	.617	1				93.3	1.7
1905	Bos-A*	153	78	74	.513	4				77.6	0.4
1906	Bos-A*	115	35	79	.307	8	8		1/2	37.3	-2.3
6		842	455	376	.548						-0.4

Collins, John Francis "Shano"

YEAR	TM/L	G	W	L	PCT	STANDING			M/Y	W-EXP	A-E
1931	Bos-A	153	62	90	.408	6				58.8	3.2
1932	Bos-A	55	11	44	.200	8	8		1/2	15.4	-4.4
2		208	73	134	.353						-1.2

Collins, Terry Lee

YEAR	TM/L	G	W	L	PCT	STANDING			M/Y	W-EXP	A-E
1994	Hou-N	115	66	49	.574	2 C				67.1	-1.1
1995	Hou-N	144	76	68	.528	2 C				79.0	-3.0
1996	Hou-N	162	82	80	.506	2 C				77.2	4.8
3		421	224	197	.532						0.7

Comiskey, Charles Albert "Charlie"

YEAR	TM/L	G	W	L	PCT	STANDING			M/Y	W-EXP	A-E
1883	StL-a*	19	12	7	.632	2	2		2/2	12.1	-0.1
1884	StL-a*	25	16	7	.696	5	4		2/2	13.8	2.2
1885	StL-a*	112	79	33	.705	1				76.3	2.7
1886	StL-a*	139	93	46	.669	1				101.3	-8.3
1887	StL-a*	138	95	40	.704	1				97.5	-2.5
1888	StL-a*	137	92	43	.681	1				95.7	-3.7
1889	StL-a*	141	89	46	.659	2				91.9	-1.9
1890	Chi-P*	138	75	62	.547	4				78.5	-3.5
1891	StL-a*	141	86	52	.623	2				88.1	-2.1
1892(1)	Cin-N*	77	44	31	.587	4				78.4	3.6
(2)	Cin-N*	78	38	37	.507	8					
1893	Cin-N*	131	65	63	.508	●6				59.2	5.8
1894	Cin-N*	134	55	75	.423	10				51.5	3.5
12		1410	839	542	.608						-4.3

Connor, Roger

YEAR	TM/L	G	W	L	PCT	STANDING			M/Y	W-EXP	A-E
1896	StL-N*	46	8	37	.178	11	11	11	4/5	12.3	-4.3

Cooke, Allen Lindsey "Dusty"

YEAR	TM/L	G	W	L	PCT	STANDING			M/Y	W-EXP	A-E
1948	Phi-N	13	6	6	.500	7	6	6	2/3	4.9	1.1

Coombs, John Wesley "Jack"

YEAR	TM/L	G	W	L	PCT	STANDING			M/Y	W-EXP	A-E
1919	Phi-N	63	18	44	.290	8	8		1/2	22.3	-4.3

Cooney, John Walter "Johnny"

YEAR	TM/L	G	W	L	PCT	STANDING			M/Y	W-EXP	A-E
1949	Bos-N	46	20	25	.444	4	4		2/2	22.1	-2.1

Corrales, Patrick "Pat"

YEAR	TM/L	G	W	L	PCT	STANDING			M/Y	W-EXP	A-E
1978	Tex-A	1	1	0	1.000	●2 W	●2 W		2/2	0.5	0.5
1979	Tex-A	162	83	79	.512	3 W				86.2	-3.2
1980	Tex-A	163	76	85	.472	4 W				80.9	-4.9
1982	Phi-N	162	89	73	.549	2 E				82.1	6.9
1983	Phi-N	86	43	42	.506	1 E	♦1 E		1/2	45.9	-2.9
	Cle-A	62	30	32	.484	7 E	7 E		2/2	27.9	2.1
1984	Cle-A	163	75	87	.463	6 E				80.5	-5.5
1985	Cle-A	162	60	102	.370	7 E				68.4	-8.4
1986	Cle-A	163	84	78	.519	5 E				80.1	3.9
1987	Cle-A	87	31	56	.356	7 E	7 E		1/2	32.8	-1.8
9		1211	572	634	.474						-13.2

Corriden, John Michael Sr. "Red"

YEAR	TM/L	G	W	L	PCT	STANDING			M/Y	W-EXP	A-E
1950	Chi-A	125	52	72	.419	8	6		2/2	51.9	0.1

Cottier, Charles Keith "Chuck"

YEAR	TM/L	G	W	L	PCT	STANDING			M/Y	W-EXP	A-E
1984	Sea-A	27	15	12	.556	7 W	●5 W		2/2	12.0	3.0
1985	Sea-A	162	74	88	.457	6 W				71.4	2.6
1986	Sea-A	28	9	19	.321	6 W	7 W		1/3	12.0	-3.0
3		217	98	119	.452						2.6

Cox, Robert Joseph "Bobby"

YEAR	TM/L	G	W	L	PCT	STANDING			M/Y	W-EXP	A-E
1978	Atl-N	162	69	93	.426	6 W				65.4	3.6
1979	Atl-N	160	66	94	.412	6 W				70.6	-4.6
1980	Atl-N	161	81	80	.503	4 W				77.3	3.7
1981(1)	Atl-N	55	25	29	.463	4 W					
(2)	Atl-N	52	25	27	.481	5 W				50.7	-0.7
1982	Tor-A	162	78	84	.481	●6 E				75.8	2.2
1983	Tor-A	162	89	73	.549	4 E				87.8	1.2
1984	Tor-A	163	89	73	.549	2 E				86.4	2.6
1985	Tor-A	161	99	62	.615	1 E				98.2	0.8
1990	Atl-N	97	40	57	.412	6 W	6 W		2/2	40.3	-0.3
1991	Atl-N	162	94	68	.580	♦1 W				91.7	2.3
1992	Atl-N	162	98	64	.605	♦1 W				93.2	4.8
1993	Atl-N	162	104	58	.642	1 W				102.8	1.2
1994	Atl-N	114	68	46	.596	2 E				66.6	1.4
1995	Atl-N	144	90	54	.625	★1 E				83.0	7.0
1996	Atl-N	162	96	66	.593	♦1 E				93.7	2.3
15		2241	1211	1028	.541						27.5

Craft, Harry Francis

YEAR	TM/L	G	W	L	PCT	STANDING			M/Y	W-EXP	A-E
1957	KC-A	50	23	27	.460	8	7		2/2	20.0	3.0
1958	KC-A	156	73	81	.474	7				69.8	3.2
1959	KC-A	154	66	88	.429	7				69.3	-3.3
1961	Chi-N	12	4	8	.333	●6	7	7	2/9	5.2	-1.2
	Chi-N	4	3	1	.750	7	7	7	5/9	1.7	1.3
1962	Hou-N	162	64	96	.400	8				66.8	-2.8
1963	Hou-N	162	66	96	.407	9				60.8	5.2
1964	Hou-N	149	61	88	.409	9	9		1/2	60.6	0.4
7		849	360	485	.426						6.0

Craig, Roger Lee

YEAR	TM/L	G	W	L	PCT	STANDING			M/Y	W-EXP	A-E
1978	SD-N	162	84	78	.519	4 W				80.2	3.8
1979	SD-N	161	68	93	.422	5 W				72.2	-4.2
1985	SF-N	18	6	12	.333	6 W	6 W		2/2	7.6	-1.6
1986	SF-N	162	83	79	.512	3 W				89.4	-6.4
1987	SF-N	162	90	72	.556	1 W				92.4	-2.4
1988	SF-N	162	83	79	.512	4 W				85.7	-2.7
1989	SF-N	162	92	70	.568	♦1 W				91.5	0.5
1990	SF-N	162	85	77	.525	3 W				81.9	3.1
1991	SF-N	162	75	87	.463	4 W				76.0	-1.0
1992	SF-N	162	72	90	.444	5 W				73.0	-1.0
10		1475	738	737	.500						-11.9

Crandall, Delmar Wesley "Del"

YEAR	TM/L	G	W	L	PCT	STANDING			M/Y	W-EXP	A-E
1972	Mil-A	124	54	70	.435	6 E	6 E		3/3	52.8	1.2
1973	Mil-A	162	74	88	.457	5 E				78.7	-4.7
1974	Mil-A	162	76	86	.469	5 E				79.6	-3.6
1975	Mil-A	161	67	94	.416	5 E	5 E		1/2	68.9	-1.9
1983	Sea-A	89	34	55	.382	7 W	7 W		2/2	33.9	0.1
1984	Sea-A	135	59	76	.437	7 W	●5 W		1/2	59.8	-0.8
6		833	364	469	.437						-9.7

Crane, Samuel Newhall "Sam"

YEAR	TM/L	G	W	L	PCT	STANDING			M/Y	W-EXP	A-E
1880	Buf-N*	84	24	58	.293	7				24.6	-0.6
1884	Cin-U*	70	49	21	.700	5	3		2/2	49.2	-0.2
2		154	73	79	.480						-0.8

Cravath, Clifford Carlton "Gavvy"

YEAR	TM/L	G	W	L	PCT	STANDING			M/Y	W-EXP	A-E
1919	Phi-N*	75	29	46	.387	8	8		2/2	27.0	2.0
1920	Phi-N*	153	62	91	.405	8				61.0	1.0
2		228	91	137	.399						2.9

Craver, William H. "Bill"

YEAR	TM/L	G	W	L	PCT	STANDING			M/Y	W-EXP	A-E
1871	Tro-n*	25	12	12	.500	7	6		2/2	11.4	0.6
1872	Bal-n*	41	27	13	.675	2	2		1/2	29.6	-2.6
1875	Cen-n*	14	2	12	.143	11				1.7	0.3
1876	NY-N*	57	21	35	.375	6				14.7	6.3
4		137	62	72	.463						4.6

Creamer, George W.

YEAR	TM/L	G	W	L	PCT	STANDING			M/Y	W-EXP	A-E
1884	Pit-a*	8	0	8	.000	10	10	10	4/5	1.8	-1.8

Cronin, Joseph Edward "Joe"

YEAR	TM/L	G	W	L	PCT	STANDING			M/Y	W-EXP	A-E
1933	Was-A*	153	99	53	.651	1				93.6	5.4
1934	Was-A*	155	66	86	.434	7				68.7	-2.7
1935	Bos-A*	154	78	75	.510	4				75.1	2.9
1936	Bos-A*	155	74	80	.481	6				78.0	-0.4
1937	Bos-A*	154	80	72	.526	5				80.3	-0.3
1938	Bos-A*	150	88	61	.591	2				88.1	-0.1

YEAR	TM/L	G	W	L	PCT	STANDING			M/Y	W-EXP	A-E
1939	Bos-A*	152	89	62	.589	2				84.1	4.9
1940	Bos-A*	154	82	72	.532	●4				81.2	0.8
1941	Bos-A*	155	84	70	.545	2				87.7	-3.7
1942	Bos-A*	152	93	59	.612	2				92.8	0.2
1943	Bos-A*	155	68	84	.447	7				71.2	-3.2
1944	Bos-A*	156	77	77	.500	4				83.3	-6.3
1945	Bos-A*	157	71	83	.461	7				69.1	1.9
1946	Bos-A	156	104	50	.675	1				96.9	7.1
1947	Bos-A	157	83	71	.539	3				82.1	0.9
15		2315	1236	1055	.540						3.7

Crooks, John Charles

YEAR	TM/L	G	W	L	PCT	STANDING			M/Y	W-EXP	A-E
1892(1)	StL-N*	47	24	22	.522	11	9		3/3		
(2)	StL-N*	15	3	11	.214	12	11		1/3	21.9	5.1

Cross, Lafayette Napoleon "Lave"

1899	Cle-N*	38	8	30	.211	12	12		1/2	3.3	4.7

Cubbage, Michael Lee "Mike"

1991	NY-N	7	3	4	.429	3 E	5 E		2/2	3.5	-0.5

Curtis, Edwin R. "Ed"

1884	Alt-U	25	6	19	.240	6				1.7	4.3

Cushman, Charles H. "Charlie"

1891	Mil-a	36	21	15	.583	5				24.5	-3.5

Cuthbert, Edgar Edward "Ned"

1882	StL-a*	80	37	43	.463	5				31.3	5.7

Dahlen, William Frederick "Bill"

YEAR	TM/L	G	W	L	PCT	STANDING			M/Y	W-EXP	A-E
1910	Bro-N*	156	64	90	.416	6				62.9	1.1
1911	Bro-N*	154	64	86	.427	7				62.1	1.9
1912	Bro-N	153	58	95	.379	7				66.3	-8.3
1913	Bro-N	152	65	84	.436	6				72.6	-7.6
4		615	251	355	.414						-12.9

Dark, Alvin Ralph

YEAR	TM/L	G	W	L	PCT	STANDING			M/Y	W-EXP	A-E
1961	SF-N	155	85	69	.552	3				88.7	-3.7
1962	SF-N	165	103	62	.624	▲1				100.8	2.2
1963	SF-N	162	88	74	.543	3				89.7	-1.7
1964	SF-N	162	90	72	.556	4				88.5	1.5
1966	KC-A	160	74	86	.463	7				70.8	3.2
1967	KC-A	121	52	69	.430	10	10		1/2	50.0	2.0
1968	Cle-A	162	86	75	.534	3				81.9	4.1
1969	Cle-A	161	62	99	.385	6 E				65.2	-3.2
1970	Cle-A	162	76	86	.469	5 E				78.3	-2.3
1971	Cle-A	103	42	61	.408	6 E	6 E		1/2	37.7	4.3
1974	Oak-A	162	90	72	.556	★1 W				96.0	-6.0
1975	Oak-A	162	98	64	.605	1 W				96.7	1.3
1977	SD-N	113	48	65	.425	4 W	5 W		3/3	46.8	1.2
13		1950	994	954	.510						2.9

Davenport, James Houston "Jim"

1985	SF-N	144	56	88	.389	6 W	6 W		1/2	60.6	-4.6

Davidson, Mordecai H.

YEAR	TM/L	G	W	L	PCT	STANDING			M/Y	W-EXP	A-E
1888	Lou-a	3	1	2	.333	8	8	7	2/4	1.1	-0.1
	Lou-a	90	34	52	.395	8	7		4/4	32.7	1.3

Davis, George Stacey

1895	NY-N*	33	16	17	.485	8	9		1/3	16.9	-0.9
1900	NY-N*	78	39	37	.513	8	8		2/2	32.5	6.5
1901	NY-N*	141	52	85	.380	7				47.6	4.4
3		252	107	139	.435						10.0

Davis, Harry H

1912	Cle-A*	127	54	71	.432	6	5		1/2	62.2	-8.2

Davis, Virgil Lawrence "Spud"

1946	Pit-N	3	1	2	.333	7	7		2/2	1.3	-0.3

Day, John B.

1899	NY-N	66	29	35	.453	9	10		1/2	26.9	2.1

Deane, John Henry "Harry"

1871	Kek-n*	5	2	3	.400	7	8		2/2	0.6	1.4

Dent, Russell Earl "Bucky"

1989	NY-A	40	18	22	.450	6 E	5 E		2/2	17.7	0.3
1990	NY-A	49	18	31	.367	7 E	7 E		1/2	19.9	-1.9
2		89	36	53	.404						-1.6

Dickey, William Malcolm "Bill"

1946	NY-A*	105	57	48	.543	2	3	3	2/3	62.4	-5.4

Diddlebock, Henry H. "Harry"

1896	StL-N	17	7	10	.412	10	11		1/5	4.6	0.3

Doby, Lawrence Eugene "Larry"

1978	Chi-A	87	37	50	.425	5 W	5 W		2/2	38.1	-1.1

Donovan, Patrick Joseph "Patsy"

YEAR	TM/L	G	W	L	PCT	STANDING			M/Y	W-EXP	A-E
1897	Pit-N*	135	60	71	.458	8				51.2	8.8
1899	Pit-N*	131	69	58	.543	10	7		2/2	69.0	0.0
1901	StL-N*	142	76	64	.543	4				79.6	-3.6
1902	StL-N*	140	56	78	.418	6				48.8	7.2
1903	StL-N*	139	43	94	.314	8				40.0	3.0
1904	Was-A*	139	37	97	.276	8	8		2/2	37.3	-0.3
1906	Bro-N*	153	66	86	.434	5				61.7	4.3
1907	Bro-N*	153	65	83	.439	5				64.9	0.1
1908	Bro-N	154	53	101	.344	7				59.7	-6.7
1910	Bos-A	158	81	72	.529	4				84.5	-3.5
1911	Bos-A	153	78	75	.510	5				80.3	-2.3
11		1597	684	879	.438						6.9

Donovan, William Edward "Bill"

YEAR	TM/L	G	W	L	PCT	STANDING			M/Y	W-EXP	A-E
1915	NY-A*	154	69	83	.454	5				75.6	-6.6
1916	NY-A*	156	80	74	.519	4				78.8	1.2
1917	NY-A	155	71	82	.464	6				72.6	-1.6
1921	Phi-N	87	25	62	.287	8	8		1/2	27.3	-2.3
4		552	245	301	.449						-9.3

Dooin, Charles Sebastian "Red"

1910	Phi-N*	157	78	75	.510	4				80.1	-2.1
1911	Phi-N*	153	79	73	.520	4				74.9	4.1
1912	Phi-N*	152	73	79	.480	5				74.2	-1.2
1913	Phi-N*	159	88	63	.583	2				81.4	6.6
1914	Phi-N*	154	74	80	.481	6				73.3	0.7
5		775	392	370	.514						8.0

Dorgan, Michael Cornelius "Mike"

1879	Syr-N*	43	17	26	.395	6	7		1/3	10.9	6.1
1880	Pro-N*	39	26	12	.684	3	2		3/3	24.7	1.3
1881	Wor-N*	56	24	32	.429	7	8		1/2	22.9	1.1
3		138	67	70	.489						8.6

Dowd, Thomas Jefferson "Tom"

1896	StL-N*	63	25	38	.397	11	11		5/5	17.2	7.8
1897	StL-N*	29	6	22	.214	12	12		1/4	5.1	0.9
2		92	31	60	.341						8.8

Doyle, John Joseph "Jack"

YEAR	TM/L	G	W	L	PCT	STANDING			M/Y	W-EXP	A-E
1895	NY-N*	64	32	31	.508	8	9	9	2/3	32.2	-0.2
	Was-										
1898	N*	17	8	9	.471	11	10	11	2/4	6.1	1.9
2		81	40	40	.500						1.7

Dressen, Charles Walter "Chuck"

YEAR	TM/L	G	W	L	PCT	STANDING			M/Y	W-EXP	A-E
1934	Cin-N	60	21	39	.350	8	8		3/3	21.7	-0.7
1935	Cin-N	154	68	85	.444	6				64.0	4.0
1936	Cin-N	154	74	80	.481	5				73.3	0.7
1937	Cin-N	130	51	78	.395	8	8		1/2	56.3	-5.3
1951	Bro-N	158	97	60	.618	▲2				96.2	0.8
1952	Bro-N	155	96	57	.627	1				93.8	2.2
1953	Bro-N	155	105	49	.682	1				101.5	3.5
1955	Was-A	154	53	101	.344	8				57.9	-4.9
1956	Was-A	155	59	95	.383	7				51.4	7.6
1957	Was-A	20	4	16	.200	8	8		1/2	7.4	-3.4
1960	Mil-N	154	88	66	.571	2				83.6	4.4
1961	Mil-N	130	71	58	.550	3	4		1/2	69.2	1.8
1963	Det-A	102	55	47	.539	9	●5		2/2	50.8	4.2
1964	Det-A	163	85	77	.525	4				83.2	1.8
1965	Det-A	120	65	55	.542	3	4		2/2	66.2	-1.2
1966	Det-A	26	16	10	.615	3	3		1/3	13.3	2.7
16		1990	1008	973	.509						18.2

Duffy, Hugh

YEAR	TM/L	G	W	L	PCT	STANDING			M/Y	W-EXP	A-E
1901	Mil-A*	139	48	89	.350	8				51.2	-3.2
1904	Phi-N*	155	52	100	.342	8				54.4	-2.4
1905	Phi-N*	155	83	69	.546	4				86.9	-3.9
1906	Phi-N*	154	71	82	.464	4				72.4	-1.4
1910	Chi-A	156	68	85	.444	6				73.8	-5.8
1911	Chi-A	154	77	74	.510	4				85.2	-8.2
1921	Bos-A	154	75	79	.487	5				74.2	0.8
1922	Bos-A	154	61	93	.396	8				59.8	1.2
8		1221	535	671	.444						-22.9

Dunlap, Frederick C. "Fred"

1882	Cle-N*	80	42	36	.538	8	5		2/2	38.2	3.8
1884	StL-U*	83	66	16	.805	1	1		2/2	70.3	-4.3
1885	StL-N*	50	21	29	.420	5	8		1/3	15.5	5.5
	StL-N*	22	9	11	.450	8	8		3/3	6.2	2.8
1889	Pit-N*	17	7	10	.412	6	7	5	2/3	7.6	-0.6
4		252	145	102	.587						7.1

Durocher, Leo Ernest

YEAR	TM/L	G	W	L	PCT	STANDING			M/Y	W-EXP	A-E
1939	Bro-N*	157	84	69	.549	3				82.9	1.1
1940	Bro-N*	156	88	65	.575	2				84.3	3.7
1941	Bro-N*	157	100	54	.649	1				99.2	0.8
1942	Bro-N	155	104	50	.675	2				101.5	2.5
1943	Bro-N	153	81	72	.529	3				80.7	0.3
1944	Bro-N	155	63	91	.409	7				63.4	-0.4
1945	Bro-N*	155	87	67	.565	3				83.8	3.2
1946	Bro-N	157	96	60	.615	▲2				91.8	4.2
1948	Bro-N	73	35	37	.486	5	3		1/3	39.6	-4.6
	NY-N	79	41	38	.519	4	5		2/2	43.3	-2.3
1949	NY-N	156	73	81	.474	5				81.3	-8.3
1950	NY-N	154	86	68	.558	3				86.2	-0.2
1951	NY-N	157	98	59	.624	▲1				92.5	5.5
1952	NY-N	154	92	62	.597	2				85.4	6.6
1953	NY-N	155	70	84	.455	5				79.0	-9.0
1954	NY-N	154	97	57	.630	★1				95.9	1.1
1955	NY-N	154	80	74	.519	3				79.9	0.1
1966	Chi-N	162	59	103	.364	10				64.5	-5.5
1967	Chi-N	162	87	74	.540	3				88.7	-1.7
1968	Chi-N	163	84	78	.519	3				81.1	2.9
1969	Chi-N	163	92	70	.568	2 E				92.4	-0.4
1970	Chi-N	162	84	78	.519	2 E				93.6	-9.6
1971	Chi-N	162	83	79	.512	●3 E				79.8	3.2
1972	Chi-N	91	46	44	.511	4 E	2 E		1/2	52.3	-6.3
	Hou-N	31	16	15	.516	2 W	2 W		3/3	17.0	-1.0
1973	Hou-N	162	82	80	.506	4 W				81.9	0.1
24		3739	2008	1709	.540						-14.0

YEAR	TM/L	G	W	L	PCT	STANDING			M/Y	W-EXP	A-E
Dwyer, John Francis "Frank"											
1902	Det-A	137	52	83	.385	7				58.4	-6.4
Dyer, Edwin Hawley "Eddie"											
1946	StL-N	156	98	58	.628	▲★1				95.7	2.3
1947	StL-N	156	89	65	.578	2				91.5	-2.5
1948	StL-N	155	85	69	.552	2				86.6	-1.6
1949	StL-N	157	96	58	.623	2				92.2	3.8
1950	StL-N	153	78	75	.510	5				78.8	-0.8
5		777	446	325	.578						1.2
Dykes, James Joseph "Jimmy"											
1934	Chi-A*	138	49	88	.358	8	8		2/2	48.6	0.4
1935	Chi-A*	153	74	78	.487	5				74.8	-0.8
1936	Chi-A*	153	81	70	.536	3				79.6	1.4
1937	Chi-A*	154	86	68	.558	3				81.8	4.2
1938	Chi-A*	149	65	83	.439	6				69.9	-4.9
1939	Chi-A*	155	85	69	.552	4				78.7	6.3
1940	Chi-A	155	82	72	.532	●4				83.3	-1.3
1941	Chi-A	156	77	77	.500	3				75.9	1.1
1942	Chi-A	148	66	82	.446	6				66.3	-0.3
1943	Chi-A	155	82	72	.532	4				74.7	7.3
1944	Chi-A	154	71	83	.461	7				64.2	6.8
1945	Chi-A	150	71	78	.477	6				70.6	0.4
1946	Chi-A	30	10	20	.333	7	5		1/2	14.3	-4.3
1951	Phi-A	154	70	84	.455	6				76.1	-6.1
1952	Phi-A	155	79	75	.513	4				71.1	7.9
1953	Phi-A	157	59	95	.383	7				60.4	-1.4
1954	Bal-A	154	54	100	.351	7				56.7	-2.7
1958	Cin-N	41	24	17	.585	8	4		2/2	22.5	1.5
1959	Det-A	137	74	63	.540	8	4		2/2	66.8	7.2
1960	Det-A	96	44	52	.458	6	6		1/3	47.3	-3.3
	Cle-A	58	26	32	.448	4	4		3/3	28.0	-2.0
1961	Cle-A	160	77	83	.481	5	5		1/2	78.5	-1.5
21		2962	1406	1541	.477						15.7
Ebbets, Charles Hercules "Charlie"											
1898	Bro-N	110	38	68	.358	9	10		3/3	40.8	-2.8
Edwards, Howard Rodney "Doc"											
1987	Cle-A	75	30	45	.400	7 E	7 E		2/2	28.3	1.7
1988	Cle-A	162	78	84	.481	6 E				74.4	3.6
1989	Cle-A	143	65	78	.455	6 E	6 E		1/2	66.7	-1.7
3		380	173	207	.455						3.6
Elberfeld, Norman Arthur "Kid"											
1908	NY-A*	98	27	71	.276	6	8		2/2	31.4	-4.4
Elia, Lee Constantine											
1982	Chi-N	162	73	89	.451	5 E				77.6	-4.6
1983	Chi-N	123	54	69	.439	5 E	5 E		1/2	60.1	-6.1
1987	Phi-N	101	51	50	.505	5 E	●4 E		2/2	47.6	3.4
1988	Phi-N	153	60	92	.395	6 E	6 E		1/2	62.5	-2.5
4		539	238	300	.442						-9.8
Ellick, Joseph J. "Joe"											
1884	Pit-U*	13	6	6	.500	5	5		2/2	5.4	0.6
Elliott, Robert Irving "Bob"											
1960	KC-A	155	58	96	.377	8				62.8	-4.8
Ens, Jewel Winklemeyer											
1929	Pit-N	35	21	14	.600	2	2		2/2	20.1	0.9
1930	Pit-N	154	80	74	.519	5				73.8	6.2
1931	Pit-N	155	75	79	.487	5				71.4	3.6
3		344	176	167	.513						10.8
Ermer, Calvin Coolidge "Cal"											
1967	Min-A	114	66	46	.589	6	●2		2/2	62.1	3.9
1968	Min-A	162	79	83	.488	7				82.8	-3.8
2		276	145	129	.529						0.1
Essian, James Sarkis "Jim"											
1991	Chi-N	122	59	63	.484	5 E	4 E		3/3	58.0	1.0
Esterbrook, Thomas Jefferson "Dude"											
1889	Lou-a*	10	2	8	.200	7	8		1/4	2.2	-0.2
Evers, John Joseph "Johnny"											
1913	Chi-N*	155	88	65	.575	3				85.6	2.4
1921	Chi-N	96	41	55	.427	6	7		1/2	41.6	-0.6
1924	Chi-A	21	10	11	.476	6			1/4	9.7	0.3
	Chi-A	103	41	61	.402	8			4/4	47.0	-6.0
3		375	180	192	.484						-3.9
Ewing, William "Buck"											
1890	NY-P*	132	74	57	.565	3				76.8	-2.8
1895	Cin-N*	132	66	64	.508	8				69.0	-3.0
1896	Cin-N*	128	77	50	.606	3				78.3	-1.3
1897	Cin-N*	134	76	56	.576	4				71.3	4.7
1898	Cin-N	157	92	60	.605	3				84.6	7.4
1899	Cin-N	157	83	67	.553	6				83.0	0.0
1900	NY-N	63	21	41	.339	8	8		1/2	26.5	-5.5
7		903	489	395	.553						-0.5
Faatz, Jayson S. "Jay"											
1890	Buf-P*	34	9	24	.273	8	8	8	2/3	8.6	0.4
Falk, Bibb August											
1933	Cle-A	1	1	0	1.000		5	5	4	2/3	0.5	0.5
Fanning, William James "Jim"											
1981(2)	Mon-N	27	16	11	.593	2 E	>1 E		2/2	14.8	1.2
1982	Mon-N	162	86	76	.531	3 E				89.5	-3.5
1984	Mon-N	30	14	16	.467	5 E	5 E		2/2	15.2	-1.2
3		219	116	103	.530						-3.5
Farrell, John A. "Jack"											
1881	Pro-N*	51	24	27	.471	4	2		1/2	26.7	-2.7
Farrell, Major Kerby "Kerby"											
1957	Cle-A	153	76	77	.497	6				72.5	3.5
Felske, John Frederick											
1985	Phi-N	162	75	87	.463	5 E				80.4	-5.4
1986	Phi-N	161	86	75	.534	2 E				83.1	2.9
1987	Phi-N	61	29	32	.475	5 E	●4 E		1/2	28.7	0.3
3		384	190	194	.495						-2.2
Ferguson, Robert V. "Bob"											
1871	Mut-n*	33	16	17	.485	4				15.7	0.3
1872	Atl-n*	37	9	28	.243	6				2.3	6.7
1873	Atl-n*	55	17	37	.315	6				13.5	3.5
1874	Atl-n*	56	22	33	.400	6				15.3	6.7
1875	Har-n*	86	54	28	.659	3				60.8	-6.8
1876	Har-N*	69	47	21	.691	3				49.9	-2.9
1877	Har-N*	60	31	27	.534	3				31.7	-0.7
1878	Chi-N*	61	30	30	.500	4				33.5	-3.5
1879	Tro-N*	30	7	22	.241	8	8		2/2	6.8	0.2
1880	Tro-N*	83	41	42	.494	4				37.1	3.9
1881	Tro-N*	85	39	45	.464	5				39.1	-0.1
1882	Tro-N*	85	35	48	.422	7				33.3	1.7
1883	Phi-N*	17	4	13	.235	8	8		1/2	2.1	1.9
1884	Pit-a*	42	11	31	.262	9	11	10	2/5	9.4	1.6
1886	NY-a	120	48	70	.407	8	7		2/2	47.7	0.3
1887	NY-a	30	6	24	.200	8	7		1/3	8.7	-2.7
16		949	417	516	.447						9.9
Ferraro, Michael Dennis "Mike"											
1983	Cle-A	100	40	60	.400	7 E	7 E		1/2	45.1	-5.1
1986	KC-A	74	36	38	.486	4 W	●3 W		2/2	36.1	-0.1
2		174	76	98	.437						-5.1
Fessenden, Wallace Clifton											
1890	Syr-a	11	4	7	.364	7	7	6	2/3	4.5	-0.5
Fitzsimmons, Frederick Landis "Freddie"											
1943	Phi-N	65	26	38	.406	7	7		2/2	27.4	-1.4
1944	Phi-N	154	61	92	.399	8				63.7	-2.7
1945	Phi-N	69	18	51	.261	8	8		1/2	20.4	-2.4
3		288	105	181	.367						-6.5
Fletcher, Arthur "Art"											
1923	Phi-N	155	50	104	.325	8				53.8	-3.8
1924	Phi-N	152	55	96	.364	7				59.1	-4.1
1925	Phi-N	153	68	85	.444	●6				66.0	2.0
1926	Phi-N	152	58	93	.384	8				55.7	2.3
1929	NY-A	11	6	5	.545	2	2		2/2	6.3	-0.3
5		623	237	383	.382						-4.0
Flint, Frank Sylvester "Silver"											
1879	Chi-N*	19	5	12	.294	2	4		2/2	9.0	-4.0
Fogarty, James G. "Jim"											
1890	Phi-P*	16	7	9	.438	5	5		1/2	8.9	-1.9
Fogel, Horace S.											
1887	Ind-N	70	20	49	.290	8	8		3/3	18.9	1.1
1902	NY-N	44	18	23	.439	4	8		1/3	14.1	3.9
2		114	38	72	.345						5.0
Fohl, Leo Alexander "Lee"											
1915	Cle-A	127	45	79	.363	6	7		2/2	50.6	-5.6
1916	Cle-A	157	77	77	.500	6				80.0	-3.0
1917	Cle-A	156	88	66	.571	3				81.6	6.4
1918	Cle-A	129	73	54	.575	2				69.8	3.2
1919	Cle-A	78	44	34	.564	3	2		1/2	44.7	-0.7
1921	StL-A	154	81	73	.526	3				76.1	4.9
1922	StL-A	154	93	61	.604	2				98.5	-5.5
1923	StL-A	103	52	49	.515	3	5		1/2	48.4	3.6
1924	Bos-A	157	67	87	.435	7				70.4	-3.4
1925	Bos-A	152	47	105	.309	8				49.5	-2.5
1926	Bos-A	154	46	107	.301	8				49.3	-3.3
11		1521	713	792	.474						-5.8
Fonseca, Lewis Albert "Lew"											
1932	Chi-A*	152	49	102	.325	7				54.0	-5.0
1933	Chi-A*	151	67	83	.447	6				62.5	4.5
1934	Chi-A	15	4	11	.267	8	8		1/2	5.3	-1.3
3		318	120	196	.380						-1.8
Foutz, David Luther "Dave"											
1893	Bro-N*	130	65	63	.508	●6				58.1	6.9
1894	Bro-N*	135	70	61	.534	5				66.6	3.4
1895	Bro-N*	134	71	60	.542	●5				68.3	2.7
1896	Bro-N*	133	58	73	.443	●9				59.0	-1.0
4		532	264	257	.507						12.1
Fox, Charles Francis "Charlie"											
1970	SF-N	120	67	53	.558	4 W	3 W		2/2	60.3	6.7
1971	SF-N	162	90	72	.556	1 W				87.4	2.6
1972	SF-N	155	69	86	.445	5 W				78.8	-9.8
1973	SF-N	162	88	74	.543	3 W				84.7	3.3
1974	SF-N	76	34	42	.447	5 W	5 W		1/2	33.7	0.3
1976	Mon-N	34	12	22	.353	6 E	6 E		2/2	12.4	-0.4

YEAR	TM/L	G	W	L	PCT	STANDING			M/Y	W-EXP	A-E
1983	Chi-N	39	17	22	.436	5 E	5 E		2/2	19.1	-2.1
	7	748	377	371	.504						0.5
Franks, Herman Louis											
1965	SF-N	163	95	67	.586	2				90.5	4.5
1966	SF-N	161	93	68	.578	2				85.7	7.3
1967	SF-N	162	91	71	.562	2				92.1	-1.1
1968	SF-N	163	88	74	.543	2				89.0	-1.0
1977	Chi-N	162	81	81	.500	4 E				76.3	4.7
1978	Chi-N	162	79	83	.488	3 E				74.8	4.2
1979	Chi-N	155	78	77	.503	5 E	5 E		1/2	77.4	0.6
	7	1128	605	521	.537						19.2
Frazer, George Kasson											
1890	Syr-a	71	31	40	.437	7	6		1/3	29.0	2.0
	Syr-a	46	20	25	.444	7	6		3/3	18.4	1.6
Frazier, Joseph Filmore "Joe"											
1976	NY-N	162	86	76	.531	3 E				89.7	-3.7
1977	NY-N	45	15	30	.333	6 E	6 E		1/2	20.2	-5.2
	2	207	101	106	.488						-8.9
Fregosi, James Louis "Jim"											
1978	Cal-A	117	62	55	.530	3 W	●2 W		2/2	60.4	1.6
1979	Cal-A	162	88	74	.543	1 W				90.3	-2.3
1980	Cal-A	160	65	95	.406	6 W				70.3	-5.3
1981(1)	Cal-A	47	22	25	.468	4 W	4 W		1/2	24.5	-2.5
1986	Chi-A	96	45	51	.469	5 W	5 W		3/3	44.6	0.4
1987	Chi-A	162	77	85	.475	5 W				81.2	-4.2
1988	Chi-A	161	71	90	.441	5 W				67.6	3.4
1991	Phi-N	149	74	75	.497	6 E	3 E		2/2	69.5	4.5
1992	Phi-N	162	70	92	.432	6 E				77.8	-7.8
1993	Phi-N	162	97	65	.599	◆1 E				94.0	3.0
1994	Phi-N	115	54	61	.470	4 E				59.9	-5.9
1995	Phi-N	144	69	75	.479	●2 E				67.7	1.3
1996	Phi-N	162	67	95	.414	5 E				66.9	0.1
	13	1799	861	938	.479						-13.7
Frey, James Gottfried "Jim"											
1980	KC-A	162	97	65	.599	◆1 W				92.3	4.7
1981(1)	KC-A	50	20	30	.400	5 W					
(2)	KC-A	20	10	10	.500	○2 W	1 W		1/2	34.4	-4.4
1984	Chi-N	161	96	65	.596	1 E				91.0	5.0
1985	Chi-N	162	77	84	.478	4 E				76.1	0.9
1986	Chi-N	56	23	33	.411	5 E	5 E		1/3	24.5	-1.5
	5	611	323	287	.530						4.6
Frisch, Frank Francis "Frankie"											
1933	StL-N*	63	36	26	.581	5	5		2/2	34.3	1.7
1934	StL-N*	154	95	58	.621	★1				90.5	4.5
1935	StL-N*	154	96	58	.623	2				96.9	-0.9
1936	StL-N*	155	87	67	.565	●2				77.1	9.9
1937	StL-N*	157	81	73	.526	4				82.4	-1.4
1938	StL-N*	139	63	72	.467	6	6		1/2	67.9	-4.9
1940	Pit-N	156	78	76	.506	4				79.4	-1.4
1941	Pit-N	156	81	73	.526	4				81.8	-0.8
1942	Pit-N	151	66	81	.449	5				68.6	-2.6
1943	Pit-N	157	80	74	.519	4				83.7	-3.7
1944	Pit-N	158	90	63	.588	2				84.7	5.3
1945	Pit-N	155	82	72	.532	4				83.6	-1.6
1946	Pit-N	152	62	89	.411	7	7		1/2	63.3	-1.3
1949	Chi-N	104	42	62	.404	7	8		2/2	39.8	2.2
1950	Chi-N	154	64	89	.418	7				63.7	0.3
1951	Chi-N	81	35	45	.438	7			1/2	32.9	2.1
	16	2246	1138	1078	.514						7.3
Fuchs, Emil Edmund "Judge"											
1929	Bos-N	154	56	98	.364	8				56.2	-0.2
Gaffney, John H.											
1886	Was-N	43	15	25	.375	8			2/2	9.0	6.0
1887	Was-N	126	46	76	.377	7				41.6	4.4
	2	169	61	101	.377						10.4
Galvin, James Francis "Jim"											
1885	Buf-N*	24	7	17	.292	7	7		1/2	6.9	0.1
Ganzel, John Henry											
1908	Cin-N*	155	73	81	.474	5				70.6	2.4
1915	Bro-F	35	17	18	.486	7	7		2/2	16.9	0.1
	2	190	90	99	.476						2.5
Garcia, David "Dave"											
1977	Cal-A	81	35	46	.432	5 W	5 W		2/2	39.5	-4.5
1978	Cal-A	45	25	20	.556	3 W	●2 W		1/2	23.2	1.8
1979	Cle-A	66	38	28	.576	6 E	6 E		2/2	31.2	6.8
1980	Cle-A	160	79	81	.494	6 E				73.3	5.7
1981(1)	Cle-A	50	26	24	.520	6 E					
(2)	Cle-A	53	26	27	.491	5 E				50.4	1.6
1982	Cle-A	162	78	84	.481	●6 E				74.3	3.6
	6	617	307	310	.498						14.9
Gardner, William Frederick "Billy"											
1981(1)	Min-A	20	6	14	.300	6 W	7 W		2/2		
(2)	Min-A	53	24	29	.453	4 W				28.8	1.2
1982	Min-A	162	60	102	.370	7 W				64.9	-4.9
1983	Min-A	162	70	92	.432	5 W				70.0	0.0
1984	Min-A	162	81	81	.500	2 W				80.8	0.2
1985	Min-A	62	27	35	.435	6 W	4 W		1/2	28.1	-1.1
1987	KC-A	126	62	64	.492	4 W	2 W		1/2	64.9	-2.9
	6	747	330	417	.442						-7.4
Garner, Philip Mason "Phil"											
1992	Mil-A	162	92	70	.568	2 E				95.2	-3.2
1993	Mil-A	162	69	93	.426	7 E				75.2	-6.2
1994	Mil-A	115	53	62	.461	5 C				53.8	-0.8
1995	Mil-A	144	65	79	.451	4 C				71.3	-6.3
1996	Mil-A	162	80	82	.494	3 C				80.5	-0.5
	5	745	359	386	.482						-17.1
Gaston, Clarence Edwin "Cito"											
1989	Tor-A	126	77	49	.611	6 E	1 E		2/2	69.4	7.6
1990	Tor-A	162	86	76	.531	2 E				91.7	-5.7
1991	Tor-A	120	66	54	.550	1 E	1 E		1/3	64.9	1.1
	Tor-A	9	6	3	.667	1 E	1 E		3/3	4.9	1.1
1992	Tor-A	162	96	66	.593	★1 E				90.8	5.2
1993	Tor-A	162	95	67	.586	★1 E				91.1	3.9
1994	Tor-A	115	55	60	.478	3 E				56.3	-1.3
1995	Tor-A	144	56	68	.452	5 E				59.1	-3.1
1996	Tor-A	162	74	88	.457	4 E				76.9	-2.9
	8	1162	611	531	.535						6.1
Gerhardt, John Joseph "Joe"											
1883	Lou-a*	98	52	45	.536	5				48.7	3.3
1890	StL-a*	38	20	16	.556	2	3		6/6	21.1	-1.1
	2	136	72	61	.541						2.2
Gessler, Harry Homer "Doc"											
1914	Pit-F	11	3	8	.273	8	7		1/2	4.8	-1.8
Gibson, George C. "Moon"											
1920	Pit-N	155	79	75	.513	4				74.5	4.5
1921	Pit-N	154	90	63	.588	2				86.6	3.4
1922	Pit-N	65	32	33	.492	5	●3		1/2	37.6	-5.6
1925	Chi-N	26	12	14	.462	7	8		3/3	12.2	-0.2
1932	Pit-N	154	86	68	.558	2				76.0	10.0
1933	Pit-N	154	87	67	.565	2				82.0	5.0
1934	Pit-N	51	27	24	.529	4	5		1/2	26.2	0.8
	7	759	413	344	.546						17.9
Gifford, James H. "Jim"											
1884	Ind-a	87	25	60	.294	10	11		1/2	21.5	3.5
1885	NY-a	108	44	64	.407	7				39.5	4.5
1886	NY-a	17	5	12	.294	8	7		1/2	6.9	-1.9
	3	212	74	136	.352						6.1
Glasscock, John Wesley "Jack"											
1889	Ind-N*	67	34	32	.515	7	7		2/2	29.9	4.1
1892(1)	StL-N*	4	1	3	.250	10	9		1/3	1.5	-0.5
	2	71	35	35	.500						3.6
Gleason, William J. "Kid"											
1919	Chi-A	140	88	52	.629	1				83.6	4.4
1920	Chi-A	154	96	58	.623	2				89.6	6.4
1921	Chi-A	154	62	92	.403	7				60.4	1.6
1922	Chi-A	155	77	77	.500	5				77.0	0.0
1923	Chi-A	156	69	85	.448	7				72.1	-3.1
	5	759	392	364	.519						9.3
Gomez, Pedro W. [Martinez] "Preston"											
1969	SD-N	162	52	110	.321	6 W				50.5	1.5
1970	SD-N	162	63	99	.389	6 W				70.3	-7.3
1971	SD-N	161	61	100	.379	6 W				66.2	-5.2
1972	SD-N	11	4	7	.364	4 W	6 W		1/2	4.1	-0.1
1974	Hou-N	162	81	81	.500	4 W				83.2	-2.2
1975	Hou-N	127	47	80	.370	6 W	6 W		1/2	59.7	-12.7
1980	Chi-N	90	38	52	.422	6 E	6 E		1/2	38.4	-0.4
	7	875	346	529	.395						-26.5
Gonzalez, Miguel Angel "Mike"											
1938	StL-N	17	8	8	.500	6	6		2/2	8.0	-0.0
1940	StL-N	6	1	5	.167	6	7	3	2/3	3.2	-2.2
	2	23	9	13	.409						-2.2
Gordon, Joseph Lowell "Joe"											
1958	Cle-A	86	46	40	.535	6	4		2/2	46.4	-0.4
1959	Cle-A	154	89	65	.578	2				86.9	2.1
1960	Cle-A	95	49	46	.516	4	4		1/3	45.9	3.1
	Det-A	57	26	31	.456	6	6		3/3	28.1	-2.1
1961	KC-A	60	26	33	.441	8	●9		1/2	23.1	2.9
1969	KC-A	163	69	93	.426	4 W				70.1	-1.1
	5	615	305	308	.498						4.6
Gore, George F.											
1892(2)	StL-N*	16	6	9	.400	12	12	11	2/3	5.5	0.5
Goryl, John Albert "Johnny"											
1980	Min-A	36	23	13	.639	4 W	3 W		2/2	16.8	6.2
1981(1)	Min-A	37	11	25	.306	6 W	7 W		1/2	14.2	-3.2
	2	73	34	38	.472						3.0
Gould, Charles Harvey "Charlie"											
1875	NH-n*	23	2	21	.087	11			1/3	1.9	0.1
1876	Cin-N*	65	9	56	.138	8				3.6	5.4
	2	88	11	77	.125						5.5
Gowdy, Henry Morgan "Hank"											
1946	Cin-N	4	3	1	.750	6	6		2/2	1.9	1.1
Graffen, Samuel Mason "Mase"											
1876	StL-N	56	39	17	.696	2	2		1/2	41.3	-2.3

YEAR	TM/L	G	W	L	PCT	STANDING			M/Y	W-EXP	A-E
Grammas, Alexander Peter "Alex"											
1969	Pit-N	5	4	1	.800	3 E	3 E		2/2	2.7	1.3
1976	Mil-A	161	66	95	.410	6 E				71.3	-5.3
1977	Mil-A	162	67	95	.414	6 E				68.2	-1.2
	3	328	137	191	.418						-5.1
Green, George Dallas "Dallas"											
1979	Phi-N	30	19	11	.633	5 E	4 E		2/2	14.3	4.7
1980	Phi-N	162	91	71	.562	★1 E				90.2	0.8
1981(1)	Phi-N	55	34	21	.618	○1 E					
(2)	Phi-N	52	25	27	.481	3 E				55.4	3.6
1989	NY-A	121	56	65	.463	6 E	5 E		1/2	53.5	2.5
1993	NY-N	124	46	78	.371	7 E	7 E		2/2	56.4	-10.4
1994	NY-N	113	55	58	.487	3 E				54.5	0.5
1995	NY-N	144	69	75	.479	●2 E				75.9	-6.9
1996	NY-N	131	59	72	.450	4 E	4 E		1/2	62.9	-3.9
	8	932	454	478	.487						-9.2
Griffin, Michael Joseph "Mike"											
1898	Bro-N*	4	1	3	.250	9	9	10	2/3	1.5	-0.5
Griffin, Tobias Charles "Sandy"											
1891	Was-a*	6	2	4	.333	8	8		4/4	1.6	0.4
Griffith, Clark Calvin											
1901	Chi-A*	137	83	53	.610	1				85.3	-2.3
1902	Chi-A*	138	74	60	.552	4				74.2	-0.2
1903	NY-A*	136	72	62	.537	4				67.6	4.4
1904	NY-A*	155	92	59	.609	2				83.5	8.5
1905	NY-A*	152	71	78	.477	6				70.7	0.3
1906	NY-A*	155	90	61	.596	2				86.5	3.5
1907	NY-A*	152	70	78	.473	5				67.8	2.2
1908	NY-A	57	24	32	.429	6	8		1/2	17.9	6.1
1909	Cin-N*	157	77	76	.503	4				77.3	-0.3
1910	Cin-N*	156	75	79	.487	5				70.4	4.6
1911	Cin-N	159	70	83	.458	6				74.1	-4.1
1912	Was-A*	154	91	61	.599	2				88.3	2.7
1913	Was-A*	155	90	64	.584	2				80.8	9.2
1914	Was-A*	158	81	73	.526	3				83.1	-2.1
1915	Was-A	156	85	68	.556	4				85.4	-0.4
1916	Was-A	159	76	77	.497	7				75.7	0.3
1917	Was-A	158	74	79	.484	5				73.9	0.1
1918	Was-A	130	72	56	.563	3				69.7	2.3
1919	Was-A	142	56	84	.400	7				66.0	-10.0
1920	Was-A	153	68	84	.447	6				68.5	-0.5
	20	2918	1491	1367	.522						24.4
Grimes, Burleigh Arland											
1937	Bro-N	155	62	91	.405	6				60.9	1.1
1938	Bro-N	151	69	80	.463	7				73.9	-4.9
	2	306	131	171	.434						-3.8
Grimm, Charles John "Charlie"											
1932	Chi-N*	55	37	18	.673	2	1		2/2	30.6	6.4
1933	Chi-N*	154	86	68	.558	3				88.9	-2.9
1934	Chi-N*	152	86	65	.570	3				82.2	3.8
1935	Chi-N*	154	100	54	.649	1				101.5	-1.5
1936	Chi-N*	154	87	67	.565	●2				92.4	-5.4
1937	Chi-N	154	93	61	.604	2				89.4	3.6
1938	Chi-N	81	45	36	.556	3	1		1/2	46.8	-1.8
1944	Chi-N	146	74	69	.517	8	4		3/3	74.6	-0.6
1945	Chi-N	155	98	56	.636	1				98.3	-0.3
1946	Chi-N	155	82	71	.536	3				81.3	0.7
1947	Chi-N	155	69	85	.448	6				60.9	8.1
1948	Chi-N	155	64	90	.416	8				65.7	-1.7
1949	Chi-N	50	19	31	.380	7	8		1/2	19.1	-0.1
1952	Bos-N	120	51	67	.432	7	7		2/2	52.2	-1.2
1953	Mil-N	157	92	62	.597	2				92.4	-0.4
1954	Mil-N	154	89	65	.578	3				89.1	-0.1
1955	Mil-N	154	85	69	.552	2				84.4	0.6
1956	Mil-N	46	24	22	.522	5	2		1/2	27.4	-3.4
1960	Chi-N	17	6	11	.353	7	7		1/2	6.9	-0.9
	19	2368	1287	1067	.547						2.8
Groh, Henry Knight "Heinie"											
1918	Cin-N*	10	7	3	.700	4	3		2/2	5.3	1.7
Gutteridge, Donald Joseph "Don"											
1969	Chi-A	145	60	85	.414	4 W	5 W		2/2	63.4	-3.4
1970	Chi-A	136	49	87	.360	6 W	6 W		1/3	52.1	-3.1
	2	281	109	172	.388						-6.5
Haas, George Edwin "Eddie"											
1985	Atl-N	121	50	71	.413	5 W	5 W		1/2	49.2	0.8
Hack, Stanley Camfield "Stan"											
1954	Chi-N	154	64	90	.416	7				70.6	-6.6
1955	Chi-N	154	72	81	.471	6				67.6	4.4
1956	Chi-N	157	60	94	.390	8				65.4	-5.4
1958	StL-N	10	3	7	.300	5	●5		2/2	4.4	-1.4
	4	475	199	272	.423						-9.1
Hackett, Charles M. "Charlie"											
1884	Cle-N	113	35	77	.313	7				32.0	3.0
1885	Bro-a	37	15	22	.405	7	●5		1/2	17.7	-2.7
	2	150	50	99	.336						0.3
Hallman, William Wilson "Bill"											
1897	StL-N*	50	13	36	.265	12	12	12	3/4	8.9	4.1
Haney, Fred Girard											
1939	StL-A	156	43	111	.279	8				50.1	-7.1
1940	StL-A	156	67	87	.435	6				65.4	1.6
1941	StL-A	44	15	29	.341	7	●6		1/2	20.4	-5.4
1953	Pit-N	154	50	104	.325	8				51.6	-1.6
1954	Pit-N	154	53	101	.344	8				48.4	4.6
1955	Pit-N	154	60	94	.390	8				55.8	4.2
1956	Mil-N	109	68	40	.630	5	2		2/2	64.3	3.7
1957	Mil-N	155	95	59	.617	★1				93.0	2.0
1958	Mil-N	154	92	62	.597	1				91.3	0.7
1959	Mil-N	157	86	70	.551	▲2				88.3	-2.3
	10	1393	629	757	.454						0.4
Hanlon, Edward Hugh "Ned"											
1889	Pit-N*	46	26	18	.591	7	5		3/3	19.8	6.2
1890	Pit-P*	131	60	68	.469	6				59.3	0.7
1891	Pit-N*	78	31	47	.397	8	8		1/2	35.5	-4.5
1892(1)	Bal-N*	56	17	39	.304	12	12		3/3	45.7	-2.7
(2)	Bal-N*	77	26	46	.361	10				45.9	1.0
1893	Bal-N	130	60	70	.462	8				59.0	1.0
1894	Bal-N	129	89	39	.695	1				90.9	-1.9
1895	Bal-N	132	87	43	.669	1				95.8	-8.8
1896	Bal-N	132	90	39	.698	1				92.7	-2.7
1897	Bal-N	136	90	40	.692	2				90.1	-0.1
1898	Bal-N	154	96	53	.644	2				103.8	-7.8
1899	Bro-N	150	101	47	.682	1				95.8	5.2
1900	Bro-N	142	82	54	.603	1				76.6	5.4
1901	Bro-N	137	79	57	.581	3				81.8	-2.8
1902	Bro-N	141	75	63	.543	2				73.9	1.1
1903	Bro-N	139	70	66	.515	5				66.6	3.4
1904	Bro-N	154	56	97	.366	6				63.4	-7.4
1905	Bro-N	155	48	104	.316	8				45.0	3.0
1906	Cin-N	155	64	87	.424	6				70.0	-6.0
1907	Cin-N	156	66	87	.431	6				77.3	-11.3
	19	2530	1313	1164	.530						-29.8
Harder, Melvin Leroy "Mel"											
1961	Cle-A	1	1	0	1.000	5	5		2/2	0.5	0.5
1962	Cle-A	2	2	0	1.000	6	6		2/2	0.9	1.1
	2	3	3	0	1.000						1.6
Hargrove, Dudley Michael "Mike"											
1991	Cle-A	85	32	53	.376	7 E	7 E		2/2	32.5	-0.5
1992	Cle-A	162	76	86	.469	●4 E				73.7	2.3
1993	Cle-A	162	76	86	.469	6 E				78.8	-2.8
1994	Cle-A	113	66	47	.584	2 C				67.1	-1.1
1995	Cle-A	144	100	44	.694	◆1 C				94.1	5.9
1996	Cle-A	161	99	62	.615	○1 C				97.3	1.7
	6	827	449	378	.543						5.6
Harrah, Colbert Dale "Toby"											
1992	Tex-A	76	32	44	.421	3 W	4 W		2/2	34.6	-2.6
Harrelson, Derrel Mc Kinley "Bud"											
1990	NY-N	120	71	49	.592	4 E	2 E		2/2	72.3	-1.3
1991	NY-N	154	74	80	.481	3 E	5 E		1/2	76.4	-2.4
	2	274	145	129	.529						-3.7
Harris, Chalmer Luman "Lum"											
1961	Bal-A	27	17	10	.630	3	3		2/2	15.3	1.7
1964	Hou-N	13	5	8	.385	9	9		2/2	5.3	-0.3
1965	Hou-N	162	65	97	.401	9				65.8	-0.8
1968	Atl-N	163	81	81	.500	5				76.9	4.1
1969	Atl-N	162	93	69	.574	1 W				87.3	5.7
1970	Atl-N	162	76	86	.469	5 W				77.5	-1.5
1971	Atl-N	162	82	80	.506	3 W				75.2	6.8
1972	Atl-N	105	47	57	.452	4 W	4 W		1/2	45.0	2.0
	8	956	466	488	.488						17.7
Harris, Stanley Raymond "Bucky"											
1924	Was-A*	156	92	62	.597	★1				91.4	0.6
1925	Was-A*	152	96	55	.636	1				90.7	5.3
1926	Was-A*	152	81	69	.540	4				78.8	2.2
1927	Was-A*	157	85	69	.552	3				82.0	3.0
1928	Was-A*	155	75	79	.487	4				78.3	-3.3
1929	Det-A*	155	70	84	.455	6				76.8	-6.8
1930	Det-A	154	75	79	.487	5				72.4	2.6
1931	Det-A	154	61	93	.396	7				59.1	1.9
1932	Det-A	153	76	75	.503	5				76.6	-0.6
1933	Det-A	153	73	79	.480	5	5		1/2	74.9	-1.9
1934	Bos-A	153	76	76	.500	4				80.2	-4.2
1935	Was-A	154	67	86	.438	6				69.3	-2.3
1936	Was-A	153	82	71	.536	4				84.6	-2.6
1937	Was-A	158	73	80	.477	6				68.6	4.4
1938	Was-A	152	75	76	.497	5				70.2	4.8
1939	Was-A	153	65	87	.428	6				66.9	-1.9
1940	Was-A	154	64	90	.416	7				62.9	1.1
1941	Was-A	156	70	84	.455	●6				70.3	-0.3
1942	Was-A	151	62	89	.411	7				59.7	2.3
1943	Phi-N	92	38	52	.422	7	7		1/2	38.5	-0.5
1947	NY-A	155	97	57	.630	★1				99.9	-2.9
1948	NY-A	154	94	60	.610	3				98.6	-4.6
1950	Was-A	155	67	87	.435	5				65.1	1.9
1951	Was-A	154	62	92	.403	7				68.0	-6.0
1952	Was-A	157	78	76	.506	5				75.9	2.1
1953	Was-A	152	76	76	.500	5				83.5	-7.5
1954	Was-A	155	66	88	.429	6				72.1	-6.1

YEAR	TM/L	G	W	L	PCT	STANDING			M/Y	W-EXP	A-E
1955	Det-A	154	79	75	.513	5				88.5	-9.5
1956	Det-A	155	82	72	.532	5				85.7	-3.7
29		4408	2157	2218	.493						-32.5

Hart, James Aristotle "Jim"

1885	Lou-a	112	53	59	.473	●5				52.8	0.2
1886	Lou-a	138	66	70	.485	4				70.4	-4.4
1889	Bos-N	133	83	45	.648	2				82.2	0.8
3		383	202	174	.537						-3.4

Hart, John Henry

| 1989 | Cle-A | 19 | 8 | 11 | .421 | 6 E | 6 E | | 2/2 | 8.9 | -0.9 |

Hartnett, Charles Leo "Gabby"

1938	Chi-N*	73	44	27	.620	3	1		2/2	41.0	3.0
1939	Chi-N*	156	84	70	.545	4				81.6	2.4
1940	Chi-N*	154	75	79	.487	5				81.6	-6.6
3		383	203	176	.536						-1.2

Hartsfield, Roy Thomas

1977	Tor-A	161	54	107	.335	7 E				58.6	-4.6
1978	Tor-A	161	59	102	.366	7 E				61.4	-2.4
1979	Tor-A	162	53	109	.327	7 E				56.2	-3.2
3		484	166	318	.343						-10.3

Hastings, Winfield Scott "Scott"

1871	Rok-n*	25	4	21	.160	9				8.8	-4.8
1872	Cle-n*	20	6	14	.300	6	7		1/2	5.1	0.9
2		45	10	35	.222						-3.9

Hatfield, John Van Buren

1872	Mut-n*	40	24	14	.632	4	3		2/2	27.6	-3.6
1873	Mut-n*	28	11	17	.393	5	4		1/2	15.6	-4.6
2		68	35	31	.530						-8.1

Hatton, Grady Edgebert

1966	Hou-N	163	72	90	.444	8				72.2	-0.2
1967	Hou-N	162	69	93	.426	9				69.0	-0.0
1968	Hou-N	61	23	38	.377	10	10		1/2	27.1	-4.1
3		386	164	221	.426						-4.3

Hecker, Guy Jackson

| 1890 | Pit-N* | 138 | 23 | 113 | .169 | 8 | | | | 15.5 | 7.5 |

Heffner, Donald Henry "Don"

| 1966 | Cin-N | 83 | 37 | 46 | .446 | 8 | 7 | | 1/2 | 41.0 | -4.0 |

Heilbroner, Louis Wilbur "Louie"

| 1900 | StL-N | 50 | 23 | 25 | .479 | 7 | ●5 | | 2/2 | 23.9 | -0.9 |

Helms, Tommy Vann

1988	Cin-N	27	12	15	.444	4 W	4 W	2 W	2/3	14.3	-2.3
1989	Cin-N	37	16	21	.432	●4 W	5 W		2/2	17.1	-1.1
2		64	28	36	.438						-3.4

Hemus, Solomon Joseph "Solly"

1959	StL-N*	154	71	83	.461	7				68.5	2.5
1960	StL-N*	155	86	68	.558	3				79.4	6.6
1961	StL-N	75	33	41	.446	6	5		1/2	38.7	-5.7
3		384	190	192	.497						3.3

Henderson, William C. "Bill"

| 1884 | Bal-U | 106 | 58 | 47 | .552 | 4 | | | | 55.5 | 2.5 |

Hendricks, John Charles "Jack"

1918	StL-N	133	51	78	.395	8				56.5	-5.5
1924	Cin-N	153	83	70	.542	4				83.9	-0.9
1925	Cin-N	153	80	73	.523	3				81.3	-1.3
1926	Cin-N	157	87	67	.565	2				86.7	0.3
1927	Cin-N	153	75	78	.490	5				75.5	-0.5
1928	Cin-N	153	78	74	.513	5				72.1	5.9
1929	Cin-N	155	66	88	.429	7				69.7	-3.7
7		1057	520	528	.496						-5.7

Hengle, Edward S. "Ed"

| 1884 | Chi-U | 74 | 34 | 39 | .466 | 5 | | | | 41.3 | -0.3 |

Herman, William Jennings Bryan "Billy"

1947	Pit-N*	155	61	92	.399	8	●7		1/2	69.6	-8.6
1964	Bos-A	2	2	0	1.000	8	8		2/2	0.9	1.1
1965	Bos-A	162	62	100	.383	9				68.8	-6.8
1966	Bos-A	146	64	82	.438	9	9		1/2	66.0	-2.0
4		465	189	274	.408						-16.3

Herzog, Charles Lincoln "Buck"

1914	Cin-N*	157	60	94	.390	8				63.8	-3.8
1915	Cin-N*	160	71	83	.461	7				69.1	1.9
1916	Cin-N*	84	34	49	.410	8	●7		1/3	34.7	-0.7
3		401	165	226	.422						-2.6

Herzog, Dorrel Norman Elvert "Whitey"

1973	Tex-A	138	47	91	.341	6 W	6 W		1/3	49.9	-2.9
1974	Cal-A	4	2	2	.500	6 W	6 W	6 W	2/3	1.9	0.1
1975	KC-A	66	41	25	.621	2 W	2 W		2/2	35.6	5.4
1976	KC-A	162	90	72	.556	1 W				91.7	-1.7
1977	KC-A	162	102	60	.630	1 W				98.0	4.0
1978	KC-A	162	92	70	.568	1 W				92.2	-0.2
1979	KC-A	162	85	77	.525	2 W				84.3	0.7
1980	StL-N	73	38	35	.521	6 E	5 E	4 E	3/4	37.8	0.2
1981(1)	StL-N	51	30	20	.600	2 E					
(2)	StL-N	52	29	23	.558	2 E				55.8	3.2
1982	StL-N	162	92	70	.568	★1 E				89.1	2.9
1983	StL-N	162	79	83	.488	4 E				77.8	1.2
1984	StL-N	162	84	78	.519	3 E				81.7	2.3

YEAR	TM/L	G	W	L	PCT	STANDING			M/Y	W-EXP	A-E
1985	StL-N	162	101	61	.623	♦1 E				99.4	1.6
1986	StL-N	161	79	82	.491	3 E				79.4	-0.4
1987	StL-N	162	95	67	.586	♦1 E				91.4	3.6
1988	StL-N	162	76	86	.469	5 E				75.0	1.0
1989	StL-N	164	86	76	.531	3 E				83.6	2.4
1990	StL-N	80	33	47	.412	6 E	6 E		1/3	34.8	-1.8
18		2409	1281	1125	.532						21.6

Hewett, Walter F.

| 1888 | Was-N | 40 | 10 | 29 | .256 | 8 | 8 | | 1/2 | 12.2 | -2.2 |

Hicks, Nathaniel Woodhull "Nat"

1874	Phi-n*	58	29	29	.500	4				32.6	-3.6
1875	Mut-n*	71	30	38	.441	7				25.1	4.9
2		129	59	67	.468						1.3

Higgins, Michael Franklin "Pinky"

1955	Bos-A	154	84	70	.545	4				87.2	-3.2
1956	Bos-A	155	84	70	.545	4				79.8	4.2
1957	Bos-A	154	82	72	.532	3				82.3	-0.3
1958	Bos-A	155	79	75	.513	3				77.6	1.4
1959	Bos-A	73	31	42	.425	8	8		1/3	37.9	-6.9
1960	Bos-A	105	48	57	.457	8	7		3/3	44.7	3.3
1961	Bos-A	163	76	86	.469	6				74.8	1.2
1962	Bos-A	160	76	84	.475	8				75.1	0.9
8		1119	560	556	.502						0.6

Higham, Richard "Dick"

| 1874 | Mut-n* | 40 | 29 | 11 | .725 | 3 | 2 | | 2/2 | 26.2 | 2.8 |

Himsl, Avitus Bernard "Vedie"

1961	Chi-N	11	5	6	.455	6	●6		1/9	4.7	0.3
	Chi-N	17	5	12	.294	7	7	7	3/9	7.3	-2.3
	Chi-N	4	0	3	.000	7	7	7	6/9	1.3	-1.3

Hitchcock, William Clyde "Billy"

1960	Det-A	1	1	0	1.000	6	6	6	2/3	0.5	0.5
1962	Bal-A	162	77	85	.475	7				78.1	-1.1
1963	Bal-A	162	86	76	.531	4				83.5	2.5
1966	Atl-N	51	33	18	.647	7	5		2/2	28.6	4.4
1967	Atl-N	159	77	82	.484	7	6		1/2	78.6	-1.6
5		535	274	261	.512						4.8

Hobson, Clell Lavern "Butch"

1992	Bos-A	162	73	89	.451	7 E				73.5	-0.5
1993	Bos-A	162	80	82	.494	5 E				79.8	0.2
1994	Bos-A	115	54	61	.470	4 E				51.0	3.0
3		439	207	232	.472						2.7

Hodges, Gilbert Raymond "Gil"

1963	Was-A	121	42	79	.347	10	10		3/3	42.6	-0.6
1964	Was-A	162	62	100	.383	9				64.7	-2.7
1965	Was-A	162	70	92	.432	8				67.3	2.7
1966	Was-A	159	71	88	.447	8				68.4	2.6
1967	Was-A	161	76	85	.472	●6				70.9	5.1
1968	NY-N	163	73	89	.451	9				77.8	-4.8
1969	NY-N	162	100	62	.617	★1 E				91.1	8.9
1970	NY-N	162	83	79	.512	3 E				87.8	-4.8
1971	NY-N	162	83	79	.512	●3 E				85.3	-2.3
9		1414	660	753	.467						4.1

Hoey, Frederick C. "Fred"

| 1899 | NY-N | 87 | 31 | 55 | .360 | 9 | 10 | | 2/2 | 36.2 | -5.2 |

Holbert, William H. "Bill"

| 1879 | Syr-N* | 1 | 0 | 1 | .000 | 6 | 6 | 7 | 2/3 | 0.3 | -0.3 |

Hollingshead, John Samuel "Holly"

1875	Was-n*	20	4	16	.200	8	10		1/2	-2.4	6.4
1884	Was-a	62	12	50	.194	12	12		1/2	10.8	1.2
2		82	16	66	.195						7.6

Holmes, Thomas Francis "Tommy"

1951	Bos-N*	95	48	47	.505	5	4		2/2	51.3	-3.3
1952	Bos-N	35	13	22	.371	7	7		1/2	15.5	-2.5
2		130	61	69	.469						-5.8

Hornsby, Rogers

1925	StL-N*	115	64	51	.557	8	4		2/2	62.0	2.0
1926	StL-N*	156	89	65	.578	★1				90.5	-1.5
1927	NY-N*	33	22	10	.688	4	3		2/2	17.9	4.1
1928	Bos-N*	122	39	83	.320	7	7		2/2	42.2	-3.2
1930	Chi-N*	4	4	0	1.000	2	2		2/2	2.3	1.7
1931	Chi-N*	156	84	70	.545	3				88.3	-4.3
1932	Chi-N*	99	53	46	.535	2	1		1/2	55.2	-2.2
1933	StL-A*	54	19	33	.365	8	8		1/2	21.0	-2.0
1934	StL-A*	154	67	85	.441	6				63.8	3.2
1935	StL-A*	155	65	87	.428	7				56.5	8.5
1936	StL-A*	155	57	95	.375	7				53.5	3.5
1937	StL-A*	78	25	52	.325	7	8		1/2	24.7	0.3
1952	StL-A	51	22	29	.431	7	7		1/2	21.1	0.6
	Cin-N	51	27	24	.529	7	6		3/3	26.0	3.0
1953	Cin-N	147	64	82	.438	6	6		1/2	66.2	-2.2
14		1530	701	812	.463						11.9

Houk, Ralph George "Ralph"

1961	NY-A	163	109	53	.673	★1				102.7	6.3
1962	NY-A	162	96	66	.593	★1				94.5	1.5
1963	NY-A	161	104	57	.646	1				98.4	5.6
1966	NY-A	140	66	73	.475	10	10		2/2	69.4	-3.4
1967	NY-A	163	72	90	.444	9				69.8	2.2

YEAR	TM/L	G	W	L	PCT	STANDING			M/Y	W-EXP	A-E
1968	NY-A	164	83	79	.512	5				81.6	1.4
1969	NY-A	162	80	81	.497	5 E				77.7	2.3
1970	NY-A	163	93	69	.574	2 E				88.2	4.8
1971	NY-A	162	82	80	.506	4 E				81.7	0.3
1972	NY-A	155	79	76	.510	4 E				80.9	-1.9
1973	NY-A	162	80	82	.494	4 E				84.3	-4.3
1974	Det-A	162	72	90	.444	6 E				65.8	6.2
1975	Det-A	159	57	102	.358	6 E				57.3	-0.3
1976	Det-A	161	74	87	.460	5 E				70.0	4.0
1977	Det-A	162	74	88	.457	4 E				77.3	-3.3
1978	Det-A	162	86	76	.531	5 E				87.3	-1.3
1981(1)	Bos-A	56	30	26	.536	5 E					
(2)	Bos-A	52	29	23	.558	●2 E				57.7	1.3
1982	Bos-A	162	89	73	.549	3 E				85.0	4.0
1983	Bos-A	162	78	84	.481	6 E				76.0	2.0
1984	Bos-A	162	86	76	.531	4 E				85.4	0.6
	20	3157	1619	1531	.514						27.8

Howard, Frank Oliver

YEAR	TM/L	G	W	L	PCT	STANDING			M/Y	W-EXP	A-E
1981(1)	SD-N	56	23	33	.411	6 W					
(2)	SD-N	54	18	36	.333	6 W				47.1	-6.1
1983	NY-N	116	52	64	.448	6 E	6 E		2/2	49.9	2.1
	2	226	93	133	.412						-4.0

Howe, Arthur Henry "Art"

YEAR	TM/L	G	W	L	PCT	STANDING			M/Y	W-EXP	A-E
1989	Hou-N	162	86	76	.531	3 W				78.7	7.3
1990	Hou-N	162	75	87	.463	●4 W				72.0	3.0
1991	Hou-N	162	65	97	.401	6 W				69.2	-4.2
1992	Hou-N	162	81	81	.500	4 W				74.6	6.4
1993	Hou-N	162	85	77	.525	3 W				90.0	-5.0
1996	Oak-A	162	78	84	.481	3 W				77.5	0.5
	6	972	470	502	.484						8.1

Howley, Daniel Philip "Dan"

YEAR	TM/L	G	W	L	PCT	STANDING			M/Y	W-EXP	A-E
1927	StL-A	155	59	94	.386	7				59.8	-0.8
1928	StL-A	154	82	72	.532	3				79.9	2.1
1929	StL-A	154	79	73	.520	4				78.0	1.0
1930	Cin-N	154	59	95	.383	7				58.7	0.3
1931	Cin-N	154	58	96	.377	8				61.7	-3.7
1932	Cin-N	155	60	94	.390	8				62.4	-2.4
	6	926	397	524	.431						-3.5

Howser, Richard Dalton "Dick"

YEAR	TM/L	G	W	L	PCT	STANDING			M/Y	W-EXP	A-E
1978	NY-A	1	0	1	.000	3 E	4 E	▲★E	2/3	0.6	-0.6
1980	NY-A	162	103	59	.636	1 E				96.7	6.3
1981(2)	KC-A	33	20	13	.606	●2 W	1 W		2/2	16.2	3.8
1982	KC-A	162	90	72	.556	2 W				87.6	2.4
1983	KC-A	163	79	83	.488	2 W				73.9	5.1
1984	KC-A	162	84	78	.519	1 W				79.7	4.3
1985	KC-A	162	91	71	.562	★1 W				86.0	5.0
1986	KC-A	88	40	48	.455	4 W	●3 W		1/2	42.9	-2.9
	8	933	507	425	.544						23.4

Huff, George A.

YEAR	TM/L	G	W	L	PCT	STANDING			M/Y	W-EXP	A-E
1907	Bos-A	8	2	6	.250	●4	6	7	2/4	3.4	-1.4

Huggins, Miller James

YEAR	TM/L	G	W	L	PCT	STANDING			M/Y	W-EXP	A-E
1913	StL-N*	153	51	99	.340	8				51.5	-0.5
1914	StL-N*	157	81	72	.529	3				78.5	2.5
1915	StL-N*	157	72	81	.471	6				75.3	-3.3
1916	StL-N*	153	60	93	.392	●7				59.4	0.6
1917	StL-N	154	82	70	.539	3				72.0	10.0
1918	NY-A	126	60	63	.488	4				63.4	-3.4
1919	NY-A	141	80	59	.576	3				77.3	2.7
1920	NY-A	154	95	59	.617	3				97.3	-2.3
1921	NY-A	153	98	55	.641	1				98.4	-0.4
1922	NY-A	154	94	60	.610	1				91.1	2.9
1923	NY-A	152	98	54	.645	★1				95.6	2.4
1924	NY-A	153	89	63	.586	2				88.7	0.3
1925	NY-A	156	69	85	.448	7				70.4	-1.4
1926	NY-A	155	91	63	.591	1				89.7	1.3
1927	NY-A	155	110	44	.714	★1				112.4	-2.4
1928	NY-A	154	101	53	.656	★1				96.6	4.4
1929	NY-A	143	82	61	.573	2	2		1/2	82.0	0.0
	17	2570	1413	1134	.555						13.5

Hunter, Gordon William "Billy"

YEAR	TM/L	G	W	L	PCT	STANDING			M/Y	W-EXP	A-E
1977	Tex-A	93	60	33	.645	5 W	2 W		4/4	52.9	7.1
1978	Tex-A	161	86	75	.534	●2 W	●2 W		1/2	86.8	-0.8
	2	254	146	108	.575						6.4

Hurst, Timothy Carroll "Tim"

YEAR	TM/L	G	W	L	PCT	STANDING			M/Y	W-EXP	A-E
1898	StL-N	154	39	111	.260	12				40.6	-1.6

Hutchinson, Frederick Charles "Fred"

YEAR	TM/L	G	W	L	PCT	STANDING			M/Y	W-EXP	A-E
1952	Det-A*	83	27	55	.329	8	8		2/2	31.0	-4.0
1953	Det-A*	158	60	94	.390	6				55.6	4.4
1954	Det-A	155	68	86	.442	5				68.5	-0.5
1956	StL-N	156	76	78	.494	4				75.0	1.0
1957	StL-N	154	87	67	.565	2				84.1	2.9
1958	StL-N	144	69	75	.479	5	●5		1/2	63.9	5.1
1959	Cin-N	74	39	35	.527	7	●5		2/2	38.2	0.8
1960	Cin-N	154	67	87	.435	6				71.7	-4.7
1961	Cin-N	154	93	61	.604	1				82.7	10.3
1962	Cin-N	162	98	64	.605	3				92.6	5.4
1963	Cin-N	162	86	76	.531	5				86.9	-0.9
1964	Cin-N	100	54	45	.545	1	●2		1/4	52.0	-1.8
	Cin-N	10	6	4	.600	4	3	●2	3/4	5.6	0.4

YEAR	TM/L	G	W	L	PCT	STANDING			M/Y	W-EXP	A-E
	12	1666	830	827	.501						18.5

Irwin, Arthur Albert

YEAR	TM/L	G	W	L	PCT	STANDING			M/Y	W-EXP	A-E
	Was-										
1889	N*	76	28	45	.384	8	8		2/2	23.2	4.8
1891	Bos-a*	139	93	42	.689	1				97.8	-4.8
1892(1)	Was-N	74	35	39	.473	●11	7		2/2		
(2)	Was-N	34	11	21	.344	11	12		1/2	44.0	2.0
1894	Phi-N*	132	71	57	.555	4				77.1	-6.1
1895	Phi-N	133	78	53	.595	3				74.0	4.0
1896	NY-N	90	36	53	.404	10	7		1/2	45.0	-9.0
1898	Was-N	30	10	19	.345	11	11		4/4	10.4	-0.4
1899	Was-N	155	54	98	.355	11				54.4	-0.4
	8	863	416	427	.493						-9.9

Jennings, Hugh Ambrose "Hughie"

YEAR	TM/L	G	W	L	PCT	STANDING			M/Y	W-EXP	A-E
1907	Det-A*	153	92	58	.613	1				92.2	-0.2
1908	Det-A*	154	90	63	.588	1				87.3	2.7
1909	Det-A*	158	98	54	.645	1				95.2	2.8
1910	Det-A	155	86	68	.558	3				87.2	-1.2
1911	Det-A	154	89	65	.578	2				82.1	6.9
1912	Det-A*	154	69	84	.451	6				71.0	-2.0
1913	Det-A	153	66	87	.431	6				67.2	-1.2
1914	Det-A	157	80	73	.523	4				76.2	3.8
1915	Det-A	156	100	54	.649	2				95.3	4.7
1916	Det-A	155	87	67	.565	3				84.9	2.1
1917	Det-A	155	78	75	.510	4				83.1	-5.1
1918	Det-A*	128	55	71	.437	7				54.4	0.6
1919	Det-A	140	80	60	.571	4				74.1	5.9
1920	Det-A	155	61	93	.396	7				59.5	1.5
1924	NY-N	44	32	12	.727	3	1	1	2/3	28.0	4.0
1925	NY-N	32	21	11	.656	1	1	2	2/3	16.7	4.3
	16	2203	1184	995	.543						29.7

Johnson, Darrell Dean

YEAR	TM/L	G	W	L	PCT	STANDING			M/Y	W-EXP	A-E
1974	Bos-A	162	84	78	.519	3 E				84.6	-0.6
1975	Bos-A	160	95	65	.594	◆1 E				88.5	6.5
1976	Bos-A	86	41	45	.477	5 E	3 E		1/2	46.1	-5.1
1977	Sea-A	162	64	98	.395	6 W				58.1	5.9
1978	Sea-A	160	56	104	.350	7 W				58.1	-2.1
1979	Sea-A	162	67	95	.414	6 W				70.4	-3.4
1980	Sea-A	105	39	65	.375	6 W	7 W		1/2	40.0	-1.0
1982	Tex-A	66	26	40	.394	6 W	6 W		2/2	26.2	-0.2
	8	1063	472	590	.444						0.1

Johnson, David Allen "Davey"

YEAR	TM/L	G	W	L	PCT	STANDING			M/Y	W-EXP	A-E
1984	NY-N	162	90	72	.556	2 E				78.5	11.5
1985	NY-N	162	98	64	.605	2 E				94.6	3.4
1986	NY-N	162	108	54	.667	★1 E				102.2	5.8
1987	NY-N	162	92	70	.568	2 E				93.2	-1.2
1988	NY-N	160	100	60	.625	1 E				98.5	1.5
1989	NY-N	162	87	75	.537	2 E				90.4	-3.4
1990	NY-N	42	20	22	.476	4 E	2 E		1/2	25.3	-5.3
1993	Cin-N	118	53	65	.449	5 W	5 W		2/2	54.5	-1.5
1994	Cin-N	115	66	48	.579	1 C				68.5	-2.5
1995	Cin-N	144	85	59	.590	1 C				84.1	0.9
1996	Bal-A	163	88	74	.543	■2 E				85.1	2.9
	11	1552	887	663	.572						12.0

Johnson, Roy J

YEAR	TM/L	G	W	L	PCT	STANDING			M/Y	W-EXP	A-E
1944	Chi-N	1	0	1	.000	8	8	4	2/3	0.5	-0.5

Johnson, Walter Perry

YEAR	TM/L	G	W	L	PCT	STANDING			M/Y	W-EXP	A-E
1929	Was-A	153	71	81	.467	5				71.6	-0.6
1930	Was-A	154	94	60	.610	2				96.0	-2.0
1931	Was-A	156	92	62	.597	3				91.5	0.5
1932	Was-A	154	93	61	.604	3				88.7	4.3
1933	Cle-A	99	48	51	.485	5	4		3/3	48.5	-0.5
1934	Cle-A	154	85	69	.552	3				81.8	3.2
1935	Cle-A	96	46	48	.489	5			1/2	49.2	-3.2
	7	966	529	432	.550						1.7

Jones, Fielder Allison

YEAR	TM/L	G	W	L	PCT	STANDING			M/Y	W-EXP	A-E
1904	Chi-A*	114	66	47	.584	4	3		2/2	66.4	-0.4
1905	Chi-A*	158	92	60	.605	2				94.6	-2.6
1906	Chi-A*	154	93	58	.616	★1				88.3	4.7
1907	Chi-A*	157	87	64	.576	3				88.7	-1.7
1908	Chi-A*	156	88	64	.579	3				83.9	4.1
1914	StL-F*	40	12	26	.316	7	8		2/2	15.5	-3.5
1915	StL-F*	159	87	67	.565	2				88.9	-1.9
1916	StL-A	158	79	75	.513	5				81.8	-2.8
1917	StL-A	155	57	97	.370	7				57.9	-0.9
1918	StL-A	46	22	24	.478	5	5		1/3	22.1	-0.1
	10	1297	683	582	.540						-5.0

Joost, Edwin David "Eddie"

YEAR	TM/L	G	W	L	PCT	STANDING			M/Y	W-EXP	A-E
1954	Phi-A*	156	51	103	.331	8				43.8	7.2

Jorgensen, Michael "Mike"

YEAR	TM/L	G	W	L	PCT	STANDING			M/Y	W-EXP	A-E
1995	StL-N	96	42	54	.438	4 C	4 C		2/2	41.5	0.5

Joyce, William Michael "Bill"

YEAR	TM/L	G	W	L	PCT	STANDING			M/Y	W-EXP	A-E
1896	NY-N*	43	28	14	.667	10	7		2/2	21.2	6.8
1897	NY-N*	138	83	48	.634	3				83.1	-0.1
1898	NY-N*	43	22	21	.512	6			1/3	22.5	-0.5
	NY-N*	92	46	39	.541	7	7		3/3	44.4	1.6
	3	316	179	122	.595						7.7

YEAR	TM/L	G	W	L	PCT	STANDING			M/Y	W-EXP	A-E
Jurges, William Frederick "Billy"											
1959	Bos-A	80	44	36	.550	8	5		3/3	41.5	2.5
1960	Bos-A	42	15	27	.357	8	7		1/3	17.9	-2.9
	2	122	59	63	.484						-0.4
Kasko, Edward Michael "Eddie"											
1970	Bos-A	162	87	75	.537	3 E				87.3	-0.3
1971	Bos-A	162	85	77	.525	3 E				83.5	1.5
1972	Bos-A	155	85	70	.548	2 E				79.6	5.4
1973	Bos-A	161	88	73	.547	2 E	2 E		1/2	89.8	-1.8
	4	640	345	295	.539						4.8
Keane, John Joseph "Johnny"											
1961	StL-N	80	47	33	.587	6	5		2/2	41.8	5.2
1962	StL-N	163	84	78	.519	6				92.1	-8.1
1963	StL-N	162	93	69	.574	2				93.3	-0.3
1964	StL-N	162	93	69	.574	★1				87.5	5.5
1965	NY-A	162	77	85	.475	6				81.8	-4.8
1966	NY-A	20	4	16	.200	10	10		1/2	10.0	-6.0
	6	749	398	350	.532						-8.5
Kelley, Joseph James "Joe"											
1902	Cin-N*	60	34	26	.567	6	4		3/3	33.0	1.0
1903	Cin-N*	141	74	65	.532	4				79.8	-5.8
1904	Cin-N*	157	88	65	.575	3				92.3	-4.3
1905	Cin-N*	155	79	74	.516	5				80.2	-1.2
1908	Bos-N*	156	63	91	.409	6				67.6	-4.6
	5	669	338	321	.513						-14.8
Kelly, Jay Thomas "Tom"											
1986	Min-A	23	12	11	.522	7 W	6 W		2/2	10.2	1.8
1987	Min-A	162	85	77	.525	★1 W				79.1	5.9
1988	Min-A	162	91	71	.562	2 W				89.8	1.2
1989	Min-A	162	80	82	.494	5 W				81.2	-1.2
1990	Min-A	162	74	88	.457	7 W				74.6	-0.6
1991	Min-A	162	95	67	.586	★1 W				93.5	1.5
1992	Min-A	162	90	72	.556	2 W				90.6	-0.6
1993	Min-A	162	71	91	.438	●5 W				67.6	3.4
1994	Min-A	113	53	60	.469	4 C				48.1	4.9
1995	Min-A	144	56	88	.389	5 C				55.2	0.8
1996	Min-A	162	78	84	.481	4 C				78.9	-0.9
	11	1576	785	791	.498						16.2
Kelly, John O.											
1887	Lou-a	139	76	60	.559	4				76.5	-0.5
1888	Lou-a	39	10	29	.256	8	7		1/4	14.8	-4.8
	2	178	86	89	.491						-5.3
Kelly, Michael Joseph "King"											
1887	Bos-N*	95	49	43	.533	5	5		1/2	48.5	0.5
1890	Bos-P*	133	81	48	.628	1				82.9	-1.9
1891	Cin-a*	102	43	57	.430	6				41.7	1.3
	3	330	173	148	.539						-0.1
Kennedy, James C. "Jim"											
1890	Bro-a	100	26	73	.263	8				28.8	-2.8
Kennedy, Kevin Curtis											
1993	Tex-A	162	86	76	.531	2 W				89.1	-3.1
1994	Tex-A	114	52	62	.456	1 W				49.6	2.4
1995	Bos-A	144	86	58	.597	○1 E				80.7	5.3
1996	Bos-A	162	85	77	.525	3 E				81.6	3.4
	4	582	309	273	.531						8.1
Kennedy, Robert Daniel "Bob"											
1963	Chi-N	162	82	80	.506	7				80.1	1.9
1964	Chi-N	162	76	86	.469	8				73.3	2.7
1965	Chi-N	58	24	32	.429	9	8		1/2	24.8	-0.8
1968	Oak-A	163	82	80	.506	6				83.9	-1.9
	4	545	264	278	.487						1.9
Kerins, John Nelson											
1888	Lou-a*	7	3	4	.429	8	8	7	3/4	2.7	0.3
1890	StL-a*	17	9	8	.529	4	4	3	2/6	10.0	-1.0
	2	24	12	12	.500						-0.6
Kessinger, Donald Eulon "Don"											
1979	Chi-A*	106	46	60	.434	5 W	5 W		1/2	51.8	-5.8
Killefer, William Lavier "Bill"											
1921	Chi-N*	57	23	34	.404	6	7		2/2	24.7	-1.7
1922	Chi-N	156	80	74	.519	5				73.5	6.5
1923	Chi-N	154	83	71	.539	4				82.1	0.9
1924	Chi-N	154	81	72	.529	5				76.4	4.6
1925	Chi-N	75	33	42	.440	7	8		1/3	35.2	-2.2
1930	StL-A	154	64	90	.416	6				64.6	-0.6
1931	StL-A	154	63	91	.409	5				63.2	-0.2
1932	StL-A	154	63	91	.409	6				62.1	0.9
1933	StL-A	91	34	57	.374	8	8		1/3	36.7	-2.7
	9	1149	524	622	.457						5.6
King, Clyde Edward											
1969	SF-N	162	90	72	.556	2 W				89.0	1.0
1970	SF-N	42	19	23	.452	4 W	3 W		1/2	21.1	-2.1
1974	Atl-N	64	38	25	.603	4 W	3 W		2/2	35.7	2.3
1975	Atl-N	134	58	76	.433	5 W	5 W		1/2	53.4	4.6
1982	NY-A	62	29	33	.468	●5 E	5 E		3/3	30.7	-1.7
	5	464	234	229	.505						4.1
Kittridge, Malachi J.											
1904	Was-A*	18	1	16	.059	8	8		1/2	4.7	-3.7

YEAR	TM/L	G	W	L	PCT	STANDING			M/Y	W-EXP	A-E
Klein, Louis Frank "Lou"											
1961	Chi-N	11	5	6	.455	7	7	7	8/9	4.7	0.3
1962	Chi-N	30	12	18	.400	9	9	9	2/3	11.4	0.6
1965	Chi-N	106	48	58	.453	9	8		2/2	47.0	1.0
	3	147	65	82	.442						1.9
Kling, John "Johnny"											
1912	Bos-N*	155	52	101	.340	8				60.6	-8.6
Knabe, Franz Otto "Otto"											
1914	Bal-F*	160	84	70	.545	3				78.8	5.2
1915	Bal-F*	155	47	107	.305	8				55.4	-8.4
	2	315	131	177	.425						-3.2
Knight, Alonzo P. "Lon"											
1883	Phi-a*	98	66	32	.673	1				63.4	2.6
1884	Phi-a*	109	61	46	.570	7				67.1	-6.1
	2	207	127	78	.620						-3.5
Knight, Charles Ray "Ray"											
1996	Cin-N	162	81	81	.500	3 C				81.5	-0.5
Knoop, Robert Frank "Bobby"											
1994	Cal-A	2	1	1	.500	3 W	2 W	4 W	2/3	0.8	0.2
Krol, John Thomas "Jack"											
1978	StL-N	2	1	1	.500	6 E	6 E	5 E	2/3	0.9	0.1
1980	StL-N	1	0	1	.000	6 E	6 E	4 E	2/4	0.5	-0.5
	2	3	1	2	.333						-0.4
Kuehl, Karl Otto											
1976	Mon-N	128	43	85	.336	6 E	6 E		1/2	46.8	-3.8
Kuenn, Harvey Edward											
1975	Mil-A	1	1	0	1.000	5 E	5 E		2/2	0.4	0.6
1982	Mil-A	116	72	43	.626	5 E	◆1 E		2/2	69.3	2.7
1983	Mil-A	162	87	75	.537	5 E				86.6	0.4
	3	279	160	118	.576						3.7
Kuhel, Joseph Anthony "Joe"											
1948	Was-A	154	56	97	.366	7				54.6	1.4
1949	Was-A	154	50	104	.325	8				49.3	0.7
	2	308	106	201	.345						2.1
Lachemann, Marcel Ernest											
1994	Cal-A	74	30	44	.405	2 W	4 W		3/3	30.0	-0.0
1995	Cal-A	145	78	67	.538	▲2 W				82.2	-4.2
1996	Cal-A	117	53	64	.453	4 W			1/2	46.4	6.6
	3	336	161	175	.479						2.4
Lachemann, Rene George											
1981(1)	Sea-A	33	15	18	.455	7 W	6 W		2/2		
(2)	Sea-A	52	23	29	.442	5 W				34.9	3.1
1982	Sea-A	162	76	86	.469	4 W				74.7	1.3
1983	Sea-A	73	26	47	.356	7 W	7 W		1/2	27.8	-1.8
1984	Mil-A	161	67	94	.416	7 E				71.0	-4.0
1993	Fla-N	162	64	98	.395	6 E				65.9	-1.9
1994	Fla-N	115	51	54	.486	5 E				46.7	4.3
1995	Fla-N	143	67	76	.469	4 E				71.5	-4.5
1996	Fla-N	86	39	47	.453	4 E	3 E		1/3	42.2	-3.2
	8	987	428	549	.438						-6.7
Lajoie, Napoleon "Nap"											
1905	Cle-A*	58	37	21	.638	●1	5		1/3	28.2	8.8
	Cle-A*	56	19	36	.345	2	5		3/3	26.7	-7.7
1906	Cle-A*	157	89	64	.582	3				96.6	-7.6
1907	Cle-A*	158	85	67	.559	4				76.6	8.4
1908	Cle-A*	157	90	64	.584	2				90.0	-0.0
1909	Cle-A*	114	57	57	.500	4	6		1/2	53.6	3.4
	5	700	377	309	.550						5.3
Lake, Frederick Lovett "Fred"											
1908	Bos-A	40	22	17	.564	6	5		2/2	21.0	1.0
1909	Bos-A	152	88	63	.583	3				80.6	7.4
1910	Bos-N*	157	53	100	.346	8				54.1	-1.1
	3	349	163	180	.475						7.3
Lamont, Gene William											
1992	Chi-A	162	86	76	.531	3 W				85.9	0.1
1993	Chi-A	162	94	68	.580	1 W				92.3	1.7
1994	Chi-A	113	67	46	.593	1 C				69.3	-2.3
1995	Chi-A	31	11	20	.355	4 C	3 C		1/2	15.4	-4.4
	4	468	258	210	.551						-4.9
Lanier, Harold Clifton "Hal"											
1986	Hou-N	162	96	66	.593	1 W				90.3	5.7
1987	Hou-N	162	76	86	.469	3 W				77.9	-1.9
1988	Hou-N	162	82	80	.506	5 W				79.5	2.5
	3	486	254	232	.523						6.4
Larkin, Henry E. "Ted"											
1890	Cle-P*	79	34	45	.430	7	7		1/2	30.9	3.1
LaRussa, Anthony "Tony"											
1979	Chi-A	54	27	27	.500	5 W	5 W		2/2	26.4	0.6
1980	Chi-A	162	70	90	.438	5 W				65.8	4.2
1981(1)	Chi-A	53	31	22	.585	3 W					
(2)	Chi-A	53	23	30	.434	6 W				58.5	-4.5
1982	Chi-A	162	87	75	.537	3 W				88.5	-1.5
1983	Chi-A	162	99	63	.611	1 W				96.0	3.0
1984	Chi-A	162	74	88	.457	●5 W				75.2	-1.2
1985	Chi-A	163	85	77	.525	3 W				82.6	2.4
1986	Chi-A	64	26	38	.406	6 W	5 W		1/3	29.7	-3.7

YEAR	TM/L	G	W	L	PCT	STANDING			M/Y	W-EXP	A-E
	Oak-A	79	45	34	.570	7 W	●3 W		3/3	38.1	6.9
1987	Oak-A	162	81	81	.500	3 W				82.6	-1.6
1988	Oak-A	162	104	58	.642	♦1 W				99.2	4.8
1989	Oak-A	162	99	63	.611	★1 W				95.5	3.5
1990	Oak-A	162	103	59	.636	♦1 W				98.2	4.8
1991	Oak-A	162	84	78	.519	4 W				79.4	4.6
1992	Oak-A	162	96	66	.593	1 W				88.4	7.6
1993	Oak-A	162	68	94	.420	7 W				68.3	-0.3
1994	Oak-A	114	51	63	.447	2 W				53.2	-2.2
1995	Oak-A	144	67	77	.465	4 W				69.1	-2.1
1996	StL-N	162	88	74	.543	>1 C				86.3	1.7
18		2668	1408	1257	.528						26.8
Lasorda, Thomas Charles "Tom"											
1976	LA-N	4	2	2	.500	2 W	2 W		2/2	2.2	-0.2
1977	LA-N	162	98	64	.605	♦1 W				100.4	-2.4
1978	LA-N	162	95	67	.586	♦1 W				97.3	-2.3
1979	LA-N	162	79	83	.488	3 W				83.2	-4.2
1980	LA-N	163	92	71	.564	▲2 W				89.3	2.7
1981(1)	LA-N	57	36	21	.632	★1 W				65.4	-2.4
(2)	LA-N	53	27	26	.509	4 W					
1982	LA-N	162	88	74	.543	2 W				89.4	-1.4
1983	LA-N	163	91	71	.562	1 W				85.9	5.1
1984	LA-N	162	79	83	.488	4 W				78.8	0.2
1985	LA-N	162	95	67	.586	1 W				92.1	2.9
1986	LA-N	162	73	89	.451	5 W				76.7	-3.7
1987	LA-N	162	73	89	.451	4 W				76.8	-3.8
1988	LA-N	162	94	67	.584	★1 W				89.9	4.1
1989	LA-N	160	77	83	.481	4 W				82.1	-5.1
1990	LA-N	162	86	76	.531	2 W				85.4	0.6
1991	LA-N	162	93	69	.574	2 W				91.9	1.1
1992	LA-N	162	63	99	.389	6 W				71.2	-8.2
1993	LA-N	162	81	81	.500	4 W				82.4	-1.4
1994	LA-N	114	58	56	.509	1 W				59.3	-1.3
1995	LA-N	144	78	66	.542	o1 W				74.6	3.4
1996	LA-N	86	41	35	.539	1 W	o■2 W		1/2	40.5	0.5
21		3050	1599	1439	.526						-15.5
Latham, George Warren "Juice"											
1875	NH-n*	18	4	14	.222	11	8	8	2/3	1.5	2.5
1882	Phi-a*	75	41	34	.547	2				39.1	1.9
2		93	45	48	.484						4.4
Latham, Walter Arlington "Arlie"											
1896	StL-N*	3	0	3	.000	10	10	11	2/5	0.8	-0.8
Lavagetto, Harry Arthur "Cookie"											
1957	Was-A	134	51	83	.381	8	8		2/2	49.3	1.7
1958	Was-A	156	61	93	.396	8				56.8	4.2
1959	Was-A	154	63	91	.409	8				68.6	-5.6
1960	Was-A	154	73	81	.474	5				74.6	-1.6
1961	Min-A	49	19	30	.388	8	7		1/4	22.4	-3.4
	Min-A	10	4	6	.400	9	9	7	3/4	4.6	-0.6
5		657	271	384	.414						-5.3
Leadley, Robert H. "Bob"											
1888	Det-N	40	19	19	.500	3	5		2/2	21.5	-2.5
1890	Cle-N	58	23	33	.411	7	7		2/2	20.2	2.8
1891	Cle-N	68	34	34	.500	4	5		1/2	31.8	2.2
3		166	76	86	.469						2.5
Lefebvre, James Kenneth "Jim"											
1989	Sea-A	162	73	89	.451	6 W				77.6	-4.6
1990	Sea-A	162	77	85	.475	5 W				76.8	0.2
1991	Sea-A	162	83	79	.512	5 W				83.9	-0.9
1992	Chi-N	162	78	84	.481	4 E				77.6	0.4
1993	Chi-N	163	84	78	.519	4 E				80.9	3.1
5		811	395	415	.488						-1.7
Lemon, James Robert "Jim"											
1968	Was-A	161	65	96	.404	10				64.9	0.1
Lemon, Robert Granville "Bob"											
1970	KC-A	110	46	64	.418	5 W	●4 W		2/2	48.3	-2.3
1971	KC-A	161	85	76	.528	2 W				84.6	0.4
1972	KC-A	154	76	78	.494	4 W				80.9	-4.9
1977	Chi-A	162	90	72	.556	3 W				87.9	2.1
1978	Chi-A	74	34	40	.459	5 W	5 W		1/2	32.4	1.6
	NY-A	68	48	20	.706	4 E	▲★1 E		3/3	40.7	7.3
1979	NY-A	65	34	31	.523	4 E	4 E		1/2	35.0	-1.0
1981(2)	NY-A	25	11	14	.440	4 E	6 E		2/2	14.5	-3.5
1982	NY-A	14	6	8	.429	●4 E	5 E		1/3	6.9	-0.9
8		833	430	403	.516						-1.4
Lennon, William F. "Bill"											
1871	Kek-n*	14	5	9	.357	7	8		1/2	1.8	3.2
Leyland, James Richard "Jim"											
1986	Pit-N	162	64	98	.395	6 E				77.2	-13.2
1987	Pit-N	162	80	82	.494	●4 E				78.9	1.1
1988	Pit-N	160	85	75	.531	2 E				83.7	1.3
1989	Pit-N	164	74	88	.457	5 E				76.4	-2.4
1990	Pit-N	162	95	67	.586	1 E				92.8	2.2
1991	Pit-N	162	98	64	.605	1 E				94.9	3.1
1992	Pit-N	162	96	66	.593	1 E				91.4	4.6
1993	Pit-N	162	75	87	.463	5 E				71.3	3.7
1994	Pit-N	114	53	61	.465	●3 C				45.7	7.3
1995	Pit-N	144	58	86	.403	5 C				61.6	-3.6
1996	Pit-N	162	73	89	.451	5 C				75.6	-2.6
11		1716	851	863	.496						1.5
Leyva, Nicolas Tomas "Nick"											
1989	Phi-N	163	67	95	.414	6 E				70.0	-3.0
1990	Phi-N	162	77	85	.475	●4 E				72.5	4.5
1991	Phi-N	13	4	9	.308	6 E	3 E		1/2	6.1	-2.1
3		338	148	189	.439						-0.5
Lillis, Robert Perry "Bob"											
1982	Hou-N	51	28	23	.549	5 W	5 W		2/2	23.7	4.3
1983	Hou-N	162	85	77	.525	3 W				80.7	4.3
1984	Hou-N	162	80	82	.494	●2 W				87.6	-7.6
1985	Hou-N	162	83	79	.512	●3 W				82.5	0.5
4		537	276	261	.514						1.5
Lipon, John Joseph "Johnny"											
1971	Cle-A	59	18	41	.305	6 E	6 E		2/2	21.6	-3.6
Lobert, John Bernard "Hans"											
1938	Phi-N	2	0	0	.000	8	8		2/2	0.6	-0.6
1942	Phi-N	151	42	109	.278	8				40.8	1.2
2		153	42	111	.275						0.6
Lockman, Carroll Walter "Whitey"											
1972	Chi-N	65	39	26	.600	4 E	2 E		2/2	37.7	1.3
1973	Chi-N	161	77	84	.478	5 E				76.1	0.9
1974	Chi-N	93	41	52	.441	5 E	6 E		1/2	37.6	3.4
3		319	157	162	.492						5.5
Loftus, Thomas Joseph "Tom"											
1884	Mil-U	12	8	4	.667	2				8.1	-0.1
1888	Cle-a	71	30	38	.441	8	6		2/2	25.3	4.7
1889	Cle-N	136	61	72	.459	6				60.5	0.5
1890	Cin-N	134	77	55	.583	4				77.2	-0.2
1891	Cin-N	138	56	81	.409	7				55.1	0.9
1900	Chi-N	146	65	75	.464	●5				58.7	6.3
1901	Chi-N	140	53	86	.381	6				57.5	-4.5
1902	Was-A	138	61	75	.449	6				60.4	0.6
1903	Was-A	140	43	94	.314	8				41.7	1.3
9		1055	454	580	.439						9.6
Lopat, Edmund Walter "Ed"											
1963	KC-A	162	73	89	.451	8				71.6	1.4
1964	KC-A	52	17	35	.327	10	10		1/2	19.1	-2.1
2		214	90	124	.421						-0.7
Lopez, Alfonso Ramon "Al"											
1951	Cle-A	155	93	61	.604	2				87.6	5.4
1952	Cle-A	155	93	61	.604	2				92.8	0.2
1953	Cle-A	155	92	62	.597	2				91.3	0.7
1954	Cle-A	156	111	43	.721	1				102.7	8.3
1955	Cle-A	154	93	61	.604	2				87.0	6.0
1956	Cle-A	155	88	66	.571	2				90.6	-2.6
1957	Chi-A	155	90	64	.584	2				91.8	-1.8
1958	Chi-A	155	82	72	.532	2				79.0	3.0
1959	Chi-A	156	94	60	.610	1				85.6	8.4
1960	Chi-A	154	87	67	.565	3				89.5	-2.5
1961	Chi-A	163	86	76	.531	4				84.9	1.1
1962	Chi-A	162	85	77	.525	5				86.1	-1.1
1963	Chi-A	162	94	68	.580	2				96.2	-2.2
1964	Chi-A	162	98	64	.605	2				96.9	1.1
1965	Chi-A	162	95	67	.586	2				91.3	3.9
1968	Chi-A	11	6	5	.545	9	9	●8	3/5	5.0	1.0
	Chi-A	36	15	21	.417	9	●8		5/5	16.3	-1.3
1969	Chi-A	17	8	9	.471	4 W	5 W		1/2	7.4	0.6
17		2425	1410	1004	.584						28.3
Lord, Harry Donald											
1915	Buf-F*	110	60	49	.550	8	6		3/3	49.9	10.1
Lowe, Robert Lincoln "Bobby"											
1904	Det-A*	78	30	44	.405	7	7		2/2	30.3	-0.3
Lucchesi, Frank Joseph											
1970	Phi-N	161	73	88	.453	5 E				66.3	6.7
1971	Phi-N	162	67	95	.414	6 E				66.9	0.1
1972	Phi-N	76	26	50	.342	6 E			1/2	30.9	-4.9
1975	Tex-A	67	35	32	.522	4 W	3 W		2/2	32.7	2.3
1976	Tex-A	162	76	86	.469	●4 W				77.1	-1.1
1977	Tex-A	62	31	31	.500	●3 W	2 W		1/4	35.3	-4.3
1987	Chi-N	25	8	17	.320	5 E	6 E		2/2	11.3	-3.3
7		715	316	399	.442						-4.4
Lumley, Harry G											
1909	Bro-N*	155	55	98	.359	6				55.6	-0.6
Lyons, Theodore Amar "Ted"											
1946	Chi-A	125	64	60	.516	7	5		2/2	59.1	4.9
1947	Chi-A	155	70	84	.455	6				65.4	4.6
1948	Chi-A	154	51	101	.336	8				50.4	0.6
3		434	185	245	.430						10.1
Mack, Cornelius Alexander "Connie"											
1894	Pit-N*	23	12	11	.545	7	7		2/2	10.8	1.2
1895	Pit-N*	135	71	61	.538	7				68.1	2.9
1896	Pit-N*	131	66	63	.512	6				68.5	-2.5
1901	Phi-A	137	74	62	.544	4				71.9	2.1
1902	Phi-A	137	83	53	.610	1				81.0	2.0
1903	Phi-A	137	75	60	.556	2				75.7	-0.7
1904	Phi-A	155	81	70	.536	5				81.7	-0.7
1905	Phi-A	152	92	56	.622	1				88.5	3.5

YEAR	TM/L	G	W	L	PCT	STANDING			M/Y	W-EXP	A-E
1906	Phi-A	149	78	67	.538	4				74.5	3.5
1907	Phi-A	150	88	57	.607	2				80.4	7.6
1908	Phi-A	157	68	85	.444	6				67.7	0.3
1909	Phi-A	153	95	58	.621	2				99.5	-4.5
1910	Phi-A	155	102	48	.680	★1				101.0	1.0
1911	Phi-A	152	101	50	.669	★1				100.7	0.3
1912	Phi-A	153	90	62	.592	3				87.8	2.2
1913	Phi-A	153	96	57	.627	★1				96.6	-0.6
1914	Phi-A	158	99	53	.651	1				99.2	-0.2
1915	Phi-A	154	43	109	.283	8				42.3	0.7
1916	Phi-A	154	36	117	.235	8				41.5	-5.5
1917	Phi-A	154	55	98	.359	8				59.2	-4.2
1918	Phi-A	130	52	76	.406	8				50.0	2.0
1919	Phi-A	140	36	104	.257	8				40.8	-4.8
1920	Phi-A	156	48	106	.312	8				49.3	-1.3
1921	Phi-A	155	53	100	.346	8				54.0	-1.0
1922	Phi-A	155	65	89	.422	7				65.1	-0.1
1923	Phi-A	153	69	83	.454	6				66.2	2.8
1924	Phi-A	152	71	81	.467	5				67.0	4.0
1925	Phi-A	153	88	64	.579	2				87.1	0.9
1926	Phi-A	150	83	67	.553	3				86.1	-3.1
1927	Phi-A	155	91	63	.591	2				87.9	3.1
1928	Phi-A	153	98	55	.641	2				97.4	0.6
1929	Phi-A	151	104	46	.693	★1				102.1	1.9
1930	Phi-A	154	102	52	.662	★1				95.0	7.0
1931	Phi-A	153	107	45	.704	1				98.4	8.6
1932	Phi-A	154	94	60	.610	2				97.5	-3.5
1933	Phi-A	152	79	72	.523	3				77.5	1.5
1934	Phi-A	153	68	82	.453	5				68.1	-0.1
1935	Phi-A	149	58	91	.389	8				59.8	-1.8
1936	Phi-A	154	53	100	.346	8				47.1	5.9
1937	Phi-A	120	39	80	.328	7	7		1/2	48.0	-9.0
1938	Phi-A	154	53	99	.349	8				55.1	-2.1
1939	Phi-A	62	25	37	.403	6	7		1/2	19.7	5.3
1940	Phi-A	154	54	100	.351	8				55.9	-1.9
1941	Phi-A	154	64	90	.416	8				65.0	-1.0
1942	Phi-A	154	55	99	.357	8				51.5	3.5
1943	Phi-A	155	49	105	.318	8				53.4	-4.4
1944	Phi-A	155	72	82	.468	●5				69.3	2.7
1945	Phi-A	153	52	98	.347	8				59.1	-7.1
1946	Phi-A	155	49	105	.318	8				60.8	-11.8
1947	Phi-A	156	78	76	.506	5				79.0	-1.0
1948	Phi-A	154	84	70	.545	4				76.4	7.6
1949	Phi-A	154	81	73	.526	5				77.1	3.9
1950	Phi-A	154	52	102	.338	8				54.3	-2.3
53		7755	3731	3948	.486						13.6

Mack, Dennis Joseph "Denny"

YEAR	TM/L	G	W	L	PCT	STANDING			M/Y	W-EXP	A-E
1882	Lou-a*	80	42	38	.525	3				48.7	-6.7

Mack, Earle Thaddeus

YEAR	TM/L	G	W	L	PCT	STANDING			M/Y	W-EXP	A-E
1937	Phi-A	34	15	17	.469	7	7		2/2	12.9	2.1
1939	Phi-A	91	30	60	.333	6	7		2/2	28.6	1.4
2		125	45	77	.369						3.5

Macullar, James F. "Jimmy"

YEAR	TM/L	G	W	L	PCT	STANDING			M/Y	W-EXP	A-E
1879	Syr-N*	27	5	21	.192	6	7		3/3	6.6	-1.6

Magee, Leo Christopher "Lee"

YEAR	TM/L	G	W	L	PCT	STANDING			M/Y	W-EXP	A-E
1915	Bro-F*	118	53	64	.453	7	7		1/2	56.5	-3.5

Malone, Ferguson G. "Fergy"

YEAR	TM/L	G	W	L	PCT	STANDING			M/Y	W-EXP	A-E
1873	Phi-n*	53	36	27	.571					35.9	0.1
1874	Chi-n*	36	18	18	.500	4	5		1/2	15.1	2.9
1884	Phi-U*	67	21	46	.313	7				23.1	-2.1
3		156	75	91	.452						0.9

Manning, James H. "Jimmy"

YEAR	TM/L	G	W	L	PCT	STANDING			M/Y	W-EXP	A-E
1901	Was-A	138	61	73	.455					58.3	2.7

Manning, John E. "Jack"

YEAR	TM/L	G	W	L	PCT	STANDING			M/Y	W-EXP	A-E
1877	Cin-N*	20	7	12	.368	6	6		3/3	4.2	2.8

Maranville, Walter James Vincent "Rabbit"

YEAR	TM/L	G	W	L	PCT	STANDING			M/Y	W-EXP	A-E
1925	Chi-N*	53	23	30	.434	7	7	8	2/3	24.8	-1.8

Marion, Martin Whitford "Marty"

YEAR	TM/L	G	W	L	PCT	STANDING			M/Y	W-EXP	A-E
1951	StL-N	155	81	73	.526	3				78.2	2.8
1952	StL-A*	104	42	61	.408	8	7		2/2	42.7	-0.7
1953	StL-A*	154	54	100	.351	8				54.3	-0.3
1954	Chi-A	9	3	6	.333	3	3		2/2	5.7	-2.7
1955	Chi-A	155	91	63	.591	3				94.5	-3.5
1956	Chi-A	154	85	69	.552	3				91.1	-6.1
6		731	356	372	.489						-10.5

Marshall, Rufus James "Jim"

YEAR	TM/L	G	W	L	PCT	STANDING			M/Y	W-EXP	A-E
1974	Chi-N	69	25	44	.362	5 E	6 E		2/2	27.9	-2.9
1975	Chi-N	162	75	87	.463	●5 E				69.8	5.2
1976	Chi-N	162	75	87	.463	4 E				68.8	6.2
1979	Oak-A	162	54	108	.333	7 W				52.0	0.2
4		555	229	326	.413						10.5

Martin, Alfred Manuel "Billy"

YEAR	TM/L	G	W	L	PCT	STANDING			M/Y	W-EXP	A-E
1969	Min-A	162	97	65	.599	1 W				98.5	-1.5
1971	Det-A	162	91	71	.562	2 E				86.8	4.2
1972	Det-A	156	86	70	.551	1 E				83.0	3.0
1973	Det-A	134	71	63	.530	3 E	3 E		1/2	64.2	6.8
	Tex-A	23	9	14	.391	6 W	6 W		3/3	8.3	0.7
1974	Tex-A	161	84	76	.525	2 W				79.2	4.8
1975	Tex-A	95	44	51	.463	4 W	3 W		1/2	46.4	-2.4
	NY-A	56	30	26	.536	3 E	3 E		2/2	31.5	-1.5
1976	NY-A	159	97	62	.610	◆1 E				95.7	1.3
1977	NY-A	162	100	62	.617	★1 E				98.9	1.1
1978	NY-A	94	52	42	.553	3 E	▲★1 E		1/3	56.3	-4.3
1979	NY-A	95	55	40	.579	4 E	4 E		2/2	51.2	3.8
1980	Oak-A	162	83	79	.512	2 W				85.6	-2.6
1981(1)	Oak-A	60	37	23	.617	>1 W					
(2)	Oak-A	49	27	22	.551	2 W				60.4	3.6
1982	Oak-A	162	68	94	.420	5 W				68.4	-0.4
1983	NY-A	162	91	71	.562	3 E				87.7	3.3
1985	NY-A	145	91	54	.628	7 E	2 E		2/2	88.4	2.6
1988	NY-A	68	40	28	.588	2 E	5 E		1/2	35.0	5.0
16		2267	1253	1013	.553						27.5

Martin, Alphonse Case "Phonney"

YEAR	TM/L	G	W	L	PCT	STANDING			M/Y	W-EXP	A-E
1872	Eck-n*	9	1	8	.111	10	9		3/3	-1.0	2.0

Martinez, Orlando iva] "Marty"

YEAR	TM/L	G	W	L	PCT	STANDING			M/Y	W-EXP	A-E
1986	Sea-A	1	0	1	.000	6 W	6 W	7 W	2/3	0.4	-0.4

Mason, Charles E. "Charlie"

YEAR	TM/L	G	W	L	PCT	STANDING			M/Y	W-EXP	A-E
1887	Phi-a	82	38	40	.487	6	5		2/2	39.1	-1.1

Mathews, Edwin Lee "Eddie"

YEAR	TM/L	G	W	L	PCT	STANDING			M/Y	W-EXP	A-E
1972	Atl-N	50	23	27	.460	4 W	4 W		2/2	21.6	1.4
1973	Atl-N	162	76	85	.472	5 W				82.9	-6.9
1974	Atl-N	99	50	49	.505	4 W	3 W		1/2	56.1	-6.1
3		311	149	161	.481						-11.6

Mathewson, Christopher "Christy"

YEAR	TM/L	G	W	L	PCT	STANDING			M/Y	W-EXP	A-E
1916	Cin-N*	69	25	43	.368	8	●7		3/3	28.4	-3.4
1917	Cin-N	157	78	76	.506	4				75.9	2.1
1918	Cin-N	120	61	57	.517	4	3		1/2	62.3	-1.3
3		346	164	176	.482						-2.7

Mattick, Robert James "Bobby"

YEAR	TM/L	G	W	L	PCT	STANDING			M/Y	W-EXP	A-E
1980	Tor-A	162	67	95	.414	7 E				66.8	0.2
1981(1)	Tor-A	58	16	42	.276	7 E					
(2)	Tor-A	48	21	27	.438	7 E				38.0	-1.0
2		268	104	164	.388						-0.8

Mauch, Gene William

YEAR	TM/L	G	W	L	PCT	STANDING			M/Y	W-EXP	A-E
1960	Phi-N	152	58	94	.382	●4	8		3/3	60.8	-2.8
1961	Phi-N	155	47	107	.305	8				55.7	-8.7
1962	Phi-N	161	81	80	.503	7				75.1	5.9
1963	Phi-N	162	87	75	.537	4				88.0	-1.0
1964	Phi-N	162	92	70	.568	●2				87.4	4.6
1965	Phi-N	162	85	76	.528	6				79.1	5.9
1966	Phi-N	162	87	75	.537	4				86.9	0.1
1967	Phi-N	162	82	80	.506	5				84.4	-2.4
1968	Phi-N	54	27	27	.500	●6	●7		1/3	24.3	2.7
1969	Mon-N	162	52	110	.321	6 E				59.5	-7.5
1970	Mon-N	162	73	89	.451	6 E				69.1	3.9
1971	Mon-N	162	71	90	.441	5 E				69.4	1.6
1972	Mon-N	156	70	86	.449	5 E				67.3	2.7
1973	Mon-N	162	79	83	.488	4 E				77.5	1.5
1974	Mon-N	161	79	82	.491	4 E				81.0	-2.0
1975	Mon-N	162	75	87	.463	●5 E				71.5	3.5
1976	Min-A	162	85	77	.525	3 W				84.9	0.1
1977	Min-A	161	84	77	.522	4 W				89.0	-5.0
1978	Min-A	162	73	89	.451	4 W				79.8	-6.8
1979	Min-A	162	82	80	.506	4 W				84.9	-2.9
1980	Min-A	125	54	71	.432	4 W	3 W		1/2	58.2	-4.2
1981(1)	Cal-A	13	9	4	.692	4 W	4 W		2/2		
(2)	Cal-A	50	20	30	.400	7 W				32.9	-3.9
1982	Cal-A	162	93	69	.574	1 W				95.3	-2.3
1985	Cal-A	162	90	72	.556	2 W				83.9	6.1
1986	Cal-A	162	92	70	.568	1 W				91.2	0.8
1987	Cal-A	162	75	87	.463	●6 W				77.8	-2.8
26		3942	1902	2037	.483						-12.9

McAleer, James Robert "Jimmy'

YEAR	TM/L	G	W	L	PCT	STANDING			M/Y	W-EXP	A-E
1901	Cle-A*	138	55	82	.401	7				53.1	0.9
1902	StL-A*	140	78	58	.574	2				69.2	8.8
1903	StL-A	139	65	74	.468	6				66.7	-1.7
1904	StL-A	156	65	87	.428	6				62.0	3.0
1905	StL-A	156	54	99	.353	8				65.6	-11.6
1906	StL-A	154	76	73	.510	5				81.4	-5.4
1907	StL-A*	155	69	83	.454	6				74.5	-5.5
1908	StL-A	155	83	69	.546	4				83.1	-0.1
1909	StL-A	154	61	89	.407	7				59.3	1.7
1910	Was-A	157	66	85	.437	7				69.8	-3.8
1911	Was-A	154	64	90	.416	7				62.9	1.1
11		1658	736	889	.453						-12.8

McBride, George Florian

YEAR	TM/L	G	W	L	PCT	STANDING			M/Y	W-EXP	A-E
1921	Was-A	154	80	73	.523	4				73.2	6.8

McBride, James Dickson "Dick"

YEAR	TM/L	G	W	L	PCT	STANDING			M/Y	W-EXP	A-E
1871	Ath-n*	28	21	7	.750	1				20.9	0.1
1872	Ath-n*	47	30	14	.682	4				35.1	-5.1
1873	Ath-n*	52	28	23	.549	5				30.7	-2.7
1874	Ath-n*	56	33	23	.589	3				35.2	-2.2
1875	Ath-n*	69	49	18	.731	2	2		1/2	55.1	-6.1
5		252	161	85	.654						-16.0

McCallister, John "Jack"

YEAR	TM/L	G	W	L	PCT	STANDING			M/Y	W-EXP	A-E
1927	Cle-A	153	66	87	.431	6				66.9	-0.9

McCarthy, Joseph Vincent "Joe"

YEAR	TM/L	G	W	L	PCT	STANDING			M/Y	W-EXP	A-E
1926	Chi-N	155	82	72	.532	4				85.3	-3.3
1927	Chi-N	153	85	68	.556	4				85.3	-0.3
1928	Chi-N	154	91	63	.591	3				87.1	3.9
1929	Chi-N	156	98	54	.645	1				96.1	1.9
1930	Chi-N	152	86	64	.573	2	2		1/2	85.8	0.2
1931	NY-A	155	94	59	.614	2				103.3	-9.3
1932	NY-A	156	107	47	.695	★1				102.1	4.9
1933	NY-A	152	91	59	.607	2				89.3	1.7
1934	NY-A	154	94	60	.610	2				93.6	0.4
1935	NY-A	149	89	60	.597	2				92.4	-3.4
1936	NY-A	155	102	51	.667	★1				105.9	-3.9
1937	NY-A	157	102	52	.662	★1				105.5	-3.5
1938	NY-A	157	99	53	.651	★1				99.5	-0.5
1939	NY-A	152	106	45	.702	★1				114.5	-8.5
1940	NY-A	155	88	66	.571	3				91.1	-3.1
1941	NY-A	156	101	53	.656	★1				96.5	4.5
1942	NY-A	154	103	51	.669	1				107.3	-4.3
1943	NY-A	155	98	56	.636	★1				90.6	7.4
1944	NY-A	154	83	71	.539	3				82.9	0.1
1945	NY-A	152	81	71	.533	4				83.2	-2.2
1946	NY-A	35	22	13	.629	2	3		1/3	20.8	1.2
1948	Bos-A	155	96	59	.619	▲2				94.8	1.2
1949	Bos-A	155	96	58	.623	2				98.6	-2.6
1950	Bos-A	59	31	28	.525	4	3		1/2	36.9	-5.9
24		3487	2125	1333	.615						-23.6

McCarthy, Thomas Francis "Tommy"

YEAR	TM/L	G	W	L	PCT	STANDING			M/Y	W-EXP	A-E
1890	StL-a*	22	11	11	.500	4	3		1/6	12.9	-1.9
	StL-a*	5	4	1	.800	2	2	3	5/6	2.9	1.1

McCloskey, John Joseph

YEAR	TM/L	G	W	L	PCT	STANDING			M/Y	W-EXP	A-E
1895	Lou-N	133	35	96	.267	12				33.4	1.6
1896	Lou-N	19	2	17	.105	12	12		1/2	5.2	-3.2
1906	StL-N	154	52	98	.347	7				59.5	-7.5
1907	StL-N	155	52	101	.340	8				54.5	-2.5
1908	StL-N	154	49	105	.318	8				46.9	2.1
5		615	190	417	.313						-9.5

McCormick, James "Jim"

YEAR	TM/L	G	W	L	PCT	STANDING			M/Y	W-EXP	A-E
1879	Cle-N*	82	27	55	.329	6				27.5	-0.5
1880	Cle-N*	85	47	37	.560	3				47.1	-0.1
1882	Cle-N*	4	0	4	.000	8	5		1/2	2.0	-2.0
3		171	74	96	.435						-2.6

McGaha, Fred Melvin "Mel"

YEAR	TM/L	G	W	L	PCT	STANDING			M/Y	W-EXP	A-E
1962	Cle-A	160	78	82	.488	6	6		1/2	73.7	4.3
1964	KC-A	111	40	70	.364	10	10		2/2	40.3	-0.3
1965	KC-A	26	5	21	.192	10	10		1/2	10.2	-5.2
3		297	123	173	.416						-1.2

McGeary, Michael Henry "Mike"

YEAR	TM/L	G	W	L	PCT	STANDING			M/Y	W-EXP	A-E
1875	Phi-n*	63	34	27	.557	4	5		1/2	37.8	-3.8
1880	Pro-N*	16	8	7	.533	4	2		1/3	9.7	-1.7
1881	Cle-N*	11	4	7	.364	6	7		1/2	5.2	-1.2
3		90	46	41	.529						-6.7

McGraw, John Joseph

YEAR	TM/L	G	W	L	PCT	STANDING			M/Y	W-EXP	A-E
1899	Bal-N*	152	86	62	.581	4				86.9	-0.9
1901	Bal-A*	135	68	65	.511	5				67.4	0.6
1902	Bal-A*	58	26	31	.456	7	8		1/2	23.5	2.5
	NY-N*	65	25	38	.397	8	8		3/3	21.7	3.3
1903	NY-N*	142	84	55	.604	2				85.6	-1.6
1904	NY-N*	158	106	47	.693	1				105.4	0.6
1905	NY-N*	155	105	48	.686	★1				105.2	-0.2
1906	NY-N*	153	96	56	.632	2				88.7	7.3
1907	NY-N	155	82	71	.536	4				83.8	-1.8
1908	NY-N	157	98	56	.636	●2				99.1	-1.1
1909	NY-N	158	92	61	.601	3				85.0	7.0
1910	NY-N	155	91	63	.591	2				92.4	-1.4
1911	NY-N	154	99	54	.647	1				98.6	0.4
1912	NY-N	154	103	48	.682	1				100.6	2.4
1913	NY-N	156	101	51	.664	1				94.3	6.7
1914	NY-N	156	84	70	.545	2				87.2	-3.2
1915	NY-N	155	69	83	.454	8				71.1	-2.1
1916	NY-N	155	86	66	.566	4				86.5	-0.5
1917	NY-N	158	98	56	.636	1				97.3	0.7
1918	NY-N	124	71	53	.573	2				69.3	1.7
1919	NY-N	140	87	53	.621	2				84.6	2.4
1920	NY-N	155	86	68	.558	2				91.8	-5.8
1921	NY-N	153	94	59	.614	★1				96.1	-2.1
1922	NY-N	156	93	61	.604	★1				95.7	-2.7
1923	NY-N	153	95	58	.621	1				93.1	1.9
1924	NY-N	29	16	13	.552	3	1		1/3	18.4	-2.4
	NY-N	81	45	35	.563	1	1		3/3	50.9	-5.9
1925	NY-N	14	10	4	.714	1	2		1/3	7.3	2.7
	NY-N	106	55	51	.519	1	2		3/3	55.3	-0.3
1926	NY-N	151	74	77	.490	5				75.0	-1.0
1927	NY-N	122	70	52	.574	4	3		1/2	68.3	1.7
1928	NY-N	155	93	61	.604	2				92.1	0.9
1929	NY-N	152	84	67	.556	3				92.9	-8.9
1930	NY-N	154	87	67	.565	3				89.8	-2.8
1931	NY-N	153	87	65	.572	2				93.0	-6.0
1932	NY-N	40	17	23	.425	8	●6		1/2	21.2	-4.2
33		4769	2763	1948	.586						-12.0

McGuire, James Thomas "Deacon"

YEAR	TM/L	G	W	L	PCT	STANDING			M/Y	W-EXP	A-E
	Was-										
1898	N*	70	21	47	.309	10	11	11	3/4	24.3	-3.3
1907	Bos-A*	112	45	61	.425	8	7		4/4	45.2	-0.2
1908	Bos-A*	115	53	62	.461	6	5		1/2	61.8	-8.8
1909	Cle-A	41	14	25	.359	4	6		2/2	18.3	-4.3
1910	Cle-A*	161	71	81	.467	5				64.0	7.0
1911	Cle-A	17	6	11	.353	7	3		1/2	8.3	-2.3
6		516	210	287	.423						-12.0

McGunnigle, William Henry "Bill"

YEAR	TM/L	G	W	L	PCT	STANDING			M/Y	W-EXP	A-E
1888	Bro-a	143	88	52	.629	2				87.0	1.0
1889	Bro-a	140	94	43	.686	1				93.4	-0.4
1890	Bro-N	129	86	43	.667	1				87.7	-1.7
1891	Pit-N	59	24	33	.421	8	8		2/2	25.9	-1.9
1896	Lou-N	115	36	76	.321	12	12		2/2	30.9	5.1
5		586	328	247	.570						2.1

McInnis, John Phalen "Stuffy"

YEAR	TM/L	G	W	L	PCT	STANDING			M/Y	W-EXP	A-E
1927	Phi-N*	155	51	103	.331	8				55.9	-4.9

McKechnie, William Boyd "Bill"

YEAR	TM/L	G	W	L	PCT	STANDING			M/Y	W-EXP	A-E
1915	New-F*	102	54	45	.545	6	5		2/2	51.2	2.8
1922	Pit-N	90	53	36	.596	5	●3		2/2	51.5	1.5
1923	Pit-N	154	87	67	.565	3				85.7	1.3
1924	Pit-N	153	90	63	.588	3				90.4	-0.4
1925	Pit-N	153	95	58	.621	★1				94.6	0.4
1926	Pit-N	157	84	69	.549	3				84.4	-0.4
1928	StL-N	154	95	59	.617	1				93.8	1.2
1929	StL-N	63	34	29	.540	4	4		3/3	32.5	1.5
1930	Bos-N	154	70	84	.455	6				63.5	6.5
1931	Bos-N	156	64	90	.416	7				61.2	2.8
1932	Bos-N	155	77	77	.500	5				76.4	0.6
1933	Bos-N	156	83	71	.539	4				79.4	3.6
1934	Bos-N	152	78	73	.517	4				72.4	5.6
1935	Bos-N	153	38	115	.248	8				49.3	-11.3
1936	Bos-N	157	71	83	.461	6				68.4	2.6
1937	Bos-N	152	79	73	.520	5				78.5	0.5
1938	Cin-N	151	82	68	.547	4				83.9	-1.9
1939	Cin-N	156	97	57	.630	1				94.5	2.5
1940	Cin-N	155	100	53	.654	★1				95.5	4.5
1941	Cin-N	154	88	66	.571	3				82.6	5.4
1942	Cin-N	154	76	76	.500	4				74.0	2.0
1943	Cin-N	155	87	67	.565	2				84.2	2.8
1944	Cin-N	155	89	65	.578	3				81.0	8.0
1945	Cin-N	154	61	93	.396	7				60.2	0.8
1946	Cin-N	152	64	86	.427	6	6		1/2	69.8	-5.8
25		3647	1896	1723	.524						37.3

McKeon, John Aloysius "Jack"

YEAR	TM/L	G	W	L	PCT	STANDING			M/Y	W-EXP	A-E
1973	KC-A	162	88	74	.543	2 W				81.3	6.7
1974	KC-A	162	77	85	.475	5 W				81.5	-4.5
1975	KC-A	96	50	46	.521	2 W	2 W		1/2	51.7	-1.7
1977	Oak-A	53	26	27	.491	●5 W	7 W		1/2	21.6	4.4
1978	Oak-A	123	45	78	.366	1 W	6 W		2/2	48.4	-3.4
1988	SD-N	115	67	48	.583	5 W	3 W		2/2	58.4	8.6
1989	SD-N	162	89	73	.549	2 W				82.7	6.3
1990	SD-N	80	37	43	.463	4 W	5 W		1/2	40.0	-3.0
8		953	479	474	.503						13.4

McKinnon, Alexander J. "Alex"

YEAR	TM/L	G	W	L	PCT	STANDING			M/Y	W-EXP	A-E
1885	StL-N*	39	6	32	.158	5	8	8	2/3	11.8	-5.8

McKnight, Dennis Hamar "Denny"

YEAR	TM/L	G	W	L	PCT	STANDING			M/Y	W-EXP	A-E
1884	Pit-a	12	4	8	.333	9	10		1/5	2.7	1.3

McManus, George

YEAR	TM/L	G	W	L	PCT	STANDING			M/Y	W-EXP	A-E
1876	StL-N	8	6	2	.750	2	2		2/2	5.9	0.1
1877	StL-N	60	28	32	.467	4				26.8	1.2
2		68	34	34	.500						1.3

McManus, Martin Joseph "Marty"

YEAR	TM/L	G	W	L	PCT	STANDING			M/Y	W-EXP	A-E
1932	Bos-A*	99	32	67	.323	8	8		2/2	27.8	4.2
1933	Bos-A*	149	63	86	.423	7				68.9	-5.9
2		248	95	153	.383						-1.7

McMillan, Roy David

YEAR	TM/L	G	W	L	PCT	STANDING			M/Y	W-EXP	A-E
1972	Mil-A	2	1	1	.500	6 E	6 E	6 E	2/3	0.9	0.1
1975	NY-N	53	26	27	.491	3 E	●3 E		2/2	27.2	-1.2
2		55	27	28	.491						-1.1

McNamara, John Francis

YEAR	TM/L	G	W	L	PCT	STANDING			M/Y	W-EXP	A-E
1969	Oak-A	13	8	5	.615	2 W	2 W		2/2	7.0	1.0
1970	Oak-A	162	89	73	.549	2 W				90.1	-1.1
1974	SD-N	162	60	102	.370	6 W				51.2	8.8
1975	SD-N	162	71	91	.438	4 W				66.8	4.2
1976	SD-N	162	73	89	.451	5 W				71.0	2.0
1977	SD-N	48	20	28	.417	4 W	5 W		1/3	19.9	0.1
1979	Cin-N	160	90	71	.559	1 W				89.4	0.6
1980	Cin-N	163	89	73	.549	3 W				84.8	4.2
1981(1)	Cin-N	56	35	21	.625	2 W					
(2)		52	31	21	.596	2 W				56.5	9.5
1982	Cin-N	92	34	58	.370	6 W	6 W		1/2	38.8	-4.8
1983	Cal-A	162	70	92	.432	●5 W				75.4	-5.4
1984	Cal-A	162	81	81	.500	●2 W				80.9	0.1
1985	Bos-A	163	81	81	.500	5 E				88.9	-7.9
1986	Bos-A	161	95	66	.590	♦1 E				90.2	4.8
1987	Bos-A	162	78	84	.481	5 E				82.6	-4.6
1988	Bos-A	85	43	42	.506	4 E	1 E		1/2	48.9	-5.9

YEAR	TM/L	G	W	L	PCT	STANDING			M/Y	W-EXP	A-E
1990	Cle-A	162	77	85	.475	4 E				80.5	-3.5
1991	Cle-A	77	25	52	.325	7 E	7 E		1/2	29.4	-4.4
1996	Cal-A	44	17	27	.386	4 W			2/2	17.4	-0.4
	19	2411	1167	1242	.484						-2.6

McPhee, John Alexander "Bid"

YEAR	TM/L	G	W	L	PCT	STANDING			M/Y	W-EXP	A-E
1901	Cin-N	142	52	87	.374	8				44.8	7.2
1902	Cin-N	65	27	37	.422	6	4		1/3	35.2	-8.2
	2	207	79	124	.389						-0.9

McRae, Harold Abraham "Hal"

YEAR	TM/L	G	W	L	PCT	STANDING			M/Y	W-EXP	A-E
1991	KC-A	124	66	58	.532	7 W	6 W		3/3	62.4	3.6
1992	KC-A	162	72	90	.444	●5 W				74.9	-2.9
1993	KC-A	162	84	78	.519	3 W				79.0	5.0
1994	KC-A	115	64	51	.557	3 C				61.6	2.4
	4	563	286	277	.508						8.1

McVey, Calvin Alexander "Cal"

YEAR	TM/L	G	W	L	PCT	STANDING			M/Y	W-EXP	A-E
1873	Bal-n*	33	20	13	.606	3	3		1/2	24.3	-4.3
1878	Cin-N*	61	37	23	.617	2				34.9	2.1
1879	Cin-N*	63	34	28	.548	4	5		2/2	32.4	1.6
	3	157	91	64	.587						-0.6

Mele, Sabath Anthony "Sam"

YEAR	TM/L	G	W	L	PCT	STANDING			M/Y	W-EXP	A-E
1961	Min-A	7	2	5	.286	8	9	7	2/4	3.2	-1.2
	Min-A	95	45	49	.479	9	7		4/4	42.9	2.1
1962	Min-A	163	91	71	.562	2				89.4	1.6
1963	Min-A	161	91	70	.565	3				97.5	-6.5
1964	Min-A	163	79	83	.488	●6				87.0	-8.0
1965	Min-A	162	102	60	.630	1				98.9	3.1
1966	Min-A	162	89	73	.549	2				89.9	-0.9
1967	Min-A	50	25	25	.500	6	●2		1/2	27.7	-2.7
	7	963	524	436	.546						-12.4

Melillo, Oscar Donald "Ski"

YEAR	TM/L	G	W	L	PCT	STANDING			M/Y	W-EXP	A-E
1938	StL-A	10	2	7	.222	7	7		2/2	3.4	-1.4

Merrill, Carl Harrison "Stump"

YEAR	TM/L	G	W	L	PCT	STANDING			M/Y	W-EXP	A-E
1990	NY-A	113	49	64	.434	7 E	7 E		2/2	45.9	3.1
1991	NY-A	162	71	91	.438	5 E				70.7	0.3
	2	275	120	155	.436						3.4

Metro, Charles "Charlie"

YEAR	TM/L	G	W	L	PCT	STANDING			M/Y	W-EXP	A-E
1962	Chi-N	112	43	69	.384	9	9		3/3	42.5	0.5
1970	KC-A	52	19	33	.365	5 W	●4 W		1/2	22.8	-3.8
	2	164	62	102	.378						-3.3

Meyer, William Adam "Billy"

YEAR	TM/L	G	W	L	PCT	STANDING			M/Y	W-EXP	A-E
1948	Pit-N	156	83	71	.539	4				77.7	5.3
1949	Pit-N	154	71	83	.461	6				69.3	1.7
1950	Pit-N	154	57	96	.373	8				59.8	-2.8
1951	Pit-N	155	64	90	.416	7				62.1	1.9
1952	Pit-N	155	42	112	.273	8				48.3	-6.3
	5	774	317	452	.412						-0.2

Michael, Eugene Richard "Gene"

YEAR	TM/L	G	W	L	PCT	STANDING			M/Y	W-EXP	A-E
1981(1)	NY-A	56	34	22	.607	♦1 E				47.7	0.3
(2)	NY-A	26	14	12	.538	4 E	6 E		1/2		
1982	NY-A	86	44	42	.512	●4 E	●5 E	5 E	2/3	42.6	1.4
1986	Chi-N	102	46	56	.451	5 E	5 E		3/3	44.6	1.4
1987	Chi-N	136	68	68	.500	5 E	6 E		1/2	61.3	6.7
	4	406	206	200	.507						9.7

Milan, Jesse Clyde "Clyde"

YEAR	TM/L	G	W	L	PCT	STANDING			M/Y	W-EXP	A-E
1922	Was-A*	154	69	85	.448	6				71.3	-2.3

Miller, George Frederick

YEAR	TM/L	G	W	L	PCT	STANDING			M/Y	W-EXP	A-E
1894	StL-N*	133	56	76	.424	9				50.8	5.2

Miller, Raymond Roger "Ray"

YEAR	TM/L	G	W	L	PCT	STANDING			M/Y	W-EXP	A-E
1985	Min-A	100	50	50	.500	6 W	4 W		2/2	45.3	4.7
1986	Min-A	139	59	80	.424	7 W	6 W		1/2	61.4	-2.4
	2	239	109	130	.456						2.3

Mills, Colonel Buster "Buster"

YEAR	TM/L	G	W	L	PCT	STANDING			M/Y	W-EXP	A-E
1953	Cin-N	8	4	4	.500	6	6		2/2	3.6	0.4

Mills, Everett

YEAR	TM/L	G	W	L	PCT	STANDING			M/Y	W-EXP	A-E
1872	Bal-n*	17	8	6	.571	2	2		2/2	10.3	-2.3

Mitchell, Frederick Francis "Fred"

YEAR	TM/L	G	W	L	PCT	STANDING			M/Y	W-EXP	A-E
1917	Chi-N	157	74	80	.481	5				75.3	-1.3
1918	Chi-N	131	84	45	.651	1				80.8	3.2
1919	Chi-N	140	75	65	.536	3				75.7	-0.7
1920	Chi-N	154	75	79	.487	●5				75.3	-0.3
1921	Bos-N	153	79	74	.516	4				78.9	0.1
1922	Bos-N	154	53	100	.346	8				54.2	-1.2
1923	Bos-N	155	54	100	.351	7				61.0	-7.0
	7	1044	494	543	.476						-7.2

Moore, Jackie Spencer

YEAR	TM/L	G	W	L	PCT	STANDING			M/Y	W-EXP	A-E
1984	Oak-A	118	57	61	.483	5 W	4 W		2/2	54.9	2.1
1985	Oak-A	162	77	85	.475	●4 W				78.1	-1.1
1986	Oak-A	73	29	44	.397	●6 W	●3 W		1/3	35.2	-6.2
	3	353	163	190	.462						-5.2

Moore, Terry Bluford

YEAR	TM/L	G	W	L	PCT	STANDING			M/Y	W-EXP	A-E
1954	Phi-N	77	35	42	.455	3	4		2/2	40.8	-5.8

Moran, Patrick Joseph "Pat"

YEAR	TM/L	G	W	L	PCT	STANDING			M/Y	W-EXP	A-E
1915	Phi-N	153	90	62	.592	1				90.4	-0.4
1916	Phi-N	154	91	62	.595	2				87.0	4.0
1917	Phi-N	155	87	65	.572	2				84.8	2.2
1918	Phi-N	125	55	68	.447	6				53.1	1.9

YEAR	TM/L	G	W	L	PCT	STANDING			M/Y	W-EXP	A-E
1919	Cin-N	140	96	44	.686	★1				90.0	6.0
1920	Cin-N	154	82	71	.536	3				84.0	-2.0
1921	Cin-N	153	70	83	.458	6				73.3	-3.3
1922	Cin-N	156	86	68	.558	2				85.8	0.2
1923	Cin-N	154	91	63	.591	2				85.0	6.0
	9	1344	748	586	.561						14.6

Morgan, Joseph Michael "Joe"

YEAR	TM/L	G	W	L	PCT	STANDING			M/Y	W-EXP	A-E
1988	Bos-A	77	46	31	.597	4 E	1 E		2/2	44.3	1.7
1989	Bos-A	162	83	79	.512	3 E				84.8	-1.8
1990	Bos-A	162	88	74	.543	1 E				84.6	3.4
1991	Bos-A	162	84	78	.519	●2 E				82.9	1.1
	4	563	301	262	.535						4.3

Moriarty, George Joseph

YEAR	TM/L	G	W	L	PCT	STANDING			M/Y	W-EXP	A-E
1927	Det-A	156	82	71	.536	4				80.2	1.8
1928	Det-A	154	68	86	.442	6				71.3	-3.3
	2	310	150	157	.489						-1.5

Morrill, John Francis

YEAR	TM/L	G	W	L	PCT	STANDING			M/Y	W-EXP	A-E
1882	Bos-N*	85	45	39	.536	●3				47.4	-2.4
1883	Bos-N*	44	33	11	.750	4	1		2/2	30.5	2.5
1884	Bos-N*	116	73	38	.658	2				76.1	-3.1
1885	Bos-N*	113	46	66	.411	5				50.2	-4.2
1886	Bos-N*	118	56	61	.479	5				58.1	-2.1
1887	Bos-N*	32	12	17	.414	5	5		2/2	15.3	-3.3
1888	Bos-N*	137	70	64	.522	4				71.9	-1.9
1889	Was-N*	51	13	38	.255	8	8		1/2	16.2	-3.2
	8	696	348	334	.510						-17.7

Morton, Charles Hazen "Charlie"

YEAR	TM/L	G	W	L	PCT	STANDING			M/Y	W-EXP	A-E
1884	Tol-a*	110	46	58	.442	8				41.4	4.6
1885	Det-N*	38	7	31	.184	8	6		1/2	16.7	-9.7
1890	Tol-a	134	68	64	.515	4				70.6	-2.6
	3	282	121	153	.442						-7.8

Moses, Felix I.

YEAR	TM/L	G	W	L	PCT	STANDING			M/Y	W-EXP	A-E
1884	Ric-a	46	12	30	.286	12				11.8	0.2

Moss, John Lester "Les"

YEAR	TM/L	G	W	L	PCT	STANDING			M/Y	W-EXP	A-E
1968	Chi-A	2	0	2	.000	9	9	●8	2/5	0.9	-0.9
	Chi-A	34	12	22	.353	9	9	●8	4/5	15.4	-3.4
1979	Det-A	53	27	26	.509	5 E	5 E		1/3	27.5	-0.5
	2	89	39	50	.438						-4.8

Murnane, Timothy Hayes "Tim"

YEAR	TM/L	G	W	L	PCT	STANDING			M/Y	W-EXP	A-E
1884	Bos-U*	111	58	51	.532	5				61.6	-3.6

Murray, William Jeremiah "Billy"

YEAR	TM/L	G	W	L	PCT	STANDING			M/Y	W-EXP	A-E
1907	Phi-N	149	83	64	.565	3				77.7	5.3
1908	Phi-N	155	83	71	.539	4				84.2	-1.2
1909	Phi-N	154	74	79	.484	5				76.3	-2.3
	3	458	240	214	.529						1.9

Murtaugh, Daniel Edward "Danny"

YEAR	TM/L	G	W	L	PCT	STANDING			M/Y	W-EXP	A-E
1957	Pit-N	51	26	25	.510	7	●7		2/2	21.7	4.3
1958	Pit-N	154	84	70	.545	2				82.7	1.3
1959	Pit-N	155	78	76	.506	4				74.0	4.0
1960	Pit-N	155	95	59	.617	★1				91.5	3.5
1961	Pit-N	154	75	79	.487	6				78.9	-3.9
1962	Pit-N	161	93	68	.578	4				88.8	4.2
1963	Pit-N	162	74	88	.457	8				77.9	-3.9
1964	Pit-N	162	80	82	.494	●6				83.9	-3.9
1967	Pit-N	79	39	39	.500	6	6		2/2	38.3	0.7
1970	Pit-N	162	89	73	.549	1 E				87.7	1.3
1971	Pit-N	162	97	65	.599	★1 E				100.4	-3.4
1973	Pit-N	26	13	13	.500	2 E	3 E		2/2	13.2	-0.2
1974	Pit-N	162	88	74	.543	1 E				90.6	-2.6
1975	Pit-N	161	92	69	.571	1 E				96.2	-4.2
1976	Pit-N	162	92	70	.568	2 E				89.1	2.9
	15	2068	1115	950	.540						0.2

Mutrie, James J. "Jim"

YEAR	TM/L	G	W	L	PCT	STANDING			M/Y	W-EXP	A-E
1883	NY-a	97	54	42	.563	4				57.1	-3.1
1884	NY-a	112	75	32	.701	1				82.5	-7.5
1885	NY-N	112	85	27	.759	2				87.3	-2.3
1886	NY-N	124	75	44	.630	3				72.2	2.8
1887	NY-N	129	68	55	.553	4				69.6	-1.6
1888	NY-N	138	84	47	.641	1				84.3	-0.3
1889	NY-N	131	83	43	.659	1				82.2	0.8
1890	NY-N	135	63	68	.481	6				66.9	-3.9
1891	NY-N	136	71	61	.538	3				69.9	1.1
	9	1114	658	419	.611						-14.1

Myatt, George Edward "George"

YEAR	TM/L	G	W	L	PCT	STANDING			M/Y	W-EXP	A-E
1968	Phi-N	1	1	0	1.000	●6	5	●7	2/3	0.5	0.5
1969	Phi-N	54	19	35	.352	5 E	5 E		2/2	23.6	-4.6
	2	55	20	35	.364						-4.0

Myers, Henry C.

YEAR	TM/L	G	W	L	PCT	STANDING			M/Y	W-EXP	A-E
1882	Bal-a*	74	19	54	.260	6				14.2	4.8

Nash, William Mitchell "Billy"

YEAR	TM/L	G	W	L	PCT	STANDING			M/Y	W-EXP	A-E
1896	Phi-N*	130	62	68	.477	8				64.9	-2.9

Neun, John Henry "Johnny"

YEAR	TM/L	G	W	L	PCT	STANDING			M/Y	W-EXP	A-E
1946	NY-A	14	8	6	.571	3	3		3/3	8.3	-0.3
1947	Cin-N	154	73	81	.474	5				69.7	3.3
1948	Cin-N	100	44	56	.440	7	7		1/2	39.1	4.9
	3	268	125	143	.466						7.8

YEAR	TM/L	G	W	L	PCT	STANDING			M/Y	W-EXP	A-E
Newman, Jeffrey Lynn "Jeff"											
1986	Oak-A	10	2	8	.200	●6 W	7 W	●3W	2/3	4.8	-2.8
Nichols, Charles Augustus "Kid"											
1904	StL-N*	155	75	79	.487	5				77.8	-2.8
1905	StL-N*	14	5	9	.357	7	6		1/3	5.1	-0.1
	2	169	80	88	.476						-2.9
Nicol, Hugh											
1897	StL-N	40	8	32	.200	12	12	12	2/4	7.3	0.7
Nixon, Russell Eugene "Russ"											
1982	Cin-N	70	27	43	.386	6 W	6 W		2/2	29.5	-2.5
1983	Cin-N	162	74	88	.457	6 W				71.9	2.1
1988	Atl-N	121	42	79	.347	6 W	6 W		2/2	45.7	-3.7
1989	Atl-N	161	63	97	.394	6 W				69.7	-6.7
1990	Atl-N	65	25	40	.385	6 W	6 W		1/2	27.0	-2.0
	5	579	231	347	.400						-12.8
Norman, Henry Willis Patrick "Bill"											
1958	Det-A	105	56	49	.533	8	5		2/2	56.3	-0.3
1959	Det-A	17	2	15	.118	8	4		1/2	8.3	-6.3
	2	122	58	64	.475						-6.6
Oakes, Ennis Telfair "Rebel"											
1914	Pit-F*	143	61	78	.439	8	7		2/2	60.6	0.4
1915	Pit-F*	156	86	67	.562	3				84.1	1.9
	2	299	147	145	.503						2.3
Oates, Johnny Lane											
1991	Bal-A	125	54	71	.432	7 E	6 E		2/2	54.1	-0.1
1992	Bal-A	162	89	73	.549	3 E				86.1	2.9
1993	Bal-A	162	85	77	.525	●3 E				85.0	-0.0
1994	Bal-A	112	63	49	.563	2 E				64.9	-1.9
1995	Tex-A	144	74	70	.514	3 W				69.2	4.8
1996	Tex-A	163	90	72	.556	o1 W				92.9	-2.9
	6	868	455	412	.525						2.9
O'Connor, John Joseph "Jack"											
1910	StL-A*	158	47	107	.305	8				45.1	1.9
O'Day, Henry Francis "Hank"											
1912	Cin-N	155	75	78	.490	4				69.9	5.1
1914	Chi-N	156	78	76	.506	4				73.5	4.5
	2	311	153	154	.498						9.6
O'Farrell, Robert Arthur "Bob"											
1927	StL-N*	153	92	61	.601	2				85.3	6.7
1934	Cin-N*	91	30	60	.333	8	8		1/3	32.5	-2.5
	2	244	122	121	.502						4.2
O'Leary, Daniel "Dan"											
1884	Cin-U*	35	20	15	.571	5	3		1/2	24.6	-4.6
O'Neill, Stephen Francis "Steve"											
1935	Cle-A	60	36	23	.610	5	3		2/2	30.9	5.1
1936	Cle-A	157	80	74	.519	5				82.3	-2.3
1937	Cle-A	156	83	71	.539	4				81.6	1.4
1943	Det-A	155	78	76	.506	5				84.8	-6.8
1944	Det-A	156	88	66	.571	2				85.2	2.8
1945	Det-A	155	88	65	.575	★1				83.8	4.2
1946	Det-A	155	92	62	.597	2				91.4	0.6
1947	Det-A	158	85	69	.552	2				84.4	0.6
1948	Det-A	154	78	76	.506	5				74.4	3.6
1950	Bos-A	95	63	32	.663	4	3		2/2	59.5	3.5
1951	Bos-A	154	87	67	.565	3				84.5	2.5
1952	Phi-N	91	59	32	.648	6	4		2/2	52.1	6.9
1953	Phi-N	156	83	71	.539	●3				82.0	1.0
1954	Phi-N	77	40	37	.519	3	4		1/2	40.8	-0.8
	14	1879	1040	821	.559						22.2
Onslow, John James "Jack"											
1949	Chi-A	154	63	91	.409	6				68.1	-5.1
1950	Chi-A	31	8	22	.267	8	6		1/2	12.6	-4.6
	2	185	71	113	.386						-9.7
O'Rourke, James Henry "Jim"											
1881	Buf-N*	83	45	38	.542	3				40.9	4.1
1882	Buf-N*	84	45	39	.536	●3				45.5	-0.5
1883	Buf-N*	98	52	45	.536	5				51.8	0.2
1884	Buf-N*	115	64	47	.577	3				62.0	2.0
	Was-										
1893	N*	130	40	89	.310	12				39.2	0.8
	5	510	246	258	.488						6.7
Orr, David L. "Dave"											
1887	NY-a*	8	3	5	.375	8	7	7	2/3	2.3	0.7
Ott, Melvin Thomas "Mel"											
1942	NY-N*	154	85	67	.559	3				83.8	1.2
1943	NY-N*	156	55	98	.359	8				60.2	-5.2
1944	NY-N*	155	67	87	.435	5				68.1	-1.1
1945	NY-N*	154	78	74	.513	5				72.8	5.2
1946	NY-N*	154	61	93	.396	8				69.5	-8.5
1947	NY-N*	155	81	73	.526	4				83.5	-2.5
1948	NY-N	76	37	38	.493	4	5		1/2	41.1	-4.1
	7	1004	464	530	.467						-14.9
Owens, Paul Francis											
1972	Phi-N	80	33	47	.412	6 E	6 E		2/2	32.5	0.5
1983	Phi-N	77	47	30	.610	1 E	♦1 E		2/2	41.5	5.5
1984	Phi-N	162	81	81	.500	4̇ E				84.1	-3.1

YEAR	TM/L	G	W	L	PCT	STANDING			M/Y	W-EXP	A-E
	3	319	161	158	.505						2.9
Ozark, Daniel Leonard "Danny"											
1973	Phi-N	162	71	91	.438	6 E				73.2	-2.2
1974	Phi-N	162	80	82	.494	3 E				78.4	1.6
1975	Phi-N	162	86	76	.531	2 E				85.1	0.9
1976	Phi-N	162	101	61	.623	1 E				103.3	-2.3
1977	Phi-N	162	101	61	.623	1 E				98.6	2.4
1978	Phi-N	162	90	72	.556	1 E				94.0	-4.0
1979	Phi-N	133	65	67	.492	5 E	4 E		1/2	63.1	1.9
1984	SF-N	56	24	32	.429	6 W	6 W		2/2	23.7	0.3
	8	1161	618	542	.533						-1.4
Pabor, Charles Henry "Charlie"											
1871	Cle-n*	29	10	19	.345	7				8.4	1.6
1875	Atl-n*	42	2	40	.048	12	12		1/2	-3.3	5.3
	NH-n*	6	1	5	.167	8	8		3/3	0.5	0.5
	2	77	13	64	.169						7.5
Parker, Francis James "Salty"											
1967	NY-N	11	4	7	.364	10	10		2/2	4.2	-0.2
1972	Hou-N	1	1	0	1.000	2 W	2 W		2/3	0.5	0.5
	2	12	5	7	.417						0.3
Parks, William Robert "Bill"											
1875	Was-n*	8	1	7	.125	8	10		2/2	-1.0	2.0
Pearce, Richard J. "Dickey"											
1872	Mut-n*	16	10	6	.625	4	3		1/2	11.6	-1.6
1875	StL-n*	70	39	29	.574	4				35.6	3.4
	2	86	49	35	.583						1.8
Peckinpaugh, Roger Thorpe											
1914	NY-A*	20	10	10	.500	7	●6		2/2	9.8	0.2
1928	Cle-A	155	62	92	.403	7				62.0	0.0
1929	Cle-A	152	81	71	.533	3				74.2	6.8
1930	Cle-A	154	81	73	.526	4				74.8	6.2
1931	Cle-A	155	78	76	.506	4				81.7	-3.7
1932	Cle-A	153	87	65	.572	4				85.1	1.9
1933	Cle-A	51	26	25	.510	5	4		1/3	25.0	1.0
1941	Cle-A	155	75	79	.487	●4				77.9	-2.9
	8	995	500	491	.505						9.5
Perez, Atanasio "Tony"											
1993	Cin-N	44	20	24	.455	5 W	5 W		1/2	20.3	-0.3
Perkins, Ralph Foster "Cy"											
1937	Det-A	15	6	9	.400	2	2		5/5	8.3	-2.3
Pesky, John Michael "Johnny"											
1963	Bos-A	161	76	85	.472	7				76.6	-0.6
1964	Bos-A	160	70	90	.438	8	8		1/2	69.7	0.3
1980	Bos-A	5	1	4	.200	3 E	4 E		2/2	2.5	-1.5
	3	326	147	179	.451						-1.8
Pfeffer, Nathaniel Frederick "Fred"											
1892(1)	Lou-N*	23	9	14	.391	10	11		2/2		
(2)	Lou-N*	77	33	42	.440	9				39.2	2.8
Phelan, Lewis G. "Lew"											
1895	StL-N	45	11	30	.268	11	11		4/4	13.1	-2.1
Phillips, Harold Ross "Lefty"											
1969	Cal-A	124	60	63	.488	6 W	3 W		2/2	51.0	9.0
1970	Cal-A	162	86	76	.531	3 W				81.1	4.9
1971	Cal-A	162	76	86	.469	4 W				73.5	2.5
	3	448	222	225	.497						16.4
Phillips, Horace B.											
1879	Tro-N	47	12	34	.261	8	8		1/2	10.8	1.2
1883	Col-a	97	32	65	.330	6				32.4	-0.4
1884	Pit-a	35	9	24	.273	10	10		5/5	7.4	1.6
1885	Pit-a	111	56	55	.505	3				56.3	-0.3
1886	Pit-a	140	80	57	.584	2				83.7	-3.7
1887	Pit-N	125	55	69	.444	6				50.3	4.7
1888	Pit-N	139	66	68	.493	6				62.1	3.9
1889	Pit-N	71	28	43	.394	6	5		1/3	31.9	-3.9
	8	765	338	415	.449						3.1
Phillips, William Corcoran "Bill"											
1914	Ind-F	157	88	65	.575	1				90.6	-2.6
1915	New-F	53	26	27	.491	6	5		1/2	27.4	-1.4
	2	210	114	92	.553						-4.0
Pike, Lipman Emanuel "Lip"											
1871	Tro-n*	4	1	3	.250	7	6		1/2	1.9	-0.9
1874	Har-n*	53	16	37	.302	7				19.0	-0.3
1877	Cin-N*	14	3	11	.214	6	6		1/3	3.1	-0.1
	3	71	20	51	.282						-4.0
Piniella, Louis Victor "Lou"											
1986	NY-A	162	90	72	.556	2 E				86.8	3.2
1987	NY-A	162	89	73	.549	4 E				83.9	5.1
1988	NY-A	93	45	48	.484	2 E	5 E		2/2	47.9	-2.9
1990	Cin-N	162	91	71	.562	★1 W				91.2	-0.2
1991	Cin-N	162	74	88	.457	5 W				80.8	-6.8
1992	Cin-N	162	90	72	.556	2 W				86.5	3.5
1993	Sea-A	162	82	80	.506	4 W				81.3	0.7
1994	Sea-A	112	49	63	.438	3 W				51.7	-2.1
1995	Sea-A	145	79	66	.545	▲1 W				80.7	-1.7
1996	Sea-A	161	85	76	.528	2 W				89.1	-4.1
	10	1483	774	709	.522						-5.7

Plummer, William Francis "Bill"

YEAR	TM/L	G	W	L	PCT	STANDING			M/Y	W-EXP	A-E
1992	Sea-A	162	64	98	.395	7 W				69.1	-5.1

Popowski, Edward Joseph "Eddie"

YEAR	TM/L	G	W	L	PCT	STANDING			M/Y	W-EXP	A-E
1969	Bos-A	9	5	4	.556	3 E	3 E		2/2	4.5	0.5
1973	Bos-A	1	1	0	1.000	2 E	2 E		2/2	0.6	0.4
2		10	6	4	.600						0.9

Porter, Matthew S. "Matt"

YEAR	TM/L	G	W	L	PCT	STANDING			M/Y	W-EXP	A-E
1884	KC-U*	16	3	13	.188	8	8	8	2/3	2.5	0.5

Powers, Patrick Thomas "Pat"

YEAR	TM/L	G	W	L	PCT	STANDING			M/Y	W-EXP	A-E
1890	Roc-a	133	63	63	.500	5				62.8	0.2
1892(1)	NY-N	74	31	43	.419	10					
(2)	NY-N	79	40	37	.519	6				74.1	-3.1
2		286	134	143	.484						-2.9

Pratt, Albert George "Al"

YEAR	TM/L	G	W	L	PCT	STANDING			M/Y	W-EXP	A-E
1882	Pit-a	79	39	39	.500	4				39.9	-0.9
1883	Pit-a	32	12	20	.375	6	7		1/3	10.4	1.6
2		111	51	59	.464						0.6

Price, James L. "Jim"

YEAR	TM/L	G	W	L	PCT	STANDING			M/Y	W-EXP	A-E
1884	NY-N	100	56	42	.571	4	●4		1/2	54.5	1.5

Prothro, James Thompson "Doc"

YEAR	TM/L	G	W	L	PCT	STANDING			M/Y	W-EXP	A-E
1939	Phi-N	152	45	106	.298	8				45.6	-0.6
1940	Phi-N	153	50	103	.327	8				49.6	0.4
1941	Phi-N	155	43	111	.279	8				46.7	-3.7
3		460	138	320	.301						-3.9

Purcell, William Aloysius "Blondie"

YEAR	TM/L	G	W	L	PCT	STANDING			M/Y	W-EXP	A-E
1883	Phi-N*	82	13	68	.160	8	8		2/2	10.0	3.0

Quilici, Francis Ralph "Frank"

YEAR	TM/L	G	W	L	PCT	STANDING			M/Y	W-EXP	A-E
1972	Min-A	84	41	43	.488	3 W	3 W		2/2	42.1	-1.1
1973	Min-A	162	81	81	.500	3 W				85.6	-4.6
1974	Min-A	163	82	80	.506	3 W				81.4	0.6
1975	Min-A	159	76	83	.478	4 W				78.3	-2.3
4		568	280	287	.494						-7.5

Quinn, Joseph J. "Joe"

YEAR	TM/L	G	W	L	PCT	STANDING			M/Y	W-EXP	A-E
1895	StL-N*	40	11	28	.282	11	11	11	3/4	12.5	-1.5
1899	Cle-N*	116	12	104	.103	12	12		2/2	10.0	2.0
2		156	23	132	.148						0.6

Rader, Douglas Lee "Doug"

YEAR	TM/L	G	W	L	PCT	STANDING			M/Y	W-EXP	A-E
1983	Tex-A	163	77	85	.475	3 W				84.3	-7.3
1984	Tex-A	161	69	92	.429	7 W				74.5	-5.5
1985	Tex-A	32	9	23	.281	7 W	7 W		1/2	12.6	-3.6
1986	Chi-A	2	1	1	.500	6 W	5 W	5 W	2/3	0.9	0.1
1989	Cal-A	162	91	71	.562	3 W				90.8	0.2
1990	Cal-A	162	80	82	.494	4 W				79.4	0.6
1991	Cal-A	124	61	63	.492	7 W	7 W		1/2	62.3	-1.3
7		806	388	417	.482						-16.9

Rapp, Vernon Fred "Vern"

YEAR	TM/L	G	W	L	PCT	STANDING			M/Y	W-EXP	A-E
1977	StL-N	162	83	79	.512	3 E				86.0	-3.0
1978	StL-N	17	6	11	.353	6 E	5 E		1/3	7.9	-1.9
1984	Cin-N	121	51	70	.421	5 W	5 W		1/2	51.3	-0.3
3		300	140	160	.467						-5.1

Reach, Alfred James "Al"

YEAR	TM/L	G	W	L	PCT	STANDING			M/Y	W-EXP	A-E
1890	Phi-N	11	4	7	.364	2	3	3	3/5	6.4	-2.4

Regan, Philip Raymond "Phil"

YEAR	TM/L	G	W	L	PCT	STANDING			M/Y	W-EXP	A-E
1995	Bal-A	144	71	73	.493	3 E				78.3	-7.3

Rice, Delbert "Del"

YEAR	TM/L	G	W	L	PCT	STANDING			M/Y	W-EXP	A-E
1972	Cal-A	155	75	80	.484	5 W				68.1	6.9

Richards, Paul Rapier

YEAR	TM/L	G	W	L	PCT	STANDING			M/Y	W-EXP	A-E
1951	Chi-A	155	81	73	.526	4				84.1	-3.1
1952	Chi-A	156	81	73	.526	3				81.6	-0.6
1953	Chi-A	156	89	65	.578	3				89.8	-0.8
1954	Chi-A	146	91	54	.628	3	3		1/2	91.5	-0.5
1955	Bal-A	156	57	97	.370	7				54.7	2.3
1956	Bal-A	154	69	85	.448	6				63.0	6.0
1957	Bal-A	154	76	76	.500	5				77.0	-1.0
1958	Bal-A	154	74	79	.484	6				70.4	3.6
1959	Bal-A	155	74	80	.481	6				69.4	4.6
1960	Bal-A	154	89	65	.578	2				84.9	4.1
1961	Bal-A	136	78	57	.578	3	3		1/2	76.7	1.3
1976	Chi-A	161	64	97	.398	6 W				63.9	0.1
12		1837	923	901	.506						15.9

Richardson, Daniel "Danny"

YEAR	TM/L	G	W	L	PCT	STANDING			M/Y	W-EXP	A-E
(2)	Was-										
1892	N*	43	12	31	.279	11	12		2/2	17.9	-5.9

Rickey, Wesley Branch "Branch"

YEAR	TM/L	G	W	L	PCT	STANDING			M/Y	W-EXP	A-E
1913	StL-A	12	5	6	.455	7	8		3/3	4.6	0.4
1914	StL-A*	159	71	82	.464	5				66.2	4.8
1915	StL-A	159	63	91	.409	6				59.6	3.4
1919	StL-N	138	54	83	.394	7				58.7	-4.7
1920	StL-N	155	75	79	.487	●5				76.3	-1.3
1921	StL-N	154	87	66	.569	3				88.8	-1.8
1922	StL-N	154	85	69	.552	●3				81.0	4.0
1923	StL-N	154	79	74	.516	5				77.9	1.1
1924	StL-N	154	65	89	.422	6				76.0	-11.0
1925	StL-N	38	13	25	.342	8	4		1/2	20.5	-7.5
10		1277	597	664	.473						-12.6

Riddoch, Gregory Lee "Greg"

YEAR	TM/L	G	W	L	PCT	STANDING			M/Y	W-EXP	A-E
1990	SD-N	82	38	44	.463	4 W	5 W		2/2	41.0	-3.0
1991	SD-N	162	84	78	.519	3 W				79.9	4.1
1992	SD-N	150	78	72	.520	3 W	3 W		1/2	73.1	4.9
3		394	200	194	.508						6.0

Riggleman, James David "Jim"

YEAR	TM/L	G	W	L	PCT	STANDING			M/Y	W-EXP	A-E
1992	SD-N	12	4	8	.333	3 W	3 W		2/2	5.8	-1.8
1993	SD-N	162	61	101	.377	7 W				71.7	-10.7
1994	SD-N	117	47	70	.402	4 W				53.2	-6.2
1995	Chi-N	144	68	76	.472	3 C				74.1	-1.1
1996	Chi-N	162	76	86	.469	4 C				81.1	-5.1
5		597	256	341	.429						-25.0

Rigney, William Joseph "Bill"

YEAR	TM/L	G	W	L	PCT	STANDING			M/Y	W-EXP	A-E
1956	NY-N	154	67	87	.435	6				65.1	1.9
1957	NY-N	154	69	85	.448	6				71.1	-2.1
1958	SF-N	154	80	74	.519	3				79.9	0.1
1959	SF-N	154	83	71	.539	3				86.4	-3.4
1960	SF-N	58	33	25	.569	2	5		1/2	30.6	2.4
1961	LA-A	162	70	91	.435	8				76.6	-6.6
1962	LA-A	162	86	76	.531	3				82.2	3.8
1963	LA-A	161	70	91	.435	9				73.7	-3.7
1964	LA-A	162	82	80	.506	5				80.2	1.8
1965	Cal-A	162	75	87	.463	7				76.2	-1.2
1966	Cal-A	162	80	82	.494	6				76.8	3.2
1967	Cal-A	161	84	77	.522	5				78.3	5.7
1968	Cal-A	162	67	95	.414	8				67.6	-0.6
1969	Cal-A	39	11	28	.282	6 W	3 W		1/2	16.2	-5.2
1970	Min-A	162	98	64	.605	1 W				95.5	2.4
1971	Min-A	160	74	86	.463	5				78.3	-4.3
1972	Min-A	70	36	34	.514	3 W	3 W		1/2	35.1	0.9
1976	SF-N	162	74	88	.457	4 W				71.3	2.7
18		2561	1239	1321	.484						-2.0

Ripken, Calvin Edwin Sr. "Cal"

YEAR	TM/L	G	W	L	PCT	STANDING			M/Y	W-EXP	A-E
1985	Bal-A	1	1	0	1.000	4 E	4 E	4 E	2/3	0.5	0.5
1987	Bal-A	162	67	95	.414	6 E				66.6	0.4
1988	Bal-A	6	0	6	.000	7 E	7 E		1/2	2.1	-2.1
3		169	68	101	.402						-1.2

Robinson, Frank

YEAR	TM/L	G	W	L	PCT	STANDING			M/Y	W-EXP	A-E
1975	Cle-A*	159	79	80	.497	4 E				78.0	1.0
1976	Cle-A*	159	81	78	.509	4 E				79.5	1.5
1977	Cle-A	57	26	31	.456	5 E	5 E		1/2	26.2	-0.2
1981(1)	SF-N	59	27	32	.458	5 W					
(2)	SF-N	52	29	23	.558	3 W				56.9	-0.9
1982	SF-N	162	87	75	.537	3 W				79.6	7.4
1983	SF-N	162	79	83	.488	5 W				80.0	-1.0
1984	SF-N	106	42	64	.396	6 W	6 W		1/2	44.9	-2.9
1988	Bal-A	155	54	101	.348	7 E	7 E		2/2	53.6	0.4
1989	Bal-A	162	87	75	.537	2 E				83.3	3.7
1990	Bal-A	162	76	85	.472	5 E				77.5	-1.5
1991	Bal-A	37	13	24	.351	7 E	6 E		1/2	16.0	-3.0
11		1432	680	751	.475						4.6

Robinson, Wilbert

YEAR	TM/L	G	W	L	PCT	STANDING			M/Y	W-EXP	A-E
1902	Bal-A*	83	24	57	.296	7	8		2/2	33.5	-9.5
1914	Bro-N	154	75	79	.487	5				77.4	-2.4
1915	Bro-N	154	80	72	.526	3				73.3	6.7
1916	Bro-N	156	94	60	.610	1				90.1	3.9
1917	Bro-N	156	70	81	.464	7				70.0	-0.0
1918	Bro-N	127	57	69	.452	5				50.9	6.1
1919	Bro-N	141	69	71	.493	5				71.3	-2.3
1920	Bro-N	155	93	61	.604	1				91.3	1.7
1921	Bro-N	152	77	75	.507	5				74.6	2.4
1922	Bro-N	155	76	78	.494	6				75.9	0.1
1923	Bro-N	155	76	78	.494	6				78.2	-2.2
1924	Bro-N	154	92	62	.597	2				81.2	10.8
1925	Bro-N	153	68	85	.444	●6				69.2	-1.2
1926	Bro-N	155	71	82	.464	6				68.1	2.9
1927	Bro-N	154	65	88	.425	6				68.0	-3.0
1928	Bro-N	155	77	76	.503	6				79.1	-2.1
1929	Bro-N	153	70	83	.458	6				64.3	5.7
1930	Bro-N	154	86	68	.558	4				89.3	-3.3
1931	Bro-N	153	79	73	.520	4				76.8	2.2
19		2819	1399	1398	.500						16.4

Robison, Matthew Stanley "Stanley"

YEAR	TM/L	G	W	L	PCT	STANDING			M/Y	W-EXP	A-E
1905	StL-N	50	19	31	.380	6	6		3/3	18.2	0.8

Rodgers, Robert Leroy "Buck"

YEAR	TM/L	G	W	L	PCT	STANDING			M/Y	W-EXP	A-E
1980	Mil-A	47	26	21	.553	2 E	3 E		1/3	27.2	-1.2
	Mil-A	23	13	10	.565	4 E	3 E		3/3	13.3	-0.3
1981(1)	Mil-A	56	31	25	.554	3 E					
(2)	Mil-A	53	31	22	.585	o1 E				58.0	4.0
1982	Mil-A	47	23	24	.489	5 E	♦1 E		1/2	28.3	-5.3
1985	Mon-N	161	84	77	.522	3 E				80.2	3.8
1986	Mon-N	161	78	83	.484	4 E				75.2	2.8
1987	Mon-N	162	91	71	.562	3 E				83.1	7.9
1988	Mon-N	163	81	81	.500	3 E				84.9	-3.9
1989	Mon-N	162	81	81	.500	4 E				81.2	-0.2
1990	Mon-N	162	85	77	.525	3 E				87.9	-2.9
1991	Mon-N	49	20	29	.408	6 E	6 E		1/2	22.0	-2.1
	Cal-A	38	20	18	.526	7 W	7 W		2/2	19.1	0.9
1992	Cal-A	39	19	20	.487	5 W	●5 W		1/3	17.1	1.9
	Cal-A	34	14	20	.412	5 W	●5 W		3/3	14.9	-0.9

YEAR	TM/L	G	W	L	PCT	STANDING			M/Y	W-EXP	A-E
1993	Cal-A	162	71	91	.438	●5 W				72.4	-1.4
1994	Cal-A	39	16	23	.410	3 W	4 W		1/3	15.8	0.2
	13	1558	784	773	.504						3.4

Rogers, James F. "Jim"

| 1897 | Lou-N* | 44 | 17 | 24 | .415 | 9 | 11 | | 1/2 | 15.2 | 1.8 |

Rojas, Octavio Victor "Cookie"

1988	Cal-A	154	75	79	.487	4 W	4 W		1/2	71.6	3.4
1996	Fla-N	1	1	0	1.000	4 E	4 E	3 E	2/3	0.5	0.5
	2	155	76	79	.490						3.9

Rolfe, Robert Abial "Red"

1949	Det-A	155	87	67	.565	4				86.6	0.4
1950	Det-A	157	95	59	.617	2				88.8	6.2
1951	Det-A	154	73	81	.474	5				71.5	1.5
1952	Det-A	73	23	49	.319	8	8		1/2	27.2	-4.2
	4	539	278	256	.521						3.9

Rose, Peter Edward "Pete"

1984	Cin-N*	41	19	22	.463	5 W	5 W		2/2	17.4	1.6
1985	Cin-N*	162	89	72	.553	2 W				81.6	7.4
1986	Cin-N*	162	86	76	.531	2 W				82.5	3.5
1987	Cin-N	162	84	78	.519	2 W				84.0	-0.0
1988	Cin-N	23	11	12	.478	4 W	2 W		1/3	12.2	-1.2
	Cin-N	111	64	47	.577	4 W	2 W		3/3	58.9	5.1
1989	Cin-N	125	59	66	.472	●4 W	5 W		1/2	57.7	1.3
	6	786	412	373	.525						17.7

Roseman, James John "Chief"

| 1890 | StL-a* | 15 | 7 | 8 | .467 | 4 | 5 | 3 | 3/6 | 8.8 | -1.8 |

Rowe, David E. "Dave"

1886	KC-N*	126	30	91	.248	7				26.1	3.9
1888	KC-a*	50	14	36	.280	8	8		1/3	14.2	-0.2
	2	176	44	127	.257						3.7

Rowe, John Charles "Jack"

| 1890 | Buf-P* | 81 | 22 | 58 | .275 | 8 | 8 | | 1/3 | 20.9 | 1.1 |
| | Buf-P* | 19 | 5 | 14 | .263 | 8 | 8 | | 3/3 | 5.0 | 0.0 |

Rowland, Clarence Henry "Pants"

1915	Chi-A	156	93	61	.604	3				99.2	-6.2
1916	Chi-A	155	89	65	.578	2				88.7	0.3
1917	Chi-A	156	100	54	.649	★1				98.5	1.5
1918	Chi-A	124	57	67	.460	6				63.2	-6.2
	4	591	339	247	.578						-10.6

Ruel, Herold Dominic "Muddy"

| 1947 | StL-A | 154 | 59 | 95 | .383 | 8 | | | | 58.5 | 0.5 |

Runnells, Thomas William "Tom"

1991	Mon-N	112	51	61	.455	6 E	6 E		2/2	50.3	0.7
1992	Mon-N	37	17	20	.459	4 E	2 E		1/2	20.2	-3.2
	2	149	68	81	.456						-2.4

Runnels, James Edward "Pete"

| 1966 | Bos-A | 16 | 8 | 8 | .500 | 9 | 9 | | 2/2 | 7.2 | 0.8 |

Russell, William Ellis "Bill"

| 1996 | LA-N | 76 | 49 | 37 | .570 | 1 W | ■○2 W | | 2/2 | 45.8 | 3.2 |

Ryan, Cornelius Joseph "Connie"

1975	Atl-N	27	9	18	.333	5 W	5 W		2/2	10.8	-1.8
1977	Tex-A	6	2	4	.333	3 W	5 W	2 W	3/4	3.4	-1.4
	2	33	11	22	.333						-3.2

Sawyer, Edwin Milby "Eddie"

1948	Phi-N	63	23	40	.365	6	6		3/3	25.7	-2.7
1949	Phi-N	154	81	73	.526	3				76.4	4.6
1950	Phi-N	157	91	63	.591	1				87.0	4.0
1951	Phi-N	154	73	81	.474	5				77.4	-4.4
1952	Phi-N	63	28	35	.444	6	4		1/2	36.1	-8.1
1958	Phi-N	70	30	40	.429	8	8		2/2	30.6	-0.6
1959	Phi-N	155	64	90	.416	8				64.1	-0.1
1960	Phi-N	1	0	1	.000	●6	8		1/3	0.4	-0.4
	8	817	390	423	.480						-7.7

Scanlon, Michael B. "Mike"

1884	Was-U	114	47	65	.420	6				46.3	0.7
1886	Was-N	82	13	67	.162	8	8		1/2	18.0	-5.0
	2	196	60	132	.313						-4.3

Schaefer, Robert Wald "Bob"

| 1991 | KC-A | 1 | 1 | 0 | 1.000 | 7 W | 7 W | 6 W | 2/3 | 0.5 | 0.5 |

Schalk, Raymond William "Ray"

1927	Chi-A*	153	70	83	.458	5				71.9	-1.9
1928	Chi-A*	75	32	42	.432	6	5		1/2	33.7	-1.7
	2	228	102	125	.449						-3.6

Scheffing, Robert Boden "Bob"

1957	Chi-N	156	62	92	.403	●7				67.4	-5.4
1958	Chi-N	154	72	82	.468	●5				75.4	-3.4
1959	Chi-N	155	74	80	.481	●5				75.5	-1.5
1961	Det-A	163	101	61	.623	2				97.7	3.3
1962	Det-A	161	85	76	.528	4				87.1	-2.1
1963	Det-A	60	24	36	.400	9	●5		1/2	29.9	-5.9
	6	849	418	427	.495						-15.1

Schlafly, Harry Linton "Larry"

1914	Buf-F*	156	80	71	.530	4				77.4	2.6
1915	Buf-F	41	13	28	.317	8	6		1/3	18.8	-5.8
	2	197	93	99	.484						-3.2

YEAR	TM/L	G	W	L	PCT	STANDING			M/Y	W-EXP	A-E

Schmelz, Gustavius Heinrich "Gus"

1884	Col-a	110	69	39	.639	2				66.3	2.7
1886	StL-N	126	43	79	.352	6				45.3	-2.3
1887	Cin-a	136	81	54	.600	2				80.2	0.8
1888	Cin-a	137	80	54	.597	4				78.1	1.9
1889	Cin-a	141	76	63	.547	4				80.7	-4.7
1890	Cle-N	78	21	55	.276	7	7		1/2	27.4	-6.4
	Col-a	57	38	13	.745	5	2		2/3	33.1	4.9
1891	Col-a	138	61	76	.445	6				61.6	-0.6
1894	Was-N	132	45	87	.341	11				47.5	-2.5
1895	Was-N	133	43	85	.336	10				47.2	-4.2
1896	Was-N	133	58	73	.443	●9				57.0	1.0
1897	Was-N	36	9	25	.265	11	●6		1/2	16.7	-7.7
	11	1357	624	703	.470						-17.2

Schoendienst, Albert Fred "Red"

1965	StL-N	162	80	81	.497	7				83.9	-3.9
1966	StL-N	162	83	79	.512	6				80.3	2.7
1967	StL-N	161	101	60	.627	★1				95.3	5.7
1968	StL-N	162	97	65	.599	1				94.1	2.9
1969	StL-N	162	87	75	.537	4 E				87.2	-0.2
1970	StL-N	162	76	86	.469	4 E				80.7	-4.7
1971	StL-N	163	90	72	.556	2 E				85.0	5.0
1972	StL-N	156	75	81	.481	4 E				74.5	0.5
1973	StL-N	162	81	81	.500	2 E				85.3	-4.3
1974	StL-N	161	86	75	.534	2 E				84.1	1.9
1975	StL-N	163	82	80	.506	●3 E				78.2	3.8
1976	StL-N	162	72	90	.444	5 E				76.6	-4.6
1980	StL-N	37	18	19	.486	5 E	4 E		4/4	19.1	-1.1
1990	StL-N	24	13	11	.542	6 E	6 E	6 E	2/3	10.4	2.6
	14	1999	1041	955	.522						6.2

Schultz, Joseph Charles Jr. "Joe"

1969	Sea-A	163	64	98	.395	6 W				64.8	-0.8
1973	Det-A	28	14	14	.500	3 E	3 E		2/2	13.4	0.6
	2	191	78	112	.411						-0.3

Selee, Frank Gibson

1890	Bos-N	134	76	57	.571	5				82.5	-6.5
1891	Bos-N	140	87	51	.630	1				86.3	0.7
1892(1)	Bos-N	75	52	22	.703	1				95.3	6.7
(2)	Bos-N	77	50	26	.658	2				95.3	6.7
1893	Bos-N	131	86	43	.667	1				81.7	4.3
1894	Bos-N	133	83	49	.629	3				82.0	1.0
1895	Bos-N	133	71	60	.542	●5				72.2	-1.2
1896	Bos-N	132	74	57	.565	4				74.0	0.0
1897	Bos-N	135	93	39	.705	1				96.5	-3.5
1898	Bos-N	152	102	47	.685	1				99.3	2.7
1899	Bos-N	153	95	57	.625	2				96.4	-1.4
1900	Bos-N	142	66	72	.478	4				72.6	-6.6
1901	Bos-N	140	69	69	.500	5				66.3	2.7
1902	Chi-N	143	68	69	.496	5				71.7	-3.7
1903	Chi-N	139	82	56	.594	3				78.4	3.6
1904	Chi-N	156	93	60	.608	2				85.7	7.3
1905	Chi-N	65	37	28	.569	4	3		1/2	43.2	-6.2
	16	2180	1284	862	.598						-0.1

Sewell, James Luther "Luke"

1941	StL-A	113	55	55	.500	7	●6		2/2	51.1	3.9
1942	StL-A*	151	82	69	.543	3				84.8	-2.8
1943	StL-A	153	72	80	.474	6				75.1	-3.1
1944	StL-A	154	89	65	.578	1				87.1	1.9
1945	StL-A	154	81	70	.536	3				80.9	0.1
1946	StL-A	125	53	71	.427	7	7		1/2	54.6	-1.6
1949	Cin-N	3	1	2	.333	7	7		2/2	1.2	-0.2
1950	Cin-N	153	66	87	.431	6				68.5	-2.5
1951	Cin-N	155	68	86	.442	6				65.5	2.5
1952	Cin-N	98	39	59	.398	7	6		1/3	46.1	-7.1
	10	1259	606	644	.485						-9.0

Shannon, Daniel W. "Dan"

1889	Lou-a*	58	10	46	.179	8	8	8	3/4	12.1	-2.1
1891	Was-a*	51	15	34	.306	7	8	8	3/4	13.0	2.0
	2	109	25	80	.238						-0.1

Sharsig, William A. "Bill"

1886	Phi-a	41	22	17	.564	6	6		2/2	15.3	6.7
1888	Phi-a	137	81	52	.609	3				88.1	-7.1
1889	Phi-a	138	75	58	.564	3				74.5	0.5
1890	Phi-a	132	54	78	.409	7				45.4	8.6
1891	Phi-a	18	6	11	.353	7	4		1/2	8.8	-2.8
	5	466	238	216	.524						5.9

Shawkey, James Robert "Bob"

| 1930 | NY-A | 154 | 86 | 68 | .558 | 3 | | | | 90.8 | -4.8 |

Sheehan, Thomas Clancy "Tom"

| 1960 | SF-N | 98 | 46 | 50 | .479 | 2 | 5 | | 2/2 | 50.6 | -4.6 |

Shepard, Lawrence William "Larry"

1968	Pit-N	163	80	82	.494	6				86.9	-6.9
1969	Pit-N	157	84	73	.535	3 E	3 E		1/2	85.8	-1.8
	2	320	164	155	.514						-8.6

Sherry, Norman Burt "Norm"

1976	Cal-A	66	37	29	.561	6 W	●4 W		2/2	29.3	7.7
1977	Cal-A	81	39	42	.481	5 W	5 W		1/2	39.5	-0.5
	2	147	76	71	.517						7.2

YEAR	TM/L	G	W	L	PCT	STANDING			M/Y	W-EXP	A-E
Shettsline, William Joseph "Bill"											
1898	Phi-N	104	59	44	.573	●8	6		2/2	54.0	5.0
1899	Phi-N	154	94	58	.618	3				91.8	2.2
1900	Phi-N	141	75	63	.543	3				70.6	4.4
1901	Phi-N	140	83	57	.593	2				82.8	0.2
1902	Phi-N	138	56	81	.409	7				51.2	4.8
	5	677	367	303	.548						16.6
Shotton, Burton Edwin "Burt"											
1928	Phi-N	152	43	109	.283	8				48.7	-5.7
1929	Phi-N	154	71	82	.464	5				65.1	5.9
1930	Phi-N	156	52	102	.338	8				56.4	-4.4
1931	Phi-N	155	66	88	.429	6				63.2	2.8
1932	Phi-N	154	78	76	.506	4				81.4	-3.4
1933	Phi-N	152	60	92	.395	7				60.7	-0.7
1934	Cin-N	1	1	0	1.000	8	8	8	2/3	0.4	0.6
1947	Bro-N	153	92	60	.605	●1	1		2/2	86.3	5.7
1948	Bro-N	81	48	33	.593	5	3		3/3	44.5	3.3
1949	Bro-N	156	97	57	.630	1				98.8	-1.8
1950	Bro-N	155	89	65	.578	2				88.6	0.4
	11	1469	697	764	.477						3.0
Showalter, William Nathaniel "Buck"											
1992	NY-A	162	76	86	.469	●4 E				79.7	-3.7
1993	NY-A	162	88	74	.543	2 E				86.8	1.2
1994	NY-A	113	70	43	.619	1 E				69.0	1.0
1995	NY-A	144	79	65	.549	■●2 E				77.8	1.2
	4	581	313	268	.539						-0.3
Silvestri, Kenneth Joseph "Ken"											
1967	Atl-N	3	0	3	.000	7	7		2/2	1.5	-1.5
Simmons, Joseph S. "Joe"											
1875	Wes-n*	13	1	12	.077	13				2.5	-1.5
1884	Wil-U	18	2	16	.111	8				0.8	1.2
	2	31	3	28	.097						-0.2
Simmons, Lewis "Lew"											
1886	Phi-a	98	41	55	.427	6	6		1/2	37.7	3.3
Sisler, George Harold											
1924	StL-A*	153	74	78	.487	4				72.3	1.7
1925	StL-A*	154	82	71	.536	3				76.0	6.0
1926	StL-A*	155	62	92	.403	7				61.4	0.6
	3	462	218	241	.475						8.3
Sisler, Richard Allan "Dick"											
1964	Cin-N	6	3	3	.500	3	4	●2	2/4	3.4	-0.4
	Cin-N	47	29	18	.617	3	●2		4/4	26.5	2.5
1965	Cin-N	162	89	73	.549	4				92.8	-3.8
	2	215	121	94	.563						-1.7
Skaff, Francis Michael "Frank"											
1966	Det-A	79	40	39	.506	2	3		3/3	40.5	-0.5
Skinner, Robert Ralph "Bob"											
1968	Phi-N	107	48	59	.449	5	●7		3/3	48.2	-0.2
1969	Phi-N	108	44	64	.407	5 E	5 E		1/2	47.2	-3.2
1977	SD-N	1	1	0	1.000	4 W	4 W	5 W	2/3	0.4	0.6
	3	216	93	123	.431						-2.7
Slattery, John Terrence "Jack"											
1928	Bos-N	31	11	20	.355	7	7		1/2	10.7	0.3
Smith, Edward Mayo "Mayo"											
1955	Phi-N	154	77	77	.500	4				77.9	-0.9
1956	Phi-N	154	71	83	.461	5				70.0	1.0
1957	Phi-N	156	77	77	.500	3				73.5	3.5
1958	Phi-N	84	39	45	.464	8	8		1/2	36.7	2.3
1959	Cin-N	80	35	45	.438	7	●5		1/2	41.3	-6.3
1967	Det-A	163	91	71	.562	●2				91.3	-0.3
1968	Det-A	164	103	59	.636	★1				101.2	1.8
1969	Det-A	162	90	72	.556	2 E				91.6	-1.6
1970	Det-A	162	79	83	.488	4 E				74.4	4.6
	9	1279	662	612	.520						4.0
Smith, George Henry "Heinie"											
1902	NY-N*	32	5	27	.156	4	8	8	2/3	11.0	-6.0
Smith, Harry Thomas											
1909	Bos-N*	79	23	54	.299	8	8		2/2	24.6	-1.6
Smith, William J. "Bill"											
1873	Mar-n*	6	0	6	.000	9				-3.9	3.9
Snyder, Charles N. "Pop"											
1882	Cin-a*	80	55	25	.688	1				61.6	-6.6
1883	Cin-a*	98	61	37	.622	3				71.6	-10.6
1884	Cin-a*	40	24	14	.632	5	5		2/2	26.5	-2.5
1891	Was-a*	70	23	46	.333	6	7	8	2/4	18.3	4.7
	4	288	163	122	.572						-14.9
Snyder, James Robert "Jim"											
1988	Sea-A	105	45	60	.429	6 W	7 W		2/2	47.2	-2.2
Sothoron, Allen Sutton											
1933	StL-A	8	2	6	.250	8	8	8	2/3	3.2	-1.2
Southworth, William Harrison "Billy"											
1929	StL-N*	90	43	45	.489	4	4		1/3	45.3	-2.3
1940	StL-N	111	69	40	.633	7	3		3/3	57.9	11.1
1941	StL-N	155	97	56	.634	2				91.4	5.6
1942	StL-N	156	106	48	.688	★1				106.1	-0.1
1943	StL-N	157	105	49	.682	1				99.6	5.4
1944	StL-N	157	105	49	.682	★1				106.8	-1.8
1945	StL-N	155	95	59	.617	2				94.7	0.3
1946	Bos-N	154	81	72	.529	4				80.5	0.5
1947	Bos-N	154	86	68	.558	3				85.1	0.9
1948	Bos-N	154	91	62	.595	1				92.4	-1.4
1949	Bos-N	111	55	54	.505	4	4		1/2	53.6	1.4
1950	Bos-N	156	83	71	.539	4				81.7	1.3
1951	Bos-N	60	28	31	.475	5	4		1/2	31.8	-3.8
	13	1770	1044	704	.597						17.1
Spalding, Albert Goodwill "Al"											
1876	Chi-N*	66	52	14	.788	1				63.1	-11.1
1877	Chi-N*	60	26	33	.441	5				28.7	-2.7
	2	126	78	47	.624						-13.9
Speaker, Tristram E "Tris"											
1919	Cle-A*	61	40	21	.656	3	2		2/2	35.0	5.0
1920	Cle-A*	154	98	56	.636	★1				97.7	0.3
1921	Cle-A*	154	94	60	.610	2				96.6	-2.6
1922	Cle-A*	155	78	76	.506	4				72.4	5.6
1923	Cle-A*	153	82	71	.536	3				89.5	-7.5
1924	Cle-A*	153	67	86	.438	6				71.0	-4.0
1925	Cle-A*	153	70	84	.455	6				73.7	-3.7
1926	Cle-A*	154	88	66	.571	2				89.8	-1.8
	8	1139	617	520	.543						-8.7
Spence, Harrison L. "Harry"											
1888	Ind-N	136	50	85	.370	7				55.2	-5.2
Stahl, Charles Sylvester "Chick"											
1906	Bos-A*	40	14	26	.350	8	8		2/2	13.1	0.9
Stahl, Garland "Jake"											
1905	Was-A*	154	64	87	.424	7				68.6	-4.6
1906	Was-A*	151	55	95	.367	7				59.3	-4.3
1912	Bos-A*	154	105	47	.691	★1				101.9	3.1
1913	Bos-A*	81	39	41	.488	5	4		1/2	41.2	-2.2
	4	540	263	270	.493						-8.0
Stallings, George Tweedy											
1897	Phi-N*	134	55	77	.417	10				62.5	-7.5
1898	Phi-N*	46	19	27	.413	●8	6		1/2	24.1	-5.1
1901	Det-A	136	74	61	.548	3				71.8	2.2
1909	NY-A	153	74	77	.490	5				75.8	-1.8
1910	NY-A	142	78	59	.569	3	2		1/2	75.3	2.7
1913	Bos-N	154	69	82	.457	5				70.5	-1.5
1914	Bos-N	158	94	59	.614	★1				88.3	5.7
1915	Bos-N	157	83	69	.546	2				80.1	2.9
1916	Bos-N	158	89	63	.586	3				86.6	2.4
1917	Bos-N	158	72	81	.471	6				74.7	-2.7
1918	Bos-N	124	53	71	.427	7				57.0	-4.0
1919	Bos-N	140	57	82	.410	6				58.6	-1.6
1920	Bos-N	153	62	90	.408	7				60.2	1.8
	13	1813	879	898	.495						-6.7
Stanky, Edward Raymond "Eddie"											
1952	StL-N*	154	88	66	.571	3				81.8	6.2
1953	StL-N*	157	83	71	.539	●3				82.4	0.6
1954	StL-N	154	72	82	.468	6				77.8	-5.8
1955	StL-N	36	17	19	.472	5	7		1/2	15.6	1.4
1966	Chi-A	163	83	79	.512	4				87.6	-4.6
1967	Chi-A	162	89	73	.549	4				85.8	3.2
1968	Chi-A	79	34	45	.430	9	8		1/5	35.7	-1.7
1977	Tex-A	1	1	0	1.000	●3 W	3 W	2 W	2/4	0.6	0.4
	8	906	467	435	.518						-0.3
Start, Joseph "Joe"											
1873	Mut-n*	25	18	7	.720	5	4		2/2	13.9	4.1
Stengel, Charles Dillon "Casey"											
1934	Bro-N	153	71	81	.467	6				71.6	-0.6
1935	Bro-N	154	70	83	.458	5				71.1	-1.1
1936	Bro-N	156	67	87	.435	7				68.0	-1.0
1938	Bos-N	153	77	75	.507	5				69.8	7.2
1939	Bos-N	152	63	88	.417	7				66.3	-3.3
1940	Bos-N	152	65	87	.428	7				63.8	1.2
1941	Bos-N	156	62	92	.403	7				63.8	-1.8
1942	Bos-N	150	59	89	.399	7				60.0	-1.0
1943	Bos-N	107	47	60	.439	6	6		2/2	41.9	5.1
1949	NY-A	155	97	57	.630	★1				95.7	1.3
1950	NY-A	155	98	56	.636	★1				97.8	0.2
1951	NY-A	154	98	56	.636	★1				94.5	3.5
1952	NY-A	154	95	59	.617	★1				94.7	0.3
1953	NY-A	151	99	52	.656	★1				101.0	-2.0
1954	NY-A	155	103	51	.669	2				101.4	1.6
1955	NY-A	154	96	58	.623	1				96.7	-0.7
1956	NY-A	154	97	57	.630	★1				98.8	-1.8
1957	NY-A	154	98	56	.636	1				96.8	1.2
1958	NY-A	155	92	62	.597	★1				95.6	-3.6
1959	NY-A	155	79	75	.513	3				81.1	-2.1
1960	NY-A	155	97	57	.630	1				89.0	8.0
1962	NY-N	161	40	120	.250	10				48.1	-8.1
1963	NY-N	162	51	111	.315	10				51.8	-0.8
1964	NY-N	163	53	109	.327	10				59.4	-6.4
1965	NY-N	96	31	64	.326	10	10		1/2	31.1	-0.1
	25	3766	1905	1842	.508						-4.8
Stovall, George Thomas											
1911	Cle-A*	139	74	62	.544	7	3		2/2	66.1	7.9

YEAR	TM/L	G	W	L	PCT	STANDING			M/Y	W-EXP	A-E
1912	StL-A*	117	41	74	.357	8	7		2/2	41.1	-0.1
1913	StL-A*	135	50	84	.373	7	8		1/3	56.1	-6.1
1914	KC-F*	154	67	84	.444	6				71.5	-4.5
1915	KC-F*	153	81	72	.529	4				76.1	4.9
	5	698	313	376	.454						2.1

Stovey, Harry Duffield
YEAR	TM/L	G	W	L	PCT	STANDING			M/Y	W-EXP	A-E
1881	Wor-N*	27	8	18	.308	7	8		2/2	10.6	-2.6
1885	Phi-a*	113	55	57	.491	4				62.1	-7.1
	2	140	63	75	.457						-9.7

Street, Charles Evard "Gabby"
YEAR	TM/L	G	W	L	PCT	STANDING			M/Y	W-EXP	A-E
1929	StL-N	1	1	0	1.000	4	4	4	2/3	0.5	0.5
1930	StL-N	154	92	62	.597	1				96.4	-4.4
1931	StL-N*	154	101	53	.656	★1				96.8	4.2
1932	StL-N	156	72	82	.468	●6				73.7	-1.7
1933	StL-N	91	46	45	.505	5	5		1/2	50.3	-4.3
1938	StL-A	146	53	90	.371	7	7		1/2	53.9	-0.9
	6	702	365	332	.524						-6.6

Stricker, John A. "Cub"
YEAR	TM/L	G	W	L	PCT	STANDING			M/Y	W-EXP	A-E
1892(1)	StL-N*	23	6	17	.261	10	11	9	2/3	8.4	-2.4

Strickland, George Bevan
YEAR	TM/L	G	W	L	PCT	STANDING			M/Y	W-EXP	A-E
1964	Cle-A	73	33	39	.458	8	●6		1/2	35.8	-2.8
1966	Cle-A	39	15	24	.385	3	5		2/2	19.2	-4.2
	2	112	48	63	.432						-7.0

Stubing, Lawrence George "Moose"
YEAR	TM/L	G	W	L	PCT	STANDING			M/Y	W-EXP	A-E
1988	Cal-A	8	0	8	.000	4 W	4 W		2/2	3.7	-3.7

Sukeforth, Clyde Leroy
YEAR	TM/L	G	W	L	PCT	STANDING			M/Y	W-EXP	A-E
1947	Bro-N	2	2	0	1.000	●1	1		1/2	1.1	0.9

Sullivan, Haywood Cooper
YEAR	TM/L	G	W	L	PCT	STANDING			M/Y	W-EXP	A-E
1965	KC-A	136	54	82	.397	10	10		2/2	53.1	0.9

Sullivan, James Patrick "Pat"
YEAR	TM/L	G	W	L	PCT	STANDING			M/Y	W-EXP	A-E
1890	Col-a	3	2	1	.667	5	5	2	3/3	1.9	0.1

Sullivan, Timothy Paul "Ted"
YEAR	TM/L	G	W	L	PCT	STANDING			M/Y	W-EXP	A-E
1883	StL-a	79	53	26	.671	2	2		1/2	50.3	2.7
1884	StL-U	31	28	3	.903	1	1		1/2	26.6	1.4
	KC-U*	62	13	46	.220	8	8		3/3	9.1	3.9
1888	Was-N	96	38	57	.400	8	8		2/2	29.8	8.2
	3	268	132	132	.500						16.2

Sullivan, William Joseph Sr. "Billy"
YEAR	TM/L	G	W	L	PCT	STANDING			M/Y	W-EXP	A-E
1909	Chi-A*	159	78	74	.513	4				79.6	-1.6

Sweasy, Charles James "Charlie"
YEAR	TM/L	G	W	L	PCT	STANDING			M/Y	W-EXP	A-E
1875	RS-n*	19	4	15	.211	9				0.6	3.4

Swift, Robert Virgil "Bob"
YEAR	TM/L	G	W	L	PCT	STANDING			M/Y	W-EXP	A-E
1965	Det-A	42	24	18	.571	3	4		1/2	23.2	0.8
1966	Det-A	57	32	25	.561	3	2	3	2/3	29.2	2.8
	2	99	56	43	.566						3.6

Tanner, Charles William "Chuck"
YEAR	TM/L	G	W	L	PCT	STANDING			M/Y	W-EXP	A-E
1970	Chi-A	16	3	13	.188	6 W	6 W		3/3	6.1	-3.1
1971	Chi-A	162	79	83	.488	3 W				83.2	-4.2
1972	Chi-A	154	87	67	.565	2 W				80.1	6.9
1973	Chi-A	162	77	85	.475	5 W				75.5	1.5
1974	Chi-A	163	80	80	.500	4 W				76.2	3.8
1975	Chi-A	161	75	86	.466	5 W				75.5	-0.5
1976	Oak-A	161	87	74	.540	2 W				89.8	-2.8
1977	Pit-N	162	96	66	.593	2 E				88.0	8.0
1978	Pit-N	161	88	73	.547	2 E				85.4	2.6
1979	Pit-N	163	98	64	.605	★1 E				94.4	3.6
1980	Pit-N	162	83	79	.512	3 E				83.1	-0.1
1981(1)	Pit-N	49	25	23	.521	4 E					
(2)	Pit-N	54	21	33	.389	6 E				49.1	-3.1
1982	Pit-N	162	84	78	.519	4 E				83.8	0.2
1983	Pit-N	162	84	78	.519	2 E				82.2	1.8
1984	Pit-N	162	75	87	.463	6 E				86.3	-11.3
1985	Pit-N	161	57	104	.354	6 E				65.6	-8.6
1986	Atl-N	161	72	89	.447	6 W				69.7	2.3
1987	Atl-N	161	69	92	.429	5 W				72.6	-3.6
1988	Atl-N	39	12	27	.308	6 W	6 W		1/2	14.7	-2.7
	19	2738	1352	1381	.495						-9.6

Tappe, Elvin Walter "El"
YEAR	TM/L	G	W	L	PCT	STANDING			M/Y	W-EXP	A-E
1961	Chi-N	2	2	0	1.000	7	7	7	4/9	0.9	1.1
	Chi-N	79	35	43	.449	7	7	7	7/9	33.5	1.5
	Chi-N	16	5	11	.313	7	7		9/9	6.9	-1.9
1962	Chi-N	20	4	16	.200	9	9		1/3	7.6	-3.6
	2	117	46	70	.397						-2.9

Taylor, George J.
YEAR	TM/L	G	W	L	PCT	STANDING			M/Y	W-EXP	A-E
1884	Bro-a	109	40	64	.385	9				36.3	3.7

Taylor, James Wren "Zack"
YEAR	TM/L	G	W	L	PCT	STANDING			M/Y	W-EXP	A-E
1946	StL-A	31	13	17	.433	7	7		2/2	13.2	-0.2
1948	StL-A	155	59	94	.386	6				59.4	-0.4
1949	StL-A	155	53	101	.344	7				53.9	-0.9
1950	StL-A	154	58	96	.377	7				55.4	2.6
1951	StL-A	154	52	102	.338	8				50.9	1.1
	5	649	235	410	.364						2.2

Tebbetts, George Robert "Birdie"
YEAR	TM/L	G	W	L	PCT	STANDING			M/Y	W-EXP	A-E
1954	Cin-N	154	74	80	.481	5				73.7	0.3
1955	Cin-N	154	75	79	.487	5				84.5	-9.5
1956	Cin-N	155	91	63	.591	3				88.5	2.5
1957	Cin-N	154	80	74	.519	4				73.8	6.2
1958	Cin-N	113	52	61	.460	8	4		1/2	62.1	-10.1
1961	Mil-N	25	12	13	.480	3	4		2/2	13.4	-1.4
1962	Mil-N	162	86	76	.531	5				87.6	-1.6
1963	Cle-A	162	79	83	.488	●5				74.0	5.0
1964	Cle-A	91	46	44	.511	8	●6		2/2	44.8	1.2
1965	Cle-A	162	87	75	.537	5				86.3	0.7
1966	Cle-A	123	66	57	.537	3	5		1/2	60.5	5.5
	11	1455	748	705	.515						-1.3

Tebeau, Oliver Wendell "Patsy"
YEAR	TM/L	G	W	L	PCT	STANDING			M/Y	W-EXP	A-E
1890	Cle-P*	52	21	30	.412	7	7		2/2	20.0	1.0
1891	Cle-N*	73	31	40	.437	4	5		2/2	33.2	-2.2
1892(1)	Cle-N*	74	40	33	.548	5					
(2)	Cle-N*	79	53	23	.697	1				97.9	-4.9
1893	Cle-N*	129	73	55	.570	3				75.0	-2.0
1894	Cle-N*	130	68	61	.527	6				67.4	0.6
1895	Cle-N*	132	84	46	.646	2				81.7	2.3
1896	Cle-N*	135	80	48	.625	2				81.2	-1.2
1897	Cle-N*	132	69	62	.527	5				73.9	-4.9
1898	Cle-N*	156	81	68	.544	5				79.2	1.8
1899	StL-N*	155	84	67	.556	5				83.1	0.9
1900	StL-N*	92	42	50	.457	7	●5		1/2	45.8	-3.8
	11	1339	726	583	.555						-12.2

Tenace, Fury Gene "Gene"
YEAR	TM/L	G	W	L	PCT	STANDING			M/Y	W-EXP	A-E
1991	Tor-A	33	19	14	.576	1 E	1 E	1 E	2/3	17.8	1.2

Tenney, Frederick "Fred"
YEAR	TM/L	G	W	L	PCT	STANDING			M/Y	W-EXP	A-E
1905	Bos-N*	156	51	103	.331	7				48.3	2.7
1906	Bos-N*	152	49	102	.325	8				48.1	0.9
1907	Bos-N*	152	58	90	.392	7				57.7	0.3
1911	Bos-N*	156	44	107	.291	8				46.4	-2.4
	4	616	202	402	.334						1.5

Terry, William Harold "Bill"
YEAR	TM/L	G	W	L	PCT	STANDING			M/Y	W-EXP	A-E
1932	NY-N*	114	55	59	.482	8	●6		2/2	60.5	-5.5
1933	NY-N*	156	91	61	.599	★1				89.4	1.6
1934	NY-N*	153	93	60	.608	2				94.4	-1.4
1935	NY-N*	156	91	62	.595	3				85.9	5.1
1936	NY-N*	154	92	62	.597	1				89.2	2.8
1937	NY-N	152	95	57	.625	1				89.2	5.8
1938	NY-N	152	83	67	.553	3				81.9	1.1
1939	NY-N	151	77	74	.510	5				77.3	-0.3
1940	NY-N	152	72	80	.474	6				76.4	-4.4
1941	NY-N	156	74	79	.484	5				72.6	1.4
	10	1496	823	661	.555						6.3

Thomas, Frederick L. "Fred"
YEAR	TM/L	G	W	L	PCT	STANDING			M/Y	W-EXP	A-E
1887	Ind-N	29	11	18	.379	8	8	8	2/3	7.9	3.1

Thompson, Andrew M. "A. M."
YEAR	TM/L	G	W	L	PCT	STANDING			M/Y	W-EXP	A-E
1884	Stp-U	9	2	6	.250	7				0.7	1.3

Tighe, John Thomas "Jack"
YEAR	TM/L	G	W	L	PCT	STANDING			M/Y	W-EXP	A-E
1957	Det-A	154	78	76	.506	4				77.0	1.0
1958	Det-A	49	21	28	.429	8	5		1/2	26.3	-5.3
	2	203	99	104	.488						-4.3

Tinker, Joseph Bert "Joe"
YEAR	TM/L	G	W	L	PCT	STANDING			M/Y	W-EXP	A-E
1913	Cin-N*	156	64	89	.418	7				65.2	-1.2
1914	Chi-F*	158	87	67	.565	2				88.6	-1.6
1915	Chi-F*	156	86	66	.566	1				87.1	-1.1
1916	Chi-N*	156	67	86	.438	5				74.1	-7.1
	4	626	304	308	.497						-10.9

Torborg, Jeffrey Allen "Jeff"
YEAR	TM/L	G	W	L	PCT	STANDING			M/Y	W-EXP	A-E
1977	Cle-A	104	45	59	.433	5 E	5 E		2/2	47.9	-2.9
1978	Cle-A	159	69	90	.434	6 E				73.8	-4.8
1979	Cle-A	95	43	52	.453	6 E	6 E		1/2	44.9	-1.9
1989	Chi-A	161	69	92	.429	7 W				74.8	-5.8
1990	Chi-A	162	94	68	.580	2 W				86.2	7.8
1991	Chi-A	162	87	75	.537	2 W				88.8	-1.8
1992	NY-N	162	72	90	.444	5 E				75.2	-3.2
1993	NY-N	38	13	25	.342	7 E	7 E		1/2	17.3	-4.3
	8	1043	492	551	.472						-16.8

Torre, Joseph Paul "Joe"
YEAR	TM/L	G	W	L	PCT	STANDING			M/Y	W-EXP	A-E
1977	NY-N*	117	49	68	.419	6 E	6 E		2/2	52.6	-3.6
1978	NY-N	162	66	96	.407	6 E				72.2	-6.2
1979	NY-N	163	63	99	.389	6 E				69.0	-6.0
1980	NY-N	162	67	95	.414	5 E				71.4	-4.4
1981(1)	NY-N	52	17	34	.333	5 E					
(2)	NY-N	53	24	28	.462	4 E				42.3	-1.3
1982	Atl-N	162	89	73	.549	1 W				84.7	4.3
1983	Atl-N	162	88	74	.543	2 W				91.9	-3.9
1984	Atl-N	162	80	82	.494	●2 W				78.6	1.4
1990	StL-N	58	24	34	.414	6 E	6 E		3/3	25.2	-1.2
1991	StL-N	162	84	78	.519	2 E				81.3	2.7
1992	StL-N	162	83	79	.512	3 E				83.9	-0.9
1993	StL-N	162	87	75	.537	3 E				82.4	4.6
1994	StL-N	115	53	61	.465	●3 C				48.9	4.1
1995	StL-N	47	20	27	.426	4 C	4 C		1/2	20.3	-0.3
1996	NY-A	162	92	70	.568	★1 E				88.9	3.1
	15	2063	986	1073	.479						-7.5

Tracewski, Richard Joseph "Dick"
YEAR	TM/L	G	W	L	PCT	STANDING			M/Y	W-EXP	A-E
1979	Det-A	2	2	0	1.000	5 E	5 E	5 E	2/3	1.0	1.0

Traynor, Harold Joseph "Pie"

YEAR	TM/L	G	W	L	PCT	STANDING			M/Y	W-EXP	A-E
1934	Pit-N*	100	47	52	.475	4	5		2/2	50.9	-3.9
1935	Pit-N	153	86	67	.562	4				86.1	-0.1
1936	Pit-N	156	84	70	.545	4				85.3	-1.3
1937	Pit-N*	154	86	68	.558	3				82.9	3.1
1938	Pit-N	152	86	64	.573	2				82.8	3.2
1939	Pit-N	153	68	85	.444	6				71.0	-3.0
6		868	457	406	.530						-1.9

Trebelhorn, Thomas Lynn "Tom"

YEAR	TM/L	G	W	L	PCT	STANDING			M/Y	W-EXP	A-E
1986	Mil-A	9	6	3	.667	6 E	6 E		2/2	4.1	1.9
1987	Mil-A	162	91	71	.562	3 E				85.2	5.8
1988	Mil-A	162	87	75	.537	●3 E				88.0	-1.0
1989	Mil-A	162	81	81	.500	4 E				83.9	-2.9
1990	Mil-A	162	74	88	.457	6 E				78.2	-4.2
1991	Mil-A	162	83	79	.512	3 E				86.3	-3.3
1994	Chi-N	113	49	64	.434	5 C				51.7	-2.7
7		932	471	461	.505						-6.4

Trott, Samuel W. "Sam"

YEAR	TM/L	G	W	L	PCT	STANDING			M/Y	W-EXP	A-E
1891	Was-a	12	4	7	.364	6	9		1/4	2.9	1.1

Turner, Robert Edward "Ted"

YEAR	TM/L	G	W	L	PCT	STANDING			M/Y	W-EXP	A-E
1977	Atl-N	1	0	1	.000	6 W	6 W	6 W	2/4	0.4	-0.4

Unglaub, Robert Alexander "Bob"

YEAR	TM/L	G	W	L	PCT	STANDING			M/Y	W-EXP	A-E
1907	Bos-A*	29	9	20	.310	6	8	7	3/4	12.4	-3.4

Valentine, Robert John "Bobby"

YEAR	TM/L	G	W	L	PCT	STANDING			M/Y	W-EXP	A-E
1985	Tex-A	129	53	76	.411	7 W	7 W		2/2	50.8	2.2
1986	Tex-A	162	87	75	.537	2 W				83.7	3.3
1987	Tex-A	162	75	87	.463	●6 W				78.6	-3.6
1988	Tex-A	161	70	91	.435	6 W				70.4	-0.4
1989	Tex-A	162	83	79	.512	4 W				79.1	3.9
1990	Tex-A	162	83	79	.512	3 W				78.9	4.1
1991	Tex-A	162	85	77	.525	3 W				82.4	2.6
1992	Tex-A	86	45	41	.523	3 W	4 W		1/2	39.2	5.8
1996	NY-N	31	12	19	.387	4 E	4 E		2/2	14.9	-2.9
9		1217	593	624	.487						14.9

Van Haltren, George Edward

YEAR	TM/L	G	W	L	PCT	STANDING			M/Y	W-EXP	A-E
1892(1)	Bal-N*	11	1	10	.091	12	12		1/3	3.9	-2.9

Vernon, James Barton "Mickey"

YEAR	TM/L	G	W	L	PCT	STANDING			M/Y	W-EXP	A-E
1961	Was-A	161	61	100	.379	●9				64.4	-3.4
1962	Was-A	162	60	101	.373	10				68.2	-8.2
1963	Was-A	40	14	26	.350	10	10		1/3	14.1	-0.1
3		363	135	227	.373						-11.7

Virdon, William Charles "Bill"

YEAR	TM/L	G	W	L	PCT	STANDING			M/Y	W-EXP	A-E
1972	Pit-N	155	96	59	.619	1 E				96.8	-0.8
1973	Pit-N	136	67	69	.493	2 E	3 E		1/2	68.9	-1.9
1974	NY-A	162	89	73	.549	2 E				86.1	2.9
1975	NY-A	104	53	51	.510	3 E	3 E		1/2	58.4	-5.4
	Hou-N	35	17	17	.500	6 W	6 W		2/2	16.0	1.0
1976	Hou-N	162	80	82	.494	3 W				77.6	2.4
1977	Hou-N	162	81	81	.500	3 W				84.1	-3.1
1978	Hou-N	162	74	88	.457	5 W				77.9	-3.9
1979	Hou-N	162	89	73	.549	2 W				81.1	7.9
1980	Hou-N	163	93	70	.571	▲1 W				86.8	6.2
1981(1)	Hou-N	57	28	29	.491	3 W					
(2)	Hou-N	53	33	20	.623	○1 W				62.4	-1.4
1982	Hou-N	111	49	62	.441	5 W	5 W		1/2	51.6	-2.6
1983	Mon-N	163	82	80	.506	3 E				84.3	-2.3
1984	Mon-N	131	64	67	.489	5 E	5 E		1/2	66.2	-2.2
13		1918	995	921	.519						-3.2

Vitt, Oscar Joseph "Ossie"

YEAR	TM/L	G	W	L	PCT	STANDING			M/Y	W-EXP	A-E
1938	Cle-A	153	86	66	.566	3				82.0	4.0
1939	Cle-A	154	87	67	.565	3				86.3	0.7
1940	Cle-A	155	89	65	.578	2				84.4	4.6
3		462	262	198	.570						9.3

Von Der Ahe, Christian Frederick Wilhelm "Chris"

YEAR	TM/L	G	W	L	PCT	STANDING			M/Y	W-EXP	A-E
1895	StL-N	1	1	0	1.000	11	11	11	2/4	0.3	0.7
1896	StL-N	2	0	2	.000	10	11	11	3/5	0.5	-0.5
1897	StL-N	14	2	12	.143	12	12		4/4	2.5	-0.5
3		17	3	14	.176						-0.4

Vukovich, John Christopher

YEAR	TM/L	G	W	L	PCT	STANDING			M/Y	W-EXP	A-E
1986	Phi-N	2	1	1	.500	5 E	5 E	5 E	2/3	0.9	0.1
1988	Phi-N	9	5	4	.556	6 E	6 E		2/2	3.7	1.3
2		11	6	5	.545						1.4

Wagner, Charles F. "Heinie"

YEAR	TM/L	G	W	L	PCT	STANDING			M/Y	W-EXP	A-E
1930	Bos-A	154	52	102	.338	8				57.1	-5.1

Wagner, John Peter "Honus"

YEAR	TM/L	G	W	L	PCT	STANDING			M/Y	W-EXP	A-E
1917	Pit-N*	5	1	4	.200	8	8	8	2/3	2.0	-1.0

Walker, Harry William

YEAR	TM/L	G	W	L	PCT	STANDING			M/Y	W-EXP	A-E
1955	StL-N*	118	51	67	.432	5	7		2/2	51.2	-0.2
1965	Pit-N	163	90	72	.556	3				91.3	-1.3
1966	Pit-N	162	92	70	.568	3				93.0	-1.0
1967	Pit-N	84	42	42	.500	6	6		1/2	41.2	0.8
1968	Hou-N	101	49	52	.485	10	10		2/2	44.9	4.1
1969	Hou-N	162	81	81	.500	5 W				81.8	-0.8
1970	Hou-N	162	79	83	.488	4 W				79.1	-0.1
1971	Hou-N	162	79	83	.488	●4 W				83.0	-4.0
1972	Hou-N	121	67	54	.554	2 W	2 W		1/3	66.3	0.7
9		1235	630	604	.511						-1.9

Wallace, Roderick John "Bobby"

YEAR	TM/L	G	W	L	PCT	STANDING			M/Y	W-EXP	A-E
1911	StL-A*	152	45	107	.296	8				51.6	-6.6
1912	StL-A*	40	12	27	.308	8	7		1/2	13.9	-1.9
1937	Cin-N	25	5	20	.200	8	8		2/2	10.9	-5.9
3		217	62	154	.287						-14.4

Walsh, Edward Augustine "Ed"

YEAR	TM/L	G	W	L	PCT	STANDING			M/Y	W-EXP	A-E
1924	Chi-A	3	1	2	.333	6			2/4	1.4	-0.4

Walsh, Michael John "Mike"

YEAR	TM/L	G	W	L	PCT	STANDING			M/Y	W-EXP	A-E
1884	Lou-a	110	68	40	.630	3				68.7	-0.7

Walters, William Henry "Bucky"

YEAR	TM/L	G	W	L	PCT	STANDING			M/Y	W-EXP	A-E
1948	Cin-N*	53	20	33	.377	7	7		2/2	20.7	-0.7
1949	Cin-N	153	61	90	.404	7	7		1/2	61.4	-0.4
2		206	81	123	.397						-1.2

Waltz, John J.

YEAR	TM/L	G	W	L	PCT	STANDING			M/Y	W-EXP	A-E
1892(1)	Bal-N	8	2	6	.250	12	12	12	2/3	2.9	-0.9

Ward, John Montgomery "Monte"

YEAR	TM/L	G	W	L	PCT	STANDING			M/Y	W-EXP	A-E
1880	Pro-N*	32	18	13	.581	4	3	2	2/3	20.1	-2.1
1884	NY-N*	16	6	8	.429	4	●4		2/2	7.8	-1.8
1890	Bro-P*	133	76	56	.576	2				71.7	4.3
1891	Bro-N*	137	61	76	.445	6				63.6	-2.6
1892(1)	Bro-N*	78	51	26	.662	2					
(2)	Bro-N*	80	44	33	.571	3				95.7	-0.7
1893	NY-N*	136	68	64	.515	5				73.9	-5.9
1894	NY-N*	139	88	44	.667	2				78.8	9.2
7		751	412	320	.563						0.4

Waterman, Frederick A. "Fred"

YEAR	TM/L	G	W	L	PCT	STANDING			M/Y	W-EXP	A-E
1872	Oly-n*	9	2	7	.222	10				-1.1	3.1

Wathan, John David

YEAR	TM/L	G	W	L	PCT	STANDING			M/Y	W-EXP	A-E
1987	KC-A	36	21	15	.583	4 W	2 W		2/2	18.5	2.5
1988	KC-A	161	84	77	.522	3 W				86.3	-2.3
1989	KC-A	162	92	70	.568	2 W				86.8	5.2
1990	KC-A	161	75	86	.466	6 W				80.3	-5.3
1991	KC-A	37	15	22	.405	7 W	6 W		1/3	18.6	-3.6
1992	Cal-A	89	39	50	.438	5 W	5 W	●5 W	2/3	39.0	-0.0
6		646	326	320	.505						-3.6

Watkins, Harvey L.

YEAR	TM/L	G	W	L	PCT	STANDING			M/Y	W-EXP	A-E
1895	NY-N	35	18	17	.514	9	9		3/3	17.9	0.1

Watkins, William Henry "Bill"

YEAR	TM/L	G	W	L	PCT	STANDING			M/Y	W-EXP	A-E
1884	Ind-a*	23	4	18	.182	10	11		2/2	5.6	-1.6
1885	Det-N	70	34	36	.486	8	6		2/2	30.8	3.2
1886	Det-N	126	87	36	.707	2				88.0	-1.0
1887	Det-N	127	79	45	.637	1				83.0	-4.0
1888	Det-N	94	49	44	.527	3	5		1/2	52.7	-3.7
	KC-a	25	8	17	.320	8	8		3/3	7.1	0.9
1889	KC-a	139	55	82	.401	7				53.9	1.1
1893	StL-N	135	57	75	.432	10				58.6	-1.6
1898	Pit-N	151	72	76	.486	8				67.9	4.1
1899	Pit-N	24	7	15	.318	10	7		1/2	11.9	-4.9
9		914	452	444	.504						-7.6

Weaver, Earl Sidney

YEAR	TM/L	G	W	L	PCT	STANDING			M/Y	W-EXP	A-E
1968	Bal-A	82	48	34	.585	3	2		2/2	45.8	2.2
1969	Bal-A	162	109	53	.673	◆1 E				108.8	0.2
1970	Bal-A	162	108	54	.667	★1 E				103.5	4.5
1971	Bal-A	158	101	57	.639	◆1 E				101.4	-0.4
1972	Bal-A	154	80	74	.519	3 E				87.8	-7.8
1973	Bal-A	162	97	65	.599	1 E				101.3	-4.3
1974	Bal-A	162	91	71	.562	1 E				86.0	5.0
1975	Bal-A	159	90	69	.566	2 E				93.4	-3.4
1976	Bal-A	162	88	74	.543	2 E				83.3	4.7
1977	Bal-A	161	97	64	.602	●2 E				87.3	9.7
1978	Bal-A	161	90	71	.559	4 E				83.3	6.7
1979	Bal-A	159	102	57	.642	◆1 E				97.6	4.4
1980	Bal-A	162	100	62	.617	2 E				97.6	2.4
1981(1)	Bal-a	54	31	23	.574	2 E					
(2)	Bal-A	51	28	23	.549	4 E				51.7	7.3
1982	Bal-A	163	94	68	.580	2 E				89.7	4.3
1985	Bal-A	105	53	52	.505	4 E	4 E		3/3	55.9	-2.9
1986	Bal-A	162	73	89	.451	7 E				75.8	-2.8
17		2541	1480	1060	.583						29.9

Westrum, Wesley Noreen "Wes"

YEAR	TM/L	G	W	L	PCT	STANDING			M/Y	W-EXP	A-E
1965	NY-N	68	19	48	.284	10	10		2/2	21.9	-2.9
1966	NY-N	161	66	95	.410	9				62.5	3.5
1967	NY-N	151	57	94	.377	10	10		1/2	57.4	-0.4
1974	SF-N	86	38	48	.442	5 W	5 W		2/2	38.1	-0.1
1975	SF-N	161	80	81	.497	3 W				79.2	0.8
5		627	260	366	.415						0.9

Wheeler, Harry Eugene

YEAR	TM/L	G	W	L	PCT	STANDING			M/Y	W-EXP	A-E
1884	KC-U*	4	0	4	.000				1/3	0.6	-0.6

White, James Laurie "Deacon"

YEAR	TM/L	G	W	L	PCT	STANDING			M/Y	W-EXP	A-E
1872	Cle-n*	2	0	2	.000	6	7		2/2	0.5	-0.5
1879	Cin-N*	18	9	9	.500	4	5		1/2	9.4	-0.4
2		20	9	11	.450						-0.9

White, Joyner Clifford "Jo-Jo"

YEAR	TM/L	G	W	L	PCT	STANDING			M/Y	W-EXP	A-E
1960	Cle-A	1	0	1	1.000	4	4	4	2/3	0.5	0.5

White, William Henry "Will"

YEAR	TM/L	G	W	L	PCT	STANDING			M/Y	W-EXP	A-E
1884	Cin-a*	72	44	27	.620	5			1/2	49.6	-5.6

YEAR	TM/L	G	W	L	PCT	STANDING			M/Y	W-EXP	A-E
White, William Warren "Warren"											
1872	Nat-n*	11	0	11	.000	11				-1.2	1.2
1874	Bal-n*	47	9	38	.191	8				2.4	6.6
2		58	9	49	.155						7.8
Wilber, Delbert Quentin "Del"											
1973	Tex-A	1	1	0	1.000	6 W	6 W	6 W	2/3	0.4	0.6
Wilhelm, Irvin Key "Kaiser"											
1921	Phi-N*	67	26	41	.388	8	8		2/2	21.0	5.0
1922	Phi-N	154	57	96	.373	7				59.9	-2.9
2		221	83	137	.377						2.1
Williams, James A. "Jimmy"											
1884	StL-a	85	51	33	.607	5	4		1/2	50.5	0.5
1887	Cle-a	133	39	92	.298	8				34.6	4.4
1888	Cle-a	64	20	44	.313	8	6		1/2	23.8	-3.8
3		282	110	169	.394						1.1
Williams, James Francis "Jimy"											
1986	Tor-A	163	86	76	.531	4 E				88.4	-2.4
1987	Tor-A	162	96	66	.593	2 E				99.7	-3.7
1988	Tor-A	162	87	75	.537	●3 E				89.3	-2.3
1989	Tor-A	36	12	24	.333	6 E	1 E		1/2	19.8	-7.8
4		523	281	241	.538						-16.3
Williams, Richard Hirschfeld "Dick"											
1967	Bos-A	162	92	70	.568	1				92.3	-0.3
1968	Bos-A	162	86	76	.531	4				81.3	4.7
1969	Bos-A	153	82	71	.536	3 E	3 E		1/2	77.2	4.8
1971	Oak-A	161	101	60	.627	1 W				94.1	6.9
1972	Oak-A	155	93	62	.600	★1 W				94.4	-1.4
1973	Oak-A	162	94	68	.580	★1 W				95.7	-1.7
1974	Cal-A	84	36	48	.429	6 W	6 W		3/3	39.8	-3.8
1975	Cal-A	161	72	89	.447	6 W				70.7	1.3
1976	Cal-A	96	39	57	.406	6 W	●4 W		1/2	42.7	-3.7
1977	Mon-N	162	75	87	.463	5 E				73.8	1.2
1978	Mon-N	162	76	86	.469	4 E				83.4	-7.4
1979	Mon-N	160	95	65	.594	2 E				92.7	2.3
1980	Mon-N	162	90	72	.556	2 E				87.8	2.2
1981(1)	Mon-N	55	30	25	.545	3 E					
(2)	Mon-N	26	14	12	.538	2 E	1 E		1/2	44.5	-0.5
1982	SD-N	162	81	81	.500	4 W				81.8	-1.8
1983	SD-N	163	81	81	.500	4 W				81.0	0.0
1984	SD-N	162	92	70	.568	♦1 W				86.5	5.5
1985	SD-N	162	83	79	.512	●3 W				84.0	-1.0
1986	Sea-A	133	58	75	.436	6 W	7 W		3/3	57.2	0.8
1987	Sea-A	162	78	84	.481	4 W				77.0	1.0
1988	Sea-A	56	23	33	.411	6 W	7 W		1/2	25.2	-2.2
21		3023	1571	1451	.520						7.0
Williams, Theodore Samuel "Ted"											
1969	Was-A	162	86	76	.531	4 E				86.2	-0.2
1970	Was-A	162	70	92	.432	6 E				74.4	-4.4
1971	Was-A	159	63	96	.396	5 E				66.1	-3.1
1972	Tex-A	154	54	100	.351	6 W				58.2	-4.2
4		637	273	364	.429						-11.8
Wills, Maurice Morning "Maury"											
1980	Sea-A	58	20	38	.345	6 W	7 W		2/2	22.3	-2.3
1981(1)	Sea-A	25	6	18	.250	7 W	6 W		1/2	9.9	-3.9
2		83	26	56	.317						-6.2
Wilson, James "Jimmie"											
1934	Phi-N*	149	56	93	.376	7				63.1	-7.1
1935	Phi-N*	156	64	89	.418	7				58.8	5.2
1936	Phi-N*	154	54	100	.351	8				63.2	-9.2
1937	Phi-N*	155	61	92	.399	7				62.9	-1.9
1938	Phi-N*	149	45	103	.304	8	8		1/2	45.7	-0.7
1941	Chi-N	155	70	84	.455	6				76.6	-6.6
1942	Chi-N	155	68	86	.442	6				69.2	-1.2
1943	Chi-N	154	74	79	.484	5				79.9	-5.9
1944	Chi-N	10	1	9	.100	8	4		1/3	5.2	-4.2
9		1237	493	735	.401						-31.7
Wine, Robert Paul Sr. "Bobby"											
1985	Atl-N	41	16	25	.390	5 W	5 W		2/2	16.7	-0.7
Wingo, Ivey Brown											
1916	Cin-N*	2	1	1	.500	8	8	●7	2/3	0.8	0.2
Winkles, Bobby Brooks											
1973	Cal-A	162	79	83	.488	4 W				78.0	1.0
1974	Cal-A	75	30	44	.405	6 W				35.1	-5.1
1977	Oak-A	108	37	71	.343	●5 W	7 W		2/2	44.0	-7.0
1978	Oak-A	39	24	15	.615	1 W	6 W		1/2	15.3	8.7
4		384	170	213	.444						-2.5

YEAR	TM/L	G	W	L	PCT	STANDING			M/Y	W-EXP	A-E
Wolf, William Van Winkle "Chicken"											
1889	Lou-a*	65	14	51	.215	8	8	8	2/4	14.0	-0.0
Wolverton, Harry Sterling											
1912	NY-A*	153	50	102	.329	8				55.5	-5.5
Wood, George A.											
1891	Phi-a*	125	67	55	.549	7	4		2/2	62.8	4.2
Wood, James Leon "Jimmy"											
1871	Chi-n*	28	19	9	.679	2				18.2	0.8
1872	Tro-n*	25	15	10	.600	5				18.2	-3.2
	Eck-n*	9	2	7	.222	10	10	9	2/3	-1.0	3.0
1874	Chi-n	23	10	13	.435	4	5		2/2	9.6	0.4
1875	Chi-n	69	30	37	.448	6				30.2	-0.2
4		154	76	76	.500						0.8
Wright, Alfred Hector "Al"											
1876	Phi-N	60	14	45	.237	7				17.5	-3.5
Wright, George											
1879	Pro-N*	85	59	25	.702	1				64.9	-5.9
Wright, William Henry "Harry"											
1871	Bos-n*	31	20	10	.667	3				21.2	-1.2
1872	Bos-n*	48	39	8	.830	1				45.0	-6.0
1873	Bos-n*	60	43	16	.729	1				48.2	-5.2
1874	Bos-n*	71	52	18	.743	1				58.9	-6.9
1875	Bos-n*	82	71	8	.899	1				78.2	-7.2
1876	Bos-N*	70	39	31	.557	4				36.7	2.3
1877	Bos-N*	61	42	18	.700	1				44.0	-2.0
1878	Bos-N	60	41	19	.683	1				35.7	5.3
1879	Bos-N	84	54	30	.643	2				61.5	-7.5
1880	Bos-N	86	40	44	.476	6				38.2	1.8
1881	Bos-N	83	38	45	.458	6				35.4	2.6
1882	Pro-N	84	52	32	.619	2				52.3	-0.3
1883	Pro-N	98	58	40	.592	3				67.1	-9.1
1884	Phi-N	113	39	73	.348	6				32.3	6.7
1885	Phi-N	111	56	54	.509	3				55.2	0.8
1886	Phi-N	119	71	43	.623	4				69.0	2.0
1887	Phi-N	128	75	48	.610	2				78.4	-3.4
1888	Phi-N	132	69	61	.531	3				67.8	1.2
1889	Phi-N	130	63	64	.496	3				63.0	0.0
1890	Phi-N	22	13	8	.636	1	3		1/5	12.7	1.3
	Phi-N	46	22	23	.489	2	3		5/5	26.0	-4.0
1891	Phi-N	138	68	69	.496	4				67.0	1.0
1892(1)	Phi-N	77	46	30	.605	3				92.6	-5.6
(2)	Phi-N	78	41	36	.532	5				78.2	-6.2
23		2145	1225	885	.581						-39.7
York, Preston Rudolph "Rudy"											
1959	Bos-A	1	0	1	.000	8	8	5	2/3	0.5	-0.5
York, Thomas J. "Tom"											
1878	Pro-N*	62	33	27	.550	3				31.4	1.6
1881	Pro-N*	34	23	10	.697	4	2		2/2	17.3	5.7
2		96	56	37	.602						7.3
Yost, Edward Frederick "Eddie"											
1963	Was-A	1	0	1	.000	10	10	10	2/3	0.4	-0.4
Young, Denton True "Cy"											
1907	Bos-A*	6	3	3	.500	●4	7		1/4	2.6	0.4
Young, Nicholas Ephraim "Nick"											
1871	Oly-n	32	15	15	.500	5				15.5	-0.5
1873	Was-n	39	8	31	.205	7				5.8	2.2
2		71	23	46	.333						1.7
Zimmer, Charles Louis "Chief"											
1903	Phi-N*	139	49	86	.363	7				55.9	-6.9
Zimmer, Donald William "Don"											
1972	SD-N	142	54	88	.380	4 W	6 W		2/2	53.0	1.0
1973	SD-N	162	60	102	.370	6 W				57.6	2.4
1976	Bos-A	76	42	34	.553	3 E	3 E		2/2	40.7	1.3
1977	Bos-A	161	97	64	.602	●2 E				94.6	2.4
1978	Bos-A	163	99	64	.607	▲2 E				95.5	3.5
1979	Bos-A	160	91	69	.569	3 E				92.5	-1.5
1980	Bos-A	155	82	73	.529	3 E	4 E		2/2	76.6	5.4
1981(1)	Tex-A	55	33	22	.600	2 W					
(2)	Tex-A	50	24	26	.480	3 W				59.2	-2.2
1982	Tex-A	96	38	58	.396	6 W	6 W		1/2	38.2	-0.2
1988	Chi-N	163	77	85	.475	4 E				77.5	-0.5
1989	Chi-N	162	93	69	.574	1 E				89.3	3.7
1990	Chi-N	162	77	85	.475	●4 E				72.6	4.4
1991	Chi-N	37	18	19	.486	4 E	4 E		1/3	17.6	0.4
13		1744	885	858	.508						20.1

Biographical Data for Managers Not Appearing in the Player/Pitcher Registers

BILL ADAIR Adair, Marion Danne b: 2/10/13, Mobile, Ala.

BILL ARMOUR Armour, William Clark b: 9/3/1869, Homestead, Pa. d: 12/2/22, Minneapolis, Minn.

FRANK BANCROFT Bancroft, Frank Carter b: 5/9/1846, Lancaster, Mass. d: 3/30/21, Cincinnati, Ohio

ED BARROW Barrow, Edward Grant "Cousin Ed" b: 5/10/1868, Springfield, Ill. d: 12/15/53, Port Chester, N.Y.

TERRY BEVINGTON Bevington, Terry Paul b: 7/7/56, Akron, Ohio

HUGO BEZDEK Bezdek, Hugo Frank b: 4/1/1884, Prague, Czechoslovakia d: 9/19/52, Atlantic City, N.J.

BICKERSON Bickerson

JOHN BOLES Boles, John b: 8/19/48, Chicago, Ill.

DAVE BRISTOL Bristol, James David b: 6/23/33, Macon, Ga.

FREEMAN BROWN Brown, Freeman b: 1/31/1845, Hubbardstown, Mass d: 12/27/16, Worcester, Mass.

AL BUCKENBERGER Buckenberger, Albert C. b: 1/31/1861, Detroit, Mich. d: 7/1/17, Syracuse, N.Y.

GEORGE BURNHAM Burnham, George Walter "Watch" b: 5/20/1860, Albion, Mich. d: 11/18/02, Detroit, Mich.

ORMOND BUTLER Butler, Ormond Hook b: 11/1854, West Virginia d: 9/12/15, Mt.Hope, Md.

CHARLIE BYRNE Byrne, Charles H. b: 9/1843, New York, N.Y. d: 1/4/1898, New York, N.Y.

JOE CANTILLON Cantillon, Joseph D. "Pongo Joe" b: 8/19/1861, Janesville, Wis. d: 1/31/30, Hickman, Ky.

O. P. CAYLOR Caylor, Oliver Perry b: 12/17/1849, Near Dayton, Ohio d: 10/19/1897, Winona, Minn.

TERRY COLLINS Collins, Terry Lee b: 5/27/49, Midland, Mich.

ED CURTIS Curtis, Edwin R.

CHARLIE CUSHMAN Cushman, Charles H. b: 5/25/1850, New York, N.Y. d: 6/29/09, Milwaukee, Wis.

MORDECAI DAVIDSON Davidson, Mordecai H. b: 11/30/1846, Port Washington, O d: 9/6/40, Louisville, Ky.

JOHN DAY Day, John B. b: 9/23/47, Colchester, Mass. d: 1/25/25, Cliffside, N.J.

HARRY DIDDLEBOCK Diddlebock, Henry H. b: 6/27/1854, Philadelphia, Pa. d: 2/5/1900, Philadelphia, Pa.

CHARLIE EBBETS Ebbets, Charles Hercules b: 10/29/1859, New York, N.Y. d: 4/18/25, New York, N.Y.

WALLACE FESSENDEN Fessenden, Wallace Clifton b: 10/5/1860, Windham, N.H.

HORACE FOGEL Fogel, Horace S. b: 3/2/1861, Macungie, Pa. d: 11/15/28, Philadelphia, Pa.

GEORGE FRAZER Frazer, George Kasson b: 1/7/1861, Syracuse, N.Y. d: 2/5/13, Philadelphia, Pa.

JIM FREY Frey, James Gottfried b: 5/26/31, Cleveland, Ohio

JUDGE FUCHS Fuchs, Emil Edwin b: 4/17/1878, Hamburg, Germany d: 12/5/61, Boston, Mass.

JOHN GAFFNEY Gaffney, John H. b: 6/29/1855, Roxbury, Mass. d: 8/8/13, New York, N.Y.

DAVE GARCIA Garcia, David b: 9/15/20, E.St.Louis, Mo.

JIM GIFFORD Gifford, James H. b: 10/18/1845, Warren, N.Y. d: 12/19/01, Columbus, Ohio

MASE GRAFFEN Graffen, Samuel Mason b: 1845, Philadelphia, Pa. d: 11/18/1883, Silver City, N.Mex

CHARLIE HACKETT Hackett, Charles M. b: 1855, Lee, Mass. d: 8/1/1898, Holyoke, Mass.

JIM HART Hart, James Aristotle b: 7/10/1855, Fairview, Pa. d: 7/18/19, Chicago, Ill.

JOHN HART Hart, John Henry (born John Henry Reen) b: 7/21/48, Tampa, Fla.

LOUIE HEILBRONER Heilbroner, Louis Wilbur b: 7/4/1861, Ft.Wayne, Ind. d: 12/21/33, Ft.Wayne, Ind.

BILL HENDERSON Henderson, William C.

ED HENGLE Hengle, Edward Siegfried b: Chicago, Ill. d: 11/4/27, Norwich, England

WALTER HEWETT Hewett, Walter F. b: 1861, Washington, D.C. d: 10/7/44, Washington, D.C.

VEDIE HIMSL Himsl, Avitus Bernard b: 4/2/17, Plevna, Mont.

FRED HOEY Hoey, Frederick Chamberlain b: 1866, New York, N.Y. d: 12/7/33, Paris, France

GEORGE HUFF Huff, George A. "Gee" b: 6/11/1872, Champaign, Ill. d: 10/1/36, Champaign, Ill.

TIM HURST Hurst, Timothy Carroll b: 6/30/1865, Ashland, Pa. d: 6/4/15, Pottsville, Pa.

JOHNNY KEANE Keane, John Joseph b: 11/3/11, St.Louis, Mo. d: 1/6/67, Houston, Tex.

JIM KENNEDY Kennedy, James C. b: 1867, New York, N.Y. d: 4/20/04, Brighton Beach, N.Y.

KEVIN KENNEDY Kennedy, Kevin Curtis b: 9/26/54, Los Angeles, Cal.

JACK KROL Krol, John Thomas b: 7/5/36, Chicago, Ill. d: 5/30/94, Winston-Salem, N.C.

KARL KUEHL Kuehl, Karl Otto b: 9/5/37, Monterey Park, Cal.

BOB LEADLEY Leadley, Robert H. b: 1858, Brooklyn, N.Y.

JIM LEYLAND Leyland, James Richard b: 12/15/44, Toledo, Ohio

NICK LEYVA Leyva, Nicholas Tomas b: 8/16/53, Ontario, Cal.

FRANK LUCCHESI Lucchesi, Frank Joseph b: 4/24/27, San Francisco, Cal.

JACK McCALLISTER McCallister, John b: 1/19/1879, Marietta, Ohio d: 10/18/46, Columbus, Ohio

JOE McCARTHY McCarthy, Joseph Vincent "Marse Joe" b: 4/21/1887, Philadelphia, Pa. d: 1/13/78, Buffalo, N.Y.

JOHN McCLOSKEY McCloskey, John Joseph "Honest John" b: 4/4/1862, Louisville, Ky. d: 11/17/40, Louisville, Ky.

MEL McGAHA McGaha, Fred Melvin b: 9/26/26, Bastrop, La.

JACK McKEON McKeon, John Aloysius b: 11/23/30, South Amboy, N.J.

DENNY McKNIGHT McKnight, Dennis Hamar b: 1847, Pittsburgh, Pa. d: 5/5/1900, Pittsburgh, Pa.

GEORGE McMANUS McManus, George b: 1846, Ireland d: 10/2/18, New York, N.Y.

JOHN McNAMARA McNamara, John Francis b: 6/4/32, Sacramento, Cal.

STUMP MERRILL Merrill, Carl Harrison b: 2/25/44, Brunswick, Me.

RAY MILLER Miller, Raymond Roger b: 4/30/45, Takoma Park, Md.

FELIX MOSES Moses, Felix I. b: Richmond, Va.

BILLY MURRAY Murray, William Jeremiah b: 4/13/1864, Peabody, Mass. d: 3/25/37, Youngstown, Ohio

JIM MUTRIE Mutrie, James J. "Truthful Jim" b: 6/13/1851, Chelsea, Mass. d: 1/24/38, New York, N.Y.

PAUL OWENS Owens, Paul Francis b: 2/7/24, Salamanca, N.Y.

DANNY OZARK Ozark, Daniel Leonard (born Daniel Leonard Orzechowski) b: 11/26/23, Buffalo, N.Y.

LEW PHELAN Phelan, Lewis G.

LEFTY PHILLIPS Phillips, Harold Ross b: 6/16/19, Los Angeles, Cal. d: 6/12/72, Fullerton, Cal.

HORACE PHILLIPS Phillips, Horace B. b: 5/14/1853, Salem, Ohio

EDDIE POPOWSKI Popowski, Edward Joseph b: 8/20/13, Sayerville, N.J.

PAT POWERS Powers, Patrick Thomas b: 6/27/1860, Trenton, N.J. d: 8/29/25, Belmar, N.J.

JIM PRICE Price, James L. b: 1847, New York, N.Y. d: 10/6/31, Chicago, Ill.

VERN RAPP Rapp, Vernon Fred b: 5/11/28, St.Louis, Mo.

GREG RIDDOCH Riddoch, Gregory Lee b: 7/17/45, Greeley, Colo.

JIM RIGGLEMAN Riggleman, James David b: 11/9/52, Fort Dix, N.J.

CAL RIPKEN Ripken, Calvin Edwin Sr. b: 12/17/35, Aberdeen, Md.

STAN ROBISON Robison, Matthew Stanley b: 3/30/1859, Pittsburgh, Pa. d: 3/24/11, Cleveland, Ohio

PANTS ROWLAND Rowland, Clarence Henry b: 2/12/1879, Platteville, Wis. d: 5/17/69, Chicago, Ill.

EDDIE SAWYER Sawyer, Edwin Milby b: 9/10/10, Westerly, R.I.

MIKE SCANLON Scanlon, Michael B. b: 1847, Cork, Ireland d: 1/18/29, Washington, D.C.

BOB SCHAEFER Schaefer, Robert Walden b: 5/22/44, Putnam, Conn. 5'11", 180 lbs. Deb: 5/22/91 M

GUS SCHMELZ Schmelz, Gustavius Heinrich b: 9/26/1850, Columbus, Ohio d: 10/13/25, Columbus, Ohio

FRANK SELEE Selee, Frank Gibson b: 10/26/1859, Amherst, N.Y. d: 7/5/09, Denver, Colo.

BILL SHARSIG Sharsig, William A. b: 1855, Philadelphia, Pa. d: 2/1/02, Philadelphia, Pa.

LARRY SHEPARD Shepard, Lawrence William b: 4/3/19, Lakewood, Ohio

BILL SHETTSLINE Shettsline, William Joseph b: 10/25/1863, Philadelphia, Pa. d: 2/22/33, Philadelphia, Pa.

BUCK SHOWALTER Showalter, William Nathaniel b: 5/23/56, DeFuniak Springs, Fla.

LEW SIMMONS Simmons, Lewis b: 8/27/1838, New Castle, Pa. d: 9/2/11, Jamestown, Pa.

HARRY SPENCE Spence, Harrison L. b: 1858, Virginia d: 5/17/08, Chicago, Ill.

PAT SULLIVAN Sullivan, James Patrick d: 5/22/1898.

GEORGE TAYLOR Taylor, George J. b: 11/22/1853, New York

FRED THOMAS Thomas, Frederick L. b: Indiana

JACK TIGHE Tighe, John Thomas b: 8/9/13, Kearny, N.J.

TOM TREBELHORN Trebelhorn, Thomas Lynn b: 1/27/48, Portland, Ore.

TED TURNER Turner, Robert Edward b: 11/19/38, Cincinnati, Ohio

CHRIS VonDER AHE Von Der Ahe, Christian Frederick Wilhelm b: 10/7/1851, Hille, Germany d: 6/5/13, St.Louis, Mo.

MIKE WALSH Walsh, Michael John b: 4/29/1850, Ireland d: 2/2/29, Louisville, Ky.

JOHN WALTZ Waltz, John J.

HARVEY WATKINS Watkins, Harvey L.
EARL WEAVER Weaver, Earl Sidney b: 8/14/30, St.Louis, Mo.
JIMMY WILLIAMS Williams, James Andrews b: 1/3/1848, Columbus, Ohio d: 10/24/18, N.Hempstead, N.Y.
BOBBY WINKLES Winkles, Bobby Brooks b: 3/11/30, Tuckerman, Ark.
AL WRIGHT Wright, Alfred Hector b: 3/30/1842, Cedar Grove, N.J. d: 4/20/05, New York, N.Y.
NICK YOUNG Young, Nicholas Ephraim b: 9/12/1840, Fort Johnson, N.Y. d: 10/31/16, Washington, D.C.

The Coach Roster

In an age of ever greater specialization in baseball, coaches have become increasingly important to the successful management of a team. The need for such assistance did not occur to any manager until John McGraw took on Arlie Latham as baseball's first full-time coach in 1909; today, teams employ separate coaches for first base, third base, pitching, the bullpen, hitting, baserunning, strength, conditioning, and more. Some coaches, like Charlie Lau and Roger Craig, have achieved fame exceeding that of the managers under whom they served. But coaches leave no statistical trail by which to track them. Players and pitchers have official records, and so do managers, but the accomplishments of coaches (and umpires) have until now resided largely in memory.

In the first edition of *Total Baseball,* the Coach Roster that follows represented a first attempt in a baseball encyclopedia to recognize these foot soldiers, who too often serve as scapegoats when a team fails but are invisible when it succeeds. We offered the roster in full knowledge that there were gaps and probably gaffes in our research; we hoped that our readers would advise us of omissions so that we could improve this roster in future editions of *Total Baseball*—and they have. We owe particular thanks to Bob Hoie and Walt Wilson. An additional feature, besides the inclusion of many new names, is full biographical data for all coaches who did not play at the major-league level and so are absent from the Registers.

The principal sources of the data herein are, for 1921–1939, the *Baseball Blue Book*; for 1940–1981, *The Sporting News Dope Book of 1961,* the *Baseball Register*, and for years since 1982, the *American League Red Book* and the *National League Green Book.* We have done our best to reconcile the many differences among the lists. The team and league abbreviations used in the Coach Roster are found on the final page of this book.

Aaron, Tommie Lee   Atl-N 1979-83

Abbott, Spencer   Was-A 1935

Adair, James A. "Jimmy"   Chi-A 1951-52, Bal-A 1957-61, Hou-N 1962-65

Adair, K. Jerry   Oak-A 1972-74, Cal-A 1975

Adair, Marion D. "Bill"   Mil-N 1962, Atl-N 1967, Chi-A 1970, Mon-N 1976

Adair, M. Richard "Rick"   Cle-A 1992-93, DE-T 1996

Adams, Charles D. "Red"   LA-N 1969-80

Adams, Robert H. "Bobby"   Chi-N 1961-65, 1973

Aguirre, Henry J. "Hank"   Chi-N 1972-74

Aker, Jackie D. "Jack"   Cle-A 1985-87

Alfonso, Carlos   SF-N 1992

Allenson, Gary M.   Bos-A 1992-94

Alomar, Santos C. "Sandy"   SD-N 1986-90

Alou, Felipe R.   Mon-N 1979-80, 1984, 1992

Alou, Jesus M. R.   Hou-N 1979

Altobelli, Joseph S. "Joe"   NY-A 1981-82, 1986, Chi-N 1988-91

Altrock, Nicholas "Nick"   Was-A 1912-53

Amalfitano, J. Joseph "Joey"   Chi-N 1967-71, SF-N 1972-75, SD-N 1976-77, Chi-N 1978-80, Cin-N 1982, LA-N 1983-96

Amaro, Ruben   Phi-N 1980-81, Chi-N 1983-86

Anderson, George L. "Sparky"   SD-N 1969

Apodaca, Robert J. "Bob"   NY-N 1996

Appling, Lucius B. "Luke"   Det-A 1960, Cle-A 1960-61, Bal-A 1963, KC-A 1964-67, Chi-A 1970-71

Arsenault, Pierre J.   Mon-N 1992-96

Auferio, Anthony P. "Tony"   StL-N 1973

Austin, James P. "Jimmy"   StL-A 1923-32, Chi-A 1933-40

Babe, Loren R.   NY-A 1967, Chi-A 1980-81, 1983

Bader, Lore V.   Bos-N 1926

Bailor, Robert M. "Bob"   Tor-A 1992-95

Baker, Delmer D. "Del"   Det-A 1933-38, Cle-A 1943-44, Bos-A 1945-48, 1953-60

Baker, Eugene W. "Gene"   Pit-N 1963

Baker, Floyd W.   Min-A 1961-64

Baker, Johnnie B "Dusty"   SF-N 1988-92

Baker, William P. "Bill"   Chi-N 1950

Bamberger, George I.   Bal-A 1968-77

Bancroft, David J. "Dave"   NY-N 1930-32

Bando, Christopher M. "Chris"   Mil-A 1996

Bando, Salvatore L. "Sal"   Mil-A 1980-81

Banks, Ernest "Ernie"   Chi-N 1967-73

Barfield, Jesse L.   Hou-N 1995

Bartell, Richard W. "Dick"   NY-A 1946, Det-A 1949-52, Cin-N 1954-55

Bartirome, Anthony J. "Tony"   Atl-N 1986-88

Basgall, Romanus "Monty"   LA-N 1973-86

Bassler, John L. "Johnny"   Cle-A 1938-40, StL-A 1941

Baylor, Don E.   Mil-A 1990-91, StL-N 1992

Bauer, Henry A. "Hank"   Bal-A 1963

Beauchamp, James E. "Jim"   Atl-N 1991-96

Bearnarth, Lawrence D. "Larry"   Mon-N 1976, 1985-91, Col-N 1993-95

Beck, Walter W. "Boom-Boom"   Was-A 1957-59

Becker, Joseph E. "Joe"   Bro-N 1955-57, LA-N 1958-64, StL-N 1965-66, Chi-N 1967-70

Bedell, Howard W. "Howie"   KC-A 1984, SE-A 1988

Bell, David G. "Buddy"   Cle-A 1994-95

Bender, Charles A. "Chief"   Chi-A 1925-26, NY-N 1931, Phi-A 1951-53

Bengough, Bernard O. "Benny"   Was-A 1940-43, Bos-N 1944-45, Phi-N 1946-58

Benson, Vernon A. "Vern"   StL-N 1961-64, NY-A 1965-66, Cin-N 1966-69, StL-N 1970-75, Atl-N 1976-77, SF-N 1980

Berardino, John "Johnny"   StL-A 1951

Berardino, Richard J. "Dick"   Bos-A 1989-91

Berg, Morris "Moe"   Bos-A 1940-41

Beringer, Carroll J. "C. B."   LA-N 1967-72, Phi-N 1973-78

Berra, Lawrence P. "Yogi"   NY-A 1963, NY-N 1965-71, NY-A 1976-83, Hou-N 1986-89

Berres, Raymond F. "Ray"   Chi-A 1949-66, 1968-69

Berry, Charles F. "Charlie"   Phi-A 1936-40

Bevington, Terry Paul   Chi-A 1989-95

Biagini, Gregory P. "Greg"   Bal-A 1992-94

Bialas, David B. "Dave"   SD-N 1993-94, Chi-N 1995-96

Bissonette, Adelphia L. "Del"   Bos-N 1945, Pit-N 1946

Blackburn, Wayne C.   Det-A 1963-64

Blackburne, Russell A. "Lena"   Chi-A 1927-28, StL-A 1930, Phi-A 1933-40, 1942-43

Blades, F. Raymond "Ray"   StL-N 1930-32, Cin-N 1942, Bro-N 1947-48, StL-N 1951, Chi-N 1953-56

Blaylock, Gary N.   KC-A 1984-87

Bloomfield, Gordon L. "Jack"   SD-N 1974, Chi-N 1975-76, 1977

Bluege, Oswald L. "Ossie"   Was-A 1940-42

Bochy, Bruce D.   SD-N 1993-94

Bombard, Marc   Cin-N 1996

Bonds, Bobby L.   Cle-A 1984-87, SF-N 1993-96

Boone, Robert R. "Bob"   Cin-N 1994

Boros, Stephen "Steve"   KC-A 1975-79, Mon-N 1981-82, KC-A 1993-94, Bal-A 1995

Bosman, Richard A. "Dick"   Chi-A 1986-87, Bal-A 1992-94, TE-X 1995-96

Bottomley, James L. "Jim"   StL-A 1937

Bowa, Lawrence R. "Larry"   Phi-N 1988-96

Boyer, Cletis L. "Clete"   Oak-A 1980-85, NY-A 1988, 1992-94

Boyer, Cloyd V.   NY-A 1975, 1977, Atl-N 1978-81, KC-A 1982-83

Boyer, Kenton L. "Ken"   StL-N 1971-72

Bragan, James A. "Jimmy"   Cin-N 1967-69, Mon-N 1970-72, Mil-A 1976-77

Bragan, Robert R. "Bobby"   LA-N 1960, Hou-N 1962

Braun, Stephen R. "Steve"   StL-N 1990

Brecheen, Harry D.   Bal-A 1954-67

Breeden, H. Scott   Cin-N 1986-89

Breeden, Joseph T. "Joe"   Fla-N 1995-96

Brenly, Robert E. "Bob"   SF-N 1992-96

Bresnahan, Roger P.   NY-N 1925-28, Det-A 1930-31

Brewer, James T. "Jim"   Mon-N 1977-79

Bridges, Everett L. "Rocky"   LA-N 1962-63, Cal-A 1968-71, SF-N 1985

Bridges, Thomas J. "Tommy"   Det-A 1946, Cin-N 1951

Brinkman, Edwin A. "Ed"   Det-A 1979, SD-N 1981, Chi-A 1983-88

Bristol, J. David "Dave"   Cin-N 1966, Mon-N 1973-75, SF-N 1978-79, Phi-N 1982-85, 1988, Cin-N 1989, 1993

Brown, H. Harold "Hal"   Bal-A 1964

Brown, Jackie G.   Tex-A 1979-82, Chi-A 1992-95

Brown, James R. "Jimmy"   Bos-N 1949-51

Brown, Mace S.   Bos-A 1965

Brown, William J. "Gates"   Det-A 1978-84

Brucker, Earle F., Sr.   Phi-A 1941-49, StL-A 1950, Cin-N 1952

Bryant, Claiborne H. "Clay"   LA-N 1961, Cle-A 1967, 1974

Bryant, Donald R. "Don"   Bos-A 1974-76, Sea-A 1977-80

Buckner, William J. "Bill"   Chi-A 1996

Buford, Donald A. "Don"   SF-N 1981-84, Bal-A 1994

Bumbry, Alonza B. "Al"   Bos-A 1988-93, Bal-A 1995

Burdette, S. Lewis "Lew"   Atl-N 1972-73

Burgess, Thomas R. "Tom"   NY-N 1977, Atl-N 1978

Burgmeier, Thomas H. "Tom"   KC-A 1991

Burke, James T. "Jimmy"   Det-A 1914-17, Bos-A 1921-23, Chi-N 1926-30, NY-A 1931-33

Burkett, Jesse C.   NY-N 1921

Burleson, Richard P. "Rick"   Oak-A 1991, Bos-A 1992-93, Cal-A 1995-96

Burns, George J.   NY-N 1931

Burns, John I. "Jack"   Bos-A 1955-59

Burris, B. Ray   Mil-A 1990-91, Tex-A 1992

Burwell, William E. "Bill"   Bos-A 1944, Pit-N 1947-48, 1958-62

Busby, James F. "Jim"   Bal-A 1961, Hou-N 1962, 1963-67, Atl-N 1968-75, Chi-A 1976, Sea-A 1977-78

Butler, John S. "Johnny"   Chi-A 1932

Butterfield, Brian J.   NY-A 1994-95

Camacho, Joseph G. "Joe"   Was-A 1969-71, Tex-A 1972

Camilli, Douglas J. "Doug"   Was-A 1968-69, Bos-A 1970-73

Cannizzaro, Christopher J. "Chris"   Atl-N 1976-78

Cardenal, Jose R. D.   Cin-N 1993, StL-N 1994-95, NY-A 1996

Carew, Rodney C. "Rod"   Cal-A 1992-96

Carey, Max G.   Pit-N 1930

Carey, Thomas F. "Tom"   Bos-A 1946-47

Carisch, Frederick B. "Fred"   Det-A 1923-24

Carlucci, David M. "Dave"   Cal-A 1996

Carnevale, Daniel J. "Danny"   KC-A 1970

Carrion, Leonel S,   Mon-N 1988

Carter, Richard J. "Dick"   Phi-N 1959-60

Case, George W.   Was-A 1961-63, Min-A 1968

Cash, David "Dave"   Phi-N 1996

Castro, William R. "Bill"   Mil-A 1992-95, NY-A 1996

Cavarretta, Philip J. "Phil"   Det-A 1961-63, NY-N 1978

Cepeda, Orlando M.   Chi-A 1980

Chambliss, C. Christopher "Chris"   NY-A 1988, StL-N 1993-95

Chandler, Spurgeon F. "Spud"   KC-A 1957-58

Chapman, W. Benjamin "Ben"   Cin-N 1952

Chesbro, John D. "Jack"   Was-A 1924

Chiti, H. Dominic "Dom"   Cle-A 1991-93

Cisco, Galen B.   KC-A 1971-79, Mon-N 1980-84, SD-N 1985-87, Tor-A 1988, 1990-95

Clark, Ronald B. "Ron"   Chi-A 1988-90, Sea-A 1991, Cle-A 1992-93

Clarke, Fred C.   Pit-N 1925

Clarke, Thomas A. "Tommy"   NY-N 1932-35, 1938

Clary, Ellis   Was-A 1955-60, Tor-A 1989

Clear, E. Robert "Bob"   Cal-A 1976-87

Clines, Eugene A. "Gene"   Chi-N 1979-81, Hou-N 1988, Sea-A 1989-92, Mil-A 1993-94

Cloninger, Tony L.   NY-A 1992-96

Cluck, Robert A. "Bob"   Hou-N 1979, 1990-93, Oak-A 1996

Clymer, William J. "Bill"   Cin-N 1925

Cochrane, Gordon S. "Mickey"   Phi-A 1950

Cohen, Andrew H. "Andy"   Phi-N 1960

Colavito, Rocco D. "Rocky"   Cle-A 1973, 1976-78, KC-A 1982-83

Cole, Richard R. "Dick"   Chi-N 1961

Coleman, Joseph H. "Joe"   Cal-A 1988-90, StL-N 1991-94, Cal-A 1996

Coleman, Robert H. "Bob"   Bos-A 1926, Det-A 1932, Bos-N 1943

Collins, David S "Dave"   StL-N 1991-92

Collins, Edward T. "Eddie"   Phi-A 1931-32

Collins, James A. "Ripper"   Chi-N 1961-63

Collins, Terry L.   Pit-N 1992-93

Combs, Earle B.   NY-A 1936-44, StL-A 1947, Bos-A 1948-52, Phi-N 1954

Combs, Merrill R. "Merl"   Tex-A 1974-75

Comer, Stephen M. "Steve"   Cle-A 1987

Connor, Mark P.   NY-A 1984-85, 1986-87, 1990-93

Connors, William J. "Billy"   KC-A 1980-81, Chi-N 1982-86, Sea-A 1987-88, NY-A 1989-90, Chi-N 1991-93, NY-A 1994-95

Conroy, William E. "Wid"   Phi-N 1922

Consolo, William A. "Billy"   Det-A 1979-92, 1995

Contreras, Arnaldo J. "Nardi"   NY-A 1995

Cooke, Allen L. "Dusty"   Phi-N 1948-52

Coombs, John W. "Jack"   Det-A 1920

Cooney, John W. "Johnny"   Bos-N 1940-42, 1946-49, 1950-52, Mil-N 1953-55, Chi-A 1957-64

Cooper, Donald J. "Don"   Chi-A 1995

Cooper, W. Walker   StL-N 1957, KC-A 1960

Corrales, Patrick "Pat"   Tex-A 1975-78, NY-A 1989, Atl-N 1990-96

Corriden, John M., Sr "Red"   Chi-N 1932-40, Bro-N 1941-46, NY-A 1947-48, Chi-A 1950

Cottier, Charles K. "Chuck"   NY-A 1979-81, Sea-A 1982-84, Chi-N 1988-94, Bal-A 1995

Couchee, Michael "Mike"   Cal-A 1996

Courtney, Clinton D. "Clint"   Hou-N 1965

Cox, Jeffrey L. "Jeff"   KC-A 1995

Cox, Larry E.   Chi-N 1988-89

Cox, Robert J. "Bobby"   NY-A 1977

Crabtree, Estel C.   Cin-N 1943-44

Craft, Harry F.   KC-A 1955-57, Chi-N 1960-61

Craig, Roger L.   SD-N 1969-72, Hou-N 1974-75, SD-N 1976-77, Det-A 1980-84

Cramer, Roger M. "Doc"   Det-A 1948, Chi-A 1951-53

Crandall, Delmar W. "Del"   Cal-A 1977

Crandall, J. Otis "Doc"   Pit-N 1931-34

Crandall, James M. "Jim"   StL-A 1953

Cravath, Clifford C. "Gavvy"   Phi-N 1923

Cresse, Mark E.   LA-N 1977-96

Crosetti, Frank P. J. "Frankie"   NY-A 1947-68, Sea-A 1969, Min-A 1970-71

Crowley, Terrence M. "Terry"   Bal-A 1985-88, Min-A 1991-96

Cubbage, Michael L. "Mike"   NY-N 1990-91, 1992-96

Cuccinello, Anthony F. "Tony"   Cin-N 1949-51, Cle-A 1952-56, Chi-A 1957-66, Det-A 1967-68, Chi-A 1969

Cuellar, Robert "Bobby"   Sea-A 1995-96

Culp, Benjamin B. "Benny"   Phi-N 1946-47

Cumberland, John S.   Bos-A 1995

Cunningham, Joseph R. "Joe"   StL-N 1982

Cunningham, William A. "Bill"   Chi-A 1932

Cuyler, Hazen S. "Kiki"   Chi-N 1941-43, Bos-A 1949

Dahlgren, Ellsworth T. "Babe"   KC-A 1964

Dal Canton, J. Bruce   Chi-A 1978, Atl-N 1987-90

Daly, Thomas D. "Tom" Bos-A 1933-46

Dark, Alvin R. Chi-N 1965, 1977

Dauer, Richard F. "Rich" Cle-A 1990-91

Davenport, James H. "Jim" SF-N 1970, SD-N 1974-75, SF-N 1976-82, 1984, Phi-N 1986-87, Cle-A 1989, SF-N 1995

Davis, Harry H. Phi-A 1913-17, 1919

Davis, H. Thomas "Tommy" Sea-A 1981

Davis, R. Brandon "Brandy" Phi-N 1972

Davis, Virgil L. "Spud" Pit-N 1942-46, Chi-N 1950-53

Deal, Ellis F. "Cot" Cin-N 1959-60, Hou-N 1962-64, NY-A 1965, KC-A 1966-67, Cle-A 1970-71, Det-A 1973-74, Hou-N 1983-85

Dean, Jay H. "Dizzy" Chi-N 1941

DeArmas, Rolando J. "Roly" Chi-A 1995-96

DeJohn, Mark S. StL-N 1996

DeMars, William L. "Billy" Phi-N 1969-81, Mon-N 1982-84, Cin-N 1985-87

DeMerritt, Martin G. "Marty" SF-N 1989

Demeter, Stephen "Steve" Pit-N 1985

Dent, Russell E. "Bucky" StL-N 1991-94, Tex-A 1995-96

Detore, George F. Pit-N 1959

Devlin, Arthur M. "Art" Bos-N 1926, 1928

Dews, Robert W. "Bobby" Atl-N 1979-81, 1985

Dickey, William M. "Bill" NY-A 1949-57, 1960

Didier, Robert D. "Bob" Oak-A 1984-86, Sea-A 1989-90

DiMaggio, Joseph P. "Joe" Oak-A 1968-69

Dixon, Walter "Walt" Chi-N 1964-65

Dobson, Patrick E. "Pat" Mil-A 1982-84, SD-N 1988-90, KC-A 1991, Bal-A 1996

Doby, Lawrence E. "Larry" Mon-N 1971-73, Cle-A 1974, Mon-N 1976, Chi-A 1977-78

Doerr, Robert P. "Bobby" Bos-A 1967-69, Tor-A 1977-81

Dolan, Albert J. "Cozy" NY-N 1922-24

Donnelly, Richard F. "Rich" Tex-A 1980, 1983-85, Pit-N 1986-95

Donovan, William E. "Bill" Det-A 1918

Doolan, Michael J. "Mickey" Chi-N 1926-29, Cin-N 1930-32

Dorish, Harry "Fritz" Bos-A 1963, Atl-N 1968-71

Douglas, Otis W. Cin-N 1961-62

Down, Richard J. "Rick" Cal-A 1987-88, NY-A 1993-95, Bal-A 1996

Drabowsky, Myron W. "Moe" Chi-A 1986, Chi-N 1994

Dressen, Charles W. "Chuck" Bro-N 1939-42, 1943-46, NY-A 1947-48, LA-N 1958-59

Dubuc, Jean J. Det-A 1930-31

Duffy, Hugh Bos-A 1932

Dugey, Oscar J. Bos-N 1920, Chi-N 1921-24

Duncan, David E. "Dave" Cle-A 1978-81, Sea-A 1982, Chi-A 1983-86, Oak-A 1986-95, StL-N 1996

Dunlop, Harry A. KC-A 1969-75, Chi-N 1976, Cin-N 1979-82, SD-N 1983-86

Durocher, Leo E. LA-N 1961-64

Dusan, Eugene P. "Gene" NY-N 1983

Dyer, Don R. "Duffy" Chi-N 1983, Mil-A 1989-95, Oak-A 1996

Dykes, James J. "Jimmy" Phi-A 1949-50, Cin-N 1955-58, Pit-N 1959, Mil-N 1962, KC-A 1963-64

Earnshaw, George L. Phi-N 1949-50

Easler, Michael A. "Mike" Mil-A 1992, Bos-A 1993-94

Easter, L. Luke Cle-A 1969

Edwards, Howard R. "Doc" Phi-N 1970-72, Cle-A 1985-87, NY-N 1990-91

Egan, Arthur A. "Ben" Bro-N 1925, Chi-A 1926

Egan, Richard W. "Dick" Tex-A 1988-89

Elia, Lee C. Phi-N 1980-81, 1985-87, NY-A 1989, Sea-A 1993-96

Elliott, Robert I. "Bob" LA-A 1961

Ellis, Samuel J. "Sammy" NY-A 1982, 1983-84, 1986, Chi-A 1989-91, Chi-N 1992, Sea-A 1993-94, Bos-A 1996

Emery, Calvin W. "Cal" Chi-A 1988

Ens, Jewel W. Pit-N 1926-29, Det-A 1932, Cin-N 1933, Bos-N 1934, Pit-N 1935-39, Cin-N 1941

Ermer, Calvin C. "Cal" Bal-A 1962, Mil-A 1970-71, Oak-A 1977

Estrada, Charles L. "Chuck" Tex-A 1973, SD-N 1978-81, Cle-A 1983

Etchebarren, Andrew A. "Andy" Cal-A 1977, Mil-A 1985-91, Bal-A 1996

Evans, Darrell W. NY-A 1990

Evans, Dwight M. Col-N 1994

Evers, John J. "Johnny" NY-N 1920, Chi-A 1922-23, Bos-N 1929-32

Evers, Walter A. "Hoot" Cle-A 1970

Ezell, Glenn W. Tex-A 1983-85, KC-A 1989-94, Det-A 1996

Faber, Urban C. "Red" Chi-A 1946-48

Fahey, William R. "Bill" SF-N 1986-91

Falk, Bibb A. Cle-A 1933, Bos-A 1934

Fanning, W. James "Jim" Atl-N 1967

Farrell, M. Kerby Chi-A 1966-69, Cle-A 1970-71

Felske, John F. Tor-A 1980-81, Phi-N 1984

Ferguson, Joseph V. "Joe" Tex-A 1986-87, LA-N 1988-89, 1992-93

Ferraro, Michael D. "Mike" NY-A 1979-82, KC-A 1984-86, NY-A 1987-88, 1989-91, Bal-A 1993

Ferrell, Richard B. "Rick" Was-A 1946-49, Det-A 1950-53

Ferrick, Thomas J. "Tom" Cin-N 1954-58, Phi-N 1959, Det-A 1960-63, KC-A 1964-65

Ferriss, David M. "Dave" Bos-A 1955-59

Fischer, Bradley J. "Brad" Oak-A 1996

Fischer, William C. "Bill" Cin-N 1979-83, Bos-A 1985-91

Fitzgerald, Edward R. "Ed" Cle-A 1960, KC-A 1961, Min-A 1962-64

Fitzgerald, Joseph P. "Joe" Was-A 1947-56

Fitzpatrick, John A. Pit-N 1953-56, Mil-N 1958-59

Fitzsimmons, Frederick "Freddie" Bro-N 1942, Bos-N 1948, NY-N 1949-53, 1954-55, Chi-N 1957-59, KC-A 1960, Chi-N 1966

Flanagan, Michael K. "Mike" Bal-A 1995

Flannery, Timothy E. "Tim" SD-N 1996

Fletcher, Arthur "Art" NY-A 1927-45

Flowers, D'Arcy R. "Jake" Pit-N 1940-45, Bos-N 1946, Cle-A 1951-52

Fohl, Leo A. "Lee" StL-A 1920

Foley, Marvis E. "Marv" Chi-N 1994

Foli, Timothy J. "Tim" Tex-A 1986-87, Mil-A 1992-95, KC-A 1996

Foote, Barry C. Chi-A 1991, NY-N 1992-93

Ford, Edward C. "Whitey" NY-A 1964, 1968, 1974-75

Fowler, J. Arthur "Art" LA-A 1964, Min-A 1969, Det-A 1971-73, Tex-A 1973-75, NY-A 1977-79, Oak-A 1980-82, NY-A 1983, 1988

Fox, Charles F. "Charlie" SF-N 1965-68, NY-A 1989

Fox, J. Nelson "Nellie" Hou-N 1965, 1966-67, Was-A 1968-71, Tex-A 1972

Foxx, James E. "Jimmie" Chi-N 1944

Francona, Terry J. Det-A 1996

Franks, Herman L. NY-N 1949-55, SF-N 1958, 1964, Chi-N 1970

Fraser, Charles C. "Chick" Pit-N 1923

Freese, George W. Chi-N 1964-65

Frey, James G. "Jim" Bal-A 1970-79, NY-N 1982-83

Friel, William E. "Bill" StL-A 1920

Friend, Owen L. KC-A 1969

Frisch, Frank F. "Frankie" NY-N 1949

Funk, Franklin R. "Frank" SF-N 1976, Sea-A 1980-81, 1983-84, KC-A 1988-90, Col-N 1996

Galan, August J. "Augie" Phi-A 1954

Galante, Matthew "Matt" Hou-N 1985-96

Gale, Richard B. "Rich" Bos-A 1992-93

Gantner, James E. "Jim" Mil-A 1996

Garcia, David "Dave" SD-N 1970-73, Cle-A 1975-76, Cal-A 1977, Cle-A 1979, Mil-A 1983-84

Gardenhire, Ronald C. "Ron" Min-A 1991-96

Gardner, William F. "Billy" Bos-A 1965-66, Mon-N 1977-78, Min-A 1981

Garner, Philip M. "Phil" Hou-N 1989-91

Garrett, H. Adrian KC-A 1988-92

Garrison, R. Ford Cin-N 1953

Gaston, Clarence E. "Cito" Tor-A 1982-89

Gebhard, Robert H. "Bob" Mon-N 1982

Gehringer, Charles L. "Charlie" Det-A 1942

Gernert, Richard E. "Dick" Tex-A 1975-76

Gharrity, E. Patrick "Patsy" Was-A 1929-32, Cle-A 1933-35

Gibson, George C. Was-A 1923, Chi-N 1925, 1926

Gibson, Robert "Bob" NY-N 1981, Atl-N 1982-84, StL-N 1995

Gilbert, Andrew "Andy" SF-N 1972-75

Gilliam, James W. "Jim" LA-N 1965-78

Gladding, Fred E. Det-A 1976-78

Gleason, William J. "Kid" Phi-N 1908-11, Chi-A 1912-14, 1916-17, Phi-A 1926-32

Gleeson, James J. "Jim" KC-A 1957, NY-A 1964

Glynn, Eugene P. "Gene" Col-N 1994, 1995-96

Gomez, Juan A. "Orlando" Tex-A 1991-92

Gomez, Pedro "Preston" LA-N 1965-68, Hou-N 1973, StL-N 1976, LA-N 1977-79, Cal-A 1981-84

Gonzalez, Miguel A. "Mike" StL-N 1934-46

Gooch, John B. "Johnny" Pit-N 1937-39

Goodman, William D. "Billy" Atl-N 1968-70

Gordon, Joseph L. "Joe" Det-A 1956

Goryl, John A. "Johnny" Min-A 1968-69, 1979-80, Cle-A 1982-88

Gowdy, Henry M. "Hank" Bos-A 1929-37, Cin-N 1938-42, 1945-46, NY-N 1947-48

Graff, Milton E. "Milt" Pit-N 1985

Grammas, Alexander P. "Alex" Chi-N 1964, Pit-N 1965-69, Cin-N 1970-75, 1978, Atl-N 1979, Det-A 1980-91

Griffey, G. Kenneth Sr. "Ken" Sea-A 1993-94, Col-N 1996

Griffin, Alfredo C. Tor-A 1996

Grimes, Burleigh A. KC-A 1955

Grimm, Charles J. "Charlie" Chi-N 1941, 1961-63

Grissom, Marvin E. "Marv" LA-A 1961-65, Cal-A 1966, Chi-A 1967-68, Cal-A 1969, Min-A 1970-71, Chi-N 1975-76, Cal-A 1977-78

Grodzicki, John "Johnny" Det-A 1979

Guerrero, Epifanio O. "Epy" Tor-A 1981

Gullett, Donald E. "Don" Cin-N 1993-96

Gustine, Frank W. "Frankie" Pit-N 1950

Gutteridge, Donald J. "Don" Chi-A 1955-66, 1968-69

Haas, G. Edward "Eddie" Atl-N 1974-77, 1984

Haas, George W. "Mule" Chi-A 1940-46

Hack, Stanley C. "Stan" StL-N 1957-58, Chi-N 1965

Hacker, Richard W. "Rich" StL-N 1986-90, Tor-A 1991-94

Haddix, Harvey NY-N 1966-67, Cin-N 1969, Bos-A 1971, Cle-A 1975-78, Pit-N 1979-84

Haines, Jesse J. Bro-N 1938

Hairston, Samuel "Sammy" Chi-A 1978

Haller, Thomas F. "Tom" SF-N 1977-79

Hamilton, Steve A. Det-A 1975

Hancken, Morris M. "Buddy" Hou-N 1968-72

Haney, Fred G. Mil-N 1956

Haney, W. Larry Mil-A 1978-91

Hansen, Guy C. KC-A 1991-93, 1996

Hansen, Roger C. Sea-A 1992

Hansen, Ronald L. "Ron" Mil-A 1980-83, Mon-N 1985-89

Harder, Melvin L. "Mel" Cle-A 1947, 1948-63, NY-N 1964, Chi-N 1965, Cin-N 1966-68, KC-A 1969

Hardy, H. Lawrence "Larry" Tex-A 1995-96

Hargrove, D. Michael "Mike" Cle-A 1990-91

Harmon, Thomas "Tom" Chi-N 1982

Harper, Tommy Bos-A 1980-84, Mon-N 1990-96

Harrah, Colbert D. "Toby" Tex-A 1989-92, Cle-A 1996

Harrelson, Derrel M. "Bud" NY-N 1982, 1985-90

Harris, C. Luman "Lum" Chi-A 1951-54, Bal-A 1955-61, Hou-N 1962-64

Hart, John H. Bal-A 1988

Hartenstein, Charles O. "Chuck" Cle-A 1979, Mil-A 1987-89

Hartley, Grover A. Cle-A 1928-30, Pit-N 1931-33, StL-A 1934-36, NY-N 1946

Hartnett, Charles L. "Gabby" Chi-N 1938, NY-N 1941, KC-A 1965

Hartsfield, Roy T. LA-N 1969-72, Atl-N 1973

Hassey, Ronald W. "Ron" Col-N 1993-95, StL-N 1996

Hatcher, Michael V. "Mickey" Tex-A 1993-94

Hatfield, Fred J. Det-A 1977-78

Hatton, Grady E. Chi-N 1960, Hou-N 1973-74

Haynes, Joseph W. "Joe" Was-A 1953-55

Hayworth, Raymond H. "Ray" Bro-N 1945, Chi-N 1955

Hebner, Richard J. "Richie" Bos-A 1989-91

Heffner, Donald H. "Don" KC-A 1958-60, Det-A 1961, NY-N 1964-65, Cal-A 1967-68

Hegan, James E. "Jim" NY-A 1960-73, 1974-78, NY-A 1979-80

Heilmann, Harry E. Cin-N 1932

Heist, Alfred M. "Al" Hou-N 1966-67, SD-N 1980

Helms, Tommy V. Tex-A 1981-82, Cin-N 1983-89

Hemsley, Ralston B. "Rollie" Phi-A 1954, Was-A 1961-62

Hemus, Solomon J. "Solly" NY-N 1962-63, Cle-A 1964-65

Henderson, Stephen C. "Steve" Hou-N 1994-96

Hendrick, George A. StL-N 1996

Hendricks, Elrod J. Bal-A 1978-96

Henrich, Thomas D. "Tommy" NY-A 1951, NY-N 1957, Det-A 1958-59

Herman, Floyd C. "Babe" Pit-N 1951

Herman, William J. "Billy" Bro-N 1952-57, Mil-N 1958-59, Bos-A 1960-64, Cal-A 1967, SD-N 1978-79

Hernandez, Carlo A "Chuck" Cal-A 1992-96

Herndon, Larry D. Det-A 1992-96

Herzog, Dorrel N. "Whitey" KC-A 1965, NY-N 1966, Cal-A 1974-75

Hiatt, Jack E   Chi-N 1981
High, Andrew A. "Andy"   Bro-N 1937-38
Hill, Marc K.   Hou-N 1988, NY-A 1991
Hill, Perry W.   Tex-A 1992-94, 1995
Hiller, Charles J. "Chuck"   Tex-A 1973, KC-A 1976-79, StL-N 1981-83, SF-N 1985, NY-N 1990
Hilton, J. David "Dave"   Mil-A 1987-88
Himsl, Avitus B. "Vedie"   Chi-N 1960-64
Hinchman, William W. "Bill"   Pit-N 1923
Hines, Benjamin T. "Ben"   Sea-A 1984, LA-N 1986, 1988-93, Hou-N 1994
Hines, Bruce E.   Cal-A 1991
Hisle, Larry E.   Tor-A 1992-95
Hitchcock, William C. "Billy"   Det-A 1955-60, Atl-N 1966
Hoak, Donald A. "Don"   Phi-N 1967
Hofman, Robert G. "Bobby"   KC-A 1966-67, Was-A 1968, Oak-A 1969-70, Cle-A 1971-72, Oak-A 1974-75, 1978
Hofmann, Fred   StL-A 1938-49, 1951
Holke, Walter H.   StL-A 1940
Hollingsworth, Albert W. "Al"   StL-N 1957-58
Holt, Golden D. "Goldie"   Pit-N 1948-50, Chi-N 1961-65
Holmberg, Dennis   Tor-A 1994-95
Holmquist, Douglas L. "Doug"   NY-A 1984, 1985
Hopp, John L. "Johnny"   Det-A 1954, StL-N 1956
Hornsby, Rogers   Chi-N 1958-59, NY-N 1962
Horton, Willie W.   NY-A 1985, Chi-A 1986
Hoscheit, Vernard A. "Vern"   Bal-A 1968, Oak-A 1969-74, Cal-A 1976, NY-N 1984-87
Houk, Ralph G.   NY-A 1954, 1958-60
House, Thomas R. "Tom"   Tex-A 1985-92
Howard, Elston G.   NY-A 1969-79
Howard, Frank O.   Mil-A 1977-80, NY-N 1982-83, 1984, Mil-A 1985-86, Sea-A 1987-88, NY-A 1989, 1991-92, NY-N 1994-96
Howe, Arthur H. "Art"   Tex-A 1985-88, Col-N 1995
Howley, Daniel P. "Dan"   Det-A 1919, 1921-22
Howser, Richard D. "Dick"   NY-A 1969-78
Hriniak, Walter J. "Walt"   Mon-N 1974-75, Bos-A 1977-88, Chi-A 1989-95
Hudlin, G. Willis   Det-A 1957-59
Hubbard, John H. "Jack"   StL-N 1993
Hudson, Sidney C. "Sid"   Was-A 1961-65, 1968-71, Tex-A 1972, 1975-78
Hulswitt, Rudolph E. "Rudy"   Bos-A 1931-33
Hundley, C. Randolph "Randy"   Chi-N 1977
Hunter, Frederick C. "Newt"   Phi-N 1928-31, 1933
Hunter, G. William "Billy"   Bal-A 1964-77
Isaac, Luis   Cle-A 1987-91, 1994-96
Jackson, Alvin N. "Al"   Bos-A 1977-79, Bal-A 1989-91
Jackson, Grant D.   Pit-N 1984-85, Cin-N 1994-95
Jackson, Roland T. "Sonny"   Atl-N 1982-83
Jackson, Ronnie D. "Ron"   Chi-A 1995-96
Jackson, Travis C.   NY-N 1939-40, 1947-48
Jansen, Lawrence J. "Larry"   NY-N 1954, SF-N 1961-71, Chi-N 1972-73
Jaramillo, Rudolph "Rudy"   Hou-N 1990-93, Tex-A 1995-96
Jenkins, Ferguson A. "Fergie"   Chi-N 1995-96
Jennings, Hugh A. "Hughie"   NY-N 1921-25
Johnson, Darrell D.   StL-N 1960-61, Bal-A 1962, Bos-A 1968-69, Tex-A 1981-82, NY-N 1993
Johnson, Deron R.   Cal-A 1979-80, NY-N 1981, Phi-N 1982-84, Sea-A 1985-86, Chi-A 1987, Cal-A 1989-91
Johnson, Lamar   Mil-A 1995-96
Johnson, Roy J   Chi-N 1935-39, 1944-53
Johnson, Sylvester W. "Syl"   Phi-N 1937-40
Johnson, Timothy E. "Tim"   Mon-N 1993-94, Bos-A 1995-96
Johnston, James H. "Jimmy"   Bro-N 1931
Jones, Clarence W.   Atl-N 1985, 1988-96
Jones, Gordon B.   Hou-N 1966-67
Jones, Grover W. "Deacon"   Hou-N 1976-82, SD-N 1984-87
Jones, Jeffrey A. "Jeff"   Det-A 1995
Jones, Lynn M.   KC-A 1991-92
Jones, Joseph C. "Joe"   KC-A 1987, 1992
Jonnard, Clarence J. "Bubber"   Phi-N 1935, NY-N 1942-46
Judge, Joseph I. "Joe"   Was-A 1945-46
Jurges, William F. "Billy"   Chi-A 1947-48, Was-A 1956-59
Kaat, James L. "Jim"   Cin-N 1984-85
Kahn, Louis "Lou"   StL-N 1955
Katt, Raymond F. "Ray"   StL-N 1959-60, Cle-A 1962
Kaufmann, Anthony C. "Tony"   StL-N 1947-50
Keane, John J. "Johnny"   StL-N 1959-61
Keefe, David E. "Dave"   Phi-A 1940-49

Keely, Robert W. "Bob"   Bos-N 1946-52, Mil-N 1953-57
Kelleher, Michael D. "Mick"   Pit-N 1986
Keller, Charles E. "Charlie"   NY-A 1957, 1959
Kelley, Joseph J. "Joe"   Bro-N 1926
Kelly, Bernard F. "Mike"   Chi-N 1930-31, Chi-N 1934, Bos-N 1937-39, Pit-N 1940-41
Kelly, George L.   Cin-N 1935-37, Bos-N 1938-43, Cin-N 1947-48
Kelly, J. Thomas "Tom"   Min-A 1983-86
Kendall, Fred L.   Det-A 1996
Kennedy, Kevin   Mon-N 1992
Kennedy, Robert D. "Bob"   Chi-N 1962-65, Atl-N 1967
Kerr, John F.   Was-A 1935
Kerrigan, Joseph T. "Joe"   Mon-N 1983-86, 1992-96
Killefer, William L. "Bill"   StL-N 1926, StL-A 1927-29, Bro-N 1939, Phi-N 1942
Kim, Wendell K.   SF-N 1989-96
Kimm, Bruce E.   Cin-N 1984-88, Pit-N 1989, SD-N 1991-92
King, Clyde E.   Cin-N 1959, Pit-N 1965-67, NY-A 1978, 1981, 1988
Kison, Bruce E.   KC-A 1992-96
Kissell, George M.   StL-N 1969-75
Kittle, Hubert M. "Hub"   Hou-N 1971-75, StL-N 1981-83
Klein, Charles H. "Chuck"   Phi-N 1942-45
Klein, Louis F. "Lou"   Chi-N 1960-65
Kluszewski, Theodore B. "Ted"   Cin-N 1970-78
Knight, C. Ray   Cin-N 1993-95
Knoop, Robert F. "Bobby"   Chi-A 1977-78, Cal-A 1979-96
Knowles, Darold D.   StL-N 1983, Phi-N 1989-90
Koenig, Fred Carl   Cal-A 1970-71, StL-N 1976, Tex-A 1977-82, Chi-N 1983, Cle-A 1985-86
Kress, Ralph "Red"   Det-A 1940, NY-N 1946-49, Cle-A 1953-60, LA-A 1961, NY-N 1962
Krol, John T. "Jack"   StL-N 1977-80, SD-N 1981-86
Krug, Everett B. "Chris"   SD-N 1969
Kuehl, Karl O.   Min-A 1977-82
Kuenn, Harvey E.   Mil-A 1971-82
Kuntz, Russell J. "Rusty"   Sea-A 1989-92, Fla-N 1995-96
Kusnyer, Arthur W. "Art"   Chi-A 1980-87, Oak-A 1989-95
Lachemann, Marcel E.   Cal-A 1984-92, Fla-N 1993-94
Lachemann, Rene G.   Bos-A 1985-86, Oak-A 1987-92
Lachemann, William C. "Bill"   Cal-A 1995-96
Lakeman, Albert W. "Al"   Bos-A 1963-64, 1967-69
Lamont, Gene W.   Pit-N 1986-91, 1996
Land, Grover C.   Pit-N 1914, Cin-N 1925-28, Chi-N 1929-30
Landestoy, Rafael S.   Mon-N 1989, NY-N 1996
Landrith, Hobert N. "Hobie"   Was-A 1964
Lanier, Harold C. "Hal"   StL-N 1981-85, Phi-N 1990-91
Lansford, Carney R.   Oak-A 1995
LaRoche, David E. "Dave"   Chi-A 1989-91, NY-N 1992-93
LaRussa, Anthony "Tony"   Chi-A 1978
Lasorda, Thomas C. "Tommy"   LA-N 1973-76
Latham, W. Arlington "Arlie"   Cin-N 1900, NY-N 1909
Lau, Charles R. "Charley"   Bal-A 1969, Oak-A 1970, KC-A 1971-74, 1975-78, NY-A 1979-81, Chi-A 1982-83
Lauder, William "Billy"   Chi-A 1925
Lavagetto, Harry A. "Cookie"   Bro-N 1951-53, Was-A 1955-57, NY-N 1962-63, SF-N 1964-67
Law, Vernon S. "Vern"   Pit-N 1968-69
Lazzeri, Anthony M. "Tony"   Chi-N 1938
Lefebvre, James K. "Jim"   LA-N 1978-79, SF-N 1980-82, Oak-A 1987-88, 1994-95
Leifield, Albert P. "Lefty"   StL-N 1920-23, Bos-A 1924-26, Det-A 1927-28
Lemon, James R. "Jim"   Min-A 1965-67, 1981-84
Lemon, Robert G. "Bob"   Cle-A 1960, Phi-N 1961, Cal-A 1967-68, KC-A 1970, NY-A 1976
Lenhardt, Donald E. "Don"   Bos-A 1970-73
Leonard, Emil J. "Dutch"   Chi-N 1954-56
Leppert, Donald G. "Don"   Pit-N 1968-76, Tor-A 1977-79, Hou-N 1980-85
Lett, James C. "Jim"   Cin-N 1988-89, 1996
Levy, Leonard "Len"   Pit-N 1957-63
Lewis, George E. "Duffy"   Bos-N 1931-35
Lewis, Johnny J.   StL-N 1973-76, 1985-89
Leyland, James R. "Jim"   Chi-A 1982-85
Leyva, Nicolas T. "Nick"   StL-N 1984-88, Tor-A 1993-96

Lillis, Robert P. "Bob"   Hou-N 1967, 1973-82, SF-N 1986-96
Linares, Julio   Hou-N 1994-96
Lipon, John J. "Johnny"   Cle-A 1968-71
Little, W. Grady   SD-N 1996
Litwhiler, Daniel W. "Danny"   Cin-N 1951
Livingston, Patrick J. "Paddy"   Phi-A 1919
Llenas, Winston E.   Tor-A 1988
Lobe, William C. "Bill"   Cle-A 1951-56
Lobert, John B. "Hans"   NY-N 1928, Phi-N 1934-41, Cin-N 1943-44
Lockman, Carroll W. "Whitey"   Cin-N 1960, SF-N 1961-64, Chi-N 1965-66
Lodigiani, Dario A.   KC-A 1961-62
Lollar, J. Sherman "Sherm"   Bal-A 1964-67, Oak-A 1968
Long, R. Dale   NY-A 1963
Lonnett, Joseph P. "Joe"   Chi-A 1971-75, Oak-A 1976, Pit-N 1977-84
Lopat, Edmund W. "Ed"   NY-A 1960, Min-A 1961, KC-A 1962
Lopes, David E. "Davey"   Tex-A 1988-91, Bal-A 1992-94, SD-N 1995-96
Lowe, Q. V. "Q. V."   Chi-N 1972
Lowrey, Harry L. "Peanuts"   Phi-N 1960-66, SF-N 1967-68, Mon-N 1969, Chi-N 1970-71, Cal-A 1972, Chi-N 1977-79, 1981
Lucchesi, Frank J.   Tex-A 1974-75, 1979-80
Lum, Michael K. "Mike"   Chi-A 1985, KC-A 1988-89
Lumpe, Jerry D.   Oak-A 1971
Lund, Donald A. "Don"   Det-A 1957-58
Luque, Adolfo "Dolf"   NY-N 1935-38, 1941-45
Lutz, R. Joseph "Joe"   Cle-A 1971-73
Luzinski, Gregory M. "Greg"   Oak-A 1993, KC-A 1995-96
Lyons, Edward H. "Eddie"   Min-A 1976
Lyons, Theodore A. "Ted"   Det-A 1949-53, Bro-N 1954
Macha, Kenneth E. "Ken"   Mon-N 1986-91, Cal-A 1992-94
Mack, Earle T.   Phi-A 1924-50
Macko, Joseph "Joe"   Chi-N 1964
MacKenzie, H. Gordon "Gordy"   KC-A 1980-81, Chi-N 1982, SF-N 1986-88, Cle-A 1991
Maddon, Joseph J. "Joe"   Cal-A 1995-96
Maglie, Salvatore A. "Sal"   Bos-A 1960-62, 1966-67, Sea-A 1969
Mahoney, James T. "Jim"   Chi-A 1972-76, Sea-A 1985-86
Majtyka, LeRoy W. "Roy"   Atl-N 1988-90
Malmberg, Harry W.   Bos-A 1963-64
Maloof, Jack G.   SD-N 1990
Maltzberger, Gordon R.   Min-A 1962-64
Mancuso, August R. "Gus"   Cin-N 1950
Mansolino, Doug   Chi-A 1992-96
Mantle, Mickey C.   NY-A 1970
Manuel, Charles F. "Charlie"   Cle-A 1988-89, 1994-96
Manuel, Jerry   Mon-N 1991-96
Manush, Henry E. "Heinie"   Was-A 1953-54
Marion, Martin W. "Marty"   StL-A 1952, Chi-A 1954
Marshall, R. James "Jim"   Chi-N 1974
Martin, Alfred M. "Billy"   Min-A 1965-68, Tex-A 1974
Martin, Fred T.   Chi-N 1961-65, Chi-A 1979
Martin, John L. "Pepper"   Chi-N 1956
Martin, Joseph C. "J. C."   Chi-N 1974
Martinez, Jose   KC-A 1980-87, Chi-N 1988-94
Martinez, Orlando "Marty"   Sea-A 1984-86, 1992
Mathews, Edwin L. "Eddie"   Atl-N 1971-72
Mathews, Henry "Harry"   Cle-A 1926-27, NY-A 1929
Mathews, Rick R.   Col-N 1993, 1995
Mathewson, Christopher "Christy"   NY-N 1919-20
Matlack, Jonathan T. "Jon"   Det-A 1996
Mauch, Gene W.   KC-A 1995
Maxvill, C. Dallan "Dal"   Oak-A 1975, NY-N 1978, StL-N 1979-80, Atl-N 1982-84
May, Lee A.   KC-A 1984-86, Cin-N 1988-89, KC-A 1992-93, Bal-A 1995
May, Milton S. "Milt"   Pit-N 1987-96
Mayberry, John C.   KC-A 1989-90
Mayo, Edward J. "Eddie"   Bos-A 1951, Phi-N 1952-54
Mays, Willie H.   NY-N 1974-79
Mazeroski, William S. "Bill"   Pit-N 1973, Sea-A 1979-80
Mazzone, Leo D.   Atl-N 1985, 1990-96
McBride, George F.   Det-A 1925-26, 1929
McBride, Kenneth F. "Ken"   Mil-A 1975
McCallister, John "Jack"   Cle-A 1920-26, Bos-N 1930

McClure, Robert C. "Bob"   Fla-N 1994

McCormick, Frank A.   Cin-N 1956-57

McCrabb, Lester W. "Les"   Phi-A 1950-54

McCraw, Tommy L.   Cle-A 1975, 1979-82, SF-N 1983-85, Bal-A 1989-91, NY-N 1992-96

McCullough, Clyde E.   Was-A 1960, Min-A 1961, NY-N 1963, SD-N 1982

McDermott, Maurice J. "Mickey"   Cal-A 1968

McDonnell, Robert A. "Maje"   Phi-N 1951-57

McGaha, F. Melvin "Mel"   Cle-A 1961, KC-A 1963-64, Hou-N 1968-70

McGinnity, Joseph J. "Joe"   Bro-N 1926

McGuire, James T. "Deacon"   Det-A 1911-16

McKay, David L. "Dave"   Oak-A 1984-95, StL-N 1996

McKechnie, William B. "Bill"   Pit-N 1922, StL-N 1927, Cle-A 1947-49, Bos-A 1952-53

McKee, J. R.   Pit-N 1947

McKeon, John A. "Jack"   Oak-A 1978

McLaren, John L.   Tor-A 1986-90, Bos-A 1991, Cin-N 1992, Sea-A 1993-96

McLish, Calvin C. "Cal"   Phi-N 1965-66, Mon-N 1969-75, Mil-A 1976-82

McMahon, Donald J. "Don"   SF-N 1973-75, Min-A 1976-77, SF-N 1980-82, Cle-A 1983-85

McMillan, Roy D.   Mil-A 1970-72, NY-N 1973-76

McNamara, John F.   Oak-A 1968-69, SF-N 1971-73, Cal-A 1978

McNeely, G. Earl   StL-A 1931, Was-A 1936-37

McNertney, Gerald E. "Jerry"   Bos-A 1988

McRae, Harold A. "Hal"   KC-A 1987, Mon-N 1990-91, Cin-N 1995-96

Mejias, Samuel E. "Sammy"   Sea-A 1993-96

Mele, Sabath A. "Sam"   Was-A 1959-60, Min-A 1961

Melillo, Oscar D. "Ski"   StL-A 1938, Cle-A 1939-40, 1942, 1945-48, 1950, Bos-A 1952-53, KC-A 1955-56

Mendoza, C. Rigoberto "Minnie"   Bal-A 1988

Menke, Denis J.   Tor-A 1980-81, Hou-N 1983-88, Phi-N 1989-96

Merkle, Frederick C. "Fred"   NY-A 1925-26

Merrill, Carl H. "Stump"   NY-A 1985, 1986-87

Metro, Charles "Charlie"   Chi-N 1962, Chi-A 1965, Oak-A 1982

Meusel, Emil F. "Irish"   NY-N 1930

Meyer, Bernhard "Benny"   Phi-N 1924-26, Det-A 1928-30

Meyer, Russell C. "Russ" Or "Monk"   NY-A 1992

Michael, Eugene R. "Gene"   NY-A 1976-77, 1978, 1984-86, 1988, 1989

Milan, J. Clyde   Was-A 1928-29, 1938-52

Miley, David A. "Dave"   Cin-N 1993

Miller, Dyar K   Chi-A 1987-88

Miller, Edmund J. "Bing"   Bos-A 1937, Det-A 1938-41, Chi-A 1942-49, Phi-A 1950-53

Miller, L. Otto   Bro-N 1926-36

Miller, Raymond R. "Ray"   Bal-A 1978-85, Pit-N 1987-96

Miller, Robert L. "Bob"   Tor-A 1977-79, SF-N 1985

Milliken, Robert F. "Bob"   StL-N 1965-70, 1976

Mills, Arthur G. "Art"   Det-A 1944-48

Mills, C. Buster   Cle-A 1946, Chi-A 1947-50, Cin-N 1953, Bos-A 1954

Minoso, S. Orestes "Minnie"   Chi-A 1976-78, 1980-81

Mitchell, Clarence E.   NY-N 1932-33

Mitchell, Frederick F. "Fred"   Bos-N 1914-16

Mitterwald, George E.   Oak-A 1979-82, NY-A 1988

Mize, John R. "Johnny"   KC-A 1961

Monbouquette, William C. "Bill"   NY-N 1982-83, NY-A 1985

Monchak, Alex "Al"   Chi-A 1971-75, Oak-A 1976, Pit-N 1977-84, Atl-N 1986-88

Moon, Wallace W. "Wally"   SD-N 1969

Moore, Jackie W.   Mil-A 1970-72, Tex-A 1973-74, 1975-76, Tor-A 1977-79, Tex-A 1980, Oak-A 1981-84, Mon-N 1987-89, Cin-N 1990-92, Tex-A 1993-94, Col-N 1996

Moore, Terry B.   StL-N 1949-52, 1956-58

Morales, Jose M.   SF-N 1986-88, Cle-A 1990-93, Fla-N 1995-96

Morales, Richard A. "Rich"   Atl-N 1986-87

Morgan, Joseph M. "Joe"   Pit-N 1972, Bos-A 1985-88

Morgan, Tom S.   Cal-A 1972-74, SD-N 1975, NY-N 1979, Cal-A 1981-83

Morgan, Vernon T. "Vern"   Min-A 1969-75

Moses, Wallace "Wally"   Phi-A 1952-54, Phi-N 1955-58, Cin-N 1959-60, NY-A 1961-62, 1966, Det-A 1967-70

Moss, J. Lester "Les"   Chi-A 1967-68, 1969-70, Chi-N 1981, Hou-N 1982-84, 1985-89

Mota, Manuel R. "Manny"   LA-N 1980-89

Motton, Curtell H. "Curt"   Bal-A 1991

Mozzali, Maurice J. "Mo"   StL-N 1977-78

Mueller, Ray C.   NY-N 1956, Chi-N 1957

Muffett, Billy A.   StL-N 1967-70, Cal-A 1974-77, Det-A 1985-94

Mulcahy, Hugh N.   Chi-A 1970

Mulleavy, Gregory T. "Greg"   Bro-N 1957, LA-N 1958-60, 1962-64

Mullin, Patrick J. "Pat"   Det-A 1963-66, Cle-A 1967, Mon-N 1979-81

Mungo, Van Lingle   Bro-N 1940

Murphy, Daniel F. "Danny"   Phi-A 1920-24, Phi-N 1927

Murtaugh, Daniel E. "Danny"   Pit-N 1956-57

Muser, Anthony J. "Tony"   Mil-A 1985-89, Chi-N 1993-96

Myatt, George E.   Was-A 1950-54, Chi-A 1955-56, Chi-N 1957-59, Mil-N 1960-61, Det-A 1962-63, Phi-N 1964-72

Napoleon, Edward G. "Ed"   Cle-A 1983-85, KC-A 1987-88, Hou-N 1989, NY-A 1992-93, Tex-A 1995-96

Naragon, Harold R. "Hal"   Min-A 1963-66, Det-A 1967-69

Narron, Jerry A.   Bal-A 1993-94, Tex-A 1995-96

Narron, Samuel "Sam"   Pit-N 1952-64

Neale, A. Earle "Greasy"   StL-N 1929

Nelson, David E. "Dave"   Chi-A 1981-84, Cle-A 1992-96

Nettles, Graig   NY-A 1991, SD-N 1995

Neun, John H. "Johnny"   NY-A 1944-46

Newman, Jeffrey L. "Jeff"   Oak-A 1986, Cle-A 1992-96

Niarhos, C. Gus   KC-A 1962-64

Niehoff, J. Albert "Bert"   NY-N 1929

Nipper, Albert S, "Al"   Bos-A 1995-96

Nixon, Russell E. "Russ"   Cin-N 1976-82, Mon-N 1984-85, Atl-N 1986-87, Sea-A 1992

Noren, Irving A. "Irv"   Oak-A 1971-74, Chi-N 1975

Norman, H. Willis P. "Bill"   StL-A 1952-53

Northey, Ronald J. "Ron"   Pit-N 1961-63

Nossek, Joseph R. "Joe"   Mil-A 1973-75, Min-A 1976, Cle-A 1977-81, KC-A 1982-83, Chi-A 1984-85, 1986, 1991-96

Nottle, Edward W. "Ed"   Oak-A 1983

Oates, Johnny L.   Chi-N 1984-87, Bal-A 1989-91

O'Brien, Edward J. "Eddie"   Sea-A 1969

Oceak, Frank J.   Pit-N 1958-64, Cin-N 1965, Pit-N 1970-72

O'Connell, Daniel F. "Danny"   Was-A 1963-64

O'Connor, Patrick F. "Paddy"   NY-A 1918-21

Oester, Ronald J. "Ron"   Cin-N 1993, Det-A 1996

Okrie, Leonard J. "Len"   Bos-A 1961-62, 1965-66, Det-A 1970

Oldis, Robert C. "Bob"   Phi-N 1964-66, Min-A 1968, Mon-N 1969

O'Leary, Charles T. "Charley"   StL-N 1913, NY-A 1920-30, Chi-N 1931-33, StL-A 1934-37

Oliva, Pedro "Tony"   Min-A 1976-78, 1985-91

Oliveras, Max "Mako"   Cal-A 1994, Chi-N 1995-96

Oliver, David J. "Dave"   Tex-A 1987-94, Bos-A 1995-96

Oliver, Thomas N. "Tom"   Phi-A 1951-53, Bal-A 1954

Olson, Ivan M. "Ivy"   Bro-N 1924, 1930-31, NY-N 1932

O'Neil, G. Michael "Mickey"   Cle-A 1930

O'Neil, John S. "Buck"   Chi-N 1962-65

O'Neill, Stephen F. "Steve"   Cle-A 1935, Det-A 1941, Cle-A 1949, Bos-A 1950

Onslow, John J. "Jack"   Pit-N 1925-26, Was-A 1927, Min-A 1928, Phi-N 1931-32, Bos-A 1934

Osborn, Donald E. "Don"   Pit-N 1963-64, 1970-72, 1974-76

Osteen, Claude W.   StL-N 1977-80, Phi-N 1982-88, Tex-A 1993-94

Otero, Regino J. "Regie"   Cin-N 1959-65, Cle-A 1966

Otis, Amos J.   SD-N 1988-90, Col-N 1993

Ott, N. Edward "Ed"   Hou-N 1989-93

Overmire, Frank "Stubby"   Det-A 1963-66

Owen, Arnold M. "Mickey"   Bos-A 1955-56

Owens, James P. "Jim"   Hou-N 1967-72

Ozark, Daniel L. "Danny"   LA-N 1965-72, 1980-82, SF-N 1983-84

Pacheco, Antonio A. "Tony"   Cle-A 1974, Hou-N 1976-79, 1982

Paepke, Jack   LA-A 1961-64, Cal-A 1965-66

Pafko, Andrew "Andy"   Mil-N 1960-62

Pagan, Jose A.   Pit-N 1974-78

Page, Mitchell O.   KC-A 1995-96

Page, Philippe R. "Phil"   Cin-N 1947-52

Paige, Leroy R. "Satchell"   Atl-N 1968-69

Parker, Francis J. "Salty"   SF-N 1958-61, Cle-A 1962, LA-A 1964, Cal-A 1965-66, NY-N 1967, Hou-N 1968-72, Cal-A 1973-74

Pascual, Camilo A.   Min-A 1978-80

Patkin, Max   Cle-A 1946-47, StL-A 1951, Chi-A 1976, 1978

Patterson, Henry J. C. "Hank"   Bos-A 1932

Pattin, Martin W. "Marty"   Tor-A 1989

Paul, Michael G. "Mike"   Oak-A 1987-88, Sea-A 1989-91, Oak-A 1993

Pavlick, Gregory M. "Greg"   NY-N 1985-86, 1988-91, 1994-96

Pazik, Michael J. "Mike"   Chi-A 1995-96

Peden, Leslie E. "Les"   Chi-N 1965

Peitz, Henry C. "Heinie"   StL-N 1913

Pennock, Herbert J. "Herb"   Bos-A 1936-39

Pentland, Jeffrey "Jeff"   Fla-N 1996

Pepitone, Joseph A. "Joe"   NY-A 1982

Perez, Atanacio R. "Tony"   Cin-N 1987-92

Perkins, Ralph F. "Cy"   NY-A 1932-33, Det-A 1934-39, Phi-N 1946-54

Perlozzo, Samuel B. "Sam"   NY-N 1987-89, Cin-N 1990-92, Sea-A 1993-95, Bal-A 1996

Perranoski, Ronald P. "Ron"   LA-N 1981-94

Pesky, John M. "Johnny"   Pit-N 1965-67, Bos-A 1975-84

Peterson, Eric H. "Rick"   Pit-N 1984-85, Chi-A 1995

Pfister, George E.   Bro-N 1952

Phillips, Harold R. "Lefty"   LA-N 1965-68, Cal-A 1969

Phillips, Richard E. "Dick"   SD-N 1980

Picciolo, Robert M. "Rob"   SD-N 1990-96

Piche, Ronald J. "Ron"   Mon-N 1976

Picinich, Valentine J. "Val"   Cin-N 1934

Piersall, James A. "Jimmy"   Tex-A 1975

Pignatano, Joseph B. "Joe"   Was-A 1965-67, NY-N 1968-81, Atl-N 1982-85

Piniella, Louis V. "Lou"   NY-A 1984-85

Pinson, Vada E.   Sea-A 1977-80, Chi-A 1981, Sea-A 1982-83, Det-A 1985-91, Fla-N 1993-94

Pitler, Jacob A. "Jake"   Bro-N 1947-57

Pitts, Gaylen R.   StL-N 1991-95

Plaza, Ronald C. "Ron"   Sea-A 1969, Cin-N 1978-83, Oak-A 1986

Plummer, William F. "Bill"   Sea-A 1982-83, 1988-91, Col-N 1993

Podres, John J. "Johnny"   SD-N 1973, Bos-A 1980, Min-A 1981-85, Phi-N 1991-96

Pole, Richard H. "Dick"   Chi-N 1988-91, SF-N 1993-96

Pollet, Howard J. "Howie"   StL-N 1959-64, Hou-N 1965

Popowski, Edward J. "Eddie"   Bos-A 1967-76

Posedel, William J. "Bill"   Pit-N 1949-53, StL-N 1954-57, Phi-N 1958, SF-N 1959-60, Oak-A 1968-72, SD-N 1974

Pujols, Luis B.   Mon-N 1993-96

Queen, Melvin D. "Mel"   Cle-A 1982, Tor-A 1996

Quilici, Francis R. "Frank"   Min-A 1971-72

Quirk, James P. "Jamie"   StL-N 1984, KC-A 1994-96

Rader, Douglas L. "Doug"   SD-N 1978-79, Chi-A 1986-87, Oak-A 1992, Fla-N 1993-94

Radison, Daniel J. "Dan"   SD-N 1993-94, Chi-N 1995-96

Ragan, D. C. Patrick "Pat"   Phi-N 1924

Randall, Robert L. "Bobby"   Min-A 1980

Randolph, Willie L.   NY-A 1994-96

Rapp, Vernon F. "Vern"   Mon-N 1979-83

Reberger, Frank B.   Cal-A 1991, Fla-N 1993-94

Redys, Edward "Ed"   StL-A 1950-51

Reese, Harold H. "Pee Wee"   LA-N 1959

Reese, James H. "Jimmie"   Cal-A 1973-94

Regan, Philip R. "Phil"   Sea-A 1984-86, Cle-A 1994

Reiser, Harold P. "Pete"   LA-N 1960-64, Chi-N 1966-69, Cal-A 1970-71, Chi-N 1972-74

Renick, W. Richard "Rick"   KC-A 1981, Mon-N 1985-86, Min-A 1987-90

Resinger, Grover S.   Atl-N 1966, Chi-A 1967-68, Det-A 1969-70, Cal-A 1975-76

Rettenmund, Mervin W. "Merv"   Cal-A 1980-82, Tex-A 1983-85, Oak-A 1989-90, SD-N 1991-96

Reyes, Benjamin "Cananea"   Sea-A 1981

Reynolds, Tommie D   Oak-A 1989-95, StL-N 1996

Rice, Delbert "Del"   StL-N 1959, LA-A 1962-64, Cal-A 1965-66, Cle-A 1967

Rice, James E. "Jim"   Bos-A 1994-96

Ricketts, David W. "Dave"   Pit-N 1971-73, StL-N 1974-75, 1978-91

Riddle, John L. "Johnny"   Pit-N 1948-50, StL-N 1952-55, Mil-N 1956-57, Cin-N 1958, Phi-N 1959

Riddoch, Gregory L. "Greg"   SD-N 1987-90

Riggins, Mark A. StL-N 1995

Riggleman, James D. "Jim" StL-N 1989-90

Rigney, William J. "Bill" SD-N 1975

Ripken, Calvin E., Sr. "Cal" Bal-A 1976-86, 1989-92

Rippelmeyer, Raymond R. "Ray" Phi-N 1970-78

Roarke, Michael T. "Mike" Det-A 1965-66, Cal-A 1967-69, Det-A 1970, Chi-N 1978-80, StL-N 1984-90, SD-N 1991-93, Bos-A 1994

Roberts, David W. "Dave" Cle-A 1987

Roberts, Melvin H. "Mel" Phi-N 1992-95

Robertson, Sherrard A. "Sherry" Min-A 1970

Robinson, Brooks C. Bal-A 1977

Robinson, Dewey E. Chi-A 1993-94

Robinson, Frank Cal-A 1977, Bal-A 1978-80, 1985-87

Robinson, Warren G. "Sheriff" NY-N 1964, 1965-67, 1972

Robinson, Wilbert NY-N 1911-13

Robinson, William H. "Bill" NY-N 1984-89

Robinson, W. Edward "Eddie" Bal-A 1957-59

Robson, Thomas J. "Tom" Tex-A 1986-92

Rodgers, Robert L. "Bob" Min-A 1970-74, SF-N 1976, Mil-A 1978-80

Rodriguez, Eddie Cal-A 1996

Rojas, Octavio V. "Cookie" Chi-N 1978-81, Fla-N 1993-96

Rolfe, Robert A. "Red" NY-A 1946

Rommel, Edwin A. "Eddie" Phi-A 1933-34

Roof, Eugene L. "Gene" Det-A 1992-95

Roof, Phillip A. "Phil" SD-N 1978, Sea-A 1983-88, Chi-N 1990-91

Root, Charles H. "Charlie" Chi-N 1951-53, Mil-N 1956-57, Chi-N 1960

Roseboro, John J. Was-A 1970-71, Cal-A 1972-74

Rosenbaum, Glen O. Chi-A 1973-75, 1986-88

Roth, Francis C. "Frank" Pit-N 1917, NY-A 1921-22, Cle-A 1923-25, Chi-A 1927

Rothschild, Lawrence L. "Larry" Cin-N 1990-93, Fla-N 1995-96

Roush, Edd J Cin-N 1938

Rowe, Donald H. "Don" Chi-A 1988, Mil-A 1992-96

Rowe, Kenneth D. "Ken" Bal-A 1985-86

Rowe, Lynwood T. "Schoolboy" Det-A 1954-55

Rowe, Ralph E. Min-A 1972-75, Bal-A 1981-84

Royster, Jeron K. "Jerry: Col-N 1993

Ruberto, John E. "Sonny" StL-N 1977-78

Rudi, Joseph O. "Joe" Oak-A 1986-87

Rudolph, Richard "Dick" Bos-N 1921-27

Ruel, Herold D. "Muddy" Chi-A 1935-45, Cle-A 1948-50

Ruffing, Charles H. "Red" NY-N 1962

Runnels, James E. "Pete" Bos-A 1965-66

Runnells, Thomas W. "Tom" Mon-N 1990-91

Russell, William E. "Bill" LA-N 1987-91, 1994-96

Ruth, George H. "Babe" Bro-N 1938

Ryan, Cornelius J. "Connie" Mil-N 1957, Atl-N 1971, 1973-75, Tex-A 1977-79

Ryan, John B. "Jack" Was-A 1912-13, Bos-A 1923-27

Ryan, Michael J. "Mike" Phi-N 1980-95

Ryba, Dominic J. "Mike" StL-N 1951-54

Sain, John F. "Johnny" KC-A 1959, NY-A 1961-63, Min-A 1965-66, Det-A 1967-69, Chi-A 1971-75, Atl-N 1977, 1985-86

Sanford, John A. "Jack" Cle-A 1968-69

Sandt, Thomas J. "Tommy" Pit-N 1987-96

Sarni, William F. "Bill" NY-N 1957

Sauer, Henry J. "Hank" SF-N 1959

Saul, James A. "Jim" Chi-A 1975-76, Oak-A 1979

Scarborough, Ray W. Bal-A 1968

Schacht, Alexander "Al" Was-A 1925-34, Bos-A 1935-36

Schaefer, Robert W. "Bob" KC-A 1988-91

Schaffer, Jimmie R. "Jim" Tex-A 1978, KC-A 1980-88

Schalk, Raymond W. "Ray" Chi-A 1930-31

Schang, Walter H. "Wally" Cle-A 1936-38

Scheffing, Robert B. "Bob" StL-A 1952-53, Chi-N 1954-55, Mil-N 1960

Scherger, George R. Cin-N 1970-78, 1982-86

Schoendienst, Albert F. "Red" StL-N 1961-64, Oak-A 1977-78, StL-N 1979-89

Schreiber, Paul F. NY-A 1942, Bos-A 1947-58

Schueler, Ronald R. "Ron" Chi-A 1979-82, Oak-A 1983-84, Chi-A 1986

Schulte, John C. "Johnny" Chi-N 1933, NY-A 1934-48, Bos-A 1949-50

Schultz, George W. "Barney" StL-N 1971-75, Chi-N 1977

Schultz, Joseph C., Jr. "Joe" StL-A 1949, StL-N 1963-68, KC-A 1970, Det-A 1971-76

Seminick, Andrew W. "Andy" Phi-N 1957-58, 1967-69

Sewell, J. Luther "Luke" Cle-A 1939-41, Cin-N 1949

Sewell, Joseph W. "Joe" NY-A 1934-35

Sewell, Truett B. "Rip" Pit-N 1948

Shanks, Howard S. "Howie" Cle-A 1928-32

Shaughnessy, Francis J. "Shag" Det-A 1928

Shaw, Robert J. "Bob" Mil-A 1973

Shawkey, J. Robert "Bob" NY-A 1929

Shea, Mervyn D. "Merv" Det-A 1939-42, Phi-N 1944-45, Chi-N 1948-49

Sheehan, Thomas C. "Tom" Cin-N 1935-37, Bro-N 1938, Bos-N 1944

Shellenback, Frank V. StL-A 1939, Bos-A 1940-44, Det-A 1946-47, NY-N 1949-55

Shellenback, James P. "Jim" Min-A 1983

Shepard, Robert E. "Bert" Was-A 1946

Shepard, Lawrence W. "Larry" Phi-N 1967, Cin-N 1970-78, SF-N 1979

Sherry, Lawrence "Larry" Pit-N 1977-78, Cal-A 1979-80

Sherry, Norman B. "Norm" Cal-A 1970-71, 1976, Mon-N 1978-81, SD-N 1982-84, SF-N 1986-91

Shore, Raymond E. "Ray" Cin-N 1963-67

Shotton, Burton E. "Burt" StL-N 1923-25, Cin-N 1934, Cle-A 1942-45

Showalter, William N. "Buck" NY-A 1990-91

Siebert, Wilfred C. "Sonny" SD-N 1994-95

Sievers, Roy E. Cin-N 1966

Silvera, Charles A. "Charlie" Min-A 1969, Det-A 1971-73, Tex-A 1973-75

Silvestri, Kenneth J. "Ken" Phi-N 1959-60, Mil-N 1963-65, Atl-N 1966-75, Chi-A 1976, 1982

Simmons, Aloysius H. "Al" Phi-A 1940-42, 1944-49, Cle-A 1950-51

Sinatro, Matthew Stephen "Matt" Sea-A 1995-96

Sisler, George H. Bos-N 1930

Sisler, Richard A. "Dick" Cin-N 1961-64, StL-N 1966-70, SD-N 1975-76, NY-N 1979-80

Sisti, Sebastian D. "Sibby" Mil-N 1954, Sea-A 1969

Skaff, Francis M. "Frank" Bal-A 1954, Det-A 1965-66, 1971

Skinner, Robert R. "Bob" SD-N 1970-73, Pit-N 1974-76, SD-N 1977, Cal-A 1978, Pit-N 1979-85, Atl-N 1986-88

Slattery, John T. "Jack" Bos-N 1918-19

Slider, Rachel W. "Rac" Bos-N 1987-90

Smith, Alfred J. "Al" NY-N 1933

Smith, Billy F. Tor-A 1984-88

Smith, C. Reginald "Reggie" LA-N 1994-96

Smith, Harold R. "Hal" StL-N 1962, Pit-N 1965-67, Cin-N 1968-69, Mil-A 1976-77

Smith, Richard P. "Red" Chi-A 1945-48

Smith, Steven J. "Steve" Sea-A 1996

Snider, Edwin D. "Duke" Mon-N 1974-75

Snitker, Brian G. Atl-N 1985, 1988-90

Snyder, Francis E. "Frank" NY-N 1933-41

Snyder, James R. "Jim" Chi-N 1987, Sea-A 1988, SD-N 1991-92

Sommers, Dennis J. "Denny" NY-N 1977-78, Cle-A 1980-85, SD-N 1988-90

Sothoron, Allen S. StL-N 1927-28, StL-A 1932-33

Southworth, William H. "Billy" NY-N 1933

Spahn, Warren E. NY-N 1965, Cle-A 1972-73

Spalding, Charles H. "Dick" Phi-N 1934-36, Chi-N 1941-43

Spangler, Albert D. "Al" Chi-N 1970-71, 1974

Sparks, Joseph E. "Joe" Cal-A 1979, Cin-N 1984, Mon-N 1989, NY-A 1990

Spencer, H. Thomas "Tom" Cle-A 1988-89, NY-N 1991, Hou-N 1992-93

Squires, Michael L. "Mike" Tor-A 1989-91, Chi-A 1992

Staller, George W. Bal-A 1962, 1969-75

Stanage, Oscar H. Pit-N 1927-31

Stange, A. Lee Bos-A 1969, 1972-74, Min-A 1975, Oak-A 1977-79, Bos-A 1981-84

Stanky, Edward R. "Eddie" Cle-A 1957-58

Stanley, Frederick B. "Fred" Mil-A 1991

Stargell, Wilver D. "Willie" Pit-N 1985, Atl-N 1986-88

Starrette, Herman P. "Herm" Atl-N 1974-76, SF-N 1977-78, Phi-N 1979-81, SF-N 1983-84, Mil-A 1985-86, Chi-N 1987, Bal-A 1988, Bos-A 1995, 1996

Staub, Daniel J. "Rusty" NY-N 1982

Stearns, John H. NY-A 1989, Bal-A 1996

Stelmaszek, Richard J. "Rick" Min-A 1981-96

Stengel, Charles D. "Casey" Bro-N 1932-33

Stevens, Edward L. "Ed" SD-N 1981

Stock, Milton J. "Milt" Chi-N 1944-48, Bro-N 1949-50, Pit-N 1951-52

Stock, Wesley G. "Wes" KC-A 1967, Mil-A 1970-72, Oak-A 1972-76, Sea-A 1977-81, Oak-A 1984-86

Stottlemyre, Melvin L. "Mel" NY-N 1984-93, Hou-N 1994-95, NY-A 1996

Stratton, Monty F. Chi-A 1939-41

Street, Charles E. "Gabby" StL-N 1929, StL-A 1937

Strickland, George B. Min-A 1962, Cle-A 1963-69, KC-A 1970-72

Strom, Brent T. Hou-N 1996

Stubing, Lawrence G. "Moose" Cal-A 1985-88, 1989-90

Such, Richard S. "Dick" Tex-A 1983-85, Min-A 1985-96

Sugden, Joseph "Joe" StL-N 1921-25, Phi-N 1926-27

Sukeforth, Clyde L. Bro-N 1943-51, Pit-N 1952-57

Sullivan, John P. KC-A 1979, Atl-N 1980-81, Tor-A 1982-93

Summers, John J. "Champ" NY-A 1989-90

Susce, George C. M. Cle-A 1941-47, 1948-49, Bos-A 1950-54, KC-A 1955-56, Mil-N 1958-59, Was-A 1961-67, 1969-71, Tex-A 1972

Sweeney, William J. "Bill" Det-A 1947-48

Sweet, Ricky J. "Rick" Sea-A 1984, Hou-N 1996

Swift, Robert V. "Bob" Det-A 1953-54, KC-A 1957-59, Was-A 1960, Det-A 1963-66

Swisher, Steven E. "Steve" NY-N 1993-96

Tannehill, Jesse N. Phi-N 1920

Tappe, Elvin W. "El" Chi-N 1958-65

Taylor, Antonio N. "Tony" Phi-N 1977-79, 1988-89

Taylor, James W. "Zack" Bro-N 1936, StL-A 1941-46, Pit-N 1947

Temple, John E. "Johnny" Cin-N 1964

Tenace, F. Gene Hou-N 1986-87, Tor-A 1990-96

Terwilliger, W. Wayne Was-A 1969-71, Tex-A 1972, 1981-85, Min-A 1986-94

Testa, Nicholas "Nick" SF-N 1958

Thomas, George E. Bos-A 1970

Thomas, Ira F. Phi-A 1914-17, 1925-26

Thomas, J. Leroy "Lee" StL-N 1972, 1983

Thomas, Roy A. StL-N 1922

Thompson, Charles L. "Tim" StL-N 1981

Tiefenauer, Bobby G. Phi-N 1979

Tighe, John T. "Jack" Det-A 1942, 1955-56

Tincup, A. Ben Bro-N 1940

Tobin, John T. "Jack" StL-A 1949-51

Tolan, Robert "Bobby" SD-N 1980-83, Sea-A 1987

Torborg, Jeffrey A. "Jeff" Cle-A 1975-77, NY-A 1979-88

Torchia, Anthony L. "Tony" Bos-A 1985

Torgeson, C. Earl NY-A 1961

Torres, Hector E. Tor-A 1991

Tracewski, Richard J. "Dick" Det-A 1972-95

Tracy, James E. "Jim" Mon-N 1995-96

Trebelhorn, Thomas L. "Tom" Mil-A 1984, 1986, Chi-N 1992-93

Treuel, Ralph M. Det-A 1995

Trucks, Virgil O. Pit-N 1963

Turley, Robert L. "Bob" Bos-A 1964

Turner, James R. "Jim" NY-A 1949-59, Cin-N 1961-65, NY-A 1966-73

Turner, Terrence L. "Terry" StL-N 1924

Uhle, George E. Cle-A 1936-37, Chi-N 1940, Was-A 1944

Ullger, Scott M. Min-A 1995-96

Unser, Delbert B. "Del" Phi-N 1985-88

Upshaw, Willie C. Tex-A 1993-94, Tor-A 1996

Valentine, Robert J. "Bobby" NY-N 1983-85, Cin-N 1993

Valo, Elmer W. Cle-A 1963-64

Van Ornum, John C. SF-N 1980-84

Vernon, James B. "Mickey" Pit-N 1960, 1964, StL-N 1965, Mon-N 1977-78, NY-A 1982

Vincent, Albert L. "Al" Det-A 1943-44, Bal-A 1955-59, Phi-N 1961-63, KC-A 1966-67

Virdon, William C. "Bill" Pit-N 1968-71, 1986

Virgil, Osvaldo Jose Sr. "Ozzie" SF-N 1969-72, 1974-75, Mon-N 1976-81, SD-N 1982-85, Sea-A 1986-88

Vukovich, John C. Chi-N 1982-87, Phi-N 1988, 1989-96

Wagner, Charles F. "Heinie" Bos-A 1916-19, 1927-29

Wagner, Charles T. "Charley" Bos-A 1970

Wagner, John P. "Honus" Pit-N 1933-51

Walker, Albert B. "Rube" LA-N 1958, Was-A 1965-67, NY-N 1968-81, Atl-N 1982-84

Walker, Fred "Dixie" StL-N 1953, 1955, Mil-N 1963-65

Walker, Gerald H. "Gee" Cin-N 1946

Walker, Harry W. StL-N 1959-62
Walker, Jerry A. NY-A 1981-82, Hou-N 1983-85
Walker, Verlon L. Chi-N 1961-70
Wallace, David W. "Dave" LA-N 1995-96
Wallace, Roderick J. "Bobby" Cin-N 1926
Waller, Tyrone E. "Tye" SD-N 1995
Walling, Dennis M. "Denny" Oak-A 1996
Walls, R. Lee Oak-A 1979-82, NY-A 1983
Walsh, Edward A. "Ed" Chi-A 1923-25, 1928-30
Walters, William H. "Bucky" Bos-N 1950-52,
  Mil-N 1953-55, NY-N 1956-57
Walton, James R. "Jim" Mil-A 1973-75
Waner, Paul G. Phi-N 1965
Ward, John F. "Jay" NY-A 1987, Mon-N 1991-92
Ward, Peter T. "Pete" Atl-N 1978
Wares, Clyde E. "Buzzy" StL-N 1930-35,
  1937-52
Warner, Harry C. Tor-A 1977-79, 1980, Mil-A
  1981-82
Warthen, Daniel D. "Dan" Sea-A 1991-92, SD-N
  1996
Washington, Ronald "Ron" Oak-A 1996
Wathan, John D. KC-A 1986, Cal-A 1992-93,
  Bos-A 1994
Watson, Robert J. "Bob" Oak-A 1986-88
Weaver, Earl S. Bal-A 1968
Webb, William J. "Billy" Chi-A 1935-39
Werle, William G. "Bill" SF-N 1966
West, Samuel F. "Sam" Was-A 1947-49
Westrum, Wesley N. "Wes" SF-N 1958-63, NY-N
  1964-65, SF-N 1968-71
Whisenant, T. Peter "Pete" Cin-N 1961-62
White, Ernest D. "Ernie" Bos-N 1947-48, NY-N
  1963
White, Frank Bos-A 1994-96

White, Joyner C. "Jo-Jo" Cle-A 1958-60, Det-A
  1960, KC-A 1961-62, Mil-N 1963-65, Atl-N 1966,
  KC-A 1969
White, Roy H. NY-A 1983-84, 1986
Whitehill, Earl O. Cle-A 1941, Phi-N 1943
Whitmer, Daniel C. "Dan" Det-A 1992-94
Widmar, Albert J. "Al" Phi-N 1962-64, 1968-69,
  Mil-A 1973-74, Tor-A 1980-88, 1989
Wietelmann, William F. "Whitey" Cin-N 1966-67,
  SD-N 1969-79
Wilber, Delbert Q. "Del" Chi-A 1955-56, Was-A
  1970, Tex-A 1973
Wiley, Mark E. Bal-A 1987, Cle-A 1988-91,
  1995-96
Wilhelm, Irvin K. "Kaiser" Phi-N 1921
Wilks, Theodore "Ted" Cle-A 1960, KC-A 1961
Williams, Billy L. Chi-N 1980-82, Oak-A 1983-85,
  Chi-N 1986-87, 1992-96
Williams, Dan Cle-A 1993
Williams, David C. "Davey" NY-N 1956-57
Williams, Donald E. "Don" SD-N 1977-80
Williams, Donald R. "Spin" Pit-N 1994-96
Williams, James B. "Jimmy" Hou-N 1975, Bal-A
  1981-87
Williams, James F. "Jimy" Tor-A 1980-85, Atl-N
  1990-96
Williams, Otto G. Det-A 1925, StL-N 1926, StL-A
  1927, Cin-N 1930
Williams, Richard A. "Rick" Fla-N 1995-96
Williams, Richard H. "Dick" Mon-N 1970
Williams, Stanley W. "Stan" Bos-A 1975-76,
  Chi-A 1977-78, NY-A 1980-81, 1982, Cin-N 1984,
  NY-A 1987, 1988, Cin-N 1990-91
Williams, Walter A. "Walt" Chi-A 1988

Wilson, James "Jimmy" Cin-N 1939-40, 1944-46
Wiltse, George L. "Hooks" NY-A 1925
Wine, Robert P. Sr. "Bobby" Phi-N 1972-83,
  Atl-N 1985, 1988-90, NY-N 1993-96
Winegarner, Ralph L. StL-A 1948-51
Wingo, Ivey B. Cin-N 1928-29, 1936
Winkles, Bobby B. Cal-A 1972, Oak-A 1974-75,
  SF-N 1976-77, Chi-A 1979-81, Mon-N 1986-88
Wolgamot, C. Earl Cle-A 1931-33
Woodall, C. Lawrence "Larry" Bos-A 1942-48
Woodling, Eugene R. "Gene" Bal-A 1964-67
Worthington, Allan F. "Al" Min-A 1972-73
Wright, James I. "Jim" Phi-N 1996
Wright, Melvin J. "Mel" Chi-N 1963-64, 1971,
  Pit-N 1973, NY-A 1974-75, Hou-N 1976-82
Wyatt, J. Whitlow "Whit" Phi-N 1955-57, Mil-N
  1958-65, Atl-N 1966-67
Wynn, Early Cle-A 1964-66, Min-A 1967-69
York, P. Rudolph "Rudy" Bos-A 1959-62
Yost, Edgar F. "Ned" Atl-N 1991-96
Yost, Edward F. "Eddie" LA-N 1962, Was-A
  1963-67, NY-N 1968-76, Bos-A 1977-84
Youngblood, Joel R. Cin-N 1994-96
Zarilla, Allen L. "Al" Was-A 1971
Zeller, Barton W. "Bart" StL-N 1970
Zimmer, Donald W. "Don" Mon-N 1971, SD-N
  1972, Bos-A 1974-76, Tex-A 1981, Chi-N
  1984-86, NY-A 1986, SF-N 1987, Bos-A 1992,
  Col-N 1993-95, NY-A 1996
Zimmer, Thomas J. "Tom" StL-N 1976
Zimmerman, Gerald R. "Gerry" Min-A 1967,
  Mon-N 1969-75, Min-A 1976-80
Zuvella, Paul Col-N 1996
Zwilling, Edward H. "Dutch" Cle-A 1941

Biographical Data for Coaches Not Appearing in the Player/Pitcher Registers or Manager Roster

SPENCER ABBOTT Abbott, Spencer Arthur b: 8/27/1877, Chicago, Ill. d: 12/18/51, Washington, D.C. BL/TL, (1B)
RICK ADAIR Adair, Michael Richard b: 1/19/58, Spartanburg, S.Car. BL/TL, 6', 185 lbs. (P)
CARLOS ALFONSO Alfonso, Carlos b: 12/18/50, Havana, Cuba BR/TR, 6'2", 205 lbs. (P)
PIERRE ARSENAULT Arsenault, Pierre Jean b: 10/12/63, Roberval, Que., Can. BR/TR, 5'11", 180 lbs. (C)
TONY AUFERIO Auferio, Anthony Patrick b: 6/13/47, Orange, N.J. BR/TR, 5'10", 185 lbs. (3B)
DICK BERARDINO Berardino, Richard J. b: 7/2/37, Cambridge, Mass. BR/TR, 6'1", 190 lbs. (OF)
C. B. BERINGER Beringer, Carroll James b: 8/14/28, Bellwood, Neb. BR/TR, 6', 195 lbs. (P)
GREG BIAGINI Biagini, Gregory Peter b: 5/12/52, Chicago, Ill. BB/TR, 6'2", 205 lbs. (1B-OF)
DAVE BIALAS Bialas, David Bruce b: 3/6/54, Houston, Tex. BR/TR, 6'1", 210 lbs. (OF)
WAYNE BLACKBURN Blackburn, Wayne Clark b: 7/10/16, My.Joy, Ohio BL/TR, 5'10", 165 lbs. (OF-3B-2B)
JACK BLOOMFIELD Bloomfield, Gordon Leigh b: 8/7/32, Monte Alto, Tex. BR/TR, 6'2", 185 lbs. (2B)
MARC BOMBARD Bombard, Marc b: 11/15/49, Tampa, Fla. BR/TL, 5'8", 180 lbs. (P)
JIMMY BRAGAN Bragan, James Alton b: 3/12/29, Birmingham, Ala. BR/TR, 6', 198 lbs. (2B) (Brother of Bobby Bragan)
SCOTT BREEDEN Breeden, Harold Scott b: 9/17/37, Charlottesville, Va. BR/TR, 6'2", 210 lbs. (P)
JOSEPH BREEDEN Breeden, Joseph Thomas b: 10/11/56, Newport News, Va. BR/TR, 5'11", 195 lbs. (C)
BRIAN BUTTERFIELD Butterfield, Brian James b: 3/9/58, Bangor, Maine BB/TR, 6', 200 lbs. (2B)
JOE CAMACHO Camacho, Joseph Gomes b: 5/29/28, New Bedford, Mass. BR/TR, 6', 185 lbs. (SS-2B)
DAVE CARLUCCI Carlucci, David Mario b: 5/1/63, Milford, Mass. BR/TR, 6'1", 195 lbs. (C)
DANNY CARNEVALE Carnevale, Daniel Joseph b: 2/8/18, Buffalo, N.Y. BR/TR, 6', 195 lbs. (SS)
LEONEL CARRION Carrion, Leonel Santiago (Matheus) b: 2/15/52, Maracaibo, Venez. BR/TR, 5'11", 185 lbs. (OF)
DICK CARTER Carter, Richard Joseph b: 8/31/16, Philadelphia, Pa. d: 9/11/69, Philadelphia, Pa. BR/TR, 5'10", 190 lbs. (P-OF)
DOM CHITI Chiti, Harry Dominic b: 12/10/58, Independence, Mo. BL/TL, 6'2", 200 lbs. (P)
BOB CLEAR Clear, Elwood Robert b: 12/14/27, Denver, Colo. BR/TR, 5'10", 170 lbs. (P)
BOB CLUCK Cluck, Robert Alton b: 1/10/46, San Diego, Cal. BL/TL, 6'2", 195 lbs. (P)
MARK CONNOR Connor, Mark Peter b: 5/27/49, Brooklyn, N.Y. BR/TR, 6'3", 195 lbs. (P)
JIMMIE CRANDALL Crandall, James Mark b: 12/7/12, Wadena, Ind. d: 2/83, Bullhead City, Ariz. BB/TR, 5'11", 190 lbs. (P-C) (Son of Doc Crandall)
MARK CRESSE Cresse, Mark Emery b: 9/21/51, St.Albans, N.Y. BR/TR, 6'3", 220 lbs. (C)
ROLY DeARMAS DeArmas, Rolando Jesus b: 12/29/51, New York, N.Y. BR/TR, 6'1", 190 lbs. (C)
MARTY DeMERRITT DeMerritt, Martin Gordon b: 3/4/53, San Francisco, Cal. BR/TR, 6'2.5", 205 lbs. (P)
BOBBY DEWS Dews, Robert Walter b: 3/23/38, Clinton, Iowa BR/TR, 6'1", 175 lbs. (SS)
WALT DIXON Dixon, Walter
RICH DONNELLY Donnelly, Richard Francis b: 8/3/46, Steubenville, Ohio BL/TR, 6', 185 lbs. (C)
OTIS DOUGLAS Douglas, Otis W. b: 7/25/11, Reedville, Va. d: 3/21/89, Kilmarnock, Va. BR/TR, 6'1", 230 lbs. (DNP)
RICK DOWN Down, Richard John b: 12/14/50, Wyandotte, Mich. BR/TR, 5'11", 220 lbs. (OF)
HARRY DUNLOP Dunlop, Harry Alexander b: 9/6/33, Sacramento, Cal. BL/TR, 6'3", 200 lbs. (C)
GENE DUSAN Dusan, Eugene Paul b: 11/9/49, Los Angeles, Cal. BB/TR, 6', 200 lbs. (C)
GLENN EZZELL Ezzell, Glenn Wayne b: 10/29/44, Kentwood, La. BR/TR, 6', 190 lbs. (C)
BRAD FISCHER Fischer, Bradley James b: 6/28/56, Toledo, Ohio BR/TR, 6'3", 198 lbs. (C)
JOE FITZGERALD Fitzgerald, Joseph Patrick b: 3/17/1897, Washington, D.C. d: 8/29/67, Orlando, Fla. BR/TR, 5'11", 200 lbs. (C)
JOHN FITZPATRICK Fitzpatrick, John Arthur b: 3/19/04, LaSalle, Ill. BR/TR, 6'1.5", 185 lbs. (C)
MATT GALANTE Galante, Matthew Joseph b: 3/2/44, Brooklyn, N.Y. BR/TR, 5'6", 175 lbs. (2B)
GENE GLYNN Glynn, Eugene Patrick b: 9/22/56, Waseca, Minn. BR/TR, 5'9", 165 lbs. (SS)
ORLANDO GOMEZ Gomez, Juan Alejandro b: 6/24/46, Juana Diaz, P.R. BR/TR, 6', 190 lbs. (C)
EPY GUERRERO Guerrero, Epifanio Obdulio (Abud) b: 1/3/42, Santo Domingo, D.R. BR/TR, 5'11", 168 lbs. (OF) (Brother of Mario Guerrero)
GUY HANSEN Hansen, Guy Christopher b: 11/12/47, Los Angeles, Cal. BR/TR, 6', 170 lbs. (P)
ROGER HANSEN Hansen, Roger Christian b: 8/28/61, Johnstown, Pa. BR/TR, 6', 200 lbs. (C)
TOM HARMON Harmon, Thomas Harold b: 12/16/48, Lubbock, Tex. BL/TR, 5'11", 185 lbs. (C)
CHUCK HERNANDEZ Hernandez, Carlo Amado b: 11/11/60, Tampa, Fla. BL/TL, 6'3", 200 lbs. (P)
PERRY HILL Hill, Perry Wendell b: 3/19/52, Salina, Kan. BR/TR, 5'10", 170 lbs. (2B)
BEN HINES Hines, Benjamin Thortan b: 11/7/35, Yeager, Okla. BR/TR, 5'11", 205 lbs. (3B-C) (Father of Bruce Hines)
BRUCE HINES Hines, Bruce Edwin b: 11/7/57, Pomona, Cal. BB/TR, 5'10", 180 lbs. (2B) (Son of Ben Hines)
DENNIS HOLMBERG Holmberg, Dennis b: 8/2/51, Fremond, Neb. BL/TR, 6', 200 lbs. (3B)
DOUG HOLMQUIST Holmquist, Douglas Leonard b: 10/4/41, Bridgeport, Conn. d: 2/27/88, Altamonte Springs, Fla. BR/TR, 6'2", 195 lbs. (C)
GOLDIE HOLT Holt, Golden Desmond b: 3/22/02, Enloe, Tex. d: 6/11/91, Sherman Oaks, Cal. BR/TR, 5'7.5", 165 lbs. (3B-OF-2B)
VERN HOSCHEIT Hoscheit, Vernard Arthur b: 4/1/22, Brunswick, Neb. BR/TR, 5'9", 185 lbs. (C)
JACK HUBBARD Hubbard, John H. b: 10/4/50, Rock Hall, Md. BR/TR, 5'11", 175 lbs. (DNP)

LUIS ISAAC Isaac, Luis (Aponte) b: 6/19/46, Rio Piedras, P.R. BR/TR, 5'11.5", 195 lbs. (C)
RUDY JARAMILLO Jaramillo, Rudolph b: 9/20/50, Beeville, Tex. BL/TR, 5'11", 180 lbs. (OF)
JOE JONES Jones, Joseph Carmack b: 12/13/41, Lebanon, Tenn. BR/TR, 5'9", 155 lbs. (2B)
LOU KAHN Kahn, Louis b: 12/4/16, St.Louis, Mo. BR/TR, 5'11", 195 lbs. (C)
MIKE KELLY Kelly, Bernard Francis b: 5/1/1896, Indianapolis, Ind. d: 10/23/68, Indianapolis, Ind. BR/TR, 6', 198 lbs. (1B)
WENDELL KIM Kim, Wendell Kealohapauloe b: 3/9/51, Honolulu, Hawaii BR/TR, 5'5", 160 lbs. (2B)
GEORGE KISSELL Kissell, George Marshall b: 9/9/21, Watertown, N.Y. BR/TR, 5'8", 175 lbs. (3B)
HUB KITTLE Kittle, Hubert Milton b: 2/19/17, Los Angeles, Cal. BR/TR, 6'1", 195 lbs. (C)
FRED KOENIG Koenig, Fred Carl b: 4/27/31, St.Louis, Mo. d: 1/12/93, Wagoner, Okla. BR/TR, 6'3", 200 lbs. (1B-3B)
BILL LACHEMANN Lachemann, William Charles b: 4/5/34, Los Angeles, Cal. BL/TR, 5'9", 195 lbs. (C)
JIM LETT Lett, James Curtis b: 1/3/51, Charleston, W.Va. BR/TR, 6'2", 185 lbs. (3B)
LENNY LEVY Levy, Leonard Howard b: 6/11/13, Pittsburgh, Pa. d: 2/2/93, Palm Desert, Cal. BR/TR, 5'10.5", 190 lbs. (C)
JULIO LINARES Linares, Julio b: 12/26/41, San Pedro De Macoris, D.R. BR/TR, 5'9", 165 lbs. (3B)
GRADY GRADY Grady, William Grady b: 3/30/50, Abilene, Tex. BR/TR, 5'11", 190 lbs. (C)
BILL LOBE Lobe, William Charles b: 3/24/12, Cleveland, Ohio d: 1/7/69, Cleveland, Ohio BR/TR, 5'9.5", 178 lbs. (C)
Q. V. LOWE Lowe, Q. V. b: 1/15/45, Red Level, Ala. BR/TR, 6'1", 185 lbs. (P)
JOE MACKO Macko, Joseph
JOE MADDON Maddon, Joseph John b: 2/8/54, Hazelton, Pa. BR/TR, 5'11", 190 lbs. (C)
ROY MAJTYKA Majtyka, Le Roy W. b: 6/1/39, Buffalo, N.Y. BR/TR, 5'11", 170 lbs. (2B)
JACK MALOOF Maloof, Jack Garth b: 10/12/49, Redlands, Cal. BL/TL, 6', 175 lbs. (1B-OF)
DOUG MANSOLINO Mansolino, Douglas b: 9/20/56, Plainfield, N.J. BR/TR, 5'7", 155 lbs. (IF)
HARRY MATHEWS Mathews, Henry
RICK MATHEWS Mathews, Rick Ray b: 10/9/47, Centerville, Iowa BR/TR, 5'11", 180 lbs. (P)
LEO MAZZONE Mazzone, Leo David b: 10/16/48, Keyser, W.Va. BL/TL, 5'10", 185 lbs. (P)
MAJE McDONNELL McDonnell, Robert A. b: 7/20/20, Philadelphia, Pa. BR/TR, 5'6", 135 lbs. (P)
J. R. McKEE McKee, John R.
JOHN McLAREN McLaren, John Lowell b: 9/29/51, Galveston, Tex. BR/TR, 6', 200 lbs. (C)
DAVE MILEY Miley, David Allen b: 4/3/62, Tampa, Fla. BL/TR, 6'3", 220 lbs. (C)
MO MOZZALI Mozzali, Maurice Joseph b: 12/12/22, Louisville, Ky. d: 3/2/87, Lakeland, Fla. BL/TL, 5'10", 160 lbs. (1B)
JACK MULL Mull, Jack Leroy b: 9/29/43, Chambersburg, Pa. BR/TR, 5'10", 188 lbs. (C)
ED NAPOLEON Napoleon, Edward George b: 9/17/37, Baltimore, Md. BR/TR, 5'8", 165 lbs. (OF-3B-1B)
ED NOTTLE Nottle, Edward William b: 10/22/39, Philadelphia, Pa. BR/TR, 5'10", 180 lbs. (P)
FRANK OCEAK Oceak, Frank John "Fez" b: 9/8/12, Pocahontas, Va. d: 3/19/83, Johnstown, Pa. BR/TR, 5'9", 172 lbs. (2B)
MAX OLIVARES Olivares, Max b: 9/10/46, Santurce, P.R. BR/TR, 6', 195 lbs. (2B)
BUCK O'NEIL O'Neil, John Jordan b: 11/13/11, Carrabele, Fla. BR/TR, 6'2", 190 lbs. (1B)
DON OSBORN Osborn, Donald Edwin b: 6/3/08, Sandpoint, Idaho d: 3/23/79, Torrance, Cal. BR/TR, 6', 185 lbs. (P)
TONY PACHECO Pacheco, Antonio Aristides b: 8/9/27, Havana, Cuba d: 87, Miami, Fla. BR/TR, 6', 190 lbs. (2B)
JACK PAEPKE Paepke, Jack b: 8/28/22, Provo, Utah BR/TR, 6'2.5", 220 lbs. (C-P) (Father of Dennis Paepke)
GREG PAVLICK Pavlick, Gregory Michael b: 3/10/50, Washington, D.C. BR/TR, 6'3", 205 lbs. (P)
MAX PATKIN Patkin, Max b: 1/10/20, Philadelphia, Pa. BR/TR, 6'3", 185 lbs. (P)
JEFF PENTLAND Pentland, Jeffrey BL/TL, (1B)
RICK PETERSON Peterson, Eric Harding b: 10/30/54, Brunswick, N.J. BL/TL, 6', 175 lbs. (P) (Son of Harding Peterson)
RON PLAZA Plaza, Ronald Charles b: 8/24/34, Passaic, N.J. BL/TR, 6', 180 lbs. (3B)
DAN RADISON Radison, Daniel J. b: 8/24/50, St.Louis, Mo. BR/TR, 6'2", 190 lbs. (C)
ED REDYS Redys, Edward b: 6/23/21, Detroit, Mich. BR/TR, 6', 185 lbs. (P)
GROVER RESINGER Resinger, Grover S b: 10/20/15, St.Louis, Mo. d: 1/11/86, St.Louis, Mo. BR/TR, 5'9", 180 lbs. (3B)
CANANEA REYES Reyes, Benjamin (Chavez) b: 2/18/37, Nacosari, Sonora, Mexico d: 11/11/91, Hermosillo, Mexico BR/TR, (OF)
MARK RIGGINS Riggins, Mark Alan b: 1/3/57, Jasper, Ind. BL/TL, 5'10", 180 lbs. (P)
MEL ROBERTS Roberts, Melvin Henry b: 1/18/43, Abington, Pa. BR/TR, 6', 180 lbs. (OF)
DEWEY ROBINSON Robinson, Dewey Everett b: 4/28/55, Evanston, Ill. BR/TR, 6', 190 lbs. (P)
SHERIFF ROBINSON Robinson, Warren Grant b: 9/8/21, Cambridge, Md. BR/TR, 6'1", 195 lbs. (C)
EDDIE RODRIGUEZ Rodriguez, Eduardo b: 3/11/59, Havana, Cuba BR/TR, 5'8", 165 lbs. (SS)
GLEN ROSENBAUM Rosenbaum, Glen Otis b: 6/14/36, Union Mills, Ind. BR/TR, 5'11", 180 lbs. (P)
RALPH ROWE Rowe, Ralph Emanuel b: 7/14/24, Newberry, S.C. BL/TR, 5'6", 160 lbs. (OF)
JIM SAUL Saul, James Allen b: 11/24/39, Bristol, Va. BL/TR, 6'3", 210 lbs. (C)
GEORGE SCHERGER Scherger, George Richard b: 11/20/20, Dickinson, N.D. BR/TR, 5'8", 183 lbs. (2B)
RAC SLIDER Slider, Rachel W. b: 12/23/33, Simms, Tex. BL/TR, 5'8", 160 lbs. (SS)
BILLY SMITH Smith, Billy Franklin b: 1/14/30, High Point, N.C. BL/TL, 5'9", 160 lbs. (1B-OF)
STEVE SMITH Smith, Steven J. b: 7/21/53, Canton, Ohio BR/TR, 5'11", 180 lbs. (2B-SS)
BRIAN SNITKER Snitker, Brian Gerald b: 10/17/55, Decatur, Ill. BR/TR, 6'1", 192 lbs. (C)
DENNY SOMMERS Sommers, Dennis James b: 7/12/40, New London, Wis. BL/TR, 6'2", 205 lbs. (C)
JOE SPARKS Sparks, Joseph Everett b: 3/15/38, McComas, W.Va. BR/TL, 5'10", 180 lbs. (3B-2B)
TONY TORCHIA Torchia, Anthony Lewis b: 12/13/43, Chicago, Ill. BR/TL, 5'10", 180 lbs. (1B-OF)
RALPH TREUEL Treuel, Ralph Martin b: 6/7/55, Elyria, Ohio BR/TR, 6'4", 220 lbs. (P)
JOHN VanORNUM Van Ornum, John Clayton b: 10/20/39, Pasadena, Cal. BR/TR, 5'11", 175 lbs. (2B)
AL VINCENT Vincent, Albert Linder b: 12/23/06, Birmingham, Ala. BR/TR, 5'9.5", 170 lbs. (C)
VERLON WALKER Walker, Verlon Lee "Rube" b: 3/7/29, Lenoir, N.C. d: 3/24/71, Chicago, Ill. BL/TR, 6', 210 lbs. (C) (Brother of Rube Walker)
JIM WALTON Walton, James Robert b: 9/5/35, Shattuck, Okla. BR/TR, 6'2", 190 lbs. (P)
HARRY WARNER Warner, Harry Clinton b: 12/11/28, Reeders, Pa. BL/TR, 6'2", 215 lbs. (1B)
DANA WILLIAMS Williams, Dana b: 3/20/63, Weirton, W.Va. BR/TR, 5'10", 170 lbs. (OF)
DON WILLIAMS Williams, Donald Ellis b: 12/24/37, Paragould, Ark. BR/TR, 5'10", 185 lbs. (SS)
SPIN WILLIAMS Williams, Donald Ray b: 1/5/56, Davenport, Iowa BL/TL, 6'3", 230 lbs. (P)
JIMMY WILLIAMS Williams, James Bernard b: 5/15/26, Toronto, Ont., Can. BR/TR, 5'10", 180 lbs. (OF)
RICK WILLIAMS Williams, Richard Anthony b: 11/21/56, Ft. Worth, Tex. BL/TL, 6'1", 105 lbs. (P) (Son of Dick Williams)
EARL WOLGAMOT Wolgamot, Clinton Earl b: 12/21/1895, Fairbank, Iowa d: 4/25/70, Independence, Iowa BR/TR, 5'8", 155 lbs. (C)
TOM ZIMMER Zimmer, Thomas Jeffrey b: 6/30/52, Mobile, Ala. BR/TR, 5'8", 165 lbs. (C) (Son of Don Zimmer)

The Umpire Roster

The men in blue have been rebuked and scorned since the Knickerbockers cavorted on the Elysian Fields of Hoboken. The first to incur an umpire's wrath in return was Knickerbocker player Davis, fined six cents for swearing, perhaps understandably since his team was being trounced by the New York Club, 23–1. The name of the umpire in that historic game of June 19, 1846—the first match game under Alexander Cartwright's new rules—was not recorded. Ever since, a handful of researchers have scrambled to find out who umpired the league games of baseball's early history.

Larry Gerlach, who knows more about umpires and umpiring than anybody, has created the Umpire Roster that follows. The basis of his roster is the list compiled by S. C. Thompson in the 1930s and 1940s, but his research has corrected several errors and omissions in that list and has scrupulously brought the umpire roster up to date. In *Total Baseball I* he hoped that "by the next edition we will have finished a complete re-study of the umpire roster. . . . I am going to try to fashion a biographical encyclopedia of major league umpires—vital statistics; minor and major league service; All-Star, World Series, Playoff games; special achievements; and so on. One of the more frustrating things about the Turkin/Thompson roster (and even

ours) is how years of service are noted in terms of seasons; it really is misleading to identify someone as working from 1980–1987 when he may have broken into the majors on September 24, 1980."

The data presented here does not meet those lofty goals, but it is vastly increased and improved, as well as reorganized. Umpires are now divided not only by league but also by: regular, league-employed umpires; substitutes; player-umpires, pressed into emergency service; and those subs used during the recent strikes. New leads continue to flow in, especially about the early days, when umpires were not assigned by the leagues but were supplied by the teams, recruited from among the fans in attendance (this explains why so many given names are lacking for pre-1900 arbiters), or, not infrequently, plucked from the team's reserve players. A feature unique to *Total Baseball* is the identification of substitute umpires in the National Association years 1871-75. An instance of this last practice occurred as late as 1935, when Chicago White Sox outfielder Jocko Conlan was recruited to fill in for umpire Red Ormsby in a game between the Sox and the St. Louis Browns. Conlan, of course, went on to a Hall of Fame career as a man in blue.

Let's call the roll.

REGULAR UMPIRES

National Association (1871-75)

Avery, C. Hamilton 1875
Beardslee, John J. 1871
Blodgett, C. W. 1875
Boardman, Frederick "Fred" 1875
Bomeisler, Theodore 1871-73
Boyd, William J. "Bill" 1875
Burdock, John J. "Jack" 1872-74
Carey, Thomas J. "Tom" 1874
Clapp, John E. 1874-75
Cone, J. Frederick "Fred" 1875
Daniels, Charles F. 1874-75
Dehlman, Herman J. 1874
Dole, Lester C. 1875
Ferguson, Robert V. "Bob" 1872-73, 1875
Fulmer, Charles J. "Chick" 1873
Heubel, George A. 1875
Hodges, Amory G. 1874-75
Holly, Samuel J. "Sam" 1871
Lennon, William F. "Bill" 1871-72, 1873-74
Mack, Dennis J. "Denny" 1875
Martin, Alphonse C. "Phonney" 1875
Mathews, Robert T. "Bobby" 1873-75
McLean, William H. "Billy" 1874-75
Mills, Charles "Charlie" 1872-73
Patterson, Daniel T. "Dan" 1874
Rogers, M. Mortimer "Mort" 1871
Sensenderfer, John P. J. "Count" 1874
Swandell, J. Martin "Marty" 1872-73
Tate, William 1874
Walsh, Michael F. "Mike" 1875
Young, Nicholas E. "Nick" 1871-75

National League (1876-)

Andrews, G. Edward "Ed" 1895, 1898-99
Baker, William P. "Bill" 1957
Ballanfant, E. Lee 1936-57
Barlick, Albert J. "Al" 1940-43, 1946-55, 1958-71
Barnes, Ronald E. "Ron" 1990-94, 1996
Barnie, William S. "Billy" 1892
Barr, George M. 1931-49
Barron, Mark E. 1992-96
Battin, Joseph V. "Joe" 1891
Bausewine, George 1905
Behle, Frank 1901
Bell, Wally 1992-96
Betts, William G. 1894-6, 1898-99
Betz, Edwin J. 1961
Boggess, Lynton R. "Dusty" 1944-48, 1950-62
Boles, Charles 1877
Bond, Thomas H. "Tommy" 1883, 1885
Bonin, Gregory "Greg" 1986-96
Bradley, George H. "Foghorn" 1879-83
Brady, Jackson 1887
Bransfield, William E. "Kitty" 1917
Bredburg, George W. 1877
Brennan, John E. "Jack" 1899
Brennan, William T. "Bill" 1909-13, 1921

Brocklander, Fred W. 1979-90
Brown, Thomas T. "Tom" 1898-99, 1901-02
Bucknor, C. B. 1996
Bunce, Joshua 1877
Burkhart, W. Kenneth "Ken" 1957-73
Burnham, George W. 1883, 1889, 1895
Burns, John S. 1884
Burns, Thomas E. "Tom" 1892
Burns, Thomas P. "Oyster" 1899
Burtis, L. W. 1876-77
Bush, Garnet C. 1911-12
Byron, William J. "Bill" or "Lord" 1913-19
Callahan, Edward J. 1881
Campbell, Daniel "Dan" 1894-96
Campbell, William M. "Bick" 1939-40
Cantillon, Joseph D. "Joe" 1902
Carpenter, William B. "Bill" 1897, 1904, 1906-07
Chapman, John C. "Jack" 1880
Chipman, Harry F. 1883, 1885
Clarke, Robert M. "Bob" 1930-31
Cockill, George W. 1915
Colgan, Harry W. 1901
Colosi, Nicholas "Nick" 1968-82
Conahan, Edward J. "Ed" 1896
Cone, J. F. "Fred" 1877
Conlan, John B. "Jocko" 1941-64
Connolly, John M. 1886
Connolly, Thomas H. "Tommy" 1898-1900
Conway, John H. 1906
Crandall, Robert 1877
Crawford, Gerald J. "Jerry" 1976-96
Crawford, Henry C. "Shag" 1956-75
Cross, John A. 1878
Cunningham, Elmer E. "Bert" 1901
Curry, Wesley "Wes" 1885-86, 1889, 1898
Cusack, Stephen P. 1909
Cushman, Charles H. "Charley" 1885, 1898
Cuzzi, Phil 1991-93
Dailey, John J. 1882
Dale, Jerry P. 1970-85
Daniels, Charles F. 1876, 1878-80, 1887-88
Danley, Kerwin 1991-96
Darling, Gary R. 1988-96
Dascoli, Frank 1948-62
Davidson, David L. "Satch" 1969-84
Davidson, Robert A. "Bob" 1983-96
Davis, Gerald "Gerry" 1985-96
Decker, Stewart M. 1883-85, 1888
Delmore, Victor "Vic" 1956-59
DeMuth, Dana A. 1986-96
Derr, Doll 1923
Devinney, P. H. "Dan" 1877
Dezelan, Frank J. 1966-68, 1969-71
Dixon, Hal H. 1953-59
Donatelli, August J. "Augie" 1950-73
Donnelly, Charles H. 1931-32
Donohue, Michael R. 1930
Doscher, John H. Sr. "Herm" 1880-81, 1887
Doyle, John J. "Jack" 1911
Dreckman, Bruce M. 1996
Ducharme, — 1876-77
Dunn, Thomas P. "Tom" 1939-46
Dunnigan, Joseph 1881-82
Dwyer, J. Francis "Frank" 1899, 1901
Eagan, John J. 1878, 1886

Eason, Malcolm W. "Mal" 1902, 1910-16
Ellick, Joseph J. "Joe" 1886
Emslie, Robert D. "Bob" 1891-1924
Engel, Robert A. "Bob" 1965-90
Engeln, William R. "Bill" 1952-56
Ferguson, Robert V. "Bob" 1879, 1884-85
Fessenden, Wallace C. "Wally" 1889-90
Fields, Stephen H. "Steve" 1979-82
Finneran, William F. 1911-12, 1924
Forman, Allen S. "Al" 1961-65
Fountain, Edward G. 1879
Frary, Ralph 1911
Froemming, Bruce N. 1971-96
Fulmer, Charles J. "Chick" 1886
Furlong, William E. "Bill" 1878-79, 1883-84
Fyfe, Lee C. 1920
Gaffney, John H. 1884-86, 1891-94, 1899-1900
Galvin, James F. "Jim" 1895
Gibbons, Brian 1994-1996
Gillean, Thomas 1879-80
Goetz, Lawrence J. "Larry" 1936-57
Gore, Arthur J. "Artie" 1947-56
Gorman, Brian 1991-96
Gorman, Thomas D. "Tom" 1951-76
Gregg, Eric E. 1977-91, 1993-96
Guglielmo, A. Augie 1952
Gunning, Thomas F. "Tom" 1887
Guthrie, William J. "Bill" 1913-15
Hallion, Thomas F. "Tom" 1986-96
Harris, Lannie D. 1979-85
Harrison, Peter A. "Pete" 1916-20
Hart, Eugene F. "Bob" 1920-29
Hart, William F. "Bill" 1914-15
Harvey, H. Douglas "Doug" 1962-92
Hautz, Charles A. "Charlie" 1876, 1879
Henderson, J. Harding "Hardie" 1895-96
Hengle, Edward S. "Ed" 1887
Henline, Walter J. "Butch" 1945-48
Hernandez, Angel 1991-96
Heuble, George A. 1876
Heydler, John A. 1898
Higham, Richard "Dick" 1881-82
Hirschbeck, Mark 1988-96
Hoagland, Willard A. 1894
Hodges, A. D. 1876
Hohn, William J. "Bill" 1987-96
Holland, John A. 1887
Holliday, James W. "Bug" 1903
Holmes, Howard E. "Ducky" 1921
Hornung, M. Joseph "Joe" 1893, 1896
Hunt, John T. 1895, 1898-99
Hurst, Timothy C. "Tim" 1891-97, 1900, 1903
Irwin, Arthur A. 1902
Jackowski, William A. "Bill" 1952-68
Jeffers, W. W. 1881
Jevne, Frederick "Fred" 1895
Johnson, Henry S. "Steamboat" 1914
Johnstone, James E. "Jim" 1903-12

Jorda, Louis D. "Lou" 1927-31, 1940-52
Julian, Joseph O. 1878
Kane, Stephen J. 1909-10
Keefe, Timothy J. "Tim" 1894-96
Kellogg, Jeffery "Jeff" 1991-96
Kelly, John O. 1882, 1888, 1897
Kennedy, Charles 1904
Kenney, John 1877
Kibler, John W. 1963-89
Klem, William J. "Bill" 1905-41
Knight, Alonzo P. "Lon" 1889
Lally, Bud 1896
Landes, Stanley A. "Stan" 1955-72
Lane, Frank H. 1883
Latham, W. Arlington "Arlie" 1899, 1902
Layne, Jerry B. 1989-96
Libby, Stephen A. 1880
Lincoln, Frederick H. 1914, 1917
Long, "Robert "Bob" 1992
Long, William H. "Billy" 1895
Lynch, Thomas J. "Tom" 1888-99
Macullar, James F. "Jimmy" 1892
Magee, Sherwood R. "Sherry" 1928
Magerkurth, George L. 1929-47
Mahoney, Michael J. 1892
Malone, Ferguson G. "Fergy" 1884
Manassau, Alfred S. "Al" 1899
Marsh, Randall G. "Randy" 1983-96
Mathews, Robert T. "Bobby" 1880
McCafferty, Charles 1921, 1923
McCormick, William J. "Barry" 1919-29
McDermott, Michael J. "Sandy" 1890, 1897
McDonald, James F. 1895, 1897-99
McElwee, Harvey 1877
McFarland, Horace 1896-97
McGarr, James B. "Chippy" 1899
McGrew, Harry T. "Ted" 1930-31, 1933-34
McLaughlin, Edward J. 1929
McLaughlin, Michael 1893
McLaughlin, Peter J. 1924-28
McLean, William H. "Billy" 1876, 1878-80, 1882-84
McQuaid, John H. "Jack" 1889-94
McSherry, John P. 1971-96
Miller, George E. 1879
Mitchell, Charles 1892
Montague, Edward M. "Ed" 1976-96
Moran, August "Augie" 1903-04, 1910, 1918
Moran, Charles B. "Charlie" 1917-39
Mullin, John 1909
Nash, William M. "Billy" 1901
Nauert, Paul 1995-96
O'Connor, Arthur 1914
O'Day, Henry F. "Hank" 1895, 1897-1911, 1913, 1915-27
Odlin, Albert F. 1883
O'Hara, — 1915
Olsen, Andrew H. "Andy" 1968-81
O'Rourke, James H. "Jim" 1894
Orth, Albert L. "Al" 1912-17
O'Sullivan, John J. 1922
Owens, Clarence B. "Brick" 1908, 1912-13
Pallone, David M. "Dave" 1979-88

Parker, George L. 1936-38
Pearce, Richard J. "Dicky" 1878, 1882
Pears, Frank 1897, 1905
Pelekoudas, Christos G. "Chris" 1960-75
Pfirman, Charles H. "Cy" 1922-36
Pierce, Grayson S. "Gracie" 1886-87
Pinelli, Ralph A. "Babe" 1935-56
Poncino, Larry L. 1986-88, 1991-96
Potter, Scott 1991-95
Powell, Cornelius J. "Jack" 1923-24, 1933
Power, Charles B. 1902
Powers, Philip J. "Phil" 1879, 1881, 1886-91
Pratt, Albert G. "Al" 1879
Pratt, Thomas J. "Tom" 1886
Pryor, J. Paul 1961-81
Pulli, Frank V. 1972-96
Quest, Joseph L. "Joe" 1886-87
Quick, James E. "Jim" 1976-96
Quigley, Ernest C. "Ernie" 1913-37
Quinn, Joseph C. "Joe" 1882
Rapuano, Edward "Ed" 1990-96
Reardon, John E. "Beans" 1926-49
Reliford, Charles "Charlie" 1989-96
Rennert, Laurence H. "Dutch" 1973-92
Rieker, Richard "Rich" 1992-96
Rigler, Charles "Cy" 1906-22, 1924-35
Riley, William J. 1880
Rippley, T. Steven "Steve" 1985-96
Robb, Douglas W. "Scotty" 1948-52
Roberts, Leonard W. "Lenny" 1953-55
Rudderham, John E. 1908
Runge, Paul E. 1973-96
Ryan, Walter 1946
Scott, James "Jim" 1930-31
Sears, John W. "Ziggy" 1934-45
Secory, Frank E. 1952-70
Sentelle, Leopold T. "Paul" 1922-23
Seward, Edward W. "Ed" 1893
Seward, George E. 1876, 1878
Sheridan, John F. "Jack" 1892, 1896-97
Smith, Charles M. "Pop" 1881
Smith, Vincent A. "Vinnie" 1957-65
Smith, William W. "Billy" 1898-99
Snyder, Charles N. "Pop" 1892-93, 1898-1901
Stage, Charles W. "Billy" 1894
Stambaugh, Calvin G. 1877-78
Stark, Albert D. "Dolly" 1928-35, 1937-39, 1942
Steiner, Melvin J. "Mel" 1961-72
Steinfeldt, Harry M. 1905
Stello, Richard J. "Dick" 1969-87
Sternburg, Paul 1909
Stewart, William J. "Bill" 1933-54
Stockdale, M. J. 1915
Strief, George A. 1890
Sudol, Edward L. "Ed" 1957-77
Sullivan, David F. "Dave" 1882, 1885
Sullivan, Jeremiah "Jerry" 1887
Sullivan, T. P. 1880
Summer, James G. 1877

Swartwood, C. Edward "Ed" 1894, 1898-1900
Sweeney, James M. "Jim" 1924-26
Tata, Terry A. 1973-96
Terry, William H. "Adonis" 1900
Tilden, Otis 1880
Tremblay, Richard H. "Dick" 1971
Truby, Harry G. 1909
Valentine, John G. 1887-88
Van Court, Eugene 1884
Vanover, Larry 1991, 1993-96
Vargo, Edward P. "Ed" 1960-83
Venzon, Anthony "Tony" 1957-71
Walker, William E. 1876-77
Walsh, Francis D. "Frank" 1961-63
Walsh, Michael F. "Mike" 1876, 1878, 1880
Warneke, Lonnie "Lon" 1949-55
Warner, Albert "Al" 1898-1900
Wendelstedt, Harry H. 1966-96
West, Joseph H. "Joe" 1976, 1978-96
Westervelt, Frederick E. 1922
Weyer, Lee H. 1961, 1963-88
White, Gideon F. 1878
Wickham, Daniel "Dan" 1990-92
Wiedman, George E. "Stump" 1896
Wilbur, Charles E. 1879
Williams, Arthur "Art" 1972-77
Williams, Charles H. "Charlie" 1978, 1983-96
Williams, William G. "Bill" 1963-87
Wilson, Frank 1922-28
Wilson, John A. 1887
Winters, Michael J. "Mike" 1990-96
Wise, Samuel W. "Sam" 1889, 1893
Wood, George A. 1898
York, Thomas J. "Tom" 1886
Young, Joseph 1879
Zacharias, Thomas 1890
Zimmer, Charles L. "Chief" 1904

American Association (1882-91)

Barnum, George W. 1890
Bauers, Albert J. "Al" 1887
Becannon, William H. 1883
Bradley, George H. "Foghorn" 1886
Brennan, John E. "Jack" 1884
Butler, Ormond H. 1883
Carey, Thomas J. "Tom" 1882
Clinton, James L. "Jim" 1886
Connell, Terence G. 1884, 1890
Connelly, John M. 1885, 1887
Connelly, William 1884
Curry, Wesley "Wes" 1887, 1890
Cuthbert, Edgar E. "Ned" 1887
Dailey, John J. 1884
Daniels, Charles F. 1883-85, 1889
Davis, James J. "Jumbo" 1891
Devinney, P. H. "Dan" 1884
Doscher, John H. Sr. "Herm" 1888, 1890
Dyler, John F. 1884
Emslie, Robert D. "Bob" 1890
Ferguson, Robert V. "Bob" 1886-89, 1891
Gaffney, John H. 1888-89

Gleason, William G. "Bill" 1891
Goldsmith, Frederick E. "Fred" 1888-89
Griffith, E. A. 1884
Hautz, Charles A. "Charlie" 1882
Hecker, Guy J. 1889
Holland, John A. 1884
Holland, Willard A. 1889
Hurley, Daniel "Dan" 1887
Jennings, Alfred J. "Al" 1887
Jones, Charles W. "Charley" 1891
Kelly, John O. 1883-86
Kerins, John A. "Jack" 1889-91
Knight, Alonzo P. "Lon" 1887
Lawler, John F. 1884
Macullar, James F. "Jimmy" 1891
Mack, Dennis J. "Denny" 1886
Magner, John T. 1883
Mahoney, Michael J. 1891
Mathews, Robert T. "Bobby" 1891
McLaughlin, Thomas 1891
McLean, William H. "Billy" 1885
McNichol, Robert T. 1883
McQuaid, John H. "Jack" 1886-88
Morton, Charles H. "Charlie" 1886
O'Brien, Frank 1890
Peoples, James E. "Jimmy" 1890
Pike, Lipman. E. "Lip" 1889
Pratt, Albert G. "Al" 1883
Quinn, A. J. 1886
Riley, William J. 1882
Ross, Robert T. 1882
Seward, George E. 1884
Simmons, Joseph S. "Joe" 1882
Smith, Charles M. "Pop" 1882
Snyder, Charles N. "Pop" 1891
Sommer, Benjamin F. 1883
Sullivan, Jeremiah "Jerry" 1887
Sullivan, Theodore P. "Ted" 1887
Taylor, Walter 1890
Toole, Stephen J. "Steve" 1890
Tunnison, William 1885-86
Valentine, John G. 1884-87
Walsh, Michael F. "Mike" 1882-83, 1885-86
York, Thomas J. "Tom" 1886
Young, Benjamin F. "Ben" 1886

Union Association (1884)

Crawford, Alexander 1884
Devinney, P. H. "Dan" 1884
Dutton, Patrick J. 1884
Hengle, Emory J. "Moxie" 1884
Holland, John A. 1884
Hooper, Michael H. 1884
Jennings, Alfred "Al" 1884
Jordan, William H. "Bill" 1884
Mapledoram, Blake A. 1884
McCaffrey, Harry 1884
Seward, George E. 1884
Stearns, D. Eckford "Ecky" 1884
Sullivan, David F. "Dave" 1884

Players League (1890)

Barnes, Roscoe C. "Ross" 1890
Ferguson, Robert V. "Bob" 1890
Gaffney, John H. 1890
Gunning, Thomas F. "Tom" 1890
Holbert, William H. "Bill" 1890

Jones, Charles W. "Charley" 1890
Knight, Alonzo P. "Lon" 1890
Leach, Henry 1890
Matthews, John 1890
Pierce, Grayson S. "Gracie" 1890
Sheridan, John F. "Jack" 1890
Snyder, Charles N. "Pop" 1890

American League (1901-)

Adams, John H. 1903
Anthony, G. Merlyn 1969-75
Ashford, Emmett L. 1966-70
Avants, Nick R. 1969-71
Barrett, Ted 1994-1996
Barnett, Lawrence R. "Larry" 1968-96
Barry, Daniel "Dan" 1928
Basil, Stephen J. "Steve" 1936-42
Bean, Ed 1994
Berry, Charles F. "Charlie" 1942-62
Betts, William G. 1901
Boyer, James M. "Jim" 1944-50
Bremigan, Nicholas G. "Nick" 1974-88
Brinkman, Joseph N. "Joe" 1973-96
Campbell, William M. "Bick" 1928-31
Cantillon, Joseph D. "Joe" 1901
Carrigan, H. Sam 1961-65
Carpenter, William B. "Bill" 1904
Caruthers, Robert L. "Bob" 1902-03
Cederstrom, Gary 1989-96
Chill, Oliver P. "Ollie" 1914-16, 1919-22
Chylak, Nestor L. 1954-78
Clark, Alan M. "Al" 1976-96
Coble, G. Drew 1983-96
Colliflower, James H. 1910
Connolly, Thomas H. "Tommy" 1901-31
Connor, Thomas "Tom" 1905-06
Cooney, Terrance J. "Terry" 1975-92
Cooper, Eric R. 1996
Cousins, Derryl 1979-96
Craft, Terry 1989-96
Culbreth, Fieldin 1993-96
Deegan, William E. J. "Bill" 1970-80
Denkinger, Donald A. "Don" 1968-96
Diaz, Lazaro 1995
DiMuro, Louis J. "Lou" 1963-80
DiMuro, Raymond "Ray" 1996
Dinneen, William H. "Bill" 1909-37
Donnelly, Charles H. 1934-35
Doyle, Walter J. 1963
Drummond, Calvin T. "Cal" 1960-69
Duffy, James F. "Jim" 1951-55
Dwyer, J. Francis "Frank" 1904
Egan, John J. "Rip" 1903, 1907-14
Eldridge, Clarence E. 1914-15
Evans, James B. "Jim" 1971-96
Evans, William G. "Billy" 1906-27
Everitt, Michael "Mike" 1996
Ferguson, Charles A. 1913
Flaherty, John F. "Red" 1953-73
Ford, R. Dale 1975-96
Foster, Martin "Mark" 1996
Frantz, Arthur F. "Art" 1969-77

Friel, William E. "Bill" 1920
Froese, Grover A. 1952-53
Garcia, Richard R. "Rich" 1975-96
Geisel, Harry C. 1925-42
Goetz, Russell L. "Russ" 1968-83
Grieve, William T. T. "Bill" 1938-55
Guthrie, William J. "Bill" 1922, 1928-32
Haller, William E. "Bill" 1961, 1963-82
Hart, Robert F. "Bertie" 1912-13
Hart, William F. "Bill" 1901
Haskell, John E. 1901
Hassett, James E. 1903
Hayes, Gerald 1925-26
Hendry, Eugene "Ted" 1978-96
Henrichs, Jeff 1993
Hickox, Edward "Ed" 1990-96
Hildebrand, George A. 1912-34
Hirschbeck, John F. 1984-96
Holbrook, Sam 1996
Holmes, Howard E. "Ducky" 1923-24
Honochick, G. James "Jim" 1949-73
Hubbard, R. Cal 1936-51
Hurley, Edwin H. "Eddie" 1947-65
Hurst, Timothy C. "Tim" 1905-09
Johnson, Mark S. 1980-96
Johnston, Charles E. 1936-37
Johnstone, James E. "Jim" 1902
Jones, Nicholas I. "Red" 1944-49
Joyce, James A. "Jim" 1989-96
Kaiser, Kenneth J. "Ken" 1977-96
Kelly, Thomas B. 1905
Kerin, John 1909-10
King, Charles F. 1904
Kinnamon, William E. "Bill" 1960-69
Kolls, Louis C. "Lou" 1933-40
Kosc, Gregory J. "Greg" 1976-96
Kunkel, William G. "Bill" 1968-84
Leppart, Thomas E. "Tom" 1984-86
Linsalata, Joseph N. "Joe" 1961-62
Luciano, Ronald M. "Ron" 1968-80
Maloney, George P. 1969-83
Manassau, Alfred S. "Al" 1901
Marberry, Frederick "Firpo" 1935
McCarthy, John "Jack" 1905
McClelland, Timothy R. "Tim" 1984-96
McCormick, William J. "Barry" 1917
McCoy, Larry S. 1970-96
McGowan, William A. "Bill" 1925-54
McGreevy, Edward 1912-13
McKean, James G. "Jim" 1974-96
McKinley, William F. "Bill" 1946-65
Meriwether, Julius "Chuck" 1988-96
Merrill, E. Durwood 1977-96
Morgenweck, Henry C. "Hank" 1972-75
Moriarty, George J. 1917-26, 1929-40
Morrison, Daniel G. "Dan" 1979-96
Mullaney, Dominic J. 1915
Mullin, John 1911-12

Nallin, Richard F. "Dick" 1915-32
Napp, Larry A. 1951-74
Neudecker, Jerome A. "Jerry" 1965-85
O'Brien, Joseph "Joe" 1912, 1914
Odom, James C. "Jim" 1965-74
O'Donnell, James M. "Jake" 1968-71
O'Loughlin, Francis H. "Silk" 1902-18
O'Nora, Brian 1992-96
Ormsby, Emmett T. "Red" 1923-41
Owens, Clarence B. "Brick" 1916-37
Palermo, Stephen M. "Steve" 1977-91
Paparella, Joseph J. "Joe" 1946-65
Parker, Harley P. 1911
Parks, Dallas F. 1979-83
Passarella, Arthur M. "Art" 1941-42, 1945-53
Perrine, Fred "Bull" 1909-12
Phillips, David R. "Dave" 1971-96
Pipgras, George W. 1938-46
Quinn, John A. 1935-42
Reed, Rick A. 1984-96
Reilly, Michael E. "Mike" 1978-96
Rice, John L. 1955-73
Robb, Douglas W. "Scotty" 1952-53
Rodriguez, Armando H. 1974-75
Roe, John A. "Rocky" 1979-96
Rommel, Edwin A. "Eddie" 1938-59
Rowland, Clarence H. "Pants" 1923-27
Rue, Joseph W. "Joe" 1938-47
Runge, Edward P. "Ed" 1954-70
Salerno, Alexander J. "Al" 1961-68
Schwarts, Harry C. 1960-62
Scott, Dale A. 1986-96
Sheridan, John F. "Jack" 1901-14
Shulock, John R. 1979-96
Smith, W. Alaric "Al" 1960-65
Soar, A. Henry "Hank" 1950-73
Spenn, Frederick C. "Fred" 1979-80
Springstead, Martin J. "Marty" 1965-86
Stafford, John H. "Jack" 1907
Stevens, John W. "Johnny" 1948-71
Stewart, Ernest D. 1941-45
Stewart, Robert W. "Bob" 1959-70
Summers, William R. "Bill" 1933-59
Tabacchi, Frank T. 1956-59
Tschida, Timothy J. "Tim" 1986-96
Umont, Frank W. 1954-73
Valentine, William T. "Bill" 1963-68
Van Graflan, Roy 1927-33
Voltaggio, Vito H. "Vic" 1977-96
Wallace, Roderick J. "Bobby" 1915-16
Walsh, Edward A. "Ed" 1922
Walton, Bennie 1996
Weafer, Harold L. "Hal" 1943-47
Welke, Timothy J. "Tim" 1985-96
Westervelt, Frederick E. 1911-12
Wilson, Frank 1921-22
Winans, Mark 1994
Young, Larry E. 1985-96

Federal League (1914-15)

Anderson, Oliver O. "Ollie" 1914
Brennan, William T. "Bill" 1914-15
Bush, Garnet C. 1914
Corcoran, Thomas W. "Tommy" 1915
Cross, Montford M. "Monte" 1914
Cusack, Stephen P. 1914
Finneran, William E. 1915
Fyfe, Louis 1915
Goeckel, E. 1914
Howell, H. Harry 1915
Johnstone, James E. "Jim" 1915
Kane, Stephen J. 1914
Langden, Joseph 1915
Mannassau, Alfred S. "Al" 1914
McCormick, William J. "Barry" 1914-15
Mullin, John 1915
O'Brien, Joseph "Joe" 1915
Quisser, —, 1914
Shannon, William P. "Spike" 1914-15
Stocksdale, Otis H. 1915
Van Sickle, Charles F. 1914
Westervelt, Frederick E. 1915
Wilhelm, Irving K. "Kaiser" 1915

SUBSTITUTE UMPIRES

National Association (1871-75)

Addy, Robert E. "Bob" 1875
Allison, Andrew K. "Andy" 1872, 1874
Allison, Arthur A. "Art" 1872
Allison, Douglas L. "Doug" 1872-73, 1875
Alston, David 1871-72, 1875
Annan, William H. 1873
Arnold, Willis S. "Billy" 1875
Avery, C. Hamilton 1874
Barlow, Thomas H. "Tom" 1875
Barnes, Roscoe C. "Ross" 1874
Barrett, William "Bill" 1872, 1874
Barron, James "Jim" 1875
Barrows, Franklin L. "Frank" 1872
Battin, Joseph V. "Joe" 1874
Beals, Thomas L. "Tommy" 1872, 1874-75
Beardslee, John J. 1872-73
Bechtel, George A. 1874
Beck, W. S. 1872
Berthrong, Hnery W. "Harry" 1872
Bielaski, Oscar 1874-75
Bigelow, W. J. 1875
Birdsall, David S. "Dave" 1873-74
Blair, William J. 1873
Boake, John L. 1871
Bomeisler, Theodore 1874-75
Bond, Thomas H. 'Tommy" 1875
Bonse, Nicholas 1871
Boyd, William J. "Bill" 1873
Bradley, George H. "Foghorn" 1875
Brainard, Asa 1872, 1875
Briggs, Warren R. 1874
Brown, William 1872, 1875
Bruce, D. W. 1875
Buck, William F. 1871
Bunce, Frederick L. "Fred" 1874
Bunce, H. C. 1872
Bush, Archibald M. "Archie" 1871
Carey, Thomas J. "Tom" 1873, 1875

Carpenter, John R. 1874
Cassidy, John P. 1875
Cavanaugh, J. H. "Harry" 1875
Chandler, Moses E. 1872-1875
Chapman, John C. "Jack" 1871, 1873-74
Clifton, — 1872
Clinton, James L. "Jim" 1873, 1875
Colby, — 1873
Collins, Daniel T. "Dan" 1875
Cone, J. Frederick "Fred" 1873-74
Cope, Elias 1871
Craver, William H. "Bill" 1873
Cuthbert, Edgar E. "Ned" 1875
Daubney, Thomas 1871
David, L. N. 1874
Dawson, Mort 1871
Deane, J. Henry "Harry" 1871, 1874
Dehlman, Herman J. 1873, 1875
Demorest, D. P. 1872-73
Dobson, H. A. 1871
Dornlach, D. E. 1872
Draper, John H. 1871
Ellis, William R. 1871-72, 1875
English, John W. 1874-75
Erby, Frederick 1872
Evans, George 1872
Fellows, T. E. 1871
Ferguson, Robert V. "Bob" 1871, 1874
Fisher, William C. "Cherokee" 1871, 1875
Foley, Thomas J. "Tom" 1874-75
Force, David W. "Davy" 1873
Fulmer, Charles J. "Chick" 1872, 1874-75
Garrigan, Charles 1873
Geer, William H. "Billy" 1874-75
Gerhardt, Joseph J. "Joe" 1875
Glenn, John W. 1874
Glover, Frank 1873
Goodwin, J. Cheever 1871-72
Gould, Charles H. "Charlie" 1874-75
Graham, J. S. 1871-72
Halback, A. C. N. 1871, 1873-75
Hall, George W. 1873-75
Hall, James "Jim" 1872-73
Hall, N. Samuel 1873
Hanna, Dr. 1872
Hartenstein, Isaac 1875
Hastings, W. Scott 1871-74
Hatfield, John V. B. 1872-73
Hayhurst, E. Hicks 1875
Haynie, James L. 1871
Hegeman, William H. 1871
Helm, J. 1871-72
Higham, Richard "Dick" 1872-75
Hodes, Charles "Charlie" 1874
Hooper, Michael H. "Mike" 1872-74
Hosworth, —, 1872-74
Hough, Pliny 1875
Howard, Charles 1872
Jennings, Alfred J. "Al" 1873
Johns, William R. 1873
Kahn, S. L. 1875
Keerl, George W. 1872
Kenney, John 1872
Kent, John 1875
Knight, George H. 1875
Kohler, Henry C. 1873
Lamb, Henry W. "Harry" 1875
Laughlin, Benjamin "Ben" 1873
Leonard, Andrew J. "Andy" 1872-73, 1875
Leonard, J. 1872
Leroy, Isaac 1871

Locke, Marshall 1873-74
Lovett, James D. 1871
Lowell, John A. 1872-73
Lush, M. R. 1873
MacDiarmed, Thomas 1872
Mack, Dennis J. "Denny" 1873-74
Malone, — 1875
Malone, Ferguson G. "Fergy" 1875
Martin, Alphonse C. "Phonney" 1871, 1873
Martin, Lewis G. 1871, 1873-74
Mathews, Robert T. "Bobby" 1871
Mawny, J. H. 1871
Maxwell, Cortez "Corty" 1875
Mays, — 1871
McCrea, — 1872
McDonald, James F. 1872
McGeary, Michael H. 1872, 1875
McLean, Harry C. 1871, 1873
McLean, William H. "Billy" 1872-73
McMahon, William 1871
McMullin, John F. 1874
McVey, Calvin A. "Cal" 1871, 1873, 1875
Meacham, — 1875
Miller, Joseph W. "Joe" 1872-73
Mills, Charles "Charlie" 1871
Mincher, Edward J. "Ed" 1872, 1875
Mincher, William E. 1875
Mitchell, Franklin B. 1874-75
Murnane, Timothy H. "Tim" 1873-75
Nelson, John W. "Candy" 1872
Nichols, A. N. 1871
Norton, Frank P. 1872
O'Brien, P. 1875
Pabor, Charles H. "Charlie" 1875
Parks, William R. "Bill" 1875
Patterson, Daniel T. "Dan" 1872
Peak, Frank 1871
Pearson, S. W. 1872
Phelps, Cornelius C. "Neal" 1874
Pike, Jacob Emanuel "Jay" 1875
Porter, — 1874
Powers, W. 1872-73, 1875
Pratt, Thomas J. "Tom" 1871-73
Quinn, — 1875
Radcliff, John Y. 1873
Ramsey, R. 1875
Rastall, Joseph H. 1872
Reach, Albert J. 1872-75
Reed, Hugh 1871, 1873-74
Remsen, John J. "Jack" 1873-74
Robinson, A. Valentine "Val" 1872
Robinson, Miley 1873
Rockwell, Horace T. 1874
Rogers, George R. 1871-72
Ryan, John J. 1872, 1875
Sawyer, Dent 1871
Schafer, Harry C. 1875
Schrader, Louis 1875
Schuester, John A. 1874-75
Scofield, John W. 1871
Sears, John K. 1873
Selman, Frank C. 1873
Sensenderfer, John P. J. "Count" 1872-73, 1875
Simmons, Joseph S. "Joe" 1871, 1873-74
Smith, Eb 1872
Smith, George 1872
Smith, Gustavus 1872
Snyder, Charles N. "Pop" 1875
Stahl, George 1875
Stanwood, —, 1872-73
Stires, Garrett "Gat" 1875
Stophlet, J. 1871

Sutton, Ezra B. 1875
Swandell, J. Martin "Marty" 1871, 1874
Sweasy, Charles J. "Charlie" 1871, 1873-74
Tighe, Edward 1871
Treacey, Frederick S. "Fred" 1871, 1873, 1875
Tyler, Columbus T. 1871-73
Urell, M. E. 1873
Van Delft, —, 1875
Voltz, Edward "Ed" 1871-72
Walk, Frank 1871
Wardell, — 1874
Waterman, Frederick A. "Fred" 1873
Weaver, Charles 1873
Weigel, William H. 1873-74
White, Horatio S. 1873
White, W. Warren 1874
White, William H. "Will" 1875
Wiggins, — 1875
Wildey, John 1871
Willard, Gardner 1871
Wirth, Adam 1872, 1875
Wood, James B. "Jimmy" 1871
Worth, Herb 1872
Wright, W. Harrison "Harry" 1875
York, Thomas J. "Tom" 1874

National League (1876-)

Adams, James 1897
Allen, Hezekiah "Ham" 1876
Ayers, — 1876
Baker, Charles 1884
Barker, Alfred L. 1881
Barnie, William S. "Billy" 1882
Barnum, George W. 1896
Barton, — 1876
Battin, Joseph V. "Joe" 1895-96
Beard, Oliver P. "Ollie" 1894
Becannon, James M. "Buck" 1885
Behle, Frank 1895-96
Berger, Frederick 1886
Bigelow, — 1877
Bittman, Henry P. "Red" 1892, 1894-95, 1897
Blakiston, Robert J. "Bob" 1884
Blodgett, C. W. 1876
Bradley, George H. "Foghorn" 1877
Brady, — 1877
Bredburg, George W. 1878-79
Brennan, John E. "Jack" 1887
Brockway, John 1877, 1879
Bullymore, Charles L. 1882
Burke, — 1892
Burlingame, Frank A. 1878
Burnham, George W. 1886-87
Campbell, Al 1886
Campbell, Daniel "Dan" 1897
Carsey, Wilfred "Kid" 1901
Caruthers, Robert L. "Bob" 1886, 1893
Chandler, Moses E. 1877
Chapman, John C. "Jack" 1876, 1882
Chill, Oliver P. "Ollie" 1916
Cheppy, John T. 1876
Chipman, Harry F. 1886
Clack, Robert H. "Bobby" 1897
Cohen, — 1893
Colgan, Harry W. 1899
Collins, Daniel T. "Dan" 1876
Cone, J. F. "Fred" 1876
Connell, Terence G. 1885, 1887
Connolly, John M. 1885, 1887, 1892-93
Cook, W. H. 1879
Crandall, Robert 1876, 1878

Crane, Edward N. "Ed" 1893
Crane, Samuel N. "Sam" 1879, 1887
Cray, P. C. 1893
Cross, John A. 1876
Cudworth, Al 1880
Curren, Peter 1876
Cushman, Charles H. "Charley" 1894
Daniels, — 1885
Deane, J. Henry "Harry" 1876, 1878
Devinney, P. H. "Dan" 1876
Doscher, John H. Sr. "Herm" 1879
Draper, John H. 1877
Dunlap, Frederick C. "Fred" 1879
Dyler, John F. 1892, 1897
Eagan, John J. 1879
Earle, William M. "Billy" 1892
Eason, Malcolm W. "Mal" 1901
English, John W. 1876
Evans, Jacob "Jake" 1886
Fenno, Norman 1876
Finneran, William F. 1923
Fisher, William C. "Cherokee" 1876
Flaherty, — 1882
Flaherty, Patrick J. "Patsy" 07
Flynn, John A. "Jocko" 1893
Fouser, William C. 1876
Fulmer, Charles J. "Chick" 1881
Furlong, William E. "Bill" 1877, 1880, 1888
Gaffney, John H. 1887, 1898
Galvin, James F. "Jim" 1886
Ganzel, Charles W. "Charlie" 1901
Gifford, James H. 1881
Gillean, Thomas 1881
Gleason, John D. 1877
Gleason, William G. "Bill" 1877
Glenn, John W. 1880
Goldsmith, Frederick E. "Fred" 1886
Graves, Frank M. 1895
Griffiths, — 1884
Gross, Edward M. 1881
Guinney, Daniel 1882
Hardie, Louis W. "Lou" 1887
Hartley, John "Jack" 1894
Hastings, W. Scott 1877
Hatfield, John V. B. 1876
Hawes, William A. 1880-82
Hegeman, William H. 1881
Hernon, Thomas H. "Tom" 1894
Heydler, John A. 1895-97
Hickey, James L. 1882
Hodges, A. D. 1877
Hogan, — 1897
Hogriever, George C. 1893
Hornung, M. Joseph "Joe" 1892
Howard, C. F. 1884
Hurll, George 1876
Hurst, Timothy C. "Tim" 1904
Jevne, Frederick "Fred" 1892, 1894
Jose, — 1889
Joyce, C. E. 1879
Kane, Stephen J. 1906
Keefe, Timothy J. "Tim" 1893
Keenan, James W. "Jim" 1893
Kelley, J. P. 1879
Kelley, W. W. 1877
Kelly, John O. 1884-85
Kennedy, — 1893
Kennedy, Michael J. 1884
Kenney, John 1876
Kerins, John A. "Jack" 1888
Kipp, Eden 1881
Kling, William "Bill" 1892
Klusman, William F. "Billy" 1893

Knight, Alonzo P. "Lon"
　　1876, 1888
Lanigan, Charles 1908
Latham, W. Arlington
　　"Arlie" 1900
Laughlin, —, 1876
Lawler, Michael H. 1882
Leary, — 1879
Libby, Stephen A. 1879
Long, William H. "Billy"
　　1893, 1897
Lynch, F. G. 1892
Lynch, Thomas J. "Tom"
　　1902
Maddox, Charles 1882
Maginnis, Jim 1910
Malone, Ferguson G.
　　"Fergy" 1892
Maloney, James "Jim"
　　1893
Manning, James H. "Jim"
　　1893
Manning, John E. "Jack"
　　1881
Mapledoram, Blake A. 1886
Martin, Alphonse C.
　　"Phonney" 1876
Mason, Charles E. "Charlie"
　　1876
Mathews, Robert T.
　　"Bobby" 1876
Mayer, — 1893
McCaffrey, Harry 1885-86
McCrum, — 1892
McGee, — 1876
McGinty, — 1897
McGunnigle, Edward 1888
McKinney, — 1883
McLeod, — 1895
McMullen, John F. 1876
Meagher, John 1877
Mears, Charles W. 1894
Medart, William 1876-77
Megrue, Cliff 1876
Mills, Abraham G. 1877
Montague, — 1877
Morrill, John F. 1891, 1896
Morris, Edward 1895, 1897
Morris, John S. 1876
Muir, Thomas 1876
Mullane, Anthony J. "Tony"
　　1897
Mullen, Peter C. 1893
Murnane, Timothy H. "Tim"
　　1886
Murphy, Henry 1880
Murphy, Martin W. 1886
Murray, Jeremiah J. "Miah"
　　1894, 1900, 1905, 1910
Myers, Henry C. 1890
Nicol, Hugh N. 1894
O'Brien, William 1876
O'Day, Henry F. "Hank"
　　1896
Orr, David L. "Dave" 1891
Osborne, William 1876
Pfeffer, Nathaniel F. "Nate"
　　1897
Phelan, — 1896
Pierce, — 1884
Pierce, Grayson S. "Gracie"
　　1892
Pike, Lipman E. "Lip" 1890
Power, Charles B. 1893-95
Pratt, Albert G. "Al" 1880,
　　1887
Quincy, W. 1893
Quinn, Joseph C. "Joe"
　　1881
Quinn, P. J. 1876
Quinn, William H. "Billy"
　　1887, 1889
Redheffer, — 1895
Reid, William A. 1882
Reilly, Charles 1880
Remsen, John J. "Jack"
　　1880
Rhodes, Eugene A. 1887
Richards, J. E. 1880
Ritchie, F. 1876
Rocap, Adam 1876
Roll, — 1876
Rowe, John C. "Jack" 1881
Rudderham, Francis F.
　　"Frank" 1907
Say, Louis I. "Lou" 1879
Schofield, J. W. 1879
Seward, Edward W. "Ed"
　　1892
Seward, George E. 1877

Shepard, W. L. 1879
Sheridan, John F. "Jack"
　　1893
Sick, — 1884
Simmons, Joseph S. "Joe"
　　1876
Skelly, — 1880
Skinner, S. A. 1886
Smith, — 1876
Sneeden, — 1895
Snodd, Carey 1877
Snyder, Charles N. "Pop"
　　1895
Sommers, Joseph A. "Joe"
　　1893
Stack, W. Edward "Eddie"
　　1934
Stafford, John H. "Jack"
　　1906
Stage, Charles W. "Billy"
　　1895
Stambaugh, Calvin G. 1879
Strief, George A. 1880
Sullivan, — 1889
Sullivan, David F. "Dave"
　　1883, 1887-88
Summer, James G. 1876,
　　1878
Supple, William N. 1906
Sutton, Ezra B. 1876
Sweasy, Charles J.
　　"Charlie" 1879
Tilden, Otis 1876
Tindall, — 1890, 1896
Toole, Stephen J. "Steve"
　　1888
Tuthill, Benjamin "Ben"
　　1895
Twitchell, Lawrence G.
　　"Larry" 1894
Wade, Ben F. 1879-80
Walker, William E. 1878
Walsh, Michael F. "Mike"
　　1879
Walters, —, 1892-93
Walton, G. W. 1876
Warren, L. B. 1876
Wash, Frank 1877
Weeden, —, 1889-90
West, — 1885
West, George 1878
West, Milton D. "Buck"
　　1890
White, Gideon F. 1876-77
White, W. Warren 1876
Williams, Elisha A. "Dale"
　　1876
Wilson, William G. "Bill"
　　1892-93
Witham, C. B. 1879
Wolf, William V. "Jimmy"
　　1893, 1895-97
Wood, George A. 1899
Wood, James B. "Jimmy"
　　1876
Wright, W. Harrison "Harry"
　　1885
Wycoff, — 1892

**American Association
(1882-91)**

Arnold, Frank W. 1889
Austin, Ed 1890
Barnie, William S. "Billy"
　　1882, 1884, 1887, 1889
Battin, Joseph V. "Joe"
　　1882, 1886
Bauers, Albert J. "Al" 1890
Bell, Frank G. 1889
Bittman, Henry P. "Red"
　　1889
Blogg, Wesley C. "Wes"
　　1886
Bloom, — 1887
Bond, Thomas H. "Tommy"
　　1891
Bowes, Frank C. 1890
Burdock, John J. "Jack"
　　1887
Burkalow, Isaac 1888
Burns, — 1882
Butler, Charles 1889
Butler, Ormond H. 1886
Campbell, Daniel "Dan"
　　1890
Carlin, William J. "Billy"
　　1885, 1888-89
Connell, Terence G.
　　1885-86, 1889

Connell, Terence G.
　　1885-86, 1889
Cornell, — 1884
Crandall, Robert 1882
Creighton, — 1889-90
Critchley, Morris A.
　　"Morrie" 1884-85
Curry, Frank 1884, 1886
Cuthbert, Edgar E. "Ned"
　　1888
Dailey, John J. 1889
Daniels, Lawrence 1887
Devine, W. James "Jim"
　　1890
Devinney, P. H. "Dan" 1887
Devlin, Charles "Charlie"
　　1888
Dolan, Thomas J. "Tom"
　　1890-91
Dow, Clarence 1891
Dugan, — 1887
Duke, Martin F. 1890
Dunlevy, Hugh 1887
Dyler, John F. 1883,
　　1885-86
Ellick, Joseph J. "Joe"
　　1888-89
Ewing, William "Buck" 1882
Fell, — 1885
Fountain, Henry V. 1888
Galvin, James F. "Jim"
　　1885
Geer, William H. "Billy"
　　1887
Gill, Thomas H. "Tommy"
　　1886
Helburn, Hugo 1887
Henderson, J. Harding
　　"Hardie" 1889
Hengle, Edward S. "Ed"
　　1889
Hicks, Nathaniel W. "Nat"
　　1885
Holliday, James W. "Bug"
　　1888
Irwin, — 1882
Irwin, John 1885
Jennings, Alfred J. "Al"
　　1882, 1884-85, 1889
Julian, Joseph O. 1888
Kelly, John O. 1887
Kelly, William 1884
Kleinbacker, —, 1886
Levis, Charles H. "Charlie"
　　1882
Lilly, J. 1884
Little, — 1884
Loughlin, —, 1885
Loughlin, William 1882
Lyons, Toby A. 1891
Lyston, William E. 1890
Magner, John T. 1882,
　　1884, 1887
Malone, J. R. 1888
Marshall, — 1887
Mathews, Robert T.
　　"Bobby" 1888
McCartney, Joseph 1882
McCormick, —, 1888
McGee, Patrick 1882, 1884
McGinnis, George W.
　　"Jumbo" 1888-89
McIntosh, — 1882
McLaughlin, William 1882
McLean, William H. "Billy"
　　1882, 1889-90
McQuade, James H. 1891
McSorley, John B. "Trick"
　　1888
Medart, William 1887
Miller, Charles A. 1884
Mitchell, — 1887
Morgan, Henry W. 1884
Morton, Charles H.
　　"Charlie" 1884
Mullen, Peter C. 1891
O'Dea, Lawrence 1890
Paasch, William 1887-89
Parker, — 1887
Phillips, Horace B. 1882
Pierce, Grayson S. "Gracie"
　　1884
Pike, Lipman. E. "Lip" 1887
Pratt, Albert G. "Al" 1886
Quinn, William H. "Billy"
　　1884-85
Ramsey, Dick 1887
Reeder, James E. 1884
Reising, Charles 1882
Rice, — 1885

Riley, William J. 1885
Robb, John 1886
Ross, Robert T. 1884
Ruhl, Gus 1882
Ryan, John 1882
Selman, Frank C. 1882
Sherman, Sharon L.
　　"Shang" 1890
Shraeder, Louis 1890
Simpson, Lew 1882
Skinner, — 1884, 1886
Smith, George 1887
Sneed, Jonathon L. 1885
Sullivan, David F. "Dave"
　　1884
Talbot, — 1887
Tinney, — 1882
Walsh, Michael F. "Mike"
　　1887-88
West, — 1885, 1887
Wood, George A. 1886
Wright, — 1884
Young, Benjamin F. "Ben"
　　1887
Young, Joseph 1890

Union Association (1884)

Adler, — 1884
Burlingame, F. A. 1884
Donovan, E. S. 1884
Furlong, William E. "Bill"
　　1884
Hudson, Vincent D. 1884
Lee, Thomas F. 1884
McGunningle, William H.
　　"Bill" 1884
McManaway, D. 1884
McMinimum, Dennis 1884
Montgomery, — 1884
Powers, Charles B. 1884
Timblin, — 1884
Torry, — 1884

Players' League (1890)

Caskin, Edward J. "Ed"
　　1890

American League (1901-)

Betts, William G. 1903
Bierhalter, Bits 1924
Brown, Thomas T. "Tom"
　　1907
Carney, "Red" 1924
Connolly, Thomas H.
　　"Tommy" 1932
Donlin, Michael J. "Mike"
　　1918
Howley, — 1922
Kennedy, — 1910
Kerin, John 1908
Kerins, John A. "Jack"
　　1903
Mace, Harry L. 1903
Monahan, Pat 1931
Nallin, Richard F. "Dick"
　　1933
Pears, Frank 1903
Quigley, Ernest C. "Ernie"
　　1906
Soar, A. Henry "Hank" 1975
Stevens, John W. "Johnny"
　　1975
Terry, William H. "Adonis"
　　1901

Federal League (1914-15)

Murphy, J. A. 1914

**ACTIVE PLAYERS WHO
UMPIRED**

National League (1876-)

Abbey, Charles S. "Charlie"
　　1897
Abbott, Frederick H. "Fred"
　　1905
Andrews, G. Edward "Ed"
　　1889
Arundel, John T. "Tug"
　　1888
Baker, Philip "Phil" 1889
Baldwin, Marcus E. "Mark"
　　1892

Bannon, James H. "Jimmy"
　　1894
Beatin, Ebenezer "Ed" 1889
Beck, Erwin T. "Erve" 1902
Beckley, Jacob P. "Jake"
　　1906
Beebe, Fred L. 1907
Berger, John H. "Tun" 1891
Bonner, Frank J. 1894
Boyle, Henry J. 1886
Boyle, John A. "Jack"
　　1892, 1897
Breitenstein, Theodore P.
　　"Ted" 1900
Briody, Charles F. "Fatty"
　　1881
Brown, Samuel W. "Sam"
　　1907
Brown, Thomas T. "Tom"
　　1896
Brown, Willard 1891
Buelow, Charles J.
　　"Charlie" 1901
Buffinton, Charles G.
　　"Charlie" 1883, 1888-89,
　　1892
Burdock, John J. "Jack"
　　1881
Burns, Thomas P. "Oyster"
　　1895
Bushong, Albert J. "Doc"
　　1880, 1890
Butler, Richard H. "Dick"
　　1897
Carrick, William M. "Bill"
　　1900
Carroll, Frederick H. "Fred"
　　1887
Carsey, Wilfred "Kid" 1894,
　　1896
Caruthers, Robert L. "Bob"
　　1891
Casey, Daniel M. "Dan"
　　1888
Caskin, Edward J. "Ed"
　　1884
Cassidy, John P. 1882
Chamberlain, Elton P. 1894
Chance, Frank L. 1902
Clack, Robert H. "Bobby"
　　1876
Clarke, Arthur F. "Artie"
　　1890
Clarke, William J.
　　"Boileryard" 1893-94,
　　1896
Clarkson, Arthur H. "Dad"
　　1893-96
Clarkson, John G. 1888,
　　1892-93
Clements, John J. "Jack"
　　1892
Coleman, John F. 1884
Coogan, Daniel G. "Dan"
　　1895
Cooney, John W. "Johnny"
　　1941
Crane, Edward N. "Ed"
　　1892
Crane, Samuel N. "Sam"
　　1886, 1890
Crolius, Frederick J. "Fred"
　　1901
Cronin, John J. "Jack"
　　1902-03
Cross, Lafayette N. "Lave"
　　1892
Culler, Richard B. "Dick"
　　1947
Cunningham, Elmer E.
　　"Bert" 1896-97, 1900
Cuppy, George M. 1894
Cusick, Andrew D. "Tony"
　　1886-87
Daily, Cornelius F. "Con"
　　1886, 1891, 1894, 1896
Daly, Thomas P. "Tom"
　　1901
Darling, Conrad "Dell" 1887
Dealy, Patrick E. "Pat" 1886
Dexter, Charles D. "Charlie"
　　1896-97
Donahue, Francis R. "Red"
　　1897
Donahue, Timothy C. "Tim"
　　1895-96
Donlin, Michael J. "Mike"
　　1900
Donnelly, James B. "Jim"
　　1896

Donovan, William E. "Bill" 1902

Dooin, Charles S. "Red" 1904

Douglass, William B. "Klondike" 1903

Dowse, Thomas J. "Tom" 1890

Duggleby, William J. "Bill" 1905

Dwyer, J. Francis "Frank" 1889, 1893-94, 1896-97

Earle, William M. "Billy" 1894

Ehret, Philip S. "Phil" 1892, 1895-97

Farrell, Charles A. "Duke" 1901-02

Ferguson, Charles J. "Charlie" 1886

Fitzsimmons, Frederick "Freddie" 1941

Flaherty, Patrick J. "Patsy" 1904

Force, David W. "Davy" 1881

Foreman, Francis I. "Frank" 1895

Foreman, John D. "Brownie" 1896

Foster, Clarence F. "Pop" 1900

Freeman, John F. "Buck" 1900

Galvin, James F. "Jim" 1881, 1887, 1889

Gardner, James A. "Jim" 1899

George, William M. "Bill" 1889

German, Lester S. "Les" 1895

Gleason, William J. "Kid" 1890, 1892

Grady, Michael W. "Mike" 1895

Graves, Frank M. 1886

Griffith, Clark C. 1894-95

Grim, John H. 1892, 1895-96

Gruber, Henry J. 1889

Gumbert, Addison C. "Ad" 1892, 1895-96

Gunning, Thomas F. "Tom" 1884-85

Gunson, Joseph B. "Joe" 1892

Hackett, Mortimer M. "Mert" 1886

Haddock, George S. 1889

Hallman, William W. "Bill" 1903

Hanlon, Edward H. "Ned" 1892

Hart, William F. "Bill" 1896-97

Hatfield, Gilbert "Gil" 1889

Healy, John J. 1887

Hemming, George E. 1895-96

Hines, Michael P. "Mike" 1884

Hoffer, William L. "Bill" 1896

Holliday, James W. "Bug" 1897

Howe, John "Shorty" 1890

Hurst, Timothy C. "Tim" 1898

Hyatt, R. Hamilton "Ham" 1912

Irwin, Arthur A. 1881

Jacklitsch, Fred L. 1901

Jennings, Hugh A. "Hughie" 1893, 1900

Johnson, Sylvester "Syl" 1934

Jones, Henry M. 1890

Kahoe, Michael J. "Mike" 1905

Karger, Edwin "Ed" 1906

Keefe, Timothy J. "Tim" 1880-82, 1884-85, 1887, 1892

Keeler, William H. "Willie" 1910

Kellum, Winford A. "Win" 1905

Kelly, Michael J. "King" 1892-93

Killen, Frank B. 1896-97

Kinslow, Thomas F. "Tom" 1892

Kittridge, Malachi J. 1890, 1899

Kitson, Frank R. 1902

Klein, Charles H. "Chuck" 1942

Kling, John G. "Johnny" 1901

Knell, Philip H. "Phil" 1895

Knowles, James "Jimmy" 1892

Krieg, William F. "Bill" 1887

Leever, Samuel W. "Sam" 1900, 1904

Lindeman, Vivian A. "Vive" 1907

Lundgren, Carl L. 1905-06

Maloney, William A. "Billy" 1902

Manning, James H. "Jim" 1886

Mathews, Robert T. "Bobby" 1882

Mathewson, Christopher "Christy" 1901, 1907

McAleer, James R. "Jim" 1893

McAllister, Lewis W. "Sport" 1899

McCarthy, Thomas F. M. "Tommy" 1896

McCauley, Allen A. "Al" 1890

McCauley, Patrick M. "Pat" 1896

McCormick, James "Jim" 1885

McFarland, Edward W. "Ed" 1896

McGarr, James B. "Chippy" 1895

McGinnity, Joseph J. "Joe" 1900

McGuire, James T. "Deacon" 1886, 1894, 1896-97, 1901

McKinnon, Alexander J. "Alex" 1886

McMahon, John J. "Sadie" 1893

Meekin, Jouette 1895-96

Menefee, John "Jock" 1903

Mercer, George B. "Win" 1896

Mertes, Samuel B. "Sam" 1905

Miller, George F. "Doggie" 1893, 1896

Miller, Joseph H. 1884

Miller, L. Otto 1934

Moran, Patrick J. "Pat" 1901

Mullane, Anthony J. "Tony" 1893

Mulvey, Joseph H. "Joe" 1895

Murphy, Morgan E. 1893, 1896, 1898

Murphy, William H. "Yale" 1895, 1897

Murray, Jeremiah J. "Miah" 1895

Myers, George D. 1886

Needham, Thomas J. "Tom" 1904, 1907

Newton, Eustace J. "Doc" 1902

Nichols, Charles A. "Kid" 1900-01

Nolan, Edward S. "The Only" 1881

Noonan, Peter J. "Pete" 1906-07

O'Brien, John F. "Darby" 1889

O'Connor, John J. "Jack" 1893, 1901

O'Day, Henry F. "Hank" 1888-89

O'Neill, Michael J. "Mike" 1904

O'Rourke, James H. "Jim" 1893

Orth, Albert L. "Al" 1901

Overall, Orval 1905, 1910

Peitz, Henry C. "Heinie" 1901, 1906

Phelps, Edward J. "Ed" 1912

Phillippe, Charles L. "Deacon" 1903

Quinn, Joseph J. "Joe" 1894, 1896

Reilly, Charles T. "Charlie" 1892, 1894-95

Reitz, Henry P. "Heinie" 1895

Rhines, William P. "Billy" 1891, 1896

Richardson, A. Harding "Hardie" 1892

Richmond, J. Lee 1883

Robinson, Wilbert 1898

Ryan, James E. "Jimmy" 1892

Sanders, A. Bennett "Ben" 1889

Schmidt, Henry M. 1903

Schriver, William F. "Pop" 1901

Serad, William I. "Billy" 1884

Smith, A. Edgar 1883

Smith, Edgar E. 1890

Smith, George H. "Heinie" 1901

Smith, Harry T. 1903

Smith, William E. "Bill" 1886

Sommers, Joseph A. "Joe" 1889

Staley, Harry E. 1892, 1895

Stearns, D. Eckford "Ecky" 1881

Stein, Edward F. "Ed" 1890, 1894, 1896

Stivetts, John C. "Jack" 1894

Stocksdale, Otis H. 1895

Stricker, John A. "Cub" 1892

Stricklett, Elmer E. 1907

Sugden, Joseph "Joe" 1897

Sullivan, James E. "Jim" 1896

Sullivan, Martin C. "Marty" 1889

Sullivan, Michael J. "Mike" 1897

Sullivan, Thomas J. "Sleeper" 1881

Sutcliffe, Elmer E. "Sy" 1889, 1892

Tannehill, Jesse N. 1897, 1901-02

Tate, Edward C. "Pop" 1888

Taylor, John B. "Jack" 1899

Taylor, John W. "Jack" 1901, 1905

Tener, John K. 1889

Terry, William H. "Adonis" 1892, 1895-96

Tiernan, Michael J. "Mike" 1895

Vaughn, Harry F. "Farmer" 1892, 1899

Viau, Leon "Lee" 1891

Vickery, Thomas G. "Tom" 1890

Walker, Thomas W. "Tom" 1905

Wall, Joseph F. "Joe" 1901

Wallace, Roderick J. "Bobby" 1895

Walters, William H. "Bucky" 1942, 1947

Ward, John M. "Monte" 1888

Warneke, Lonnie "Lon" 1940

Warner, John J. "Jack" 1896-97, 1901, 1903

Weaver, William B. "Farmer" 1893

Weimer, Jacob W. "Jake" 1905, 1907

Welch, Michael F. "Mickey" 1881-82, 1885-86, 1888

Weyhing, August "Gus" 1899-1900

Whistler, Lewis "Lew" 1891

White, Guy H. "Doc" 1901-02

White, James L. "Deacon" 1880

Whitney, James E. "Jim" 1884, 1886

Wilhelm, Irving K. "Kaiser" 1904-05

Williamson, Edward N. "Ned" 1878, 1880

Willis, Victor G. "Vic" 1903

Wilmot, Walter R. "Walt" 1897

Wilson, Frank A. "Zeke" 1896, 1899

Wilson, James "Jimmie" 1942

Wilson, Parke A. 1894-96, 1899

Wilson, William G. "Bill" 1890

Wright, W. Harrison "Harry" 1876-77

Yeager, George J. 1901

Young, Denton T. "Cy" 1896

Young, Irving M. "Irv" 1905, 1907

Zimmer, Charles L. "Chief" 1889, 1901

American Association (1882-91)

Baldwin, Clarence G. "Kid" 1887

Becannon, James M. "Buck" 1884

Bond, Thomas H. "Tommy" 1884

Booth, Amos S. 1882

Boyle, John A. "Jack" 1888

Brennan, John G. "Jack" 1888

Briody, Charles F. "Fatty" 1888

Burns, Thomas P. "Oyster" 1888

Bushong, Albert J. "Doc" 1888-89

Carlin, William J. "Billy" 1886

Carsey, Wilfred "Kid" 1891

Cassidy, John P. 1884

Chamberlain, Elton P. 1887, 1891

Cross, Lafayette N. "Lave" 1889

Crowell, William T. "Billy" 1888

Darling, Conrad "Dell" 1891

Donahue, James A. "Jim" 1888

Easton, John S. "Jack" 1891

Ehret, Philip S. "Phil" 1890

Ewing, John 1889

Fulmer, Charles J. "Chick" 1888

Galvin, James F. "Jim" 1886

Ganzel, Charles W. "Charlie" 1886

Goldsby, Walton H. "Walt" 1888

Greenwood, William F. "Bill" 1884

Griffith, Clark C. 1891

Gunning, Thomas F. "Tom" 1888-89

Healy, John J. 1890

Hecker, Guy J. 1888

Herr, Edward J. "Ed" 1888

Higgins, William E. "Bill" 1890

Holbert, William H. "Bill" 1888

Johnston, Richard F. "Dick" 1884

Keefe, Timothy J. "Tim" 1884

Keenan, James W. "Jim" 1887-88

Kilroy, Matthew A. "Matt" 1891

Kirby, John F. 1888

Knell, Philip H. "Phil" 1891

Latham, George W. "Juice" 1884

Lynch, John H. "Jack" 1884

Macullar, James F. "Jimmy" 1886

Mattimore, Michael J. "Mike" 1888

Mays, Albert C. "Al" 1887

McCarthy, Thomas F. M. "Tommy" 1889

McKelvy, Russell E. "Russ" 1882

McMahon, John J. "Sadie" 1890

McSorley, John B. "Trick" 1884

Merrill, Edward M. "Ed" 1884

Mountain, Frank H. 1884

Mullane, Anthony J. "Tony" 1888

Murphy, Joseph A. "Joe" 1887

O'Brien, William D. "Darby" 1887-88

O'Connor, John J. "Jack" 1889

O'Day, Henry F. "Hank" 1884

Peoples, James E. "Jimmy" 1888-89

Pierce, Grayson S. "Gracie" 1882

Sage, Harry 1890

Serad, William I. "Billy" 1888

Smith, Charles M. "Pop" 1886

Smith, Frederick C. "Fred" 1890

Smith, John F. "Phenomenal" 1888

Snyder, Charles N. "Pop" 1886

Sommer, Joseph J. "Joe" 1888

Sprague, Charles W. "Charlie" 1890

Stivetts, John C. "Jack" 1891

Sweeney, Charles J. "Charley" 1887

Sylvester, Louis J. "Lou" 1888

Terry, William H. "Adonis" 1884, 1888

Townsend, George H. 1890

Traffley, William F. "Bill" 1884

Vaughn, Harry F. "Farmer" 1891

Weyhing, August "Gus" 1891

Wheeler, Harry E. 1882

Wood, George A. 1891

Zimmer, Charles L. "Chief" 1888

Union Association (1884)

Bradley, George W. 1884

Callahan, Edward J. "Ed" 1884

Carroll, Patrick "Pat" 1884

Cuthbert, Edgar E. "Ned" 1884

Kelly, John F. 1884

McLaughlin, James C. "Jim" 1884

Oberbeck, Henry A. 1884

Wheeler, Harry E. 1884

Williams, Washington J. "Wash" 1884

Players League (1890)

Bakely, Edward E. "Ed" 1890

Carney, John J. 1890

Comiskey, Charles A. "Charlie" 1890

Daily, Cornelius F. "Con" 1890

Gumbert, Addison C. "Ad" 1890

Haddock, George S. 1890

Hallman, William W. "Bill" 1890

Keefe, Timothy J. "Tim" 1890

Kelly, Michael J. "King" 1890

Madden, Michael J. "Kid" 1890

Milligan, John "Jocko" 1890

O'Day, Henry F. "Hank" 1890
Tener, John K. 1890

American League (1901-)

Altrock, Nicholas "Nick" 1907
Bejma, Alojzy F. "Ollie" 1935
Bender, Charles A. "Chief" 1907
Bernhard, William H. "Bill" 1903, 1907
Beville, H. Monte 1903-04
Blankenship, Clifford D. "Cliff" 1907
Buelow, Frederick W. "Fritz" 1906
Callahan, James J. "Nixey" 1901
Conlan, John B. "Jocko" 1935
Coughlin, William P. "Bill" 1904
Cronin, John J. "Jack" 1901
Davis, Harry H. 1903
Dinneen, William H. "Bill" 1907
Donahue, Francis R. "Red" 1903, 1906
Donovan, William E. "Bill" 1903, 1906
Drill, Lewis L. "Lew" 1903-04
Flaherty, Patrick J. "Patsy" 1903
Foreman, Francis I. "Frank" 1901
Grady, Michael W. "Mike" 1901
Griffith, Clark C. 1903
Harris, Joseph W. "Joe" 1906
Hartley, Grover A. 1935
Hickman, Charles T. "Charlie" 1907
Howell, H. Harry 1904, 1906-07
Kittridge, Malachi J. 1905-06
Leahy, Thomas J. "Tom" 1901
Leppert, Donald G. "Don" 1978
Lowe, Robert L. "Bobby" 1905
McAllister, Lewis W. "Sport" 1901-02
McGuire, James T> "Deacon" 1905
Moore, Earl A. 1903
O'Brien, Peter J. "Pete" 1907
Patten, Case L. 1903
Pelty, Barney 1906
Powers, Michael R. "Mike" 1902
Schmidt, Charles "Boss" 1907
Schreckengost, Ossee F. 1903
Siever, Edward T. "Ed" 1901
Warner, John J. "Jack" 1908
White, Guy H. "Doc" 1903
Winter, George L. 1903, 1905
Young, Denton T. "Cy" 1903
Zimmerman, Gerald R. "Jerry" 1978

UMPIRES DURING STRIKES

National League (1876-)

Anderson, Lewis E. "Andy" 1978-79
Andress, William J. "Bill" 1979

Baird, John 1979
Ballino, Frank 1991, 1995
Barston, Michael "Mike" 1979
Baswell, Jack S. 1979
Beck, Robert "Bob" 1979
Bendekovits, Joseph "Joe" 1979
Betcher, Ralph A. 1976
Blandford, Fred 1970
Bovey, Terry R. 1979, 1984, 1995
Bruns, Randy 1991
Campagna, Frank J. 1979, 1984
Cavenaugh, Richard P. "Dick" 1979, 1984
Cohen, Alfred A. "Al" 1976
Cote, Emilien 1979
Cuneo, James "Jim" 1978-79
Davidson, — 1995
Davis, Bill 1995
Deniston, Shannon W. "Shan" 1978
Dierking, Roger A. 1978
Edwards, Larry 1978
Fick, Jerry D. 1978-79
Fisher, Frank 1979, 1984
Fleming, Thomas E. "Tom" 1979
Floras, John 1991
Ford, Wade 1995
Fowler, A. Wheeler 1978
Freels, Robert L. "Bob" 1979
Garman, Jim 1995
Gisondi, Tony 1991
Graham, Scott 1991, 1995
Grimsley, John 1970
Grinder, Scott 1976
Grooms, Roger C. 1979
Grygiel, George R. 1970
Guckert, Elmer 1976
Hadry, Merrill A. 1979
Hamil, Ray 1979
Hansen, Howard 1978-79
Hantak, H. Robert "Bob" 1979
Harris, Vance 1995
Henry, William E. "Bill" 1979
Hernandez, Bob 1995
Holoka, Mike 1991, 1995
Homolka, Bob 1995
Humphrey, Rick 1995
Hutson, Ronald "Ron" 1979
Jackson, Dick 1995
January, Don 1991, 1995
Jeffers, Ronald L. "Ron" 1979
Jenkins, Jeff 1995
Jones, Bob 1995
Jones, James "Jim" 1979
Jumper, Howard 1979
Lambeth, Jim 1995
Lauzon, Jacques 1979
Lawson, William R. "Bill" 1979
Loeber, Gerald G. "Jerry" 1979
Lospitalier, Philip A. "Phil" 1979
Lupo, Charles "Charlie" 1978-79
Maher, Robert J. "Bob" 1979, 1984
Martine, Bruce 1991
Mauer, Boyd 1978-79
Melton, David "Dave" 1978
Miller, Marvin G. "Bud" 1979
Mills, Greg 1979
Morgenweck, Henry C. "Hank" 1970
Mrvos, Joseph S. "Joe" 1979
Myers, Joseph "Joe" 1979
Negri, Peter "Pete" 1979
Nelson, Robert "Bob" 1979, 1991, 1995
Norris, Edward E. "Ed" 1978-79
Oliger, Edward C. "Ed" 1979

Pacheco, Jim 1995
Padilla, Joe 1995
Patch, Tony D. 1978-79
Perez, J. Ray 1979
Pomponi, Joseph L. "Joe" 1979, 1984
Rains, James "Jim" 1978-79
Randall, Larry 1995
Riccio, Dennis R. 1979
Riccio, L. Leonard "Len" 1979
Riggers, Mike 1995
Rodriguez, Gus 1995
Rosenberry, Bill 1995
Roth, Roy 1978-79
Rountree, Henry J. "Hank" 1978-79
Ryberg, Sy 1995
Schaff, Fred 1995
Schaller, Cliff 1978-79
Schleyer, John 1979
Schratz, Joseph "Joe" 1979
Schroeder, Robert L. "Bobby" 1978-79
Scott, James "Jim" 1978-79
Sharkey, Michael E. "Mick" 1978-79
Sharp, Robert C. "Bob" 1979
Siroka, Harold L. 1979
Slattery, Donald L. "Don" 1979
Slickenmeyer, David W. "Dave" 1979, 1984
Smail, Harry F. 1979
Spange, John 1991
Spinelli, Michel 1979
Stansell, B. Jack 1979
Stewart, John 1979, 1984
Strey, Murray W. 1978-79
Sylvester, Frank 1995
Telford, Thomas "Tom" 1979
Tillman, Henry T. "Hank" 1978-79
Treitel, Leslie J. "Les" 1978-79
Tremblay, Richard H. "Dick" 1979
Urlage, Richard C. "Dick" 1979, 1991
Waller, James "Jim" 1979
Whaley, — 1995
Williams, Dale 1978-79
Willman, Bob 1991, 1995
Yeast, Dave 1995

American League (1901-)

Arata, Mark 1991
Berry, Charles F. "Charlie" 1970
Bialorucko, Larry 1995
Bible, Jonathan D. "Jon" 1984
Bishop, Homer L. 1979
Bohn, Matt 1995
Borga, Steven A. "Steve" 1979
Briscese, Michael L. "Mike" 1979
Brown, Buddy Lee "Bud" 1979
Brown, Douglas D. "Doug" 1979
Brown, Jeff 1978-79
Camp, John W. 1979
Campbell, Robert "Bob" 1979
Carcao, Joe 1995
Clegg, Richard "Dick" 1979
Clement, Robert F. "Bob" 1978-79
Compton, Craig 1995
Contant, Alan 1978-79
Cossey, Douglas C. "Doug" 1978-79, 1984
Cuneo, James "Jim" 1979
Cristal, W. Randle "Randy" 1984
Davidson, Dale F. 1979

Deegan, William E. J. "Bill" 1970, 1984, 1991, 1995
DeFlesco, Pete 1991
Denny, Richard 1984
Dreke, Roy 1995
Dresser, Al 1995
Driscoll, Joseph M. "Joe" 1978
Duncan, Robert 1995
Dunne, James "Jim" 1978-79
Easley, Harold L. 1979
Eshelman, George R. 1979
Evans, Jeff 1991
Farmer, Michael "Mike" 1979
Farnsworth, Harry 1979
Feaser, Richard L. "Dick" 1979
Fitzpatrick, Michael N. "Mike" 1979
Follmer, William A. "Bill" 1979
Forman, Allen S. "Al" 1978-79
Freese, Todd 1995
Fuchs, Lester 1978-79
Gallagher, Lawrence E. "Larry" 1979
George, Edward "Ed" 1979
Giard, Robert "Bob" 1978
Gustafson, G. David "Dave" 1978
Hafner, William F. "Bill" 1979
Hadry, Merrill A. 1979
Harris, Vance 1995
Harvey, Randy 1991, 1995
Heitzer, Richard "Dick" 1979
Henrichs, Jeff 1995
Henry, William E. "Bill" 1979
Higgins, John 1991, 1995
Huber, Mike 1995
Ivory, William J. "Bill" 1979
Jackson, Charles L. 1979
James, John F. "Johnny" 1978-79
Jones, Robert G. "Bob" 1979, 1984
Jordan, Harold E. 1984
Kaplan, Al 1995
Kavulich, Joseph "Joe" 1978-79
Keister, R. Wayne 1978-79
Kelly, Eugene C. "Gene" 1979
Kimball, Shawn 1991
Kirby, Kenneth "Ken" 1979
Klein, Gus 1991, 1995
Knauss, Jim 1991
LaPierre, Richard 1979
Laude, William F. "Bill" 1978-79
Lazar, Richard R. "Richie" 1978-79
Levet, Jay 1979
Loeber, Gerald G. "Jerry" 1979
Lospitalier, Philip A. "Phil" 1979
Luker, Dale 1995
Lupo, Charles "Charlie" 1979
Mabbot, Frederick J. "Fred" 1979
Mackin, John F. 1979
Mann, Terry 1995
Marino, James H. "Jimmy" 1979
Mason, Danny 1995
Mauer, Boyd 1979
McDougall, Scott 1991
McNally, James "Jim" 1979
Merritt, Clarence 1979
Miller, Gale 1979
Miller, John A. "Jack" 1979
Moyer, Robert "Bob" 1979
Mulcahy, James "Jim" 1979
Murray, Ed 1991
Nelson, Richard "Dick" 1979
Nothhnagel, Carl L. 1984

Novack, Lester A. "Les" 1979
O'Brien, James D. "Jim" 1979
O'Connor, James "Jim" 1978-79
O'Connor, Thomas M. "Tom" 1979
O'Dell, Mikel R. "Mike" 1984
Panas, Richard J. "Rich" 1978-79
Parks, Dallas F. 1991, 1995
Patch, Tony D. 1979
Paylor, Jim 1995
Perez, David A. "Dave" 1979
Phipps, George H. "Jerry" 1978-79
Pilato, Mike 1995
Pratt, Lester 1979
Purduski, Al J. 1979
Ravan, Bruce 1995
Ravashiere, Thomas "Tom" 1979
Riccio, L. Leonard "Len" 1979
Rice, Robert W. "Bob" 1979
Robinson, William N. "Bill" 1978-79
Roesner, Robert A. "Bob" 1978-79
Roth, Roy 1979
Rountree, Henry J. "Hank" 1991
Runchey, Richard D. "Dick" 1979, 1984
Satchell, Darold L. 1970
Sawchuk, Joseph W. "Joe" 1978-79
Schaly, Jim 1995
Scheel, Alfred M. "Al" 1979
Schirmer, Donald A. "Don" 1979
Schulte, Donald E. "Don" 1979
Schwarz, Henry "Hank" 1995
Shaw, A. Duane 1979
Shewmake, James B. "Jim" 1978
Siroka, Harold L. 1979
Slattery, Donald L. "Don" 1979
Slickenmeyer, David W. "Dave" 1979, 1991, 1995
Spenn, Frederick C. "Fred" 1991
Sprincz, William "Bill" 1978-79
Stevens, John W. "Johnny" 1970
Sweeney, George P. 1979
Swenson, Charles H. 1979
Taylor, Joe Bob 1979
Terlop, Russell F. "Russ" 1979
Theilander, Theodore "Ted" 1979
Thompson, Michael G. "Mike" 1978-79
Tillman, Henry T. "Hank" 1979
Travis, Vic 1995
Trimmer, Harry 1979
Turner, Leo I. 1978
Ulrich, George 1995
Urchak, Woody J. 1978-79
Uremovich, Jim 1991, 1995
Walding, Larry 1995
Williams, Dale 1979
Wright, Marvin 1995
Zirbel, Lawrence A. "Larry" 1979, 1984
Zivic, Richard J. "Dick" 1984
Zuccaro, Amerigo J. "Rico" 1978-79

The Owners and Officials Roster

Although Major League Baseball began in 1871 with the National Association, it is undeniable that with the founding of the National League in 1876 something dramatic occurred that altered forevermore the character of professional baseball: the division of the game into two classes, labor and management.

The National Association of Professional Base Ball Players was an outgrowth of the amateur association of the same name, in which baseball clubs were formed as organizations devoted to social intercourse and fraternal competition. Amateur clubs were organized along the same lines as today's Elks or Odd Fellows, with elected officials and dues-paying members. As players of special skill were invited into these clubs, their dues might be forgiven or "emoluments" offered—no-show jobs or under-the-table payments. The abuses of the amateur system of the mid-1860s led to the declaration by several clubs of their openly professional status; players would sometimes draw salaries and as often would share in gate receipts. By the end of the decade gambling and game-fixing were rife.

Despite the formation of the National Association, these evils continued largely unabated into the 1870s. A monopolization of talent, largely in Boston, rendered Western clubs uncompetitive, and spectator rowdyism spawned by gambling interest, and the open sale of hard liquor burdened the new league. Clubs were admitted into the NA for paltry fees and fulfilled their schedules half-heartedly. Some of the member clubs had active presidents who functioned much as owners later would; other clubs were "cooperative nines," managed by the players themselves; still others were hybrids, born of civic boosterism. By 1876, the odd amalgam of the NA, presided over by Brooklyn Atlantics star Bob Ferguson, was failing.

Thus in 1876 William Hulbert, president of the Chicago club, combined with seven other team representatives to form the National League, a circuit run entirely by owners. Since then, fan interest has focused on the players, of course, and to a lesser extent on the managers, coaches, and umpires. But it can be said with some justice that while the on-field personnel and personalities "are" the game, it is the club owners, presidents, and league officials who make the game possible and ensure its continuity.

The Owners and Officials Roster that follows represents a first attempt in a baseball encyclopedia to recognize these individuals. As we did with the Coach Roster in the first edition of *Total Baseball*, we offered this section in *Total Baseball*'s second, third and fourth editions with the full knowledge that there were gaps and probably gaffes in our research; we hope that our readers will advise us of omissions so that we can continue to improve the roster in future editions. (The names of National Association club presidents and officials are listed below despite our understanding that these individuals were, by and large, not owners in the sense used after 1876.)

Commissioners, Major League Baseball

1920–1944	Kenesaw M. Landis
1945–1951	Albert B. Chandler
1951–1965	Ford C. Frick
1965–1968	William D. Eckert
1969–1984	Bowie K. Kuhn
1984–1989	Peter Ueberroth
1989	A. Bartlett Giamatti
1989–1992	Francis T. Vincent, Jr.
1993–	Alan H. Selig (interim commissioner)

National Association

Association President

1871	James W. Kerns
1872–1875	Robert W. Ferguson

Club Presidents and/or NA Convention Delegates

Baltimore Lord Baltimores

1872	—
1873	R. C. Hall
1874	C. A. Hadel

Baltimore Marylands

1873	W. J. Smith

Boston Red Stockings

1871	Ivers Whitney Adams
1872	Col. Charles H. Porter
1873–1875	Nathan Taylor Appolonio

Brooklyn Atlantics

1872–1873	Robert W. Ferguson
1874	—
1875	B. Van Delft

Brooklyn Eckfords

1872	William H. Ray

Chicago White Stockings

1871	J. M. Thatcher
1874	Mr. Gassette
	George W. Gage
1875	William A. Hulbert

Cleveland Forest City

1871	J. F. Evans
1872	H. C. Doolittle

Elizabeth Resolutes

1873	Charles N. Garrighan

Fort Wayne Kekiongas

1871	George J. E. Mayers

Hartford Dark Blues

1874	G. B. Hubbell
1875	Morgan G. Bulkeley

Keokuk Westerns

1875	W. Trimble

Middletown Mansfields

1872	B. Douglass, Jr.
	T. W. Ratcliff

New Haven Elm City

1875	W. S. Arnold

New York Mutuals

1871–1872	Alexander V. Davidson
1873	Robert Mathews
1874	Alexander V. Davidson
1875	William H. Cammeyer

Philadelphia Athletics

1871	James W. Kerns
1872–1873	E. H. Hayhurst
1874	D. F. Houston
1875	George W. Thompson
	C. Spering

Philadelphia White Stockings

1873	Frank McBride
1874	D. L. Reid
1875	George Concannon

Philadelphia Centennials

1875	E. H. Hayhurst

Rockford Forest City

1871	Hiram Waldo

St. Louis Brown Stockings

1875	C. O. Bishop

St. Louis Red Stockings

1875	A. Blong

Troy Haymakers

1871	J. W. Scofield

1872	C. C. Clark

Washington Nationals

1872	Mr. Millar
	R. Hough

Washington Olympics

1871	Nicholas E. Young
1872	Mr. Pike

Washington

1873	Nicholas E. Young
1875	D. W. Bruce
	A. F. Childs

National League

Presidents

1876	Morgan G. Bulkeley
1877–1882	William A. Hulbert
1882	Arthur H. Soden
1883–1884	Abraham G. Mills
1885–1902	Nicholas E. Young
1903–1909	Harry C. Pulliam
1909	John A. Heydler
1910–1913	Thomas J. Lynch
1913–1918	John K. Tener
1918–1934	John A. Heydler
1934–1951	Ford C. Frick
1951–1969	Warren C. Giles
1970–1986	Charles S. Feeney
1986–1989	A. Bartlett Giamatti
1989–1994	William White
1994–	Leonard S. Coleman, Jr.

Vice Presidents

1929–1932	Barney Dreyfuss
1933–1936	Charles A. Stoneham
1936–1947	Samuel Breadon
1947–1966	Philip K. Wrigley
1966–1969	Horace C. Stoneham
1970–1986	John J. McHale
1987–1994	Phyllis Collins
1994–	Katy Feeney

Club Presidents

Atlanta

1966	John J. McHale
1967–1972	William C. Bartholomay
1973–1975	Daniel J. Donahue
1976–1986	R. E. (Ted) Turner
1987–	William C. Bartholomay (Ch. of Bd.)

Baltimore

1892	Harry B. Von der Horst
1893–1899	Edward H. Hanlon

Boston (to Milwaukee)

1876	Nathan Taylor Appolonio
1907–1909	George B. Dovey
1909–1910	John S. Dovey
1911	W. Hepburn Russell
1912	John M. Ward
1913–1915	James E. Gaffney
1916–1918	Percy D. Haughton
1919–1922	George W. Grant
1923	Christopher Mathewson
1924	J. A. Robert Quinn
1925	Christopher Mathewson
1926	J. A. Robert Quinn
1927–1935	Emil E. Fuchs (Pres.)
1936–1944	J. A. Robert Quinn (Pres.)
1945–1952	Louis R. Perini (Pres.)

Brooklyn (to L.A.)

1890–1897	Charles H. Byrne
1898–1925	Charles H. Ebbets
1925	Edward J. McKeever
1925–1929	Wilbert Robinson (Pres.)
1930–1932	Frank B. York (Pres.)
1933–1938	Stephen W. McKeever
1939–1942	Leland S. MacPhail, Sr. (Exec. VP)
1943–1950	W. Branch Rickey (Pres./GM)
1950–1957	Walter F. O'Malley (Pres.)

Buffalo

1879–1880	E. B. Smith
1880	John B. Sage
1881–1885	Josiah Jewett

Chicago

1876–1881	William A. Hulbert
1882–1891	Albert G. Spalding
1892–1905	James A. Hart
1906–1913	Charles W. Murphy
1914–1915	Charles H. Thomas
1916–1918	Charles H. Weeghman

1919	Fred F. Mitchell
1919–1933	William L. Veeck, Sr. (Pres.)
1934	William M. Walker
1934–1977	Philip K. Wrigley (Pres.)
1977–1981	William J. Hagenah, Jr. (Pres./CEO/Treas.)
1982–1983	Andrew J. McKenna (Ch. of Bd.)
1984	James E. Finks (Pres./CEO)
1985–1987	Dallas Green (Pres./GM)
1988	John W. Madigan (Ch. of Bd.)
1989–1994	Stanton Cook (Ch. of Bd.)
1994–	Andy MacPhail (Pres./CEO)

Cincinnati

1876–1877	Josiah L. Keck
1878–1879	J. Wayne Neff
1880	Justus Thorner

Cincinnati

1890	Aaron A. Stern
1891–1902	John T. Brush
1902–1927	August Hermann (Pres.)
1928–1929	C. J. McDiarmid (Pres.)
1930–1933	Sidney Weil (Pres.)
1934–1946	Powel Crosley, Jr. (Pres.)
1946–1951	Warren C. Giles (Pres.)
1951–1961	Powel Crosley, Jr. (Pres.)
1961–1966	William O. DeWitt (Pres./GM/Treas.)
1967–1973	Francis L. Dale (Pres.)
1973–1978	Robert L. Howsam (Pres./CEO)
1979–1983	Richard Wagner (Pres./CEO)
1984–1985	Robert L. Howsam (Pres./CEO)
1986–	Marge Schott (Gen. Partner/Pres.)

Cleveland

1879–1881	J. Ford Evans
1882–1884	C. H. Bulkley

Cleveland

1889–1898	Frank D. Robison
1899	M. Stanley Robison

Colorado

1992	John Antonucci (Ch./CEO)
1993–	Jerry McMorris (Ch./CEO/Pres.)

Detroit

1881–1884	William G. Thompson
1885–1886	Joseph H. Marsh
1887–1888	Fred K. Stearns
1888	Charles W. Smith

Florida

1992–	Wayne Huizenga (Chairman)

Hartford

1876–1877	Morgan G. Bulkeley

Houston

1962	Craig F. Cullinan, Jr. (Pres.)
1963–1971	Roy Hofheinz (Pres.)
1972–1973	Reuben W. Askanase (Pres./Ch. of Bd.)
1974–1975	T. H. Neyland (Pres.)
1976	Sidney L. Shlenker (Pres.)
1976–1980	Talbot M. Smith (Pres./GM)
1981–1985	Albert L. Rosen (Pres./GM)
1986–1987	Dick Wagner
1988	Fred Stanley
1980–1992	Dr. John J. McMullen (Ch. of Bd.)
1992–	Drayton McLane, Jr. (Ch. of Bd./CEO)

Indianapolis

1878	William D. Perritt

Indianapolis

1887–1889	John T. Brush

Kansas City

1886	Joseph J. Heim

Los Angeles

1958–1969	Walter F. O'Malley (Pres.)
1970–	Peter O'Malley (Pres.)

Louisville

1876–1877	Walter N. Haldeman

Louisville

1892	T. Hunt Stucky
1893–1896	Fred Drexler
1897–1899	Harry C. Pulliam
1899	Barney Dreyfuss

Milwaukee
1878   J. R. Kaine

Milwaukee Braves (to Atlanta Braves)
1953–1956   Louis R. Perini (Pres.)
1957–1961   Joseph F. Cairnes (Pres.)
1962–1966   John J. McHale (Pres.)

Montreal Expos
1969–1986   John J. McHale (Pres./CEO)
1986–   Claude R. Brochu
     (Pres./CEO)

Mutual Club (N.Y.)
1876   William H. Cammeyer

New York Giants (to San Francisco)
1883–1892   John B. Day
1893–1894   C. C. Van Cott
1895–1902   Andrew Freedman
1903–1912   John T. Brush
1912–1918   Harry N. Hempstead
1919–1935   Charles A. Stoneham (Pres.)
1936–1957   Horace C. Stoneham (Pres.)

New York Mets
1962–1966   George M. Weiss (Pres.)
1966–1967   Vaughan P. Devine (Pres.)
1968–1975   Mrs. Joan W. Payson (Pres.)
1976–1979   Mrs. Lorinda de Roulet (Pres.)
1980–   Fred Wilpon (Pres./CEO)

Philadelphia Athletics
1876   Thomas J. Smith

Philadelphia Phillies
1883–1902   Alfred J. Reach
1903–1904   James Potter
1905–1908   William J. Shettsline
1909   Israel W. Durham
1909–1912   Horace S. Fogel
1912   Alfred D. Wiler
1913   William H. Locke
1913–1930   William F. Baker (Pres.)
1931–1932   L. Charles Ruch
1933–1942   Gerald P. Nugent (Pres.)
1943   William D. Cox
1943–1972   Robert M. Carpenter, Jr.
     (Pres.)
1973–1981   Robert M. Carpenter III (Pres.)
1982–   Bill Giles (Pres./CEO)

Pittsburgh
1887–1890   William A. Nimick
1891   J. Palmer O'Neill
1892   William C. Temple
1893   Albert C. Buckenberger
1894–1897   William W. Kerr
1898   William H. Watkins
1899   William W. Kerr
1900–1932   Barney Dreyfuss (Pres.)
1932–1946   William E. Benswanger (Pres./
     Treas.)
1946–1950   Frank E. McKinney (Pres.)
1951–1969   John W. Galbreath (Pres.)
1970–1985   Daniel M. Galbreath (Pres.)
1986–1987   Malcolm Prine
1988–1990   Carl Barger (Pres.)
1988–1991   Douglas D. Danforth
     (Chairman/CEO)
1992   Vincent Sarni (Pres./CEO)
1992–1996   Mark Sauer (Pres./CEO)
1996–   Kevin S. McClatchy (CEO/
     Man. Gen. Partner)

Providence
1878   John D. Thurston
1879–1881   Henry J. Root
1882–1883   Henry B. Winship
1884–1885   Henry J. Root

St. Louis Brown Stockings
1876–1877   John R. Lucas

St. Louis Maroons
1885–1886   Henry V. Lucas

St. Louis Cardinals
1892–1897   Chris Von der Ahe
1898   Benjamin S. Muckenfuss
1899–1906   Frank D. Robison
1907–1910   M. Stanley Robison
1911–1912   E. A. Steininger
1912   James C. Jones
1913–1916   Schuyler P. Britton
1916   Mrs. Schuyler P. Britton
1917–1919   W. Branch Rickey
1920–1947   Samuel Breadon (Pres.)
1947–1949   Robert E. Hannegan
1949–1952   Fred M. Saigh, Jr. (Pres.)
1953–1989   August A. Busch, Jr. (Pres.)

1990–1991   Fred L. Kuhlmann
     (Pres./CEO)
1992–1994   Stuart Meyer (Pres./CEO)
1994–   Mark C. Lamping (Pres.)

San Diego
1969–1977   Emil J. Bavasi (Pres.)
1977–1980   Ray A. Kroc
1981–1983   Ray A. Kroc (owner)
1980–1987   Ballard F. Smith, Jr.
1988   Chub Feeney
1990   Dick Freeman
1984–1990   Joan Kroc (owner)
1991–1994   Tom Werner (Prin. Owner/Ch.)
1994–   John Moores (Ch. of the Bd.)

San Francisco
1958–1975   Horace C. Stoneham (Pres.)
1976–1979   Robert A. Lurie/Bud Herseth
     (Co-Chairmen)
1980–1985   Robert A. Lurie (Pres.)
1986–1990   Robert A. Lurie (owner)
1986–1992   Albert L. Rosen (Pres./GM)
1993–   Peter A. Magowan (Pres.)

Syracuse
1879   Hamilton S. White

Troy
1879–1880   Gardner Earl
1881–1882   A. L. Hotchkin
1882   Francis N. Mann

Washington
1886–1888   Robert C. Hewitt
1889   Walter F. Hewitt

Washington
1892–1899   George W. Wagner

Worcester
1880–1882   Elbert B. Pratt

American Association

League Presidents
1882–1885   H. D. McKnight
1886–1889   Wheeler C. Wyckoff
1890   Zach Phelps
1891   Louis Kramer
     Ed Renau
     Zach Phelps

Club Presidents

Baltimore
1882   H. C. Myers (?)
1883   William Barnie (?)
1884   H. T. Houck
1885–1887   William Barnie
1888   Harry Von der Horst
1889   William Barnie
1891   Harry Von der Horst

Boston
1891   Charles A. Prince

Brooklyn
1884–1889   Charles H. Byrne

Brooklyn–Baltimore
1890   James M. Kennedy
     Wm. Barnie (?)

Cincinnati
1882   Justus Thorner
1883–1884   Aaron S. Stern
1885   George L. Herancourt
1886   John Hauck
1887–1889   Aaron S. Stern

Cincinnati-Milwaukee
1891   Albert Johnson

Cleveland
1887–1888   Frank Robison

Columbus
1883–1884   H. T. Crittendon (?)
1889–1891   Conrad Born, Jr.

Indianapolis
1884   Joseph Schwabacher

Kansas City
1888   Joseph J. Heim
1889   John W. Speas

Louisville
1882–1883   J. H. Pank
1884   William L. Jackson, Jr.
1885–1887   Zach Phelps
1888   W. L. Lyons
1889   M. H. Davidson
1890   Lawrence S. Parsons

1891   Julian B. Hart

New York
1883–1884   John B. Day
1885   Frank Rhouer
1886–1887   Erastus Wiman

Philadelphia
1882   Lew Simmons (?)
1883–1886   William Sharsig
1887   Lew Simmons
1888–1890   H. C. Pennypacker
1891   J. Earle Wagner

Pittsburgh
1882–1883   H. D. McKnight
1884   E. E. Converse
1885–1886   William A. Nimick

Richmond
1884   W. C. Seddon

Rochester
1890   Henry Brinker

St. Louis
1882–1891   Chris Von der Ahe

Syracuse
1890   George K. Frazier

Toledo
1884   W. J. Colburn
1890   V. H. Ketcham

Washington
1884   L. Moxley
1891   H. B. Bennett

Union Association

League Presidents
1883   H. B. Bennett
1883–1885   Henry V. Lucas

Club Presidents

Altoona
1884   W. W. Rich

Baltimore
1884   J. W. Lowe

Boston
1884   Frank E. Winslow

Chicago-Pittsburgh
1884   A. H. Henderson

Cincinnati
1884   Justus Thorner

Kansas City
1884   Americus V. McKim

Milwaukee
1884   Charles Kippen (?)

Philadelphia
1884   Thomas J. Pratt

St. Louis
1884   H. V. Lucas

St. Paul
1884   A. M. Thompson (?)

Washington
1884   H. B. Bennett

Wilmington
1884   John T. West

Players League

League President
1890   Col. Edward A. McAlpin

Club Presidents

Boston
1890   Col. Charles H. Porter

Brooklyn
1890   Wendell Goodwin

Buffalo
1890   Moses Shire

Chicago
1890   John Addison

Cleveland
1890   Albert L. Johnson

New York
1890   Cornelius Van Cott

Philadelphia
1890   H. M. Love

Pittsburgh
1890   William McCallin

American League

Presidents

1901–1927	B. Bancroft Johnson
1927–1931	Ernest S. Barnard
1931–1959	William Harridge
1959–1973	Joseph E. Cronin
1974–1984	Leland S. MacPhail, Jr.
1984–1994	Robert W. Brown, M.D.
1994–	Dr. Gene A. Budig

Vice Presidents

1901–1916	Charles W. Somers
1917–1919	Charles A. Comiskey
1921–1935	Frank J. Navin
1935–1938	Jacob Ruppert
1939–1955	Clark C. Griffith
1955–1976	Thomas A. Yawkey
1976–1982	Calvin R. Griffith
1983–1984	Calvin R. Griffith
	John Fetzer
	Gene Autry
1985	John Fetzer and Gene Autry
1986–1989	Calvin R. Griffith
	John Fetzer
	Gene Autry
1990	John Fetzer and Gene Autry
1991	Jean Yawkey and Gene Autry
1992–	Gene Autry

Club Presidents

Baltimore (to New York)

1901	Sidney W. Frank
1902	John J. Mahon

Baltimore

1954–1955	Clarence W. Miles (Pres.)
1956–1959	James Keelty, Jr. (Pres.)
1960–1965	Leland S. MacPhail, Jr. (Pres./GM)
1966–1979	Jerold C. Hoffberger (Ch. of Bd.)
1980–1982	Jerold C. Hoffberger (as Pres.)
1983–1988	Edward B. Williams (Ch. of Bd./Pres.)
1989–1992	Lawrence Lucchino (Pres./CEO)
1994–	Peter Angelos (Managing Gen. Partner)

Boston

1901–1902	Charles W. Somers
1903–1904	Henry J. Killilea
1904–1911	John I. Taylor
1912–1913	James R. McAleer
1913–1916	Joseph J. Lannin
1917–1923	Harry H. Frazee
1923–1932	Robert Quinn (Pres.)
1933–1976	Thomas A. Yawkey (Pres.)
1977–1988	Jean R. Yawkey (majority owner)
1989–	John L. Harrington (General Partner)

California (includes Los Angeles, 1961–64)

1961–1974	Robert Reynolds (Pres.)
1975–1977	Arthur E. Patterson (Pres.)
1977–1990	Gene Autry (owner/president)
1990–	Richard M. Brown (Pres./CEO)

Chicago

1901–1931	Charles A. Comiskey (Pres.)
1932–1939	J. Louis Comiskey (Pres./Treas.)
1940	Harry Grabiner (VP)
1941–1956	Mrs. Grace Comiskey (Pres.)
1957–1959	Charles A. Comiskey II/John Rigney (VPs)
1959–1961	William L. Veeck, Jr. (Pres.)
1961–1969	Arthur C. Allyn, Jr. (Pres.)
1970–1975	John W. Allyn (Pres.)
1976–1980	William L. Veeck, Jr. (Pres.)
1981–	Jerry M. Reinsdorf (Chairman)

Cleveland

1901–1909	John F. Kilfoyl
1910–1915	Charles W. Somers
1916–1922	James C. Dunn
1922–1927	Ernest S. Barnard (Pres.)
1928–1946	Alva Bradley (Pres./Treas.)
1946–1949	William L. Veeck, Jr. (Pres.)
1950–1952	Ellis W. Ryan (Pres.)
1953–1962	Myron H. Wilson, Jr. (Pres.)
1963–1971	Gabriel H. Paul (Pres./Treas./GM)
1972–1975	Nick Mileti (Pres.)
1975–1977	Alva T. Bonda (Pres.)
1978–1985	Gabriel H. Paul (Pres./CEO)
1986–	Patrick J. O'Neill (Chairman)
1987–	Richard E. Jacobs (Ch. of Bd./CEO)

Detroit

1901	James D. Burns (Pres.)
1902–1903	Samuel F. Angus (Pres.)
1904–1907	William H. Yawkey (Pres.)
1908–1935	Frank J. Navin (Pres.)
1936–1952	Walter O. Briggs, Sr. (Pres.)
1952–1956	Walter O. Briggs, Jr. (Pres.)
1957	Frederick A. Knorr (Pres.)
1957–1959	Harvey R. Hansen (Pres.)
1960	William O. DeWitt (Pres.)
1961–1989	John E. Fetzer (Pres.)
1978–1989	James Campbell (Pres.)
1984–1990	Thomas S. Monaghan (Pres.)
1990–1992	Glenn E. (Bo) Schembechler (Pres.)
1992–	Michael Ilitch (Owner and Chairman)

Kansas City A's (to Oakland)

1955–1959	Arnold Johnson (Pres.)
1960	Parke Carroll (VP)
1961–1967	Charles O. Finley (Pres.)

Kansas City Royals

1969–1993	Ewing Kauffman (Ch. of Bd.)
1993–	David D. Glass (Ch./CEO)

Milwaukee (to St. Louis)

1901	Matthew Killilea

Milwaukee Brewers

1970–	Allan H. "Bud" Selig (Pres./CEO)

Minnesota

1961–1984	Calvin R. Griffith (Chairman/Pres.)
1985–1986	Howard T. Fox, Jr.
1987–1989	Jerry Bell
1985–	Carl Pohlad (owner)

New York

1903–1906	Joseph W. Gordon
1903–1915	Frank J. Farrell and William S. Devery (owners)
1907–1914	Frank J. Farrell
1915–1938	Jacob Ruppert (Pres.)
1939–1944	Edward G. Barrow (Pres./GM)
1945–1947	Leland S. MacPhail, Sr. (Pres./GM/Treas.)
1948–1953	Daniel R. Topping (Pres.)
1954-1966	Daniel R. Topping/Del E. Webb (co-owners)
1966–1973	Michael Burke (Ch. of the Bd./Pres.)
1973–1977	Gabriel H. Paul (Pres.)
1978–1980	Albert L. Rosen (Pres./CEO)
1980–1990	George M. Steinbrenner (Ch. of Bd.)
1990–1991	Robert Nederlander (Man. Gen. Part.)
1992	Daniel McCarthy (Man. Gen. Part.)
1993–	George M. Steinbrenner (Prin. owner)

Oakland

1968–1980	Charles O. Finley (Pres.)
1981–1990	Roy Eisenhardt (Pres.)
1990–1995	Walter J. Haas (Chairman/CEO)
1995-	Steven C. Schott (Owner/Pres.)

Philadelphia (to Kansas City)

1901–1921	Benjamin F. Shibe (Pres.)
1922–1935	Thomas S. Shibe (Pres.)
1936	John D. Shibe
1937–1954	Connie Mack (Pres.)

Seattle Pilots (to Milwaukee)

1969	Dewey Soriano (Pres.)

Seattle Mariners

1977–1979	Danny Kaye and Lester Smith (Man. Gen. Partners)
1980–1983	Daniel F. O'Brien (Pres./CEO)
1981–1989	George L. Argyros (Ch. of Bd./CEO)
1984–1989	Charles G. Armstrong
1990–1991	Jeff Smulyan (Ch. of Bd.)
1992–	John W. Ellis (Ch. of Bd./CEO)

St. Louis (to Baltimore)

1902	Ralph T. Orthwein
1903–1915	Robert L. Hedges
1916–1933	Philip D. Ball (Pres.)
1934–1936	Louis B. Von Weise
1937–1945	Donald L. Barnes (Pres.)
1946–1948	Richard C. Muckerman (Pres.)
1949–1951	William O. DeWitt (Pres.)
1951–1953	William L. Veeck, Jr. (Pres.)

Texas

1972–1974	Robert E. Short (Pres.)
1974	Robert W. Brown, M.D.
1975–1980	Bradford G. Corbett (Pres.)
1980–1987	Eddie Chiles (Owner/Ch. of Bd./CEO)
1984–1990	Michael H. Stone (Pres./COO)
1991–	J. Thomas Schieffer (Pres.)

Toronto

1977–1981	Peter Bavasi (Exec. VP/GM)
1977–1988	R. Howard Webster (Ch. of Bd.)
1989–	Paul Beeston (Pres./CEO)

Washington (to Minnesota)

1901–1903	Frederick Postal
1904	Thomas J. Loftus
1904	Harry B. Lambert
1905–1912	Thomas C. Noyes
1920–1955	Clark C. Griffith (Pres.)
1956–1960	Calvin R. Griffith (Pres.)

Washington

1961–1962	Elwood R. Quesada (Pres.)
1963–1967	James M. Johnston (Ch. of Bd.)
1968	James H. Lemon (Ch. of Bd.)
1969–1971	Robert E. Short (Pres.)

Federal League

League President

1914–1915	James A. Gilmore

Club Presidents

Baltimore

1914–1915	Carrol W. Rasin

Brooklyn

1914–1915	Robert B. Ward

Buffalo

1914	Walter F. Mullen
	William E. Robertson
1915	William E. Robertson

Chicago

1914–1915	Charles A. Weeghman

Indianapolis

1914	J. E. Krause

Kansas City

1914	C. C. Madison
1915	Charles Baird
	Conrad H. Mann

Newark

1915	P. T. Powers
	Harry Sinclair

Pittsburgh

1914	John R. Barbour
1915	Edward W. Gwinner

St. Louis

1914	E. A. Steininger
1915	Lloyd H. Rickart

Appendixes

Rules and Scoring
Dennis Bingham and Thomas R. Heitz

The chronologies presented here trace the evolution of baseball's playing and scoring rules from those governing the first properly organized baseball club (1845) to the present major league clubs (through 1994).

Playing Rules

As a starting point, the rules of the 1845 Knickerbocker Base Ball Club of New York City are provided. During earlier decades, rules had been published for popular bat-and-ball and baserunning games played by eighteenth- and early nineteenth-century youths (indeed, some basic baseball principles can be traced back for centuries), but the codified Knickerbocker rules serve as a direct link to the rules of today. Their rules were the model for the hundreds of organized amateur clubs that sprang up in the 1850s.

Following the 1845 rules is an outline listing the significant rule changes made in the next eleven years. This brief outline illustrates how little the rules had changed in more than a decade.

In 1857, however, several baseball clubs, led by the old Knickerbockers, held a convention with the purpose of changing the rules to make baseball less a mere recreation and more a "scientific and manly" exercise and competition. At this convention, the club delegates greatly expanded, refined, clarified, and polished the rule book. The following year, the baseball clubs held another convention, made some rule changes, and formed themselves into a permanent body—the National Association of Base Ball Players. Although these baseball clubs were composed primarily of amateurs, their rule book became the core of every rule book for every baseball league that followed. The 1857 rules are set forth in their entirety and are followed by changes to the rules under annual headings through 1996.

The work of the Nineteenth Century Committee of the Society for American Baseball Research (SABR) was instrumental in compiling these chronologies.

The first major league, the National Association of Professional Base-Ball Players, was formed in 1871 and used essentially the same rule book as its predecessor. In 1876 the National League dethroned the professional players' association and adopted their rule book, with their amendments to the rules noted under that year's heading.

Rule differences for subsequent major leagues are also listed in the chronology and are noted under the annual heading in which they were introduced, e.g. Union Association (1884) and Players League (1890).

In most cases, the actual text of a new rule or change has been taken verbatim from original sources. However, to reduce verbiage, the references to section numbering and headings, which have varied widely over the years, have been deleted along with other extraneous spacing and punctuation. In many cases, primarily in the early years, the wording has been slightly changed to convey the meaning of the rule more clearly. In a few cases the technical wording of complex rules has been summa-

rized for ease of reading. Researchers requiring precise quotations of rules are advised to consult original sources, e.g., the *Spalding* and *Reach Baseball Guides*.

Individual headings have been added to each of the changes under the annual headings to assist the reader. By consulting the index and headings, readers may follow the evolution of any one particular rule through the years.

The chronology includes practically *all* changes to the playing rules—certainly all those of significance and substance. However, numerous minor changes in wording not affecting meaning, or changes in punctuation and spelling which had no purpose other than grammatical correctness, have been ignored. Also, the chronology includes only those rules and regulations found in the official baseball rule book, not those found in other baseball documents such as league constitutions and the Basic Agreement. Thus rules and subject matter that may have been dropped from the early rule books and inserted in the league's constitution, such as those concerning player eligibility and discipline, may still govern baseball for years later.

In some instances, rule changes, such as those affecting umpires and little-used rules regarding suspended games or batting out of order, have been summarized or simply alluded to in the interests of brevity. If a passage is preceded by the word "Note," it indicates additional information supplied by the compiler. If preceded by the words "casebook note," the passage is an actual note taken from the rule book.

The scoring rules are presented in a separate section of this appendix because of their length and special interest.

Baseball's rules continue to evolve in the twentieth century despite the perception of many that "the game remains pretty much the same as it always has been." The most far-reaching revision of baseball's playing rules came in 1950 when the entire code was virtually rewritten. Additional changes and refinements were added throughout the 1950s, and it is the rules of 1950 for the most part that we use today.

The rules of baseball are commonly considered the means of keeping the game in that delicate balance between offense and defense with neither side enjoying a marked advantage. This balance is the dynamic force of competition, which drives the game and ultimately creates interest and motivation for players and spectators alike.

But changes to the playing rules can also be categorized in terms of response to various social, economic, and technological factors as well as to the need for competitive balance. For example, when the uncouth language of hard-bitten nineteenth-century players became offensive to female rooters, appropriate rules were adopted (in an attempt) to modify player behavior. Likewise, gloves were introduced gradually in the 1870s and 1880s to protect the players' catching hands from injury. However, when glove design clearly departed from the goal of protection and extended to aiding in the catching process, effectively making the glove an extension of the hand, it became necessary to invoke standards for gloves in the rules.

In terms of competitive balance, perhaps the most striking evolution is that of the pitching rules, which have undergone a remarkable transformation from the days of simple underhanded hurling from a boxlike enclosure to today's complex series of physical motions from which almost any deviation may elicit a call of "balk."

In many cases, the introduction of a playing rule followed several years of development on the field of play. Like state and federal legislative bodies, baseball's rule-making authorities are often slow to respond to changing conditions or perhaps justifiably cautious about making such changes before the effects are fully understood. For example, there is no mention of pitching mounds in the playing rules until 1903, when the maximum elevation was fixed at 15 inches. However, pitching mounds were in general use many years prior to 1903 and may have come into vogue as early as the 1880s. The lifting of restrictions on the angle of pitching delivery in 1884 made overhanded throwing legal, and it was not long before the hurlers realized the mechanical advantages of stepping off a short incline as they directed the ball toward the plate. Presumably, by 1903 the lack of uniformity in certain parks had become a problem, and so the rules set a standard.

Another point that should be kept in mind while reading this chronology is that just because a particular rule is "in the book" doesn't necessarily mean that it was (or is) always enforced.

The researcher is advised to scan the Index to Playing Rule Changes prior to consulting the chronology.

Scoring Rules

The chronology presented after that of the playing rules traces the evolution of professional baseball's scoring rules from 1877 through 1996.

The Knickerbockers kept score in the 1840s and, in the decades that followed, other clubs, sportswriters, and fans kept score and compiled statistics. The scoring rules of 1877, however, are presented as a starting point, in their entirety, because they are the first official scoring rules included in the rule book. Thereafter changes to the scoring rules are noted under annual headings.

In most cases, as with the playing rules, the actual text of a new scoring rule or change has been taken verbatim from original sources.

The scoring rules are at the heart of baseball's accountability to itself and to the millions of fans who follow the game day by day. Through the use of these rules the daily performance of players and teams is described and measured in a uniform and meaningful way. Baseball is unique in publishing the performance records of its key personnel, and in so doing it subjects the individual, the team, and its management to the scrutiny and judgment of anyone who has the price of a daily newspaper.

Like the playing rules, they have evolved from a rather primitive code to a complex, legalistic document. The scoring rules have been transformed over the decades from the simple recording of hits, outs, errors, and assists in the 1870s into a highly technical set of rules and guidelines used to record almost every significant offensive and defensive event that transpires on the field of play.

Although the collection of such statistics as "caught stealing" did not commence until later years, still baseball's major performance records can be traced in an unbroken skein well back into the nineteenth century. As a result, no other professional sport can claim such a rich resource of historical statistics.

The researcher is advised to scan the Index to Scoring Rule Changes prior to consulting the chronology.

Playing Rules for 1845

1. Members must strictly observe the time agreed upon for exercise, and be punctual in their attendance.

2. When assembled for exercise, the President, or in his absence the Vice-President, shall appoint an Umpire, who shall keep the game in a book provided for that purpose, and note all violations of the By-Laws and Rules during the time of exercise.

3. The presiding officer shall designate two members as Captains, who shall retire and make the match to be played, observing at the same time that the players put opposite to each other should be as nearly equal as possible; the choice of sides to be then tossed for, and the first in hand to be decided in like manner.

4. The bases shall be from "home" to second base, forty-two paces; from first to third base, forty-two paces, equidistant.

5. No stump match shall be played on a regular day of exercise.

6. If there should not be a sufficient number of members of the Club present at the time agreed upon to commence exercise, gentlemen not members may be chosen in to make up the match, which shall not be broken up to take in members that may afterwards appear; but, in all cases, members shall have the preference, when present, at the making of a match.

7. If members appear after the game is commenced they may be chosen in if mutually agreed upon.

8. The game to consist of twenty-one counts, or aces; but at the conclusion an equal number of hands must be played.

9. The ball must be pitched, and not thrown, for the bat.

10. A ball knocked out of the field, or outside the range of the first or third base, is foul.

11. Three balls being struck at and missed and the last one caught, is a hand out; if not caught is considered fair, and the striker bound to run.

12. If a ball be struck, or tipped, and caught, either flying or on the first bound, it is a hand out.

13. A player running the bases shall be out, if the ball is in the hands of an adversary on the base, or the runner is touched with it before he makes his base; it being understood, however, that in no instance is a ball to be thrown at him.

14. A player running who shall prevent an adversary from catching or getting the ball before making his base, is a hand out.

15. Three hands out, all out.

16. Players must take their strike in regular turn.

17. All disputes and differences relative to the game, to be decided by the Umpire, from which there is no appeal.

18. No ace or base can be made on a foul strike.

19. A runner cannot be put out in making one base, when a balk is made by the pitcher.

20. But one base allowed when a ball bounds out of the field when struck.

Rule Changes 1846–1856

In 1848 a rule was amended declaring that the batter-runner was out if the ball was held on first base before he reached it; previously, the rule applied the situation to *all* bases. By 1852, the captains of each club had been given the authority to position each player in the field, which could not be changed without their consent, and that each club member would take turns as umpire.

The 1854 rule book included the following: "When a fair ball is struck and the striker not put out, the first base must be vacated as well as the next base or bases if similarly occupied; players may be put out, under these circumstances, in the same manner as when running to first base." In other words, the force out had been introduced. Also in 1854, it was specified that the pitcher was to be "not less than 15 paces" from home plate.

The dimensions of the ball had also been established—from 5½ to 6 ounces in weight and from 2¾ to 3½ inches in diameter. Rule books also included the description of the bat as being round and from 2½ to 3 inches in diameter.

A player was also now called out if he *intentionally* prevented an opponent from catching the ball. Rules preventing obstruction had also been added with the case of his being prevented by their occupation by an adversary, he shall be entitled to that base. It had also been established that the game would be controlled by two umpires, and a referee (who would make the final ruling should the two umpires disagree).

It should be remembered that, during this period, baseball clubs played under their own individual rule books which may have differed on various points from other clubs. It's probable that some clubs of this day played under rules that would later be adopted into the mainstream rule book but, alas, had never been put into written form and are now lost to history.

Playing Rules for 1857

Section 1. Ball. The ball must weigh not less than 6 nor more than 6¼ ounces avoirdupois. It must measure not less than 10 nor more than 10¼ inches in circumference. It must be composed of India rubber and yarn, and covered with leather. It shall be furnished by the challenging club, and become the property of the winning club as a trophy of victory.

Section 2. Bat. The bat must be round and must not exceed 2½ half inches in diameter in the thickest part. It must be made of wood and may be of any length to suit the striker.

Section 3. Bases. The bases must be four in number, placed at equal distances from each other, and securely fastened upon the four corners of a square whose sides are respectively thirty yards. They must be so constructed as to be distinctly seen by the umpires and referee, and must cover a space equal to one square foot of surface. The first, second, and third bases shall be canvas bags, painted white, and filled with sand or sawdust; the home base and pitcher's points to be each marked with a flat circular iron plate, painted or enameled white.

Section 4. Bases/Position. The base from which the ball is struck shall be designated the home base and must be directly opposite the second base; the first base must always be that upon the right hand, and the third base that upon the left hand side of the striker when occupying his position at the home base.

Section 5. Pitcher/Position. The pitcher's position shall be designated by a line four yards in length, drawn at right angles to a line from home to the second base, having its center upon that line, at a fixed iron plate placed at a point 15 yards distant from the home base.

Section 6. Pitcher/Delivery. The ball must be pitched, not jerked or thrown, to the bat; and whenever the pitcher draws back his hand, with the apparent purpose or pretension to deliver the ball, he shall so deliver it. The pitcher must deliver the ball as near as possible over the center of the home base, and must have neither foot in advance of the line at the time of delivering the ball; and if he fails in either of these particulars, then it shall be declared a balk.

Section 7. Balk. When a balk is made by the pitcher, every player running the bases is entitled to one base without being put out.

Section 8. Fair/Foul Balls. If the ball, from a stroke of the bat, is caught behind the range of home and the first base or home and the third base, without having touched the ground, or first touches the ground behind those bases, it shall be termed foul and must be so declared by the umpire unasked. If the ball first touches the ground, or is caught without having touched the ground, either upon or in front of the range of those bases, it shall be considered fair.

Section 9. Run Scored. A player making the home base shall be entitled to score one run.

Section 10. Strikeout. If three balls are struck at and missed, and the last one is not caught either flying or upon the first bound, it shall be considered fair and the striker must attempt to make his run.

Section 11. Batter/Caught Foul. The striker is out if a foul ball is caught, either before touching the ground or upon the first bound;

Section 12. Strikeout. Or if three balls are struck at and missed, and the last is caught either before touching the ground or upon the first bound;

Section 13. Batter/Caught Fair Fly. Or if a fair ball is struck, and the ball is caught either without having touched the ground or upon the first bound;

Section 14. Batter/Out at First. Or if a fair ball is struck, and the ball is held by an adversary on the first base before the striker touches that base;

Section 15. Batter/Tagged. Or if, at any time, he is touched by the ball while in play in the hands of an adversary, without some part of his person being on a base.

Section 16. Runner/Advancing. No ace nor base can be made upon a foul ball, nor when a fair ball has been caught without having touched the ground; and the ball shall, in both instances, be considered dead and not in play until it shall first have been settled in the hands of the pitcher. When a fair ball has been caught without having touched the ground, the players running the bases shall have the privilege of returning to them.

Section 17. Batter/Position. Players must stand on a line drawn through the center of the home base, not exceeding in length three feet from either side thereof, and such line shall be parallel with the line occupied by the pitcher. They shall strike in regular rotation and, after the first inning is played, the turn commences with the player who stands on the list next to the one who lost the third hand.

Section 18. Runner/Forced. Players must take their bases in the order of striking; and when a fair ball is struck, and not caught flying nor on the first bound, the first base must be vacated, as also the second and third bases if they are occupied at the same time. Players may be put out upon any base, under these circumstances, in the same manner as the striker when running to the first base.

Section 19. Runner/Out of Baseline. Players running the bases must, as far as possible, keep upon the direct line between the bases; and should any player run three feet out of this line, for the purpose of avoiding the ball in the hands of an adversary, he shall be declared out.

Section 20. Interference/Offensive. Any player who shall intentionally prevent an adversary from catching or fielding the ball, shall be declared out.

Section 21. Obstruction. If a player is prevented from making a base by the intentional obstruction of an adversary, he shall be entitled to that base and not be put out.

Section 22. Fielder/Illegal Act. If any adversary stops the ball with his hat or cap, or takes it from the hands of a party not engaged in the game, no player can be put out unless the ball shall first have been settled in the hands of the pitcher.

Section 23. Catch. If a ball, from the strike of a bat, is held under any other circumstances than as enumerated in Section 22, and without having touched the ground more than once, the striker is out.

Section 24. Run Scored. If two hands are already out, no player running home at the time a ball is struck can make an ace if the striker is put out.

Section 25. Inning. An inning must be concluded at the time the third hand is put out.

Section 26. Game. The game shall consist of nine innings to each side, when, should the number of runs be equal, the innings shall be continued until a majority of runs, upon an equal number of innings shall be declared, which shall conclude the game.

Section 27. Player/Eligible, Substitute, Positions. In playing all matches, nine players from each club shall constitute a full field, and they must have been regular members of the club which they represent, for thirty days prior to the match. No changes or substitution shall be made after the game has been commenced, unless for reason of illness or injury. Positions of players shall be determined by captains previously appointed for that purpose by the respective clubs.

Section 28. Player/Eligible. Any player holding membership in more than one club at the same time shall not be permitted to play in the matches of either club.

Section 29. Umpire/Duties. The umpires in all matches shall take care that the regulations respecting the ball, bats, bases, and the pitcher's and striker's positions are strictly observed. They shall be the judge of fair and unfair play, and shall determine all differences which may occur during the game. They shall take especial care to declare all fair balls and balks immediately on their occurrence. They shall together select a referee from whose decision—in case of a disagreement between them—there shall be no appeal.

Section 30. Gambling/Substitute. No person engaged in a match, either as umpire, referee, or player, shall be directly or indirectly interested in any bet upon the game. Neither umpire, referee, nor player shall be changed during a match, unless with the consent of both parties, except for a violation of this law, and except as provided in Section 27, and then the referee may dismiss any transgressor.

Section 31. Game/Legal. The umpires and referee in any match shall determine when play shall be suspended; and if the game cannot be concluded, it shall be decided by the last even innings, provided five innings have been played, and the party having the greatest number of runs shall be declared the winner.

Section 32. Ground Rules. Clubs may adopt such rules respecting balls knocked beyond or outside the bounds of the field, as the circumstances of the ground may demand, and these rules shall govern all matches played upon the ground, provided that they are distinctly made known to every player and umpire, and the referee, previous to the commencement of the game.

Section 33. Interference. No person shall be permitted to approach or to speak with the referee, umpires, or players, or in any manner to interrupt or interfere during the progress of the game, unless by special request of the umpires or referee.

Section 34. Umpire. No person shall be permitted to act as umpire or referee in any match, unless he shall be a member of a base ball club governed by these rules.

Section 35. Game/Start, Forfeit. Whenever a match shall have been determined upon between two clubs, play shall be called at the exact hour appointed; and should either party fail to produce their players within fifteen minutes thereafter, the party so failing shall admit a defeat.

Chronology of Rule Changes 1858-1996

1858

Pitcher/Delivery   The pitcher must deliver the ball as near as possible over the center of the plate and for the striker.

Player/Eligible   No person who may be in arrears to any club he may have belonged to previous to the one he is then a member of shall be competent to play in a match unless such arrears are paid.

Runner/Returning   Players running the bases shall return to them following foul balls and fair balls caught on the fly, and shall not be put out in so running unless the ball has been first pitched to the striker.

Strike Zone   Should a striker stand at the bat without striking at good balls repeatedly pitched to him, for the purpose of delaying the game or of giving advantage to a player, the umpire, after warning him, shall call one strike; and if he persists in such action, two and three strikes. When three strikes are called, he shall be subject to the same rules as if he had struck at the three balls.

Umpire   The umpire in all matches shall take care that the regulations respecting the ball, bats, bases, and the pitcher's and striker's positions are strictly observed. He shall keep a record of the game in a book prepared for the purpose. He shall be the judge of fair and unfair play, and shall determine all disputes and differences which may occur during the game. He shall take especial care to declare all foul balls and balks immediately upon occurrence, unasked, and in a district and audible manner.

Note: All references to a "referee" and "umpires" in the plural sense have been deleted. The game is now under control of a single umpire, rather than a tribunal.

Umpire/Scorer   In all matches, the umpire shall be selected by the captains of the respective sides, and shall perform all duties enumerated in Section 28, except recording the game, which shall be done by two scorers, appointed by each of the contending clubs.

Note: "Section 28" is the paragraph under the heading "Umpire" above. Also, the rules prohibiting gambling and requiring participants to be members of a baseball club now applied to scorers as well as umpires and players.

1859

Ball   The ball must weigh 5¾ to 6 ounces and measure 9¾ to 10 inches in circumference.

Player/Eligible   No person who receives compensation for his services as a player shall be competent to play in any match.

Game/Number   Every match shall be decided by a single game.

Note: In previous years, a series of games often determined the winner of a "match."

Runner/Advancing   Caught fly balls which do not touch the ground are no longer considered dead balls.

Note: With this amendment it was understood that runners, following caught fly balls, could now advance after returning to their original base. This, however, was not as yet written into the rules.

1860

Game/Number   Every match shall be decided by a single game unless otherwise mutually agreed upon by the contesting clubs.

Runner/Returning   Runners, returning to their bases following foul balls and caught fly balls not touching the ground, may be put out in the same manner as the batter when running to first base.

Note: At the 1857 meeting of baseball clubs, the progressive Knickerbockers proposed that in order to retire the batter the ball must be caught on the fly and not on one bounce. It became a hotly debated topic during the next several conventions but, although it gained more support each year, the "fly rule" continued to be defeated when put to a vote. In 1860, however, the "fly game" was allowed if both contesting clubs agreed. This concession was not officially written into the rule book.

1861

Ball   The ball must weigh 5½ to 5¾ ounces and measure 9½ to 9¾ inches in circumference.

Foul Ball   If the ball, from the stroke of the bat, first touches the ground, the person of a player, or any object behind the range of home and first or home and third base, it shall be a foul ball.

Grounds   A line connecting home and first base and home and third base shall be marked by chalk, or other suitable material, so as to be distinctly seen by the umpire.

Runner   Players running the bases must make them in the following order: first, second, third, and home, and in returning must reverse this order.

Umpire   The umpire, before leaving the grounds, must declare the winning club and record his decision in the scorebooks of the two clubs.

1862

There were no changes to the playing rules this year.

1863

Base on Balls When three "balls" have been called, the striker is entitled to first base, and each player occupying a base is entitled to one base without being put out.

Note: In actuality it took more than three balls to be awarded first base; see 1863, *Strike Zone*.

Pitcher/Delivery If the pitcher, at the time of delivery, has either foot off the ground or in advance of the front line of his position, it shall be declared a balk.

Pitcher/Position The pitcher's position shall be two lines, each twelve feet in length, with the front line forty-five feet and the back line forty-eight feet distant from home base. Both pitcher's lines are to be marked by a flat, circular iron plate.

Note: This introduces the pitcher's box (a "box" with only two lines), which replaces the single twelve-foot line.

Runner/Advancing Runners, after returning to their respective bases, may advance immediately after a fair fly ball has been settled in the hands of a fielder.

Note: This put into words what had been understood for the past four years; see 1859 rule.

Runner/Bases Each runner must touch each base in making the circuit.

Note: Runners were previously allowed to go around or near the bases.

Strike Zone Should the pitcher repeatedly fail to deliver "fair" balls, for the purpose of delaying the game or for any cause, the umpire, after warning him, shall call one "ball"; and if the pitcher persists, two and three balls.

1864

There were no changes to the playing rules this year.

1865

Batter/Caught Foul A batted ball in foul territory must be caught on the fly to be declared an out.

Note: The "fly game" has been adopted; fair balls caught on one bounce are no longer outs.

Interference/Spectator If a ball is stopped by any person not engaged in the game, no player may be put out unless the ball has first been settled in the hands of the pitcher.

Umpire The umpire is no longer responsible for keeping a record of the game in the scorebook.

Note: This amendment corrects a contradiction in earlier rule books in which one rule held the umpire responsible for keeping score and another rule instructed the umpire not to perform the duty.

1866

Bases First, second, and third bases shall be canvas bags, painted white and filled with some soft material.

Game/Legal Any game played in contravention of National Association rules shall be considered null and void and shall not be counted in the list of games won or lost; unless a game is delayed by rain beyond the appointed start. Any game may be put off by mutual consent of the two clubs. No game shall be commenced in the rain.

Game/Number Every game shall be decided by the best two games out of three, unless a single game is mutually agreed upon by the two clubs.

Pitcher/Position The back line of the pitcher's box is moved back one foot, increasing the depth to 4 feet while remaining 12 feet in width.

1867

Batter/Position The batter, when in the act of striking, shall not step forward or backward but must stand on the three-foot line drawn through the center of home base.

Batter-Runner The batter shall be considered a baserunner as soon as he hits a fair ball.

Dead Ball Any pitch on which a "balk" or "ball" has been called is considered a dead ball, and the batter cannot be put out if he hits such a ball. Dead balls are returned to play when the ball has been settled in the hands of the pitcher while he stands within the pitcher's box.

Forfeited Game A club failing to produce their players within thirty minutes of the start of the game shall admit a defeat. The opposing club receives a win and is entitled to nine runs, and the game is counted in the list of games played. The game shall not be forfeited if the club fails to play because of the recent death of one of its members and there hasn't been sufficient time to notify the opposing club.

Pitcher/Delivery The pitcher must deliver the ball as near as possible over the center of home base and fairly for the striker.

The ball must be pitched, not jerked or thrown, to the bat. The ball shall be considered jerked if the pitcher's arm touches his person when the arm is swung forward to deliver the ball; and it is a throw if the arm is bent at the elbow at an angle from the body or horizontally from the shoulder when the arm is swung forward in delivery. A pitched ball is one delivered with arm straight and swinging perpendicularly and free from the body.

Note: The word *perpendicular* was used in the rule but the word *parallel* was intended. This error would be repeated for several years.

Pitcher/Position The pitcher's box is reduced in size to six feet in width and four feet in length.

Player/Eligible All players who play baseball for money, place, or emolument are regarded as professional players and shall not take part in any game. Any club giving compensation to a player or having knowledge that one of their players is playing for compensation shall be expelled from the National Association. Any club engaging in a game with an expelled club shall also forfeit membership.

Run Scored If there are two outs, no player can score a run if the batter is put out by a legal catch, forced between home and first base, or the ball is held by an adversary on first base before the batter reaches it.

Strikeout The batter is out if three balls are swung at and missed and the last one is caught either on the fly or on the first bound; provided the pitches are not those on which "balks" or "balls" have been called, or if the batter swings for the purpose of willfully striking out.

Strike Zone All pitches striking the ground in front of home base, over the head of the batter, or to the side opposite to that which the batter swings from, shall be considered unfair "balls."

Substitute An umpire, scorer, or player shall not be changed during a game except for reason of illness or injury and with the consent of both clubs; or when the umpire dismisses a transgressor for violation of the rules.

Umpire The umpire must declare when a player is out and in what position and manner.

Note: For example, if a batter is out on a caught fly to center, the umpire must yell, "Striker is out on the fly by the center fielder." This rule lasted only one year.

1868

Ball The ball must weigh from 5 to 5¼ ounces and measure from 9¼ to 9½ inches in circumference.

The challenging club must furnish a ball with the size, weight, and maker's name on it.

Bases The base-bag shall be considered the base and not the part to which it is or should be fastened.

Note: This rule was dropped in 1876.

The home base and pitcher's points must be flat plates, painted white.

Bat The bat shall not exceed forty inches in length.

Batter/Position The batter, when about to strike the ball, must stand astride the three-foot line which is drawn through the center of home base and parallel with the front line of the pitcher's box.

The batter must not take any backward step when striking at the ball. The penalty is the calling of "foul strike," and when three such strikes are called, the batter is out. The batter is also out if he hits such a "strike" and the ball is caught, either fair or foul. No base may be run, but the baserunner is allowed to return to his base without being put out.

Catch If a fair ball is held by a fielder before touching the ground after it has rebounded from the hands or person of another player, it shall be considered a catch. A foul ball, if similarly held but touches the ground once, is also a catch.

Dead Ball No base may be run or player put out on a dead ball. If the batter hits a pitch on which a "balk" or "ball" has been called, no "strike" or foul ball shall be called, or a player put out; except bases may be taken on balks and calls of ball three.

Forfeited Game Any club failing to take their positions within five minutes after the umpire calls "play" shall forfeit the game.

Game/Rain No game shall be started when rain is falling and no game shall be continued when rain has fallen for five minutes.

Game/Scheduled When a challenge has been accepted for a series of games, each of the three games must be played at least within fifteen days of the previous game. The first game is played on the grounds of the challenger, the second game on the grounds of the challenged, and the third game, if necessary, on grounds mutually agreed upon. When a first-nine match is to be played, the clubs must play their recognized first nine, as far as practicable.

Note: This rule was dropped the next season.

Game/"Time" When the umpire calls "play," the game must begin at once. When the umpire calls "time," play shall be suspended until he calls "play" again. When the umpire "calls" a game, it shall end, but when he merely suspends play for any stated period, it may be resumed at the point at which it was suspended, provided it does not extend to the next day.

Obstruction If a runner is prevented from making a base by the intentional obstruction of an adversary, he shall be entitled to that base and not be put out. Any obstruction that could readily have been avoided shall be considered intentional.

Pitcher/Delivery The pitcher is no longer required to keep both feet on the ground when delivering the ball.

Player Every player taking part in a regular match game, no matter how many innings have been played, shall be, in the meaning of these rules, considered a member of the club with which he plays.

Runner/Bases If a runner fails to touch each base, he shall be declared out unless he returns to the base before the ball is held on it.

Run Scored When there are two outs, no runner may score if the batter is put out.

Substitute No player may be substituted after the third inning except in cases of illness and injury.

Umpire/Decisions Only the captain of each club is allowed to appeal for the reversal of a decision by the umpire. No decision by the umpire shall be reversed by the testimony of any player; and no decision whatever shall be reversed except for a palpable infringement of the rules, and then only on an appeal by the captain.

Time See *Game/Time*

Umpire/Scorer The umpire shall require that the game be recorded by a scorer for each of the contesting clubs.

Note: This rule was dropped from the rule book in 1874.

1869

Ball In the first and third games of a series the ball shall be furnished by the challenging club, and in the second game by the challenged club.

Base on Balls When the batter is awarded first base after three called balls, no other runner shall take a base unless he is obliged to vacate the base he occupies.

Bat The bat shall not exceed forty-two inches in length.

Batter/Fails to Bat Any player failing to take his turn at bat, unless for reason of illness or injury or by consent of the opposing captain, shall be declared out.

Note: In 1870, the rule was amended: Any player failing to bat "after the umpire has called for the striker . . . shall be declared out."

Batter/Position When in the act of striking at the ball, the batsman is required to stand astride the batter's line.

Catch It is not a catch if the ball is caught after touching any object [fence, building, tree] other than a player, even if the ball does not touch the ground.

Club/Eligible Any club willfully infringing any rule shall be suspended for a period not to exceed one year for the first offense, and expulsion from membership for the second offense, after trial by the judiciary committee.

Forfeited Game No game shall be forfeited because of the failure of the umpire to discharge his duties or for failing to declare the winning club of a match.

There must be at least a two-day notice for postponement of a game because of the death of a club member or the club is liable to forfeit.

Game/Drawn If the score is tied at the end of nine innings, the captains may mutually agree to consider the game a draw. In case of no such agreement, the club refusing to continue play shall forfeit the ball.

Game/Winner If the game cannot be continued, it shall be decided by the score of the last equal innings and the club having the greater number of runs is the winner; unless one club has completed their inning and the other club has exceeded their opponent's score in their uncompleted inning, in which case the club with the higher score is the winner. But no game shall be considered as played unless five innings on each side have been completed.

Pitcher/Delivery When about to deliver the ball or at the actual time of delivery, the pitcher cannot have either foot outside the pitcher's box.

Pitcher/Position The pitcher's box is enlarged to a six-foot square.

Player/Eligible Players must not have been members of any other National Association club (college clubs excepted) for sixty days immediately prior to the game.

All players who play baseball for money or who at any time receive compensation for their services as players shall be considered professional players; and all others shall be regarded as amateur players.

Note: This rule officially recognized two distinct classes of players—professional and amateur—and permitted the participation of professional players.

Runner/Forced   No baserunner shall be forced to vacate a base unless as provided in these rules.

Note: This amendment prevented a runner, not forced to vacate his own base, from forcing another to vacate his base. For example, if a runner attempts to steal third base, changes his mind before reaching third, and returns to second base to find the runner from first now standing on the bag, the original runner still has the right to the base.

Run Scored   When there are two outs, no runner may score a run if the batter or player running the bases is put out before touching first base.

Strike Zone   Balls and strikes may not be called unless there has first been issued a warning and they may not be called until the pitch has crossed the plate. All "balls" *must* be called by the umpire after the pitcher has been warned of the penalty. One warning for each batter shall suffice.

Substitute/Runner   No player shall be allowed to have a substitute run the bases for him except in cases of illness or injury.

1870

Ball   The challenged club must supply the means of ascertaining the size and weight of the ball furnished by the other club.

Note: This rule was dropped in 1871 and replaced with the previous rule requiring the challenging club to furnish a ball on which its size, weight, and the name of the manufacturer is stamped.

Base on Balls   Any player awarded a base on balls is allowed to advance, at his own risk, beyond the base awarded him.

Note: This rule was inexplicably left out of the 1871 rule book but was back in 1872.

Dead Ball   Called "balls" not hit by the batter are no longer dead balls, and any base can be run or player put out on such pitches.

Fair Ball   If the ball, from the stroke of the bat, first touches the ground, the person of a player or any other object, either upon or in front of the foul lines, it shall be declared a fair ball.

Forfeited Game   All games in which any rule is infringed shall be considered forfeited games and shall be recorded as games won by a score of 9 to 0 against the club infringing the rules.

No forfeit shall be declared if a club fails to play a game because of the recent death of one of its members.

Note: The requirement of two days notice has been dropped.

Grounds   The lines of the batter's and pitcher's positions must be marked with chalk or other suitable material so as to be distinctly seen by the umpire.

Runner/Forced   The moment the player running to first base is out, other baserunners previously forced to vacate their bases shall cease to be forced and may return to their bases.

Note: In 1872 the rule was amended and clarified that runners could still be put out in returning to their base.

Strike Zone   The umpire no longer issues a warning before calling a pitch, but "balls" and "strikes" may not be called on the first pitch delivered.

All pitches which are not within the fair reach of the striker, such as pitches over the striker's head, on the ground in front of home base, to the side opposite to that the batsman strikes from, or which hit the striker while he is standing in his proper

position, are considered unfair "balls" and must be called whenever delivered (except for the first pitch). (See also *Dead Ball*)

Umpire/Decisions   No decision given by the umpire shall be reversed by the testimony of any player, and the umpire shall not be guided in his decisions by any such testimony.

1871

The rule book is adopted by the National Association of Professional Base-Ball Players.

Ball   The ball must weigh from 5 to 5¼ ounces and must measure exactly 9¼ inches in circumference.

Batter/Overrunning First   A baserunner touching and overrunning first base shall be allowed to return at once to the base without being put out, provided he does not attempt to make second base.

Batter/Position   The batter must stand at least one foot from home base and astride the three-foot line drawn through the center of home base. When striking at the ball, he may take a forward step but must keep one foot behind the line.

Dead Ball   It is a dead ball whenever a pitch touches the umpire, or is accidentally stopped by him.

Game/Legal   Under no circumstances shall a game be considered played unless five innings have been completed. Should darkness or rain prevent the continuing of the game before the end of the fifth inning, the umpire shall declare "no game."

Note: This made clearer what had long been understood by most.

Grounds   No fence may be erected within ninety feet of home base, unless the fence marks the boundary line of the field. Baserunners are entitled to one base whenever the ball passes the catcher and touches a fence located closer than ninety feet behind home base.

Pitcher/Delivery   The penalty for pitches thrown, jerked, or delivered other than with a straight arm swinging perpendicular [parallel] to the body shall be the calling of a "ball." If, after a warning by the umpire, three men are awarded first base in one inning on such called balls, the game shall be declared a forfeit.

Player/Eligible   Players who have been constitutionally expelled from another club for dishonorable conduct shall not be permitted to play in any game during the year they were expelled.

Player/Position   The fielders may take any position in the field their captain may choose to assign them.

Note: This rule made it clear that the captains could position their players anywhere in the field they wished, including foul territory. The rule, with an obvious omission, was rectified in 1874 with the added phrase, "with the exception of the pitcher, who must occupy his appointed position."

Runner/Advancing   Baserunners, on caught fly balls, may advance after they return to their original base after the ball has been settled momentarily in the hands of the pitcher. Baserunners shall not be entitled to any base touched after a fair fly ball has been hit and prior to the catch being made.

Runner/Fielder   When a fielder, holding the ball, tags a runner who is off a base but the ball is knocked out of his hand by the runner, the runner is still out.

Strike Zone   The batter is allowed to call for either a "high" or "low" pitch, and the pitcher must deliver the ball as required. A "high" ball is one pitched between the waist and the shoulder of the batter; a "low" ball is one pitched between the knee and the waist. Should the batter refuse to swing at balls pitched over the home base and within the specified reach of the bat, it shall be a called "strike." All pitches over the home base that are between the batter's knee and shoulder are considered "fair" pitches.

No strike shall be called when the pitch is struck at for the purpose of willfully striking out.

Note: This sentence was deleted from the rules in 1874.

No strike shall be called on the first pitch delivered unless the batter swings at the pitch.

Note: This one was dropped in 1875.

Substitute/Runner   No player shall be allowed to have a substitute run the bases for him, except for illness or injury, unless by special consent of the opposing captain.

Umpire   See *Dead Ball*

1872

Ball   The ball must weigh from 5 to 5¼ ounces and measure from 9 to 9¼ inches in circumference.

Note: These are the dimensions of today's ball.

The ball shall contain one ounce of vulcanized rubber in mold form.

If the ball becomes ripped, out of shape, or, in the umpire's opinion, unfit for play, the umpire shall call for a new ball at the end of a complete inning.

Bases   Home base shall be made of white marble or stone and fixed in the ground so as to be even with the surface.

Bat   A batter shall be privileged to use his own private bat exclusively. No player of the opposing club shall have any claim to the use of the bat except by consent of the owner.

Note: This rule was dropped in 1874.

Batter/Illegal Act   The batter is out if he willfully "balks" [interferes with] the catcher.

Batter/Overrunning First   A runner may overrun first base without being put out if, after touching first, he runs straight down the line or to the right of the bag. Should he turn to the left or attempt to make second base, he shall be at risk of being put out.

Batter/Position   When striking at the ball, the batter is allowed to make a backward step as well as a forward step as long as he keeps one foot on either side of the line.

Coach   The umpire shall require members of the side at bat to remain a reasonable distance (at least fifteen feet) from the foul lines while directing the movements of baserunners to prevent the interference of fielders. If a club persists in infringing this rule, the umpire shall declare a forfeit.

Dead Balls   Foul balls are dead and are not in play until the ball has been settled in the hands of the pitcher, no matter in what part of the field the pitcher may happen to be.

Forfeited Game   It is not a forfeit if a club fails to play because of the death of a club member or because of an unavoidable accident.

Note: This rule was dropped in 1876. See also *Coach*

Foul Ball   (See *Dead Ball* and *Umpire/Duties*)

Game/Drawn   Clubs are no longer allowed to mutually agree to call a game a draw. Drawn games may only be declared if, after five or more innings, the game is prevented from being continued because of darkness, rain, or other cause, and the score is equal on the even innings played.

Game/Rain   Should rain begin to fall during a game, the umpire must promptly note the time and should the rain continue to fall for five minutes, the umpire shall suspend play and the game shall not continue until, in the umpire's opinion, the ground is fit for fair fielding.

Interference/Offensive   Any player who designedly [*willfully*

and *intentionally* are used in subsequent years] lets the ball hit him or kicks the ball while at bat or running the bases, thus preventing an opponent from holding or fielding the ball, shall be declared out. Any baserunner who, in any way, prevents a fielder from catching a batted fly ball, fair or foul, shall be called out. (See also *Batter/Illegal Act*)

Pitcher/Delivery   The pitcher must deliver the ball while within the lines of his position and must remain within them until the ball has left his hand. He shall not make any motion to deliver the ball while outside the box.

Whenever the pitcher delivers the pitch with an overhand or roundarm throw, the umpire shall call a "foul balk." Should the pitcher persist in such action, the umpire, after warning him of the penalty, shall declare the game forfeited. Baserunners are awarded one base on "foul balks" as on any other balk.

Note: This rule legalized the jerk, wrist snap, and bent-elbow deliveries and, thus, the curveball. It was now legal for the pitcher to snap his wrist as long as he kept his hand, while in the forward motion, below the hip.

Pitcher/Position   In addition to the iron plates marking the center of the two pitcher lines, iron plates must be placed at each end of the front line of the pitcher's box.

Player/Eligible   Any player who has willfully broken a written engagement to a club shall not be eligible to play in any game during the year the engagement was made. No engagement shall be considered binding unless made in writing and signed by at least two witnesses. This rule shall be binding unless rescinded by the judiciary committee.

Strike Zone   All pitches that come within one foot of the batter shall be called "balls."

All pitches that are sent in over home base at the height called for by the batter and are not delivered with an overhand throw or round-arm delivery as in cricket are "fair" pitches. Should the batter fail to call either a "high" or "low" pitch, no "ball" shall be called for "fair" pitches.

A "low" ball is a pitch between the waist of the batter and one foot from the ground.

Substitute/Runner   No player shall be allowed a substitute in running the bases, except for illness or injury, unless by special consent of the opposing captain; and in such case the captain shall select the player to run as substitute.

Umpire/Duties   The umpire is required to call all foul balls, while the ball is still in the air, as soon as he sees the ball is falling in foul territory.

Umpire/Replacing   The umpire shall not be changed during the game, unless with the consent of both captains, except for illness or injury or for violation of the rules.

1873

Interference/Spectator   If a ball is stopped in any way by a person not engaged in the game, no player can be put out until the ball has been first settled in the hands of the pitcher while he stands within the lines of his position.

Fielder/Illegal Act   If a fielder stops the ball with his hat or cap, no player can be put out and each baserunner shall be entitled to one base.

1874

Ball   The yarn used in the composition of the ball must be woolen.

The visiting club furnishes the ball for a series of games; the home team when only a single game is played.

Base   Home base must have one corner facing the pitcher's position.

Base on Balls   Note: In 1874 there were two classifications of base on balls. See explanation under *Strike Zone*.

Bat   The bat must be made wholly of wood.

Note: This made it clear that the bat must be made entirely of wood. Any metal or other material on it renders it illegal.

Batter/Fails to Bat   Any batter refusing to bat within three minutes after the umpire has called for him shall be declared out.

Batter/Position   The batter's position shall be a space on either side of home base, six feet long by three feet wide, which extends three feet in front and three feet behind the line drawn through the center of home base, and its nearest line one foot from home base. Batters must stand within this position when in the act of striking the ball.

Note: This introduces the batter's box.

Batter/Runner   When the batsman has fairly struck a fair ball, he shall vacate his position and is considered a baserunner until he is put out or scores his run.

Runner/Overrunning First   The batter may overrun first base without risk of being put out provided he makes no attempt to run to second base and returns at once to first base.

Batting Order   The batsmen must take their positions in the order in which they are named on the scorebook.

Any batsman failing to take his position in the order of striking, unless by reason of illness or injury or by consent of the opposing captain, shall be declared out, unless the error is discovered before a fair ball has been hit or the batter is put out.

Catch   Should the umpire be unable to see whether a catch has been fairly made, he shall be privileged to appeal to the bystanders and render his decision according to the fairest testimony at command.

Coach/Offensive Team   The umpire shall require members of the batting side, who are not at bat or running the bases, to keep at a distance of at least fifty feet from the foul lines, or farther if the umpire desires. The captain and one assistant only are permitted to approach the foul lines, and not nearer than fifteen feet, to coach baserunners. If a club persists in infringing this rule, the umpire shall declare a forfeit.

Dead Ball   All pitches that touch the striker's bat without being swung at, or touch the batter while he is standing in his box, or which hit the umpire, shall be considered dead balls. No base shall be run or run scored on such balls. Pitches that strike the umpire are not dead balls unless the ball passes the catcher.

Should the batter swing at or hit any pitch on which a "ball" has been called, the umpire shall disregard his call and render his decision on the swing or hit made. It is not a dead ball.

Fielder/Illegal Act   Should any fielder stop the ball with his hat, cap, or any other part of his dress, the umpire shall call "dead ball" and the ball shall not be in play again until the umpire calls "ball in play." Baserunners are entitled to the base they were running for.

Forfeited Game   Any game in which the umpire declares any section of these rules to have been willfully violated, he shall at once declare the game a forfeit.

Foul Ball   See *Runner/Foul Ball*

Gambling   Any player who shall, in any way, be interested in any bet or wager on the game in which he takes part, either as umpire, player, or scorer, or who purchases or has purchased for him any "pool" or chance, sold or given away, on the game in which he takes part, he shall be dishonorably expelled from both his club and the association [league in 1876]. Umpires, players, and scorers who have wagers on any other association [league] game shall be suspended for the season.

Ground Rules   Before calling "play," the umpire shall ask the home field captain whether there are any special ground rules and shall take note of such rules and see that they are enforced, provided they do not conflict with any regular rules of the game. Should the umpire not be notified of any ground rules, the rules shall not be enforced.

Note: This last sentence was dropped from the 1876 rule book.

Grounds   The foul ball lines shall be unlimited in length and shall run from the center of home base through the center of first and third bases to the foul ball posts, which shall be located at the boundary of the field and within the range of home and first base, and home and third base. Said lines shall be marked from base to base with chalk, or some other white substance, so as to be plainly seen by the umpire.

Interference/Spectator   Should the ball be willfully stopped by any outside person not engaged in the game, the ball shall be dead until settled in the hands of the pitcher while standing in his box. Baserunners at the time shall be entitled to the base they were running for.

Pitcher/Delivery   The ball must be delivered with the arm swinging nearly perpendicular [parallel] to the side of the body.

Should the pitcher deliver the ball by an overhand throw, outward swing of the arm, roundarm bowling, or any other swing other than nearly perpendicular to the body, it shall be a "foul balk." When a foul balk is called, the umpire shall warn the pitcher of the penalty and should three foul balks be called in one inning, the umpire shall declare a forfeit.

If the pitcher makes any motion to deliver the ball and fails to do so—except if the ball is accidentally dropped—the umpire shall call a balk.

Pitcher/Position   Each corner of the pitcher's box must be marked by a flat six-inch square iron plate.

Player/Eligible   Players must not have been members of any other club in the association for sixty days prior to the date of the game, unless their previous club has disbanded and their contract with such club has been canceled.

The rules of 1874 also include other rules concerning contracts including disciplinary actions for players who violate them. See also *Gambling*

Runner   A player running the bases shall be considered holding a base—entitled to occupy it—until he has regularly touched the next base in order.

Note: This new rule is inaccurate because it neglects to mention the important exception of runners forced off their base. This correction would not be made until 1880.

Runner/Foul Ball   In the case of a foul ball, the baserunner returning to touch the base must remain on it until the ball is held by the pitcher, no matter in what part of the field the pitcher happens to be.

Run Scored   No run shall score unless the home base is touched before three players have been put out; and if the third player is put out before reaching first base, the run shall not be scored.

Spectators   No person not engaged in the game shall be permitted to occupy any position within the lines of the field, or in any way interrupt the umpire during the game.

Strike Zone   There are now two classifications of unfair pitches: "balls" and "wide balls."

"Balls" are pitches not at the height called for by the batter ("high" or "low") or are not exactly over home base. "Wide balls" are pitches that are out of the reach of the striker's bat, such as those that hit the ground or the batter, or are over the batter's head. The umpire shall call every third "ball." When three "balls" [actually nine pitches] have been called, the batter is awarded first base. With the exception of the first pitch, all "wides" are called in the order of their delivery. When three "wides" have been called, the batter is awarded first base.

Note: When you consider that one type of base on balls required three (and sometimes four) pitches, while another required nine pitches—not to mention calling strikes—it's no wonder they started paying the unfortunate umpire of 1874. "Wide balls" as a special classification of unfair pitches lasted only one year and was dropped from the rule book in 1875.

Substitute   No player not in position on the field or ready to bat after the close of the third inning and before the start of the fourth, shall be substituted for another player, except in running the bases.

Substitute/Runner   A player serving as substitute for another in running the bases must cross the batter's position in front of home base, and must not start to run until the batter strikes at the ball.

Note: This clarified the position in which the substitute runner must stand. In previous years, substitute runners often ran behind the batter and interfered with the catcher.

Umpire   See *Catch, Dead Ball, Gambling, Ground Rules* as well as the entries below.

Umpire/Decisions   The umpire shall render no decision except when appealed to by a player, unless expressly required to do so by the rules of the game, as in calling "balls," etc.

No player shall be permitted to converse with the umpire during the game, except to make a legal appeal for his decision in giving a player out.

No decision by the umpire on any point of play in baserunning shall be reversed upon the testimony of any player. But if it is shown by the two captains that the umpire has misinterpreted the rules or has given an erroneous decision, the umpire shall be allowed to reverse his decision.

Umpire/Payment   The umpire may receive compensation for his services as the clubs deem advisable, provided he receives the same amount from both clubs.

Note: This was dropped from the rule book in 1876.

Umpire/Replacing   The umpire shall not be changed during the game, except for illness or injury, or by consent of both captains if the umpire has willfully violated the written rules of the game.

Should the umpire fail to enforce any section of the rules or should he interpret the rules other than the express letter of the rule, he shall cease to be eligible to act in the position and shall at once be dismissed.

Note: This last paragraph was dropped from the 1876 rule book.

1875

Ball   When the ball becomes out of shape, cut or ripped to expose the yarn, or in any way injured to be unfit for fair use, the umpire, at the close of an even inning at the request of either captain, shall call for a new ball.

Base   The corner of home base facing the pitcher's position must touch the intersection of the foul lines.

Note: This places home base entirely in foul territory.

Base on Balls   See *Strike Zone*.

Batter/Position   The batsman's position is six feet long by three feet wide, extending two feet in front of and four feet behind the center of home base. Its nearest line is one foot from home base.

Note: With the placement of home base in foul territory, the batter's box has also been moved back.

Should the batter step outside the batter's box while striking the ball, the umpire shall call "foul strike," and two such foul strikes shall put the batter out. All baserunners are allowed to return to their original base.

Game/Rain   After rain has fallen for five minutes, the umpire shall suspend play at the request of either captain.

Pitcher/Position   The pitcher's points may be made of either iron or stone and must be laid even with the ground.

Note: With the movement of home plate into foul territory, the entire pitcher's box was required to be moved forward 8½ inches to maintain the 45 foot distance from the box to the center of home plate.

Strike Zone   All pitches not over home base or at the height called for by the batter are considered unfair "balls." Every third consecutive "ball" must be called by the umpire. When three "balls" [nine pitches] have been called, the batter is awarded first base.

Note: The term "wide balls" has been dropped from the rule book. In 1876, the word "consecutive" was dropped.

Umpire   The umpire shall not enter the infield while the ball is in play.

1876

The National League is founded and adopts the rule book.

Ball   In all regular match games, the balls are furnished by the home club. Should any ball used in a game prove, on examination by the umpire, to be illegal in size, weight, or materials, balls of the same manufacture shall not be used thereafter in regular match games.

The rubber used in the composition of the ball must weigh not more than one ounce.

Should the ball be lost during a game, the umpire, at the expiration of five minutes, shall call for a new ball.

Batter/Position   If the batter steps outside the batter's box when he strikes at the ball, the umpire shall call "foul balk and out" and baserunners shall return to their original base.

Fielder/Illegal Act   Baserunners are entitled to two bases for any fair hit ball stopped or caught by a fielder with his hat, cap, or any part of his dress. The ball is dead.

Foul Ball   See *Runner/Advancing*.

Game/Rain   If a game cannot be concluded, it shall be decided by the score of the last equal innings played, unless one club has completed an inning and the other club has equaled or exceeded their opponent's score in an incomplete inning, in which case the game shall be decided by the total score.

Obstruction   If a baserunner is prevented from making a base by the obstruction of an adversary, he shall be entitled to that base and shall not be put out.

Pitcher/Delivery   It shall be a balk if the pitcher unnecessarily delays the game by not delivering the ball.

Player/Eligible   Many rules and regulations concerning eligibility of players, contracts, and disciplinary actions are removed from the rule book.

Player/Illegal Act   No manager, captain, or player shall address the audience except in case of necessary explanation. Any manager, captain, or player who uses abusive, threatening, or improper language to the audience shall be punished by suspension from play for twenty days and forfeiture of his salary for such period.

Rules   No section of these rules shall be construed as conflicting with or affecting any article of the league's constitution.

Runner/Advancing   Following caught fly balls, both foul or fair, runners may advance after returning to their original base. On all foul balls, not caught on the fly, caught on one bounce, runners may not advance but may return to their original base without being put out.

Run Scored If the third out is forced out or is put out before reaching first base, no run shall be scored.

Strikeout Should the batter, with two strikes, not swing at the next "good ball," the umpire shall not call a "strike" but warn him by calling "good ball." But should the batter swing and miss or fail to swing at the next good ball, "three strikes" must be called and the batter must run to first as in the case of hitting a fair ball.

Strike Zone The batsman, on taking his position, must call for a "high," "low," or "fair" pitch, and the umpire shall notify the pitcher to deliver the ball as required; such call cannot be changed after the first pitch is delivered.

Substitute No player taking part in the game shall be replaced by another after the start of the fourth inning, except in running the bases.

Umpire No player shall be permitted to converse with the umpire during the game, except the two captains and then only to appeal a misinterpretation of the rules or an erroneous decision.

1877

Ball No ball is to be used except those furnished by the secretary of the league.

Bases First, second, and third bases must cover a space equal to 15 inches square.

Home base is to be placed entirely into fair territory with two of its sides forming part of the foul lines.

Batter/Fails to Bat Any batsman who fails to take his position at bat within one minute after the umpire has called for him shall be out.

Batter/Position The batter's box is six feet long by three feet wide with the line of home base running through its center.

Note: This arrangement permitted a batter to stand three feet in front of or three feet behind home base.

Coach See *Grounds*.

Foul/Fair Balls A batted ball striking in foul territory and then in fair is fair; a batted ball striking fair and then foul is foul.

Gambling See *Player Expulsion*

Game The home club shall first take the bat.

Game/Rain Should rain continue to fall for 10 minutes (following suspension of play) the game shall terminate.

Grounds Lines parallel to the foul lines and 15 feet back are to be drawn to delineate a boundary for the captain and one assistant to coach baserunners. Lines parallel to the foul lines and 50 feet back are to be drawn to delineate a boundary for players on the batting side.

Note: In the rules of 1880, these lines are referred to as the "Captain's Lines" and the "Players' Lines" respectively.

Interference/Offensive When a fielder occupies the basepath in the act of fielding a ball, the baserunner shall run out of the path and behind the fielder to avoid interference.

A baserunner struck by a batted ball is out.

A baserunner, from home to first base, shall not run inside the foul line or more than three feet outside of it, or he shall be declared out.

Pitcher/Position Note: With home plate being placed entirely in fair territory, the entire pitcher's box must be moved back to maintain the 45-foot distance from the box's front line to the center of home plate.

Player/Expulsion Any player who shall, in any way, be interested in any bet or wager on any league game or who shall purchase or have purchased for him any "pool" or chance, sold or given away, shall be expelled.

The club is entitled to the best services of the player, and players who become indifferent or careless in play or who become unable to render satisfactory service to the club from any cause may have their salaries suspended or their contracts canceled.

Players conspiring against the interest of their clubs or who "manifest a disposition" to obstruct club management may be expelled.

Note: These three rules were removed from the rule book in 1878.

Runner/Fielder A baserunner who knocks the ball out of the hand of a fielder while in the act of running to a base is no longer out.

Strike Zone A "low" pitch is one thrown belt high or below the belt and above the knee. A "high" pitch is one above the belt to the shoulder.

A ball pitched and called "dead" by reason of having struck the umpire shall be counted as one of nine called balls entitling the batter to a base if it is also an "unfair" ball.

Substitute No substitution is to be made after the start of the second inning except in cases of illness or injury.

Three-Foot Lane See *Interference/Offensive*

1878

Batting Order The batsmen must take their positions in the order in which they are directed by their captain, and after each player has had one time at bat, the order established shall not be changed during the game.

Batter/Position The batter must actually hit the ball while outside the batter's box to commit a "foul strike" and be called out.

Game The club that bats first shall be determined by the two captains.

Grounds The foul lines shall be continued to the limits of the field beyond and back of home base. This triangular area shall be for the exclusive use of the catcher, umpire, and batsman; and no offensive player (except the batsman) shall occupy it.

Note: In the rules of 1880, these lines are referred to as the "Catcher's Lines."

Pitcher/Delivery The pitcher's hand must pass below the waist in delivering the ball.

Substitute/Runner No player shall be allowed a substitute in running the bases except for illness or injury incurred in the game then being played, and then such substitute shall take the player's place only after the latter has reached first base.

1879

Ball The "Spalding League Ball" is adopted as the official ball, which is indicated in the footnotes of some rule books.

Base on Balls Note: The amount of unfair pitches is still the same for the awarding of a base on balls but, to everyone's delight, the terminology is finally changed from "every third ball must be called" to "every ball must be called." The result is the same, nine "balls" and the batter is awarded first base.

Batter/Caught Foul A batted ball in foul territory must be caught on the fly to be declared an out.

Note: This rule was dropped in 1880 but was again added in 1883.

Batter-Runner The batter is out after three strikes if the ball is caught before touching the ground.

Batting Order After the first inning, the first striker in each inning shall be the batsman whose name follows that of the last man who has completed his turn (time) at bat in the preceding inning.

Pitcher/Delivery The pitcher, when taking his position to deliver the ball, must face the batter.

Pitcher/Illegal Act If a pitcher delivers the ball to intentionally strike the batter, in the judgment of the umpire, the umpire shall fine the pitcher not less than $10 nor more than $50.

Pitcher/Position The pitcher's box is now four feet wide and six feet long.

Run Scored See *Interference/Offensive*

Strikeout See *Batter-Runner*

Strikeout The batter is out after three strikes if the ball is caught before touching the ground.

1880

Alcohol/Grounds No club shall sell or allow to be sold on its grounds, nor in any building owned or occupied by it, any spirituous, vinous or malt liquors.

Note: It usually doesn't take too long for profits to triumph over morality. Six years later, this rule was dropped.

Appeal/Runner A baserunner who fails to touch intervening bases when returning to a base shall not be declared out unless the opposing captain appeals to the umpire before the pitcher delivers the ball to the batter.

Base on Balls A base on balls is awarded to the batter when eight balls have been called by the umpire.

Grounds The ground must be an enclosed field sufficient in size to enable each player to play in his position as required by the rules.

Interference/Offensive No run can be scored if a baserunner is declared out for being hit with a fair hit batted ball.

Runner/Returning The baserunner is out if he fails to return to the base he occupied after a foul fly has been caught and the runner is touched with the ball or the ball is returned to the base the runner occupied before he returns.

Strikeout The batter becomes a runner immediately when three strikes have been called by the umpire.

Umpire No player except the captain or his assistant shall address the umpire concerning any point of play. Violators are subject to a fine.

1881

Base on Balls A batter is awarded first base after seven balls are called by the umpire.

Forfeited Game Every club shall furnish sufficient police force upon its own grounds to preserve order. In the event of a crowd entering the field during the progress of a game, and interfering with play in any manner, the visiting club may refuse to play further until the field is cleared; if the ground is not cleared within 15 minutes, the visiting club is entitled to a forfeit by a score of 9–0, regardless of the number of innings played.

Pitcher/Position The pitcher's box is to be fifty feet from the center of home base.

Security See *Forfeited Game*.

Spectators No person shall be allowed upon any part of the field during the progress of the game, in addition to the nine players on each side and the umpire, except such officers of the law who are present in uniform to preserve the peace.

Strikeout The batter, on a called third strike, is no longer given a warning of "good ball" by the umpire. (See 1876 *Strikeout*)

Substitute A substitute is not permitted unless a player is disabled by injury or illness in the game being played.

Substitute/Runner A player shall not have a substitute run the bases for him.

Umpire/Decisions The umpire shall *not* reverse his decision on any point of play upon the testimony of any player or bystander.

1882

The American Association begins its first season and makes several modifications to the rule book to meet its own needs and wants. Among the rules not included in the AA rule book are the prohibition of liquor being sold on club grounds, and the fining of pitchers who, in the umpire's judgment, purposely hit batters with pitched balls. Other changes and amendments particular to the AA are noted below.

Ball Should the ball become so injured as to be unfit for fair use in the opinion of the umpire, on being appealed to by either captain, a new ball shall be called for by the umpire at the end of an even inning.

Note: The AA's rule doesn't require an appeal by a captain.

Ball (American Association) The ball must be stamped "American Association." Each ball shall be enclosed in a paper box and sealed by the manufacturer. The seal shall not be broken except by the umpire in the presence of the two captains after "play" has been called.

Note: The AA selected the Mahn Sporting Company's ball as its official ball.

Batter The two players following the batsman, in the order in which they are named on the scorebook, must be ready with bat in hand to promptly take their position as batsmen.

Note: This rule was not adopted by the AA.

Bench The players' bench must be furnished by the home club and placed on a portion of the ground outside the players' lines. It must be twelve feet in length and fastened to the ground. Bat racks sufficient in size to hold twenty bats are to be adjacent to the players' bench.

Note: This is not in the AA rule book.

Interference/Offensive A baserunner is out if he obstructs a fielder attempting to field a batted ball; provided that if two or more fielders attempt to field the ball and the runner comes in contact with one of them, the umpire shall determine which fielder is entitled to the benefit of the rule and shall not call the runner out for coming in contact with the other fielder.

Note: This provision isn't included in the AA rules.

The batter is out if he plainly attempts to hinder the catcher from catching the ball, without effort to make a fair hit.

Note: Not outlined in the AA rules.

Interference/Spectator A "blocked ball" is a batted or thrown ball that is stopped or handled by any person not engaged in the game. Whenever a block is called, baserunners may run the bases without being put out until the ball is returned to and held by the pitcher standing in his position. Exception: When the person not engaged in the game retains possession of the ball or throws or kicks it beyond reach of fielders, the umpire should call time and require baserunners to stop at the last base touched by them.

Note: The AA does not use the term *blocked ball* and uses the following rule for spectator interference: "If a batted or thrown ball is stopped by any person not engaged in the game, the ball shall not be considered in play until it is held by the pitcher standing in his position. The baserunner shall be entitled to take one base."

Spectators   Spectators hissing or hooting at the umpire are to be promptly ejected from the grounds.

Three-Foot Line   The three-foot line area, in which the batter-runner must run to avoid interference, must be marked on the field.

Note: The rules of the AA do not require the actual markings.

Time   The umpire shall suspend play for an accident to himself or a player; but in case of an accident to a fielder, time shall not be called until the ball is returned and held by the pitcher standing in his position.

Note: The AA rule book does not include this important exception.

1883

Ball   In calling for a new ball, replacing one unfit for fair play, the umpire may call for one "at once" and does not have to wait until the end of the inning.

Note: The AA here still requires the umpire to wait until the close of an inning before calling for a new ball.

Ball (American Association)   The ball must be manufactured by A. J. Reach, according to the specifications, and stamped "American Association."

Note: The Mahn ball was found unsatisfactory.

Batter/Caught Foul   A batted ball in foul territory must be caught on the fly to be declared an out.

Note: Foul balls caught on one bounce are no longer outs. The AA refuses to go along with the rule and continues with the one-bound foul flyout.

Batter/Overrunning First   In the American Association a runner touching and overrunning first base is at risk of being put out while off the base if he turns to the left from the foul line while returning to the bag.

Batting Order   The batter is out if he fails to take his position at bat in the order of batting, unless the error is discovered and the proper batsman takes his position before a fair hit has been made. In such case, the "balls" and "strikes" called will be counted in the time at bat of the proper batsman.

Note: This last sentence is not included in the AA rule book.

Forfeited Game   See *Pitcher/Delivery*

Pitcher/Delivery   A fair ball is a ball delivered by the pitcher, while wholly within the lines of his position, and while facing the batsman and his hand, in delivering the ball, must not pass above the line of his shoulder.

When the umpire has called two "foul balks," the batter and all baserunners are awarded one base. Three foul balks in one inning no longer constitutes a forfeited game.

Note: The AA discards the term "foul balk."

Runner/Returning   A baserunner who fails to return to his base at a run following a foul ball is liable to be put out by being touched by the ball while off his base.

Substitute/Runner   The American Association allows a substitute to run the bases for a player if the player is injured in the game being played and the opposing club consents to the use of a substitute runner.

Umpire   Umpires are to be salaried employees.

1884

In 1884 the Union Association became operational and adopted virtually the same rule book used by the American Association. The few exceptions include the additional rule requiring foul balls to be caught on the fly to record an out, and the Wright & Ditson ball as the league's official ball. The Union Association folded after one season.

Base on Balls   The batter is awarded a base on balls after six balls have been called by the umpire. Note: The AA and UA retain the seven-ball base on balls.

Bat Boy/Girl   The American Association allows "a person to take charge of the bats of each club" to be on the playing field.

Note: Not in the UA rule book.

Fair/Foul Balls   When a batted ball passes outside the grounds, the umpire shall declare it fair should it disappear within, or foul should it disappear outside of the range of the foul lines.

Note: This is not found in the AA and UA rule books.

Hit by Pitch   The American Association adds the following rule: If a batsman be solidly hit by a ball from the pitcher when he evidently cannot avoid the same, he shall be given his base by the umpire.

Note: The AA is the first league to award a batter first base for being hit with a pitch; not in the UA rule book.

Home Run   See *Fair/Foul Balls*

Pitcher/Delivery   All restrictions on the delivery of the ball are lifted except that the pitcher must be entirely within the lines of his position and must face the batter.

Note: The overhanded delivery was thus permitted for the first time. The AA and UA kept the shoulder-high delivery.

1885

Bases   The home base may be made of white rubber or stone.

Note: In the AA, home base must be made of white rubber only.

Bat   The handle of the bat may be wound with twine not to exceed 18 inches from the end.

Note: No such rule in the AA rule book.

The bat must be round except that a portion of the surface on one side may be flat.

Note: The AA nixed this one also.

Batter/Caught Foul   In a special midseason meeting held on June 7, 1885, the American Association adopts the rule that a foul ball must be caught on the fly to be declared an out.

Batter/Position   The batter's box is now six feet long by four feet wide with its nearest line six inches from home base.

Note: The AA keeps the six by three foot box that is one foot from the plate.

Game   The American Association gives the option of which club bats first to the home team captain.

Grounds/Fence   A fair batted ball that goes over the fence at a distance less than 210 feet from home base shall entitle the batsman to two bases. A distinctive line shall be marked on the fence at this point.

Note: This is not in the AA rule book.

Grounds/Three-Foot Lane   The American Association requires the marking of the three-foot area in which the batsman must run to avoid interference.

Home Run/Double   See *Grounds/Fence*.

Pitcher/Delivery   The pitcher must have both feet touching the ground while making any one of the series of motions he is accustomed to make in the delivery of the ball. A violation of this rule shall be a "foul balk" and two foul balks shall entitle the batter and each runner to one base.

Note: At a special National League meeting held on June 7, 1885, this rule was dropped. The term "foul balk" was also dropped from the rules. (The AA never required its pitchers to keep both feet on the ground during delivery.) However, in a special meeting of their own, also held on June 7, the AA adopted the rule allowing the overhand delivery, conforming with the NL rule.

A balk is made whenever the pitcher, when about to deliver

the ball to the bat while standing in his position, makes any one of the series of actions he habitually makes in delivery, and he fails to deliver the ball to the bat.

Uniforms (American Association) Every club shall be required to adopt a neat and attractive uniform for its players, and shall at all times be required to present the same upon the field in a clean and attractive condition.

1886

Ball Should the ball be knocked outside of the enclosure or lost during the game, the umpire shall call at once for another ball.

Base on Balls The NL increases the number to seven balls for the awarding of a base on balls. The AA drops the number to six balls.

Bat Handle A granulated substance may be applied to the bat handle not to exceed 18 inches from the end.

Batter/Position The AA adopts the NL batter's box, which is six feet long by four feet wide and six inches from home plate.

Pitcher/Delivery The pitcher is no longer required to keep both feet on the ground while delivering the ball.

Note: The term "foul balk" is dropped from the rules.

Pitcher/Position The pitcher's lines must be straight lines forming a box seven feet long by four feet wide.

The AA requires that a flat, stone slab, four feet wide by one foot deep, be placed in front of the pitcher's box and level with the playing surface. This rule is dropped the following year.

1887

The National League and the American Association agree to be governed by the same rule book after several rules are rewritten.

Ball In all games, the ball or balls played with shall be furnished by the home club, and the last ball in play becomes the property of the winning club. Each ball to be used in championship games shall be examined, measured, and weighed by the Secretary of the Association, enclosed in a paper box, and sealed with the seal of the Secretary, which seal shall not be broken except by the umpire in the presence of the captains of the two contesting nines after play has been called.

Note: The Spalding and Reach balls respectively remain the official balls of the National League and the American Association.

For each championship game, two balls shall be furnished by the home club to the umpire for use. When the ball in play is batted over the fence or stands, onto foul ground out of sight of the players, the other ball shall be immediately put into play by the umpire. As often as one of the two in use shall be lost, a new one must be substituted, so that the umpire may at all times, after the game begins, have two for use. The moment the umpire delivers the alternate ball to the catcher or pitcher, it comes into play, and shall not be exchanged until it, in turn, passes out of sight onto foul ground.

Base on Balls The batter is entitled to one base when five balls have been called by the umpire.

Bases Home base must be made of whitened rubber.

Second base shall be upon its corner of the infield, and the center of the first and third bases shall be on lines running to and from second base and 7½ inches from the foul lines, providing that each base shall be entirely within the foul lines.

Note: This placed first and third bases, for the first time, entirely in foul territory and entirely within the 90-foot square—the way it remains today. If you carefully read the rule, however, you realize that the precise description actually places first and third base 7½ inches farther toward the outfield than they are today, and thus not entirely within the 90-foot square. In fact, the

bases were never placed as outlined in this rule. It wasn't until 1894 that the rule was rewritten to reflect the proper placement of the bases on the field.

Batter/Overrunning First If the baserunner overruns first base and turns to his left from the foul line, he may be put out in returning to the base or in attempting to advance.

Batter/Position The batter's box is again made four feet wide by six feet long.

Coach/Position The captain's or coacher's lines must be 15 feet from and parallel with the foul lines and should commence 75 feet distant from the catcher's line. Should the captain or coacher willfully fail to remain in said bounds, he shall be fined by the umpire $5 for each such offense, except upon an appeal by the captain from the umpire's decision upon a misinterpretation of the rules.

The captains and coachers are restricted in coaching to the baserunner only, and are not allowed to address any remarks except to the baserunner, and then only in words of necessary direction; no player shall use language which will, in any manner, refer to or reflect upon a player of the opposing club or the audience. To enforce the above, the captain of the opposing side may call the attention of the umpire to the offense and upon a repetition of the same the club shall be debarred from further coaching during the game.

Foul Ball See last paragraph under *Strike Zone*.

Foul Lines/Grounds The foul lines must be drawn in straight lines from the outer corner of home base along the outer edges of the first and third bases to the boundaries of the ground.

Note: Also see *Coach* for "Coacher's Lines."

Game The choice of innings is given to the home team captain.

No game is to be begun later than two hours before sunset.

The players of each club in a match game shall be nine in number, and in no case shall less than nine men be allowed to play on each side.

Game/Rain The home club captain shall be the sole judge of the fitness of the ground for beginning a game after rain.

Hit by Pitch The batter is entitled to take first base if his person or clothing is hit by a ball from the pitcher, unless in the umpire's opinion he intentionally permitted himself to be hit.

Interference/Offensive The baserunner is out if he intentionally interferes with a thrown ball.

Pitcher/Delivery The pitcher shall take his position facing the batsman, with both feet squarely on the ground, the right foot on the rear line of the "box," his left foot in advance of the right, and to the left of an imaginary line from his right foot to the center of the home base. He shall not raise his right foot, unless in the act of delivering the ball, nor make more than one step in such delivery. He shall hold the ball, before delivery, fairly in front of his body, and in sight of the umpire. In the case of a lefthanded pitcher, the above words "left" and "right" are to be reversed. When the pitcher feigns to throw the ball to a base, he must resume the above position and pause momentarily before delivering the ball to the bat.

Any motion made by the pitcher to deliver the ball to the bat without delivering it is a balk, and shall be held to include any and every accustomed motion with the hands, arms, or feet, or position of the body assumed by the pitcher in his delivery of the ball, and any motion calculated to deceive a baserunner, except the ball be accidentally dropped.

It is a balk if the ball be held by the pitcher so long as to delay the game unnecessarily. It is a balk if the pitcher makes any motion to deliver the ball to the bat when any part of his person is upon grounds outside of the lines of his position, including all preliminary motions with the hands, arms, and feet. The batter becomes a baserunner after any illegal delivery of a ball by the pitcher.

Pitcher/Position   The pitcher's box is now 5½ feet long by four feet wide.

Player/Illegal Act   No umpire, manager, captain, or player shall address the audience during the progress of a game, except in case of necessary explanation.

Runner/Returning   Baserunners need not return to their bags on the run following a foul ball etc., provided they do not unnecessarily delay the game.

Spectators   No person shall be allowed upon any part of the field during the progress of a game, in addition to the players in uniform, the manager on each side, and the umpire; except such officers of the law as may be present in uniform, and such officials of the home club as may be necessary to preserve the peace. See also *Player/Illegal Act*

Strikeout   The batter is out after four strikes are declared by the umpire.

Strike Zone   The batter can no longer call for a "high" or "low" pitch.

A "fair" ball (strike) is defined as a legally pitched ball that passes over home base "not lower than the batsman's knee, nor higher than his shoulder."

A strike is called when the batter makes any obvious attempt to make a foul hit.

Time   The umpire may call "timeout" to enforce order in case of annoyance from spectators.

Umpire/Decisions   No one except the captains of the contending teams can question an umpire's decision; no player other than a captain can approach or address the umpire unless required to do so. Violators may be fined $10.

The umpire cannot reverse his decision by the testimony of a player or spectator. However, the umpire may consult a player on the question before rendering his decision.

Uniforms/Shoes   Every club shall be required to adopt uniforms for its players. Each player shall be required to present himself upon the field during the game in a neat and clean condition, but no player shall attach anything to the sole or heel of his shoes other than the ordinary baseball shoe plate.

1888

Hit by Pitch   See *Strikeout*

Interference/Offensive   If a fair hit ball strikes the baserunner before touching a fielder, the runner shall be declared out—however, in such case, no base shall be run unless forced by the batter becoming a baserunner, and no run shall be scored.

Note: In 1890, the rule was amended with the additional phrase, "and no other baserunner put out." This clarified that the batter could not be thrown out nor any possible double play could be made on such a play.

Strikeout   The batter is out after three strikes are declared by the umpire.

The batter is out if, while making the third strike, the ball hits his person or clothing.

1889

Base on Balls   A batter is entitled to take first base when four balls have been called by the umpire.

Foul Tip   A foul tip is defined as a foul hit not rising above the batter's head and caught by the catcher playing within 10 feet of home base. In the case of a foul tip, the batter is not out and any baserunners may return to their bases without being put out.

Pitcher/Delivery   The pitcher shall take his position facing the batsman with both feet square on the ground, one foot on the rear line of the "box." He shall not raise either foot, unless in the act of delivering the ball, nor make more than one step in such delivery. He shall hold the ball, before the delivery fairly in front of his body, and in sight of the umpire. When the pitcher feigns to throw the ball to a base, he must resume the above position and pause momentarily before delivering the ball to the bat.

Substitute   One player, whose name shall be printed on the scorecard as an extra player, may be substituted at the end of any complete inning by either club, but the player retired shall not thereafter participate in the game. In addition thereto, a substitute may be allowed at any time in place of a player disabled in the game then being played, by reason of illness or injury, of the nature and extent of which the umpire shall be the sole judge.

Substitute/Runner   The baserunner shall not have a substitute run for him, except by consent of the captains of the contesting teams.

1890

In 1890, the Players League was in operation for its one and only season, for which they adopted the rule book and made several modifications.

Ball   The Players League used the "Keefe ball" as its official ball.

Ball/Defacing   At no time shall the ball be intentionally discolored by rubbing it with the soil or otherwise.

Note: This rule was not in the Players League rule book.

Forfeited Game (Players League)   If a club fails to begin play within one minute after the umpire calls "play" at the start of the game, unless such delay is unavoidable, the game shall be declared a forfeit.

If the club fails to resume play within five minutes after the umpire has called "play" (following suspension of play), the game shall be declared a forfeit.

Note: The NL and AA rule book allowed for just the opposite before declaring a forfeit—five minutes at the start of the game, one minute after suspended play.

Pitcher/Delivery   The Players League deleted the following line from its rule book: "He [the pitcher] shall not raise either foot, unless in the act of delivering the ball."

Note: See 1889 *Pitcher/Delivery*.

Pitcher/Position (Players League)   The pitcher's lines must be six feet long by four feet wide, its forward line distant fifty-one feet from the center of home base. Each corner of the "box" must be marked by a wooden peg.

The NL and AA require the pitcher's points to be flat, round, rubber plates, six inches in diameter.

Substitute   Two players, whose names shall be printed on the scorecard as extra players, may be substituted at any time by either club, but no player so retired shall thereafter participate in the game.

Note: The Players League applied this rule but required the substitution to be made at the end of a complete inning.

Umpire (Players League)   There shall be two umpires at every championship game; one shall stand behind the bat and the other shall stand in the field.

Note: Leave it to the players to understand the importance of having at least two umpires on the field of play.

1891

Substitute   Each team is required to have one or more substitutes available.

1892

Bench/Player Players' benches must be located at least 25 feet back of the players' lines.

Coach A team is permitted to have not more than two coaches who may be one player participating in the game and any other player under contract to the club.

Coachers are not to use language which in any manner refers to or reflects upon spectators.

Dead/Live Ball A legally delivered fair ball that touches the bat of the batter in his position shall be considered a batted ball and in play.

Forfeited Game A forfeit shall be declared if a team resorts to dilatory practices in order to gain time, for the purpose of having the game called on account of darkness or rain or for any reason whatsoever.

Game "No Game" shall be declared by the umpire if he shall terminate play on account of rain or darkness before five innings on each side are completed, except in a case when the game is called, the club second at bat shall have more runs at the end of its fourth inning than the club first at bat made in its five innings, then the umpire shall award the game to the club having made the greatest number of runs, and it shall be a game and be so counted in the championship record.

Grounds/Fence A fair batted ball that goes over the fence shall entitle the batter to a home run; except that should it go over the fence at a distance less than 235 feet from home base, the batter is entitled to only two bases. A distinctive line is to be marked on the fence showing the required point.

Hit by Pitch The batter becomes a baserunner if, while he be a batsman, his person—excepting hands or forearm, which makes it a dead ball—or clothing be hit by a ball from the pitcher, unless, in the opinion of the umpire, he intentionally permits himself to be so hit.

Home Run/Double See *Grounds/Fence*.

Interference/Offensive The batter is out if he attempts to hinder the catcher from fielding or throwing the ball by stepping outside the lines of his position or otherwise obstructing or interfering with the catcher.

Spectators See *Coach*

1893

Bat The bat must be made wholly of hard wood except that the handle may be wound with twine, or a granulated substance applied, not to exceed 18 inches from the end. It must be round, not to exceed 2½ inches in diameter in the thickest part, and must not exceed 42 inches in length.

Note: Bats with a flat side are now illegal.

Batting Order The batsmen must take their positions within the batsmen's lines in the order in which they are named in the batting order, which batting order must be submitted by the captains of the opposing teams to the umpire before the game, and when approved by him this batting order must be followed except in the case of a substitute player, in which case the substitute must take the place of the original player in the batting order. After the first inning the first striker (batter) in each inning shall be the batsman whose name follows that of the last man who has completed his turn—time at bat—in the preceding inning.

Pitcher/Delivery The pitcher shall take his position facing the batter with both feet square on the ground, and in front of the pitcher's plate but in the act of delivering the ball one foot must be in contact with the pitcher's plate.

A balk is any motion in delivering the ball to the bat by the pitcher while not in the required position.

Pitcher/Position The pitcher's boundary shall be marked by a white rubber plate 12 inches long and 4 inches wide so fixed in the ground as to be even with the surface at the distance of 60 feet 6 inches from the outer corner of the home plate, so that a line drawn from the center of the home base and the center of the second base shall give 6 inches on either side.

Substitute See *Batting Order*

1894

Foul Ball See *Strike Zone*.

Grounds Detailed, and often confusing, directions for laying out a baseball field are included in the rules of 1894.

Strike Zone A strike is called when the batter makes a foul hit, other than a foul tip, while attempting a bunt hit that falls or rolls upon foul ground between home base and first or third bases.

1895

Bat The bat cannot exceed 2¾ inches in diameter.

Batting Order The batsman is out if he fails to take his position at the bat in his order of batting, unless the error be discovered and the proper batsman takes his position before a time "at bat" recorded; and in such case the balls and strikes called must be counted in the time "at bat" of the proper batsman, and only the proper batsman shall be declared out. This rule shall not take effect unless the out is declared before the ball is delivered to the succeeding batsman, and no runs shall be scored or bases run, and further, no outs shall be counted other than that of the proper batsman.

Foul Tip A strike is called when a ball is tipped by the batter and caught by the catcher within the 10-foot lines.

Glove The catcher and first baseman are permitted to wear a glove or mitt of any size, shape or weight. All other players are restricted to the use of a glove or mitt weighing not over 10 ounces, and measuring in circumference around the palm of the hand not over 14 inches.

Infield Fly The batter is out if he hits a fly ball that can be handled by an infielder while first and second bases are occupied, or first, second, and third, with only one out. If the third strike is called (on attempted bunt in foul territory) the umpire shall declare infield or outfield hit.

Pitcher/Position The pitcher's plate is enlarged to 24 by 6 inches, its current size.

Strike Zone See *Foul Tip*.

Umpire Umpires may assess fines of $25 to $100 for specified misconduct by players.

1896

Ball The home club shall have at least a dozen regulation balls on the field ready for use on the call of the umpire during each game.

Bench No one is to occupy the players' bench under any circumstances except the club president, managers, and players in uniform.

Game/Rain The choice of innings shall be given to the captain of the home club, who shall also be the sole judge of the fitness of the ground for beginning a game after rain, but after play has been called by the umpire he alone shall be the judge as to the fitness of the ground for resuming play after the game has been suspended on account of rain.

Pitcher/Delivery The pitcher is no longer required to hold the ball before the delivery fairly in front of his body and in the sight of the umpire.

Player/Illegal Act Players guilty of indecent or vulgar language or conduct shall be removed from the game and fined $25.

Umpire Umpires may assess fines of $5 to $10 for specified misconduct; repeat violators are to be fined $25.

1897

Ball/Defacing At no time shall the ball be intentionally discolored by rubbing it with the soil or otherwise. In the event of a new ball being intentionally discolored, or otherwise injured by a player, the umpire shall, upon appeal from the captain of the opposite side, forthwith demand the return of that ball and shall substitute another new ball and impose a fine of $5 upon the offending player.

Bunt A bunt hit is a ball delivered by the pitcher to the batsman who, while standing within the lines of his position, makes a deliberate attempt to hit the ball so slowly within the infield that it cannot be fielded in time to retire the batsman. If such a bunt hit goes to foul ground a strike shall be called by the umpire.

Defense/Illegal Act See *Ball/Defacing*.

Fair/Foul Ball A fair hit is a ball batted by the batsman—while he is standing within the lines of his position—that first touches "fair" ground, or the person of a player or the umpire while standing on fair ground, and then settles on fair ground before passing the line of first or third base.

A foul hit is a similarly batted ball that first touches "foul" ground or the person of a player or the umpire while standing on foul ground.

Should such "fair hit" ball bound or roll to foul ground before passing the line of first or third base and settle on foul ground, it shall be declared by the umpire a foul ball.

Should such "foul hit" ball bound or roll to fair ground and settle there before passing the line of first or third base, it shall be declared by the umpire a "fair ball."

Foul Tip A foul tip is a ball batted by the batsman while standing within the lines of his position that goes foul sharp from the bat to the catcher's hands.

Obstruction The baserunner shall be entitled, without being put out, to take a base in the following cases: (1) If he is prevented from making a base by the obstruction of an adversary, unless the latter be a fielder having the ball in his hand ready to meet the baserunner; (2) If the fielder stop or catch a batted ball with his hat or any part of his uniform except his gloved hand.

Runner/Bases The baserunner must touch each base in regular order, viz., first, second, third, and home bases, and when obliged to return (except on a foul hit) must retouch the base or bases in reverse order. He shall only be considered as holding a base after touching it, and shall then be entitled to hold such base until he has legally touched the next base in order or has been legally forced to vacate it for a succeeding baserunner. However, no baserunner shall score a run to count in the game until the baserunner preceding him in the batting list (provided there has been such a baserunner who has not been put out in that inning) shall have first touched home base without being put out.

Runs Scored See *Runner/Bases* above

Substitute In every championship game, each side shall be required to have present on the field, in uniform, a sufficient number of substitute players to carry out the provision which requires that not less than nine players shall occupy the field in any inning of a game.

Umpire The umpire shall not address the spectators at any time, except in case of necessary explanation of misunderstood decision or points of play.

Umpire/Decisions No decision, rendered by the umpire, shall be reversed by him in which the question of an error of judgment is alone involved.

Should the umpire render any decision based on an illegal interpretation of any rule of the game, the same shall be reversed on the appeal of either of the two captains, but not otherwise.

1898

Batting Order The batsman is out if he fails to take his position at the bat in his order of batting, unless the error is discovered and the proper batsman takes his position before a time "at bat" is recorded, and, in such case, the balls and strikes called must be counted in the time "at bat" of the proper batsman, and only the proper batsman shall be declared out, and no runs shall be scored or bases run because of any act of the improper batsman. Provided, this rule shall not take effect unless the out is declared before the ball is delivered to the succeeding batsman. Should the batsman declared out by this rule be sufficient to retire the side, the proper batsman the next inning is the player who would have come to bat had the players been out by ordinary play.

Pitcher/Delivery A balk shall be: (1) Any motion made by the pitcher to deliver the ball to the bat without delivering it; (2) Any delivery of the ball to the bat while his pivot foot is not in contact with the pitcher's plate; (3) Any motion in delivering the ball to the bat by the pitcher while not in the position required by the rules; (4) The holding of the ball by the pitcher so long as, in the opinion of the umpire, to delay the game unnecessarily; (5) Standing in position and making any motion to pitch without having the ball in his possession, except in the case of a "block ball"; (6) The making of any motion the pitcher habitually makes in his method of delivery, without his immediately delivering the ball to the bat; (7) If the pitcher feigns to throw the ball to a base and does not resume his legal position and pause momentarily before delivering the ball to the bat. When the pitcher feigns to throw the ball to a base he must resume the required position and pause momentarily before delivering the ball to the bat.

Player/Illegal Act Players in uniform shall not be permitted to occupy seats in the stands or to stand among the spectators.

Umpire The rules of 1898 describe in detail the responsibilities of each umpire in games where two umpires are assigned.

1899

Bench The players' benches must be furnished by the home club and placed upon a portion of the ground not less than 25 feet outside of the players' lines. One such bench shall be for the exclusive use of the visiting club, and one for the exclusive use of the home club. The benches must be covered by a roof and closed at the back and each end; a space, however, not more than six inches wide may be left just under the roof for ventilation. All players of the side at bat must be seated on their bench, except such as are legally assigned to coach baserunners, and also the batsman, except when called to the bat by the umpire, and under no circumstances shall the umpire permit any person, except managers and players in uniform to occupy seats on the benches.

Catcher/Position The catcher must stand within the lines of his position whenever the pitcher delivers the ball to the bat.

Foul Tip A foul tip by the batter, caught by the catcher while standing within the lines of his position is a strike.

Game If the umpire calls "Game" on account of darkness or rain at any time after five innings have been completed, the score shall be that of the last equal innings played, but if the side second at bat shall have scored in an unequal number of innings or before the completion of its unfinished inning one or more runs than the side first at bat, the score of the game shall be the total number of runs made.

Interference/Defensive The batter becomes a baserunner if the catcher interferes with him, preventing him from striking the ball.

Pitcher/Delivery In addition to the rules for "balk" promulgated in 1898, the rules of 1899 state: A balk shall be: (1) The throwing of the ball by the pitcher to any base to catch the baserunner without first stepping directly towards said base immediately before throwing the ball; (2) Any delivery of the ball to the bat by the pitcher while his pivot foot is not in contact with the pitcher's plate, and he is not facing the batsman; (3) If the pitcher delivers the ball to the bat when the catcher is standing outside the lines of the catcher's position as defined by the rules.

The batter becomes a baserunner when a balk is called by the umpire.

Strike Zone See *Foul Tip*.

Substitute In any championship game, each side shall be required to have present on the field, in uniform, conforming to the suits worn by their teammates, a sufficient number of substitute players to carry out the provision which requires that not less than nine players shall occupy the field in any innings of a game.

Uniforms Every club shall adopt uniforms for its players, and the suit of each team shall conform in color and style. No player who shall attach anything to the sole or heel of his shoes other than the ordinary baseball shoe plate, or who shall appear in a uniform not conforming to the suits of the other members of his team, shall be permitted to take part in the game.

1900

Bases The shape of home base is changed from a 12-inch square to a five-sided shape, 17 inches wide.

Pitcher/Delivery The batter does not become a runner when the pitcher balks in throwing to pick off a runner on the bases.

Any motion made by the pitcher to deliver the ball to the bat or to first base without delivering it is a balk.

Note: This rule previously specified "any base."

1901

The American League begins operation and adopts the rule book with only a few modifications.

Catcher/Position The catcher must stand within the lines of his position whenever the pitcher delivers the ball to the bat and within 10 feet of the home base.

Note: This rule was adopted by the National League in 1901. The American League adopted the rule in 1902.

Foul Ball A foul hit ball not caught on the fly is a strike unless two strikes have already been called.

Note: This rule was used by the National League in 1901 and 1902. The American League adopted the rule in 1903. See 1902 summary for further elaboration of this rule by the National League.

A "bunt hit" which sends the ball to foul ground either directly or by bounding or rolling from fair ground to foul ground and which settles on foul ground is a strike.

Infield Fly The batter is out if he hits a fly ball that can be handled by an infielder while first and second bases are occupied, or first, second, and third, unless two hands are out. In such case the umpire shall, as soon as the ball is hit, declare infield or outfield hit.

Pitcher/Delivery If the ball is thrown by the pitcher to any player other than the catcher (except to retire a baserunner) and

the batsman is standing in his proper position ready to strike at a pitched ball, each ball so delivered shall be called a ball.

The umpire shall call a ball on the pitcher each time he delays the game by failing to deliver the ball to the batsman when in position for a longer period than 20 seconds.

Strike Zone See *Foul Ball* and *Pitcher/Delivery*.

1902

Foul Ball The batter is out if after two strikes have been called he obviously attempts to make a foul hit.

Hit by Pitch The batsman becomes a baserunner if while he be a batsman, without making any attempt to strike at the ball, his person or clothing be hit by a ball from the pitcher, unless in the opinion of the umpire he plainly avoids making any effort to get out of the way of the ball from the pitcher and thereby permits himself to be so hit.

Pitcher/Delivery The umpire shall call a ball on the pitcher each time he delays the game by failing to deliver the ball to the batsman when in position for a longer period than 20 seconds, excepting that in the case of the first batsman in each inning, the pitcher may occupy not more than one minute in delivering [warm-up pitches] not to exceed five balls to a baseman.

Strike Zone/Strikeout See *Foul Ball* and *Pitcher/Delivery*.

1903

Pitcher/Position The pitcher's box shall be no more than 15 inches higher than the baselines and home plate. The baselines and home plate shall be on a perfect level, and the slope from the pitcher's box towards the baselines and home plate shall be gradual.

Note: In 1904, the phrase "pitcher's box" was deleted from this rule and replaced by the phrase "pitcher's plate."

Umpire The rules of 1903 contain an extensive reorganization and rewriting of the rules pertaining to umpires.

1904

Ball Two regulation balls of the make adopted by the league of which the contesting clubs are members shall be delivered by the home club to the umpire at or before the hour for the commencement of a championship game. If the ball first placed in play be batted or thrown out of the grounds or into one of the stands for spectators or, in the judgment of the umpire, become unfit for play from any cause, the umpire shall at once deliver the alternate ball to the pitcher and another legal ball shall be supplied to him, so that he shall at all times have in his control one or more alternate balls to substitute for the ball in play in any of the contingencies above set forth. Provided, however, that all balls batted or thrown out of the ground or into a stand, shall, when returned to the field, be given into the custody of the umpire immediately and become alternate balls, and so long as he has in his possession two or more alternate balls, he shall not call for a new ball to replace a ball that has gone out of play. The alternate balls shall become the ball in play in the order in which they were delivered to the umpire.

Bench/Dugout See *Interference/Offensive*

Bunt A bunt hit is a legally batted ball, not swung at, but met with the bat and tapped slowly within the infield by the batsman with the expectation of reaching first base before the ball can be fielded to that base. If the attempt to bunt result in a foul, a strike shall be called by the umpire.

Coach/Illegal Act The baserunner is out if, before two hands are out and while third base is occupied, the coacher stationed near that base shall run in the direction of home base on or near the baseline while a fielder is making or trying to make a play on a batted ball not caught on the fly, or on a thrown ball, and thereby draws a throw to home base. The baserunner entitled to third base shall be declared out by the umpire for the coacher's interference with and prevention of the legitimate play.

Note: In 1914, the words "on a fly ball" were inserted in this rule.

Dead/Live Ball   Immediately upon the delivery to him of the alternate ball by the umpire, the pitcher shall take his position and on the call of "Play," by the umpire, it shall become the ball in play. Provided, however, that play shall not be resumed with the alternate ball when a fair batted ball or a ball thrown by a fielder goes out of the ground or into a stand for spectators until the baserunners have completed the circuit of the bases unless compelled to stop at second or third base in compliance with a ground rule.

Grounds/Fences   To obviate the necessity for ground rules, the shortest distance from a fence or stand on fair territory to home base should be 235 feet and from home base to the grandstand 90 feet.

Interference/Offensive   The baserunner is out if one or more members of the team at bat stand or collect at or around a base for which a baserunner is trying, thereby confusing the fielding side and adding to the difficulty of making such play. The baserunner shall be declared out for the interference of his teammate or teammates.

The players of the side at bat must speedily abandon their bench and hasten to another part of the field when by remaining upon or near it they or any of them would interfere with a fielder in an attempt to catch or handle a thrown ball.

Player   The players of each club, actively engaged in a game at one time, shall be nine in number, one of whom shall act as captain; and in no case shall more or less than nine men be allowed to play on a side in a game.

Note: The previous rule read, "in no case shall less than nine men be allowed to play."

Runner   The baserunner is out if he touches home base before a baserunner preceding him in the batting order, and such preceding baserunner loses his right to third base.

Uniform   Every club shall adopt two uniforms for its players, one to be worn in games at home and the other in games abroad, and the suits of each of the uniforms of a team shall conform in color and style.

1905

There were no changes in the playing rules this year.

1906

Bunt   A bunt hit is a legally batted ball, not swung at, but met with the bat and tapped slowly within the infield by the batsman. If the attempt to bunt result in a foul not legally caught, a strike shall be called by the umpire.

Game/Rain   The choice of innings shall be given to the captain of the home club, who shall be the sole judge of the fitness of the ground for beginning a game after a rain; but, after play has been called by the umpire, he alone shall be the judge as to the fitness of the ground for resuming play after the game has been suspended on account of rain, and when time is so called the groundskeeper and sufficient assistants shall be under the control of the umpire for the purpose of putting the ground in proper shape for play, under penalty of forfeiture of the game by the home team.

Ground/Foul Lines   Foul lines are to be clearly visible from any part of the diamond, and no wood or other hard substance shall be used in the construction of such lines.

1907

Ball/Defaced   In the event of a ball being intentionally discolored by rubbing it with the soil or otherwise by any player except the pitcher, or otherwise damaged by any player, the umpire shall, upon appeal by the captain of the opposite side, forthwith demand the return of that ball and substitute for it another legal ball and impose a fine of $5 on the offending player.

Batter/Awarded Bases   The baserunner shall be entitled to advance one base without liability to be put out if, while the batsman, he becomes a baserunner by reason of "four balls" or for being hit by a pitched ball, or for being interfered with by the catcher in striking at a pitched ball.

Batter/Position   The batter is out if he steps from one batsman's box to the other after the pitcher has taken his position.

Batter-Runner   The batter becomes a baserunner if a fair hit ball strike the person or clothing of the umpire or a baserunner on fair ground.

Defense/Illegal Act   See *Ball/Defaced*.

Game/Legal   If the umpire calls a game at any time after five innings have been completed, the score shall be that of the last equal innings played, except that if the side second at bat shall have scored in an unequal number of innings, or before the completion of the unfinished inning, at least one run more than the side first at bat, the score of the game shall be the total number of runs each team has made.

Game/Rain   If the game be called by the umpire on account of darkness, rain, fire, panic, or for other cause which puts patrons or players in peril, the game shall terminate.

Interference/Offensive   The baserunner is out if with one or no one out and a baserunner on third base, the batsman interferes with a play being made at home plate.

See also *Batter/Runner*.

Interference/Umpire   See *Batter/Runner*.

Pitcher/Delivery   A fairly delivered ball is a ball pitched or thrown to the bat by the pitcher while standing in his position and facing the batsman that passes over any portion of the home base, before touching the ground, not lower than the batsman's knee, nor higher than his shoulder. For every such fairly delivered ball, the umpire shall call one strike.

An unfairly delivered ball is a ball delivered to the bat by the pitcher while standing in his position and facing the batsman that does not pass over any portion of the home base between the batsman's shoulder and knees, or that touches the ground before passing home base, unless struck at by the batsman. For every unfairly delivered ball the umpire shall call one ball.

Runner/Illegal Act   The baserunner is out if he passes a baserunner who is caught between two bases. He shall be declared out immediately upon passing the preceding baserunner.

Strike Zone   See *Pitcher/Delivery*

1908

Ball/Defacing   The rule prohibiting the discoloring of the ball by rubbing it with the soil was amended to include the pitcher as well as all other players.

1909

Dead/Live Ball   In case of a foul strike, foul hit ball not legally caught, dead ball, interference with the fielder or batsman, or a fair hit ball touching a baserunner, the ball shall not be considered in play until it be held by the pitcher standing in his position and the umpire shall have called "Play."

Fair/Foul Ball   A fair hit is a legally batted ball that settles on fair ground between home and first base or between home and third base or that is on fair ground when bounding to the outfield past first or third base or that first falls on fair territory beyond first or third base or that, while on or over fair ground, touches the person of the umpire or a player.

A foul hit is a legally batted ball that settles on foul territory between home and first base or home and third base or that bounds past first or third base in foul territory or that falls on foul territory beyond first or third base or while on or over foul ground, touches the person of the umpire or a player.

Ground Rules Before the commencement of a game the umpire shall see that the rules governing all the materials of the game are strictly observed. He shall ask the captain of the home club whether there are any special ground rules, and if there be, he shall acquaint himself with them, advise the captain of the visiting team of their scope, and see that each is duly enforced, provided that it does not conflict with any of these rules, and are acceptable to the captain of the visiting team. If the latter object to a proposed ground rule, the umpire shall have authority to adopt or reject it.

Pitcher When the umpire announces the pitcher prior to commencement of the game, the player announced must pitch until the first batsman has either been put out or has reached first base. See also *Relief Pitcher*.

Player/Ejected In the event of removal of player or manager by the umpire, he shall go direct to the club house and remain there during progress of the game, or leave the grounds; and a failure to do so will warrant a forfeiture of the game by the umpire.

Relief Pitcher In event of the pitcher being taken from the game by either manager or captain, the player substituted for him shall continue to pitch until the batsman then at bat has either been put out or has reached first base. See also *Pitcher*.

1910

Batter/Awarded Bases The baserunner shall be entitled, without liability to be put out, to advance a base if, while the batsman, he becomes a baserunner by reason of "four balls" or for being hit by a pitched ball, or if a fair hit ball strike the person or clothing of the umpire or a baserunner on fair ground.

Batter/Position The batter is out if he steps from one batsman's box to the other while the pitcher is in his position ready to pitch.

An illegally batted ball is a ball batted by the batsman when either or both of his feet are upon the ground outside the lines of the batsman's position.

Note: This rule replaced the term "foul strike."

Batting Order The batting order of each team must be on the scorecard and must be delivered before the game by its captain to the umpire at home plate, who shall submit it to the inspection of the captain of the other side. The batting order delivered to the umpire must be followed throughout the game unless a player be substituted for another, in which case the substitute must take the place in the batting order of the retired player.

Dead/Live Ball In case of an illegally batted ball, a balk, foul hit ball not legally caught, dead ball, interference with the fielder or batsman, or a fair hit ball striking a baserunner or umpire before touching a fielder, the ball shall not be considered in play until it be held by the pitcher standing in his position and the umpire shall have called "Play."

Fielder/Illegal Act If the fielder stop or catch a batted ball with his cap, glove, or any part of his uniform, while detached from its proper place on his person, the runner or runners shall be entitled to three bases.

Ground Rules/Spectators In case of spectators overflowing on the playing field, the home captain shall make special ground rules to cover balls batted or thrown into the crowd, provided such rules be acceptable to the captain of the visiting club. If the latter object, then the umpire shall have full authority to make and enforce such special rules, and he shall announce the scope of same to the spectators.

Interference/Offensive The baserunner shall return to his base without liability to be put out if the umpire declares the batsman or another baserunner out for interference.

Interference/Umpire If a thrown or pitched ball strike the person or clothing of an umpire on foul ground the ball shall be considered in play and the runner or runners shall be entitled to all the bases they can make.

The baserunner shall return to his base without liability to be put out if the umpire be struck by a fair hit ball before touching a fielder; in which case no base shall be run unless necessitated by the batsman becoming a baserunner, and no run shall be scored unless all the bases are occupied.

Pitcher/Delivery With the bases unoccupied, any ball delivered by the pitcher while either foot is not in contact with the pitcher's plate shall be called a ball by the umpire.

Player/Position The players of the team not at bat may be stationed at any points of the field on fair ground their captain may elect, regardless of their respective positions, except that the pitcher, while in the act of delivering the ball to the bat must take his position as defined in the rules and the catcher likewise must be within the lines of his position and within 10 feet of home base whenever the pitcher delivers the ball to the bat.

Run Scored See *Interference/Umpire*

Runner/Awarded Bases In all cases where there are no spectators on the playing field, and where a thrown ball goes into a stand for spectators, or over or through any fence surrounding the playing field, into the players' bench (whether the ball rebounds into the field or not), the runner or runners shall be entitled to two bases. The umpire in awarding such bases shall be governed by the position of the runner or runners at the time the throw is made.

Strike Zone See *Pitcher/Delivery*

Substitute Whenever one player is substituted for another, whether as batsman, baserunner, or fielder, the captain of the side making the change must immediately notify the umpire, who in turn must announce the same to the spectators. A fine of $5 shall be assessed by the umpire against the captain for each violation of this rule, and the president of the League shall impose a similar fine against the umpire who, after having been notified of a change, fails to make proper announcement. Play shall be suspended while announcement is being made, and the player substituted shall become actively engaged in the game immediately upon his captain's notice of the change to the umpire.

Umpire The rules of 1910 contain new provisions for umpires and describe the respective duties of the Umpire-in-Chief and the Field Umpire.

1911

Ball Cork-center balls are used for the first time as regulation balls in all games.

1912-13

There were no changes in the playing rules in these years.

1914

The Federal League begins operation and adopts virtually the entire rule book. The Victor Sporting Goods Company provides the new league's official ball. The Federal League folded after the 1915 season.

Ball League presidents are no longer required to examine, measure, and weigh baseballs for use in championship games.

Coach   A coach may address words of assistance and direction to the baserunners and to the batter.

Coach/Illegal Acts   If, while third base is occupied, the coacher stationed near that base shall run in the direction of home base on or near the base line while a fielder is making or trying to make a play on a batted ball not caught on the fly or on a thrown ball or a fly ball [see note below], and thereby draws a throw to home base, the baserunner entitled to third base shall be declared out by the umpire for the coacher's interference with and prevention of the legitimate play.

Note: This rule was first adopted in 1904 but did not include the phrase "or a fly ball."

If a coach at third base touches or holds a baserunner at third base or a baserunner who is rounding third base for home plate, such baserunner is out.

Fielder/Illegal Acts   The baserunner is entitled to advance a base without liability to be put out if the fielder stop or catch a batted ball or a thrown ball with his cap, glove, or any part of his uniform, while detached from its proper place on his person, the runner or runners shall be entitled to three bases if a batted ball or to two bases if a thrown ball.

Home Run/Double   See *Runner/Bases.*

Interference/Offensive   The batter is out if he obstructs or interferes with the catcher except when he does so with a runner on third base (with one out or no one out) in which case the baserunner is out.

Interference/Umpire   The baserunner shall return to his base without liability to be put out if the person or clothing of the umpire, while stationed back of the bat, interfere with the catcher in an attempt to throw.

The baserunner is entitled to advance a base if a thrown or pitched ball strike the person or clothing of an umpire. The ball shall be considered in play and the baserunner or runners shall be entitled to all the bases they can make.

Note: Under the previous rule only balls striking the umpire in foul territory entitled the baserunner to advance.

Pitcher/Delivery   The pitcher is permitted to have his feet on top of the pitcher's plate or in front of the plate preliminary to pitching.

Runner/Awarded Bases   Should an errant thrown ball remain in the meshes of a wire screen protecting the spectators, the runner or runners shall be entitled to two bases. The umpire in awarding such bases shall be governed by the position of the runner or runners at the time the throw is made.

Runner/Bases   A batter who hits a home run or a ground-rule double must touch all of the bases in regular order.

1915–19

There were no changes in the playing rules in these years.

1920

Ball   The President of the League of which the contesting clubs are members shall specify the number of baseballs which the home club must deliver to the umpire prior to the hour set for the commencement of a championship game, and all of such baseballs shall be of the regulation make adopted by the league.

The seal on boxes of new balls is not to be broken by the umpire except prior to game time and for the purpose of inspecting the ball and removing the gloss therefrom.

Ball/Defacing   In event of the ball being intentionally discolored by any player, either by rubbing it with the soil, or by applying rosin, paraffin, licorice, or any other foreign substance to it, or otherwise intentionally damaging or roughening the same with sandpaper or emery paper, or other substance, the umpire shall forthwith demand the return of that ball and substitute for it another legal ball, and the offending player shall be disbarred from further participation in the game. If, however, the umpire cannot detect the violator of this rule, and the ball is delivered to the bat by the pitcher, then the latter shall be at once removed from the game, and as an additional penalty shall be automatically suspended for a period of 10 days.

At no time during the progress of the game shall the pitcher be allowed to: (1) Apply a foreign substance of any kind to the ball; (2) Expectorate either on the ball or his glove; (3) Rub the ball on his glove, person, or clothing; (4) Deface the ball in any manner; (5) or to deliver what is called the "shine" ball, "spit" ball, "mud" ball, or "emery" ball. For violation of any part of this rule the umpire shall at once order the pitcher from the game, and in addition he shall be automatically suspended for a period of 10 days, on notice from the president of the league.

Note: In adopting the foregoing rule against "freak" deliveries on February 9, 1920, it was understood and agreed that all bona fide spitball pitchers would be certified to the respective presidents of the National and American leagues at least 10 days prior to April 14, 1920, and that the pitchers so certified would be exempt from the operation of the rule, as far as it related to the spitball only.

Batter/Awarded Bases   The baserunner shall be entitled to advance one base if, while the batsman, a fair hit ball strike the person or clothing of the umpire or a baserunner on fair ground before touching a fielder. Provided, that if a fair hit ball strikes the umpire after having passed a fielder or having been touched by a fielder, the ball shall be considered in play. Also, if a fair hit ball strike the umpire on foul ground, the ball shall be in play.

Catcher/Position   It shall be illegal for the catcher to leave his natural position immediately and directly back of the plate for the purpose of aiding the pitcher to intentionally give a base on balls to a batsman. If the catcher shall move out of position prior to the time of the ball leaving the pitcher's hand, all runners on bases shall be entitled to advance one base.

Also see *Interference/Defensive.*

Coach   See *Interference/Offensive.*

Dead Ball   The baserunner shall return to his base without liability to be put out if the umpire declares a dead ball, unless it also be the fourth unfair ball, and he be thereby forced to take the next base as provided in the rules. Provided, such fourth unfair ball shall not be called if the umpire declare the ball "dead" because of a pitched ball accidentally hitting the bat.

Doubleheader   Whenever necessity demands that two games be played in one afternoon, the first game shall be the regularly scheduled game for that day.

Fair/Foul Ball   A fair or foul fly must be judged according to the relative position of the ball and the foul line, and not as to whether the fielder is on fair or foul ground at the time he touches the ball.

Fielder   See *Runner Tagged.*

Force Out   A force out can be made only when a baserunner legally loses the right to the base he occupies by reason of the batsman becoming a baserunner, and he is thereby obliged to advance.

Game/Drawn   A drawn game shall be declared by the umpire if the score is equal on the last even inning played when he terminates play in accordance with the rules after five or more equal innings have been played by each team. But if the side that went second to bat is at bat when the game is terminated, and has scored the same number of runs as the other side, the umpire shall declare the game drawn without regard to the score of the last equal inning. Provided, that if the side last at bat shall, before the completion of the fifth inning, equal the score made by the opposing side in five complete innings then the game shall be declared as legally drawn, and the individual and team averages shall be incorporated in the Official Playing Records.

Game/Legal "No Game" shall be declared by the umpire if he terminates play in accordance with the rules before five innings are completed by each team. Provided, however, that if the club second at bat shall have made more runs at the end of its fourth inning, or before the completion of its fifth inning, than the club first at bat made in five completed innings of a game so terminated, the umpire shall award the game to the club having made the greater number of runs, and it shall count as a legal game in the championship record.

Hit by Pitch A "dead" ball is a ball delivered to the bat by the pitcher, not struck at by the batsman, that touches any part of the batsman's person or clothing while he is standing in his position or a wildly pitched ball which the batsman plainly makes an attempt to dodge to avoid being hit, but which ball accidentally hits his bat.

Home Run/Game-Ending If a batsman, in the last half of the final inning of any game, hit a home run over the fence or into a stand, all runners on the bases at the time, as well as the batsman, shall be entitled to score, and in such event all bases must be touched in order, and the final score of the game shall be the total number of runs made.

Infield Fly If, before two hands are out, while first and second or first, second, and third bases are occupied, he hit a fair fly ball, other than a line drive, that can be handled by an infielder, the batter is out. In such case, the umpire shall, as soon as the ball be hit, declare it an infield or outfield hit; but the runners may be off their bases or advance at the risk of the ball being caught, the same as on any other fly ball. Provided, that, with first and second bases occupied, with less than two out, any attempt to bunt which results in a fair fly ball shall not be regarded as an infield fly.

Interference/Defensive In the event a baserunner is trying to score from third base on a pitched ball or the "squeeze" play, a "balk" and also an "interference" should be called if the catcher runs out in front of the plate to catch the ball; the runner shall be allowed to score and the batsman entitled to first base. The same penalties must be imposed in case the catcher pushes the batsman out of the way or tips his bat.

Interference/Offensive The baserunner is out if, in the judgment of the umpire, the coacher at third base by touching or holding the runner physically assists him in returning to or leaving third base. The runner, however, should not be declared out if no play is being made.

The baserunner shall be entitled to advance one base if a thrown ball strike a coacher on foul ground and the ball shall be considered in play. Provided, that if in the opinion of the umpire the coacher intentionally interfere with such thrown ball, the runner or runners must return to the last bases touched, and the coacher penalized by removal from the playing field.

The baserunner is *not* out if a fair hit ball goes through an infielder, and hits a runner immediately back of him. The umpire must be convinced that the ball passed through the infield and that no other infielder had the chance to make a play on the ball. If, in the judgment of the umpire, the runner deliberately and intentionally kicks such a hit ball, on which the infielder has missed a play, then the runner must be called out for interference.

Interference/Umpire See *Batter/Awarded Bases*.

Pitcher/Delivery The following prohibitions were added to the previous balk rule in 1920:

A balk shall be: Making any motion to pitch while standing in his position without having the ball in his possession; or, regardless of whether he makes any motion to pitch or not, if the pitcher takes a legal position on the rubber without the ball in his possession, or if he takes a position off the rubber and feints to deliver the ball to the bat.

A balk shall be: After the pitcher has taken position, with both hands holding the ball in front of him, he cannot take either hand off the ball except in the act of delivering the ball to the batsman or in throwing to bases.

A balk shall be: If, with one or more runners on bases, the pitcher, in the act of delivering the ball to the batsman or in throwing to first base, drop the ball, either intentionally or accidentally, the umpire shall call it a "balk" and advance runner or runners. No penalty shall be imposed if, with no one on bases, the pitcher drop the ball while delivering it to the batsman.

If the pitcher steps off the rubber, after being in position, for the purpose either of drying his hands or rubbing his eyes, or for other reasons, and it is a legitimate action not understood or interpreted by the umpire to deceive the baserunner, then the umpire shall call "Time."

In case a balk is called, the ball shall be considered "dead" when announcement is made, and no play can be made until the runner or runners reach the base or bases to which they are entitled.

If, with no one on base, the pitcher deliver the ball while off the rubber, the umpire shall call a "ball" whether it goes over the plate fair or not. If, however, the batsman strikes at such illegally delivered ball it counts either for a strike or whatever play may follow.

Pitcher/Illegal Act See *Ball/Defacing*.

Player/Position The players of the team not at bat may be stationed at any points of the field on fair ground their captain may elect, regardless of their respective positions, except that the pitcher, while in the act of delivering the ball to the bat must take his position and the catcher must be within the lines of his position, and within 10 feet of home base, whenever the pitcher delivers the ball to the bat; nor shall the catcher leave his natural position immediately and directly back of the plate for the purpose of aiding the pitcher to intentionally give a base on balls to a batsman.

Runner/Advancing A baserunner who holds his base on a fly ball shall have the right to advance the moment such fly ball touches the hands of a fielder.

Runner/Bases The failure of a preceding runner to touch a base (and who is declared out therefore) shall not affect the status of a succeeding runner who touches each base in proper order.

Runner/Illegal Act A baserunner having acquired legal title to a base cannot run bases in reverse order for the purpose either of confusing the fielders or making a travesty of the game. A runner violating this rule is out if touched with the ball, or the ball held on the base said runner was entitled to hold.

Runner/Returning In case a runner is being run down between bases, and the following runner occupies the same base the first runner has left, the second man cannot be put out while holding said base. If the first runner, however, returns safely to the base he left, and both runners are then occupying the same base, the second runner is the man out, if touched with the ball.

Run Scored See *Interference/Defensive*

Runner/Tagged The baserunner is out if at any time while the ball is in play, he be touched by the ball in the hands of a fielder, unless some part of his person be touching the base he is entitled to occupy; provided, however, that the ball be held by the fielder after touching him, unless the baserunner deliberately knock it out of his hand. The ball must be firmly held by the fielder after touching the runner. The ball cannot be juggled, even though the fielder may retain possession of the ball and prevent same from dropping to the ground.

Substitute When a substitution is made but no announcement of the substitution is made as required by the rules the substitute will nevertheless be considered in the game as follows: if a pitcher, when he takes his place on the rubber; if a batter, when he takes his place in the batsman's box; if a fielder, when he takes the place of the fielder substituted for; if a runner, when the substitute replaces him on the base he is holding, and any play made by such unannounced substitute shall be legal under the rules.

Time The rules of 1920 contain several new provisions governing the calling of "Time" by the umpire, the most important of which is the following: That in case of an accident to a player or players in attempting to make a play on either a batted or a thrown ball, "Time" shall not be called until, in the judgment of the umpire, no further play is possible.

Umpire The rules of 1920 contain various new provisions governing umpires and their respective duties.

1921

Pitcher Note: By concurrent action of the National and American leagues taken at their respective annual meetings held in New York in December 1920, it was agreed that all bona fide spitball pitchers then remaining in the National and American leagues be exempt from the operation of the rule against the use of the spitball during the balance of their major league careers. The pitchers so exempted were: National League—Bill Doak, Phil Douglas, Dana Fillingim, Ray Fisher, Marv Goodwin, Burleigh Grimes, Clarence Mitchell, and Dick Rudolph (8). American League—Doc Ayers, Ray Caldwell, Stan Coveleskie, Urban "Red" Faber, Hubert "Dutch" Leonard, Jack Quinn, Allan Russell, Urban Shocker, and Allen Sothoron (9).

1922–25

There were no changes to the playing rules in these years.

1926

Grounds/Fences A fair batted ball that goes over the fence or into a stand shall entitle the batsman to a home run, unless it should pass out of the ground or into a stand at a distance less than 250 feet from the home base, in which case the batsman shall be entitled to two bases only. In either event the batsman must touch the bases in regular order. The point at which a fence or stand is less than 250 feet from the home base shall be plainly indicated by a white or black sign or mark for the umpire's guidance.

Rosin Bag Under the supervision and control of the umpire, the pitcher may use to dry his hands a small, finely meshed sealed bag containing powdered rosin, furnished by the League.
Note: This rule was first adopted by the National League only.

1927–30

There were no changes to the playing rules in these years.

1931

Batter The rules of 1931 provide new wording for the rule governing when the batter is out without changing the substance of the rule.

Batter/Awarded Bases A fair hit ball that bounds into a stand or over a fence shall be a two-base hit.
Note: There is no reference to distance in this rule and any fair hit ball bounding over the fence or into the stand is a two-base hit.

Coach See *Interference/Offensive*.

Dead Ball The rules of 1931 merge two previous rules governing dead balls in one differently worded rule without changing the substance of the old rules.

Double See *Batter/Awarded Bases*.

Fair/Foul Ball When a batted ball passes outside the playing field the umpire shall decide it fair or foul according to where it leaves the playing field.

Game The rules of 1931 merge four previous rules governing regulation games in one differently worded rule without changing the substance of the old rules.

Game/Legal "No game" shall be declared by the umpire if he terminates play in accordance with the rules before five innings have been completed by each team; but if the team last at bat is at bat in the last half of the fifth inning and has equaled before the completion of that inning the score of the side first at bat, the umpire shall declare the game "legally drawn" in accordance with the rules. If the team second at bat shall have made more runs at the end of its fourth inning or before the completion of its fifth inning, than the team first at bat has made in five completed innings of a game so terminated, the umpire shall award the game to the team having made the greater number of runs, and it shall count as a legal game in the championship record.

Glove/Pitcher The pitcher's glove must be uniform in color.

Interference/Offensive The players or coaches of the side at bat must immediately vacate any space occupied by them if it is needed by a fielder attempting to handle a batted or thrown ball. See also *Three-Foot Lane*.

Obstruction The baserunner shall advance one base if he be prevented from making a base by the obstruction of a fielder, except when a fielder is trying to field a batted ball unless the latter has the ball in his hand ready to touch the baserunner. The ball is still in play so far as other baserunners are concerned.

Pitcher/Delivery Preliminary to pitching, the pitcher shall take his position facing the batsman, with both feet squarely on the ground and on top of the pitcher's plate, or one foot on top of the pitcher's plate and the other foot in contact with same, or one foot in front of the pitcher's plate and the other foot on top of same, and in the act of delivering the ball to the batsman he must keep one foot in contact with the pitcher's plate. He shall not raise either foot until in the act of delivering the ball to the batsman, or in throwing to a base; nor may he make more than one step in such delivery. With a runner on first base or on second base, the pitcher must face the batsman with both hands holding the ball in front of him. If he indulges in a preliminary stretch by raising his arms above his head or out in front, he must return to a natural pitcher's position and stop before starting his delivery of the ball to the batsman.

Runner/Awarded Bases In all cases where there are no spectators on the playing field and where a thrown ball goes into a stand for spectators or over or through any fence surrounding the playing field or into the players' bench (whether the ball rebounds into the field or not) or remains in the meshes of a wire screen protecting the spectators, the runner or runners shall be entitled to two bases. When the throw is made by an infielder, the umpire, in awarding such bases, shall be governed by the position of the runner or runners at the time the ball was pitched; when the throw is made by an outfielder, the award shall be governed by the position of the runner or runners at the time the throw was made.
The baserunner shall advance one base without liability to be put out if a ball delivered by the pitcher pass the catcher and touch any fence or building within 60 feet of the home base. The ball shall be dead in such case.

Runner/Bases The baserunner is out if, when advancing bases or obliged to return to a base while the ball is in play, he fail to touch the intervening base or bases, if any, in the regular or reverse order, as the case may be, he may be put out by the ball being held by a fielder on any base he failed to touch or by being touched by the ball in the hand of a fielder in the same manner as in running to first base; provided, that the baserunner shall not be out in such case if the ball be delivered to the bat by the pitcher before the fielder hold it on said base or touch the baserunner with it; however, after a fly ball other than a foul tip be legally caught by a fielder, the baserunner who complies with this rule can only be retired by the ball being held by a fielder on the base occupied by the runner when such ball was batted or by being touched by the ball in the hand of the fielder.

The failure of a preceding runner to touch a base (and who is declared out therefore) shall not affect the status of a succeeding runner who touches each base in proper order; except that, after two are out, a succeeding runner cannot score a run when a preceding runner is declared out for failing to touch a base as provided in the rules. This exception also applies to a batsman who hits the ball out of the playing field for an apparent home run.

Substitute   Substitutions shall not be in effect until the manager or captain of the team making the change notifies the umpire.

Substitute/Runner   The manager or the captain of the opposing team must consent before a runner can be substituted for another baserunner.

Note: Previously this rule referred only to the captain. Throughout the rules of 1931, wherever authority or decision-making authority is granted to the captain, the words "or manager" have been added.

Three-Foot Lane   The baserunner is out if, in running the last half of the distance from home base to first base, while the ball is being fielded to first base, he runs outside the three-foot lines, and, in the opinion of the umpire, interferes with the fielder taking the throw at first base; except that he may run outside the three-foot lines to avoid a fielder attempting to field a batted ball.

Uniform   Glass buttons or polished metal must not be used on a uniform.

1932–38

There were no changes to the playing rules in these years.

1939

Batter/Caught Fly   The baserunner is out if, having made a fair hit while batsman, such fair hit ball be caught by a fielder before touching the ground or any object other than a fielder; provided, it be not caught in a fielder's hat, cap, protector, pocket, or other part of his uniform.

Fielder/Drops Fly Ball   If, before two are out, while first and second or first, second, and third bases are occupied, an outfielder, in the judgment of the umpire, intentionally drops a fly ball or a line drive, he shall immediately rule the ball has been caught.

Note: Baserunners are obliged to "tag up" after the out has been declared before they can advance.

Gloves   The catcher may wear a leather glove or mitt of any size, shape or weight.

The first baseman may wear a leather glove or mitt not more than 12 inches from top to bottom and not more than 8 inches wide across the palm, with thumb and palm connected by leather lacing of not more than 4 inches from thumb to palm, which lacing shall not be enlarged, extended or reinforced by any process or material whatever.

Every other player is restricted to the use of a leather glove weighing not over 10 ounces and measuring not over 14 inches around the palm. The pitcher's glove must be uniform in color.

Pitcher/Delivery   Preliminary to pitching, the pitcher shall take his position facing the batsman with both feet squarely on the ground, but his pivot foot must be on or in front in contact with the pitcher's plate.

Note: After the pitcher takes legal position for delivery of the ball to the batsman, he can take but one step and that must be forward.

A balk will be called (entitling the runner or runners to advance one base) if the pitcher makes any delivery of the ball to the bat while his pivot foot is back of and not in contact with the pitcher's plate.

1940

Bat   The bat must be made entirely of hardwood in one piece.

Coach   No fines are to be assessed for violations of the coaching rules.

Dead Ball   A batted or thrown ball touched, stopped, or handled by a person not engaged in the game is dead and not in play. If a fair hit, the batsman making the hit shall be entitled to two bases and each baserunner shall be entitled to advance two bases. If a thrown ball, each baserunner shall be entitled to advance in accordance with the rules governing a thrown ball.

Note: This rule replaces the rule regarding "blocked balls."

Fielder   See *Runner/Tagged*.

Fielder/Drops Fly Ball   See *Runner/Advancing*.

Foul Ball   A foul hit is a legally batted ball that settles on foul territory between home and first base or home and third base or that bounds past first or third base on or over foul territory or that falls on foul territory beyond first or third base or, while on or over foul ground, touches the person of the umpire or a player or any object foreign to the natural ground. A foul fly must be judged according to the relative position of the ball and the foul line, and not as to whether the fielder is on foul or fair ground at the time he touches the ball.

Game/Doubleheader   No club or clubs shall engage in more than two championship games within a period of one day.

Game/Start   No inning of any night game shall be started after 11:50 P.M. standard time.

Grounds   The ball ground must be enclosed. To obviate the necessity for ground rules, the shortest distance from a fence or stand on fair territory to the home base should be 250 feet and from home base to the grandstand 60 feet.

Grounds/Foul Lines   The foul lines are to be continued until they reach the boundary lines of the ground and not less than 10 feet above the top of the fence or stand. The foul lines are to be made, on the playing field, of lime, chalk, or other powder or paint.

Infield Fly   The batter is out if, before two are out, while first and second or first, second, and third bases are occupied, he hit a fair fly ball, other than a line drive, that can reasonably be caught by an infielder. In such case, the umpire shall declare it an infield fly. However, the runners may be off their bases or advance at the risk of the ball being caught, the same as on any other fly ball; but if hit by the ball while standing on base, that baserunner shall not be called out, but the ball is dead and the batsman shall be called out and if the baserunner be hit while off base, both that baserunner and the batsman shall be called out and the ball is dead. Provided, that, with first and second bases occupied or first, second, and third bases occupied, with less than two out, any attempt to bunt which results in a fair fly ball shall not be regarded as an infield fly.

Interference/Defensive   The batter becomes a baserunner if the catcher interferes with him, unless he makes a safe hit.

The baserunner is entitled to advance one base if the catcher interferes with the batsman while a baserunner is attempting to steal a base.

Interference/Offensive   If one or more members of the team at bat stand or collect at or around a base for which a baserunner is trying, thereby confusing the team in the field and adding to the difficulty of making such play or if a batsman or baserunner who has just been retired obstructs or interferes with any following play being made on a baserunner, the baserunner shall be declared out for the interference of his teammate or teammates.

The baserunner is out if, after having hit or bunted a ball to fair territory, his bat again hits the ball on or over fair territory and deflects its course. Other baserunners cannot advance.

Pitcher/Delivery   Preliminary to pitching, the pitcher shall take his position facing the batsman with his pivot foot always on or in front of and in contact with the pitcher's plate. In the act of delivering the ball to the batsman, the pitcher's other foot is free, except that he cannot step to either side of the pitcher's plate. He shall not raise either foot until in the act of delivering the ball to the batsman or in throwing to a base. With a runner on first or second base, the pitcher must face the batsman with both hands holding the ball in front of him. If he raises his arms above his head or out in front he must return to a natural pitcher's position and stop before starting the delivery of the ball to the batsman.

Note: After pitcher takes legal position for delivery of ball to batsman, he may take one step backward and one step forward, but not to either side.

It is a balk if the pitcher, in the act of delivering the ball to the batsman or in throwing to first base, drop the ball, either intentionally or accidentally.

Note: With no one on base, it is not a balk if the pitcher drops the ball while delivering it to the batsman.

A balk (entitling the runner or runners to advance one base) shall be called for: (1) Throwing the ball by the pitcher to any base to catch the baserunner without first stepping directly toward such base in the act of making such throw; or throwing or feinting to throw to an unoccupied base; (2) Making any motion of the arm, shoulder, hip, knee, foot, or body the pitcher habitually makes in his method of delivery, without immediately delivering the ball to the bat.

Runner/Advancing   A baserunner who holds his base on a fly ball shall have the right to advance the moment such fly ball touches the person or uniform of a fielder.

The baserunner may "tag up" and advance if, before two are out, while first, or first and second, or first, second, and third bases are occupied, any player, in the judgment of the umpire, intentionally drops a fly ball or a line drive, the umpire shall immediately rule the ball has been caught.

Runner/Awarded Bases   In all cases where there are no spectators on the playing field, and where a thrown ball goes into a stand for spectators, or over or through any fence surrounding the playing field, or into the players' bench (whether the ball rebounds into the field or not), or remains in the meshes of a wire screen protecting the spectators, the runner or runners shall be entitled to two bases. When a first throw made by an infielder, the umpire, in awarding such bases, shall be governed by the position of the runner or runners at the time the ball was pitched; when the throw is made by an outfielder or is the result of any following plays or attempted plays, the award shall be governed by the position of the runner or runners at the time the last throw was made.

Runner/Overrunning First   The baserunner is permitted to "overslide" as well as overrun first base without liability to be put out.

Runner/Tagged   The baserunner is out if at any time while the ball is in play, he be touched by the ball in the hand of a fielder, unless some part of his person be touching the base he is entitled to occupy; provided, however, that the ball be held by the fielder after touching him, unless the baserunner deliberately knock it out of his hand. The ball must be firmly held by the fielder after touching the runner. The ball cannot be juggled, even though the

fielder may regain possession of the ball and prevent same from dropping to the ground.

Note: The previous rule read: "even though the fielder may *retain* possession of the ball."

Trainer   Trainers are permitted to occupy the players' bench.

Trainer/Umpire   Umpires are given authority over trainers.

Umpire   The rules of 1940 describe the procedures to be used when more than two umpires are assigned.

The Umpire-in-Chief is to make all decisions regarding batters.

1941

There were no changes to the playing rules this year.

1942

Game/Start   No inning of any night game shall be started after 12:50 A.M. war time.

1943–48

There were no changes to the playing rules in these years.

1949

Catcher/Position   The catcher must stand with both feet inside the catcher's lines until the ball leaves the pitcher's hand.

Coach   First base coaches as well as third base coaches must refrain from touching or holding the runner physically or the runner is out.

Foul/Fair Ball   A foul fly must be judged according to the relative position of the ball and the foul line, including the foul pole, and not as to whether the fielder is on foul or fair ground at the time he touches the ball.

Game/Start   No inning of any night game shall be started after 12:50 A.M. local city time.

Pitcher/Delivery   No balk can be committed with all bases empty.

Player/Illegal Act   No manager, captain, coach, or player shall address the spectators before or during a game except in reply to a request for information about the progress or state of the game or to give the name of a player.

1950

In 1950, the rule book was entirely recodified and greatly rewritten, refined, and clarified. Although the essence of many of the rules remained the same as in previous years, the rewritten passages are included below.

Bases   The home plate and the pitcher's plate shall be of whitened rubber, anchored in the ground, even with its surface. The home plate, with beveled edges, shall be level with the baselines. The pitcher's plate shall be on an 18-foot-diameter mound, exactly 15 inches above the level of home plate. The plate shall be placed six inches from the front of a two-foot by five-foot leveled area atop the mound. The slope from the pitcher's plate to the baselines shall be gradual.

First, second, and third bases shall be approved bags of white canvas, securely anchored in the ground. They shall be 15 inches square and not less than three, nor more than five inches thick and shall be filled with soft material.

Bat   The bat shall be round, not over 2¾ inches in diameter at the thickest part, not more than 42 inches in length, and entirely of hard, solid wood in one piece. Twine may be wound around it or a granulated substance applied to it, for a distance of 18 inches from the end of the handle, but not elsewhere.

Batter/Awarded Bases   Each runner including the batter-runner may, without liability of being put out, advance to home base, scoring a run, if a fair ball goes over the field fence in flight and he touch all bases legally; or if a fair ball which, in the umpire's judgment, would have cleared the field fence in flight, is deflected by the act of a defensive player in throwing his glove, cap, or any article of his apparel, the runner shall be awarded a home run.

The rules of 1950 include various new provisions for baserunners when balls are hit or thrown into the stands.

The batter becomes a baserunner when a fair ball, after touching the ground, bounds into the stands or passes through or under a fence or through or under a scoreboard or through or under shrubbery or vines on the fence, in which case the batter and the baserunners shall be entitled to advance two bases.

The batter becomes a baserunner when any fair ball which, either before or after striking the ground, passes through or under a fence or through or under a scoreboard or through any opening in the fence or scoreboard or through or under shrubbery or vines on the fence, in which case the batter and the baserunners shall be entitled to two bases.

The batter becomes a baserunner when any bounding fair ball is deflected by the fielder into the stands or over or under a fence on fair or foul ground, in which case the batter and all baserunners shall be entitled to advance two bases.

The batter becomes a baserunner when any fair fly ball is deflected by the fielder into the stands or over the fence into foul territory, in which case the batter shall be entitled to advance to second base; but if deflected into the stands or over the fence in fair territory, the batter shall be entitled to a home run.

Batter/Illegal Act   The batter is out for illegal action when he fails to take his position in the batter's box promptly. If he persists in unwarranted delay in taking his position the umpire shall direct the pitcher to deliver the ball to the bat and every such pitch shall be called "strike" by the umpire. If he enters the batter's box in the interval between any such pitches, the ball and strike count shall continue regularly, but if he has not entered the batter's box when three strikes are called he shall be declared "out."

Catch   A catch is the act of a defensive player in receiving, and holding firmly in his hand or glove, a batted or thrown ball. It is not a catch, however, if simultaneously or immediately following his contact with the ball, he collide with a player or with a wall or if he fall down, and as a result of such collision or falling, drops the ball. If the player has made the catch and drops the ball while in the act of making a throw following the catch, the ball shall be adjudged to have been caught. In establishing the validity of the catch, the player shall hold the ball long enough to prove that he has complete control of the ball and that his release of the ball is voluntary and intentional.

Dead/Live Ball   See *Time* and *Pitcher-Infielder.*

Definitions   Rule Two of the rules of 1950 includes the definitions of 69 baseball terms as used in the rules. Several of the key definitions are quoted throughout this year's rule entries.

Doubleheader   The rules of 1950 include a series of new provisions governing the conduct of doubleheaders.

Fair Territory   Fair territory is that part of the playing field within, and including the first and third baselines, from home base to the bottom of the playing field fence and perpendicularly upwards. All foul lines are in fair territory.

Foul Tip   A foul tip is a ball batted by the batter that goes sharp and direct from the bat to the catcher's hands and is legally caught. It is not a foul tip unless caught and any foul tip that is caught is a strike, and the ball is in play. It is not a catch if it is a rebound from any part of the catcher's equipment other than the catcher's glove or hand.

Game   Baseball is a game between two teams of nine players, each with adequate substitutes, coaches, and trainers, under the direction of a manager, played in accordance with these rules, under jurisdiction of an umpire or umpires on an enclosed field.

The object of each team is to win by scoring the more runs.

A game consists of nine innings, except as otherwise provided, and an inning is that portion of the game during which each team shall play both offensively and defensively.

The winner of the game shall be that team which shall have scored, in accordance with these rules, the greater number of runs at the conclusion of a regulation game.

Game/Rain   The manager of the home team shall be the sole judge of the fitness of the playing field for the beginning of any game other than the second game of a doubleheader. Exception: Any league may permanently authorize its president to suspend the application of this rule as to that league during the closing weeks of its championship season in order to ensure that the championship is decided each year on its merits. When the postponement of, and possible failure to play, a game in the final series of a championship season between any two teams might affect the final standing of any club in the league, the president, on appeal from any league member, may assume the authority granted the home team manager by this rule.

Game/Start   The players of the home team shall take their defensive positions, the first batter of the visiting team shall take his position in the batter's box, the umpire shall call "Play," and the game shall proceed.

The rules of 1950 include a series of new provisions governing the preliminaries before championship games.

Glove/Fielder   Each player, other than the first baseman and the catcher, is restricted to the use of a leather glove not more than twelve inches long nor more than eight inches wide, measured from the base of the thumb crotch to the outside edge of the glove. The space between the thumb and the forefinger shall not exceed 4½ inches at the top nor more than 3½ inches at the base of the thumb crotch. The webbing may be standard leather or lacing and shall not be enlarged, extended, or reinforced by any process or materials whatever. The webbing cannot be constructed of wound or wrapped lacing to make a net type of trap. The glove may be of any weight.

Glove/First Baseman   The first baseman may wear a leather glove or mitt not more than 12 inches long from top to bottom and not more than eight inches wide across the palm, measured from base of thumb crotch to outer edge of the mitt. The space between the thumb section and the finger section of the mitt shall not exceed four inches at the top of the mitt and 3½ inches at the base of the thumb crotch. The mitt shall be constructed so that this space is permanently fixed and cannot be enlarged, extended, widened, or deepened by the use of any materials or process whatever. The web of the mitt shall measure not more than five inches from its top to the base of the thumb crotch. The web may be either a lacing, lacing through leather tunnels, or a center piece of leather which may be an extension of the palm connected to the mitt with lacing and constructed so that it will not exceed the above-mentioned measurements. The webbing cannot be constructed of wound or wrapped lacing or deepened to make a net type of trap.

Glove/Pitcher   The pitcher's glove shall be uniform in color and cannot be white or gray.

Home Run   See *Batter/Awarded Bases.*

Infield Fly   An infield fly is an out called by the umpire on the batter—if, before two are out, while first and second or first, second, and third bases are occupied, he hit a fair fly ball, other than a line drive, that in the judgment of the umpire can reasonably be caught by an infielder. Where a defensive player who normally plays in the outfield places himself in the infield, he shall for the purpose of the infield fly rule be considered an infielder. In such case, the umpire shall declare it an infield fly.

However, the runners may be off their bases or advance at the risk of the ball being caught, the same as on any other fly ball. If a runner is hit by the ball while standing on base, he shall not be called out, but the ball is dead and the batter shall be called out; but if a baserunner is hit while off base, both he and the batter shall be called out and the ball is dead. Provided, that, with first and second bases occupied, or first, second, and third bases occupied, before two are out, any attempt to bunt which results in a fair fly ball shall not be regarded as an infield fly.

Interference/Offensive   The rules of 1950 include several new provisions describing the circumstances under which a baserunner is out for interference.

The batter is out when a preceding runner shall, in the umpire's judgment, intentionally interfere with the play of a defensive player who is attempting to catch a thrown ball or to throw the ball in an attempt to complete any play.

The batter is out when with two out, a runner on third base, and two strikes on the batter, the runner attempts to steal home base on a legal pitch and the ball strikes the runner in the strike zone. The umpire shall call "strike three," the batter is out and the run shall not count; with less than two out the umpire shall call "strike three," the ball is dead, and the run counts.

The batter is out when after striking or bunting the ball he intentionally strikes the ball a second time, or strikes it with a thrown bat or deflects its course in any manner while running to first base. The ball is dead and no runners may advance. If the runner drops his bat and the ball rolls against the bat and, in the umpire's judgment, there was no intention to interfere with the course of the ball, the ball is alive and in play.

Obstruction   A batter who has become a runner is entitled to unimpeded progress as he advances around the bases. Whenever a defensive player impedes the runner in any way, unless he is attempting to field a batted ball or has the ball in his possession, the umpire shall call "obstruction," the ball shall remain in play, and all runners shall be permitted to advance, without liability to be put out, to the bases which, in the judgment of the umpire, the runners would have reached had obstruction not been called.

In a "run-down" play, if the runner's progress is impeded by any defensive player who does not have the ball in his possession, the umpire shall call "obstruction" and the runner shall be entitled to occupy the base he is attempting to reach when the obstruction occurred.

Pitcher/Delivery   There are two legal pitching positions: The "Wind-up" position and the "Set" position. Either position may be used at any time.

Pivot Foot   The pitcher's pivot foot is that foot which is in contact with the pitcher's plate as he delivers the pitch.

Set Position   Set position is the pitcher's position when he stands facing the batter with his entire pivot foot on or in front of and in contact with, and not off the end of the pitcher's plate, and his other foot in front of the pitcher's plate, holding the ball in both hands in front of his body and coming to a complete stop of at least one second.

Wind-up Position   Wind-up position is the pitcher's position when he stands facing the batter, his pivot foot on or in front of and touching the pitcher's plate, and the other foot free.

From the set position, the pitcher may deliver the ball to the batter, throw to a base, or step backward off the pitcher's plate with his pivot foot. Before assuming set position the pitcher may elect to make any natural preliminary motion such as that known as "the stretch." But if he so elects, he must come to set position before delivering the ball to the batter. After assuming set position, any natural motion associated with his delivery of the ball to the batter commits him to the pitch without alteration or interruption.

If there is a runner or runners it is a balk if the pitcher delivers the pitch from "set position" without coming to a stop of one full second. See also *Pitcher/Pickoff*.

Pitcher/Illegal Act   The pitcher shall not be allowed to pitch at a batter's head, and if, in the umpire's opinion, such violation occurs, he shall call "Time" and warn the pitcher and the manager of the defensive team that another such pitch will mean the immediate expulsion of the pitcher from the game. If such pitch is repeated, the umpire shall inflict the penalty as follows: The pitcher shall be removed from the game and from the grounds. The president of the League shall impose such fine and suspension as his judgment warrants.

See also *Pitcher/Uniform*.

Pitcher/Illegal Pitches   If the pitcher makes an illegal pitch with the bases unoccupied it shall be called a ball, unless the batter shall make a fair hit or reaches first base on an error or otherwise.

The pitcher shall not be allowed to pitch the "quick return ball." Whenever such pitch is attempted the umpire shall call "Time." If the offense is repeated the umpire shall call each such repeated offense a "ball," unless the batter reaches first base on a fair hit, an error, or otherwise, and no other runner is forced by his reaching first base, in which case the play proceeds.

Pitcher-Infielder   If the pitcher removes his pivot foot from contact with the pitcher's plate by stepping backward with that foot, he thereby becomes an infielder and, if his subsequent throw to a base, when off the pitcher's plate, goes into a stand or over, through, or under a fence or into a bench or dugout (whether the ball rebounds or not) or remains in the meshes of a wire screen protecting the spectators, the ball is dead and all runners shall be entitled to advance two bases.

Pitcher/Pick-Off   At any time during the pitcher's preliminary movements and until his natural pitching motion commits him to the pitch, he may throw to any base provided he step directly toward such base before making the throw.

Pitcher/Position   See *Bases* for pitcher's plate.

Pitcher/Uniform   The pitcher shall not be allowed to wear a garment with ragged, frayed or slit sleeves, and shall not be permitted to attach tape or other material of a color different from his uniform or glove to his glove or clothing.

Pitcher/Warm-Ups   When a pitcher takes his position at the beginning of each inning or when he relieves another pitcher, he shall be permitted to pitch not to exceed eight preparatory pitches to his catcher during which play shall be suspended. Such preparatory pitches shall not consume more than one minute of time.

Player/Illegal Acts   Players in uniform shall not address nor mingle with spectators, nor sit in the stands before or during a game. No manager, captain, coach, or player shall address any spectator before or during a game. Players of opposing teams shall not fraternize at any time while in uniform. Penalty: The president of the league shall impose fines for violation of this rule at his discretion.

No manager, player, substitute, coach, trainer, or batboy shall at any time, whether from the bench, the coacher's box, or on the playing field, or elsewhere call "Time," or employ any other word or phrase while the ball is alive and in play for the obvious purpose of confusing an umpire or an opposing player.

Except the batter, or a runner attempting to score, no offensive player shall cross the catcher's lines when the ball is in play.

Runner   See *Batter/Awarded Bases* and *Pitcher-Infielder*.

Runner/Out   The baserunner is out if, after he has acquired legal possession of a base, he or that base is tagged while he is running the bases in reverse order for the purpose of confusing the defense or making a travesty of the game. No runner may advance in this situation in the event of an error on this play by the defensive team.

The baserunner is out if, in running or sliding for home base, he fails to touch home base and makes no attempt to return to the base, when a defensive player holds the ball in his hand while touching home base and appeals to the umpire for the decision.

Strike Zone The strike zone is that space over home plate which is between the batter's armpits and the top of his knees when he assumes his natural stance.

Substitute A player or players may be substituted during a game at any time the ball is dead. A substituted player shall bat in the replaced player's position in the team's batting order. A player once removed from a game shall not re-enter that game. If a substitute enters the game in place of a manager, the manager may thereafter go to the coaching lines at his discretion. When two or more substitute players of the defensive team enter the game at the same time, the manager, or his designated representative, shall, immediately before they take their position as defensive players, designate to the umpire-in-chief such players' positions in the team's batting order and the umpire-in-chief shall so notify the official scorer. If this information is not immediately given to the umpire-in-chief, he shall have authority to designate the substitutes' places in the batting order.

Substitute/Runner A player whose name is on his team's batting order may not become a substitute runner for another member of his team.

Time The ball is dead when the umpire-in-chief suspends play by calling "Time" when a manager requests "Time" for a substitution or for conference with his player.

The ball is dead when the umpire-in-chief suspends play by calling "Time" when a fielder, after catching a fly ball, falls into a bench, dugout, or stand or falls across ropes into a crowd (when spectators are on the field), and baserunners may advance one base without liability to be put out.

Note: If player after making the catch steps into the dugout but does not fall, the ball is alive and in play and runners may advance at their own peril.

After the umpire calls "Play" the ball is alive and in play and remains alive and in play until for legal cause, or at the umpire's call of "Time" suspending play, the ball becomes dead. While the ball is dead no player may be put out, no bases may be run, and no runs may be scored, except that runners may advance as legally provided.

Umpire Each umpire is the representative of the president of the league, the president of the National Association and the Commissioner of Baseball.

The umpire-in-chief shall enforce the rules from the moment he receives the batting order from the manager of the home team until termination of the game. This shall include control of ground crews, newsmen, and photographers, and any other persons whose duties require their presence upon the field.

Uniform See *Pitcher/Uniform*

1951–53

There were no changes to the playing rules in these years.

1954

Balk In the event a balk is called, the ball is dead, and each runner shall advance one base without liability to be put out unless the batter hits the pitch on which the balk is made, in which case the manager of the offensive team may elect to accept either the balk penalty or the result of the batter's action.

Bat The bat shall be a smooth, rounded stick not more than 2¾ inches in diameter at the thickest part and not more than 42 inches in length. The bat shall be one piece of solid wood or formed from a block of wood consisting of two or more pieces of wood bonded together with an adhesive in such a way that the grain direction of all pieces is essentially parallel to the length of

the bat. Any such laminated bat shall contain only wood or adhesive, except for a clear finish.

For a distance of 18 inches from the end by which the bat is gripped, it may be roughened or wrapped with tape or twine.

Note: Approval of the laminated bat is experimental for the 1954 season, and no laminated bat shall be used in a professional game until the manufacturer has secured approval from the Rules Committee of his design and method of manufacture. In giving or withholding such approval, the Rules Committee will be guided by comparison of the laminated bat with one-piece solid wood bats. Laminated bats which are inferior to one-piece solid wood bats in safety or durability will not be approved. A design or method of manufacture which produces a "loaded" or "freak" type of bat or which produces a substantially greater reaction or distance factor than one-piece solid wood bats will not be approved.

Batter/Illegal Act See *Interference/Offensive*.

Catch A catch is the act of a fielder in getting secure possession in his hand or glove of a ball in flight and firmly holding it; providing he does not use his cap, protector, pocket, or any other part of his uniform in getting possession.

Dead/Live Ball See *Time*.

Definitions Rules Two and Three of the rules of 1954 contain several new definitions of baseball terms as used in the rules.

Fielder/Drops Fly Ball The batter is out when, with less than two out and first, first and second, first and third, or first, second, and third bases occupied, a fielder intentionally drops a fair fly ball or line drive. Runners need not re-touch and may advance at their own peril.

Fielder/Illegal Act No fielder shall take a position in the batter's line of vision, and with deliberate unsportsmanlike intent, act in a manner to distract the batter.

Game The rules of 1954 contain a series of new provisions governing suspended games.

Gloves/Equipment Members of the offensive team shall carry all gloves and other equipment off the field and to the dugout while their team is at bat. No equipment shall be left lying on the field, either in fair or foul territory.

Interference/Defensive Defensive interference is an illegal act by a fielder which hinders or prevents a batter from hitting a pitch.

Interference/Offensive The batter is out after hitting or bunting a fair ball, when his bat hits the ball a second time in fair territory. The ball is dead and no runners may advance. If the batter-runner drops his bat and the ball rolls against the bat in fair territory and, in the umpire's judgment, there was no intention to interfere with the course of the ball, the ball is alive and in play.

The batter is out after hitting or bunting a foul ball, when he intentionally deflects the course of the ball in any manner while running to first base. The ball is dead and no runners may advance.

The batter is out when his fair ball touches him before touching a fielder.

It is interference by a batter or runner when he intentionally deflects the course of a foul ball in any manner.

Interference/Spectator The batter is out when spectator interference clearly prevents a fielder from catching his fly ball.

Spectator interference occurs when a spectator reaches out of the stands, or goes on the playing field and touches a live ball. When there is spectator interference with any thrown ball, except a throw by the pitcher, the ball shall be dead at the moment of interference and the umpire shall impose such penalties as in his opinion will nullify the act of interference.

Pitcher/Delivery See *Balk*

Pitcher/Illegal Pitch A quick return pitch is a pitch made with obvious intent to catch a batter off balance.

Pitcher/Starter The pitcher named in the batting order handed the umpire-in-chief shall pitch to the first batter or any substitute batter until the batter is put out or reaches first base, unless the pitcher sustains injury or illness which, in the judgment of the umpire-in-chief, incapacitates him from pitching further.

If the pitcher is replaced, the substitute pitcher shall pitch to the batter then at bat, or any substitute batter, until such batter is retired or reaches first base, or until the offensive team is retired, unless the substitute pitcher sustains injury or illness which, in the umpire-in-chief's judgment, incapacitates him for further play as a pitcher.

Relief Pitcher See above, *Pitcher/Starter.*

Runner The rules of 1954 include several new provisions awarding baserunners additional bases in various circumstances.

Time After the umpire calls "Play" the ball is alive and in play and remains alive and in play until for legal cause, or at the umpire's call of "Time" suspending play, the ball becomes dead. While the ball is dead no player may be put out, no bases may be run, and no runs may be scored, except that runners may advance one or more bases as the result of acts which occurred while the ball was alive (such as, but not limited to, a balk, an overthrow, interference, or a home run or other fair hit out of the playing field).

Umpire The umpire's authority to act in legal manner on all matters pertaining to a game shall not be questioned. The umpire shall have power to make decisions on any points not specifically covered in the rules.

1955

Balk See *Catcher/Position*

Ball The ball shall be a sphere formed by yarn wound around a small core of cork, rubber or similar material, covered with two strips of white horsehide, tightly stitched together. It shall weigh not less than 5 nor more than 5¼ ounces avoirdupois and measure not less than 9 nor more than 9¼ inches in circumference.

Batter/Position (Illegal) An illegally batted ball is one hit by the batter with one or both feet outside of the batter's box.

Batting Order The umpire-in-chief shall make certain that the original and copies of the respective batting orders are identical, and then tender a copy of each batting order to the opposing manager. The copy retained by the umpire shall be the official batting order. The tender of the batting order by the umpire shall establish the batting orders. Thereafter, no substitutions shall be made by either manager, except as provided in the rules.

Catcher/Position The catcher shall stand with both feet within the lines of the catcher's box, directly back of the plate, until the ball leaves the pitcher's hand. The intent of this rule is to deter the giving of intentional bases on balls. If the catcher has either foot outside his box when the pitcher delivers the ball, it is a balk.

Dead/Live Ball See *Time.*

Interference/Defensive The batter becomes a runner and is entitled to first base when the catcher or any other fielder interferes with him, unless the batter reaches first base on a hit, an error, or otherwise, and all other runners advance at least one base, in which case the play proceeds without reference to the interference.

Interference/Offensive It is interference by a batter or runner when any member or members of the offensive team stand or gather around any base to which a runner is advancing, to confuse, hinder, or add to the difficulty of the fielders. Such runner shall be declared out for the interference of his teammate or teammates.

It is interference by a batter or runner when any batter or runner who has just been retired hinders or impedes any following play being made on a runner. Such runner shall be declared out for the interference of his teammate.

Forfeited Game A game shall be forfeited in favor of the opposing team when a team is unable or refuses to place nine players on the field.

Game The rules of 1955 include new provisions for determining a suspended game and its resumption.

Game/Rain The manager of the home team shall be the sole judge as to whether a game shall be started because of unsuitable weather conditions or the unfit condition of the playing field, except for the second game of a doubleheader.

Pitcher/Delivery When the bases are unoccupied, the pitcher shall deliver the ball to the batter within 20 seconds after taking his pitching position. Each time the pitcher delays the game by violating this rule, the umpire shall call "Ball."

Time The ball becomes dead when the umpire-in-chief suspends play by calling "Time" when an accident incapacitates a player or umpire, or if it is necessary to remove a player or spectator from the grounds. The umpire shall not call "Time" because of an accident to player or umpire during a play, until in his judgment, no further action is possible in that play, unless an accident to a runner is such as to prevent him from proceeding to a base to which he is legally entitled, as on a home run hit out of the playing field, or an award of one or more bases, in which case a substitute runner shall be permitted to complete the play.

1956

There were no changes to the playing rules this year.

1957

The rules of 1957 contain new wording and explanation for the rules governing a batter who bats out of order.

Ball/Defacing See *Pitcher/Illegal Act.*

Balk If there is a runner or runners, it is a balk if the pitcher makes an illegal pitch. See *Catcher/Position.*

Batter/Position The batter shall take his position in the batter's box promptly when it is his time at bat.

The batter shall not leave his position in the batter's box after the pitcher comes to the Set Position, or starts his windup. Penalty: If the pitcher pitches, the umpire shall call "Ball" or "Strike," as the case may be.

Catcher/Position When the ball is put in play at the start of or during a game, all fielders other than the catcher shall be on fair territory. The catcher shall station himself directly back of the plate. He may leave his position at any time to catch a pitch or make a play except that when the batter is being given an intentional base on balls, the catcher must stand with both feet within the lines of the catcher's box until the ball leaves the pitcher's hand. Penalty: Balk.

Coach The offensive team shall station two coaches on the field during its term at bat, one near first base and one near third base. Failure to place two coaches on the field shall subject the manager to fine or suspension or both by the league president.

Coaches shall be limited to two in number and shall (1) be in team uniform; (2) remain within the coach's box at all times; and (3) address players of their own team only. Penalty: The offending coach shall be removed from the game, and shall leave the playing field.

Doubleheader A league may adopt a rule providing that one game of a doubleheader shall be seven innings in length. In such games, any of these rules applying to the ninth inning shall apply to the seventh inning.

The second game of a doubleheader shall start 20 minutes after the first game is completed, unless a longer interval (not to exceed 30 minutes) is declared by the umpire-in-chief and announced to the opposing managers at the end of the first game. Exception: If the league president has approved a request of the home club for a longer interval between games for some special event, the umpire-in-chief shall declare such longer interval and announce it to the opposing managers. The umpire-in-chief of the first game shall be the timekeeper controlling the interval between games.

Game When the winning run is scored in the last half-inning of a regulation game, or in the last half of an extra inning, as the result of a base on balls, hit batsman, or any other play with the bases full which forces the runner on third to advance, the umpire shall not declare the game ended until the runner forced to advance from third has touched home base and the batter-runner has touched first base. Penalty: If the runner on third refuses to advance to and touch home base in a reasonable time, the umpire shall disallow the run, call out the offending player, and order the game resumed. If, with less than two out, the batter-runner refuses to advance to and touch first base, the run shall count, but the offending player shall be called out.

The rules of 1957 include a rewording of the rules governing suspended games and the resumption of suspended games.

Hit by Pitch The batter becomes a runner and is entitled to first base without liability to be put out (provided he advances to and touches first base) when he is touched by a pitched ball which he is not attempting to hit unless: (1) The ball is in the strike zone when it touches the batter, or (2) The batter makes no attempt to avoid being touched by the ball.

Note: If the ball is in the strike zone when it touches the batter, it shall be called a strike, whether or not the batter tries to avoid the ball. If the ball is outside the strike zone when it touches the batter, it shall be called a ball if he makes no attempt to avoid being touched.

Infield Fly An infield fly is a fair fly ball (not including a line drive nor an attempted bunt) which can be caught by an infielder with ordinary effort when first and second, or first, second, and third bases are occupied, before two are out. The pitcher, catcher, and any outfielder who stations himself in the infield on the play shall be considered infielders for the purpose of this rule.

When it seems apparent that a batted ball will be an infield fly, the umpire shall immediately declare "Infield Fly" for the benefit of the runners. If the ball is near the baselines, the umpire shall declare "Infield Fly, if Fair."

The ball is alive and runners may advance at the risk of the ball being caught, or re-touch and advance after the ball is touched, the same as on any fly ball. If the hit becomes a foul ball, it is treated the same as any foul.

Note: If a declared infield fly is allowed to fall untouched to the ground, and bounces foul, it is a foul ball. If a declared infield fly falls untouched to the ground outside the baseline, and bounces fair, it is an infield fly.

Interference/Defensive If, with a runner on third base and trying to score by means of a squeeze play or a steal, the catcher or any other fielder steps on, or in front of home base without possession of the ball, or touches the batter or his bat, the pitcher shall be charged with a balk, the batter shall be awarded first base on the interference, and the ball is dead.

Each runner, other than the batter, may without liability to be put out, advance one base when he is attempting to steal a base, if the batter is interfered with by the catcher or any other fielder.

Note: When a runner is entitled to a base without liability to be put out, while the ball is in play, or under any rule in which the ball is in play after the runner reaches the base to which he is entitled, and the runner fails to touch the base to which he is entitled before attempting to advance to the next base, the runner shall forfeit his exemption from liability to be put out, and he may be put out by tagging the base or by tagging the runner before he returns to the missed base.

Obstruction In a rundown play, if the runner is obstructed by any fielder who does not have the ball in his possession (unless the fielder is in the act of fielding the ball), the umpire shall call "Obstruction" and the runner shall be entitled to occupy the base he is attempting to reach when the obstruction occurs. If such base is held by a following runner, any following runner forced to vacate his base by the obstructed runner's return shall be permitted to return to his last-held base without liability to be put out.

Pitcher/Delivery When the bases are unoccupied, the pitcher shall deliver the ball to the batter within 20 seconds after he receives the ball. Each time the pitcher delays the game by violating this rule, the umpire shall call "Ball."

Note: The intent of this rule is to avoid unnecessary delays. The umpire shall insist that the catcher return the ball promptly to the pitcher, and that the pitcher take his position on the rubber promptly. Obvious delay by the pitcher should instantly be penalized by the umpire. See also *Balk* and *Catcher/Positions.*

Pitcher/Illegal Act The pitcher shall not (1) apply a foreign substance of any kind to the ball; (2) expectorate either on the ball or his glove; (3) rub the ball on his glove, person, or clothing; (4) deface the ball in any manner; (5) deliver what is called the "shine" ball, "spit" ball, "mud" ball or "emery" ball. The pitcher, of course, is allowed to rub the ball between his bare hands. Penalty: For violation of any part of this rule, the umpire shall immediately disqualify the pitcher, and the league president shall suspend the pitcher for a period of 10 days. If a pitch is delivered in violation of this rule, it shall be treated as an illegal pitch.

Player/Illegal Act Players in uniform shall not address nor mingle with spectators, nor sit in the stands before, during, or after a game. No manager, captain, coach, or player shall address any spectator before or during a game.

Players of opposing teams shall not fraternize at any time while in uniform. Penalty: The league president shall impose fines for violation of this rule at his discretion.

Player/Position See *Catcher/Position.*

Relief Pitcher If an improper substitution is made for the pitcher, the umpire shall direct the proper pitcher to return to the game until the provisions of this rule are fulfilled. If the improper pitcher is permitted to pitch, any play that results is legal. The improper pitcher becomes the proper pitcher as soon as he makes his first pitch to the batter, or as soon as any runner is retired.

Strike Zone A strike is a legal pitch when so called by the umpire which (a) is struck at by the batter and is missed; (b) enters the strike zone in flight and is not struck at; (c) is fouled by the batter when he has less than two strikes; (d) is bunted foul; (e) touches the batter as he strikes at it; (f) touches the batter in flight in the strike zone; or (g) becomes a foul tip. Note: (f) was added to the former rule and definition.

Touch/Definition To touch a player or umpire is to touch any part of his body, clothing, or his equipment.

Umpire Each umpire has authority to disqualify any player, coach, manager, or substitute for objecting to decisions or for unsportsmanlike conduct or language, and to remove such disqualified person from the playing field. If an umpire disqualifies a player while a play is in progress, the disqualification shall not take effect until no further action is possible in that play.

Each umpire has authority at his discretion to remove from the playing field (1) any person whose duties permit his presence on the field, such as ground-crew members, ushers, photographers, newsmen, broadcasting-crew members, etc., or (2) any spectator or other person not authorized to be on the playing field.

Umpire/Decisions If different decisions should be made on one play by different umpires, the umpire-in-chief shall call all the umpires into consultation, with no manager or player present. After consultation, the umpire-in-chief (unless another umpire may have been designated by the league president) shall determine which decision shall prevail, based on which umpire was in best position and which decision was most likely correct. Play shall proceed as if only the final decision had been made.

1958

Appeal/Runner Any runner shall be called out, on appeal, when (a) after a fly ball is caught, he fails to re-touch his base before he or his base is tagged; (b) with the ball in play, while advancing or returning to a base, he fails to touch each base in order before he, or a missed base is tagged; (c) he overruns or overslides first base and fails to return to the base immediately, and he or the base is tagged; (d) he fails to touch home base and makes no attempt to return to that base, and home base is tagged. Any appeal under this rule must be made before the next legal pitch. If the violation occurs during a play which ends a half-inning, the appeal must be made before the defensive team leaves the field.

Note: Appeal plays may require an umpire to recognize an apparent "fourth out." If the third out is made during a play in which an appeal play is sustained on another runner, the appeal play decision takes precedence in determining the out. If there is more than one appeal during a play that ends a half-inning, the defense may elect to take the out that gives it the advantage. If the third out on appeal is a force play or failure of the batter-runner to touch first base, no runs can score on the play. Otherwise runs made before the appeal is sustained shall count. For the purposes of this rule, the defensive team has "left the field" when the pitchers and all infielders have left fair territory on their way to the bench or clubhouse.

1959

Grounds Any playing field constructed by a professional club after June 1, 1958, shall provide a minimum distance of 325 feet from home base to the nearest fence, stand, or other obstruction on the right and left field foul lines, and a minimum distance of 400 feet to the center field fence. No existing playing fields shall be remodeled after June 1, 1958, in such manner as to reduce the distance from home base to the foul poles and to the center field fence below the minimum distances.

Interference/Spectator When there is spectator interference with any thrown ball, the ball shall be dead at the moment of interference, and the umpire shall impose such penalties as in his opinion will nullify the act of interference.

Runner/Awarded Bases The runner is entitled to advance one base, if a ball, pitched to the batter, or thrown by the pitcher from his position on the pitcher's plate to a base to catch a runner, goes into a stand, or players' bench, or over or through a field fence or backstop. The ball is dead.

Note: If such a wild pitch is ball four, the batter-runner is entitled to first base only.

Each runner, including the batter-runner, may advance two bases, if a fair ball bounces or is deflected into the stands outside the first or third base foul lines; or if it goes through or under a field fence, or through or under a scoreboard, or through or

under shrubbery or vines on the fence; or if it sticks in such fence, scoreboard, shrubbery, or vines.

1960–62

There were no changes to the playing rules in these years.

1963

Interference/Offensive Offensive interference is an act by the team at bat which interferes with, obstructs, impedes, hinders, or confuses any fielder attempting to make a play. If the umpire declares the batter, batter-runner, or a runner out for interference, all other runners shall return to the last base that was, in the judgment of the umpire, legally touched at the time of the interference, unless otherwise provided by these rules.

Pitcher/Delivery Wind-up Position Note: When a pitcher holds the ball with both hands in front of his body, with his entire pivot foot on, or in front of and touching but not off the end of the pitcher's plate, and his other foot free, he will be considered in a Windup Position.

If there is a runner, or runners, it is a balk when the pitcher, after coming to a legal pitching position, removes one hand from the ball other than in an actual pitch, or in throwing to a base.

Pitcher/Warm-Up Pitches A league by its own action may limit the number of preparatory pitches to less than eight preparatory pitches. If a sudden emergency causes a pitcher to be summoned into the game without any opportunity to warm up, the umpire-in-chief shall allow him as many pitches as the umpire deems necessary.

Runner A runner acquires the right to an unoccupied base when he touches it before he is out. He is then entitled to it until he is put out, or forced to vacate it for another runner. If a runner legally acquires title to a base, and the pitcher assumes his pitching position, the runner may not return to a previously occupied base.

Unless two are out, the status of a following runner is not affected by a preceding runner's failure to touch or re-touch a base. If, upon appeal, the preceding runner is the third out, no runners following him shall score. If such third out is the result of a force play, neither preceding nor following runners shall score.

Strike Zone The strike zone is that space over home plate which is between the top of the batter's shoulders and his knees when he assumes his natural stance. The umpire shall determine the strike zone according to the batter's usual stance when he swings at a pitch.

1964

Bat No colored bat may be used in a professional game unless approved by the rules committee.

Interference/Defensive The batter becomes a runner and is entitled to first base when the catcher or any fielder interferes with him. If a play follows the interference, the manager of the offense may advise the plate umpire that he elects to decline the interference penalty and accept the play. Such election shall be made immediately at the end of the play. However, if the batter reaches first base on a hit, an error, a base on balls, a hit batsman, or otherwise, and all other runners advance at least one base, the play proceeds without reference to the interference.

Interference/Offensive It is interference when a batter-runner willfully and deliberately interferes with a batted ball or a fielder in the act of fielding a batted ball, with the obvious intent to break up a double play. The ball is dead. The umpire shall call the batter-runner out for interference and also call out the next preceding runner for the action of his teammate. In no event may bases be run or runs scored because of such action by a runner.

Note: In 1964, this rule was significantly changed. The batter-runner is still called out, of course, but rather than the next preceding runner also being called out, the runner who had advanced closest to the home plate, regardless where the double play might have been possible is also called out. In 1967, words were added to the rule clarifying that interference is determined by the umpire's judgment.

It is interference by a runner when, in the judgment of the umpire, a baserunner willfully and deliberately interferes with a batted ball or a fielder in the act of fielding a batted ball with the obvious intent to break up a double play. The ball is dead. The umpire shall call the runner out for interference and also call out the runner because of the action of his teammate. In no event may bases be run or runs scored because of such action by a runner.

Pitcher/Delivery The Set Position Note: The pitcher, in coming to the set position, must now come merely to a complete stop, rather than a complete stop of at least one second.

Uniforms Any part of an undershirt exposed to view shall be of a uniform solid color for all players on a team. Any player other than the pitcher may have numbers, letters, insignia attached to the sleeve of an undershirt.

1965

Appeal See *Runner/Bases*

Glove/Catcher The catcher may wear a leather glove or mitt no more than 38 inches in circumference, nor more than 15½ inches from top to bottom. Such limits shall include all lacing and any leather band or facing attached to the outer edge of the mitt. The space between the thumb section and the finger section of the mitt shall not exceed six inches at the top of the mitt and four inches at the base of the thumb crotch. The web shall measure not more than seven inches across the top or more than six inches from its top to the base of the thumb crotch. The web may be either a lacing or lacing through leather tunnels, or a center piece of leather which may be an extension of the palm, connected to the mitt with lacing and constructed so that it will not exceed any of the above mentioned requirements. The glove may be of any weight.

Interference/Offensive See 1964 *Interference/Offensive*

Runner/Bases Any runner shall be called out, on appeal, when with the ball in play, while advancing or returning to a base, he fails to touch each base in order before he, or a missed base, is tagged. Approved Ruling: (1) No runner may return to touch a missed base after a following runner has scored. (2) When the ball is dead, no runner may return to touch a missed base or one he has left after he has advanced to and touched a base beyond the missed base.

1966

There were no changes to the playing rules this year.

1967

Catch It is not a catch, however, if simultaneously or immediately following his contact with the ball, he collides with a player, or with a wall, or if he falls down, and as a result of such collision or falling, drops the ball. It is not a catch if a fielder touches a fly ball which then hits a member of the offensive team or an umpire and then is caught by another defensive player.

Coach/Manager See *Pitcher/Visits.*

Interference/Offensive The players, coaches, or any member of an offensive team shall vacate any space (including both dugouts) needed by a fielder who is attempting to field a batted or thrown ball. Penalty: Interference shall be called and the batter or runner on whom the play is being made shall be declared out.

The batter becomes a runner when a fair ball, after having

passed a fielder other than the pitcher, or after having been touched by a fielder, *including the pitcher,* shall touch an umpire or runner on fair territory.

Note: A runner who is adjudged to have hindered a fielder who is attempting to make a play on a batted ball is out whether it was intentional or not. If, however, the runner has contact with a legally occupied base when he hinders the fielder, he shall not be called out unless, in the umpire's judgment, such hindrance is intentional.

See also *Interference/Offensive.*

Interference/Umpire See above, *Interference/Offensive.*

Pitcher/Delivery Pitchers shall take signs from the catcher while standing on the rubber.

Pitcher/Visits A professional league shall adopt the following rule pertaining to the visit of the manager or coach to the pitcher: (a) This rule limits the number of trips a manager or coach may make to any one pitcher in any one inning; (b) A second trip to the same pitcher in the same inning will cause the pitcher's automatic removal; (c) The manager or coach is prohibited from making a second visit to the mound while the same batter is at bat; but (d) If a pinch-hitter is substituted for this batter, the manager or coach may make a second visit to the mound, but must remove the pitcher.

A manager or coach is considered to have concluded his visit to the mound when he leaves the 18-foot circle surrounding the pitcher's rubber.

Runner A runner acquires the right to an unoccupied base when he touches it before he is out. He is then entitled to it until he is put out, or forced to vacate it for another runner legally entitled to that base.

1968

Ball/Defaced See *Pitcher/Illegal Act.*

Coach See *Interference/Offensive.*

Interference/Offensive The ball becomes dead and runners advance one base or return to their bases without liability to be put out when a base coach intentionally interferes with a thrown ball. Runners return to the base last legally touched.

See also 1967 *Interference/Offensive.*

Pitcher/Illegal Act The pitcher shall not (1) bring his pitching hand in contact with his mouth or lips. Penalty: For violating this part of this rule the umpire shall warn the pitcher and if this action is repeated the umpire shall immediately disqualify the pitcher; (2) apply a foreign substance of any kind to the ball; (3) expectorate on the ball, his pitching hand, or his glove; (4) rub the ball on his glove, person, or clothing; (5) deface the ball in any manner; (6) deliver what is called the "shine" ball, "spit" ball, "mud" ball, or "emery" ball. The pitcher, of course, is allowed to rub the ball between his bare hands. Penalty: For violation of any part of this rule the umpire shall immediately disqualify the pitcher.

1969

Appeal/Runner Any runner is out when he fails to re-touch the base after a fair or foul ball is legally caught before he or his base is tagged by a fielder. He shall not be called out for failure to re-touch his base after the first following pitch, or any play or attempted play. This is an appeal play.

Game A game called at the end of a completed inning with the score tied after nine innings shall be a tie game.

Pitcher/Position The pitcher's plate shall be 10 inches above the level of home plate. The degree of slope from a point six inches in front of the pitcher's plate to a point six feet toward home plate shall be one inch to one foot, and such degree of slope shall be uniform. The leveled area atop the mound is enlarged to 34 inches by 5 feet, with the added 10 inches placed behind the pitcher's plate.

Strike Zone The strike zone is that space over home plate which is between the batter's armpits and the top of his knees when he assumes his natural stance. The umpire shall determine the strike zone according to the batter's usual stance when he swings at a pitch.

1970

There were no changes to the playing rules this year.

1971

Helmet All players shall use some type of protective helmet while at bat.

1972

Appeal An appeal is not to be interpreted as a play or an attempted play.

Successive appeals may not be made on a runner at the same base. If the defensive team on its first appeal errs, a request for a second appeal on the same runner at the same base shall not be allowed by the umpire.

Helmet All players in Class AA, Class A, and rookie leagues shall wear ear-flap helmets while at bat starting in 1972; and in 1973 all Class AAA players shall wear ear-flap helmets while at bat.

Interference/Offensive In the event offensive interference in which the batter-runner has not reached first base, all runners shall return to the base last occupied at the time of the pitch.

Suspended Game A game shall be suspended to be completed at a future date by reason of light failure or malfunction of a mechanical field device, under control of the home club, this shall include automatic tarpaulin or water-removal equipment.

1973

Designated Hitter Any league may elect to use the Designated Hitter (DH) rule as follows: (1) A hitter may be designated to bat for the starting pitcher and all subsequent pitchers in any game without otherwise affecting the status of the pitcher or pitcher in the game. A DH for the pitcher must be selected prior to the game and must be included in the lineup cards presented to the umpire-in-chief; (2) It is not mandatory that a club designate a hitter for the pitcher, but failure to do so prior to the game precludes the use of a DH for that game; (3) Pinch hitters for a DH may be used. Any substitute hitter for a DH becomes the DH. A replaced DH shall not re-enter the game in any capacity; (4) The DH may be used defensively, continuing to bat in the same position in the batting order, but the pitcher must then bat in the place of the substituted defensive player, unless more than one substitution is made, and the manager then must designate their spots in the batting order; (5) A runner may be substituted for the DH and the runner assumes the role of DH; (6) A DH is "locked" into the batting order. No multiple substitutions may be made that will alter the batting rotation of the DH; (7) Once the game-pitcher is switched from the mound to a defensive position this move shall terminate the DH role for the remainder of the game; (8) Once the game-pitcher bats for the DH this move shall terminate the DH's role for the remainder of the game. The game pitcher may only pinch-hit for the DH; (9) Once a DH assumes a defensive position this move shall terminate the DH role for the remainder of the game.

Note: The DH rule was adopted only by the American League.

Game In all protested games, the decision of the league president shall be final.

1974

Ball/Defaced See *Pitcher/Illegal Act.*

Helmet All players are required to wear batting helmets with ear flaps.

Pitcher/Illegal Act If, in his judgment, the umpire determines that a foreign substance has been applied to the ball, he shall (a) call the pitch a ball, warn the pitcher and have announced by the public address system the reason for the action; (b) in the case of a second offense by the same pitcher any time later in the game, the pitcher shall be disqualified from the game and may additionally be subject to such action as may be imposed by the league office; (c) if a play follows the violation called by the umpire, the manager of the offensive team may advise the plate umpire that he elects to decline the penalty and accept the play. Such election shall be made immediately at the end of the play. However, if a batter reaches first base on a hit, an error, a base on balls, a hit batsman, or otherwise, and no other runner is put out before advancing at least one base, the play shall proceed without reference to the violation; (d) even though the offense elects to take the play, the violation shall be recognized and the penalties in (a) and (b) will still be in effect; (e) the umpire shall be the sole judge on whether any portion of this rule has been violated.

1975

Ball The ball may be covered with white cowhide as well as horsehide.

Bat/Cupped An indentation in the end of the bat up to one inch in depth is permitted and may be no wider than two inches and no less than one inch in diameter. The indentation must be curved with no foreign substance added.

Bat/Illegal A batter is out for illegal action when he hits a fair ball with a filled, doctored, or flat-surfaced bat in which event he shall be immediately ejected from the game and suspended by his league president for three days.

Fielder/Drops Fly Ball A batter is out when an infielder intentionally drops a fair fly ball or line drive, with first, first and second, first and third, or first, second, and third bases occupied before two are out. The ball is dead and runner or runners shall return to their original base or bases.

Infield Fly See *Fielder/Drops Fly Ball.*

Pitcher/Illegal Act The pitcher shall not have on his person, or in his possession, any foreign substance. For such infraction of this section the penalty shall be immediate ejection from the game.

Appeal/Runner Any runner shall be called out, on appeal, when after a fly ball is caught, he fails to re-touch his *original* base before he or his *original* base is tagged.

Runner/Awarded Bases Approved Ruling: When a wild pitch or passed ball goes through or by the catcher, or deflects off the catcher, and goes directly into the dugout, stands, above the break, or any area where the ball is dead, the awarding of bases shall be one base. One base shall also be awarded if the pitcher, while in contact with the rubber, throws to a base, and the throw goes directly into the stands or into any area where the ball is dead.

If, however, the pitched or thrown ball goes through or by the catcher or through the fielder, and remains on the playing field, and is subsequently kicked or deflected into the dugout, stands or other area where the ball is dead, the awarding of bases shall be two bases from position of runners at the time of the pitch or throw.

Suspended Game A game may be suspended if local law prohibits the use of lights and it is too dark to continue.

1976

Bat The bat handle, for not more than 18 inches from the end, may be covered or treated with any material (including pine tar) to improve the grip. Any such material, including pine tar, which extends past the 18-inch limitation, in the umpire's judgment, shall cause the bat to be removed from the game. No such material shall improve the reaction or distance factor of the bat.

Bat/Illegal The batter is out for illegal action when he uses or attempts to use a bat that, in the umpire's judgment, has been altered or tampered with in such a way to improve the distance factor or cause an unusual reaction on the baseball. This includes, bats that are filled, flat-surfaced, nailed, hollowed, grooved, or covered with a substance such as paraffin, wax, etc. No advancement on the bases will be allowed and any out or outs made during a play shall stand. In addition to being called out, the player shall be ejected from the game and may be subject to additional penalties as determined by the league president.

Designated Hitter A Designated Hitter (DH) may not pinch run.

Once a pinch hitter bats for any player in the batting order and then enters the game to pitch, this move shall terminate the DH role for the remainder of the game.

A substitute for the DH need not be announced until it is the DH's turn to bat.

Player/Illegal Act No manager, player, substitute, coach, trainer, or batboy shall at any time, whether from the bench, the coach's box or on the playing field, or elsewhere make intentional contact with the umpire in any manner.

Umpire See *Player/Illegal Act.*

Uniform/Shoes No player shall attach anything to the heel or toe of his shoe other than the ordinary shoe plate or toe plate. Shoes with pointed spikes similar to golf or track shoes shall not be worn.

1977

There were no changes to the playing rules this year.

1978

Designated Hitter In the event of interleague competition between clubs of leagues using the Designated Hitter rule and clubs of leagues not using the Designated Hitter rule, the rule will be used as follows: (1) In exhibition games, the rule will be used or not used as is the practice of the home team; (2) In All-Star Games, the rule will only be used if both teams and both leagues so agree; (3) In World Series play, the rule will be used every other year. It will not be used in 1977, but will be used in 1978, etc.

Pitcher/Illegal Act The pitcher shall not intentionally pitch at the batter. If, in the umpire's judgment, such a violation occurs, the umpire shall warn the pitcher and his manager that another such pitch will mean immediate expulsion of the pitcher. At the same time the umpire shall warn the opposing manager that such an infraction by his pitcher shall result in that pitcher's expulsion. If, in the umpire's judgment, there is another such pitch during the game by any pitcher, the umpire shall eject the pitcher from the game. If, in the umpire's judgment circumstances warrant, one or both teams may be officially "warned" prior to the game or an actual violation during the game in progress. League presidents may take additional action under the rules.

To pitch at a batter's head is unsportsmanlike and highly dangerous. It should be—and is—condemned by everybody. Umpires should act without hesitation in enforcement of this rule.

1979

There were no changes to the playing rules this year.

1980

Equipment Playing Equipment including but not limited to the bases, pitcher's plate, baseball, bats, uniforms, catcher's mitts, first baseman's gloves, infielders and outfielders gloves and protective helmets, as detailed in the provisions of this rule, shall not contain and undue commercialization of the product. Designations by the manufacturer on any such equipment must be in good taste as to the size and content of the manufacturer's logo or the brand of the item. The provisions of this section shall apply to professional leagues only.

[Casebook] Note: Manufacturers who plan innovative changes in baseball equipment for professional baseball leagues should submit same to the Official Playing Rules Committee prior to production.

Game The rules of 1980 include several amendments to the rules governing suspended games and protested games.

Substitute/Fielder If no announcement of a substitution is made, the substitute shall be considered as having entered the game when, if a fielder, he reaches the position usually occupied by the fielder he has replaced and play commences.

Uniforms All players' uniforms shall include minimal six-inch numbers on their backs. See also *Equipment* above.

1981

Designated Hitter The Designated Hitter (DH) named in the starting lineup must come to bat at least one time, unless the opposing club changes pitchers.

1982

Pitcher Under extreme cold weather conditions a pitcher may warm his throwing hand by blowing on it provided that both managers and umpires have agreed to this before the game begins.

1983

Helmet All players shall use some type of protective helmet while at bat. All players in National Association Leagues shall wear a double ear-flap helmet while at bat. All players entering the major leagues commencing with the 1983 championship season and every succeeding season thereafter must wear a single ear-flap helmet (or at the player's option, a double ear-flap helmet), except those players who were in the major leagues during the 1982 season, and who, as recorded in that season, objected to wearing a single ear-flap helmet. If the umpire observes any violation of these rules, he shall direct the violation to be corrected. If the violation is not corrected within a reasonable time, in the umpire's judgment, the umpire shall eject the offender from the game.

1984

Bat The bat handle, for not more than 18 inches from its end, may be covered or treated with any material or substance to improve the grip. Any such material or substance, which extends past the 18-inch limitation, shall cause the bat to be removed from the game.

1985

Uniform No part of the uniform shall include patches or designs relating to commercial advertisements.

A league may provide that the uniforms of its member teams include the names of its players on their backs. Any name other than the last name of the player must be approved by the league president. If adopted, all uniforms for a team must have the names of its players.

1986

Designated Hitter The Designated Hitter (DH) rule will be

used or not used in World Series or exhibition games according to the practice of the home team.

1987

There were no changes to the playing rules this year.

1988

Bases Note: Although the shape and position remains the same as it has always been since 1900, the following is added to provide a more accurate description: It shall be a 17-inch square with two of the corners removed so that one edge is 17 inches long, two adjacent sides are 8½ inches and the remaining two sides are 12 inches and set at an angle to make a point.

Helmet All catchers shall wear a catcher's protective helmet, while fielding their position.

All bat/ballboys or girls shall wear a protective helmet while performing their duties.

Pitcher/Delivery The Set Position The pitcher must come to a single complete and discernible stop before throwing the ball. A complete stop shall not be construed as occurring because of a change in direction of the hands and arms.

The pitcher, following his stretch, must (a) hold the ball in both hands in front of his body and (b) come to a complete and discernible stop, with both feet on the ground. This must be enforced. Umpires should watch this closely, and should immediately call a "balk" for any violation.

Note: After this new wording resulted in a huge increase in the number of balks, it was decided, after only one year, to revert to the previous language. The entire text of the set position rule may be found in the 1989 Pitcher/Delivery entry.

Pitcher/Illegal Act The pitcher shall not intentionally pitch at the batter. If, in the umpire's judgment, such a violation occurs, the umpire may elect either to: (1) expel the pitcher, or the manager and the pitcher, from the game, or; (2) may warn the pitcher and the manager of both teams that another such pitch will result in the immediate expulsion of that pitcher (or a replacement) and the manager. If, in the umpire's judgment, and circumstances warrant, both teams may be officially "warned" prior to the game or at any time during the game. League presidents may take additional action under the rules.

Strike Zone The Strike Zone is that area over home plate the upper limit of which is a horizontal line at the midpoint between the top of the shoulders and the top of the uniform pants, and the lower level is a line at the top of the knees. The Strike Zone shall be determined from the batter's stance as the batter is prepared to swing at a pitched ball.

1989

Bat The bat shall be a smooth, *round* stick not more than 2¾ inches in diameter at the thickest part and not more than 42 inches in length. The bat shall be one piece of solid wood.

Note: No laminated or experimental bats shall be used in a professional game (either championship or exhibition games) until the manufacturer has secured approval from the Rules Committee of his design and methods of manufacture.

Pitcher/Delivery The Set Position Set Position shall be indicated by the pitcher when he stands facing the batter with his entire pivot foot on, or in front of, and in contact with, and not off the end of the pitcher's plate, and his other foot in front of the pitcher's plate, holding the ball in both hands in front of his body and coming to a complete stop. From such Set Position he may deliver the ball to the batter, throw to a base, or step backward off the pitcher's plate with his pivot foot. Before assuming Set Position, the pitcher may elect to make any natural preliminary motion such as that known as "the stretch." But if he so elects, he shall come to Set Position before delivering the ball to the batter. After assuming Set Position, any natural motion associated with his delivery of the ball to the batter commits him to the pitch without alteration or interruption.

Preparatory to coming to a set position, the pitcher shall have one hand on his side; from this position he shall go to his set position as defined above without interruption and in one continuous motion.

The whole width of the foot in contact with the rubber must be on the rubber. A pitcher cannot pitch from off the end of the rubber with just the side of his foot touching the rubber.

The pitcher, following his stretch, must (a) hold the ball in both hands in front of his body and (b) come to a complete stop. This must be enforced. Umpires should watch this closely. Pitchers are constantly attempting to "beat the rule" in their efforts to hold runners on bases and in cases where the pitcher fails to make a complete "stop" called for in the rules, the umpire should immediately call a "balk."

See also 1988 *Pitcher/Delivery*.

1990–94

There were no changes to the playing rules in these years.

1995

Strike Zone The Strike Zone is that area over home plate the upper limit of which is a horizontal line at the midpoint between the top of the shoulders and the top of the uniform pants, and the lower level is a line at the hallow beneath the kneecap. The Strike Zone shall be determined from the batter's stance as the batter is prepared to swing at a pitched ball.

Index to Playing Rule Changes 1845–1996

Note: Dates shown following an entry refer to the year a rule change or amendment was adopted. Rule changes and summaries of rules are to be found in the chronology.

Scoring Rules for 1877

Batting

Section 1. Time at Bat   The first item in the tabulated score, after the player's name and position, shall be the number of times he has been at bat during the game. Any time or times where the player has been sent to base on called balls shall not be included in this column.

Section 2. Runs Scored   In the second column should be set down the runs made by each player.

Section 3. Base Hits   In the third column should be placed the first-base hits made by each player. A base hit should be scored in the following cases:

When the ball from the bat strikes the ground between the foul lines and out of the reach of the fielders.

When a hit is partially or wholly stopped by a fielder in motion, but such player cannot recover himself in time to handle the ball before the striker reaches first base.

When the ball is hit so sharply to an infielder that he cannot handle it in time to put out a man. In case of doubt over this class of hits, score a base hit and exempt the fielder from the charge of an error.

When a ball is hit so slowly toward a fielder that he cannot reach it before the batsman is safe.

Section 4. Total Bases   In the fourth column should be placed to the credit of each player the total bases made off his hits. The unit, or base, consists in getting from any one base to any other base without being put out, and the striker is to be credited not only with the number of bases which he himself makes after a hit, but, in addition, with those safely made by every other player who is on base at the time he runs toward first. It should be understood that a base or bases made off an error of a fielder count toward the score of the player who ran from home base toward first base when the error was made. All the bases made off such error, whether by the striker or by some other player then on base, shall go to the credit of the striker. The striker shall be credited with a base when he is sent to base on called balls, and, in addition, with all the bases made by other players who may be advanced on the play under the rules.

A base or bases shall be given to the runner for a successful steal, whether made on an error of his opponents, or without error.

Bases shall not be given to a striker when any player, other than himself, shall be put out on his strike.

Fielding

Section 5. Putout   The number of opponents put out by each player shall be set down in the fifth column. Where a striker is given out by the umpire for a foul strike or because he struck out of his turn, the putout shall be scored to the catcher.

Section 6. Assist   The number of times a player assists shall be set down in the sixth column. An assist should be given to each player who handles the ball in a runout or other play of the kind.

An assist should be given to the pitcher when a batsman fails to hit the ball on the third strike.

An assist should be given to the pitcher in each case where the batsman is declared out for making a foul strike or striking out of turn.

An assist should be given to a player who makes a play in time to put a runner out, even if the player who should complete the play fails, through no fault of the player assisting.

An assist should not be given to a player who muffs the ball, or allows it to bound off his body toward a player who then assists or puts out a player.

And, generally, an assist should be given to each player who handles the ball from the time it leaves the bat until it reaches the player who makes the putout, or in case of a thrown ball, to each player who throws or handles it cleanly, and in such way that a putout results, or would result, if no error were made by the receiver.

Section 7.   An error should be given for each misplay, which allows the striker or baserunner to make one or more bases, when perfect play would have insured his being put out. In scoring errors off batted balls, see Sec. 3 of this Article.

Chronology of Scoring Rules 1878–1996

1878

Assist An assist is no longer denied a player who has a ball bounce off him toward a player who then makes the play.

On-Base In the fourth column should be placed to the credit of each player the number of times he reaches first base during the game, whether upon hits, errors, called balls, or in any other way he is not put out.

Total Bases The statistic crediting players with total bases is dropped from the rule book (Section 4 in 1877).

1879

There were no changes to the scoring rules this year.

1880

Base Hit Score a base hit when a ball is hit so slowly toward a fielder that he cannot handle it in time to put out a man.

Force Out See *Total Bases*

Total Bases In the fourth column should be placed to the credit of each player the total bases run during the game. In scoring "bases run" where a player has reached first base as the result of the putting out of another player, such first base shall not be credited to the striker as one of the bases run by him.

Total Chances/Fielding In the seventh column should be placed the "total chances offered" to retire players, which should include each perfect play, as well as each misplay or failure to accept a chance to retire a batsman or baserunner. "Chances offered" should not include "passed balls," "called balls," or "wild pitches." In scoring "chances offered" off batted balls, see Sec. 3 of the Scoring Rules.

Note: This rule does not appear in the scoring rules following 1880.

1881

Total Bases In the fourth column should be placed to the credit of each player the total bases made by him off his hits.

1882

In 1882 the American Association was founded, adopted the rule book, and made the following addition and deletion for their scoring rules:

Assist (American Association) An assist should be given to the pitcher on every chance offered to the catcher for a putout on a foul ball.

Total Bases (American Association) Total bases were not credited to the player's record.

1883

Assist (American Association) The pitcher is no longer credited with an assist when the batsman fails to hit the ball on the third strike, or when the batsman is declared out for making a foul strike or for striking out of turn.

Assist (American Association) An assist should be given to the pitcher when a batsman fails to hit the ball on the third strike. An assist should be given to the pitcher in each case where the batsman is declared out for making a foul strike, or striking out of turn. Such assistance is to be placed in the summary of the score.

Note: These two rules were dropped by the AA in 1884.

Error An error should be given to the pitcher when the batsman is given first base on "called balls."

Scoring Summary In the summary of the game should be credited to the pitcher the number of times a batsman fails to hit the ball on the third strike.

Scoring Summary (American Association) The summary shall contain: (1) The number of earned runs made by each side; (2) The number of two-base hits made by each player; (3) The number of three-base hits made by each player; (4) The number of home runs made by each player; (5) The number of men on each side left on bases; (6) The number of double and triple plays made by each side; (7) The number of men struck out by each pitcher; (8) The number of men given base on balls by each pitcher; (9) The number of passed balls by each catcher; (10) The number of wild pitches by each pitcher; (11) The time of game; (12) The name of the umpire.

1884

In 1884 the Union Association was formed and adopted the same scoring rules used by the American Association, with the exception that the new league credited assists to the pitcher for strikeouts, batters called out for batting out of turn, and batters striking the ball while out of the batter's box. The Union Association existed for one season.

Scoring Summary (American Association) The number of men given bases from being hit by pitched balls is added to the summary.

Note: The Union Association did not include this in their summary.

Strikeout (American Association) A strikeout should be given to the pitcher when a batsman fails to hit the ball on the third strike, and in each case where the batsman is declared out for making a foul strike, or striking out of turn.

1885

Assist An assist shall be given the pitcher when the batsman fails to hit the ball on the third strike, and the same shall also be entered in the summary under the head of "struck out."

Note: This rule was dropped in 1889.

Error Wild pitches and passed balls shall be charged to the pitcher and catcher respectively in the error column, and shall also appear in the summary.

Note: This rule was dropped in 1886.

Error (American Association) An error shall be given for each misplay which allows the striker or baserunner to make one or more bases, when perfect play would have insured his being put out; except that wild pitches, bases on called balls, bases on the batsman being struck by a pitched ball, balks, and passed balls shall not be included in said column.

Note: The National League adopted this rule in 1887 and added the term "illegal pitched ball" to the exceptions. The phrase "bases on called balls" was deleted from the exceptions in 1888 only.

1886

Stolen Base Bases stolen by players shall appear to their credit in the summary of the game.

1887

In 1887 the National League and the American Association agreed to use the same scoring rules.

Assist An assist shall be given the pitcher when the batsman fails to hit the ball on the fourth [third in 1888] strike, and the same shall be entered in the summary under the head of "struck out."

Note: This rule was dropped in 1889.

Base Hit A base hit is to be scored when the batsman is awarded a base on balls.

Note: This rule was dropped in 1888.

Scoring Summary The summary shall contain: (1) The number of earned runs made by each side; (2) The number of two-base hits made by each player; (3) The number of three-base hits made by each player; (4) The number of home runs made by each player; (5) The number of double and triple plays made by each side, with the names of the players assisting in the same; (6) The number of men given bases on called balls by each pitcher; (7) The number of men given bases from being hit by pitched balls; (8) The number of passed balls by each catcher; (9) The number of wild pitches by each pitcher; (10) The time of the game; (11) The name of the umpire.

Stolen Base In the fourth column shall be scored bases stolen, and shall include every base made after first base has been reached by a baserunner, except those made by reason of, or with the aid of, a "battery" error, or by batting, "balks" or by being forced off. In short, shall include all bases made by a "clean steal," or through a wild throw or muff of the ball by a fielder who is directly trying to put the baserunner out while attempting to steal a base.

Time at Bat The first item in the tabulated score, after the player's name and position, shall be the number of times he has been at bat during the game. No time at bat shall be scored if the batsman be hit by a pitched ball while standing in his position, and after trying to avoid being so hit, or in case of the pitcher's illegal delivery of the ball to the bat which gives the batsman his base, or when he intentionally hits the ball to the field, purposely to be put out, or if he is given first base on called balls.

1888

Base Hit In all cases where a baserunner is retired by being hit by a batted ball, the batsman should be credited with a base hit.

That when a player reaches first base through an error of judgment such as two fielders allowing the ball to drop between them, the batter shall not be credited with a base hit, nor the fielder charged with an error, but it shall be scored as an unaccepted chance, and the batter shall be charged with a time at the bat.

Note: This rule was dropped in 1889.

Earned Run An earned run shall be scored every time the player reaches the home base unaided by errors before chances have been offered to retire the side, but bases on balls, though summarized as errors, shall be credited as factors in earned runs.

Note: This rule was deleted in 1898 but reappears in 1917. Also see 1912.

Stolen Base In the fourth column shall be scored bases stolen, and shall be governed as follows: Any attempt to steal a base must go to the credit of the baserunner, but any manifest error is to be charged to the fielder making the same. If the baserunner advances another base he shall not be credited with a stolen base, and the fielder allowing the advancement is also to be charged with an error. If a baserunner makes a start and a battery error is made, the runner secures the credit of a stolen base, and the battery error is scored against the player making it. Should a baserunner overrun a base and then be put out, he should receive the credit for the stolen base.

Time at Bat The first item in the tabulated score, after the player's name and position, shall be the number of times he has been at bat during the game. At any time or times where the player has been sent to base by being hit by a pitched ball, by the pitcher's illegal delivery, or by a base on balls shall not be included in this column.

1889

Base Hit A base hit should be scored when a batted ball hits the person or clothing of the umpire as provided in the playing rules.

Earned Run An earned run shall be scored every time the player reaches the home base unaided by errors before chances have been offered to retire the side.

Note: See entries under 1888, 1912, and 1917.

Sacrifice In the fourth column shall be placed sacrifice hits, which shall be credited to the batsman, who when but one man is out advances a runner on base on a fly to the outfield or a ground hit, which results in putting out the batsman, or would so result if handled without error.

Scoring Summary The number of bases stolen is added to the scoring summary.

1890

Assist Assistances on strikes are not to be included in the record of fielding assistances.

Earned Run Earned runs should be charged against the pitcher only on the basis of base hits made off the pitching, and should not include stolen bases or bases scored in any other way.

1891

Scoring Summary The number of runs batted in by base hits by each batsman is added to the scoring summary.

1892

Stolen Base The following sentence is added to the 1888 rule for scoring stolen bases: If a baserunner advances a base on a fly out, or gains two bases on a single base hit, or an infield out, or attempted out, he shall be credited with a stolen base, provided there is a possible chance and a palpable attempt made to retire him.

Note: This sentence was dropped from the rule in 1897.

1893

There were no changes to the scoring rules this year.

1894

Sacrifice A sacrifice hit is to be credited to the batsman who advances a runner with no one out or one out by a bunt sacrifice which results in putting out the batsman.

Note: Previously the rule applied only with one out. See 1889.

Time at Bat The batter is not charged with a time at bat for a sacrifice hit purposely made to the infield which advances a runner without resulting in a putout except to the batsman.

1895–6

There were no changes to the scoring rules in these years.

1897

Earned Run An earned run shall be scored every time the player reaches the home base by the aid of base hits only before chances have been offered to retire the side.

Note: See entries under 1888, 1912 and 1917.

Sacrifice In the fourth column shall be placed the sacrifice hits, which shall be credited to the batsman who, when no one is out or when but one man is out, advances a runner a base by a bunt hit, which results in putting out the batsman, or would so result if the ball were handled without error.

Scoring Summary The summary shall contain: (1) The number of earned runs made off each pitcher; (2) The number of two-base hits made by each player; (3) The number of three-base hits made by each player; (4) The number of home runs made by each player; (5) The number of bases stolen by each player; (6) The number of double and triple plays made by each side and the names of the players assisting in the same; (7) The number of men given bases on called balls by each pitcher and the names of the players who were thus given bases; (8) The number of men given bases from being hit by pitched balls by each pitcher and the names of the players who are thus given bases; (9) The number of men struck out by each pitcher and the names of the players struck out; (10) The number of passed balls by each catcher; (11) The number of wild pitches by each pitcher; (12) The number of baserunners left on bases by each side; (13) The number of innings each pitcher played; (14) The number of base hits made off each pitcher; (15) The number of bases on balls given by each pitcher; (16) The number of batsmen hit by each pitcher; (17) The number of batsmen struck out by each pitcher [Note: This requirement apparently duplicates Sec. 9 above]; (18) The number of baserunners of each side who reached first base by fielding errors; (19) The time it took to play the game; (20) The condition of the weather; (21) The condition of the playing field; (22) The name of the umpire.

Stolen Base   The rule regarding stolen bases is now the same as that used between 1888 through 1891. Additional language adopted in 1892 and included through 1896 has been deleted. See 1892.

Time at Bat   The first item in the tabulated score, after the player's name and position, shall be the number of times he has been at bat during the game. The time or times when the player has been sent to base by being hit by a pitched ball, by the pitcher's illegal delivery, or by a base on balls, or has made a sacrifice hit which was manifestly intentional, shall not be included in this column.

1898

Assist   Assists should be credited to every player who handles the ball in the play which results in a baserunner being called out for interference or for running out of line.

Base Hit   A base hit should be scored when a ball is hit with such force to an infielder that he cannot handle it in time to put out the batsman. In case of doubt over this class of hits, score a base hit and exempt the fielder from the charge of an error.

In no case shall a base hit be scored when a baserunner has been forced out by the play.

Error   An error shall be given in the seventh column for each misplay which allows the striker or baserunner to make one or more bases when perfect play would have insured his being put out, except that "wild pitches," "bases on balls," bases on the batsman being struck by a "pitched ball," or in case of illegal pitched balls, balks and passed balls, all of which comprise battery errors, shall not be included in said column. In scoring errors of batted balls see Sec. 3 of this rule.

An error shall not be scored against the catcher for a wild throw to prevent a stolen base, unless the baserunner advances an extra base because of the error.

No error shall be scored against an infielder who attempts to complete a double play, unless the throw is so wild that an additional base is gained.

Putout   The number of opponents put out by each player shall be set down in the fifth column. Where a batsman is given out by the umpire for a foul strike, or where the batsman fails to bat in proper order, the putout shall be scored to the catcher. In all cases of "out" for interference, running out of line, or infield fly dropped, the "out" should be credited to the player who would have made the play but for the action of the baserunner or batsman.

Scoring Summary   The summary shall contain: (1) The score made in each inning of the game; (2) The number of bases stolen by each player; (3) The number of two-base hits made by each player; (4) The number of three-base hits made by each player; (5) The number of home runs made by each player; (6) The number of double and triple plays made by each side and the names of the players assisting in the same; (7) The number of innings each pitcher pitched in; (8) The number of base hits made off each pitcher; (9) The number of times the pitcher strikes out the opposing batsmen; (10) The number of times the

pitcher gives bases on balls; (11) The number of wild pitches charged to the pitcher; (12) The number of times the pitcher hits batsmen with pitched ball; (13) The number of passed balls by each catcher; (14) The time of the game; (15) The names and positions of each umpire.

Stolen Base   A stolen base shall be credited to the baserunner whenever he reaches the base he attempts to steal unaided by a fielding or by a battery error or a hit by the batsman.

Time at Bat   The first item in the tabulated score, after the player's name and position, shall be the number of times he has been at bat during the game. No time at bat shall be scored if the batsman be hit by a pitched ball while standing in his position, and after trying to avoid being so hit, or in case of the pitcher's illegal delivery of the ball to the bat which gives the batsman his base, or when he intentionally hits the ball to the field, purposely to be put out, or if he is given first base on called balls.

1899–1903

There were no changes to the scoring rules in these years.

1904

Assist   The number of times, if any, each player assists in putting out an opponent shall be set down in the sixth column. An assist should be given to each player who handles the ball in aiding in a run-out or any other play of the kind, except the one who completes it.

Note: The rule remains unchanged except to clarify that the fielder completing a run-down play by making the putout is not to be credited with an assist even if he handled the ball prior to receiving it again to make the putout. But see the entry under 1910.

Base Hit   A base hit should be scored when the ball is hit so slowly toward a fielder that he cannot handle it in time to put out the batsman or force out a baserunner.

Note: The phrase "or force out a baserunner" has been added to the original rule. See 1878.

Error   An error shall be given in the seventh column for each misplay which prolongs the time at bat of the batsman or allows a baserunner to make one or more bases when perfect play would have insured his being put out. But a wild pitch, a base on balls, a base awarded to a batsman by being struck by a pitched ball, an illegal pitch, a balk and a passed ball, each of which is a battery and not a fielding error, shall not be included in the seventh column.

In case a baserunner advance a base through the failure of a baseman to stop or try to stop a ball accurately thrown to his base, he shall be charged with an error and not the player who made such throw, provided there were occasion for it. If such throw be made to second base, the scorer shall determine whether the second baseman or shortstop shall be charged with an error.

Putout   The number of opponents, if any, put out by each player shall be set down in the fifth column. Where the batsman is given out by the umpire for a foul strike, or fails to bat in proper order, the putout shall be scored to the catcher. In cases of the baserunner being declared "out" for interference, running out of line, or on an infield fly, the "out" should be credited to the player who would have made the play but for the action of the baserunner or the announcement of the umpire.

Note: The phrase "or the announcement of the umpire" has been added in place of "or batsman." See 1898.

Sacrifice   In the fourth column shall be placed the sacrifice hits. A sacrifice hit shall be credited to the batsman who, when no one is out or when but one man is out, advances a runner a base by a bunt hit, which results in the batsman being put out before reaching first, or would so result if it were handled without error.

Note: The phrase "before reaching first" has been added to the rule. See 1889.

Scoring Summary   The scoring summary is to include the total runs by each side as well as the score made in each inning.

Stolen Base   A stolen base shall be credited to the baserunner whenever he advances a base unaided by a base hit, a putout, a fielding or a battery error.

Time at Bat   The first item in the tabulated score, after the player's name and position, shall be the number of times he has been at bat during the game.

"A Time at Bat" is the term at-bat of a batsman. It begins when he takes his position, and continues until he is put out or becomes a baserunner. But a time at bat shall not be charged against a batsman who is awarded first base by the umpire for being hit by a pitched ball or for the illegal delivery of the pitcher, or on called balls, or when he makes a sacrifice hit.

1905–06

There were no changes to the scoring rules in these years.

1907

Base Hit   In all cases where a baserunner is retired by being hit by a batted ball, unless batted by himself, the batsman should be credited with a base hit.

Game Played   All appearances by a player in a championship game count as a game played in the American League, which prior to 1907 had not so credited the appearances of pinch hitters, pinch runners, and defensive substitutes in most cases. See 1912 for National League.

1908

Sacrifice   A sacrifice hit shall be credited to a batsman who, when no one is out or when but one man is out, hits a fly ball that is caught but results in a run being scored.

1909

Double Play   A double play shall mean any two continuous putouts that take place between the time the ball leaves the pitcher's hands until it is returned to him again standing in the pitcher's box.

Error   In case a runner advances a base through the failure of a baseman to stop or try to stop a ball accurately thrown to his base, the latter shall be charged with an error and not the player who made such throw, provided there was occasion for it. If such throw be made to second base, the scorer shall determine whether the second baseman or shortstop shall be charged with an error.

An error shall be given in the sixth column for each misplay which prolongs the time at bat of the batsman or allows a baserunner to make one or more bases when perfect play would have insured his being put out. But a base on balls, a base awarded to a batsman by being struck by a pitched ball, an illegal pitch, a balk, a passed ball or wild pitch, unless such wild pitch or passed ball be on the third strike and allow the batter to reach first base, shall not be included in the sixth column. In case of a wild pitch or a passed ball allowing the batter to reach first base, the pitcher or the catcher, as the case may be, shall be charged with an error.

In event of a fielder dropping a fly but recovering the ball in time to force a batter at another base, he shall be exempted from an error, the play being scored as a "force-out."

Putout   The number of opponents, if any, put out by each player shall be set down in the fourth column. Where the batsman is given out by the umpire for a foul strike, or fails to bat in proper order, or is declared out on third bunt strike, the putout shall be scored to the catcher. In cases of the baserunner being declared "out" for interference, running out of line, or on an infield fly, the "out" should be credited to the player who would have made the play but for the action of the baserunner or the announcement of the umpire.

Sacrifice   A sacrifice hit shall be credited to a batsman who, when no one is out or when but one man is out, hits a fly ball that is caught but results in a run being scored, or would in the judgment of the scorer so result if caught.

Scoring Summary   The summary shall contain: (1) The score made in each inning of the game and the total runs of each side in the game; (2) The number of stolen bases, if any, by each player; (3) The number of sacrifice hits, if any, made by each player; (4) The number of sacrifice flies, if any, made by each player; (5) The number of two-base hits, if any, made by each player; (6) The number of three-base hits, if any, made by each player; (7) The number of home runs, if any, made by each player; (8) The number of double and triple plays, if any, made by each club and the players participating in same; (9) The number of innings each pitcher pitched in; (10) The number of base hits, if any, made off each pitcher and the number of legal at-bats scored against each pitcher; (11) The number of times, if any, the pitcher strikes out the opposing batsmen; (12) The number of times, if any, the pitcher gives bases on balls; (13) The number of wild pitches, if any, charged against the pitcher; (14) The number of times, if any, the pitcher hits a batsman with a pitched ball, the name or names of the batsman or batsmen so hit to be given; (15) The number of passed balls by each catcher; (16) The time of the game; (17) The name of the umpires.

Stolen Base   A stolen base shall be credited to the baserunner whenever he advances a base unaided by a base hit, a putout, a fielding or a battery error, subject to the following exceptions: (1) In event of a double steal being attempted from bases one and two to bases two and three, where either is thrown out, the other shall not be credited with a stolen base; (2) In event of a baserunner being touched out after sliding over a base, he shall not be regarded as having stolen the base in question; (3) In event of a baserunner making his start to steal a base prior to a battery error, he shall be credited with a stolen base; (4) In event of a palpable muff of a ball thrown by the catcher, when the baserunner is clearly blocked, the infielder making the muff shall be charged with an error and the baserunner shall not be credited with a stolen base.

1910

Assist   The number of times, if any, each player assists in putting out an opponent shall be set down in the fifth column. An assist should be given to each player who handles the ball in aiding in a run-out or any other play of the kind, even though he complete the play by making the putout.

Note: Compare to the 1904 rule.

Error   An error shall be given in the sixth column for each misplay which prolongs the time at bat of the batsman or allows a baserunner to make one or more bases when perfect play would have insured his being put out. But a base on balls, a base awarded to a batsman by being struck by a pitched ball, a balk, a passed ball, or wild pitch shall not be included in the sixth column.

Passed Ball   A passed ball is a legally delivered ball that the catcher should hold or control with ordinary effort, but his failure to do so enables the batsman, who becomes a baserunner on such pitched ball, to reach first base or a baserunner to advance.

Stolen Base   In event of a double or triple steal being attempted, where either runner is thrown out, the other or others shall not be credited with a stolen base.

Wild Pitch   A wild pitch is a legally delivered ball, so high, low or wide of the plate that the catcher cannot or does not stop and control it with ordinary effort, and as a result the batsman, who becomes a baserunner on such pitched ball, reaches first base or a baserunner advances.

1911

There were no changes to the scoring rules this year.

1912

Earned Run   An earned run is charged to the pitcher every time a player scores by the aid of safe hits, sacrifice hits, bases on balls, hit batters, wild pitches, and balks before fielding chances have been offered to retire the side.

Note: This rule is not included in the scoring rules for 1912 but earned runs were compiled in the official pitching records of the National League (1912) and American League (1913). The earned run scoring rule does not appear in the scoring rules until 1917.

Game Played   All appearances by a player in a championship game count as a game played in the National League, which prior to 1912 had not so credited the appearances of pinch hitters, pinch runners, and defensive substitutes, with certain exceptions.

1913

There were no changes to the scoring rules this year.

1914

Assist   The number of times, if any, each player assists in putting out an opponent shall be set down in the fifth column. One assist and no more shall be given to each player who handles the ball in aiding in a run-out or any other play of the kind even though he complete the play by making the putout.

Note: Compare to 1910 and 1904.

Base Hit   A base hit should be scored when the ball from the bat strikes the ground on or within the foul lines and out of reach of the fielders, provided the batter reaches first base safely.

When a fielder, after handling a batted ball, elects to try to retire a baserunner instead of the batter, the play is known as a "fielder's choice." In case the runner is retired, or would be retired but for an error, the batter shall be charged with a time at bat, but no hit. If the runner is not retired, and no error is made, the batter shall be charged with a time at bat, but no hit, provided he swung at the ball, and shall be credited with a sacrifice hit, provided he bunted the ball; if, however, in the judgment of the scorer, the batter could not have been retired at first base by perfect fielding, he shall be credited with a base hit.

Error   In event of a baserunner making his start to steal a base prior to a battery error, he shall be credited with a stolen base and the battery error shall also be charged.

An error shall not be scored against the catcher or an infielder who attempts to complete a double play, unless the throw be so wild that an additional base be gained. This, however, does not exempt from an error a player who drops a thrown ball when by holding it he would have completed a double play.

An error shall be given in the sixth column for each misplay which prolongs the time at bat of the batsman or prolongs the life of the baserunner or allows a baserunner to make one or more bases when perfect play would have insured his being put out. But a base on balls, a base awarded to a batsman by being struck with a pitched ball, a balk, a passed ball, or wild pitch shall not be included in the sixth column.

Note: The phrase "or prolongs the life of the baserunner" has been added to the existing rule.

Fielder's Choice   See *Base Hit.*

1915–16

There were no changes to the scoring rules in these years.

1917

Earned Run   A run earned off the pitcher shall be scored every time a player reaches home base by the aid of safe hits, sacrifice hits, stolen bases, bases on balls, hit batsmen, wild pitches, and balks, before fielding chances have been offered to retire the side.

The pitcher shall be given the benefit of doubt whenever fielding errors are made and in determining the base to which a runner should have been held with perfect support on part of fielders. A fielding error made by the pitcher shall be considered the same as any other fielding error. No run can be earned that scores as a result of the batsman having reached first base on a fielding error or passed ball; nor can any run be earned after the fielding side has failed to accept chances offered to retire the side.

Percentage   To determine the pitcher's percentage for the season, the total number of runs earned off his pitching shall be divided by the total number of innings he has pitched; then multiplied by nine, to find his average effectiveness for a complete game.

1918–19

There were no changes to the scoring rules in these years.

1920

Error   An error shall be charged to the first baseman if, on receiving a throw in ample time to retire the batsman, he fail to touch first base.

An error shall be charged to the catcher if he drop a third strike, allowing the runner to reach first base; except this rule is not to apply in case of a wild pitch.

Game Ending Hit   If, in the last half of the final inning, with the winning run on base, the batsman drives home that run, credit shall be given him for as many bases on his hit as the runner advances; except, however, that in case of the batsman driving a fair ball out of the playing field, he shall receive credit for a home run.

Percentage   To determine the percentage of games won and lost, divide the total number of games won and lost into the number won.

To determine batting averages, divide the total "Times at Bat" into the total number of base hits.

To determine fielding averages, divide the total of putouts, assists, and errors into the total of putouts and assists.

In all cases where the remaining fraction is one-half or over, a point is added to the average.

Sacrifice   No distinction shall be made in the summary as between bunted or fly-ball sacrifices.

Scoring Summary   The scoring summary is to include sacrifice flies (within the category of sacrifice hits) and the number of runs batted in by each batsman.

Stolen Base   No stolen base shall be credited to a runner who is allowed to advance without any effort being made to stop him.

Wild Pitch   See *Error*, second paragraph.

1921–25

There were no changes to the scoring rules in these years.

1926

Error   See *Wild Pitch.*

Passed Ball   The catcher shall be charged with a passed ball when a baserunner is enabled to advance by the catcher's failure to hold or control a legally delivered ball that should have been held or controlled with ordinary effort.

Sacrifice Fly   Awarded if any runner is advanced.

Wild Pitch An error shall be charged to the pitcher if he make a wild pitch for the third strike, and the batsman reach first base; in such case the pitcher shall not have credit for a strikeout.

A wild pitch is a legally delivered ball, so high, low, or wide of the plate that the catcher cannot or does not stop and control it with ordinary effort, and as a result the batsman reaches first base or a baserunner advances.

1927–30

There were no changes to the scoring rules in these years.

1931

Assist Credit an assist to a player who, by deflecting a batted ball with his glove or any part of his body, aids in retiring the batsman or another baserunner.

Credit an assist to each player who handles and throws the ball in such a way that a putout would have resulted except for the error of a teammate.

Do not credit an assist to a fielder who makes a bad throw, even when a runner trying to advance on it is subsequently retired. A play that follows an error is a new play and the player making an error is not entitled to an assist unless he takes part in the new play.

Do not credit an assist to the pitcher when, in legally delivering the ball to the batsman, he helps to retire a runner attempting to steal home.

Base Hit A base hit shall be scored in the following cases: (1) When a fair hit is made, as defined in the Playing Rules, and the batsman reaches first base safely; (2) When a fair hit ball is partially or wholly stopped by a fielder in motion, but such player cannot recover himself in time to field the ball to first before the batsman reaches that base, or to some other base in time to force out another runner; (3) When a ball is hit with such force to an infielder or pitcher that he cannot handle it in time to put out the batsman or force out a baserunner; except when the ball is recovered by another fielder in time to retire the batsman or force out a baserunner. In case of doubt over this kind of hit, a base hit should be scored and the fielder be exempted from the charge of an error.

Earned Run A run earned off the pitcher shall be scored every time a player reaches home base by the aid of safe hits, sacrifice hits, stolen bases, putouts, bases on balls, hit batsman, wild pitches, or balks, before fielding chances have been offered to retire the side.

The pitcher shall be given the benefit of doubt whenever fielding errors are made and in determining the base to which a runner should have been held with perfect support on part of fielders. A fielding error made by the pitcher shall be considered the same as any other fielding error. No run can be earned that scores as a result of the batsman having reached first base on a catcher's interference, a fielding error, or passed ball; nor can any run be earned after the fielding side has failed to accept chances offered to retire the side.

Note: The phrase "catcher's interference" has been added to the prior rule. See entry for 1917.

Error An error, but not a passed ball, shall be charged to the catcher if he drops or misses a third strike, allowing the batsman to reach first base. Credit the pitcher with a strikeout.

An error shall be charged to the first baseman (or the pitcher or second baseman when covering first base) if, on receiving a throw in ample time to retire the batsman, he does not touch first base as required by rule. The same rule shall be followed with respect to any fielder covering any other base on a force play.

Forfeited Game In a regulation game which the umpire shall declare forfeited after four and one-half innings have been played, all individual and team averages shall be incorporated in the official playing records.

Game-Ending Hit If, in the last half of the final inning, with the winning run on base, the batsman drives home that run, credit shall be given him for as many bases as, in the judgment of the official scorer, he would have made under normal conditions; the number, however, not to exceed the number of bases advanced by the runner; except when the batsman drives a fair ball out of the playing field, he shall receive credit for a home run, provided he legally touches each base in proper order.

Hit by Pitch When a batsman is hit by what would have been the fourth called ball, it shall be scored as a "hit by pitcher."

Passed Ball See *Error*.

Percentage In determining averages where the remaining fraction is one-half or over, a full point is to be added to the average.

Putout The number of opponents, if any, put out by each player shall be set down in the fourth column. When the batsman is called out by the umpire for an illegally batted ball, or for a foul third strike bunt, or for being hit by his own batted ball, or for interference with the catcher, or for failing to bat in proper turn, the putout shall be credited to the catcher. When a baserunner is declared out on an infield fly, the putout shall be credited to the player who would have made the play except for the action of the runner or the announcement of the umpire. When a baserunner is declared out because of being hit by a batted ball, the putout shall be credited to the fielder nearest to the ball at the time of the occurrence.

Run Batted In Runs batted in should include runs scored on safe hits (including home runs), sacrifice hits, infield outs, and when the run is forced over by reason of batsman becoming a baserunner. With less than two out, if an error is made on a play on which a runner from third would ordinarily score, credit the batsman with a run batted in.

Sacrifice Rule Awarding of sacrifice flies is abolished.

Stolen Base In the event of a palpable muff of a ball thrown by the catcher, when, in the judgment of the scorer, the baserunner would have been out if the ball had been held, the infielder making the muff shall be charged with an error and the baserunner shall not be credited with a stolen base.

When a wild pitch or a passed ball occurs after a runner has started to steal, do not credit the runner with a stolen base but charge the wild pitch or passed ball.

Do not give a stolen base to a runner who has started to steal and the pitcher balks.

Time at Bat A "Time at Bat" is the term at bat of a batsman. It begins when he takes his position, and continues until he is put out or becomes a baserunner. But a time at bat shall not be charged against a batsman who is awarded first base by the umpire for being hit by a pitched ball, or on called balls, or when he makes a sacrifice hit, or for interference by the catcher.

Note: This rule is Rule 69, Sec. 5, of the Playing Rules.

The first item in the tabulated score, after the player's name and position, shall be the number of times he has been at bat during the game, but the exceptions made in Rule 69, Sec. 5, must not be included.

Note: See above entry for Rule 69, Sec. 5.

Wild Pitch A wild pitch is a legally delivered ball, so high, low, or wide of the plate that the catcher cannot or does not stop and control it with ordinary effort, and as a result the batsman reaches first base or a baserunner advances. Any pitched ball that strikes the ground before reaching the home plate and passes the catcher, allowing runners to advance, shall be scored as a wild pitch.

1932–38

There were no changes to the scoring rules in these years.

1939

Base Hit/Value   In event of a batsman oversliding second or third bases and being tagged by the opposing fielder when said batsman is attempting to stretch a single into a two-base hit or a two-base hit into a three-base hit, the play should be scored the same as when a baserunner attempts to steal, overslides the base and is tagged out. In other words, the batsman oversliding second base and is tagged out shall be credited only with a single, while one who overslides third base and is tagged out shall be credited only with a two-base hit.

Earned Run   A wild pitch which is a third strike is to be used in determining earned runs charged to the pitcher.

Run Batted In   The batsman shall not be credited with driving in a run when a runner scores as he hits into a force infield double play or a double play in which the first baseman picks up a fair hit ground ball, touches first base and then throws to second retiring the runner who had been on first, said runner not being forced, has to be tagged out.

Sacrifice   A sacrifice hit also shall be credited to the batsman who, when no one is out or when but one man is out, hits a fly ball that is caught but which results in a baserunner scoring, or would have scored a runner if said fly ball had not been dropped for an error, in the judgment of the scorer; but no distinction shall be made in the summary as between bunted or fly ball sacrifices.

1940

Base Hit   In all cases where a baserunner is retired by being hit by a batted ball, unless batted by himself, the batsman should be credited with a base hit, except if the runner is hit by an infield fly, the play should be scored as provided in the Playing Rules (Sec. 8 of Rule 44).

Earned Run   A run earned off the pitcher shall be scored every time a player reaches home base by the aid of safe hits, sacrifice hits, stolen bases, putouts, bases on balls, hit batsman, wild pitches, or balks, even though the wild pitch be a third strike, before fielding chances have been offered to retire the team. The preceding pitcher, and not a relieving pitcher shall be charged with runs scored by any runners on base when such relief pitcher entered the game. The relieving pitcher shall not be charged with his first batsman reaching first base if such batsman had any advantage because of poor pitching by the preceding pitcher. With the count two or three balls and one or no strikes, or three balls and two strikes, charge preceding pitcher if batsman reaches first base, but credit relieving pitcher if batsman is retired. With count one or two balls and two strikes, charge relieving pitcher if batsman reaches first base and credit him if batsman is retired.

Forfeited Game   In a regulation game which the umpire shall declare forfeited after four and one-half innings have been played, all individual and team averages shall be incorporated in the official playing records, except that no pitcher shall be credited with a victory or charged with a loss in said game.

1941–49

There were no changes to the scoring rules in these years.

1950

Assist   An assist shall be credited to each player who throws or deflects a batted or thrown ball in such a way that a putout results, or would have resulted except for a subsequent error by a teammate, but only one assist and no more shall be credited to each player who throws or deflects the ball in a rundown play which results in a putout, or would have resulted in a putout, except for a subsequent error.

Credit an assist to each player who throws or deflects the ball during a play which results in a baserunner being called out for interference, or for running out of line.

Situations will arise in which a wild throw shall be scored as an assist and not as an error while on some plays a wild throw shall be scored both as an assist and as an error.

Note: The scoring rules for 1950 then present four detailed examples illustrating the application of the assist provisions.

Base Hit   A base hit shall be scored under these circumstances: (1) When a batter reaches first base (or any succeeding base) safely on a legally batted ball which settles on fair ground or strikes a fence behind fair ground before being touched by a fielder, or which clears a fence behind fair territory; (2) When a batter reaches first base after hitting a ball with such force, or so slowly, that the pitcher or fielder attempting to make a play with it has no opportunity to do so; (3) When a batter reaches first base safely on a batted ball which strikes either first base, second, or third base before being touched by a fielder and bounces away from the reach of the fielder; (4) When a batter reaches first base safely on a legally batted ball which has not been touched by a fielder and which is in fair territory when it bounds into the outfield unless in the scorer's judgment it could have been handled with ordinary effort; (5) When a legally batted ball which has not been touched by a fielder becomes "dead" by reason of touching the person or clothing of a runner or umpire, except that when a runner is called out for having been struck by an "infield fly" the batter shall not be credited with a hit; (6) When, in the scorer's judgment, the batter could not have been retired at first base by perfect fielding, when the fielder fails in an attempt to retire a preceding baserunner; (7) Always give the batter the benefit of the doubt. A safe course to follow being to score a hit when exceptionally good fielding of a batted ball fails to result in a putout; (8) In no case shall a base hit be scored when a runner is forced out by a batted ball, or would have been forced out except for a fielding error. Nor shall a hit be scored when an infield batted ball results in another runner, who is attempting to advance one base, being retired, whether forced out or not; (9) Score the play as a "fielder's choice" when a fielder uses a batted ball to retire a preceding baserunner, or would have retired one with ordinary effort except for a fielding error, charging the batter with time at bat, but no hit.

Base Hit/Value   Whether a safe hit shall be scored as a one-base hit, two-base hit or a three-base hit when no error or putout results shall be determined as follows:

It is a one-base hit if the batter stops at first base; it is a two-base hit if the batter stops at second base; it is a three-base hit if the batter stops at third base, but note this exception: the batter must, if attempting to take two or three bases on a safe hit by sliding, hold the last base to which he advances. If he overslides and is tagged out before getting back to the base safely he shall be given credit for only as many bases as he safely attained. If he overslides second base and is tagged out he shall be given a one-base hit; if he overslides third base and is tagged out, he shall be given a two-base hit. If he runs past second base after reaching that base on his feet, attempts to return and is tagged out, he shall be given credit for a two-base hit. If he runs past third base after reaching that base on his feet, attempts to return and is tagged out, he shall be given credit for a three-base hit.

If a batter is awarded three bases on a batted or bunted ball because a fielder has touched the ball with his glove, cap, or any other part of his uniform while such article is detached from its proper place on his person, the scorer's judgment shall dictate whether the batter shall be given credit for a one-base hit, a two-base hit, a three-base hit, or a home run. If the scorer believes the fielder could have, by ordinary effort, kept the hit from being good for more than one, two, or three bases he shall score it as a one-base hit or as a two-base hit or as a three-base hit and charge the fielder with an error. If, however, the scorer believes the hit would have been a legitimate home run, despite illegal use of equipment, he shall so score it if the batter touches all bases in the proper order.

In no instance shall the batter be credited with a two-base hit or a three-base hit if he fail to advance a preceding runner whose advance is necessary to permit the batter to reach second or third base. Example: Runner on first, batter makes a long hit and reaches second but runner is thrown out at third. Score a one-base hit and credit batter with reaching second on the play.

Should a batter, after making a safe hit, be called out for having failed to touch a base, the last base he reached safely shall determine if his hit is scored as a one-base hit, a two-base hit, or a three-base hit. If he is called out for missing second base, the hit shall be scored as a one-base hit. If he is called out for missing third base, his hit shall be scored as a two-base hit. If he is tagged out after missing home base, his hit shall be scored as a three-base hit. If he is called out for missing first base, he shall be charged with a time at bat but no hit.

When a batter ends a game with a safe hit, other than a home run, which drives in as many runs as are necessary to put his team in the lead, he shall be credited with only as many bases on his hit as are advanced by the runner who scores the winning run, and then only if the batter runs out his hit for as many bases as are advanced by the runner who scores the winning run, touching each base in the proper order.

If a batter ends a game with a home run out of the playing field and touches all the bases in their proper order, his run, and also the runs of all other runners who were on base when the home run was hit, shall count in the final score even though this gives the team last at bat a winning margin in excess of one run.

Base on Balls   A base on balls shall be scored whenever a batter is awarded first base by the umpire because of four balls having been pitched outside the strike zone, but when the fourth such ball strike the batter it shall be scored as a "hit batter."

Championship   To be eligible for the individual batting championship of any minor league, a player must have appeared in at least two-thirds of the games played by his team. Thus, if a team plays 154 games, a player must appear in 102 games. If his team plays 150 games he must appear in 100. If his team plays 140 games he must appear in 93, etc.

To be eligible for the individual batting championship of a major league, a player must be credited with at least 400 official "times at bat."

Double Play   A double play is any two successive putouts which take place between the time a ball leaves a pitcher's hand and is returned to him while he is standing in the pitcher's box.

Earned Run   An earned run is a run for which the pitching is held accountable.

An earned run shall be scored every time a player reaches home base by the aid of safe hits, sacrifices, stolen bases, putouts, bases on balls, hit batters, balks, or wild pitches (even though a wild pitch be a third strike which enables a batter to reach first base), before fielding chances have been offered to retire the offensive team.

Since a wild pitch on which a batter reaches first base is the pitcher's fault, solely, even though it is scored as a fielding error, it shall be disregarded as an error and considered as a wild pitch in computing earned runs and is the only instance in which an error is so disregarded.

In computing earned runs, any type of fielding error made by a pitcher (other than the one mentioned in the preceding two paragraphs) shall be considered in the same light as an error by any other fielder.

Whenever a fielding error occurs the pitcher shall be given the benefit of the doubt in determining to which bases any baserunners would have advanced had the fielding by the defensive team been errorless.

No run can be earned which scores as a result of a batter having reached first base safely because of a catcher's interference, or because of any fielding error, except a wild pitch.

When pitchers are changed during an inning, the preceding pitcher, and not the relieving pitcher, shall be charged with any earned or unearned runs scored by any runners on base when such relief pitcher entered the game. There is, however, this exception: If the action of any batter to whom the relieving pitcher pitches results in the retirement of a runner left on base by the preceding pitcher, the batter whose action resulted in the retirement of that runner shall be considered as having been left on base by the preceding pitcher and any run scored by such runner shall be charged to the preceding pitcher.

A relieving pitcher shall not be held accountable for the first batter to whom he pitches reaching first base if that batter had a decided advantage because of ineffective pitching by the pitcher whom the relieving pitcher succeeded. Thus, if the count is two or three balls and one or no strikes, or if the count is three balls and two strikes when pitchers are changed, and the batter reaches first base safely, charge that batter to the pitcher who was replaced. If such a batter is retired, or would have been retired except for a fielding error, the batter shall be credited to the relieving pitcher. Likewise, if such a batter hits into a force-out or into a fielder's choice on which a runner is retired, or would have been retired except for a fielding error, credit the action of such a batter to the relieving pitcher. (The foregoing sentence is not to be construed as affecting or conflicting with the exception noted.) If pitchers are changed when the count is two balls and one or no strikes, or one ball and one or no strikes, the relieving pitcher shall be held accountable for whatever the batter does.

Error   An error shall be scored for each misplay (fumble, muff, or wild throw) which prolongs the time at bat of a batter, or which prolongs the life of a runner, or which permits a runner to advance one or more bases when perfect play would have resulted in the batter or the runner being retired.

Certain misplays by the catcher and pitcher known as "passed balls" and "wild pitches" are not errors but items for the summary and are defined elsewhere in these rules.

Errors are not charged when a batter is awarded first base because of a base on balls, or for being struck by a pitched ball, or if a runner, or runners, advance because of a passed ball or because of the pitcher making a balk or a wild pitch, except: If a batter swings at a wild pitch for his third strike and thereby is enabled to reach first base, it shall be scored as a strikeout and also as an error for the pitcher and not a wild pitch; when a catcher muffs a third strike, thereby permitting a batter to reach first base, it shall be scored as an error for the catcher, not a passed ball, and as a strikeout.

No error shall be charged against the catcher or any other player for making a wild throw in attempting to prevent a stolen base or any other advance by a runner, unless the scorer is convinced such wild throw permitted the runner to advance one or more bases. If the wild throw permits a runner to advance an extra base, or bases, one error shall be charged to the player making the wild throw.

When any player throws wildly in attempting to complete a double play, or a triple play, no error shall be scored unless the throw is so wild that at least one additional base be gained. However, if a fielder muff a thrown ball which, if held, would have completed a double play or a triple play, score an error for the player who drops the ball.

An error shall be scored against any player who, on receiving a thrown ball in ample time to retire a batter or any other baserunner on a force play, does not touch the base as required by the rules.

When a runner advances because of the failure of a fielder to stop, or try to stop, an accurately thrown ball, the fielder failing to stop the ball shall be charged with an error and not the player making the throw, provided there was occasion for the throw. If such throw be made to second base the scorer shall determine whether it was the duty of the second baseman or the shortstop to stop the ball, and he shall charge the error to the negligent player.

No error shall be scored if any fielder, after dropping a fly ball, a line drive or a thrown ball recovers the ball in time to force out a runner at another base.

Accurately directed throws, especially from the outfield, which strike a baserunner or an umpire, or which take an unnatural bounce and permit a baserunner or baserunners to advance, shall be scored as errors for the player making the throw, even though it appears to be doing an injustice to the thrower. Every base advanced by a baserunner must be accounted for.

Game-Ending Hit   See last two paragraphs, *Base Hit/Value*.

Hit by Pitch   See *Base on Balls*.

Innings Pitched   In giving a pitcher credit for the number of innings pitched divide each inning into three parts. Thus, if a pitcher is replaced, with one opponent out, in the sixth inning the pitcher so replaced shall be credited with having pitched $5\frac{1}{3}$ innings. If a pitcher is replaced with none out in the opposing team's sixth inning he shall be credited with having pitched 5 innings and a notation made to the effect that there were none out in the sixth inning.

Passed Ball   A catcher shall be charged with a passed ball when a runner, or runners, advance because of the catcher's failure to hold or to control a legally pitched ball which should have been held or controlled with ordinary effort.

Percentage   To determine a pitcher's earned run prevention average for a season, the total number of earned runs charged against his pitching shall be divided by the total number of innings he has pitched, then multiplied by nine to find his average effectiveness for a complete game.

(a) To determine the percentage of games won and lost divide the total number of games won and lost into the number won.

(b) To determine a batting average, divide the total "times at bat" into the total number of safe hits.

(c) To determine a slugging percentage, divide the total "times at bat" into the total bases of all safe hits.

(d) To determine a fielding average, divide the total of put-outs, assists, and errors into the total of putouts and assists.

Putout   A putout shall be recorded each time a defensive player catches a fly ball, whether fair or foul, a line drive or a thrown ball which retires a batter or runner, or when a fielder tags a runner with the ball when the runner is off the base to which he legally is entitled.

Automatic putouts shall be credited to the catcher as follows: (1) When a batter is called out by the umpire for an illegally batted ball; when a batter is called out by the umpire for bunting foul for his third strike; when a batter is called out by an umpire for being struck by his own batted ball; when a batter is called out by an umpire for interfering with the catcher; when a batter is called out by an umpire for failing to bat in his proper turn. (Note exception in 10.14 (a).) (2) Other automatic putouts shall be credited as follows: (3) When a batter is called out on an infield fly which is not caught, the putout shall be credited to the fielder whom the scorer believes could have made the putout; (4) When a runner is called out for being struck by a fair ball (including an infield fly) the putout shall be credited to the fielder nearest the ball; (5) When a runner is declared out by an umpire for running out of line to avoid being tagged by the ball in the hands of a fielder, the putout shall be credited to the fielder whom the runner avoided; (6) When a runner is declared out by the umpire for having interfered with a fielder, credit the putout to the fielder with whom the runner interfered, unless the fielder was in the act of throwing the ball when interfered with, in which case the putout shall be credited to the fielder for whom the throw was intended, and the fielder whose throw was interfered with shall be credited with an assist.

Relief Pitcher   See last two paragraphs, *Earned Run*.

Runs Batted In   A run batted in is a run which reaches home base safely because of a safe hit, sacrifice hit, infield putout or outfield putout, or which is forced over home plate by reason of the batter being struck by a pitched ball, or being awarded a base on balls, or being awarded first base because of interference by the catcher. If a batter hit a home run with the bases empty, score both a home run and a run batted in. If, with less than two out, an error is made on a play on which a runner from third base ordinarily would score and does score, credit the batter with a run batted in.

The batter shall not be credited with a run batted in if a run scores when he hits into a force double play, or into a double play in which the first baseman fields a fair hit ground ball, touches first base ahead of the batter for an out, then throws to second or third base, retiring a second runner who has to be tagged.

Sacrifice   Score a sacrifice if, with less than two out, the batter advances one or more runners with a bunt and is retired at first base, or would have been retired except for a fielding error. In case a runner is forced out at any base on a bunt, it shall be scored as a time at bat but no sacrifice.

Scorer   The scorer is an actual official of the game he is scoring, is an accredited representative of the league, is entitled to the respect and dignity of his office and shall be accorded full protection by the president of the league.

The scorer shall report to the President of the league any indignity expressed by manager, player, club employee or club official in the course of, or as the result of, the discharge of his duties.

To promote uniformity in keeping the records of championship games, scorers shall conform to the instructions of this scoring code.

Scoring Summary   In making a box score of a game, each player's name and the fielding position or positions he has played shall be listed in the order in which he batted, or would have batted if the game ends before he gets to bat, followed by a tabulated record of each player's batting and fielding. (a) The first column shall show the number of times each player batted during the game, but no time at bat shall be charged against a player when he is awarded first base on four called balls, for being hit by a pitched ball, or because of being interfered with by the catcher, or for being obstructed by the catcher or any other player, while en route to first base. A sacrifice also exempts a player from being charged with a time at bat. (b) The second column shall show the number of runs, if any, made by each player. (c) The third column shall show the number of safe hits, if any, made by each player. (d) The fourth column shall show the number of putouts, if any, made by each player. (e) The fifth column shall show the number of fielding assists, if any, made by each player. (f) The sixth column shall show the number of fielding errors, if any, made by each player. (g) All players inserted into each team's lineup as substitute batters or substitute runners shall be so designated by special symbols plus notations at the bottom of their team's tabulated record. The symbols a, b, c, d, etc., are recommended. It also is recommended that the notations should describe what the extra batters did, such as—a-Singled for _____ in sixth inning; b-Flied out for _____ in third inning; c-Forced _____ for _____ in seventh inning; d-Grounded out for _____ in ninth inning. (h) The score by innings of each team follows the box score tabulations and precedes the summary in which should be listed the following items in this order: (1) Runs batted in; (2) Two-base hits; (3) Three-base hits; (4) Home runs, together with the names of the pitchers off whom hit; (5) Stolen bases; (6) Sacrifices; (7) Double plays; (8) Triple plays; (9) Number of runners left on base by each team; (10) Number of bases on balls issued by each pitcher; (11) Number of batters struck out by each pitcher. These shall be listed as "strikeouts"; (12) Number of hits and runs (also earned runs) allowed by each pitcher (if one or both teams use more than one pitcher), together with the number of innings pitched by each pitcher. If a team uses only one pitcher, list the number of earned runs he allowed; (13) The names of any hit batters together with the names of the pitchers who hit them, if a team uses more than one pitcher; (14) The number of wild pitches made; (15) The number of passed balls made by the catchers; (16) The name of the winning pitcher, if the winning team uses more than one pitcher; (17) The name of the losing pitcher, if the losing team uses more than one pitcher; (18) The names of the umpires, listed in this order: (a) plate umpire; (b) first base umpire; (c) second base umpire; (d) third base umpire; (19) The time of game with any delays for rain, fog, snow, light failure or violent wind storm deducted; (20) All individual and team records of any forfeited or tied game which has reached or exceeded legal length when ended shall become a part of the official averages except that no pitcher shall be credited with a victory or charged with a defeat; (21) A box score is in balance (or proved) when the total of a team's times at bat, bases on balls received, hit batters, sacrifices and batters awarded first base because of interference or obstruction equals the total of that team's runs, players left on base, and the other team's putouts.

Stolen Base A stolen base shall be credited to a runner whenever he advances one base unaided by a base hit, a putout, a forceout, a fielder's choice, a passed ball, a wild pitch or a balk, subject to the following exceptions:

If a double or triple steal is attempted and one runner is thrown out before reaching and holding the base he is attempting to steal, no other runner shall be credited with a stolen base;

A runner who is touched out after oversliding a base shall not be regarded as having stolen that base.

If it is the scorer's judgment that a palpable muff of a thrown ball prevents a runner who is attempting to steal from being retired, it shall be scored as an error for the player muffing the throw, an assist for the player throwing the ball, and not a stolen base.

No stolen base shall be scored when a runner advances solely because of the defensive team's indifference to his advancement.

If a runner advances while the defensive team, unsuccessfully, is attempting to retire another runner who, in attempting to steal, evades being put out in a rundown play and returns to the base he originally occupied, a stolen base shall be credited to the runner who so advances.

If a runner has started for a succeeding base before the pitcher delivers the ball and the pitch results in a wild pitch or a passed ball, credit the runner with a stolen base with this exception: If another runner also advances because of the pitch becoming a wild pitch or passed ball, the wild pitch or passed ball also shall be scored.

If a runner, attempting to steal, is well advanced toward the base he is attempting to steal and a balk is called on the pitcher, credit the runner with a stolen base and do not score the balk unless another runner who is not attempting to steal is advanced by the balk.

Note: This paragraph was dropped in 1951.

Squeeze Play "Squeeze play" is the term designating a play when a team, with a runner on third base, attempts to score that runner by means of a bunt. It also is a "squeeze play" if an attempt is made to score a runner from second base by means of a bunt.

Strikeout A strikeout shall be scored whenever a pitcher delivers three legal pitches at which the batter swings and misses, or which the umpire decrees are strikes even though the batter may reach first base safely after the third strike by reason of a wild pitch or the catcher's failure to hold the ball.

A strikeout shall be scored whenever a batter bunts foul when there are two strikes against him, except that should the bunt result in a foul fly caught by the catcher or any other player it shall not be scored as a strikeout but as a regular foul-fly putout.

When a batter goes out of the game with two strikes against him and the substitute batter completes a strikeout, score it as a strikeout for the first batter. If the substitute batter completes the turn at bat in any other manner, score the action as having been that of the substitute batter.

Substitute Batter See last paragraph, *Strikeout*.

Triple Play A triple play is any three successive putouts which take place between the time a ball leaves a pitcher's hand and is returned to him while he is standing in the pitcher's box.

Wild Pitch A wild pitch shall be scored when a legally delivered ball is so high, or so wide, or so low that the catcher does not stop and control the ball by ordinary effort and, as a result, a runner, or runners, advance.

Any legally pitched ball which strikes the ground before reaching home plate and passes the catcher, permitting a runner, or runners, to advance shall be scored as a wild pitch.

Winning and Losing Pitcher Determining the winning and losing pitcher of a game often calls for much careful consideration.

Do not give the starting pitcher credit for a game won, even if the score is in his favor, unless he has pitched at least five innings when replaced.

The five-inning rule to determine a winning pitcher shall be in effect for all games of six or more innings. When a game is called after five innings of play the starting pitcher must have pitched at least four innings to be credited with the victory. If the starting pitcher is replaced (except in a five-inning game) before he has pitched five complete innings when his team is ahead, remains ahead to win, and more than one relief pitcher is used by his team, the scorer shall credit the victory (as among all relieving pitchers) to the pitcher whom the scorer considers to have done the most effective pitching. If, in a five-inning game, the starting pitcher is replaced before pitching four complete innings when his team is ahead, remains ahead to win, and more than one relief pitcher is used by his team, the scorer shall credit the victory (as among all relieving pitchers) to the pitcher whom the scorer considers to have done the most effective pitching.

Regardless of how many innings the first pitcher has pitched, he shall be charged with the loss of the game if he is replaced when his team is behind in the score, and his team thereafter fails to either tie the score or gain the lead.

If a pitcher retires from the game for a substitute batter, or a substitute runner, after pitching five or more innings and his team scores enough runs in the inning in which he is replaced to take the lead, those runs shall be credited to his benefit. Thus, if a pitcher is removed for a substitute batter or a substitute baserunner in any inning after the pitcher has pitched at least five complete innings and during the inning in which he is removed his team assumes the lead, he shall be credited with the victory if his team remains ahead until the finish of the game.

Examples: If the pitcher of the team first at bat is removed in the first half of the sixth inning for a substitute batter, or a substitute runner, and his team gains the lead in that inning and the relieving pitcher holds the lead through the last half of the ninth inning, the pitcher who was removed shall be credited with the victory; if the pitcher of the team last at bat is removed in the last half of the fifth inning for a substitute batter, or a substitute runner, and his team gains the lead in that inning with the relieving pitcher holding the lead through the ninth inning, the pitcher who was removed shall be credited with the victory.

1951

Base Hit When a batter apparently hits safely and a runner who is obliged to advance by reason of the batter becoming a baserunner misses touching the first base to which he is advancing and is called out on appeal, charge the batter with a time at bat but no hit.

Caught Stealing When records are kept of players caught stealing by catchers, credit the catcher with preventing a stolen base each time he traps a runner off any base with a thrown ball and, as a result of such throw, the runner is retired or would have been except for a subsequent error by any fielder, including the catcher. Runners who are retired in rundown plays started by the catcher trapping a runner off any base, or whose baserunning life is prolonged by an error after they have been trapped off base by the catcher, are to be included among those prevented from stealing by the catcher.

Championship To be designated as the leader of his league's pitchers in the minimum average number of earned runs allowed, a pitcher is required to pitch at least as many innings as the number of games scheduled for each team in his league. (This would be 154 innings in a major league.)

Error If a batter is awarded first base by an umpire because of interference by the catcher, charge the catcher with an error; if an umpire awards a runner or runners one or more bases because of interference or obstruction by any defensive player, charge the player who committed the interference or obstruction with one error, no matter how many bases the runner or runners are advanced.

An error is to be charged when a fielder, in violation of the playing rules, touches a thrown ball with his cap, glove, or uniform while such article is detached from its proper place.

Sacrifice Also score a sacrifice if, with less than two out, the fielders handle a bunted ball without error in attempting to force a preceding runner but fail to do so. Exception: When such an attempt is made to turn a bunt into a force-out of a preceding runner and fails and it is the scorer's judgment that perfect play would not have retired the batter at first base, it shall be scored as a one-base hit and not as a sacrifice.

Shutout No pitcher shall be credited with pitching a shutout unless he pitches the complete game. When two or more pitchers combine to pitch a shutout, a notation to that effect should be included in the league's official pitching records.

Stolen Base See *Caught Stealing*; also see 1950 *Stolen Base* entry.

Time at Bat See *Base Hit*.

Winning and Losing Pitcher Determining the winning and losing pitcher of a game in which a team uses more than one pitcher often calls for careful consideration. Scorers can be guided by these rules: (1) Credit the starting pitcher with a game won only if he has pitched at least five complete innings and his team not only is in the lead when he is replaced but remains in the lead the remainder of the game; (2) They "must pitch five complete innings" rule in respect to the starting pitcher shall be in effect for all games of six or more innings. When a game is ended after five innings of play the starting pitcher must have pitched at least four complete innings to be credited with a victory. As stated in 10.16 (a), the starting pitcher in a five-inning game can be credited with a victory only if his team is in the lead when he is replaced (after pitching at least four complete innings) and his team remains in the lead to the finish of the game; (3) Except in a five-inning game (when they "must pitch at least four complete innings" rule applies) if the winning team uses more than two pitchers and the starting pitcher has not pitched at least five complete innings the victory shall be awarded one of the relieving pitchers on this basis: (a) Once the opposing team assumes the lead, all pitchers who have pitched for the winning team up to that point are excluded from being credited with the victory with the exception that if the pitcher against whose pitching the opposing team gained the lead con-

tinues to pitch until his team regains the lead which it holds to the finish of the game that pitcher would be the winning pitcher; (b) If, after the starting pitcher is replaced before pitching at least five complete innings, the opposing team does not tie the score or take the lead, credit the victory to the relief pitcher deemed by the scorer to have done the most effective pitching; (c) Whenever the score is tied, the game becomes a new contest insofar as determining the winning and losing pitchers are concerned; (d) With one exception, no pitcher can be credited with a victory unless he is the pitcher of record when his team assumes a lead and maintains the lead to the finish of the game; (e) The exception to the foregoing is: Do not credit a game won to a relief pitcher who pitches briefly and ineffectively and is the pitcher of record when his team assumes a lead which it maintains over a period of innings to the finish of the game. If a succeeding relief pitcher pitches effectively in helping to maintain his team in the lead credit such relief pitcher with the victory.

1952

Championship The individual batting champion of any league shall be the player with the highest batting average, if he is credited with as many or more times at bat as the number of games scheduled for one club in his league during the season, multiplied by 2.6. However, if there is any player in a league with fewer than the required number of times at bat whose average would be the highest if he were charged with this required at-bat total, then that player shall be awarded the batting championship.

Putout When a runner is declared out by an umpire for running out of line to avoid being tagged by the ball in the hands of a fielder, the putout shall be credited to the fielder whom the runner avoided; when a runner is called out for passing another runner, credit the putout to the fielder nearest the spot at which the violation took place.

1953

There were no changes to the scoring rules this year.

1954

Double Play A double play is a play by the defense in which two offensive players are legally put out as a result of continuous action, providing there is no error between putouts.

Sacrifice The following section was added to the rule regarding sacrifice bunts and flies: Also score a sacrifice if, with less than two out, the batter hits a fair fly ball which is caught, and a runner scores after the catch, or is dropped for an error, and a runner scores, if in the scorer's judgment, the runner could have scored after the catch had the fly been caught.

Scorer To promote uniformity in keeping the records of championship games, scorers shall conform to the instructions of this scoring code, but in no case shall the scorer's decisions conflict with the playing rules.

Scoring Summary Sacrifice flies and bunts are to be listed separately in the scoring summary.

1955

Assist Mere ineffective contact with the ball shall not be considered an assist. "Deflect" shall mean to slow down or change the direction of the ball and thereby effectively assist in retiring a batter or runner.

Do not credit an assist to the pitcher when, as the result of a legal pitch caught by the catcher, a runner is retired, as when the catcher picks a runner off base, throws out a runner trying to steal or tags a runner trying to steal home.

Do not credit an assist to a fielder whose wild throw permits a runner to advance, even though the runner subsequently is retired as a result of a continuous play. A play which follows an error is a new play, and the player making an error is not entitled to an assist unless he takes part in the new play.

Base Hit   A base hit shall be scored when a batter reaches first base safely on a fair ball which takes an unnatural bounce so that a fielder cannot handle it with ordinary effort, or which strikes the pitcher's plate or any base (including home plate) before being touched by a fielder and bounces so that a fielder cannot handle it with ordinary effort.

A base hit shall be scored when the fielder throws to another base in an unsuccessful attempt to retire a preceding runner, and in the scorer's judgment the batter-runner would not have been retired at first base by perfect fielding.

A base hit shall not be scored when a fielder fails in an attempt to retire a preceding runner, and in the scorer's judgment the batter-runner could have been retired at first base.

A base hit shall not be scored when a fielder handles a batted ball and retires a preceding runner, or would have retired one with ordinary effort except for a fielding error. Charge the batter with a time at bat but no hit.

Note: This shall not apply if the fielder merely looks toward or feints toward another base before attempting to make the putout at first base.

Base Hit/Value   Whether a safe hit shall be scored as a one-base hit, two-base hit, or three-base hit when no error or putout results, shall be determined as follows: When, with one or more runners on base, the batter advances more than one base on a safe hit and the defensive team makes an attempt to retire a preceding runner, the scorer shall determine whether the batter made a legitimate two-base hit or three-base hit, or whether he advanced beyond first base on the fielder's choice.

Note: The rules of 1955 include a series of examples to illustrate the application of this rule for the guidance of the scorer.

When the batter attempts to make a two-base hit or a three-base hit by sliding, he must hold the last base to which he advances. If he overslides and is tagged out before getting back to the base safely, he shall be credited with only as many bases as he attained safely. If he overslides second base and is tagged out, he shall be credited with a one-base hit; if he overslides third base and is tagged out he shall be credited with a two-base hit.

Note: If the batter overruns second or third base and is tagged out trying to return, he shall be credited with the last base he touched. If he runs past second base after reaching that base on his feet, attempts to return and is tagged out, he shall be credited with a two-base hit. If he runs past third base after reaching that base on his feet, attempts to return and is tagged out, he shall be credited with a three-base hit.

Subject to provisions of the playing rules, when the batter ends a game with a safe hit which drives in as many runs as are necessary to put his team in the lead, he shall be credited with only as many bases on his hit as are advanced by the runner who scores the winning run, and then only if the batter runs out his hit for as many bases as are advanced by the runner who scores the winning run, touching each base in proper order.

Note: Apply this rule even when the batter is theoretically entitled to more bases because of being awarded an "automatic" extra-base hit under various provisions of the playing rules.

Base on Balls   A base on balls shall be scored whenever a batter is awarded first base because of four balls having been pitched outside the strike zone, but when the fourth such ball strikes the batter it shall be scored as a "hit batter."

Note: The scoring rules contain detailed instructions for charging runners who receive a base on balls when the pitcher is changed in mid-batter.

Batter/Out of Turn   When a player bats out of turn, and is put out, and the proper batter is called out before the ball is pitched to the next batter, charge the proper batter with a time at bat and

score the putout and any assists the same as if the correct batting order had been followed. If an improper batter becomes a runner by reason of a hit, error, fielder's choice, hit batter, base on balls, interference or obstruction, and the proper batter is called out for having missed his turn at bat, charge the proper batter with a time at bat, credit the putout to the catcher, and ignore everything entering into the improper batter's safe arrival on base. If more than one batter bats out of turn in succession, score all plays just as they occur, skipping the turn at bat of the player or players who first missed batting in the proper order.

Box Score   A box score is in balance (or proved) when the total of the team's times at bat, bases on balls received, hit batters, sacrifice bunts, sacrifice flies, and batters awarded first base because of interference or obstruction, equals the total of that team's runs, players left on base, and the opposing team's putouts.

Caught Stealing   Do not credit the catcher with a man "caught stealing" when he traps a runner off base after fielding a batted ball or on any play started by another fielder.

Championship   The individual fielding champions shall be the fielders with the highest fielding average at each position, subject to the following: (1) A catcher must have participated as a catcher in at least 90 games (80 games in leagues playing schedules of 140 games or less); (2) An infielder or outfielder must have participated at his position in at least 100 games (90 games in leagues playing schedules of 140 games or less); (3) A pitcher must have pitched in at least as many innings as the number of games scheduled for each club in his league that season.

Earned Run   The scoring rules of 1955 contain detailed provisions for charging runners and runs to starting pitchers and relief pitchers where pitching changes are made in mid-batter.

No run can be earned which scores as a result of the batter reaching first base (1) on a hit or otherwise after his time at bat is prolonged by a muffed foul fly; (2) because of interference or obstruction; or (3) because of any fielding error, except for a wild pitch charged as an error.

Error   Slow handling of the ball which does not involve mechanical misplay shall not be construed as an error.

An error shall be charged against any fielder when he muffs a foul fly, to prolong the time at bat of the batter, whether the batter subsequently reaches first base or is retired.

If a runner advances on a throw by a fielder, and in the scorer's judgment there was no occasion for the throw, an error shall be charged to the fielder making the unnecessary throw.

An error shall be charged against any fielder whose throw takes an unnatural bounce, or strikes a base or the pitcher's plate, or strikes a runner, a fielder or an umpire, thereby permitting any runner to advance.

Note: Apply this rule even when it appears to be an injustice to a fielder whose throw was accurately directed. Every base advanced by a runner must be accounted for.

When an umpire awards the batter or any runner or runners one or more bases because of interference or obstruction, charge the fielder who committed the interference or obstruction with one error, no matter how many bases the batter, or runner or runners, may be advanced.

No error shall be charged against the catcher when he makes a wild throw in attempting to prevent a stolen base, unless such wild throw permits the base stealer to advance one or more extra bases, or in the scorer's judgment permits another runner to advance one or more bases. Charge only one error on such a wild throw, regardless of the number of bases advanced by the runner or runners.

No error shall be charged against any fielder when he makes a wild throw in attempting to prevent a runner's advance, unless in the scorer's judgment such wild throw permits the runner to advance beyond the base he would have reached had the throw not been wild, or permits any other runner to advance one or more bases beyond the base he would have reached had the throw not been wild. Charge only one error on such wild throw, regardless of the number of bases advanced by the runner or runners.

See also *Wild Pitch*.

Fielder's Choice   Fielder's choice is the act of a fielder who handles a fair grounder and, instead of throwing to first base to retire the batter-runner, throws to another base in an attempt to retire a preceding runner. The term is also used by scorers (1) to account for the advance of the batter-runner who takes one or more extra bases when the fielder who handles his safe hit attempts to retire a preceding runner; and (2) to account for the advance of a runner (other than by stolen base or error) while a fielder is attempting to retire another runner.

Note: This definition appears in the Playing Rules for 1955.

Game-Ending Hit   See last paragraph, *Base Hit/Value*.

Putout   When a runner is called out for running the bases in reverse order, credit the putout to the fielder covering the base he left in starting his reverse run. Do not credit any assist on such plays.

When the batter-runner is called out because of interference by a preceding runner, credit the putout to the first baseman. If the fielder interfered with was in the act of throwing the ball, credit him with an assist, but credit only one assist on any one play.

Run Batted In   A run batted in is a run which reaches home base safely because of a safe hit, a sacrifice bunt, a sacrifice fly, a putout via a foul fly, an infield putout, or a fielder's choice; or which is forced over home plate by reason of the batter being struck by a pitched ball, or being awarded a base on balls, or being awarded first base because of interference or obstruction. If a batter hits a home run always score the home run as a run batted in. Also count all other runs which score ahead of the batter who hit the home run as runs batted in. If, with less than two out, an error is made on a play on which a runner from third base ordinarily would score and does score, credit the batter with a run batted in.

Sacrifice   Score a sacrifice bunt when, with less than two outs, the fielders handle a bunted ball without error in an unsuccessful attempt to retire a preceding runner advancing one base. Exception: When an attempt to turn a bunt into a putout of a preceding runner fails, and in the scorer's judgment perfect play would not have retired the batter at first base, the batter shall be credited with a one-base hit and not a sacrifice.

Do not score a sacrifice bunt when a runner is retired attempting to advance one base on a bunt. Charge the batter with a time at bat.

Scorer   The Official Scorer shall keep records of each game as outlined in the scoring rules. He shall have sole authority to make all decisions involving judgment, such as whether a batter's advance to first base is the result of a hit or an error. In no event shall a scorer make a decision conflicting with the Official Playing Rules or with an umpire's decision.

Scoring Summary   The scoring summary shall contain: (1) Number of runners left on base by each team. This total shall include all runners who get on base by any means and who do not score and are not put out. Include in this total a batter-runner whose batted ball results in another runner being retired for the third out; (2) Total number of bases on balls issued by each pitcher and a separate listing of the number of intentional bases on balls issued by each pitcher.

The scoring rules of 1955 also include detailed instructions for notations to the tabulated game records. It is recommended that letters a, b, c, d, etc., be used in the notations as symbols for

substitute batters and that numerals 1, 2, 3, 4, etc., be used as symbols for substitute runners. Also the instructions detail notations needed when a substitute is announced but removed for another substitute before he actually enters the game.

Stolen Base   A stolen base shall be credited to a runner whenever he advances one base unaided by a base hit, a putout, an error, a force-out, a fielder's choice, a passed ball, a wild pitch or a balk, subject to the following: When a runner, attempting to steal, evades being put out in a rundown play and advances to the next base without the aid of an error, credit the runner with a stolen base. If another runner also advances on the play, credit both runners with stolen bases. If a runner advances while another runner, attempting to steal, evades being put out in a rundown play and returns safely, without the aid of an error, to the base he originally occupied, credit a stolen base to the runner who advances.

Strikeout   A strikeout shall be scored whenever a pitcher delivers three legal pitches at which the batter swings and misses, or which the umpire decrees are strikes. A strikeout shall be scored even though the batter reaches first base safely after the third strike because of an error by the pitcher or catcher as defined in the scoring rules.

Wild Pitch   When the batter's fourth called ball is a wild pitch and as a result (1) the batter-runner advances to a base beyond first base; (2) any runner, forced to advance by reason of the batter becoming a runner, advances more than one base; or (3) any runner, not forced to advance by reason of the batter becoming a runner, advances one or more bases, score the base on balls and also an error for the pitcher and do not score a wild pitch.

When the batter swings at a wild pitch for his third strike and thereby is enabled to reach first base, score a strikeout and also an error for the pitcher, and do not score a wild pitch.

When the batter swings at a wild pitch for his third strike or when the catcher muffs a third strike, if the catcher recovers the ball and throws out the batter-runner trying to reach first base, but another runner or runners advance, score the strikeout and error the same as if the batter had reached first base. Credit an assist to the catcher, and a putout to the fielder taking the throw at first base.

Winning and Losing Pitcher   In some non-championship games (such as the Major League All-Star Game) it is provided in advance that each pitcher shall work a stated number of innings, usually two or three. In such games, it is customary to credit the victory to the pitcher of record, whether starter or reliever, when the winning team takes a lead which it maintains to the end of the game, unless such pitcher is knocked out after the winning team has a commanding lead, and the scorer believes a subsequent pitcher is entitled to credit for the victory.

1956

Base Hit   A base hit should be scored when the fielder unsuccessfully attempts to retire a preceding runner, and, in the scorer's judgment, the batter-runner would not have been retired at first base by perfect fielding.

Also see *Time at Bat*.

Run Batted In   The batter shall not be credited with a run batted in if a run scores when he grounds into a force double play, or grounds into a double play in which the first out is made at first base and the second out made by tagging a runner who was originally forced, attempting to advance one base.

Time at Bat   When a fielder handles a batted ball and retires a preceding runner who is attempting to advance one base, or would have retired one with ordinary effort except for a fielding error, charge the batter with a time at bat but no hit.

1957

Base Hit   A base hit shall be scored when a batter reaches first base safely on a fair ball hit with such force, or so slowly, that any fielder attempting to make a play with it has no opportunity to do so.

Note: A hit shall be scored if the fielder attempting to handle the ball cannot make a play, even if such fielder deflects the ball from or cuts off another fielder who could have retired a runner.

Championship To assure uniformity in establishing the batting, pitching and fielding championship of professional leagues, such champions shall meet the following minimum performance standards: The individual batting champion shall be the player with the highest batting average, provided he is credited with as many or more total appearances at the plate in league championship games as the number of games scheduled for each club in the league that season, multiplied by 3.1. Total appearances at the plate shall include official times at bat, plus bases on balls, times hit by pitcher, sacrifice hits, sacrifice flies and times awarded first base because of interference or obstruction.

Earned Run An earned run shall be scored every time a runner reaches home base by the aid of safe hits, sacrifice bunts, a sacrifice fly, stolen bases, putouts, fielder's choices, bases on balls, hit batters, balks or wild pitches (including a wild pitch on third strike which permits a batter to reach first base) before fielding chances have been offered to retire the offensive team.

Note: A wild pitch is solely the pitcher's fault, and contributes to an earned run just as a base on balls or a balk.

No run can be earned which scores as a result of the batter reaching base (1) on a hit or otherwise after his time at bat is prolonged by a muffed foul fly; (2) because of interference or obstruction; or (3) because of any fielding error.

An error by the pitcher is treated exactly the same as an error by any other fielder in computing earned runs.

Error No error shall be charged to any fielder who permits a foul fly to fall safe with a runner on third base before two are out, if in the scorer's judgment the fielder deliberately refuses the catch in order that the runner on third shall not score after the catch.

Because the pitcher and catcher handle the ball much more than other fielders, certain misplays on pitched balls are called "wild pitches" and "passed balls," and are defined elsewhere in the scoring rules. No error shall be charged when a wild pitch or passed ball is scored. No error shall be charged when the batter is awarded first base on four called balls or because he was touched by a pitched ball, or when he reaches first base as the result of a wild pitch or passed ball. When the third strike is a wild pitch, permitting the batter to reach first base, score a strikeout and a wild pitch. When the third strike is a passed ball, permitting the batter to reach first base, score a strikeout and a passed ball.

Passed Ball See second paragraph, *Error.*

Run Batted In Scorer's judgment must determine whether a run batted in shall be credited for a run which scores when a fielder holds the ball, or throws to a wrong base. Ordinarily, if the runner keeps going, credit a run batted in; if the runner stops and takes off again when he notices the misplay, credit the run as scored on a fielder's choice.

Scorer The league president shall appoint an official scorer for each league championship game. The official scorer shall observe the game from a position in the press box. The scorer shall have sole authority to make all decisions involving judgment, such as whether a batter's advance to first base is the result of a hit or an error. He shall communicate such decisions to the press box and broadcasting booths by hand signals or over the press box loudspeaker system, and shall advise the public address announcer of such decisions if requested.

After each game, including drawn, forfeited and called games, the scorer shall prepare a report, on a form prescribed by the league president, listing the date of the game, where it was played, the names of the competing clubs and the umpires, the full score of the game, and all records of individual players compiled according to the system specified in these Official Scoring Rules. He shall forward this report to the league office within 36 hours after the game ends. He shall forward the report of any suspended game within 36 hours after the game has been completed, or after it becomes an official game because it cannot be completed, as provided by the Official Playing Rules.

To achieve uniformity in keeping the records of championship games, the scorer shall conform strictly to the Official Scoring Rules.

If the teams change sides before three men are put out, the scorer shall immediately inform the umpire of the mistake.

If the game is protested or suspended, the scorer shall make note of the exact situation at the time of the protest or suspension, including the score, the number of outs, the position of any runners, and the ball and strike count on the batter.

Note: It is important that a suspended game resume with exactly the same situation as existed at the time of suspension. If a protested game is ordered replayed from the point of protest, it must be resumed with exactly the situation that existed just before the protested play.

The scorer shall not make any decision conflicting with the Official Playing Rules or with an umpire's decision.

The scorer shall not call the attention of the umpire or of any member of either team to the fact that a player is batting out of turn.

The scorer is an official representative of the league, and is entitled to the respect and dignity of his office, and shall be accorded full protection by the league president. The scorer shall report to the president any indignity expressed by any manager, player, club employee or club officer in the course of, or as the result of, the discharge of his duties.

The umpire-in-chief shall inform the official scorer of the official batting order, and any changes in the lineups and batting order, on request.

Wild Pitch See second paragraph, *Error.*

Winning and Losing Pitcher Regardless of how many innings the first pitcher has pitched, he shall be charged with the loss of the game if he is replaced when his team is behind in the score, and his team thereafter fails either to tie the score or gain the lead.

1958

Championship The individual fielding champions shall be the fielders with the highest fielding average at each position, provided: (1) A catcher must have participated as a catcher in at least one-half the number of games scheduled for each club in his league that season; (2) An infielder or outfielder must have participated at his position in at least two-thirds of the number of games scheduled for each club in his league that season; (3) A pitcher must have pitched at least as many innings as the number of games scheduled for each club in his league that season.

Percentage To compute the pitcher's earned run average, multiply the total earned runs charged against his pitching by 9, and divide the result by the total number of innings he pitched.

Sacrifice Score a sacrifice fly when, before two are out, the batter hits a fair fly ball which: (1) is caught, and a runner scores after the catch, or (2) is dropped, and a runner scores, if, in the scorer's judgment, the runner could have scored after the catch had the fly been caught.

Note: Score a sacrifice fly in accordance with the scoring rules even though another runner is forced out by reason of the batter becoming a runner.

1959–64

There were no changes to the scoring rules in these years.

1965

Championship To qualify for the fielding championship at his position a pitcher must have pitched at least as many innings as the number of games scheduled for each club in his league that season. Exception: If another pitcher has a fielding average as high or higher, and has handled more total chances in a lesser number of innings, he shall be the fielding champion.

1966

There were no changes to the scoring rules this year.

1967

Championship The individual batting champion shall be the player with the highest batting average, provided he is credited with as many or more total appearances at the plate in league championship games as the number of games scheduled for each club in his league that season, multiplied by 3.1. Exception: However, if there is any player with fewer than the required number of plate appearances whose average would be highest if he were charged with the required number of plate appearances or official at-bats, then that player shall be awarded the batting championship.

Error Mental mistakes or misjudgments are not to be scored as errors unless specifically covered in the rules.

No error shall be charged against any fielder when, after fumbling a ground ball or dropping a fly ball, a line drive or a thrown ball, he recovers the ball in time to force out a runner at any base.

Sacrifice Do not score a sacrifice bunt when, in the judgment of the scorer, the batter is bunting for a base hit and not solely for the purpose of advancing a runner or runners. Charge the batter with a time at bat.

Note: In applying this rule always give the batter the benefit of the doubt.

Stolen Base When a runner, attempting to steal, or after being picked off base, evades being put out in a rundown play and advances to the next base without the aid of an error, credit the runner with a stolen base. If another runner also advances on the play, credit both runners with stolen bases. If a runner advances while another runner, attempting to steal, evades being put out in a rundown play and returns safely, without the aid of an error, to the base he originally occupied, credit a stolen base to the runner who advances.

1968

There were no changes to the scoring rules this year.

1969

Double Play/Triple Play Credit participation in the double play or triple play to each fielder who earns a putout or an assist when two or three players are put out between the time a pitch is delivered and the time the ball next becomes dead or is next in possession of the pitcher in pitching position, unless an error or misplay intervenes between putouts.

Note: Credit the double play or triple play also if an appeal play after the ball is in possession of the pitcher results in an additional putout.

Earned Run An earned run is a run for which the pitcher is held accountable. In determining earned runs, the inning should be reconstructed without the errors and passed balls, and the benefit of the doubt should always be given to the pitcher in determining which bases would have been reached by errorless play.

When pitchers are changed during an inning, the relief pitcher shall not have the benefit of previous chances for outs not accepted in determining earned runs.

Note: It is the intent of this rule to prevent relief pitchers from not being charged with earned runs for which they are solely responsible.

Error When an umpire awards the batter or any runner or runners one or more bases because of interference or obstruction, charge the fielder who committed the interference or obstruction with one error, no matter how many bases the batter, or runner or runners, may be advanced.

Note: Do not charge an error if obstruction does not change the play in the opinion of the scorer.

Relief Pitcher See *Earned Run*, second paragraph.

Sacrifice Do not score a sacrifice bunt when, in the judgment of the scorer, the batter is bunting *primarily* for a base hit and not for the purpose of advancing a runner or runners. Charge the batter with a time at bat.

Note: In applying this rule always give the batter the benefit of the doubt.

Note: The rule is the same as that appearing in the 1967 scoring rules with the addition of the word *primarily*.

Save Credit a save to a relief pitcher who enters a game with his team in the lead if he holds the lead the remainder of the game, provided he is not credited with the victory. A relief pitcher cannot be credited with a save if he does not finish the game unless he is removed for a pinch hitter or pinch runner. When more than one relief pitcher qualifies for a save under the provisions of this rule, credit the save to the relief pitcher judged by the scorer to have been the most effective. Only one save can be credited in any game.

1970–72

There were no changes to the scoring rules in these years.

1973

Save A pitcher shall be credited with a save when, in entering a game as a relief pitcher, he finds the potential tying or winning run either on base or at the plate or pitches at least three or more effective innings and, in either case, preserves the lead.

1974

Hitting/Playing Streaks A consecutive hitting streak shall not be terminated if the plate appearance results in a base on balls, hit batsman, defensive interference or a sacrifice bunt.

A sacrifice fly shall terminate the streak.

A consecutive-game hitting streak shall not be terminated if all the player's plate appearances (one or more) result in a base on balls, hit batsman, defensive interference or a sacrifice bunt. The streak shall terminate if the player has a sacrifice fly and no hit.

A consecutive-game playing streak shall be extended if the player plays one half-inning on defense, or if he completes a time at bat by reaching base or being put out. A pinch-running appearance only shall not extend the streak. If a player is ejected from a game by an umpire before he can comply with the requirements of this rule, his streak shall continue.

Suspended Game For the purpose of the scoring rules, all performances in the completion of a suspended game shall be considered as occurring on the original date of the game.

1975

Sacrifice Score a sacrifice fly when, before two are out, the batter hits a fly ball or a line drive handled by an outfielder or an infielder running in the outfield which: (1) is caught, and a runner scores after the catch, or (2) is dropped, and a runner scores, if in the scorer's judgment the runner could have scored after the catch had the fly been caught.

Note: Score a sacrifice fly in accordance with the scoring rules even though another runner is forced out by reason of the batter becoming a runner.

Save Credit a pitcher with a save when he meets all three of the following conditions: (1) He is the finishing pitcher in a game won by his club; and (2) He is not the winning pitcher; and (3) He qualifies under one of the following conditions: (a) He enters the game with a lead of no more than three runs and pitches for at least one inning; or (b) He enters the game with the potential tying run either on base, or at bat, or on deck (that is, the potential tying run is either already on base or is one of the first two batsmen he faces); or (c) He pitches effectively for at least three innings. No more than one save may be credited in each game.

1976

Base on Balls See *Strikeout*.

Earned Run An earned run is a run for which the pitcher is held accountable. In determining earned runs, the inning should be reconstructed without the errors (which includes catcher's interference) and passed balls, and the benefit of the doubt should always be given to the pitcher in determining which bases would have been reached by errorless play.

When pitchers are changed during an inning, the relief pitcher shall not be charged with any run (earned or unearned) scored by a runner who was on base at the time he entered the game, nor for runs scored by any runner who reaches base on a fielder's choice which puts out a runner left on base by the preceding pitcher.

Note: It is the intent of this rule to charge each pitcher with the number of runners he put on base, rather than with the individual runners. When a pitcher puts runners on base and is relieved, he shall be charged with all runs subsequently scored up to and including the number of runners he left on base when he left the game, unless such runners are put out without action by the batter, i.e., caught stealing, picked off base, or called out for interference when a batter-runner does not reach first base on the play. Exception: The pitcher walks batter A and is relieved. The relief pitcher allows B to single, but runner A is out trying for third. Runner B takes second on the throw. Batter C singles, scoring runner B. Charge the run to the relief pitcher rather than the preceding pitcher.

Game Played When a player listed in the starting lineup for the visiting club is substituted for before he plays defensively, he shall not receive credit in the defensive statistics (fielding), unless he actually plays that position during a game. All such players, however, shall be credited with one game played (in batting statistics) as long as they are announced into the game or listed on the official lineup card.

Percentage For purposes of earned run average calculations and innings pitched totals, innings pitched shall be rounded off to the nearest whole inning. Examples: 200⅓ innings becomes 200; 200⅔ becomes 201.

Note: This standard was changed in 1982 and fractions were no longer rounded off but counted for their full value. Also see rule addition under 1981.

Relief Pitcher See *Earned Run*, second paragraph.

Scoring Summary The name of a pitcher credited with a save is to be shown on the scoring summary.

Strikeout When the batter leaves the game with two strikes against him, and the substitute batter completes a strikeout, charge the strikeout and the time at bat to the first batter. If the substitute batter completes the turn at bat in any other manner, including a base on balls, score the action as having been that of the substitute batter.

Substitute Batter See *Strikeout*.

1977

Base on Balls Intentional base on balls shall be scored when the pitcher makes no attempt to throw the last pitch to the batter into the strike zone but purposely throws the ball wide to the catcher outside the catcher's box.

1978

There were no changes to the scoring rules this year.

1979

Caught Stealing A runner shall be charged as "caught stealing" if he is put out, or would have been put out by errorless play, when he (1) tries to steal; (2) is picked off a base and tries to advance (any move toward the next base shall be considered an attempt to advance); (3) overslides while stealing.

Note: In those instances where a pitched ball eludes the catcher and the runner is put out trying to advance, no caught stealing shall be charged.

Earned Run An earned run is a run for which the pitcher is held accountable. In determining earned runs, the inning should be reconstructed without the errors (which include catcher's interference) and passed balls, and the benefit of the doubt should always be given to the pitcher in determining which bases would have been reached by errorless play. For the purpose of determining earned runs, an intentional base on balls, regardless of the circumstances, shall be construed in exactly the same manner as any other base on balls.

Scorer The official scorer must make all decisions concerning judgment calls within twenty-four (24) hours after a game has been officially concluded. No judgment decision shall be changed thereafter except, upon immediate application to the league president, the scorer may request a change, citing the reasons for such. In all cases the official scorer is not permitted to make a scoring decision which is in conflict with the scoring rules.

1980

Run Batted In Game-winning RBI is credited for the RBI that gives a club the lead it never relinquishes.

Note: There does not have to be a game-winning RBI in every game and all game-winning RBIs must conform to the scoring rule governing RBIs.

1981

Percentage For purposes of earned run average calculations and innings pitched totals, do not round off the fraction where a pitcher has only ⅓ of an inning for the entire season. In such cases carry his total for innings pitched as ⅓.

1982

Percentage Earned run averages shall be calculated on the basis of total innings pitched, including fractional innings. Example: 9⅓ innings pitched and three earned runs is an earned run average of 2.89 (3 ER times 9 divided by 9⅓ equals 2.89).

1983

Championship The individual batting champion or slugging champion shall be the player with the highest batting average or slugging percentage, provided he is credited with as many or more total appearances at the plate in League championship games as the number of games scheduled for each club in his League that season, multiplied by 3.1 in the case of a major league player. Exception: However, if there is any player with fewer than the required number of plate appearances or official at-bats, but who, when credited with an out for each of his deficient at-bats, still has the highest average, then that player shall be awarded the batting championship or slugging championship.

1984

Percentage To compute on-base percentage, divide the total of hits, all bases on balls, and hit by pitch, by the total of at-bats, all bases on balls, hit by pitch, and sacrifice flies.

[Casebook] Note: For the purpose of computing on-base percentage, ignore being awarded first base on interference or obstruction.

1985–88

There were no changes to the scoring rules this year.

1989

Run Batted In The game-winning RBI is dropped from the rule book.

1990–1996

There were no changes to the scoring rules in these years.

Index to Scoring Rule Changes 1877–1996

Note: Dates shown following an entry refer to the year a rule change or amendment was adopted. Rule changes and summaries of rules are to be found in the chronology.

Jackie Robinson's Signing: The Real, Untold Story

John Thorn and Jules Tygiel

October 1945. As the Detroit Tigers and Chicago Cubs faced off in the World Series, photographer Maurice Terrell arrived at an almost deserted minor league park in San Diego, California, to carry out a top-secret assignment: to surreptitiously photograph three black baseball players.

Terrell shot hundreds of motion-picture frames of Jackie Robinson and the two other players. A few photos appeared in print but the existence of the additional images remained unknown for four decades. In April 1987, as Major League Baseball prepared a lavish commemoration of the fortieth anniversary of Robinson's debut, John Thorn unearthed a body of contact sheets and unprocessed film from a previously unopened carton donated in 1954 by *Look* magazine to the Baseball Hall of Fame in Cooperstown, New York. This discovery triggered an investigation which led to startling revelations regarding Branch Rickey, the president of the Brooklyn Dodgers, and his signing of Jackie Robinson to shatter baseball's longstanding color line; the relationship between these two historic figures; and the still controversial issue of black managers in baseball.

The popular "frontier" image of Jackie Robinson as a lone gunman facing down a hostile mob has always dominated the story of the integration of baseball. But new information related to the Terrell photos reveals that while Robinson was the linchpin in Branch Rickey's strategy, in October 1945 Rickey intended to announce the signing of not just Jackie Robinson, but of several other Negro League stars. Political pressure, however, forced Rickey's hand, thrusting Robinson alone into the spotlight. And in 1950, after only three years in the major leagues, Robinson pressed Rickey to consider him for a position as field manager or front office executive, raising an issue with which the baseball establishment still grapples.

The story of these revelations began with the discovery of the Terrell photographs. The photos show a youthful, muscular Robinson in a battered cap and baggy uniform fielding from his position at shortstop, batting with a black catcher crouched behind him, trapping a third black player in a rundown between third and home, and sprinting along the basepaths more like a former track star than a baseball player. All three players wore uniforms emblazoned with the name "Royals." A woman with her back to the action is the only figure visible amid the vacant stands. The contact sheets are dated October 7, 1945.

The photos were perplexing. The momentous announcement of Jackie Robinson's signing with the Montreal Royals took place on October 23, 1945. Before that date his recruitment had been a tightly guarded secret. Why, then, had a *Look* photographer taken such an interest in Robinson two weeks earlier? Where had the pictures been taken? And why was Robinson already wearing a Royals uniform?

Thorn called Jules Tygiel, the author of *Baseball's Great Experiment: Jackie Robinson and His Legacy,* to see if he could shed some light on the photos. Tygiel knew nothing about them,

but he did have in his files a 1945 manuscript by newsman Arthur Mann, who frequently wrote for *Look*. The article, drafted with Rickey's cooperation, had been intended to announce the Robinson signing but had never been published. The pictures, they concluded, were to have accompanied Mann's article; they decided to find out the story behind the photo session.

The clandestine nature of the photo session did not surprise the researchers. From the moment he had arrived in Brooklyn in 1942, determined to end baseball's Jim Crow traditions, Rickey had feared that premature disclosure of his intentions might doom his bold design. No blacks had appeared in the major leagues since 1884 when two brothers, Welday and Moses Fleetwood Walker, had played for Toledo in the American Association. Not since the 1890s had black players appeared on a minor league team. During the ensuing half century all-black teams and leagues featuring legendary figures like pitcher Satchel Paige and catcher Josh Gibson had performed on the periphery of Organized Baseball. Baseball executives, led by Commissioner Kenesaw Mountain Landis, had strictly policed the color line, barring blacks from both major and minor leagues. In 1943 when young Bill Veeck attempted to buy the Philadelphia Phillies and stock the team with Negro League stars, Landis had quietly but decisively blocked the move. Rickey therefore moved slowly and secretly to explore the issue and cover up his attempts to scout black players during his first three years in Brooklyn. He informed the Dodger owners of his plans but took few others into his confidence.

In the spring of 1945, as Rickey prepared to accelerate his scouting efforts, advocates of integration, emboldened by the impending end of World War II and the recent death of Commissioner Landis, escalated their campaign to desegregate baseball. On April 6, 1945, black sportswriter Joe Bostic appeared at the Dodgers' Bear Mountain training camp with Negro League stars Terris McDuffie and Dave "Showboat" Thomas and forced Rickey to hold tryouts for the two players. Ten days later black journalist Wendell Smith, white sportswriter Dave Egan, and Boston city councilman Isadore Muchnick engineered an unsuccessful audition with the Red Sox for Robinson and two other black athletes. In response to these events the major leagues announced the formation of a Committee on Baseball Integration. (Reflecting Organized Baseball's true intentions on the matter, the group never met.)

In the face of this heightened activity, Rickey created an elaborate smokescreen to obscure his scouting of black players. In May 1945 he announced the formation of a new franchise, the Brooklyn Brown Dodgers, and a new Negro League, the United States League. Rickey then dispatched his best talent hunters to observe black ballplayers, ostensibly for the Brown Dodgers, but in reality for the Brooklyn National League club.

A handwritten memorandum in the Rickey Papers offers a rare glimpse of Rickey's emphasis on secrecy in his instructions to Dodger scouts. The document, signed by Chas. D. Clark and accompanied by a Negro National League schedule for April-May 1945, is headlined "Job Analysis," and defines the following "Duties: under supervision of management of club":

1. To establish contact (silent) with all clubs (local or general).
2. To gain knowledge and abilities of all players.
3. To report all possible material (players).
4. Prepare weekly reports of activities.
5. Keep composite report of outstanding players . . . To travel and cover player whenever management so desire.

Clark's "Approch" [sic] was to "Visit game and loose [sic] self in stands; Keep statistical report (speed, power, agility, ability, fielding, batting, etc.) by score card"; and "Leave immediately after game."

Clark's directions, however, contain one major breach in Rickey's elaborate security precautions. According to his later accounts, Rickey had told most Dodger scouts that they were evaluating talent for a new "Brown Dodger" franchise. But Clark's first "Objective" was "To Cover Negro teams for possible major league talent." Had Rickey confided in Clark, a figure so obscure as to escape prior mention in the voluminous Robinson literature? Dodger superscout and Rickey confidante Clyde Sukeforth has no recollection of Clark, raising the possibility that Clark was not part of the Dodger family, but perhaps someone connected with black baseball. Had Clark himself interpreted his instructions in this manner?

Whatever the answer, Rickey successfully diverted attention from his true motives. Nonetheless, mounting interest in the integration issue threatened Rickey's careful planning. In the summer of 1945 Rickey constructed yet another facade. The Dodger President took Dan Dodson, a New York University sociologist who chaired Mayor Fiorello LaGuardia's Committee on Unity, into his confidence and requested that Dodson form a Committee on Baseball ostensibly to study the possibility of integration. In reality, the committee would provide the illusion of action while Rickey quietly completed his own preparations. "This was one of the toughest decisions I ever had to make while in office," Dodson later confessed. "The major purpose I could see for the committee was that it was a stall for time. . . . Yet had Mr. Rickey not delivered . . . I would have been totally discredited."

Thus by late August, even as Rickey's extensive scouting reports had led him to focus on Jackie Robinson as his standard bearer, few people in or out of the Dodger organization suspected that a breakthrough was imminent. On August 28 Rickey and Robinson held their historic meeting at the Dodgers' Montague Street offices in downtown Brooklyn. Robinson signed an agreement to accept a contract with the Montreal Royals, the top Dodger affiliate, by November 1. Rickey, still concerned with secrecy, impressed upon Robinson the need to maintain silence. Robinson could tell the momentous news to his family and fiancee, but no one else.

For the conspiratorial Rickey, keeping the news sheltered while continuing arrangements required further subterfuge. Rumors about Robinson's visit had already spread through the world of black baseball. To stifle speculation Rickey "leaked" an adulterated version of the incident to black sportswriter Wendell Smith. Smith, who had recommended Robinson to Rickey and advised Rickey on the integration project, doubtless knew the true story behind the meeting. On September 8, however, he reported in the Pittsburgh *Courier* that the "sensational shortstop" and "colorful major league dynamo" had met behind "closed doors. . . . The nature of the conference has not been revealed," Smith continued. Rickey claimed that he and Robinson had assessed "the organization of Negro baseball," but Smith noted that "it does not seem logical [Rickey] should call in a rookie player to discuss the future organization of Negro baseball." He closed with the tantalizing thought that "it appears that the Brooklyn boss has a plan on his mind that extends

further than just the future of Negro baseball as an organization." The subterfuge succeeded. Neither black nor white reporters pursued the issue.

Rickey, always sensitive to criticism by New York sports reporters and understanding the historic significance of his actions, also wanted to be sure that his version of the integration breakthrough and his role in it be accurately portrayed. To guarantee this he persuaded Arthur Mann, his close friend and later a Dodger employee, to write a 3,000 word manuscript to be published simultaneously with the announcement of the signing.

Although it was impossible to confirm this in 1987 (it has since been confirmed by Maurice Terrell himself, who was eventually located), it seemed highly likely that Terrell's photos, commissioned by *Look,* were destined to accompany Mann's article. Clearer prints of the negatives revealed that Terrell had taken the pictures in San Diego's Lane Stadium. This fit in with Robinson's autumn itinerary. After his meeting with Rickey, Robinson had returned briefly to the Kansas City Monarchs. With the Dodger offer securing his future and the relentless bus trips of the Negro League schedule wearing him down, he had left the Monarchs before season's end and returned home to Pasadena, California. In late September he hooked up with Chet Brewer's Kansas City Royals, a postseason barnstorming team which toured the Pacific Coast, competing against other Negro League teams and major and minor league all-star squads. Thus the word "Royals" on Robinson's uniform, which had so piqued the interest of Thorn and Tygiel, ironically turned out to relate not to Robinson's future team in Montreal, but rather to his interim employment in California.

For further information Tygiel contacted Chet Brewer, who at age eighty still lived in Los Angeles. Brewer, one of the great pitchers of the Jim Crow era, had known Robinson well. He had followed Robinson's spectacular athletic career at UCLA and in 1945 they became teammates on the Monarchs. "Jackie was major league all the way," recalled Brewer. "He had the fastest reflexes I ever saw in a player."

Robinson particularly relished facing major league all-star squads. Against Bob Feller, Robinson once slashed two doubles. "Jack was running crazy on the bases," a Royal teammate remembered. In one game he upended Gerry Priddy, Washington Senator infielder. Priddy angrily complained about the hard slide in an exhibition game. "Any time I put on a uniform," retorted Robinson, "I play to win."

Brewer recalled that Robinson and two other Royals journeyed from Los Angeles to San Diego on a day when the team was not scheduled to play. He identified the catcher in the photos as Buster Haywood and the other player as Royals third baseman Herb Souell. Souell was no longer living, but Haywood, who, like Brewer lived in Los Angeles, vaguely recalled the event, which he incorrectly remembered as occurring in Pasadena. Robinson recruited the catcher and Souell, his former Monarch teammate, to "work out" with him. All three wore their Royal uniforms. Haywood found neither Robinson's request nor the circumstances unusual. Although he was unaware that they were being photographed, Haywood described the session accurately. "We didn't know what was going on," he stated. "We'd hit and throw and run from third base to home plate."

The San Diego pictures provide a rare glimpse of the pre-Montreal Robinson. The article which they were to accompany and related correspondence in the Library of Congress offer even rarer insights into Rickey's thinking. The unpublished Mann manuscript was entitled "The Negro and Baseball: "The National Game Faces a Racial Challenge Long Ignored." As Mann doubtless based his account on conversations with Rickey and since Rickey's handwritten comments appear in the margin, it stands as the earliest "official" account of the Rickey-Robinson story and reveals many of the concerns confronting Rickey in September 1945.

One of the most striking features of the article is the language used to refer to Robinson. Mann, reflecting the racism typical of postwar America, portrays Robinson as the "first Negro chattel in the so-called National pastime." At another point he writes, "Rickey felt the boy's sincerity," appropriate language perhaps for an 18-year-old prospect, but not for a 26-year-old former army officer.

"The Negro and Baseball" consists largely of the now familiar Rickey–Robinson story. Mann recreated Rickey's haunting 1904 experience as collegiate coach when one of his black baseball players, Charlie Thomas, was denied access to a hotel. Thomas cried and rubbed his hands, chanting, "Black skin! Black skin! If I could only make 'em white." Mann described Rickey's search for the "right" man, the formation of the United States League as a cover for scouting operations, the reasons for selecting Robinson, and the fateful Rickey–Robinson confrontation. Other sections, however, graphically illustrate additional issues Rickey deemed significant. Mann repeatedly cites the costs the Dodgers incurred: $5,000 to scout Cuba, $6,000 to scout Mexico, $5,000 to establish the "Brooklyn Brown Dodgers." The final total reaches $25,000, a modest sum considering the ultimate returns, but one which Rickey felt would counter his skinflint image.

Rickey's desire to show that he was not motivated by political pressures also emerges clearly. Mann had suggested that upon arriving in Brooklyn in 1942, Rickey "was beseiged by telephone calls, telegrams and letters of petition in behalf of black ball players," and that this "staggering pile of missives [was] so inspired to convince him that he and the Dodgers had been selected as a kind of guinea pig." In his marginal comments, Rickey vehemently wrote "No!" in a strong dark script. "I began all this as soon as I went to Brooklyn." Explaining why he had never attacked the subject during his two decades as general manager of the St. Louis Cardinals, Rickey referred to the segregation in that city. "St. Louis never permitted Negro patrons in the grandstand," he wrote, describing a policy he apparently had felt powerless to change.

Mann also devoted two of his twelve pages to a spirited attack on the Negro Leagues, repeating Rickey's charges that "they are the poorest excuse for the word league" and documented the prevalence of barnstorming, the uneven scheduling, absence of contracts, and dominance of booking agents. Mann revealingly traces Rickey's distaste for the Negro Leagues to the "outrageous" guarantees demanded by New York booking agent William Leuschner to place black teams in Ebbets Field while the Dodgers were on the road.

Rickey's misplaced obsession with the internal disorganization of the Negro Leagues had substantial factual basis. But Rickey had an ulterior motive. In his September 8 article, Wendell Smith addressed the issue of "player tampering," asking, "Would [Rickey] not first approach the owners of these Negro teams who have these stars under contract?" Rickey, argued Smith in what might have been an unsuccessful preemptive strike, "is obligated to do so and his record as a businessman indicated that he would." As Smith may have known, Rickey maintained that Negro League players did not sign valid contracts and so became free agents at the end of each season. Thus the Mahatma had no intention of compensating Negro League teams for the players he signed. His repeated attacks on black baseball, including the Mann article, served to justify this questionable position.

The one respect in which "The Negro and Baseball" departs radically from common picture of the Robinson legend is in its report of Robinson as one of a group of blacks about to be signed by the Dodgers. Mann's manuscript and subsequent correspondence from Rickey reveal that Rickey did not intend for Robinson to withstand the pressures alone. "Determined not to be charged with merely nibbling at the problem," wrote Mann, "Rickey went all out and brought in two more Negro players," and "consigned them, with Robinson, to the Dodgers' top farm club, the Montreal Royals." Mann named pitcher Don Newcombe and, surprisingly, outfielder Sam Jethroe as Robinson's

future teammates. Whether the recruitment of additional blacks had always been Rickey's intention or whether he had reached his decision after meeting with Robinson in August is unclear. But by late September, when he provided information to Mann for his article, Rickey had clearly decided to bring in other Negro League stars.

During the first weekend in October, Dodger coach Chuck Dressen fielded a major league all-star team in a series of exhibition games against Negro League standouts at Ebbets Field. Rickey took the opportunity to interview at least three black pitching prospects, Newcombe, Roy Partlow and John Wright. The following week he met with catcher Roy Campanella. Campanella and Newcombe, at least, believed they had been approached to play for the "Brown Dodgers."

At the same time Rickey decided to postpone publication of Mann's manuscript. In a remarkable letter sent from the World Series in Chicago on October 7, Rickey informed Mann:

We just can't go now with the article. The thing isn't dead,-not at all. It is more alive than ever and that is the reason we can't go with any publicity at this time. There is more involved in the situation than I had contemplated. Other players are in it and it may be that I can't clear these players until after the December meetings, possibly not until after the first of the year. You must simply sit in the boat. . . .

There is a November 1 deadline on Robinson,-you know that. I am undertaking to extend that date until January 1st so as to give me time to sign plenty of players and make one break on the complete story. Also, quite obviously it might not be good to sign Robinson with other and possibly better players unsigned.

The revelations and tone of this letter surprised Robinson's widow, Rachel, forty years after the event. Rickey "was such a deliberate man," she recalled, "and this letter is so urgent. He must have been very nervous as he neared his goal. Maybe he was nervous that the owners would turn him down and having five people at the door instead of just one would have been more powerful."

Events in the weeks after October 7 justified Rickey's nervousness and forced him to deviate from the course stated in the Mann letter. Candidates in New York City's upcoming November elections, most notably black Communist City Councilman Ben Davis, made baseball integration a major issue in the campaign. Mayor LaGuardia's Democratic party also sought to exploit the issue. The Committee on Baseball had prepared a report outlining a modest, long-range strategy for bringing blacks into the game and describing the New York teams, because of the favorable political and racial climate in the city, as in a "choice position to undertake this pattern of integration." LaGuardia wanted Rickey's permission to make a pre-election announcement that "baseball would shortly begin signing Negro players," as a result of the committee's work.

Rickey, a committee member, had long ago subverted the panel to his own purposes. By mid-October, however, the committee had become "an election football." Again unwilling to risk the appearance of succumbing to political pressure and thereby surrendering what he viewed as his rightful role in history, Rickey asked LaGuardia to delay his comments. Rickey hurriedly contacted Robinson, who had joined a barnstorming team in New York en route to play winter ball in Venezuela, and dispatched him to Montreal. On October 23, 1945, with Rickey's carefully laid plans scuttled, the Montreal Royals announced the signing of Robinson, and Robinson alone.

Mann's article never appeared. *Look,* having lost its exclusive, published two strips of the Terrell pictures in its November 27, 1945 issue accompanying a brief summary of the Robinson story, by then old news. The unprocessed film and contact sheets were loaded into a box and nine years later shipped to the National Baseball Hall of Fame, where they remained, along with a picture of Jethroe, unpacked until April 1987.

Newcombe, Campanella, Wright and Partlow all joined the Dodger organization the following spring. Jethroe became a victim of the "deliberate speed" of baseball integration. Rickey did not interview Jethroe in 1945. Since few teams followed the Dodger lead, the fleet, powerful outfielder remained in the Negro Leagues until 1948, when Rickey finally bought his contract from the Cleveland Buckeyes for $5,000. Jethroe had two spectacular seasons at Montreal before Rickey, fearing a "surfeit of colored boys on the Brooklyn club," profitably sold him to the Boston Braves for $100,000. Jethroe won the Rookie of the Year Award in 1950, but his delayed entry into Organized Baseball foreshortened what should have been a stellar career. Until informed by the authors of this essay, Jethroe remained unaware of how close he came to joining Robinson, Newcombe and Campanella in the pantheon of integration pioneers.

For Robinson, who had always occupied center stage in Rickey's thinking, the early announcement intensified the pressures and enhanced the legend. The success or failure of integration rested disproportionately on his capable shoulders. He became the lightning rod for supporter and opponent alike, attracting the responsibility, the opprobrium, and ultimately the acclaim for his historic achievement.

Beyond these revelations about the Robinson signing, the Library of Congress documents add surprisingly little to the familiar story of the integration of baseball. The Rickey Papers copiously detail his post-Dodger career as general manager of the Pittsburgh Pirates, but are strangely silent about the criticial 1944–1948 period. Records for these years probably remained with the Dodger organization, which claims to have no knowledge of their whereabouts. National League documents for these years remain closed to the public.

In light of the controversy engendered by former Dodger General Manager Al Campanis's remarks about blacks in management, however, one exchange between Rickey and Robinson becomes particularly relevant. In 1950, after his fourth season with the Dodgers, Robinson appears to have written Rickey about the possibility of employment in baseball when his playing days ended. Robinson's original letter cannot be found in either the Rickey papers or the Robinson family archives. However, Rickey's reply, dated December 31, 1950, survives. Rickey, who had recently left the Dodgers after an unsuccessful struggle to wrest control of the team from Walter O'Malley, responded to Robinson's inquiry with a long and equivocal answer.

"It is not at all because of lack of appreciation that I have not acknowledged your good letter of some time ago," began Rickey. "Neither your writing, nor sending the letter, nor its contents gave me very much surprise." On the subject of managing, Rickey replied optimistically, "I hope that the day will soon come when it will be entirely possible, as it is entirely right, that you can be considered for administrative work in baseball, particularly in the direction of field management." Rickey claimed to have told several writers that "I do not know of any player in the game today who could, in my judgement, manage a major league team better than yourself," but that the news media had inexplicably ignored these comments.

Yet Rickey tempered his encouragement with remarks that to a reader today seem gratuitous. "As I have often expressed to you," he wrote, "I think you carry a great responsibility for your people . . . and I cannot close this letter without admonishing you to prepare yourself to do a widely useful work, and, at the same time, dignifed and effective in the field of public relations. A part of this preparation, and I know you are smiling, for you have already guessed my oft repeated suggestion—to finish your college course meritoriously and get your degree." This advice, according to Rachel Robinson, was a "matter of routine" between the two men ever since their first meeting. Nonetheless, to the thirty-one-year-old Robinson, whose nonathletic academic career had been marked by indifferent success and whose endorsements and business acumen had already established the

promise of a secure future, Rickey's response may have seemed to beg the question.

Rickey concluded with the promise, which seems to hinge on the completion of a college degree, that "It would be a great pleasure for me to be your agent in placing you in a big job after your playing days are finished. Believe me always." Shortly after writing this letter Rickey became the general manager of the Pittsburgh Pirates. Had Robinson ended his playing career before Rickey left the Pirates, perhaps the Mahatma would have made good on his pledge. But Rickey resigned from the Pirates at the end of the 1955 season, one year before Robinson's retirement, and never again had the power to hire a manager.

Robinson's 1950 letter to Rickey marked only the beginning of his quest to see a black manager in the major leagues. In 1952 he hoped to gain experience by managing in the Puerto Rican winter league, but, according to the New York *Post*, Commissioner Happy Chandler withheld his approval, forcing Robinson to cancel his plans. On November 30, 1952, the Dodger star raised the prospect of a black manager in a televised interview on "Youth Wants to Know," stating that both he and Campanella had been "approached" on the subject. In 1954, after the Dodgers had fired manager Chuck Dressen, speculation arose that either Robinson or Pee Wee Reese might be named to the post. But the team bypassed both men and selected veteran minor league manager Walter Alston, who held the job for more than two decades.

Upon his retirement in 1956, Robinson, who had begun to manifest signs of the diabetes that would plague the rest of his life, had lost much of his enthusiasm for the prospect of managing, but nonetheless would probably have accepted another pioneering role. "He had wearied of the travel," states Rachel, "and no longer wanted to manage. He just wanted to be asked as a recognition of his accomplishments, his abilities as a strategist, and to show that white men could be led by a black."

Ironically, in the early years of integration Organized Baseball had bypassed a large pool of qualified and experienced black managers: former Negro League players and managers like Chet Brewer, Ray Dandridge, and Quincy Trouppe. In the early 1950s Brewer and several other Negro League veterans managed all-black minor league teams, but no interracial club at any level offered a managerial position to a black until 1961, when former Negro League and major league infielder Gene Baker assumed the reins of a low-level Pittsburgh Pirate farm team, one of only three blacks to manage a major league affiliate before 1975.

This lack of opportunity loomed as a major frustration for those who had broken the color line. "We bring dollars into club treasuries while we play," protested Larry Doby, the first black American Leaguer, in 1964, "but when we stop playing, our dollars stop. When I retired in '59 I wanted to stay in the game, to be a coach or in some other capacity, or to manage in the minors until I'd qualify for a big league job. Baseball owners are missing the boat by not considering Negroes for such jobs." Monte Irvin, who had integrated the New York Giants in 1949 and clearly possessed managerial capabilities, concurred. "Among retired and active players [there] are Negroes with backgrounds suited to these jobs," wrote Irvin. "Owning a package liquor store, bowling alley or selling insurance is hardly the vocation for an athlete who has accumulated a lifetime knowledge of the game."

Had Robinson, Doby, Irvin, or another black been offered a managerial position in the 1950s or early 1960s, and particularly if the first black manager had experienced success, it is possible that this would have opened the doors for other black candidates. As with Robinson's ascension to the major leagues, this example might ultimately have made the hiring and firing of a black manager more or less routine. Robinson dismissed the notion that a black manager might experience extraordinary difficulties. "Many people believe that white athletes will not play for a Negro manager," he argued in 1964. "A professional athlete will play with or for anyone who helps him make more money. He will respect ability, first, last, and all the time. This is something that baseball's executives must learn—that any experienced player with leadership qualities can pilot a ball club to victory, no matter what the color of his skin."

On the other hand, the persistent biases of major league owners and their subsequent history of discriminatory hiring indicate that the solitary example of a Jackie Robinson regime would probably not have been enough to shake the complacency of the baseball establishment. Few baseball executives considered hiring blacks as managers even in the 1960s and 1970s. In 1960 Chicago White Sox owner Bill Veeck, who had hired Doby in 1947 and represented the most enlightened thinking in the game, raised the issue, but even Veeck defined special qualifications needed for a black to manage. "A man will have to have more stability to be a Negro coach or manager and be slower to anger than if he were white," stated Veeck. "The first major

league manager will have to be a fellow who has been playing extremely well for a dozen years or so so that he becomes a byword for excellence." The following year Veeck sold the White Sox; other owners ignored the issue entirely.

Robinson himself never flagged in his determination to see a black manager. In 1972 baseball commemorated the 25th anniversary of Robinson's major league debut at the World Series at Riverfront Stadium in Cincinnati. A graying, almost blind, but still defiant Robinson told a nationwide television audience, "I'd like to live to see a black manager." Nine days later he was dead.

"I would have eagerly welcomed the challenge of a managerial job before I left the game," Robinson revealed in his 1972 autobiography, *I Never Had It Made.* "I know I could have been a good manager." But despite his obvious qualifications, no one offered him a job. Thus, Jackie Robinson once again had been the first—the first of many worthy black baseball players denied the chance to manage in the major leagues.

Baseball, Computers, and New Statistics

Gary Gillette

With the coming of age of the personal computer, the sea of baseball statistics in recent years has become a veritable flood. With the baseball world seemingly inundated with numbers, there has been a backlash against statistics and statisticians. Many fans—especially those of the "old school"—believe that baseball already had enough stats, and that the newer numbers served mostly to obscure the game they love, rather than to illuminate it.

Which is true? Certainly, baseball has been blessed over the years with a wealth of numbers. Far more than any other major sport, baseball has been described and preserved in the script of Arabic numerals—it is the primary way in which the stars of yesterday are remembered. All sports have their legends, with their apocryphal stories about their superstars. Where baseball transcends other sports, however, is in the numbers. Baseball statistics give clarity and perspective to the hallowed yet hazy pictures of the past; numbers make almost tangible the exploits of players long gone. It is, in fact, the accuracy and scope of these numbers which make meaningful comparisons of players across eras at all possible.

Who is responsible for this flood of numbers? First, the fans, who have always looked for evidence to buttress their opinions. Second, the media, who have latched onto this trend and exploited it commercially. Third, Major League Baseball, which has aided and abetted the trend for publicity. Fourth, fantasy baseball players, many of whom were only casual fans before the advent of Rotisserie leagues. Fifth, authors and analysts, who use these new numbers to examine and explain the seemingly simple game of baseball.

Of all the new statistics, the type which has become most popular is the situational. In contrast to traditional baseball totals or averages like home runs and batting average, situational stats are an attempt to break baseball statistics into how and when they happened. The most important situational breakdowns are how batters perform versus lefthanded and righthanded pitchers (and pitchers vs. same and opposite handed batters) and how players perform in their home park as opposed to when they are on the road. In reality, these situational stats have been part of the game for decades, as generations of fans have argued about the effect of Yankee Stadium on sluggers like Babe Ruth and Roger Maris, while generations of managers have platooned their hitters. Aside from these two key categories, several other types of breakdowns have become prominent: "clutch" hitting measures, grass/turf splits, and individual pitcher-batter match-ups.

The biggest problem with this flood of data is that very little analysis has been done. For example, when a manager chooses to start a right-handed batter (who would normally be platooned) against a right-handed pitcher, he can justify it statistically in any number of ways. He could base his decisions on that hitter's past performance against the opposing team, or by his performance against the opposing pitcher, or by his performance in day games, or by his performance against ground-ball pitchers, or even by his performance in the past week if he's

been on a hot streak. All of these statistics (and many more) are now available to teams on a daily basis. Of course, many of these numbers will be contradictory: a hitter might have done poorly against right-handed pitchers, but have done well against that team. He could also carry a pitiful average against that day's starting pitcher, but have done excellently in day games.

The real problem, then, is not a lack of available *data*—the problem is too little *information*. Whether you are managing the 1993 World Champion Toronto Blue Jays or playing armchair manager while watching the home team on cable, which statistics do you rely upon? Literally everyone these days comes armed with reams of statistics—managers, teams, players and their agents, the media, and the fans. Unfortunately, the answer is that no one really knows. Precious little work has been done in understanding what these numbers mean; most of the work that has been done is in generating still more numbers. No one really knows if individual pitcher-batter matchups are more reliable predictors of performance than left/right breakdowns, and while everyone talks about "clutch" hitters, there are a dozen ways of measuring what might be called "clutch" hitting. Indeed, many studies have been done which fail to show any consistent, measurable effect which could be labeled as "clutch" hitting. Just what is true and what isn't?

The answer is both true and false. Most of the statistics quoted and published are literally true. That is, they are accounts of events which actually happened on the field, and therefore must be true. Stating that a player batted .390 with runners in scoring position doesn't leave anything to argue over, other than whether the arithmetic was done properly. Manifestly false, however, are most of the claims made about these statistics. If one argues that batting .390 with runners in scoring position means that the player is a good "clutch" hitter, the validity of that statement depends not on the actual numbers, but on the *interpretation* of those numbers. The interpretation and misinterpretation of the numbers—and the predictions based on these interpretations and misinterpretations—are what cause the arguments.

At their best, these new statistics illuminate the various aspects of the game, making it easier to understand how and why players and teams win and lose games. The fact that they describe performances in specific situations (hence their name) is both their strength and their weakness. At their worst, situational stats divide up the game into irrelevant categories which hinder understanding. The common parody of situational statistics—how a player hits "in Tuesday night games at home when facing a southpaw in July with the bases loaded"—is sometimes all too close to reality. In Game Seven of the 1992 World Series, for example, more than five hundred stats were bandied about by the network broadcasters or displayed on the screen during the game; in recent years, it has only gotten worse. With so many numbers coming fast and furious, the significant ones get lost in the trivial, and the currency of all analytical statistics is debased.

The schizoid attitudes in baseball toward new statistics and analysis are shown by the fact that there isn't even general agreement on the use of the word sabermetrics: many fans have never heard of the term, and while some professionals in the field call themselves sabermetricians, others eschew the word and call themselves statistical analysts. The word *sabermetrics* was coined by author Bill James, who took the acronym for the Society for American Baseball Research *(SABR)* for the root of the word and added the suffix *-metrics* to denote measurement.

While SABR may have lent these new statistics its name, the Society for American Baseball Research is not the primary purveyor of these new statistics. There are many outlets for statistics today, but most of these statistics come from only a few sources. The Major League Baseball Information System, which operates out of the Commissioner's office in New York City, now compiles baseball's official statistics. This system was set up in the late 1980s to provide statistics to major-league teams, and it now also provides much of the material used by the media. The Elias Sports Bureau, also headquartered in New York, remains the official statistician for both major leagues and is another major source of statistics. Howe News Bureau, which had previously served for many years as the official statistician of the American League, became the official statisticians in the late 1980s for all minor leagues and most of the Latin and Caribbean leagues. Signifying its new business orientation was a change in name to Howe Sportsdata International, which now provides minor-league statistics to numerous publications, making the records of tomorrow's stars available to fans today.

In the front offices of baseball teams, there have been two primary usages of these new statistics. Team public relations departments, aided by the MLB Information System, have become increasingly more proficient and prolific at churning out special stats about their players. Most of these find their way to the fans via the media, who publicize these stats in print and on the air. The other way in which the new statistics have penetrated the business end of baseball is through salary arbitration, a quasilegal proceeding which directly sets salaries for a few dozen players each year. Indirectly, however, salary arbitration has a much broader impact on the game's salary structure. Newer statistical measures have been used by both management and labor in arbitration in recent years, although many analytical stats are still not admissible in arbitration proceedings by the mutual agreement of disputing parties.

Outside the arbitration hearing room, new analytical measures have had a greater impact. Several major-league teams have employed full-time professional statistical analysts in the past decade, and other teams have employed statistical analysts as consultants. Of these analysts, Eddie Epstein, now Director of Baseball Operations for the San Diego Padres, has risen the highest and had the most influence. Some other teams have employed computer systems to compile and analyze performance data, with veteran managers Tony LaRussa and Davey Johnson getting the most credit for successfully using these tools. It is clear that the impact of computers—and the analytical statistics they make possible—will continue to grow in baseball's executive suites in the future.

In the publishing world, the main effect of the new statistics has been to create a new subgenre of baseball books. The number of statistically oriented titles released each year in the early 1990s was truly astounding. Bill James, a Kansan who was not a sportswriter, made the best-seller lists year after year in the 1980s on the strength of his detailed statistical analysis as well as his witty and satirical prose. Pete Palmer, a computer programmer by trade, blazed the way for accurate historical comparisons of players and teams by combining his tireless research and top-notch computer skills to produce a comprehensive historical database. The publication of this database in the first edition of *Total Baseball* (1989) was almost as important as the publication of the first comprehensive baseball encyclopedia in 1969. A first in a comprehensive historical reference work, Palmer and co-editor John Thorn brought sabermetrics and serious analytical measures to the general baseball public.

Many other authors have made a living in the last decade by publishing baseball books which relied on the numbers. By 1990, well over a hundred baseball books were being released by major publishers each spring; several dozen of these were devoted to statistical analysis or intended as reference works. However, the number of such reference works has declined dramatically in recent years due to a slump in the sports publishing industry, the devastating 1994-95 strike, and the availability of baseball statistics on computer disk and on-line. The Elias Sports Bureau, longtime official statisticians of the National League, made their mark by publishing their annual eponymous book of situational stats starting in 1985. These stats, previously available only to major-league teams, instantly became part of the baseball public's consciousness. The *Elias Baseball Analyst* became the best-seller of the annual statistical tomes and was very widely quoted by the media, though it ceased publication after 1993.

Just as James, Palmer, and Elias were preceded by the members of the Society for American Baseball Research, they were also followed by many others. Project Scoresheet, a nonprofit organization founded by James in 1984, coordinated the efforts of hundreds of volunteers and produced the first and only publicly available database of contemporary baseball. Retrosheet, another volunteer group founded by David Smith (a longtime SABR member and professor at the University of Delaware), is now collecting scoresheets from pre-1984 games. Armed with copies of more than 75,000 scoresheets donated by teams, sportswriters and fans, Retrosheet has started distributing detailed play-by-play data for seasons from the 1960s through the early 1980s, with much more to come as the exhaustive work of computerizing and proofing these scoresheets progresses.

As the official statisticians, Major League Baseball and the Elias Sports Bureau are the primary sources from which both the electronic and the print media get their baseball statistics. Two independent organizations also maintain baseball data bases, providing both the media and the fans with ready access to almost any conceivable baseball statistic: Stats, Inc., of Chicago (run by John Dewan and Dick Cramer), and The Baseball Workshop of Philadelphia (run by the author). Stats, Inc., has provided greatly improved and expanded box scores to USA Today, Baseball Weekly, and other newspapers since 1990. Stats also provides statistics to ESPN and other media outlets, produces the annual Scouting Report, and self-publishes other baseball reference books. The Baseball Workshop maintains and updates the former Project Scoresheet data base while providing statistics and analysis to publishers and to media clients. The Workshop's annual Great American Baseball Stat Book features comprehensive situational statistics for all active major-league players.

On the periodical side, media conglomerate Gannett founded a weekly newspaper in 1990 devoted solely to baseball—more specifically to baseball statistics, which take up a large portion of the paper. While the hundred-year-old *Sporting News* has deemphasized baseball, *USA Today Baseball Weekly* has found a market hundreds of thousands strong by focusing exclusively on baseball. It is true, though, that a very large share of the *Baseball Weekly* audience is composed of fantasy baseball players, and the format of the statistics published in *BBW* is designed for their convenience. *Baseball America,* a biweekly newspaper which focuses on minor-league and college baseball, has also gained a large following among dedicated fans and fantasy baseball players. The ready availability of information about thousands of minor leaguers in *Baseball America,* and the regular publication by *BBW* in 1992 of OPS (On-Base plus Slugging, an analytical measure developed by Pete Palmer) show just how far the new statistics have come.

Probably the most high-profile and controversial element of this new statistical trend has been the explosion in popularity of fantasy baseball, a pastime that occupies several million players. An undeniable attraction of fantasy baseball is that it brings to baseball one element which football has had for decades: gambling. It is probably true that without the wager, there would be very few fantasy leagues. The excitement of betting on football is one of the main reasons for its spectacular growth in popularity, and fantasy games give baseball fans a chance to partake of the action during the summer as well as in the fall. Gamblers, both fantasy players and others, make extensive use of the new stats, and fantasy baseball is firmly established and likely to increase in popularity.

Another area of great growth has been in baseball games. Baseball board games, using dice as the element of chance and statistics to recreate performance, have been played by a small but devoted group since the birth of APBA Baseball in the early 1950s. In the mid-1980s computer baseball games took hold and now appear to be the future of baseball gaming. While board games still have their audience, computer games are much more flexible and are able to provide fans with a variety of simulated experiences which board games cannot. Furthermore, the virtues of a computer opponent, when a flesh-and-blood one is unavailable, are understandable.

The latest computer games simulate sophisticated opposing managers as well as recreating player performance. Moreover, the era of almost real-time baseball games has already dawned. In 1991 the computer service Prodigy debuted a bseball game which used last night's real-life performances to play simulated games. The participants in "Big League Manager" send in their lineups by modem before they go to bed; the next morning, they dial up the Prodigy computer and see a boxscore for last night's game for their team displayed along with current league standings. Compuserve and other major computer on-line services also provide an electronic forum which connects baseball fans across the country. These services run hundreds of electronic fantasy baseball leagues which attract thousands of players. Fantasy baseball contests, made possible by the combination of computers and "800" and "900"phone lines, have also become big business in the 1990s.

Yet another electronic milestone was reached in 1991-1992 with the debut of the electronic baseball encyclopedia, in two forms: Total Baseball became available in compact disc, read-only memory form (CD-ROM)—in a mini-disc for Sony's palmtop DataDiscman player and for the desktop computer, MS-DOS or Macintosh, in a conventional size disc published by CMC; also, Big League Baseball, a handheld reference device

published by Franklin Electronics which fit into a shirt pocket. The most recent development, as of 1994, is Microsoft Baseball, which incorporates the statistical database and prose features of Total Baseball within a larger reference framework, created for the Windows graphical environment. The advantage of an electronic baseball encyclopedia is not simply its portability or its compact data storage and retrieval. These electronic editions invite the user to manipulate the numbers, to make customized lists and complicated research requests, all of which make the numbers more meaningful and accessible to the fan than they are on the printed page.

Last, and least, is the negative reaction to the new statistics. There has been a definite backlash to this flood of new data. Many writers, broadcasters, and fans believe that the game has suffered from these stats and their purveyors. However, these new statistics don't change the grand old game—they just provide new ways of looking at it. After all, most traditional baseball statistics (e.g., batting average, earned run average, errors, etc.) were invented in the nineteenth century, and they reflect the way the game was played at that time. The game on the field is quite different now, and it is certainly appropriate that the statistics used to describe and analyze the contemporary game reflect the way the game is played now.

As with new strategies on the field, the old stats will persist for awhile while their replacements become established. During this time, the improvement in analysis will be obscured by the clash of stats and the arguments of the analysts. Inevitably, though, the best of the new stats will oust the worst of the old, and the game will look a little different in the future. The tremendous advances in computer technology in the past decade have given us the capacity to produce these new statistics, and it is now time to separate the statistical wheat from the chaff. If this is done, the best of the new statistics will enhance our understanding of the game. If this winnowing is not done, the explosion of data will obscure the game itself, fulfilling the predictions of the Luddites.

Not too long ago, you know, nobody bothered to count such silly things as runs batted in, batter strikeouts, times caught stealing, or saves. Players change, teams change, ballparks change, strategies change—even "the unchanging game" itself changes. Why shouldn't baseball statistics change along with them?

Forfeit and No-Decision Games
Pete Palmer

A forfeited game is one in which the umpire, having observed any one of a number of specified flagrant violations of the rules, declares the game over and awards the decision to the offended team by a score of 9–0. Such games are relatively rare in major league history, but they have provided scoring problems—whether to award wins and losses to the contending pitchers, whether to include batting, fielding, and pitching statistics in the player and team records, and whether to count such games as victories/defeats for the opposing manager.

Originally there was no rule that covered wins and losses for pitchers in forfeits. However, practices indicate that the present rule was followed, except that wins and losses were also awarded in tie games.

In 1904 forfeits were covered by Rule 26, which made no mention of whether player stats should be recorded or not. In 1931 the standard covering forfeits was changed to Rule 24; section 24-11 specified that all stats in a regulation forfeit should be counted. From 1931 through 1939 there were no instances of a losing team being ahead at the time of forfeit, so no decisions were awarded in a manner contrary to present rules. In 1940 Rule 24-11 was changed; now no win or loss would be accorded a pitcher in a forfeit, regardless of score. In 1950, a year of massive rules modification, rules were revised and the question of forfeited games was shifted to Section 10.03. In 1963 this rule was revised to give a win if the team was ahead at the time of the forfeit, but no decision was to be recorded for pitchers or managers if the score was tied. During the 1941–62 period, the only case in which the winning team was ahead at the time of the forfeit was the Giants-Phillies game in 1949.

This section details the conclusions the editors have reached regarding how the totals for these forfeit games should be recorded, if at all; in some cases reference is made to the Macmillan *Baseball Encyclopedia* to illustrate differences between how a game has been previously regarded and how it is counted in *Total Baseball*. We follow with an evaluation of no-decision games, that is, games that were terminated without a win or loss awarded to either club.

Forfeit Games

All forfeit games show the winner listed first. For games in which no win or loss was awarded, the appended comment "no game" means it was not a regulation game;

otherwise, the loser was ahead at the time of forfeit. In those cases in which the team that was ahead at the time of forfeit won, and the game was a regulation game, the appended comment is "OK" followed by the score. In a game noted as "OK," a win and loss should be awarded to individual pitchers. The research of Frank Williams into early scoring practices has shown that the rules of the day indicated that in some years tied forfeit games should also have wins and losses awarded to the pitchers.

In the lists below, the victorious team is presented first. If that team was the home team, it is followed by "vs" and the visiting team; if the visiting team was victorious, it is presented first, followed by "at" and the name of the home team. For a key to the abbreviations used in these tables, see the last page of the book. The official score of all these games is 9–0.

Year	Date	League	Teams	Notes
1871	May 11	NA	Chi at Cle	Game OK, Chi ahead 18–10 FtW forfeited 9 unplayed games and Mut forfeited 1. These unplayed games were not counted by Macmillan or *Total Baseball*.
	May 17	NA	Oly at Rok	Later ruled a forfeit because Rok used ineligible player Scott Hastings
	May 23	NA	Kek vs Rok	Later ruled a forfeit because Rok used ineligible player Scott Hastings
	June 5	NA	Ath vs Rok	Later ruled a forfeit because Rok used ineligible player Scott Hastings
	June 15	NA	Ath vs Rok	Later ruled a forfeit because Rok used ineligible player Scott Hastings
	June 19	NA	Tro vs Kek	Kek ahead 6–3, no pitcher win/loss
1872	Aug. 31	NA	Ath vs Eck	Game OK, score tied 5–5
1874	Sept. 28	NA	Ath vs Chi	Game OK, Ath ahead 15–7
1875	May 29	NA	Was vs NH	Game OK, Was ahead 11–10 NH walked off the field with one out left.
1876	Aug. 3	N	Chi at Lou	No game (Chicago was 4–1 in the fifth when Lou began to stall, hoping for rain; game was forfeited to Chi but later thrown out; researcher Jim Smith claims it should have been counted as a forfeit with stats included; the stats are not counted in *Total Baseball*.
	Aug. 21	N	StL vs Chi	Game OK, StL ahead 7–6 The score was tied in the last of the ninth. McGeary of StL was on third with one out when Cuthbert hit a grounder to third which hit McGeary. The umpire ruled it was accidental and allowed McGeary to score the winning run. Chi refused to continue and the umpire awarded a forfeit to StL.

Year	Date	League	Teams	Notes
1877	May 15	N	Cin vs Lou	Lou ahead 8–5 (game later thrown out) The league decided not to count any games involving Cin, but Macmillan decided to put them back in. However, this game remained thrown out.
1880	Sept. 10	N	Buf vs Cin	Score tied 11–11 (game later thrown out, however Macmillan counted it as a tie; counted as a tie in *Total Baseball*, since Tattersall stats included it, and these do not have day-by-day breakdowns)
1882	June 29	A	StL vs Lou	No game (later thrown out; however, it was counted as a no-game forfeit by Macmillan, which did not count either the StL vs Lou tie (6–6) on Oct 3 or the StL vs Lou win (6–2) on Oct 5, which were treated as if they were exhibition games. They should have been counted, and *Total Baseball* does.)
	Aug. 16	N	Cle at Wor	No game (game later thrown out)
1883	July 4	N	Phi vs Pro	Game OK, Pro won 11–9 in AM game (Pro had to leave for PM game in NY after 7 innings), no pitcher win/loss
	July 27	AA	NY vs Phi	No game (game later thrown out)
	Aug. 1	N	Bos at Cle	Bos refused to allow a substitute for Cle, so Cle walked off.
1884	May 31	AA	Cin at Was	Game OK, Cin ahead 6–0
	July 5	U	Bal vs Cin	No game (umpire late, Cin refused to play)
	Aug. 11	N	Buf at Chi	No game (1st game; argument in first inning; the second game, a makeup, ended in a 6–6 tie)
	Aug. 22	U	StL at KC	Game OK, KC ahead 6–3, no pitcher win/loss
	Aug. 23	N	Bos vs Det	Game OK, Bos ahead 7–5 (Macmillan gave no win or loss in this game, should be Whitney-W, Meinke-L)
	Aug. 25	U	Bos vs Wil	No game (1st game; Wil arrived late)
	Aug. 30	AA	Tol at StL	Game OK, Tol ahead 2–1 (PM game)
	Sept. 8	U	Was vs Pit	No game (Pit failed to appear)
	Sept. 20	U	Was vs Cin	No game (Cin failed to appear) (This game not counted by Macmillan or *Total Baseball*)
	Sept. 24	AA	Tol vs Ric	No game (Ric failed to appear)
	Sept. 24	A	Bal at Pit	Game OK, Bal ahead 8–6
	Oct. 11	U	StL vs Was	No game (Was refused to continue) Was called for a new ball after a foul, and wouldn't play with the old one.
	Oct. 11	U	Bos at Cin	No game
1885	Aug. 5	AA	Bal vs. Phi	Game OK, Bal ahead 8–7
1886	July 30	N	Det at Was	Game OK, Det ahead 13–9 (Macmillan gave no win or loss in this game. Win should go to Hardy Richardson in relief, loss to George Keefe; Getzien started for Det but left in the 5th behind 9–6. Det got 7 in 7th. There is some controversy on this game because a lot of runs were scored before the game was actually forfeited)
	Sept. 29	N	Was vs StL	Score tied 2–2
	Oct. 7	N	Was vs KC	No game (1st game, AM)
	Oct. 8	N	Was vs KC	No game (1st game, AM)
	Oct. 9	N	Was vs KC	No game (1st game, AM; KC refused to play morning games on these three dates)
1887	Apr. 30	AA	Lou vs Cin	No game (Cin arrived late)
	June 27	N	Det vs NY	No game (1st game; game thrown out on Aug. 14)
	July 3	AA	Lou at StL	No game
	July 22	AA	Phi vs Cle	Game OK, Cle ahead 6–4 (no pitcher win/loss)
	Aug. 12	AA	NY at Phi	Game OK, NY ahead 9–7
1888	May 31	N	NY vs Pit	No game (Pit did not appear)
	July 14	AA	KC vs Bro	Game OK, KC ahead 5–4
	Sept. 12	N	Chi vs NY	Game OK, Chi ahead 8–2 (Macmillan awarded no win or loss in this game, should be Krock-W, Keefe-L)

Year	Date	League	Teams	Notes
	Oct. 13	N	Phi vs Chi	No game (Chi did not appear; Macmillan has extra win for Phi, extra loss for Pit—they counted a Phi win over Pit May 5 which was later thrown out; Buffington should have one less win, Morris one less loss; *Total Baseball* counts stats for May 5th game except for wins and losses)
1889	May 5	AA	Phi at Bro	Game OK, Phi ahead 11–1
	June 24	AA	Bro vs Col	No game (1st game; Col refused to play with sub ump; 2nd game was played)
	Sept. 7	AA	Bro vs StL	StL ahead 4–2 (this forfeit later overruled and given back to StL as normal game)
	Sept. 8	AA	Bro vs StL	No game (StL did not appear)
	Sept. 26	AA	Cle vs Was	No game (Washington's train delayed; game later thrown out, played on Sept 28)
1890	Apr. 20	AA	Lou vs StL	No game
	Apr. 24	N	Bos vs NY	Game OK, score tied 2–2
	June 17	N	Pit vs Cle	No game (train delay; game later thrown out)
	July 2	AA	Phi at Tol	Game OK; score tied 5–5
	July 27	AA	Col vs Bro	Game OK; Bro ahead 13–8 (no pitcher win/loss)
	Aug. 3	AA	Syr vs Lou	No game
	Aug. 5	AA	Tol vs Roc	Game OK, Tol ahead 7–3
	Sept. 2	N	Chi at Bos	No game (1st game; umpire late, game not started; later forfeited to Bos and then thrown out)
	Sept. 21	AA	Stl at Roc	Game OK (2nd game), StL ahead 10–3
1891	Apr. 8	AA	StL vs Cin	No game, tied 7–7 (overruled and replayed on Apr. 13; counted by Macmillan and *Total Baseball* as a tie)
	Sept. 12	AA	StL vs Bos	Game OK, StL ahead 4–2
	Sept. 20	AA	Lou vs Phi	No game; Phi refused to continue (2nd game)
	Sept. 25	N	Chi vs Pit	Game OK, score tied 4–4
	Sept. 25	AA	StL at Lou	
	Oct. 2	AA	StL vs Lou	(These two games were exhibitions but are counted by *Total Baseball* but should not have been. Meekin beat McGill, 7–4, in the first one, McGill beat Fitzgerald, 13–8, in the second)
	Oct. 5	AA	Was vs Bal	Game OK, Bal ahead 4–1, no pitcher win/loss (counted as a win for Bal in Macmillan; there should be win for Healy or loss for Foreman)
1892	Apr. 20	N	NY at Bal	Game OK, Balt ahead 6–5, no pitcher win/loss
	Apr. 23	N	Lou at Chi	Game OK, Chi ahead 4–2, no pitcher win/loss (Macmillan has extra loss for Chi, extra win for NY. They gave a loss to Luby on Apr. 23 and a win to King on Apr. 20, although the opposing team pitcher in each case had his decision removed)
	May 10	N	Pit vs NY	No game (NY refused to play in rain)
	May 21	N	Cle vs StL	No game (1st game; StL arrived late)
	Aug. 16	N	Pit vs Was	Game OK, score tied 2–2
	Sept. 22	N	Pit vs Chi	No game (Chi trying to delay for rain)
	Oct. 12	N	Pit vs Cle	No game (Cle did not appear)
1893	May 25	N	Lou vs Chi	No game (Chi did not appear) (This game later thrown out)
	Sept. 16	N	Cle vs Bal	Game OK, Cle ahead 15–11
1894	May 1	N	Bro vs Was	Game OK, Was ahead 2–1; no pitcher win/loss (Macmillan gave a loss (and shutout!) to Stephens of Was in this game)
	May 26	N	Pit at Cle	Game OK, Pit ahead 12–3
	July 17	N	Phi vs Bos	Game OK, Phi ahead 12–2
	Aug. 3	N	Lou vs Chi	No game (Chi refused to play)
	Sept. 5	N	Was vs StL	Game OK, Washington ahead 7–4
1895	May 23	N	Bro at Lou	No game
	Aug. 28	N	Bal vs Pit	No game (1st game; Pit arrived late)

Year	Date	League	Teams	Notes
1896	May 13	N	Bos at Chi	Game OK, score tied 4–4 Research by Frank Williams indicates that Bos scored 5 runs before the forfeit (making it 9–4). Then Chi tried to delay the game by throwing the ball around and not making outs. Bos got two more runs before the umpire forfeited the game to Bos. These 5 runs should be added to official stats.
	July 24	N	Bal vs StL	Game OK, Bal ahead 13–8
1897	May 3	N	NY at Was	No game
	June 1	N	NY vs Pit	Game OK, Pit ahead 7–4, no pitcher win/loss
	June 4	N	Phi vs Pit	No game
	July 24	N	Cle vs Phi	Game OK, Phi ahead 4–3, no pitcher win/loss
	Aug. 1	N	StL vs Lou	Lou ahead 5–4 (2nd game, later thrown out). This was an overruled forfeit. Cunningham kept rubbing new balls in the dirt in the ninth and umpire Donahue forfeited the game to Lou. This game was umped by players because the regular ump did not show up.
	Aug. 4	N	Lou vs Cle	No game (1st game; Cle refused to continue)
	Sept. 8	N	Was vs Cle	No game (2nd game) Was ahead 6–2 in the top of the 5th
	Sept. 10	N	Bal vs Lou	Game OK, Bal ahead 6–5
1898	July 25	N	Bal vs NY	No game (NY refused to continue) (1st game) Chi ahead 2–1
	Sept. 16	N	Phi vs Chi	(Macmillan gave Donahue, Phi a win in this game, but this was not a regulation game and should have no stats counted)
1899	May 19	N	StL vs NY	Game OK, NY ahead 10–9, no pitcher win/loss
	June 16	N	Bro at NY	No game
	Oct. 14	N	Bro vs Bal	No game (1st game) The league voted not to count this game and 15 games played by Zeke Wrigley for Bro, however, Macmillan decided to bring them back in.
1900	June 22	N	Bro at Phi	Game OK, Bro ahead 20–13
	Sept. 19	N	Bro vs StL	No game (StL refused to continue)
1901	May 2	A	Det at Chi	Game OK, Det ahead 7–5
	May 13	NL	NY vs Bro	Game OK, score tied 7–7
	May 31	AL	Det vs Bal	Game OK, score tied 5–5
	June 9	NL	NY at Cin	Game OK, NY ahead 25–13
	July 23	AL	Cle vs Was	Game OK, score tied 4–4 (This game ruled a tie by the league and so counted by *Total Baseball*, but counted as a forfeit by Macmillan/ICI)
	Aug. 21	AL	Det vs Bal	No game (crowd swarmed on field)
1902	June 16	NL	Pit at Bos	No game (Bos trying to delay for rain)
	June 28	AL	Bos vs Bal	Game OK, Bos ahead 9–4
	July 17	AL	StL at Bal	No game (Bal did not appear)
1903	Aug. 9	AL	Det at Cle	Game OK, Det ahead 6–5
1904	Oct. 4	NL	StL at NY	No game (2nd game; NY refused to continue)
1905	Aug. 5	NL	Pit vs NY	Game OK, score tied 5–5
	Aug. 22	AL	Was at Det	Game OK, Washington ahead 2–1
1906	June 9	NL	Pit vs Phi	Game OK, Pit ahead 7–1
	July 2	AL	NY at Phi	Game OK, NY ahead 5–1
	Aug. 7	NL	Chi at NY	No game (umpire not allowed into park)
	Sept. 3	AL	NY vs Phi	Game OK (2nd game, score tied 3–3)
1907	Apr. 11	NL	Phi at NY	Game OK, Phi ahead 3–0
	Oct. 5	NL	StL vs Chi	No game (1st game, Chi refused to continue) This was not a regulation game but was included in the official stats. The game was called in the last of the fourth with Chi ahead 2–0.
1909	Oct. 4	NL	NY vs Phi	No game (2nd game, score tied 1–1 in 4th inning; this was not a regulation game but was included in the official stats)
1913	July 6	NL	StL at Chi	No game (2nd game, Chi tried to stall so that curfew would be invoked; this was not a regulation game but was included in the official stats)
1914	June 26	AL	Phi vs Was	No game (1st game, Washington refused to continue)
1916	July 18	NL	Bro at Chi	Game OK, score tied 4–4
1917	Sept. 9	AL	Chi vs Cle	Game OK, score tied 3–3
1918	July 20	AL	Cle at Phi	Game OK (2nd game, Cle ahead 9–1)
	Sept. 2	A	Cle at StL	No games (doubleheader; Cle did not show up for last games of war-shortened season, not wanting to bear expense of trip to StL; two losses for Cle were counted at time but later thrown out; no league umpires were present to forfeit games)
1920	Aug. 20	AL	Chi at Phi	Game OK (2nd game, Chi ahead 5–2)
1924	June 13	AL	NY at Det	Game OK, NY ahead 10–6
1925	Apr. 26	AL	Cle at Chi	Game OK, Cle ahead 7–2
1937	June 6	NL	StL vs Phi	No game (2nd game, Phi tried to stall so that curfew would be invoked)
1939	Sept. 3	A	NY at Bos	Game OK (2nd game, NY ahead 7–5 when curfew near, so Yanks tried to make outs to get game in; Bos fans littered field in protest, umpire forfeited game to NY, later overruled; game declared a tie and NY players fined)
1941	Aug. 15	AL	Bos at Was	Game OK, Washington ahead 6–3, no pitcher win/loss
1942	Sept. 26	NL	Bos at NY	Game OK (2nd game, NY ahead 5–2, no pitcher win/loss)
1949	Aug. 21	NL	NY at Phi	Game OK (2nd game, NY ahead 4–2 in top of ninth; no win or loss given, per rules of day; Larry Jansen pitched for NY, Schoolboy Rowe for Phi)
1954	July 18	NL	Phi at StL	No game (2nd game, StL tried to stall for darkness)
1971	Sept. 30	AL	NY at Was	Game OK (Washington ahead 7–5, no pitcher win/loss; this was the last game in Washington and fans vandalized the field in the ninth)
1974	June 4	AL	Tex at Cle	Game OK, scored tied 5–5 (crowd invaded field)
1977	Sept. 15	AL	Tor vs Bal	Game OK, Tor ahead 4–0 (Bal refused to continue)
1979	July 12	AL	Det at Chi	No game (2nd game, crowd littered field between games)
1995	Aug. 10	NL	StL at LA	Game OK, StL ahead 2–0 (fans threw complimentary baseballs on the field for the third time in the ninth inning)

No-Decision Games

In the National Association of 1871–75, no-decision games were counted in the records by researcher Michael Stagno and thus are adopted in *Total Baseball*. In the National League of 1876–1890, no-decision games were counted by researcher John Tattersall and thus were adopted by the Macmillan *Baseball Encyclopedia* and *Total Baseball*. In the ensuing period, covered by ICI research and the computer printouts that ICI deposited at the Hall of Fame, protested games were not counted. Although they may have been included in the official averages, source data for these has been lost. In the 1910–19 period, protested games were not counted at all. From 1920–92, protested games were counted. Because of the effect these games had on the records of the teams' managers, the managers are listed. For more on this, see the Introduction to the Manager Roster, criterion number 7.

This list of no-decision games does not include protests that were upheld in which the game was resumed from the point of protest; it includes only those games that were thrown out entirely. These games did ultimately come to a decision.

This was counted by Michael Stagno:

Year	Date	League	Teams	Notes/Managers
1872	May 20	NA	Ath at Bal	Game disallowed (McBride–Craver)

These were counted by Tattersall:

Year	Date	League	Teams	Notes/Managers
1880	Sept. 10	NL	Cin at Buf	Forfeit to Buf overruled; this game counted as a tie with all stats in by Macmillan (Clapp–Crane)
1887	Sept. 23	NL	Bos at Chi	Second game
1887	Sept. 24	NL	Bos at Chi	First and second games; these two games plus the one of the day before were ties replayed without proper consent; counted as no-decisions but included in averages by Tattersall and Macmillan (Morrill–Anson)
	July 4	NL	Bos at Det	2nd game was a 4½-inning, 7–7 tie; since it did not go five innings, it should not have counted in the records, but it was included by Tattersall and Macmillan. It was not protested (Kelly–Watkins)
1888	May 5	NL	Phi at Pit	Phi ahead 4–3; this game counted by Tattersall and Macmillan as a win for Phi (however, this game was protested, replayed and not counted in the league standings) (Wright–Phillips)
1890	May 23	NL	Chi vs Phi	This was a protested game not counted in the league standings, but Macmillan and Tattersall counted it as a win for Chi. (Anson–Clements)

These were not counted by Macmillan:

Year	Date	League	Teams	Notes/Managers
1884	Sept. 3	AA	Phi at Bal	This was a makeup game which was not cleared with the league office, it was replayed on October 10. (Knight–Barnie)
1884	Oct. 4	NL	Bos vs Cle	This was not a protested game. It was an exhibition game at Akron, Ohio which was listed as a league game by *Sporting Life*. (Barnie–Sharsig)
1888	June 10	AA	Bal at Phi	This was a rescheduled rainout without league approval.
1888	July 8	AA	Bal at KC	This was a game in which the umpire did not show up so two players umpired. They did a poor job, Bal protested and KC agreed to replay the game. (Barnie–Barkley)
1890	July 10, 11, 12	PL	Pit at Bos	Three games in which Bos used Gil Hatfield, on loan from NY, against league rules (Hanlon–Kelly)
1891	Apr. 8	AA	Cin at StL	Forfeit overruled (Kelly–Comiskey)
1894	Apr. 26	NL	Phi at Bro	(Irwin–Foutz)
	May 23	NL	Pit at Chi	Forfeit overruled (Buckenberger–Anson)
	Aug. 18	NL	Chi at NY	1st game (Anson–Ward)
	Aug. 25	NL	Lou at NY	1st game (Barnie–Ward)
	Aug. 27	NL	Cin at Phi	1st game (Comiskey–Irwin)
	Sept. 6	NL	Cin at Phi	1st game (Comiskey–Irwin) (Macmillan threw out the first game and counted the second game; four games above were transferred without league approval; Jim Smith claims that first game should count and second game be thrown out) (Mack–Foutz)
1895	June 1	NL	Pit at Bro	After a rain delay in the third, Donovan of Pit was called out after taking his spot at second because he didn't tag first on the way.

Year	Date	League	Teams	Notes/Managers
	July 14	NL	Cle at StL	(Schmelz–Selee) Sub umpires Staley and Wallace allowed the winning run to score on a play in which the runner was hit by a batted ball, not allowed in the rules.
	Aug. 12	NL	Was at Bos	(Tebeau–Quinn) There was a batting out of order mixup involving Hassamaer.
1897	June 3	NL	Lou at NY	1st game (Rogers–Joyce) This was a makeup for a rainout that was not approved by the league.
	Aug. 1	NL	Lou at StL	2nd game (Clarke–Hallman) This was an overruled forfeit. Cunningham kept rubbing new balls in the dirt in the ninth and umpire Donahue forfeited the game to Lou. This game was umped by players because the regular ump did not show up. (Clarke–Watkins)
1899	May 3	NL	Lou at Pit	Pit scored the winning run when an employee opened a door in the outfield fence and made off with the ball as it rolled through.
	May 30	NL	NY at Cin	PM game (Ewing–Day) Umpire Gaffney allowed Gleason, NY to score the winning run without touching the plate.
1902	May 7	NL	NY at Chi	(Fogel–Selee)
	May 8	NL	NY at Chi	Pitching distance too short; this game and the one above may have been included in the official averages, but no record exists (Fogel–Selee)

These were not counted in the official averages or by Macmillan:

Year	Date	League	Teams	Notes/Managers
1911	May 30	NL	Chi at Pit	1st game (Chance–Clarke)
1912	Oct. 2	NL	Pit at Chi	(Clarke–Chance)
1915	May 14	FL	Chi at Buf	(Tinker–Schafly)
	June 19	FL	Chi at Bal	(Tinker–Knabe)
	Sept. 3	AL	Cle at Chi	2nd game (Fohl–Rowland)
	Aug. 17	NL	Chi at Pit	1st game; Benton pitched for Pit (Bresnahan–Clarke)
1917	Apr. 17	NL	Bos at Phi	(Stallings–Moran)
	Aug. 19	AL	Was vs Det	(Griffith–Jennings)
1918	Apr. 29	NL	StL at Cin	(Hendricks–Mathewson)
	June 3	NL	StL at Bro	(Hendricks–Robinson)

These were counted by both the offical averages and Macmillan:

Year	Date	League	Teams	Notes/Managers
1890	May 23	N	Chi vs Phi	(Researcher Joe Wayman claims this is a protested game not counted in standings, per baseball guide for 1891; however, Tattersall and Macmillan have counted game as win for Chi)
1909	Apr. 23	NL	Cin at Pit	(Griffith–Clarke)
1924	July 15	NL	NY at Chi	(McGraw–Killefer)
1924	July 28	AL	Bos at StL	Individual data counted, team data not counted; Macmillan originally took out the individual records; later editions have added the batting records, but omitted the pitching records (Fohl–Sisler)
1932	Aug. 19	AL	NY at Det	All data counted except in the games-played column in official records; games played added by Macmillan (McCarthy–Harris)
1937	Aug. 6	AL	NY vs Cle	(McCarthy–O'Neill)
1938	May 14	NL	StL vs Cin	(7–6, this game later declared a tie)
1939	Sept. 12	AL	Chi at Was	(Dykes–Harris)
1940	June 20	AL	Chi vs NY	(Dykes–McCarthy)
1947	July 20	NL	Bro vs StL	(3–2, this game later declared a tie)

Famous Firsts

David Pietrusza

1845 Alexander Cartwright and the Knickerbocker Base Ball Club codify playing rules; also, first box score of baseball game, eight men to the side, is printed in *New York Morning News.*

1846 At Elysian Fields on June 19 in Hoboken, New Jersey the N.Y. Knickerbockers lose to the New York Club in first match game under Cartwright's rules.

1849 Knickerbockers develop first uniforms (colors: blue & white).

1853 First box score of Knickerbocker-style game is printed in *New York Clipper.*

1856 Henry Chadwick becomes the first regular baseball reporter.

1858 First admission (50 cents) charged, for game between All-Star teams representing New York and Brooklyn played at Long Island's Fashion Race Course on July 20.

1859 At Pittsfield, Massachusetts, on July 1, Amherst defeats Williams College 73-32 in first college game.

1860 The Excelsiors of Brooklyn make the first "road trip." Their first stop: Albany's Washington Parade Grounds on July 2.

1862 William Cammeyer's Union Grounds in Brooklyn is the first enclosed ballpark; it opens on May 15.

1863 First calling of balls and strikes.

1865 Ed Cuthbert of the Keystones steals the first base.

1866 Bob Addy of Rockford employs the first slide to steal a base; the Brooklyn Atlantics' Tom Barlow lays down the first bunt.

1867 First use of curve ball, by W. A. "Candy" Cummings.

1869 The Cincinnati Red Stockings are the first fully professional team; they are also the first team to wear knickers.

1870 First listing of at bats in box scores, in the *Clipper.*

1871 First professional league is formed—the National Association; first game: Cleveland Forest Citys lose 2-0 at Fort Wayne on May 4; first batting averages printed in *The Dime Base Ball Player.*

1873 First doubleheader: Resolutes vs. Boston, July 4.

1874 Boston Red Stockings and Philadelphia Athletics conduct first foreign tour.

1875 Philadelphia's Joe Borden hurls first no-hitter in pro ranks on July 28.

1876 National League's first game: Boston at Philadelphia on April 22.

1877 International League becomes the first minor league; Tecumsehs and Maple Leafs are the first foreign professional teams; first professional gambling scandal—four Louisville players expelled from game; Will White is the first player to wear eyeglasses.

1878 Turnstiles introduced (at Providence); Paul Hines of Providence wins first triple crown and executes first unassisted triple play (May 8); Bud Fowler is first black in pro ball, for Lynn Live Oaks of International Association.

1879 Reserve clause first used.

1880 First night game—between two department store teams, at Nantasket Beach in Massachusetts; Worcester's Lee Richmond hurls first perfect game, against Cleveland on June 12.

1882 American Association introduces first salaried umpiring staff; first postseason playoff; first professional doubleheader, Providence vs. Worcester, September 25; Paul Hines is first player to wear sunglasses in field.

1884 First "third major league," the Union Association; first blacks in Major League Baseball—Moses and Weldy Walker of Toledo (AA); hit by pitch allows batter to take first base in AA.

1885 Umpires and catchers use first chest protectors.

1886 Players organize first union, "The Brotherhood of Ball Players"; first spring training camp (Chicago White Stockings at Hot Springs, Arkansas).

1887 Charles Zimmer is first catcher to play consistently behind the batter; Baltimore's Mike Griffin of Baltimore and Cincinnati's George "White Wings" Tebeau are the first to homer in their first major league at-bat; both do it on the same day, April 16.

1887 The Cleveland Blues' James Toy becomes the first American Indian to play in the major leagues.

1888 First round-the-world baseball tour, by Chicago White Stockings and all-star squad; "Casey at the Bat" makes its first debut in print and on the stage; Washington Nationals are the first ML club to train in Florida.

1892 National League allows Sunday baseball; first pinch homer, by Brooklyn's Tom Daly on May 24.

1894 Boston's Bobby Lowe is first major league player to smash four homers in one game.

1896 Prof. Charles Hinton demonstrates the first pitching machine.

1900 First pinch-hit grand slam, by St. Louis pitcher Mike O'Neill on September 4.

1901 First American League game, Cleveland loses 8-7 at Chicago on April 24.

1903 First modern World Series—Boston defeats Pittsburgh five games to three.

1905 The first "sanitary hose" are introduced.

1907 Giants catcher Roger Bresnahan introduces shin guards.

1909 First concrete-and-steel-park opens—Philadelphia's Shibe Park; Cleveland's Neal Ball turns first modern unassisted major league triple play in majors, on July 19; William Howard

Taft is first President to throw out "first ball"; Arlie Latham of the N.Y. Giants is baseball's first full-time coach.

1910 First cork-centered ball.

1911 First MVP Awards to the Cubs' Frank Schulte and the Tigers' Ty Cobb.

1916 Fred Clarke patents the first flip-up sunglasses.

1917 First "knothole gang" organized in St. Louis.

1920 First Japanese pro team, the Nihon Undo Kyokai; first team to draw 1 million fans, Yankees with 1,289,422.

1921 First baseball commissioner, Kenesaw Mountain Landis; First radio broadcast of a game, by Harold Arlin of KDKA from Forbes Field on August 5; first World Series broadcast (Yankees vs. Giants).

1923 Babe Ruth becomes first player to earn $50,000 in a season.

1926 First amplifiers used (at Polo Grounds).

1929 Tigers are the first ML club to train in Arizona.

1930 First successful night ball in minors.

1933 First All-Star Game, Chicago's Comiskey Park on July 6.

1935 First major league night game; Phils at Reds, May 24 at Cincinnati's Crosley Field.

1936 First pro league in Japan; first players elected to Hall of Fame (Cobb, Ruth, Mathewson, Wagner, Johnson); the Reds are the first team to fly—from St. Louis to Chicago on July 30.

1939 First AL night game, at Philadelphia Shibe Park on May 16; first televised game, from Ebbets Field on August 26.

1941 Dodgers are first club to wear batting helmets.

1946 Montreal's Jackie Robinson is the century's first black professional player; first team to draw 2 million fans, Yankees with 2,265,512.

1947 Robinson becomes first modern major league black player; Cleveland's Larry Doby is first black player in AL; first BBWAA Rookie-of-the-Year Awards; Hank Greenberg becomes the first $100,000 player.

1951 Emmett Ashford is first black pro umpire (Southwestern International League); first game televised coast-to-coast (last game of NL Playoff); first nationally televised World Series (Yankees vs. Giants); first true baseball encyclopedia, Turkin & Thompson's *The Official Encyclopedia of Baseball*; Paul Pettit is the first $100,000 bonus baby.

1952 Clint Courtney is the first catcher to wear glasses.

1956 Don Larsen hurls first World Series perfect game, on October 8.

1956 Frank Umont and Ed Rommel are first major league umps to wear eyeglasses on field.

1957 First Gold Glove Awards.

1959 Joe Cronin becomes first player to become league president when he assumes leadership of American League.

1962 Jackie Robinson becomes the first black elected to the Hall of Fame.

1965 First enclosed stadium, the Astrodome, opens on April 9; First amateur draft; Rick Monday is first player selected.

1966 First major league black umpire, Emmett Ashford of AL.

1969 First major league game outside U.S., St. Louis at Montreal's Jarry Park on April 14.

1970 First strike by major league umpires occurs during playoffs; first World Series game on artificial turf—Baltimore at Cincinnati on October 10.

1971 First night World Series game—Baltimore at Pittsburgh on October 13; aluminum bats first approved for use in Little League.

1972 First major league player strike; Bernice Gera is first female professional umpire.

1973 The Yankees' Ron Blomberg becomes the first designated hitter, on April 6.

1974 First major league Hispanic umpire: Armando Rodriguez in AL; aluminum bats first approved for use by NCAA.

1975 Indians hire Frank Robinson as first black manager; first players declared free-agents (on December 23), Andy Messersmith and Dave McNally; Danny Litwhiler introduces the first radar gun.

1977 Mike Schmidt earns the first $500,000 salary.

1978 First team to draw 3 million fans, Los Angeles Dodgers with 3,347,945.

1980 Nolan Ryan earns the first $1,000,000 salary (a 4-season contract).

1982 Joel Youngblood becomes first major league player to play for two different teams (Mets & Expos) in two different cities (Chicago & Philadelphia) on same day, August 4; George Foster earns the first $2,000,000 salary, $2.04 million a year for 5 seasons.

1989 Bill White becomes first black league president (NL); the Griffeys become first father-son duo to perform simultaneously.

1990 Kirby Puckett earns the first $3,000,000 salary.

1991 First modern teams to go from last to first (Twins and Braves) meet in World Series; first team to draw 4 million fans, the Toronto Blue Jays with 4,001,527; Roger Clemens becomes first player to top $5 million mark, with $5.38 million salary per year for 5 seasons; Brien Taylor becomes first $1 million bonus baby.

1992 First non-US world champion, Toronto Blue Jays.

1993 Carey Schueler, 18-year-old daughter of White Sox General Manager Ron Schueler, becomes the first woman chosen in the amateur free agent draft, when the Sox select her in the 43rd round.

1994 First year of three divisions in each league.

1995 First use of "wild cards" in post season play; Yankees are first team to have average salary of over $2 million.

1996 First major league game in Mexico, Mets vs. Padres.

1997 Albert Belle earns the first $10 million salary, $11 million a year for 5 seasons.

Notes on Contributors

Paul Adomites was born and raised in Pittsburgh, and lives there now. He was publications director for the Society for American Baseball Research from 1987-1990. He is the founding editor of *The SABR Review of Books* and its successor, *The Cooperstown Review.*

Larry Amman was born and raised in the suburbs of Detroit. He graduated from Wayne State University with a B.A. in history and political science in 1967, then served in the U.S. Army Intelligence in Vietnam and Germany. Although he has lived in the Washington, D.C., area for the last ten years, the Detroit Tigers remain his favorite team. He has published several articles on the Tigers, and has compiled all their game-winning RBI from 1901–1980.

Dennis Bingham is a writer for the Chicago Police Department, a freelance cartoonist, and an umpire for several adult and youth baseball leagues in the Chicago area. (His umpiring partner is often his father, Bill, who taught him the rules.) Bingham served as a historical adviser for the movie *Eight Men Out*, in which he also played a bit part as umpire Billy Evans. He was associate editor of the SABR publication *Baseball in Chicago*. One of the three founding members of SABR's Umpires and Rules Committee, Bingham lives with his wife, Diane, and sons Sean, Kevin, and Dennis on Chicago's South Side.

Bob Carroll, a former high school teacher, is a freelance writer and illustrator who lives in North Huntingdon, Pennsylvania. He is the founder and executive director of PFRA (the Professional Football Researchers Association) and a longtime member of SABR. He regularly writes and illustrates for *Oldtyme Baseball News*. His baseball books include *Baseball Between the Lies, The Whole Baseball Catalogue* (with John Thorn), *The Dodgers Trivia Book,* and *The Major League Way to Play Baseball.* Among his football credits are *Total Football*, *The Hidden Game of Football* (with Pete Palmer and John Thorn) and *When the Grass Was Real*. He regularly provides cartoons for *Pro Football Weekly*. His hobbies are listening to classical music, cleaning the Augean stables, and writing threatening letters.

Jim Charlton is a writer and editor with more than three dozen books to his credit, including four on baseball. Mr. Charlton is also a literary agent and book packager, as well as a lifetime Cubs fan, all frustrating occupations. He is married and lives in Greenwich Village, five blocks from where he was born.

Garth Chouteau is an associate producer and marketing executive with Stormfront Studios, makers of *Old Time Baseball* and the *Tony La Russa Baseball* line of entertainment software. Chouteau has more than ten years experience in the computer hardware and software markets, as well as a lifelong love of baseball. The only film during which Mr. Chouteau has ever cried is *It's Good to Be Alive, the Roy Campanella Story*.

Merritt Clifton edits *Animal People: News for People Who Care about Animals.* Clifton also is author of numerous works on "outlaw" baseball, especially as played in Quebec, Vermont, Japan, and Mexico, and *Relative Baseball*, a pioneering sabermetric study and a history and statistical analysis of *The Sporting News*/Topps All-Star Rookie teams, 1958-1983.

Don Daglow is founder and president of Stormfront Studios Inc. a California multimedia developer that publishes *Old Time Baseball* and the *Tony LaRussa Baseball* line of entertainment software. In 1971 he was the first person to simulate a complete baseball season on a computer, and as the computer and video game business developed he became particularly known for successful baseball simulations. Games designed or produced by Don and the Stormfront team include *Intellivision World Series Baseball* (Mattel, 1983), *Earl Weaver Baseball* (Electronic Arts, 1987), *ESPN Baseball Tonight* (Sony Imagesoft, 1995), *Tony La Russa Baseball 3* (Stormfront Studios, 1995), *Old Time Baseball* (Stormfront Studios, 1995), and *Tony La Russa Baseball 3: 1996 Edition* (Stormfront Studios, 1996).

Bill Deane is a freelance baseball researcher and writer stationed near Cooperstown, New York, where he spent eight years as Senior Research Associate for the National Baseball Library & Archive. He has published two books and more than one hundred articles for such publications as *Street & Smith's Official Baseball Yearbook* and *USA Today Baseball Weekly,* and was a recipient of the 1989 SABR-Macmillan Baseball Research Award. Deane resides in Fly Creek, New York, with his wife, Pam, and daughter, Sarah.

Rob Edelman is the author of *Great Baseball Films* (Citadel Press). He is co-author (with his wife, Audrey Kupferberg) of *Angela Lansbury: A Life on Stage and Screen* (Birch Lane) and *The John Travolta Scrapbook* (Citadel Press). He is a Contributing Editor of Leonard Maltin's *Movie and Video Guide,* and has written essays in *A Political Companion to American Film, The International Dictionary of Films and Filmmakers* and the *International Film Guide*. His byline has appeared in dozens of publications, from *American Film* to *The Washington Post*.

Eddie Epstein is currently director of research and statistics for the San Diego Padres. In that capacity he evaluates professional talent, participates in the negotiation of major league player contracts, and provides information to the team's manager about upcoming opponents. His work has been published in Bill James' *The Baseball Book* and *Baseball Abstract*, *Sports Illustrated*, *USA Today Baseball Weekly*, and *The Sporting News*. A Baltimore native, Eddie earned a BA (1981) and an MA (1985) from the University of Delaware.

Myles E. Friedman is editor and vice president of Vanguard Publications, which has published the annual *Spring Training Baseball Yearbook* since 1988. He also publishes historical wall charts on baseball, football, and World Cup soccer.

Warner Fusselle is the voice behind numerous television and radio programs and films on the subject of baseball. He worked with Mel Allen on *This Week in Baseball* since its inception in 1977 until Mel's death in 1996 and continues on that program. He continues to host ESPN's *Major League Baseball Magazine*, which he commenced in 1990. In addition to his baseball narration, Fusselle's play-by-play announcing can be heard on WABC Radio in New York City. He is the author of *Baseball . . . A Laughing Matter!* and has produced two albums of baseball music for Rhino Records: *Baseball's Greatest Hits* and *Baseball's Greatest Hits . . . Let's Play II*.

Larry R. Gerlach is professor of American sports history at the University of Utah. He is a member of the editorial board of *Nine*, the board of directors of SABR, and has served as chair of SABR's Umpires and Rules Committee. He has published numerous articles in journals and reference works, as well as *The Men in Blue: Conversations with Umpires*.

Mike Gershman is known among baseball fans for his series of *Baseball Card Engagement Books* and the *Baseball Stadium Postcard Albums*. *Diamonds*, his book about the evolution of the ballpark, was published by Houghton-Mifflin in the fall of 1993 and received both the SABR-Macmillan Award and the Casey Award. He is also, with John Thorn, the co-founder of Total Sports and he is co-editor of *Total Football*.

Gary Gillette is the author of the annual *Great American Baseball Stat Book*. He served as executive director or chairman of Project Scoresheet in 1987–1992. The Baseball Workshop, over which he presides, continues the work of Project Scoresheet under license by collecting and publishing computerized play-by-play data for all major league games. Gillette also acts as a consultant in arbitration cases for several prominent player agents, and has written for *USA Today*, *USA Today Baseball Weekly*, *Baseball Today* magazine, and several daily newspapers. He provides baseball commentary for WHYY in Philadelphia and several Public Radio stations.

Gary Hailey is a Washington, D.C. attorney and the author of "Anatomy of a Murder: The Federal League and the Courts," which appeared in the Spring 1985 issue of *The National Pastime*. He is a native of Joplin, Missouri, and a graduate of Rice University and Harvard Law School. Although he now realizes that he will never achieve his childhood ambition of playing center field for the New York Yankees, he still daydreams about one day being the Yankees' general counsel.

Donald Hall is the author of many books of verse, nineteen books of prose and anthologies, and editor for numerous publications. His poetry has won the National Book Critics Circle Award and the Robert Frost Medal of the Poetry Society of America. His most recent book of verse is *The Museum of Clear Ideas*.

Barry Halper, born in Newark, New Jersey, in 1939, began collecting baseball material twenty years ago and now holds the largest single collection of baseball memorabilia, surpassing even Cooperstown's. His collection includes over one million baseball cards and approximately a thousand baseball uniforms. Halper and his wife, Sharon, have three children and reside in Livingston, New Jersey.

Tom Heitz, born in Kansas City, Missouri, in 1940, has been a lifelong baseball fan. He learned the National Pastime from his father, a law professor and Little League coach, and from Harry Caray, the voice of the St. Louis Cardinals. Heitz received his formal education at the University of Kansas (B.A., 1962), the University of Missouri at Kansas City School of Law (J.D., 1965), and the University of Washington, where he studied library science under renowned law librarian Marian Gallagher. Heitz served as Librarian at the National Baseball Library & Archive from 1983 through 1994. He now writes and lectures on baseball subjects.

Bob Hoie has long been an active member of the Society for American Baseball Research, receiving the Society's Bob Davids Award for meritorious service in 1987. He has served as chairman of SABR's Minor League Committee, was a principal contributor to *Minor League Baseball Stars*, volumes 1, 2 and 3, and contributed to *The Encyclopedia of Minor League Baseball*. A native of Los Angeles and a fan of the Pacific Coast League Angels until their demise in 1957, Hoie is retired after thirty years of service as an urban planner for Los Angeles County.

John B. Holway has written for numerous magazines and newspapers, including *American Heritage, The Sporting News, The New York Times,* and the *Washington Post.* He is the author of *Voices from the Great Black Baseball Leagues, Blackball Stars, The Pitcher* with John Thorn, and *The Last .400 Hitter.* He has written about Ted Williams, whom he saw in 1941, the Negro leagues, which he saw in 1944, Japanese baseball, which he saw in 1948, and pitching, which he has spent a lifetime swinging at and missing. He won *Spitball* magazine's Casey Award and SABR's Bob Davids Award, both in 1990.

Frederick Ivor-Campbell turned to baseball research and writing after many years in religious publishing (editor/writer, Gospel Light Publications, California), public information (Barrington College, Rhode Island), and college teaching (English, at the University of Rhode Island and The King's College, New York). He has written baseball history and biography for several periodicals and reference works. Ivor-Campbell has served on the board of directors of the Society for American Baseball Research, and chairs SABR's Nineteenth Century Committee. He lives with his wife, Alma, in Warren, Rhode Island.

Clifford S. Kachline, following a stint as sports editor of the North Penn *Reporter* of Lansdale, Pennsylvania, joined the editorial staff of *The Sporting News* at age twenty-one in April 1943. He remained there for twenty-four years. Besides writing for *TSN,* for twenty years he was the compiler and editor of the *Official Baseball Guide* and *The Dope Book.* Kachline left *TSN* in May 1967 to become public relations director of the North American Soccer League; he then served as Baseball Hall of Fame historian (1969–1982), and then, until his retirement in 1985, as the first executive director of the Society for American Baseball Research.

Jack Kavanagh has given up the pretense of retirement for a writer's life in Rhode Island. His books have focused on such diverse subjects as Shoeless Joe Jackson and Robert E. Lee. In 1995 he celebrated his seventy-fifth birthday with his first adult, full-scale biography, a treatment of Walter Johnson (Diamond Communications); the following year saw him win SABR's Bob Davids Award and publish a biography of Grover Cleveland Alexander. He enjoys his five nearby grandchildren and the health to sniff the roses while they bloom. He has wonderful memories of a fifty-year marriage to his late wife Sally.

Jack Lang has reported on major league baseball for half a century, starting in 1946 when he covered the Brooklyn Dodgers for the *Long Island Press.* His last thirteen years on the beat were for the *New York Daily News,* where he was the senior major league baseball writer in 1987, when he retired. In 1966 he began conducting the annual Hall of Fame election and was elected Secretary-Treasurer of the Baseball Writers Association of America, for whom he conducted the annual polls for the Most Valuable Player, Cy Young, Rookie, and Manager Awards. In 1987 Lang himself was elected to the Hall of Fame when he was named winner of the J.G. Taylor Spink Award for meritorious contributions to baseball writing.

Philip J. Lowry is author of *Green Cathedrals*, the definitive study of all ballparks ever used for Major League and Negro League games since 1871, and of *Green Gridirons,* a similar study on all pro football stadiums. He has served on the Board of Directors and as Ballparks Chair and Negro Leagues Chair for SABR. Phil received B.A. and M.B.A. degrees from Harvard University, served in the U.S. Army airborne for six years as an infantry captain, and now resides in Minnetonka, Minnesota with his wife, Ellen, and their children, Evan and Megan.

Bill Madden majored in journalism at the University of South Carolina and launched his sportswriting career at United Press International in New York in 1970. From 1980-1988, Madden was *The Daily News*'s New York Yankees beat writer. He became that publication's national baseball columnist in 1989. In 1990 he collaborated on the bestselling book, *Damned Yankees*. In his years at *The Daily News* he was responsible for breaking numerous baseball stories, including the National League's surprise election of Bill White as its president in February 1989. In addition to writing for *The Daily News* Madden also has contributed freelance articles to numerous sports publications and a semiweekly sports collecting column for *The Sporting News*.

Yoichi Nagata holds a B.A. from Osaka University in Japan and an M.A. from the University of Pennsylvania. He has been a freelance sports journalist, writing numerous articles on sports for Japanese magazines. He is an avid baseball fan of the now-defunct Nishitetsu Lions of Fukuoka and of the Philadelphia Phillies.

Joseph M. Overfield was born in 1916 in Buffalo, where he has lived all his life, except for three years in the Air Force in World War Two. Historian for the Buffalo Bisons and a member of the Buffalo Baseball Hall of Fame Committee, he wrote *100 Seasons of Buffalo Baseball* in 1985, and has written for *Baseball Digest*, *The Sporting News*, Buffalo's *Courier-Express* and *News*, *Niagara Frontier*, and SABR's *Baseball Research Journal* and *The National Pastime*. Overfield was honored in 1986 by SABR for his contributions to minor league history. He is now semiretired after fifty-one years with a Buffalo real-estate title firm.

Pete Palmer is the former editor of the Barnes *Official Encyclopedia of Baseball*. He began compiling his historical and analytical data in the mid-1960s, and from 1978–1987 he was chairman of SABR's statistical analysis committee. In that time he also served as a consultant for the Sports Information Center, the official statisticians of the American League. He was on the board of directors of Project Scoresheet. Palmer has contributed articles to *Sport*, *USA Today*, *Sports Heritage*, *The National Pastime*, and *Baseball Research Journal*. He is coauthor, with John Thorn, of *The Hidden Game of Baseball* and *The Official Major League Baseball Record Book*; with Thorn and Bob Carroll of *The Hidden Game of Football* and *The Football Abstract*; and with Thorn and Eliot Cohen of *The Baseball Annual 1990*. He won SABR's Bob Davids Award in 1989.

Douglas R. Pappas is an attorney in New York. He founded SABR's Business of Baseball Committee and serves as its chairman, as well as SABR's legal advisor. Baseball, in the form of the Amazing Mets, seduced him at age eight; the affair has now lasted a quarter century, through The University of Chicago (A.B. 1982) and The University of Michigan Law School (J.D. 1985).

David Pietrusza, president of the Society for American Baseball Research (SABR) and Editorial Director of Total Sports, is the author of *Judge & Jury: The Life and Times of Judge Kenesaw Mountain Landis*, *Lights On!*, *Minor Miracles: The Legends & Lures of Minor League Baseball*; *Major Leagues*; and *Baseball's Canadian-American League*. He has been a research consultant for *Ballparks of North America* and *All My Octobers* and a contributor to *Collier's Encyclopedia*. Pietrusza served as producer for the documentary *Local Heroes: Baseball on Capital Region Diamonds* for PBS-television station WMHT (Schenectady, NY) and as consultant for the Baseball Online segment of the PBS LearningLink system. A columnist for *Oldtyme Baseball News*, he has written for such other periodicals as *USA Today*, *Baseball Weekly*, *Baseball America*, *Elysian Fields Quarterly*, *The National Pastime*, *New Mexico Magazine*, and *The Baseball Research Journal*. Pietrusza was also a writer for Microsoft's multimedia product *Complete Baseball*. A former member of the Amsterdam (N.Y.) City Council, he holds an M.A. in history and has also written extensively on American and world history.

Bruce L. Prentice was born and raised in Toronto, Ontario, Canada, and was a top amateur baseball player before turning to coaching and instruction. In the late 1970s he assisted the introduction of the first high school baseball programs in Canada. He was founder of Canada's first college baseball program at Seneca College in Toronto and was an area scout for the Blue Jays from 1980–1986. Prentice is the owner and operator of Proway Baseball Schools, the founder and long-time president of the Canadian Baseball Hall of Fame and Museum, and was instrumental in forming the World Baseball Hall of Fame in 1989.

Rob Ruck is the author of *Sandlot Seasons: Sport in Black Pittsburgh* and *The Tropic of Baseball: Baseball in the Dominican Republic*, a 1991 MacMillan–SABR Award Winner. He produced *Kings on the Hill: Baseball's Forgotten Men*, a documentary on the Negro Leagues. He is on the faculty of the Center for Latin American Studies and the History Department at the University of Pittsburgh.

Matthew Silverman is marketing director as well as an editor for Total Sports in Connecticut. He has provided research and biographies for *Total Baseball*, *Total Football* and the team books produced by the company. He started his journalism career at eighteen as a part-time editor at *Variety* in New York and worked at three New England newspapers following his graduation from Roanoke College.

Allan Simpson is the founding editor of *Baseball America* and is recognized as the expert on baseball's amateur free-agent draft. *Baseball America* is based in Durham, North Carolina, and specializes in the coverage of player development.

David Spaner was born in Toronto and grew up in Vancouver. A graduate of Simon Fraser University (history) and Langara College (journalism), he has worked as a feature writer, reporter, and editor for numerous publications, and is currently employed at the *Vancouver Province* newspaper. David is at work on a book about Canadian comedy.

John Thorn is the author/editor of many baseball books, including *The Game for All America*, *The Armchair Books of Baseball*, *Ted Williams: Seasons of the Kid* (with Richard Ben Cramer and Mark Rucker), *The National Pastime*, and *The Relief Pitcher*. He coauthored *The Pitcher* with John Holway, and *The Hidden Game of Baseball* and *The Baseball Record Book* with Pete Palmer. With Palmer and Bob Carroll he also coauthored *The Hidden Game of Football* and *The Football Abstract*. He has written for several periodicals, among them *The Sporting News*, *Sport*, and *American Heritage*. Thorn was Senior Creative Consultant to *Baseball*, Ken Burns's nine-part film for the Public Broadcasting System, and serves as a consultant to the National Baseball Hall of Fame Committee on Baseball Veterans. The publisher of Total Sports and Total Baseball Online, Thorn is also a co-editor of *Total Football*.

Robert L. Tiemann served as chairman of the nineteenth-century research committee of the Society for American Baseball Research and is the author of *Cardinal Classics* and *Dodger Classics*. He headed the SABR research project that reconstructed from newspaper play-by-play accounts much of the missing data for the National Association of 1871–1875. With Rich Topp, Tiemann shared a SABR award for his redevelopment of the Manager Roster as it appears in *Total Baseball*, and in 1992 won SABR's Bob Davids Award.

Jules Tygiel is a professor of history at San Francisco State University. He is the author of *Baseball's Great Experiment: Jackie Robinson and his Legacy* (Oxford University Press, 1983; Vintage Paperback edition, 1984) and has contributed articles to many periodicals.

Eduardo Valero, Chairman of the Latin America Committee of SABR, is also President of the Puerto Rico Professional Baseball Hall of Fame and the Puerto Rico Amateur Baseball Hall of Fame. A former Vice President of the Sportswriter Federation of America and President of the Puerto Rico Professional Sportswriters Association, Valero is also a feature writer of the sports supplement of the daily newspaper *El Vocero de Puerto Rico*. Over the past thirty-five years he has covered major and minor league baseball, the Caribbean Baseball Series, the Olympics, and the Panamerican and Centroamerican Caribbean Games for newspapers, news agencies, and radio/TV stations.

Joseph M. Wayman, publisher and editor of *Grandstand Baseball Annual,* which he founded in 1985, has been the subject of a "SABR Salute," which commended him for his steadfast "investigative reporting of questionable baseball records." Several of his discoveries have been accepted as fact by *Total Baseball* and the Elias Sports Bureau and have resulted in a rewriting of the baseball record books. His writings have also appeared in the *Baseball Research Journal* and *Baseball Bulletin*.

With appreciation to these readers of *Total Baseball 1* who sent in corrections or made suggestions on how to improve the second edition:

Larry Amman, Ray Andreotti, Mel Bailey, Craig Barbarino, Edgar K. Beatty, James M. Beck, Joseph R. Bender, Robert Beukelher, John Booth, Jim Bostain, Therese R. Brown, J. Paul Browne, Bob Cambris, Kevin A. Carleton, Bob Carroll, Anthony M. Chieco, Ken Coleman, Steve Cooper, Owen Curtis, Clay Davenport, L. Robert Davids, Bill Deane, Harold Dellinger, Ted D. DeVries, Don Dewey, Raymond A. DiSanto, Sam Elfand, Don Elliott, John Emerson, Eddie Epstein, Kenneth Fink, Robert L. Franz, Andrew Fussner, Cam Gibson, Steven Goldberg, Ray Gonzalez, Dan Greenia, Bill Haber, Rod Hay, Bob Hoie, Fred Ivor-Campbell, Tom Jennings, Bill Jensen, Warren Johnson, Cliff Kachline, James Kaufman, Dave Kemp, Larry Kempster, Randall Kleinman, Jack Lang, Ron Liebman, Jerry Malloy, James F. Maxfield, Bob McConnell, Joe M. McGowan, David Molnar, George S. Moskal, Frank J. Mueller, Neil Munro, Thomas L. Nester, Dave Nichols, Tom O'Brien, Yoshio Ohno, S. Mark Parker, Paul E. Pennebaker, Peretz Perl, Dave Pietrusza, Mike Post, Jorgen Rasmussen, Allan Rausch, Andrew Richardson, John Rickert, John M. Roca, Winslow Rogers, Tom Ruane, Bill Rubenstein, David Schermer, Leon Schmerhold, John Schwartz, Alfred Secondi, Sy Siegel, Richard Siegelman, Al Smith, David M. Snyder, David Stephan, Mike Sparks, Lyle Spatz, Dean Sullivan, Isaac Thorn, Richard Topp, Stephen Toth, T. Brook Treakle III, Jim Troisi, Jim Tuttle, Jim Vail, Cullen P. Vane, David Vincent, Joseph M. Wayman, Jim Weigand, Bernard Weisberger, Christopher Williams, Frank Williams, Joseph C. Williams, Ralph Winnie, Jim Wright, and Ed Yerha.

And to those whose suggestions have improved the third edition:

David Aceto, Tim Anderson, Andrew J. Balog, Robert Browning, Chuck Carey, Keith Carlson, Garrett M. Casey, Jim Conroy, Bob Davids, Bill Deane, Dennis DeValeria, Ted DiTullio, Robert Downer, Tom Dunken, Jules Egyrd, Eddie Epstein, Ken Fetterman, Bob Franzosa, Gary Gillette, Jay Gregory, Charlie Harville, Jeffrey Hatt, Ralph Horton, Jeff James, Darlene Kadlecik, Jerry Kahn, John Kenyon, Patrick Kinas, D.C. Larkin, II, Matthew Lesniewski, Morris Levin, Don Luce, Michael Lucich, Ed Luteran, Jeff Magalif, E.H. Marshall, Richard A. Marston, Ronald A. Mayer, John P. McBride, John McClaran, Randy Messel, Scott Messinger, Steve Moore, Neil Munro, John O'Malley, Ed Oswalt, Douglas R. Pappas, Richard Pardoe, Danny Radakovich, Matt Rapacz, Louis Rauco, Matt Reese, Eric Reinholdt, Dennis Repp, John Richards, Bob Richardson, John M. Roca, Seth D. Rodgers, Robert Schulz, John Schwartz, John Scott, Jamie Selko, Jim Smith, Dave Smith, Lewis J. Snyder, Lyle Spatz, Alan Steinberg, David Stephan, A.D. Suehsdorf, James Swetnam, Blair D. Tarr, Robert Tiemann, Harry L. Turtledove, Bill Wallace, Patrick K. Walsh, Joe Wayman, Jim Weigand, Frank Williams, Walt Wilson, and Edgar M. Wyatt.

The fourth edition has benefited from the comments of:

Tim Anderson, Arnie Braunstein, Chuck Carey, Bill Carle, Tim Cashion, Tom Chase, Ed Coen, Bob Davids, Bill Deane, Dan Dischley, Ted DiTullio, Jules Egyrd, Eddie Epstein, Bill French, Campbell Gibson, Gary Gillette, Herb Goldman, Albert A. Gunnell, Robert Kern, Joe Kinsman, Joe Klein, Joe Marchetto, Jeff Marcus, Bob McConnell, Randy Messell, Scott Messinger, Neil Munro, John O'Malley, Ed Oswalt, Doug Pappas, Jeffrey Platt, Frank Phelps, Bob Richardson, Win Rogers, Bob Rosiek, Jim Sargent, Robert Schulz, John Schwartz, Jamie Selko, Dave Smith, Jim Smith, David Stephan, Chuck Stevens, David Stone, Adie Suehsdorf, Bob Tiemann, David Vincent, Bill Way, Joe Wayman, Jim Weigand, Roy White, Alan Whitney, Frank Williams, Walt Wilson, and Ed Yerha.

This fifth edition has benefited from the comments of:

Arnie Braunstein, Chuck Carey, Keith Carlson, Bill Carle, Bill Carr, Tim Cashion, Tom Chase, Bob Davids, Bill Deane, Dan Dischley, Bill Doig, Jeff Fox, Tate Giersdorf, Gary Gillette, Herb Goldberg, Ed Hartig, Bob Hoie, Fred Ivor-Campbell, Herm Krabbenhoft, Dan Levitt, Fred Lenger, David Marasco, John Matthew IV, Neil Munro, John O'Malley, David Neft, Doug Pappas, Bob Richardson, Patrick Rock, Jim Sargent, John Schultz, John Schwartz, Jamie Selko, Joe Simenic, Allan Simpson, Lyle Spatz, Dick Thompson, Bob Tiemann, Dixie Torangeau, Jim Troisi, Frank Vaccaro, Paul Walker, Bill Way, Joe Wayman, Jim Weigand, Frank Williams, Walt Wilson, and Dave Zeman.

Glossary of Statistical Terms

This Glossary contains definitions of the statistical terms and measures that may be unfamiliar to the average baseball fan or that represent what today might seem odd scoring practices. The Glossary will also be of value to the advanced fan who wishes to know more about the mathematical and theoretical foundations of certain statistics.

/A "Adjusted"; means that the statistic to the immediate left of this mark has been normalized to league average and adjusted for home park factor. Stats that are normalized in this book are Batting Runs, Production, Batting Average, On Base Percentage, Slugging Average, Earned Run Average, and Pitcher Runs.

Assist Although credited to pitchers on strikeouts in some of baseball's early years, not counted as such in this volume.

Assist Average Assists divided by games played. Stat created by Philadelphia baseball writer Al Wright in 1875.

At-Bats Charged to batters on sacrifice hits, 1889–1893; on sacrifice-fly situations, 1931–1938 and 1940–1953; bases on balls, 1876, 1887. However, we did not count at-bats for bases on balls.

Average and Over Early form of expressing averages for base hits, runs, and outs. The average of a batter with 23 hits in six games would be not 3.83 but 3–5 (an average of 3 with an overage, or remainder, of 5); borrowed from cricket.

Average Bases Allowed A pitcher's total bases allowed, divided by his innings pitched—what might be termed Opponents' Slugging Average. Created by Alfred P. Berry in 1951.

Average Batting (Pitching, Fielding) Skill The great philosophical as well as statistical puzzler: after one has normalized a player's performance to that of his league, how does one compare one season's league average with that of another far removed in time? Does a .266 batting average in the NL of 1902 mean the same thing as a .266 batting average in the AL of 1977?

Bases on Balls Counted as outs for batters in 1876 and as hits for batters in 1887, but as neither throughout this book. Awarded for a varying number of errant pitches since 1876, from nine in that year to the current four (standardized in 1889). (After 1887, the batter was no longer allowed to specify strike zone as waist to shoulders or waist to shins.)

Bases on Balls Percentage Batters' stat: most walks per 100 at-bats plus bases on balls.

Bases on Balls Per Game Game defined as nine innings; league-leading pitchers calculated on basis of lowest mark; computed as bases on balls times nine, divided by innings.

Base-Out Percentage Barry Codell's stat for measuring complete offensive performance, in which the elements of the numerator represent bases gained while the events in the denominator represent outs produced (sacrifices and sacrifice flies appear in both because they achieve both—gaining a base for the team while costing it an out). The formula:

Total Bases + Walks + HBP + Steals + Sacrifices + Sacrifice Flies

At-bats − Hits + Caught Stealing + GIDP + Sac. + Sac. Flies

(GIDP, in the equation above, stands for Grounded Into Double Play; HBP for Hit By Pitch.)

Batters Facing Pitcher Unavailable before 1903 in the National League. The 1903 and 1908 data was not published and has been reconstructed. BFP was unavailable for the American League of 1901-1907. Excepting the NL of 1876-1888 and the AA of 1882 and 1884-1887, for which John Tattersall calculated BFP from box scores, earlier years in both leagues have had their BFP constructed from available data in this manner: subtract league base hits from league at-bats, divide by league innings pitched, multiply by the pitcher's innings, and add his hits allowed, walks, hit by pitch, and sacrifice hits, if available. Abbreviated as BFP.

Batter's Park Factor The Park Factor shown in the batters' section of the team statistics in the Annual Record, Player Register, and Home-Road Statistics. Above 100 means batters benefited from playing half their games in a good hitting park. Abbreviated as BPF or, in what are clearly batters' stats (as in the Player Register) simply as PF. See entry for *Park Factor* for the computation.

Battery Errors In baseball's early years, wild pitches, passed balls, and hit batsmen were lumped together in the statistical summary of a game as *battery errors* and were charged against the fielding percentage of the pitcher or catcher. Such battery errors have been removed from individual and team stats for this book.

Batting Average Calculated as base hits divided by at-bats ever since its first appearance in print in 1874. In 1876 walks were counted as at-bats, and in 1887 they were counted as at-bats and as hits. For this book, batting averages are computed in uniform fashion throughout baseball history. Abbreviated in Part 2 of this volume as AVG, although it is also commonly abbreviated BA.

Batting Runs The Linear Weights measure of runs contributed *beyond* those of a league-average batter or team, such league average defined as zero. The formula depends upon the run values for each offensive event that resulted from Pete Palmer's 1978 computer simulation of all major league games played since 1901. Run values change marginally with changing conditions of play (an out costs a team more in a hitters' year, such as 1930, than in a pitchers' year, such as 1908), and they differ slightly up and down the batting order (a homer is not worth as much to the leadoff hitter as it is to the fifth-place batter; a walk is worth more for the man batting second than for the man batting eighth); however, these differences have been averaged out historically in the figures below.

$$\text{Runs} = (.47)1B + (.78)2B + (1.09)3B + (1.40)HR + (.33)(BB + HB) - (.25)(AB - H) - (.50)OOB$$

(An out is considered to be a hitless at-bat and its value is set so that the sum of all events times their frequency is zero, thus establishing zero as the baseline, or norm, for performance.)

Some events one might expect to see included in this formula but that do not appear are sacrifices, sacrifice hits, grounded into double plays, and reached on error. The last is not known for most years and in the official statistics is indistinguishable from outs on base (OOB). The sacrifice has values that essentially cancel one another, trading an out for an advanced base which, often as not, leaves the team in a situation with poorer run potential than it had before the sacrifice. The sacrifice fly has dubious run value because it is entirely dependent on a situation not under the batter's control: while a single or a walk or a hit by pitch always has potential run value, a long fly does not unless a man happens to be poised at third base. Last, the grounded into double play is to a far greater extent a function of one's place in the batting order than it is of poor speed or failure in the clutch, and thus it does not find a home in a formula applicable to all batters. It is no accident that Hank Aaron, who ran well for most of his long career and wasn't too shabby in the clutch, hit into more DPs than anyone else, nor that Roberto Clemente, Al Kaline, and Frank Robinson, who fit the same description, are also among the ten "worst" in this department.

The Batting Runs formula can be condensed by eliminating the components for steals, caught stealing, and outs on base. Outs on base (calculated as *Hits + Walks + Hit Batsman − Left on Base − Runs − Caught Stealing*) is meaningful only for teams, not individuals. We eliminate steals from the formula in those years in which caught-stealing figures are not available, but the surviving data for the early years indicate that few of the men with high base-stealing totals exceeded the break-even point of 66.7 percent by a margin large enough to produce even one additional Batting Win. A further condensation that we have used for our historical data, as indicated in the formula above, involves setting the value of a single at .47 runs and each extra base at .31, making a double .78, a triple 1.09, and a homer 1.40. (This tends to even out the fluctuations in run values for base hits and extra bases over time: a double, for example, was in fact worth .82 runs from 1901–1920, .80 runs from 1941–1960, and .77 runs from 1961–1977.) Subtract the hits from the total bases and multiply the resulting extra bases by .31 and the hits by .47. This may introduce small variations from a more rigorous formula that includes differing run values for the differing periods or even for single years (generally amounting to a fraction of a run), but the calculation is much snappier for those without a computer.

The Batting Runs formula may be long, even in its condensed form, but it calls for only addition, subtraction, and multiplication and thus is as simple as Slugging Average, whose incorrect weights (1, 2, 3, and 4) it revises and expands upon. Each event has a value and frequency, just as in Slugging Average, yet in Batting Runs outs are treated as offensive events with a run value of their own (albeit a negative one). Just as the run potential for a team in a given half-inning is boosted by a man reaching base, it is diminished by a man being retired; not only has he failed to brighten the situation on the bases but he has deprived his team of the services of a man further down the order who might have come up in this half-inning, either with men on base and/or with scores already in.

The Batting Runs stat treats every offensive event in terms of its impact upon the team—an *average* team, so that a man does not benefit in his individual record for having the good fortune to bat cleanup with the Rockies or suffer for batting cleanup with the White Sox. The relationship of individual performance to team play is stated poorly or not at all in conventional baseball statistics. In Batting Runs it is crystal clear.

Recognizing that some readers will wish to keep track of batting performance by compiling Batting Runs themselves over the course of a season and that they may be frustrated by the difficulty of separating out pitcher batting or of calculating the (At-Bats − Hits) factor for the league, we advise that using the fixed value of − .25 for outs will tend to work quite well if you wish to include pitcher batting performance, and a fixed value of − .27 will serve if you wish to exclude it. Actually, any fixed value will suffice in midseason; it's only when all the numbers are in and you care to compare this year's results with last year's (or, e.g., with those of the 1927 Yankees) that more precision is desirable. At that point the value of the out may be calculated by the more ambitious among you, but, ideally, the sporting press will provide accurate Batting Runs figures. (Who calculates ERA for himself?) Batting Runs are abbreviated as BR.

Batting Wins Adjusted Batting Runs divided by the number of runs required to create an additional win beyond average (see *Runs Per Win*). That average is defined as a team record of .500 because a league won-lost average must be .500, or as an individual record of zero because the value of the out for a given year is calculated to establish a baseline of zero. Abbreviated as BW.

Calculated Stat One or more counting stats (see below) subjected to a mathematical process such as averaging.

Chances Accepted Putouts and assists, minus errors.

Clutch Hitting Index Calculated for individuals, actual RBIs over expected RBIs, adjusted for league average and slot in batting order; 100 is a league-average performance. The spot in the batting order is figured as

$$5 - (9 \times BFPGP - BFPGT)$$

where BFPGP is the batters facing pitcher per game for the player, or plate appearances divided by games, and BFPGT is the batters facing pitcher per game of the entire team.

Expected RBIs are calculated as

$$(.25 \text{ singles} + .50 \text{ doubles} + .75 \text{ triples} + 1.75 \text{ homers}) \times$$
$$LGAV \times EXPSL$$

where LGAV (league average) = league RBIs divided by (.25 singles + .50 doubles + .75 triples + 1.75 homers), and EXPSL (expected RBI by slot number) = .88 for the leadoff batter, and for the remaining slots, descending to ninth, .90, .98, 1.08, 1.08, 1.04, 1.04, 1.04, and 1.02.

Calculated for teams, Clutch Hitting Index is actual runs scored over Batting Runs. Abbreviated as CHI.

Clutch Pitching Index Expected runs allowed over actual runs allowed, with 100 being a league-average performance. Expected runs are figured on the basis of the pitcher's opposing at-bats, hits, walks, and hit batsmen (doubles and triples estimated at league average). Abbreviated as CPI.

Counting Stat A raw figure that tells how many of an item have been accumulated, as opposed to a calculated or derived figure such as an average.

Differential The difference between a team's actual won-lost record and that predicted by the total of its Pitching Wins, Batting Wins, Fielding Wins, and Stolen Base Wins; this measure indicates the extent to which a team outperformed or underperformed its talent. Abbreviated as DIF.

Earned Run Average Calculated as earned runs times nine, divided by innings pitched. For a few years after being introduced as an official stat in the National League in 1912 and the American League in 1913, runs aided by stolen bases were not counted as earned (see Chronology of Scoring Rules in Appendix 1, Rules and Scoring). For years before 1912, ERA has been constructed from raw data, but for some teams in some seasons, earned runs cannot be identified with perfect certainty. For those teams, we use the estimating procedure created by Information Concepts, Inc., of assigning to those runs whose earned/unearned status is unknown the percentage of earned runs to runs that characterize the team's known runs. In *Total Baseball*, we have created an Adjusted ERA by normalizing to the league average—which is done by dividing the league average ERA by the individual ERA—and then factoring in home park.

Expected Wins Calculated for the team based on its actual runs scored and allowed, not its predicted runs scored and allowed. A team that allows exactly as many runs as it scores is predicted to play .500 ball. The equation for expected wins is:

$$\frac{(\text{Runs Scored} - \text{Runs Allowed})}{\text{Runs Per Win}} + \frac{(\text{Wins} + \text{Losses})}{2}$$

Abbreviated as W− EXP.

Fielding Average Defined as putouts and assists divided by the total of putouts, assists, and errors. The weakness of this stat is that it values a player with minimal range but good hands over another player who may accept many more chances but mishandle a few of these. Abbreviated as FA. See *Range Factor, Total Chances*.

Fielding Runs The Linear Weights measure of runs saved *beyond* what a league-average player at that position might have saved, defined as zero; this stat is calculated to take account of the particular demands of the different positions.

For second basemen, shortstops, and third basemen, the formula begins by calculating the league average for the position:

$$AVG \begin{array}{c} \text{pos.} \\ \text{lg.} \end{array} = \left(\frac{.20 \, (PO + 2A - E + DP) \text{ league at position}}{PO \text{ league total} - K \text{ league total}} \right)$$

where A = assists, PO = putouts, E = errors, DP = double plays, and K = strikeouts. Then we estimate the number of innings for each player at each position based upon each player's entire fielding record and his number of plate appearances. So, if the team played 1,500 innings and one player was calculated to have played 1,000 of those innings at a given position, his Fielding Runs (FR) would be calculated as:

$$FR = .20 \, (PO + 2A - E + DP) \, \text{player} - \text{avg. pos. lg.} \times \left(\frac{PO}{\text{team}} - \frac{K}{\text{team}} \right) \frac{\text{innings, player}}{\text{innings, team}}$$

Assists are doubly weighted because more fielding skill is generally required to get one than to record a putout.

For catchers, the above formula is modified by removing strikeouts from their formulas and subtracting not only errors but also passed balls divided by two. Also incorporated in the catcher's Fielding Runs is one tenth of the adjusted Pitching Runs for the team, times the percentage of games behind the plate by that catcher.

For pitchers, the above formula is modified to subtract individual pitcher strikeouts from the total number of potential outs (otherwise, exceptional strikeout pitchers like Nolan Ryan or Bob Feller would see their Fielding Runs artificially depressed). Also, pitchers' chances are weighted less than infielders' assists because a pitcher's style may produce fewer ground balls. Thus the formula for pitchers is .10(PO + 2A − E + DP), whereas for second basemen, shortstops, and third basemen it is .20(PO + 2A − E + DP).

For first basemen, because putouts and double plays require so little skill in all but the odd case, these plays are eliminated, leaving only .20(2A − E) in the numerator.

For outfielders, the formula becomes .20(PO + 4A − E + 2DP). The weighting for assists is boosted here because a good outfielder can prevent runs through the threat of assists that are never made; for them, unlike infielders, the assist is essentially an elective play, like the stolen base. Outfielders' Fielding Runs were subject to some degree of error because outfielders sometimes switch fields within a game or season (Babe Ruth, for example, was positioned in the field that required the lesser range—right field in Yankee Stadium, left field in most road parks). Also, short distances to left- or right-field walls in some parks tend to depress putout totals.

Since the third edition of *Total Baseball*, however, we have researched and obtained breakouts of all outfielders' games in left, center, and right fields. Center fielders now have higher ratings than they did in the first and second editions. Abbreviated as FR.

Fielding Wins Fielding Runs divided by the number of runs required to create an additional win beyond average. That average is defined as a team record of .500 because a league won-lost average must be .500. Abbreviated as FW. See *Runs Per Win*.

Games Behind Figured by adding the difference in wins between a trailing team and the leader to the difference in losses, and dividing by two. Thus a team that is three games behind may trail by three in the win column and three in the loss column, or four and two, or any other combination of wins and losses totaling six. Abbreviated as GB.

Game-Winning Run Batted In Credited to the batter who drives in a run that gives his club a lead that it never relinquishes, no matter when that run is driven in nor what the final score is. Introduced in 1980 as an official stat and later disowned, the GWRBI is not recorded in this volume.

Grounded into Double Play Kept officially since 1993 in the NL and 1939 in the AL (though the NL data of 1933-38 made no distinction between lined-into double plays and grounded-into double plays, and the AL data of 1939 was not published). This stat tends to be overvalued by the general public as an indicator of rally-killing ineptitude. Instead, it is largely a function of high totals of at-bats, which tend to be accumulated by the game's best players, not its worst. Abbreviated as GIDP.

Hands Out The original 1840s scoring term for batters producing outs either at the plate or on the bases. On a force out, the runner retired on the bases would be charged with a hand out, not the batter. Also called Hands Lost, and abbreviated as HO or HL.

Hit by Pitch A batter struck by a pitched ball was not awarded

first base until 1884 in the American Association and 1887 in the National League. Reconstruction of stats for batters and pitchers in the years 1897-1908 has been accomplished. Abbreviated as HBP.

Hits Bases on balls originally counted as hits in 1887, but are recorded in this volume as neither hits nor at-bats.

Home Run Factor A measure of the home runs hit in a given ballpark, with 100 representing the average home park and the highest figure above that representing the best home-run park. Computed in the same manner as Home Run Batter Rating (see above). Abbreviated as HRF.

Home Run Percentage Home runs per 100 at-bats.

Home Run Pitcher Rating A measure of a team's ability to prevent home runs, taking into account the Home Run Factor (see above) of the park and the team's not having to face its own batters. The average mark is represented as 100, and the lowest figure beneath that indicates the best.

Home Runs When is a home run not a home run? Before 1920, not if it came with men on base in the ultimate inning and created a margin of victory greater than one run. A ruling of the Special Baseball Records Committee in 1969 reversed its earlier decision that had made home runs of 37 disputed final-inning, game-winning base hits. In accordance with the practice of the day, such a hit, even if it sailed out of the park, would be credited with only as many bases as necessary to plate the winning run. Thus Babe Ruth's "715th home run," hit on July 8, 1918, to win a game against Cleveland, remained a triple, and Jimmy Collins and Sherry Magee were each deprived of two home runs.

Innings Pitched Official baseball practice was, until 1982, to round off fractional innings for individuals to the next highest inning. Since then fractional innings have been kept for individuals and teams. In this volume fractional innings are supplied for all individuals and all teams in all years. Those men who took a turn on the mound but failed to retire a batter are credited with no innings pitched and, if they allowed a runner or runners to score, an ERA of infinity.

Intentional Bases on Balls Recorded only since 1955.

Isolated Power Total bases minus hits, divided by at-bats; in other words, Slugging Average minus Batting Average. Appears to have been created by Allan Roth and Branch Rickey in the 1950s.

League-Average Replacement Player That model player who performs at precisely the league average, creating a baseline against which to measure others.

League Performance: Because the caliber of play in the Union Association of 1884 and the Federal League of 1914-15 was substantially below that of its rivals in those years, we have made an upward adjustment to overall league performance, thus lowering individual ratings or computed stats, while leaving unaffected the raw statistics of Organized Baseball. League at bats were reduced to 80 percent for the UA and 90 percent for the FL.

We tested all players who appeared in at least 30 games for the UA in 1884 and 30 or more games in the NL or AA in the 1883-85 period. There were 31 players who played 2,182 games in the UA and had a Total Player Rating 2.6 wins higher per 112 games in the UA. There were 17 pitchers who pitched 3,678 innings in the UA with at least 30 innings in the UA and 30 innings in other leagues in the 1883-85 period). These pitchers had a Total Pitcher Index 0.8 wins higher in the UA per 112 innings.

For the Federal League, there were 54 players with 30 games in the FL and at least 30 games in other leagues in the 1913-16 period. These players had 10,401 games in the FL and had a Total Player Rating 1.26 wins higher per 154 games. For pitchers, there were 39 with 30 or more innings in the FL and 30 innings in other leagues in the 1913-16 period). These pitchers had 13,872 innings and a Total Pitcher Index .49 wins higher in the FL per 154 innings.

Actually, the calculations for the UA produced a .76 multiplier for on base percentage and slugging, which we have rounded to .80. The calculations for the FL produced a .90 multiplier for on base percentage and slugging, which we have incorporated. UA pitchers had an .875 multiplier for earned run average, which we have expressed as .80 for consistency with the batting figure. FL pitchers had a multiplier of .924, which we have rounded to .90.

Linear Weights A system created by Pete Palmer to measure all the events on a ballfield in terms of runs. At the root of this system, as with other sabermetric figures such as Runs Created, is the knowledge that wins and losses are what the game of baseball is about, that wins and losses are proportional in some way to runs scored and runs allowed, and that runs in turn are proportional to the events that go into their making.

Normalizing Restating a figure as a ratio by comparing it to the league average, or norm.

On Base Percentage Created by Roth and Rickey in its current form—hits plus walks plus hit by pitch, divided by at-bats plus walks plus hit by pitch—in the early 1950s, although there were nineteenth-century forebears such as "Reached First Base." When OBP, as it is abbreviated, was adopted as an official stat in 1984, the denominator was expanded to include sacrifice flies. The effect is to penalize a batter in his on base percentage by giving him a plate appearance while at the same time crediting him in his batting average by deleting the plate appearance. In this book we calculate OBP without considering sacrifice flies, which in any event are calculable on a continuing basis only since 1954.

On Base plus Slugging See *Production*.

Opponents' Batting Average Hits allowed divided by at-bats allowed (or, if at-bats allowed is unknown, then at-bats equals hits plus inning times "K," where "K" is the league average of at-bats minus hits, all over innings). Abbreviated as OAV.

Opponents' On Base Percentage For years before 1908 in the American League and 1903 in the National League, the number of batters facing a pitcher has been constructed from the available raw data. We have subtracted league base hits from league at-bats, divided by league innings pitched, multiplied by the pitcher's innings, and added his hits and walks allowed and hit by pitch and sacrifices, if available. Abbreviated as OOB.

Outs Until 1883, included catching a ball on one bounce in foul ground. Not credited after three strikes in 1887, when the rule was "four strikes and yer out"—as it was, in fact, from 1871–1881, when batters commonly received "warning pitches" rather than called strikes.

Outs Per Game The 1860s successor to Hands Out (see above), it joined with Runs Per Game to form the batting record before the rise of professional league play.

Park Factor Calculated separately for batters and pitchers. Above 100 signifies a park favorable to hitters; below 100 signifies a park favorable to pitchers. The computation of PF is admittedly daunting, and what follows is probably of interest to the merest handful of readers, but we feel obliged to state the mathematical underpinnings for those few who may care. We use a three-year average Park Factor for players and teams unless they change home parks. Then a two-year average is used, unless the park existed for only one year. Then a one-year mark is used. If a team started up in Year 1, played two years in the first park, one in the next, and three in the park after that and then stopped play, the average would be as follows (where F*n* is the one-year park factor for year *n*):

Year 1 and 2 = (F1 + F2)/2   Year 4 = (F4 + F5)/2
Year 3 = F3   Year 5 = (F4 + F5 + F6)/3
     Year 6 = (F5 + F6)/2

Step 1. Find games, losses, and runs scored and allowed for each team at home and on the road. Take runs per game scored and allowed at home over runs per game scored and allowed on the road. This is the initial figure, but we must make two corrections to it.

Step 2. The first correction is for innings pitched at home and on the road. This is a bit complicated, so the mathematically faint of heart may want to head back at this point. First, find the team's home winning percentage (wins at home over games at home). Do the same for road games. Calculate the Innings Pitched Corrector (IPC) shown below. If it is greater than 1, this means the innings pitched on the road are higher because the other team is batting more often in the last of the ninth. This rating is divided by the Innings Pitched Corrector, like so:

$$IPC = \frac{(18.5 - \text{Wins at home} / \text{Games at home})}{(18.5 - \text{Losses on road} / \text{Games on road})}$$

Note: 18.5 is the average number of half-innings per game if the home team always bats in the ninth.

Step 3. Make corrections for the fact that the other road parks' total difference from the league average is offset by the park rating of the club that is being rated. Multiply rating by this Other Parks Corrector (OPC):

$$OPC = \frac{\text{No. of teams}}{\text{No. of teams} - 1 + \text{Run Factor, team}}$$

(Note that this OPC differs from that presented earlier in *The Hidden Game of Baseball*, for in preparing the pre-1900 data for *Total Baseball*, we discovered that for some parks with extreme characteristics, like Chicago's Lake Front Park of 1884, which had a Home Run Factor of nearly 5, the earlier formula produced wrong results. For parks with factors of 1.5 or less, either formula works well.)

Example. In 1982, Atlanta scored 388 runs and allowed 387 runs at home in 81 games, and scored 351 and allowed 315 on the road in 81 games. The initial factor is (775/81) ÷ (666/81) = 1.164. The Braves' home record was 42–39, or .519, and their road record was 47–34, or .580. Thus the IPC = (18.5 − .519) ÷ (18.5 − .420) = .995. The team rating is now 1.164/.995 = 1.170. The OPC = (12) ÷ (12 − 1 + 1.170) = .986. The final runs-allowed rating is 1.170 × .986, or 1.154.

We warned you it wouldn't be easy!

The batter adjustment factor is composed of two parts, one the park factor and the other the fact that a batter does not have to face his own team's pitchers. The initial correction takes care of only the second factor. Start with the following (SF = Scoring Factor, previously determined [for Atlanta, 1.154], and SF1 = Scoring Factor of the other clubs [NT = number of teams]):

$$1 - \frac{SF - 1}{NT - 1}$$

Next is an iterative process in which the initial team pitching rating is assumed to be 1, and the following factors are employed:

RHT, RAT = Runs per game scored at home (H) and away (A), by team

OHT, OAT = Runs per game allowed at home, away, by team

RAL = Runs per game by both teams

Now, with the Team Pitching Rating (TPR) = 1, we proceed to calculate Team Batting Rating (TBR):

$$TBR = \left(\frac{RAT}{SF1} + \frac{RHT}{SF}\right)\left(1 + \frac{TPR - 1}{NT - 1}\right)\bigg/RAL$$

$$TPR = \left(\frac{OAT}{SF1} + \frac{OHT}{SF}\right)\left(1 + \frac{TBR - 1}{NT - 1}\right)\bigg/RAL$$

The last two steps are repeated three more times. The final Batting Corrector, or Batters' Park Factor (BPF) is

$$BPF = \frac{(SF + SF1)}{\left(2 \times \left[1 + \frac{TPR - 1}{NT - 1}\right]\right)}$$

Similarly, the final Pitching Corrector, or Pitchers' Park Factor (PPF) is

$$PPF = \frac{(SF + SF1)}{\left(2 \times \left[1 + \frac{TBR - 1}{NT - 1}\right]\right)}$$

Now an example, using the 1982 Atlanta Braves once again.

$$RHT = \frac{388}{81} = 4.79 \qquad RAT = \frac{351}{81} = 4.33$$

$$OHT = \frac{387}{81} = 4.78 \qquad OAT = \frac{315}{81} = 3.89$$

$$RAL = \frac{7947}{972} = 8.18 \qquad NT = 12$$

$$SF = 1.154 \qquad SF1 = 1 - \left(\frac{1.154 - 1}{11}\right) = .986$$

$$TBR = \left(\frac{4.33}{.986} + \frac{4.79}{1.154}\right)\left(1 + \frac{1 - 1}{11}\right)\Big/ 8.18 = 1.044$$

$$TPR = \left(\frac{3.89}{.986} + \frac{4.78}{1.154}\right)\left(1 + \frac{1.044 - 1}{11}\right)\Big/ 8.18 = .993$$

Repeating these steps gives a TBR of 1.04 and a TPR of .97. The Batters' Park Factor is

$$BPF = \frac{(1.170 + .986)}{\left(2 \times \left[1 + \frac{.99 - 1}{11}\right]\right)} = 1.07$$

This is not a great deal removed from taking the original ratio,

$$\frac{1.170 + 1}{2}, \text{ which is } 1.08.$$

The Pitchers' Park Factor may be calculated in analogous fashion.

To apply the Batters' Park Factor to Batting Runs, one must use this formula:

$$\frac{BR}{corr.} = \frac{BR}{uncorr.}\Bigg/ \frac{Runs\,(league)}{AB+BB+HBP} - \frac{Runs\,(league)}{AB+BB+HBP} \times (BPF - 1) \times \frac{AB+BB+HBP}{(player\,or\,team)}$$
$$(league) \qquad\qquad (league)$$

For example, if a player produces 20 runs above average in 700 plate appearances with a Batters' Park Factor of 1.10, and the league average of runs produced per plate appearance is .11, this means that the player's uncorrected Batting Runs is 20 over the zero point of 700 × .11 (77 runs). In other words, 77 runs is the average run contribution expected of this batter were he playing in an average home park. But because his Batters' Park Factor is 1.10, which means his home park was 10 percent kinder to hitters (than the average), you would really expect an average run production of 1.1 × 77, or 85 runs. Thus the player whose uncorrected Batting Runs is 97 with a BF of 1.1 is only +10 runs rather than +20, and 10 is his Park Adjusted Batting Runs (in the Player Register, BR/A):

$$10 = 20/1.10 - .11 \times (1.10 - 1) \times 700.$$

Percentage of Team Wins A simple but deceiving measure of a good pitcher's contribution to a bad club; in this, it shares the virtues and flaws of Ted Oliver's Weighted Rating System and, to a lesser degree, our own Wins Above Team (both of which see). Steve Carlton had the highest single-season rating in this century when, in 1972, he went 27–10 for a Phillie club that won only 59 games. Yet his mark of 45.8 percent of his team's wins would not make the top 100 list of seasons since 1876, making this stat nearly useless for historical analysis.

Pitcher Defense Abbreviated as PD. See *Fielding Runs*.

Pitchers' Park Factor The same as the Park Factor shown in the pitchers' section of the team statistics portion of the Annual Record and in the Pitcher Register; above 100 means a pitcher was hurt by playing half his games in a good hitting park. See *Park Factor*.

Pitcher Strikeouts Made tougher or easier by cyclically varying rules and conditions. For instance, foul tips did not count as strikes for many years, even when deliberate, as with bunts; fouls caught on a bounce were outs until 1883; the ball-strike count underwent much experimentation until settling at four balls and three strikes in

1889; not to mention the high-low strike zone, warning pitches, varying pitching distances, and restricted deliveries. It helps to know some history before rattling off stats to prove this or that, but normalizing a stat to its league helps, even with counting stats such as strikeouts.

Pitching Runs The Linear Weights measure of runs saved *beyond* what a league-average pitcher or team might have saved, defined as zero. The math is simple: *Pitching Runs = Innings Pitched × (League ERA/9) − Earned Runs Allowed*. An alternate version is: *Innings Pitched/9 × (League ERA − Individual ERA)*. Abbreviated as PR.

Pitching Wins Park Adjusted Pitching Runs divided by the number of runs required to create an additional win beyond average. That average is defined as a team record of .500 because a league won-lost average must be .500. Abbreviated as PW. See *Pitching Runs*, above, and *Runs Per Win*.

Player Win Averages The title of a 1970 book issued by the Mills brothers, Harlan and Eldon, as well as the name of their overall method of determining not only the *what* of baseball statistics but also the *when*, or clutch element. Computerizing complete play-by-play data for a full season for their book, they assigned "Win Points"—reflective of that event's potential impact on the team's prospects of victory—to *every* event on a baseball field.

Positional Adjustment A key factor in the Total Player Rating that addresses the relative worth to a ball club of the defensive positions. A man who bats .270, hits 25 homers, and drives in 80 runs may be an average performer in left field, no matter how good his glove; but credit those batting stats to a shortstop or second baseman and you have a star, because the defensive demands of the position are so much greater. To balance the abundance of good-hitting outfielders or first basemen against the scarcity of such players at catcher or shortstop, we created a positional adjustment expressed in terms of the average batting skill needed to hold down a major league spot at that position.

To determine the average defensive skill required of a position, simply subtract the average batting skill at that position from his Total Player Rating. This may seem strange at first glance, but it does put, for example, shortstops, first basemen, and left fielders on the same footing. The explanation that follows represents a change from previous editions, in which players were measured against only those who played their position in their league in that year. We have now redefined the positional adjustment as an average over *both* leagues for a three-year period centered on the measured year. This raised the ratings for Lou Gehrig and Jimmie Foxx by a win or two, as they are now compared with sixteen first basemen over three years (a total of forty-eight) rather than just eight. In the 1950–1970 period, AL outfielders averaged a few more Batting Runs per season than their counterparts in the NL. When both leagues were counted, NL players dropped a few Wins and AL players gained. Hank Aaron lost 4 Wins for this reason.

In the years since 1977 the positional adjustment for, say a National League first baseman, will be in the context of the batting records of not merely twelve men, but twenty-six—times three, or seventy-eight—obviously, a much broader base of comparison. For each edition, the concluding season's positional adjustments are based on the average of that year and the preceding season.

Let's say that last year all major league left fielders accounted for 198 batting runs. The positional adjustment, or factor for average defensive skill, for a left fielder who played in all 162 games would be 162 × 198/3,202 (which calculates to 10), where 3,202 is the number of games played in both leagues by all left fielders (or any other position, obviously). Thus a left fielder who played in all his team's games would have 10 runs subtracted from the sum of his Batting Runs, Stolen Base Runs, and Fielding Runs. If all major league shortstops last year accounted for 158 Batting Runs below average, the adjustment for a shortstop would be figured in the same way, multiplying his games played by − 158/3,202, or − 8 runs, meaning that 8 runs (minus a minus 8) would be *added* to his Total Player Rating.

Production On Base Percentage plus Slugging Average: a simple but elegant measure of batting prowess, in that the weaknesses of one-half of the formulation, On Base Percentage, are countered by the strengths of the other, Slugging Average, and vice versa. When PRO, as it is abbreviated, is adjusted for home park and normalized to league average to become PRO⁺, the calculation is modified slightly to create a baseline of 100 for a league-average performance. For PRO⁺, the calculation is

$$\frac{\text{Player On Base Pct.}}{\text{League On Base Pct.}} + \frac{\text{Player Slugging Avg.}}{\text{League Slugging Avg.}} - 1$$

This produces a figure with a decimal point—an above-average figure, like 1.46, or a below-average figure, like 0.82. For ease of display, in this book we drop the decimal and express these as 146 and 82.

Putout Average Putouts divided by games played; a stat created by Philadelphia baseball writer Al Wright in 1875.

Quality Start A game started in which a pitcher lasts for six innings or more and allows three runs or less.

Ratio Hits plus walks plus hit batsmen allowed per nine innings. Abbreviated as RAT.

RBI Opportunities An official American League stat for the first three weeks of 1918, until the league saw how much work it involved and scrapped it. Still a good idea, sort of, and the folks at the Elias Sports Bureau have tracked this type of "situational stat" since 1975.

Reached First Base A precursor of the On Base Percentage, this stat was introduced as an official National League measure in 1879, its one and only year of existence. It included times reached via hits, walks, and errors, but not hit by pitch because putting their bodies on the line did not yet, in 1879, send batters to first base. Trivia: the league leader in this stat's lone year of life was Paul Hines, with 193.

Relative Batting Average Pioneered by David Shoebotham in a *Baseball Research Journal* article in 1976, this was the first traditional stat normalized to league average so as to permit cross-era comparison. Most folks who have employed this measure simply divide individual batting average by league batting average. Shoebotham's original computation was more precise:

$$RBA = \frac{\text{player's hits}}{\text{player's AB}} \Big/ \frac{\text{league hits} - \text{player's hits}}{\text{league AB} - \text{player's AB}}$$

In this manner a player's own performance would not be compared with itself.

Relief Points Relief wins plus saves minus losses was the original formula used as the basis for the Rolaids Company's annual award to the top reliever in each league. Recently the formula has been changed to include a debit for blown saves.

Relief Ranking Takes *Relief Runs* (which see), adjusts them for home park, then weights them by a factor (F in the formula below) reflecting the greater value of the innings pitched by a bullpen "closer." Relief Runs, which weights all innings identically, will tend to benefit long and middle relievers who are effective over many innings, while Relief Ranking—which was initially designed for those men who pitch less than three innings per game over a season or career—will tend to benefit relievers who may have fewer innings but who have more saves and decisions. The formula is

$$(\text{Relief Runs}) \times F \text{ where the Factor} = \frac{9 \times (\text{Wins} + \text{Losses} + K* [\text{Saves}])}{IP}$$

*K = either .25 or 1 over 10 times fraction of league wins that are saved, whichever is smaller.

The multiplier, or Factor, is usually around 1, but can get up to 1.5 or even 2 for some relievers, and can get down as low as 0.8 for some starters who have a lot of no-decision games.

Relief Runs Identical to Pitching Runs but confined to relief pitchers, defined as those who average less than three innings per appearance. Abbreviated as RR. See *Relief Ranking*.

Run Batted In Though widely regarded as a good measure of a

batter's overall productivity and value to his team, the RBI is extremely situation-dependent, denying equal access to opportunity on the basis of a player's team, slot in the batting order, and particularly the men surrounding him in the batting order.

Run Factor A measure of the run scoring in a given ballpark compared to other ballparks, with 100 representing the average home park and the highest figure above that representing the best hitters' park. Abbreviated as RF, it is computed on the basis of comparing runs scored and allowed per inning at home and on the road. Innings are estimated from the number of games and games won, allowing for the home team not batting in the final inning of a game in which it leads. The resulting Run Factor is then compared to the league average.

Run Rating for Batters A measure of a team's run-scoring ability, taking into account the park's *Run Factor* (see above) and the team's batters not having to face its own pitchers, with 100 representing the average and the highest figure above that representing the best. Abbreviated as RB.

Run Rating for Pitchers A measure of a team's run-prevention ability, taking into account the *Run Factor* (see above) and the team's pitchers not having to face its own batters, with 100 representing the average and the lowest figure beneath that representing the best. Abbreviated as RP.

Runs Created Bill James's formulation for run contribution from a variety of batting and baserunning events. Many different formulas are used, depending upon data available. In its basic expression, the formula is:

$$\frac{(\text{Hits} + \text{Walks})\,(\text{Total Bases})}{\text{At-Bats} + \text{Walks}}$$

The essence of this formulation is that the ability to get on base and the ability to push baserunners around fairly describes offensive ability. James later refined the formula with a "stolen base version":

$$\frac{(\text{Hits} + \text{Walks} - \text{Caught Stealing})\,(\text{Total Bases} + .55 \times \text{Stolen Bases})}{\text{At-Bats} + \text{Walks}}$$

Next came the "technical version": a longer formulation, presented below using the standard abbreviations for the various offensive events (the two elements multiplied in the numerator are referred to below as "A" and "B," and the denominator is referred to as "C"):

$$\frac{(H + BB + HBP - CS - GIDP)\,(TB + .26[BB - IBB + HBP] + .52[SH + SF + SB])}{AB + BB + HBP + SH + SF}$$

From this technical version (Tech-1), James spun off 13 additional technical versions. "The reason that we have to do this," he wrote in *The Bill James Historical Baseball Abstract*, "is that the data set changes and evolves rapidly throughout the century, or at least up until about 1955, when the progress of evolution in statistical information came to a temporary halt (it stopped moving forward until Bill James and Pete Palmer came around, about twenty years later). In 1900 we have no data for how many times a player grounded into a double play, how many times he was hit by a pitch, how many of his walks might have been intentional, how many times he was caught stealing, or how many sacrifice flies he hit." Accordingly, James adjusted his Runs Created formula to fit the available data; some versions, such as Tech-3, cover as much as a decade in a given league, while others, such as Tech-4, are in force for only a single league season. In *Total Baseball*, we have computed Runs Created values for all players since 1876 using the version most applicable to the period, with the single exception of Tech-9, which James applied only to the American League of 1916 but which we use for 1914–1916 in the AL and 1915–1916 in the NL because we have discovered additional caught-stealing data. (For those players whose careers began before 1900, James used the Tech-11 formula "to estimate how many runs they had created," but appended a note saying that "these estimates were of indeterminate accuracy.")

Here are the formulas for Runs Created (RC) technical versions 2–14 (Tech-1 was used for both leagues in 1955–1988):

Tech-2 (1954)
Factors A and C of Tech-1 remain the same, while Part B simply drops Intentional Bases on Balls.

Tech-3 (AL 1940–1953; NL 1951–1953)
Factor A remains the same, while SF is dropped from Factor C; Factor B changes to: 1.025 TB + .26(BB + HBP) + .52(SH + SB).

Tech-4 (AL 1939)
Factors A and C remain the same, while B becomes: TB + .26(BB + HBP) + .52(SH + SB).

Tech-5 (AL 1931–1938)
Factors B and C remain the same, while A becomes: .96(H + BB + HBP – CS).

Tech-6 (AL 1920–1930; NL 1920–1925)
Factors A and C remain the same, while B changes only in the value placed on the sacrifice hit and stolen base, which declines from .52 to .51.

Tech-7 (NL 1926–1930)
C remains the same, while A changes to: .93(H + BB + HBP), and B becomes: TB + .26(BB + HBP) + .46(SH).

Tech-8 (AL 1913, 1917–1919; NL 1913–1914, 1917–1919)
C remains the same, while A becomes: H + W + HBP – .02(AB), and B becomes: TB + .85(SH + SB).

Tech-9 (AL 1914–1916; NL 1915–1916)
B and C are the same, while A becomes: H + BB + HBP – CS.

Tech-10 (AL, NL 1908–1912)
A and C remain the same, while B becomes: 1.025(TB + SB) + .75(SH).

Tech-11 (AL, NL 1900–1907)
B and C remain the same, while A becomes: H + BB + HBP.

Tech-12 (NL 1939–1950)
A Factor: H + BB + HBP – GIDP
B Factor: TB + .26(BB +HBP) + .52(SH)

Tech-13 (NL 1933–1938)
A and C remain the same as above, while B becomes: 1.025(TB) + .26(BB + HBP) + .52(SH)

Tech-14 (NL 1931–1932)
B and C remain the same, but A becomes: .95(H + BB + HBP).

Runs Per Game With its mate *Outs Per Game* (which see), this was the precursor, in the 1860s, of the batting average; by the end of that decade it gave way to Hits Per Game.

Runs Per Win Branch Rickey and Allan Roth first stated the proportional nature of runs and wins in their 1954 article in *Life*. Since then the point has been expanded upon by George Lindsey, Pete Palmer, Bill James, and every sabermetrician worth his salt: the point being that just as runs scored and allowed are the key to victory in a given game, so are they the key to success over the course of a season and the predictors of won-lost record with a surprising degree of precision. In 1982, Palmer wrote in *The National Pastime*, "My work showed that as a rough rule of thumb, each additional ten runs scored (or ten less runs allowed) produced one extra win. . . . However, breaking the teams into groups showed that high-scoring teams needed more runs to produce a win. This runs-per-win factor I determined to be ten times the square root of the average number of runs scored per inning by both teams. Thus in normal play, when 4.5 runs per game are scored by each club, each team scores .5 runs per inning—totaling one run, the square root of which is one, times ten."

For *Total Baseball*, we have improved the Runs Per Win figure used in calculating the overall win figures in the Total Player Rating

and the Total Pitcher Index. Rather than using 10 times the square root of the average number of runs scored per inning by both teams, we use adjusted runs per inning based on what the player or pitcher rating is. A hitter will increase the figure by adding in his rating over the number of games played, while a pitcher will have his rating subtracted. Say the average number of runs scored per inning is 1, as in the model above; then Runs Per Win = 10. Take a pitcher who allows 45 runs less than average in 25 games. This lowers the runs per game by 1.8, or runs per inning by .2, so the new Runs Per Win figure is 10 times the square root of the average number of runs scored per inning by both teams, *minus the pitcher's rating*. So we take from the one run per inning the .2 run saved by the pitcher, giving a result of 0.8. Ten times the square root of 0.8 is 8.9, so the pitcher gets 45/8.9, or 5.1, wins instead of 4.5. A hitter with plus 45 runs in 150 games, or .3 runs per game, contributes .03 runs per inning. His Runs Per Win is now 10 times the square root of the average number of runs scored per inning *plus the batter's rating*. So we add to the 1 run per inning the .03 runs added by the batter, giving a result of 10.1. Ten times the square root of 10.1 gives the batter 4.4 wins. (This method makes makes more of a difference in pitching because the runs are contributed over fewer games. With the same run contribution—45 beyond average—the pitcher gains 0.7 wins over the batter. This is because when the total number of runs scored is lowered, the value of each run is greater).

Runs Produced Runs batted in plus runs scored minus home runs.

Sabermetrics Defined by Bill James, who coined the term in honor of the Society for American Baseball Research, as "the search for objective knowledge about baseball" and, earlier, as "the mathematical and statistical analysis of baseball records."

SABR Pronounced "saber," this is the acronym for the Society for American Baseball Research, the organization that has, since its founding by Bob Davids in 1971, steadily advanced the state of baseball knowledge.

Sacrifice Fly First recognized as an event in 1908 but indistinguishable in the official records from sacrifice hits until 1954. There has been much flip-flopping since 1930 on whether to credit the sacrifice flier with an at-bat or an RBI or whether a fly ball that advances a runner to a base other than home plate also should exempt a man from an at-bat.

Sacrifice Hits Invented in the 1860s, recorded since 1889; sacrificer charged with an at-bat until 1894. Sabermetricians frown on the strategy because all the studies show that the trading of an out for a base advanced is a losing strategy—lowering the run expectations of the team that attempts it—in all but the most unusual of cases . . . even if the sacrifice "succeeds."

Sacrifice Hits Allowed Computed officially in the National League since 1913 but not published until 1916, and kept in the American League since 1921 but not published until 1922; what it signified about anything is unclear.

Save Created by Jerome Holtzman of the Chicago *Sun-Times*, the save began to be reported by *The Sporting News* on a regular basis in 1960. The major leagues adopted the save in 1969, at which time it was credited to a reliever who finished a game that his team won. In 1973 the save was redefined so that a reliever had not only to finish the game but also to find the potential tying or winning run on base or at the plate, or, alternately, to pitch the final three innings of a victorious contest. In 1975 the rule was liberalized to include a reliever's appearance of one inning or more in which he protects a lead of three runs or less; or he enters the game with the tying or winning run on base, at bat, or on deck; or he pitches three innings to the game's conclusion. In this book, the 1969 definition is applied to all games before 1969; otherwise the rule in force at the time prevails. Abbreviated as SV.

Shutouts On an individual basis, credited only to pitchers of complete-game scoreless victories or ties; former practice was to credit combined shutouts to the starting pitcher if he had pitched most of the way. Abbreviated as SH.

Situational Statistics How does a batter perform with the bases loaded? At night? On artificial turf? With no one on base? After the seventh inning when his team is tied or trails? The specialty of Baseball Workshop, Stats, Inc., and the Elias Sports Bureau.

Slugging Average Total bases divided by at-bats; combines nicely with On Base Percentage to create *Production* (which see). Abbreviated as SLG.

Starter Runs Identical to *Pitching Runs* (which see) but confined to starting pitchers, defined as those who average more than three innings per appearance. Abbreviated as SR.

Stolen Base Average Stolen bases divided by attempts; its computation is dependent upon the availability of caught-stealing numbers. Abbreviated as SBA.

Stolen Base Runs For teams, the Linear Weights measure of runs contributed *beyond* what a league-average basestealing team might have gained, defined as zero; for individuals, Stolen Base Runs are calculated on the basis of the 66.7 percent success rate that sabermetric studies have shown to be the break-even point for producing runs beyond the average. Availability dependent upon caught stealing data as with Stolen Base Average. The formula is simple: .30(Stolen Bases) − .60(Caught Stealing). A man who steals two bases in three attempts is merely spinning his wheels in terms of value to his team, and even a man who succeeds at an 80 percent clip will have to steal a lot of bases—about 65—to create just one win beyond average. Abbreviated as SBR.

Stolen Base Wins Stolen Base Runs divided by the number of runs required to create an additional win beyond average. Those runs are generally around around 10—historically in the range of 9–11. Abbreviated as SBW. See *Runs Per Win*.

Stolen Bases Recorded since 1886, but until 1898 steals are thought to have included a variety of daring baserunning exploits, such as going from first to third on a single or advancing an extra base on an out. Abbreviated as SB.

Strikeouts Varying rules concerning the strike zone, the foul strike, and the warning pitch—not to mention the fourth strike of 1887—all contribute to making the cross-era comparison of strikeout accomplishments a very sticky business. Abbreviated as SO.

Strikeout Percentage A batters' stat: fewest strikeouts per 100 at bats.

Total Average Tom Boswell's formulation for offensive contribution from a variety of batting and baserunning events; as with Runs Created, we have calculated Total Average to make use of the maximum available data in a given year. The concept of the numerator is bases gained, that of the denominator is outs made:

$$\frac{\text{(Total Bases + Steals + Walks + HBP − Caught Stealing)}}{\text{(At-Bats − Hits + Caught Stealing + GIDP)}}$$

Abbreviated as TA. See *Base-Out Percentage*.

Total Baseball Ranking The "MVP" of statistics, this ranks pitchers and position players by their total wins contributed in all their endeavors, revealing the most valuable performers in a given year. Abbreviated as TBR, it is not a computed stat but a sorting of players and pitchers by, respectively, the sum of their Total Batter Rating and Total Pitcher Index.

Total Bases Average Henry Chadwick's measure that divided total bases by games played; a forerunner of the Slugging Average.

Total Bases Run A silly stat of one year's duration, 1880, this was sort of an RBI in reverse, from the runner's perspective. Also called "Bases Touched," it was nothing more than that and signified nothing about individual talent. Trivia: the National League's leader in 1880 was Abner Dalrymple, with 501 bases touched.

Total Chances Putouts plus assists plus errors; in other words, total chances offered, not total chances accepted.

Total Pitcher Index The sum of a pitcher's Pitching Runs—expressed as Ranking Runs, employing the same formula used to compute Relief Ranking Runs—Batting Runs (in the AL since 1973, zero), and Fielding Runs, all divided by the Runs Per Win factor for that year (generally around 10, historically in the 9–11 range); abbreviated as TPI. See *Runs Per Win, Relief Ranking*.

Total Player Rating The sum of a player's Adjusted Batting Runs, Fielding Runs, and Base Stealing Runs, minus his positional

adjustment, all divided by the Runs Per Win factor for t̶ (generally around 10, historically in the 9–11 range). See *R̶ Win*.

Triple Crown Long regarded as consisting of batting ave̶ home runs, and RBIs, but was not always so. In the early year̶ this century, newspapers spoke of Ty Cobb shooting for the "tri̶ crown" of batting average, runs, and hits.

Weighted Average The next step in statistical sophistication̶ after first, counting and, next, averaging. Chadwick's Total Bases̶ Average was probably the first weighted average, in that it assigned̶ values of 1 to a single, 2 to a double, 3 to a triple, and 4 to a home̶ run.

Weighted Rating System Ted Oliver's invention, promoted in a̶ 1944 self-published booklet called *Kings of the Mound*. We have̶ modified Oliver's pioneering effort to create *Wins Above Team* (see̶ below), which entry presents a discussion of Oliver's effort.

Win Points See *Player Win Averages*.

Wins Above League A pitcher's won-lost record restated by adding his Pitching Wins above the league average to the record that a league-average pitcher would have had with his number of decisions. Example: Tom Seaver has a hard-luck season, going only 16–14 despite a 1.76 ERA and five Pitching Wins; applying the five wins to a league-average 15–15 mark in the same 30 decisions results in a WAL of 20-10.

Wins Above Team How many wins a pitcher garnered beyond those expected of an average pitcher for that team. As the editors of this volume, in their earlier *Hidden Game of Baseball*, modified Ted Oliver's *Weighted Rating System* (see above), they now improve this statistic thanks to Bill Deane's corrective for its tendency to overvalue the contributions of good pitchers on awful teams.

Oliver's Weighted Rating System for pitchers was motivated by the inadequacies of both the won-lost percentage and the ERA when it came to evaluating pitchers laboring for poor teams. The Oliver formula, ingenious if flawed, was: pitcher's won-lost percentage minus the team's won-lost percentage—after removing the pitcher's decisions from the team's record—then multiplying the difference by the pitcher's number of decisions. Here is an example of the Oliver method as applied to Bobby Castillo, who in 1982 pitched very well in going 13–11 for a very bad Minnesota club (60–102; without him, 47–91):

$$\left(\frac{13}{24} - \frac{47}{138}\right) \times 24$$

or

$$(.542 - .341) \times 24$$

or

$$.201 \times 24 = 4.824$$

The figure of 4.824 would have been represented by Ted Oliver as "4,824 points"; he did not seem to recognize that had he retained the decimal point, his rating would have been expressed directly in *wins*. Thus the number of wins Castillo accounted for in his 24 decisions that an average Minnesota pitcher would *not* have gained was 4.8.

Thanks to a key modification of our earlier formula for Wins Above Team, abbreviated as WAT, we now propose the following: calculate the pitcher's won-lost percentage and the team's winning percentage after his decisions have been set aside. If the pitcher's percentage is higher, then WAT is

$$\text{Pitcher decisions} \times \left(\frac{\text{Pitcher pct. − Team pct.}}{2 - 2 \times \text{Team pct.}}\right)$$

If the pitcher's percentage is lower, then WAT is

$$\text{Pitcher decisions} \times \left(\frac{\text{Pitcher pct. − Team pct.}}{2 \times \text{Team pct.}}\right)$$

Won-lost percentage Computed as wins over decisions.

Team and League Abbreviations

These are the 145 franchises, seven principal leagues and their abbreviations as used throughout this book.

		own as n or NA)	
		Athletics	
		antics	
		e Lord Baltimores	
		n Red Stockings	
		adelphia Centennials	
		chicago White Stockings	
		Chicago White Stockings	
		Cleveland Forest City	
	572	Brooklyn Eckfords	
	1875	Hartford Dark Blues	
	1871	Fort Wayne Kekiongas	
2	1872	Middletown (Conn.) Mansfields	
871	1875	New York Mutuals	
1872	1872	Washington, D.C., Nationals	
1875	1875	New Haven Elm City	
1871	1872	Washington, D.C., Olympics	
1873	1875	Philadelphia White Stockings	
ES n	1873	1873	Elizabeth (N.J.) Resolutes
ROK n	1871	1871	Rockford (Ill.) Forest City
RS n	1875	1875	St. Louis Red Stockings
STL n	1875	1875	St. Louis Brown Stockings
TRO n	1871	1872	Troy Haymakers
WAS n	1873	1873	Washington Washingtons
WAS n	1875	1875	Washington Washingtons
WES n	1875	1875	Keokuk (Iowa) Westerns

NATIONAL LEAGUE, 1876– (Shown as N or NL)

Abbrev.	First	Last	Team
ATL N	1966		Atlanta
BAL N	1892	1899	Baltimore
BOS N	1876	1952	Boston (transferred to Milwaukee)
BRO N	1890	1957	Brooklyn (transferred to Los Angeles)
BUF N	1879	1885	Buffalo
CHI N	1876		Chicago
CIN N	1876	1880	Cincinnati
CIN N	1890		Cincinnati
CLE N	1879	1884	Cleveland
CLE N	1889	1899	Cleveland
COL N	1993		Colorado
DET N	1881	1888	Detroit
FLA N	1993		Florida
HAR N	1876	1877	Hartford (played in Brooklyn in 1877)
HOU N	1962		Houston
IND N	1878	1878	Indianapolis
IND N	1887	1889	Indianapolis
KC N	1886	1886	Kansas City
LA N	1958		Los Angeles
LOU N	1876	1877	Louisville
LOU N	1892	1899	Louisville
MIL N	1878	1878	Milwaukee
MIL N	1953	1965	Milwaukee (transferred to Atlanta)
MON N	1969		Montreal
NY N	1876	1876	New York (played in Brooklyn)
NY N	1883	1957	New York (transferred to San Francisco)
NY N	1962		New York
PHI N	1876	1876	Philadelphia
PHI N	1883		Philadelphia
PIT N	1887		Pittsburgh
PRO N	1878	1885	Providence
STL N	1876	1877	St. Louis
STL N	1885	1886	St. Louis
STL N	1892		St. Louis
SD N	1969		San Diego
SF N	1958		San Francisco
SYR N	1879	1879	Syracuse
TRO N	1879	1882	Troy (N.Y.)
WAS N	1886	1889	Washington, D.C.
WAS N	1892	1899	Washington, D.C.
WOR N	1880	1882	Worcester (Mass.)

AMERICAN ASSOCIATION, 1882-1891 (Shown as a or AA)

Abbrev.	First	Last	Team
BAL a	1882	1889	Baltimore
BAL a	1890	1890	Baltimore (combined with Brooklyn, shown as BB)
BAL a	1891	1891	Baltimore (transferred to National League)
BOS a	1891	1891	Boston
BRO a	1884	1889	Brooklyn (transferred to National League)
BRO a	1890	1890	Brooklyn (combined with Baltimore, shown as BB)
CIN a	1882	1889	Cincinnati (transferred to National League)
CIN a	1891	1891	Cincinnati
CLE a	1887	1888	Cleveland (transferred to National League)

COL a	1883	1884	Columbus (Ohio)
COL a	1889	1891	Columbus (Ohio)
IND a	1884	1884	Indianapolis
KC a	1888	1889	Kansas City
LOU a	1882	1891	Louisville (transferred to National League)
MIL a	1891	1891	Milwaukee
NY a	1883	1887	New York
PHI a	1882	1891	Philadelphia
PIT a	1882	1886	Pittsburgh (transferred to National League)
RIC a	1884	1884	Richmond
ROC a	1890	1890	Rochester
STL a	1882	1891	St. Louis (transferred to National League)
SYR a	1890	1890	Syracuse
TOL a	1884	1884	Toledo
TOL a	1890	1890	Toledo
WAS a	1884	1884	Washington, D.C.
WAS a	1891	1891	Washington, D.C. (transferred to National League)

UNION ASSOCIATION, 1884 (Shown as U or UA)

Abbrev.	First	Last	Team
ALT U	1884	1884	Altoona (Pa.)
BAL U	1884	1884	Baltimore
BOS U	1884	1884	Boston
CHI U	1884	1884	Chicago (combined with Pittsburgh, shown as CP)
CIN U	1884	1884	Cincinnati
KC U	1884	1884	Kansas City
MIL U	1884	1884	Milwaukee
PHI U	1884	1884	Philadelphia
PIT U	1884	1884	Pittsburgh (combined with Chicago, shown as CP)
STL U	1884	1884	St. Louis
STP U	1884	1884	St. Paul (Minn.)
WAS U	1884	1884	Washington, D.C.
WIL U	1884	1884	Wilmington (Del.)

PLAYERS LEAGUE, 1890 (Shown as P or PL)

Abbrev.	First	Last	Team
BOS P	1890	1890	Boston
BRO P	1890	1890	Brooklyn
BUF P	1890	1890	Buffalo
CHI P	1890	1890	Chicago
CLE P	1890	1890	Cleveland
NY P	1890	1890	New York
PHI P	1890	1890	Philadelphia
PIT P	1890	1890	Pittsburgh

AMERICAN LEAGUE, 1901– (Shown as A or AL)

Abbrev.	First	Last	Team
BAL A	1901	1902	Baltimore (replaced by New York)
BAL A	1954		Baltimore
BOS A	1901		Boston
CAL A	1965		California
CHI A	1901		Chicago
CLE A	1901		Cleveland
DET A	1901		Detroit
KC A	1955	1967	Kansas City (transferred to Oakland)
KC A	1969		Kansas City
LA A	1961	1964	Los Angeles (transferred to California)
MIL A	1901	1901	Milwaukee (replaced by St. Louis)
MIL A	1970		Milwaukee
MIN A	1961		Minnesota
NY A	1903		New York
OAK A	1968		Oakland
PHI A	1901	1954	Philadelphia (transferred to Kansas City)
STL A	1902	1953	St. Louis (transferred to Baltimore)
SEA A	1969	1969	Seattle (transferred to Milwaukee)
SEA A	1977		Seattle
TEX A	1972		Texas
TOR A	1977		Toronto
WAS A	1901	1960	Washington, D.C. (transferred to Minnesota)
WAS A	1961	1971	Washington, D.C. (transferred to Texas)

FEDERAL LEAGUE, 1914-1915 (Shown as F or FL)

Abbrev.	First	Last	Team
BAL F	1914	1915	Baltimore
BRO F	1914	1915	Brooklyn
BUF F	1914	1915	Buffalo
CHI F	1914	1915	Chicago
IND F	1914	1914	Indianapolis (transferred to Newark)
KC F	1914	1915	Kansas City
NEW F	1915	1915	Newark
PIT F	1914	1915	Pittsburgh
STL F	1914	1915	St. Louis